CONTENTS

**ACADEMIC AND
PROFESSIONAL PROGRAMS IN
INTERDISCIPLINARY STUDIES**

**ACADEMIC AND PROFESSIONAL
PROGRAMS IN THE SOCIAL SCIENCES**

APPENDIXES

INDEXES

SPECIAL ADVERTISING SECTION

A Note from the Peterson's Editors

The six volumes of Peterson's *Graduate and Professional Programs*, the only annually updated reference work of its kind, provide wide-ranging information on the graduate and professional programs offered by accredited colleges and universities in the United States, U.S. territories, and Canada and by those institutions outside the United States that are accredited by U.S. accrediting bodies. More than 44,000 individual academic and professional programs at more than 2,200 institutions are listed. Peterson's *Graduate and Professional Programs* have been used for more than forty years by prospective graduate and professional students, placement counselors, faculty advisers, and all others interested in postbaccalaureate education.

Graduate & Professional Programs: An Overview contains information on institutions as a whole, while the other books in the series are devoted to specific academic and professional fields:

Graduate Programs in the Humanities, Arts & Social Sciences
Graduate Programs in the Biological Sciences
Graduate Programs in the Physical Sciences, Mathematics, Agricultural Sciences, the Environment & Natural Resources
Graduate Programs in Engineering & Applied Sciences
Graduate Programs in Business, Education, Health, Information Studies, Law & Social Work

The books may be used individually or as a set. For example, if you have chosen a field of study but do not know what institution you want to attend or if you have a college or university in mind but have not chosen an academic field of study, it is best to begin with the Overview guide.

Graduate & Professional Programs: An Overview presents several directories to help you identify programs of study that might interest you; you can then research those programs further in the other books in the series by using the Directory of Graduate and Professional Programs by Field, which lists 500 fields and gives the names of those institutions that offer graduate degree programs in each.

For geographical or financial reasons, you may be interested in attending a particular institution and will want to know what it has to offer. You should turn to the Directory of Institutions and Their Offerings, which lists the degree programs available at each institution. As in the Directory of Graduate and Professional Programs by Field, the level of degrees offered is also indicated.

All books in the series include advice on graduate education, including topics such as admissions tests, financial aid, and accreditation. **The Graduate Adviser** includes two essays and information about accreditation. The first essay, "The Admissions Process," discusses general admission requirements, admission tests, factors to consider when selecting a graduate school or program, when and how to apply, and how admission decisions are made. Special information for international students and tips for minority students are also included. The second essay, "Financial Support," is an overview of the broad range of support available at the graduate level. Fellowships, scholarships, and grants; assistantships and internships; federal and private loan programs, as well as Federal Work-Study; and the GI bill are detailed. This essay concludes with advice on applying for need-based financial aid. "Accreditation and Accrediting Agencies" gives information on accreditation and its purpose and lists institutional accrediting agencies first and then specialized accrediting agencies relevant to each volume's specific fields of study.

With information on more than 44,000 graduate programs in 500 disciplines, Peterson's *Graduate and Professional Programs* give you all the information you need about the programs that are of interest to you in three formats: **Profiles** (capsule summaries of basic information), **Displays** (information that an institution or program wants to emphasize), and **Close-Ups** (written by administrators, with more expansive information than the **Profiles**, emphasizing different aspects of the programs). By using these various formats of program information, coupled with **Appendixes** and **Indexes** covering directories and subject areas for all six books, you will find that these guides provide the most comprehensive, accurate, and up-to-date graduate study information available.

At the end of the book, you'll find a special section of ads placed by Peterson's preferred clients. Their financial support makes it possible for Peterson's Publishing to continue to provide you with the highest-quality educational exploration, test-prep, financial aid, and career-preparation resources you need to succeed on your educational journey.

Find Us on Facebook®

Join the grad school conversation on Facebook® at www.facebook.com/petersonspublishing. Peterson's expert resources are available to help you as you search for the right graduate program for you.

Peterson's publishes a full line of resources with information you need to guide you through the graduate admissions process. Peterson's publications can be found at college libraries and career centers and your local bookstore or library—or visit us on the Web at www.petersonspublishing.com. Peterson's books are now also available as eBooks.

Colleges and universities will be pleased to know that Peterson's helped you in your selection. Admissions staff members are more than happy to answer questions, address specific problems, and help in any way they can. The editors at Peterson's wish you great success in your graduate program search!

THE GRADUATE ADVISER

The Admissions Process

Generalizations about graduate admissions practices are not always helpful because each institution has its own set of guidelines and procedures. Nevertheless, some broad statements can be made about the admissions process that may help you plan your strategy.

Factors Involved in Selecting a Graduate School or Program

Selecting a graduate school and a specific program of study is a complex matter. Quality of the faculty; program and course offerings; the nature, size, and location of the institution; admission requirements; cost; and the availability of financial assistance are among the many factors that affect one's choice of institution. Other considerations are job placement and achievements of the program's graduates and the institution's resources, such as libraries, laboratories, and computer facilities. If you are to make the best possible choice, you need to learn as much as you can about the schools and programs you are considering before you apply.

The following steps may help you narrow your choices.

- Talk to alumni of the programs or institutions you are considering to get their impressions of how well they were prepared for work in their fields of study.
- Remember that graduate school requirements change, so be sure to get the most up-to-date information possible.
- Talk to department faculty members and the graduate adviser at your undergraduate institution. They often have information about programs of study at other institutions.
- Visit the Web sites of the graduate schools in which you are interested to request a graduate catalog. Contact the department chair in your chosen field of study for additional information about the department and the field.
- Visit as many campuses as possible. Call ahead for an appointment with the graduate adviser in your field of interest and be sure to check out the facilities and talk to students.

General Requirements

Graduate schools and departments have requirements that applicants for admission must meet. Typically, these requirements include undergraduate transcripts (which provide information about undergraduate grade point average and course work applied toward a major), admission test scores, and letters of recommendation. Most graduate programs also ask for an essay or personal statement that describes your personal reasons for seeking graduate study. In some fields, such as art and music, portfolios or auditions may be required in addition to other evidence of talent. Some institutions require that the applicant have an undergraduate degree in the same subject as the intended graduate major.

Most institutions evaluate each applicant on the basis of the applicant's total record, and the weight accorded any given factor varies widely from institution to institution and from program to program.

The Application Process

You should begin the application process at least one year before you expect to begin your graduate study. Find out the application deadline for each institution (many are provided in the **Profile** section of this guide). Go to the institution's Web site and find out if you can apply online. If not, request a paper application form. Fill out this form thoroughly and neatly. Assume that the school needs all the information it is requesting and that the admissions officer will be sensitive to the neatness and overall quality of what you submit. Do not supply more information than the school requires.

The institution may ask at least one question that will require a three- or four-paragraph answer. Compose your response on the assumption that the admissions officer is interested in both what you think and how you express yourself. Keep your statement brief and to the point, but, at the same time, include all pertinent information about your past experiences and your educational goals. Individual statements vary greatly in style and content, which helps admissions officers differentiate among applicants. Many graduate departments give considerable weight to the statement in making their admissions decisions, so be sure to take the time to prepare a thoughtful and concise statement.

If recommendations are a part of the admissions requirements, carefully choose the individuals you ask to write them. It is generally best to ask current or former professors to write the recommendations, provided they are able to attest to your intellectual ability and motivation for doing the work required of a graduate student. It is advisable to provide stamped, preaddressed envelopes to people being asked to submit recommendations on your behalf.

Completed applications, including references, transcripts, and admission test scores, should be received at the institution by the specified date.

Be advised that institutions do not usually make admissions decisions until all materials have been received. Enclose a self-addressed postcard with your application, requesting confirmation of receipt. Allow at least ten days for the return of the postcard before making further inquiries.

If you plan to apply for financial support, it is imperative that you file your application early.

ADMISSION TESTS

The major testing program used in graduate admissions is the Graduate Record Examinations (GRE) testing program, sponsored by the GRE Board and administered by Educational Testing Service, Princeton, New Jersey.

The Graduate Record Examinations testing program consists of a General Test and eight Subject Tests. The General Test measures critical thinking, verbal reasoning, quantitative reasoning, and analytical writing skills. It is offered as an Internet-based test (iBT) in the United States, Canada, and many other countries.

The typical computer-based General Test consists of one 30-minute verbal reasoning section, one 45-minute quantitative reasoning sections, one 45-minute issue analysis (writing) section, and one 30-minute argument analysis (writing) section. In addition, an unidentified verbal or quantitative section that doesn't count toward a score may be included and an identified research section that is not scored may also be included.

The Subject Tests measure achievement and assume undergraduate majors or extensive background in the following eight disciplines:

- Biochemistry, Cell and Molecular Biology
- Biology
- Chemistry
- Computer Science
- Literature in English
- Mathematics
- Physics
- Psychology

The Subject Tests are available three times per year as paper-based administrations around the world. Testing time is approximately 2 hours and 50 minutes. You can obtain more information about the GRE by visiting the ETS Web site at www.ets.org or consulting the *GRE Information and Registration Bulletin*. The *Bulletin* can be obtained at many undergraduate colleges. You can also download it from the ETS Web site or obtain it by contacting Graduate Record Examinations, Educational Testing Service, P.O. Box 6000, Princeton, NJ 08541-6000; phone: 609-771-7670.

If you expect to apply for admission to a program that requires any of the GRE tests, you should select a test date well in advance of the application deadline. Scores on the computer-based General Test are reported within ten to fifteen days; scores on the paper-based Subject Tests are reported within six weeks.

Another testing program, the Miller Analogies Test (MAT), is administered at more than 500 Controlled Testing Centers, licensed by Harcourt Assessment, Inc., in the United States, Canada, and other countries. The MAT computer-based test is now available. Testing time is 60 minutes. The test consists of 120 partial analogies. You can obtain the *Candidate Information Booklet,* which contains a list of test centers and instructions for taking the test, from http://www.milleranalogies.com or by calling 800-622-3231 (toll-free).

Check the specific requirements of the programs to which you are applying.

How Admission Decisions Are Made

The program you apply to is directly involved in the admissions process. Although the final decision is usually made by the graduate dean (or an associate) or the faculty admissions committee, recommendations from faculty members in your intended field are important. At some institutions, an interview is incorporated into the decision process.

A Special Note for International Students

In addition to the steps already described, there are some special considerations for international students who intend to apply for graduate study in the United States. All graduate schools require an indication of competence in English. The purpose of the Test of English as a Foreign Language (TOEFL) is to evaluate the English proficiency of people who are nonnative speakers of English and want to study at colleges and universities where English is the language of instruction. The TOEFL is administered by Educational Testing Service (ETS) under the general direction of a policy board established by the College Board and the Graduate Record Examinations Board.

The TOEFL iBT assesses the four basic language skills: listening, reading, writing, and speaking. It was administered for the first time in September 2005, and ETS continues to introduce the TOEFL iBT in selected cities. The Internet-based test is administered at secure, official test centers. The testing time is approximately 4 hours. Because the TOEFL iBT includes a speaking section, the Test of Spoken English (TSE) is no longer needed.

The TOEFL is also offered in the paper-based format in areas of the world where Internet-based testing is not available. The paper-based TOEFL consists of three sections—listening comprehension, structure and written expression, and reading comprehension. The testing time is approximately 3 hours. The Test of Written English (TWE) is also given. The TWE is a 30-minute essay that measures the examinee's ability to compose in English. Examinees receive a TWE score separate from their TOEFL score. The *Information Bulletin* contains information on local fees and registration procedures.

Additional information and registration materials are available from TOEFL Services, Educational Testing Service, P.O. Box 6151, Princeton, New Jersey 08541-6151. Phone: 609-771-7100. Web site: www.toefl.org.

International students should apply especially early because of the number of steps required to complete the admissions process. Furthermore, many United States graduate schools have a limited number of spaces for international students, and many more students apply than the schools can accommodate.

International students may find financial assistance from institutions very limited. The U.S. government requires international applicants to submit a certification of support, which is a statement attesting to the applicant's financial resources. In addition, international students *must* have health insurance coverage.

Tips for Minority Students

Indicators of a university's values in terms of diversity are found both in its recruitment programs and its resources directed to student success. Important questions: Does the institution vigorously recruit minorities for its graduate programs? Is there funding available to help with the costs associated with visiting the school? Are minorities represented in the institution's brochures or Web site or on their faculty rolls? What campus-based resources or services (including assistance in locating housing or career counseling and placement) are available? Is funding available to members of underrepresented groups?

At the program level, it is particularly important for minority students to investigate the "climate" of a program under consideration. How many minority students are enrolled and how many have graduated? What opportunities are there to work with diverse faculty and mentors whose research interests match yours? How are conflicts resolved or concerns addressed? How interested are faculty in building strong and supportive relations with students? "Climate" concerns should be addressed by posing questions to various individuals, including faculty members, current students, and alumni.

Information is also available through various organizations, such as the Hispanic Association of Colleges & Universities (HACU), and publications such as *Diverse Issues in Higher Education* and *Hispanic Outlook* magazine. There are also books devoted to this topic, such as *The Multicultural Student's Guide to Colleges* by Robert Mitchell.

Financial Support

The range of financial support at the graduate level is very broad. The following descriptions will give you a general idea of what you might expect and what will be expected of you as a financial support recipient.

Fellowships, Scholarships, and Grants

These are usually outright awards of a few hundred to many thousands of dollars with no service to the institution required in return. Fellowships and scholarships are usually awarded on the basis of merit and are highly competitive. Grants are made on the basis of financial need or special talent in a field of study. Many fellowships, scholarships, and grants not only cover tuition, fees, and supplies but also include stipends for living expenses with allowances for dependents. However, the terms of each should be examined because some do not permit recipients to supplement their income with outside work. Fellowships, scholarships, and grants may vary in the number of years for which they are awarded.

In addition to the availability of these funds at the university or program level, many excellent fellowship programs are available at the national level and may be applied for before and during enrollment in a graduate program. A listing of many of these programs can be found at the Council of Graduate Schools' Web site: http://www.cgsnet.org. There is a wealth of information in the "Programs" and "Awards" sections.

Assistantships and Internships

Many graduate students receive financial support through assistantships, particularly involving teaching or research duties. It is important to recognize that such appointments should not be viewed simply as employment relationships but rather should constitute an integral and important part of a student's graduate education. As such, the appointments should be accompanied by strong faculty mentoring and increasingly responsible apprenticeship experiences. The specific nature of these appointments in a given program should be considered in selecting that graduate program.

TEACHING ASSISTANTSHIPS

These usually provide a salary and full or partial tuition remission and may also provide health benefits. Unlike fellowships, scholarships, and grants, which require no service to the institution, teaching assistantships require recipients to provide the institution with a specific amount of undergraduate teaching, ideally related to the student's field of study. Some teaching assistants are limited to grading papers, compiling bibliographies, taking notes, or monitoring laboratories. At some graduate schools, teaching assistants must carry lighter course loads than regular full-time students.

RESEARCH ASSISTANTSHIPS

These are very similar to teaching assistantships in the manner in which financial assistance is provided. The difference is that recipients are given basic research assignments in their disciplines rather than teaching responsibilities. The work required is normally related to the student's field of study; in most instances, the assistantship supports the student's thesis or dissertation research.

ADMINISTRATIVE INTERNSHIPS

These are similar to assistantships in application of financial assistance funds, but the student is given an assignment on a part-time basis, usually as a special assistant with one of the university's administrative offices. The assignment may not necessarily be directly related to the recipient's discipline.

RESIDENCE HALL AND COUNSELING ASSISTANTSHIPS

These assistantships are frequently assigned to graduate students in psychology, counseling, and social work, but they may be offered to students in other disciplines, especially if the student has worked in this capacity during his or her undergraduate years. Duties can vary from being available in a dean's office for a specific number of hours for consultation with undergraduates to living in campus residences and being responsible for both counseling and administrative tasks or advising student activity groups. Residence hall assistantships often include a room and board allowance and, in some cases, tuition assistance and stipends. Contact the Housing and Student Life Office for more information.

Health Insurance

The availability and affordability of health insurance is an important issue and one that should be considered in an applicant's choice of institution and program. While often included with assistantships and fellowships, this is not always the case and, even if provided, the benefits may be limited. It is important to note that the U.S. government requires international students to have health insurance.

The GI Bill

This provides financial assistance for students who are veterans of the United States armed forces. If you are a veteran, contact your local Veterans Administration office to determine your eligibility and to get full details about benefits. There are a number of programs that offer educational benefits to current military enlistees. Some states have tuition assistance programs for members of the National Guard. Contact the VA office at the college for more information.

Federal Work-Study Program (FWS)

Employment is another way some students finance their graduate studies. The federally funded Federal Work-Study Program provides eligible students with employment opportunities, usually in public and private nonprofit organizations. Federal funds pay up to 75 percent of the wages, with the remainder paid by the employing agency. FWS is available to graduate students who demonstrate financial need. Not all schools have these funds, and some only award them to undergraduates. Each school sets its application deadline and work-study earnings limits. Wages vary and are related to the type of work done. You must file the Free Application for Federal Student Aid (FAFSA) to be eligible for this program.

Loans

Many graduate students borrow to finance their graduate programs when other sources of assistance (which do not have to be repaid) prove insufficient. You should always read and understand the terms of any loan program before submitting your application.

FEDERAL DIRECT LOANS

Federal Direct Stafford Loans. The Federal Direct Stafford Loan Program offers low-interest loans to students with the Department of Education acting as the lender.

There are two components of the Federal Stafford Loan program. Under the *subsidized* component of the program, the federal government pays the interest on the loan while you are enrolled in graduate school on at least a half-time basis, during the six-month grace period after you drop below half-time enrollment, as well as during any period of deferment. Under the *unsubsidized* component of the program, you pay the interest on the loan from the day proceeds are issued. Eligibility for the federal subsidy is based on demonstrated financial need as determined by the financial aid office from the information you provide on the FAFSA. A cosigner is not required, since the loan is not based on creditworthiness.

Although *unsubsidized* Federal Direct Stafford Loans may not be as desirable as *subsidized* Federal Direct Stafford Loans from the student's perspective, they are a useful source of support for those who may not qualify for the subsidized loans or who need additional financial assistance.

Graduate students may borrow up to $20,500 per year through the Direct Stafford Loan Program, up to a cumulative maximum of $138,500, including undergraduate borrowing. This may include up to $8,500 in *subsidized* Direct Stafford Loans annually, depending on eligibility, up to a cumulative maximum of $65,500, including undergraduate borrowing. The amount of the loan borrowed through the *unsubsidized* Direct Stafford Loan Program equals the total amount of the loan (as much as $20,500) minus your eligibility for a *subsidized* Direct Stafford Loan (as much as $8,500). You may borrow up to the cost of attendance at the school in which you are enrolled or will attend, minus estimated financial assistance from other federal, state, and private sources, up to a maximum of $20,500.

Direct Stafford Loans made on or after July 1, 2006, carry a fixed interest rate of 6.8% both for in-school and in-repayment borrowers.

A fee is deducted from the loan proceeds upon disbursement. Loans with a first disbursement on or after July 1, 2010, have a borrower origination fee of 1 percent. The Department of Education offers a 0.5 percent origination fee rebate incentive. Borrowers must make their first twelve payments on time in order to retain the rebate.

Under the *subsidized* Federal Direct Stafford Loan Program, repayment begins six months after your last date of enrollment on at least a half-time basis. Under the *unsubsidized* program, repayment of interest begins within thirty days from disbursement of the loan proceeds, and repayment of the principal begins six months after your last enrollment on at least a half-time basis. Some borrowers may choose to defer interest payments while they are in school. The accrued interest is added to the loan balance when the borrower begins repayment. There are several repayment options.

Federal Perkins Loans. The Federal Perkins Loan is available to students demonstrating financial need and is administered directly by the school. Not all schools have these funds, and some may award them to undergraduates only. Eligibility is determined from the information you provide on the FAFSA. The school will notify you of your eligibility.

Eligible graduate students may borrow up to $6,000 per year, up to a maximum of $40,000, including undergraduate borrowing (even if your previous Perkins Loans have been repaid). The interest rate for Federal Perkins Loans is 5 percent, and no interest accrues while you remain in school at least half-time. There are no guarantee, loan, or disbursement fees. Repayment begins nine months after your last date of enrollment on at least a half-time basis and may extend over a maximum of ten years with no prepayment penalty.

Federal Direct Graduate PLUS Loans. Effective July 1, 2006, graduate and professional students are eligible for Graduate PLUS loans. This program allows students to borrow up to the cost of attendance, less any other aid received. These loans have a fixed interest rate of 7.9 percent, and interest begins to accrue at the time of disbursement. The PLUS loans do involve a credit check; a PLUS borrower may obtain a loan with a cosigner if his or her credit is not good enough. Grad PLUS loans may be deferred while a student in school and for the six months following a drop below half-time enrollment. For more information, contact your college financial aid office.

Deferring Your Federal Loan Repayments. If you borrowed under the Federal Direct Stafford Loan Program, Federal Direct PLUS Loan Program, or the Federal Perkins Loan Program for previous undergraduate or graduate study, your payments may be deferred when you return to graduate school, depending on when you borrowed and under which program.

There are other deferment options available if you are temporarily unable to repay your loan. Information about these deferments is provided at your entrance and exit interviews. If you believe you are eligible for a deferment of your loan payments, you must contact your lender or loan servicer to request a deferment. The deferment must be filed prior to the time your payment is due, and it must be refiled when it expires if you remain eligible for deferment at that time.

SUPPLEMENTAL (PRIVATE) LOANS

Many lending institutions offer supplemental loan programs and other financing plans, such as the ones described here, to students seeking additional assistance in meeting their education expenses. Some loan programs target all types of graduate students; others are designed specifically for business, law, or medical students. In addition, you can use private loans not specifically designed for education to help finance your graduate degree.

If you are considering borrowing through a supplemental or private loan program, you should carefully consider the terms and be sure to "read the fine print." Check with the program sponsor for the most current terms that will be applicable to the amounts you intend to borrow for graduate study. Most supplemental loan programs for graduate study offer unsubsidized, credit-based loans. In general, a credit-ready borrower is one who has a satisfactory credit history or no credit history at all. A creditworthy borrower generally must pass a credit test to be eligible to borrow or act as a cosigner for the loan funds.

Many supplemental loan programs have minimum and maximum annual loan limits. Some offer amounts equal to the cost of attendance minus any other aid you will receive for graduate study. If you are planning to borrow for several years of graduate study, consider whether there is a cumulative or aggregate limit on the amount you may borrow. Often this cumulative or aggregate limit will include any amounts you borrowed and have not repaid for undergraduate or previous graduate study.

The combination of the annual interest rate, loan fees, and the repayment terms you choose will determine how much you will repay over time. Compare these features in combination before you decide which loan program to use. Some loans offer interest rates that are adjusted monthly, some quarterly, some annually. Some offer interest rates that are lower during the in-school, grace, and deferment periods and then increase when you begin repayment. Some programs include a loan "origination" fee, which is usually deducted from the principal amount you receive when the loan is disbursed and must be repaid along with the interest and other principal when you graduate, withdraw from school, or drop below half-time study. Sometimes the loan fees are reduced if you borrow with a qualified cosigner. Some programs allow you to defer interest and/or principal payments while you are enrolled in graduate school. Many programs allow you to capitalize your interest payments; the interest due on your loan is added to the outstanding balance of your loan, so you don't have to repay immediately, but this increases the amount you owe. Other programs allow you to pay the interest as you go, which reduces the amount you later have to repay. The private loan market is very competitive, and your financial aid office can help you evaluate these programs.

Applying for Need-Based Financial Aid

Schools that award federal and institutional financial assistance based on need will require you to complete the FAFSA and, in some cases, an institutional financial aid application.

If you are applying for federal student assistance, you **must** complete the FAFSA. A service of the U.S. Department of Education, the FAFSA is free to all applicants. Most applicants apply online at www.fafsa.ed.gov. Paper applications are available at the financial aid office of your local college.

After your FAFSA information has been processed, you will receive a Student Aid Report (SAR). If you provided an e-mail address on the FAFSA, this will be sent to you electronically; otherwise, it will be mailed to your home address.

Follow the instructions on the SAR if you need to correct information reported on your original application. If your situation changes after you file your FAFSA, contact your financial aid officer to discuss amending your information. You can also appeal your financial aid award if you have extenuating circumstances.

If you would like more information on federal student financial aid, visit the FAFSA Web site or download the most recent version of *Funding Education Beyond High School: The Guide to Federal Student Aid* at http://studentaid.ed.gov/students/publications/student_guide/index.html. This guide is also available in Spanish.

The U.S. Department of Education also has a toll-free number for questions concerning federal student aid programs. The number is 1-800-4-FED AID (1-800-433-3243). If you are hearing impaired, call toll-free, 1-800-730-8913.

Summary

Remember that these are generalized statements about financial assistance at the graduate level. Because each institution allots its aid differently, you should communicate directly with the school and the specific department of interest to you. It is not unusual, for example, to find that an endowment vested within a specific department supports one or more fellowships. You may fit its requirements and specifications precisely.

Accreditation and Accrediting Agencies

Colleges and universities in the United States, and their individual academic and professional programs, are accredited by nongovernmental agencies concerned with monitoring the quality of education in this country. Agencies with both regional and national jurisdictions grant accreditation to institutions as a whole, while specialized bodies acting on a nationwide basis—often national professional associations—grant accreditation to departments and programs in specific fields.

Institutional and specialized accrediting agencies share the same basic concerns: the purpose an academic unit—whether university or program—has set for itself and how well it fulfills that purpose, the adequacy of its financial and other resources, the quality of its academic offerings, and the level of services it provides. Agencies that grant institutional accreditation take a broader view, of course, and examine university-wide or college-wide services with which a specialized agency may not concern itself.

Both types of agencies follow the same general procedures when considering an application for accreditation. The academic unit prepares a self-evaluation, focusing on the concerns mentioned above and usually including an assessment of both its strengths and weaknesses; a team of representatives of the accrediting body reviews this evaluation, visits the campus, and makes its own report; and finally, the accrediting body makes a decision on the application. Often, even when accreditation is granted, the agency makes a recommendation regarding how the institution or program can improve. All institutions and programs are also reviewed every few years to determine whether they continue to meet established standards; if they do not, they may lose their accreditation.

Accrediting agencies themselves are reviewed and evaluated periodically by the U.S. Department of Education and the Council for Higher Education Accreditation (CHEA). Recognized agencies adhere to certain standards and practices, and their authority in matters of accreditation is widely accepted in the educational community.

This does not mean, however, that accreditation is a simple matter, either for schools wishing to become accredited or for students deciding where to apply. Indeed, in certain fields the very meaning and methods of accreditation are the subject of a good deal of debate. For their part, those applying to graduate school should be aware of the safeguards provided by regional accreditation, especially in terms of degree acceptance and institutional longevity. Beyond this, applicants should understand the role that specialized accreditation plays in their field, as this varies considerably from one discipline to another. In certain professional fields, it is necessary to have graduated from a program that is accredited in order to be eligible for a license to practice, and in some fields the federal government also makes this a hiring requirement. In other disciplines, however, accreditation is not as essential, and there can be excellent programs that are not accredited. In fact, some programs choose not to seek accreditation, although most do.

Institutions and programs that present themselves for accreditation are sometimes granted the status of candidate for accreditation, or what is known as "preaccreditation." This may happen, for example, when an academic unit is too new to have met all the requirements for accreditation. Such status signifies initial recognition and indicates that the school or program in question is working to fulfill all requirements; it does not, however, guarantee that accreditation will be granted.

Institutional Accrediting Agencies—Regional

MIDDLE STATES ASSOCIATION OF COLLEGES AND SCHOOLS
Accredits institutions in Delaware, District of Columbia, Maryland, New Jersey, New York, Pennsylvania, Puerto Rico, and the Virgin Islands.
Dr. Elizabeth Sibolski, President
Middle States Commission on Higher Education
3624 Market Street, Second Floor West
Philadelphia, Pennsylvania 19104
Phone: 267-284-5000
Fax: 215-662-5501
E-mail: info@msche.org
Web: www.msche.org

NEW ENGLAND ASSOCIATION OF SCHOOLS AND COLLEGES
Accredits institutions in Connecticut, Maine, Massachusetts, New Hampshire, Rhode Island, and Vermont.
Barbara E. Brittingham, Director
Commission on Institutions of Higher Education
209 Burlington Road, Suite 201
Bedford, Massachusetts 01730-1433
Phone: 781-271-0022
Fax: 781-271-0950
E-mail: kwillis@neasc.org
Web: www.neasc.org

NORTH CENTRAL ASSOCIATION OF COLLEGES AND SCHOOLS
Accredits institutions in Arizona, Arkansas, Colorado, Illinois, Indiana, Iowa, Kansas, Michigan, Minnesota, Missouri, Nebraska, New Mexico, North Dakota, Ohio, Oklahoma, South Dakota, West Virginia, Wisconsin, and Wyoming.
Dr. Sylvia Manning, President
The Higher Learning Commission
230 South LaSalle Street, Suite 7-500
Chicago, Illinois 60604-1413
Phone: 312-263-0456
Fax: 312-263-7462
E-mail: smanning@hlcommission.org
Web: www.ncahlc.org

NORTHWEST COMMISSION ON COLLEGES AND UNIVERSITIES
Accredits institutions in Alaska, Idaho, Montana, Nevada, Oregon, Utah, and Washington.
Dr. Sandra E. Elman, President
8060 165th Avenue, NE, Suite 100
Redmond, Washington 98052
Phone: 425-558-4224
Fax: 425-376-0596
E-mail: selman@nwccu.org
Web: www.nwccu.org

SOUTHERN ASSOCIATION OF COLLEGES AND SCHOOLS
Accredits institutions in Alabama, Florida, Georgia, Kentucky, Louisiana, Mississippi, North Carolina, South Carolina, Tennessee, Texas, and Virginia.
Belle S. Wheelan, President
Commission on Colleges
1866 Southern Lane
Decatur, Georgia 30033-4097
Phone: 404-679-4500
Fax: 404-679-4558
E-mail: questions@sacscoc.org
Web: www.sacscoc.org

WESTERN ASSOCIATION OF SCHOOLS AND COLLEGES
Accredits institutions in California, Guam, and Hawaii.
Ralph A. Wolff, President and Executive Director
Accrediting Commission for Senior Colleges and Universities
985 Atlantic Avenue, Suite 100
Alameda, California 94501
Phone: 510-748-9001
Fax: 510-748-9797
E-mail: www.wascsenior.org/contact
Web: www.wascweb.org/contact

Institutional Accrediting Agencies—Other

ACCREDITING COUNCIL FOR INDEPENDENT COLLEGES AND SCHOOLS
Albert C. Gray, Ph.D., Executive Director and CEO
750 First Street, NE, Suite 980
Washington, DC 20002-4241
Phone: 202-336-6780
Fax: 202-842-2593
E-mail: info@acics.org
Web: www.acics.org

DISTANCE EDUCATION AND TRAINING COUNCIL (DETC)
Accrediting Commission
Michael P. Lambert, Executive Director
1601 18th Street, NW, Suite 2
Washington, DC 20009
Phone: 202-234-5100
Fax: 202-332-1386
E-mail: Brianna@detc.org
Web: www.detc.org

Specialized Accrediting Agencies

[Only *Graduate & Professional Programs: An Overview* of *Peterson's Graduate and Professional Programs* Series includes the complete list of specialized accrediting groups recognized by the U.S. Department of Education and the Council on Higher Education Accreditation (CHEA). The list in this book is abridged.]

ART AND DESIGN
Samuel Hope, Executive Director
Karen P. Moynahan, Associate Director
National Association of Schools of Art and Design (NASAD)
Commission on Accreditation
11250 Roger Bacon Drive, Suite 21
Reston, Virginia 20190-5243
Phone: 703-437-0700
Fax: 703-437-6312
E-mail: info@arts-accredit.org
Web: www.arts-accredit.org

CLINICAL PASTORAL EDUCATION
Teresa E. Snorton, Executive Director
Accreditation Commission
Association for Clinical Pastoral Education, Inc.
1549 Claremont Road, Suite 103
Decatur, Georgia 30033-4611
Phone: 404-320-1472
Fax: 404-320-0849
E-mail: acpe@acpe.edu
Web: www.acpe.edu

DANCE
Samuel Hope, Executive Director
Karen P. Moynahan, Associate Director
National Association of Schools of Dance (NASD)
Commission on Accreditation
11250 Roger Bacon Drive, Suite 21
Reston, Virginia 20190-5248
Phone: 703-437-0700
Fax: 703-437-6312
E-mail: info@arts-accredit.org
Web: www.arts-accredit.org

DIETETICS
Ulric K. Chung, Ph.D., Executive Director
American Dietetic Association
Commission on Accreditation for Dietetics Education (CADE-ADA)
120 South Riverside Plaza, Suite 2000
Chicago, Illinois 60606-6995
Phone: 800-877-1600
Fax: 312-899-4817
E-mail: cade@eatright.org
Web: www.eatright.org/cade

INTERIOR DESIGN
Holly Mattson, Executive Director
Council for Interior Design Accreditation
206 Grandview Avenue, Suite 350
Grand Rapids, Michigan 49503-4014
Phone: 616-458-0400
Fax: 616-458-0460
E-mail: info@accredit-id.org
Web: www.accredit-id.org

JOURNALISM AND MASS COMMUNICATIONS
Susanne Shaw, Executive Director
Accrediting Council on Education in Journalism and Mass Communications (ACEJMC)
School of Journalism
Stauffer-Flint Hall
University of Kansas
1435 Jayhawk Boulevard
Lawrence, Kansas 66045-7575
Phone: 785-864-3973
Fax: 785-864-5225
E-mail: sshaw@ku.edu
Web: www2.ku.edu/~acejmc

LANDSCAPE ARCHITECTURE
Ronald C. Leighton, Executive Director
Landscape Architectural Accreditation Board
American Society of Landscape Architects
636 Eye Street, NW
Washington, DC 20001-3736
Phone: 202-898-2444
Fax: 202-898-1185
E-mail: info@asla.org
Web: www.asla.org

MARRIAGE AND FAMILY THERAPY
Jeff S. Harmon, Director of Accreditation Services
Commission on Accreditation for Marriage and Family Therapy Education
American Association for Marriage and Family Therapy
112 South Alfred Street
Alexandria, Virginia 22314-3061
Phone: 703-838-9808
Fax: 703-838-9805
E-mail: coa@aamft.org
Web: www.aamft.org

MEDICAL ILLUSTRATION
Commission on Accreditation of Allied Health Education Programs (CAAHEP)
Kathleen Megivern, Executive Director
1361 Park Street
Clearwater, Florida 33756
Phone: 727-210-2350
Fax: 727-210-2354
E-mail: mail@caahep.org
Web: www.caahep.org

MUSIC
Samuel Hope, Executive Director
Karen P. Moynahan, Associate Director
National Association of Schools of Music (NASM)
Commission on Accreditation
11250 Roger Bacon Drive, Suite 21
Reston, Virginia 20190-5248
Phone: 703-437-0700
Fax: 703-437-6312
E-mail: info@arts-accredit.org
Web: www.arts-accredit.org

PLANNING
Shonagh Merits, Executive Director
American Institute of Certified Planners/Association of Collegiate Schools of Planning/American Planning Association
Planning Accreditation Board (PAB)
53 W. Jackson Boulevard, Suite 1315
Chicago, Illinois 60604
Phone: 312-334-1271
Fax: 312-334-1273
E-mail: pab@planning.org
Web: www.planningaccreditationboard.org

PSYCHOLOGY AND COUNSELING
Susan Zlotlow, Executive Director
Office of Program Consultation and Accreditation
American Psychological Association
750 First Street, NE
Washington, DC 20002-4242
Phone: 202-336-5979
Fax: 202-336-5978
E-mail: apaaccred@apa.org
Web: www.apa.org/ed/accreditation

Carol L. Bobby, Executive Director
Council for Accreditation of Counseling and Related Educational Programs (CACREP)
1001 North Fairfax Street, Suite 510
Alexandria, Virginia 22314
Phone: 703-535-5990
Fax: 703-739-6209
E-mail: cacrep@cacrep.org
Web: www.cacrep.org

PUBLIC AFFAIRS AND ADMINISTRATION
Crystal Calarusse, Executive Director
Commission on Peer Review and Accreditation
National Association of Schools of Public Affairs and Administration
1029 Vermont Avenue, NW, Suite 1100
Washington, DC 20005
Phone: 202-628-8965
Fax: 202-626-4978
E-mail: copra@naspaa.org
Web: www.naspaa.org

SPEECH-LANGUAGE PATHOLOGY AND AUDIOLOGY
Patrima L. Tice, Director of Credentialing
American Speech-Language-Hearing Association
Council on Academic Accreditation in Audiology and Speech-Language Pathology
2200 Research Boulevard
Rockville, Maryland 20850-3289
Phone: 301-296-5796
Fax: 301-296-8750
E-mail: ptice@asha.org
Web: www.asha.org/academic/accreditation/default.htm

TECHNOLOGY
Michale S. McComis, Ed.D., Executive Director
Accrediting Commission of Career Schools and Colleges
2101 Wilson Boulevard, Suite 302
Arlington, Virginia 22201
Phone: 703-247-4212
Fax: 703-247-4533
E-mail: mccomis@accsc.org
Web: www.accsc.org

THEATER
Samuel Hope, Executive Director
Karen P. Moynahan, Associate Director
National Association of Schools of Theatre
Commission on Accreditation
11250 Roger Bacon Drive, Suite 21
Reston, Virginia 20190
Phone: 703-437-0700
Fax: 703-437-6312
E-mail: info@arts-accredit.org
Web: www.arts-accredit.org

THEOLOGY
Bernard Fryshman, Executive Vice President
Association of Advanced Rabbinical and Talmudic Schools (AARTS)
Accreditation Commission
11 Broadway, Suite 405
New York, New York 10004
Phone: 212-363-1991
Fax: 212-533-5335
E-mail: BFryshman@nyit.edu

Daniel O. Aleshire, Executive Director
Association of Theological Schools in the United States and Canada (ATS)
Commission on Accrediting
10 Summit Park Drive
Pittsburgh, Pennsylvania 15275-1110
Phone: 412-788-6505
Fax: 412-788-6510
E-mail: ats@ats.edu
Web: www.ats.edu

T. Paul Boatner, President
Transnational Association of Christian Colleges and Schools (TRACS)
Accreditation Commission
15935 Forest Road
Forest, Virginia 24551
Phone: 434-525-9539
Fax: 434-525-9538
E-mail: info@tracs.org
Web: www.tracs.org

How to Use These Guides

As you identify the particular programs and institutions that interest you, you can use both the *Graduate & Professional Programs: An Overview* volume and the specialized volumes in the series to obtain detailed information.

- *Graduate Programs in the Physical Sciences, Mathematics, Agricultural Sciences, the Environment & Natural Resources*
- *Graduate Programs in Engineering & Applied Sciences*
- *Graduate Programs the Humanities, Arts & Social Sciences*
- *Graduate Programs in the Biological Sciences*
- *Graduate Programs in Business, Education, Health, Information Studies, Law & Social Work*

Each of the specialized volumes in the series is divided into sections that contain one or more directories devoted to programs in a particular field. If you do not find a directory devoted to your field of interest in a specific volume, consult "Directories and Subject Areas" (located at the end of each volume). After you have identified the correct volume, consult the "Directories and Subject Areas in This Book" index, which shows (as does the more general directory) what directories cover subjects not specifically named in a directory or section title.

Each of the specialized volumes in the series has a number of general directories. These directories have entries for the largest unit at an institution granting graduate degrees in that field. For example, the general Engineering and Applied Sciences directory in the *Graduate Programs in Engineering & Applied Sciences* volume consists of **Profiles** for colleges, schools, and departments of engineering and applied sciences.

General directories are followed by other directories, or sections, that give more detailed information about programs in particular areas of the general field that has been covered. The general Engineering and Applied Sciences directory, in the previous example, is followed by nineteen sections with directories in specific areas of engineering, such as Chemical Engineering, Industrial/Management Engineering, and Mechanical Engineering.

Because of the broad nature of many fields, any system of organization is bound to involve a certain amount of overlap. Environmental studies, for example, is a field whose various aspects are studied in several types of departments and schools. Readers interested in such studies will find information on relevant programs in the *Graduate Programs in the Biological Sciences* volume under Ecology and Environmental Biology; in the *Graduate Programs in the Physical Sciences, Mathematics, Agricultural Sciences, the Environment & Natural Resources* volume under Environmental Management and Policy and Natural Resources; in the *Graduate Programs in Engineering & Applied Sciences* volume under Energy Management and Policy and Environmental Engineering; and in the *Graduate Programs in Business, Education, Health, Information Studies, Law & Social Work* volume under Environmental and Occupational Health. To help you find all of the programs of interest to you, the introduction to each section within the specialized volumes includes, if applicable, a paragraph suggesting other sections and directories with information on related areas of study.

Directory of Institutions with Programs in the Humanities, Arts & Social Sciences

This directory lists institutions in alphabetical order and includes beneath each name the academic fields in which each institution offers graduate programs. The degree level in each field is also indicated, provided that the institution has supplied that information in response to Peterson's Annual Survey of Graduate and Professional Institutions. An M indicates that a master's degree program is offered; a D indicates that a doctoral degree program is offered; a P indicates that the first professional degree is offered; an O signifies that other advanced degrees (e.g., certificates or specialist degrees) are offered; and an *

(asterisk) indicates that a **Close-Up** and/or **Display** is located in this volume. See the index, "Close-Ups and Displays," for the specific page number.

Profiles of Academic and Professional Programs in the Specialized Volumes

Each section of **Profiles** has a table of contents that lists the Program Directories, **Displays**, and **Close-Ups**. Program Directories consist of the **Profiles** of programs in the relevant fields, with **Displays** following if programs have chosen to include them. **Close-Ups,** which are more individualized statements, again if programs have chosen to submit them, are also listed.

The **Profiles** found in the 500 directories in the specialized volumes provide basic data about the graduate units in capsule form for quick reference. To make these directories as useful as possible, **Profiles** are generally listed for an institution's smallest academic unit within a subject area. In other words, if an institution has a College of Liberal Arts that administers many related programs, the **Profile** for the individual program (e.g., Program in History), not the entire College, appears in the directory.

There are some programs that do not fit into any current directory and are not given individual **Profiles**. The directory structure is reviewed annually in order to keep this number to a minimum and to accommodate major trends in graduate education.

The following outline describes the **Profile** information found in the guides and explains how best to use that information. Any item that does not apply to or was not provided by a graduate unit is omitted from its listing. The format of the **Profiles** is constant, making it easy to compare one institution with another and one program with another.

Identifying Information. The institution's name, in boldface type, is followed by a complete listing of the administrative structure for that field of study. (For example, University of Akron, Buchtel College of Arts and Sciences, Department of Theoretical and Applied Mathematics, Program in Mathematics.) The last unit listed is the one to which all information in the **Profile** pertains. The institution's city, state, and zip code follow.

Offerings. Each field of study offered by the unit is listed with all postbaccalaureate degrees awarded. Degrees that are not preceded by a specific concentration are awarded in the general field listed in the unit name. Frequently, fields of study are broken down into subspecializations, and those appear following the degrees awarded; for example, "Offerings in secondary education (M.Ed.), including English education, mathematics education, science education." Students enrolled in the M.Ed. program would be able to specialize in any of the three fields mentioned.

Professional Accreditation. Some **Profiles** indicate whether a program is professionally accredited. Because it is possible for a program to receive or lose professional accreditation at any time, students entering fields in which accreditation is important to a career should verify the status of programs by contacting either the chairperson or the appropriate accrediting association.

Jointly Offered Degrees. Explanatory statements concerning programs that are offered in cooperation with other institutions are included in the list of degrees offered. This occurs most commonly on a regional basis (for example, two state universities offering a cooperative Ph.D. in special education) or where the specialized nature of the institutions encourages joint efforts (a J.D./M.B.A. offered by a law school at an institution with no formal business programs and an institution with a business school but lacking a law school). Only programs that are truly cooperative are listed; those involving only limited course work at another institution are not. Interested students should contact the heads of such units for further information.

Part-Time and Evening/Weekend Programs. When information regarding the availability of part-time or evening/weekend study appears in the **Profile**, it means that students are able to earn a degree exclusively through such study.

Postbaccalaureate Distance Learning Degrees. A postbaccalaureate distance learning degree program signifies that course requirements can be fulfilled with minimal or no on-campus study.

Faculty. Figures on the number of faculty members actively involved with graduate students through teaching or research are separated into full-and part-time as well as men and women whenever the information has been supplied.

Students. Figures for the number of students enrolled in graduate and professional programs pertain to the semester of highest enrollment from the 2010–11 academic year. These figures are broken down into full-and part-time and men and women whenever the data have been supplied. Information on the number of matriculated students enrolled in the unit who are members of a minority group or are international students appears here. The average age of the matriculated students is followed by the number of applicants, the percentage accepted, and the number enrolled for fall 2010.

Degrees Awarded. The number of degrees awarded in the calendar year is listed. Many doctoral programs offer a terminal master's degree if students leave the program after completing only part of the requirements for a doctoral degree; that is indicated here. All degrees are classified into one of four types: master's, doctoral, first professional, and other advanced degrees. A unit may award one or several degrees at a given level; however, the data are only collected by type and may therefore represent several different degree programs.

Degree Requirements. The information in this section is also broken down by type of degree, and all information for a degree level pertains to all degrees of that type unless otherwise specified. Degree requirements are collected in a simplified form to provide some very basic information on the nature of the program and on foreign language, thesis or dissertation, comprehensive exam, and registration requirements. Many units also provide a short list of additional requirements, such as fieldwork or an internship. For complete information on graduation requirements, contact the graduate school or program directly.

Entrance Requirements. Entrance requirements are broken down into the four degree levels of master's, doctoral, first professional, and other advanced degrees. Within each level, information may be provided in two basic categories: entrance exams and other requirements. The entrance exams are identified by the standard acronyms used by the testing agencies, unless they are not well known. Other entrance requirements are quite varied, but they often contain an undergraduate or graduate grade point average (GPA). Unless otherwise stated, the GPA is calculated on a 4.0 scale and is listed as a minimum required for admission. Additional exam requirements/recommendations for international students may be listed here. Application deadlines for domestic and international students, the application fee, and whether electronic applications are accepted may be listed here. Note that the deadline should be used for reference only; these dates are subject to change, and students interested in applying should always contact the graduate unit directly about application procedures and deadlines.

Expenses. The typical cost of study for the 2010–11 academic year is given in two basic categories: tuition and fees. Cost of study may be quite complex at a graduate institution. There are often sliding scales for part-time study, a different cost for first-year students, and other variables that make it impossible to completely cover the cost of study for each graduate program. To provide the most usable information, figures are given for full-time study for a full year where available and for part-time study in terms of a per-unit rate (per credit, per semester hour, etc.). Occasionally, variances may be noted in tuition and fees for reasons such as the type of program, whether courses are taken during the day or evening, whether courses are at the master's or doctoral level, or other institution-specific reasons. Expenses are usually subject to change; for exact costs at any given time, contact your chosen schools and programs directly. Keep in mind that the tuition of Canadian institutions is usually given in Canadian dollars.

Financial Support. This section contains data on the number of awards administered by the institution and given to graduate students during the 2010–11 academic year. The first figure given represents the total number of students receiving financial support enrolled in that unit. If the unit has provided information on graduate appoint-

ments, these are broken down into three major categories: fellowships give money to graduate students to cover the cost of study and living expenses and are not based on a work obligation or research commitment, research assistantships provide stipends to graduate students for assistance in a formal research project with a faculty member, and teaching assistantships provide stipends to graduate students for teaching or for assisting faculty members in teaching undergraduate classes. Within each category, figures are given for the total number of awards, the average yearly amount per award, and whether full or partial tuition reimbursements are awarded. In addition to graduate appointments, the availability of several other financial aid sources is covered in this section. Tuition waivers are routinely part of a graduate appointment, but units sometimes waive part or all of a student's tuition even if a graduate appointment is not available. Federal Work-Study is made available to students who demonstrate need and meet the federal guidelines; this form of aid normally includes 10 or more hours of work per week in an office of the institution. Institutionally sponsored loans are low-interest loans available to graduate students to cover both educational and living expenses. Career-related internships or fieldwork offer money to students who are participating in a formal off-campus research project or practicum. Grants, scholarships, traineeships, unspecified assistantships, and other awards may also be noted. The availability of financial support to part-time students is also indicated here.

Some programs list the financial aid application deadline and the forms that need to be completed for students to be eligible for financial awards. There are two forms: FAFSA, the Free Application for Federal Student Aid, which is required for federal aid, and the CSS PROFILE®.

Faculty Research. Each unit has the opportunity to list several keyword phrases describing the current research involving faculty members and graduate students. Space limitations prevent the unit from listing complete information on all research programs. The total expenditure for funded research from the previous academic year may also be included.

Unit Head and Application Contact. The head of the graduate program for each unit is listed with academic title and telephone and fax numbers and e-mail address if available. In addition to the unit head, many graduate programs list a separate contact for application and admission information, which follows the listing for the unit head. If no unit head or application contact is given, you should contact the overall institution for information on graduate admissions. ✎

Displays and Close-Ups

The **Displays** and **Close-Ups** are supplementary insertions submitted by deans, chairs, and other administrators who wish to offer an additional, more individualized statement to readers. A number of graduate school and program administrators have attached a **Display** ad near the **Profile** listing. Here you will find information that an institution or program wants to emphasize. The **Close-Ups** are by their very nature more expansive and flexible than the **Profiles**, and the administrators who have written them may emphasize different aspects of their programs. All of the **Close-Ups** are organized in the same way (with the exception of a few that describe research and training opportunities instead of degree programs), and in each one you will find information on the same basic topics, such as programs of study, research facilities, tuition and fees, financial aid, and application procedures. If an institution or program has submitted a **Close-Up**, a boldface cross-reference appears below its **Profile**. As with the **Displays**, all of the **Close-Ups** in the guides have been submitted by choice; the absence of a **Display** or **Close-Up** does not reflect any type of editorial judgment on the part of Peterson's, and their presence in the guides should not be taken as an indication of status, quality, or approval. Statements regarding a university's objectives and accomplishments are a reflection of its own beliefs and are not the opinions of the Peterson's editors.

Appendixes

This section contains two appendixes. The first, "Institutional Changes Since the 2011 Edition," lists institutions that have closed, merged, or changed their name or status since the last edition of the guides. The second, "Abbreviations Used in the Guides," gives abbreviations of degree names, along with what those abbreviations stand for. These appendixes are identical in all six volumes of *Peterson's Graduate and Professional Programs*.

Indexes

There are three indexes presented here. The first index, "Close-Ups and Displays," gives page references for all programs that have chosen to place **Close-Ups** and **Displays** in this volume. It is arranged alphabetically by institution; within institutions, the arrangement is alphabetical by subject area. It is not an index to all programs in the book's directories of **Profiles**; readers must refer to the directories themselves for **Profile** information on programs that have not submitted the additional, more individualized statements. The second index, "Directories and Subject Areas in Other Books in This Series", gives book references for the directories in the specialized volumes and also includes cross-references for subject area names not used in the directory structure, for example, "Computing Technology (see Computer Science)." The third index, "Directories and Subject Areas in This Book," gives page references for the directories in this volume and cross-references for subject area names not used in this volume's directory structure.

Data Collection Procedures

The information published in the directories and **Profiles** of all the books is collected through Peterson's Annual Survey of Graduate and Professional Institutions. The survey is sent each spring to nearly 2,400 institutions offering postbaccalaureate degree programs, including accredited institutions in the United States, U.S. territories, and Canada and those institutions outside the United States that are accredited by U.S. accrediting bodies. Deans and other administrators complete these surveys, providing information on programs in the 500 academic and professional fields covered in the guides as well as overall institutional information. While every effort has been made to ensure the accuracy and completeness of the data, information is sometimes unavailable or changes occur after publication deadlines. All usable information received in time for publication has been included. The omission of any particular item from a directory or **Profile** signifies either that the item is not applicable to the institution or program or that information was not available. **Profiles** of programs scheduled to begin during the 2011–12 academic year cannot, obviously, include statistics on enrollment or, in many cases, the number of faculty members. If no usable data were submitted by an institution, its name, address, and program name appear in order to indicate the availability of graduate work.

Criteria for Inclusion in This Guide

To be included in this guide, an institution must have full accreditation or be a candidate for accreditation (preaccreditation) status by an institutional or specialized accrediting body recognized by the U.S. Department of Education or the Council for Higher Education Accreditation (CHEA). Institutional accrediting bodies, which review each institution as a whole, include the six regional associations of schools and colleges (Middle States, New England, North Central, Northwest, Southern, and Western), each of which is responsible for a specified portion of the United States and its territories. Other institutional accrediting bodies are national in scope and accredit specific kinds of institutions (e.g., Bible colleges, independent colleges, and rabbinical and Talmudic schools). Program registration by the New York State Board of Regents is considered to be the equivalent of institutional accreditation, since the board requires that all programs offered by an institution meet its standards before recognition is granted. A Canadian institution must be chartered and authorized to grant degrees by the provincial government, affiliated with a chartered institution, or accredited by a recognized U.S. accrediting body. This guide also includes institutions outside the United States that are accredited by these U.S. accrediting bodies. There are recognized specialized or professional accrediting bodies in more than fifty different fields, each of which is authorized to accredit institutions or specific programs in its particular field. For specialized institutions that offer programs in one field only, we designate this to be the equivalent of institutional accreditation. A full explanation of the accrediting process and complete information on recognized institutional (regional and national) and specialized accrediting bodies can be found online at www.chea.org or at www.ed.gov/admins/finaid/accred/index.html.

NOTICE: Certain portions of or information contained in this book have been submitted and paid for by the educational institution identified, and such institutions take full responsibility for the accuracy, timeliness, completeness and functionality of such contents. Such portions or information include (i) each display ad that comprises a half page of information covering a single educational institution or program and (ii) each two-page description or Close-Up of a graduate school or program that appear in the different sections of this guide. The "Close-Ups and Displays" are listed in various sections throughout the book.

DIRECTORY OF INSTITUTIONS WITH PROGRAMS IN HUMANITIES, ARTS & SOCIAL SCIENCES

ABILENE CHRISTIAN UNIVERSITY

Clinical Psychology	M
Communication— General	M
Conflict Resolution and Mediation/Peace Studies	M,O
Counseling Psychology	M
English	M
Liberal Studies	M
Marriage and Family Therapy	M
Missions and Missiology	M
Pastoral Ministry and Counseling	M,D
Psychology—General	M
Rhetoric	M
School Psychology	O
Theology	P,M
Writing	M

ACADEMY OF ART UNIVERSITY

Applied Arts and Design—General	M
Architecture	M
Art/Fine Arts	M
Clothing and Textiles	M
Computer Art and Design	M
Film, Television, and Video Production	M
Graphic Design	M
Illustration	M
Industrial Design	M
Interior Design	M
Internet and Interactive Multimedia	M
Music	M
Photography	M
Textile Design	M

ACADIA UNIVERSITY

Clinical Psychology	M
English	M
Geographic Information Systems	M
Political Science	M
Psychology—General	M
Sociology	M
Theology	P,M,D

ADAMS STATE COLLEGE

Art/Fine Arts	M
History	M

ADELPHI UNIVERSITY

Art/Fine Arts	M*
Clinical Psychology	D
Counseling Psychology	M
Emergency Management	O
Gerontology	M,O
Psychology—General	M,D*
Public Administration	O
School Psychology	M
Writing	M*

ADLER GRADUATE SCHOOL

Art Therapy	M,O
Clinical Psychology	M,O
Counseling Psychology	M,O
Marriage and Family Therapy	M,O
Psychoanalysis and Psychotherapy	M,O

ADLER SCHOOL OF PROFESSIONAL PSYCHOLOGY

Addictions/Substance Abuse Counseling	M,D,O
Art Therapy	M,D,O

Clinical Psychology	M,D,O
Counseling Psychology	M,D,O
Criminal Justice and Criminology	M,D,O
Forensic Psychology	M,D,O
Gerontology	M,D,O
Health Psychology	M,D,O
Industrial and Organizational Psychology	M,D,O
Marriage and Family Therapy	M,D,O
Psychoanalysis and Psychotherapy	M,D,O
Psychology—General	M,D,O*
Rehabilitation Counseling	M,D,O
Social Psychology	M,D,O
Sport Psychology	M,D,O

ALABAMA AGRICULTURAL AND MECHANICAL UNIVERSITY

Agricultural Economics and Agribusiness	M
Clinical Psychology	M,O
Counseling Psychology	M,O
Family and Consumer Sciences-General	M,D
Music	M
Psychology—General	M,O
School Psychology	M,O
Urban and Regional Planning	M

ALABAMA STATE UNIVERSITY

Music	M

ALASKA PACIFIC UNIVERSITY

Counseling Psychology	M
Interdisciplinary Studies	M
Liberal Studies	M

ALBANY STATE UNIVERSITY

Criminal Justice and Criminology	M
Economic Development	M
Economics	M
Forensic Sciences	M
Public Administration	M
Public Policy	M

ALBERTUS MAGNUS COLLEGE

Art Therapy	M
Liberal Studies	M
Writing	M

ALCORN STATE UNIVERSITY

Agricultural Economics and Agribusiness	M

ALFRED UNIVERSITY

Applied Arts and Design—General	M
Art/Fine Arts	M,D
Computer Art and Design	M
Internet and Interactive Multimedia	M
School Psychology	M,D,O

ALLIANT INTERNATIONAL UNIVERSITY–FRESNO

Clinical Psychology	D
Forensic Psychology	D
Industrial and Organizational Psychology	M,D
Psychology—General	D

ALLIANT INTERNATIONAL UNIVERSITY–IRVINE

Forensic Psychology	D

Forensic Sciences	D
Marriage and Family Therapy	M,D
School Psychology	M,D,O

ALLIANT INTERNATIONAL UNIVERSITY–LOS ANGELES

Addictions/Substance Abuse Counseling	M
Clinical Psychology	D
Forensic Psychology	D
Gerontology	M
Industrial and Organizational Psychology	M,D
Marriage and Family Therapy	M
Psychology—General	M,D
School Psychology	M,D,O

ALLIANT INTERNATIONAL UNIVERSITY–MÉXICO CITY

Counseling Psychology	M
International Affairs	M

ALLIANT INTERNATIONAL UNIVERSITY–SACRAMENTO

Clinical Psychology	D
Industrial and Organizational Psychology	D
Marriage and Family Therapy	M
Psychology—General	M,D

ALLIANT INTERNATIONAL UNIVERSITY–SAN DIEGO

Clinical Psychology	M,D
Industrial and Organizational Psychology	M,D
International Affairs	M
Marriage and Family Therapy	M,D
Psychology—General	M,D
School Psychology	M,D,O

ALLIANT INTERNATIONAL UNIVERSITY–SAN FRANCISCO

Clinical Psychology	D,O
Industrial and Organizational Psychology	M,D
Psychology—General	M,D,O
School Psychology	M,D,O

ALVERNIA UNIVERSITY

Liberal Studies	M
Social Psychology	M

AMBERTON UNIVERSITY

Counseling Psychology	M
Interdisciplinary Studies	M

AMBROSE UNIVERSITY COLLEGE

Cultural Studies	P,M,O
Missions and Missiology	P,M,O
Religion	P,M,O
Theology	P,M,O

AMERICAN BAPTIST SEMINARY OF THE WEST

Pastoral Ministry and Counseling	P,M
Theology	P,M

AMERICAN CONSERVATORY THEATER

Theater	M,O

AMERICAN FILM INSTITUTE CONSERVATORY

Film, Television, and Video Production	M

AMERICAN GRADUATE SCHOOL IN PARIS

International Affairs	M,D

AMERICAN INTERCONTINENTAL UNIVERSITY ONLINE

Industrial and Organizational Psychology	M

AMERICAN INTERNATIONAL COLLEGE

Clinical Psychology	M
Corporate and Organizational Communication	M
Forensic Psychology	M
Psychology—General	M,D
Public Administration	M

AMERICAN JEWISH UNIVERSITY

Jewish Studies	M
Theology	M

AMERICAN PUBLIC UNIVERSITY SYSTEM

Conflict Resolution and Mediation/Peace Studies	M
Criminal Justice and Criminology	M
Emergency Management	M
History	M
Homeland Security	M
Humanities	M
International Affairs	M
Military and Defense Studies	M
National Security	M
Political Science	M
Psychology—General	M
Public Administration	M

AMERICAN UNIVERSITY

American Studies	M,D,O
Anthropology	M,D,O
Applied Economics	M,D,O
Applied Social Research	M,O
Art History	M
Art/Fine Arts	M
Arts Administration	M,O
Broadcast Journalism	M
Clinical Psychology	M,D
Communication— General	M,D
Comparative Literature	M
Conflict Resolution and Mediation/Peace Studies	M,D,O
Criminal Justice and Criminology	M,D
Cultural Studies	M,D,O
Economics	M,D,O
Ethics	M,D,O
Experimental Psychology	M,D
Film, Television, and Video Production	M
French	M,O
History	M,D
Interdisciplinary Studies	M
International Affairs	M,D,O
International Development	M,D,O
Journalism	M

Latin American Studies — M,O
Mass Communication — M,D,O
Media Studies — M,D
Philosophy — M
Political Science — M,D,O
Psychology—General — M,D
Public Administration — M,D,O
Public Affairs — M
Public Policy — M
Russian — M,O
Social Psychology — M,D
Sociology — M,O
Spanish — M,O
Sustainable
  Development — M,D,O
Translation and
  Interpretation — M,O
Western European
  Studies — M,D,O
Writing — M

THE AMERICAN UNIVERSITY IN CAIRO

Anthropology — M
Broadcast Journalism — M
Communication—
  General — M
Comparative Literature — M
Demography and
  Population Studies — M,O
Economics — M
English — M
Gender Studies — M,O
Journalism — M
Mass Communication — M
Near and Middle
  Eastern Languages — M,O
Near and Middle
  Eastern Studies — M,O
Political Science — M
Public Administration — M,O
Public Policy — M,O
Sociology — M
Women's Studies — M,O

THE AMERICAN UNIVERSITY OF ATHENS

Corporate and
  Organizational
  Communication — M
Political Science — M

AMERICAN UNIVERSITY OF BEIRUT

Agricultural Economics
  and Agribusiness — M
Anthropology — M
Archaeology — M
Economics — M
English — M
History — M
Near and Middle
  Eastern Languages — M
Near and Middle
  Eastern Studies — M
Philosophy — M
Political Science — M
Psychology—General — M
Public Administration — M
Sociology — M
Urban and Regional
  Planning — M,D
Urban Design — M,D

THE AMERICAN UNIVERSITY OF PARIS

Communication—
  General — M
Conflict Resolution and
  Mediation/Peace
  Studies — M
Cultural Studies — M
International Affairs — M

Near and Middle
  Eastern Studies — M
Public Policy — M

AMERICAN UNIVERSITY OF PUERTO RICO

Art History — M,O
Criminal Justice and
  Criminology — M

AMERICAN UNIVERSITY OF SHARJAH

Public Administration — M
Translation and
  Interpretation — M
Urban and Regional
  Planning — M

AMRIDGE UNIVERSITY

Counseling Psychology — P,M,D
Marriage and Family
  Therapy — P,M,D
Pastoral Ministry and
  Counseling — P,M,D
Religion — P,M,D
Theology — P,M,D

ANDERSON UNIVERSITY (IN)

Missions and Missiology — P,M,D
Theology — P,M,D

ANDERSON UNIVERSITY (SC)

Criminal Justice and
  Criminology — M
Pastoral Ministry and
  Counseling — M

ANDOVER NEWTON THEOLOGICAL SCHOOL

Theology — P,M,D

ANDREW JACKSON UNIVERSITY

Criminal Justice and
  Criminology — M
Public Administration — M

ANDREWS UNIVERSITY

Architecture — M
Communication—
  General — M
Counseling Psychology — D
Developmental
  Psychology — M,D
Economics — M
English — M
History — M
International
  Development — M
Music — M
Pastoral Ministry and
  Counseling — P,M,D,O
Psychology—General — M,D,O
School Psychology — M,O
Social Psychology — M
Theology — P,M,D,O

ANGELO STATE UNIVERSITY

Applied Psychology — M
Communication—
  General — M
Counseling Psychology — M
English — M
History — M
Industrial and
  Organizational
  Psychology — M
Interdisciplinary Studies — M
Journalism — M
Psychology—General — M
Public Administration — M

ANNA MARIA COLLEGE

Art/Fine Arts — M,O
Counseling Psychology — M
Criminal Justice and
  Criminology — M
Emergency
  Management — M,O
Pastoral Ministry and
  Counseling — M
Public Administration — M

ANTIOCH UNIVERSITY LOS ANGELES

Clinical Psychology — M
Psychology—General — M
Writing — M,O

ANTIOCH UNIVERSITY MIDWEST

Art/Fine Arts — M
Comparative Literature — M
Conflict Resolution and
  Mediation/Peace
  Studies — M
Counseling Psychology — M
Film, Television, and
  Video Production — M
Liberal Studies — M
Psychology—General — M
Theater — M
Writing — M

ANTIOCH UNIVERSITY NEW ENGLAND

Applied Psychology — M,D,O
Clinical Psychology — M,D
Counseling Psychology — M
Interdisciplinary Studies — M
Marriage and Family
  Therapy — M,D
Therapies—Dance,
  Drama, and Music — M

ANTIOCH UNIVERSITY SANTA BARBARA

Clinical Psychology — D
Psychology—General — M

ANTIOCH UNIVERSITY SEATTLE

Corporate and
  Organizational
  Communication — M
Industrial and
  Organizational
  Psychology — M
Psychology—General — M,D

APEX SCHOOL OF THEOLOGY

Theology — P,M,D

APPALACHIAN BIBLE COLLEGE

Pastoral Ministry and
  Counseling — M

APPALACHIAN STATE UNIVERSITY

American Studies — M
Clinical Psychology — M,O
Counseling Psychology — M
Criminal Justice and
  Criminology — M
Cultural Studies — M
English — M
Experimental
  Psychology — M,O
Geographic Information
  Systems — M
Geography — M
Health Psychology — M,O
History — M
Industrial and
  Organizational
  Psychology — M,O
International Affairs — M

Marriage and Family
  Therapy — M
Music — M
Political Science — M
Psychology—General — M,O
Public Administration — M
Public History — M
Romance Languages — M
School Psychology — M
Sustainable
  Development — M
Therapies—Dance,
  Drama, and Music — M

AQUINAS INSTITUTE OF THEOLOGY

Pastoral Ministry and
  Counseling — P,M,D,O
Theology — P,M,D,O

ARCADIA UNIVERSITY

Child Development — M,D,O
Conflict Resolution and
  Mediation/Peace
  Studies — M*
English — M
Forensic Sciences — M*
Genetic Counseling — M
Humanities — M
Psychology—General — M,D,O
School Psychology — M
Social Psychology — M
Theater — M,D,O

ARGOSY UNIVERSITY, ATLANTA

Clinical Psychology — M,D,O
Forensic Psychology — M,D,O
Health Psychology — M,D,O
Industrial and
  Organizational
  Psychology — M,D,O
Marriage and Family
  Therapy — M,D,O
Psychology—General — M,D,O*
Social Psychology — M,D,O
Sport Psychology — M,D,O

ARGOSY UNIVERSITY, CHICAGO

Clinical Psychology — M,D*
Counseling Psychology — D
Forensic Psychology — D
Health Psychology — D
Human Development — D
Industrial and
  Organizational
  Psychology — M,D
Marriage and Family
  Therapy — D
Psychoanalysis and
  Psychotherapy — D
Psychology—General — M,D
Public Administration — M,D
Social Psychology — M,D

ARGOSY UNIVERSITY, DALLAS

Clinical Psychology — M,D*
Forensic Psychology — M
Industrial and
  Organizational
  Psychology — M
Psychology—General — M,D
Public Administration — M,D,O
School Psychology — M,D
Social Psychology — M

ARGOSY UNIVERSITY, DENVER

Clinical Psychology — M,D
Counseling Psychology — M,D
Forensic Psychology — M,D
Industrial and
  Organizational
  Psychology — M,D

Marriage and Family Therapy	M,D
Psychology—General	M,D
Public Administration	M,D
Social Psychology	M,D*

ARGOSY UNIVERSITY, HAWAI'I

Addictions/Substance Abuse Counseling	O
Clinical Psychology	M,D,O
Counseling Psychology	D
Forensic Psychology	M
Marriage and Family Therapy	M
Psychology—General	M,D,O*
School Psychology	M

ARGOSY UNIVERSITY, INLAND EMPIRE

Clinical Psychology	M,D
Counseling Psychology	M,D
Forensic Psychology	M,D
Industrial and Organizational Psychology	M,D
Marriage and Family Therapy	M,D
Psychology—General	M,D*
Public Administration	M,D
Sport Psychology	M,D

ARGOSY UNIVERSITY, LOS ANGELES

Clinical Psychology	M,D*
Counseling Psychology	M,D
Forensic Psychology	M,D
Marriage and Family Therapy	M,D
Psychology—General	M,D
Public Administration	M,D

ARGOSY UNIVERSITY, NASHVILLE

Counseling Psychology	M,D*
Psychology—General	M,D

ARGOSY UNIVERSITY, ORANGE COUNTY

Clinical Psychology	M,D
Counseling Psychology	M,D
Forensic Psychology	M
Marriage and Family Therapy	M,D
Psychology—General	M,D*
Public Administration	M,D,O
Sport Psychology	M

ARGOSY UNIVERSITY, PHOENIX

Clinical Psychology	M,D
Counseling Psychology	M
Forensic Psychology	M
Industrial and Organizational Psychology	M
Psychology—General	M,D*
Public Administration	M,D
School Psychology	M,D
Sport Psychology	M,D

ARGOSY UNIVERSITY, SALT LAKE CITY

Counseling Psychology	M,D
Forensic Psychology	M,D
Marriage and Family Therapy	M,D
Psychology—General	M,D*
Public Administration	M,D

ARGOSY UNIVERSITY, SAN DIEGO

Clinical Psychology	M,D

Counseling Psychology	M,D*
Forensic Psychology	M,D
Marriage and Family Therapy	M,D
Psychology—General	M,D
Public Administration	M,D

ARGOSY UNIVERSITY, SAN FRANCISCO BAY AREA

Clinical Psychology	M,D
Counseling Psychology	M,D
Forensic Psychology	M
Psychology—General	M,D*
Public Administration	M,D
Sport Psychology	M,D

ARGOSY UNIVERSITY, SARASOTA

Counseling Psychology	M,D
Forensic Psychology	M,D
Marriage and Family Therapy	M,D
Pastoral Ministry and Counseling	M,D
Psychology—General	M,D*
Public Administration	M,D,O
School Psychology	M,D,O
Social Psychology	M,D,O

ARGOSY UNIVERSITY, SCHAUMBURG

Clinical Psychology	M,D,O*
Corporate and Organizational Communication	M,D,O
Counseling Psychology	M,D,O
Forensic Psychology	M,D,O
Health Psychology	M,D,O
Industrial and Organizational Psychology	M,D,O
Marriage and Family Therapy	M,D,O
Psychology—General	M,D,O
Public Administration	M,D,O
Social Psychology	M,D,O

ARGOSY UNIVERSITY, SEATTLE

Clinical Psychology	M,D,O*
Counseling Psychology	M,D
Psychology—General	M,D,O
Public Administration	M,D

ARGOSY UNIVERSITY, TAMPA

Clinical Psychology	M,D
Counseling Psychology	M,D
Industrial and Organizational Psychology	M,D
Marriage and Family Therapy	M,D
Psychology—General	M,D*
Public Administration	M,D

ARGOSY UNIVERSITY, TWIN CITIES

Clinical Psychology	M,D,O
Forensic Psychology	M,D,O
Health Psychology	M,D,O
Industrial and Organizational Psychology	M,D,O
Marriage and Family Therapy	M,D,O
Psychology—General	M,D,O*
Public Administration	M,D

ARGOSY UNIVERSITY, WASHINGTON DC

Clinical Psychology	M,D*
Counseling Psychology	M,D
Forensic Psychology	M,D

Health Psychology	M,D
Marriage and Family Therapy	M,D
Psychology—General	M,D
Public Administration	M,D,O
Social Psychology	M,D

ARIZONA STATE UNIVERSITY

African-American Studies	M,D,O
Agricultural Economics and Agribusiness	M,D
Anthropology	M,D,O
Applied Psychology	M
Archaeology	M,D,O
Architectural History	D
Architecture	M,D
Art History	M,D
Art/Fine Arts	M,D
Building Science	M,D
Child and Family Studies	M,D
Chinese	M,D
Clinical Psychology	D
Cognitive Sciences	M,D
Communication—General	M,D
Comparative Literature	M,D,O
Counseling Psychology	D
Criminal Justice and Criminology	M,D
Cultural Studies	M,D
Dance	M
Developmental Psychology	D
Economics	D
English	M,D,O
Environmental Design	D
Ethics	M,D
Film, Television, and Video Production	M
French	M
Gender Studies	M,D,O
Geographic Information Systems	M,D,O
Geography	M,D,O
German	M
Gerontology	M,D,O
History of Science and Technology	D
History	M,D,O
Human Development	M,D
Interdisciplinary Studies	M
Interior Design	M,D
Japanese	M
Journalism	M,D
Landscape Architecture	M,D
Latin American Studies	M,D,O
Liberal Studies	M
Linguistics	M,D,O
Marriage and Family Therapy	M,D
Mass Communication	M,D
Media Studies	M,D
Medieval and Renaissance Studies	M,D,O
Museum Studies	M,D,O
Music	M,D
Philosophy	M,D,O
Political Science	M,D
Psychology—General	M,D
Public Affairs	M,D
Public History	M,D,O
Public Policy	P,M,D
Publishing	M,D,O
Religion	M,D,O
Social Psychology	D
Sociology	M,D
Spanish	M,D
Sustainable Development	M,D,O
Theater	M,D

Therapies—Dance, Drama, and Music	M,D
Urban and Regional Planning	M,D,O
Urban Design	M,D
Writing	M

ARKANSAS STATE UNIVERSITY

Art/Fine Arts	M
Communication—General	M,O
Counseling Psychology	M,O
Criminal Justice and Criminology	M,O
English	M,O
Gerontology	M,O
Health Communication	M,O
Historic Preservation	M,D
History	M,O
Journalism	M
Media Studies	M
Music	M,O
Political Science	M,O
Public Administration	M,O
Rehabilitation Counseling	M,O
School Psychology	M,O
Sociology	M,O
Speech and Interpersonal Communication	M,O
Theater	M,O

ARKANSAS TECH UNIVERSITY

Art/Fine Arts	M
Communication—General	M
Emergency Management	M
English	M
History	M
Journalism	M
Psychology—General	M
Social Sciences	M
Spanish	M

ARMSTRONG ATLANTIC STATE UNIVERSITY

Criminal Justice and Criminology	M
History	M
Liberal Studies	M

ART CENTER COLLEGE OF DESIGN

Applied Arts and Design—General	M*
Art/Fine Arts	M
Computer Art and Design	M
Environmental Design	M
Film, Television, and Video Production	M
Industrial Design	M

THE ART INSTITUTE OF BOSTON AT LESLEY UNIVERSITY

Art/Fine Arts	M

THE ART INSTITUTE OF CALIFORNIA–SAN FRANCISCO

Art/Fine Arts	M
Film, Television, and Video Production	M

ASBURY THEOLOGICAL SEMINARY

Missions and Missiology	M,D,O
Pastoral Ministry and Counseling	M,D,O
Theology	M,D,O

*M—master's degree; P—first professional degree; D—doctorate; O—other advanced degree; *—Close-Up and / or Display*

ASBURY UNIVERSITY

Child and Family Studies	M
Classics	M
English	M
French	M
Spanish	M
Writing	M

ASHLAND THEOLOGICAL SEMINARY

History	P,M,D,O
Pastoral Ministry and Counseling	P,M,D,O
Theology	P,M,D,O

ASHLAND UNIVERSITY

History	M
Political Science	M
Writing	M

ASHWORTH COLLEGE

Criminal Justice and Criminology	M

ASSEMBLIES OF GOD THEOLOGICAL SEMINARY

Cultural Studies	P,M,D
Missions and Missiology	P,M,D
Pastoral Ministry and Counseling	P,M,D
Theology	P,M,D

ASSOCIATED MENNONITE BIBLICAL SEMINARY

Conflict Resolution and Mediation/Peace Studies	P,M,O
Missions and Missiology	P,M,O
Theology	P,M,O

ASSUMPTION COLLEGE

Child and Family Studies	M,O
Counseling Psychology	M,O
Economics	M,O
Psychology—General	M,O
Rehabilitation Counseling	M,O
School Psychology	M,O

ATHABASCA UNIVERSITY

Applied Psychology	M,O
Art Therapy	M,O
Counseling Psychology	M,O
Cultural Studies	M
Interdisciplinary Studies	M
International Development	M

THE ATHENAEUM OF OHIO

Pastoral Ministry and Counseling	P,M,O
Theology	P,M,O

ATLANTIC COLLEGE

Graphic Design	M

ATLANTIC SCHOOL OF THEOLOGY

Pastoral Ministry and Counseling	P,M,O
Theology	P,M,O

ATLANTIC UNIVERSITY

Transpersonal and Humanistic Psychology	M

A.T. STILL UNIVERSITY OF HEALTH SCIENCES

Gerontology	M,D

AUBURN UNIVERSITY

Agricultural Economics and Agribusiness	M,D
Applied Behavior Analysis	M,D
Applied Economics	M,D
Architecture	M
Building Science	M
Child and Family Studies	M,D
Clothing and Textiles	M
Communication—General	M
Economics	M
English	M,D
Experimental Psychology	M,D
Geography	M
History	M,D
Human Development	M,D
Industrial and Organizational Psychology	M,D
Industrial Design	M
Landscape Architecture	M
Mass Communication	M
Political Science	M,D
Psychology—General	M,D
Public Administration	M,D
Rehabilitation Counseling	M,D
Rural Sociology	M
Sociology	M
Spanish	M
Urban and Regional Planning	M

AUBURN UNIVERSITY MONTGOMERY

Criminal Justice and Criminology	M
Liberal Studies	M
Political Science	M,D
Psychology—General	M
Public Administration	M,D

AUGUSTA STATE UNIVERSITY

Political Science	M
Psychology—General	M

AURORA UNIVERSITY

Criminal Justice and Criminology	M,D

AUSTIN COLLEGE

Theater	M

AUSTIN GRADUATE SCHOOL OF THEOLOGY

Theology	M

AUSTIN PEAY STATE UNIVERSITY

Communication—General	M
English	M
Military and Defense Studies	M
Music	M
Psychology—General	M,O

AUSTIN PRESBYTERIAN THEOLOGICAL SEMINARY

Pastoral Ministry and Counseling	P,M,D
Theology	P,M,D

AVE MARIA UNIVERSITY

Pastoral Ministry and Counseling	M,D
Theology	M,D

AVILA UNIVERSITY

Counseling Psychology	M
Psychology—General	M

AZUSA PACIFIC UNIVERSITY

Art/Fine Arts	M
Clinical Psychology	M,D
Ethics	M
International Affairs	M
Marriage and Family Therapy	M,D
Music	M
Pastoral Ministry and Counseling	P,M
Psychology—General	M,D
Public Administration	M
School Psychology	M
Theology	M,D
Urban Studies	M

BABEL UNIVERSITY SCHOOL OF TRANSLATION

Translation and Interpretation	M

BAKER UNIVERSITY

Conflict Resolution and Mediation/Peace Studies	M
Liberal Studies	M

BAKKE GRADUATE UNIVERSITY

Pastoral Ministry and Counseling	M,D

BALL STATE UNIVERSITY

Anthropology	M
Applied Behavior Analysis	M,D,O
Architecture	M
Art/Fine Arts	M
Clinical Psychology	M
Cognitive Sciences	M
Communication—General	M
Counseling Psychology	M,D
Criminal Justice and Criminology	M
English	M,D
Family and Consumer Sciences-General	M
Geography	M
Gerontology	M
Historic Preservation	M
History	M
Journalism	M
Landscape Architecture	M
Linguistics	M,D
Political Science	M
Psychology—General	M
Public Administration	M
Rhetoric	M
School Psychology	M,D,O
Social Psychology	M
Sociology	M
Speech and Interpersonal Communication	M
Urban and Regional Planning	M
Urban Design	M
Writing	M,D

BANGOR THEOLOGICAL SEMINARY

Theology	P,M,D

BANK STREET COLLEGE OF EDUCATION

Child and Family Studies	M

BAPTIST BIBLE COLLEGE

Cultural Studies	P,M
Pastoral Ministry and Counseling	P,M
Theology	P,M

BAPTIST BIBLE COLLEGE OF PENNSYLVANIA

Missions and Missiology	P,M,D
Pastoral Ministry and Counseling	P,M,D
Religion	P,M,D
Theology	P,M,D

BAPTIST MISSIONARY ASSOCIATION THEOLOGICAL SEMINARY

Theology	P,M

BAPTIST THEOLOGICAL SEMINARY AT RICHMOND

Pastoral Ministry and Counseling	P,M,D
Religion	P,M,D
Theology	P,M,D

BARD COLLEGE

Art/Fine Arts	M
Museum Studies	M
Music	M
Photography	M

BARD GRADUATE CENTER: DECORATIVE ARTS, DESIGN HISTORY, MATERIAL CULTURE

Art History	M,D*
Decorative Arts	M,D

BARRY UNIVERSITY

Art/Fine Arts	M
Clinical Psychology	M,O
Communication—General	M,O
Corporate and Organizational Communication	M,O
Liberal Studies	M
Marriage and Family Therapy	M,O
Pastoral Ministry and Counseling	M,D
Photography	M
Psychology—General	M,O*
Public Administration	M
Rehabilitation Counseling	M,O
School Psychology	M,O
Sport Psychology	M
Theology	M,D

BASTYR UNIVERSITY

Health Psychology	M

BAYAMÓN CENTRAL UNIVERSITY

Industrial and Organizational Psychology	M
Marriage and Family Therapy	M,O
Rehabilitation Counseling	M,O

BAYLOR UNIVERSITY

American Studies	M
Clinical Psychology	M,D
Communication—General	M
Economics	M
English	M,D
History	M
Interdisciplinary Studies	M,D
International Affairs	M,D

Journalism	M
Museum Studies	M
Music	M
Philosophy	M,D
Political Science	M,D
Psychology—General	M,D*
Public Administration	M,D
Public Policy	M,D
Religion	M,D
Sociology	M,D
Spanish	M
Theater	M
Theology	P,M,D

BELHAVEN UNIVERSITY (MS)

Public Administration	M

BELLARMINE UNIVERSITY

Communication— General	M
Religion	M

BELLEVUE UNIVERSITY

Criminal Justice and Criminology	M,D
Public Administration	M,D

BELMONT UNIVERSITY

English	M
Music	M
Writing	M

BEMIDJI STATE UNIVERSITY

Counseling Psychology	M
English	M

BENEDICTINE UNIVERSITY

Clinical Psychology	M
Emergency Management	M

BENNINGTON COLLEGE

Dance	M
English	M
French	M
Music	M
Spanish	M
Theater	M
Writing	M

BERNARD M. BARUCH COLLEGE OF THE CITY UNIVERSITY OF NEW YORK

Corporate and Organizational Communication	M
Economics	M
Industrial and Labor Relations	M
Industrial and Organizational Psychology	M,D,O
Public Administration	M
Public Policy	M

BETHANY THEOLOGICAL SEMINARY

Conflict Resolution and Mediation/Peace Studies	P,M,O
Pastoral Ministry and Counseling	P,M,O
Religion	P,M,O
Theology	P,M,O

BETHANY UNIVERSITY

Clinical Psychology	M

BETHEL COLLEGE

Pastoral Ministry and Counseling	M
Theology	M

BETHEL SEMINARY

Classics	P,M,D,O
Marriage and Family Therapy	P,M,D,O

Missions and Missiology	P,M,D,O
Near and Middle Eastern Languages	P,M,D,O
Pastoral Ministry and Counseling	P,M,D,O
Religion	P,M,D,O
Theology	P,M,D,O

BETHEL UNIVERSITY (MN)

Communication— General	M,O
Counseling Psychology	M
Developmental Psychology	M
Gerontology	M
Social Psychology	M

BETHEL UNIVERSITY (TN)

Conflict Resolution and Mediation/Peace Studies	M

BETHESDA CHRISTIAN UNIVERSITY

Music	P,M
Religion	P,M
Theology	P,M

BETH HAMEDRASH SHAAREI YOSHER INSTITUTE

Theology	

BETH HATALMUD RABBINICAL COLLEGE

Theology	

BETH MEDRASH GOVOHA

Theology	

BETHUNE-COOKMAN UNIVERSITY

Theology	M

BEULAH HEIGHTS UNIVERSITY

Religion	M

BEXLEY HALL EPISCOPAL SEMINARY

Theology	P,M

BIBLICAL THEOLOGICAL SEMINARY

Missions and Missiology	P,M,D,O
Pastoral Ministry and Counseling	P,M,D,O
Theology	P,M,D,O

BIOLA UNIVERSITY

Anthropology	M,D,O
Cultural Studies	M,D,O
Ethics	P,M,D
Linguistics	M,D,O
Missions and Missiology	M,D,O
Psychology—General	D
Religion	P,M,D
Theology	P,M,D

BLESSED JOHN XXIII NATIONAL SEMINARY

Theology	P

BOB JONES UNIVERSITY

Art/Fine Arts	P,M,D,O
English	P,M,D,O
Film, Television, and Video Production	P,M,D,O
Graphic Design	P,M,D,O
History	P,M,D,O
Illustration	P,M,D,O
Journalism	P,M,D,O
Media Studies	P,M,D,O

Music	P,M,D,O
Pastoral Ministry and Counseling	P,M,D,O
Religion	P,M,D,O
Rhetoric	P,M,D,O
Speech and Interpersonal Communication	P,M,D,O
Theater	P,M,D,O
Theology	P,M,D,O

BOISE STATE UNIVERSITY

Art/Fine Arts	M
Communication— General	M
Criminal Justice and Criminology	M
English	M
History	M
Interdisciplinary Studies	M
Music	M
Public Administration	M
Public Policy	M
Technical Communication	M
Writing	M

BORICUA COLLEGE

Latin American Studies	M

BOSTON ARCHITECTURAL COLLEGE

Architecture	M
Interior Design	M

BOSTON COLLEGE

Applied Psychology	M,D
Classics	M
Counseling Psychology	M,D
Developmental Psychology	M,D
East European and Russian Studies	M
Economics	D
English	M,D
French	M,D
History	M,D
Italian	M,D
Linguistics	M
Pastoral Ministry and Counseling	P,M,D,O
Philosophy	M,D
Political Science	M,D
Psychology—General	M,D
Russian	M
Slavic Languages	M
Sociology	M,D
Spanish	M,D
Theology	P,M,D,O
Western European Studies	M,D

THE BOSTON CONSERVATORY

Music	M,O
Theater	M

BOSTON GRADUATE SCHOOL OF PSYCHOANALYSIS

Counseling Psychology	M
Psychoanalysis and Psychotherapy	M,D,O
Psychology—General	M

BOSTON UNIVERSITY

African Studies	M,O
African-American Studies	M
American Studies	D
Anthropology	M,D
Archaeology	M,D
Art History	M,D,O
Art/Fine Arts	M

Arts Administration	M,O
Broadcast Journalism	M
Classics	M,D,O
Cognitive Sciences	M,D
Communication— General	M
Corporate and Organizational Communication	M
Counseling Psychology	M,D,O
Criminal Justice and Criminology	M
Cultural Studies	M
Economic Development	M
Economics	M,D
Emergency Management	M
English	M,D,O
Film, Television, and Video Production	M
Film, Television, and Video Theory and Criticism	M
Forensic Sciences	M
French	M,D,O
Geographic Information Systems	M,D
Geography	M,D
Graphic Design	M
Hispanic and Latin American Languages	M,D
Historic Preservation	M
History	M,D,O
Human Development	M,D,O
International Affairs	M,D,O
Journalism	M
Linguistics	M,D
Mass Communication	M
Media Studies	M
Museum Studies	M,D,O
Music	M,D,O
Philosophy	M,D
Political Science	M,D,O
Psychology—General	M,D
Public Administration	M,D,O
Public Policy	M,D,O
Religion	M,D
Romance Languages	M,D
School Psychology	M,D,O
Social Psychology	M,D,O
Sociology	M,D
Spanish	M,D,O
Sport Psychology	M,D,O
Theater	M,O
Theology	P,M,D
Urban and Regional Planning	M
Urban Studies	M
Writing	M,D

BOWIE STATE UNIVERSITY

Corporate and Organizational Communication	M,O
Counseling Psychology	M
English	M
Public Administration	M

BOWLING GREEN STATE UNIVERSITY

American Studies	M,D
Applied Arts and Design—General	M
Art History	M
Art/Fine Arts	M
Child and Family Studies	M
Clinical Psychology	M,D
Communication— General	M,D
Computer Art and Design	M

*M—master's degree; P—first professional degree; D—doctorate; O—other advanced degree; *—Close-Up and/or Display*

Counseling Psychology	M
Criminal Justice and Criminology	M
Demography and Population Studies	M,D
Developmental Psychology	M,D
Economics	M
English	M,D
Experimental Psychology	M,D
Family and Consumer Sciences—General	M
Film, Television, and Video Production	M,D
French	M
German	M
Graphic Design	M
History	M,D
Human Development	M
Industrial and Organizational Psychology	M,D
Interdisciplinary Studies	M,D
Music	M,D
Philosophy	M,D
Political Science	M
Psychology—General	M,D
Public Administration	M
Rehabilitation Counseling	M
Rhetoric	M,D
School Psychology	M,O
Social Psychology	M,D
Sociology	M,D
Spanish	M
Speech and Interpersonal Communication	M
Technical Communication	M,D
Theater	M,D
Writing	M,D

BRADLEY UNIVERSITY

Applied Arts and Design—General	M
Art/Fine Arts	M
Comparative and Interdisciplinary Arts	M
English	M
Human Development	M
Illustration	M
Liberal Studies	M
Photography	M

BRANDEIS UNIVERSITY

Anthropology	M,D
Art/Fine Arts	O
Child and Family Studies	M,D
Classics	M,O
Cognitive Sciences	M,D
Communication—General	M,O
Developmental Psychology	M,D
Disability Studies	D
Economics	M
English	M,D
Gender Studies	M,D
Genetic Counseling	M
History	M,D
International Affairs	M,D
International Development	M
Jewish Studies	M,D
Linguistics	M
Music	M,D
Near and Middle Eastern Languages	M
Near and Middle Eastern Studies	M,D
Philosophy	M

Political Science	M,D
Psychology—General	M,D
Public Policy	M
Social Psychology	M,D
Sociology	M,D
Sustainable Development	M
Theater	M
Women's Studies	M,D

BRANDON UNIVERSITY

Music	M
Rural Planning and Studies	M,O

BRENAU UNIVERSITY

Interior Design	M
Psychology—General	M

BRIDGEWATER STATE UNIVERSITY

Criminal Justice and Criminology	M
English	M
Psychology—General	M
Public Administration	M

BRIERCREST SEMINARY

Marriage and Family Therapy	M
Missions and Missiology	M
Pastoral Ministry and Counseling	P,M
Religion	P,M
Theology	P,M

BRIGHAM YOUNG UNIVERSITY

Anthropology	M
Art History	M
Art/Fine Arts	M
Child and Family Studies	M,D
Clinical Psychology	M,D
Communication—General	M
Comparative and Interdisciplinary Arts	M
Comparative Literature	M
Counseling Psychology	M,D,O
English	M
Film, Television, and Video Production	M
French	M
Geography	M
Hispanic and Latin American Languages	M
Human Development	M,D
Humanities	M
Industrial Design	M
Linguistics	M,O
Marriage and Family Therapy	M,D
Mass Communication	M
Music	M
Political Science	M
Portuguese	M
Psychology—General	M,D
Public Administration	M
Public Policy	M
Rhetoric	M
School Psychology	M,D,O
Social Psychology	M,D
Sociology	M
Spanish	M
Theater	M
Writing	M

BROCK UNIVERSITY

Child and Family Studies	M
Classics	M
Comparative Literature	M
Cultural Studies	M

Disability Studies	M,O
Economics	M
English	M
Geography	M
History	M
Human Development	M,D
International Affairs	M
Philosophy	M
Political Science	M
Psychology—General	M,D
Public Policy	M
Social Psychology	M,D
Sociology	M

BROOKLYN COLLEGE OF THE CITY UNIVERSITY OF NEW YORK

Art History	M,D
Art/Fine Arts	M,D
Counseling Psychology	M,D,O
Economics	M
English	M,D
Experimental Psychology	M,D
Film, Television, and Video Production	M
French	M,D
History	M,D
Industrial and Organizational Psychology	M
International Affairs	M,D
Internet and Interactive Multimedia	M,O
Jewish Studies	M
Liberal Studies	M
Media Studies	M
Music	M,D,O
Photography	M,D
Political Science	M,D
Psychology—General	M,D
Public Policy	M,D
School Psychology	M,O
Social Psychology	M
Sociology	M,D
Spanish	M,D
Speech and Interpersonal Communication	M,D
Thanatology	M
Theater	M,D
Urban Studies	M,D
Writing	M

BROOKS INSTITUTE

Photography	M

BROWN UNIVERSITY

American Studies	M,D
Anthropology	M,D
Archaeology	M,D
Art History	M,D
Classics	M,D
Cognitive Sciences	M,D
Comparative Literature	D
Developmental Psychology	D
East European and Russian Studies	M,D
Economics	D
English	M,D
French	D
German	D
Hispanic Studies	M,D
History	M,D
Italian	D
Jewish Studies	D
Latin American Studies	M,D
Linguistics	M,D
Museum Studies	M,D
Music	D
Philosophy	M,D
Political Science	D
Psychology—General	D

Public Policy	M
Religion	D
Russian	M,D
Slavic Languages	M,D
Social Psychology	D
Sociology	M,D
Theater	M,D
Western European Studies	M,D
Writing	M

BRYN ATHYN COLLEGE OF THE NEW CHURCH

Religion	P,M
Theology	P,M

BRYN MAWR COLLEGE

Archaeology	M,D*
Art History	M,D*
Classics	M,D*
French	M,D

BUCKNELL UNIVERSITY

English	M
Psychology—General	M
School Psychology	M

BUFFALO STATE COLLEGE, STATE UNIVERSITY OF NEW YORK

Applied Economics	M
Criminal Justice and Criminology	M
Economics	M
English	M
Historic Preservation	M,O
History	M
Interdisciplinary Studies	M

BUTLER UNIVERSITY

English	M
History	M
Music	M

CALDWELL COLLEGE

Applied Behavior Analysis	M,D
Art Therapy	M
Counseling Psychology	M
Pastoral Ministry and Counseling	M

CALIFORNIA BAPTIST UNIVERSITY

Counseling Psychology	M
English	M
Forensic Psychology	M
Music	M
Pastoral Ministry and Counseling	M
Public Administration	M
School Psychology	M

CALIFORNIA COAST UNIVERSITY

Criminal Justice and Criminology	M
Psychology—General	M

CALIFORNIA COLLEGE OF THE ARTS

Applied Arts and Design—General	M
Architecture	M
Art/Fine Arts	M
Film, Television, and Video Production	M
Film, Television, and Video Theory and Criticism	M
Museum Studies	M
Photography	M

Textile Design | M
Writing | M

CALIFORNIA INSTITUTE OF INTEGRAL STUDIES

Art Therapy | M,D
Asian Studies | M,D
Clinical Psychology | M,D
Counseling Psychology | M,D
Cultural Anthropology | M,D
Health Psychology | M,D
Humanities | M,D
Interdisciplinary Studies | M,D
Philosophy | M,D
Psychology—General | M,D
Religion | M,D
Social Psychology | M,D
Theology | M,D
Therapies—Dance, Drama, and Music | M,D
Women's Studies | M,D
Writing | M,D

CALIFORNIA INSTITUTE OF TECHNOLOGY

Social Sciences | M,D

CALIFORNIA INSTITUTE OF THE ARTS

Applied Arts and Design—General | M,O
Art/Fine Arts | M,O
Dance | M,O
Film, Television, and Video Production | M,O
Graphic Design | M,O
Music | M,O
Photography | M,O
Theater | M,O
Writing | M,O

CALIFORNIA LUTHERAN UNIVERSITY

Clinical Psychology | M,D
Economics | M,O
Marriage and Family Therapy | M,D
Psychology—General | M,D
Public Administration | M
Public Policy | M

CALIFORNIA POLYTECHNIC STATE UNIVERSITY, SAN LUIS OBISPO

Agricultural Economics and Agribusiness | M
Architecture | M
English | M
History | M
Political Science | M
Psychology—General | M
Urban and Regional Planning | M

CALIFORNIA STATE POLYTECHNIC UNIVERSITY, POMONA

Architecture | M
Economics | M
English | M
History | M
Landscape Architecture | M
Psychology—General | M
Public Administration | M
Urban and Regional Planning | M

CALIFORNIA STATE UNIVERSITY, BAKERSFIELD

Anthropology | M
Counseling Psychology | M

English | M
History | M
Interdisciplinary Studies | M
Psychology—General | M
Public Administration | M
Sociology | M
Spanish | M

CALIFORNIA STATE UNIVERSITY, CHICO

Anthropology | M
Applied Psychology | M
Art History | M
Art/Fine Arts | M
Communication—General | M
English | M
Geography | M
History | M
Interdisciplinary Studies | M
Marriage and Family Therapy | M
Museum Studies | M
Music | M
Political Science | M
Psychology—General | M
Public Administration | M
Rural Planning and Studies | M
Social Sciences | M
Urban and Regional Planning | M

CALIFORNIA STATE UNIVERSITY, DOMINGUEZ HILLS

Applied Social Research | M,O
Clinical Psychology | M
Conflict Resolution and Mediation/Peace Studies | M
English | M,O
Humanities | M*
Marriage and Family Therapy | M
Psychology—General | M
Public Administration | M
Rhetoric | M,O
Sociology | M,O

CALIFORNIA STATE UNIVERSITY, EAST BAY

Anthropology | M
Communication—General | M
Economics | M
English | M
Geography | M
History | M
Humanities | M
Interdisciplinary Studies | M
Internet and Interactive Multimedia | M
Music | M
Public Administration | M
Sport Psychology | M

CALIFORNIA STATE UNIVERSITY, FRESNO

Applied Arts and Design—General | M
Art/Fine Arts | M
Communication—General | M
Criminal Justice and Criminology | M
English | M
Family and Consumer Sciences-General | M
History | M
International Affairs | M
Journalism | M
Linguistics | M

Marriage and Family Therapy | M
Mass Communication | M
Music | M
Psychology—General | M
Public Administration | M
Rehabilitation Counseling | M
Spanish | M
Sport Psychology | M
Writing | M

CALIFORNIA STATE UNIVERSITY, FULLERTON

American Studies | M
Anthropology | M
Applied Arts and Design—General | M
Art History | M
Art/Fine Arts | M
Clinical Psychology | M
Communication—General | M
Comparative Literature | M
Dance | M
Economics | M
English | M
Film, Television, and Video Production | M
French | M
Geography | M
German | M
Gerontology | M
History | M
Journalism | M
Linguistics | M
Media Studies | M
Music | M
Photography | M
Political Science | M
Psychology—General | M
Public Administration | M
Social Psychology | M
Sociology | M
Spanish | M
Speech and Interpersonal Communication | M
Theater | M

CALIFORNIA STATE UNIVERSITY, LONG BEACH

African Studies | M
American Studies | M
Anthropology | M
Art History | M
Art/Fine Arts | M
Asian Studies | M
Asian-American Studies | M
Communication—General | M
Consumer Economics | M
Criminal Justice and Criminology | M
Dance | M
Economics | M
Emergency Management | M
English | M
Family and Consumer Sciences-General | M
French | M
Geography | M
German | M
Gerontology | M
History | M
Industrial and Organizational Psychology | M
Interdisciplinary Studies | M
Latin American Studies | M
Linguistics | M

Marriage and Family Therapy | M
Medieval and Renaissance Studies | M
Music | M
Near and Middle Eastern Studies | M
Philosophy | M
Political Science | M
Psychology—General | M
Public Administration | M
Public Policy | M
Religion | M
Spanish | M
Sport Psychology | M
Theater | M
Western European Studies | M
Writing | M

CALIFORNIA STATE UNIVERSITY, LOS ANGELES

Anthropology | M
Applied Arts and Design—General | M
Art History | M
Art Therapy | M
Art/Fine Arts | M
Child and Family Studies | M
Child Development | M
Communication—General | M
Criminal Justice and Criminology | M
Economics | M
English | M
Film, Television, and Video Production | M
French | M
Geography | M
Graphic Design | M
Hispanic Studies | M
History | M
Latin American Studies | M
Music | M
Philosophy | M
Photography | M
Political Science | M
Psychology—General | M
Public Administration | M
Rehabilitation Counseling | M,D
School Psychology | M,D
Sociology | M
Spanish | M
Speech and Interpersonal Communication | M
Textile Design | M
Theater | M

CALIFORNIA STATE UNIVERSITY, MONTEREY BAY

Interdisciplinary Studies | M
Public Policy | M

CALIFORNIA STATE UNIVERSITY, NORTHRIDGE

Anthropology | M
Applied Psychology | M
Archaeology | M
Art History | M
Art/Fine Arts | M
Clinical Psychology | M
Communication—General | M
Comparative Literature | M
English | M
Experimental Psychology | M

---

*M—master's degree; P—first professional degree; D—doctorate; O—other advanced degree; *—Close-Up and / or Display*

Family and Consumer Sciences-General	M
Film, Television, and Video Production	M
Geography	M
Hispanic Studies	M
History	M
Interdisciplinary Studies	M
Journalism	M
Linguistics	M
Marriage and Family Therapy	M
Mass Communication	M
Music	M
Political Science	M
Psychology—General	M
Public Administration	M
Rhetoric	M
School Psychology	M
Sociology	M
Spanish	M
Speech and Interpersonal Communication	M
Theater	M
Writing	M

CALIFORNIA STATE UNIVERSITY, SACRAMENTO

Anthropology	M
Art/Fine Arts	M
Communication—General	M
Counseling Psychology	M
Criminal Justice and Criminology	M
Dance	M
English	M
French	M
German	M
International Affairs	M
Liberal Studies	M
Music	M
Political Science	M
Psychology—General	M
Public Administration	M
Public History	M
Public Policy	M
School Psychology	M
Sociology	M
Spanish	M
Theater	M
Writing	M

CALIFORNIA STATE UNIVERSITY, SAN BERNARDINO

Art/Fine Arts	M
Child Development	M
Clinical Psychology	M
Communication—General	M
Corporate and Organizational Communication	M
Counseling Psychology	M
Criminal Justice and Criminology	M
English	M
Experimental Psychology	M
Human Development	M
Industrial and Organizational Psychology	M
Interdisciplinary Studies	M
National Security	M
Psychology—General	M
Public Administration	M
Rehabilitation Counseling	M
Social Sciences	M
Spanish	M
Theater	M
Writing	M

CALIFORNIA STATE UNIVERSITY, SAN MARCOS

English	M
Psychology—General	M
Sociology	M
Spanish	M
Writing	M

CALIFORNIA STATE UNIVERSITY, STANISLAUS

Applied Behavior Analysis	M
Counseling Psychology	M
Criminal Justice and Criminology	M
English	M,O
Genetic Counseling	M
History	M
Interdisciplinary Studies	M
International Affairs	M
Psychology—General	M
Public Administration	M
Rhetoric	M,O
Sustainable Development	M
Writing	M,O

CALIFORNIA UNIVERSITY OF PENNSYLVANIA

Criminal Justice and Criminology	M
School Psychology	M
Social Sciences	M
Sport Psychology	M

CALUMET COLLEGE OF SAINT JOSEPH

Criminal Justice and Criminology	M

CALVARY BAPTIST THEOLOGICAL SEMINARY

Theology	P,M,D

CALVARY BIBLE COLLEGE AND THEOLOGICAL SEMINARY

Pastoral Ministry and Counseling	P,M
Theology	P,M

CALVIN THEOLOGICAL SEMINARY

Missions and Missiology	P,M,D
Pastoral Ministry and Counseling	P,M,D
Religion	P,M,D
Theology	P,M,D

CAMBRIDGE COLLEGE

Addictions/Substance Abuse Counseling	M,O
Conflict Resolution and Mediation/Peace Studies	M
Counseling Psychology	M,O
Forensic Psychology	M,O
Interdisciplinary Studies	M,D,O
Marriage and Family Therapy	M,O
Psychology—General	M,O
School Psychology	M,D,O

CAMERON UNIVERSITY

Psychology—General	M

CAMPBELLSVILLE UNIVERSITY

Music	M
Social Sciences	M
Theology	M

CAMPBELL UNIVERSITY

Interdisciplinary Studies	M
Theology	P,M,D

CANADIAN SOUTHERN BAPTIST SEMINARY

Theology	P,M

CANISIUS COLLEGE

Corporate and Organizational Communication	M
School Psychology	M
Social Psychology	M

CAPELLA UNIVERSITY

Addictions/Substance Abuse Counseling	M,D,O
Child and Family Studies	M,D,O
Clinical Psychology	M,D,O
Counseling Psychology	M,D,O
Criminal Justice and Criminology	M,D,O
Developmental Psychology	M,D,O
Emergency Management	M,D
Gerontology	M,D
Industrial and Organizational Psychology	M,D,O
Marriage and Family Therapy	M,D,O
Psychology—General	M,D,O
Public Administration	M,D
School Psychology	M,D,O
Sport Psychology	M,D,O

CAPITAL BIBLE SEMINARY

Pastoral Ministry and Counseling	P,M,O
Theology	P,M,O

CAPITAL UNIVERSITY

Music	M

CARDINAL STRITCH UNIVERSITY

Applied Arts and Design—General	M
Clinical Psychology	M
Graphic Design	M
History	M
Liberal Studies	M
Music	M
Pastoral Ministry and Counseling	M
Psychology—General	M
Religion	M

CAREY THEOLOGICAL COLLEGE

Theology	P,M,D

CARIBBEAN UNIVERSITY

Art History	M,D
Criminal Justice and Criminology	M,D
Museum Studies	M,D

CARLETON UNIVERSITY

Anthropology	M
Architecture	M
Art History	M
Canadian Studies	M,D
Cognitive Sciences	D
Communication—General	M,D
Comparative Literature	D
Conflict Resolution and Mediation/Peace Studies	M,O

East European and Russian Studies	M,O
Economics	M,D
English	M,D
Film, Television, and Video Production	M
French	M
Geography	M,D
History	M,D
Industrial Design	M
International Affairs	M,D
Journalism	M,D
Linguistics	M
Music	M
Philosophy	M
Political Science	M,D
Psychology—General	M,D
Public Administration	M,D
Public Policy	M,D
Sociology	M,D
Western European Studies	M,O

CARLOS ALBIZU UNIVERSITY

Clinical Psychology	M,D
Industrial and Organizational Psychology	M,D
Psychology—General	M,D

CARLOS ALBIZU UNIVERSITY, MIAMI CAMPUS

Clinical Psychology	M,D
Counseling Psychology	M,D
Industrial and Organizational Psychology	M,D
Marriage and Family Therapy	M,D
Psychology—General	M,D
School Psychology	M,D

CARLOW UNIVERSITY

Counseling Psychology	M,D
Humanities	M
Writing	M

CARNEGIE MELLON UNIVERSITY

African Studies	M,D
African-American Studies	M,D
Applied Arts and Design—General	D
Architecture	M,D
Art/Fine Arts	M
Arts Administration	M
Building Science	M,D
Cognitive Sciences	D
Communication—General	M,D
Comparative Literature	M,D
Computer Art and Design	M,D
Corporate and Organizational Communication	M
Criminal Justice and Criminology	M
Cultural Studies	M,D
Developmental Psychology	D
Economics	D
English	M,D
Film, Television, and Video Production	M
Gender Studies	M,D
History of Science and Technology	M,D
History	M,D
Industrial and Labor Relations	M,D
Linguistics	D

Media Studies	M
Music	M
Philosophy	M,D
Psychology—General	D
Public Administration	M
Public Policy	M,D
Publishing	M
Rhetoric	M,D
Social Psychology	D
Social Sciences	D
Technical Writing	M
Theater	M
Urban Design	M,D
Writing	M

CAROLINA EVANGELICAL DIVINITY SCHOOL

Pastoral Ministry and Counseling	D
Theology	P,M

CARSON-NEWMAN COLLEGE

Theology	M

CASE WESTERN RESERVE UNIVERSITY

Anthropology	M,D
Art History	M,D
Clinical Psychology	D
Cognitive Sciences	M
Comparative Literature	M
Dance	M
Economics	M
English	M,D
Experimental Psychology	D
French	M
Genetic Counseling	M
History	M,D
Industrial and Labor Relations	M
Linguistics	M
Museum Studies	M,D
Music	M,D
Political Science	M,D
Psychology—General	D
Sociology	M,D
Theater	M

CASTLETON STATE COLLEGE

Forensic Psychology	M
Psychology—General	M

THE CATHOLIC DISTANCE UNIVERSITY

Theology	M

CATHOLIC THEOLOGICAL UNION AT CHICAGO

Missions and Missiology	P,M,D,O
Pastoral Ministry and Counseling	P,M,D,O
Theology	P,M,D,O

THE CATHOLIC UNIVERSITY OF AMERICA

Anthropology	M
Applied Psychology	M,D
Architecture	M
Classics	M,D,O
Clinical Psychology	M,D
Cultural Studies	M
Economics	M
English	M,D,O
Experimental Psychology	D
History	M,D
International Affairs	M,D
Medieval and Renaissance Studies	M,D,O
Music	M,D,O

Near and Middle Eastern Languages	M,D
Near and Middle Eastern Studies	M,D
Pastoral Ministry and Counseling	P,M,D,O
Philosophy	M,D,O
Political Science	M,D
Psychology—General	M,D
Religion	P,M,D,O
Rhetoric	M,D,O
Sociology	M
Spanish	M,D
Sustainable Development	M
Theater	M
Theology	P,M,D,O
Urban and Regional Planning	M
Western European Studies	M,D

CEDAR CREST COLLEGE

Forensic Sciences	M

CENTENARY COLLEGE

Counseling Psychology	M

CENTRAL BAPTIST THEOLOGICAL SEMINARY

Missions and Missiology	P,M,O
Theology	P,M,O

CENTRAL BAPTIST THEOLOGICAL SEMINARY OF VIRGINIA BEACH

Theology	P,M

CENTRAL CONNECTICUT STATE UNIVERSITY

Communication— General	M,O
Corporate and Organizational Communication	M,O
Criminal Justice and Criminology	M
English	M,O
French	M,O
Geography	M
German	M,O
Health Psychology	M
Hispanic and Latin American Languages	M,O
History	M,O
International Affairs	M
Italian	M,O
Marriage and Family Therapy	M,O
Psychology—General	M
Rehabilitation Counseling	M,O
School Psychology	M,O
Social Psychology	M
Spanish	M,O

CENTRAL EUROPEAN UNIVERSITY

Anthropology	M,D
Economics	M,D
Gender Studies	M,D
History	M,D
Humanities	M,D
International Affairs	M,D
Medieval and Renaissance Studies	M,D
Philosophy	M,D
Political Science	M,D
Public Policy	M,D
Social Sciences	M,D
Sociology	M,D

CENTRAL MICHIGAN UNIVERSITY

American Indian/Native American Studies	M
American Studies	M,D,O
Applied Psychology	M,D
Child and Family Studies	M,O
Clinical Psychology	M,D
Clothing and Textiles	M,O
Communication— General	M
Corporate and Organizational Communication	M,O
Counseling Psychology	M,D,O
Cultural Studies	M
Economics	M
English	M
Experimental Psychology	M,D
Family and Consumer Sciences-General	M,O
Film, Television, and Video Production	M
Film, Television, and Video Theory and Criticism	M
Gender Studies	M
Gerontology	M,O
Health Psychology	M,D
History	M,D,O
Human Development	M,O
Humanities	M
Industrial and Organizational Psychology	M,D
International Affairs	M,O
Mass Communication	M
Media Studies	M
Music	M
Political Science	M,O
Psychology—General	M,D,O
Public Administration	M,O
School Psychology	D,O
Spanish	M
Speech and Interpersonal Communication	M
Western European Studies	M,D,O
Writing	M

CENTRAL WASHINGTON UNIVERSITY

Art/Fine Arts	M
Child and Family Studies	M
Counseling Psychology	M
English	M
Experimental Psychology	M
Family and Consumer Sciences-General	M
History	M
Interdisciplinary Studies	M
Music	M
Psychology—General	M
School Psychology	M
Theater	M

CENTRAL YESHIVA TOMCHEI TMIMIM-LUBAVITCH

Theology	M

CENTRO DE ESTUDIOS AVANZADOS DE PUERTO RICO Y EL CARIBE

History	M,D
Latin American Studies	M,D

CHAMINADE UNIVERSITY OF HONOLULU

Conflict Resolution and Mediation/Peace Studies	M
Counseling Psychology	M
Criminal Justice and Criminology	M,O
Forensic Sciences	M
Homeland Security	M,O
Pastoral Ministry and Counseling	M
Theology	M

CHAMPLAIN COLLEGE

Conflict Resolution and Mediation/Peace Studies	M
Forensic Sciences	M

CHAPMAN UNIVERSITY

Cultural Studies	D
Disability Studies	D
Economics	P,M
English	M
Film, Television, and Video Production	M
Health Communication	M
International Affairs	M
Marriage and Family Therapy	M
School Psychology	M,D,O
Writing	M

CHARLESTON SOUTHERN UNIVERSITY

Criminal Justice and Criminology	M

CHATHAM UNIVERSITY

Computer Art and Design	M
Counseling Psychology	M,D
Developmental Psychology	M,D
Film, Television, and Video Production	M
Health Psychology	M,D
Industrial and Organizational Psychology	M,D
Interior Design	M
Landscape Architecture	M
Marriage and Family Therapy	M,D
Sport Psychology	M,D
Writing	M

CHESTNUT HILL COLLEGE

Clinical Psychology	M,D,O
Counseling Psychology	M,O
Psychology—General	M,D,O
Religion	M,O

CHEYNEY UNIVERSITY OF PENNSYLVANIA

Public Administration	M

THE CHICAGO SCHOOL OF PROFESSIONAL PSYCHOLOGY

Applied Behavior Analysis	M,D
Applied Psychology	M,D
Clinical Psychology	M,D
Forensic Psychology	M,D
Industrial and Organizational Psychology	M,D
Psychology—General	D
School Psychology	O

*M—master's degree; P—first professional degree; D—doctorate; O—other advanced degree; *—Close-Up and / or Display*

THE CHICAGO SCHOOL OF PROFESSIONAL PSYCHOLOGY AT DOWNTOWN LOS ANGELES

Applied Behavior Analysis	M,D
Clinical Psychology	M,D
Forensic Psychology	D
Industrial and Organizational Psychology	M
Marriage and Family Therapy	M,D

THE CHICAGO SCHOOL OF PROFESSIONAL PSYCHOLOGY AT GRAYSLAKE

Clinical Psychology	M
Counseling Psychology	M
School Psychology	O

THE CHICAGO SCHOOL OF PROFESSIONAL PSYCHOLOGY AT IRVINE

Clinical Psychology	D
Forensic Psychology	D
Marriage and Family Therapy	M,D
Psychology—General	D

THE CHICAGO SCHOOL OF PROFESSIONAL PSYCHOLOGY AT WESTWOOD

Clinical Psychology	M
Marriage and Family Therapy	M,D
Psychology—General	D

THE CHICAGO SCHOOL OF PROFESSIONAL PSYCHOLOGY: ONLINE

Applied Psychology	M,O
Forensic Psychology	M,O
Industrial and Organizational Psychology	M,D,O
Psychology—General	M,D

CHICAGO STATE UNIVERSITY

Criminal Justice and Criminology	M
Economic Development	M
English	M
Geography	M
History	M
Writing	M

CHICAGO THEOLOGICAL SEMINARY

Ethics	P,M,D
Pastoral Ministry and Counseling	P,M,D
Religion	P,M,D
Theology	P,M,D

CHRISTENDOM COLLEGE

Theology	M

CHRISTIAN BROTHERS UNIVERSITY

Religion	M

CHRISTIAN THEOLOGICAL SEMINARY

Marriage and Family Therapy	P,M,D
Pastoral Ministry and Counseling	P,M,D
Religion	P,M,D
Theology	P,M,D

CHRISTIE'S EDUCATION

Art History	M
Museum Studies	M

CHRIST THE KING SEMINARY

Pastoral Ministry and Counseling	P,M
Theology	P,M

CHURCH DIVINITY SCHOOL OF THE PACIFIC

Theology	P,M,D,O

CINCINNATI CHRISTIAN UNIVERSITY

Pastoral Ministry and Counseling	M
Religion	P,M
Theology	P,M

THE CITADEL, THE MILITARY COLLEGE OF SOUTH CAROLINA

English	M
History	M
Psychology—General	M,O
School Psychology	O
Social Sciences	M

CITY COLLEGE OF THE CITY UNIVERSITY OF NEW YORK

Architecture	M
Art History	M
Art/Fine Arts	M
Clinical Psychology	M,D
Counseling Psychology	M
Economics	M
English	M
Experimental Psychology	M,D
Graphic Design	M
History	M
International Affairs	M
Landscape Architecture	M
Media Studies	M
Museum Studies	M
Music	M
Psychology—General	M,D
Public Administration	M,D
Sociology	M
Spanish	M
Sustainable Development	M
Urban Design	M
Writing	M

CITY UNIVERSITY OF SEATTLE

Counseling Psychology	M
School Psychology	M,O

CLAREMONT GRADUATE UNIVERSITY

African Studies	M,D,O
American Studies	M,D,O
Art/Fine Arts	M
Arts Administration	M
Cognitive Sciences	M,D,O
Comparative Literature	M,D
Computer Art and Design	M
Cultural Studies	M,D,O
Developmental Psychology	M,D,O
Economic Development	M,D,O
Economics	M,D,O
English	M,D
Ethics	M,D
Film, Television, and Video Theory and Criticism	M,D
Health Psychology	M,D,O
History	M,D,O
Human Development	M,D,O
Humanities	M,D,O
Industrial and Organizational Psychology	M,D,O
International Affairs	M,D
International Economics	M,D,O
Media Studies	M,D,O
Museum Studies	M,D,O
Music	M,D
Philosophy	M,D
Photography	M
Political Science	M,D
Psychology—General	M,D,O
Public Policy	M,D,O
Religion	M,D
Social Psychology	M,D,O
Theology	M,D
Western European Studies	M,D,O
Women's Studies	M,D
Writing	M,D

CLAREMONT SCHOOL OF THEOLOGY

Ethics	M,D
Pastoral Ministry and Counseling	M,D
Religion	M,D
Theology	P,M,D

CLARION UNIVERSITY OF PENNSYLVANIA

Communication— General	M
English	M

CLARK ATLANTA UNIVERSITY

African-American Studies	M,D
Criminal Justice and Criminology	M
Economics	M
English	M,D
History	M,D
Political Science	M,D
Public Administration	M
Romance Languages	M,D
Sociology	M
Women's Studies	M,D

CLARKSON UNIVERSITY

Sustainable Development	M,D

CLARK UNIVERSITY

American Studies	M,D
Clinical Psychology	D
Communication— General	M
Developmental Psychology	D
Economics	D
English	M
Geographic Information Systems	M
Geography	M,D
History	M,D,O
Holocaust and Genocide Studies	D
International Development	M
Liberal Studies	M
Public Administration	M,O
Social Psychology	D
Sustainable Development	M
Urban and Regional Planning	M

CLAYTON STATE UNIVERSITY

Liberal Studies	M

CLEMSON UNIVERSITY

Applied Economics	M,D

Applied Psychology	M
Architecture	M
Art/Fine Arts	M
Communication— General	M,D
Computer Art and Design	M
Counseling Psychology	M
Economics	M,D
English	M
Environmental Design	D
Historic Preservation	M
History	M
Human Development	M
Humanities	D
Industrial and Organizational Psychology	D
Landscape Architecture	M
Psychology—General	D
Public Administration	M
Public Affairs	D
Public Policy	D,O
Rhetoric	D
Social Sciences	D
Sociology	M
Urban and Regional Planning	M
Writing	M

CLEVELAND INSTITUTE OF MUSIC

Music	M,D,O

CLEVELAND STATE UNIVERSITY

Addictions/Substance Abuse Counseling	M,O
Art History	M
Art/Fine Arts	M
Clinical Psychology	M,D,O
Communication— General	M,O
Counseling Psychology	M,D,O
Economic Development	M,D,O
Economics	M,D,O
English	M
Experimental Psychology	M,D,O
French	M
Geographic Information Systems	M,D,O
Gerontology	M,D,O
Health Communication	M,O
History	M
Industrial and Labor Relations	P,M,O
Industrial and Organizational Psychology	M,D,O
Latin American Studies	M
Linguistics	M
Museum Studies	M,D
Music	M
Philosophy	M,O
Psychology—General	M,D,O
Public Administration	M,O
School Psychology	M,D,O
Sociology	M
Spanish	M
Sport Psychology	M
Urban and Regional Planning	M,O
Urban Design	M,O
Urban Studies	M,D,O
Writing	M

COASTAL CAROLINA UNIVERSITY

Writing	M

COLGATE ROCHESTER CROZER DIVINITY SCHOOL

Theology	P,M,D,O

THE COLLEGE AT BROCKPORT, STATE UNIVERSITY OF NEW YORK

American Studies	M
Art/Fine Arts	M
Arts Administration	M,O
Communication— General	M
Counseling Psychology	M,O
Dance	M
English	M
History	M
Liberal Studies	M
Psychology—General	M
Public Administration	M,O
Writing	M

COLLÈGE DOMINICAIN DE PHILOSOPHIE ET DE THÉOLOGIE

Philosophy	M,D
Theology	M,D,O

COLLEGE OF CHARLESTON

Arts Administration	M,O
Communication— General	M
English	M
Historic Preservation	M
History	M
Public Administration	M
Urban and Regional Planning	O

COLLEGE OF EMMANUEL AND ST. CHAD

Theology	P,M

COLLEGE OF MOUNT ST. JOSEPH

Pastoral Ministry and Counseling	M,O
Theology	M,O

THE COLLEGE OF NEW JERSEY

Addictions/Substance Abuse Counseling	M,O
English	M
Marriage and Family Therapy	O

THE COLLEGE OF NEW ROCHELLE

Art Therapy	M
Art/Fine Arts	M
Communication— General	M,O
Counseling Psychology	M,O
Gerontology	M,O
Graphic Design	M
School Psychology	M
Social Psychology	M

COLLEGE OF NOTRE DAME OF MARYLAND

Communication— General	M
Liberal Studies	M

COLLEGE OF SAINT ELIZABETH

Counseling Psychology	M,O
Criminal Justice and Criminology	M
Forensic Psychology	M,O
Psychology—General	M,O
Public Administration	M
Theology	M

COLLEGE OF ST. JOSEPH

Addictions/Substance Abuse Counseling	M
Clinical Psychology	M
Counseling Psychology	M
Psychology—General	M
School Psychology	M
Social Psychology	M

THE COLLEGE OF SAINT ROSE

English	M
History	M
Mass Communication	M
Music	M
Political Science	M
School Psychology	M,O

COLLEGE OF STATEN ISLAND OF THE CITY UNIVERSITY OF NEW YORK

Counseling Psychology	M
English	M
Film, Television, and Video Theory and Criticism	M
History	M
Liberal Studies	M
Media Studies	M

COLLEGE OF THE HUMANITIES AND SCIENCES, HARRISON MIDDLETON UNIVERSITY

Comparative Literature	M,D
Humanities	M,D
Interdisciplinary Studies	M,D
Philosophy	M,D
Religion	M,D
Social Sciences	M,D

THE COLLEGE OF WILLIAM AND MARY

Addictions/Substance Abuse Counseling	M,D
American Studies	M,D
Anthropology	M,D
Experimental Psychology	M
History	M,D
Marriage and Family Therapy	M,D
Public Policy	M
School Psychology	M,O

COLLÈGE UNIVERSITAIRE DE SAINT-BONIFACE

Canadian Studies	M

COLORADO CHRISTIAN UNIVERSITY

Counseling Psychology	M

THE COLORADO COLLEGE

American Studies	M
Humanities	M
Liberal Studies	M

COLORADO SCHOOL OF MINES

International Affairs	M,O
Mineral Economics	M,D

COLORADO STATE UNIVERSITY

Agricultural Economics and Agribusiness	M,D
Anthropology	M
Art/Fine Arts	M
Child and Family Studies	M,D
Consumer Economics	M
Economics	M,D
English	M
History	M

Human Development	M,D
Landscape Architecture	M,D
Mass Communication	M,D
Music	M
Philosophy	M
Political Science	M,D
Psychology—General	M,D
Sociology	M,D
Speech and Interpersonal Communication	M
Technical Communication	M,D
Technical Writing	M,D
Writing	M

COLORADO TECHNICAL UNIVERSITY COLORADO SPRINGS

Conflict Resolution and Mediation/Peace Studies	M,D
Criminal Justice and Criminology	M

COLORADO TECHNICAL UNIVERSITY DENVER

Conflict Resolution and Mediation/Peace Studies	M
Criminal Justice and Criminology	M

COLORADO TECHNICAL UNIVERSITY SIOUX FALLS

Criminal Justice and Criminology	M

COLUMBIA COLLEGE (MO)

Criminal Justice and Criminology	M
Military and Defense Studies	M

COLUMBIA COLLEGE (SC)

Conflict Resolution and Mediation/Peace Studies	M,O

COLUMBIA COLLEGE CHICAGO

Arts Administration	M
Comparative and Interdisciplinary Arts	M
Film, Television, and Video Production	M
Journalism	M
Media Studies	M
Music	M
Photography	M
Therapies—Dance, Drama, and Music	M,O
Writing	M

COLUMBIA INTERNATIONAL UNIVERSITY

Cultural Studies	P,M,D,O
Missions and Missiology	P,M,D,O
Pastoral Ministry and Counseling	P,M,D,O
Theology	P,M,D,O

COLUMBIA SOUTHERN UNIVERSITY

Criminal Justice and Criminology	M

COLUMBIA THEOLOGICAL SEMINARY

Theology	P,M,D

COLUMBIA UNIVERSITY

African Studies	O
African-American Studies	M
American Studies	M
Anthropology	M,D
Archaeology	M,D
Architecture	M,D
Art History	M,D
Art/Fine Arts	M
Asian Languages	M,D
Asian Studies	M,D,O
Classics	M,D
Communication— General	M,D
Comparative Literature	M,D
Conflict Resolution and Mediation/Peace Studies	M
Corporate and Organizational Communication	M
East European and Russian Studies	M,O
Economics	M,D
English	M,D
Environmental Design	M
Ethics	M
Experimental Psychology	M,D
Film, Television, and Video Production	M
French	M,D
German	M,D
Historic Preservation	M,O
History	M,D
Interdisciplinary Studies	M
International Affairs	M
Italian	M,D
Jewish Studies	M,D
Journalism	M,D,O
Landscape Architecture	M
Latin American Studies	M,O
Liberal Studies	M
Medieval and Renaissance Studies	M
Music	M,D
Near and Middle Eastern Languages	M,D
Near and Middle Eastern Studies	M,D,O
Philosophy	M,D
Photography	M
Political Science	M,D
Psychology—General	M,D
Public Administration	M
Public Policy	M
Religion	M,D
Romance Languages	M,D
Russian	M,D
Slavic Languages	M,D
Social Psychology	M,D
Social Sciences	M
Sociology	M,D
Spanish	M,D
Sustainable Development	M,D
Theater	M,D*
Urban and Regional Planning	M,D
Western European Studies	M,O
Writing	M

COLUMBUS STATE UNIVERSITY

Counseling Psychology	M,D,O
Criminal Justice and Criminology	M
Public Administration	M

---

*M—master's degree; P—first professional degree; D—doctorate; O—other advanced degree; *—Close-Up and / or Display*

CONCORDIA LUTHERAN SEMINARY

Theology	P,O

CONCORDIA SEMINARY

Theology	P,M,D,O

CONCORDIA THEOLOGICAL SEMINARY

Theology	P,M,D

CONCORDIA UNIVERSITY (CA)

Applied Social Research	M
Cultural Studies	M
International Affairs	M
Religion	M
Theology	M

CONCORDIA UNIVERSITY (CANADA)

Anthropology	M
Applied Arts and Design—General	O
Art History	M,D
Art Therapy	M
Art/Fine Arts	M
Child and Family Studies	M
Clinical Psychology	M,D,O
Communication—General	M,D,O
Computer Art and Design	O
Cultural Anthropology	M
Economic Development	O
Economics	M,D,O
English	M
Film, Television, and Video Production	M
Film, Television, and Video Theory and Criticism	M
French	M,O
Geography	M,D,O
History	M,D
Humanities	D
Interdisciplinary Studies	M,D
Internet and Interactive Multimedia	M,O
Jewish Studies	M
Journalism	O
Linguistics	M,O
Media Studies	M,D,O
Music	O
Philosophy	M
Political Science	M,D
Psychology—General	M,D
Public Administration	M,D
Public Affairs	O
Public Policy	M,D
Religion	M,D
Rural Planning and Studies	M,D,O
Sociology	M
Theology	M
Translation and Interpretation	M,O
Urban and Regional Planning	O
Urban Studies	M,O
Writing	M

CONCORDIA UNIVERSITY CHICAGO

Counseling Psychology	M
Gerontology	M
Liberal Studies	M
Music	M
Psychology—General	M
Religion	M

CONCORDIA UNIVERSITY COLLEGE OF ALBERTA

Religion	M
Theology	M

CONCORDIA UNIVERSITY, NEBRASKA

Pastoral Ministry and Counseling	M

CONCORDIA UNIVERSITY, ST. PAUL

Child and Family Studies	M,O
Corporate and Organizational Communication	M
Criminal Justice and Criminology	M
Pastoral Ministry and Counseling	M,O
Theology	M,O

CONCORDIA UNIVERSITY WISCONSIN

Child and Family Studies	M
Corporate and Organizational Communication	M
Counseling Psychology	M
Music	M
Psychology—General	M
Public Administration	M

CONCORD UNIVERSITY

Geography	M

CONNECTICUT COLLEGE

Psychology—General	M

CONSERVATORIO DE MUSICA

Music	O

CONVERSE COLLEGE

English	M
History	M
Liberal Studies	M
Marriage and Family Therapy	O
Music	M
Political Science	M

CONWAY SCHOOL OF LANDSCAPE DESIGN

Landscape Architecture	M

COOPER UNION FOR THE ADVANCEMENT OF SCIENCE AND ART

Architecture	M

COPPIN STATE UNIVERSITY

Addictions/Substance Abuse Counseling	M
Applied Psychology	M
Criminal Justice and Criminology	M
Rehabilitation Counseling	M

CORBAN UNIVERSITY

Pastoral Ministry and Counseling	M

CORCORAN COLLEGE OF ART AND DESIGN

Decorative Arts	M
Interior Design	M

CORNELL UNIVERSITY

African Studies	M,D
African-American Studies	M,D
Agricultural Economics and Agribusiness	M
American Studies	M,D
Anthropology	D
Applied Economics	M,D
Archaeology	M,D
Architectural History	M,D
Architecture	M,D
Art History	D
Art/Fine Arts	M
Asian Languages	M,D
Asian Studies	M,D
Building Science	M,D
Child and Family Studies	D
Chinese	M,D
Classics	D
Clothing and Textiles	D
Cognitive Sciences	D
Communication—General	M,D
Comparative Literature	D
Computer Art and Design	M,D
Conflict Resolution and Mediation/Peace Studies	M,D
Consumer Economics	M,D
Cultural Anthropology	D
Cultural Studies	M,D
Demography and Population Studies	M,D
Developmental Psychology	D
East European and Russian Studies	M,D
Economic Development	M,D
Economics	M,D
English	M,D
Environmental Design	M
Ethnic Studies	M,D
Experimental Psychology	D
French	D
Gender Studies	M,D
German	M,D
Hispanic and Latin American Languages	D
Historic Preservation	M,D
History of Science and Technology	M,D
History	M,D
Human Development	D
Industrial and Labor Relations	M,D*
Interior Design	M
International Affairs	D
International Development	M
Italian	D
Japanese	M,D
Jewish Studies	M,D
Landscape Architecture	M
Latin American Studies	M,D
Linguistics	M,D
Medieval and Renaissance Studies	M,D
Music	M,D
Near and Middle Eastern Studies	M,D
Philosophy	D
Photography	M
Political Science	D
Psychology—General	D
Public Affairs	M
Public Policy	M,D
Religion	D
Romance Languages	M,D
Rural Planning and Studies	M
Rural Sociology	M,D
Scandinavian Languages	M,D
Slavic Languages	M,D
Social Psychology	M,D
Sociology	M,D
Spanish	D
Textile Design	M,D
Theater	D
Urban and Regional Planning	M,D
Urban Design	M,D
Western European Studies	M,D
Women's Studies	M,D
Writing	M,D

COVENANT THEOLOGICAL SEMINARY

Theology	P,M,D,O

CRANBROOK ACADEMY OF ART

Applied Arts and Design—General	M
Architecture	M
Art/Fine Arts	M
Graphic Design	M
Photography	M
Textile Design	M

CREIGHTON UNIVERSITY

Conflict Resolution and Mediation/Peace Studies	M,O
English	M
International Affairs	M
Liberal Studies	M
Social Psychology	M
Theology	M
Writing	M

THE CRISWELL COLLEGE

Jewish Studies	P,M
Pastoral Ministry and Counseling	P,M
Theology	P,M

CROWN COLLEGE

Theology	M

CUMBERLAND UNIVERSITY

Public Administration	M

CUNY GRADUATE SCHOOL OF JOURNALISM

Journalism	M

CURRY COLLEGE

Criminal Justice and Criminology	M

CURTIS INSTITUTE OF MUSIC

Music	M

DALHOUSIE UNIVERSITY

Anthropology	M,D
Architecture	M
Classics	M,D
Clinical Psychology	M,D
Economics	M,D
English	M,D
French	M,D
German	M
History	M,D
Interdisciplinary Studies	D
International Development	M
Music	M
Philosophy	M,D
Political Science	M,D
Psychology—General	M,D
Public Administration	M,O

Rural Planning and
  Studies — M
Sociology — M,D
Urban and Regional
  Planning — M

DALLAS BAPTIST UNIVERSITY

Conflict Resolution and
  Mediation/Peace
  Studies — M
Corporate and
  Organizational
  Communication — M
Counseling Psychology — M
Criminal Justice and
  Criminology — M
Experimental
  Psychology — M
Interdisciplinary Studies — M
Liberal Studies — M
Missions and Missiology — M
Pastoral Ministry and
  Counseling — M

DALLAS THEOLOGICAL SEMINARY

Media Studies — M,D,O
Missions and Missiology — M,D,O
Pastoral Ministry and
  Counseling — M,D,O
Theology — M,D,O

DARKEI NOAM RABBINICAL COLLEGE

Theology — M

DARTMOUTH COLLEGE

Cognitive Sciences — D
Comparative Literature — M
Liberal Studies — M
Music — M
Psychology—General — D

DEFIANCE COLLEGE

Criminal Justice and
  Criminology — M

DELAWARE STATE UNIVERSITY

Historic Preservation — M

DELAWARE VALLEY COLLEGE

Agricultural Economics
  and Agribusiness — M

DELL'ARTE INTERNATIONAL SCHOOL OF PHYSICAL THEATRE

Theater — M

DELTA STATE UNIVERSITY

Criminal Justice and
  Criminology — M
Urban and Regional
  Planning — M

DENVER SEMINARY

Marriage and Family
  Therapy — P,M,D,O
Pastoral Ministry and
  Counseling — P,M,D,O
Religion — P,M,D,O
Theology — P,M,D,O

DEPAUL UNIVERSITY

Clinical Psychology — M,D
Communication—
  General — M
Computer Art and
  Design — M,D

Corporate and
  Organizational
  Communication — M
Economics — M
English — M
Experimental
  Psychology — M,D
Film, Television, and
  Video Production — M,D
History — M
Human Development — M,D
Industrial and
  Organizational
  Psychology — M,D
Interdisciplinary Studies — M
Internet and Interactive
  Multimedia — M,D
Journalism — M
Media Studies — M
Music — M,O
Philosophy — M,D
Psychology—General — M,D
Public Administration — M,O
Public Affairs — M,O
Public Policy — M,O
Publishing — M
Social Psychology — M,D
Sociology — M
Theater — M
Urban and Regional
  Planning — M,O
Writing — M

DESALES UNIVERSITY

Criminal Justice and
  Criminology — M
Forensic Sciences — M

DEVRY UNIVERSITY

Communication—
  General — M
Public Administration — M

DIGITAL MEDIA ARTS COLLEGE

Computer Art and
  Design — M
Graphic Design — M
Media Studies — M

DOMINICAN HOUSE OF STUDIES, PONTIFICAL FACULTY OF THE IMMACULATE CONCEPTION

Theology — P,M,O

DOMINICAN SCHOOL OF PHILOSOPHY AND THEOLOGY

Philosophy — M
Theology — P,M,O

DOMINICAN UNIVERSITY

Pastoral Ministry and
  Counseling — M

DOMINICAN UNIVERSITY OF CALIFORNIA

Counseling Psychology — M
Humanities — M
Marriage and Family
  Therapy — M
Sustainable
  Development — M

DOWLING COLLEGE

Liberal Studies — M

DRAKE UNIVERSITY

Communication—
  General — M
Public Administration — M

DREW UNIVERSITY

English — M
French — M
History — M,D
Holocaust and Genocide
  Studies — M,D,O
Humanities — M,D,O
Interdisciplinary Studies — M,D,O
Italian — M
Spanish — M
Theater — M
Theology — P,M,D,O
Translation and
  Interpretation — M
Writing — M

DREXEL UNIVERSITY

Applied Arts and
  Design—General — M
Art Therapy — M,O
Arts Administration — M
Clinical Psychology — D
Communication—
  General — M
Computer Art and
  Design — M
Corporate and
  Organizational
  Communication — M
Economics — M,D,O
Emergency
  Management — M
Film, Television, and
  Video Production — M
Forensic Psychology — D
Health Psychology — D
History of Science and
  Technology — M
Homeland Security — M
Interior Design — M
Journalism — M
Marriage and Family
  Therapy — M,D
Mass Communication — M
Psychology—General — M,D
Publishing — M
Technical
  Communication — M
Technical Writing — M
Textile Design — M
Therapies—Dance,
  Drama, and Music — M,O

DRURY UNIVERSITY

Architecture — M
Art/Fine Arts — M
Communication—
  General — M
Criminal Justice and
  Criminology — M

DUKE UNIVERSITY

Art History — D
Art/Fine Arts — D
Asian Studies — M,O
Biological Anthropology — D
Classics — D
Clinical Psychology — D
Cognitive Sciences — D
Comparative Literature — D
Cultural Anthropology — D
Developmental
  Psychology — D
Economics — M,D
English — D
Experimental
  Psychology — D
French — D
German — D
Health Psychology — D
History — M,D
Human Development — D

Humanities — M
International
  Development — M,O
Latin American Studies — M,D
Liberal Studies — M
Media Studies — M
Music — M,D
Philosophy — M,D
Political Science — M,D
Psychology—General — D
Public Policy — M,D,O
Religion — M,D
Slavic Languages — M,O
Sociology — M,D
Spanish — D
Theology — P,M,D

DUQUESNE UNIVERSITY

Clinical Psychology — D
Communication—
  General — M,D
Conflict Resolution and
  Mediation/Peace
  Studies — M,O
English — M,D
Ethics — M
Forensic Sciences — M
History — M
Internet and Interactive
  Multimedia — M,O
Liberal Studies — M
Museum Studies — M
Music — M,O
Philosophy — M,D
Psychology—General — D
Public Administration — M,O
Public Policy — M,O
Rhetoric — M,D
School Psychology — M,D,O
Theology — M,D

EARLHAM SCHOOL OF RELIGION

Religion — P,M
Theology — P,M

EAST CAROLINA UNIVERSITY

Addictions/Substance
  Abuse Counseling — M
American Studies — M
Anthropology — M
Art/Fine Arts — M
Child and Family
  Studies — M
Child Development — M
Clinical Psychology — M
Criminal Justice and
  Criminology — M
Economics — M
English — M
Geography — M
Health Communication — M
Health Psychology — D
History — M
International Affairs — M
Marriage and Family
  Therapy — M
Music — M
Political Science — M
Psychology—General — M
Public Administration — M
Rehabilitation
  Counseling — M
School Psychology — M
Sociology — M
Therapies—Dance,
  Drama, and Music — M
Western European
  Studies — M

---

*M—master's degree; P—first professional degree; D—doctorate; O—other advanced degree; *—Close-Up and/or Display*

EAST CENTRAL UNIVERSITY

Criminal Justice and Criminology	M
Psychology—General	M
Rehabilitation Counseling	M

EASTERN ILLINOIS UNIVERSITY

Art/Fine Arts	M
Clinical Psychology	M,O
Consumer Economics	M
Economics	M
English	M
Family and Consumer Sciences-General	M
Gerontology	M
History	M
Music	M
Political Science	M
Psychology—General	M,O
Public History	M
School Psychology	M,O
Speech and Interpersonal Communication	M

EASTERN KENTUCKY UNIVERSITY

Clinical Psychology	M,O
Criminal Justice and Criminology	M
English	M
History	M
Industrial and Organizational Psychology	M,O
Music	M
Political Science	M
Psychology—General	M,O
Public Administration	M
School Psychology	M,O
Urban and Regional Planning	M
Writing	M

EASTERN MENNONITE UNIVERSITY

Conflict Resolution and Mediation/Peace Studies	M,O
Pastoral Ministry and Counseling	P,M,O
Religion	P,M,O
Theology	P,M,O

EASTERN MICHIGAN UNIVERSITY

Addictions/Substance Abuse Counseling	M
African-American Studies	O
American Studies	M,O
Applied Economics	M
Art/Fine Arts	M
Arts Administration	M
Child and Family Studies	M
Clinical Psychology	M,D
Clothing and Textiles	M
Communication—General	M
Criminal Justice and Criminology	M
Cultural Studies	M
Economic Development	M
Economics	M
English	M,O
French	M,O
Gender Studies	M,O
Geographic Information Systems	M,O
Geography	M,O
German	M,O

Gerontology	M,O
Hispanic and Latin American Languages	M,O
Hispanic Studies	M,O
Historic Preservation	M,O
History	M,O
Interior Design	M
International Economics	M
Japanese	M,O
Linguistics	M
Music	M
Psychology—General	M,D
Public Administration	M,O
Public Policy	M,O
Social Psychology	M,O
Social Sciences	M,O
Sociology	M
Spanish	M,O
Technical Communication	M,O
Theater	M
Urban and Regional Planning	M,O
Women's Studies	M,O
Writing	M,O

EASTERN NAZARENE COLLEGE

Counseling Psychology	M
Marriage and Family Therapy	M

EASTERN NEW MEXICO UNIVERSITY

Anthropology	M
Communication—General	M
English	M

EASTERN UNIVERSITY

Counseling Psychology	M,O
Economic Development	M
International Development	M
Marriage and Family Therapy	D
Missions and Missiology	D
Pastoral Ministry and Counseling	D
School Psychology	M,O
Social Psychology	M,O
Theology	P,M,D
Urban and Regional Planning	M
Urban Studies	M

EASTERN VIRGINIA MEDICAL SCHOOL

Art Therapy	M
Clinical Psychology	D

EASTERN WASHINGTON UNIVERSITY

Applied Psychology	M
Clinical Psychology	M
Communication—General	M
Counseling Psychology	M
English	M
Experimental Psychology	M
History	M
Interdisciplinary Studies	M
Music	M
Psychology—General	M
Public Administration	M
Rhetoric	M
School Psychology	M
Sport Psychology	M
Technical Communication	M
Urban and Regional Planning	M
Writing	M

EAST STROUDSBURG UNIVERSITY OF PENNSYLVANIA

History	M
Political Science	M

EAST TENNESSEE STATE UNIVERSITY

Art/Fine Arts	M
Clinical Psychology	M,D
Communication—General	M
Computer Art and Design	M,O
Criminal Justice and Criminology	M,O
Economics	M,O
English	M,O
Gerontology	M,D,O
History	M
Human Development	M,D
Liberal Studies	M,O
Marriage and Family Therapy	M,D
Political Science	M
Psychology—General	M,D
Sociology	M
Urban and Regional Planning	M,O
Urban Studies	M,O

ECUMENICAL THEOLOGICAL SEMINARY

Pastoral Ministry and Counseling	D
Theology	P

EDEN THEOLOGICAL SEMINARY

Theology	P,M,D

EDGEWOOD COLLEGE

Marriage and Family Therapy	M
Religion	M

EDINBORO UNIVERSITY OF PENNSYLVANIA

Art/Fine Arts	M
Communication—General	M,O
Conflict Resolution and Mediation/Peace Studies	M,O
Music	M,O
Rehabilitation Counseling	M,O
School Psychology	M,O
Social Sciences	M

ELMHURST COLLEGE

English	M
Industrial and Organizational Psychology	M

ELMS COLLEGE

Religion	M

ELON UNIVERSITY

Internet and Interactive Multimedia	M

EMBRY-RIDDLE AERONAUTICAL UNIVERSITY–DAYTONA

Interdisciplinary Studies	M

EMERSON COLLEGE

Broadcast Journalism	M
Communication—General	M
Corporate and Organizational Communication	M
Health Communication	M

Journalism	M
Media Studies	M
Publishing	M
Theater	M
Writing	M

EMILY CARR UNIVERSITY OF ART + DESIGN

Applied Arts and Design—General	M
Art/Fine Arts	M
Computer Art and Design	M

EMMANUEL CHRISTIAN SEMINARY

Missions and Missiology	P,M,D
Pastoral Ministry and Counseling	P,M,D
Religion	P,M,D
Theology	P,M,D

EMORY & HENRY COLLEGE

American Studies	M
History	M

EMORY UNIVERSITY

Anthropology	D
Art History	D
Clinical Psychology	D
Cognitive Sciences	D
Comparative Literature	D,O
Demography and Population Studies	M
Developmental Psychology	D
Economics	D
English	D,O
Ethics	P,M,D
Film, Television, and Video Theory and Criticism	M,D,O
French	D,O
Gerontology	M
History	D
Interdisciplinary Studies	D
Jewish Studies	M
Music	M
Near and Middle Eastern Studies	D,O
Pastoral Ministry and Counseling	P,M,D
Philosophy	D,O
Political Science	D
Portuguese	D,O
Psychology—General	D
Religion	D,O
Sociology	M,D
Spanish	D,O
Sustainable Development	M
Theology	P,M,D
Women's Studies	D,O

EMPORIA STATE UNIVERSITY

Art Therapy	M
Clinical Psychology	M
Counseling Psychology	M
English	M
History	M
Industrial and Organizational Psychology	M
Music	M
Psychology—General	M
Rehabilitation Counseling	M
School Psychology	M,O

ENDICOTT COLLEGE

Interior Design	M

EPISCOPAL DIVINITY SCHOOL

Theology	P,M,D,O

ERIKSON INSTITUTE

Child Development	M
Developmental Psychology	M,O
Human Development	M,O

ERSKINE THEOLOGICAL SEMINARY

Theology	P,M,D

EVANGELICAL SEMINARY OF PUERTO RICO

Theology	P,M,D

EVANGELICAL THEOLOGICAL SEMINARY

Marriage and Family Therapy	P,M
Missions and Missiology	P,M
Pastoral Ministry and Counseling	P,M
Theology	P,M

EVANGEL UNIVERSITY

Clinical Psychology	M
Counseling Psychology	M
Psychology—General	M
School Psychology	M

EVEREST UNIVERSITY

Criminal Justice and Criminology	M

EVEREST UNIVERSITY

Criminal Justice and Criminology	M

EVEREST UNIVERSITY

Criminal Justice and Criminology	M

EVEREST UNIVERSITY

Criminal Justice and Criminology	M

THE EVERGREEN STATE COLLEGE

Public Administration	M

EXCELSIOR COLLEGE

Liberal Studies	M

FAIRFIELD UNIVERSITY

American Studies	M
Applied Psychology	M,O
Child and Family Studies	M
Clinical Psychology	M,O
Communication— General	M
Counseling Psychology	M,O
Industrial and Organizational Psychology	M,O
Marriage and Family Therapy	M
School Psychology	M,O
Writing	M

FAIRLEIGH DICKINSON UNIVERSITY, COLLEGE AT FLORHAM

Clinical Psychology	M
Corporate and Organizational Communication	M
Counseling Psychology	M

Industrial and Organizational Psychology	M
Psychology—General	M,O
Public Administration	M
Writing	M

FAIRLEIGH DICKINSON UNIVERSITY, METROPOLITAN CAMPUS

Art/Fine Arts	M
Clinical Psychology	M,D
Communication— General	M
Comparative Literature	M
Criminal Justice and Criminology	M
English	M
Experimental Psychology	M,O
Forensic Psychology	M
History	M
Homeland Security	M
International Affairs	M
Media Studies	M
Political Science	M
Psychology—General	M,D,O
Public Administration	M,O
School Psychology	M,D

FAIRMONT STATE UNIVERSITY

Criminal Justice and Criminology	M

FAITH BAPTIST BIBLE COLLEGE AND THEOLOGICAL SEMINARY

Pastoral Ministry and Counseling	P,M
Religion	P,M
Theology	P,M

FAITH EVANGELICAL LUTHERAN SEMINARY

Theology	P,M,D

FAITH THEOLOGICAL SEMINARY

Theology	P,D

FASHION INSTITUTE OF TECHNOLOGY

Applied Arts and Design—General	M*
Art History	M
Arts Administration	M*
Exhibition Design	M*
Fashion and Textile Studies	M*
Illustration	M*
Sustainable Interior Environments	M*

FAULKNER UNIVERSITY

Criminal Justice and Criminology	M
History	M
Liberal Studies	M
Missions and Missiology	M
Pastoral Ministry and Counseling	M
Theology	M

FAYETTEVILLE STATE UNIVERSITY

Criminal Justice and Criminology	M
English	M
History	M
Political Science	M

Psychology—General	M
Sociology	M

FELICIAN COLLEGE

Counseling Psychology	M*

FERRIS STATE UNIVERSITY

Applied Arts and Design—General	M
Art/Fine Arts	M
Criminal Justice and Criminology	M

FIELDING GRADUATE UNIVERSITY

Clinical Psychology	M,D,O
Human Development	M,D,O
Psychology—General	M,D,O

FISK UNIVERSITY

Clinical Psychology	M
Psychology—General	M

FITCHBURG STATE UNIVERSITY

Communication— General	M,O
Counseling Psychology	M
English	M,O
Health Communication	M,O
History	M,O
Interdisciplinary Studies	O
Technical Writing	M,O

FIVE TOWNS COLLEGE

Music	M,D

FLORIDA AGRICULTURAL AND MECHANICAL UNIVERSITY

African-American Studies	M
Agricultural Economics and Agribusiness	M
Architecture	M
Criminal Justice and Criminology	M
Economics	M
History	M
International Affairs	M
Journalism	M
Landscape Architecture	M
Political Science	M
Psychology—General	M
Public Administration	M
School Psychology	M
Social Psychology	M
Social Sciences	M
Sociology	M

FLORIDA ATLANTIC UNIVERSITY

Anthropology	M
Applied Arts and Design—General	M
Art/Fine Arts	M
Communication— General	M,O
Comparative and Interdisciplinary Arts	D
Comparative Literature	M
Computer Art and Design	M
Counseling Psychology	M,D,O
Criminal Justice and Criminology	M
Economic Development	M,O
Economics	M
English	M
Environmental Design	M,O
Film, Television, and Video Production	M,O

Film, Television, and Video Theory and Criticism	M,O
French	M
Geography	M,D
Graphic Design	M
History	M,O
Journalism	M,O
Liberal Studies	M
Linguistics	M
Marriage and Family Therapy	M,D,O
Music	M
Political Science	M
Psychology—General	M,D
Public Administration	M,D
Rehabilitation Counseling	M,D,O
Sociology	M
Spanish	M
Sustainable Development	M,O
Theater	M
Urban and Regional Planning	M,O
Women's Studies	M,O
Writing	M

FLORIDA GULF COAST UNIVERSITY

Criminal Justice and Criminology	M
English	M
Forensic Sciences	M
History	M
Interdisciplinary Studies	M
Public Administration	M

FLORIDA INSTITUTE OF TECHNOLOGY

Applied Behavior Analysis	M,D
Clinical Psychology	M,D
Communication— General	M
Corporate and Organizational Communication	M
Emergency Management	M
Industrial and Organizational Psychology	M,D
Interdisciplinary Studies	M,D
Psychology—General	M,D
Public Administration	M
Technical Communication	M

FLORIDA INTERNATIONAL UNIVERSITY

African Studies	M
Architecture	M
Art/Fine Arts	M
Asian Studies	M
Clinical Psychology	M,D,O
Conflict Resolution and Mediation/Peace Studies	M,D,O
Counseling Psychology	M,D,O
Criminal Justice and Criminology	M
Economics	M,D
English	M
Forensic Sciences	M
History	M,D
Interior Design	M
International Affairs	M,D
Landscape Architecture	M
Latin American Studies	M
Liberal Studies	M
Linguistics	M

M—master's degree; P—first professional degree; D—doctorate; O—other advanced degree; *—Close-Up and / or Display

Mass Communication	M
Music	M
Political Science	M,D
Psychology—General	M,D
Public Administration	M,D
Rehabilitation Counseling	M,D,O
Religion	M,D
School Psychology	M,D,O
Sociology	M,D
Spanish	M,D
Writing	M

FLORIDA STATE UNIVERSITY

Applied Behavior Analysis	M
Archaeology	M,D
Art History	M,D,O
Art/Fine Arts	M
Arts Administration	M,D
Asian Studies	M
Child and Family Studies	M,D
Classics	M,D
Clinical Psychology	D
Cognitive Sciences	D
Communication— General	M,D
Corporate and Organizational Communication	M,D
Counseling Psychology	M,D,O
Criminal Justice and Criminology	M,D
Dance	M
Demography and Population Studies	M
Developmental Psychology	D
East European and Russian Studies	M
Economics	M,D
English	M,D
Family and Consumer Sciences-General	M,D
Film, Television, and Video Production	M
French	M,D
Geographic Information Systems	M,D
Geography	M,D
German	M
History	M,D
Interior Design	M
International Affairs	M
Italian	M
Marriage and Family Therapy	M,D
Mass Communication	M,D
Media Studies	M,D
Museum Studies	M,D,O
Music	M,D
Philosophy	M,D
Political Science	M,D
Psychology—General	M,D
Public Administration	M,D,O
Public History	M,D
Public Policy	M,D,O
Rehabilitation Counseling	M,D,O
Religion	M,D
Rhetoric	M,D
School Psychology	M,O
Slavic Languages	M
Social Psychology	D
Sociology	M,D
Spanish	M,D
Speech and Interpersonal Communication	M,D
Sport Psychology	M,D,O
Theater	M,D
Therapies—Dance, Drama, and Music	M,D

Urban and Regional Planning	M,D
Writing	M,D

FONTBONNE UNIVERSITY

Art/Fine Arts	M
Family and Consumer Sciences-General	M
Theater	M

FORDHAM UNIVERSITY

Applied Psychology	D
Classics	M,D
Clinical Psychology	D
Communication— General	M
Corporate and Organizational Communication	M
Counseling Psychology	M,D,O
Developmental Psychology	D
Economic Development	M,O
Economics	M,D,O
Emergency Management	M
English	M,D
Ethics	M,O
History	M,D
International Affairs	M,O
International Development	M,O
International Economics	M,O
Latin American Studies	M,O
Liberal Studies	M
Mass Communication	M
Media Studies	M
Medieval and Renaissance Studies	M,O
Pastoral Ministry and Counseling	M,D,O
Philosophy	M,D
Political Science	M
Psychology—General	D
Religion	M,D,O
School Psychology	M,D,O
Sociology	M
Theology	M,D
Urban Studies	M

FORT HAYS STATE UNIVERSITY

Art/Fine Arts	M
Communication— General	M
English	M
Geography	M
History	M
Liberal Studies	M
Psychology—General	M,O
School Psychology	O

FORT VALLEY STATE UNIVERSITY

Counseling Psychology	M
Rehabilitation Counseling	M

FRAMINGHAM STATE UNIVERSITY

Art/Fine Arts	M
Psychology—General	M
Public Administration	M
Spanish	M

FRANCISCAN SCHOOL OF THEOLOGY

Theology	P,M

FRANCISCAN UNIVERSITY OF STEUBENVILLE

Counseling Psychology	M
Philosophy	M
Theology	M

FRANCIS MARION UNIVERSITY

Applied Psychology	M,O
Clinical Psychology	M,O
Counseling Psychology	M,O
Psychology—General	M,O
School Psychology	M,O

FRANKLIN PIERCE UNIVERSITY

Interdisciplinary Studies	M,D,O

FRANKLIN UNIVERSITY

Corporate and Organizational Communication	M

FRANK LLOYD WRIGHT SCHOOL OF ARCHITECTURE

Architecture	M

FREDERICK S. PARDEE RAND GRADUATE SCHOOL

Public Policy	D

FREED-HARDEMAN UNIVERSITY

Ethics	M
Pastoral Ministry and Counseling	M
Theology	P,M

FRESNO PACIFIC UNIVERSITY

Conflict Resolution and Mediation/Peace Studies	M
Interdisciplinary Studies	M
Marriage and Family Therapy	M,O
Missions and Missiology	M
Pastoral Ministry and Counseling	M
School Psychology	M
Theology	P,M

FRIENDS UNIVERSITY

Marriage and Family Therapy	M
Theology	M

FROSTBURG STATE UNIVERSITY

Counseling Psychology	M
Interdisciplinary Studies	M
Psychology—General	M

FULLER THEOLOGICAL SEMINARY

Clinical Psychology	D
Marriage and Family Therapy	M,O
Missions and Missiology	P,M,D
Music	P,M,D
Pastoral Ministry and Counseling	P,M,D
Psychology—General	M,D,O
Theology	P,M,D

FULL SAIL UNIVERSITY

Art/Fine Arts	M
Computer Art and Design	M
Graphic Design	M
Internet and Interactive Multimedia	M
Journalism	M
Media Studies	M
Writing	M

FUTURE GENERATIONS GRADUATE SCHOOL

Social Psychology	M

GALLAUDET UNIVERSITY

Clinical Psychology	M,D,O

Counseling Psychology	M,D,O
Linguistics	M,D,O
School Psychology	M,D,O
Translation and Interpretation	M,D,O

GANNON UNIVERSITY

Counseling Psychology	D
English	M
Gerontology	O
Pastoral Ministry and Counseling	M,O
Public Administration	M,O

GARDNER-WEBB UNIVERSITY

Counseling Psychology	M
English	M
Missions and Missiology	P,D
Pastoral Ministry and Counseling	P,D
Psychology—General	M
Religion	M
School Psychology	M
Theology	P,D

GARRETT-EVANGELICAL THEOLOGICAL SEMINARY

Music	P,M,D
Pastoral Ministry and Counseling	P,M,D
Theology	P,M,D

GENERAL THEOLOGICAL SEMINARY

Pastoral Ministry and Counseling	P,M,D,O
Religion	P,M,D,O
Theology	P,M,D,O

GENEVA COLLEGE

Counseling Psychology	M
Marriage and Family Therapy	M
Psychology—General	M

GEORGE FOX UNIVERSITY

Clinical Psychology	M,D,O
Counseling Psychology	M,O
Marriage and Family Therapy	M,O
Missions and Missiology	P,M,D,O
Pastoral Ministry and Counseling	P,M,D,O
School Psychology	M,O
Theology	P,M,D,O

GEORGE MASON UNIVERSITY

Anthropology	M,D
Art History	M
Arts Administration	M,O
Cognitive Sciences	M,D,O
Communication— General	M,D
Conflict Resolution and Mediation/Peace Studies	M,D,O
Criminal Justice and Criminology	M,D
Cultural Studies	M,D,O
Dance	M
Economics	M,D,O
Emergency Management	M,D,O
English	M,D,O
Ethics	M,D,O
Folklore	M,D,O
Forensic Sciences	M,D,O
Geographic Information Systems	M,D,O
Geography	M,D,O
Gerontology	M,O
Graphic Design	M
History	M,D

Homeland Security	M,D,O
Interdisciplinary Studies	M
International Affairs	M
Internet and Interactive Multimedia	M,D,O
Linguistics	M,D,O
Music	M,D,O
National Security	M,D,O
Philosophy	M
Political Science	M,D,O
Psychology—General	M,D,O
Public Administration	M,D,O
Public Affairs	M,D,O
Public Policy	M,D*
Rural Planning and Studies	M,O
School Psychology	O
Sociology	M,D
Sustainable Development	M,D,O
Writing	M

GEORGETOWN UNIVERSITY

American Studies	M,D
Communication—General	M
Comparative Literature	M,D
Conflict Resolution and Mediation/Peace Studies	M
East European and Russian Studies	M
Economic Development	D
Economics	D
English	M
Ethics	M,D
German	M,D
History	M,D
Humanities	M,D
Industrial and Labor Relations	D
Interdisciplinary Studies	M,D
International Affairs	P,M,D
Internet and Interactive Multimedia	M
Journalism	M,D
Latin American Studies	M
Liberal Studies	M,D
Linguistics	M,D,O
Media Studies	M,D
Medieval and Renaissance Studies	M,D
Near and Middle Eastern Languages	M,D
Near and Middle Eastern Studies	M,D,O
Philosophy	M,D
Political Science	M,D
Psychology—General	D
Public Policy	M,D
Religion	M,D
Spanish	M,D
Theology	D
Western European Studies	M

THE GEORGE WASHINGTON UNIVERSITY

American Studies	M,D
Anthropology	M,D
Applied Psychology	D
Art History	M
Art Therapy	M
Art/Fine Arts	M
Asian Studies	M
Clinical Psychology	D
Cognitive Sciences	D
Communication—General	M
Criminal Justice and Criminology	M
Dance	M

East European and Russian Studies	M
Economics	M,D
Emergency Management	M,D,O
English	M,D
Folklore	M,D
Forensic Sciences	M
Geography	M
Historic Preservation	M,D
History	M,D
Human Development	M
Industrial and Organizational Psychology	M,D
Interior Design	M
International Affairs	M
International Development	M
International Trade Policy	M
Latin American Studies	M
Mass Communication	M
Military and Defense Studies	M
Museum Studies	M,O
Near and Middle Eastern Studies	M
Philosophy	M
Photography	M
Political Science	M,D
Psychology—General	D
Public Administration	M
Public Affairs	M
Public Policy	M,D
Publishing	M
Rehabilitation Counseling	M
Religion	M
Social Psychology	M,D
Sociology	M
Theater	M
Western European Studies	M
Women's Studies	M,O

GEORGIA COLLEGE & STATE UNIVERSITY

Criminal Justice and Criminology	M
English	M
History	M
Public Administration	M
Public History	M
Therapies—Dance, Drama, and Music	M
Writing	M

GEORGIA HEALTH SCIENCES UNIVERSITY

Medical Illustration	M

GEORGIA INSTITUTE OF TECHNOLOGY

Architecture	M,D
Building Science	M,D
Computer Art and Design	M,D
Economic Development	M,D
Economics	M
Experimental Psychology	M,D
Geographic Information Systems	M,D
History of Science and Technology	M,D
Industrial and Organizational Psychology	M,D
International Affairs	M,D
Internet and Interactive Multimedia	M,D

Psychology—General	M,D
Public Policy	M,D
Urban and Regional Planning	M,D
Urban Design	M,D

GEORGIAN COURT UNIVERSITY

Clinical Psychology	M,O
Counseling Psychology	M,O
Health Psychology	M,O
Pastoral Ministry and Counseling	M,O
School Psychology	M,O
Theology	M,O

GEORGIA SOUTHERN UNIVERSITY

Applied Economics	M
Art/Fine Arts	M
English	M
History	M
Music	M
Psychology—General	M,D
Public Administration	M
School Psychology	M,O
Sociology	M
Spanish	M

GEORGIA STATE UNIVERSITY

Anthropology	M
Art History	M
Art/Fine Arts	M
Communication—General	M,D
Counseling Psychology	M,D,O
Criminal Justice and Criminology	M,D,O
Economic Development	M,D,O
Economics	M,D
Emergency Management	M,D,O
English	M,D
Film, Television, and Video Production	M,D
French	M,O
Geographic Information Systems	O
Geography	M
German	M,O
Gerontology	M
Historic Preservation	M,O
History	M,D
Latin American Studies	M,D,O
Linguistics	M,D
Mass Communication	M,D
Music	M
Philosophy	M
Photography	M,D
Political Science	M,D
Psychology—General	M,D
Public Administration	M,D,O
Public Policy	M,D,O
Rehabilitation Counseling	M
Religion	M
Rhetoric	M,D
School Psychology	M,D,O
Sociology	M,D
Spanish	M,O
Speech and Interpersonal Communication	M,D
Translation and Interpretation	O
Urban and Regional Planning	M,D,O
Women's Studies	M,O
Writing	M,D

GLOBAL UNIVERSITY

Missions and Missiology	P,M
Theology	P,M

GODDARD COLLEGE

Comparative and Interdisciplinary Arts	M
Counseling Psychology	M
Industrial and Organizational Psychology	M
Interdisciplinary Studies	M
Writing	M

GOLDEN GATE BAPTIST THEOLOGICAL SEMINARY

Pastoral Ministry and Counseling	P,M,D,O
Theology	P,M,D,O

GOLDEN GATE UNIVERSITY

Forensic Sciences	M,O
Psychology—General	M,D,O
Public Administration	M,D,O

GONZAGA UNIVERSITY

Communication—General	M
Counseling Psychology	M
Pastoral Ministry and Counseling	M
Philosophy	M
Religion	M

GORDON-CONWELL THEOLOGICAL SEMINARY

Archaeology	P,M,D
Missions and Missiology	P,M,D
Pastoral Ministry and Counseling	P,M,D
Religion	P,M,D
Theology	P,M,D

GOUCHER COLLEGE

Arts Administration	M
Computer Art and Design	M
Cultural Studies	M
Historic Preservation	M
Writing	M

GOVERNORS STATE UNIVERSITY

Addictions/Substance Abuse Counseling	M
Art/Fine Arts	M
Communication—General	M
Counseling Psychology	M
English	M
Media Studies	M
Political Science	M
Psychology—General	M
Public Administration	M

GRACE COLLEGE

Counseling Psychology	M

GRACELAND UNIVERSITY (IA)

Pastoral Ministry and Counseling	M
Religion	M
Theology	M

GRACE THEOLOGICAL SEMINARY

Cultural Studies	P,M,D,O
Missions and Missiology	P,M,D,O
Pastoral Ministry and Counseling	P,M,D,O
Theology	P,M,D,O

GRACE UNIVERSITY

Counseling Psychology	M

*M—master's degree; P—first professional degree; D—doctorate; O—other advanced degree; *—Close-Up and/or Display*

Pastoral Ministry and
  Counseling — M
Theology — M

GRADUATE INSTITUTE OF APPLIED LINGUISTICS

Linguistics — M,O

GRADUATE SCHOOL AND UNIVERSITY CENTER OF THE CITY UNIVERSITY OF NEW YORK

Anthropology — D
Archaeology — D
Architectural History — D
Art History — D
Classics — M,D
Clinical Psychology — D
Cognitive Sciences — D
Comparative Literature — M,D
Criminal Justice and
  Criminology — D
Cultural Anthropology — D
Developmental
  Psychology — D
Economics — D
English — D
Experimental
  Psychology — D
French — D
German — M,D
Hispanic and Latin
  American Languages — D
History — D
Industrial and
  Organizational
  Psychology — D
Interdisciplinary Studies — M,D
Italian — M,D
Liberal Studies — M
Linguistics — M,D
Medieval and
  Renaissance Studies — M,D
Music — D
Philosophy — M,D
Political Science — M,D
Psychology—General — D
Public Policy — M,D
Social Psychology — D
Sociology — D
Theater — D
Urban Studies — M,D
Women's Studies — M,D

GRADUATE THEOLOGICAL UNION

Art History — M,D,O
Cultural Studies — M,D,O
Ethics — M,D,O
Jewish Studies — M,D,O
Religion — M,D,O
Social Sciences — M,D,O
Theology — M,D,O

GRAMBLING STATE UNIVERSITY

Criminal Justice and
  Criminology — M
English — M,D
Mass Communication — M
Political Science — M
Public Administration — M

GRAND CANYON UNIVERSITY

Addictions/Substance
  Abuse Counseling — M
Cognitive Sciences — D
Counseling Psychology — M
Emergency
  Management — M
Industrial and
  Organizational
  Psychology — D

Marriage and Family
  Therapy — M
Psychology—General — D
Public Administration — M

GRAND RAPIDS THEOLOGICAL SEMINARY OF CORNERSTONE UNIVERSITY

Missions and Missiology — P,M
Pastoral Ministry and
  Counseling — P,M
Religion — P,M
Theology — P,M

GRAND VALLEY STATE UNIVERSITY

Communication—
  General — M
Criminal Justice and
  Criminology — M
English — M
Public Administration — M
School Psychology — M

GRATZ COLLEGE

Holocaust and Genocide
  Studies — M,O
Jewish Studies — M,O
Music — M,O

GREENVILLE COLLEGE

Pastoral Ministry and
  Counseling — M

HAMLINE UNIVERSITY

Liberal Studies — M,O
Public Administration — M,D
Writing — M,O

HAMPTON UNIVERSITY

Architecture — M
Pastoral Ministry and
  Counseling — M

HARDING UNIVERSITY

Counseling Psychology — M
Marriage and Family
  Therapy — M
Pastoral Ministry and
  Counseling — M

HARDING UNIVERSITY GRADUATE SCHOOL OF RELIGION

Pastoral Ministry and
  Counseling — P,M,D
Religion — P,M,D
Theology — P,M,D

HARDIN-SIMMONS UNIVERSITY

English — M
History — M
Marriage and Family
  Therapy — M
Music — M
Pastoral Ministry and
  Counseling — M,D
Psychology—General — M
Religion — M
Theology — P,M,D

HARRINGTON COLLEGE OF DESIGN

Interior Design — M

HARRISBURG UNIVERSITY OF SCIENCE AND TECHNOLOGY

Public Administration — M

HARTFORD SEMINARY

Pastoral Ministry and
  Counseling — M,D,O

Religion — M,D,O
Theology — M,D,O

HARVARD UNIVERSITY

African Studies — D
African-American
  Studies — D
American Studies — D
Anthropology — M,D
Archaeology — M,D
Architectural History — D
Architecture — M,D
Art History — D
Asian Languages — M,D
Asian Studies — M,D
Celtic Languages — D
Chinese — D
Classics — D
Cognitive Sciences — M,D
Communication—
  General — M,O
Comparative Literature — D
Demography and
  Population Studies — M,D
Developmental
  Psychology — D
East European and
  Russian Studies — M
Economics — D
English — M,D,O
Experimental
  Psychology — D
French — M,D
German — D
History of Science and
  Technology — M,D
History — D
Human Development — M,D
International Affairs — P,D
International
  Development — M
Italian — M,D
Japanese — D
Jewish Studies — M,D
Journalism — M,O
Landscape Architecture — M,D
Liberal Studies — M,O
Linguistics — D
Medieval and
  Renaissance Studies — D
Museum Studies — M,O
Music — M,D
Near and Middle
  Eastern Languages — M,D
Near and Middle
  Eastern Studies — M,D
Philosophy — M,D
Political Science — M,D
Portuguese — M,D
Psychology—General — D
Public Administration — M
Public Policy — M,D
Religion — D
Russian — D
Scandinavian
  Languages — D
Slavic Languages — D
Social Psychology — D
Sociology — D
Spanish — M,D
Technical
  Communication — M
Theology — P,M,D
Urban and Regional
  Planning — M,D
Urban Design — M

HAWAI'I PACIFIC UNIVERSITY

Clinical Psychology — M
Communication—
  General — M*
Economics — M
Military and Defense
  Studies — M*

Sustainable
  Development — M*

HAZELDEN GRADUATE SCHOOL OF ADDICTION STUDIES

Addictions/Substance
  Abuse Counseling — M,O

HEBREW COLLEGE

Jewish Studies — M,O
Music — M,O
Theology — M

HEBREW UNION COLLEGE–JEWISH INSTITUTE OF RELIGION (NY)

Jewish Studies — M
Music — M
Near and Middle
  Eastern Languages — D
Theology — P,D

HEC MONTREAL

Applied Economics — M
Arts Administration — O
Corporate and
  Organizational
  Communication — O
Sustainable
  Development — O

HEIDELBERG UNIVERSITY

Counseling Psychology — M

HENDERSON STATE UNIVERSITY

Counseling Psychology — M
Liberal Studies — M

HENLEY-PUTNAM UNIVERSITY

Homeland Security — M
Military and Defense
  Studies — M
National Security — D

HERITAGE BAPTIST COLLEGE AND HERITAGE THEOLOGICAL SEMINARY

Pastoral Ministry and
  Counseling — P,M,D,O
Theology — P,M,D,O

HERITAGE CHRISTIAN UNIVERSITY

Classics — M
Pastoral Ministry and
  Counseling — M
Religion — M

HERITAGE UNIVERSITY

English — M

HIGH POINT UNIVERSITY

Corporate and
  Organizational
  Communication — M
History — M

HILLSDALE FREE WILL BAPTIST COLLEGE

Pastoral Ministry and
  Counseling — M

HIRAM COLLEGE

Interdisciplinary Studies — M

HODGES UNIVERSITY

Counseling Psychology — M
Criminal Justice and
  Criminology — M
Interdisciplinary Studies — M

Psychology—General M
Public Administration M

HOFSTRA UNIVERSITY

Applied Psychology D
Applied Social Research M
Art Therapy M,O
Art/Fine Arts M,O
Clinical Psychology D
Communication—
General M
Comparative Literature M
Counseling Psychology M,O
English M
Family and Consumer
Sciences-General M,O
Film, Television, and
Video Production M
French M,O
German M,O
Gerontology M,O
Human Development D
Humanities D
Industrial and
Organizational
Psychology M,D
Journalism M
Linguistics M,D
Marriage and Family
Therapy M,O
Music M,O
Rehabilitation
Counseling M,O
Russian M,O
School Psychology D
Social Psychology D
Sociology M
Spanish M,O
Speech and
Interpersonal
Communication M
Writing M,D,O

HOLLINS UNIVERSITY

Art/Fine Arts M,O
Dance M
English M
Film, Television, and
Video Production M
Film, Television, and
Video Theory and
Criticism M
Humanities M,O
Interdisciplinary Studies M,O
Liberal Studies M,O
Music M,O
Social Sciences M,O
Theater M
Writing M

HOLMES INSTITUTE

Pastoral Ministry and
Counseling M

**HOLY APOSTLES COLLEGE
AND SEMINARY**

Theology P,M,O

**HOLY CROSS GREEK
ORTHODOX SCHOOL OF
THEOLOGY**

Theology P,M

HOLY FAMILY UNIVERSITY

Counseling Psychology M*
Criminal Justice and
Criminology M*

HOLY NAMES UNIVERSITY

Counseling Psychology M,O
Forensic Psychology M,O
Music M,O

Pastoral Ministry and
Counseling M,O
Religion M,O
Writing M

HOOD COLLEGE

Art/Fine Arts M,O
Human Development M,O
Humanities M
Psychology—General M,O
Public Administration M
Thanatology M,O

**HOOD THEOLOGICAL
SEMINARY**

Theology P,M,D

**HOPE INTERNATIONAL
UNIVERSITY**

International
Development M
Marriage and Family
Therapy M
Missions and Missiology M
Music M
Religion M

HOUGHTON COLLEGE

Music M

HOUSTON BAPTIST UNIVERSITY

Counseling Psychology M
Liberal Studies M
Pastoral Ministry and
Counseling M
Psychology—General M
Theology M

**HOUSTON GRADUATE SCHOOL
OF THEOLOGY**

Pastoral Ministry and
Counseling P,M,D
Theology P,M,D

HOWARD PAYNE UNIVERSITY

Pastoral Ministry and
Counseling M

HOWARD UNIVERSITY

African Studies M,D
Applied Arts and
Design—General M
Art History M
Art/Fine Arts M
Clinical Psychology M,D
Communication—
General M,D
Corporate and
Organizational
Communication M,D
Counseling Psychology M,D
Developmental
Psychology M,D
Economics M,D
English M,D
Experimental
Psychology M,D
Film, Television, and
Video Production M
French M,D
History M,D
Mass Communication M,D
Media Studies M,D
Music M
Philosophy M
Photography M
Political Science M,D
Psychology—General M,D
Public Administration M
School Psychology M,D
Social Psychology M,D
Sociology M,D

Spanish M
Theology P,M,D

**HULT INTERNATIONAL
BUSINESS SCHOOL (UNITED
STATES)**

Conflict Resolution and
Mediation/Peace
Studies M
International Affairs M
National Security M
Political Science M

HUMBOLDT STATE UNIVERSITY

Counseling Psychology M
English M
Film, Television, and
Video Production M
Psychology—General M
School Psychology M
Social Sciences M
Sociology M
Theater M

**HUNTER COLLEGE OF THE CITY
UNIVERSITY OF NEW YORK**

Anthropology M
Applied Psychology M,D
Applied Social Research M
Art History M
Art/Fine Arts M
Classics M
Cognitive Sciences M,D
Economics M
English M
French M
Geographic Information
Systems M,O
Geography M,O
History M
Italian M
Media Studies M
Music M
Psychology—General M,D
Rehabilitation
Counseling M
Romance Languages M
Social Psychology M,D
Sociology M
Spanish M
Theater M
Urban and Regional
Planning M
Urban Studies M
Writing M

HUNTINGTON UNIVERSITY

Pastoral Ministry and
Counseling M

HUSSON UNIVERSITY

Counseling Psychology M
Criminal Justice and
Criminology M

IDAHO STATE UNIVERSITY

Anthropology M
Art/Fine Arts M
Clinical Psychology D
Counseling Psychology M,D,O
English M,D,O
Geographic Information
Systems M,O
History M
Interdisciplinary Studies M
Marriage and Family
Therapy M,D,O
Political Science M,D
Psychology—General M,D
Public Administration M
Rhetoric M
School Psychology M,D,O

Sociology M
Speech and
Interpersonal
Communication M
Theater M

ILIFF SCHOOL OF THEOLOGY

Pastoral Ministry and
Counseling P,M,D
Religion P,M,D
Theology P,M,D

**ILLINOIS INSTITUTE OF
TECHNOLOGY**

Applied Arts and
Design—General M,D
Architecture M,D
Clinical Psychology M,D
Communication—
General M,D
Corporate and
Organizational
Communication M
Industrial and
Organizational
Psychology M,D
Landscape Architecture M,D
Psychology—General M,D
Public Administration M
Rehabilitation
Counseling M,D
Technical Writing M,D

ILLINOIS STATE UNIVERSITY

Agricultural Economics
and Agribusiness M
Archaeology M
Art History M
Art/Fine Arts M
Clinical Psychology M,D,O
Communication—
General M
Counseling Psychology M,D,O
Criminal Justice and
Criminology M
Developmental
Psychology M,D,O
Economics M
English M,D
Experimental
Psychology M,D,O
Family and Consumer
Sciences-General M
French M
German M
Graphic Design M
History M
Industrial and
Organizational
Psychology M,D,O
Music M
Photography M
Political Science M
Psychology—General M,D,O
School Psychology D,O
Sociology M
Spanish M
Textile Design M
Theater M
Writing M

IMMACULATA UNIVERSITY

Clinical Psychology M,D,O
Communication—
General M
Counseling Psychology M,D,O
Psychology—General M,D,O
School Psychology M,D,O
Therapies—Dance,
Drama, and Music M

*M—master's degree; P—first professional degree; D—doctorate; O—other advanced degree; *—Close-Up and / or Display*

INDIANA STATE UNIVERSITY

Art/Fine Arts	M
Clinical Psychology	M,D
Communication— General	M
Comparative Literature	M
Consumer Economics	M
Counseling Psychology	M,D,O
Criminal Justice and Criminology	M
English	M
Family and Consumer Sciences-General	M
Geography	M,D
Graphic Design	M
History	M
Linguistics	M,O
Media Studies	M
Music	M
Photography	M
Political Science	M
Psychology—General	M,D
Public Administration	M
School Psychology	M,D,O
Writing	M

INDIANA TECH

Criminal Justice and Criminology	M

INDIANA UNIVERSITY BLOOMINGTON

African Studies	M
African-American Studies	M
Anthropology	M,D
Art History	M,D
Art/Fine Arts	M,D
Arts Administration	M
Asian Languages	M,D
Asian Studies	M,D
Child and Family Studies	M,D
Chinese	M,D
Classics	M,D
Cognitive Sciences	M,D
Communication— General	M,D
Comparative Literature	M,D
Computer Art and Design	M,D
Criminal Justice and Criminology	M,D
Developmental Psychology	M,D
East European and Russian Studies	M,O
Economic Development	M,D,O
Economics	M,D
English	M,D
Film, Television, and Video Theory and Criticism	M,D
Folklore	M,D
French	M,D
Gender Studies	D
Geography	M,D
German	M,D
Hispanic and Latin American Languages	M,D
History of Science and Technology	M,D
History	M,D
Human Development	M,D
International Affairs	M,D,O
Italian	M,D
Japanese	M,D
Journalism	M,D
Latin American Studies	M
Linguistics	M,D
Mass Communication	M,D
Media Studies	M,D

Medieval and Renaissance Studies	M,D
Music	M,D,O
Near and Middle Eastern Languages	M,D
Philosophy	M,D
Political Science	M,D
Portuguese	M,D
Psychology—General	M,D
Public Administration	M,D,O
Public Affairs	M,D,O*
Public Policy	M,D,O
Religion	M,D
Rhetoric	M,D
School Psychology	M,D,O
Slavic Languages	M,D
Social Psychology	M,D
Social Sciences	P,M,D,O
Sociology	M,D
Spanish	M,D
Speech and Interpersonal Communication	M,D
Theater	M,D
Western European Studies	M
Writing	M,D

INDIANA UNIVERSITY KOKOMO

Liberal Studies	M
Public Administration	M,O

INDIANA UNIVERSITY NORTHWEST

Criminal Justice and Criminology	M,O
Public Administration	M,O
Public Affairs	M,O

INDIANA UNIVERSITY OF PENNSYLVANIA

Archaeology	M
Art/Fine Arts	M
Clinical Psychology	D
Communication— General	M,D
Criminal Justice and Criminology	M,D
Emergency Management	M
English	M,D
Geography	M
History	M
Industrial and Labor Relations	M
Linguistics	M,D
Media Studies	M,D
Music	M
Psychology—General	M,D
Public Affairs	M
Rhetoric	M,D
School Psychology	D,O
Sociology	M
Writing	M,D

INDIANA UNIVERSITY–PURDUE UNIVERSITY FORT WAYNE

Communication— General	M
English	M,O
Liberal Studies	M
Marriage and Family Therapy	M,O
Public Affairs	M,O
Sociology	M

INDIANA UNIVERSITY–PURDUE UNIVERSITY INDIANAPOLIS

Addictions/Substance Abuse Counseling	M,D
Applied Arts and Design—General	M
Art/Fine Arts	M

Child and Family Studies	M
Clinical Psychology	M,D
Criminal Justice and Criminology	M,O
Economics	M
English	M
Gender Studies	M
Geographic Information Systems	M,O
History	M
Industrial and Organizational Psychology	M
Internet and Interactive Multimedia	M,D
Liberal Studies	M,D,O
Museum Studies	M,O
Music	M
Philanthropic Studies	M,D
Philosophy	M,O
Political Science	M,O
Psychology—General	M,D
Public Administration	M,O
Public Affairs	M,O
Public History	M
Public Policy	M,O
Rehabilitation Counseling	M,D
Sociology	M

INDIANA UNIVERSITY SOUTH BEND

Applied Psychology	M
English	M
Liberal Studies	M
Music	M
Public Administration	M,O
Public Affairs	M,O

INDIANA UNIVERSITY SOUTHEAST

Liberal Studies	M

INDIANA WESLEYAN UNIVERSITY

Addictions/Substance Abuse Counseling	M
Counseling Psychology	M
Marriage and Family Therapy	M
Pastoral Ministry and Counseling	M
Social Psychology	M
Theology	P

INSTITUTE FOR CHRISTIAN STUDIES

Philosophy	M,D
Political Science	M,D
Theology	M,D

INSTITUTE FOR DOCTORAL STUDIES IN THE VISUAL ARTS

Art/Fine Arts	D
Philosophy	D

THE INSTITUTE FOR THE PSYCHOLOGICAL SCIENCES

Clinical Psychology	M,D

INSTITUTE OF PUBLIC ADMINISTRATION

Public Administration	M,O

INSTITUTE OF TRANSPERSONAL PSYCHOLOGY

Clinical Psychology	M,D
Counseling Psychology	M,D
Pastoral Ministry and Counseling	M
Psychology—General	M,D,O

Transpersonal and Humanistic Psychology	M,D,O
Women's Studies	M

THE INSTITUTE OF WORLD POLITICS

Military and Defense Studies	M,O
National Security	M,O
Political Science	M,O
Public Affairs	M,O
Public Policy	M,O

INSTITUTO CENTROAMERICANO DE ADMINISTRACIÓN DE EMPRESAS

Agricultural Economics and Agribusiness	M
Sustainable Development	M

INSTITUTO TECNOLOGICO DE SANTO DOMINGO

Communication— General	M,O
Counseling Psychology	M,O
Economics	M,O
Gender Studies	M,O
Humanities	M,O
International Affairs	M,O
Linguistics	M,O
Marriage and Family Therapy	M,O
Sustainable Development	M,O

INSTITUTO TECNOLÓGICO Y DE ESTUDIOS SUPERIORES DE MONTERREY, CAMPUS CENTRAL DE VERACRUZ

Humanities	M

INSTITUTO TECNOLÓGICO Y DE ESTUDIOS SUPERIORES DE MONTERREY, CAMPUS CIUDAD DE MÉXICO

Economics	M,D
Humanities	M,D

INSTITUTO TECNOLÓGICO Y DE ESTUDIOS SUPERIORES DE MONTERREY, CAMPUS CIUDAD JUÁREZ

Humanities	M
Public Administration	M

INSTITUTO TECNOLÓGICO Y DE ESTUDIOS SUPERIORES DE MONTERREY, CAMPUS CIUDAD OBREGÓN

Communication— General	M
International Affairs	M

INSTITUTO TECNOLÓGICO Y DE ESTUDIOS SUPERIORES DE MONTERREY, CAMPUS ESTADO DE MÉXICO

Architecture	M,D
Humanities	M,D

INSTITUTO TECNOLÓGICO Y DE ESTUDIOS SUPERIORES DE MONTERREY, CAMPUS IRAPUATO

Architecture	M,D
Humanities	M,D

INSTITUTO TECNOLÓGICO Y DE ESTUDIOS SUPERIORES DE MONTERREY, CAMPUS MONTERREY

Communication— General	M,D

INTER AMERICAN UNIVERSITY OF PUERTO RICO, AGUADILLA CAMPUS

Counseling Psychology	M
Criminal Justice and Criminology	M

INTER AMERICAN UNIVERSITY OF PUERTO RICO, METROPOLITAN CAMPUS

American Studies	M,D
Counseling Psychology	M,D
Criminal Justice and Criminology	M
English	M
History	M,D
Industrial and Labor Relations	M,D
Industrial and Organizational Psychology	M,D
Pastoral Ministry and Counseling	D
Psychology—General	M,D
School Psychology	M,D
Spanish	M
Theology	D
Women's Studies	M

INTER AMERICAN UNIVERSITY OF PUERTO RICO, PONCE CAMPUS

Criminal Justice and Criminology	M
Spanish	M

INTER AMERICAN UNIVERSITY OF PUERTO RICO, SAN GERMÁN CAMPUS

Art/Fine Arts	M
Counseling Psychology	M,D
Photography	M
Psychology—General	M,D
School Psychology	M,D

INTERDENOMINATIONAL THEOLOGICAL CENTER

Theology	P,M,D

INTERIOR DESIGNERS INSTITUTE

Interior Design	M

INTERNATIONAL BAPTIST COLLEGE

Pastoral Ministry and Counseling	M,D
Theology	M

INTERNATIONAL TECHNOLOGICAL UNIVERSITY

Computer Art and Design	M

IONA COLLEGE

Counseling Psychology	M
Criminal Justice and Criminology	M
English	M
Experimental Psychology	M
History	M

Industrial and Organizational Psychology	M
Italian	M
Journalism	M
Marriage and Family Therapy	M,O
Mass Communication	M
Pastoral Ministry and Counseling	M,O
Psychology—General	M
School Psychology	M
Spanish	M

IOWA STATE UNIVERSITY OF SCIENCE AND TECHNOLOGY

Agricultural Economics and Agribusiness	M,D
Anthropology	M
Applied Arts and Design—General	M
Architecture	M
Child and Family Studies	M,D
Clothing and Textiles	M,D
Cognitive Sciences	D
Consumer Economics	M,D
Corporate and Organizational Communication	M,D
Counseling Psychology	D
Economics	M,D
English	M,D
Family and Consumer Sciences-General	M
Graphic Design	M
History of Science and Technology	M,D
History	M,D
Human Development	M,D
Interdisciplinary Studies	M
Interior Design	M
Journalism	M
Landscape Architecture	M
Mass Communication	M
Political Science	M
Psychology—General	D
Public Administration	M
Rhetoric	M,D
Rural Planning and Studies	M,D
Rural Sociology	M,D
Social Psychology	D
Sociology	M,D
Sustainable Development	M,D
Urban and Regional Planning	M
Writing	M,D

ITHACA COLLEGE

Communication— General	M
Music	M

JACKSON STATE UNIVERSITY

Clinical Psychology	D
Criminal Justice and Criminology	M
English	M
History	M
Mass Communication	M
Political Science	M
Psychology—General	D
Public Administration	M,D
Public Affairs	M,D
Public Policy	M,D
Rehabilitation Counseling	M
Sociology	M
Urban and Regional Planning	M,D

JACKSONVILLE STATE UNIVERSITY

Criminal Justice and Criminology	M
Emergency Management	M,D
English	M
History	M
Liberal Studies	M
Music	M
Political Science	M
Psychology—General	M

JAMES MADISON UNIVERSITY

Art History	M
Art/Fine Arts	M
Clinical Psychology	M,D,O
Counseling Psychology	M,O
English	M
History	M
Music	D
Photography	M
Political Science	M
Psychology—General	M,D,O
Public Administration	M
School Psychology	M,D,O
Technical Writing	M
Textile Design	M

THE JEWISH THEOLOGICAL SEMINARY

Jewish Studies	M,D
Music	M
Religion	M,D
Theology	M,D,O
Women's Studies	M,D

JEWISH UNIVERSITY OF AMERICA

Jewish Studies	P,D
Pastoral Ministry and Counseling	M,D

JOHN BROWN UNIVERSITY

Ethics	M
International Development	M
Marriage and Family Therapy	M
Pastoral Ministry and Counseling	M
Urban and Regional Planning	M

JOHN CARROLL UNIVERSITY

Corporate and Organizational Communication	M
Counseling Psychology	M,O
English	M
History	M
Humanities	M
Religion	M

JOHN F. KENNEDY UNIVERSITY

Art/Fine Arts	M
Comparative and Interdisciplinary Arts	M
Counseling Psychology	M
Health Psychology	M
Industrial and Organizational Psychology	M,O
Interdisciplinary Studies	M
Museum Studies	M,O
Psychology—General	M,D,O
Sport Psychology	M
Transpersonal and Humanistic Psychology	M

JACKSONVILLE STATE UNIVERSITY

JOHN JAY COLLEGE OF CRIMINAL JUSTICE OF THE CITY UNIVERSITY OF NEW YORK

Criminal Justice and Criminology	M,D
Forensic Psychology	M,D
Forensic Sciences	M,D
Public Administration	M
Public Policy	M,D

THE JOHNS HOPKINS UNIVERSITY

Addictions/Substance Abuse Counseling	M,D
Anthropology	D
Applied Economics	M
Art History	M,D
Asian Studies	M,D,O
Classics	D
Clinical Psychology	M,D
Cognitive Sciences	D
Communication— General	M
Comparative Literature	D
Criminal Justice and Criminology	M
Demography and Population Studies	M,D
Economics	D
Emergency Management	M,O
English	D
French	D
Genetic Counseling	M,D
Geography	M,D
German	D
Health Communication	M,D
History of Science and Technology	M,D
History	D
Homeland Security	M,O
International Affairs	M,D,O
International Development	M,D,O
International Economics	M,D,O
Italian	D
Liberal Studies	M,O
Medical Illustration	M
Military and Defense Studies	M
Museum Studies	M
Music	M,D,O
Near and Middle Eastern Studies	D
Philosophy	M,D
Political Science	M,D,O
Psychology—General	D
Public Policy	M
Romance Languages	D
School Psychology	M,O
Social Sciences	M,D
Sociology	M,D
Spanish	D
Technical Writing	M
Writing	M

JOHNSON STATE COLLEGE

Applied Behavior Analysis	M
Art/Fine Arts	M

JOHNSON UNIVERSITY

Marriage and Family Therapy	M
Theology	M

---

*M—master's degree; P—first professional degree; D—doctorate; O—other advanced degree; *—Close-Up and / or Display*

JONES INTERNATIONAL UNIVERSITY

Conflict Resolution and Mediation/Peace Studies	M
Corporate and Organizational Communication	M

THE JUDGE ADVOCATE GENERAL'S SCHOOL, U.S. ARMY

Military and Defense Studies	M

JUDSON UNIVERSITY

Architecture	M

THE JUILLIARD SCHOOL

Music	M,D,O

KANSAS STATE UNIVERSITY

Agricultural Economics and Agribusiness	M,D
Applied Arts and Design—General	M
Architecture	M
Art/Fine Arts	M
Child and Family Studies	M,D
Clothing and Textiles	M,D
Communication—General	M
Consumer Economics	D
Economics	M,D
English	M
Family and Consumer Sciences-General	M,D
French	M
Geography	M,D
German	M
History	M,D
Human Development	M,D
International Affairs	M
Landscape Architecture	M
Marriage and Family Therapy	M,D
Mass Communication	M
Music	M
National Security	M,D
Political Science	M
Psychology—General	M,D
Public Administration	M
Rhetoric	M
Sociology	M,D
Spanish	M
Speech and Interpersonal Communication	M
Theater	M
Urban and Regional Planning	M

KAPLAN UNIVERSITY, DAVENPORT CAMPUS

Criminal Justice and Criminology	M
Political Science	M,O

KEAN UNIVERSITY

Addictions/Substance Abuse Counseling	M
Art/Fine Arts	M
Clinical Psychology	M,D
Communication—General	M
Counseling Psychology	M
Criminal Justice and Criminology	M
Holocaust and Genocide Studies	M

Industrial and Organizational Psychology	M
Liberal Studies	M
Marriage and Family Therapy	O
Political Science	M
Psychology—General	M
Public Administration	M
School Psychology	D,O
Sociology	M
Spanish	M
Writing	M

KEENE STATE COLLEGE

School Psychology	M,O

KEHILATH YAKOV RABBINICAL SEMINARY

Theology	M

KEISER UNIVERSITY

Criminal Justice and Criminology	M

KENNESAW STATE UNIVERSITY

American Studies	M
Conflict Resolution and Mediation/Peace Studies	M,D
International Affairs	M
Public Administration	M
Writing	M

KENRICK-GLENNON SEMINARY

Theology	P,M

KENT STATE UNIVERSITY

Anthropology	M
Architecture	M,O
Art History	M
Art/Fine Arts	M
Biological Anthropology	D
Child and Family Studies	M
Classics	M,D
Clinical Psychology	M,D
Communication—General	M,D
Comparative Literature	M,D
Counseling Psychology	M
Criminal Justice and Criminology	M
Economics	M
English	M,D
Experimental Psychology	M,D
French	M,D
Geography	M,D
German	M,D
Gerontology	M
Graphic Design	M
Historic Preservation	M,O
History	M,D
Human Development	M,D
Illustration	M
Japanese	M,D
Journalism	M
Liberal Studies	M
Mass Communication	M
Music	M,D
Philosophy	M
Political Science	M,D
Psychology—General	M,D
Public Administration	M
Public Policy	M,D
Rehabilitation Counseling	M,O
Rhetoric	M,D
Russian	M
School Psychology	M,D,O
Sociology	M,D
Spanish	M,D

Textile Design	M
Theater	M
Translation and Interpretation	M,D
Urban Design	M,O
Writing	M,D

KENTUCKY CHRISTIAN UNIVERSITY

Religion	M
Theology	M

KENTUCKY STATE UNIVERSITY

International Affairs	M
Public Administration	M

KEUKA COLLEGE

Criminal Justice and Criminology	M

KNOX COLLEGE

Theology	P,M,D

KNOX THEOLOGICAL SEMINARY

Missions and Missiology	M
Pastoral Ministry and Counseling	D
Religion	M
Theology	P,M,O

KOL YAAKOV TORAH CENTER

Theology	O

KONA UNIVERSITY

Transpersonal and Humanistic Psychology	M

KUTZTOWN UNIVERSITY OF PENNSYLVANIA

Counseling Psychology	M
English	M
Marriage and Family Therapy	M
Media Studies	M
Public Administration	M

LAGUNA COLLEGE OF ART & DESIGN

Art/Fine Arts	M

LAKE FOREST COLLEGE

Liberal Studies	M

LAKEHEAD UNIVERSITY

Clinical Psychology	M,D
Economics	M
English	M
Experimental Psychology	M,D
Gerontology	M,D
History	M
Psychology—General	M,D
Sociology	M
Women's Studies	M,D

LAKELAND COLLEGE

Theology	M

LAMAR UNIVERSITY

Applied Arts and Design—General	M
Art History	M
Art/Fine Arts	M
Clinical Psychology	M
Criminal Justice and Criminology	M
English	M
Family and Consumer Sciences-General	M,O
History	M

Industrial and Organizational Psychology	M
Music	M
Photography	M
Political Science	M
Psychology—General	M
Public Administration	M
Social Psychology	M
Theater	M

LANCASTER BIBLE COLLEGE

Counseling Psychology	M,D
Marriage and Family Therapy	M,D
Pastoral Ministry and Counseling	M,D
Theology	M,D

LANCASTER THEOLOGICAL SEMINARY

Art History	P,M,D,O
Ethics	P,M,D,O
Religion	P,M,D,O
Theology	P,M,D,O

LANGSTON UNIVERSITY

Rehabilitation Counseling	M

LA SALLE UNIVERSITY

Clinical Psychology	M,D
Corporate and Organizational Communication	M
Counseling Psychology	M
East European and Russian Studies	M
Hispanic Studies	M
History	M
Latin American Studies	M
Marriage and Family Therapy	D
Pastoral Ministry and Counseling	M
Psychology—General	D
Rehabilitation Counseling	D
Religion	M
Theology	M

LASELL COLLEGE

Communication—General	M,O
Corporate and Organizational Communication	M,O

LA SIERRA UNIVERSITY

Communication—General	M
English	M
Pastoral Ministry and Counseling	P,M
Religion	P,M
School Psychology	M,O
Writing	M

LAURA AND ALVIN SIEGAL COLLEGE OF JUDAIC STUDIES

Holocaust and Genocide Studies	M
Humanities	M
Jewish Studies	M

LAURENTIAN UNIVERSITY

Applied Psychology	M
Applied Social Research	M
Experimental Psychology	M
History	M
Human Development	M
Humanities	M

Psychology—General M
Sociology M
Technical Writing O

LAWRENCE TECHNOLOGICAL UNIVERSITY

Architecture M
Corporate and
  Organizational
  Communication M
Interior Design M
Technical
  Communication M
Urban Design M

LEBANESE AMERICAN UNIVERSITY

International Affairs M

LEE UNIVERSITY

Child Development M
Counseling Psychology M
Marriage and Family
  Therapy M
Music M
Pastoral Ministry and
  Counseling M
Religion M
Theology M

LEHIGH UNIVERSITY

American Studies M,D
Counseling Psychology M,D,O
Economics M,D
English M,D
History M,D
Human Development M,D
Interdisciplinary Studies M,D
International
  Development M,O
Political Science M
Psychology—General M,D
School Psychology D,O
Sociology M

LEHMAN COLLEGE OF THE CITY UNIVERSITY OF NEW YORK

Art/Fine Arts M
English M
History M
Spanish M

LE MOYNE COLLEGE

Urban Studies M,O

LENOIR-RHYNE UNIVERSITY

School Psychology M
Social Psychology M

LESLEY UNIVERSITY

Art Therapy M,D,O
Art/Fine Arts M
Clinical Psychology M,D,O
Counseling Psychology M
Health Psychology M
Interdisciplinary Studies M
International Affairs M,O
Psychology—General M,D,O
School Psychology M
Social Psychology M,D,O
Sustainable
  Development M
Therapies—Dance,
  Drama, and Music M,D,O
Urban and Regional
  Planning M
Women's Studies M
Writing M

LETOURNEAU UNIVERSITY

Psychology—General M

LEWIS & CLARK COLLEGE

Addictions/Substance
  Abuse Counseling M
Counseling Psychology M,O
Cultural Studies M,O
Marriage and Family
  Therapy M
Psychology—General M,O
School Psychology M,O
Social Psychology M

LEWIS UNIVERSITY

Counseling Psychology M
Criminal Justice and
  Criminology M
Public Administration M

LEXINGTON THEOLOGICAL SEMINARY

Theology P,M,D

LIBERTY UNIVERSITY

Communication—
  General M
Counseling Psychology M,D
Pastoral Ministry and
  Counseling M,D
Religion P,M,D
Theology P,M,D

LIM COLLEGE

Textile Design M

LINCOLN CHRISTIAN SEMINARY

Pastoral Ministry and
  Counseling P,M,D
Theology P,M,D

LINCOLN UNIVERSITY (MO)

Criminal Justice and
  Criminology M,O
History M,O
Political Science M,O
Public Administration M,O
Public Policy M,O
Social Sciences M,O
Sociology M,O

LINDENWOOD UNIVERSITY

American Studies M
Art/Fine Arts M
Communication—
  General M,O
Counseling Psychology M,D,O
Criminal Justice and
  Criminology M,O
Gerontology M,O
International Affairs M
Public Administration M
School Psychology M,D,O
Theater M
Writing M,O

LINDSEY WILSON COLLEGE

Counseling Psychology M
Human Development M

LIPSCOMB UNIVERSITY

Conflict Resolution and
  Mediation/Peace
  Studies M,O
Counseling Psychology M,O
Psychology—General M,O
Religion P,M
Sustainable
  Development M
Theology P,M

LOCK HAVEN UNIVERSITY OF PENNSYLVANIA

Liberal Studies M

LOGOS EVANGELICAL SEMINARY

Theology P,M,D

LOMA LINDA UNIVERSITY

Child and Family
  Studies M,D,O
Pastoral Ministry and
  Counseling M,O
Psychology—General D
Religion M

LONG ISLAND UNIVERSITY AT RIVERHEAD

Applied Behavior
  Analysis M,O
Homeland Security M,O

LONG ISLAND UNIVERSITY, BRENTWOOD CAMPUS

Counseling Psychology M
Criminal Justice and
  Criminology M

LONG ISLAND UNIVERSITY, BROOKLYN CAMPUS

Clinical Psychology D
Comparative Literature M
Computer Art and
  Design M
Economics M
English M
History M,O
International Affairs M,O
Political Science M
Psychology—General M,D
Public Administration M
School Psychology M
Social Sciences M,O
Urban Studies M
Writing M

LONG ISLAND UNIVERSITY, C.W. POST CAMPUS

Addictions/Substance
  Abuse Counseling M
Art Therapy M
Art/Fine Arts M
Clinical Psychology D
Computer Art and
  Design M
Criminal Justice and
  Criminology M
English M
Forensic Sciences M
Genetic Counseling M
Gerontology M,O
History M
Interdisciplinary Studies M
International Affairs M
Internet and Interactive
  Multimedia M
Music M
Political Science M
Psychology—General M,D
Public Administration M,O
Social Sciences M
Spanish M
Theater M

LONG ISLAND UNIVERSITY, ROCKLAND GRADUATE CAMPUS

Counseling Psychology M
Gerontology M,O
Public Administration M,O

LONG ISLAND UNIVERSITY, WESTCHESTER GRADUATE CAMPUS

Counseling Psychology M
School Psychology M

LONGWOOD UNIVERSITY

Criminal Justice and
  Criminology M
English M
Writing M

LONGY SCHOOL OF MUSIC

Music M,O

LORAS COLLEGE

Applied Psychology M
Pastoral Ministry and
  Counseling M
Theology M

LOUISIANA STATE UNIVERSITY AND AGRICULTURAL AND MECHANICAL COLLEGE

Agricultural Economics
  and Agribusiness M,D
Anthropology M,D
Applied Arts and
  Design—General M
Architecture M
Art History M
Art/Fine Arts M
Clinical Psychology M,D
Cognitive Sciences M,D
Communication—
  General M,D
Comparative Literature M,D
Developmental
  Psychology M,D
Economics M,D
English M,D
Family and Consumer
  Sciences-General M,D
French M,D
Geography M,D
Graphic Design M
Hispanic Studies M
History M,D
Industrial and
  Organizational
  Psychology M,D
Landscape Architecture M
Liberal Studies M
Linguistics M,D
Mass Communication M,D
Media Studies M,D
Music M,D
Philosophy M
Photography M
Political Science M,D
Psychology—General M,D
Public Administration M,D
School Psychology M,D
Sociology M,D
Theater M,D
Writing M,D

LOUISIANA STATE UNIVERSITY HEALTH SCIENCES CENTER

Rehabilitation
  Counseling M

LOUISIANA STATE UNIVERSITY IN SHREVEPORT

Counseling Psychology M
Liberal Studies M
School Psychology O

LOUISIANA TECH UNIVERSITY

Applied Arts and
  Design—General M

---

*M—master's degree; P—first professional degree; D—doctorate; O—other advanced degree; *—Close-Up and/or Display*

Art/Fine Arts	M
Counseling Psychology	M,D
Economics	M,D
English	M
Family and Consumer Sciences-General	M
Graphic Design	M
History	M
Industrial and Organizational Psychology	M,D
Interior Design	M
Photography	M
Psychology—General	M,D
Speech and Interpersonal Communication	M

LOUISVILLE PRESBYTERIAN THEOLOGICAL SEMINARY

Religion	P,M,D
Theology	P,M,D

LOYOLA MARYMOUNT UNIVERSITY

English	M
Film, Television, and Video Production	M
Marriage and Family Therapy	M
Pastoral Ministry and Counseling	M
Philosophy	M
School Psychology	M
Theology	M
Writing	M

LOYOLA UNIVERSITY CHICAGO

Applied Psychology	M,D
Clinical Psychology	M,D
Corporate and Organizational Communication	M
Counseling Psychology	D
Criminal Justice and Criminology	M
Developmental Psychology	M,D
English	M,D
History	M,D
Industrial and Labor Relations	M
Pastoral Ministry and Counseling	M,O
Philosophy	M,D
Political Science	M,D
Psychology—General	M,D
Public History	M,D
School Psychology	D,O
Social Psychology	M,D
Sociology	M,D
Spanish	M
Theology	P,M,D,O
Urban and Regional Planning	M,O
Urban Studies	M,D

LOYOLA UNIVERSITY MARYLAND

Clinical Psychology	M,D,O
Counseling Psychology	M,O
Liberal Studies	M
Pastoral Ministry and Counseling	M,D,O
Psychology—General	M,D,O

LOYOLA UNIVERSITY NEW ORLEANS

Criminal Justice and Criminology	M
Music	M
Theology	M,O

Therapies—Dance, Drama, and Music	M

LUBBOCK CHRISTIAN UNIVERSITY

Theology	M

LUTHERAN SCHOOL OF THEOLOGY AT CHICAGO

Pastoral Ministry and Counseling	P,M,D
Theology	P,M,D

LUTHERAN THEOLOGICAL SEMINARY

Ethics	P,M,D
Pastoral Ministry and Counseling	P,M,D
Religion	P,M,D
Theology	P,M,D

LUTHERAN THEOLOGICAL SEMINARY AT GETTYSBURG

Pastoral Ministry and Counseling	P,M,D
Religion	P,M,D
Theology	P,M,D

THE LUTHERAN THEOLOGICAL SEMINARY AT PHILADELPHIA

Pastoral Ministry and Counseling	P,M,D,O
Religion	P,M,D,O
Theology	P,M,D,O

LUTHERAN THEOLOGICAL SOUTHERN SEMINARY

Theology	P,M,D

LUTHER RICE UNIVERSITY

Missions and Missiology	P,M,D
Pastoral Ministry and Counseling	P,M,D
Theology	P,M,D

LUTHER SEMINARY

Theology	P,M,D

LYNCHBURG COLLEGE

Clinical Psychology	M
Counseling Psychology	M
English	M
History	M
Music	M
School Psychology	M
Social Psychology	M

LYNN UNIVERSITY

Applied Psychology	M,O
Criminal Justice and Criminology	M,O
Emergency Management	M,O
Mass Communication	M
Media Studies	M
Music	M,O

MACHZIKEI HADATH RABBINICAL COLLEGE

Theology	O

MADONNA UNIVERSITY

Clinical Psychology	M
Criminal Justice and Criminology	M
Liberal Studies	M
Pastoral Ministry and Counseling	M
Psychology—General	M
Theology	M

MAHARISHI UNIVERSITY OF MANAGEMENT

Asian Studies	M,D

MAINE COLLEGE OF ART

Art/Fine Arts	M

MALONE UNIVERSITY

Theology	M

MANHATTAN SCHOOL OF MUSIC

Music	M,D,O

MANHATTANVILLE COLLEGE

Liberal Studies	M
Writing	M

MANSFIELD UNIVERSITY OF PENNSYLVANIA

Music	M
Psychology—General	M

MAPLE SPRINGS BAPTIST BIBLE COLLEGE AND SEMINARY

Pastoral Ministry and Counseling	P,M,D,O
Theology	P,M,D,O

MARANATHA BAPTIST BIBLE COLLEGE

Cultural Studies	M
Pastoral Ministry and Counseling	M
Religion	M
Theology	P,M

MARIETTA COLLEGE

Corporate and Organizational Communication	M
Psychology—General	M

MARIST COLLEGE

Corporate and Organizational Communication	M
Counseling Psychology	M,O
Psychology—General	M,O
Public Administration	M
School Psychology	M,O

MARLBORO COLLEGE

Internet and Interactive Multimedia	M

MARQUETTE UNIVERSITY

Clinical Psychology	M,D,O
Communication—General	M,O
Conflict Resolution and Mediation/Peace Studies	M,O
Counseling Psychology	M,D,O
Criminal Justice and Criminology	M,O
Economics	M
English	M,D
Ethics	M,D
Health Communication	M,O
History	M,D
Interdisciplinary Studies	M,D
International Affairs	M,D
Jewish Studies	M,D
Journalism	M,O
Mass Communication	M,O
Media Studies	M,O
Philosophy	M,D
Political Science	M
Psychology—General	D
Public Administration	M,O

Religion	M,D
Spanish	M
Speech and Interpersonal Communication	M,O
Theology	M,D

MARSHALL UNIVERSITY

Art/Fine Arts	M
Classics	M
Clinical Psychology	M,D
Communication—General	M
Criminal Justice and Criminology	M
English	M
Family and Consumer Sciences-General	M
Geography	M
History	M
Humanities	M
Industrial and Organizational Psychology	M,D
Journalism	M
Mass Communication	M
Music	M
Political Science	M
Psychology—General	M,D
School Psychology	O
Sociology	M
Spanish	M

MARS HILL GRADUATE SCHOOL

Counseling Psychology	M
Religion	M
Theology	M

MARTIN UNIVERSITY

Pastoral Ministry and Counseling	M
Psychology—General	M
Social Psychology	M

MARY BALDWIN COLLEGE

English	M
Theater	M

MARYGROVE COLLEGE

English	M
Translation and Interpretation	O

MARYLAND INSTITUTE COLLEGE OF ART

Applied Arts and Design—General	M
Art/Fine Arts	M,O
Graphic Design	M
Illustration	M
Museum Studies	M
Photography	M

MARYLHURST UNIVERSITY

Art Therapy	M,O
Counseling Psychology	M,O
Interdisciplinary Studies	M
Public Administration	M
Public Policy	M
Sustainable Development	M
Theology	P,M

MARYMOUNT UNIVERSITY

Counseling Psychology	M,O
English	M
Forensic Psychology	M
Humanities	M
Interior Design	M
Pastoral Ministry and Counseling	M,O

MARYVILLE UNIVERSITY OF SAINT LOUIS

Addictions/Substance Abuse Counseling	M,O
Marriage and Family Therapy	M,O
Rehabilitation Counseling	M,O
Therapies—Dance, Drama, and Music	M

MARYWOOD UNIVERSITY

Architecture	M
Art Therapy	M,O
Art/Fine Arts	M
Clinical Psychology	M,D
Communication—General	M
Corporate and Organizational Communication	M,O
Counseling Psychology	M
Criminal Justice and Criminology	M
Film, Television, and Video Production	M
Gerontology	M
Graphic Design	M
Health Communication	M,O
Human Development	D
Illustration	M
Interdisciplinary Studies	M
Interior Design	M
Media Studies	M
Photography	M
Psychology—General	M
Public Administration	M
School Psychology	O
Textile Design	M
Therapies—Dance, Drama, and Music	M,O

MASSACHUSETTS COLLEGE OF ART AND DESIGN

Applied Arts and Design—General	M
Architecture	M
Art/Fine Arts	M
Film, Television, and Video Production	M
Photography	M
Textile Design	M
Theater	M

MASSACHUSETTS INSTITUTE OF TECHNOLOGY

Archaeology	M,D,O
Architectural History	M,D
Architecture	M,D
Art History	M,D
Cognitive Sciences	D
Economics	M,D
History of Science and Technology	D
Linguistics	D
Media Studies	M,D
Philosophy	D
Political Science	M,D
Social Sciences	D
Technical Writing	M
Urban and Regional Planning	M,D
Urban Studies	M,D
Writing	M

MASSACHUSETTS MARITIME ACADEMY

Emergency Management	M

MASSACHUSETTS SCHOOL OF PROFESSIONAL PSYCHOLOGY

Applied Psychology	M,D,O
Clinical Psychology	M,D,O
Counseling Psychology	M,D,O
Forensic Psychology	M,D,O
Industrial and Organizational Psychology	M,D,O
Psychology—General	M,D,O
School Psychology	M,D,O

THE MASTER'S COLLEGE AND SEMINARY

Pastoral Ministry and Counseling	P,M,D
Theology	P,M,D

MCCORMICK THEOLOGICAL SEMINARY

Pastoral Ministry and Counseling	P,M,D,O
Theology	P,M,D,O

MCDANIEL COLLEGE

Liberal Studies	M

MCGILL UNIVERSITY

Agricultural Economics and Agribusiness	M
Anthropology	M,D
Architecture	M,D,O
Art History	M,D
Asian Studies	M,D
Clinical Psychology	M,D
Communication—General	M,D
Counseling Psychology	M,D,O
Developmental Psychology	M,D,O
Economics	M,D
English	M,D
Experimental Psychology	M,D
Forensic Sciences	M,D,O
French	M,D
Genetic Counseling	M,D
Geography	M,D
German	M,D
Hispanic Studies	M,D
History of Medicine	M,D
History	M,D
International Development	M,D,O
Italian	M,D
Jewish Studies	M
Linguistics	M,D
Music	M,D
Near and Middle Eastern Studies	M,D,O
Philosophy	M,D
Political Science	M,D
Psychology—General	M,D
Religion	M,D
Russian	M,D
School Psychology	M,D,O
Sociology	M,D,O
Theology	M,D
Urban and Regional Planning	M,D

MCKENDREE UNIVERSITY

Counseling Psychology	M

MCMASTER UNIVERSITY

Anthropology	M,D
Classics	M,D
Cultural Studies	M,D
Economics	M,D
English	M,D
French	M

Geography	M,D
History	M,D
Industrial and Labor Relations	M
International Affairs	M,D
Pastoral Ministry and Counseling	P,M,D,O
Philosophy	M,D
Political Science	M,D
Psychology—General	M,D
Public Administration	M,D
Public Affairs	M,D
Public Policy	M,D
Religion	M,D
Sociology	M,D
Theology	P,M,D,O

MCNEESE STATE UNIVERSITY

Addictions/Substance Abuse Counseling	M
Applied Behavior Analysis	M
Counseling Psychology	M
English	M
Experimental Psychology	M
Psychology—General	M
School Psychology	M,O
Writing	M

MEADVILLE LOMBARD THEOLOGICAL SCHOOL

Pastoral Ministry and Counseling	P,M,D
Theology	P,M,D

MEDAILLE COLLEGE

Counseling Psychology	M
Psychology—General	M

MEMORIAL UNIVERSITY OF NEWFOUNDLAND

Anthropology	M,D
Applied Psychology	M,D
Archaeology	M,D
Classics	M
Cultural Anthropology	M,D
Economics	M
English	M,D
Experimental Psychology	M,D
Folklore	M,D
French	M
Gender Studies	M,D
Geography	M,D
German	M
History	M,D
Humanities	M
Industrial and Labor Relations	M
Linguistics	M,D
Music	M,D
Philosophy	M
Political Science	M
Psychology—General	M,D
Religion	M
Social Psychology	M,D
Sociology	M,D
Sport Psychology	M
Women's Studies	M

MEMPHIS COLLEGE OF ART

Applied Arts and Design—General	M
Art/Fine Arts	M*

MEMPHIS THEOLOGICAL SEMINARY

Theology	P,M,D

MERCER UNIVERSITY

Music	P,M
Theology	P,M,D

MERCY COLLEGE

Addictions/Substance Abuse Counseling	M,O
Applied Behavior Analysis	O
Counseling Psychology	M,O
English	M
Internet and Interactive Multimedia	M,O
Marriage and Family Therapy	M,O
Psychology—General	M
School Psychology	M

MERCYHURST COLLEGE

Biological Anthropology	M
Criminal Justice and Criminology	M,O
Forensic Sciences	M

MESIVTA OF EASTERN PARKWAY–YESHIVA ZICHRON MEILECH

Theology	

MESIVTA TIFERETH JERUSALEM OF AMERICA

Theology	

MESIVTA TORAH VODAATH RABBINICAL SEMINARY

Theology	

MESSIAH COLLEGE

Clinical Psychology	M,O
Counseling Psychology	M,O
Marriage and Family Therapy	M,O
Music	M
Pastoral Ministry and Counseling	M

METHODIST THEOLOGICAL SCHOOL IN OHIO

Theology	P,M,D

METHODIST UNIVERSITY

Criminal Justice and Criminology	M

METROPOLITAN COLLEGE OF NEW YORK

Corporate and Organizational Communication	M
Media Studies	M
Public Administration	M

METROPOLITAN STATE UNIVERSITY

Liberal Studies	M
Psychology—General	M,O
Public Administration	M,D,O
Technical Writing	M

MIAMI INTERNATIONAL UNIVERSITY OF ART & DESIGN

Art/Fine Arts	M
Computer Art and Design	M
Film, Television, and Video Production	M
Graphic Design	M*
Interior Design	M

MIAMI UNIVERSITY

Architecture	M

*M—master's degree; P—first professional degree; D—doctorate; O—other advanced degree; *—Close-Up and/or Display*

Art/Fine Arts	M
Child and Family Studies	M
Economics	M
English	M,D
French	M
Geography	M
Gerontology	M,D
History	M
Music	M
Philosophy	M
Political Science	M
Psychology—General	D
Religion	M
School Psychology	M,O
Theater	M

MICHIGAN SCHOOL OF PROFESSIONAL PSYCHOLOGY

Clinical Psychology	M,D
Psychology—General	M,D
Transpersonal and Humanistic Psychology	M,D

MICHIGAN STATE UNIVERSITY

African Studies	M,D
African-American Studies	M,D
Agricultural Economics and Agribusiness	M,D
American Studies	M,D
Anthropology	M,D
Art/Fine Arts	M
Child and Family Studies	M,D
Child Development	M,D
Communication—General	M,D
Computer Art and Design	M
Criminal Justice and Criminology	M,D
Economics	M,D
English	M,D
Environmental Design	M,D
Forensic Sciences	M,D
French	M,D
Geography	M,D
German	M,D
Health Communication	M
Hispanic and Latin American Languages	M,D
Hispanic Studies	M,D
History	M,D
Industrial and Labor Relations	M,D
Interior Design	M,D
Journalism	M
Latin American Studies	D
Linguistics	M,D
Marriage and Family Therapy	M,D
Media Studies	M,D
Music	M,D
Philosophy	M,D
Political Science	M,D
Portuguese	M,D
Psychology—General	M,D
Rehabilitation Counseling	M,D,O
Rhetoric	M,D
Romance Languages	M,D
School Psychology	M,D,O
Sociology	M,D
Spanish	M,D
Theater	M
Therapies—Dance, Drama, and Music	M,D
Urban and Regional Planning	M,D
Writing	M,D

MICHIGAN TECHNOLOGICAL UNIVERSITY

Archaeology	M,D
Historic Preservation	D
Mineral Economics	M
Rhetoric	M,D
Sustainable Development	O
Technical Communication	M,D

MICHIGAN THEOLOGICAL SEMINARY

Counseling Psychology	P,M,O
Religion	P,M,O
Theology	P,M,O

MID-AMERICA BAPTIST THEOLOGICAL SEMINARY

Theology	P,M,D

MID-AMERICA BAPTIST THEOLOGICAL SEMINARY NORTHEAST BRANCH

Theology	P

MID-AMERICA CHRISTIAN UNIVERSITY

Counseling Psychology	M
Marriage and Family Therapy	M
Pastoral Ministry and Counseling	M
Public Administration	M

MIDAMERICA NAZARENE UNIVERSITY

Counseling Psychology	M,O

MID-AMERICA REFORMED SEMINARY

Theology	P,M

MIDDLEBURY COLLEGE

Chinese	M
English	M
French	M,D
German	M,D
Italian	M,D
Russian	M,D
Spanish	M,D

MIDDLE TENNESSEE STATE UNIVERSITY

Child and Family Studies	M
Child Development	M
Clinical Psychology	M,O
Counseling Psychology	M,O
Criminal Justice and Criminology	M
Economics	M,D
English	M,D
Experimental Psychology	M,O
Gerontology	O
History	M
Industrial and Organizational Psychology	M,O
Mass Communication	M
Music	M
Psychology—General	M
Public History	M,D
School Psychology	M,O
Social Sciences	M,O
Sociology	M

MIDWESTERN BAPTIST THEOLOGICAL SEMINARY

Archaeology	P,M,D,O
Linguistics	P,M,D,O

Missions and Missiology	P,M,D,O
Music	P,M,D,O
Pastoral Ministry and Counseling	P,M,D,O
Religion	P,M,D,O
Theology	P,M,D,O

MIDWESTERN STATE UNIVERSITY

Criminal Justice and Criminology	M
English	M
History	M
Political Science	M
Psychology—General	M
Public Administration	M

MIDWESTERN UNIVERSITY, DOWNERS GROVE CAMPUS

Clinical Psychology	M,D

MIDWESTERN UNIVERSITY, GLENDALE CAMPUS

Clinical Psychology	D

MIDWEST UNIVERSITY

Theology	P,M,D

MILLERSVILLE UNIVERSITY OF PENNSYLVANIA

Clinical Psychology	M
Emergency Management	M
English	M
French	M
German	M
History	M
Psychology—General	M
School Psychology	M
Spanish	M

MILLS COLLEGE

Art/Fine Arts	M
Dance	M
English	M
Illustration	M
Interdisciplinary Studies	M,O
Music	M
Photography	M
Public Policy	M
Writing	M

MINNEAPOLIS COLLEGE OF ART AND DESIGN

Applied Arts and Design—General	M
Art/Fine Arts	M,O
Computer Art and Design	O
Film, Television, and Video Production	M
Graphic Design	M,O
Illustration	M
Photography	M
Sustainable Development	O

MINNESOTA STATE UNIVERSITY MANKATO

Anthropology	M
Art/Fine Arts	M
Clinical Psychology	M,D
Communication—General	M,O
Corporate and Organizational Communication	M,O
Counseling Psychology	M,D,O
English	M,O
Ethnic Studies	M,O
French	M
Gender Studies	M,O

Geographic Information Systems	M,O
Geography	M,O
Gerontology	M,O
History	M
Industrial and Organizational Psychology	M,D
Interdisciplinary Studies	M
Marriage and Family Therapy	M,D,O
Music	M
Psychology—General	M,D
Public Administration	M
Rehabilitation Counseling	M
School Psychology	M,D
Sociology	M
Spanish	M
Technical Communication	M,O
Theater	M
Urban and Regional Planning	M,O
Urban Studies	M,O
Women's Studies	M,O
Writing	M,O

MINNESOTA STATE UNIVERSITY MOORHEAD

Liberal Studies	M
Public Administration	M
School Psychology	M,O
Writing	M

MINOT STATE UNIVERSITY

Criminal Justice and Criminology	M
School Psychology	O

MIRRER YESHIVA

Theology	

MISSISSIPPI COLLEGE

Art/Fine Arts	M
Communication—General	M
Corporate and Organizational Communication	M
Counseling Psychology	M,O
Criminal Justice and Criminology	M,O
English	M
History	M,O
Liberal Studies	M
Marriage and Family Therapy	M,O
Music	M
Political Science	M
Social Sciences	M,O

MISSISSIPPI STATE UNIVERSITY

Agricultural Economics and Agribusiness	M
American Studies	M,D
Anthropology	M
Applied Economics	M,D
Architecture	M
Clinical Psychology	M,D
Cognitive Sciences	M,D
Computer Art and Design	M
Economics	M,D
English	M
Experimental Psychology	M,D
French	M
German	M
History	M,D
Interdisciplinary Studies	M,D
Landscape Architecture	M
Political Science	M,D

Psychology—General	M,D
Public Administration	M,D
Public Policy	M,D
School Psychology	M,D,O
Sociology	M,D
Spanish	M
Western European Studies	M,D

MISSISSIPPI VALLEY STATE UNIVERSITY

Criminal Justice and Criminology	M

MISSOURI BAPTIST UNIVERSITY

Pastoral Ministry and Counseling	M,O

MISSOURI SOUTHERN STATE UNIVERSITY

Criminal Justice and Criminology	M

MISSOURI STATE UNIVERSITY

Anthropology	M
Art/Fine Arts	M
Child and Family Studies	M
Clinical Psychology	M
Communication—General	M
Criminal Justice and Criminology	M
English	M
Experimental Psychology	M
Family and Consumer Sciences-General	M
Geography	M
History	M
Industrial and Organizational Psychology	M
Interior Design	M
International Affairs	M
Military and Defense Studies	M
Music	M
Political Science	M
Psychology—General	M
Public Administration	M
Religion	M
Social Psychology	M
Spanish	M
Textile Design	M
Theater	M
Urban and Regional Planning	M

MISSOURI WESTERN STATE UNIVERSITY

Forensic Sciences	M
Media Studies	M
Rhetoric	M
Technical Communication	M
Writing	M

MOLLOY COLLEGE

Criminal Justice and Criminology	M
Therapies—Dance, Drama, and Music	M

MONMOUTH UNIVERSITY

American Studies	M
Communication—General	M,O
Corporate and Organizational Communication	M,O
Counseling Psychology	M,O

Criminal Justice and Criminology	M,O
English	M
History	M
Homeland Security	M,O
Liberal Studies	M
Psychology—General	M,O
Public Policy	M
Rhetoric	M
Western European Studies	M
Writing	M

MONTANA STATE UNIVERSITY

American Indian/Native American Studies	M
Architecture	M
Art History	M
Art/Fine Arts	M
English	M
Film, Television, and Video Production	M
History	M,D
Human Development	M
Psychology—General	M
Public Administration	M
School Psychology	M,D,O

MONTANA STATE UNIVERSITY BILLINGS

Communication—General	M
Interdisciplinary Studies	M
Psychology—General	M
Public Administration	M
Rehabilitation Counseling	M

MONTANA TECH OF THE UNIVERSITY OF MONTANA

Interdisciplinary Studies	M
Technical Communication	M

MONTCLAIR STATE UNIVERSITY

Addictions/Substance Abuse Counseling	M,D,O
Anthropology	O
Art/Fine Arts	M,O
Arts Administration	M
Clinical Psychology	M,O
Communication—General	M
Conflict Resolution and Mediation/Peace Studies	M,O
Corporate and Organizational Communication	M
Counseling Psychology	M,D,O
English	M,O
French	M,O
Geographic Information Systems	M,D,O
History	M,O
Industrial and Organizational Psychology	M,O
Italian	M,O
Linguistics	M,O
Marriage and Family Therapy	M,O
Museum Studies	M,O
Music	M,O
Philosophy	D,O
Political Science	M,O
Psychology—General	M,O
School Psychology	M,O
Social Psychology	M,D,O
Social Sciences	M,O
Sociology	M
Spanish	M,O

Theater	M
Therapies—Dance, Drama, and Music	M,O
Translation and Interpretation	M,O
Urban and Regional Planning	O
Writing	M,O

MONTEREY INSTITUTE OF INTERNATIONAL STUDIES

International Affairs	M
International Trade Policy	M
Public Administration	M
Translation and Interpretation	M

MOODY BIBLE INSTITUTE

Pastoral Ministry and Counseling	P,M,O
Theology	P,M,O
Urban Studies	P,M,O

MOORE COLLEGE OF ART & DESIGN

Art/Fine Arts	M
Interior Design	M

MORAVIAN THEOLOGICAL SEMINARY

Pastoral Ministry and Counseling	P,M
Theology	P,M

MOREHEAD STATE UNIVERSITY

Art/Fine Arts	M
Clinical Psychology	M
Communication—General	M
Counseling Psychology	M
Criminal Justice and Criminology	M
English	M
Experimental Psychology	M
Gerontology	M
Graphic Design	M
Music	M
Psychology—General	M
Public Administration	M
Public Policy	M
Sociology	M

MORGAN STATE UNIVERSITY

African-American Studies	M,D
Architecture	M
Economics	M
English	M,D
History	M,D
International Affairs	M
Landscape Architecture	M
Music	M
Psychology—General	M,D
Sociology	M
Urban and Regional Planning	M

MOUNTAIN STATE UNIVERSITY

Criminal Justice and Criminology	M
Interdisciplinary Studies	M
Psychology—General	M,O

MOUNT ALOYSIUS COLLEGE

Criminal Justice and Criminology	M
Psychology—General	M
Social Psychology	M

MOUNT ANGEL SEMINARY

Theology	P,M

MOUNT HOLYOKE COLLEGE

Psychology—General	M

MOUNT IDA COLLEGE

Interior Design	M

MOUNT MARTY COLLEGE

Pastoral Ministry and Counseling	M

MOUNT MARY COLLEGE

Art Therapy	M
English	M
Pastoral Ministry and Counseling	M
Social Psychology	M

MOUNT ST. MARY'S COLLEGE

Counseling Psychology	M
Humanities	M
Marriage and Family Therapy	M
Psychology—General	M
Religion	M

MOUNT ST. MARY'S UNIVERSITY

Philosophy	M
Theology	P,M

MOUNT SAINT VINCENT UNIVERSITY

Child and Family Studies	M
Gerontology	M
School Psychology	M
Women's Studies	M

MOUNT SINAI SCHOOL OF MEDICINE

Genetic Counseling	M,D

MOUNT VERNON NAZARENE UNIVERSITY

Theology	M

MURRAY STATE UNIVERSITY

Clinical Psychology	M
Corporate and Organizational Communication	M
Economics	M
English	M
History	M
Mass Communication	M
Music	M
Psychology—General	M
Public Affairs	M
Writing	M

NAROPA UNIVERSITY

Art Therapy	M
Asian Languages	M
Clinical Psychology	M
Counseling Psychology	M
Psychoanalysis and Psychotherapy	M
Religion	M
Social Psychology	M
Theater	M
Theology	P
Therapies—Dance, Drama, and Music	M
Transpersonal and Humanistic Psychology	M
Writing	M

---

*M—master's degree; P—first professional degree; D—doctorate; O—other advanced degree; *—Close-Up and / or Display*

NASHOTAH HOUSE

Theology	P,M,O

NATIONAL DEFENSE INTELLIGENCE COLLEGE

Military and Defense Studies	M

NATIONAL DEFENSE UNIVERSITY

Conflict Resolution and Mediation/Peace Studies	M
Homeland Security	M
Military and Defense Studies	M
National Security	M

NATIONAL-LOUIS UNIVERSITY

Human Development	M,D,O
Psychology—General	M,D,O
Public Policy	M,D,O
School Psychology	M,D,O
Writing	M,D,O

NATIONAL THEATRE CONSERVATORY

Theater	M,O

NATIONAL UNIVERSITY

Art/Fine Arts	M
Communication— General	M
Computer Art and Design	M
Conflict Resolution and Mediation/Peace Studies	M
Corporate and Organizational Communication	M
Counseling Psychology	M
Criminal Justice and Criminology	M
Economics	M
English	M
Forensic Sciences	M
History	M
Homeland Security	M
Humanities	M
Internet and Interactive Multimedia	M
Media Studies	M
Psychology—General	M
Public Administration	M
School Psychology	M
Writing	M

NATIONAL UNIVERSITY OF SINGAPORE

Public Administration	M,D
Public Affairs	M,D
Public Policy	M,D

NAVAL POSTGRADUATE SCHOOL

International Affairs	M
Military and Defense Studies	M,D
National Security	M
Political Science	M

NAVAL WAR COLLEGE

National Security	M

NAZARENE THEOLOGICAL SEMINARY

Missions and Missiology	P,M,O
Theology	P,M,D

NAZARETH COLLEGE OF ROCHESTER

Art Therapy	M
Liberal Studies	M
Therapies—Dance, Drama, and Music	M

NEBRASKA WESLEYAN UNIVERSITY

Forensic Sciences	M
History	M

NER ISRAEL RABBINICAL COLLEGE

Theology	M,D,O

NER ISRAEL YESHIVA COLLEGE OF TORONTO

Theology	

NEUMANN UNIVERSITY

Pastoral Ministry and Counseling	M,O

NEW BRUNSWICK THEOLOGICAL SEMINARY

Pastoral Ministry and Counseling	D
Theology	P,M,D

NEW ENGLAND COLLEGE

Counseling Psychology	M
International Affairs	M
Public Policy	M
Writing	M

NEW ENGLAND COLLEGE OF BUSINESS AND FINANCE

Ethics	M

NEW ENGLAND CONSERVATORY OF MUSIC

Music	M,D,O

NEW JERSEY CITY UNIVERSITY

Art/Fine Arts	M
Counseling Psychology	M
Criminal Justice and Criminology	M
Music	M
School Psychology	M,O
Urban Studies	M

NEW JERSEY INSTITUTE OF TECHNOLOGY

Architecture	M
Emergency Management	M,D
History	M
Technical Communication	M
Urban Studies	D

NEW LIFE THEOLOGICAL SEMINARY

Religion	M

NEWMAN THEOLOGICAL COLLEGE

Theology	P,M

NEWMAN UNIVERSITY

Theology	M

NEW MEXICO HIGHLANDS UNIVERSITY

American Studies	M
Anthropology	M
Clinical Psychology	M
English	M
Internet and Interactive Multimedia	M

Media Studies	M
Psychology—General	M
Public Affairs	M
Rhetoric	M
School Psychology	M
Writing	M

NEW MEXICO STATE UNIVERSITY

Agricultural Economics and Agribusiness	M,D
Anthropology	M
Applied Arts and Design—General	M
Art History	M
Art/Fine Arts	M
Communication— General	M
Corporate and Organizational Communication	M,D
Counseling Psychology	M,D,O
Criminal Justice and Criminology	M
Economic Development	M,D
Economics	M,D
English	M,D
Family and Consumer Sciences-General	M
Geography	M
History	M
Interdisciplinary Studies	M,D
Music	M
Photography	M
Political Science	M
Psychology—General	M,D
Rhetoric	M,D
School Psychology	M,D,O
Spanish	M
Writing	M,D

NEW ORLEANS BAPTIST THEOLOGICAL SEMINARY

Music	P,M,D
Pastoral Ministry and Counseling	P,M,D
Theology	P,M,D

NEW SAINT ANDREWS COLLEGE

Religion	M,O
Theology	M,O

THE NEW SCHOOL: A UNIVERSITY

Anthropology	M,D
Applied Arts and Design—General	M
Applied Social Research	M,D
Architecture	M
Art/Fine Arts	M
Clinical Psychology	M,D
Cognitive Sciences	M,D
Computer Art and Design	M
Decorative Arts	M
Developmental Psychology	M,D
Economics	M,D
History	M,D
Interior Design	M
International Affairs	M
International Economics	M,D
Liberal Studies	M
Lighting Design	M
Media Studies	M,O
Music	M
Philosophy	M,D
Photography	M
Political Science	M,D
Psychology—General	M,D
Public Policy	D
Social Sciences	M,D

Sociology	M,D
Textile Design	M
Theater	M
Urban Design	M
Urban Studies	M
Writing	M

NEWSCHOOL OF ARCHITECTURE & DESIGN

Architecture	M

NEW YORK ACADEMY OF ART

Art/Fine Arts	M

NEW YORK FILM ACADEMY

Film, Television, and Video Production	M
Photography	M

NEW YORK INSTITUTE OF TECHNOLOGY

Architecture	M
Art/Fine Arts	M
Communication— General	M
Computer Art and Design	M
Counseling Psychology	M
Graphic Design	M
Industrial and Labor Relations	M,O
Urban Design	M

NEW YORK MEDICAL COLLEGE

Emergency Management	O

NEW YORK SCHOOL OF INTERIOR DESIGN

Interior Design	M
Lighting Design	M
Sustainable Development	M

NEW YORK STUDIO SCHOOL OF DRAWING, PAINTING AND SCULPTURE

Art/Fine Arts	M,O

NEW YORK THEOLOGICAL SEMINARY

Theology	P,M,D

NEW YORK UNIVERSITY

African Studies	M,D,O
American Studies	M,D
Anthropology	M,D
Applied Arts and Design—General	M
Applied Economics	M,D,O
Applied Psychology	M,D,O
Archaeology	M,D
Art History	M,D
Art Therapy	M
Art/Fine Arts	M,D,O
Arts Administration	M
Asian Studies	M,D
Classics	M,D,O
Cognitive Sciences	M,D,O
Communication— General	M,D
Comparative Literature	M,D
Computer Art and Design	M
Conflict Resolution and Mediation/Peace Studies	M
Corporate and Organizational Communication	M
Counseling Psychology	M,D,O
Cultural Studies	M,D,O
Dance	M,D

Developmental Psychology	M,D
Economics	M,D,O
English	M,D,O
Film, Television, and Video Production	M
Film, Television, and Video Theory and Criticism	M,D
French	M,D,O
German	M,D
Gerontology	D
Graphic Design	M
Hispanic Studies	M,D
Historic Preservation	
History	M,D,O
Human Development	M,D,O
Humanities	M,O
Industrial and Organizational Psychology	M,D,O
Interdisciplinary Studies	M
International Affairs	M,D,O
Internet and Interactive Multimedia	M
Italian	M,D
Jewish Studies	M,D,O
Journalism	M,D,O
Latin American Studies	M,D,O
Linguistics	M,D,O
Media Studies	M,D
Museum Studies	M,O
Music	M,D,O
National Security	M
Near and Middle Eastern Studies	M,D,O
Philosophy	M,D
Political Science	M,D
Portuguese	M,D
Psychoanalysis and Psychotherapy	M,D,O
Psychology—General	M,D,O
Public Administration	M,D,O
Public History	M,D,O
Publishing	M
Religion	M,O
Romance Languages	M,D
Russian	M
Slavic Languages	M
Social Psychology	M,D,O
Social Sciences	M,O
Sociology	M,D
Spanish	M,D
Speech and Interpersonal Communication	M,D
Sustainable Development	M,O
Theater	M,D,O
Therapies—Dance, Drama, and Music	M
Translation and Interpretation	M,D
Urban and Regional Planning	M,O
Western European Studies	M
Writing	M,D

NIAGARA UNIVERSITY

Criminal Justice and Criminology	M
Interdisciplinary Studies	M
School Psychology	M,O

NICHOLLS STATE UNIVERSITY

Counseling Psychology	M,O
School Psychology	M,O

NICHOLS COLLEGE

Criminal Justice and Criminology	M

THE NIGERIAN BAPTIST THEOLOGICAL SEMINARY

Music	P,M,D,O
Pastoral Ministry and Counseling	P,M,D,O
Theology	P,M,D,O

NORFOLK STATE UNIVERSITY

Art/Fine Arts	M
Clinical Psychology	M
Communication— General	M
Criminal Justice and Criminology	M
Media Studies	M
Music	M
Psychology—General	M,D
Social Psychology	M
Sociology	M
Urban Studies	M

NORTH CAROLINA AGRICULTURAL AND TECHNICAL STATE UNIVERSITY

African-American Studies	M
Agricultural Economics and Agribusiness	M
Applied Economics	M
English	M
Rehabilitation Counseling	M,D

NORTH CAROLINA CENTRAL UNIVERSITY

Criminal Justice and Criminology	M
English	M
Family and Consumer Sciences-General	M
History	M
Music	M
Psychology—General	M
Public Administration	M
Social Psychology	M
Sociology	M

NORTH CAROLINA STATE UNIVERSITY

Agricultural Economics and Agribusiness	M
Anthropology	M
Applied Arts and Design—General	M,D
Architecture	M
Clothing and Textiles	D
Communication— General	M
Computer Art and Design	D
Cultural Anthropology	M
Developmental Psychology	D
Economics	M,D
English	M
Experimental Psychology	D
French	M
Geographic Information Systems	M,D
Graphic Design	M
History	M
Industrial and Organizational Psychology	D
Industrial Design	M
International Affairs	M
Landscape Architecture	M
Liberal Studies	M
Psychology—General	D
Public Administration	M,D

Public History	M
Rhetoric	D
School Psychology	D
Social Psychology	M
Sociology	M,D
Spanish	M
Technical Communication	M
Writing	M

NORTH CENTRAL COLLEGE

Internet and Interactive Multimedia	M
Liberal Studies	M
Technical Communication	M

NORTHCENTRAL UNIVERSITY

Marriage and Family Therapy	M,D,O
Psychology—General	M,D,O

NORTH DAKOTA STATE UNIVERSITY

Agricultural Economics and Agribusiness	M
Child and Family Studies	M,D
Child Development	M,D
Clinical Psychology	M,D
Cognitive Sciences	M,D
Communication— General	M,D
Consumer Economics	M,D
Criminal Justice and Criminology	M,D
Emergency Management	M,D
English	M
Family and Consumer Sciences-General	M
Gerontology	M,D
Health Psychology	M,D
History	M,D
Human Development	D
Marriage and Family Therapy	M,D
Mass Communication	M,D
Music	M,D
Psychology—General	M,D
Social Psychology	M,D
Social Sciences	M,D
Sociology	M,D
Speech and Interpersonal Communication	M,D

NORTHEASTERN ILLINOIS UNIVERSITY

English	M
Geography	M
Gerontology	M
History	M
Linguistics	M
Music	M
Political Science	M
Rehabilitation Counseling	M
Speech and Interpersonal Communication	M
Writing	M

NORTHEASTERN SEMINARY AT ROBERTS WESLEYAN COLLEGE

Theology	P,M,D

NORTHEASTERN STATE UNIVERSITY

Addictions/Substance Abuse Counseling	M

American Studies	M
Communication— General	M
Counseling Psychology	M
Criminal Justice and Criminology	M
English	M
Psychology—General	M

NORTHEASTERN UNIVERSITY

Applied Behavior Analysis	M
Applied Economics	M,D
Applied Psychology	M,D,O
Architecture	M
Art/Fine Arts	M
Communication— General	M
Counseling Psychology	M,D,O
Criminal Justice and Criminology	M,D
Cultural Studies	M
Economics	M,D
English	M,D
Experimental Psychology	M,D
History	M,D
Interdisciplinary Studies	D
International Affairs	M,D,O
Media Studies	M
Political Science	M,D,O
Public Administration	M,D,O
Public Affairs	M,D,O
Public History	M,D
Public Policy	M,D
School Psychology	M,D,O
Sociology	M,D
Speech and Interpersonal Communication	D
Urban and Regional Planning	M,D,O
Urban Studies	M,D,O

NORTHERN ARIZONA UNIVERSITY

Anthropology	M
Archaeology	M
Clinical Psychology	M
Communication— General	M
Counseling Psychology	M,D,O
Criminal Justice and Criminology	M
Cultural Anthropology	M
English	M,D,O
Ethnic Studies	O
Gender Studies	O
Geographic Information Systems	M,O
Geography	M,O
History	M,D
Human Development	O
Liberal Studies	M
Linguistics	M,D,O
Music	M,O
Political Science	M,D,O
Psychology—General	M
Public Administration	M,D,O
School Psychology	M,D,O
Sociology	M
Spanish	M
Sustainable Development	M
Technical Writing	M,D,O
Women's Studies	O
Writing	M,D,O

*M—master's degree; P—first professional degree; D—doctorate; O—other advanced degree; *—Close-Up and / or Display*

NORTHERN BAPTIST THEOLOGICAL SEMINARY

Pastoral Ministry and Counseling	P,M,D
Theology	P,M,D

NORTHERN ILLINOIS UNIVERSITY

Anthropology	M
Art/Fine Arts	M
Child and Family Studies	M
Communication—General	M
Dance	M
Economics	M,D
English	M,D
French	M
Geography	M,D
History	M,D
Music	M,O
Philosophy	M
Political Science	M,D
Psychology—General	M,D
Public Administration	M
Romance Languages	M
Sociology	M
Spanish	M
Theater	M

NORTHERN KENTUCKY UNIVERSITY

Clinical Psychology	M,O
Communication—General	M,O
Counseling Psychology	M,O
Cultural Studies	M,O
English	M,O
Geographic Information Systems	M,O
Health Psychology	M,O
Industrial and Organizational Psychology	M,O
Liberal Studies	M,O
Marriage and Family Therapy	M,O
Media Studies	M,O
Music	M,O
Public Administration	M,O
Public History	M,O
Rhetoric	M,O
Social Psychology	M,O
Writing	M,O

NORTHERN MICHIGAN UNIVERSITY

Criminal Justice and Criminology	M
English	M
Psychology—General	M
Public Administration	M
Writing	M

NORTH GEORGIA COLLEGE & STATE UNIVERSITY

Public Administration	M
Social Psychology	M

NORTH GREENVILLE UNIVERSITY

Pastoral Ministry and Counseling	M

NORTH PARK THEOLOGICAL SEMINARY

Pastoral Ministry and Counseling	M,O
Theology	P,M,D

NORTH PARK UNIVERSITY

Music	M

NORTHWEST BAPTIST SEMINARY

Theology	P,M,D,O

NORTHWESTERN COLLEGE

Theology	M

NORTHWESTERN OKLAHOMA STATE UNIVERSITY

Counseling Psychology	M

NORTHWESTERN STATE UNIVERSITY OF LOUISIANA

Archaeology	M
Art/Fine Arts	M
Clinical Psychology	M
English	M
Historic Preservation	M
Music	M
Psychology—General	M

NORTHWESTERN UNIVERSITY

African Studies	O
African-American Studies	D
American Studies	M
Anthropology	D
Art History	D
Art/Fine Arts	M
Broadcast Journalism	M
Clinical Psychology	D
Cognitive Sciences	D
Communication—General	M,D
Comparative Literature	M,D,O
Corporate and Organizational Communication	M
Counseling Psychology	M
Economics	M,D
English	M,D
Ethics	M
Film, Television, and Video Production	M,D
French	D,O
Gender Studies	M
Genetic Counseling	M
German	D
History	M,D
Human Development	D
International Affairs	P,M,O
Internet and Interactive Multimedia	M
Italian	D,O
Journalism	M
Liberal Studies	M
Linguistics	M,D
Marriage and Family Therapy	M
Media Studies	M,D
Music	M,D,O
Philosophy	D
Political Science	M,D
Psychology—General	D
Public Administration	M
Public Policy	M,D
Publishing	M
Religion	M
Slavic Languages	D
Social Psychology	D
Social Sciences	M,O
Sociology	D
Speech and Interpersonal Communication	M,D
Theater	M,D
Writing	M

NORTHWEST MISSOURI STATE UNIVERSITY

Agricultural Economics and Agribusiness	M
English	M

Geographic Information Systems	M,O
Geography	M,O
History	M
Psychology—General	M

NORTHWEST NAZARENE UNIVERSITY

Marriage and Family Therapy	M
Missions and Missiology	P,M
Pastoral Ministry and Counseling	P,M
Religion	P,M
School Psychology	M
Social Psychology	M

NORTHWEST UNIVERSITY

Counseling Psychology	M,D
Cultural Studies	M
Missions and Missiology	M
Pastoral Ministry and Counseling	M
Psychology—General	M,D
Theology	M

NORWICH UNIVERSITY

American Studies	M
Conflict Resolution and Mediation/Peace Studies	M
Criminal Justice and Criminology	M
Ethnic Studies	M
Gender Studies	M
International Affairs	M
Military and Defense Studies	M
Public Administration	M

NOTRE DAME COLLEGE (OH)

Homeland Security	M,O
Pastoral Ministry and Counseling	M,O

NOTRE DAME DE NAMUR UNIVERSITY

Art Therapy	M
Clinical Psychology	M
English	M,O
Marriage and Family Therapy	M
Music	M,O
Psychology—General	M
Public Administration	M
Public Affairs	M

NOTRE DAME SEMINARY

Theology	P,M

NOVA SOUTHEASTERN UNIVERSITY

Child and Family Studies	M,D
Clinical Psychology	D,O
Conflict Resolution and Mediation/Peace Studies	M,D
Counseling Psychology	M
Criminal Justice and Criminology	M
Humanities	M,O
Interdisciplinary Studies	M
Marriage and Family Therapy	M,D,O
National Security	M,O
Psychology—General	M,D,O
Public Administration	M
School Psychology	O
Social Sciences	M,O
Spanish	M,O

NSCAD UNIVERSITY

Applied Arts and Design—General	M
Art/Fine Arts	M

NYACK COLLEGE

Counseling Psychology	M
Marriage and Family Therapy	M
Pastoral Ministry and Counseling	P,M,D
Theology	P,M,D

OAKLAND CITY UNIVERSITY

Theology	P,D

OAKLAND UNIVERSITY

Counseling Psychology	M,D,O
Economics	O
English	M
History	M
Liberal Studies	M
Linguistics	M,O
Music	M,D
Public Administration	M

OAKWOOD UNIVERSITY

Pastoral Ministry and Counseling	M

OBERLIN COLLEGE

Music	M,O

OBLATE SCHOOL OF THEOLOGY

Pastoral Ministry and Counseling	P,M,D,O
Religion	P,M,D,O
Theology	P,M,D,O

OCCIDENTAL COLLEGE

Liberal Studies	M

OHIO DOMINICAN UNIVERSITY

Liberal Studies	M
Theology	M

THE OHIO STATE UNIVERSITY

African Studies	M
African-American Studies	M
Agricultural Economics and Agribusiness	M,D
Anthropology	M,D
Architecture	M,D
Art History	M,D
Art/Fine Arts	M
Arts Administration	M
Asian Languages	M,D
Child and Family Studies	M,D
Chinese	M,D
Classics	M,D
Clinical Psychology	M,D
Clothing and Textiles	M,D
Cognitive Sciences	M,D
Communication—General	M,D
Consumer Economics	M,D
Dance	M,D
Developmental Psychology	M,D
East European and Russian Studies	M,D
Economics	M,D
English	M,D
French	M,D
Geography	M,D
German	M,D
History	M,D
Human Development	M,D
Industrial and Labor Relations	M,D

Industrial Design	M
Interdisciplinary Studies	M,D
Interior Design	M
Italian	M,D
Japanese	M,D
Landscape Architecture	M,D
Linguistics	M,D
Music	M,D
Near and Middle Eastern Languages	M,D
Philosophy	M,D
Political Science	M,D
Portuguese	M,D
Psychology—General	M,D
Public Administration	M,D
Public Affairs	M,D
Public Policy	M,D
Rural Sociology	M,D
Russian	M,D
Slavic Languages	M,D
Social Psychology	M,D
Sociology	M,D
Spanish	M,D
Theater	M,D
Urban and Regional Planning	M,D
Women's Studies	M,D

OHIO UNIVERSITY

African Studies	M
Applied Economics	M
Art History	M
Art/Fine Arts	M
Asian Studies	M
Child and Family Studies	M
Child Development	M
Clinical Psychology	D
Clothing and Textiles	M
Communication—General	M,D
Comparative and Interdisciplinary Arts	D
Corporate and Organizational Communication	M,D
Economics	M
English	M,D
Experimental Psychology	D
Family and Consumer Sciences-General	M
Film, Television, and Video Production	M
Film, Television, and Video Theory and Criticism	M
French	M
Geography	M
Graphic Design	M
Health Communication	M,D
History	M,D
Industrial and Organizational Psychology	D
International Affairs	M
International Development	M
Journalism	M,D
Latin American Studies	M
Linguistics	M
Media Studies	M,D
Music	M,O
Philosophy	M
Photography	M
Political Science	M
Psychology—General	D
Public Administration	M
Rehabilitation Counseling	M,D
Rhetoric	M,D
Social Sciences	M

Sociology	M
Spanish	M
Speech and Interpersonal Communication	M,D
Theater	M
Therapies—Dance, Drama, and Music	M,O

OHR HAMEIR THEOLOGICAL SEMINARY

Theology	M

OKLAHOMA CHRISTIAN UNIVERSITY

Pastoral Ministry and Counseling	P,M
Theology	P,M

OKLAHOMA CITY UNIVERSITY

Applied Behavior Analysis	M
Art/Fine Arts	M
Comparative Literature	M
Corporate and Organizational Communication	M
Criminal Justice and Criminology	M
Dance	M
Liberal Studies	M
Mass Communication	M
Music	M
Philosophy	M
Religion	M
Sociology	M
Theater	M
Writing	M

OKLAHOMA STATE UNIVERSITY

Agricultural Economics and Agribusiness	M,D
Applied Arts and Design—General	M,D
Applied Behavior Analysis	M,D,O
Applied Psychology	M,D,O
Child and Family Studies	M,D
Clinical Psychology	M,D
Clothing and Textiles	M,D
Consumer Economics	M,D
Economics	M,D
Emergency Management	M,D
English	M,D
Family and Consumer Sciences-General	M,D
Geography	M,D
History	M,D
Human Development	M,D
International Affairs	M,D,O
Landscape Architecture	M,D
Marriage and Family Therapy	M,D
Mass Communication	M
Music	M
Philosophy	M
Political Science	M,D
Psychology—General	M,D
Sociology	M,D
Theater	M
Writing	M,D

OKLAHOMA STATE UNIVERSITY CENTER FOR HEALTH SCIENCES

Forensic Psychology	M,O
Forensic Sciences	M,O

OLD DOMINION UNIVERSITY

Applied Economics	M

Applied Psychology	D
Clinical Psychology	D
Computer Art and Design	M
Criminal Justice and Criminology	D
Economics	M
English	M,D
Experimental Psychology	D
History	M
Humanities	M
Industrial and Organizational Psychology	D
International Affairs	M,D
Linguistics	M
Psychology—General	M,D
Public Administration	M,D
Sociology	M
Speech and Interpersonal Communication	M
Urban Studies	D
Women's Studies	M,D
Writing	M

OLIVET NAZARENE UNIVERSITY

Religion	M
Theology	M

ORAL ROBERTS UNIVERSITY

Marriage and Family Therapy	P,M,D
Missions and Missiology	P,M,D
Near and Middle Eastern Languages	P,M,D
Pastoral Ministry and Counseling	P,M,D
Theology	P,M,D

OREGON HEALTH & SCIENCE UNIVERSITY

Gerontology	M,O

OREGON STATE UNIVERSITY

Agricultural Economics and Agribusiness	M,D
Anthropology	M
Child and Family Studies	M,D
Clothing and Textiles	M,D
Economics	M,D
English	M
Family and Consumer Sciences-General	M
Geography	M,D
Gerontology	M
History of Science and Technology	M,D
History	M,D
Human Development	M,D
Interdisciplinary Studies	M

OREGON STATE UNIVERSITY–CASCADES

School Psychology	M
Social Psychology	M

OTIS COLLEGE OF ART AND DESIGN

Art/Fine Arts	M
Graphic Design	M
Photography	M
Writing	M

OTTAWA UNIVERSITY

Art Therapy	M
Counseling Psychology	M
Marriage and Family Therapy	M

Pastoral Ministry and Counseling	M
School Psychology	M

OUR LADY OF HOLY CROSS COLLEGE

Marriage and Family Therapy	M

OUR LADY OF THE LAKE UNIVERSITY OF SAN ANTONIO

Communication—General	M
Counseling Psychology	M,D
English	M
Human Development	M
Marriage and Family Therapy	M,D
Psychology—General	M,D
School Psychology	M,D
Writing	M

OXFORD GRADUATE SCHOOL

Child and Family Studies	M,D
Religion	M,D
Sociology	M,D

PACE UNIVERSITY

Addictions/Substance Abuse Counseling	M
Clinical Psychology	M,D
Counseling Psychology	M
Economics	M
Forensic Sciences	M
Homeland Security	M
Internet and Interactive Multimedia	M,D,O
Psychology—General	M
Public Administration	M
Publishing	M,O
School Psychology	M,D
Sustainable Development	P,M,D
Theater	M

PACIFICA GRADUATE INSTITUTE

Clinical Psychology	M,D
Counseling Psychology	M,D
Psychology—General	M,D

PACIFIC LUTHERAN THEOLOGICAL SEMINARY

Theology	P,M,D,O

PACIFIC LUTHERAN UNIVERSITY

Marriage and Family Therapy	M
Writing	M

PACIFIC NORTHWEST COLLEGE OF ART

Applied Arts and Design—General	M
Art/Fine Arts	M

PACIFIC OAKS COLLEGE

Human Development	M
Marriage and Family Therapy	M

PACIFIC SCHOOL OF RELIGION

Religion	P,M,D,O
Theology	P,M,D,O

PACIFIC UNIVERSITY

Psychology—General	M,D
Writing	M

*M—master's degree; P—first professional degree; D—doctorate; O—other advanced degree; *—Close-Up and/or Display*

PALM BEACH ATLANTIC UNIVERSITY

Addictions/Substance Abuse Counseling	M
Counseling Psychology	M
Marriage and Family Therapy	M

PALO ALTO UNIVERSITY

Clinical Psychology	D
Psychology—General	M,D

PARK UNIVERSITY

Emergency Management	M
Public Administration	M
Public Affairs	M

PAYNE THEOLOGICAL SEMINARY

Theology	P

PENN STATE HARRISBURG

American Studies	M,D
Humanities	M,D
Psychology—General	M,D
Public Affairs	M,D

PENN STATE UNIVERSITY PARK

Agricultural Economics and Agribusiness	M,D
Anthropology	M,D
Architecture	M,D
Art History	M,D
Art/Fine Arts	M,D
Child and Family Studies	M,D
Communication— General	M,D
Counseling Psychology	M,D
Economics	M,D
English	M,D
French	M,D
Geography	M,D
German	M,D
History	M,D
Homeland Security	M,D
Human Development	M,D
Industrial and Labor Relations	M
Landscape Architecture	M
Linguistics	M,D
Music	M,D
Philosophy	M,D
Political Science	M,D
Psychology—General	M,D
Rural Sociology	M,D
School Psychology	M,D
Sociology	M,D
Spanish	M,D
Theater	M
Writing	M,D

PENNSYLVANIA ACADEMY OF THE FINE ARTS

Art/Fine Arts	M,O

PENTECOSTAL THEOLOGICAL SEMINARY

Pastoral Ministry and Counseling	P,M,D
Theology	P,M,D

PEPPERDINE UNIVERSITY

American Studies	M
Clinical Psychology	M
Communication— General	M
Conflict Resolution and Mediation/Peace Studies	M
Economics	M

Film, Television, and Video Production	M
History	M
Humanities	M
International Affairs	M
Marriage and Family Therapy	M
Pastoral Ministry and Counseling	M
Political Science	M
Psychology—General	D
Public Administration	M
Public Policy	M
Religion	P,M
Theology	P
Writing	M

PERELANDRA COLLEGE

Counseling Psychology	M
Writing	M

PERU STATE COLLEGE

Economics	M

PFEIFFER UNIVERSITY

Theology	M

PHILADELPHIA BIBLICAL UNIVERSITY

Pastoral Ministry and Counseling	M
Theology	P,M

PHILADELPHIA COLLEGE OF OSTEOPATHIC MEDICINE

Clinical Psychology	M,D,O
Counseling Psychology	M,D,O
Forensic Sciences	M
Health Psychology	M,D,O
Industrial and Organizational Psychology	M,D,O
Psychology—General	M,D,O*
School Psychology	M,D,O

PHILADELPHIA UNIVERSITY

Architecture	M
Clothing and Textiles	M
Computer Art and Design	M
Emergency Management	M
Sustainable Development	M
Textile Design	M

PHILLIPS GRADUATE INSTITUTE

Marriage and Family Therapy	M
School Psychology	M

PHILLIPS THEOLOGICAL SEMINARY

Ethics	P,M,D
Missions and Missiology	P,M,D
Music	P,M,D
Pastoral Ministry and Counseling	D
Theology	P,M,D

PHOENIX SEMINARY

Counseling Psychology	P,M,D,O
Pastoral Ministry and Counseling	P,M,D,O
Theology	P,M,D,O

PIEDMONT BAPTIST COLLEGE AND GRADUATE SCHOOL

Theology	M,D

PITTSBURGH THEOLOGICAL SEMINARY

Theology	P,M,D

PITTSBURG STATE UNIVERSITY

Art/Fine Arts	M
Communication— General	M
English	M
Graphic Design	M
History	M
Music	M
Psychology—General	M
School Psychology	O
Social Psychology	M
Theater	M

POINT LOMA NAZARENE UNIVERSITY

Religion	M

POINT PARK UNIVERSITY

Communication— General	M
Criminal Justice and Criminology	M
Journalism	M
Mass Communication	M
Music	M
Theater	M

POLYTECHNIC INSTITUTE OF NYU

Communication— General	O
Criminal Justice and Criminology	M,D,O
Film, Television, and Video Production	O
History of Science and Technology	M
Humanities	M,O
Interdisciplinary Studies	M
Internet and Interactive Multimedia	M,O
Journalism	M
Psychology—General	M,O
Technical Writing	M
Urban and Regional Planning	M
Urban Studies	M

POLYTECHNIC INSTITUTE OF NYU, LONG ISLAND GRADUATE CENTER

Interdisciplinary Studies	M

POLYTECHNIC INSTITUTE OF NYU, WESTCHESTER GRADUATE CENTER

Criminal Justice and Criminology	M
Interdisciplinary Studies	M

POLYTECHNIC UNIVERSITY OF PUERTO RICO

Landscape Architecture	M

PONCE SCHOOL OF MEDICINE

Clinical Psychology	D

PONTIFICAL CATHOLIC UNIVERSITY OF PUERTO RICO

Art/Fine Arts	M
Clinical Psychology	D
Criminal Justice and Criminology	M
Hispanic Studies	M,O
History	M
Industrial and Organizational Psychology	D
Psychology—General	M,D
Public Administration	M
Rehabilitation Counseling	M

Spanish	M,O
Theology	P

PONTIFICAL COLLEGE JOSEPHINUM

Theology	P,M

PONTIFICIA UNIVERSIDAD CATOLICA MADRE Y MAESTRA

Architecture	M
Building Science	M
Clinical Psychology	M
Criminal Justice and Criminology	M
Developmental Psychology	M
Forensic Psychology	M
Interior Design	M
International Affairs	M
Landscape Architecture	M
Psychology—General	M

PORTLAND STATE UNIVERSITY

Anthropology	M,D,O
Applied Economics	M,D
Applied Social Research	M,D
Art/Fine Arts	M
Conflict Resolution and Mediation/Peace Studies	M
Criminal Justice and Criminology	M,D
Economics	M,D,O
English	M
French	M,D
Geography	M
German	M
Gerontology	O
History	M
Japanese	M
Music	M
Political Science	M,D
Psychology—General	M,D,O
Public Administration	M,D
Sociology	M,D,O
Spanish	M
Speech and Interpersonal Communication	M,O
Theater	M
Urban and Regional Planning	M
Urban Studies	M,D

PRAIRIE VIEW A&M UNIVERSITY

Agricultural Economics and Agribusiness	M
Architecture	M
Clinical Psychology	M,D
English	M
Family and Consumer Sciences-General	M
Forensic Psychology	M,D
Sociology	M
Urban Design	M

PRATT INSTITUTE

Applied Arts and Design—General	M,O*
Architecture	M*
Art History	M
Art Therapy	M
Art/Fine Arts	M
Arts Administration	M
Graphic Design	M
Historic Preservation	M
Industrial Design	M
Interior Design	M
Internet and Interactive Multimedia	M
Photography	M
Sustainable Development	M

Therapies—Dance,
Drama, and Music   M
Urban and Regional
Planning   M
Urban Design   M

PRESCOTT COLLEGE

Art Therapy   M
Counseling Psychology   M
Health Psychology   M
Humanities   M
Psychoanalysis and
Psychotherapy   M

PRINCETON THEOLOGICAL SEMINARY

Religion   P,M,D
Theology   P,M,D

PRINCETON UNIVERSITY

Anthropology   D
Archaeology   D
Architecture   M,D
Asian Studies   D
Classics   D
Comparative Literature   D
Demography and
Population Studies   D,O
Economics   D,O
English   D
French   D
German   D
History of Science and
Technology   D
History   D
International Affairs   M,D
Music   D
Near and Middle
Eastern Studies   M,D
Philosophy   D
Political Science   D
Portuguese   D
Psychology—General   D
Public Affairs   M,D,O
Public Policy   M,D
Religion   D
Russian   D
Slavic Languages   D
Sociology   D,O
Spanish   D

PROVIDENCE COLLEGE

American Studies   M
History   M
Religion   M
Theology   M

PROVIDENCE COLLEGE AND THEOLOGICAL SEMINARY

Counseling Psychology   P,M,D,O
Missions and Missiology   P,M,D,O
Pastoral Ministry and
Counseling   P,M,D,O
Theology   P,M,D,O

PURCHASE COLLEGE, STATE UNIVERSITY OF NEW YORK

Art History   M
Art/Fine Arts   M
Dance   M
Music   M
Theater   M

PURDUE UNIVERSITY

Agricultural Economics
and Agribusiness   M,D
American Studies   M,D
Anthropology   M,D
Applied Arts and
Design—General   M
Art/Fine Arts   M

Child and Family
Studies   M,D
Child Development   M,D
Clothing and Textiles   M,D
Communication—
General   M,D
Comparative Literature   M,D
Consumer Economics   M,D
Economics   D
English   M,D
Family and Consumer
Sciences-General   M,D
French   M,D
German   M,D
History   M,D
Human Development   M,D
Linguistics   M,D
Marriage and Family
Therapy   M,D
Philosophy   M,D
Political Science   M,D
Psychology—General   D
Sociology   M,D
Spanish   M,D
Sport Psychology   M,D
Theater   M
Writing   M,D

PURDUE UNIVERSITY CALUMET

Child and Family
Studies   M
Child Development   M
Communication—
General   M
Counseling Psychology   M
English   M
History   M
Marriage and Family
Therapy   M
School Psychology   M

QUEENS COLLEGE OF THE CITY UNIVERSITY OF NEW YORK

Art History   M
Art/Fine Arts   M
Clinical Psychology   M
English   M
Family and Consumer
Sciences-General   M
French   M
Hispanic and Latin
American Languages   M
History   M
Italian   M
Liberal Studies   M
Linguistics   M
Music   M
Psychology—General   M
Romance Languages   M
School Psychology   M,O
Social Sciences   M
Sociology   M
Spanish   M
Urban Studies   M
Writing   M

QUEEN'S UNIVERSITY AT KINGSTON

Canadian Studies   M,D
Classics   M
Clinical Psychology   M,D
Cognitive Sciences   M,D
Communication—
General   M,D
Developmental
Psychology   M,D
English   M,D
French   M,D
Gender Studies   M,D
Geography   M,D
German   M,D

Hispanic Studies   M
Industrial and Labor
Relations   M
International Affairs   M,D
Philosophy   M,D
Political Science   M,D
Psychology—General   M,D
Public Policy   M
Religion   M
Social Psychology   M,D
Sociology   M,D
Spanish   M
Sport Psychology   M,D
Theology   P,M,O
Urban and Regional
Planning   M
Women's Studies   M,D

QUEENS UNIVERSITY OF CHARLOTTE

Corporate and
Organizational
Communication   M
Writing   M

QUINCY UNIVERSITY

Clinical Psychology   M
Counseling Psychology   M
School Psychology   M
Theology   M

QUINNIPIAC UNIVERSITY

Communication—
General   M
Interdisciplinary Studies   D
Internet and Interactive
Multimedia   M
Journalism   M

RABBI ISAAC ELCHANAN THEOLOGICAL SEMINARY

Theology   O

RABBINICAL ACADEMY MESIVTA RABBI CHAIM BERLIN

Theology   O

RABBINICAL COLLEGE BETH SHRAGA

Theology   M

RABBINICAL COLLEGE BOBOVER YESHIVA B'NEI ZION

Theology   M

RABBINICAL COLLEGE CH'SAN SOFER

Theology   M

RABBINICAL COLLEGE OF LONG ISLAND

Theology   M

RABBINICAL SEMINARY M'KOR CHAIM

Theology   M

RABBINICAL SEMINARY OF AMERICA

Theology   M

RADFORD UNIVERSITY

Art/Fine Arts   M
Clinical Psychology   M
Corporate and
Organizational
Communication   M
Counseling Psychology   M,D
Criminal Justice and
Criminology   M
English   M

Experimental
Psychology   M
Industrial and
Organizational
Psychology   M
Music   M
Psychology—General   M
School Psychology   M,O
Therapies—Dance,
Drama, and Music   M

RAMAPO COLLEGE OF NEW JERSEY

Liberal Studies   M
Sustainable
Development   M

RECONSTRUCTIONIST RABBINICAL COLLEGE

Jewish Studies   P,M,D,O
Theology   P,M,D,O
Women's Studies   P,M,D,O

REED COLLEGE

Liberal Studies   M

REFORMED PRESBYTERIAN THEOLOGICAL SEMINARY

Theology   P,M,D

REFORMED THEOLOGICAL SEMINARY–ATLANTA CAMPUS

Theology   P,M,D,O

REFORMED THEOLOGICAL SEMINARY–CHARLOTTE CAMPUS

Pastoral Ministry and
Counseling   P,M,D
Religion   P,M,D
Theology   P,M,D

REFORMED THEOLOGICAL SEMINARY–JACKSON CAMPUS

Marriage and Family
Therapy   P,M,D,O
Missions and Missiology   P,M,D,O
Pastoral Ministry and
Counseling   P,M,D,O
Theology   P,M,D,O

REFORMED THEOLOGICAL SEMINARY–ORLANDO CAMPUS

Pastoral Ministry and
Counseling   P,M,D
Theology   P,M,D

REFORMED THEOLOGICAL SEMINARY–WASHINGTON D.C.

Religion   P,M
Theology   P,M

REGENT COLLEGE

Theology   P,M,O

REGENT'S AMERICAN COLLEGE LONDON

International Affairs   M

REGENT UNIVERSITY

American Studies   M
Clinical Psychology   M,D,O
Communication—
General   M,D
Computer Art and
Design   M,D
Counseling Psychology   M,D,O
Film, Television, and
Video Production   M,D
Journalism   M,D
Missions and Missiology   P,M,D

M—master's degree; P—first professional degree; D—doctorate; O—other advanced degree; *—Close-Up and / or Display

Pastoral Ministry and
Counseling — P,M,D
Political Science — M
Psychoanalysis and
Psychotherapy — M,D
Public Administration — M
Social Psychology — M,D,O
Theater — M,D
Theology — P,M,D

REGIS COLLEGE (CANADA)

Pastoral Ministry and
Counseling — P,M,D,O
Philosophy — P,M,D,O
Theology — P,M,D,O

REGIS COLLEGE (MA)

Corporate and
Organizational
Communication — M

REGIS UNIVERSITY

Arts Administration — M,O
Communication—
General — M,O
Conflict Resolution and
Mediation/Peace
Studies — M,O
Counseling Psychology — M,O
Criminal Justice and
Criminology — M
Interdisciplinary Studies — M,O
Marriage and Family
Therapy — M,O
Psychology—General — M,O
Social Psychology — M,O
Technical Writing — M,O

REINHARDT UNIVERSITY

Music — M

RENSSELAER POLYTECHNIC INSTITUTE

Applied Arts and
Design—General — M,D
Art/Fine Arts — M,D
Building Science — M,D
Cognitive Sciences — M,D
Computer Art and
Design — M,D
History of Science and
Technology — M,D
Interdisciplinary Studies — M,D
Lighting Design — M,D
Rhetoric — M,D
Speech and
Interpersonal
Communication — M,D
Sustainable
Development — M,D
Technical
Communication — M

RHODE ISLAND COLLEGE

Art/Fine Arts — M
Arts Administration — M
Counseling Psychology — M,O
English — M,O
Health Psychology — M,O
History — M
Psychology—General — M,O
Public Administration — M
School Psychology — M,O
Writing — M,O

RHODE ISLAND SCHOOL OF DESIGN

Applied Arts and
Design—General — M
Architecture — M
Art/Fine Arts — M
Computer Art and
Design — M

Graphic Design — M
Industrial Design — M
Interior Design — M
Landscape Architecture — M
Photography — M
Textile Design — M

RICE UNIVERSITY

African Studies — D
American Studies — D
Anthropology — M,D
Archaeology — M,D
Architecture — M,D
Art History — D
Cognitive Sciences — M,D
Cultural Anthropology — M,D
Economics — M,D
English — M,D
History — M,D
Industrial and
Organizational
Psychology — M,D
Jewish Studies — D
Liberal Studies — M
Linguistics — M,D
Music — M,D
Near and Middle
Eastern Studies — D
Philosophy — M,D
Political Science — D
Psychology—General — M,D
Religion — D
Sociology — D
Urban Design — M,D

THE RICHARD STOCKTON COLLEGE OF NEW JERSEY

Criminal Justice and
Criminology — M
Holocaust and Genocide
Studies — M

RICHMOND, THE AMERICAN INTERNATIONAL UNIVERSITY IN LONDON

Art History — M
International Affairs — M

RICHMONT GRADUATE UNIVERSITY

Counseling Psychology — M
Marriage and Family
Therapy — M
Psychology—General — M

RIDER UNIVERSITY

French — O
German — O
Music — M
School Psychology — O
Spanish — O

RIVIER COLLEGE

Clinical Psychology — M
Counseling Psychology — M,D,O
English — M
Experimental
Psychology — M
Psychology—General — M
Writing — M

THE ROBERT E. WEBBER INSTITUTE FOR WORSHIP STUDIES

Religion — M,D

ROBERT MORRIS UNIVERSITY

Internet and Interactive
Multimedia — M,D

ROBERTS WESLEYAN COLLEGE

Child and Family
Studies — M
Pastoral Ministry and
Counseling — M
School Psychology — M

ROCHESTER COLLEGE

Missions and Missiology — M

ROCHESTER INSTITUTE OF TECHNOLOGY

Architecture — M
Art/Fine Arts — M
Communication—
General — M
Computer Art and
Design — M
Criminal Justice and
Criminology — M
Film, Television, and
Video Production — M
Gerontology — M,O
Graphic Design — M
Industrial Design — M
Interdisciplinary Studies — M
Internet and Interactive
Multimedia — M,O
Media Studies — M
Medical Illustration — M
Photography — M
Psychology—General — M
Public Policy — M
Sustainable
Development — M,D
Technical
Communication — O

ROGER WILLIAMS UNIVERSITY

Architecture — M
Criminal Justice and
Criminology — M
Forensic Psychology — M
Public Administration — M

ROLLINS COLLEGE

Liberal Studies — M
Sustainable
Development — M
Urban Design — M

ROOSEVELT UNIVERSITY

Anthropology — M
Applied Economics — M
Clinical Psychology — M
Communication—
General — M
Corporate and
Organizational
Communication — M
Economics — M
English — M
Gender Studies — M,O
History — M
Industrial and
Organizational
Psychology — M,D
Journalism — M
Music — M,O
Political Science — M
Psychology—General — M,D
Public Administration — M
Sociology — M
Spanish — M
Theater — M
Women's Studies — M,O
Writing — M

ROBERTS WESLEYAN COLLEGE (right col)

ROSALIND FRANKLIN UNIVERSITY OF MEDICINE AND SCIENCE

Interdisciplinary Studies — D
Psychology—General — M,D

ROSEMONT COLLEGE

Counseling Psychology — M
English — M
Publishing — M
Writing — M

ROWAN UNIVERSITY

Applied Behavior
Analysis — M
Applied Psychology — M
Clinical Psychology — M
Counseling Psychology — M
Criminal Justice and
Criminology — M
Music — M
Psychology—General — M
School Psychology — M,O
Theater — M
Writing — M

ROYAL MILITARY COLLEGE OF CANADA

Military and Defense
Studies — M,D

ROYAL ROADS UNIVERSITY

Conflict Resolution and
Mediation/Peace
Studies — M,O
Emergency
Management — M,O

RUTGERS, THE STATE UNIVERSITY OF NEW JERSEY, CAMDEN

Child Development — M,D
Criminal Justice and
Criminology — M
English — M
History — M
International Affairs — M
International
Development — M
Liberal Studies — M
Psychology—General — M
Public Administration — M
Public History — M
Public Policy — M
Writing — M

RUTGERS, THE STATE UNIVERSITY OF NEW JERSEY, NEWARK

American Studies — M,D
Cognitive Sciences — D*
Criminal Justice and
Criminology — M,D
Economics — M,D
English — M
History — M
International Affairs — M,D
Music — M
Political Science — M
Psychology—General — D
Public Administration — M,D
Public Policy — M,D
Social Psychology — D
Urban Studies — M,D
Writing — M

RUTGERS, THE STATE UNIVERSITY OF NEW JERSEY, NEW BRUNSWICK

African Studies — D
African-American
Studies — D

Agricultural Economics and Agribusiness	M
Anthropology	M,D
Applied Arts and Design—General	M
Applied Psychology	M,D
Art History	M,D,O
Art/Fine Arts	M
Asian Studies	D
Classics	M,D
Clinical Psychology	M,D
Cognitive Sciences	D
Communication—General	D
Comparative Literature	M,D
Counseling Psychology	M
Economics	M,D
English	D
French	M,D
Gender Studies	M,D
Geography	M,D
German	M,D
Health Psychology	D
Historic Preservation	M,D,O
History of Medicine	D
History of Science and Technology	D
History	D
Industrial and Labor Relations	M,D
Interdisciplinary Studies	D
International Affairs	D
Italian	M,D
Linguistics	D
Media Studies	D
Medieval and Renaissance Studies	D
Music	M,D,O
Philosophy	D
Political Science	D
Psychology—General	D
Public Policy	M,D
School Psychology	M,D
Social Psychology	D
Sociology	M,D
Spanish	M,D
Theater	M
Translation and Interpretation	M,D
Urban and Regional Planning	M,D
Women's Studies	M,D
Writing	M

RYERSON UNIVERSITY

Arts Administration	M

SACRED HEART MAJOR SEMINARY

Pastoral Ministry and Counseling	P,M
Theology	P,M

SACRED HEART SCHOOL OF THEOLOGY

Theology	P,M

SACRED HEART UNIVERSITY

Criminal Justice and Criminology	M
Gerontology	M
Internet and Interactive Multimedia	M,O
Religion	M

SAGE GRADUATE SCHOOL

Applied Behavior Analysis	M,O
Child and Family Studies	M
Counseling Psychology	M
Forensic Psychology	M,O

Gerontology	M,O
Psychology—General	M
Public Administration	M
Social Psychology	M

SAGINAW VALLEY STATE UNIVERSITY

Communication—General	M
Media Studies	M
Public Administration	M

ST. AMBROSE UNIVERSITY

Criminal Justice and Criminology	M
Pastoral Ministry and Counseling	M

ST. ANDREW'S COLLEGE

Theology	P,M

ST. ANDREW'S COLLEGE IN WINNIPEG

Theology	P

ST. AUGUSTINE'S SEMINARY OF TORONTO

Pastoral Ministry and Counseling	P,M,O
Theology	P,M,O

SAINT BERNARD'S SCHOOL OF THEOLOGY AND MINISTRY

Pastoral Ministry and Counseling	P,M,O
Theology	P,M,O

ST. BONAVENTURE UNIVERSITY

Corporate and Organizational Communication	M
Counseling Psychology	M,O
English	M
Religion	M
Social Psychology	M,O

ST. CATHERINE UNIVERSITY

Pastoral Ministry and Counseling	M,O
Theology	M,O

ST. CHARLES BORROMEO SEMINARY, OVERBROOK

Religion	M
Theology	P,M

ST. CLOUD STATE UNIVERSITY

Applied Behavior Analysis	M
Applied Economics	M
Archaeology	M
Child and Family Studies	M
Criminal Justice and Criminology	M
Economics	M
English	M
Geography	M
Gerontology	M
Historic Preservation	M
History	M
Industrial and Organizational Psychology	M
Marriage and Family Therapy	M
Mass Communication	M
Music	M
Psychology—General	M,D

Rehabilitation Counseling	M
Social Psychology	M

ST. EDWARD'S UNIVERSITY

Computer Art and Design	M
Conflict Resolution and Mediation/Peace Studies	M,O
Counseling Psychology	M
Ethics	M
Humanities	M,O
Liberal Studies	M,O
Media Studies	M
Social Sciences	M,O

SAINT FRANCIS SEMINARY

Pastoral Ministry and Counseling	P,M
Theology	P,M

ST. FRANCIS XAVIER UNIVERSITY

Cultural Studies	M

ST. JOHN FISHER COLLEGE

Counseling Psychology	M
International Affairs	M

ST. JOHN'S COLLEGE (MD)

Liberal Studies	M

ST. JOHN'S COLLEGE (NM)

Asian Languages	M
Asian Studies	M
Liberal Studies	M

ST. JOHN'S SEMINARY (CA)

Pastoral Ministry and Counseling	P,M
Theology	P,M

SAINT JOHN'S SEMINARY (MA)

Religion	P,M
Theology	P,M

SAINT JOHN'S UNIVERSITY (MN)

Music	P,M
Pastoral Ministry and Counseling	P,M
Theology	P,M

ST. JOHN'S UNIVERSITY (NY)

African Studies	M,O
Asian Studies	M,O
Clinical Psychology	M,D
Criminal Justice and Criminology	M
English	M,D
Experimental Psychology	M
History	M,D
International Affairs	M
Liberal Studies	M
Pastoral Ministry and Counseling	P,M,O
Philosophy	M
Political Science	M
Psychology—General	M,D
Rehabilitation Counseling	M,D,O
School Psychology	M,D
Sociology	M
Spanish	M
Theology	P,M,O

SAINT JOSEPH COLLEGE

Counseling Psychology	M
Gerontology	M,O
Human Development	M,O

Marriage and Family Therapy	M
Social Psychology	M

SAINT JOSEPH'S COLLEGE

Music	M,O

ST. JOSEPH'S SEMINARY

Theology	P,M

SAINT JOSEPH'S UNIVERSITY

Criminal Justice and Criminology	M,O
Gerontology	M,O
Homeland Security	M,O
Industrial and Organizational Psychology	M,O
Psychology—General	M,O
Writing	M

ST. LAWRENCE UNIVERSITY

Human Development	M,O

SAINT LEO UNIVERSITY

Criminal Justice and Criminology	M
Forensic Sciences	M
Pastoral Ministry and Counseling	M
Theology	M

SAINT LOUIS UNIVERSITY

American Studies	M,D
Clinical Psychology	M,D
Communication—General	M
English	M,D
Experimental Psychology	M,D
French	M
Geographic Information Systems	M,D,O
History	M,D
Human Development	M,D,O
Industrial and Organizational Psychology	M,D
Marriage and Family Therapy	M,D,O
Philosophy	M,D
Political Science	M
Psychology—General	M,D
Public Administration	M,D,O
Public Policy	M,D,O
Spanish	M
Theology	M,D
Urban Studies	M,D,O

SAINT LOUIS UNIVERSITY–MADRID CAMPUS

English	M
Spanish	M

SAINT MARTIN'S UNIVERSITY

Counseling Psychology	M
Social Psychology	M

SAINT MARY-OF-THE-WOODS COLLEGE

Art Therapy	M,O
Pastoral Ministry and Counseling	M,O
Theology	M,O
Therapies—Dance, Drama, and Music	M

SAINT MARY'S COLLEGE OF CALIFORNIA

Marriage and Family Therapy	M
Writing	M

*M—master's degree; P—first professional degree; D—doctorate; O—other advanced degree; *—Close-Up and/or Display*

SAINT MARY SEMINARY AND GRADUATE SCHOOL OF THEOLOGY

Theology	P,M,D

ST. MARY'S SEMINARY AND UNIVERSITY

Theology	P,M,D,O

SAINT MARY'S UNIVERSITY (CANADA)

Applied Psychology	M,D
Canadian Studies	M,O
Criminal Justice and Criminology	M
Gender Studies	M
History	M
Industrial and Organizational Psychology	M,D
International Development	M,O
Philosophy	M
Psychology—General	M,D
Religion	M
Theology	M
Women's Studies	M

ST. MARY'S UNIVERSITY (UNITED STATES)

Addictions/Substance Abuse Counseling	M,D,O
Clinical Psychology	M
Communication—General	M
Counseling Psychology	M
English	M
Industrial and Organizational Psychology	M
International Affairs	M
Marriage and Family Therapy	M,D
Pastoral Ministry and Counseling	M
Political Science	M
Psychology—General	M
Public Administration	M
Social Psychology	M
Theology	M

SAINT MARY'S UNIVERSITY OF MINNESOTA

Arts Administration	M
Counseling Psychology	M,D,O
Geographic Information Systems	M,O
Human Development	M
Marriage and Family Therapy	M,O
Pastoral Ministry and Counseling	M,O
Philanthropic Studies	M

SAINT MEINRAD SCHOOL OF THEOLOGY

Theology	P,M

SAINT MICHAEL'S COLLEGE

Clinical Psychology	M
Theology	M,O

ST. NORBERT COLLEGE

Liberal Studies	M
Theology	M

ST. PATRICK'S SEMINARY & UNIVERSITY

Theology	P,M

SAINT PAUL SCHOOL OF THEOLOGY

Theology	P,M,D

SAINT PAUL UNIVERSITY

Conflict Resolution and Mediation/Peace Studies	M
Counseling Psychology	M
Marriage and Family Therapy	M
Missions and Missiology	M
Pastoral Ministry and Counseling	M,D,O
Theology	M,D,O

SAINT PETER'S COLLEGE

Applied Behavior Analysis	M,D,O
Criminal Justice and Criminology	M

ST. PETER'S SEMINARY

Theology	P,M

SAINTS CYRIL AND METHODIUS SEMINARY

Pastoral Ministry and Counseling	P,M
Theology	P,M

ST. STEPHEN'S COLLEGE

Pastoral Ministry and Counseling	M,D
Theology	M,D

ST. THOMAS UNIVERSITY

Arts Administration	M
Communication—General	M,D,O
Counseling Psychology	M
Criminal Justice and Criminology	M,O
Film, Television, and Video Production	M
Hispanic Studies	M,O
Marriage and Family Therapy	M,O
Pastoral Ministry and Counseling	M,D,O
Public Administration	M,O
Theology	M,D,O

ST. TIKHON'S ORTHODOX THEOLOGICAL SEMINARY

Theology	P

SAINT VINCENT DE PAUL REGIONAL SEMINARY

Theology	P,M

SAINT VINCENT SEMINARY

Theology	P,M

ST. VLADIMIR'S ORTHODOX THEOLOGICAL SEMINARY

Music	P,M,D
Theology	P,M,D

SAINT XAVIER UNIVERSITY

Counseling Psychology	M,O
English	M,O
Psychology—General	M,O
Writing	M,O

SALEM STATE UNIVERSITY

Counseling Psychology	M,O
Criminal Justice and Criminology	M
English	M
Geography	M
History	M
Psychology—General	M,O
Spanish	M

SALISBURY UNIVERSITY

Conflict Resolution and Mediation/Peace Studies	M
English	M
Geographic Information Systems	M
History	M
Writing	M

SALVE REGINA UNIVERSITY

Art Therapy	M,O
Counseling Psychology	M,O
Criminal Justice and Criminology	M
Homeland Security	M,O
Humanities	M,D,O
International Affairs	M,O
Rehabilitation Counseling	M,O

SAMFORD UNIVERSITY

Music	M
Theology	P,M,D

SAM HOUSTON STATE UNIVERSITY

Clinical Psychology	M,D
Criminal Justice and Criminology	M,D
Dance	M
English	M
Family and Consumer Sciences-General	M
Forensic Sciences	M,D
History	M
Humanities	M,D
Music	M
Political Science	M
Psychology—General	M,D
Public Administration	M
Sociology	M
Speech and Interpersonal Communication	M,D

SAN DIEGO STATE UNIVERSITY

Anthropology	M
Applied Arts and Design—General	M
Art History	M
Art/Fine Arts	M
Asian Studies	M
Child and Family Studies	M
Child Development	M
Clinical Psychology	M,D
Communication—General	M
Criminal Justice and Criminology	M
Economics	M
Emergency Management	M,D
English	M
Environmental Design	M
Film, Television, and Video Production	M
Geography	M,D
Gerontology	M
Graphic Design	M
Health Psychology	M,D
History	M
Industrial and Organizational Psychology	M,D
Interdisciplinary Studies	M
Interior Design	M
Internet and Interactive Multimedia	M

Latin American Studies	M
Liberal Studies	M
Linguistics	M,O
Media Studies	M
Music	M
Philosophy	M
Political Science	M
Psychology—General	M,D
Public Administration	M
Rehabilitation Counseling	M
Rhetoric	M
Romance Languages	M
School Psychology	M
Sociology	M
Spanish	M
Theater	M
Urban and Regional Planning	M
Western European Studies	M
Women's Studies	M
Writing	M

SAN FRANCISCO ART INSTITUTE

Applied Arts and Design—General	M,O
Art History	M
Art/Fine Arts	M,O
Film, Television, and Video Production	M,O
Museum Studies	M
Photography	M,O
Urban Studies	M

SAN FRANCISCO CONSERVATORY OF MUSIC

Music	M

SAN FRANCISCO STATE UNIVERSITY

Anthropology	M
Archaeology	M
Art/Fine Arts	M
Asian-American Studies	M
Chinese	M
Classics	M
Clinical Psychology	M
Comparative Literature	M
Counseling Psychology	M
Cultural Anthropology	M
Cultural Studies	M
Developmental Psychology	M
Economics	M
English	M
Ethnic Studies	M
Family and Consumer Sciences-General	M
Film, Television, and Video Production	M
Film, Television, and Video Theory and Criticism	M
French	M
Geographic Information Systems	M
Geography	M
German	M
Gerontology	M
History	M
Humanities	M
Industrial and Organizational Psychology	M
Industrial Design	M
International Affairs	M
Italian	M
Japanese	M
Linguistics	M
Marriage and Family Therapy	M

Media Studies	M
Museum Studies	M
Music	M
Philosophy	M,O
Political Science	M
Psychology—General	M
Public Administration	M
Public Policy	M
Rehabilitation Counseling	M
School Psychology	M
Social Psychology	M
Spanish	M
Speech and Interpersonal Communication	M
Theater	M
Women's Studies	M
Writing	M

SAN FRANCISCO THEOLOGICAL SEMINARY

Theology	P,M,D

SAN JOSE STATE UNIVERSITY

Anthropology	M
Applied Arts and Design—General	M
Applied Economics	M
Art History	M
Art/Fine Arts	M
Child and Family Studies	M
Clinical Psychology	M
Communication—General	M
Comparative Literature	M
Computer Art and Design	M
Criminal Justice and Criminology	M
Economics	M
English	M
Experimental Psychology	M
Film, Television, and Video Production	M
French	M
Geographic Information Systems	M,O
Geography	M,O
Gerontology	M,O
Hispanic Studies	M
History	M
Illustration	M
Industrial and Organizational Psychology	M
Interdisciplinary Studies	M
Linguistics	M,O
Mass Communication	M
Music	M
Philosophy	M
Photography	M
Psychology—General	M
Public Administration	M
Sociology	M
Spanish	M
Speech and Interpersonal Communication	M
Theater	M
Urban and Regional Planning	M,O

SANTA CLARA UNIVERSITY

Agricultural Economics and Agribusiness	M
Counseling Psychology	M
Pastoral Ministry and Counseling	M
Theology	P,M,D,O

SARAH LAWRENCE COLLEGE

Child Development	M
Dance	M
Genetic Counseling	M
History	M
Interdisciplinary Studies	M
Theater	M
Women's Studies	M
Writing	M

SAVANNAH COLLEGE OF ART AND DESIGN

Applied Arts and Design—General	M,O
Architectural History	M
Architecture	M
Art History	M*
Art/Fine Arts	M*
Arts Administration	M
Clothing and Textiles	M,O
Computer Art and Design	M,O
Cultural Studies	M,O
Film, Television, and Video Production	M
Film, Television, and Video Theory and Criticism	M
Graphic Design	M
Historic Preservation	M,O
Illustration	M
Industrial Design	M
Interior Design	M
Internet and Interactive Multimedia	M,O
Media Studies	M
Music	M,O
Photography	M
Textile Design	M
Theater	M
Urban Design	M
Writing	M

SAVANNAH STATE UNIVERSITY

Public Administration	M
Urban Studies	M

SAYBROOK UNIVERSITY

Clinical Psychology	M,D
Counseling Psychology	M
Health Psychology	M,D
Marriage and Family Therapy	M,D
Psychology—General	M,D
Sustainable Development	M,D
Transpersonal and Humanistic Psychology	M,D

SCHILLER INTERNATIONAL UNIVERSITY

International Affairs	M

SCHILLER INTERNATIONAL UNIVERSITY (UNITED KINGDOM)

Corporate and Organizational Communication	M
International Affairs	M

SCHOOL OF ADVANCED AIR AND SPACE STUDIES

Military and Defense Studies	M

THE SCHOOL OF PROFESSIONAL PSYCHOLOGY AT FOREST INSTITUTE

Applied Behavior Analysis	M,D,O
Clinical Psychology	M,D,O

Counseling Psychology	M,D,O
Marriage and Family Therapy	M,D,O
Psychology—General	M,D,O

SCHOOL OF THE ART INSTITUTE OF CHICAGO

Applied Arts and Design—General	M
Architecture	M
Art History	M
Art Therapy	M
Art/Fine Arts	M*
Arts Administration	M
Arts Journalism	M
Film, Television, and Video Production	M
Graphic Design	M
Historic Preservation	M
Interior Design	M
Journalism	M
Music	M
Photography	M
Textile Design	M,O
Writing	M,O

SCHOOL OF THE MUSEUM OF FINE ARTS, BOSTON

Art/Fine Arts	M

SCHOOL OF VISUAL ARTS (NY)

Applied Arts and Design—General	M
Art Therapy	M
Art/Fine Arts	M
Computer Art and Design	M
Film, Television, and Video Production	M
Illustration	M
Internet and Interactive Multimedia	M
Photography	M

SEABURY-WESTERN THEOLOGICAL SEMINARY

Music	P,M,D,O
Theology	P,M,D,O

SEATTLE PACIFIC UNIVERSITY

Clinical Psychology	D
Industrial and Organizational Psychology	M,D
Marriage and Family Therapy	M,O
Theology	P,M
Writing	M

SEATTLE UNIVERSITY

Criminal Justice and Criminology	M
Pastoral Ministry and Counseling	M
Psychology—General	M
Public Administration	M
School Psychology	M,O
Theology	P,M,O
Transpersonal and Humanistic Psychology	M

SEMINARY OF THE IMMACULATE CONCEPTION

Pastoral Ministry and Counseling	P,M,D,O
Theology	P,M,D,O

SEMINARY OF THE SOUTHWEST

Pastoral Ministry and Counseling	P,M,O

Religion	P,M,O
Theology	P,M,O

SETON HALL UNIVERSITY

Art/Fine Arts	M
Asian Languages	M
Asian Studies	M
Chinese	M
Communication—General	M
Corporate and Organizational Communication	M
Counseling Psychology	M,D
English	M
Experimental Psychology	M
History	M
Holocaust and Genocide Studies	M
International Affairs	M
Jewish Studies	M
Marriage and Family Therapy	M,D,O
Museum Studies	M
Pastoral Ministry and Counseling	P,M,O
Psychology—General	M,D,O
Public Administration	M,O
Public Policy	M,O
Religion	P,M,O
School Psychology	O
Speech and Interpersonal Communication	M
Theology	P,M,O
Writing	M

SETON HILL UNIVERSITY

Art Therapy	M
Holocaust and Genocide Studies	O
Marriage and Family Therapy	M
Writing	M,O

SEWANEE: THE UNIVERSITY OF THE SOUTH

English	M
Theology	P,M,D
Writing	M

SHASTA BIBLE COLLEGE

Pastoral Ministry and Counseling	M

SHAW UNIVERSITY

Theology	P,M

SHENANDOAH UNIVERSITY

Arts Administration	M,D,O
Music	M,D,O
Public Administration	M,D,O
Therapies—Dance, Drama, and Music	M,D,O

SHIPPENSBURG UNIVERSITY OF PENNSYLVANIA

Addictions/Substance Abuse Counseling	M,O
Applied Psychology	M
Clinical Psychology	M,O
Communication—General	M
Counseling Psychology	M,O
Criminal Justice and Criminology	M
Geography	M
Gerontology	M,O
History	M,O
Marriage and Family Therapy	M,O

---

*M—master's degree; P—first professional degree; D—doctorate; O—other advanced degree; *—Close-Up and / or Display*

Psychology—General M
Public Administration M
Public History M,O
Sociology M

SH'OR YOSHUV RABBINICAL COLLEGE

Theology

SIMMONS COLLEGE

Applied Behavior
  Analysis M,D,O
Corporate and
  Organizational
  Communication M
Cultural Studies M
English M
Gender Studies M
History M
Psychology—General M,D
Public History O
Spanish M

SIMON FRASER UNIVERSITY

Anthropology M,D
Archaeology M,D
Communication—
  General M,D
Comparative and
  Interdisciplinary Arts M
Criminal Justice and
  Criminology M,D
Economics M,D
English M,D
French M
Geography M,D
Gerontology M,D
History M,D
Internet and Interactive
  Multimedia M,D
Latin American Studies M
Liberal Studies M
Linguistics M,D
Philosophy M,D
Political Science M,D
Psychology—General M,D
Public Policy M
Publishing M
Sociology M,D
Urban Studies M,O
Women's Studies M,D

SIMPSON COLLEGE

Criminal Justice and
  Criminology M

SIMPSON UNIVERSITY

Counseling Psychology M
Missions and Missiology P,M
Pastoral Ministry and
  Counseling P,M

SIOUX FALLS SEMINARY

Marriage and Family
  Therapy M
Pastoral Ministry and
  Counseling P,M
Religion M
Theology M,D,O

SIT GRADUATE INSTITUTE

Conflict Resolution and
  Mediation/Peace
  Studies M
International Affairs M
Sustainable
  Development M

SKIDMORE COLLEGE

Liberal Studies M

SLIPPERY ROCK UNIVERSITY OF PENNSYLVANIA

Criminal Justice and
  Criminology M
History M
Sustainable
  Development M

SMITH COLLEGE

Dance M
French M
History M
Theater M
Women's Studies O

SOJOURNER-DOUGLASS COLLEGE

Public Administration M

SOKA UNIVERSITY OF AMERICA

Japanese O

SONOMA STATE UNIVERSITY

Anthropology M
Counseling Psychology M
English M
History M
Interdisciplinary Studies M
Marriage and Family
  Therapy M
Political Science M
Public Administration M
Public History M
Writing M

SOTHEBY'S INSTITUTE OF ART–LONDON

Art/Fine Arts M
Arts Administration M
Decorative Arts M
Photography M

SOTHEBY'S INSTITUTE OF ART–NEW YORK

Art/Fine Arts M
Arts Administration M
Decorative Arts M

SOUTH CAROLINA STATE UNIVERSITY

Agricultural Economics
  and Agribusiness M
Child and Family
  Studies M
Family and Consumer
  Sciences-General M
Rehabilitation
  Counseling M

SOUTH DAKOTA STATE UNIVERSITY

Clothing and Textiles M
Communication—
  General M
Economics M
English M
Family and Consumer
  Sciences-General M
Geography M
Human Development M
Interior Design M
Journalism M
Rural Sociology M,D

SOUTHEASTERN BAPTIST THEOLOGICAL SEMINARY

Ethics P,M,D
Missions and Missiology P,M,D
Music P,M,D
Philosophy P,M,D
Psychology—General P,M,D
Theology P,M,D
Women's Studies P,M,D

SOUTHEASTERN LOUISIANA UNIVERSITY

Addictions/Substance
  Abuse Counseling M
Communication—
  General M
Criminal Justice and
  Criminology M
English M
History M
Marriage and Family
  Therapy M
Music M
Psychology—General M
Public Policy M
Social Psychology M
Sociology M
Writing M

SOUTHEASTERN OKLAHOMA STATE UNIVERSITY

Clinical Psychology M
Counseling Psychology M

SOUTHEASTERN UNIVERSITY (FL)

Counseling Psychology M
Pastoral Ministry and
  Counseling M

SOUTHEAST MISSOURI STATE UNIVERSITY

Counseling Psychology M,O
Criminal Justice and
  Criminology M
English M
Historic Preservation M,O
History M,O
Public Administration M
Public History M,O
School Psychology M,O
Social Psychology M,O

SOUTHERN ADVENTIST UNIVERSITY

Counseling Psychology M
Missions and Missiology M
Psychology—General M
Religion M
Theology M

SOUTHERN ARKANSAS UNIVERSITY–MAGNOLIA

Public Administration M

SOUTHERN BAPTIST THEOLOGICAL SEMINARY

Missions and Missiology P,M,D
Music P,M,D
Pastoral Ministry and
  Counseling P,M,D
Philosophy P,M,D
Religion P,M,D
Theology P,M,D

SOUTHERN CALIFORNIA INSTITUTE OF ARCHITECTURE

Architecture M

SOUTHERN CALIFORNIA SEMINARY

Counseling Psychology P,M,D
Marriage and Family
  Therapy P,M,D
Psychology—General P,M,D
Religion P,M,D
Theology P,M,D

SOUTHERN CONNECTICUT STATE UNIVERSITY

English M
History M

Political Science M
Psychology—General M
School Psychology M,O
Sociology M
Sport Psychology M
Urban Studies M
Women's Studies M

SOUTHERN EVANGELICAL SEMINARY

Jewish Studies P,M,D,O
Missions and Missiology P,M,D,O
Near and Middle
  Eastern Studies P,M,D,O
Pastoral Ministry and
  Counseling P,M,D,O
Philosophy P,M,D,O
Religion P,M,D,O
Theology P,M,D,O

SOUTHERN ILLINOIS UNIVERSITY CARBONDALE

Agricultural Economics
  and Agribusiness M
Anthropology M,D
Applied Arts and
  Design—General M
Architecture M
Art/Fine Arts M
Clinical Psychology M,D
Communication—
  General M,D
Counseling Psychology M,D
Criminal Justice and
  Criminology M
Cultural Studies M
Economics M,D
English M,D
Experimental
  Psychology M,D
Geography M,D
History M,D
Human Development M,D
Journalism D
Linguistics M
Mass Communication M
Media Studies M
Music M
Philosophy M,D
Political Science M,D
Psychology—General M,D
Public Administration M
Rehabilitation
  Counseling M,D
Rhetoric M,D
Sociology M,D
Speech and
  Interpersonal
  Communication M,D
Theater M,D
Writing M

SOUTHERN ILLINOIS UNIVERSITY EDWARDSVILLE

Art Therapy M
Art/Fine Arts M
Clinical Psychology M
Corporate and
  Organizational
  Communication M,O
Economics M
English M,O
Geography M
Health Communication M
History M
Industrial and
  Organizational
  Psychology M
Mass Communication M
Media Studies O
Museum Studies O
Music M
Psychology—General M,O

Public Administration	M
School Psychology	O
Sociology	M
Speech and Interpersonal Communication	M
Writing	M

SOUTHERN METHODIST UNIVERSITY

Anthropology	M,D
Applied Economics	M,D
Art History	M
Art/Fine Arts	M
Arts Administration	
Clinical Psychology	D
Communication— General	M
Conflict Resolution and Mediation/Peace Studies	M,O
Dance	M
Economics	M,D
English	M,D
Film, Television, and Video Production	M
History	M,D
Liberal Studies	M
Medieval and Renaissance Studies	M
Music	M,O
Photography	M
Psychology—General	D
Religion	M,D
Theater	M
Theology	P,M,D

SOUTHERN NAZARENE UNIVERSITY

Counseling Psychology	M
Marriage and Family Therapy	M
Psychology—General	M
Religion	M
Theology	M

SOUTHERN NEW HAMPSHIRE UNIVERSITY

Addictions/Substance Abuse Counseling	M,O
Child Development	M,O
Clinical Psychology	M,O
Economic Development	M,D
Psychology—General	M,O
Public Policy	M,D
Writing	M,O

SOUTHERN OREGON UNIVERSITY

Counseling Psychology	M
Interdisciplinary Studies	M
Psychology—General	M

SOUTHERN POLYTECHNIC STATE UNIVERSITY

Communication— General	M,O
Graphic Design	M,O
Internet and Interactive Multimedia	M,O
Technical Communication	M,O

SOUTHERN UNIVERSITY AND AGRICULTURAL AND MECHANICAL COLLEGE

Criminal Justice and Criminology	M
History	M
Mass Communication	M
Political Science	M
Psychology—General	M

Public Administration	M
Public Policy	D
Rehabilitation Counseling	M
Social Sciences	M

SOUTHERN UTAH UNIVERSITY

Arts Administration	M
Communication— General	M
Forensic Sciences	M
Public Administration	M

SOUTHERN WESLEYAN UNIVERSITY

Pastoral Ministry and Counseling	M

SOUTH UNIVERSITY (AL)

Counseling Psychology	M*

SOUTH UNIVERSITY (FL)

Counseling Psychology	M*

SOUTH UNIVERSITY (GA)

Counseling Psychology	M*
Criminal Justice and Criminology	M*

SOUTH UNIVERSITY (MI)

Counseling Psychology	M*

SOUTH UNIVERSITY (SC)

Counseling Psychology	M*
Criminal Justice and Criminology	M*

SOUTH UNIVERSITY (VA)

Counseling Psychology	M*

SOUTH UNIVERSITY (VA)

Counseling Psychology	M*

SOUTHWESTERN ASSEMBLIES OF GOD UNIVERSITY

Counseling Psychology	M
History	M
Missions and Missiology	P,M
Pastoral Ministry and Counseling	P,M
Religion	P,M
Theology	P,M

SOUTHWESTERN BAPTIST THEOLOGICAL SEMINARY

Music	M,D,O
Theology	P,M,D,O

SOUTHWESTERN CHRISTIAN UNIVERSITY

Missions and Missiology	M
Pastoral Ministry and Counseling	M

SOUTHWESTERN COLLEGE (KS)

Criminal Justice and Criminology	M
Music	M
Theology	M

SOUTHWESTERN COLLEGE (NM)

Art Therapy	M
Counseling Psychology	M,O
Health Psychology	O
Psychology—General	O
Social Psychology	O
Thanatology	M,O

SOUTHWESTERN OKLAHOMA STATE UNIVERSITY

Music	M
School Psychology	M

SOUTHWEST UNIVERSITY

Criminal Justice and Criminology	M

SPALDING UNIVERSITY

Applied Behavior Analysis	M
Clinical Psychology	M,D
Communication— General	M
Corporate and Organizational Communication	M
Psychology—General	M,D
Writing	M

SPERTUS INSTITUTE OF JEWISH STUDIES

Jewish Studies	M,D

SPRING ARBOR UNIVERSITY

Child and Family Studies	M
Communication— General	M
Counseling Psychology	M
Pastoral Ministry and Counseling	M
Theology	M

SPRINGFIELD COLLEGE

Addictions/Substance Abuse Counseling	M
Art Therapy	M,O
Counseling Psychology	M,O
Industrial and Organizational Psychology	M,O
Marriage and Family Therapy	M,O
Rehabilitation Counseling	M
Social Psychology	M
Sport Psychology	M,D,O

SPRING HILL COLLEGE

Art/Fine Arts	M
English	M
Ethics	M
History	M
Liberal Studies	M
Pastoral Ministry and Counseling	M
Theology	M

STANFORD UNIVERSITY

Anthropology	M,D
Art/Fine Arts	M,D
Asian Studies	M
Child and Family Studies	D
Chinese	M,D
Classics	M,D
Communication— General	M,D
Comparative Literature	D
Counseling Psychology	D
Cultural Anthropology	M,D
Developmental Psychology	D
East European and Russian Studies	M
Economics	D
English	M,D
French	M,D
German	M,D

History	M,D
Humanities	M
Interdisciplinary Studies	M,D
International Affairs	M
Italian	M,D
Japanese	M,D
Journalism	M,D
Linguistics	M,D
Music	M,D
Philosophy	M,D
Political Science	M,D
Psychology—General	D
Religion	M,D
Russian	M,D
Slavic Languages	M,D
Sociology	D
Spanish	M,D
Theater	D

STARR KING SCHOOL FOR THE MINISTRY

Theology	P

STATE UNIVERSITY OF NEW YORK AT BINGHAMTON

Anthropology	M,D
Art History	M,D
Clinical Psychology	M,D
Cognitive Sciences	M,D
Comparative Literature	M,D
Cultural Studies	M,D
Economics	M,D
English	M,D
French	M
Geography	M
History	M,D
Italian	M
Music	M
Philosophy	M,D
Political Science	M,D
Psychology—General	M,D
Public Administration	M
Public Policy	M,D
Sociology	M,D
Spanish	M,O
Theater	M
Translation and Interpretation	M,O

STATE UNIVERSITY OF NEW YORK AT FREDONIA

English	M
Interdisciplinary Studies	M
Music	M

STATE UNIVERSITY OF NEW YORK AT NEW PALTZ

Art/Fine Arts	M
Counseling Psychology	M
English	M
French	M
Music	M
Psychology—General	M
Spanish	M
Therapies—Dance, Drama, and Music	M

STATE UNIVERSITY OF NEW YORK AT OSWEGO

Art/Fine Arts	M
Child and Family Studies	M
Consumer Economics	M
Counseling Psychology	M,O
English	M
History	M
School Psychology	M,O

STATE UNIVERSITY OF NEW YORK AT PLATTSBURGH

Liberal Studies	M

*M—master's degree; P—first professional degree; D—doctorate; O—other advanced degree; *—Close-Up and/or Display*

Psychology—General | M,O
School Psychology | M,O

STATE UNIVERSITY OF NEW YORK COLLEGE AT CORTLAND

American Studies | O
English | M
History | M

STATE UNIVERSITY OF NEW YORK COLLEGE AT ONEONTA

Family and Consumer
Sciences-General | M
Museum Studies | M

STATE UNIVERSITY OF NEW YORK COLLEGE AT POTSDAM

Communication—
General | M
English | M
Music | M

STATE UNIVERSITY OF NEW YORK COLLEGE OF ENVIRONMENTAL SCIENCE AND FORESTRY

Communication—
General | M,D
Geographic Information
Systems | M,D
Landscape Architecture | M
Urban and Regional
Planning | M,D
Urban Design | M

STATE UNIVERSITY OF NEW YORK EMPIRE STATE COLLEGE

Industrial and Labor
Relations | M
Liberal Studies | M
Public Policy | M

STATE UNIVERSITY OF NEW YORK INSTITUTE OF TECHNOLOGY

Sociology | M

STEPHEN F. AUSTIN STATE UNIVERSITY

Applied Arts and
Design—General | M
Art/Fine Arts | M
Communication—
General | M
English | M
Family and Consumer
Sciences-General | M
History | M
Interdisciplinary Studies | M
Mass Communication | M
Music | M
Psychology—General | M
Public Administration | M
School Psychology | M

STEPHENS COLLEGE

Counseling Psychology | M
Marriage and Family
Therapy | M

STETSON UNIVERSITY

English | M
Marriage and Family
Therapy | M

STEVENS INSTITUTE OF TECHNOLOGY

Communication—
General | M,D,O
Computer Art and
Design | M,D,O

Corporate and
Organizational
Communication | O
Internet and Interactive
Multimedia | M,D,O

STEVENSON UNIVERSITY

Forensic Sciences | M

STONY BROOK UNIVERSITY, STATE UNIVERSITY OF NEW YORK

Addictions/Substance
Abuse Counseling | M
African Studies | M
Anthropology | M,D
Art History | M,D
Art/Fine Arts | M
Clinical Psychology | D
Comparative Literature | M,D
Cultural Studies | M,D
Economics | M,D
English | M,D,O
Experimental
Psychology | D
French | M
Health Psychology | D
Hispanic and Latin
American Languages | M,D
History | M,D
Italian | M
Liberal Studies | M,O
Linguistics | M,D
Music | M,D
Philosophy | M,D
Political Science | M,D
Psychology—General | D
Public Policy | M
Romance Languages | M
Social Psychology | D
Social Sciences | M,O
Sociology | M,D
Theater | M
Women's Studies | O
Writing | M,O

STRAYER UNIVERSITY

Public Administration | M

SUFFOLK UNIVERSITY

Applied Arts and
Design—General | M
Clinical Psychology | D
Communication—
General | M
Corporate and
Organizational
Communication | M
Counseling Psychology | M,O
Criminal Justice and
Criminology | M
Economics | M,D
Ethics | M
Graphic Design | M
Interior Design | M
Political Science | M,O
Psychology—General | D
Public Administration | M,O
Public Policy | M
Women's Studies | M

SULLIVAN UNIVERSITY

Conflict Resolution and
Mediation/Peace
Studies | P,M,D

SUL ROSS STATE UNIVERSITY

Applied Arts and
Design—General | M
Art History | M
Art/Fine Arts | M
Criminal Justice and
Criminology | M

English | M
History | M
Political Science | M
Psychology—General | M
Public Administration | M
Textile Design | M

SYRACUSE UNIVERSITY

Addictions/Substance
Abuse Counseling | O
African Studies | M
African-American
Studies | M
Anthropology | M,D
Applied Arts and
Design—General | M
Architecture | M
Art History | M
Art/Fine Arts | M*
Arts Journalism | M
Broadcast Journalism | M
Child and Family
Studies | M,D
Clinical Psychology | M,D
Communication—
General | M,D
Computer Art and
Design | M
Conflict Resolution and
Mediation/Peace
Studies | O
Disability Studies | O
Economics | M,D,O
English | M,D
Experimental
Psychology | D
Film, Television, and
Video Production | M
Film, Television, and
Video Theory and
Criticism | M
Forensic Sciences | M
French | M
Gender Studies | O
Geography | M,D
Historic Preservation | O
History | M,D
Illustration | M
International Affairs | M
Journalism | M
Latin American Studies | O
Linguistics | M
Marriage and Family
Therapy | M
Mass Communication | M,D
Media Studies | M
Museum Studies | M
Music | M
Near and Middle
Eastern Studies | O
Philosophy | M,D
Photography | M
Political Science | M,D,O
Public Administration | M,D,O
Public Policy | O
Religion | M,D
Rhetoric | M,D
School Psychology | M,D,O
Social Psychology | D
Social Sciences | M,D
Sociology | M,D
Spanish | M
Western European
Studies | O
Women's Studies | O
Writing | M,D

TALMUDIC COLLEGE OF FLORIDA

Theology | M

TARLETON STATE UNIVERSITY

Counseling Psychology | M,O

Criminal Justice and
Criminology | M
Economics | M
English | M
History | M
Liberal Studies | M
Political Science | M
School Psychology | M,O

TAYLOR COLLEGE AND SEMINARY

Cultural Studies | P,M,O
Missions and Missiology | P,M,O
Theology | P,M,O

TAYLOR UNIVERSITY

Religion | M

TEACHERS COLLEGE, COLUMBIA UNIVERSITY

Anthropology | M,D
Applied Behavior
Analysis | M,D
Applied Psychology | M,D
Arts Administration | M
Clinical Psychology | D
Communication—
General | M,D
Counseling Psychology | M,D
Developmental
Psychology | M,D
Economics | M,D
History | M,D
Industrial and
Organizational
Psychology | M
Interdisciplinary Studies | M,D
Linguistics | M,D
Political Science | M,D
Rehabilitation
Counseling | M
School Psychology | M,D
Social Psychology | M
Sociology | M,D

TELSHE YESHIVA–CHICAGO

Jewish Studies | O

TEMPLE BAPTIST SEMINARY

Archaeology | P,M,D
Religion | P,M,D
Theology | P,M,D

TEMPLE UNIVERSITY

African-American
Studies | M,D
Anthropology | D
Applied Behavior
Analysis | M,D
Architecture | M
Art History | M,D
Art/Fine Arts | M
Arts Administration | M,D
Clinical Psychology | M,D
Cognitive Sciences | M,D
Communication—
General | M,D
Corporate and
Organizational
Communication | M
Counseling Psychology | M,D
Criminal Justice and
Criminology | M,D
Dance | M,D
Developmental
Psychology | M,D
Economics | M,D
English | M,D
Film, Television, and
Video Production | M
Geography | M,D
Graphic Design | M
History | M,D

Industrial and Organizational Psychology	M
Journalism	M
Landscape Architecture	M
Liberal Studies	M
Linguistics	M,D
Mass Communication	D
Media Studies	M,D
Music	M,D
Philosophy	M,D
Photography	M
Political Science	M,D
Psychology—General	M,D
Religion	M,D
School Psychology	M,D
Social Psychology	M,D
Sociology	M,D
Spanish	M,D
Textile Design	M
Theater	M
Therapies—Dance, Drama, and Music	M,D
Urban and Regional Planning	M
Urban Design	M,D
Urban Studies	M,D
Writing	M

TENNESSEE STATE UNIVERSITY

Counseling Psychology	M,D
Criminal Justice and Criminology	M
English	M
Family and Consumer Sciences-General	M
Psychology—General	M,D
Public Administration	M,D
School Psychology	M,D

TENNESSEE TECHNOLOGICAL UNIVERSITY

Applied Behavior Analysis	D
English	M

TEXAS A&M INTERNATIONAL UNIVERSITY

Counseling Psychology	M
Criminal Justice and Criminology	M
English	M,D
Hispanic Studies	M,D
History	M
Political Science	M
Psychology—General	M
Public Administration	M
Social Sciences	M
Sociology	M
Spanish	M,D

TEXAS A&M UNIVERSITY

Agricultural Economics and Agribusiness	M,D
Anthropology	M,D
Architecture	M,D
Art/Fine Arts	M,D
Asian Studies	M,O
Clinical Psychology	D
Cognitive Sciences	D
Communication—General	M,D
Counseling Psychology	M,D
Cultural Studies	M,D
Developmental Psychology	D
Economics	M,D
English	M,D
Geography	M,D
History	M,D
Homeland Security	M,O
Human Development	M,D

Industrial and Organizational Psychology	D
International Affairs	M,O
Journalism	M
Landscape Architecture	M,D
National Security	M,O
Philosophy	M,D
Political Science	D
Psychology—General	D
Public Administration	M,O
Public Affairs	M,O
School Psychology	M,D
Social Psychology	D
Sociology	M,D
Spanish	M,D
Urban and Regional Planning	M,D

TEXAS A&M UNIVERSITY–COMMERCE

Art History	M
Art/Fine Arts	M
Cognitive Sciences	M,D
Counseling Psychology	M,D
Economics	M
English	M,D
History	M
Music	M
Psychology—General	M,D
Social Sciences	M
Sociology	M
Spanish	M,D
Speech and Interpersonal Communication	M
Theater	M

TEXAS A&M UNIVERSITY–CORPUS CHRISTI

Art/Fine Arts	M
English	M
History	M
Psychology—General	M
Public Administration	M

TEXAS A&M UNIVERSITY–KINGSVILLE

Agricultural Economics and Agribusiness	M
Art/Fine Arts	M
English	M
Family and Consumer Sciences-General	M
Gerontology	M
History	M
Political Science	M
Psychology—General	M
Sociology	M
Spanish	M

TEXAS A&M UNIVERSITY–SAN ANTONIO

English	M

TEXAS A&M UNIVERSITY–TEXARKANA

Counseling Psychology	M
English	M
Interdisciplinary Studies	M
Psychology—General	M

TEXAS CHRISTIAN UNIVERSITY

Art History	M
Art/Fine Arts	M
Cognitive Sciences	M,D
English	M,D
Experimental Psychology	M,D
History	M,D
Journalism	M
Liberal Studies	M

Music	M,D,O
Psychology—General	M,D
Rhetoric	M,D
Social Psychology	M,D
Speech and Interpersonal Communication	M

TEXAS SOUTHERN UNIVERSITY

Art/Fine Arts	M
Communication—General	M
Criminal Justice and Criminology	M,D
English	M
Family and Consumer Sciences-General	M
History	M
Music	M
Psychology—General	M
Public Administration	M
Sociology	M
Urban and Regional Planning	M,D

TEXAS STATE UNIVERSITY–SAN MARCOS

Anthropology	M
Child and Family Studies	M
Communication—General	M
Computer Art and Design	M
Criminal Justice and Criminology	M,D
English	M
Geographic Information Systems	M,D
Geography	M,D
Graphic Design	M
Health Psychology	M
History	M
Interdisciplinary Studies	M
International Affairs	M
Mass Communication	M
Music	M
Political Science	M
Psychology—General	M
Public Administration	M
Rhetoric	M
School Psychology	O
Sociology	M
Spanish	M
Technical Communication	M
Theater	M
Writing	M

TEXAS TECH UNIVERSITY

Agricultural Economics and Agribusiness	M,D
Anthropology	M
Applied Economics	M,D
Architecture	M
Art History	M
Art/Fine Arts	M,D
Child and Family Studies	M,D
Classics	M
Clinical Psychology	M,D
Communication—General	M
Consumer Economics	M,D
Counseling Psychology	M,D
Dance	D
Economics	M,D
English	M,D
Environmental Design	M,D
Experimental Psychology	M,D

Family and Consumer Sciences-General	M,D
French	M
German	M
Gerontology	M,D
Historic Preservation	M
History	M,D
Human Development	M,D
Humanities	M,D
Interdisciplinary Studies	M
Interior Design	M,D*
Landscape Architecture	M
Linguistics	M
Marriage and Family Therapy	M,D
Mass Communication	M,D
Museum Studies	M
Music	M,D
Philosophy	M
Political Science	M,D
Psychology—General	M,D
Rhetoric	M,D
Romance Languages	M,D
Sociology	M
Spanish	M,D
Technical Writing	M,D
Theater	M,D

TEXAS TECH UNIVERSITY HEALTH SCIENCES CENTER

Rehabilitation Counseling	M

TEXAS WESLEYAN UNIVERSITY

Counseling Psychology	M,D
Marriage and Family Therapy	M,D

TEXAS WOMAN'S UNIVERSITY

Art/Fine Arts	M
Child and Family Studies	M,D
Child Development	M,D
Counseling Psychology	M,D,O
Dance	M,D
English	M,D
History	M
Marriage and Family Therapy	M,D
Music	M
Political Science	M
Psychology—General	M,D,O
Rhetoric	M,D
School Psychology	M,D,O
Sociology	M,D
Theater	M
Women's Studies	M,D

THOMAS EDISON STATE COLLEGE

Homeland Security	O
Liberal Studies	M
Public Administration	O

THOMAS JEFFERSON UNIVERSITY

Marriage and Family Therapy	M

THOMAS UNIVERSITY

Rehabilitation Counseling	M
Social Psychology	M

TIFFIN UNIVERSITY

Criminal Justice and Criminology	M
Forensic Psychology	M
Homeland Security	M
Humanities	M

M—master's degree; P—first professional degree; D—doctorate; O—other advanced degree; *—Close-Up and / or Display

TORONTO SCHOOL OF THEOLOGY

Theology	P,M,D

TOURO COLLEGE

Jewish Studies	M

TOWSON UNIVERSITY

Art/Fine Arts	M
Child and Family Studies	M,O
Clinical Psychology	M
Communication—General	M,O
Corporate and Organizational Communication	M
Counseling Psychology	O
Forensic Sciences	M
Geography	M
Gerontology	M,O
Homeland Security	M,O
Humanities	M
Internet and Interactive Multimedia	M,D,O
Jewish Studies	M,D,O
Liberal Studies	M
Music	M
School Psychology	O
Social Sciences	M
Theater	M
Women's Studies	M,O
Writing	M

TRENT UNIVERSITY

American Indian/Native American Studies	M,D
Anthropology	M
Canadian Studies	M,D
Cultural Studies	D
Geography	M,D

TREVECCA NAZARENE UNIVERSITY

Counseling Psychology	M
Marriage and Family Therapy	M
Psychology—General	M,D
Religion	M
Theology	M

TRINE UNIVERSITY

Criminal Justice and Criminology	M

TRINITY BAPTIST COLLEGE

Pastoral Ministry and Counseling	M

TRINITY COLLEGE

American Studies	M
Economics	M
English	M
Public Policy	M

TRINITY INTERNATIONAL UNIVERSITY

Archaeology	P,M,D,O
Communication—General	M
Counseling Psychology	P,M,D,O
Missions and Missiology	P,M,D,O
Pastoral Ministry and Counseling	P,M,D,O
Theology	P,M,D,O

TRINITY INTERNATIONAL UNIVERSITY, SOUTH FLORIDA CAMPUS

Counseling Psychology	M
Religion	M,O

TRINITY LUTHERAN SEMINARY

Music	P,M
Pastoral Ministry and Counseling	P,M
Theology	P,M

TRINITY SCHOOL FOR MINISTRY

Missions and Missiology	P,M,D,O
Pastoral Ministry and Counseling	P,M,D,O
Religion	P,M,D,O
Theology	P,M,D,O

TRINITY UNIVERSITY

School Psychology	M

TRINITY (WASHINGTON) UNIVERSITY

Communication—General	M
National Security	M

TRINITY WESTERN UNIVERSITY

Counseling Psychology	M
English	M
History	M
Humanities	M
Interdisciplinary Studies	M
Linguistics	M
Pastoral Ministry and Counseling	P,M,D
Philosophy	M
Theology	P,M,D

TROPICAL AGRICULTURE RESEARCH AND HIGHER EDUCATION CENTER

Agricultural Economics and Agribusiness	M,D

TROY UNIVERSITY

Addictions/Substance Abuse Counseling	M,O
Clinical Psychology	M,O
Criminal Justice and Criminology	M,O
Economic Development	M
History	M
International Affairs	M
Music	M
National Security	M
Political Science	M
Public Administration	M
Rehabilitation Counseling	M,O
School Psychology	M,O
Social Psychology	M,O

TRUMAN STATE UNIVERSITY

English	M
Music	M

TUFTS UNIVERSITY

Archaeology	M
Art History	M
Art/Fine Arts	M
Child and Family Studies	M,D,O
Child Development	M,D,O
Classics	M
Conflict Resolution and Mediation/Peace Studies	M,D
Economics	M
English	M,D
Family and Consumer Sciences-General	M,D,O
French	M
German	M
Health Communication	M
History	M,D
International Affairs	M,D

International Development	M,D
Museum Studies	O
Music	M
Philosophy	M
Psychology—General	M,D
Public Administration	O
Public Policy	M
School Psychology	M,O
Theater	M,D
Urban and Regional Planning	M
Urban Studies	M

TUI UNIVERSITY

Conflict Resolution and Mediation/Peace Studies	M,D
Criminal Justice and Criminology	M,D
Emergency Management	M,D,O
Public Administration	M,D

TULANE UNIVERSITY

Anthropology	M,D
Architecture	M
Art History	M
Art/Fine Arts	M
Classics	M
Dance	M
Economics	M,D
English	M,D
French	M,D
Health Communication	M
History	M,D
Interdisciplinary Studies	D
International Development	M,D
Latin American Studies	M,D*
Liberal Studies	M
Music	M
Philosophy	M,D
Political Science	M,D
Portuguese	M,D
Psychology—General	M,D
Sociology	M,D
Spanish	M,D
Theater	M

TUSKEGEE UNIVERSITY

Agricultural Economics and Agribusiness	M

TYNDALE UNIVERSITY COLLEGE & SEMINARY

Missions and Missiology	P,M,O
Pastoral Ministry and Counseling	P,M,O
Theology	P,M,O

UNIFICATION THEOLOGICAL SEMINARY

Pastoral Ministry and Counseling	P,M,D
Religion	P,M,D
Theology	P,M,D

UNIFORMED SERVICES UNIVERSITY OF THE HEALTH SCIENCES

Clinical Psychology	D
Psychology—General	D

UNION COLLEGE (KY)

Clinical Psychology	M
Counseling Psychology	M
Psychology—General	M
School Psychology	M

UNION GRADUATE COLLEGE

Chinese	M,O
Classics	M,O

UNION INSTITUTE & UNIVERSITY

Clinical Psychology	M,D,O
Counseling Psychology	M,D,O
Cultural Studies	M
Developmental Psychology	M,D,O
Ethics	D
History	M
Human Development	M,D,O
Humanities	D
Industrial and Organizational Psychology	M,D,O
Interdisciplinary Studies	M,D
Psychology—General	M,D,O
Public Policy	M,D
Writing	M

UNION THEOLOGICAL SEMINARY IN THE CITY OF NEW YORK

Theology	P,M,D

UNION UNIVERSITY

Cultural Studies	M
Pastoral Ministry and Counseling	M,D
Religion	M,D

UNITED STATES ARMY COMMAND AND GENERAL STAFF COLLEGE

Military and Defense Studies	M

UNITED STATES INTERNATIONAL UNIVERSITY

Addictions/Substance Abuse Counseling	M
Conflict Resolution and Mediation/Peace Studies	M
Counseling Psychology	M
Health Psychology	M
International Affairs	M

UNITED TALMUDICAL SEMINARY

Theology	

UNITED THEOLOGICAL SEMINARY

Theology	P,M,D

UNITED THEOLOGICAL SEMINARY OF THE TWIN CITIES

Art/Fine Arts	P,M,D,O
Asian Studies	P,M,D,O
Conflict Resolution and Mediation/Peace Studies	P,M,D,O
Ethnic Studies	P,M,D,O
Humanities	P,M,D,O
Pastoral Ministry and Counseling	P,M,D,O
Religion	P,M,D,O
Theology	P,M,D,O
Women's Studies	P,M,D,O

UNIVERSIDAD ADVENTISTA DE LAS ANTILLAS

Pastoral Ministry and Counseling	P,M

UNIVERSIDAD AUTONOMA DE GUADALAJARA

Architecture	M,D
Computer Art and Design	M,D

Corporate and
Organizational
Communication — M,D
Film, Television, and
Video Production — M,D
Internet and Interactive
Multimedia — M,D
Philosophy — M,D
Public Policy — M,D
Spanish — M,D
Translation and
Interpretation — M,D

UNIVERSIDAD CENTRAL DEL CARIBE

Addictions/Substance
Abuse Counseling — M

UNIVERSIDAD DE IBEROAMERICA

Clinical Psychology — P,M,D
Forensic Psychology — P,M,D

UNIVERSIDAD DE LAS AMERICAS, A.C.

International Affairs — M
Marriage and Family
Therapy — M
Psychology—General — M

UNIVERSIDAD DE LAS AMÉRICAS–PUEBLA

American Studies — M
Anthropology — M
Archaeology — M
Computer Art and
Design — M
Economics — M
English — M
Linguistics — M
Psychology—General — M

UNIVERSIDAD DEL ESTE

Agricultural Economics
and Agribusiness — M
Criminal Justice and
Criminology — M
Public Policy — M

UNIVERSIDAD DEL TURABO

Art/Fine Arts — M
Arts Administration — M
Conflict Resolution and
Mediation/Peace
Studies — M
Counseling Psychology — M,D,O
Criminal Justice and
Criminology — M
Forensic Sciences — M

UNIVERSIDAD FLET

Theology — M

UNIVERSIDAD METROPOLITANA

Counseling Psychology — M

UNIVERSIDAD NACIONAL PEDRO HENRIQUEZ URENA

Architecture — M
Historic Preservation — M
International Affairs — M
Political Science — M

UNIVERSITÉ DE MONCTON

Economics — M
French — M,D
History — M
Public Administration — M

UNIVERSITÉ DE MONTRÉAL

Anthropology — M,D

Art History — M,D
Classics — M
Communication—
General — M,D
Comparative Literature — M,D
Criminal Justice and
Criminology — M,D
Demography and
Population Studies — M,D
Developmental
Psychology — M,D
Economics — M,D,O
Emergency
Management — O
English — M,D
Environmental Design — M,D,O
Film, Television, and
Video Theory and
Criticism — M,D
French — M,D
Genetic Counseling — O
Geography — M,D,O
German — M
Hispanic and Latin
American Languages — M,D
History — M,D
Industrial and Labor
Relations — M,D,O
International Affairs — M,O
Linguistics — M,D,O
Museum Studies — M
Music — M,D,O
Philosophy — M,D
Political Science — M,D
Psychology—General — M,D
Public Policy — O
Religion — M,D,O
Sociology — M,D
Spanish — M
Theology — M,D,O
Translation and
Interpretation — M,D,O
Urban and Regional
Planning — M,D,O

UNIVERSITÉ DE SHERBROOKE

Canadian Studies — M,D
Comparative Literature — M,D
Conflict Resolution and
Mediation/Peace
Studies — P,M,D,O
Corporate and
Organizational
Communication — M
Economic Development — D
Economics — M
Ethics — M,D,O
French — M,D
Geography — M,D
Gerontology — M
History — M
Linguistics — M,D
Philosophy — M,D,O
Psychology—General — M
Public Administration — M
Religion — M,D,O
Theater — M,D
Theology — M,D,O

UNIVERSITÉ DU QUÉBEC À CHICOUTIMI

Art/Fine Arts — M
Canadian Studies — M
Comparative Literature — M
Ethics — O
French — O
Linguistics — M
Theology — M,D

UNIVERSITÉ DU QUÉBEC À MONTRÉAL

Art History — M,D

Art/Fine Arts — M
Communication—
General — M,D
Comparative Literature — M,D
Dance — M
Economics — M,D
Geographic Information
Systems — O
Geography — M
History — M,D
Linguistics — M,D
Museum Studies — M
Philosophy — M,D
Political Science — M,D
Psychology—General — D
Public Administration — M
Religion — M,D
Sociology — M,D
Urban Studies — M,D

UNIVERSITÉ DU QUÉBEC À RIMOUSKI

Comparative Literature — M,D
Ethics — M,O
Social Psychology — M
Urban and Regional
Planning — M,D,O

UNIVERSITÉ DU QUÉBEC À TROIS-RIVIÈRES

Communication—
General — M,O
Comparative Literature — M
Industrial and Labor
Relations — O
Philosophy — M,D
Psychology—General — D,O

UNIVERSITÉ DU QUÉBEC, ÉCOLE NATIONALE D'ADMINISTRATION PUBLIQUE

Public Administration — D,O
Urban Studies — M

UNIVERSITÉ DU QUÉBEC EN OUTAOUAIS

Industrial and Labor
Relations — M,D,O
Urban and Regional
Planning — M

UNIVERSITÉ DU QUÉBEC, INSTITUT NATIONAL DE LA RECHERCHE SCIENTIFIQUE

Demography and
Population Studies — M,D
Urban Studies — M,D

UNIVERSITÉ LAVAL

Agricultural Economics
and Agribusiness — M
Anthropology — M,D
Archaeology — M,D
Architecture — M
Art History — M,D
Art/Fine Arts — M
Clinical Psychology — D
Comparative Literature — M,D
Consumer Economics — O
Economics — M,D
English — M,D
Ethics — O
Ethnic Studies — M,D
Film, Television, and
Video Theory and
Criticism — M,D
Geographic Information
Systems — M,O
Geography — M,D
Gerontology — O
Graphic Design — M
History — M,D

Industrial and Labor
Relations — M,D
International Affairs — M,D
Journalism — O
Linguistics — M,D
Mass Communication — M,D
Museum Studies — O
Music — M,D
Philosophy — M,D
Political Science — M,D
Psychology—General — D
Religion — M,D
Rural Planning and
Studies — O
Social Psychology — D
Sociology — M,D
Spanish — M,D
Theater — M,D
Theology — M,D
Translation and
Interpretation — M,O
Urban and Regional
Planning — M,D
Women's Studies — O

UNIVERSITY AT ALBANY, STATE UNIVERSITY OF NEW YORK

African Studies — M
African-American
Studies — M
Anthropology — M,D
Art/Fine Arts — M
Clinical Psychology — M,D,O
Communication—
General — M,D
Counseling Psychology — M,D,O
Criminal Justice and
Criminology — M,D
Demography and
Population Studies — M,D,O
Economics — M,D,O
English — M,D
Experimental
Psychology — M,D,O
Forensic Sciences — M,D
French — M,D
Geographic Information
Systems — M,O
Geography — M,O
History — M,D,O
Industrial and
Organizational
Psychology — M,D,O
Italian — M
Latin American Studies — M,O
Liberal Studies — M
Philosophy — M,D
Political Science — M,D
Psychology—General — M,D,O
Public Administration — M,D,O
Public History — M,D,O
Public Policy — M,D,O
Rehabilitation
Counseling — M
Russian — M,O
School Psychology — M,D,O
Social Psychology — M,D,O
Sociology — M,D,O
Spanish — M,D
Theater — M
Translation and
Interpretation — M,O
Urban and Regional
Planning — M
Urban Studies — M,D,O
Women's Studies — M,D

UNIVERSITY AT BUFFALO, THE STATE UNIVERSITY OF NEW YORK

American Studies — M,D
Anthropology — M,D

*M—master's degree; P—first professional degree; D—doctorate; O—other advanced degree; *—Close-Up and/or Display*

Architecture	M
Art History	M,O
Art/Fine Arts	M,O
Classics	M,D,O
Clinical Psychology	M,D
Cognitive Sciences	M,D
Communication—General	M,D
Comparative Literature	M,D
Counseling Psychology	M,D,O
Cultural Studies	M
Economics	M,D,O
English	M,D
French	M,D,O
Geographic Information Systems	M,D,O
Geography	M,D,O
German	M,D,O
History	M,D
Latin American Studies	M
Linguistics	M,D
Media Studies	M,D,O
Museum Studies	M,O
Music	M,D
Philosophy	M,D
Political Science	M,D
Psychology—General	M,D
Rehabilitation Counseling	M,D,O
Romance Languages	M,D
Social Psychology	M,D
Sociology	M,D
Spanish	M,D,O
Urban and Regional Planning	M
Urban Design	M

UNIVERSITY OF ADVANCING TECHNOLOGY

Internet and Interactive Multimedia	M

THE UNIVERSITY OF AKRON

Arts Administration	M
Child and Family Studies	M
Child Development	M
Clothing and Textiles	M
Communication—General	M
Counseling Psychology	M,D
Economics	M
English	M
Geographic Information Systems	M
Geography	M
History	M,D
Industrial and Organizational Psychology	M,D
Marriage and Family Therapy	M
Music	M
Political Science	M
Psychology—General	M,D
Public Administration	M
School Psychology	M
Social Psychology	M
Sociology	M,D
Spanish	M
Theater	M
Urban and Regional Planning	M
Urban Studies	M,D
Writing	M

THE UNIVERSITY OF ALABAMA

American Studies	M
Anthropology	M,D
Art History	M
Art/Fine Arts	M
Child and Family Studies	M
Clinical Psychology	D

Clothing and Textiles	M
Communication—General	M,D
Consumer Economics	M
Criminal Justice and Criminology	M
Economics	M,D
English	M,D
Experimental Psychology	D
Family and Consumer Sciences-General	M,D
Film, Television, and Video Production	M
French	M,D
Geography	M
German	M,D
History	M,D
Human Development	M
Interdisciplinary Studies	D
Interior Design	M
Journalism	M
Mass Communication	D
Media Studies	M
Music	M,D
Photography	M
Political Science	M,D
Psychology—General	D
Public Administration	M,D
Rhetoric	M,D
Romance Languages	M,D
Spanish	M,D
Speech and Interpersonal Communication	M
Theater	M
Women's Studies	M
Writing	M,D

THE UNIVERSITY OF ALABAMA AT BIRMINGHAM

Anthropology	M
Art History	M
Communication—General	M
Criminal Justice and Criminology	M
English	M
Forensic Sciences	M
Genetic Counseling	M
History	M
Interdisciplinary Studies	D
Psychology—General	M,D
Public Administration	M
Sociology	M,D

THE UNIVERSITY OF ALABAMA IN HUNTSVILLE

Criminal Justice and Criminology	M,O
English	M,O
Experimental Psychology	M
History	M
Industrial and Organizational Psychology	M
Interdisciplinary Studies	M,D,O
Psychology—General	M
Public Affairs	M
Technical Writing	M,O

UNIVERSITY OF ALASKA ANCHORAGE

Anthropology	M
Clinical Psychology	M,D
English	M
Interdisciplinary Studies	M
Psychology—General	M,D
Public Administration	M
Social Psychology	M,D
Writing	M

UNIVERSITY OF ALASKA FAIRBANKS

Anthropology	M,D
Art/Fine Arts	M
Clinical Psychology	D
Communication—General	M
Computer Art and Design	M
Corporate and Organizational Communication	M
Criminal Justice and Criminology	M
Cultural Studies	M
Economics	M
English	M
Geography	M,D
History	M
Interdisciplinary Studies	M,D
Linguistics	M
Music	M
Northern Studies	M
Photography	M
Psychology—General	D
Rural Planning and Studies	M
Social Psychology	M,D
Sustainable Development	M,D
Writing	M

UNIVERSITY OF ALASKA SOUTHEAST

Public Administration	M

UNIVERSITY OF ALBERTA

Agricultural Economics and Agribusiness	M,D
Anthropology	M,D
Applied Arts and Design—General	M
Archaeology	M,D
Art History	M
Art/Fine Arts	M
Asian Studies	M
Chinese	M
Classics	M,D
Clothing and Textiles	M,D
Communication—General	M
Counseling Psychology	M,D
Criminal Justice and Criminology	M,D
Demography and Population Studies	M,D
East European and Russian Studies	M,D
Economics	M,D
English	M,D
Family and Consumer Sciences-General	M,D
Folklore	M,D
French	M,D
German	M,D
Hispanic Studies	M,D
History	M,D
Industrial and Labor Relations	D
Italian	M,D
Japanese	M
Linguistics	M,D
Music	M,D
Philosophy	M,D
Political Science	M,D
Psychology—General	M,D
Rural Sociology	M,D
School Psychology	M,D
Slavic Languages	M,D
Sociology	M,D
Theater	M

THE UNIVERSITY OF ARIZONA

Agricultural Economics and Agribusiness	M
American Indian/Native American Studies	M,D
Anthropology	M,D
Architecture	M
Art History	M,D
Art/Fine Arts	M
Asian Studies	M,D
Child and Family Studies	M
Classics	M
Communication—General	M,D
Dance	M
Economics	M,D
English	M,D
Family and Consumer Sciences-General	M,D
French	M
Gender Studies	M,D
Geography	M,D
German	M
History	M,D
Human Development	M
Interdisciplinary Studies	M,D
Landscape Architecture	M
Latin American Studies	M
Linguistics	M,D
Media Studies	M
Music	M,D
Near and Middle Eastern Studies	M,D
Philosophy	M,D
Political Science	M,D
Psychology—General	M,D
Public Administration	M,D
Public Policy	M,D
Rehabilitation Counseling	M,D
Rhetoric	D
Russian	M
School Psychology	D,O
Sociology	D
Spanish	M,D
Theater	M
Urban and Regional Planning	M
Women's Studies	M,D
Writing	M

UNIVERSITY OF ARKANSAS

Agricultural Economics and Agribusiness	M
Anthropology	M,D
Art/Fine Arts	M
Communication—General	M
Comparative Literature	M,D
Economics	M,D
English	M,D
Family and Consumer Sciences-General	M
French	M
Geography	M
German	M
History	M,D
Interdisciplinary Studies	M,D
Journalism	M
Music	M
Philosophy	M,D
Political Science	M
Psychology—General	M,D
Public Administration	M
Public Policy	D
Rehabilitation Counseling	M,D
Sociology	M
Spanish	M
Theater	M

Translation and
  Interpretation — M
Writing — M

UNIVERSITY OF ARKANSAS AT LITTLE ROCK

Applied Psychology — M
Art History — M
Art/Fine Arts — M
Conflict Resolution and
  Mediation/Peace
  Studies — O
Criminal Justice and
  Criminology — M,D
Gerontology — O
Journalism — M
Liberal Studies — M
Marriage and Family
  Therapy — O
Mass Communication — M
Psychology—General — M
Public Administration — M
Public Affairs — M,O
Public History — M
Rehabilitation
  Counseling — M,O
Rhetoric — M
Speech and
  Interpersonal
  Communication — M
Technical Writing — M
Writing — M

UNIVERSITY OF ARKANSAS AT PINE BLUFF

Addictions/Substance
  Abuse Counseling — M

UNIVERSITY OF ARKANSAS FOR MEDICAL SCIENCES

Genetic Counseling — M

UNIVERSITY OF ATLANTA

Social Sciences — P,M,D,O

UNIVERSITY OF BALTIMORE

Applied Arts and
  Design—General — M
Applied Psychology — M
Computer Art and
  Design — M,D
Conflict Resolution and
  Mediation/Peace
  Studies — M
Counseling Psychology — M
Criminal Justice and
  Criminology — M
Ethics — M
Graphic Design — M,D
Industrial and
  Organizational
  Psychology — M
Public Administration — M,D
Publishing — M
Writing — M

UNIVERSITY OF BRIDGEPORT

Conflict Resolution and
  Mediation/Peace
  Studies — M
International Affairs — M

THE UNIVERSITY OF BRITISH COLUMBIA

Agricultural Economics
  and Agribusiness — M
Anthropology — M,D
Archaeology — M,D
Architecture — M
Art History — M,D,O
Art/Fine Arts — M,D,O
Asian Studies — M,D

Classics — M,D
Clinical Psychology — M,D
Cognitive Sciences — M,D
Counseling Psychology — M,D,O
Developmental
  Psychology — M,D
East European and
  Russian Studies — M,D
Economics — M,D
English — M,D
Film, Television, and
  Video Production — M,O
Film, Television, and
  Video Theory and
  Criticism — M,O
French — M,D
Genetic Counseling — M
Geography — M,D
German — M,D
Health Psychology — M,D
Hispanic Studies — M,D
History — M,D
Human Development — M,D,O
Interdisciplinary Studies — M
International Affairs — M
Journalism — M
Landscape Architecture — M
Linguistics — M,D
Museum Studies — M,D,O
Music — M,D
Philosophy — M,D
Political Science — M,D
Psychology—General — M,D
Religion — M,D
School Psychology — M,D,O
Social Psychology — M,D
Sociology — M,D
Theater — M,D
Urban and Regional
  Planning — M,D
Writing — M,O

UNIVERSITY OF CALGARY

Anthropology — M,D
Applied Psychology — M,D
Archaeology — M,D
Architecture — M,D
Art/Fine Arts — M
Classics — M,D
Clinical Psychology — M,D
Communication—
  General — M,D
Counseling Psychology — M,D
Economics — M,D
English — M,D
Environmental Design — M,D
Geography — M,D
German — M
History — M,D
Human Development — M,D
Linguistics — M,D
Military and Defense
  Studies — M,D
Music — M,D
Philosophy — M,D
Political Science — M,D
Psychology—General — M,D
Religion — M,D
School Psychology — M,D
Sociology — M,D
Theater — M

UNIVERSITY OF CALIFORNIA, BERKELEY

Addictions/Substance
  Abuse Counseling — O
African-American
  Studies — D
Agricultural Economics
  and Agribusiness — D
Anthropology — D

Applied Arts and
  Design—General — M,O
Archaeology — M,D
Architectural History — M,D
Architecture — M,D
Art History — D
Art/Fine Arts — M,O
Asian Languages — M,D
Asian Studies — M,D
Building Science — M,D
Chinese — D
Classics — M,D
Comparative Literature — D
Counseling Psychology — O
Demography and
  Population Studies — M,D
Economics — D
English — D
Environmental Design — M,D
Ethnic Studies — D
Folklore — M
French — D
Geography — D
German — D
Hispanic and Latin
  American Languages — D
History of Science and
  Technology — D
History — M,D
Human Development — M,D
Industrial and Labor
  Relations — D
Interior Design — O
International Affairs — M,D
Italian — D
Japanese — D
Jewish Studies — D
Journalism — M
Landscape Architecture — M,D,O
Latin American Studies — M
Linguistics — D
Music — D
Near and Middle
  Eastern Studies — M,D
Philosophy — D
Political Science — D
Psychology—General — D
Public Policy — M,D
Religion — D
Rhetoric — D
Romance Languages — D
Russian — D
Scandinavian
  Languages — D
Slavic Languages — D
Sociology — D
Spanish — D
Sustainable
  Development — O
Theater — D
Urban and Regional
  Planning — M,D
Urban Design — M,D
Writing — O

UNIVERSITY OF CALIFORNIA, DAVIS

Agricultural Economics
  and Agribusiness — M,D
American Indian/Native
  American Studies — M,D
Anthropology — M,D
Art History — M
Art/Fine Arts — M
Child Development — M
Clothing and Textiles — M
Communication—
  General — M
Comparative Literature — D
Cultural Studies — M,D
Economics — M,D
English — M,D

Forensic Sciences — M
French — D
Geography — M,D
German — M,D
History — M,D
Human Development — D
Linguistics — M,D
Music — M,D
Philosophy — M,D
Political Science — M,D
Psychology—General — D
Sociology — M,D
Spanish — M,D
Textile Design — M
Theater — M,D
Urban and Regional
  Planning — M
Writing — M,D

UNIVERSITY OF CALIFORNIA, IRVINE

Anthropology — M,D
Art History — M,D
Art/Fine Arts — M,D
Asian Languages — M,D
Chinese — M,D
Classics — M,D
Comparative Literature — M,D
Criminal Justice and
  Criminology — M,D
Cultural Studies — D
Dance — M
Demography and
  Population Studies — M
Economics — M,D
English — M,D
Environmental Design — D
French — M,D
Genetic Counseling — M
German — M,D
History — M,D
Japanese — M,D
Music — M
Philosophy — M,D
Political Science — D
Psychology—General — D
Social Sciences — M,D
Sociology — M,D
Spanish — M,D
Theater — M,D
Urban and Regional
  Planning — M,D
Urban Studies — M,D
Writing — M

UNIVERSITY OF CALIFORNIA, LOS ANGELES

African Studies — M
African-American
  Studies — M
American Indian/Native
  American Studies — M
Anthropology — M,D
Applied Arts and
  Design—General — M
Applied Social Research — M,D
Archaeology — M,D
Architecture — M,D
Art History — M,D
Art/Fine Arts — M
Asian Languages — M,D
Asian Studies — M,D
Asian-American Studies — M
Classics — M,D
Comparative Literature — M,D
Dance — M,D
Economics — M,D
English — M,D
Film, Television, and
  Video Production — M,D
French — M,D
Geography — M,D

*M—master's degree; P—first professional degree; D—doctorate; O—other advanced degree; *—Close-Up and/or Display*

Peterson's Graduate Programs in the Humanities, Arts & Social Sciences 2012   www.facebook.com/petersonspublishing   **63**

German	M,D
Hispanic and Latin American Languages	D
Historic Preservation	M
History	M,D
Italian	M,D
Latin American Studies	M
Linguistics	M,D
Music	M,D
Near and Middle Eastern Languages	M,D
Near and Middle Eastern Studies	M,D
Philosophy	M,D
Political Science	M,D
Portuguese	M
Psychology—General	M,D
Public Policy	M
Scandinavian Languages	M
Slavic Languages	M,D
Sociology	M,D
Spanish	M
Theater	M,D
Urban and Regional Planning	M,D
Urban Design	M,D
Women's Studies	M,D

UNIVERSITY OF CALIFORNIA, MERCED

Cognitive Sciences	M,D
Social Sciences	M,D

UNIVERSITY OF CALIFORNIA, RIVERSIDE

Anthropology	M,D
Art History	M
Art/Fine Arts	M
Asian Studies	M
Classics	D
Comparative Literature	M,D
Dance	M,D
Economics	M,D
English	M,D
Ethnic Studies	D
Hispanic Studies	M,D
Historic Preservation	M,D
History	M,D
Museum Studies	M,D
Music	M,D
Philosophy	M,D
Political Science	M,D
Psychology—General	M,D
School Psychology	M,D
Sociology	M,D
Spanish	M,D
Writing	M

UNIVERSITY OF CALIFORNIA, SAN DIEGO

Anthropology	D
Art/Fine Arts	M,D
Clinical Psychology	D
Cognitive Sciences	D
Communication—General	M,D
Comparative Literature	M,D
Economics	M,D
English	M
Ethnic Studies	M,D
French	M
German	M
History of Science and Technology	M,D
History	M,D
International Affairs	M,D
Jewish Studies	M,D
Latin American Studies	M
Linguistics	D
Music	M,D
Pacific Area/Pacific Rim Studies	M,D

Philosophy	D
Political Science	M,D
Psychology—General	D
Sociology	D
Spanish	M
Theater	M,D

UNIVERSITY OF CALIFORNIA, SAN FRANCISCO

Anthropology	D
History of Science and Technology	M,D
Sociology	D

UNIVERSITY OF CALIFORNIA, SANTA BARBARA

Agricultural Economics and Agribusiness	M,D
Anthropology	M,D
Archaeology	M,D
Art History	D
Art/Fine Arts	M,D
Asian Languages	M,D
Asian Studies	M,D
Child and Family Studies	M,D
Classics	M,D
Clinical Psychology	M,D
Cognitive Sciences	M,D
Communication—General	D
Comparative Literature	D
Counseling Psychology	M,D
Cultural Anthropology	M,D
Cultural Studies	M
Developmental Psychology	M,D
Economics	M,D
English	D
Film, Television, and Video Production	M,D
French	D
Geography	M,D
Hispanic and Latin American Languages	M,D
Hispanic Studies	M,D
History	D
International Affairs	M,D
Latin American Studies	M
Linguistics	M,D
Media Studies	M,D
Medieval and Renaissance Studies	M,D
Music	M,D
Philosophy	D
Political Science	M,D
Portuguese	M,D
Psychology—General	D
Religion	M,D
School Psychology	M,D
Social Sciences	D
Sociology	M,D
Spanish	M,D
Speech and Interpersonal Communication	D
Sustainable Development	M
Theater	M,D
Translation and Interpretation	M,D
Women's Studies	M,D

UNIVERSITY OF CALIFORNIA, SANTA CRUZ

Anthropology	D
Applied Economics	M
Art/Fine Arts	M,D
Communication—General	O
Comparative Literature	M,D
Computer Art and Design	M,D

Cultural Anthropology	D
Economics	D
English	M,D
Film, Television, and Video Theory and Criticism	D
History	M,D
Humanities	D
Interdisciplinary Studies	M,D
International Affairs	D
Linguistics	M,D
Music	M,D
Philosophy	M,D
Political Science	D
Psychology—General	D
Social Sciences	D
Sociology	D
Theater	O
Writing	M

UNIVERSITY OF CENTRAL ARKANSAS

Computer Art and Design	M
Counseling Psychology	M
Economic Development	M,O
Economics	M
English	M
Family and Consumer Sciences-General	M
Film, Television, and Video Production	M
Geographic Information Systems	M,O
Geography	M,O
History	M
Music	M
Psychology—General	M,D
School Psychology	M,D
Social Psychology	M
Urban and Regional Planning	M,O

UNIVERSITY OF CENTRAL FLORIDA

Anthropology	M
Applied Psychology	M,D
Art/Fine Arts	M
Child and Family Studies	M,O
Clinical Psychology	M,D
Communication—General	M
Computer Art and Design	M
Criminal Justice and Criminology	M,O
Emergency Management	M,O
English	M,O
Experimental Psychology	M,D
Film, Television, and Video Production	M
Forensic Sciences	M,D,O
Gerontology	M,O
History	M
Homeland Security	M,O
Industrial and Organizational Psychology	M,D
Interdisciplinary Studies	M
Latin American Studies	M,D,O
Marriage and Family Therapy	M,O
Music	M
Political Science	M
Psychology—General	M,D
Public Administration	M,O
Public Affairs	D
School Psychology	O
Sociology	M,D,O
Spanish	M
Theater	M

Urban and Regional Planning	M,O
Writing	M,O

UNIVERSITY OF CENTRAL MISSOURI

Counseling Psychology	M,D,O
Criminal Justice and Criminology	M
English	M
Gerontology	M
History	M
Mass Communication	M
Music	M
Psychology—General	M
Sociology	M
Speech and Interpersonal Communication	M
Theater	M

UNIVERSITY OF CENTRAL OKLAHOMA

Addictions/Substance Abuse Counseling	M
American Studies	M
Applied Arts and Design—General	M
Counseling Psychology	M
Criminal Justice and Criminology	M
English	M
Family and Consumer Sciences-General	M
Gerontology	M
History	M
Human Development	M
Interior Design	M
International Affairs	M
Museum Studies	M
Music	M
Political Science	M
Psychology—General	M
Urban Studies	M
Writing	M

UNIVERSITY OF CHICAGO

Anthropology	M,D
Archaeology	M,D
Art History	M,D
Art/Fine Arts	M
Asian Languages	M,D
Asian Studies	M,D
Classics	M,D
Comparative Literature	M,D
Economics	M,D
English	M,D
Film, Television, and Video Theory and Criticism	M,D
French	M,D
German	M,D
History	D
Human Development	D
Humanities	M
Interdisciplinary Studies	D
International Affairs	M
Italian	M,D
Latin American Studies	M
Linguistics	M,D
Media Studies	M,D
Music	M,D
Near and Middle Eastern Languages	M,D
Near and Middle Eastern Studies	M,D
Philosophy	M,D
Political Science	D
Psychology—General	D
Public Policy	M
Religion	P,M,D
Romance Languages	M,D
Slavic Languages	M,D
Social Sciences	M,D

Sociology	D
Spanish	M,D
Theology	P,M,D

UNIVERSITY OF CINCINNATI

Anthropology	M
Applied Arts and Design—General	M
Architecture	M
Art History	M
Art/Fine Arts	M
Arts Administration	M,D
Classics	M,D
Clinical Psychology	D
Communication— General	M
Criminal Justice and Criminology	M,D
Economics	M
English	M,D
Experimental Psychology	D
French	M,D
Genetic Counseling	M
Geography	M,D
German	M,D
Graphic Design	M
History	M,D
Industrial and Labor Relations	M
Industrial Design	M
Interdisciplinary Studies	D
Interior Design	M
Music	M,D,O
Philosophy	M,D
Political Science	M,D
Psychology—General	D
Romance Languages	M,D
School Psychology	D,O
Sociology	M,D
Spanish	M,D
Textile Design	M
Theater	M,D
Urban and Regional Planning	M
Women's Studies	M,O

UNIVERSITY OF COLORADO AT COLORADO SPRINGS

Communication— General	M
Criminal Justice and Criminology	M
Geography	M
History	M
Psychology—General	M,D
Public Administration	M
Public Affairs	M
Sociology	M

UNIVERSITY OF COLORADO BOULDER

Anthropology	M,D
Art History	M
Art/Fine Arts	M
Asian Studies	M,D
Chinese	M,D
Classics	M,D
Communication— General	M,D
Comparative Literature	M,D
Dance	M,D
Economics	M,D
English	M,D
French	M,D
Geography	M,D
German	M
Hispanic and Latin American Languages	M,D
History	M,D
International Affairs	M,D
Japanese	M,D

Journalism	M,D
Linguistics	M,D
Mass Communication	M,D
Media Studies	D
Museum Studies	M
Music	M,D
Philosophy	M,D
Photography	M
Political Science	M,D
Psychology—General	M,D
Public Policy	M,D
Religion	M
Sociology	D
Spanish	M
Theater	M,D
Writing	M,D

UNIVERSITY OF COLORADO DENVER

American Studies	M
Anthropology	M
Archaeology	M
Architectural History	D
Clinical Psychology	M,D
Communication— General	M
Corporate and Organizational Communication	M
Counseling Psychology	M
Criminal Justice and Criminology	M,D
Economic Development	M
Economics	M
Emergency Management	M,D
English	M
Forensic Sciences	M
Gender Studies	M
Genetic Counseling	M
Geographic Information Systems	M,D
Historic Preservation	M
History	M
Homeland Security	M,D
Human Development	M,O
Humanities	M
International Affairs	M
Landscape Architecture	M
Linguistics	M
Military and Defense Studies	M,D
Music	M
Political Science	M,D
Public Administration	M,D
Public Affairs	M,D
Public History	M
Rhetoric	M
School Psychology	M,O
Social Sciences	M
Sociology	M
Spanish	M
Sustainable Development	M,D
Technical Communication	M
Urban and Regional Planning	M,D
Urban Design	M,D
Western European Studies	M
Women's Studies	M
Writing	M

UNIVERSITY OF CONNECTICUT

African Studies	M
Agricultural Economics and Agribusiness	M,D
Anthropology	M,D
Art History	M
Art/Fine Arts	M

Child and Family Studies	M,D,O
Clinical Psychology	M,D,O
Cognitive Sciences	M,D,O
Communication— General	M
Comparative Literature	M,D
Corporate and Organizational Communication	D
Counseling Psychology	M,D,O
Developmental Psychology	M,D,O
Economics	M,D
English	M,D
Experimental Psychology	M,D,O
French	M,D
Geographic Information Systems	M,D,O
Geography	M,D,O
German	M,D
Health Psychology	M,D,O
History	M,D
Homeland Security	M
Human Development	M,D,O
Industrial and Organizational Psychology	M,D,O
International Affairs	M
Italian	M,D
Jewish Studies	M
Latin American Studies	M
Linguistics	M,D
Medieval and Renaissance Studies	M,D
Music	M,D,O
Philosophy	M,D
Political Science	M,D
Psychology—General	M,D,O
Public Administration	M,O
School Psychology	M,D,O
Social Psychology	M,D,O
Sociology	M,D
Spanish	M,D
Sustainable Development	M
Theater	M
Western European Studies	M

UNIVERSITY OF DALLAS

American Studies	M
Art/Fine Arts	M
Comparative Literature	D
English	M
Humanities	M
Pastoral Ministry and Counseling	M
Philosophy	M,D
Political Science	M,D
Psychology—General	M
Theology	M,D

UNIVERSITY OF DAYTON

Clinical Psychology	M
Communication— General	M
English	M
Human Development	M,O
Pastoral Ministry and Counseling	M,D
Psychology—General	M
Public Administration	M
School Psychology	M,O
Social Psychology	M,O
Theology	M,D

UNIVERSITY OF DELAWARE

Agricultural Economics and Agribusiness	M
American Studies	M

Applied Arts and Design—General	M
Art History	M,D
Art/Fine Arts	M
Child and Family Studies	M,D
Chinese	M
Clinical Psychology	D
Clothing and Textiles	M
Cognitive Sciences	D
Communication— General	M
Criminal Justice and Criminology	M,D
Economics	M,D
English	M,D
French	M
Geography	M,D
German	M
Historic Preservation	M,D
History of Science and Technology	M,D
History	M,D
Human Development	M,D
International Affairs	M,D
Liberal Studies	M
Linguistics	M,D
Music	M
Political Science	M,D
Psychology—General	D
Public Administration	M*
Public Policy	M,D*
School Psychology	M,D,O
Social Psychology	D
Sociology	M,D
Spanish	M
Theater	M
Translation and Interpretation	M
Urban Studies	M,D

UNIVERSITY OF DENVER

Anthropology	M
Archaeology	M
Art History	M
Art/Fine Arts	M,O
Arts Administration	M,O
Child and Family Studies	M,D,O
Clinical Psychology	M,D
Computer Art and Design	M
Conflict Resolution and Mediation/Peace Studies	M,O
Corporate and Organizational Communication	M,O
Counseling Psychology	M,D,O
Criminal Justice and Criminology	M,O
Cultural Anthropology	M
Cultural Studies	M,O
Developmental Psychology	D
Economics	M
Emergency Management	M,O
English	M,D
Forensic Psychology	M,D
Geographic Information Systems	M,D,O
Geography	M,D
History	M,O
Homeland Security	M,D,O
Interdisciplinary Studies	M,D
International Affairs	M,D,O
International Development	M,D,O
International Economics	M,D,O
Internet and Interactive Multimedia	M,O

M—master's degree; P—first professional degree; D—doctorate; O—other advanced degree; *—Close-Up and / or Display

Mass Communication — M
Media Studies — M
Museum Studies — M
Music — M,O
National Security — M,D,O
Psychology—General — M,D
Public Policy — M
Religion — M,D
Rhetoric — M,D
School Psychology — M,D,O
Social Psychology — D
Speech and
 Interpersonal
 Communication — M,D
Sport Psychology — M,D
Theology — D
Translation and
 Interpretation — M,O
Writing — M,D,O

UNIVERSITY OF DETROIT MERCY

Addictions/Substance
 Abuse Counseling — M,O
Clinical Psychology — M,D
Criminal Justice and
 Criminology — M
Industrial and
 Organizational
 Psychology — M
Liberal Studies — M
Military and Defense
 Studies — M
Psychology—General — M,D,O
Religion — M
School Psychology — O

UNIVERSITY OF DUBUQUE

Communication—
 General — M
Theology — P,M,D

UNIVERSITY OF EVANSVILLE

Public Administration — M

THE UNIVERSITY OF FINDLAY

Public Administration — M

UNIVERSITY OF FLORIDA

African Studies — M,D,O
Agricultural Economics
 and Agribusiness — M,D
American Studies — M,D
Anthropology — M,D
Architecture — M,D
Art History — M,D
Art/Fine Arts — M,D
Arts Administration — M
Asian Studies — M,D
Building Science — M,D
Classics — M,D
Clinical Psychology — D
Cognitive Sciences — M,D
Communication—
 General — M,D
Computer Art and
 Design — M,D
Counseling Psychology — M,D
Criminal Justice and
 Criminology — M,D
Developmental
 Psychology — M,D
Economics — M,D
English — M,D
Family and Consumer
 Sciences-General — M
Forensic Sciences — M,O
French — M,D
Gender Studies — M,O
Geography — M,D
German — M,D
Graphic Design — M,D
Health Communication — M,D,O

Health Psychology — D
Historic Preservation — D
History — M,D
Interior Design — M,D
International Affairs — M
International
 Development — M,D,O
Internet and Interactive
 Multimedia — M,D
Journalism — M
Landscape Architecture — M
Latin American Studies — M,D,O
Linguistics — M,D,O
Marriage and Family
 Therapy — M,D,O
Mass Communication — M,D
Media Studies — M
Museum Studies — M,D
Music — M,D
Philosophy — M,D
Photography — M,D
Political Science — M,D,O
Psychology—General — M,D
Public Affairs — M,D,O
Religion — M,D
School Psychology — M,D,O
Social Psychology — M,D
Social Sciences — M
Sociology — M,D
Spanish — M,D
Theater — M
Urban and Regional
 Planning — M
Western European
 Studies — M,D
Women's Studies — M,O
Writing — M,D

UNIVERSITY OF GEORGIA

Agricultural Economics
 and Agribusiness — M,D
Anthropology — M,D
Applied Economics — M,D
Archaeology — M,D
Art History — M
Art/Fine Arts — M
Child and Family
 Studies — M,D,O
Classics — M
Clothing and Textiles — M,D
Communication—
 General — M,D
Comparative Literature — M,D
Consumer Economics — M,D
Economics — M,D
English — M,D
Environmental Design — M
Family and Consumer
 Sciences-General — M,D
French — M
Geography — M,D
German — M
Gerontology — O
Historic Preservation — M
History — M,D
Interior Design — M,D
Internet and Interactive
 Multimedia — M
Journalism — M,D
Landscape Architecture — M
Linguistics — M,D
Mass Communication — M,D
Music — M,D
Philosophy — M,D
Political Science — M,D
Psychology—General — M,D
Public Administration — M,D
Public Policy — M,D
Religion — M
Romance Languages — M,D
Sociology — M,D
Spanish — M

Speech and
 Interpersonal
 Communication — M,D
Sustainable
 Development — M,D
Theater — M,D
Women's Studies — O
Writing — M

UNIVERSITY OF GREAT FALLS

Counseling Psychology — M
Criminal Justice and
 Criminology — M

UNIVERSITY OF GUAM

Art/Fine Arts — M
English — M
Graphic Design — M
Pacific Area/Pacific Rim
 Studies — M
Public Administration — M

UNIVERSITY OF GUELPH

Agricultural Economics
 and Agribusiness — M,D
Anthropology — M,D
Applied Psychology — M,D
Art/Fine Arts — M
Child and Family
 Studies — M,D
Clinical Psychology — M,D
Cognitive Sciences — M,D
Comparative Literature — D
Consumer Economics — M
Criminal Justice and
 Criminology — M,D
Demography and
 Population Studies — M,D
Economics — M,D
English — M
French — M
Geography — M,D
History — M,D
Human Development — M,D
Industrial and
 Organizational
 Psychology — M,D
International
 Development — M,D
Landscape Architecture — M
Marriage and Family
 Therapy — M,D
Medieval and
 Renaissance Studies — D
Philosophy — M,D
Political Science — M
Psychology—General — M
Public Administration — M
Public Policy — M
Rural Planning and
 Studies — M,D
Social Psychology — M,D
Sociology — M,D
Theater — M
Western European
 Studies — M

UNIVERSITY OF HARTFORD

Architecture — M
Art/Fine Arts — M
Clinical Psychology — M,D
Communication—
 General — M
Experimental
 Psychology — M
Music — M,D,O
Psychology—General — M,D
School Psychology — M

UNIVERSITY OF HAWAII AT HILO

Asian Studies — M

Counseling Psychology — M
Cultural Studies — M,D

UNIVERSITY OF HAWAII AT MANOA

American Studies — M,D,O
Anthropology — M,D
Architecture — D
Art History — M
Art/Fine Arts — M
Asian Languages — M,D
Asian Studies — O
Chinese — M,D,O
Clinical Psychology — M,D,O
Communication—
 General — M,O
Conflict Resolution and
 Mediation/Peace
 Studies — O
Cultural Studies — O
Dance — M,D
Demography and
 Population Studies — O
Disability Studies — O
Economics — M,D
Emergency
 Management — O
English — M,D
French — M
Geography — M,D,O
Historic Preservation — O
History — M,D
International Affairs — O
Japanese — M,D,O
Linguistics — M,D
Museum Studies — O
Music — M,D
Pacific Area/Pacific Rim
 Studies — M,O
Philosophy — M,D
Political Science — M,D
Psychology—General — M,D,O
Public Administration — M,O
Public Policy — O
Religion — M
Social Psychology — M,D,O
Sociology — M,D
Spanish — M
Speech and
 Interpersonal
 Communication — M
Theater — M,D
Urban and Regional
 Planning — M,D,O
Women's Studies — O

UNIVERSITY OF HOUSTON

Anthropology — M
Applied Economics — M,D
Architecture — M
Art History — M
Art/Fine Arts — M
Clinical Psychology — M,D
Communication—
 General — M
Comparative Literature — M
Counseling Psychology — M,D
Cultural Studies — M
Developmental
 Psychology — M,D
Economics — M,D
Family and Consumer
 Sciences-General — M
Health Communication — M
Hispanic Studies — M,D
History — M,D
Industrial and
 Organizational
 Psychology — M,D
Linguistics — M,D
Mass Communication — M
Music — M
Philosophy — M
Political Science — M,D

Peterson's Graduate Programs in the Humanities, Arts & Social Sciences 2012

Psychology—General	M,D
Public Administration	M,D
Social Psychology	M,D
Sociology	M
Spanish	M,D
Speech and Interpersonal Communication	M
Theater	M
Writing	M,D

UNIVERSITY OF HOUSTON–CLEAR LAKE

Clinical Psychology	M
Criminal Justice and Criminology	M
Cultural Studies	M
English	M
History	M
Humanities	M
Marriage and Family Therapy	M
Psychology—General	M
School Psychology	M
Sociology	M

UNIVERSITY OF HOUSTON–DOWNTOWN

Criminal Justice and Criminology	M
English	M
Technical Communication	M
Writing	M

UNIVERSITY OF HOUSTON–VICTORIA

Counseling Psychology	M
Economic Development	M
Interdisciplinary Studies	M
Psychology—General	M
Publishing	M
School Psychology	M

UNIVERSITY OF IDAHO

Agricultural Economics and Agribusiness	M
American Indian/Native American Studies	P
Anthropology	M
Applied Economics	M
Architecture	M
Art/Fine Arts	M
Consumer Economics	M
Economics	M
English	M
Geography	M,D
Graphic Design	M
History	M,D
Interdisciplinary Studies	M
Landscape Architecture	M
Music	M
Political Science	M,D
Psychology—General	M
Public Administration	M
Public Affairs	M,D
School Psychology	O
Social Sciences	M,D
Theater	M
Urban and Regional Planning	M
Urban Design	M
Writing	M

UNIVERSITY OF ILLINOIS AT CHICAGO

Anthropology	M,D
Architecture	M
Art History	M,D
Art/Fine Arts	M
Communication—General	M,D

Criminal Justice and Criminology	M,D
Disability Studies	M,D
Economics	M,D
English	M,D
Forensic Sciences	M
French	M
Geography	M
German	M,D
Graphic Design	M
Hispanic and Latin American Languages	M,D
Hispanic Studies	M,D
History	M,D
Human Development	M,D
Industrial Design	M
Linguistics	M
Medical Illustration	M
Philosophy	M,D
Photography	M
Political Science	M,D
Psychology—General	D
Public Administration	M,D
Sociology	M,D
Spanish	M,D
Urban and Regional Planning	M,D
Writing	M,D

UNIVERSITY OF ILLINOIS AT SPRINGFIELD

Addictions/Substance Abuse Counseling	M
Child and Family Studies	M
Communication—General	M
English	M
Gerontology	M
History	M
Human Development	M
Interdisciplinary Studies	M
Journalism	M
Political Science	M
Public Administration	M,D
Public History	M
Social Sciences	M

UNIVERSITY OF ILLINOIS AT URBANA–CHAMPAIGN

African Studies	M
Agricultural Economics and Agribusiness	M,D
Anthropology	M,D
Applied Arts and Design—General	M,D
Applied Economics	M,D
Architecture	M,D
Art History	M,D
Art/Fine Arts	M
Asian Languages	M,D
Asian Studies	M,D
Classics	M,D
Communication—General	M,D
Comparative Literature	M,D
Consumer Economics	M,D
Dance	M
East European and Russian Studies	M
Economics	M,D
English	M,D
French	M,D
Geography	M,D
German	M,D
Graphic Design	M
History	M,D
Human Development	M,D
Industrial and Labor Relations	M,D
Industrial Design	M
Italian	M,D

Journalism	M
Landscape Architecture	M,D
Latin American Studies	M
Linguistics	M,D
Media Studies	M,D
Music	M,D,O
Philosophy	M,D
Photography	M
Political Science	M,D
Portuguese	M,D
Psychology—General	M,D
Slavic Languages	M,D
Sociology	M,D
Spanish	M,D
Theater	M,D
Urban and Regional Planning	M,D
Western European Studies	M
Writing	M,D

UNIVERSITY OF INDIANAPOLIS

Anthropology	M
Art/Fine Arts	M
Clinical Psychology	M,D
Counseling Psychology	M,D
English	M
Gerontology	M,O
History	M
International Affairs	M
Psychology—General	M,D
Sociology	M

THE UNIVERSITY OF IOWA

African-American Studies	M
American Studies	M,D
Anthropology	M,D
Art History	M,D
Art/Fine Arts	M
Asian Studies	M
Classics	M,D
Communication—General	M,D
Comparative Literature	M,D
Counseling Psychology	M,D,O
Dance	M
Economics	D
English	M,D
Film, Television, and Video Production	M
Film, Television, and Video Theory and Criticism	M,D
French	M,D
Geography	M,D
German	M,D
History	M,D
Journalism	M
Linguistics	M,D
Mass Communication	M,D
Media Studies	M,D
Music	M,D
Philosophy	M,D
Political Science	M,D
Psychology—General	M,D,O
Rehabilitation Counseling	M,D
Religion	M,D
Rhetoric	M,D
School Psychology	M,D,O
Social Psychology	M,D
Sociology	M,D
Spanish	M,D
Sport Psychology	M,D
Theater	M
Translation and Interpretation	M
Urban and Regional Planning	M
Women's Studies	D
Writing	M,D

THE UNIVERSITY OF KANSAS

African Studies	M,O
African-American Studies	M,O
American Indian/Native American Studies	M
American Studies	M,D
Anthropology	M,D
Applied Arts and Design—General	M
Applied Behavior Analysis	M,D
Architecture	M,D,O
Art History	M,D
Art/Fine Arts	M
Asian Languages	M
Asian Studies	M
Classics	M
Clinical Psychology	M,D
Cognitive Sciences	M,D
Communication—General	M,D
Computer Art and Design	M
Counseling Psychology	M,D
Developmental Psychology	M,D
East European and Russian Studies	M
Economics	M,D
English	M,D
Film, Television, and Video Theory and Criticism	M,D
French	M,D
Geography	M,D
German	M,D
Gerontology	M,D,O
History	M,D
Interdisciplinary Studies	M,D
International Affairs	M
Journalism	M
Latin American Studies	M,O
Linguistics	M,D
Media Studies	M,D
Museum Studies	M
Music	M,D
Near and Middle Eastern Studies	M
Philosophy	M,D
Political Science	M,D
Psychology—General	M,D
Public Administration	M,D
Rehabilitation Counseling	M,D
Religion	M
School Psychology	D,O
Slavic Languages	M,D
Social Psychology	M,D
Sociology	M,D
Spanish	M,D
Theater	M,D
Therapies—Dance, Drama, and Music	M
Urban and Regional Planning	M
Writing	M,D

UNIVERSITY OF KENTUCKY

Agricultural Economics and Agribusiness	M,D
Anthropology	M,D
Applied Arts and Design—General	M
Architecture	M
Art History	M
Art/Fine Arts	M
Child and Family Studies	M,D
Classics	M
Clinical Psychology	M,D
Clothing and Textiles	M

*M—master's degree; P—first professional degree; D—doctorate; O—other advanced degree; *—Close-Up and/or Display*

Communication—
General — M,D
Counseling Psychology — M,D,O
Economics — M,D
English — M,D
Experimental
Psychology — M,D
French — M
Geography — M,D
German — M
Gerontology — D
Hispanic Studies — M,D
Historic Preservation — M
History — M,D
Interior Design — M
International Affairs — M
Music — M
Philosophy — M,D
Political Science — M,D
Psychology—General — M,D
Public Administration — M,D
Rehabilitation
Counseling — M,D
School Psychology — M,D,O
Sociology — M,D
Theater — M

UNIVERSITY OF LA VERNE

Child and Family
Studies — M
Child Development — M
Clinical Psychology — D
Counseling Psychology — M
Gerontology — M,O
Marriage and Family
Therapy — M
Psychology—General — M,D
Public Administration — M,D
Social Psychology — D

UNIVERSITY OF LETHBRIDGE

Addictions/Substance
Abuse Counseling — M,D
American Indian/Native
American Studies — M,D
Anthropology — M,D
Archaeology — M,D
Art/Fine Arts — M,D
Canadian Studies — M,D
Counseling Psychology — M,D
Economics — M,D
English — M,D
French — M,D
Geographic Information
Systems — M,D
Geography — M,D
German — M,D
History — M,D
Media Studies — M,D
Music — M,D
Philosophy — M,D
Political Science — M,D
Psychology—General — M,D
Religion — M,D
Social Sciences — M,D
Sociology — M,D
Spanish — M,D
Theater — M,D
Urban Studies — M,D
Women's Studies — M,D

UNIVERSITY OF LOUISIANA AT LAFAYETTE

American Studies — D
Cognitive Sciences — D
Communication—
General — M
English — M
Folklore — M,D
French — M,D
History — M
Mass Communication — M
Music — M
Psychology—General — M

Rehabilitation
Counseling — M
Rhetoric — M,D
Writing — M,D

UNIVERSITY OF LOUISIANA AT MONROE

Addictions/Substance
Abuse Counseling — M
Communication—
General — M
Criminal Justice and
Criminology — M
English — M
Experimental
Psychology — M
Gerontology — M,O
History — M
Marriage and Family
Therapy — M,D
Music — M
Psychology—General — M,O
School Psychology — M,O

UNIVERSITY OF LOUISVILLE

Addictions/Substance
Abuse Counseling — M,D,O
African Studies — M
African-American
Studies — M
Anthropology — M
Art History — M,D
Art/Fine Arts — M,D
Clinical Psychology — D
Communication—
General — M
Criminal Justice and
Criminology — M
English — M,D
Experimental
Psychology — D
French — M
Geography — M
Gerontology — M,D,O
History — M,O
Humanities — M,D
Interdisciplinary Studies — M,D
Marriage and Family
Therapy — M,D,O
Museum Studies — M,D
Music — M
Philosophy — M
Political Science — M
Psychology—General — D
Public Administration — M,D
Public Affairs — M,D
Public History — M,O
Public Policy — M,D
Rhetoric — M,D
Sociology — M
Spanish — M
Theater — M
Urban and Regional
Planning — M,D
Urban Studies — M,D
Women's Studies — M,O
Writing — M,D

UNIVERSITY OF MAINE

Agricultural Economics
and Agribusiness — M
American Studies — M,D
Asian Studies — M,D
Canadian Studies — M,D
Clinical Psychology — M,D
Communication—
General — M,D
Conflict Resolution and
Mediation/Peace
Studies — M
Developmental
Psychology — M,D
English — M

Experimental
Psychology — M,D
French — M
Gender Studies — M
History of Science and
Technology — M,D
History — M,D
Human Development — M
Interdisciplinary Studies — M,D
Liberal Studies — M
Mass Communication — M,D
Media Studies — M
Music — M
Psychology—General — M,D
Public Administration — M,D
Western European
Studies — M,D
Writing — M

UNIVERSITY OF MANAGEMENT AND TECHNOLOGY

Criminal Justice and
Criminology — M
Public Administration — M,O

THE UNIVERSITY OF MANCHESTER

Anthropology — M,D
Archaeology — M,D
Architecture — M,D
Art History — D
Art/Fine Arts — M,D
Arts Administration — D
Asian Studies — M,D
Chinese — M,D
Classics — D
Clinical Psychology — M,D
Clothing and Textiles — M,D
Conflict Resolution and
Mediation/Peace
Studies — D
Counseling Psychology — M,D
Criminal Justice and
Criminology — M,D
Cultural Studies — M,D
Developmental
Psychology — M,D
Economics — D
English — D
Environmental Design — M,D
French — M,D
Geography — M,D
German — M,D
Hispanic Studies — M,D
History of Medicine — M,D
History of Science and
Technology — M,D
History — D
International Affairs — D
International
Development — M,D
Italian — M,D
Japanese — M,D
Landscape Architecture — M,D
Latin American Studies — M,D
Linguistics — M,D
Museum Studies — D
Music — D
Near and Middle
Eastern Languages — M,D
Near and Middle
Eastern Studies — M,D
Philosophy — M,D
Political Science — M,D
Psychology—General — M,D
Religion — D
Russian — M,D
Slavic Languages — M,D
Social Sciences — M,D
Sociology — M,D
Spanish — M,D
Textile Design — M,D
Theater — D
Theology — D

Translation and
Interpretation — M,D
Writing — D

UNIVERSITY OF MANITOBA

Agricultural Economics
and Agribusiness — M,D
American Indian/Native
American Studies — M
Anthropology — M,D
Architecture — M
Canadian Studies — M
Child and Family
Studies — M
Classics — M
Clinical Psychology — M,D
Clothing and Textiles — M
Disability Studies — M
Economics — M,D
English — M,D
Family and Consumer
Sciences-General — M
French — M,D
Geography — M,D
German — M
History — M,D
Interdisciplinary Studies — M,D
Interior Design — M
Landscape Architecture — M
Linguistics — M,D
Music — M
Northern Studies — M
Philosophy — M
Political Science — M
Psychology—General — M,D
Public Administration — M
Religion — M,D
School Psychology — M,D
Slavic Languages — M
Sociology — M,D
Urban and Regional
Planning — M

UNIVERSITY OF MARY

Addictions/Substance
Abuse Counseling — M
School Psychology — M
Social Psychology — M

UNIVERSITY OF MARY HARDIN-BAYLOR

Clinical Psychology — M
Counseling Psychology — M
Marriage and Family
Therapy — M
Psychology—General — M
School Psychology — M

UNIVERSITY OF MARYLAND, BALTIMORE

Genetic Counseling — M
Gerontology — M,D

UNIVERSITY OF MARYLAND, BALTIMORE COUNTY

Applied Behavior
Analysis — M,D
Applied Psychology — D
Art/Fine Arts — M
Cognitive Sciences — D
Communication—
General — M
Dance — M
Developmental
Psychology — D
Economics — M,D
Geographic Information
Systems — M,O
Geography — M,D
Gerontology — M,D
History — M

Industrial and Organizational Psychology	M
Linguistics	M
Music	O
Psychology—General	M,D
Public History	M,D
Public Policy	M,D
Social Sciences	D
Sociology	M,O
Theater	M
Urban Studies	M,D
Women's Studies	O

UNIVERSITY OF MARYLAND, COLLEGE PARK

Agricultural Economics and Agribusiness	M,D
American Studies	M,D
Anthropology	M
Architecture	M
Art History	M,D
Art Therapy	M,D,O
Art/Fine Arts	M
Broadcast Journalism	M,D
Child and Family Studies	M,D
Classics	M
Clinical Psychology	M,D
Cognitive Sciences	D
Communication—General	M,D
Comparative Literature	M,D
Counseling Psychology	M,D,O
Criminal Justice and Criminology	M,D
Dance	M,D
Developmental Psychology	M,D
Economics	M,D
English	M,D
Experimental Psychology	M,D
Family and Consumer Sciences-General	M,D
French	M,D
Geography	M,D
German	M,D
Historic Preservation	M,O
History	M,D
Human Development	M,D
Industrial and Organizational Psychology	M,D
Jewish Studies	M
Journalism	M,D
Landscape Architecture	M
Linguistics	M,D
Marriage and Family Therapy	M,D
Media Studies	M,D
Music	M,D
Near and Middle Eastern Languages	M,O
Philosophy	M,D
Political Science	D
Portuguese	M,D
Psychology—General	M,D
Public Administration	M
Public Policy	M,D
Rehabilitation Counseling	M,D,O
School Psychology	M,D,O
Social Psychology	M,D
Sociology	M,D
Spanish	M,D
Speech and Interpersonal Communication	M,D
Survey Methodology	M,D
Sustainable Development	M

Theater	M
Urban and Regional Planning	M,D
Women's Studies	M,D
Writing	M,D

UNIVERSITY OF MARYLAND EASTERN SHORE

Criminal Justice and Criminology	M
Rehabilitation Counseling	M

UNIVERSITY OF MASSACHUSETTS AMHERST

African-American Studies	M,D
Agricultural Economics and Agribusiness	M,D
Anthropology	M,D
Applied Arts and Design—General	M
Architecture	M
Art History	M
Art/Fine Arts	M
Child and Family Studies	M,D,O
Chinese	M
Classics	M
Clinical Psychology	M,D
Cognitive Sciences	M,D
Communication—General	M,D
Comparative Literature	M,D
Conflict Resolution and Mediation/Peace Studies	M,D
Developmental Psychology	M,D
Economics	M,D
English	M,D
French	M
Geography	M
German	M,D
Hispanic and Latin American Languages	M,D
Historic Preservation	M
History of Science and Technology	M,D
History	M,D
Industrial and Labor Relations	M
Interior Design	M
Italian	M
Japanese	M
Landscape Architecture	M
Linguistics	M,D
Music	M,D
Philosophy	M,D
Political Science	M,D
Portuguese	M,D
Psychology—General	M,D
Public Administration	M
Public History	M,D
Public Policy	M
Scandinavian Languages	M,D
School Psychology	M,D,O
Social Psychology	M,D
Sociology	M,D
Spanish	M,D
Theater	M
Urban and Regional Planning	M,D
Writing	M,D

UNIVERSITY OF MASSACHUSETTS BOSTON

American Studies	M
Archaeology	M
Clinical Psychology	D

Conflict Resolution and Mediation/Peace Studies	M,O
Counseling Psychology	M,O
English	M
Forensic Psychology	M,O
Gerontology	M,D,O
History	M
Linguistics	M
Marriage and Family Therapy	M,O
Political Science	M,D,O
Public Affairs	M
Public Policy	D
Rehabilitation Counseling	M,O
School Psychology	M,O
Sociology	M
Women's Studies	M,D,O

UNIVERSITY OF MASSACHUSETTS DARTMOUTH

Applied Arts and Design—General	M
Art/Fine Arts	M,O
Clinical Psychology	M,O
Computer Art and Design	M
Graphic Design	M
Illustration	M
Latin American Studies	M,D
Photography	M
Portuguese	M,D
Psychology—General	M,O
Public Policy	M,O
Textile Design	M,O
Writing	M,O

UNIVERSITY OF MASSACHUSETTS LOWELL

Criminal Justice and Criminology	M
Economic Development	M,O
Economics	M,O
Music	M
Psychology—General	M
Social Psychology	M
Sociology	M,O
Sustainable Development	M,D,O

UNIVERSITY OF MASSACHUSETTS WORCESTER

Interdisciplinary Studies	M,D

UNIVERSITY OF MEDICINE AND DENTISTRY OF NEW JERSEY

Counseling Psychology	M,D,O
Emergency Management	M,D,O
Interdisciplinary Studies	M,D
Public Policy	M,O
Rehabilitation Counseling	M,D

UNIVERSITY OF MEMPHIS

African-American Studies	M,D,O
Anthropology	M
Archaeology	M,D,O
Architecture	M
Art History	M,O
Art/Fine Arts	M,O
Clinical Psychology	M,D,O
Communication—General	M,D
Comparative Literature	M,D
Counseling Psychology	M,D
Criminal Justice and Criminology	M
Economics	M,D
English	M,D,O

Experimental Psychology	M,D,O
Family and Consumer Sciences-General	M
Film, Television, and Video Production	M,D
French	M
Geographic Information Systems	M,D,O
Geography	M,D,O
Graphic Design	M,O
History	M,D
Interdisciplinary Studies	M,D,O
Interior Design	M,O
Journalism	M
Liberal Studies	M
Linguistics	M,D,O
Music	M,D
Near and Middle Eastern Studies	M,D
Philosophy	M,D
Photography	M,O
Political Science	M
Psychology—General	M,D,O
Public Administration	M
Public Policy	M
Rehabilitation Counseling	M,D
School Psychology	M,D,O
Social Sciences	M
Sociology	M
Spanish	M
Theater	M
Urban and Regional Planning	M
Writing	M,D,O

UNIVERSITY OF MIAMI

Architecture	M
Art History	M
Art/Fine Arts	M
Broadcast Journalism	M,D
Clinical Psychology	M,D
Communication—General	M,D
Counseling Psychology	D
Developmental Psychology	M,D
Economic Development	M,D
Economics	M,D
English	M,D
Film, Television, and Video Production	M,D
Film, Television, and Video Theory and Criticism	M,D
French	D
Geography	M
Graphic Design	M
History	M,D
International Affairs	M,D
International Economics	M,D
Internet and Interactive Multimedia	M
Journalism	M,D
Latin American Studies	M
Liberal Studies	M
Marriage and Family Therapy	M,O
Music	M,D,O
Philosophy	M,D
Photography	M
Political Science	M
Psychology—General	M,D
Romance Languages	D
Sociology	M,D
Spanish	M,D
Therapies—Dance, Drama, and Music	M,D,O
Urban Design	M
Writing	M,D

*M—master's degree; P—first professional degree; D—doctorate; O—other advanced degree; *—Close-Up and/or Display*

UNIVERSITY OF MICHIGAN

American Studies	M,D
Anthropology	D
Applied Arts and Design—General	M
Applied Economics	M
Archaeology	D
Architecture	M,D
Art History	D
Art/Fine Arts	M
Asian Languages	M,D
Asian Studies	M,D,O
Classics	M,D,O
Clinical Psychology	D
Communication—General	D
Comparative Literature	D
Dance	M
Developmental Psychology	D
East European and Russian Studies	M,O
Economics	M,D
English	M,D,O
Experimental Psychology	D
Film, Television, and Video Theory and Criticism	D,O
French	D
Genetic Counseling	M,D
German	M,D
History	D,O
Italian	D
Jewish Studies	M,D,O
Landscape Architecture	M,D
Linguistics	D
Mass Communication	D
Media Studies	M
Medieval and Renaissance Studies	O
Music	M,D,O
Near and Middle Eastern Languages	M,D
Near and Middle Eastern Studies	M,D
Philosophy	M,D
Political Science	M,D
Psychology—General	D,O
Public Policy	M,D
Religion	M,D
Romance Languages	D
Russian	M,D
Slavic Languages	M,D
Social Psychology	D
Social Sciences	D
Sociology	D,O
Spanish	D
Survey Methodology	M,D,O
Sustainable Development	M,D
Theater	M,D
Urban and Regional Planning	M,D,O
Urban Design	M
Women's Studies	D,O
Writing	M

UNIVERSITY OF MICHIGAN–DEARBORN

Clinical Psychology	M
Health Psychology	M
Liberal Studies	M
Public Administration	M,O
Public Policy	M

UNIVERSITY OF MICHIGAN–FLINT

American Studies	M
English	M
Public Administration	M
Social Sciences	M

UNIVERSITY OF MINNESOTA, DULUTH

Anthropology	M
Art/Fine Arts	M
Criminal Justice and Criminology	M
English	M
Graphic Design	M
Liberal Studies	M
Music	M
Sociology	M

UNIVERSITY OF MINNESOTA, TWIN CITIES CAMPUS

American Studies	D
Anthropology	M,D
Applied Arts and Design—General	M,D,O
Applied Economics	M,D
Archaeology	M,D
Architecture	M
Art History	M,D
Art/Fine Arts	M
Asian Languages	D
Asian Studies	D
Child and Family Studies	M,D
Child Development	M,D
Classics	M,D
Clinical Psychology	D
Clothing and Textiles	M,D,O
Cognitive Sciences	D
Communication—General	M,D,O
Comparative Literature	D
Counseling Psychology	D
Cultural Studies	D
Dance	M,D
Economic Development	M
Economics	D
English	M,D
French	M,D
Genetic Counseling	M,D
Geographic Information Systems	M
German	M,D
Hispanic and Latin American Languages	M,D
History of Medicine	M,D
History of Science and Technology	M,D
History	M,D
Industrial and Labor Relations	M,D
Industrial and Organizational Psychology	D
Interdisciplinary Studies	D
Interior Design	M,D,O
International Development	M
Landscape Architecture	M
Linguistics	M,D
Marriage and Family Therapy	M,D
Mass Communication	M,D
Medieval and Renaissance Studies	M,D
Music	M,D
Philosophy	M,D
Political Science	D
Portuguese	M
Psychology—General	D
Public Affairs	M
Public Policy	M
Religion	M,D
Scandinavian Languages	M,D
School Psychology	M,D,O
Social Psychology	D
Sociology	M,D
Spanish	M,D
Textile Design	M,D,O

Theater	M,D
Urban and Regional Planning	M
Women's Studies	D

UNIVERSITY OF MISSISSIPPI

American Studies	M
Anthropology	M
Art History	M
Art/Fine Arts	M
Clinical Psychology	M,D
Economics	M
English	M,D
Experimental Psychology	M,D
Family and Consumer Sciences-General	M
French	M
German	M
History	M,D
Journalism	M
Music	M,D
Philosophy	M
Political Science	M,D
Psychology—General	M,D
Sociology	M
Spanish	M

UNIVERSITY OF MISSOURI

Agricultural Economics and Agribusiness	M,D
Anthropology	M,D
Archaeology	M,D
Architecture	M
Art History	M,D
Art/Fine Arts	M
Child and Family Studies	M,D
Classics	M,D
Clothing and Textiles	M
Communication—General	M,D
Comparative Literature	M,D
Computer Art and Design	M
Conflict Resolution and Mediation/Peace Studies	M
Consumer Economics	M
Counseling Psychology	M,D,O
Economics	M,D
English	M,D
Environmental Design	M
Family and Consumer Sciences-General	M,D
French	M,D
Geography	M
German	M
History	M,D
Human Development	M,D
Journalism	M,D
Music	M
Philosophy	M,D
Political Science	M,D
Psychology—General	M,D
Public Affairs	M
Religion	M
Romance Languages	M,D
Rural Sociology	M,D
School Psychology	M,D,O
Sociology	M,D
Spanish	M,D
Theater	M,D

UNIVERSITY OF MISSOURI–KANSAS CITY

Art History	M,D
Art/Fine Arts	M,D
Clinical Psychology	M,D
Counseling Psychology	M,D,O
Criminal Justice and Criminology	M
Economics	M,D
English	M,D

Health Psychology	M,D
History	M,D
Interdisciplinary Studies	D
Media Studies	M,D
Music	M,D
Political Science	M,D
Psychology—General	M,D
Public Administration	M,D
Public Affairs	M,D
Romance Languages	M
Social Psychology	M,D
Sociology	M,D
Theater	M
Writing	M,D

UNIVERSITY OF MISSOURI–ST. LOUIS

American Studies	M,D
Clinical Psychology	M,D,O
Communication—General	M
Criminal Justice and Criminology	M,D
Cultural Studies	O
Economics	M
English	M,O
Gender Studies	O
Gerontology	M,O
Industrial and Organizational Psychology	M,D,O
Interdisciplinary Studies	O
Linguistics	M,O
Museum Studies	M,O
Philosophy	M
Political Science	M,D,O
Psychology—General	M,D,O
Public Administration	M,D,O
Public Policy	M,D,O
School Psychology	O
Social Psychology	M,D,O
Writing	M,O

UNIVERSITY OF MOBILE

Marriage and Family Therapy	M
Religion	M
Theology	M

THE UNIVERSITY OF MONTANA

Anthropology	M,D
Art/Fine Arts	M
Clinical Psychology	M,D,O
Communication—General	M
Counseling Psychology	M,D,O
Criminal Justice and Criminology	M
Developmental Psychology	M,D,O
Economics	M
English	M
Experimental Psychology	M,D,O
French	M
Geographic Information Systems	M
Geography	M
German	M
History	M,D
Interdisciplinary Studies	M,D
Jewish Studies	M
Journalism	M
Linguistics	M,D
Music	M
Philosophy	M
Political Science	M
Psychology—General	M,D,O
Public Administration	M
Rural Planning and Studies	M
Rural Sociology	M
School Psychology	M,D,O
Sociology	M

Spanish	M
Theater	M
Writing	M

UNIVERSITY OF MONTEVALLO

English	M
Marriage and Family Therapy	M
Social Psychology	M

UNIVERSITY OF NEBRASKA AT KEARNEY

English	M
History	M
School Psychology	M,O
Writing	M

UNIVERSITY OF NEBRASKA AT OMAHA

Communication—General	M
Criminal Justice and Criminology	M,D
Developmental Psychology	M,D,O
Economics	M
English	M,O
Geography	M,O
Gerontology	M,O
History	M
Industrial and Organizational Psychology	M,D,O
Music	M
Political Science	M
Psychology—General	M,D,O
Public Administration	M,D,O
School Psychology	M,D,O
Technical Communication	M,O
Theater	M
Writing	M,O

UNIVERSITY OF NEBRASKA–LINCOLN

Agricultural Economics and Agribusiness	M,D
Anthropology	M
Archaeology	M,D
Architecture	M,D
Art History	M
Art/Fine Arts	M
Child and Family Studies	M,D
Child Development	M,D
Classics	M
Clinical Psychology	M,D
Clothing and Textiles	M,D
Cognitive Sciences	M,D,O
Communication—General	M,D
Comparative Literature	M,D
Consumer Economics	M,D
Corporate and Organizational Communication	M,D
Counseling Psychology	M,D,O
Developmental Psychology	M,D,O
Economics	M,D
English	M,D
Family and Consumer Sciences-General	M,D
French	M,D
Geography	M,D
German	M,D
Gerontology	M,D
History	M,D
Human Development	M,D,O
Interior Design	M,D
Journalism	M

Marriage and Family Therapy	M,D
Mass Communication	M
Music	M,D
Philosophy	M,D
Political Science	M,D,O
Psychology—General	M,D
Public Policy	M,D,O
Rhetoric	M,D
School Psychology	M,D,O
Social Psychology	M,D
Sociology	M,D
Spanish	M,D
Speech and Interpersonal Communication	M,D
Survey Methodology	M,D
Theater	M
Urban and Regional Planning	M,D
Writing	M,D

UNIVERSITY OF NEVADA, LAS VEGAS

Anthropology	M,D
Architecture	M
Art/Fine Arts	M
Clinical Psychology	M,O
Communication—General	M
Criminal Justice and Criminology	M
Economics	M
Emergency Management	M,D,O
English	M,D
Ethics	M
Ethnic Studies	M,D
Film, Television, and Video Production	M
Forensic Sciences	M,O
Hispanic Studies	M
History	M,D
Journalism	M,O
Marriage and Family Therapy	M
Media Studies	M
Music	M,D
Political Science	M,D
Psychology—General	M,D
Public Administration	M,D,O
Public Affairs	M,D,O
Public Policy	M
Rehabilitation Counseling	M,O
Sociology	M,D
Theater	M
Women's Studies	O
Writing	M,D

UNIVERSITY OF NEVADA, RENO

Agricultural Economics and Agribusiness	M,D
Anthropology	M,D
Applied Economics	M,D
Art/Fine Arts	M
Child and Family Studies	M
Clinical Psychology	D
Cognitive Sciences	M,D
Criminal Justice and Criminology	M
Economics	M
English	M,D
French	M
Geography	M,D
German	M
History	M,D
Human Development	M
Journalism	M
Music	M
Philosophy	M

Political Science	M,D
Psychology—General	M,D
Public Administration	M
Social Psychology	D
Sociology	M
Spanish	M
Speech and Interpersonal Communication	M
Western European Studies	D

UNIVERSITY OF NEW BRUNSWICK FREDERICTON

Anthropology	M
Applied Economics	M
Classics	M
Conflict Resolution and Mediation/Peace Studies	M
Economics	M
English	M,D
History	M,D
Interdisciplinary Studies	M,D
Philosophy	M
Political Science	M
Public Administration	M
Public Policy	M
Sociology	M,D
Sustainable Development	M

UNIVERSITY OF NEW BRUNSWICK SAINT JOHN

Applied Psychology	M,D
Clinical Psychology	M,D
Experimental Psychology	M,D
Psychology—General	M,D

UNIVERSITY OF NEW ENGLAND

Addictions/Substance Abuse Counseling	M,O
Ethics	M,O
Gerontology	M,O

UNIVERSITY OF NEW HAMPSHIRE

Art/Fine Arts	M
Child and Family Studies	M
Comparative Literature	M,D
Economics	M,D
English	M,D
History	M,D
International Development	M,D,O
Liberal Studies	M
Linguistics	M,D
Marriage and Family Therapy	M
Museum Studies	M,D
Music	M
Political Science	M
Psychology—General	D
Public Administration	M,O
Sociology	M,D
Spanish	M
Writing	M,D

UNIVERSITY OF NEW HAVEN

Conflict Resolution and Mediation/Peace Studies	M,O
Criminal Justice and Criminology	M,D,O
Emergency Management	M,O
Forensic Psychology	M,D,O
Forensic Sciences	M,D,O
Geographic Information Systems	M,O

Political Science	M,D
Psychology—General	M,D
Public Administration	M
Social Psychology	D
Sociology	M
Spanish	M
Speech and Interpersonal Communication	M
Western European Studies	D

UNIVERSITY OF NEW MEXICO

American Studies	M,D
Anthropology	M,D
Architecture	M
Art History	M,D
Art/Fine Arts	M
Child and Family Studies	M,D
Clinical Psychology	M,D
Communication—General	M,D
Comparative Literature	M,D
Dance	M
Economics	M,D
English	M,D
French	M,D
Geography	M
German	M,D
Historic Preservation	O
History	M,D
Industrial and Labor Relations	M,D
International Development	M,D
International Economics	M,D
Landscape Architecture	M
Latin American Studies	M,D
Linguistics	M,D
Music	M
Philosophy	M,D
Political Science	M,D
Portuguese	M,D
Psychology—General	M,D
Public Administration	M
Sociology	M,D
Spanish	M,D
Theater	M
Urban and Regional Planning	M
Urban Design	O
Women's Studies	O
Writing	M,D

UNIVERSITY OF NEW ORLEANS

Art/Fine Arts	M
Arts Administration	M
Economics	D
English	M
Film, Television, and Video Production	M
Geography	M
History	M
Music	M
Political Science	M,D
Psychology—General	M,D
Public Administration	M
Romance Languages	M
Sociology	M
Theater	M
Urban and Regional Planning	M
Urban Studies	M,D

UNIVERSITY OF NORTH ALABAMA

Criminal Justice and Criminology	M
English	M
History	M

Homeland Security	M,O
Industrial and Labor Relations	M,O
Industrial and Organizational Psychology	M,O
National Security	M,O
Public Administration	M,O
Social Psychology	M,O
Urban and Regional Planning	M,O

*M—master's degree; P—first professional degree; D—doctorate; O—other advanced degree; *—Close-Up and/or Display*

THE UNIVERSITY OF NORTH CAROLINA AT ASHEVILLE

Liberal Studies	M

THE UNIVERSITY OF NORTH CAROLINA AT CHAPEL HILL

Anthropology	M,D
Archaeology	M,D
Art History	M,D
Art/Fine Arts	M
Classics	M,D
Clinical Psychology	D
Cognitive Sciences	D
Communication— General	D
Developmental Psychology	D
East European and Russian Studies	M
Economics	M,D
English	M,D
Experimental Psychology	D
Folklore	M
French	M,D
Geography	M,D
German	M,D
History	M,D
Italian	M,D
Latin American Studies	M,D,O
Linguistics	M,D
Mass Communication	M,D
Music	M,D
Philosophy	M,D
Political Science	M,D,O
Portuguese	M,D
Psychology—General	D
Public Administration	M
Public Policy	D
Rehabilitation Counseling	M,D
Religion	M,D
Romance Languages	M,D
Russian	M,D
School Psychology	M,D
Slavic Languages	M,D
Social Psychology	D
Sociology	M,D
Spanish	M,D
Theater	M
Urban and Regional Planning	M,D

THE UNIVERSITY OF NORTH CAROLINA AT CHARLOTTE

Architecture	M
Arts Administration	M,D,O
Child Development	M,D
Clinical Psychology	M,D,O
Communication— General	M
Corporate and Organizational Communication	M
Criminal Justice and Criminology	M
Dance	M,D
Economics	M
Emergency Management	M,D,O
English	M,O
Ethics	M,O
Ethnic Studies	M
Gender Studies	M
Geographic Information Systems	M,D
Geography	M,D
Gerontology	M,O
Health Communication	M
Health Psychology	M,D,O
History	M

Industrial and Organizational Psychology	M,D,O
Interdisciplinary Studies	M,O
Latin American Studies	M,O
Liberal Studies	M,O
Media Studies	M
Philosophy	M,O
Political Science	M
Psychology—General	M,D,O
Public Administration	M,D,O
Public Policy	M,D,O
Religion	M
Rhetoric	M
Social Psychology	M,D,O
Social Sciences	M
Sociology	M
Spanish	M
Theater	M,D
Urban and Regional Planning	M,D,O
Urban Design	M
Women's Studies	M,O
Writing	M,O

THE UNIVERSITY OF NORTH CAROLINA AT GREENSBORO

Applied Economics	M
Architecture	M,O
Art/Fine Arts	M
Child and Family Studies	M,D
Classics	M
Clinical Psychology	M,D
Cognitive Sciences	M,D
Communication— General	M
Conflict Resolution and Mediation/Peace Studies	M,O
Counseling Psychology	M,D,O
Criminal Justice and Criminology	M
Dance	M
Developmental Psychology	M,D
Economic Development	M,D,O
Economics	D
English	M,D
Family and Consumer Sciences-General	M,D,O
Film, Television, and Video Production	M
French	M
Gender Studies	M,O
Genetic Counseling	M
Geographic Information Systems	M,D,O
Geography	M,D,O
Gerontology	M,O
Hispanic and Latin American Languages	M,O
Hispanic Studies	M,O
Historic Preservation	M,O
History	M,D,O
Human Development	M,D
Interior Design	M,O
Liberal Studies	M
Marriage and Family Therapy	M,D,O
Media Studies	M
Museum Studies	M,D,O
Music	M,D
Political Science	M,O
Psychology—General	M,D
Public Affairs	M,O
Rhetoric	M,D
School Psychology	M,D,O
Social Psychology	M,D
Sociology	M
Spanish	M,O
Technical Writing	M,D,O
Textile Design	M,D
Theater	M

Women's Studies	M,D,O
Writing	M

THE UNIVERSITY OF NORTH CAROLINA AT PEMBROKE

Public Administration	M

UNIVERSITY OF NORTH CAROLINA SCHOOL OF THE ARTS

Arts Administration	M
Film, Television, and Video Production	M
Music	M
Theater	M

THE UNIVERSITY OF NORTH CAROLINA WILMINGTON

Criminal Justice and Criminology	M
English	M
Gerontology	M
Hispanic Studies	M,O
History	M
Liberal Studies	M
Psychology—General	M
Public Administration	M
Sociology	M
Spanish	M,O
Writing	M

UNIVERSITY OF NORTH DAKOTA

Applied Economics	M
Art/Fine Arts	M
Clinical Psychology	M,D
Communication— General	M,D
Counseling Psychology	M
Criminal Justice and Criminology	D
English	M,D
Experimental Psychology	M,D
Forensic Psychology	M,D
Geography	M
History	M,D
Linguistics	M
Music	M,D
Psychology—General	M,D
Public Administration	M
Sociology	M
Theater	M

UNIVERSITY OF NORTHERN BRITISH COLUMBIA

Disability Studies	M,D,O
Gender Studies	M,D,O
History	M,D,O
Interdisciplinary Studies	M,D,O
International Affairs	M,D,O
Political Science	M,D,O
Psychology—General	M,D,O

UNIVERSITY OF NORTHERN COLORADO

Art/Fine Arts	M
Communication— General	M
Criminal Justice and Criminology	M
English	M
Gerontology	M
History	M
Music	M,D
Psychology—General	M,D
Rehabilitation Counseling	M,D
School Psychology	D,O
Sociology	M
Spanish	M

UNIVERSITY OF NORTHERN IOWA

Art/Fine Arts	M
Communication— General	M
Counseling Psychology	M
Criminal Justice and Criminology	M
English	M
French	M
Gender Studies	M
Geography	M
German	M
History	M
Music	M
Political Science	M
Psychology—General	M
Public History	M
Public Policy	M
School Psychology	M,O
Social Sciences	M
Sociology	M
Spanish	M
Women's Studies	M
Writing	M

UNIVERSITY OF NORTH FLORIDA

Applied Behavior Analysis	M
Counseling Psychology	M
Criminal Justice and Criminology	M
Economics	M
English	M
Ethics	M,O
Gerontology	M,O
History	M
Philosophy	M,O
Psychology—General	M
Public Administration	M,O
Rehabilitation Counseling	M,O
Translation and Interpretation	M
Writing	M

UNIVERSITY OF NORTH TEXAS

Anthropology	M
Applied Arts and Design—General	M
Applied Economics	M
Art History	M,D,O
Art/Fine Arts	M
Child and Family Studies	M,O
Clinical Psychology	M,D
Clothing and Textiles	M
Communication— General	M
Counseling Psychology	M,D
Criminal Justice and Criminology	M
Economics	M
English	M,D
Experimental Psychology	M,D
Film, Television, and Video Production	M
French	M
Geography	M
Gerontology	M,D,O
Health Psychology	M,D
History	M,D
Human Development	M,O
Industrial and Labor Relations	M
Interdisciplinary Studies	M
Journalism	M,O
Museum Studies	M,D,O
Music	M,D
Philosophy	M,D
Political Science	M,D

Psychology—General	M,D
Public Administration	M,D
Rehabilitation Counseling	M
Religion	M,D
School Psychology	M
Sociology	M,D
Spanish	M
Writing	M,D

UNIVERSITY OF NORTH TEXAS HEALTH SCIENCE CENTER AT FORT WORTH

Forensic Sciences	M,D

UNIVERSITY OF NOTRE DAME

Applied Arts and Design—General	M
Architecture	M
Art History	M
Art/Fine Arts	M
Cognitive Sciences	D
Comparative Literature	D
Conflict Resolution and Mediation/Peace Studies	M,D
Counseling Psychology	D
Developmental Psychology	D
Economics	M,D
English	M,D
French	M
Graphic Design	M
History of Science and Technology	M,D
History	M,D
Industrial Design	M
Italian	M
Latin American Studies	M
Medieval and Renaissance Studies	M,D
Philosophy	D
Photography	M
Political Science	D
Psychology—General	D
Religion	M
Romance Languages	M
Sociology	D
Spanish	M
Theology	P,M,D
Writing	M

UNIVERSITY OF OKLAHOMA

Addictions/Substance Abuse Counseling	M,O
American Indian/Native American Studies	M
Anthropology	M,D
Applied Arts and Design—General	M
Applied Economics	M,D
Architecture	M
Art History	M,D
Art/Fine Arts	M
Child and Family Studies	M,O
Communication—General	M,D
Counseling Psychology	D
Dance	M
Economics	M,D
English	M,D
Film, Television, and Video Production	M
French	M,D
Gender Studies	O
Geography	M,D
German	M
History of Science and Technology	M,D
History	M,D

Industrial and Organizational Psychology	M,D
Interdisciplinary Studies	M,D
International Affairs	M,O
Journalism	M
Landscape Architecture	M
Liberal Studies	M
Mass Communication	M
Museum Studies	M
Music	M,D
Philosophy	M,D
Photography	M
Political Science	M,D
Psychology—General	M,D
Public Administration	M
Social Psychology	M
Sociology	M,D
Spanish	M,D
Theater	M
Urban and Regional Planning	M
Women's Studies	O
Writing	M,D

UNIVERSITY OF OKLAHOMA HEALTH SCIENCES CENTER

Genetic Counseling	M

UNIVERSITY OF OREGON

Anthropology	M,D
Architecture	M
Art History	M,D
Art/Fine Arts	M
Arts Administration	M
Asian Languages	M,D
Asian Studies	M
Chinese	M,D
Classics	M
Clinical Psychology	D
Cognitive Sciences	M,D
Communication—General	M,D
Comparative Literature	M,D
Dance	M
Developmental Psychology	M,D
Economics	M,D
English	M,D
Folklore	M
French	M
Geography	M,D
German	M,D
Historic Preservation	M
History	M,D
Interdisciplinary Studies	M
Interior Design	M
International Affairs	M
Italian	M
Japanese	M,D
Journalism	M,D
Landscape Architecture	M
Linguistics	M,D
Media Studies	M
Music	M,D
Philosophy	M,D
Political Science	M,D
Psychology—General	M,D
Public Policy	M
Romance Languages	M,D
Russian	M
Social Psychology	M,D
Sociology	M,D
Spanish	M
Theater	M,D
Urban and Regional Planning	M
Writing	M

UNIVERSITY OF OTTAWA

Anthropology	M
Canadian Studies	D

Classics	M,D
Communication—General	M
Criminal Justice and Criminology	M,D
Economics	M,D
English	M,D
French	M,D
Geography	M,D
History	M,D
Interdisciplinary Studies	D,O
International Development	M
Linguistics	M,D
Music	M,O
Philosophy	M,D
Political Science	M,D
Psychology—General	D
Public Administration	D,O
Religion	M,D
Sociology	M
Spanish	M,D
Theater	M
Translation and Interpretation	M,D
Women's Studies	M

UNIVERSITY OF PENNSYLVANIA

African Studies	M,D
Anthropology	M,D
Applied Economics	D
Applied Psychology	M,D
Archaeology	M,D
Architecture	M,D,O
Art History	M,D
Art/Fine Arts	M
Asian Studies	M,D
Classics	M,D
Communication—General	D
Comparative Literature	M,D
Computer Art and Design	M
Counseling Psychology	M,D
Criminal Justice and Criminology	M,D
Demography and Population Studies	M,D
Economics	M,D
English	M,D
Ethics	M,D
French	M,D
German	M,D
Historic Preservation	M,O
History of Science and Technology	M,D
History	M,D
Human Development	M,D
International Affairs	M
Italian	M,D
Landscape Architecture	M,O
Liberal Studies	M
Linguistics	M,D
Music	M,D
Near and Middle Eastern Studies	M,D
Philosophy	M,D
Political Science	M,D
Psychology—General	D
Public Administration	M
Public Policy	M,D
Religion	D
Romance Languages	M,D
Sociology	M,D
Spanish	M,D
Urban and Regional Planning	M,D,O
Urban Design	D
Writing	M,D

UNIVERSITY OF PHILOSOPHICAL RESEARCH

Psychology—General	M
Theology	M

UNIVERSITY OF PHOENIX

Clinical Psychology	M
Counseling Psychology	M
Criminal Justice and Criminology	M
Gerontology	M
Industrial and Organizational Psychology	D,O
Psychology—General	M
Public Administration	M
Social Psychology	M

UNIVERSITY OF PHOENIX– ATLANTA CAMPUS

Public Administration	M

UNIVERSITY OF PHOENIX– AUGUSTA CAMPUS

Criminal Justice and Criminology	M
Public Administration	M

UNIVERSITY OF PHOENIX– AUSTIN CAMPUS

Criminal Justice and Criminology	M
Public Administration	M

UNIVERSITY OF PHOENIX– BIRMINGHAM CAMPUS

Criminal Justice and Criminology	M
Gerontology	M
Psychology—General	M
Public Administration	M

UNIVERSITY OF PHOENIX– CENTRAL FLORIDA CAMPUS

Public Administration	M

UNIVERSITY OF PHOENIX– CENTRAL VALLEY CAMPUS

Gerontology	M
Marriage and Family Therapy	M
Public Administration	M

UNIVERSITY OF PHOENIX– CHARLOTTE CAMPUS

Gerontology	M

UNIVERSITY OF PHOENIX– CHATTANOOGA CAMPUS

Gerontology	M
Industrial and Organizational Psychology	M,D
Psychology—General	M,D
Public Administration	M

UNIVERSITY OF PHOENIX– CHEYENNE CAMPUS

Criminal Justice and Criminology	M
Public Administration	M

UNIVERSITY OF PHOENIX– CINCINNATI CAMPUS

Psychology—General	M
Public Administration	M

UNIVERSITY OF PHOENIX– CLEVELAND CAMPUS

Public Administration	M

*M—master's degree; P—first professional degree; D—doctorate; O—other advanced degree; *—Close-Up and / or Display*

UNIVERSITY OF PHOENIX–COLUMBUS GEORGIA CAMPUS

Public Administration	M

UNIVERSITY OF PHOENIX–COLUMBUS OHIO CAMPUS

Public Administration	M

UNIVERSITY OF PHOENIX–DALLAS CAMPUS

Criminal Justice and Criminology	M
Public Administration	M

UNIVERSITY OF PHOENIX–DENVER CAMPUS

Public Administration	M
School Psychology	M

UNIVERSITY OF PHOENIX–DES MOINES CAMPUS

Criminal Justice and Criminology	M
Gerontology	M,D
Public Administration	M

UNIVERSITY OF PHOENIX–EASTERN WASHINGTON CAMPUS

Public Administration	M

UNIVERSITY OF PHOENIX–HARRISBURG CAMPUS

Criminal Justice and Criminology	M
Public Administration	M

UNIVERSITY OF PHOENIX–HAWAII CAMPUS

Gerontology	M
Public Administration	M

UNIVERSITY OF PHOENIX–HOUSTON CAMPUS

Public Administration	M

UNIVERSITY OF PHOENIX–IDAHO CAMPUS

Public Administration	M

UNIVERSITY OF PHOENIX–INDIANAPOLIS CAMPUS

Public Administration	M

UNIVERSITY OF PHOENIX–JERSEY CITY CAMPUS

Criminal Justice and Criminology	M
Psychology—General	M
Public Administration	M

UNIVERSITY OF PHOENIX–KANSAS CITY CAMPUS

Criminal Justice and Criminology	M
Public Administration	M

UNIVERSITY OF PHOENIX–LAS VEGAS CAMPUS

Counseling Psychology	M
Marriage and Family Therapy	M
Public Administration	M
School Psychology	M

UNIVERSITY OF PHOENIX–LOUISIANA CAMPUS

Public Administration	M

UNIVERSITY OF PHOENIX–LOUISVILLE CAMPUS

Gerontology	M

UNIVERSITY OF PHOENIX–MADISON CAMPUS

Internet and Interactive Multimedia	M
Public Administration	M

UNIVERSITY OF PHOENIX–MARYLAND CAMPUS

Public Administration	M

UNIVERSITY OF PHOENIX–MEMPHIS CAMPUS

Criminal Justice and Criminology	M
Public Administration	M

UNIVERSITY OF PHOENIX–MILWAUKEE CAMPUS

Criminal Justice and Criminology	M
Gerontology	M,D
Industrial and Organizational Psychology	M,D
Psychology—General	M,D
Public Administration	M,D

UNIVERSITY OF PHOENIX–MINNEAPOLIS/ST. LOUIS PARK CAMPUS

Public Administration	M
Social Psychology	M

UNIVERSITY OF PHOENIX–NORTHERN NEVADA CAMPUS

Criminal Justice and Criminology	M
Public Administration	M

UNIVERSITY OF PHOENIX–NORTHERN VIRGINIA CAMPUS

Criminal Justice and Criminology	M
Public Administration	M

UNIVERSITY OF PHOENIX–NORTH FLORIDA CAMPUS

Public Administration	M

UNIVERSITY OF PHOENIX–NORTHWEST ARKANSAS CAMPUS

Criminal Justice and Criminology	M
Public Administration	M

UNIVERSITY OF PHOENIX–OMAHA CAMPUS

Criminal Justice and Criminology	M
Public Administration	M

UNIVERSITY OF PHOENIX–OREGON CAMPUS

Public Administration	M

UNIVERSITY OF PHOENIX–PHILADELPHIA CAMPUS

Psychology—General	M
Public Administration	M

UNIVERSITY OF PHOENIX–PHOENIX CAMPUS

Counseling Psychology	M
Psychology—General	M
Social Psychology	M

UNIVERSITY OF PHOENIX–PITTSBURGH CAMPUS

Public Administration	M

UNIVERSITY OF PHOENIX–PUERTO RICO CAMPUS

Counseling Psychology	M
Marriage and Family Therapy	M
School Psychology	M

UNIVERSITY OF PHOENIX–RALEIGH CAMPUS

Gerontology	M,D

UNIVERSITY OF PHOENIX–RICHMOND CAMPUS

Public Administration	M

UNIVERSITY OF PHOENIX–SACRAMENTO VALLEY CAMPUS

Public Administration	M

UNIVERSITY OF PHOENIX–ST. LOUIS CAMPUS

Criminal Justice and Criminology	M
Public Administration	M

UNIVERSITY OF PHOENIX–SAN ANTONIO CAMPUS

Criminal Justice and Criminology	M
Public Administration	M

UNIVERSITY OF PHOENIX–SAN DIEGO CAMPUS

Public Administration	M

UNIVERSITY OF PHOENIX–SAVANNAH CAMPUS

Criminal Justice and Criminology	M
Public Administration	M

UNIVERSITY OF PHOENIX–SOUTHERN ARIZONA CAMPUS

Psychology—General	M

UNIVERSITY OF PHOENIX–SOUTHERN CALIFORNIA CAMPUS

Counseling Psychology	M
Criminal Justice and Criminology	M
Marriage and Family Therapy	M
Psychology—General	M
School Psychology	M
Social Psychology	M

UNIVERSITY OF PHOENIX–SOUTHERN COLORADO CAMPUS

Gerontology	M
Public Administration	M
School Psychology	M,O

UNIVERSITY OF PHOENIX–SOUTH FLORIDA CAMPUS

Public Administration	M

UNIVERSITY OF PHOENIX–SPRINGFIELD CAMPUS

Criminal Justice and Criminology	M
Public Administration	M

UNIVERSITY OF PHOENIX–UTAH CAMPUS

School Psychology	M

UNIVERSITY OF PHOENIX–WASHINGTON CAMPUS

Criminal Justice and Criminology	M

UNIVERSITY OF PHOENIX–WASHINGTON D.C. CAMPUS

Criminal Justice and Criminology	M
Gerontology	M,D
Industrial and Organizational Psychology	M,D
Psychology—General	M,D
Public Administration	M,D

UNIVERSITY OF PHOENIX–WEST FLORIDA CAMPUS

Public Administration	M

UNIVERSITY OF PITTSBURGH

African Studies	O
Anthropology	M,D
Applied Psychology	M,D
Architectural History	M,D
Art History	M,D
Asian Studies	M,O
Classics	M,D
Cognitive Sciences	D
Communication—General	M,D
Criminal Justice and Criminology	M,D
Cultural Studies	M,D,O
Developmental Psychology	M,D
East European and Russian Studies	O
Economics	M,D
English	M,D
Film, Television, and Video Theory and Criticism	O
French	M,D
Genetic Counseling	M,D,O
Geographic Information Systems	M,D
German	M,D
Gerontology	M,D,O
Hispanic and Latin American Languages	M,D
History of Science and Technology	M,D
History	M,D
Interdisciplinary Studies	D
International Affairs	M,D,O
International Development	M,O
Italian	M
Latin American Studies	O
Linguistics	M,D
Medieval and Renaissance Studies	O
Military and Defense Studies	M
Music	M,D
National Security	M
Philosophy	M,D
Political Science	M,D
Psychology—General	M,D
Public Administration	M,D,O
Public Policy	M,D,O
Rehabilitation Counseling	M
Religion	M,D
Slavic Languages	M,D
Sociology	M,D
Spanish	M,D
Theater	M,D

Urban and Regional
  Planning — M,O
Western European
  Studies — O
Women's Studies — O
Writing — M,D

UNIVERSITY OF PORTLAND

Communication—
  General — M
Corporate and
  Organizational
  Communication — M
Pastoral Ministry and
  Counseling — M
Theater — M

UNIVERSITY OF PRINCE EDWARD ISLAND

Geography — M

UNIVERSITY OF PUERTO RICO, MAYAGÜEZ CAMPUS

Agricultural Economics
  and Agribusiness — M
English — M
Hispanic Studies — M

UNIVERSITY OF PUERTO RICO, MEDICAL SCIENCES CAMPUS

Demography and
  Population Studies — M
Gerontology — M,O

UNIVERSITY OF PUERTO RICO, RÍO PIEDRAS

Architecture — M
Clinical Psychology — M,D
Communication—
  General — M
Comparative Literature — M
Economic Development — M
Economics — M
English — M,D
Family and Consumer
  Sciences-General — M
Hispanic Studies — M,D
History — M,D
Industrial and
  Organizational
  Psychology — M,D
Journalism — M
Linguistics — M,D
Mass Communication — M
Philosophy — M
Psychology—General — M,D
Public Administration — M
Public Policy — M
Rehabilitation
  Counseling — M
Social Psychology — M,D
Sociology — M
Translation and
  Interpretation — M,O
Urban and Regional
  Planning — M

UNIVERSITY OF PUGET SOUND

Counseling Psychology — M
Pastoral Ministry and
  Counseling — M

UNIVERSITY OF REDLANDS

Geographic Information
  Systems — M
Music — M

UNIVERSITY OF REGINA

Anthropology — M
Applied Psychology — M,D
Art/Fine Arts — M
Canadian Studies — M,D

Clinical Psychology — M,D
Criminal Justice and
  Criminology — M
Economics — M,D,O
English — M
Experimental
  Psychology — M,D
French — M
Geography — M
Gerontology — M
History — M
Linguistics — M
Media Studies — M
Music — M
Philosophy — M
Political Science — M
Psychology—General — M,D
Public Administration — M,D,O
Public Policy — M,D,O
Religion — M
Social Sciences — M
Sociology — M
Women's Studies — M

UNIVERSITY OF RHODE ISLAND

Child and Family
  Studies — M
Clinical Psychology — M,D
Clothing and Textiles — M
Communication—
  General — M
Counseling Psychology — M
Economics — M,D
English — M,D
Forensic Sciences — M,D,O
Gerontology — M,D
History — M
Industrial and Labor
  Relations — M
International Affairs — M
Music — M
Political Science — M
Psychology—General — M,D
Public Administration — M
Public Policy — M
School Psychology — M,D
Spanish — M
Sport Psychology — M

UNIVERSITY OF ROCHESTER

Art History — M,D
Art/Fine Arts — M,D
Clinical Psychology — M
Cognitive Sciences — M,D
Comparative Literature — M
Cultural Studies — M
Developmental
  Psychology — M
Economics — M,D
Emergency
  Management — M,D,O
English — M
French — M
German — M
History — M,D
Human Development — M
Linguistics — M
Marriage and Family
  Therapy — M
Music — M
Philosophy — M,D
Political Science — M,D
Psychology—General — M
Romance Languages — M
Social Psychology — M,D
Spanish — M
Translation and
  Interpretation — M

UNIVERSITY OF SAINT FRANCIS (IN)

Art/Fine Arts — M

Counseling Psychology — M
Pastoral Ministry and
  Counseling — M
Psychology—General — M

UNIVERSITY OF SAINT MARY

Psychology—General — M

UNIVERSITY OF SAINT MARY OF THE LAKE–MUNDELEIN SEMINARY

Theology — P,M,D

UNIVERSITY OF ST. MICHAEL'S COLLEGE

Jewish Studies — P,M,D,O
Pastoral Ministry and
  Counseling — P,M,D,O
Theology — P,M,D,O

UNIVERSITY OF ST. THOMAS (MN)

Art History — M
Corporate and
  Organizational
  Communication — M
Counseling Psychology — M,D,O
English — M
Human Development — M,D,O
Marriage and Family
  Therapy — M,D,O
Music — M
Pastoral Ministry and
  Counseling — P,M
Psychology—General — M,D,O
Religion — M
Theology — P,M

UNIVERSITY OF ST. THOMAS (TX)

Liberal Studies — M
Philosophy — M,D
Religion — M
Theology — P,M

UNIVERSITY OF SAN DIEGO

Conflict Resolution and
  Mediation/Peace
  Studies — M
Counseling Psychology — M
History — M
International Affairs — M
Marriage and Family
  Therapy — M
Theater — M

UNIVERSITY OF SAN FRANCISCO

Asian Studies — M
Counseling Psychology — M,D
Economics — M
International Affairs — M
International
  Development — M
Internet and Interactive
  Multimedia — M
Marriage and Family
  Therapy — M,D
Pacific Area/Pacific Rim
  Studies — M
Public Administration — M
Public Affairs — M
Writing — M

UNIVERSITY OF SASKATCHEWAN

Agricultural Economics
  and Agribusiness — M,D,O
Anthropology — M
Archaeology — M,D
Art/Fine Arts — M

Canadian Studies — M,D
East European and
  Russian Studies — M
Economics — M,O
English — M,D
French — M
Gender Studies — M,D
Geography — M,D
German — M
History — M,D
Industrial and Labor
  Relations — M
Music — M
Philosophy — M
Political Science — M
Psychology—General — M,D
Public Affairs — M,D
Public Policy — M,D
Religion — M
Sociology — M,D
Theater — M
Women's Studies — M,D

THE UNIVERSITY OF SCRANTON

Counseling Psychology — M,O
History — M
Rehabilitation
  Counseling — M
Social Psychology — M
Theology — M

UNIVERSITY OF SOUTH AFRICA

Anthropology — M,D
Archaeology — M,D
Art History — M,D
Classics — M,D
Clinical Psychology — M,D
Communication—
  General — M,D
Counseling Psychology — M,D
Criminal Justice and
  Criminology — M,D
Economics — M,D
English — M,D
Ethics — M,D
Family and Consumer
  Sciences-General — M,D
French — M,D
Geography — M,D
German — M,D
History — M,D
Human Development — M,D
Industrial and
  Organizational
  Psychology — M,D
Italian — M,D
Linguistics — M,D
Missions and Missiology — M,D
Music — M,D
Near and Middle
  Eastern Languages — M,D
Near and Middle
  Eastern Studies — M,D
Pastoral Ministry and
  Counseling — M,D
Philosophy — M,D
Political Science — M,D
Portuguese — M,D
Psychology—General — M,D
Public Administration — M,D
Religion — M,D
Romance Languages — M,D
Russian — M,D
Sociology — M,D
Spanish — M,D
Theology — M,D

UNIVERSITY OF SOUTH ALABAMA

Clinical Psychology — M,D

---

*M—master's degree; P—first professional degree; D—doctorate; O—other advanced degree; *—Close-Up and/or Display*

Communication—	
General	M
Counseling Psychology	M,D
English	M
Gerontology	O
History	M
Psychology—General	M,D
Public Administration	M
Rehabilitation	
Counseling	M,D
School Psychology	M,D
Sociology	M

UNIVERSITY OF SOUTH CAROLINA

Anthropology	M,D
Art History	M
Art/Fine Arts	M
Clinical Psychology	M,D
Comparative Literature	M,D
Consumer Economics	M
Criminal Justice and	
Criminology	M,D
Economics	M,D
English	M,D
Experimental	
Psychology	M,D
French	M,D
Genetic Counseling	M
Geography	M,D
German	M,D
Gerontology	O
Historic Preservation	M,O
History	M,D,O
International Affairs	M,D
Journalism	M,D
Linguistics	M,D,O
Media Studies	M
Museum Studies	M,O
Music	M,D,O
Philosophy	M,D
Political Science	M,D
Psychology—General	M,D
Public Administration	M
Public History	M,O
Rehabilitation	
Counseling	M,O
Religion	M
School Psychology	D
Social Psychology	M,D
Sociology	M,D
Spanish	M,D
Speech and	
Interpersonal	
Communication	M,D
Theater	M,D
Women's Studies	O
Writing	M,D

UNIVERSITY OF SOUTH CAROLINA AIKEN

Applied Psychology	M
Clinical Psychology	M

THE UNIVERSITY OF SOUTH DAKOTA

Art/Fine Arts	M
Clinical Psychology	M,D
Communication—	
General	M
English	M,D
History	M
Interdisciplinary Studies	M
Music	M
Political Science	M,D
Psychology—General	M,D
Public Administration	M,D
Theater	M

UNIVERSITY OF SOUTHERN CALIFORNIA

American Studies	D
Architecture	M,D

Art History	M,D,O
Art/Fine Arts	M,D,O
Arts Administration	M
Asian Languages	M,D
Asian Studies	M,D
Broadcast Journalism	M
Child and Family	
Studies	M,D
Classics	M,D
Clinical Psychology	M,D
Cognitive Sciences	M,D
Communication—	
General	M,D*
Comparative Literature	D
Computer Art and	
Design	M
Corporate and	
Organizational	
Communication	M,D
Cultural Studies	D
Developmental	
Psychology	M,D
Economic Development	M,D
Economics	M,D
English	M,D
Film, Television, and	
Video Production	M
Film, Television, and	
Video Theory and	
Criticism	M,D
Geographic Information	
Systems	M,O
Geography	M,O
Gerontology	M,D,O
Health Communication	M,D
History	M,D
Homeland Security	M,O
International Affairs	M,D
Internet and Interactive	
Multimedia	M,D,O
Journalism	M
Latin American Studies	D
Linguistics	M,D
Marriage and Family	
Therapy	M
Mass Communication	M,D
Media Studies	M,D
Music	M,D,O
Philosophy	M,D
Photography	M
Political Science	M,D
Psychology—General	M,D
Public Administration	M,O
Public Policy	M,D,O
Slavic Languages	M,D
Social Psychology	M,D
Sociology	D
Spanish	D
Speech and	
Interpersonal	
Communication	M,D
Sustainable	
Development	M,D,O
Theater	M
Urban and Regional	
Planning	M,D,O
Writing	M,D

UNIVERSITY OF SOUTHERN INDIANA

Communication—	
General	M
Liberal Studies	M
Public Administration	M

UNIVERSITY OF SOUTHERN MAINE

American Studies	M
Applied Behavior	
Analysis	M,O
Counseling Psychology	M,O
Music	M
Public Policy	M,D,O

Rehabilitation	
Counseling	M,O
School Psychology	M,D
Urban and Regional	
Planning	M,O
Writing	M

UNIVERSITY OF SOUTHERN MISSISSIPPI

Anthropology	M
Child and Family	
Studies	M
Clinical Psychology	M,D
Counseling Psychology	M,D
Criminal Justice and	
Criminology	M,D
Economic Development	M,D
Economics	M,D
English	M,D
Experimental	
Psychology	M,D
Forensic Sciences	M,D
Geography	M,D
History	M,D
International Affairs	M,D
International	
Development	M,D
Marriage and Family	
Therapy	M
Mass Communication	M,D
Music	M,D
Political Science	M,D
Psychology—General	M,D
School Psychology	M,D
Speech and	
Interpersonal	
Communication	M,D
Theater	M
Writing	M,D

UNIVERSITY OF SOUTH FLORIDA

African Studies	M
American Studies	M
Anthropology	M,D
Applied Behavior	
Analysis	M
Architecture	M
Art History	M
Art/Fine Arts	M
Classics	M
Clinical Psychology	D
Cognitive Sciences	D
Communication—	
General	M,D
Criminal Justice and	
Criminology	M,D
Economics	M,D
English	M,D
Film, Television, and	
Video Theory and	
Criticism	M
French	M
Geography	M,D
Gerontology	M,D
History	M,D
Humanities	M
Industrial and	
Organizational	
Psychology	D
Interdisciplinary Studies	M,D
International Affairs	M,D
Latin American Studies	M,D
Linguistics	M
Mass Communication	M
Music	M,D
Philosophy	M,D
Political Science	M,D
Psychology—General	D
Public Administration	M,D
Rehabilitation	
Counseling	M
Religion	M
School Psychology	M,D,O

Sociology	M,D
Spanish	M
Women's Studies	M

THE UNIVERSITY OF TENNESSEE

Anthropology	M,D
Applied Psychology	M,D
Archaeology	M,D
Architecture	M
Art/Fine Arts	M
Child and Family	
Studies	M,D
Clinical Psychology	M,D
Clothing and Textiles	M,D
Communication—	
General	M,D
Consumer Economics	M,D
Counseling Psychology	M,D
Criminal Justice and	
Criminology	M,D
Cultural Anthropology	M,D
Economics	M,D
English	M,D
Experimental	
Psychology	M,D
Family and Consumer	
Sciences-General	D
French	M,D
Geography	M,D
German	M,D
Gerontology	M
Graphic Design	M
History	M,D
Industrial and	
Organizational	
Psychology	D
Italian	D
Journalism	M,D
Landscape Architecture	M
Linguistics	D
Media Studies	M,D
Music	M
Philosophy	M,D
Photography	M
Political Science	M,D
Portuguese	D
Psychology—General	M,D
Public Administration	M
Rehabilitation	
Counseling	M,D
Religion	M,D
Russian	D
School Psychology	M,D,O
Sociology	M,D
Spanish	M,D
Speech and	
Interpersonal	
Communication	M,D
Theater	M

THE UNIVERSITY OF TENNESSEE AT CHATTANOOGA

Criminal Justice and	
Criminology	M
English	M,O
Experimental	
Psychology	M
Industrial and	
Organizational	
Psychology	M
Music	M
Psychology—General	M
Public Administration	M,O
Rhetoric	M,O
School Psychology	O
Social Psychology	M
Writing	M,O

THE UNIVERSITY OF TENNESSEE AT MARTIN

Child and Family	
Studies	M

Child Development — M
Family and Consumer
  Sciences-General — M
Social Psychology — M

THE UNIVERSITY OF TEXAS AT ARLINGTON

Anthropology — M
Architecture — M
Art/Fine Arts — M
Communication—
  General — M
Criminal Justice and
  Criminology — M
Economics — M
English — M,D
Experimental
  Psychology — M,D
Film, Television, and
  Video Production — M
French — M
Health Psychology — M,D
History — M,D
Industrial and
  Organizational
  Psychology — M,D
Interdisciplinary Studies — M
Landscape Architecture — M
Linguistics — M,D
Music — M
Political Science — M
Psychology—General — M,D
Public Administration — M
Public Affairs — D
Sociology — M
Spanish — M
Urban and Regional
  Planning — M

THE UNIVERSITY OF TEXAS AT AUSTIN

African Studies — M,D
American Studies — M,D
Anthropology — M,D
Applied Arts and
  Design—General — M
Archaeology — M,D
Architectural History — M,D
Architecture — M,D
Art History — M,D
Art/Fine Arts — M
Asian Languages — M,D
Asian Studies — M,D
Child and Family
  Studies — M,D
Child Development — M,D
Classics — M,D
Cognitive Sciences — M,D
Communication—
  General — M,D
Comparative Literature — M,D
Counseling Psychology — M,D
Dance — M,D
East European and
  Russian Studies — M
Economics — M,D
English — M,D
Family and Consumer
  Sciences-General — M,D
Film, Television, and
  Video Production — M,D
Folklore — M,D
French — M,D
Geography — M,D
German — M,D
Hispanic and Latin
  American Languages — M,D
Hispanic Studies — M
Historic Preservation — M,D
History — M,D
Human Development — M,D
Italian — M,D

Journalism — M,D
Landscape Architecture — M,D
Latin American Studies — M,D
Linguistics — M,D
Media Studies — M,D
Mineral Economics — M
Music — M,D
Near and Middle
  Eastern Languages — M,D
Near and Middle
  Eastern Studies — M,D
Philosophy — D
Political Science — D
Portuguese — M,D
Psychology—General — D
Public Affairs — M,D
Public History — M,D
Public Policy — M,D
Romance Languages — M,D
School Psychology — M,D
Slavic Languages — M,D
Sociology — M,D
Spanish — M,D
Sport Psychology — M,D
Theater — M,D
Urban and Regional
  Planning — M,D
Urban Design — M,D
Writing — M,D

THE UNIVERSITY OF TEXAS AT BROWNSVILLE

English — M
History — M
Interdisciplinary Studies — M
Political Science — M
Psychology—General — M
Public Administration — M
Public Policy — M
Spanish — M

THE UNIVERSITY OF TEXAS AT DALLAS

Child and Family
  Studies — M,D
Cognitive Sciences — M,D
Communication—
  General — M,D
Comparative Literature — M,D
Criminal Justice and
  Criminology — M,D
Economics — M,D*
English — M,D
Geographic Information
  Systems — M,D
History — M,D
Humanities — M,D
Interdisciplinary Studies — M
Internet and Interactive
  Multimedia — M,D
Latin American Studies — M,D
Philosophy — M,D
Political Science — M,D
Psychology—General — M,D
Public Affairs — M,D
Public Policy — M,D
Sociology — M

THE UNIVERSITY OF TEXAS AT EL PASO

Art/Fine Arts — M
Clinical Psychology — M,D
Communication—
  General — M
Economics — M
English — M,D,O
Experimental
  Psychology — M,D
Gender Studies — O
History — M,D
Homeland Security — M,O
Interdisciplinary Studies — M

Latin American Studies — M,O
Liberal Studies — M
Linguistics — M,O
Military and Defense
  Studies — M,O
Music — M
National Security — M,O
Philosophy — M
Political Science — M
Psychology—General — M,D
Public Administration — M,O
Public Policy — M,O
Rehabilitation
  Counseling — M
Rhetoric — M,D,O
Sociology — M,O
Spanish — M,O
Women's Studies — O
Writing — M,D,O

THE UNIVERSITY OF TEXAS AT SAN ANTONIO

Anthropology — M,D
Architecture — M
Art History — M
Art/Fine Arts — M
Communication—
  General — M
Criminal Justice and
  Criminology — M
Cultural Studies — M,D
Demography and
  Population Studies — D
Economics — M
English — M,D
History — M
Interdisciplinary Studies — M,D
Music — M,O
Political Science — M
Psychology—General — M
Public Administration — M
School Psychology — M*
Sociology — M
Spanish — M

THE UNIVERSITY OF TEXAS AT TYLER

Art History — M
Art/Fine Arts — M
Clinical Psychology — M
Communication—
  General — M
Counseling Psychology — M
Criminal Justice and
  Criminology — M
English — M
History — M
Interdisciplinary Studies — M
Marriage and Family
  Therapy — M
Political Science — M
Psychology—General — M
Public Administration — M
School Psychology — M
Social Sciences — M
Sociology — M

THE UNIVERSITY OF TEXAS HEALTH SCIENCE CENTER AT HOUSTON

Genetic Counseling — M

THE UNIVERSITY OF TEXAS MEDICAL BRANCH

Humanities — M,D

THE UNIVERSITY OF TEXAS OF THE PERMIAN BASIN

Applied Psychology — M
Clinical Psychology — M
Criminal Justice and
  Criminology — M

English — M
Experimental
  Psychology — M
History — M
Political Science — M
Psychology—General — M
Spanish — M

THE UNIVERSITY OF TEXAS–PAN AMERICAN

Art/Fine Arts — M
Clinical Psychology — M
Communication—
  General — M
Criminal Justice and
  Criminology — M
Economics — D
English — M
Experimental
  Psychology — M
History — M
Interdisciplinary Studies — M
Music — M
Psychology—General — M
Public Administration — M
Rehabilitation
  Counseling — M,D
School Psychology — M
Sociology — M
Spanish — M
Theater — M

THE UNIVERSITY OF TEXAS SOUTHWESTERN MEDICAL CENTER AT DALLAS

Clinical Psychology — D
Medical Illustration — M
Rehabilitation
  Counseling — M

THE UNIVERSITY OF THE ARTS

Art/Fine Arts — M*
Industrial Design — M
Museum Studies — M
Music — M

UNIVERSITY OF THE CUMBERLANDS

Clinical Psychology — D
Counseling Psychology — M
Religion — M
Theater — M,D,O

UNIVERSITY OF THE DISTRICT OF COLUMBIA

Clinical Psychology — M
Counseling Psychology — M
English — M
Public Administration — M

UNIVERSITY OF THE FRASER VALLEY

Criminal Justice and
  Criminology — M

UNIVERSITY OF THE INCARNATE WORD

Communication—
  General — M,O
Interdisciplinary Studies — M
Religion — M

UNIVERSITY OF THE PACIFIC

Communication—
  General — M
Criminal Justice and
  Criminology — P,M,D
International Affairs — P,M,D
Music — M
Psychology—General — M
Public Policy — P,M,D

M—master's degree; P—first professional degree; D—doctorate; O—other advanced degree; *—Close-Up and/or Display

School Psychology — M,D,O
Therapies—Dance,
  Drama, and Music — M

UNIVERSITY OF THE ROCKIES

Psychology—General — M,D

UNIVERSITY OF THE SACRED HEART

Broadcast Journalism — M,O
Communication—
  General — M,O
Conflict Resolution and
  Mediation/Peace
  Studies — M
Cultural Studies — M
Film, Television, and
  Video Production — M,O
Internet and Interactive
  Multimedia — M,O
Writing — M,O

UNIVERSITY OF THE SCIENCES IN PHILADELPHIA

Health Psychology — M
Technical Writing — M,O

UNIVERSITY OF THE SOUTHWEST

Counseling Psychology — M

UNIVERSITY OF THE VIRGIN ISLANDS

Public Administration — M

UNIVERSITY OF THE WEST

Psychology—General — M
Religion — M,D

THE UNIVERSITY OF TOLEDO

Clinical Psychology — M,D
Communication—
  General — O
Criminal Justice and
  Criminology — M,O
Economics — M,D,O
English — M,O
Experimental
  Psychology — M,D
French — M
Geographic Information
  Systems — M,D,O
Geography — M,D,O
German — M
Gerontology — M,O
History — M,D
Homeland Security — M,O
Liberal Studies — M
Music — M
Philosophy — M
Political Science — M,O
Psychology—General — M,D
Public Administration — M,O
School Psychology — M,D,O
Social Psychology — M,D,O
Sociology — M
Spanish — M
Urban and Regional
  Planning — M,D,O
Writing — M,O

UNIVERSITY OF TORONTO

Anthropology — M,D
Architecture — M
Art History — M,D
Art/Fine Arts — M,D
Asian Studies — M,D
Classics — M,D
Comparative Literature — M,D
Criminal Justice and
  Criminology — M,D
East European and
  Russian Studies — M

Economics — M,D
English — M,D
Film, Television, and
  Video Theory and
  Criticism — M
French — M,D
Gender Studies — M
Genetic Counseling — M,D
Geography — M,D
German — M,D
History of Science and
  Technology — M,D
History — M,D
Industrial and Labor
  Relations — M,D
International Affairs — M
Italian — M,D
Linguistics — M,D
Medieval and
  Renaissance Studies — M,D
Museum Studies — M,D
Music — M,D
Near and Middle
  Eastern Studies — M,D
Philosophy — M,D
Political Science — M,D
Portuguese — M,D
Psychology—General — M,D
Religion — M,D
Slavic Languages — M,D
Sociology — M,D
Spanish — M,D
Theater — M,D
Urban and Regional
  Planning — M,D
Urban Design — M,D
Women's Studies — M

UNIVERSITY OF TRINITY COLLEGE

Music — P,M,D,O
Pastoral Ministry and
  Counseling — P,M,D,O
Theology — P,M,D,O

UNIVERSITY OF TULSA

American Indian/Native
  American Studies — M
Anthropology — M
Art/Fine Arts — M
Clinical Psychology — M,D
English — M,D
History — M
Industrial and
  Organizational
  Psychology — M,D
Museum Studies — M
Psychology—General — M,D
Public Policy — P,M,O
Theater — M

UNIVERSITY OF UTAH

American Studies — M,D
Anthropology — M,D
Architecture — M
Art History — M
Art/Fine Arts — M
Asian Studies — M
Child and Family
  Studies — M
Clinical Psychology — D
Communication—
  General — M,D
Comparative Literature — M,D
Consumer Economics — M
Counseling Psychology — M,D
Dance — M
Economics — M,D
English — M,D
Film, Television, and
  Video Production — M
French — M,D
Geography — M,D
German — M,D

Gerontology — M,O
Graphic Design — M
History — M,D
Human Development — M
Humanities — M
International Affairs — M
Linguistics — M,D
Music — M,D
Near and Middle
  Eastern Languages — M,D
Near and Middle
  Eastern Studies — M,D
Philosophy — M,D
Photography — M
Political Science — M,D
Psychology—General — D
Public Administration — M
Rhetoric — M,D
School Psychology — M,D
Sociology — M,D
Spanish — M,D
Urban and Regional
  Planning — M,D
Writing — M,D

UNIVERSITY OF VERMONT

Agricultural Economics
  and Agribusiness — M
Applied Economics — M
Classics — M
Clinical Psychology — D
Communication—
  General — M
Counseling Psychology — M
English — M
French — M
German — M
Historic Preservation — M
History — M
Interdisciplinary Studies — M
Psychology—General — D
Public Administration — M

UNIVERSITY OF VICTORIA

Anthropology — M
Art History — M,D
Art/Fine Arts — M
Asian Studies — M
Child and Family
  Studies — M,D
Classics — M,D
Clinical Psychology — M,D
Computer Art and
  Design — M
Conflict Resolution and
  Mediation/Peace
  Studies — M,D
Counseling Psychology — M,D
Developmental
  Psychology — M,D
Economics — M,D
English — M,D
Experimental
  Psychology — M,D
Film, Television, and
  Video Production — M
French — M
Geography — M,D
German — M
Hispanic Studies — M
History — M,D
Human Development — M,D
Italian — M
Linguistics — M,D
Music — M,D
Pacific Area/Pacific Rim
  Studies — M
Philosophy — M
Photography — M
Political Science — M,D
Psychology—General — M,D
Public Administration — M,D
Social Psychology — M,D
Sociology — M,D

Theater — M
Writing — M

UNIVERSITY OF VIRGINIA

Anthropology — M,D
Architectural History — M,D
Art History — M,D
Asian Studies — M
Classics — M,D
Clinical Psychology — D
Economics — M,D
English — M,D,O
French — M,D
German — M,D
History — M,D
Interdisciplinary Studies — M,D
International Affairs — M,D
Italian — M
Landscape Architecture — M
Linguistics — M
Music — M,D
Near and Middle
  Eastern Studies — M
Philosophy — M,D
Political Science — M,D
Psychology—General — M,D
Public Policy — M
Religion — M,D
Romance Languages — M,D
School Psychology — M,D
Slavic Languages — M,D
Sociology — M,D
Spanish — M,D
Theater — M
Urban and Regional
  Planning — M,O
Writing — M

UNIVERSITY OF WASHINGTON

Anthropology — M,D
Applied Arts and
  Design—General — M
Architecture — M,D,O
Art History — M,D
Art/Fine Arts — M
Asian Languages — M,D
Asian Studies — M,D
Chinese — M,D
Classics — M,D
Clinical Psychology — D
Cognitive Sciences — D
Communication—
  General — M,D
Comparative Literature — M,D
Dance — M
Demography and
  Population Studies — M,D
Developmental
  Psychology — D
East European and
  Russian Studies — M
Economics — M,D
English — M,D
French — M,D
Geography — M,D
German — M,D
Hispanic and Latin
  American Languages — M
Hispanic Studies — M,D
Historic Preservation — O
History — M,D
Human Development — M,D
Industrial Design — M
International Affairs — M
Italian — M,D
Japanese — M,D
Landscape Architecture — M
Lighting Design — M,D,O
Linguistics — M,D
Museum Studies — M
Music — M,D
Near and Middle
  Eastern Studies — M,D
Philosophy — M,D

Photography	M
Political Science	M,D
Portuguese	M
Psychology—General	D
Public Administration	M,D
Public Affairs	M,D
Public Policy	M,D
Religion	M,D
Romance Languages	M,D
Russian	M,D
Scandinavian Languages	M,D
School Psychology	M,D
Slavic Languages	M,D
Social Psychology	D
Social Sciences	M,D
Sociology	M,D
Spanish	M
Sustainable Development	P,M,D
Technical Communication	M,D
Theater	M,D
Urban and Regional Planning	M,D
Urban Design	M,D,O
Women's Studies	D
Writing	M

UNIVERSITY OF WASHINGTON, BOTHELL

Cultural Studies	M
Public Policy	M

UNIVERSITY OF WASHINGTON, TACOMA

Interdisciplinary Studies	M

UNIVERSITY OF WATERLOO

Anthropology	M
Architecture	M
Art/Fine Arts	M
Economic Development	M
Economics	M,D
English	M,D
French	M,D
Geography	M,D
German	M,D
History	M,D
International Affairs	M,D
Near and Middle Eastern Studies	M
Philosophy	M,D
Political Science	M,D
Psychology—General	M,D
Public Affairs	M
Religion	D
Russian	M,D
Sociology	M,D
Technical Writing	M,D
Urban and Regional Planning	M,D

THE UNIVERSITY OF WESTERN ONTARIO

Anthropology	M,D
Classics	M
Comparative Literature	M,D
Counseling Psychology	M
Economics	M,D
English	M,D
French	M,D
Geography	M,D
History	M,D
Interdisciplinary Studies	M,D
Journalism	M
Media Studies	M,D
Music	M,D
Philosophy	M,D
Political Science	M,D
Psychology—General	M,D
Sociology	M,D

Spanish	M,D
Sustainable Development	M,D

UNIVERSITY OF WEST FLORIDA

Anthropology	M
Archaeology	M
Communication—General	M
Counseling Psychology	M
Criminal Justice and Criminology	M
English	M
Gerontology	M
History	M
Industrial and Organizational Psychology	M
Military and Defense Studies	M
Political Science	M
Psychology—General	M
Public Administration	M
Public History	M
Sociology	M
Writing	M

UNIVERSITY OF WEST GEORGIA

Criminal Justice and Criminology	M
English	M
French	M,O
History	M,O
Museum Studies	M,O
Music	M
Political Science	M,D
Psychology—General	M,D
Public Administration	M,O
Public History	M,O
Rural Planning and Studies	M,O
Sociology	M
Spanish	M,O

UNIVERSITY OF WINDSOR

Applied Psychology	M,D
Art/Fine Arts	M
Clinical Psychology	M,D
Communication—General	M
Criminal Justice and Criminology	M,D
Economics	M
English	M
History	M
Philosophy	M
Political Science	M
Psychology—General	M,D
Social Psychology	M,D
Sociology	M,D
Writing	M

THE UNIVERSITY OF WINNIPEG

History	M
Marriage and Family Therapy	P,M,O
Public Administration	M
Religion	M
Theology	P,M,O

UNIVERSITY OF WISCONSIN–EAU CLAIRE

English	M
History	M
Psychology—General	M,O
School Psychology	M,O
Writing	M

UNIVERSITY OF WISCONSIN–LA CROSSE

Psychology—General	M,O
School Psychology	M,O

UNIVERSITY OF WISCONSIN–MADISON

African Studies	M,D
African-American Studies	M
Agricultural Economics and Agribusiness	M,D
American Studies	M,D
Anthropology	D
Applied Arts and Design—General	M,D
Applied Economics	M,D
Archaeology	D
Art History	M,D
Art/Fine Arts	M
Arts Administration	M
Asian Languages	M,D
Asian Studies	M,D
Child and Family Studies	M,D
Chinese	M,D
Classics	M,D
Clinical Psychology	D
Cognitive Sciences	D
Communication—General	M,D
Comparative Literature	M,D
Consumer Economics	M,D
Counseling Psychology	D
Cultural Anthropology	D
Developmental Psychology	D
Economics	D
English	M,D
Family and Consumer Sciences-General	M,D
Film, Television, and Video Theory and Criticism	M,D
Folklore	M,D
French	M,D,O
Genetic Counseling	M
Geographic Information Systems	M,D,O
Geography	M,D,O
German	M,D
History of Science and Technology	M,D
History	M,D
Human Development	M,D
Italian	M,D
Japanese	M,D
Jewish Studies	M,D
Journalism	M,D
Landscape Architecture	M
Latin American Studies	M,D
Linguistics	M,D
Mass Communication	M,D
Media Studies	M,D
Music	M,D
Near and Middle Eastern Languages	M,D
Near and Middle Eastern Studies	M,D
Philosophy	M,D
Political Science	D
Portuguese	M,D
Psychology—General	D
Public Affairs	M
Rehabilitation Counseling	M,D
Rhetoric	M,D
Rural Sociology	M,D
Scandinavian Languages	M,D
Slavic Languages	M,D
Social Psychology	D
Social Sciences	D
Sociology	M,D
Spanish	M,D

Speech and Interpersonal Communication	M,D
Sustainable Development	M
Theater	M,D
Urban and Regional Planning	M,D
Women's Studies	M,D
Writing	M,D

UNIVERSITY OF WISCONSIN–MILWAUKEE

African Studies	D
Anthropology	M,D,O
Architecture	M,D,O
Art History	M,O
Art/Fine Arts	M
Classics	M,O
Clinical Psychology	M,D
Communication—General	M,D,O
Comparative Literature	M,D,O
Conflict Resolution and Mediation/Peace Studies	M,D,O
Counseling Psychology	M,D
Criminal Justice and Criminology	M
Dance	M
Developmental Psychology	M,D
Economics	M,D
English	M,D,O
Film, Television, and Video Production	M
French	M,O
Geographic Information Systems	M,O
Geography	M,D
German	M,O
Gerontology	M,D,O
Historic Preservation	M,D,O
History	M,D
Industrial and Labor Relations	M,O
Interdisciplinary Studies	D
Italian	M,O
Jewish Studies	M,O
Liberal Studies	M
Linguistics	M,D,O
Marriage and Family Therapy	M,D,O
Media Studies	M,O
Museum Studies	M,D,O
Music	M,O
Philosophy	M
Political Science	M,D
Psychology—General	M,D
Public Administration	M
Rhetoric	M,D,O
School Psychology	D,O
Slavic Languages	M,O
Social Psychology	M,D
Sociology	M
Spanish	M,O
Technical Communication	M,D,O
Theater	M
Translation and Interpretation	M,O
Urban and Regional Planning	M,O
Urban Studies	M,D
Women's Studies	M
Writing	M,D,O

UNIVERSITY OF WISCONSIN–OSHKOSH

English	M
Experimental Psychology	M

*M—master's degree; P—first professional degree; D—doctorate; O—other advanced degree; *—Close-Up and/or Display*

Industrial and Organizational Psychology — M
Psychology—General — M
Public Administration — M

UNIVERSITY OF WISCONSIN–PLATTEVILLE

Criminal Justice and Criminology — M

UNIVERSITY OF WISCONSIN–RIVER FALLS

Art/Fine Arts — M
School Psychology — M,O

UNIVERSITY OF WISCONSIN–STEVENS POINT

Communication— General — M
Corporate and Organizational Communication — M
English — M
Family and Consumer Sciences-General — M
History — M
Human Development — M
Mass Communication — M
Speech and Interpersonal Communication — M

UNIVERSITY OF WISCONSIN–STOUT

Applied Psychology — M
Child and Family Studies — M
Counseling Psychology — M
Human Development — M
Marriage and Family Therapy — M
Rehabilitation Counseling — M
School Psychology — M,O

UNIVERSITY OF WISCONSIN–SUPERIOR

Art History — M
Art Therapy — M
Art/Fine Arts — M
Communication— General — M
Mass Communication — M
School Psychology — M
Social Psychology — M
Speech and Interpersonal Communication — M
Theater — M

UNIVERSITY OF WISCONSIN–WHITEWATER

Communication— General — M
Corporate and Organizational Communication — M
Mass Communication — M
Psychology—General — M,O
School Psychology — M,O
Social Psychology — M

UNIVERSITY OF WYOMING

Agricultural Economics and Agribusiness — M
American Studies — M
Anthropology — M,D
Applied Economics — M
Child Development — M
Communication— General — M
Consumer Economics — M

Economics — M,D
English — M
French — M
Geography — M
German — M
History — M
International Affairs — M
Music — M
Philosophy — M
Political Science — M
Psychology—General — M,D
Public Administration — M
Rural Planning and Studies — M
Sociology — M
Spanish — M
Writing — M

UPPER IOWA UNIVERSITY

Criminal Justice and Criminology — M
Homeland Security — M
Public Administration — M

URBANA UNIVERSITY

Criminal Justice and Criminology — M

URSULINE COLLEGE

Art Therapy — M
Historic Preservation — M
Liberal Studies — M
Theology — M

UTAH STATE UNIVERSITY

American Studies — M
Applied Economics — M
Art/Fine Arts — M
Child and Family Studies — M,D
Clinical Psychology — M,D
Communication— General — M
Consumer Economics — M
Counseling Psychology — M,D
Disability Studies — M,D,O
Economics — M,D
English — M
Family and Consumer Sciences-General — M,D
Folklore — M
Geography — M,D
History — M
Human Development — M,D
Interior Design — M
Landscape Architecture — M
Marriage and Family Therapy — M,D
Political Science — M
Psychology—General — M,D
Rehabilitation Counseling — M
School Psychology — M,D
Sociology — M,D
Theater — M
Urban and Regional Planning — M,D
Writing — M

UTICA COLLEGE

Criminal Justice and Criminology — M
Forensic Sciences — M
Liberal Studies — M

VALDOSTA STATE UNIVERSITY

Clinical Psychology — M,O
Counseling Psychology — M,O
Criminal Justice and Criminology — M
English — M
History — M

Industrial and Organizational Psychology — M,O
Marriage and Family Therapy — M
Psychology—General — M,O
School Psychology — M,O
Sociology — M

VALLEY FORGE CHRISTIAN COLLEGE

Music — M
Religion — M
Theology — M

VALPARAISO UNIVERSITY

Arts Administration — M
Asian Studies — M
Clinical Psychology — M,O
Communication— General — M,O
Counseling Psychology — M,O
English — M,O
Ethics — M,O
Gerontology — M,O
History — M,O
International Economics — M
Liberal Studies — M,O
Media Studies — M,O
Psychology—General — M,O
School Psychology — M,O
Theology — M,O

VANCOUVER SCHOOL OF THEOLOGY

Theology — P,M,O

VANDERBILT UNIVERSITY

Anthropology — M,D
Child and Family Studies — M
Classics — M
Economic Development — M,D
Economics — P,M,D
English — M,D
French — M,D
German — M,D
History — M,D
Human Development — M
Latin American Studies — M
Liberal Studies — M
Philosophy — M,D
Political Science — M,D
Portuguese — M,D
Psychology—General — M,D
Public Policy — M,D
Religion — M,D
Sociology — M,D
Spanish — M,D
Theology — P,M
Urban and Regional Planning — M
Writing — M

VANGUARD UNIVERSITY OF SOUTHERN CALIFORNIA

Clinical Psychology — M
Religion — M
Theology — M

VERMONT COLLEGE OF FINE ARTS

Art/Fine Arts — M
Graphic Design — M
Music — M
Writing — M

VICTORIA UNIVERSITY

Theology — P,M,D,O

VILLANOVA UNIVERSITY

American Studies — M,O

Communication— General — M
English — M
Hispanic Studies — M
History — M
Humanities — M
Liberal Studies — M,O
Missions and Missiology — M
Philosophy — D
Political Science — M
Psychology—General — M
Public Administration — M
Theater — M
Theology — M

VIRGINIA COLLEGE AT BIRMINGHAM

Criminal Justice and Criminology — M

VIRGINIA COMMONWEALTH UNIVERSITY

Applied Arts and Design—General — M
Applied Social Research — M,O
Architectural History — M,D
Art History — M,D
Art/Fine Arts — M,D
Clinical Psychology — D
Communication— General — D
Counseling Psychology — M,D,O
Criminal Justice and Criminology — M,O
Developmental Psychology — D
Economics — M
Emergency Management — M,O
English — M
Forensic Sciences — M
Geographic Information Systems — O
Gerontology — M,D,O
Health Psychology — D
Historic Preservation — O
History — M,D
Homeland Security — M,O
Humanities — M,D,O
Interdisciplinary Studies — M
Interior Design — M
Internet and Interactive Multimedia — M
Journalism — M
Mass Communication — M
Media Studies — M,D
Museum Studies — M,D
Music — M
Photography — M,D
Political Science — M,D,O
Psychology—General — D
Public Administration — M,O
Public Affairs — M,D,O
Public Policy — D
Rehabilitation Counseling — M,O
Rhetoric — M
Social Psychology — D
Sociology — M,O
Theater — M
Urban and Regional Planning — M
Writing — M

VIRGINIA POLYTECHNIC INSTITUTE AND STATE UNIVERSITY

Agricultural Economics and Agribusiness — M,D
Applied Arts and Design—General — M,D
Applied Economics — M,D
Architecture — M,D

Art/Fine Arts	D,O
Clothing and Textiles	M,D
Cognitive Sciences	M,D,O
Communication— General	M
Consumer Economics	M,D
Economic Development	M,D,O
Economics	D
English	M,D
Environmental Design	D
Gender Studies	M,D,O
Geographic Information Systems	D,O
Geography	M,D
History of Science and Technology	M,D,O
History	M
Homeland Security	M,D,O
Humanities	D,O
Interdisciplinary Studies	M,D,O
Interior Design	M,D
International Affairs	M,D,O
Internet and Interactive Multimedia	M
Landscape Architecture	M,D,O
Liberal Studies	M,O
Marriage and Family Therapy	M,D,O
National Security	M,O
Philosophy	M
Political Science	M,D,O
Psychology—General	M,D
Public Administration	M,D,O
Public Affairs	M,D,O
Public Policy	M,O
Religion	O
Sociology	M,D,O
Theater	M
Urban and Regional Planning	M,D,O
Women's Studies	M,D,O

VIRGINIA STATE UNIVERSITY

Clinical Psychology	M,D
Economics	M
English	M
Health Psychology	M,D
History	M
Interdisciplinary Studies	M
Psychology—General	M,D

VIRGINIA THEOLOGICAL SEMINARY

Theology	P,M,D

VIRGINIA UNION UNIVERSITY

Theology	P,D

VIRGINIA UNIVERSITY OF LYNCHBURG

Religion	P

WAKE FOREST UNIVERSITY

Communication— General	M
English	M
Liberal Studies	M
Psychology—General	M
Religion	M
Speech and Interpersonal Communication	M

WALDEN UNIVERSITY

Child and Family Studies	M,D
Clinical Psychology	M,D,O
Conflict Resolution and Mediation/Peace Studies	M,D,O
Counseling Psychology	M,D,O

Criminal Justice and Criminology	M,D,O
Developmental Psychology	M,D,O
Emergency Management	M,D,O
Forensic Psychology	M,D,O
Health Psychology	M,D,O
Homeland Security	M,D,O
Industrial and Organizational Psychology	M,D,O
International Affairs	M,D,O
International Development	M,D,O
Marriage and Family Therapy	M,D
Psychology—General	M,D,O
Public Administration	M,D,O
Public Policy	M,D,O
Social Psychology	M,D,O
Sustainable Development	M,D,O

WALLA WALLA UNIVERSITY

Counseling Psychology	M

WALSH UNIVERSITY

Corporate and Organizational Communication	M
Counseling Psychology	M
Theology	M

WARNER PACIFIC COLLEGE

Ethics	M
Pastoral Ministry and Counseling	M
Religion	M
Theology	M

WARREN WILSON COLLEGE

Writing	M

WARTBURG THEOLOGICAL SEMINARY

Theology	P,M

WASHBURN UNIVERSITY

Clinical Psychology	M
Criminal Justice and Criminology	M
Liberal Studies	M
Psychology—General	M

WASHINGTON ADVENTIST UNIVERSITY

Counseling Psychology	M
Public Administration	M
Religion	M

WASHINGTON COLLEGE

English	M
History	M
Psychology—General	M

WASHINGTON STATE UNIVERSITY

Agricultural Economics and Agribusiness	M,D,O
American Studies	M,D
Anthropology	M,D
Applied Economics	M,D,O
Archaeology	M,D
Architecture	M
Art/Fine Arts	M
Asian Studies	M,D
Clinical Psychology	M,D
Clothing and Textiles	M,D
Communication— General	M,D

Computer Art and Design	M
Corporate and Organizational Communication	M,D
Counseling Psychology	M,D,O
Criminal Justice and Criminology	M,D
Cultural Anthropology	M,D
Cultural Studies	M,D
Demography and Population Studies	M,D
Economics	M,D,O
English	M,D
Ethnic Studies	M,D
Experimental Psychology	M,D
Health Communication	M,D
History	M,D
Human Development	M
Interdisciplinary Studies	D
Interior Design	M,D
International Affairs	M,D
Landscape Architecture	M,D
Media Studies	M,D
Music	M
Philosophy	M
Photography	M
Political Science	M,D
Psychology—General	M,D
Public History	M,D
Public Policy	M,D
School Psychology	M,D,O
Social Psychology	M,D
Sociology	M,D
Spanish	M
Western European Studies	M,D
Women's Studies	M,D

WASHINGTON STATE UNIVERSITY SPOKANE

Architecture	M,D
Criminal Justice and Criminology	M,D
Interior Design	M,D
Landscape Architecture	M,D

WASHINGTON STATE UNIVERSITY VANCOUVER

History	M
Public Affairs	M

WASHINGTON THEOLOGICAL UNION

Theology	P,M,D

WASHINGTON UNIVERSITY IN ST. LOUIS

Anthropology	D
Archaeology	M,D
Architecture	M
Art History	M,D
Art/Fine Arts	M*
Asian Languages	M,D
Asian Studies	M
Chinese	M,D
Classics	M
Clinical Psychology	D
Comparative Literature	M,D
Economics	D
English	M,D
Experimental Psychology	D
French	M,D
German	M,D
History	M,D
Japanese	M,D
Music	M,D
Philosophy	M,D
Political Science	M,D
Psychology—General	D

Public Policy	M
Romance Languages	M,D
Social Psychology	D
Spanish	M,D
Speech and Interpersonal Communication	M,D
Urban Design	M
Writing	M

WAYLAND BAPTIST UNIVERSITY

Counseling Psychology	M
Criminal Justice and Criminology	M
Homeland Security	M
Interdisciplinary Studies	M
Pastoral Ministry and Counseling	M
Public Administration	M
Religion	M

WAYNESBURG UNIVERSITY

Addictions/Substance Abuse Counseling	M,D
Clinical Psychology	M,D
Counseling Psychology	M,D

WAYNE STATE COLLEGE

Communication— General	M

WAYNE STATE UNIVERSITY

Anthropology	M,D
Applied Arts and Design—General	M
Art History	M
Art/Fine Arts	M
Classics	M
Clinical Psychology	M,D,O
Communication— General	M,D
Comparative Literature	M
Conflict Resolution and Mediation/Peace Studies	M,O
Corporate and Organizational Communication	M,D
Criminal Justice and Criminology	M
Economics	M,D
English	M,D
French	M,D
Genetic Counseling	M
Geography	M
German	M,D
History	M,D
Industrial and Organizational Psychology	M,D
Italian	M
Linguistics	M
Media Studies	M,D
Music	M,O
Near and Middle Eastern Languages	M
Near and Middle Eastern Studies	M
Philosophy	M,D
Political Science	M,D
Psychology—General	M,D
Public Administration	M
Rehabilitation Counseling	M,D,O
Russian	M,D
School Psychology	M,D,O
Sociology	M,D
Spanish	M,D
Speech and Interpersonal Communication	M,D

*M—master's degree; P—first professional degree; D—doctorate; O—other advanced degree; *—Close-Up and / or Display*

Sustainable
  Development   O
Theater   M,D
Urban and Regional
  Planning   M
Writing   M,D

WEBBER INTERNATIONAL UNIVERSITY

Criminal Justice and
  Criminology   M

WEBER STATE UNIVERSITY

English   M

WEBSTER UNIVERSITY

Art/Fine Arts   M
Arts Administration   M
Communication—
  General   M
Corporate and
  Organizational
  Communication   M
Counseling Psychology   M
Criminal Justice and
  Criminology   M,D,O
Gerontology   M
International Affairs   M
Media Studies   M
Music   M
Public Administration   M,D,O

WENTWORTH INSTITUTE OF TECHNOLOGY

Architecture   M*

WESLEYAN UNIVERSITY

Liberal Studies   M,O
Music   M,D

WESLEY BIBLICAL SEMINARY

Marriage and Family
  Therapy   P,M
Missions and Missiology   P,M
Pastoral Ministry and
  Counseling   P,M
Religion   P,M
Theology   P,M

WESLEY THEOLOGICAL SEMINARY

Theology   P,M,D

WEST CHESTER UNIVERSITY OF PENNSYLVANIA

Anthropology   M,O
Clinical Psychology   M,O
Communication—
  General   M
Criminal Justice and
  Criminology   M
Emergency
  Management   M,O
English   M,O
Ethics   M,O
French   M,O
Geographic Information
  Systems   M,O
Geography   M,O
Gerontology   M,O
Health Psychology   M,O
History   M,O
Holocaust and Genocide
  Studies   M,O
Industrial and
  Organizational
  Psychology   M,O
Music   M,O
Philosophy   M,O
Political Science   M,O
Psychology—General   M,O
Public Administration   M,O
Public Affairs   M,O

Sociology   M,O
Spanish   M,O
Sustainable
  Development   M,O
Urban and Regional
  Planning   M,O

WESTERN CAROLINA UNIVERSITY

Applied Arts and
  Design—General   M
Art/Fine Arts   M
English   M
History   M
Music   M
Psychology—General   M
Public Affairs   M
School Psychology   M
Social Psychology   M

WESTERN CONNECTICUT STATE UNIVERSITY

Art/Fine Arts   M
Criminal Justice and
  Criminology   M
English   M
History   M
Illustration   M
Social Psychology   M
Writing   M

WESTERN ILLINOIS UNIVERSITY

Applied Arts and
  Design—General   M
Clinical Psychology   M,O
Communication—
  General   M
Criminal Justice and
  Criminology   M,O
Economic Development   M,O
Economics   M,O
English   M,O
Geographic Information
  Systems   M,O
Geography   M,O
Graphic Design   M,O
History   M
Internet and Interactive
  Multimedia   M,O
Liberal Studies   M
Museum Studies   M,O
Music   M
Political Science   M
Psychology—General   M,O
School Psychology   M,O
Social Psychology   M,O
Sociology   M
Sustainable
  Development   M,O
Theater   M
Writing   M,O

WESTERN INTERNATIONAL UNIVERSITY

Public Administration   M

WESTERN KENTUCKY UNIVERSITY

Anthropology   M
Applied Economics   M
Clinical Psychology   M,O
Communication—
  General   M,O
Comparative Literature   M
Corporate and
  Organizational
  Communication   M,O
Counseling Psychology   M
Criminal Justice and
  Criminology   M
English   M
Experimental
  Psychology   M,O

French   M
German   M
History   M
Homeland Security   M
Industrial and
  Organizational
  Psychology   M,O
Interdisciplinary Studies   M,O
Marriage and Family
  Therapy   M
Political Science   M
Psychology—General   M,O
Public Administration   M
School Psychology   M,O
Sociology   M
Spanish   M
Writing   M

WESTERN MICHIGAN UNIVERSITY

Anthropology   M
Applied Arts and
  Design—General   M
Applied Economics   M,D
Art/Fine Arts   M
Clinical Psychology   M,D
Communication—
  General   M
Corporate and
  Organizational
  Communication   M
Counseling Psychology   M,D
Economics   M,D
English   M,D
Family and Consumer
  Sciences-General   M
Geographic Information
  Systems   M,O
Geography   M,O
History   M,D
Industrial and
  Organizational
  Psychology   M,D
International Affairs   M
Medieval and
  Renaissance Studies   M
Music   M
Philosophy   M
Political Science   M,D
Psychology—General   M,D
Public Administration   M,D,O
Public Affairs   M,D,O
Rehabilitation
  Counseling   M
Religion   M
Sociology   M,D
Spanish   M,D
Therapies—Dance,
  Drama, and Music   M
Writing   M,D

WESTERN NEW ENGLAND UNIVERSITY

Applied Behavior
  Analysis   D,O

WESTERN NEW MEXICO UNIVERSITY

Interdisciplinary Studies   M
School Psychology   M

WESTERN OREGON UNIVERSITY

Criminal Justice and
  Criminology   M
Music   M
Rehabilitation
  Counseling   M

WESTERN SEMINARY

Pastoral Ministry and
  Counseling   P,M,D,O
Religion   M,O

Theology   P,M,O
Women's Studies   M

WESTERN SEMINARY–SACRAMENTO CAMPUS

Marriage and Family
  Therapy   M
Pastoral Ministry and
  Counseling   M,O
Theology   P,M,O
Women's Studies   O

WESTERN SEMINARY–SAN JOSE CAMPUS

Marriage and Family
  Therapy   P,M,O
Pastoral Ministry and
  Counseling   P,M,O
Theology   P,M,O

WESTERN STATE COLLEGE OF COLORADO

Film, Television, and
  Video Production   M
Writing   M*

WESTERN THEOLOGICAL SEMINARY

Theology   P,M,D

WESTERN WASHINGTON UNIVERSITY

Anthropology   M
Counseling Psychology   M
English   M
Experimental
  Psychology   M
Geography   M
History   M
Music   M
Political Science   M
Psychology—General   M
Rehabilitation
  Counseling   M

WESTFIELD STATE UNIVERSITY

Applied Behavior
  Analysis   M
Counseling Psychology   M
Criminal Justice and
  Criminology   M
English   M
History   M
Psychology—General   M

WESTMINSTER COLLEGE (UT)

Communication—
  General   M
Counseling Psychology   M
Writing   M

WESTMINSTER SEMINARY CALIFORNIA

Religion   P,M
Theology   P,M

WESTMINSTER THEOLOGICAL SEMINARY

Missions and Missiology   P,M,D,O
Pastoral Ministry and
  Counseling   P,M,D,O
Religion   P,M,D,O
Theology   P,M,D,O

WEST TEXAS A&M UNIVERSITY

Agricultural Economics
  and Agribusiness   M
Art/Fine Arts   M
Communication—
  General   M
Criminal Justice and
  Criminology   M
Economics   M

English	M
History	M
Interdisciplinary Studies	M
Music	M
Political Science	M
Psychology—General	M

WEST VIRGINIA STATE UNIVERSITY

Media Studies	M

WEST VIRGINIA UNIVERSITY

African Studies	M,D
African-American Studies	M,D
Agricultural Economics and Agribusiness	M
American Studies	M,D
Applied Social Research	M
Art History	M
Art/Fine Arts	M
Asian Studies	M,D
Child and Family Studies	M
Clinical Psychology	M,D
Communication—General	M,D
Corporate and Organizational Communication	M,D,O
Counseling Psychology	D
Developmental Psychology	M,D
Economic Development	M,D
Economics	M,D
English	M,D
Forensic Sciences	M,D
French	M
Geographic Information Systems	M,D
Geography	M,D
Graphic Design	M
History of Science and Technology	M,D
History	M,D
Human Development	M,D
Industrial and Labor Relations	M
International Affairs	M,D
International Economics	M,D
Journalism	M,O
Latin American Studies	M,D
Liberal Studies	M
Linguistics	M
Music	M,D
Political Science	M,D
Psychology—General	M,D
Public Administration	M
Public Policy	M,D
Rehabilitation Counseling	M
Sociology	M
Spanish	M
Sport Psychology	M,D
Sustainable Development	D
Theater	M
Urban and Regional Planning	M,D
Writing	M

WHEATON COLLEGE

American Studies	M
Archaeology	M
Clinical Psychology	M,D
Cultural Studies	M,O
Missions and Missiology	M,O
Pastoral Ministry and Counseling	M,D
Psychology—General	M,D
Religion	M
Theology	M,D

WHEELOCK COLLEGE

Child and Family Studies	M
Human Development	M

WHITTIER COLLEGE

Child Development	M

WHITWORTH UNIVERSITY

Theology	M

WICHITA STATE UNIVERSITY

Anthropology	M
Art/Fine Arts	M
Clinical Psychology	D
Communication—General	M
Criminal Justice and Criminology	M
Economics	M
English	M
Gerontology	M
History	M
Liberal Studies	M
Music	M
Psychology—General	D
Public Administration	M
School Psychology	M,O
Social Psychology	D
Sociology	M
Spanish	M
Writing	M

WIDENER UNIVERSITY

Clinical Psychology	D
Criminal Justice and Criminology	M
Liberal Studies	M
Psychology—General	M
Public Administration	M

WILBERFORCE UNIVERSITY

Rehabilitation Counseling	M

WILFRID LAURIER UNIVERSITY

American Studies	M,D
Archaeology	M
Canadian Studies	M,D
Classics	M
Cognitive Sciences	M,D
Communication—General	M
Conflict Resolution and Mediation/Peace Studies	D
Criminal Justice and Criminology	M
Cultural Studies	M,D
Developmental Psychology	M,D
Economics	M,D
English	M,D
Film, Television, and Video Theory and Criticism	M,D
Gender Studies	M,D
Geography	M,D
History	M,D
International Affairs	M,D
International Economics	M
Media Studies	M,D
Near and Middle Eastern Studies	M
Pastoral Ministry and Counseling	P,M,D,O
Philosophy	M
Political Science	M,D
Psychology—General	M,D
Public Policy	M
Religion	M,D
Social Psychology	M,D

Social Sciences	M
Sociology	M
Theology	P,M,D,O
Therapies—Dance, Drama, and Music	M

WILKES UNIVERSITY

Writing	M

WILLIAM CAREY UNIVERSITY

Counseling Psychology	M
Psychology—General	M

WILLIAM PATERSON UNIVERSITY OF NEW JERSEY

Art/Fine Arts	M
Clinical Psychology	M
Communication—General	M
Counseling Psychology	M
English	M
History	M
Music	M
Public Policy	M
Sociology	M

WILLIAMS COLLEGE

Art History	M

WILLIAM WOODS UNIVERSITY

Agricultural Economics and Agribusiness	M,O

WILMINGTON UNIVERSITY

Criminal Justice and Criminology	M
Gerontology	M
Homeland Security	M
Internet and Interactive Multimedia	M
Public Administration	M
Social Psychology	M

WINEBRENNER THEOLOGICAL SEMINARY

Theology	P,M,D

WINONA STATE UNIVERSITY

English	M

WINSTON-SALEM STATE UNIVERSITY

Rehabilitation Counseling	M

WINTHROP UNIVERSITY

Art/Fine Arts	M
Arts Administration	M
English	M
History	M
Liberal Studies	M
Music	M
Psychology—General	M,O
Spanish	M

WISCONSIN SCHOOL OF PROFESSIONAL PSYCHOLOGY

Clinical Psychology	M,D
Psychology—General	M,D

WON INSTITUTE OF GRADUATE STUDIES

Religion	M

WOODBURY UNIVERSITY

Architecture	M
Urban Design	M

WORCESTER POLYTECHNIC INSTITUTE

Interdisciplinary Studies	M,D,O
Social Sciences	M,D,O

WORCESTER STATE UNIVERSITY

History	M
School Psychology	M,O
Spanish	M

WRIGHT INSTITUTE

Clinical Psychology	D
Counseling Psychology	M
Psychology—General	D

WRIGHT STATE UNIVERSITY

Applied Behavior Analysis	M
Applied Economics	M
Clinical Psychology	D
Criminal Justice and Criminology	M
Economics	M
English	M
History	M
Humanities	M
Industrial and Organizational Psychology	M,D
Interdisciplinary Studies	M
Music	M
Psychology—General	M,D
Public Administration	M
Rehabilitation Counseling	M
Rhetoric	M
Urban Studies	M
Writing	M

WYCLIFFE COLLEGE

Religion	P,M,D,O
Theology	P,M,D,O

XAVIER UNIVERSITY

Clinical Psychology	M,D
Criminal Justice and Criminology	M
English	M
Experimental Psychology	M,D
Industrial and Organizational Psychology	M,D
Pastoral Ministry and Counseling	M
Psychology—General	M,D
Theology	M

XAVIER UNIVERSITY OF LOUISIANA

Pastoral Ministry and Counseling	M
Theology	M

YALE UNIVERSITY

African Studies	M
African-American Studies	D
American Studies	D
Anthropology	M,D
Applied Arts and Design—General	M
Archaeology	M,D
Architecture	M,D
Art History	D
Art/Fine Arts	M
Asian Languages	D
Asian Studies	M
Classics	M,D
Clinical Psychology	D

*M—master's degree; P—first professional degree; D—doctorate; O—other advanced degree; *—Close-Up and/or Display*

Cognitive Sciences	D	Psychology—General	D
Comparative Literature	D	Religion	D
Developmental Psychology	D	Russian	D
East European and Russian Studies	M,D	Slavic Languages	D
Economic Development	M	Social Psychology	D
Economics	M,D	Social Sciences	M,D,O
English	M,D	Sociology	D
Environmental Design	M,D	Spanish	D
Film, Television, and Video Theory and Criticism	D	Theater	M,D,O
French	M,D	Theology	P,M
German	D		
Graphic Design	M	**YESHIVA BETH MOSHE**	
History of Medicine	M,D	Theology	O
History of Science and Technology	M,D	**YESHIVA DERECH CHAIM**	
History	M,D	Religion	D
International Affairs	M		
International Economics	M	**YESHIVA KARLIN STOLIN RABBINICAL INSTITUTE**	
Italian	D	Theology	O
Latin American Studies	D		
Linguistics	D	**YESHIVA OF NITRA RABBINICAL COLLEGE**	
Medieval and Renaissance Studies	M,D	Theology	D
Music	M,D,O		
Near and Middle Eastern Languages	M,D	**YESHIVA SHAAR HATORAH TALMUDIC RESEARCH INSTITUTE**	
Near and Middle Eastern Studies	M,D	Theology	D
Philosophy	D		
Photography	M	**YESHIVATH ZICHRON MOSHE**	
Political Science	D	Theology	O
Portuguese	D		

YESHIVA TORAS CHAIM TALMUDICAL SEMINARY

Theology	

YESHIVA UNIVERSITY

Clinical Psychology	D
Conflict Resolution and Mediation/Peace Studies	P,M
Counseling Psychology	M
Health Psychology	D
Jewish Studies	M,D
Psychology—General	M,D
School Psychology	D

YORKTOWN UNIVERSITY

American Studies	M
Economics	M
Political Science	M

YORK UNIVERSITY

Anthropology	M,D
Applied Arts and Design—General	M
Art History	M,D
Art/Fine Arts	M,D
Communication—General	M,D
Dance	M
Disability Studies	M,D
Economics	M,D
Emergency Management	M
English	M,D

Film, Television, and Video Production	M,D
French	M
Geography	M,D
History	M,D
Humanities	M,D
Interdisciplinary Studies	M
International Affairs	M
Linguistics	M,D
Music	M,D
Philosophy	M,D
Political Science	M,D
Psychology—General	M,D
Public Administration	M,D
Public Affairs	M
Public Policy	M
Social Sciences	M
Sociology	M,D
Theater	M,D
Translation and Interpretation	M
Women's Studies	M,D

YOUNGSTOWN STATE UNIVERSITY

Applied Behavior Analysis	M
Counseling Psychology	M
Criminal Justice and Criminology	M
Economics	M
English	M
History	M
Music	M
Psychology—General	M
School Psychology	M

ACADEMIC AND PROFESSIONAL
PROGRAMS IN ARTS AND ARCHITECTURE

Section 1
Applied Arts and Design

This section contains a directory of institutions offering graduate work in applied arts and design, followed by in-depth entries submitted by institutions that chose to prepare detailed program descriptions. Additional information about programs listed in the directory but not augmented by an in-depth entry may be obtained by writing directly to the dean of a graduate school or chair of a department at the address given in the directory.

For programs offering related work, see also in this book *Architecture* and *Art and Art History.* In another guide in this series: **Graduate Programs in Business, Education, Health, Information Studies, Law & Social Work**

See *Advertising and Public Relations*

CONTENTS

Program Directories

Close-Ups and Displays

See also:

Applied Arts and Design—General

Academy of Art University, Graduate Program, School of Advertising, San Francisco, CA 94105-3410. Offers MFA. Part-time programs available. Postbaccalaureate distance learning degree programs offered (no on-campus study). *Faculty:* 9 full-time (2 women), 51 part-time/adjunct (17 women). *Students:* 201 full-time (123 women), 95 part-time (64 women); includes 24 Black or African American, non-Hispanic/Latino; 20 Asian, non-Hispanic/Latino; 14 Hispanic/Latino, 115 international. Average age 28. 87 applicants. In 2010, 38 master's awarded. *Degree requirements:* For master's, thesis, final review. *Entrance requirements:* For master's, minimum GPA of 3.0, portfolio. *Application deadline:* For fall admission, 9/7 for domestic and international students; for spring admission, 2/2 for domestic and international students. Applications are processed on a rolling basis. Application fee: $100 ($500 for international students). Electronic applications accepted. *Expenses:* Tuition: Full-time $20,160; part-time $840 per semester hour. Required fees: $45 per semester. *Financial support:* Career-related internships or fieldwork and Federal Work-Study available. Support available to part-time students. Financial award application deadline: 8/10; financial award applicants required to submit FAFSA. *Application contact:* 800-544-ARTS, Fax: 415-263-4130, E-mail: info@academyart.edu.

Alfred University, Graduate School, New York State College of Ceramics, School of Art and Design, Alfred, NY 14802-1205. Offers ceramic art (MFA); electronic integrated arts (MFA); glass art (MFA); sculpture (MFA). *Accreditation:* NASAD. *Degree requirements:* For master's, exhibit. *Entrance requirements:* For master's, portfolio. Additional exam requirements/recommendations for international students: Required—TOEFL (minimum score 550 paper-based; 213 computer-based; 80 iBT), IELTS (minimum score 6). Electronic applications accepted. *Faculty research:* Ceramic sculpture, functional ceramics, wood, mixed media, hot and cold glass.

Art Center College of Design, Graduate Division, Pasadena, CA 91103. Offers MFA, MS. *Accreditation:* NASAD. *Faculty:* 15 full-time (4 women), 32 part-time/adjunct (12 women). *Students:* 130 full-time (47 women), 51 part-time (16 women); includes 49 minority (10 Black or African American, non-Hispanic/Latino; 23 Asian, non-Hispanic/Latino; 9 Hispanic/Latino; 4 Native Hawaiian or other Pacific Islander, non-Hispanic/Latino; 3 Two or more races, non-Hispanic/Latino), 55 international. Average age 30. *Degree requirements:* For master's, thesis, studio project. *Entrance requirements:* For master's, portfolio. Additional exam requirements/recommendations for international students: Required—TOEFL (minimum score 100 iBT). *Application deadline:* For fall admission, 2/1 priority date for domestic and international students; for spring admission, 10/1 priority date for domestic and international students. Applications are processed on a rolling basis. *Expenses:* Tuition: Part-time $17,220 per term. *Financial support:* In 2010–11, 149 students received support; teaching assistantships, career-related internships or fieldwork, Federal Work-Study, and scholarships/grants available. Financial award application deadline: 3/1. *Faculty research:* Computer graphics, automobile aerodynamics. *Unit head:* Kit Baron, Vice President of Admission and Enrollment Management, 626-396-2373. *Application contact:* Kit Baron, Vice President of Admission and Enrollment Management, 626-396-2373.

See Display on next page and Close-Up on page 119.

Bowling Green State University, Graduate College, College of Arts and Sciences, School of Art, Bowling Green, OH 43403. Offers 2-D studio art (MA, MFA); 3-D studio art (MA, MFA); art education (MA); art history (MA); computer art (MA); design (MFA); digital arts (MFA); graphics (MFA). *Accreditation:* NASAD. Part-time programs available. *Degree requirements:* For master's, thesis or alternative, final exhibit (MFA). *Entrance requirements:* For master's, GRE General Test (MA), slide portfolio (15-20 slides). Additional exam requirements/recommendations for international students: Required—TOEFL. Electronic applications accepted. *Faculty research:* Computer animation and virtual reality, Spanish still-life painting from 1600 to 1800, art and psychotherapy, Japanese wood-firing techniques in ceramics, non-toxic printmaking technologies.

Bradley University, Graduate School, Slane College of Communications and Fine Arts, Department of Art, Peoria, IL 61625-0002. Offers ceramics (MA, MFA); drawing/illustration (MA, MFA); interdisciplinary art (MA, MFA); painting (MA, MFA); photography (MA, MFA); printmaking (MA, MFA); sculpture (MA, MFA); visual communication and design (MA, MFA). *Accreditation:* NASAD. Part-time programs available. *Degree requirements:* For master's, comprehensive exam, thesis, final exhibit. *Entrance requirements:* For master's, portfolio, 2 letters of recommendation. Additional exam requirements/recommendations for international students: Required—TOEFL (minimum score 550 paper-based; 213 computer-based; 79 iBT).

California College of the Arts, Graduate Programs, Program in Design, San Francisco, CA 94107. Offers MFA. *Accreditation:* NASAD. *Faculty:* 8 full-time (2 women), 26 part-time/adjunct (10 women). *Students:* 69 full-time (45 women), 1 part-time (0 women); includes 26 minority (1 Black or African American, non-Hispanic/Latino; 16 Asian, non-Hispanic/Latino; 9 Hispanic/Latino), 14 international. Average age 29. 188 applicants, 44% accepted, 33 enrolled. In 2010, 20 master's awarded. *Degree requirements:* For master's, thesis, exhibit. *Entrance requirements:* For master's, appropriate bachelor's degree, portfolio, resume, letters of recommendation, transcripts. Additional exam requirements/recommendations for international students: Required—TOEFL (minimum score 600 paper-based; 250 computer-based; 100 iBT). *Application deadline:* For fall admission, 1/5 for domestic and international students. Application fee: $70. Electronic applications accepted. *Expenses:* Tuition: Full-time $38,550; part-time $1285 per unit. One-time fee: $185 full-time. *Financial support:* In 2010–11, 10 fellowships (averaging $18,000 per year), teaching assistantships (averaging $2,000 per year) were awarded; career-related internships or fieldwork, Federal Work-Study, scholarships/grants, and health care benefits also available. Financial award application deadline: 3/2. *Unit head:* Brenda Laurel, Graduate Chair, 415-551-9283, Fax: 415-703-9539, E-mail: blaurel@cca.edu. *Application contact:* Heidi Geis, Assistant Director of Graduate Admissions, 415-703-9523 Ext. 9533, Fax: 415-703-9539, E-mail: hgeis@cca.edu.

California College of the Arts, Graduate Programs, Program in Design Strategy, San Francisco, CA 94107. Offers MBA. *Accreditation:* NASAD. *Faculty:* 4 full-time (1 woman), 17 part-time/adjunct (6 women). *Students:* 72 full-time (39 women), 2 part-time (both women); includes 26 minority (5 Black or African American, non-Hispanic/Latino; 15 Asian, non-Hispanic/Latino; 6 Hispanic/Latino), 8 international. Average age 32. 151 applicants, 58% accepted, 51 enrolled. In 2010, 23 master's awarded. *Degree requirements:* For master's, thesis. *Entrance requirements:* Additional exam requirements/recommendations for international students: Required—TOEFL (minimum score 600 paper-based; 250 computer-based; 100 iBT). *Application deadline:* For fall admission, 1/5 for domestic and international students. Application fee: $70. *Expenses:* Tuition: Full-time $38,550; part-time $1285 per unit. One-time fee: $185 full-time. *Financial support:* In 2010–11, 3 fellowships (averaging $18,000 per year) were awarded. *Unit head:* Nathan Shedroff, Program Chair, 800-447-1ART, E-mail: nshedroff@cca.edu. *Application contact:* Heidi Geis, Assistant Director of Graduate Admissions, 415-703-9523 Ext. 9533, Fax: 415-703-9539, E-mail: hgeis@cca.edu.

California Institute of the Arts, School of Art, Valencia, CA 91355-2340. Offers art (MFA, Adv C); graphic design (MFA, Adv C); photography (MFA, Adv C). *Accreditation:* NASAD (one or more programs are accredited). *Degree requirements:* For master's, final project. *Entrance requirements:* For master's, portfolio. Additional exam requirements/recommendations for international students: Required—TOEFL. Electronic applications accepted.

California State University, Fresno, Division of Graduate Studies, College of Arts and Humanities, Department of Art and Design, Fresno, CA 93740-8027. Offers art (MA). Part-time and evening/weekend programs available. *Degree requirements:* For master's, thesis or alternative. *Entrance requirements:* For master's, GRE General Test, minimum GPA of 3.0, portfolio. Additional exam requirements/recommendations for international students: Required—TOEFL. Electronic applications accepted. *Faculty research:* Art history, graphic design, studio art.

California State University, Fullerton, Graduate Studies, College of the Arts, Department of Art, Fullerton, CA 92834-9480. Offers art (MA, MFA), including ceramics (MFA), crafts, creative photography (MFA), design (MFA), drawing and painting, printmaking (MFA), sculpture; art history (MA); design (MA). *Accreditation:* NASAD (one or more programs are accredited). Part-time programs available. *Students:* 50 full-time (34 women), 38 part-time (24 women); includes 1 Black or African American, non-Hispanic/Latino; 12 Asian, non-Hispanic/Latino; 11 Hispanic/Latino, 8 international. Average age 35. 113 applicants, 26% accepted, 26 enrolled. In 2010, 14 master's awarded. *Degree requirements:* For master's, project or thesis. *Entrance requirements:* For master's, minimum GPA of 2.5 in last 60 units of course work, portfolio. Application fee: $55. *Financial support:* Career-related internships or fieldwork, Federal Work-Study, institutionally sponsored loans, and scholarships/grants available. Support available to part-time students. Financial award application deadline: 3/1; financial award applicants required to submit FAFSA. *Unit head:* Larry Johnson, Chair, 657-278-3471. *Application contact:* Admissions/Applications, 657-278-2371.

California State University, Los Angeles, Graduate Studies, College of Arts and Letters, Department of Art, Los Angeles, CA 90032-8530. Offers art (MA), including art education, art history, art therapy, ceramics, metals, and textiles, design (MA, MFA), painting, sculpture, and graphic arts, photography; fine arts (MFA), including crafts, design (MA, MFA), studio arts. *Accreditation:* NASAD (one or more programs are accredited). Part-time and evening/weekend programs available. *Faculty:* 9 full-time (5 women), 3 part-time/adjunct (2 women). *Students:* 27 full-time (19 women), 33 part-time (22 women); includes 24 minority (3 Black or African American, non-Hispanic/Latino; 7 Asian, non-Hispanic/Latino; 13 Hispanic/Latino; 1 Two or more races, non-Hispanic/Latino), 9 international. Average age 36. 19 applicants, 100% accepted, 13 enrolled. In 2010, 26 master's awarded. *Degree requirements:* For master's, comprehensive exam, project or thesis. *Entrance requirements:* For master's, portfolio. Additional exam requirements/recommendations for international students: Required—TOEFL (minimum score 500 paper-based; 173 computer-based). *Application deadline:* For fall admission, 5/1 for domestic and international students. Applications are processed on a rolling basis. Application fee: $55. Electronic applications accepted. *Financial support:* Federal Work-Study available. Support available to part-time students. Financial award application deadline: 3/1. *Faculty research:* The artist and the book, conceptual art, ceramic processes, computer graphics, architectural graphics. *Unit head:* Dr. Abbas Daneshvari, Chair, 323-343-4010, Fax: 323-343-4045, E-mail: adanesh@calstatela.edu. *Application contact:* Dr. Alan Muchlinski, Dean of Graduate Studies, 323-343-3820, Fax: 323-343-5653, E-mail: amuchli@exchange.calstatela.edu.

Cardinal Stritch University, College of Arts and Sciences, Department of Art, Milwaukee, WI 53217-3985. Offers visual studies (MA). Part-time and evening/weekend programs available. *Degree requirements:* For master's, thesis, portfolio, exhibit. *Entrance requirements:* For master's, minimum GPA of 2.75; 3 letters of recommendation.

Carnegie Mellon University, College of Fine Arts, School of Design, Program in Design, Pittsburgh, PA 15213-3891. Offers PhD. *Accreditation:* NASAD. *Degree requirements:* For doctorate, one foreign language, comprehensive exam, thesis/dissertation. *Entrance requirements:* For doctorate, GRE, portfolio of relevant work. Additional exam requirements/recommendations for international students: Required—TOEFL (minimum score 600 paper-based; 250 computer-based). *Faculty research:* Design theory, typography and information design, new product development, organizational behavior, interaction design.

Concordia University, School of Graduate Studies, Faculty of Fine Arts, Department of Design and Computation Arts, Montréal, QC H3G 1M8, Canada. Offers digital technologies in design art practice (Certificate).

Cranbrook Academy of Art, Graduate School, Program in Fine Arts, Bloomfield Hills, MI 48303-0801. Offers ceramics (MFA); design (MFA), including graphic design; fiber arts (MFA); metalsmithing (MFA); painting (MFA); photography (MFA); printmaking (MFA); sculpture (MFA). *Accreditation:* NASAD. *Degree requirements:* For master's, thesis, exhibit. *Entrance requirements:* Additional exam requirements/recommendations for international students: Required—TOEFL (minimum score 550 paper-based; 213 computer-based).

Drexel University, Antoinette Westphal College of Media Arts and Design, Philadelphia, PA 19104-2875. Offers arts administration (MS); digital media (MS); fashion design (MS); interior architecture and design (MS); television management (MS); MS/MBA. *Accreditation:* NASAD. Part-time and evening/weekend programs available. *Entrance requirements:* For master's, interview. Additional exam requirements/recommendations for international students: Required—TOEFL. Electronic applications accepted. *Expenses:* Contact institution.

Emily Carr University of Art + Design, Program in Applied Arts, Vancouver, BC V6H 3R9, Canada. Offers design (MAA); media arts (MAA); visual arts (MAA). *Degree requirements:* For master's, internship, thesis project. *Entrance requirements:* For master's, minimum overall GPA of 3.0, visual portfolio, 3 letters of recommendation. Additional exam requirements/recommendations for international students: Required—TOEFL (minimum score 570 paper-based; 230 computer-based; 84 iBT), IELTS (minimum score 6.5), Michigan English Language Assessment Battery (minimum score 81). Electronic applications accepted.

Fashion Institute of Technology, School of Graduate Studies, New York, NY 10001-5992. Offers MA, MPS. *Accreditation:* NASAD. Part-time and evening/weekend programs available. *Degree requirements:* For master's, one foreign language, thesis, internship. *Entrance requirements:* For master's, GRE or GMAT, portfolio, letters of recommendation, resume. Additional exam requirements/recommendations for international students: Required—TOEFL (minimum score 550 paper-based; 213 computer-based). Electronic applications accepted. *Faculty research:* Fashion history, material conservation, international marketing and global sourcing, sustainable economic development, luxury braiding in China.

See Display on page 90 and Close-Up on page 123.

Fashion Institute of Technology, School of Graduate Studies, Program in Exhibition Design, New York, NY 10001-5992. Offers MA. *Entrance requirements:* Additional exam requirements/recommendations for international students: Required—TOEFL (minimum score 550 paper-based; 213 computer-based). Electronic applications accepted.

See Display on page 90 and Close-Up on page 123.

Ferris State University, Kendall College of Art and Design, Big Rapids, MI 49307. Offers MFA. *Accreditation:* NASAD. Part-time programs available. *Faculty:* 15 full-time (10 women). *Students:* 29 full-time (19 women), 15 part-time (10 women); includes 1 American Indian or Alaska Native, non-Hispanic/Latino; 1 Asian, non-Hispanic/Latino; 1 Two or more races, non-Hispanic/Latino. Average age 31. 37 applicants, 70% accepted, 13 enrolled. In 2010, 15 master's awarded. *Degree requirements:* For master's, thesis, seminars. *Entrance requirements:* For master's, portfolio, 3 letters of recommendation, curriculum vitae. Additional exam requirements/recommendations for international students: Required—TOEFL (minimum score 500 paper-based; 173 computer-based; 61 iBT). *Application deadline:* For fall admission, 2/15 priority date for domestic and international students; for spring admission, 11/1 priority date for domestic and international students. Applications are processed on a rolling basis. Application fee: $30. *Financial support:* In 2010–11, 30 students received support, including 7 fellowships (averaging $13,370 per year); scholarships/grants, unspecified assistantships, and half-tuition scholarships ($6317 average), graduate assistantships ($5309 average) also available. Support available to part-time students. Financial award application deadline: 2/15; financial award applicants required to submit FAFSA. *Unit head:* Dr. Oliver H. Evans, President and Vice

Chancellor, 616-451-2787. *Application contact:* Sandra Britton, Director of Enrollment Management, 616-451-2787, Fax: 616-831-9689, E-mail: kcadadmissions@ferris.edu.

Florida Atlantic University, Dorothy F. Schmidt College of Arts and Letters, Department of Visual Arts and Art History, Boca Raton, FL 33431-0991. Offers art education (MAT); ceramics (MFA); computer art (MFA); graphic design (MFA); painting (MFA). *Faculty:* 17 full-time (11 women), 9 part-time/adjunct (7 women). *Students:* 19 full-time (12 women), 7 part-time (2 women); includes 8 minority (all Hispanic/Latino), 1 international. Average age 30. 33 applicants, 30% accepted, 6 enrolled. In 2010, 5 master's awarded. *Degree requirements:* For master's, one foreign language, project. *Entrance requirements:* For master's, GRE General Test, minimum GPA of 3.0 during last 60 hours of course work, slide portfolio. *Application deadline:* For fall admission, 2/21 for domestic and international students; for spring admission, 10/1 for domestic and international students. Application fee: $30. Electronic applications accepted. *Expenses:* Tuition, area resident: Part-time $319.96 per credit. Tuition, state resident: part-time $319.96 per credit. Tuition, nonresident: part-time $926.42 per credit. *Financial support:* Research assistantships with full tuition reimbursements, teaching assistantships with full tuition reimbursements, career-related internships or fieldwork, Federal Work-Study, and institutionally sponsored loans available. Financial award applicants required to submit FAFSA. *Faculty research:* Painting, ceramics (traditional and non-traditional), installation, video and interactive sculpture. *Unit head:* Dr. Linda Johnson, Chair, 561-297-3870, Fax: 561-297-3078, E-mail: ljohnson@fau.edu. *Application contact:* James A. Novak, Associate Professor/Graduate Coordinator/Advisor, 561-297-2430, Fax: 561-297-3078, E-mail: jnovak@fau.edu.

Howard University, Graduate School, Division of Fine Arts, Department of Art, Program in Fine Arts, Washington, DC 20059-0002. Offers 3D reality (sculpture and ceramics) (MFA); design (MFA); electronic studio (MFA); painting (MFA); photography (MFA). *Accreditation:* NASAD. *Degree requirements:* For master's, comprehensive exam, thesis, exhibit. *Entrance requirements:* For master's, minimum GPA of 3.0, portfolio.

Illinois Institute of Technology, Graduate College, Institute of Design, Chicago, IL 60616-3793. Offers M Des, MDM, PhD, M Des/MBA. Part-time programs available. *Faculty:* 13 full-time (2 women), 31 part-time/adjunct (10 women). *Students:* 128 full-time (64 women), 18 part-time (8 women); includes 33 minority (5 Black or African American, non-Hispanic/Latino; 1 American Indian or Alaska Native, non-Hispanic/Latino; 21 Asian, non-Hispanic/Latino; 4 Hispanic/Latino; 2 Two or more races, non-Hispanic/Latino), 40 international. Average age 31. 144 applicants, 74% accepted, 51 enrolled. In 2010, 54 master's, 1 doctorate awarded. Terminal master's awarded for partial completion of doctoral program. *Degree requirements:* For master's, comprehensive exam (for some programs), thesis (for some programs); for doctorate, one foreign language, comprehensive exam, thesis/dissertation. *Entrance requirements:* For master's, GRE General Test (minimum score 1000 Quantitative and Verbal, 3.5 Analytical Writing), bachelor's degree, minimum GPA of 3.0, official transcripts, portfolio, prior work experience, 3 letters of recommendation from professional contacts, statement of education and career goals, interview; for doctorate, GRE General Test, master's degree in design from accredited institution, official transcripts, portfolio, 2-5 years of work experience, 3 letters of recommendation, statement of research interests, interview. Additional exam requirements/recommendations for international students: Required—TOEFL (minimum score 550 paper-based; 213 computer-based; 80 iBT), Test for Spoken English (TSE): 24; Recommended—IELTS (minimum score 5.5). *Application deadline:* For fall admission, 2/15 for domestic and international students; for spring admission, 10/15 for domestic students, 9/15 for international students. Application fee: $100. Electronic applications accepted. *Expenses:* Contact institution. *Financial support:* In 2010–11, 1 research assistantship (averaging $2,000 per year) was awarded; fellowships with full and partial tuition reimbursements, career-related internships or fieldwork, Federal Work-Study, institutionally sponsored loans, scholarships/grants, health care benefits, tuition waivers (partial), and unspecified assistantships also available. Support available to part-time students. Financial award applicants required to submit FAFSA. *Faculty research:* Users' interactions with their environments, methods of innovation within organizations, the value of design for business and strategy. Total annual research expenditures: $739,289. *Unit head:* Patrick Whitney, Dean, 312-595-4900, Fax: 312-595-4901, E-mail: patrick.whitney@iit.edu. *Application contact:* Rachel Dean, Director of Admissions and Retention, 312-595-4906, Fax: 312-596-4901, E-mail: rdean@id.iit.edu.

Indiana University–Purdue University Indianapolis, Herron School of Art and Design, Indianapolis, IN 46202-2896. Offers art education (MAE); furniture design (MFA); printmaking (MFA); sculpture (MFA); visual communication (MFA). *Accreditation:* NASAD. Part-time and evening/weekend programs available. *Faculty:* 2 full-time (both women). *Students:* 32 full-time (18 women), 14 part-time (all women); includes 5 minority (2 Asian, non-Hispanic/Latino; 3 Hispanic/Latino), 6 international. Average age 30. 57 applicants, 42% accepted, 11 enrolled. In 2010, 14 master's awarded. *Entrance requirements:* For master's, portfolio, 44 hours of course work in art history and studio art. *Application deadline:* For fall admission, 6/1 priority date for domestic students, 3/15 priority date for international students; for spring admission, 11/1 priority date for domestic students, 10/15 priority date for international students. Applications are processed on a rolling basis. Application fee: $55 ($65 for international students). Electronic applications accepted. *Financial support:* Career-related internships or fieldwork, Federal Work-Study, institutionally sponsored loans, scholarships/grants, and tuition waivers (partial) available. Support available to part-time students. Total annual research expenditures: $6,097. *Unit head:* Valerie Eickmeier, Dean, 317-278-9470, Fax: 317-278-9471, E-mail: herron@iupui.edu. *Application contact:* Herron Student Services Office, 317-378-9400, E-mail: herrart@iupui.edu.

Iowa State University of Science and Technology, Graduate College, College of Design, Department of Art and Design, Ames, IA 50011. Offers art and design (MA); graphic design (MFA); integrated visual arts (MFA); interior design (MFA). Part-time programs available. *Faculty:* 36 full-time (20 women), 1 (woman) part-time/adjunct. *Students:* 52 full-time (39 women), 22 part-time (11 women); includes 1 Black or African American, non-Hispanic/Latino; 1 Asian, non-Hispanic/Latino; 1 Hispanic/Latino, 18 international. 48 applicants, 71% accepted, 19 enrolled. In 2010, 15 master's awarded. *Degree requirements:* For master's, thesis (for some programs). *Entrance requirements:* For master's, GRE General Test, resume. Additional exam requirements/recommendations for international students: Required—TOEFL (minimum score 550 paper-based; 79 iBT), IELTS (minimum score 6.5). *Application deadline:* For fall admission, 4/15 priority date for domestic and international students; for spring admission, 4/15 for domestic and international students. Applications are processed on a rolling basis. Application fee: $40 ($90 for international students). Electronic applications accepted. *Financial support:* Research assistantships with tuition reimbursements, teaching assistantships with tuition reimbursements, career-related internships or fieldwork, Federal Work-Study, institutionally sponsored loans, and tuition waivers (partial) available. Support available to part-time students. Financial award application deadline: 2/15; financial award applicants required to submit FAFSA. *Faculty research:* Computer applications, fire safety, human factors in design, art and design education, fine arts, craft design. *Unit head:* Dr. Roger Baer, Chair, 515-294-6724, Fax: 515-294-2725, E-mail: artdn@iastate.edu. *Application contact:* Dr. Roger Baer, Chair, 515-294-6724, Fax: 515-294-2725, E-mail: artdn@iastate.edu.

Kansas State University, Graduate School, College of Human Ecology, Department of Apparel, Textiles, and Interior Design, Manhattan, KS 66506. Offers design (MS); general apparel and textile (MS); marketing (MS); merchandising (MS); product development (MS). *Degree requirements:* For master's, thesis optional, residency. *Entrance requirements:* For master's, GRE General Test, minimum undergraduate GPA of 3.0. Additional exam requirements/recommendations for international students: Required—TOEFL (minimum score 600 paper-based; 250 computer-based). Electronic applications accepted. *Faculty research:* Apparel marketing and consumer behavior, protective and functional clothing and textiles, social and environmental responsibility, apparel design, new product development.

Lamar University, College of Graduate Studies, College of Fine Arts and Communication, Department of Art, Beaumont, TX 77710. Offers art history (MA); photography (MA); studio art

Applied Arts and Design—General

Lamar University (continued)
(MA); visual design (MA). Part-time and evening/weekend programs available. *Faculty:* 5 full-time (3 women). *Students:* 2 full-time (1 woman), 3 part-time (2 women). Average age 42. 3 applicants, 33% accepted, 0 enrolled. *Degree requirements:* For master's, thesis. *Entrance requirements:* For master's, GRE General Test, minimum GPA of 2.5 in last 60 hours of undergraduate course work. Additional exam requirements/recommendations for international students: Required—TOEFL. *Application deadline:* For fall admission, 8/1 priority date for domestic students; for spring admission, 12/1 for domestic students. Applications are processed on a rolling basis. Application fee: $25 ($50 for international students). *Expenses:* Tuition, state resident: full-time $4160; part-time $208 per credit hour. Tuition, nonresident: full-time $10,360; part-time $518 per credit hour. *Financial support:* Fellowships, career-related internships or fieldwork, Federal Work-Study, and scholarships/grants available. Financial award application deadline: 4/1. *Faculty research:* Nineteenth century academic paintings, metal casting, pigment color stability, computer-modified photography, manipulated photography. *Unit head:* Donna M. Meeks, Chair, 409-880-8141, Fax: 409-880-1799, E-mail: meeksdm@lub002.lamar.edu. *Application contact:* Debbie Piper, Coordinator of Graduate Admissions, 409-880-8356, Fax: 409-880-8414, E-mail: gradmissions@hal.lamar.edu.

Louisiana State University and Agricultural and Mechanical College, Graduate School, College of Art and Design, Baton Rouge, LA 70803. Offers M Arch, MA, MFA, MLA. *Accreditation:* ASLA (one or more programs are accredited); NASAD (one or more programs are accredited). Part-time programs available. *Students:* 129 full-time (71 women), 8 part-time (5 women); includes 4 Asian, non-Hispanic/Latino; 3 Hispanic/Latino; 1 Native Hawaiian or other Pacific Islander, non-Hispanic/Latino, 16 international. Average age 28. 270 applicants, 41% accepted, 49 enrolled. In 2010, 42 master's awarded. *Degree requirements:* For master's, thesis. *Entrance requirements:* For master's, GRE General Test, minimum GPA of 3.0. Additional exam requirements/recommendations for international students: Required—TOEFL (minimum score 550 paper-based; 213 computer-based; 79 iBT) or IELTS (minimum score 6.5). *Application deadline:* For fall admission, 1/25 priority date for domestic students, 5/15 for international students; for spring admission, 10/15 for international students. Applications are processed on a rolling basis. Application fee: $50 ($70 for international students). Electronic applications accepted. *Financial support:* In 2010–11, 114 students received support, including 24 research assistantships with partial tuition reimbursements available (averaging $7,389 per year), 45 teaching assistantships with partial tuition reimbursements available (averaging $7,044 per year); fellowships, career-related internships or fieldwork, Federal Work-Study, institutionally sponsored loans, scholarships/grants, health care benefits, tuition waivers (full and partial), and unspecified assistantships also available. Support available to part-time students. Financial award applicants required to submit FAFSA. *Faculty research:* Creative studio work, site-design, computer applications, historic preservation, energy conservation. Total annual research expenditures: $57,960. *Unit head:* Kenneth Carpenter, Dean, 225-578-5400, Fax: 225-578-5040, E-mail: dc1@lsu.edu. *Application contact:* Theresa Mooney, Academic Counselor, 225-578-5400, Fax: 225-578-1445, E-mail: deacon1@lsu.edu.

Louisiana Tech University, Graduate School, College of Liberal Arts, School of Art, Ruston, LA 71272. Offers art and graphic design (MFA); photography (MFA); studio art (MFA). *Accreditation:* NASAD. Part-time programs available. *Degree requirements:* For master's, exhibit. *Entrance requirements:* For master's, GRE General Test, portfolio.

Maryland Institute College of Art, Graduate Studies, The Business of Art and Design Program, Baltimore, MD 21217. Offers MPS. Part-time programs available. Postbaccalaureate distance learning degree programs offered (minimal on-campus study). *Entrance requirements:* Additional exam requirements/recommendations for international students: Required—TOEFL (minimum score 550 paper-based; 213 computer-based; 80 iBT). *Application deadline:* For spring admission, 1/15 for domestic and international students. Application fee: $60. *Expenses:* Tuition: Full-time $34,550; part-time $1440 per credit hour. Required fees: $1140; $570 per term. *Financial support:* Applicants required to submit FAFSA. *Unit head:* Heather Bradbury, Manager, 410-225-2220, Fax: 410-225-2229, E-mail: hbradbury@mica.edu. *Application contact:*

Scott G. Kelly, Associate Dean of Graduate Admission, 410-225-2256, Fax: 410-225-2408, E-mail: graduate@mica.edu.

Massachusetts College of Art and Design, Graduate Programs, Master of Fine Arts (MFA) Program, Boston, MA 02115-5882. Offers ceramics (MFA); design (MFA); fibers (MFA); film/video (MFA); glass (MFA); media and performing arts (MFA); metals/jewelry (MFA); painting (MFA); photography (MFA); printmaking (MFA); sculpture (MFA). *Accreditation:* NASAD. *Faculty:* 14 full-time (7 women), 16 part-time/adjunct (10 women). *Students:* 86 full-time (51 women), 9 part-time (5 women); includes 10 minority (1 Asian, non-Hispanic/Latino; 6 Hispanic/Latino; 3 Two or more races, non-Hispanic/Latino), 14 international. Average age 34. 298 applicants, 28% accepted, 41 enrolled. In 2010, 40 master's awarded. *Degree requirements:* For master's, thesis, exhibit. *Entrance requirements:* For master's, 12 units of course work in art history, portfolio, resume, letters of reference, interview. Additional exam requirements/recommendations for international students: Required—TOEFL (minimum score 563 paper-based; 223 computer-based; 85 iBT); Recommended—IELTS (minimum score 6.5). *Application deadline:* For fall admission, 1/15 for domestic and international students. Application fee: $85. Electronic applications accepted. *Expenses:* Tuition, state resident: part-time $665 per credit. Tuition, nonresident: part-time $665 per credit. *Financial support:* In 2010–11, 19 fellowships (averaging $5,000 per year), 43 research assistantships (averaging $2,000 per year), 44 teaching assistantships (averaging $2,000 per year) were awarded; career-related internships or fieldwork and Federal Work-Study also available. Support available to part-time students. Financial award application deadline: 5/1; financial award applicants required to submit FAFSA. *Unit head:* George Creamer, Dean of Graduate Programs, 617-879-7163, Fax: 617-879-7171, E-mail: creamer@massart.edu. *Application contact:* George Creamer, Dean of Graduate Programs, 617-879-7163, Fax: 617-879-7171, E-mail: creamer@massart.edu.

Memphis College of Art, Graduate Programs, Memphis, TN 38104-2764. Offers art education (MA, MAT); studio art (MFA). *Accreditation:* NASAD. Part-time and evening/weekend programs available. *Faculty:* 26 full-time (15 women), 13 part-time/adjunct (8 women). *Students:* 28 full-time (18 women), 42 part-time (27 women); includes 13 minority (11 Black or African American, non-Hispanic/Latino; 1 Asian, non-Hispanic/Latino; 1 Hispanic/Latino), 2 international. Average age 28. 68 applicants, 56% accepted, 22 enrolled. In 2010, 28 master's awarded. *Degree requirements:* For master's, thesis. *Entrance requirements:* For master's, portfolio, interview, resume. Additional exam requirements/recommendations for international students: Required—TOEFL (minimum score 525 paper-based; 195 computer-based). *Application deadline:* For fall admission, 3/1 for domestic and international students; for spring admission, 11/1 for domestic and international students. Applications are processed on a rolling basis. Application fee: $50. Electronic applications accepted. *Expenses:* Tuition: Full-time $24,300; part-time $1012 per credit hour. Required fees: $650; $325 per semester. Tuition and fees vary according to course load. *Financial support:* Application deadline: 8/1. *Unit head:* Ken Strickland, Vice President for Academic Affairs, 901-272-5107, Fax: 901-272-5158, E-mail: kstrickland@mca.edu. *Application contact:* Annette Moore, Dean of Admissions, 901-272-5153, Fax: 901-272-5158, E-mail: amoore@mca.edu.

See Display on page 173 and Close-Up on page 221.

Minneapolis College of Art and Design, Program in Visual Studies, Minneapolis, MN 55404-4347. Offers animation (MFA); comic art (MFA); drawing (MFA); filmmaking (MFA); fine arts (MFA); furniture design (MFA); graphic design (MFA); illustration (MFA); interactive media (MFA); painting (MFA); photography (MFA); printmaking (MFA); sculpture (MFA). *Accreditation:* NASAD. Part-time programs available. *Degree requirements:* For master's, thesis, thesis exhibit. *Entrance requirements:* For master's, portfolio of visual artwork, resume, 3 letters of recommendation. Additional exam requirements/recommendations for international students: Required—TOEFL (minimum score 550 paper-based; 213 computer-based; 79 iBT). Electronic applications accepted. *Faculty research:* Visual arts: animation, comic art, drawing, film-making, furniture design, graphic design, illustration, interactive media, painting, photography, printmaking, sculpture.

New Mexico State University, Graduate School, College of Arts and Sciences, Department of Art, Las Cruces, NM 88003-8001. Offers art history (MA); ceramics (MA, MFA); design (MA, MFA); drawing (MFA); metals (MA, MFA); painting (MFA); photography (MFA); sculpture (MA, MFA). *Faculty:* 9 full-time (5 women), 3 part-time/adjunct (1 woman). *Students:* 18 full-time (10 women), 2 part-time (both women); includes 6 minority (1 American Indian or Alaska Native, non-Hispanic/Latino; 1 Asian, non-Hispanic/Latino; 4 Hispanic/Latino), 1 international. Average age 34. 26 applicants, 77% accepted, 11 enrolled. In 2010, 11 master's awarded. *Degree requirements:* For master's, comprehensive exam (for some programs), thesis, thesis exhibit. *Entrance requirements:* For master's, portfolio, 10-page paper (art history). *Application deadline:* For fall admission, 2/15 for domestic students; for winter admission, 10/15 for domestic students; for spring admission, 7/15 for domestic students. Application fee: $30 ($50 for international students). Electronic applications accepted. *Expenses:* Tuition, state resident: full-time $4536; part-time $242 per credit. Tuition, nonresident: full-time $15,816; part-time $712 per credit. Required fees: $636 per term. *Financial support:* In 2010–11, 17 teaching assistantships (averaging $6,640 per year) were awarded; research assistantships, Federal Work-Study and health care benefits also available. Support available to part-time students. Financial award application deadline: 3/1; financial award applicants required to submit FAFSA. *Faculty research:* Painting, graphic design, sculpture, ceramics, photography, jewelry. *Unit head:* Dr. Thom Brown, Head, 575-646-1705, Fax: 575-646-8036, E-mail: artdept@nmsu.edu. *Application contact:* Dr. Thom Brown, Head, 575-646-1705, Fax: 575-646-8036, E-mail: artdept@nmsu.edu.

The New School: A University, Parsons The New School for Design, Program in Design Studies, New York, NY 10011. Offers MA.

The New School: A University, Parsons The New School for Design, Program in Transdisciplinary Design (TransDesign), New York, NY 10011. Offers MFA. *Degree requirements:* For master's, thesis.

New York University, Tisch School of the Arts Asia, Singapore, NY 248923, Singapore. Offers animation and digital arts (MFA); dramatic writing (MFA); film production (MFA). *Entrance requirements:* Additional exam requirements/recommendations for international students: Required—TOEFL (minimum score 610 paper-based; 250 computer-based; 105 iBT). Electronic applications accepted.

New York University, Tisch School of the Arts, Department of Design for Stage and Film, New York, NY 10012-1019. Offers MFA. *Faculty:* 10 full-time, 11 part-time/adjunct. *Students:* 58 full-time (35 women); includes 2 Black or African American, non-Hispanic/Latino; 1 American Indian or Alaska Native, non-Hispanic/Latino; 3 Asian, non-Hispanic/Latino; 1 Hispanic/Latino. Average age 28. 139 applicants, 22% accepted, 20 enrolled. In 2010, 20 master's awarded. *Degree requirements:* For master's, thesis. *Entrance requirements:* For master's, interview, portfolio. Additional exam requirements/recommendations for international students: Required—TOEFL (minimum score 620 paper-based; 260 computer-based; 105 iBT), IELTS. *Application deadline:* For fall admission, 1/1 priority date for domestic and international students. Application fee: $60. Electronic applications accepted. *Financial support:* In 2010–11, 28 students received support, including 12 fellowships with full and partial tuition reimbursements available; Federal Work-Study, institutionally sponsored loans, tuition waivers (partial), and unspecified assistantships also available. Financial award application deadline: 2/15; financial award applicants required to submit FAFSA. *Unit head:* Susan Hilferty, Chair, 212-998-1950, Fax: 212-998-1953, E-mail: tisch.design@nyu.edu. *Application contact:* Dan Sandford, Director of Graduate Admissions, 212-998-1918, Fax: 212-995-4060, E-mail: tisch.gradadmissions@nyu.edu.

North Carolina State University, Graduate School, College of Design, Program in Art and Design, Raleigh, NC 27695. Offers MAD. *Degree requirements:* For master's, thesis optional. Electronic applications accepted.

North Carolina State University, Graduate School, College of Design, Program in Design, Raleigh, NC 27695. Offers PhD. *Degree requirements:* For doctorate, thesis/dissertation. *Entrance requirements:* For doctorate, GRE. Electronic applications accepted. *Faculty research:* Design and cognition, children's environments, community design, ecological design, sustainable communities and urban spatial development.

NSCAD University, Program in Fine Arts, Halifax, NS B3J 3J6, Canada. Offers craft (MFA); design (M Des); fine and media arts (MFA). *Degree requirements:* For master's, thesis, exhibit. *Entrance requirements:* For master's, portfolio, at least 5 art history classes. Additional exam requirements/recommendations for international students: Required—Michigan English Language Assessment Battery (minimum score: 80), CanTEST (minimum score: 4.5), CAEL (minimum score: 70); Recommended—TOEFL (minimum score 575 paper-based; 233 computer-based; 90 iBT), IELTS (minimum score 6.5).

Oklahoma State University, College of Human Sciences, Department of Design, Housing and Merchandising, Stillwater, OK 74078. Offers MS, PhD. *Faculty:* 16 full-time (12 women). *Students:* 10 full-time (9 women), 17 part-time (15 women); includes 1 Black or African American, non-Hispanic/Latino; 1 Asian, non-Hispanic/Latino; 1 Hispanic/Latino, 6 international. Average age 31. 21 applicants, 38% accepted, 4 enrolled. In 2010, 7 master's, 6 doctorates awarded. *Degree requirements:* For master's, thesis (for some programs); for doctorate, comprehensive exam, thesis/dissertation. *Entrance requirements:* For master's and doctorate, GRE or GMAT. Additional exam requirements/recommendations for international students: Required—TOEFL (minimum score 550 paper-based; 79 iBT). *Application deadline:* For fall admission, 3/1 priority date for international students; for spring admission, 8/1 priority date for international students. Applications are processed on a rolling basis. Application fee: $40 ($75 for international students). Electronic applications accepted. *Expenses:* Tuition, state resident: full-time $3716; part-time $154.85 per credit hour. Tuition, nonresident: full-time $14,892; part-time $621 per credit hour. Required fees: $2044; $85.20 per credit hour. One-time fee: $50. Tuition and fees vary according to course load and campus/location. *Financial support:* In 2010–11, 8 research assistantships (averaging $10,343 per year), 10 teaching assistantships (averaging $11,369 per year) were awarded; career-related internships or fieldwork, Federal Work-Study, scholarships/grants, health care benefits, tuition waivers (partial), and unspecified assistantships also available. Support available to part-time students. Financial award application deadline: 3/1; financial award applicants required to submit FAFSA. *Faculty research:* Environmental sciences design, housing and merchandising; creativity and physical environment; product development, production and evaluation; experimental learning and critical thinking; technology strategies and assessment; customer expectation and satisfaction. *Unit head:* Dr. Randall Russ, Interim Head, 405-744-5049, Fax: 405-744-6910. *Application contact:* Dr. Gordon Emslie, Dean, 405-744-6368, Fax: 405-744-0355, E-mail: grad-i@okstate.edu.

Pacific Northwest College of Art, Program in Applied Craft and Design, Portland, OR 97209. Offers MFA. Program offered in collaboration with Oregon College of Art & Craft. *Accreditation:* NASAD. *Entrance requirements:* For master's, resume, 2 letters of recommendation, portfolio.

Pratt Institute, School of Art and Design, Brooklyn, NY 11205-3899. Offers MFA, MID, MPS, MS, Adv C, MS/MFA, MS/MS. *Accreditation:* NASAD (one or more programs are accredited). Part-time programs available. *Faculty:* 41 full-time (17 women), 200 part-time/adjunct (99 women). *Students:* 952 full-time (728 women), 47 part-time (36 women); includes 34 Black or African American, non-Hispanic/Latino; 82 Asian, non-Hispanic/Latino; 61 Hispanic/Latino; 14 Two or more races, non-Hispanic/Latino, 288 international. Average age 28. 1,882 applicants, 47% accepted, 394 enrolled. In 2010, 347 master's awarded. *Degree requirements:* For master's, thesis. *Entrance requirements:* Additional exam requirements/recommendations for international students: Required—TOEFL. *Application deadline:* For fall admission, 1/5 for domestic and international students; for spring admission, 10/1 for domestic and international students. Application fee: $50 ($90 for international students). Electronic applications accepted. *Expenses:* Tuition: Full-time $22,734; part-time $1263 per credit. Required fees: $1280. *Financial support:* Career-related internships or fieldwork, Federal Work-Study, institutionally sponsored loans, scholarships/grants, health care benefits, and unspecified assistantships available. Support available to part-time students. Financial award application deadline: 2/1; financial award applicants required to submit FAFSA. *Faculty research:* Painting, sculpture, and printmaking; package, interior, and communications design; art therapy; graphic and industrial design; four-dimensional design. *Unit head:* Concetta Stewart, Dean, 718-636-3619. *Application contact:* Young Hah, Director of Graduate Admissions, 718-636-3683, Fax: 718-399-4242, E-mail: yhah@pratt.edu.

See Display on next page and Close-Up on page 131.

Purdue University, Graduate School, College of Liberal Arts, Department of Visual and Performing Arts, West Lafayette, IN 47907. Offers art and design (MA); theatre (MA, MFA). *Accreditation:* NASAD; NAST. Part-time programs available. *Degree requirements:* For master's, terminal exhibit, project, or thesis. *Entrance requirements:* Additional exam requirements/recommendations for international students: Required—TOEFL. Electronic applications accepted. *Faculty research:* Design, fine arts, photography, acting, directing, theatre technology.

Rensselaer Polytechnic Institute, Graduate School, School of Humanities, Arts, and Social Sciences, Program in Science and Technology Studies, Troy, NY 12180-3590. Offers design studies (MS, PhD); policy studies (MS, PhD); science studies (MS, PhD); sustainability studies (MS, PhD); technology studies (MS, PhD). *Faculty:* 15 full-time (5 women). *Students:* 20 full-time (5 women), 4 part-time (2 women); includes 2 Black or African American, non-Hispanic/Latino; 1 Asian, non-Hispanic/Latino, 4 international. Average age 27. 19 applicants, 42% accepted, 5 enrolled. In 2010, 2 master's, 1 doctorate awarded. Terminal master's awarded for partial completion of doctoral program. *Degree requirements:* For master's, thesis (for some programs); for doctorate, comprehensive exam, thesis/dissertation. *Entrance requirements:* For master's and doctorate, GRE General Test. Additional exam requirements/recommendations for international students: Required—TOEFL (minimum score 600 paper-based; 250 computer-based). *Application deadline:* For fall admission, 1/15 priority date for domestic students, 1/15 for international students. Applications are processed on a rolling basis. Application fee: $75. Electronic applications accepted. *Expenses:* Tuition: Full-time $39,600; part-time $1650 per credit. Required fees: $1896. *Financial support:* In 2010–11, 22 students received support, including 6 fellowships with tuition reimbursements available (averaging $19,800 per year), 2 research assistantships with full tuition reimbursements available (averaging $19,800 per year), 11 teaching assistantships with full tuition reimbursements available (averaging $19,800 per year); career-related internships or fieldwork, institutionally sponsored loans, and tuition waivers (partial) also available. Financial award application deadline: 1/15. *Faculty research:* Communities and technology, social dimensions of IT and biotechnology, ethics and policy, design. Total annual research expenditures: $75,000. *Unit head:* Dr. Sharon Anderson-Gold, Chair, 518-276-8837, Fax: 518-276-2659, E-mail: anders@rpi.edu. *Application contact:* Dr. Edward J. Woodhouse, Director of Graduate Studies, 518-276-8506, Fax: 518-276-2659, E-mail: woodhouse@rpi.edu.

Rhode Island School of Design, Graduate Studies, Providence, RI 02903-2784. Offers M Arch, MA, MAT, MFA, MIA, MID, MLA. *Accreditation:* NASAD (one or more programs are accredited). *Degree requirements:* For master's, thesis, exhibit. *Entrance requirements:* For master's, portfolio, 3 letters of recommendation. Additional exam requirements/recommendations for international students: Required—TOEFL (minimum score 580 paper-based; 237 computer-based), IELTS (minimum score 6.5). Electronic applications accepted. *Faculty research:* Ceramics, glass, graphic design, sculpture, jewelry/metalsmithing, photography, painting, industrial design, architecture.

Rutgers, The State University of New Jersey, New Brunswick, Mason Gross School of the Arts, Theater Arts Department, New Brunswick, NJ 08901. Offers acting (MFA); design (MFA); directing (MFA); playwriting (MFA); stage management (MFA). *Faculty:* 13 full-time (8 women), 21 part-time/adjunct (6 women). *Students:* 67 full-time (41 women); includes 10 Black or African American, non-Hispanic/Latino; 1 Hispanic/Latino. Average age 27. 183 applicants, 17% accepted, 27 enrolled. In 2010, 22 master's awarded. *Degree requirements:* For master's, thesis (for some programs), performance project. *Entrance requirements:* For master's, audition, interview, portfolio. Additional exam requirements/recommendations for international students: Required—TOEFL (minimum score 550 paper-based; 213 computer-based), IELTS (minimum score 7). *Application deadline:* For fall admission, 3/1 for domestic and international students. Application fee: $65. Electronic applications accepted. *Expenses:* Tuition, state resident: full-time $7200; part-time $600 per credit. Tuition, nonresident: full-time $11,124; part-time $927 per credit. *Financial support:* In 2010–11, 16 fellowships (averaging $1,000 per year), 62 teaching assistantships with partial tuition reimbursements (averaging $3,700 per year) were awarded; career-related internships or fieldwork, Federal Work-Study, scholarships/grants, and health care benefits also available. Financial award application deadline: 3/1; financial award applicants required to submit FAFSA. *Faculty research:* Faculty of working professional. *Unit head:* Michael Miller, Interim Chair, 732-932-9891 Ext. 10, Fax: 732-932-1409. *Application contact:* Barbara Harwanko, Administrative Assistant, 732-932-9891 Ext. 10, Fax: 732-932-1409, E-mail: harwanko@masongross.rutgers.edu.

San Diego State University, Graduate and Research Affairs, College of Professional Studies and Fine Arts, School of Art, Design and Art History, San Diego, CA 92182. Offers art history (MA); studio arts (MA, MFA), including applied design, environmental design, graphic design, interior design, painting and printmaking, sculpture. *Accreditation:* NASAD (one or more programs are accredited). *Degree requirements:* For master's, variable foreign language requirement, thesis. *Entrance requirements:* For master's, GRE General Test, bachelor's degree in related field, slide portfolio, typed slide information sheet, 2 letters of recommendation. Additional exam requirements/recommendations for international students: Required—TOEFL. Electronic applications accepted.

San Francisco Art Institute, Graduate Program, Department of Design and Technology, San Francisco, CA 94133. Offers MFA, Certificate. Part-time programs available. *Degree requirements:* For master's and Certificate, oral reviews. *Entrance requirements:* For master's and Certificate, portfolio. Additional exam requirements/recommendations for international students: Required—TOEFL (minimum score 580 paper-based; 237 computer-based). Electronic applications accepted.

San Jose State University, Graduate Studies and Research, College of Humanities and the Arts, School of Art and Design, San Jose, CA 95192-0001. Offers animation/illustration (MA); art history (MA); digital media arts (MFA); photography (MFA); pictorial arts (MFA); spatial arts (MFA). *Accreditation:* NASAD (one or more programs are accredited). *Entrance requirements:* For master's, GRE. Electronic applications accepted.

Savannah College of Art and Design, Graduate School, Savannah, GA 31402-3146. Offers accessory design (MA, MFA); advertising design (MA, MFA); animation (MA, MFA); architectural history (MA, MFA); architecture (M Arch); art history (MA); arts administration (MA); broadcast design (MA, MFA); cinema studies (MA); commercial photography (MA); digital photography (MA); documentary photography (MA); fashion (MA, MFA); fibers (MA, MFA); film and television (MA, MFA); furniture design (MA, MFA); graphic design (MA, MFA); historic preservation (MA, MFA, Graduate Certificate); illustration (MA, MFA); illustration design (MA); industrial design (MA, MFA); interactive design and game development (MA, MFA, Graduate Certificate); interior design (MA, MFA); international preservation (MA); luxury and fashion management (MA, MFA); metals and jewelry (MA, MFA); painting (MA, MFA); performing arts (MFA); photography (MA, MFA); printmaking (MA, MFA); production design (MA, MFA); professional education (MAT), including art, drama; professional writing (MFA); sculpture (MA, MFA); sequential art (MA, MFA); service design (MFA); sound design (MA, MFA); urban design and development (MUD); visual effects (MA, MFA). Part-time programs available. Postbaccalaureate distance learning degree programs offered (no on-campus study). *Students:* 1,576 full-time (898 women), 407 part-time (240 women); includes 208 minority (115 Black or African American, non-Hispanic/Latino; 8 American Indian or Alaska Native, non-Hispanic/Latino; 29 Asian, non-Hispanic/Latino; 45 Hispanic/Latino; 2 Native Hawaiian or other Pacific Islander, non-Hispanic/Latino; 9 Two or more races, non-Hispanic/Latino), 435 international. Average age

28. 2,826 applicants, 36% accepted, 642 enrolled. In 2010, 534 master's, 8 other advanced degrees awarded. *Degree requirements:* For master's, thesis, internship. *Entrance requirements:* For master's, interview, 3 letters of recommendation. Additional exam requirements/recommendations for international students: Required—TOEFL (minimum score 550 paper-based; 133 computer-based). *Application deadline:* For fall admission, 4/1 priority date for domestic and international students. Applications are processed on a rolling basis. Application fee: $35. Electronic applications accepted. *Expenses:* Tuition: Full-time $29,520; part-time $3280 per quarter. Tuition and fees vary according to campus/location. *Financial support:* Fellowships, career-related internships or fieldwork, Federal Work-Study, and scholarships/grants available. Financial award application deadline: 4/1; financial award applicants required to submit FAFSA. *Unit head:* Edward Dupuy, Dean of Graduate Studies, 912-525-5838, E-mail: edupuy@scad.edu. *Application contact:* Elizabeth Mathis, Director of Graduate Recruitment, 912-525-5965, Fax: 912-525-5985, E-mail: emathis@scad.edu.

See Display on page 177 and Close-Up on page 223

School of the Art Institute of Chicago, Graduate Division, Department of Architecture, Interior Architecture, and Designed Objects, Program in Designed Objects, Chicago, IL 60603-3103. Offers M Des. *Entrance requirements:* Additional exam requirements/recommendations for international students: Required—TOEFL, IELTS.

See Close-Up on page 225.

School of the Art Institute of Chicago, Graduate Division, Department of Architecture, Interior Architecture, and Designed Objects, Program in Design for Emerging Technologies, Chicago, IL 60603-3103. Offers MFA. *Entrance requirements:* Additional exam requirements/recommendations for international students: Required—TOEFL, IELTS.

See Close-Up on page 225.

School of the Art Institute of Chicago, Graduate Division, Department of Architecture, Interior Architecture, and Designed Objects, Program in Interior Architecture, Chicago, IL 60603-3103. Offers M Arc. *Entrance requirements:* Additional exam requirements/recommendations for international students: Required—TOEFL, IELTS.

See Close-Up on page 225.

School of Visual Arts, Graduate Programs, Branding Department, New York, NY 10010-3994. Offers MPS.

School of Visual Arts, Graduate Programs, Design Department, New York, NY 10010-3994. Offers MFA. *Accreditation:* NASAD. *Degree requirements:* For master's, final review, project or thesis. *Entrance requirements:* For master's, portfolio. Additional exam requirements/recommendations for international students: Required—TOEFL (minimum score 550 paper-based; 213 computer-based; 79 iBT). Electronic applications accepted. *Expenses:* Contact institution.

School of Visual Arts, Graduate Programs, Program in Design Criticism, New York, NY 10010-3994. Offers MFA.

Southern Illinois University Carbondale, Graduate School, College of Liberal Arts, School of Art and Design, Carbondale, IL 62901-4701. Offers ceramics (MFA); drawing (MFA); fiber/weaving (MFA); glass (MFA); jewelry (MFA); metalsmithing/blacksmithing (MFA); painting (MFA); printmaking (MFA); sculpture (MFA). *Accreditation:* NASAD. *Degree requirements:* For master's, thesis or alternative. *Entrance requirements:* For master's, minimum GPA of 2.7, portfolio, slides. Additional exam requirements/recommendations for international students: Required—TOEFL. *Faculty research:* Prints/woodcuts, foundry, watercolor.

Stephen F. Austin State University, Graduate School, College of Fine Arts, School of Art, Nacogdoches, TX 75962. Offers art (MA); design (MFA); drawing (MFA); painting (MFA); sculpture (MFA). *Accreditation:* NASAD. Part-time programs available. *Degree requirements:* For master's, comprehensive exam, thesis, exhibit. *Entrance requirements:* For master's, GRE General Test, portfolio. Additional exam requirements/recommendations for international students: Required—TOEFL. *Faculty research:* Printmaking, jewelry, photography, ceramics, art history.

Suffolk University, New England School of Art and Design, Boston, MA 02108-2770. Offers graphic design (MA); interior architecture (MFA); interior design (MA). *Accreditation:* CIDA; NASAD. Part-time and evening/weekend programs available. *Faculty:* 21 full-time (12 women), 7 part-time/adjunct (2 women). *Students:* 56 full-time (45 women), 76 part-time (65 women); includes 2 Black or African American, non-Hispanic/Latino; 5 Asian, non-Hispanic/Latino; 5 Hispanic/Latino, 13 international. Average age 30. 113 applicants, 67% accepted, 48 enrolled. In 2010, 30 master's awarded. *Entrance requirements:* For master's, GRE (for MFA), art portfolio, interview, 2 letters of recommendation, resume; letter of intent (for MFA). Additional exam requirements/recommendations for international students: Required—TOEFL (minimum score 550 paper-based; 213 computer-based; 80 iBT). *Application deadline:* For fall admission, 6/15 priority date for domestic students, 6/15 for international students; for spring admission, 11/1 priority date for domestic students, 11/1 for international students. Applications are processed on a rolling basis. Application fee: $50. Electronic applications accepted. *Expenses:* Contact institution. *Financial support:* In 2010–11, 83 students received support, including 39 fellowships with partial tuition reimbursements available (averaging $7,001 per year). Financial award application deadline: 4/1. *Faculty research:* Adaptive re-use of historical structures, universal design, American architecture history, interior design to reduce inefficiency, meditation SPA. *Unit head:* William Davis, Director, 617-994-4264, Fax: 617-994-4250, E-mail: wdavis@suffolk.edu. *Application contact:* Judith Reynolds, Director of Graduate Admissions, 617-573-8302, Fax: 617-305-1733, E-mail: grad.admission@suffolk.edu.

Sul Ross State University, School of Arts and Sciences, Department of Fine Arts and Communication, Alpine, TX 79832. Offers art education (M Ed); art history (M Ed); studio art (M Ed), including ceramics, design, drawing, jewelry, painting, printmaking, sculpture, weaving. Part-time programs available. *Degree requirements:* For master's, oral or written exam. *Entrance requirements:* For master's, GRE General Test, minimum GPA of 2.5 in last 60 hours of undergraduate work. *Faculty research:* Ceramic sculpture, watercolor, wood sculpture, rock art.

Syracuse University, College of Visual and Performing Arts, Program in Art Video, Syracuse, NY 13244. Offers MFA. *Accreditation:* NASAD. Part-time programs available. Postbaccalaureate distance learning degree programs offered (no on-campus study). *Students:* 5 full-time (3 women), 1 (woman) part-time, 5 international. Average age 27. 8 applicants, 25% accepted, 2 enrolled. In 2010, 4 master's awarded. *Degree requirements:* For master's, thesis or alternative. *Entrance requirements:* For master's, portfolio. Additional exam requirements/recommendations for international students: Required—TOEFL (minimum score 100 iBT). *Application deadline:* For fall admission, 2/1 priority date for domestic and international students. Application fee: $75. Electronic applications accepted. *Expenses:* Tuition: Part-time $1162 per credit. *Financial support:* Fellowships with full tuition reimbursements, teaching assistantships with full and partial tuition reimbursements, tuition waivers (partial) available. Financial award application deadline: 1/1; financial award applicants required to submit FAFSA. *Unit head:* Heath Hanlin, Dept. Chair, 315-443-2103, E-mail: hahanlin@syr.edu. *Application contact:* Harriett Conti, Assistant Dean for Recruitment and Admissions, 315-443-5755, E-mail: hmconti@syr.edu.

See Display on page 179 and Close-Up on page 227.

Syracuse University, College of Visual and Performing Arts, Program in Collaborative Design, Syracuse, NY 13244. Offers MFA. *Entrance requirements:* For master's, portfolio. Additional exam requirements/recommendations for international students: Required—TOEFL (minimum score 100 iBT). *Application deadline:* For fall admission, 2/1 priority date for domestic and international students. Application fee: $75. Electronic applications accepted. *Expenses:* Tuition:

Part-time $1162 per credit. *Financial support:* Fellowships with full tuition reimbursements, teaching assistantships, tuition waivers (partial) available. Financial award application deadline: 1/1. *Unit head:* Ann Clarke, Chair, 315-443-5889. *Application contact:* Harriett Conti, Assistant Dean for Recruitment and Admissions, 315-443-5755, E-mail: hmconti@syr.edu.

See Display on page 179 and Close-Up on page 227.

University of Alberta, Faculty of Graduate Studies and Research, Department of Art and Design, Edmonton, AB T6G 2E1, Canada. Offers drawing (MFA); history of art, design, and visual culture (MA); industrial design (M Des); painting (MFA); printmaking (MFA); sculpture (MFA); visual communication design (M Des). *Degree requirements:* For master's, thesis. *Entrance requirements:* For master's, portfolio (MFA and MDES). Additional exam requirements/recommendations for international students: Required—TOEFL (minimum score 550 paper-based; 213 computer-based).

University of Baltimore, Graduate School, The Yale Gordon College of Liberal Arts, Program in Integrated Design, Baltimore, MD 21201-5779. Offers MFA. Part-time and evening/weekend programs available. *Entrance requirements:* Additional exam requirements/recommendations for international students: Required—TOEFL (minimum score 550 paper-based; 213 computer-based). Electronic applications accepted. *Expenses:* Contact institution. *Faculty research:* Information and graphics design, economics, hypermedia communications.

University of California, Berkeley, Graduate Division, College of Environmental Design, Master of Arts in Design Program, Berkeley, CA 94720-1500. Offers MA. *Degree requirements:* For master's, thesis. *Entrance requirements:* For master's, GRE General Test, minimum GPA of 3.0, portfolio, 3 letters of recommendation. Additional exam requirements/recommendations for international students: Required—TOEFL.

University of California, Berkeley, UC Berkeley Extension, Certificate Programs in Art and Design, Berkeley, CA 94720-1500. Offers interior design and interior architecture (Certificate); landscape architecture (Certificate); visual arts (Postbaccalaureate Certificate).

University of California, Los Angeles, Graduate Division, School of the Arts and Architecture, Department of Design/Media Arts, Los Angeles, CA 90095. Offers MFA. *Faculty:* 12 full-time (4 women). *Students:* 21 full-time (6 women); includes 4 minority (1 Black or African American, non-Hispanic/Latino; 2 Asian, non-Hispanic/Latino; 1 Hispanic/Latino), 6 international. Average age 27. 164 applicants, 8% accepted, 12 enrolled. In 2010, 6 master's awarded. *Degree requirements:* For master's, comprehensive exam. *Entrance requirements:* For master's, portfolio, 20 slides and/or videotape, minimum GPA of 3.0. Additional exam requirements/recommendations for international students: Required—TOEFL. *Application deadline:* For fall admission, 12/15 for domestic students. Application fee: $70 ($90 for international students). Electronic applications accepted. *Financial support:* In 2010–11, 14 fellowships, 15 teaching assistantships were awarded; research assistantships, Federal Work-Study, institutionally sponsored loans, scholarships/grants, tuition waivers (full and partial), and unspecified assistantships also available. Financial award application deadline: 3/2. *Unit head:* Willem Henri Lucas, Chair, 310-825-0925, E-mail: whlucas@ucla.edu. *Application contact:* Department Office, 310-267-4907, E-mail: dmainfo@arts.ucla.edu.

University of Central Oklahoma, College of Graduate Studies and Research, College of Fine Arts and Design, Department of Design and Interior Design, Edmond, OK 73034-5209. Offers MFA. Part-time programs available. Postbaccalaureate distance learning degree programs offered (minimal on-campus study). *Entrance requirements:* Additional exam requirements/recommendations for international students: Required—TOEFL (minimum score 550 paper-based; 213 computer-based). Electronic applications accepted.

University of Cincinnati, Graduate School, College of Design, Architecture, Art, and Planning, School of Design, Cincinnati, OH 45221. Offers fashion design (M Des); graphic design (M Des); industrial design (M Des); interaction design (M Des); product development (M Des). *Accreditation:* NASAD. *Degree requirements:* For master's, thesis. *Entrance requirements:* For master's, undergraduate degree in design or related field, 2 years of work experience in design or related field. Additional exam requirements/recommendations for international students: Required—TOEFL. Electronic applications accepted. *Faculty research:* Design theory, interdisciplinary design topics.

University of Delaware, College of Arts and Sciences, Department of Art, Newark, DE 19716. Offers MA, MFA. *Degree requirements:* For master's, exposition paper final exhibition. *Entrance requirements:* For master's, portfolio of creative work. Electronic applications accepted. *Faculty research:* Painting, printmaking, ceramics, photography, sculpture.

University of Illinois at Urbana–Champaign, Graduate College, College of Fine and Applied Arts, School of Art and Design, Champaign, IL 61820. Offers Ed M, MA, MFA, PhD. *Accreditation:* NASAD. *Faculty:* 45 full-time (20 women), 4 part-time/adjunct (2 women). *Students:* 80 full-time (56 women), 12 part-time (5 women); includes 2 Asian, non-Hispanic/Latino; 4 Hispanic/Latino; 2 Two or more races, non-Hispanic/Latino, 26 international. 299 applicants, 11% accepted, 31 enrolled. In 2010, 28 master's, 4 doctorates awarded. *Entrance requirements:* For master's, minimum GPA of 3.0. *Application deadline:* Applications are processed on a rolling basis. Application fee: $75 ($90 for international students). Electronic applications accepted. *Financial support:* In 2010–11, 12 fellowships, 10 research assistantships, 51 teaching assistantships were awarded; tuition waivers (full and partial) also available. *Unit head:* Nan Goggin, Director, 217-333-0855, Fax: 217-244-7688, E-mail: goggin@illinois.edu. *Application contact:* Marsha K. Biddle, Coordinator of Graduate Academic Affairs, 217-333-0642, Fax: 217-244-7688, E-mail: mbiddle@illinois.edu.

The University of Kansas, Graduate Studies, School of Architecture, Design, and Planning, Department of Design, Lawrence, KS 66045. Offers design (MA, MFA); design management (MA); interaction design (MA). *Accreditation:* NASAD (one or more programs are accredited). *Students:* 11 full-time (7 women), 24 part-time (14 women), 5 international. Average age 33. 18 applicants, 72% accepted, 12 enrolled. In 2010, 4 master's awarded. *Degree requirements:* For master's, thesis. *Entrance requirements:* For master's, portfolio, 3 letters of recommendation, minimum GPA of 3.0. Additional exam requirements/recommendations for international students: Required—TOEFL, IELTS. *Application deadline:* For fall admission, 2/1 for domestic and international students; for spring admission, 10/15 for domestic students. Application fee: $55 ($65 for international students). Electronic applications accepted. *Expenses:* Tuition, state resident: full-time $7092; part-time $295.50 per credit hour. Tuition, nonresident: full-time $16,590; part-time $691.25 per credit hour. Required fees: $858; $71.49 per credit hour. Tuition and fees vary according to course load, campus/location and program. *Financial support:* Fellowships, teaching assistantships with full and partial tuition reimbursements, Federal Work-Study, scholarships/grants, and unspecified assistantships available. Financial award application deadline: 2/1; financial award applicants required to submit FAFSA. *Faculty research:* Interaction design, design management, photography, graphic design, industrial design. *Unit head:* Lois Greene, Interim Chair and Associate Dean, 785-864-4401, E-mail: design@ku.edu. *Application contact:* Brian Hanabury, Coordinator of Student Services, 785-864-4401, E-mail: design@ku.edu.

University of Kentucky, Graduate School, College of Design, Lexington, KY 40506-0032. Offers M Arch, MAIDM, MHP, MSIDM. *Accreditation:* NASAD. *Entrance requirements:* For master's, GRE, minimum GPA of 2.75. Additional exam requirements/recommendations for international students: Required—TOEFL (minimum score 550 paper-based; 213 computer-based). Electronic applications accepted.

University of Massachusetts Amherst, Graduate School, College of Humanities and Fine Arts, Department of Art, Programs in Art, Amherst, MA 01003. Offers art education (MA); design (MA); studio art (MFA). Part-time programs available. *Students:* 18 full-time (12 women), 16 part-time (13 women); includes 3 minority (1 American Indian or Alaska Native, non-Hispanic/Latino; 1 Asian, non-Hispanic/Latino; 1 Hispanic/Latino). Average age 33. 83 applicants, 19% accepted, 10 enrolled. In 2010, 12 master's awarded. *Degree requirements:* For master's, comprehensive exam (for some programs), thesis (for some programs). *Entrance requirements:* For master's, portfolio. Additional exam requirements/recommendations for international students: Required—TOEFL (minimum score 530 paper-based; 213 computer-based; 80 iBT), IELTS (minimum score 6.5). *Application deadline:* For fall admission, 2/1 for domestic and international students. Applications are processed on a rolling basis. Application fee: $50 ($65 for international students). Electronic applications accepted. *Expenses:* Tuition, state resident: full-time $2640. Required fees: $8282. One-time fee: $357 full-time. *Financial support:* In 2010–11, 1 fellowship with full tuition reimbursement (averaging $3,629 per year), 1 research assistantship with full tuition reimbursement (averaging $2,903 per year), 27 teaching assistantships with full tuition reimbursements (averaging $5,943 per year) were awarded; career-related internships or fieldwork, Federal Work-Study, scholarships/grants, traineeships, health care benefits, tuition waivers (full), and unspecified assistantships also available. Support available to part-time students. Financial award application deadline: 2/1; financial award applicants required to submit FAFSA. *Unit head:* Dr. Young Min Moon, Graduate Program Director, 413-545-1903, Fax: 413-545-3929. *Application contact:* Jean M. Ames, Supervisor of Admissions, 413-545-0722, Fax: 413-577-0100, E-mail: gradadm@grad.umass.edu.

University of Massachusetts Dartmouth, Graduate School, College of Visual and Performing Arts, Program in Visual Design, North Dartmouth, MA 02747-2300. Offers digital media (MFA); graphic design (MFA); illustration (MFA); photography (MFA); typography (MFA). *Accreditation:* NASAD. *Faculty:* 17 full-time (7 women), 4 part-time/adjunct (1 woman). *Students:* 12 full-time (8 women), 5 part-time (4 women); includes 1 Two or more races, non-Hispanic/Latino, 1 international. Average age 35. 33 applicants, 48% accepted, 7 enrolled. In 2010, 1 master's awarded. *Degree requirements:* For master's, visual thesis. *Entrance requirements:* For master's, portfolio, interview, minimum GPA of 3.0, 3 letters of recommendation. Additional exam requirements/recommendations for international students: Required—TOEFL (minimum score 500 paper-based). *Application deadline:* For fall admission, 2/1 priority date for domestic students, 12/1 priority date for international students. Applications are processed on a rolling basis. Application fee: $40 ($60 for international students). Electronic applications accepted. *Expenses:* Tuition, state resident: full-time $2071; part-time $86 per credit. Tuition, nonresident: full-time $8099; part-time $337 per credit. Required fees: $9446; $394 per credit. One-time fee: $75. Part-time tuition and fees vary according to class time, course load, degree level and reciprocity agreements. *Financial support:* In 2010–11, 5 teaching assistantships with full tuition reimbursements (averaging $3,088 per year) were awarded; Federal Work-Study and unspecified assistantships also available. Support available to part-time students. Financial award application deadline: 3/1; financial award applicants required to submit FAFSA. *Faculty research:* Typography. Total annual research expenditures: $5,898. *Unit head:* Memory Holloway, Director, 508-999-8554, E-mail: mholloway@umassd.edu. *Application contact:* Elan Turcotte-Shamski, Graduate Admissions Officer, 508-999-8604, Fax: 508-999-8183, E-mail: graduate@umassd.edu.

University of Michigan, Horace H. Rackham School of Graduate Studies, School of Art and Design, Ann Arbor, MI 48109. Offers art and design (MFA). *Accreditation:* NASAD. *Degree requirements:* For master's, thesis, exhibit (MFA), slide lecture. *Entrance requirements:* For master's, portfolio. Additional exam requirements/recommendations for international students: Required—TOEFL, IELTS. Electronic applications accepted. *Expenses:* Tuition, state resident: full-time $17,784; part-time $1116 per credit hour. Tuition, nonresident: full-time $35,944; part-time $2125 per credit hour. International tuition: $35,994 full-time. Required fees: $95 per semester. Tuition and fees vary according to course load, degree level and program. *Faculty research:* Creative expression, commercial design, preparation for teaching.

University of Minnesota, Twin Cities Campus, Graduate School, College of Design, Department of Design, Housing, and Apparel, Minneapolis, MN 55455-0213. Offers apparel (MA, MS, PhD); design communication (MA, MS, PhD); housing studies (MA, MS, PhD, Postbaccalaureate Certificate); interactive design (MFA); interior design (MA, MS, PhD). Part-time programs available. *Degree requirements:* For master's and Postbaccalaureate Certificate, comprehensive exam, thesis (for some programs); for doctorate, comprehensive exam, thesis/dissertation. *Entrance requirements:* For master's, GRE General Test, minimum GPA of 3.0 (preferred), portfolio, 3 letters of recommendation; for doctorate, GRE General Test, minimum GPA of 3.0 (preferred), portfolio, 3 letters of recommendation, writing sample; for Post-baccalaureate Certificate, GRE General Test, minimum GPA of 3.0 (preferred). Additional exam requirements/recommendations for international students: Required—TOEFL (minimum score 550 paper-based; 213 computer-based; 79 iBT). Electronic applications accepted. *Faculty research:* Housing policy and community development; consumer behavior; interactive design; design history; social, cultural, and behavioral issues related to designed environments.

University of North Texas, Toulouse Graduate School, College of Visual Arts and Design, Department of Design, Denton, TX 76203. Offers MFA. *Accreditation:* NASAD. *Degree requirements:* For master's, problem or thesis. *Entrance requirements:* Additional exam requirements/recommendations for international students: Recommended—TOEFL (minimum score 550 paper-based; 213 computer-based; 79 iBT). *Application deadline:* Applications are processed on a rolling basis. Electronic applications accepted. *Expenses:* Tuition, state resident: full-time $4298; part-time $239 per credit hour. Tuition, nonresident: full-time $10,782; part-time $549 per credit hour. Required fees: $1292; $270 per credit hour. *Financial support:* Fellowships, teaching assistantships available. Financial award applicants required to submit FAFSA. *Faculty research:* Color, lighting, sustainable design, hand sewing techniques, ethics.

University of Notre Dame, Graduate School, College of Arts and Letters, Division of Humanities, Department of Art, Art History, and Design, Notre Dame, IN 46556. Offers art history (MA); design (MFA), including graphic design, industrial design; studio art (MFA), including ceramics, painting, photography, printmaking, sculpture. *Accreditation:* NASAD. *Degree requirements:* For master's, comprehensive exam (for some programs), thesis. *Entrance requirements:* For master's, GRE General Test, minimum GPA of 3.0. Additional exam requirements/recommendations for international students: Required—TOEFL (minimum score 600 paper-based; 250 computer-based; 80 iBT). Electronic applications accepted. *Faculty research:* Studio art practice in ceramics, printing, photography, printmaking and sculpture, graphic design and industrial design, digital imaging in design and photography, Renaissance and American art history, contemporary art theory and criticism.

University of Oklahoma, Weitzenhoffer Family College of Fine Arts, School of Drama, Norman, OK 73019. Offers drama (MA, MFA), including acting/directing/design (MFA), design (MFA), directing (MFA). *Accreditation:* NAST. Part-time programs available. *Faculty:* 9 full-time (4 women). *Students:* 9 full-time (4 women); includes 1 minority (Two or more races, non-Hispanic/Latino). Average age 32. 6 applicants, 33% accepted, 2 enrolled. In 2010, 5 master's awarded. *Degree requirements:* For master's, comprehensive exam, thesis (MA), departmental qualifying exam. *Entrance requirements:* For master's, BA with 36 hours in drama, auditions. Additional exam requirements/recommendations for international students: Required—TOEFL (minimum score 550 paper-based; 213 computer-based; 79 iBT). *Application deadline:* For fall admission, 3/1 for domestic and international students; for spring admission, 11/1 for domestic students, 9/1 for international students. Applications are processed on a rolling basis. Application fee: $40 ($90 for international students). Electronic applications accepted. *Expenses:* Tuition, state resident: full-time $3893; part-time $162.20 per credit hour. Tuition, nonresident: full-time $14,167; part-time $590.30 per credit hour. Required fees: $2523; $94.60 per credit hour. Tuition and fees vary according to course load and degree level. *Financial support:* In 2010–11, 1 research assistantship with partial tuition reimbursement (averaging $9,586 per year), 6 teaching assistantships with partial tuition reimbursements (averaging $9,586 per year) were awarded; Federal Work-Study also available. Financial award application deadline: 4/7; financial award applicants required to submit FAFSA. *Faculty research:* Directing, design, acting, dramaturgy, stage management, theatre pedagogy. *Unit head:* Dr. Tom Orr, Director, 405-325-4021, Fax: 405-325-0400, E-mail: thorr@ou.edu. *Application contact:* Dr. Kae Koger, Graduate Liaison, 405-325-4021, Fax: 405-325-0400, E-mail: akoger@ou.edu.

Applied Arts and Design—General

The University of Texas at Austin, Graduate School, College of Fine Arts, Department of Art and Art History, Program in Design, Austin, TX 78712-1111. Offers MFA. *Accreditation:* NASAD. *Degree requirements:* For master's, thesis, oral exam, exhibition. *Entrance requirements:* For master's, minimum GPA of 3.0, portfolio. Electronic applications accepted.

University of Washington, Graduate School, College of Arts and Sciences, School of Art, Division of Design, Seattle, WA 98195. Offers industrial design (MFA); visual communication design (MFA).

University of Wisconsin–Madison, Graduate School, School of Human Ecology, Program in Design Studies, Madison, WI 53706. Offers MFA, MS, PhD. *Faculty:* 11 full-time (6 women). *Students:* 21 full-time (18 women). Average age 34. 27 applicants, 15% accepted, 4 enrolled. *Degree requirements:* For master's, thesis (for some programs); for doctorate, comprehensive exam, thesis/dissertation. *Entrance requirements:* For master's, portfolio, scholarly paper, 3 letters of recommendation from faculty; for doctorate, letters of recommendation, scholarly paper. Additional exam requirements/recommendations for international students: Required—TOEFL (minimum score 580 paper-based; 237 computer-based; 92 iBT). *Application deadline:* For fall admission, 1/3 for domestic and international students. Application fee: $56. *Expenses:* Tuition, state resident: full-time $9887; part-time $617.96 per credit. Tuition, nonresident: full-time $24,054; part-time $1503.40 per credit. Required fees: $67.63 per credit. Tuition and fees vary according to reciprocity agreements. *Financial support:* Fellowships with full tuition reimbursements, research assistantships with full tuition reimbursements, teaching assistantships with full tuition reimbursements, institutionally sponsored loans, scholarships/grants, health care benefits, and unspecified assistantships available. *Faculty research:* Feng shui, material culture, behavior and environment, use of pattern to enhance environment, design visualization. *Application contact:* Lori Ushman, Department Administrator, 608-262-2651, Fax: 608-265-5099, E-mail: ushman@wisc.edu.

Virginia Commonwealth University, Graduate School, School of the Arts, Department of Graphic Design, Richmond, VA 23284-9005. Offers design/visual communications (MFA); interior environment (MFA). *Accreditation:* NASAD. *Faculty:* 15 full-time (3 women). *Students:* 35 full-time (27 women), 4 part-time (2 women); includes 3 minority (all Asian, non-Hispanic/Latino), 1 international. 212 applicants, 19% accepted, 25 enrolled. In 2010, 13 master's awarded. *Degree requirements:* For master's, thesis, exhibition. *Entrance requirements:* For master's, portfolio. Additional exam requirements/recommendations for international students: Required—TOEFL (minimum score 600 paper-based; 250 computer-based; 100 iBT). *Application deadline:* For fall admission, 2/1 for domestic students. Application fee: $50. Electronic applications accepted. *Expenses:* Tuition, state resident: full-time $4308; part-time $479 per credit hour. Tuition, nonresident: full-time $8942; part-time $994 per credit hour. Required fees: $2000; $85 per credit hour. Tuition and fees vary according to course level, course load, degree level, campus/location and program. *Financial support:* Fellowships, teaching assistantships, career-related internships or fieldwork, Federal Work-Study, institutionally sponsored loans, and tuition waivers (full and partial) available. Support available to part-time students. Financial award application deadline: 3/15. *Faculty research:* Conducting visual or theoretical research, and in investigating the intersection of function and expression in design problem solving. *Unit head:* John DeMao, Chair, 804-828-1709, E-mail: jdemao@vcu.edu. *Application contact:* John DeMao, Chair, 804-828-1709, E-mail: jdemao@vcu.edu.

Virginia Polytechnic Institute and State University, Graduate School, College of Architecture and Urban Studies, School of Architecture and Design, Blacksburg, VA 24061. Offers architecture (M Arch, MS); architecture and design research (PhD). *Faculty:* 57 full-time (18 women), 2 part-time/adjunct (1 woman). *Students:* 184 full-time (85 women), 27 part-time (13 women); includes 12 Black or African American, non-Hispanic/Latino; 12 Asian, non-Hispanic/Latino; 9 Hispanic/Latino, 50 international. Average age 28. 488 applicants, 34% accepted, 75 enrolled. In 2010, 48 master's awarded. *Degree requirements:* For master's, comprehensive exam (for some programs), thesis (for some programs); for doctorate, comprehensive exam (for some programs), thesis/dissertation (for some programs). *Entrance requirements:* For master's and doctorate, GRE. Additional exam requirements/recommendations for international students: Required—TOEFL (minimum score 550 paper-based; 213 computer-based). *Application deadline:* For fall admission, 7/1 for domestic and international students; for spring admission, 12/1 for domestic and international students. Applications are processed on a rolling basis. Application fee: $65. Electronic applications accepted. *Expenses:* Tuition, state resident: full-time $9399; part-time $488 per credit hour. Tuition, nonresident: full-time $17,854; part-time $957.75 per credit hour. Required fees: $1534. Full-time tuition and fees vary according to program. *Financial support:* In 2010–11, 2 fellowships with full tuition reimbursements (averaging $4,875 per year), 11 teaching assistantships with full tuition reimbursements (averaging $15,546 per year) were awarded; career-related internships or fieldwork, Federal Work-Study, scholarships/grants, health care benefits, and unspecified assistantships also available. Financial award application deadline: 1/15. *Faculty research:* Computer applications in design, building technology, architectural design theory, solar/passive energy design, building assembly. Total annual research expenditures: $605,652. *Unit head:* Dr. Steve R. Thompson, UNIT HEAD, 540-231-9931, Fax: 540-231-9938, E-mail: stthomp2@vt.edu. *Application contact:* Dr. Steve R. Thompson, UNIT HEAD, 540-231-9931, Fax: 540-231-9938, E-mail: stthomp2@vt.edu.

Wayne State University, College of Fine, Performing and Communication Arts, Department of Art and Art History, Program in Design and Merchandising, Detroit, MI 48202. Offers MA. *Faculty:* 19 full-time (9 women), 2 part-time/adjunct (0 women). *Students:* 2 full-time (both women), 1 (woman) part-time; includes 1 minority (Black or African American, non-Hispanic/Latino). Average age 25. 8 applicants, 25% accepted, 2 enrolled. *Degree requirements:* For master's, one foreign language. *Entrance requirements:* Additional exam requirements/recommendations for international students: Required—TOEFL (minimum score 550 paper-based; 213 computer-based); Recommended—TWE (minimum score 6). *Application deadline:* For fall admission, 4/1 for domestic students, 6/1 for international students; for winter admission, 10/1 for international students; for spring admission, 2/1 for international students. Application fee: $30 ($50 for international students). Electronic applications accepted. *Expenses:* Tuition, state resident: full-time $7662; part-time $478.85 per credit hour. Tuition, nonresident: full-time $16,920; part-time $1057.55 per credit hour. Required fees: $571.20; $35.70 per credit hour. $188.05 per semester. Tuition and fees vary according to course load and program. *Financial support:* In 2010–11, 1 teaching assistantship (averaging $14,620 per year) was awarded. *Unit head:* Dr. John Richardson, Chair, 313-577-2980, Fax: 313-577-3491, E-mail: af5343@wayne.edu. *Application contact:* Brian Madigan, Associate Professor, 313-577-2685, E-mail: bmadigan@wayne.edu.

Western Carolina University, Graduate School, College of Fine and Performing Arts, School of Art and Design, Cullowhee, NC 28723. Offers MFA. *Accreditation:* NASAD. Part-time programs available. *Degree requirements:* For master's, thesis. *Entrance requirements:* For master's, GRE, appropriate undergraduate degree, portfolio, letters of recommendation. Additional exam requirements/recommendations for international students: Required—TOEFL (minimum score 550 paper-based; 270 computer-based; 79 iBT). *Faculty research:* Art and society, visual literacy, vernacular cultural studies and oral history, environments for aging, health and leisure.

Western Illinois University, School of Graduate Studies, College of Fine Arts and Communication, Department of Theatre and Dance, Macomb, IL 61455-1390. Offers acting (MFA); design (MFA); directing (MFA). *Accreditation:* NAST. Part-time programs available. *Students:* 23 full-time (11 women), 5 part-time (1 woman), 1 international. Average age 29. 36 applicants, 33% accepted. In 2010, 12 master's awarded. *Degree requirements:* For master's, comprehensive exam, thesis or alternative, creative project, written exam. *Entrance requirements:* For master's, audition or interview. Additional exam requirements/recommendations for international students: Required—TOEFL (minimum score 550 paper-based; 213 computer-based; 80 iBT). *Application deadline:* Applications are processed on a rolling basis. Application fee: $30. Electronic applications accepted. *Expenses:* Tuition, state resident: full-time $6370; part-time $265.40 per credit hour. Tuition, nonresident: full-time $12,740; part-time $530.80 per credit hour. Required fees: $75.67 per credit hour. *Financial support:* In 2010–11, 25 students received support, including 19 research assistantships with full tuition reimbursements available (averaging $7,280 per year), 6 teaching assistantships with full tuition reimbursements available (averaging $8,400 per year). Financial award applicants required to submit FAFSA. *Unit head:* Dr. David Patrick, Chairperson, 309-298-1543. *Application contact:* Evelyn Hoing, Assistant Director of Graduate Studies, 309-298-1806, Fax: 309-298-2345, E-mail: grad-office@wiu.edu.

Western Michigan University, Graduate College, College of Fine Arts, Gwen Frostic School of Art, Kalamazoo, MI 49008. Offers art education (MA); studio art (MFA). *Accreditation:* NASAD (one or more programs are accredited). *Degree requirements:* For master's, thesis or alternative.

Yale University, School of Art, New Haven, CT 06520-8339. Offers graphic design (MFA); painting/printmaking (MFA); photography (MFA); sculpture (MFA). *Faculty:* 9 full-time (4 women), 35 part-time/adjunct (12 women). *Students:* 121 full-time (64 women); includes 32 minority (7 Black or African American, non-Hispanic/Latino; 10 Asian, non-Hispanic/Latino; 15 Hispanic/Latino), 32 international. Average age 28. 1,222 applicants, 5% accepted, 57 enrolled. In 2010, 57 master's awarded. *Degree requirements:* For master's, thesis (for some programs). *Entrance requirements:* Additional exam requirements/recommendations for international students: Required—TOEFL (minimum score 550 paper-based; 250 computer-based; 100 iBT). *Application deadline:* For fall admission, 1/4 for domestic and international students. Application fee: $100. Electronic applications accepted. *Expenses:* Contact institution. *Financial support:* In 2010–11, 90 students received support, including 54 teaching assistantships (averaging $1,900 per year); Federal Work-Study, scholarships/grants, and unspecified assistantships also available. Financial award application deadline: 3/1; financial award applicants required to submit FAFSA. *Unit head:* Robert Storr, Dean, 203-432-2606. *Application contact:* Patricia Ann DeChiara, Director of Academic Affairs, 203-432-2600, E-mail: artschool.info@yale.edu.

York University, Faculty of Graduate Studies, Faculty of Fine Arts, Program in Design, Toronto, ON M3J 1P3, Canada. Offers M Des. Electronic applications accepted.

Computer Art and Design

Academy of Art University, Graduate Program, School of Web Design and New Media, San Francisco, CA 94105-3410. Offers MFA. Part-time and evening/weekend programs available. Postbaccalaureate distance learning degree programs offered (no on-campus study). *Faculty:* 5 full-time (2 women), 58 part-time/adjunct (17 women). *Students:* 224 full-time (117 women), 222 part-time (134 women); includes 27 Black or African American, non-Hispanic/Latino; 1 American Indian or Alaska Native, non-Hispanic/Latino; 35 Asian, non-Hispanic/Latino; 20 Hispanic/Latino, 149 international. Average age 31. 108 applicants. In 2010, 37 master's awarded. *Degree requirements:* For master's, thesis, final review. *Entrance requirements:* For master's, portfolio. *Application deadline:* For fall admission, 9/7 for domestic and international students; for spring admission, 2/2 for domestic students, 9/2 for international students. Applications are processed on a rolling basis. Application fee: $100 ($500 for international students). Electronic applications accepted. *Expenses:* Tuition: Full-time $20,160; part-time $840 per semester hour. Required fees: $45 per semester. *Financial support:* Career-related internships or fieldwork and Federal Work-Study available. Support available to part-time students. Financial award application deadline: 8/10; financial award applicants required to submit FAFSA. *Application contact:* 800-544-ARTS, Fax: 415-263-4130, E-mail: info@academyart.edu.

Alfred University, Graduate School, New York State College of Ceramics, School of Art and Design, Alfred, NY 14802-1205. Offers ceramic art (MFA); electronic integrated arts (MFA); glass art (MFA); sculpture (MFA). *Accreditation:* NASAD. *Degree requirements:* For master's, exhibit. *Entrance requirements:* For master's, portfolio. Additional exam requirements/recommendations for international students: Required—TOEFL (minimum score 550 paper-based; 213 computer-based; 80 iBT), IELTS (minimum score 6). Electronic applications accepted. *Faculty research:* Ceramic sculpture, functional ceramics, wood, mixed media, hot and cold glass.

Art Center College of Design, Graduate Division, Department of Media Design, Pasadena, CA 91103. Offers MFA. *Accreditation:* NASAD. *Faculty:* 3 full-time (0 women). *Students:* 39 full-time (22 women); includes 19 minority (1 Black or African American, non-Hispanic/Latino; 11 Asian, non-Hispanic/Latino; 3 Hispanic/Latino; 2 Native Hawaiian or other Pacific Islander, non-Hispanic/Latino; 2 Two or more races, non-Hispanic/Latino), 10 international. Average age 29. 93 applicants, 35% accepted, 15 enrolled. In 2010, 13 master's awarded. *Degree requirements:* For master's, thesis, studio project. *Entrance requirements:* For master's, portfolio. Additional exam requirements/recommendations for international students: Required—TOEFL (minimum score 600 paper-based; 250 computer-based; 100 iBT). *Application deadline:* For fall admission, 2/1 for domestic students, 2/1 priority date for international students. Application fee: $50 ($70 for international students). *Expenses:* Tuition: Part-time $17,220 per term. *Financial support:* Teaching assistantships, career-related internships or fieldwork, Federal Work-Study, and scholarships/grants available. Support available to part-time students. Financial award application deadline: 2/1; financial award applicants required to submit FAFSA. *Unit head:* Anne Burdick, Chair, 626-396-2359, E-mail: anne.burdick@artcenter.edu. *Application contact:* Kevin Wingate, 626-396-2469.

See Display on page 89 and Close-Up on page 119.

Bowling Green State University, Graduate College, College of Arts and Sciences, School of Art, Bowling Green, OH 43403. Offers 2-D studio art (MA, MFA); 3-D studio art (MA, MFA); art education (MA); art history (MA); computer art (MA); design (MFA); digital arts (MFA); graphics (MFA). *Accreditation:* NASAD. Part-time programs available. *Degree requirements:* For master's, thesis or alternative, final exhibit (MFA). *Entrance requirements:* For master's, GRE General Test (MA), slide portfolio (15-20 slides). Additional exam requirements/recommendations for international students: Required—TOEFL. Electronic applications accepted. *Faculty research:* Computer animation and virtual reality, Spanish still-life painting from 1600 to 1800, art and psychotherapy, Japanese wood-firing techniques in ceramics, non-toxic printmaking technologies.

Carnegie Mellon University, College of Fine Arts, School of Design, Program in Interaction Design, Pittsburgh, PA 15213-3891. Offers M Des, PhD. Part-time programs available. *Degree requirements:* For master's, thesis. *Entrance requirements:* For master's, GRE, portfolio of relevant work. Additional exam requirements/recommendations for international students: Required—TOEFL (minimum score 600 paper-based; 250 computer-based). *Faculty research:*

interaction and emotion, visual interface design, robotics, visualization and diagramming, design theory.

Chatham University, Program in Film and Digital Technology, Pittsburgh, PA 15232-2826. Offers emerging media (MFA). Part-time and evening/weekend programs available. *Degree requirements:* For master's, thesis, capstone project. *Entrance requirements:* Additional exam requirements/recommendations for international students: Required—TOEFL (minimum score 600 paper-based; 250 computer-based; 100 iBT), IELTS (minimum score 6.5), TWE. Electronic applications accepted.

Claremont Graduate University, Graduate Programs, School of Arts and Humanities, Department of Art, Claremont, CA 91711. Offers digital media (MA, MFA); drawing (MA, MFA); installation (MA, MFA); new genre (MA, MFA); painting (MA, MFA); performance (MA, MFA); photography (MA, MFA); sculpture (MA, MFA). Part-time programs available. *Faculty:* 4 full-time (1 woman). *Students:* 60 full-time (33 women); includes 5 Asian, non-Hispanic/Latino; 7 Hispanic/Latino, 3 international. Average age 34. In 2010, 29 master's awarded. *Degree requirements:* For master's, final project show. *Entrance requirements:* For master's, BA in art or BFA, slide review. Additional exam requirements/recommendations for international students: Required—TOEFL (minimum score 550 paper-based; 213 computer-based; 80 iBT). *Application deadline:* For fall admission, 2/1 priority date for domestic students. Applications are processed on a rolling basis. Application fee: $60. Electronic applications accepted. *Expenses:* Contact institution. *Financial support:* Fellowships, research assistantships, teaching assistantships, Federal Work-Study, institutionally sponsored loans, and scholarships/grants available. Support available to part-time students. Financial award application deadline: 2/15; financial award applicants required to submit FAFSA. *Faculty research:* Acoustic sculpture, feminization of abstraction, installation sculpture. *Unit head:* David Pagel, Chair, 909-607-2479, Fax: 909-607-1276, E-mail: david.pagel@cgu.edu. *Application contact:* Pat Evans, Program Administrator, 909-607-9292, Fax: 909-607-1276, E-mail: patricia.evans@cgu.edu.

Clemson University, Graduate School, College of Engineering and Science, School of Computing, Program in Digital Production Arts, Clemson, SC 29634. Offers MFA. *Accreditation:* NASAD. *Students:* 20 full-time (5 women), 8 part-time (0 women); includes 3 Black or African American, non-Hispanic/Latino; 2 Asian, non-Hispanic/Latino; 1 Hispanic/Latino, 5 international. Average age 29. 25 applicants, 80% accepted, 10 enrolled. In 2010, 7 master's awarded. *Degree requirements:* For master's, thesis. *Entrance requirements:* For master's, GRE General Test, portfolio. Additional exam requirements/recommendations for international students: Required—TOEFL. *Application deadline:* For fall admission, 4/15 for domestic and international students; for spring admission, 9/15 for international students. Applications are processed on a rolling basis. Application fee: $70 ($80 for international students). Electronic applications accepted. *Expenses:* Tuition, state resident: full-time $6492; part-time $400 per credit hour. Tuition, nonresident: full-time $13,634; part-time $800 per credit hour. Required fees: $262 per semester. Part-time tuition and fees vary according to course load and program. *Financial support:* In 2010–11, 16 students received support, including 4 research assistantships with partial tuition reimbursements available (averaging $10,800 per year); fellowships with full and partial tuition reimbursements available, teaching assistantships with partial tuition reimbursements available, career-related internships or fieldwork, institutionally sponsored loans, scholarships/grants, health care benefits, and unspecified assistantships also available. Support available to part-time students. *Faculty research:* Volume rendering, fluid dynamics, 3D reconstruction. *Unit head:* Dr. Jerry A. Tessendorf, Director, 864-656-6977, Fax: 864-656-0145, E-mail: jtessen@clemson.edu. *Application contact:* April Bowen, Administrative Coordinator, 864-656-5577, Fax: 864-656-0145, E-mail: abowen@clemson.edu.

Concordia University, School of Graduate Studies, Faculty of Fine Arts, Department of Design and Computation Arts, Montréal, QC H3G 1M8, Canada. Offers digital technologies in design art practice (Certificate).

Cornell University, Graduate School, Graduate Fields of Architecture, Art and Planning, Field of Architecture, Ithaca, NY 14853-0001. Offers architectural design (M Arch); architectural science (MS); building technology and environmental science (MS); computer graphics (MS); history of architecture (MA, PhD); history of urban development (MA, PhD); theory and criticism of architecture (M Arch); urban design (M Arch). *Faculty:* 26 full-time (8 women). *Students:* 113 full-time (55 women); includes 2 Black or African American, non-Hispanic/Latino; 15 Asian, non-Hispanic/Latino; 8 Hispanic/Latino, 47 international. Average age 26. 545 applicants, 26% accepted, 65 enrolled. In 2010, 26 master's, 1 doctorate awarded. *Degree requirements:* For master's, one foreign language, thesis (MA, MS); for doctorate, 2 foreign languages, comprehensive exam, thesis/dissertation. *Entrance requirements:* For master's, GRE General Test, 5 year bachelor's degree in architecture, portfolio (M Arch), 3 letters of recommendation; for doctorate, GRE General Test, 3 letters of recommendation. Additional exam requirements/recommendations for international students: Required—TOEFL (minimum score 600 paper-based; 250 computer-based; 77 iBT). *Application deadline:* For fall admission, 1/15 priority date for domestic students. Application fee: $70. Electronic applications accepted. *Expenses:* Tuition: Full-time $29,500. Required fees: $76. Tuition and fees vary according to degree level and program. *Financial support:* In 2010–11, 11 fellowships with full tuition reimbursements, 19 teaching assistantships with full tuition reimbursements were awarded; research assistantships with full tuition reimbursements, institutionally sponsored loans, scholarships/grants, health care benefits, tuition waivers (full and partial), and unspecified assistantships also available. Financial award applicants required to submit FAFSA. *Faculty research:* Architectural design and urban design, theory and criticism of architecture, computer graphics, building technology and environmental science, history of architecture and history of urban-development. *Unit head:* Director of Graduate Studies, 607-255-6701, Fax: 607-255-0291. *Application contact:* Graduate Field Assistant, 607-255-6701, Fax: 607-255-0291, E-mail: cuarch@cornell.edu.

DePaul University, College of Computing and Digital Media, Chicago, IL 60604. Offers animation (MA, MFA); applied technology (MS); business information technology (MS); cinema (MFA); cinema production (MS); computational finance (MS); computer and information sciences (PhD); computer game development (MS); computer graphics and motion technology (MS); computer information and network security (MS); computer science (MS); e-commerce technology (MS); human-computer interaction (MS); information systems (MS); information technology (MA); information technology project management (MS); network engineering and management (MS); predictive analytics (MS); screenwriting (MFA); software engineering (MS); JD/MA; JD/MS. Part-time and evening/weekend programs available. Postbaccalaureate distance learning degree programs offered (no on-campus study). *Faculty:* 51 full-time (11 women), 50 part-time/adjunct (9 women). *Students:* 952 full-time (230 women), 927 part-time (226 women); includes 557 minority (205 Black or African American, non-Hispanic/Latino; 2 American Indian or Alaska Native, non-Hispanic/Latino; 167 Asian, non-Hispanic/Latino; 136 Hispanic/Latino; 7 Native Hawaiian or other Pacific Islander, non-Hispanic/Latino; 40 Two or more races, non-Hispanic/Latino), 292 international. Average age 31. 896 applicants, 70% accepted, 324 enrolled. In 2010, 417 master's, 6 doctorates awarded. *Degree requirements:* For master's, thesis (for some programs); for doctorate, comprehensive exam, thesis/dissertation. *Entrance requirements:* For master's, GRE or GMAT (MS in computational finance only), bachelor's degree, resume (MS in predictive analytics only), IT experience (MS in information technology project management only), portfolio review (MFA); for doctorate, GRE, master's degree in computer science. Additional exam requirements/recommendations for international students: Required—TOEFL (minimum score 550 paper-based; 213 computer-based; 80 iBT), IELTS (minimum score 6.5), Pearson Test of English (minimum score 53). *Application deadline:* For fall admission, 8/15 priority date for domestic students, 6/1 priority date for international students; for winter admission, 12/15 priority date for domestic students, 9/15 priority date for international students; for spring admission, 3/1 priority date for domestic students, 12/15 priority date for international students. Applications are processed on a rolling basis. Application fee: $25. Electronic applications accepted. *Expenses:* Contact institution. *Financial support:* In 2010–11, 102 students received support, including 4 fellowships with full tuition reimbursements available (averaging $24,435 per year), 6 research assistantships (averaging $21,100 per year), 92 teaching assistantships with full and partial tuition reimbursements available (averaging $6,904 per year); Federal Work-Study, scholarships/grants, tuition waivers (full and partial), and unspecified assistantships also available. Support available to part-time students. Financial award application deadline: 4/30; financial award applicants required to submit FAFSA. *Faculty research:* Bioinformatics, visual computing, graphics and animation, high performance and scientific computing, databases. Total annual research expenditures: $1.4 million. *Unit head:* Dr. David Miller, Dean, 312-362-8381, Fax: 312-362-5185. *Application contact:* Dr. Liz Friedman, Assistant Dean of Student Services, 312-362-8714, Fax: 312-362-5179, E-mail: efriedm2@cdm.depaul.edu.

Digital Media Arts College, Graduate Programs, Boca Raton, FL 33431. Offers graphic design (MFA); special FX animation (MFA).

Drexel University, Antoinette Westphal College of Media Arts and Design, Program in Digital Media, Philadelphia, PA 19104-2875. Offers MS. *Degree requirements:* For master's, thesis (including oral presentation, written statement, and copy of completed media work). *Entrance requirements:* For master's, interview. Additional exam requirements/recommendations for international students: Required—TOEFL. Electronic applications accepted.

East Tennessee State University, School of Graduate Studies, College of Business and Technology, Department of Technology and Geomatics, Johnson City, TN 37614. Offers digital media (MS); engineering technology (MS); entrepreneurial leadership (MS, Certificate). Part-time programs available. *Faculty:* 19 full-time (2 women). *Students:* 22 full-time (5 women), 27 part-time (8 women); includes 13 minority (8 Black or African American, non-Hispanic/Latino; 2 Asian, non-Hispanic/Latino; 2 Hispanic/Latino; 1 Two or more races, non-Hispanic/Latino), 3 international. Average age 35. 34 applicants, 71% accepted, 8 enrolled. In 2010, 21 master's, 2 other advanced degrees awarded. *Degree requirements:* For master's, comprehensive exam, thesis optional, strategic experience, capstone. *Entrance requirements:* For master's, bachelor's degree in technical or related area, minimum GPA of 3.0. Additional exam requirements/recommendations for international students: Required—TOEFL (minimum score 550 paper-based; 213 computer-based; 79 iBT). *Application deadline:* For fall admission, 6/1 priority date for domestic students, 4/30 for international students; for spring admission, 11/1 for domestic students, 9/30 for international students. Application fee: $25 ($35 for international students). Electronic applications accepted. *Financial support:* In 2010–11, 10 research assistantships with full tuition reimbursements (averaging $5,500 per year), 1 teaching assistantship with full tuition reimbursement (averaging $5,500 per year) were awarded; career-related internships or fieldwork, institutionally sponsored loans, scholarships/grants, and unspecified assistantships also available. Financial award application deadline: 7/1; financial award applicants required to submit FAFSA. *Faculty research:* Computer-integrated manufacturing, technology education, CAD/CAM, organizational change. Total annual research expenditures: $136,039. *Unit head:* Dr. Keith V. Johnson, Chair, 423-439-7813, Fax: 423-439-7750, E-mail: johnsonk@etsu.edu. *Application contact:* Dr. Keith V. Johnson, Chair, 423-439-7813, Fax: 423-439-7750, E-mail: johnsonk@etsu.edu.

Emily Carr University of Art + Design, Program in Digital Media, Vancouver, BC V5T 1E1, Canada. Offers MDM. *Degree requirements:* For master's, internship. *Entrance requirements:* For master's, portfolio, minimum undergraduate B+ average, 3 reference letters. Additional exam requirements/recommendations for international students: Required—TOEFL (minimum score 86 iBT). Electronic applications accepted.

Florida Atlantic University, Dorothy F. Schmidt College of Arts and Letters, Department of Visual Arts and Art History, Boca Raton, FL 33431-0991. Offers art education (MAT); ceramics (MFA); computer art (MFA); graphic design (MFA); painting (MFA). *Faculty:* 17 full-time (11 women), 9 part-time/adjunct (7 women). *Students:* 19 full-time (12 women), 7 part-time (2 women); includes 8 minority (all Hispanic/Latino), 1 international. Average age 30. 33 applicants, 30% accepted, 6 enrolled. In 2010, 5 master's awarded. *Degree requirements:* For master's, one foreign language, project. *Entrance requirements:* For master's, GRE General Test, minimum GPA of 3.0 during last 60 hours of course work, slide portfolio. *Application deadline:* For fall admission, 2/21 for domestic and international students; for spring admission, 10/1 for domestic and international students. Application fee: $30. Electronic applications accepted. *Expenses:* Tuition, area resident: Part-time $319.96 per credit. Tuition, state resident: part-time $319.96 per credit. Tuition, nonresident: part-time $926.42 per credit. *Financial support:* Research assistantships with full tuition reimbursements, teaching assistantships with full tuition reimbursements, career-related internships or fieldwork, Federal Work-Study, and institutionally sponsored loans available. Financial award applicants required to submit FAFSA. *Faculty research:* Painting, ceramics (traditional and non-traditional), installation, video and interactive sculpture. *Unit head:* Dr. Linda Johnson, Chair, 561-297-3870, Fax: 561-297-3078, E-mail: ljohnson@fau.edu. *Application contact:* James A. Novak, Associate Professor/Graduate Coordinator/Advisor, 561-297-2430, Fax: 561-297-3078, E-mail: jnovak@fau.edu.

Full Sail University, Game Design Master of Science Program—Campus, Winter Park, FL 32792-7437. Offers MS.

Georgia Institute of Technology, Graduate Studies and Research, Ivan Allen College of Policy and International Affairs, School of Literature, Communication and Culture, Atlanta, GA 30332-0001. Offers digital media (MS, PhD); human computer interaction (MSHCI). *Degree requirements:* For master's, thesis or alternative. *Entrance requirements:* Additional exam requirements/recommendations for international students: Required—TOEFL. Electronic applications accepted. *Faculty research:* New media studies.

Goucher College, Program in Digital Arts, Baltimore, MD 21204-2794. Offers MA. Part-time programs available. Postbaccalaureate distance learning degree programs offered (minimal on-campus study). *Faculty:* 5 part-time/adjunct (1 woman). *Degree requirements:* For master's, portfolio, practicum. *Application deadline:* For fall admission, 4/20 for domestic students; for spring admission, 10/15 for domestic students. *Expenses:* Contact institution. *Financial support:* Application deadline: 3/15. *Unit head:* Michael E. Scott-Nelson, Academic Director, 410-337-6200, Fax: 410-337-6085, E-mail: michael.scott-nelson@goucher.edu. *Application contact:* Megan Cornett, Director of Marketing and Communications, 410-337-6200, Fax: 410-337-6085, E-mail: mcornett@goucher.edu.

Indiana University Bloomington, School of Informatics, Bloomington, IN 47408. Offers bioinformatics (MS); chemical informatics (MS); computer science (MS, PhD); health informatics (MS); human computer interaction (MS); informatics (PhD); laboratory informatics (MS); media arts and science (MS); music informatics (MS); security informatics (MS); MS/PhD. PhD offered through University Graduate School. Part-time programs available. Postbaccalaureate distance learning degree programs offered (no on-campus study). *Faculty:* 63 full-time (12 women). *Students:* 372 full-time (88 women), 34 part-time (10 women); includes 7 Black or African American, non-Hispanic/Latino; 1 American Indian or Alaska Native, non-Hispanic/Latino; 10 Asian, non-Hispanic/Latino; 3 Hispanic/Latino; 3 Two or more races, non-Hispanic/Latino, 261 international. Average age 27. 746 applicants, 40% accepted, 131 enrolled. In 2010, 117 master's, 20 doctorates awarded. Terminal master's awarded for partial completion of doctoral program. *Degree requirements:* For master's, thesis optional; for doctorate, comprehensive exam, thesis/dissertation, oral and written exams. *Entrance requirements:* For master's and doctorate, GRE, letters of reference. Additional exam requirements/recommendations for international students: Required—TOEFL. *Application deadline:* For fall admission, 1/15 for domestic students, 12/1 for international students. Application fee: $55 ($65 for international students). Electronic applications accepted. *Financial support:* In 2010–11, fellowships with full and partial tuition reimbursements (averaging $20,000 per year), research assistantships (averaging $14,000 per year), teaching assistantships (averaging $13,000 per year) were awarded; Federal Work-Study, institutionally sponsored loans, scholarships/grants, health care benefits, tuition waivers (full and partial), and unspecified assistantships also available. Support available to part-time students. Total annual research expenditures: $2 million. *Unit head:* Dr. David Leake, Associate Dean for Graduate Studies, 812-855-9756,

Computer Art and Design

Indiana University Bloomington (continued)
E-mail: leake@cs.indiana.edu. *Application contact:* Rachel Lawmaster, Manager of Graduate Admissions and Graduate Studies, 812-856-3622, Fax: 812-856-3825, E-mail: raclee@indiana.edu.

International Technological University, Program in Digital Arts, Santa Clara, CA 95050. Offers MA.

Long Island University, Brooklyn Campus, Richard L. Conolly College of Liberal Arts and Sciences, Department of Media Arts, Brooklyn, NY 11201-8423. Offers MA. Part-time and evening/weekend programs available. *Degree requirements:* For master's, integrated thesis project. *Entrance requirements:* For master's, 2 letters of recommendation. Additional exam requirements/recommendations for international students: Required—TOEFL (minimum score 500 paper-based; 173 computer-based). *Faculty research:* Film noir, art and photography, new media/new aesthetic.

Long Island University, C.W. Post Campus, School of Visual and Performing Arts, Department of Theatre, Film, Dance and Arts Management, Brookville, NY 11548-1300. Offers interactive multimedia (MA); theatre (MA). Part-time and evening/weekend programs available. *Degree requirements:* For master's, thesis. *Entrance requirements:* For master's, placement exam. Electronic applications accepted. *Faculty research:* Playwriting, intercultural dance and theatre, translation, Suzuki, set and costume design.

Miami International University of Art & Design, Program in Computer Animation, Miami, FL 33132-1418. Offers MA. Postbaccalaureate distance learning degree programs offered. *Application contact:* Office of Graduate Admissions, 305-428-5700.

See Close-Up on page 129.

Michigan State University, The Graduate School, College of Communication Arts and Sciences, Department of Telecommunication, Information Studies, and Media, East Lansing, MI 48824. Offers digital media arts and technology (MA); information and telecommunication management (MA); information, policy and society (MA); serious game design (MA). *Entrance requirements:* Additional exam requirements/recommendations for international students: Required—TOEFL. Electronic applications accepted.

Minneapolis College of Art and Design, Certificate Programs, Minneapolis, MN 55404-4347. Offers design (Certificate); fine arts (Certificate); graphic design (Certificate); media (Certificate); sustainable design (Certificate). Part-time programs available. Postbaccalaureate distance learning degree programs offered. *Degree requirements:* For Certificate, final project. *Entrance requirements:* For degree, resume, portfolio, letter of recommendation. Additional exam requirements/recommendations for international students: Required—TOEFL (minimum score 550 paper-based; 213 computer-based; 79 iBT). Electronic applications accepted. *Faculty research:* Visual arts.

Mississippi State University, College of Architecture, Art and Design, Mississippi State, MS 39762. Offers MS. *Faculty:* 18 full-time (6 women). *Students:* 4 full-time (all women), 1 (woman) part-time; includes 2 minority (both Black or African American, non-Hispanic/Latino), 1 international. Average age 30. 8 applicants, 25% accepted, 2 enrolled. In 2010, 2 master's awarded. *Degree requirements:* For master's, comprehensive exam, thesis, final written and oral exam. *Entrance requirements:* For master's, GRE General Test, essay stating intent and aspirations for study, portfolio, minimum GPA of 3.0. Additional exam requirements/recommendations for international students: Required—TOEFL (minimum score 600 paper-based; 250 computer-based; 100 iBT); Recommended—IELTS (minimum score 7.5). *Application deadline:* For fall admission, 7/1 for domestic students, 5/1 for international students; for spring admission, 11/1 for domestic students, 9/1 for international students. Applications are processed on a rolling basis. Application fee: $40. Electronic applications accepted. *Expenses:* Tuition, state resident: full-time $2730.50; part-time $304 per credit hour. Tuition, nonresident: full-time $6901; part-time $767 per credit hour. *Financial support:* Career-related internships or fieldwork, Federal Work-Study, institutionally sponsored loans, and unspecified assistantships available. Financial award application deadline: 4/1; financial award applicants required to submit FAFSA. *Faculty research:* Digital art in architecture, process change and management, multi-media databases, 3-D modeling and animation, virtual archaeology. *Unit head:* Jim West, Dean/Professor, 662-325-2202, Fax: 662-325-8872, E-mail: jwest@caad.msstate.edu. *Application contact:* Dr. David C. Lewis, Associate Dean and Graduate Coordinator, 662-325-2202, Fax: 662-325-8872, E-mail: dlewis@caad.msstate.edu.

National University, Academic Affairs, School of Media and Communication, Department of Media, La Jolla, CA 92037-1011. Offers digital cinema (MFA); educational and instructional technology (MS); video game production and design (MFA). Part-time and evening/weekend programs available. Postbaccalaureate distance learning degree programs offered (no on-campus study). *Faculty:* 9 full-time (3 women), 61 part-time/adjunct (21 women). *Students:* 72 full-time (23 women), 131 part-time (63 women); includes 71 minority (31 Black or African American, non-Hispanic/Latino; 1 American Indian or Alaska Native, non-Hispanic/Latino; 7 Asian, non-Hispanic/Latino; 23 Hispanic/Latino; 1 Native Hawaiian or other Pacific Islander, non-Hispanic/Latino; 8 Two or more races, non-Hispanic/Latino), 10 international. Average age 39. 121 applicants, 100% accepted, 81 enrolled. In 2010, 47 master's awarded. *Degree requirements:* For master's, thesis. *Entrance requirements:* For master's, interview, minimum GPA of 2.5. Additional exam requirements/recommendations for international students: Required—TOEFL (minimum score 550 paper-based; 213 computer-based; 79 iBT), IELTS (minimum score 6). *Application deadline:* Applications are processed on a rolling basis. Application fee: $60 ($65 for international students). Electronic applications accepted. *Expenses:* Tuition: Full-time $9450; part-time $350 per unit. Required fees: $350 per unit. One-time fee: $60. *Financial support:* Career-related internships or fieldwork, institutionally sponsored loans, scholarships/grants, and tuition waivers (partial) available. Support available to part-time students. Financial award application deadline: 6/30; financial award applicants required to submit FAFSA. *Unit head:* Dr. Cynthia Sistek-Chandler, Department Chair, 858-309-3457, E-mail: cchandler@nu.edu. *Application contact:* Dominick Giovanniello, Associate Regional Dean—San Diego, 800-NAT-UNIV, Fax: 858-541-7792, E-mail: dgiovann@nu.edu.

The New School: A University, Parsons The New School for Design, Program in Design and Technology, New York, NY 10011. Offers MFA. *Accreditation:* NASAD. *Degree requirements:* For master's, thesis, exam, written essay. *Entrance requirements:* For master's, portfolio. Additional exam requirements/recommendations for international students: Required—TOEFL (minimum score 580 paper-based; 237 computer-based; 92 iBT). Electronic applications accepted.

New York Institute of Technology, Graduate Division, School of Arts and Sciences, Program in Fine Arts, Old Westbury, NY 11568-8000. Offers computer graphics and animation (MFA); fine arts and technology (MFA); graphic design (MFA). Part-time and evening/weekend programs available. *Students:* 34 full-time (21 women), 6 part-time (1 woman); includes 14 minority (7 Black or African American, non-Hispanic/Latino; 2 Asian, non-Hispanic/Latino; 4 Hispanic/Latino; 1 Two or more races, non-Hispanic/Latino), 11 international. Average age 32. In 2010, 5 master's awarded. *Degree requirements:* For master's, thesis or alternative. *Entrance requirements:* Additional exam requirements/recommendations for international students: Required—TOEFL (minimum score 550 paper-based; 213 computer-based). *Application deadline:* For fall admission, 7/1 priority date for domestic students; for spring admission, 12/1 priority date for domestic students. Applications are processed on a rolling basis. Application fee: $50. Electronic applications accepted. *Expenses:* Tuition: Part-time $835 per credit. *Financial support:* Research assistantships, career-related internships or fieldwork, Federal Work-Study, institutionally sponsored loans, tuition waivers (partial), and unspecified assistantships available. Support available to part-time students. Financial award applicants required to submit FAFSA. *Unit head:* Dr. Roger Yu, Dean, 516-686-7700, Fax: 516-686-1192, E-mail: ryu@nyit.edu. *Application contact:* Dr. Jacquelyn Nealon, Vice President for Enrollment Services, 516-686-7925, Fax: 516-686-7597, E-mail: jnealon@nyit.edu.

New York University, School of Continuing and Professional Studies, Division for Media Industry Studies and Design, Center for Advanced Digital Applications, New York, NY 10012-1019. Offers digital imaging and design (MS), including 2D or 3D production. Part-time programs available. *Faculty:* 2 full-time (1 woman), 21 part-time/adjunct (3 women). *Students:* 22 full-time (9 women), 26 part-time (12 women); includes 2 Asian, non-Hispanic/Latino; 4 Hispanic/Latino, 9 international. Average age 31. 41 applicants, 63% accepted, 15 enrolled. In 2010, 25 master's awarded. *Degree requirements:* For master's, thesis, project. *Entrance requirements:* For master's, portfolio, 2 letters of recommendation, resume, essay, professional experience. Additional exam requirements/recommendations for international students: Required—TOEFL (minimum score 600 paper-based; 250 computer-based; 100 iBT). *Application deadline:* For fall admission, 2/1 priority date for domestic and international students; for spring admission, 8/15 priority date for domestic and international students. Applications are processed on a rolling basis. Application fee: $75. Electronic applications accepted. *Financial support:* In 2010–11, 37 students received support, including 37 fellowships with tuition reimbursements available (averaging $2,757 per year); career-related internships or fieldwork and scholarships/grants also available. Support available to part-time students. Financial award application deadline: 3/1; financial award applicants required to submit FAFSA. *Unit head:* Patricia Heard-Greene, Director, 212-992-3370, Fax: 212-992-3386, E-mail: patricia.heard-greene@nyu.edu. *Application contact:* Wang Kathy, Assistant Director, 212-992-3370, Fax: 212-992-3386, E-mail: cada@nyu.edu.

New York University, School of Continuing and Professional Studies, Division for Media Industry Studies and Design, Program in Graphic Communications Management and Technology, New York, NY 10012-1019. Offers MA. Part-time and evening/weekend programs available. *Faculty:* 1 (woman) full-time, 15 part-time/adjunct (4 women). *Students:* 15 full-time (10 women), 47 part-time (29 women); includes 6 Black or African American, non-Hispanic/Latino; 6 Asian, non-Hispanic/Latino; 4 Hispanic/Latino, 11 international. Average age 31. 43 applicants, 65% accepted, 18 enrolled. In 2010, 36 master's awarded. *Degree requirements:* For master's, thesis, capstone, research course. *Entrance requirements:* For master's, GRE General Test or GMAT (for recent graduates), resume, 2 letters of recommendation, essay, professional experience. Additional exam requirements/recommendations for international students: Required—TOEFL (minimum score 600 paper-based; 250 computer-based; 100 iBT). *Application deadline:* For fall admission, 2/1 priority date for domestic and international students; for spring admission, 10/15 priority date for domestic students, 8/15 priority date for international students. Applications are processed on a rolling basis. Application fee: $75. Electronic applications accepted. *Financial support:* In 2010–11, 46 students received support, including 46 fellowships (averaging $1,744 per year); scholarships/grants and tuition waivers (partial) also available. Support available to part-time students. Financial award application deadline: 3/1; financial award applicants required to submit FAFSA. *Unit head:* Bonnie Blake, Academic Director, 212-992-3222, Fax: 212-992-3386, E-mail: bonnie.blake@nyu.edu. *Application contact:* Ansley Dunn, Program Administrator, 212-992-3283, Fax: 212-992-3233, E-mail: ansley.dunn@nyu.edu.

New York University, Tisch School of the Arts Asia, Singapore, NY 248923, Singapore. Offers animation and digital arts (MFA); dramatic writing (MFA); film production (MFA). *Entrance requirements:* Additional exam requirements/recommendations for international students: Required—TOEFL (minimum score 610 paper-based; 250 computer-based; 105 iBT). Electronic applications accepted.

North Carolina State University, Graduate School, College of Humanities and Social Sciences, Program in Communication, Rhetoric, and Digital Media, Raleigh, NC 27695. Offers PhD.

Old Dominion University, College of Arts and Letters, Program in Lifespan and Digital Communication, Norfolk, VA 23529. Offers MA. *Accreditation:* NASAD. Part-time programs available. *Faculty:* 15 full-time (5 women). *Degree requirements:* For master's, thesis optional, comprehensive exam (for non-thesis students of a project). *Entrance requirements:* For master's, GRE. *Expenses:* Tuition, state resident: full-time $8592; part-time $358 per credit. Tuition, nonresident: full-time $21,672; part-time $903 per credit. Required fees: $119 per semester. One-time fee: $50. *Faculty research:* Family communication, digital media studies, lifespan communication, social media, screenwriting. *Unit head:* Dr. Thomas J. Socha, Graduate Program Director, 757-683-3828, E-mail: tsocha@odu.edu. *Application contact:* Dr. Robert Wojtowicz, Associate Dean, 757-683-6077, Fax: 757-683-5746, E-mail: rwojtowi@odu.edu.

Philadelphia University, School of Design and Media, Program in Digital Design, Philadelphia, PA 19144. Offers MS. *Entrance requirements:* For master's, portfolio. Additional exam requirements/recommendations for international students: Required—TOEFL (minimum score 550 paper-based; 213 computer-based; 79 iBT). Electronic applications accepted.

Regent University, Graduate School, School of Communication and the Arts, Virginia Beach, VA 23464-9800. Offers acting (MFA); cinema arts/television arts (MA); communication (MA, PhD); digital media (MA); directing for cinema/television (MA, MFA); editing for cinema/television (MA); journalism (MA); producing for cinema/television (MA, MFA); script and screenwriting (MFA); theatre (MA). Part-time programs available. Postbaccalaureate distance learning degree programs offered (minimal on-campus study). *Faculty:* 29 full-time (4 women), 25 part-time/adjunct (5 women). *Students:* 93 full-time (48 women), 167 part-time (80 women); includes 45 Black or African American, non-Hispanic/Latino; 2 American Indian or Alaska Native, non-Hispanic/Latino; 3 Asian, non-Hispanic/Latino; 9 Hispanic/Latino, 11 international. Average age 32. 247 applicants, 45% accepted, 65 enrolled. In 2010, 82 master's, 17 doctorates awarded. *Degree requirements:* For master's, thesis or alternative; for doctorate, thesis/dissertation. *Entrance requirements:* For master's, GRE General Test or MAT, minimum undergraduate GPA of 3.0, writing sample, computer literacy survey, recommendation, resume, interview, audition (MFA programs); for doctorate, GRE General Test, minimum graduate GPA of 3.0, writing sample, computer literacy survey, recommendation, interview, transcripts. Additional exam requirements/recommendations for international students: Required—TOEFL (minimum score 577 paper-based; 233 computer-based). *Application deadline:* For fall admission, 3/1 priority date for domestic students; for spring admission, 10/1 priority date for domestic students. Applications are processed on a rolling basis. Application fee: $50. Electronic applications accepted. *Expenses:* Contact institution. *Financial support:* Fellowships with full and partial tuition reimbursements, career-related internships or fieldwork, scholarships/grants, tuition waivers (full and partial), and unspecified assistantships available. Support available to part-time students. Financial award application deadline: 9/1; financial award applicants required to submit FAFSA. *Faculty research:* Southern gospel music, education and entertainment, celebrities and the media, journalism and ethics, C. S. Lewis. *Unit head:* Dr. Emmanuel Ayee, Interim Dean, 757-352-4945, Fax: 757-352-4291, E-mail: eayee@regent.edu. *Application contact:* Matthew Chadwick, Director of Enrollment Support Services, 800-373-5504, Fax: 757-352-4381, E-mail: admissions@regent.edu.

Rensselaer Polytechnic Institute, Graduate School, School of Humanities, Arts, and Social Sciences, Program in Electronic Arts, Troy, NY 12180-3590. Offers MFA, PhD. *Faculty:* 15 full-time (8 women). *Students:* 13 full-time (6 women), 2 part-time (both women); includes 1 American Indian or Alaska Native, non-Hispanic/Latino; 2 Asian, non-Hispanic/Latino; 1 Hispanic/Latino, 2 international. Average age 28. 76 applicants, 20% accepted, 3 enrolled. In 2010, 5 master's, 1 doctorate awarded. *Degree requirements:* For master's, thesis in the form of a large-scale creative project; for doctorate, comprehensive exam, dissertation or creative project and dissertation text. *Entrance requirements:* For master's, portfolio; for doctorate, MA, MM, MS or MFA; portfolio; scholarly writing sample (previous thesis or publication); evidence of research-based creative orientation. Additional exam requirements/recommendations for international students: Required—TOEFL (minimum score 570 paper-based; 230 computer-based; 89 iBT), IELTS (minimum score 6.5). *Application deadline:* For fall admission, 1/1 for domestic and international students. Applications are processed on a rolling basis. Application fee: $75.

Electronic applications accepted. *Expenses:* Tuition: Full-time $39,600; part-time $1650 per credit. Required fees: $1896. *Financial support:* In 2010–11, 12 students received support, including 4 fellowships with full tuition reimbursements available (averaging $20,500 per year), 8 teaching assistantships with full tuition reimbursements available (averaging $17,500 per year); unspecified assistantships also available. Financial award application deadline: 1/1. *Faculty research:* Computer music, video art, Internet art, interactivity, bio art. *Unit head:* Caren Canier, Acting Head, 518-276-4784, Fax: 518-276-4370, E-mail: caniec@rpi.edu. *Application contact:* Jennifer Mumby, Graduate Program Administrator, 518-276-4784, Fax: 518-276-4370, E-mail: mumbyj@rpi.edu.

Rhode Island School of Design, Graduate Studies, Program in Digital Media, Providence, RI 02903-2784. Offers MFA. *Entrance requirements:* Additional exam requirements/recommendations for international students: Required—TOEFL (minimum score 580 paper-based; 237 computer-based), IELTS (minimum score 6.5).

Rochester Institute of Technology, Graduate Enrollment Services, College of Imaging Arts and Sciences, School of Design, Program in Computer Graphics Design, Rochester, NY 14623-5603. Offers MFA. *Accreditation:* NASAD. Part-time programs available. *Students:* 53 full-time (25 women), 26 part-time (12 women); includes 3 Black or African American, non-Hispanic/Latino; 1 American Indian or Alaska Native, non-Hispanic/Latino; 5 Asian, non-Hispanic/Latino; 1 Hispanic/Latino; 1 Native Hawaiian or other Pacific Islander, non-Hispanic/Latino, 43 international. Average age 29. 59 applicants, 49% accepted, 16 enrolled. In 2010, 11 master's awarded. *Degree requirements:* For master's, thesis. *Entrance requirements:* For master's, portfolio, minimum GPA of 3.0. Additional exam requirements/recommendations for international students: Required—TOEFL (minimum score 550 paper-based; 213 computer-based; 79 iBT) or IELTS (minimum score 6.5). *Application deadline:* For fall admission, 2/15 priority date for domestic and international students. Applications are processed on a rolling basis. Application fee: $50. Electronic applications accepted. *Expenses:* Tuition: Full-time $33,234; part-time $924 per credit hour. Required fees: $219. *Financial support:* In 2010–11, 50 students received support; research assistantships with partial tuition reimbursements available, teaching assistantships with partial tuition reimbursements available, career-related internships or fieldwork, institutionally sponsored loans, scholarships/grants, and unspecified assistantships available. Support available to part-time students. Financial award application deadline: 8/30; financial award applicants required to submit FAFSA. *Unit head:* Chris Jackson, Graduate Program Director, 585-475-5823, Fax: 585-475-7533, E-mail: cbjpgd@rit.edu. *Application contact:* Diane Ellison, Assistant Vice President, Graduate Enrollment Services, 585-475-2229, Fax: 585-475-7164, E-mail: gradinfo@rit.edu.

St. Edward's University, School of Management and Business, Area of Digital Media Management, Austin, TX 78704. Offers MBA. *Students:* 46 full-time (18 women); includes 14 minority (1 Black or African American, non-Hispanic/Latino; 2 Asian, non-Hispanic/Latino; 11 Hispanic/Latino). Average age 27. 36 applicants, 72% accepted, 25 enrolled. In 2010, 12 master's awarded. *Entrance requirements:* For master's, GRE or GMAT, interview, 2 letters of recommendation, minimum GPA of 3.0 in last 60 hours of course work. Additional exam requirements/recommendations for international students: Required—TOEFL (minimum score 550 paper-based; 213 computer-based; 79 iBT) or IELTS (minimum score 6). *Application deadline:* For fall admission, 2/15 priority date for domestic and international students. Applications are processed on a rolling basis. Application fee: $45 ($50 for international students). Electronic applications accepted. *Expenses:* Contact institution. *Financial support:* Scholarships/grants available. *Unit head:* Russell Rains, Director, 512-428-1220, Fax: 512-448-8492, E-mail: russellr@stedwards.edu. *Application contact:* Kay L. Arnold, Assistant Director of Admissions, 512-233-1661, Fax: 512-428-1032, E-mail: kayla@stedwards.edu.

San Jose State University, Graduate Studies and Research, College of Humanities and the Arts, School of Art and Design, San Jose, CA 95192-0001. Offers animation/illustration (MA); art history (MA); digital media arts (MFA); photography (MFA); pictorial arts (MFA); spatial arts (MFA). *Accreditation:* NASAD (one or more programs are accredited). *Entrance requirements:* For master's, GRE. Electronic applications accepted.

Savannah College of Art and Design, Graduate School, Program in Animation, Savannah, GA 31402-3146. Offers MA, MFA. Part-time programs available. *Faculty:* 21 full-time (4 women), 1 part-time/adjunct (0 women). *Students:* 112 full-time (49 women), 19 part-time (9 women); includes 6 Black or African American, non-Hispanic/Latino; 1 American Indian or Alaska Native, non-Hispanic/Latino; 2 Asian, non-Hispanic/Latino; 1 Hispanic/Latino, 47 international. Average age 26. In 2010, 34 master's awarded. *Degree requirements:* For master's, thesis, internships. *Entrance requirements:* For master's, interview, portfolio. Additional exam requirements/recommendations for international students: Required—TOEFL (minimum score 450 paper-based; 133 computer-based). *Application deadline:* For fall admission, 4/1 priority date for domestic and international students. Applications are processed on a rolling basis. Application fee: $35. Electronic applications accepted. *Expenses:* Tuition: Full-time $29,520; part-time $3280 per quarter. Tuition and fees vary according to campus/location. *Financial support:* Fellowships, career-related internships or fieldwork, Federal Work-Study, and scholarships/grants available. Financial award application deadline: 4/1; financial award applicants required to submit FAFSA. *Unit head:* Jeremy Moorshead, Chair, 912-525-8527, Fax: 912-525-8597, E-mail: jmoorshe@scad.edu. *Application contact:* Elizabeth Mathis, Director of Graduate and International Enrollment, 912-525-5965, Fax: 912-525-5985, E-mail: admission@scad.edu.

Savannah College of Art and Design, Graduate School, Program in Broadcast Design, Savannah, GA 31402-3146. Offers MA, MFA. Part-time programs available. Postbaccalaureate distance learning degree programs offered (no on-campus study). *Faculty:* 9 full-time (1 woman), 7 part-time/adjunct (2 women). *Students:* 38 full-time (14 women), 6 part-time (2 women); includes 1 Black or African American, non-Hispanic/Latino; 2 Asian, non-Hispanic/Latino; 2 Hispanic/Latino; 1 Native Hawaiian or other Pacific Islander, non-Hispanic/Latino, 13 international. Average age 30. In 2010, 24 master's awarded. *Degree requirements:* For master's, thesis, internships. *Entrance requirements:* For master's, interview, portfolio. Additional exam requirements/recommendations for international students: Required—TOEFL (minimum score 450 paper-based; 133 computer-based). *Application deadline:* For fall admission, 4/1 priority date for domestic and international students. Applications are processed on a rolling basis. Application fee: $35. Electronic applications accepted. *Expenses:* Tuition: Full-time $29,520; part-time $3280 per quarter. Tuition and fees vary according to campus/location. *Financial support:* Research assistantships, career-related internships or fieldwork, Federal Work-Study, and scholarships/grants available. Financial award application deadline: 4/1; financial award applicants required to submit FAFSA. *Unit head:* John Colette, Chair, 912-525-5000, E-mail: jcolette@scad.edu. *Application contact:* Elizabeth Mathis, Director of Graduate Recruitment, 912-525-5965, Fax: 912-525-5985, E-mail: emathis@scad.edu.

Savannah College of Art and Design, Graduate School, Program in Digital Photography, Savannah, GA 31402-3146. Offers MA. Part-time programs available. *Faculty:* 4 full-time (2 women). *Students:* 10 full-time (6 women), 13 part-time (3 women), 1 international. 54 applicants, 35% accepted, 10 enrolled. In 2010, 1 master's awarded. *Degree requirements:* For master's, thesis. *Entrance requirements:* For master's, interview, portfolio. Additional exam requirements/recommendations for international students: Required—TOEFL (minimum score 450 paper-based; 133 computer-based). *Application deadline:* For fall admission, 4/1 priority date for domestic and international students. Applications are processed on a rolling basis. Application fee: $50. Electronic applications accepted. *Expenses:* Tuition: Full-time $29,520; part-time $3280 per quarter. Tuition and fees vary according to campus/location. *Financial support:* Fellowships, career-related internships or fieldwork, Federal Work-Study, and scholarships/grants available. Financial award application deadline: 4/1; financial award applicants required to submit FAFSA. *Unit head:* Thomas Fischer, Chair, 912-525-6570, Fax: 912-525-3507, E-mail: tfischer@scad.edu. *Application contact:* Darrell Tutchton, Director of Graduate and International Enrollment, 912-525-5961, Fax: 912-525-5985, E-mail: admission@scad.edu.

Savannah College of Art and Design, Graduate School, Program in Interactive Design and Game Development, Savannah, GA 31402-3146. Offers MA, MFA, Graduate Certificate. Part-time programs available. *Faculty:* 16 full-time (4 women), 4 part-time/adjunct (0 women). *Students:* 64 full-time (20 women), 34 part-time (15 women); includes 7 Black or African American, non-Hispanic/Latino; 3 Asian, non-Hispanic/Latino; 4 Hispanic/Latino, 19 international. Average age 29. In 2010, 19 master's, 1 other advanced degree awarded. *Degree requirements:* For master's, thesis, internships. *Entrance requirements:* For master's, interview, portfolio. Additional exam requirements/recommendations for international students: Required—TOEFL (minimum score 450 paper-based; 133 computer-based). *Application deadline:* For fall admission, 4/1 priority date for domestic and international students. Applications are processed on a rolling basis. Application fee: $35. Electronic applications accepted. *Expenses:* Tuition: Full-time $29,520; part-time $3280 per quarter. Tuition and fees vary according to campus/location. *Financial support:* Fellowships, career-related internships or fieldwork, Federal Work-Study, and scholarships/grants available. Financial award application deadline: 4/1; financial award applicants required to submit FAFSA. *Unit head:* Luis Cataldi, Chair, 912-525-8523, E-mail: lcataldi@scad.edu. *Application contact:* Elizabeth Mathis, Director of Graduate Recruitment, 912-525-5965, Fax: 912-525-5985, E-mail: emathis@scad.edu.

School of Visual Arts, Graduate Programs, Computer Art Department, New York, NY 10010-3994. Offers MFA. *Accreditation:* NASAD. *Degree requirements:* For master's, final review, project or thesis. *Entrance requirements:* For master's, portfolio. Additional exam requirements/recommendations for international students: Required—TOEFL (minimum score 550 paper-based; 213 computer-based; 79 iBT). Electronic applications accepted.

Stevens Institute of Technology, Graduate School, Charles V. Schaefer Jr. School of Engineering, Department of Computer Science, Hoboken, NJ 07030. Offers computer graphics (Certificate); computer science (MS, PhD); computer systems (Certificate); database management systems (Certificate); distributed systems (Certificate); elements of computer science (Certificate); enterprise computing (Certificate); enterprise security and information assurance (Certificate); health informatics (Certificate); multimedia experience and management (Certificate); networks and systems administration (Certificate); security and privacy (Certificate); service oriented computing (Certificate); software design (Certificate); theoretical computer science (Certificate). Part-time and evening/weekend programs available. *Faculty:* 12 full-time (5 women). *Students:* 117 full-time (42 women), 88 part-time (17 women); includes 4 Black or African American, non-Hispanic/Latino; 21 Asian, non-Hispanic/Latino; 3 Hispanic/Latino, 99 international. Average age 28. 327 applicants, 57% accepted. In 2010, 72 master's, 2 doctorates awarded. Terminal master's awarded for partial completion of doctoral program. *Degree requirements:* For master's, thesis optional; for doctorate, variable foreign language requirement, comprehensive exam, thesis/dissertation. *Entrance requirements:* For master's and doctorate, GRE, minimum GPA of 3.0. Additional exam requirements/recommendations for international students: Required—TOEFL. *Application deadline:* Applications are processed on a rolling basis. Application fee: $50. Electronic applications accepted. *Financial support:* Fellowships, Federal Work-Study available. Financial award application deadline: 4/15. *Faculty research:* Semantics, reliability theory, programming language, cyber security. *Unit head:* Daniel Duchamp, Director, 201-216-5390, Fax: 201-216-8249, E-mail: djd@cs.stevens.edu. *Application contact:* Graduate Admissions, 800-496-4935, Fax: 201-216-8044, E-mail: gradadmissions@stevens.edu.

Syracuse University, College of Visual and Performing Arts, Program in Computer Art and Animation, Syracuse, NY 13244. Offers MFA. *Students:* 3 full-time (1 woman), 1 part-time (0 women); includes 1 minority (Asian, non-Hispanic/Latino). Average age 25. 25 applicants, 20% accepted, 3 enrolled. In 2010, 3 master's awarded. *Degree requirements:* For master's, thesis or alternative. *Entrance requirements:* For master's, portfolio. Additional exam requirements/recommendations for international students: Required—TOEFL (minimum score 100 iBT). *Application deadline:* For fall admission, 2/1 priority date for domestic and international students. Application fee: $75. Electronic applications accepted. *Expenses:* Tuition: Part-time $1162 per credit. *Financial support:* Fellowships with full tuition reimbursements, teaching assistantships with full and partial tuition reimbursements available. Financial award application deadline: 1/1; financial award applicants required to submit FAFSA. *Unit head:* Heath Hanlin, Chair, 315-443-1033, E-mail: hahanlin@syr.edu. *Application contact:* Harriett Conti, Assistant Dean for Recruitment and Admissions, 315-443-5755, E-mail: hmconti@syr.edu.

See Display on page 179 and Close-Up on page 227.

Texas State University–San Marcos, Graduate School, College of Fine Arts and Communication, School of Art and Design, Program in Communication Design, San Marcos, TX 78666. Offers MFA. *Faculty:* 9 full-time (3 women). *Students:* 16 full-time (7 women), 31 part-time (13 women); includes 1 Black or African American, non-Hispanic/Latino; 2 Asian, non-Hispanic/Latino; 8 Hispanic/Latino, 2 international. Average age 32. 36 applicants, 67% accepted, 20 enrolled. In 2010, 3 master's awarded. *Degree requirements:* For master's, comprehensive exam, thesis (for some programs). *Entrance requirements:* For master's, minimum GPA of 2.75 on last 60 hours of undergraduate work, 20-work portfolio. Additional exam requirements/recommendations for international students: Required—TOEFL (minimum score 550 paper-based; 213 computer-based; 78 iBT). *Application deadline:* For fall admission, 4/30 for domestic and international students; for spring admission, 10/31 for domestic and international students. Applications are processed on a rolling basis. Application fee: $40 ($90 for international students). Electronic applications accepted. *Expenses:* Tuition, state resident: full-time $6024; part-time $251 per credit hour. Tuition, nonresident: full-time $13,536; part-time $564 per credit hour. Required fees: $1776; $50 per credit hour. $306 per semester. *Financial support:* In 2010–11, 14 students received support, including 6 teaching assistantships (averaging $5,526 per year); Federal Work-Study, institutionally sponsored loans, scholarships/grants, and unspecified assistantships also available. Support available to part-time students. Financial award application deadline: 4/1; financial award applicants required to submit FAFSA. *Unit head:* Claudia Roschmann, Program Advisor, 512-245-2646, E-mail: cr29@txstate.edu. *Application contact:* Dr. J. Michael Willoughby, Dean of Graduate School, 512-245-2581, Fax: 512-245-8365, E-mail: gradcollege@txstate.edu.

Universidad Autonoma de Guadalajara, Graduate Programs, Guadalajara, Mexico. Offers administrative law and justice (LL M); advertising and corporate communications (MA); architecture (M Arch); business (MBA); computational science (MCC); education (Ed M, Ed D); English-Spanish translation (MA); entrepreneurship and management (MBA); integrated management of digital animation (MA); international business (MIB); international corporate law (LL M); internet technologies (MS); manufacturing systems (MMS); occupational health (MS); philosophy (MA, PhD); power electronics (MS); quality systems (MQS); renewable energy (MS); social evaluation of projects (MBA); strategic market research (MBA); tax law (MA); teaching mathematics (MA).

Universidad de las Américas–Puebla, Division of Graduate Studies, School of Humanities, Program in Information Design, Puebla, Mexico. Offers MA. Part-time and evening/weekend programs available. *Degree requirements:* For master's, one foreign language, thesis. *Entrance requirements:* Additional exam requirements/recommendations for international students: Required—TOEFL. *Faculty research:* Typography, project development, organizational image.

University of Alaska Fairbanks, College of Liberal Arts, Department of Art, Fairbanks, AK 99775-5640. Offers art (MFA); ceramics (MFA); computer art (MFA); drawing (MFA); Native arts (MFA); painting (MFA); photography (MFA); printmaking (MFA); sculpture (MFA). Part-time programs available. *Faculty:* 7 full-time (2 women). *Students:* 8 full-time (4 women), 1 part-time (0 women), 1 international. Average age 33. 11 applicants, 9% accepted, 0 enrolled. In 2010, 3 master's awarded. *Degree requirements:* For master's, comprehensive exam, thesis, oral exam, oral defense. *Entrance requirements:* For master's, portfolio. Additional exam requirements/recommendations for international students: Required—TOEFL (minimum score 550 paper-based; 213 computer-based; 80 iBT). *Application deadline:* For fall admission, 6/1 for domestic students, 3/1 for international students; for spring admission, 10/15 for domestic students, 9/1 for international students. Applications are processed on a rolling basis. Application

Computer Art and Design

University of Alaska Fairbanks (continued)
fee: $60. Electronic applications accepted. *Expenses:* Tuition, state resident: full-time $5688; part-time $316 per credit. Tuition, nonresident: full-time $11,628; part-time $646 per credit. Required fees: $289 per semester. Tuition and fees vary according to course load and reciprocity agreements. *Financial support:* In 2010–11, 7 teaching assistantships with tuition reimbursements (averaging $8,174 per year) were awarded; fellowships with tuition reimbursements, research assistantships with tuition reimbursements, Federal Work-Study, scholarships/grants, health care benefits, and unspecified assistantships also available. Support available to part-time students. Financial award application deadline: 7/1; financial award applicants required to submit FAFSA. *Faculty research:* Computer art, survey of arts in Alaska, found object art, visualization and animation, painting from the wilderness. Total annual research expenditures: $8,543. *Unit head:* David Mollett, Chair, 907-474-7530, Fax: 907-474-5853, E-mail: fyart@uaf.edu. *Application contact:* David Mollett, Chair, 907-474-7530, Fax: 907-474-5853, E-mail: fyart@uaf.edu.

University of Baltimore, Graduate School, The Yale Gordon College of Liberal Arts, School of Information Arts and Technologies, Baltimore, MD 21201-5779. Offers communications design (DCD); human-computer interaction (MS); interaction design and information technology (MS). Part-time and evening/weekend programs available. *Entrance requirements:* For master's, GRE or MAT, minimum undergraduate GPA of 3.0. Additional exam requirements/recommendations for international students: Required—TOEFL (minimum score 550 paper-based; 213 computer-based).

University of California, Santa Cruz, Division of Graduate Studies, Division of the Arts, Department of Film and Digital Media, Santa Cruz, CA 95064. Offers PhD. *Students:* 4 full-time (1 woman); includes 2 minority (both Asian, non-Hispanic/Latino). Average age 33. 61 applicants, 10% accepted, 4 enrolled. *Degree requirements:* For doctorate, one foreign language, thesis/dissertation, qualifying exams. *Entrance requirements:* For doctorate, GRE. Additional exam requirements/recommendations for international students: Required—TOEFL (minimum score 550 paper-based; 220 computer-based; 83 iBT); Recommended—IELTS (minimum score 8). *Application deadline:* For fall admission, 12/2 for domestic and international students. Application fee: $70 ($90 for international students). Electronic applications accepted. *Financial support:* Fellowships, research assistantships, teaching assistantships, institutionally sponsored loans and tuition waivers available. Financial award applicants required to submit FAFSA. *Faculty research:* Integrating critical and creative practice, working across media, pursuing new modes of social and political engagement, fostering global cultural citizenship. *Unit head:* Robert Valiente-Neighbours, Graduate Program Coordinator, 831-459-4706, E-mail: fdmphd@ucsc.edu. *Application contact:* Robert Valiente-Neighbours, Graduate Program Coordinator, 831-459-4706, E-mail: fdmphd@ucsc.edu.

University of California, Santa Cruz, Division of Graduate Studies, Division of the Arts, Program in Digital Arts and New Media, Santa Cruz, CA 95064. Offers MFA. *Students:* 22 full-time (9 women); includes 4 minority (2 Asian, non-Hispanic/Latino; 2 Hispanic/Latino). Average age 32. 64 applicants, 30% accepted, 12 enrolled. In 2010, 19 master's awarded. *Degree requirements:* For master's, thesis, written paper. *Entrance requirements:* Additional exam requirements/recommendations for international students: Required—TOEFL (minimum score 550 paper-based; 220 computer-based; 83 iBT); Recommended—IELTS (minimum score 8). *Application deadline:* For fall admission, 2/1 for domestic and international students. Application fee: $70 ($90 for international students). Electronic applications accepted. *Financial support:* Fellowships, research assistantships, teaching assistantships, tuition waivers available. Financial award applicants required to submit FAFSA. *Faculty research:* Mechatronics, participatory culture, performative technologies, playable media. *Unit head:* Felicia Rice, Graduate Program Coordinator, 831-459-1554, E-mail: fsrice@ucsc.edu. *Application contact:* Felicia Rice, Graduate Program Coordinator, 831-459-1554, E-mail: fsrice@ucsc.edu.

University of Central Arkansas, Graduate School, College of Fine Arts and Communication, Program in Digital Filmmaking, Conway, AR 72035-0001. Offers MFA. *Students:* 18 full-time (6 women), 8 part-time (0 women); includes 2 minority (1 Black or African American, non-Hispanic/Latino; 1 Asian, non-Hispanic/Latino), 1 international. Average age 29. In 2010, 4 master's awarded. *Degree requirements:* For master's, thesis. *Entrance requirements:* For master's, GRE General Test, minimum GPA of 2.7. Additional exam requirements/recommendations for international students: Required—TOEFL (minimum score 550 paper-based; 213 computer-based). *Application deadline:* For fall admission, 3/1 priority date for domestic and international students; for spring admission, 10/1 priority date for domestic and international students. Applications are processed on a rolling basis. Application fee: $25 ($50 for international students). *Financial support:* Unspecified assistantships available. *Unit head:* Dr. Bruce Hutchinson, Chair, 501-450-3162, E-mail: josepha@uca.edu. *Application contact:* Susan Wood, Admissions Assistant, 501-450-3124, Fax: 501-450-5678, E-mail: swood@uca.edu.

University of Central Florida, College of Arts and Humanities, Department of Art, Orlando, FL 32816. Offers digital media (MA); emerging media (MFA). *Faculty:* 41 full-time (11 women), 13 part-time/adjunct (3 women). *Students:* 28 full-time (13 women), 8 part-time (3 women); includes 4 Asian, non-Hispanic/Latino; 2 Hispanic/Latino, 2 international. Average age 32. 63 applicants, 48% accepted, 15 enrolled. In 2010, 3 master's awarded. Application fee: $30. Electronic applications accepted. *Expenses:* Tuition, state resident: part-time $256.56 per credit hour. Tuition, nonresident: part-time $1011.52 per credit hour. Part-time tuition and fees vary according to program. *Financial support:* In 2010–11, 12 students received support, including 3 fellowships (averaging $10,000 per year), 3 research assistantships (averaging $3,200 per year), 7 teaching assistantships (averaging $5,600 per year); scholarships/grants and unspecified assistantships also available. *Unit head:* Dr. Paul Lartonoix, Interim Director, 407-823-3253, E-mail: plartonoix@mail.ucf.edu. *Application contact:* Dr. Paul Lartonoix, Interim Director, 407-823-3253, E-mail: plartonoix@mail.ucf.edu.

University of Central Florida, College of Arts and Humanities, Division of Film and Digital Media, Orlando, FL 32816. Offers MFA. *Faculty:* 16 full-time (5 women), 3 part-time/adjunct (2 women). *Students:* 14 full-time (3 women), 4 part-time (0 women); includes 1 Black or African American, non-Hispanic/Latino; 2 Hispanic/Latino, 1 international. Average age 27. 21 applicants, 38% accepted, 7 enrolled. In 2010, 5 master's awarded. Application fee: $30. *Expenses:* Tuition, state resident: part-time $256.56 per credit hour. Tuition, nonresident: part-time $1011.52 per credit hour. Part-time tuition and fees vary according to program. *Financial support:* In 2010–11, 10 students received support, including 2 fellowships with partial tuition reimbursements available (averaging $5,900 per year), 9 teaching assistantships (averaging $5,500 per year). *Unit head:* Stephen Schlow, Interim Chair, 407-823-2845, Fax: 407-823-3659, E-mail: sschlow@mail.ucf.edu. *Application contact:* Stephen Schlow, Interim Chair, 407-823-2845, Fax: 407-823-3659, E-mail: sschlow@mail.ucf.edu.

University of Denver, Division of Arts, Humanities and Social Sciences, Department of Digital Media Studies, Denver, CO 80208. Offers MA. Part-time programs available. *Faculty:* 7 full-time (3 women), 5 part-time/adjunct (2 women). *Students:* 10 part-time (4 women). Average age 34. 23 applicants, 70% accepted, 6 enrolled. In 2010, 5 master's awarded. *Degree requirements:* For master's, project or thesis. *Entrance requirements:* For master's, GRE General Test. Additional exam requirements/recommendations for international students: Required—TOEFL (minimum score 620 paper-based; 105 iBT). *Application deadline:* For fall admission, 2/18 priority date for domestic students. Applications are processed on a rolling basis. Application fee: $60. Electronic applications accepted. *Expenses:* Tuition: Full-time $35,604; part-time $29,670 per year. Required fees: $687 per year. Tuition and fees vary according to program. *Financial support:* In 2010–11, 2 teaching assistantships with full and partial tuition reimbursements (averaging $7,000 per year) were awarded; Federal Work-Study, scholarships/grants, and unspecified assistantships also available. Financial award application deadline: 2/16; financial award applicants required to submit FAFSA. *Unit head:* Dr. Trace E. Reddell, Director, 303-871-3874, E-mail: treddell@du.edu. *Application contact:* Chris Coleman, Graduate Director, 303-871-7716, E-mail: ccolem22@du.edu.

University of Denver, Division of Arts, Humanities and Social Sciences, School of Art and Art History, Denver, CO 80208. Offers art history (MA); art history/museum studies (MA); electronic media arts and design (MFA). *Accreditation:* NASAD. Part-time programs available. *Faculty:* 13 full-time (7 women), 10 part-time/adjunct (3 women). *Students:* 14 full-time (12 women), 11 part-time (10 women); includes 2 minority (both Hispanic/Latino). Average age 29. 61 applicants, 46% accepted, 11 enrolled. In 2010, 19 master's awarded. *Degree requirements:* For master's, one foreign language, comprehensive exam, research paper. *Entrance requirements:* For master's, GRE General Test. Additional exam requirements/recommendations for international students: Required—TOEFL (minimum score 550 paper-based; 80 iBT). *Application deadline:* Applications are processed on a rolling basis. Application fee: $60. Electronic applications accepted. *Expenses:* Tuition: Full-time $35,604; part-time $29,670 per year. Required fees: $687 per year. Tuition and fees vary according to program. *Financial support:* In 2010–11, 2 teaching assistantships with full and partial tuition reimbursements (averaging $10,500 per year) were awarded; career-related internships or fieldwork, Federal Work-Study, institutionally sponsored loans, scholarships/grants, and unspecified assistantships also available. Support available to part-time students. Financial award application deadline: 3/1; financial award applicants required to submit FAFSA. *Faculty research:* Images of women in alchemical manuscripts and books, Giovanni Benedetto, Salvatore Castiglione. *Unit head:* Dr. M. E. Warlick, Director, 303-871-2371, E-mail: mwarlick@du.edu. *Application contact:* Dr. Annabeth Headrick, Graduate Admissions Coordinator, 303-871-3574, E-mail: saah-interest@du.edu.

University of Florida, Graduate School, College of Engineering and College of Liberal Arts and Sciences, Department of Computer and Information Science and Engineering, Gainesville, FL 32611. Offers computer engineering (ME, MS, PhD); computer science (MS); digital arts and sciences (MS). Part-time programs available. Postbaccalaureate distance learning degree programs offered (minimal on-campus study). *Faculty:* 32 full-time (4 women), 2 part-time/adjunct (0 women). *Students:* 439 full-time (104 women), 81 part-time (19 women); includes 4 Black or African American, non-Hispanic/Latino; 11 Asian, non-Hispanic/Latino; 7 Hispanic/Latino, 445 international. Average age 24. 816 applicants, 60% accepted, 224 enrolled. In 2010, 156 master's, 25 doctorates awarded. Terminal master's awarded for partial completion of doctoral program. *Degree requirements:* For master's, comprehensive exam, thesis optional; for doctorate, comprehensive exam, thesis/dissertation. *Entrance requirements:* For master's and doctorate, GRE General Test, minimum GPA of 3.0. Additional exam requirements/recommendations for international students: Required—TOEFL (minimum score 550 paper-based; 213 computer-based; 80 iBT), IELTS (minimum score 6). *Application deadline:* For fall admission, 6/1 priority date for domestic students, 2/1 for international students; for spring admission, 9/1 for domestic and international students. Applications are processed on a rolling basis. Application fee: $30. Electronic applications accepted. *Expenses:* Tuition, state resident: full-time $10,915.92. Tuition, nonresident: full-time $28,309. *Financial support:* In 2010–11, 164 students received support, including 5 fellowships, 90 research assistantships (averaging $15,999 per year), 69 teaching assistantships (averaging $10,640 per year); unspecified assistantships also available. Financial award application deadline: 2/1; financial award applicants required to submit FAFSA. *Faculty research:* Computer systems, database, computer networks, graphics and vision, algorithm and parallel processing. Total annual research expenditures: $5.7 million. *Unit head:* Dr. Sartaj Sahni, Chair, 352-392-1527, Fax: 352-392-1220, E-mail: sahni@cise.ufl.edu. *Application contact:* Dr. Jih-Kwon Peir, Graduate Coordinator, 352-450-3446, Fax: 352-392-1220, E-mail: peir@cise.ufl.edu.

University of Florida, Graduate School, College of Fine Arts, School of Art and Art History, Gainesville, FL 32611. Offers art (MFA), including ceramics, creative photography, drawing, electronic intermedia, graphic design, painting, printmaking, sculpture; art education (MA); art history (MA, PhD); digital arts and sciences (MA); museology (museum studies) (MA). *Accreditation:* NASAD. Postbaccalaureate distance learning degree programs offered (minimal on-campus study). *Faculty:* 29 full-time (14 women). *Students:* 107 full-time (72 women), 57 part-time (52 women); includes 6 Black or African American, non-Hispanic/Latino; 1 American Indian or Alaska Native, non-Hispanic/Latino; 5 Asian, non-Hispanic/Latino; 13 Hispanic/Latino, 14 international. Average age 31. 282 applicants, 30% accepted, 61 enrolled. In 2010, 24 master's, 3 doctorates awarded. *Degree requirements:* For master's, thesis, project or thesis (MFA); 1 foreign language (MA in art history); for doctorate, 2 foreign languages, comprehensive exam, thesis/dissertation. *Entrance requirements:* For master's, GRE General Test, portfolio (MFA), writing sample (MA), minimum GPA of 3.0; for doctorate, GRE General Test, minimum GPA of 3.0. Additional exam requirements/recommendations for international students: Required—TOEFL (minimum score 550 paper-based; 213 computer-based; 80 iBT), IELTS (minimum score 6). *Application deadline:* For fall admission, 1/1 priority date for domestic students, 1/1 for international students; for spring admission, 11/1 for domestic and international students. Applications are processed on a rolling basis. Application fee: $30. Electronic applications accepted. *Expenses:* Tuition, state resident: full-time $10,915.92. Tuition, nonresident: full-time $28,309. *Financial support:* In 2010–11, 36 students received support, including 9 fellowships, 3 research assistantships with tuition reimbursements available (averaging $12,789 per year), 24 teaching assistantships with tuition reimbursements available (averaging $10,512 per year); Federal Work-Study, institutionally sponsored loans, and unspecified assistantships also available. Financial award applicants required to submit FAFSA. *Faculty research:* Studio production, art historical studies of style context. *Unit head:* Laura Robertsoon, SR Associate in Graduate Studies, 352-846-3425, E-mail: laurar@ufl.edu. *Application contact:* Lauren G. Lake, Coordinator, 352-273-3032, Fax: 352-392-8453, E-mail: lglake@arts.ufl.edu.

The University of Kansas, Graduate Studies, School of Architecture, Design, and Planning, Department of Design, Lawrence, KS 66045. Offers design (MA, MFA); design management (MA); interaction design (MA). *Accreditation:* NASAD (one or more programs are accredited). *Students:* 11 full-time (7 women), 24 part-time (14 women), 5 international. Average age 33. 18 applicants, 72% accepted, 12 enrolled. In 2010, 4 master's awarded. *Degree requirements:* For master's, thesis. *Entrance requirements:* For master's, portfolio, 3 letters of recommendation, minimum GPA of 3.0. Additional exam requirements/recommendations for international students: Required—TOEFL, IELTS. *Application deadline:* For fall admission, 2/1 for domestic and international students; for spring admission, 10/15 for domestic students. Application fee: $55 ($65 for international students). Electronic applications accepted. *Expenses:* Tuition, state resident: full-time $7092; part-time $295.50 per credit hour. Tuition, nonresident: full-time $16,590; part-time $691.25 per credit hour. Required fees: $858; $71.49 per credit hour. Tuition and fees vary according to course load, campus/location and program. *Financial support:* Fellowships, teaching assistantships with full and partial tuition reimbursements, Federal Work-Study, scholarships/grants, and unspecified assistantships available. Financial award application deadline: 2/1; financial award applicants required to submit FAFSA. *Faculty research:* Interaction design, design management, photography, graphic design, industrial design. *Unit head:* Lois Greene, Interim Chair and Associate Dean, 785-864-4401, E-mail: design@ku.edu. *Application contact:* Brian Hanabury, Coordinator of Student Services, 785-864-4401, E-mail: design@ku.edu.

University of Massachusetts Dartmouth, Graduate School, College of Visual and Performing Arts, Program in Visual Design, North Dartmouth, MA 02747-2300. Offers digital media (MFA); graphic design (MFA); illustration (MFA); photography (MFA); typography (MFA). *Accreditation:* NASAD. *Faculty:* 17 full-time (7 women), 4 part-time/adjunct (1 woman). *Students:* 12 full-time (8 women), 5 part-time (4 women); includes 1 Two or more races, non-Hispanic/Latino, 1 international. Average age 35. 33 applicants, 48% accepted, 7 enrolled. In 2010, 1 master's awarded. *Degree requirements:* For master's, visual thesis. *Entrance requirements:* For master's, portfolio, interview, minimum GPA of 3.0, 3 letters of recommendation. Additional exam requirements/recommendations for international students: Required—TOEFL (minimum score 500 paper-based). *Application deadline:* For fall admission, 2/1 priority date for domestic students, 12/1 priority date for international students. Applications are processed on a rolling basis. Application fee: $40 ($60 for international students). Electronic applications accepted. *Expenses:* Tuition, state resident: full-time $2071; part-time $86 per credit. Tuition, nonresident: full-time $8099; part-time $337 per credit. Required fees: $9446; $394 per credit. One-time fee: $75. Part-time tuition and fees vary according to class time, course load, degree level and reciprocity agreements. *Financial support:* In 2010–11, 5 teaching assistantships with full tuition reimbursements (averaging $3,088 per year) were awarded; Federal Work-Study and unspecified assistantships also available. Support available to part-time students. Financial award application deadline: 3/1; financial award applicants required to submit FAFSA. *Faculty research:* Typography. Total annual research expenditures: $5,898. *Unit head:* Memory Holloway, Director, 508-999-8554, E-mail: mholloway@umassd.edu. *Application contact:* Elan Turcotte-Shamski, Graduate Admissions Officer, 508-999-8604, Fax: 508-999-8183, E-mail: graduate@umassd.edu.

University of Missouri, Graduate School, College of Human Environmental Science, Department of Architectural Studies, Columbia, MO 65211. Offers design with digital media (MA, MS); environmental design (MS). *Entrance requirements:* For master's, GRE General Test, minimum GPA of 3.0. Additional exam requirements/recommendations for international students: Required—TOEFL (minimum score 500 paper-based; 173 computer-based; 61 iBT).

University of Pennsylvania, School of Engineering and Applied Science, Computer Graphics and Game Technology Program, Philadelphia, PA 19104. Offers MSE. *Students:* 27 full-time (2 women), 4 part-time (2 women); includes 7 Asian, non-Hispanic/Latino, 16 international. 88 applicants, 39% accepted, 20 enrolled. In 2010, 17 master's awarded. Application fee: $70. *Expenses:* Tuition: Full-time $25,660; part-time $4758 per course. Required fees: $2152; $270 per course. Tuition and fees vary according to course load, degree level and program. *Application contact:* Stephen H. Lane, 215-898-8560, E-mail: cggt@cis.upenn.edu.

University of Southern California, Graduate School, School of Cinematic Arts, Division of Animation and Digital Arts, Los Angeles, CA 90089. Offers MFA. *Faculty:* 9 full-time (5 women), 20 part-time/adjunct (7 women). *Students:* 44 full-time (21 women); includes 17 minority (4 Black or African American, non-Hispanic/Latino; 3 Asian, non-Hispanic/Latino; 8 Hispanic/Latino; 2 Two or more races, non-Hispanic/Latino), 9 international. In 2010, 13 master's awarded. *Degree requirements:* For master's, thesis, digital media and research documentation. *Application deadline:* For fall admission, 12/1 for domestic and international students. Electronic applications accepted. *Expenses:* Contact institution. *Financial support:* In 2010–11, 17 students received support, including 3 fellowships with partial tuition reimbursements available; career-related internships or fieldwork, scholarships/grants, and tuition waivers (partial) also available. Financial award applicants required to submit FAFSA. *Faculty research:* Character animation, visual effects, motion graphics, documentary animation, experimental animation. *Unit head:* Kathy Evelyn Smith, Chair and Associate Professor, 213-821-1348, Fax: 213-740-5869, E-mail: kates@usc.edu. *Application contact:* Daphne M. Sigismondi, Program Specialist, 213-740-3986, Fax: 213-740-5869, E-mail: dsigismondi@cinema.usc.edu.

University of Victoria, Faculty of Graduate Studies, Faculty of Fine Arts, Department of Visual Arts, Victoria, BC V8W 2Y2, Canada. Offers digital multimedia (MFA); drawing (MFA); painting (MFA); photography (MFA); sculpture (MFA); video (MFA). *Degree requirements:* For master's, exhibit, oral exam. *Entrance requirements:* For master's, portfolio, BFA. Additional exam requirements/recommendations for international students: Required—TOEFL (minimum score 575 paper-based; 233 computer-based), IELTS (minimum score 7). Electronic applications accepted.

Washington State University, Graduate School, College of Liberal Arts, Department of Fine Arts, Pullman, WA 99164. Offers ceramics (MFA); digital media (MFA); drawing (MFA); painting (MFA); photography (MFA); print making (MFA); sculpture (MFA). *Faculty:* 10. *Students:* 15 full-time (8 women); includes 1 Black or African American, non-Hispanic/Latino; 1 Hispanic/Latino. Average age 29. 30 applicants, 20% accepted, 5 enrolled. In 2010, 5 master's awarded. *Degree requirements:* For master's, comprehensive exam (for some programs), thesis, exhibit, oral exam. *Entrance requirements:* For master's, GRE, statement of intent, portfolio of no more than 15 images on CD/DVD. Additional exam requirements/recommendations for international students: Required—TOEFL (minimum score 550 paper-based; 213 computer-based), IELTS. *Application deadline:* For fall admission, 1/10 for domestic and international students. Application fee: $50. Electronic applications accepted. *Expenses:* Tuition, state resident: full-time $8552; part-time $443 per credit. Tuition, nonresident: full-time $21,650; part-time $1083 per credit. Required fees: $846. *Financial support:* In 2010–11, fellowships with full and partial tuition reimbursements (averaging $3,114 per year), research assistantships with full and partial tuition reimbursements (averaging $13,917 per year), teaching assistantships with full and partial tuition reimbursements (averaging $13,056 per year) were awarded; career-related internships or fieldwork, Federal Work-Study, institutionally sponsored loans, tuition waivers (partial), and unspecified assistantships also available. Financial award application deadline: 2/15; financial award applicants required to submit FAFSA. *Faculty research:* Polynesian art, museum representation, number theory. *Unit head:* Dr. Chris Watts, Interim Chair, 509-335-7107, Fax: 509-335-7742, E-mail: cjwatts@wsu.edu. *Application contact:* Graduate School Admissions, 800-GRADWSU, Fax: 509-335-1949, E-mail: gradsch@wsu.edu.

Graphic Design

Academy of Art University, Graduate Program, School of Graphic Design, San Francisco, CA 94105-3410. Offers MFA. *Accreditation:* NASAD. Part-time programs available. Post-baccalaureate distance learning degree programs offered (no on-campus study). *Faculty:* 9 full-time (3 women), 64 part-time/adjunct (28 women). *Students:* 184 full-time (128 women), 217 part-time (158 women); includes 18 Black or African American, non-Hispanic/Latino; 1 American Indian or Alaska Native, non-Hispanic/Latino; 26 Asian, non-Hispanic/Latino; 18 Hispanic/Latino, 138 international. Average age 30. 170 applicants. In 2010, 15 master's awarded. *Degree requirements:* For master's, thesis, final review. *Entrance requirements:* For master's, minimum GPA of 3.0, portfolio. *Application deadline:* For fall admission, 9/7 for domestic and international students; for spring admission, 2/2 for domestic and international students. Applications are processed on a rolling basis. Application fee: $100 ($500 for international students). Electronic applications accepted. *Expenses:* Tuition: Full-time $20,160; part-time $840 per semester hour. Required fees: $45 per semester. *Financial support:* Career-related internships or fieldwork and Federal Work-Study available. Support available to part-time students. Financial award application deadline: 8/10; financial award applicants required to submit FAFSA. *Application contact:* Prospective Student Services, 800-544-ARTS, Fax: 415-263-4130, E-mail: info@academyart.edu.

Atlantic College, Program in Graphic Arts, Guaynabo, PR 00970. Offers digital graphic design (MGD). Part-time programs available. *Degree requirements:* For master's, thesis. *Entrance requirements:* For master's, minimum GPA of 3.0, 2 letters of recommendation, portfolio, interview. *Faculty research:* Digital design, technology.

Bob Jones University, Graduate Programs, Greenville, SC 29614. Offers accountancy (MS); Bible (MA); Bible translation (MA); Biblical studies (Certificate); broadcast management (MS); business administration (MBA); church history (MA, PhD); church ministries (MA); church music (MM); cinema and video production (MA); counseling (MS); curriculum and instruction (Ed D); divinity (M Div); dramatic production (MA); educational leadership (MS, Ed D, Ed S); elementary education (M Ed, MAT); English (M Ed, MA, MAT); fine arts (MA); graphic design (MA); history (M Ed, MA); illustration (MA); interpretative speech (MA); mathematics (M Ed, MAT); medical missions (Certificate); ministry (MM, D Min); multi-categorical special education (M Ed, MAT); music (M Ed); New Testament interpretation (PhD); Old Testament interpretation (PhD); orchestral instrument performance (MM); organ performance (MM); pastoral studies (MA); personnel services (MS, Ed S); piano pedagogy (MM); piano performance (MM); platform arts (MA); radio and television broadcasting (MS); rhetoric and public address (MA); secondary education (M Ed); studio art (MA); teaching Bible (MA); theology (MA, PhD); voice performance (MM); youth ministries (MA); M Div/MM.

Boston University, College of Fine Arts, School of Visual Arts, Boston, MA 02215. Offers art education (MA); graphic design (MFA); painting (MFA); sculpture (MFA); studio teaching (MA). *Faculty:* 17 full-time, 4 part-time/adjunct. *Students:* 34 full-time (19 women); includes 7 minority (2 Black or African American, non-Hispanic/Latino; 2 Asian, non-Hispanic/Latino; 3 Hispanic/Latino), 4 international. Average age 27. 281 applicants, 28% accepted. In 2010, 130 master's awarded. *Entrance requirements:* For master's, portfolio. Additional exam requirements/recommendations for international students: Required—TOEFL. *Application deadline:* For fall admission, 2/15 for domestic and international students. Applications are processed on a rolling basis. Application fee: $70. *Expenses:* Tuition: Full-time $39,314; part-time $1228 per credit. Required fees: $40 per semester. *Financial support:* Fellowships, teaching assistantships available. Financial award application deadline: 2/15. *Unit head:* Lynne Allen, Director, 617-353-3371. *Application contact:* Mark Krone, Manager, Graduate Admissions, 617-353-3350, E-mail: arts@bu.edu.

Bowling Green State University, Graduate College, College of Arts and Sciences, School of Art, Bowling Green, OH 43403. Offers 2-D studio art (MA, MFA); 3-D studio art (MA, MFA); art education (MA); art history (MA); computer art (MA); design (MFA); digital arts (MFA); graphics (MFA). *Accreditation:* NASAD. Part-time programs available. *Degree requirements:* For master's, thesis or alternative, final exhibit (MFA). *Entrance requirements:* For master's, GRE General Test (MA), slide portfolio (15-20 slides). Additional exam requirements/recommendations for international students: Required—TOEFL. Electronic applications accepted. *Faculty research:* Computer animation and virtual reality, Spanish still-life painting from 1600 to 1800, art and psychotherapy, Japanese wood-firing techniques in ceramics, non-toxic printmaking technologies.

California Institute of the Arts, School of Art, Valencia, CA 91355-2340. Offers art (MFA, Adv C); graphic design (MFA, Adv C); photography (MFA, Adv C). *Accreditation:* NASAD (one or more programs are accredited). *Degree requirements:* For master's, final project. *Entrance requirements:* For master's, portfolio. Additional exam requirements/recommendations for international students: Required—TOEFL. Electronic applications accepted.

California State University, Los Angeles, Graduate Studies, College of Arts and Letters, Department of Art, Los Angeles, CA 90032-8530. Offers art (MA), including art education, art history, art therapy, ceramics, metals, and textiles, design (MA, MFA), painting, sculpture, and graphic arts, photography; fine arts (MFA), including crafts, design (MA, MFA), studio arts. *Accreditation:* NASAD (one or more programs are accredited). Part-time and evening/weekend programs available. *Faculty:* 9 full-time (5 women), 3 part-time/adjunct (2 women). *Students:* 27 full-time (19 women), 33 part-time (22 women); includes 24 minority (3 Black or African American, non-Hispanic/Latino; 7 Asian, non-Hispanic/Latino; 13 Hispanic/Latino; 1 Two or more races, non-Hispanic/Latino), 9 international. Average age 36. 19 applicants, 100% accepted, 13 enrolled. In 2010, 26 master's awarded. *Degree requirements:* For master's, comprehensive exam, project or thesis. *Entrance requirements:* For master's, portfolio. Additional exam requirements/recommendations for international students: Required—TOEFL (minimum score 500 paper-based; 173 computer-based). *Application deadline:* For fall admission, 5/1 for domestic and international students. Applications are processed on a rolling basis. Application fee: $55. Electronic applications accepted. *Financial support:* Federal Work-Study available. Support available to part-time students. Financial award application deadline: 3/1. *Faculty research:* The artist and the book, conceptual art, ceramic processes, computer graphics, architectural graphics. *Unit head:* Dr. Abbas Daneshvari, Chair, 323-343-4010, Fax: 323-343-4045, E-mail: adanesh@calstatela.edu. *Application contact:* Dr. Alan Muchlinski, Dean of Graduate Studies, 323-343-3820, Fax: 323-343-5653, E-mail: amuchli@exchange.calstatela.edu.

Cardinal Stritch University, College of Arts and Sciences, Department of Art, Milwaukee, WI 53217-3985. Offers visual studies (MA). Part-time and evening/weekend programs available. *Degree requirements:* For master's, thesis, portfolio, exhibit. *Entrance requirements:* For master's, minimum GPA of 2.75; 3 letters of recommendation.

City College of the City University of New York, Graduate School, College of Liberal Arts and Science, Division of the Humanities and Arts, Department of Art, Program in Fine Arts, New York, NY 10031-9198. Offers advertising design (MFA); ceramic design (MFA); painting (MFA); printmaking (MFA); sculpture (MFA); wood and metal design (MFA). *Degree requirements:* For master's, thesis exhibit. *Entrance requirements:* For master's, 20 slide portfolio. Additional exam requirements/recommendations for international students: Required—TOEFL (minimum score 577 paper-based; 90 iBT). Electronic applications accepted.

The College of New Rochelle, Graduate School, Division of Art and Communication Studies, Program in Studio Art, New Rochelle, NY 10805-2308. Offers MS. Part-time and evening/weekend programs available. *Degree requirements:* For master's, apprenticeship. *Entrance requirements:* For master's, portfolio, 36 credits of course work in studio art. *Faculty research:* Experimental computer graphics.

Cranbrook Academy of Art, Graduate School, Program in Fine Arts, Bloomfield Hills, MI 48303-0801. Offers ceramics (MFA); design (MFA), including graphic design; fiber arts (MFA); metalsmithing (MFA); painting (MFA); photography (MFA); printmaking (MFA); sculpture (MFA). *Accreditation:* NASAD. *Degree requirements:* For master's, thesis, exhibit. *Entrance requirements:* Additional exam requirements/recommendations for international students: Required—TOEFL (minimum score 550 paper-based; 213 computer-based).

Digital Media Arts College, Graduate Programs, Boca Raton, FL 33431. Offers graphic design (MFA); special FX animation (MFA).

Florida Atlantic University, Dorothy F. Schmidt College of Arts and Letters, Department of Visual Arts and Art History, Boca Raton, FL 33431-0991. Offers art education (MAT); ceramics (MFA); computer art (MFA); graphic design (MFA); painting (MFA). *Faculty:* 17 full-time (11 women), 9 part-time/adjunct (7 women). *Students:* 19 full-time (12 women), 7 part-time (2 women); includes 8 minority (all Hispanic/Latino), 1 international. Average age 30. 33 applicants, 30% accepted, 6 enrolled. In 2010, 5 master's awarded. *Degree requirements:* For master's, one foreign language, project. *Entrance requirements:* For master's, GRE General Test, minimum GPA of 3.0 during last 60 hours of course work, slide portfolio. *Application deadline:* For fall admission, 2/21 for domestic and international students; for spring admission, 10/1 for domestic and international students. Application fee: $30. Electronic applications accepted. *Expenses:* Tuition, area resident: Part-time $319.96 per credit. Tuition, state resident: part-time $319.96 per credit. Tuition, nonresident: part-time $926.42 per credit. *Financial support:* Research assistantships with full tuition reimbursements, teaching assistantships with full tuition reimbursements, career-related internships or fieldwork, Federal Work-Study, and institutionally sponsored loans available. Financial award applicants required to submit FAFSA. *Faculty research:* Painting, ceramics (traditional and non-traditional), installation, video and interactive sculpture. *Unit head:* Dr. Linda Johnson, Chair, 561-297-3870, Fax: 561-297-3078, E-mail: ljohnson@

Graphic Design

Florida Atlantic University (continued)
fau.edu. *Application contact:* James A. Novak, Associate Professor/Graduate Coordinator/ Advisor, 561-297-2430, Fax: 561-297-3078, E-mail: jnovak@fau.edu.

Full Sail University, Game Design Master of Science Program—Campus, Winter Park, FL 32792-7437. Offers MS.

George Mason University, College of Visual and Performing Arts, Program in Visual Technologies, Fairfax, VA 22030. Offers art and visual technology (MFA); art education (MAT). *Accreditation:* NASAD. *Faculty:* 21 full-time (11 women), 34 part-time/adjunct (21 women). *Students:* 15 full-time (9 women), 5 part-time (3 women); includes 2 Asian, non-Hispanic/ Latino; 1 Hispanic/Latino; 1 Two or more races, non-Hispanic/Latino, 2 international. Average age 33. 41 applicants, 27% accepted, 7 enrolled. In 2010, 5 master's awarded. *Degree requirements:* For master's, apprenticeship in business; dissertation or project. *Entrance requirements:* For master's, BA or BFA, portfolio, resume, 3 letters of reference. Additional exam requirements/recommendations for international students: Required—TOEFL (minimum score 570 paper-based; 230 computer-based; 88 iBT). *Application deadline:* For fall admission, 1/15 for domestic students. Application fee: $100. Electronic applications accepted. *Expenses:* Tuition, state resident: full-time $8192; part-time $440 per credit hour. Tuition, nonresident: full-time $22,952; part-time $1055 per credit hour. Required fees: $2364; $99 per credit hour. *Financial support:* Career-related internships or fieldwork, Federal Work-Study, scholarships/ grants, unspecified assistantships, and health care benefits (full-time research or teaching assistantship recipients) available. Financial award application deadline: 3/1; financial award applicants required to submit FAFSA. *Faculty research:* Digital arts, painting, photography, print-making, sculpture; combined art forms in in-disciplinary projects including installation, performance, publishing, time or writing-based; combined creative and critical approaches. *Unit head:* Dr. Scott M. Martin, Director, 703-993-4574, Fax: 703-993-8995, E-mail: smartin4@ gmu.edu. *Application contact:* Dr. Scott M. Martin, Director, 703-993-4574, Fax: 703-993-8995, E-mail: smartin4@gmu.edu.

Illinois State University, Graduate School, College of Fine Arts, School of Art, Normal, IL 61790-2200. Offers art history (MA, MS); ceramics (MFA, MS); drawing (MFA, MS); fibers (MFA, MS); glass (MFA, MS); graphic design (MFA, MS); metals (MFA, MS); painting (MFA, MS); photography (MFA, MS); printmaking (MFA, MS); sculpture (MFA, MS). *Accreditation:* NASAD (one or more programs are accredited). *Degree requirements:* For master's, thesis or alternative, internship. *Entrance requirements:* For master's, portfolio, sample of scholarly writing. *Faculty research:* General operations support: Normal Editions Workshop for FY2007.

Indiana State University, College of Graduate and Professional Studies, College of Arts and Sciences, Department of Art, Terre Haute, IN 47809. Offers ceramics (MA, MFA); drawing (MA, MFA); graphic design (MA, MFA); painting (MA, MFA); photography (MA, MFA); printmaking (MA, MFA); sculpture (MA, MFA). *Accreditation:* NASAD (one or more programs are accredited). Part-time programs available. *Degree requirements:* For master's, thesis or alternative, departmental qualifying exam. *Entrance requirements:* For master's, portfolio. Additional exam requirements/recommendations for international students: Required—TOEFL (minimum score 550 paper-based).

Iowa State University of Science and Technology, Graduate College, College of Design, Department of Art and Design, Ames, IA 50011. Offers art and design (MA); graphic design (MFA); integrated visual arts (MFA); interior design (MFA). Part-time programs available. *Faculty:* 36 full-time (20 women), 1 (woman) part-time/adjunct. *Students:* 52 full-time (39 women), 22 part-time (11 women); includes 1 Black or African American, non-Hispanic/Latino; 1 Asian, non-Hispanic/Latino; 1 Hispanic/Latino, 18 international. 48 applicants, 71% accepted, 19 enrolled. In 2010, 15 master's awarded. *Degree requirements:* For master's, thesis (for some programs). *Entrance requirements:* For master's, GRE General Test, resume. Additional exam requirements/recommendations for international students: Required—TOEFL (minimum score 550 paper-based; 79 iBT), IELTS (minimum score 6.5). *Application deadline:* For fall admission, 4/15 priority date for domestic and international students; for spring admission, 4/15 for domestic and international students. Applications are processed on a rolling basis. Application fee: $40 ($90 for international students). Electronic applications accepted. *Financial support:* Research assistantships with tuition reimbursements, teaching assistantships with tuition reimbursements, career-related internships or fieldwork, Federal Work-Study, institutionally sponsored loans, and tuition waivers (partial) available. Support available to part-time students. Financial award application deadline: 2/15; financial award applicants required to submit FAFSA. *Faculty research:* Computer applications, fire safety, human factors in design, art and design education, fine arts, craft design. *Unit head:* Dr. Roger Baer, Chair, 515-294-6724, Fax: 515-294-2725, E-mail: artdn@iastate.edu. *Application contact:* Dr. Roger Baer, Chair, 515-294-6724, Fax: 515-294-2725, E-mail: artdn@iastate.edu.

Kent State University, College of Communication and Information, School of Visual Communication Design, Kent, OH 44242-0001. Offers MA, MFA. *Accreditation:* NASAD. Part-time programs available. *Degree requirements:* For master's, thesis, portfolios. *Entrance requirements:* For master's, portfolio (studio majors), minimum GPA of 2.75, GPA of 3.0 in major. *Expenses:* Tuition, state resident: full-time $7866; part-time $437 per credit hour. Tuition, nonresident: full-time $14,022; part-time $779 per credit hour. *Faculty research:* Graphic design.

Louisiana State University and Agricultural and Mechanical College, Graduate School, College of Art and Design, School of Art, Program in Studio Art, Baton Rouge, LA 70803. Offers ceramics (MFA); graphic design (MFA); painting and drawing (MFA); photography (MFA); printmaking (MFA); sculpture (MFA). *Accreditation:* NASAD. *Students:* 45 full-time (29 women), 3 part-time (all women); includes 1 Black or African American, non-Hispanic/Latino; 4 Asian, non-Hispanic/Latino, 4 international. Average age 29. 114 applicants, 21% accepted, 14 enrolled. In 2010, 15 master's awarded. *Degree requirements:* For master's, thesis. *Entrance requirements:* For master's, minimum GPA of 3.0. Additional exam requirements/ recommendations for international students: Required—TOEFL (minimum score 550 paper-based; 213 computer-based; 79 iBT), IELTS (minimum score 6.5). *Application deadline:* For fall admission, 1/25 priority date for domestic students, 5/15 for international students; for spring admission, 10/15 for international students. Applications are processed on a rolling basis. Electronic applications accepted. *Financial support:* In 2010–11, 25 students received support; research assistantships with partial tuition reimbursements available, teaching assistantships, career-related internships or fieldwork, Federal Work-Study, institutionally sponsored loans, scholarships/grants, and unspecified assistantships available. Support available to part-time students. Financial award application deadline: 3/15. *Unit head:* Tom Neff, Graduate Coordinator, 225-578-5411, Fax: 225-578-1445, E-mail: tneff@lsu.edu.

Louisiana Tech University, Graduate School, College of Liberal Arts, School of Art, Ruston, LA 71272. Offers art and graphic design (MFA); photography (MFA); studio art (MFA). *Accreditation:* NASAD. Part-time programs available. *Degree requirements:* For master's, exhibit. *Entrance requirements:* For master's, GRE General Test, portfolio.

Maryland Institute College of Art, Graduate Studies, Program in Graphic Design, Baltimore, MD 21217. Offers MFA. *Faculty:* 2 full-time (both women), 10 part-time/adjunct (5 women). *Students:* 28 full-time (18 women); includes 5 minority (2 Asian, non-Hispanic/Latino; 3 Hispanic/ Latino), 6 international. Average age 27. In 2010, 6 master's awarded. *Degree requirements:* For master's, thesis, exhibit. *Entrance requirements:* For master's, 40 credits in studio art, 6 credits in art history, portfolio. Additional exam requirements/recommendations for international students: Required—TOEFL (minimum score 550 paper-based; 213 computer-based). *Application deadline:* For fall admission, 1/15 for domestic and international students. Application fee: $60. *Expenses:* Tuition: Full-time $34,550; part-time $1440 per credit hour. Required fees: $1140; $570 per term. *Financial support:* In 2010–11, 28 students received support, including 28 fellowships (averaging $10,000 per year), 25 teaching assistantships (averaging $1,800 per year); career-related internships or fieldwork and scholarships/grants also available. Financial award application deadline: 3/1; financial award applicants required to submit FAFSA. *Unit head:* Ellen Lupton, Director, 410-225-2382, Fax: 410-669-1141. *Application contact:* Scott G. Kelly, Associate Dean of Graduate Admission, 410-225-2256, Fax: 410-225-2408, E-mail: graduate@mica.edu.

Marywood University, Academic Affairs, Insalaco College of Creative and Performing Arts, Art Department, Program in Studio Art, Scranton, PA 18509-1598. Offers advertising design (MA); ceramics (MA); clay (MA); graphic design (MA); illustration (MA); painting (MA); photography (MA); printmaking (MA); sculpture (MA); weaving (MA). *Accreditation:* NASAD. *Entrance requirements:* Additional exam requirements/recommendations for international students: Required—TOEFL (minimum score 550 paper-based; 213 computer-based; 79 iBT). Electronic applications accepted. *Expenses:* Tuition: Part-time $735 per credit. Required fees: $470 per semester. Tuition and fees vary according to degree level and campus/location. *Faculty research:* Texture and line in clay, cast bronze sculpture, color theories, book art and illustration, sculptural form.

Marywood University, Academic Affairs, Insalaco College of Creative and Performing Arts, Art Department, Program in Visual Arts, Scranton, PA 18509-1598. Offers advertising design (MFA); clay (MFA); graphic design (MFA); illustration (MFA); metals (MFA); painting (MFA); photography (MFA); printmaking (MFA). *Accreditation:* NASAD. *Entrance requirements:* Additional exam requirements/recommendations for international students: Required—TOEFL (minimum score 550 paper-based; 213 computer-based; 79 iBT). Electronic applications accepted. *Expenses:* Contact institution. *Faculty research:* Mariology, exploration of visual imagery, explorations involving drawing on the loom, clay as sculptural medium, oil paintings.

Miami International University of Art & Design, Program in Graphic Design, Miami, FL 33132-1418. Offers MFA. Postbaccalaureate distance learning degree programs offered. *Application contact:* Office of Graduate Admissions, 305-428-5700.

See Close-Up on page 129.

Minneapolis College of Art and Design, Certificate Programs, Minneapolis, MN 55404-4347. Offers design (Certificate); fine arts (Certificate); graphic design (Certificate); media (Certificate); sustainable design (Certificate). Part-time programs available. Postbaccalaureate distance learning degree programs offered. *Degree requirements:* For Certificate, final project. *Entrance requirements:* For degree, resume, portfolio, letter of recommendation. Additional exam requirements/recommendations for international students: Required—TOEFL (minimum score 550 paper-based; 213 computer-based; 79 iBT). Electronic applications accepted. *Faculty research:* Visual arts.

Minneapolis College of Art and Design, Program in Visual Studies, Minneapolis, MN 55404-4347. Offers animation (MFA); comic art (MFA); drawing (MFA); filmmaking (MFA); fine arts (MFA); furniture design (MFA); graphic design (MFA); illustration (MFA); interactive media (MFA); painting (MFA); photography (MFA); printmaking (MFA); sculpture (MFA). *Accreditation:* NASAD. Part-time programs available. *Degree requirements:* For master's, thesis, thesis exhibit. *Entrance requirements:* For master's, portfolio of visual artwork, resume, 3 letters of recommendation. Additional exam requirements/recommendations for international students: Required—TOEFL (minimum score 550 paper-based; 213 computer-based; 79 iBT). Electronic applications accepted. *Faculty research:* Visual arts: animation, comic art, drawing, filmmaking, furniture design, graphic design, illustration, interactive media, painting, photography, printmaking, sculpture.

Morehead State University, Graduate Programs, Caudill College of Arts, Humanities and Social Sciences, Department of Art and Design, Morehead, KY 40351. Offers art education (MA); graphic design (MA); studio art (MA). Part-time and evening/weekend programs available. *Degree requirements:* For master's, comprehensive exam, thesis (for some programs), oral exam during exhibition. *Entrance requirements:* For master's, GRE General Test, minimum undergraduate GPA of 3.0 in major, 2.5 overall; portfolio; bachelor's degree in art. Additional exam requirements/recommendations for international students: Required—TOEFL (minimum score 500 paper-based; 173 computer-based). Electronic applications accepted. *Faculty research:* Computer art, painting, drawing, ceramics, photography.

New York Institute of Technology, Graduate Division, School of Arts and Sciences, Program in Fine Arts, Old Westbury, NY 11568-8000. Offers computer graphics and animation (MFA); fine arts and technology (MFA); graphic design (MFA). Part-time and evening/weekend programs available. *Students:* 34 full-time (21 women), 6 part-time (1 woman); includes 14 minority (7 Black or African American, non-Hispanic/Latino; 2 Asian, non-Hispanic/Latino; 4 Hispanic/ Latino; 1 Two or more races, non-Hispanic/Latino), 11 international. Average age 32. In 2010, 5 master's awarded. *Degree requirements:* For master's, thesis or alternative. *Entrance requirements:* Additional exam requirements/recommendations for international students: Required—TOEFL (minimum score 550 paper-based; 213 computer-based). *Application deadline:* For fall admission, 7/1 priority date for domestic students; for spring admission, 12/1 priority date for domestic students. Applications are processed on a rolling basis. Application fee: $50. Electronic applications accepted. *Expenses:* Tuition: Part-time $835 per credit. *Financial support:* Research assistantships, career-related internships or fieldwork, Federal Work-Study, institutionally sponsored loans, tuition waivers (partial), and unspecified assistantships available. Support available to part-time students. Financial award applicants required to submit FAFSA. *Unit head:* Dr. Roger Yu, Dean, 516-686-7700, Fax: 516-686-1192, E-mail: ryu@nyit.edu. *Application contact:* Dr. Jacquelyn Nealon, Vice President for Enrollment Services, 516-686-7925, Fax: 516-686-7597, E-mail: jnealon@nyit.edu.

New York University, School of Continuing and Professional Studies, Division for Media Industry Studies and Design, Program in Graphic Communications Management and Technology, New York, NY 10012-1019. Offers MA. Part-time and evening/weekend programs available. *Faculty:* 1 (woman) full-time, 15 part-time/adjunct (4 women). *Students:* 15 full-time (10 women), 47 part-time (29 women); includes 6 Black or African American, non-Hispanic/Latino; 6 Asian, non-Hispanic/Latino; 4 Hispanic/Latino, 11 international. Average age 31. 43 applicants, 65% accepted, 18 enrolled. In 2010, 36 master's awarded. *Degree requirements:* For master's, thesis, capstone, research course. *Entrance requirements:* For master's, GRE General Test or GMAT (for recent graduates), resume, 2 letters of recommendation, essay, professional experience. Additional exam requirements/recommendations for international students: Required—TOEFL (minimum score 600 paper-based; 250 computer-based; 100 iBT). *Application deadline:* For fall admission, 2/1 priority date for domestic and international students; for spring admission, 10/15 priority date for domestic students, 8/15 priority date for international students. Applications are processed on a rolling basis. Application fee: $75. Electronic applications accepted. *Financial support:* In 2010–11, 46 students received support, including 46 fellowships (averaging $1,744 per year); scholarships/grants and tuition waivers (partial) also available. Support available to part-time students. Financial award application deadline: 3/1; financial award applicants required to submit FAFSA. *Unit head:* Bonnie Blake, Academic Director, 212-992-3222, Fax: 212-992-3386, E-mail: bonnie.blake@nyu.edu. *Application contact:* Ansley Dunn, Program Administrator, 212-992-3283, Fax: 212-992-3233, E-mail: ansley.dunn@ nyu.edu.

North Carolina State University, Graduate School, College of Design, Department of Graphic Design, Raleigh, NC 27695. Offers MGD. *Accreditation:* NASAD. *Degree requirements:* For master's, thesis optional, oral exam. *Entrance requirements:* For master's, GRE General Test, portfolio. Electronic applications accepted. *Faculty research:* Typography, graphic design, interaction design, design and cognition, design and culture.

Ohio University, Graduate College, College of Fine Arts, School of Art, Athens, OH 45701-2979. Offers art history (MA); ceramics (MFA); graphic design (MFA); painting (MFA); photography (MFA); printmaking (MFA); sculpture (MFA). Part-time programs available. *Students:* 62 full-time (35 women), 4 part-time (3 women); includes 5 minority (1 American Indian or Alaska Native, non-Hispanic/Latino; 1 Asian, non-Hispanic/Latino; 3 Hispanic/Latino), 7 international. 181 applicants, 19% accepted, 28 enrolled. In 2010, 14 master's awarded. *Degree requirements:* For master's, thesis. *Entrance requirements:* For master's, portfolio.

Additional exam requirements/recommendations for international students: Required—TOEFL (minimum score 550 paper-based; 80 iBT) or IELTS (minimum score 6.5). *Application deadline:* For fall admission, 2/1 for domestic and international students. Application fee: $50 ($55 for international students). Electronic applications accepted. *Financial support:* Teaching assistantships with full and partial tuition reimbursements, career-related internships or fieldwork, Federal Work-Study, institutionally sponsored loans, scholarships/grants, tuition waivers (partial), and unspecified assistantships available. Financial award application deadline: 2/1. *Faculty research:* Vapor-fired ceramics, video installation, art theory, digital photography, mixed and interdisciplinary media work. *Unit head:* David LaPalombara, Director, 740-593-4290, Fax: 740-593-0457, E-mail: lapalomb@ohio.edu. *Application contact:* Melissa Haviland, Chair, Graduate Programs, 740-593-9996, Fax: 740-593-0457, E-mail: haviland@ohio.edu.

Otis College of Art and Design, Program in Graphic Design, Los Angeles, CA 90045-9785. Offers MFA. *Faculty:* 3 part-time/adjunct (2 women). *Students:* 19 full-time (8 women), 6 part-time (5 women); includes 9 minority (2 Black or African American, non-Hispanic/Latino; 2 Asian, non-Hispanic/Latino; 5 Hispanic/Latino), 6 international. 75 applicants, 29% accepted, 14 enrolled. In 2010, 9 master's awarded. *Entrance requirements:* Additional exam requirements/recommendations for international students: Required—TOEFL (minimum score 600 paper-based; 250 computer-based). *Application deadline:* For fall admission, 1/15 for domestic students. Application fee: $60. Electronic applications accepted. *Expenses:* Tuition: Full-time $33,900; part-time $1107 per unit. Required fees: $700. *Unit head:* Kali Nikitas, Chair, Graduate Studies, 310-665-6820, Fax: 310-665-6843, E-mail: jhayes@otis.edu. *Application contact:* Information Contact, 310-665-6820, Fax: 310-665-6821, E-mail: admissions@otis.edu.

Pittsburg State University, Graduate School, College of Technology, Department of Graphics and Imaging Technologies, Pittsburg, KS 66762. Offers commercial graphics (MST); printing management (MST). *Degree requirements:* For master's, thesis or alternative.

Pratt Institute, School of Art and Design, Program in Communications Design, New York, NY 10011. Offers MFA, MS. *Accreditation:* NASAD. Part-time programs available. *Faculty:* 5 full-time (2 women), 33 part-time/adjunct (9 women). *Students:* 183 full-time (137 women), 18 part-time (12 women); includes 5 Black or African American, non-Hispanic/Latino; 23 Asian, non-Hispanic/Latino; 12 Hispanic/Latino, 76 international. Average age 27. 316 applicants, 50% accepted, 72 enrolled. In 2010, 76 master's awarded. *Degree requirements:* For master's, thesis. *Entrance requirements:* For master's, portfolio, letters of recommendation. Additional exam requirements/recommendations for international students: Required—TOEFL (minimum score 575 paper-based; 233 computer-based; 90 iBT). *Application deadline:* For fall admission, 1/5 for domestic and international students; for spring admission, 10/1 for domestic and international students. Application fee: $50 ($90 for international students). Electronic applications accepted. *Expenses:* Tuition: Full-time $22,734; part-time $1263 per credit. Required fees: $1280. *Financial support:* Career-related internships or fieldwork, Federal Work-Study, institutionally sponsored loans, scholarships/grants, and unspecified assistantships available. Support available to part-time students. Financial award application deadline: 2/1; financial award applicants required to submit FAFSA. *Faculty research:* Graphics, film, photography, media presentations, computer graphics for community service organizations. *Unit head:* Jeffrey Bellantoni, Chairperson, 212-647-7573, E-mail: jbell189@pratt.edu. *Application contact:* Young Hah, Director of Graduate Admissions, 718-636-3683, Fax: 718-399-4242, E-mail: yhah@pratt.edu.

See Display on page 92 and Close-Up on page 131.

Pratt Institute, School of Art and Design, Program in Digital Arts, Brooklyn, NY 11205-3899. Offers MFA, MS/MFA. *Accreditation:* NASAD. *Faculty:* 6 full-time (1 woman), 17 part-time/adjunct (8 women). *Students:* 60 full-time (33 women); includes 2 Black or African American, non-Hispanic/Latino; 3 Asian, non-Hispanic/Latino; 4 Hispanic/Latino, 34 international. Average age 27. 126 applicants, 52% accepted, 27 enrolled. In 2010, 19 master's awarded. *Degree requirements:* For master's, thesis, exhibit. *Entrance requirements:* For master's, portfolio or video tape, letters of recommendation. Additional exam requirements/recommendations for international students: Required—TOEFL (minimum score 550 paper-based; 213 computer-based; 79 iBT). *Application deadline:* For fall admission, 1/5 for domestic and international students; for spring admission, 10/1 for domestic and international students. Applications are processed on a rolling basis. Application fee: $50 ($90 for international students). Electronic applications accepted. *Expenses:* Tuition: Full-time $22,734; part-time $1263 per credit. Required fees: $1280. *Financial support:* Career-related internships or fieldwork, Federal Work-Study, institutionally sponsored loans, scholarships/grants, health care benefits, and unspecified assistantships available. Support available to part-time students. Financial award application deadline: 2/1; financial award applicants required to submit FAFSA. *Unit head:* Peter Patchen, Chair, 718-636-3693, E-mail: ppatchen@pratt.edu. *Application contact:* Young Hah, Director of Graduate Admissions, 718-636-3683, Fax: 718-399-4242, E-mail: yhah@pratt.edu.

See Display on page 92 and Close-Up on page 131.

Rhode Island School of Design, Graduate Studies, Division of Architecture and Design, Department of Graphic Design, Providence, RI 02903-2784. Offers MFA. *Accreditation:* NASAD. *Degree requirements:* For master's, thesis, exhibit. *Entrance requirements:* For master's, portfolio, 3 letters of recommendation. Additional exam requirements/recommendations for international students: Required—TOEFL (minimum score 580 paper-based; 237 computer-based), IELTS (minimum score 6.5).

Rochester Institute of Technology, Graduate Enrollment Services, College of Imaging Arts and Sciences, School of Design, Program in Computer Graphics Design, Rochester, NY 14623-5603. Offers MFA. *Accreditation:* NASAD. Part-time programs available. *Students:* 53 full-time (25 women), 26 part-time (12 women); includes 3 Black or African American, non-Hispanic/Latino; 1 American Indian or Alaska Native, non-Hispanic/Latino; 5 Asian, non-Hispanic/Latino; 1 Hispanic/Latino; 1 Native Hawaiian or other Pacific Islander, non-Hispanic/Latino, 43 international. Average age 29. 59 applicants, 49% accepted, 16 enrolled. In 2010, 11 master's awarded. *Degree requirements:* For master's, thesis. *Entrance requirements:* For master's, portfolio, minimum GPA of 3.0. Additional exam requirements/recommendations for international students: Required—TOEFL (minimum score 550 paper-based; 213 computer-based; 79 iBT) or IELTS (minimum score 6.5). *Application deadline:* For fall admission, 2/15 priority date for domestic and international students. Applications are processed on a rolling basis. Application fee: $50. Electronic applications accepted. *Expenses:* Tuition: Full-time $33,234; part-time $924 per credit hour. Required fees: $219. *Financial support:* In 2010–11, 50 students received support; research assistantships with partial tuition reimbursements available, teaching assistantships with partial tuition reimbursements available, career-related internships or fieldwork, institutionally sponsored loans, scholarships/grants, and unspecified assistantships available. Support available to part-time students. Financial award application deadline: 8/30; financial award applicants required to submit FAFSA. *Unit head:* Chris Jackson, Graduate Program Director, 585-475-5823, Fax: 585-475-7533, E-mail: cbjpgd@rit.edu. *Application contact:* Diane Ellison, Assistant Vice President, Graduate Enrollment Services, 585-475-2229, Fax: 585-475-7164, E-mail: gradinfo@rit.edu.

Rochester Institute of Technology, Graduate Enrollment Services, College of Imaging Arts and Sciences, School of Design, Program in Graphic Design, Rochester, NY 14623-5603. Offers MFA. *Accreditation:* NASAD. Part-time programs available. *Students:* 20 full-time (16 women); includes 1 Hispanic/Latino, 8 international. Average age 27. 79 applicants, 28% accepted, 6 enrolled. In 2010, 2 master's awarded. *Degree requirements:* For master's, thesis (for some programs). *Entrance requirements:* For master's, portfolio, minimum GPA of 3.0. Additional exam requirements/recommendations for international students: Required—TOEFL (minimum score 550 paper-based; 213 computer-based; 79 iBT) or IELTS (minimum score 6.5). *Application deadline:* For fall admission, 2/15 priority date for domestic and international students. Applications are processed on a rolling basis. Application fee: $50. *Expenses:* Tuition: Full-time $33,234; part-time $924 per credit hour. Required fees: $219. *Financial support:* In 2010–11, 15 students received support; teaching assistantships with partial tuition reimbursements available, career-related internships or fieldwork, institutionally sponsored loans, scholarships/grants, and unspecified assistantships available. Support available to part-time students. Financial award application deadline: 2/15; financial award applicants required to submit FAFSA. *Unit head:* Chris Jackson, Graduate Program Director, 585-475-5823, Fax: 585-475-7533, E-mail: cbjpgd@rit.edu. *Application contact:* Diane Ellison, Assistant Vice President, Graduate Enrollment Services, 585-475-2229, Fax: 585-475-7164, E-mail: gradinfo@rit.edu.

Rochester Institute of Technology, Graduate Enrollment Services, College of Imaging Arts and Sciences, School of Print Media, Program in Print Media, Rochester, NY 14623-5603. Offers MS. Part-time programs available. Postbaccalaureate distance learning degree programs offered (minimal on-campus study). *Students:* 25 full-time (12 women), 3 part-time; includes 1 Black or African American, non-Hispanic/Latino; 1 Asian, non-Hispanic/Latino, 20 international. Average age 26. 30 applicants, 60% accepted, 14 enrolled. In 2010, 8 master's awarded. *Entrance requirements:* For master's, minimum GPA of 3.0. Additional exam requirements/recommendations for international students: Required—TOEFL (minimum score 550 paper-based; 213 computer-based; 79 iBT) or IELTS (minimum score 6.5). *Application deadline:* For fall admission, 2/15 priority date for domestic and international students. Applications are processed on a rolling basis. Application fee: $50. Electronic applications accepted. *Expenses:* Tuition: Full-time $33,234; part-time $924 per credit hour. Required fees: $219. *Financial support:* In 2010–11, 12 students received support; research assistantships with partial tuition reimbursements available, teaching assistantships with partial tuition reimbursements available, career-related internships or fieldwork, institutionally sponsored loans, scholarships/grants, and unspecified assistantships available. Support available to part-time students. Financial award applicants required to submit FAFSA. *Unit head:* Dr. Scott Williams, Graduate Program Chair, 585-475-2728, Fax: 585-475-5336, E-mail: sawppr@rit.edu. *Application contact:* Diane Ellison, Assistant Vice President, Graduate Enrollment Services, 585-475-2229, Fax: 585-475-7164, E-mail: gradinfo@rit.edu.

San Diego State University, Graduate and Research Affairs, College of Professional Studies and Fine Arts, School of Art, Design and Art History, San Diego, CA 92182. Offers art history (MA); studio arts (MA, MFA), including applied design, environmental design, graphic design, interior design, painting and printmaking, sculpture. *Accreditation:* NASAD (one or more programs are accredited). *Degree requirements:* For master's, variable foreign language requirement, thesis. *Entrance requirements:* For master's, GRE General Test, bachelor's degree in related field, slide portfolio, typed slide information sheet, 2 letters of recommendation. Additional exam requirements/recommendations for international students: Required—TOEFL. Electronic applications accepted.

Savannah College of Art and Design, Graduate School, Program in Advertising Design, Savannah, GA 31402-3146. Offers MA, MFA. Part-time programs available. *Faculty:* 12 full-time (4 women), 5 part-time/adjunct (2 women). *Students:* 37 full-time (22 women), 9 part-time (8 women); includes 2 Black or African American, non-Hispanic/Latino; 1 Hispanic/Latino, 12 international. Average age 26. In 2010, 30 master's awarded. *Degree requirements:* For master's, thesis, internships. *Entrance requirements:* For master's, interview, portfolio. Additional exam requirements/recommendations for international students: Required—TOEFL (minimum score 450 paper-based; 133 computer-based). *Application deadline:* For fall admission, 4/1 priority date for domestic and international students. Applications are processed on a rolling basis. Application fee: $35. Electronic applications accepted. *Expenses:* Tuition: Full-time $29,520; part-time $3280 per quarter. Tuition and fees vary according to campus/location. *Financial support:* Fellowships, career-related internships or fieldwork, Federal Work-Study, and scholarships/grants available. Financial award application deadline: 4/1; financial award applicants required to submit FAFSA. *Unit head:* Stephen Hall, Chair, 912-525-5974. *Application contact:* Elizabeth Mathis, Director of Graduate and International Enrollment, 912-525-5965, Fax: 912-525-5985, E-mail: emathis@scad.edu.

Savannah College of Art and Design, Graduate School, Program in Graphic Design, Savannah, GA 31402-3146. Offers MA, MFA. Part-time programs available. Postbaccalaureate distance learning degree programs offered. *Faculty:* 28 full-time (9 women), 21 part-time/adjunct (10 women). *Students:* 146 full-time (100 women), 68 part-time (42 women); includes 8 Black or African American, non-Hispanic/Latino; 1 American Indian or Alaska Native, non-Hispanic/Latino; 3 Asian, non-Hispanic/Latino; 3 Hispanic/Latino, 49 international. Average age 30. In 2010, 71 master's awarded. *Degree requirements:* For master's, thesis, exhibit, internships. *Entrance requirements:* For master's, interview, portfolio. Additional exam requirements/recommendations for international students: Required—TOEFL (minimum score 450 paper-based; 133 computer-based). *Application deadline:* For fall admission, 4/1 priority date for domestic and international students. Applications are processed on a rolling basis. Application fee: $35. Electronic applications accepted. *Expenses:* Tuition: Full-time $29,520; part-time $3280 per quarter. Tuition and fees vary according to campus/location. *Financial support:* Fellowships, career-related internships or fieldwork, Federal Work-Study, and scholarships/grants available. Financial award application deadline: 4/1; financial award applicants required to submit FAFSA. *Unit head:* John Waters, Chair, 917-685-0680, Fax: 912-525-5994, E-mail: jwaters@scad.edu. *Application contact:* Elizabeth Mathis, Director of Graduate Recruitment, 912-525-5965, Fax: 912-525-5985, E-mail: emathis@scad.edu.

See Display on page 177 and Close-Up on page 223

School of the Art Institute of Chicago, Graduate Division, Department of Visual Communication, Chicago, IL 60603-3103. Offers MFA. *Entrance requirements:* Additional exam requirements/recommendations for international students: Required—TOEFL, IELTS.

See Close-Up on page 225.

Southern Polytechnic State University, School of Arts and Sciences, Department of English, Technical Communication, and Media Arts, Marietta, GA 30060-2896. Offers communications management (AGC); content development (AGC); information and instructional design (MSIID); information design and communication (MS); instructional design (AGC); technical communication (Graduate Certificate); visual communication and graphics (AGC). Part-time and evening/weekend programs available. Postbaccalaureate distance learning degree programs offered (no on-campus study). *Faculty:* 4 full-time (3 women), 1 (woman) part-time/adjunct. *Students:* 2 full-time (both women), 61 part-time (40 women); includes 19 Black or African American, non-Hispanic/Latino; 1 Two or more races, non-Hispanic/Latino, 3 international. Average age 38. 37 applicants, 100% accepted, 29 enrolled. In 2010, 6 master's, 5 other advanced degrees awarded. *Degree requirements:* For master's, thesis or internship; for other advanced degree, thesis optional, 18 hours completed through thesis option (6 hours), internship option (6 hours) or advanced coursework option (6 hours). *Entrance requirements:* For master's, GRE, statement of purpose, writing sample, professional recommendations, timed essay; for other advanced degree, writing sample, professional recommendations. Additional exam requirements/recommendations for international students: Required—TOEFL (minimum score 550 paper-based; 213 computer-based; 79 iBT), IELTS (minimum score 6.5). *Application deadline:* For fall admission, 5/1 priority date for domestic students, 7/1 priority date for international students; for spring admission, 9/1 priority date for domestic students, 11/1 priority date for international students. Applications are processed on a rolling basis. Application fee: $20. Electronic applications accepted. *Expenses:* Tuition, state resident: full-time $3690; part-time $205 per semester hour. Tuition, nonresident: full-time $13,428; part-time $746 per semester hour. Required fees: $598 per semester. *Financial support:* Research assistantships with tuition reimbursements, teaching assistantships with tuition reimbursements, career-related internships or fieldwork, Federal Work-Study, scholarships/grants, and unspecified assistantships available. Support available to part-time students. Financial award application deadline: 5/1; financial award applicants required to submit FAFSA. *Faculty research:* Usability, user-centered design, instructional design, information architecture, information design. *Unit head:* Dr. Mark Nunes, Chair, 678-915-7202, Fax: 678-915-7425, E-mail: mnunes@spsu.edu. *Application contact:* Nikki Palamiotis, Director of Graduate Studies, 678-915-4276, Fax: 678-915-7292, E-mail: npalamio@spsu.edu.

Graphic Design

Suffolk University, New England School of Art and Design, Boston, MA 02108-2770. Offers graphic design (MA); interior architecture (MFA); interior design (MA). *Accreditation:* CIDA; NASAD. Part-time and evening/weekend programs available. *Faculty:* 21 full-time (12 women), 7 part-time/adjunct (2 women). *Students:* 56 full-time (45 women), 76 part-time (65 women); includes 2 Black or African American, non-Hispanic/Latino; 5 Asian, non-Hispanic/Latino; 5 Hispanic/Latino, 13 international. Average age 30. 113 applicants, 67% accepted, 48 enrolled. In 2010, 30 master's awarded. *Entrance requirements:* For master's, GRE (for MFA), art portfolio, interview, 2 letters of recommendation, resume; letter of intent (for MFA). Additional exam requirements/recommendations for international students: Required—TOEFL (minimum score 550 paper-based; 213 computer-based; 80 iBT). *Application deadline:* For fall admission, 6/15 priority date for domestic students, 6/15 for international students; for spring admission, 11/1 priority date for domestic students, 11/1 for international students. Applications are processed on a rolling basis. Application fee: $50. Electronic applications accepted. *Expenses:* Contact institution. *Financial support:* In 2010–11, 83 students received support, including 39 fellowships with partial tuition reimbursements available (averaging $7,001 per year). Financial award application deadline: 4/1. *Faculty research:* Adaptive re-use of historical structures, universal design, American architecture history, interior design to reduce inefficiency, meditation SPA. *Unit head:* William Davis, Director, 617-994-4264, Fax: 617-994-4250, E-mail: wdavis@suffolk.edu. *Application contact:* Judith Reynolds, Director of Graduate Admissions, 617-573-8302, Fax: 617-305-1733, E-mail: grad.admission@suffolk.edu.

Temple University, Tyler School of Art, Department of Graphic Arts and Design, Philadelphia, PA 19122-6096. Offers graphic and interactive design (MFA); photography (MFA); printmaking (MFA). *Faculty:* 13 full-time (6 women). *Students:* 18 full-time (13 women), 2 international. 149 applicants, 13% accepted, 10 enrolled. In 2010, 11 master's awarded. *Degree requirements:* For master's, essay, exhibit. *Entrance requirements:* For master's, minimum GPA of 3.0; slide portfolio, 40 credits in studio art; 12 credits in art history. Additional exam requirements/recommendations for international students: Required—TOEFL (minimum score 550 paper-based; 213 computer-based; 79 iBT). *Application deadline:* For fall admission, 1/15 for domestic students, 12/15 for international students. Application fee: $50. Electronic applications accepted. *Financial support:* Fellowships with full tuition reimbursements, research assistantships with full tuition reimbursements, teaching assistantships with full tuition reimbursements, Federal Work-Study available. Support available to part-time students. Financial award application deadline: 1/15; financial award applicants required to submit FAFSA. *Unit head:* Stephanie Knopp, Chair, 215-782-2932, Fax: 215-782-2799, E-mail: stephanie.knopp@temple.edu. *Application contact:* Carmina Cianciulli, Assistant Dean for Admissions, 215-782-2875, Fax: 215-782-2711, E-mail: tylerart@temple.edu.

Texas State University–San Marcos, Graduate School, College of Fine Arts and Communication, School of Art and Design, Program in Communication Design, San Marcos, TX 78666. Offers MFA. *Faculty:* 9 full-time (3 women). *Students:* 16 full-time (7 women), 31 part-time (13 women); includes 1 Black or African American, non-Hispanic/Latino; 2 Asian, non-Hispanic/Latino; 8 Hispanic/Latino, 2 international. Average age 32. 36 applicants, 67% accepted, 20 enrolled. In 2010, 3 master's awarded. *Degree requirements:* For master's, comprehensive exam, thesis (for some programs). *Entrance requirements:* For master's, minimum GPA of 2.75 on last 60 hours of undergraduate work, 20-work portfolio. Additional exam requirements/recommendations for international students: Required—TOEFL (minimum score 550 paper-based; 213 computer-based; 78 iBT). *Application deadline:* For fall admission, 4/30 for domestic and international students; for spring admission, 10/31 for domestic and international students. Applications are processed on a rolling basis. Application fee: $40 ($90 for international students). Electronic applications accepted. *Expenses:* Tuition, state resident: full-time $6024; part-time $251 per credit hour. Tuition, nonresident: full-time $13,536; part-time $564 per credit hour. Required fees: $1776; $50 per credit hour. $306 per semester. *Financial support:* In 2010–11, 14 students received support, including 6 teaching assistantships (averaging $5,526 per year); Federal Work-Study, institutionally sponsored loans, scholarships/grants, and unspecified assistantships also available. Support available to part-time students. Financial award application deadline: 4/1; financial award applicants required to submit FAFSA. *Unit head:* Claudia Roschmann, Program Advisor, 512-245-2646, E-mail: cr29@txstate.edu. *Application contact:* Dr. J. Michael Willoughby, Dean of Graduate School, 512-245-2581, Fax: 512-245-8365, E-mail: gradcollege@txstate.edu.

Université Laval, Faculty of Architecture, Planning and Visual Arts, School of Visual Arts, Programs in Visual Arts, Québec, QC G1K 7P4, Canada. Offers graphic design and multimedia (MA); visual arts (MA). *Degree requirements:* For master's, thesis (for some programs). *Entrance requirements:* For master's, technical exam, interview, mastery of pertinent software, knowledge of French. Electronic applications accepted.

University of Baltimore, Graduate School, The Yale Gordon College of Liberal Arts, Program in Publications Design, Baltimore, MD 21201-5779. Offers MA. Part-time and evening/weekend programs available. *Degree requirements:* For master's, seminar project. *Entrance requirements:* For master's, minimum GPA of 3.0, portfolio, interview. Additional exam requirements/recommendations for international students: Required—TOEFL (minimum score 550 paper-based; 213 computer-based). Electronic applications accepted. *Faculty research:* Communication theory, graphic design, media technology.

University of Baltimore, Graduate School, The Yale Gordon College of Liberal Arts, School of Information Arts and Technologies, Doctoral Program in Communications Design, Baltimore, MD 21201-5779. Offers DCD. Part-time and evening/weekend programs available. *Entrance requirements:* For doctorate, minimum GPA of 3.2, previous graduate study in related discipline, portfolio, resume. Electronic applications accepted.

University of Cincinnati, Graduate School, College of Design, Architecture, Art, and Planning, School of Design, Cincinnati, OH 45221. Offers fashion design (M Des); graphic design (M Des); industrial design (M Des); interaction design (M Des); product development (M Des). *Accreditation:* NASAD. *Degree requirements:* For master's, thesis. *Entrance requirements:* For master's, undergraduate degree in design or related field, 2 years of work experience in design or related field. Additional exam requirements/recommendations for international students: Required—TOEFL. Electronic applications accepted. *Faculty research:* Design theory, interdisciplinary design topics.

University of Florida, Graduate School, College of Fine Arts, School of Art and Art History, Gainesville, FL 32611. Offers art (MFA), including ceramics, creative photography, drawing, electronic intermedia, graphic design, painting, printmaking, sculpture; art education (MA); art history (MA, PhD); digital arts and sciences (MA); museology (museum studies) (MA). *Accreditation:* NASAD. Postbaccalaureate distance learning degree programs offered (minimal on-campus study). *Faculty:* 29 full-time (14 women). *Students:* 107 full-time (72 women), 57 part-time (52 women); includes 6 Black or African American, non-Hispanic/Latino; 1 American Indian or Alaska Native, non-Hispanic/Latino; 5 Asian, non-Hispanic/Latino; 13 Hispanic/Latino, 14 international. Average age 31. 282 applicants, 30% accepted, 61 enrolled. In 2010, 24 master's, 3 doctorates awarded. *Degree requirements:* For master's, thesis, project or thesis (MFA); 1 foreign language (MA in art history); for doctorate, 2 foreign languages, comprehensive exam, thesis/dissertation. *Entrance requirements:* For master's, GRE General Test, portfolio (MFA), writing sample (MA), minimum GPA of 3.0; for doctorate, GRE General Test, minimum GPA of 3.0. Additional exam requirements/recommendations for international students: Required—TOEFL (minimum score 550 paper-based; 213 computer-based; 80 iBT), IELTS (minimum score 6). *Application deadline:* For fall admission, 1/1 priority date for domestic students, 1/1 for international students; for spring admission, 11/1 for domestic and international students. Applications are processed on a rolling basis. Application fee: $30. Electronic applications accepted. *Expenses:* Tuition, state resident: full-time $10,915.92. Tuition, nonresident: full-time $28,309. *Financial support:* In 2010–11, 36 students received support, including 9 fellowships, 3 research assistantships with tuition reimbursements available (averaging $12,789 per year), 24 teaching assistantships with tuition reimbursements available (averaging $10,512 per year); Federal Work-Study, institutionally sponsored loans, and unspecified assistantships also available. Financial award applicants required to submit FAFSA. *Faculty research:* Studio production, art historical studies of style context. *Unit head:* Laura Robertsoon, SR Associate in Graduate Studies, 352-846-3425, E-mail: laurar@ufl.edu. *Application contact:* Lauren G. Lake, Coordinator, 352-273-3032, Fax: 352-392-8453, E-mail: lglake@arts.ufl.edu.

University of Guam, Office of Graduate Studies, College of Liberal Arts and Social Sciences, Division of Fine Arts, Mangilao, GU 96923. Offers ceramics (MA); graphics (MA); painting (MA). *Degree requirements:* For master's, thesis or alternative, exhibit, final oral exam. *Entrance requirements:* For master's, GRE General Test, portfolio. Additional exam requirements/recommendations for international students: Required—TOEFL.

University of Idaho, College of Graduate Studies, College of Art and Architecture, Moscow, ID 83844-2282. Offers architecture (MS), including community planning, compution and visualization studies, environment and behavior studies, urban design; architecture (professional degree) (M Arch); landscape architecture (MS); studio art (MFA), including graphic design, interactive and information design, interface, painting, printmaking, sculpture; teaching art (MAT). *Accreditation:* NASAD. *Faculty:* 19 full-time, 1 part-time/adjunct. *Students:* 102 full-time, 15 part-time. Average age 27. In 2010, 31 master's awarded. *Application deadline:* For fall admission, 8/1 for domestic students; for spring admission, 12/15 for domestic students. Applications are processed on a rolling basis. Application fee: $60. Electronic applications accepted. *Expenses:* Tuition, nonresident: part-time $580 per credit. Required fees: $306 per credit. *Financial support:* Applicants required to submit FAFSA. *Faculty research:* Sustainability in communities, urban research, virtual technology, bioregional planning, environment and behavior interaction. *Unit head:* Dr. Mark Elison Hoversten, Dean, 208-885-5423, E-mail: caa@uidaho.edu. *Application contact:* Dr. Mark Elison Hoversten, Dean, 208-885-5423, E-mail: caa@uidaho.edu.

University of Illinois at Chicago, Graduate College, College of Architecture and Art, School of Art and Design, Chicago, IL 60607-7128. Offers electronic visualization (MFA); film animation (MFA); graphic design (MFA); industrial design (MFA); photography (MFA); studio arts (MFA). *Accreditation:* NASAD. *Degree requirements:* For master's, thesis, exhibit. *Entrance requirements:* For master's, MAT, portfolio. Additional exam requirements/recommendations for international students: Required—TOEFL. Electronic applications accepted.

University of Illinois at Urbana–Champaign, Graduate College, College of Fine and Applied Arts, School of Art and Design, Program in Design and Media, Champaign, IL 61820. Offers art and design (MFA), including new media; graphic design (MFA); industrial design (MFA). *Accreditation:* NASAD. *Students:* 14 full-time (4 women), 3 part-time (1 woman); includes 1 Asian, non-Hispanic/Latino, 10 international. 156 applicants, 3% accepted, 5 enrolled. In 2010, 3 master's awarded. *Entrance requirements:* For master's, minimum GPA of 3.0. Additional exam requirements/recommendations for international students: Required—TOEFL (minimum score 550 paper-based; 213 computer-based; 79 iBT). *Application deadline:* Applications are processed on a rolling basis. Application fee: $75 ($90 for international students). Electronic applications accepted. *Financial support:* Fellowships, research assistantships, teaching assistantships, tuition waivers (full and partial) available. *Unit head:* Ernest Scott, Chair, 217-333-1579, E-mail: ernscott@illinois.edu. *Application contact:* Marsha Biddle, Coordinator of Graduate Academic Affairs, 217-333-0642, Fax: 217-244-7688, E-mail: mbiddle@illinois.edu.

University of Massachusetts Dartmouth, Graduate School, College of Visual and Performing Arts, Program in Visual Design, North Dartmouth, MA 02747-2300. Offers digital media (MFA); graphic design (MFA); illustration (MFA); photography (MFA); typography (MFA). *Accreditation:* NASAD. *Faculty:* 17 full-time (7 women), 4 part-time/adjunct (1 woman). *Students:* 12 full-time (8 women), 5 part-time (4 women); includes 1 Two or more races, non-Hispanic/Latino, 1 international. Average age 35. 33 applicants, 48% accepted, 7 enrolled. In 2010, 1 master's awarded. *Degree requirements:* For master's, visual thesis. *Entrance requirements:* For master's, portfolio, interview, minimum GPA of 3.0, 3 letters of recommendation. Additional exam requirements/recommendations for international students: Required—TOEFL (minimum score 500 paper-based). *Application deadline:* For fall admission, 2/1 priority date for domestic students, 12/1 priority date for international students. Applications are processed on a rolling basis. Application fee: $40 ($60 for international students). Electronic applications accepted. *Expenses:* Tuition, state resident: full-time $2071; part-time $86 per credit. Tuition, nonresident: full-time $8099; part-time $337 per credit. Required fees: $9446; $394 per credit. One-time fee: $75. Part-time tuition and fees vary according to class time, course load, degree level and reciprocity agreements. *Financial support:* In 2010–11, 5 teaching assistantships with full tuition reimbursements (averaging $3,088 per year) were awarded; Federal Work-Study and unspecified assistantships also available. Support available to part-time students. Financial award application deadline: 3/1; financial award applicants required to submit FAFSA. *Faculty research:* Typography. Total annual research expenditures: $5,898. *Unit head:* Memory Holloway, Director, 508-999-8554, E-mail: mholloway@umassd.edu. *Application contact:* Elan Turcotte-Shamski, Graduate Admissions Officer, 508-999-8604, Fax: 508-999-8183, E-mail: graduate@umassd.edu.

University of Memphis, Graduate School, College of Communication and Fine Arts, Department of Art, Memphis, TN 38152. Offers art (Graduate Certificate); art history (MA), including Egyptian art and archaeology, general art history; ceramics (MFA); graphic design (MFA); interior design (MFA); painting (MFA); printmaking/photography (MFA); sculpture (MFA). *Accreditation:* NASAD (one or more programs are accredited). *Faculty:* 20 full-time (7 women), 4 part-time/adjunct (2 women). *Students:* 39 full-time (26 women), 10 part-time (8 women); includes 4 Black or African American, non-Hispanic/Latino; 1 Asian, non-Hispanic/Latino, 1 international. Average age 29. 44 applicants, 77% accepted, 22 enrolled. In 2010, 16 master's, 5 other advanced degrees awarded. *Degree requirements:* For master's, 2 foreign languages, comprehensive exam, thesis. *Entrance requirements:* For master's, GRE General Test or MAT, portfolio (MFA). *Application deadline:* For fall admission, 8/1 for domestic students; for spring admission, 12/1 for domestic students. Applications are processed on a rolling basis. Application fee: $35 ($60 for international students). *Financial support:* In 2010–11, 38 students received support; research assistantships with full tuition reimbursements available, teaching assistantships with full tuition reimbursements available, Federal Work-Study, scholarships/grants, and unspecified assistantships available. Financial award application deadline: 2/15; financial award applicants required to submit FAFSA. *Faculty research:* Online collaborative learning, advanced art history studies, electronic publishing/design, studio arts, architectural studies. *Unit head:* Prof. Richard Lou, Chair, 901-678-2216, Fax: 901-678-2735, E-mail: gmyatt@memphis.edu. *Application contact:* Greely Myat, Graduate Studies Coordinator, 901-678-2650.

University of Miami, Graduate School, College of Arts and Sciences, Department of Art and Art History, Coral Gables, FL 33124. Offers art history (MA); ceramics/glass (MFA); graphic design/multimedia (MFA); painting (MFA); photography/digital imaging (MFA); printmaking (MFA); sculpture (MFA). Part-time programs available. *Degree requirements:* For master's, variable foreign language requirement, thesis, exhibit (MFA), comprehensive exam (MA). *Entrance requirements:* For master's, GRE General Test (MA), research paper (MA), slide portfolio (MFA). Additional exam requirements/recommendations for international students: Required—TOEFL. Electronic applications accepted. *Faculty research:* Installation art, public art.

University of Minnesota, Duluth, Graduate School, School of Fine Arts, Department of Art and Design, Duluth, MN 55812-2496. Offers graphic design (MFA). Part-time programs available. *Degree requirements:* For master's, final exhibit, project, supporting paper. *Entrance requirements:* For master's, minimum GPA of 3.0, writing sample, slide portfolio. Additional exam requirements/recommendations for international students: Required—TOEFL (minimum score 550 paper-based; 213 computer-based). *Faculty research:* Motion graphics, graphic design history, interactive design, typography, education.

University of Notre Dame, Graduate School, College of Arts and Letters, Division of Humanities, Department of Art, Art History, and Design, Notre Dame, IN 46556. Offers art history (MA); design (MFA), including graphic design, industrial design; studio art (MFA), including ceramics, painting, photography, printmaking, sculpture. *Accreditation:* NASAD. *Degree requirements:* For master's, comprehensive exam (for some programs), thesis. *Entrance requirements:* For master's, GRE General Test, minimum GPA of 3.0. Additional exam requirements/recommendations for international students: Required—TOEFL (minimum score 600 paper-based; 250 computer-based; 80 iBT). Electronic applications accepted. *Faculty research:* Studio art practice in ceramics, printing, photography, printmaking and sculpture, graphic design and industrial design, digital imaging in design and photography, Renaissance and American art history, contemporary art theory and criticism.

The University of Tennessee, Graduate School, College of Arts and Sciences, School of Art, Knoxville, TN 37996. Offers ceramics (MFA); drawing (MFA); graphic design (MFA); inter-area studies (MFA); media arts (MFA); painting (MFA); printmaking (MFA); sculpture (MFA); watercolor (MFA). *Accreditation:* NASAD. *Degree requirements:* For master's, thesis or alternative, exhibit. *Entrance requirements:* For master's, portfolio, minimum GPA of 2.7. Additional exam requirements/recommendations for international students: Required—TOEFL. Electronic applications accepted. *Expenses:* Tuition, state resident: full-time $7440; part-time $414 per credit hour. Tuition, nonresident: full-time $22,478; part-time $1250 per credit hour. Required fees: $922; $43 per credit hour. Tuition and fees vary according to program.

University of Utah, Graduate School, College of Fine Arts, Department of Art and Art History, Salt Lake City, UT 84112-0380. Offers art history (MA); ceramics (MFA); community-based art education (MFA); drawing (MFA); graphic design (MFA); painting (MFA); photography/digital imaging (MFA); printmaking (MFA); sculpture/intermedia (MFA). *Faculty:* 23 full-time (10 women). *Students:* 17 full-time (12 women), 1 (woman) part-time; includes 2 minority (both Hispanic/Latino), 1 international. Average age 29. 54 applicants, 20% accepted, 7 enrolled. In 2010, 5 master's awarded. *Degree requirements:* For master's, variable foreign language requirement, comprehensive exam (for some programs), thesis or alternative, exhibit and final project paper (for MFA). *Entrance requirements:* For master's, CD portfolio (MFA), writing sample (MA), curriculum vitae, letters of recommendation. Additional exam requirements/recommendations for international students: Required—TOEFL (minimum score 575 paper-based; 183 computer-based; 75 iBT). *Application deadline:* For fall admission, 1/2 priority date for domestic and international students. Application fee: $55 ($65 for international students). Electronic applications accepted. *Expenses:* Tuition, area resident: Part-time $179.19 per credit hour. Tuition, state resident: full-time $4384. Tuition, nonresident: full-time $16,684; part-time $630.67 per credit hour. Required fees: $350 per semester. Tuition and fees vary according to course load, degree level and program. *Financial support:* In 2010–11, 2 fellowships, 6 research assistantships with partial tuition reimbursements, 34 teaching assistantships with partial tuition reimbursements were awarded; Federal Work-Study, institutionally sponsored loans, scholarships/grants, tuition waivers (partial), unspecified assistantships, and stipends also available. Financial award application deadline: 1/2; financial award applicants required to submit FAFSA. *Faculty research:* Studio art, European art history, Asian art history, Latin American art history, twentieth century/contemporary art history. Total annual research expenditures: $23,714. *Unit head:* Prof. Brian Snapp, Chair, 801-581-8677, Fax: 801-585-6171, E-mail: b.snapp@utah.edu. *Application contact:* Prof. Paul Stout, Director of Graduate Studies, 801-581-8677, Fax: 801-585-6171, E-mail: pls@utah.edu.

Vermont College of Fine Arts, Program in Graphic Design, Montpelier, VT 05602. Offers MFA. Postbaccalaureate distance learning degree programs offered (minimal on-campus study). *Application deadline:* For fall admission, 8/15 for domestic students. *Expenses:* Tuition: Full-time $17,820. Required fees: $270. *Unit head:* Jennifer Renko, Program Director, 866-934-8232 Ext. 8896, E-mail: jennifer.renko@vermontcollege.edu. *Application contact:* Debbie New, Assistant Director of Admissions, 802-828-8636, E-mail: debbie.new@vermontcollege.edu.

Western Illinois University, School of Graduate Studies, College of Education and Human Services, Department of Instructional Design and Technology, Macomb, IL 61455-1390. Offers distance learning (Certificate); educational technology specialist (Certificate); graphic applications (Certificate); instructional design and technology (MS); multimedia (Certificate); technology integration in education (Certificate); training development (Certificate). Part-time programs available. Postbaccalaureate distance learning degree programs offered (no on-campus study). *Students:* 18 full-time (12 women), 48 part-time (30 women); includes 7 minority (5 Black or African American, non-Hispanic/Latino; 2 American Indian or Alaska Native, non-Hispanic/Latino), 7 international. Average age 38. 23 applicants, 74% accepted. In 2010, 25 master's awarded. *Degree requirements:* For master's, thesis or alternative. *Entrance requirements:* Additional exam requirements/recommendations for international students: Required—TOEFL (minimum score 550 paper-based; 213 computer-based; 80 iBT). *Application deadline:* Applications are processed on a rolling basis. Application fee: $30. Electronic applications accepted. *Expenses:* Tuition, state resident: full-time $6370; part-time $265.40 per credit hour. Tuition, nonresident: full-time $12,740; part-time $530.80 per credit hour. Required fees: $75.67 per credit hour. *Financial support:* In 2010–11, 10 students received support, including 6 research assistantships with full tuition reimbursements available (averaging $7,280 per year), 4 teaching assistantships with full tuition reimbursements available (averaging $8,400 per year). Financial award applicants required to submit FAFSA. *Unit head:* Dr. Hoyet Hemphill, Chairperson, 309-298-1952. *Application contact:* Evelyn Hoing, Assistant Director of Graduate Studies, 309-298-1806, Fax: 309-298-2345, E-mail: grad-office@wiu.edu.

West Virginia University, College of Creative Arts, Division of Art and Design, Morgantown, WV 26506. Offers art education (MA); art history (MA); ceramics (MFA); graphic design (MFA); painting (MFA); printmaking (MFA); sculpture (MFA); studio art (MA). *Accreditation:* NASAD. *Degree requirements:* For master's, thesis, exhibit. *Entrance requirements:* For master's, minimum GPA of 2.75, portfolio. Additional exam requirements/recommendations for international students: Required—TOEFL. *Expenses:* Contact institution. *Faculty research:* Medieval art history.

Yale University, School of Art, New Haven, CT 06520-8339. Offers graphic design (MFA); painting/printmaking (MFA); photography (MFA); sculpture (MFA). *Faculty:* 9 full-time (4 women), 35 part-time/adjunct (12 women). *Students:* 121 full-time (64 women); includes 32 minority (7 Black or African American, non-Hispanic/Latino; 10 Asian, non-Hispanic/Latino; 15 Hispanic/Latino), 32 international. Average age 28. 1,222 applicants, 5% accepted, 57 enrolled. In 2010, 57 master's awarded. *Degree requirements:* For master's, thesis (for some programs). *Entrance requirements:* Additional exam requirements/recommendations for international students: Required—TOEFL (minimum score 550 paper-based; 250 computer-based; 100 iBT). *Application deadline:* For fall admission, 1/4 for domestic and international students. Application fee: $100. Electronic applications accepted. *Expenses:* Contact institution. *Financial support:* In 2010–11, 90 students received support, including 54 teaching assistantships (averaging $1,900 per year); Federal Work-Study, scholarships/grants, and unspecified assistantships also available. Financial award application deadline: 3/1; financial award applicants required to submit FAFSA. *Unit head:* Robert Storr, Dean, 203-432-2606. *Application contact:* Patricia Ann DeChiara, Director of Academic Affairs, 203-432-2600, E-mail: artschool.info@yale.edu.

Illustration

Academy of Art University, Graduate Program, School of Illustration, San Francisco, CA 94105-3410. Offers MFA. *Accreditation:* NASAD. Part-time programs available. Postbaccalaureate distance learning degree programs offered (no on-campus study). *Faculty:* 12 full-time (2 women), 45 part-time/adjunct (5 women). *Students:* 158 full-time (103 women), 185 part-time (95 women); includes 12 Black or African American, non-Hispanic/Latino; 5 American Indian or Alaska Native, non-Hispanic/Latino; 17 Asian, non-Hispanic/Latino; 11 Hispanic/Latino; 1 Native Hawaiian or other Pacific Islander, non-Hispanic/Latino, 87 international. Average age 32. 114 applicants. In 2010, 31 master's awarded. *Degree requirements:* For master's, thesis, final review. *Entrance requirements:* For master's, minimum GPA of 3.0, portfolio. *Application deadline:* For fall admission, 9/7 for domestic and international students; for spring admission, 2/2 for domestic and international students. Applications are processed on a rolling basis. Application fee: $100 ($500 for international students). Electronic applications accepted. *Expenses:* Tuition: Full-time $20,160; part-time $840 per semester hour. Required fees: $45 per semester. *Financial support:* Career-related internships or fieldwork and Federal Work-Study available. Support available to part-time students. Financial award application deadline: 8/10; financial award applicants required to submit FAFSA. *Application contact:* Prospective Student Services, 800-544-ARTS, Fax: 415-263-4130, E-mail: info@academyart.edu.

Bob Jones University, Graduate Programs, Greenville, SC 29614. Offers accountancy (MS); Bible (MA); Bible translation (MA); Biblical studies (Certificate); broadcast management (MS); business administration (MBA); church history (MA, PhD); church ministries (MA); church music (MM); cinema and video production (MA); counseling (MS); curriculum and instruction (Ed D); divinity (M Div); dramatic production (MA); educational leadership (MS, Ed D, Ed S); elementary education (M Ed, MAT); English (M Ed, MA, MAT); fine arts (MA); graphic design (MA); history (M Ed, MA); illustration (MA); interpretative speech (MA); mathematics (M Ed, MAT); medical missions (Certificate); ministry (MM, D Min); multi-categorical special education (M Ed, MAT); music (M Ed); New Testament interpretation (PhD); Old Testament interpretation (PhD); orchestral instrument performance (MM); organ performance (MM); pastoral studies (MA); personnel services (MS, Ed S); piano pedagogy (MM); piano performance (MM); platform arts (MA); radio and television broadcasting (MS); rhetoric and public address (MA); secondary education (M Ed); studio art (MA); teaching Bible (MA); theology (MA, PhD); voice performance (MM); youth ministries (MA); M Div/MM.

Bradley University, Graduate School, Slane College of Communications and Fine Arts, Department of Art, Peoria, IL 61625-0002. Offers ceramics (MA, MFA); drawing/illustration (MA, MFA); interdisciplinary art (MA, MFA); painting (MA, MFA); photography (MA, MFA); printmaking (MA, MFA); sculpture (MA, MFA); visual communication and design (MA, MFA). *Accreditation:* NASAD. Part-time programs available. *Degree requirements:* For master's, comprehensive exam, thesis, final exhibit. *Entrance requirements:* For master's, portfolio, 2 letters of recommendation. Additional exam requirements/recommendations for international students: Required—TOEFL (minimum score 550 paper-based; 213 computer-based; 79 iBT).

Fashion Institute of Technology, School of Graduate Studies, Program in Illustration, New York, NY 10001-5992. Offers MA. *Entrance requirements:* Additional exam requirements/recommendations for international students: Required—TOEFL (minimum score 550 paper-based; 213 computer-based). Electronic applications accepted.

See Display on next page and Close-Up on page 127.

Kent State University, College of Communication and Information, School of Visual Communication Design, Kent, OH 44242-0001. Offers MA, MFA. *Accreditation:* NASAD. Part-time programs available. *Degree requirements:* For master's, thesis, portfolios. *Entrance requirements:* For master's, portfolio (studio majors), minimum GPA of 2.75, GPA of 3.0 in major. *Expenses:* Tuition, state resident: full-time $7866; part-time $437 per credit hour. Tuition, nonresident: full-time $14,022; part-time $779 per credit hour. *Faculty research:* Graphic design.

Maryland Institute College of Art, Graduate Studies, Program in Illustration Practice, Baltimore, MD 21217. Offers MFA. *Entrance requirements:* Additional exam requirements/recommendations for international students: Required—TOEFL (minimum score 550 paper-based; 213 computer-based; 80 iBT). *Application deadline:* For fall admission, 1/15 for domestic and international students. *Expenses:* Tuition: Full-time $34,550; part-time $1440 per credit hour. Required fees: $1140; $570 per term. *Financial support:* Application deadline: 3/1. *Unit head:* Whitney Sherman, Director, 410-225-5273, Fax: 410-225-5275, E-mail: graduate@mica.edu. *Application contact:* Scott G. Kelly, Associate Dean of Graduate Admission, 410-225-2256, Fax: 410-225-2408, E-mail: graduate@mica.edu.

Marywood University, Academic Affairs, Insalaco College of Creative and Performing Arts, Art Department, Program in Studio Art, Scranton, PA 18509-1598. Offers advertising design (MA); ceramics (MA); clay (MA); graphic design (MA); illustration (MA); painting (MA); photography (MA); printmaking (MA); sculpture (MA); weaving (MA). *Accreditation:* NASAD. *Entrance requirements:* Additional exam requirements/recommendations for international students: Required—TOEFL (minimum score 550 paper-based; 213 computer-based; 79 iBT). Electronic applications accepted. *Expenses:* Tuition: Part-time $735 per credit. Required fees: $470 per semester. Tuition and fees vary according to degree level and campus/location. *Faculty research:* Texture and line in clay, cast bronze sculpture, color theories, book art and illustration, sculptural form.

Marywood University, Academic Affairs, Insalaco College of Creative and Performing Arts, Art Department, Program in Visual Arts, Scranton, PA 18509-1598. Offers advertising design (MFA); clay (MFA); graphic design (MFA); illustration (MFA); metals (MFA); painting (MFA); photography (MFA); printmaking (MFA). *Accreditation:* NASAD. *Entrance requirements:* Additional exam requirements/recommendations for international students: Required—TOEFL (minimum score 550 paper-based; 213 computer-based; 79 iBT). Electronic applications accepted. *Expenses:* Contact institution. *Faculty research:* Mariology, exploration of visual imagery, explorations involving drawing on the loom, clay as sculptural medium, oil paintings.

Mills College, Graduate Studies, Department of English, Oakland, CA 94613-1000. Offers book art and creative writing (MFA); creative writing, poetry (MFA); creative writing, prose (MFA); English and American literature (MA). Part-time programs available. *Faculty:* 14 full-time (11 women), 15 part-time/adjunct (12 women). *Students:* 94 full-time (81 women), 2 part-time (both women); includes 8 Black or African American, non-Hispanic/Latino; 4 Asian, non-Hispanic/Latino; 7 Hispanic/Latino; 1 Native Hawaiian or other Pacific Islander, non-Hispanic/Latino; 1 Two or more races, non-Hispanic/Latino. Average age 31. 155 applicants, 88% accepted, 48 enrolled. In 2010, 63 master's awarded. *Degree requirements:* For master's, comprehensive exam, thesis. *Entrance requirements:* For master's, manuscript, writing sample. Additional exam requirements/recommendations for international students: Required—TOEFL (minimum score 600 paper-based; 250 computer-based; 100 iBT), IELTS (minimum score 7). *Application deadline:* For fall admission, 12/15 priority date for domestic students, 12/15 for international students. Applications are processed on a rolling basis. Application fee: $50. Electronic applications accepted. *Expenses:* Tuition: Full-time $28,280; part-time $7070 per course. Required fees: $1058; $1058 per year. Tuition and fees vary according to program. *Financial support:* In 2010–11, 120 fellowships (averaging $5,723 per year), 37 teaching assistantships with partial

Illustration

Mills College (continued)
tuition reimbursements (averaging $3,081 per year) were awarded; scholarships/grants also available. Support available to part-time students. Financial award application deadline: 2/1; financial award applicants required to submit FAFSA. *Faculty research:* Creative writing, African-American literature, Victorian women writers, theories of sexuality, Shakespeare. *Unit head:* Dr. Cynthia Scheinberg, Chair, 510-430-2213, E-mail: cyns@mills.edu. *Application contact:* Jessica King, Graduate Admission Specialist, 510-430-3305, Fax: 510-430-2159, E-mail: grad-studies@mills.edu.

Mills College, Graduate Studies, Program in Book Art and Creative Writing, Oakland, CA 94613-1000. Offers MFA. *Faculty:* 1 (woman) full-time, 1 (woman) part-time/adjunct. *Students:* 6 full-time (5 women). 22 applicants, 59% accepted, 5 enrolled. *Degree requirements:* For master's, thesis project. *Application deadline:* For fall admission, 12/15 priority date for domestic students, 12/15 for international students. *Expenses:* Tuition: Full-time $28,280; part-time $7070 per course. Required fees: $1058; $1058 per year. Tuition and fees vary according to program. *Financial support:* In 2010–11, 9 fellowships (averaging $6,167 per year), 3 teaching assistantships (averaging $3,000 per year) were awarded. *Unit head:* Carol Langlois, Administrative Dean for Graduate Recruitment and Enrollment, 510-430-3118, Fax: 510-430-2159, E-mail: clangloi@mills.edu. *Application contact:* Jessica King, Graduate Admission Specialist, 510-430-3305, Fax: 510-430-2159, E-mail: grad-studies@mills.edu.

Minneapolis College of Art and Design, Program in Visual Studies, Minneapolis, MN 55404-4347. Offers animation (MFA); comic art (MFA); drawing (MFA); filmmaking (MFA); fine arts (MFA); furniture design (MFA); graphic design (MFA); illustration (MFA); interactive media (MFA); painting (MFA); photography (MFA); printmaking (MFA); sculpture (MFA). *Accreditation:* NASAD. Part-time programs available. *Degree requirements:* For master's, thesis, thesis exhibit. *Entrance requirements:* For master's, portfolio of visual artwork, resume, 3 letters of recommendation. Additional exam requirements/recommendations for international students: Required—TOEFL (minimum score 550 paper-based; 213 computer-based; 79 iBT). Electronic applications accepted. *Faculty research:* Visual arts: animation, comic art, drawing, film-making, furniture design, graphic design, illustration, interactive media, painting, photography, printmaking, sculpture.

San Jose State University, Graduate Studies and Research, College of Humanities and the Arts, School of Art and Design, San Jose, CA 95192-0001. Offers animation/illustration (MA); art history (MA); digital media arts (MFA); photography (MFA); pictorial arts (MFA); spatial arts (MFA). *Accreditation:* NASAD (one or more programs are accredited). *Entrance requirements:* For master's, GRE. Electronic applications accepted.

Savannah College of Art and Design, Graduate School, Program in Illustration, Savannah, GA 31402-3146. Offers MA, MFA. Part-time programs available. *Faculty:* 15 full-time (4 women), 6 part-time/adjunct (2 women). *Students:* 64 full-time (38 women), 10 part-time (5 women); includes 2 Black or African American, non-Hispanic/Latino; 1 Hispanic/Latino, 16 international. Average age 28. In 2010, 27 master's awarded. *Degree requirements:* For master's, thesis, exhibit, internships. *Entrance requirements:* For master's, interview, portfolio. Additional exam requirements/recommendations for international students: Required—TOEFL (minimum score 450 paper-based; 133 computer-based). *Application deadline:* For fall admission, 4/1 priority date for domestic and international students. Applications are processed on a rolling basis. Application fee: $35. Electronic applications accepted. *Expenses:* Tuition: Full-time $29,520; part-time $3280 per quarter. Tuition and fees vary according to campus/location. *Financial support:* In 2010–11, 4 fellowships were awarded; career-related internships or fieldwork, Federal Work-Study, and scholarships/grants also available. Financial award application deadline: 4/1; financial award applicants required to submit FAFSA. *Unit head:* Allan Drummond, Chair, 912-525-5187, Fax: 912-525-5981, E-mail: adrummon@scad.edu. *Application contact:* Elizabeth Mathis, Director of Graduate Recruitment, 912-525-5965, Fax: 912-525-5985, E-mail: emathis@scad.edu.

See Display on page 177 and Close-Up on page 223

Savannah College of Art and Design, Graduate School, Program in Illustration Design, Savannah, GA 31402-3146. Offers MA. Part-time programs available. *Faculty:* 2 full-time (0 women). *Students:* 7 full-time (2 women), 5 part-time (3 women); includes 1 Black or African American, non-Hispanic/Latino; 1 Asian, non-Hispanic/Latino. Average age 36. In 2010, 10 master's awarded. *Degree requirements:* For master's, thesis. *Entrance requirements:* For master's, interview, portfolio. Additional exam requirements/recommendations for international students: Required—TOEFL (minimum score 450 paper-based; 133 computer-based). *Application deadline:* For fall admission, 4/1 priority date for domestic and international students. Applications are processed on a rolling basis. Application fee: $35. Electronic applications accepted. *Expenses:* Tuition: Full-time $29,520; part-time $3280 per quarter. Tuition and fees vary according to campus/location. *Financial support:* Fellowships, career-related internships or fieldwork, Federal Work-Study, and scholarships/grants available. Financial award application deadline: 4/1; financial award applicants required to submit FAFSA. *Unit head:* Allan Drummond, Chair, 912-525-5817, Fax: 912-525-5981, E-mail: adrummond@scad.edu. *Application contact:* Elizabeth Mathis, Director of Graduate Recruitment, 912-525-5965, Fax: 912-525-5985, E-mail: emathis@scad.edu.

Savannah College of Art and Design, Graduate School, Program in Sequential Art, Savannah, GA 31402-3146. Offers MA, MFA. Part-time programs available. *Faculty:* 14 full-time (1 woman), 4 part-time/adjunct (2 women). *Students:* 43 full-time (19 women), 4 part-time (1 woman); includes 2 Black or African American, non-Hispanic/Latino; 2 Hispanic/Latino, 2 international. Average age 26. In 2010, 10 master's awarded. *Degree requirements:* For master's, thesis, exhibit, internships. *Entrance requirements:* For master's, interview, portfolio. Additional exam requirements/recommendations for international students: Required—TOEFL (minimum score 450 paper-based; 133 computer-based). *Application deadline:* For fall admission, 4/1 priority date for domestic and international students. Applications are processed on a rolling basis. Application fee: $35. Electronic applications accepted. *Expenses:* Tuition: Full-time $29,520; part-time $3280 per quarter. Tuition and fees vary according to campus/location. *Financial support:* Fellowships, career-related internships or fieldwork, Federal Work-Study, and scholarships/grants available. Financial award application deadline: 4/1; financial award applicants required to submit FAFSA. *Unit head:* Anthony Fisher, Chair, 912-525-4895, Fax: 912-525-5996, E-mail: afisher@scad.edu. *Application contact:* Elizabeth Mathis, Director of Graduate Recruitment, 912-525-5965, Fax: 912-525-5985, E-mail: admission@scad.edu.

See Display on page 177 and Close-Up on page 223

School of Visual Arts, Graduate Programs, Illustration Department, New York, NY 10010-3994. Offers MFA. *Accreditation:* NASAD. *Degree requirements:* For master's, final review, project or thesis. *Entrance requirements:* For master's, portfolio. Additional exam requirements/recommendations for international students: Required—TOEFL (minimum score 550 paper-based; 213 computer-based; 79 iBT). Electronic applications accepted.

Syracuse University, College of Visual and Performing Arts, Program in Illustration, Syracuse, NY 13244. Offers MFA. *Students:* 4 full-time (2 women); includes 1 minority (Asian, non-Hispanic/Latino), 1 international. Average age 30. 22 applicants, 23% accepted, 2 enrolled. *Entrance requirements:* For master's, portfolio. Additional exam requirements/recommendations for international students: Required—TOEFL (minimum score 100 iBT). *Application deadline:* For fall admission, 2/1 priority date for domestic and international students. Application fee: $75. Electronic applications accepted. *Expenses:* Tuition: Part-time $1162 per credit. *Financial support:* Fellowships with full tuition reimbursements, teaching assistantships with full and partial tuition reimbursements available. Financial award application deadline: 1/1. *Unit head:* Errol Willett, Chair, 315-443-3830, E-mail: eswillett@syr.edu. *Application contact:* Harriett Conti, Assistant Dean for Recruitment & Admissions, 315-443-5755, E-mail: hmconti@syr.edu.

See Display on page 179 and Close-Up on page 227.

University of Massachusetts Dartmouth, Graduate School, College of Visual and Performing Arts, Program in Visual Design, North Dartmouth, MA 02747-2300. Offers digital media (MFA);

graphic design (MFA); illustration (MFA); photography (MFA); typography (MFA). *Accreditation:* NASAD. *Faculty:* 17 full-time (7 women), 4 part-time/adjunct (1 woman). *Students:* 12 full-time (8 women), 5 part-time (4 women); includes 1 Two or more races, non-Hispanic/Latino, 1 international. Average age 35. 33 applicants, 48% accepted, 7 enrolled. In 2010, 1 master's awarded. *Degree requirements:* For master's, visual thesis. *Entrance requirements:* For master's, portfolio, interview, minimum GPA of 3.0, 3 letters of recommendation. Additional exam requirements/recommendations for international students: Required—TOEFL (minimum score 500 paper-based). *Application deadline:* For fall admission, 2/1 priority date for domestic students, 12/1 priority date for international students. Applications are processed on a rolling basis. Application fee: $40 ($60 for international students). Electronic applications accepted. *Expenses:* Tuition, state resident: full-time $2071; part-time $86 per credit. Tuition, nonresident: full-time $8099; part-time $337 per credit. Required fees: $9446; $394 per credit. One-time fee: $75. Part-time tuition and fees vary according to class time, course load, degree level and reciprocity agreements. *Financial support:* In 2010–11, 5 teaching assistantships with full tuition reimbursements (averaging $3,088 per year) were awarded; Federal Work-Study and unspecified assistantships also available. Support available to part-time students. Financial award application deadline: 3/1; financial award applicants required to submit FAFSA. *Faculty research:* Typography. Total annual research expenditures: $5,898. *Unit head:* Memory Holloway, Director, 508-999-8554, E-mail: mholloway@umassd.edu. *Application contact:* Elan Turcotte-Shamski, Graduate Admissions Officer, 508-999-8604, Fax: 508-999-8183, E-mail: graduate@umassd.edu.

Western Connecticut State University, Division of Graduate Studies and External Programs, School of Visual and Performing Arts, Department of Art, Danbury, CT 06810-6885. Offers illustration (MFA); painting (MFA). Part-time programs available. *Students:* 17 full-time (12 women); includes 2 minority (1 Black or African American, non-Hispanic/Latino; 1 Asian, non-Hispanic/Latino). Average age 34. In 2010, 12 master's awarded. *Degree requirements:* For master's, individual exhibition of artwork, review of student's progress prior to admission to final semester, completion of program in 6 years. *Entrance requirements:* For master's, portfolio review, minimum GPA of 2.5. Additional exam requirements/recommendations for international students: Recommended—TOEFL (minimum score 550 paper-based; 213 computer-based; 79 iBT), IELTS (minimum score 6). *Application deadline:* For fall admission, 8/5 priority date for domestic students; for spring admission, 1/5 priority date for domestic students. Application fee: $50. *Expenses:* Tuition, state resident: full-time $5012; part-time $417 per credit hour. Tuition, nonresident: full-time $13,962; part-time $423 per credit hour. Required fees: $3886. Full-time tuition and fees vary according to course load, degree level and program. *Financial support:* In 2010–11, 8 students received support. Scholarships/grants available. Financial award application deadline: 5/1; financial award applicants required to submit FAFSA. *Unit head:* Margaret Grimes, Graduate Coordinator, 203-837-8402, Fax: 203-837-8945, E-mail: grimesm@wcsu.edu. *Application contact:* Chris Shankle, Associate Director of Graduate Studies, 203-837-9005, Fax: 203-837-8326, E-mail: shanklec@wcsu.edu.

Industrial Design

Academy of Art University, Graduate Program, School of Industrial Design, San Francisco, CA 94105-3410. Offers MFA. Part-time programs available. Postbaccalaureate distance learning degree programs offered (no on-campus study). *Faculty:* 5 full-time (0 women), 41 part-time/adjunct (9 women). *Students:* 149 full-time (59 women), 53 part-time (19 women); includes 2 Black or African American, non-Hispanic/Latino; 12 Asian, non-Hispanic/Latino; 10 Hispanic/Latino, 120 international. Average age 28. 85 applicants. In 2010, 18 master's awarded. *Degree requirements:* For master's, thesis, final review. *Entrance requirements:* For master's, portfolio. *Application deadline:* For fall admission, 9/7 for domestic and international students; for spring admission, 2/2 for domestic and international students. Applications are processed on a rolling basis. Application fee: $100 ($500 for international students). Electronic applications accepted. *Expenses:* Tuition: Full-time $20,160; part-time $840 per semester hour. Required fees: $45 per semester. *Financial support:* Career-related internships or fieldwork and Federal Work-Study available. Support available to part-time students. Financial award application deadline: 8/10; financial award applicants required to submit FAFSA. *Application contact:* 800-544-ARTS, Fax: 415-263-4130, E-mail: info@academyart.edu.

Art Center College of Design, Graduate Division, Industrial Design Department, Pasadena, CA 91103. Offers environmental design (MS); product design (MS). *Accreditation:* NASAD. *Faculty:* 2 full-time (0 women), 8 part-time/adjunct (1 woman). *Students:* 25 full-time (7 women), 22 part-time (7 women); includes 9 minority (2 Black or African American, non-Hispanic/Latino; 6 Asian, non-Hispanic/Latino; 1 Hispanic/Latino), 24 international. Average age 30. 87 applicants, 25% accepted, 9 enrolled. In 2010, 9 master's awarded. *Degree requirements:* For master's, thesis, studio project. *Entrance requirements:* For master's, portfolio. Additional exam requirements/recommendations for international students: Required—TOEFL (minimum score 600 paper-based; 250 computer-based; 100 iBT). *Application deadline:* For fall admission, 2/1 for domestic and international students. Application fee: $50 ($70 for international students). *Expenses:* Tuition: Part-time $17,220 per term. *Financial support:* Teaching assistantships, career-related internships or fieldwork, Federal Work-Study, and scholarships/grants available. Financial award application deadline: 2/1. *Unit head:* Andrew Ogden, Chair, 626-396-2464. *Application contact:* Maritza Hererra, Coordinator, 626-396-2464.

See Display on page 89 and Close-Up on page 119.

Auburn University, Graduate School, College of Architecture, Design, and Construction, Department of Industrial Design, Auburn University, AL 36849. Offers MID. *Accreditation:* NASAD. Part-time programs available. *Faculty:* 17 full-time (3 women). *Students:* 11 full-time (7 women), 7 part-time (3 women); includes 1 Black or African American, non-Hispanic/Latino; 1 Asian, non-Hispanic/Latino, 5 international. Average age 26. 31 applicants, 35% accepted, 7 enrolled. In 2010, 6 master's awarded. *Entrance requirements:* For master's, GRE General Test. *Application deadline:* For fall admission, 9/1 for domestic students; for spring admission, 3/1 for domestic students. Applications are processed on a rolling basis. Application fee: $50 ($60 for international students). Electronic applications accepted. *Expenses:* Tuition, state resident: full-time $7002. Tuition, nonresident: full-time $21,898. International tuition: $22,116 full-time. Required fees: $892. Tuition and fees vary according to course load and program. *Financial support:* Federal Work-Study available. Support available to part-time students. Financial award application deadline: 3/15; financial award applicants required to submit FAFSA. *Faculty research:* Design of space living facilities, color use in business communications. *Unit head:* Clark E. Lundell, Head, 334-844-2364. *Application contact:* Dr. George Flowers, Dean of the Graduate School, 334-844-2125.

Brigham Young University, Graduate Studies, Ira A. Fulton College of Engineering and Technology, School of Technology, Provo, UT 84602-1001. Offers construction management (MS); information technology (MS); manufacturing systems (MS); technology and engineering education (MS). *Faculty:* 26 full-time (0 women). *Students:* 29 full-time (3 women), 6 part-time (0 women); includes 1 Black or African American, non-Hispanic/Latino; 7 American Indian or Alaska Native, non-Hispanic/Latino; 1 Asian, non-Hispanic/Latino; 3 Hispanic/Latino, 3 international. Average age 25. 14 applicants, 71% accepted, 6 enrolled. In 2010, 10 master's awarded. *Degree requirements:* For master's, thesis. *Entrance requirements:* For master's, GRE General Test, GMAT of GRE (Construction Management emphasis), minimum GPA of 3.0 in last 60 hours of course work. Additional exam requirements/recommendations for international students: Required—TOEFL (minimum score 580 paper-based; 237 computer-based; 85 iBT). *Application deadline:* For fall admission, 2/15 for domestic and international students; for winter admission, 9/15 for domestic and international students; for spring admission, 2/15 for domestic and international students. Application fee: $50. Electronic applications accepted. *Expenses:* Tuition: Full-time $5580; part-time $310 per credit hour. Tuition and fees vary according to program and student's religious affiliation. *Financial support:* In 2010–11, 34 students received support, including 13 research assistantships (averaging $3,498 per year), 6 teaching assistantships (averaging $3,000 per year); fellowships, career-related internships or fieldwork and scholarships/grants also available. Financial award application deadline: 2/1; financial award applicants required to submit FAFSA. *Faculty research:* Real time process control in IT, electronic physical design, processing and non-linear systems, networking, computerized systems in CM. Total annual research expenditures: $238,500. *Unit head:* Val D. Hawks, Director, 801-422-6300, Fax: 801-422-0490, E-mail: hawksv@byu.edu. *Application contact:* Ronald E. Terry, Graduate Coordinator, 801-422-4297, Fax: 801-422-0490, E-mail: ralowe@byu.edu.

Carleton University, Faculty of Graduate Studies, Faculty of Engineering and Design, School of Industrial Design, Ottawa, ON K1S 5B6, Canada. Offers M Des. *Degree requirements:* For master's, thesis optional. *Entrance requirements:* For master's, honors degree. Additional exam requirements/recommendations for international students: Required—TOEFL.

North Carolina State University, Graduate School, College of Design, Department of Industrial Design, Raleigh, NC 27695. Offers MID. *Accreditation:* NASAD. Part-time programs available. *Degree requirements:* For master's, thesis optional, oral exam, project. *Entrance requirements:* For master's, GRE General Test (recommended), portfolio. Electronic applications accepted. *Faculty research:* Computer graphics, ergonomics, product design.

The Ohio State University, Graduate School, College of Arts and Sciences, Division of Arts and Humanities, Department of Industrial, Interior, and Visual Communication Design, Columbus, OH 43210. Offers MA, MFA. *Accreditation:* NASAD. Part-time programs available. *Faculty:* 14. *Students:* 31 full-time (14 women), 6 part-time (2 women); includes 2 Black or African American, non-Hispanic/Latino; 1 Asian, non-Hispanic/Latino, 8 international. Average age 32. In 2010, 10 master's awarded. *Degree requirements:* For master's, project or thesis. *Entrance requirements:* For master's, bachelor's degree in interior space, graphics, product design, or related field. Additional exam requirements/recommendations for international students: Recommended—TOEFL (minimum score 600 paper-based; 250 computer-based). *Application deadline:* For fall admission, 8/15 priority date for domestic students, 7/1 priority date for international students; for winter admission, 12/1 priority date for domestic students, 11/1 priority date for international students; for spring admission, 3/1 priority date for domestic students, 2/1 priority date for international students. Applications are processed on a rolling basis. Application fee: $40 ($50 for international students). Electronic applications accepted. *Expenses:* Tuition, state resident: full-time $10,605. Tuition, nonresident: full-time $26,535. Tuition and fees vary according to course load and program. *Financial support:* Fellowships, research assistantships, teaching assistantships, career-related internships or fieldwork, Federal Work-Study, institutionally sponsored loans, and unspecified assistantships available. Support available to part-time students. Financial award application deadline: 5/1. *Unit head:* Paul Nini, Interim Chair, 614-292-1077, E-mail: nini.1@osu.edu. *Application contact:* 614-292-9444, Fax: 614-292-3895, E-mail: domestic.grad@osu.edu.

Pratt Institute, School of Art and Design, Program in Industrial Design, Brooklyn, NY 11205-3899. Offers MID. *Accreditation:* NASAD. Part-time programs available. *Faculty:* 6 full-time (1 woman), 26 part-time/adjunct (8 women). *Students:* 80 full-time (48 women), 1 (woman) part-time; includes 4 Black or African American, non-Hispanic/Latino; 11 Asian, non-Hispanic/Latino; 4 Hispanic/Latino; 1 Two or more races, non-Hispanic/Latino, 15 international. Average age 29. 244 applicants, 30% accepted, 35 enrolled. In 2010, 30 master's awarded. *Degree requirements:* For master's, thesis. *Entrance requirements:* For master's, portfolio, letters of recommendation. Additional exam requirements/recommendations for international students: Required—TOEFL (minimum score 575 paper-based; 233 computer-based; 100 iBT). *Application deadline:* For fall admission, 1/5 for domestic and international students; for spring admission, 10/1 for domestic and international students. Application fee: $50 ($90 for international students). Electronic applications accepted. *Expenses:* Tuition: Full-time $22,734; part-time $1263 per credit. Required fees: $1280. *Financial support:* Career-related internships or fieldwork, Federal Work-Study, institutionally sponsored loans, scholarships/grants, health care benefits, and unspecified assistantships available. Support available to part-time students. Financial award application deadline: 2/1; financial award applicants required to submit FAFSA. *Faculty research:* Universal design, design ethics, sustainability in design. *Unit head:* Matthew Burger, Chairperson, 718-636-3520, Fax: 718-636-3553, E-mail: mburger@pratt.edu. *Application contact:* Young Hah, Director of Graduate Admissions, 718-636-3683, Fax: 718-399-4242, E-mail: yhah@pratt.edu.

See Display on page 92 and Close-Up on page 131.

Pratt Institute, School of Art and Design, Program in Package Design, New York, NY 10011. Offers MS. *Accreditation:* NASAD. Part-time programs available. *Faculty:* 5 full-time (2 women), 33 part-time/adjunct (9 women). *Students:* 30 full-time (26 women), 2 part-time (both women); includes 2 Black or African American, non-Hispanic/Latino; 3 Asian, non-Hispanic/Latino; 1 Hispanic/Latino; 1 Two or more races, non-Hispanic/Latino, 11 international. Average age 27. 38 applicants, 89% accepted, 18 enrolled. In 2010, 11 master's awarded. *Degree requirements:* For master's, thesis. *Entrance requirements:* For master's, portfolio, letters of recommendation. Additional exam requirements/recommendations for international students: Required—TOEFL (minimum score 575 paper-based; 233 computer-based; 90 iBT). *Application deadline:* For fall admission, 1/5 for domestic and international students; for spring admission, 10/1 for domestic and international students. Application fee: $50 ($90 for international students). Electronic applications accepted. *Expenses:* Tuition: Full-time $22,734; part-time $1263 per credit. Required fees: $1280. *Financial support:* Career-related internships or fieldwork, Federal Work-Study, institutionally sponsored loans, scholarships/grants, health care benefits, and unspecified assistantships available. Support available to part-time students. Financial award application deadline: 2/1; financial award applicants required to submit FAFSA. *Unit head:* Jeffrey Bellantoni, Chairperson, 212-647-7573, E-mail: jbell189@pratt.edu. *Application contact:* Young Hah, Director of Graduate Admissions, 718-636-3683, Fax: 718-399-4242, E-mail: yhah@pratt.edu.

See Display on page 92 and Close-Up on page 131.

Rhode Island School of Design, Graduate Studies, Division of Architecture and Design, Department of Industrial Design, Providence, RI 02903-2784. Offers MID. *Accreditation:* NASAD. *Degree requirements:* For master's, thesis, exhibit. *Entrance requirements:* For master's, portfolio, 3 letters of recommendation. Additional exam requirements/recommendations for international students: Required—TOEFL (minimum score 580 paper-based; 237 computer-based), IELTS (minimum score 6.5).

Rochester Institute of Technology, Graduate Enrollment Services, College of Imaging Arts and Sciences, School of Design, Program in Industrial Design, Rochester, NY 14623-5603. Offers MFA. *Accreditation:* NASAD. Part-time programs available. *Students:* 16 full-time (7

Industrial Design

Rochester Institute of Technology (continued)
women), 9 part-time (5 women); includes 1 Asian, non-Hispanic/Latino, 16 international. Average age 29. 120 applicants, 33% accepted, 12 enrolled. In 2010, 5 master's awarded. *Degree requirements:* For master's, thesis (for some programs). *Entrance requirements:* For master's, portfolio, minimum GPA of 3.0. Additional exam requirements/recommendations for international students: Required—TOEFL (minimum score 550 paper-based; 213 computer-based; 79 iBT) or IELTS (minimum score 6.5). *Application deadline:* For fall admission, 2/15 priority date for domestic and international students. Applications are processed on a rolling basis. Application fee: $50. Electronic applications accepted. *Expenses:* Tuition: Full-time $33,234; part-time $924 per credit hour. Required fees: $219. *Financial support:* In 2010–11, 15 students received support; teaching assistantships with partial tuition reimbursements available, career-related internships or fieldwork, institutionally sponsored loans, scholarships/grants, and unspecified assistantships available. Support available to part-time students. Financial award application deadline: 8/30; financial award applicants required to submit FAFSA. *Unit head:* Stan Rickel, Graduate Program Director, 585-475-4745, E-mail: srrfaa@rit.edu. *Application contact:* Diane Ellison, Assistant Vice President, Graduate Enrollment Services, 585-475-2229, Fax: 585-475-7164, E-mail: gradinfo@rit.edu.

San Francisco State University, Division of Graduate Studies, College of Creative Arts, Department of Design and Industry, San Francisco, CA 94132-1722. Offers industrial arts (MA). *Unit head:* Jane Veeder, Interim Chair, 415-338-2211. *Application contact:* Shirl Buss, Graduate Coordinator, 415-338-2211.

Savannah College of Art and Design, Graduate School, Program in Industrial Design, Savannah, GA 31402-3146. Offers MA, MFA. Part-time programs available. *Faculty:* 10 full-time (2 women), 2 part-time/adjunct (0 women). *Students:* 60 full-time (19 women), 11 part-time (6 women); includes 1 Black or African American, non-Hispanic/Latino; 2 Asian, non-Hispanic/Latino; 1 Hispanic/Latino; 2 Two or more races, non-Hispanic/Latino, 49 international. Average age 26. In 2010, 14 master's awarded. *Degree requirements:* For master's, thesis, exhibit, internships. *Entrance requirements:* For master's, interview, portfolio. Additional exam requirements/recommendations for international students: Required—TOEFL (minimum score 450 paper-based; 133 computer-based). *Application deadline:* For fall admission, 4/1 priority date for domestic students, 4/1 for international students. Applications are processed on a rolling basis. Application fee: $35. Electronic applications accepted. *Expenses:* Tuition: Full-time $29,520; part-time $3280 per quarter. Tuition and fees vary according to campus/location. *Financial support:* Fellowships, career-related internships or fieldwork, Federal Work-Study, and scholarships/grants available. Financial award application deadline: 4/1; financial award applicants required to submit FAFSA. *Unit head:* Peter Solomon, Chair, 912-525-6432, Fax: 912-525-6437, E-mail: psolomon@scad.edu. *Application contact:* Elizabeth Mathis, Director of Graduate Recruitment, 912-525-5965, Fax: 912-525-5985, E-mail: emathis@scad.edu.

See Display on page 177 and Close-Up on page 223

University of Cincinnati, Graduate School, College of Design, Architecture, Art, and Planning, School of Design, Cincinnati, OH 45221. Offers fashion design (M Des); graphic design (M Des); industrial design (M Des); interaction design (M Des); product development (M Des). *Accreditation:* NASAD. *Degree requirements:* For master's, thesis. *Entrance requirements:* For master's, undergraduate degree in design or related field, 2 years of work experience in design or related field. Additional exam requirements/recommendations for international students: Required—TOEFL. Electronic applications accepted. *Faculty research:* Design theory, interdisciplinary design topics.

University of Illinois at Chicago, Graduate College, College of Architecture and Art, School of Art and Design, Chicago, IL 60607-7128. Offers electronic visualization (MFA); film animation (MFA); graphic design (MFA); industrial design (MFA); photography (MFA); studio arts (MFA). *Accreditation:* NASAD. *Degree requirements:* For master's, thesis, exhibit. *Entrance requirements:* For master's, MAT, portfolio. Additional exam requirements/recommendations for international students: Required—TOEFL. Electronic applications accepted.

University of Illinois at Urbana–Champaign, Graduate College, College of Fine and Applied Arts, School of Art and Design, Program in Design and Media, Champaign, IL 61820. Offers art and design (MFA), including new media; graphic design (MFA); industrial design (MFA). *Accreditation:* NASAD. *Students:* 14 full-time (4 women), 3 part-time (1 woman); includes 1 Asian, non-Hispanic/Latino, 10 international. 156 applicants, 3% accepted, 5 enrolled. In 2010, 3 master's awarded. *Entrance requirements:* For master's, minimum GPA of 3.0. Additional exam requirements/recommendations for international students: Required—TOEFL (minimum score 550 paper-based; 213 computer-based; 79 iBT). *Application deadline:* Applications are processed on a rolling basis. Application fee: $75 ($90 for international students). Electronic applications accepted. *Financial support:* Fellowships, research assistantships, teaching assistantships, tuition waivers (full and partial) available. *Unit head:* Ernest Scott, Chair, 217-333-1579, E-mail: ernscott@illinois.edu. *Application contact:* Marsha Biddle, Coordinator of Graduate Academic Affairs, 217-333-0642, Fax: 217-244-7688, E-mail: mbiddle@illinois.edu.

University of Notre Dame, Graduate School, College of Arts and Letters, Division of Humanities, Department of Art, Art History, and Design, Notre Dame, IN 46556. Offers art history (MA); design (MFA), including graphic design, industrial design; studio art (MFA), including ceramics, painting, photography, printmaking, sculpture. *Accreditation:* NASAD. *Degree requirements:* For master's, comprehensive exam (for some programs), thesis. *Entrance requirements:* For master's, GRE General Test, minimum GPA of 3.0. Additional exam requirements/recommendations for international students: Required—TOEFL (minimum score 600 paper-based; 250 computer-based; 80 iBT). Electronic applications accepted. *Faculty research:* Studio art practice in ceramics, printing, photography, printmaking and sculpture, graphic design and industrial design, digital imaging in design and photography, Renaissance and American art history, contemporary art theory and criticism.

The University of the Arts, College of Art, Media and Design, Department of Industrial Design, Philadelphia, PA 19102-4944. Offers MID. *Accreditation:* NASAD. *Degree requirements:* For master's, thesis. *Entrance requirements:* For master's, portfolio of 20 pieces that showcases self-generated projects, professional assignments or projects developed in a previous program; official transcripts; three letters of recommendation; one- to two-page statement of professional plans and goals; personal interview; resume or curriculum vitae; statement of intent. Additional exam requirements/recommendations for international students: Required—TOEFL (minimum score 580 paper-based, 92 iBT) or IELTS (minimum score 6.5).

See Display on page 187 and Close-Up on page 229.

University of Washington, Graduate School, College of Arts and Sciences, School of Art, Division of Design, Seattle, WA 98195. Offers industrial design (MFA); visual communication design (MFA).

Interior Design

Academy of Art University, Graduate Program, School of Interior Architecture and Design, San Francisco, CA 94105-3410. Offers MFA. Part-time programs available. Postbaccalaureate distance learning degree programs offered (no on-campus study). *Faculty:* 5 full-time (3 women), 55 part-time/adjunct (28 women). *Students:* 181 full-time (146 women), 185 part-time (160 women); includes 13 Black or African American, non-Hispanic/Latino; 21 Asian, non-Hispanic/Latino; 17 Hispanic/Latino, 107 international. Average age 32. 127 applicants. In 2010, 10 master's awarded. *Degree requirements:* For master's, thesis, final review. *Entrance requirements:* For master's, portfolio. *Application deadline:* For fall admission, 9/7 for domestic and international students; for spring admission, 2/2 for domestic and international students. Applications are processed on a rolling basis. Application fee: $100 ($500 for international students). Electronic applications accepted. *Expenses:* Tuition: Full-time $20,160; part-time $840 per semester hour. Required fees: $45 per semester. *Financial support:* Career-related internships or fieldwork and Federal Work-Study available. Support available to part-time students. Financial award application deadline: 8/10; financial award applicants required to submit FAFSA. *Application contact:* 800-544-ARTS, Fax: 415-263-4130, E-mail: info@academyart.edu.

Arizona State University, Herberger Institute for Design and the Arts, School of Architecture and Landscape Architecture, Tempe, AZ 85287-1605. Offers architecture (M Arch); building design/built environment (MS); design (arts, media, and engineering) (MSD); design (healthcare and healing environments) (MSD); design (industrial design) (MSD); design (interior design) (MSD); design (new product innovation) (MSD); design (visual communication design) (MSD); design, environment and the arts (PhD), including design, environment and the arts (design), design, environment and the arts (healthcare and healing environments), design, environment and the arts (history, theory, and criticism); landscape architecture (MLA); urban design (MUD); MA/MBA. *Accreditation:* NASAD. *Faculty:* 41 full-time (9 women), 6 part-time/adjunct (3 women). *Students:* 252 full-time (111 women), 45 part-time (21 women); includes 61 minority (3 Black or African American, non-Hispanic/Latino; 2 American Indian or Alaska Native, non-Hispanic/Latino; 13 Asian, non-Hispanic/Latino; 41 Hispanic/Latino; 1 Native Hawaiian or other Pacific Islander, non-Hispanic/Latino; 1 Two or more races, non-Hispanic/Latino), 58 international. Average age 29. 420 applicants, 61% accepted, 117 enrolled. In 2010, 60 master's, 8 doctorates awarded. Terminal master's awarded for partial completion of doctoral program. *Degree requirements:* For master's, thesis optional, interactive Program of Study (iPOS) submitted before completing 50 percent of required credit hours; for doctorate, comprehensive exam, thesis/dissertation, interactive Program of Study (iPOS) submitted before completing 50 percent of required credit hours. *Entrance requirements:* For master's, GRE General Test, minimum GPA of 3.0 or equivalent in last 2 years of work leading to bachelor's degree, design/creative works portfolio, 3 references, statement of intent; for doctorate, GRE, master's degree in architecture, graphic design, industrial design, interior design, landscape architecture, or art history or equivalent standing; statement of purpose; 3 letters of recommendation; indication of potential faculty mentor; sample of written work. Additional exam requirements/recommendations for international students: Required—TOEFL (minimum score 600 paper-based; 250 computer-based; 100 iBT). *Application deadline:* For fall admission, 1/15 priority date for domestic and international students. Application fee: $70 ($90 for international students). Electronic applications accepted. *Expenses:* Tuition, state resident: full-time $8510; part-time $608 per credit. Tuition, nonresident: full-time $16,542; part-time $919 per credit. Required fees: $339; $110 per credit. Part-time tuition and fees vary according to course load. *Financial support:* In 2010–11, 9 research assistantships with full and partial tuition reimbursements (averaging $11,913 per year), 76 teaching assistantships with full and partial tuition reimbursements (averaging $6,294 per year) were awarded; fellowships with full and partial tuition reimbursements, scholarships/grants and tuition waivers (full and partial) also available. Financial award application deadline: 3/1; financial award applicants required to submit FAFSA. Total annual research expenditures: $410,956. *Unit head:* Darren Petrucci, Director, 480-965-3536, E-mail: darren.petrucci@asu.edu. *Application contact:* Graduate Admissions, 480-965-6113.

Boston Architectural College, Graduate Programs, Boston, MA 02115-2795. Offers architecture (M Arch); interior design (MID). *Accreditation:* CIDA. *Degree requirements:* For master's, thesis. *Entrance requirements:* For master's, portfolio (recommended). Electronic applications accepted.

Brenau University, Sydney O. Smith Graduate School, School of Fine Arts and Humanities, Gainesville, GA 30501. Offers interior design (MID). *Accreditation:* CIDA. Part-time programs available. *Faculty:* 3 full-time (all women). *Students:* 7 full-time (all women), 6 part-time (all women); includes 2 Black or African American, non-Hispanic/Latino; 1 Hispanic/Latino. Average age 42. In 2010, 6 master's awarded. *Degree requirements:* For master's, internship; portfolio. *Entrance requirements:* For master's, portfolio review, minimum GPA of 3.0, resume. Additional exam requirements/recommendations for international students: Required—TOEFL (minimum score 500 paper-based; 173 computer-based; 61 iBT); Recommended—IELTS (minimum score 5). *Application deadline:* Applications are processed on a rolling basis. Application fee: $35. Electronic applications accepted. *Expenses:* Tuition: Part-time $494 per credit hour. Required fees: $130 per semester. Tuition and fees vary according to campus/location and program. *Unit head:* Dr. Andrea Birch, Dean, 710-718-5325, E-mail: abirch@brenau.edu. *Application contact:* Christina White, Dean of Admissions, 770-718-5320, Fax: 770-718-5338.

Chatham University, Program in Interior Architecture, Pittsburgh, PA 15232-2826. Offers MIA. *Accreditation:* CIDA. Part-time and evening/weekend programs available. Postbaccalaureate distance learning degree programs offered (no on-campus study). *Entrance requirements:* Additional exam requirements/recommendations for international students: Required—TOEFL (minimum score 600 paper-based; 250 computer-based; 100 iBT), IELTS (minimum score 6.5), TWE. Electronic applications accepted. *Faculty research:* Sustainability.

Corcoran College of Art and Design, Graduate Programs, Washington, DC 20006-4804. Offers art education (MAT); history of decorative arts (MA); interior design (MA). *Accreditation:* NASAD. Part-time programs available. *Entrance requirements:* Additional exam requirements/recommendations for international students: Required—TOEFL.

Cornell University, Graduate School, Graduate Fields of Human Ecology, Field of Design and Environmental Analysis, Ithaca, NY 14853. Offers applied research in human-environment relations (MS); facilities planning and management (MS); housing and design (MS); human factors and ergonomics (MS); human-environment relations (MS); interior design (MA, MPS). *Faculty:* 15 full-time (6 women). *Students:* 27 full-time (22 women); includes 2 Black or African American, non-Hispanic/Latino; 6 Asian, non-Hispanic/Latino, 7 international. Average age 25. 83 applicants, 27% accepted, 21 enrolled. In 2010, 29 master's awarded. *Degree requirements:* For master's, thesis. *Entrance requirements:* For master's, GRE General Test, portfolio or slides of recent work; bachelor's degree in interior design, architecture or related design discipline; 2 letters of recommendation. Additional exam requirements/recommendations for international students: Required—TOEFL (minimum score 600 paper-based; 250 computer-based; 105 iBT). *Application deadline:* For fall admission, 2/1 priority date for domestic students. Application fee: $70. Electronic applications accepted. *Expenses:* Tuition: Full-time $29,500. Required fees: $76. Tuition and fees vary according to degree level and program. *Financial support:* In 2010–11, 13 students received support, including 3 fellowships with full tuition reimbursements available, 2 research assistantships with full tuition reimbursements available, 13 teaching assistantships with full tuition reimbursements available; institutionally sponsored loans, scholarships/grants, health care benefits, tuition waivers (full and partial), and unspecified assistantships also available. Financial award applicants required to submit FAFSA. *Faculty research:* Facility planning and management, environmental psychology, housing, interior design, ergonomics and human factors. *Unit head:* Director of Graduate Studies, 607-255-2168, Fax: 607-255-0305. *Application contact:* Graduate Field Assistant, 607-255-2168, Fax: 607-255-0305, E-mail: deagrad@cornell.edu.

Drexel University, Antoinette Westphal College of Media Arts and Design, Program in Interior Architecture and Design, Philadelphia, PA 19104-2875. Offers MS. *Accreditation:* NASAD. *Degree requirements:* For master's, comprehensive exam, thesis, graduate review. *Entrance requirements:* For master's, interview. Additional exam requirements/recommendations for international students: Required—TOEFL. Electronic applications accepted. *Faculty research:* History of commercial interiors, hospice spaces, environmental sculpture, painting.

Eastern Michigan University, Graduate School, College of Technology, School of Engineering Technology, Program in Interior Design, Ypsilanti, MI 48197. Offers MS. Part-time and evening/weekend programs available. Postbaccalaureate distance learning degree programs offered (minimal on-campus study). *Students:* 11 full-time (9 women), 19 part-time (16 women); includes 4 minority (3 Black or African American, non-Hispanic/Latino; 1 Asian, non-Hispanic/Latino), 5 international. Average age 35. In 2010, 3 master's awarded. *Entrance requirements:* Additional exam requirements/recommendations for international students: Required—TOEFL. *Application deadline:* Applications are processed on a rolling basis. Application fee: $35. *Financial support:* Fellowships, research assistantships with full tuition reimbursements, teaching assistantships with full tuition reimbursements, career-related internships or fieldwork, Federal Work-Study, institutionally sponsored loans, scholarships/grants, tuition waivers (partial), and unspecified assistantships available. Support available to part-time students. Financial award applicants required to submit FAFSA. *Unit head:* Dr. Shinming Shyu, Program Coordinator, 734-487-6419, Fax: 734-487-8755, E-mail: sshyu@emich.edu. *Application contact:* Dr. Shinming Shyu, Program Coordinator, 734-487-6419, Fax: 734-487-8755, E-mail: sshyu@emich.edu.

Endicott College, Van Loan School of Graduate and Professional Studies, Program in Interior Design, Beverly, MA 01915-2096. Offers MA, MFA. *Faculty:* 1 full-time (0 women), 4 part-time/adjunct (0 women). *Students:* 8 full-time (7 women), 2 part-time (both women); includes 1 Asian, non-Hispanic/Latino. Average age 40. 8 applicants, 100% accepted, 7 enrolled. *Entrance requirements:* For master's, MAT or GRE, statement of professional goals, two letters of recommendation, design portfolio, interview. Additional exam requirements/recommendations for international students: Required—TOEFL (minimum score 550 paper-based; 79 iBT). Application fee: $50. *Financial support:* Applicants required to submit FAFSA. *Application contact:* Dr. Mary Huegel, Dean of Graduate and Professional Studies, 978-232-2084, Fax: 978-232-3000, E-mail: mhuegel@endicott.edu.

Fashion Institute of Technology, School of Graduate Studies, Program in Sustainable Interior Environments, New York, NY 10001-5992. Offers MA.

See Display below and Close-Up on page 125.

Florida International University, College of Architecture and the Arts, School of Architecture, Interior Design Program, Miami, FL 33199. Offers MA, MID. *Accreditation:* CIDA. *Faculty:* 1 (woman) full-time, 2 part-time/adjunct (1 woman). *Students:* 51 full-time (47 women), 13 part-time (all women); includes 5 Black or African American, non-Hispanic/Latino; 1 Asian, non-Hispanic/Latino; 37 Hispanic/Latino, 2 international. Average age 28. 47 applicants, 19% accepted, 5 enrolled. In 2010, 14 master's awarded. *Entrance requirements:* For master's, GRE or minimum GPA of 3.0 in upper-level undergraduate work, portfolio. Additional exam requirements/recommendations for international students: Required—TOEFL (minimum score 550 paper-based; 80 iBT). *Application deadline:* For fall admission, 2/1 for domestic and international students. Application fee: $30. Electronic applications accepted. *Financial support:* Institutionally sponsored loans and scholarships/grants available. Financial award application deadline: 3/1; financial award applicants required to submit FAFSA. *Unit head:* Dr. Brian Schriner, Interim Dean, 305-348-6742, Fax: 305-348-2650, E-mail: schriner@fiu.edu. *Application*

contact: Prof. Janine King, Graduate Program Director, 305-348-6630, Fax: 305-348-2650, E-mail: janine.king@fiu.edu.

Florida State University, The Graduate School, College of Visual Arts, Theatre and Dance, Department of Interior Design, Tallahassee, FL 32306. Offers MA, MFA, MS. *Accreditation:* NASAD (one or more programs are accredited). *Faculty:* 8 full-time (3 women), 4 part-time/adjunct (3 women). *Students:* 36 full-time (31 women), 36 part-time (32 women); includes 4 Black or African American, non-Hispanic/Latino; 1 Asian, non-Hispanic/Latino; 1 Hispanic/Latino. Average age 30. 13 applicants, 92% accepted, 12 enrolled. In 2010, 14 master's awarded. *Degree requirements:* For master's, thesis or alternative. *Entrance requirements:* For master's, GRE General Test, minimum GPA of 3.0 during previous 2 years. Additional exam requirements/recommendations for international students: Required—TOEFL (minimum score 550 paper-based). Application fee: $30. Electronic applications accepted. *Expenses:* Tuition, state resident: full-time $8238.24. *Financial support:* In 2010–11, 1 fellowship (averaging $18,000 per year), 2 research assistantships with tuition reimbursements (averaging $3,200 per year), 10 teaching assistantships with tuition reimbursements (averaging $3,200 per year) were awarded; career-related internships or fieldwork and unspecified assistantships also available. Financial award applicants required to submit FAFSA. *Faculty research:* Graphics techniques, history of interiors, technical proficiencies, computer-aided design and drafting, historic restoration. *Unit head:* Eric Wiedegreen, Chairman, 850-645-2504, Fax: 850-644-3112, E-mail: ewiedegr@fsu.edu. *Application contact:* Dr. Jill Pable, Director of Graduate Studies, 850-645-6831, Fax: 850-644-3112, E-mail: jpable@fsu.edu.

The George Washington University, Columbian College of Arts and Sciences, Department of Fine Arts and Art History, Program in Interior Design, Washington, DC 20052. Offers MFA. *Students:* 27 full-time (26 women), 30 part-time (27 women); includes 3 Black or African American, non-Hispanic/Latino; 3 Asian, non-Hispanic/Latino; 3 Hispanic/Latino, 4 international. Average age 31. 62 applicants, 79% accepted, 20 enrolled. In 2010, 13 master's awarded. *Entrance requirements:* Additional exam requirements/recommendations for international students: Required—TOEFL (minimum score 550 paper-based; 213 computer-based; 80 iBT). *Application deadline:* For fall admission, 3/1 for domestic students, 1/15 for international students; for spring admission, 10/1 for domestic students, 9/1 for international students. *Financial support:* Application deadline: 1/15. *Unit head:* Thomas K. Brown, Chair, 202-994-9067, E-mail: thbrown@gwu.edu. *Application contact:* Information Contact, 202-994-6085, Fax: 202-994-8657, E-mail: art@gwu.edu.

Harrington College of Design, Programs in Interior Design, Chicago, IL 60605-1496. Offers MA, MID.

Interior Designers Institute, Graduate Program, Newport Beach, CA 92660. Offers MA.

Iowa State University of Science and Technology, Graduate College, College of Design, Department of Art and Design, Ames, IA 50011. Offers art and design (MA); graphic design (MFA); integrated visual arts (MFA); interior design (MFA). Part-time programs available. *Faculty:* 36 full-time (20 women), 1 (woman) part-time/adjunct. *Students:* 52 full-time (39 women), 22 part-time (11 women); includes 1 Black or African American, non-Hispanic/Latino; 1 Asian, non-Hispanic/Latino; 1 Hispanic/Latino, 18 international. 48 applicants, 71% accepted, 19 enrolled. In 2010, 15 master's awarded. *Degree requirements:* For master's, thesis (for some programs). *Entrance requirements:* For master's, GRE General Test, resume. Additional exam requirements/recommendations for international students: Required—TOEFL (minimum score 550 paper-based; 79 iBT), IELTS (minimum score 6.5). *Application deadline:* For fall admission, 4/15 priority date for domestic and international students; for spring admission, 4/15 for domestic and international students. Applications are processed on a rolling basis. Application fee: $40 ($90 for international students). Electronic applications accepted. *Financial support:* Research assistantships with tuition reimbursements, teaching assistantships with tuition reimbursements, career-related internships or fieldwork, Federal Work-Study, institutionally sponsored loans, and tuition waivers (partial) available. Support available to part-time students. Financial award application deadline: 2/15; financial award applicants required to submit

Interior Design

Iowa State University of Science and Technology (continued)

FAFSA. *Faculty research:* Computer applications, fire safety, human factors in design, art and design education, fine arts, craft design. *Unit head:* Dr. Roger Baer, Chair, 515-294-6724, Fax: 515-294-2725, E-mail: artdn@iastate.edu. *Application contact:* Dr. Roger Baer, Chair, 515-294-6724, Fax: 515-294-2725, E-mail: artdn@iastate.edu.

Lawrence Technological University, College of Architecture and Design, Southfield, MI 48075-1058. Offers architecture (M Arch); architecture 3+ (M Arch); interior design (MID); interior design 3+ (MID); urban design (MUD). *Accreditation:* NASAD. Part-time and evening/weekend programs available. *Faculty:* 9 full-time (2 women), 12 part-time/adjunct (3 women). *Students:* 11 full-time (5 women), 225 part-time (89 women); includes 13 Black or African American, non-Hispanic/Latino; 11 Asian, non-Hispanic/Latino; 7 Hispanic/Latino; 1 Native Hawaiian or other Pacific Islander, non-Hispanic/Latino; 2 Two or more races, non-Hispanic/Latino, 23 international. Average age 31. 174 applicants, 55% accepted, 68 enrolled. In 2010, 47 master's awarded. *Degree requirements:* For master's, thesis. *Entrance requirements:* For master's, portfolio. Additional exam requirements/recommendations for international students: Required—TOEFL (minimum score 550 paper-based; 213 computer-based; 79 iBT). *Application deadline:* For fall admission, 6/30 priority date for domestic students, 6/30 for international students; for spring admission, 1/15 priority date for domestic students, 1/15 for international students. Applications are processed on a rolling basis. Application fee: $50. Electronic applications accepted. *Financial support:* In 2010–11, 83 students received support. Federal Work-Study available. Financial award application deadline: 4/1; financial award applicants required to submit FAFSA. *Unit head:* Glen LeRoy, Dean, 248-204-2800, Fax: 248-204-2900, E-mail: archdean@ltu.edu. *Application contact:* Jane Rohrback, Director of Admissions, 248-204-3160, Fax: 248-204-2228, E-mail: admissions@ltu.edu.

Louisiana Tech University, Graduate School, College of Liberal Arts, School of Architecture, Ruston, LA 71272. Offers interior design (MFA). *Entrance requirements:* For master's, GRE General Test.

Marymount University, School of Arts and Sciences, Program in Interior Design, Arlington, VA 22207-4299. Offers MA. *Accreditation:* CIDA. Part-time and evening/weekend programs available. *Degree requirements:* For master's, thesis or alternative. *Entrance requirements:* For master's, GRE, National Council for Interior Design Qualification (NCIDQ) exam, or National Council of Architectural Registration Boards (NCARB) Architectural Registration Exam, 2 letters of recommendation, interview, resume, personal statement, portfolio. Additional exam requirements/recommendations for international students: Required—TOEFL (minimum score 600 paper-based; 250 computer-based; 96 iBT), IELTS (minimum score 6.5). Electronic applications accepted.

Marywood University, Academic Affairs, School of Architecture, Scranton, PA 18509-1598. Offers architecture (M Arch); studio art (MA), including interior design. *Entrance requirements:* Additional exam requirements/recommendations for international students: Required—TOEFL (minimum score 550 paper-based; 213 computer-based; 79 iBT). *Expenses:* Tuition: Part-time $735 per credit. Required fees: $470 per semester. Tuition and fees vary according to degree level and campus/location.

Miami International University of Art & Design, Program in Interior Design, Miami, FL 33132-1418. Offers MFA. *Application contact:* Office of Graduate Admissions, 305-428-5700.

See Close-Up on page 129.

Michigan State University, The Graduate School, College of Agriculture and Natural Resources and College of Social Science, School of Planning, Design and Construction, East Lansing, MI 48824. Offers construction management (MS, PhD); environmental design (MA); interior design and facilities management (MA); international planning studies (MIPS); urban and regional planning (MURP). *Degree requirements:* For master's, thesis or alternative. *Entrance requirements:* Additional exam requirements/recommendations for international students: Required—TOEFL. Electronic applications accepted.

Missouri State University, Graduate College, College of Natural and Applied Sciences, Department of Fashion and Interior Design, Springfield, MO 65897. Offers secondary education (MS Ed), including consumer sciences. Part-time programs available. *Degree requirements:* For master's, comprehensive exam, thesis or alternative. *Entrance requirements:* For master's, 9-12 teaching certification (MS Ed), minimum GPA of 3.0 (MNAS). Additional exam requirements/recommendations for international students: Required—TOEFL (minimum score 550 paper-based; 213 computer-based; 79 iBT). Electronic applications accepted. *Expenses:* Tuition, state resident: full-time $3348; part-time $186 per credit hour. Tuition, nonresident: full-time $6696; part-time $372 per credit hour. Required fees: $238 per semester. Tuition and fees vary according to course level, course load and program.

Moore College of Art & Design, Program in Interior Design, Philadelphia, PA 19103. Offers MFA. *Accreditation:* NASAD. Evening/weekend programs available. *Degree requirements:* For master's, thesis, internship, thesis exhibition. *Entrance requirements:* For master's, minimum GPA of 3.0, on-site interview, portfolio, 3 letters of recommendation, resume.

Mount Ida College, Program in Interior Design, Newton, MA 02459-3310. Offers MSM. Part-time and evening/weekend programs available. Postbaccalaureate distance learning degree programs offered (minimal on-campus study). *Entrance requirements:* For master's, portfolio. Additional exam requirements/recommendations for international students: Required—TOEFL (minimum score 550 paper-based; 220 computer-based; 79 iBT); Recommended—IELTS (minimum score 5.5). Electronic applications accepted.

The New School: A University, Parsons The New School for Design, Program in Interior Design, New York, NY 10011. Offers MFA. *Degree requirements:* For master's, thesis. *Entrance requirements:* For master's, portfolio. Additional exam requirements/recommendations for international students: Required—TOEFL (minimum score 580 paper-based; 237 computer-based; 92 iBT). Electronic applications accepted.

The New School: A University, Parsons The New School for Design, Program in Lighting Design, New York, NY 10011. Offers MFA. *Accreditation:* NASAD. *Degree requirements:* For master's, thesis. *Entrance requirements:* For master's, portfolio. Additional exam requirements/recommendations for international students: Required—TOEFL (minimum score 580 paper-based; 237 computer-based; 92 iBT). Electronic applications accepted.

New York School of Interior Design, Program in Interior Design, New York, NY 10021-5110. Offers MFA. *Accreditation:* NASAD. *Faculty:* 24 part-time/adjunct (10 women). *Students:* 68 full-time (56 women); includes 22 minority (3 Black or African American, non-Hispanic/Latino; 18 Asian, non-Hispanic/Latino; 1 Hispanic/Latino). Average age 30. 128 applicants, 77% accepted, 36 enrolled. In 2010, 1 master's awarded. *Degree requirements:* For master's, thesis. *Entrance requirements:* For master's, portfolio, undergraduate degree in interior design or closely related field. Additional exam requirements/recommendations for international students: Required—TOEFL (minimum score 550 paper-based; 213 computer-based; 79 iBT). *Application deadline:* For fall admission, 2/1 for domestic and international students. Application fee: $60 ($100 for international students). Electronic applications accepted. *Expenses:* Tuition: Full-time $26,500. Required fees: $335. One-time fee: $60 full-time. *Financial support:* In 2010–11, 2 research assistantships (averaging $10,000 per year) were awarded; career-related internships or fieldwork, Federal Work-Study, institutionally sponsored loans, and scholarships/grants also available. Financial award application deadline: 8/1; financial award applicants required to submit FAFSA. *Faculty research:* History, theory, aesthetics, sociology, and green design; landscape, lighting, furniture, product, and set design. *Unit head:* Scott Ageloff, Dean, 212-472-1500 Ext. 301, Fax: 212-288-6577, E-mail: sageloff@nysid.edu. *Application contact:* David T. Sprouls, Director of Admissions, 212-472-1500 Ext. 202, Fax: 212-472-1867, E-mail: dsprouls@nysid.edu.

New York School of Interior Design, Program in Interior Design (Post-Professional Level), New York, NY 10021-5110. Offers MFA. *Faculty:* 24 part-time/adjunct (10 women). *Students:* 25 full-time (18 women); includes 13 minority (12 Asian, non-Hispanic/Latino; 1 Hispanic/Latino). Average age 27. 47 applicants, 68% accepted, 14 enrolled. In 2010, 1 master's awarded. *Degree requirements:* For master's, thesis. *Entrance requirements:* For master's, portfolio. Additional exam requirements/recommendations for international students: Required—TOEFL (minimum score 550 paper-based; 213 computer-based; 79 iBT). *Application deadline:* For fall admission, 2/1 priority date for domestic and international students. Application fee: $60 ($100 for international students). Electronic applications accepted. *Expenses:* Tuition: Full-time $26,500. Required fees: $335. One-time fee: $60 full-time. *Financial support:* In 2010–11, 3 research assistantships (averaging $10,000 per year) were awarded; career-related internships or fieldwork, Federal Work-Study, institutionally sponsored loans, and scholarships/grants also available. Financial award application deadline: 8/1; financial award applicants required to submit FAFSA. *Application contact:* Scott Ageloff, Dean, 212-472-1500 Ext. 301, Fax: 212-288-6577, E-mail: sageloff@nysid.edu.

The Ohio State University, Graduate School, College of Arts and Sciences, Division of Arts and Humanities, Department of Industrial, Interior, and Visual Communication Design, Columbus, OH 43210. Offers MA, MFA. *Accreditation:* NASAD. Part-time programs available. *Faculty:* 14. *Students:* 31 full-time (14 women), 6 part-time (2 women); includes 2 Black or African American, non-Hispanic/Latino; 1 Asian, non-Hispanic/Latino, 8 international. Average age 32. In 2010, 10 master's awarded. *Degree requirements:* For master's, project or thesis. *Entrance requirements:* For master's, bachelor's degree in interior space, graphics, product design, or related field. Additional exam requirements/recommendations for international students: Recommended—TOEFL (minimum score 600 paper-based; 250 computer-based). *Application deadline:* For fall admission, 8/15 priority date for domestic students, 7/1 priority date for international students; for winter admission, 12/1 priority date for domestic students, 11/1 priority date for international students; for spring admission, 3/1 priority date for domestic students, 2/1 priority date for international students. Applications are processed on a rolling basis. Application fee: $40 ($50 for international students). Electronic applications accepted. *Expenses:* Tuition, state resident: full-time $10,605. Tuition, nonresident: full-time $26,535. Tuition and fees vary according to course load and program. *Financial support:* Fellowships, research assistantships, teaching assistantships, career-related internships or fieldwork, Federal Work-Study, institutionally sponsored loans, and unspecified assistantships available. Support available to part-time students. Financial award application deadline: 5/1. *Unit head:* Paul Nini, Interim Chair, 614-292-1077, E-mail: nini.1@osu.edu. *Application contact:* 614-292-9444, Fax: 614-292-3895, E-mail: domestic.grad@osu.edu.

Pontificia Universidad Catolica Madre y Maestra, Graduate School, Faculty of Sciences and Humanities, Santiago, Dominican Republic. Offers architecture (M Arch), including architecture of interiors, architecture of tourist lodgings, landscaping; early childhood education (M Ed).

Pratt Institute, School of Art and Design, Program in Interior Design, Brooklyn, NY 11205-3899. Offers MS. *Accreditation:* NASAD. Part-time programs available. *Faculty:* 4 full-time (1 woman), 27 part-time/adjunct (10 women). *Students:* 182 full-time (156 women), 8 part-time (all women); includes 3 Black or African American, non-Hispanic/Latino; 18 Asian, non-Hispanic/Latino; 19 Hispanic/Latino; 2 Two or more races, non-Hispanic/Latino, 65 international. Average age 28. 273 applicants, 57% accepted, 70 enrolled. In 2010, 53 master's awarded. *Degree requirements:* For master's, thesis. *Entrance requirements:* For master's, portfolio, letters of recommendation. Additional exam requirements/recommendations for international students: Required—TOEFL (minimum score 575 paper-based; 233 computer-based; 90 iBT). *Application deadline:* For fall admission, 1/5 for domestic and international students; for spring admission, 10/1 for domestic and international students. Application fee: $50 ($90 for international students). Electronic applications accepted. *Expenses:* Tuition: Full-time $22,734; part-time $1263 per credit. Required fees: $1280. *Financial support:* Career-related internships or fieldwork, Federal Work-Study, institutionally sponsored loans, scholarships/grants, health care benefits, and unspecified assistantships available. Support available to part-time students. Financial award application deadline: 2/1; financial award applicants required to submit FAFSA. *Unit head:* Anita Cooney, Chairperson, 718-636-3630, Fax: 718-636-3553, E-mail: acooney@pratt.edu. *Application contact:* Young Hah, Director of Graduate Admissions, 718-636-3683, Fax: 718-399-4242, E-mail: yhah@pratt.edu.

See Display on page 92 and Close-Up on page 131.

Rhode Island School of Design, Graduate Studies, Division of Architecture and Design, Department of Interior Architecture, Providence, RI 02903-2784. Offers MIA. *Degree requirements:* For master's, thesis, exhibit. *Entrance requirements:* For master's, portfolio, 3 letters of recommendation. Additional exam requirements/recommendations for international students: Required—TOEFL (minimum score 580 paper-based; 237 computer-based), IELTS (minimum score 6.5).

San Diego State University, Graduate and Research Affairs, College of Professional Studies and Fine Arts, School of Art, Design and Art History, San Diego, CA 92182. Offers art history (MA); studio arts (MA, MFA), including applied design, environmental design, graphic design, interior design, painting and printmaking, sculpture. *Accreditation:* NASAD (one or more programs are accredited). *Degree requirements:* For master's, variable foreign language requirement, thesis. *Entrance requirements:* For master's, GRE General Test, bachelor's degree in related field, slide portfolio, typed slide information sheet, 2 letters of recommendation. Additional exam requirements/recommendations for international students: Required—TOEFL. Electronic applications accepted.

Savannah College of Art and Design, Graduate School, Program in Interior Design, Savannah, GA 31402-3146. Offers MA, MFA. Part-time programs available. *Faculty:* 20 full-time (15 women), 12 part-time/adjunct (10 women). *Students:* 100 full-time (82 women), 20 part-time (16 women); includes 6 Black or African American, non-Hispanic/Latino; 2 Asian, non-Hispanic/Latino; 1 Hispanic/Latino; 1 Two or more races, non-Hispanic/Latino, 35 international. Average age 30. In 2010, 49 master's awarded. *Degree requirements:* For master's, thesis, internship. *Entrance requirements:* For master's, interview, portfolio. Additional exam requirements/recommendations for international students: Required—TOEFL (minimum score 450 paper-based; 133 computer-based). *Application deadline:* For fall admission, 4/1 priority date for domestic and international students. Applications are processed on a rolling basis. Application fee: $35. Electronic applications accepted. *Expenses:* Tuition: Full-time $29,520; part-time $3280 per quarter. Tuition and fees vary according to campus/location. *Financial support:* Fellowships, career-related internships or fieldwork, Federal Work-Study, and scholarships/grants available. Financial award application deadline: 4/1; financial award applicants required to submit FAFSA. *Unit head:* Khoi Nguyen Vo, Acting Chair, 912-525-6910, Fax: 912-525-6904, E-mail: kvo@scad.edu. *Application contact:* Elizabeth Mathis, Director of Graduate Recruitment, 912-525-5965, Fax: 912-525-5985, E-mail: emathis@scad.edu.

See Display on page 177 and Close-Up on page 223

School of the Art Institute of Chicago, Graduate Division, Department of Architecture, Interior Architecture, and Designed Objects, Chicago, IL 60603-3103. Offers architecture (M Arc); design for emerging technologies (MFA); designed objects (M Des); interior architecture (M Arc). *Entrance requirements:* Additional exam requirements/recommendations for international students: Required—TOEFL, IELTS.

See Close-Up on page 225.

South Dakota State University, Graduate School, College of Education and Human Sciences, Department of Apparel Merchandising and Interior Design, Brookings, SD 57007. Offers MFCS. Part-time and evening/weekend programs available. Postbaccalaureate distance learning degree programs offered. *Entrance requirements:* Additional exam requirements/recommendations for international students: Required—TOEFL (minimum score 550 paper-based; 213 computer-based; 79 iBT). *Faculty research:* Rural internet shopping, professional development in apparel merchandising, gender, aesthetics.

Suffolk University, New England School of Art and Design, Boston, MA 02108-2770. Offers graphic design (MA); interior architecture (MFA); interior design (MA). *Accreditation:* CIDA; NASAD. Part-time and evening/weekend programs available. *Faculty:* 21 full-time (12 women), 7 part-time/adjunct (2 women). *Students:* 56 full-time (45 women), 76 part-time (65 women); includes 2 Black or African American, non-Hispanic/Latino; 5 Asian, non-Hispanic/Latino; 5 Hispanic/Latino, 13 international. Average age 30. 113 applicants, 67% accepted, 48 enrolled. In 2010, 30 master's awarded. *Entrance requirements:* For master's, GRE (for MFA), art portfolio, interview, 2 letters of recommendation, resume; letter of intent (for MFA). Additional exam requirements/recommendations for international students: Required—TOEFL (minimum score 550 paper-based; 213 computer-based; 80 iBT). *Application deadline:* For fall admission, 6/15 priority date for domestic students, 6/15 for international students; for spring admission, 11/1 priority date for domestic students, 11/1 for international students. Applications are processed on a rolling basis. Application fee: $50. Electronic applications accepted. *Expenses:* Contact institution. *Financial support:* In 2010–11, 83 students received support, including 39 fellowships with partial tuition reimbursements available (averaging $7,001 per year). Financial award application deadline: 4/1. *Faculty research:* Adaptive re-use of historical structures, universal design, American architecture history, interior design to reduce inefficiency, meditation SPA. *Unit head:* William Davis, Director, 617-994-4264, Fax: 617-994-4250, E-mail: wdavis@suffolk.edu. *Application contact:* Judith Reynolds, Director of Graduate Admissions, 617-573-8302, Fax: 617-305-1733, E-mail: grad.admission@suffolk.edu.

Texas Tech University, Graduate School, College of Human Sciences, Department of Design, Lubbock, TX 79409. Offers environmental design (MS); interior and environmental design (PhD). *Faculty:* 4 full-time (2 women). *Students:* 18 full-time (16 women), 7 part-time (5 women); includes 1 Asian, non-Hispanic/Latino; 1 Hispanic/Latino, 8 international. Average age 27. 16 applicants, 69% accepted, 8 enrolled. In 2010, 3 master's awarded. *Degree requirements:* For master's, thesis or alternative; for doctorate, thesis/dissertation. *Entrance requirements:* For master's and doctorate, GRE, 3 letters of recommendation, design portfolio, resume. Additional exam requirements/recommendations for international students: Required—TOEFL (minimum score 550 paper-based; 213 computer-based; 79 iBT). *Application deadline:* For fall admission, 6/1 priority date for domestic students, 1/15 priority date for international students; for spring admission, 9/1 priority date for domestic students, 6/15 priority date for international students. Applications are processed on a rolling basis. Application fee: $50 ($75 for international students). Electronic applications accepted. *Expenses:* Tuition, state resident: full-time $5495.76; part-time $228.99 per credit hour. Tuition, nonresident: full-time $12,936; part-time $538.99 per credit hour. Required fees: $2674; $36 per credit hour. $905 per semester. *Financial support:* In 2010–11, 3 students received support, including 2 research assistantships with partial tuition reimbursements available (averaging $1,479 per year). Financial award application deadline: 4/15; financial award applicants required to submit FAFSA. *Faculty research:* Healthcare and the built environment, sustainability, ergonomics, environmental design, evidence-based design. Total annual research expenditures: $150,144. *Unit head:* Dr. Cherif M. Amor, Chair, 806-742-3050, Fax: 806-742-1639, E-mail: cherif.amor@ttu.edu. *Application contact:* Dr. Su-Jeong Hwang Shin, Graduate Programs Director, 806-742-3050 Ext. 262, Fax: 806-742-1639, E-mail: su.hwang@ttu.edu.

See Display on this page and Close-Up on page 133.

The University of Alabama, Graduate School, College of Human Environmental Sciences, Department of Clothing, Textiles, and Interior Design, Tuscaloosa, AL 35487. Offers MSHES. *Faculty:* 6 full-time (all women), 1 (woman) part-time/adjunct. *Students:* 3 full-time (all women), 1 (woman) part-time. Average age 31. 3 applicants, 100% accepted, 2 enrolled. *Degree requirements:* For master's, comprehensive exam, thesis optional. *Entrance requirements:* For master's, GRE General Test or MAT, minimum GPA of 3.0. *Application deadline:* For fall admission, 7/6 for domestic students. Applications are processed on a rolling basis. Application fee: $50 ($60 for international students). *Expenses:* Tuition, state resident: full-time $7900. Tuition, nonresident: full-time $20,500. *Financial support:* In 2010–11, 1 research assistantship with full tuition reimbursement (averaging $8,100 per year), 2 teaching assistantships with full tuition reimbursements (averaging $8,100 per year) were awarded; fellowships, career-related internships or fieldwork, Federal Work-Study, and scholarships/grants also available. Financial award application deadline: 3/15. *Faculty research:* Archeological textiles, textile science, material culture, social psychology, international trade. *Unit head:* Dr. Carolyn Callis, Chair and Associate Professor, 205-348-6176, Fax: 205-348-0022, E-mail: ccallis@ches.ua.edu. *Application contact:* Dr. Carolyn Callis, Chair and Associate Professor, 205-348-6176, Fax: 205-348-0022, E-mail: ccallis@ches.ua.edu.

University of California, Berkeley, UC Berkeley Extension, Certificate Programs in Art and Design, Berkeley, CA 94720-1500. Offers interior design and interior architecture (Certificate); landscape architecture (Certificate); visual arts (Postbaccalaureate Certificate).

University of Central Oklahoma, College of Graduate Studies and Research, College of Education, Department of Human Environmental Sciences, Edmond, OK 73034-5209. Offers family and child studies (MS); family and consumer science education (MS); interior design (MS); nutrition-food management (MS). Part-time programs available. *Entrance requirements:* Additional exam requirements/recommendations for international students: Required—TOEFL (minimum score 550 paper-based; 213 computer-based). Electronic applications accepted. *Faculty research:* Dietetics and food science.

University of Central Oklahoma, College of Graduate Studies and Research, College of Fine Arts and Design, Department of Design and Interior Design, Edmond, OK 73034-5209. Offers MFA. Part-time programs available. Postbaccalaureate distance learning degree programs offered (minimal on-campus study). *Entrance requirements:* Additional exam requirements/recommendations for international students: Required—TOEFL (minimum score 550 paper-based; 213 computer-based). Electronic applications accepted.

University of Cincinnati, Graduate School, College of Design, Architecture, Art, and Planning, School of Architecture and Interior Design, Cincinnati, OH 45221. Offers architecture (M Arch). *Accreditation:* NASAD. *Degree requirements:* For master's, one foreign language, thesis. *Entrance requirements:* Additional exam requirements/recommendations for international students: Required—TOEFL. *Faculty research:* Theory and history of architecture.

University of Florida, Graduate School, College of Design, Construction and Planning, Department of Interior Design, Gainesville, FL 32611. Offers MID, PhD. *Faculty:* 6 full-time (4 women). *Students:* 17 full-time (15 women), 4 part-time (all women); includes 2 Asian, non-Hispanic/Latino; 1 Hispanic/Latino, 4 international. Average age 29. 18 applicants, 33% accepted, 4 enrolled. In 2010, 1 master's awarded. *Degree requirements:* For master's, thesis; for doctorate, comprehensive exam, thesis/dissertation. *Entrance requirements:* For master's, GRE General Test, minimum GPA of 3.0. Additional exam requirements/recommendations for international students: Required—TOEFL (minimum score 550 paper-based; 213 computer-based; 80 iBT), IELTS (minimum score 6). *Application deadline:* For fall admission, 4/1 for domestic students, 2/1 for international students. Application fee: $30. *Expenses:* Tuition, state resident: full-time $10,915.92. Tuition, nonresident: full-time $28,309. *Financial support:* In 2010–11, 4 students received support, including 2 research assistantships (averaging $6,893 per year), 2 teaching assistantships (averaging $6,893 per year). Financial award applicants required to submit FAFSA. *Faculty research:* Sustainable design and environmentally significant behaviors; design innovation, creativity, methods and pedagogy; lighting and color design and perception; historic preservation; design for special populations. Total annual research expenditures: $150,000. *Unit head:* Dr. Margaret Portillo, Chair, 352-392-0252 Ext. 334, Fax: 352-392-7266, E-mail: mportill@ufl.edu. *Application contact:* Dr. Maruja Torress-Antonini, Graduate Coordinator, 352-392-0252 Ext. 335, Fax: 352-392-7266, E-mail: mta@ufl.edu.

Interior Design

University of Georgia, College of Family and Consumer Sciences, Department of Textiles, Merchandising, and Interiors, Athens, GA 30602. Offers historic costume and textiles (MS); merchandising/international trade (MS); textile analysis (PhD); textile chemical processes (PhD); textile products and standards (PhD); textile science (MS). *Faculty:* 13 full-time (9 women). *Students:* 18 full-time (16 women), 2 part-time (both women); includes 2 Black or African American, non-Hispanic/Latino; 1 Hispanic/Latino, 8 international. 23 applicants, 52% accepted, 5 enrolled. In 2010, 8 master's awarded. *Degree requirements:* For master's, thesis; for doctorate, thesis/dissertation. *Entrance requirements:* For master's and doctorate, GRE General Test. *Application deadline:* For fall admission, 7/1 priority date for domestic students; for spring admission, 11/15 for domestic students. Application fee: $50. Electronic applications accepted. *Expenses:* Tuition, state resident: full-time $7200; part-time $344 per credit hour. Tuition, nonresident: full-time $21,900; part-time $944 per credit hour. Tuition and fees vary according to course load and program. *Financial support:* Fellowships, research assistantships, teaching assistantships, unspecified assistantships available. *Unit head:* Dr. Patricia K. Hunt-Hurst, Department Head, 706-542-4891, Fax: 706-542-4862, E-mail: phunt@fcs.uga.edu. *Application contact:* Dr. Soyoung Kim, Graduate Coordinator, 706-542-4887, E-mail: skim@fcs.uga.edu.

University of Kentucky, Graduate School, College of Design, Program in Interior Design, Merchandising, and Textiles, Lexington, KY 40506-0032. Offers MAIDM, MSIDM. *Degree requirements:* For master's, comprehensive exam, thesis optional. *Entrance requirements:* For master's, GRE General Test, minimum undergraduate GPA of 2.75. Additional exam requirements/recommendations for international students: Required—TOEFL (minimum score 550 paper-based; 213 computer-based). Electronic applications accepted. *Faculty research:* Interior design, apparel merchandising, textile evaluation, creativity in design, social-psychological aspects of dress and interiors.

University of Manitoba, Faculty of Graduate Studies, Faculty of Architecture, Department of Interior Design, Winnipeg, MB R3T 2N2, Canada. Offers MID. *Accreditation:* CIDA.

University of Massachusetts Amherst, Graduate School, College of Humanities and Fine Arts, Department of Art, Programs in Architecture and Design, Amherst, MA 01003. Offers architecture and design (M Arch); historic preservation (MS); interior design (MS). Part-time programs available. *Students:* 55 full-time (25 women), 5 part-time (4 women); includes 4 minority (1 Asian, non-Hispanic/Latino; 2 Hispanic/Latino; 1 Native Hawaiian or other Pacific Islander, non-Hispanic/Latino), 7 international. Average age 32. 131 applicants, 65% accepted, 33 enrolled. In 2010, 13 master's awarded. *Degree requirements:* For master's, thesis or alternative, project. *Entrance requirements:* For master's, GRE General Test (M Arch only), portfolio (MS only). Additional exam requirements/recommendations for international students: Required—TOEFL (minimum score 550 paper-based; 213 computer-based; 80 iBT), IELTS (minimum score 6.5). *Application deadline:* For fall admission, 2/1 for domestic and international students. Applications are processed on a rolling basis. Application fee: $50 ($65 for international students). Electronic applications accepted. *Expenses:* Tuition, state resident: full-time $2640. Required fees: $8282. One-time fee: $357 full-time. *Financial support:* Fellowships, research assistantships, teaching assistantships, career-related internships or fieldwork, Federal Work-Study, scholarships/grants, traineeships, health care benefits, tuition waivers (full), and unspecified assistantships available. Support available to part-time students. Financial award application deadline: 2/1; financial award applicants required to submit FAFSA. *Unit head:* Dr. Max Page, Graduate Program Director, 413-545-0943, Fax: 413-545-3929. *Application contact:* Jean M. Ames, Supervisor of Admissions, 413-545-0722, Fax: 413-577-0100, E-mail: gradadm@grad.umass.edu.

University of Memphis, Graduate School, College of Communication and Fine Arts, Department of Art, Memphis, TN 38152. Offers art (Graduate Certificate); art history (MA), including Egyptian art and archaeology, general art history; ceramics (MFA); graphic design (MFA); interior design (MFA); painting (MFA); printmaking/photography (MFA); sculpture (MFA). *Accreditation:* NASAD (one or more programs are accredited). *Faculty:* 20 full-time (7 women), 4 part-time/adjunct (2 women). *Students:* 39 full-time (26 women), 10 part-time (8 women); includes 4 Black or African American, non-Hispanic/Latino; 1 Asian, non-Hispanic/Latino, 1 international. Average age 29. 44 applicants, 77% accepted, 22 enrolled. In 2010, 16 master's, 5 other advanced degrees awarded. *Degree requirements:* For master's, 2 foreign languages, comprehensive exam, thesis. *Entrance requirements:* For master's, GRE General Test or MAT, portfolio (MFA). *Application deadline:* For fall admission, 8/1 for domestic students; for spring admission, 12/1 for domestic students. Applications are processed on a rolling basis. Application fee: $35 ($60 for international students). *Financial support:* In 2010–11, 38 students received support; research assistantships with full tuition reimbursements available, teaching assistantships with full tuition reimbursements available, Federal Work-Study, scholarships/grants, and unspecified assistantships available. Financial award application deadline: 2/15; financial award applicants required to submit FAFSA. *Faculty research:* Online collaborative learning, advanced art history studies, electronic publishing/design, studio arts, architectural studies. *Unit head:* Prof. Richard Lou, Chair, 901-678-2216, Fax: 901-678-2735, E-mail: gmyatt@memphis.edu. *Application contact:* Greely Myat, Graduate Studies Coordinator, 901-678-2650.

University of Minnesota, Twin Cities Campus, Graduate School, College of Design, Department of Design, Housing, and Apparel, Minneapolis, MN 55455-0213. Offers apparel (MA, MS, PhD); design communication (MA, MS, PhD); housing studies (MA, MS, PhD, Postbaccalaureate Certificate); interactive design (MFA); interior design (MA, MS, PhD). Part-time programs available. *Degree requirements:* For master's and Postbaccalaureate Certificate, comprehensive exam, thesis (for some programs); for doctorate, comprehensive exam, thesis/dissertation. *Entrance requirements:* For master's, GRE General Test, minimum GPA of 3.0 (preferred), portfolio, 3 letters of recommendation; for doctorate, GRE General Test, minimum GPA of 3.0 (preferred), portfolio, 3 letters of recommendation, writing sample; for Postbaccalaureate Certificate, GRE General Test, minimum GPA of 3.0 (preferred). Additional exam requirements/recommendations for international students: Required—TOEFL (minimum score 550 paper-based; 213 computer-based; 79 iBT). Electronic applications accepted. *Faculty research:* Housing policy and community development; consumer behavior; interactive design; design history; social, cultural, and behavioral issues related to designed environments.

University of Nebraska–Lincoln, Graduate College, College of Architecture, Department of Architecture, Lincoln, NE 68588. Offers architecture (M Arch, MS, PhD); interior design (MS); M Arch/MBA; M Arch/MCRP. *Entrance requirements:* Additional exam requirements/recommendations for international students: Required—TOEFL. Electronic applications accepted.

The University of North Carolina at Greensboro, Graduate School, School of Human Environmental Sciences, Department of Interior Architecture, Greensboro, NC 27412-5001. Offers historic preservation (Certificate); interior architecture (MS); museum studies (Certificate). *Degree requirements:* For master's, thesis. *Entrance requirements:* For master's, GRE General Test or MAT, bachelor's degree in interior design, interview, portfolio. Additional exam requirements/recommendations for international students: Required—TOEFL. Electronic applications accepted.

University of Oregon, Graduate School, School of Architecture and Allied Arts, Department of Architecture, Eugene, OR 97403. Offers architecture (M Arch); interior architecture (MI Arch). *Accreditation:* CIDA. *Degree requirements:* For master's, thesis (for some programs). *Entrance requirements:* For master's, GRE General Test. Additional exam requirements/recommendations for international students: Required—TOEFL. *Faculty research:* Innovation in housing design and design production, climate responsive design, passive heating and cooling, computer software development for design applications, vernacular architecture.

Utah State University, School of Graduate Studies, College of Humanities, Arts and Social Sciences, Program in Interior Design, Logan, UT 84322. Offers MS. Part-time programs available. Postbaccalaureate distance learning degree programs offered. *Entrance requirements:* For master's, GRE General Test, MAT, minimum GPA of 3.0. Additional exam requirements/recommendations for international students: Required—TOEFL.

Virginia Commonwealth University, Graduate School, School of the Arts, Department of Graphic Design, Richmond, VA 23284-9005. Offers design/visual communications (MFA); interior environment (MFA). *Accreditation:* NASAD. *Faculty:* 15 full-time (3 women). *Students:* 35 full-time (27 women), 4 part-time (2 women); includes 3 minority (all Asian, non-Hispanic/Latino), 1 international. 212 applicants, 19% accepted, 25 enrolled. In 2010, 13 master's awarded. *Degree requirements:* For master's, thesis, exhibition. *Entrance requirements:* For master's, portfolio. Additional exam requirements/recommendations for international students: Required—TOEFL (minimum score 600 paper-based; 250 computer-based; 100 iBT). *Application deadline:* For fall admission, 2/1 for domestic students. Application fee: $50. Electronic applications accepted. *Expenses:* Tuition, state resident: full-time $4308; part-time $479 per credit hour. Tuition, nonresident: full-time $8942; part-time $994 per credit hour. Required fees: $2000; $85 per credit hour. Tuition and fees vary according to course level, course load, degree level, campus/location and program. *Financial support:* Fellowships, teaching assistantships, career-related internships or fieldwork, Federal Work-Study, institutionally sponsored loans, and tuition waivers (full and partial) available. Support available to part-time students. Financial award application deadline: 3/15. *Faculty research:* Conducting visual or theoretical research, and in investigating the intersection of function and expression in design problem solving. *Unit head:* John DeMao, Chair, 804-828-1709, E-mail: jdemao@vcu.edu. *Application contact:* John DeMao, Chair, 804-828-1709, E-mail: jdemao@vcu.edu.

Virginia Polytechnic Institute and State University, Graduate School, College of Liberal Arts and Human Sciences, Department of Apparel, Housing, and Resource Management, Blacksburg, VA 24061. Offers apparel business and economics (MS, PhD); apparel product design and analysis (MS, PhD); apparel quality analysis (MS, PhD); consumer studies (MS, PhD); family financial management (MS, PhD); household equipment (MS, PhD); housing (MS, PhD); interior design (MS, PhD); resource management (MS, PhD). *Faculty:* 13 full-time (all women). *Students:* 7 full-time (all women), 2 part-time (both women); includes 1 Black or African American, non-Hispanic/Latino; 1 Asian, non-Hispanic/Latino; 1 Hispanic/Latino, 4 international. Average age 39. In 2010, 3 master's, 2 doctorates awarded. *Degree requirements:* For master's, comprehensive exam (for some programs), thesis (for some programs); for doctorate, comprehensive exam (for some programs), thesis/dissertation (for some programs). *Entrance requirements:* For master's and doctorate, GRE. Additional exam requirements/recommendations for international students: Required—TOEFL (minimum score 550 paper-based; 213 computer-based). *Application deadline:* For fall admission, 7/1 for domestic and international students; for spring admission, 12/1 for domestic and international students. Applications are processed on a rolling basis. Application fee: $65. Electronic applications accepted. *Expenses:* Tuition, state resident: full-time $9399; part-time $488 per credit hour. Tuition, nonresident: full-time $17,854; part-time $957.75 per credit hour. Required fees: $1534. Full-time tuition and fees vary according to program. *Financial support:* In 2010–11, 6 teaching assistantships with full tuition reimbursements (averaging $12,561 per year) were awarded; career-related internships or fieldwork, Federal Work-Study, scholarships/grants, health care benefits, and unspecified assistantships also available. Financial award application deadline: 1/15. *Faculty research:* Housing for elderly, affordable housing, household time use, phosphate laundry study, economic well-living. Total annual research expenditures: $11,651. *Unit head:* Dr. LuAnn R. Gaskill, UNIT HEAD, 540-231-4781, Fax: 540-231-3250, E-mail: lagaskil@vt.edu. *Application contact:* Julia Beemish, Contact, 540-231-8881, Fax: 540-231-3250, E-mail: jbeamish@vt.edu.

Washington State University, Graduate School, College of Agricultural, Human, and Natural Resource Sciences, Department of Apparel, Merchandising, Design, and Textiles, Pullman, WA 99164. Offers apparel, merchandising, design and textiles (MA); interdisciplinary (PhD); interior design (MA). Part-time programs available. *Faculty:* 8. *Students:* 7 full-time (6 women), 2 part-time (both women); includes 2 minority (1 Asian, non-Hispanic/Latino; 1 Native Hawaiian or other Pacific Islander, non-Hispanic/Latino), 2 international. Average age 33. 16 applicants, 31% accepted, 5 enrolled. In 2010, 6 master's awarded. *Degree requirements:* For master's, comprehensive exam (for some programs), thesis, oral exam; for doctorate, comprehensive exam, thesis/dissertation. *Entrance requirements:* For master's, GRE, minimum GPA of 3.0, 3 writing samples, 3 letters of recommendation, portfolio. Additional exam requirements/recommendations for international students: Required—TOEFL, IELTS. *Application deadline:* For fall admission, 1/11 priority date for domestic students, 1/10 for international students; for spring admission, 7/1 for domestic and international students. Applications are processed on a rolling basis. Application fee: $50. Electronic applications accepted. *Expenses:* Tuition, state resident: full-time $8552; part-time $443 per credit. Tuition, nonresident: full-time $21,650; part-time $1083 per credit. Required fees: $846. *Financial support:* In 2010–11, research assistantships with full and partial tuition reimbursements (averaging $18,204 per year), 5 teaching assistantships with full and partial tuition reimbursements (averaging $18,204 per year) were awarded; career-related internships or fieldwork, Federal Work-Study, institutionally sponsored loans, and scholarships/grants also available. Financial award application deadline: 2/15; financial award applicants required to submit FAFSA. *Faculty research:* Product development, design theory, cultural diversity, computer design accessibility. Total annual research expenditures: $26,000. *Unit head:* Dr. Karen K. Leonas, Department Chair, 509-335-1233, Fax: 509-355-7299, E-mail: kleonas@wsu.edu. *Application contact:* Graduate School Admissions, 800-GRADWSU, Fax: 509-335-1949, E-mail: gradsch@wsu.edu.

Washington State University Spokane, Graduate Programs, Interdisciplinary Design Institute, Spokane, WA 99210. Offers architecture (M Arch, MS); design (Dr DES); interior design (MA); landscape architecture (MS). Part-time programs available. *Faculty:* 7. *Students:* 9 full-time (6 women), 2 part-time (both women); includes 1 Asian, non-Hispanic/Latino, 5 international. Average age 35. In 2010, 18 master's awarded. *Degree requirements:* For master's, comprehensive exam (for some programs), thesis (for some programs); for doctorate, comprehensive exam, thesis/dissertation. *Entrance requirements:* For master's, minimum GPA of 3.0, portfolio of design work, 3 letters of recommendation (M Arch); for doctorate, minimum graduate GPA of 3.5. Additional exam requirements/recommendations for international students: Required—TOEFL (minimum score 550 paper-based; 213 computer-based). *Application deadline:* For fall admission, 1/10 priority date for domestic students, 1/10 for international students; for spring admission, 7/1 priority date for domestic students, 7/1 for international students. Application fee: $50. *Financial support:* In 2010–11, research assistantships with full and partial tuition reimbursements (averaging $14,634 per year), teaching assistantships with full and partial tuition reimbursements (averaging $13,383 per year) were awarded. Financial award application deadline: 2/15. *Faculty research:* Environment-behavior relationships, land use and environmental planning, urban space as interior design, art and architectural aesthetics. Total annual research expenditures: $84,000. *Unit head:* Dr. Nancy H. Blossom, Director, 509-358-7513, E-mail: blossom@wsu.edu. *Application contact:* Graduate School Admissions, 800-GRADWSU, Fax: 509-335-1949, E-mail: gradsch@wsu.edu.

Medical Illustration

Georgia Health Sciences University, College of Graduate Studies, Program in Medical Illustration, Augusta, GA 30912. Offers MS. *Accreditation:* ARCMI. *Faculty:* 2 full-time (0 women), 2 part-time/adjunct (0 women). *Students:* 17 full-time (11 women); includes 1 Black or African American, non-Hispanic/Latino; 2 Asian, non-Hispanic/Latino; 1 Two or more races, non-Hispanic/Latino. Average age 26. 18 applicants, 56% accepted, 8 enrolled. In 2010, 10 master's awarded. *Degree requirements:* For master's, thesis or alternative, project. *Entrance requirements:* For master's, GRE General Test, portfolio. Additional exam requirements/recommendations for international students: Required—TOEFL (minimum score 550 paper-based; 213 computer-based; 79 iBT). *Application deadline:* For fall admission, 1/31 for domestic and international students. Application fee: $30. Electronic applications accepted. *Expenses:* Tuition, state resident: full-time $7500; part-time $313 per semester hour. Tuition, nonresident: full-time $24,772; part-time $1033 per semester hour. Required fees: $1112. *Financial support:* In 2010–11, 11 students received support. Federal Work-Study and institutionally sponsored loans available. Support available to part-time students. Financial award application deadline: 5/31; financial award applicants required to submit FAFSA. *Faculty research:* Digital visual communication modalities, information science education, Southwestern Native American art pedagogy, medical illustration pedagogy, public health/visual education. *Unit head:* Dr. Douglas Keskula, Acting Chair, 706-721-2621, Fax: 706-721-7312, E-mail: dkeskula@georgiahealth.edu. *Application contact:* Dr. Steven Harrison, Chair, Associate Professor and Graduate Program Director, 706-721-3266, E-mail: sharriso@georgiahealth.edu.

The Johns Hopkins University, School of Medicine, Graduate Programs in Medicine, Department of Art as Applied to Medicine, Baltimore, MD 21205. Offers medical and biological illustration (MA). *Accreditation:* ARCMI. *Faculty:* 8 full-time (2 women), 15 part-time/adjunct (7 women). *Students:* 13 full-time (10 women), 1 (woman) part-time, 2 international. Average age 24. 48 applicants, 15% accepted, 6 enrolled. In 2010, 6 master's awarded. *Degree requirements:* For master's, thesis. *Application deadline:* For fall admission, 1/15 for domestic and international students. Applications are processed on a rolling basis. Application fee: $85. Electronic applications accepted. *Financial support:* In 2010–11, 13 students received support, including 12 fellowships with partial tuition reimbursements available (averaging $17,000 per year), 4 teaching assistantships (averaging $500 per year); institutionally sponsored loans, scholarships/grants, tuition waivers (partial), and unspecified assistantships also available. Financial award application deadline: 5/31; financial award applicants required to submit FAFSA. *Faculty research:* Visualization, digital media, animation and 3D modeling, instructional design, facial prosthetics and anaplastology. *Unit head:* Gary Lees, Chairman and Director, 410-955-3213, Fax: 410-955-1085, E-mail: medart-info@jhmi.edu. *Application contact:* Dacia M. Balch, Administrative Coordinator, 410-955-3213, Fax: 410-955-1085, E-mail: medart-info@jhmi.edu.

Rochester Institute of Technology, Graduate Enrollment Services, College of Imaging Arts and Sciences, School of Art, Program in Medical Illustration, Rochester, NY 14623-5603. Offers MFA. Part-time programs available. *Students:* 7 full-time (6 women), 3 part-time (2 women); includes 1 Asian, non-Hispanic/Latino. Average age 34. 14 applicants, 71% accepted, 6 enrolled. In 2010, 2 master's awarded. *Degree requirements:* For master's, thesis. *Entrance requirements:* For master's, portfolio, minimum GPA of 3.0. Additional exam requirements/recommendations for international students: Required—TOEFL (minimum score 550 paper-based; 213 computer-based; 79 iBT) or IELTS (minimum score 6.5). *Application deadline:* For fall admission, 2/15 priority date for domestic and international students. Applications are processed on a rolling basis. Application fee: $50. Electronic applications accepted. *Expenses:* Tuition: Full-time $33,234; part-time $924 per credit hour. Required fees: $219. *Financial support:* In 2010–11, 3 students received support; teaching assistantships with partial tuition reimbursements available, career-related internships or fieldwork, institutionally sponsored loans, scholarships/grants, and unspecified assistantships available. Support available to part-time students. Financial award applicants required to submit FAFSA. *Unit head:* Glen Hintz, Graduate Program Director, 585-475-2443, Fax: 585-475-6447, E-mail: grhfad@rit.edu. *Application contact:* Diane Ellison, Assistant Vice President, Graduate Enrollment Services, 585-475-2229, Fax: 585-475-7164, E-mail: gradinfo@rit.edu.

University of Illinois at Chicago, Graduate College, College of Applied Health Sciences, Program in Biomedical Visualization, Chicago, IL 60607-7128. Offers MS. *Accreditation:* ARCMI. *Degree requirements:* For master's, thesis. *Entrance requirements:* For master's, GRE General Test, minimum GPA of 2.75. Additional exam requirements/recommendations for international students: Required—TOEFL. Electronic applications accepted. *Expenses:* Contact institution. *Faculty research:* Medical illustration, graphics, reconstruction, anatomical modeling.

The University of Texas Southwestern Medical Center at Dallas, Southwestern School of Health Professions, Biomedical Communications Program, Dallas, TX 75390. Offers MA. *Accreditation:* ARCMI. *Students:* 9 full-time (7 women), 6 part-time (5 women); includes 3 minority (2 Asian, non-Hispanic/Latino; 1 Hispanic/Latino), 1 international. Average age 26. 33 applicants, 27% accepted, 4 enrolled. In 2010, 8 master's awarded. *Degree requirements:* For master's, thesis. *Entrance requirements:* For master's, GRE General Test, minimum GPA of 3.0. *Application deadline:* For spring admission, 9/1 priority date for domestic students. Applications are processed on a rolling basis. Application fee: $0. Electronic applications accepted. *Financial support:* In 2010–11, 4 teaching assistantships were awarded; career-related internships or fieldwork and institutionally sponsored loans also available. Financial award application deadline: 3/1; financial award applicants required to submit FAFSA. *Faculty research:* Breast self-examination to indigent populations. *Unit head:* Lewis E. Calver, Chair, 214-648-4699, Fax: 214-648-5353, E-mail: lcalve@mednet.swmed.edu. *Application contact:* Sonja Shryer, Education Coordinator, 214-648-4634, Fax: 214-648-5353, E-mail: marcelle.hanson@utsouthwestern.edu.

Photography

Academy of Art University, Graduate Program, School of Photography, San Francisco, CA 94105-3410. Offers MFA. *Accreditation:* NASAD. Part-time programs available. Post-baccalaureate distance learning degree programs offered (no on-campus study). *Faculty:* 16 full-time (6 women), 85 part-time/adjunct (28 women). *Students:* 199 full-time (127 women), 275 part-time (167 women); includes 24 Black or African American, non-Hispanic/Latino; 3 American Indian or Alaska Native, non-Hispanic/Latino; 14 Asian, non-Hispanic/Latino; 23 Hispanic/Latino, 64 international. Average age 34. 143 applicants. In 2010, 48 master's awarded. *Degree requirements:* For master's, thesis, final review. *Entrance requirements:* For master's, portfolio. *Application deadline:* For fall admission, 9/7 for domestic and international students; for spring admission, 2/2 for domestic and international students. Applications are processed on a rolling basis. Application fee: $100 ($500 for international students). Electronic applications accepted. *Expenses:* Tuition: Full-time $20,160; part-time $840 per semester hour. Required fees: $45 per semester. *Financial support:* Career-related internships or fieldwork and Federal Work-Study available. Support available to part-time students. Financial award application deadline: 8/10; financial award applicants required to submit FAFSA. *Application contact:* 800-544-ARTS, Fax: 415-263-4130, E-mail: info@academyart.edu.

Bard College, International Center of Photography, Annandale-on-Hudson, NY 12504. Offers advanced photographic studies (MFA).

Barry University, School of Arts and Sciences, Department of Fine Arts, Miami Shores, FL 33161-6695. Offers photography (MA, MFA). *Degree requirements:* For master's, thesis (for some programs). *Entrance requirements:* For master's, GRE General Test, minimum GPA of 3.0. Electronic applications accepted. *Faculty research:* Inclusion education, exceptional education, art-based assessments.

Bradley University, Graduate School, Slane College of Communications and Fine Arts, Department of Art, Peoria, IL 61625-0002. Offers ceramics (MA, MFA); drawing/illustration (MA, MFA); interdisciplinary art (MA, MFA); painting (MA, MFA); photography (MA, MFA); printmaking (MA, MFA); sculpture (MA, MFA); visual communication and design (MA, MFA). *Accreditation:* NASAD. Part-time programs available. *Degree requirements:* For master's, comprehensive exam, thesis, final exhibit. *Entrance requirements:* For master's, portfolio, 2 letters of recommendation. Additional exam requirements/recommendations for international students: Required—TOEFL (minimum score 550 paper-based; 213 computer-based; 79 iBT).

Brooklyn College of the City University of New York, Division of Graduate Studies, Department of Art, Brooklyn, NY 11210-2889. Offers art history (MA, PhD); digital art (MFA); drawing and painting (MFA); photography (MFA); printmaking (MFA); sculpture (MFA). Part-time programs available. *Students:* 23 full-time (16 women), 26 part-time (20 women); includes 13 minority (5 Black or African American, non-Hispanic/Latino; 3 Asian, non-Hispanic/Latino; 5 Hispanic/Latino), 2 international. Average age 30. 119 applicants, 45% accepted, 17 enrolled. In 2010, 9 master's awarded. *Degree requirements:* For master's, thesis. *Entrance requirements:* For master's, bachelor's degree in art, portfolio, 2 letters of recommendation. Additional exam requirements/recommendations for international students: Required—TOEFL (minimum score 500 paper-based; 173 computer-based; 61 iBT). *Application deadline:* For fall admission, 2/1 priority date for domestic students, 2/1 for international students. Applications are processed on a rolling basis. Application fee: $125. Electronic applications accepted. *Expenses:* Tuition, state resident: full-time $7360; part-time $310 per credit hour. Tuition, nonresident: full-time $13,800; part-time $575 per credit hour. Required fees: $190 per semester. *Financial support:* Career-related internships or fieldwork, Federal Work-Study, institutionally sponsored loans, scholarships/grants, and painting awards available. Support available to part-time students. Financial award application deadline: 5/1; financial award applicants required to submit FAFSA. *Unit head:* Dr. Michael Mallory, Chairperson, 718-951-5181, E-mail: mmallory@brooklyn.cuny.edu. *Application contact:* Hernan Sierra, Graduate Admissions Coordinator, 718-951-4536, Fax: 718-951-4506, E-mail: grads@brooklyn.cuny.edu.

Brooks Institute, Graduate Program in Professional Photography, Santa Barbara, CA 93101. Offers MFA. Evening/weekend programs available. *Degree requirements:* For master's, thesis. *Entrance requirements:* For master's, portfolio review testing procedure (written exam), minimum GPA of 3.0, 3 letters of recommendation. Additional exam requirements/recommendations for international students: Required—TOEFL (minimum score 580 paper-based; 237 computer-based). Electronic applications accepted.

California College of the Arts, Graduate Programs, Programs in Fine Art, San Francisco, CA 94107. Offers ceramics (MFA); film/video/performance (MFA); glass (MFA); jewelry/metal arts (MFA); painting/drawing (MFA); photography (MFA); printmaking (MFA); sculpture (MFA); textiles (MFA); wood/furniture (MFA). *Accreditation:* NASAD. *Faculty:* 20 full-time (10 women), 25 part-time/adjunct (14 women). *Students:* 95 full-time (66 women), 12 part-time (9 women); includes 3 Black or African American, non-Hispanic/Latino; 1 American Indian or Alaska Native, non-Hispanic/Latino; 5 Asian, non-Hispanic/Latino; 20 Hispanic/Latino; 2 Native Hawaiian or other Pacific Islander, non-Hispanic/Latino, 7 international. Average age 30. 462 applicants, 37% accepted, 55 enrolled. In 2010, 173 master's awarded. *Degree requirements:* For master's, thesis, exhibit. *Entrance requirements:* For master's, appropriate bachelor's degree, portfolio, resume, 2 letters of recommendation, transcript. Additional exam requirements/recommendations for international students: Required—TOEFL (minimum score 600 paper-based; 250 computer-based; 100 iBT). *Application deadline:* For fall admission, 1/5 for domestic and international students. Application fee: $70. Electronic applications accepted. *Expenses:* Tuition: Full-time $38,550; part-time $1285 per unit. One-time fee: $185 full-time. *Financial support:* In 2010–11, 12 fellowships (averaging $27,000 per year), teaching assistantships (averaging $2,000 per year) were awarded; career-related internships or fieldwork, Federal Work-Study, scholarships/grants, and health care benefits also available. Financial award application deadline: 3/1; financial award applicants required to submit FAFSA. *Unit head:* Ted Purves, Chair, 415-551-9214, Fax: 415-703-9539, E-mail: tpurves@cca.edu. *Application contact:* Heidi Geis, Assistant Director of Graduate Admissions, 415-703-9523 Ext. 9533, Fax: 415-703-9539, E-mail: hgeis@cca.edu.

California Institute of the Arts, School of Art, Valencia, CA 91355-2340. Offers art (MFA, Adv C); graphic design (MFA, Adv C); photography (MFA, Adv C). *Accreditation:* NASAD (one or more programs are accredited). *Degree requirements:* For master's, final project. *Entrance requirements:* For master's, portfolio. Additional exam requirements/recommendations for international students: Required—TOEFL. Electronic applications accepted.

California State University, Fullerton, Graduate Studies, College of the Arts, Department of Art, Fullerton, CA 92834-9480. Offers art (MA, MFA), including ceramics (MFA), crafts, creative photography (MFA), design (MFA), drawing and painting, printmaking (MFA), sculpture; art history (MA); design (MA). *Accreditation:* NASAD (one or more programs are accredited). Part-time programs available. *Students:* 50 full-time (34 women), 38 part-time (24 women); includes 1 Black or African American, non-Hispanic/Latino; 12 Asian, non-Hispanic/Latino; 11 Hispanic/Latino, 8 international. Average age 35. 113 applicants, 26% accepted, 26 enrolled. In 2010, 14 master's awarded. *Degree requirements:* For master's, project or thesis. *Entrance requirements:* For master's, minimum GPA of 2.5 in last 60 units of course work, portfolio. Application fee: $55. *Financial support:* Career-related internships or fieldwork, Federal Work-Study, institutionally sponsored loans, and scholarships/grants available. Support available to part-time students. Financial award application deadline: 3/1; financial award applicants required to submit FAFSA. *Unit head:* Larry Johnson, Chair, 657-278-3471. *Application contact:* Admissions/Applications, 657-278-2371.

California State University, Los Angeles, Graduate Studies, College of Arts and Letters, Department of Art, Los Angeles, CA 90032-8530. Offers art (MA), including art education, art history, art therapy, ceramics, metals, and textiles, design (MA, MFA), painting, sculpture, and graphic arts, photography; fine arts (MFA), including crafts, design (MA, MFA), studio arts. *Accreditation:* NASAD (one or more programs are accredited). Part-time and evening/weekend programs available. *Faculty:* 9 full-time (5 women), 3 part-time/adjunct (2 women). *Students:* 27 full-time (19 women), 33 part-time (22 women); includes 24 minority (3 Black or African American, non-Hispanic/Latino; 7 Asian, non-Hispanic/Latino; 13 Hispanic/Latino; 1 Two or more races, non-Hispanic/Latino), 9 international. Average age 36. 19 applicants, 100% accepted, 13 enrolled. In 2010, 26 master's awarded. *Degree requirements:* For master's, comprehensive exam, project or thesis. *Entrance requirements:* For master's, portfolio. Additional exam requirements/recommendations for international students: Required—TOEFL (minimum

Photography

California State University, Los Angeles (continued)
score 500 paper-based; 173 computer-based). *Application deadline:* For fall admission, 5/1 for domestic and international students. Applications are processed on a rolling basis. Application fee: $55. Electronic applications accepted. *Financial support:* Federal Work-Study available. Support available to part-time students. Financial award application deadline: 3/1. *Faculty research:* The artist and the book, conceptual art, ceramic processes, computer graphics, architectural graphics. *Unit head:* Dr. Abbas Daneshvari, Chair, 323-343-4010, Fax: 323-343-4045, E-mail: adanesh@calstatela.edu. *Application contact:* Dr. Alan Muchlinski, Dean of Graduate Studies, 323-343-3820, Fax: 323-343-5653, E-mail: amuchli@exchange.calstatela.edu.

Claremont Graduate University, Graduate Programs, School of Arts and Humanities, Department of Art, Claremont, CA 91711. Offers digital media (MA, MFA); drawing (MA, MFA); installation (MA, MFA); new genre (MA, MFA); painting (MA, MFA); performance (MA, MFA); photography (MA, MFA); sculpture (MA, MFA). Part-time programs available. *Faculty:* 4 full-time (1 woman). *Students:* 60 full-time (33 women); includes 5 Asian, non-Hispanic/Latino; 7 Hispanic/Latino, 3 international. Average age 34. In 2010, 29 master's awarded. *Degree requirements:* For master's, final project show. *Entrance requirements:* For master's, BA in art or BFA, slide review. Additional exam requirements/recommendations for international students: Required—TOEFL (minimum score 550 paper-based; 213 computer-based; 80 iBT). *Application deadline:* For fall admission, 2/1 priority date for domestic students. Applications are processed on a rolling basis. Application fee: $60. Electronic applications accepted. *Expenses:* Contact institution. *Financial support:* Fellowships, research assistantships, teaching assistantships, Federal Work-Study, institutionally sponsored loans, and scholarships/grants available. Support available to part-time students. Financial award application deadline: 2/15; financial award applicants required to submit FAFSA. *Faculty research:* Acoustic sculpture, feminization of abstraction, installation sculpture. *Unit head:* David Pagel, Chair, 909-607-2479, Fax: 909-607-1276, E-mail: david.pagel@cgu.edu. *Application contact:* Pat Evans, Program Administrator, 909-607-9292, Fax: 909-607-1276, E-mail: patricia.evans@cgu.edu.

Columbia College Chicago, Graduate School, Department of Photography, Chicago, IL 60605-1996. Offers MA, MFA. *Students:* 20 full-time (12 women), 2 part-time (1 woman); includes 1 American Indian or Alaska Native, non-Hispanic/Latino; 1 Asian, non-Hispanic/Latino; 3 Hispanic/Latino. Average age 26. 97 applicants, 20% accepted, 7 enrolled. In 2010, 8 master's awarded. *Degree requirements:* For master's, thesis, project. *Entrance requirements:* For master's, minimum GPA of 3.0, portfolio. Additional exam requirements/recommendations for international students: Required—TOEFL (minimum score 550 paper-based; 213 computer-based). *Application deadline:* For fall admission, 1/14 for domestic and international students. Application fee: $55. Electronic applications accepted. *Expenses:* Tuition: Full-time $16,966; part-time $684 per credit. Required fees: $520; $113 per semester. One-time fee: $150 full-time. Tuition and fees vary according to course load and program. *Financial support:* Fellowships, Federal Work-Study and scholarships/grants available. Support available to part-time students. Financial award application deadline: 8/13; financial award applicants required to submit FAFSA. *Unit head:* Paul D'Amato, Coordinator, MFA Program, 312-369-7036, E-mail: pdamato@colum.edu. *Application contact:* Cate Lagueux, Director of Graduate Admissions, 312-369-7260, Fax: 312-369-8047, E-mail: gradstudy@colum.edu.

Columbia University, School of the Arts, Visual Arts Division, New York, NY 10027. Offers new genres (MFA); painting (MFA); photography (MFA); printmaking (MFA); sculpture (MFA). *Degree requirements:* For master's, thesis. *Entrance requirements:* For master's, 3 letters of recommendation, portfolio, resume. Additional exam requirements/recommendations for international students: Required—TOEFL (minimum score 600 paper-based; 250 computer-based; 100 iBT). Electronic applications accepted.

See Close-Up on page 295.

Cornell University, Graduate School, Graduate Fields of Architecture, Art and Planning, Field of Art, Ithaca, NY 14853-0001. Offers creative visual arts (MFA), including painting, photography, printmaking, sculpture. *Faculty:* 12 full-time (5 women). *Students:* 11 full-time (6 women); includes 1 Asian, non-Hispanic/Latino; 1 Hispanic/Latino, 2 international. Average age 31. 148 applicants, 5% accepted, 5 enrolled. In 2010, 3 master's awarded. *Degree requirements:* For master's, thesis, exhibit. *Entrance requirements:* For master's, slide portfolio of 10-20 slides, 3 letters of recommendation, resume. Additional exam requirements/recommendations for international students: Required—TOEFL (minimum score 550 paper-based; 213 computer-based; 77 iBT). *Application deadline:* For fall admission, 2/15 for domestic students. Application fee: $70. Electronic applications accepted. *Expenses:* Tuition: Full-time $29,500. Required fees: $76. Tuition and fees vary according to degree level and program. *Financial support:* In 2010–11, 11 teaching assistantships with full tuition reimbursements were awarded; fellowships with full tuition reimbursements, research assistantships with full tuition reimbursements, institutionally sponsored loans, scholarships/grants, health care benefits, tuition waivers (full and partial), and unspecified assistantships also available. Financial award applicants required to submit FAFSA. *Faculty research:* Painting, sculpture, photography, printmaking. *Unit head:* Director of Graduate Studies, 607-255-6730, Fax: 607-255-3462. *Application contact:* Graduate Field Assistant, 607-255-6730, Fax: 607-255-3462, E-mail: artinfo@cornell.edu.

Cranbrook Academy of Art, Graduate School, Program in Fine Arts, Bloomfield Hills, MI 48303-0801. Offers ceramics (MFA); design (MFA), including graphic design; fiber arts (MFA); metalsmithing (MFA); painting (MFA); photography (MFA); printmaking (MFA); sculpture (MFA). *Accreditation:* NASAD. *Degree requirements:* For master's, thesis, exhibit. *Entrance requirements:* Additional exam requirements/recommendations for international students: Required—TOEFL (minimum score 550 paper-based; 213 computer-based).

The George Washington University, Columbian College of Arts and Sciences, Department of Fine Arts and Art History, Washington, DC 20052. Offers art history (MA), including art history, museum training; ceramics (MFA); drawing/painting (MFA); interior design (MFA); new media (MFA); photography (MFA); sculpture (MFA). *Accreditation:* CIDA. Part-time and evening/weekend programs available. *Faculty:* 18 full-time (9 women), 34 part-time/adjunct (25 women). *Students:* 49 full-time (44 women), 41 part-time (38 women); includes 5 Black or African American, non-Hispanic/Latino; 4 Asian, non-Hispanic/Latino; 4 Hispanic/Latino, 5 international. Average age 30. 144 applicants, 66% accepted, 40 enrolled. In 2010, 24 master's awarded. *Entrance requirements:* For master's, GRE General Test, bachelor's degree in field, minimum GPA of 3.0. Additional exam requirements/recommendations for international students: Required—TOEFL (minimum score 550 paper-based; 213 computer-based; 80 iBT). *Application deadline:* For fall admission, 3/1 priority date for domestic students, 1/15 priority date for international students; for spring admission, 10/1 priority date for domestic students, 9/1 priority date for international students. Applications are processed on a rolling basis. Application fee: $75. Electronic applications accepted. *Financial support:* In 2010–11, 12 students received support; fellowships, teaching assistantships, career-related internships or fieldwork, Federal Work-Study, and tuition waivers available. Financial award application deadline: 1/15. *Unit head:* Thomas K. Brown, Chair, 202-994-9067, E-mail: thbrown@gwu.edu. *Application contact:* Information Contact, 202-994-6085, Fax: 202-994-8657, E-mail: art@gwu.edu.

Georgia State University, College of Arts and Sciences, Department of Communication, Atlanta, GA 30302-3083. Offers film/video/digital imaging (MA); human communication and social influence (MA); mass communication (MA); moving image studies (PhD); public communication (PhD). Part-time programs available. *Degree requirements:* For master's, one foreign language, thesis or alternative; for doctorate, comprehensive exam, thesis/dissertation. *Entrance requirements:* For master's and doctorate, GRE General Test. Additional exam requirements/recommendations for international students: Required—TOEFL (minimum score 80 computer-based). Electronic applications accepted. *Faculty research:* Critical/cultural studies, rhetoric studies, film/media studies, mass communications/journalism, audience studies.

Howard University, Graduate School, Division of Fine Arts, Department of Art, Program in Fine Arts, Washington, DC 20059-0002. Offers 3D reality (sculpture and ceramics) (MFA); design (MFA); electronic studio (MFA); painting (MFA); photography (MFA). *Accreditation:* NASAD. *Degree requirements:* For master's, comprehensive exam, thesis, exhibit. *Entrance requirements:* For master's, minimum GPA of 3.0, portfolio.

Illinois State University, Graduate School, College of Fine Arts, School of Art, Normal, IL 61790-2200. Offers art history (MA, MS); ceramics (MFA, MS); drawing (MFA, MS); fibers (MFA, MS); glass (MFA, MS); graphic design (MFA, MS); metals (MFA, MS); painting (MFA, MS); photography (MFA, MS); printmaking (MFA, MS); sculpture (MFA, MS). *Accreditation:* NASAD (one or more programs are accredited). *Degree requirements:* For master's, thesis or alternative, internship. *Entrance requirements:* For master's, portfolio, sample of scholarly writing. *Faculty research:* General operations support: Normal Editions Workshop for FY2007.

Indiana State University, College of Graduate and Professional Studies, College of Arts and Sciences, Department of Art, Terre Haute, IN 47809. Offers ceramics (MA, MFA); drawing (MA, MFA); graphic design (MA, MFA); painting (MA, MFA); photography (MA, MFA); printmaking (MA, MFA); sculpture (MA, MFA). *Accreditation:* NASAD (one or more programs are accredited). Part-time programs available. *Degree requirements:* For master's, thesis or alternative, departmental qualifying exam. *Entrance requirements:* For master's, portfolio. Additional exam requirements/recommendations for international students: Required—TOEFL (minimum score 550 paper-based).

Inter American University of Puerto Rico, San Germán Campus, Graduate Studies Center, Program in Fine Arts, San Germán, PR 00683-5008. Offers ceramics (MFA); drawing (MFA); engraving (MFA); painting (MFA); photography (MFA); sculpture (MFA). *Degree requirements:* For master's, comprehensive exam, thesis. *Entrance requirements:* For master's, GRE General Test or EXADEP, minimum GPA of 3.0. *Expenses:* Tuition: Part-time $202 per credit. Required fees: $258 per semester.

James Madison University, The Graduate School, College of Visual and Performing Arts, School of Art and Art History, Harrisonburg, VA 22807. Offers art education (MA); art history (MA); ceramics (MFA); drawing/painting (MFA); metal/jewelry (MFA); photography (MFA); printmaking (MFA); sculpture (MFA); studio art (MA); weaving/fibers (MFA). *Accreditation:* NASAD. Part-time programs available. *Faculty:* 8 full-time (5 women). *Students:* 10 full-time (6 women); includes 1 minority (Black or African American, non-Hispanic/Latino). Average age 27. In 2010, 3 master's awarded. *Degree requirements:* For master's, thesis (for some programs). *Entrance requirements:* For master's, GRE General Test, language exam in French or German, portfolio, 3 letters of recommendation, research paper. Additional exam requirements/recommendations for international students: Required—TOEFL. *Application deadline:* For fall admission, 2/15 priority date for domestic students, 2/15 for international students; for spring admission, 10/15 priority date for domestic students, 10/15 for international students. Applications are processed on a rolling basis. Application fee: $55. Electronic applications accepted. *Financial support:* In 2010–11, 9 students received support, including 3 teaching assistantships with full tuition reimbursements available (averaging $8,664 per year); Federal Work-Study and 6 graduate assistantships ($7382) also available. Financial award application deadline: 3/1; financial award applicants required to submit FAFSA. *Unit head:* William Srightman, Director, 540-568-6216. *Application contact:* Lynette M. Bible, Director of Graduate Admissions, 540-568-6395, Fax: 540-568-7860, E-mail: biblelm@jmu.edu.

Lamar University, College of Graduate Studies, College of Fine Arts and Communication, Department of Art, Beaumont, TX 77710. Offers art history (MA); photography (MA); studio art (MA); visual design (MA). Part-time and evening/weekend programs available. *Faculty:* 5 full-time (3 women). *Students:* 2 full-time (1 woman), 3 part-time (2 women). Average age 42. 3 applicants, 33% accepted, 0 enrolled. *Degree requirements:* For master's, thesis. *Entrance requirements:* For master's, GRE General Test, minimum GPA of 2.5 in last 60 hours of undergraduate course work. Additional exam requirements/recommendations for international students: Required—TOEFL. *Application deadline:* For fall admission, 8/1 priority date for domestic students; for spring admission, 12/1 for domestic students. Applications are processed on a rolling basis. Application fee: $25 ($50 for international students). *Expenses:* Tuition, state resident: full-time $4160; part-time $208 per credit hour. Tuition, nonresident: full-time $10,360; part-time $518 per credit hour. *Financial support:* Fellowships, career-related internships or fieldwork, Federal Work-Study, and scholarships/grants available. Financial award application deadline: 4/1. *Faculty research:* Nineteenth century academic paintings, metal casting, pigment color stability, computer-modified photography, manipulated photography. *Unit head:* Donna M. Meeks, Chair, 409-880-8141, Fax: 409-880-1799, E-mail: meeksdm@lub002.lamar.edu. *Application contact:* Debbie Piper, Coordinator of Graduate Admissions, 409-880-8356, Fax: 409-880-8414, E-mail: gradmissions@hal.lamar.edu.

Louisiana State University and Agricultural and Mechanical College, Graduate School, College of Art and Design, School of Art, Program in Studio Art, Baton Rouge, LA 70803. Offers ceramics (MFA); graphic design (MFA); painting and drawing (MFA); photography (MFA); printmaking (MFA); sculpture (MFA). *Accreditation:* NASAD. *Students:* 45 full-time (29 women), 3 part-time (all women); includes 1 Black or African American, non-Hispanic/Latino; 4 Asian, non-Hispanic/Latino, 4 international. Average age 29. 114 applicants, 21% accepted, 14 enrolled. In 2010, 15 master's awarded. *Degree requirements:* For master's, thesis. *Entrance requirements:* For master's, minimum GPA of 3.0. Additional exam requirements/recommendations for international students: Required—TOEFL (minimum score 550 paper-based; 213 computer-based; 79 iBT), IELTS (minimum score 6.5). *Application deadline:* For fall admission, 1/25 priority date for domestic students, 5/15 for international students; for spring admission, 10/15 for international students. Applications are processed on a rolling basis. Electronic applications accepted. *Financial support:* In 2010–11, 25 students received support; research assistantships with partial tuition reimbursements available, teaching assistantships, career-related internships or fieldwork, Federal Work-Study, institutionally sponsored loans, scholarships/grants, and unspecified assistantships available. Support available to part-time students. Financial award application deadline: 3/15. *Unit head:* Tom Neff, Graduate Coordinator, 225-578-5411, Fax: 225-578-1445, E-mail: tneff@lsu.edu.

Louisiana Tech University, Graduate School, College of Liberal Arts, School of Art, Ruston, LA 71272. Offers art and graphic design (MFA); photography (MFA); studio art (MFA). *Accreditation:* NASAD. Part-time programs available. *Degree requirements:* For master's, exhibit. *Entrance requirements:* For master's, GRE General Test, portfolio.

Maryland Institute College of Art, Graduate Studies, Program in Photographic and Electronic Media, Baltimore, MD 21217. Offers MFA. *Accreditation:* NASAD. *Faculty:* 1 full-time (0 women), 4 part-time/adjunct (1 woman). *Students:* 22 full-time (10 women); includes 3 minority (2 Hispanic/Latino; 1 Two or more races, non-Hispanic/Latino), 3 international. Average age 29. In 2010, 11 master's awarded. *Degree requirements:* For master's, thesis, exhibit. *Entrance requirements:* For master's, portfolio, 40 studio credits, 6 credits in art history. Additional exam requirements/recommendations for international students: Required—TOEFL (minimum score 550 paper-based; 213 computer-based; 80 iBT). *Application deadline:* For fall admission, 1/15 for domestic and international students. Application fee: $60. *Expenses:* Tuition: Full-time $34,550; part-time $1440 per credit hour. Required fees: $1140; $570 per term. *Financial support:* In 2010–11, 22 students received support, including 22 fellowships (averaging $10,000 per year), 22 teaching assistantships (averaging $1,800 per year); career-related internships or fieldwork and scholarships/grants also available. Financial award application deadline: 3/1; financial award applicants required to submit FAFSA. *Unit head:* Timothy Druckrey, Director, 410-225-2405, Fax: 410-669-1141. *Application contact:* Scott G. Kelly, Associate Dean of Graduate Admission, 410-225-2256, Fax: 410-225-2408, E-mail: graduate@mica.edu.

Marywood University, Academic Affairs, Insalaco College of Creative and Performing Arts, Art Department, Program in Studio Art, Scranton, PA 18509-1598. Offers advertising design (MA); ceramics (MA); clay (MA); graphic design (MA); illustration (MA); painting (MA); photography (MA); printmaking (MA); sculpture (MA); weaving (MA). *Accreditation:* NASAD. *Entrance requirements:* Additional exam requirements/recommendations for international students: Required—TOEFL (minimum score 550 paper-based; 213 computer-based; 79 iBT). Electronic applications accepted. *Expenses:* Tuition: Part-time $735 per credit. Required fees:

$470 per semester. Tuition and fees vary according to degree level and campus/location. *Faculty research:* Texture and line in clay, cast bronze sculpture, color theories, book art and illustration, sculptural form.

Marywood University, Academic Affairs, Insalaco College of Creative and Performing Arts, Art Department, Program in Visual Arts, Scranton, PA 18509-1598. Offers advertising design (MFA); clay (MFA); graphic design (MFA); illustration (MFA); metals (MFA); painting (MFA); photography (MFA); printmaking (MFA). *Accreditation:* NASAD. *Entrance requirements:* Additional exam requirements/recommendations for international students: Required—TOEFL (minimum score 550 paper-based; 213 computer-based; 79 iBT). Electronic applications accepted. *Expenses:* Contact institution. *Faculty research:* Mariology, exploration of visual imagery, explorations involving drawing on the loom, clay as sculptural medium, oil paintings.

Massachusetts College of Art and Design, Graduate Programs, Master of Fine Arts (MFA) Program, Boston, MA 02115-5882. Offers ceramics (MFA); design (MFA); fibers (MFA); film/video (MFA); glass (MFA); media and performing arts (MFA); metals/jewelry (MFA); painting (MFA); photography (MFA); printmaking (MFA); sculpture (MFA). *Accreditation:* NASAD. *Faculty:* 14 full-time (7 women), 16 part-time/adjunct (10 women). *Students:* 86 full-time (51 women), 9 part-time (5 women); includes 10 minority (1 Asian, non-Hispanic/Latino; 6 Hispanic/Latino; 3 Two or more races, non-Hispanic/Latino), 14 international. Average age 34. 298 applicants, 28% accepted, 41 enrolled. In 2010, 40 master's awarded. *Degree requirements:* For master's, thesis, exhibit. *Entrance requirements:* For master's, 12 units of course work in art history, portfolio, resume, letters of reference, interview. Additional exam requirements/recommendations for international students: Required—TOEFL (minimum score 563 paper-based; 223 computer-based; 85 iBT); Recommended—IELTS (minimum score 6.5). *Application deadline:* For fall admission, 1/15 for domestic and international students. Application fee: $85. Electronic applications accepted. *Expenses:* Tuition, state resident: part-time $665 per credit. Tuition, nonresident: part-time $665 per credit. *Financial support:* In 2010–11, 19 fellowships (averaging $5,000 per year), 43 research assistantships (averaging $2,000 per year), 44 teaching assistantships (averaging $2,000 per year) were awarded; career-related internships or fieldwork and Federal Work-Study also available. Support available to part-time students. Financial award application deadline: 5/1; financial award applicants required to submit FAFSA. *Unit head:* George Creamer, Dean of Graduate Programs, 617-879-7163, Fax: 617-879-7171, E-mail: creamer@massart.edu. *Application contact:* George Creamer, Dean of Graduate Programs, 617-879-7163, Fax: 617-879-7171, E-mail: creamer@massart.edu.

Mills College, Graduate Studies, Department of Art, Oakland, CA 94613-1000. Offers ceramics (MFA); intermedia (MFA); painting (MFA); photography (MFA); sculpture (MFA). *Faculty:* 5 full-time (4 women), 9 part-time/adjunct (5 women). *Students:* 24 full-time (15 women); includes 7 minority (1 Black or African American, non-Hispanic/Latino; 2 Asian, non-Hispanic/Latino; 1 Hispanic/Latino; 3 Two or more races, non-Hispanic/Latino). Average age 33. 83 applicants, 35% accepted, 12 enrolled. In 2010, 10 master's awarded. *Degree requirements:* For master's, thesis or alternative, exhibit. *Entrance requirements:* For master's, portfolio, artist statement. Additional exam requirements/recommendations for international students: Required—TOEFL. *Application deadline:* For fall admission, 2/1 for domestic students, 12/15 for international students. Application fee: $50. *Expenses:* Contact institution. *Financial support:* In 2010–11, 19 students received support, including 19 fellowships (averaging $12,615 per year), 13 teaching assistantships with partial tuition reimbursements available (averaging $15,009 per year); scholarships/grants and unspecified assistantships also available. Financial award application deadline: 2/1; financial award applicants required to submit FAFSA. *Faculty research:* Experimental film and video, public art projects, ecological design, contemporary art philosophy, sound installations. *Unit head:* Mary-Ann Milford, Chairperson, 510-430-3142, Fax: 510-430-3314. *Application contact:* Jessica King, Graduate Admission Specialist, 510-430-3305, Fax: 510-430-2159, E-mail: grad-studies@mills.edu.

Minneapolis College of Art and Design, Program in Visual Studies, Minneapolis, MN 55404-4347. Offers animation (MFA); comic art (MFA); drawing (MFA); filmmaking (MFA); fine arts (MFA); furniture design (MFA); graphic design (MFA); illustration (MFA); interactive media (MFA); painting (MFA); photography (MFA); printmaking (MFA); sculpture (MFA). *Accreditation:* NASAD. Part-time programs available. *Degree requirements:* For master's, thesis, thesis exhibit. *Entrance requirements:* For master's, portfolio of visual artwork, resume, 3 letters of recommendation. Additional exam requirements/recommendations for international students: Required—TOEFL (minimum score 550 paper-based; 213 computer-based; 79 iBT). Electronic applications accepted. *Faculty research:* Visual arts: animation, comic art, drawing, filmmaking, furniture design, graphic design, illustration, interactive media, painting, photography, printmaking, sculpture.

New Mexico State University, Graduate School, College of Arts and Sciences, Department of Art, Las Cruces, NM 88003-8001. Offers art history (MA); ceramics (MA, MFA); design (MA, MFA); drawing (MFA); metals (MA, MFA); painting (MFA); photography (MFA); sculpture (MA, MFA). *Faculty:* 9 full-time (5 women), 3 part-time/adjunct (1 woman). *Students:* 18 full-time (10 women), 2 part-time (both women); includes 6 minority (1 American Indian or Alaska Native, non-Hispanic/Latino; 1 Asian, non-Hispanic/Latino; 4 Hispanic/Latino), 1 international. Average age 34. 26 applicants, 77% accepted, 11 enrolled. In 2010, 11 master's awarded. *Degree requirements:* For master's, comprehensive exam (for some programs), thesis, thesis exhibit. *Entrance requirements:* For master's, portfolio, 10-page paper (art history). *Application deadline:* For fall admission, 2/15 for domestic students; for winter admission, 10/15 for domestic students; for spring admission, 7/15 for domestic students. Application fee: $30 ($50 for international students). Electronic applications accepted. *Expenses:* Tuition, state resident: full-time $4536; part-time $242 per credit. Tuition, nonresident: full-time $15,816; part-time $712 per credit. Required fees: $636 per term. *Financial support:* In 2010–11, 17 teaching assistantships (averaging $6,640 per year) were awarded; research assistantships, Federal Work-Study and health care benefits also available. Support available to part-time students. Financial award application deadline: 3/1; financial award applicants required to submit FAFSA. *Faculty research:* Painting, graphic design, sculpture, ceramics, photography, jewelry. *Unit head:* Dr. Thom Brown, Head, 575-646-1705, Fax: 575-646-8036, E-mail: artdept@nmsu.edu. *Application contact:* Dr. Thom Brown, Head, 575-646-1705, Fax: 575-646-8036, E-mail: artdept@nmsu.edu.

The New School: A University, Parsons The New School for Design, Program in Photography, New York, NY 10011. Offers MFA. *Degree requirements:* For master's, thesis. *Entrance requirements:* For master's, portfolio. Additional exam requirements/recommendations for international students: Required—TOEFL (minimum score 580 paper-based; 237 computer-based; 93 iBT). Electronic applications accepted.

New York Film Academy, Program in Filmmaking–Hollywood, Los Angeles, CA 90068. Offers acting for film (MFA); cinematography (MFA); filmmaking (MFA); photography (MFA); producing (MFA); screenwriting (MFA). *Accreditation:* NASAD.

Ohio University, Graduate College, College of Fine Arts, School of Art, Athens, OH 45701-2979. Offers art history (MA); ceramics (MFA); graphic design (MFA); painting (MFA); photography (MFA); printmaking (MFA); sculpture (MFA). Part-time programs available. *Students:* 62 full-time (35 women), 4 part-time (3 women); includes 5 minority (1 American Indian or Alaska Native, non-Hispanic/Latino; 1 Asian, non-Hispanic/Latino; 3 Hispanic/Latino), 7 international. 181 applicants, 19% accepted, 28 enrolled. In 2010, 14 master's awarded. *Degree requirements:* For master's, thesis. *Entrance requirements:* For master's, portfolio. Additional exam requirements/recommendations for international students: Required—TOEFL (minimum score 550 paper-based; 80 iBT) or IELTS (minimum score 6.5). *Application deadline:* For fall admission, 2/1 for domestic and international students. Application fee: $50 ($55 for international students). Electronic applications accepted. *Financial support:* Teaching assistantships with full and partial tuition reimbursements, career-related internships or fieldwork, Federal Work-Study, institutionally sponsored loans, scholarships/grants, tuition waivers (partial), and unspecified assistantships available. Financial award application deadline: 2/1. *Faculty research:* Vapor-fired ceramics, video installation, art theory, digital photography, mixed and interdisciplinary media work. *Unit head:* David LaPalombara, Director, 740-593-4290, Fax: 740-593-0457, E-mail: lapalomb@ohio.edu. *Application contact:* Melissa Haviland, Chair, Graduate Programs, 740-593-9996, Fax: 740-593-0457, E-mail: haviland@ohio.edu.

Ohio University, Graduate College, Scripps College of Communication, School of Visual Communication, Athens, OH 45701-2979. Offers MA. *Accreditation:* NASAD. *Students:* 32 full-time (17 women), 4 part-time (2 women); includes 3 minority (1 Black or African American, non-Hispanic/Latino; 2 Hispanic/Latino), 5 international. 43 applicants, 91% accepted, 21 enrolled. In 2010, 21 master's awarded. *Entrance requirements:* For master's, minimum GPA of 2.5, portfolio. Additional exam requirements/recommendations for international students: Required—TOEFL (minimum score 600 paper-based; 100 iBT) or IELTS (minimum score 7). *Application deadline:* For fall admission, 2/1 for domestic students, 12/14 for international students. Application fee: $50 ($55 for international students). Electronic applications accepted. *Financial support:* Federal Work-Study, institutionally sponsored loans, and tuition waivers (partial) available. Financial award applicants required to submit FAFSA. *Faculty research:* Photojournalism (including documentary photography), commercial photography (including illustrative photography), picture editing, informational graphics/publication design, interactive multimedia, visual media management. *Unit head:* Terry Eiler, Director, 740-595-4895, Fax: 740-593-0190, E-mail: eiler@ohio.edu. *Application contact:* Stan Alost, Assistant Director, 740-597-1756, Fax: 740-593-0190, E-mail: alost@ohio.edu.

Otis College of Art and Design, Program in Fine Arts, Los Angeles, CA 90045-9785. Offers new genres (MFA); painting (MFA); photography (MFA); sculpture (MFA). *Accreditation:* NASAD. *Faculty:* 1 (woman) full-time, 6 part-time/adjunct (3 women). *Students:* 23 full-time (14 women); includes 2 minority (1 Asian, non-Hispanic/Latino; 1 Hispanic/Latino), 3 international. Average age 32. 140 applicants, 26% accepted, 15 enrolled. In 2010, 7 master's awarded. *Degree requirements:* For master's, thesis. *Entrance requirements:* For master's, portfolio. Additional exam requirements/recommendations for international students: Required—TOEFL (minimum score 600 paper-based; 250 computer-based). *Application deadline:* For fall admission, 1/15 for domestic and international students; for spring admission, 11/15 for domestic and international students. Application fee: $60. Electronic applications accepted. *Expenses:* Tuition: Full-time $33,900; part-time $1107 per unit. Required fees: $700. *Financial support:* Career-related internships or fieldwork, Federal Work-Study, scholarships/grants, and tuition waivers (partial) available. Financial award applicants required to submit FAFSA. *Unit head:* Roy Dowell, Chair, 310-665-6893, Fax: 310-665-6998, E-mail: grads@otis.edu. *Application contact:* Information Contact, 310-665-6820, Fax: 310-665-6821, E-mail: admissions@otis.edu.

Pratt Institute, School of Art and Design, Program in Fine Arts, Brooklyn, NY 11205-3899. Offers new forms (MFA); painting and drawing (MFA); photography (MFA); printmaking (MFA); sculpture (MFA). *Accreditation:* NASAD. Part-time programs available. *Faculty:* 8 full-time (2 women), 30 part-time/adjunct (15 women). *Students:* 141 full-time (94 women), 5 part-time (2 women); includes 3 Black or African American, non-Hispanic/Latino; 6 Asian, non-Hispanic/Latino; 4 Hispanic/Latino; 4 Two or more races, non-Hispanic/Latino, 45 international. Average age 28. 355 applicants, 46% accepted, 65 enrolled. In 2010, 43 master's awarded. *Degree requirements:* For master's, thesis, exhibit. *Entrance requirements:* For master's, portfolio, letters of recommendation. Additional exam requirements/recommendations for international students: Required—TOEFL (minimum score 550 paper-based; 213 computer-based; 79 iBT). *Application deadline:* For fall admission, 1/5 for domestic and international students; for spring admission, 10/1 for domestic and international students. Application fee: $50 ($90 for international students). Electronic applications accepted. *Expenses:* Tuition: Full-time $22,734; part-time $1263 per credit. Required fees: $1280. *Financial support:* Career-related internships or fieldwork, Federal Work-Study, institutionally sponsored loans, scholarships/grants, health care benefits, and unspecified assistantships available. Support available to part-time students. Financial award application deadline: 2/1; financial award applicants required to submit FAFSA. *Unit head:* Donna Moran, Chairperson, 718-636-3602, E-mail: dmoran@pratt.edu. *Application contact:* Young Hah, Director of Graduate Admissions, 718-636-3683, Fax: 718-399-4242, E-mail: yhah@pratt.edu.

See Display on page 92 and Close-Up on page 131.

Rhode Island School of Design, Graduate Studies, Division of Fine Arts, Department of Photography, Providence, RI 02903-2784. Offers MFA. *Accreditation:* NASAD. *Degree requirements:* For master's, thesis, exhibit. *Entrance requirements:* For master's, portfolio, 3 letters of recommendation. Additional exam requirements/recommendations for international students: Required—TOEFL (minimum score 580 paper-based; 237 computer-based), IELTS (minimum score 6.5).

Rochester Institute of Technology, Graduate Enrollment Services, College of Imaging Arts and Sciences, School of Photographic Arts and Sciences, Program in Imaging Arts, Rochester, NY 14623-5603. Offers MFA. *Accreditation:* NASAD. Part-time programs available. *Students:* 64 full-time (30 women), 32 part-time (22 women); includes 2 Black or African American, non-Hispanic/Latino; 2 Asian, non-Hispanic/Latino; 3 Hispanic/Latino; 1 Two or more races, non-Hispanic/Latino, 40 international. Average age 29. 207 applicants, 33% accepted, 35 enrolled. In 2010, 21 master's awarded. *Degree requirements:* For master's, thesis, exhibit. *Entrance requirements:* For master's, portfolio, minimum GPA of 3.0. Additional exam requirements/recommendations for international students: Required—TOEFL (minimum score 550 paper-based; 213 computer-based; 79 iBT) or IELTS (minimum score 6.5). *Application deadline:* For fall admission, 2/15 priority date for domestic and international students. Applications are processed on a rolling basis. Application fee: $50. Electronic applications accepted. *Expenses:* Tuition: Full-time $33,234; part-time $924 per credit hour. Required fees: $219. *Financial support:* In 2010–11, 45 students received support; fellowships with partial tuition reimbursements available, research assistantships with partial tuition reimbursements available, teaching assistantships with partial tuition reimbursements available, career-related internships or fieldwork, institutionally sponsored loans, scholarships/grants, tuition waivers (partial), and unspecified assistantships available. Support available to part-time students. Financial award application deadline: 8/30; financial award applicants required to submit FAFSA. *Unit head:* Angela Kelly, Graduate Program Director, 585-475-2616, Fax: 585-475-5804, E-mail: amkpph@rit.edu. *Application contact:* Diane Ellison, Assistant Vice President, Graduate Enrollment Services, 585-475-2229, Fax: 585-475-7164, E-mail: gradinfo@rit.edu.

San Francisco Art Institute, Graduate Program, Department of Photography, San Francisco, CA 94133. Offers MFA, Certificate. *Accreditation:* NASAD. Part-time programs available. *Degree requirements:* For master's and Certificate, oral reviews. *Entrance requirements:* For master's and Certificate, portfolio. Additional exam requirements/recommendations for international students: Required—TOEFL (minimum score 580 paper-based; 237 computer-based). Electronic applications accepted.

San Jose State University, Graduate Studies and Research, College of Humanities and the Arts, School of Art and Design, San Jose, CA 95192-0001. Offers animation/illustration (MA); art history (MA); digital media arts (MFA); photography (MFA); pictorial arts (MFA); spatial arts (MFA). *Accreditation:* NASAD (one or more programs are accredited). *Entrance requirements:* For master's, GRE. Electronic applications accepted.

Savannah College of Art and Design, Graduate School, Program in Commercial Photography, Savannah, GA 31402-3146. Offers MA. Part-time programs available. *Faculty:* 4 full-time (2 women). *Students:* 5 full-time (1 woman); includes 1 Black or African American, non-Hispanic/Latino, 2 international. 7 applicants, 57% accepted, 2 enrolled. *Degree requirements:* For master's, thesis. *Entrance requirements:* For master's, interview, portfolio. Additional exam requirements/recommendations for international students: Required—TOEFL (minimum score 450 paper-based; 133 computer-based). *Application deadline:* For fall admission, 4/1 priority date for domestic and international students. Applications are processed on a rolling basis. Application fee: $50. Electronic applications accepted. *Expenses:* Tuition: Full-time $29,520; part-time $3280 per quarter. Tuition and fees vary according to campus/location. *Financial support:* Fellowships, career-related internships or fieldwork, Federal Work-Study, and

Photography

Savannah College of Art and Design *(continued)*

scholarships/grants available. Financial award application deadline: 4/1; financial award applicants required to submit FAFSA. *Unit head:* Jenny Kuhla, Chair, 912-525-6502. *Application contact:* Darrell Tutchton, Director of Graduate and International Enrollment, 912-525-5961, Fax: 912-525-5985, E-mail: admission@scad.edu.

Savannah College of Art and Design, Graduate School, Program in Digital Photography, Savannah, GA 31402-3146. Offers MA. Part-time programs available. *Faculty:* 4 full-time (2 women). *Students:* 10 full-time (6 women), 13 part-time (3 women), 1 international. 54 applicants, 35% accepted, 10 enrolled. In 2010, 1 master's awarded. *Degree requirements:* For master's, thesis. *Entrance requirements:* For master's, interview, portfolio. Additional exam requirements/recommendations for international students: Required—TOEFL (minimum score 450 paper-based; 133 computer-based). *Application deadline:* For fall admission, 4/1 priority date for domestic and international students. Applications are processed on a rolling basis. Application fee: $50. Electronic applications accepted. *Expenses:* Tuition: Full-time $29,520; part-time $3280 per quarter. Tuition and fees vary according to campus/location. *Financial support:* Fellowships, career-related internships or fieldwork, Federal Work-Study, and scholarships/grants available. Financial award application deadline: 4/1; financial award applicants required to submit FAFSA. *Unit head:* Thomas Fischer, Chair, 912-525-6570, Fax: 912-525-3507, E-mail: tfischer@scad.edu. *Application contact:* Darrell Tutchton, Director of Graduate and International Enrollment, 912-525-5961, Fax: 912-525-5985, E-mail: admission@scad.edu.

Savannah College of Art and Design, Graduate School, Program in Documentary Photography, Savannah, GA 31402-3146. Offers MA. Part-time programs available. *Faculty:* 1 full-time (0 women). *Students:* 1 part-time (0 women), all international. 8 applicants, 13% accepted, 1 enrolled. *Degree requirements:* For master's, thesis. *Entrance requirements:* For master's, interview, portfolio. Additional exam requirements/recommendations for international students: Required—TOEFL (minimum score 450 paper-based; 133 computer-based). *Application deadline:* For fall admission, 4/1 priority date for domestic and international students. Applications are processed on a rolling basis. Electronic applications accepted. *Expenses:* Tuition: Full-time $29,520; part-time $3280 per quarter. Tuition and fees vary according to campus/location. *Financial support:* Fellowships, career-related internships or fieldwork, Federal Work-Study, and scholarships/grants available. Financial award application deadline: 4/1; financial award applicants required to submit FAFSA. *Unit head:* Jenny Kuhla, Chair, 912-525-6502. *Application contact:* Darrell Tutchton, Director of Graduate and International Enrollment, 912-525-5961, Fax: 912-525-5985, E-mail: admission@scad.edu.

Savannah College of Art and Design, Graduate School, Program in Photography, Savannah, GA 31402-3146. Offers MA, MFA. Part-time programs available. Postbaccalaureate distance learning degree programs offered (no on-campus study). *Faculty:* 23 full-time (9 women), 11 part-time/adjunct (7 women). *Students:* 80 full-time (47 women), 13 part-time (3 women); includes 4 Black or African American, non-Hispanic/Latino; 3 Asian, non-Hispanic/Latino; 1 Hispanic/Latino, 10 international. Average age 30. In 2010, 20 master's awarded. *Degree requirements:* For master's, thesis, exhibit, internships. *Entrance requirements:* For master's, interview, portfolio. Additional exam requirements/recommendations for international students: Required—TOEFL (minimum score 450 paper-based; 133 computer-based). *Application deadline:* For fall admission, 4/1 priority date for domestic and international students. Applications are processed on a rolling basis. Application fee: $35. Electronic applications accepted. *Expenses:* Tuition: Full-time $29,520; part-time $3280 per quarter. Tuition and fees vary according to campus/location. *Financial support:* Fellowships, career-related internships or fieldwork, Federal Work-Study, and scholarships/grants available. Financial award application deadline: 4/1; financial award applicants required to submit FAFSA. *Unit head:* Steven Mosch, Chair, 912-525-6515, E-mail: smosch@scad.edu. *Application contact:* Elizabeth Mathis, Director of Graduate Recruitment, 912-525-5965, Fax: 912-525-5985, E-mail: emathis@scad.edu.

See Display on page 177 and Close-Up on page 223

School of the Art Institute of Chicago, Graduate Division, Department of Photography, Chicago, IL 60603-3103. Offers MFA. *Accreditation:* NASAD. *Entrance requirements:* Additional exam requirements/recommendations for international students: Required—TOEFL.

See Close-Up on page 225.

School of Visual Arts, Graduate Programs, Digital Photography Department, New York, NY 10010-3994. Offers MPS. *Degree requirements:* For master's, thesis or project. *Entrance requirements:* For master's, portfolio. Additional exam requirements/recommendations for international students: Required—TOEFL (minimum score 550 paper-based; 213 computer-based; 79 iBT). Electronic applications accepted.

School of Visual Arts, Graduate Programs, Program in Photography, Video and Related Media, New York, NY 10010-3994. Offers MFA. *Accreditation:* NASAD. *Degree requirements:* For master's, final review, project or thesis. *Entrance requirements:* For master's, portfolio. Additional exam requirements/recommendations for international students: Required—TOEFL (minimum score 550 paper-based; 213 computer-based; 79 iBT). Electronic applications accepted.

Sotheby's Institute of Art–London, Graduate Programs, London, United Kingdom. Offers art business (MA); contemporary art (MA); contemporary design (MA); East Asian art (MA); fine and decorative art (MA); photography (MA).

Southern Methodist University, Meadows School of the Arts, Division of Art, Dallas, TX 75275. Offers studio art (MFA), including ceramics, drawing, painting, photography, printmaking, sculpture. *Accreditation:* NASAD. *Faculty:* 11 full-time (2 women), 5 part-time/adjunct (3 women). *Students:* 8 full-time (5 women), 1 part-time (0 women); includes 1 Hispanic/Latino, 1 international. Average age 30. 35 applicants, 20% accepted, 6 enrolled. In 2010, 4 master's awarded. *Degree requirements:* For master's, thesis or alternative, exhibit. *Entrance requirements:* For master's, BFA or equivalent, letters of recommendation, portfolio. Additional exam requirements/recommendations for international students: Required—TOEFL (minimum score 550 paper-based; 213 computer-based; 80 iBT). *Application deadline:* For fall admission, 2/15 for domestic and international students. Application fee: $75. *Financial support:* In 2010–11, 5 fellowships (averaging $32,914 per year), 5 teaching assistantships (averaging $3,000 per year) were awarded; scholarships/grants and unspecified assistantships also available. Financial award application deadline: 3/1; financial award applicants required to submit FAFSA. *Faculty research:* American stoneware, Southwestern furniture traditions, photographic apparatus and techniques, American ceramists, architecture. Total annual research expenditures: $20,000. *Unit head:* James W. Sullivan, Chair, 214-768-2489, E-mail: jsulliva@smu.edu. *Application contact:* Jean Cherry, Director of Graduate Admissions and Records, 214-768-3765, Fax: 214-768-3272, E-mail: jcherry@smu.edu.

Syracuse University, College of Visual and Performing Arts, Program in Art Photography, Syracuse, NY 13244. Offers MFA. *Accreditation:* NASAD. *Students:* 11 full-time (6 women), 2 international. Average age 29. 29 applicants, 31% accepted, 2 enrolled. In 2010, 2 master's awarded. *Degree requirements:* For master's, thesis or alternative. *Entrance requirements:* For master's, portfolio. Additional exam requirements/recommendations for international students: Required—TOEFL (minimum score 100 iBT). *Application deadline:* For fall admission, 2/1 priority date for domestic and international students. Application fee: $75. Electronic applications accepted. *Expenses:* Tuition: Part-time $1162 per credit. *Financial support:* Fellowships with full tuition reimbursements, teaching assistantships with full and partial tuition reimbursements, tuition waivers (partial) available. Financial award application deadline: 1/1; financial award applicants required to submit FAFSA. *Unit head:* Heath Hanlin, Department Chair, 315-443-1033, E-mail: hahanlin@syr.edu. *Application contact:* Harriett Conti, Assistant Dean for Recruitment and Admissions, 315-443-5755, E-mail: hmconti@syr.edu.

Syracuse University, S. I. Newhouse School of Public Communications, Program in Photography, Syracuse, NY 13244. Offers MS. *Students:* 15 full-time (7 women), 3 part-time (2 women); includes 3 minority (1 Black or African American, non-Hispanic/Latino; 2 Asian, non-Hispanic/Latino), 2 international. Average age 30. 13 applicants, 77% accepted, 5 enrolled. In 2010, 8 master's awarded. *Degree requirements:* For master's, thesis optional, special project. *Entrance requirements:* For master's, GRE General Test, portfolio. Additional exam requirements/recommendations for international students: Required—TOEFL (minimum score 600 paper-based; 250 computer-based; 100 iBT). *Application deadline:* For fall admission, 2/1 priority date for domestic and international students. Application fee: $45. Electronic applications accepted. *Expenses:* Tuition: Part-time $1162 per credit. *Financial support:* Fellowships with full tuition reimbursements, research assistantships with partial tuition reimbursements, teaching assistantships with partial tuition reimbursements, Federal Work-Study available. Financial award application deadline: 2/1. *Unit head:* Anthony R. Golden, Director, 315-443-2304, Fax: 315-443-3946, E-mail: argolden@syr.edu. *Application contact:* Martha Coria, Graduate Admissions, 315-443-5749, Fax: 315-443-1834, E-mail: pcgrad@syr.edu.

See Display on page 179 and Close-Up on page 227.

Temple University, Tyler School of Art, Department of Graphic Arts and Design, Philadelphia, PA 19122-6096. Offers graphic and interactive design (MFA); photography (MFA); printmaking (MFA). *Faculty:* 13 full-time (6 women). *Students:* 18 full-time (13 women), 2 international. 149 applicants, 13% accepted, 10 enrolled. In 2010, 11 master's awarded. *Degree requirements:* For master's, essay, exhibit. *Entrance requirements:* For master's, minimum GPA of 3.0; slide portfolio, 40 credits in studio art; 12 credits in art history. Additional exam requirements/recommendations for international students: Required—TOEFL (minimum score 550 paper-based; 213 computer-based; 79 iBT). *Application deadline:* For fall admission, 1/15 for domestic students, 12/15 for international students. Application fee: $50. Electronic applications accepted. *Financial support:* Fellowships with full tuition reimbursements, research assistantships with full tuition reimbursements, teaching assistantships with full tuition reimbursements, Federal Work-Study available. Support available to part-time students. Financial award application deadline: 1/15; financial award applicants required to submit FAFSA. *Unit head:* Stephanie Knopp, Chair, 215-782-2932, Fax: 215-782-2799, E-mail: stephanie.knopp@temple.edu. *Application contact:* Carmina Cianciulli, Assistant Dean for Admissions, 215-782-2875, Fax: 215-782-2711, E-mail: tylerart@temple.edu.

The University of Alabama, Graduate School, College of Arts and Sciences, Department of Art, Tuscaloosa, AL 35487. Offers art history (MA); studio art (MA, MFA), including ceramics, painting, photography, printmaking, sculpture. *Accreditation:* NASAD. Part-time programs available. *Faculty:* 16 full-time (8 women). *Students:* 17 full-time (13 women), 7 part-time (4 women); includes 2 minority (1 Black or African American, non-Hispanic/Latino; 1 Asian, non-Hispanic/Latino), 2 international. Average age 33. 21 applicants, 67% accepted, 7 enrolled. In 2010, 5 master's awarded. *Degree requirements:* For master's, one foreign language, comprehensive exam (for some programs), oral exam, thesis statement, exhibit (studio art), thesis (art history). *Entrance requirements:* For master's, GRE General Test or MAT (art history), minimum GPA of 3.0, BFA or equivalent (studio art). Additional exam requirements/recommendations for international students: Required—TOEFL (minimum score 550 paper-based; 213 computer-based). *Application deadline:* For fall admission, 3/15 for domestic and international students; for spring admission, 10/15 for domestic and international students. Applications are processed on a rolling basis. Application fee: $50 ($60 for international students). Electronic applications accepted. *Expenses:* Tuition, state resident: full-time $7900. Tuition, nonresident: full-time $20,500. *Financial support:* In 2010–11, 2 fellowships with full tuition reimbursements (averaging $14,000 per year), 13 teaching assistantships with full and partial tuition reimbursements (averaging $9,206 per year) were awarded; career-related internships or fieldwork, institutionally sponsored loans, scholarships/grants, and unspecified assistantships also available. Financial award application deadline: 7/14. *Faculty research:* Nineteenth century American art history, Chinese art history, Baroque art history, twentieth century art history, Asian art history. *Unit head:* William T. Dooley, Chairperson, 205-348-1890, Fax: 205-348-0287, E-mail: wtdooley@bama.ua.edu. *Application contact:* Craig R. Wedderspoon, Graduate Coordinator, 205-348-1898, Fax: 205-348-0287, E-mail: cwedders@bama.edu.

University of Alaska Fairbanks, College of Liberal Arts, Department of Art, Fairbanks, AK 99775-5640. Offers art (MFA); ceramics (MFA); computer art (MFA); drawing (MFA); Native arts (MFA); painting (MFA); photography (MFA); printmaking (MFA); sculpture (MFA). Part-time programs available. *Faculty:* 7 full-time (2 women). *Students:* 8 full-time (4 women), 1 part-time (0 women), 1 international. Average age 33. 11 applicants, 9% accepted, 0 enrolled. In 2010, 3 master's awarded. *Degree requirements:* For master's, comprehensive exam, thesis, oral exam, oral defense. *Entrance requirements:* For master's, portfolio. Additional exam requirements/recommendations for international students: Required—TOEFL (minimum score 550 paper-based; 213 computer-based; 80 iBT). *Application deadline:* For fall admission, 6/1 for domestic students, 3/1 for international students; for spring admission, 10/15 for domestic students, 9/1 for international students. Applications are processed on a rolling basis. Application fee: $60. Electronic applications accepted. *Expenses:* Tuition, state resident: full-time $5688; part-time $316 per credit. Tuition, nonresident: full-time $11,628; part-time $646 per credit. Required fees: $289 per semester. Tuition and fees vary according to course load and reciprocity agreements. *Financial support:* In 2010–11, 7 teaching assistantships with tuition reimbursements (averaging $8,174 per year) were awarded; fellowships with tuition reimbursements, research assistantships with tuition reimbursements, Federal Work-Study, scholarships/grants, health care benefits, and unspecified assistantships also available. Support available to part-time students. Financial award application deadline: 7/1; financial award applicants required to submit FAFSA. *Faculty research:* Computer art, survey of arts in Alaska, found object art, visualization and animation, painting from the wilderness. Total annual research expenditures: $8,543. *Unit head:* David Mollett, Chair, 907-474-7530, Fax: 907-474-5853, E-mail: fyart@uaf.edu. *Application contact:* David Mollett, Chair, 907-474-7530, Fax: 907-474-5853, E-mail: fyart@uaf.edu.

University of Colorado Boulder, Graduate School, College of Arts and Sciences, Department of Art and Art History, Boulder, CO 80309. Offers art history (MA), including contemporary art criticism, early twentieth century art, nineteenth century art, Russian and Soviet art; ceramics (MFA); drawing (MFA); painting (MFA); photography and media arts (MFA); printmaking (MFA); sculpture (MFA). *Faculty:* 26 full-time (12 women). *Students:* 50 full-time (36 women), 2 part-time (both women); includes 7 minority (1 American Indian or Alaska Native, non-Hispanic/Latino; 2 Asian, non-Hispanic/Latino; 3 Hispanic/Latino; 1 Two or more races, non-Hispanic/Latino), 2 international. Average age 30. 265 applicants, 18 enrolled. In 2010, 16 master's awarded. *Degree requirements:* For master's, variable foreign language requirement, comprehensive exam, thesis (for some programs). *Entrance requirements:* For master's, GRE General Test, minimum undergraduate GPA of 3.0, portfolio. *Application deadline:* For fall admission, 1/15 priority date for domestic students, 12/1 for international students. Application fee: $50 ($60 for international students). *Financial support:* In 2010–11, 6 fellowships (averaging $1,713 per year), 13 research assistantships (averaging $5,087 per year) were awarded; Federal Work-Study, scholarships/grants, and tuition waivers (full) also available. Financial award application deadline: 1/15. *Faculty research:* Drawing, painting, ceramics, sculpture, photography and media arts, printmaking, Russian and Soviet art, early twentieth century art, contemporary art criticism, nineteenth century art.

University of Florida, Graduate School, College of Fine Arts, School of Art and Art History, Gainesville, FL 32611. Offers art (MFA), including ceramics, creative photography, drawing, electronic intermedia, graphic design, painting, printmaking, sculpture; art education (MA); art history (MA, PhD); digital arts and sciences (MA); museology (museum studies) (MA). *Accreditation:* NASAD. Postbaccalaureate distance learning degree programs offered (minimal on-campus study). *Faculty:* 29 full-time (14 women). *Students:* 107 full-time (72 women), 57 part-time (52 women); includes 6 Black or African American, non-Hispanic/Latino; 1 American Indian or Alaska Native, non-Hispanic/Latino; 5 Asian, non-Hispanic/Latino; 13 Hispanic/Latino, 14 international. Average age 31. 282 applicants, 30% accepted, 61 enrolled. In 2010, 24 master's, 3 doctorates awarded. *Degree requirements:* For master's, thesis, project or thesis (MFA); 1 foreign language (MA in art history); for doctorate, 2 foreign languages, comprehensive exam, thesis/dissertation. *Entrance requirements:* For master's, GRE General Test, portfolio (MFA), writing sample (MA), minimum GPA of 3.0; for doctorate, GRE General Test, minimum GPA of 3.0. Additional exam requirements/recommendations for international students: Required—TOEFL (minimum score 550 paper-based; 213 computer-based; 80 iBT), IELTS (minimum score 6). *Application deadline:* For fall admission, 1/1 priority date for domestic students, 1/1 for international students; for spring admission, 11/1 for domestic and international students. Applications are processed on a rolling basis. Application fee: $30. Electronic applications accepted. *Expenses:* Tuition, state resident: full-time $10,915.92. Tuition, nonresident: full-time $28,309. *Financial support:* In 2010–11, 36 students received support, including 9 fellowships, 3 research assistantships with tuition reimbursements available (averaging $12,789 per year), 24 teaching assistantships with tuition reimbursements available (averaging $10,512 per year); Federal Work-Study, institutionally sponsored loans, and unspecified assistantships also available. Financial award applicants required to submit FAFSA. *Faculty research:* Studio production, art historical studies of style context. *Unit head:* Laura Robertsoon, SR Associate in Graduate Studies, 352-846-3425, E-mail: laurar@ufl.edu. *Application contact:* Lauren G. Lake, Coordinator, 352-273-3032, Fax: 352-392-8453, E-mail: lglake@arts.ufl.edu.

University of Illinois at Chicago, Graduate College, College of Architecture and Art, School of Art and Design, Chicago, IL 60607-7128. Offers electronic visualization (MFA); film animation (MFA); graphic design (MFA); industrial design (MFA); photography (MFA); studio arts (MFA). *Accreditation:* NASAD. *Degree requirements:* For master's, thesis, exhibit. *Entrance requirements:* For master's, MAT, portfolio. Additional exam requirements/recommendations for international students: Required—TOEFL. Electronic applications accepted.

University of Illinois at Urbana–Champaign, Graduate College, College of Fine and Applied Arts, School of Art and Design, Program in Studio Arts, Champaign, IL 61820. Offers art and design (MFA); crafts (MFA); metals (MFA); painting (MFA); photography (MFA); sculpture (MFA). *Accreditation:* NASAD. *Students:* 20 full-time (12 women), 1 (woman) part-time; includes 1 Hispanic/Latino; 2 Two or more races, non-Hispanic/Latino, 2 international. 64 applicants, 13% accepted, 7 enrolled. In 2010, 5 master's awarded. *Entrance requirements:* For master's, minimum GPA of 3.0. Additional exam requirements/recommendations for international students: Required—TOEFL (minimum score 550 paper-based; 213 computer-based; 79 iBT). *Application deadline:* Applications are processed on a rolling basis. Application fee: $75 ($90 for international students). Electronic applications accepted. *Financial support:* Fellowships, research assistantships, teaching assistantships, tuition waivers (full and partial) available. *Unit head:* Timothy Van Laar, Chair, 217-333-6611, E-mail: tvanlaar@illinois.edu. *Application contact:* Marsha Biddle, Assistant to the Associate Director, 217-333-0642, Fax: 217-244-7688, E-mail: mbiddle@illinois.edu.

University of Massachusetts Dartmouth, Graduate School, College of Visual and Performing Arts, Program in Visual Design, North Dartmouth, MA 02747-2300. Offers digital media (MFA); graphic design (MFA); illustration (MFA); photography (MFA); typography (MFA). *Accreditation:* NASAD. *Faculty:* 17 full-time (7 women), 4 part-time/adjunct (1 woman). *Students:* 12 full-time (8 women), 5 part-time (4 women); includes 1 Two or more races, non-Hispanic/Latino, 1 international. Average age 35. 33 applicants, 48% accepted, 7 enrolled. In 2010, 1 master's awarded. *Degree requirements:* For master's, visual thesis. *Entrance requirements:* For master's, portfolio, interview, minimum GPA of 3.0, 3 letters of recommendation. Additional exam requirements/recommendations for international students: Required—TOEFL (minimum score 500 paper-based). *Application deadline:* For fall admission, 2/1 priority date for domestic students, 12/1 priority date for international students. Applications are processed on a rolling basis. Application fee: $40 ($60 for international students). Electronic applications accepted. *Expenses:* Tuition, state resident: full-time $2071; part-time $86 per credit. Tuition, nonresident: full-time $8099; part-time $337 per credit. Required fees: $9446; $394 per credit. One-time fee: $75. Part-time tuition and fees vary according to class time, course load, degree level and reciprocity agreements. *Financial support:* In 2010–11, 5 teaching assistantships with full tuition reimbursements (averaging $3,088 per year) were awarded; Federal Work-Study and unspecified assistantships also available. Support available to part-time students. Financial award application deadline: 3/1; financial award applicants required to submit FAFSA. *Faculty research:* Typography. Total annual research expenditures: $5,898. *Unit head:* Memory Holloway, Director, 508-999-8554, E-mail: mholloway@umassd.edu. *Application contact:* Elan Turcotte-Shamski, Graduate Admissions Officer, 508-999-8604, Fax: 508-999-8183, E-mail: graduate@umassd.edu.

University of Memphis, Graduate School, College of Communication and Fine Arts, Department of Art, Memphis, TN 38152. Offers art (Graduate Certificate); art history (MA), including Egyptian art and archaeology, general art history; ceramics (MFA); graphic design (MFA); interior design (MFA); painting (MFA); printmaking/photography (MFA); sculpture (MFA). *Accreditation:* NASAD (one or more programs are accredited). *Faculty:* 20 full-time (7 women), 4 part-time/adjunct (2 women). *Students:* 39 full-time (26 women), 10 part-time (8 women); includes 4 Black or African American, non-Hispanic/Latino; 1 Asian, non-Hispanic/Latino, 1 international. Average age 29. 44 applicants, 77% accepted, 22 enrolled. In 2010, 16 master's, 5 other advanced degrees awarded. *Degree requirements:* For master's, 2 foreign languages, comprehensive exam, thesis. *Entrance requirements:* For master's, GRE General Test or MAT, portfolio (MFA). *Application deadline:* For fall admission, 8/1 for domestic students; for spring admission, 12/1 for domestic students. Applications are processed on a rolling basis. Application fee: $35 ($60 for international students). *Financial support:* In 2010–11, 38 students received support; research assistantships with full tuition reimbursements available, teaching assistantships with full tuition reimbursements available, Federal Work-Study, scholarships/grants, and unspecified assistantships available. Financial award application deadline: 2/15; financial award applicants required to submit FAFSA. *Faculty research:* Online collaborative learning, advanced art history studies, electronic publishing/design, studio arts, architectural studies. *Unit head:* Prof. Richard Lou, Chair, 901-678-2216, Fax: 901-678-2735, E-mail: gmyatt@memphis.edu. *Application contact:* Greely Myat, Graduate Studies Coordinator, 901-678-2650.

University of Miami, Graduate School, College of Arts and Sciences, Department of Art and Art History, Coral Gables, FL 33124. Offers art history (MA); ceramics/glass (MFA); graphic design/multimedia (MFA); painting (MFA); photography/digital imaging (MFA); printmaking (MFA); sculpture (MFA). Part-time programs available. *Degree requirements:* For master's, variable foreign language requirement, thesis, exhibit (MFA), comprehensive exam (MA). *Entrance requirements:* For master's, GRE General Test (MA), research paper (MA), slide portfolio (MFA). Additional exam requirements/recommendations for international students: Required—TOEFL. Electronic applications accepted. *Faculty research:* Installation art, public art.

University of Notre Dame, Graduate School, College of Arts and Letters, Division of Humanities, Department of Art, Art History, and Design, Notre Dame, IN 46556. Offers art history (MA); design (MFA), including graphic design, industrial design; studio art (MFA), including ceramics, painting, photography, printmaking, sculpture. *Accreditation:* NASAD. *Degree requirements:* For master's, comprehensive exam (for some programs), thesis. *Entrance requirements:* For master's, GRE General Test, minimum GPA of 3.0. Additional exam requirements/recommendations for international students: Required—TOEFL (minimum score 600 paper-based; 250 computer-based; 80 iBT). Electronic applications accepted. *Faculty research:* Studio art practice in ceramics, printing, photography, printmaking and sculpture, graphic design and industrial design, digital imaging in design and photography, Renaissance and American art history, contemporary art theory and criticism.

University of Oklahoma, Weitzenhoffer Family College of Fine Arts, School of Art and Art History, Program in Art, Norman, OK 73019. Offers art (MFA), including ceramics, film, painting, photography, printmaking, sculpture, video, visual communication. MA applicants admitted fall/spring; MFA applicants admitted fall only. *Students:* 17 full-time (9 women), 2 part-time (1 woman); includes 5 minority (3 American Indian or Alaska Native, non-Hispanic/Latino; 2 Native Hawaiian or other Pacific Islander, non-Hispanic/Latino), 3 international. Average age 29. 27 applicants, 41% accepted, 8 enrolled. In 2010, 3 master's awarded. *Degree requirements:* For master's, thesis (MA), exhibit (MFA), departmental qualifying exam. *Entrance requirements:* For master's, GRE General Test (MA). Additional exam requirements/recommendations for international students: Required—TOEFL (minimum score 550 paper-based; 213 computer-based; 79 iBT). *Application deadline:* For fall admission, 2/1 for domestic and international students; for spring admission, 10/1 for domestic and international students. Applications are processed on a rolling basis. Application fee: $40 ($90 for international students). Electronic applications accepted. *Expenses:* Tuition, state resident: full-time $3893; part-time $162.20 per credit hour. Tuition, nonresident: full-time $14,167; part-time $590.30 per credit hour. Required fees: $2523; $94.60 per credit hour. Tuition and fees vary according to course load and degree level. *Financial support:* Career-related internships or fieldwork, scholarships/grants, tuition waivers (full and partial), and unspecified assistantships available. Financial award application deadline: 4/7; financial award applicants required to submit FAFSA. *Faculty research:* Interactions between technology and art; propaganda banners relating to the nuclear age; investigation of the nature of structures; relationships between history, myth and culture; gestural vase forms and slabbed formed architectural vessels. *Unit head:* Mary Jo Watson, Director, 405-325-2691, Fax: 405-325-1668, E-mail: mjwatson@ou.edu. *Application contact:* Andrew Strout, Graduate Liaison, 405-325-4094, Fax: 405-325-1668, E-mail: aestrout@ou.edu.

University of Southern California, Graduate School, Roski School of Fine Arts, Graduate Programs in Fine Arts, Los Angeles, CA 90089. Offers new genres (MFA); painting/drawing (MFA); photography (MFA); sculpture (MFA). *Faculty:* 5 full-time (3 women), 1 part-time/adjunct (0 women). *Students:* 17 full-time (6 women), 3 international. Average age 27. 312 applicants, 3% accepted, 8 enrolled. In 2010, 8 master's awarded. *Degree requirements:* For master's, thesis. *Entrance requirements:* For master's, Not Required, portfolio, artist statement, 3 letters of recommendation. Additional exam requirements/recommendations for international students: Required—TOEFL (minimum score 600 paper-based; 250 computer-based; 100 iBT). *Application deadline:* For fall admission, 2/1 for domestic and international students. Application fee: $85. Electronic applications accepted. *Expenses:* Tuition: Full-time $31,240; part-time $1420 per unit. Required fees: $600. One-time fee: $35 full-time. Full-time tuition and fees vary according to degree level and program. *Financial support:* In 2010–11, 16 students received support, including 16 teaching assistantships with full tuition reimbursements available (averaging $9,625 per year); Federal Work-Study, health care benefits, and unspecified assistantships also available. Financial award application deadline: 2/1; financial award applicants required to submit FAFSA. *Faculty research:* Fine art production in the areas of photography, video, sculpture, drawing, and performance. *Unit head:* Jud Fine, Director, MFA program, 213-743-1804, Fax: 213-743-4563. *Application contact:* Dwayne Moser, MFA Program Coordinator, 213-743-1804, Fax: 213-743-4563, E-mail: dmoser@usc.edu.

The University of Tennessee, Graduate School, College of Arts and Sciences, School of Art, Knoxville, TN 37996. Offers ceramics (MFA); drawing (MFA); graphic design (MFA); inter-area studies (MFA); media arts (MFA); painting (MFA); printmaking (MFA); sculpture (MFA); watercolor (MFA). *Accreditation:* NASAD. *Degree requirements:* For master's, thesis or alternative, exhibit. *Entrance requirements:* For master's, portfolio, minimum GPA of 2.7. Additional exam requirements/recommendations for international students: Required—TOEFL. Electronic applications accepted. *Expenses:* Tuition, state resident: full-time $7440; part-time $414 per credit hour. Tuition, nonresident: full-time $22,478; part-time $1250 per credit hour. Required fees: $922; $43 per credit hour. Tuition and fees vary according to program.

University of Utah, Graduate School, College of Fine Arts, Department of Art and Art History, Salt Lake City, UT 84112-0380. Offers art history (MA); ceramics (MFA); community-based art education (MFA); drawing (MFA); graphic design (MFA); painting (MFA); photography/digital imaging (MFA); printmaking (MFA); sculpture/intermedia (MFA). *Faculty:* 23 full-time (10 women). *Students:* 17 full-time (12 women), 1 (woman) part-time; includes 2 minority (both Hispanic/Latino), 1 international. Average age 29. 54 applicants, 20% accepted, 7 enrolled. In 2010, 5 master's awarded. *Degree requirements:* For master's, variable foreign language requirement, comprehensive exam (for some programs), thesis or alternative, exhibit and final project paper (for MFA). *Entrance requirements:* For master's, CD portfolio (MFA), writing sample (MA), curriculum vitae, letters of recommendation. Additional exam requirements/recommendations for international students: Required—TOEFL (minimum score 575 paper-based; 183 computer-based; 75 iBT). *Application deadline:* For fall admission, 1/2 priority date for domestic and international students. Application fee: $55 ($65 for international students). Electronic applications accepted. *Expenses:* Tuition, area resident: Part-time $179.19 per credit hour. Tuition, state resident: full-time $4384. Tuition, nonresident: full-time $16,684; part-time $630.67 per credit hour. Required fees: $350 per semester. Tuition and fees vary according to course load, degree level and program. *Financial support:* In 2010–11, 2 fellowships, 6 research assistantships with partial tuition reimbursements, 34 teaching assistantships with partial tuition reimbursements were awarded; Federal Work-Study, institutionally sponsored loans, scholarships/grants, tuition waivers (partial), unspecified assistantships, and stipends also available. Financial award application deadline: 1/2; financial award applicants required to submit FAFSA. *Faculty research:* Studio art, European art history, Asian art history, Latin American art history, twentieth century/contemporary art history. Total annual research expenditures: $23,714. *Unit head:* Prof. Brian Snapp, Chair, 801-581-8677, Fax: 801-585-6171, E-mail: b.snapp@utah.edu. *Application contact:* Prof. Paul Stout, Director of Graduate Studies, 801-581-8677, Fax: 801-585-6171, E-mail: pls@utah.edu.

University of Victoria, Faculty of Graduate Studies, Faculty of Fine Arts, Department of Visual Arts, Victoria, BC V8W 2Y2, Canada. Offers digital multimedia (MFA); drawing (MFA); painting (MFA); photography (MFA); sculpture (MFA); video (MFA). *Degree requirements:* For master's, exhibit, oral exam. *Entrance requirements:* For master's, portfolio, BFA. Additional exam requirements/recommendations for international students: Required—TOEFL (minimum score 575 paper-based; 233 computer-based), IELTS (minimum score 7). Electronic applications accepted.

University of Washington, Graduate School, College of Arts and Sciences, School of Art, Division of Art, Seattle, WA 98195. Offers painting and drawing (MFA); photography (MFA). *Degree requirements:* For master's, thesis, exhibit. *Entrance requirements:* For master's, BFA or equivalent academic work in art, 20 slide portfolio. Additional exam requirements/recommendations for international students: Required—TOEFL. Electronic applications accepted.

Virginia Commonwealth University, Graduate School, School of the Arts, Richmond, VA 23284-9005. Offers art education (MAE); art history (MA, PhD), including architectural history (MA), art history, historical studies (MA), museum studies (MA); ceramics (MFA); fibers (MFA); furniture design (MFA); glassworking (MFA); graphic design (MFA), including design/visual communications, interior environment, photography and film; jewelry/metalworking (MFA); kinetic imaging (MFA); music (MM), including education; painting (MFA); printmaking (MFA); sculpture (MFA); theatre (MFA), including acting, costume design, directing, pedagogy, scene design/technical theater. Part-time programs available. *Students:* 158 full-time (103 women), 116 part-time (96 women); includes 31 minority (10 Black or African American, non-Hispanic/Latino; 7 Asian, non-Hispanic/Latino; 11 Hispanic/Latino; 3 Two or more races, non-Hispanic/Latino), 9 international. 907 applicants, 18% accepted, 92 enrolled. In 2010, 87 master's, 5 doctorates awarded. *Entrance requirements:* For doctorate, GRE General Test, writing sample. Additional exam requirements/recommendations for international students: Required—TOEFL (minimum score 600 paper-based; 250 computer-based; 100 iBT). *Application deadline:* For fall admission, 1/15 priority date for domestic students. Application fee: $50. Electronic applications accepted. *Expenses:* Tuition, state resident: full-time $4308; part-time $479 per credit hour. Tuition, nonresident: full-time $8942; part-time $994 per credit hour. Required fees: $2000; $85 per credit hour. Tuition and fees vary according to course level, course load, degree level, campus/location and program. *Financial support:* Fellowships, teaching assistantships, career-related internships or fieldwork, Federal Work-Study, institutionally sponsored loans, and tuition waivers (full and partial) available. Support available to part-time students.

Virginia Commonwealth University (continued)
Financial award applicants required to submit FAFSA. *Unit head:* Joseph H. Seipel, Dean, 804-828-2787, Fax: 804-828-6469, E-mail: arts@vcu.edu. *Application contact:* Jack H. Risley, Associate Dean for Academic Affairs, 804-828-2787, Fax: 804-828-6469, E-mail: jhrisley@vcu.edu.

Washington State University, Graduate School, College of Liberal Arts, Department of Fine Arts, Pullman, WA 99164. Offers ceramics (MFA); digital media (MFA); drawing (MFA); painting (MFA); photography (MFA); print making (MFA); sculpture (MFA). *Faculty:* 10. *Students:* 15 full-time (8 women); includes 1 Black or African American, non-Hispanic/Latino; 1 Hispanic/Latino. Average age 29. 30 applicants, 20% accepted, 5 enrolled. In 2010, 5 master's awarded. *Degree requirements:* For master's, comprehensive exam (for some programs), thesis, exhibit, oral exam. *Entrance requirements:* For master's, GRE, statement of intent, portfolio of no more than 15 images on CD/DVD. Additional exam requirements/recommendations for international students: Required—TOEFL (minimum score 550 paper-based; 213 computer-based), IELTS. *Application deadline:* For fall admission, 1/10 for domestic and international students. Application fee: $50. Electronic applications accepted. *Expenses:* Tuition, state resident: full-time $8552; part-time $443 per credit. Tuition, nonresident: full-time $21,650; part-time $1083 per credit. Required fees: $846. *Financial support:* In 2010–11, fellowships with full and partial tuition reimbursements (averaging $3,114 per year), research assistantships with full and partial tuition reimbursements (averaging $13,917 per year), teaching assistantships with full and partial tuition reimbursements (averaging $13,056 per year) were awarded; career-related internships or fieldwork, Federal Work-Study, institutionally sponsored loans, tuition waivers (partial), and unspecified assistantships also available. Financial award application deadline: 2/15; financial award applicants required to submit FAFSA. *Faculty research:* Polynesian art, museum representation, number theory. *Unit head:* Dr. Chris Watts, Interim Chair, 509-335-7107, Fax: 509-335-7742, E-mail: cjwatts@wsu.edu. *Application contact:* Graduate School Admissions, 800-GRADWSU, Fax: 509-335-1949, E-mail: gradsch@wsu.edu.

Yale University, School of Art, New Haven, CT 06520-8339. Offers graphic design (MFA); painting/printmaking (MFA); photography (MFA); sculpture (MFA). *Faculty:* 9 full-time (4 women), 35 part-time/adjunct (12 women). *Students:* 121 full-time (64 women); includes 32 minority (7 Black or African American, non-Hispanic/Latino; 10 Asian, non-Hispanic/Latino; 15 Hispanic/Latino), 32 international. Average age 28. 1,222 applicants, 5% accepted, 57 enrolled. In 2010, 57 master's awarded. *Degree requirements:* For master's, thesis (for some programs). *Entrance requirements:* Additional exam requirements/recommendations for international students: Required—TOEFL (minimum score 550 paper-based; 250 computer-based; 100 iBT). *Application deadline:* For fall admission, 1/4 for domestic and international students. Application fee: $100. Electronic applications accepted. *Expenses:* Contact institution. *Financial support:* In 2010–11, 90 students received support, including 54 teaching assistantships (averaging $1,900 per year); Federal Work-Study, scholarships/grants, and unspecified assistantships also available. Financial award application deadline: 3/1; financial award applicants required to submit FAFSA. *Unit head:* Robert Storr, Dean, 203-432-2606. *Application contact:* Patricia Ann DeChiara, Director of Academic Affairs, 203-432-2600, E-mail: artschool.info@yale.edu.

Textile Design

Academy of Art University, Graduate Program, School of Fashion, San Francisco, CA 94105-3410. Offers fashion design (MFA); fashion merchandising (MFA); fashion textiles (MFA); knitwear (MFA). Part-time programs available. Postbaccalaureate distance learning degree programs offered (no on-campus study). *Faculty:* 23 full-time (13 women), 110 part-time/adjunct (87 women). *Students:* 487 full-time (445 women), 260 part-time (237 women); includes 73 Black or African American, non-Hispanic/Latino; 6 American Indian or Alaska Native, non-Hispanic/Latino; 45 Asian, non-Hispanic/Latino; 35 Hispanic/Latino, 310 international. Average age 29. 218 applicants. In 2010, 107 master's awarded. *Degree requirements:* For master's, thesis, final review. *Entrance requirements:* For master's, minimum GPA of 3.0, portfolio. *Application deadline:* For fall admission, 9/7 for domestic and international students; for spring admission, 2/2 for domestic and international students. Applications are processed on a rolling basis. Application fee: $100 ($500 for international students). Electronic applications accepted. *Expenses:* Tuition: Full-time $20,160; part-time $840 per semester hour. Required fees: $45 per semester. *Financial support:* Career-related internships or fieldwork and Federal Work-Study available. Support available to part-time students. Financial award application deadline: 8/10; financial award applicants required to submit FAFSA. *Application contact:* Prospective Student Services, 800-544-ARTS, Fax: 415-263-4130, E-mail: info@academyart.edu.

California College of the Arts, Graduate Programs, Programs in Fine Art, San Francisco, CA 94107. Offers ceramics (MFA); film/video/performance (MFA); glass (MFA); jewelry/metal arts (MFA); painting/drawing (MFA); photography (MFA); printmaking (MFA); sculpture (MFA); textiles (MFA); wood/furniture (MFA). *Accreditation:* NASAD. *Faculty:* 20 full-time (10 women), 25 part-time/adjunct (14 women). *Students:* 95 full-time (66 women), 12 part-time (9 women); includes 3 Black or African American, non-Hispanic/Latino; 1 American Indian or Alaska Native, non-Hispanic/Latino; 5 Asian, non-Hispanic/Latino; 20 Hispanic/Latino; 2 Native Hawaiian or other Pacific Islander, non-Hispanic/Latino, 7 international. Average age 30. 462 applicants, 37% accepted, 55 enrolled. In 2010, 173 master's awarded. *Degree requirements:* For master's, thesis, exhibit. *Entrance requirements:* For master's, appropriate bachelor's degree, portfolio, resume, 2 letters of recommendation, transcript. Additional exam requirements/recommendations for international students: Required—TOEFL (minimum score 600 paper-based; 250 computer-based; 100 iBT). *Application deadline:* For fall admission, 1/5 for domestic and international students. Application fee: $70. Electronic applications accepted. *Expenses:* Tuition: Full-time $38,550; part-time $1285 per unit. One-time fee: $185 full-time. *Financial support:* In 2010–11, 12 fellowships (averaging $27,000 per year), teaching assistantships (averaging $2,000 per year) were awarded; career-related internships or fieldwork, Federal Work-Study, scholarships/grants, and health care benefits also available. Financial award application deadline: 3/1; financial award applicants required to submit FAFSA. *Unit head:* Ted Purves, Chair, 415-551-9214, Fax: 415-703-9539, E-mail: tpurves@cca.edu. *Application contact:* Heidi Geis, Assistant Director of Graduate Admissions, 415-703-9523 Ext. 9533, Fax: 415-703-9539, E-mail: hgeis@cca.edu.

California State University, Los Angeles, Graduate Studies, College of Arts and Letters, Department of Art, Los Angeles, CA 90032-8530. Offers art (MA), including art education, art history, art therapy, ceramics, metals, and textiles, design (MA, MFA), painting, sculpture, and graphic arts, photography; fine arts (MFA), including crafts, design (MA, MFA), studio arts. *Accreditation:* NASAD (one or more programs are accredited). Part-time and evening/weekend programs available. *Faculty:* 9 full-time (5 women), 3 part-time/adjunct (2 women). *Students:* 27 full-time (19 women), 33 part-time (22 women); includes 24 minority (3 Black or African American, non-Hispanic/Latino; 7 Asian, non-Hispanic/Latino; 13 Hispanic/Latino; 1 Two or more races, non-Hispanic/Latino), 9 international. Average age 36. 19 applicants, 100% accepted, 13 enrolled. In 2010, 26 master's awarded. *Degree requirements:* For master's, comprehensive exam, project or thesis. *Entrance requirements:* For master's, portfolio. Additional exam requirements/recommendations for international students: Required—TOEFL (minimum score 500 paper-based; 173 computer-based). *Application deadline:* For fall admission, 5/1 for domestic and international students. Applications are processed on a rolling basis. Application fee: $55. Electronic applications accepted. *Financial support:* Federal Work-Study available. Support available to part-time students. Financial award application deadline: 3/1. *Faculty research:* The artist and the book, conceptual art, ceramic processes, computer graphics, architectural graphics. *Unit head:* Dr. Abbas Daneshvari, Chair, 323-343-4010, Fax: 323-343-4045, E-mail: adanesh@calstatela.edu. *Application contact:* Dr. Alan Muchlinski, Dean of Graduate Studies, 323-343-3820, Fax: 323-343-5653, E-mail: amuchli@exchange.calstatela.edu.

Cornell University, Graduate School, Graduate Fields of Human Ecology, Field of Textiles, Ithaca, NY 14853. Offers apparel design (MA, MPS); fiber science (MS, PhD); polymer science (MS, PhD); textile science (MS, PhD). *Faculty:* 19 full-time (7 women). *Students:* 20 full-time (15 women); includes 1 Black or African American, non-Hispanic/Latino; 1 Asian, non-Hispanic/Latino, 9 international. Average age 28. 41 applicants, 29% accepted, 9 enrolled. In 2010, 5 master's, 3 doctorates awarded. *Degree requirements:* For master's, thesis (MA, MS), project paper (MPS); for doctorate, comprehensive exam, thesis/dissertation. *Entrance requirements:* For master's, GRE General Test, 2 letters of recommendation, portfolio (functional apparel design); for doctorate, GRE General Test, 2 letters of recommendation. Additional exam requirements/recommendations for international students: Required—TOEFL (minimum score 600 paper-based; 250 computer-based; 77 iBT). *Application deadline:* For fall admission, 3/1 for domestic students; for spring admission, 10/1 for domestic students. Application fees: $70. Electronic applications accepted. *Expenses:* Tuition: Full-time $29,500. Required fees: $76. Tuition and fees vary according to degree level and program. *Financial support:* In 2010–11, 19 students received support, including 2 fellowships with full tuition reimbursements available, 7 research assistantships with full tuition reimbursements available, 8 teaching assistantships with full tuition reimbursements available; institutionally sponsored loans, scholarships/grants, health care benefits, tuition waivers (full and partial), and unspecified assistantships also available. Financial award applicants required to submit FAFSA. *Faculty research:* Apparel design, consumption, mass customization, 3-D body scanning. *Unit head:* Director of Graduate Studies, 607-255-3151, Fax: 607-255-1093. *Application contact:* Graduate Field Assistant, 607-255-3151, Fax: 607-255-1093, E-mail: textiles_grad@cornell.edu.

Cranbrook Academy of Art, Graduate School, Program in Fine Arts, Bloomfield Hills, MI 48303-0801. Offers ceramics (MFA); design (MFA), including graphic design; fiber arts (MFA); metalsmithing (MFA); painting (MFA); photography (MFA); printmaking (MFA); sculpture (MFA). *Accreditation:* NASAD. *Degree requirements:* For master's, thesis, exhibit. *Entrance requirements:* Additional exam requirements/recommendations for international students: Required—TOEFL (minimum score 550 paper-based; 213 computer-based).

Drexel University, Antoinette Westphal College of Media Arts and Design, Program in Fashion Design, Philadelphia, PA 19104-2875. Offers MS. *Accreditation:* NASAD. *Degree requirements:* For master's, thesis, portfolio review. *Entrance requirements:* For master's, interview. Additional exam requirements/recommendations for international students: Required—TOEFL. Electronic applications accepted.

Illinois State University, Graduate School, College of Fine Arts, School of Art, Normal, IL 61790-2200. Offers art history (MA, MS); ceramics (MFA, MS); drawing (MFA, MS); fibers (MFA, MS); glass (MFA, MS); graphic design (MFA, MS); metals (MFA, MS); painting (MFA, MS); photography (MFA, MS); printmaking (MFA, MS); sculpture (MFA, MS). *Accreditation:* NASAD (one or more programs are accredited). *Degree requirements:* For master's, thesis or alternative, internship. *Entrance requirements:* For master's, portfolio, sample of scholarly writing. *Faculty research:* General operations support: Normal Editions Workshop for FY2007.

James Madison University, The Graduate School, College of Visual and Performing Arts, School of Art and Art History, Harrisonburg, VA 22807. Offers art education (MA); art history (MA); ceramics (MFA); drawing/painting (MFA); metal/jewelry (MFA); photography (MFA); printmaking (MFA); sculpture (MFA); studio art (MA); weaving/fibers (MFA). *Accreditation:* NASAD. Part-time programs available. *Faculty:* 8 full-time (5 women). *Students:* 10 full-time (6 women); includes 1 minority (Black or African American, non-Hispanic/Latino). Average age 27. In 2010, 3 master's awarded. *Degree requirements:* For master's, thesis (for some programs). *Entrance requirements:* For master's, GRE General Test, language exam in French or German, portfolio, 3 letters of recommendation, research paper. Additional exam requirements/recommendations for international students: Required—TOEFL. *Application deadline:* For fall admission, 2/15 priority date for domestic students, 2/15 for international students; for spring admission, 10/15 priority date for domestic students, 10/15 for international students. Applications are processed on a rolling basis. Application fee: $55. Electronic applications accepted. *Financial support:* In 2010–11, 9 students received support, including 3 teaching assistantships with full tuition reimbursements available (averaging $8,664 per year); Federal Work-Study and 6 graduate assistantships ($7382) also available. Financial award application deadline: 3/1; financial award applicants required to submit FAFSA. *Unit head:* William Srightman, Director, 540-568-6216. *Application contact:* Lynette M. Bible, Director of Graduate Admissions, 540-568-6395, Fax: 540-568-7860, E-mail: biblelm@jmu.edu.

Kent State University, College of the Arts, School of Art, Kent, OH 44242-0001. Offers art education (MA); art history (MA); crafts (MA, MFA), including ceramics (MA), glass, jewelry/metals, textiles/art; fine art (MA, MFA), including drawing/painting, printmaking, sculpture. *Accreditation:* NASAD (one or more programs are accredited). *Degree requirements:* For master's, one foreign language, thesis. *Entrance requirements:* For master's, undergraduate degree in proposed area of study (for fine arts and crafts programs); minimum overall GPA of 2.75 (3.0 for art major); 3 letters of recommendation; portfolio (15-20 slides for MA, 20-25 for MFA). Additional exam requirements/recommendations for international students: Required—TOEFL. Electronic applications accepted. *Expenses:* Tuition, state resident: full-time $7866; part-time $437 per credit hour. Tuition, nonresident: full-time $14,022; part-time $779 per credit hour.

LIM College, MBA Program, New York, NY 10022-5268. Offers entrepreneurship (MBA); fashion management (MBA).

Marywood University, Academic Affairs, Insalaco College of Creative and Performing Arts, Art Department, Program in Studio Art, Scranton, PA 18509-1598. Offers advertising design (MA); ceramics (MA); clay (MA); graphic design (MA); illustration (MA); painting (MA); photography (MA); printmaking (MA); sculpture (MA); weaving (MA). *Accreditation:* NASAD. *Entrance requirements:* Additional exam requirements/recommendations for international students: Required—TOEFL (minimum score 550 paper-based; 213 computer-based; 79 iBT). Electronic applications accepted. *Expenses:* Tuition: Part-time $735 per credit. Required fees: $470 per semester. Tuition and fees vary according to degree level and campus/location. *Faculty research:* Texture and line in clay, cast bronze sculpture, color theories, book art and illustration, sculptural form.

Massachusetts College of Art and Design, Graduate Programs, Master of Fine Arts (MFA) Program, Boston, MA 02115-5882. Offers ceramics (MFA); design (MFA); fibers (MFA); film/video (MFA); glass (MFA); media and performing arts (MFA); metals/jewelry (MFA); painting (MFA); photography (MFA); printmaking (MFA); sculpture (MFA). *Accreditation:* NASAD. *Faculty:* 14 full-time (7 women), 16 part-time/adjunct (10 women). *Students:* 86 full-time (51 women), 9 part-time (5 women); includes 10 minority (1 Asian, non-Hispanic/Latino; 6 Hispanic/Latino; 3 Two or more races, non-Hispanic/Latino), 14 international. Average age 34. 298 applicants, 28% accepted, 41 enrolled. In 2010, 40 master's awarded. *Degree requirements:* For master's, thesis, exhibit. *Entrance requirements:* For master's, 12 units of course work in art history, portfolio, resume, letters of reference, interview. Additional exam requirements/recommendations for international students: Required—TOEFL (minimum score 563 paper-based; 223 computer-based; 85 iBT); Recommended—IELTS (minimum score 6.5). *Application deadline:* For fall admission, 1/15 for domestic and international students. Application fee: $85. Electronic applications accepted. *Expenses:* Tuition, state resident: part-time $665 per credit. Tuition, nonresident: part-time $665 per credit. *Financial support:* In 2010–11, 19 fellowships (averaging $5,000 per year), 43 research assistantships (averaging $2,000 per year), 44 teaching assistantships (averaging $2,000 per year) were awarded; career-related internships or fieldwork and Federal Work-Study also available. Support available to part-time students. Financial award application deadline: 5/1; financial award applicants required to submit FAFSA. *Unit head:* George Creamer, Dean of Graduate Programs, 617-879-7163, Fax: 617-879-7171, E-mail: creamer@massart.edu. *Application contact:* George Creamer, Dean of Graduate Programs, 617-879-7163, Fax: 617-879-7171, E-mail: creamer@massart.edu.

Missouri State University, Graduate College, College of Natural and Applied Sciences, Department of Fashion and Interior Design, Springfield, MO 65897. Offers secondary education (MS Ed), including consumer sciences. Part-time programs available. *Degree requirements:* For master's, comprehensive exam, thesis or alternative. *Entrance requirements:* For master's, 9-12 teaching certification (MS Ed), minimum GPA of 3.0 (MNAS). Additional exam requirements/recommendations for international students: Required—TOEFL (minimum score 550 paper-based; 213 computer-based; 79 iBT). Electronic applications accepted. *Expenses:* Tuition, state resident: full-time $3348; part-time $186 per credit hour. Tuition, nonresident: full-time $6696; part-time $372 per credit hour. Required fees: $238 per semester. Tuition and fees vary according to course level, course load and program.

The New School: A University, Parsons The New School for Design, Program in Fashion Design and Society, New York, NY 10011. Offers MFA.

The New School: A University, Parsons The New School for Design, Program in Fashion Studies, New York, NY 10011. Offers MA. *Degree requirements:* For master's, thesis.

Philadelphia University, School of Engineering and Textiles, Program in Textile Design, Philadelphia, PA 19144. Offers MS. Part-time programs available. *Entrance requirements:* For master's, GRE or MAT, minimum GPA of 2.8. Additional exam requirements/recommendations for international students: Required—TOEFL (minimum score 550 paper-based; 213 computer-based; 79 iBT). Electronic applications accepted.

Rhode Island School of Design, Graduate Studies, Division of Fine Arts, Department of Textiles, Providence, RI 02903-2784. Offers MFA. *Accreditation:* NASAD. *Degree requirements:* For master's, thesis, exhibit. *Entrance requirements:* For master's, portfolio, 3 letters of recommendation. Additional exam requirements/recommendations for international students: Required—TOEFL (minimum score 580 paper-based; 237 computer-based), IELTS (minimum score 6.5).

Savannah College of Art and Design, Graduate School, Program in Fashion, Savannah, GA 31402-3146. Offers MA, MFA. Part-time programs available. *Faculty:* 20 full-time (13 women), 6 part-time/adjunct (5 women). *Students:* 27 full-time (24 women), 5 part-time (all women); includes 3 Black or African American, non-Hispanic/Latino, 10 international. Average age 27. In 2010, 13 master's awarded. *Degree requirements:* For master's, thesis, internship. *Entrance requirements:* For master's, interview, portfolio. Additional exam requirements/recommendations for international students: Required—TOEFL (minimum score 450 paper-based; 133 computer-based). *Application deadline:* For fall admission, 4/1 priority date for domestic and international students. Applications are processed on a rolling basis. Application fee: $35. Electronic applications accepted. *Expenses:* Tuition: Full-time $29,520; part-time $3280 per quarter. Tuition and fees vary according to campus/location. *Financial support:* Fellowships, career-related internships or fieldwork, Federal Work-Study, and scholarships/grants available. Financial award application deadline: 4/1; financial award applicants required to submit FAFSA. *Unit head:* Carmela Spinelli, Chair, 912-525-6637, E-mail: cspinellir@scad.edu. *Application contact:* Elizabeth Mathis, Director of Graduate Recruitment, 912-525-5965, Fax: 912-525-5985, E-mail: emathis@scad.edu.

See Display on page 177 and Close-Up on page 223

Savannah College of Art and Design, Graduate School, Program in Fibers, Savannah, GA 31402-3146. Offers MA, MFA. Part-time programs available. *Faculty:* 8 full-time (7 women), 1 (woman) part-time/adjunct. *Students:* 10 full-time (9 women), 5 part-time (all women), 1 international. Average age 27. In 2010, 9 master's awarded. *Degree requirements:* For master's, thesis, internship. *Entrance requirements:* For master's, interview, portfolio. Additional exam requirements/recommendations for international students: Required—TOEFL (minimum score 450 paper-based; 133 computer-based). *Application deadline:* For fall admission, 4/1 priority date for domestic and international students. Applications are processed on a rolling basis. Application fee: $35. Electronic applications accepted. *Expenses:* Tuition: Full-time $29,520; part-time $3280 per quarter. Tuition and fees vary according to campus/location. *Financial support:* Fellowships, career-related internships or fieldwork, Federal Work-Study, and scholarships/grants available. Financial award application deadline: 4/1; financial award applicants required to submit FAFSA. *Unit head:* Cayoweh Easley, Chair, 912-525-4136, E-mail: ceasley@scad.edu. *Application contact:* Elizabeth Mathis, Director of Graduate Recruitment, 912-525-5965, Fax: 912-525-5985, E-mail: emathis@scad.edu.

See Display on page 177 and Close-Up on page 223

School of the Art Institute of Chicago, Graduate Division, Program in Fashion, Body, and Garment, Chicago, IL 60603-3103. Offers M Des, Certificate.

See Close-Up on page 225.

Sul Ross State University, School of Arts and Sciences, Department of Fine Arts and Communication, Alpine, TX 79832. Offers art education (M Ed); art history (M Ed); studio art (M Ed), including ceramics, design, drawing, jewelry, painting, printmaking, sculpture, weaving. Part-time programs available. *Degree requirements:* For master's, oral or written exam. *Entrance requirements:* For master's, GRE General Test, minimum GPA of 2.5 in last 60 hours of undergraduate work. *Faculty research:* Ceramic sculpture, watercolor, wood sculpture, rock art.

Temple University, Tyler School of Art, Department of Crafts, Philadelphia, PA 19122-6096. Offers ceramics/glass (MFA); fibers and fabric design (MFA); metals/jewelry/CAD-CAM (MFA). *Faculty:* 6 full-time (3 women). *Students:* 22 full-time (15 women), 1 (woman) part-time; includes 1 Black or African American, non-Hispanic/Latino; 1 American Indian or Alaska Native, non-Hispanic/Latino; 1 Hispanic/Latino, 2 international. 67 applicants, 25% accepted, 15 enrolled. In 2010, 11 master's awarded. *Degree requirements:* For master's, essay, exhibit. *Entrance requirements:* For master's, minimum GPA of 3.0, slide portfolio, 40 credits in studio art, 12 credits in art history. Additional exam requirements/recommendations for international students: Required—TOEFL (minimum score 550 paper-based; 213 computer-based; 79 iBT). *Application deadline:* For fall admission, 12/15 for international students. Application fee: $50. Electronic applications accepted. *Financial support:* Fellowships with full tuition reimbursements, research assistantships with full tuition reimbursements, teaching assistantships with full tuition reimbursements, Federal Work-Study available. Support available to part-time students. Financial award application deadline: 1/15; financial award applicants required to submit FAFSA. *Unit head:* Nicholas Kripal, Chair, 215-782-2790, Fax: 215-782-2799, E-mail: nkripal@temple.edu. *Application contact:* Carmina Cianciulli, Assistant Dean for Admissions, 215-782-2875, Fax: 215-782-2711, E-mail: tylerart@temple.edu.

University of California, Davis, Graduate Studies, Program in Textile Arts and Costume Design, Davis, CA 95616. Offers MFA. *Degree requirements:* For master's, presentation of an individual project/body of work. *Entrance requirements:* For master's, minimum GPA of 3.0, portfolio. Additional exam requirements/recommendations for international students: Required—TOEFL (minimum score 550 paper-based; 213 computer-based). Electronic applications accepted. *Faculty research:* Historic ethnographic and contemporary costume and textile design, computer-aided design.

University of Cincinnati, Graduate School, College of Design, Architecture, Art, and Planning, School of Design, Cincinnati, OH 45221. Offers fashion design (M Des); graphic design (M Des); industrial design (M Des); interaction design (M Des); product development (M Des). *Accreditation:* NASAD. *Degree requirements:* For master's, thesis. *Entrance requirements:* For master's, undergraduate degree in design or related field, 2 years of work experience in design or related field. Additional exam requirements/recommendations for international students: Required—TOEFL. Electronic applications accepted. *Faculty research:* Design theory, interdisciplinary design topics.

The University of Manchester, School of Materials, Manchester, United Kingdom. Offers advanced aerospace materials engineering (M Sc); advanced metallic systems (PhD); biomedical materials (M Phil, M Sc, PhD); ceramics and glass (M Phil, M Sc, PhD); composite materials (M Sc, PhD); corrosion and protection (M Phil, M Sc, PhD); materials (M Phil, PhD); metallic materials (M Phil, M Sc, PhD); nanostructural materials (M Phil, M Sc, PhD); paper science (M Phil, M Sc, PhD); polymer science and engineering (M Phil, M Sc, PhD); technical textiles (M Sc); textile design, fashion and management (M Phil, M Sc, PhD); textile science and technology (M Phil, M Sc, PhD); textiles (M Phil, PhD); textiles and fashion (M Ent).

University of Massachusetts Dartmouth, Graduate School, College of Visual and Performing Arts, Program in Artisanry, North Dartmouth, MA 02747-2300. Offers ceramics (MFA, Postbaccalaureate Certificate); fibers (MFA); fibers/textiles (Postbaccalaureate Certificate); jewelry/metals (MFA, Postbaccalaureate Certificate); wood/furniture design (MFA, Postbaccalaureate Certificate). *Accreditation:* NASAD. *Faculty:* 7 full-time (4 women). *Students:* 17 full-time (12 women), 9 part-time (all women); includes 1 Asian, non-Hispanic/Latino; 1 Hispanic/Latino, 2 international. Average age 29. 47 applicants, 47% accepted, 10 enrolled. In 2010, 9 master's awarded. *Degree requirements:* For master's, thesis, visual thesis. *Entrance requirements:* For master's, portfolio, interview, minimum GPA of 3.0, 3 letters of recommendation. Additional exam requirements/recommendations for international students: Required—TOEFL (minimum score 500 paper-based). *Application deadline:* For fall admission, 2/1 for domestic students, 12/1 for international students. Applications are processed on a rolling basis. Application fee: $40 ($60 for international students). Electronic applications accepted. *Expenses:* Tuition, state resident: full-time $2071; part-time $86 per credit. Tuition, nonresident: full-time $8099; part-time $337 per credit. Required fees: $9446; $394 per credit. One-time fee: $75. Part-time tuition and fees vary according to class time, course load, degree level and reciprocity agreements. *Financial support:* In 2010–11, 2 fellowships with full tuition reimbursements (averaging $5,333 per year), 1 research assistantship with full tuition reimbursement (averaging $7,400 per year), 14 teaching assistantships with full tuition reimbursements (averaging $3,088 per year) were awarded; Federal Work-Study and unspecified assistantships also available. Support available to part-time students. Financial award application deadline: 3/1; financial award applicants required to submit FAFSA. Total annual research expenditures: $831. *Unit head:* Memory Holloway, Director, 508-999-8554, E-mail: mholloway@umassd.edu. *Application contact:* Elan Turcotte-Shamski, Graduate Admissions Officer, 508-999-8604, Fax: 508-999-8183, E-mail: graduate@umassd.edu.

University of Minnesota, Twin Cities Campus, Graduate School, College of Design, Department of Design, Housing, and Apparel, Minneapolis, MN 55455-0213. Offers apparel (MA, MS, PhD); design communication (MA, MS, PhD); housing studies (MA, MS, PhD, Postbaccalaureate Certificate); interactive design (MFA); interior design (MA, MS, PhD). Part-time programs available. *Degree requirements:* For master's and Postbaccalaureate Certificate, comprehensive exam, thesis (for some programs); for doctorate, comprehensive exam, thesis/dissertation. *Entrance requirements:* For master's, GRE General Test, minimum GPA of 3.0 (preferred), portfolio, 3 letters of recommendation; for doctorate, GRE General Test, minimum GPA of 3.0 (preferred), portfolio, 3 letters of recommendation, writing sample; for Postbaccalaureate Certificate, GRE General Test, minimum GPA of 3.0 (preferred). Additional exam requirements/recommendations for international students: Required—TOEFL (minimum score 550 paper-based; 213 computer-based; 79 iBT). Electronic applications accepted. *Faculty research:* Housing policy and community development; consumer behavior; interactive design; design history; social, cultural, and behavioral issues related to designed environments.

The University of North Carolina at Greensboro, Graduate School, School of Human Environmental Sciences, Department of Consumer, Apparel, and Retail Studies, Greensboro, NC 27412-5001. Offers MS, PhD. *Degree requirements:* For master's, one foreign language; for doctorate, one foreign language, thesis/dissertation. *Entrance requirements:* For master's and doctorate, GRE General Test. Additional exam requirements/recommendations for international students: Required—TOEFL. Electronic applications accepted. *Faculty research:* Impact of phosphate removal, protective clothing for pesticide workers, fabric hand: subjective and objective measurements.

ArtCenter

ART CENTER COLLEGE OF DESIGN

Programs of Study	Art Center's graduate programs provide a framework in which students can pursue advanced studies in media design, broadcast cinema (film), art, and industrial design. The graduate programs enable students to broaden their practical, conceptual, and analytical skills by providing a balance between professional and theoretical approaches to art and design practice.
	Future graduate programs in transportation design and environmental design are being planned. Every program has its own graduate seminar, which brings artists, designers, and critics to the campus regularly. Each program's curriculum allows students to follow their own interests and direction, yet is designed to ensure that every student covers comprehensive course material and receives critical feedback. In addition to regular meetings with graduate faculty members, students benefit from interaction with visiting artists and designers.
	Broadcast Cinema, Art Center's M.F.A. program for filmmakers, is focused on the creation of works for existing, emerging, and future forms of broadcast and theatrical distribution. The traditional term "broadcast" represents the College's exploration of the vast potential of satellite distribution and "cinema" represents innovation in visual aesthetics and content. Early development of each student's individual creative identity is a priority. Students may choose to specialize in any creative leadership roles in filmmaking. The program encourages students to explore new content, forms, and methods of storytelling.
	The M.F.A. program in Media Design is for students who are interested in exploring the future of communication in an information-saturated, media-driven world. This interdisciplinary program encourages innovation and experimentation, theoretical research, the development of technological sophistication, and individual creativity. Students work in state-of-the-art facilities under the direction of a diverse faculty of accomplished designers, technology specialists, theorists, and thought leaders, and meet regularly with visiting artists, scholars, and entrepreneurs. In addition, there is a Media Design Matters program that allows students to focus on issues of significant social and environmental relevance. More details are available at Art Center's Web site.
	An M.S. degree is offered in Industrial Design. This graduate program encourages students with a background in product or environmental design to expand their knowledge and expertise while emphasizing experimentation, innovation, and multidisciplinary research. Particular emphasis is placed on broadening students' intellectual grasp of design issues, using digital and written media for communication, and realizing the full potential of the creative process. The first year of the program is spent in a joint multidisciplinary project. Students work closely with a distinguished core faculty and with many visiting specialists.
	The M.F.A. program in Art brings together students and a varied faculty composed of internationally known artists. The size of the program—about 35 students and 7 graduate advisers—allows for intensive one-on-one dialogue while offering sufficient diversity to generate critical exchange and controversy. The program emphasizes both making and theorizing the art object and provides studios for independent work as well as classes in theory and technique.
Research Facilities	The James Lemont Fogg Memorial Library contains 92,000 volumes of books and periodicals, and 9,000 videotapes and DVDs of rare features, animation, documentaries, advertising, computer graphics, and instructional programs. A photo reference collection contains more than 90,000 pictures. The Rare Book Room houses limited and signed editions, portfolios, and other materials. Subscriptions are maintained for more than 400 magazines, and online subscriptions provide access to thousands of magazine articles and images. A CD-ROM workstation can be used to view a collection of more than 350 interactive CD-ROMs. Occidental College's library of more than 1 million volumes serves as another resource for Art Center students.
	Art Center maintains state-of-the-art studios and shops, including a rapid-modeling machine that creates three-dimensional prototype models. Archetype Press, a 3,000-square-foot facility, houses fourteen presses and 2,400 drawers of rare type from American and European foundries. Students have access to a wide range of interactive multimedia and digital resources for exploring and refining their ideas, including sixty Silicon Graphics workstations, 140 Apple Macintosh computers, twelve Compaq Professional NT workstations, and the latest design software available.
	In addition, the Wind Tunnel facility at Art Center's South Campus includes the New Ecology of Things (N.E.T.) research lab, dedicated to exploring a future world of interactive networked technologies. The lab includes a collection of experimental media and technologies, including custom hardware and software created by the media design faculty.
Financial Aid	Graduate students may apply for scholarships by meeting priority deadlines. Scholarships are awarded by a graduate scholarship committee. Candidates must demonstrate financial need and present an exceptional portfolio of work for scholarship consideration. Grants and loans, including the California Graduate Fellowship and FFELP Loan Program, are available. Teaching assistantships are also available.
Cost of Study	The cost of tuition for 2011 is $17,724 per fifteen-week semester.
Living and Housing Costs	The College does not currently maintain dormitories. A wide variety of housing is available in Pasadena and neighboring communities. The average cost of rent and food per semester is approximately $5000.
Student Group	Approximately 130 graduate students, of whom 60 percent are men and 40 percent are women, are enrolled in the College.
Student Outcomes	Most students pursue careers as practicing artists and designers within their professions.
Location	Art Center is located in Pasadena, California, a residential community near Los Angeles. With two campuses, one in a striking glass and steel facility on the hillsides of Pasadena and the other near old town Pasadena, the College is a short distance from greater Los Angeles. Students benefit from their proximity to art galleries, advertising and design agencies, and the entertainment industry.
The College	A private, nonprofit institution, Art Center College of Design was founded in 1930 with the purpose of educating students for distinguished careers in the visual arts professions. The total enrollment, including undergraduates, is 1,600. Eighteen percent of students are international and represent forty-seven different countries. The College is accredited by WASC and NASAD.
Applying	Applicants for the Art program may apply for entry in fall or spring. Applications are accepted on a rolling admissions basis, with consideration given as long as space is available in a class. Spaces in most graduate programs are extremely limited and may require application a number of semesters in advance. Media Design and Industrial Design applicants may apply only for the fall semester, and the application deadline for these programs is February 1. Broadcast Cinema students start in the fall only and applications are reviewed on a rolling basis. The Art program is six semesters in length and the Broadcast Cinema is four semesters in length. The media design program offers a two- and three-year option. Applicants may consult the Admissions Office about the status of any entering class.
Correspondence and Information	Admissions Office Art Center College of Design 1700 Lida Street Pasadena, California 91103 Phone: 626-396-2373 Fax: 626-795-0578 E-mail: admissions@artcenter.edu Web site: http://www.artcenter.edu

Art Center College of Design

THE FACULTY

The faculty members are core faculty advisers for graduate programs. Graduate students have access to a wide variety of classes and additional faculty members at Art Center.

Media Design Program

Anne Burdick, Chair; M.F.A., California Institute of the Arts. Designer, writer, editor. Work is included in the Museum of Modern Art in New York and the San Francisco Museum of Modern Art. Publications include *Eye, I.D., Idea, Adobe Think Tank,* and *Emigre* magazines. Awards include the Leipzig Award (Most Beautiful Book in the World), AIGA 50 Books/50 Covers, I.D. Interactive Design Annual, Webby Award, ACD 100, and others. Projects include electronic corpora and text-dictionaries with the Austrian Academy of Sciences, experimental fiction at the Walker Art Center's Gallery 9, and books of literary/media criticism by authors such as Marshall McLuhan and N. Katherine Hayles. Burdick has been the design editor of *Electronic Book Review* since 1995.

Sean Donahue, M.F.A., Art Center College of Design. Principal of ResearchCenteredDesign, a Los Angeles–based design practice. His practice consists of professional commissions, self-initiated research, design advocacy, education, and publishing. Donahue has lectured and published internationally at RISD, RCA, and North Carolina State University, where he was also the 2004 Designer-in-Residence. Published research: the University of Cambridge, Princeton Architectural Press, MIT Press, and *I.D.* magazine.

Tim Durfee, M.Arch., Yale. He is a partner of the Los Angeles firm of Durfee | Regn which has created—in collaboration with other designers—award-winning exhibitions for LACMA, the Hammer, Huntington Library, Pacific Design Center, UCLA, the Indianapolis Museum of Art, the International Center for Photography in New York, and a permanent exhibition for Target Corporation's headquarters in Minneapolis. He also collaborates with artists, including Ultraworld at the Centre Pompidou's L'ARC in Paris with Doug Aitken in 2005. He has developed interface prototypes and production designs for SF MOMA and LAUNCH and an award-winning Web site for LACMA.

Ben Hooker, M.A., B.Sc., Royal College of Art (London). Collaborates with architects, industrial designers, and computer scientists working in the field of human-computer interaction, resulting in computer-generated data landscapes merging with real, physical spaces. He is also a member of the Visiting Faculty at Intel's Research Lab in Berkeley. Clients include Shona Kitchen; San Jose International Airport, and projects for Vitra Design Museum and Art Center College of Design.

Philip Van Allen, B.A., California, Santa Cruz. Interaction designer/producer/technologist for experimental information and entertainment systems with a research focus on interactive objects and spaces, productive interaction (productiveinteraction.com) and interactive audio. Background in music recording and software development. Principal: Commotion New Media. Clients: Infiniti, George P. Johnson, Interval Research, Philips, Yahoo/Launch Media, Virgin Interactive Entertainment, Art Center College of Design, Nestlé, U2, The Germs. Teacher: ACCD, Santa Monica College, McGill University. Interactive art collaborations: Yoko Ono, Kim Abeles. Exhibitions: Nucleus Gallery, SIGGRAPH Virtual Lounge. Publications: Founded mid-nineties magazine ArtCommotion.com, DIS 2004 ACM conference proceedings, USC Annenberg Online Journalism Review.

Industrial Design Program

Andrew Ogden, Chair; B.S., Art Center College of Design. Vice president and executive designer, Walt Disney Imagineering; designer, Honda R&D North America.

Mark Andersen, B.S., Art Center College of Design. Designer; founder/owner, ZoomOutDesign. Clients: Zaca Inc. and BioControl Inc. Exhibitions: *Brewery Art Walk 2005–06,* Los Angeles. Awards: IDSA silver for Zaca SpaceCab, IDSA bronze for Hycore Biomedical accuPINCH, and honorable mention, "Why Design?", Art Center faculty grant for 3-D digital modeling research.

Katherine Bennett, B.S.I.D., Philadelphia College of Art. Design research, product development, information architecture, strategic planning. Clients: Johnson Controls International, Avery Dennison. Formerly with Donald Chadwick Associates, Hauser, Saul Bass, Henry Dreyfuss Associates. Projects: contract and residential furniture, consumer products, equipment and instrumentation, communications. Publications (periodicals): *Los Angeles Times, Innovation, Modern Photography.*

Richard Keyes, B.F.A., Art Center College of Design. Owner, Keyes Design; former designer, Steven Jacobs, Fulton & Green, the Graphics Studio. Clients: Warner Brothers Records, Atlantic Richfield, Guess? Jeans, Convergent Technologies, His Holiness the Dalai Lama, Empire Berol (color consulting), Homebody, Los Angeles Housing Department, Parson's Engineering (design consultant). Former instructor: California State University, Los Angeles; Los Angeles Valley College; UCLA Extension.

Steven Montgomery, B.A., Michigan State. Industrial designer; principal, BioDesign, specializing in medical and consumer product design; former project manager for S. G. Hauser Associates, Inc.; designer, Huck & Studer Design, KMH Associates. Clients: Johnson & Johnson, Baxter Healthcare Corporation, Becton Dickinson, Omron Healthcare, Cepheid, Panasonic, Technicolor, Boeing/Teague, Bissell, Thomson Electronics, Reebok, Acer, Whirlpool, Hyundai, Honda R&D, Goldstar, Caterpillar, DaimlerChrysler, Nokia, Microsoft, Disney. Awards: IDSA.

Geoff Wardle, M.Des., Royal College of Art (London). Corporate design experience: British Leyland, Chrysler Europe, Saab, Ford Asia Pacific. Design consultant: Tatra, Czech Republic; TVS-Suzuki, India. Former chair of Transportation Design, Art Center Europe.

Broadcast Cinema Program

Robert W. Peterson, Chair; B.F.A., Art Center College of Design. Director/Director of Photography. Production design, visual effects design, commercials, music videos, documentary films, television, theater. Clients: 20th Century Fox, Paramount, Columbia, Universal, United Artists. Awards: Clio, Belding, Council for Advancement of Secondary Education, New York Film Festival.

Jean-Pierre Geuens, Ph.D., USC. Professor of Cinema, Los Angeles City College. Author: *Film Production Theory.* Publications: *Film Quarterly, Film Criticism, Spectator, LA/CA Journal.*

John Hartzog, Ph.D., USC. Director, Learning Resource Center, California State University, Northridge. Publications: *Film Quarterly, Magill Cinema Annual, Academe.*

Victoria Hochberg, B.A., Antioch College. Fulbright Fellowship. Writer/director: feature films, television, documentaries, music videos. Television: *Sex and the City, Ghost Whisperer, Kitchen Confidential, Reaper.* Feature writer: *The Love of Good Women,* performed with the San Francisco Mime Troupe, Pantomime Theatre of New York. Awards: two Emmy awards for writing and directing, four nominations and two Directors Guild of America awards, Writers Guild of America Award nomination. Member: National Board of the Directors Guild of America, including the Special Projects and Creative Rights Committees.

Eric Sherman, B.A., Yale. Director, cinematographer, producer: *Pep Squad, Mystic Nights & Pirate Fights, After Freedom.* President, Film Transform. Author: *The Director's Event, Directing the Film, Frame by Frame, Selling Your Film, Home Entertainment–The Ultimate Movie Marketplace.* Publications: *Moviemaker.* Awards: Montreal Film Festival, Audience Award, Methodfest *(After Freedom),* New York, Bilbao, Columbus Film Festivals, Peabody Broadcasting Award. Member: Board of Trustees, American Cinematheque; Board of Directors, Film Forum.

Fine Art Program

Jeremy Gilbert-Rolfe, Chair; M.F.A., Florida State. Paintings exhibited nationally and internationally since 1971. Major publications include *Immanence and Contradiction: Recent Essays on the Artistic Device* and *Beyond Piety: Critical Essays on the Visual Arts, 1986–1993.* Recipient, John Simon Guggenheim Memorial Fellowship and the Frank Jewett Mather Award for distinction in art or architectural criticism.

Lita Albuquerque, B.A., UCLA. In the 1970s and 1980s, Albuquerque was a seminal part of the California Light and Space movement and a pioneer in Process Art, Environmental Art, and Earth Art. In recent years, she completed an installation on the pyramids in Egypt called Sol Star. She is currently preparing for a global project at the North and South Poles.

Walead Beshty, M.F.A., Yale. Exhibitions: Hirschhorn Museum, Washington D.C.; Museum of Modern Art, New York; The Tate Britain, U.K.; Armand Hammer Museum of Art, Los Angeles; Whitney Museum of American Art, New York; Wallspace, New York. Faculty: Art Institute of Chicago, Bard College, Roski Graduate School of Fine Arts–UCLA, CalArts.

Stan Douglas, M.F.A., Emily Carr Institute. Exhibitions: Vancouver Art Gallery; Waterloo Art Gallery, Ontario; Joslyn Art Museum, Omaha; The Art Institute of Chicago; Institute of Contemporary Arts, London; Galerie Nationale du Jeu de Paume, Paris. Faculty: Professor of Photography and Digital Media, Universität der Künste, Berlin, 2004–06.

Diana Maria Thater, M.F.A., Art Center College of Design. Exhibitions: Dia Center for the Arts, the Museum of Modern Art, the Saint Louis Art Museum, the Renaissance Society at the University of Chicago, Walker Center for the Arts, Portland Art Museum, Vienna Secession, the Basel Kunsthalle, and the Salzburger Kunstverein, among many others. Grants: NEA and the Etants-Donnes Foundation, Guggenheim Fellowship, 2005–06.

Annette Weisser, M.A., Academy of Media Arts (Cologne). Solo exhibitions include *Annette Weisser/Ingo Vetter: Works 1996–2006,* Westphalian State Museum of Art and Culture, Munster (2006); *NameGame,* Hall for Art, Luneburg (2003); *NameGame,* platform ev, Berlin and Forum Citypark, , Graz (2002); *What counts is to absorb all the antitheses at once, rather than resolving them,* Bethany Arthouse, Berlin (1998); *Tableau,* Current Art Society, Munster (1998).

Located on 175 wooded acres in Pasadena, Hillside Campus has been home to Art Center since 1976. The main building is a dramatic postmodern steel-and-glass bridge structure spanning an arroyo in the San Raphael Hills, just above the Rose Bowl.

Fashion Institute of Technology
State University of New York

FASHION INSTITUTE OF TECHNOLOGY

State University of New York

School of Graduate Studies

Programs of Study

The Fashion Institute of Technology (FIT), a State University of New York (SUNY) college of art and design, business, and technology, is home to a mix of innovative achievers, creative thinkers, and industry pioneers. FIT fosters interdisciplinary initiatives, advances research, and provides access to an international network of professionals. With selective admissions and a reputation for excellence, FIT offers its diverse student body access to world-class faculty, dynamic and relevant curricula, and a superior education at an affordable cost. It offers seven programs of graduate study. The programs in Art Market: Principles and Practices; Exhibition Design; Fashion and Textile Studies: History, Theory, Museum Practice; and Sustainable Interior Environments lead to the Master of Arts (M.A.) degree. The Illustration program leads to the Master of Fine Arts (M.F.A.) degree. The Master of Professional Studies (M.P.S.) degree programs are Cosmetics and Fragrance Marketing and Management, and Global Fashion Management.

Art Market: Principles and Practices is a 48-credit, full- or part-time M.A. program preparing students for careers in the business, collection, and exhibition of art. The curriculum includes art history, writing for the art market, gallery design and operation, business practices, computer technology for the art world, marketing, valuation and appraisal, exhibition theory, and art law and professional ethics. Students are required to complete a relevant internship and to research and write a master's qualifying paper. Graduating students must also complete a practicum in which they assemble a group show from concept to execution at a New York City gallery.

Cosmetics and Fragrance Marketing and Management is a 36-credit, part-time M.P.S. program providing industry professionals with high-level management skills and an interdisciplinary, global perspective. The curriculum is designed to encompass three skill sets that leaders in the cosmetics and fragrance industries have identified as crucial to managerial success: core business skills such as management, corporate finance, international business, and management communication; marketing skills such as advanced marketing theory, marketing communications, and market research and strategy; and technical and creative competencies such as cosmetics and fragrance product knowledge, retail and creative management, and an intellectual foundation in beauty and fashion culture. A global component sends students abroad for an intensive week of meetings with industry leaders. The program culminates in a capstone seminar.

The 36-credit, full-time Exhibition Design M.A. program prepares students for careers in the exhibition design and visual display production industry. The studio-driven, one-year course of study focuses on the designer's role within the exhibition team, with emphasis on the development of both design and fabrication skills. Studio projects—such as museum and gallery design, traveling exhibits, and corporate collections—are linked to graphic, lighting, and presentation courses. All graduating students complete an independent, theme-driven design project. Students are also required to complete a related internship.

The 48-credit, full- or part-time Fashion and Textile Studies: History, Theory, Museum Practice M.A. program prepares students for professional curatorial, conservation, education, and other scholarly careers that focus on historic clothing, accessories, textiles, and related materials. The curriculum incorporates conservation skills, current collections management methods, exhibition techniques, art historical methodologies, material culture studies, and gender studies and utilizes the resources of The Museum at FIT, one of the world's largest collections of clothing, textiles, and accessories. Students may elect either a conservation or curatorial emphasis; they may also select up to two independent study courses with an appropriate focus on their chosen specialization. All students are required to complete an internship in the field, write a master's qualifying paper based on original research, and take an active role in a yearlong course culminating in a professional exhibition.

Global Fashion Management is a 36-credit, full-time M.P.S. program offered in collaboration with Hong Kong Polytechnic University in Hong Kong and the Institut Français de la Mode in Paris, preparing current fashion executives for senior managerial positions. The course of study is completed in a three-semester period and includes one intensive seminar course taught in each of the three participating institutions. The curriculum includes courses in production management and the supply chain, global marketing and fashion brand management, current technologies in the fashion industry, international team management, international culture and business, challenges to profitability, and politics and world trade.

The 60-credit evening and weekend Illustration M.F.A. program is designed for working professionals seeking advanced study to further develop their skills as master illustrators. The program focuses on high-level techniques, new media applications, and illustration business practices. The curriculum encompasses digital and traditional studio methods, entrepreneurial research and writing, and opportunities in new and emerging markets. The program features assignments that mirror marketplace demands and specifications, regular guest lecturers, a visit to West Coast film and entertainment studios, and regular off-campus involvement in New York City's art and design world. Students complete a visual thesis project and an independently researched and written master's thesis.

Sustainable Interior Environments is a 36-credit, two-year, part-time evening and weekend M.A. program for established professionals, including practicing interior designers, architects, facilities planners, and managers. The program's intensive, hands-on curriculum focuses on the principles and theories of sustainable design as they apply to the built environment. Through experiential learning, specialized science courses, case studies, and research, students acquire a deep understanding of human psychological, physiological, and ergonomic needs, as well as information about toxic substances, pollution prevention, environmental systems, energy efficiency, and resource conservation. A graduate seminar guides students toward their research-oriented capstone project.

Research Facilities

The School of Graduate Studies is primarily located in the campus's Shirley Goodman Resource Center, which also houses the Gladys Marcus Library and The Museum at FIT. School of Graduate Studies facilities include conference rooms; a fully equipped conservation laboratory; a multipurpose laboratory for conservation projects and the dressing of mannequins; storage facilities for costume and textile materials; a graduate student lounge with computer and printer access; a graduate student library reading room with computers, reference materials, and copies of past classes' qualifying and thesis papers; specialized wireless classrooms; and classrooms equipped with model stands, easels, and drafting tables.

The Gladys Marcus Library houses more than 300,000 volumes of print, nonprint, and digital resources. Specialized holdings include industry reference materials, manufacturers' catalogues, original fashion sketches and scrapbooks, portfolios of plates, photographs, and sample books. The FIT Digital Library provides access to over 90 searchable online databases.

The Museum at FIT houses one of the world's most important collections of clothing and textiles and is the only museum in New York City dedicated to the art of fashion. The permanent collection encompasses more than 50,000 garments and accessories dating from the eighteenth century, with particular strength in twentieth-century fashion, as well as 30,000 textiles and 100,000 textile swatches. Each year, nearly 100,000 visitors are drawn to the museum's award-winning exhibitions and public programs.

Financial Aid

FIT directly administers its institutional grants, scholarships, and loans. Federal funding administered by the college may include Federal Perkins Loans, federally subsidized and unsubsidized Direct Loans for students, Grad PLUS loans, and the Federal Work-Study Program. Priority for institutionally administered funds is given to students enrolled and designated as full-time.

Cost of Study

Tuition for New York State residents is $4099 per semester, or $342 per credit. Out-of-state residents' tuition is $6972 per semester, or $581 per credit. Tuition and fees are subject to change at the discretion of FIT's Board of Trustees. Additional expenses—for class materials, textbooks, and travel—may apply and vary per program.

Living and Housing Costs

Residence facilities are available to graduate students. Traditional residence hall accommodations (including meal plan) cost from $5920 to $6095 per semester. Apartment-style housing options (not including meal plan) cost from $5065 to $9880 per semester.

Student Group

Enrollment in the School of Graduate Studies is approximately 200 students per academic year, allowing considerable individualized advisement. Students come to FIT from throughout the country and around the world.

Student Outcomes

Art Market: Principles and Practices graduates find employment as art gallery directors, public art program directors, art consultants for private and corporate collections, art foundation administrators, museum marketing and development directors, independent curators, auction house department heads, and artists' representatives. Students in the Cosmetics and Fragrance Marketing and Management and Global Fashion Management programs maintain full-time employment in the industry while working toward their degree, which provides the basis for advancement to positions of upper-level managerial responsibility. Graduates of the Exhibition Design program find employment with architectural and exhibition design firms, museums, historic trusts, and special-events companies. Graduates of the Fashion and Textile Studies: History, Theory, Museum Practice program find positions as museum curators, research specialists, collections managers and registrars, historic house directors, museum educators, independent exhibition curators, corporate curators, fashion and textile historians, costume and textile conservators, auction house department specialists and researchers, vintage clothing and textile dealers, and consultants. Students in the Illustration program graduate with a personal vision, an entrepreneurial spirit, and the skills needed to succeed as freelance illustrators. Students in the Sustainable Interior Environments program gain highly marketable expertise that enables them to advance in their current employment, as well as assume leadership positions in the design industry, educational institutions, and research centers.

Location

FIT is connected to New York City, to students, and to careers. Located in Manhattan's Chelsea neighborhood, it places students at the heart of the advertising, visual arts, marketing, fashion, business, design, and communications industries. Students gain unparalleled exposure to their field through guest lectures, field trips, internships, and sponsored competitions. The location provides access to major museums, galleries, and auction houses as well as dining, entertainment, and shopping options. The campus is near subway, bus, and commuter rail lines.

Applying

Applicants to all School of Graduate Studies programs must hold a baccalaureate degree in an appropriate major from a college or university, with a cumulative GPA of 3.0 or higher. International students from non-English-speaking countries are required to submit minimum TOEFL scores of 550 on the written test, 213 on the computer test, or 80 on the Internet test. Students applying to the Art Market: Principles and Practices; Fashion and Textile Studies: History, Theory, Museum Practice; and Global Fashion Management programs must submit GRE scores. Each major has additional, specialized prerequisites for admission; for detailed information, students should visit the School of Graduate Studies on FIT's Web site.

Domestic and international students use the same application when seeking admission. The deadline for completed applications with transcripts and supplemental materials is February 15 for Art Market: Principles and Practices; Exhibition Design; Fashion and Textile Studies: History, Theory, Museum Practice; Illustration; Global Fashion Management; and Sustainable Interior Environments. The deadline for Cosmetics and Fragrance Marketing and Management is March 15. After the deadline dates, applicants are considered on a rolling admissions basis. Candidates may apply online at www.fitnyc.edu/gradstudies.

Correspondence and Information

School of Graduate Studies
Room E315
Fashion Institute of Technology
227 West 27th Street
New York, New York 10001-5992

Phone: 212-217-4300
Fax: 212-217-4301
E-mail: gradinfo@fitnyc.edu
Web site: http://www.fitnyc.edu/gradstudies

Fashion Institute of Technology

THE FACULTY

The faculty members listed below constitute a partial listing. Guest lecturers are not included.

Art Market: Principles and Practices
Katherine Jánszky Michaelsen, Associate Chairperson; Ph.D., Columbia.
Catherine Hannah Behrend, M.A., M.B.A., NYU; Certificate in Executive Education, INSEAD (France).
Ágnes Berecz, Ph.D., Sorbonne (Paris).
Elizabeth M. Grady, M.A.,Ph.D., Northwestern.
John Lee, B.A., Vassar.
Donald McMichael, M.B.A., Duke.
Sheri L. Pasquarella, B.A., Stony Brook, SUNY.
Lucille A. Roussin, Ph.D., Columbia; J.D., Yeshiva.
Martha Schwendener, M.A., Texas at Austin.
Beth Miller Servetar, M.F.A., Bennington.
Gayle M. Skluzacek, B.A., Barat.
Courtney Strimple, M.A., Fashion Institute of Technology.
Andrew Weinstein, Ph.D., NYU.

Cosmetics and Fragrance Marketing and Management
Stephan Kanlian, Associate Chairperson; M.P.A., Pennsylvania.
Brooke Carlson, Sc.D., New Haven.
Dorothy C. Foster, J.D., Fordham.
Judy Galloway, A.B., Mary Baldwin.
Leslie Harris, M.P.S., Fashion Institute of Technology.
Mark Polson, M.P.S., Fashion Institute of Technology.
Cynthia Strite, Ph.D. candidate, Columbia Teachers College.
Mary Tumolo, former Vice President, Promotional Marketing, Lancôme, L'Oreal USA.
Rochelle Udell, M.S., Pratt.
Pamela Vaile, M.B.A., Pace.
Karen Young, B.A., Denver.
Jean Zimmerman, B.A., Florida.

Exhibition Design
Brenda Cowan, Associate Chairperson; M.S.Ed., Bank Street College of Education.
Norman Bleckner, B.I.D., Pratt.
Robin Drake, B.S., Pratt.
Ran Lerner, M.I.D., Domus Academy (Italy).
Scott Lundberg, M.I.D., Pratt.
Karl Matsuda, Certificate in Art, Cooper Union.
Matthew Moore, President, Hipbone Design.
John Newman, M.A., Parsons; IES.
Rick Orlosky, B.F.A., Hartford.
Michael Stiller, B.A., Bard.
Michele Y. T. Washington, StudioFlow9.

Fashion and Textile Studies: History, Theory, Museum Practice
Denyse Montegut, Associate Chairperson; Ph.D. candidate, Delaware.
June Burns Bové, M.A., NYU.
Nancy Deihl, M.A., NYU.
Judith Eisenberg, M.A., Wichita State.

Rebecca Fifield, M.A., George Washington.
Lourdes M. Font, Ph.D., NYU.
Donna Ghelerter, M.A., Fashion Institute of Technology.
Désirée Koslin, M.F.A., CUNY, City College; Ph.D., NYU.
Diane Maglio, M.A., Fashion Institute of Technology.
Elizabeth McMahon, Ph.D. candidate, Bard Graduate Center.
Sarah Scaturro, B.A., Colorado.
Rebecca Shea, M.A., Fashion Institute of Technology.
Valerie Soll, B.A., Oregon.
Denise Stone, M.A., Fashion Institute of Technology.
Tanya Wetenhall, M.A., Fashion Institute of Technology.

Global Fashion Management
Pamela Ellsworth, Associate Chairperson; M.P.S., Fashion Institute of Technology.
Brooke Carlson, Sc.D., New Haven.
Praveen K. Chaudhry, Ph.D., Pennsylvania.
Robert Day, M.A., Berkeley.
Robin Lewis, B.S., Northwestern.
Tom Nastos, B.S., Fashion Institute of Technology.
Jeanette Nostra, B.S., Goddard.

Illustration
Melanie Reim, Associate Chairperson; M.F.A., Syracuse.
Daniel Abraham, J.D., Miami (Florida).
Steve Brodner, B.F.A., Cooper Union.
Peter Cusack, M.A., Syracuse.
Dayna D'Eletto, M.F.A., SUNY, Purchase.
Michael De Feo, Temple.
Dennis Dittrich, M.F.A., Syracuse.
Daniel Filippone, M.F.A., New York Academy of Art.
Michael Hyde, M.F.A., Columbia; Ph.D., NYU.
Amy Lemmon, Ph.D., Cincinnati.
Albert Lorenz, M.S., Columbia.
Monika Maniecki, M.A., Fashion Institute of Technology.
Anelle Miller, B.F.A., Parsons.
Daniel Pelavin, M.F.A., Cranbrook Academy of Art.
Cheryl Phelps, B.F.A., Memphis College of Art.
Zina Saunders, Cooper Union.
Chris Spollen, B.F.A., Parsons.
Nancy Stahl, Arizona.
Murray Tinkelman, Cooper Union.
Carmile S. Zaino, B.F.A., Parsons.

Sustainable Interior Environments
Grazyna Pilatowicz, Associate Chairperson, M.A., Lublin (Poland).
Susan Kaplan, B.A., CUNY, Queens; B.Arch., CUNY, City College.
John Katimaris, M.F.A., Parsons, RA, AIA, IES, IIDA.
Arthur H. Kopelman, M.Phil., Ph.D., CUNY Graduate Center.
Karen R. Pearson, Ph.D., Washington State.

FIT provides students with classrooms, laboratories, and studios that reflect the most advanced educational and industry practices.

The FIT campus is a tightly knit community in Manhattan's Chelsea neighborhood. It's one of the most vibrant areas of New York City, with cafes, art galleries, boutiques, theaters, museums, and restaurants within walking distance.

**Fashion Institute
of Technology**
State University of New York

FASHION INSTITUTE OF TECHNOLOGY
State University of New York

M.A. in Exhibition Design

Programs of Study	The Fashion Institute of Technology (FIT), a State University of New York (SUNY) college of art and design, business, and technology, is home to a mix of innovative achievers, creative thinkers, and industry pioneers. FIT fosters interdisciplinary initiatives, advances research, and provides access to an international network of professionals. With selective admissions and a reputation for excellence, FIT offers its diverse student body access to world-class faculty, dynamic and relevant curricula, and a superior education at an affordable cost. It offers seven programs of graduate study. The programs in Art Market: Principles and Practices; Exhibition Design; Fashion and Textile Studies: History, Theory, Museum Practice; and Sustainable Interior Environments lead to the Master of Arts (M.A.) degree. The Illustration program leads to the Master of Fine Arts (M.F.A.) degree. The Master of Professional Studies (M.P.S.) degree programs are Cosmetics and Fragrance Marketing and Management, and Global Fashion Management.
	The 36-credit, full-time Exhibition Design M.A. program prepares students for careers in the exhibition design and visual display production industry. The studio-driven, one-year course of study focuses on the designer's role within the exhibition team, with emphasis on the development of both design and fabrication skills. Studio projects—such as museum and gallery design, traveling exhibits, and corporate collections—are linked to graphic, lighting, and presentation courses. All graduating students complete an independent, theme-driven design project. Students are also required to complete a related internship.
Research Facilities	The School of Graduate Studies is primarily located in the campus's Shirley Goodman Resource Center, which also houses the Gladys Marcus Library and The Museum at FIT. School of Graduate Studies facilities include conference rooms; a fully equipped conservation laboratory; a multipurpose laboratory for conservation projects and the dressing of mannequins; storage facilities for costume and textile materials; a graduate student lounge with computer and printer access; a graduate student library reading room with computers, reference materials, and copies of past classes' qualifying and thesis papers; specialized wireless classrooms; and classrooms equipped with model stands, easels, and drafting tables.
	The Gladys Marcus Library houses more than 300,000 volumes of print, nonprint, and digital resources. Specialized holdings include industry reference materials, manufacturers' catalogues, original fashion sketches and scrapbooks, portfolios of plates, photographs, and sample books. The FIT Digital Library provides access to over 90 searchable online databases.
	The Museum at FIT houses one of the world's most important collections of clothing and textiles and is the only museum in New York City dedicated to the art of fashion. The permanent collection encompasses more than 50,000 garments and accessories dating from the eighteenth century, with particular strength in twentieth-century fashion, as well as 30,000 textiles and 100,000 textile swatches. Each year, nearly 100,000 visitors are drawn to the museum's award-winning exhibitions and public programs.
Financial Aid	FIT directly administers its institutional grants, scholarships, and loans. Federal funding administered by the college may include Federal Perkins Loans, federally subsidized and unsubsidized Direct Loans for students, Grad PLUS loans, and the Federal Work-Study Program. Priority for institutionally administered funds is given to students enrolled and designated as full-time.
Cost of Study	Tuition for New York State residents is $4099 per semester, or $342 per credit. Out-of-state residents' tuition is $6972 per semester, or $581 per credit. Tuition and fees are subject to change at the discretion of FIT's Board of Trustees. Additional expenses—for class materials, textbooks, and travel—may apply and vary per program.
Living and Housing Costs	Residence facilities are available to graduate students. Traditional residence hall accommodations (including meal plan) cost from $5920 to $6095 per semester. Apartment-style housing options (not including meal plan) cost from $5065 to $9880 per semester.
Student Group	Enrollment in the School of Graduate Studies is approximately 200 students per academic year, allowing considerable individualized advisement. Students come to FIT from throughout the country and around the world.
Student Outcomes	Graduates of the Exhibition Design program find employment with architectural and exhibition design firms, museums, historic trusts, and special-events companies.
Location	FIT is connected to New York City, to students, and to careers. Located in Manhattan's Chelsea neighborhood, it places students at the heart of the advertising, visual arts, marketing, fashion, business, design, and communications industries. Students gain unparalleled exposure to their field through guest lectures, field trips, internships, and sponsored competitions. The location provides access to major museums, galleries, and auction houses as well as dining, entertainment, and shopping options. The campus is near subway, bus, and commuter rail lines.
Applying	Applicants to all School of Graduate Studies programs must hold a baccalaureate degree in an appropriate major from a college or university, with a cumulative GPA of 3.0 or higher. International students from non-English-speaking countries are required to submit minimum TOEFL scores of 550 on the written test, 213 on the computer test, or 80 on the Internet test. Each major has additional, specialized prerequisites for admission; for detailed information, students should visit the School of Graduate Studies on FIT's Web site.
	Domestic and international students use the same application when seeking admission. The deadline for completed applications with transcripts and supplemental materials is February 15 for the Exhibition Design program. After the deadline date, applicants are considered on a rolling admissions basis. Candidates may apply online at www.fitnyc.edu/gradstudies.
Correspondence and Information	School of Graduate Studies Room E315 Fashion Institute of Technology 227 West 27 Street New York, New York 10001-5992
	Phone: 212-217-4300 Fax: 212-217-4301 E-mail: gradinfo@fitnyc.edu Web site: http://www.fitnyc.edu/gradstudies 　　　　　http://www.fitnyc.edu/exhibitiondesign

Fashion Institute of Technology

THE FACULTY

The faculty members listed below constitute a partial listing. Guest lecturers are not included.

Brenda Cowan, Associate Chairperson; M.S.Ed., Bank Street College of Education.

Norman Bleckner, B.I.D., Pratt.
Robin Drake, B.S., Pratt.
Ran Lerner, M.I.D., Domus Academy (Italy).
Scott Lundberg, M.I.D., Pratt.
Karl Matsuda, Certificate in Art, Cooper Union.
Matthew Moore, Principal, Hipbone Design.
John Newman, M.A., Parsons; IES.
Rick Orlosky, B.F.A., Hartford.
Michael Stiller, B.A., Bard.
Michele Y.T. Washington, Principal, studioflow9.

Fashion Institute of Technology
State University of New York

FASHION INSTITUTE OF TECHNOLOGY
State University of New York

M.A. in Sustainable Interior Environments

Programs of Study

The Fashion Institute of Technology (FIT), a State University of New York (SUNY) college of art and design, business, and technology, is home to a mix of innovative achievers, creative thinkers, and industry pioneers. FIT fosters interdisciplinary initiatives, advances research, and provides access to an international network of professionals. With selective admissions and a reputation for excellence, FIT offers its diverse student body access to world-class faculty, dynamic and relevant curricula, and a superior education at an affordable cost. It offers seven programs of graduate study. The programs in Art Market: Principles and Practices; Exhibition Design; Fashion and Textile Studies: History, Theory, Museum Practice; and Sustainable Interior Environments lead to the Master of Arts (M.A.) degree. The Illustration program leads to the Master of Fine Arts (M.F.A.) degree. The Master of Professional Studies (M.P.S.) degree programs are Cosmetics and Fragrance Marketing and Management, and Global Fashion Management.

Sustainable Interior Environments is a 36-credit, two-year, part-time evening and weekend M.A. program for established professionals, including practicing interior designers, architects, facilities planners, and managers. The program's intensive, hands-on curriculum focuses on the principles and theories of sustainable design as they apply to the built environment. Through experiential learning, specialized science courses, case studies, and research, students acquire a deep understanding of human psychological, physiological, and ergonomic needs, as well as information about toxic substances, pollution prevention, environmental systems, energy efficiency, and resource conservation. A graduate seminar guides students toward their research-oriented capstone project.

Research Facilities

The School of Graduate Studies is primarily located in the campus's Shirley Goodman Resource Center, which also houses the Gladys Marcus Library and The Museum at FIT. School of Graduate Studies facilities include conference rooms; a fully equipped conservation laboratory; a multipurpose laboratory for conservation projects and the dressing of mannequins; storage facilities for costume and textile materials; a graduate student lounge with computer and printer access; a graduate student library reading room with computers, reference materials, and copies of past classes' qualifying and thesis papers; specialized wireless classrooms; and classrooms equipped with model stands, easels, and drafting tables.

The Gladys Marcus Library houses more than 300,000 volumes of print, nonprint, and digital resources. Specialized holdings include industry reference materials, manufacturers' catalogues, original fashion sketches and scrapbooks, portfolios of plates, photographs, and sample books. The FIT Digital Library provides access to over 90 searchable online databases.

The Museum at FIT houses one of the world's most important collections of clothing and textiles and is the only museum in New York City dedicated to the art of fashion. The permanent collection encompasses more than 50,000 garments and accessories dating from the eighteenth century, with particular strength in twentieth-century fashion, as well as 30,000 textiles and 100,000 textile swatches. Each year, nearly 100,000 visitors are drawn to the museum's award-winning exhibitions and public programs.

Financial Aid

FIT directly administers its institutional grants, scholarships, and loans. Federal funding administered by the college may include Federal Perkins Loans, federally subsidized and unsubsidized Direct Loans for students, Grad PLUS loans, and the Federal Work-Study Program. Priority for institutionally administered funds is given to students enrolled and designated as full-time.

Cost of Study

Tuition for New York State residents is $4099 per semester, or $342 per credit. Out-of-state residents' tuition is $6972 per semester, or $581 per credit. Tuition and fees are subject to change at the discretion of FIT's Board of Trustees. Additional expenses—for class materials, textbooks, and travel—may apply and vary per program.

Living and Housing Costs

Residence facilities are available to graduate students. Traditional residence hall accommodations (including meal plan) cost from $5920 to $6095 per semester. Apartment-style housing options (not including meal plan) cost from $5065 to $9880 per semester.

Student Group

Enrollment in the School of Graduate Studies is approximately 200 students per academic year, allowing considerable individualized advisement. Students come to FIT from throughout the country and around the world.

Student Outcomes

Students in the Sustainable Interior Environments program gain highly marketable expertise that enables them to advance in their current employment, as well as assume leadership positions in the design industry, educational institutions, and research centers.

Location

FIT is connected to New York City, to students, and to careers. Located in Manhattan's Chelsea neighborhood, it places students at the heart of the advertising, visual arts, marketing, fashion, business, design, and communications industries. Students gain unparalleled exposure to their field through guest lectures, field trips, internships, and sponsored competitions. The location provides access to major museums, galleries, and auction houses as well as dining, entertainment, and shopping options. The campus is near subway, bus, and commuter rail lines.

Applying

Applicants to all School of Graduate Studies programs must hold a baccalaureate degree in an appropriate major from a college or university, with a cumulative GPA of 3.0 or higher. International students from non-English-speaking countries are required to submit minimum TOEFL scores of 550 on the written test, 213 on the computer test, or 80 on the Internet test. Each major has additional, specialized prerequisites for admission; for detailed information, students should visit the School of Graduate Studies on FIT's Web site.

Domestic and international students use the same application when seeking admission. The deadline for completed applications with transcripts and supplemental materials is February 15 for the Sustainable Interior Environments program. After the deadline date, applicants are considered on a rolling admissions basis. Candidates may apply online at www.fitnyc.edu/gradstudies.

Correspondence and Information

School of Graduate Studies
Room E315
Fashion Institute of Technology
227 West 27 Street
New York, New York 10001-5992

Phone: 212-217-4300
Fax: 212-217-4301
E-mail: gradinfo@fitnyc.edu
Web site: http://www.fitnyc.edu/gradstudies
　　　　http://www.fitnyc.edu/SIE

Fashion Institute of Technology

THE FACULTY

The faculty members listed below constitute a partial listing. Guest lecturers are not included.

Grazyna Pilatowicz, Associate Chairperson; M.A., Lublin (Poland).

Susan Kaplan, B.Arch., CUNY, City College.
John Katimaris, M.F.A., Parsons; RA, AIA, IES, IIDA.
Arthur H. Kopelman, Ph.D., CUNY Graduate Center.
Karen R. Pearson, Ph.D., Washington State.

FASHION INSTITUTE OF TECHNOLOGY
State University of New York

M.F.A. in Illustration

Programs of Study	The Fashion Institute of Technology (FIT), a State University of New York (SUNY) college of art and design, business, and technology, is home to a mix of innovative achievers, creative thinkers, and industry pioneers. FIT fosters interdisciplinary initiatives, advances research, and provides access to an international network of professionals. With selective admissions and a reputation for excellence, FIT offers its diverse student body access to world-class faculty, dynamic and relevant curricula, and a superior education at an affordable cost. It offers seven programs of graduate study. The programs in Art Market: Principles and Practices; Exhibition Design; Fashion and Textile Studies: History, Theory, Museum Practice; and Sustainable Interior Environments lead to the Master of Arts (M.A.) degree. The Illustration program leads to the Master of Fine Arts (M.F.A.) degree. The Master of Professional Studies (M.P.S.) degree programs are Cosmetics and Fragrance Marketing and Management, and Global Fashion Management.

The 60-credit evening and weekend Illustration M.F.A. program is designed for working professionals seeking advanced study to further develop their skills as master illustrators. The program focuses on high-level techniques, new media applications, and illustration business practices. The curriculum encompasses digital and traditional studio methods, entrepreneurial research and writing, and opportunities in new and emerging markets. The program features assignments that mirror marketplace demands and specifications, regular guest lecturers, a visit to West Coast film and entertainment studios, and regular off-campus involvement in New York City's art and design world. Students complete a visual thesis project and an independently researched and written master's thesis.

Research Facilities The School of Graduate Studies is primarily located in the campus's Shirley Goodman Resource Center, which also houses the Gladys Marcus Library and The Museum at FIT. School of Graduate Studies facilities include conference rooms; a fully equipped conservation laboratory; a multipurpose laboratory for conservation projects and the dressing of mannequins; storage facilities for costume and textile materials; a graduate student lounge with computer and printer access; a graduate student library reading room with computers, reference materials, and copies of past classes' qualifying and thesis papers; specialized wireless classrooms; and classrooms equipped with model stands, easels, and drafting tables.

The Gladys Marcus Library houses more than 300,000 volumes of print, nonprint, and digital resources. Specialized holdings include industry reference materials, manufacturers' catalogues, original fashion sketches and scrapbooks, portfolios of plates, photographs, and sample books. The FIT Digital Library provides access to over 90 searchable online databases.

The Museum at FIT houses one of the world's most important collections of clothing and textiles and is the only museum in New York City dedicated to the art of fashion. The permanent collection encompasses more than 50,000 garments and accessories dating from the eighteenth century, with particular strength in twentieth-century fashion, as well as 30,000 textiles and 100,000 textile swatches. Each year, nearly 100,000 visitors are drawn to the museum's award-winning exhibitions and public programs.

Financial Aid FIT directly administers its institutional grants, scholarships, and loans. Federal funding administered by the college may include Federal Perkins Loans, federally subsidized and unsubsidized Direct Loans for students, Grad PLUS loans, and the Federal Work-Study Program. Priority for institutionally administered funds is given to students enrolled and designated as full-time.

Cost of Study Tuition for New York State residents is $4099 per semester, or $342 per credit. Out-of-state residents' tuition is $6972 per semester, or $581 per credit. Tuition and fees are subject to change at the discretion of FIT's Board of Trustees. Additional expenses—for class materials, textbooks, and travel—may apply and vary per program.

Living and Housing Costs Residence facilities are available to graduate students. Traditional residence hall accommodations (including meal plan) cost from $5920 to $6095 per semester. Apartment-style housing options (not including meal plan) cost from $5065 to $9880 per semester.

Student Group Enrollment in the School of Graduate Studies is approximately 200 students per academic year, allowing considerable individualized advisement. Students come to FIT from throughout the country and around the world.

Student Outcomes Students in the Illustration program graduate with a personal vision, an entrepreneurial spirit, and the skills needed to succeed as freelance illustrators.

Location FIT is connected to New York City, to students, and to careers. Located in Manhattan's Chelsea neighborhood, it places students at the heart of the advertising, visual arts, marketing, fashion, business, design, and communications industries. Students gain unparalleled exposure to their field through guest lectures, field trips, internships, and sponsored competitions. The location provides access to major museums, galleries, and auction houses as well as dining, entertainment, and shopping options. The campus is near subway, bus, and commuter rail lines.

Applying Applicants to all School of Graduate Studies programs must hold a baccalaureate degree in an appropriate major from a college or university, with a cumulative GPA of 3.0 or higher. International students from non-English-speaking countries are required to submit minimum TOEFL scores of 550 on the written test, 213 on the computer test, or 80 on the Internet test. Each major has additional, specialized prerequisites for admission; for detailed information, students should visit the School of Graduate Studies on FIT's Web site.

Domestic and international students use the same application when seeking admission. The deadline for completed applications with transcripts and supplemental materials is February 15 for the Illustration program. After the deadline date, applicants are considered on a rolling admissions basis. Candidates may apply online at www.fitnyc.edu/gradstudies.

Correspondence and Information
School of Graduate Studies
Room E315
Fashion Institute of Technology
227 West 27 Street
New York, New York 10001-5992
Phone: 212-217-4300
Fax: 212-217-4301
E-mail: gradinfo@fitnyc.edu
Web site: http://www.fitnyc.edu/gradstudies
http://www.fitnyc.edu/gradillustration

Fashion Institute of Technology

THE FACULTY

The faculty members listed below constitute a partial listing. Guest lecturers are not included.

Melanie Reim, Associate Chairperson; M.F.A., Syracuse.

Daniel Abraham, J.D., Miami (Florida).
Steve Brodner, B.F.A., Cooper Union.
Peter Cusack, M.A., Syracuse.
Dayna D'Eletto, M.F.A., Purchase, SUNY.
Michael De Feo, Temple.
Dennis Dittrich, M.F.A., Syracuse.
Daniel Filippone, M.F.A., New York Academy of Art.
Michael Hyde, M.F.A., Columbia; Ph.D., NYU.
Amy Lemmon, Ph.D., Cincinnati.
Albert Lorenz, M.S., Columbia.
Monika Maniecki, M.A., Fashion Institute of Technology.
Anelle Miller, B.F.A., Parsons.
Daniel Pelavin, M.F.A., Cranbrook Academy of Art.
Cheryl Phelps, B.F.A., Memphis College of Art.
Zina Saunders, Cooper Union.
Chris Spollen, B.F.A., Parsons.
Nancy Stahl, Arizona.
Murray Tinkelman, Cooper Union.
Carmile S. Zaino, B.F.A., Parsons.

Ai Miami International University
of Art & Design™

MIAMI INTERNATIONAL UNIVERSITY
OF ART & DESIGN
Master's Programs

Programs of Study

Miami International University of Art & Design offers master's degree programs in design and media management, film, graphic design, interior design, and visual arts. No matter which course of study a student may choose, the professionals at Miami International University of Art & Design will guide, support, and help each student as their talents evolve on their journey of personal and professional transformation.

Research Facilities

Miami International University of Art & Design provides a learning environment with professional-grade technology applicable to a student's course of study. Students are able to build a portfolio of work that shows employers they've been trained to use the software, hardware, or equipment utilized within the industry. Depending upon the course of study, students are immersed in a creative environment—from classrooms to computer labs to studios—focused on relevant, hands-on education that prepares them for the real world.

Financial Aid

Financial aid is available for those who qualify. Students who require financial assistance should first complete and submit the Free Application for Federal Student Aid (FAFSA) and meet with a financial aid officer.

Cost of Study

Tuition cost varies by program. Prospective students should contact the University for current tuition costs. Other charges include a starting kit for all first-quarter students. Kits vary in price, depending on the program of study.

**Living and
Housing Costs**

Students should contact the University for information on housing options and living expenses.

Student Group

Individuals enrolled in graduate programs at Miami International University of Art & Design come from a variety of backgrounds. Students (graduate and undergraduate) at the University are from all across America; many also come from other countries.

Student Outcomes

A focused education from Miami International University of Art & Design can help students turn their creative energy into a powerful tool that can make a difference in the world. Students become a part of a collaborative and supportive community, where experienced instructors provide the guidance and skills needed to get started on careers in the creative economy.

Location

Miami is a culturally rich region that celebrates events year-round, including the African-American Heritage Festival, Haitian Heritage week, the Viva Mexico celebration, the Israel Independence celebration, and Asian Cultural Festival. The city is home to professional sports teams, and residents enjoy the sandy beaches, international cuisine, local clubs, the historic Art Deco District, Coral Gables, and Key Biscayne. The Florida Keys, Disney World, and the Bahamas are all just a short trip away.

The University

Miami International University of Art & Design and its branch campuses, The Art Institute of Jacksonville and The Art Institute of Tampa, are accredited by the Commission on Colleges of the Southern Association of Colleges and Schools to award diplomas and associate, baccalaureate, and master's degrees. Contact the Commission on Colleges at 1866 Southern Lane, Decatur, Georgia 30033-4097 or call 404-679-4500 for questions about the accreditation of Miami International University of Art & Design.

Miami International University of Art & Design is licensed by the Commission for Independent Education, Florida Department of Education. Additional information regarding this institution may be obtained by contacting the commission at 325 West Gaines Street, Suite 1414, Tallahassee, Florida 32399-0400; phone: 888-224-6684 (toll-free).

Applying

Applicants must provide proof of high school graduation or achievement of a General Educational Development (GED) certificate as a prerequisite for admission. In lieu of documenting high school graduation or a GED certificate, applicants may provide proof of attaining an associate degree or higher from an accredited institution. An official transcript indicating date of high school graduation, GED certificate (including test scores), or date of college graduation (including degree granted) is required as proof.

All individuals seeking admission to the University are interviewed in person or by phone by an assistant director of admissions, and each applicant must create an original essay of at least 150 words stating how an education at Miami International University of Art & Design would help them to achieve career goals. There is a $50 application fee.

**Correspondence
and Information**

Miami International University of Art & Design
1501 Biscayne Boulevard, Suite 100
Miami, Florida 33132-1418
Phone: 305-428-5700
         800-225-9023 (toll-free)
Fax: 305-374-5933
Web site: http://www.artinstitutes.edu/miami

Miami International University of Art & Design

THE FACULTY AND THEIR RESEARCH

The faculty members at Miami International University of Art & Design are experienced professionals who create a learning environment that's similar to the professional world students are ready to join after graduation. Instructors are focused on giving students the tools they need to transform their creative potential into marketable skills.

The Art Institute of Atlanta; The Art Institute of Atlanta–Decatur[1]; The Art Institute of Austin[2]; The Art Institute of California–Hollywood; The Art Institute of California–Inland Empire; The Art Institute of California–Los Angeles; The Art Institute of California–Orange County; The Art Institute of California–Sacramento; The Art Institute of California–San Diego; The Art Institute of California–San Francisco; The Art Institute of California–Sunnyvale; The Art Institute of Charleston[1]; The Art Institute of Charlotte; The Art Institute of Colorado; The Art Institute of Dallas[3]; The Art Institute of Fort Lauderdale; The Art Institute of Fort Worth[3]; The Art Institute of Houston; The Art Institute of Houston–North[2]; The Art Institute of Indianapolis[4]; The Art Institute of Jacksonville[5]; The Art Institute of Las Vegas; The Art Institute of Michigan; The Art Institute of New York City; The Art Institute of Ohio–Cincinnati[6]; The Art Institute of Philadelphia; The Art Institute of Phoenix; The Art Institute of Pittsburgh; The Art Institute of Portland; The Art Institute of Raleigh–Durham; The Art Institute of Salt Lake City; The Art Institute of San Antonio[2]; The Art Institute of Seattle; The Art Institute of Tampa[5]; The Art Institute of Tennessee–Nashville[1]; The Art Institute of Tucson; The Art Institute of Vancouver; The Art Institute of Virginia Beach[1,7]; The Art Institute of Washington[1,7]; The Art Institute of Washington–Northern Virginia[1,7]; The Art Institute of Wisconsin; The Art Institute of York–Pennsylvania; The Art Institutes International–Kansas City; The Art Institutes International Minnesota; The Illinois Institute of Art–Chicago; The Illinois Institute of Art–Schaumburg; The Illinois Institute of Art–Tinley Park; Miami International University of Art & Design; The New England Institute of Art.

[1]A branch of The Art Institute of Atlanta

[2]A branch of The Art Institute of Houston

[3]A campus of South University

[4]The Art Institute of Indianapolis is regulated by the Indiana Commission on Proprietary Education, 302 West Washington Street, Room E201, Indianapolis, Indiana 46204, AC-0080

[5]A branch of Miami International University of Art & Design

[6]The Art Institute of Ohio–Cincinnati, 8845 Governors Hill Drive, Suite 100, Cincinnati, Ohio 45249-3317, OH Reg. #04-01-1698B

[7]Certified by the State Council of Higher Education to operate in Virginia.

PRATT INSTITUTE

School of Art and Design

Programs of Study	Pratt has been educating professionals for productive careers in the fields of art and design since its founding in 1887. Pratt's School of Art and Design, one of the largest of its kind, offers an outstanding professional art and design education taught by a faculty of working professionals who bring high standards and current practices to the classroom. Faculty members have received more than eighteen Tiffany, Fulbright, and Guggenheim awards as well as other prestigious professional awards. Pratt's graduate interior design program was ranked first nationally by *DesignIntelligence* in 2011; graduate industrial design was ranked seventh. *U.S. News and World Report* ranked Pratt's interior design program first in the country; graduate fine art was ranked fifteenth, and industrial design was ranked fourth.
	Pratt offers master's degrees in a variety of programs, including Master of Fine Arts in digital arts, history of art and design, or studio arts (new forms–nontraditional investigations, painting and drawing, photography, printmaking, sculpture); Master of Science in art and design education (teacher certification), communications and package design, dance/movement therapy, history of art and design, or interior design; Master of Industrial Design; and Master of Professional Studies in art therapy, art therapy–special education, arts and cultural management, or design management. A postbaccalaureate New York State certification program for the teaching of art in grades pre-K–12 is available for fine arts graduate students. Art therapy majors electing a special education concentration are eligible for provisional New York State teaching certification. Pratt also offers a dual degree in fine arts and library and information science, a dual degree in art history and library science, and a dual degree in digital arts and library science as well as various certificates for holders of the M.S. in library science including museum studies, archives, and library and information studies.
	Graduates of Pratt's design programs have the competitive edge needed to obtain top administrative and creative positions in design studios, businesses, various industries, and arts organizations; graduates of the digital arts program may also work in interactive media or computer animation. Art and design education graduates are prepared to pursue teaching careers in pre-K–12 schools, museums and cultural institutions, or colleges. Graduates of the creative arts therapy program work in psychiatric, medical rehabilitation, geriatric and family therapy, school, substance abuse, and child-life settings. They also learn to work with a variety of patient populations, including patients with eating disorders and the homeless.
	All graduate art and design curricula include supportive course work in the humanities. Students can choose from a wide array of course offerings, including art and design history, comparative literature, philosophy, foreign languages, and social sciences. The graduate programs require the completion of 34 to 68 credits (75 credits for the M.S./M.F.A. dual-degree program) and last from 2 to 3 years, depending on the curriculum and the number of prerequisites that have not been met at the time of admission. For the granting of degrees, all of the graduate programs require the submission of a thesis or a comparable effort. For the M.F.A., an exhibition and supporting corollary statement are required. Candidates for the M.S. and the M.I.D. degrees must present a thesis project that demonstrates a meaningful contribution to design and documents the supportive research that informs all phases of design and construction. For the M.P.S. in art therapy and the M.S. in dance/movement therapy, the thesis project may involve research, an extended case study, the development of a project implementing innovative techniques in therapy, or the opportunity to publish an article. For the M.P.S. in design management, the thesis project is the preparation of a business case study.
Research Facilities	The Pratt Library contains 186,589 bound volumes, serial backfiles, and other material (including government documents); 251,603 audiovisual materials; and 3,996 microforms and subscribes to 925 periodicals.
	Pratt maintains numerous studios, shops, and technical facilities for work in all media as well as state-of-the-art computer facilities. Computer graphics labs include state-of-the-art Macintosh, PC/NT, and UNIX operating systems as well as digital video and audio systems. Pratt also has extensive gallery space for exhibitions.
Financial Aid	Financial aid awards are offered through a variety of institutional, state, and federally funded programs. These include Graduate Scholarships awarded by departments to incoming students on the basis of merit, endowed and restricted scholarships for continuing students, Federal Perkins Loan and Federal Work-Study Programs, the Tuition Assistance Program of New York State, and Pratt loans and student help. Assistantships are awarded on a competitive basis to continuing students in all departments. Special alumni-sponsored fellowships are also available.
Cost of Study	Graduate tuition for 2011–12 is $24,084 per year (full-time 18 credits, $1338 per credit) and student fees are $1740 per year. The cost of books and supplies varies widely, depending on the program in which the student is enrolled. Updated cost information is available at http://www.pratt.edu/costs_and_budgeting.
Living and Housing Costs	Campus housing continues to be expanded to meet students' needs and is available for single students on a first-come, first-served basis. Housing costs average $17,594 per academic year. Pratt offers limited graduate student housing two blocks away from the campus. There is a plentiful supply of moderately priced rentals in the immediate area and in adjacent neighborhoods for married students seeking housing and for those students choosing to reside off campus.
Student Group	In educating more than four generations of students to be creative, technically skilled, and adaptable professionals, Pratt has gained an international reputation that attracts more than 4,700 undergraduate and graduate students annually from forty-seven states and over eighty countries.
Location	Pratt Institute's 25-acre, parklike main campus is situated among the turn-of-the-century mansions, Victorian brownstones, and wide, tree-lined boulevards of Clinton Hill, one of Brooklyn's landmark-designated historic neighborhoods. Midtown Manhattan, the heart of New York City, is only 25 minutes away by subway and offers students a vast array of professional, cultural, and recreational opportunities. Pratt also maintains a satellite facility in Manhattan's Chelsea district. Pratt Manhattan houses the Institute's graduate arts and cultural management, communications/packaging design, design management, facilities management, historic preservation, library and information science, and urban design; it also offers Associate of Occupational Studies (A.O.S.) and Associate of Applied Science (A.A.S.) degree programs.
The Institute	A private, nonsectarian institute of higher education, Pratt Institute was founded by the industrialist and philanthropist Charles Pratt. Changing with the needs and requirements of the professional world for which it prepares its graduates, Pratt today educates 3,008 undergraduate and 1,725 graduate students for careers in art and design, architecture, and library and information science.
Applying	The deadline for applications and all supporting materials, including portfolio, is January 5. Applicants should include everything in one package, including recommendations in sealed envelopes with the reference's signature across the flap. Early submission of applications with all necessary credentials is highly desirable. For applicants who intend to file for financial aid, applications and all supporting documents should be received no later than January 5 for the fall semester and October 1 for the spring semester. Applications received after these dates are considered if openings exist in a particular program.

Correspondence and Information	Graduate Admissions Office
	Pratt Institute
	200 Willoughby Avenue
	Brooklyn, New York 11205
	Phone: 718-636-3514
	      800-331-0834 (toll-free)
	Fax: 718-399-4242
	E-mail: admissions@pratt.edu
	Web site: http://www.pratt.edu
	      http://www.pratt.edu/admiss/request (to request information)

Pratt Institute

THE FACULTY

Concetta Stewart, Dean; Ph.D., Rutgers.

Art and Design Education
Amir Parsa, Chair. Lisa Baumwell, Associate Professor; Ph.D., NYU. Allison Berkoy, Visiting Instructor; M.A., NYU. Lisa Capone, Adjunct Instructor; M.F.A., Pratt. Mary Elmer-Dewitt, Adjunct Instructor; M.S., Pratt. Shari Fischberg (Lederman), Assistant Professor; M.F.A., CUNY, Queens. Dahn Hiuni, Visiting Professor; Ph.D., Penn State. Tonya Leslie, Visiting Instructor; M.A., NYU. Heather Lewis, Assistant Professor; Ph.D., NYU. Josh Millis, Visiting Instructor; M.F.A., Art Institute of Chicago. Kristina Lamour Sansone, Visiting Professor; M.F.A., Yale. Shervone Neckles, Visiting Instructor; M.F.A., CUNY, Queens. Theodora Skipitares, Associate Professor; M.F.A., NYU. Aileen Wilson, Associate Professor; M.A., Chelsea School of Art, London.

Arts and Cultural Management
Mary McBride, Chair; Ph.D., NYU. Sally Block, Visiting Assistant Professor. Catherine Cacho-Leary, Visiting Assistant Professor; M.B.A., Keller Graduate School of Management. Ada Ciniglio, Visiting Assistant Professor; M.S., SUNY at New Paltz. Laurie Cumbo, Visiting Assistant Professor; M.A., NYU. Radiah Harper, Visiting Assistant Professor; M.S., Bank Street College of Education. Jeffrey Klein, Visiting Assistant Professor. Bonita Kolb, Visiting Assistant Professor; Ph.D., Golden Gate. Bradley McCallum, Visiting Assistant Professor; M.F.A. Yale. Elissa Moorhead, Visiting Assistant Professor. Mario Moorhead, Visiting Assistant Professor. Judith Olch Richards, Visiting Assistant Professor; M.A. New Mexico. Susan Schear, Visiting Assistant Professor. Vida Schreibman, Visiting Associate Professor; M.A., NYU. Jennifer Scott, Visiting Assistant Professor; M.A., Michigan–Dearborn. Christopher Shrum, Visiting Assistant Professor; M.A.; NYU. Denise Tahara, Visiting Assistant Professor; Ph.D., NYU. Jacqueline Tarry, Visiting Assistant Professor. Yolanda Trincere, Visiting Assistant Professor; Ph.D., NYU.

Communications/Package Design
Jeff Bellantoni, Chair; M.F.A., Virginia Commonwealth. Michelle Hinebrook, Assistant Chair and Adjunct Instructor; M.F.A., Cranbrook Academy of Art. Pooja Badlani, Visiting Insturctor; M.S., Pratt. Inbar Barak, Visiting Assistant Professor; M.P.S., NYU. Chava Ben-Amos, Professor; B.A., Bezalel Art Academy (Jerusalem, Israel). Warren Bernard, Adjunct Assistant Instructor; M.S., Pratt. Andrew Brenits, Visiting Assistant Professor; M.P.S., Pratt. Jean Brennan, Adjunct Associate Professor; M.S., Pratt. Tom Delaney, Visiting Instructor. Antonio Dispigna, Professor; M.S., Pratt. Tom Dolle, Adjunct Professor; B.F.A., Rhode Island School of Design; CCE. Debra Drodvillo, Visiting Associate Professor; M.F.A., Yale. David Frisco, Adjunct Associate Professor; M.F.A., Yale. Carla Gannis, Adjunct Instructor (Digital Arts Dept.); M.F.A., Boston University. Kevin Gatta, Professor; M.S., Pratt. Bob Gill, Adjunct Associate Professor.

J. Roger Guilfoyle, Adjunct Professor; B.A., Creighton; CCE. J. Graham Hanson, Adjunct Associate Professor; B.F.A., Iowa State. William Hilson, Adjunct Professor; CCE. D. K. Holland, Visiting Professor. Alvin Katz, Visiting Associate Professor; B.F.A. Ohio State. Jeong Hoon Kim, Visiting Assistant Professor; M.F.A., Rhode Island School of Design. Kimberly Kiser, Visiting Instructor; M.S., Pratt. Tom Klinkowstein, Adjunct Professor; M.S., Syracuse; CCE. Gusty Lange, Adjunct Associate Professor; M.P.S., Pratt; CCE. Eunsun Lee, Adjunct Associate Professor; M.S., Pratt. Alex Liebergesell, Adjunct Assistant Professor; M.F.A., Yale. Sandie Maxa, Visiting Assistant Professor; M.F.A., Virginia Commonwealth. Brenda McManus, Visiting Assistant Professor; M.S. Pratt. Scott Menchin, Visiting Associate Professor. Manuel Miranda, Visiting Assistant Professor; M.F.A. Yale. Katya Moorman, Visiting Assistant Professor; M.F.A., Cranbrook. Ann Morris, Visiting Assistant Professor; M.A., CUNY, Hunter. Katherine Muth, Visiting Assistant Profesor; M.F.A., New School. Gala Narezo, Visiting Assistant Professor; B.F.A., Art Center College of Design. Eric O'Toole, Adjunct Assistant Professor; B.I.D., Pratt. Peter Jay Pultorak, Visiting Instructor; B.A., Notre Dame. Marc Rosen, Visiting Associate Professor; M. S., Pratt. Mark Sanders, Visiting Assistant Professor; M.F.A., Virginia Commonwealth. Ashish Shah, Visiting Instructor; M.S., Baroda, India. Christie Shin, Visiting Instructor; M.S., Pratt. Pirco Wolfframm, Adjunct Assistant Professor; M.F.A., California Institute of the Arts. Edwin Yegir, Visiting Associate Professor; M.F.A., Yale. Alisa Zamir, Professor; M.S., Pratt.

Creative Arts Therapy
Jean Davis, Chair, Adjunct Associate Professor; M.P.S. Pratt. Linda Siegel, Director of Graduate Art Therapy Program, Assistant Professor. Joan Wittig, Director of Graduate Dance/Movement Therapy Program, Assistant Professor; M.S., CUNY, Hunter. Josephine Abbenante, Adjunct Assistant Professor; M.A., Louisville. Claudia Bader, Visiting Instructor; M.P.S., Pratt. Donna Bassin, Visiting Associate Professor. Beate Becker, Adjunct Associate Professor; M.S., CUNY, Hunter. Joachim Boenig, Adjunct Assistant Professor. Corinna Brown, Visiting Instructor; M.S., CUNY, Hunter. Kimberly Bush, Visiting Instructor; M.F.A., Parsons. Barbara Cooper, Adjunct Associate Professor. Carol Cox, Visiting Assistant Professor. Christina Devereaux, Visiting Assistant Professor; M.A., UCLA. Alison Gigl-George, Adjunct Assistant Professor. Blair Glaser, Visiting Instructor. Stephanie Gorski, Visiting Instructor; M.P.S., Pratt. Valerie Hubbs, Visiting Instructor; M.S., CUNY, Hunter. Melissa Klay, Visiting Instructor; Ph.D., Pacifica Graduate. Judith Luongo, Adjunct Associate Professor. Julie Miller, Visiting Instructor. Madeline Rugh, Visiting Associate Professor; Ph.D., Oklahoma. Dina Schapiro, Adjunct Instructor. Jean Seibel, Visiting Instructor. Ann Smith, Visiting Instructor; Ph.D., Fielding Graduate University. Laurel Thompson, Professor; Ph.D., Union (Ohio). Susan Tortora, Visiting Assistant Professor. Elissa White, Visiting Assistant Professor. Robert Wolf, Visiting Assistant Professor. Eva Young, Visiting Instructor.

Design Management
Mary McBride, Chair; Ph.D., NYU. Christopher Collette, Adjunct Assistant Professor; M.A., Denison University. Laurence DeGaetano, Adjunct Assistant Professor; M.B.A., NYU. Roger Dunbar, Visiting Professor; Ph.D., Cornell. Scott Fiaschetti, Visiting Associate Professor. Larry Gibbs, Visiting Assistant Professor. Richard Green, Professor. Jacqueline McCormack, Adjunct Associate Professor; M.P.S., Pratt. James Murray, Visiting Assistant Professor; M.P.S., Pratt. Jo Ann Stonier, Visiting Assistant Professor; J.D., St. John's (New York). Marvin Waldman, Visiting Assistant Professor; M.B.A., CUNY, Baruch. Eric Wilmot, Visting Assistant Professor.

Digital Arts
Peter Patchen, Chair; M.F.A., Oregon. Rick Barry, Professor; M.F.A., Pratt. Thomas Bone, Visiting Assistant Professor. Liubomir Borissov, Associate Professor; Ph.D., Columbia. Svjetlana Bukvich-Nichols, Visiting Associate Professor; M.F.A., Rensselaer. Edward Darino, Adjunct Associate Professor; Ph.D., Udako Euskal Unibertsitatea (Basque Country). Marianna Ellenberg, Visiting Instructor; M.A., Slade School of Art. Carla Gannis, Visiting Instructor; M.F.A., Boston University. Kay Hines, Visiting Instructor; B.A., Barnard. Everett Kane, Visiting Associate Professor; M.F.A., Art Center College of Design. Lara Kohl, Adjunct Assistant Professor; M.F.A., Art Institute of Chicago. Linda Lauro-Lazin, Adjunct Associate Professor. Peter Mackey, Professor; M.F.A., USC. Michael O'Rourke, Professor; Ed.M., Harvard. Samantha Olschan, Visiting Instructor; M.F.A., Art Institute of Chicago. Gap-Yuel Seo, Visiting Instructor; B.F.A., Pratt. Claudia Tait, Associate Professor; M.F.A., Maryland.

Fine Arts
Donna Moran, Chair; M.F.A., Pratt. Sheila Pepe, Assistant Chair; M.F.A., School of the Museum of Fine Arts. David Alban, Visiting Assistant Professor; M.F.A., Cranbrook Academy of Art. Adam Apostolos, Visiting Instructor. Michael Brennan, Adjunct Instructor; M.F.A., Pratt. Mona Brody, Visiting Assistant Professor; M.F.A., Norwich. Richard Budelis, Associate Professor. James Costanzo, Adjunct Associate Professor; M.F.A., Iowa. Kelly Driscoll, Assistant Professor; M.F.A., CUNY, City College. Allen Frame, Adjunct Associate Professor. Linda Francis, Adjunct Professor; M.A., CUNY, Hunter. Joseph Fyfe, Visiting Assistant Professor; B.F.A., University of the Arts. Jonathan Goodman, Adjunct Associate Professor. Eric Heist, Visiting Assistant Professor; M.F.A., CUNY, Hunter. Licio Isolani, Professor. Shirley Kaneda, Associate Professor; B.F.A., Parsons. Catherine Lecleire, Adjunct Assistant Professor; M.F.A., USC. Jenny Lee, Adjunct Professor. Marc Lepson, Visiting Associate Professor; M.F.A., Art Institute of Chicago. Frank Lind, Professor; M.F.A., Pratt. Naohisa Matsumoto, Visiting Instructor. J. Martin Mazorra, Visiting Assistant Professor; M.F.A., American. Dennis McNett, Adjunct Assistant Professor; M.F.A., Pratt. Jennifer Melby, Visiting Assistant Professor. Anne Messner, Adjunct Professor; B.F.A., Pratt. Robert Morgan, Adjunct Professor; Ph.D., NYU. Cyrilla Mozenter, Adjunct Professor; M.F.A., Pratt. Dominique Nahas, Visiting Assistant Professor. Ross Neher, Adjunct Professor. Thirwell Nolen, Adjunct Assistant Professor. Catherine Redmond, Adjunct Associate Professor; B.A., Harpur College. Howard Rosenthal, Visiting Associate Professor; M.F.A., Pratt. Miriam Schaer, Visiting Assistant Professor; B.F.A., School of Visual Arts. Linda Schrank, Adjunct Professor; M.A., NYU. Carla Shapiro, Visiting Assistant Professor. Elise Siegel, Visiting Assistant Professor. Lori Sikorski, Adjunct Assistant Professor; M.F.A., Pratt. Robbin Silverberg, Adjunct Assistant Professor; B.A., Princeton. Joseph Smith, Professor; B.F.A., Pratt. Judith Solodkin, Visiting Associate Professor; M.F.A. Columbia. Marjorie Welish, Adjunct Professor. Elizabeth Whalley, Visiting Assistant Professor; M.F.A., CUNY, Brooklyn. Christopher White, Adjunct Assistant Professor; B.A., Harvard. Robert Zakarian, Professor.

History of Art and Design
Steven Zucker, Chair; Ph.D., CUNY Graduate Center. Gayle Rodda Kurtz, Assistant Chair; Ph.D., CUNY Graduate Center. Agnes Berecz, Visiting Assistant Professor; Ph.D, Universite Paris I. Sam Bryan, Adjunct Associate Professor; D.A., Carnegie Mellon. Edward DeCarbo, Adjunct Associate Professor; Ph.D., Indiana. Eva Diaz, Assistant Professor; M.A., Princeton. Mary Edwards, Adjunct Professor; Ph.D., Columbia. Diana Gisolfi, Professor; Ph.D., Yale. Dimitri Hazzikostas, Assistant Professor; Ph.D., Columbia. Frima Fox Hofrichter; Ph.D., Rutgers. Vivien Knussi, Adjunct Assistant Instructor; M.A., Tufts. Marilyn Kushner, Visiting Professor; Ph.D., Northwestern. Marsha Morton, Professor; Ph.D., NYU. Nick Napoli, Visiting Assistant Professor; Ph.D., Princeton. Antoinette Owen, Visiting Associate Professor; M.A., SUNY College at Oneonta. Joyce Polistena, Adjunct Associate Professor; Ph.D., Columbia. Katarina V. Posch, Associate Professor; Ph.D., Tokyo National University of the Arts. Vanessa Rocco, Adjunct Assistant Professor; Ph.D., CUNY Graduate Center. Ann Schoenfeld, Adjunct Assistant Professor; Ph.D., CUNY Graduate Center. Dorothy Shepard, Adjunct Professor; Ph.D., Bryn Mawr. Jack Toolin, Visiting Assistant Professor; M.F.A., San Jose State. Tom Tredway, Visiting Assistant Professor; M.A., Bard. Borhua Wang, Adjunct Associate Professor; Ph.D., Columbia.

Industrial Design
Steve Diskin, Chair; Ph.D., Ecole Polytechnique Federale de Lausanne. Laurel Voss, Acting Assistant Chair/Visiting Instructor; M.F.A., California College of the Arts. Harvey Bernstein, Adjunct Professor; M.S., Pratt; CCE. Fred Blumlein, Adjunct Professor; CCE. Meri Bourgard-Rohrs, Adjunct Professor; M.F.A., Pratt; CCE. Gina Caspi, Visiting Professor; M.I.D., Pratt. Gihyun Cho, Adjunct Professor; M.I.D., Syracuse. Kevin Crowley, Visiting Assistant Professor; B.I.D., Pratt. Lucia DeRespinis, Adjunct Professor; B.I.D., Pratt; CCE. Peter Erickson, Visiting Instructor. Stephen Faletti, Visiting Instructor; B.I.D., Pratt. Patrick Fenton, Visiting Instructor; M.F.A., Stanford. Colin Gentle, Visiting Assistant Professor; B.Eng., Connecticut. Mark Goetz, Adjunct Professor; B.I.D., Pratt. Bruce Hannah, Professor; B.I.D., Pratt. Lloyd Hicks, Adjunct Associate Professor; M.S., Lund (Sweden). Kate Hixon, Adjunct Associate Professor. Robert Langhorn, Visiting Assistant Professor; Royal College of Art. Jay Levy, Visiting Assistant Professor; M.Arch Columbia. Jong Lim, Adjunct Professor; M.F.A., Pratt. Scott Lundberg, Adjunct Assistant Professor; M.I.D., Pratt. Steven Mercurio, Visiting Associate Professor; M.A., SUNY at Stony Brook. Katrin Mueller-Russo, Adjunct Associate Professor. Shigeru Natsume, Visiting Associate Professor; M.F.A., Cranbrook. Jeanne Pfordresher, Adjunct Instructor; B.F.A., Cleveland Institute of Art. Russell Robertson, Adjunct Professor; B.F.A., Cleveland Institute of Art. Andrew Schloss, Adjunct Associate Professor; M.I.D., Pratt. Arthur Sempliner, Adjunct Professor; M.B.A., Michigan. Martin Skalski, Professor; M.I.D., Pratt. Jordan Steckel, Adjunct Professor; B.F.A., Yale. Irvin Tepper, Adjunct Professor; M.F.A., Washington (Seattle). Jonathan Thayer, Assistant Professor; B.I.D., Pratt. Rebecca Welz, Adjunct Professor; B.A., SUNY Empire State College; CCE. Joel Wennerstrom, Adjunct Associate Professor; M.I.D., Pratt. Hyukjae Yoo, Adjunct Professor; M.I.D., Pratt.

Interior Design
Anita Cooney, Chair; B.A., Brown, B.Arch., Pratt. Jennifer Logun, Assistant Chair; M.Arch., Florida. Eric Ansel, Visiting Assistant Professor; M.F.A., Art Institute of Chicago, M.Arch., Pratt. Tarek Ashkar, Visiting Assistant Professor; M.Arch., Harvard. Harvey Bernstein, Adjunct Professor; M.S., Pratt. Meri Bourgard, Adjunct Professor; M.F.A., Pratt; CCE. Jennifer Broutin, Visiting Associate Professor; M.S., Columbia. Mary Burke, Visiting Assistant Professor. Mateo Antonio de Cardenas, Visiting Assistant Professor; B.Arch, Cooper Union. Ike Cheung, Visiting Assistant Professor; B.Arch., Pratt. Melissa Ciccetti, Visiting Assistant Professor; M.Arch., Pennsylvania. James Conti, Adjunct Associate Professor; M.F.A., Ohio State. Carol Crawford, Adjunct Assistant Professor. Ron Eng, Visiting Assistant Professor; M.Arch., MIT. Philip Farrell, Adjunct Professor; M.S., Pratt. David C. C. Foley, Visiting Assistant Professor; M.A., Notre Dame. Antonio Furgiuele, Visiting Assistant Professor. Pavlina Gantcheva, Visiting Assistant Professor; M.S., Columbia. Jennifer Hanlin, Visiting Assistant Professor; M.Arch., Harvard. John Heida, Visiting Assistant Professor; B.Arch., California College of the Arts. Moia Henry, Visiting Assistant Professor; M.A., Southern California Institute of Architecture. Claudia Hernandez, Visiting Assistant Professor; M.S., Columbia. Stephen Horner, Visiting Assistant Professor; M.A., Parsons. Aki Ishida, Visiting Professor; M.S., Columbia. Eric Kachelhofer, Visiting Professor. Mi-Young Kang, Visiting Assistant Professor; M.S., Pratt. Sheryl Kasak, Visiting Assistant Professor; M.A., Columbia. Komal Kehar, Visting Assistant Professor; M.A., Parsons. Vanessa Keith, Visiting Assistant Professor; M.Arch., Pennsylvania. Margaret Kirk, Visiting Instructor; M.Arch., Pratt. Eugene Kwak, Visiting Assistant Professor; M.A., Columbia. Annie Kwon, Visiting Assistant Professor; M.S., Columbia. Scott Larrabee, Visiting Assistant Professor.Jason Livingston, Visiting Assistant Professor; M.F.A., NYU. Cam Lorendo, Visiting Assistant Professor; B.A., Parsons. William Mangold, Adjunct Assistant Professor; Ph.D., CUNY Graduate Center. T. Camille Martin, Visting Assistant Professor; M.A., Washington (St. Louis). Anthony Mekel, Adjunct Assistant Professor; B.Arch., Pratt. Francine Monaco, Adjunct Associate Professor; B.Arch., Cincinnati. Julie Torres Moskovitz, Visiting Assistant Professor; M.Arch., Pennsylvania. Stephen Mullins, Visiting Assistant Professor; M.F.A., Architectural Association (London). Robert Nassar, Visiting Assistant Professor; B.F.A., Syracuse. Tetsu Ohara, Visiting Assistant Professor; M.Arch., Harvard. Brian Osborn, Visiting Assistant Professor; M.A., Pratt. Jon Otis, Professor; M.S., Massachusetts. Andrew Pettit, Adjunct Associate Professor; B.Arch., Pratt. Salvatore Raffone, Visiting Assistant Professor; M.Arch., Harvard. Woodson Rainey, Visiting Assistant Professor; B.F.A., B.Arch., Utah. Christian Rietzke, Visiting Assistant Professor. Gustav Rohrs, Professor; B.Arch., MIT. Edward Russell, Adjunct Assistant Professor; M.F.A., Parsons. Mary-Jo Schlachter, Visiting Assistant Professor; M.A., Pennsylvania. Hazel Siegel, Visiting Assistant Professor; M.F.A., CUNY, Hunter. Andrew Simons, Visiting Assistant Professor; B.F.A., Carnegie Mellon. Steve Smith, Adjunct Associate Professor; B.S., Pratt. Joanna Sohn, Visiting Assistant Professor; M.S., Pratt. Jina Y. Son, Visiting Assocaite Professor; B.S., Cincinnati. Elizabeth Stoel, Visiting Associate Professor; M.A., Harvard. Sara Strauss, Visiting Associate Professor; M.A., Yale. Brent Stringfellow, Visiting Assistant Professor; M.A., Harvard. Keena Suh, Adjunct Assistant Professor; M.Arch., Columbia. Myonggi Sul, Professor; M.S., Pratt. Yutaka Takiura, Visiting Associate Professor; M.Arch., Pennsylvania. Madeleine Taylor, Visiting Assistant Professor; M.S., Columbia. Karin Tehve, Visiting Assistant Professor; M.Arch., Harvard. Omar Toro-Vaca, Visiting Assistant Professor; B.Arch., Pratt. Jack Travis, Adjunct Assistant Professor; M.Arch., Illinois at Urbana–Champaign. Michael Zuckerman, Adjunct Associate Professor; B.Arch., CUNY, City College.

TEXAS TECH UNIVERSITY

Department of Design
Programs in Interior and Environmental Design

Programs of Study	The **Ph.D. Degree Program** provides study opportunities in the areas of Interior and Environmental Design. A minimum of 65 semester credit hours of graduate work beyond the bachelor's degree, exclusive of credit for the dissertation, is required. Students develop a course of study in consultation with an advisory committee. A preliminary examination is required before the end of the second semester of work. Leveling course work may be required to remove subject matter deficiencies revealed by the preliminary examination. Following the completion of course work, a qualifying examination is administered
	The **Master of Science Degree Program** emphasizes environmental design. The master's degree includes two options: the thesis and report options. While the report option offers the possibility of addressing a line of inquiry based on a phenomenological approach-basic research; the thesis option paves the way for inquiries based on applied research, which constitute an excellent preparation towards the doctoral degree. Appropriate leveling course work may be required when the degree plan is designed. A minimum of 30 semester credit hours including 6 credit hours for the thesis/report is required.
Research Facilities	The Texas Tech University Library maintains a collection of 2.3 million volumes, nearly 22 million microforms that hold images from specialized collections, and more than 30,000 industry-related journals. It is one of two regional depositories for U.S. government documents in Texas. Students also have access to more than 500 online and CD-ROM databases.
Financial Aid	Financial assistance is available from a number of sources on campus. A partial listing of assistance and information is as follows. To qualify for a graduate assistantship and/or scholarship, the student must be admitted to a degree program in the Department.
	For scholarships, graduate students are encouraged to stay well-informed of sources of information on University scholarships. As a general rule, the graduate school accepts applications early in the spring semester for awards for the upcoming academic year. Applicants do not have to be officially admitted to a TTU graduate program when applying for scholarships. In addition, applying to the Graduate School does not automatically qualify a student for University scholarships. Students need to fill out the online application. For more details, check the scholarship listing, including award amount and duration as well as eligibility requirements at http://www.depts.ttu.edu/gradschool/funding/assistantships.php.
	For graduate assistantships, including graduate research or teaching assistantships, applications may be submitted at any time and will be considered when vacancies occur. Priority is given to graduate students with prior industry, teaching, or research experience. A copy of the application form may be found in the Department of Design Graduate Programs Web site: http://www.depts.ttu.edu/hs/dod/ied/.
	For other scholarship, grant, and loan opportunities, students should contact the Office of Student Financial Aid. Ask Raider Red, or phone 806-742-3681 to speak with a financial aid adviser. Graduate students may borrow up to $20,500 annually in the Federal Direct Loan Program and may borrow up to the total cost of education less any other financial aid through the Federal Graduate PLUS Loan Program. Student must complete the Free Application for Federal Student Aid (FAFSA) for grant consideration. Information regarding loan application is available at http://www.depts.ttu.edu/financialaid/.
Cost of Study	For up-to-date information of tuition costs and fees, prospective students should visit the Web site at http://www.depts.ttu.edu/officialpublications/catalog/_financialinfo.php#Tuition.
Living and Housing Costs	Students can live on campus in a residence hall or apartment complex. Rates per academic year range from $2820 for a non–air conditioned one-bedroom apartment to $4684 for a three-bedroom town house. Other rates vary depending on apartment size and location. Flexible dining plans range from $2845 to $3345. Students can also live off-campus; rents average from $300 to $700 per month for a one- or two-bedroom apartment.
Student Group	Texas Tech University prides itself on being a major comprehensive research university that retains the sense of a smaller liberal arts institution. Although enrollment is over 30,000, Texas Tech students boast of one-on-one interaction with top faculty and an environment that stresses student accomplishment above all else. The University is large enough to provide the best in facilities and academics, but small enough to focus on the student. It is committed to enhancing the cultural and economic development of the state, nation, and world. Texas Tech students come from every county in Texas, all fifty states and more than ninety other countries.
Location	The University is located in Lubbock, in the heart of West Texas. With a population of more than 200,000, Lubbock is a major regional center for business and industry and the major medical center for the surrounding 300-mile area. The climate in Lubbock is excellent, with dry winters and an average annual rainfall of 18 inches.
The University and The College	Texas Tech University, the largest higher education institution in the western region of Texas, serves an area larger than forty-six of the nation's fifty states and is the only campus in Texas to have a major university, law school, and medical school. Originally named Texas Technological College, the school formally became Texas Tech University in 1969. Today, nearly 29,000 students attend classes on the 1,839-acre Lubbock campus. The University also operates research centers in the Texas Panhandle and New Deal as well as branch campuses in Junction and the scenic hill country region.
	The College of Human Sciences at TTU is among the three largest colleges of its kind in the nation. The Department of Design is one of four departments within the College. The Department includes undergraduate programs in apparel design and manufacturing, and interior design. The Interior Design program is CIDA accredited.
Applying	Admission to the graduate school must be obtained through the graduate admissions office. For the online application, prospective students should visit http://www.depts.ttu.edu/gradschool/admissions/how.php. Application to the Department of Design graduate programs in the areas of Interior and Environmental Design is located at http://www.depts.ttu.edu/hs/dod/ied.
	The acceptance process is based on a review of the following criteria: GPA from undergraduate/graduate study; TOEFL scores (international students); letters of recommendation; design portfolio; unique contributions as evidenced in the applicant's resume or vita, such as the following: special accomplishments in industry or academic pursuits, leadership experience and potential, and other unique life experiences relevant to the pursuit of a graduate degree.

Correspondence and Information

Kristi Gaines, Ph.D.
Director of the Graduate Programs
Department of Design
College of Human Sciences
Texas Tech University
Lubbock, Texas 79409-1162
Phone: 806-742-3050 Ext. 223
Fax: 806-742-1639
E-mail: Kristi.Gaines@ttu.edu
Web site: http://www.depts.ttu.edu/hs/dod/

Cherif Amor, Ph.D., Department Chair
Department of Design
College of Human Sciences
Texas Tech University
Lubbock, Texas 79409-1162
Phone: 806-742-3050
Fax: 806-742-1639
E-mail: Cherif.Amor@ttu.edu

Texas Tech University

THE FACULTY AND THEIR RESEARCH

The Department of Design graduate faculty members are nationally and internationally recognized for achievements in evidence-based design, healthcare and the built environment, ergonomics, sustainability, and adaptive re-use. For additional information, prospective students should visit the faculty Web page at http://www.depts.ttu.edu/hs/dod/faculty.php.

Cherif Amor, Associate Professor of Interior and Environmental Design; Ph.D., Missouri (Columbia), Evidence-based design and sustainability.
Don Collier, Associate Professor of Interior Design; M.F.A., Austin State. Historical restoration and adaptive reuse.
Kristi Gaines, Assistant Professor in Interior Design; Ph.D., Texas Tech. Therapeutic environments for Individuals with neurodiversity.
Debajyoti Pati, Associate Professor of Interior and Environmental Design; Ph.D., Georgia Tech. Healthcare and the built environment.
Su Shin, Associate Professor; Ph.D., North Carolina State, Ergonomics using 3-D body scan technology.

Section 2
Architecture

This section contains a directory of institutions offering graduate work in architecture, followed by in-depth entries submitted by institutions that chose to prepare detailed program descriptions. Additional information about programs listed in the directory but not augmented by an in-depth entry may be obtained by writing directly to the dean of a graduate school or chair of a department at the address given in the directory.

For programs offering related work, see also in this book *Applied Arts and Design, Art and Art History,* and *Public, Regional, and Industrial Affairs. In another guide in this series:*
Graduate Programs in Engineering & Applied Sciences
See *Civil and Environmental Engineering*

CONTENTS

Program Directories

Close-Ups and Displays

Architectural History

Arizona State University, Herberger Institute for Design and the Arts, School of Architecture and Landscape Architecture, PhD Program in Design, Environment and the Arts, Tempe, AZ 85287-2105. Offers design, environment and the arts (design) (PhD); design, environment and the arts (healthcare and healing environments) (PhD); design, environment and the arts (history, theory, and criticism) (PhD). *Faculty:* 25 full-time (13 women). *Students:* 17 full-time (4 women), 15 part-time (7 women); includes 4 minority (2 Asian, non-Hispanic/Latino; 2 Hispanic/Latino), 17 international. Average age 36. 19 applicants, 53% accepted, 4 enrolled. In 2010, 8 doctorates awarded. *Degree requirements:* For doctorate, comprehensive exam, thesis/dissertation, interactive Program of Study (iPOS) submitted before completing 50 percent of required credit hours. *Entrance requirements:* For doctorate, GRE, master's degree in architecture, graphic design, industrial design, interior design, landscape architecture, or art history or equivalent standing; statement of purpose; 3 letters of recommendation; indication of potential faculty mentor; sample of written work. Additional exam requirements/recommendations for international students: Required—TOEFL, IELTS, or Pearson Test of English. *Application deadline:* For fall admission, 12/15 for domestic and international students. Application fee: $70 ($90 for international students). Electronic applications accepted. *Expenses:* Contact institution. *Financial support:* In 2010–11, 3 research assistantships with full and partial tuition reimbursements (averaging $16,365 per year), 9 teaching assistantships with full and partial tuition reimbursements (averaging $10,384 per year) were awarded; institutionally sponsored loans, scholarships/grants, and tuition waivers (partial) also available. Financial award application deadline: 3/1; financial award applicants required to submit FAFSA. *Unit head:* Dr. Michael D. Kroelinger, Executive Dean/Director, 480-965-5561, E-mail: design.phd@asu.edu. *Application contact:* Graduate Admissions, 480-965-6113.

Cornell University, Graduate School, Graduate Fields of Architecture, Art and Planning, Field of Architecture, Ithaca, NY 14853-0001. Offers architectural design (M Arch); architectural science (MS); building technology and environmental science (MS); computer graphics (MS); history of architecture (MA, PhD); history of urban development (MA, PhD); theory and criticism of architecture (M Arch); urban design (M Arch). *Faculty:* 26 full-time (8 women). *Students:* 113 full-time (55 women); includes 2 Black or African American, non-Hispanic/Latino; 15 Asian, non-Hispanic/Latino; 8 Hispanic/Latino, 47 international. Average age 26. 545 applicants, 26% accepted, 65 enrolled. In 2010, 26 master's, 1 doctorate awarded. *Degree requirements:* For master's, one foreign language, thesis (MA, MS); for doctorate, 2 foreign languages, comprehensive exam, thesis/dissertation. *Entrance requirements:* For master's, GRE General Test, 5 year bachelor's degree in architecture, portfolio (M Arch), 3 letters of recommendation; for doctorate, GRE General Test, 3 letters of recommendation. Additional exam requirements/recommendations for international students: Required—TOEFL (minimum score 600 paper-based; 250 computer-based; 77 iBT). *Application deadline:* For fall admission, 1/15 priority date for domestic students. Application fee: $70. Electronic applications accepted. *Expenses:* Tuition: Full-time $29,500. Required fees: $76. Tuition and fees vary according to degree level and program. *Financial support:* In 2010–11, 11 fellowships with full tuition reimbursements, 19 teaching assistantships with full tuition reimbursements were awarded; research assistantships with full tuition reimbursements, institutionally sponsored loans, scholarships/grants, health care benefits, tuition waivers (full and partial), and unspecified assistantships also available. Financial award applicants required to submit FAFSA. *Faculty research:* Architectural design and urban design, theory and criticism of architecture, computer graphics, building technology and environmental science, history of architecture and history of urban-development. *Unit head:* Director of Graduate Studies, 607-255-6701, Fax: 607-255-0291. *Application contact:* Graduate Field Assistant, 607-255-6701, Fax: 607-255-0291, E-mail: cuarch@cornell.edu.

Graduate School and University Center of the City University of New York, Graduate Studies, Program in Art History, New York, NY 10016-4039. Offers architecture (PhD); graphic arts (PhD); painting (PhD); photography (PhD); sculpture (PhD). *Degree requirements:* For doctorate, 2 foreign languages, thesis/dissertation. *Entrance requirements:* For doctorate, GRE General Test. Additional exam requirements/recommendations for international students: Required—TOEFL. Electronic applications accepted.

Harvard University, Graduate School of Arts and Sciences, Department of History of Art and Architecture, Cambridge, MA 02138. Offers ancient art (PhD); ancient Near Eastern art (PhD); baroque art (PhD); Byzantine art (PhD); classical art (PhD); Indian art (PhD); Islamic art (PhD); Japanese and Chinese art (PhD); medieval art (PhD); modern art (PhD); Renaissance and modern architecture (PhD); Renaissance art (PhD). *Degree requirements:* For doctorate, variable foreign language requirement, thesis/dissertation, general exams; reading exams in French, German, and Italian. *Entrance requirements:* For doctorate, GRE General Test. Additional exam requirements/recommendations for international students: Required—TOEFL. *Expenses:* Tuition: Full-time $34,976. Required fees: $1166. Full-time tuition and fees vary according to program.

Massachusetts Institute of Technology, School of Architecture and Planning, Department of Architecture, Cambridge, MA 02139. Offers architecture (M Arch, PhD), including building technology (PhD), design and computation (PhD), history and theory of architecture (PhD), history and theory of art (PhD); architecture studies (SM Arch S); building technology (SMBT); visual studies (SM Vis S). *Faculty:* 30 full-time (7 women). *Students:* 241 full-time (111 women), 1 (woman) part-time; includes 54 minority (6 Black or African American, non-Hispanic/Latino; 2 American Indian or Alaska Native, non-Hispanic/Latino; 31 Asian, non-Hispanic/Latino; 10 Hispanic/Latino; 5 Two or more races, non-Hispanic/Latino), 84 international. Average age 28. 1,166 applicants, 13% accepted, 94 enrolled. In 2010, 63 master's, 6 doctorates awarded. *Degree requirements:* For master's, thesis; for doctorate, comprehensive exam, thesis/dissertation. *Entrance requirements:* For master's, GRE General Test (for some programs), portfolio (for some programs); for doctorate, GRE General Test (for some programs). Additional exam requirements/recommendations for international students: Required—TOEFL (minimum score 650 paper-based; 280 computer-based; 114 iBT), IELTS (minimum score 7). *Application deadline:* For fall admission, 12/15 for domestic and international students. Application fee: $75. Electronic applications accepted. *Expenses:* Tuition: Full-time $38,940; part-time $605 per unit. Required fees: $272. *Financial support:* In 2010–11, 195 students received support, including 155 fellowships with tuition reimbursements available (averaging $18,267 per year), 32 research assistantships with tuition reimbursements available (averaging $24,642 per year), 25 teaching assistantships with tuition reimbursements available (averaging $29,366 per year); career-related internships or fieldwork, Federal Work-Study, institutionally sponsored loans, scholarships/grants, health care benefits, and unspecified assistantships also available. *Faculty research:* Architecture and urbanism; building technology and sustainability; computation and design; history, theory, and criticism; contemporary visual art practice; digital fabrication. Total annual research expenditures: $2.4 million. *Unit head:* Prof. Nader Tehrani, Department Head, 617-253-7791, E-mail: arch@mit.edu. *Application contact:* Admissions Coordinator, 617-715-4490, Fax: 617-253-8993, E-mail: arch@mit.edu.

Savannah College of Art and Design, Graduate School, Program in Architectural History, Savannah, GA 31402-3146. Offers MA, MFA. Part-time programs available. *Faculty:* 8 full-time (1 woman), 1 part-time/adjunct (0 women). *Students:* 7 full-time (6 women), 4 part-time (3 women). Average age 25. In 2010, 3 master's awarded. *Degree requirements:* For master's, one foreign language, thesis, internship. *Entrance requirements:* For master's, interview, research paper. Additional exam requirements/recommendations for international students: Required—TOEFL (minimum score 450 paper-based; 133 computer-based). *Application deadline:* For fall admission, 4/1 priority date for domestic and international students. Applications are processed on a rolling basis. Application fee: $35. Electronic applications accepted. *Expenses:* Tuition: Full-time $29,520; part-time $3280 per quarter. Tuition and fees vary according to campus/location. *Financial support:* In 2010–11, 1 fellowship was awarded; career-related internships or fieldwork, Federal Work-Study, and scholarships/grants also available. Financial award application deadline: 4/1; financial award applicants required to submit FAFSA. *Unit head:* Dr. Robin Williams, Chair, 912-525-6058, Fax: 912-525-6050, E-mail: rwilliam@scad.edu. *Application contact:* Darrell Tutchton, Director of Graduate and International Enrollment, 912-525-5965, Fax: 912-525-5985, E-mail: emathis@scad.edu.

University of California, Berkeley, Graduate Division, College of Environmental Design, Department of Architecture, Berkeley, CA 94720-1500. Offers architecture (M Arch); building science (MS, PhD); building structures, construction and materials (MS, PhD); design theories, methods, and practices (MS, PhD); environmental design in developing countries (MS, PhD); history of architecture and urbanism (MS, PhD); social and cultural processes in architecture and urbanism (MS, PhD); M Arch/MCP; M Arch/MS; MLA/M Arch. *Degree requirements:* For master's, thesis; for doctorate, thesis/dissertation, qualifying exam. *Entrance requirements:* For master's and doctorate, GRE General Test, minimum GPA of 3.0, 3 letters of recommendation. Additional exam requirements/recommendations for international students: Required—TOEFL. Electronic applications accepted.

University of Colorado Denver, College of Architecture and Planning, Program in Design and Planning, Denver, CO 80217-3364. Offers history of architecture, landscape and urbanism (PhD); sustainable and healthy environments (PhD). Part-time programs available. *Students:* 25 full-time (15 women), 11 part-time (7 women); includes 2 Black or African American, non-Hispanic/Latino; 1 Asian, non-Hispanic/Latino; 2 Hispanic/Latino, 7 international. Average age 40. 60 applicants, 15% accepted, 6 enrolled. In 2010, 2 doctorates awarded. *Degree requirements:* For doctorate, comprehensive exam, thesis/dissertation. *Entrance requirements:* For doctorate, GRE, minimum undergraduate GPA of 3.0, graduate 3.5; writing sample. Additional exam requirements/recommendations for international students: Required—TOEFL (minimum score 575 paper-based). *Application deadline:* For fall admission, 2/1 for domestic students; for spring admission, 10/1 for domestic students. Application fee: $50 ($75 for international students). Electronic applications accepted. *Expenses:* Contact institution. *Financial support:* Fellowships, research assistantships, teaching assistantships, career-related internships or fieldwork, Federal Work-Study, scholarships/grants, tuition waivers, and unspecified assistantships available. Support available to part-time students. Financial award application deadline: 4/1; financial award applicants required to submit FAFSA. *Faculty research:* Land use and environmental planning and design; design and planning processes and practices; history, theory, and criticism of the built environment. *Unit head:* Dr. Kevin Krizek, Director, 303-556-3282, Fax: 303-556-3687, E-mail: kevin.krizek@colorado.edu. *Application contact:* Michael Harper, Administrative Coordinator, 303-556-6042, Fax: 303-556-3687, E-mail: michael.t.harper@ucdenver.edu.

University of Pittsburgh, School of Arts and Sciences, Department of History of Art and Architecture, Pittsburgh, PA 15260. Offers MA, PhD. *Faculty:* 13 full-time (7 women). *Students:* 31 full-time (26 women); includes 5 Asian, non-Hispanic/Latino; 1 Hispanic/Latino. Average age 33. 51 applicants, 12% accepted, 5 enrolled. In 2010, 3 master's, 6 doctorates awarded. Terminal master's awarded for partial completion of doctoral program. *Degree requirements:* For master's, one foreign language, thesis; for doctorate, 2 foreign languages, comprehensive exam, thesis/dissertation. *Entrance requirements:* For doctorate, GRE General Test, 3 letters of recommendation, writing sample, foreign language questionnaire, statement of purpose. Additional exam requirements/recommendations for international students: Required—TOEFL (minimum score 550 paper-based; 213 computer-based; 80 iBT). *Application deadline:* For fall admission, 1/15 for domestic and international students. Application fee: $50. Electronic applications accepted. *Expenses:* Tuition, state resident: full-time $17,304; part-time $701 per credit. Tuition, nonresident: full-time $29,554; part-time $1210 per credit. Required fees: $740; $214 per term. Tuition and fees vary according to program. *Financial support:* In 2010–11, 29 students received support, including 16 fellowships with full tuition reimbursements available (averaging $17,972 per year), 13 teaching assistantships with full tuition reimbursements available (averaging $15,064 per year); research assistantships with full tuition reimbursements available, career-related internships or fieldwork, Federal Work-Study, scholarships/grants, health care benefits, and tuition waivers (partial) also available. Financial award application deadline: 1/15. *Faculty research:* Asian, medieval, Renaissance/Baroque, modern art and architecture, contemporary. *Unit head:* Dr. Kirk Savage, Chair, 412-648-2405, Fax: 412-648-2792, E-mail: ksa@pitt.edu. *Application contact:* Dr. Josh Ellenbogen, Director, Graduate Studies, 412-648-8530, Fax: 412-648-2792, E-mail: jme23@pitt.edu.

The University of Texas at Austin, Graduate School, School of Architecture, Austin, TX 78712-1111. Offers architecture (M Arch); community and regional planning (MSCRP, PhD); historic preservation (MS); history of architecture (MA, PhD); landscape architecture (MLA); urban design (MSUD); JD/MSCRP; MSCRP/MA; MSCRP/PhD. *Degree requirements:* For doctorate, thesis/dissertation. *Entrance requirements:* For master's and doctorate, GRE General Test. Additional exam requirements/recommendations for international students: Required—TOEFL (minimum score 550 paper-based; 213 computer-based). Electronic applications accepted.

University of Virginia, School of Architecture, Department of Architectural History, Charlottesville, VA 22903. Offers M Arch H, PhD. *Faculty:* 6 full-time (3 women). *Students:* 24 full-time (18 women), 1 part-time (0 women); includes 1 Black or African American, non-Hispanic/Latino; 1 Hispanic/Latino, 2 international. Average age 29. 26 applicants, 77% accepted, 5 enrolled. In 2010, 12 master's, 2 doctorates awarded. *Degree requirements:* For master's, one foreign language, thesis. *Entrance requirements:* For master's, GRE General Test, 3 letters of recommendation. Additional exam requirements/recommendations for international students: Required—TOEFL (minimum score 600 paper-based; 250 computer-based; 90 iBT). *Application deadline:* For fall admission, 1/5 for domestic and international students. Applications are processed on a rolling basis. Application fee: $60. Electronic applications accepted. *Financial support:* Career-related internships or fieldwork, Federal Work-Study, and institutionally sponsored loans available. Financial award applicants required to submit FAFSA. *Faculty research:* Urban form, nineteenth and twentieth century American architecture. *Unit head:* Louis Nelson, Chair, 434-924-1428, Fax: 434-982-2678, E-mail: lnelson@virginia.edu. *Application contact:* Graduate Admissions Officer, 434-924-6442, E-mail: arch-admissions@virginia.edu.

Virginia Commonwealth University, Graduate School, School of the Arts, Department of Art History, Richmond, VA 23284-9005. Offers architectural history (MA); art history (MA, PhD); historical studies (MA); museum studies (MA). *Accreditation:* NASAD. *Faculty:* 10 full-time (4 women). *Students:* 15 full-time (13 women), 27 part-time (24 women); includes 4 minority (1 Asian, non-Hispanic/Latino; 3 Hispanic/Latino), 1 international. 52 applicants, 48% accepted, 12 enrolled. In 2010, 9 master's, 5 doctorates awarded. *Degree requirements:* For master's, thesis; for doctorate, comprehensive exam, thesis/dissertation. *Entrance requirements:* For master's and doctorate, GRE General Test. *Application deadline:* For fall admission, 1/15 for domestic students. Application fee: $50. Electronic applications accepted. *Expenses:* Tuition, state resident: full-time $4308; part-time $479 per credit hour. Tuition, nonresident: full-time $8942; part-time $994 per credit hour. Required fees: $2000; $85 per credit hour. Tuition and fees vary according to course level, course load, degree level, campus/location and program. *Financial support:* Fellowships, teaching assistantships, career-related internships or fieldwork, Federal Work-Study, and institutionally sponsored loans available. Support available to part-time students. Financial award application deadline: 3/15; financial award applicants required to submit FAFSA. *Faculty research:* Modern, nineteenth-century, Renaissance, American, and medieval art. *Unit head:* Dr. Dina Bangdel, Director of Graduate Studies, 804-628-7027, Fax: 804-828-7468, E-mail: dbangdel@vcu.edu. *Application contact:* Dr. Dina Bangdel, Director of Graduate Studies, 804-628-7027, Fax: 804-828-7468, E-mail: dbangdel@vcu.edu.

Architecture

Academy of Art University, Graduate Program, School of Architecture, San Francisco, CA 94105-3410. Offers M Arch. Part-time programs available. Postbaccalaureate distance learning degree programs offered (no on-campus study). *Faculty:* 2 full-time (1 woman), 27 part-time/adjunct (8 women). *Students:* 153 full-time (70 women), 36 part-time (11 women); includes 7 Black or African American, non-Hispanic/Latino; 19 Asian, non-Hispanic/Latino; 10 Hispanic/Latino, 90 international. Average age 29. 147 applicants. In 2010, 7 master's awarded. *Degree requirements:* For master's, thesis, final review. *Entrance requirements:* For master's, portfolio, bachelor's degree in architecture or related field. *Application deadline:* For fall admission, 9/7 for domestic and international students; for spring admission, 2/2 for domestic and international students. Applications are processed on a rolling basis. Application fee: $100 ($500 for international students). Electronic applications accepted. *Expenses:* Tuition: Full-time $20,160; part-time $840 per semester hour. Required fees: $45 per semester. *Financial support:* Career-related internships or fieldwork and Federal Work-Study available. Support available to part-time students. Financial award application deadline: 8/10; financial award applicants required to submit FAFSA. *Application contact:* Prospective Students Services, 800-544-ARTS, Fax: 415-263-4131, E-mail: info@academyart.edu.

Andrews University, School of Graduate Studies, Division of Architecture, Berrien Springs, MI 49104. Offers M Arch. *Entrance requirements:* For master's, GRE. Additional exam requirements/recommendations for international students: Required—TOEFL (minimum score 550 paper-based).

Arizona State University, Herberger Institute for Design and the Arts, School of Architecture and Landscape Architecture, Tempe, AZ 85287-1605. Offers architecture (M Arch); building design/built environment (MS); design (arts, media, and engineering) (MSD); design (healthcare and healing environments) (MSD); design (industrial design) (MSD); design (interior design) (MSD); design (new product innovation) (MSD); design (visual communication design) (MSD); design, environment and the arts (PhD), including design, environment and the arts (design), design, environment and the arts (healthcare and healing environments), design, environment and the arts (history, theory, and criticism); landscape architecture (MLA); urban design (MUD); MA/MBA. *Accreditation:* NASAD. *Faculty:* 41 full-time (9 women), 6 part-time/adjunct (3 women). *Students:* 252 full-time (111 women), 45 part-time (21 women); includes 61 minority (3 Black or African American, non-Hispanic/Latino; 2 American Indian or Alaska Native, non-Hispanic/Latino; 13 Asian, non-Hispanic/Latino; 41 Hispanic/Latino; 1 Native Hawaiian or other Pacific Islander, non-Hispanic/Latino; 1 Two or more races, non-Hispanic/Latino), 58 international. Average age 29. 420 applicants, 61% accepted, 117 enrolled. In 2010, 60 master's, 8 doctorates awarded. Terminal master's awarded for partial completion of doctoral program. *Degree requirements:* For master's, thesis optional, interactive Program of Study (iPOS) submitted before completing 50 percent of required credit hours; for doctorate, comprehensive exam, thesis/dissertation, interactive Program of Study (iPOS) submitted before completing 50 percent of required credit hours. *Entrance requirements:* For master's, GRE General Test, minimum GPA of 3.0 or equivalent in last 2 years of work leading to bachelor's degree, design/creative works portfolio, 3 references, statement of intent; for doctorate, GRE, master's degree in architecture, graphic design, industrial design, interior design, landscape architecture, or art history or equivalent standing; statement of purpose; 3 letters of recommendation; indication of potential faculty mentor; sample of written work. Additional exam requirements/recommendations for international students: Required—TOEFL (minimum score 600 paper-based; 250 computer-based; 100 iBT). *Application deadline:* For fall admission, 1/15 priority date for domestic and international students. Application fee: $70 ($90 for international students). Electronic applications accepted. *Expenses:* Tuition, state resident: full-time $8510; part-time $608 per credit. Tuition, nonresident: full-time $16,542; part-time $919 per credit. Required fees: $339; $110 per credit. Part-time tuition and fees vary according to course load. *Financial support:* In 2010–11, 9 research assistantships with full and partial tuition reimbursements (averaging $11,913 per year), 76 teaching assistantships with full and partial tuition reimbursements (averaging $6,294 per year) were awarded; fellowships with full and partial tuition reimbursements, scholarships/grants and tuition waivers (full and partial) also available. Financial award application deadline: 3/1; financial award applicants required to submit FAFSA. Total annual research expenditures: $410,956. *Unit head:* Darren Petrucci, Director, 480-965-3536, E-mail: darren.petrucci@asu.edu. *Application contact:* Graduate Admissions, 480-965-6113.

Auburn University, Graduate School, College of Architecture, Design, and Construction, Auburn University, AL 36849. Offers MBS, MCP, MDB, MID, MLA, MPA/MCP. Part-time programs available. *Faculty:* 61 full-time (12 women), 6 part-time/adjunct (2 women). *Students:* 111 full-time (41 women), 43 part-time (12 women); includes 8 Black or African American, non-Hispanic/Latino; 1 Asian, non-Hispanic/Latino; 3 Hispanic/Latino, 22 international. Average age 26. 250 applicants, 58% accepted, 97 enrolled. In 2010, 37 master's awarded. *Entrance requirements:* For master's, GRE General Test. *Application deadline:* For fall admission, 7/7 for domestic students; for spring admission, 11/24 for domestic students. Applications are processed on a rolling basis. Application fee: $50 ($60 for international students). Electronic applications accepted. *Expenses:* Contact institution. *Financial support:* Fellowships, Federal Work-Study available. Support available to part-time students. Financial award application deadline: 3/15; financial award applicants required to submit FAFSA. *Unit head:* Dr. Vini Nathan, Dean, 334-844-4285. *Application contact:* Dr. George Flowers, Dean of the Graduate School, 334-844-2125.

Ball State University, Graduate School, College of Architecture and Planning, Department of Architecture, Program in Architecture, Muncie, IN 47306-1099. Offers M Arch. *Faculty:* 25. *Students:* 71 full-time (24 women), 17 part-time (5 women); includes 4 minority (3 Asian, non-Hispanic/Latino; 1 Two or more races, non-Hispanic/Latino), 18 international. Average age 27. 97 applicants, 59% accepted, 27 enrolled. In 2010, 42 master's awarded. *Degree requirements:* For master's, thesis. *Entrance requirements:* For master's, minimum undergraduate B average, portfolio, writing sample. Application fee: $50. *Expenses:* Tuition, state resident: full-time $6160; part-time $299 per credit hour. Tuition, nonresident: full-time $16,020; part-time $783 per credit hour. Required fees: $2278; $95 per credit hour. *Financial support:* Research assistantships with full tuition reimbursements available. Financial award application deadline: 3/1. *Unit head:* Dr. Mahesh Senagala, Department Chairperson, 765-285-1900, Fax: 765-285-1765, E-mail: msenagala@bsu.edu. *Application contact:* Dr. Joshua Coggeshall, Graduate Program Director, 765-285-1900, Fax: 765-285-1765.

Boston Architectural College, Graduate Programs, Boston, MA 02115-2795. Offers architecture (M Arch); interior design (MID). *Accreditation:* CIDA. *Degree requirements:* For master's, thesis. *Entrance requirements:* For master's, portfolio (recommended). Electronic applications accepted.

California College of the Arts, Graduate Programs, Program in Architecture, San Francisco, CA 94107. Offers M Arch. *Faculty:* 12 full-time (5 women), 40 part-time/adjunct (14 women). *Students:* 97 full-time (47 women), 4 part-time (1 woman); includes 3 Black or African American, non-Hispanic/Latino; 3 American Indian or Alaska Native, non-Hispanic/Latino; 11 Asian, non-Hispanic/Latino; 10 Hispanic/Latino, 7 international. Average age 27. 221 applicants, 64% accepted, 46 enrolled. In 2010, 26 master's awarded. *Degree requirements:* For master's, thesis. *Entrance requirements:* For master's, appropriate bachelor's degree, portfolio, resume, minimum 2 letters of recommendation, essay, transcripts. Additional exam requirements/recommendations for international students: Required—TOEFL (minimum score 600 paper-based; 250 computer-based; 100 iBT). *Application deadline:* For fall admission, 1/15 for domestic and international students. Application fee: $70. *Expenses:* Tuition: Full-time $38,550; part-time $1285 per unit. One-time fee: $185 full-time. *Financial support:* In 2010–11, 12 fellowships (averaging $14,000 per year), teaching assistantships (averaging $2,000 per year) were awarded; career-related internships or fieldwork, Federal Work-Study, scholarships/grants, and health care benefits also available. *Unit head:* Ila Berman, Chair, 415-703-9516,

E-mail: iberman@cca.edu. *Application contact:* Heidi Geis, Assistant Director of Graduate Admissions, 415-703-9523 Ext. 9533, Fax: 415-703-9539, E-mail: hgeis@cca.edu.

California Polytechnic State University, San Luis Obispo, College of Architecture and Environmental Design, Department of Architecture, San Luis Obispo, CA 93407. Offers MS. Part-time programs available. *Faculty:* 1 full-time (0 women), 1 part-time/adjunct (0 women). *Students:* 19 full-time (6 women), 6 part-time (3 women); includes 9 minority (2 Asian, non-Hispanic/Latino; 5 Hispanic/Latino; 2 Two or more races, non-Hispanic/Latino), 2 international. Average age 30. 34 applicants, 59% accepted, 16 enrolled. In 2010, 12 master's awarded. *Degree requirements:* For master's, thesis. *Entrance requirements:* For master's, GRE, minimum GPA of 3.0, 2 letters of recommendation. Additional exam requirements/recommendations for international students: Required—TOEFL (minimum score 550 paper-based; 213 computer-based) or IELTS (minimum score 6). *Application deadline:* For fall admission, 7/1 for domestic students, 11/30 for international students; for winter admission, 11/1 for domestic students, 6/30 for international students. Applications are processed on a rolling basis. Application fee: $55. Electronic applications accepted. *Expenses:* Tuition, state resident: full-time $5386; part-time $3124 per year. Tuition, nonresident: full-time $11,160; part-time $248 per unit. Required fees: $2250; $614 per term. One-time fee: $2250 full-time; $1842 part-time. *Financial support:* Research assistantships, teaching assistantships, Federal Work-Study and institutionally sponsored loans available. Support available to part-time students. Financial award application deadline: 3/2; financial award applicants required to submit FAFSA. *Faculty research:* Computer-assisted design, decision support systems, building science, facilities management. Total annual research expenditures: $2.4 million. *Unit head:* Dr. Jens Pohl, Graduate Coordinator, 805-756-2841, Fax: 805-756-1500, E-mail: jpohl@calpoly.edu. *Application contact:* Dr. James Maraviglia, Assistant Vice President for Admissions, Recruitment and Financial Aid, 805-756-2311, Fax: 805-756-5400, E-mail: admissions@calpoly.edu.

California State Polytechnic University, Pomona, Academic Affairs, College of Environmental Design, Program in Architecture, Pomona, CA 91768-2557. Offers M Arch. Part-time programs available. *Students:* 57 full-time (31 women), 8 part-time (5 women); includes 20 minority (11 Asian, non-Hispanic/Latino; 7 Hispanic/Latino; 2 Two or more races, non-Hispanic/Latino), 6 international. Average age 29. 164 applicants, 19% accepted, 21 enrolled. In 2010, 12 master's awarded. *Degree requirements:* For master's, thesis or alternative. *Application deadline:* For fall admission, 5/1 for domestic students; for winter admission, 10/15 priority date for domestic students; for spring admission, 1/20 priority date for domestic students. Applications are processed on a rolling basis. Application fee: $55. Electronic applications accepted. *Expenses:* Tuition, state resident: full-time $5386; part-time $2850 per year. Tuition, nonresident: full-time $12,082; part-time $248 per credit. Required fees: $577; $248 per credit. $577 per year. Tuition and fees vary according to course load and program. *Financial support:* Career-related internships or fieldwork, Federal Work-Study, and institutionally sponsored loans available. Support available to part-time students. Financial award application deadline: 3/2; financial award applicants required to submit FAFSA. *Unit head:* Kip A. Dickson, Graduate Coordinator, 909-869-2682, Fax: 909-869-4331, E-mail: kadickson@csupomona.edu. *Application contact:* Scott J. Duncan, Director, Admissions, 909-869-3258, Fax: 909-869-4529, E-mail: sjduncan@csupomona.edu.

Carleton University, Faculty of Graduate Studies, Faculty of Engineering and Design, School of Architecture, Ottawa, ON K1S 5B6, Canada. Offers design studies (M Arch). *Degree requirements:* For master's, thesis. *Entrance requirements:* For master's, honors degree. Additional exam requirements/recommendations for international students: Required—TOEFL. *Faculty research:* Theoretical issues in architecture and culture, cultural diversity, architecture and technoscientific culture.

Carnegie Mellon University, College of Fine Arts, School of Architecture, Pittsburgh, PA 15213-3891. Offers architectural engineering construction management (M Sc); architecture (MSA); architecture, engineering, and construction management (PhD); building performance and diagnostics (M Sc, PhD); computational design (M Sc, PhD); sustainable design (M Sc); urban design (M Sc). Terminal master's awarded for partial completion of doctoral program. *Degree requirements:* For doctorate, thesis/dissertation. *Entrance requirements:* For master's and doctorate, GRE General Test. Additional exam requirements/recommendations for international students: Required—TOEFL.

The Catholic University of America, School of Architecture and Planning, Washington, DC 20064. Offers architecture studies (MS Arch St); sustainable design (MSSD). Part-time programs available. *Faculty:* 25 full-time (6 women), 38 part-time/adjunct (9 women). *Students:* 116 full-time (55 women), 31 part-time (13 women); includes 11 Black or African American, non-Hispanic/Latino; 6 Asian, non-Hispanic/Latino; 11 Hispanic/Latino, 11 international. Average age 27. 167 applicants, 70% accepted, 56 enrolled. In 2010, 55 master's awarded. *Degree requirements:* For master's, thesis. *Entrance requirements:* For master's, GRE (minimum score: 1000), minimum GPA of 2.8, portfolio, statement of purpose, official copies of academic transcripts, three letters of recommendation. Additional exam requirements/recommendations for international students: Required—TOEFL (minimum score 580 paper-based; 237 computer-based). *Application deadline:* For fall admission, 1/15 priority date for domestic students, 1/15 for international students; for spring admission, 10/15 priority date for domestic students, 10/15 for international students. Applications are processed on a rolling basis. Application fee: $55. Electronic applications accepted. *Expenses:* Contact institution. *Financial support:* Fellowships, research assistantships, teaching assistantships, Federal Work-Study, scholarships/grants, tuition waivers (full and partial), and unspecified assistantships available. Financial award application deadline: 2/1; financial award applicants required to submit FAFSA. *Faculty research:* Architectural history, cultural studies/sacred space, design technologies, digital media, real estate development, urban design. *Unit head:* Randall Ott, Dean, 202-319-5784, Fax: 202-319-2023, E-mail: ott@cua.edu. *Application contact:* Andrew Woodall, Director of Graduate Admissions, 202-319-5057, Fax: 202-319-6533, E-mail: cua-admissions@cua.edu.

City College of the City University of New York, Graduate School, School of Architecture and Environmental Studies, Program in Architecture, New York, NY 10031-9198. Offers M Arch. *Entrance requirements:* For master's, GRE. Additional exam requirements/recommendations for international students: Required—TOEFL (minimum score 550 paper-based; 213 computer-based).

Clemson University, Graduate School, College of Architecture, Arts, and Humanities, Department of Architecture, Clemson, SC 29634. Offers architecture (M Arch, MS). *Faculty:* 21 full-time (4 women), 8 part-time/adjunct (2 women). *Students:* 108 full-time (48 women), 1 (woman) part-time; includes 4 Black or African American, non-Hispanic/Latino; 2 American Indian or Alaska Native, non-Hispanic/Latino; 4 Asian, non-Hispanic/Latino; 4 Hispanic/Latino; 2 Two or more races, non-Hispanic/Latino, 8 international. Average age 27. 272 applicants, 45% accepted, 47 enrolled. In 2010, 21 master's awarded. Terminal master's awarded for partial completion of doctoral program. *Degree requirements:* For master's, thesis. *Entrance requirements:* For master's, GRE General Test (including Analytical Writing), design portfolio. Additional exam requirements/recommendations for international students: Required—TOEFL. *Application deadline:* 1/15 for domestic and international students. Applications are processed on a rolling basis. Application fee: $70 ($80 for international students). Electronic applications accepted. *Expenses:* Tuition, state resident: full-time $6492; part-time $400 per credit hour. Tuition, nonresident: full-time $13,634; part-time $800 per credit hour. Required fees: $262 per semester. Part-time tuition and fees vary according to course load and program. *Financial support:* In 2010–11, 53 students received support, including 27 fellowships with partial tuition reimbursements available (averaging $2,521 per year), 6 research assistantships with partial tuition reimbursements available (averaging $4,222 per year), 20 teaching assistantships with partial tuition reimbursements available (averaging $3,924 per year); career-related internships or fieldwork, institutionally sponsored loans, scholarships/grants, health care benefits,

Architecture

Clemson University (continued)
and unspecified assistantships also available. Financial award application deadline: 1/15. *Faculty research:* Architecture and health, sustainable design, community design-build, architectural robotics, architectural and urban history and theory, digital fabrication. Total annual research expenditures: $402,234. *Unit head:* Dr. Kate Schwennsen, Chair, 864-656-3898, Fax: 864-656-0204, E-mail: kschwen@clemson.edu. *Application contact:* Michelle McLane, Student Services Coordinator, 864-656-3938, Fax: 864-656-1810, E-mail: wking@clemson.edu.

Columbia University, Graduate School of Architecture, Planning, and Preservation, Program in Advanced Architectural Design, New York, NY 10027. Offers MS. *Entrance requirements:* For master's, GRE General Test.

Columbia University, Graduate School of Architecture, Planning, and Preservation, Program in Architecture, New York, NY 10027. Offers M Arch, PhD, M Arch/MS. PhD offered through the Graduate School of Arts and Science. *Degree requirements:* For master's, thesis optional. *Entrance requirements:* For master's, GRE General Test.

Cooper Union for the Advancement of Science and Art, Irwin S. Chanin School of Architecture, New York, NY 10003-7120. Offers M Arch II. *Faculty:* 14 full-time (3 women), 19 part-time/adjunct (6 women). *Students:* 8 full-time (3 women), 4 international. Average age 25. 122 applicants, 10% accepted, 8 enrolled. In 2010, 7 master's awarded. *Degree requirements:* For master's, thesis. *Entrance requirements:* For master's, GRE, 1 year of work experience, 3 letters of recommendation, resume or curriculum vitae, essay, portfolio, interview. Additional exam requirements/recommendations for international students: Required—TOEFL. *Application deadline:* For fall admission, 2/1 for domestic students. Application fee: $65. *Expenses:* Tuition: Full-time $35,000; part-time $1100 per credit. Required fees: $825 per semester. *Financial support:* In 2010–11, 7 students received support. Tuition waivers and all admitted students receive a full-tuition scholarship for the length of their study available. Financial award application deadline: 5/1; financial award applicants required to submit CSS PROFILE or FAFSA. *Unit head:* Dr. Anthony Vidler, Dean. *Application contact:* Susan Cohen, Student Contact, 212-353-4120, E-mail: admissions@cooper.edu.

Cornell University, Graduate School, Graduate Fields of Architecture, Art and Planning, Field of Architecture, Ithaca, NY 14853-0001. Offers architectural design (M Arch); architectural science (MS); building technology and environmental science (MS); computer graphics (MS); history of architecture (MA, PhD); history of urban development (MA, PhD); theory and criticism of architecture (M Arch); urban design (M Arch). *Faculty:* 26 full-time (8 women). *Students:* 113 full-time (55 women); includes 2 Black or African American, non-Hispanic/Latino; 15 Asian, non-Hispanic/Latino; 8 Hispanic/Latino, 47 international. Average age 26. 545 applicants, 26% accepted, 65 enrolled. In 2010, 26 master's, 1 doctorate awarded. *Degree requirements:* For master's, one foreign language, thesis (MA, MS); for doctorate, 2 foreign languages, comprehensive exam, thesis/dissertation. *Entrance requirements:* For master's, GRE General Test, 5 year bachelor's degree in architecture, portfolio (M Arch), 3 letters of recommendation; for doctorate, GRE General Test, 3 letters of recommendation. Additional exam requirements/recommendations for international students: Required—TOEFL (minimum score 600 paper-based; 250 computer-based; 77 iBT). *Application deadline:* For fall admission, 1/15 priority date for domestic students. Application fee: $70. Electronic applications accepted. *Expenses:* Tuition: Full-time $29,500. Required fees: $76. Tuition and fees vary according to degree level and program. *Financial support:* In 2010–11, 11 fellowships with full tuition reimbursements, 19 teaching assistantships with full tuition reimbursements were awarded; research assistantships with full tuition reimbursements, institutionally sponsored loans, scholarships/grants, health care benefits, tuition waivers (full and partial), and unspecified assistantships also available. Financial award applicants required to submit FAFSA. *Faculty research:* Architectural design and urban design, theory and criticism of architecture, computer graphics, building technology and environmental science, history of architecture and history of urban-development. *Unit head:* Director of Graduate Studies, 607-255-6701, Fax: 607-255-0291. *Application contact:* Graduate Field Assistant, 607-255-6701, Fax: 607-255-0291, E-mail: cuarch@cornell.edu.

Cranbrook Academy of Art, Graduate School, Program in Architecture, Bloomfield Hills, MI 48303-0801. Offers M Arch. *Degree requirements:* For master's, thesis, exhibit. *Entrance requirements:* Additional exam requirements/recommendations for international students: Required—TOEFL (minimum score 550 paper-based; 213 computer-based).

Dalhousie University, Faculty of Architecture and Planning, Halifax, NS B3J 2X4, Canada. Offers M Arch, M Eng, M Plan, MEDS, MPS. *Degree requirements:* For master's, thesis. *Entrance requirements:* Additional exam requirements/recommendations for international students: Required—TOEFL, IELTS, 1 of 5 approved tests: TOEFL, IELTS, CANTEST, CAEL, Michigan English Language Assessment Battery. Electronic applications accepted.

Drury University, Hammons School of Architecture, Springfield, MO 65802. Offers M Arch. *Degree requirements:* For master's, thesis project.

Florida Agricultural and Mechanical University, Division of Graduate Studies, Research, and Continuing Education, School of Architecture, Tallahassee, FL 32307-3200. Offers architectural studies (MS Arch); architecture (professional) (M Arch); landscape architecture (MLA). Part-time programs available. *Degree requirements:* For master's, thesis. *Entrance requirements:* For master's, GRE General Test, minimum GPA of 3.0, portfolio. Additional exam requirements/recommendations for international students: Required—TOEFL (minimum score 550 paper-based). *Faculty research:* Environmental technology, post-occupancy evaluation, building economics, design methods, computer-aided design.

Florida International University, College of Architecture and the Arts, Miami, FL 33199. Offers M Arch, MA, MFA, MID, MLA, MM, MS. *Accreditation:* ASLA. Part-time and evening/weekend programs available. *Faculty:* 64 full-time (21 women), 80 part-time/adjunct (38 women). *Students:* 404 full-time (227 women), 61 part-time (35 women); includes 23 Black or African American, non-Hispanic/Latino; 2 American Indian or Alaska Native, non-Hispanic/Latino; 11 Asian, non-Hispanic/Latino; 292 Hispanic/Latino, 21 international. Average age 26. 315 applicants, 29% accepted, 81 enrolled. In 2010, 70 master's awarded. *Degree requirements:* For master's, thesis (for some programs). *Entrance requirements:* For master's, GRE (depending on program), minimum GPA of 3.0 (upper-level coursework). Additional exam requirements/recommendations for international students: Required—TOEFL (minimum score 550 paper-based; 80 iBT). *Application deadline:* For fall admission, 6/1 for domestic students, 4/1 for international students; for spring admission, 10/1 for domestic students, 9/1 for international students. Applications are processed on a rolling basis. Application fee: $30. Electronic applications accepted. *Financial support:* Institutionally sponsored loans and scholarships/grants available. Financial award application deadline: 3/1; financial award applicants required to submit FAFSA. *Unit head:* Dr. Brian Schriner, Dean, 305-348-3181, Fax: 305-348-6716, E-mail: brian.schriner@fiu.edu. *Application contact:* Nanett Rojas, Assistant Director of Graduate Admissions, 305-348-7442, Fax: 305-348-7441, E-mail: gradadm@fiu.edu.

Florida International University, College of Architecture and the Arts, School of Architecture, Architecture Program, Miami, FL 33199. Offers M Arch, MA. Part-time and evening/weekend programs available. *Faculty:* 12 full-time (3 women). *Students:* 257 full-time (136 women), 23 part-time (8 women); includes 12 Black or African American, non-Hispanic/Latino; 1 American Indian or Alaska Native, non-Hispanic/Latino; 7 Asian, non-Hispanic/Latino; 195 Hispanic/Latino, 10 international. Average age 25. 141 applicants, 36% accepted, 48 enrolled. In 2010, 30 master's awarded. *Entrance requirements:* For master's, GRE or minimum GPA of 3.0 in upper-level undergraduate work, portfolio. Additional exam requirements/recommendations for international students: Required—TOEFL (minimum score 550 paper-based; 80 iBT). *Application deadline:* For fall admission, 2/1 for domestic and international students. Application fee: $30. Electronic applications accepted. *Financial support:* Institutionally sponsored loans and scholarships/grants available. Financial award application deadline: 3/1; financial award applicants required to submit FAFSA. *Unit head:* Prof. Brian Schriner, Interim Dean, 305-348-6442, Fax: 305-348-2650, E-mail: schriner@fiu.edu. *Application contact:* Prof. Adam Drisin, Graduate Program Director, 305-348-7077, Fax: 305-348-2650, E-mail: drisina@fiu.edu.

Frank Lloyd Wright School of Architecture, Graduate Program, Scottsdale, AZ 85261-4430. Offers M Arch. Summer session held in Spring Green, WI. *Degree requirements:* For master's, thesis or alternative. *Entrance requirements:* For master's, interviews, portfolio. Additional exam requirements/recommendations for international students: Required—TOEFL.

Georgia Institute of Technology, Graduate Studies and Research, College of Architecture, City and Regional Planning Program, Atlanta, GA 30332-0001. Offers city and regional planning (PhD); economic development (MCRP); environmental planning and management (MCRP); geographic information systems (MCRP); land and community development (MCRP); land use planning (MCRP); transportation (MCRP); urban design (MCRP); MCP/MSCE. *Accreditation:* ACSP. *Degree requirements:* For master's, thesis, internship. *Entrance requirements:* For master's, GRE General Test, minimum GPA of 2.7. Additional exam requirements/recommendations for international students: Required—TOEFL. Electronic applications accepted.

Georgia Institute of Technology, Graduate Studies and Research, College of Architecture, Doctoral Program in Architecture, Atlanta, GA 30332-0001. Offers PhD. Part-time programs available. Postbaccalaureate distance learning degree programs offered. *Degree requirements:* For doctorate, comprehensive exam, thesis/dissertation. *Entrance requirements:* For doctorate, GRE General Test. Additional exam requirements/recommendations for international students: Required—TOEFL (minimum score 600 paper-based; 250 computer-based). Electronic applications accepted.

Georgia Institute of Technology, Graduate Studies and Research, College of Architecture, Master's Program in Architecture, Atlanta, GA 30332-0001. Offers M Arch, MS, M Arch/MCRP. Part-time programs available. *Degree requirements:* For master's, thesis or alternative. *Entrance requirements:* For master's, GRE General Test. Additional exam requirements/recommendations for international students: Required—TOEFL (minimum score 600 paper-based; 250 computer-based). Electronic applications accepted.

Georgia Institute of Technology, Graduate Studies and Research, College of Architecture, Program in Building Construction, Atlanta, GA 30332-0001. Offers building construction (PhD); integrated facility management (MS); integrated project delivery systems (MS); residential construction development (MS). Part-time and evening/weekend programs available. *Entrance requirements:* For master's and doctorate, GRE or GMAT. Additional exam requirements/recommendations for international students: Required—TOEFL (minimum score 550 paper-based; 213 computer-based). Electronic applications accepted. *Faculty research:* Design-build, mold, indoor air quality, real estate.

Hampton University, School of Engineering and Technology, Hampton, VA 23668. Offers architecture (M Arch).

Harvard University, Graduate School of Arts and Sciences, Committee on Architecture, Landscape Architecture, and Urban Planning, Cambridge, MA 02138. Offers architecture (PhD); landscape architecture (PhD); urban planning (PhD). *Degree requirements:* For doctorate, one foreign language, thesis/dissertation, oral exam. *Entrance requirements:* For doctorate, GRE General Test. Additional exam requirements/recommendations for international students: Required—TOEFL. *Expenses:* Tuition: Full-time $34,976. Required fees: $1166. Full-time tuition and fees vary according to program.

Harvard University, Graduate School of Design, Department of Architecture, Cambridge, MA 02138. Offers M Arch. *Degree requirements:* For master's, thesis (for some programs). *Entrance requirements:* For master's, GRE General Test. Additional exam requirements/recommendations for international students: Required—TOEFL (minimum score 600 paper-based; 250 computer-based; 104 iBT). Electronic applications accepted. *Expenses:* Tuition: Full-time $34,976. Required fees: $1166. Full-time tuition and fees vary according to program.

Harvard University, Graduate School of Design, Program in Design, Cambridge, MA 02138. Offers Dr DES. *Entrance requirements:* For doctorate, GRE General Test. Additional exam requirements/recommendations for international students: Required—TOEFL (minimum score 600 paper-based; 250 computer-based; 104 iBT). Electronic applications accepted. *Expenses:* Tuition: Full-time $34,976. Required fees: $1166. Full-time tuition and fees vary according to program.

Harvard University, Graduate School of Design, Program in Design Studies, Cambridge, MA 02138. Offers M Des S. *Entrance requirements:* For master's, GRE General Test. Additional exam requirements/recommendations for international students: Required—TOEFL (minimum score 600 paper-based; 250 computer-based; 104 iBT). Electronic applications accepted. *Expenses:* Tuition: Full-time $34,976. Required fees: $1166. Full-time tuition and fees vary according to program.

Illinois Institute of Technology, Graduate College, College of Architecture, Chicago, IL 60616-3793. Offers M Arch, M IBD, MLA, MS Arch, PhD. *Accreditation:* ASLA. Part-time programs available. *Faculty:* 39 full-time (5 women), 54 part-time/adjunct (15 women). *Students:* 234 full-time (103 women), 14 part-time (7 women); includes 20 minority (3 Black or African American, non-Hispanic/Latino; 7 Asian, non-Hispanic/Latino; 9 Hispanic/Latino; 1 Two or more races, non-Hispanic/Latino), 97 international. Average age 28. 500 applicants, 65% accepted, 114 enrolled. In 2010, 84 master's, 1 doctorate awarded. Terminal master's awarded for partial completion of doctoral program. *Degree requirements:* For master's, comprehensive exam (for some programs), thesis (for some programs); for doctorate, comprehensive exam, thesis/dissertation. *Entrance requirements:* For master's, GRE General Test (minimum score 900 Quantitative and Verbal, 2.5 Analytical Writing), minimum college GPA of 3.0, official transcripts, portfolio, 3 letters of recommendation, professional statement; personal interview (recommended); for doctorate, GRE General Test (minimum score 900 Quantitative and Verbal, 2.5 Analytical Writing), minimum GPA of 3.5, official transcripts, portfolio, 3 letters of recommendation, professional statement. Additional exam requirements/recommendations for international students: Required—TOEFL (minimum score 550 paper-based; 80 iBT); Recommended—IELTS (minimum score 5.5). *Application deadline:* For fall admission, 4/15 for domestic and international students; for spring admission, 11/15 for domestic and international students. Applications are processed on a rolling basis. Application fee: $50. Electronic applications accepted. *Expenses:* Tuition: Full-time $18,576; part-time $1032 per credit hour. Required fees: $583 per semester. One-time fee: $150. Tuition and fees vary according to program and student level. *Financial support:* In 2010–11, 1 research assistantship (averaging $5,000 per year), 39 teaching assistantships with full and partial tuition reimbursements (averaging $1,566 per year) were awarded; fellowships with full and partial tuition reimbursements, career-related internships or fieldwork, Federal Work-Study, institutionally sponsored loans, scholarships/grants, health care benefits, tuition waivers (partial), and unspecified assistantships also available. Support available to part-time students. Financial award applicants required to submit FAFSA. *Faculty research:* Sustainable design and efficiency; the influence of climate and environment on building form; emerging ubanisms; computer applications (such as 3-D modeling); the design, planning and structure of high-rise buildings. Total annual research expenditures: $49,595. *Unit head:* Donna V. Robertson, Dean, 312-567-3230, Fax: 312-567-5820, E-mail: robertson@iit.edu. *Application contact:* Katherine Fitzgibbon, Director, Graduate Academic Affairs, 312-567-5858, Fax: 312-567-5820, E-mail: kfitzgib@iit.edu.

Instituto Tecnológico y de Estudios Superiores de Monterrey, Campus Estado de México, Professional and Graduate Division, Estado de Mexico, Mexico. Offers administration of information technologies (MITA); architecture (M Arch); business administration (GMBA, MBA); computer sciences (MCS, PhD); education (M Ed); educational institution administration (MAD); educational technology and innovation (PhD); electronic commerce (MEC); environmental systems (MS); finance (MAF); humanistic studies (MHS); information sciences and knowledge management (MISKM); information systems (MS); manufacturing systems (MS); marketing (MEM); quality systems and productivity (MS); science and materials engineering (PhD);

telecommunications management (MTM). Part-time programs available. Postbaccalaureate distance learning degree programs offered (minimal on-campus study). *Degree requirements:* For master's, one foreign language, thesis (for some programs); for doctorate, one foreign language, thesis/dissertation. *Entrance requirements:* For master's, E-PAEP 500, interview; for doctorate, E-PAEP 500, research proposal. Additional exam requirements/recommendations for international students: Required—TOEFL (minimum score 550 paper-based). *Faculty research:* Surface treatments by plasmas, mechanical properties, robotics, graphical computing, mechatronics security protocols.

Instituto Tecnológico y de Estudios Superiores de Monterrey, Campus Irapuato, Graduate Programs, Irapuato, Mexico. Offers administration (MBA); administration of information technology (MAIT); administration of telecommunications (MAT); architecture (M Arch); computer science (MCS); education (M Ed); educational administration (MEA); educational innovation and technology (DEIT); educational technology (MET); electronic commerce (MBA); environmental administration and planning (MEAP); environmental systems (MES); finances (MBA); humanistic studies (MHS); international management for Latin American executives (MIMLAE); library and information science (MLIS); manufacturing quality management (MMQM); marketing research (MBA).

Iowa State University of Science and Technology, Graduate College, College of Design, Department of Architecture, Ames, IA 50011. Offers architectural studies (MSAS); architecture (M Arch); M Arch/MBA; M Arch/MCRP; M Arch/MS. *Faculty:* 26 full-time (8 women). *Students:* 66 full-time (27 women), 6 part-time (4 women); includes 1 Black or African American, non-Hispanic/Latino; 6 Hispanic/Latino, 19 international. 79 applicants, 65% accepted, 29 enrolled. In 2010, 15 master's awarded. *Degree requirements:* For master's, thesis (for some programs). *Entrance requirements:* For master's, GRE General Test, portfolio, letters of reference. Additional exam requirements/recommendations for international students: Required—TOEFL (minimum score 600 paper-based; 79 iBT), IELTS (minimum score 7). *Application deadline:* For fall admission, 1/4 priority date for domestic and international students. Applications are processed on a rolling basis. Application fee: $40 ($90 for international students). Electronic applications accepted. *Financial support:* In 2010–11, 30 students received support, including 1 research assistantship with partial tuition reimbursement available (averaging $3,262 per year), 27 teaching assistantships with partial tuition reimbursements available (averaging $3,049 per year); career-related internships or fieldwork, Federal Work-Study, institutionally sponsored loans, tuition waivers (partial), and unspecified assistantships also available. Support available to part-time students. Financial award application deadline: 2/1; financial award applicants required to submit FAFSA. *Faculty research:* Computer-aided architectural design, social dimensions of urban architecture, designing for the elderly, energy utilization in buildings, architectural theory. *Unit head:* Dr. Calvin F. Lewis, Chair, 515-294-2665, Fax: 515-294-1440, E-mail: calewis@iastate.edu. *Application contact:* Dr. Marwan Ghandour, Director of Graduate Education, 515-294-3543, E-mail: jejonas@iastate.edu.

Judson University, Graduate Programs, Elgin, IL 60123-1498. Offers architecture (M Arch); literacy (M Ed); organizational leadership (MA); teaching (M Ed). Part-time and evening/weekend programs available. Postbaccalaureate distance learning degree programs offered (no on-campus study). *Faculty:* 18 full-time (7 women), 27 part-time/adjunct (9 women). *Students:* 59 full-time (38 women), 46 part-time (23 women); includes 16 minority (8 Black or African American, non-Hispanic/Latino; 1 Asian, non-Hispanic/Latino; 7 Hispanic/Latino), 2 international. Average age 32. In 2010, 76 master's awarded. *Degree requirements:* For master's, comprehensive exam (for some programs), thesis. *Entrance requirements:* For master's, interviews, written essays, portfolios (depending on program of study). Additional exam requirements/recommendations for international students: Required—TOEFL (minimum score 550 paper-based; 213 computer-based). *Application deadline:* Applications are processed on a rolling basis. Application fee: $40. Electronic applications accepted. *Expenses:* Tuition: Full-time $18,000; part-time $1000 per credit hour. Required fees: $200 per term. Tuition and fees vary according to course load, program and student level. *Financial support:* Applicants required to submit FAFSA. *Faculty research:* Leadership, sustainable design, sustainability management, bilingual education, literacy. *Unit head:* Dr. Dale H. Simmons, Provost and Vice-President for Academic Affairs, 847-628-1000, E-mail: dsimmons@judsonu.edu. *Application contact:* Maria Aguirre, Assistant to the Registrar for Graduate Programs, 847-628-1160, E-mail: maguirre@judsonu.edu.

Kansas State University, Graduate School, College of Architecture, Planning and Design, Department of Architecture, Manhattan, KS 66506. Offers M Arch. Part-time programs available. *Degree requirements:* For master's, thesis optional, residency. *Entrance requirements:* For master's, portfolio, minimum GPA of 3.0. Additional exam requirements/recommendations for international students: Required—TOEFL (minimum score 600 paper-based). Electronic applications accepted. *Faculty research:* Design theory, environment behavior and place studies, ecological and sustainable design.

Kent State University, College of Architecture and Environmental Design, Kent, OH 44242-0001. Offers architecture (M Arch); preservation architecture (Certificate); urban design (M Arch, MUD, Certificate). Part-time programs available. *Degree requirements:* For master's, thesis optional. *Entrance requirements:* For master's, GRE, portfolio, minimum GPA of 2.75, 3 letters of reference, resume, undergraduate architecture degree. Additional exam requirements/recommendations for international students: Required—TOEFL (minimum score 550 paper-based). Electronic applications accepted. *Expenses:* Tuition, state resident: full-time $7866; part-time $437 per credit hour. Tuition, nonresident: full-time $14,022; part-time $779 per credit hour. *Faculty research:* History and theory, building technology, landscape architecture and urbanism, urbanism, sustainable development.

Lawrence Technological University, College of Architecture and Design, Southfield, MI 48075-1058. Offers architecture (M Arch); architecture 3+ (M Arch); interior design (MID); interior design 3+ (MID); urban design (MUD). *Accreditation:* NASAD. Part-time and evening/weekend programs available. *Faculty:* 9 full-time (2 women), 12 part-time/adjunct (3 women). *Students:* 11 full-time (5 women), 225 part-time (89 women); includes 13 Black or African American, non-Hispanic/Latino; 11 Asian, non-Hispanic/Latino; 7 Hispanic/Latino; 1 Native Hawaiian or other Pacific Islander, non-Hispanic/Latino; 2 Two or more races, non-Hispanic/Latino, 23 international. Average age 31. 174 applicants, 55% accepted, 68 enrolled. In 2010, 47 master's awarded. *Degree requirements:* For master's, thesis. *Entrance requirements:* For master's, portfolio. Additional exam requirements/recommendations for international students: Required—TOEFL (minimum score 550 paper-based; 213 computer-based; 79 iBT). *Application deadline:* For fall admission, 6/30 priority date for domestic students, 6/30 for international students; for spring admission, 1/15 priority date for domestic students, 1/15 for international students. Applications are processed on a rolling basis. Application fee: $50. Electronic applications accepted. *Financial support:* In 2010–11, 83 students received support. Federal Work-Study available. Financial award application deadline: 4/1; financial award applicants required to submit FAFSA. *Unit head:* Glen LeRoy, Dean, 248-204-2800, Fax: 248-204-2900, E-mail: archdean@ltu.edu. *Application contact:* Jane Rohrback, Director of Admissions, 248-204-3160, Fax: 248-204-2228, E-mail: admissions@ltu.edu.

Louisiana State University and Agricultural and Mechanical College, Graduate School, College of Art and Design, School of Architecture, Baton Rouge, LA 70803. Offers M Arch. Part-time programs available. *Faculty:* 12 full-time (3 women). *Students:* 34 full-time (15 women), 2 part-time (1 woman); includes 1 Black or African American, non-Hispanic/Latino; 2 Hispanic/Latino; 1 Native Hawaiian or other Pacific Islander, non-Hispanic/Latino, 1 international. Average age 27. 55 applicants, 42% accepted, 12 enrolled. In 2010, 8 master's awarded. *Degree requirements:* For master's, thesis. *Entrance requirements:* For master's, GRE General Test, minimum GPA of 3.0. Additional exam requirements/recommendations for international students: Required—TOEFL (minimum score 550 paper-based; 213 computer-based; 79 iBT) or IELTS (minimum score 6.5). *Application deadline:* For fall admission, 1/25 priority date for domestic students, 5/15 for international students; for spring admission, 10/15 for international students. Applications are processed on a rolling basis. Application fee: $50 ($70 for inter-

national students). Electronic applications accepted. *Financial support:* In 2010–11, 27 students received support, including 6 research assistantships with full and partial tuition reimbursements available (averaging $6,930 per year), 2 teaching assistantships with full and partial tuition reimbursements available (averaging $9,300 per year); fellowships, career-related internships or fieldwork, Federal Work-Study, institutionally sponsored loans, scholarships/grants, health care benefits, tuition waivers (full and partial), and unspecified assistantships also available. Support available to part-time students. Financial award application deadline: 3/1; financial award applicants required to submit FAFSA. *Faculty research:* Architectural design, history of architecture, sustainable design, digital fabrication, community design. Total annual research expenditures: $33,449. *Unit head:* Jori Erdman, Director, 225-578-6885, Fax: 225-578-2168, E-mail: jerdman@lsu.edu. *Application contact:* David Bertolini, Graduate Coordinator, 225-578-6885, Fax: 225-578-2168, E-mail: dbertoli@lsu.edu.

Marywood University, Academic Affairs, School of Architecture, Scranton, PA 18509-1598. Offers architecture (M Arch); studio art (MA), including interior design. *Entrance requirements:* Additional exam requirements/recommendations for international students: Required—TOEFL (minimum score 550 paper-based; 213 computer-based; 79 iBT). *Expenses:* Tuition: Part-time $735 per credit. Required fees: $470 per semester. Tuition and fees vary according to degree level and campus/location.

Massachusetts College of Art and Design, Graduate Programs, Program in Architecture, Boston, MA 02115-5882. Offers M Arch. Part-time programs available. *Faculty:* 4 full-time (2 women), 13 part-time/adjunct (4 women). *Students:* 31 full-time (15 women); includes 5 minority (1 Black or African American, non-Hispanic/Latino; 1 Hispanic/Latino; 3 Two or more races, non-Hispanic/Latino), 4 international. 35 applicants, 71% accepted, 9 enrolled. *Degree requirements:* For master's, thesis. *Entrance requirements:* For master's, portfolio, resume, college transcripts, statement of purpose, letters of reference, interview. Additional exam requirements/recommendations for international students: Required—TOEFL (minimum score 563 paper-based; 223 computer-based; 85 iBT); Recommended—IELTS (minimum score 6.5). *Application deadline:* For fall admission, 1/15 for domestic and international students. Application fee: $85. Electronic applications accepted. *Expenses:* Contact institution. *Financial support:* In 2010–11, 16 research assistantships (averaging $2,000 per year), 5 teaching assistantships (averaging $2,000 per year) were awarded. Financial award application deadline: 3/1; financial award applicants required to submit FAFSA. *Unit head:* George Creamer, Dean of Graduate Programs, 617-879-7163, Fax: 617-879-7171, E-mail: creamer@massart.edu. *Application contact:* George Creamer, Dean of Graduate Programs, 617-879-7163, Fax: 617-879-7171, E-mail: creamer@massart.edu.

Massachusetts Institute of Technology, School of Architecture and Planning, Department of Architecture, Cambridge, MA 02139. Offers architecture (M Arch, PhD), including building technology (PhD), design and computation (PhD), history and theory of architecture (PhD), history and theory of art (PhD); architecture studies (SM Arch S); building technology (SMBT); visual studies (SM Vis S). *Faculty:* 30 full-time (7 women). *Students:* 241 full-time (111 women), 1 (woman) part-time; includes 54 minority (6 Black or African American, non-Hispanic/Latino; 2 American Indian or Alaska Native, non-Hispanic/Latino; 31 Asian, non-Hispanic/Latino; 10 Hispanic/Latino; 5 Two or more races, non-Hispanic/Latino), 84 international. Average age 28. 1,166 applicants, 13% accepted, 94 enrolled. In 2010, 63 master's, 6 doctorates awarded. *Degree requirements:* For master's, thesis; for doctorate, comprehensive exam, thesis/dissertation. *Entrance requirements:* For master's, GRE General Test (for some programs), portfolio (for some programs); for doctorate, GRE General Test (for some programs). Additional exam requirements/recommendations for international students: Required—TOEFL (minimum score 650 paper-based; 280 computer-based; 114 iBT), IELTS (minimum score 7). *Application deadline:* For fall admission, 12/15 for domestic and international students. Application fee: $75. Electronic applications accepted. *Expenses:* Tuition: Full-time $38,940; part-time $605 per unit. Required fees: $272. *Financial support:* In 2010–11, 195 students received support, including 155 fellowships with tuition reimbursements available (averaging $18,267 per year), 32 research assistantships with tuition reimbursements available (averaging $24,642 per year), 25 teaching assistantships with tuition reimbursements available (averaging $29,366 per year); career-related internships or fieldwork, Federal Work-Study, institutionally sponsored loans, scholarships/grants, health care benefits, and unspecified assistantships also available. *Faculty research:* Architecture and urbanism; building technology and sustainability; computation and design; history, theory, and criticism; contemporary visual art practice; digital fabrication. Total annual research expenditures: $2.4 million. *Unit head:* Prof. Nader Tehrani, Department Head, 617-253-7791, E-mail: arch@mit.edu. *Application contact:* Admissions Coordinator, 617-715-4490, Fax: 617-253-8993, E-mail: arch@mit.edu.

McGill University, Faculty of Graduate and Postdoctoral Studies, Faculty of Engineering, School of Architecture, Montréal, QC H3A 2T5, Canada. Offers affordable homes (M Arch II, Diploma); architectural history and theory (M Arch II); architecture (PhD); domestic environment (M Arch II); domestic environments (Diploma); minimum cost housing in developing countries (M Arch II, Diploma); professional architecture (M Arch I).

Miami University, Graduate School, School of Fine Arts, Department of Architecture, Oxford, OH 45056. Offers M Arch. *Students:* 35 full-time (12 women), 1 (woman) part-time; includes 3 minority (1 Black or African American, non-Hispanic/Latino; 1 Hispanic/Latino; 1 Native Hawaiian or other Pacific Islander, non-Hispanic/Latino), 5 international. Average age 26. In 2010, 8 master's awarded. *Entrance requirements:* For master's, portfolio, minimum undergraduate GPA of 3.0 during previous 2 years or overall. Additional exam requirements/recommendations for international students: Required—TOEFL. Application fee: $50. *Expenses:* Tuition, state resident: full-time $11,616; part-time $484 per credit hour. Tuition, nonresident: full-time $25,656; part-time $1069 per credit hour. Required fees: $528. *Financial support:* Fellowships with full tuition reimbursements, research assistantships, teaching assistantships, Federal Work-Study, health care benefits, tuition waivers (full), and unspecified assistantships available. Financial award application deadline: 3/1. *Unit head:* Dr. John Weigand, Chair, 513-529-4903. *Application contact:* Craig Hinrichs, Associate Professor/Director of Graduate Studies, 513-529-7210, E-mail: arcid@muohio.edu.

Mississippi State University, College of Architecture, Art and Design, Mississippi State, MS 39762. Offers MS. *Faculty:* 18 full-time (6 women). *Students:* 4 full-time (all women), 1 (woman) part-time; includes 2 minority (both Black or African American, non-Hispanic/Latino), 1 international. Average age 30. 8 applicants, 25% accepted, 2 enrolled. In 2010, 2 master's awarded. *Degree requirements:* For master's, comprehensive exam, thesis, final written and oral exam. *Entrance requirements:* For master's, GRE General Test, essay stating intent and aspirations for study, portfolio, minimum GPA of 3.0. Additional exam requirements/recommendations for international students: Required—TOEFL (minimum score 600 paper-based; 250 computer-based; 100 iBT); Recommended—IELTS (minimum score 7.5). *Application deadline:* For fall admission, 7/1 for domestic students, 5/1 for international students; for spring admission, 11/1 for domestic students, 9/1 for international students. Applications are processed on a rolling basis. Application fee: $40. Electronic applications accepted. *Expenses:* Tuition, state resident: full-time $2730.50; part-time $304 per credit hour. Tuition, nonresident: full-time $6901; part-time $767 per credit hour. *Financial support:* Career-related internships or fieldwork, Federal Work-Study, institutionally sponsored loans, and unspecified assistantships available. Financial award application deadline: 4/1; financial award applicants required to submit FAFSA. *Faculty research:* Digital art in architecture, process change and management, multi-media databases, 3-D modeling and animation, virtual archaeology. *Unit head:* Jim West, Dean/Professor, 662-325-2202, Fax: 662-325-8872, E-mail: jwest@caad.msstate.edu. *Application contact:* Dr. David C. Lewis, Associate Dean and Graduate Coordinator, 662-325-2202, Fax: 662-325-8872, E-mail: dlewis@caad.msstate.edu.

Montana State University, College of Graduate Studies, College of Arts and Architecture, School of Architecture, Bozeman, MT 59717. Offers M Arch. Part-time programs available. *Faculty:* 19 full-time (4 women), 4 part-time/adjunct (2 women). *Students:* 59 full-time (21 women), 15 part-time (5 women); includes 5 minority (1 American Indian or Alaska Native,

Architecture

Montana State University (continued)
non-Hispanic/Latino; 2 Hispanic/Latino; 1 Native Hawaiian or other Pacific Islander, non-Hispanic/Latino; 1 Two or more races, non-Hispanic/Latino), 3 international. Average age 25. 53 applicants, 43% accepted, 16 enrolled. In 2010, 67 master's awarded. *Degree requirements:* For master's, comprehensive exam. *Entrance requirements:* For master's, GRE General Test, minimum cumulative GPA of 3.0, portfolio, 3 letters of recommendation. Additional exam requirements/recommendations for international students: Required—TOEFL (minimum score 550 paper-based; 213 computer-based). *Application deadline:* For fall admission, 7/15 priority date for domestic students, 5/15 priority date for international students; for spring admission, 12/1 priority date for domestic students, 10/1 priority date for international students. Applications are processed on a rolling basis. Application fee: $30. Electronic applications accepted. *Expenses:* Tuition, state resident: full-time $5553.90. Tuition, nonresident: full-time $14,646. Required fees: $1233. *Financial support:* In 2010–11, 48 students received support, including 38 teaching assistantships with partial tuition reimbursements available; Federal Work-Study and scholarships/grants also available. Financial award application deadline: 3/1; financial award applicants required to submit FAFSA. *Faculty research:* Sustainability, architecture as craft, visualization, stewardship, community design, design build. Total annual research expenditures: $117,002. *Unit head:* Steven Juroszek, Interim Director, 406-994-3921, Fax: 406-994-4257, E-mail: stevej@montana.edu. *Application contact:* Dr. Carl A. Fox, Vice Provost for Graduate Education, 406-994-4145, Fax: 406-994-7433, E-mail: gradstudy@montana.edu.

Morgan State University, School of Graduate Studies, Institute of Architecture and Planning, Program in Architecture, Baltimore, MD 21251. Offers M Arch. *Degree requirements:* For master's, thesis. *Entrance requirements:* Additional exam requirements/recommendations for international students: Required—TOEFL (minimum score 550 paper-based; 213 computer-based).

New Jersey Institute of Technology, Office of Graduate Studies, School of Architecture, Program in Architecture, Newark, NJ 07102. Offers M Arch, MS, M Arch/MIP, M Arch/MS. Part-time and evening/weekend programs available. *Students:* 66 full-time (31 women), 9 part-time (4 women); includes 4 Black or African American, non-Hispanic/Latino; 1 American Indian or Alaska Native, non-Hispanic/Latino; 6 Asian, non-Hispanic/Latino; 8 Hispanic/Latino, 14 international. Average age 29. 163 applicants, 40% accepted, 29 enrolled. In 2010, 20 master's awarded. *Degree requirements:* For master's, thesis (for some programs). *Entrance requirements:* For master's, GRE General Test, minimum GPA of 3.0. Additional exam requirements/recommendations for international students: Required—TOEFL (minimum score 550 paper-based; 213 computer-based; 79 iBT). *Application deadline:* For fall admission, 6/5 priority date for domestic students, 4/1 for international students; for spring admission, 11/15 for domestic and international students. Applications are processed on a rolling basis. Application fee: $65. Electronic applications accepted. *Expenses:* Tuition, state resident: full-time $14,724; part-time $818 per credit. Tuition, nonresident: full-time $20,304; part-time $1128 per credit. Required fees: $2272; $209 per credit. $103 per semester. One-time fee: $312 full-time; $212 part-time. *Financial support:* Fellowships with full and partial tuition reimbursements, research assistantships with full and partial tuition reimbursements, teaching assistantships with full and partial tuition reimbursements, career-related internships or fieldwork, Federal Work-Study, institutionally sponsored loans, and unspecified assistantships available. Financial award application deadline: 3/15. *Faculty research:* Management of new technologies, information systems management, operations management systems, marketing management, human resource management. *Unit head:* Dr. Frederick A. Little, Graduate Program Manager, 973-642-7576, E-mail: frederick.a.little@njit.edu. *Application contact:* Kathryn Kelly, Director of Admissions, 973-596-3300, Fax: 973-596-3461, E-mail: admissions@njit.edu.

New Jersey Institute of Technology, Office of Graduate Studies, School of Architecture, Program in Infrastructure Planning, Newark, NJ 07102. Offers MIP. Part-time and evening/weekend programs available. *Students:* 11 full-time (5 women), 1 (woman) part-time; includes 1 Black or African American, non-Hispanic/Latino; 1 Asian, non-Hispanic/Latino; 4 Hispanic/Latino, 4 international. Average age 35. 25 applicants, 48% accepted, 7 enrolled. In 2010, 9 master's awarded. *Degree requirements:* For master's, thesis (for some programs). *Entrance requirements:* For master's, GRE General Test, minimum GPA of 3.0. Additional exam requirements/recommendations for international students: Required—TOEFL (minimum score 550 paper-based; 213 computer-based; 79 iBT). *Application deadline:* For fall admission, 6/5 priority date for domestic students, 4/1 for international students; for spring admission, 11/15 for domestic and international students. Applications are processed on a rolling basis. Application fee: $65. Electronic applications accepted. *Expenses:* Tuition, state resident: full-time $14,724; part-time $818 per credit. Tuition, nonresident: full-time $20,304; part-time $1128 per credit. Required fees: $2272; $209 per credit. $103 per semester. One-time fee: $312 full-time; $212 part-time. *Financial support:* Fellowships with full and partial tuition reimbursements, research assistantships with full and partial tuition reimbursements, teaching assistantships with full and partial tuition reimbursements, career-related internships or fieldwork, Federal Work-Study, institutionally sponsored loans, and unspecified assistantships available. Financial award application deadline: 3/15. *Unit head:* Dr. Fred Little, Graduate Program and Admissions Coordinator, 973-596-3078, Fax: 973-596-3073, E-mail: frederick.a.little@njit.edu. *Application contact:* Kathryn Kelly, Director of Admissions, 973-596-3300, Fax: 973-596-3461, E-mail: admissions@njit.edu.

The New School: A University, Parsons The New School for Design, Program in Architecture, New York, NY 10011. Offers M Arch. *Degree requirements:* For master's, thesis. *Entrance requirements:* For master's, GRE General Test, portfolio. Additional exam requirements/recommendations for international students: Required—TOEFL (minimum score 580 paper-based; 237 computer-based; 92 iBT). Electronic applications accepted.

Newschool of Architecture & Design, Program in Architecture, San Diego, CA 92101-6634. Offers M Arch, MS. Part-time and evening/weekend programs available. *Degree requirements:* For master's, thesis. *Entrance requirements:* For master's, portfolio, interview. *Faculty research:* Urban studies, regional studies, environmental design, structures, cross-cultural studies.

New York Institute of Technology, Graduate Division, School of Architecture and Design, Old Westbury, NY 11568-8000. Offers urban and regional design (M Arch). Part-time programs available. *Students:* 24 full-time (11 women), 3 part-time (all women); includes 6 minority (3 Asian, non-Hispanic/Latino; 3 Hispanic/Latino), 16 international. Average age 27. In 2010, 12 master's awarded. *Degree requirements:* For master's, thesis. *Entrance requirements:* For master's, minimum QPA of 2.85, portfolio. Additional exam requirements/recommendations for international students: Required—TOEFL (minimum score 550 paper-based; 213 computer-based). *Application deadline:* For fall admission, 7/1 priority date for domestic students; for spring admission, 12/1 priority date for domestic students. Applications are processed on a rolling basis. Application fee: $50. Electronic applications accepted. *Expenses:* Tuition: Part-time $835 per credit. *Financial support:* Research assistantships with partial tuition reimbursements, institutionally sponsored loans and tuition waivers (full and partial) available. Support available to part-time students. Financial award applicants required to submit FAFSA. *Faculty research:* Affordable housing, urban modeling and simulation, transport systems and infrastructure, relationships of policy and form. *Unit head:* Judith DiMaio, Dean, 516-686-7594, Fax: 516-686-7921, E-mail: jdimaio@nyit.edu. *Application contact:* Dr. Jacquelyn Nealon, Vice President for Enrollment Services, 516-686-7925, Fax: 516-686-7597, E-mail: jnealon@nyit.edu.

North Carolina State University, Graduate School, College of Design, School of Architecture, Raleigh, NC 27695. Offers M Arch. *Degree requirements:* For master's, thesis optional, oral exam, project. *Entrance requirements:* For master's, GRE General Test, portfolio. Electronic applications accepted. *Faculty research:* Architectural design, architectural history and theory, construction materials, sustainable design.

Northeastern University, College of Arts, Media and Design, School of Architecture, Boston, MA 02115-5096. Offers M Arch. *Faculty:* 12 full-time (4 women), 26 part-time/adjunct (10 women). *Students:* 39 full-time (17 women). 138 applicants, 47% accepted, 36 enrolled. In 2010, 27 master's awarded. *Entrance requirements:* Additional exam requirements/recommendations for international students: Required—TOEFL or IELTS. *Application deadline:* For fall admission, 2/1 priority date for domestic and international students. Applications are processed on a rolling basis. Application fee: $50. Electronic applications accepted. *Financial support:* Federal Work-Study and scholarships/grants available. Support available to part-time students. Financial award application deadline: 3/1; financial award applicants required to submit FAFSA. *Unit head:* Peter Wiederspahn, Chair, 617-373-4637, Fax: 617-373-7080, E-mail: p.wiederspahn@neu.edu. *Application contact:* Jo-Anne Dickinson, Administrative Assistant, 617-373-5990, Fax: 617-373-7281, E-mail: gsas@neu.edu.

The Ohio State University, Graduate School, College of Engineering, Austin E. Knowlton School of Architecture, Columbus, OH 43210. Offers architecture (M Arch); city and regional planning (MCRP, PhD); landscape architecture (M Land Arch). *Accreditation:* ACSP; ASLA. *Faculty:* 35. *Students:* 204 full-time (81 women), 27 part-time (14 women); includes 9 Black or African American, non-Hispanic/Latino; 1 American Indian or Alaska Native, non-Hispanic/Latino; 8 Asian, non-Hispanic/Latino; 8 Hispanic/Latino; 1 Two or more races, non-Hispanic/Latino, 26 international. Average age 28. In 2010, 76 master's, 6 doctorates awarded. *Degree requirements:* For doctorate, thesis/dissertation. *Entrance requirements:* Additional exam requirements/recommendations for international students: Recommended—TOEFL (minimum score 600 paper-based; 250 computer-based). *Application deadline:* For fall admission, 8/15 priority date for domestic students, 7/1 priority date for international students; for winter admission, 12/1 priority date for domestic students, 11/1 priority date for international students; for spring admission, 3/1 priority date for domestic students, 2/1 priority date for international students. Applications are processed on a rolling basis. Application fee: $40 ($50 for international students). Electronic applications accepted. *Expenses:* Tuition, state resident: full-time $10,605. Tuition, nonresident: full-time $26,535. Tuition and fees vary according to course load and program. *Financial support:* Fellowships, research assistantships, Federal Work-Study, institutionally sponsored loans, and unspecified assistantships available. Support available to part-time students. *Unit head:* Ann Pendleton-Jullian, Director, 614-292-9811, Fax: 614-292-7106, E-mail: pendleton-jullia@osu.edu. *Application contact:* 614-292-9444, Fax: 614-292-3895, E-mail: domestic.grad@osu.edu.

Penn State University Park, Graduate School, College of Arts and Architecture, Department of Architecture, State College, University Park, PA 16802-1503. Offers M Arch, PhD.

Philadelphia University, School of Architecture, Philadelphia, PA 19144. Offers MS.

Pontificia Universidad Catolica Madre y Maestra, Graduate School, Faculty of Sciences and Humanities, Santiago, Dominican Republic. Offers architecture (M Arch), including architecture of interiors, architecture of tourist lodgings, landscaping; early childhood education (M Ed).

Prairie View A&M University, School of Architecture, Prairie View, TX 77446-0519. Offers architecture (M Arch); community development (MCD). Part-time and evening/weekend programs available. *Faculty:* 4 full-time (1 woman), 6 part-time/adjunct (2 women). *Students:* 31 full-time (6 women), 38 part-time (18 women); includes 55 Black or African American, non-Hispanic/Latino; 1 Asian, non-Hispanic/Latino; 6 Hispanic/Latino, 5 international. Average age 31. 63 applicants, 100% accepted. In 2010, 35 master's awarded. *Entrance requirements:* For master's, GRE General Test, portfolio (M Arch). Additional exam requirements/recommendations for international students: Required—TOEFL (minimum score 550 paper-based). *Application deadline:* For fall admission, 6/1 priority date for domestic and international students; for spring admission, 11/1 priority date for domestic students, 10/1 priority date for international students. Applications are processed on a rolling basis. Application fee: $50. Electronic applications accepted. *Expenses:* Tuition, state resident: full-time $3586.14; part-time $119.06 per credit hour. Tuition, nonresident: part-time $511.23 per credit hour. *Financial support:* In 2010–11, 1 research assistantship (averaging $6,792 per year) was awarded; career-related internships or fieldwork, Federal Work-Study, institutionally sponsored loans, scholarships/grants, tuition waivers (full and partial), and unspecified assistantships also available. Support available to part-time students. Financial award application deadline: 3/1; financial award applicants required to submit FAFSA. *Faculty research:* Community management, sustainable design. *Unit head:* Dr. Ikhlas Sabouni, Dean, 936-261-9800, Fax: 936-261-2350, E-mail: isabouni@pvamu.edu. *Application contact:* Dr. Ikhlas Sabouni, Dean, 936-261-9800, Fax: 936-261-2350, E-mail: isabouni@pvamu.edu.

Pratt Institute, School of Architecture, Program in Architecture, Brooklyn, NY 11205-3899. Offers architecture (first-professional) (M Arch); architecture (post-professional) (MS Arch). *Faculty:* 10 full-time (3 women), 47 part-time/adjunct (18 women). *Students:* 206 full-time (93 women); includes 10 Black or African American, non-Hispanic/Latino; 16 Asian, non-Hispanic/Latino; 18 Hispanic/Latino; 2 Two or more races, non-Hispanic/Latino, 52 international. Average age 26. 658 applicants, 44% accepted, 74 enrolled. In 2010, 58 master's awarded. *Degree requirements:* For master's, thesis. *Entrance requirements:* For master's, GRE (M Arch only), B Arch, portfolio, letters of recommendation. Additional exam requirements/recommendations for international students: Required—TOEFL (minimum score 550 paper-based; 213 computer-based; 79 iBT). *Application deadline:* For fall admission, 1/5 for domestic and international students; for spring admission, 10/1 for domestic and international students. Application fee: $50 ($90 for international students). Electronic applications accepted. *Expenses:* Tuition: Full-time $22,734; part-time $1263 per credit. Required fees: $1280. *Financial support:* Career-related internships or fieldwork, Federal Work-Study, institutionally sponsored loans, scholarships/grants, health care benefits, and unspecified assistantships available. Support available to part-time students. Financial award application deadline: 2/1; financial award applicants required to submit FAFSA. *Faculty research:* Design theory, advanced structural systems, urban investigations. *Unit head:* William J. Mac Donald, Chairperson, 718-636-4308, E-mail: wmacdona@pratt.edu. *Application contact:* Young Hah, Director of Graduate Admissions, 718-636-3683, Fax: 718-399-4242, E-mail: yhah@pratt.edu.

See Display on next page and Close-Up on page 161.

Princeton University, Graduate School, School of Architecture, Princeton, NJ 08544-1019. Offers M Arch, PhD. Terminal master's awarded for partial completion of doctoral program. *Degree requirements:* For master's, thesis; for doctorate, 2 foreign languages, comprehensive exam, thesis/dissertation. *Entrance requirements:* For master's, GRE General Test, design portfolio, math, 2 semesters of physics, and art/architecture survey; for doctorate, GRE General Test, samples of written work. Additional exam requirements/recommendations for international students: Required—TOEFL (minimum score 600 paper-based; 260 computer-based). Electronic applications accepted. *Faculty research:* Design, urban studies, landscape architecture, media and information technologies in architecture.

Rhode Island School of Design, Graduate Studies, Division of Architecture and Design, Department of Architecture, Providence, RI 02903-2784. Offers M Arch. *Degree requirements:* For master's, thesis, exhibit. *Entrance requirements:* For master's, portfolio, 3 letters of recommendation. Additional exam requirements/recommendations for international students: Required—TOEFL (minimum score 580 paper-based; 237 computer-based), IELTS (minimum score 6.5).

Rice University, Graduate Programs, School of Architecture, Houston, TX 77251-1892. Offers architecture (M Arch, D Arch); urban design (M Arch). *Degree requirements:* For master's, thesis optional; for doctorate, thesis/dissertation. *Entrance requirements:* For master's and doctorate, GRE. Additional exam requirements/recommendations for international students: Required—TOEFL (minimum score 600 paper-based; 250 computer-based; 100 iBT). Electronic applications accepted.

Rochester Institute of Technology, Graduate Enrollment Services, Golisano Institute for Sustainability, Program in Architecture, Rochester, NY 14623-5603. Offers M Arch. *Degree*

requirements: For master's, thesis. *Entrance requirements:* For master's, GRE, portfolio. Additional exam requirements/recommendations for international students: Required—TOEFL (minimum score 600 paper-based; 250 computer-based; 100 iBT). *Application deadline:* Applications are processed on a rolling basis. Application fee: $50. Electronic applications accepted. *Expenses:* Tuition: Full-time $33,234; part-time $924 per credit hour. Required fees: $219. *Financial support:* Applicants required to submit FAFSA. *Faculty research:* Sustainable design and practice, practices and principles of preservation and adaptive reuse. *Unit head:* Dr. Alex Bitterman, Graduate Program Director, 585-475-5397, E-mail: aebfaa@rit.edu. *Application contact:* Diane Ellison, Assistant Vice President, Graduate Enrollment Services, 585-475-2229, Fax: 585-475-7164, E-mail: gradinfo@rit.edu.

Roger Williams University, School of Architecture, Art and Historic Preservation, Bristol, RI 02809. Offers architecture (M Arch). Students often begin 5-6 year dual degree sequence as undergraduates. *Degree requirements:* For master's, thesis. *Entrance requirements:* For master's, portfolio, 2 letters of recommendation. Additional exam requirements/recommendations for international students: Recommended—IELTS. Electronic applications accepted. *Expenses:* Contact institution.

Savannah College of Art and Design, Graduate School, Program in Architecture, Savannah, GA 31402-3146. Offers M Arch. Part-time programs available. *Faculty:* 25 full-time (9 women), 12 part-time/adjunct (1 woman). *Students:* 126 full-time (56 women), 26 part-time (10 women); includes 4 Black or African American, non-Hispanic/Latino; 1 American Indian or Alaska Native, non-Hispanic/Latino; 2 Asian, non-Hispanic/Latino; 7 Hispanic/Latino, 29 international. Average age 25. In 2010, 81 master's awarded. *Degree requirements:* For master's, thesis, internship. *Entrance requirements:* For master's, interview, portfolio. Additional exam requirements/recommendations for international students: Required—TOEFL (minimum score 450 paper-based; 133 computer-based). *Application deadline:* For fall admission, 4/1 priority date for domestic and international students. Applications are processed on a rolling basis. Application fee: $35. Electronic applications accepted. *Expenses:* Tuition: Full-time $29,520; part-time $3280 per quarter. Tuition and fees vary according to campus/location. *Financial support:* Fellowships, career-related internships or fieldwork, Federal Work-Study, and scholarships/grants available. Financial award application deadline: 4/1; financial award applicants required to submit FAFSA. *Faculty research:* Computer-aided design, photovoltaics-powered environmental control. *Unit head:* Scott Singeisen, Chair, 912-525-6871, E-mail: ssingeis@scad.edu. *Application contact:* Elizabeth Mathis, Director of Graduate and International Enrollment, 912-525-5965, Fax: 912-525-5985, E-mail: emathis@scad.edu.

See Display on page 177 and Close-Up on page 223

School of the Art Institute of Chicago, Graduate Division, Department of Architecture, Interior Architecture, and Designed Objects, Chicago, IL 60603-3103. Offers architecture (M Arc); design for emerging technologies (MFA); designed objects (M Des); interior architecture (M Arc). *Entrance requirements:* Additional exam requirements/recommendations for international students: Required—TOEFL, IELTS.

See Close-Up on page 225.

Southern California Institute of Architecture, Graduate Program in Architecture, Los Angeles, CA 90013. Offers M Arch. *Faculty:* 43 full-time (12 women), 43 part-time/adjunct (15 women). *Students:* 230 full-time (81 women); includes 86 minority (8 Black or African American, non-Hispanic/Latino; 4 American Indian or Alaska Native, non-Hispanic/Latino; 34 Asian, non-Hispanic/Latino; 38 Hispanic/Latino; 2 Native Hawaiian or other Pacific Islander, non-Hispanic/Latino), 85 international. Average age 27. 506 applicants, 63% accepted, 103 enrolled. In 2010, 93 master's awarded. *Degree requirements:* For master's, thesis, final project. *Entrance requirements:* For master's, GRE General Test, portfolio of architectural and creative work, 3 letters of recommendation. Additional exam requirements/recommendations for international students: Required—TOEFL (minimum score 560 paper-based; 90 iBT), IELTS (minimum score 6.5), IELTS or TOEFL. *Application deadline:* For fall admission, 12/15 for domestic students. Application fee: $75. Electronic applications accepted. *Expenses:* Tuition: Full-time $13,750; part-time $764 per credit hour. Required fees: $350. *Financial support:* In 2010–11, 32 students received support; teaching assistantships, Federal Work-Study and scholarships/grants available. Financial award application deadline: 2/15. *Unit head:* Hernan Diaz Alonso, Graduate Program Chair, 213-613-2200, Fax: 213-613-2260, E-mail: hernan@sciarc.edu. *Application contact:* J. J. Jackman, Director of Admissions, 213-356-5321, Fax: 213-613-2260, E-mail: jj@sciarc.edu.

Southern Illinois University Carbondale, Graduate School, College of Applied Science, School of Architecture, Carbondale, IL 62901-4701. Offers M Arch.

Syracuse University, School of Architecture, Syracuse, NY 13244. Offers M Arch I, M Arch II. *Faculty:* 37 full-time (12 women), 7 part-time/adjunct (3 women). *Students:* 112 full-time (42 women), 4 part-time (3 women); includes 23 minority (6 Black or African American, non-Hispanic/Latino; 8 Asian, non-Hispanic/Latino; 8 Hispanic/Latino; 1 Two or more races, non-Hispanic/Latino), 17 international. Average age 26. 256 applicants, 42% accepted, 44 enrolled. In 2010, 17 master's awarded. *Degree requirements:* For master's, thesis. *Entrance requirements:* For master's, GRE General Test, interview, portfolio. Additional exam requirements/recommendations for international students: Required—TOEFL (minimum score 100 iBT). *Application deadline:* For fall admission, 2/1 priority date for domestic and international students. Application fee: $75. Electronic applications accepted. *Expenses:* Tuition: Part-time $1162 per credit. *Financial support:* Fellowships with full tuition reimbursements, research assistantships with full and partial tuition reimbursements, teaching assistantships with full and partial tuition reimbursements available. Financial award application deadline: 1/1. *Faculty research:* Urban design, urban mapping, building systems, landscape, theory. *Unit head:* Mark Robbins, Dean, 315-443-1041, Fax: 315-443-5082. *Application contact:* Prof. Francisco Sanin, Graduate Director, 315-443-1041, Fax: 315-443-5082, E-mail: fesanin@syr.edu.

Temple University, Tyler School of Art, Department of Architecture, Philadelphia, PA 19122-6096. Offers M Arch. Part-time and evening/weekend programs available. *Faculty:* 3 full-time (1 woman). *Students:* 9 full-time (4 women); includes 1 Black or African American, non-Hispanic/Latino; 1 Asian, non-Hispanic/Latino. 20 applicants, 70% accepted, 9 enrolled. *Entrance requirements:* Additional exam requirements/recommendations for international students: Required—TOEFL. Application fee: $50. Electronic applications accepted. *Financial support:* Career-related internships or fieldwork, Federal Work-Study, and institutionally sponsored loans available. Support available to part-time students. Financial award application deadline: 1/15; financial award applicants required to submit FAFSA. *Unit head:* Kate Wingert-Playdon, Chair, 215-204-8813, Fax: 215-204-5481, E-mail: architecture@temple.edu. *Application contact:* Carmina Cianciulli, Assistant Dean for Admissions, 215-782-2875, Fax: 215-782-2711, E-mail: tylerart@temple.edu.

Texas A&M University, College of Architecture, Department of Architecture, College Station, TX 77843. Offers M Arch, MS Arch, PhD. *Faculty:* 35. *Students:* 150 full-time (67 women), 13 part-time (4 women); includes 30 minority (4 Black or African American, non-Hispanic/Latino; 2 American Indian or Alaska Native, non-Hispanic/Latino; 9 Asian, non-Hispanic/Latino; 15 Hispanic/Latino), 67 international. Average age 24. In 2010, 48 master's, 6 doctorates awarded. *Degree requirements:* For master's, comprehensive exam, thesis; for doctorate, comprehensive exam, thesis/dissertation. *Entrance requirements:* For master's, GRE General Test, portfolio, letters of recommendation; for doctorate, GRE General Test. Additional exam requirements/recommendations for international students: Required—TOEFL. *Application deadline:* For fall admission, 1/15 priority date for domestic and international students. Applications are processed on a rolling basis. Application fee: $50 ($75 for international students). Electronic applications accepted. *Financial support:* Fellowships, research assistantships, teaching assistantships, career-related internships or fieldwork, Federal Work-Study, institutionally sponsored loans, and scholarships/grants available. Financial award application deadline: 1/15; financial award applicants required to submit FAFSA. *Faculty research:* Energy optimization, architecture pedagogy, environment and behavior. *Unit head:* Ward Wells, Interim Head, 979-845-1015, Fax: 979-862-1571, E-mail: ward-wells@tamu.edu.

Architecture

Texas Tech University, Graduate School, College of Architecture, Post-Professional Program in Architecture, Lubbock, TX 79409. Offers MS. Part-time programs available. *Students:* 4 full-time (0 women), 3 part-time (2 women); includes 2 Hispanic/Latino, 3 international. Average age 27. 18 applicants, 11% accepted, 1 enrolled. In 2010, 2 master's awarded. *Degree requirements:* For master's, thesis. *Entrance requirements:* For master's, GRE General Test, portfolio. Additional exam requirements/recommendations for international students: Required—TOEFL (minimum score 550 paper-based; 213 computer-based; 79 iBT). *Application deadline:* For fall admission, 6/1 priority date for domestic students, 1/15 priority date for international students; for spring admission, 9/1 priority date for domestic students, 6/15 priority date for international students. Applications are processed on a rolling basis. Application fee: $50 ($75 for international students). Electronic applications accepted. *Expenses:* Tuition, state resident: full-time $5495.76; part-time $228.99 per credit hour. Tuition, nonresident: full-time $12,936; part-time $538.99 per credit hour. Required fees: $2674; $36 per credit hour. $905 per semester. *Financial support:* Application deadline: 4/15. *Faculty research:* Historic preservation, digital design and fabrication, urban and community design, vernacular architecture, healthcare facilities. *Unit head:* Saif Haq, Associate Dean of Research and Post-Professional Graduate Studies, 806-742-3136 Ext. 284, Fax: 806-742-4604, E-mail: saif.haq@ttu.edu. *Application contact:* Lori Rodriguez, Academic Program Assistant, 806-742-3136 Ext. 272, Fax: 806-742-2855, E-mail: lori.rodriguez@ttu.edu.

Texas Tech University, Graduate School, College of Architecture, Professional Program in Architecture, Lubbock, TX 79409. Offers M Arch, M Arch/MBA. Part-time programs available. *Students:* 95 full-time (22 women), 20 part-time (6 women); includes 1 American Indian or Alaska Native, non-Hispanic/Latino; 4 Asian, non-Hispanic/Latino; 27 Hispanic/Latino; 1 Two or more races, non-Hispanic/Latino, 8 international. Average age 23. 74 applicants, 53% accepted, 31 enrolled. In 2010, 58 master's awarded. *Degree requirements:* For master's, thesis. *Entrance requirements:* For master's, GRE General Test, portfolio. Additional exam requirements/recommendations for international students: Required—TOEFL (minimum score 550 paper-based; 213 computer-based; 79 iBT). *Application deadline:* For fall admission, 6/1 priority date for domestic students, 1/15 priority date for international students; for spring admission, 9/1 priority date for domestic students, 6/15 priority date for international students. Applications are processed on a rolling basis. Application fee: $50 ($75 for international students). Electronic applications accepted. *Expenses:* Tuition, state resident: full-time $5495.76; part-time $228.99 per credit hour. Tuition, nonresident: full-time $12,936; part-time $538.99 per credit hour. Required fees: $2674; $36 per credit hour. $905 per semester. *Financial support:* Application deadline: 4/15. *Faculty research:* Digital design and construction, urban design, healthcare facilities, architectural history, historic preservation. *Unit head:* Dr. Clifton Ellis, Associate Dean for Academics, 806-742-3136, Fax: 806-742-2855, E-mail: architecture.programs@ttu.edu. *Application contact:* Lori Rodriguez, Academic Program Assistant, 806-742-3136 Ext. 247, Fax: 806-742-2855, E-mail: lori.rodriguez@ttu.edu.

Tulane University, School of Architecture, New Orleans, LA 70118-5669. Offers M Arch, MPS. Part-time programs available. *Degree requirements:* For master's, thesis. *Entrance requirements:* For master's, GRE, portfolio. Additional exam requirements/recommendations for international students: Required—TOEFL. *Expenses:* Contact institution. *Faculty research:* Design topics, preservation and environmental conservation, architecture and human health, computing.

Universidad Autonoma de Guadalajara, Graduate Programs, Guadalajara, Mexico. Offers administrative law and justice (LL M); advertising and corporate communications (MA); architecture (M Arch); business (MBA); computational science (MCC); education (Ed M, Ed D); English-Spanish translation (MA); entrepreneurship and management (MBA); integrated management of digital animation (MA); international business (MIB); international corporate law (LL M); internet technologies (MS); manufacturing systems (MMS); occupational health (MS); philosophy (MA, PhD); power electronics (MS); quality systems (MQS); renewable energy (MS); social evaluation of projects (MBA); strategic market research (MBA); tax law (MA); teaching mathematics (MA).

Universidad Nacional Pedro Henriquez Urena, Graduate School, Santo Domingo, Dominican Republic. Offers agricultural diversity (MS), including horticultural/fruit production, tropical animal production; conservation of monuments and cultural assets (M Arch); ecology and environment (MS); environmental engineering (MEE); international relations (MA); natural resource management (MS); political science (MA); project optimization (MPM); project feasibility (MPM); project management (MPM); sanitation engineering (ME); science for teachers (MS); tropical Caribbean architecture (M Arch).

Université Laval, Faculty of Architecture, Planning and Visual Arts, School of Architecture, Program in Architecture, Québec, QC G1K 7P4, Canada. Offers M Arch, M Sc. Part-time programs available. *Degree requirements:* For master's, thesis (for some programs). *Entrance requirements:* For master's, mastery of software (CAO), knowledge of French and English. Electronic applications accepted.

University at Buffalo, the State University of New York, Graduate School, School of Architecture and Planning, Department of Architecture, Buffalo, NY 14260. Offers M Arch, MS, M Arch/MBA, M Arch/MFA, M Arch/MUP. *Faculty:* 24 full-time (7 women), 18 part-time/adjunct (5 women). *Students:* 118 full-time (48 women), 4 part-time (2 women); includes 1 Black or African American, non-Hispanic/Latino; 4 Asian, non-Hispanic/Latino; 2 Hispanic/Latino, 23 international. Average age 25. 287 applicants, 36% accepted, 44 enrolled. In 2010, 40 master's awarded. *Degree requirements:* For master's, thesis or alternative, project. *Entrance requirements:* For master's, GRE, portfolio, 3 letters of recommendation, minimum GPA of 3.0. Additional exam requirements/recommendations for international students: Required—TOEFL (minimum score 213 computer-based; 79 iBT), IELTS (minimum score 6.5). *Application deadline:* For fall admission, 1/15 for domestic and international students. Application fee: $75. Electronic applications accepted. *Financial support:* In 2010–11, 4 fellowships with full tuition reimbursements (averaging $9,600 per year), 4 research assistantships with full and partial tuition reimbursements (averaging $6,573 per year), 28 teaching assistantships with partial tuition reimbursements (averaging $4,800 per year) were awarded; career-related internships or fieldwork, Federal Work-Study, institutionally sponsored loans, scholarships/grants, health care benefits, tuition waivers (partial), and unspecified assistantships also available. Support available to part-time students. Financial award application deadline: 3/1; financial award applicants required to submit FAFSA. *Faculty research:* Inclusive design, material culture, situated technologies, sustainable urban and natural environments. Total annual research expenditures: $1.2 million. *Unit head:* Prof. Omar Khan, Chair, 716-829-3483 Ext. 105, Fax: 716-829-3256, E-mail: omar.khan@buffalo.edu. *Application contact:* Debbie Eggebrecht, Assistant to the Chair, 716-829-3485 Ext. 105, Fax: 716-829-3256, E-mail: dle2@buffalo.edu.

The University of Arizona, College of Architecture and Landscape Architecture, School of Architecture, Tucson, AZ 85721. Offers M Arch. *Faculty:* 10 full-time (3 women). *Students:* 29 full-time (8 women), 8 part-time (5 women); includes 2 Black or African American, non-Hispanic/Latino; 6 Hispanic/Latino; 4 Two or more races, non-Hispanic/Latino, 9 international. Average age 30. 64 applicants, 45% accepted, 16 enrolled. In 2010, 12 master's awarded. *Entrance requirements:* For master's, GRE, 3 letters of recommendation, statement of purpose, portfolio, resume. Additional exam requirements/recommendations for international students: Required—TOEFL (minimum score 550 paper-based; 213 computer-based; 79 iBT). *Application deadline:* For fall admission, 2/1 for domestic students, 12/1 for international students; for spring admission, 2/1 for domestic and international students. Application fee: $75. Electronic applications accepted. *Expenses:* Tuition, state resident: full-time $7692. *Financial support:* In 2010–11, 17 research assistantships with full tuition reimbursements (averaging $13,000 per year), 9 teaching assistantships with full tuition reimbursements (averaging $13,000 per year) were awarded; health care benefits and unspecified assistantships also available. Total annual research expenditures: $41,435. *Unit head:* Mary Hardin, Interim Director, 520-621-6752, E-mail: mchardin@u.arizona.edu. *Application contact:* Linda Erasmus, 520-621-9819, Fax: 520-621-8700, E-mail: erasmus@email.arizona.edu.

The University of British Columbia, Faculty of Applied Science, School of Architecture and Landscape Architecture, Vancouver, BC V6T 1Z2, Canada. Offers architecture (M Arch, MASA); landscape architecture (MASLA, MLA). *Degree requirements:* For master's, thesis. *Entrance requirements:* For master's, portfolio, resume, 3 reference letters. Additional exam requirements/recommendations for international students: Required—TOEFL (minimum score 600 paper-based; 250 computer-based; 100 iBT). Electronic applications accepted. *Expenses:* Contact institution. *Faculty research:* Energy and resource use of buildings, advanced design research, urban design and community activism, advanced research in computer applications, cultural studies.

University of Calgary, Faculty of Graduate Studies, Faculty of Environmental Design, Calgary, AB T2N 1N4, Canada. Offers architecture (M Arch); environmental design (M Env Des, PhD). *Degree requirements:* For master's, thesis; for doctorate, thesis/dissertation. *Entrance requirements:* For master's, minimum GPA of 3.0; for doctorate, minimum GPA of 3.5. Additional exam requirements/recommendations for international students: Required—TOEFL (minimum score 550 paper-based; 213 computer-based). *Faculty research:* Sustainable development in architecture, planning and product design, energy and environment, impact assessment, ecotourism.

University of California, Berkeley, Graduate Division, College of Environmental Design, Department of Architecture, Berkeley, CA 94720-1500. Offers architecture (M Arch); building science (MS, PhD); building structures, construction and materials (MS, PhD); design theories, methods, and practices (MS, PhD); environmental design in developing countries (MS, PhD); history of architecture and urbanism (MS, PhD); social and cultural processes in architecture and urbanism (MS, PhD); M Arch/MCP; M Arch/MS; MLA/M Arch. *Degree requirements:* For master's, thesis; for doctorate, thesis/dissertation, qualifying exam. *Entrance requirements:* For master's and doctorate, GRE General Test, minimum GPA of 3.0, 3 letters of recommendation. Additional exam requirements/recommendations for international students: Required—TOEFL. Electronic applications accepted.

University of California, Los Angeles, Graduate Division, School of the Arts and Architecture, Department of Architecture and Urban Design, Los Angeles, CA 90095. Offers M Arch, MA, PhD. *Faculty:* 14 full-time (6 women). *Students:* 165 full-time (60 women); includes 39 minority (4 Black or African American, non-Hispanic/Latino; 24 Asian, non-Hispanic/Latino; 9 Hispanic/Latino; 1 Native Hawaiian or other Pacific Islander, non-Hispanic/Latino; 1 Two or more races, non-Hispanic/Latino), 27 international. Average age 28. 648 applicants, 23% accepted, 51 enrolled. In 2010, 43 master's awarded. *Degree requirements:* For master's, thesis or alternative, comprehensive exam or design project; for doctorate, 2 foreign languages, thesis/dissertation, oral and written qualifying exams. *Entrance requirements:* For master's and doctorate, GRE General Test, portfolio. Additional exam requirements/recommendations for international students: Required—TOEFL. *Application deadline:* For fall admission, 1/5 for domestic students. Application fee: $70 ($90 for international students). Electronic applications accepted. *Financial support:* In 2010–11, 137 students received support, including 34 fellowships, 13 research assistantships, 45 teaching assistantships; Federal Work-Study, institutionally sponsored loans, tuition waivers (full and partial), and unspecified assistantships also available. Financial award application deadline: 3/2. *Faculty research:* Urban poverty and low wage labor markets; environmental planning and politics; international political economy; physical planning, urban design, planning history; housing and land development; transportation and land use; critical urban and regional studies. *Unit head:* Dr. Hitoshi Abe, Chair, 310-206-3495. *Application contact:* Jim Kies, Information Contact, 310-825-0525, Fax: 310-825-8959, E-mail: admissions@aud.ucla.edu.

University of Cincinnati, Graduate School, College of Design, Architecture, Art, and Planning, School of Architecture and Interior Design, Cincinnati, OH 45221. Offers architecture (M Arch). *Accreditation:* NASAD. *Degree requirements:* For master's, one foreign language, thesis. *Entrance requirements:* Additional exam requirements/recommendations for international students: Required—TOEFL. *Faculty research:* Theory and history of architecture.

University of Florida, Graduate School, College of Design, Construction and Planning, Doctoral Program in Design, Construction and Planning, Gainesville, FL 32611. Offers design, construction and planning (PhD); historic preservation (PhD). *Faculty:* 15 full-time (2 women). *Students:* 60 full-time (25 women), 16 part-time (6 women); includes 4 Black or African American, non-Hispanic/Latino; 3 Asian, non-Hispanic/Latino; 2 Hispanic/Latino, 35 international. Average age 29. 68 applicants, 46% accepted, 17 enrolled. In 2010, 6 doctorates awarded. *Degree requirements:* For doctorate, thesis/dissertation. *Entrance requirements:* For doctorate, GRE General Test minimum of 1200 combined Verbal and Quantitative score. Minimum GPA 3.0. Additional exam requirements/recommendations for international students: Required—TOEFL (minimum score 550 paper-based; 213 computer-based; 80 iBT), IELTS (minimum score 6). *Application deadline:* For fall admission, 2/1 for domestic and international students. Applications are processed on a rolling basis. Application fee: $30. Electronic applications accepted. *Expenses:* Tuition, state resident: full-time $10,915.92. Tuition, nonresident: full-time $28,309. *Financial support:* In 2010–11, 48 students received support, including 16 fellowships, 26 research assistantships (averaging $10,928 per year), 6 teaching assistantships (averaging $12,314 per year); unspecified assistantships also available. Financial award applicants required to submit FAFSA. *Faculty research:* Architecture, building construction, urban and regional planning. *Unit head:* Dr. Christopher Silver, Dean, 352-392-0997 Ext. 433, Fax: 352-392-3308, E-mail: silver2@dcp.ufl.edu. *Application contact:* Dr. Paul D. Zwick, Associate Dean for Research and Graduate Programs, 352-392-0997 Ext. 427, Fax: 352-392-3308, E-mail: pdzwick@ufl.edu.

University of Florida, Graduate School, College of Design, Construction and Planning, School of Architecture, Gainesville, FL 32611. Offers M Arch, MSAS. *Faculty:* 20 full-time (5 women), 1 (woman) part-time/adjunct. *Students:* 121 full-time (54 women), 8 part-time (3 women); includes 10 Black or African American, non-Hispanic/Latino; 2 American Indian or Alaska Native, non-Hispanic/Latino; 7 Asian, non-Hispanic/Latino; 18 Hispanic/Latino, 12 international. Average age 27. 270 applicants, 38% accepted, 36 enrolled. In 2010, 41 master's awarded. *Entrance requirements:* For master's, GRE General Test, Minimum GPA of 3.0. Additional exam requirements/recommendations for international students: Required—TOEFL (minimum score 550 paper-based; 213 computer-based; 80 iBT), IELTS (minimum score 6). Application fee: $30. *Expenses:* Tuition, state resident: full-time $10,915.92. Tuition, nonresident: full-time $28,309. *Financial support:* In 2010–11, 35 students received support, including 2 research assistantships (averaging $6,692 per year), 33 teaching assistantships (averaging $7,219 per year). Financial award applicants required to submit FAFSA. *Unit head:* Prof. Martin Gold, Director, 352-392-0205 Ext. 209, E-mail: mgold@ufl.edu. *Application contact:* Prof. Nancy M. Clark, Assistant Director for Graduate Program, 352-392-0205 Ext. 220, E-mail: nmclark@ufl.edu.

University of Hartford, College of Engineering, Technology and Architecture, Program in Architecture, West Hartford, CT 06117-1599. Offers M Arch. *Entrance requirements:* For master's, 3 letters of recommendation, portfolio. Additional exam requirements/recommendations for international students: Required—TOEFL (minimum score 550 paper-based; 213 computer-based).

University of Hawaii at Manoa, School of Architecture, Honolulu, HI 96822. Offers D Arch. Part-time programs available. *Faculty:* 10 full-time (3 women). *Students:* 130 full-time (67 women), 21 part-time (6 women); includes 3 Black or African American, non-Hispanic/Latino; 62 Asian, non-Hispanic/Latino; 4 Hispanic/Latino; 12 Native Hawaiian or other Pacific Islander, non-Hispanic/Latino; 16 Two or more races, non-Hispanic/Latino, 16 international. Average age 33. *Entrance requirements:* Additional exam requirements/recommendations for international students: Required—TOEFL, IELTS. *Application deadline:* For fall admission, 5/1 for domestic and international students; for spring admission, 9/1 for domestic students, 8/1 for international students. Application fee: $60. *Financial support:* In 2010–11, 31 students received support, including 11 fellowships (averaging $3,020 per year), 2 research assistantships with full tuition reimbursements available (averaging $17,496 per year); teaching assistantships with full tuition reimbursements available, institutionally sponsored loans, scholarships/grants, and unspecified assistantships also available. Financial award applicants required to submit FAFSA. *Faculty research:* Housing, future cities, environmental studies, preservation, professional practice. Total annual research expenditures: $182,200. *Application contact:* Spencer Leineweber, Graduate Field Chairperson, 808-956-7228, Fax: 808-956-7778, E-mail: aspencer@hawaii.edu.

University of Houston, College of Architecture, Houston, TX 77204. Offers architecture (MS); architecture studies (MA); space architecture (MS). *Faculty:* 18 full-time (3 women), 13 part-time/adjunct (2 women). *Students:* 92 full-time (40 women), 6 part-time (2 women); includes 1 Black or African American, non-Hispanic/Latino; 1 American Indian or Alaska Native, non-Hispanic/Latino; 9 Asian, non-Hispanic/Latino; 8 Hispanic/Latino; 3 Two or more races, non-Hispanic/Latino, 19 international. Average age 28. 192 applicants, 45% accepted, 47 enrolled. In 2010, 21 master's awarded. *Entrance requirements:* For master's, GRE General Test. Additional exam requirements/recommendations for international students: Required—TOEFL (minimum score 550 paper-based; 79 iBT), IELTS (minimum score 6.5). *Application deadline:* For fall admission, 2/1 priority date for domestic students, 2/1 for international students. Applications are processed on a rolling basis. Application fee: $50. Electronic applications accepted. *Expenses:* Tuition, state resident: full-time $8592; part-time $358 per credit hour. Tuition, nonresident: full-time $16,032; part-time $668 per credit hour. Required fees: $2889. Tuition and fees vary according to course load and program. *Financial support:* In 2010–11, 1 research assistantship with partial tuition reimbursement (averaging $7,720 per year), 11 teaching assistantships with partial tuition reimbursements (averaging $5,264 per year) were awarded; career-related internships or fieldwork, Federal Work-Study, institutionally sponsored loans, scholarships/grants, health care benefits, and unspecified assistantships also available. Support available to part-time students. Financial award application deadline: 2/1. *Faculty research:* Community-based design; twentieth century architecture, urbanism, and design; extreme environments; design build; green building components and digital technology. *Unit head:* Dr. Patricia Oliver, Dean, 713-743-2400, Fax: 713-743-2358, E-mail: poliver@central.uh.edu. *Application contact:* Trang Phan, Assistant Dean, 713-743-2400, Fax: 713-743-2358, E-mail: tphan@uh.edu.

University of Idaho, College of Graduate Studies, College of Art and Architecture, Moscow, ID 83844-2282. Offers architecture (MS), including community planning, compution and visualization studies, environment and behavior studies, urban design; architecture (professional degree) (M Arch); landscape architecture (MS); studio art (MFA), including graphic design, interactive and information design, interface, painting, printmaking, sculpture; teaching art (MAT). *Accreditation:* NASAD. *Faculty:* 19 full-time, 1 part-time/adjunct. *Students:* 102 full-time, 15 part-time. Average age 27. In 2010, 31 master's awarded. *Application deadline:* For fall admission, 8/1 for domestic students; for spring admission, 12/15 for domestic students. Applications are processed on a rolling basis. Application fee: $60. Electronic applications accepted. *Expenses:* Tuition, nonresident: part-time $580 per credit. Required fees: $306 per credit. *Financial support:* Applicants required to submit FAFSA. *Faculty research:* Sustainability in communities, urban research, virtual technology, bioregional planning, environment and behavior interaction. *Unit head:* Dr. Mark Elison Hoversten, Dean, 208-885-5423, E-mail: caa@uidaho.edu. *Application contact:* Dr. Mark Elison Hoversten, Dean, 208-885-5423, E-mail: caa@uidaho.edu.

University of Illinois at Chicago, Graduate College, College of Architecture and Art, School of Architecture, Chicago, IL 60607-7128. Offers architecture (M Arch, MS Arch); architecture in health design (MS Arch). *Entrance requirements:* For master's, GRE General Test, portfolio, minimum GPA of 3.0. Additional exam requirements/recommendations for international students: Required—TOEFL. Electronic applications accepted. *Faculty research:* Housing values, elderly housing, design theory, deconstructivism.

University of Illinois at Urbana–Champaign, Graduate College, College of Fine and Applied Arts, School of Architecture, Champaign, IL 61820. Offers architectural studies (MS); architecture (M Arch, PhD); M Arch/MBA; M Arch/MS; M Arch/MUP; MCS/M Arch; MRP/JD. *Faculty:* 33 full-time (7 women), 8 part-time/adjunct (1 woman). *Students:* 188 full-time (87 women), 2 part-time (0 women); includes 7 Black or African American, non-Hispanic/Latino; 13 Asian, non-Hispanic/Latino; 15 Hispanic/Latino; 2 Two or more races, non-Hispanic/Latino, 31 international. 470 applicants, 23% accepted, 86 enrolled. In 2010, 83 master's awarded. *Entrance requirements:* For master's, minimum GPA of 3.0; portfolio; for doctorate, GRE, minimum GPA of 3.0; portfolio. Additional exam requirements/recommendations for international students: Required—TOEFL (minimum score 590 paper-based; 243 computer-based; 96 iBT) or IELTS (minimum score 6.5). *Application deadline:* Applications are processed on a rolling basis. Application fee: $75 ($90 for international students). Electronic applications accepted. *Financial support:* In 2010–11, 19 fellowships, 20 research assistantships, 24 teaching assistantships were awarded; tuition waivers (full and partial) also available. *Unit head:* David Chasco, Director, 217-333-1331, Fax: 217-244-8866, E-mail: dchasco@illinois.edu. *Application contact:* Christopher R. Wilcock, Admissions and Records Officer, 217-244-4723, Fax: 217-244-8866, E-mail: cwilcock@illinois.edu.

The University of Kansas, Graduate Studies, School of Architecture, Design, and Planning, Program in Architecture, Lawrence, KS 66045. Offers academic track (MA); architecture (PhD); facility management (Certificate); management track (MA); professional track (M Arch); M Arch/MBA; M Arch/MUP. *Faculty:* 20 full-time (5 women). *Students:* 187 full-time (88 women), 24 part-time (10 women); includes 22 minority (4 Black or African American, non-Hispanic/Latino; 1 American Indian or Alaska Native, non-Hispanic/Latino; 3 Asian, non-Hispanic/Latino; 8 Hispanic/Latino; 6 Two or more races, non-Hispanic/Latino), 18 international. Average age 26. 137 applicants, 64% accepted, 47 enrolled. In 2010, 67 master's awarded. Terminal master's awarded for partial completion of doctoral program. *Degree requirements:* For master's, thesis or alternative, 1 summer abroad; for doctorate, comprehensive exam, thesis/dissertation. *Entrance requirements:* For master's, portfolio, minimum GPA of 3.0; for doctorate, GRE, portfolio. Additional exam requirements/recommendations for international students: Required—TOEFL. *Application deadline:* For fall admission, 3/1 priority date for domestic and international students; for spring admission, 11/1 priority date for domestic and international students. Applications are processed on a rolling basis. Application fee: $55 ($65 for international students). Electronic applications accepted. *Expenses:* Tuition, state resident: full-time $7092; part-time $295.50 per credit hour. Tuition, nonresident: full-time $16,590; part-time $691.25 per credit hour. Required fees: $858; $71.49 per credit hour. Tuition and fees vary according to course load, campus/location and program. *Financial support:* Fellowships, research assistantships with partial tuition reimbursements, teaching assistantships with full and partial tuition reimbursements, scholarships/grants, health care benefits, and unspecified assistantships available. Financial award application deadline: 2/1; financial award applicants required to submit FAFSA. *Faculty research:* Design build, sustainability, emergent technology, healthy places, urban design. *Unit head:* Prof. Nils Gore, Interim Chair, 785-864-2700, Fax: 785-864-5185, E-mail: archku@ku.edu. *Application contact:* Gera Elliott, Admissions Coordinator, 785-864-3167, Fax: 785-864-5185, E-mail: archku@ku.edu.

University of Kentucky, Graduate School, College of Design, School of Architecture, Lexington, KY 40506-0032. Offers M Arch. *Degree requirements:* For master's, comprehensive exam. *Entrance requirements:* For master's, GRE General Test, minimum undergraduate GPA of 2.75. Additional exam requirements/recommendations for international students: Required—TOEFL (minimum score 550 paper-based; 213 computer-based). Electronic applications accepted.

The University of Manchester, School of Environment and Development, Manchester, United Kingdom. Offers architecture (M Phil, PhD); development policy and management (M Phil, PhD); human geography (M Phil, PhD); physical geography (M Phil, PhD); planning and landscape (M Phil, PhD).

University of Manitoba, Faculty of Graduate Studies, Faculty of Architecture, Department of Architecture, Winnipeg, MB R3T 2N2, Canada. Offers M Arch. *Degree requirements:* For master's, thesis or alternative.

University of Maryland, College Park, Academic Affairs, School of Architecture, Planning and Preservation, Program in Architecture, College Park, MD 20742. Offers M Arch, M Arch/MCP. Part-time and evening/weekend programs available. *Students:* 86 full-time (49 women); includes 20 minority (2 Black or African American, non-Hispanic/Latino; 7 Asian, non-Hispanic/Latino; 8 Hispanic/Latino; 3 Two or more races, non-Hispanic/Latino), 6 international. 267 applicants, 23% accepted, 22 enrolled. In 2010, 12 master's awarded. *Entrance requirements:* For master's, GRE General Test, portfolio, minimum GPA of 3.0, letters of recommendation. Additional exam requirements/recommendations for international students: Required—TOEFL. *Application deadline:* For fall admission, 12/15 for domestic and international students. Applications are processed on a rolling basis. Application fee: $75. Electronic applications accepted. *Expenses:* Tuition, state resident: part-time $471 per credit hour. Tuition, nonresident: part-time $1016 per credit hour. Required fees: $337 per term. *Financial support:* In 2010–11, 50 teaching assistantships (averaging $15,253 per year) were awarded; fellowships, research assistantships, career-related internships or fieldwork, Federal Work-Study, and scholarships/grants also available. Support available to part-time students. Financial award applicants required to submit FAFSA. *Faculty research:* Design, history, theory. *Unit head:* Madlen Simon, Director, 301-405-8677, Fax: 301-314-9583, E-mail: mgsimon@umd.edu. *Application contact:* Dr. Charles A. Caramello, Dean of Graduate School, 301-405-0358, Fax: 301-314-9305.

University of Massachusetts Amherst, Graduate School, College of Humanities and Fine Arts, Department of Art, Programs in Architecture and Design, Amherst, MA 01003. Offers architecture and design (M Arch); historic preservation (MS); interior design (MS). Part-time programs available. *Students:* 55 full-time (25 women), 5 part-time (4 women); includes 4 minority (1 Asian, non-Hispanic/Latino; 2 Hispanic/Latino; 1 Native Hawaiian or other Pacific Islander, non-Hispanic/Latino), 7 international. Average age 32. 131 applicants, 65% accepted, 33 enrolled. In 2010, 13 master's awarded. *Degree requirements:* For master's, thesis or alternative, project. *Entrance requirements:* For master's, GRE General Test (M Arch only), portfolio (MS only). Additional exam requirements/recommendations for international students: Required—TOEFL (minimum score 550 paper-based; 213 computer-based; 80 iBT), IELTS (minimum score 6.5). *Application deadline:* For fall admission, 2/1 for domestic and international students. Applications are processed on a rolling basis. Application fee: $50 ($65 for international students). Electronic applications accepted. *Expenses:* Tuition, state resident: full-time $2640. Required fees: $8282. One-time fee: $357 full-time. *Financial support:* Fellowships, research assistantships, teaching assistantships, career-related internships or fieldwork, Federal Work-Study, scholarships/grants, traineeships, health care benefits, tuition waivers (full), and unspecified assistantships available. Support available to part-time students. Financial award application deadline: 2/1; financial award applicants required to submit FAFSA. *Unit head:* Dr. Max Page, Graduate Program Director, 413-545-0943, Fax: 413-545-3929. *Application contact:* Jean M. Ames, Supervisor of Admissions, 413-545-0722, Fax: 413-577-0100, E-mail: gradadm@grad.umass.edu.

University of Memphis, Graduate School, College of Communication and Fine Arts, Department of Architecture, Memphis, TN 38152. Offers M Arch. *Faculty:* 4 full-time (1 woman), 1 part-time/adjunct (0 women). *Students:* 27 full-time (12 women), 16 part-time (11 women); includes 11 minority (all Black or African American, non-Hispanic/Latino), 5 international. Average age 29. 42 applicants, 62% accepted, 13 enrolled. *Financial support:* In 2010–11, 7 students received support; research assistantships with full tuition reimbursements available, teaching assistantships with full tuition reimbursements available, Federal Work-Study, scholarships/grants, and unspecified assistantships available. Financial award application deadline: 2/15; financial award applicants required to submit FAFSA. *Unit head:* Dr. Michael D. Hagge, Chair, 901-678-2724, Fax: 901-678-1755, E-mail: mdhagge@memphis.edu. *Application contact:* Sherry Brian, Coordinator of Graduate Studies, 901-678-3302, Fax: 901-678-1755.

University of Miami, Graduate School, School of Architecture, Coral Gables, FL 33124. Offers architecture (M Arch); suburb and town design (M Arch). *Entrance requirements:* For master's, GRE General Test, minimum GPA of 3.0, portfolio. Additional exam requirements/recommendations for international students: Required—TOEFL. Electronic applications accepted. *Faculty research:* Housing, town planning, retrofit.

University of Michigan, Taubman College of Architecture and Urban Planning, Doctoral Studies in Architecture, Ann Arbor, MI 48109. Offers PhD. Offered through the Horace H. Rackham School of Graduate Studies. Terminal master's awarded for partial completion of doctoral program. *Degree requirements:* For doctorate, comprehensive exam, thesis/dissertation, oral defense of dissertation, preliminary exam, practicum. *Entrance requirements:* For doctorate, GRE General Test. Additional exam requirements/recommendations for international students: Required—TOEFL (minimum score 560 paper-based; 220 computer-based; 100 iBT). Electronic applications accepted. *Expenses:* Contact institution. *Faculty research:* Environment and behavior, environmental technology, history-theory, design process and methods.

University of Michigan, Taubman College of Architecture and Urban Planning, Master of Architecture Program, Ann Arbor, MI 48109-2069. Offers M Arch, M Sc, M Arch/M Eng, M Arch/MSE, M Arch/MUP, MBA/M Arch. *Entrance requirements:* For master's, GRE, 3 recommendations, resume, portfolio. Additional exam requirements/recommendations for international students: Required—TOEFL (minimum score 600 paper-based; 250 computer-based; 100 iBT). Electronic applications accepted. *Expenses:* Contact institution.

University of Minnesota, Twin Cities Campus, Graduate School, College of Design, School of Architecture, Minneapolis, MN 55455-0213. Offers architecture (M Arch); sustainable design (MS). First professional and post-professional tracks available in M Arch program. *Degree requirements:* For master's, thesis (for some programs). *Entrance requirements:* For master's, GRE General Test, suggested GPA of 3.0, portfolio. Additional exam requirements/recommendations for international students: Required—TOEFL (minimum score 550 paper-based; 213 computer-based; 79 iBT). *Expenses:* Contact institution. *Faculty research:* History, daylighting, computer-aided design, sustainable design, structures.

University of Missouri, Graduate School, College of Human Environmental Science, Department of Architectural Studies, Columbia, MO 65211. Offers design with digital media (MA, MS); environmental design (MS). *Entrance requirements:* For master's, GRE General Test, minimum GPA of 3.0. Additional exam requirements/recommendations for international students: Required—TOEFL (minimum score 500 paper-based; 173 computer-based; 61 iBT).

University of Nebraska–Lincoln, Graduate College, College of Architecture, Department of Architecture, Graduate Program in Architecture, Lincoln, NE 68588. Offers MS, PhD. *Degree requirements:* For master's, comprehensive exam, thesis. *Entrance requirements:* For master's, GRE General Test. Additional exam requirements/recommendations for international students: Required—TOEFL (minimum score 550 paper-based; 213 computer-based). Electronic applications accepted. *Faculty research:* Housing, environmental design, architectural history, sustainable design, rural architecture.

University of Nebraska–Lincoln, Graduate College, College of Architecture, Department of Architecture, Professional Program in Architecture, Lincoln, NE 68588. Offers M Arch, M Arch/MBA, M Arch/MCRP. *Entrance requirements:* For master's, GRE General Test. Additional exam requirements/recommendations for international students: Required—TOEFL. *Faculty research:* Housing, environmental design, architectural history, sustainable design, rural architecture.

University of Nevada, Las Vegas, Graduate College, College of Fine Arts, School of Architecture, Las Vegas, NV 89154. Offers M Arch. Part-time programs available. *Faculty:* 10 full-time (1 woman), 3 part-time/adjunct (0 women). *Students:* 37 full-time (15 women), 10

Architecture

University of Nevada, Las Vegas (continued)
part-time (3 women); includes 17 minority (1 Black or African American, non-Hispanic/Latino; 3 Asian, non-Hispanic/Latino; 4 Hispanic/Latino; 9 Two or more races, non-Hispanic/Latino), 2 international. Average age 32. 43 applicants, 86% accepted, 17 enrolled. In 2010, 12 master's awarded. *Degree requirements:* For master's, thesis (for some programs), professional project. *Entrance requirements:* For master's, GRE General Test (minimum score 410 verbal, 430 quantitative). Additional exam requirements/recommendations for international students: Required—TOEFL (minimum score 550 paper-based; 213 computer-based; 80 iBT), IELTS (minimum score 7). *Application deadline:* For fall admission, 7/1 priority date for domestic and international students. Applications are processed on a rolling basis. Application fee: $60 ($95 for international students). Electronic applications accepted. *Expenses:* Tuition, area resident: Part-time $239.50 per credit. Tuition, state resident: part-time $239.50 per credit. Tuition, nonresident: part-time $503 per credit. Required fees: $108 per semester. Tuition and fees vary according to course load, program and reciprocity agreements. *Financial support:* In 2010–11, 10 students received support, including 6 research assistantships with partial tuition reimbursements available (averaging $12,500 per year), 4 teaching assistantships with partial tuition reimbursements available (averaging $12,500 per year); institutionally sponsored loans, scholarships/grants, health care benefits, and unspecified assistantships also available. Financial award application deadline: 3/1. *Faculty research:* Sustainability, hospitality/entertainment design, educational design, urban studies/design. Total annual research expenditures: $11,424. *Unit head:* Dr. David Baird, Director/Professor, 702-895-0939, Fax: 702-895-1119, E-mail: david.baird@unlv.edu. *Application contact:* Graduate College Admissions Evaluator, 702-895-3320, Fax: 702-895-4180, E-mail: gradcollege@unlv.edu.

University of New Mexico, Graduate School, School of Architecture and Planning, Program in Architecture, Albuquerque, NM 87131-2039. Offers M Arch. *Students:* 83 full-time (25 women), 10 part-time (3 women); includes 45 minority (10 American Indian or Alaska Native, non-Hispanic/Latino; 2 Asian, non-Hispanic/Latino; 33 Hispanic/Latino), 2 international. Average age 30. 133 applicants, 26% accepted, 30 enrolled. In 2010, 28 master's awarded. *Degree requirements:* For master's, thesis (for some programs), review. *Entrance requirements:* For master's, experience in field. Additional exam requirements/recommendations for international students: Required—TOEFL (minimum score 550 paper-based; 213 computer-based; 79 iBT). *Application deadline:* For fall admission, 2/1 priority date for domestic students. Application fee: $50. Electronic applications accepted. *Expenses:* Tuition, state resident: full-time $5991; part-time $251 per credit hour. Tuition, nonresident: full-time $14,405; part-time $800.20 per credit hour. Tuition and fees vary according to course level, course load, program and reciprocity agreements. *Financial support:* In 2010–11, 77 students received support, including 1 research assistantship with partial tuition reimbursement available (averaging $7,500 per year); fellowships, scholarships/grants, health care benefits, and unspecified assistantships also available. Financial award application deadline: 3/1; financial award applicants required to submit FAFSA. *Faculty research:* Professional practice, design theory, sustainable environments, architecture and children, environment and behavior. *Unit head:* Geraldine Forbes Isais, Director, 505-277-3303, Fax: 505-277-0076, E-mail: gforbes@unm.edu. *Application contact:* Elizabeth Rowe, Senior Academic Advisor, 505-277-1303, Fax: 505-277-0076, E-mail: mitziv@unm.edu.

The University of North Carolina at Charlotte, Graduate School, College of Arts and Architecture, Charlotte, NC 28223-0001. Offers architecture (M Arch); urban design (MUD). *Faculty:* 34 full-time (12 women), 3 part-time/adjunct (0 women). *Students:* 76 full-time (36 women), 6 part-time (5 women); includes 8 minority (5 Black or African American, non-Hispanic/Latino; 2 Asian, non-Hispanic/Latino; 1 Hispanic/Latino), 1 international. Average age 27. 72 applicants, 67% accepted, 32 enrolled. In 2010, 29 master's awarded. *Degree requirements:* For master's, project or thesis. *Entrance requirements:* For master's, GRE General Test or GMAT, portfolio, resume. Additional exam requirements/recommendations for international students: Required—TOEFL (minimum score 557 paper-based; 220 computer-based; 83 iBT). *Application deadline:* For fall admission, 2/15 for domestic students, 1/31 for international students. Application fee: $55. Electronic applications accepted. *Expenses:* Tuition, state resident: full-time $3464. Tuition, nonresident: full-time $14,297. Required fees: $2094. Tuition and fees vary according to course load. *Financial support:* In 2010–11, 12 students received support, including 5 research assistantships (averaging $9,032 per year), 7 teaching assistantships (averaging $8,451 per year); career-related internships or fieldwork, institutionally sponsored loans, scholarships/grants, and unspecified assistantships also available. Support available to part-time students. Financial award application deadline: 4/1; financial award applicants required to submit FAFSA. *Faculty research:* Daylighting and energy control, urban design, history and theory, construction techniques. Total annual research expenditures: $131,220. *Unit head:* Kenneth A. Lambla, Dean, 704-687-4024, Fax: 704-687-3353, E-mail: kalambla@uncc.edu. *Application contact:* Kathy B. Giddings, Director of Graduate Admissions, 704-687-5503, Fax: 704-687-3279, E-mail: gradadm@uncc.edu.

The University of North Carolina at Greensboro, Graduate School, School of Human Environmental Sciences, Department of Interior Architecture, Greensboro, NC 27412-5001. Offers historic preservation (Certificate); interior architecture (MS); museum studies (Certificate). *Degree requirements:* For master's, thesis. *Entrance requirements:* For master's, GRE General Test or MAT, bachelor's degree in interior design, interview, portfolio. Additional exam requirements/recommendations for international students: Required—TOEFL. Electronic applications accepted.

University of Notre Dame, Graduate School, School of Architecture, Notre Dame, IN 46556. Offers architectural design and urbanism (M ADU); architecture (M Arch). *Degree requirements:* For master's, thesis or alternative. *Entrance requirements:* For master's, GRE General Test, portfolio. Additional exam requirements/recommendations for international students: Required—TOEFL (minimum score 600 paper-based; 250 computer-based; 80 iBT). Electronic applications accepted. *Faculty research:* Architectural theory, urban design, classical and traditional architecture and urbanism.

University of Oklahoma, College of Architecture, Division of Architecture, Norman, OK 73019-0390. Offers M Arch, MS. *Faculty:* 26 full-time (7 women). *Students:* 26 full-time (7 women), 10 part-time (5 women); includes 6 minority (1 American Indian or Alaska Native, non-Hispanic/Latino; 2 Asian, non-Hispanic/Latino; 1 Native Hawaiian or other Pacific Islander, non-Hispanic/Latino; 2 Two or more races, non-Hispanic/Latino), 8 international. Average age 31. 26 applicants, 69% accepted, 12 enrolled. In 2010, 11 master's awarded. Terminal master's awarded for partial completion of doctoral program. *Degree requirements:* For master's, thesis or alternative, portfolio, project. *Entrance requirements:* For master's, GRE General Test, portfolio. Additional exam requirements/recommendations for international students: Required—TOEFL (minimum score 550 paper-based; 213 computer-based; 79 iBT). *Application deadline:* For fall admission, 4/1 for domestic and international students; for spring admission, 11/1 for domestic students, 9/1 for international students. Applications are processed on a rolling basis. Application fee: $40 ($90 for international students). Electronic applications accepted. *Expenses:* Tuition, state resident: full-time $3893; part-time $162.20 per credit hour. Tuition, nonresident: full-time $14,167; part-time $590.30 per credit hour. Required fees: $2523; $94.60 per credit hour. Tuition and fees vary according to course load and degree level. *Financial support:* In 2010–11, 23 students received support, including 4 teaching assistantships with partial tuition reimbursements available (averaging $9,586 per year); unspecified assistantships also available. Financial award applicants required to submit FAFSA. *Faculty research:* Sustainability, energy research, energy analysis, alternative materials. Total annual research expenditures: $488,708. *Unit head:* Joel K. Dietrich, Interim Director, 405-325-6792, Fax: 405-325-7558, E-mail: dietrich@ou.edu. *Application contact:* Lee Fithian, Associate Professor, 405-325-2444, Fax: 405-325-7558, E-mail: leefithian@ou.edu.

University of Oregon, Graduate School, School of Architecture and Allied Arts, Department of Architecture, Eugene, OR 97403. Offers architecture (M Arch); interior architecture (MI Arch). *Accreditation:* CIDA. *Degree requirements:* For master's, thesis (for some programs). *Entrance requirements:* For master's, GRE General Test. Additional exam requirements/recommendations for international students: Required—TOEFL. *Faculty research:* Innovation in housing design and design production, climate responsive design, passive heating and cooling, computer software development for design applications, vernacular architecture.

University of Pennsylvania, School of Design, Graduate Group in Architecture, Philadelphia, PA 19104. Offers architecture (PhD); real estate design and development (PhD); urban design (PhD). Part-time programs available. *Faculty:* 15 full-time (5 women), 13 part-time/adjunct (3 women). *Students:* 277 full-time (120 women), 9 part-time (3 women); includes 4 Black or African American, non-Hispanic/Latino; 2 American Indian or Alaska Native, non-Hispanic/Latino; 31 Asian, non-Hispanic/Latino; 11 Hispanic/Latino, 95 international. 963 applicants, 34% accepted, 112 enrolled. In 2010, 4 doctorates awarded. *Degree requirements:* For doctorate, 2 foreign languages, comprehensive exam, thesis/dissertation, qualifying exam, final exam. *Entrance requirements:* For doctorate, GRE General Test, B Arch, M Arch, portfolio, writing sample. Additional exam requirements/recommendations for international students: Required—TOEFL. *Application deadline:* For fall admission, 1/2 priority date for domestic students. Application fee: $70. *Expenses:* Tuition: Full-time $25,660; part-time $4758 per course. Required fees: $2152; $270 per course. Tuition and fees vary according to course load, degree level and program. *Financial support:* Fellowships, research assistantships, teaching assistantships, institutionally sponsored loans, scholarships/grants, traineeships, health care benefits, and unspecified assistantships available. *Faculty research:* Theory, history, technology, representation, visualization, landscape, urban design, historic preservation.

University of Pennsylvania, School of Design, Master of Architecture Program, Philadelphia, PA 19104. Offers architecture (M Arch); real estate design and development (Certificate); urban design (Certificate). *Degree requirements:* For master's, thesis (for some programs). *Entrance requirements:* For master's and Certificate, GRE, portfolio. Additional exam requirements/recommendations for international students: Required—TOEFL. *Expenses:* Tuition: Full-time $25,660; part-time $4758 per course. Required fees: $2152; $270 per course. Tuition and fees vary according to course load, degree level and program. *Faculty research:* Computer modeling, metropolitan and regional urbanism, contemporary architectural theory structure and technology.

University of Puerto Rico, Río Piedras, School of Architecture, San Juan, PR 00931-3300. Offers M Arch. Part-time programs available. *Degree requirements:* For master's, comprehensive exam, thesis, design project. *Entrance requirements:* For master's, PAEG or GRE, bachelor's degree in architecture, interview, minimum GPA of 3.0, portfolio, 2 letters of recommendation.

University of Southern California, Graduate School, School of Architecture, Los Angeles, CA 90089. Offers M Arch, MBS, MHP, MLA, PhD, M Arch/M Pl, MLA/M Pl. *Faculty:* 12 full-time (2 women), 31 part-time/adjunct (9 women). *Students:* 203 full-time (119 women), 20 part-time (6 women); includes 45 minority (5 Black or African American, non-Hispanic/Latino; 1 American Indian or Alaska Native, non-Hispanic/Latino; 22 Asian, non-Hispanic/Latino; 15 Hispanic/Latino; 1 Native Hawaiian or other Pacific Islander, non-Hispanic/Latino; 1 Two or more races, non-Hispanic/Latino), 105 international. 424 applicants, 56% accepted, 88 enrolled. In 2010, 40 master's awarded. Terminal master's awarded for partial completion of doctoral program. *Degree requirements:* For master's, thesis (for some programs); for doctorate, thesis/dissertation. *Entrance requirements:* For master's and doctorate, GRE. Additional exam requirements/recommendations for international students: Required—TOEFL (minimum score 100 iBT). *Application deadline:* For fall admission, 1/15 priority date for domestic and international students. Application fee: $85. Electronic applications accepted. *Expenses:* Tuition: Full-time $31,240; part-time $1420 per unit. Required fees: $600. One-time fee: $35 full-time. Full-time tuition and fees vary according to degree level and program. *Financial support:* In 2010–11, 95 students received support. Federal Work-Study and scholarships/grants available. Financial award application deadline: 5/1; financial award applicants required to submit CSS PROFILE or FAFSA. *Faculty research:* Urban housing; advanced digital simulation, computation, and representation; building skins; parametric design; advanced seismic research. *Unit head:* Dean Qingyun Ma, Dean, 213-740-2420, Fax: 213-740-8884, E-mail: archdean@usc.edu. *Application contact:* Laarni Cutidioc, Graduate Admissions Coordinator, 213-821-2168, Fax: 213-740-8884, E-mail: archgrad@usc.edu.

University of South Florida, Graduate School, College of The Arts, School of Architecture and Community Design, Tampa, FL 33620-9951. Offers M Arch. *Faculty:* 9 full-time (0 women), 4 part-time/adjunct (1 woman). *Students:* 87 full-time (37 women), 42 part-time (16 women); includes 4 Black or African American, non-Hispanic/Latino; 2 American Indian or Alaska Native, non-Hispanic/Latino; 8 Asian, non-Hispanic/Latino; 30 Hispanic/Latino, 4 international. Average age 28. 88 applicants, 34% accepted, 23 enrolled. In 2010, 39 master's awarded. *Degree requirements:* For master's, comprehensive exam, thesis. *Entrance requirements:* For master's, GRE General Test, minimum GPA of 3.0 in last 60 hours of coursework. Additional exam requirements/recommendations for international students: Required—TOEFL (minimum score 550 paper-based; 213 computer-based). *Application deadline:* For fall admission, 2/1 priority date for domestic students, 1/2 for international students. Applications are processed on a rolling basis. Application fee: $30. Electronic applications accepted. *Financial support:* In 2010–11, 20 students received support, including 4 research assistantships with tuition reimbursements available (averaging $9,360 per year), 2 teaching assistantships with tuition reimbursements available (averaging $9,750 per year); Federal Work-Study, scholarships/grants, and unspecified assistantships also available. *Faculty research:* Community design, sustainability, portable classrooms. Total annual research expenditures: $49,327. *Unit head:* Prof. Robert MacLeod, School Director, 813-974-6015, Fax: 813-974-2557, E-mail: rmacleod@arch.usf.edu. *Application contact:* Mildred Abreu, Academic Advisor, 813-974-1216, Fax: 813-974-2557, E-mail: abreu@arch.usf.edu.

The University of Tennessee, Graduate School, College of Architecture and Design, Program in Architecture, Knoxville, TN 37996. Offers architecture (professional) (M Arch); architecture (research) (M Arch). *Degree requirements:* For master's, thesis. *Entrance requirements:* For master's, GRE General Test, minimum GPA of 3.0, 3 letters of recommendation, samples of portfolio work (highly recommended for professional track). Additional exam requirements/recommendations for international students: Required—TOEFL (minimum score 550 paper-based). *Expenses:* Tuition, state resident: full-time $7440; part-time $414 per credit hour. Tuition, nonresident: full-time $22,478; part-time $1250 per credit hour. Required fees: $922; $43 per credit hour. Tuition and fees vary according to program.

The University of Texas at Arlington, Graduate School, School of Architecture, Program in Architecture, Arlington, TX 76019. Offers M Arch, M Arch/MCRP. *Faculty:* 16 full-time (2 women), 1 part-time/adjunct (0 women). *Students:* 148 full-time (56 women), 35 part-time (12 women); includes 65 minority (6 Black or African American, non-Hispanic/Latino; 22 Asian, non-Hispanic/Latino; 32 Hispanic/Latino; 5 Two or more races, non-Hispanic/Latino), 18 international. 141 applicants, 60% accepted, 57 enrolled. In 2010, 49 master's awarded. *Degree requirements:* For master's, thesis. *Entrance requirements:* For master's, GRE General Test, minimum GPA of 3.0, portfolio (for those with previous design degrees). Additional exam requirements/recommendations for international students: Required—TOEFL (minimum score 575 paper-based; 233 computer-based; 91 iBT). *Application deadline:* For fall admission, 6/1 for domestic students, 4/1 for international students; for spring admission, 10/15 for domestic students, 9/15 for international students. Applications are processed on a rolling basis. Application fee: $35 ($60 for international students). *Expenses:* Tuition, state resident: full-time $7500. Tuition, nonresident: full-time $13,080. International tuition: $13,250 full-time. *Financial support:* In 2010–11, 19 students received support, including 12 research assistantships with partial tuition reimbursements available (averaging $4,824 per year), 16 teaching assistantships with full tuition reimbursements available (averaging $4,824 per year); career-related internships or fieldwork, scholarships/grants, and unspecified assistantships also available. Financial award application deadline: 6/1; financial award applicants required to submit FAFSA. *Faculty research:* Regional landscapes/native materials, urban densification, urban design, sustainable design principles. *Unit head:* Dr. Pat Taylor, Program Director, 817-272-2801, Fax: 817-272-5098,

E-mail: pdt@uta.edu. *Application contact:* Ana Maria Peredo-Manor, Administrative Assistant, 817-272-2801, Fax: 817-272-5098, E-mail: ampmanor@uta.edu.

The University of Texas at Austin, Graduate School, School of Architecture, Austin, TX 78712-1111. Offers architecture (M Arch); community and regional planning (MSCRP, PhD); historic preservation (MS); history of architecture (MA, PhD); landscape architecture (MLA); urban design (MSUD); JD/MSCRP; MSCRP/MA; MSCRP/PhD. *Degree requirements:* For doctorate, thesis/dissertation. *Entrance requirements:* For master's and doctorate, GRE General Test. Additional exam requirements/recommendations for international students: Required—TOEFL (minimum score 550 paper-based; 213 computer-based). Electronic applications accepted.

The University of Texas at San Antonio, College of Architecture, San Antonio, TX 78249-0617. Offers M Arch, MS Arch. *Faculty:* 19 full-time (6 women). *Students:* 89 full-time (28 women), 21 part-time (9 women); includes 40 minority (2 Black or African American, non-Hispanic/Latino; 2 Asian, non-Hispanic/Latino; 35 Hispanic/Latino; 1 Two or more races, non-Hispanic/Latino), 11 international. Average age 29. 92 applicants, 54% accepted, 31 enrolled. In 2010, 28 master's awarded. *Degree requirements:* For master's, comprehensive exam (for some programs), thesis (for some programs). *Entrance requirements:* For master's, GRE General Test, minimum GPA of 3.0 in last 60 hours and in all architecture courses. Additional exam requirements/recommendations for international students: Required—TOEFL (minimum score 500 paper-based; 173 computer-based; 61 iBT), IELTS (minimum score 5). *Application deadline:* For fall admission, 7/1 for domestic students, 4/1 for international students; for spring admission, 11/1 for domestic students, 9/1 for international students. Applications are processed on a rolling basis. Application fee: $45 ($80 for international students). Electronic applications accepted. *Expenses:* Tuition, state resident: full-time $4172; part-time $231.75 per credit hour. Tuition, nonresident: full-time $15,332; part-time $851.75 per credit hour. *Financial support:* In 2010–11, 22 students received support, including 119 research assistantships (averaging $7,416 per year); career-related internships or fieldwork, scholarships/grants, and unspecified assistantships also available. Total annual research expenditures: $60,720. *Unit head:* Dr. John D. Murphy, Dean, 210-458-3090, Fax: 210-458-3016, E-mail: john.murphy@utsa.edu. *Application contact:* Veronica Ramirez, Assistant Dean of the Graduate School, 210-458-4330, Fax: 210-458-4332, E-mail: graduatestudies@utsa.edu.

University of Toronto, School of Graduate Studies, Social Sciences Division, Faculty of Architecture, Landscape and Design, Toronto, ON M5S 1A1, Canada. Offers M Arch, MLA, MUD. *Accreditation:* ASLA. *Entrance requirements:* For master's, minimum B average; 3 letters of reference; resume; 3 writing samples; 5 samples of design work, drawing, or work in a related field. Additional exam requirements/recommendations for international students: Required—TOEFL (minimum score 580 paper-based; 237 computer-based), TWE (minimum score 5), Michigan English Language Assessment Battery (minimum score: 85), IELTS (minimum score: 7) or COPE (minimum score: 4). *Expenses:* Contact institution.

University of Utah, Graduate School, College of Architecture and Planning, School of Architecture, Salt Lake City, UT 84112. Offers architectural studies (MS); architecture (M Arch); M Arch/MBA. Part-time programs available. *Faculty:* 16 full-time (6 women), 7 part-time/adjunct (1 woman). *Students:* 99 full-time (36 women), 5 part-time (2 women); includes 10 minority (3 Asian, non-Hispanic/Latino; 5 Hispanic/Latino; 1 Native Hawaiian or other Pacific Islander, non-Hispanic/Latino; 1 Two or more races, non-Hispanic/Latino), 5 international. Average age 27. 66 applicants, 70% accepted, 30 enrolled. In 2010, 45 master's awarded. *Degree requirements:* For master's, thesis (for some programs), comprehensive project. *Entrance requirements:* For master's, minimum undergraduate GPA of 3.0; portfolio. Additional exam requirements/recommendations for international students: Required—TOEFL (minimum score 550 paper-based; 173 computer-based). *Application deadline:* For fall admission, 1/1 for domestic and international students. Application fee: $55 ($65 for international students). Electronic applications accepted. *Expenses:* Contact institution. *Financial support:* In 2010–11, 36 students received support, including 15 fellowships with partial tuition reimbursements available (averaging $2,875 per year), 1 research assistantship with partial tuition reimbursement available (averaging $2,875 per year), 22 teaching assistantships with partial tuition reimbursements available (averaging $2,875 per year); career-related internships or fieldwork, Federal Work-Study, and scholarships/grants also available. Financial award application deadline: 3/1; financial award applicants required to submit FAFSA. *Faculty research:* History, design, acoustics, photography, structures, architecture of American West, architectural communication and representation, impact of technology, design build. Total annual research expenditures: $87,880. *Unit head:* Prescott Muir, Director, 801-585-5354. *Application contact:* Mayra Focht, Administrative Assistant/Advisor, 801-585-5354, Fax: 801-581-8217, E-mail: focht@arch.utah.edu.

University of Washington, Graduate School, College of Built Environments, Department of Architecture, Seattle, WA 98195. Offers architecture (M Arch, MS); built environment (PhD); design computing (Certificate); design firm leadership and management (Certificate); historic preservation (Certificate); lighting (Certificate); urban design (Certificate). *Degree requirements:* For master's, thesis. *Entrance requirements:* For master's, GRE General Test, minimum GPA of 3.0, portfolio, 3 letters of recommendation. Additional exam requirements/recommendations for international students: Required—TOEFL. *Faculty research:* Lighting, materials, computing theory, media, culture, environment.

University of Waterloo, Graduate Studies, Faculty of Engineering, School of Architecture, Waterloo, ON N2L 3G1, Canada. Offers M Arch. Part-time programs available. *Degree requirements:* For master's, thesis. *Entrance requirements:* For master's, bachelor's degree in pre-professional architecture. Electronic applications accepted.

University of Wisconsin–Milwaukee, Graduate School, School of Architecture and Urban Planning, Department of Architecture, Milwaukee, WI 53201-0413. Offers architecture (PhD); preservation studies (Certificate); M Arch/MUP. *Faculty:* 26 full-time (4 women). *Students:* 194 full-time (64 women), 13 part-time (5 women); includes 3 Black or African American, non-Hispanic/Latino; 5 Asian, non-Hispanic/Latino; 5 Hispanic/Latino, 16 international. Average age 28. 193 applicants, 67% accepted, 61 enrolled. In 2010, 15 master's awarded. *Degree requirements:* For master's, comprehensive exam, thesis; for doctorate, comprehensive exam, thesis/dissertation. *Entrance requirements:* For master's, GRE General Test, portfolio. Additional exam requirements/recommendations for international students: Required—TOEFL (minimum score 600 paper-based; 250 computer-based; 100 iBT), IELTS (minimum score 7). *Application deadline:* For fall admission, 1/1 priority date for domestic students; for spring admission, 9/1 for domestic students. Applications are processed on a rolling basis. Application fee: $56 ($96 for international students). Electronic applications accepted. *Financial support:* In 2010–11, 3 fellowships, 20 teaching assistantships were awarded; career-related internships or fieldwork, health care benefits, unspecified assistantships, and project assistantships also available. Support available to part-time students. Financial award application deadline: 4/15; financial award applicants required to submit FAFSA. *Unit head:* Joan Simuncak, Representative, 414-229-4015, Fax: 414-229-6976, E-mail: joanarch@uwm.edu. *Application contact:* Josef Stagg, General Information Contact, 414-229-4032, Fax: 414-229-6967, E-mail: jstagg@uwm.edu.

Virginia Polytechnic Institute and State University, Graduate School, College of Architecture and Urban Studies, School of Architecture and Design, Blacksburg, VA 24061. Offers architecture (M Arch, MS); architecture and design research (PhD). *Faculty:* 57 full-time (18 women), 2 part-time/adjunct (1 woman). *Students:* 184 full-time (85 women), 27 part-time (13 women); includes 12 Black or African American, non-Hispanic/Latino; 12 Asian, non-Hispanic/Latino; 9 Hispanic/Latino, 50 international. Average age 28. 488 applicants, 34% accepted, 75 enrolled. In 2010, 48 master's awarded. *Degree requirements:* For master's, comprehensive exam (for some programs), thesis (for some programs); for doctorate, comprehensive exam (for some programs), thesis/dissertation (for some programs). *Entrance requirements:* For master's and doctorate, GRE. Additional exam requirements/recommendations for international students: Required—TOEFL (minimum score 550 paper-based; 213 computer-based). *Application deadline:* For fall admission, 7/1 for domestic and international students; for spring admission, 12/1 for domestic and international students. Applications are processed on a rolling basis. Application fee: $65. Electronic applications accepted. *Expenses:* Tuition, state resident: full-time $9399; part-time $488 per credit hour. Tuition, nonresident: full-time $17,854; part-time $957.75 per credit hour. Required fees: $1534. Full-time tuition and fees vary according to program. *Financial support:* In 2010–11, 2 fellowships with full tuition reimbursements (averaging $4,875 per year), 11 teaching assistantships with full tuition reimbursements (averaging $15,546 per year) were awarded; career-related internships or fieldwork, Federal Work-Study, scholarships/grants, health care benefits, and unspecified assistantships also available. Financial award application deadline: 1/15. *Faculty research:* Computer applications in design, building technology, architectural design theory, solar/passive energy design, building assembly. Total annual research expenditures: $605,652. *Unit head:* Dr. Steve R. Thompson, UNIT HEAD, 540-231-9931, Fax: 540-231-9938, E-mail: stthomp2@vt.edu. *Application contact:* Dr. Steve R. Thompson, UNIT HEAD, 540-231-9931, Fax: 540-231-9938, E-mail: stthomp2@vt.edu.

Washington State University, Graduate School, College of Engineering and Architecture, School of Architecture and Construction Management, Pullman, WA 99164. Offers architecture (M Arch); architecture design theory (MS). *Faculty:* 19. *Students:* 4 full-time (2 women), 97 part-time (23 women); includes 18 minority (7 Black or African American, non-Hispanic/Latino; 1 American Indian or Alaska Native, non-Hispanic/Latino; 7 Asian, non-Hispanic/Latino; 2 Hispanic/Latino; 1 Native Hawaiian or other Pacific Islander, non-Hispanic/Latino), 6 international. Average age 37. 265 applicants, 15% accepted, 20 enrolled. In 2010, 19 master's awarded. *Degree requirements:* For master's, comprehensive exam (for some programs), thesis, oral exam. *Entrance requirements:* For master's, GRE General Test, minimum GPA of 3.0, 3 letters of recommendation. Additional exam requirements/recommendations for international students: Required—TOEFL, IELTS. *Application deadline:* For fall admission, 1/10 priority date for domestic and international students. Applications are processed on a rolling basis. Application fee: $50. *Expenses:* Tuition, state resident: full-time $8552; part-time $443 per credit. Tuition, nonresident: full-time $21,650; part-time $1083 per credit. Required fees: $846. *Financial support:* In 2010–11, 6 research assistantships with full and partial tuition reimbursements (averaging $18,204 per year), 1 teaching assistantship with full and partial tuition reimbursement (averaging $18,204 per year) were awarded; career-related internships or fieldwork, Federal Work-Study, institutionally sponsored loans, and tuition waivers (partial) also available. Financial award application deadline: 3/1; financial award applicants required to submit FAFSA. *Faculty research:* Cultural, technological, and environmental design. *Unit head:* Dr. Greg Kessler, Director, 509-335-5539, Fax: 509-335-6132, E-mail: gkessler@acm.wsu.edu. *Application contact:* Graduate School Admissions, 800-GRADWSU, Fax: 509-335-1949, E-mail: gradsch@wsu.edu.

Washington State University Spokane, Graduate Programs, Interdisciplinary Design Institute, Spokane, WA 99210. Offers architecture (M Arch, MS); design (Dr DES); interior design (MA); landscape architecture (MS). Part-time programs available. *Faculty:* 7. *Students:* 9 full-time (6 women), 2 part-time (both women); includes 1 Asian, non-Hispanic/Latino, 5 international. Average age 35. In 2010, 18 master's awarded. *Degree requirements:* For master's, comprehensive exam (for some programs), thesis (for some programs); for doctorate, comprehensive exam, thesis/dissertation. *Entrance requirements:* For master's, minimum GPA of 3.0, portfolio of design work, 3 letters of recommendation (M Arch); for doctorate, minimum graduate GPA of 3.5. Additional exam requirements/recommendations for international students: Required—TOEFL (minimum score 550 paper-based; 213 computer-based). *Application deadline:* For fall admission, 1/10 priority date for domestic students, 1/10 for international students; for spring admission, 7/1 priority date for domestic students, 7/1 for international students. Application fee: $50. *Financial support:* In 2010–11, research assistantships with full and partial tuition reimbursements (averaging $14,634 per year), teaching assistantships with full and partial tuition reimbursements (averaging $13,383 per year) were awarded. Financial award application deadline: 2/15. *Faculty research:* Environment-behavior relationships, land use and environmental planning, urban space as interior design, art and architectural aesthetics. Total annual research expenditures: $84,000. *Unit head:* Dr. Nancy H. Blossom, Director, 509-358-7513, E-mail: blossom@wsu.edu. *Application contact:* Graduate School Admissions, 800-GRADWSU, Fax: 509-335-1949, E-mail: gradsch@wsu.edu.

Washington University in St. Louis, Sam Fox School of Design and Visual Arts, Program in Architecture, St. Louis, MO 63130-4899. Offers M Arch, MLA, M Arch/MBA, M Arch/MCM, M Arch/MSW, M Arch/MUD, MLA/M Arch. *Degree requirements:* For master's, final project. *Entrance requirements:* For master's, GRE General Test, portfolio. Additional exam requirements/recommendations for international students: Required—TOEFL (minimum score 550 paper-based; 213 computer-based; 80 iBT), TWE. Electronic applications accepted. *Faculty research:* Urban design development issues.

Wentworth Institute of Technology, Department of Architecture, Boston, MA 02115-5998. Offers M Arch. *Faculty:* 17 full-time (4 women), 22 part-time/adjunct (5 women). *Students:* 78 full-time (26 women); includes 3 Asian, non-Hispanic/Latino; 2 Hispanic/Latino; 1 Two or more races, non-Hispanic/Latino, 6 international. Average age 23. 108 applicants, 78% accepted, 78 enrolled. *Degree requirements:* For master's, thesis project. *Entrance requirements:* For master's, GRE (external candidates), portfolio, references, minimum GPA of 3.0. Additional exam requirements/recommendations for international students: Required—TOEFL (minimum score 525 paper-based; 197 computer-based). *Application deadline:* For fall admission, 1/15 priority date for domestic and international students. Applications are processed on a rolling basis. Application fee: $50. Electronic applications accepted. *Expenses:* Tuition: Full-time $31,200; part-time $1130 per credit hour. Required fees: $1000. *Financial support:* In 2010–11, 78 students received support, including 78 fellowships (averaging $4,475 per year); Federal Work-Study and scholarships/grants also available. Financial award applicants required to submit FAFSA. *Unit head:* Dr. Glenn Wiggins, Dean of the College of Architecture, Design and Construction Management, 617-989-4470, E-mail: wigginsg@wit.edu. *Application contact:* Maureen Dischino, Executive Director of Admissions, 617-989-4009, Fax: 617-989-4010, E-mail: dischinom@wit.edu.

See Display on next page and Close-Up on page 163.

Woodbury University, School of Architecture, Burbank, CA 91504-1099. Offers architecture (M Arch); landscape and urbanism (M Arch); post-professional (M Arch). *Faculty:* 6 full-time (4 women), 19 part-time/adjunct (6 women). *Students:* 54 full-time (16 women); includes 21 minority (2 Black or African American, non-Hispanic/Latino; 8 Asian, non-Hispanic/Latino; 11 Hispanic/Latino), 9 international. Average age 28. 72 applicants, 60% accepted, 36 enrolled. In 2010, 13 master's awarded. *Degree requirements:* For master's, thesis. *Entrance requirements:* For master's, GRE (if undergraduate GPA is below 3.0), 3 letters of recommendation, portfolio, essay, interview, resume, academic transcripts. Additional exam requirements/recommendations for international students: Required—TOEFL (minimum score 550 paper-based; 220 computer-based; 83 iBT), IELTS (minimum score 6.5). *Application deadline:* For fall admission, 3/1 priority date for domestic and international students. Application fee: $60. *Expenses:* Contact institution. *Financial support:* In 2010–11, 52 students received support, including 36 fellowships (averaging $6,000 per year), 10 research assistantships (averaging $2,000 per year), 23 teaching assistantships (averaging $2,000 per year); scholarships/grants also available. *Unit head:* Norman Millar, Dean, 318-767-0888 Ext. 130, Fax: 318-504-9320, E-mail: norman.millar@woodbury.edu. *Application contact:* Glisery Colon, Director, Graduate Admissions, 818-252-5234, Fax: 818-252-5221, E-mail: glisery.colon@woodbury.edu.

Yale University, School of Architecture, New Haven, CT 06520. Offers M Arch, M Env Des, MEM, PhD, M Arch/M Env Des, M Arch/MBA. *Entrance requirements:* For master's, GRE General Test, design portfolio. Additional exam requirements/recommendations for international students: Required—TOEFL. *Expenses:* Contact institution.

Building Science

Arizona State University, Herberger Institute for Design and the Arts, School of Architecture and Landscape Architecture, Tempe, AZ 85287-1605. Offers architecture (M Arch); building design/built environment (MS); design (arts, media, and engineering) (MSD); design (healthcare and healing environments) (MSD); design (industrial design) (MSD); design (interior design) (MSD); design (new product innovation) (MSD); design (visual communication design) (MSD); design, environment and the arts (PhD), including design, environment and the arts (design), design, environment and the arts (healthcare and healing environments), design, environment and the arts (history, theory, and criticism); landscape architecture (MLA); urban design (MUD); MA/MBA. *Accreditation:* NASAD. *Faculty:* 41 full-time (9 women), 6 part-time/adjunct (3 women). *Students:* 252 full-time (111 women), 45 part-time (21 women); includes 61 minority (3 Black or African American, non-Hispanic/Latino; 2 American Indian or Alaska Native, non-Hispanic/Latino; 13 Asian, non-Hispanic/Latino; 41 Hispanic/Latino; 1 Native Hawaiian or other Pacific Islander, non-Hispanic/Latino; 1 Two or more races, non-Hispanic/Latino), 58 international. Average age 29. 420 applicants, 61% accepted, 117 enrolled. In 2010, 60 master's, 8 doctorates awarded. Terminal master's awarded for partial completion of doctoral program. *Degree requirements:* For master's, thesis optional, interactive Program of Study (iPOS) submitted before completing 50 percent of required credit hours; for doctorate, comprehensive exam, thesis/dissertation, interactive Program of Study (iPOS) submitted before completing 50 percent of required credit hours. *Entrance requirements:* For master's, GRE General Test, minimum GPA of 3.0 or equivalent in last 2 years of work leading to bachelor's degree, design/creative works portfolio, 3 references, statement of intent; for doctorate, GRE, master's degree in architecture, graphic design, industrial design, interior design, landscape architecture, or art history or equivalent standing; statement of purpose; 3 letters of recommendation; indication of potential faculty mentor; sample of written work. Additional exam requirements/recommendations for international students: Required—TOEFL (minimum score 600 paper-based; 250 computer-based; 100 iBT). *Application deadline:* For fall admission, 1/15 priority date for domestic and international students. Application fee: $70 ($90 for international students). Electronic applications accepted. *Expenses:* Tuition, state resident: full-time $8510; part-time $608 per credit. Tuition, nonresident: full-time $16,542; part-time $919 per credit. Required fees: $339; $110 per credit. Part-time tuition and fees vary according to course load. *Financial support:* In 2010–11, 9 research assistantships with full and partial tuition reimbursements (averaging $11,913 per year), 76 teaching assistantships with full and partial tuition reimbursements (averaging $6,294 per year) were awarded; fellowships with full and partial tuition reimbursements, scholarships/grants and tuition waivers (full and partial) also available. Financial award application deadline: 3/1; financial award applicants required to submit FAFSA. Total annual research expenditures: $410,956. *Unit head:* Darren Petrucci, Director, 480-965-3536, E-mail: darren.petrucci@asu.edu. *Application contact:* Graduate Admissions, 480-965-6113.

Auburn University, Graduate School, College of Architecture, Design, and Construction, Department of Building Science, Auburn University, AL 36849. Offers building science (MBS); construction management (MBS). *Faculty:* 18 full-time (1 woman), 3 part-time/adjunct (1 woman). *Students:* 23 full-time (6 women), 25 part-time (3 women); includes 1 Black or African American, non-Hispanic/Latino; 2 Hispanic/Latino, 4 international. Average age 27. 83 applicants, 60% accepted, 42 enrolled. In 2010, 7 master's awarded. *Entrance requirements:* For master's, GRE General Test. *Application deadline:* For fall admission, 7/7 for domestic students; for spring admission, 11/24 for domestic students. Applications are processed on a rolling basis. Application fee: $50 ($60 for international students). Electronic applications accepted. *Expenses:* Tuition, state resident: full-time $7002. Tuition, nonresident: full-time $21,898. International tuition: $22,116 full-time. Required fees: $892. Tuition and fees vary according to course load

and program. *Financial support:* Application deadline: 3/15. *Unit head:* Dr. Richard Burt, Head, 334-844-5260. *Application contact:* Dr. George Flowers, Dean of the Graduate School, 334-844-2125.

Auburn University, Graduate School, College of Architecture, Design, and Construction, Program in Design-Build, Auburn University, AL 36849. Offers MDB. *Faculty:* 10 full-time (1 woman). *Students:* 20 full-time (4 women), 1 part-time (0 women), 1 international. Average age 25. 41 applicants, 54% accepted, 21 enrolled. In 2010, 10 master's awarded. Application fee: $50 ($60 for international students). *Expenses:* Tuition, state resident: full-time $7002. Tuition, nonresident: full-time $21,898. International tuition: $22,116 full-time. Required fees: $892. Tuition and fees vary according to course load and program. *Financial support:* Applicants required to submit FAFSA. *Unit head:* Dr. Vini Nathan, Dean, 334-844-4524. *Application contact:* Dr. George Flowers, Dean of the Graduate School, 334-844-2125.

Carnegie Mellon University, College of Fine Arts, School of Architecture, Pittsburgh, PA 15213-3891. Offers architectural engineering construction management (M Sc); architecture (MSA); architecture, engineering, and construction management (PhD); building performance and diagnostics (M Sc, PhD); computational design (M Sc, PhD); sustainable design (M Sc); urban design (M Sc). Terminal master's awarded for partial completion of doctoral program. *Degree requirements:* For doctorate, thesis/dissertation. *Entrance requirements:* For master's and doctorate, GRE General Test. Additional exam requirements/recommendations for international students: Required—TOEFL.

Cornell University, Graduate School, Graduate Fields of Architecture, Art and Planning, Field of Architecture, Ithaca, NY 14853-0001. Offers architectural design (M Arch); architectural science (MS); building technology and environmental science (MS); computer graphics (MS); history of architecture (MA, PhD); history of urban development (MA, PhD); theory and criticism of architecture (M Arch); urban design (M Arch). *Faculty:* 26 full-time (8 women). *Students:* 113 full-time (55 women); includes 2 Black or African American, non-Hispanic/Latino; 15 Asian, non-Hispanic/Latino; 8 Hispanic/Latino, 47 international. Average age 26. 545 applicants, 26% accepted, 65 enrolled. In 2010, 26 master's, 1 doctorate awarded. *Degree requirements:* For master's, one foreign language, thesis (MA, MS); for doctorate, 2 foreign languages, comprehensive exam, thesis/dissertation. *Entrance requirements:* For master's, GRE General Test, 5 year bachelor's degree in architecture, portfolio (M Arch), 3 letters of recommendation; for doctorate, GRE General Test, 3 letters of recommendation. Additional exam requirements/recommendations for international students: Required—TOEFL (minimum score 600 paper-based; 250 computer-based; 77 iBT). *Application deadline:* For fall admission, 1/15 priority date for domestic students. Application fee: $70. Electronic applications accepted. *Expenses:* Tuition: Full-time $29,500. Required fees: $76. Tuition and fees vary according to degree level and program. *Financial support:* In 2010–11, 11 fellowships with full tuition reimbursements, 19 teaching assistantships with full tuition reimbursements were awarded; research assistantships with full tuition reimbursements, institutionally sponsored loans, scholarships/grants, health care benefits, tuition waivers (full and partial), and unspecified assistantships also available. Financial award applicants required to submit FAFSA. *Faculty research:* Architectural design and urban design, theory and criticism of architecture, computer graphics, building technology and environmental science, history of architecture and history of urban-development. *Unit head:* Director of Graduate Studies, 607-255-6701, Fax: 607-255-0291. *Application contact:* Graduate Field Assistant, 607-255-6701, Fax: 607-255-0291, E-mail: cuarch@cornell.edu.

Georgia Institute of Technology, Graduate Studies and Research, College of Architecture, Program in Building Construction, Atlanta, GA 30332-0001. Offers building construction (PhD); integrated facility management (MS); integrated project delivery systems (MS); residential construction development (MS). Part-time and evening/weekend programs available. *Entrance requirements:* For master's and doctorate, GRE or GMAT. Additional exam requirements/recommendations for international students: Required—TOEFL (minimum score 550 paper-based; 213 computer-based). Electronic applications accepted. *Faculty research:* Design-build, mold, indoor air quality, real estate.

Pontificia Universidad Catolica Madre y Maestra, Graduate School, Faculty of Engineering Sciences, Santiago, Dominican Republic. Offers earthquake engineering (ME); logistics management (ME).

Rensselaer Polytechnic Institute, Graduate School, School of Architecture, PhD Program in Architectural Sciences, Troy, NY 12180-3590. Offers acoustics (PhD); built ecologies (PhD); lighting (PhD). *Faculty:* 12 full-time (4 women), 7 part-time/adjunct (3 women). *Students:* 25 full-time (7 women), 4 part-time (1 woman); includes 2 Black or African American, non-Hispanic/Latino; 1 Hispanic/Latino; 1 Two or more races, non-Hispanic/Latino, 9 international. Average age 31. 50 applicants, 28% accepted, 7 enrolled. In 2010, 4 doctorates awarded. *Degree requirements:* For doctorate, comprehensive exam (for some programs), thesis/dissertation. *Entrance requirements:* For doctorate, GRE General Test, resume, portfolio, research writing sample. Additional exam requirements/recommendations for international students: Required—TOEFL (minimum score 570 paper-based; 230 computer-based; 89 iBT), IELTS (minimum score 6.5). *Application deadline:* For fall admission, 1/1 priority date for domestic students, 1/1 for international students. Applications are processed on a rolling basis. Application fee: $75. Electronic applications accepted. *Expenses:* Tuition: Full-time $39,600; part-time $1650 per credit. Required fees: $1896. *Financial support:* In 2010–11, 23 students received support, including 5 fellowships with full tuition reimbursements available (averaging $23,000 per year), 17 research assistantships with tuition reimbursements available (averaging $17,500 per year), 1 teaching assistantship with full tuition reimbursement available (averaging $17,500 per year); career-related internships or fieldwork, institutionally sponsored loans, scholarships/grants and unspecified assistantships also available. Financial award application deadline: 1/1. *Faculty research:* Lighting, acoustics, computation, building systems. *Unit head:* Prof. Ted Krueger, Head, Graduate Programs, 518-276-2562, Fax: 518-276-3034, E-mail: krueger@rpi.edu. *Application contact:* Erin Bermingham, Senior Graduate Programs Administrator, 518-276-3986, Fax: 518-276-3034, E-mail: bermie@rpi.edu.

Rensselaer Polytechnic Institute, Graduate School, School of Architecture, Program in Built Ecologies, Troy, NY 12180-3590. Offers MS. *Faculty:* 3 full-time (1 woman), 2 part-time/adjunct (0 women). *Students:* 15 full-time (7 women), 2 part-time (0 women); includes 1 Black or African American, non-Hispanic/Latino; 1 Hispanic/Latino; 1 Two or more races, non-Hispanic/Latino, 5 international. Average age 31. 49 applicants, 24% accepted, 6 enrolled. In 2010, 4 master's awarded. *Degree requirements:* For master's, thesis. *Entrance requirements:* Additional exam requirements/recommendations for international students: Required—TOEFL (minimum score 570 paper-based; 230 computer-based; 89 iBT), IELTS (minimum score 6.5). *Application deadline:* For fall admission, 1/1 for domestic and international students. Applications are processed on a rolling basis. Application fee: $75. Electronic applications accepted. *Expenses:* Tuition: Full-time $39,600; part-time $1650 per credit. Required fees: $1896. *Financial support:* In 2010–11, 11 students received support, including 4 fellowships with full tuition reimbursements available (averaging $23,500 per year), 6 research assistantships with full tuition reimbursements available (averaging $17,500 per year), 1 teaching assistantship with full tuition reimbursement available (averaging $17,500 per year); institutionally sponsored loans, scholarships/grants, and unspecified assistantships also available. Financial award application deadline: 1/1. *Faculty research:* Emerging materials and technologies, sustainable built environments. Total annual research expenditures: $450,000. *Unit head:* Prof. Ted Krueger, Head, Graduate Programs, 518-276-2562, Fax: 518-276-3034, E-mail: krueger@rpi.edu. *Application contact:* Erin Bermingham, Senior Program Administrator, 518-276-3986, Fax: 518-276-3034, E-mail: bermie@rpi.edu.

University of California, Berkeley, Graduate Division, College of Environmental Design, Department of Architecture, Berkeley, CA 94720-1500. Offers architecture (M Arch); building science (MS, PhD); building structures, construction and materials (MS, PhD); design theories, methods, and practices (MS, PhD); environmental design in developing countries (MS, PhD); history of architecture and urbanism (MS, PhD); social and cultural processes in architecture and urbanism (MS, PhD); M Arch/MCP; M Arch/MS; MLA/M Arch. *Degree requirements:* For master's, thesis; for doctorate, thesis/dissertation, qualifying exam. *Entrance requirements:* For master's and doctorate, GRE General Test, minimum GPA of 3.0, 3 letters of recommendation. Additional exam requirements/recommendations for international students: Required—TOEFL. Electronic applications accepted.

University of Florida, Graduate School, College of Design, Construction and Planning, M. E. Rinker, Sr. School of Building Construction, Gainesville, FL 32611. Offers MBC, MICM, MSBC, PhD. Part-time programs available. *Faculty:* 15 full-time (2 women). *Students:* 175 full-time (57 women), 45 part-time (16 women); includes 6 Black or African American, non-Hispanic/Latino; 9 Asian, non-Hispanic/Latino; 16 Hispanic/Latino, 60 international. Average age 26. 90 applicants, 70% accepted, 30 enrolled. In 2010, 64 master's, 6 doctorates awarded. *Degree requirements:* For master's, thesis; for doctorate, comprehensive exam, thesis/dissertation. *Entrance requirements:* For master's, GRE General Test, minimum GPA of 3.0; for doctorate, GRE General Test combined verbal and quantitative score of 1200, minimum GPA of 3.0. Additional exam requirements/recommendations for international students: Required—TOEFL (minimum score 550 paper-based; 213 computer-based; 80 iBT), IELTS (minimum score 6). *Application deadline:* Applications are processed on a rolling basis. Application fee: $30. Electronic applications accepted. *Expenses:* Tuition, state resident: full-time $10,915.92. Tuition, nonresident: full-time $28,309. *Financial support:* In 2010–11, 13 students received support, including 7 research assistantships with full tuition reimbursements available (averaging $8,836 per year), 6 teaching assistantships with full tuition reimbursements available (averaging $9,363 per year); career-related internships or fieldwork and unspecified assistantships also available. Financial award applicants required to submit FAFSA. *Faculty research:* Safety, affordable housing, construction management, environmental issues, sustainable construction. *Unit head:* Dr. Abdol R. Chini, Director, 352-273-1165, Fax: 352-392-9606, E-mail: chini@ufl.edu. *Application contact:* Dr. Ian Flood, Coordinator of PhD program, 352-273-1159, Fax: 352-392-7266, E-mail: flood@ufl.edu.

Environmental Design

Arizona State University, Herberger Institute for Design and the Arts, School of Architecture and Landscape Architecture, PhD Program in Design, Environment and the Arts, Tempe, AZ 85287-2105. Offers design, environment and the arts (design) (PhD); design, environment and the arts (healthcare and healing environments) (PhD); design, environment and the arts (history, theory, and criticism) (PhD). *Faculty:* 25 full-time (13 women). *Students:* 17 full-time (4 women), 15 part-time (7 women); includes 4 minority (2 Asian, non-Hispanic/Latino; 2 Hispanic/Latino), 17 international. Average age 36. 19 applicants, 53% accepted, 4 enrolled. In 2010, 8 doctorates awarded. *Degree requirements:* For doctorate, comprehensive exam, thesis/dissertation, interactive Program of Study (iPOS) submitted before completing 50 percent of required credit hours. *Entrance requirements:* For doctorate, GRE, master's degree in architecture, graphic design, industrial design, interior design, landscape architecture, or art history or equivalent standing; statement of purpose; 3 letters of recommendation; indication of potential faculty mentor; sample of written work. Additional exam requirements/recommendations for international students: Required—TOEFL, IELTS, or Pearson Test of English. *Application deadline:* For fall admission, 12/15 for domestic and international students. Application fee: $70 ($90 for international students). Electronic applications accepted. *Expenses:* Contact institution. *Financial support:* In 2010–11, 3 research assistantships with full and partial tuition reimbursements (averaging $16,365 per year), 9 teaching assistantships with full and partial tuition reimbursements (averaging $10,384 per year) were awarded; institutionally sponsored loans, scholarships/grants, and tuition waivers (partial) also available. Financial award application deadline: 3/1; financial award applicants required to submit FAFSA. *Unit head:* Dr. Michael D. Kroelinger, Executive Dean/Director, 480-965-5561, E-mail: design.phd@asu.edu. *Application contact:* Graduate Admissions, 480-965-6113.

Art Center College of Design, Graduate Division, Industrial Design Department, Pasadena, CA 91103. Offers environmental design (MS); product design (MS). *Accreditation:* NASAD. *Faculty:* 2 full-time (0 women), 8 part-time/adjunct (1 woman). *Students:* 25 full-time (7 women), 22 part-time (7 women); includes 9 minority (2 Black or African American, non-Hispanic/Latino; 6 Asian, non-Hispanic/Latino; 1 Hispanic/Latino), 24 international. Average age 30. 87 applicants, 25% accepted, 9 enrolled. In 2010, 9 master's awarded. *Degree requirements:* For master's, thesis, studio project. *Entrance requirements:* For master's, portfolio. Additional exam requirements/recommendations for international students: Required—TOEFL (minimum score 600 paper-based; 250 computer-based; 100 iBT). *Application deadline:* For fall admission, 2/1 for domestic and international students. Application fee: $50 ($70 for international students). *Expenses:* Tuition: Part-time $17,220 per term. *Financial support:* Teaching assistantships, career-related internships or fieldwork, Federal Work-Study, and scholarships/grants available. Financial award application deadline: 2/1. *Unit head:* Andrew Ogden, Chair, 626-396-2464. *Application contact:* Maritza Hererra, Coordinator, 626-396-2464.

See Display on page 89 and Close-Up on page 119.

Clemson University, Graduate School, College of Architecture, Arts, and Humanities, Program in Planning, Design and the Built Environment, Clemson, SC 29634. Offers PhD. *Students:* 18 full-time (3 women), 4 part-time (0 women); includes 1 Black or African American, non-Hispanic/Latino, 4 international. Average age 39. 36 applicants, 33% accepted, 6 enrolled. In 2010, 2 doctorates awarded. *Entrance requirements:* For doctorate, GRE General Test. Additional exam requirements/recommendations for international students: Required—TOEFL. *Application deadline:* For fall admission, 1/1 for domestic and international students. Applications are processed on a rolling basis. Application fee: $70 ($80 for international students). Electronic applications accepted. *Expenses:* Tuition, state resident: full-time $6492; part-time $400 per credit hour. Tuition, nonresident: full-time $13,634; part-time $800 per credit hour. Required fees: $262 per semester. Part-time tuition and fees vary according to course load and program. *Financial support:* In 2010–11, 17 students received support, including 1 research assistantship with partial tuition reimbursement available (averaging $18,000 per year), 15 teaching assistantships with partial tuition reimbursements available (averaging $17,520 per year); career-related internships or fieldwork, institutionally sponsored loans, scholarships/grants, health care benefits, and unspecified assistantships also available. Support available to part-time students. *Unit head:* Roger Liska, Interim Director, 864-656-3878, E-mail: riggor@clemson.edu. *Application contact:* Mickey Lauria, Concentration Coordinator, 864-656-0520, E-mail: mlauria@clemson.edu.

Columbia University, School of Continuing Education, Program in Landscape Design, New York, NY 10027. Offers MS. Part-time programs available. *Entrance requirements:* For master's, minimum undergraduate GPA of 3.0. Additional exam requirements/recommendations for international students: Required—American Language Program placement test.

Cornell University, Graduate School, Graduate Fields of Human Ecology, Field of Design and Environmental Analysis, Ithaca, NY 14853. Offers applied research in human-environment relations (MS); facilities planning and management (MS); housing and design (MS); human factors and ergonomics (MS); human-environment relations (MS); interior design (MA, MPS). *Faculty:* 15 full-time (6 women). *Students:* 27 full-time (22 women); includes 2 Black or African American, non-Hispanic/Latino; 6 Asian, non-Hispanic/Latino, 7 international. Average age 25. 83 applicants, 27% accepted, 21 enrolled. In 2010, 29 master's awarded. *Degree requirements:* For master's, thesis. *Entrance requirements:* For master's, GRE General Test, portfolio or slides of recent work; bachelor's degree in interior design, architecture or related design discipline; 2 letters of recommendation. Additional exam requirements/recommendations for international students: Required—TOEFL (minimum score 600 paper-based; 250 computer-based; 105 iBT). *Application deadline:* For fall admission, 2/1 priority date for domestic students. Application fee: $70. Electronic applications accepted. *Expenses:* Tuition: Full-time $29,500. Required fees: $76. Tuition and fees vary according to degree level and program. *Financial support:* In 2010–11, 13 students received support, including 3 fellowships with full tuition reimbursements available, 2 research assistantships with full tuition reimbursements available, 13 teaching assistantships with full tuition reimbursements available; institutionally sponsored loans, scholarships/grants, health care benefits, tuition waivers (full and partial), and unspecified assistantships also available. Financial award applicants required to submit FAFSA. *Faculty research:* Facility planning and management, environmental psychology, housing, interior design, ergonomics and human factors. *Unit head:* Director of Graduate Studies, 607-255-2168, Fax: 607-255-0305. *Application contact:* Graduate Field Assistant, 607-255-2168, Fax: 607-255-0305, E-mail: deagrad@cornell.edu.

Florida Atlantic University, College of Design and Social Inquiry, School of Urban and Regional Planning, Boca Raton, FL 33431-0991. Offers economic development and tourism (Certificate); environmental planning (Certificate); sustainable community planning (Certificate); urban and regional planning (MURP); visual planning technology (Certificate). *Accreditation:* ACSP. Part-time and evening/weekend programs available. *Faculty:* 8 full-time (5 women), 2 part-time/adjunct (1 woman). *Students:* 24 full-time (18 women), 12 part-time (1 woman); includes 17 minority (4 Black or African American, non-Hispanic/Latino; 1 American Indian or Alaska Native, non-Hispanic/Latino; 12 Hispanic/Latino), 2 international. Average age 30. 55 applicants, 35% accepted, 12 enrolled. In 2010, 13 master's awarded. *Entrance requirements:* For master's, GRE General Test, minimum GPA of 3.0. Additional exam requirements/recommendations for international students: Required—TOEFL. *Application deadline:* For fall admission, 7/1 priority date for domestic students, 2/15 for international students; for spring admission, 11/1 priority date for domestic students, 7/15 for international students. Applications are processed on a rolling basis. Application fee: $30. *Expenses:* Tuition, area resident: Part-time $319.96 per credit. Tuition, state resident: part-time $319.96 per credit. Tuition, nonresident: part-time $926.42 per credit. *Financial support:* Fellowships with full tuition reimbursements, research assistantships, career-related internships or fieldwork, Federal Work-Study, institutionally sponsored loans, and tuition waivers (partial) available. Financial award application deadline: 4/1. *Faculty research:* Growth management, urban design, computer applications/geographical information systems, environmental planning. *Unit head:* Dr. Jaap

Environmental Design

Florida Atlantic University (continued)
Vos, Chair, 954-762-5653, Fax: 954-762-5673, E-mail: jvos@fau.edu. *Application contact:* Dr. Jaap Vos, Chair, 954-762-5653, Fax: 954-762-5673, E-mail: jvos@fau.edu.

Michigan State University, The Graduate School, College of Agriculture and Natural Resources and College of Social Science, School of Planning, Design and Construction, East Lansing, MI 48824. Offers construction management (MS, PhD); environmental design (MA); interior design and facilities management (MA); international planning studies (MIPS); urban and regional planning (MURP). *Degree requirements:* For master's, thesis or alternative. *Entrance requirements:* Additional exam requirements/recommendations for international students: Required—TOEFL. Electronic applications accepted.

San Diego State University, Graduate and Research Affairs, College of Professional Studies and Fine Arts, School of Art, Design and Art History, San Diego, CA 92182. Offers art history (MA); studio arts (MA, MFA), including applied design, environmental design, graphic design, interior design, painting and printmaking, sculpture. *Accreditation:* NASAD (one or more programs are accredited). *Degree requirements:* For master's, variable foreign language requirement, thesis. *Entrance requirements:* For master's, GRE General Test, bachelor's degree in related field, slide portfolio, typed slide information sheet, 2 letters of recommendation. Additional exam requirements/recommendations for international students: Required—TOEFL. Electronic applications accepted.

Texas Tech University, Graduate School, College of Human Sciences, Department of Design, Lubbock, TX 79409. Offers environmental design (MS); interior and environmental design (PhD). *Faculty:* 4 full-time (2 women). *Students:* 18 full-time (16 women), 7 part-time (5 women); includes 1 Asian, non-Hispanic/Latino; 1 Hispanic/Latino, 8 international. Average age 27. 16 applicants, 69% accepted, 8 enrolled. In 2010, 3 master's awarded. *Degree requirements:* For master's, thesis or alternative; for doctorate, thesis/dissertation. *Entrance requirements:* For master's and doctorate, GRE, 3 letters of recommendation, design portfolio, resume. Additional exam requirements/recommendations for international students: Required—TOEFL (minimum score 550 paper-based; 213 computer-based; 79 iBT). *Application deadline:* For fall admission, 6/1 priority date for domestic students, 1/15 priority date for international students; for spring admission, 9/1 priority date for domestic students, 6/15 priority date for international students. Applications are processed on a rolling basis. Application fee: $50 ($75 for international students). Electronic applications accepted. *Expenses:* Tuition, state resident: full-time $5495.76; part-time $228.99 per credit hour. Tuition, nonresident: full-time $12,936; part-time $538.99 per credit hour. Required fees: $2674; $36 per credit hour. $905 per semester. *Financial support:* In 2010–11, 3 students received support, including 2 research assistantships with partial tuition reimbursements available (averaging $1,479 per year). Financial award application deadline: 4/15; financial award applicants required to submit FAFSA. *Faculty research:* Healthcare and the built environment, sustainability, ergonomics, environmental design, evidence-based design. Total annual research expenditures: $150,144. *Unit head:* Dr. Cherif M. Amor, Chair, 806-742-3050, Fax: 806-742-1639, E-mail: cherif.amor@ttu.edu. *Application contact:* Dr. Su-Jeong Hwang Shin, Graduate Programs Director, 806-742-3050 Ext. 262, Fax: 806-742-1639, E-mail: su.hwang@ttu.edu.

See Display on page 109 and Close-Up on page 133.

Université de Montréal, Faculty of Environmental Design and Planning, Montréal, QC H3C 3J7, Canada. Offers environmental design and planning (M Sc A, PhD); environmental planning and design projects (DESS); game design (DESS); urban management for developing countries (DESS); urban planning (M Urb). DESS programs offered jointly with HEC Montreal and École Polytechnique de Montréal. *Accreditation:* ACSP. *Degree requirements:* For doctorate, thesis/dissertation, general exam. Electronic applications accepted. *Expenses:* Contact institution. *Faculty research:* Wayfinding, environmental evaluation, housing studies, urban design, urban and regional planning.

University of Calgary, Faculty of Graduate Studies, Faculty of Environmental Design, Calgary, AB T2N 1N4, Canada. Offers architecture (M Arch); environmental design (M Env Des, PhD). *Degree requirements:* For master's, thesis; for doctorate, thesis/dissertation. *Entrance requirements:* For master's, minimum GPA of 3.0; for doctorate, minimum GPA of 3.5. Additional exam requirements/recommendations for international students: Required—TOEFL (minimum score 550 paper-based; 213 computer-based). *Faculty research:* Sustainable development in architecture, planning and product design, energy and environment, impact assessment, ecotourism.

University of California, Berkeley, Graduate Division, College of Environmental Design, Department of Landscape Architecture and Environmental Planning, Berkeley, CA 94720-1500. Offers landscape architecture (MLA), including environmental planning, landscape design and site planning, urban and community design; landscape architecture and environmental planning (PhD); MLA/M Arch; MLA/MCP. *Accreditation:* ASLA (one or more programs are accredited). *Degree requirements:* For master's, professional project or thesis; for doctorate, one foreign language, thesis/dissertation, qualifying exam. *Entrance requirements:* For master's, GRE General Test, minimum GPA of 3.0, portfolio; for doctorate, GRE General Test, master's degree (strongly recommended), minimum GPA of 3.0, sample of written work, 3 letters of recommendation.

University of California, Berkeley, Graduate Division, College of Environmental Design, Master of Arts in Design Program, Berkeley, CA 94720-1500. Offers MA. *Degree requirements:* For master's, thesis. *Entrance requirements:* For master's, GRE General Test, minimum GPA of 3.0, portfolio, 3 letters of recommendation. Additional exam requirements/recommendations for international students: Required—TOEFL.

University of California, Irvine, School of Social Ecology, Programs in Social Ecology, Irvine, CA 92697. Offers environmental analysis and design (PhD); epidemiology and public health (PhD); social ecology (PhD). *Students:* 13 full-time (10 women); includes 3 minority (1 Asian, non-Hispanic/Latino; 2 Hispanic/Latino), 2 international. Average age 28. 24 applicants, 17% accepted, 4 enrolled. In 2010, 1 doctorate awarded. Application fee: $80 ($100 for international students). *Unit head:* Valerie Jenness, Dean, 949-824-6094, Fax: 949-824-1845, E-mail: jenness@uci.edu. *Application contact:* Maria Victoria Dela Cruz, Director, Graduate Services, 949-824-5918, Fax: 949-824-1845, E-mail: mvdelacr@uci.edu.

University of Georgia, College of Environment and Design, Athens, GA 30602. Offers environmental planning and design (MEPD); historic preservation (MHP); landscape architecture (MLA). *Faculty:* 29 full-time (8 women). *Students:* 111 full-time (69 women), 25 part-time (15 women); includes 2 Black or African American, non-Hispanic/Latino; 1 Asian, non-Hispanic/Latino; 3 Two or more races, non-Hispanic/Latino, 9 international. 200 applicants, 56% accepted, 58 enrolled. In 2010, 26 master's awarded. *Application deadline:* For fall admission, 7/1 priority date for domestic students; for spring admission, 11/15 for domestic students. Application fee: $50. *Expenses:* Tuition, state resident: full-time $7200; part-time $344 per credit hour. Tuition, nonresident: full-time $21,900; part-time $944 per credit hour. Tuition and fees vary according to course load and program. *Unit head:* Dean Daniels J. Nadenicek, Acting Dean, 706-542-1100, Fax: 706-542-4485, E-mail: dnadeni@uga.edu. *Application contact:* Prof. Brian J. LaHaie, Director of Enrolled Student Services, 706-542-4704, Fax: 706-542-4236, E-mail: blahaie@uga.edu.

The University of Manchester, School of Environment and Development, Manchester, United Kingdom. Offers architecture (M Phil, PhD); development policy and management (M Phil, PhD); human geography (M Phil, PhD); physical geography (M Phil, PhD); planning and landscape (M Phil, PhD).

University of Missouri, Graduate School, College of Human Environmental Science, Department of Architectural Studies, Columbia, MO 65211. Offers design with digital media (MA, MS); environmental design (MS). *Entrance requirements:* For master's, GRE General Test, minimum GPA of 3.0. Additional exam requirements/recommendations for international students: Required—TOEFL (minimum score 500 paper-based; 173 computer-based; 61 iBT).

Virginia Polytechnic Institute and State University, Graduate School, College of Architecture and Urban Studies, Program in Environmental Design and Planning, Blacksburg, VA 24061. Offers PhD. *Students:* 13 full-time (4 women), 7 part-time (1 woman); includes 1 Black or African American, non-Hispanic/Latino; 2 Asian, non-Hispanic/Latino, 5 international. Average age 35. 3 applicants, 67% accepted, 2 enrolled. In 2010, 6 doctorates awarded. *Degree requirements:* For doctorate, comprehensive exam (for some programs), thesis/dissertation (for some programs). *Entrance requirements:* For doctorate, GRE. Additional exam requirements/recommendations for international students: Required—TOEFL (minimum score 550 paper-based; 213 computer-based). *Application deadline:* For fall admission, 7/1 for domestic and international students; for spring admission, 12/1 for domestic and international students. Applications are processed on a rolling basis. Application fee: $65. Electronic applications accepted. *Expenses:* Tuition, state resident: full-time $9399; part-time $488 per credit hour. Tuition, nonresident: full-time $17,854; part-time $957.75 per credit hour. Required fees: $1534. Full-time tuition and fees vary according to program. *Financial support:* Career-related internships or fieldwork, Federal Work-Study, scholarships/grants, health care benefits, and unspecified assistantships available. Financial award application deadline: 1/15. *Faculty research:* Urban studies, architecture, landscape planning. *Unit head:* Dr. Patrick Miller, UNIT HEAD, 540-231-5582, Fax: 540-231-9938, E-mail: pmiller@vt.edu. *Application contact:* Chris Coon, Contact, 540-231-6416, Fax: 540-231-9938, E-mail: garch@vt.edu.

Yale University, School of Architecture, New Haven, CT 06520. Offers M Arch, M Env Des, MEM, PhD, M Arch/M Env Des, M Arch/MBA. *Entrance requirements:* For master's, GRE General Test, design portfolio. Additional exam requirements/recommendations for international students: Required—TOEFL. *Expenses:* Contact institution.

Historic Preservation

Arkansas State University, Graduate School, College of Humanities and Social Sciences, Heritage Studies Program, Jonesboro, State University, AR 72467. Offers MA, PhD. Part-time programs available. *Faculty:* 2 full-time (1 woman), 2 part-time/adjunct (1 woman). *Students:* 14 full-time (9 women), 24 part-time (12 women); includes 5 minority (4 Black or African American, non-Hispanic/Latino; 1 Two or more races, non-Hispanic/Latino), 1 international. Average age 43. 17 applicants, 71% accepted, 10 enrolled. In 2010, 7 master's, 2 doctorates awarded. *Degree requirements:* For master's, comprehensive exam, thesis or alternative, portfolio; for doctorate, comprehensive exam, thesis/dissertation, portfolio. *Entrance requirements:* For master's, GRE, MAT or GMAT, appropriate bachelor's degree, letters of reference, official transcript, interview, letter of interest, writing sample, immunization records; for doctorate, GRE, MAT, or GMAT, appropriate bachelor's or master's degree, interview, letters of reference, official transcript, letter of interest, writing sample, immunization records. Additional exam requirements/recommendations for international students: Required—TOEFL (minimum score 550 paper-based; 213 computer-based; 79 iBT), IELTS (minimum score 6), PTE: Pearson Test of English Academic (56). *Application deadline:* For fall admission, 7/1 for domestic and international students. Applications are processed on a rolling basis. Application fee: $50. Electronic applications accepted. *Expenses:* Tuition, state resident: full-time $3888; part-time $216 per credit hour. Tuition, nonresident: full-time $9918; part-time $551 per credit hour. International tuition: $8376 full-time. Required fees: $932; $49 per credit hour. $25 per term. One-time fee: $30. Tuition and fees vary according to course load and program. *Financial support:* In 2010–11, 12 students received support; fellowships, teaching assistantships, career-related internships or fieldwork, scholarships/grants, tuition waivers (partial), and unspecified assistantships available. Financial award application deadline: 7/1; financial award applicants required to submit FAFSA. *Unit head:* Dr. Clyde Milner, Director, 870-972-3509, Fax: 870-972-3207, E-mail: cmilner@astate.edu. *Application contact:* Dr. Andrew Sustich, Dean of the Graduate School, 870-972-3029, Fax: 870-972-3857, E-mail: sustich@astate.edu.

Ball State University, Graduate School, College of Architecture and Planning, Department of Architecture, Program in Historic Preservation, Muncie, IN 47306-1099. Offers M Arch, MS. *Faculty:* 25. *Students:* 24 full-time (16 women), 7 part-time (3 women). Average age 31. 32 applicants, 53% accepted, 10 enrolled. In 2010, 4 master's awarded. *Degree requirements:* For master's, thesis. *Entrance requirements:* For master's, minimum undergraduate B average, portfolio, writing sample. Application fee: $50. *Expenses:* Tuition, state resident: full-time $6160; part-time $299 per credit hour. Tuition, nonresident: full-time $16,020; part-time $783 per credit hour. Required fees: $2278; $95 per credit hour. *Financial support:* In 2010–11, 14 research assistantships with full tuition reimbursements (averaging $6,912 per year) were awarded. Financial award application deadline: 3/1. *Unit head:* Dr. Mahesh Senagala, Director, 765-285-1900, Fax: 765-285-1765, E-mail: msenagala@bsu.edu. *Application contact:* Dr. Duncan Campbell, Graduate Program Director, 765-285-1900, Fax: 765-285-1765, E-mail: dcambell@bsu.edu.

Boston University, Graduate School of Arts and Sciences, Program in Preservation Studies, Boston, MA 02215. Offers MA, JD/MA. *Students:* 2 full-time (both women), 10 part-time (9 women). Average age 32. 26 applicants, 62% accepted, 3 enrolled. *Degree requirements:* For master's, one foreign language, thesis or alternative, internship. *Entrance requirements:* For master's, GRE General Test, scholarly writing sample, 3 letters of recommendation. Additional exam requirements/recommendations for international students: Required—TOEFL (minimum score 550 paper-based; 213 computer-based). *Application deadline:* For fall admission, 4/1 for domestic and international students; for spring admission, 11/15 for domestic and international students. Application fee: $70. Electronic applications accepted. *Expenses:* Tuition: Full-time $39,314; part-time $1228 per credit. Required fees: $40 per semester. *Financial support:* In 2010–11, 2 research assistantships with partial tuition reimbursements were awarded; career-related internships or fieldwork, Federal Work-Study, and unspecified assistantships also available. Support available to part-time students. Financial award application deadline: 1/15; financial award applicants required to submit FAFSA. *Unit head:* Claire Dempsey, Director, 617-353-9910, Fax: 617-353-2556, E-mail: dempseyc@bu.edu. *Application contact:* Benjamin Tocchi, Senior Program Coordinator, 617-353-2948, Fax: 617-353-2556, E-mail: btocchi@bu.edu.

Buffalo State College, State University of New York, The Graduate School, Faculty of Arts and Humanities, Department of Art Conservation, Buffalo, NY 14222-1095. Offers art conservation (CAS); conservation of historic works and art works (MA). *Degree requirements:* For master's, final oral exam; for CAS, internship. *Entrance requirements:* For master's, GRE General Test, minimum GPA of 2.8. Additional exam requirements/recommendations for international students: Required—TOEFL (minimum score 550 paper-based; 213 computer-based). *Faculty research:* Mechanics of deterioration of art, conservation of materials.

Clemson University, Graduate School, College of Architecture, Arts, and Humanities, Department of Planning and Landscape Architecture, Program in Historic Preservation, Clemson, SC 29634. Offers MS. *Students:* 25 full-time (20 women), 3 international. Average age 27. 54 applicants, 57% accepted, 15 enrolled. In 2010, 10 master's awarded. *Entrance requirements:* For master's, GRE General Test. Additional exam requirements/recommendations for international students: Required—TOEFL. *Application deadline:* For fall admission, 2/15 for domestic and international students. Applications are processed on a rolling basis. Application fee: $70 ($80 for international students). Electronic applications accepted. *Expenses:* Tuition, state resident: full-time $6492; part-time $400 per credit hour. Tuition, nonresident: full-time $13,634; part-time $800 per credit hour. Required fees: $262 per semester. Part-time tuition and fees vary according to course load and program. *Financial support:* In 2010–11, 24 students received support, including 24 fellowships with partial tuition reimbursements available (averaging $5,833 per year); research assistantships with partial tuition reimbursements available, teaching assistantships with partial tuition reimbursements available, career-related internships or fieldwork, institutionally sponsored loans, scholarships/grants, health care benefits, and unspecified assistantships also available. Support available to part-time students. *Unit head:* Dr. Elaine M. Worzala, Chair, 864-656-3657, Fax: 864-656-0204, E-mail: eworzal@clemson.edu. *Application contact:* Ashley Robbins, Coordinator, 864-937-9596, Fax: 864-656-0204, E-mail: arobbin@clemson.edu.

College of Charleston, Graduate School, School of the Arts, Program in Historic Preservation, Charleston, SC 29424-0001. Offers MS. *Faculty:* 9 full-time (1 woman), 2 part-time/adjunct (both women). *Students:* 25 full-time (19 women); includes 1 minority (Asian, non-Hispanic/Latino). Average age 25. In 2010, 10 master's awarded. *Degree requirements:* For master's, thesis optional. *Entrance requirements:* For master's, GRE. Additional exam requirements/recommendations for international students: Required—TOEFL (minimum score 81 iBT). *Application fee:* $45. Electronic applications accepted. *Financial support:* Career-related internships or fieldwork, Federal Work-Study, scholarships/grants, and unspecified assistantships available. Support available to part-time students. Financial award application deadline: 4/1; financial award applicants required to submit FAFSA. *Unit head:* Dr. Carter L. Hudgins, Director, 843-937-9596, E-mail: chudgin@clemson.edu. *Application contact:* Susan Hallatt, Director of Graduate Admissions, 843-953-5614, Fax: 843-953-1434, E-mail: hallatts@cofc.edu.

Columbia University, Graduate School of Architecture, Planning, and Preservation, Program in Historic Preservation, New York, NY 10027. Offers MS, Certificate, M Arch/MS, MS/MS. *Degree requirements:* For master's, thesis. *Entrance requirements:* For master's, GRE General Test.

Cornell University, Graduate School, Graduate Fields of Architecture, Art and Planning, Field of City and Regional Planning, Ithaca, NY 14853-0001. Offers city and regional planning (MRP, PhD); environmental planning and design (MRP, PhD); historic preservation planning (MA); international development planning (MRP, PhD); planning theory and systems analysis (MRP, PhD); regional economics and development planning (MRP, PhD); regional science (MRP, PhD); social and health systems planning (MRP, PhD); urban and regional theory (MRP, PhD); urban planning history (MRP, PhD). *Accreditation:* ACSP (one or more programs are accredited). *Faculty:* 31 full-time (10 women). *Students:* 136 full-time (66 women); includes 6 Black or African American, non-Hispanic/Latino; 10 Asian, non-Hispanic/Latino; 9 Hispanic/Latino, 20 international. Average age 27. 452 applicants, 32% accepted, 64 enrolled. In 2010, 42 master's, 4 doctorates awarded. *Degree requirements:* For master's, thesis (MA); for doctorate, comprehensive exam, thesis/dissertation. *Entrance requirements:* For master's and doctorate, GRE General Test, 2 letters of recommendation. Additional exam requirements/recommendations for international students: Required—TOEFL (minimum score 600 paper-based; 250 computer-based; 77 iBT). *Application deadline:* For fall admission, 1/10 for domestic students. Application fee: $70. Electronic applications accepted. *Expenses:* Tuition: Full-time $29,500. Required fees: $76. Tuition and fees vary according to degree level and program. *Financial support:* In 2010–11, 9 fellowships with full tuition reimbursements, 2 research assistantships with full tuition reimbursements, 13 teaching assistantships with full tuition reimbursements were awarded; institutionally sponsored loans, scholarships/grants, health care benefits, tuition waivers (full and partial), and unspecified assistantships also available. Financial award applicants required to submit FAFSA. *Faculty research:* Land use planning, economic development, international development, historic preservation, community development. *Unit head:* Director of Graduate Studies, 607-255-6848, Fax: 607-255-1971. *Application contact:* Graduate Field Assistant, 607-255-6848, Fax: 607-255-1971, E-mail: crp_admissions@cornell.edu.

Delaware State University, Graduate Programs, Department of History, Philosophy and Political Sciences, Dover, DE 19901-2277. Offers historic preservation (MA). *Entrance requirements:* Additional exam requirements/recommendations for international students: Required—TOEFL (minimum score 550 paper-based). Electronic applications accepted.

Eastern Michigan University, Graduate School, College of Arts and Sciences, Department of Geography and Geology, Program in Historic Preservation, Ypsilanti, MI 48197. Offers heritage interpretation and tourism (MS); historic preservation (MS, Graduate Certificate). Part-time and evening/weekend programs available. Postbaccalaureate distance learning degree programs offered (minimal on-campus study). *Students:* 17 full-time (14 women), 59 part-time (44 women); includes 2 minority (both Black or African American, non-Hispanic/Latino), 1 international. Average age 35. In 2010, 14 master's, 4 other advanced degrees awarded. *Entrance requirements:* Additional exam requirements/recommendations for international students: Required—TOEFL. *Application deadline:* Applications are processed on a rolling basis. Application fee: $35. *Financial support:* Fellowships, research assistantships with full tuition reimbursements, teaching assistantships with full tuition reimbursements, career-related internships or fieldwork, Federal Work-Study, institutionally sponsored loans, scholarships/grants, tuition waivers (partial), and unspecified assistantships available. Support available to part-time students. Financial award applicants required to submit FAFSA. *Application contact:* Dr. Ted Ligibel, Program Advisor, 734-487-0232, Fax: 734-487-6979, E-mail: tligibel@emich.edu.

The George Washington University, Columbian College of Arts and Sciences, Department of American Studies, Washington, DC 20052. Offers American studies (PhD); folklife (MA); historic preservation (MA); material culture (MA). Part-time and evening/weekend programs available. *Faculty:* 11 full-time (5 women), 4 part-time/adjunct (2 women). *Students:* 24 full-time (17 women), 29 part-time (13 women); includes 4 Black or African American, non-Hispanic/Latino; 2 Asian, non-Hispanic/Latino; 1 Hispanic/Latino, 1 international. Average age 29. 134 applicants, 49% accepted, 19 enrolled. In 2010, 8 master's, 7 doctorates awarded. Terminal master's awarded for partial completion of doctoral program. *Degree requirements:* For master's, comprehensive exam; for doctorate, one foreign language, thesis/dissertation, general exam. *Entrance requirements:* For master's and doctorate, GRE General Test, minimum GPA of 3.0. Additional exam requirements/recommendations for international students: Required—TOEFL (minimum score 550 paper-based; 213 computer-based; 80 iBT). *Application deadline:* For fall admission, 1/15 priority date for domestic and international students; for spring admission, 10/1 for domestic students. Application fee: $75. *Financial support:* In 2010–11, 22 students received support; fellowships, research assistantships, teaching assistantships, career-related internships or fieldwork, Federal Work-Study, institutionally sponsored loans, and tuition waivers available. Financial award application deadline: 1/15. *Unit head:* James A. Miller, Chair, 202-994-6743, E-mail: jam@gwu.edu. *Application contact:* Information Contact, 202-994-6070, Fax: 202-994-8651, E-mail: amst@gwu.edu.

Georgia State University, College of Arts and Sciences, Department of History, Program in Heritage Preservation, Atlanta, GA 30302-3083. Offers MHP, Certificate. Part-time and evening/weekend programs available. *Degree requirements:* For master's, exam, internship or thesis. *Entrance requirements:* For master's, GRE General Test, minimum GPA of 3.0. Additional

exam requirements/recommendations for international students: Required—TOEFL. Electronic applications accepted. *Faculty research:* Historic preservation, local history, public history, museum studies.

Goucher College, Historic Preservation Program, Baltimore, MD 21204-2794. Offers MA. Part-time and evening/weekend programs available. Postbaccalaureate distance learning degree programs offered (minimal on-campus study). *Faculty:* 18 part-time/adjunct (8 women). *Students:* 3 full-time (2 women), 31 part-time (24 women); includes 2 Black or African American, non-Hispanic/Latino, 1 international. Average age 42. In 2010, 7 master's awarded. *Degree requirements:* For master's, thesis. *Entrance requirements:* For master's, 2 years of post-baccalaureate work or volunteer experience. *Application deadline:* For fall admission, 2/18 for domestic students. Application fee: $50. *Expenses:* Contact institution. *Financial support:* Career-related internships or fieldwork available. Support available to part-time students. Financial award application deadline: 3/15; financial award applicants required to submit FAFSA. *Unit head:* Richard Wagner, Director, 410-337-6200, Fax: 410-337-6085, E-mail: rwagner@goucher.edu. *Application contact:* Megan Cornett, Director of Marketing and Communications, 410-337-6200, Fax: 410-337-6085, E-mail: mcornett@goucher.edu.

Kent State University, College of Architecture and Environmental Design, Kent, OH 44242-0001. Offers architecture (M Arch); preservation architecture (Certificate); urban design (M Arch, MUD, Certificate). Part-time programs available. *Degree requirements:* For master's, thesis optional. *Entrance requirements:* For master's, GRE, portfolio, minimum GPA of 2.75, 3 letters of reference, resume, undergraduate architecture degree. Additional exam requirements/recommendations for international students: Required—TOEFL (minimum score 550 paper-based). Electronic applications accepted. *Expenses:* Tuition, state resident: full-time $7866; part-time $437 per credit hour. Tuition, nonresident: full-time $14,022; part-time $779 per credit hour. *Faculty research:* History and theory, building technology, landscape architecture and urbanism, urbanism, sustainable development.

Michigan Technological University, Graduate School, College of Sciences and Arts, Department of Social Sciences, Program in Industrial Heritage and Archeology, Houghton, MI 49931. Offers PhD. Part-time programs available. *Degree requirements:* For doctorate, comprehensive exam, thesis/dissertation. *Entrance requirements:* Additional exam requirements/recommendations for international students: Required—TOEFL (minimum score 550 paper-based; 213 computer-based). Electronic applications accepted.

New York University, Graduate School of Arts and Science, Institute of Fine Arts, Program in Conservation Training, New York, NY 10012-1019. Offers MA/Diploma. *Application deadline:* For fall admission, 1/4 for domestic students. Application fee: $90. *Financial support:* Career-related internships or fieldwork, Federal Work-Study, and institutionally sponsored loans available. Financial award application deadline: 1/4; financial award applicants required to submit FAFSA. *Unit head:* Hannelore Roemich, Chair, Conservation Center, 212-992-5800, Fax: 212-992-5807, E-mail: ifa.program@nyu.edu. *Application contact:* Michele Marincola, Director, 212-992-5800, Fax: 212-992-5807, E-mail: ifa.program@nyu.edu.

Northwestern State University of Louisiana, Graduate Studies and Research, Program in Heritage Resources, Natchitoches, LA 71497. Offers MA. *Degree requirements:* For master's, comprehensive exam, thesis or alternative. *Entrance requirements:* For master's, GRE General Test, minimum undergraduate GPA of 2.5.

Pratt Institute, School of Architecture, Program in Historic Preservation, New York, NY 10011. Offers MS. Part-time programs available. *Faculty:* 4 part-time/adjunct (1 woman). *Students:* 31 full-time (25 women), 3 part-time (all women); includes 1 Asian, non-Hispanic/Latino; 2 Hispanic/Latino, 1 international. Average age 29. 46 applicants, 89% accepted, 8 enrolled. In 2010, 11 master's awarded. *Entrance requirements:* For master's, writing sample, bachelor's degree, transcripts, letters of recommendation, portfolio. Additional exam requirements/recommendations for international students: Required—TOEFL (minimum score 550 paper-based; 213 computer-based; 79 iBT). *Application deadline:* For fall admission, 1/5 for domestic and international students; for spring admission, 10/1 for domestic and international students. Application fee: $50 ($90 for international students). Electronic applications accepted. *Expenses:* Tuition: Full-time $22,734; part-time $1263 per credit. Required fees: $1280. *Financial support:* Career-related internships or fieldwork, Federal Work-Study, institutionally sponsored loans, scholarships/grants, health care benefits, and unspecified assistantships available. Support available to part-time students. Financial award application deadline: 2/1; financial award applicants required to submit FAFSA. *Unit head:* Eric Allison, Coordinator, 212-647-7532, E-mail: eallison@pratt.edu. *Application contact:* Young Hah, Director of Graduate Admissions, 718-636-3683, Fax: 718-399-4242, E-mail: yhah@pratt.edu.

See Display on page 141 and Close-Up on page 161.

Rutgers, The State University of New Jersey, New Brunswick, Graduate School-New Brunswick, Program in Art History, Piscataway, NJ 08854-8097. Offers art history (MA, PhD); curatorial studies (Certificate); historic preservation (Certificate). Part-time programs available. Terminal master's awarded for partial completion of doctoral program. *Degree requirements:* For master's, one foreign language, comprehensive exam; for doctorate, 2 foreign languages, comprehensive exam, thesis/dissertation. *Entrance requirements:* For master's and doctorate, GRE General Test, writing sample. Additional exam requirements/recommendations for international students: Required—TOEFL (minimum score 550 paper-based; 213 computer-based). Electronic applications accepted. *Expenses:* Tuition, state resident: full-time $7200; part-time $600 per credit. Tuition, nonresident: full-time $11,124; part-time $927 per credit. *Faculty research:* Ancient and medieval art and architecture; Renaissance and Baroque art and architecture; modern and contemporary art and architecture; Italian studies; the arts of Asia, Africa, and the Americas.

St. Cloud State University, School of Graduate Studies, College of Social Sciences, Program in Cultural Resource Management Archeology, St. Cloud, MN 56301-4498. Offers MS. *Entrance requirements:* For master's, GRE General Test, minimum GPA of 2.75. Additional exam requirements/recommendations for international students: Required—Michigan English Language Assessment Battery; Recommended—TOEFL (minimum score 550 paper-based; 213 computer-based).

Savannah College of Art and Design, Graduate School, Program in Historic Preservation, Savannah, GA 31402-3146. Offers MA, MFA, Graduate Certificate. Part-time programs available. Postbaccalaureate distance learning degree programs offered (no on-campus study). *Faculty:* 6 full-time (2 women), 4 part-time/adjunct (2 women). *Students:* 53 full-time (47 women), 22 part-time (18 women); includes 2 Black or African American, non-Hispanic/Latino; 2 American Indian or Alaska Native, non-Hispanic/Latino. Average age 31. In 2010, 39 master's, 7 other advanced degrees awarded. *Degree requirements:* For master's, thesis, internship. *Entrance requirements:* For master's, interview, research paper. Additional exam requirements/recommendations for international students: Required—TOEFL (minimum score 450 paper-based; 133 computer-based). *Application deadline:* For fall admission, 4/1 priority date for domestic and international students. Applications are processed on a rolling basis. Application fee: $35. Electronic applications accepted. *Expenses:* Tuition: Full-time $29,520; part-time $3280 per quarter. Tuition and fees vary according to campus/location. *Financial support:* Fellowships, career-related internships or fieldwork, Federal Work-Study, and scholarships/grants available. Financial award application deadline: 4/1; financial award applicants required to submit FAFSA. *Unit head:* Jeanne Lambin, Chair, 912-525-6852, E-mail: jlambin@scad.edu. *Application contact:* Elizabeth Mathis, Director of Graduate Recruitment, 912-525-5965, Fax: 912-525-5985, E-mail: emathis@scad.edu.

See Display on page 177 and Close-Up on page 223

School of the Art Institute of Chicago, Graduate Division, Program in Historic Preservation, Chicago, IL 60603-3103. Offers MSHP. *Entrance requirements:* Additional exam requirements/recommendations for international students: Required—TOEFL, IELTS.

See Close-Up on page 225.

Historic Preservation

Southeast Missouri State University, School of Graduate Studies, Department of History, Cape Girardeau, MO 63701-4799. Offers heritage education (Certificate); historic preservation (Certificate); history (MA); public history (MA), including heritage education, historic preservation. Part-time and evening/weekend programs available. *Faculty:* 10 full-time (2 women). *Students:* 5 full-time (all women), 9 part-time (3 women). Average age 31. 9 applicants, 100% accepted, 4 enrolled. In 2010, 5 master's awarded. *Degree requirements:* For master's, comprehensive exam (for some programs), thesis (for some programs), paper (for history); for Certificate, internship, advanced project in applied history, exam, and paper (for historic preservation). *Entrance requirements:* For master's, GRE, minimum undergraduate GPA of 2.75; 3 reference letters; writing sample; letter of intent. Additional exam requirements/recommendations for international students: Required—TOEFL (minimum score 550 paper-based; 213 computer-based; 79 iBT); Recommended—IELTS (minimum score 6). *Application deadline:* For fall admission, 8/1 for domestic students, 6/1 for international students; for spring admission, 11/21 for domestic students, 10/1 for international students. Applications are processed on a rolling basis. Application fee: $25 ($35 for international students). Electronic applications accepted. *Expenses:* Tuition, state resident: full-time $4698; part-time $261 per credit hour. Tuition, nonresident: full-time $8379; part-time $465.50 per credit hour. *Financial support:* In 2010–11, 4 students received support, including 5 teaching assistantships with full tuition reimbursements available (averaging $7,600 per year); career-related internships or fieldwork, Federal Work-Study, institutionally sponsored loans, scholarships/grants, tuition waivers (full), and unspecified assistantships also available. Financial award application deadline: 6/30; financial award applicants required to submit FAFSA. *Faculty research:* Modern America, historic preservation, world history. *Unit head:* Dr. Wayne H. Bowen, Chairperson, 573-651-2179, E-mail: wbowen@semo.edu. *Application contact:* Gail Amick, Administrative Secretary, 573-651-2049, Fax: 573-651-2001, E-mail: gamick@semo.edu.

Syracuse University, School of Information Studies, Program in Cultural Heritage Preservation, Syracuse, NY 13244. Offers CAS. Part-time programs available. *Students:* 14 applicants, 100% accepted. *Degree requirements:* For CAS, internships. *Entrance requirements:* Additional exam requirements/recommendations for international students: Required—TOEFL (minimum score 100 iBT). *Application deadline:* For fall admission, 2/1 priority date for domestic and international students; for spring admission, 10/15 for domestic students, 10/15 priority date for international students. Applications are processed on a rolling basis. Application fee: $75. Electronic applications accepted. *Expenses:* Tuition: Part-time $1162 per credit. *Unit head:* Kenneth Lavender, Dean, 315-443-6890, E-mail: klavende@syr.edu. *Application contact:* Susan Corieri, Director of Enrollment Management, 315-443-2575, E-mail: ischool@syr.edu.

Texas Tech University, Graduate School, Programs in Museum Science and Heritage Management, Lubbock, TX 79409. Offers heritage management (MS); museum science (MA). Part-time programs available. *Faculty:* 6 full-time (4 women). *Students:* 38 full-time (33 women), 3 part-time (all women); includes 1 Black or African American, non-Hispanic/Latino; 1 American Indian or Alaska Native, non-Hispanic/Latino; 6 Hispanic/Latino. Average age 25. 35 applicants, 74% accepted, 20 enrolled. In 2010, 18 master's awarded. *Degree requirements:* For master's, thesis. *Entrance requirements:* For master's, GRE General Test. Additional exam requirements/recommendations for international students: Required—TOEFL (minimum score 550 paper-based; 213 computer-based; 79 iBT). *Application deadline:* For fall admission, 6/1 priority date for domestic students, 1/15 priority date for international students; for spring admission, 9/1 priority date for domestic students, 6/15 priority date for international students. Applications are processed on a rolling basis. Application fee: $50 ($75 for international students). Electronic applications accepted. *Expenses:* Tuition, state resident: full-time $5495.76; part-time $228.99 per credit hour. Tuition, nonresident: full-time $12,936; part-time $538.99 per credit hour. Required fees: $2674; $36 per credit hour. $905 per semester. *Financial support:* In 2010–11, 4 students received support, including 2 research assistantships with partial tuition reimbursements available (averaging $2,393 per year); teaching assistantships with partial tuition reimbursements available. Financial award application deadline: 4/15; financial award applicants required to submit FAFSA. *Faculty research:* Lubbock Lake Landmark, regional American fine art, museum education, Southern Plains cultural and natural heritage, natural science research. Total annual research expenditures: $143,295. *Unit head:* Dr. Eileen Johnson, Chair, 806-742-2442, Fax: 806-742-1136, E-mail: eileen.johnson@ttu.edu. *Application contact:* Claudia Cory, Assistant to the Director, 806-742-2442 Ext. 222, Fax: 806-742-1136, E-mail: claudia.cory@ttu.edu.

Universidad Nacional Pedro Henriquez Urena, Graduate School, Santo Domingo, Dominican Republic. Offers agricultural diversity (MS), including horticultural/fruit production, tropical animal production; conservation of monuments and cultural assets (M Arch); ecology and environment (MS); environmental engineering (MEE); international relations (MA); natural resource management (MS); political science (MA); project optimization (MPM); project feasibility (MPM); project management (MPM); sanitation engineering (ME); science for teachers (MS); tropical Caribbean architecture (M Arch).

University of California, Los Angeles, Graduate Division, College of Letters and Science, Interdepartmental Program in Conservation of Archaeological and Ethnographic Materials, Los Angeles, CA 90095. Offers MA. *Students:* 7 full-time (all women); includes 2 minority (1 Asian, non-Hispanic/Latino; 1 Hispanic/Latino), 1 international. Average age 27. In 2010, 4 master's awarded. Application fee: $70 ($90 for international students). *Financial support:* In 2010–11, 7 fellowships, 7 research assistantships were awarded; teaching assistantships. *Unit head:* Dr. David A. Scott, Chair, 310-794-4855, E-mail: dascott@ucla.edu. *Application contact:* Amber Cordts-Cole, Program Coordinator, 310-825-1711, E-mail: acordts@ucla.edu.

University of California, Riverside, Graduate Division, Department of History, Riverside, CA 92521-0102. Offers archival management (MA); historic preservation (MA); history (MA, PhD); museum curatorship (MA). Part-time programs available. Terminal master's awarded for partial completion of doctoral program. *Degree requirements:* For master's, one foreign language, comprehensive exam, internship report and oral exams, or thesis; for doctorate, 2 foreign languages, thesis/dissertation, qualifying exams, teaching experience. *Entrance requirements:* For master's, GRE General Test, minimum GPA of 3.2; for doctorate, GRE General Test, MA in history, minimum GPA of 3.2. Additional exam requirements/recommendations for international students: Required—TOEFL (minimum score 550 paper-based; 213 computer-based; 80 iBT). Electronic applications accepted. *Faculty research:* Native American history, United States, public history, Russia, Europe.

University of Colorado Denver, College of Architecture and Planning, Program in Historic Preservation, Denver, CO 80217. Offers MS. *Students:* 9 full-time (7 women), 2 part-time. Average age 35. 5 applicants, 80% accepted, 4 enrolled. *Degree requirements:* For master's, thesis or alternative, 45 credit hours. *Entrance requirements:* For master's, GRE (recommended), brief statement of interest (500-word maximum); compact portfolio of writing samples (maximum 20 pages). Additional exam requirements/recommendations for international students: Required—TOEFL. *Expenses:* Contact institution. *Financial support:* Application deadline: 4/1. *Faculty research:* Rural cultural landscapes; vernacular architecture; cultural preservation; architectural conservation, heritage, and policy. *Unit head:* Dr. Christopher Koziol, Director, 303-556-6516, E-mail: christopher.koziol@ucdenver.edu. *Application contact:* Pam Erickson, Student Services Officer, 303-556-3387, E-mail: pam.erickson@ucdenver.edu.

University of Delaware, College of Arts and Sciences, Program in Art Conservation, Newark, DE 19716. Offers practicing art conservation (MS). *Degree requirements:* For master's, internship, portfolio, oral exam, oral presentation. *Entrance requirements:* For master's, GRE General Test, course work in chemistry, art history/anthropology and studio art; minimum of 400 hours of conservation experience. Electronic applications accepted. *Faculty research:* Emergency response cleaning techniques, degradation process, art history, artists, materials, techniques of preservation and treatment.

University of Delaware, College of Human Services, Education and Public Policy, Center for Energy and Environmental Policy, Program in Urban Affairs and Public Policy, Newark, DE 19716. Offers community development and nonprofit leadership (MA); energy and environmental policy (MA); governance, planning and management (PhD); historic preservation (MA); social and urban policy (PhD); technology, environment and society (PhD). Part-time programs available. Terminal master's awarded for partial completion of doctoral program. *Degree requirements:* For master's, analytical paper or thesis; for doctorate, thesis/dissertation. *Entrance requirements:* For master's, GRE General Test, minimum GPA of 3.0; for doctorate, GRE General Test, minimum GPA of 3.5. Additional exam requirements/recommendations for international students: Required—TOEFL. Electronic applications accepted. *Faculty research:* Political economy; social policy analysis; technology and society; historic preservation; urban policy.

University of Florida, Graduate School, College of Design, Construction and Planning, Doctoral Program in Design, Construction and Planning, Gainesville, FL 32611. Offers design, construction and planning (PhD); historic preservation (PhD). *Faculty:* 15 full-time (2 women). *Students:* 60 full-time (25 women), 16 part-time (6 women); includes 4 Black or African American, non-Hispanic/Latino; 3 Asian, non-Hispanic/Latino; 2 Hispanic/Latino, 35 international. Average age 29. 68 applicants, 46% accepted, 17 enrolled. In 2010, 6 doctorates awarded. *Degree requirements:* For doctorate, thesis/dissertation. *Entrance requirements:* For doctorate, GRE General Test, minimum of 1200 combined Verbal and Quantitative score. Minimum GPA 3.0. Additional exam requirements/recommendations for international students: Required—TOEFL (minimum score 550 paper-based; 213 computer-based; 80 iBT), IELTS (minimum score 6). *Application deadline:* For fall admission, 2/1 for domestic and international students. Applications are processed on a rolling basis. Application fee: $30. Electronic applications accepted. *Expenses:* Tuition, state resident: full-time $10,915.92. Tuition, nonresident: full-time $28,309. *Financial support:* In 2010–11, 48 students received support, including 16 fellowships, 26 research assistantships (averaging $10,928 per year), 6 teaching assistantships (averaging $12,314 per year); unspecified assistantships also available. Financial award applicants required to submit FAFSA. *Faculty research:* Architecture, building construction, urban and regional planning. *Unit head:* Dr. Christopher Silver, Dean, 352-392-0997 Ext. 433, Fax: 352-392-3308, E-mail: silver2@dcp.ufl.edu. *Application contact:* Dr. Paul D. Zwick, Associate Dean for Research and Graduate Programs, 352-392-0997 Ext. 427, Fax: 352-392-3308, E-mail: pdzwick@ufl.edu.

University of Georgia, College of Environment and Design, Program in Historic Preservation, Athens, GA 30602. Offers MHP. *Students:* 28 full-time (19 women), 15 part-time (8 women); includes 1 Asian, non-Hispanic/Latino. 42 applicants, 71% accepted, 16 enrolled. In 2010, 21 master's awarded. *Degree requirements:* For master's, thesis. *Entrance requirements:* For master's, GRE General Test. *Application deadline:* For fall admission, 7/1 priority date for domestic students; for spring admission, 11/15 for domestic students. Application fee: $50. Electronic applications accepted. *Expenses:* Tuition, state resident: full-time $7200; part-time $344 per credit hour. Tuition, nonresident: full-time $21,900; part-time $944 per credit hour. Tuition and fees vary according to course load and program. *Financial support:* Fellowships, research assistantships, teaching assistantships, unspecified assistantships available. *Unit head:* Prof. John C. Waters, Graduate Coordinator, 706-542-4706, Fax: 706-542-4236, E-mail: jcwaters@uga.edu. *Application contact:* Graduate Coordinator.

University of Hawaii at Manoa, Graduate Division, College of Arts and Humanities, Department of American Studies, Program in Historic Preservation, Honolulu, HI 96822. Offers Graduate Certificate. Part-time programs available. *Students:* 9 full-time (7 women), 14 part-time (9 women); includes 10 minority (1 Black or African American, non-Hispanic/Latino; 3 Asian, non-Hispanic/Latino; 2 Native Hawaiian or other Pacific Islander, non-Hispanic/Latino; 4 Two or more races, non-Hispanic/Latino), 3 international. Average age 36. 17 applicants, 88% accepted, 15 enrolled. In 2010, 8 Graduate Certificates awarded. *Entrance requirements:* Additional exam requirements/recommendations for international students: Required—TOEFL (minimum score 600 paper-based; 250 computer-based; 100 iBT), IELTS (minimum score 7). *Application deadline:* For fall admission, 3/1 for domestic and international students; for spring admission, 9/1 for domestic and international students. Application fee: $60. *Financial support:* In 2010–11, 1 research assistantship (averaging $16,176 per year), 3 teaching assistantships (averaging $14,774 per year) were awarded; fellowships also available. *Application contact:* William Chapman, Graduate Chair, 808-956-8826, Fax: 808-956-4733, E-mail: amstuh@hawaii.edu.

University of Kentucky, Graduate School, College of Design, Department of Historic Preservation, Lexington, KY 40506-0032. Offers MHP. *Degree requirements:* For master's, comprehensive exam. *Entrance requirements:* For master's, GRE General Test, minimum undergraduate GPA of 2.75. Additional exam requirements/recommendations for international students: Required—TOEFL (minimum score 550 paper-based; 213 computer-based). Electronic applications accepted.

University of Maryland, College Park, Academic Affairs, School of Architecture, Planning and Preservation, Program in Historic Preservation, College Park, MD 20742. Offers MHP, Certificate. *Faculty:* 4 full-time (2 women), 3 part-time/adjunct (1 woman). *Students:* 15 full-time (9 women), 7 part-time (5 women); includes 1 minority (Black or African American, non-Hispanic/Latino), 2 international. 58 applicants, 43% accepted, 9 enrolled. In 2010, 10 master's awarded. *Degree requirements:* For Certificate, thesis. *Entrance requirements:* For master's, GRE, minimum GPA of 3.0, 3 letters of recommendation, writing sample. Additional exam requirements/recommendations for international students: Required—TOEFL. *Application deadline:* For fall admission, 12/15 for domestic and international students. Applications are processed on a rolling basis. Application fee: $75. Electronic applications accepted. *Expenses:* Tuition, state resident: part-time $471 per credit hour. Tuition, nonresident: part-time $1016 per credit hour. Required fees: $337 per term. *Financial support:* In 2010–11, 16 teaching assistantships (averaging $16,040 per year) were awarded; career-related internships or fieldwork and tuition waivers also available. *Unit head:* Donald Linebaugh, Director, 301-405-6309, Fax: 301-314-9583, E-mail: dwline@umd.edu. *Application contact:* Dr. Charles A. Caramello, Dean of Graduate School, 301-405-0358, Fax: 301-314-9305.

University of Massachusetts Amherst, Graduate School, College of Humanities and Fine Arts, Department of Art, Programs in Architecture and Design, Amherst, MA 01003. Offers architecture and design (M Arch); historic preservation (MS); interior design (MS). Part-time programs available. *Students:* 55 full-time (25 women), 5 part-time (4 women); includes 4 minority (1 Asian, non-Hispanic/Latino; 2 Hispanic/Latino; 1 Native Hawaiian or other Pacific Islander, non-Hispanic/Latino), 7 international. Average age 32. 131 applicants, 65% accepted, 33 enrolled. In 2010, 13 master's awarded. *Degree requirements:* For master's, thesis or alternative, project. *Entrance requirements:* For master's, GRE General Test (M Arch only), portfolio (MS only). Additional exam requirements/recommendations for international students: Required—TOEFL (minimum score 550 paper-based; 213 computer-based; 80 iBT), IELTS (minimum score 6.5). *Application deadline:* For fall admission, 2/1 for domestic and international students. Applications are processed on a rolling basis. Application fee: $50 ($65 for international students). Electronic applications accepted. *Expenses:* Tuition, state resident: full-time $2640. Required fees: $8282. One-time fee: $357 full-time. *Financial support:* Fellowships, research assistantships, teaching assistantships, career-related internships or fieldwork, Federal Work-Study, scholarships/grants, traineeships, health care benefits, tuition waivers (full), and unspecified assistantships available. Support available to part-time students. Financial award application deadline: 2/1; financial award applicants required to submit FAFSA. *Unit head:* Dr. Max Page, Graduate Program Director, 413-545-0943, Fax: 413-545-3929. *Application contact:* Jean M. Ames, Supervisor of Admissions, 413-545-0722, Fax: 413-577-0100, E-mail: gradadm@grad.umass.edu.

University of New Mexico, Graduate School, School of Architecture and Planning, Program in Historic Preservation and Regionalism, Albuquerque, NM 87131-2039. Offers Graduate Certificate. Part-time and evening/weekend programs available. *Students:* 1 (woman) full-time, 8 part-time (6 women); includes 1 minority (Hispanic/Latino). Average age 47. 13 applicants, 92% accepted, 3 enrolled. In 2010, 8 Graduate Certificates awarded. *Application deadline:* For fall admission, 11/1 priority date for domestic students; for spring admission, 3/1 priority date for domestic students. Application fee: $50. Electronic applications accepted. *Expenses:* Tuition, state resident: full-time $5991; part-time $251 per credit hour. Tuition, nonresident: full-time $14,405; part-time $800.20 per credit hour. Tuition and fees vary according to course level, course load, program and reciprocity agreements. *Financial support:* In 2010–11, 1 student received support, including 1 research assistantship (averaging $7,500 per year); career-related internships or fieldwork and scholarships/grants also available. Support available to part-time students. *Unit head:* Chris Wilson, Director, 505-277-3303, Fax: 505-277-0897, E-mail: chwilson@unm.edu. *Application contact:* Chris Wilson, Director, 505-277-3303, Fax: 505-277-0897, E-mail: chwilson@unm.edu.

The University of North Carolina at Greensboro, Graduate School, School of Human Environmental Sciences, Department of Interior Architecture, Greensboro, NC 27412-5001. Offers historic preservation (Certificate); interior architecture (MS); museum studies (Certificate). *Degree requirements:* For master's, thesis. *Entrance requirements:* For master's, GRE General Test or MAT, bachelor's degree in interior design, interview, portfolio. Additional exam requirements/recommendations for international students: Required—TOEFL. Electronic applications accepted.

University of Oregon, Graduate School, School of Architecture and Allied Arts, Program in Historic Preservation, Eugene, OR 97403. Offers MS. *Degree requirements:* For master's, thesis, internship. *Entrance requirements:* For master's, participation in Pacific Northwest Field School. Additional exam requirements/recommendations for international students: Required—TOEFL. *Faculty research:* Vernacular architecture, Native American architecture, masonry structure and details, wood construction systems, cultural landscapes.

University of Pennsylvania, School of Design, Graduate Group in Historic Preservation, Philadelphia, PA 19104. Offers conservation and heritage management (Certificate); historic conservation (Certificate); historic preservation (MS). Part-time programs available. *Faculty:* 2 full-time (0 women), 2 part-time/adjunct (0 women). *Students:* 55 full-time (42 women); includes 2 Black or African American, non-Hispanic/Latino; 3 Asian, non-Hispanic/Latino; 5 Hispanic/Latino, 4 international. 93 applicants, 74% accepted, 35 enrolled. In 2010, 21 master's, 9 other advanced degrees awarded. *Degree requirements:* For master's, thesis. *Entrance requirements:* For master's, GRE. Additional exam requirements/recommendations for international students: Required—TOEFL. *Application deadline:* For fall admission, 1/2 priority date for domestic students. Application fee: $70. *Expenses:* Tuition: Full-time $25,660; part-time $4758 per course. Required fees: $2152; $270 per course. Tuition and fees vary according to course load, degree level and program. *Financial support:* Fellowships, research assistantships, teaching assistantships, career-related internships or fieldwork, Federal Work-Study, institutionally sponsored loans, scholarships/grants, and tuition waivers (partial) available. Support available to part-time students. Financial award applicants required to submit FAFSA. *Faculty research:* Historic building technology, architectural conservation, architectural theory, preservation in the Third World.

University of South Carolina, The Graduate School, College of Arts and Sciences, Department of History, Program in Public History, Columbia, SC 29208. Offers archives (MA); historic preservation (MA); museum (MA); museum management (Certificate); MLIS/MA. *Degree requirements:* For master's, one foreign language, thesis, internship. *Entrance requirements:* For master's, GRE General Test, writing sample. Additional exam requirements/recommendations for international students: Required—TOEFL. Electronic applications accepted. *Faculty research:* Museum studies, historic preservation, archives administration.

The University of Texas at Austin, Graduate School, School of Architecture, Austin, TX 78712-1111. Offers architecture (M Arch); community and regional planning (MSCRP, PhD); historic preservation (MS); history of architecture (MA, PhD); landscape architecture (MLA); urban design (MSUD); JD/MSCRP; MSCRP/MA; MSCRP/PhD. *Degree requirements:* For doctorate, thesis/dissertation. *Entrance requirements:* For master's and doctorate, GRE General Test. Additional exam requirements/recommendations for international students: Required—TOEFL (minimum score 550 paper-based; 213 computer-based). Electronic applications accepted.

University of Vermont, Graduate College, College of Arts and Sciences, Program in Historic Preservation, Burlington, VT 05405. Offers MS. *Students:* 24 (16 women); includes 1 American Indian or Alaska Native, non-Hispanic/Latino. 39 applicants, 64% accepted, 10 enrolled. In 2010, 10 master's awarded. *Entrance requirements:* For master's, GRE General Test, sample project or equivalent. Additional exam requirements/recommendations for international students: Required—TOEFL (minimum score 550 paper-based; 213 computer-based; 80 iBT). *Application*

deadline: For fall admission, 3/1 for domestic students. Application fee: $40. Electronic applications accepted. *Expenses:* Tuition, state resident: part-time $537 per credit hour. Tuition, nonresident: part-time $1355 per credit hour. *Financial support:* Fellowships, teaching assistantships available. Financial award application deadline: 3/1. *Faculty research:* Architectural environment. *Unit head:* T. Visser, Director, 802-656-3180. *Application contact:* T. Visser, Director, 802-656-3180.

University of Washington, Graduate School, College of Built Environments, Interdisciplinary Program in Historic Preservation, Seattle, WA 98195. Offers Certificate. Offered in cooperation with the Departments of Architecture, Landscape Architecture, and Urban Design and Planning. Part-time programs available. Electronic applications accepted. *Faculty research:* History of the built environment, historic preservation planning, vernacular architecture, ethnic and gender issues in preservation, restoration.

University of Wisconsin–Milwaukee, Graduate School, School of Architecture and Urban Planning, Department of Architecture, Milwaukee, WI 53201-0413. Offers architecture (PhD); preservation studies (Certificate); M Arch/MUP. *Faculty:* 26 full-time (4 women). *Students:* 194 full-time (64 women), 13 part-time (5 women); includes 3 Black or African American, non-Hispanic/Latino; 5 Asian, non-Hispanic/Latino; 5 Hispanic/Latino, 16 international. Average age 28. 193 applicants, 67% accepted, 61 enrolled. In 2010, 15 master's awarded. *Degree requirements:* For master's, comprehensive exam, thesis; for doctorate, comprehensive exam, thesis/dissertation. *Entrance requirements:* For master's, GRE General Test, portfolio. Additional exam requirements/recommendations for international students: Required—TOEFL (minimum score 600 paper-based; 250 computer-based; 100 iBT), IELTS (minimum score 7). *Application deadline:* For fall admission, 1/1 priority date for domestic students; for spring admission, 9/1 for domestic students. Applications are processed on a rolling basis. Application fee: $56 ($96 for international students). Electronic applications accepted. *Financial support:* In 2010–11, 3 fellowships, 20 teaching assistantships were awarded; career-related internships or fieldwork, health care benefits, unspecified assistantships, and project assistantships also available. Support available to part-time students. Financial award application deadline: 4/15; financial award applicants required to submit FAFSA. *Unit head:* Joan Simuncak, Representative, 414-229-4015, Fax: 414-229-6976, E-mail: joanarch@uwm.edu. *Application contact:* Josef Stagg, General Information Contact, 414-229-4032, Fax: 414-229-6967, E-mail: jstagg@uwm.edu.

Ursuline College, School of Graduate Studies, Program in Historic Preservation, Pepper Pike, OH 44124-4398. Offers MA. Part-time programs available. *Faculty:* 1 (woman) full-time, 2 part-time/adjunct (0 women). *Students:* 8 full-time (7 women), 3 part-time (all women); includes 2 minority (both Black or African American, non-Hispanic/Latino). Average age 34. 3 applicants, 100% accepted, 1 enrolled. In 2010, 2 master's awarded. *Degree requirements:* For master's, thesis. *Entrance requirements:* For master's, minimum undergraduate GPA of 3.0. Additional exam requirements/recommendations for international students: Required—TOEFL (minimum score 500 paper-based; 173 computer-based). *Application deadline:* For fall admission, 8/1 priority date for domestic students. Applications are processed on a rolling basis. Application fee: $25. *Expenses:* Tuition: Full-time $15,138; part-time $841 per credit. Required fees: $240; $120 per semester. *Financial support:* In 2010–11, 4 students received support. Federal Work-Study available. Financial award application deadline: 3/1. *Unit head:* Dr. Bari Stith, 440-646-8135, Fax: 440-684-6088, E-mail: bstith@ursuline.edu. *Application contact:* Melanie Steele, Graduate Admission Assistant, 440-646-8199, Fax: 440-684-6138, E-mail: graduateadmissions@ursuline.edu.

Virginia Commonwealth University, Graduate School, College of Humanities and Sciences, Wilder School of Government and Public Affairs, Department of Urban Studies and Planning, Program in Historic Preservation Planning, Richmond, VA 23284-9005. Offers Certificate. *Students:* 6 applicants, 83% accepted, 4 enrolled. *Entrance requirements:* Additional exam requirements/recommendations for international students: Required—TOEFL (minimum score 600 paper-based; 250 computer-based; 100 iBT); Recommended—IELTS (minimum score 6.5). *Application deadline:* For fall admission, 7/25 for domestic students; for spring admission, 11/30 for domestic students. Applications are processed on a rolling basis. Application fee: $50. Electronic applications accepted. *Expenses:* Tuition, state resident: full-time $4308; part-time $479 per credit hour. Tuition, nonresident: full-time $8942; part-time $994 per credit hour. Required fees: $2000; $85 per credit hour. Tuition and fees vary according to course level, course load, degree level, campus/location and program. *Unit head:* Dr. I-Shian Suen, Program Chair, 804-828-2721, E-mail: isuen@vcu.edu. *Application contact:* Dr. John Accordino, Associate Professor, 804-827-0525, E-mail: jaccordi@vcu.edu.

Landscape Architecture

Arizona State University, Herberger Institute for Design and the Arts, School of Architecture and Landscape Architecture, Tempe, AZ 85287-1605. Offers architecture (M Arch); building design/built environment (MS); design (arts, media, and engineering) (MSD); design (healthcare and healing environments) (MSD); design (industrial design) (MSD); design (interior design) (MSD); design (new product innovation) (MSD); design (visual communication design) (MSD); design, environment and the arts (PhD), including design, environment and the arts (design), design, environment and the arts (healthcare and healing environments), design, environment and the arts (history, theory, and criticism); landscape architecture (MLA); urban design (MUD); MA/MBA. *Accreditation:* NASAD. *Faculty:* 41 full-time (9 women), 6 part-time/adjunct (3 women). *Students:* 252 full-time (111 women), 45 part-time (21 women); includes 61 minority (3 Black or African American, non-Hispanic/Latino; 2 American Indian or Alaska Native, non-Hispanic/Latino; 13 Asian, non-Hispanic/Latino; 41 Hispanic/Latino; 1 Native Hawaiian or other Pacific Islander, non-Hispanic/Latino; 1 Two or more races, non-Hispanic/Latino), 58 international. Average age 29. 420 applicants, 61% accepted, 117 enrolled. In 2010, 60 master's, 8 doctorates awarded. Terminal master's awarded for partial completion of doctoral program. *Degree requirements:* For master's, thesis optional, interactive Program of Study (iPOS) submitted before completing 50 percent of required credit hours; for doctorate, comprehensive exam, thesis/dissertation, interactive Program of Study (iPOS) submitted before completing 50 percent of required credit hours. *Entrance requirements:* For master's, GRE General Test, minimum GPA of 3.0 or equivalent in last 2 years of work leading to bachelor's degree, design/creative works portfolio, 3 references, statement of intent; for doctorate, GRE, master's degree in architecture, graphic design, industrial design, interior design, landscape architecture, or art history or equivalent standing; statement of purpose; 3 letters of recommendation; indication of potential faculty mentor; sample of written work. Additional exam requirements/recommendations for international students: Required—TOEFL (minimum score 600 paper-based; 250 computer-based; 100 iBT). *Application deadline:* For fall admission, 1/15 priority date for domestic and international students. Application fee: $70 ($90 for international students). Electronic applications accepted. *Expenses:* Tuition, state resident: full-time $8510; part-time $608 per credit. Tuition, nonresident: full-time $16,542; part-time $919 per credit. Required fees: $339; $110 per credit. Part-time tuition and fees vary according to course load. *Financial support:* In 2010–11, 9 research assistantships with full and partial tuition reimbursements (averaging $11,913 per year), 76 teaching assistantships with full and partial tuition reimbursements (averaging $6,294 per year) were awarded; fellowships with full and partial tuition reimbursements, scholarships/grants and tuition waivers (full and partial) also available. Financial award application deadline: 3/1; financial award applicants required to submit FAFSA. Total annual research expenditures: $410,956. *Unit head:* Darren Petrucci,

Director, 480-965-3536, E-mail: darren.petrucci@asu.edu. *Application contact:* Graduate Admissions, 480-965-6113.

Auburn University, Graduate School, College of Architecture, Design, and Construction, Program in Landscape Architecture, Auburn University, AL 36849. Offers MLA. *Accreditation:* ASLA. *Faculty:* 26 full-time (6 women), 3 part-time/adjunct (1 woman). *Students:* 33 full-time (11 women), 4 part-time (3 women); includes 1 Black or African American, non-Hispanic/Latino; 1 Hispanic/Latino, 10 international. Average age 26. 56 applicants, 70% accepted, 17 enrolled. In 2010, 7 master's awarded. *Entrance requirements:* For master's, 3 letters of recommendation. Application fee: $50 ($60 for international students). *Expenses:* Tuition, state resident: full-time $7002. Tuition, nonresident: full-time $21,898. International tuition: $22,116 full-time. Required fees: $892. Tuition and fees vary according to course load and program. *Financial support:* Applicants required to submit FAFSA. *Unit head:* Charlene Lebleu, Chair, 334-844-4516. *Application contact:* Dr. George Flowers, Dean of the Graduate School, 334-844-2125.

Ball State University, Graduate School, College of Architecture and Planning, Department of Landscape Architecture, Muncie, IN 47306-1099. Offers MLA. *Accreditation:* ASLA. *Faculty:* 13. *Students:* 29 full-time (17 women), 11 part-time (8 women); includes 4 minority (1 American Indian or Alaska Native, non-Hispanic/Latino; 2 Hispanic/Latino; 1 Two or more races, non-Hispanic/Latino), 15 international. Average age 29. 62 applicants, 53% accepted, 6 enrolled. In 2010, 5 master's awarded. *Degree requirements:* For master's, thesis. *Entrance requirements:* For master's, writing sample. Application fee: $50. *Expenses:* Tuition, state resident: full-time $6160; part-time $299 per credit hour. Tuition, nonresident: full-time $16,020; part-time $783 per credit hour. Required fees: $2278; $95 per credit hour. *Financial support:* In 2010–11, 26 teaching assistantships with full tuition reimbursements (averaging $6,622 per year) were awarded; research assistantships with full tuition reimbursements. Financial award application deadline: 3/1. *Unit head:* Jody Rosenblatt, Chairperson, 765-285-1982, Fax: 765-285-1983. *Application contact:* Dr. Joseph Blalock, 765-285-4258, E-mail: jblalock@bsu.edu.

California State Polytechnic University, Pomona, Academic Affairs, College of Environmental Design, Program in Landscape Architecture, Pomona, CA 91768-2557. Offers M Land Arch. *Accreditation:* ASLA. Part-time programs available. *Students:* 44 full-time (25 women), 14 part-time (6 women); includes 17 minority (1 Black or African American, non-Hispanic/Latino; 9 Asian, non-Hispanic/Latino; 2 Hispanic/Latino; 5 Two or more races, non-Hispanic/Latino), 5 international. Average age 32. 101 applicants, 30% accepted, 24 enrolled. In 2010, 19 master's awarded. *Degree requirements:* For master's, thesis or alternative. *Application deadline:* For fall admission, 5/1 priority date for domestic students; for winter

Landscape Architecture

California State Polytechnic University, Pomona (continued)
admission, 10/15 priority date for domestic students; for spring admission, 1/20 priority date for domestic students. Applications are processed on a rolling basis. Application fee: $55. Electronic applications accepted. *Expenses:* Tuition, state resident: full-time $5386; part-time $2850 per year. Tuition, nonresident: full-time $12,082; part-time $248 per credit. Required fees: $577; $248 per credit. $577 per year. Tuition and fees vary according to course load and program. *Financial support:* Career-related internships or fieldwork, Federal Work-Study, and institutionally sponsored loans available. Support available to part-time students. Financial award application deadline: 3/2; financial award applicants required to submit FAFSA. *Unit head:* Dr. Gerald O. Taylor, Graduate Program Coordinator, 909-869-6891, Fax: 909-869-4460, E-mail: lagradprog@csupomona.edu. *Application contact:* Scott J. Duncan, Director, Admissions, 909-869-3258, Fax: 909-869-4529, E-mail: sjduncan@csupomona.edu.

Chatham University, Program in Landscape Architecture, Pittsburgh, PA 15232-2826. Offers landscape architecture (ML Arch); landscape studies (MA). *Accreditation:* ASLA. Part-time and evening/weekend programs available. *Degree requirements:* For master's, thesis, capstone project. *Entrance requirements:* Additional exam requirements/recommendations for international students: Required—TOEFL (minimum score 600 paper-based; 250 computer-based; 100 iBT), IELTS (minimum score 6.5), TWE. Electronic applications accepted. *Faculty research:* Sustainability.

City College of the City University of New York, Graduate School, School of Architecture and Environmental Studies, New York, NY 10031-9198. Offers architecture (M Arch); landscape architecture (MLA); urban design (MUP). Part-time programs available. *Degree requirements:* For master's, thesis. *Entrance requirements:* For master's, portfolio, professional degree in architecture or equivalent. Additional exam requirements/recommendations for international students: Required—TOEFL (minimum score 550 paper-based; 213 computer-based).

Clemson University, Graduate School, College of Architecture, Arts, and Humanities, Department of Planning and Landscape Architecture, Program in Landscape Architecture, Clemson, SC 29634. Offers MLA. *Accreditation:* ASLA. *Students:* 27 full-time (12 women), 2 part-time (both women); includes 2 Hispanic/Latino; 1 Two or more races, non-Hispanic/Latino, 7 international. Average age 31. 41 applicants, 76% accepted, 11 enrolled. In 2010, 10 master's awarded. *Entrance requirements:* For master's, GRE General Test. Additional exam requirements/recommendations for international students: Required—TOEFL. *Application deadline:* For fall admission, 2/15 for domestic students, 4/15 for international students. Applications are processed on a rolling basis. Application fee: $70 ($80 for international students). Electronic applications accepted. *Expenses:* Tuition, state resident: full-time $6492; part-time $400 per credit hour. Tuition, nonresident: full-time $13,634; part-time $800 per credit hour. Required fees: $262 per semester. Part-time tuition and fees vary according to course load and program. *Financial support:* In 2010–11, 15 students received support, including 15 teaching assistantships with partial tuition reimbursements available (averaging $3,480 per year); fellowships with partial tuition reimbursements available, research assistantships with partial tuition reimbursements available, career-related internships or fieldwork, institutionally sponsored loans, scholarships/grants, health care benefits, and unspecified assistantships also available. Support available to part-time students. *Unit head:* Dr. Elaine M. Worzala, Chair, 864-656-3657, Fax: 864-656-7519, E-mail: eworzal@clemson.edu. *Application contact:* Dr. Umit Yilmaz, Coordinator, 864-656-7349, Fax: 864-656-7519, E-mail: uyilmaz@clemson.edu.

Colorado State University, Graduate School, College of Agricultural Sciences, Department of Horticulture and Landscape Architecture, Fort Collins, CO 80523-1173. Offers horticulture (MS, PhD); landscape architecture (MLA). Part-time programs available. *Faculty:* 24 full-time (4 women). *Students:* 16 full-time (5 women), 12 part-time (4 women); includes 5 minority (1 Black or African American, non-Hispanic/Latino; 1 American Indian or Alaska Native, non-Hispanic/Latino; 1 Hispanic/Latino; 2 Two or more races, non-Hispanic/Latino), 6 international. Average age 33. 22 applicants, 68% accepted, 8 enrolled. In 2010, 3 master's, 5 doctorates awarded. *Degree requirements:* For master's, thesis (for some programs); for doctorate, comprehensive exam, thesis/dissertation. *Entrance requirements:* For master's, GRE General Test (minimum upper 50th percentile, minimum score 1100 verbal and quantitative), minimum GPA of 3.0, letters of reference, related bachelor's degree or experience; for doctorate, GRE General Test (upper 50th percentile and combined minimum score of 1100 for the Verbal and Quantitative sections), minimum GPA of 3.0, letters of reference, statement of purpose, related bachelor's degree or experience. Additional exam requirements/recommendations for international students: Required—TOEFL (minimum score 550 paper-based; 213 computer-based; 80 iBT). *Application deadline:* Applications are processed on a rolling basis. Application fee: $50. Electronic applications accepted. *Expenses:* Tuition, state resident: full-time $7434; part-time $413 per credit. Tuition, nonresident: full-time $19,022; part-time $1057 per credit. Required fees: $1729; $88 per credit. *Financial support:* In 2010–11, 12 students received support, including 2 fellowships with full tuition reimbursements available (averaging $16,489 per year), 6 research assistantships with partial tuition reimbursements available (averaging $7,679 per year), 4 teaching assistantships with partial tuition reimbursements available (averaging $8,657 per year); scholarships/grants, unspecified assistantships, and fellowships also available. Financial award applicants required to submit FAFSA. *Faculty research:* Antioxidants in food crops, environmental physiology, water conservation, tissue culture, rhizosphere biology, cancer prevention through dietary intervention. Total annual research expenditures: $2.5 million. *Unit head:* Dr. Stephen J. Wallner, Head, 970-491-7018, Fax: 970-491-7745, E-mail: stephen.wallner@colostate.edu. *Application contact:* Kathi Nietfeld, Coordinator, 970-491-7018, Fax: 970-491-7745, E-mail: kathi.nietfeld@colostate.edu.

Columbia University, School of Continuing Education, Program in Landscape Design, New York, NY 10027. Offers MS. Part-time programs available. *Entrance requirements:* For master's, minimum undergraduate GPA of 3.0. Additional exam requirements/recommendations for international students: Required—American Language Program placement test.

Conway School of Landscape Design, Graduate Program in Landscape Design, Conway, MA 01341-0179. Offers MA. *Degree requirements:* For master's, projects. *Faculty research:* Restoration of native plant communities; integration of humanities, environment, and design.

Cornell University, Graduate School, Graduate Fields of Agriculture and Life Sciences and Graduate Fields of Architecture, Art and Planning, Field of Landscape Architecture, Ithaca, NY 14853-0001. Offers MLA. *Accreditation:* ASLA. *Faculty:* 18 full-time (8 women). *Students:* 53 full-time (26 women); includes 4 Asian, non-Hispanic/Latino; 1 Hispanic/Latino, 7 international. Average age 29. 160 applicants, 37% accepted, 28 enrolled. In 2010, 18 master's awarded. *Degree requirements:* For master's, project or thesis. *Entrance requirements:* For master's, GRE General Test (recommended), portfolio, 2 letters of recommendation. Additional exam requirements/recommendations for international students: Required—TOEFL (minimum score 550 paper-based; 213 computer-based; 77 iBT). *Application deadline:* For fall admission, 2/15 priority date for domestic students. Applications are processed on a rolling basis. Application fee: $70. Electronic applications accepted. *Expenses:* Tuition: Full-time $29,500. Required fees: $76. Tuition and fees vary according to degree level and program. *Financial support:* In 2010–11, 2 fellowships with full tuition reimbursements, 10 teaching assistantships with full tuition reimbursements were awarded; research assistantships with full tuition reimbursements, institutionally sponsored loans, scholarships/grants, health care benefits, tuition waivers (full and partial), and unspecified assistantships also available. Financial award applicants required to submit FAFSA. *Faculty research:* Urban horticulture and landscape design, urban design research, cultural landscape history, women in landscape architecture, landscape design language, Japanese landscape architecture. *Unit head:* Director of Graduate Studies, 607-254-9552. *Application contact:* Graduate School Application Requests, Caldwell Hall, 607-254-9552, E-mail: lafield@cornell.edu.

Florida Agricultural and Mechanical University, Division of Graduate Studies, Research, and Continuing Education, School of Architecture, Tallahassee, FL 32307-3200. Offers architectural studies (MS Arch); architecture (professional) (M Arch); landscape architecture (MLA). Part-time programs available. *Degree requirements:* For master's, thesis. *Entrance requirements:* For master's, GRE General Test, minimum GPA of 3.0, portfolio. Additional exam requirements/recommendations for international students: Required—TOEFL (minimum score 550 paper-based). *Faculty research:* Environmental technology, post-occupancy evaluation, building economics, design methods, computer-aided design.

Florida International University, College of Architecture and the Arts, School of Architecture, Landscape Architecture Program, Miami, FL 33199. Offers MA, MLA. Part-time programs available. *Faculty:* 3 full-time (1 woman), 4 part-time/adjunct (1 woman). *Students:* 56 full-time (24 women), 10 part-time (8 women); includes 4 Black or African American, non-Hispanic/Latino; 2 Asian, non-Hispanic/Latino; 36 Hispanic/Latino, 4 international. Average age 26. 51 applicants, 22% accepted, 9 enrolled. In 2010, 7 master's awarded. *Entrance requirements:* For master's, GRE or minimum GPA of 3.0 in upper-level undergraduate work, portfolio. Additional exam requirements/recommendations for international students: Required—TOEFL (minimum score 550 paper-based; 80 iBT). *Application deadline:* For fall admission, 2/1 for domestic and international students. Application fee: $30. Electronic applications accepted. *Financial support:* Institutionally sponsored loans and scholarships/grants available. Financial award application deadline: 3/1; financial award applicants required to submit FAFSA. *Unit head:* Dr. Brian Schriner, Interim Dean, 305-348-6442, Fax: 305-348-6716, E-mail: schriner@fiu.edu. *Application contact:* Prof. Marta Canaves, Graduate Program Director, 305-348-1886, Fax: 305-348-6716, E-mail: marta.canaves@fiu.edu.

Harvard University, Graduate School of Arts and Sciences, Committee on Architecture, Landscape Architecture, and Urban Planning, Cambridge, MA 02138. Offers architecture (PhD); landscape architecture (PhD); urban planning (PhD). *Degree requirements:* For doctorate, one foreign language, thesis/dissertation, oral exam. *Entrance requirements:* For doctorate, GRE General Test. Additional exam requirements/recommendations for international students: Required—TOEFL. *Expenses:* Tuition: Full-time $34,976. Required fees: $1166. Full-time tuition and fees vary according to program.

Harvard University, Graduate School of Design, Department of Landscape Architecture, Cambridge, MA 02138. Offers MLA. *Accreditation:* ASLA. *Entrance requirements:* For master's, GRE General Test. Additional exam requirements/recommendations for international students: Required—TOEFL (minimum score 600 paper-based; 250 computer-based; 104 iBT). Electronic applications accepted. *Expenses:* Tuition: Full-time $34,976. Required fees: $1166. Full-time tuition and fees vary according to program.

Illinois Institute of Technology, Graduate College, College of Architecture, Chicago, IL 60616-3793. Offers M Arch, M IBD, MLA, MS Arch, PhD. *Accreditation:* ASLA. Part-time programs available. *Faculty:* 39 full-time (5 women), 54 part-time/adjunct (15 women). *Students:* 234 full-time (103 women), 14 part-time (7 women); includes 20 minority (3 Black or African American, non-Hispanic/Latino; 7 Asian, non-Hispanic/Latino; 9 Hispanic/Latino; 1 Two or more races, non-Hispanic/Latino), 97 international. Average age 28. 500 applicants, 65% accepted, 114 enrolled. In 2010, 84 master's, 1 doctorate awarded. Terminal master's awarded for partial completion of doctoral program. *Degree requirements:* For master's, comprehensive exam (for some programs), thesis (for some programs); for doctorate, comprehensive exam, thesis/dissertation. *Entrance requirements:* For master's, GRE General Test (minimum score 900 Quantitative and Verbal, 2.5 Analytical Writing), minimum college GPA of 3.0, official transcripts, portfolio, 3 letters of recommendation, professional statement; personal interview (recommended); for doctorate, GRE General Test (minimum score 900 Quantitative and Verbal, 2.5 Analytical Writing), minimum GPA of 3.5, official transcripts, portfolio, 3 letters of recommendation, professional statement. Additional exam requirements/recommendations for international students: Required—TOEFL (minimum score 550 paper-based; 80 iBT); Recommended—IELTS (minimum score 5.5). *Application deadline:* For fall admission, 4/15 for domestic and international students; for spring admission, 11/15 for domestic and international students. Applications are processed on a rolling basis. Application fee: $50. Electronic applications accepted. *Expenses:* Tuition: Full-time $18,576; part-time $1032 per credit hour. Required fees: $583 per semester. One-time fee: $150. Tuition and fees vary according to program and student level. *Financial support:* In 2010–11, 1 research assistantship (averaging $5,000 per year), 39 teaching assistantships with full and partial tuition reimbursements (averaging $1,566 per year) were awarded; fellowships with full and partial tuition reimbursements, career-related internships or fieldwork, Federal Work-Study, institutionally sponsored loans, scholarships/grants, health care benefits, tuition waivers (partial), and unspecified assistantships also available. Support available to part-time students. Financial award applicants required to submit FAFSA. *Faculty research:* Sustainable design and efficiency; the influence of climate and environment on building form; emerging ubanisms; computer applications (such as 3-D modeling); the design, planning and structure of high-rise buildings. Total annual research expenditures: $49,595. *Unit head:* Donna V. Robertson, Dean, 312-567-3230, Fax: 312-567-5820, E-mail: robertson@iit.edu. *Application contact:* Katherine Fitzgibbon, Director, Graduate Academic Affairs, 312-567-5858, Fax: 312-567-5820, E-mail: kfitzgib@iit.edu.

Iowa State University of Science and Technology, Graduate College, College of Design, Department of Landscape Architecture, Ames, IA 50011. Offers MLA, MCRP/MLA. Part-time programs available. *Faculty:* 12 full-time (5 women), 1 part-time/adjunct (0 women). *Students:* 9 full-time (4 women), 7 part-time (4 women); includes 1 Black or African American, non-Hispanic/Latino; 1 American Indian or Alaska Native, non-Hispanic/Latino; 1 Hispanic/Latino, 2 international. 13 applicants, 54% accepted, 5 enrolled. *Degree requirements:* For master's, thesis. *Entrance requirements:* For master's, GRE (highly recommended), portfolio. Additional exam requirements/recommendations for international students: Required—TOEFL (minimum score 600 paper-based; 79 iBT), IELTS (minimum score 7). *Application deadline:* For fall admission, 2/1 priority date for domestic and international students. Applications are processed on a rolling basis. Application fee: $40 ($90 for international students). Electronic applications accepted. *Financial support:* In 2010–11, 2 research assistantships with full and partial tuition reimbursements (averaging $3,169 per year), 2 teaching assistantships with full and partial tuition reimbursements (averaging $2,113 per year) were awarded; career-related internships or fieldwork, Federal Work-Study, institutionally sponsored loans, tuition waivers (partial), and unspecified assistantships also available. Support available to part-time students. Financial award application deadline: 2/15; financial award applicants required to submit FAFSA. *Faculty research:* Landscape ecology, geographic information systems, landscape perception, historic preservation, resource management, design. Total annual research expenditures: $1.2 million. *Unit head:* Dr. Douglas Johnston, Chair, 515-294-6942, Fax: 515-294-2348, E-mail: landarch@iastate.edu. *Application contact:* Dr. Paul F. Anderson, Director of Graduate Education, 515-294-8958, E-mail: landarch@iastate.edu.

Kansas State University, Graduate School, College of Architecture, Planning and Design, Department of Landscape Architecture and Regional and Community Planning, Manhattan, KS 66506. Offers MLA. *Accreditation:* ASLA. Part-time programs available. *Degree requirements:* For master's, thesis, residency, oral exam. *Entrance requirements:* For master's, portfolio. Additional exam requirements/recommendations for international students: Required—TOEFL (minimum score 600 paper-based). Electronic applications accepted. *Faculty research:* Community planning and design, design and planning theory, geospatial technology infrastructure, watershed restoration, landscape ecology.

Louisiana State University and Agricultural and Mechanical College, Graduate School, College of Art and Design, School of Landscape Architecture, Baton Rouge, LA 70803. Offers MLA. *Accreditation:* ASLA. *Faculty:* 12 full-time (3 women). *Students:* 36 full-time (16 women); includes 1 Hispanic/Latino, 10 international. Average age 27. 82 applicants, 62% accepted, 16 enrolled. In 2010, 14 master's awarded. *Degree requirements:* For master's, thesis. *Entrance requirements:* For master's, GRE General Test, minimum GPA of 3.0. Additional exam requirements/recommendations for international students: Required—TOEFL (minimum score 550 paper-based; 213 computer-based; 79 iBT) or IELTS (minimum score 6.5). *Application deadline:* For fall admission, 1/25 priority date for domestic students, 5/15 for international students; for spring admission, 10/15 for international students. Applications are processed on a rolling basis. Application fee: $50 ($70 for international students). Electronic applications accepted. *Financial support:* In 2010–11, 28 students received support, including 15 research assistantships with full and partial tuition reimbursements available (averaging $6,552 per year); fellowships, career-related internships or fieldwork, Federal Work-Study, institutionally sponsored loans, health care benefits, and unspecified assistantships also available. Financial award application deadline: 7/1; financial award applicants required to submit FAFSA. *Faculty research:* Digital representation, cultural landscapes, urban infrastructure, community design. Total annual research expenditures: $2,491. *Unit head:* Prof. Van Cox, Interim Director, 225-578-1434, Fax: 225-578-1445, E-mail: vcox1@lsu.edu. *Application contact:* Bradly Cantrell, Graduate Coordinator, 225-578-1474, Fax: 225-578-1445, E-mail: cantrell@lsu.edu.

Mississippi State University, College of Agriculture and Life Sciences, Department of Landscape Architecture, Mississippi State, MS 39762. Offers MLA. Part-time programs available. *Faculty:* 9 full-time (0 women). *Students:* 25 full-time (6 women), 4 part-time (0 women); includes 1 minority (Native Hawaiian or other Pacific Islander, non-Hispanic/Latino), 5 international. Average age 29. 21 applicants, 57% accepted, 9 enrolled. In 2010, 5 master's awarded. *Degree requirements:* For master's, thesis. *Entrance requirements:* For master's, GRE or minimum GPA of 3.0 in upper-division major emphasis courses from an accredited university, minimum GPA of 2.8 on bachelor's degree. Additional exam requirements/recommendations for international students: Required—TOEFL (minimum score 600 paper-based; 250 computer-based; 100 iBT); Recommended—IELTS (minimum score 7.5). *Application deadline:* For fall admission, 7/1 for domestic students, 5/1 for international students; for spring admission, 10/1 for domestic students, 9/1 for international students. Applications are processed on a rolling basis. Application fee: $40. Electronic applications accepted. *Expenses:* Tuition, state resident: full-time $2730.50; part-time $304 per credit hour. Tuition, nonresident: full-time $6901; part-time $767 per credit hour. *Financial support:* In 2010–11, 3 research assistantships (averaging $14,507 per year), 4 teaching assistantships with full and partial tuition reimbursements (averaging $7,120 per year) were awarded; Federal Work-Study, institutionally sponsored loans, tuition waivers (partial), and unspecified assistantships also available. Financial award application deadline: 4/1; financial award applicants required to submit FAFSA. *Faculty research:* Design pedagogy, low impact development, conservation planning, wildlife/urban interfacing planning, sustainable communities, watershed planning, historical landscapes, decision support system development, Center for Sustainable Design. *Unit head:* Sadik C. Artunc, Professor and Head, 662-325-4554, Fax: 662-325-7893, E-mail: sartunc@lalc.msstate.edu. *Application contact:* Prof. Wayne Wilkerson, Professor and Graduate Coordinator, 662-325-3012, Fax: 662-325-7893, E-mail: gww@ra.msstate.edu.

Morgan State University, School of Graduate Studies, Institute of Architecture and Planning, Program in Landscape Architecture, Baltimore, MD 21251. Offers MLA, MSLA. *Accreditation:* ASLA. *Degree requirements:* For master's, thesis. *Entrance requirements:* Additional exam requirements/recommendations for international students: Required—TOEFL (minimum score 550 paper-based; 213 computer-based). *Faculty research:* Philosophy and design, urban design, design history and theory, computer-aided design and community design.

North Carolina State University, Graduate School, College of Design, Department of Landscape Architecture, Raleigh, NC 27695. Offers MLA. *Accreditation:* ASLA. *Degree requirements:* For master's, thesis optional, oral exam, project. *Entrance requirements:* For master's, GRE General Test (recommended), portfolio. Electronic applications accepted. *Faculty research:* Community development and co-operative engagement, landscape planning and design.

The Ohio State University, Graduate School, College of Engineering, Austin E. Knowlton School of Architecture, Columbus, OH 43210. Offers architecture (M Arch); city and regional planning (MCRP, PhD); landscape architecture (M Land Arch). *Accreditation:* ACSP; ASLA. *Faculty:* 35. *Students:* 204 full-time (81 women), 27 part-time (14 women); includes 9 Black or African American, non-Hispanic/Latino; 1 American Indian or Alaska Native, non-Hispanic/Latino; 8 Asian, non-Hispanic/Latino; 8 Hispanic/Latino; 1 Two or more races, non-Hispanic/Latino, 26 international. Average age 28. In 2010, 76 master's, 6 doctorates awarded. *Degree requirements:* For doctorate, thesis/dissertation. *Entrance requirements:* Additional exam requirements/recommendations for international students: Recommended—TOEFL (minimum score 600 paper-based; 250 computer-based). *Application deadline:* For fall admission, 8/15 priority date for domestic students, 7/1 priority date for international students; for winter admission, 12/1 priority date for domestic students, 11/1 priority date for international students; for spring admission, 3/1 priority date for domestic students, 2/1 priority date for international students. Applications are processed on a rolling basis. Application fee: $40 ($50 for international students). Electronic applications accepted. *Expenses:* Tuition, state resident: full-time $10,605. Tuition, nonresident: full-time $26,535. Tuition and fees vary according to course load and program. *Financial support:* Fellowships, research assistantships, Federal Work-Study, institutionally sponsored loans, and unspecified assistantships available. Support available to part-time students. *Unit head:* Ann Pendleton-Jullian, Director, 614-292-9811, Fax: 614-292-7106, E-mail: pendleton-jullia@osu.edu. *Application contact:* 614-292-9444, Fax: 614-292-3895, E-mail: domestic.grad@osu.edu.

Oklahoma State University, College of Agricultural Science and Natural Resources, Department of Horticulture and Landscape Architecture, Stillwater, OK 74078. Offers agriculture (M Ag); crop science (PhD); environmental science (PhD); horticulture (MS); plant science (PhD). *Faculty:* 21 full-time (2 women), 1 (woman) part-time/adjunct. *Students:* 1 (woman) full-time, 16 part-time (8 women); includes 1 Black or African American, non-Hispanic/Latino; 1 American Indian or Alaska Native, non-Hispanic/Latino; 1 Hispanic/Latino, 9 international. Average age 30. 12 applicants, 33% accepted, 4 enrolled. In 2010, 3 master's awarded. *Degree requirements:* For master's, thesis (for some programs); for doctorate, comprehensive exam, thesis/dissertation. *Entrance requirements:* For master's and doctorate, GRE or GMAT. Additional exam requirements/recommendations for international students: Required—TOEFL (minimum score 550 paper-based; 79 iBT). *Application deadline:* For fall admission, 3/1 priority date for international students; for spring admission, 8/1 priority date for international students. Applications are processed on a rolling basis. Application fee: $40 ($75 for international students). Electronic applications accepted. *Expenses:* Tuition, state resident: full-time $3716; part-time $154.85 per credit hour. Tuition, nonresident: full-time $14,892; part-time $621 per credit hour. Required fees: $2044; $85.20 per credit hour. One-time fee: $50. Tuition and fees vary according to course load and campus/location. *Financial support:* In 2010–11, 14 research assistantships (averaging $14,037 per year) were awarded; career-related internships or fieldwork, Federal Work-Study, scholarships/grants, health care benefits, tuition waivers (partial), and unspecified assistantships also available. Support available to part-time students. Financial award application deadline: 3/1; financial award applicants required to submit FAFSA. *Faculty research:* Stress and postharvest physiology; water utilization and runoff; IPM systems and nursery, turf, floriculture, vegetable, net and fruit products and natural resources, food extraction, and processing; public garden management. *Unit head:* Dr. Dale Maronek, Head, 405-744-5414, Fax: 405-744-9709. *Application contact:* Dr. Gordon Emslie, Dean, 405-744-6368, Fax: 405-744-0355, E-mail: grad-i@okstate.edu.

Penn State University Park, Graduate School, College of Arts and Architecture, Department of Landscape Architecture, State College, University Park, PA 16802-1503. Offers MLA, MS.

Polytechnic University of Puerto Rico, Graduate School, Hato Rey, PR 00919. Offers business administration (MBA), including computer information systems, general management, management of information systems, management of international enterprises; civil engineering (ME, MS); computer engineering (ME, MS); computer science (MCS, MS); electrical engineering (ME, MS); engineering management (MEM); environmental management (MEM); landscape architecture (M Land Arch); manufacturing competitiveness (MMC, MS); manufacturing engineering (ME, MS); mechanical engineering (M Mech E). Part-time and evening/weekend programs available. *Entrance requirements:* For master's, 3 letters of recommendation.

Pontificia Universidad Catolica Madre y Maestra, Graduate School, Faculty of Sciences and Humanities, Santiago, Dominican Republic. Offers architecture (M Arch), including architecture of interiors, architecture of tourist lodgings, landscaping; early childhood education (M Ed).

Rhode Island School of Design, Graduate Studies, Division of Architecture and Design, Department of Landscape Architecture, Providence, RI 02903-2784. Offers MLA. *Accreditation:* ASLA. *Degree requirements:* For master's, thesis, exhibit. *Entrance requirements:* For master's, portfolio, 3 letters of recommendation. Additional exam requirements/recommendations for international students: Required—TOEFL (minimum score 580 paper-based; 237 computer-based), IELTS (minimum score 6.5).

State University of New York College of Environmental Science and Forestry, Department of Landscape Architecture, Syracuse, NY 13210-2779. Offers community design and planning (MLA, MS); cultural landscape conservation (MLA, MS); landscape and urban ecology (MLA, MS). *Accreditation:* ASLA (one or more programs are accredited). *Degree requirements:* For master's, comprehensive exam (for some programs), thesis (for some programs). *Entrance requirements:* For master's, GRE General Test, minimum GPA of 3.0. Additional exam requirements/recommendations for international students: Required—TOEFL (paper-based 550, computer-based 213, iBT 80) or IELTS (6) or STEP Aiken (Grade 1). *Expenses:* Tuition, state resident: full-time $8370; part-time $349 per credit hour. Tuition, nonresident: full-time $13,780. Required fees: $30.30 per credit hour. $20 per year. *Faculty research:* Site analysis and design, city and regional planning, community environments.

Temple University, School of Environmental Design, Department of Landscape Architecture and Horticulture, Philadelphia, PA 19122-6096. Offers landscape architecture (ML Arch). Part-time and evening/weekend programs available. *Faculty:* 5 full-time (2 women). *Students:* 23 full-time (15 women), 6 part-time (4 women); includes 1 Black or African American, non-Hispanic/Latino; 1 Asian, non-Hispanic/Latino, 1 international. 48 applicants, 77% accepted, 29 enrolled. *Entrance requirements:* Additional exam requirements/recommendations for international students: Required—TOEFL (minimum score 550 paper-based; 213 computer-based; 79 iBT). *Application deadline:* For fall admission, 7/1 for domestic students, 12/15 for international students; for spring admission, 11/1 for domestic students, 8/1 for international students. Applications are processed on a rolling basis. Application fee: $50. *Financial support:* Application deadline: 1/15. *Unit head:* Dr. Mary Myers, Chairperson, 267-468-8181, E-mail: mary.myers@temple.edu. *Application contact:* Tara Schumacher, Coordinator of Outreach, 215-204-6575, Fax: 215-204-8781, E-mail: tara.schumacher@temple.edu.

Texas A&M University, College of Architecture, Department of Landscape Architecture and Urban Planning, College Station, TX 77843. Offers land development (MSLD); landscape architecture (MLA); urban and regional science (PhD); urban planning (MUP). *Accreditation:* ACSP (one or more programs are accredited); ASLA (one or more programs are accredited). *Faculty:* 29. *Students:* 166 full-time (69 women), 19 part-time (7 women); includes 18 minority (5 Black or African American, non-Hispanic/Latino; 1 American Indian or Alaska Native, non-Hispanic/Latino; 3 Asian, non-Hispanic/Latino; 9 Hispanic/Latino), 97 international. Average age 31. In 2010, 46 master's, 6 doctorates awarded. Terminal master's awarded for partial completion of doctoral program. *Degree requirements:* For master's, thesis optional, professional internship; for doctorate, comprehensive exam, thesis/dissertation, methods statistics seminar. *Entrance requirements:* For master's, GMAT or GRE General Test, portfolio (MLA), minimum GPA of 3.0; for doctorate, GMAT or GRE General Test. Additional exam requirements/recommendations for international students: Required—TOEFL. *Application deadline:* For fall admission, 2/1 priority date for domestic students; for spring admission, 8/1 for domestic students. Applications are processed on a rolling basis. Application fee: $50 ($75 for international students). Electronic applications accepted. *Financial support:* In 2010–11, fellowships with tuition reimbursements (averaging $1,000 per year), research assistantships with partial tuition reimbursements (averaging $8,100 per year), teaching assistantships with partial tuition reimbursements (averaging $11,250 per year) were awarded; career-related internships or fieldwork, institutionally sponsored loans, and scholarships/grants also available. Financial award application deadline: 4/1; financial award applicants required to submit FAFSA. *Faculty research:* Erosion control/water quality, geographic information systems/spatial information technology, transport hazards, international sustainable development. *Unit head:* Dr. Forster Ndubisi, Head, 979-845-1019, Fax: 979-862-1784. *Application contact:* Thena Morris, Administrative Assistant, 979-845-6582, Fax: 979-845-4491, E-mail: t-morris@tamu.edu.

Texas Tech University, Graduate School, College of Agricultural Sciences and Natural Resources, Department of Landscape Architecture, Lubbock, TX 79409. Offers MLA. *Accreditation:* ASLA. Part-time programs available. *Faculty:* 4 full-time (0 women). *Students:* 12 full-time (5 women), 7 part-time (0 women); includes 1 Hispanic/Latino, 3 international. Average age 30. 18 applicants, 78% accepted, 8 enrolled. In 2010, 1 master's awarded. *Entrance requirements:* For master's, GRE General Test, formal approval from departmental committee. Additional exam requirements/recommendations for international students: Required—TOEFL (minimum score 550 paper-based; 213 computer-based; 79 iBT). *Application deadline:* For fall admission, 6/1 priority date for domestic students, 1/15 priority date for international students; for spring admission, 9/1 priority date for domestic students, 6/15 priority date for international students. Applications are processed on a rolling basis. Application fee: $50 ($75 for international students). Electronic applications accepted. *Expenses:* Tuition, state resident: full-time $5495.76; part-time $228.99 per credit hour. Tuition, nonresident: full-time $12,936; part-time $538.99 per credit hour. Required fees: $2674; $36 per credit hour. $905 per semester. *Financial support:* In 2010–11, 1 student received support, including 1 research assistantship with partial tuition reimbursement available (averaging $1,699 per year). Financial award application deadline: 4/15; financial award applicants required to submit FAFSA. *Faculty research:* Computer-aided design, environmental planning and design, therapeutic landscapes, geographic information systems in planning, creative problem solving, site planning. *Unit head:* Alon Kvashny, Chair, 806-742-2894, Fax: 806-742-0770, E-mail: alon.kvashny@ttu.edu. *Application contact:* John C. Billing, Graduate Coordinator, 806-742-2858, Fax: 806-742-0770, E-mail: john.billing@ttu.edu.

The University of Arizona, College of Architecture and Landscape Architecture, School of Landscape Architecture, Tucson, AZ 85721. Offers ML Arch. *Accreditation:* ASLA. *Faculty:* 3 full-time (2 women). *Students:* 47 full-time (28 women), 3 part-time (2 women); includes 1 Black or African American, non-Hispanic/Latino; 1 American Indian or Alaska Native, non-Hispanic/Latino; 2 Asian, non-Hispanic/Latino; 3 Hispanic/Latino; 4 Two or more races, non-Hispanic/Latino, 6 international. Average age 35. 57 applicants, 65% accepted, 17 enrolled. In 2010, 13 master's awarded. *Degree requirements:* For master's, thesis. *Entrance requirements:* For master's, minimum GPA of 3.2, 3 letters of reference, statement of intent, portfolio, transcripts. Additional exam requirements/recommendations for international students: Required—TOEFL (minimum score 600 paper-based). *Application deadline:* For fall admission, 1/15 for domestic and international students. Application fee: $75. Electronic applications accepted. *Expenses:* Tuition, state resident: full-time $7692. *Financial support:* In 2010–11, 6 research assistantships with full tuition reimbursements (averaging $13,290 per year), 2 teaching assistantships with full tuition reimbursements (averaging $13,290 per year) were awarded; career-related internships or fieldwork, scholarships/grants, health care benefits, tuition waivers (full), and unspecified assistantships also available. Financial award application deadline: 1/31. *Faculty research:* Children's environments, cultural landscapes, arid lands plant communities, geographic information systems and science (GS), computer-aided drafting and design (CAD). Total annual research expenditures: $80,123. *Unit head:* Prof. Ronald R. Stoltz, Director, 520-626-7730, Fax: 520-626-6448, E-mail: rstoltz@u.arizona.edu. *Application contact:* Debi A. Romero, Administrative Assistant, 520-621-1004, Fax: 520-626-6448, E-mail: landarch@u.arizona.edu.

The University of British Columbia, Faculty of Applied Science, School of Architecture and Landscape Architecture, Program in Landscape Architecture, Vancouver, BC V6T 1Z1, Canada. Offers MASLA, MLA. *Accreditation:* ASLA (one or more programs are accredited). *Degree requirements:* For master's, comprehensive exam or thesis. *Entrance requirements:* For master's, portfolio. Additional exam requirements/recommendations for international students: Required—TOEFL (minimum score 560 paper-based; 220 computer-based). Electronic applications accepted. Tuition charges are reported in Canadian dollars. *Expenses:* Tuition, area resident: Full-time $4179 Canadian dollars. International tuition: $7344 Canadian dollars full-time. *Faculty*

Landscape Architecture

The University of British Columbia (continued)
research: Landscape design, urban-rural interface, urban ecology, sustainable development, collaborative planning and community forestry.

University of California, Berkeley, Graduate Division, College of Environmental Design, Department of Landscape Architecture and Environmental Planning, Berkeley, CA 94720-1500. Offers landscape architecture (MLA), including environmental planning, landscape design and site planning, urban and community design; landscape architecture and environmental planning (PhD); MLA/M Arch; MLA/MCP. *Accreditation:* ASLA (one or more programs are accredited). *Degree requirements:* For master's, professional project or thesis; for doctorate, one foreign language, thesis/dissertation, qualifying exam. *Entrance requirements:* For master's, GRE General Test, minimum GPA of 3.0, portfolio; for doctorate, GRE General Test, master's degree (strongly recommended), minimum GPA of 3.0, sample of written work, 3 letters of recommendation.

University of California, Berkeley, UC Berkeley Extension, Certificate Programs in Art and Design, Berkeley, CA 94720-1500. Offers interior design and interior architecture (Certificate); landscape architecture (Certificate); visual arts (Postbaccalaureate Certificate).

University of Colorado Denver, College of Architecture and Planning, Program in Landscape Architecture, Denver, CO 80217-3364. Offers MLA. *Accreditation:* ASLA. Part-time programs available. *Students:* 97 full-time (56 women), 2 part-time (both women); includes 1 Black or African American, non-Hispanic/Latino; 1 Asian, non-Hispanic/Latino; 4 Hispanic/Latino, 9 international. Average age 30. 116 applicants, 69% accepted, 38 enrolled. In 2010, 28 master's awarded. *Degree requirements:* For master's, thesis optional, six-semester sequence of course work totaling 90 semester hours. *Entrance requirements:* For master's, GRE or minimum GPA of 3.0, portfolio. Additional exam requirements/recommendations for international students: Required—TOEFL (minimum score 550 paper-based; 213 computer-based). *Application deadline:* For fall admission, 2/15 for domestic students; for spring admission, 10/1 for domestic students. Application fee: $50 ($75 for international students). Electronic applications accepted. *Expenses:* Contact institution. *Financial support:* Teaching assistantships, career-related internships or fieldwork, Federal Work-Study, and scholarships/grants available. Financial award application deadline: 4/1; financial award applicants required to submit FAFSA. *Faculty research:* Landscape architectural design theory and process, urban design, advanced landscape technologies, landscape planning. *Unit head:* Ann Komara, Associate Professor and Chair, 303-315-2428, E-mail: ann.komara@ucdenver.edu. *Application contact:* Michael Harper, Administrative Coordinator, Graduate Admissions and PhD Program, 303-556-6042, E-mail: michael.t.harper@ucdenver.edu.

University of Florida, Graduate School, College of Design, Construction and Planning, Department of Landscape Architecture, Gainesville, FL 32611. Offers MLA. *Accreditation:* ASLA. Part-time programs available. *Faculty:* 8 full-time (3 women). *Students:* 32 full-time (19 women), 3 part-time (2 women); includes 1 Black or African American, non-Hispanic/Latino; 1 Asian, non-Hispanic/Latino; 1 Hispanic/Latino, 13 international. Average age 27. 60 applicants, 60% accepted, 9 enrolled. In 2010, 5 master's awarded. *Degree requirements:* For master's, thesis, internship. *Entrance requirements:* For master's, GRE General Test, minimum GPA of 3.0. Additional exam requirements/recommendations for international students: Required—TOEFL (minimum score 550 paper-based; 213 computer-based; 80 iBT), IELTS (minimum score 6). *Application deadline:* For fall admission, 2/15 priority date for domestic students. Applications are processed on a rolling basis. Application fee: $30. Electronic applications accepted. *Expenses:* Tuition, state resident: full-time $10,915.92. Tuition, nonresident: full-time $28,309. *Financial support:* In 2010–11, 2 students received support, including 2 teaching assistantships (averaging $6,692 per year); career-related internships or fieldwork also available. Financial award applicants required to submit FAFSA. *Faculty research:* Landscape reclamation, community development, landscape ethics, land-use planning, international conservation. *Unit head:* Prof. Maria C. Gurucharri, Chair, 352-392-6098 Ext. 328, Fax: 352-392-7266, E-mail: guruch@ufl.edu. *Application contact:* Prof. Kevin R. Thompson, Graduate Coordinator, 352-392-6098 Ext. 329, Fax: 352-392-7266, E-mail: gday@ufl.edu.

University of Georgia, College of Environment and Design, Program in Landscape Architecture, Athens, GA 30602. Offers MLA. *Accreditation:* ASLA. *Students:* 50 full-time (35 women), 8 part-time (2 women); includes 1 Asian, non-Hispanic/Latino, 9 international. 61 applicants, 38% accepted, 17 enrolled. In 2010, 11 master's awarded. *Degree requirements:* For master's, thesis. *Entrance requirements:* For master's, GRE General Test. Additional exam requirements/recommendations for international students: Required—TOEFL. *Application deadline:* For fall admission, 7/1 for domestic students; for spring admission, 11/15 priority date for domestic students. Application fee: $50. Electronic applications accepted. *Expenses:* Contact institution. *Financial support:* In 2010–11, 20 students received support; fellowships, research assistantships, teaching assistantships, tuition waivers (partial) and unspecified assistantships available. *Unit head:* Dr. Brian LaHaie, Graduate Coordinator, 706-542-4704, Fax: 706-542-4236, E-mail: blahaie@uga.edu. *Application contact:* Graduate Coordinator.

University of Guelph, Graduate Studies, Ontario Agricultural College, School of Environmental Design and Rural Development, Landscape Architecture Program, Guelph, ON N1G 2W1, Canada. Offers MLA. *Accreditation:* ASLA. *Degree requirements:* For master's, thesis. *Entrance requirements:* For master's, minimum B- average during previous 2 years of honors degree, portfolio and questionnaire. Additional exam requirements/recommendations for international students: Required—TOEFL (minimum score 600 paper-based; 250 computer-based; 89 iBT), IELTS (minimum score 7), Canadian Academic Language Assessment, Michigan English Language Assessment Battery. Electronic applications accepted. *Faculty research:* Land planning, human factors in design, landscape assessment (biophysical and cultural), landscape ecology and restoration, community design.

University of Idaho, College of Graduate Studies, College of Art and Architecture, Moscow, ID 83844-2282. Offers architecture (MS), including community planning, compution and visualization studies, environment and behavior studies, urban design; architecture (professional degree) (M Arch); landscape architecture (MS); studio art (MFA), including graphic design, interactive and information design, interface, painting, printmaking, sculpture; teaching art (MAT). *Accreditation:* NASAD. *Faculty:* 19 full-time, 1 part-time/adjunct. *Students:* 102 full-time, 15 part-time. Average age 27. In 2010, 31 master's awarded. *Application deadline:* For fall admission, 8/1 for domestic students; for spring admission, 12/15 for domestic students. Applications are processed on a rolling basis. Application fee: $60. Electronic applications accepted. *Expenses:* Tuition, nonresident: part-time $580 per credit. Required fees: $306 per credit. *Financial support:* Applicants required to submit FAFSA. *Faculty research:* Sustainability in communities, urban research, virtual technology, bioregional planning, environment and behavior interaction. *Unit head:* Dr. Mark Elison Hoversten, Dean, 208-885-5423, E-mail: caa@uidaho.edu. *Application contact:* Dr. Mark Elison Hoversten, Dean, 208-885-5423, E-mail: caa@uidaho.edu.

University of Illinois at Urbana–Champaign, Graduate College, College of Fine and Applied Arts, Department of Landscape Architecture, Champaign, IL 61820. Offers MLA, PhD, MLA/MUP. *Accreditation:* ASLA. *Faculty:* 11 full-time (5 women). *Students:* 38 full-time (20 women), 5 part-time (3 women); includes 2 minority (1 Black or African American, non-Hispanic/Latino; 1 Hispanic/Latino), 16 international. 145 applicants, 22% accepted, 9 enrolled. In 2010, 13 master's, 1 doctorate awarded. *Entrance requirements:* For master's, GRE, minimum GPA of 3.0; portfolio; for doctorate, GRE, minimum GPA of 3.0. Additional exam requirements/recommendations for international students: Required—TOEFL (minimum score 570 paper-based; 230 computer-based; 89 iBT). *Application deadline:* Applications are processed on a rolling basis. Application fee: $75 ($90 for international students). Electronic applications accepted. *Financial support:* In 2010–11, 7 fellowships, 10 research assistantships, 15 teaching assistantships were awarded; tuition waivers (full and partial) also available. *Unit head:* Margaret Elen Deming, Head, 217-333-0176, Fax: 217-244-4568, E-mail: medeming@illinois.edu. *Application contact:* Carol Emmerling-DiNovo, Assistant Head, 214-244-0994, Fax: 214-244-4568, E-mail: cemmer@illinois.edu.

The University of Manchester, School of Environment and Development, Manchester, United Kingdom. Offers architecture (M Phil, PhD); development policy and management (M Phil, PhD); human geography (M Phil, PhD); physical geography (M Phil, PhD); planning and landscape (M Phil, PhD).

University of Manitoba, Faculty of Graduate Studies, Faculty of Architecture, Department of Landscape Architecture, Winnipeg, MB R3T 2N2, Canada. Offers M Land Arch. *Accreditation:* ASLA. *Degree requirements:* For master's, thesis or alternative.

University of Maryland, College Park, Academic Affairs, College of Agriculture and Natural Resources, Department of Plant Science and Landscape Architecture, Landscape Architecture Program, College Park, MD 20742. Offers MLA. *Students:* 22 full-time (14 women), 5 international. 59 applicants, 31% accepted, 10 enrolled. *Entrance requirements:* Additional exam requirements/recommendations for international students: Required—TOEFL. *Application deadline:* For fall admission, 2/1 for domestic and international students; for spring admission, 10/1 for domestic students, 6/1 for international students. Applications are processed on a rolling basis. Application fee: $75. Electronic applications accepted. *Expenses:* Tuition, state resident: part-time $471 per credit hour. Tuition, nonresident: part-time $1016 per credit hour. Required fees: $337 per term. *Financial support:* In 2010–11, 1 research assistantship (averaging $16,363 per year), 14 teaching assistantships (averaging $16,437 per year) were awarded; fellowships, career-related internships or fieldwork also available. Financial award applicants required to submit FAFSA. *Faculty research:* Cereal crop production, soil and water conservation, turf management, x-ray defraction. *Unit head:* Dr. William Kenworthy, Acting Chair, 301-405-6244, Fax: 301-314-9308, E-mail: wkenwort@umd.edu. *Application contact:* Dr. Charles A. Caramello, Dean of Graduate School, 301-405-0358, Fax: 301-314-9305, E-mail: ccaramel@umd.edu.

University of Massachusetts Amherst, Graduate School, College of Social and Behavioral Sciences, Department of Landscape Architecture and Regional Planning, Program in Landscape Architecture, Amherst, MA 01003. Offers MLA, MLA/MRP. *Accreditation:* ASLA. Part-time programs available. *Students:* 30 full-time (14 women), 9 part-time (8 women), 9 international. Average age 33. 105 applicants, 51% accepted, 14 enrolled. In 2010, 9 master's awarded. *Degree requirements:* For master's, thesis or alternative. *Entrance requirements:* For master's, GRE General Test, portfolio. Additional exam requirements/recommendations for international students: Required—TOEFL (minimum score 550 paper-based; 213 computer-based; 80 iBT), IELTS (minimum score 6.5). *Application deadline:* For fall admission, 2/1 for domestic and international students. Applications are processed on a rolling basis. Application fee: $50 ($65 for international students). Electronic applications accepted. *Expenses:* Tuition, state resident: full-time $2640. Required fees: $8282. One-time fee: $357 full-time. *Financial support:* Fellowships, research assistantships, teaching assistantships, career-related internships or fieldwork, Federal Work-Study, scholarships/grants, traineeships, health care benefits, tuition waivers (full), and unspecified assistantships available. Support available to part-time students. Financial award application deadline: 2/1; financial award applicants required to submit FAFSA. *Unit head:* Dr. Mark S. Lindhult, Graduate Program Director, 413-545-2266, Fax: 413-545-1772. *Application contact:* Jean M. Ames, Supervisor of Admissions, 413-545-0722, Fax: 413-577-0010, E-mail: gradadm@grad.umass.edu.

University of Massachusetts Amherst, Graduate School, College of Social and Behavioral Sciences, Department of Landscape Architecture and Regional Planning, Program in Landscape Architecture and Regional Planning, Amherst, MA 01003. Offers MLA/MRP. *Accreditation:* ACSP; ASLA. Part-time programs available. *Students:* 9 full-time (6 women), 1 international. Average age 32. 12 applicants, 83% accepted, 4 enrolled. *Entrance requirements:* Additional exam requirements/recommendations for international students: Required—TOEFL (minimum score 550 paper-based; 213 computer-based; 80 iBT), IELTS (minimum score 6.5). *Application deadline:* For fall admission, 2/1 for domestic and international students. Applications are processed on a rolling basis. Application fee: $50 ($65 for international students). Electronic applications accepted. *Expenses:* Tuition, state resident: full-time $2640. Required fees: $8282. One-time fee: $357 full-time. *Financial support:* Fellowships, research assistantships, teaching assistantships, career-related internships or fieldwork, Federal Work-Study, scholarships/grants, traineeships, health care benefits, tuition waivers (full), and unspecified assistantships available. Support available to part-time students. Financial award application deadline: 2/1; financial award applicants required to submit FAFSA. *Unit head:* Dr. Robert L. Ryan, Graduate Program Director, 413-545-2266, Fax: 413-545-1772. *Application contact:* Jean M. Ames, Supervisor of Admissions, 413-545-0721, Fax: 413-577-0010, E-mail: gradadm@grad.umass.edu.

University of Michigan, School of Natural Resources and Environment, Program in Landscape Architecture, Ann Arbor, MI 48109. Offers MLA, PhD, MLA/M Arch, MLA/MBA, MLA/MUP. Offered through the Horace H. Rackham School of Graduate Studies. *Accreditation:* ASLA (one or more programs are accredited). *Faculty:* 5 full-time (3 women), 1 part-time/adjunct (0 women). *Students:* 40 full-time (28 women); includes 3 Asian, non-Hispanic/Latino; 2 Two or more races, non-Hispanic/Latino, 5 international. Average age 27. 82 applicants. In 2010, 14 master's awarded. *Degree requirements:* For master's, thesis, practicum or group project; for doctorate, comprehensive exam, thesis/dissertation, oral defense of dissertation, preliminary exam. *Entrance requirements:* For master's, GRE General Test; for doctorate, GRE General Test, master's degree, portfolio. Additional exam requirements/recommendations for international students: Required—TOEFL (minimum score 560 paper-based; 220 computer-based; 84 iBT) or IELTS (minimum score 6.5). *Application deadline:* For fall admission, 1/5 priority date for domestic and international students. Applications are processed on a rolling basis. Application fee: $65 ($75 for international students). *Expenses:* Tuition, state resident: full-time $17,784; part-time $1116 per credit hour. Tuition, nonresident: full-time $35,944; part-time $2125 per credit hour. International tuition: $35,994 full-time. Required fees: $95 per semester. Tuition and fees vary according to course load, degree level and program. *Financial support:* Fellowships with tuition reimbursements, research assistantships with tuition reimbursements, teaching assistantships with tuition reimbursements, career-related internships or fieldwork, Federal Work-Study, institutionally sponsored loans, scholarships/grants, health care benefits, unspecified assistantships, and Peace Corps Fellows available. Support available to part-time students. Financial award application deadline: 1/5; financial award applicants required to submit FAFSA. *Faculty research:* Historic landscape documentation, landscape architecture, landscape perception, sustainable design, ecological design. Total annual research expenditures: $139,000. *Unit head:* Chris Ellis, Professor, 734-764-6453, Fax: 734-734-2195, E-mail: cdellis@umich.edu. *Application contact:* Adam Ancira, Recruiting and Admissions Coordinator, 734-764-6453, Fax: 734-936-2195, E-mail: snre.admissions@umich.edu.

University of Minnesota, Twin Cities Campus, Graduate School, College of Design, Department of Landscape Architecture, Minneapolis, MN 55455-0213. Offers MLA, MS. *Accreditation:* ASLA (one or more programs are accredited). *Degree requirements:* For master's, thesis (MS). *Entrance requirements:* For master's, GRE General Test (MS), suggested GPA of 3.0. Additional exam requirements/recommendations for international students: Required—TOEFL (minimum score 550 paper-based; 213 computer-based; 79 iBT). Electronic applications accepted. *Expenses:* Contact institution. *Faculty research:* Landscape history, landscape ecology, urban design, sustainable design, public art/space.

University of New Mexico, Graduate School, School of Architecture and Planning, Program in Landscape Architecture, Albuquerque, NM 87131-2039. Offers MLA. *Accreditation:* ASLA. Part-time programs available. *Students:* 47 full-time (26 women), 3 part-time (2 women); includes 1 Black or African American, non-Hispanic/Latino; 1 American Indian or Alaska Native, non-Hispanic/Latino; 1 Asian, non-Hispanic/Latino; 2 Hispanic/Latino, 5 international. Average age 33. 46 applicants, 37% accepted, 12 enrolled. In 2010, 15 master's awarded. *Degree requirements:* For master's, comprehensive exam, thesis optional, portfolio review, thesis studio. *Entrance requirements:* For master's, minimum GPA of 3.0. Additional exam requirements/recommendations for international students: Required—TOEFL. *Application deadline:* For fall admission, 2/15 priority date for domestic students, 2/15 for international students; for spring admission, 11/1 for domestic and international students. Applications are processed on a rolling basis. Application fee: $50. Electronic applications accepted. *Expenses:* Contact institution. *Financial support:* In 2010–11, 43 students received support, including 4 research assistantships with partial tuition reimbursements available (averaging $7,306 per year), 1 teaching assistantship with partial tuition reimbursement available (averaging $3,698 per year); scholarships/grants, health care benefits, tuition waivers (partial), and unspecified assistantships also available. Financial award application deadline: 3/1; financial award applicants required to submit FAFSA. *Faculty research:* Cultural landscape studies, urban design and sustainability, landscape and infrastructure. *Unit head:* Dr. Alfred Simon, Director, 505-277-4120, Fax: 505-277-0897, E-mail: asimon@unm.edu. *Application contact:* Beth Rowe, Senior Academic Advisor, 505-277-1303, Fax: 505-277-0076, E-mail: erowe@unm.edu.

University of Oklahoma, College of Architecture, Division of Landscape Architecture, Norman, OK 73019-0390. Offers MLA, MRCP/MLA. *Accreditation:* ASLA. Part-time programs available. *Faculty:* 2 full-time (0 women). *Students:* 11 full-time (6 women), 6 part-time (2 women); includes 2 minority (1 American Indian or Alaska Native, non-Hispanic/Latino; 1 Asian, non-Hispanic/Latino), 1 international. Average age 31. 20 applicants, 90% accepted, 5 enrolled. In 2010, 2 master's awarded. *Degree requirements:* For master's, comprehensive exam, portfolio, project. *Entrance requirements:* For master's, GRE General Test, portfolio. Additional exam requirements/recommendations for international students: Required—TOEFL (minimum score 550 paper-based; 213 computer-based; 79 iBT). *Application deadline:* For fall admission, 4/1 for domestic and international students; for spring admission, 11/1 for domestic students, 9/1 for international students. Applications are processed on a rolling basis. Application fee: $40 ($90 for international students). Electronic applications accepted. *Expenses:* Tuition, state resident: full-time $3893; part-time $162.20 per credit hour. Tuition, nonresident: full-time $14,167; part-time $590.30 per credit hour. Required fees: $2523; $94.60 per credit hour. Tuition and fees vary according to course load and degree level. *Financial support:* In 2010–11, 3 research assistantships with partial tuition reimbursements (averaging $9,586 per year) were awarded; career-related internships or fieldwork, Federal Work-Study, institutionally sponsored loans, scholarships/grants, and unspecified assistantships also available. Financial award applicants required to submit FAFSA. *Faculty research:* Sustainable urban design, greenways, community-based design and planning, site design and site planning, meaning in built environments. *Unit head:* Thomas Woodfin, Interim Director of Landscape Architecture, 405-325-2299, Fax: 405-325-7558, E-mail: twoodfin@ou.edu. *Application contact:* Thomas Woodfin, Interim Director of Landscape Architecture, 405-325-2299, Fax: 405-325-7558, E-mail: twoodfin@ou.edu.

University of Oregon, Graduate School, School of Architecture and Allied Arts, Department of Landscape Architecture, Eugene, OR 97403. Offers MLA. *Accreditation:* ASLA. *Degree requirements:* For master's, thesis or alternative, project. *Entrance requirements:* For master's, portfolio. Additional exam requirements/recommendations for international students: Required—TOEFL. *Faculty research:* Design, landscape planning analysis, history and theory, computer applications.

University of Pennsylvania, School of Design, Program in Landscape Architecture and Regional Planning, Philadelphia, PA 19104. Offers landscape architecture and regional planning (MLA); landscape studies (Certificate). *Accreditation:* ASLA (one or more programs are accredited). Part-time programs available. *Faculty:* 7 full-time (3 women), 4 part-time/adjunct (2 women). *Students:* 98 full-time (68 women); includes 2 Black or African American, non-Hispanic/Latino; 6 Asian, non-Hispanic/Latino; 2 Hispanic/Latino, 32 international. 274 applicants, 39% accepted, 34 enrolled. In 2010, 46 master's, 6 Certificates awarded. *Degree requirements:* For master's, thesis optional. *Entrance requirements:* For master's, GRE, portfolio. Additional exam requirements/recommendations for international students: Required—TOEFL. *Application deadline:* For fall admission, 1/2 priority date for domestic students. Application fee: $70. *Expenses:* Tuition: Full-time $25,660; part-time $4758 per course. Required fees: $2152; $270 per course. Tuition and fees vary according to course load, degree level and program. *Financial support:* Fellowships, research assistantships, teaching assistantships, career-related internships or fieldwork, Federal Work-Study, and institutionally sponsored loans available. Financial award applicants required to submit FAFSA. *Faculty research:* Early landscape architecture, natural distribution through landslides, urban gardens, landscape registration, watershed studies. *Application contact:* Diane Pringle, Coordinator, 215-898-6591, E-mail: dianep@design.upenn.edu.

The University of Tennessee, Graduate School, College of Architecture and Design, Program in Landscape Architecture, Knoxville, TN 37996. Offers landscape architecture (MLA); landscape architecture (research) (MA, MS). *Degree requirements:* For master's, oral exam, project and thesis optional (MLA), oral exam and thesis (MA, MS). *Entrance requirements:* For master's, GRE General Test, minimum GPA of 3.0, 3 letters of recommendation, samples of portfolio work. Additional exam requirements/recommendations for international students: Required—TOEFL (minimum score 550 paper-based). *Expenses:* Tuition, state resident: full-time $7440; part-time $414 per credit hour. Tuition, nonresident: full-time $22,478; part-time $1250 per credit hour. Required fees: $922; $43 per credit hour. Tuition and fees vary according to program.

The University of Texas at Arlington, Graduate School, School of Architecture, Program in Landscape Architecture, Arlington, TX 76019. Offers MLA. *Accreditation:* ASLA. Part-time and evening/weekend programs available. *Faculty:* 7 full-time (0 women). *Students:* 41 full-time (27 women), 3 part-time (2 women); includes 10 minority (3 Black or African American, non-Hispanic/Latino; 3 Asian, non-Hispanic/Latino; 4 Hispanic/Latino), 14 international. 31 applicants, 97% accepted, 19 enrolled. In 2010, 8 master's awarded. *Degree requirements:* For master's, thesis. *Entrance requirements:* For master's, GRE General Test, minimum GPA of 3.0, portfolio. Additional exam requirements/recommendations for international students: Required—TOEFL (minimum score 550 paper-based; 213 computer-based). *Application deadline:* For fall admission, 1/15 for domestic and international students. Applications are processed on a rolling basis. Application fee: $35 ($50 for international students). *Expenses:* Tuition, state resident: full-time $7500. Tuition, nonresident: full-time $13,080. International tuition: $13,250 full-time. *Financial support:* In 2010–11, 1 research assistantship with partial tuition reimbursement (averaging $4,824 per year), 2 teaching assistantships with partial tuition reimbursements (averaging $4,824 per year) were awarded; fellowships, career-related internships or fieldwork and tuition waivers (partial) also available. Financial award application deadline: 6/1; financial award applicants required to submit FAFSA. *Unit head:* Dr. Pat D. Taylor, Program Director, 817-272-2801, Fax: 817-272-5098, E-mail: pdt@uta.edu. *Application contact:* David Jones, Associate Dean, 817-272-2801, Fax: 817-272-5098, E-mail: djonesarch@uta.edu.

The University of Texas at Austin, Graduate School, School of Architecture, Austin, TX 78712-1111. Offers architecture (M Arch); community and regional planning (MSCRP, PhD); historic preservation (MS); history of architecture (MA, PhD); landscape architecture (MLA); urban design (MSUD); JD/MSCRP; MSCRP/MA; MSCRP/PhD. *Degree requirements:* For doctorate, thesis/dissertation. *Entrance requirements:* For master's and doctorate, GRE General Test. Additional exam requirements/recommendations for international students: Required—TOEFL (minimum score 550 paper-based; 213 computer-based). Electronic applications accepted.

University of Virginia, School of Architecture, Program in Landscape Architecture, Charlottesville, VA 22903. Offers M Land Arch. *Accreditation:* ASLA. *Faculty:* 7 full-time (5 women). *Students:* 49 full-time (31 women); includes 1 Black or African American, non-Hispanic/Latino; 1 Asian, non-Hispanic/Latino; 1 Hispanic/Latino, 5 international. Average age 28. 136 applicants, 14% accepted, 4 enrolled. In 2010, 13 master's awarded. *Entrance requirements:* For master's, GRE General Test, 3 letters of recommendation; portfolio. Additional exam requirements/recommendations for international students: Required—TOEFL (minimum score 600 paper-based; 250 computer-based; 90 iBT). *Application deadline:* For fall admission, 1/15 for domestic students, 1/16 for international students. Applications are processed on a rolling basis. Application fee: $60. Electronic applications accepted. *Financial support:* Applicants required to submit FAFSA. *Faculty research:* History of landscape architecture. *Unit head:* Kristina Hill, Director, 434-924-1044, Fax: 434-982-2678, E-mail: kzhill@virginia.edu. *Application contact:* Graduate Admissions Officer, 434-924-6442, Fax: 434-982-2678, E-mail: arch-admissions@virginia.edu.

University of Washington, Graduate School, College of Built Environments, Department of Landscape Architecture, Seattle, WA 98195. Offers MLA. *Accreditation:* ASLA. *Degree requirements:* For master's, thesis. *Entrance requirements:* For master's, GRE, minimum GPA of 3.0. Additional exam requirements/recommendations for international students: Required—TOEFL. *Faculty research:* Cultural landscape, history of gardens, urban stream restoration, campus master planning, urban ecology.

University of Wisconsin–Madison, Graduate School, College of Agricultural and Life Sciences, Department of Landscape Architecture, Madison, WI 53076. Offers MA, MS. Part-time programs available. *Degree requirements:* For master's, thesis. *Entrance requirements:* For master's, GRE (recommended), samples of creative work. Additional exam requirements/recommendations for international students: Required—TOEFL (minimum score 580 paper-based; 237 computer-based). Electronic applications accepted. *Expenses:* Tuition, state resident: full-time $9887; part-time $617.96 per credit. Tuition, nonresident: full-time $24,054; part-time $1503.40 per credit. Required fees: $67.63 per credit. Tuition and fees vary according to reciprocity agreements. *Faculty research:* Urban/landscape ecology, land restoration, cultural resource preservation, community design, conservation design.

Utah State University, School of Graduate Studies, College of Humanities, Arts and Social Sciences, Department of Landscape Architecture and Environmental Planning, Logan, UT 84322. Offers bioregional planning (MS); landscape architecture (MLA). *Accreditation:* ASLA (one or more programs are accredited). *Degree requirements:* For master's, thesis. *Entrance requirements:* For master's, GRE General Test, minimum GPA of 3.0. Additional exam requirements/recommendations for international students: Required—TOEFL. *Faculty research:* Visual resource management, planning for wildlife, agricultural land preservation, watershed planning, community planning and design.

Virginia Polytechnic Institute and State University, Graduate School, College of Architecture and Urban Studies, Department of Landscape Architecture, Blacksburg, VA 24061. Offers MLA, PhD. *Accreditation:* ASLA. *Students:* 33 full-time (19 women), 15 part-time (7 women); includes 1 Black or African American, non-Hispanic/Latino; 2 Asian, non-Hispanic/Latino; 1 Hispanic/Latino, 10 international. Average age 29. 54 applicants, 43% accepted, 14 enrolled. In 2010, 7 master's awarded. *Degree requirements:* For master's, comprehensive exam (for some programs), thesis (for some programs); for doctorate, comprehensive exam (for some programs), thesis/dissertation (for some programs). *Entrance requirements:* For master's and doctorate, GRE. Additional exam requirements/recommendations for international students: Required—TOEFL (minimum score 550 paper-based; 213 computer-based). *Application deadline:* For fall admission, 7/1 for domestic and international students; for spring admission, 12/1 for domestic and international students. Applications are processed on a rolling basis. Application fee: $65. Electronic applications accepted. *Expenses:* Tuition, state resident: full-time $9399; part-time $488 per credit hour. Tuition, nonresident: full-time $17,854; part-time $957.75 per credit hour. Required fees: $1534. Full-time tuition and fees vary according to program. *Financial support:* Career-related internships or fieldwork, Federal Work-Study, scholarships/grants, health care benefits, and unspecified assistantships available. Financial award application deadline: 1/15. *Faculty research:* Land planning issues in rural areas, landscape perception and visual management theory, universal design, accessibility, ecological and cultural processes. *Unit head:* Dr. Brian F. Katen, UNIT HEAD, 540-231-7505, Fax: 540-231-3367, E-mail: bkaten@vt.edu. *Application contact:* Mintai Kim, Contact, 540-231-9872, Fax: 540-231-3367, E-mail: mintkim@vt.edu.

Virginia Polytechnic Institute and State University, Graduate School, College of Architecture and Urban Studies, School of Public and International Affairs, Blacksburg, VA 24061. Offers economic development (Certificate); government and international affairs (MPIA, PhD); homeland security policy (Certificate); local government management (Certificate); nonprofit and nongovernmental organization management (Certificate); planning, governance and globalization (PhD); public administration and public affairs (MPA, PhD); urban and regional planning (MURPL). *Accreditation:* ACSP. *Faculty:* 31 full-time (9 women). *Students:* 114 full-time (66 women), 105 part-time (54 women); includes 11 Black or African American, non-Hispanic/Latino; 1 American Indian or Alaska Native, non-Hispanic/Latino; 7 Asian, non-Hispanic/Latino; 8 Hispanic/Latino, 19 international. Average age 31. 166 applicants, 67% accepted, 53 enrolled. In 2010, 41 master's, 3 doctorates awarded. *Degree requirements:* For master's, comprehensive exam (for some programs), thesis (for some programs); for doctorate, comprehensive exam (for some programs), thesis/dissertation (for some programs). *Entrance requirements:* For master's and doctorate, GRE. Additional exam requirements/recommendations for international students: Required—TOEFL (minimum score 550 paper-based; 213 computer-based). *Application deadline:* For fall admission, 7/1 for domestic and international students; for spring admission, 12/1 for domestic and international students. Applications are processed on a rolling basis. Application fee: $65. Electronic applications accepted. *Expenses:* Tuition, state resident: full-time $9399; part-time $488 per credit hour. Tuition, nonresident: full-time $17,854; part-time $957.75 per credit hour. Required fees: $1534. Full-time tuition and fees vary according to program. *Financial support:* In 2010–11, 1 teaching assistantship with full tuition reimbursement (averaging $21,395 per year) was awarded; career-related internships or fieldwork, Federal Work-Study, scholarships/grants, health care benefits, and unspecified assistantships also available. Financial award application deadline: 1/15. *Faculty research:* Design theory, environmental planning, town planning, transportation planning. Total annual research expenditures: $610,749. *Unit head:* Dr. Karen M. Hult, UNIT HEAD, 540-231-5351, Fax: 540-231-9938, E-mail: khult@vt.edu. *Application contact:* Krystal D. Wright, Contact, 540-231-2291, Fax: 540-231-9938, E-mail: garch@vt.edu.

Washington State University, Graduate School, College of Agricultural, Human, and Natural Resource Sciences, Department of Horticulture and Landscape Architecture, Pullman, WA 99164. Offers horticulture (MS, PhD); landscape architecture (MSLA). Part-time programs available. *Faculty:* 18. *Students:* 26 full-time (21 women), 1 (woman) part-time; includes 1 minority (Black or African American, non-Hispanic/Latino), 10 international. Average age 28. 43 applicants, 33% accepted, 10 enrolled. In 2010, 7 master's awarded. *Degree requirements:* For master's, comprehensive exam (for some programs), thesis (for some programs), oral exam; for doctorate, comprehensive exam, thesis/dissertation, oral exam, written exam. *Entrance requirements:* For master's and doctorate, GRE General Test, GRE Subject Test, minimum GPA of 3.0, 3 letters of recommendation. Additional exam requirements/recommendations for international students: Required—TOEFL (minimum score 550 paper-based). *Application deadline:* For fall admission, 2/1 priority date for domestic students, 3/1 for international students; for spring admission, 9/1 for domestic students, 7/1 for international students. Applications are processed on a rolling basis. Application fee: $50. Electronic applications accepted. *Expenses:* Tuition, state resident: full-time $8552; part-time $443 per credit. Tuition, nonresident: full-time $21,650; part-time $1083 per credit. Required fees: $846. *Financial support:* In 2010–11, 16 students received support, including fellowships (averaging $2,275 per year), 10 research assistantships with full and partial tuition reimbursements available (averaging $18,204 per year), 2 teaching assistantships with full and partial tuition reimbursements available (averaging $18,204 per year); career-related internships or fieldwork, Federal Work-Study, institutionally sponsored loans, and health care benefits also available. Financial award application deadline: 4/1; financial award applicants required to submit FAFSA. *Faculty research:* Post-harvest physiology, genetics/plant breeding, molecular biology. Total annual research expenditures: $3.9 million. *Unit head:* Dr. N. Richard Knowles, Chair, 509-335-9502, Fax: 509-335-8690, E-mail: rknowles@wsu.edu. *Application contact:* Graduate School Admissions, 800-GRADWSU, Fax: 509-335-1949, E-mail: gradsch@wsu.edu.

Landscape Architecture

Washington State University Spokane, Graduate Programs, Interdisciplinary Design Institute, Spokane, WA 99210. Offers architecture (M Arch, MS); design (Dr DES); interior design (MA); landscape architecture (MS). Part-time programs available. *Faculty:* 7. *Students:* 9 full-time (6 women), 2 part-time (both women); includes 1 Asian, non-Hispanic/Latino, 5 international. Average age 35. In 2010, 18 master's awarded. *Degree requirements:* For master's, comprehensive exam (for some programs), thesis (for some programs); for doctorate, comprehensive exam, thesis/dissertation. *Entrance requirements:* For master's, minimum GPA of 3.0, portfolio of design work, 3 letters of recommendation (M Arch); for doctorate, minimum graduate GPA of 3.5. Additional exam requirements/recommendations for international students: Required—TOEFL (minimum score 550 paper-based; 213 computer-based). *Application*

deadline: For fall admission, 1/10 priority date for domestic students, 1/10 for international students; for spring admission, 7/1 priority date for domestic students, 7/1 for international students. Application fee: $50. *Financial support:* In 2010–11, research assistantships with full and partial tuition reimbursements (averaging $14,634 per year), teaching assistantships with full and partial tuition reimbursements (averaging $13,383 per year) were awarded. Financial award application deadline: 2/15. *Faculty research:* Environment-behavior relationships, land use and environmental planning, urban space as interior design, art and architectural aesthetics. Total annual research expenditures: $84,000. *Unit head:* Dr. Nancy H. Blossom, Director, 509-358-7513, E-mail: blossom@wsu.edu. *Application contact:* Graduate School Admissions, 800-GRADWSU, Fax: 509-335-1949, E-mail: gradsch@wsu.edu.

Lighting Design

The New School: A University, Parsons The New School for Design, Program in Lighting Design, New York, NY 10011. Offers MFA. *Accreditation:* NASAD. *Degree requirements:* For master's, thesis. *Entrance requirements:* For master's, portfolio. Additional exam requirements/recommendations for international students: Required—TOEFL (minimum score 580 paper-based; 237 computer-based; 92 iBT). Electronic applications accepted.

New York School of Interior Design, Program in Interior Lighting Design, New York, NY 10021-5110. Offers MPS. In 2010, 1 master's awarded. *Entrance requirements:* For master's, portfolio. Additional exam requirements/recommendations for international students: Required—TOEFL (minimum score 213 computer-based; 79 iBT). *Application deadline:* For fall admission, 2/1 for domestic and international students. Application fee: $60 ($100 for international students). Electronic applications accepted. *Expenses:* Tuition: Full-time $26,500. Required fees: $335. One-time fee: $60 full-time. *Financial support:* Fellowships available. Financial award application deadline: 8/1; financial award applicants required to submit FAFSA. *Application contact:* Scott Ageloff, Dean, 212-472-1500 Ext. 301, Fax: 212-288-6577, E-mail: sageloff@nysid.edu.

Rensselaer Polytechnic Institute, Graduate School, School of Architecture, PhD Program in Architectural Sciences, Troy, NY 12180-3590. Offers acoustics (PhD); built ecologies (PhD); lighting (PhD). *Faculty:* 12 full-time (4 women), 7 part-time/adjunct (3 women). *Students:* 25 full-time (7 women), 4 part-time (1 woman); includes 2 Black or African American, non-Hispanic/Latino; 1 Hispanic/Latino; 1 Two or more races, non-Hispanic/Latino, 9 international. Average age 31. 50 applicants, 28% accepted, 7 enrolled. In 2010, 4 doctorates awarded. *Degree requirements:* For doctorate, comprehensive exam (for some programs), thesis/dissertation. *Entrance requirements:* For doctorate, GRE General Test, resume, portfolio, research writing sample. Additional exam requirements/recommendations for international students: Required—TOEFL (minimum score 570 paper-based; 230 computer-based; 89 iBT), IELTS (minimum score 6.5). *Application deadline:* For fall admission, 1/1 priority date for domestic students, 1/1 for international students. Applications are processed on a rolling basis. Application fee: $75. Electronic applications accepted. *Expenses:* Tuition: Full-time $39,600; part-time $1650 per credit. Required fees: $1896. *Financial support:* In 2010–11, 23 students received support, including 5 fellowships with full tuition reimbursements available (averaging $23,000 per year), 17 research assistantships with tuition reimbursements available (averaging $17,500 per year), 1 teaching assistantship with full tuition reimbursement available (averaging $17,500 per year); career-related internships or fieldwork, institutionally sponsored loans, scholarships/grants, and unspecified assistantships also available. Financial award application deadline:

1/1. *Faculty research:* Lighting, acoustics, computation, building systems. *Unit head:* Prof. Ted Krueger, Head, Graduate Programs, 518-276-2562, Fax: 518-276-3034, E-mail: krueger@rpi.edu. *Application contact:* Erin Bermingham, Senior Graduate Programs Administrator, 518-276-3986, Fax: 518-276-3034, E-mail: bermie@rpi.edu.

Rensselaer Polytechnic Institute, Graduate School, School of Architecture, Program in Lighting, Troy, NY 12180-3590. Offers MS. Part-time programs available. *Faculty:* 5 full-time (2 women), 5 part-time/adjunct (3 women). *Students:* 15 full-time (6 women), 3 part-time (1 woman); includes 2 Asian, non-Hispanic/Latino, 10 international. Average age 29. 30 applicants, 37% accepted, 5 enrolled. In 2010, 6 master's awarded. *Degree requirements:* For master's, comprehensive exam, thesis. *Entrance requirements:* For master's, GRE General Test, letters of recommendation, resume, statement of research interests. Additional exam requirements/recommendations for international students: Required—TOEFL (minimum score 570 paper-based; 230 computer-based; 89 iBT), IELTS (minimum score 6.5). *Application deadline:* For fall admission, 1/1 priority date for domestic and international students. Applications are processed on a rolling basis. Application fee: $75. Electronic applications accepted. *Expenses:* Tuition: Full-time $39,600; part-time $1650 per credit. Required fees: $1896. *Financial support:* In 2010–11, 10 students received support, including 10 research assistantships with full tuition reimbursements available (averaging $17,500 per year); fellowships, teaching assistantships, career-related internships or fieldwork, institutionally sponsored loans, scholarships/grants, and unspecified assistantships also available. Financial award application deadline: 1/1. *Faculty research:* Energy-efficient lighting, lighting product development, lighting design demonstration, daylighting, transportation lighting. Total annual research expenditures: $3.3 million. *Unit head:* Prof. Ted Krueger, Head, Graduate Programs, 518-276-6466. *Application contact:* Erin Bermingham, Senior Graduate Programs Administrator, 518-276-3986, Fax: 518-276-3034, E-mail: bermie@rpi.edu.

University of Washington, Graduate School, College of Built Environments, Department of Architecture, Seattle, WA 98195. Offers architecture (M Arch, MS); built environment (PhD); design computing (Certificate); design firm leadership and management (Certificate); historic preservation (Certificate); lighting (Certificate); urban design (Certificate). *Degree requirements:* For master's, thesis. *Entrance requirements:* For master's, GRE General Test, minimum GPA of 3.0, portfolio, 3 letters of recommendation. Additional exam requirements/recommendations for international students: Required—TOEFL. *Faculty research:* Lighting, materials, computing theory, media, culture, environment.

Urban Design

American University of Beirut, Graduate Programs, Faculty of Engineering and Architecture, Beirut, Lebanon. Offers applied energy (MME); civil engineering (ME, PhD); electrical and computer engineering (ME, PhD); engineering management (MEM); environmental and water resources (ME); environmental and water resources engineering (PhD); environmental technology (MSES); mechanical engineering (ME, PhD); urban design (MUD); urban planning and policy (MUP). Part-time programs available. *Faculty:* 57 full-time (12 women), 3 part-time/adjunct (0 women). *Students:* 261 full-time (92 women), 58 part-time (20 women). Average age 25. 272 applicants, 79% accepted, 108 enrolled. In 2010, 70 master's, 1 doctorate awarded. *Degree requirements:* For master's, one foreign language, comprehensive exam, thesis (for some programs); for doctorate, one foreign language, comprehensive exam, thesis/dissertation, publications. *Entrance requirements:* For master's, GRE (for electrical and computer engineering), letters of recommendation; for doctorate, GRE, letters of recommendation, master's degree, transcripts, curriculum vitae, interview. Additional exam requirements/recommendations for international students: Required—TOEFL (minimum score 600 paper-based; 250 computer-based; 100 iBT), IELTS (minimum score 7.5). *Application deadline:* For fall admission, 2/5 priority date for domestic and international students; for spring admission, 11/1 priority date for domestic students, 11/1 for international students. Applications are processed on a rolling basis. Application fee: $50. Electronic applications accepted. *Expenses:* Tuition: Full-time $12,294; part-time $683 per credit. Required fees: $499; $499 per credit. Tuition and fees vary according to course load and program. *Financial support:* In 2010–11, 10 fellowships with full tuition reimbursements (averaging $24,800 per year), 33 research assistantships with full tuition reimbursements (averaging $24,800 per year), 70 teaching assistantships with full tuition reimbursements (averaging $9,800 per year) were awarded; career-related internships or fieldwork, institutionally sponsored loans, scholarships/grants, health care benefits, and unspecified assistantships also available. Total annual research expenditures: $586,131. *Unit head:* Fadl H. Moukalled, Acting Dean, 961-135-0000 Ext. 3400, Fax: 961-174-4462, E-mail: memouk@aub.edu.lb. *Application contact:* Dr. Salim Kanaan, Director, Admissions Office, 961-135-0000 Ext. 2594, Fax: 961-175-0775, E-mail: sk00@aub.edu.lb.

Arizona State University, Herberger Institute for Design and the Arts, School of Architecture and Landscape Architecture, Tempe, AZ 85287-1605. Offers architecture (M Arch); building design/built environment (MS); design (arts, media, and engineering) (MSD); design (healthcare and healing environments) (MSD); design (industrial design) (MSD); design (interior design) (MSD); design (new product innovation) (MSD); design (visual communication design) (MSD); design, environment and the arts (PhD), including design, environment and the arts (design), design, environment and the arts (healthcare and healing environments), design, environment and the arts (history, theory, and criticism); landscape architecture (MLA); urban design (MUD); MA/MBA. *Accreditation:* NASAD. *Faculty:* 41 full-time (9 women), 6 part-time/adjunct (3 women). *Students:* 252 full-time (111 women), 45 part-time (21 women); includes 61 minority (3 Black or African American, non-Hispanic/Latino; 2 American Indian or Alaska Native, non-Hispanic/Latino; 13 Asian, non-Hispanic/Latino; 41 Hispanic/Latino; 1 Native Hawaiian or other Pacific Islander, non-Hispanic/Latino; 1 Two or more races, non-Hispanic/Latino), 58 international. Average age 29. 420 applicants, 61% accepted, 117 enrolled. In 2010, 60 master's, 8 doctorates awarded. Terminal master's awarded for partial completion of doctoral program. *Degree requirements:* For master's, thesis optional, interactive Program of

Study (iPOS) submitted before completing 50 percent of required credit hours; for doctorate, comprehensive exam, thesis/dissertation, interactive Program of Study (iPOS) submitted before completing 50 percent of required credit hours. *Entrance requirements:* For master's, GRE General Test, minimum GPA of 3.0 or equivalent in last 2 years of work leading to bachelor's degree, design/creative works portfolio, 3 references, statement of intent; for doctorate, GRE, master's degree in architecture, graphic design, industrial design, interior design, landscape architecture, or art history or equivalent standing; statement of purpose; 3 letters of recommendation; indication of potential faculty mentor; sample of written work. Additional exam requirements/recommendations for international students: Required—TOEFL (minimum score 600 paper-based; 250 computer-based; 100 iBT). *Application deadline:* For fall admission, 1/15 priority date for domestic and international students. Application fee: $70 ($90 for international students). Electronic applications accepted. *Expenses:* Tuition, state resident: full-time $8510; part-time $608 per credit. Tuition, nonresident: full-time $16,542; part-time $919 per credit. Required fees: $339; $110 per credit. Part-time tuition and fees vary according to course load. *Financial support:* In 2010–11, 9 research assistantships with full and partial tuition reimbursements (averaging $11,913 per year), 76 teaching assistantships with full and partial tuition reimbursements (averaging $6,294 per year) were awarded; fellowships with full and partial tuition reimbursements, scholarships/grants and tuition waivers (full and partial) also available. Financial award application deadline: 3/1; financial award applicants required to submit FAFSA. Total annual research expenditures: $410,956. *Unit head:* Darren Petrucci, Director, 480-965-3536, E-mail: darren.petrucci@asu.edu. *Application contact:* Graduate Admissions, 480-965-6113.

Ball State University, Graduate School, College of Architecture and Planning, Department of Architecture, Program in Urban Design, Muncie, IN 47306-1099. Offers MUD. *Students:* 11 full-time (5 women); includes 1 Black or African American, non-Hispanic/Latino. 25 applicants, 64% accepted, 8 enrolled. In 2010, 11 master's awarded. Application fee: $50. *Expenses:* Tuition, state resident: full-time $6160; part-time $299 per credit hour. Tuition, nonresident: full-time $16,020; part-time $783 per credit hour. Required fees: $2278; $95 per credit hour. *Financial support:* In 2010–11, 2 research assistantships (averaging $6,496 per year) were awarded. *Unit head:* Dr. Michele Mounayar, Head, 765-285-5188. *Application contact:* Dr. Brad Beaubien, Graduate Program Director, 765-285-1900, Fax: 765-285-1765.

Carnegie Mellon University, College of Fine Arts, School of Architecture, Pittsburgh, PA 15213-3891. Offers architectural engineering construction management (M Sc); architecture (MSA); architecture, engineering, and construction management (PhD); building performance and diagnostics (M Sc, PhD); computational design (M Sc, PhD); sustainable design (M Sc); urban design (M Sc). Terminal master's awarded for partial completion of doctoral program. *Degree requirements:* For doctorate, thesis/dissertation. *Entrance requirements:* For master's and doctorate, GRE General Test. Additional exam requirements/recommendations for international students: Required—TOEFL.

City College of the City University of New York, Graduate School, School of Architecture and Environmental Studies, Program in Urban Design, New York, NY 10031-9198. Offers MUP. Part-time programs available. *Degree requirements:* For master's, thesis. *Entrance requirements:* For master's, portfolio, professional degree in architecture or equivalent. Additional exam requirements/recommendations for international students: Required—TOEFL (minimum score 550 paper-based; 213 computer-based). *Faculty research:* Real estate, planning, law.

Cleveland State University, College of Graduate Studies, Maxine Goodman Levin College of Urban Affairs, Program in Urban Planning, Design, and Development, Cleveland, OH 44115. Offers geographic information systems (Certificate); local and urban management (Certificate); urban economic development (Certificate); urban planning, design, and development (MUPDD); urban real estate development and finance (Certificate); JD/MUPDD. *Accreditation:* ACSP. Part-time and evening/weekend programs available. *Faculty:* 32 full-time (19 women), 8 part-time/adjunct (4 women). *Students:* 30 full-time (10 women), 28 part-time (17 women); includes 6 Black or African American, non-Hispanic/Latino; 3 Hispanic/Latino, 5 international. Average age 38. 72 applicants, 56% accepted, 21 enrolled. In 2010, 24 master's, 9 Certificates awarded. *Degree requirements:* For master's, thesis or alternative, project or thesis. *Entrance requirements:* For master's, GRE General Test (minimum 50th percentile verbal and quantitative, 4.0 analytical writing), minimum GPA of 3.0. Additional exam requirements/recommendations for international students: Required—TOEFL (minimum score 525 paper-based; 197 computer-based; 65 iBT). *Application deadline:* For fall admission, 7/15 priority date for domestic students, 5/15 for international students; for spring admission, 11/1 for international students. Applications are processed on a rolling basis. Application fee: $30. Electronic applications accepted. *Expenses:* Tuition, state resident: full-time $8447; part-time $469 per credit hour. Tuition, nonresident: full-time $16,020; part-time $890 per credit hour. Required fees: $50. *Financial support:* In 2010–11, 15 students received support, including 10 research assistantships with full and partial tuition reimbursements available (averaging $6,960 per year), 5 teaching assistantships with full and partial tuition reimbursements available (averaging $6,960 per year); career-related internships or fieldwork, Federal Work-Study, tuition waivers (full and partial), and unspecified assistantships also available. Support available to part-time students. Financial award application deadline: 3/1. *Faculty research:* Housing and neighborhood development, urban housing policy, environmental sustainability, economic development, metropolitan change, GIS and planning decision support, PPGIS. *Unit head:* Dr. Dennis Keating, Director, 216-687-2298, Fax: 216-687-2013, E-mail: w.keating@csuohio.edu. *Application contact:* Joan Demkow, Graduate Program Coordinator, 216-523-7522, Fax: 216-687-5398, E-mail: urbanprograms@csuohio.edu.

Cornell University, Graduate School, Graduate Fields of Architecture, Art and Planning, Field of Architecture, Ithaca, NY 14853-0001. Offers architectural design (M Arch); architectural science (MS); building technology and environmental science (MS); computer graphics (MS); history of architecture (MA, PhD); history of urban development (MA, PhD); theory and criticism of architecture (M Arch); urban design (M Arch). *Faculty:* 26 full-time (8 women). *Students:* 113 full-time (55 women); includes 2 Black or African American, non-Hispanic/Latino; 15 Asian, non-Hispanic/Latino; 8 Hispanic/Latino, 47 international. Average age 26. 545 applicants, 26% accepted, 65 enrolled. In 2010, 26 master's, 1 doctorate awarded. *Degree requirements:* For master's, one foreign language, thesis (MA, MS); for doctorate, 2 foreign languages, comprehensive exam, thesis/dissertation. *Entrance requirements:* For master's, GRE General Test, 5 year bachelor's degree in architecture, portfolio (M Arch), 3 letters of recommendation; for doctorate, GRE General Test, 3 letters of recommendation. Additional exam requirements/recommendations for international students: Required—TOEFL (minimum score 600 paper-based; 250 computer-based; 77 iBT). *Application deadline:* For fall admission, 1/15 priority date for domestic students. Application fee: $70. Electronic applications accepted. *Expenses:* Tuition: Full-time $29,500. Required fees: $76. Tuition and fees vary according to degree level and program. *Financial support:* In 2010–11, 11 fellowships with full tuition reimbursements, 19 teaching assistantships with full tuition reimbursements were awarded; research assistantships with full tuition reimbursements, institutionally sponsored loans, scholarships/grants, health care benefits, tuition waivers (full and partial), and unspecified assistantships also available. Financial award applicants required to submit FAFSA. *Faculty research:* Architectural design and urban design, theory and criticism of architecture, computer graphics, building technology and environmental science, history of architecture and history of urban-development. *Unit head:* Director of Graduate Studies, 607-255-6701, Fax: 607-255-0291. *Application contact:* Graduate Field Assistant, 607-255-6701, Fax: 607-255-0291, E-mail: cuarch@cornell.edu.

Georgia Institute of Technology, Graduate Studies and Research, College of Architecture, City and Regional Planning Program, Atlanta, GA 30332-0001. Offers city and regional planning (PhD); economic development (MCRP); environmental planning and management (MCRP); geographic information systems (MCRP); land and community development (MCRP); land use planning (MCRP); transportation (MCRP); urban design (MCRP); MCP/MSCE. *Accreditation:* ACSP. *Degree requirements:* For master's, thesis, internship. *Entrance requirements:* For master's, GRE General Test, minimum GPA of 2.7. Additional exam requirements/recommendations for international students: Required—TOEFL. Electronic applications accepted.

Harvard University, Graduate School of Design, Department of Urban Planning and Design, Cambridge, MA 02138. Offers urban planning (MUP); urban planning and design (MAUD, MLAUD). *Accreditation:* ACSP (one or more programs are accredited). *Entrance requirements:* For master's, GRE General Test. Additional exam requirements/recommendations for international students: Required—TOEFL (minimum score 600 paper-based; 250 computer-based; 104 iBT). Electronic applications accepted. *Expenses:* Tuition: Full-time $34,976. Required fees: $1166. Full-time tuition and fees vary according to program.

Kent State University, College of Architecture and Environmental Design, Kent, OH 44242-0001. Offers architecture (M Arch); preservation architecture (Certificate); urban design (M Arch, MUD, Certificate). Part-time programs available. *Degree requirements:* For master's, thesis optional. *Entrance requirements:* For master's, GRE, portfolio, minimum GPA of 2.75, 3 letters of reference, resume, undergraduate architecture degree. Additional exam requirements/recommendations for international students: Required—TOEFL (minimum score 550 paper-based). Electronic applications accepted. *Expenses:* Tuition, state resident: full-time $7866; part-time $437 per credit hour. Tuition, nonresident: full-time $14,022; part-time $779 per credit hour. *Faculty research:* History and theory, building technology, landscape architecture and urbanism, urbanism, sustainable development.

Lawrence Technological University, College of Architecture and Design, Southfield, MI 48075-1058. Offers architecture (M Arch); architecture 3+ (M Arch); interior design (MID); interior design 3+ (MID); urban design (MUD). *Accreditation:* NASAD. Part-time and evening/weekend programs available. *Faculty:* 9 full-time (2 women), 12 part-time/adjunct (3 women). *Students:* 11 full-time (5 women), 225 part-time (89 women); includes 13 Black or African American, non-Hispanic/Latino; 11 Asian, non-Hispanic/Latino; 7 Hispanic/Latino; 1 Native Hawaiian or other Pacific Islander, non-Hispanic/Latino; 2 Two or more races, non-Hispanic/Latino, 23 international. Average age 31. 174 applicants, 55% accepted, 68 enrolled. In 2010, 47 master's awarded. *Degree requirements:* For master's, thesis. *Entrance requirements:* For master's, portfolio. Additional exam requirements/recommendations for international students: Required—TOEFL (minimum score 550 paper-based; 213 computer-based; 79 iBT). *Application deadline:* For fall admission, 6/30 priority date for domestic students, 6/30 for international students; for spring admission, 1/15 priority date for domestic students, 1/15 for international students. Applications are processed on a rolling basis. Application fee: $50. Electronic applications accepted. *Financial support:* In 2010–11, 83 students received support. Federal Work-Study available. Financial award application deadline: 4/1; financial award applicants required to submit FAFSA. *Unit head:* Glen LeRoy, Dean, 248-204-2800, Fax: 248-204-2900, E-mail: archdean@ltu.edu. *Application contact:* Jane Rohrback, Director of Admissions, 248-204-3160, Fax: 248-204-2228, E-mail: admissions@ltu.edu.

The New School: A University, Parsons The New School for Design, Program in Design and Urban Ecologies, New York, NY 10011. Offers MS.

The New School: A University, Parsons The New School for Design, Program in Theories of Urban Practice, New York, NY 10011. Offers MA.

New York Institute of Technology, Graduate Division, School of Architecture and Design, Old Westbury, NY 11568-8000. Offers urban and regional design (M Arch). Part-time programs available. *Students:* 24 full-time (11 women), 3 part-time (all women); includes 6 minority (3 Asian, non-Hispanic/Latino; 3 Hispanic/Latino), 16 international. Average age 27. In 2010, 12 master's awarded. *Degree requirements:* For master's, thesis. *Entrance requirements:* For master's, minimum QPA of 2.85, portfolio. Additional exam requirements/recommendations for international students: Required—TOEFL (minimum score 550 paper-based; 213 computer-based). *Application deadline:* For fall admission, 7/1 priority date for domestic students; for spring admission, 12/1 priority date for domestic students. Applications are processed on a rolling basis. Application fee: $50. Electronic applications accepted. *Expenses:* Tuition: Part-time $835 per credit. *Financial support:* Research assistantships with partial tuition reimbursements, institutionally sponsored loans and tuition waivers (full and partial) available. Support available to part-time students. Financial award applicants required to submit FAFSA. *Faculty research:* Affordable housing, urban modeling and simulation, transport systems and infrastructure, relationships of policy and form. *Unit head:* Judith DiMaio, Dean, 516-686-7594, Fax: 516-686-7921, E-mail: jdimaio@nyit.edu. *Application contact:* Dr. Jacquelyn Nealon, Vice President for Enrollment Services, 516-686-7925, Fax: 516-686-7597, E-mail: jnealon@nyit.edu.

Prairie View A&M University, School of Architecture, Prairie View, TX 77446-0519. Offers architecture (M Arch); community development (MCD). Part-time and evening/weekend programs available. *Faculty:* 4 full-time (1 woman), 6 part-time/adjunct (2 women). *Students:* 31 full-time (6 women), 38 part-time (18 women); includes 55 Black or African American, non-Hispanic/Latino; 1 Asian, non-Hispanic/Latino; 6 Hispanic/Latino, 5 international. Average age 31. 63 applicants, 100% accepted. In 2010, 35 master's awarded. *Entrance requirements:* For master's, GRE General Test, portfolio (M Arch). Additional exam requirements/recommendations for international students: Required—TOEFL (minimum score 550 paper-based). *Application deadline:* For fall admission, 6/1 priority date for domestic and international students; for spring admission, 11/1 priority date for domestic students, 10/1 priority date for international students. Applications are processed on a rolling basis. Application fee: $50. Electronic applications accepted. *Expenses:* Tuition, state resident: full-time $3586.14; part-time $119.06 per credit hour. Tuition, nonresident: part-time $511.23 per credit hour. *Financial support:* In 2010–11, 1 research assistantship (averaging $6,792 per year) was awarded; career-related internships or fieldwork, Federal Work-Study, institutionally sponsored loans, scholarships/grants, tuition waivers (full and partial), and unspecified assistantships also available. Support available to part-time students. Financial award application deadline: 3/1; financial award applicants required to submit FAFSA. *Faculty research:* Community management, sustainable design. *Unit head:* Dr. Ikhlas Sabouni, Dean, 936-261-9800, Fax: 936-261-2350, E-mail: isabouni@pvamu.edu. *Application contact:* Dr. Ikhlas Sabouni, Dean, 936-261-9800, Fax: 936-261-2350, E-mail: isabouni@pvamu.edu.

Pratt Institute, School of Architecture, Program in Architecture and Urban Design, Brooklyn, NY 11205-3899. Offers architecture and urban design (post-profession) (MS). *Faculty:* 4 part-time/adjunct (2 women). *Students:* 19 full-time (5 women); includes 1 Black or African American, non-Hispanic/Latino, 14 international. Average age 27. 62 applicants, 56% accepted, 9 enrolled. In 2010, 7 master's awarded. *Degree requirements:* For master's, thesis. *Entrance requirements:* For master's, portfolio, letters of recommendation. Additional exam requirements/recommendations for international students: Required—TOEFL (minimum score 550 paper-based; 213 computer-based; 79 iBT). *Application deadline:* For fall admission, 1/5 for domestic and international students; for spring admission, 10/1 for domestic and international students. Applications are processed on a rolling basis. Application fee: $50 ($90 for international students). Electronic applications accepted. *Expenses:* Tuition: Full-time $22,734; part-time $1263 per credit. Required fees: $1280. *Financial support:* Career-related internships or fieldwork, Federal Work-Study, institutionally sponsored loans, scholarships/grants, health care benefits, and unspecified assistantships available. Support available to part-time students. Financial award application deadline: 2/1; financial award applicants required to submit FAFSA. *Faculty research:* Urban development process; historical, social, and economic implications of planning. *Unit head:* William J. Mac Donald, Chairperson, 718-399-4357, E-mail: wmacdona@pratt.edu. *Application contact:* Young Hah, Director of Graduate Admissions, 718-636-3683, Fax: 718-399-4242, E-mail: yhah@pratt.edu.

See Display on page 141 and Close-Up on page 161.

Rice University, Graduate Programs, School of Architecture, Houston, TX 77251-1892. Offers architecture (M Arch, D Arch); urban design (M Arch). *Degree requirements:* For master's, thesis optional; for doctorate, thesis/dissertation. *Entrance requirements:* For master's and doctorate, GRE. Additional exam requirements/recommendations for international students: Required—TOEFL (minimum score 600 paper-based; 250 computer-based; 100 iBT). Electronic applications accepted.

Rollins College, Hamilton Holt School, Program in Civic Urbanism, Winter Park, FL 32789. Offers M Pl. Part-time and evening/weekend programs available. *Faculty:* 2 full-time (0 women). *Students:* 26 part-time (13 women); includes 4 minority (1 Asian, non-Hispanic/Latino; 3 Hispanic/Latino). Average age 32. 44 applicants, 64% accepted, 24 enrolled. *Entrance requirements:* For master's, GRE. Additional exam requirements/recommendations for international students: Required—TOEFL (minimum score 550 paper-based; 213 computer-based; 80 iBT). *Application deadline:* For fall admission, 4/1 for domestic students. Application fee: $50. *Expenses:* Contact institution. *Financial support:* Career-related internships or fieldwork, scholarships/grants, and unspecified assistantships available. Support available to part-time students. Financial award applicants required to submit FAFSA. *Unit head:* Dr. Bruce Stephenson, Chair, 407-646-2232. *Application contact:* Graduate Program Admission, 407-646-2232, Fax: 407-646-1551.

Savannah College of Art and Design, Graduate School, Program in Urban Design and Development, Savannah, GA 31402-3146. Offers MUD. Part-time programs available. *Faculty:* 1 full-time (0 women), 1 part-time/adjunct (0 women). *Students:* 16 full-time (3 women), 2 part-time (both women), 12 international. Average age 27. In 2010, 1 master's awarded. *Degree requirements:* For master's, thesis. *Entrance requirements:* For master's, interview, portfolio. Additional exam requirements/recommendations for international students: Required—TOEFL (minimum score 450 paper-based; 133 computer-based). *Application deadline:* For fall admission, 4/1 priority date for domestic and international students. Application fee: $35. *Expenses:* Tuition: Full-time $29,520; part-time $3280 per quarter. Tuition and fees vary according to campus/location. *Financial support:* Fellowships, career-related internships or fieldwork, Federal Work-Study, and scholarships/grants available. Financial award application deadline: 4/1; financial award applicants required to submit FAFSA. *Unit head:* Brian Wishne, Chair, 912-525-6110, E-mail: bwishne@scad.edu. *Application contact:* Elizabeth Mathis, Director of Graduate Recruitment, 912-525-5965, Fax: 912-525-5985, E-mail: emathis@scad.edu.

State University of New York College of Environmental Science and Forestry, Department of Landscape Architecture, Syracuse, NY 13210-2779. Offers community design and planning (MLA, MS); cultural landscape conservation (MLA, MS); landscape and urban ecology (MLA, MS). *Accreditation:* ASLA (one or more programs are accredited). *Degree requirements:* For master's, comprehensive exam (for some programs), thesis (for some programs). *Entrance requirements:* For master's, GRE General Test, minimum GPA of 3.0. Additional exam requirements/recommendations for international students: Required—TOEFL (paper-based 550, computer-based 213, iBT 80) or IELTS (6) or STEP Aiken (Grade 1). *Expenses:* Tuition, state resident: full-time $8370; part-time $349 per credit hour. Tuition, nonresident: full-time $13,780. Required fees: $30.30 per credit hour. $20 per year. *Faculty research:* Site analysis and design, city and regional planning, community environments.

Temple University, College of Liberal Arts, Department of Geography and Urban Studies, Philadelphia, PA 19122-6096. Offers geography (MA); geography and urban studies (MA); urban studies (MA, PhD). *Faculty:* 25 full-time (16 women). *Students:* 19 full-time (11 women), 12 part-time (6 women); includes 3 Black or African American, non-Hispanic/Latino; 2 Asian,

Urban Design

Temple University (continued)
non-Hispanic/Latino; 1 Hispanic/Latino, 3 international. 69 applicants, 41% accepted, 11 enrolled. In 2010, 13 master's awarded. *Degree requirements:* For master's, comprehensive exam, thesis or alternative. *Entrance requirements:* For master's, GRE General Test, minimum GPA of 3.0. Additional exam requirements/recommendations for international students: Required—TOEFL (minimum score 550 paper-based; 213 computer-based; 79 iBT). *Application deadline:* For fall admission, 1/15 for domestic students, 12/15 for international students; for spring admission, 10/15 for domestic students, 8/1 for international students. Applications are processed on a rolling basis. Application fee: $50. Electronic applications accepted. *Financial support:* Fellowships, teaching assistantships, career-related internships or fieldwork, Federal Work-Study, and tuition waivers (partial) available. Financial award application deadline: 1/15; financial award applicants required to submit FAFSA. *Faculty research:* Environmental issues, urban political economy, poverty and unemployment, neighborhood development, African and Asian urbanization, housing, computer cartography. Total annual research expenditures: $400,000. *Unit head:* Dr. Michele Masucci, Chair, 215-204-7692, Fax: 215-204-7833, E-mail: masucci@temple.edu. *Application contact:* Dr. Michele Masucci, Chair, 215-204-7692, Fax: 215-204-7833, E-mail: masucci@temple.edu.

University at Buffalo, the State University of New York, Graduate School, School of Architecture and Planning, Department of Urban and Regional Planning, Buffalo, NY 14260. Offers MUP, JD/MUP, M Arch/MUP. *Accreditation:* ACSP. Part-time programs available. *Faculty:* 14 full-time (3 women), 8 part-time/adjunct (2 women). *Students:* 81 full-time (35 women), 13 part-time (7 women); includes 9 Black or African American, non-Hispanic/Latino; 1 American Indian or Alaska Native, non-Hispanic/Latino; 3 Asian, non-Hispanic/Latino; 6 Hispanic/Latino, 20 international. Average age 28. 214 applicants, 39% accepted, 40 enrolled. In 2010, 39 master's awarded. *Degree requirements:* For master's, thesis or alternative, project. *Entrance requirements:* For master's, minimum GPA of 3.0, resume, 3 letters of recommendation. Additional exam requirements/recommendations for international students: Required—TOEFL (minimum score 213 computer-based; 79 iBT), IELTS (minimum score 6.5). *Application deadline:* For fall admission, 3/1 priority date for domestic and international students; for spring admission, 10/31 priority date for domestic students, 10/1 priority date for international students. Applications are processed on a rolling basis. Application fee: $75. Electronic applications accepted. *Financial support:* In 2010–11, 5 fellowships with full tuition reimbursements (averaging $9,600 per year), 15 research assistantships with full and partial tuition reimbursements (averaging $5,044 per year), 14 teaching assistantships with partial tuition reimbursements (averaging $4,800 per year) were awarded; career-related internships or fieldwork, Federal Work-Study, institutionally sponsored loans, scholarships/grants, health care benefits, tuition waivers (partial), and unspecified assistantships also available. Support available to part-time students. Financial award application deadline: 3/1; financial award applicants required to submit FAFSA. *Faculty research:* Community development and urban management, economic and international development, environmental and land use planning, GIS and spatial modeling, urban design and physical planning. Total annual research expenditures: $204,853. *Unit head:* Dr. Ernest Sternberg, Professor and Chair, 716-829-2133 Ext. 109, Fax: 716-829-3256, E-mail: ezs@buffalo.edu. *Application contact:* Donna M. Rogalski, Assistant to the Chair, 716-829-2133 Ext. 109, Fax: 716-829-3256, E-mail: dmr1@buffalo.edu.

University of California, Berkeley, Graduate Division, College of Environmental Design, Department of Architecture, Berkeley, CA 94720-1500. Offers architecture (M Arch); building science (MS, PhD); building structures, construction and materials (MS, PhD); design theories, methods, and practices (MS, PhD); environmental design in developing countries (MS, PhD); history of architecture and urbanism (MS, PhD); social and cultural processes in architecture and urbanism (MS, PhD); M Arch/MCP; M Arch/MS; MLA/M Arch. *Degree requirements:* For master's, thesis; for doctorate, thesis/dissertation, qualifying exam. *Entrance requirements:* For master's and doctorate, GRE General Test, minimum GPA of 3.0, 3 letters of recommendation. Additional exam requirements/recommendations for international students: Required—TOEFL. Electronic applications accepted.

University of California, Berkeley, Graduate Division, College of Environmental Design, Department of Landscape Architecture and Environmental Planning, Berkeley, CA 94720-1500. Offers landscape architecture (MLA), including environmental planning, landscape design and site planning, urban and community design; landscape architecture and environmental planning (PhD); MLA/M Arch; MLA/MCP. *Accreditation:* ASLA (one or more programs are accredited). *Degree requirements:* For master's, professional project or thesis; for doctorate, one foreign language, thesis/dissertation, qualifying exam. *Entrance requirements:* For master's, GRE General Test, minimum GPA of 3.0, portfolio; for doctorate, GRE General Test, master's degree (strongly recommended), minimum GPA of 3.0, sample of written work, 3 letters of recommendation.

University of California, Berkeley, Graduate Division, College of Environmental Design, Group in Urban Design, Berkeley, CA 94720-1500. Offers MUD. *Degree requirements:* For master's, professional project or thesis. *Entrance requirements:* For master's, GRE General Test, minimum GPA of 3.0, portfolio, 3 letters of recommendation.

University of California, Los Angeles, Graduate Division, School of the Arts and Architecture, Department of Architecture and Urban Design, Los Angeles, CA 90095. Offers M Arch, MA, PhD. *Faculty:* 14 full-time (6 women). *Students:* 165 full-time (60 women); includes 39 minority (4 Black or African American, non-Hispanic/Latino; 24 Asian, non-Hispanic/Latino; 9 Hispanic/Latino; 1 Native Hawaiian or other Pacific Islander, non-Hispanic/Latino; 1 Two or more races, non-Hispanic/Latino), 27 international. Average age 28. 648 applicants, 23% accepted, 51 enrolled. In 2010, 43 master's awarded. *Degree requirements:* For master's, thesis or alternative, comprehensive exam or design project; for doctorate, 2 foreign languages, thesis/dissertation, oral and written qualifying exams. *Entrance requirements:* For master's and doctorate, GRE General Test, portfolio. Additional exam requirements/recommendations for international students: Required—TOEFL. *Application deadline:* For fall admission, 1/5 for domestic students. Application fee: $70 ($90 for international students). Electronic applications accepted. *Financial support:* In 2010–11, 137 students received support, including 34 fellowships, 13 research assistantships, 45 teaching assistantships; Federal Work-Study, institutionally sponsored loans, tuition waivers (full and partial), and unspecified assistantships also available. Financial award application deadline: 3/2. *Faculty research:* Urban poverty and low wage labor markets; environmental planning and politics; international political economy; physical planning, urban design, planning history; housing and land development; transportation and land use; critical urban and regional studies. *Unit head:* Dr. Hitoshi Abe, Chair, 310-206-3495. *Application contact:* Jim Kies, Information Contact, 310-825-0525, Fax: 310-825-8959, E-mail: admissions@aud.ucla.edu.

University of Colorado Denver, College of Architecture and Planning, Program in Design and Planning, Denver, CO 80217-3364. Offers history of architecture, landscape and urbanism (PhD); sustainable and healthy environments (PhD). Part-time programs available. *Students:* 25 full-time (15 women), 11 part-time (7 women); includes 2 Black or African American, non-Hispanic/Latino; 1 Asian, non-Hispanic/Latino; 2 Hispanic/Latino, 7 international. Average age 40. 60 applicants, 15% accepted, 6 enrolled. In 2010, 2 doctorates awarded. *Degree requirements:* For doctorate, comprehensive exam, thesis/dissertation. *Entrance requirements:* For doctorate, GRE, minimum undergraduate GPA of 3.0, graduate 3.5; writing sample. Additional exam requirements/recommendations for international students: Required—TOEFL (minimum score 575 paper-based). *Application deadline:* For fall admission, 2/1 for domestic students; for spring admission, 10/1 for domestic students. Application fee: $50 ($75 for international students). Electronic applications accepted. *Expenses:* Contact institution. *Financial support:* Fellowships, research assistantships, teaching assistantships, career-related internships or fieldwork, Federal Work-Study, scholarships/grants, tuition waivers, and unspecified assistantships available. Support available to part-time students. Financial award application deadline: 4/1; financial award applicants required to submit FAFSA. *Faculty research:* Land use and environmental planning and design; design and planning processes and practices; history, theory, and criticism of the built environment. *Unit head:* Dr. Kevin Krizek, Director, 303-556-3282, Fax: 303-556-3687, E-mail: kevin.krizek@colorado.edu. *Application contact:* Michael Harper, Administrative Coordinator, 303-556-6042, Fax: 303-556-3687, E-mail: michael.t.harper@ucdenver.edu.

University of Colorado Denver, College of Architecture and Planning, Program in Urban Design, Denver, CO 80217. Offers MUD. Part-time programs available. *Students:* 10 full-time (5 women), 4 part-time (3 women); includes 3 Hispanic/Latino, 3 international. Average age 36. 26 applicants, 54% accepted, 8 enrolled. In 2010, 25 master's awarded. *Degree requirements:* For master's, thesis optional, 36 credits. *Entrance requirements:* For master's, GRE (recommended), BA in architecture, minimum GPA of 3.0, portfolio. Additional exam requirements/recommendations for international students: Required—TOEFL (minimum score 550 paper-based; 213 computer-based). *Application deadline:* For fall admission, 2/15 for domestic students; for spring admission, 10/1 for domestic students. Applications are processed on a rolling basis. Application fee: $50 ($75 for international students). Electronic applications accepted. *Expenses:* Contact institution. *Financial support:* Federal Work-Study and scholarships/grants available. Financial award application deadline: 4/1; financial award applicants required to submit FAFSA. *Faculty research:* Architecture of the city, architectural experimentation and exploration, composition and decomposition, intervention and transformation in the urban and rural landscape. *Unit head:* Jeremy Nemeth, Assistant Professor of Planning/Program Director, 303-556-3688, E-mail: jeremy.nemeth@ucdenver.edu. *Application contact:* Michael Harper, Administrative Coordinator, Graduate Admissions and PhD Program, 303-556-6042, E-mail: michael.t.harper@ucdenver.edu.

University of Colorado Denver, School of Education and Human Development, Program in Educational Leadership and Innovation, Denver, CO 80217-3364. Offers educational studies and research (PhD), including administrative leadership and policy, assessment and measurement, math education, science education, urban ecologies; leadership for educational equity (Ed D), including executive leadership, instructional leadership. Part-time and evening/weekend programs available. *Students:* 42 full-time (29 women), 27 part-time (18 women); includes 4 Black or African American, non-Hispanic/Latino; 1 American Indian or Alaska Native, non-Hispanic/Latino; 2 Asian, non-Hispanic/Latino; 3 Hispanic/Latino, 1 international. Average age 42. 1 applicant, 100% accepted, 0 enrolled. In 2010, 11 doctorates awarded. *Degree requirements:* For doctorate, comprehensive exam, thesis/dissertation, 75 credit hours (for PhD), 69 (for EdD). *Entrance requirements:* For doctorate, GRE or equivalent, resume or curriculum vitae, written statement, letters of recommendation, master's degree or equivalent, completion of basic or advanced statistics course with minimum B grade. Additional exam requirements/recommendations for international students: Required—TOEFL (minimum score 525 paper-based; 197 computer-based). *Application deadline:* For fall admission, 9/15 for domestic students. Applications are processed on a rolling basis. Application fee: $50 ($75 for international students). Electronic applications accepted. *Expenses:* Contact institution. *Financial support:* Fellowships, research assistantships, teaching assistantships, scholarships/grants and unspecified assistantships available. Financial award application deadline: 4/1; financial award applicants required to submit FAFSA. *Faculty research:* Administrative leadership and policy studies, early childhood education, research in diversity, paraprofessionals in education, urban schools lab. *Unit head:* Dr. Deanna Sands, Associate Dean, Research and Professional Development, 303-315-4931, E-mail: deanna.sands@ucdenver.edu. *Application contact:* Student Services Center, 303-315-6300, Fax: 303-315-6311, E-mail: education@ucdenver.edu.

University of Idaho, College of Graduate Studies, College of Art and Architecture, Moscow, ID 83844-2282. Offers architecture (MS), including community planning, computation and visualization studies, environment and behavior studies, urban design; architecture (professional degree) (M Arch); landscape architecture (MS); studio art (MFA), including graphic design, interactive and information design, interface, painting, printmaking, sculpture; teaching art (MAT). *Accreditation:* NASAD. *Faculty:* 19 full-time, 1 part-time/adjunct. *Students:* 102 full-time, 15 part-time. Average age 27. In 2010, 31 master's awarded. *Application deadline:* For fall admission, 8/1 for domestic students; for spring admission, 12/15 for domestic students. Applications are processed on a rolling basis. Application fee: $60. Electronic applications accepted. *Expenses:* Tuition, nonresident: part-time $580 per credit. Required fees: $306 per credit. *Financial support:* Applicants required to submit FAFSA. *Faculty research:* Sustainability in communities, urban research, virtual technology, bioregional planning, environment and behavior interaction. *Unit head:* Dr. Mark Elison Hoversten, Dean, 208-885-5423, E-mail: caa@uidaho.edu. *Application contact:* Dr. Mark Elison Hoversten, Dean, 208-885-5423, E-mail: caa@uidaho.edu.

University of Miami, Graduate School, School of Architecture, Program in Suburb and Town Design, Coral Gables, FL 33124. Offers M Arch. *Entrance requirements:* For master's, GRE General Test, minimum GPA of 3.0, portfolio. Additional exam requirements/recommendations for international students: Required—TOEFL. Electronic applications accepted.

University of Michigan, Taubman College of Architecture and Urban Planning, Master of Urban Design Program, Ann Arbor, MI 48109-2069. Offers MUD. *Entrance requirements:* For master's, GRE General Test, 5 year bachelor of architecture, M Arch, bachelor of landscape architecture, master of landscape architecture, or MUP; portfolio. Additional exam requirements/recommendations for international students: Required—TOEFL (minimum score 560 paper-based; 220 computer-based; 84 iBT). *Expenses:* Contact institution.

University of New Mexico, Graduate School, School of Architecture and Planning, Program in Town Design, Albuquerque, NM 87131-2039. Offers Graduate Certificate. Part-time programs available. In 2010, 2 Graduate Certificates awarded. *Application deadline:* For fall admission, 3/1 for domestic students; for spring admission, 11/1 for domestic students. Application fee: $50. Electronic applications accepted. *Expenses:* Tuition, state resident: full-time $5991; part-time $251 per credit hour. Tuition, nonresident: full-time $14,405; part-time $800.20 per credit hour. Tuition and fees vary according to course level, course load, program and reciprocity agreements. *Unit head:* Mark C. Childs, Director, 505-277-5059, Fax: 505-277-0076, E-mail: mchilds@unm.edu. *Application contact:* Mark C. Childs, Director, 505-277-5059, Fax: 505-277-0076, E-mail: mchilds@unm.edu.

The University of North Carolina at Charlotte, Graduate School, College of Arts and Architecture, Charlotte, NC 28223-0001. Offers architecture (M Arch); urban design (MUD). *Faculty:* 34 full-time (12 women), 3 part-time/adjunct (0 women). *Students:* 76 full-time (36 women), 6 part-time (5 women); includes 8 minority (5 Black or African American, non-Hispanic/Latino; 2 Asian, non-Hispanic/Latino; 1 Hispanic/Latino), 1 international. Average age 27. 72 applicants, 67% accepted, 32 enrolled. In 2010, 29 master's awarded. *Degree requirements:* For master's, project or thesis. *Entrance requirements:* For master's, GRE General Test or GMAT, portfolio, resume. Additional exam requirements/recommendations for international students: Required—TOEFL (minimum score 557 paper-based; 220 computer-based; 83 iBT). *Application deadline:* For fall admission, 2/15 for domestic students, 1/31 for international students. Application fee: $55. Electronic applications accepted. *Expenses:* Tuition, state resident: full-time $3464. Tuition, nonresident: full-time $14,297. Required fees: $2094. Tuition and fees vary according to course load. *Financial support:* In 2010–11, 12 students received support, including 5 research assistantships (averaging $9,032 per year), 7 teaching assistantships (averaging $8,451 per year); career-related internships or fieldwork, institutionally sponsored loans, scholarships/grants, and unspecified assistantships also available. Support available to part-time students. Financial award application deadline: 4/1; financial award applicants required to submit FAFSA. *Faculty research:* Daylighting and energy control, urban design, history and theory, construction techniques. Total annual research expenditures: $131,220. *Unit head:* Kenneth A. Lambla, Dean, 704-687-4024, Fax: 704-687-3353, E-mail: kalambla@uncc.edu. *Application contact:* Kathy B. Giddings, Director of Graduate Admissions, 704-687-5503, Fax: 704-687-3279, E-mail: gradadm@uncc.edu.

University of Pennsylvania, School of Design, Graduate Group in Architecture, Philadelphia, PA 19104. Offers architecture (PhD); real estate design and development (PhD); urban design (PhD). Part-time programs available. *Faculty:* 15 full-time (5 women), 13 part-time/adjunct (3 women). *Students:* 277 full-time (120 women), 9 part-time (3 women); includes 4 Black or African American, non-Hispanic/Latino; 2 American Indian or Alaska Native, non-Hispanic/Latino; 31 Asian, non-Hispanic/Latino; 11 Hispanic/Latino, 95 international. 963 applicants, 34% accepted, 112 enrolled. In 2010, 4 doctorates awarded. *Degree requirements:* For doctorate, 2 foreign languages, comprehensive exam, thesis/dissertation, qualifying exam, final exam. *Entrance requirements:* For doctorate, GRE General Test, B Arch, M Arch, portfolio, writing sample. Additional exam requirements/recommendations for international students: Required—TOEFL. *Application deadline:* For fall admission, 1/2 priority date for domestic students. Application fee: $70. *Expenses:* Tuition: Full-time $25,660; part-time $4758 per course. Required fees: $2152; $270 per course. Tuition and fees vary according to course load, degree level and program. *Financial support:* Fellowships, research assistantships, teaching assistantships, institutionally sponsored loans, scholarships/grants, traineeships, health care benefits, and unspecified assistantships available. *Faculty research:* Theory, history, technology, representation, visualization, landscape, urban design, historic preservation.

The University of Texas at Austin, Graduate School, School of Architecture, Austin, TX 78712-1111. Offers architecture (M Arch); community and regional planning (MSCRP, PhD); historic preservation (MS); history of architecture (MA, PhD); landscape architecture (MLA); urban design (MSUD); JD/MSCRP; MSCRP/MA; MSCRP/PhD. *Degree requirements:* For doctorate, thesis/dissertation. *Entrance requirements:* For master's and doctorate, GRE General Test. Additional exam requirements/recommendations for international students: Required—TOEFL (minimum score 550 paper-based; 213 computer-based). Electronic applications accepted.

University of Toronto, School of Graduate Studies, Social Sciences Division, Department of Geography, Toronto, ON M5S 1A1, Canada. Offers geography (M Sc, MA, PhD); planning (M Sc Pl); urban design studies (MUD). Part-time programs available. *Degree requirements:* For master's, thesis optional; for doctorate, thesis/dissertation. *Entrance requirements:* For master's, bachelor's degree or equivalent in geography or a closely related field, minimum B+ average in each of 2 final years of degree, 3 letters of reference; for doctorate, master of geography degree, minimum A–average.

University of Washington, Graduate School, College of Built Environments, Department of Urban Design and Planning, Seattle, WA 98195. Offers strategic planning for critical infrastructures (MSCPI); urban design and planning (PhD); urban planning (MUP). *Accreditation:* ACSP (one or more programs are accredited). *Degree requirements:* For master's, thesis or alternative; for doctorate, thesis/dissertation. *Entrance requirements:* For master's and doctorate, GRE General Test, minimum GPA of 3.0. Additional exam requirements/recommendations for international students: Required—TOEFL. *Faculty research:* Land-use and growth management, urban form and travel behavior, geographic information systems/remote sensing, historic preservation, urban ecology and environmental planning.

University of Washington, Graduate School, College of Built Environments, Interdisciplinary Program in Urban Design, Seattle, WA 98195. Offers Certificate. Electronic applications accepted. *Faculty research:* Urban design process; urban form; place theory; place analysis; race, class, and gender in community design.

Washington University in St. Louis, Sam Fox School of Design and Visual Arts, Program in Urban Design, St. Louis, MO 63130-4899. Offers MUD, M Arch/MUD, MUD/MSW. *Entrance requirements:* For master's, GRE General Test, portfolio. Additional exam requirements/recommendations for international students: Required—TOEFL (minimum score 600 paper-based; 250 computer-based; 100 iBT), TWE. *Faculty research:* Urban design development issues: city revitalization, sustainability and suburbanization; urban history and visualization of urban form.

Woodbury University, School of Architecture, Burbank, CA 91504-1099. Offers architecture (M Arch); landscape and urbanism (M Arch); post-professional (M Arch). *Faculty:* 6 full-time (4 women), 19 part-time/adjunct (6 women). *Students:* 54 full-time (16 women); includes 21 minority (2 Black or African American, non-Hispanic/Latino; 8 Asian, non-Hispanic/Latino; 11 Hispanic/Latino), 9 international. Average age 28. 72 applicants, 60% accepted, 36 enrolled. In 2010, 13 master's awarded. *Degree requirements:* For master's, thesis. *Entrance requirements:* For master's, GRE (if undergraduate GPA is below 3.0), 3 letters of recommendation, portfolio, essay, interview, resume, academic transcripts. Additional exam requirements/recommendations for international students: Required—TOEFL (minimum score 550 paper-based; 220 computer-based; 83 iBT), IELTS (minimum score 6.5). *Application deadline:* For fall admission, 3/1 priority date for domestic and international students. Application fee: $60. *Expenses:* Contact institution. *Financial support:* In 2010–11, 52 students received support, including 36 fellowships (averaging $6,000 per year), 10 research assistantships (averaging $2,000 per year), 23 teaching assistantships (averaging $2,000 per year); scholarships/grants also available. *Unit head:* Norman Millar, Dean, 318-767-0888 Ext. 130, Fax: 318-504-9320, E-mail: norman.millar@woodbury.edu. *Application contact:* Glisery Colon, Director, Graduate Admissions, 818-252-5234, Fax: 818-252-5221, E-mail: glisery.colon@woodbury.edu.

PRATT INSTITUTE

School of Architecture

Programs of Study	The School of Architecture is dedicated to maintaining the connection between design theory and practice and to extending the range of knowledge necessary to an understanding of the built environment. The diversity of programs within the School and the accessibility of other programs within the Institute enable students to pursue a wide range of interests. Students can take electives in fine arts, film, digital arts, industrial design, furniture design, interior design, and photography as well as electives in advanced architectural theory, design, technology, and management. The School has many internationally recognized faculty members who bring to the graduate programs a strong theoretical base and the high standards of their professional work. The programs are distinguished by strong studio cultures and creative approaches to architectural design. Many special courses are offered in contemporary theoretical and critical issues, advanced computing and media, building technology, architectural history, and experimental structures. The electronic laboratory is a fifty-station PC-based facility that offers instruction in a wide variety of two-dimensional and three-dimensional design programs. Students are exposed to the professional world through optional internship programs that place them in outstanding New York architectural offices, public agencies, and nonprofit design institutions, giving them firsthand work experience and credit towards their degree.

The School of Architecture offers a total of seven graduate programs. There are two graduate architecture programs: the first-professional accredited Master of Architecture (M.Arch.) and the postprofessional Master of Architecture (M.S.Arch.). There are also five Master of Science programs: architecture and urban design, city and regional planning, environmental systems management, facilities management, and historic preservation.

The three-year M.Arch. first-professional program is designed for students holding a four-year undergraduate program in any field, including architecture. Graduate courses and seminars are designed to familiarize students with all aspects of the discipline and practice of architecture. Design studios at Pratt find many of their coordinates within the rich territory of New York City. However, the program also reaches into areas worldwide and into other frames, such as global marketplaces, digital worlds, and historical, theoretical, and political networks. This program is fully accredited by NAAB. Students with a B.S. in architecture or other nonprofessional degree should apply for this M.Arch. program. The postprofessional M.S.Arch., a summer/fall/spring program, is for those who hold an accredited architecture degree or the equivalent. The program takes three semesters to complete. Students with significant professional experience can also apply for work credit, which reduces total credit-hour requirements. The postprofessional M.S.Arch. allows intensive theoretical and technical engagement of architecture and the city and stresses research and experimentation concentrating on the relations between architecture and other urban forms, scales, and forces. Research is conducted primarily within the analytic and synthetic content of the design studio and culminates in a required thesis.

The Master of Science in architecture and urban design program is intended for students who are interested in careers that enhance the growth and development of the built urban environments, the context for an urban laboratory. The 33-credit program requires 17 hours of design studio and research, with the balance of the credits in required courses in urban history, theory, infrastructure, and implementation and electives in law, transportation, housing, and preservation. The program is open to those with professional undergraduate degrees in architecture and is a summer/fall/spring program.

The four programs offered by Pratt's Programs for Sustainable Planning and Development (PSPD)—the M.S. in city and regional planning (CRP), the M.S. in environmental systems management (ESM), the M.S. in historic preservation, and the M.S. in facilities management—emphasize planning and preservation practice rooted in the principles of sustainability, equity, and public participation.

The curricula are designed to build the professional skills and knowledge of students who desire to affect the built, natural, and social environments of the nation's cities and communities in positive ways. CRP and ESM courses are offered in the evenings, enabling students to work full-time. The city and regional planning program offers specializations in community development, environmental planning, physical planning, and preservation planning. The CRP program requires the completion of 60 credits, including the thesis or the Demonstration of Professional Competence course. The ESM program requires 40 credits of course work.

Students with undergraduate degrees in architecture and engineering may have up to 9 credits waived in either the CRP or ESM program.

PSPD's historic preservation program is a two-year graduate program leading to the M.S. in historic preservation. The program, designed primarily for full-time students and based at the Manhattan campus, is a 44-credit sequence of courses that provides studies in community planning, history, interpretation, design, policy, and regulatory practice.

Recognizing that today's field of preservation requires more than curatorial management, the program fosters the knowledge preservationists must have in order to participate in policy-making to revitalize urban areas, suburban communities, and rural landscapes. With its urban focus, the program emphasizes hands-on work and makes extensive use of New York City's rich resources.

All four graduate programs in the PSPD maintain strong ties with Pratt's architecture and design programs and with the Pratt Center for Community Development, an innovative center for the practice of planning, design, and policy work that focuses on increasing quality of life and affecting social change in New York City's diverse communities.

The M.S. in facilities management program prepares individuals to assume leadership roles in corporations, institutions, and government. The degree requires the completion of 45 credits of course work and the 5-credit Demonstration of Professional Competence course, for a total of 50 credits. Students entering the program with prior professional experience or graduate work in related fields may be eligible for advanced standing; up to 12 credits may be waived. The facilities management program, accredited by IFMA, is offered at the Pratt Manhattan Center on an evening schedule, allowing maximum flexibility to combine full-time work with study and research. Students may take courses in any of the programs in PSPD.

Research Facilities	The Pratt Library has grown with the Institute to house one of the finest collections of reference material on art, design, and architecture. Recently remodeled and expanded to accommodate its growing collection, the library contains 186,589 bound volumes, serial backfiles, and other material, including government documents; 251,603 audiovisual materials; and 3,996 microforms and subscribes to 925 periodicals.

Pratt maintains numerous studios, shops, and technical facilities for work in all media, as well as state-of-the-art computer facilities. Pratt also has extensive gallery space for the exhibition of works by the student body, alumni, faculty members, and well-known architects and designers.

Financial Aid	Financial aid is offered through a variety of programs funded by the institution and the federal and state governments. These include Federal Perkins Loan and Federal Work-Study programs, the Tuition Assistance Program of New York State, and Pratt loans and student help. Graduate scholarships are awarded to entering students on a competitive basis. Fellowships and assistantships are awarded on a competitive basis to continuing students in all departments. Special alumni-sponsored fellowships are also available.
Cost of Study	Graduate tuition for 2011–12 is $24,084 per year (full-time 18 credits, $1338 per credit). Student fees are $1740 per semester. The cost of books and supplies varies widely, depending on the program in which the student is enrolled.
Living and Housing Costs	Campus housing continues to be expanded to meet student needs and is available for single students on a first-come, first-served basis. Housing costs average $17,594 per academic year. There is a plentiful supply of moderately priced rentals in the immediate area and in adjacent neighborhoods for married students seeking housing as well as for those students choosing to reside off campus.
Student Group	There are 395 students enrolled in Pratt's School of Architecture graduate programs; 50 percent are women. They come from all parts of the United States and the world. The graduate programs are noted for an exceptional placement ratio, with more than 85 percent of the graduating students finding employment before graduation.
Location	Pratt Institute is located in the Clinton Hill section of Brooklyn, on a 25-acre park-like campus. Pratt's Manhattan campus houses the Institute's graduate arts and cultural management, communications design, design management, facilities management, historic preservation, and library and information science programs as well as offering courses in architecture, city and regional planning, creative arts therapy, and urban design.
The Institute	A private, nonsectarian institute of higher education, Pratt Institute was founded in 1887 by the industrialist and philanthropist Charles Pratt. Today, Pratt educates 3,008 undergraduates and 1,725 graduate students for careers in art and design, architecture, and library and information science.
Applying	The application deadline is January 5. Early submission of applications, together with all necessary credentials, is highly desirable. For the applicant who intends to file for merit-based scholarships, applications and all supporting documents need to be received no later than January 5 for the fall semester and October 1 for the spring semester. All application materials must be received by January 5, or soon thereafter. Materials should be submitted in one package that includes the three letters of recommendation in sealed envelopes with the reference's signature across the flap.
Correspondence and Information	Graduate Admissions Office Pratt Institute 200 Willoughby Avenue Brooklyn, New York 11205 Phone: 718-636-3514 800-331-0834 (toll-free outside New York State) Fax: 718-399-4242 E-mail: admissions@pratt.edu Web site: http://www.pratt.edu

Pratt Institute

THE FACULTY

Thomas Hanrahan, Dean; M.Arch., Harvard; AIA, NCARB.

Architecture
William MacDonald, Professor and Chair; M.S., Columbia.
Philip Parker, Assistant Chair; M.Arch., Yale.
Vito Acconci, Adjunct Associate Professor; M.F.A., Iowa.
Nick Agneta, Visiting Assistant Professor; B.Arch., Cooper Union; AIA.
Gilland Akos, Visiting Assistant Professor.
Ezra Ardolino, Adjunct Assistant Professor; M.Arch., Pratt.
Kutan Ayata, Adjunct Assistant Professor; M.Arch., Princeton.
Alexandra Barker, Adjunct Assistant Professor; M.Arch., Harvard.
Elizabeth Ellen Barry, Adjunct Assistant Professor; M.S.A.U.D., Columbia.
Stephanie Bayard, Adjunct Assistant Professor; M.A., Columbia.
Karen Brandt, Visiting Professor; M.Arch., Harvard.
Theodore Calvin, Visiting Professor; M.S., Columbia.
Erick Carcamo, Adjunct Assistant Professor; M.S.A.A.D., Columbia.
Robert Cervellione, Visiting Instructor; M.Arch., Pratt.
Steven J. Change, Adjunct Assistant Professor; B.Arch., Berkeley; AIA.
Theo David, Professor; M.Arch., Yale.
Manuel DeLanda, Adjunct Professor; B.F.A., School of Visual Arts.
Hernan Diaz-Alonso, Adjunct Assistant Professor; M.S., Columbia.
Matthew Flannery, Adjunct Assistant Professor; B.S., Penn State.
Deborah Gans, Associate Professor; M.Arch., Princeton
James Garrison, Adjunct Associate Professor; B.Arch., Syracuse.
Erik Ghenoiu, Visiting Assistant Professor; Ph.D., Harvard.
Jose Gonzalez, Visiting Assistant Professor; M.S., Columbia.
Matthew Herman, Visiting Assistant Professor; M.Arch., Pennsylvania.
Catherine Ingraham, Professor; Ph.D., Johns Hopkins.
Hina Jamelle, Visiting Assistant Professor; M.Arch., Michigan.
Robert Kearns, Visiting Assistant Professor; M.A.E., Penn State.
Karel Klein, Adjunct Associate Professor; M.Arch., Columbia.
Carisima Koenig, Visiting Instructor; M.Arch., Iowa State.
M. Ferda Kolatan, Visiting Assistant Professor; M.S.A.A.D., Columbia.
A. Sulan Kolatan, Adjunct Assistant Professor; M.S.Arch., Columbia.
Craig Konyk, Adjunct Associate Professor; M.Arch., Columbia.
David Christopher Kroner, Visiting Assistant Professor; M.Arch., Columbia.
Sameer Kumar, Adjunct Assistant Professor; M.Arch., Pennsylvania.
Franklin Lee, Visiting Instructor; M.S.Arch., Columbia.
Thomas Leeser, Adjunct Associate Professor.
Carla Leitao, Adjunct Assistant Professor; M.S.Arch., Columbia.
Teresa Llorente, Adjunct Assistant Professor; M.S., Columbia.
John Lobell, Professor; M.Arch., Pennsylvania.
Peter Macapia, Adjunct Assistant Professor; Ph.D., Columbia.
Radhi Majmuder, Visiting Assistant Professor.
Elliott Maltby, Adjunct Associate Professor; M.L.A., Berkeley.
Benjamin Martinson, Visiting Instructor; M.Arch., Pratt.
Audrey Matlock, Adjunct Assistant Professor; M.Arch.
Tali Mejicovsky, Visiting Instructor; B.S., B.A., Pennsylvania.
Signe Nielsen, Adjunct Professor; B.S., Pratt.
Gregory Okshteyn, Adjunct Assistant Professor; M.S., Columbia; Assoc. AIA.
Chris Perry, Adjunct Assistant Professor; M.Arch., Columbia.
David Ruy, Adjunct Associate Professor; M.Arch., Columbia.
Anne Save de Beaurecueil, Adjunct Assistant Professor; M.S., Columbia.
Richard Scherr, Director, Facilities Planning; M.S.Arch., Columbia.
Erich Schoenenberger, Adjunct Assistant Professor; M.S.A.A.D., Columbia.
Paul Segal, Adjunct Professor; M.F.A., Princeton; FAIA.
Benjamin Shepherd, Adjunct Assistant Professor; M.A., Yale.
Daniel Sherer, Adjunct Assistant Professor; Ph.D., Harvard.
Maria Sieira, Adjunct Instructor; M.Arch., Pennsylvania.
Henry Smith-Miller, Adjunct Professor; M.Arch., Pennsylvania.
Roland Snooks, Adjunct Assistant Professor; M.S.A.A.D., Columbia.
Jeremy Siegel, Visiting Assistant Professor.
Michael Szivos, Visiting Assistant Professor; M.S.A.A.D., Columbia.
Jeffrey Taras, Visiting Instructor; M.Arch., Columbia.
Meredith Tenhoor, Visiting Instructor; Ph.D. candidate, Princeton.
Maria Ludovica Tramontin, Adjunct Assistant Professor; Ph.D., Cagliari (Italy).
Jason Vigneri-Beane, Adjunct Assistant Professor; M.Arch., Iowa State.
John Whitelaw, Visiting Instructor; M.Arch., Columbia.
Lebbeus Woods, Adjunct Professor.

Urban Design
William MacDonald, Professor and Chair; M.S., Columbia.
Philip Parker, Assistant Chair; M.Arch., Yale.
Vito Acconci, Adjunct Associate Professor; M.F.A., Iowa.
Maria Aiolova, Adjunct Assistant Professor; M.A.U.D., Harvard.
Ramon Carlos Arnaiz, Adjunct Assistant Professor; M.Arch., Harvard.
Meta Brunzema, Adjunct Assistant Professor; M.Arch., Columbia.
Jose Gonzales, Visiting Assistant Professor; M.S.Arch., Columbia.
Mitchell Joachim, Adjunct Assistant Professor; Ph.D., MIT.
M. Ferda Kolatan, Visiting Assistant Professor; M.S.A.A.D, Columbia.
A. Sulan Kolatan, Adjunct Assistant Professor; M.S.Arch., Columbia.
Carla Leitao, Adjunct Assistant Professor; M.S.Arch., Columbia.
Elliot Maltby, Adjunct Associate Professor; M.L.A., Berkeley.
Signe Nielsen, Adjunct Professor; B.S., Pratt.
David Ruy, Adjunct Associate Professor; M.Arch., Columbia.
Erich Schoenenberger, Adjunct Assistant Professor; M.S.A.A.D., Columbia.

Nanako Umemoto, Adjunct Professor; B.Arch., Cooper Union.

Planning and the Environment (City and Regional Planning and Environmental Systems Management)
John Shapiro, Chair, Associate Professor; M.S.C.R.P., Pratt; AICP.
Moshe Adler, Visiting Associate Professor; Ph.D., UCLA.
Caron Atlas, Visiting Assistant Professor; M.A., Chicago.
Eve Baron, Ph.D., Visiting Associate Professor; Ph.D., Rutgers.
Eddie Bautista, Visiting Assistant Professor; M.S.C.R.P., Pratt.
David Burney, Visiting Assistant Professor; M.S., London.
Joan Byron, Visiting Assistant Professor; B.Arch, Pratt.
Carter Craft, Visiting Assistant Professor; M.U.P., NYU.
Mike Flynn, Visiting Assistant Professor; M.S.C.R.P, Pratt.
Adam Friedman, Visiting Assistant Professor; J.D., Yeshiva.
Eva Hanhardt, Adjunct Assistant Professor; M.U.P., NYU.
Justine Heilner, Visiting Assistant Professor; M.L.A., Pennsylvania.
Daniel Hernandez, Visiting Assistant Professor; M.Arch., UCLA.
George Jacquemart, Visiting Assistant Professor; M.S.U.P., Stanford; PE.
Urvashi Kaul, Visiting Assistant Professor; M.P.A., Columbia.
Brad Lander, Visiting Assistant Professor; M.S.C.R.P., Pratt.
Rob Lane, Visiting Assistant Professor; M.Arch., Columbia.
Frank Lang, Visiting Assistant Professor; M.Arch., Pennsylvania.
Matthew Lister, Visiting Assistant Professor.
Tina Lund, Visiting Assistant Professor; B.A., Grinnell College.
Elliott Maltby, Adjunct Associate Professor; M.L.A., Berkeley.
Jonathan Martin, Associate Professor; Ph.D., Cornell.
William Menking, Professor; M.S.C.R.P., Pratt.
Mercedes Narciso, Adjunct Associate Professor; M.S.C.R.P., Pratt.
Ellen Neises, Visiting Assistant Professor; M.L.A., Pennsylvania.
Signe Nielsen, Adjunct Professor; B.L.Arch., CUNY, City College.
Juan Camilo Osorio, Visiting Assistant Professor; M.S., Massachusetts.
Stuart Pertz, Visiting Assistant Professor; M.Arch., Princeton.
David Reiss, Visiting Assistant Professor; J.D., NYU.
Damon Rich, Visiting Assistant Professor; Graduate School of Design, Harvard.
Steven Romalewski, Visiting Assistant Professor; M.S., Columbia.
Alison Schneider, Visiting Assistant Professor; M.S.C.R.P., Pratt.
Ron Shiffman, Professor; M.S.C.R.P., Pratt; FAICP, FAIA.
Toby Snyder, Visiting Assistant Professor; M.Arch., Rhode Island School of Design.
Samara Swanston, Visiting Assistant Professor; J.D., St. John's (New York).
Petra Todorovich, Visiting Assistant Professor; M.S.C.R.P., Rutgers.
Meenakshi Varandani, Visiting Assistant Professor; M.S., Pratt.
Meg Walker, Visiting Assistant Professor; M.Arch., Columbia.
Joseph Weisbord, Visiting Assistant Professor; M.S.C.R.P. Pratt.
Sarah Wick, Visiting Assistant Professor; M.S.C.R.P., Pratt.
Andrew Wiley-Schwartz, Visiting Assistant Professor; B.A., Hampshire College.
Edward Perry Winston, Visiting Assistant Professor; M.Arch., Rice; RA.
Ayse Yonder, Associate Professor; Ph.D., Berkeley.
Catherine Zidar, Visiting Assistant Professor; M.S.C.R.P., Pratt.

Historic Preservation
William MacDonald, Chair; M.S., Columbia.
Eric Allison, Adjunct Associate Professor and Coordinator; Ph.D., Columbia; AICP.
Lacey Tauber, Visiting Assistant Professor and Assistant to the Chair; M.S., Pratt.
Lisa Ackerman, Visiting Assistant Professor; M.B.A. NYU.
Carol Clark, Visiting Associate Professor; M.S., Columbia.
Pat Fisher-Olsen, Visiting Assistant Professor; M.S., Pratt.
Bill Higgins, Visiting Assistant Professor; M.S. Columbia.
Jeanne Houch, Ph.D., Visiting Assistant Professor; Ph.D., NYU.
Anne Hrychuk, Visiting Assistant Professor; Ph.D., NYU.
Keenan Hughes, Visiting Assistant Professor; M.S., Pratt.
Ned Kaufman, Adjunct Associate Professor; Ph.D., Yale.
Jon Meyers, Visiting Assistant Professor; M.B.A., Columbia.
Norman Mintz, Visiting Associate Professor; M.S., Columbia.
Christopher Neville, Visiting Assistant Professor; M.S., Columbia.
Theodore Prudon, Adjunct Professor; Ph.D., Columbia; FAIA.
Vicki Weiner, Adjunct Assistant Professor; M.S., Columbia.
Kevin Wolfe, Visiting Assistant Professor; M.Arch., Columbia.

Facilities Management and Construction Management
Harriet Markis, Adjunct Associate Professor and Chair; M.Eng., Cornell.
Matthias Ebinger, Visiting Assistant Professor; M.S., NYU.
William Henry, Visiting Assistant Professor; B.Arch., NYU.
Stephen Lograsso, Visiting Assistant Professor; B.S., NYIT.
Mary J. Matthews, Professor; M.S., Boston College.
Gerald F. McGowan, Visiting Associate Professor; M.B.A., NYU.
Martin J. McManus, Visiting Assistant Professor; B.B.A., Pace.
Russell Olson, Visiting Assistant Professor; M.S., Pratt.
John Osborn, Visiting Associate Professor; J.D., South Carolina.
Edward D. Re Jr., Adjunct Associate Professor; M.S., Pratt.
Carol Reznikoff, Adjunct Associate Professor; M.S., Pratt.
Marjorie St. Ellin, Visiting Assistant Professor; B.S., Pratt.

WENTWORTH INSTITUTE OF TECHNOLOGY

College of Architecture, Design, and Construction Management
Master of Architecture Program

Programs of Study	Wentworth Institute of Technology offers the Master of Architecture (M.Arch.) degree, a first professional degree accredited by the National Architectural Accreditation Board (NAAB). The M.Arch. program is open to students who have completed a four-year NAAB-based preprofessional Bachelor of Arts or Bachelor of Science in architecture degree or its international equivalent (as established by the Canberra Accord on Architectural Education). The program includes two options: a one-year degree for students who received a Bachelor of Science in architecture from Wentworth and a two-year degree for external candidates who have successfully completed a four-year, NAAB-based program at another school of architecture. Wentworth's M.Arch. program encompasses both the art and science of architecture by examining the history, culture, and technology of the built environment. The graduate curriculum promotes research and design investigations on the linkage between theoretical frameworks; design intentions; and the tangible, material nature of architecture. A rigorous process of critical thinking is instilled through studios, seminars, and thesis preparation course work.
Research Facilities	The Alumni Library, with over 75,000 volumes, supports the Wentworth community in teaching, learning, and scholarship by providing resources and services that anticipate and respond to changing information and research needs. The Alumni Library's architecture collection covers the history, theory, and criticism of the built environment from its beginnings to the present day including such major subheadings as ancient architecture, medieval architecture, classicism, eclecticism, functionalism, international style, constructivism, and postmodernism. As part of the consortium Fenway Libraries Online (FLO), Wentworth has access to the New England Library Information Network (NELINET), a regional member of OCLC, an international bibliographic service which is shared by about 60,000 libraries in 96 countries around the world, and a member of the cataloguing services of the Library of Congress.
Financial Aid	Financial aid is available in the form of loans. Students interested in pursuing financial aid should submit the Free Application for Federal Student Aid (FAFSA) form online at www.fafsa.ed.gov.
Cost of Study	Tuition for full-time M.Arch. students is $31,200 per year. This amount includes a laptop computer with industry-specific software.
Living and Housing Costs	On-campus housing is available for students in the program and off-campus housing options are also available. Students should contact Wentworth's Office of Housing and Residential Life at 617-989-4160 for more specific housing information.
Student Group	Wentworth's current enrollment is 3,721 undergraduate students (3,285 full-time) and 124 graduate students (78 full-time) from 33 states and 46 countries.
Student Outcomes	Wentworth's M.Arch. program provides graduates with the insight, skills, and perspective to pursue distinguished and rewarding careers in architecture and the allied design fields while also supplying the academic credentials required for registration as an architect. Graduate study in architecture is an exhilarating and challenging enterprise, an opportunity for students to develop a focused position within a broad and rapidly evolving field.
Location	Wentworth Institute of Technology is located in Boston, Massachusetts. The city offers students many different cultural, entertainment, and educational options. Public transportation in the form of the Massachusetts Bay Transit Authority (MBTA or "the T") is conveniently located next to the Wentworth campus.
The Institute	Founded in 1904, Wentworth Institute of Technology is an independent, coeducational, nationally ranked institution offering career-focused education through eighteen undergraduate degree programs and two graduate degree programs. Wentworth's 31-acre campus offers both academic and residential facilities with four separate colleges housing over fifteen departments in areas such as architecture, computer science, construction management, design, engineering, engineering technology, and management. Wentworth is a leader in technical education and is well known for its academic excellence and cooperative (co-op) education program, community service, and support for the economic growth of the region.
Applying	All application materials must be completed in English, and the candidate should keep a copy of all application materials. The following application materials must be delivered to the Admissions Office by January 15 as a complete application packet: (1) Official transcripts from all institutions attended after high school graduation, along with a statement of rank in the class, and in the department, if available. Students who are currently enrolled in a program should ask their college's registrar to include a list of classes in which they are currently registered. The transcript(s) must be sealed in an envelope from the registrar's office; loose or opened transcripts will not be accepted. (2) GRE general test scores for external candidates only. They are not required for internal candidates. (3) Completed online application (www.wit.edu) and a $50 nonrefundable application fee. (4) A statement of intent detailing interest in studying architecture on the graduate level and intended career/professional goals. (5) References/letters of recommendation: Internal candidates must include on the application form the names and contact information (address, phone, and e-mail) for 2 people who may be contacted as references in lieu of letters of recommendation. References should be individuals who can judge the candidate's potential success in the study of architecture on the graduate level. Letters of recommendation should not be submitted by internal candidates. External candidates must submit two letters of recommendation with their application, using the recommendation form available for download with the online application. Recommendations should come from individuals who can judge the candidate's potential success in the study of architecture at the graduate level. Each recommender must return the recommendation in a sealed envelope with their signature across the back flap of the envelope; loose or opened letters of recommendation will not be accepted. Professional portfolios should contain work that demonstrates a student's proficiency in architecture and reflects the full range of their creative, research, and technical skills. Portfolios may be no smaller than 6 x 9 inches and no larger than 9 x 12 inches and must lay flat; attached objects, foldouts, unbound pages, CDs, DVDs, or other nonprinted materials are not permitted. Portfolios must have a front and back cover, be bound on one side using professional quality binding techniques, and may not contain more than fifteen interior pages. The applicant's name must be clearly printed on the front cover. Note that portfolios will not be returned, and electronic portfolios are not accepted.
Correspondence and Information	Admissions Office Maureen Dischino, Executive Director of Admissions Wentworth Institute of Technology 550 Huntington Avenue Boston, Massachusetts 02115 Phone: 617-989-4000 Fax: 617-989-4010 E-mail: admissions@wit.edu Web site: http://www.wit.edu/admissions	College of Architecture, Design, and Construction Management Glenn Wiggins, Dean, College of Architecture, Design, and Construction Management John Ellis, Department Chair, Architecture Wentworth Institute of Technology 550 Huntington Avenue Boston, Massachusetts 02115 Phone: 617-989-4450 Fax: 617-989-4591 E-mail: architecture@wit.edu Web site: http://www.wit.edu/arch

Wentworth Institute of Technology

THE FACULTY

Wentworth's architecture faculty and staff members have a broad range of backgrounds, scholarly interests, and areas of expertise. They are united by a shared enthusiasm for architecture as an art grounded in the materials and methods of building. Faculty members bring substantial achievement in professional practice and research into the classroom setting. More information about the following faculty members can be found at http://www.wit.edu/arch/faculty-staff/index.html.

Glenn Wiggins, Professor and Dean, College of Architecture, Design, and Construction Management.

Ann Borst, Professor and Chair of Undergraduate Studies.
John Ellis, Professor and Chair of Graduate Studies.
Michael MacPhail, Associate Professor and Chair of Foundation Studies.
Rolf Backmann, Associate Professor and Director of Study Abroad.
Carol Burns, Associate Professor and Director of Research.
Charles Cimino, Associate Professor.
Phillip Comeau, Associate Professor.
Robert Cowherd, Associate Professor.
Manuel Delgado, Associate Professor.
Elizabeth Gibb, Associate Professor.
Garrick Goldenberg, Professor.
Andrew Johnston, Associate Professor.
Patricia Kendall, Associate Professor.
Lora Kim, Associate Professor.
Mark Klopfer, Associate Professor.
Anthony Kurneta, Associate Professor.
Thomas Lesko, Professor.
Terry Moor, Professor.
Mark Pasnik, Associate Professor.
Ann Pitt, Associate Professor.
Weldon Pries, Professor.
Ingrid Strong, Assistant Professor.
Robert Trumbour, Assistant Professor.

Study architecture at Wentworth Institute of Technology, located in the heart of Boston.

Section 3
Art and Art History

This section contains a directory of institutions offering graduate work in art and art history, followed by in-depth entries submitted by institutions that chose to prepare detailed program descriptions. Additional information about programs listed in the directory but not augmented by an in-depth entry may be obtained by writing directly to the dean of a graduate school or chair of a department at the address given in the directory.

For programs offering related work, see also in this book *Applied Arts and Design; Architecture; Area and Cultural Studies; Film, Television, and Video; Performing Arts;* and *Sociology, Anthropology, and Archaeology.* In another guide in this series:
Graduate Programs in Business, Education, Health, Information Studies, Law & Social Work
See *Subject Areas (Art Education)*

CONTENTS

Art/Fine Arts

Academy of Art University, Graduate Program, School of Fine Art, San Francisco, CA 94105-3410. Offers figurative painting (MFA); non-figurative painting (MFA); printmaking (MFA); sculpture (MFA). *Accreditation:* NASAD. Part-time programs available. Postbaccalaureate distance learning degree programs offered (no on-campus study). *Faculty:* 19 full-time (7 women), 65 part-time/adjunct (28 women). *Students:* 151 full-time (93 women), 266 part-time (193 women); includes 15 Black or African American, non-Hispanic/Latino; 1 American Indian or Alaska Native, non-Hispanic/Latino; 29 Asian, non-Hispanic/Latino; 22 Hispanic/Latino, 58 international. Average age 40. 115 applicants. In 2010, 38 master's awarded. *Degree requirements:* For master's, thesis, final review. *Entrance requirements:* For master's, minimum GPA of 3.0, portfolio. *Application deadline:* For fall admission, 9/7 for domestic and international students; for spring admission, 2/2 for domestic and international students. Applications are processed on a rolling basis. Application fee: $100 ($500 for international students). Electronic applications accepted. *Expenses:* Tuition: Full-time $20,160; part-time $840 per semester hour. Required fees: $45 per semester. *Financial support:* Career-related internships or fieldwork and Federal Work-Study available. Support available to part-time students. Financial award application deadline: 8/10; financial award applicants required to submit FAFSA. *Application contact:* Prospective Student Services, 800-544-ARTS, Fax: 415-263-4130, E-mail: info@academyart.edu.

Adams State College, The Graduate School, Department of Art, Alamosa, CO 81102. Offers MA. Part-time programs available. *Degree requirements:* For master's, thesis, departmental qualifying exam. *Entrance requirements:* For master's, GRE General Test or MAT, minimum undergraduate GPA of 2.75.

Adelphi University, Graduate School of Arts and Sciences, Department of Art and Art History, Garden City, NY 11530-0701. Offers MA. Part-time programs available. *Students:* 1 (woman) full-time, 8 part-time (5 women), 2 international. Average age 40. In 2010, 3 master's awarded. *Degree requirements:* For master's, art exhibit. *Entrance requirements:* For master's, portfolio, 2 letters of recommendation. Additional exam requirements/recommendations for international students: Required—TOEFL (minimum score 550 paper-based; 213 computer-based; 80 iBT). *Application deadline:* For fall admission, 5/1 for international students; for spring admission, 12/1 for international students. Applications are processed on a rolling basis. Application fee: $50. Electronic applications accepted. *Financial support:* Research assistantships with full and partial tuition reimbursements, career-related internships or fieldwork, Federal Work-Study, institutionally sponsored loans, and unspecified assistantships available. Financial award application deadline: 2/15; financial award applicants required to submit FAFSA. *Unit head:* David Hornung, Chairperson, 516-877-4458, E-mail: hornung@adelphi.edu. *Application contact:* Christine Murphy, Director of Admissions, 516-877-3050, Fax: 516-877-3039, E-mail: graduateadmissions@adelphi.edu.

See Close-Up on page 213.

Alfred University, Graduate School, New York State College of Ceramics, School of Art and Design, Alfred, NY 14802-1205. Offers ceramic art (MFA); electronic integrated arts (MFA); glass art (MFA); sculpture (MFA). *Accreditation:* NASAD. *Degree requirements:* For master's, exhibit. *Entrance requirements:* For master's, portfolio. Additional exam requirements/recommendations for international students: Required—TOEFL (minimum score 550 paper-based; 213 computer-based; 80 iBT), IELTS (minimum score 6). Electronic applications accepted. *Faculty research:* Ceramic sculpture, functional ceramics, wood, mixed media, hot and cold glass.

Alfred University, Graduate School, New York State College of Ceramics, School of Engineering, Alfred, NY 14802-1205. Offers biomedical materials engineering science (MS); ceramic engineering (MS); ceramics (PhD); electrical engineering (MS); glass science (MS, PhD); materials science and engineering (MS, PhD); mechanical engineering (MS). *Degree requirements:* For master's, thesis; for doctorate, thesis/dissertation. *Entrance requirements:* Additional exam requirements/recommendations for international students: Required—TOEFL (minimum score 590 paper-based; 243 computer-based). Electronic applications accepted. *Expenses:* Contact institution. *Faculty research:* Fine-particle technology, x-ray diffraction, superconductivity, electronic materials.

American University, College of Arts and Sciences, Department of Art, Washington, DC 20016-8004. Offers art history (MA); painting, sculpture and printmaking (MFA). Part-time programs available. *Faculty:* 18 full-time (12 women), 16 part-time/adjunct (10 women). *Students:* 26 full-time (19 women), 26 part-time (all women); includes 2 minority (1 Asian, non-Hispanic/Latino; 1 Hispanic/Latino), 1 international. Average age 28. 82 applicants, 60% accepted, 15 enrolled. In 2010, 16 master's awarded. *Degree requirements:* For master's, comprehensive exam. *Entrance requirements:* For master's, GRE, portfolio or writing sample. Additional exam requirements/recommendations for international students: Required—TOEFL. *Application deadline:* For fall admission, 10/15 for domestic students. Application fee: $80. *Financial support:* Fellowships, research assistantships with full and partial tuition reimbursements, teaching assistantships with full and partial tuition reimbursements, career-related internships or fieldwork, Federal Work-Study, and institutionally sponsored loans available. Support available to part-time students. Financial award application deadline: 1/15. *Faculty research:* Studio artists, painting, Renaissance, Impressionism, twentieth century. *Unit head:* Jose-Maria Montes-Armenteros, Chair, 202-885-1697, Fax: 202-885-1132, E-mail: cmontes@american.edu. *Application contact:* Glenna K. Haynie, Administrative Coordinator, 202-885-1671.

Anna Maria College, Graduate Division, Program in Education, Paxton, MA 01612. Offers early childhood education (M Ed); education (CAGS); elementary education (M Ed); English language arts (M Ed); visual arts (M Ed). Part-time and evening/weekend programs available. *Entrance requirements:* For master's, bachelor's degree in liberal arts or sciences, minimum GPA of 3.0. Additional exam requirements/recommendations for international students: Required—TOEFL (minimum score 500 paper-based). Electronic applications accepted.

Anna Maria College, Graduate Division, Program in Visual Arts, Paxton, MA 01612. Offers art and visual art (MA); teacher of visual art (M Ed). Part-time and evening/weekend programs available. *Degree requirements:* For master's, thesis. *Entrance requirements:* For master's, minimum GPA of 2.7, undergraduate major in art, portfolio. Additional exam requirements/recommendations for international students: Required—TOEFL (minimum score 500 paper-based). Electronic applications accepted.

Antioch University Midwest, Graduate Programs, Individualized Liberal and Professional Studies Program, Yellow Springs, OH 45387-1609. Offers liberal and professional studies (MA), including counseling, creative writing, education, film studies, liberal studies, management, modern literature, psychology, theatre, visual arts. Part-time and evening/weekend programs available. Postbaccalaureate distance learning degree programs offered (minimal on-campus study). *Faculty:* 2 full-time (1 woman), 2 part-time/adjunct (both women). *Students:* 15 full-time (11 women), 34 part-time (22 women); includes 11 minority (8 Black or African American, non-Hispanic/Latino; 3 Hispanic/Latino). Average age 40. 13 applicants, 69% accepted, 5 enrolled. In 2010, 18 master's awarded. *Degree requirements:* For master's, thesis or alternative. *Entrance requirements:* For master's, resume, goal statement, interview. *Application deadline:* For fall admission, 8/1 for domestic students; for winter admission, 12/1 for domestic students; for spring admission, 3/10 for domestic students. Applications are processed on a rolling basis. Application fee: $50. Electronic applications accepted. *Expenses:* Contact institution. *Financial support:* Federal Work-Study available. Financial award applicants required to submit FAFSA. *Unit head:* Dr. Joseph Cronin, Chair, 937-769-1894, Fax: 937-769-1807, E-mail: jcronin@antioch.edu. *Application contact:* Seth Gordon, Assistant Director of Admissions, 937-769-1800 Ext. 1825, Fax: 937-769-1804, E-mail: sgordon@antioch.edu.

Arizona State University, Herberger Institute for Design and the Arts, School of Art, Tempe, AZ 85287-1505. Offers art (art education) (MA); art (art history) (MA); art (ceramics) (MFA); art (digital technology) (MFA); art (drawing) (MFA); art (fibers) (MFA); art (intermedia) (MFA); art (metals) (MFA); art (painting) (MFA); art (printmaking) (MFA); art (sculpture) (MFA); art (wood) (MFA); design, environment and the arts (history, theory and criticism) (PhD). *Faculty:* 46 full-time (28 women). *Students:* 98 full-time (56 women), 21 part-time (18 women); includes 13 minority (2 American Indian or Alaska Native, non-Hispanic/Latino; 3 Asian, non-Hispanic/Latino; 8 Hispanic/Latino), 7 international. Average age 31. 206 applicants, 32% accepted, 37 enrolled. In 2010, 26 master's, 1 doctorate awarded. Terminal master's awarded for partial completion of doctoral program. *Degree requirements:* For master's, thesis/exhibition (MFA, MA in art education); interactive Program of Study (iPOS) submitted before completing 50 percent of required credit hours; for doctorate, comprehensive exam, thesis/dissertation, interactive Program of Study (iPOS) submitted before completing 50 percent of required credit hours. *Entrance requirements:* For master's, GRE or MAT, minimum GPA of 3.0 or equivalent in last 2 years of work leading to bachelor's degree; for doctorate, GRE, master's degree in architecture, graphic design, industrial design, interior design, landscape architecture, or art history or equivalent standing; statement of purpose; 3 letters of recommendation; indication of potential faculty mentor; sample of written work. Additional exam requirements/recommendations for international students: Required—TOEFL, IELTS, or Pearson Test of English. *Application deadline:* For fall admission, 1/15 priority date for domestic and international students. Applications are processed on a rolling basis. Application fee: $70 ($90 for international students). Electronic applications accepted. *Expenses:* Tuition, state resident: full-time $8510; part-time $608 per credit. Tuition, nonresident: full-time $16,542; part-time $919 per credit. Required fees: $339; $110 per credit. Part-time tuition and fees vary according to course load. *Financial support:* In 2010–11, 4 research assistantships with full and partial tuition reimbursements (averaging $7,475 per year), 55 teaching assistantships with full and partial tuition reimbursements (averaging $6,553 per year) were awarded; fellowships with full and partial tuition reimbursements, scholarships/grants and tuition waivers (full and partial) also available. Financial award application deadline: 3/1; financial award applicants required to submit FAFSA. Total annual research expenditures: $26,418. *Unit head:* Adriene Jenik, Director, 480-965-8521, Fax: 480-965-8338, E-mail: ajenik@mainex1.asu.edu. *Application contact:* Graduate Admissions, 480-965-6113.

Arkansas State University, Graduate School, College of Fine Arts, Department of Art, Jonesboro, State University, AR 72467. Offers MA. *Accreditation:* NASAD. Part-time programs available. *Faculty:* 9 full-time (4 women). *Students:* 4 full-time (2 women), 2 part-time (both women), 1 international. Average age 29. 10 applicants, 70% accepted, 3 enrolled. In 2010, 3 master's awarded. *Degree requirements:* For master's, comprehensive exam, thesis. *Entrance requirements:* For master's, GRE General Test or MAT, portfolio, appropriate bachelor's degree, letters of reference, writing sample, official transcript, immunization records. Additional exam requirements/recommendations for international students: Required—TOEFL (minimum score 550 paper-based; 213 computer-based; 79 iBT), IELTS (minimum score 6), PTE: Pearson Test of English Academic (56). *Application deadline:* For fall admission, 4/8 for domestic and international students; for spring admission, 11/11 for domestic and international students. Applications are processed on a rolling basis. Application fee: $30 ($40 for international students). Electronic applications accepted. *Expenses:* Tuition, state resident: full-time $3888; part-time $216 per credit hour. Tuition, nonresident: full-time $9918; part-time $551 per credit hour. International tuition: $8376 full-time. Required fees: $932; $49 per credit hour. $25 per term. One-time fee: $30. Tuition and fees vary according to course load and program. *Financial support:* In 2010–11, 4 students received support; teaching assistantships, career-related internships or fieldwork, scholarships/grants, and unspecified assistantships available. Financial award application deadline: 7/1; financial award applicants required to submit FAFSA. *Unit head:* Curtis Steele, Chair, 870-972-3050, Fax: 870-972-3932, E-mail: csteele@astate.edu. *Application contact:* Dr. Andrew Sustich, Dean of the Graduate School, 870-972-3029, Fax: 870-972-3857, E-mail: sustich@astate.edu.

Arkansas Tech University, Graduate College, College of Arts and Humanities, Russellville, AR 72801. Offers communication (MLA); English (M Ed, MA); fine arts (MLA); history (MA); multi-media journalism (MA); psychology (MS); social science (MLA); Spanish (MA, MLA); teaching English as a second language (MA, MLA). Part-time programs available. *Students:* 39 full-time (23 women), 87 part-time (69 women); includes 13 minority (3 Black or African American, non-Hispanic/Latino; 1 American Indian or Alaska Native, non-Hispanic/Latino; 1 Asian, non-Hispanic/Latino; 8 Hispanic/Latino), 14 international. Average age 32. In 2010, 54 master's awarded. *Degree requirements:* For master's, comprehensive exam (for some programs), thesis (for some programs), project. *Entrance requirements:* For master's, GRE General Test or MAT. Additional exam requirements/recommendations for international students: Required—TOEFL (minimum score 550 paper-based; 213 computer-based; 79 iBT), IELTS (minimum score 6). *Application deadline:* For fall admission, 3/1 priority date for domestic students, 5/1 priority date for international students; for spring admission, 10/1 priority date for domestic and international students. Applications are processed on a rolling basis. Application fee: $0 ($50 for international students). Electronic applications accepted. *Expenses:* Tuition, state resident: full-time $4680; part-time $195 per credit hour. Tuition, nonresident: full-time $9360; part-time $390 per credit hour. Required fees: $714; $14 per credit hour. One-time fee: $326 part-time. Tuition and fees vary according to course load. *Financial support:* In 2010–11, teaching assistantships with full tuition reimbursements (averaging $4,000 per year); research assistantships, career-related internships or fieldwork, Federal Work-Study, scholarships/grants, health care benefits, and unspecified assistantships also available. Support available to part-time students. Financial award application deadline: 4/15; financial award applicants required to submit FAFSA. *Unit head:* Dr. Micheal Tarver, Dean, 479-968-0274, Fax: 479-964-0812, E-mail: mtarver@atu.edu. *Application contact:* Dr. Mary B. Gunter, Dean of Graduate College, 479-968-0398, Fax: 479-964-0542, E-mail: graduate.school@atu.edu.

Art Center College of Design, Graduate Division, Fine Arts Department, Pasadena, CA 91103. Offers MFA. *Accreditation:* NASAD. *Faculty:* 10 full-time (4 women), 21 part-time/adjunct (11 women). *Students:* 25 full-time (11 women); includes 2 minority (1 Asian, non-Hispanic/Latino; 1 Hispanic/Latino), 3 international. Average age 31. *Degree requirements:* For master's, thesis. *Entrance requirements:* Additional exam requirements/recommendations for international students: Required—TOEFL. *Application deadline:* For fall admission, 3/1 for domestic students; for winter admission, 9/15 for domestic students. Applications are processed on a rolling basis. *Expenses:* Tuition: Part-time $17,220 per term. *Unit head:* Dr. Jeremy Gilbert-Rolfe, Chair, 626-584-8424. *Application contact:* Dr. Jeremy Gilbert-Rolfe, Chair, 626-584-8424.

See Display on page 89 and Close-Up on page 119.

The Art Institute of Boston at Lesley University, Program in Visual Arts, Boston, MA 02215-2598. Offers MFA. *Accreditation:* NASAD.

The Art Institute of California–San Francisco, Master of Fine Arts Program, San Francisco, CA 94102. Offers computer animation (MFA).

Azusa Pacific University, College of Liberal Arts and Sciences, Program in Fine Arts in Visual Art, Azusa, CA 91702-7000. Offers MFA. *Accreditation:* NASAD. *Students:* 27 part-time (16 women); includes 7 minority (1 Asian, non-Hispanic/Latino; 5 Hispanic/Latino; 1 Native Hawaiian or other Pacific Islander, non-Hispanic/Latino). Average age 36. In 2010, 9 master's awarded. *Unit head:* William Catling, Chair, 626-969-3434. *Application contact:* Director of Graduate Admissions, 626-812-3037, Fax: 626-969-7180.

Ball State University, Graduate School, College of Fine Arts, Department of Art, Muncie, IN 47306-1099. Offers art (MA); art education (MA, MAE). *Accreditation:* NASAD. *Faculty:* 18. *Students:* 9 full-time (2 women), 13 part-time (4 women); includes 3 minority (1 Black or

African American, non-Hispanic/Latino; 1 American Indian or Alaska Native, non-Hispanic/Latino; 1 Hispanic/Latino). Average age 27. 15 applicants, 73% accepted, 8 enrolled. In 2010, 5 master's awarded. Application fee: $50. *Expenses:* Tuition, state resident: full-time $6160; part-time $299 per credit hour. Tuition, nonresident: full-time $16,020; part-time $783 per credit hour. Required fees: $2278; $95 per credit hour. *Financial support:* In 2010–11, 5 teaching assistantships with full tuition reimbursements (averaging $7,000 per year) were awarded; research assistantships with full tuition reimbursements. Financial award application deadline: 3/1. *Unit head:* Thomas Riesing, Head, 765-285-5838, Fax: 765-285-5275. *Application contact:* Kenton Hall, Director, 765-285-5838, Fax: 765-285-5275, E-mail: khall@bsu.edu.

Bard College, Milton Avery Graduate School of the Arts, Annandale-on-Hudson, NY 12504. Offers MFA. *Degree requirements:* For master's, thesis, project, 8-week summer residency, independent study. *Entrance requirements:* For master's, interview, portfolio, 2 letters of recommendation, history of work in the arts. Additional exam requirements/recommendations for international students: Required—TOEFL (minimum score 550 paper-based; 213 computer-based). Electronic applications accepted. *Faculty research:* Original work in painting, writing, sculpture, photography, video/film, sound/music.

Barry University, School of Arts and Sciences, Department of Fine Arts, Miami Shores, FL 33161-6695. Offers photography (MA, MFA). *Degree requirements:* For master's, thesis (for some programs). *Entrance requirements:* For master's, GRE General Test, minimum GPA of 3.0. Electronic applications accepted. *Faculty research:* Inclusion education, exceptional education, art-based assessments.

Bob Jones University, Graduate Programs, Greenville, SC 29614. Offers accountancy (MS); Bible (MA); Bible translation (MA); Biblical studies (Certificate); broadcast management (MS); business administration (MBA); church history (MA, PhD); church ministries (MA); church music (MM); cinema and video production (MA); counseling (MS); curriculum and instruction (Ed D); divinity (M Div); dramatic production (MA); educational leadership (MS, Ed D, Ed S); elementary education (M Ed, MAT); English (M Ed, MA, MAT); fine arts (MA); graphic design (MA); history (M Ed, MA); illustration (MA); interpretative speech (MA); mathematics (M Ed, MAT); medical missions (Certificate); ministry (MM, D Min); multi-categorical special education (M Ed, MAT); music (M Ed); New Testament interpretation (PhD); Old Testament interpretation (PhD); orchestral instrument performance (MM); organ performance (MM); pastoral studies (MA); personnel services (MS, Ed S); piano pedagogy (MM); piano performance (MM); platform arts (MA); radio and television broadcasting (MS); rhetoric and public address (MA); secondary education (M Ed); studio art (MA); teaching Bible (MA); theology (MA, PhD); voice performance (MM); youth ministries (MA); M Div/MM.

Boise State University, Graduate College, College of Arts and Sciences, Department of Art, Program in Visual Arts, Boise, ID 83725-0399. Offers MFA. *Accreditation:* NASAD. Part-time programs available. *Degree requirements:* For master's, thesis. *Entrance requirements:* For master's, minimum GPA of 3.0, portfolio. Additional exam requirements/recommendations for international students: Required—TOEFL (minimum score 587 paper-based; 240 computer-based). Electronic applications accepted.

Boston University, College of Fine Arts, School of Visual Arts, Boston, MA 02215. Offers art education (MA); graphic design (MFA); painting (MFA); sculpture (MFA); studio teaching (MA). *Faculty:* 17 full-time, 4 part-time/adjunct. *Students:* 34 full-time (19 women); includes 7 minority (2 Black or African American, non-Hispanic/Latino; 2 Asian, non-Hispanic/Latino; 3 Hispanic/Latino), 4 international. Average age 27. 281 applicants, 28% accepted. In 2010, 130 master's awarded. *Entrance requirements:* For master's, portfolio. Additional exam requirements/recommendations for international students: Required—TOEFL. *Application deadline:* For fall admission, 2/15 for domestic and international students. Applications are processed on a rolling basis. Application fee: $70. *Expenses:* Tuition: Full-time $39,314; part-time $1228 per credit. Required fees: $40 per semester. *Financial support:* Fellowships, teaching assistantships available. Financial award application deadline: 2/15. *Unit head:* Lynne Allen, Director, 617-353-3371. *Application contact:* Mark Krone, Manager, Graduate Admissions, 617-353-3350, E-mail: arts@bu.edu.

Bowling Green State University, Graduate College, College of Arts and Sciences, School of Art, Bowling Green, OH 43403. Offers 2-D studio art (MA, MFA); 3-D studio art (MA, MFA); art education (MA); art history (MA); computer art (MA); design (MFA); digital arts (MFA); graphics (MFA). *Accreditation:* NASAD. Part-time programs available. *Degree requirements:* For master's, thesis or alternative, final exhibit (MFA). *Entrance requirements:* For master's, GRE General Test (MA), slide portfolio (15-20 slides). Additional exam requirements/recommendations for international students: Required—TOEFL. Electronic applications accepted. *Faculty research:* Computer animation and virtual reality, Spanish still-life painting from 1600 to 1800, art and psychotherapy, Japanese wood-firing techniques in ceramics, non-toxic printmaking technologies.

Bradley University, Graduate School, Slane College of Communications and Fine Arts, Department of Art, Peoria, IL 61625-0002. Offers ceramics (MA, MFA); drawing/illustration (MA, MFA); interdisciplinary art (MA, MFA); painting (MA, MFA); photography (MA, MFA); printmaking (MA, MFA); sculpture (MA, MFA); visual communication and design (MA, MFA). *Accreditation:* NASAD. Part-time programs available. *Degree requirements:* For master's, comprehensive exam, thesis, final exhibit. *Entrance requirements:* For master's, portfolio, 2 letters of recommendation. Additional exam requirements/recommendations for international students: Required—TOEFL (minimum score 550 paper-based; 213 computer-based; 79 iBT).

Brandeis University, Graduate School of Arts and Sciences, Program in Studio Art, Waltham, MA 02454-9110. Offers Certificate. *Faculty:* 14 full-time (6 women), 2 part-time/adjunct (0 women). *Students:* 14 full-time (12 women); includes 1 Black or African American, non-Hispanic/Latino; 1 Asian, non-Hispanic/Latino, 1 international. 20 applicants, 100% accepted, 11 enrolled. In 2010, 3 Certificates awarded. *Degree requirements:* For Certificate, thesis, exhibit of work. *Entrance requirements:* For degree, resume, sample of work, studio work, letters of recommendation. Additional exam requirements/recommendations for international students: Required—TOEFL (minimum score 600 paper-based; 250 computer-based; 100 iBT); Recommended—IELTS (minimum score 7). *Application deadline:* Applications are processed on a rolling basis. Application fee: $75. Electronic applications accepted. *Expenses:* Contact institution. *Financial support:* In 2010–11, 14 teaching assistantships with partial tuition reimbursements were awarded; scholarships/grants and tuition waivers (partial) also available. Financial award application deadline: 4/15; financial award applicants required to submit FAFSA. *Faculty research:* Painting, sculpture, three-dimensional design, printmaking, drawing. *Unit head:* Prof. Sean Downey, Faculty Coordinator, 781-736-2660, Fax: 781-736-2672, E-mail: sdowney@brandeis.edu. *Application contact:* Joy Vlachos, Department Administrator, 781-736-2655, Fax: 781-736-2672, E-mail: vlachos@brandeis.edu.

Brigham Young University, Graduate Studies, College of Fine Arts and Communications, Department of Visual Arts, Provo, UT 84602-6414. Offers art education (MA); art history (MA); studio art (MFA). Art education applications accepted biennially. *Accreditation:* NASAD. *Faculty:* 27 full-time (7 women), 1 (woman) part-time/adjunct. *Students:* 36 full-time (26 women); includes 1 Asian, non-Hispanic/Latino; 2 Native Hawaiian or other Pacific Islander, non-Hispanic/Latino. Average age 26. 33 applicants, 33% accepted, 10 enrolled. In 2010, 5 master's awarded. *Degree requirements:* For master's, one foreign language, thesis (art history), selected project (MFA), curriculum project (art education). *Entrance requirements:* For master's, GRE (art history), minimum GPA of 3.0 (MFA, MA in art education), 3.3 (MA in art history), portfolio in CD format (MFA), writing samples (MA in art education, art history). Additional exam requirements/recommendations for international students: Required—TOEFL (minimum score 500 paper-based). *Application deadline:* For fall admission, 2/1 for domestic and international students. Application fee: $50. Electronic applications accepted. *Expenses:* Tuition: Full-time $5580; part-time $310 per credit hour. Tuition and fees vary according to program and student's religious affiliation. *Financial support:* In 2010–11, 32 students received support; research assistantships, teaching assistantships with partial tuition reimbursements available, scholarships/grants and tuition waivers (partial) available. Financial award application deadline: 2/1. *Faculty research:* Methodology-standards-assessment, medieval architecture, classical/Islamic eighteenth and nineteenth century art, Netherlandish art, contemporary art, modern art, history of photography. Total annual research expenditures: $83,932. *Unit head:* Prof. Linda A. Reynolds, Chair, 801-422-4429, Fax: 801-422-0695, E-mail: sullivan@byu.edu. *Application contact:* Sharon Lyn Heelis, Secretary, 801-422-4429, Fax: 801-422-0695, E-mail: sharon_heelis@byu.edu.

Brooklyn College of the City University of New York, Division of Graduate Studies, Department of Art, Brooklyn, NY 11210-2889. Offers art history (MA, PhD); digital art (MFA); drawing and painting (MFA); photography (MFA); printmaking (MFA); sculpture (MFA). Part-time programs available. *Students:* 23 full-time (16 women), 26 part-time (20 women); includes 13 minority (5 Black or African American, non-Hispanic/Latino; 3 Asian, non-Hispanic/Latino; 5 Hispanic/Latino), 2 international. Average age 30. 119 applicants, 45% accepted, 17 enrolled. In 2010, 9 master's awarded. *Degree requirements:* For master's, thesis. *Entrance requirements:* For master's, bachelor's degree in art, portfolio, 2 letters of recommendation. Additional exam requirements/recommendations for international students: Required—TOEFL (minimum score 500 paper-based; 173 computer-based; 61 iBT). *Application deadline:* For fall admission, 2/1 priority date for domestic students, 2/1 for international students. Applications are processed on a rolling basis. Application fee: $125. Electronic applications accepted. *Expenses:* Tuition, state resident: full-time $7360; part-time $310 per credit hour. Tuition, nonresident: full-time $13,800; part-time $575 per credit hour. Required fees: $190 per semester. *Financial support:* Career-related internships or fieldwork, Federal Work-Study, institutionally sponsored loans, scholarships/grants, and painting awards available. Support available to part-time students. Financial award application deadline: 5/1; financial award applicants required to submit FAFSA. *Unit head:* Dr. Michael Mallory, Chairperson, 718-951-5181, E-mail: mmallory@brooklyn.cuny.edu. *Application contact:* Hernan Sierra, Graduate Admissions Coordinator, 718-951-4536, Fax: 718-951-4506, E-mail: grads@brooklyn.cuny.edu.

California College of the Arts, Graduate Programs, Program in Visual and Critical Studies, San Francisco, CA 94107. Offers MA. *Faculty:* 8 full-time (6 women), 5 part-time/adjunct (all women). *Students:* 21 full-time (17 women), 1 part-time (0 women). Average age 29. 221 applicants, 64% accepted. In 2010, 4 master's awarded. *Degree requirements:* For master's, thesis. *Entrance requirements:* For master's, appropriate bachelor's degree, portfolio, resume, 2 letters of recommendation, transcripts. Additional exam requirements/recommendations for international students: Required—TOEFL (minimum score 600 paper-based; 250 computer-based; 100 iBT). *Application deadline:* For fall admission, 1/5 for domestic and international students. Application fee: $70. Electronic applications accepted. *Expenses:* Tuition: Full-time $38,550; part-time $1285 per unit. One-time fee: $185 full-time. *Financial support:* In 2010–11, 2 fellowships (averaging $11,000 per year), teaching assistantships (averaging $2,000 per year) were awarded; career-related internships or fieldwork, Federal Work-Study, scholarships/grants, and health care benefits also available. Financial award application deadline: 3/2; financial award applicants required to submit FAFSA. *Unit head:* Tirza Latimer, Chair, 415-551-9250, E-mail: tlatimer@cca.edu. *Application contact:* Heidi Geis, Assistant Director of Graduate Admissions, 415-703-9523 Ext. 9533, Fax: 415-703-9539, E-mail: hgeis@cca.edu.

California College of the Arts, Graduate Programs, Programs in Fine Art, San Francisco, CA 94107. Offers ceramics (MFA); film/video/performance (MFA); glass (MFA); jewelry/metal arts (MFA); painting/drawing (MFA); photography (MFA); printmaking (MFA); sculpture (MFA); textiles (MFA); wood/furniture (MFA). *Accreditation:* NASAD. *Faculty:* 20 full-time (10 women), 25 part-time/adjunct (14 women). *Students:* 95 full-time (66 women), 12 part-time (9 women); includes 3 Black or African American, non-Hispanic/Latino; 1 American Indian or Alaska Native, non-Hispanic/Latino; 5 Asian, non-Hispanic/Latino; 20 Hispanic/Latino; 2 Native Hawaiian or other Pacific Islander, non-Hispanic/Latino, 7 international. Average age 30. 462 applicants, 37% accepted, 55 enrolled. In 2010, 173 master's awarded. *Degree requirements:* For master's, thesis, exhibit. *Entrance requirements:* For master's, appropriate bachelor's degree, portfolio, resume, 2 letters of recommendation, transcript. Additional exam requirements/recommendations for international students: Required—TOEFL (minimum score 600 paper-based; 250 computer-based; 100 iBT). *Application deadline:* For fall admission, 1/5 for domestic and international students. Application fee: $70. Electronic applications accepted. *Expenses:* Tuition: Full-time $38,550; part-time $1285 per unit. One-time fee: $185 full-time. *Financial support:* In 2010–11, 12 fellowships (averaging $27,000 per year), teaching assistantships (averaging $2,000 per year) were awarded; career-related internships or fieldwork, Federal Work-Study, scholarships/grants, and health care benefits also available. Financial award application deadline: 3/1; financial award applicants required to submit FAFSA. *Unit head:* Ted Purves, Chair, 415-551-9214, Fax: 415-703-9539, E-mail: tpurves@cca.edu. *Application contact:* Heidi Geis, Assistant Director of Graduate Admissions, 415-703-9523 Ext. 9533, Fax: 415-703-9539, E-mail: hgeis@cca.edu.

California Institute of the Arts, School of Art, Valencia, CA 91355-2340. Offers art (MFA, Adv C); graphic design (MFA, Adv C); photography (MFA, Adv C). *Accreditation:* NASAD (one or more programs are accredited). *Degree requirements:* For master's, final project. *Entrance requirements:* For master's, portfolio. Additional exam requirements/recommendations for international students: Required—TOEFL. Electronic applications accepted.

California State University, Chico, Graduate School, College of Humanities and Fine Arts, Department of Art and Art History, Program in Fine Arts, Chico, CA 95929-0722. Offers MFA. *Accreditation:* NASAD. *Students:* 14 full-time (9 women), 3 part-time (2 women); includes 2 Hispanic/Latino, 1 international. Average age 33. 14 applicants, 29% accepted, 3 enrolled. In 2010, 2 master's awarded. *Degree requirements:* For master's, thesis or alternative. *Entrance requirements:* For master's, 2 letters of recommendation. Additional exam requirements/recommendations for international students: Required—TOEFL (minimum score 550 paper-based; 213 computer-based; 80 iBT), IELTS (minimum score 6.5). *Application deadline:* For fall admission, 3/1 priority date for domestic students, 3/1 for international students; for spring admission, 9/15 priority date for domestic students, 9/15 for international students. Applications are processed on a rolling basis. Application fee: $55. Electronic applications accepted. *Unit head:* Dr. Cameron Crawford, Graduate Coordinator, 530-898-6860. *Application contact:* Dr. Cameron Crawford, Graduate Coordinator, 530-898-6860.

California State University, Fresno, Division of Graduate Studies, College of Arts and Humanities, Department of Art and Design, Fresno, CA 93740-8027. Offers art (MA). Part-time and evening/weekend programs available. *Degree requirements:* For master's, thesis or alternative. *Entrance requirements:* For master's, GRE General Test, minimum GPA of 3.0, portfolio. Additional exam requirements/recommendations for international students: Required—TOEFL. Electronic applications accepted. *Faculty research:* Art history, graphic design, studio art.

California State University, Fullerton, Graduate Studies, College of the Arts, Department of Art, Fullerton, CA 92834-9480. Offers art (MA, MFA), including ceramics (MFA), crafts, creative photography (MFA), design (MFA), drawing and painting, printmaking (MFA), sculpture; art history (MA); design (MA). *Accreditation:* NASAD (one or more programs are accredited). Part-time programs available. *Students:* 50 full-time (34 women), 38 part-time (24 women); includes 1 Black or African American, non-Hispanic/Latino; 12 Asian, non-Hispanic/Latino; 11 Hispanic/Latino, 8 international. Average age 35. 113 applicants, 26% accepted, 26 enrolled. In 2010, 14 master's awarded. *Degree requirements:* For master's, project or thesis. *Entrance requirements:* For master's, minimum GPA of 2.5 in last 60 units of course work, portfolio. Application fee: $55. *Financial support:* Career-related internships or fieldwork, Federal Work-Study, institutionally sponsored loans, and scholarships/grants available. Support available to part-time students. Financial award application deadline: 3/1; financial award applicants required to submit FAFSA. *Unit head:* Larry Johnson, Chair, 657-278-3471. *Application contact:* Admissions/Applications, 657-278-2371.

California State University, Long Beach, Graduate Studies, College of the Arts, Department of Art, Long Beach, CA 90840. Offers art education (MA); art history (MA); studio art (MA, MFA). *Accreditation:* NASAD. Part-time programs available. *Faculty:* 36 full-time (16 women),

Art/Fine Arts

California State University, Long Beach (continued)
5 part-time/adjunct (4 women). *Students:* 86 full-time (49 women), 26 part-time (21 women); includes 1 American Indian or Alaska Native, non-Hispanic/Latino; 10 Asian, non-Hispanic/Latino; 17 Hispanic/Latino, 9 international. Average age 33. 222 applicants, 20% accepted, 29 enrolled. In 2010, 35 master's awarded. *Degree requirements:* For master's, thesis (for some programs). *Entrance requirements:* For master's, minimum GPA of 3.0 in last 60 hours. *Application deadline:* For fall admission, 7/1 for domestic students; for spring admission, 12/1 for domestic students. Applications are processed on a rolling basis. Application fee: $55. Electronic applications accepted. *Financial support:* Federal Work-Study, institutionally sponsored loans, and scholarships/grants available. Financial award application deadline: 3/2. *Unit head:* Prof. David Hadlock, Chair, 562-985-7908, Fax: 562-985-1650, E-mail: dhadlock@csulb.edu. *Application contact:* Margaret Black, Graduate Advisor, 562-985-7910, Fax: 562-985-1650.

California State University, Los Angeles, Graduate Studies, College of Arts and Letters, Department of Art, Los Angeles, CA 90032-8530. Offers art (MA), including art education, art history, art therapy, ceramics, metals, and textiles, design (MA, MFA), painting, sculpture, and graphic arts, photography; fine arts (MFA), including crafts, design (MA, MFA), studio arts. *Accreditation:* NASAD (one or more programs are accredited). Part-time and evening/weekend programs available. *Faculty:* 9 full-time (5 women), 3 part-time/adjunct (2 women). *Students:* 27 full-time (19 women), 33 part-time (22 women); includes 24 minority (3 Black or African American, non-Hispanic/Latino; 7 Asian, non-Hispanic/Latino; 13 Hispanic/Latino; 1 Two or more races, non-Hispanic/Latino), 9 international. Average age 36. 19 applicants, 100% accepted, 13 enrolled. In 2010, 26 master's awarded. *Degree requirements:* For master's, comprehensive exam, project or thesis. *Entrance requirements:* For master's, portfolio. Additional exam requirements/recommendations for international students: Required—TOEFL (minimum score 500 paper-based; 173 computer-based). *Application deadline:* For fall admission, 5/1 for domestic and international students. Applications are processed on a rolling basis. Application fee: $55. Electronic applications accepted. *Financial support:* Federal Work-Study available. Support available to part-time students. Financial award application deadline: 3/1. *Faculty research:* The artist and the book, conceptual art, ceramic processes, computer graphics, architectural graphics. *Unit head:* Dr. Abbas Daneshvari, Chair, 323-343-4010, Fax: 323-343-4045, E-mail: adanesh@calstatela.edu. *Application contact:* Dr. Alan Muchlinski, Dean of Graduate Studies, 323-343-3820, Fax: 323-343-5653, E-mail: amuchli@exchange.calstatela.edu.

California State University, Northridge, Graduate Studies, College of Arts, Media, and Communication, Department of Art, Northridge, CA 91330. Offers art education (MA); art history (MA); studio art (MA, MFA); visual communications (MA, MFA). *Accreditation:* NASAD.

California State University, Sacramento, Graduate Studies, College of Arts and Letters, Department of Art, Sacramento, CA 95819. Offers studio art (MA). *Accreditation:* NASAD. Part-time programs available. *Degree requirements:* For master's, thesis or alternative, departmental qualifying exam, writing proficiency exam. *Entrance requirements:* For master's, minimum GPA of 3.0 during previous 2 years. Additional exam requirements/recommendations for international students: Required—TOEFL. Electronic applications accepted.

California State University, San Bernardino, Graduate Studies, College of Arts and Letters, Department of Art, San Bernardino, CA 92407-2397. Offers art (MA); art/graphics (MA). *Accreditation:* NASAD. *Entrance requirements:* Additional exam requirements/recommendations for international students: Required—TOEFL.

Carnegie Mellon University, College of Fine Arts, School of Art, Pittsburgh, PA 15213-3891. Offers MFA. *Accreditation:* NASAD. *Degree requirements:* For master's, thesis, exhibit. *Entrance requirements:* For master's, portfolio. Additional exam requirements/recommendations for international students: Required—TOEFL.

Central Washington University, Graduate Studies and Research, College of Arts and Humanities, Department of Art, Ellensburg, WA 98926. Offers MA, MFA. *Degree requirements:* For master's, thesis or alternative. *Entrance requirements:* For master's, minimum GPA of 3.0, portfolio. Additional exam requirements/recommendations for international students: Required—TOEFL (minimum score 550 paper-based; 213 computer-based; 79 iBT). Electronic applications accepted.

City College of the City University of New York, Graduate School, College of Liberal Arts and Science, Division of the Humanities and Arts, Department of Art, Program in Fine Arts, New York, NY 10031-9198. Offers advertising design (MFA); ceramic design (MFA); painting (MFA); printmaking (MFA); sculpture (MFA); wood and metal design (MFA). *Degree requirements:* For master's, thesis exhibit. *Entrance requirements:* For master's, 20 slide portfolio. Additional exam requirements/recommendations for international students: Required—TOEFL (minimum score 577 paper-based; 90 iBT). Electronic applications accepted.

Claremont Graduate University, Graduate Programs, School of Arts and Humanities, Department of Art, Claremont, CA 91711. Offers digital media (MA, MFA); drawing (MA, MFA); installation (MA, MFA); new genre (MA, MFA); painting (MA, MFA); performance (MA, MFA); photography (MA, MFA); sculpture (MA, MFA). Part-time programs available. *Faculty:* 4 full-time (1 woman). *Students:* 60 full-time (33 women); includes 5 Asian, non-Hispanic/Latino; 7 Hispanic/Latino, 3 international. Average age 34. In 2010, 29 master's awarded. *Degree requirements:* For master's, final project show. *Entrance requirements:* For master's, BA in art or BFA, slide review. Additional exam requirements/recommendations for international students: Required—TOEFL (minimum score 550 paper-based; 213 computer-based; 80 iBT). *Application deadline:* For fall admission, 2/1 priority date for domestic students. Applications are processed on a rolling basis. Application fee: $60. Electronic applications accepted. *Expenses:* Contact institution. *Financial support:* Fellowships, research assistantships, teaching assistantships, Federal Work-Study, institutionally sponsored loans, and scholarships/grants available. Support available to part-time students. Financial award application deadline: 2/15; financial award applicants required to submit FAFSA. *Faculty research:* Acoustic sculpture, feminization of abstraction, installation sculpture. *Unit head:* David Pagel, Chair, 909-607-2479, Fax: 909-607-1276, E-mail: david.pagel@cgu.edu. *Application contact:* Pat Evans, Program Administrator, 909-607-9292, Fax: 909-607-1276, E-mail: patricia.evans@cgu.edu.

Clemson University, Graduate School, College of Architecture, Arts, and Humanities, Department of Art, Clemson, SC 29634. Offers visual arts (MFA). *Accreditation:* NASAD. *Faculty:* 8 full-time (4 women), 5 part-time/adjunct (2 women). *Students:* 14 full-time (5 women), 1 (woman) part-time. Average age 30. 26 applicants, 19% accepted, 2 enrolled. In 2010, 7 master's awarded. *Entrance requirements:* For master's, portfolio. Additional exam requirements/recommendations for international students: Required—TOEFL. *Application deadline:* For fall admission, 3/15 for domestic students, 4/15 for international students; for spring admission, 9/15 for international students. Application fee: $70 ($80 for international students). Electronic applications accepted. *Expenses:* Tuition, state resident: full-time $6492; part-time $400 per credit hour. Tuition, nonresident: full-time $13,634; part-time $800 per credit hour. Required fees: $262 per semester. Part-time tuition and fees vary according to course load and program. *Financial support:* In 2010–11, 15 students received support, including 5 fellowships with partial tuition reimbursements available (averaging $2,320 per year), 13 teaching assistantships with partial tuition reimbursements available (averaging $3,508 per year); career-related internships or fieldwork, institutionally sponsored loans, scholarships/grants, health care benefits, and unspecified assistantships also available. Support available to part-time students. Financial award applicants required to submit FAFSA. *Unit head:* Michael V. Vatalaro, Chair, 864-656-3881, E-mail: vatalam@clemson.edu. *Application contact:* Dave Detrich, Coordinator, 864-656-3890, Fax: 864-656-0204, E-mail: ddavid@clemson.edu.

Cleveland State University, College of Graduate Studies, College of Liberal Arts and Social Sciences, Department of Art, Cleveland, OH 44115. Offers art education (M Ed); art history (MA). *Faculty:* 6 full-time (4 women), 2 part-time/adjunct (1 woman). *Students:* 1 (woman) full-time, 4 part-time (all women). 2 applicants, 0% accepted, 0 enrolled. In 2010, 2 master's awarded. *Expenses:* Tuition, state resident: full-time $8447; part-time $469 per credit hour. Tuition, nonresident: full-time $16,020; part-time $890 per credit hour. Required fees: $50. *Unit head:* Howie Smith, Chair, 212-523-7546, E-mail: art.chair@csuohio.edu. *Application contact:* Dr. Giannina Pianalto, Director of Graduate Admissions, 216-687-5599, Fax: 216-687-5400, E-mail: g.pianalto@csuohio.edu.

The College at Brockport, State University of New York, School of the Arts, Humanities and Social Sciences, Visual Studies Workshop, Brockport, NY 14420-2997. Offers visual studies (MFA). *Students:* 9 full-time (7 women), 4 part-time (3 women); includes 1 minority (Hispanic/Latino). 24 applicants, 54% accepted, 13 enrolled. In 2010, 8 master's awarded. *Degree requirements:* For master's, thesis or alternative, internship, final project. *Entrance requirements:* For master's, slides, portfolio, video or CD/DVD, including work description; letters of recommendation; minimum GPA of 3.0; statement of objectives. Additional exam requirements/recommendations for international students: Required—TOEFL (minimum score 550 paper-based; 213 computer-based; 79 iBT). *Application deadline:* For fall admission, 2/15 priority date for domestic and international students. Application fee: $50. Electronic applications accepted. *Financial support:* Federal Work-Study and scholarships/grants available. Support available to part-time students. Financial award application deadline: 3/15; financial award applicants required to submit FAFSA. *Faculty research:* Photography, film, video, digital media, artists' books. *Unit head:* Tate Shaw, Executive Director, 585-442-8676, Fax: 585-442-1992, E-mail: tshaw@brockport.edu. *Application contact:* Kristen Merola, MFA Coordinator, 585-442-8676, Fax: 585-442-1992, E-mail: kmerola@brockport.edu.

The College of New Rochelle, Graduate School, Division of Art and Communication Studies, Program in Studio Art, New Rochelle, NY 10805-2308. Offers MS. Part-time and evening/weekend programs available. *Degree requirements:* For master's, apprenticeship. *Entrance requirements:* For master's, portfolio, 36 credits of course work in studio art. *Faculty research:* Experimental computer graphics.

Colorado State University, Graduate School, College of Liberal Arts, Department of Art, Fort Collins, CO 80523-1779. Offers MFA. *Faculty:* 23 full-time (10 women). *Students:* 17 full-time (13 women), 1 part-time (0 women), 1 international. Average age 34. 80 applicants, 14% accepted, 5 enrolled. In 2010, 10 master's awarded. *Degree requirements:* For master's, comprehensive exam (for some programs), thesis (for some programs), exhibition. *Entrance requirements:* For master's, portfolio, letters of recommendation. Additional exam requirements/recommendations for international students: Required—TOEFL (minimum score 550 paper-based; 213 computer-based; 80 iBT). *Application deadline:* For fall admission, 2/1 priority date for domestic students; for spring admission, 10/15 priority date for domestic students. Applications are processed on a rolling basis. Application fee: $50. Electronic applications accepted. *Expenses:* Contact institution. *Financial support:* In 2010–11, 9 students received support, including 9 teaching assistantships with tuition reimbursements available (averaging $7,535 per year); fellowships, research assistantships, Federal Work-Study, institutionally sponsored loans, scholarships/grants, health care benefits, and unspecified assistantships also available. Support available to part-time students. Financial award application deadline: 3/1; financial award applicants required to submit FAFSA. *Faculty research:* African art history, bronze castings, etching/lithography, pre-Columbian art history, contemporary crafts. Total annual research expenditures: $8,200. *Unit head:* Gary W. Voss, Chair, 970-491-5192, E-mail: gary.voss@colostate.edu. *Application contact:* Tom Lundberg, Graduate Coordinator, 970-491-5734, E-mail: thomas.lundberg@colostate.edu.

Columbia University, School of the Arts, Visual Arts Division, New York, NY 10027. Offers new genres (MFA); painting (MFA); photography (MFA); printmaking (MFA); sculpture (MFA). *Degree requirements:* For master's, thesis. *Entrance requirements:* For master's, 3 letters of recommendation, portfolio, resume. Additional exam requirements/recommendations for international students: Required—TOEFL (minimum score 600 paper-based; 250 computer-based; 100 iBT). Electronic applications accepted.

See Close-Up on page 295.

Concordia University, School of Graduate Studies, Faculty of Fine Arts, Department of Studio Arts, Montréal, QC H3G 1M8, Canada. Offers studio arts (MFA), including film production, open media, painting, photography, print media, sculpture, ceramics and fibers. *Degree requirements:* For master's, thesis or alternative. *Entrance requirements:* For master's, portfolio.

Cornell University, Graduate School, Graduate Fields of Architecture, Art and Planning, Field of Art, Ithaca, NY 14853-0001. Offers creative visual arts (MFA), including painting, photography, printmaking, sculpture. *Faculty:* 12 full-time (5 women). *Students:* 11 full-time (6 women); includes 1 Asian, non-Hispanic/Latino; 1 Hispanic/Latino, 2 international. Average age 31. 148 applicants, 5% accepted, 5 enrolled. In 2010, 3 master's awarded. *Degree requirements:* For master's, thesis, exhibit. *Entrance requirements:* For master's, slide portfolio of 10-20 slides, 3 letters of recommendation, resume. Additional exam requirements/recommendations for international students: Required—TOEFL (minimum score 550 paper-based; 213 computer-based; 77 iBT). *Application deadline:* For fall admission, 2/15 for domestic students. Application fee: $70. Electronic applications accepted. *Expenses:* Tuition: Full-time $29,500. Required fees: $76. Tuition and fees vary according to degree level and program. *Financial support:* In 2010–11, 11 teaching assistantships with full tuition reimbursements were awarded; fellowships with full tuition reimbursements, research assistantships with full tuition reimbursements, institutionally sponsored loans, scholarships/grants, health care benefits, tuition waivers (full and partial), and unspecified assistantships also available. Financial award applicants required to submit FAFSA. *Faculty research:* Painting, sculpture, photography, printmaking. *Unit head:* Director of Graduate Studies, 607-255-6730, Fax: 607-255-3462. *Application contact:* Graduate Field Assistant, 607-255-6730, Fax: 607-255-3462, E-mail: artinfo@cornell.edu.

Cranbrook Academy of Art, Graduate School, Program in Fine Arts, Bloomfield Hills, MI 48303-0801. Offers ceramics (MFA); design (MFA), including graphic design; fiber arts (MFA); metalsmithing (MFA); painting (MFA); photography (MFA); printmaking (MFA); sculpture (MFA). *Accreditation:* NASAD. *Degree requirements:* For master's, thesis, exhibit. *Entrance requirements:* Additional exam requirements/recommendations for international students: Required—TOEFL (minimum score 550 paper-based; 213 computer-based).

Drury University, Program in Studio Art and Theory, Springfield, MO 65802. Offers MA. *Entrance requirements:* For master's, GRE or MAT. Additional exam requirements/recommendations for international students: Required—TOEFL. Electronic applications accepted.

Duke University, Graduate School, Department of Art, Art History and Visual Studies, Durham, NC 27708-0764. Offers PhD. *Faculty:* 16 full-time. *Students:* 41 full-time (35 women); includes 2 Black or African American, non-Hispanic/Latino; 1 Asian, non-Hispanic/Latino; 3 Hispanic/Latino, 11 international. 78 applicants, 13% accepted, 4 enrolled. In 2010, 1 doctorate awarded. *Degree requirements:* For doctorate, thesis/dissertation. *Entrance requirements:* For doctorate, GRE General Test. Additional exam requirements/recommendations for international students: Required—TOEFL (minimum score 550 paper-based; 213 computer-based; 83 iBT), IELTS (minimum score 7). *Application deadline:* For fall admission, 12/8 priority date for domestic and international students. Application fee: $75. Electronic applications accepted. *Financial support:* Fellowships, teaching assistantships available. Financial award application deadline: 12/8. *Unit head:* Gennifer Weisenfeld, Director of Graduate Studies, 919-684-2224, Fax: 919-684-4398, E-mail: gennifer.weisenfeld@duke.edu. *Application contact:* Elizabeth Hutton, Director of Admissions, 919-684-3913, Fax: 919-684-2277, E-mail: grad-admissions@duke.edu.

East Carolina University, Graduate School, College of Fine Arts and Communication, School of Art and Design, Greenville, NC 27858-4353. Offers MA, MA Ed, MFA. *Accreditation:* NASAD (one or more programs are accredited). Part-time and evening/weekend programs available. *Degree requirements:* For master's, comprehensive exam, thesis (for some programs). *Entrance requirements:* For master's, GRE General Test or MAT, portfolio. Additional exam requirements/recommendations for international students: Required—TOEFL. *Expenses:* Tuition, state resident: full-time $3130; part-time $391.25 per credit hour. Tuition, nonresident: full-time

$13,817; part-time $1727.13 per credit hour. Required fees: $1916; $239.50 per credit hour. Tuition and fees vary according to campus/location and program.

Eastern Illinois University, Graduate School, College of Arts and Humanities, Department of Art, Charleston, IL 61920-3099. Offers art (MA); art education (MA). *Accreditation:* NASAD. *Degree requirements:* For master's, thesis or alternative, portfolio.

Eastern Michigan University, Graduate School, College of Arts and Sciences, Department of Art, Program in Studio Art, Ypsilanti, MI 48197. Offers MA, MFA. Part-time and evening/weekend programs available. Postbaccalaureate distance learning degree programs offered (minimal on-campus study). *Students:* 12 full-time (7 women), 15 part-time (12 women); includes 2 minority (1 Black or African American, non-Hispanic/Latino; 1 Asian, non-Hispanic/Latino), 1 international. Average age 41. In 2010, 3 master's awarded. *Application deadline:* Applications are processed on a rolling basis. Application fee: $35. *Financial support:* Fellowships, research assistantships with full tuition reimbursements, teaching assistantships with full tuition reimbursements, career-related internships or fieldwork, Federal Work-Study, institutionally sponsored loans, scholarships/grants, and unspecified assistantships available. Support available to part-time students.

East Tennessee State University, School of Graduate Studies, College of Arts and Sciences, Department of Art and Design, Johnson City, TN 37614. Offers studio art (MFA). *Accreditation:* NASAD. *Faculty:* 14 full-time (6 women). *Students:* 17 full-time (5 women), 3 part-time (2 women); includes 2 minority (1 Black or African American, non-Hispanic/Latino; 1 Hispanic/Latino), 2 international. Average age 35. 36 applicants, 22% accepted, 7 enrolled. In 2010, 6 master's awarded. *Degree requirements:* For master's, thesis, exhibit, oral exam (MFA). *Entrance requirements:* For master's, GRE General Test, portfolio (MFA), bachelor's degree in art, minimum GPA of 3.0. Additional exam requirements/recommendations for international students: Required—TOEFL (minimum score 550 paper-based; 213 computer-based; 79 iBT). *Application deadline:* For fall admission, 2/1 priority date for domestic students, 2/1 for international students. Application fee: $25 ($35 for international students). Electronic applications accepted. *Financial support:* In 2010–11, 2 research assistantships with full tuition reimbursements (averaging $5,000 per year), 4 teaching assistantships with full tuition reimbursements (averaging $5,000 per year) were awarded; career-related internships or fieldwork, institutionally sponsored loans, scholarships/grants, and unspecified assistantships also available. Financial award application deadline: 7/1; financial award applicants required to submit FAFSA. *Faculty research:* History of sculpture, art and senior citizens, encaustic paintings, digital media in art history. *Unit head:* Dr. M. Wayne Dyer, Chair, 423-439-5296, Fax: 423-439-4393, E-mail: dyerm@etsu.edu. *Application contact:* Admissions and Records Clerk, 423-439-4221, Fax: 423-439-5624, E-mail: gradsch@etsu.edu.

Edinboro University of Pennsylvania, College of Arts and Sciences, Department of Art, Edinboro, PA 16444. Offers art (MA); fine arts (MFA), including ceramics, jewelry/metalsmithing, painting, printmaking, sculpture. *Accreditation:* NASAD. Evening/weekend programs available. *Faculty:* 19 full-time (8 women), 1 (woman) part-time/adjunct. *Students:* 35 full-time (18 women), 46 part-time (38 women); includes 3 minority (1 Black or African American, non-Hispanic/Latino; 1 Hispanic/Latino; 1 Native Hawaiian or other Pacific Islander, non-Hispanic/Latino). Average age 31. In 2010, 5 master's awarded. *Degree requirements:* For master's, comprehensive exam, thesis or alternative, competency exam, exhibit, portfolio. *Entrance requirements:* For master's, GRE or MAT, interview, minimum QPA of 2.5, portfolio. *Application deadline:* Applications are processed on a rolling basis. Application fee: $30. Electronic applications accepted. *Expenses:* Tuition, state resident: full-time $6966; part-time $387 per credit. Tuition, nonresident: full-time $11,146; part-time $619 per credit. Required fees: $2401.70; $96.25 per credit. *Financial support:* In 2010–11, 23 research assistantships with full and partial tuition reimbursements (averaging $4,050 per year) were awarded; Federal Work-Study, scholarships/grants, and unspecified assistantships also available. Financial award application deadline: 2/15; financial award applicants required to submit FAFSA. *Unit head:* Prof. Lee Rexrode, Program Head, 814-732-2309, E-mail: lrexrode@edinboro.edu. *Application contact:* Prof. Lee Rexrode, Program Head, 814-732-2309, E-mail: lrexrode@edinboro.edu.

Emily Carr University of Art + Design, Program in Applied Arts, Vancouver, BC V6H 3R9, Canada. Offers design (MAA); media arts (MAA); visual arts (MAA). *Degree requirements:* For master's, internship, thesis project. *Entrance requirements:* For master's, minimum overall GPA of 3.0, visual portfolio, 3 letters of recommendation. Additional exam requirements/recommendations for international students: Required—TOEFL (minimum score 570 paper-based; 230 computer-based; 84 iBT), IELTS (minimum score 6.5), Michigan English Language Assessment Battery (minimum score 81). Electronic applications accepted.

Fairleigh Dickinson University, Metropolitan Campus, University College: Arts, Sciences, and Professional Studies, School of Art and Media Studies, Teaneck, NJ 07666-1914. Offers MA. *Students:* 14 full-time (9 women), 10 part-time (8 women), 5 international. Average age 29. 16 applicants, 81% accepted, 7 enrolled. In 2010, 16 master's awarded. *Application deadline:* Applications are processed on a rolling basis. Application fee: $40. *Application contact:* Susan Brooman, University Director of Graduate Admissions, 201-692-2554, Fax: 201-692-2560, E-mail: globaleducation@fdu.edu.

Ferris State University, Kendall College of Art and Design, Big Rapids, MI 49307. Offers MFA. *Accreditation:* NASAD. Part-time programs available. *Faculty:* 15 full-time (10 women). *Students:* 29 full-time (19 women), 15 part-time (10 women); includes 1 American Indian or Alaska Native, non-Hispanic/Latino; 1 Asian, non-Hispanic/Latino; 1 Two or more races, non-Hispanic/Latino. Average age 31. 37 applicants, 70% accepted, 13 enrolled. In 2010, 15 master's awarded. *Degree requirements:* For master's, thesis, seminars. *Entrance requirements:* For master's, portfolio, 3 letters of recommendation, curriculum vitae. Additional exam requirements/recommendations for international students: Required—TOEFL (minimum score 500 paper-based; 173 computer-based; 61 iBT). *Application deadline:* For fall admission, 2/15 priority date for domestic and international students; for spring admission, 11/1 priority date for domestic and international students. Applications are processed on a rolling basis. Application fee: $30. *Financial support:* In 2010–11, 30 students received support, including 7 fellowships (averaging $13,370 per year); scholarships/grants, unspecified assistantships, and half-tuition scholarships ($6317 average), graduate assistantships ($5309 average) also available. Support available to part-time students. Financial award application deadline: 2/15; financial award applicants required to submit FAFSA. *Unit head:* Dr. Oliver H. Evans, President and Vice Chancellor, 616-451-2787. *Application contact:* Sandra Britton, Director of Enrollment Management, 616-451-2787, Fax: 616-831-9689, E-mail: kcadadmissions@ferris.edu.

Florida Atlantic University, Dorothy F. Schmidt College of Arts and Letters, Department of Visual Arts and Art History, Boca Raton, FL 33431-0991. Offers art education (MAT); ceramics (MFA); computer art (MFA); graphic design (MFA); painting (MFA). *Faculty:* 17 full-time (11 women), 9 part-time/adjunct (7 women). *Students:* 19 full-time (12 women), 7 part-time (2 women); includes 8 minority (all Hispanic/Latino), 1 international. Average age 30. 33 applicants, 30% accepted, 6 enrolled. In 2010, 5 master's awarded. *Degree requirements:* For master's, one foreign language, project. *Entrance requirements:* For master's, GRE General Test, minimum GPA of 3.0 during last 60 hours of course work, slide portfolio. *Application deadline:* For fall admission, 2/21 for domestic and international students; for spring admission, 10/1 for domestic and international students. Application fee: $30. Electronic applications accepted. *Expenses:* Tuition, area resident: Part-time $319.96 per credit. Tuition, state resident: part-time $319.96 per credit. Tuition, nonresident: part-time $926.42 per credit. *Financial support:* Research assistantships with full tuition reimbursements, teaching assistantships with full tuition reimbursements, career-related internships or fieldwork, Federal Work-Study, and institutionally sponsored loans available. Financial award applicants required to submit FAFSA. *Faculty research:* Painting, ceramics (traditional and non-traditional), installation, video and interactive sculpture. *Unit head:* Dr. Linda Johnson, Chair, 561-297-3870, Fax: 561-297-3078, E-mail: ljohnson@fau.edu. *Application contact:* James A. Novak, Associate Professor/Graduate Coordinator/Advisor, 561-297-2430, Fax: 561-297-3078, E-mail: jnovak@fau.edu.

Florida International University, College of Architecture and the Arts, School of Art and Art History, Miami, FL 33199. Offers visual arts (MFA). *Accreditation:* NASAD. Part-time and evening/weekend programs available. *Faculty:* 14 full-time (6 women), 4 part-time/adjunct (0 women). *Students:* 10 full-time (6 women), 1 (woman) part-time; includes 1 Black or African American, non-Hispanic/Latino; 4 Hispanic/Latino, 1 international. Average age 27. 34 applicants, 12% accepted, 4 enrolled. In 2010, 4 master's awarded. *Entrance requirements:* For master's, minimum GPA of 3.0 (upper level coursework), 3 letters of recommendation, 20 slides of creative work. Additional exam requirements/recommendations for international students: Required—TOEFL (minimum score 550 paper-based; 80 iBT). *Application deadline:* For fall admission, 2/1 for domestic and international students. Application fee: $30. Electronic applications accepted. *Financial support:* Institutionally sponsored loans and scholarships/grants available. Financial award application deadline: 3/1; financial award applicants required to submit FAFSA. *Unit head:* Dr. Juan Martinez, Chair, 305-348-3539, Fax: 305-348-0513, E-mail: juan.martinez@fiu.edu. *Application contact:* Evelyn Martinez, Graduate Secretary, 305-348-6268, Fax: 305-348-0513, E-mail: emart022@fiu.edu.

Florida State University, The Graduate School, College of Visual Arts, Theatre and Dance, Department of Art, Tallahassee, FL 32306. Offers MFA. *Accreditation:* NASAD. *Faculty:* 20 full-time (13 women), 22 part-time/adjunct (10 women). *Students:* 29 full-time (14 women); includes 5 minority (2 Black or African American, non-Hispanic/Latino; 3 Hispanic/Latino). Average age 26. 53 applicants, 28% accepted. In 2010, 2 master's awarded. *Degree requirements:* For master's, thesis, culminating exhibition show. *Entrance requirements:* Additional exam requirements/recommendations for international students: Required—TOEFL (minimum score 550 paper-based). *Application deadline:* For fall admission, 2/1 for domestic and international students. Application fee: $30. *Expenses:* Tuition, state resident: full-time $8238.24. *Financial support:* Fellowships, research assistantships, teaching assistantships, tuition waivers (full) and unspecified assistantships available. *Faculty research:* Photography, painting, sculpture, printmaking, ceramics. *Unit head:* Carolyn Henne, Chair, 850-644-8254, E-mail: chenne@fsu.edu. *Application contact:* Sara Howard, Academic Advisor, 850-644-8262, E-mail: sshoward@admin.fsu.edu.

Fontbonne University, Graduate Programs, Department of Fine Arts, St. Louis, MO 63105-3098. Offers art (MA); fine arts (MFA); theater education (MA). Part-time and evening/weekend programs available. *Faculty:* 7 full-time (2 women), 8 part-time/adjunct (7 women). *Students:* 8 full-time (2 women), 7 part-time (5 women); includes 1 Black or African American, non-Hispanic/Latino; 3 Asian, non-Hispanic/Latino. Average age 41. In 2010, 10 master's awarded. *Degree requirements:* For master's, thesis exhibit (MFA). *Entrance requirements:* For master's, minimum GPA of 3.0, portfolio. *Application deadline:* For fall admission, 8/1 priority date for domestic students. Applications are processed on a rolling basis. Application fee: $25. *Expenses:* Tuition: Full-time $11,328. Full-time tuition and fees vary according to program. *Financial support:* In 2010–11, teaching assistantships (averaging $2,500 per year). Support available to part-time students. Financial award application deadline: 4/1; financial award applicants required to submit FAFSA. *Unit head:* Catherine Connor-Talasek, Chairperson, 314-889-1431, Fax: 314-889-4545, E-mail: cconnor@fontbonne.edu. *Application contact:* Catherine Connor-Talasek, Chairperson, 314-889-1431, Fax: 314-889-4545, E-mail: cconnor@fontbonne.edu.

Fort Hays State University, Graduate School, College of Arts and Sciences, Department of Art, Hays, KS 67601-4099. Offers studio art (MFA). Part-time programs available. *Degree requirements:* For master's, comprehensive exam, thesis. *Entrance requirements:* For master's, slides. Additional exam requirements/recommendations for international students: Required—TOEFL (minimum score 550 paper-based; 213 computer-based; 79 iBT). Electronic applications accepted. *Faculty research:* Migration art of Germanic tribes, iconographic and stylistic development, graphic design, photography, lithography.

Framingham State University, Division of Graduate and Continuing Education, Program in Art, Framingham, MA 01701-9101. Offers M Ed.

Full Sail University, Education Media Design and Technology Master of Science Program—Online, Winter Park, FL 32792-7437. Offers MS. Postbaccalaureate distance learning degree programs offered (no on-campus study). *Entrance requirements:* Additional exam requirements/recommendations for international students: Required—TOEFL (minimum score 550 paper-based; 213 computer-based; 79 iBT).

Full Sail University, Media Design Master of Fine Arts Program—Online, Winter Park, FL 32792-7437. Offers MFA. Postbaccalaureate distance learning degree programs offered.

The George Washington University, Columbian College of Arts and Sciences, Department of Fine Arts and Art History, Washington, DC 20052. Offers art history (MA), including art history, museum training; ceramics (MFA); drawing/painting (MFA); interior design (MFA); new media (MFA); photography (MFA); sculpture (MFA). *Accreditation:* CIDA. Part-time and evening/weekend programs available. *Faculty:* 18 full-time (9 women), 34 part-time/adjunct (25 women). *Students:* 49 full-time (44 women), 41 part-time (38 women); includes 5 Black or African American, non-Hispanic/Latino; 4 Asian, non-Hispanic/Latino; 4 Hispanic/Latino, 5 international. Average age 30. 144 applicants, 66% accepted, 40 enrolled. In 2010, 24 master's awarded. *Entrance requirements:* For master's, GRE General Test, bachelor's degree in field, minimum GPA of 3.0. Additional exam requirements/recommendations for international students: Required—TOEFL (minimum score 550 paper-based; 213 computer-based; 80 iBT). *Application deadline:* For fall admission, 3/1 priority date for domestic students, 1/15 priority date for international students; for spring admission, 10/1 priority date for domestic students, 9/1 priority date for international students. Applications are processed on a rolling basis. Application fee: $75. Electronic applications accepted. *Financial support:* In 2010–11, 12 students received support; fellowships, teaching assistantships, career-related internships or fieldwork, Federal Work-Study, and tuition waivers available. Financial award application deadline: 1/15. *Unit head:* Thomas K. Brown, Chair, 202-994-9067, E-mail: thbrown@gwu.edu. *Application contact:* Information Contact, 202-994-6085, Fax: 202-994-8657, E-mail: art@gwu.edu.

Georgia Southern University, Jack N. Averitt College of Graduate Studies, College of Liberal Arts and Social Sciences, Department of Art, Statesboro, GA 30460. Offers fine arts (MFA). *Accreditation:* NASAD. Part-time programs available. *Students:* 20 full-time (10 women), 8 part-time (5 women); includes 3 Black or African American, non-Hispanic/Latino; 2 Hispanic/Latino, 1 international. Average age 34. 9 applicants, 67% accepted, 4 enrolled. In 2010, 5 master's awarded. *Degree requirements:* For master's, thesis, exhibition. *Entrance requirements:* For master's, minimum GPA of 3.0; 18 semester hours of course work in studio art, 9 in art history; portfolio; letters of reference. Additional exam requirements/recommendations for international students: Required—TOEFL (minimum score 550 paper-based; 213 computer-based). *Application deadline:* For fall admission, 3/1 priority date for domestic and international students; for spring admission, 10/1 priority date for domestic students, 10/1 for international students. Applications are processed on a rolling basis. Application fee: $50. Electronic applications accepted. *Expenses:* Tuition, state resident: full-time $6000; part-time $250 per semester hour. Tuition, nonresident: full-time $23,976; part-time $999 per semester hour. Required fees: $1644. *Financial support:* In 2010–11, 23 students received support, including research assistantships with partial tuition reimbursements available (averaging $7,200 per year), teaching assistantships with partial tuition reimbursements available (averaging $7,200 per year); career-related internships or fieldwork, Federal Work-Study, scholarships/grants, tuition waivers (partial), and unspecified assistantships also available. Support available to part-time students. Financial award application deadline: 4/15; financial award applicants required to submit FAFSA. *Faculty research:* International design trends; graphic design social awareness campaigns; functional design; public sculpture; fine art painting, drawing, printmaking, paper and book arts; folk art; Georgia artists archive. *Unit head:* Dr. Patricia Carter, Chair, 912-478-5472, Fax: 912-478-5104, E-mail: pwcarter@georgiasouthern.edu. *Application contact:* Dr. Charles Ziglar, Coordinator for Graduate Student Recruitment, 912-478-5635, Fax: 912-478-0740, E-mail: gradadmissions@georgiasouthern.edu.

Art/Fine Arts

Georgia State University, College of Arts and Sciences, Ernest G. Welch School of Art and Design, Program in Studio Art, Atlanta, GA 30302-3083. Offers MFA. *Accreditation:* NASAD. *Degree requirements:* For master's, thesis, exhibit, presentations, screening. *Entrance requirements:* For master's, portfolio. Additional exam requirements/recommendations for international students: Required—TOEFL (minimum score 550 paper-based; 213 computer-based). Electronic applications accepted. *Faculty research:* Photography, drawing/painting, printmaking, sculpture, ceramics.

Governors State University, College of Arts and Sciences, Program in Art, University Park, IL 60466-0975. Offers MA. Part-time and evening/weekend programs available. *Degree requirements:* For master's, thesis or alternative. *Entrance requirements:* For master's, portfolio, bachelor's degree in humanities. *Expenses:* Tuition, state resident: full-time $5400; part-time $225 per credit hour. Tuition, nonresident: full-time $16,200; part-time $675 per credit hour. Required fees: $1358; $46 per credit hour. $126 per term. Tuition and fees vary according to degree level and program. *Faculty research:* Historical study of art of selected ethnic groups of southwestern Zaire.

Hofstra University, School of Education, Health, and Human Services, Programs in Teaching K-12, Hempstead, NY 11549. Offers bilingual education (MS Ed); bilingual extension (CAS), including education/speech language pathology, intensive teacher institute; family and consumer science (MS Ed); fine art and music education (Advanced Certificate); fine arts education (MA, MS Ed); middle childhood extension (Advanced Certificate), including grades 5-6 or 7-9; music education (MA, MS Ed); teaching languages other than English and TESOL (MS Ed); TESOL (MS Ed); wind conducting (MA). Part-time and evening/weekend programs available. *Students:* 65 full-time (55 women), 67 part-time (52 women); includes 8 Black or African American, non-Hispanic/Latino; 8 Asian, non-Hispanic/Latino; 16 Hispanic/Latino; 1 Two or more races, non-Hispanic/Latino, 1 international. Average age 30. 102 applicants, 87% accepted, 41 enrolled. In 2010, 56 master's, 24 other advanced degrees awarded. *Degree requirements:* For master's, one foreign language, thesis (for some programs), completion of electronic and Tk20 portfolios. *Entrance requirements:* For master's, 2 letters of recommendation, portfolio, teacher certification (MA), essay; for other advanced degree, 2 letters of recommendation, interview, teaching certificate, essay. Additional exam requirements/recommendations for international students: Required—TOEFL (minimum score 550 paper-based; 213 computer-based; 80 iBT). *Application deadline:* Applications are processed on a rolling basis. Application fee: $70 ($75 for international students). Electronic applications accepted. *Expenses:* Tuition: Full-time $18,000; part-time $1000 per credit hour. Required fees: $970; $145 per term. Tuition and fees vary according to program. *Financial support:* In 2010–11, 49 students received support, including 14 fellowships with full and partial tuition reimbursements available (averaging $2,750 per year), 2 research assistantships with full and partial tuition reimbursements available (averaging $9,091 per year); career-related internships or fieldwork, Federal Work-Study, institutionally sponsored loans, scholarships/grants, tuition waivers (full and partial), unspecified assistantships, and scholarships also available. Support available to part-time students. Financial award applicants required to submit FAFSA. *Faculty research:* The teacher/artist, interdisciplinary curriculum, applied linguistics, structural inequalities, creativity. *Unit head:* Dr. Esther Fusco, Chairperson, 516-463-7704, Fax: 516-463-6196, E-mail: catezf@hofstra.edu. *Application contact:* Carol Drummer, Dean of Graduate Admissions, 516-463-4876, Fax: 516-463-4664, E-mail: gradstudent@hofstra.edu.

Hollins University, Graduate Programs, Program in Liberal Studies, Roanoke, VA 24020-1603. Offers humanities (MALS); interdisciplinary studies (MALS); justice and legal studies (MALS); liberal studies (CAS); social science (MALS); visual and performing arts (MALS). Part-time and evening/weekend programs available. *Degree requirements:* For master's, thesis. *Entrance requirements:* For master's, letters of recommendation, interview. Additional exam requirements/recommendations for international students: Required—TOEFL (minimum score 550 paper-based; 213 computer-based; 79 iBT). Electronic applications accepted. *Faculty research:* Elderly blacks, film, feminist economics, US voting patterns, Wagner, diversity.

Hood College, Graduate School, Program in Ceramic Arts, Frederick, MD 21701-8575. Offers ceramic arts (Certificate); ceramics (MFA). Part-time and evening/weekend programs available. *Faculty:* 1 (woman) full-time, 4 part-time/adjunct (2 women). *Students:* 3 full-time (2 women), 15 part-time (11 women); includes 1 Black or African American, non-Hispanic/Latino; 1 Asian, non-Hispanic/Latino; 2 Two or more races, non-Hispanic/Latino. Average age 36. 5 applicants, 40% accepted, 1 enrolled. In 2010, 1 master's, 7 other advanced degrees awarded. *Degree requirements:* For master's, comprehensive exam. *Entrance requirements:* For master's, minimum GPA of 2.75; for Certificate, portfolio. Additional exam requirements/recommendations for international students: Required—TOEFL (minimum score 575 paper-based; 231 computer-based; 89 iBT). *Application deadline:* For fall admission, 7/15 for domestic and international students; for spring admission, 12/15 for domestic and international students. Applications are processed on a rolling basis. Application fee: $35. Electronic applications accepted. *Expenses:* Tuition: Full-time $6480; part-time $360 per credit. Required fees: $100; $50 per term. *Financial support:* Applicants required to submit FAFSA. *Unit head:* Joyce Michaud, Director, 301-696-3526, E-mail: jmichaud@hood.edu. *Application contact:* Dr. Allen P. Flora, Dean of Graduate School, 301-696-3811, Fax: 301-696-3597, E-mail: gofurther@hood.edu.

Howard University, Graduate School, Division of Fine Arts, Department of Art, Program in Fine Arts, Washington, DC 20059-0002. Offers 3D reality (sculpture and ceramics) (MFA); design (MFA); electronic studio (MFA); painting (MFA); photography (MFA). *Accreditation:* NASAD. *Degree requirements:* For master's, comprehensive exam, thesis, exhibit. *Entrance requirements:* For master's, minimum GPA of 3.0, portfolio.

Hunter College of the City University of New York, Graduate School, School of Arts and Sciences, Department of Art, Program in Studio Art, New York, NY 10021-5085. Offers fine arts (MFA). Part-time and evening/weekend programs available. *Faculty:* 14 full-time (6 women), 1 part-time/adjunct (0 women). *Students:* 53 full-time (51 women), 68 part-time (62 women); includes 4 Black or African American, non-Hispanic/Latino; 6 Asian, non-Hispanic/Latino; 9 Hispanic/Latino, 14 international. Average age 30. 766 applicants, 5% accepted, 22 enrolled. In 2010, 49 master's awarded. *Degree requirements:* For master's, exhibit, project. *Entrance requirements:* For master's, minimum of 24 credits of course work in studio art, 9 in art history; portfolio. Additional exam requirements/recommendations for international students: Required—TOEFL. *Application deadline:* For fall admission, 2/1 for domestic students; for spring admission, 10/1 for domestic students. Application fee: $125. *Financial support:* Career-related internships or fieldwork, Federal Work-Study, scholarships/grants, and tuition waivers (partial) available. Support available to part-time students. Financial award application deadline: 4/15. *Faculty research:* Color theory, public printmaking and environmental commissions in painting and sculpture, graphics, ceramics, contemporary film and video. *Unit head:* Joel Carreiro, Graduate Adviser, 212-650-3398, E-mail: grad.arthistoryadvisor@hunter.cuny.edu. *Application contact:* William Zlata, Director for Graduate Admissions, 212-772-4482, Fax: 212-650-3336, E-mail: admissions@hunter.cuny.edu.

Idaho State University, Office of Graduate Studies, College of Arts and Sciences, Department of Art and Pre-Architecture, Pocatello, ID 83209-8004. Offers art (MFA). Part-time programs available. *Degree requirements:* For master's, comprehensive exam, thesis, exhibit, 2 year minimum participation in program, oral exam. *Entrance requirements:* For master's, GRE General Test, GMAT or MAT, minimum GPA of 3.0 in all upper-division classes, portfolio of work, 3 letters of recommendation. Additional exam requirements/recommendations for international students: Required—TOEFL (minimum score 550 paper-based; 213 computer-based; 80 iBT). Electronic applications accepted. *Faculty research:* Computerized weaving, anodizing refractory metals, viscosity printing, neon, ceramic shell casting.

Illinois State University, Graduate School, College of Fine Arts, Program in Arts Technology, Normal, IL 61790-2200. Offers MS. *Accreditation:* NASAD. *Degree requirements:* For master's, thesis or alternative.

Illinois State University, Graduate School, College of Fine Arts, School of Art, Normal, IL 61790-2200. Offers art history (MA, MS); ceramics (MFA, MS); drawing (MFA, MS); fibers (MFA, MS); glass (MFA, MS); graphic design (MA, MS); metals (MFA, MS); painting (MFA, MS); photography (MFA, MS); printmaking (MFA, MS); sculpture (MFA, MS). *Accreditation:* NASAD (one or more programs are accredited). *Degree requirements:* For master's, thesis or alternative, internship. *Entrance requirements:* For master's, portfolio, sample of scholarly writing. *Faculty research:* General operations support: Normal Editions Workshop for FY2007.

Indiana State University, College of Graduate and Professional Studies, College of Arts and Sciences, Department of Art, Terre Haute, IN 47809. Offers ceramics (MA, MFA); drawing (MA, MFA); graphic design (MA, MFA); painting (MA, MFA); photography (MA, MFA); printmaking (MA, MFA); sculpture (MA, MFA). *Accreditation:* NASAD (one or more programs are accredited). Part-time programs available. *Degree requirements:* For master's, thesis or alternative, departmental qualifying exam. *Entrance requirements:* For master's, portfolio. Additional exam requirements/recommendations for international students: Required—TOEFL (minimum score 550 paper-based).

Indiana University Bloomington, University Graduate School, College of Arts and Sciences, Henry Radford Hope School of Fine Arts, Bloomington, IN 47405-7000. Offers MA, MFA, PhD. *Accreditation:* NASAD (one or more,programs are accredited). *Faculty:* 17 full-time (10 women). *Students:* 133 full-time (94 women), 11 part-time (9 women); includes 11 minority (1 Black or African American, non-Hispanic/Latino; 1 American Indian or Alaska Native, non-Hispanic/Latino; 2 Asian, non-Hispanic/Latino; 3 Hispanic/Latino; 4 Two or more races, non-Hispanic/Latino), 10 international. Average age 29. 300 applicants, 27% accepted, 37 enrolled. In 2010, 32 master's, 3 doctorates awarded. *Degree requirements:* For doctorate, 2 foreign languages, thesis/dissertation. *Entrance requirements:* For master's, portfolio (MFA); for doctorate, minimum GPA of 3.0. Additional exam requirements/recommendations for international students: Required—TOEFL. *Application deadline:* For fall admission, 1/15 priority date for domestic students, 12/15 for international students; for spring admission, 9/1 for domestic and international students. Applications are processed on a rolling basis. Application fee: $55 ($65 for international students). *Financial support:* In 2010–11, 9 fellowships with tuition reimbursements (averaging $15,000 per year), 1 research assistantship with tuition reimbursement (averaging $11,000 per year), 11 teaching assistantships with tuition reimbursements (averaging $11,700 per year) were awarded; career-related internships or fieldwork, Federal Work-Study, scholarships/grants, tuition waivers (full and partial), and stipends also available. Financial award application deadline: 2/15. *Faculty research:* Infrared reflectography, Italian Renaissance painters, hand papermaking, British Romantic landscape painting, late nineteenth century American art. *Unit head:* Paul Brown, Director, 812-855-7498. *Application contact:* Brad Wicklund, Graduate Services Coordinator, 812-855-7766, E-mail: bwicklun@indiana.edu.

Indiana University of Pennsylvania, School of Graduate Studies and Research, College of Fine Arts, Department of Art, Program in Art, Indiana, PA 15705-1087. Offers MA, MFA. *Accreditation:* NASAD. Part-time programs available. *Faculty:* 9 full-time (2 women). *Students:* 12 full-time (4 women), 15 part-time (6 women); includes 4 minority (1 Black or African American, non-Hispanic/Latino; 2 Asian, non-Hispanic/Latino; 1 Hispanic/Latino), 3 international. Average age 29. 28 applicants, 32% accepted, 8 enrolled. In 2010, 10 master's awarded. *Degree requirements:* For master's, thesis optional. *Entrance requirements:* For master's, 3 letters of recommendation, portfolio. Additional exam requirements/recommendations for international students: Required—TOEFL. *Application deadline:* For fall admission, 7/1 priority date for domestic students; for spring admission, 11/1 for domestic students. Applications are processed on a rolling basis. Application fee: $40. *Financial support:* In 2010–11, 11 research assistantships with full and partial tuition reimbursements (averaging $4,080 per year) were awarded; fellowships, career-related internships or fieldwork and Federal Work-Study also available. Support available to part-time students. Financial award application deadline: 3/15; financial award applicants required to submit FAFSA. *Unit head:* Dr. James Nestor, 724-357-2593, E-mail: nestor@iup.edu. *Application contact:* Dr. James Nestor, Graduate Coordinator, 724-357-2593, E-mail: nestor@iup.edu.

Indiana University–Purdue University Indianapolis, Herron School of Art and Design, Indianapolis, IN 46202-2896. Offers art education (MAE); furniture design (MFA); printmaking (MFA); sculpture (MFA); visual communication (MFA). *Accreditation:* NASAD. Part-time and evening/weekend programs available. *Faculty:* 2 full-time (both women). *Students:* 32 full-time (18 women), 14 part-time (all women); includes 5 minority (2 Asian, non-Hispanic/Latino; 3 Hispanic/Latino), 6 international. Average age 30. 57 applicants, 42% accepted, 11 enrolled. In 2010, 14 master's awarded. *Entrance requirements:* For master's, portfolio, 44 hours of course work in art history and studio art. *Application deadline:* For fall admission, 6/1 priority date for domestic students, 3/15 priority date for international students; for spring admission, 11/1 priority date for domestic students, 10/15 priority date for international students. Applications are processed on a rolling basis. Application fee: $55 ($65 for international students). Electronic applications accepted. *Financial support:* Career-related internships or fieldwork, Federal Work-Study, institutionally sponsored loans, scholarships/grants, and tuition waivers (partial) available. Support available to part-time students. Total annual research expenditures: $6,097. *Unit head:* Valerie Eickmeier, Dean, 317-278-9470, Fax: 317-278-9471, E-mail: herron@iupui.edu. *Application contact:* Herron Student Services Office, 317-378-9400, E-mail: herrart@iupui.edu.

Institute for Doctoral Studies in the Visual Arts, PhD Program in Visual Art: Philosophy, Aesthetics, and Art Theory, Portland, ME 04102. Offers aesthetics (PhD); art theory (PhD); philosophy (PhD). Postbaccalaureate distance learning degree programs offered (minimal on-campus study). *Faculty:* 2 full-time (1 woman), 11 part-time/adjunct (3 women). *Students:* 24 full-time (19 women); includes 3 Black or African American, non-Hispanic/Latino; 1 Asian, non-Hispanic/Latino; 1 Hispanic/Latino. Average age 38. *Degree requirements:* For doctorate, comprehensive exam, thesis/dissertation, dissertation defense. *Entrance requirements:* For doctorate, curriculum vitae, writing sample, letter of purpose, portfolio, artist's statement, interview. *Application deadline:* Applications are processed on a rolling basis. Application fee: $50. Electronic applications accepted. *Expenses:* Tuition: Full-time $24,000. *Financial support:* In 2010–11, 22 students received support, including 1 fellowship (averaging $2,000 per year); scholarships/grants also available. *Faculty research:* Visual culture, sonic art, cultural studies, feminism, contemporary art. *Unit head:* Amy Curtis, Executive Vice President, 207-879-8757, E-mail: acurtis@idsva.org. *Application contact:* Diane Einsiedler, Assistant to the Executive Vice President, 207-771-8887, E-mail: info@idsva.org.

Inter American University of Puerto Rico, San Germán Campus, Graduate Studies Center, Program in Fine Arts, San Germán, PR 00683-5008. Offers ceramics (MFA); drawing (MFA); engraving (MFA); painting (MFA); photography (MFA); sculpture (MFA). *Degree requirements:* For master's, comprehensive exam, thesis. *Entrance requirements:* For master's, GRE General Test or EXADEP, minimum GPA of 3.0. *Expenses:* Tuition: Part-time $202 per credit. Required fees: $258 per semester.

James Madison University, The Graduate School, College of Visual and Performing Arts, School of Art and Art History, Harrisonburg, VA 22807. Offers art education (MA); art history (MA); ceramics (MFA); drawing/painting (MFA); metal/jewelry (MFA); photography (MFA); printmaking (MFA); sculpture (MFA); studio art (MA); weaving/fibers (MFA). *Accreditation:* NASAD. Part-time programs available. *Faculty:* 8 full-time (5 women). *Students:* 10 full-time (6 women); includes 1 minority (Black or African American, non-Hispanic/Latino). Average age 27. In 2010, 3 master's awarded. *Degree requirements:* For master's, thesis (for some programs). *Entrance requirements:* For master's, GRE General Test, language exam in French or German, portfolio, 3 letters of recommendation, research paper. Additional exam requirements/recommendations for international students: Required—TOEFL. *Application deadline:* For fall admission, 2/15 priority date for domestic students, 2/15 for international students; for spring admission, 10/15 priority date for domestic students, 10/15 for international students. Applications are processed on a rolling basis. Application fee: $55. Electronic applications accepted. *Financial support:* In 2010–11, 9 students received support, including 3 teaching assistantships with full tuition reimbursements available (averaging $8,664 per year); Federal Work-Study and 6 graduate assistantships ($7382) also available. Financial award application deadline: 3/1; financial award applicants required to submit FAFSA. *Unit head:* William Srightman, Director, 540-568-6216. *Application contact:* Lynette M. Bible, Director of Graduate Admissions, 540-568-6395, Fax: 540-568-7860, E-mail: biblelm@jmu.edu.

John F. Kennedy University, Graduate School of Holistic Studies, Department of Arts and Consciousness, Program in Studio Arts, Pleasant Hill, CA 94523-4817. Offers MFA. Part-time and evening/weekend programs available. *Degree requirements:* For master's, thesis or alternative. *Entrance requirements:* For master's, interview, portfolio. Additional exam requirements/recommendations for international students: Required—TOEFL. *Expenses:* Contact institution.

Johnson State College, Program in Studio Arts, Johnson, VT 05656. Offers drawing (MFA); mixed media (MFA); painting (MFA); sculpture (MFA). Part-time programs available. Postbaccalaureate distance learning degree programs offered (minimal on-campus study). *Entrance requirements:* For master's, portfolio. Additional exam requirements/recommendations for international students: Required—TOEFL. *Expenses:* Contact institution.

Kansas State University, Graduate School, College of Arts and Sciences, Department of Art, Manhattan, KS 66506. Offers MFA. *Accreditation:* NASAD. Part-time programs available. *Degree requirements:* For master's, thesis, gallery exhibit. *Entrance requirements:* For master's, slides of artistic work, portfolio. Additional exam requirements/recommendations for international students: Required—TOEFL (minimum score 550 paper-based; 213 computer-based). Electronic applications accepted. *Faculty research:* Drawing, painting, sculpture, metalsmithing, visual communication.

Kean University, College of Visual and Performing Arts, Union, NJ 07083. Offers MA. Part-time and evening/weekend programs available. *Faculty:* 23 full-time (8 women). *Students:* 20 full-time (15 women), 54 part-time (41 women); includes 7 Black or African American, non-Hispanic/Latino; 5 Asian, non-Hispanic/Latino; 7 Hispanic/Latino; 1 Two or more races, non-Hispanic/Latino, 4 international. Average age 37. 39 applicants, 97% accepted, 21 enrolled. In 2010, 30 master's awarded. *Degree requirements:* For master's, comprehensive exam (for some programs), thesis (for some programs). *Entrance requirements:* For master's, minimum GPA of 3.0, 3 letters of recommendation, portfolio. *Application deadline:* For fall admission, 6/1 for domestic students; for spring admission, 11/1 for domestic students. Application fee: $75 ($150 for international students). Electronic applications accepted. *Expenses:* Tuition, state resident: full-time $10,872; part-time $500 per credit. Tuition, nonresident: full-time $14,736; part-time $614 per credit. Required fees: $2740.80; $125 per credit. Part-time tuition and fees vary according to course load and degree level. *Financial support:* In 2010–11, 3 research assistantships with full tuition reimbursements (averaging $3,263 per year) were awarded; unspecified assistantships also available. Financial award applicants required to submit FAFSA. *Unit head:* Dr. Holly Logue, Dean, 908-737-4376, Fax: 908-737-4377, E-mail: hlogue@kean.edu. *Application contact:* Ann-Marie Kay, Assistant Director for Graduate Admissions, 908-737-5922, Fax: 908-737-5925, E-mail: akay@kean.edu.

Kent State University, College of the Arts, School of Art, Kent, OH 44242-0001. Offers art education (MA); art history (MA); crafts (MA, MFA), including ceramics (MA), glass, jewelry/metals, textiles/art; fine art (MA, MFA), including drawing/painting, printmaking, sculpture. *Accreditation:* NASAD (one or more programs are accredited). *Degree requirements:* For master's, one foreign language, thesis. *Entrance requirements:* For master's, undergraduate degree in proposed area of study (for fine arts and crafts programs); minimum overall GPA of 2.75 (3.0 for art major); 3 letters of recommendation; portfolio (15-20 slides for MA, 20-25 for MFA). Additional exam requirements/recommendations for international students: Required—TOEFL. Electronic applications accepted. *Expenses:* Tuition, state resident: full-time $7866; part-time $437 per credit hour. Tuition, nonresident: full-time $14,022; part-time $779 per credit hour.

Laguna College of Art & Design, Graduate Program, Laguna Beach, CA 92651-1136. Offers painting (MFA). *Accreditation:* NASAD. *Entrance requirements:* For master's, BA with a studio concentration or BFA, minimum GPA of 3.0 in studio subjects, portfolio, resume. Additional exam requirements/recommendations for international students: Required—TOEFL (minimum score 550 paper-based). Electronic applications accepted.

Lamar University, College of Graduate Studies, College of Fine Arts and Communication, Department of Art, Beaumont, TX 77710. Offers art history (MA); photography (MA); studio art (MA); visual design (MA). Part-time and evening/weekend programs available. *Faculty:* 5 full-time (3 women). *Students:* 2 full-time (1 woman), 3 part-time (2 women). Average age 42. 3 applicants, 33% accepted, 0 enrolled. *Degree requirements:* For master's, thesis. *Entrance requirements:* For master's, GRE General Test, minimum GPA of 2.5 in last 60 hours of undergraduate course work. Additional exam requirements/recommendations for international students: Required—TOEFL. *Application deadline:* For fall admission, 8/1 priority date for domestic students; for spring admission, 12/1 for domestic students. Applications are processed on a rolling basis. Application fee: $25 ($50 for international students). *Expenses:* Tuition, state resident: full-time $4160; part-time $208 per credit hour. Tuition, nonresident: full-time $10,360; part-time $518 per credit hour. *Financial support:* Fellowships, career-related internships or fieldwork, Federal Work-Study, and scholarships/grants available. Financial award application deadline: 4/1. *Faculty research:* Nineteenth century academic paintings, metal casting, pigment color stability, computer-modified photography, manipulated photography. *Unit head:* Donna M. Meeks, Chair, 409-880-8141, Fax: 409-880-1799, E-mail: meeksdm@lub002.lamar.edu. *Application contact:* Debbie Piper, Coordinator of Graduate Admissions, 409-880-8356, Fax: 409-880-8414, E-mail: gradmissions@hal.lamar.edu.

Lehman College of the City University of New York, Division of Arts and Humanities, Department of Art, Bronx, NY 10468-1589. Offers MA, MFA. Part-time and evening/weekend programs available. *Entrance requirements:* For master's, 33 undergraduate credits in art, interview, portfolio. *Faculty research:* Graphic art, modern and contemporary art, sculpture, primitive and pre-Columbian art, medieval art.

Lesley University, Graduate School of Arts and Social Sciences, Program in Visual Arts, Cambridge, MA 02138-2790. Offers MFA. Postbaccalaureate distance learning degree programs offered. *Entrance requirements:* For master's, portfolio. Additional exam requirements/recommendations for international students: Required—TOEFL (minimum score 550 paper-based; 213 computer-based; 80 iBT). *Expenses:* Contact institution.

Lindenwood University, Graduate Programs, School of Fine and Performing Arts, St. Charles, MO 63301-1695. Offers arts management (MA); communication arts (MA); studio art (MA, MFA); theatre (MA, MFA). Part-time programs available. *Faculty:* 15 full-time (6 women), 5 part-time/adjunct (2 women). *Students:* 24 full-time (14 women), 16 part-time (12 women); includes 3 minority (all Black or African American, non-Hispanic/Latino), 3 international. Average age 30. 6 applicants, 2 enrolled. In 2010, 9 master's awarded. *Degree requirements:* For master's, thesis (for some programs). *Entrance requirements:* For master's, audition or interview, minimum GPA of 3.0, submission of portfolio, letter of recommendation. Additional exam requirements/recommendations for international students: Required—TOEFL (minimum score 550 paper-based; 213 computer-based; 80 iBT). *Application deadline:* For fall admission, 8/27 priority date for domestic and international students; for spring admission, 1/28 priority date for domestic and international students. Applications are processed on a rolling basis. Application fee: $30 ($100 for international students). Electronic applications accepted. *Expenses:* Tuition: Full-time $13,260; part-time $380 per credit hour. Required fees: $340. One-time fee: $30. Tuition and fees vary according to course level and course load. *Financial support:* In 2010–11, 10 students received support. Career-related internships or fieldwork, institutionally sponsored loans, tuition waivers (partial), and unspecified assistantships available. Financial award application deadline: 6/30; financial award applicants required to submit FAFSA. *Unit head:* Donnell Walsh, Dean of Fine Arts, 636-949-4853, Fax: 636-949-4910, E-mail: dwalsh@lindenwood.edu. *Application contact:* Brett Barger, Dean of Evening Admissions and Extension Campuses, 636-949-4934, Fax: 636-949-4109, E-mail: adultadmissions@lindenwood.edu.

Long Island University, C.W. Post Campus, School of Visual and Performing Arts, Department of Art, Brookville, NY 11548-1300. Offers art (MA); art education (MS); clinical art therapy (MA); fine art and design (MFA). Part-time and evening/weekend programs available. *Degree requirements:* For master's, thesis. Electronic applications accepted. *Faculty research:* Painting, sculpture, installation, computers, video.

Louisiana State University and Agricultural and Mechanical College, Graduate School, College of Art and Design, School of Art, Program in Studio Art, Baton Rouge, LA 70803. Offers ceramics (MFA); graphic design (MFA); painting and drawing (MFA); photography (MFA); printmaking (MFA); sculpture (MFA). *Accreditation:* NASAD. *Students:* 45 full-time (29 women), 3 part-time (all women); includes 1 Black or African American, non-Hispanic/Latino; 4 Asian, non-Hispanic/Latino, 4 international. Average age 29. 114 applicants, 21% accepted, 14 enrolled. In 2010, 15 master's awarded. *Degree requirements:* For master's, thesis. *Entrance requirements:* For master's, minimum GPA of 3.0. Additional exam requirements/recommendations for international students: Required—TOEFL (minimum score 550 paper-based; 213 computer-based; 79 iBT), IELTS (minimum score 6.5). *Application deadline:* For fall admission, 1/25 priority date for domestic students, 5/15 for international students; for spring admission, 10/15 for international students. Applications are processed on a rolling basis. Electronic applications accepted. *Financial support:* In 2010–11, 25 students received support; research assistantships with partial tuition reimbursements available, teaching assistantships, career-related internships or fieldwork, Federal Work-Study, institutionally sponsored loans, scholarships/grants, and unspecified assistantships available. Support available to part-time students. Financial award application deadline: 3/15. *Unit head:* Tom Neff, Graduate Coordinator, 225-578-5411, Fax: 225-578-1445, E-mail: tneff@lsu.edu.

Louisiana Tech University, Graduate School, College of Liberal Arts, School of Art, Ruston, LA 71272. Offers art and graphic design (MFA); photography (MFA); studio art (MFA). *Accreditation:* NASAD. Part-time programs available. *Degree requirements:* For master's, exhibit. *Entrance requirements:* For master's, GRE General Test, portfolio.

Maine College of Art, Program in Studio Arts, Portland, ME 04101. Offers MFA. *Accreditation:* NASAD. *Faculty:* 1 (woman) full-time, 26 part-time/adjunct (14 women). *Students:* 23 full-time (19 women). Average age 30. 56 applicants, 12 enrolled. In 2010, 11 master's awarded. *Entrance requirements:* Additional exam requirements/recommendations for international students: Required—TOEFL (minimum score 550 paper-based; 213 computer-based). *Application deadline:* Applications are processed on a rolling basis. Application fee: $40 ($60 for international students). Electronic applications accepted. *Expenses:* Tuition: Full-time $27,695. Required fees: $250. One-time fee: $50 full-time. *Financial support:* Application deadline: 3/1. *Unit head:* Rachel A. Katz, Administrative Director, MFA in Studio Art, 207-699-5030, Fax: 207-775-5087, E-mail: rkatz@meca.edu. *Application contact:* Rachel A. Katz, Administrative Director, MFA in Studio Art, 207-699-5030, Fax: 207-775-5087, E-mail: rkatz@meca.edu.

Marshall University, Academic Affairs Division, College of Fine Arts, Department of Art, Huntington, WV 25755. Offers MA. Evening/weekend programs available. *Faculty:* 12 full-time (7 women). *Students:* 5 full-time (2 women), 4 part-time (3 women). Average age 30. In 2010, 3 master's awarded. *Degree requirements:* For master's, thesis optional. *Entrance requirements:* For master's, GRE General Test, portfolio. Application fee: $40. *Unit head:* Prof. Byron Clercx, Chair, 304-696-5451, Fax: 304-696-6505, E-mail: clercx@marshall.edu. *Application contact:* Information Contact, 304-746-1900, Fax: 304-746-1902, E-mail: services@marshall.edu.

Maryland Institute College of Art, Graduate Studies, The Business of Art and Design Program, Baltimore, MD 21217. Offers MPS. Part-time programs available. Postbaccalaureate distance learning degree programs offered (minimal on-campus study). *Entrance requirements:* Additional exam requirements/recommendations for international students: Required—TOEFL (minimum score 550 paper-based; 213 computer-based; 80 iBT). *Application deadline:* For spring admission, 1/15 for domestic and international students. Application fee: $60. *Expenses:* Tuition: Full-time $34,550; part-time $1440 per credit hour. Required fees: $1140; $570 per term. *Financial support:* Applicants required to submit FAFSA. *Unit head:* Heather Bradbury, Manager, 410-225-2220, Fax: 410-225-2229, E-mail: hbradbury@mica.edu. *Application contact:* Scott G. Kelly, Associate Dean of Graduate Admission, 410-225-2256, Fax: 410-225-2408, E-mail: graduate@mica.edu.

Maryland Institute College of Art, Graduate Studies, Fine Arts Post Baccalaureate Certificate Program, Baltimore, MD 21217. Offers Certificate. *Faculty:* 1 full-time (0 women), 1 (woman) part-time/adjunct. *Students:* 23 full-time (15 women), 1 (woman) part-time; includes 4 minority (3 Asian, non-Hispanic/Latino; 1 Two or more races, non-Hispanic/Latino), 2 international. Average age 26. In 2010, 20 Certificates awarded. *Degree requirements:* For Certificate, thesis. *Entrance requirements:* For degree, portfolio, 40 studio credits, 6 credits in art history. Additional exam requirements/recommendations for international students: Required—TOEFL (minimum score 550 paper-based; 213 computer-based; 80 iBT). *Application deadline:* For fall admission, 1/15 for domestic and international students; for spring admission, 10/1 for domestic and international students. Application fee: $60. *Expenses:* Tuition: Full-time $34,550; part-time $1440 per credit hour. Required fees: $1140; $570 per term. *Financial support:* In 2010–11, 18 students received support, including 18 fellowships with partial tuition reimbursements available (averaging $5,500 per year); scholarships/grants also available. Financial award application deadline: 3/1; financial award applicants required to submit FAFSA. *Unit head:* William Schmidt, Director, 410-230-0568, Fax: 410-225-2408. *Application contact:* Scott G. Kelly, Associate Dean of Graduate Admission, 410-225-2256, Fax: 410-225-2408, E-mail: graduate@mica.edu.

Maryland Institute College of Art, Graduate Studies, Hoffberger School of Painting, Baltimore, MD 21217. Offers MFA. *Accreditation:* NASAD. *Faculty:* 1 (woman) full-time, 1 part-time/adjunct (0 women). *Students:* 16 full-time (8 women); includes 2 minority (1 Asian, non-Hispanic/Latino; 1 Hispanic/Latino), 2 international. Average age 27. In 2010, 6 master's awarded. *Degree requirements:* For master's, thesis, exhibit. *Entrance requirements:* For master's, portfolio, 40 studio credits, 6 credits in art history. Additional exam requirements/recommendations for international students: Required—TOEFL (minimum score 550 paper-based; 213 computer-based; 80 iBT). *Application deadline:* For fall admission, 1/15 for domestic and international students. Application fee: $60. *Expenses:* Tuition: Full-time $34,550; part-time $1440 per credit hour. Required fees: $1140; $570 per term. *Financial support:* In 2010–11, 16 students received support, including 16 fellowships with partial tuition reimbursements available (averaging $16,000 per year), 8 teaching assistantships (averaging $1,800 per year); career-related internships or fieldwork and scholarships/grants also available. Financial award application deadline: 3/1; financial award applicants required to submit FAFSA. *Unit head:* Joan Waltemath, Director, 410-225-2255, Fax: 410-225-2408, E-mail: graduate@mica.edu. *Application contact:* Scott G. Kelly, Associate Dean of Graduate Admission, 410-225-2256, Fax: 410-225-2408, E-mail: graduate@mica.edu.

Maryland Institute College of Art, Graduate Studies, Mount Royal School of Art, Baltimore, MD 21217. Offers painting (MFA). *Faculty:* 1 (woman) full-time, 4 part-time/adjunct (1 woman). *Students:* 25 full-time (16 women); includes 2 minority (1 Asian, non-Hispanic/Latino; 1 Two or more races, non-Hispanic/Latino), 3 international. Average age 27. In 2010, 15 master's awarded. *Degree requirements:* For master's, thesis, exhibit. *Entrance requirements:* For master's, 40 credits in studio art, 6 credits in art history, portfolio. Additional exam requirements/recommendations for international students: Required—TOEFL (minimum score 550 paper-based; 213 computer-based; 80 iBT). *Application deadline:* For fall admission, 1/15 for domestic and international students. Application fee: $60. *Expenses:* Tuition: Full-time $34,550; part-time $1440 per credit hour. Required fees: $1140; $570 per term. *Financial support:* In 2010–11, 15 students received support, including 15 fellowships with partial tuition reimbursements available (averaging $10,000 per year), 1 teaching assistantship (averaging $1,800 per year); career-related internships or fieldwork and scholarships/grants also available. Financial award application deadline: 3/1; financial award applicants required to submit FAFSA. *Unit head:*

Art/Fine Arts

Maryland Institute College of Art (continued)
Frances Barth, Director, 410-225-2347, Fax: 410-225-5275, E-mail: graduate@mica.edu. *Application contact:* Scott G. Kelly, Associate Dean of Graduate Admission, 410-225-2256, Fax: 410-225-2408, E-mail: graduate@mica.edu.

Maryland Institute College of Art, Graduate Studies, Program in Community Arts, Baltimore, MD 21217. Offers MA, MFA. Part-time programs available. *Faculty:* 2 full-time (1 woman), 3 part-time/adjunct (all women). *Students:* 1 (woman) full-time, 27 part-time (24 women); includes 5 minority (3 Black or African American, non-Hispanic/Latino; 1 American Indian or Alaska Native, non-Hispanic/Latino; 1 Asian, non-Hispanic/Latino), 1 international. Average age 30. In 2010, 15 master's awarded. *Degree requirements:* For master's, thesis. *Entrance requirements:* For master's, portfolio, 40 studio credits, 6 credits in art history. Additional exam requirements/recommendations for international students: Required—TOEFL (minimum score 550 paper-based; 213 computer-based). *Application deadline:* For fall admission, 1/15 for domestic and international students. Application fee: $60. *Expenses:* Tuition: Full-time $34,550; part-time $1440 per credit hour. Required fees: $1140; $570 per term. *Financial support:* In 2010–11, 9 students received support, including 9 fellowships with partial tuition reimbursements available (averaging $10,000 per year), 4 teaching assistantships; career-related internships or fieldwork and scholarships/grants also available. Financial award application deadline: 3/1; financial award applicants required to submit FAFSA. *Unit head:* Ken Krafchek, Director, 410-225-2587, Fax: 410-225-2574. *Application contact:* Scott G. Kelly, Associate Dean of Graduate Admission, 410-225-2256, Fax: 410-225-2408, E-mail: graduate@mica.edu.

Maryland Institute College of Art, Graduate Studies, Program in Studio Art, Baltimore, MD 21217. Offers MFA. Offered during summer only. Part-time programs available. *Faculty:* 2 full-time (1 woman), 1 (woman) part-time/adjunct. *Students:* 9 full-time (6 women), 28 part-time (15 women); includes 4 minority (1 Asian, non-Hispanic/Latino; 2 Hispanic/Latino; 1 Two or more races, non-Hispanic/Latino), 2 international. Average age 37. In 2010, 8 master's awarded. *Degree requirements:* For master's, thesis. *Entrance requirements:* For master's, portfolio, 40 studio credits, 6 credits in art history. Additional exam requirements/recommendations for international students: Required—TOEFL (minimum score 550 paper-based; 213 computer-based; 80 iBT). *Application deadline:* For fall admission, 1/15 for domestic and international students. Application fee: $60. *Expenses:* Tuition: Full-time $34,550; part-time $1440 per credit hour. Required fees: $1140; $570 per term. *Financial support:* In 2010–11, 37 students received support, including 37 fellowships with partial tuition reimbursements available (averaging $5,500 per year); teaching assistantships, career-related internships or fieldwork and scholarships/grants also available. Financial award application deadline: 3/1; financial award applicants required to submit FAFSA. *Unit head:* Zlata Baum, Director, 410-225-2297, Fax: 410-225-2257. *Application contact:* Scott G. Kelly, Associate Dean of Graduate Admission, 410-225-2256, Fax: 410-225-2408, E-mail: graduate@mica.edu.

Maryland Institute College of Art, Graduate Studies, Rinehart School of Sculpture, Baltimore, MD 21217. Offers MFA. *Accreditation:* NASAD. *Faculty:* 2 full-time (1 woman), 1 (woman) part-time/adjunct. *Students:* 9 full-time (5 women), 1 part-time (0 women); includes 1 minority (Asian, non-Hispanic/Latino), 3 international. Average age 31. In 2010, 6 master's awarded. *Degree requirements:* For master's, thesis, exhibit. *Entrance requirements:* For master's, portfolio, 40 studio credits, 6 credits in art history. Additional exam requirements/recommendations for international students: Required—TOEFL (minimum score 550 paper-based; 213 computer-based; 80 iBT). *Application deadline:* For fall admission, 1/15 for domestic and international students. Application fee: $60. *Expenses:* Tuition: Full-time $34,550; part-time $1440 per credit hour. Required fees: $1140; $570 per term. *Financial support:* In 2010–11, 10 students received support, including 10 fellowships with partial tuition reimbursements available (averaging $10,000 per year), 9 teaching assistantships (averaging $1,800 per year); career-related internships or fieldwork and scholarships/grants also available. Financial award application deadline: 3/1; financial award applicants required to submit FAFSA. *Unit head:* Maren Hassinger, Director, 410-225-2271, Fax: 410-225-2408. *Application contact:* Scott G. Kelly, Associate Dean of Graduate Admission, 410-225-2256, Fax: 410-225-2408, E-mail: graduate@mica.edu.

Marywood University, Academic Affairs, Insalaco College of Creative and Performing Arts, Art Department, Program in Studio Art, Scranton, PA 18509-1598. Offers advertising design (MA); ceramics (MA); clay (MA); graphic design (MA); illustration (MA); painting (MA); photography (MA); printmaking (MA); sculpture (MA); weaving (MA). *Accreditation:* NASAD. *Entrance requirements:* Additional exam requirements/recommendations for international students: Required—TOEFL (minimum score 550 paper-based; 213 computer-based; 79 iBT). Electronic applications accepted. *Expenses:* Tuition: Part-time $735 per credit. Required fees: $470 per semester. Tuition and fees vary according to degree level and campus/location. *Faculty research:* Texture and line in clay, cast bronze sculpture, color theories, book art and illustration, sculptural form.

Marywood University, Academic Affairs, Insalaco College of Creative and Performing Arts, Art Department, Program in Visual Arts, Scranton, PA 18509-1598. Offers advertising design (MFA); clay (MFA); graphic design (MFA); illustration (MFA); metals (MFA); painting (MFA); photography (MFA); printmaking (MFA). *Accreditation:* NASAD. *Entrance requirements:* Additional exam requirements/recommendations for international students: Required—TOEFL (minimum score 550 paper-based; 213 computer-based; 79 iBT). Electronic applications accepted. *Expenses:* Contact institution. *Faculty research:* Mariology, exploration of visual imagery, explorations involving drawing on the loom, clay as sculptural medium, oil paintings.

Marywood University, Academic Affairs, School of Architecture, Scranton, PA 18509-1598. Offers architecture (M Arch); studio art (MA), including interior design. *Entrance requirements:* Additional exam requirements/recommendations for international students: Required—TOEFL (minimum score 550 paper-based; 213 computer-based; 79 iBT). *Expenses:* Tuition: Part-time $735 per credit. Required fees: $470 per semester. Tuition and fees vary according to degree level and campus/location.

Massachusetts College of Art and Design, Graduate Programs, Master of Fine Arts (MFA) Program, Boston, MA 02115-5882. Offers ceramics (MFA); design (MFA); fibers (MFA); film/video (MFA); glass (MFA); media and performing arts (MFA); metals/jewelry (MFA); painting (MFA); photography (MFA); printmaking (MFA); sculpture (MFA). *Accreditation:* NASAD. *Faculty:* 14 full-time (7 women), 16 part-time/adjunct (10 women). *Students:* 86 full-time (51 women), 9 part-time (5 women); includes 10 minority (1 Asian, non-Hispanic/Latino; 6 Hispanic/Latino; 3 Two or more races, non-Hispanic/Latino), 14 international. Average age 34. 298 applicants, 28% accepted, 41 enrolled. In 2010, 40 master's awarded. *Degree requirements:* For master's, thesis, exhibit. *Entrance requirements:* For master's, 12 units of course work in art history, portfolio, resume, letters of reference, interview. Additional exam requirements/recommendations for international students: Required—TOEFL (minimum score 563 paper-based; 223 computer-based; 85 iBT); Recommended—IELTS (minimum score 6.5). *Application deadline:* For fall admission, 1/15 for domestic and international students. Application fee: $85. Electronic applications accepted. *Expenses:* Tuition, state resident: part-time $665 per credit. Tuition, nonresident: part-time $665 per credit. *Financial support:* In 2010–11, 19 fellowships (averaging $5,000 per year), 43 research assistantships (averaging $2,000 per year), 44 teaching assistantships (averaging $2,000 per year) were awarded; career-related internships or fieldwork and Federal Work-Study also available. Support available to part-time students. Financial award application deadline: 5/1; financial award applicants required to submit FAFSA. *Unit head:* George Creamer, Dean of Graduate Programs, 617-879-7163, Fax: 617-879-7171, E-mail: creamer@massart.edu. *Application contact:* George Creamer, Dean of Graduate Programs, 617-879-7163, Fax: 617-879-7171, E-mail: creamer@massart.edu.

Memphis College of Art, Graduate Programs, Program in Studio Art, Memphis, TN 38104-2764. Offers MFA. *Accreditation:* NASAD. *Faculty:* 26 full-time (15 women), 13 part-time/adjunct (8 women). *Students:* 27 full-time (17 women); includes 4 minority (2 Black or African American, non-Hispanic/Latino; 1 Asian, non-Hispanic/Latino; 1 Hispanic/Latino), 1 international. Average age 28. 53 applicants, 43% accepted, 13 enrolled. In 2010, 8 master's awarded. *Degree requirements:* For master's, thesis. *Entrance requirements:* For master's, portfolio, interview, resume. Additional exam requirements/recommendations for international students: Required—TOEFL (minimum score 525 paper-based; 195 computer-based). *Application deadline:* For fall admission, 2/15 priority date for domestic and international students; for spring admission, 11/1 priority date for domestic and international students. Application fee: $50. Electronic applications accepted. *Expenses:* Tuition: Full-time $24,300; part-time $1012 per credit hour. Required fees: $650; $325 per semester. Tuition and fees vary according to course load. *Financial support:* Application deadline: 8/1. *Unit head:* Howard Paine, Director, 901-272-5100, E-mail: hpaine@mca.edu. *Application contact:* Annette Moore, Dean of Admissions, 901-272-5153, Fax: 901-272-5158, E-mail: amoore@mca.edu.

See Display on next page and Close-Up on page 221.

Miami International University of Art & Design, Program in Visual Arts, Miami, FL 33132-1418. Offers MFA. Postbaccalaureate distance learning degree programs offered. *Application contact:* Office of Graduate Admissions, 305-428-5700.

See Close-Up on page 129.

Miami University, Graduate School, School of Fine Arts, Department of Art, Program in Studio Art, Oxford, OH 45056. Offers MFA. *Accreditation:* NASAD. *Degree requirements:* For master's, thesis, final project. *Entrance requirements:* For master's, portfolio, minimum undergraduate GPA of 3.0 during previous 2 years or 2.75 overall. *Application deadline:* For fall admission, 2/1 priority date for domestic students. Applications are processed on a rolling basis. Application fee: $35. *Expenses:* Tuition, state resident: full-time $11,616; part-time $484 per credit hour. Tuition, nonresident: full-time $25,656; part-time $1069 per credit hour. Required fees: $528. *Financial support:* Application deadline: 3/1. *Unit head:* Prof. Ellen Price, Graduate Director, 513-529-7128, E-mail: priceej@muohio.edu. *Application contact:* Prof. Ellen Price, Graduate Director, 513-529-7128, E-mail: priceej@muohio.edu.

Michigan State University, The Graduate School, College of Arts and Letters, Department of Art and Art History, East Lansing, MI 48824. Offers studio art (MFA). *Entrance requirements:* For master's, minimum GPA of 3.0, portfolio, resume. Additional exam requirements/recommendations for international students: Required—TOEFL, Michigan State University ELT (minimum score 85), Michigan English Language Assessment Battery (minimum score 83). Electronic applications accepted.

Mills College, Graduate Studies, Department of Art, Oakland, CA 94613-1000. Offers ceramics (MFA); intermedia (MFA); painting (MFA); photography (MFA); sculpture (MFA). *Faculty:* 5 full-time (4 women), 9 part-time/adjunct (5 women). *Students:* 24 full-time (15 women); includes 7 minority (1 Black or African American, non-Hispanic/Latino; 2 Asian, non-Hispanic/Latino; 1 Hispanic/Latino; 3 Two or more races, non-Hispanic/Latino). Average age 33. 83 applicants, 35% accepted, 12 enrolled. In 2010, 10 master's awarded. *Degree requirements:* For master's, thesis or alternative, exhibit. *Entrance requirements:* For master's, portfolio, artist statement. Additional exam requirements/recommendations for international students: Required—TOEFL. *Application deadline:* For fall admission, 2/1 for domestic students, 12/15 for international students. Application fee: $50. *Expenses:* Contact institution. *Financial support:* In 2010–11, 19 students received support, including 19 fellowships (averaging $12,615 per year), 13 teaching assistantships with partial tuition reimbursements available (averaging $15,009 per year); scholarships/grants and unspecified assistantships also available. Financial award application deadline: 2/1; financial award applicants required to submit FAFSA. *Faculty research:* Experimental film and video, public art projects, ecological design, contemporary art philosophy, sound installations. *Unit head:* Mary-Ann Milford, Chairperson, 510-430-3142, Fax: 510-430-3314. *Application contact:* Jessica King, Graduate Admission Specialist, 510-430-3305, Fax: 510-430-2159, E-mail: grad-studies@mills.edu.

Minneapolis College of Art and Design, Certificate Programs, Minneapolis, MN 55404-4347. Offers design (Certificate); fine arts (Certificate); graphic design (Certificate); media (Certificate); sustainable design (Certificate). Part-time programs available. Postbaccalaureate distance learning degree programs offered. *Degree requirements:* For Certificate, final project. *Entrance requirements:* For degree, resume, portfolio, letter of recommendation. Additional exam requirements/recommendations for international students: Required—TOEFL (minimum score 550 paper-based; 213 computer-based; 79 iBT). Electronic applications accepted. *Faculty research:* Visual arts.

Minneapolis College of Art and Design, Program in Visual Studies, Minneapolis, MN 55404-4347. Offers animation (MFA); comic art (MFA); drawing (MFA); filmmaking (MFA); fine arts (MFA); furniture design (MFA); graphic design (MFA); illustration (MFA); interactive media (MFA); painting (MFA); photography (MFA); printmaking (MFA); sculpture (MFA). *Accreditation:* NASAD. Part-time programs available. *Degree requirements:* For master's, thesis, thesis exhibit. *Entrance requirements:* For master's, portfolio of visual artwork, resume, 3 letters of recommendation. Additional exam requirements/recommendations for international students: Required—TOEFL (minimum score 550 paper-based; 213 computer-based; 79 iBT). Electronic applications accepted. *Faculty research:* Visual arts: animation, comic art, drawing, filmmaking, furniture design, graphic design, illustration, interactive media, painting, photography, printmaking, sculpture.

Minnesota State University Mankato, College of Graduate Studies, College of Arts and Humanities, Department of Art, Mankato, MN 56001. Offers studio art (MA); teaching art (MAT). *Accreditation:* NASAD (one or more programs are accredited). Part-time programs available. *Students:* 4 full-time (0 women), 4 part-time (2 women). *Degree requirements:* For master's, one foreign language, comprehensive exam, thesis or alternative. *Entrance requirements:* For master's, minimum GPA of 3.0 during previous 2 years, portfolio (MA). Additional exam requirements/recommendations for international students: Required—TOEFL. *Application deadline:* For fall admission, 7/1 priority date for domestic students, 5/1 for international students; for spring admission, 11/1 for domestic students, 10/1 for international students. Applications are processed on a rolling basis. Application fee: $40. Electronic applications accepted. *Financial support:* Research assistantships, teaching assistantships with full tuition reimbursements, unspecified assistantships available. Financial award application deadline: 3/15; financial award applicants required to submit FAFSA. *Faculty research:* Photographic documentation. *Unit head:* Brian Frink, Graduate Coordinator, 507-389-6412. *Application contact:* 507-389-2321, E-mail: grad@mnsu.edu.

Mississippi College, Graduate School, College of Arts and Sciences, School of Christian Studies and the Arts, Department of Art, Clinton, MS 39058. Offers M Ed, MA, MFA. Part-time and evening/weekend programs available. *Degree requirements:* For master's, one foreign language, comprehensive exam, thesis (for some programs). *Entrance requirements:* For master's, GRE or NTE, minimum GPA of 2.5. Additional exam requirements/recommendations for international students: Recommended—IELTS. Electronic applications accepted.

Missouri State University, Graduate College, College of Arts and Letters, Department of Art and Design, Springfield, MO 65897. Offers secondary education (MS Ed), including art. Part-time programs available. *Entrance requirements:* For master's, minimum GPA of 3.0, 9-12 teaching certification. Additional exam requirements/recommendations for international students: Required—TOEFL (minimum score 550 paper-based; 213 computer-based; 79 iBT). Electronic applications accepted. *Expenses:* Tuition, state resident: full-time $3348; part-time $186 per credit hour. Tuition, nonresident: full-time $6696; part-time $372 per credit hour. Required fees: $238 per semester. Tuition and fees vary according to course level, course load and program.

Montana State University, College of Graduate Studies, College of Arts and Architecture, School of Art, Bozeman, MT 59717. Offers art (MFA); art history (MA). *Accreditation:* NASAD (one or more programs are accredited). Part-time programs available. *Faculty:* 15 full-time (6 women), 8 part-time/adjunct (4 women). *Students:* 14 full-time (10 women), 3 part-time (all women); includes 1 minority (Hispanic/Latino). Average age 28. 49 applicants, 16% accepted,

6 enrolled. *Degree requirements:* For master's, comprehensive exam, thesis. *Entrance requirements:* For master's, GRE General Test, undergraduate degree in art. Additional exam requirements/recommendations for international students: Required—TOEFL (minimum score 550 paper-based; 213 computer-based). *Application deadline:* For fall admission, 7/15 priority date for domestic students, 5/15 priority date for international students; for spring admission, 12/1 priority date for domestic students, 10/1 priority date for international students. Applications are processed on a rolling basis. Application fee: $30. Electronic applications accepted. *Expenses:* Tuition, state resident: full-time $5553.90. Tuition, nonresident: full-time $14,646. Required fees: $1233. *Financial support:* In 2010–11, 15 students received support, including 15 teaching assistantships with partial tuition reimbursements available (averaging $7,725 per year); Federal Work-Study, scholarships/grants, health care benefits, tuition waivers (partial), and unspecified assistantships also available. Financial award application deadline: 3/1; financial award applicants required to submit FAFSA. *Faculty research:* Encaustic painting, wild clay research, environmentally friendly kiln fuel, Roman wall paintings, French revolutionary portraiture. *Unit head:* Vaughan Judge, Head, 406-994-4501, Fax: 406-994-3680, E-mail: vaughan.judge@montana.edu. *Application contact:* Dr. Carl A. Fox, Vice Provost for Graduate Education, 406-994-4145, Fax: 406-994-7433, E-mail: gradstudy@montana.edu.

Montclair State University, The Graduate School, School of the Arts, Department of Art and Design, Montclair, NJ 07043-1624. Offers art (Certificate); fine arts (MA), including museum management, studio; studio art (MFA). *Accreditation:* NASAD (one or more programs are accredited). Part-time and evening/weekend programs available. *Faculty:* 28 full-time (12 women), 91 part-time/adjunct (50 women). *Students:* 37 full-time (25 women), 30 part-time (24 women); includes 2 Black or African American, non-Hispanic/Latino; 4 Asian, non-Hispanic/Latino; 5 Hispanic/Latino; 2 Two or more races, non-Hispanic/Latino, 3 international. Average age 34. 49 applicants, 71% accepted, 18 enrolled. In 2010, 16 master's awarded. *Degree requirements:* For master's, project. *Entrance requirements:* For master's, GRE General Test or MAT (MA), portfolio, undergraduate degree in fine arts or equivalent, 2 letters of recommendation, teaching certificate (art education). Additional exam requirements/recommendations for international students: Required—TOEFL (minimum iBT score of 83) or IELTS. *Application deadline:* For fall admission, 2/1 for domestic and international students. Applications are processed on a rolling basis. Application fee: $60. Electronic applications accepted. *Expenses:* Tuition, state resident: part-time $501.34 per credit. Tuition, nonresident: part-time $773.88 per credit. Required fees: $71.15 per credit. *Financial support:* In 2010–11, 4 research assistantships with full tuition reimbursements (averaging $7,000 per year) were awarded; Federal Work-Study, scholarships/grants, and unspecified assistantships also available. Support available to part-time students. Financial award application deadline: 3/1; financial award applicants required to submit FAFSA. *Unit head:* Dr. Scott Gordley, Chairperson, 973-655-7295. *Application contact:* Amy Aiello, Director of Graduate Admissions and Operations, 973-655-5147, E-mail: graduate.school@montclair.edu.

Moore College of Art & Design, Program in Studio Art, Philadelphia, PA 19103. Offers MFA. *Accreditation:* NASAD. *Degree requirements:* For master's, thesis. *Entrance requirements:* For master's, bachelor's degree in visual arts or another field with completion of 15 art history credits; minimum GPA of 3.0; on-site interview; portfolio; 3 letters of recommendation; resume.

Morehead State University, Graduate Programs, Caudill College of Arts, Humanities and Social Sciences, Department of Art and Design, Morehead, KY 40351. Offers art education (MA); graphic design (MA); studio art (MA). Part-time and evening/weekend programs available. *Degree requirements:* For master's, comprehensive exam, thesis (for some programs), oral exam during exhibition. *Entrance requirements:* For master's, GRE General Test, minimum undergraduate GPA of 3.0 in major, 2.5 overall; portfolio; bachelor's degree in art. Additional exam requirements/recommendations for international students: Required—TOEFL (minimum score 500 paper-based; 173 computer-based). Electronic applications accepted. *Faculty research:* Computer art, painting, drawing, ceramics, photography.

National University, Academic Affairs, College of Letters and Sciences, Department of Art and Humanities, La Jolla, CA 92037-1011. Offers creative writing (MFA); English (MA); history (MA). Part-time and evening/weekend programs available. Postbaccalaureate distance learning degree programs offered (no on-campus study). *Faculty:* 17 full-time (6 women), 198 part-time/adjunct (110 women). *Students:* 198 full-time (144 women), 534 part-time (364 women); includes 99 Black or African American, non-Hispanic/Latino; 6 American Indian or Alaska Native, non-Hispanic/Latino; 10 Asian, non-Hispanic/Latino; 54 Hispanic/Latino; 14 Two or more races, non-Hispanic/Latino. Average age 38. 424 applicants, 100% accepted, 289 enrolled. In 2010, 222 master's awarded. *Degree requirements:* For master's, thesis (for some programs). *Entrance requirements:* For master's, interview, minimum GPA of 2.5. Additional exam requirements/recommendations for international students: Required—TOEFL (minimum score 550 paper-based; 213 computer-based; 79 iBT), IELTS (minimum score 6). *Application deadline:* Applications are processed on a rolling basis. Application fee: $60 ($65 for international students). Electronic applications accepted. *Expenses:* Tuition: Full-time $9450; part-time $350 per unit. Required fees: $350 per unit. One-time fee: $60. *Financial support:* Career-related internships or fieldwork, institutionally sponsored loans, scholarships/grants, and tuition waivers (partial) available. Support available to part-time students. Financial award application deadline: 6/30; financial award applicants required to submit FAFSA. *Unit head:* Dr. Janet Baker, Chair, 858-642-8472, Fax: 858-642-8715, E-mail: jbaker@nu.edu. *Application contact:* Dominick Giovanniello, Associate Regional Dean—San Diego, 800-NAT-UNIV, Fax: 858-541-7792, E-mail: dgiovann@nu.edu.

New Jersey City University, Graduate Studies and Continuing Education, William J. Maxwell College of Arts and Sciences, Department of Art, Jersey City, NJ 07305-1597. Offers art (MFA); art education (MA); studio art (MFA). *Accreditation:* NASAD. Part-time and evening/weekend programs available. *Degree requirements:* For master's, thesis or alternative, exhibit. *Entrance requirements:* For master's, GRE General Test or MAT, portfolio. Additional exam requirements/recommendations for international students: Required—TOEFL.

New Mexico State University, Graduate School, College of Arts and Sciences, Department of Art, Las Cruces, NM 88003-8001. Offers art history (MA); ceramics (MA, MFA); design (MA, MFA); drawing (MFA); metals (MA, MFA); painting (MFA); photography (MFA); sculpture (MA, MFA). *Faculty:* 9 full-time (5 women), 3 part-time/adjunct (1 woman). *Students:* 18 full-time (10 women), 2 part-time (both women); includes 6 minority (1 American Indian or Alaska Native, non-Hispanic/Latino; 1 Asian, non-Hispanic/Latino; 4 Hispanic/Latino), 1 international. Average age 34. 26 applicants, 77% accepted, 11 enrolled. In 2010, 11 master's awarded. *Degree requirements:* For master's, comprehensive exam (for some programs), thesis, thesis exhibit. *Entrance requirements:* For master's, portfolio, 10-page paper (art history). *Application deadline:* For fall admission, 2/15 for domestic students; for winter admission, 10/15 for domestic students; for spring admission, 7/15 for domestic students. Application fee: $30 ($50 for international students). Electronic applications accepted. *Expenses:* Tuition, state resident: full-time $4536; part-time $242 per credit. Tuition, nonresident: full-time $15,816; part-time $712 per credit. Required fees: $636 per term. *Financial support:* In 2010–11, 17 teaching assistantships (averaging $6,640 per year) were awarded; research assistantships, Federal Work-Study and health care benefits also available. Support available to part-time students. Financial award application deadline: 3/1; financial award applicants required to submit FAFSA. *Faculty research:* Painting, graphic design, sculpture, ceramics, photography, jewelry. *Unit head:* Dr. Thom Brown, Head, 575-646-1705, Fax: 575-646-8036, E-mail: artdept@nmsu.edu. *Application contact:* Dr. Thom Brown, Head, 575-646-1705, Fax: 575-646-8036, E-mail: artdept@nmsu.edu.

The New School: A University, Parsons The New School for Design, Program in Fine Arts, New York, NY 10011. Offers MFA. *Degree requirements:* For master's, thesis. *Entrance requirements:* For master's, portfolio. Additional exam requirements/recommendations for international students: Required—TOEFL (minimum score 580 paper-based; 237 computer-based; 92 iBT). Electronic applications accepted.

Art/Fine Arts

New York Academy of Art, Program in Figurative Art, New York, NY 10013-2911. Offers MFA. *Degree requirements:* For master's, project. *Entrance requirements:* For master's, slide portfolio. Additional exam requirements/recommendations for international students: Required—TOEFL.

New York Institute of Technology, Graduate Division, School of Arts and Sciences, Program in Fine Arts, Old Westbury, NY 11568-8000. Offers computer graphics and animation (MFA); fine arts and technology (MFA); graphic design (MFA). Part-time and evening/weekend programs available. *Students:* 34 full-time (21 women), 6 part-time (1 woman); includes 14 minority (7 Black or African American, non-Hispanic/Latino; 2 Asian, non-Hispanic/Latino; 4 Hispanic/Latino; 1 Two or more races, non-Hispanic/Latino), 11 international. Average age 32. In 2010, 5 master's awarded. *Degree requirements:* For master's, thesis or alternative. *Entrance requirements:* Additional exam requirements/recommendations for international students: Required—TOEFL (minimum score 550 paper-based; 213 computer-based). *Application deadline:* For fall admission, 7/1 priority date for domestic students; for spring admission, 12/1 priority date for domestic students. Applications are processed on a rolling basis. Application fee: $50. Electronic applications accepted. *Expenses:* Tuition: Part-time $835 per credit. *Financial support:* Research assistantships, career-related internships or fieldwork, Federal Work-Study, institutionally sponsored loans, tuition waivers (partial), and unspecified assistantships available. Support available to part-time students. Financial award applicants required to submit FAFSA. *Unit head:* Dr. Roger Yu, Dean, 516-686-7700, Fax: 516-686-1192, E-mail: ryu@nyit.edu. *Application contact:* Dr. Jacquelyn Nealon, Vice President for Enrollment Services, 516-686-7925, Fax: 516-686-7597, E-mail: jnealon@nyit.edu.

New York Studio School of Drawing, Painting and Sculpture, Certificate Program, New York, NY 10011. Offers studio art (Certificate).

New York Studio School of Drawing, Painting and Sculpture, MFA Program, New York, NY 10011. Offers painting (MFA); sculpture (MFA).

New York University, Graduate School of Arts and Science, Institute of Fine Arts, New York, NY 10012-1019. Offers art history and archaeology (MA, PhD), including architectural studies (PhD), art history and archaeology, classical art and archaeology (PhD), curatorial studies (PhD), East and South Asian art (PhD), Near Eastern art and archaeology (PhD); MA/Diploma; PhD/Certificate. Part-time programs available. *Faculty:* 19 full-time (5 women). *Students:* 243 full-time (192 women), 59 part-time (47 women); includes 2 Black or African American, non-Hispanic/Latino; 20 Asian, non-Hispanic/Latino; 8 Hispanic/Latino, 29 international. Average age 32. 394 applicants, 27% accepted, 57 enrolled. In 2010, 29 master's, 12 doctorates awarded. Terminal master's awarded for partial completion of doctoral program. *Degree requirements:* For master's, 2 foreign languages, thesis or alternative, 2 qualifying papers; for doctorate, 2 foreign languages, thesis/dissertation. *Entrance requirements:* For master's, GRE General Test; for doctorate, GRE General Test, MA. Additional exam requirements/recommendations for international students: Required—TOEFL. *Application deadline:* For fall admission, 12/15 for domestic students. Application fee: $90. *Financial support:* Fellowships with tuition reimbursements, research assistantships with tuition reimbursements, teaching assistantships with tuition reimbursements, career-related internships or fieldwork, Federal Work-Study, institutionally sponsored loans, and tuition waivers (partial) available. Financial award application deadline: 12/15; financial award applicants required to submit FAFSA. *Unit head:* Patricia Rubin, Chair, 212-992-5800, Fax: 212-992-5807, E-mail: ifa.program@nyu.edu. *Application contact:* Priscilla Saucek, Director of Graduate Studies, 212-992-5800, Fax: 212-992-5807, E-mail: ifa.program@nyu.edu.

New York University, NYU in Madrid, Madrid, NY 10012-1019, Spain. Offers creative writing in Spanish (MFA); Spanish (PhD); Spanish and Latin American literatures and cultures (MA); Spanish language and translation (MA).

New York University, Steinhardt School of Culture, Education, and Human Development, Department of Art and Art Professions, Program in Studio Art, New York, NY 10003. Offers MA, MFA, Advanced Certificate. Part-time programs available. *Faculty:* 15 full-time (7 women). *Students:* 20 full-time (8 women), 9 part-time (all women); includes 2 Black or African American, non-Hispanic/Latino; 6 Asian, non-Hispanic/Latino; 3 Hispanic/Latino, 4 international. Average age 29. 301 applicants, 4% accepted, 10 enrolled. In 2010, 22 master's awarded. *Degree requirements:* For master's, thesis (for some programs). *Entrance requirements:* For master's, portfolio, interview, presentation. Additional exam requirements/recommendations for international students: Required—TOEFL. *Application deadline:* For fall admission, 12/1 priority date for domestic and international students. Applications are processed on a rolling basis. Application fee: $75. Electronic applications accepted. *Financial support:* Career-related internships or fieldwork, Federal Work-Study, institutionally sponsored loans, scholarships/grants, tuition waivers (partial), and unspecified assistantships available. Support available to part-time students. Financial award application deadline: 2/1; financial award applicants required to submit FAFSA. *Faculty research:* Media and culture, video art and digital media, multimedia works, critical theory, memory and history, performance and text. *Application contact:* 212-998-5030, Fax: 212-995-4328, E-mail: stein.hardt.gradadmissions@nyu.edu.

New York University, Steinhardt School of Culture, Education, and Human Development, Department of Art and Art Professions, Program in Visual Culture, New York, NY 10012-1019. Offers costume studies (MA). Part-time programs available. *Students:* 23 full-time (22 women), 10 part-time (9 women); includes 5 Black or African American, non-Hispanic/Latino; 2 Asian, non-Hispanic/Latino, 9 international. Average age 26. 37 applicants, 68% accepted, 17 enrolled. In 2010, 24 master's awarded. *Degree requirements:* For master's, thesis (for some programs). *Entrance requirements:* Additional exam requirements/recommendations for international students: Required—TOEFL. *Application deadline:* For fall admission, 12/1 priority date for domestic and international students. Applications are processed on a rolling basis. Application fee: $75. Electronic applications accepted. *Financial support:* Career-related internships or fieldwork, Federal Work-Study, institutionally sponsored loans, scholarships/grants, and tuition waivers available. Support available to part-time students. Financial award application deadline: 2/1; financial award applicants required to submit FAFSA. *Faculty research:* Textiles as material culture, contemporary visual culture and globalization, cultural theory. *Unit head:* Prof. Nancy Deihl, Director, 212-998-5762, E-mail: nbd2012@nyu.edu. *Application contact:* 212-998-5030, Fax: 212-995-4328, E-mail: steinhardt.gradadmissions@nyu.edu.

New York University, Tisch School of the Arts Asia, Singapore, NY 248923, Singapore. Offers animation and digital arts (MFA); dramatic writing (MFA); film production (MFA). *Entrance requirements:* Additional exam requirements/recommendations for international students: Required—TOEFL (minimum score 610 paper-based; 250 computer-based; 105 iBT). Electronic applications accepted.

New York University, Tisch School of the Arts, Program in Arts Politics, New York, NY 10012-1019. Offers MA. *Faculty:* 3 full-time (2 women), 4 part-time/adjunct (3 women). *Students:* 10 full-time (9 women), 1 (woman) part-time; includes 1 Black or African American, non-Hispanic/Latino; 3 Asian, non-Hispanic/Latino. Average age 25. 45 applicants, 58% accepted. *Degree requirements:* For master's, thesis. *Entrance requirements:* For master's, professional resume, writing sample, statement of purpose. Additional exam requirements/recommendations for international students: Required—TOEFL or IELTS. *Application deadline:* For fall admission, 1/1 for domestic and international students. Application fee: $60. *Financial support:* In 2010–11, 2 students received support. Federal Work-Study and scholarships/grants available. Financial award application deadline: 2/15; financial award applicants required to submit FAFSA. *Unit head:* Randy Martin, Director of the program, 212-992-8248. *Application contact:* Dan Sandford, Director of Graduate Admissions, 212-998-1918, Fax: 212-995-4060, E-mail: tisch.gradadmissions@nyu.edu.

Norfolk State University, School of Graduate Studies, School of Liberal Arts, Department of Fine Arts, Norfolk, VA 23504. Offers visual studies (MA, MFA). Part-time programs available. *Degree requirements:* For master's, thesis or alternative. *Entrance requirements:* For master's,

portfolio, interview, letters of recommendation. Additional exam requirements/recommendations for international students: Required—TOEFL (minimum score 500 paper-based).

Northeastern University, College of Arts, Media and Design, Department of Art + Design, Boston, MA 02115-5096. Offers studio art (MFA). Program offered jointly with School of the Museum of Fine Arts, Boston. *Faculty:* 16 full-time (10 women), 18 part-time/adjunct (10 women). *Students:* 1 full-time (0 women). *Degree requirements:* For master's, thesis exhibition. *Entrance requirements:* Additional exam requirements/recommendations for international students: Required—TOEFL. *Application deadline:* For fall admission, 1/15 for domestic and international students. Application fee: $50. Electronic applications accepted. *Financial support:* In 2010–11, 1 fellowship (averaging $17,040 per year) was awarded; Federal Work-Study and tuition waivers (partial) also available. Financial award application deadline: 2/1; financial award applicants required to submit FAFSA. *Unit head:* Prof. Russell Pensyl, Chair, 617-373-7926, E-mail: r.pensyl@neu.edu. *Application contact:* Jo-Anne Dickinson, Graduate Admissions Contact, 617-373-5990, Fax: 617-373-7281, E-mail: gsas@neu.edu.

Northern Illinois University, Graduate School, College of Visual and Performing Arts, School of Art, De Kalb, IL 60115-2854. Offers MA, MFA, MS. *Accreditation:* NASAD (one or more programs are accredited). Part-time and evening/weekend programs available. *Faculty:* 36 full-time (15 women), 1 (woman) part-time/adjunct. *Students:* 63 full-time (33 women), 36 part-time (24 women); includes 2 Black or African American, non-Hispanic/Latino; 2 Asian, non-Hispanic/Latino; 10 Hispanic/Latino; 1 Two or more races, non-Hispanic/Latino, 5 international. Average age 30. 83 applicants, 45% accepted, 22 enrolled. In 2010, 30 master's awarded. *Degree requirements:* For master's, variable foreign language requirement, comprehensive exam, thesis (for some programs), show or project. *Entrance requirements:* For master's, GRE General Test, minimum GPA of 2.75, portfolio. Additional exam requirements/recommendations for international students: Required—TOEFL (minimum score 550 paper-based; 213 computer-based). *Application deadline:* For fall and spring admission, 3/1 for domestic and international students. Applications are processed on a rolling basis. Application fee: $30. Electronic applications accepted. *Expenses:* Tuition, state resident: full-time $7200; part-time $300 per credit hour. Tuition, nonresident: full-time $14,400; part-time $600 per credit hour. Required fees: $79 per credit hour. *Financial support:* In 2010–11, 1 research assistantship with full tuition reimbursement, 65 teaching assistantships with full tuition reimbursements were awarded; fellowships with full tuition reimbursements, career-related internships or fieldwork, Federal Work-Study, scholarships/grants, tuition waivers (full), and staff assistantships also available. Support available to part-time students. Financial award applicants required to submit FAFSA. *Faculty research:* Art education, portfolio assessment, central European design history, relationship between modern art and industrialism. *Unit head:* Doug Boughton, Director, 815-753-7850, Fax: 815-753-7701, E-mail: dboughton@niu.edu. *Application contact:* Yale Factor, Graduate Coordinator, 815-753-3801, E-mail: yfactor@niu.edu.

Northwestern State University of Louisiana, Graduate Studies and Research, School of Creative and Performing Arts, Program in Art, Natchitoches, LA 71497. Offers fine and graphic arts (MA). *Accreditation:* NASAD. *Degree requirements:* For master's, comprehensive exam, thesis or alternative. *Entrance requirements:* For master's, GRE General Test, minimum undergraduate GPA of 2.5.

Northwestern University, The Graduate School, Judd A. and Marjorie Weinberg College of Arts and Sciences, Department of Art Theory and Practice, Evanston, IL 60208. Offers visual arts (MFA). Admissions and degrees offered through The Graduate School. *Degree requirements:* For master's, essay, exhibit. *Entrance requirements:* For master's, 20 slides of recent work. Additional exam requirements/recommendations for international students: Required—TOEFL. Electronic applications accepted.

NSCAD University, Program in Fine Arts, Halifax, NS B3J 3J6, Canada. Offers craft (MFA); design (M Des); fine and media arts (MFA). *Degree requirements:* For master's, thesis, exhibit. *Entrance requirements:* For master's, portfolio, at least 5 art history classes. Additional exam requirements/recommendations for international students: Required—Michigan English Language Assessment Battery (minimum score: 80), CanTEST (minimum score: 4.5), CAEL (minimum score: 70); Recommended—TOEFL (minimum score 575 paper-based; 233 computer-based; 90 iBT), IELTS (minimum score 6.5).

The Ohio State University, Graduate School, College of Arts and Sciences, Division of Arts and Humanities, Department of Art, Columbus, OH 43210. Offers MFA. *Accreditation:* NASAD. *Faculty:* 27. *Students:* 49 full-time (25 women), 1 (woman) part-time; includes 1 Black or African American, non-Hispanic/Latino; 1 American Indian or Alaska Native, non-Hispanic/Latino; 1 Asian, non-Hispanic/Latino; 1 Hispanic/Latino; 1 Two or more races, non-Hispanic/Latino, 6 international. Average age 31. In 2010, 18 master's awarded. *Degree requirements:* For master's, thesis, exhibit, oral exams. *Entrance requirements:* For master's, portfolio. Additional exam requirements/recommendations for international students: Recommended—TOEFL (minimum score 600 paper-based; 250 computer-based). *Application deadline:* For fall admission, 8/15 priority date for domestic students, 7/1 priority date for international students; for winter admission, 12/1 priority date for domestic students, 11/1 priority date for international students; for spring admission, 3/1 priority date for domestic students, 2/1 priority date for international students. Applications are processed on a rolling basis. Application fee: $40 ($50 for international students). Electronic applications accepted. *Expenses:* Tuition, state resident: full-time $10,605. Tuition, nonresident: full-time $26,535. Tuition and fees vary according to course load and program. *Financial support:* Fellowships, teaching assistantships, Federal Work-Study, institutionally sponsored loans, and unspecified assistantships available. Support available to part-time students. *Unit head:* Sergio Soave, Chair, 614-292-5072, E-mail: soave.1@osu.edu. *Application contact:* 614-292-9444, Fax: 614-292-3895, E-mail: domestic.grad@osu.edu.

Ohio University, Graduate College, College of Fine Arts, School of Art, Athens, OH 45701-2979. Offers art history (MA); ceramics (MFA); graphic design (MFA); painting (MFA); photography (MFA); printmaking (MFA); sculpture (MFA). Part-time programs available. *Students:* 62 full-time (35 women), 4 part-time (3 women); includes 5 minority (1 American Indian or Alaska Native, non-Hispanic/Latino; 1 Asian, non-Hispanic/Latino; 3 Hispanic/Latino), 7 international. 181 applicants, 19% accepted, 28 enrolled. In 2010, 14 master's awarded. *Degree requirements:* For master's, thesis. *Entrance requirements:* For master's, portfolio. Additional exam requirements/recommendations for international students: Required—TOEFL (minimum score 550 paper-based; 80 iBT) or IELTS (minimum score 6.5). *Application deadline:* For fall admission, 2/1 for domestic and international students. Application fee: $50 ($55 for international students). Electronic applications accepted. *Financial support:* Teaching assistantships with full and partial tuition reimbursements, career-related internships or fieldwork, Federal Work-Study, institutionally sponsored loans, scholarships/grants, tuition waivers (partial), and unspecified assistantships available. Financial award application deadline: 2/1. *Faculty research:* Vapor-fired ceramics, video installation, art theory, digital photography, mixed and interdisciplinary media work. *Unit head:* David LaPalombara, Director, 740-593-4290, Fax: 740-593-0457, E-mail: lapalomb@ohio.edu. *Application contact:* Melissa Haviland, Chair, Graduate Programs, 740-593-9996, Fax: 740-593-0457, E-mail: haviland@ohio.edu.

Oklahoma City University, Petree College of Arts and Sciences, Program in Liberal Arts, Oklahoma City, OK 73106-1402. Offers art (MLA); general studies (MLA); leadership/management (MLA); literature (MLA); mass communications (MLA); philosophy (MLA); writing (MLA). Part-time and evening/weekend programs available. *Degree requirements:* For master's, comprehensive exam, thesis optional. *Entrance requirements:* Additional exam requirements/recommendations for international students: Required—TOEFL (minimum score 550 paper-based).

Otis College of Art and Design, Program in Fine Arts, Los Angeles, CA 90045-9785. Offers new genres (MFA); painting (MFA); photography (MFA); sculpture (MFA). *Accreditation:* NASAD. *Faculty:* 1 (woman) full-time, 6 part-time/adjunct (3 women). *Students:* 23 full-time (14 women); includes 2 minority (1 Asian, non-Hispanic/Latino; 1 Hispanic/Latino), 3 international. Average

age 32. 140 applicants, 26% accepted, 15 enrolled. In 2010, 7 master's awarded. *Degree requirements:* For master's, thesis. *Entrance requirements:* For master's, portfolio. Additional exam requirements/recommendations for international students: Required—TOEFL (minimum score 600 paper-based; 250 computer-based). *Application deadline:* For fall admission, 1/15 for domestic and international students; for spring admission, 11/15 for domestic and international students. Application fee: $60. Electronic applications accepted. *Expenses:* Tuition: Full-time $33,900; part-time $1107 per unit. Required fees: $700. *Financial support:* Career-related internships or fieldwork, Federal Work-Study, scholarships/grants, and tuition waivers (partial) available. Financial award applicants required to submit FAFSA. *Unit head:* Roy Dowell, Chair, 310-665-6893, Fax: 310-665-6998, E-mail: grads@otis.edu. *Application contact:* Information Contact, 310-665-6820, Fax: 310-665-6821, E-mail: admissions@otis.edu.

Otis College of Art and Design, Program in Public Practice, Los Angeles, CA 90045-9785. Offers MFA. *Faculty:* 12 part-time/adjunct (7 women). *Students:* 15 full-time (12 women), 1 (woman) part-time; includes 4 minority (all Hispanic/Latino), 4 international. 23 applicants, 74% accepted, 7 enrolled. In 2010, 5 master's awarded. *Entrance requirements:* Additional exam requirements/recommendations for international students: Required—TOEFL (minimum score 600 paper-based; 250 computer-based). *Application deadline:* For fall admission, 1/15 for domestic and international students; for spring admission, 11/1 for domestic and international students. Application fee: $60. Electronic applications accepted. *Expenses:* Tuition: Full-time $33,900; part-time $1107 per unit. Required fees: $700. *Unit head:* Suzanne Lacy, Chair, Graduate Studies, 310-665-6820, Fax: 310-846-2612, E-mail: cvelasco@otis.edu. *Application contact:* Information Contact, 310-665-6820, Fax: 310-665-6821, E-mail: admissions@otis.edu.

Pacific Northwest College of Art, Program in Visual Studies, Portland, OR 97209. Offers MFA. *Accreditation:* NASAD.

Penn State University Park, Graduate School, College of Arts and Architecture, School of Visual Arts, State College, University Park, PA 16802-1503. Offers M Ed, MFA, MPS, MS, PhD. *Accreditation:* NASAD.

Pennsylvania Academy of the Fine Arts, Graduate School, Philadelphia, PA 19102. Offers drawing (MFA, Postbaccalaureate Certificate); painting (MFA, Postbaccalaureate Certificate); printmaking (MFA, Postbaccalaureate Certificate); sculpture (MFA, Postbaccalaureate Certificate). *Accreditation:* NASAD (one or more programs are accredited). *Faculty:* 9 full-time (4 women), 19 part-time/adjunct (9 women). *Students:* 104 full-time (61 women); includes 9 minority (8 Asian, non-Hispanic/Latino; 1 Hispanic/Latino). Average age 26. 115 applicants, 52% accepted, 34 enrolled. In 2010, 33 master's, 12 other advanced degrees awarded. *Degree requirements:* For master's, thesis, thesis exhibit. *Entrance requirements:* For master's, 10-20 slides of work and slide list, 3 letters of recommendation. Additional exam requirements/recommendations for international students: Required—TOEFL (minimum score 500 paper-based). *Application deadline:* For fall admission, 2/1 for domestic and international students. Application fee: $50. Electronic applications accepted. *Expenses:* Tuition: Full-time $31,000. *Financial support:* Federal Work-Study, institutionally sponsored loans, and scholarships/grants available. Financial award application deadline: 3/1; financial award applicants required to submit FAFSA. *Unit head:* Steven Connell, Graduate Program Coordinator, 215-972-2027, Fax: 215-569-0153, E-mail: sconnell@pafa.edu. *Application contact:* Stan Greidus, Vice President of Admissions and Financial Aid, 215-972-2047, Fax: 215-569-0153, E-mail: sgreidus@pafa.edu.

Pittsburg State University, Graduate School, College of Arts and Sciences, Department of Art, Pittsburg, KS 66762. Offers art education (MA); studio art (MA). *Degree requirements:* For master's, thesis or alternative.

Pontifical Catholic University of Puerto Rico, College of Arts and Humanities, Department of Fine Arts, Ponce, PR 00717-0777. Offers painting and drawing (MA).

Portland State University, Graduate Studies, School of Fine and Performing Arts, Department of Art, Portland, OR 97207-0751. Offers drawing (MFA); mixed media (MFA); painting (MFA); printmaking (MFA); sculpture (MFA). *Accreditation:* NASAD. *Faculty:* 27 full-time (15 women), 40 part-time/adjunct (26 women). *Students:* 19 full-time (10 women), 6 part-time (3 women); includes 1 Black or African American, non-Hispanic/Latino; 1 American Indian or Alaska Native, non-Hispanic/Latino; 1 Hispanic/Latino, 1 international. Average age 31. 22 applicants, 100% accepted, 17 enrolled. In 2010, 7 master's awarded. *Degree requirements:* For master's, variable foreign language requirement, thesis, exhibit. *Entrance requirements:* For master's, minimum GPA of 3.0 in upper-division course work or 2.75 overall, portfolio, 3 letters of recommendation. Additional exam requirements/recommendations for international students: Required—TOEFL (minimum score 550 paper-based; 213 computer-based). *Application deadline:* For fall admission, 3/1 for domestic and international students. Application fee: $50. *Expenses:* Tuition, state resident: full-time $8505; part-time $315 per credit. Tuition, nonresident: full-time $13,284; part-time $492 per credit. Required fees: $1482; $21 per credit. $99 per term. One-time fee: $120. Part-time tuition and fees vary according to course load and program. *Financial support:* Research assistantships with full tuition reimbursements, teaching assistantships with full tuition reimbursements, Federal Work-Study, scholarships/grants, and unspecified assistantships available. Support available to part-time students. Financial award application deadline: 3/1; financial award applicants required to submit FAFSA. *Unit head:* William LePore, Chair, 503-725-3515, Fax: 503-725-4541. *Application contact:* Ellen Wack, Administrative Coordinator, 503-725-8450, Fax: 503-725-4541, E-mail: wacke@pdx.edu.

Pratt Institute, School of Art and Design, Program in Fine Arts, Brooklyn, NY 11205-3899. Offers new forms (MFA); painting and drawing (MFA); photography (MFA); printmaking (MFA); sculpture (MFA). *Accreditation:* NASAD. Part-time programs available. *Faculty:* 8 full-time (2 women), 30 part-time/adjunct (15 women). *Students:* 141 full-time (94 women), 5 part-time (2 women); includes 3 Black or African American, non-Hispanic/Latino; 6 Asian, non-Hispanic/Latino; 4 Hispanic/Latino; 4 Two or more races, non-Hispanic/Latino, 45 international. Average age 28. 355 applicants, 46% accepted, 65 enrolled. In 2010, 43 master's awarded. *Degree requirements:* For master's, thesis, exhibit. *Entrance requirements:* For master's, portfolio, letters of recommendation. Additional exam requirements/recommendations for international students: Required—TOEFL (minimum score 550 paper-based; 213 computer-based; 79 iBT). *Application deadline:* For fall admission, 1/5 for domestic and international students; for spring admission, 10/1 for domestic and international students. Application fee: $50 ($90 for international students). Electronic applications accepted. *Expenses:* Tuition: Full-time $22,734; part-time $1263 per credit. Required fees: $1280. *Financial support:* Career-related internships or fieldwork, Federal Work-Study, institutionally sponsored loans, scholarships/grants, health care benefits, and unspecified assistantships available. Support available to part-time students. Financial award application deadline: 2/1; financial award applicants required to submit FAFSA. *Unit head:* Donna Moran, Chairperson, 718-636-3602, E-mail: dmoran@pratt.edu. *Application contact:* Young Hah, Director of Graduate Admissions, 718-636-3683, Fax: 718-399-4242, E-mail: yhah@pratt.edu.

See Display on page 92 and Close-Up on page 131.

Purchase College, State University of New York, School of Art and Design, Purchase, NY 10577-1400. Offers MFA. *Accreditation:* NASAD. *Degree requirements:* For master's, thesis, exhibit. *Entrance requirements:* For master's, portfolio. Electronic applications accepted.

Purdue University, Graduate School, College of Liberal Arts, Department of Visual and Performing Arts, West Lafayette, IN 47907. Offers art and design (MA); theatre (MA, MFA). *Accreditation:* NASAD; NAST. Part-time programs available. *Degree requirements:* For master's, terminal exhibit, project, or thesis. *Entrance requirements:* Additional exam requirements/recommendations for international students: Required—TOEFL. Electronic applications accepted. *Faculty research:* Design, fine arts, photography, acting, directing, theatre technology.

Queens College of the City University of New York, Division of Graduate Studies, Arts and Humanities Division, Department of Art, Program in Fine Arts, Flushing, NY 11367-1597.

Offers MFA. *Faculty:* 12 full-time (6 women). *Students:* 14 full-time (7 women), 5 part-time (all women); includes 1 Black or African American, non-Hispanic/Latino; 2 Asian, non-Hispanic/Latino; 7 Hispanic/Latino. 24 applicants, 21% accepted, 4 enrolled. In 2010, 4 master's awarded. *Degree requirements:* For master's, art show. *Entrance requirements:* For master's, minimum GPA of 3.0, portfolio. Additional exam requirements/recommendations for international students: Required—TOEFL. *Application deadline:* For fall admission, 3/15 for domestic students; for spring admission, 10/15 for domestic students. Application fee: $125. *Financial support:* Career-related internships or fieldwork, Federal Work-Study, institutionally sponsored loans, and tuition waivers (partial) available. Support available to part-time students. Financial award application deadline: 4/1; financial award applicants required to submit FAFSA. *Unit head:* Dr. Arthur Cohen, Graduate Advisor, 718-997-4770. *Application contact:* Mario Caruso, Director of Graduate Admissions, 718-997-5200, Fax: 718-997-5193, E-mail: graduate_admissions@qc.edu.

Radford University, College of Graduate and Professional Studies, College of Visual and Performing Arts, Department of Art, Radford, VA 24142. Offers MFA. Part-time programs available. *Faculty:* 12 full-time (5 women), 9 part-time/adjunct (6 women). *Students:* 17 full-time (7 women), 1 part-time (0 women); includes 5 minority (1 Black or African American, non-Hispanic/Latino; 2 Asian, non-Hispanic/Latino; 1 Hispanic/Latino; 1 Native Hawaiian or other Pacific Islander, non-Hispanic/Latino), 1 international. Average age 27. 14 applicants, 64% accepted, 6 enrolled. In 2010, 7 master's awarded. *Degree requirements:* For master's, comprehensive exam. *Entrance requirements:* For master's, minimum GPA of 2.75; 2 letters of reference; statement of philosophy; BFA or commensurate collegiate course work; slides or CD of recent work. Additional exam requirements/recommendations for international students: Required—TOEFL (minimum score 550 paper-based; 213 computer-based; 79 iBT). *Application deadline:* For fall admission, 2/15 priority date for domestic students, 12/1 for international students; for spring admission, 7/1 for international students. Applications are processed on a rolling basis. Application fee: $50. Electronic applications accepted. *Expenses:* Tuition, state resident: full-time $5746; part-time $239 per credit hour. Tuition, nonresident: full-time $14,174; part-time $591 per credit hour. Required fees: $2634; $111 per credit hour. *Financial support:* In 2010–11, 15 students received support, including 4 research assistantships with partial tuition reimbursements available (averaging $8,000 per year), 6 teaching assistantships with partial tuition reimbursements available (averaging $8,700 per year); career-related internships or fieldwork, Federal Work-Study, institutionally sponsored loans, scholarships/grants, and unspecified assistantships also available. Financial award application deadline: 3/1; financial award applicants required to submit FAFSA. *Unit head:* Dr. Richard J. Bay, Chair, 540-831-5475, Fax: 540-831-6799, E-mail: rjbay@radford.edu. *Application contact:* Rebecca Conner, Graduate Admissions, 540-831-5431, Fax: 540-831-6061, E-mail: gradcollege@radford.edu.

Rensselaer Polytechnic Institute, Graduate School, School of Humanities, Arts, and Social Sciences, Program in Electronic Arts, Troy, NY 12180-3590. Offers MFA, PhD. *Faculty:* 15 full-time (8 women). *Students:* 13 full-time (6 women), 2 part-time (both women); includes 1 American Indian or Alaska Native, non-Hispanic/Latino; 2 Asian, non-Hispanic/Latino; 1 Hispanic/Latino, 2 international. Average age 28. 76 applicants, 20% accepted, 3 enrolled. In 2010, 5 master's, 1 doctorate awarded. *Degree requirements:* For master's, thesis in the form of a large-scale creative project; for doctorate, comprehensive exam, dissertation or creative project and dissertation text. *Entrance requirements:* For master's, portfolio; for doctorate, MA, MM, MS or MFA; portfolio; scholarly writing sample (previous thesis or publication); evidence of research-based creative orientation. Additional exam requirements/recommendations for international students: Required—TOEFL (minimum score 570 paper-based; 230 computer-based; 89 iBT), IELTS (minimum score 6.5). *Application deadline:* For fall admission, 1/1 for domestic and international students. Applications are processed on a rolling basis. Application fee: $75. Electronic applications accepted. *Expenses:* Tuition: Full-time $39,600; part-time $1650 per credit. Required fees: $1896. *Financial support:* In 2010–11, 12 students received support, including 4 fellowships with full tuition reimbursements available (averaging $20,500 per year), 8 teaching assistantships with full tuition reimbursements available (averaging $17,500 per year); unspecified assistantships also available. Financial award application deadline: 1/1. *Faculty research:* Computer music, video art, Internet art, interactivity, bio art. *Unit head:* Caren Canier, Acting Head, 518-276-4784, Fax: 518-276-4370, E-mail: caniec@rpi.edu. *Application contact:* Jennifer Mumby, Graduate Program Administrator, 518-276-4784, Fax: 518-276-4370, E-mail: mumbyj@rpi.edu.

Rhode Island College, School of Graduate Studies, Faculty of Arts and Sciences, Department of Art, Providence, RI 02908-1991. Offers art education (MA, MAT); media studies (MA). *Accreditation:* NASAD (one or more programs are accredited). Part-time and evening/weekend programs available. *Faculty:* 10 full-time (4 women), 1 part-time/adjunct (0 women). *Students:* 7 full-time (4 women), 17 part-time (13 women). Average age 38. In 2010, 9 master's awarded. *Degree requirements:* For master's, thesis. *Entrance requirements:* For master's, GRE General Test, portfolio (MA), 3 letters of recommendation, interview. Additional exam requirements/recommendations for international students: Recommended—TOEFL (minimum score 550 paper-based; 213 computer-based; 79 iBT). *Application deadline:* For fall admission, 3/1 for domestic students. Applications are processed on a rolling basis. Application fee: $50. *Expenses:* Tuition, state resident: full-time $8208; part-time $342 per credit hour. Tuition, nonresident: full-time $16,080; part-time $670 per credit hour. Required fees: $554; $20 per credit. $72 per term. *Financial support:* Teaching assistantships with full tuition reimbursements, career-related internships or fieldwork, Federal Work-Study, scholarships/grants, health care benefits, and unspecified assistantships available. Support available to part-time students. Financial award application deadline: 5/15; financial award applicants required to submit FAFSA. *Unit head:* Prof. William Martin, Chair, 401-456-8054. *Application contact:* Graduate Studies, 401-456-8700.

Rhode Island School of Design, Graduate Studies, Division of Fine Arts, Department of Ceramics, Providence, RI 02903-2784. Offers MFA. *Accreditation:* NASAD. *Degree requirements:* For master's, thesis, exhibit. *Entrance requirements:* For master's, portfolio. Additional exam requirements/recommendations for international students: Required—TOEFL (minimum score 580 paper-based; 237 computer-based), IELTS (minimum score 6.5).

Rhode Island School of Design, Graduate Studies, Division of Fine Arts, Department of Glass, Providence, RI 02903-2784. Offers MFA. *Accreditation:* NASAD. *Degree requirements:* For master's, thesis, exhibit. *Entrance requirements:* For master's, portfolio, 3 letters of recommendation. Additional exam requirements/recommendations for international students: Required—TOEFL (minimum score 580 paper-based; 237 computer-based), IELTS (minimum score 6.5).

Rhode Island School of Design, Graduate Studies, Division of Fine Arts, Department of Jewelry and Light Metals, Providence, RI 02903-2784. Offers MFA. *Accreditation:* NASAD. *Degree requirements:* For master's, thesis, exhibit. *Entrance requirements:* For master's, portfolio, 3 letters of recommendation. Additional exam requirements/recommendations for international students: Required—TOEFL (minimum score 580 paper-based; 237 computer-based), IELTS (minimum score 6.5).

Rhode Island School of Design, Graduate Studies, Division of Fine Arts, Department of Painting, Providence, RI 02903-2784. Offers MFA. *Accreditation:* NASAD. *Degree requirements:* For master's, thesis, exhibit. *Entrance requirements:* For master's, portfolio, 3 letters of recommendation. Additional exam requirements/recommendations for international students: Required—TOEFL (minimum score 580 paper-based; 237 computer-based), IELTS (minimum score 6.5).

Rhode Island School of Design, Graduate Studies, Division of Fine Arts, Department of Printmaking, Providence, RI 02903-2784. Offers MFA. *Entrance requirements:* For master's, portfolio, 3 letters of recommendation. Additional exam requirements/recommendations for international students: Required—TOEFL (minimum score 580 paper-based; 237 computer-based), IELTS (minimum score 6.5).

Art/Fine Arts

Rhode Island School of Design, Graduate Studies, Division of Fine Arts, Department of Sculpture, Providence, RI 02903-2784. Offers MFA. *Accreditation:* NASAD. *Degree requirements:* For master's, thesis, exhibit. *Entrance requirements:* For master's, portfolio, 3 letters of recommendation. Additional exam requirements/recommendations for international students: Required—TOEFL (minimum score 580 paper-based; 237 computer-based), IELTS (minimum score 6.5).

Rochester Institute of Technology, Graduate Enrollment Services, College of Imaging Arts and Sciences, School for American Crafts, Program in Ceramics, Rochester, NY 14623. Offers MFA. *Accreditation:* NASAD. Part-time programs available. *Students:* 8 full-time (6 women). Average age 31. 12 applicants, 83% accepted, 3 enrolled. In 2010, 5 master's awarded. *Entrance requirements:* For master's, portfolio, minimum GPA of 3.0. Additional exam requirements/recommendations for international students: Required—TOEFL (minimum score 550 paper-based; 230 computer-based; 79 iBT) or IELTS (minimum score 6.5). *Application deadline:* For fall admission, 2/15 priority date for domestic students, 2/2 priority date for international students. Applications are processed on a rolling basis. Application fee: $50. Electronic applications accepted. *Expenses:* Tuition: Full-time $33,234; part-time $924 per credit hour. Required fees: $219. *Financial support:* In 2010–11, 6 students received support; teaching assistantships with partial tuition reimbursements available, career-related internships or fieldwork, institutionally sponsored loans, scholarships/grants, and unspecified assistantships available. Support available to part-time students. Financial award applicants required to submit FAFSA. *Unit head:* Robin Cass, Graduate Program Director, 585-475-2650, Fax: 585-475-6447, E-mail: sac@rit.edu. *Application contact:* Diane Ellison, Assistant Vice President, Graduate Enrollment Services, 585-475-2229, Fax: 585-475-7164, E-mail: gradinfo@rit.edu.

Rochester Institute of Technology, Graduate Enrollment Services, College of Imaging Arts and Sciences, School for American Crafts, Program in Glass, Rochester, NY 14623-5603. Offers MFA. *Accreditation:* NASAD. Part-time programs available. *Students:* 6 full-time (3 women), 2 international. Average age 27. 13 applicants, 31% accepted, 4 enrolled. In 2010, 4 master's awarded. *Entrance requirements:* For master's, portfolio, minimum GPA of 3.0. Additional exam requirements/recommendations for international students: Required—TOEFL (minimum score 550 paper-based; 230 computer-based; 79 iBT) or IELTS (minimum score 6.5). *Application deadline:* For fall admission, 2/15 priority date for domestic and international students. Applications are processed on a rolling basis. Application fee: $50. Electronic applications accepted. *Expenses:* Tuition: Full-time $33,234; part-time $924 per credit hour. Required fees: $219. *Financial support:* In 2010–11, 6 students received support; teaching assistantships with partial tuition reimbursements available, career-related internships or fieldwork, institutionally sponsored loans, scholarships/grants, and unspecified assistantships available. Support available to part-time students. Financial award application deadline: 8/30; financial award applicants required to submit FAFSA. *Unit head:* Robin Cass, Graduate Program Director, 585-475-2650, Fax: 585-475-6447, E-mail: sac@rit.edu. *Application contact:* Diane Ellison, Assistant Vice President, Graduate Enrollment Services, 585-475-2229, Fax: 585-475-7164, E-mail: gradinfo@rit.edu.

Rochester Institute of Technology, Graduate Enrollment Services, College of Imaging Arts and Sciences, School for American Crafts, Program in Metal Crafts and Jewelry, Rochester, NY 14623-5603. Offers MFA. *Accreditation:* NASAD. Part-time programs available. *Students:* 11 full-time (6 women), 1 (woman) part-time; includes 1 American Indian or Alaska Native, non-Hispanic/Latino, 8 international. Average age 32. 10 applicants, 70% accepted, 4 enrolled. In 2010, 1 master's awarded. *Entrance requirements:* For master's, portfolio, minimum GPA of 3.0. Additional exam requirements/recommendations for international students: Required—TOEFL (minimum score 550 paper-based; 230 computer-based; 79 iBT) or IELTS (minimum score 6.5). *Application deadline:* For fall admission, 2/15 priority date for domestic and international students. Applications are processed on a rolling basis. Application fee: $50. Electronic applications accepted. *Expenses:* Tuition: Full-time $33,234; part-time $924 per credit hour. Required fees: $219. *Financial support:* In 2010–11, 10 students received support; teaching assistantships with partial tuition reimbursements available, career-related internships or fieldwork, institutionally sponsored loans, scholarships/grants, and unspecified assistantships available. Support available to part-time students. Financial award application deadline: 8/30; financial award applicants required to submit FAFSA. *Unit head:* Len Urso, Graduate Program Director, 585-475-2654, Fax: 585-475-6447, E-mail: sac@rit.edu. *Application contact:* Diane Ellison, Assistant Vice President, Graduate Enrollment Services, 585-475-2229, Fax: 585-475-7164, E-mail: gradinfo@rit.edu.

Rochester Institute of Technology, Graduate Enrollment Services, College of Imaging Arts and Sciences, School for American Crafts, Program in Woodworking and Furniture Design, Rochester, NY 14623-5603. Offers MFA. Part-time programs available. *Students:* 6 full-time (2 women), 1 part-time; includes 1 Asian, non-Hispanic/Latino, 2 international. Average age 28. 13 applicants, 77% accepted, 4 enrolled. In 2010, 1 master's awarded. *Entrance requirements:* For master's, portfolio, minimum GPA of 3.0. Additional exam requirements/recommendations for international students: Required—TOEFL (minimum score 550 paper-based; 213 computer-based; 79 iBT) or IELTS (minimum score 6.5). *Application deadline:* For fall admission, 2/15 priority date for domestic and international students. Applications are processed on a rolling basis. Application fee: $50. Electronic applications accepted. *Expenses:* Tuition: Full-time $33,234; part-time $924 per credit hour. Required fees: $219. *Financial support:* In 2010–11, 4 students received support; teaching assistantships with partial tuition reimbursements available, career-related internships or fieldwork, institutionally sponsored loans, scholarships/grants, and unspecified assistantships available. Support available to part-time students. Financial award application deadline: 8/30; financial award applicants required to submit FAFSA. *Unit head:* Don Arday, Interim Chair, 585-475-6114, Fax: 585-475-6447, E-mail: sac@rit.edu. *Application contact:* Diane Ellison, Assistant Vice President, Graduate Enrollment Services, 585-475-2229, Fax: 585-475-7164, E-mail: gradinfo@rit.edu.

Rochester Institute of Technology, Graduate Enrollment Services, College of Imaging Arts and Sciences, School of Art, Program in Fine Arts, Rochester, NY 14623. Offers fine arts studio (MST); painting (MFA); printmaking (MFA). *Accreditation:* NASAD. Part-time programs available. *Students:* 24 full-time (11 women), 2 part-time (both women); includes 1 American Indian or Alaska Native, non-Hispanic/Latino; 1 Asian, non-Hispanic/Latino; 3 Hispanic/Latino, 6 international. Average age 32. 34 applicants, 74% accepted, 10 enrolled. In 2010, 9 master's awarded. *Degree requirements:* For master's, thesis (for some programs). *Entrance requirements:* For master's, portfolio, minimum GPA of 3.0. Additional exam requirements/recommendations for international students: Required—TOEFL (minimum score 550 paper-based; 213 computer-based; 79 iBT) or IELTS (minimum score 6.5). *Application deadline:* For fall admission, 2/15 priority date for domestic and international students. Applications are processed on a rolling basis. Application fee: $50. Electronic applications accepted. *Expenses:* Tuition: Full-time $33,234; part-time $924 per credit hour. Required fees: $219. *Financial support:* In 2010–11, 17 students received support; teaching assistantships, career-related internships or fieldwork, institutionally sponsored loans, scholarships/grants, and unspecified assistantships available. Support available to part-time students. Financial award application deadline: 8/30; financial award applicants required to submit FAFSA. *Unit head:* Tom Lightfoot, Graduate Program Director, 585-475-2657, Fax: 585-475-6344, E-mail: trlfad@rit.edu. *Application contact:* Diane Ellison, Assistant Vice President, Graduate Enrollment Services, 585-475-2229, Fax: 585-475-7164, E-mail: gradinfo@rit.edu.

Rutgers, The State University of New Jersey, New Brunswick, Mason Gross School of the Arts, Visual Arts Department, New Brunswick, NJ 08901. Offers drawing (MFA); painting (MFA); sculpture (MFA); visual arts (MFA). *Faculty:* 15 full-time (9 women), 2 part-time/adjunct (1 woman). *Students:* 35 full-time (16 women); includes 2 Hispanic/Latino. Average age 30. 194 applicants, 17% accepted, 19 enrolled. In 2010, 15 master's awarded. *Degree requirements:* For master's, thesis, exhibit. *Entrance requirements:* For master's, portfolio. Additional exam requirements/recommendations for international students: Required—TOEFL (minimum score 550 paper-based; 213 computer-based), IELTS (minimum score 7). *Application deadline:* For fall admission, 2/1 for domestic and international students. Application fee: $65. Electronic applications accepted. *Expenses:* Tuition, state resident: full-time $7200; part-time $600 per credit. Tuition, nonresident: full-time $11,124; part-time $927 per credit. *Financial support:* In 2010–11, 19 teaching assistantships were awarded; Federal Work-Study and scholarships/grants also available. Financial award application deadline: 3/1. *Faculty research:* Media, painting, sculpture, photography, film. *Unit head:* Diane Neumaier, Department Chair, 732-932-2222. *Application contact:* Mandy R. Feiler, Admissions Officer, 732-932-9360 Ext. 517, Fax: 732-932-8497, E-mail: mfeiler@masongross.rutgers.edu.

San Diego State University, Graduate and Research Affairs, College of Professional Studies and Fine Arts, School of Art, Design and Art History, San Diego, CA 92182. Offers art history (MA); studio arts (MA, MFA), including applied design, environmental design, graphic design, interior design, painting and printmaking, sculpture. *Accreditation:* NASAD (one or more programs are accredited). *Degree requirements:* For master's, variable foreign language requirement, thesis. *Entrance requirements:* For master's, GRE General Test, bachelor's degree in related field, slide portfolio, typed slide information sheet, 2 letters of recommendation. Additional exam requirements/recommendations for international students: Required—TOEFL. Electronic applications accepted.

San Francisco Art Institute, Graduate Program, Department of Painting, San Francisco, CA 94133. Offers MFA, Certificate. *Accreditation:* NASAD. Part-time programs available. *Degree requirements:* For master's and Certificate, oral reviews. *Entrance requirements:* For master's and Certificate, portfolio. Additional exam requirements/recommendations for international students: Required—TOEFL (minimum score 580 paper-based; 237 computer-based). Electronic applications accepted.

San Francisco Art Institute, Graduate Program, Department of Printmaking, San Francisco, CA 94133. Offers MFA, Certificate. *Accreditation:* NASAD. Part-time programs available. *Degree requirements:* For master's and Certificate, oral reviews. *Entrance requirements:* For master's and Certificate, portfolio. Additional exam requirements/recommendations for international students: Required—TOEFL (minimum score 580 paper-based; 237 computer-based). Electronic applications accepted.

San Francisco Art Institute, Graduate Program, Department of Sculpture, San Francisco, CA 94133. Offers MFA, Certificate. *Accreditation:* NASAD. Part-time programs available. *Degree requirements:* For master's and Certificate, oral reviews. *Entrance requirements:* For master's and Certificate, portfolio. Additional exam requirements/recommendations for international students: Required—TOEFL (minimum score 580 paper-based; 237 computer-based).

San Francisco State University, Division of Graduate Studies, College of Creative Arts, Department of Art, San Francisco, CA 94132-1722. Offers art (MFA). *Accreditation:* NASAD. *Unit head:* Paul Mullins, Chair, 415-338-2176. *Application contact:* Gail Dawson, Graduate Coordinator, 415-338-2176, E-mail: gdawson@sfsu.edu.

San Jose State University, Graduate Studies and Research, College of Humanities and the Arts, School of Art and Design, San Jose, CA 95192-0001. Offers animation/illustration (MA); art history (MA); digital media arts (MFA); photography (MFA); pictorial arts (MFA); spatial arts (MFA). *Accreditation:* NASAD (one or more programs are accredited). *Entrance requirements:* For master's, GRE. Electronic applications accepted.

Savannah College of Art and Design, Graduate School, Program in Metals and Jewelry, Savannah, GA 31402-3146. Offers MA, MFA. Part-time programs available. *Faculty:* 6 full-time (all women), 1 part-time/adjunct (0 women). *Students:* 9 full-time (all women), 2 part-time (both women), 8 international. Average age 26. In 2010, 4 master's awarded. *Degree requirements:* For master's, thesis, internship. *Entrance requirements:* For master's, interview, portfolio. Additional exam requirements/recommendations for international students: Required—TOEFL (minimum score 450 paper-based; 133 computer-based). *Application deadline:* For fall admission, 4/1 priority date for domestic and international students. Applications are processed on a rolling basis. Application fee: $35. Electronic applications accepted. *Expenses:* Tuition: Full-time $29,520; part-time $3280 per quarter. Tuition and fees vary according to campus/location. *Financial support:* Fellowships, career-related internships or fieldwork, Federal Work-Study, and scholarships/grants available. Financial award application deadline: 4/1; financial award applicants required to submit FAFSA. *Unit head:* Jay Song, Chair, 912-525-8458, Fax: 912-525-8453, E-mail: hsong@scad.edu. *Application contact:* Elizabeth Mathis, Director of Graduate Recruitment, 912-525-5965, Fax: 912-525-5985, E-mail: emathis@scad.edu.

See Display on next page and Close-Up on page 223.

Savannah College of Art and Design, Graduate School, Program in Painting, Savannah, GA 31402-3146. Offers MA, MFA. Part-time programs available. Postbaccalaureate distance learning degree programs offered (minimal on-campus study). *Faculty:* 12 full-time (4 women), 2 part-time/adjunct (both women). *Students:* 75 full-time (49 women), 11 part-time (5 women); includes 2 Black or African American, non-Hispanic/Latino; 4 Hispanic/Latino, 16 international. Average age 33. In 2010, 31 master's awarded. *Degree requirements:* For master's, thesis, exhibit, internships. *Entrance requirements:* For master's, interview, portfolio. Additional exam requirements/recommendations for international students: Required—TOEFL (minimum score 450 paper-based; 133 computer-based). *Application deadline:* For fall admission, 4/1 priority date for domestic and international students. Applications are processed on a rolling basis. Application fee: $35. Electronic applications accepted. *Expenses:* Tuition: Full-time $29,520; part-time $3280 per quarter. Tuition and fees vary according to campus/location. *Financial support:* Fellowships, career-related internships or fieldwork, Federal Work-Study, and scholarships/grants available. Financial award application deadline: 4/1; financial award applicants required to submit FAFSA. *Unit head:* Laura Mosquera, Chair, 912-525-6408, E-mail: lmosquer@scad.edu. *Application contact:* Elizabeth Mathis, Director of Graduate Recruitment, 912-525-5965, Fax: 912-525-5985, E-mail: emathis@scad.edu.

See Display on next page and Close-Up on page 223.

Savannah College of Art and Design, Graduate School, Program in Printmaking, Savannah, GA 31402-3146. Offers MA, MFA. Part-time programs available. *Faculty:* 5 full-time (2 women), 4 part-time/adjunct (2 women). *Students:* 8 full-time (4 women), 1 (woman) part-time. Average age 27. In 2010, 1 master's awarded. *Degree requirements:* For master's, thesis. *Entrance requirements:* For master's, interview, portfolio. Additional exam requirements/recommendations for international students: Required—TOEFL (minimum score 450 paper-based; 133 computer-based). *Application deadline:* For fall admission, 4/1 priority date for domestic and international students. Applications are processed on a rolling basis. Application fee: $35. Electronic applications accepted. *Expenses:* Tuition: Full-time $29,520; part-time $3280 per quarter. Tuition and fees vary according to campus/location. *Financial support:* Fellowships, career-related internships or fieldwork, Federal Work-Study, and scholarships/grants available. Financial award application deadline: 4/1; financial award applicants required to submit FAFSA. *Unit head:* Robert Brown, Chair, 404-775-4667, Fax: 404-253-3309, E-mail: rbrown@scad.edu. *Application contact:* Elizabeth Mathis, Director of Graduate Recruitment, 912-525-5965, Fax: 912-525-5985, E-mail: emathis@scad.edu.

See Display on next page and Close-Up on page 223.

Savannah College of Art and Design, Graduate School, Program in Professional Education, Savannah, GA 31402-3146. Offers art (MAT); drama (MAT). *Faculty:* 3 full-time (all women), 2 part-time/adjunct (both women). *Students:* 17 full-time (all women); includes 2 Hispanic/Latino; 1 Two or more races, non-Hispanic/Latino, 1 international. Average age 26. In 2010, 6 master's awarded. *Degree requirements:* For master's, comprehensive exam, student teaching. *Entrance requirements:* Additional exam requirements/recommendations for international students: Required—TOEFL (minimum score 450 paper-based; 133 computer-based). *Application deadline:* For fall admission, 4/1 priority date for domestic and international students. Applications are processed on a rolling basis. Application fee: $35. Electronic applications accepted. *Expenses:* Tuition: Full-time $29,520; part-time $3280 per quarter. Tuition and fees vary according to campus/location. *Financial support:* Fellowships, career-related internships or fieldwork, Federal Work-Study, and scholarships/grants available. Financial award application deadline: 4/1; financial award applicants required to submit FAFSA. *Unit head:* Audra Price, Chair, 877-722-3285, E-mail: aprice@scad.edu. *Application contact:* Elizabeth Mathis, Director of Graduate Recruitment, 912-525-5965, Fax: 912-525-5985, E-mail: emathis@scad.edu.

See Display below and Close-Up on page 223.

Savannah College of Art and Design, Graduate School, Program in Sculpture, Savannah, GA 31402-3146. Offers MA, MFA. Part-time programs available. *Faculty:* 4 full-time (1 woman), 5 part-time/adjunct (1 woman). *Students:* 10 full-time (4 women); includes 1 Black or African American, non-Hispanic/Latino, 2 international. Average age 30. In 2010, 4 master's awarded. *Degree requirements:* For master's, thesis. *Entrance requirements:* For master's, interview, portfolio. Additional exam requirements/recommendations for international students: Required—TOEFL (minimum score 450 paper-based; 133 computer-based). *Application deadline:* For fall admission, 4/1 priority date for domestic and international students. Applications are processed on a rolling basis. Application fee: $35. Electronic applications accepted. *Expenses:* Tuition: Full-time $29,520; part-time $3280 per quarter. Tuition and fees vary according to campus/location. *Financial support:* Fellowships, career-related internships or fieldwork, Federal Work-Study, and scholarships/grants available. Financial award application deadline: 4/1; financial award applicants required to submit FAFSA. *Unit head:* Susan Krause, Chair, 404-253-3211, Fax: 404-253-3466, E-mail: skrause@scad.edu. *Application contact:* Elizabeth Mathis, Director of Graduate Recruitment, 912-525-5965, Fax: 912-525-5985, E-mail: emathis@scad.edu.

See Display below and Close-Up on page 223.

Savannah College of Art and Design, Graduate School, Program in Visual Effects, Savannah, GA 31402-3146. Offers MA, MFA. Part-time programs available. *Faculty:* 16 full-time (5 women), 2 part-time/adjunct (0 women). *Students:* 49 full-time (6 women), 4 part-time (0 women); includes 2 Black or African American, non-Hispanic/Latino; 1 American Indian or Alaska Native, non-Hispanic/Latino; 1 Hispanic/Latino; 1 Two or more races, non-Hispanic/Latino, 22 international. Average age 27. In 2010, 18 master's awarded. *Degree requirements:* For master's, thesis, internships. *Entrance requirements:* For master's, interview, portfolio. Additional exam requirements/recommendations for international students: Required—TOEFL (minimum score 450 paper-based; 133 computer-based). *Application deadline:* For fall admission, 4/1 priority date for domestic and international students. Applications are processed on a rolling basis. Application fee: $35. Electronic applications accepted. *Expenses:* Tuition: Full-time $29,520; part-time $3280 per quarter. Tuition and fees vary according to campus/location. *Financial support:* Fellowships available. Financial award application deadline: 4/1; financial award applicants required to submit FAFSA. *Unit head:* Barbara McCullough, Chair, 912-525-8536. *Application contact:* Elizabeth Mathis, Director of Graduate and International Enrollment, 912-525-5965, Fax: 912-525-5985, E-mail: emathis@scad.edu.

See Display below and Close-Up on page 223.

School of the Art Institute of Chicago, Graduate Division, Department of Art and Technology Studies, Chicago, IL 60603-3103. Offers MFA. *Entrance requirements:* Additional exam requirements/recommendations for international students: Required—TOEFL, IELTS. Electronic applications accepted.

See Close-Up on page 225.

School of the Art Institute of Chicago, Graduate Division, Department of Ceramics, Chicago, IL 60603-3103. Offers MFA. *Accreditation:* NASAD. *Entrance requirements:* Additional exam requirements/recommendations for international students: Required—TOEFL, IELTS. Electronic applications accepted.

See Close-Up on page 225.

School of the Art Institute of Chicago, Graduate Division, Department of Fiber and Material Studies, Chicago, IL 60603-3103. Offers MFA. *Accreditation:* NASAD. *Entrance requirements:* Additional exam requirements/recommendations for international students: Required—TOEFL, IELTS.

See Close-Up on page 225.

School of the Art Institute of Chicago, Graduate Division, Department of Painting and Drawing, Chicago, IL 60603-3103. Offers MFA. *Accreditation:* NASAD. *Entrance requirements:* Additional exam requirements/recommendations for international students: Required—TOEFL, IELTS.

See Close-Up on page 225.

School of the Art Institute of Chicago, Graduate Division, Department of Printmaking, Chicago, IL 60603-3103. Offers MFA. *Accreditation:* NASAD. *Entrance requirements:* Additional exam requirements/recommendations for international students: Required—TOEFL (minimum score 550 paper-based; 213 computer-based; 80 iBT), IELTS (minimum score 6.5).

See Close-Up on page 225.

School of the Art Institute of Chicago, Graduate Division, Department of Sculpture, Chicago, IL 60603-3103. Offers MFA. *Accreditation:* NASAD. *Entrance requirements:* Additional exam requirements/recommendations for international students: Required—TOEFL, IELTS.

See Close-Up on page 225.

School of the Art Institute of Chicago, Graduate Division, Program in Visual and Critical Studies, Chicago, IL 60603-3103. Offers MA.

See Close-Up on page 225.

School of the Museum of Fine Arts, Boston, Graduate Program, Boston, MA 02115. Offers MAT, MFA, MAT offered jointly with Tufts University. *Accreditation:* NASAD (one or more programs are accredited). *Faculty:* 48 full-time (24 women), 47 part-time/adjunct (27 women). *Students:* 118 full-time (82 women); includes 22 minority (5 Black or African American, non-Hispanic/Latino; 10 Asian, non-Hispanic/Latino; 4 Hispanic/Latino; 3 Two or more races, non-Hispanic/Latino), 7 international. Average age 30. 227 applicants, 51% accepted, 51 enrolled. In 2010, 31 master's awarded. Terminal master's awarded for partial completion of doctoral program. *Degree requirements:* For master's, thesis, exhibition thesis. *Entrance requirements:* For master's, BFA or bachelor's degree in related area, portfolio. Additional exam requirements/recommendations for international students: Required—TOEFL (minimum score 550 paper-based; 213 computer-based). *Application deadline:* For fall admission, 1/15 priority date for domestic and international students. Application fee: $65. Electronic applications accepted. *Financial support:* In 2010–11, 9 fellowships (averaging $2,400 per year), 20 teaching assistantships (averaging $2,000 per year) were awarded; career-related internships or fieldwork, Federal Work-Study, scholarships/grants, tuition waivers (partial), and unspecified assistantships also available. Support available to part-time students. Financial award application deadline: 2/15; financial award applicants required to submit FAFSA. *Faculty research:* Public art commissions, National Endowment for the Arts grant recipients, international exhibitions. *Unit head:* David L. Brown, Associate Dean of Academic Affairs, Graduate Programs, 617-369-3870, E-mail: dbrown@smfa.edu. *Application contact:* Any Admissions Representative, 617-369-3626, Fax: 617-369-4264, E-mail: admissions@smfa.edu.

School of Visual Arts, Graduate Programs, Computer Art Department, New York, NY 10010-3994. Offers MFA. *Accreditation:* NASAD. *Degree requirements:* For master's, review, project or thesis. *Entrance requirements:* For master's, portfolio. Additional exam requirements/recommendations for international students: Required—TOEFL (minimum score 550 paper-based; 213 computer-based; 79 iBT). Electronic applications accepted.

School of Visual Arts, Graduate Programs, Design Department, New York, NY 10010-3994. Offers MFA. *Accreditation:* NASAD. *Degree requirements:* For master's, final review, project or

Art/Fine Arts

School of Visual Arts (continued)

thesis. *Entrance requirements:* For master's, portfolio. Additional exam requirements/recommendations for international students: Required—TOEFL (minimum score 550 paper-based; 213 computer-based; 79 iBT). Electronic applications accepted. *Expenses:* Contact institution.

School of Visual Arts, Graduate Programs, Fine Arts Department, New York, NY 10010-3994. Offers painting (MFA); printmaking (MFA); sculpture (MFA). *Accreditation:* NASAD. *Degree requirements:* For master's, final review, project or thesis. *Entrance requirements:* For master's, portfolio. Additional exam requirements/recommendations for international students: Required—TOEFL (minimum score 550 paper-based; 213 computer-based; 79 iBT). Electronic applications accepted.

School of Visual Arts, Graduate Programs, Illustration Department, New York, NY 10010-3994. Offers MFA. *Accreditation:* NASAD. *Degree requirements:* For master's, final review, project or thesis. *Entrance requirements:* For master's, portfolio. Additional exam requirements/recommendations for international students: Required—TOEFL (minimum score 550 paper-based; 213 computer-based; 79 iBT). Electronic applications accepted.

School of Visual Arts, Graduate Programs, Program in Photography, Video and Related Media, New York, NY 10010-3994. Offers MFA. *Accreditation:* NASAD. *Degree requirements:* For master's, final review, project or thesis. *Entrance requirements:* For master's, portfolio. Additional exam requirements/recommendations for international students: Required—TOEFL (minimum score 550 paper-based; 213 computer-based; 79 iBT). Electronic applications accepted.

Seton Hall University, College of Arts and Sciences, Department of Art, Music and Design, South Orange, NJ 07079-2697. Offers museum professions (MA), including exhibition development, museum education, museum management, museum registration. Part-time and evening/weekend programs available. *Degree requirements:* For master's, thesis. *Entrance requirements:* For master's, GRE General Test, previous course work in art history. Additional exam requirements/recommendations for international students: Required—TOEFL. Electronic applications accepted. *Faculty research:* History of museums, museum education, theory of museums, nineteenth century art, African-American art, Renaissance art history, museum registration, museum ethics.

Sotheby's Institute of Art–London, Graduate Programs, London, United Kingdom. Offers art business (MA); contemporary art (MA); contemporary design (MA); East Asian art (MA); fine and decorative art (MA); photography (MA).

Sotheby's Institute of Art–New York, Graduate Programs, New York, NY 10021. Offers American fine and decorative art (MA); art business (MA); contemporary art (MA). *Accreditation:* NASAD.

Southern Illinois University Carbondale, Graduate School, College of Liberal Arts, School of Art and Design, Carbondale, IL 62901-4701. Offers ceramics (MFA); drawing (MFA); fiber/weaving (MFA); glass (MFA); jewelry (MFA); metalsmithing/blacksmithing (MFA); painting (MFA); printmaking (MFA); sculpture (MFA). *Accreditation:* NASAD. *Degree requirements:* For master's, thesis or alternative. *Entrance requirements:* For master's, minimum GPA of 2.7, portfolio, slides. Additional exam requirements/recommendations for international students: Required—TOEFL. *Faculty research:* Prints/woodcuts, foundry, watercolor.

Southern Illinois University Edwardsville, Graduate School, College of Arts and Sciences, Department of Art and Design, Program in Studio Art, Edwardsville, IL 62026-0001. Offers MFA. Part-time programs available. *Students:* 18 full-time (9 women), 1 (woman) part-time. Average age 26. 32 applicants, 34% accepted. In 2010, 5 master's awarded. *Degree requirements:* For master's, thesis, exhibition. *Entrance requirements:* For master's, portfolio. Additional exam requirements/recommendations for international students: Required—TOEFL (minimum score 550 paper-based; 213 computer-based; 79 iBT), IELTS (minimum score 6.5). *Application deadline:* For fall admission, 2/1 for domestic and international students. Application fee: $30. Electronic applications accepted. *Expenses:* Tuition, state resident: full-time $6012; part-time $1503 per semester. Tuition, nonresident: full-time $15,030; part-time $3758 per semester. Required fees: $1711; $675 per semester. *Financial support:* In 2010–11, 22 teaching assistantships with full tuition reimbursements (averaging $8,064 per year) were awarded; fellowships with full tuition reimbursements, research assistantships with full tuition reimbursements, Federal Work-Study, institutionally sponsored loans, and unspecified assistantships also available. Support available to part-time students. Financial award application deadline: 3/1; financial award applicants required to submit FAFSA. *Unit head:* Dr. John Denhouter, Chair, 618-650-3074, E-mail: jdenhou@siue.edu. *Application contact:* Michelle Robinson, Coordinator for Graduate Recruitment, 618-650-2811, Fax: 618-650-3523, E-mail: michero@siue.edu.

Southern Methodist University, Meadows School of the Arts, Division of Art, Dallas, TX 75275. Offers studio art (MFA), including ceramics, drawing, painting, photography, print-making, sculpture. *Accreditation:* NASAD. *Faculty:* 11 full-time (2 women), 5 part-time/adjunct (3 women). *Students:* 8 full-time (5 women), 1 part-time (0 women); includes 1 Hispanic/Latino, 1 international. Average age 30. 35 applicants, 20% accepted, 6 enrolled. In 2010, 4 master's awarded. *Degree requirements:* For master's, thesis or alternative, exhibit. *Entrance requirements:* For master's, BFA or equivalent, letters of recommendation, portfolio. Additional exam requirements/recommendations for international students: Required—TOEFL (minimum score 550 paper-based; 213 computer-based; 80 iBT). *Application deadline:* For fall admission, 2/15 for domestic and international students. Application fee: $75. *Financial support:* In 2010–11, 5 fellowships (averaging $32,914 per year), 5 teaching assistantships (averaging $3,000 per year) were awarded; scholarships/grants and unspecified assistantships also available. Financial award application deadline: 3/1; financial award applicants required to submit FAFSA. *Faculty research:* American stoneware, Southwestern furniture traditions, photographic apparatus and techniques, American ceramists, architecture. Total annual research expenditures: $20,000. *Unit head:* James W. Sullivan, Chair, 214-768-2489, E-mail: jsulliva@smu.edu. *Application contact:* Jean Cherry, Director of Graduate Admissions and Records, 214-768-3765, Fax: 214-768-3272, E-mail: jcherry@smu.edu.

Spring Hill College, Graduate Programs, Program in Liberal Arts, Mobile, AL 36608-1791. Offers fine arts (MLA); history and social science (MLA); leadership and ethics (MLA); literature (MLA). Part-time and evening/weekend programs available. *Faculty:* 5 full-time (2 women), 2 part-time/adjunct (1 woman). *Students:* 3 full-time (2 women), 31 part-time (19 women); includes 10 minority (9 Black or African American, non-Hispanic/Latino; 1 Hispanic/Latino). Average age 37. In 2010, 12 master's awarded. *Degree requirements:* For master's, capstone course, completion of program within 6 years of initial admittance. *Entrance requirements:* For master's, bachelor's degree with minimum undergraduate GPA of 3.0 or graduate/professional degree. Additional exam requirements/recommendations for international students: Required—TOEFL (minimum score 550 paper-based; 213 computer-based; 80 iBT), IELTS (minimum score 6.5), CPE or CAE (score: C), MELAB (score: 90). *Application deadline:* For fall admission, 8/1 priority date for domestic and international students; for spring admission, 12/1 priority date for domestic and international students. Applications are processed on a rolling basis. Application fee: $25 ($35 for international students). Electronic applications accepted. *Expenses:* Contact institution. *Financial support:* Applicants required to submit FAFSA. *Unit head:* Dr. Alexander R. Landi, Director, 251-380-3056, Fax: 251-460-2115, E-mail: landi@shc.edu. *Application contact:* Donna B. Tarasavage, Director of Admissions, Graduate and Continuing Studies, 251-380-3067, Fax: 251-460-2190, E-mail: dtarasavage@shc.edu.

Stanford University, School of Humanities and Sciences, Department of Art and Art History, Stanford, CA 94305-9991. Offers art history (PhD); art practice (MFA); MS/MFA. *Degree requirements:* For master's, thesis (for some programs), faculty reviews; for doctorate, 2 foreign languages, thesis/dissertation. *Entrance requirements:* For master's and doctorate,

GRE General Test. Additional exam requirements/recommendations for international students: Required—TOEFL. Electronic applications accepted. *Expenses:* Tuition: Full-time $38,700; part-time $860 per unit. One-time fee: $200 full-time.

State University of New York at New Paltz, Graduate School, School of Fine and Performing Arts, Department of Fine Arts, New Paltz, NY 12561. Offers art studio (MA); ceramics (MFA); metal (MFA); painting/drawing (MFA); printmaking (MFA); sculpture (MFA). *Accreditation:* NASAD (one or more programs are accredited). Part-time and evening/weekend programs available. *Faculty:* 17 full-time (11 women), 3 part-time/adjunct (1 woman). *Students:* 45 full-time (30 women), 14 part-time (11 women); includes 2 Asian, non-Hispanic/Latino; 1 Hispanic/Latino; 1 Two or more races, non-Hispanic/Latino, 5 international. Average age 30. 98 applicants, 39% accepted, 21 enrolled. In 2010, 36 master's awarded. *Degree requirements:* For master's, thesis, portfolio, exhibit (MFA). *Entrance requirements:* For master's, minimum GPA of 3.0, portfolio. Additional exam requirements/recommendations for international students: Required—TOEFL (minimum score 550 paper-based; 213 computer-based; 80 iBT), IELTS (minimum score 6.5). *Application deadline:* For fall admission, 2/15 priority date for domestic and international students. Applications are processed on a rolling basis. Application fee: $50. Electronic applications accepted. *Expenses:* Tuition, state resident: full-time $8370; part-time $349 per credit hour. Tuition, nonresident: full-time $13,780; part-time $574 per credit hour. Required fees: $1165; $33.80 per credit hour. $175 per term. Tuition and fees vary according to program. *Financial support:* In 2010–11, 11 students received support, including 1 fellowship (averaging $9,000 per year), 1 research assistantship with partial tuition reimbursement available (averaging $5,000 per year), 8 teaching assistantships with partial tuition reimbursements available (averaging $5,000 per year); Federal Work-Study, institutionally sponsored loans, scholarships/grants, traineeships, tuition waivers (full), and unspecified assistantships also available. Financial award application deadline: 8/1; financial award applicants required to submit FAFSA. *Unit head:* Prof. Myra Mimlitsch-Gray, Chair, 845-257-3833, E-mail: mimlitsm@newpaltz.edu. *Application contact:* Prof. Matthew Friday, Graduate Coordinator, 845-257-2609, E-mail: fridaym@newpaltz.edu.

State University of New York at Oswego, Graduate Studies, Department of Art, Oswego, NY 13126. Offers MA. *Accreditation:* NASAD. Part-time programs available. *Faculty:* 7 full-time (4 women), 2 part-time/adjunct (1 woman). *Students:* 4 full-time (2 women), 3 part-time (1 woman), 1 international. Average age 25. 10 applicants, 60% accepted. In 2010, 10 master's awarded. *Degree requirements:* For master's, exhibit, final presentation. *Entrance requirements:* For master's, slides of previous work. Additional exam requirements/recommendations for international students: Required—TOEFL (minimum score 560 paper-based; 220 computer-based). *Application deadline:* For fall admission, 4/1 for domestic students; for spring admission, 10/1 for domestic students. Applications are processed on a rolling basis. Application fee: $50. *Expenses:* Tuition, state resident: full-time $8370; part-time $349 per credit hour. Tuition, nonresident: full-time $13,780; part-time $574 per credit hour. Required fees: $853; $22.59 per credit hour. *Financial support:* In 2010–11, 6 students received support, including 4 teaching assistantships with full and partial tuition reimbursements available (averaging $3,800 per year); career-related internships or fieldwork, Federal Work-Study, institutionally sponsored loans, scholarships/grants, health care benefits, tuition waivers (partial), and unspecified assistantships also available. Support available to part-time students. Financial award application deadline: 4/1; financial award applicants required to submit FAFSA. *Faculty research:* Ancient and primitive art, nineteenth century art, medieval art, Renaissance art. *Unit head:* Cynthia Clabough, Chair, 315-312-2111. *Application contact:* Juan Perdiguero, Program Coordinator, 315-312-2111.

Stephen F. Austin State University, Graduate School, College of Fine Arts, School of Art, Nacogdoches, TX 75962. Offers art (MA); design (MFA); drawing (MFA); painting (MFA); sculpture (MFA). *Accreditation:* NASAD. Part-time programs available. *Degree requirements:* For master's, comprehensive exam, thesis, exhibit. *Entrance requirements:* For master's, GRE General Test, portfolio. Additional exam requirements/recommendations for international students: Required—TOEFL. *Faculty research:* Printmaking, jewelry, photography, ceramics, art history.

Stony Brook University, State University of New York, Graduate School, College of Arts and Sciences, Department of Art, Program in Studio Art, Stony Brook, NY 11794. Offers MFA. *Students:* 15 full-time (7 women); includes 2 Hispanic/Latino, 5 international. Average age 32. 23 applicants, 65% accepted, 2 enrolled. In 2010, 2 master's awarded. *Degree requirements:* For master's, comprehensive exam, thesis, reading knowledge of German, French, or Italian; exhibition. *Entrance requirements:* For master's, GRE General Test, minimum undergraduate GPA of 3.0. Additional exam requirements/recommendations for international students: Required—TOEFL. *Application deadline:* For fall admission, 1/15 priority date for domestic students. Application fee: $100. *Expenses:* Tuition, state resident: full-time $8370; part-time $349 per credit. Tuition, nonresident: full-time $13,780; part-time $574 per credit. Required fees: $994. *Unit head:* Stephanie Dinkins, Director, 631-632-7254, E-mail: sdinkins@ms.cc.sunysb.edu. *Application contact:* Dr. Michele Bogart, Director, 631-632-7270.

Sul Ross State University, School of Arts and Sciences, Department of Fine Arts and Communication, Alpine, TX 79832. Offers art education (M Ed); art history (M Ed); studio art (M Ed), including ceramics, design, drawing, jewelry, painting, printmaking, sculpture, weaving. Part-time programs available. *Degree requirements:* For master's, oral or written exam. *Entrance requirements:* For master's, GRE General Test, minimum GPA of 2.5 in last 60 hours of undergraduate work. *Faculty research:* Ceramic sculpture, watercolor, wood sculpture, rock art.

Syracuse University, College of Visual and Performing Arts, Program in Ceramics, Syracuse, NY 13244. Offers MFA. *Accreditation:* NASAD. Part-time programs available. *Students:* 4 full-time (2 women). Average age 29. 12 applicants, 42% accepted, 3 enrolled. In 2010, 3 master's awarded. *Degree requirements:* For master's, thesis or alternative. *Entrance requirements:* For master's, portfolio. Additional exam requirements/recommendations for international students: Required—TOEFL (minimum score 100 iBT). *Application deadline:* For fall admission, 2/1 priority date for domestic and international students. Application fee: $75. Electronic applications accepted. *Expenses:* Tuition: Part-time $1162 per credit. *Financial support:* Fellowships with full tuition reimbursements, teaching assistantships with full and partial tuition reimbursements, tuition waivers (partial) available. Financial award application deadline: 1/1; financial award applicants required to submit FAFSA. *Unit head:* Errol Willett, Chair, 315-443-3830, E-mail: eswillett@syr.edu. *Application contact:* Harriett Conti, Assistant Dean for Recruitment and Admissions, 315-443-5755, E-mail: hmconti@syr.edu.

See Display on next page and Close-Up on page 227.

Syracuse University, College of Visual and Performing Arts, Program in Jewelry and Metalsmithing, Syracuse, NY 13244. Offers MFA. *Students:* 3 full-time (all women). Average age 30. 12 applicants, 25% accepted, 1 enrolled. *Degree requirements:* For master's, thesis or alternative. *Entrance requirements:* For master's, portfolio. Additional exam requirements/recommendations for international students: Required—TOEFL (minimum score 100 iBT). *Application deadline:* For fall admission, 2/1 priority date for domestic and international students. Application fee: $75. Electronic applications accepted. *Expenses:* Tuition: Part-time $1162 per credit. *Financial support:* Fellowships with full tuition reimbursements, teaching assistantships with full and partial tuition reimbursements available. Financial award application deadline: 1/1; financial award applicants required to submit FAFSA. *Unit head:* Errol Willett, Chair, 315-443-3830, E-mail: eswillett@syr.edu. *Application contact:* Harriett Conti, Assistant Dean for Recruitment and Admissions, 315-443-5755, E-mail: hmconti@syr.edu.

See Display on next page and Close-Up on page 227.

Syracuse University, College of Visual and Performing Arts, Program in Painting, Syracuse, NY 13244. Offers MFA. *Students:* 6 full-time (3 women). Average age 28. 35 applicants, 11% accepted, 1 enrolled. In 2010, 2 master's awarded. *Degree requirements:* For master's, thesis or alternative. *Entrance requirements:* For master's, portfolio. Additional exam requirements/

recommendations for international students: Required—TOEFL (minimum score 100 iBT). *Application deadline:* For fall admission, 2/1 priority date for domestic and international students. Application fee: $75. Electronic applications accepted. *Expenses:* Tuition: Part-time $1162 per credit. *Financial support:* Fellowships with full tuition reimbursements, teaching assistantships with full and partial tuition reimbursements available. Financial award application deadline: 1/1; financial award applicants required to submit FAFSA. *Unit head:* Errol Willett, Chair, 315-443-3830, E-mail: eswillett@syr.edu. *Application contact:* Harriett Conti, Assistant Dean for Recruitment and Admissions, 315-443-5755, E-mail: hmconti@syr.edu.

See Display on this page and Close-Up on page 227.

Syracuse University, College of Visual and Performing Arts, Program in Printmaking, Syracuse, NY 13244. Offers MFA. *Students:* 3 full-time (1 woman). Average age 29. 12 applicants, 8% accepted, 1 enrolled. *Entrance requirements:* For master's, portfolio. Additional exam requirements/recommendations for international students: Required—TOEFL (minimum score 100 iBT). *Application deadline:* For fall admission, 2/1 priority date for domestic and international students. Application fee: $75. Electronic applications accepted. *Expenses:* Tuition: Part-time $1162 per credit. *Financial support:* Fellowships with full tuition reimbursements, teaching assistantships with full and partial tuition reimbursements available. Financial award application deadline: 1/1; financial award applicants required to submit FAFSA. *Unit head:* Errol Willett, Chair, 315-443-3830, E-mail: eswillett@syr.edu. *Application contact:* Harriett Conti, Assistant Dean for Recruitment and Admissions, 315-443-5755, E-mail: hmconti@syr.edu.

See Display on this page and Close-Up on page 227.

Syracuse University, College of Visual and Performing Arts, Program in Sculpture, Syracuse, NY 13244. Offers MFA. *Students:* 9 full-time (4 women); includes 1 minority (Asian, non-Hispanic/Latino), 1 international. Average age 28. 22 applicants, 9% accepted, 2 enrolled. In 2010, 1 master's awarded. *Degree requirements:* For master's, thesis or alternative. *Entrance requirements:* For master's, portfolio. Additional exam requirements/recommendations for international students: Required—TOEFL (minimum score 100 iBT). *Application deadline:* For fall admission, 2/1 priority date for domestic and international students. Application fee: $75. Electronic applications accepted. *Expenses:* Tuition: Part-time $1162 per credit. *Financial support:* Fellowships with full tuition reimbursements, teaching assistantships with full and partial tuition reimbursements available. Financial award application deadline: 1/1; financial award applicants required to submit FAFSA. *Unit head:* Errol Willett, Chair, 315-443-3830, E-mail: eswillett@syr.edu. *Application contact:* Harriett Conti, Assistant Dean for Recruitment and Admissinos, 315-443-5755, E-mail: hmconti@syr.edu.

See Display on this page and Close-Up on page 227.

Temple University, Tyler School of Art, Department of Crafts, Philadelphia, PA 19122-6096. Offers ceramics/glass (MFA); fibers and fabric design (MFA); metals/jewelry/CAD-CAM (MFA). *Faculty:* 6 full-time (3 women). *Students:* 22 full-time (15 women), 1 (woman) part-time; includes 1 Black or African American, non-Hispanic/Latino; 1 American Indian or Alaska Native, non-Hispanic/Latino; 1 Hispanic/Latino, 2 international. 67 applicants, 25% accepted, 15 enrolled. In 2010, 11 master's awarded. *Degree requirements:* For master's, essay, exhibit. *Entrance requirements:* For master's, minimum GPA of 3.0, slide portfolio, 40 credits in studio art, 12 credits in art history. Additional exam requirements/recommendations for international students: Required—TOEFL (minimum score 550 paper-based; 213 computer-based; 79 iBT). *Application deadline:* For fall admission, 12/15 for international students. Application fee: $50. Electronic applications accepted. *Financial support:* Fellowships with full tuition reimbursements, research assistantships with full tuition reimbursements, teaching assistantships with full tuition reimbursements, Federal Work-Study available. Support available to part-time students. Financial award application deadline: 1/15; financial award applicants required to submit FAFSA. *Unit head:* Nicholas Kripal, Chair, 215-782-2790, Fax: 215-782-2799, E-mail: nkripal@temple.edu. *Application contact:* Carmina Cianciulli, Assistant Dean for Admissions, 215-782-2875, Fax: 215-782-2711, E-mail: tylerart@temple.edu.

Temple University, Tyler School of Art, Department of Graphic Arts and Design, Philadelphia, PA 19122-6096. Offers graphic and interactive design (MFA); photography (MFA); printmaking (MFA). *Faculty:* 13 full-time (6 women). *Students:* 18 full-time (13 women), 2 international. 149 applicants, 13% accepted, 10 enrolled. In 2010, 11 master's awarded. *Degree requirements:* For master's, essay, exhibit. *Entrance requirements:* For master's, minimum GPA of 3.0; slide portfolio, 40 credits in studio art; 12 credits in art history. Additional exam requirements/recommendations for international students: Required—TOEFL (minimum score 550 paper-based; 213 computer-based; 79 iBT). *Application deadline:* For fall admission, 1/15 for domestic students, 12/15 for international students. Application fee: $50. Electronic applications accepted. *Financial support:* Fellowships with full tuition reimbursements, research assistantships with full tuition reimbursements, teaching assistantships with full tuition reimbursements, Federal Work-Study available. Support available to part-time students. Financial award application deadline: 1/15; financial award applicants required to submit FAFSA. *Unit head:* Stephanie Knopp, Chair, 215-782-2932, Fax: 215-782-2799, E-mail: stephanie.knopp@temple.edu. *Application contact:* Carmina Cianciulli, Assistant Dean for Admissions, 215-782-2875, Fax: 215-782-2711, E-mail: tylerart@temple.edu.

Temple University, Tyler School of Art, Department of Painting, Drawing, and Sculpture, Philadelphia, PA 19122-6096. Offers painting (MFA); sculpture (MFA). *Faculty:* 8 full-time (4 women). *Students:* 22 full-time (9 women); includes 1 Black or African American, non-Hispanic/Latino; 1 Asian, non-Hispanic/Latino, 4 international. 310 applicants, 6% accepted, 13 enrolled. In 2010, 13 master's awarded. *Degree requirements:* For master's, essay, exhibit. *Entrance requirements:* For master's, minimum GPA of 3.0, slide portfolio, 40 credits in studio art, 12 credits in art history. Additional exam requirements/recommendations for international students: Required—TOEFL (minimum score 550 paper-based; 213 computer-based; 79 iBT). *Application deadline:* For fall admission, 1/15 for domestic students, 12/15 for international students. Application fee: $50. Electronic applications accepted. *Financial support:* In 2010–11, 19 students received support; fellowships with full tuition reimbursements available, research assistantships with full tuition reimbursements available, teaching assistantships with full tuition reimbursements available, Federal Work-Study available. Support available to part-time students. Financial award application deadline: 1/15; financial award applicants required to submit FAFSA. *Unit head:* Margo Margolis, Chair, 215-782-2870, Fax: 215-782-2799, E-mail: margom@temple.edu. *Application contact:* Carmina Cianciulli, Assistant Dean for Admissions, 215-782-2875, Fax: 215-782-2711, E-mail: tylerart@temple.edu.

Texas A&M University, College of Architecture, Department of Visualization, College Station, TX 77843. Offers MS, PhD. *Faculty:* 13. *Students:* 57 full-time (20 women), 23 part-time (6 women); includes 14 minority (5 Asian, non-Hispanic/Latino; 9 Hispanic/Latino), 14 international. In 2010, 5 master's awarded. *Unit head:* Dr. Tim McLaughlin, Department Head, 979-845-3465, E-mail: timm@viz.tamu.edu. *Application contact:* Prof. Carol LaFayette, Program Coordinator, 979-845-5691, E-mail: lurleen@viz.tamu.edu.

Texas A&M University–Commerce, Graduate School, College of Arts and Sciences, Department of Art, Commerce, TX 75429-3011. Offers art (MA, MS); art history (MA); fine arts (MFA); studio art (MA). MFA offered jointly with University of North Texas, Texas Woman's University. Part-time programs available. *Degree requirements:* For master's, comprehensive exam, thesis (for some programs). *Entrance requirements:* For master's, GRE General Test. Electronic applications accepted. *Faculty research:* Use of different art media.

Texas A&M University–Corpus Christi, Graduate Studies and Research, College of Liberal Arts, Program in Studio Arts, Corpus Christi, TX 78412-5503. Offers MA, MFA. Part-time and evening/weekend programs available. *Degree requirements:* For master's, comprehensive exam, thesis (for some programs). *Entrance requirements:* For master's, GRE General Test. Additional exam requirements/recommendations for international students: Required—TOEFL. Electronic applications accepted.

Art/Fine Arts

Texas A&M University–Kingsville, College of Graduate Studies, College of Arts and Sciences, Department of Art, Kingsville, TX 78363. Offers MA, MS. Part-time programs available. *Degree requirements:* For master's, comprehensive exam, thesis or alternative. *Entrance requirements:* For master's, GRE General Test, minimum GPA of 3.0. Additional exam requirements/recommendations for international students: Required—TOEFL.

Texas Christian University, College of Fine Arts, Department of Art and Art History, Fort Worth, TX 76129. Offers art history (MA); studio art (MFA). *Accreditation:* NASAD. Part-time programs available. *Degree requirements:* For master's, thesis, internship, foreign language exam. *Entrance requirements:* For master's, GRE General Test, writing sample. Additional exam requirements/recommendations for international students: Required—TOEFL. *Application deadline:* For fall admission, 3/15 for domestic students. Applications are processed on a rolling basis. Application fee: $0. *Expenses:* Tuition: Full-time $18,720; part-time $1040 per credit hour. Tuition and fees vary according to course load and program. *Financial support:* Unspecified assistantships available. Financial award application deadline: 3/1. *Unit head:* Ron Watson, Chairperson, 817-257-7643, E-mail: r.watson@tcu.edu. *Application contact:* Dr. Joseph Butler, Associate Dean, College of Fine Arts, 817-257-6629, E-mail: j.butler@tcu.edu.

Texas Southern University, College of Liberal Arts and Behavioral Sciences, Department of Fine Arts, Houston, TX 77004-4584. Offers fine arts (MA); music (MA). Part-time programs available. *Faculty:* 3 full-time (1 woman), 1 (woman) part-time/adjunct. *Students:* 2 full-time (0 women), 5 part-time (2 women); includes all Black or African American, non-Hispanic/Latino. Average age 42. 4 applicants, 100% accepted, 3 enrolled. *Degree requirements:* For master's, one foreign language, comprehensive exam, recital. *Entrance requirements:* For master's, GRE General Test, minimum GPA of 2.5. Additional exam requirements/recommendations for international students: Required—TOEFL. *Application deadline:* For fall admission, 7/1 for domestic and international students; for spring admission, 11/1 for domestic and international students. Applications are processed on a rolling basis. Application fee: $50 ($75 for international students). Electronic applications accepted. *Expenses:* Tuition, state resident: full-time $1875; part-time $100 per credit hour. Tuition, nonresident: full-time $6641; part-time $343 per credit hour. Tuition and fees vary according to course level, course load and degree level. *Financial support:* Fellowships, teaching assistantships, scholarships/grants and unspecified assistantships available. Support available to part-time students. Financial award application deadline: 5/1. *Faculty research:* Music theory, choral music, composition, percussion composition, ethnic musicology. *Unit head:* Dr. Dianne F. Jemison-Pollard, Chair, 713-313-7337, Fax: 713-313-1869, E-mail: jemison_dp@tsu.edu. *Application contact:* Dr. Gregory Maddox, Dean of the Graduate School, 713-313-7011 Ext. 4410, Fax: 713-639-1876, E-mail: maddox_gh@tsu.edu.

Texas Tech University, Graduate School, College of Visual and Performing Arts, Fine Arts Doctoral Program, Lubbock, TX 79409. Offers arts (PhD). *Accreditation:* NAST. Part-time programs available. *Students:* 46 full-time (22 women), 32 part-time (15 women); includes 2 Black or African American, non-Hispanic/Latino; 1 American Indian or Alaska Native, non-Hispanic/Latino; 1 Asian, non-Hispanic/Latino; 5 Hispanic/Latino, 10 international. Average age 35. 36 applicants, 44% accepted, 9 enrolled. In 2010, 14 doctorates awarded. *Degree requirements:* For doctorate, comprehensive exam, thesis/dissertation. *Entrance requirements:* For doctorate, GRE General Test. Additional exam requirements/recommendations for international students: Required—TOEFL (minimum score 550 paper-based; 213 computer-based; 79 iBT). *Application deadline:* For fall admission, 6/1 priority date for domestic students, 1/15 priority date for international students; for spring admission, 9/1 priority date for domestic students, 6/15 priority date for international students. Applications are processed on a rolling basis. Application fee: $50 ($75 for international students). Electronic applications accepted. *Expenses:* Tuition, state resident: full-time $5495.76; part-time $228.99 per credit hour. Tuition, nonresident: full-time $12,936; part-time $538.99 per credit hour. Required fees: $2674; $36 per credit hour. $905 per semester. *Financial support:* Research assistantships with partial tuition reimbursements, teaching assistantships with partial tuition reimbursements available. Financial award application deadline: 4/15; financial award applicants required to submit FAFSA. *Faculty research:* Art criticism and theory, music, theatre arts; arts education; history of arts. *Unit head:* Dr. Brian D, Steele, Director, 806-742-0700, Fax: 806-742-0695, E-mail: brian.steele@ttu.edu. *Application contact:* Dr. Brian D. Steele, Director, 806-742-0700, Fax: 806-742-0695, E-mail: brian.steele@ttu.edu.

Texas Tech University, Graduate School, College of Visual and Performing Arts, School of Art, Lubbock, TX 79409. Offers art (MFA); art education (MAE); art history (MA). *Accreditation:* NASAD (one or more programs are accredited). Part-time programs available. *Faculty:* 22 full-time (11 women). *Students:* 49 full-time (21 women), 29 part-time (19 women); includes 2 Black or African American, non-Hispanic/Latino; 2 American Indian or Alaska Native, non-Hispanic/Latino; 1 Asian, non-Hispanic/Latino; 7 Hispanic/Latino, 1 Two or more races, non-Hispanic/Latino, 8 international. Average age 33. 77 applicants, 43% accepted, 20 enrolled. In 2010, 14 master's awarded. *Degree requirements:* For master's, thesis (for some programs). *Entrance requirements:* For master's, GRE General Test. Additional exam requirements/recommendations for international students: Required—TOEFL (minimum score 550 paper-based; 213 computer-based; 79 iBT). *Application deadline:* For fall admission, 6/1 priority date for domestic students, 1/15 priority date for international students; for spring admission, 9/1 priority date for domestic students, 6/15 priority date for international students. Applications are processed on a rolling basis. Application fee: $50 ($75 for international students). Electronic applications accepted. *Expenses:* Tuition, state resident: full-time $5495.76; part-time $228.99 per credit hour. Tuition, nonresident: full-time $12,936; part-time $538.99 per credit hour. Required fees: $2674; $36 per credit hour. $905 per semester. *Financial support:* In 2010–11, 41 students received support, including 19 teaching assistantships with partial tuition reimbursements available (averaging $5,992 per year). Financial award application deadline: 4/15; financial award applicants required to submit FAFSA. *Faculty research:* Studio, art history, art education. *Unit head:* Prof. Tina Fuentes, Director, 806-742-3825 Ext. 223, Fax: 806-742-1971, E-mail: tina.fuentes@ttu.edu. *Application contact:* Sang-Mi Yoo, Graduate Advisor, 806-742-3825 Ext. 244, Fax: 806-742-1971, E-mail: sang-mi.yoo@ttu.edu.

Texas Woman's University, Graduate School, College of Arts and Sciences, School of the Arts, Department of Visual Arts, Denton, TX 76201. Offers art (MA, MFA). *Faculty:* 8 full-time (5 women). *Students:* 18 full-time (15 women), 24 part-time (23 women); includes 1 Black or African American, non-Hispanic/Latino; 2 Asian, non-Hispanic/Latino; 4 Hispanic/Latino, 3 international. Average age 40. 17 applicants, 65% accepted, 11 enrolled. In 2010, 9 master's awarded. *Degree requirements:* For master's, thesis (for some programs), exhibit (MFA), oral exam, thesis or professional paper (MA). *Entrance requirements:* For master's, portfolio, interview, curriculum vitae, letter of intent, 3 letters of recommendation (for MFA only). Additional exam requirements/recommendations for international students: Required—TOEFL (minimum score 550 paper-based; 213 computer-based; 79 iBT). *Application deadline:* For fall admission, 2/15 priority date for domestic students, 3/1 for international students; for spring admission, 10/15 priority date for domestic students, 7/1 for international students. Applications are processed on a rolling basis. Application fee: $50 ($75 for international students). Electronic applications accepted. *Expenses:* Tuition, state resident: full-time $3834; part-time $213 per credit hour. Tuition, nonresident: full-time $9468; part-time $526 per credit hour. Required fees: $1247; $220 per credit hour. *Financial support:* In 2010–11, 17 students received support, including 8 research assistantships (averaging $9,684 per year), 6 teaching assistantships (averaging $9,684 per year); career-related internships or fieldwork, Federal Work-Study, institutionally sponsored loans, scholarships/grants, traineeships, health care benefits, and unspecified assistantships also available. Support available to part-time students. Financial award application deadline: 3/1; financial award applicants required to submit FAFSA. *Faculty research:* Art education and electronic technology, film noir, handmade paper, one-of-a-kind art books, new media. *Unit head:* Gary Washmon, Acting Chair, 940-898-2530, Fax: 940-898-2496, E-mail: gwashmon@twu.edu. *Application contact:* Dr. Samuel Wheeler, Assistant Director of Admissions, 940-898-3188, Fax: 940-898-3081, E-mail: wheelersr@twu.edu.

Towson University, Program in Studio Arts, Towson, MD 21252-0001. Offers MFA. *Students:* 22 full-time (11 women), 5 part-time (3 women); includes 5 minority (2 Black or African American, non-Hispanic/Latino; 1 Asian, non-Hispanic/Latino; 2 Hispanic/Latino), 2 international. Average age 30. In 2010, 5 master's awarded. *Degree requirements:* For master's, exam. *Entrance requirements:* For master's, portfolio, minimum GPA of 3.0. Additional exam requirements/recommendations for international students: Required—TOEFL (minimum score 550 paper-based). *Application deadline:* For fall admission, 2/1 for domestic students; for spring admission, 11/1 for domestic students. Application fee: $50. Electronic applications accepted. *Expenses:* Tuition, state resident: part-time $324 per credit. Tuition, nonresident: part-time $681 per credit. Required fees: $95 per term. *Financial support:* Federal Work-Study and unspecified assistantships available. Financial award application deadline: 4/1; financial award applicants required to submit FAFSA. *Unit head:* Tonia Matthews, Graduate Program Director, 410-704-2803, E-mail: tmatthews@towson.edu. *Application contact:* 410-704-2501, Fax: 410-704-4675, E-mail: grads@towson.edu.

Tufts University, Graduate School of Arts and Sciences, Department of Art and Art History, Program in Studio Art, Medford, MA 02155. Offers MFA, MA/MFA, MFA/Certificate. Program offered jointly with School of the Museum of Fine Arts, Boston. *Degree requirements:* For master's, exhibit. *Entrance requirements:* For master's, portfolio. Additional exam requirements/recommendations for international students: Required—TOEFL (minimum score 550 paper-based; 213 computer-based; 80 iBT). *Expenses:* Tuition: Full-time $39,624; part-time $3962 per course. Required fees: $40 per year. Full-time tuition and fees vary according to degree level, program and student level. Part-time tuition and fees vary according to course load.

Tulane University, School of Liberal Arts, Department of Art, New Orleans, LA 70118-5669. Offers art (MFA); art history (MA). *Degree requirements:* For master's, one foreign language, thesis. *Entrance requirements:* For master's, GRE General Test, minimum B average in undergraduate course work. Additional exam requirements/recommendations for international students: Required—TOEFL. Electronic applications accepted.

United Theological Seminary of the Twin Cities, Graduate Programs, New Brighton, MN 55112-2598. Offers advanced theological studies (Diploma); justice and peace studies (M Div, MA); leadership toward racial justice (M Div, MA, Certificate); Methodist studies (M Div, MA, Certificate); ministry (D Min); ministry renewal and professional development (Certificate); pastoral care and counseling (M Div, MA, MARL); religion and theology (MA); theological and religious studies (Certificate); theology and the arts (M Div, MA); urban ministry (M Div, MA, MARL); women's studies: religion, theology and ministry (M Div, MA). *Accreditation:* ACIPE; ATS. Part-time and evening/weekend programs available. *Faculty:* 8 full-time (5 women), 28 part-time/adjunct (16 women). *Students:* 57 full-time (41 women), 94 part-time (61 women); includes 6 minority (5 Black or African American, non-Hispanic/Latino; 1 Hispanic/Latino), 1 international. Average age 47. 49 applicants, 98% accepted, 41 enrolled. In 2010, 10 first professional degrees, 6 master's, 4 doctorates, 2 other advanced degrees awarded. *Degree requirements:* For master's, thesis; for doctorate, comprehensive exam, thesis/dissertation; for M Div, integrative notebook, spiritual chronicle. *Entrance requirements:* For M Div and master's, minimum GPA of 2.75; strong analytical, reflective thinking and writing skills; vocational and academic goals compatible with those of Seminary; for doctorate, M Div or equivalent, minimum GPA of 3.0, 3 years experience in professional ministry; for other advanced degree, BA or equivalent life experience; strong analytical, reflective thinking and writing skills (Certificate); proficiency in English language, previous study of theology at a theological school, recommendation of student's denomination (Diploma). Additional exam requirements/recommendations for international students: Required—TOEFL (minimum score 550 paper-based). *Application deadline:* For fall admission, 7/1 priority date for domestic students, 11/1 priority date for international students; for winter admission, 11/1 priority date for domestic students; for spring admission, 11/15 priority date for domestic students. Applications are processed on a rolling basis. Application fee: $50. *Expenses:* Tuition: Full-time $13,014; part-time $482 per credit hour. One-time fee: $170. Tuition and fees vary according to course load, degree level and program. *Financial support:* In 2010–11, 120 students received support. Career-related internships or fieldwork, institutionally sponsored loans, and scholarships/grants available. Support available to part-time students. Financial award application deadline: 5/1; financial award applicants required to submit FAFSA. *Unit head:* Prof. Susan K. Ebbers, Dean of the Seminary, 651-255-6143 Ext. 108, Fax: 651-633-4315, E-mail: sebbers@unitedseminary.edu. *Application contact:* Rev. Glen Herrington-Hall, Director of Admissions, 651-255-6107 Ext. 107, Fax: 651-633-4315, E-mail: gherrington-hall@unitedseminary.edu.

Universidad del Turabo, Graduate Programs, Programs in Education, Program in Teaching of Fine Arts, Gurabo, PR 00778-3030. Offers M Ed.

Université du Québec à Chicoutimi, Graduate Programs, Program in Fine Arts, Chicoutimi, QC G7H 2B1, Canada. Offers MA. Program offered jointly with Université du Québec à Montréal. Part-time programs available. *Degree requirements:* For master's, thesis optional. *Entrance requirements:* For master's, appropriate bachelor's degree, proficiency in French.

Université du Québec à Montréal, Graduate Programs, Program in Fine Arts, Montréal, QC H3C 3P8, Canada. Offers MA. Program offered jointly with Université du Québec à Chicoutimi. Part-time programs available. *Degree requirements:* For master's, thesis optional. *Entrance requirements:* For master's, appropriate bachelor's degree or equivalent, proficiency in French.

Université Laval, Faculty of Architecture, Planning and Visual Arts, School of Visual Arts, Programs in Visual Arts, Québec, QC G1K 7P4, Canada. Offers graphic design and multimedia (MA); visual arts (MA). *Degree requirements:* For master's, thesis (for some programs). *Entrance requirements:* For master's, technical exam, interview, mastery of pertinent software, knowledge of French. Electronic applications accepted.

University at Albany, State University of New York, College of Arts and Sciences, Department of Art, Albany, NY 12222-0001. Offers MA, MFA. *Degree requirements:* For master's, exhibit. *Entrance requirements:* For master's, portfolio. Additional exam requirements/recommendations for international students: Required—TOEFL (minimum score 550 paper-based; 213 computer-based). *Faculty research:* Art history, sculpture, painting and drawing, photography, digital media.

University at Buffalo, the State University of New York, Graduate School, College of Arts and Sciences, Department of Visual Studies, Buffalo, NY 14260. Offers art (MFA), including fine arts; art history (MA, Certificate), including art history (MA), critical museum studies (Certificate). *Degree requirements:* For master's, thesis.

The University of Alabama, Graduate School, College of Arts and Sciences, Department of Art, Tuscaloosa, AL 35487. Offers art history (MA); studio art (MA, MFA), including ceramics, painting, photography, printmaking, sculpture. *Accreditation:* NASAD. Part-time programs available. *Faculty:* 16 full-time (8 women). *Students:* 17 full-time (13 women), 7 part-time (4 women); includes 2 minority (1 Black or African American, non-Hispanic/Latino; 1 Asian, non-Hispanic/Latino), 2 international. Average age 33. 21 applicants, 67% accepted, 7 enrolled. In 2010, 5 master's awarded. *Degree requirements:* For master's, one foreign language, comprehensive exam (for some programs), oral exam, thesis statement, exhibit (studio art), thesis (art history). *Entrance requirements:* For master's, GRE General Test or MAT (art history), minimum GPA of 3.0, BFA or equivalent (studio art). Additional exam requirements/recommendations for international students: Required—TOEFL (minimum score 550 paper-based; 213 computer-based). *Application deadline:* For fall admission, 3/15 for domestic and international students; for spring admission, 10/15 for domestic and international students. Applications are processed on a rolling basis. Application fee: $50 ($60 for international students). Electronic applications accepted. *Expenses:* Tuition, state resident: full-time $7900. Tuition, nonresident: full-time $20,500. *Financial support:* In 2010–11, 2 fellowships with full tuition reimbursements (averaging $14,000 per year), 13 teaching assistantships with full and partial tuition reimbursements (averaging $9,206 per year) were awarded; career-related internships or fieldwork, institutionally sponsored loans, scholarships/grants, and unspecified assistantships also available. Financial award application deadline: 7/14. *Faculty research:* Nineteenth century American art history, Chinese art history, Baroque art history, twentieth century art history, Asian art history. *Unit head:* William T. Dooley, Chairperson, 205-348-1890, Fax: 205-348-0287, E-mail: wtdooley@bama.ua.edu. *Application contact:* Craig R. Wedderspoon, Graduate Coordinator, 205-348-1898, Fax: 205-348-0287, E-mail: cwedders@bama.edu.

University of Alaska Fairbanks, College of Liberal Arts, Department of Art, Fairbanks, AK 99775-5640. Offers art (MFA); ceramics (MFA); computer art (MFA); drawing (MFA); Native arts (MFA); painting (MFA); photography (MFA); printmaking (MFA); sculpture (MFA). Part-time programs available. *Faculty:* 7 full-time (2 women). *Students:* 8 full-time (4 women), 1 part-time (0 women), 1 international. Average age 33. 11 applicants, 9% accepted, 0 enrolled. In 2010, 3 master's awarded. *Degree requirements:* For master's, comprehensive exam, thesis, oral exam, oral defense. *Entrance requirements:* For master's, portfolio. Additional exam requirements/recommendations for international students: Required—TOEFL (minimum score 550 paper-based; 213 computer-based; 80 iBT). *Application deadline:* For fall admission, 6/1 for domestic students, 3/1 for international students; for spring admission, 10/15 for domestic students, 9/1 for international students. Applications are processed on a rolling basis. Application fee: $60. Electronic applications accepted. *Expenses:* Tuition, state resident: full-time $5688; part-time $316 per credit. Tuition, nonresident: full-time $11,628; part-time $646 per credit. Required fees: $289 per semester. Tuition and fees vary according to course load and reciprocity agreements. *Financial support:* In 2010–11, 7 teaching assistantships with tuition reimbursements (averaging $8,174 per year) were awarded; fellowships with tuition reimbursements, research assistantships with tuition reimbursements, Federal Work-Study, scholarships/grants, health care benefits, and unspecified assistantships also available. Support available to part-time students. Financial award application deadline: 7/1; financial award applicants required to submit FAFSA. *Faculty research:* Computer art, survey of arts in Alaska, found object art, visualization and animation, painting from the wilderness. Total annual research expenditures: $8,543. *Unit head:* David Mollett, Chair, 907-474-7530, Fax: 907-474-5853, E-mail: fyart@uaf.edu. *Application contact:* David Mollett, Chair, 907-474-7530, Fax: 907-474-5853, E-mail: fyart@uaf.edu.

University of Alberta, Faculty of Graduate Studies and Research, Department of Art and Design, Edmonton, AB T6G 2E1, Canada. Offers drawing (MFA); history of art, design, and visual culture (MA); industrial design (M Des); painting (MFA); printmaking (MFA); sculpture (MFA); visual communication design (M Des). *Degree requirements:* For master's, thesis. *Entrance requirements:* For master's, portfolio (MFA and MDES). Additional exam requirements/recommendations for international students: Required—TOEFL (minimum score 550 paper-based; 213 computer-based).

The University of Arizona, College of Fine Arts, School of Art, Program in Studio Art, Tucson, AZ 85721. Offers MFA. *Accreditation:* NASAD. Part-time programs available. *Students:* 29 full-time (12 women), 11 part-time (8 women); includes 1 American Indian or Alaska Native, non-Hispanic/Latino; 1 Asian, non-Hispanic/Latino; 2 Hispanic/Latino; 3 Two or more races, non-Hispanic/Latino, 1 international. Average age 29. 118 applicants, 20% accepted, 15 enrolled. In 2010, 14 master's awarded. *Degree requirements:* For master's, thesis or alternative. *Entrance requirements:* For master's, portfolio, minimum GPA of 3.0 for last 60 units, 3 letters of recommendation, resume or curriculum vitae. Additional exam requirements/recommendations for international students: Required—TOEFL (minimum score 550 paper-based). *Application deadline:* For fall admission, 2/1 for domestic students, 12/1 for international students. Application fee: $75. *Expenses:* Tuition, state resident: full-time $7692. *Financial support:* In 2010–11, 2 fellowships with full and partial tuition reimbursements (averaging $10,000 per year), 15 teaching assistantships with full tuition reimbursements (averaging $5,000 per year) were awarded; career-related internships or fieldwork, Federal Work-Study, institutionally sponsored loans, scholarships/grants, and tuition waivers (full) also available. Support available to part-time students. Financial award application deadline: 4/1; financial award applicants required to submit FAFSA. *Faculty research:* Painting, photography and intermedia, sculpture, print-making, ceramics. *Unit head:* Dr. Julie Plax, Associate Director, Academic Affairs, 520-621-7000, E-mail: jplax@email.arizona.edu. *Application contact:* Kimberly Mast, Graduate Coordinator, 520-621-8518, E-mail: kmast@email.arizona.edu.

University of Arkansas, Graduate School, J. William Fulbright College of Arts and Sciences, Department of Art, Fayetteville, AR 72701-1201. Offers MFA. *Students:* 15 full-time (7 women), 1 (woman) part-time; includes 2 minority (1 Asian, non-Hispanic/Latino; 1 Hispanic/Latino), 4 international. 6 applicants, 67% accepted. In 2010, 5 master's awarded. *Degree requirements:* For master's, exhibit or thesis. *Application deadline:* For fall admission, 4/1 for international students; for spring admission, 10/1 for international students. Applications are processed on a rolling basis. Application fee: $40 ($50 for international students). Electronic applications accepted. *Financial support:* In 2010–11, 12 fellowships, 2 research assistantships, 6 teaching assistantships were awarded; career-related internships or fieldwork and Federal Work-Study also available. Support available to part-time students. Financial award application deadline: 4/1; financial award applicants required to submit FAFSA. *Unit head:* Jeannie Hulen, Department Chairperson, 479-575-5202, Fax: 479-575-2062, E-mail: jhulen@uark.edu. *Application contact:* Tom Hapgood, Graduate Coordinator, 479-575-7405, Fax: 479-575-2062, E-mail: thapgoo@uark.edu.

University of Arkansas at Little Rock, Graduate School, College of Arts, Humanities, and Social Science, Department of Art, Little Rock, AR 72204-1099. Offers art education (MA); art history (MA); studio art (MA). *Accreditation:* NASAD. Part-time programs available. *Degree requirements:* For master's, 4 foreign languages, oral exam, oral defense of thesis or exhibit. *Entrance requirements:* For master's, portfolio review or term paper evaluation, minimum GPA of 2.7.

The University of British Columbia, Faculty of Arts and Faculty of Graduate Studies, Department of Art History, Visual Art, and Theory, Vancouver, BC V6T1Z2, Canada. Offers art history (MA, PhD, Diploma); critical and curatorial studies (MA); visual art (MFA). *Degree requirements:* For master's, one foreign language, thesis, final exhibition (MFA, MA in critical and curatorial studies); for doctorate, 2 foreign languages, comprehensive exam, thesis/dissertation. *Entrance requirements:* For master's, bachelor's degree with minimum B+ average (MFA, MA in critical and curatorial studies), A- (MA in art history); for doctorate, master's degree with minimum A- average. Additional exam requirements/recommendations for international students: Required—TOEFL (minimum score 600 paper-based; 250 computer-based). Electronic applications accepted. Tuition charges are reported in Canadian dollars. *Expenses:* Tuition, area resident: Full-time $4179 Canadian dollars. International tuition: $7344 Canadian dollars full-time. *Faculty research:* Conceptual art, Asian art, indigenous North American art, post-second war art, eighteenth and nineteenth century art, curatorial, digital art.

University of Calgary, Faculty of Graduate Studies, Faculty of Fine Arts, Department of Art, Calgary, AB T2N 1N4, Canada. Offers MA, MFA. *Degree requirements:* For master's, thesis. *Entrance requirements:* Additional exam requirements/recommendations for international students: Required—TOEFL. *Faculty research:* Painting, sculpture, drawing, photography, printmaking, new media.

University of California, Berkeley, Graduate Division, College of Letters and Science, Department of Art Practice, Berkeley, CA 94720-1500. Offers MFA. *Entrance requirements:* For master's, GRE General Test, minimum GPA of 3.0, sample of work, 3 letters of recommendation. Additional exam requirements/recommendations for international students: Required—TOEFL (minimum score 570 paper-based; 230 computer-based). Electronic applications accepted.

University of California, Berkeley, UC Berkeley Extension, Certificate Programs in Art and Design, Berkeley, CA 94720-1500. Offers interior design and interior architecture (Certificate); landscape architecture (Certificate); visual arts (Postbaccalaureate Certificate).

University of California, Davis, Graduate Studies, Program in Art, Davis, CA 95616. Offers MFA. *Degree requirements:* For master's, final exhibit. *Entrance requirements:* For master's, minimum GPA of 3.0, portfolio. Additional exam requirements/recommendations for inter-

national students: Required—TOEFL (minimum score 550 paper-based; 213 computer-based). Electronic applications accepted. *Faculty research:* Drawing, painting, photography, video, interactive art.

University of California, Irvine, Claire Trevor School of the Arts, Department of Studio Art, Irvine, CA 92697. Offers MFA. *Students:* 29 full-time (15 women); includes 13 minority (1 Black or African American, non-Hispanic/Latino; 4 Asian, non-Hispanic/Latino; 7 Hispanic/Latino; 1 Two or more races, non-Hispanic/Latino), 2 international. Average age 28. 89 applicants, 25% accepted, 10 enrolled. In 2010, 10 master's awarded. *Degree requirements:* For master's, thesis. *Entrance requirements:* For master's, minimum GPA of 3.0. *Application deadline:* For fall admission, 1/15 for domestic and international students. Applications are processed on a rolling basis. Application fee: $80 ($100 for international students). Electronic applications accepted. *Financial support:* Fellowships with tuition reimbursements, research assistantships with tuition reimbursements, teaching assistantships with tuition reimbursements, institutionally sponsored loans, traineeships, health care benefits, and unspecified assistantships available. Financial award application deadline: 3/1; financial award applicants required to submit FAFSA. *Faculty research:* Experimental concepts, processes relevant to contemporary issues. *Unit head:* Prof. Miles Coolidge, Chair, 949-824-2667, Fax: 949-824-5297, E-mail: mcoolidg@uci.edu. *Application contact:* Maria T. Yanez De Inga, Administrative Analyst, 949-824-6648, Fax: 949-824-5297, E-mail: mdeinga@uci.edu.

University of California, Irvine, School of Humanities, Program in Visual Studies, Irvine, CA 92697. Offers PhD.

University of California, Los Angeles, Graduate Division, School of the Arts and Architecture, Department of Art, Los Angeles, CA 90095. Offers MA, MFA. *Faculty:* 13 full-time (6 women). *Students:* 40 full-time (17 women); includes 6 minority (4 Asian, non-Hispanic/Latino; 2 Hispanic/Latino), 7 international. Average age 29. 711 applicants, 3% accepted, 18 enrolled. In 2010, 20 master's awarded. *Degree requirements:* For master's, comprehensive exam. *Entrance requirements:* For master's, 20 slides and/or videotape, minimum GPA of 3.0. *Application deadline:* For fall admission, 12/15 for domestic students. Application fee: $70 ($90 for international students). Electronic applications accepted. *Financial support:* In 2010–11, 42 fellowships, 1 research assistantship, 41 teaching assistantships were awarded; Federal Work-Study, institutionally sponsored loans, scholarships/grants, tuition waivers (full and partial), and unspecified assistantships also available. Financial award application deadline: 3/2. *Unit head:* Dr. Russell Ferguson, Chair, 310-825-9287, E-mail: rferguson@arts.ucla.edu. *Application contact:* Caron Cronin, Graduate & Undergraduate Student Advisor, 310-206-7363, Fax: 310-206-6676, E-mail: ccronin@arts.ucla.edu.

University of California, Riverside, Graduate Division, Program in Visual Arts, Riverside, CA 92521-0102. Offers MFA. *Degree requirements:* For master's, thesis. *Entrance requirements:* For master's, portfolio, minimum GPA of 3.2. Additional exam requirements/recommendations for international students: Required—TOEFL (minimum score 550 paper-based; 213 computer-based; 80 iBT). Electronic applications accepted. *Faculty research:* Painting, photography, sculpture, digital art, video.

University of California, San Diego, Office of Graduate Studies, Department of Visual Arts, La Jolla, CA 92093. Offers MFA, PhD. *Degree requirements:* For master's, thesis, exhibit, oral exam. Electronic applications accepted. *Faculty research:* Developments within art and art theory.

University of California, Santa Barbara, Graduate Division, College of Letters and Sciences, Division of Humanities and Fine Arts, Department of Art, Santa Barbara, CA 93106-7120. Offers MFA. *Faculty:* 14 full-time (5 women), 9 part-time/adjunct (5 women). *Students:* 14 full-time (9 women); includes 2 Asian, non-Hispanic/Latino; 2 Hispanic/Latino. Average age 30. 56 applicants, 18% accepted, 9 enrolled. In 2010, 7 master's awarded. *Degree requirements:* For master's, thesis, exhibition. *Entrance requirements:* Additional exam requirements/recommendations for international students: Required—TOEFL (minimum score 550 paper-based; 80 iBT), IELTS (minimum score 7). *Application deadline:* For fall admission, 1/2 for domestic and international students. Application fee: $70 ($90 for international students). Electronic applications accepted. *Financial support:* In 2010–11, 12 students received support, including 10 fellowships with full tuition reimbursements available (averaging $8,408 per year), 12 teaching assistantships with partial tuition reimbursements available (averaging $9,243 per year); tuition waivers (full and partial) also available. Financial award application deadline: 1/2; financial award applicants required to submit FAFSA. *Faculty research:* Digital media, interactive media, spatial studies, public space art, book arts. *Unit head:* Prof. Jane Mulfinger, Chairperson, 805-893-2153, Fax: 805-893-7117, E-mail: mulfinger@arts.ucsb.edu. *Application contact:* Carol Talley, Staff Graduate Advisor, 805-893-8710, Fax: 805-893-7117, E-mail: ctalley@hfa.ucsb.edu.

University of California, Santa Barbara, Graduate Division, College of Letters and Sciences, Division of Humanities and Fine Arts, Department of Media Arts and Technology, Santa Barbara, CA 93106-6065. Offers electronic music and sound design (MA); media arts and technology (PhD); multimedia engineering (MS); technology and society (PhD); visual and spatial arts (MA). *Faculty:* 19 full-time (4 women). *Students:* 35 full-time (5 women); includes 1 American Indian or Alaska Native, non-Hispanic/Latino; 5 Asian, non-Hispanic/Latino; 4 Hispanic/Latino. Average age 32. 57 applicants, 32% accepted, 6 enrolled. In 2010, 5 master's, 2 doctorates awarded. Terminal master's awarded for partial completion of doctoral program. *Degree requirements:* For master's, thesis; for doctorate, comprehensive exam, thesis/dissertation. *Entrance requirements:* For master's and doctorate, GRE. Additional exam requirements/recommendations for international students: Required—TOEFL (minimum score 550 paper-based; 80 iBT), IELTS (minimum score 7). *Application deadline:* For fall admission, 12/15 for domestic and international students. Application fee: $70 ($90 for international students). Electronic applications accepted. *Financial support:* In 2010–11, 28 students received support, including 11 fellowships with full tuition reimbursements available (averaging $7,399 per year), 8 research assistantships with full and partial tuition reimbursements available (averaging $12,014 per year), 16 teaching assistantships with partial tuition reimbursements available (averaging $9,358 per year); career-related internships or fieldwork and tuition waivers (full and partial) also available. Financial award application deadline: 12/15; financial award applicants required to submit FAFSA. *Faculty research:* Transarchitectures and worldmaking, virtual and mixed reality, visualization, intelligent space and interactive installation, human-computer interaction. *Unit head:* Curtis Roads, Chair and Professor, 805-893-2932, Fax: 805-893-2930, E-mail: clang@create.ucsb.edu. *Application contact:* Yumi Kinoshita, Graduate Program Assistant, 805-893-2887, Fax: 805-893-2930, E-mail: yumi@mat.ucsb.edu.

University of California, Santa Cruz, Division of Graduate Studies, Division of the Arts, Program in Digital Arts and New Media, Santa Cruz, CA 95064. Offers MFA. *Students:* 22 full-time (9 women); includes 4 minority (2 Asian, non-Hispanic/Latino; 2 Hispanic/Latino). Average age 32. 64 applicants, 30% accepted, 12 enrolled. In 2010, 19 master's awarded. *Degree requirements:* For master's, thesis, written paper. *Entrance requirements:* Additional exam requirements/recommendations for international students: Required—TOEFL (minimum score 550 paper-based; 220 computer-based; 83 iBT); Recommended—IELTS (minimum score 8). *Application deadline:* For fall admission, 2/1 for domestic and international students. Application fee: $70 ($90 for international students). Electronic applications accepted. *Financial support:* Fellowships, research assistantships, teaching assistantships, tuition waivers available. Financial award applicants required to submit FAFSA. *Faculty research:* Mechatronics, participatory culture, performative technologies, playable media. *Unit head:* Felicia Rice, Graduate Program Coordinator, 831-459-1554, E-mail: fsrice@ucsc.edu. *Application contact:* Felicia Rice, Graduate Program Coordinator, 831-459-1554, E-mail: fsrice@ucsc.edu.

University of California, Santa Cruz, Division of Graduate Studies, Division of the Arts, Program in Visual Studies, Santa Cruz, CA 95064. Offers PhD. *Students:* 4 full-time (all women); includes 1 minority (Hispanic/Latino). Average age 35. 64 applicants, 11% accepted. *Degree requirements:* For doctorate, one foreign language, thesis/dissertation, qualifying exams.

Art/Fine Arts

University of California, Santa Cruz (continued)
Entrance requirements: For doctorate, GRE, writing sample under 20 pages, 3 letters of recommendation. Additional exam requirements/recommendations for international students: Required—TOEFL (minimum score 550 paper-based; 220 computer-based; 83 iBT); Recommended—IELTS (minimum score 8). *Application deadline:* For fall admission, 12/1 for domestic and international students. Application fee: $70 ($90 for international students). Electronic applications accepted. *Financial support:* Fellowships, research assistantships, teaching assistantships, institutionally sponsored loans and tuition waivers available. Financial award applicants required to submit FAFSA. *Faculty research:* Opportunity to consider the role of social and cultural forces in guiding how and what their members see, concentration on cultures in Africa, the Americas, Asia, Europe, and the Pacific Islands. *Unit head:* Robert Valiente-Neighbours, Graduate Program Coordinator, 831-502-7380, E-mail: visualstudies@ucsc.edu. *Application contact:* Robert Valiente-Neighbours, Graduate Program Coordinator, 831-502-7380, E-mail: visualstudies@ucsc.edu.

University of Central Florida, College of Arts and Humanities, Department of Art, Orlando, FL 32816. Offers digital media (MA); emerging media (MFA). *Faculty:* 41 full-time (11 women), 13 part-time/adjunct (3 women). *Students:* 28 full-time (13 women), 8 part-time (3 women); includes 4 Asian, non-Hispanic/Latino; 2 Hispanic/Latino, 2 international. Average age 32. 63 applicants, 48% accepted, 15 enrolled. In 2010, 3 master's awarded. Application fee: $30. Electronic applications accepted. *Expenses:* Tuition, state resident: part-time $256.56 per credit hour. Tuition, nonresident: part-time $1011.52 per credit hour. Part-time tuition and fees vary according to program. *Financial support:* In 2010–11, 12 students received support, including 3 fellowships (averaging $10,000 per year), 3 research assistantships (averaging $3,200 per year), 7 teaching assistantships (averaging $5,600 per year); scholarships/grants and unspecified assistantships also available. *Unit head:* Dr. Paul Lartonoix, Interim Director, 407-823-3253, E-mail: plartonoix@mail.ucf.edu. *Application contact:* Dr. Paul Lartonoix, Interim Director, 407-823-3253, E-mail: plartonoix@mail.ucf.edu.

University of Chicago, Division of the Humanities, Committee on the Visual Arts, Chicago, IL 60637-1513. Offers MFA. *Entrance requirements:* For master's, GRE General Test.

University of Cincinnati, Graduate School, College of Design, Architecture, Art, and Planning, School of Art, Program in Fine Arts, Cincinnati, OH 45221. Offers MFA. *Accreditation:* NASAD. Part-time programs available. *Degree requirements:* For master's, thesis, oral exam. *Entrance requirements:* Additional exam requirements/recommendations for international students: Required—TOEFL. Electronic applications accepted. *Faculty research:* Painting, drawing, ceramics, printmaking, sculpture.

University of Colorado Boulder, Graduate School, College of Arts and Sciences, Department of Art and Art History, Boulder, CO 80309. Offers art history (MA), including contemporary art criticism, early twentieth century art, nineteenth century art, Russian and Soviet art; ceramics (MFA); drawing (MFA); painting (MFA); photography and media arts (MFA); printmaking (MFA); sculpture (MFA). *Faculty:* 26 full-time (12 women). *Students:* 50 full-time (36 women), 2 part-time (both women); includes 7 minority (1 American Indian or Alaska Native, non-Hispanic/Latino; 2 Asian, non-Hispanic/Latino; 3 Hispanic/Latino; 1 Two or more races, non-Hispanic/Latino), 2 international. Average age 30. 265 applicants, 18 enrolled. In 2010, 16 master's awarded. *Degree requirements:* For master's, variable foreign language requirement, comprehensive exam, thesis (for some programs). *Entrance requirements:* For master's, GRE General Test, minimum undergraduate GPA of 3.0, portfolio. *Application deadline:* For fall admission, 1/15 priority date for domestic students, 12/1 for international students. Application fee: $50 ($60 for international students). *Financial support:* In 2010–11, 6 fellowships (averaging $1,713 per year), 13 research assistantships (averaging $5,087 per year) were awarded; Federal Work-Study, scholarships/grants, and tuition waivers (full) also available. Financial award application deadline: 1/15. *Faculty research:* Drawing, painting, ceramics, sculpture, photography and media arts, printmaking, Russian and Soviet art, early twentieth century art, contemporary art criticism, nineteenth century art.

University of Connecticut, Graduate School, School of Fine Arts, Department of Art and Art History, Field of Studio Art, Storrs, CT 06269. Offers MFA. *Accreditation:* NASAD. *Entrance requirements:* Additional exam requirements/recommendations for international students: Required—TOEFL (minimum score 550 paper-based; 213 computer-based). Electronic applications accepted.

University of Dallas, Braniff Graduate School of Liberal Arts, Program in Art, Irving, TX 75062-4736. Offers MA, MFA. Part-time programs available. *Degree requirements:* For master's, exhibit, oral exam. *Entrance requirements:* For master's, GRE General Test, portfolio. Additional exam requirements/recommendations for international students: Required—TOEFL (minimum score 550 paper-based; 213 computer-based). *Expenses:* Tuition: Full-time $7500; part-time $720 per credit hour. Required fees: $500; $60 per credit hour. $300 per semester. One-time fee: $150. Tuition and fees vary according to program and student level. *Faculty research:* Ceramics, printmaking, sculpture, art history, religious imagery and architecture.

University of Delaware, College of Arts and Sciences, Department of Art, Newark, DE 19716. Offers MA, MFA. *Degree requirements:* For master's, exposition paper final exhibition. *Entrance requirements:* For master's, portfolio of creative work. Electronic applications accepted. *Faculty research:* Painting, printmaking, ceramics, photography, sculpture.

University of Denver, Division of Arts, Humanities and Social Sciences, School of Art and Art History, Denver, CO 80208. Offers art history (MA); art history/museum studies (MA); electronic media arts and design (MFA). *Accreditation:* NASAD. Part-time programs available. *Faculty:* 13 full-time (7 women), 10 part-time/adjunct (3 women). *Students:* 14 full-time (12 women), 11 part-time (10 women); includes 2 minority (both Hispanic/Latino). Average age 29. 61 applicants, 46% accepted, 11 enrolled. In 2010, 19 master's awarded. *Degree requirements:* For master's, one foreign language, comprehensive exam, research paper. *Entrance requirements:* For master's, GRE General Test. Additional exam requirements/recommendations for international students: Required—TOEFL (minimum score 550 paper-based; 80 iBT). *Application deadline:* Applications are processed on a rolling basis. Application fee: $60. Electronic applications accepted. *Expenses:* Tuition: Full-time $35,604; part-time $29,670 per year. Required fees: $687 per year. Tuition and fees vary according to program. *Financial support:* In 2010–11, 2 teaching assistantships with full and partial tuition reimbursements (averaging $10,500 per year) were awarded; career-related internships or fieldwork, Federal Work-Study, institutionally sponsored loans, scholarships/grants, and unspecified assistantships also available. Support available to part-time students. Financial award application deadline: 3/1; financial award applicants required to submit FAFSA. *Faculty research:* Images of women in alchemical manuscripts and books, Giovanni Benedetto, Salvatore Castiglione. *Unit head:* Dr. M. E. Warlick, Director, 303-871-2371, E-mail: mwarlick@du.edu. *Application contact:* Dr. Annabeth Headrick, Graduate Admissions Coordinator, 303-871-3574, E-mail: saah-interest@du.edu.

University of Denver, University College, Denver, CO 80208. Offers arts and culture (MLS, Certificate), including art, literature, and culture, arts development and program management (Certificate), creative writing; environmental policy and management (MAS, Certificate), including energy and sustainability (Certificate), environmental assessment of nuclear power (Certificate), environmental health and safety (Certificate), environmental management, natural resource management (Certificate); geographic information systems (MAS, Certificate); global affairs (MLS, Certificate), including translation studies, world history and culture; healthcare leadership (MPH, Certificate), including healthcare policy, law, and ethics, medical and healthcare information technologies, strategic management of healthcare; information and communications technology (MCIS, Certificate), including database design and administration (Certificate), geographic information systems (MCIS), information security systems security (Certificate), information systems security (MCIS), project management (MCIS, MPS, Certificate), software design and administration (Certificate), software design and programming (MCIS), technology management, telecommunications technology (MCIS), Web design and development; leadership and organizations (MPS, Certificate), including human capital in organizations, philanthropic leadership, project management (MCIS, MPS, Certificate), strategic innovation and change; organizational and professional communication (MPS, Certificate), including alternative dispute resolution, organizational communication, organizational development and training, public relations and marketing; security management (MAS, Certificate), including emergency planning and response, information security (MAS), organizational security; strategic human resource management (MPS, Certificate), including global human resources (MPS), human resource management and development (MPS). Part-time and evening/weekend programs available. Postbaccalaureate distance learning degree programs offered (no on-campus study). *Faculty:* 7 full-time (2 women), 212 part-time/adjunct (83 women). *Students:* 52 full-time (19 women), 1,044 part-time (625 women); includes 196 minority (81 Black or African American, non-Hispanic/Latino; 7 American Indian or Alaska Native, non-Hispanic/Latino; 30 Asian, non-Hispanic/Latino; 66 Hispanic/Latino; 3 Native Hawaiian or other Pacific Islander, non-Hispanic/Latino; 9 Two or more races, non-Hispanic/Latino), 76 international. Average age 36. 488 applicants, 91% accepted, 339 enrolled. In 2010, 286 master's, 130 other advanced degrees awarded. *Entrance requirements:* Additional exam requirements/recommendations for international students: Required—TOEFL (minimum score 550 paper-based; 80 iBT). *Application deadline:* For fall admission, 6/22 priority date for domestic students, 6/10 priority date for international students; for winter admission, 9/15 priority date for domestic students, 9/6 priority date for international students; for spring admission, 2/3 priority date for domestic students, 12/15 priority date for international students. Applications are processed on a rolling basis. Application fee: $75. Electronic applications accepted. *Expenses:* Contact institution. *Financial support:* Applicants required to submit FAFSA. *Unit head:* Dr. James Davis, Dean, 303-871-2291, Fax: 303-871-4047, E-mail: jdavis@du.edu. *Application contact:* Information Contact, 303-871-3155, Fax: 303-871-4047, E-mail: ucolinfo@du.edu.

University of Florida, Graduate School, College of Fine Arts, School of Art and Art History, Gainesville, FL 32611. Offers art (MFA), including ceramics, creative photography, drawing, electronic intermedia, graphic design, painting, printmaking, sculpture; art education (MA); art history (MA, PhD); digital arts and sciences (MA); museology (museum studies) (MA). *Accreditation:* NASAD. Postbaccalaureate distance learning degree programs offered (minimal on-campus study). *Faculty:* 29 full-time (14 women). *Students:* 107 full-time (72 women), 57 part-time (52 women); includes 6 Black or African American, non-Hispanic/Latino; 1 American Indian or Alaska Native, non-Hispanic/Latino; 5 Asian, non-Hispanic/Latino; 13 Hispanic/Latino, 14 international. Average age 31. 282 applicants, 30% accepted, 61 enrolled. In 2010, 24 master's, 3 doctorates awarded. *Degree requirements:* For master's, thesis, project or thesis (MFA); 1 foreign language (MA in art history); for doctorate, 2 foreign languages, comprehensive exam, thesis/dissertation. *Entrance requirements:* For master's, GRE General Test, portfolio (MFA), writing sample (MA), minimum GPA of 3.0; for doctorate, GRE General Test, minimum GPA of 3.0. Additional exam requirements/recommendations for international students: Required—TOEFL (minimum score 550 paper-based; 213 computer-based; 80 iBT), IELTS (minimum score 6). *Application deadline:* For fall admission, 1/1 priority date for domestic students, 1/1 for international students; for spring admission, 11/1 for domestic and international students. Applications are processed on a rolling basis. Application fee: $30. Electronic applications accepted. *Expenses:* Tuition, state resident: full-time $10,915.92. Tuition, nonresident: full-time $28,309. *Financial support:* In 2010–11, 36 students received support, including 9 fellowships, 3 research assistantships with tuition reimbursements available (averaging $12,789 per year), 24 teaching assistantships with tuition reimbursements available (averaging $10,512 per year); Federal Work-Study, institutionally sponsored loans, and unspecified assistantships also available. Financial award applicants required to submit FAFSA. *Faculty research:* Studio production, art historical studies of style context. *Unit head:* Laura Robertsoon, SR Associate in Graduate Studies, 352-846-3425, E-mail: laurar@ufl.edu. *Application contact:* Lauren G. Lake, Coordinator, 352-273-3032, Fax: 352-392-8453, E-mail: lglake@arts.ufl.edu.

University of Georgia, College of Arts and Sciences, Lamar Dodd School of Art, Program in Art, Athens, GA 30602. Offers MFA. *Accreditation:* NASAD. *Students:* 60 full-time (38 women), 10 part-time (all women); includes 1 American Indian or Alaska Native, non-Hispanic/Latino; 5 Asian, non-Hispanic/Latino; 5 Hispanic/Latino, 2 international. 220 applicants, 14% accepted, 27 enrolled. In 2010, 14 master's awarded. *Entrance requirements:* For master's, GRE General Test. *Application deadline:* For fall admission, 7/1 priority date for domestic students; for spring admission, 11/15 for domestic students. Application fee: $50. Electronic applications accepted. *Expenses:* Tuition, state resident: full-time $7200; part-time $344 per credit hour. Tuition, nonresident: full-time $21,900; part-time $944 per credit hour. Tuition and fees vary according to course load and program. *Financial support:* Fellowships, research assistantships, teaching assistantships, unspecified assistantships available. *Unit head:* Prof. Georgia Strange, Director, 706-542-1600, Fax: 706-542-0226, E-mail: strange@uga.edu. *Application contact:* Dr. Carole Henry, Graduate Coordinator, 706-542-1624, Fax: 706-542-0226, E-mail: ckhenry@uga.edu.

University of Guam, Office of Graduate Studies, College of Liberal Arts and Social Sciences, Division of Fine Arts, Mangilao, GU 96923. Offers ceramics (MA); graphics (MA); painting (MA). *Degree requirements:* For master's, thesis or alternative, exhibit, final oral exam. *Entrance requirements:* For master's, GRE General Test, portfolio. Additional exam requirements/recommendations for international students: Required—TOEFL.

University of Guelph, Graduate Studies, College of Arts, School of Fine Art and Music, Guelph, ON N1G 2W1, Canada. Offers studio art (MFA). *Degree requirements:* For master's, exhibition, support paper, oral defense. *Entrance requirements:* For master's, minimum B-average during previous 2 years of course work. Additional exam requirements/recommendations for international students: Required—TOEFL. Electronic applications accepted. *Faculty research:* Studio practice in painting, sculpture, print, photo, drawing, video.

University of Hartford, Hartford Art School, West Hartford, CT 06117-1599. Offers MFA. *Accreditation:* NASAD. Part-time programs available. *Degree requirements:* For master's, thesis. *Entrance requirements:* For master's, portfolio, 3 letters of recommendation. Additional exam requirements/recommendations for international students: Required—TOEFL (minimum score 550 paper-based; 213 computer-based). Electronic applications accepted. *Expenses:* Contact institution.

University of Hawaii at Manoa, Graduate Division, College of Arts and Humanities, Department of Art and Art History, Honolulu, HI 96822. Offers art history (MA); visual arts (MFA). Part-time programs available. *Faculty:* 26 full-time (11 women), 1 part-time/adjunct (0 women). *Students:* 22 full-time (11 women), 8 part-time (6 women); includes 2 Asian, non-Hispanic/Latino; 1 Two or more races, non-Hispanic/Latino, 3 international. Average age 32. 47 applicants, 32% accepted, 11 enrolled. In 2010, 5 master's awarded. *Degree requirements:* For master's, thesis optional. *Entrance requirements:* For master's, GRE General Test, BFA, 18 hours of course work in art history. Additional exam requirements/recommendations for international students: Required—TOEFL (minimum score 550 paper-based; 79 iBT), IELTS (minimum score 7). *Application deadline:* For fall admission, 1/15 for domestic students, 12/15 for international students. Application fee: $60. *Financial support:* In 2010–11, 22 students received support, including 15 fellowships (averaging $5,000 per year), 7 teaching assistantships with full tuition reimbursements available (averaging $14,382 per year); Federal Work-Study, scholarships/grants, and tuition waivers (full and partial) also available. Financial award application deadline: 3/1; financial award applicants required to submit FAFSA. *Faculty research:* Painting, sculpture, glass, design, printmaking. Total annual research expenditures: $42,300. *Unit head:* Mary Babcock, Graduate Chair, 808-956-8180. *Application contact:* Charles Cohan, Graduate Field Chairperson, 808-956-8251, Fax: 808-956-9043, E-mail: gradart@hawaii.edu.

University of Houston, College of Liberal Arts and Social Sciences, Department of Art, Houston, TX 77204. Offers art history (MA); interdisciplinary practice and emerging forms (MFA); painting (MFA); studio art (MFA). *Faculty:* 14 full-time (8 women), 7 part-time/adjunct (5 women). *Students:* 33 full-time (21 women); includes 3 Black or African American, non-Hispanic/Latino; 3 Asian, non-Hispanic/Latino; 2 Hispanic/Latino, 2 international. Average age 31. 77

applicants, 26% accepted, 12 enrolled. In 2010, 11 master's awarded. *Entrance requirements:* For master's, baccalaureate degree, portfolio. *Application deadline:* For fall admission, 2/1 for domestic and international students. Application fee: $25 ($75 for international students). Electronic applications accepted. *Expenses:* Tuition, state resident: full-time $8592; part-time $358 per credit hour. Tuition, nonresident: full-time $16,032; part-time $668 per credit hour. Required fees: $2889. Tuition and fees vary according to course load and program. *Financial support:* In 2010–11, 5 teaching assistantships with full tuition reimbursements (averaging $5,161 per year) were awarded; career-related internships or fieldwork, Federal Work-Study, institutionally sponsored loans, scholarships/grants, health care benefits, and unspecified assistantships also available. Support available to part-time students. Financial award application deadline: 3/10. *Faculty research:* Painting, sculpture, photography/installation/video, graphic design and typography, art history (Pre-Columbian to Surrealism). *Unit head:* Dr. John Reed, Chairperson, 713-743-3001, Fax: 713-743-2823, E-mail: jreed@uh.edu. *Application contact:* Pat Deeves, Assistant Director, 713-743-0936, E-mail: deeves@central.uh.edu.

University of Idaho, College of Graduate Studies, College of Art and Architecture, Moscow, ID 83844-2282. Offers architecture (MS), including community planning, compution and visualization studies, environment and behavior studies, urban design; architecture (professional degree) (M Arch); landscape architecture (MS); studio art (MFA), including graphic design, interactive and information design, interface, painting, printmaking, sculpture; teaching art (MAT). *Accreditation:* NASAD. *Faculty:* 19 full-time, 1 part-time/adjunct. *Students:* 102 full-time, 15 part-time. Average age 27. In 2010, 31 master's awarded. *Application deadline:* For fall admission, 8/1 for domestic students; for spring admission, 12/15 for domestic students. Applications are processed on a rolling basis. Application fee: $60. Electronic applications accepted. *Expenses:* Tuition, nonresident: part-time $580 per credit. Required fees: $306 per credit. *Financial support:* Applicants required to submit FAFSA. *Faculty research:* Sustainability in communities, urban research, virtual technology, bioregional planning, environment and behavior interaction. *Unit head:* Dr. Mark Elison Hoversten, Dean, 208-885-5423, E-mail: caa@uidaho.edu. *Application contact:* Dr. Mark Elison Hoversten, Dean, 208-885-5423, E-mail: caa@uidaho.edu.

University of Illinois at Chicago, Graduate College, College of Architecture and Art, School of Art and Design, Chicago, IL 60607-7128. Offers electronic visualization (MFA); film animation (MFA); graphic design (MFA); industrial design (MFA); photography (MFA); studio arts (MFA). *Accreditation:* NASAD. *Degree requirements:* For master's, thesis, exhibit. *Entrance requirements:* For master's, MAT, portfolio. Additional exam requirements/recommendations for international students: Required—TOEFL. Electronic applications accepted.

University of Illinois at Urbana–Champaign, Graduate College, College of Fine and Applied Arts, School of Art and Design, Program in Design and Media, Champaign, IL 61820. Offers art and design (MFA), including new media; graphic design (MFA); industrial design (MFA). *Accreditation:* NASAD. *Students:* 14 full-time (4 women), 3 part-time (1 woman); includes 1 Asian, non-Hispanic/Latino, 10 international. 156 applicants, 3% accepted, 5 enrolled. In 2010, 3 master's awarded. *Entrance requirements:* For master's, minimum GPA of 3.0. Additional exam requirements/recommendations for international students: Required—TOEFL (minimum score 550 paper-based; 213 computer-based; 79 iBT). *Application deadline:* Applications are processed on a rolling basis. Application fee: $75 ($90 for international students). Electronic applications accepted. *Financial support:* Fellowships, research assistantships, teaching assistantships, tuition waivers (full and partial) available. *Unit head:* Ernest Scott, Chair, 217-333-1579, E-mail: ernscott@illinois.edu. *Application contact:* Marsha Biddle, Coordinator of Graduate Academic Affairs, 217-333-0642, Fax: 217-244-7688, E-mail: mbiddle@illinois.edu.

University of Illinois at Urbana–Champaign, Graduate College, College of Fine and Applied Arts, School of Art and Design, Program in Studio Arts, Champaign, IL 61820. Offers art and design (MFA); crafts (MFA); metals (MFA); painting (MFA); photography (MFA); sculpture (MFA). *Accreditation:* NASAD. *Students:* 20 full-time (12 women), 1 (woman) part-time; includes 1 Hispanic/Latino; 2 Two or more races, non-Hispanic/Latino, 2 international. 64 applicants, 13% accepted, 7 enrolled. In 2010, 5 master's awarded. *Entrance requirements:* For master's, minimum GPA of 3.0. Additional exam requirements/recommendations for international students: Required—TOEFL (minimum score 550 paper-based; 213 computer-based; 79 iBT). *Application deadline:* Applications are processed on a rolling basis. Application fee: $75 ($90 for international students). Electronic applications accepted. *Financial support:* Fellowships, research assistantships, teaching assistantships, tuition waivers (full and partial) available. *Unit head:* Timothy Van Laar, Chair, 217-333-6611, E-mail: tvanlaar@illinois.edu. *Application contact:* Marsha Biddle, Assistant to the Associate Director, 217-333-0642, Fax: 217-244-7688, E-mail: mbiddle@illinois.edu.

University of Indianapolis, Graduate Programs, College of Arts and Sciences, Department of Art, Indianapolis, IN 46227-3697. Offers MA. *Accreditation:* NASAD. Part-time and evening/weekend programs available. *Faculty:* 2 full-time (0 women). *Students:* 1 full-time (0 women), 7 part-time (5 women), 2 international. Average age 37. In 2010, 4 master's awarded. *Entrance requirements:* For master's, GRE Subject Test, 3 letters of recommendation, portfolio. Additional exam requirements/recommendations for international students: Required—TOEFL. *Application deadline:* Applications are processed on a rolling basis. Application fee: $30. Tuition and fees vary according to course load, degree level and program. *Financial support:* Federal Work-Study, scholarships/grants, and tuition waivers (full and partial) available. Support available to part-time students. Financial award application deadline: 5/1; financial award applicants required to submit FAFSA. *Unit head:* Dee Schaad, Chair, 317-788-3253, E-mail: dschaad@uindy.edu. *Application contact:* Katherine Fries, 317-788-3253, E-mail: frieskj@uindy.edu.

The University of Iowa, Graduate College, College of Liberal Arts and Sciences, School of Art and Art History, Programs in Art, Iowa City, IA 52242-1316. Offers MA, MFA. *Degree requirements:* For master's, thesis, final exam. *Entrance requirements:* For master's, portfolio. Additional exam requirements/recommendations for international students: Required—TOEFL (minimum score 550 paper-based; 213 computer-based; 81 iBT). Electronic applications accepted. *Faculty research:* Ceramics, painting and drawing, design, printmaking, photography.

The University of Kansas, Graduate Studies, College of Liberal Arts and Sciences, Department of Visual Art, Program in Visual Art Education, Lawrence, KS 66045. Offers MA. Part-time programs available. *Faculty:* 3 full-time (2 women). *Students:* 6 full-time (all women), 7 part-time (all women); includes 1 minority (Black or African American, non-Hispanic/Latino). Average age 28. 6 applicants, 50% accepted, 1 enrolled. In 2010, 2 master's awarded. *Degree requirements:* For master's, thesis or alternative. *Entrance requirements:* For master's, portfolio, 3 letters of recommendation, minimum GPA of 3.0. Additional exam requirements/recommendations for international students: Required—TOEFL (minimum score 570 paper-based; 230 computer-based) or IELTS (minimum score 6.5). *Application deadline:* For fall admission, 5/1 for domestic and international students; for spring admission, 10/15 for domestic and international students. Application fee: $55 ($65 for international students). Electronic applications accepted. *Expenses:* Tuition, state resident: full-time $7092; part-time $295.50 per credit hour. Tuition, nonresident: full-time $16,590; part-time $691.25 per credit hour. Required fees: $858; $71.49 per credit hour. Tuition and fees vary according to course load, campus/location and program. *Financial support:* Teaching assistantships with full tuition reimbursements, Federal Work-Study, scholarships/grants, and unspecified assistantships available. Financial award application deadline: 5/1. *Faculty research:* Museum education, art educator education. *Unit head:* Prof. Mary Anne Jordan, Chairperson, 785-864-4401, E-mail: majordan@ku.edu. *Application contact:* Tanya E. Hartman, Director, 785-864-2957, Fax: 785-864-4404, E-mail: thartman@ku.edu.

University of Kentucky, Graduate School, College of Fine Arts, Program in Art Studio, Lexington, KY 40506-0032. Offers MFA. *Accreditation:* NASAD. *Degree requirements:* For master's, comprehensive exam. *Entrance requirements:* For master's, GRE General Test, minimum undergraduate GPA of 2.75. Additional exam requirements/recommendations for international students: Required—TOEFL (minimum score 550 paper-based; 213 computer-based). Electronic applications accepted.

University of Lethbridge, School of Graduate Studies, Lethbridge, AB T1K 3M4, Canada. Offers accounting (MScM); addictions counseling (M Sc); agricultural biotechnology (M Sc); agricultural studies (M Sc, MA); anthropology (MA); archaeology (MA); art (MA, MFA); biochemistry (M Sc); biological sciences (M Sc); biomolecular science (PhD); biosystems and biodiversity (PhD); Canadian studies (MA); chemistry (M Sc); computer science (M Sc); computer science and geographical information science (M Sc); counseling psychology (M Ed); dramatic arts (MA); earth, space, and physical science (PhD); economics (MA); educational leadership (M Ed); English (MA); environmental science (M Sc); evolution and behavior (PhD); exercise science (M Sc); finance (MScM); French (MA); French/German (MA); French/Spanish (MA); general education (M Ed); general management (MScM); geography (M Sc, MA); German (MA); health science (M Sc); history (MA); human resource management and labour relations (MScM); individualized multidisciplinary (M Sc, MA); information systems (MScM); international management (MScM); kinesiology (M Sc, MA); management (M Sc, MA); marketing (MScM); mathematics (M Sc); music (M Mus, MA); Native American studies (MA); neuroscience (M Sc, PhD); new media (MA); nursing (M Sc); philosophy (MA); physics (M Sc); policy and strategy (MScM); political science (MA); psychology (M Sc, MA); religious studies (MA); social sciences (MA); sociology (MA); theatre and dramatic arts (MFA); theoretical and computational science (PhD); urban and regional studies (MA); women's studies (MA). Part-time and evening/weekend programs available. *Degree requirements:* For doctorate, comprehensive exam, thesis/dissertation. *Entrance requirements:* For master's, GMAT (M Sc in management), bachelor's degree in related field, minimum GPA of 3.0 during previous 20 graded semester courses, 2 years teaching or related experience (M Ed); for doctorate, master's degree, minimum graduate GPA of 3.5. Additional exam requirements/recommendations for international students: Required—TOEFL. *Faculty research:* Movement and brain plasticity, gibberellin physiology, photosynthesis, carbon cycling, molecular properties of main-group ring components.

University of Louisville, Graduate School, College of Arts and Sciences, Department of Fine Arts, Louisville, KY 40292. Offers art history (MA, PhD); creative art (MA); curatorial studies (MA). *Faculty:* 18 full-time (8 women), 3 part-time/adjunct (0 women). *Students:* 22 full-time (19 women), 12 part-time (10 women); includes 1 Black or African American, non-Hispanic/Latino, 2 international. Average age 34. 21 applicants, 48% accepted, 7 enrolled. In 2010, 8 master's, 1 doctorate awarded. *Degree requirements:* For master's, thesis; for doctorate, 2 foreign languages, comprehensive exam, thesis/dissertation. *Entrance requirements:* For master's and doctorate, GRE General Test. *Application deadline:* For fall admission, 1/15 for domestic and international students. Applications are processed on a rolling basis. Application fee: $50. *Expenses:* Tuition, state resident: full-time $9144; part-time $508 per credit hour. Tuition, nonresident: full-time $19,026; part-time $1057 per credit hour. Tuition and fees vary according to program and reciprocity agreements. *Financial support:* In 2010–11, 5 teaching assistantships with full tuition reimbursements (averaging $18,000 per year) were awarded. Financial award application deadline: 1/15. *Faculty research:* Art history in the periods from ancient to contemporary and various regions, 2-D and 3D Studio areas, intermedia, curatorial studies. *Unit head:* Prof. Ying Kit Chan, Chair, 502-852-6794, Fax: 502-852-6791, E-mail: chan@louisville.edu. *Application contact:* Libby Leggett, Director, Graduate Admissions, 502-852-3101, Fax: 502-852-6536, E-mail: gradadm@louisville.edu.

The University of Manchester, School of Arts, Histories and Cultures, Manchester, United Kingdom. Offers anthropology, media and performance (PhD); applied theatre professional (PhD); archaeology (PhD); art history and visual studies (PhD); arts management and cultural policy (PhD); classics and ancient history (PhD); composition (PhD); creative writing (PhD); drama (PhD); economic and social history (PhD); electroacoustic composition (PhD); English and American studies (PhD); history (PhD); humanitarianism and conflict response (PhD); museology (PhD); music (PhD); musicology (PhD); religions and theology (PhD).

The University of Manchester, School of Materials, Manchester, United Kingdom. Offers advanced aerospace materials engineering (M Sc); advanced metallic systems (PhD); biomedical materials (M Phil, M Sc, PhD); ceramics and glass (M Phil, M Sc, PhD); composite materials (M Sc, PhD); corrosion and protection (M Phil, M Sc, PhD); materials (M Phil, PhD); metallic materials (M Phil, M Sc, PhD); nanostructural materials (M Phil, M Sc, PhD); paper science (M Phil, M Sc, PhD); polymer science and engineering (M Phil, M Sc, PhD); technical textiles (M Sc); textile design, fashion and management (M Phil, M Sc, PhD); textile science and technology (M Phil, M Sc, PhD); textiles (M Phil, PhD); textiles and fashion (M Ent).

University of Maryland, Baltimore County, Graduate School, College of Arts, Humanities and Social Sciences, Department of Visual Arts, Baltimore, MD 21250. Offers imaging and digital arts (MFA). *Faculty:* 24 full-time (13 women), 11 part-time/adjunct (5 women). *Students:* 18 full-time (9 women); includes 1 Hispanic/Latino, 2 international. Average age 32. 35 applicants, 20% accepted, 7 enrolled. In 2010, 7 master's awarded. *Degree requirements:* For master's, thesis, oral defense, thesis exhibition. *Entrance requirements:* For master's, minimum GPA of 3.0. Additional exam requirements/recommendations for international students: Required—TOEFL. *Application deadline:* For fall admission, 2/1 for domestic and international students. Application fee: $50. Electronic applications accepted. *Financial support:* In 2010–11, 16 students received support, including 12 research assistantships with full and partial tuition reimbursements available (averaging $14,300 per year); scholarships/grants and health care benefits also available. Financial award application deadline: 2/1. *Faculty research:* Advanced visual studies, digital imaging and interactive art, studio and computer art, video art. Total annual research expenditures: $22,500. *Unit head:* Prof. Vin Grabill, Chair, 410-455-1656, Fax: 410-455-1053, E-mail: grabill@umbc.edu. *Application contact:* Prof. Steve Bradley, Graduate Program Director, 410-455-2721, Fax: 410-455-1053, E-mail: sbradley@umbc.edu.

University of Maryland, College Park, Academic Affairs, College of Arts and Humanities, Department of Art, College Park, MD 20742. Offers MFA. *Faculty:* 17 full-time (6 women), 11 part-time/adjunct (5 women). *Students:* 16 full-time (3 women); includes 2 minority (1 Black or African American, non-Hispanic/Latino; 1 Two or more races, non-Hispanic/Latino). 64 applicants, 16% accepted, 6 enrolled. In 2010, 4 master's awarded. *Degree requirements:* For master's, thesis, oral defense. *Entrance requirements:* For master's, minimum GPA of 3.0, portfolio, 15 slides, 3 letters of recommendation. *Application deadline:* For fall admission, 1/16 for domestic students, 2/1 for international students; for spring admission, 6/1 for international students. Applications are processed on a rolling basis. Application fee: $75. Electronic applications accepted. *Expenses:* Tuition, state resident: part-time $471 per credit hour. Tuition, nonresident: part-time $1016 per credit hour. Required fees: $337 per term. *Financial support:* In 2010–11, 2 fellowships with full and partial tuition reimbursements (averaging $13,750 per year), 14 teaching assistantships with tuition reimbursements (averaging $15,905 per year) were awarded; research assistantships with tuition reimbursements, Federal Work-Study and scholarships/grants also available. Support available to part-time students. Financial award applicants required to submit FAFSA. *Faculty research:* Studio art. *Unit head:* Dr. John Ruppert, Chair, 301-405-1446, Fax: 301-314-9740, E-mail: ruppertj@umd.edu. *Application contact:* Dean of Graduate School, 301-405-0376, Fax: 301-314-9305.

University of Massachusetts Amherst, Graduate School, College of Humanities and Fine Arts, Department of Art, Programs in Art, Amherst, MA 01003. Offers art education (MA); design (MA); studio art (MFA). Part-time programs available. *Students:* 18 full-time (12 women), 16 part-time (13 women); includes 3 minority (1 American Indian or Alaska Native, non-Hispanic/Latino; 1 Asian, non-Hispanic/Latino; 1 Hispanic/Latino). Average age 33. 83 applicants, 19% accepted, 10 enrolled. In 2010, 12 master's awarded. *Degree requirements:* For master's, comprehensive exam (for some programs), thesis (for some programs). *Entrance requirements:* For master's, portfolio. Additional exam requirements/recommendations for international students: Required—TOEFL (minimum score 530 paper-based; 213 computer-based; 80 iBT), IELTS (minimum score 6.5). *Application deadline:* For fall admission, 2/1 for domestic and international students. Applications are processed on a rolling basis. Application fee: $50 ($65 for international students). Electronic applications accepted. *Expenses:* Tuition, state resident: full-time $2640. Required fees: $8282. One-time fee: $357 full-time. *Financial support:* In 2010–11, 1 fellowship with full tuition reimbursement (averaging $3,629 per year), 1 research assistantship with full tuition reimbursement (averaging $2,903 per year), 27 teaching assistant-

Art/Fine Arts

University of Massachusetts Amherst (continued)
ships with full tuition reimbursements (averaging $5,943 per year) were awarded; career-related internships or fieldwork, Federal Work-Study, scholarships/grants, traineeships, health care benefits, tuition waivers (full), and unspecified assistantships also available. Support available to part-time students. Financial award application deadline: 2/1; financial award applicants required to submit FAFSA. *Unit head:* Dr. Young Min Moon, Graduate Program Director, 413-545-1903, Fax: 413-545-3929. *Application contact:* Jean M. Ames, Supervisor of Admissions, 413-545-0722, Fax: 413-577-0100, E-mail: gradadm@grad.umass.edu.

University of Massachusetts Dartmouth, Graduate School, College of Visual and Performing Arts, Program in Artisanry, North Dartmouth, MA 02747-2300. Offers ceramics (MFA, Postbaccalaureate Certificate); fibers (MFA); fibers/textiles (Postbaccalaureate Certificate); jewelry/metals (MFA, Postbaccalaureate Certificate); wood/furniture design (MFA, Postbaccalaureate Certificate). *Accreditation:* NASAD. *Faculty:* 7 full-time (4 women). *Students:* 17 full-time (12 women), 9 part-time (all women); includes 1 Asian, non-Hispanic/Latino; 1 Hispanic/Latino, 2 international. Average age 29. 47 applicants, 47% accepted, 10 enrolled. In 2010, 9 master's awarded. *Degree requirements:* For master's, thesis, visual thesis. *Entrance requirements:* For master's, portfolio, interview, minimum GPA of 3.0, 3 letters of recommendation. Additional exam requirements/recommendations for international students: Required—TOEFL (minimum score 500 paper-based). *Application deadline:* For fall admission, 2/1 for domestic students, 12/1 for international students. Applications are processed on a rolling basis. Application fee: $40 ($60 for international students). Electronic applications accepted. *Expenses:* Tuition, state resident: full-time $2071; part-time $86 per credit. Tuition, nonresident: full-time $8099; part-time $337 per credit. Required fees: $9446; $394 per credit. One-time fee: $75. Part-time tuition and fees vary according to class time, course load, degree level and reciprocity agreements. *Financial support:* In 2010–11, 2 fellowships with full tuition reimbursements (averaging $5,333 per year), 1 research assistantship with full tuition reimbursement (averaging $7,400 per year), 14 teaching assistantships with full tuition reimbursements (averaging $3,088 per year) were awarded; Federal Work-Study and unspecified assistantships also available. Support available to part-time students. Financial award application deadline: 3/1; financial award applicants required to submit FAFSA. Total annual research expenditures: $831. *Unit head:* Memory Holloway, Director, 508-999-8554, E-mail: mholloway@umassd.edu. *Application contact:* Elan Turcotte-Shamski, Graduate Admissions Officer, 508-999-8604, Fax: 508-999-8183, E-mail: graduate@umassd.edu.

University of Massachusetts Dartmouth, Graduate School, College of Visual and Performing Arts, Program in Fine Arts, North Dartmouth, MA 02747-2300. Offers drawing (MFA); painting (MFA); printmaking (MFA); sculpture (MFA). *Faculty:* 12 full-time (3 women), 4 part-time/adjunct (2 women). *Students:* 15 full-time (11 women), 3 part-time (1 woman), 1 international. Average age 31. 32 applicants, 44% accepted, 7 enrolled. In 2010, 6 master's awarded. *Degree requirements:* For master's, visual thesis. *Entrance requirements:* For master's, minimum GPA of 3.0, portfolio, 3 letters of recommendation. Additional exam requirements/recommendations for international students: Required—TOEFL (minimum score 500 paper-based). *Application deadline:* For fall admission, 2/1 priority date for domestic students, 12/1 priority date for international students. Applications are processed on a rolling basis. Application fee: $40 ($60 for international students). Electronic applications accepted. *Expenses:* Tuition, state resident: full-time $2071; part-time $86 per credit. Tuition, nonresident: full-time $8099; part-time $337 per credit. Required fees: $9446; $394 per credit. One-time fee: $75. Part-time tuition and fees vary according to class time, course load, degree level and reciprocity agreements. *Financial support:* In 2010–11, 1 fellowship with full tuition reimbursement (averaging $5,333 per year), 8 teaching assistantships with full tuition reimbursements (averaging $3,088 per year) were awarded; research assistantships, Federal Work-Study and unspecified assistantships also available. Support available to part-time students. Financial award application deadline: 3/1. Total annual research expenditures: $800. *Unit head:* Memory Holloway, Director, 508-999-8554, E-mail: mholloway@umassd.edu. *Application contact:* Elan Turcotte-Shamski, Graduate Admissions Officer, 508-999-8604, Fax: 508-999-8183, E-mail: graduate@umassd.edu.

University of Memphis, Graduate School, College of Communication and Fine Arts, Department of Art, Memphis, TN 38152. Offers art (Graduate Certificate); art history (MA), including Egyptian art and archaeology, general art history; ceramics (MFA); graphic design (MFA); interior design (MFA); painting (MFA); printmaking/photography (MFA); sculpture (MFA). *Accreditation:* NASAD (one or more programs are accredited). *Faculty:* 20 full-time (7 women), 4 part-time/adjunct (2 women). *Students:* 39 full-time (26 women), 10 part-time (8 women); includes 4 Black or African American, non-Hispanic/Latino; 1 Asian, non-Hispanic/Latino, 1 international. Average age 29. 44 applicants, 77% accepted, 22 enrolled. In 2010, 16 master's, 5 other advanced degrees awarded. *Degree requirements:* For master's, 2 foreign languages, comprehensive exam, thesis. *Entrance requirements:* For master's, GRE General Test or MAT, portfolio (MFA). *Application deadline:* For fall admission, 8/1 for domestic students; for spring admission, 12/1 for domestic students. Applications are processed on a rolling basis. Application fee: $35 ($60 for international students). *Financial support:* In 2010–11, 38 students received support; research assistantships with full tuition reimbursements available, teaching assistantships with full tuition reimbursements available, Federal Work-Study, scholarships/grants, and unspecified assistantships available. Financial award application deadline: 2/15; financial award applicants required to submit FAFSA. *Faculty research:* Online collaborative learning, advanced art history studies, electronic publishing/design, studio arts, architectural studies. *Unit head:* Prof. Richard Lou, Chair, 901-678-2216, Fax: 901-678-2735, E-mail: gmyatt@memphis.edu. *Application contact:* Greely Myat, Graduate Studies Coordinator, 901-678-2650.

University of Miami, Graduate School, College of Arts and Sciences, Department of Art and Art History, Coral Gables, FL 33124. Offers art history (MA); ceramics/glass (MFA); graphic design/multimedia (MFA); painting (MFA); photography/digital imaging (MFA); printmaking (MFA); sculpture (MFA). Part-time programs available. *Degree requirements:* For master's, variable foreign language requirement, thesis, exhibit (MFA), comprehensive exam (MA). *Entrance requirements:* For master's, GRE General Test (MA), research paper (MA), slide portfolio (MFA). Additional exam requirements/recommendations for international students: Required—TOEFL. Electronic applications accepted. *Faculty research:* Installation art, public art.

University of Michigan, Horace H. Rackham School of Graduate Studies, School of Art and Design, Ann Arbor, MI 48109. Offers art and design (MFA). *Accreditation:* NASAD. *Degree requirements:* For master's, thesis, exhibit (MFA), slide lecture. *Entrance requirements:* For master's, portfolio. Additional exam requirements/recommendations for international students: Required—TOEFL, IELTS. Electronic applications accepted. *Expenses:* Tuition, state resident: full-time $17,784; part-time $1116 per credit hour. Tuition, nonresident: full-time $35,944; part-time $2125 per credit hour. International tuition: $35,994 full-time. Required fees: $95 per semester. Tuition and fees vary according to course load, degree level and program. *Faculty research:* Creative expression, commercial design, preparation for teaching.

University of Minnesota, Duluth, Graduate School, School of Fine Arts, Department of Art and Design, Duluth, MN 55812-2496. Offers graphic design (MFA). Part-time programs available. *Degree requirements:* For master's, final exhibit, project, supporting paper. *Entrance requirements:* For master's, minimum GPA of 3.0, writing sample, slide portfolio. Additional exam requirements/recommendations for international students: Required—TOEFL (minimum score 550 paper-based; 213 computer-based). *Faculty research:* Motion graphics, graphic design history, interactive design, typography, education.

University of Minnesota, Twin Cities Campus, Graduate School, College of Liberal Arts, Department of Art, Minneapolis, MN 55455-0213. Offers MFA. *Degree requirements:* For master's, oral exam, supporting paper, thesis exhibit. *Entrance requirements:* For master's, portfolio, letters of recommendation, minimum GPA of 3.0. Additional exam requirements/recommendations for international students: Required—TOEFL (minimum score 550 paper-based; 79 iBT); Recommended—IELTS (minimum score 6.5). Electronic applications accepted. *Faculty research:* Photography as code and symbol, sculpture with an emphasis on multimedia, high-fired salt glazed and utilitarian ceramic earthenware, performance and installations contemporary theory, electronic technology and the human body.

University of Mississippi, Graduate School, College of Liberal Arts, Department of Art, Oxford, University, MS 38677. Offers art education (MA); art history (MA); fine arts (MFA). *Accreditation:* NASAD (one or more programs are accredited). Part-time programs available. *Students:* 13 full-time (6 women); includes 1 Asian, non-Hispanic/Latino; 3 Hispanic/Latino; 1 Two or more races, non-Hispanic/Latino. In 2010, 3 master's awarded. *Degree requirements:* For master's, thesis (for some programs). *Entrance requirements:* For master's, GRE General Test, minimum GPA of 3.0. Additional exam requirements/recommendations for international students: Required—TOEFL. *Application deadline:* For fall admission, 3/1 for domestic students; for spring admission, 10/1 for domestic students. Applications are processed on a rolling basis. Application fee: $25. Electronic applications accepted. *Financial support:* Fellowships, scholarships/grants and unspecified assistantships available. Financial award application deadline: 3/1; financial award applicants required to submit FAFSA. *Unit head:* Dr. Sheri Fleck Reith, Chair, 662-915-7193, Fax: 662-915-5013, E-mail: art@olemiss.edu. *Application contact:* Dr. Christy M. Wyandt, Associate Dean, 662-915-7474, Fax: 662-915-7577, E-mail: cwyandt@olemiss.edu.

University of Missouri, Graduate School, College of Arts and Sciences, Department of Art, Columbia, MO 65211. Offers MFA. *Faculty:* 13 full-time (3 women), 8 part-time/adjunct (5 women). *Students:* 16 full-time (10 women), 1 (woman) part-time, 4 international. Average age 34. 21 applicants, 19% accepted, 3 enrolled. In 2010, 5 master's awarded. *Degree requirements:* For master's, thesis. *Entrance requirements:* For master's, GRE General Test, minimum GPA of 3.0. Additional exam requirements/recommendations for international students: Required—TOEFL (minimum score 550 paper-based; 80 iBT), IELTS (minimum score 5.5). *Application deadline:* For fall admission, 2/1 priority date for domestic students; for winter admission, 9/1 for domestic students; for spring admission, 2/1 for domestic students. Applications are processed on a rolling basis. Application fee: $45 ($60 for international students). Electronic applications accepted. *Financial support:* In 2010–11, 2 research assistantships with full tuition reimbursements, 14 teaching assistantships were awarded; institutionally sponsored loans, health care benefits, and unspecified assistantships also available. Support available to part-time students. *Faculty research:* Painting, digital art, new media, photography, ceramics. *Unit head:* Dr. Lampo Leong, Department Chair, 573-882-3761, E-mail: leongl@missouri.edu. *Application contact:* Brenda J. Warren, 573-882-4037, E-mail: warrenb@missouri.edu.

University of Missouri–Kansas City, College of Arts and Sciences, Department of Art and Art History, Kansas City, MO 64110-2499. Offers art history (MA, PhD); studio art (MA). PhD (interdisciplinary) offered through the School of Graduate Studies. Part-time programs available. *Faculty:* 12 full-time (5 women), 9 part-time/adjunct (2 women). *Students:* 7 full-time (6 women), 37 part-time (33 women); includes 2 Black or African American, non-Hispanic/Latino; 1 American Indian or Alaska Native, non-Hispanic/Latino; 1 Asian, non-Hispanic/Latino; 1 Hispanic/Latino; 1 Two or more races, non-Hispanic/Latino, 1 international. Average age 34. 25 applicants, 36% accepted, 8 enrolled. In 2010, 6 master's awarded. Terminal master's awarded for partial completion of doctoral program. *Degree requirements:* For master's, thesis, qualifying exam; for doctorate, thesis/dissertation, exams. *Entrance requirements:* For master's, good general education in the humanities. Additional exam requirements/recommendations for international students: Required—TOEFL (minimum score 550 paper-based; 213 computer-based; 80 iBT). *Application deadline:* For fall admission, 3/1 priority date for domestic and international students; for spring admission, 10/15 for domestic and international students. Applications are processed on a rolling basis. Application fee: $45 ($50 for international students). Electronic applications accepted. *Expenses:* Tuition, state resident: full-time $5522.40; part-time $306.80 per credit hour. Tuition, nonresident: full-time $7128; part-time $792 per credit hour. Required fees: $261.15 per term. *Financial support:* In 2010–11, 7 teaching assistantships with partial tuition reimbursements (averaging $11,750 per year) were awarded; career-related internships or fieldwork, Federal Work-Study, institutionally sponsored loans, and tuition waivers (full and partial) also available. Support available to part-time students. Financial award application deadline: 3/1; financial award applicants required to submit FAFSA. *Faculty research:* Painting, electronic media, Western and non-Western art history, photography. *Unit head:* Kati Toivanen, Chair, 816-235-6230, Fax: 816-235-5507, E-mail: toivanenk@umkc.edu. *Application contact:* Craig Subler, Professor, 816-235-2985, Fax: 816-235-5507, E-mail: sublerc@umkc.edu.

The University of Montana, Graduate School, School of Fine Arts, Department of Art, Missoula, MT 59812-0002. Offers fine arts (MA, MFA), including art (MA), art history (MA), ceramics (MFA), integrated arts and education (MA), media arts (MFA), painting and drawing (MFA), photography (MFA), printmaking (MFA), sculpture (MFA). *Accreditation:* NASAD (one or more programs are accredited). *Degree requirements:* For master's, thesis exhibit. *Entrance requirements:* For master's, GRE General Test, portfolio.

The University of Montana, Graduate School, School of Fine Arts, Department of Drama/Dance, Missoula, MT 59812-0002. Offers fine arts (MA, MFA), including acting (MFA), design/technology (MFA), directing (MFA), drama (MA), integrated arts and education (MA), media arts (MFA). *Accreditation:* NAST (one or more programs are accredited). *Degree requirements:* For master's, thesis or alternative. *Entrance requirements:* For master's, GRE General Test, audition, portfolio, production notebook.

University of Nebraska–Lincoln, Graduate College, College of Fine and Performing Arts, Department of Art and Art History, Lincoln, NE 68588. Offers art history (MA); studio art (MFA);). *Accreditation:* NASAD. *Degree requirements:* For master's, thesis. *Entrance requirements:* For master's, slide portfolio. Additional exam requirements/recommendations for international students: Required—TOEFL (minimum score 550 paper-based; 213 computer-based). Electronic applications accepted. *Faculty research:* Classical archaeology, contemporary art, printmaking, photography.

University of Nevada, Las Vegas, Graduate College, College of Fine Arts, Department of Art, Las Vegas, NV 89154-5013. Offers MFA. *Accreditation:* NASAD. Part-time programs available. *Faculty:* 1 full-time (0 women). *Students:* 12 full-time (7 women); includes 3 minority (1 Hispanic/Latino; 2 Two or more races, non-Hispanic/Latino). Average age 32. 35 applicants, 20% accepted, 5 enrolled. In 2010, 4 master's awarded. *Degree requirements:* For master's, comprehensive exam, thesis. *Entrance requirements:* Additional exam requirements/recommendations for international students: Required—TOEFL (minimum score 550 paper-based; 213 computer-based; 80 iBT), IELTS (minimum score 7). *Application deadline:* For fall admission, 2/1 priority date for domestic and international students. Applications are processed on a rolling basis. Application fee: $60 ($95 for international students). Electronic applications accepted. *Expenses:* Tuition, area resident: Part-time $239.50 per credit. Tuition, state resident: part-time $239.50 per credit. Tuition, nonresident: part-time $503 per credit. Required fees: $108 per semester. Tuition and fees vary according to course load, program and reciprocity agreements. *Financial support:* In 2010–11, 8 research assistantships with partial tuition reimbursements (averaging $10,000 per year), 5 teaching assistantships with partial tuition reimbursements (averaging $10,000 per year) were awarded; institutionally sponsored loans, scholarships/grants, health care benefits, and unspecified assistantships also available. Financial award application deadline: 3/1. Total annual research expenditures: $1,945. *Unit head:* Dr. Mark Burns, Chair/Professor, 702-895-3892, Fax: 702-895-4194, E-mail: mark.burns@unlv.edu. *Application contact:* Graduate College Admissions Evaluator, 702-895-3320, Fax: 702-895-4180, E-mail: gradcollege@unlv.edu.

University of Nevada, Reno, Graduate School, College of Liberal Arts, Department of Fine Arts, Reno, NV 89557. Offers MFA. *Degree requirements:* For master's, thesis optional. *Entrance requirements:* For master's, minimum GPA of 2.75. Additional exam requirements/recommendations for international students: Required—TOEFL (minimum score 500 paper-based; 173 computer-based; 61 iBT), IELTS (minimum score 6). Electronic applications accepted.

Expenses: Tuition, state resident: full-time $2219; part-time $246 per credit. Tuition, nonresident: part-time $510 per credit. International tuition: $9009 full-time. Required fees: $59 per term. One-time fee: $101. Tuition and fees vary according to course load. *Faculty research:* Ceramics; digital-media; drawing; painting; performance; photography; printmaking; sculpture; video; studio program supported by a strong emphasis in the areas of contemporary art, theory and criticism.

University of New Hampshire, Graduate School, College of Liberal Arts, Program in Painting, Durham, NH 03824. Offers MFA. Program offered in fall only. Part-time programs available. *Faculty:* 12 full-time (4 women). *Students:* 4 full-time (2 women); includes 1 minority (Asian, non-Hispanic/Latino). Average age 35. 20 applicants, 30% accepted, 4 enrolled. In 2010, 3 master's awarded. *Degree requirements:* For master's, thesis or alternative. *Entrance requirements:* For master's, slide portfolio. Additional exam requirements/recommendations for international students: Required—TOEFL (minimum score 550 paper-based; 213 computer-based; 80 iBT). *Application deadline:* For fall admission, 2/15 priority date for domestic students, 2/15 for international students. Applications are processed on a rolling basis. Application fee: $65. Electronic applications accepted. *Financial support:* Fellowships, research assistantships, teaching assistantships, career-related internships or fieldwork, Federal Work-Study, and scholarships/grants available. Support available to part-time students. Financial award application deadline: 2/15. *Unit head:* Michael McConnell, Chair, 603-862-3820. *Application contact:* Eileen Wong, Administrative Assistant, 603-862-3820, E-mail: mfa.painting@unh.edu.

University of New Mexico, Graduate School, College of Fine Arts, Department of Art and Art History, Program in Studio Arts, Albuquerque, NM 87131-2039. Offers MFA. *Students:* 45 full-time (31 women), 5 part-time (3 women); includes 1 Black or African American, non-Hispanic/Latino; 1 American Indian or Alaska Native, non-Hispanic/Latino; 1 Asian, non-Hispanic/Latino; 3 Hispanic/Latino, 6 international. Average age 31. 167 applicants, 14% accepted, 16 enrolled. *Degree requirements:* For master's, comprehensive exam, thesis or alternative, studio reviews, qualifying exams. *Entrance requirements:* Additional exam requirements/recommendations for international students: Required—TOEFL (minimum score 550 paper-based; 213 computer-based). *Application deadline:* For fall admission, 1/15 for domestic students. Application fee: $50. Electronic applications accepted. *Expenses:* Tuition, state resident: full-time $5991; part-time $251 per credit hour. Tuition, nonresident: full-time $14,405; part-time $800.20 per credit hour. Tuition and fees vary according to course level, course load, program and reciprocity agreements. *Financial support:* In 2010–11, 48 students received support, including 1 fellowship (averaging $3,600 per year), 6 research assistantships with tuition reimbursements available (averaging $2,714 per year), 33 teaching assistantships with partial tuition reimbursements available (averaging $6,233 per year); Federal Work-Study, institutionally sponsored loans, scholarships/grants, health care benefits, and unspecified assistantships also available. Support available to part-time students. Financial award application deadline: 3/1; financial award applicants required to submit FAFSA. *Faculty research:* Photography, painting, drawing, printmaking, sculpture and ceramics, electronic arts, art and ecology. Total annual research expenditures: $23. *Unit head:* Dr. David Craven, Chair, 505-277-5861, Fax: 505-277-5955, E-mail: dcraven@unm.edu. *Application contact:* Kat Heatherington, Graduate Advisor, 505-277-6672, Fax: 505-277-5955, E-mail: art255@unm.edu.

University of New Orleans, Graduate School, College of Liberal Arts, Department of Fine Arts, New Orleans, LA 70148. Offers MFA. *Accreditation:* NASAD. *Degree requirements:* For master's, thesis. *Entrance requirements:* For master's, GRE General Test, slide review. Additional exam requirements/recommendations for international students: Required—TOEFL (minimum score 550 paper-based; 213 computer-based; 79 iBT). Electronic applications accepted. *Faculty research:* Large-scale painting and sculpture, black-and-white and color photography, computer graphics.

The University of North Carolina at Chapel Hill, Graduate School, College of Arts and Sciences, Department of Art, Studio Art Program, Chapel Hill, NC 27599. Offers MFA. *Degree requirements:* For master's, variable foreign language requirement. *Entrance requirements:* For master's, minimum GPA of 3.0, portfolio. Electronic applications accepted. *Faculty research:* Environmental installation, painting, photography, mixed media, printmaking.

The University of North Carolina at Greensboro, Graduate School, College of Arts and Sciences, Department of Art, Greensboro, NC 27412-5001. Offers studio arts (MFA). *Degree requirements:* For master's, thesis (for some programs). *Entrance requirements:* For master's, GRE General Test, 39 hours of course work in studio art, 15 hours of course work in art history, portfolio. Additional exam requirements/recommendations for international students: Required—TOEFL. Electronic applications accepted.

University of North Dakota, Graduate School, College of Arts and Sciences, Department of Visual Arts, Grand Forks, ND 58202. Offers MFA. *Accreditation:* NASAD. *Faculty:* 12 full-time (5 women). *Students:* 18 full-time (11 women), 4 part-time (2 women); includes 3 minority (1 American Indian or Alaska Native, non-Hispanic/Latino; 2 Asian, non-Hispanic/Latino), 1 international. Average age 35. 12 applicants, 67% accepted, 8 enrolled. In 2010, 2 master's awarded. *Degree requirements:* For master's, thesis or alternative, comprehensive evaluation, professional exhibition. *Entrance requirements:* For master's, minimum GPA of 3.0. Additional exam requirements/recommendations for international students: Required—TOEFL (minimum score 550 paper-based; 213 computer-based; 79 iBT), IELTS (minimum score 6.5). *Application deadline:* For fall admission, 8/1 priority date for domestic students, 5/1 priority date for international students; for spring admission, 12/1 priority date for domestic students, 9/1 priority date for international students. Applications are processed on a rolling basis. Application fee: $35. Electronic applications accepted. *Expenses:* Tuition, state resident: full-time $5857; part-time $306.74 per credit. Tuition, nonresident: full-time $15,666; part-time $729.77 per credit. Required fees: $53.42 per credit. Tuition and fees vary according to course load, program and reciprocity agreements. *Financial support:* In 2010–11, 16 students received support, including 6 research assistantships (averaging $10,413 per year), 9 teaching assistantships with full tuition reimbursements available (averaging $10,413 per year); fellowships with full and partial tuition reimbursements available, Federal Work-Study, institutionally sponsored loans, scholarships/grants, health care benefits, tuition waivers (full and partial), and unspecified assistantships also available. Support available to part-time students. Financial award application deadline: 3/15; financial award applicants required to submit FAFSA. *Faculty research:* Ceramics, drawing, metalsmithing, printmaking, painting. Total annual research expenditures: $12,300. *Unit head:* Dr. Anita Monsebroten, Graduate Director, 701-777-2257, Fax: 701-777-2903, E-mail: anita_monsebroten@und.nodak.edu. *Application contact:* Matt Anderson, Admissions Specialist, 701-777-2947, Fax: 701-777-3619, E-mail: matthew.anderson@gradschool.und.edu.

University of Northern Colorado, Graduate School, College of Performing and Visual Arts, School of Visual Arts, Greeley, CO 80639. Offers visual arts (MA). Part-time programs available. *Faculty:* 5 full-time (3 women). *Students:* 8 part-time (7 women). Average age 43. 10 applicants, 80% accepted, 0 enrolled. In 2010, 8 master's awarded. *Degree requirements:* For master's, comprehensive exam, thesis. *Entrance requirements:* For master's, GRE General Test, portfolio, 3 letters of recommendation, minimum undergraduate GPA of 3.0. *Application deadline:* Applications are processed on a rolling basis. Application fee: $50 ($60 for international students). Electronic applications accepted. *Expenses:* Tuition, state resident: full-time $6199; part-time $344 per credit hour. Tuition, nonresident: full-time $14,834; part-time $824 per credit hour. Required fees: $1091; $60.60 per credit hour. Tuition and fees vary according to course load, degree level and program. *Financial support:* In 2010–11, 3 teaching assistantships (averaging $5,065 per year) were awarded; fellowships, research assistantships, unspecified assistantships also available. Financial award application deadline: 3/1; financial award applicants required to submit FAFSA. *Unit head:* Dr. Dennis Morimoto, Director, 970-351-2143, Fax: 970-351-2299. *Application contact:* Linda Sisson, Graduate Student Admission Coordinator, 970-351-1807, Fax: 970-351-2371, E-mail: linda.sisson@unco.edu.

University of Northern Iowa, Graduate College, College of Humanities and Fine Arts, Department of Art, Cedar Falls, IA 50614. Offers art education (MA). *Accreditation:* NASAD. Part-time and evening/weekend programs available. *Students:* 1 full-time (0 women). 1 applicant, 0% accepted, 0 enrolled. In 2010, 6 master's awarded. *Degree requirements:* For master's, comprehensive exam (for some programs), thesis or alternative. *Entrance requirements:* For master's, minimum GPA of 3.0, portfolio. Additional exam requirements/recommendations for international students: Required—TOEFL (minimum score 500 paper-based; 180 computer-based; 61 iBT). *Application deadline:* For fall admission, 8/1 priority date for domestic students. Applications are processed on a rolling basis. Application fee: $50 ($70 for international students). Electronic applications accepted. *Financial support:* Career-related internships or fieldwork, Federal Work-Study, scholarships/grants, and tuition waivers (full and partial) available. Support available to part-time students. Financial award application deadline: 2/1. *Unit head:* Dr. Jeffery Byrd, Head/Professor, 319-273-2077, Fax: 319-273-7333, E-mail: jeffery.byrd@uni.edu. *Application contact:* Laurie S. Russell, Record Analyst, 319-273-2623, Fax: 319-273-2885, E-mail: laurie.russell@uni.edu.

University of North Texas, Toulouse Graduate School, College of Visual Arts and Design, Department of Studio Art, Denton, TX 76203. Offers metalsmithing and jewelry (MFA), including ceramics, fibers, metalsmithing and jewelry, new media, photography, printmaking, sculpture, watercolor. Part-time programs available. *Degree requirements:* For master's, exhibition, extended artists statement disk of 20 images from show, committee approval. *Entrance requirements:* For master's, resume, 2 letters of recommendation, portfolio of 20 works. Additional exam requirements/recommendations for international students: Recommended—TOEFL (minimum score 550 paper-based; 213 computer-based; 79 iBT). *Application deadline:* Applications are processed on a rolling basis. Electronic applications accepted. *Expenses:* Tuition, state resident: full-time $4298; part-time $239 per credit hour. Tuition, nonresident: full-time $10,782; part-time $549 per credit hour. Required fees: $1292; $270 per credit hour. *Financial support:* Fellowships with partial tuition reimbursements, teaching assistantships with partial tuition reimbursements, tuition waivers and unspecified assistantships available. Financial award applicants required to submit FAFSA. *Faculty research:* Altered terrain, enameling on metal, electrical and mechanical interactivity, interactive animation, environmental conservation.

University of Notre Dame, Graduate School, College of Arts and Letters, Division of Humanities, Department of Art, Art History, and Design, Notre Dame, IN 46556. Offers art history (MA); design (MFA), including graphic design, industrial design; studio art (MFA), including ceramics, painting, photography, printmaking, sculpture. *Accreditation:* NASAD. *Degree requirements:* For master's, comprehensive exam (for some programs), thesis. *Entrance requirements:* For master's, GRE General Test, minimum GPA of 3.0. Additional exam requirements/recommendations for international students: Required—TOEFL (minimum score 600 paper-based; 250 computer-based; 80 iBT). Electronic applications accepted. *Faculty research:* Studio art practice in ceramics, printing, photography, printmaking and sculpture, graphic design and industrial design, digital imaging in design and photography, Renaissance and American art history, contemporary art theory and criticism.

University of Oklahoma, Weitzenhoffer Family College of Fine Arts, School of Art and Art History, Program in Art, Norman, OK 73019. Offers art (MFA), including ceramics, film, painting, photography, printmaking, sculpture, video, visual communication. MA applicants admitted fall/spring; MFA applicants admitted fall only. *Students:* 17 full-time (9 women), 2 part-time (1 woman); includes 5 minority (3 American Indian or Alaska Native, non-Hispanic/Latino; 2 Native Hawaiian or other Pacific Islander, non-Hispanic/Latino), 3 international. Average age 29. 27 applicants, 41% accepted, 8 enrolled. In 2010, 3 master's awarded. *Degree requirements:* For master's, thesis (MA), exhibit (MFA), departmental qualifying exam. *Entrance requirements:* For master's, GRE General Test (MA). Additional exam requirements/recommendations for international students: Required—TOEFL (minimum score 550 paper-based; 213 computer-based; 79 iBT). *Application deadline:* For fall admission, 2/1 for domestic and international students; for spring admission, 10/1 for domestic and international students. Applications are processed on a rolling basis. Application fee: $40 ($90 for international students). Electronic applications accepted. *Expenses:* Tuition, state resident: full-time $3893; part-time $162.20 per credit hour. Tuition, nonresident: full-time $14,167; part-time $590.30 per credit hour. Required fees: $2523; $94.60 per credit hour. Tuition and fees vary according to course load and degree level. *Financial support:* Career-related internships or fieldwork, scholarships/grants, tuition waivers (full and partial), and unspecified assistantships available. Financial award application deadline: 4/7; financial award applicants required to submit FAFSA. *Faculty research:* Interactions between technology and art; propaganda banners relating to the nuclear age; investigation of the nature of structures; relationships between history, myth and culture; gestural vase forms and slabbed formed architectural vessels. *Unit head:* Mary Jo Watson, Director, 405-325-2691, Fax: 405-325-1668, E-mail: mjwatson@ou.edu. *Application contact:* Andrew Strout, Graduate Liaison, 405-325-4094, Fax: 405-325-1668, E-mail: aestrout@ou.edu.

University of Oregon, Graduate School, School of Architecture and Allied Arts, Department of Art, Eugene, OR 97403. Offers MFA. *Accreditation:* NASAD. *Degree requirements:* For master's, thesis or alternative. *Entrance requirements:* For master's, BFA or equivalent. Additional exam requirements/recommendations for international students: Required—TOEFL.

University of Pennsylvania, School of Design, Department of Fine Arts, Philadelphia, PA 19104. Offers MFA. *Faculty:* 3 full-time (1 woman), 1 (woman) part-time/adjunct. *Students:* 36 full-time (27 women), 3 part-time (1 woman); includes 3 Black or African American, non-Hispanic/Latino; 2 Asian, non-Hispanic/Latino; 2 Hispanic/Latino, 5 international. 165 applicants, 18% accepted, 14 enrolled. In 2010, 18 master's awarded. *Entrance requirements:* For master's, slide portfolio. Additional exam requirements/recommendations for international students: Required—TOEFL. *Application deadline:* For fall admission, 1/2 priority date for domestic students. Application fee: $70. *Expenses:* Tuition: Full-time $25,660; part-time $4758 per course. Required fees: $2152; $270 per course. Tuition and fees vary according to course load, degree level and program. *Financial support:* Fellowships, teaching assistantships available. Financial award applicants required to submit FAFSA. *Faculty research:* Painting, sculpture, printmaking, combined media.

University of Regina, Faculty of Graduate Studies and Research, Faculty of Fine Arts, Department of Visual Arts, Regina, SK S4S 0A2, Canada. Offers ceramics (MFA); drawing (MFA); intermedia (MFA); painting (MFA); sculpture (MFA). *Faculty:* 9 full-time (5 women). *Students:* 9 full-time (6 women), 1 (woman) part-time. 7 applicants, 57% accepted. In 2010, 1 master's awarded. *Degree requirements:* For master's, exhibition, support paper, oral defense. *Entrance requirements:* For master's, documentation of recent work. Additional exam requirements/recommendations for international students; Required—TOEFL (minimum score 580 paper-based; 80 iBT). *Application deadline:* For fall admission, 2/15 for domestic and international students. Application fee: $100. Electronic applications accepted. Tuition and fees charges are reported in Canadian dollars. *Expenses:* Tuition, area resident: Full-time $3244.50 Canadian dollars; part-time $180.25 Canadian dollars per credit hour. International tuition: $4744.50 Canadian dollars full-time. Required fees: $494 Canadian dollars; $115.25 Canadian dollars per credit hour. $115.25 Canadian dollars per semester. Tuition and fees vary according to program. *Financial support:* In 2010–11, 1 fellowship (averaging $18,000 per year), 2 research assistantships (averaging $16,500 per year), 2 teaching assistantships (averaging $6,759 per year) were awarded; scholarships/grants also available. Financial award application deadline: 6/15. *Faculty research:* Contemporary visual art theory and practice; art history; curatorial practice; print media; drawing/painting, sculpture, and ceramics. *Unit head:* Rachelle Viader Knowles, Head, 306-585-5552, Fax: 306-585-5526, E-mail: rachelle.viader.knowles@uregina.ca. *Application contact:* Rachelle Viader Knowles, Graduate Program Coordinator, 306-585-5552, Fax: 306-585-5526, E-mail: rachelle.viader.knowles@uregina.ca.

University of Rochester, School of Arts and Sciences, Department of Art and Art History, Rochester, NY 14627. Offers visual and cultural studies (MA, PhD). Terminal master's awarded for partial completion of doctoral program. *Degree requirements:* For master's, thesis optional; for doctorate, one foreign language, thesis/dissertation, qualifying exam. *Entrance requirements:*

Art/Fine Arts

University of Rochester (continued)
For master's and doctorate, GRE General Test. Additional exam requirements/recommendations for international students: Required—TOEFL.

University of Saint Francis, Graduate School, Department of Art and Visual Communication, Fort Wayne, IN 46808-3994. Offers fine art (MA). *Accreditation:* NASAD. Part-time and evening/weekend programs available. *Degree requirements:* For master's, thesis, exhibit. *Entrance requirements:* For master's, minimum GPA of 3.0 in art, portfolio. *Expenses:* Tuition: Part-time $770 per semester hour. Part-time tuition and fees vary according to program.

University of Saskatchewan, College of Graduate Studies and Research, College of Arts and Sciences, Department of Art and Art History, Saskatoon, SK S7N 5A2, Canada. Offers MFA. Part-time programs available. *Degree requirements:* For master's, thesis. *Entrance requirements:* Additional exam requirements/recommendations for international students: Required—TOEFL (minimum score 80 iBT); Recommended—IELTS (minimum score 6.5).

University of South Carolina, The Graduate School, College of Arts and Sciences, Department of Art, Columbia, SC 29208. Offers art education (IMA, MA, MAT); art history (MA); art studio (MA); media arts (MMA); studio art (MFA). *Accreditation:* NASAD. *Degree requirements:* For master's, comprehensive exam (for some programs), thesis (for some programs). *Entrance requirements:* For master's, GRE General Test or MAT, portfolio. Additional exam requirements/recommendations for international students: Required—TOEFL. Electronic applications accepted. *Faculty research:* Script writing, teaching art at the elementary and secondary levels of education, history of art and architecture.

The University of South Dakota, Graduate School, College of Fine Arts, Department of Art, Vermillion, SD 57069-2390. Offers MFA. *Accreditation:* NASAD. *Degree requirements:* For master's, thesis or alternative. *Entrance requirements:* For master's, portfolio, minimum GPA of 2.7. Additional exam requirements/recommendations for international students: Required—TOEFL (minimum score 550 paper-based; 213 computer-based; 79 iBT). Electronic applications accepted.

University of Southern California, Graduate School, Dana and David Dornsife College of Letters, Arts and Sciences, Department of Art History, Los Angeles, CA 90089. Offers art history (MA, PhD); visual studies (Graduate Certificate). *Faculty:* 11 full-time (7 women), 5 part-time/adjunct (2 women). *Students:* 34 full-time (27 women); includes 7 minority (6 Asian, non-Hispanic/Latino; 1 Hispanic/Latino), 4 international. 40 applicants, 10% accepted, 4 enrolled. In 2010, 6 master's, 1 doctorate, 4 other advanced degrees awarded. *Degree requirements:* For doctorate, 2 foreign languages, comprehensive exam, thesis/dissertation, 60 units. *Entrance requirements:* For doctorate, GRE. Additional exam requirements/recommendations for international students: Required—TOEFL. *Application deadline:* For fall admission, 12/1 for domestic students. Application fee: $85. *Expenses:* Tuition: Full-time $31,240; part-time $1420 per unit. Required fees: $600. One-time fee: $35 full-time. Full-time tuition and fees vary according to degree level and program. *Financial support:* In 2010–11, 31 students received support, including 10 fellowships with full tuition reimbursements available (averaging $19,000 per year), 12 teaching assistantships with full tuition reimbursements available (averaging $19,000 per year); career-related internships or fieldwork, institutionally sponsored loans, scholarships/grants, health care benefits, unspecified assistantships, and cash awards for travel and research also available. Financial award application deadline: 2/1. *Faculty research:* Ancient, medieval, Renaissance, eighteenth-nineteenth century, contemporary. *Unit head:* Dr. Carolyn Malone, Professor and Chair, 213-740-4552, Fax: 213-740-8971, E-mail: cmalone@usc.edu. *Application contact:* Jeanne Herman, Academic Advisor, 213-740-9516, Fax: 213-740-8971, E-mail: jaherman@usc.edu.

University of Southern California, Graduate School, Roski School of Fine Arts, Graduate Programs in Fine Arts, Los Angeles, CA 90089. Offers new genres (MFA); painting/drawing (MFA); photography (MFA); sculpture (MFA). *Faculty:* 5 full-time (3 women), 1 part-time/adjunct (0 women). *Students:* 17 full-time (6 women), 3 international. Average age 27. 312 applicants, 3% accepted, 8 enrolled. In 2010, 8 master's awarded. *Degree requirements:* For master's, thesis. *Entrance requirements:* For master's, Not Required, portfolio, artist statement, 3 letters of recommendation. Additional exam requirements/recommendations for international students: Required—TOEFL (minimum score 600 paper-based; 250 computer-based; 100 iBT). *Application deadline:* For fall admission, 2/1 for domestic and international students. Application fee: $85. Electronic applications accepted. *Expenses:* Tuition: Full-time $31,240; part-time $1420 per unit. Required fees: $600. One-time fee: $35 full-time. Full-time tuition and fees vary according to degree level and program. *Financial support:* In 2010–11, 16 students received support, including 16 teaching assistantships with full tuition reimbursements available (averaging $9,625 per year); Federal Work-Study, health care benefits, and unspecified assistantships also available. Financial award application deadline: 2/1; financial award applicants required to submit FAFSA. *Faculty research:* Fine art production in the areas of photography, video, sculpture, drawing, and performance. *Unit head:* Jud Fine, Director, MFA program, 213-743-1804, Fax: 213-743-4563. *Application contact:* Dwayne Moser, MFA Program Coordinator, 213-743-1804, Fax: 213-743-4563, E-mail: dmoser@usc.edu.

University of South Florida, Graduate School, College of The Arts, School of Art and Art History, Tampa, FL 33620-9951. Offers art history (MA); studio art (MFA). *Accreditation:* NASAD. Part-time programs available. *Faculty:* 8 full-time (4 women). *Students:* 40 full-time (22 women), 8 part-time (6 women); includes 1 Black or African American, non-Hispanic/Latino; 2 American Indian or Alaska Native, non-Hispanic/Latino; 5 Hispanic/Latino; 1 Two or more races, non-Hispanic/Latino, 3 international. Average age 31. 105 applicants, 25% accepted, 17 enrolled. In 2010, 12 master's awarded. *Degree requirements:* For master's, thesis, exhibition (MFA). *Entrance requirements:* For master's, GRE General Test (MA), minimum GPA of 3.0 in last 60 hours of coursework. *Application deadline:* For fall admission, 1/15 for domestic students, 1/2 for international students. Application fee: $30. *Financial support:* In 2010–11, 34 teaching assistantships with partial tuition reimbursements (averaging $9,265 per year) were awarded; scholarships/grants, health care benefits, and unspecified assistantships also available. Support available to part-time students. Financial award application deadline: 2/15; financial award applicants required to submit FAFSA. *Faculty research:* Contemporary art and role of the artist, identity strategies, political iconography, art practice and technology, construction of race in art. Total annual research expenditures: $184,644. *Unit head:* Prof. Wallace Wilson, Director, School of Art and Art History, 813-974-2360, Fax: 813-974-9226, E-mail: wwilson2@usf.edu. *Application contact:* Gloria Ann Quigley, Academic Specialist, 813-974-9249, Fax: 813-974-9226, E-mail: gquigley@usf.edu.

The University of Tennessee, Graduate School, College of Arts and Sciences, School of Art, Knoxville, TN 37996. Offers ceramics (MFA); drawing (MFA); graphic design (MFA); inter-area studies (MFA); media arts (MFA); painting (MFA); printmaking (MFA); sculpture (MFA); watercolor (MFA). *Accreditation:* NASAD. *Degree requirements:* For master's, thesis or alternative, exhibit. *Entrance requirements:* For master's, portfolio, minimum GPA of 2.7. Additional exam requirements/recommendations for international students: Required—TOEFL. Electronic applications accepted. *Expenses:* Tuition, state resident: full-time $7440; part-time $414 per credit hour. Tuition, nonresident: full-time $22,478; part-time $1250 per credit hour. Required fees: $922; $43 per credit hour. Tuition and fees vary according to program.

The University of Texas at Arlington, Graduate School, College of Liberal Arts, Department of Art and Art History, Arlington, TX 76019. Offers film and video (MFA); glass (MFA); intermedia (MFA); visual communication (MFA). *Accreditation:* NASAD. *Faculty:* 21 full-time (7 women). *Students:* 25 full-time (10 women), 3 part-time (all women); includes 5 minority (1 Black or African American, non-Hispanic/Latino; 1 American Indian or Alaska Native, non-Hispanic/Latino; 1 Asian, non-Hispanic/Latino; 2 Hispanic/Latino), 2 international. 24 applicants, 63% accepted, 10 enrolled. In 2010, 3 master's awarded. *Degree requirements:* For master's, thesis or alternative. *Entrance requirements:* For master's, minimum GPA of 3.0, 3 letters of recommendation, portfolio, resume. Additional exam requirements/recommendations for inter-

national students: Required—TOEFL (minimum score 550 paper-based; 213 computer-based). *Application deadline:* For fall admission, 1/15 priority date for domestic and international students; for spring admission, 10/15 priority date for domestic and international students. Applications are processed on a rolling basis. Electronic applications accepted. *Expenses:* Tuition, state resident: full-time $7500. Tuition, nonresident: full-time $13,080. International tuition: $13,250 full-time. *Financial support:* In 2010–11, 4 fellowships (averaging $1,000 per year), 4 research assistantships (averaging $4,000 per year), 18 teaching assistantships (averaging $6,000 per year) were awarded; scholarships/grants and unspecified assistantships also available. Financial award applicants required to submit FAFSA. *Unit head:* Prof. Robert Hower, Chair/Professor, 817-272-2891, Fax: 817-272-2805, E-mail: hower@uta.edu. *Application contact:* Prof. Nancy Palmeri, Graduate Advisor/Associate Professor, 817-272-2891, Fax: 817-272-2805, E-mail: palmeri@uta.edu.

The University of Texas at Austin, Graduate School, College of Fine Arts, Department of Art and Art History, Program in Studio Art, Austin, TX 78712-1111. Offers MFA. *Accreditation:* NASAD. *Degree requirements:* For master's, thesis, oral exam. *Entrance requirements:* For master's, minimum GPA of 3.0, portfolio of 15 slides. Electronic applications accepted. *Faculty research:* Painting, sculpture, transmedia, photography, printmaking.

The University of Texas at El Paso, Graduate School, College of Liberal Arts, Department of Art, El Paso, TX 79968-0001. Offers art education (MA); studio art (MA). Part-time and evening/weekend programs available. *Students:* 12 (8 women); includes 9 Hispanic/Latino, 2 international. Average age 34. In 2010, 1 master's awarded. *Degree requirements:* For master's, thesis optional. *Entrance requirements:* For master's, minimum GPA of 3.0, digital portfolio, letters of recommendation. Additional exam requirements/recommendations for international students: Required—TOEFL; Recommended—IELTS. *Application deadline:* For fall admission, 8/1 priority date for domestic students, 3/1 for international students; for spring admission, 11/1 priority date for domestic students, 9/1 for international students. Applications are processed on a rolling basis. Application fee: $45 ($80 for international students). Electronic applications accepted. *Financial support:* In 2010–11, research assistantships with partial tuition reimbursements (averaging $18,625 per year), teaching assistantships with partial tuition reimbursements (averaging $14,900 per year) were awarded; fellowships with partial tuition reimbursements, institutionally sponsored loans, scholarships/grants, health care benefits, tuition waivers (partial), and unspecified assistantships also available. Support available to part-time students. Financial award application deadline: 3/15; financial award applicants required to submit FAFSA. *Unit head:* Dr. J. Quinnan, Chair, 915-747-5181, Fax: 915-747-6749, E-mail: jquinnan@utep.edu. *Application contact:* Dr. Patricia D. Witherspoon, Dean of the Graduate School, 915-747-5491, Fax: 915-747-5788, E-mail: withersp@utep.edu.

The University of Texas at San Antonio, College of Liberal and Fine Arts, Department of Art and Art History, San Antonio, TX 78249-0617. Offers art (MFA); art history (MA). *Accreditation:* NASAD (one or more programs are accredited). *Faculty:* 15 full-time (7 women). *Students:* 25 full-time (16 women), 14 part-time (12 women); includes 12 minority (1 American Indian or Alaska Native, non-Hispanic/Latino; 10 Hispanic/Latino; 1 Two or more races, non-Hispanic/Latino), 2 international. Average age 30. 30 applicants, 60% accepted, 8 enrolled. In 2010, 10 master's awarded. *Degree requirements:* For master's, comprehensive exam (for some programs), thesis (for some programs). *Entrance requirements:* For master's, GRE General Test, portfolio, minimum GPA of 3.0 in last 60 hours, 3 letters of recommendation. Additional exam requirements/recommendations for international students: Required—TOEFL (minimum score 500 paper-based; 173 computer-based; 61 iBT), IELTS (minimum score 5). *Application deadline:* For fall admission, 7/1 for domestic students, 4/1 for international students; for spring admission, 11/1 for domestic students, 9/1 for international students. Applications are processed on a rolling basis. Application fee: $45 ($80 for international students). Electronic applications accepted. *Expenses:* Tuition, state resident: full-time $4172; part-time $231.75 per credit hour. Tuition, nonresident: full-time $15,332; part-time $851.75 per credit hour. *Financial support:* In 2010–11, 24 students received support, including 15 research assistantships (averaging $15,074 per year), 13 teaching assistantships (averaging $7,569 per year); career-related internships or fieldwork, scholarships/grants, tuition waivers (partial), and unspecified assistantships also available. Support available to part-time students. *Faculty research:* Artistic production in media; art history and criticism, focusing on American and Hispanic art. *Unit head:* Dr. Gregory Elliott, Department Chair, 210-458-4362, Fax: 210-458-4356, E-mail: greg.elliott@utsa.edu. *Application contact:* Veronica Ramirez, Assistant Dean of the Graduate School, 210-458-4330, Fax: 210-458-4332, E-mail: graduatestudies@utsa.edu.

The University of Texas at Tyler, College of Arts and Sciences, Department of Art and Art History, Tyler, TX 75799-0001. Offers art history (MA); interdisciplinary (MAIS); studio art (MFA). *Degree requirements:* For master's, thesis, graduate committee review. *Entrance requirements:* For master's, minimum GPA of 3.0. Additional exam requirements/recommendations for international students: Required—TOEFL (minimum score 79 computer-based). *Faculty research:* Classical myths in contemporary art, social issues in contemporary art, casting methods, Renaissance art.

The University of Texas–Pan American, College of Arts and Humanities, Department of Art, Edinburg, TX 78539. Offers MFA. Part-time programs available. *Degree requirements:* For master's, thesis, thesis show of artwork. *Entrance requirements:* For master's, bachelor's degree in fine arts, portfolio, 3 letters of reference. *Faculty research:* Creative art, ceramics, painting, sculpture, computer art.

The University of the Arts, College of Art, Media and Design, Department of Book Arts/Printmaking, Philadelphia, PA 19102-4944. Offers MFA. *Accreditation:* NASAD. *Degree requirements:* For master's, thesis. *Entrance requirements:* For master's, portfolio of 20-30 digital images showing work that represents applicant's full range of studio experience, preferably including printmaking and book arts; official transcripts from each undergraduate or graduate school attended; three letters of recommendation; one- to two-page statement of professional plans and goals; personal interview. Additional exam requirements/recommendations for international students: Required—TOEFL (minimum score 580 paper-based, 92 iBT) or IELTS (minimum score 6.5).

See Display on next page and Close-Up on page 229.

The University of the Arts, College of Art, Media and Design, Program in Ceramics, Philadelphia, PA 19102-4944. Offers MFA. Offered during summer only. *Accreditation:* NASAD. Part-time programs available. *Degree requirements:* For master's, thesis, summer residency. *Entrance requirements:* For master's, portfolio. Additional exam requirements/recommendations for international students: Required—TOEFL (minimum score 550 paper-based; 213 computer-based). Electronic applications accepted.

See Display on next page and Close-Up on page 229.

The University of the Arts, College of Art, Media and Design, Program in Painting, Philadelphia, PA 19102-4944. Offers MFA. Offered during summer only. *Accreditation:* NASAD. Part-time programs available. *Degree requirements:* For master's, thesis, summer residency. *Entrance requirements:* For master's, portfolio. Additional exam requirements/recommendations for international students: Required—TOEFL (minimum score 550 paper-based; 213 computer-based).

See Display on next page and Close-Up on page 229.

The University of the Arts, College of Art, Media and Design, Program in Sculpture, Philadelphia, PA 19102-4944. Offers MFA. Offered during summer only. *Accreditation:* NASAD. Part-time programs available. *Degree requirements:* For master's, thesis, summer residency. *Entrance requirements:* For master's, portfolio. Additional exam requirements/recommendations for international students: Required—TOEFL (minimum score 550 paper-based; 213 computer-based).

See Display on next page and Close-Up on page 229.

University of Toronto, School of Graduate Studies, Humanities Division, Department of Art, Toronto, ON M5S 1A1, Canada. Offers art history (MA, PhD); visual studies (MVS). Part-time programs available. *Degree requirements:* For master's, 2 foreign languages, language proficiency exams; for doctorate, 2 foreign languages, comprehensive exam, thesis/dissertation. *Entrance requirements:* For master's, coursework in a foreign language, 3 letters of reference, sample research paper, minimum B+ average in senior art history and/or humanities courses; for doctorate, minimum A– average in senior art history and/or humanities courses, 2 letters of reference, sample research paper.

University of Tulsa, Graduate School, College of Arts and Sciences, Department of Art, Tulsa, OK 74104-3189. Offers MA, MFA, MTA. Part-time programs available. *Faculty:* 7 full-time (5 women), 4 part-time/adjunct (0 women). *Students:* 10 full-time (6 women), 3 part-time (2 women). Average age 34. 16 applicants, 31% accepted, 3 enrolled. In 2010, 2 master's awarded. *Degree requirements:* For master's, comprehensive exam (for some programs), thesis (for some programs). *Entrance requirements:* For master's, portfolio. Additional exam requirements/recommendations for international students: Required—TOEFL (minimum score 575 paper-based; 231 computer-based; 91 iBT), IELTS (minimum score 6.5). *Application deadline:* For fall admission, 2/1 for domestic and international students. Application fee: $40. Electronic applications accepted. *Expenses:* Tuition: Full-time $16,902; part-time $939 per credit hour. Required fees: $1020; $4 per credit hour. Tuition and fees vary according to course load. *Financial support:* In 2010–11, 7 students received support, including 1 fellowship with full tuition reimbursement available (averaging $14,000 per year), 6 teaching assistantships with full and partial tuition reimbursements available (averaging $11,942 per year); research assistantships with full tuition reimbursements available, career-related internships or fieldwork, Federal Work-Study, scholarships/grants, traineeships, health care benefits, tuition waivers (full and partial), and unspecified assistantships also available. Support available to part-time students. Financial award application deadline: 2/1; financial award applicants required to submit FAFSA. *Faculty research:* Drawing, painting, printmaking, ceramics, graphic design. *Unit head:* Dr. Susan Dixon, Chairperson, 918-631-2740, Fax: 918-631-3423, E-mail: susan-dixon@utulsa.edu. *Application contact:* Prof. Michelle Martin, Adviser, 918-631-2736, Fax: 918-631-3423, E-mail: michelle-martin@utulsa.edu.

University of Tulsa, Graduate School, College of Arts and Sciences, School of Education, Program in Teaching Arts, Tulsa, OK 74104-3189. Offers art (MTA); biology (MTA); English (MTA); history (MTA); mathematics (MTA); theatre (MTA). Part-time programs available. *Students:* 2 part-time (both women); includes 1 minority (American Indian or Alaska Native, non-Hispanic/Latino). Average age 31. 1 applicant, 0% accepted, 0 enrolled. In 2010, 2 master's awarded. *Entrance requirements:* For master's, GRE General Test. Additional exam requirements/recommendations for international students: Required—TOEFL (minimum score 575 paper-based; 231 computer-based), IELTS (minimum score 6.5). *Application deadline:* Applications are processed on a rolling basis. Application fee: $40. Electronic applications accepted. *Expenses:* Tuition: Full-time $16,902; part-time $939 per credit hour. Required fees: $1020; $4 per credit hour. Tuition and fees vary according to course load. *Financial support:* In 2010–11, 2 students received support, including 2 fellowships with full and partial tuition reimbursements available (averaging $2,191 per year); research assistantships with full and partial tuition reimbursements available, teaching assistantships with full and partial tuition reimbursements available, Federal Work-Study, scholarships/grants, and tuition waivers (full and partial) also available. Support available to part-time students. Financial award application deadline: 2/1; financial award applicants required to submit FAFSA. *Unit head:* Dr. David Brown, Advisor, 918-631-2719, Fax: 918-631-2133, E-mail: david-brown@utulsa.edu. *Application contact:* Dr. David Brown, Advisor, 918-631-2719, Fax: 918-631-2133, E-mail: david-brown@utulsa.edu.

University of Utah, Graduate School, College of Fine Arts, Department of Art and Art History, Salt Lake City, UT 84112-0380. Offers art history (MA); ceramics (MFA); community-based art education (MFA); drawing (MFA); graphic design (MFA); painting (MFA); photography/digital imaging (MFA); printmaking (MFA); sculpture/intermedia (MFA). *Faculty:* 23 full-time (10 women). *Students:* 17 full-time (12 women), 1 (woman) part-time; includes 2 minority (both Hispanic/ Latino), 1 international. Average age 29. 54 applicants, 20% accepted, 7 enrolled. In 2010, 5 master's awarded. *Degree requirements:* For master's, variable foreign language requirement, comprehensive exam (for some programs), thesis or alternative, exhibit and final project paper (for MFA). *Entrance requirements:* For master's, CD portfolio (MFA), writing sample (MA), curriculum vitae, letters of recommendation. Additional exam requirements/recommendations for international students: Required—TOEFL (minimum score 575 paper-based; 183 computer-based; 75 iBT). *Application deadline:* For fall admission, 1/2 priority date for domestic and international students. Application fee: $55 ($65 for international students). Electronic applications accepted. *Expenses:* Tuition, area resident: Part-time $179.19 per credit hour. Tuition, state resident: full-time $4384. Tuition, nonresident: full-time $16,684; part-time $630.67 per credit hour. Required fees: $350 per semester. Tuition and fees vary according to course load, degree level and program. *Financial support:* In 2010–11, 2 fellowships, 6 research assistantships with partial tuition reimbursements, 34 teaching assistantships with partial tuition reimbursements were awarded; Federal Work-Study, institutionally sponsored loans, scholarships/grants, tuition waivers (partial), unspecified assistantships, and stipends also available. Financial award application deadline: 1/2; financial award applicants required to submit FAFSA. *Faculty research:* Studio art, European art history, Asian art history, Latin American art history, twentieth century/contemporary art history. Total annual research expenditures: $23,714. *Unit head:* Prof. Brian Snapp, Chair, 801-581-8677, Fax: 801-585-6171, E-mail: b.snapp@utah.edu. *Application contact:* Prof. Paul Stout, Director of Graduate Studies, 801-581-8677, Fax: 801-585-6171, E-mail: pls@utah.edu.

University of Victoria, Faculty of Graduate Studies, Faculty of Fine Arts, Department of Visual Arts, Victoria, BC V8W 2Y2, Canada. Offers digital multimedia (MFA); drawing (MFA); painting (MFA); photography (MFA); sculpture (MFA); video (MFA). *Degree requirements:* For master's, exhibit, oral exam. *Entrance requirements:* For master's, portfolio, thesis. Additional exam requirements/recommendations for international students: Required—TOEFL (minimum score 575 paper-based; 233 computer-based), IELTS (minimum score 7). Electronic applications accepted.

University of Washington, Graduate School, College of Arts and Sciences, School of Art, Division of Art, Seattle, WA 98195. Offers painting and drawing (MFA); photography (MFA). *Degree requirements:* For master's, thesis, exhibit. *Entrance requirements:* For master's, BFA or equivalent academic work in art, 20 slide portfolio. Additional exam requirements/recommendations for international students: Required—TOEFL. Electronic applications accepted.

University of Waterloo, Graduate Studies, Faculty of Arts, Department of Fine Arts, Waterloo, ON N2L 3G1, Canada. Offers studio art (MFA). *Degree requirements:* For master's, thesis exhibit. *Entrance requirements:* For master's, honors degree, minimum A- average, sample of work. Additional exam requirements/recommendations for international students: Required—TOEFL, TWE. Electronic applications accepted. *Faculty research:* Ceramic sculpture, computer imaging, painting, drawing, contemporary art theory.

University of Windsor, Faculty of Graduate Studies, Faculty of Arts and Social Sciences, School of Visual Arts, Windsor, ON N9B 3P4, Canada. Offers MFA. *Degree requirements:* For master's, thesis. *Entrance requirements:* For master's, minimum B average, portfolio. Additional exam requirements/recommendations for international students: Required—TOEFL (minimum score 560 paper-based; 220 computer-based). Electronic applications accepted.

University of Wisconsin–Madison, Graduate School, School of Education, Department of Art, Madison, WI 53706-1380. Offers art (MA, MFA); art education (MA). *Accreditation:* NASAD. *Application deadline:* For fall admission, 1/10 for domestic students. Application fee: $56. Electronic applications accepted. *Expenses:* Tuition, state resident: full-time $9887; part-time $617.96 per credit. Tuition, nonresident: full-time $24,054; part-time $1503.40 per credit. Required fees: $67.63 per credit. Tuition and fees vary according to reciprocity agreements. *Financial support:* Fellowships with full tuition reimbursements, research assistantships with full tuition reimbursements, teaching assistantships with full tuition reimbursements, project

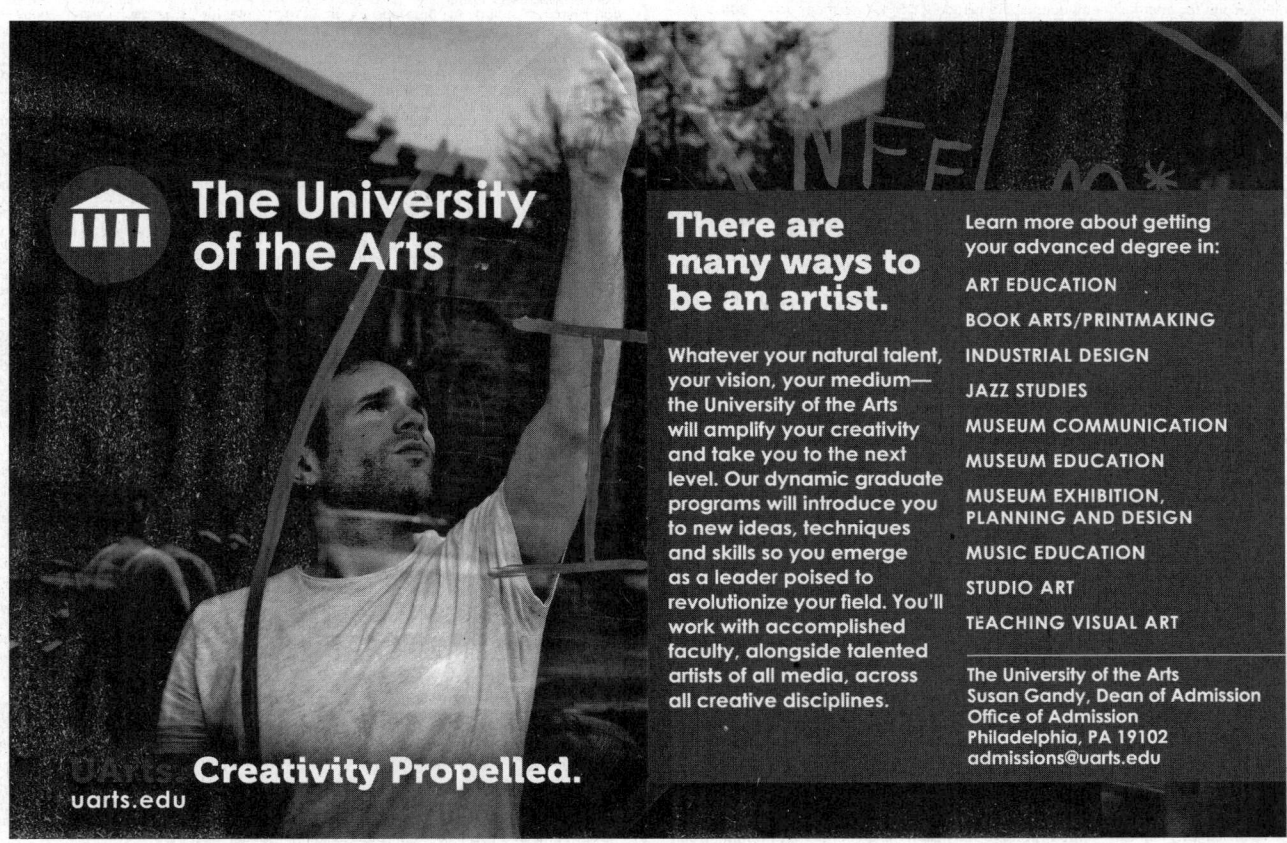

Art/Fine Arts

University of Wisconsin–Madison (continued)
assistantships available. *Unit head:* Dr. Tom Loeser, Chair, 608-262-1662, E-mail: tloeser@facstaff.wisc.edu. *Application contact:* Dr. Tom Loeser, Chair, 608-262-1662, E-mail: tloeser@facstaff.wisc.edu.

University of Wisconsin–Milwaukee, Graduate School, Peck School of the Arts, Department of Art and Design, Milwaukee, WI 53201-0413. Offers art (MA, MFA); art education (MA, MFA, MS). Part-time programs available. *Faculty:* 24 full-time (17 women). *Students:* 19 full-time (12 women), 4 part-time (3 women); includes 3 Asian, non-Hispanic/Latino; 1 Hispanic/Latino, 2 international. Average age 33. 59 applicants, 24% accepted, 9 enrolled. In 2010, 10 master's awarded. *Degree requirements:* For master's, comprehensive exam, thesis or alternative. *Entrance requirements:* For master's, portfolio. Additional exam requirements/recommendations for international students: Required—TOEFL (minimum score 550 paper-based; 79 iBT), IELTS (minimum score 6.5). *Application deadline:* For fall admission, 1/1 priority date for domestic students; for spring admission, 9/1 for domestic students. Applications are processed on a rolling basis. *Application fee:* $56 ($96 for international students). Electronic applications accepted. *Financial support:* In 2010–11, 10 teaching assistantships were awarded; career-related internships or fieldwork, health care benefits, unspecified assistantships, and project assistantships also available. Support available to part-time students. Financial award application deadline: 4/15. *Unit head:* Denis Sargent, Representative, 414-229-6053, E-mail: artgrado@uwm.edu. *Application contact:* General Information Contact, 414-229-4982, Fax: 414-229-6967, E-mail: gradschool@uwm.edu.

University of Wisconsin–River Falls, Outreach and Graduate Studies, College of Arts and Science, Program in Fine Arts, River Falls, WI 54022. Offers MSE.

University of Wisconsin–Superior, Graduate Division, Department of Visual Arts, Superior, WI 54880-4500. Offers art education (MA); art history (MA); art therapy (MA); studio arts (MA). Part-time programs available. *Degree requirements:* For master's, comprehensive exam, exhibit. *Entrance requirements:* For master's, minimum GPA of 2.75, portfolio.

Utah State University, School of Graduate Studies, College of Humanities, Arts and Social Sciences, Department of Art, Logan, UT 84322. Offers MA, MFA. *Degree requirements:* For master's, thesis, exhibit. *Entrance requirements:* For master's, GRE General Test or MAT, minimum GPA of 3.0, slide portfolio of art. Additional exam requirements/recommendations for international students: Required—TOEFL. *Faculty research:* Painting, drawing, sculpture, ceramics, photography.

Vermont College of Fine Arts, Program in Visual Art, Montpelier, VT 05602. Offers MFA. Postbaccalaureate distance learning degree programs offered (minimal on-campus study). *Faculty:* 10 full-time, 8 part-time/adjunct. *Students:* 47 full-time (33 women), 1 part-time; includes 1 Black or African American, non-Hispanic/Latino. Average age 42. 50 applicants, 68% accepted, 19 enrolled. *Application deadline:* For fall admission, 2/15 priority date for domestic students, 2/15 for international students; for spring admission, 9/1 priority date for domestic students, 9/1 for international students. Applications are processed on a rolling basis. *Application fee:* $75. Electronic applications accepted. *Expenses:* Tuition: Full-time $17,820. Required fees: $270. *Financial support:* Scholarships/grants available. Financial award applicants required to submit FAFSA. *Unit head:* Danielle Dahline, Program Director, 802-828-8703, E-mail: danielle.dahline@vermontcollege.edu. *Application contact:* Denise MacMartin, Director of Admissions, 802-828-8535, E-mail: denise.macmartin@vermontcollege.edu.

Virginia Commonwealth University, Graduate School, College of Humanities and Sciences, School of Mass Communications, Program in Media, Art, and Text, Richmond, VA 23284-9005. Offers PhD. *Students:* 20 full-time (15 women), 22 part-time (11 women); includes 10 minority (3 Black or African American, non-Hispanic/Latino; 1 American Indian or Alaska Native, non-Hispanic/Latino; 2 Asian, non-Hispanic/Latino; 3 Hispanic/Latino; 1 Two or more races, non-Hispanic/Latino), 1 international. 29 applicants, 31% accepted, 6 enrolled. In 2010, 1 doctorate awarded. *Entrance requirements:* For doctorate, GRE. Additional exam requirements/recommendations for international students: Required—TOEFL (minimum score 600 paper-based; 250 computer-based; 100 iBT); Recommended—IELTS (minimum score 6.5). *Application deadline:* For fall admission, 1/15 for domestic students. *Application fee:* $50. Electronic applications accepted. *Expenses:* Tuition, state resident: full-time $4308; part-time $479 per credit hour. Tuition, nonresident: full-time $8942; part-time $994 per credit hour. Required fees: $2000; $85 per credit hour. Tuition and fees vary according to course level, course load, degree level, campus/location and program. *Unit head:* Dr. Eric G. Garberson, Director, MATX Ph.D. Program, 804-828-7295, E-mail: eggarberson@vcu.edu. *Application contact:* Thom N. Didato, Graduate Programs Adviser, 804-828-1329, E-mail: tndidato@vcu.edu.

Virginia Commonwealth University, Graduate School, School of the Arts, Richmond, VA 23284-9005. Offers art education (MAE); art history (MA, PhD), including architectural history (MA), art history, historical studies (MA); museum studies (MA); ceramics (MFA); fibers (MFA); furniture design (MFA); glassworking (MFA); graphic design (MFA), including design/visual communications, interior environment, photography and film; jewelry/metalworking (MFA); kinetic imaging (MFA); music (MM), including education; painting (MFA); printmaking (MFA); sculpture (MFA); theatre (MFA), including acting, costume design, directing, pedagogy, scene design/technical theater. Part-time programs available. *Students:* 158 full-time (103 women), 116 part-time (96 women); includes 31 minority (10 Black or African American, non-Hispanic/Latino; 7 Asian, non-Hispanic/Latino; 11 Hispanic/Latino; 3 Two or more races, non-Hispanic/Latino), 9 international. 907 applicants, 18% accepted, 92 enrolled. In 2010, 87 master's, 5 doctorates awarded. *Entrance requirements:* For doctorate, GRE General Test, writing sample. Additional exam requirements/recommendations for international students: Required—TOEFL (minimum score 600 paper-based; 250 computer-based; 100 iBT). *Application deadline:* For fall admission, 1/15 priority date for domestic students. *Application fee:* $50. Electronic applications accepted. *Expenses:* Tuition, state resident: full-time $4308; part-time $479 per credit hour. Tuition, nonresident: full-time $8942; part-time $994 per credit hour. Required fees: $2000; $85 per credit hour. Tuition and fees vary according to course level, course load, degree level, campus/location and program. *Financial support:* Fellowships, teaching assistantships, career-related internships or fieldwork, Federal Work-Study, institutionally sponsored loans, and tuition waivers (full and partial) available. Support available to part-time students. Financial award applicants required to submit FAFSA. *Unit head:* Joseph H. Seipel, Dean, 804-828-2787, Fax: 804-828-6469, E-mail: arts@vcu.edu. *Application contact:* Jack H. Risley, Associate Dean for Academic Affairs, 804-828-2787, Fax: 804-828-6469, E-mail: jhrisley@vcu.edu.

Virginia Polytechnic Institute and State University, Graduate School, College of Liberal Arts and Human Sciences, Alliance for Social, Political, Ethical, and Cultural Thought, Blacksburg, VA 24061. Offers PhD, Certificate. *Expenses:* Tuition, state resident: full-time $9399; part-time $488 per credit hour. Tuition, nonresident: full-time $17,854; part-time $957.75 per credit hour. Required fees: $1534. Full-time tuition and fees vary according to program.

Washington State University, Graduate School, College of Liberal Arts, Department of Fine Arts, Pullman, WA 99164. Offers ceramics (MFA); digital media (MFA); drawing (MFA); painting (MFA); photography (MFA); print making (MFA); sculpture (MFA). *Faculty:* 10. *Students:* 15 full-time (8 women); includes 1 Black or African American, non-Hispanic/Latino; 1 Hispanic/Latino. Average age 29. 30 applicants, 20% accepted, 5 enrolled. In 2010, 5 master's awarded. *Degree requirements:* For master's, comprehensive exam (for some programs), thesis, exhibit, oral exam. *Entrance requirements:* For master's, GRE, statement of intent, portfolio of no more than 15 images on CD/DVD. Additional exam requirements/recommendations for international students: Required—TOEFL (minimum score 550 paper-based; 213 computer-based), IELTS. *Application deadline:* For fall admission, 1/10 for domestic and international students. *Application fee:* $50. Electronic applications accepted. *Expenses:* Tuition, state resident: full-time $8552; part-time $443 per credit. Tuition, nonresident: full-time $21,650; part-time $1083 per credit. Required fees: $846. *Financial support:* In 2010–11, fellowships with full and partial tuition

reimbursements (averaging $3,114 per year), research assistantships with full and partial tuition reimbursements (averaging $13,917 per year), teaching assistantships with full and partial tuition reimbursements (averaging $13,056 per year) were awarded; career-related internships or fieldwork, Federal Work-Study, institutionally sponsored loans, tuition waivers (partial), and unspecified assistantships also available. Financial award application deadline: 2/15; financial award applicants required to submit FAFSA. *Faculty research:* Polynesian art, museum representation, number theory. *Unit head:* Dr. Chris Watts, Interim Chair, 509-335-7107, Fax: 509-335-7742, E-mail: cjwatts@wsu.edu. *Application contact:* Graduate School Admissions, 800-GRADWSU, Fax: 509-335-1949, E-mail: gradsch@wsu.edu.

Washington University in St. Louis, Sam Fox School of Design and Visual Arts, Graduate School of Art, St. Louis, MO 63130-4899. Offers MFA. *Accreditation:* NASAD. *Degree requirements:* For master's, thesis, exhibition. *Entrance requirements:* For master's, portfolio, resume. Additional exam requirements/recommendations for international students: Required—TOEFL (minimum score 550 paper-based; 213 computer-based; 79 iBT). Electronic applications accepted. *Expenses:* Contact institution. *Faculty research:* New media, design, fine arts.

See Display on next page and Close-Up on page 231.

Wayne State University, College of Fine, Performing and Communication Arts, Department of Art and Art History, Program in Art, Detroit, MI 48202. Offers MA, MFA. *Faculty:* 19 full-time (9 women), 2 part-time/adjunct (0 women). *Students:* 17 full-time (10 women), 8 part-time (4 women); includes 1 minority (Black or African American, non-Hispanic/Latino), 3 international. Average age 40. 26 applicants, 42% accepted, 10 enrolled. In 2010, 11 master's awarded. *Degree requirements:* For master's, thesis (MFA). *Entrance requirements:* Additional exam requirements/recommendations for international students: Required—TOEFL (minimum score 550 paper-based; 213 computer-based); Recommended—TWE (minimum score 6). *Application deadline:* For fall admission, 4/1 for domestic students, 6/1 for international students; for winter admission, 10/1 for international students; for spring admission, 2/1 for international students. *Application fee:* $30 ($50 for international students). Electronic applications accepted. *Expenses:* Tuition, state resident: full-time $7662; part-time $478.85 per credit hour. Tuition, nonresident: full-time $16,920; part-time $1057.55 per credit hour. Required fees: $571.20; $35.70 per credit hour. $188.05 per semester. Tuition and fees vary according to course load and program. *Financial support:* In 2010–11, 1 fellowship (averaging $15,750 per year), 2 teaching assistantships (averaging $14,620 per year) were awarded. *Faculty research:* Painting, drawing, computer art. *Unit head:* Dr. John Richardson, Chair, 313-577-2980, Fax: 313-577-3491, E-mail: af5343@wayne.edu. *Application contact:* Brian Madigan, Associate Professor, 313-577-2685, E-mail: bmadigan@wayne.edu.

Webster University, Leigh Gerdine College of Fine Arts, Department of Art, St. Louis, MO 63119-3194. Offers art (MA); arts management and leadership (MFA). Part-time programs available. *Degree requirements:* For master's, thesis. *Entrance requirements:* For master's, BA or BFA in related field, interview, portfolio. Additional exam requirements/recommendations for international students: Required—TOEFL. *Expenses:* Tuition: Part-time $585 per credit hour. Tuition and fees vary according to degree level, campus/location and program.

Western Carolina University, Graduate School, College of Fine and Performing Arts, Cullowhee, NC 28723. Offers MA Ed, MAT, MFA, MM. *Accreditation:* NASAD. Part-time programs available. *Degree requirements:* For master's, comprehensive exam, thesis optional. *Entrance requirements:* For master's, GRE, appropriate undergraduate degree, portfolio, letters of recommendation, letter of intent, live audition and/or interview. Additional exam requirements/recommendations for international students: Required—TOEFL (minimum score 550 paper-based; 270 computer-based; 79 iBT). *Faculty research:* Vernacular cultural studies and oral history, sound mixing for television, music technology.

Western Connecticut State University, Division of Graduate Studies and External Programs, School of Visual and Performing Arts, Department of Art, Danbury, CT 06810-6885. Offers illustration (MFA); painting (MFA). Part-time programs available. *Students:* 17 full-time (12 women); includes 2 minority (1 Black or African American, non-Hispanic/Latino; 1 Asian, non-Hispanic/Latino). Average age 34. In 2010, 12 master's awarded. *Degree requirements:* For master's, individual exhibition of artwork, review of student's progress prior to admission to final semester, completion of program in 6 years. *Entrance requirements:* For master's, portfolio review, minimum GPA of 2.5. Additional exam requirements/recommendations for international students: Recommended—TOEFL (minimum score 550 paper-based; 213 computer-based; 79 iBT), IELTS (minimum score 6). *Application deadline:* For fall admission, 8/5 priority date for domestic students; for spring admission, 1/5 priority date for domestic students. *Application fee:* $50. *Expenses:* Tuition, state resident: full-time $5012; part-time $417 per credit hour. Tuition, nonresident: full-time $13,962; part-time $423 per credit hour. Required fees: $3886. Full-time tuition and fees vary according to course load, degree level and program. *Financial support:* In 2010–11, 8 students received support. Scholarships/grants available. Financial award application deadline: 5/1; financial award applicants required to submit FAFSA. *Unit head:* Margaret Grimes, Graduate Coordinator, 203-837-8402, Fax: 203-837-8945, E-mail: grimesm@wcsu.edu. *Application contact:* Chris Shankle, Associate Director of Graduate Studies, 203-837-9005, Fax: 203-837-8326, E-mail: shanklec@wcsu.edu.

Western Michigan University, Graduate College, College of Fine Arts, Gwen Frostic School of Art, Kalamazoo, MI 49008. Offers art education (MA); studio art (MFA). *Accreditation:* NASAD (one or more programs are accredited). *Degree requirements:* For master's, thesis or alternative.

West Texas A&M University, College of Fine Arts and Humanities, Department of Art, Communication, and Theater, Program in Art, Canyon, TX 79016-0001. Offers MA. Part-time programs available. *Degree requirements:* For master's, comprehensive exam, thesis optional, exhibit, portfolio review. *Entrance requirements:* For master's, GRE General Test, interview, portfolio. Additional exam requirements/recommendations for international students: Required—TOEFL (minimum score 550 paper-based). Electronic applications accepted. *Faculty research:* Ceramics, graphic design, woodblock prints, art history, aesthetics, glassblowing.

West Texas A&M University, College of Fine Arts and Humanities, Department of Art, Communication, and Theater, Program in Studio Art, Canyon, TX 79016-0001. Offers MFA. Part-time programs available. *Degree requirements:* For master's, comprehensive exam, thesis optional, exhibit, portfolio review, professional paper. *Entrance requirements:* For master's, GRE General Test, interview, portfolio. Additional exam requirements/recommendations for international students: Required—TOEFL (minimum score 550 paper-based). *Faculty research:* Ceramics, printmaking, graphic design, art history, aesthetics, glass blowing.

West Virginia University, College of Creative Arts, Division of Art and Design, Morgantown, WV 26506. Offers art education (MA); art history (MA); ceramics (MFA); graphic design (MFA); painting (MFA); printmaking (MFA); sculpture (MFA); studio art (MA). *Accreditation:* NASAD. *Degree requirements:* For master's, thesis, exhibit. *Entrance requirements:* For master's, minimum GPA of 2.75, portfolio. Additional exam requirements/recommendations for international students: Required—TOEFL. *Expenses:* Contact institution. *Faculty research:* Medieval art history.

Wichita State University, Graduate School, College of Fine Arts, School of Art and Design, Wichita, KS 67260. Offers studio arts (MFA), including ceramics, painting, printmaking, sculpture. *Accreditation:* NASAD. *Unit head:* Prof. Barry Badgett, Director, 316-978-3555, Fax: 316-978-5418, E-mail: barry.badgett@wichita.edu. *Application contact:* Prof. Ronald Christ, Graduate Coordinator, 316-978-3555, Fax: 316-978-5418, E-mail: ronald.christ@wichita.edu.

William Paterson University of New Jersey, College of the Arts and Communication, Wayne, NJ 07470-8420. Offers art (MFA); music (MM); professional communication (MA). *Accreditation:* NASAD. Part-time and evening/weekend programs available. *Entrance requirements:* For master's, minimum GPA of 2.75. Electronic applications accepted.

Winthrop University, College of Visual and Performing Arts, Department of Art, Rock Hill, SC 29733. Offers art (MFA); art administration (MA); art education (MA). *Accreditation:* NASAD. Part-time programs available. *Degree requirements:* For master's, thesis, documented exhibit, oral exam. *Entrance requirements:* For master's, GRE General Test or MAT, PRAXIS (MA), minimum GPA of 3.0, resume, slide portfolio, teaching certificate (MA). Electronic applications accepted.

Yale University, School of Art, New Haven, CT 06520-8339. Offers graphic design (MFA); painting/printmaking (MFA); photography (MFA); sculpture (MFA). *Faculty:* 9 full-time (4 women), 35 part-time/adjunct (12 women). *Students:* 121 full-time (64 women); includes 32 minority (7 Black or African American, non-Hispanic/Latino; 10 Asian, non-Hispanic/Latino; 15 Hispanic/Latino), 32 international. Average age 28. 1,222 applicants, 5% accepted, 57 enrolled. In 2010, 57 master's awarded. *Degree requirements:* For master's, thesis (for some programs). *Entrance requirements:* Additional exam requirements/recommendations for international students: Required—TOEFL (minimum score 550 paper-based; 250 computer-based; 100 iBT). *Application deadline:* For fall admission, 1/4 for domestic and international students. Application fee: $100. Electronic applications accepted. *Expenses:* Contact institution. *Financial support:* In 2010–11, 90 students received support, including 54 teaching assistantships (averaging $1,900 per year); Federal Work-Study, scholarships/grants, and unspecified assistantships also available. Financial award application deadline: 3/1; financial award applicants required to submit FAFSA. *Unit head:* Robert Storr, Dean, 203-432-2606. *Application contact:* Patricia Ann DeChiara, Director of Academic Affairs, 203-432-2600, E-mail: artschool.info@yale.edu.

York University, Faculty of Graduate Studies, Faculty of Fine Arts, Program in Visual Arts, Toronto, ON M3J 1P3, Canada. Offers MFA, PhD. *Degree requirements:* For master's, thesis. *Entrance requirements:* For master's, portfolio. Electronic applications accepted.

Art History

American University, College of Arts and Sciences, Department of Art, Washington, DC 20016-8004. Offers art history (MA); painting, sculpture and printmaking (MFA). Part-time programs available. *Faculty:* 18 full-time (12 women), 16 part-time/adjunct (10 women). *Students:* 26 full-time (19 women), 26 part-time (all women); includes 2 minority (1 Asian, non-Hispanic/Latino; 1 Hispanic/Latino), 1 international. Average age 28. 82 applicants, 60% accepted, 15 enrolled. In 2010, 16 master's awarded. *Degree requirements:* For master's, comprehensive exam. *Entrance requirements:* For master's, GRE, portfolio or writing sample. Additional exam requirements/recommendations for international students: Required—TOEFL. *Application deadline:* For fall admission, 10/15 for domestic students. Application fee: $80. *Financial support:* Fellowships, research assistantships with full and partial tuition reimbursements, teaching assistantships with full and partial tuition reimbursements, career-related internships or fieldwork, Federal Work-Study, and institutionally sponsored loans available. Support available to part-time students. Financial award application deadline: 1/15. *Faculty research:* Studio artists, painting, Renaissance, Impressionism, twentieth century. *Unit head:* Jose-Maria Montes-Armenteros, Chair, 202-885-1697, Fax: 202-885-1132, E-mail: cmontes@american.edu. *Application contact:* Glenna K. Haynie, Administrative Coordinator, 202-885-1671.

American University of Puerto Rico, Program in Education, Bayamón, PR 00960-2037. Offers art history (M Ed); elementary education (4-6) (M Ed); elementary education (K-3) (M Ed); general science education (M Ed); physical education (M Ed); special education (transition) (M Ed); youth transition to adult life (Graduate Certificate). *Faculty:* 1 full-time (0 women), 22 part-time/adjunct (6 women). *Students:* 104 full-time (83 women), 45 part-time (40 women); includes all Hispanic/Latino. *Entrance requirements:* For master's, EXADEP, GRE, or MAT, 2 letters of recommendation, minimum GPA of 2.5. *Application deadline:* For fall admission, 8/1 for domestic students; for winter admission, 10/18 for domestic students; for spring admission, 3/15 for domestic students. Applications are processed on a rolling basis. Application fee: $50. *Application contact:* Information Contact, 787-620-2040, E-mail: oficnaadmisiones@aupr.edu.

Arizona State University, Herberger Institute for Design and the Arts, School of Art, Tempe, AZ 85287-1505. Offers art (art education) (MA); art (art history) (MA); art (ceramics) (MFA); art (digital technology) (MFA); art (drawing) (MFA); art (fibers) (MFA); art (intermedia) (MFA); art (metals) (MFA); art (painting) (MFA); art (printmaking) (MFA); art (sculpture) (MFA); art (wood) (MFA); design, environment and the arts (history, theory and criticism) (PhD). *Faculty:* 46 full-time (28 women). *Students:* 98 full-time (56 women), 21 part-time (18 women); includes 13 minority (2 American Indian or Alaska Native, non-Hispanic/Latino; 3 Asian, non-Hispanic/Latino; 8 Hispanic/Latino), 7 international. Average age 31. 206 applicants, 32% accepted, 37 enrolled. In 2010, 26 master's, 1 doctorate awarded. Terminal master's awarded for partial completion of doctoral program. *Degree requirements:* For master's, thesis/exhibition (MFA, MA in art education); interactive Program of Study (iPOS) submitted before completing 50 percent of required credit hours; for doctorate, comprehensive exam, thesis/dissertation, interactive Program of Study (iPOS) submitted before completing 50 percent of required credit hours. *Entrance requirements:* For master's, GRE or MAT, minimum GPA of 3.0 or equivalent in last 2 years of work leading to bachelor's degree; for doctorate, GRE, master's degree in architecture, graphic design, industrial design, interior design, landscape architecture, or art history or equivalent standing; statement of purpose; 3 letters of recommendation; indication of potential faculty mentor; sample of written work. Additional exam requirements/recommendations for international students: Required—TOEFL, IELTS, or Pearson Test of English. *Application deadline:* For fall admission, 1/15 priority date for domestic and international students. Applications are processed on a rolling basis. Application fee: $70 ($90 for international students). Electronic applications accepted. *Expenses:* Tuition, state resident: full-time $8510; part-time $608 per credit. Tuition, nonresident: full-time $16,542; part-time $919 per credit. Required fees: $339; $110 per credit. Part-time tuition and fees vary according to course load. *Financial*

support: In 2010–11, 4 research assistantships with full and partial tuition reimbursements (averaging $7,475 per year), 55 teaching assistantships with full and partial tuition reimbursements (averaging $6,553 per year) were awarded; fellowships with full and partial tuition reimbursements, scholarships/grants and tuition waivers (full and partial) also available. Financial award application deadline: 3/1; financial award applicants required to submit FAFSA. Total annual research expenditures: $26,418. *Unit head:* Adriene Jenik, Director, 480-965-8521, Fax: 480-965-8338, E-mail: ajenik@mainex1.asu.edu. *Application contact:* Graduate Admissions, 480-965-6113.

Bard Graduate Center: Decorative Arts, Design History, Material Culture, Graduate Studies, New York, NY 10024-3602. Offers M Phil, MA, PhD. Part-time programs available. *Degree requirements:* For master's, one foreign language, internship, qualifying paper; for doctorate, 2 foreign languages, thesis/dissertation, exams. *Entrance requirements:* For master's, GRE General Test, writing sample, 3 letters of recommendation; for doctorate, GRE General Test, master's thesis or equivalent, 3 letters of recommendation. Additional exam requirements/recommendations for international students: Required—TOEFL. *Faculty research:* English craftsmen; ancient furniture; aesthetics and politics; Art Nouveau jewelry; European sculpture; New York and American material culture; modern design history; early modern Europe; history and theory of museums; comparative medieval material culture (China, Islam, Europe); archaeology, anthropology, and material culture.

See Display below and Close-Up on page 215.

Boston University, Graduate School of Arts and Sciences, Department of Art History, Boston, MA 02215. Offers art history (MA, PhD); museum studies (Certificate). *Students:* 44 full-time (39 women), 9 part-time (8 women); includes 6 minority (4 Black or African American, non-Hispanic/Latino; 1 Asian, non-Hispanic/Latino; 1 Two or more races, non-Hispanic/Latino), 7 international. Average age 32. 227 applicants, 32% accepted, 14 enrolled. In 2010, 11 master's, 6 doctorates awarded. Terminal master's awarded for partial completion of doctoral program. *Degree requirements:* For master's, one foreign language, comprehensive exam, thesis; for doctorate, 2 foreign languages, comprehensive exam, thesis/dissertation. *Entrance requirements:* For master's and doctorate, GRE General Test, 3 letters of recommendation; for Certificate, GRE General Test. Additional exam requirements/recommendations for international students: Required—TOEFL (minimum score 600 paper-based; 250 computer-based). *Application deadline:* For fall admission, 1/15 for domestic and international students; for spring admission, 10/15 for domestic and international students. Application fee: $70. *Expenses:* Tuition: Full-time $39,314; part-time $1228 per credit. Required fees: $40 per semester. *Financial support:* In 2010–11, 20 students received support, including 2 fellowships (averaging $19,300 per year), 1 research assistantship (averaging $18,800 per year), 6 teaching assistantships with full tuition reimbursements available (averaging $18,800 per year); career-related internships or fieldwork, Federal Work-Study, and unspecified assistantships also available. Support available to part-time students. Financial award application deadline: 1/15; financial award applicants required to submit FAFSA. *Unit head:* Fred S. Kleiner, Chairman, 617-353-2520, Fax: 617-353-3243, E-mail: fsk@bu.edu. *Application contact:* Cheryl Crombie, Administrative Assistant, 617-353-2522, Fax: 617-353-3243, E-mail: ccrombie@bu.edu.

Bowling Green State University, Graduate College, College of Arts and Sciences, School of Art, Bowling Green, OH 43403. Offers 2-D studio art (MA, MFA); 3-D studio art (MA, MFA); art education (MA); art history (MA); computer art (MA); design (MFA); digital arts (MFA); graphics (MFA). *Accreditation:* NASAD. Part-time programs available. *Degree requirements:* For master's, thesis or alternative, final exhibit (MFA). *Entrance requirements:* For master's, GRE General Test (MA), slide portfolio (15-20 slides). Additional exam requirements/recommendations for international students: Required—TOEFL. Electronic applications accepted. *Faculty research:*

Our MA & PhD Programs focus on the cultural history of the material world.

Areas of Special Strength
New York & American Material Culture
Modern Design History
Early Modern Europe
History and Theory of Museums
Comparative Medieval Material Culture
Archaeology and Material Culture

For More Information
please contact us at
admissions@bgc.bard.edu
or visit bgc.bard.edu/admissions

Application Deadlines
For full-time and part-time students the deadline is January 3, 2012. Fellowships and scholarships are available for qualified students.

Upcoming Exhibitions
BGC Galleries
18 West 86th Street
New York, NY 10024
T 212 501 3074
W bgc.bard.edu/gallery

Bard Graduate Center: Decorative Arts, Design History, Material Culture

Computer animation and virtual reality, Spanish still-life painting from 1600 to 1800, art and psychotherapy, Japanese wood-firing techniques in ceramics, non-toxic printmaking technologies.

Brigham Young University, Graduate Studies, College of Fine Arts and Communications, Department of Visual Arts, Provo, UT 84602-6414. Offers art education (MA); art history (MA); studio art (MFA). Art education applications accepted biennially. *Accreditation:* NASAD. *Faculty:* 27 full-time (7 women), 1 (woman) part-time/adjunct. *Students:* 36 full-time (26 women); includes 1 Asian, non-Hispanic/Latino; 2 Native Hawaiian or other Pacific Islander, non-Hispanic/Latino. Average age 26. 33 applicants, 33% accepted, 10 enrolled. In 2010, 5 master's awarded. *Degree requirements:* For master's, one foreign language, thesis (art history), selected project (MFA), curriculum project (art education). *Entrance requirements:* For master's, GRE (art history), minimum GPA of 3.0 (MFA, MA in art education), 3.3 (MA in art history), portfolio in CD format (MFA), writing samples (MA in art education, art history). Additional exam requirements/recommendations for international students: Required—TOEFL (minimum score 500 paper-based). *Application deadline:* For fall admission, 2/1 for domestic and international students. Application fee: $50. Electronic applications accepted. *Expenses:* Tuition: Full-time $5580; part-time $310 per credit hour. Tuition and fees vary according to program and student's religious affiliation. *Financial support:* In 2010–11, 32 students received support; research assistantships, teaching assistantships with partial tuition reimbursements available, scholarships/grants and tuition waivers (partial) available. Financial award application deadline: 2/1. *Faculty research:* Methodology-standards-assessment, medieval architecture, classical/Islamic eighteenth and nineteenth century art, Netherlandish art, contemporary art, modern art, history of photography. Total annual research expenditures: $83,932. *Unit head:* Prof. Linda A. Reynolds, Chair, 801-422-4429, Fax: 801-422-0695, E-mail: sullivan@byu.edu. *Application contact:* Sharon Lyn Heelis, Secretary, 801-422-4429, Fax: 801-422-0695, E-mail: sharon_heelis@byu.edu.

Brooklyn College of the City University of New York, Division of Graduate Studies, Department of Art, Program in Art History, Brooklyn, NY 11210-2889. Offers MA, PhD. Part-time programs available. *Students:* 24 part-time (19 women); includes 2 minority (both Black or African American, non-Hispanic/Latino). Average age 28. 34 applicants, 74% accepted, 4 enrolled. In 2010, 5 master's awarded. *Degree requirements:* For master's, one foreign language, 2 publishable papers or thesis. *Entrance requirements:* For master's, bachelor's degree in art, minimum GPA of 3.0, portfolio, interview. Additional exam requirements/recommendations for international students: Required—TOEFL (minimum score 500 paper-based; 173 computer-based; 61 iBT). *Application deadline:* For fall admission, 3/1 priority date for domestic students, 2/1 priority date for international students; for spring admission, 11/1 priority date for domestic students, 10/1 priority date for international students. Applications are processed on a rolling basis. Application fee: $125. Electronic applications accepted. *Expenses:* Tuition, state resident: full-time $7360; part-time $310 per credit hour. Tuition, nonresident: full-time $13,800; part-time $575 per credit hour. Required fees: $190 per semester. *Financial support:* Career-related internships or fieldwork, Federal Work-Study, institutionally sponsored loans, and scholarships/grants available. Support available to part-time students. Financial award application deadline: 5/1; financial award applicants required to submit FAFSA. *Faculty research:* Contemporary art, ancient Near East art, northern Baroque art, nineteenth century French art, Italian Renaissance art. *Unit head:* Dr. Mona Hadler, Deputy Chairperson, 718-951-5181, E-mail: mhadler@brooklyn.cuny.edu. *Application contact:* Hernan Sierra, Graduate Admissions Coordinator, 718-951-4536, Fax: 718-951-4506, E-mail: grads@brooklyn.cuny.edu.

Brown University, Graduate School, Department of History of Art and Architecture, Providence, RI 02912. Offers MA, PhD. *Degree requirements:* For master's, 2 foreign languages, thesis; for doctorate, 2 foreign languages, thesis/dissertation, oral exam. *Entrance requirements:* For master's, GRE General Test; for doctorate, GRE General Test, MA with distinction.

Brown University, Graduate School, Joukowsky Institute for Archaeology and the Ancient World, Providence, RI 02912. Offers PhD. *Degree requirements:* For doctorate, thesis/dissertation.

Bryn Mawr College, Graduate School of Arts and Sciences, Department of History of Art, Bryn Mawr, PA 19010-2899. Offers MA, PhD. Part-time programs available. *Faculty:* 8. *Students:* 23 full-time (18 women), 6 part-time (all women); includes 2 Asian, non-Hispanic/Latino; 3 Hispanic/Latino. Average age 31. 54 applicants, 24% accepted, 4 enrolled. In 2010, 4 master's, 1 doctorate awarded. *Degree requirements:* For master's, 2 foreign languages, thesis; for doctorate, 2 foreign languages, comprehensive exam, thesis/dissertation. *Entrance requirements:* For master's and doctorate, GRE General Test. Additional exam requirements/recommendations for international students: Required—TOEFL (minimum score 600 paper-based; 250 computer-based). *Application deadline:* For fall admission, 1/3 for domestic and international students. Application fee: $50. *Financial support:* In 2010–11, 17 fellowships with full tuition reimbursements (averaging $15,824 per year), 6 teaching assistantships with partial tuition reimbursements (averaging $12,833 per year) were awarded; Federal Work-Study, scholarships/grants, tuition waivers (full and partial), and unspecified assistantships also available. Support available to part-time students. Financial award application deadline: 1/3. *Unit head:* Dr. Steven Z. Levine, Chairman, 610-526-5333, E-mail: dcast@brynmawr.edu. *Application contact:* Teri R. Lobo, Administrative Assistant to the Graduate School of Arts and Sciences Dean, 610-526-5072, Fax: 610-526-5076, E-mail: lrmiller@brynmawr.edu.

See Display on page 1299 and Close-Up on page 1329.

California State University, Chico, Graduate School, College of Humanities and Fine Arts, Department of Art and Art History, Program in Art History, Chico, CA 95929-0722. Offers MA. *Accreditation:* NASAD. *Students:* 5 full-time (4 women), 1 (woman) part-time. Average age 31. 2 applicants, 100% accepted, 2 enrolled. *Degree requirements:* For master's, thesis or alternative. *Entrance requirements:* For master's, 2 letters of recommendation. Additional exam requirements/recommendations for international students: Required—TOEFL (minimum score 550 paper-based; 213 computer-based; 80 iBT), IELTS (minimum score 6.5). *Application deadline:* For fall admission, 3/1 priority date for domestic students, 3/1 for international students; for spring admission, 9/15 priority date for domestic students, 9/15 for international students. Application fee: $55. *Unit head:* Dr. Cameron Crawford, Graduate Coordinator, 530-898-6860. *Application contact:* Dr. Cameron Crawford, Graduate Coordinator, 530-898-6860.

California State University, Fullerton, Graduate Studies, College of the Arts, Department of Art, Fullerton, CA 92834-9480. Offers art (MA, MFA), including ceramics (MFA), crafts, creative photography (MFA), design (MFA), drawing and painting, printmaking (MFA), sculpture; art history (MA); design (MA). *Accreditation:* NASAD (one or more programs are accredited). Part-time programs available. *Students:* 50 full-time (34 women), 38 part-time (24 women); includes 1 Black or African American, non-Hispanic/Latino; 12 Asian, non-Hispanic/Latino; 11 Hispanic/Latino, 8 international. Average age 35. 113 applicants, 26% accepted, 26 enrolled. In 2010, 14 master's awarded. *Degree requirements:* For master's, project or thesis. *Entrance requirements:* For master's, minimum GPA of 2.5 in last 60 units of course work, portfolio. Application fee: $55. *Financial support:* Career-related internships or fieldwork, Federal Work-Study, institutionally sponsored loans, and scholarships/grants available. Support available to part-time students. Financial award application deadline: 3/1; financial award applicants required to submit FAFSA. *Unit head:* Larry Johnson, Chair, 657-278-3471. *Application contact:* Admissions/Applications, 657-278-2371.

California State University, Long Beach, Graduate Studies, College of the Arts, Department of Art, Long Beach, CA 90840. Offers art education (MA); art history (MA); studio art (MA, MFA). *Accreditation:* NASAD. Part-time programs available. *Faculty:* 36 full-time (16 women), 5 part-time/adjunct (4 women). *Students:* 86 full-time (49 women), 26 part-time (21 women); includes 1 American Indian or Alaska Native, non-Hispanic/Latino; 10 Asian, non-Hispanic/Latino; 17 Hispanic/Latino, 9 international. Average age 33. 222 applicants, 20% accepted, 29 enrolled. In 2010, 35 master's awarded. *Degree requirements:* For master's, thesis (for some programs). *Entrance requirements:* For master's, minimum GPA of 3.0 in last 60 hours. *Application deadline:* For fall admission, 7/1 for domestic students; for spring admission, 12/1 for domestic students. Applications are processed on a rolling basis. Application fee: $55. Electronic applications accepted. *Financial support:* Federal Work-Study, institutionally sponsored loans, and scholarships/grants available. Financial award application deadline: 3/2. *Unit head:* Prof. David Hadlock, Chair, 562-985-7908, Fax: 562-985-1650, E-mail: dhadlock@csulb.edu. *Application contact:* Margaret Black, Graduate Advisor, 562-985-7910, Fax: 562-985-1650.

California State University, Los Angeles, Graduate Studies, College of Arts and Letters, Department of Art, Los Angeles, CA 90032-8530. Offers art (MA), including art education, art history, art therapy, ceramics, metals, and textiles, design (MA, MFA), painting, sculpture, and graphic arts, photography; fine arts (MFA), including crafts, design (MA, MFA), studio arts. *Accreditation:* NASAD (one or more programs are accredited). Part-time and evening/weekend programs available. *Faculty:* 9 full-time (5 women), 3 part-time/adjunct (2 women). *Students:* 27 full-time (19 women), 33 part-time (22 women); includes 24 minority (3 Black or African American, non-Hispanic/Latino; 7 Asian, non-Hispanic/Latino; 13 Hispanic/Latino; 1 Two or more races, non-Hispanic/Latino), 9 international. Average age 36. 19 applicants, 100% accepted, 13 enrolled. In 2010, 26 master's awarded. *Degree requirements:* For master's, comprehensive exam, project or thesis. *Entrance requirements:* For master's, portfolio. Additional exam requirements/recommendations for international students: Required—TOEFL (minimum score 500 paper-based; 173 computer-based). *Application deadline:* For fall admission, 5/1 for domestic and international students. Applications are processed on a rolling basis. Application fee: $55. Electronic applications accepted. *Financial support:* Federal Work-Study available. Support available to part-time students. Financial award application deadline: 3/1. *Faculty research:* The artist and the book, conceptual art, ceramic processes, computer graphics, architectural graphics. *Unit head:* Dr. Abbas Daneshvari, Chair, 323-343-4010, Fax: 323-343-4045, E-mail: adanesh@calstatela.edu. *Application contact:* Dr. Alan Muchlinski, Dean of Graduate Studies, 323-343-3820, Fax: 323-343-5653, E-mail: amuchli@exchange.calstatela.edu.

California State University, Northridge, Graduate Studies, College of Arts, Media, and Communication, Department of Art, Northridge, CA 91330. Offers art education (MA); art history (MA); studio art (MA, MFA); visual communications (MA, MFA). *Accreditation:* NASAD.

Caribbean University, Graduate School, Bayamón, PR 00960-0493. Offers administration and supervision (MA Ed); criminal justice (MA); curriculum and instruction (MA Ed, PhD), including elementary education (MA Ed), English education (MA Ed), history education (MA Ed), mathematics education (MA Ed), primary education (MA Ed), science education (MA Ed), Spanish education (MA Ed); educational technology in instructional systems (MA Ed); gerontology (MSN); human resources (MBA); museology, archiving and art history (MA Ed); neonatal pediatrics (MSN); physical education (MA Ed); special education (MA Ed). *Entrance requirements:* For master's, interview, minimum GPA of 2.5.

Carleton University, Faculty of Graduate Studies, Faculty of Arts and Social Sciences, School for Studies in Art and Culture, Program in Art History: Art and its Institutions, Ottawa, ON K1S 5B6, Canada. Offers MA. *Degree requirements:* For master's, thesis. *Entrance requirements:* For master's, honors degree.

Case Western Reserve University, School of Graduate Studies, Department of Art History and Art, Program in Art History, Cleveland, OH 44106. Offers MA, PhD. MA and PhD offered jointly with the Cleveland Museum of Art. Part-time programs available. *Faculty:* 8 full-time (6 women), 12 part-time/adjunct (6 women). *Students:* 13 full-time (12 women), 1 (woman) part-time, 1 international. Average age 30. 19 applicants, 26% accepted, 3 enrolled. In 2010, 6 master's, 2 doctorates awarded. *Degree requirements:* For master's, one foreign language, thesis or alternative; for doctorate, 2 foreign languages, comprehensive exam, thesis/dissertation. *Entrance requirements:* For master's, GRE General Test, 2 samples of written work; for doctorate, GRE General Test, 2 samples of written work and MA thesis. Additional exam requirements/recommendations for international students: Required—TOEFL (minimum score 550 paper-based; 213 computer-based; 79 iBT). *Application deadline:* For fall admission, 1/1 priority date for domestic students. Applications are processed on a rolling basis. Application fee: $50. Electronic applications accepted. *Financial support:* Fellowships, research assistantships, teaching assistantships, career-related internships or fieldwork and tuition waivers available. Financial award application deadline: 1/1; financial award applicants required to submit FAFSA. *Faculty research:* Greek art and architecture, Northern Baroque art, Italian Baroque sculpture, abstract expressionism, Indian art, nineteenth century French art, American and contemporary art. *Unit head:* Catherine Scallen, Chair, 216-368-2383, Fax: 216-368-4681, E-mail: catherine.scallen@case.edu. *Application contact:* Debby Tenenbaum, Assistant, 216-368-4118, Fax: 216-368-4681, E-mail: deborah.tenenbaum@case.edu.

Christie's Education, Program in Modern Art, Connoisseurship, and the History of the Art Market, New York, NY 10036. Offers MA. *Degree requirements:* For master's, one foreign language, thesis. *Entrance requirements:* For master's, GRE, writing sample, 3 letters of recommendation. Additional exam requirements/recommendations for international students: Required—TOEFL.

City College of the City University of New York, Graduate School, College of Liberal Arts and Science, Division of the Humanities and Arts, Department of Art, Concentrations in Art History and Museum Studies, New York, NY 10031-9198. Offers art history (MA); museum studies (MA). Part-time programs available. *Degree requirements:* For master's, one foreign language, thesis. *Entrance requirements:* For master's, minimum GPA of 3.0, portfolio, art history paper. Additional exam requirements/recommendations for international students: Required—TOEFL (minimum score 577 paper-based; 90 iBT). Electronic applications accepted. *Faculty research:* Egyptian, Greek, medieval, Romanesque, and Ottoman art.

Cleveland State University, College of Graduate Studies, College of Liberal Arts and Social Sciences, Department of Art, Cleveland, OH 44115. Offers art education (M Ed); art history (MA). *Faculty:* 6 full-time (4 women), 2 part-time/adjunct (1 woman). *Students:* 1 (woman) full-time, 4 part-time (all women). 2 applicants, 0% accepted, 0 enrolled. In 2010, 2 master's awarded. *Expenses:* Tuition, state resident: full-time $8447; part-time $469 per credit hour. Tuition, nonresident: full-time $16,020; part-time $890 per credit hour. Required fees: $50. *Unit head:* Howie Smith, Chair, 212-523-7546, E-mail: art.chair@csuohio.edu. *Application contact:* Dr. Giannina Pianalto, Director of Graduate Admissions, 216-687-5599, Fax: 216-687-5400, E-mail: g.pianalto@csuohio.edu.

Cleveland State University, College of Graduate Studies, College of Liberal Arts and Social Sciences, Department of History, Cleveland, OH 44115. Offers art history (MA); history (MA); museum studies (MA). Part-time and evening/weekend programs available. *Faculty:* 18 full-time (6 women), 10 part-time/adjunct (2 women). *Students:* 14 full-time (7 women), 19 part-time (12 women); includes 2 Black or African American, non-Hispanic/Latino. Average age 34. 39 applicants, 51% accepted, 14 enrolled. In 2010, 20 master's awarded. *Degree requirements:* For master's, thesis optional. *Entrance requirements:* For master's, minimum GPA of 3.0, bachelor's degree in history. Additional exam requirements/recommendations for international students: Required—TOEFL (minimum score 525 paper-based; 197 computer-based). *Application deadline:* For fall admission, 7/15 priority date for domestic students. Applications are processed on a rolling basis. Application fee: $30. Electronic applications accepted. *Expenses:* Tuition, state resident: full-time $8447; part-time $469 per credit hour. Tuition, nonresident: full-time $16,020; part-time $890 per credit hour. Required fees: $50. *Financial support:* In 2010–11, 7 students received support, including research assistantships with full tuition reimbursements available (averaging $8,600 per year); career-related internships or fieldwork and unspecified assistantships also available. *Faculty research:* African Diaspora, social history and the city, early modern Europe, local history. *Unit head:* Dr. Elizabeth A.

Art History

Cleveland State University (continued)
Lehfeldt, Chairperson, 216-687-3920, Fax: 216-687-5592, E-mail: e.lehfeldt@csuohio.edu. *Application contact:* Dr. Robert S. Shelton, Graduate Director, 216-687-3927, E-mail: r.s. shelton@csuohio.edu.

Columbia University, Graduate School of Arts and Sciences, Division of Humanities, Department of Art History and Archaeology, New York, NY 10027. Offers archaeology (M Phil, MA, PhD); art history and archaeology (M Phil, MA, PhD); modern art (MA). *Degree requirements:* For master's, 2 foreign languages, thesis; for doctorate, 3 foreign languages, thesis/dissertation. *Entrance requirements:* For master's and doctorate, GRE General Test. Additional exam requirements/recommendations for international students: Required—TOEFL.

Concordia University, School of Graduate Studies, Faculty of Fine Arts, Department of Art History, Montréal, QC H3G 1M8, Canada. Offers MA, PhD. PhD program offered jointly with Université Laval, Université de Montréal, and Université du Québec à Montréal. *Degree requirements:* For master's, one foreign language, thesis. *Entrance requirements:* For master's, BFA or equivalent, minimum B average in major. *Faculty research:* Ancient and modern Canadian art and architecture, Canadian decorative arts, museum studies.

Cornell University, Graduate School, Graduate Fields of Arts and Sciences, Field of History of Art, Archaeology and Visual Studies, Ithaca, NY 14853. Offers American art (PhD); ancient art and archaeology (PhD); Asian art (PhD); Baroque art (PhD); medieval art (PhD); modern art (PhD); Renaissance art (PhD); Southeast Asian art (PhD); theory and criticism (PhD). *Faculty:* 24 full-time (15 women). *Students:* 21 full-time (19 women); includes 1 Black or African American, non-Hispanic/Latino; 2 American Indian or Alaska Native, non-Hispanic/Latino; 1 Hispanic/Latino, 7 international. Average age 31. 71 applicants, 7% accepted, 5 enrolled. In 2010, 2 doctorates awarded. *Degree requirements:* For doctorate, one foreign language, comprehensive exam, thesis/dissertation, general exams in 3 areas. *Entrance requirements:* For doctorate, GRE General Test, sample of written work, 3 letters of recommendation. Additional exam requirements/recommendations for international students: Required—TOEFL (minimum score 550 paper-based; 213 computer-based; 77 iBT). *Application deadline:* For fall admission, 1/15 for domestic students. Application fee: $80. Electronic applications accepted. *Expenses:* Tuition: Full-time $29,500. Required fees: $76. Tuition and fees vary according to degree level and program. *Financial support:* In 2010–11, 8 fellowships with full tuition reimbursements, 11 teaching assistantships with full tuition reimbursements were awarded; research assistantships with full tuition reimbursements, institutionally sponsored loans, scholarships/grants, health care benefits, tuition waivers (full and partial), and unspecified assistantships also available. Financial award applicants required to submit FAFSA. *Unit head:* Director of Graduate Studies, 607-255-4905, Fax: 607-255-0566, E-mail: art_history@cornell.edu. *Application contact:* Graduate Field Assistant, 607-255-4905, Fax: 607-255-0566, E-mail: art_history@cornell.edu.

Duke University, Graduate School, Department of Art, Art History and Visual Studies, Durham, NC 27708-0764. Offers PhD. *Faculty:* 16 full-time. *Students:* 41 full-time (35 women); includes 2 Black or African American, non-Hispanic/Latino; 1 Asian, non-Hispanic/Latino; 3 Hispanic/Latino, 11 international. 78 applicants, 13% accepted, 4 enrolled. In 2010, 1 doctorate awarded. *Degree requirements:* For doctorate, thesis/dissertation. *Entrance requirements:* For doctorate, GRE General Test. Additional exam requirements/recommendations for international students: Required—TOEFL (minimum score 550 paper-based; 213 computer-based; 83 iBT), IELTS (minimum score 7). *Application deadline:* For fall admission, 12/8 priority date for domestic and international students. Application fee: $75. Electronic applications accepted. *Financial support:* Fellowships, teaching assistantships available. Financial award application deadline: 12/8. *Unit head:* Gennifer Weisenfeld, Director of Graduate Studies, 919-684-2224, Fax: 919-684-

4398, E-mail: gennifer.weisenfeld@duke.edu. *Application contact:* Elizabeth Hutton, Director of Admissions, 919-684-3913, Fax: 919-684-2277, E-mail: grad-admissions@duke.edu.

Emory University, Laney Graduate School, Department of Art History, Atlanta, GA 30322-1100. Offers PhD. *Degree requirements:* For doctorate, 2 foreign languages, comprehensive exam, thesis/dissertation, oral exam. *Entrance requirements:* For doctorate, GRE General Test. Electronic applications accepted. *Expenses:* Tuition: Full-time $33,800. Required fees: $1300.

Fashion Institute of Technology, School of Graduate Studies, Program in Art Market: Principles and Practices, New York, NY 10001-5992. Offers MA. *Accreditation:* NASAD. *Degree requirements:* For master's, one foreign language, thesis. *Entrance requirements:* For master's, GRE General Test, previous course work in art history, 4 semesters of a foreign language. Additional exam requirements/recommendations for international students: Required—TOEFL (minimum score 550 paper-based; 213 computer-based). Electronic applications accepted.

See Display below and Close-Up on page 217.

Florida State University, The Graduate School, College of Visual Arts, Theatre and Dance, Department of Art History, Tallahassee, FL 32306. Offers art history (MA, PhD); museum studies (Certificate). *Accreditation:* NASAD. Part-time programs available. *Faculty:* 10 full-time (5 women), 5 part-time/adjunct (3 women). *Students:* 34 full-time (26 women), 15 part-time (14 women); includes 4 minority (1 Asian, non-Hispanic/Latino; 2 Hispanic/Latino; 1 Two or more races, non-Hispanic/Latino), 1 international. Average age 32. 54 applicants, 54% accepted, 16 enrolled. In 2010, 9 master's, 4 doctorates awarded. Terminal master's awarded for partial completion of doctoral program. *Degree requirements:* For master's, one foreign language, thesis (for some programs), first-year review; for doctorate, 2 foreign languages, comprehensive exam, thesis/dissertation, first-year review. *Entrance requirements:* For master's, GRE General Test, minimum GPA of 3.0; for doctorate, GRE General Test, minimum GPA of 3.5. Additional exam requirements/recommendations for international students: Required—TOEFL. *Application deadline:* For fall admission, 1/10 for domestic students, 1/11 for international students. Application fee: $30. Electronic applications accepted. *Expenses:* Tuition, state resident: full-time $8238.24. *Financial support:* In 2010–11, 27 students received support, including 1 fellowship with full tuition reimbursement available (averaging $18,000 per year), 21 research assistantships with full tuition reimbursements available (averaging $5,000 per year), 5 teaching assistantships with full tuition reimbursements available (averaging $13,000 per year); career-related internships or fieldwork, Federal Work-Study, institutionally sponsored loans, scholarships/grants, and unspecified assistantships also available. Financial award application deadline: 1/11; financial award applicants required to submit FAFSA. *Faculty research:* Modern art and critical theory; medieval, Renaissance and Baroque art; Pre-Colombian. *Unit head:* Dr. Adam Jolles, Professor/Chair, 850-644-7066, Fax: 850-644-7065, E-mail: ajolles@fsu.edu. *Application contact:* Kathy Braun, Programs Coordinator/Graduate Student Advisor, 850-644-8207, Fax: 850-644-7065.

George Mason University, College of Humanities and Social Sciences, Department of History and Art History, Program in Art History, Fairfax, VA 22030. Offers MA. *Accreditation:* NASAD. *Faculty:* 49 full-time (19 women), 19 part-time/adjunct (10 women). *Students:* 6 full-time (all women), 21 part-time (17 women); includes 2 Hispanic/Latino, 1 international. Average age 33. 19 applicants, 68% accepted, 8 enrolled. In 2010, 3 master's awarded. *Degree requirements:* For master's, variable foreign language requirement, comprehensive exam, thesis optional. *Entrance requirements:* For master's, GRE, 2 letters of recommendation, resume. Additional exam requirements/recommendations for international students: Required—TOEFL (minimum score 570 paper-based; 230 computer-based; 88 iBT). *Application deadline:* For fall admission,

4/15 priority date for domestic students; for spring admission, 11/1 for domestic students. Applications are processed on a rolling basis. Application fee: $100. Electronic applications accepted. *Expenses:* Tuition, state resident: full-time $8192; part-time $440 per credit hour. Tuition, nonresident: full-time $22,952; part-time $1055 per credit hour. Required fees: $2364; $99 per credit hour. *Financial support:* In 2010–11, 1 student received support, including 1 teaching assistantship with full and partial tuition reimbursement available (averaging $9,480 per year); career-related internships or fieldwork, Federal Work-Study, scholarships/grants, unspecified assistantships, and health care benefits (full-time research or teaching assistantship recipients) also available. Support available to part-time students. Financial award application deadline: 3/1; financial award applicants required to submit FAFSA. *Faculty research:* Exhibit on Pompeii—ancient art, southeast Asia—history on Buddhist art, twentieth century Latin American interchange, Silk Road project, American art on visual imagery. *Unit head:* Brian Platt, Graduate Director, 703-993-1250, E-mail: bplatt1@gmu.edu. *Application contact:* Mack Holt, Information Contact, 703-993-1259, E-mail: mholt@gmu.edu.

The George Washington University, Columbian College of Arts and Sciences, Department of Fine Arts and Art History, Program in Art History, Washington, DC 20052. Offers art history (MA); museum training (MA). Part-time and evening/weekend programs available. *Students:* 14 full-time (13 women), 11 part-time (all women); includes 1 Asian, non-Hispanic/Latino; 1 Hispanic/Latino. Average age 29. 64 applicants, 59% accepted. In 2010, 7 master's awarded. *Degree requirements:* For master's, one foreign language, comprehensive exam, thesis or alternative. *Entrance requirements:* For master's, GRE General Test, bachelor's degree in field, minimum GPA of 3.0. Additional exam requirements/recommendations for international students: Required—TOEFL (minimum score 550 paper-based; 213 computer-based; 80 iBT). *Application deadline:* For fall admission, 3/1 priority date for domestic students, 1/15 priority date for international students; for spring admission, 10/1 priority date for domestic students, 9/1 priority date for international students. Applications are processed on a rolling basis. Application fee: $75. Electronic applications accepted. *Financial support:* In 2010–11, 3 students received support; fellowships, teaching assistantships, career-related internships or fieldwork and Federal Work-Study available. Financial award application deadline: 1/15. *Application contact:* Information Contact, 202-994-6085, Fax: 202-994-8657, E-mail: art@gwu.edu.

Georgia State University, College of Arts and Sciences, Ernest G. Welch School of Art and Design, Program in Art History, Atlanta, GA 30302-3083. Offers MA. *Accreditation:* NASAD. *Degree requirements:* For master's, one foreign language, comprehensive exam, thesis. *Entrance requirements:* For master's, GRE General Test, writing sample. Additional exam requirements/recommendations for international students: Required—TOEFL (minimum score 550 paper-based; 213 computer-based). Electronic applications accepted. *Faculty research:* Latin American art, contemporary art, Egypt/Near East art, African American art, 19th/20th century art.

Graduate School and University Center of the City University of New York, Graduate Studies, Program in Art History, New York, NY 10016-4039. Offers architecture (PhD); graphic arts (PhD); painting (PhD); photography (PhD); sculpture (PhD). *Degree requirements:* For doctorate, 2 foreign languages, thesis/dissertation. *Entrance requirements:* For doctorate, GRE General Test. Additional exam requirements/recommendations for international students: Required—TOEFL. Electronic applications accepted.

Graduate Theological Union, Graduate Programs, Berkeley, CA 94709-1212. Offers art and religion (MA, PhD, Th D); biblical languages (MA); biblical studies (MA); Biblical studies (PhD, Th D); Buddhist studies (MA); Christian spirituality (MA, PhD, Th D); cultural and historical studies of religions (MA, PhD, Th D); ethics and social theory (PhD, Th D); history (MA, PhD, Th D); homiletics (MA, PhD, Th D); interdisciplinary studies (PhD, Th D); Jewish studies (MA, PhD, Th D, Certificate); liturgical studies (MA, PhD, Th D); Near Eastern religions (PhD, Th D); Orthodox Christian studies (MA); religion and psychology (MA, PhD, Th D); religion and society/ethics and social theory (MA); systematic and philosophical theology (MA, PhD, Th D). PhD programs in Jewish studies and Near Eastern religions offered jointly with University of California, Berkeley. *Accreditation:* ATS. Terminal master's awarded for partial completion of doctoral program. *Degree requirements:* For master's, one foreign language, thesis; for doctorate, one foreign language, comprehensive exam, thesis/dissertation. *Entrance requirements:* For master's, GRE General Test; for doctorate, GRE General Test, MA or M Div. Additional exam requirements/recommendations for international students: Required—TOEFL. Electronic applications accepted.

Harvard University, Graduate School of Arts and Sciences, Department of History of Art and Architecture, Cambridge, MA 02138. Offers ancient art (PhD); ancient Near Eastern art (PhD); baroque art (PhD); Byzantine art (PhD); classical art (PhD); Indian art (PhD); Islamic art (PhD); Japanese and Chinese art (PhD); medieval art (PhD); modern art (PhD); Renaissance and modern architecture (PhD); Renaissance art (PhD). *Degree requirements:* For doctorate, variable foreign language requirement, thesis/dissertation, general exams; reading exams in French, German, and Italian. *Entrance requirements:* For doctorate, GRE General Test. Additional exam requirements/recommendations for international students: Required—TOEFL. *Expenses:* Tuition: Full-time $34,976. Required fees: $1166. Full-time tuition and fees vary according to program.

Howard University, Graduate School, Division of Fine Arts, Department of Art, Program in Art History, Washington, DC 20059-0002. Offers art history (MA); history of art and visual culture (MA). *Accreditation:* NASAD. Part-time programs available. *Degree requirements:* For master's, comprehensive exam, thesis. *Entrance requirements:* For master's, GRE General Test, minimum GPA of 3.0, BA in art history or related field, portfolio.

Hunter College of the City University of New York, Graduate School, School of Arts and Sciences, Department of Art, Program in Art History, New York, NY 10021-5085. Offers MA. Part-time and evening/weekend programs available. *Faculty:* 14 full-time (6 women), 1 part-time/adjunct (0 women). *Students:* 2 full-time (both women), 136 part-time (117 women); includes 6 Black or African American, non-Hispanic/Latino; 1 American Indian or Alaska Native, non-Hispanic/Latino; 7 Asian, non-Hispanic/Latino; 7 Hispanic/Latino, 1 international. Average age 31. 115 applicants, 65% accepted, 34 enrolled. In 2010, 22 master's awarded. *Degree requirements:* For master's, one foreign language, comprehensive exam, thesis. *Entrance requirements:* For master's, GRE General Test, minimum 12 credits of course work in art history, reading knowledge of a foreign language (Italian, French or German), 2 letters of recommendation. Additional exam requirements/recommendations for international students: Required—TOEFL. *Application deadline:* For fall admission, 3/1 for domestic students; for spring admission, 10/1 for domestic students. Application fee: $125. *Financial support:* Teaching assistantships, career-related internships or fieldwork, Federal Work-Study, scholarships/grants, and tuition waivers (partial) available. Support available to part-time students. Financial award application deadline: 4/15. *Faculty research:* Islamic art, Renaissance and Baroque, Impressionism, critical theory, Modernism. *Unit head:* Dr. Richard Stapleford, Graduate Adviser, 212-650-5052, E-mail: grad.arthisotryadvisor@hunter.cuny.edu. *Application contact:* William Zlata, Director for Graduate Admissions, 212-772-4482, Fax: 212-650-3336, E-mail: admissions@hunter.cuny.edu.

Illinois State University, Graduate School, College of Fine Arts, School of Art, Normal, IL 61790-2200. Offers art history (MA, MS); ceramics (MFA, MS); drawing (MFA, MS); fibers (MFA, MS); glass (MFA, MS); graphic design (MFA, MS); metals (MFA, MS); painting (MFA, MS); photography (MFA, MS); printmaking (MFA, MS); sculpture (MFA, MS). *Accreditation:* NASAD (one or more programs are accredited). *Degree requirements:* For master's, thesis or alternative, internship. *Entrance requirements:* For master's, portfolio, sample of scholarly writing. *Faculty research:* General operations support: Normal Editions Workshop for FY2007.

Indiana University Bloomington, University Graduate School, College of Arts and Sciences, Henry Radford Hope School of Fine Arts, Department of the History of Art, Bloomington, IN 47405-7000. Offers MA, PhD. *Accreditation:* NASAD. *Faculty:* 11 full-time (7 women), 1 (woman) part-time/adjunct. *Students:* 62 full-time (54 women), 4 part-time (3 women); includes 3 minority (1 Black or African American, non-Hispanic/Latino; 1 Hispanic/Latino; 1 Two or more races, non-Hispanic/Latino), 4 international. Average age 30. 68 applicants, 49% accepted, 15 enrolled. In 2010, 8 master's, 3 doctorates awarded. *Degree requirements:* For master's, one foreign language, thesis; for doctorate, 2 foreign languages, comprehensive exam, thesis/dissertation. *Entrance requirements:* For master's, GRE, writing sample, 3 letters of recommendation; for doctorate, GRE, transcript, writing samples, 3 letters of recommendation. Additional exam requirements/recommendations for international students: Required—TOEFL (minimum score 550 paper-based; 213 computer-based). *Application deadline:* For fall admission, 1/5 for domestic and international students; for spring admission, 8/15 for domestic and international students. Application fee: $55 ($65 for international students). Electronic applications accepted. *Financial support:* In 2010–11, 5 fellowships with full tuition reimbursements (averaging $16,660 per year), 1 research assistantship with full tuition reimbursement (averaging $11,000 per year), 11 teaching assistantships with full tuition reimbursements (averaging $11,700 per year) were awarded; career-related internships or fieldwork and Federal Work-Study also available. Financial award application deadline: 2/15. *Faculty research:* Art and social history, consumer culture, feminist art and theory, classical revivals. *Unit head:* Patrick McNaughton, Chair, 812-855-4924, Fax: 812-855-7498, E-mail: mcnaught@indiana.edu. *Application contact:* Fenella Jean Alice Flinn, Administrative Assistant, 812-855-9556, Fax: 812-855-7498, E-mail: fflinn@indiana.edu.

James Madison University, The Graduate School, College of Visual and Performing Arts, School of Art and Art History, Harrisonburg, VA 22807. Offers art education (MA); art history (MA); ceramics (MFA); drawing/painting (MFA); metal/jewelry (MFA); photography (MFA); printmaking (MFA); sculpture (MFA); studio art (MA); weaving/fibers (MFA). *Accreditation:* NASAD. Part-time programs available. *Faculty:* 8 full-time (5 women). *Students:* 10 full-time (6 women); includes 1 minority (Black or African American, non-Hispanic/Latino). Average age 27. In 2010, 3 master's awarded. *Degree requirements:* For master's, thesis (for some programs). *Entrance requirements:* For master's, GRE General Test, language exam in French or German, portfolio, 3 letters of recommendation, research paper. Additional exam requirements/recommendations for international students: Required—TOEFL. *Application deadline:* For fall admission, 2/15 priority date for domestic students, 2/15 for international students; for spring admission, 10/15 priority date for domestic students, 10/15 for international students. Applications are processed on a rolling basis. Application fee: $55. Electronic applications accepted. *Financial support:* In 2010–11, 9 students received support, including 3 teaching assistantships with full tuition reimbursements available (averaging $8,664 per year); Federal Work-Study and 6 graduate assistantships ($7382) also available. Financial award application deadline: 3/1; financial award applicants required to submit FAFSA. *Unit head:* William Srightman, Director, 540-568-6216. *Application contact:* Lynette M. Bible, Director of Graduate Admissions, 540-568-6395, Fax: 540-568-7860, E-mail: biblelm@jmu.edu.

The Johns Hopkins University, Zanvyl Krieger School of Arts and Sciences, Department of History of Art, Baltimore, MD 21218. Offers MA, PhD. *Faculty:* 6 full-time (1 woman), 1 part-time/adjunct (0 women). *Students:* 14 full-time (10 women), 4 international. Average age 28. 67 applicants, 6% accepted, 4 enrolled. In 2010, 6 master's, 5 doctorates awarded. Terminal master's awarded for partial completion of doctoral program. *Degree requirements:* For master's, 2 foreign languages; for doctorate, 2 foreign languages, thesis/dissertation. *Entrance requirements:* For master's and doctorate, GRE General Test. Additional exam requirements/recommendations for international students: Required—TOEFL (minimum score 600 paper-based; 250 computer-based; 100 iBT), IELTS. *Application deadline:* For fall admission, 1/15 for domestic and international students. Application fee: $75. Electronic applications accepted. *Financial support:* In 2010–11, 14 students received support, including 6 fellowships with full tuition reimbursements available (averaging $17,500 per year), 4 research assistantships with full tuition reimbursements available (averaging $17,500 per year), 4 teaching assistantships with full tuition reimbursements available (averaging $17,500 per year). Financial award application deadline: 4/15; financial award applicants required to submit FAFSA. *Faculty research:* Modern art, Renaissance art, medieval art, Roman art. *Unit head:* Dr. Stephen Campbell, Chair, 410-516-4928, Fax: 410-516-5188, E-mail: stephen.campbell@jhu.edu. *Application contact:* Sally Hauf, Graduate Administrative Coordinator, 410-516-7117, Fax: 410-516-5188, E-mail: arthist@jhu.edu.

Kent State University, College of the Arts, School of Art, Kent, OH 44242-0001. Offers art education (MA); art history (MA); crafts (MA, MFA), including ceramics (MA), glass, jewelry/metals, textiles/art; fine art (MA, MFA), including drawing/painting, printmaking, sculpture. *Accreditation:* NASAD (one or more programs are accredited). *Degree requirements:* For master's, one foreign language, thesis. *Entrance requirements:* For master's, undergraduate degree in proposed area of study (for fine arts and crafts programs); minimum overall GPA of 2.75 (3.0 for art major); 3 letters of recommendation; portfolio (15-20 slides for MA, 20-25 for MFA). Additional exam requirements/recommendations for international students: Required—TOEFL. Electronic applications accepted. *Expenses:* Tuition, state resident: full-time $7866; part-time $437 per credit hour. Tuition, nonresident: full-time $14,022; part-time $779 per credit hour.

Lamar University, College of Graduate Studies, College of Fine Arts and Communication, Department of Art, Beaumont, TX 77710. Offers art history (MA); photography (MA); studio art (MA); visual design (MA). Part-time and evening/weekend programs available. *Faculty:* 5 full-time (3 women). *Students:* 2 full-time (1 woman), 3 part-time (2 women). Average age 42. 3 applicants, 33% accepted, 0 enrolled. *Degree requirements:* For master's, thesis. *Entrance requirements:* For master's, GRE General Test, minimum GPA of 2.5 in last 60 hours of undergraduate course work. Additional exam requirements/recommendations for international students: Required—TOEFL. *Application deadline:* For fall admission, 8/1 priority date for domestic students; for spring admission, 12/1 for domestic students. Applications are processed on a rolling basis. Application fee: $25 ($50 for international students). *Expenses:* Tuition, state resident: full-time $4160; part-time $208 per credit hour. Tuition, nonresident: full-time $10,360; part-time $518 per credit hour. *Financial support:* Fellowships, career-related internships or fieldwork, Federal Work-Study, and scholarships/grants available. Financial award application deadline: 4/1. *Faculty research:* Nineteenth century academic paintings, metal casting, pigment color stability, computer-modified photography, manipulated photography. *Unit head:* Donna M. Meeks, Chair, 409-880-8141, Fax: 409-880-1799, E-mail: meeksdm@lub002.lamar.edu. *Application contact:* Debbie Piper, Coordinator of Graduate Admissions, 409-880-8356, Fax: 409-880-8414, E-mail: gradmissions@hal.lamar.edu.

Lancaster Theological Seminary, Graduate and Professional Programs, Lancaster, PA 17603-2812. Offers biblical studies (MAR); Christian education (MAR); Christianity and the arts (MAR); church history (MAR); congregational life (MAR); lay leadership (Certificate); theological studies (M Div); theology (D Min); theology and ethics (MAR). *Accreditation:* ACIPE; ATS. *Degree requirements:* For doctorate, thesis/dissertation; for M Div, one foreign language.

Louisiana State University and Agricultural and Mechanical College, Graduate School, College of Art and Design, School of Art, Program in Art History, Baton Rouge, LA 70803. Offers MA. *Accreditation:* NASAD. *Students:* 14 full-time (11 women), 3 part-time (1 woman), 1 international. Average age 29. 19 applicants, 74% accepted, 7 enrolled. In 2010, 5 master's awarded. *Degree requirements:* For master's, one foreign language, thesis. *Entrance requirements:* For master's, GRE General Test, minimum GPA of 3.0. Additional exam requirements/recommendations for international students: Required—TOEFL (minimum score 550 paper-based; 213 computer-based; 79 iBT), IELTS (minimum score 6.5). *Application deadline:* For fall admission, 1/25 priority date for domestic students, 5/15 for international students; for spring admission, 10/15 for international students. Applications are processed on a rolling basis. Application fee: $50 ($70 for international students). Electronic applications accepted. *Financial support:* In 2010–11, 2 students received support; research assistantships with partial tuition reimbursements available, teaching assistantships with partial tuition reimbursements available, career-related internships or fieldwork, Federal Work-Study, institutionally sponsored loans, scholarships/grants, traineeships, health care benefits, and unspecified assistantships available. Support available to part-time students. Financial award

Art History

Louisiana State University and Agricultural and Mechanical College (continued)
application deadline: 3/15. *Faculty research:* Liturgical art, Greco-Roman art, Renaissance prints, American twentieth century art, performance art. *Unit head:* Dr. Susan Ryan, Coordinator, 225-578-5411, E-mail: faryan@lsu.edu. *Application contact:* Dr. Susan Ryan, Graduate Coordinator, 225-578-8813, Fax: 225-578-5424.

Massachusetts Institute of Technology, School of Architecture and Planning, Department of Architecture, Cambridge, MA 02139. Offers architecture (M Arch, PhD), including building technology (PhD), design and computation (PhD), history and theory of architecture (PhD), history and theory of art (PhD); architecture studies (SM Arch S); building technology (SMBT); visual studies (SM Vis S). *Faculty:* 30 full-time (7 women). *Students:* 241 full-time (111 women), 1 (woman) part-time; includes 54 minority (6 Black or African American, non-Hispanic/Latino; 2 American Indian or Alaska Native, non-Hispanic/Latino; 31 Asian, non-Hispanic/Latino; 10 Hispanic/Latino; 5 Two or more races, non-Hispanic/Latino), 84 international. Average age 28. 1,166 applicants, 13% accepted, 94 enrolled. In 2010, 63 master's, 6 doctorates awarded. *Degree requirements:* For master's, thesis; for doctorate, comprehensive exam, thesis/dissertation. *Entrance requirements:* For master's, GRE General Test (for some programs), portfolio (for some programs); for doctorate, GRE General Test (for some programs). Additional exam requirements/recommendations for international students: Required—TOEFL (minimum score 650 paper-based; 280 computer-based; 114 iBT), IELTS (minimum score 7). *Application deadline:* For fall admission, 12/15 for domestic and international students. Application fee: $75. Electronic applications accepted. *Expenses:* Tuition: Full-time $38,940; part-time $605 per unit. Required fees: $272. *Financial support:* In 2010–11, 195 students received support, including 155 fellowships with tuition reimbursements available (averaging $18,267 per year), 32 research assistantships with tuition reimbursements available (averaging $24,642 per year), 25 teaching assistantships with tuition reimbursements available (averaging $29,366 per year); career-related internships or fieldwork, Federal Work-Study, institutionally sponsored loans, scholarships/grants, health care benefits, and unspecified assistantships also available. *Faculty research:* Architecture and urbanism; building technology and sustainability; computation and design; history, theory, and criticism; contemporary visual art practice; digital fabrication. Total annual research expenditures: $2.4 million. *Unit head:* Prof. Nader Tehrani, Department Head, 617-253-7791, E-mail: arch@mit.edu. *Application contact:* Admissions Coordinator, 617-715-4490, Fax: 617-253-8993, E-mail: arch@mit.edu.

McGill University, Faculty of Graduate and Postdoctoral Studies, Faculty of Arts, Department of Art History and Communication Studies, Montréal, QC H3A 2T5, Canada. Offers MA, PhD.

Montana State University, College of Graduate Studies, College of Arts and Architecture, School of Art, Bozeman, MT 59717. Offers art (MFA); art history (MA). *Accreditation:* NASAD (one or more programs are accredited). Part-time programs available. *Faculty:* 15 full-time (6 women), 8 part-time/adjunct (4 women). *Students:* 14 full-time (10 women), 3 part-time (all women); includes 1 minority (Hispanic/Latino). Average age 28. 49 applicants, 16% accepted, 6 enrolled. *Degree requirements:* For master's, comprehensive exam, thesis. *Entrance requirements:* For master's, GRE General Test, undergraduate degree in art. Additional exam requirements/recommendations for international students: Required—TOEFL (minimum score 550 paper-based; 213 computer-based). *Application deadline:* For fall admission, 7/15 priority date for domestic students, 5/15 priority date for international students; for spring admission, 12/1 priority date for domestic students, 10/1 priority date for international students. Applications are processed on a rolling basis. Application fee: $30. Electronic applications accepted. *Expenses:* Tuition, state resident: full-time $5553.90. Tuition, nonresident: full-time $14,646. Required fees: $1233. *Financial support:* In 2010–11, 15 students received support, including 15 teaching assistantships with partial tuition reimbursements available (averaging $7,725 per year); Federal Work-Study, scholarships/grants, health care benefits, tuition waivers (partial), and unspecified assistantships also available. Financial award application deadline: 3/1; financial award applicants required to submit FAFSA. *Faculty research:* Encaustic painting, wild clay research, environmentally friendly kiln fuel, Roman wall paintings, French revolutionary portraiture. *Unit head:* Vaughan Judge, Head, 406-994-4501, Fax: 406-994-3680, E-mail: vaughan.judge@montana.edu. *Application contact:* Dr. Carl A. Fox, Vice Provost for Graduate Education, 406-994-4145, Fax: 406-994-7433, E-mail: gradstudy@montana.edu.

New Mexico State University, Graduate School, College of Arts and Sciences, Department of Art, Las Cruces, NM 88003-8001. Offers art history (MA); ceramics (MA, MFA); design (MA, MFA); drawing (MFA); metals (MA, MFA); painting (MFA); photography (MFA); sculpture (MA, MFA). *Faculty:* 9 full-time (5 women), 3 part-time/adjunct (1 woman). *Students:* 18 full-time (10 women), 2 part-time (both women); includes 6 minority (1 American Indian or Alaska Native, non-Hispanic/Latino; 1 Asian, non-Hispanic/Latino; 4 Hispanic/Latino), 1 international. Average age 34. 26 applicants, 77% accepted, 11 enrolled. In 2010, 11 master's awarded. *Degree requirements:* For master's, comprehensive exam (for some programs), thesis, thesis exhibit. *Entrance requirements:* For master's, portfolio, 10-page paper (art history). *Application deadline:* For fall admission, 2/15 for domestic students; for winter admission, 10/15 for domestic students; for spring admission, 7/15 for domestic students. Application fee: $30 ($50 for international students). Electronic applications accepted. *Expenses:* Tuition, state resident: full-time $4536; part-time $242 per credit. Tuition, nonresident: full-time $15,816; part-time $712 per credit. Required fees: $636 per term. *Financial support:* In 2010–11, 17 teaching assistantships (averaging $6,640 per year) were awarded; research assistantships, Federal Work-Study and health care benefits also available. Support available to part-time students. Financial award application deadline: 3/1; financial award applicants required to submit FAFSA. *Faculty research:* Painting, graphic design, sculpture, ceramics, photography, jewelry. *Unit head:* Dr. Thom Brown, Head, 575-646-1705, Fax: 575-646-8036, E-mail: artdept@nmsu.edu. *Application contact:* Dr. Thom Brown, Head, 575-646-1705, Fax: 575-646-8036, E-mail: artdept@nmsu.edu.

New York University, Graduate School of Arts and Science, Institute of Fine Arts, Program in Art History and Archaeology, New York, NY 10012-1019. Offers architectural studies (PhD); art history and archaeology (MA, PhD); classical art and archaeology (PhD); curatorial studies (PhD); East and South Asian art (PhD); Near Eastern art and archaeology (PhD); MA/Diploma; PhD/Certificate. Part-time programs available. *Students:* 243 full-time (192 women), 59 part-time (47 women); includes 2 Black or African American, non-Hispanic/Latino; 20 Asian, non-Hispanic/Latino; 8 Hispanic/Latino, 29 international. Average age 32. 394 applicants, 27% accepted, 57 enrolled. In 2010, 29 master's, 12 doctorates awarded. Terminal master's awarded for partial completion of doctoral program. *Degree requirements:* For master's, 2 foreign languages, thesis or alternative, 2 qualifying papers; for doctorate, 2 foreign languages, thesis/dissertation. *Entrance requirements:* For master's, GRE General Test; for doctorate, GRE General Test, MA. Additional exam requirements/recommendations for international students: Required—TOEFL. *Application deadline:* For fall admission, 12/15 for domestic students. Application fee: $90. *Financial support:* Fellowships with tuition reimbursements, research assistantships with tuition reimbursements, teaching assistantships with tuition reimbursements, career-related internships or fieldwork, Federal Work-Study, and institutionally sponsored loans available. Financial award application deadline: 12/15; financial award applicants required to submit FAFSA. *Unit head:* Patricia Rubin, Chair, 212-992-5800, Fax: 212-992-5807, E-mail: ifa.program@nyu.edu. *Application contact:* Priscilla Saucek, Director of Graduate Studies, 212-992-5800, Fax: 212-992-5807, E-mail: ifa.program@nyu.edu.

Northwestern University, The Graduate School, Judd A. and Marjorie Weinberg College of Arts and Sciences, Department of Art History, Evanston, IL 60208. Offers PhD. Admissions and degrees offered through The Graduate School. *Degree requirements:* For doctorate, 2 foreign languages, comprehensive exam, thesis/dissertation, major and minor field exercises. *Entrance requirements:* For doctorate, GRE General Test. Additional exam requirements/recommendations for international students: Required—TOEFL. Electronic applications accepted. *Faculty research:* Modern American and European art and architecture, prehistoric and ancient art, central Asian art, medieval manuscripts and early printed books, history of museums, art of Western Africa, theory of culture.

The Ohio State University, Graduate School, College of Arts and Sciences, Division of Arts and Humanities, Department of History of Art, Columbus, OH 43210. Offers MA, PhD. *Accreditation:* NASAD. *Faculty:* 20. *Students:* 29 full-time (18 women), 7 part-time (6 women); includes 2 Asian, non-Hispanic/Latino; 2 Hispanic/Latino; 1 Two or more races, non-Hispanic/Latino, 9 international. Average age 32. In 2010, 6 master's, 1 doctorate awarded. *Degree requirements:* For master's, one foreign language, thesis optional; for doctorate, 2 foreign languages, thesis/dissertation. *Entrance requirements:* For master's and doctorate, GRE General Test. Additional exam requirements/recommendations for international students: Recommended—TOEFL (minimum score 600 paper-based; 250 computer-based). *Application deadline:* For fall admission, 8/15 priority date for domestic students, 7/1 priority date for international students; for winter admission, 12/1 priority date for domestic students, 11/1 priority date for international students; for spring admission, 3/1 priority date for domestic students, 2/1 priority date for international students. Applications are processed on a rolling basis. Application fee: $40 ($50 for international students). Electronic applications accepted. *Expenses:* Tuition, state resident: full-time $10,605. Tuition, nonresident: full-time $26,535. Tuition and fees vary according to course load and program. *Financial support:* Fellowships, teaching assistantships, Federal Work-Study and institutionally sponsored loans available. Support available to part-time students. *Faculty research:* Western and Oriental art, African art and archaeology. *Unit head:* Andrew Shelton, Chair, 614-292-7481, E-mail: shelton.85@osu.edu. *Application contact:* 614-688-9444, Fax: 614-292-3895, E-mail: domestic.grad@osu.edu.

Ohio University, Graduate College, College of Fine Arts, School of Art, Athens, OH 45701-2979. Offers art history (MA); ceramics (MFA); graphic design (MFA); painting (MFA); photography (MFA); printmaking (MFA); sculpture (MFA). Part-time programs available. *Students:* 62 full-time (35 women), 4 part-time (3 women); includes 5 minority (1 American Indian or Alaska Native, non-Hispanic/Latino; 1 Asian, non-Hispanic/Latino; 3 Hispanic/Latino), 7 international. 181 applicants, 19% accepted, 28 enrolled. In 2010, 14 master's awarded. *Degree requirements:* For master's, thesis. *Entrance requirements:* For master's, portfolio. Additional exam requirements/recommendations for international students: Required—TOEFL (minimum score 550 paper-based; 80 iBT) or IELTS (minimum score 6.5). *Application deadline:* For fall admission, 2/1 for domestic and international students. Application fee: $50 ($55 for international students). Electronic applications accepted. *Financial support:* Teaching assistantships with full and partial tuition reimbursements, career-related internships or fieldwork, Federal Work-Study, institutionally sponsored loans, scholarships/grants, tuition waivers (partial), and unspecified assistantships available. Financial award application deadline: 2/1. *Faculty research:* Vapor-fired ceramics, video installation, art theory, digital photography, mixed and interdisciplinary media work. *Unit head:* David LaPalombara, Director, 740-593-4290, Fax: 740-593-0457, E-mail: lapalomb@ohio.edu. *Application contact:* Melissa Haviland, Chair, Graduate Programs, 740-593-9996, Fax: 740-593-0457, E-mail: haviland@ohio.edu.

Penn State University Park, Graduate School, College of Arts and Architecture, Department of Art History, State College, University Park, PA 16802-1503. Offers MA, PhD.

Pratt Institute, School of Art and Design, Program in Art History, Brooklyn, NY 11205-3899. Offers art history (MS); art history theory and criticism (MS); MS/MFA; MS/MS. *Accreditation:* NASAD. Part-time programs available. *Faculty:* 5 full-time (3 women), 12 part-time/adjunct (7 women). *Students:* 51 full-time (43 women), 2 part-time (both women); includes 3 Black or African American, non-Hispanic/Latino; 2 Asian, non-Hispanic/Latino; 4 Hispanic/Latino, 4 international. Average age 27. 75 applicants, 71% accepted, 20 enrolled. In 2010, 7 master's awarded. *Degree requirements:* For master's, one foreign language, thesis. *Entrance requirements:* For master's, GRE General Test, letters of recommendation, portfolio. Additional exam requirements/recommendations for international students: Required—TOEFL (minimum score 600 paper-based; 250 computer-based; 100 iBT). *Application deadline:* For fall admission, 1/5 for domestic and international students; for spring admission, 10/1 for domestic and international students. Application fee: $50 ($90 for international students). Electronic applications accepted. *Expenses:* Tuition: Full-time $22,734; part-time $1263 per credit. Required fees: $1280. *Financial support:* Career-related internships or fieldwork, Federal Work-Study, institutionally sponsored loans, scholarships/grants, health care benefits, and unspecified assistantships available. Support available to part-time students. Financial award application deadline: 2/1; financial award applicants required to submit CSS PROFILE or FAFSA. *Faculty research:* Conservation techniques, women artists from previous centuries, art of sixteenth century Veneto, design history, nineteenth century Germany. *Unit head:* Steven Zucker, Chairperson, 718-636-3598, E-mail: szucker@pratt.edu. *Application contact:* Young Hah, Director of Graduate Admissions, 718-636-3683, Fax: 718-399-4242, E-mail: yhah@pratt.edu.

See Display on page 92 and Close-Up on page 131.

Purchase College, State University of New York, School of Humanities, Purchase, NY 10577-1400. Offers art history (MA). *Accreditation:* NASAD. *Degree requirements:* For master's, one foreign language, thesis. *Entrance requirements:* For master's, BA or BFA, previous course work in art history.

Queens College of the City University of New York, Division of Graduate Studies, Arts and Humanities Division, Department of Art, Program in Art History, Flushing, NY 11367-1597. Offers MA. Part-time and evening/weekend programs available. *Faculty:* 6 full-time (3 women). *Students:* 1 (woman) full-time, 17 part-time (14 women); includes 1 Asian, non-Hispanic/Latino; 4 Hispanic/Latino, 1 international. 14 applicants, 71% accepted, 4 enrolled. In 2010, 3 master's awarded. *Degree requirements:* For master's, 2 foreign languages, thesis, qualifying exam. *Entrance requirements:* For master's, minimum GPA of 3.0. Additional exam requirements/recommendations for international students: Required—TOEFL. *Application deadline:* For fall admission, 4/1 for domestic students; for spring admission, 11/1 for domestic students. Applications are processed on a rolling basis. Application fee: $125. *Financial support:* Career-related internships or fieldwork, Federal Work-Study, institutionally sponsored loans, and tuition waivers (partial) available. Support available to part-time students. Financial award application deadline: 4/1; financial award applicants required to submit FAFSA. *Unit head:* Dr. Barbara Lane, Head, 718-997-4820. *Application contact:* Mario Caruso, Director of Graduate Admissions, 718-997-5200, Fax: 718-997-5193, E-mail: graduate_admissions@qc.edu.

Rice University, Graduate Programs, School of Humanities, Department of Art History, Houston, TX 77251-1892. Offers PhD.

Richmond, The American International University in London, MA in Art History Program, Richmond, United Kingdom. Offers MA. Part-time programs available. *Degree requirements:* For master's, thesis. *Entrance requirements:* For master's, minimum GPA of 3.0. Additional exam requirements/recommendations for international students: Required—TOEFL, IELTS. Electronic applications accepted. *Expenses:* Contact institution. *Faculty research:* Archaeology of art and representation, contemporary paganisms, nineteenth century modernisms, American twentieth century art, sound media.

Rutgers, The State University of New Jersey, New Brunswick, Graduate School-New Brunswick, Program in Art History, Piscataway, NJ 08854-8097. Offers art history (MA, PhD); curatorial studies (Certificate); historic preservation (Certificate). Part-time programs available. Terminal master's awarded for partial completion of doctoral program. *Degree requirements:* For master's, one foreign language, comprehensive exam; for doctorate, 2 foreign languages, comprehensive exam, thesis/dissertation. *Entrance requirements:* For master's and doctorate, GRE General Test, writing sample. Additional exam requirements/recommendations for international students: Required—TOEFL (minimum score 550 paper-based; 213 computer-based). Electronic applications accepted. *Expenses:* Tuition, state resident: full-time $7200; part-time $600 per credit. Tuition, nonresident: full-time $11,124; part-time $927 per credit. *Faculty research:* Ancient and medieval art and architecture; Renaissance and Baroque art and architecture; modern and contemporary art and architecture; Italian studies; the arts of Asia, Africa, and the Americas.

San Diego State University, Graduate and Research Affairs, College of Professional Studies and Fine Arts, School of Art, Design and Art History, San Diego, CA 92182. Offers art history (MA); studio arts (MA, MFA), including applied design, environmental design, graphic design, interior design, painting and printmaking, sculpture. *Accreditation:* NASAD (one or more programs are accredited). *Degree requirements:* For master's, variable foreign language requirement, thesis. *Entrance requirements:* For master's, GRE General Test, bachelor's degree in related field, slide portfolio, typed slide information sheet, 2 letters of recommendation. Additional exam requirements/recommendations for international students: Required—TOEFL. Electronic applications accepted.

San Francisco Art Institute, Graduate Program, Department of History and Theory of Contemporary Art, San Francisco, CA 94133. Offers MA. *Entrance requirements:* Additional exam requirements/recommendations for international students: Required—TOEFL (minimum score 580 paper-based; 237 computer-based).

San Jose State University, Graduate Studies and Research, College of Humanities and the Arts, School of Art and Design, San Jose, CA 95192-0001. Offers animation/illustration (MA); art history (MA); digital media arts (MFA); photography (MFA); pictorial arts (MFA); spatial arts (MFA). *Accreditation:* NASAD (one or more programs are accredited). *Entrance requirements:* For master's, GRE. Electronic applications accepted.

Savannah College of Art and Design, Graduate School, Program in Art History, Savannah, GA 31402-3146. Offers MA. Part-time programs available. *Faculty:* 41 full-time (24 women), 9 part-time/adjunct (7 women). *Students:* 6 full-time (all women). Average age 24. In 2010, 4 master's awarded. *Degree requirements:* For master's, one foreign language, comprehensive exam, thesis, internship. *Entrance requirements:* For master's, art history paper, interview. Additional exam requirements/recommendations for international students: Required—TOEFL (minimum score 550 paper-based; 213 computer-based). *Application deadline:* For fall admission, 4/1 priority date for domestic and international students. Applications are processed on a rolling basis. Application fee: $35. Electronic applications accepted. *Expenses:* Tuition: Full-time $29,520; part-time $3280 per quarter. Tuition and fees vary according to campus/location. *Financial support:* Fellowships, career-related internships or fieldwork, Federal Work-Study, and scholarships/grants available. Financial award application deadline: 4/1; financial award applicants required to submit FAFSA. *Faculty research:* Contemporary art. *Unit head:* Prof. Geoffrey Taylor, Chair, 912-525-6049, Fax: 912-525-6064, E-mail: gtaylor@scad.edu. *Application contact:* Elizabeth Mathis, Director of Graduate and International Enrollment, 912-525-5965, Fax: 912-525-5985, E-mail: emathis@scad.edu.

See Display on page 177 and Close-Up on page 223

School of the Art Institute of Chicago, Graduate Division, Program in Modern Art History, Theory, and Criticism, Chicago, IL 60603-3103. Offers MA. *Accreditation:* NASAD. *Entrance requirements:* For master's, GRE. Additional exam requirements/recommendations for international students: Required—TOEFL, IELTS.

See Close-Up on page 225.

Southern Methodist University, Meadows School of the Arts, Division of Art History, Dallas, TX 75275. Offers MA. Part-time and evening/weekend programs available. *Faculty:* 9 full-time (4 women). *Students:* 11 full-time (9 women), 7 part-time (all women); includes 1 Black or African American, non-Hispanic/Latino; 3 Hispanic/Latino; 1 Two or more races, non-Hispanic/Latino, 1 international. Average age 28. 32 applicants, 25% accepted, 6 enrolled. In 2010, 2 master's awarded. *Degree requirements:* For master's, one foreign language, thesis, translation exam. *Entrance requirements:* For master's, GRE, 12 upper-level hours in art history, sample research paper. Additional exam requirements/recommendations for international students: Required—TOEFL (minimum score 550 paper-based; 213 computer-based; 80 iBT). *Application deadline:* For fall admission, 2/15 priority date for domestic and international students; for spring admission, 11/1 for domestic and international students. Application fee: $75. *Financial support:* In 2010–11, 13 students received support, including 13 teaching assistantships (averaging $3,500 per year); scholarships/grants and unspecified assistantships also available. Financial award application deadline: 3/1; financial award applicants required to submit FAFSA. *Faculty research:* American art, nineteenth and twentieth century art, classical and Byzantine art, Hispanic art, Mesoamerican art, Renaissance-Baroque. *Unit head:* Dr. Janice Bergman-Carton, Chair, 214-768-2615, E-mail: jbergman@smu.edu. *Application contact:* Joe S. Hoselton, Graduate Admissions and Records Coordinator, 214-768-3765, Fax: 214-768-3272, E-mail: hoselton@smu.edu.

State University of New York at Binghamton, Graduate School, School of Arts and Sciences, Department of Art History, Binghamton, NY 13902-6000. Offers MA, PhD. *Faculty:* 5 full-time (3 women), 2 part-time/adjunct (1 woman). *Students:* 17 full-time (14 women), 14 part-time (10 women); includes 1 Asian, non-Hispanic/Latino; 2 Hispanic/Latino, 15 international. Average age 35. 28 applicants, 54% accepted, 5 enrolled. In 2010, 2 master's, 4 doctorates awarded. *Degree requirements:* For master's, one foreign language, comprehensive exam, thesis; for doctorate, 2 foreign languages, comprehensive exam, thesis/dissertation, oral exam. *Entrance requirements:* For master's and doctorate, GRE General Test, writing sample. Additional exam requirements/recommendations for international students: Required—TOEFL. *Application deadline:* For fall admission, 1/15 priority date for domestic and international students; for spring admission, 10/1 priority date for domestic and international students. Applications are processed on a rolling basis. Application fee: $60. Electronic applications accepted. *Financial support:* In 2010–11, 13 students received support, including 10 teaching assistantships with full tuition reimbursements available (averaging $14,500 per year); career-related internships or fieldwork, Federal Work-Study, institutionally sponsored loans, scholarships/grants, health care benefits, and unspecified assistantships also available. Financial award application deadline: 2/15; financial award applicants required to submit FAFSA. *Faculty research:* History of art and architecture. *Unit head:* Dr. Tom McDonough, Professor and Chair, 607-777-2847, Fax: 607-777-4466, E-mail: tmcdonou@binghamton.edu. *Application contact:* Catherine Smith, 607-777-2151, Fax: 607-777-2501, E-mail: cmsmith@binghamton.edu.

Stony Brook University, State University of New York, Graduate School, College of Arts and Sciences, Department of Art, Program in Art History and Criticism, Stony Brook, NY 11794. Offers MA, PhD. Part-time programs available. *Students:* 41 full-time (31 women), 5 part-time (3 women); includes 1 American Indian or Alaska Native, non-Hispanic/Latino; 1 Asian, non-Hispanic/Latino; 2 Hispanic/Latino, 13 international. Average age 30. 73 applicants, 59% accepted, 18 enrolled. In 2010, 9 master's, 7 doctorates awarded. *Degree requirements:* For master's, comprehensive exam, thesis, reading knowledge of German or French; for doctorate, comprehensive exam, thesis/dissertation, qualifying paper, reading knowledge of German and French, qualifying examination. *Entrance requirements:* For master's, GRE General Test, minimum undergraduate GPA of 3.0; for doctorate, GRE General Test, minimum graduate GPA of 3.0. Additional exam requirements/recommendations for international students: Required—TOEFL (minimum score 550 paper-based; 213 computer-based), IELTS (minimum score 6.5). *Application deadline:* For fall admission, 1/15 for domestic students. Application fee: $100. *Expenses:* Tuition, state resident: full-time $8370; part-time $349 per credit. Tuition, nonresident: full-time $13,780; part-time $574 per credit. Required fees: $994. *Financial support:* In 2010–11, 1 research assistantship, 17 teaching assistantships were awarded. *Unit head:* Dr. Joseph Monteyne, Director, 631-632-7264, E-mail: jmonteyne@notes.cc.sunysb.edu. *Application contact:* Dr. Michele Bogart, Director, 631-632-7270.

Sul Ross State University, School of Arts and Sciences, Department of Fine Arts and Communication, Alpine, TX 79832. Offers art education (M Ed); art history (M Ed); studio art (M Ed), including ceramics, design, drawing, jewelry, painting, printmaking, sculpture, weaving. Part-time programs available. *Degree requirements:* For master's, oral or written exam. *Entrance requirements:* For master's, GRE General Test, minimum GPA of 2.5 in last 60 hours of undergraduate work. *Faculty research:* Ceramic sculpture, watercolor, wood sculpture, rock art.

Syracuse University, College of Arts and Sciences, Program in Art History, Syracuse, NY 13244. Offers MA. *Students:* 32 full-time (30 women), 3 part-time (2 women); includes 1 minority (Hispanic/Latino). Average age 24. 55 applicants, 67% accepted, 19 enrolled. In 2010, 13 master's awarded. *Degree requirements:* For master's, one foreign language, symposium presentation. *Entrance requirements:* For master's, GRE, research writing sample; second language. Additional exam requirements/recommendations for international students: Required—TOEFL (minimum score 100 iBT). *Application deadline:* For fall admission, 1/1 priority date for domestic and international students. Application fee: $75. *Expenses:* Tuition: Part-time $1162 per credit. *Financial support:* In 2010–11, 4 fellowships were awarded; teaching assistantships. Financial award application deadline: 1/1; financial award applicants required to submit FAFSA. *Unit head:* Prof. Laurinda Dixon, Graduat Program Director, 315-443-4185. *Application contact:* Linda Straub, Information Contact, 315-443-4185, E-mail: ljstraub@syr.edu.

See Display on page 179 and Close-Up on page 227.

Temple University, Tyler School of Art, Department of Art History, Philadelphia, PA 19122-6096. Offers MA, PhD. Part-time programs available. *Faculty:* 11 full-time (7 women). *Students:* 52 full-time (46 women), 8 part-time (all women); includes 1 Asian, non-Hispanic/Latino; 1 Hispanic/Latino, 2 international. 62 applicants, 65% accepted, 18 enrolled. In 2010, 13 master's, 1 doctorate awarded. Terminal master's awarded for partial completion of doctoral program. *Degree requirements:* For master's, 2 foreign languages, thesis, comprehensive slide exam; for doctorate, thesis/dissertation, qualifying exam. *Entrance requirements:* For master's, GRE General Test, minimum GPA of 3.0; for doctorate, MA in art history. Additional exam requirements/recommendations for international students: Required—TOEFL. *Application deadline:* For fall admission, 4/15 for domestic students, 12/15 for international students; for spring admission, 11/15 for domestic students, 8/1 for international students. Applications are processed on a rolling basis. Application fee: $50. Electronic applications accepted. *Financial support:* Fellowships, research assistantships with full tuition reimbursements, teaching assistantships with full tuition reimbursements, career-related internships or fieldwork, institutionally sponsored loans, and technical assistantships available. Financial award application deadline: 1/15. *Faculty research:* Aegean, Greek, and Roman art; early Christian art; medieval art and architecture; Renaissance and Baroque painting, sculpture, and architecture; nineteenth and twentieth century painting and sculpture. *Unit head:* Dr. Gerald Silk, Chair, 215-204-7837, Fax: 215-204-6951, E-mail: gsilk@temple.edu. *Application contact:* Dr. Gerald Silk, Chair, 215-204-7837, Fax: 215-204-6951, E-mail: gsilk@temple.edu.

Texas A&M University–Commerce, Graduate School, College of Arts and Sciences, Department of Art, Commerce, TX 75429-3011. Offers art (MA, MS); art history (MA); fine arts (MFA); studio art (MA). MFA offered jointly with University of North Texas, Texas Woman's University. Part-time programs available. *Degree requirements:* For master's, comprehensive exam, thesis (for some programs). *Entrance requirements:* For master's, GRE General Test. Electronic applications accepted. *Faculty research:* Use of different art media.

Texas Christian University, College of Fine Arts, Department of Art and Art History, Fort Worth, TX 76129. Offers art history (MA); studio art (MFA). *Accreditation:* NASAD. Part-time programs available. *Degree requirements:* For master's, thesis, internship, foreign language exam. *Entrance requirements:* For master's, GRE General Test, writing sample. Additional exam requirements/recommendations for international students: Required—TOEFL. *Application deadline:* For fall admission, 3/15 for domestic students. Applications are processed on a rolling basis. Application fee: $0. *Expenses:* Tuition: Full-time $18,720; part-time $1040 per credit hour. Tuition and fees vary according to course load and program. *Financial support:* Unspecified assistantships available. Financial award application deadline: 3/1. *Unit head:* Ron Watson, Chairperson, 817-257-7643, E-mail: r.watson@tcu.edu. *Application contact:* Dr. Joseph Butler, Associate Dean, College of Fine Arts, 817-257-6629, E-mail: j.butler@tcu.edu.

Texas Tech University, Graduate School, College of Visual and Performing Arts, School of Art, Lubbock, TX 79409. Offers art (MFA); art education (MAE); art history (MA). *Accreditation:* NASAD (one or more programs are accredited). Part-time programs available. *Faculty:* 22 full-time (11 women). *Students:* 49 full-time (21 women), 29 part-time (19 women); includes 2 Black or African American, non-Hispanic/Latino; 2 American Indian or Alaska Native, non-Hispanic/Latino; 1 Asian, non-Hispanic/Latino; 7 Hispanic/Latino; 1 Two or more races, non-Hispanic/Latino, 8 international. Average age 33. 77 applicants, 43% accepted, 20 enrolled. In 2010, 14 master's awarded. *Degree requirements:* For master's, thesis (for some programs). *Entrance requirements:* For master's, GRE General Test. Additional exam requirements/recommendations for international students: Required—TOEFL (minimum score 550 paper-based; 213 computer-based; 79 iBT). *Application deadline:* For fall admission, 6/1 priority date for domestic students, 1/15 priority date for international students; for spring admission, 9/1 priority date for domestic students, 6/15 priority date for international students. Applications are processed on a rolling basis. Application fee: $50 ($75 for international students). Electronic applications accepted. *Expenses:* Tuition, state resident: full-time $5495.76; part-time $228.99 per credit hour. Tuition, nonresident: full-time $12,936; part-time $538.99 per credit hour. Required fees: $2674; $36 per credit hour. $905 per semester. *Financial support:* In 2010–11, 41 students received support, including 19 teaching assistantships with partial tuition reimbursements available (averaging $5,992 per year). Financial award application deadline: 4/15; financial award applicants required to submit FAFSA. *Faculty research:* Studio, art history, art education. *Unit head:* Prof. Tina Fuentes, Director, 806-742-3825 Ext. 223, Fax: 806-742-1971, E-mail: tina.fuentes@ttu.edu. *Application contact:* Sang-Mi Yoo, Graduate Advisor, 806-742-3825 Ext. 244, Fax: 806-742-1971, E-mail: sang-mi.yoo@ttu.edu.

Tufts University, Graduate School of Arts and Sciences, Department of Art and Art History, Program in Art History, Medford, MA 02155. Offers MA. Part-time programs available. *Degree requirements:* For master's, one foreign language, thesis (for some programs). *Entrance requirements:* For master's, GRE General Test, previous course work in art history, writing sample. Additional exam requirements/recommendations for international students: Required—TOEFL (minimum score 550 paper-based; 213 computer-based; 80 iBT). Electronic applications accepted. *Expenses:* Tuition: Full-time $39,624; part-time $3962 per course. Required fees: $40 per year. Full-time tuition and fees vary according to degree level, program and student level. Part-time tuition and fees vary according to course load.

Tulane University, School of Liberal Arts, Department of Art, Program in Art History, New Orleans, LA 70118-5669. Offers MA. *Degree requirements:* For master's, one foreign language, thesis. *Entrance requirements:* For master's, GRE General Test, minimum B average in undergraduate course work. Additional exam requirements/recommendations for international students: Required—TOEFL. Electronic applications accepted.

Université de Montréal, Faculty of Arts and Sciences, Department of Art History and Film Studies, Montréal, QC H3C 3J7, Canada. Offers art history (MA, PhD); film studies (MA, PhD). Programs offered jointly with Concordia University, Université Laval, and Université du Québec à Montréal. *Degree requirements:* For master's, thesis. Electronic applications accepted. *Faculty research:* Western art from the Middle Ages, classic and modern theory, modern and contemporary art, Canadian art.

Université du Québec à Montréal, Graduate Programs, Program in Art Studies, Montréal, QC H3C 3P8, Canada. Offers art history (PhD); art studies (MA); study and practices of the arts (PhD). Part-time programs available. *Degree requirements:* For master's, thesis; for doctorate, thesis/dissertation. *Entrance requirements:* For master's, appropriate bachelor's

Art History

Université du Québec à Montréal (continued)
degree or equivalent, proficiency in French; for doctorate, appropriate master's degree or equivalent, proficiency in French.

Université Laval, Faculty of Letters, Department of History, Programs in Art History, Québec, QC G1K 7P4, Canada. Offers MA, PhD. PhD offered jointly with Concordia University, Université de Montréal, and Université du Québec à Montréal. Terminal master's awarded for partial completion of doctoral program. *Degree requirements:* For master's, thesis; for doctorate, comprehensive exam, thesis/dissertation. *Entrance requirements:* For master's, English test (comprehension of written English), knowledge of French; for doctorate, English test (comprehension of written English), knowledge of French and English, knowledge of a third language. Electronic applications accepted.

University at Buffalo, the State University of New York, Graduate School, College of Arts and Sciences, Department of Visual Studies, Program in Art History, Buffalo, NY 14260. Offers art history (MA); critical museum studies (Certificate). Part-time programs available. *Degree requirements:* For master's, one foreign language, thesis, field exam. *Entrance requirements:* Additional exam requirements/recommendations for international students: Required—TOEFL (minimum score 79 iBT). Electronic applications accepted. *Faculty research:* Frank Lloyd Wright, non-Western art, Renaissance, Bronze Age Crete, American art.

The University of Alabama, Graduate School, College of Arts and Sciences, Department of Art, Tuscaloosa, AL 35487. Offers art history (MA); studio art (MA, MFA), including ceramics, painting, photography, printmaking, sculpture. *Accreditation:* NASAD. Part-time programs available. *Faculty:* 16 full-time (8 women). *Students:* 17 full-time (13 women), 7 part-time (4 women); includes 2 minority (1 Black or African American, non-Hispanic/Latino; 1 Asian, non-Hispanic/Latino), 2 international. Average age 33. 21 applicants, 67% accepted, 7 enrolled. In 2010, 5 master's awarded. *Degree requirements:* For master's, one foreign language, comprehensive exam (for some programs), oral exam, thesis statement, exhibit (studio art), thesis (art history). *Entrance requirements:* For master's, GRE General Test or MAT (art history), minimum GPA of 3.0, BFA or equivalent (studio art). Additional exam requirements/recommendations for international students: Required—TOEFL (minimum score 550 paper-based; 213 computer-based). *Application deadline:* For fall admission, 3/15 for domestic and international students; for spring admission, 10/15 for domestic and international students. Applications are processed on a rolling basis. Application fee: $50 ($60 for international students). Electronic applications accepted. *Expenses:* Tuition, state resident: full-time $7900. Tuition, nonresident: full-time $20,500. *Financial support:* In 2010–11, 2 fellowships with full tuition reimbursements (averaging $14,000 per year), 13 teaching assistantships with full and partial tuition reimbursements (averaging $9,206 per year) were awarded; career-related internships or fieldwork, institutionally sponsored loans, scholarships/grants, and unspecified assistantships also available. Financial award application deadline: 7/14. *Faculty research:* Nineteenth century American art history, Chinese art history, Baroque art history, twentieth century art history, Asian art history. *Unit head:* William T. Dooley, Chairperson, 205-348-1890, Fax: 205-348-0287, E-mail: wtdooley@bama.ua.edu. *Application contact:* Craig R. Wedderspoon, Graduate Coordinator, 205-348-1898, Fax: 205-348-0287, E-mail: cwedders@bama.edu.

The University of Alabama at Birmingham, College of Arts and Sciences, Program in Art History, Birmingham, AL 35294. Offers MA. Program offered jointly with The University of Alabama (Tuscaloosa). *Accreditation:* NASAD. *Students:* 7 full-time (6 women), 6 part-time (5 women); includes 2 minority (1 Black or African American, non-Hispanic/Latino; 1 Hispanic/Latino), 1 international. Average age 30. 8 applicants, 88% accepted, 3 enrolled. In 2010, 7 master's awarded. *Degree requirements:* For master's, one foreign language, comprehensive exam, thesis optional. *Entrance requirements:* For master's, GRE General Test or MAT, minimum GPA of 2.75. *Application deadline:* Applications are processed on a rolling basis. Electronic applications accepted. *Expenses:* Tuition, state resident: full-time $5482. Tuition, nonresident: full-time $12,430. Tuition and fees vary according to program. *Financial support:* Research assistantships, Federal Work-Study and tuition waivers (partial) available. Financial award application deadline: 5/1. *Unit head:* Erin Wright, Chair, 205-934-8567, Fax: 205-975-2836. *Application contact:* Julie Bryan, Director of Graduate School Operations, 205-934-8227, Fax: 205-934-8413.

University of Alberta, Faculty of Graduate Studies and Research, Department of Art and Design, Edmonton, AB T6G 2E1, Canada. Offers drawing (MFA); history of art, design, and visual culture (MA); industrial design (M Des); painting (MFA); printmaking (MFA); sculpture (MFA); visual communication design (M Des). *Degree requirements:* For master's, thesis. *Entrance requirements:* For master's, portfolio (MFA and MDES). Additional exam requirements/recommendations for international students: Required—TOEFL (minimum score 550 paper-based; 213 computer-based).

The University of Arizona, College of Fine Arts, School of Art, Program in Art History, Tucson, AZ 85721. Offers art history (MA); history and theory of art (PhD). *Accreditation:* NASAD. Part-time programs available. *Students:* 23 full-time (18 women), 9 part-time (8 women); includes 8 minority (1 American Indian or Alaska Native, non-Hispanic/Latino; 1 Asian, non-Hispanic/Latino; 2 Hispanic/Latino; 4 Two or more races, non-Hispanic/Latino). Average age 33. 32 applicants, 59% accepted, 11 enrolled. In 2010, 6 master's awarded. Terminal master's awarded for partial completion of doctoral program. *Degree requirements:* For master's, one foreign language, thesis; for doctorate, 2 foreign languages, comprehensive exam, thesis/dissertation. *Entrance requirements:* For master's, GRE, 3 letters of recommendation, resume or curriculum vitae, writing sample; for doctorate, GRE, 3 letters of recommendation, statement of purpose, resume or curriculum vitae, writing sample. Additional exam requirements/recommendations for international students: Required—TOEFL (minimum score 550 paper-based; 213 computer-based; 79 iBT). *Application deadline:* For fall admission, 2/1 for domestic students, 12/1 for international students; for spring admission, 10/1 for domestic students, 9/1 for international students. Application fee: $75. Electronic applications accepted. *Expenses:* Tuition, state resident: full-time $7692. *Financial support:* Career-related internships or fieldwork, Federal Work-Study, institutionally sponsored loans, scholarships/grants, tuition waivers (full and partial), and unspecified assistantships available. Support available to part-time students. Financial award application deadline: 4/1; financial award applicants required to submit FAFSA. *Faculty research:* American art, history of photography, Mexican art, contemporary African art. *Application contact:* Megan Bartel, Graduate Program Coordinator, 520-621-8518, Fax: 520-621-2955, E-mail: mbartel@email.arizona.edu.

University of Arkansas at Little Rock, Graduate School, College of Arts, Humanities, and Social Science, Department of Art, Little Rock, AR 72204-1099. Offers art education (MA); art history (MA); studio art (MA). *Accreditation:* NASAD. Part-time programs available. *Degree requirements:* For master's, 4 foreign languages, oral exam, oral defense of thesis or exhibit. *Entrance requirements:* For master's, portfolio review or term paper evaluation, minimum GPA of 2.7.

The University of British Columbia, Faculty of Arts and Faculty of Graduate Studies, Department of Art History, Visual Art, and Theory, Vancouver, BC V6T1Z2, Canada. Offers art history (MA, PhD, Diploma); critical and curatorial studies (MA); visual art (MFA). *Degree requirements:* For master's, one foreign language, thesis, final exhibition (MFA, MA in critical and curatorial studies); for doctorate, 2 foreign languages, comprehensive exam, thesis/dissertation. *Entrance requirements:* For master's, bachelor's degree with minimum B+ average (MFA, MA in critical and curatorial studies), A- (MA in art history); for doctorate, master's degree with minimum A- average. Additional exam requirements/recommendations for international students: Required—TOEFL (minimum score 600 paper-based; 250 computer-based). Electronic applications accepted. Tuition charges are reported in Canadian dollars. *Expenses:* Tuition, area resident: Full-time $4179 Canadian dollars. International tuition: $7344 Canadian dollars full-time. *Faculty research:* Conceptual art, Asian art, indigenous North American art, post-second war art, eighteenth and nineteenth century art, curatorial, digital art.

University of California, Berkeley, Graduate Division, College of Letters and Science, Department of History of Art, Berkeley, CA 94720-1500. Offers PhD. *Degree requirements:* For doctorate, 2 foreign languages, thesis/dissertation, qualifying exam. *Entrance requirements:* For doctorate, GRE General Test, minimum GPA of 3.0, 3 letters of recommendation. Additional exam requirements/recommendations for international students: Required—TOEFL. *Faculty research:* Modernism, Italian Renaissance art and architecture, Gothic art and architecture, women artists' representations of the body, the body in ancient Greece.

University of California, Davis, Graduate Studies, Program in Art History, Davis, CA 95616. Offers MA. *Degree requirements:* For master's, thesis. *Entrance requirements:* For master's, GRE, minimum GPA of 3.0, writing sample. Additional exam requirements/recommendations for international students: Required—TOEFL (minimum score 550 paper-based; 213 computer-based). Electronic applications accepted.

University of California, Irvine, School of Humanities, Department of Art History, Irvine, CA 92697. Offers visual studies (MA, PhD). *Students:* 37 full-time (25 women), 2 part-time (both women); includes 7 minority (2 Asian, non-Hispanic/Latino; 4 Hispanic/Latino; 1 Two or more races, non-Hispanic/Latino), 2 international. Average age 28. 116 applicants, 12% accepted, 7 enrolled. In 2010, 6 master's, 10 doctorates awarded. *Degree requirements:* For doctorate, thesis/dissertation. *Entrance requirements:* For master's, GRE, minimum GPA of 3.0; for doctorate, GRE General Test, writing sample. Additional exam requirements/recommendations for international students: Required—TOEFL (minimum score 550 paper-based; 213 computer-based). *Application deadline:* For fall admission, 12/15 for domestic and international students. Application fee: $80 ($100 for international students). Electronic applications accepted. *Financial support:* Fellowships, teaching assistantships, institutionally sponsored loans, traineeships, health care benefits, and unspecified assistantships available. Financial award application deadline: 3/1; financial award applicants required to submit FAFSA. *Faculty research:* Interdisciplinary study and research in art history, critical theory, women's studies, cultural studies, film studies. *Unit head:* Prof. Cecile Marie Whiting, Chair, 949-824-2464, E-mail: cwhiting@uci.edu. *Application contact:* Prof. Cecile Marie Whiting, Chair, 949-824-2464, E-mail: cwhiting@uci.edu.

University of California, Los Angeles, Graduate Division, College of Letters and Science, Department of Art History, Los Angeles, CA 90095. Offers MA, PhD. *Faculty:* 18 full-time (10 women). *Students:* 43 full-time (36 women); includes 13 minority (2 Black or African American, non-Hispanic/Latino; 8 Asian, non-Hispanic/Latino; 2 Hispanic/Latino; 1 Two or more races, non-Hispanic/Latino), 4 international. Average age 31. 117 applicants, 9% accepted, 4 enrolled. In 2010, 2 master's, 19 doctorates awarded. Terminal master's awarded for partial completion of doctoral program. *Degree requirements:* For master's, one foreign language, thesis; for doctorate, one foreign language, thesis/dissertation, oral and written qualifying exams. *Entrance requirements:* For doctorate, GRE General Test, 2 samples of research writing or thesis, minimum undergraduate GPA of 3.0, 3 letters of recommendation. *Application deadline:* For fall admission, 11/30 for domestic students. Application fee: $70 ($90 for international students). Electronic applications accepted. *Financial support:* In 2010–11, 40 fellowships with full and partial tuition reimbursements, 10 research assistantships with full and partial tuition reimbursements, 28 teaching assistantships with full and partial tuition reimbursements were awarded; Federal Work-Study, scholarships/grants, health care benefits, tuition waivers (full and partial), and unspecified assistantships also available. Financial award application deadline: 3/1; financial award applicants required to submit FAFSA. *Unit head:* Dr. David A. Scott, Chair, 310-794-4855, Fax: 310-206-4723, E-mail: dascott@ucla.edu. *Application contact:* Department Office, 310-825-3480, E-mail: vjohnson@humnet.ucla.edu.

University of California, Riverside, Graduate Division, Department of Art History, Riverside, CA 92521-0102. Offers MA. Part-time programs available. *Degree requirements:* For master's, one foreign language, thesis. *Entrance requirements:* For master's, GRE General Test, sample of written work, minimum GPA of 3.2. Additional exam requirements/recommendations for international students: Required—TOEFL (minimum score 550 paper-based; 213 computer-based; 80 iBT). Electronic applications accepted. *Faculty research:* Ancient, medieval, Renaissance, seventeenth and eighteenth century art; modern European art; contemporary art and theory; modern architecture and urbanism; history of photography.

University of California, Santa Barbara, Graduate Division, College of Letters and Sciences, Division of Humanities and Fine Arts, Department of History of Art and Architecture, Santa Barbara, CA 93106-2014. Offers art history (PhD), including art history, European medieval studies, feminist studies; MA/PhD. *Faculty:* 18 full-time (8 women), 6 part-time/adjunct (2 women). *Students:* 45 full-time (40 women); includes 7 Asian, non-Hispanic/Latino; 4 Hispanic/Latino. Average age 32. 93 applicants, 11% accepted, 8 enrolled. In 2010, 3 doctorates awarded. Terminal master's awarded for partial completion of doctoral program. *Degree requirements:* For doctorate, 2 foreign languages, comprehensive exam, thesis/dissertation. *Entrance requirements:* For doctorate, GRE. Additional exam requirements/recommendations for international students: Required—TOEFL (minimum score 550 paper-based; 80 iBT), IELTS (minimum score 7). *Application deadline:* For fall admission, 12/15 priority date for domestic and international students. Application fee: $70 ($90 for international students). Electronic applications accepted. *Financial support:* In 2010–11, 31 students received support, including 24 fellowships with full tuition reimbursements available (averaging $9,585 per year), 1 research assistantship with full and partial tuition reimbursement available (averaging $15,896 per year), 21 teaching assistantships with partial tuition reimbursements available (averaging $11,884 per year); career-related internships or fieldwork, institutionally sponsored loans, and tuition waivers (full and partial) also available. Financial award application deadline: 12/15; financial award applicants required to submit FAFSA. *Faculty research:* History of architecture, Renaissance-Italian, Baroque, American. Total annual research expenditures: $72,000. *Unit head:* Prof. Ulrich Keller, Chair, 805-893-8710, Fax: 805-893-7117, E-mail: ukeller@arthisory.ucsb.edu. *Application contact:* Graduate Program Administrator, 805-893-2454, Fax: 805-893-7117, E-mail: lfredrickson@hfa.ucsb.edu.

University of Chicago, Division of the Humanities, Department of Art History, Chicago, IL 60637-1513. Offers AM, PhD. *Degree requirements:* For master's, variable foreign language requirement, thesis; for doctorate, variable foreign language requirement, thesis/dissertation. *Entrance requirements:* For master's and doctorate, GRE General Test.

University of Cincinnati, Graduate School, College of Design, Architecture, Art, and Planning, School of Art, Program in Art History, Cincinnati, OH 45221. Offers MA. *Accreditation:* NASAD. Part-time programs available. *Degree requirements:* For master's, one foreign language, comprehensive exam, thesis. Electronic applications accepted.

University of Colorado Boulder, Graduate School, College of Arts and Sciences, Department of Art and Art History, Boulder, CO 80309. Offers art history (MA), including contemporary art criticism, early twentieth century art, nineteenth century art, Russian and Soviet art; ceramics (MFA); drawing (MFA); painting (MFA); photography and media arts (MFA); printmaking (MFA); sculpture (MFA). *Faculty:* 26 full-time (12 women). *Students:* 50 full-time (36 women), 2 part-time (both women); includes 7 minority (1 American Indian or Alaska Native, non-Hispanic/Latino; 2 Asian, non-Hispanic/Latino; 3 Hispanic/Latino; 1 Two or more races, non-Hispanic/Latino), 2 international. Average age 30. 265 applicants, 18 enrolled. In 2010, 16 master's awarded. *Degree requirements:* For master's, variable foreign language requirement, comprehensive exam, thesis (for some programs). *Entrance requirements:* For master's, GRE General Test, minimum undergraduate GPA of 3.0, portfolio. *Application deadline:* For fall admission, 1/15 priority date for domestic students, 12/1 for international students. Application fee: $50 ($60 for international students). *Financial support:* In 2010–11, 6 fellowships (averaging $1,713 per year), 13 research assistantships (averaging $5,087 per year) were awarded; Federal Work-Study, scholarships/grants, and tuition waivers (full) also available. Financial award application deadline: 1/15. *Faculty research:* Drawing, painting, ceramics, sculpture, photography and media arts, printmaking, Russian and Soviet art, early twentieth century art, contemporary art criticism, nineteenth century art.

University of Connecticut, Graduate School, School of Fine Arts, Department of Art and Art History, Field of Art History, Storrs, CT 06269. Offers MA. *Accreditation:* NASAD. *Degree requirements:* For master's, comprehensive exam. *Entrance requirements:* Additional exam requirements/recommendations for international students: Required—TOEFL (minimum score 550 paper-based; 213 computer-based). Electronic applications accepted.

University of Delaware, College of Arts and Sciences, Department of Art History, Newark, DE 19716. Offers MA, PhD. Part-time programs available. *Degree requirements:* For master's, one foreign language, thesis; for doctorate, 2 foreign languages, comprehensive exam, thesis/dissertation. *Entrance requirements:* For master's and doctorate, GRE General Test, writing sample. Additional exam requirements/recommendations for international students: Required—TOEFL. Electronic applications accepted. *Faculty research:* Art of Europe and the United States, art theory, vernacular architecture, medieval manuscripts, African art and architecture.

University of Denver, Division of Arts, Humanities and Social Sciences, School of Art and Art History, Denver, CO 80208. Offers art history (MA); art history/museum studies (MA); electronic media arts and design (MFA). *Accreditation:* NASAD. Part-time programs available. *Faculty:* 13 full-time (7 women), 10 part-time/adjunct (3 women). *Students:* 14 full-time (12 women), 11 part-time (10 women); includes 2 minority (both Hispanic/Latino). Average age 29. 61 applicants, 46% accepted, 11 enrolled. In 2010, 19 master's awarded. *Degree requirements:* For master's, one foreign language, comprehensive exam, research paper. *Entrance requirements:* For master's, GRE General Test. Additional exam requirements/recommendations for international students: Required—TOEFL (minimum score 550 paper-based; 80 iBT). *Application deadline:* Applications are processed on a rolling basis. Application fee: $60. Electronic applications accepted. *Expenses:* Tuition: Full-time $35,604; part-time $29,670 per year. Required fees: $687 per year. Tuition and fees vary according to program. *Financial support:* In 2010–11, 2 teaching assistantships with full and partial tuition reimbursements (averaging $10,500 per year) were awarded; career-related internships or fieldwork, Federal Work-Study, institutionally sponsored loans, scholarships/grants, and unspecified assistantships also available. Support available to part-time students. Financial award application deadline: 3/1; financial award applicants required to submit FAFSA. *Faculty research:* Images of women in alchemical manuscripts and books, Giovanni Benedetto, Salvatore Castiglione. *Unit head:* Dr. M. E. Warlick, Director, 303-871-2371, E-mail: mwarlick@du.edu. *Application contact:* Dr. Annabeth Headrick, Graduate Admissions Coordinator, 303-871-3574, E-mail: saah-interest@du.edu.

University of Florida, Graduate School, College of Fine Arts, School of Art and Art History, Gainesville, FL 32611. Offers art (MFA), including ceramics, creative photography, drawing, electronic intermedia, graphic design, painting, printmaking, sculpture; art education (MA); art history (MA, PhD); digital arts and sciences (MA); museology (museum studies) (MA). *Accreditation:* NASAD. Postbaccalaureate distance learning degree programs offered (minimal on-campus study). *Faculty:* 29 full-time (14 women). *Students:* 107 full-time (72 women), 57 part-time (52 women); includes 6 Black or African American, non-Hispanic/Latino; 1 American Indian or Alaska Native, non-Hispanic/Latino; 5 Asian, non-Hispanic/Latino; 13 Hispanic/Latino, 14 international. Average age 31. 282 applicants, 30% accepted, 61 enrolled. In 2010, 24 master's, 3 doctorates awarded. *Degree requirements:* For master's, thesis, project or thesis (MFA); 1 foreign language (MA in art history); for doctorate, 2 foreign languages, comprehensive exam, thesis/dissertation. *Entrance requirements:* For master's, GRE General Test, portfolio (MFA), writing sample (MA), minimum GPA of 3.0; for doctorate, GRE General Test, minimum GPA of 3.0. Additional exam requirements/recommendations for international students: Required—TOEFL (minimum score 550 paper-based; 213 computer-based; 80 iBT), IELTS (minimum score 6). *Application deadline:* For fall admission, 1/1 priority date for domestic students, 1/1 for international students; for spring admission, 11/1 for domestic and international students. Applications are processed on a rolling basis. Application fee: $30. Electronic applications accepted. *Expenses:* Tuition, state resident: full-time $10,915.92. Tuition, nonresident: full-time $28,309. *Financial support:* In 2010–11, 36 students received support, including 9 fellowships, 3 research assistantships with tuition reimbursements available (averaging $12,789 per year), 24 teaching assistantships with tuition reimbursements available (averaging $10,512 per year); Federal Work-Study, institutionally sponsored loans, and unspecified assistantships also available. Financial award applicants required to submit FAFSA. *Faculty research:* Studio production, art historical studies of style context. *Unit head:* Laura Robertsoon, SR Associate in Graduate Studies, 352-846-3425, E-mail: laurar@ufl.edu. *Application contact:* Lauren G. Lake, Coordinator, 352-273-3032, Fax: 352-392-8453, E-mail: lglake@arts.ufl.edu.

University of Georgia, College of Arts and Sciences, Lamar Dodd School of Art, Program in Art History, Athens, GA 30602. Offers MA. *Accreditation:* NASAD. *Students:* 9 full-time (7 women), 2 part-time (1 woman). 27 applicants, 37% accepted, 3 enrolled. In 2010, 7 master's awarded. *Degree requirements:* For master's, one foreign language, thesis. *Entrance requirements:* For master's, GRE General Test. *Application deadline:* For fall admission, 7/1 priority date for domestic students; for spring admission, 11/15 for domestic students. Application fee: $50. Electronic applications accepted. *Expenses:* Tuition, state resident: full-time $7200; part-time $344 per credit hour. Tuition, nonresident: full-time $21,900; part-time $944 per credit hour. Tuition and fees vary according to course load and program. *Financial support:* Fellowships, research assistantships, teaching assistantships, unspecified assistantships available. *Unit head:* Prof. Georgia Strange, Director, 706-542-1600, Fax: 706-542-0226, E-mail: strange@uga.edu. *Application contact:* Dr. Carole Henry, Graduate Coordinator, 706-542-1624, Fax: 706-542-0226, E-mail: ckhenry@uga.edu.

University of Hawaii at Manoa, Graduate Division, College of Arts and Humanities, Department of Art and Art History, Program in Art History, Honolulu, HI 96822. Offers MA. Part-time programs available. *Faculty:* 26 full-time (11 women), 1 part-time/adjunct (0 women). *Students:* 7 full-time (4 women), 1 (woman) part-time; includes 3 minority (2 Native Hawaiian or other Pacific Islander, non-Hispanic/Latino; 1 Two or more races, non-Hispanic/Latino), 1 international. Average age 29. 13 applicants, 54% accepted, 7 enrolled. *Entrance requirements:* Additional exam requirements/recommendations for international students: Required—TOEFL (minimum score 600 paper-based; 100 iBT); Recommended—IELTS. *Application deadline:* For fall admission, 1/15 for domestic and international students. Application fee: $60. *Financial support:* In 2010–11, 6 students received support, including 5 fellowships (averaging $3,200 per year), 2 teaching assistantships with full tuition reimbursements available (averaging $14,382 per year); Federal Work-Study, scholarships/grants, and unspecified assistantships also available. Support available to part-time students. Total annual research expenditures: $43,000. *Application contact:* Mary Babcock, Graduate Field Chairperson, 808-956-8180, Fax: 808-956-9043, E-mail: gradart@hawaii.edu.

University of Houston, College of Liberal Arts and Social Sciences, Department of Art, Houston, TX 77204. Offers art history (MA); interdisciplinary practice and emerging forms (MFA); painting (MFA); studio art (MFA). *Faculty:* 14 full-time (8 women), 7 part-time/adjunct (5 women). *Students:* 33 full-time (21 women); includes 3 Black or African American, non-Hispanic/Latino; 3 Asian, non-Hispanic/Latino; 2 Hispanic/Latino, 2 international. Average age 31. 77 applicants, 26% accepted, 12 enrolled. In 2010, 11 master's awarded. *Entrance requirements:* For master's, baccalaureate degree, portfolio. *Application deadline:* For fall admission, 2/1 for domestic and international students. Application fee: $25 ($75 for international students). Electronic applications accepted. *Expenses:* Tuition, state resident: full-time $8592; part-time $358 per credit hour. Tuition, nonresident: full-time $16,032; part-time $668 per credit hour. Required fees: $2889. Tuition and fees vary according to course load and program. *Financial support:* In 2010–11, 5 teaching assistantships with full tuition reimbursements (averaging $5,161 per year) were awarded; career-related internships or fieldwork, Federal Work-Study, institutionally sponsored loans, scholarships/grants, health care benefits, and unspecified assistantships also available. Support available to part-time students. Financial award application deadline: 3/10. *Faculty research:* Painting, sculpture, photography/installation/video, graphic design and typography, art history (Pre-Columbian to Surrealism). *Unit head:* Dr. John Reed, Chairperson, 713-743-3001, Fax: 713-743-2823, E-mail: jreed@uh.edu. *Application contact:* Pat Deeves, Assistant Director, 713-743-0936, E-mail: deeves@central.uh.edu.

University of Illinois at Chicago, Graduate College, College of Architecture and Art, Department of Art History, Chicago, IL 60607-7128. Offers MA, PhD. Part-time and evening/weekend programs available. Terminal master's awarded for partial completion of doctoral program. *Degree requirements:* For master's, one foreign language, thesis or alternative; for doctorate, thesis/dissertation. *Entrance requirements:* For master's, GRE General Test, minimum GPA of 2.75, 3 letters of recommendation; for doctorate, GRE General Test, M.A. in art history or equivalent, minimum GPA of 3.0. Additional exam requirements/recommendations for international students: Required—TOEFL. Electronic applications accepted. *Faculty research:* Modern painting and sculpture, history of architecture, city planning and design, history of photography.

University of Illinois at Urbana–Champaign, Graduate College, College of Fine and Applied Arts, School of Art and Design, Program in Art History, Champaign, IL 61820. Offers MA, PhD. *Accreditation:* NASAD. *Students:* 23 full-time (21 women), 5 part-time (2 women); includes 3 Asian, non-Hispanic/Latino, 7 international. 57 applicants, 12% accepted, 7 enrolled. In 2010, 8 master's, 2 doctorates awarded. *Entrance requirements:* For master's and doctorate, minimum GPA of 3.0. Additional exam requirements/recommendations for international students: Required—TOEFL (minimum score 550 paper-based; 213 computer-based; 79 iBT). *Application deadline:* Applications are processed on a rolling basis. Application fee: $75 ($90 for international students). Electronic applications accepted. *Financial support:* Fellowships, research assistantships, teaching assistantships, tuition waivers (full and partial) available. *Unit head:* Lisa Rosenthal, Chair, 217-265-5236, Fax: 217-244-7688, E-mail: lrosenth@illinois.edu. *Application contact:* Marsha Biddle, Coordinator of Graduate Academic Affairs, 217-333-0642, Fax: 217-244-7688, E-mail: mbiddle@illinois.edu.

The University of Iowa, Graduate College, College of Liberal Arts and Sciences, School of Art and Art History, Program in Art History, Iowa City, IA 52242-1316. Offers MA, PhD. *Degree requirements:* For master's, one foreign language, thesis, exam; for doctorate, 2 foreign languages, comprehensive exam, thesis/dissertation, final exams. *Entrance requirements:* For master's, GRE General Test; for doctorate, GRE General Test, MA in art history. Additional exam requirements/recommendations for international students: Required—TOEFL (minimum score 550 paper-based; 213 computer-based; 81 iBT). Electronic applications accepted. *Faculty research:* African (Oceanic), Asian, Ancient (3000 B.C.-300 A.D.), medieval, Renaissance, Baroque, eighteenth and nineteenth century European, American (includes Pre-Columbian, Native American, and African American), and Modern/Contemporary.

The University of Kansas, Graduate Studies, College of Liberal Arts and Sciences, History of Art Department, Lawrence, KS 66045. Offers MA, PhD. Part-time programs available. *Faculty:* 13 full-time (9 women). *Students:* 60 full-time (53 women), 7 part-time (5 women); includes 6 minority (1 American Indian or Alaska Native, non-Hispanic/Latino; 4 Asian, non-Hispanic/Latino; 1 Hispanic/Latino), 14 international. Average age 34. 48 applicants, 60% accepted, 13 enrolled. In 2010, 6 master's, 2 doctorates awarded. Terminal master's awarded for partial completion of doctoral program. *Degree requirements:* For master's, one foreign language, comprehensive exam, thesis optional; for doctorate, 2 foreign languages, comprehensive exam, thesis/dissertation, 1 year full-time enrollment. *Entrance requirements:* For master's, GRE, minimum undergraduate GPA of 3.3, 18 credit hours of art history; for doctorate, GRE, MA in art history or related field. Additional exam requirements/recommendations for international students: Required—TOEFL, TWE (minimum score 4.5). *Application deadline:* For fall admission, 1/1 for domestic and international students; for spring admission, 10/15 for domestic students, 10/1 for international students. Application fee: $55 ($65 for international students). Electronic applications accepted. *Expenses:* Tuition, state resident: full-time $7092; part-time $295.50 per credit hour. Tuition, nonresident: full-time $16,590; part-time $691.25 per credit hour. Required fees: $858; $71.49 per credit hour. Tuition and fees vary according to course load, campus/location and program. *Financial support:* Fellowships with full tuition reimbursements, research assistantships with partial tuition reimbursements, teaching assistantships with full tuition reimbursements, career-related internships or fieldwork, scholarships/grants, health care benefits, and unspecified assistantships available. Financial award application deadline: 1/1. *Faculty research:* American, African, Asian, European, and modern art; history of photography. *Unit head:* Linda Stone-Ferrier, Chair, 785-864-4713, Fax: 785-864-5091, E-mail: lsf@ku.edu. *Application contact:* Karen Brichoux, Graduate Admissions, 785-864-4713, Fax: 785-864-5091, E-mail: arthist@ku.edu.

University of Kentucky, Graduate School, College of Fine Arts, Program in Art History, Lexington, KY 40506-0032. Offers MA. *Accreditation:* NASAD. *Degree requirements:* For master's, 2 foreign languages, comprehensive exam, thesis. *Entrance requirements:* For master's, GRE General Test, minimum undergraduate GPA of 2.75. Additional exam requirements/recommendations for international students: Required—TOEFL (minimum score 550 paper-based; 213 computer-based). Electronic applications accepted. *Faculty research:* Northern European prints and drawings, nineteenth century French painting and drawing, Roman sarcophagus sculpture, manuscript illumination, history and theory of photography.

University of Louisville, Graduate School, College of Arts and Sciences, Department of Fine Arts, Louisville, KY 40292. Offers art history (MA, PhD); creative art (MA); curatorial studies (MA). *Faculty:* 18 full-time (8 women), 3 part-time/adjunct (0 women). *Students:* 22 full-time (19 women), 12 part-time (10 women); includes 1 Black or African American, non-Hispanic/Latino, 2 international. Average age 34. 21 applicants, 48% accepted, 7 enrolled. In 2010, 8 master's, 1 doctorate awarded. *Degree requirements:* For master's, thesis; for doctorate, 2 foreign languages, comprehensive exam, thesis/dissertation. *Entrance requirements:* For master's and doctorate, GRE General Test. *Application deadline:* For fall admission, 1/15 for domestic and international students. Applications are processed on a rolling basis. Application fee: $50. *Expenses:* Tuition, state resident: full-time $9144; part-time $508 per credit hour. Tuition, nonresident: full-time $19,026; part-time $1057 per credit hour. Tuition and fees vary according to program and reciprocity agreements. *Financial support:* In 2010–11, 5 teaching assistantships with full tuition reimbursements (averaging $18,000 per year) were awarded. Financial award application deadline: 1/15. *Faculty research:* Art history in the periods from ancient to contemporary and various regions, 2-D and 3D Studio areas, intermedia, curatorial studies. *Unit head:* Prof. Ying Kit Chan, Chair, 502-852-6794, Fax: 502-852-6791, E-mail: chan@louisville.edu. *Application contact:* Libby Leggett, Director, Graduate Admissions, 502-852-3101, Fax: 502-852-6536, E-mail: gradadm@louisville.edu.

The University of Manchester, School of Arts, Histories and Cultures, Manchester, United Kingdom. Offers anthropology, media and performance (PhD); applied theatre professional (PhD); archaeology (PhD); art history and visual studies (PhD); arts management and cultural policy (PhD); classics and ancient history (PhD); composition (PhD); creative writing (PhD); drama (PhD); economic and social history (PhD); electroacoustic composition (PhD); English and American studies (PhD); history (PhD); humanitarianism and conflict response (PhD); museology (PhD); music (PhD); musicology (PhD); religions and theology (PhD).

University of Maryland, College Park, Academic Affairs, College of Arts and Humanities, Department of Art History and Archaeology, College Park, MD 20742. Offers art history (MA, PhD). *Faculty:* 13 full-time (8 women), 4 part-time/adjunct (2 women). *Students:* 42 full-time (31 women), 4 part-time (all women); includes 1 Black or African American, non-Hispanic/Latino; 6 Asian, non-Hispanic/Latino; 1 Hispanic/Latino; 1 Two or more races, non-Hispanic/Latino, 3 international. 139 applicants, 6% accepted, 5 enrolled. In 2010, 4 master's, 5 doctorates awarded. *Degree requirements:* For master's, one foreign language, thesis, oral exam; for doctorate, 2 foreign languages, thesis/dissertation, oral exam. *Entrance requirements:* For master's, GRE General Test, minimum GPA of 3.0, writing sample, 3 letters of recommendation. Additional exam requirements/recommendations for international students: Required—TOEFL. *Application deadline:* For fall admission, 12/10 for domestic students, 2/1 for international students. Applications are processed on a rolling basis. Application fee: $75.

Art History

University of Maryland, College Park (continued)

Electronic applications accepted. *Expenses:* Tuition, state resident: part-time $471 per credit hour. Tuition, nonresident: part-time $1016 per credit hour. Required fees: $337 per term. *Financial support:* In 2010–11, 8 fellowships with full and partial tuition reimbursements (averaging $19,934 per year), 24 teaching assistantships with tuition reimbursements (averaging $16,115 per year) were awarded; research assistantships, Federal Work-Study and scholarships/grants also available. Support available to part-time students. Financial award applicants required to submit FAFSA. *Faculty research:* Western, African, pre-Columbian, American, and East Asian art. *Unit head:* Majorie Venit, Acting Chair, 301-405-1481, Fax: 301-314-9305, E-mail: venit@umd.edu. *Application contact:* Dean of Graduate School, 301-405-0376, Fax: 301-314-9305.

University of Massachusetts Amherst, Graduate School, College of Humanities and Fine Arts, Department of Art, Program in Art History, Amherst, MA 01003. Offers MA. Part-time programs available. *Students:* 13 full-time (all women), 7 part-time (5 women); includes 1 minority (Black or African American, non-Hispanic/Latino). Average age 27. 36 applicants, 44% accepted, 7 enrolled. In 2010, 3 master's awarded. *Degree requirements:* For master's, one foreign language, comprehensive exam, thesis or alternative, 1 journal level French, German or Italian. *Entrance requirements:* For master's, GRE General Test, 7-20 page writing sample. Additional exam requirements/recommendations for international students: Required—TOEFL (minimum score 550 paper-based; 213 computer-based; 80 iBT), IELTS (minimum score 6.5). *Application deadline:* For fall admission, 1/15 for domestic and international students; for spring admission, 10/1 for domestic and international students. Applications are processed on a rolling basis. Application fee: $50 ($65 for international students). Electronic applications accepted. *Expenses:* Tuition, state resident: full-time $2640. Required fees: $8282. One-time fee: $357 full-time. *Financial support:* In 2010–11, 14 teaching assistantships with full tuition reimbursements (averaging $6,702 per year) were awarded; fellowships with full tuition reimbursements, research assistantships, career-related internships or fieldwork, Federal Work-Study, scholarships/grants, traineeships, health care benefits, tuition waivers (full), and unspecified assistantships also available. Support available to part-time students. Financial award application deadline: 1/15; financial award applicants required to submit FAFSA. *Unit head:* Dr. Timothy Rohan, Graduate Program Director, 413-545-3595, Fax: 413-545-3880. *Application contact:* Jean M. Ames, Supervisor of Admissions, 413-545-0722, Fax: 413-577-0100, E-mail: gradadm@grad.umass.edu.

University of Memphis, Graduate School, College of Communication and Fine Arts, Department of Art, Memphis, TN 38152. Offers art (Graduate Certificate); art history (MA), including Egyptian art and archaeology, general art history; ceramics (MFA); graphic design (MFA); interior design (MFA); painting (MFA); printmaking/photography (MFA); sculpture (MFA). *Accreditation:* NASAD (one or more programs are accredited). *Faculty:* 20 full-time (7 women), 4 part-time/adjunct (2 women). *Students:* 39 full-time (26 women), 10 part-time (8 women); includes 4 Black or African American, non-Hispanic/Latino; 1 Asian, non-Hispanic/Latino, 1 international. Average age 29. 44 applicants, 77% accepted, 22 enrolled. In 2010, 16 master's, 5 other advanced degrees awarded. *Degree requirements:* For master's, 2 foreign languages, comprehensive exam, thesis. *Entrance requirements:* For master's, GRE General Test or MAT, portfolio (MFA). *Application deadline:* For fall admission, 8/1 for domestic students; for spring admission, 12/1 for domestic students. Applications are processed on a rolling basis. Application fee: $35 ($60 for international students). *Financial support:* In 2010–11, 38 students received support; research assistantships with full tuition reimbursements available, teaching assistantships with full tuition reimbursements available, Federal Work-Study, scholarships/grants, and unspecified assistantships available. Financial award application deadline: 2/15; financial award applicants required to submit FAFSA. *Faculty research:* Online collaborative learning, advanced art history studies, electronic publishing/design, studio arts, architectural studies. *Unit head:* Prof. Richard Lou, Chair, 901-678-2216, Fax: 901-678-2735, E-mail: gmyatt@memphis.edu. *Application contact:* Greely Myat, Graduate Studies Coordinator, 901-678-2650.

University of Miami, Graduate School, College of Arts and Sciences, Department of Art and Art History, Coral Gables, FL 33124. Offers art history (MA); ceramics/glass (MFA); graphic design/multimedia (MFA); painting (MFA); photography/digital imaging (MFA); printmaking (MFA); sculpture (MFA). Part-time programs available. *Degree requirements:* For master's, variable foreign language requirement, thesis, exhibit (MFA), comprehensive exam (MA). *Entrance requirements:* For master's, GRE General Test (MA), research paper (MA), slide portfolio (MFA). Additional exam requirements/recommendations for international students: Required—TOEFL. Electronic applications accepted. *Faculty research:* Installation art, public art.

University of Michigan, Horace H. Rackham School of Graduate Studies, College of Literature, Science, and the Arts, Department of History of Art, Ann Arbor, MI 48109-1357. Offers PhD. *Degree requirements:* For doctorate, 2 foreign languages, thesis/dissertation, preliminary examinations, oral defense of dissertation. *Entrance requirements:* For doctorate, GRE General Test. Electronic applications accepted. *Expenses:* Tuition, state resident: full-time $17,784; part-time $1116 per credit hour. Tuition, nonresident: full-time $35,944; part-time $2125 per credit hour. International tuition: $35,994 full-time. Required fees: $95 per semester. Tuition and fees vary according to course load, degree level and program. *Faculty research:* Asian, African and African-American, ancient, medieval and Byzantine, early modern, and modern art.

University of Michigan, Horace H. Rackham School of Graduate Studies, College of Literature, Science, and the Arts, Interdepartmental Program in Classical Art and Archaeology, Ann Arbor, MI 48109. Offers PhD. *Faculty:* 26 full-time (12 women), 1 (woman) part-time/adjunct. *Students:* 28 full-time (19 women); includes 1 Hispanic/Latino, 5 international. Average age 27. 68 applicants, 4% accepted, 3 enrolled. In 2010, 3 doctorates awarded. *Degree requirements:* For doctorate, 4 foreign languages, comprehensive exam, thesis/dissertation, ancient history exam, preliminary exam. *Entrance requirements:* For doctorate, GRE General Test. Additional exam requirements/recommendations for international students: Required—TOEFL (minimum score 560 paper-based; 84 iBT). *Application deadline:* For fall admission, 12/15 for domestic and international students. Application fee: $65 ($75 for international students). Electronic applications accepted. *Expenses:* Tuition, state resident: full-time $17,784; part-time $1116 per credit hour. Tuition, nonresident: full-time $35,944; part-time $2125 per credit hour. International tuition: $35,994 full-time. Required fees: $95 per semester. Tuition and fees vary according to course load, degree level and program. *Financial support:* In 2010–11, 27 students received support, including 16 fellowships with full tuition reimbursements available (averaging $17,000 per year), 1 research assistantship with full tuition reimbursement available (averaging $16,694 per year), 8 teaching assistantships with full tuition reimbursements available (averaging $16,694 per year); career-related internships or fieldwork and health care benefits also available. Financial award application deadline: 4/15. *Faculty research:* Greek art and archaeology, roman art and archaeology, near eastern art and archaeology, archaeological theory and methodology. Total annual research expenditures: $30,880. *Unit head:* Prof. Christopher Ratte, Director, 734-936-3888, Fax: 734-763-8976, E-mail: ratte@umich.edu. *Application contact:* Alexander Zwinak, Graduate Coordinator, 734-764-6323, Fax: 734-763-8976, E-mail: ipcaa.office@umich.edu.

University of Minnesota, Twin Cities Campus, Graduate School, College of Liberal Arts, Department of Art History, Minneapolis, MN 55455. Offers MA, PhD. *Faculty:* 10 full-time (4 women). *Students:* 28 full-time (24 women); includes 1 Hispanic/Latino, 7 international. 37 applicants, 16% accepted, 4 enrolled. In 2010, 2 master's, 2 doctorates awarded. *Degree requirements:* For master's, one foreign language, comprehensive exam, thesis; for doctorate, 2 foreign languages, comprehensive exam, thesis/dissertation. *Entrance requirements:* For master's, GRE, 3 letters of recommendation, writing sample; for doctorate, GRE, transcripts, 3 letters of recommendation, writing sample. Additional exam requirements/recommendations for international students: Required—TOEFL. *Application deadline:* For fall admission, 12/1 for domestic and international students. Application fee: $75 ($95 for international students). Electronic applications accepted. *Financial support:* In 2010–11, 17 students received support, including 2 research assistantships with full tuition reimbursements available (averaging $14,000 per year), 12 teaching assistantships with full tuition reimbursements available (averaging $14,000 per year); fellowships with full and partial tuition reimbursements available, career-related internships or fieldwork, Federal Work-Study, institutionally sponsored loans, scholarships/grants, health care benefits, and unspecified assistantships also available. Financial award application deadline: 6/30; financial award applicants required to submit FAFSA. *Faculty research:* American, Latin American, modern/contemporary, early modern, and ancient art. *Unit head:* Steven F. Ostrow, Chair, 612-624-4500, Fax: 612-626-8679, E-mail: ostro133@umn.edu. *Application contact:* Erik Farseth, Information Contact, 612-624-4500, Fax: 612-626-8679, E-mail: arthist@umn.edu.

University of Minnesota, Twin Cities Campus, Graduate School, College of Liberal Arts, Department of Classical and Near Eastern Studies, Minneapolis, MN 55455-0213. Offers ancient and medieval art and archaeology (MA, PhD); classics (MA, PhD); Greek (MA, PhD); Latin (MA, PhD); religions in antiquity (MA). Part-time programs available. Terminal master's awarded for partial completion of doctoral program. *Degree requirements:* For master's, 2 foreign languages, comprehensive exam, thesis or alternative; for doctorate, variable foreign language requirement, comprehensive exam, thesis/dissertation. *Entrance requirements:* For master's and doctorate, GRE, 3 letters of recommendation, writing sample, copies of transcripts, personal statement. Additional exam requirements/recommendations for international students: Required—TOEFL. Electronic applications accepted. *Faculty research:* Greek and Latin literature, religions in antiquity, ancient Near East.

University of Mississippi, Graduate School, College of Liberal Arts, Department of Art, Oxford, University, MS 38677. Offers art education (MA); art history (MA); fine arts (MFA). *Accreditation:* NASAD (one or more programs are accredited). Part-time programs available. *Students:* 13 full-time (6 women); includes 1 Asian, non-Hispanic/Latino; 3 Hispanic/Latino; 1 Two or more races, non-Hispanic/Latino. In 2010, 3 master's awarded. *Degree requirements:* For master's, thesis (for some programs). *Entrance requirements:* For master's, GRE General Test, minimum GPA of 3.0. Additional exam requirements/recommendations for international students: Required—TOEFL. *Application deadline:* For fall admission, 3/1 for domestic students; for spring admission, 10/1 for domestic students. Applications are processed on a rolling basis. Application fee: $25. Electronic applications accepted. *Financial support:* Fellowships, scholarships/grants and unspecified assistantships available. Financial award application deadline: 3/1; financial award applicants required to submit FAFSA. *Unit head:* Dr. Sheri Fleck Reith, Chair, 662-915-7193, Fax: 662-915-5013, E-mail: art@olemiss.edu. *Application contact:* Dr. Christy M. Wyandt, Associate Dean, 662-915-7474, Fax: 662-915-7577, E-mail: cwyandt@olemiss.edu.

University of Missouri, Graduate School, College of Arts and Sciences, Department of Art History and Archaeology, Columbia, MO 65211. Offers MA, PhD. *Faculty:* 10 full-time (5 women). *Students:* 26 full-time (21 women), 1 (woman) part-time; includes 2 minority (1 Hispanic/Latino; 1 Two or more races, non-Hispanic/Latino), 2 international. Average age 30. 33 applicants, 42% accepted, 7 enrolled. In 2010, 4 master's, 1 doctorate awarded. Terminal master's awarded for partial completion of doctoral program. *Degree requirements:* For master's, 2 foreign languages, thesis; for doctorate, 2 foreign languages, thesis/dissertation. *Entrance requirements:* For master's, GRE General Test (minimum score 1000 verbal and quantitative, 4.5 analytical), minimum GPA of 3.0, 3.3 in major field; at least 3 semesters in appropriate foreign language; for doctorate, GRE General Test, minimum GPA of 3.0; MA or equivalent in art history or classical archaeology; master's thesis. Additional exam requirements/recommendations for international students: Required—TOEFL (minimum score 500 paper-based; 173 computer-based; 61 iBT), IELTS (minimum score 5.5). *Application deadline:* For fall admission, 1/18 priority date for domestic students. Applications are processed on a rolling basis. Application fee: $45 ($60 for international students). Electronic applications accepted. *Financial support:* In 2010–11, 4 fellowships with full tuition reimbursements, 13 research assistantships with full tuition reimbursements, 5 teaching assistantships with full tuition reimbursements were awarded; institutionally sponsored loans, health care benefits, and unspecified assistantships also available. *Faculty research:* Classical Mediterranean archaeology, medieval and Renaissance art, art and architecture of modern Europe and the Americas. *Unit head:* Dr. Anne Rudloff Stanton, Department Chair, 573-882-6711, E-mail: stantona@missouri.edu. *Application contact:* Linda Garrison, 573-882-2757, E-mail: garrisonl@missouri.edu.

University of Missouri–Kansas City, College of Arts and Sciences, Department of Art and Art History, Kansas City, MO 64110-2499. Offers art history (MA, PhD); studio art (MA). PhD (interdisciplinary) offered through the School of Graduate Studies. Part-time programs available. *Faculty:* 12 full-time (5 women), 9 part-time/adjunct (2 women). *Students:* 7 full-time (6 women), 37 part-time (33 women); includes 2 Black or African American, non-Hispanic/Latino; 1 American Indian or Alaska Native, non-Hispanic/Latino; 1 Asian, non-Hispanic/Latino; 1 Hispanic/Latino; 1 Two or more races, non-Hispanic/Latino, 1 international. Average age 34. 25 applicants, 36% accepted, 8 enrolled. In 2010, 6 master's awarded. Terminal master's awarded for partial completion of doctoral program. *Degree requirements:* For master's, thesis, qualifying exam; for doctorate, thesis/dissertation, exams. *Entrance requirements:* For master's, good general education in the humanities. Additional exam requirements/recommendations for international students: Required—TOEFL (minimum score 550 paper-based; 213 computer-based; 80 iBT). *Application deadline:* For fall admission, 3/1 priority date for domestic and international students; for spring admission, 10/15 for domestic and international students. Applications are processed on a rolling basis. Application fee: $45 ($50 for international students). Electronic applications accepted. *Expenses:* Tuition, state resident: full-time $5522.40; part-time $306.80 per credit hour. Tuition, nonresident: full-time $7128; part-time $792 per credit hour. Required fees: $261.15 per term. *Financial support:* In 2010–11, 7 teaching assistantships with partial tuition reimbursements (averaging $11,750 per year) were awarded; career-related internships or fieldwork, Federal Work-Study, institutionally sponsored loans, and tuition waivers (full and partial) also available. Support available to part-time students. Financial award application deadline: 3/1; financial award applicants required to submit FAFSA. *Faculty research:* Painting, electronic media, Western and non-Western art history, photography. *Unit head:* Kati Toivanen, Chair, 816-235-6230, Fax: 816-235-5507, E-mail: toivanenk@umkc.edu. *Application contact:* Craig Subler, Professor, 816-235-2985, Fax: 816-235-5507, E-mail: sublerc@umkc.edu.

University of Nebraska–Lincoln, Graduate College, College of Fine and Performing Arts, Department of Art and Art History, Lincoln, NE 68588. Offers art history (MA); studio art (MFA);). *Accreditation:* NASAD. *Degree requirements:* For master's, thesis. *Entrance requirements:* For master's, slide portfolio. Additional exam requirements/recommendations for international students: Required—TOEFL (minimum score 550 paper-based; 213 computer-based). Electronic applications accepted. *Faculty research:* Classical archaeology, contemporary art, printmaking, photography.

University of New Mexico, Graduate School, College of Fine Arts, Department of Art and Art History, Program in Art History, Albuquerque, NM 87131-2039. Offers MA, PhD. Part-time programs available. *Students:* 28 full-time (23 women), 12 part-time (10 women); includes 2 American Indian or Alaska Native, non-Hispanic/Latino; 1 Asian, non-Hispanic/Latino; 12 Hispanic/Latino, 5 international. Average age 38. 57 applicants, 32% accepted, 12 enrolled. In 2010, 3 master's, 1 doctorate awarded. *Degree requirements:* For master's, one foreign language, comprehensive exam (for some programs), thesis, symposium; for doctorate, 2 foreign languages, comprehensive exam, thesis/dissertation, symposium. *Entrance requirements:* Additional exam requirements/recommendations for international students: Required—TOEFL (minimum score 550 paper-based; 213 computer-based). *Application deadline:* For fall admission, 1/15 for domestic students; for spring admission, 1/15 for domestic students. Application fee: $50. Electronic applications accepted. *Expenses:* Tuition, state resident: full-time $5991;

part-time $251 per credit hour. Tuition, nonresident: full-time $14,405; part-time $800.20 per credit hour. Tuition and fees vary according to course level, course load, program and reciprocity agreements. *Financial support:* In 2010–11, 30 students received support, including 3 fellowships (averaging $7,433 per year), 12 research assistantships with tuition reimbursements available (averaging $5,216 per year), 112 teaching assistantships with partial tuition reimbursements available (averaging $4,005 per year); Federal Work-Study, institutionally sponsored loans, scholarships/grants, health care benefits, and unspecified assistantships also available. Support available to part-time students. Financial award application deadline: 3/1; financial award applicants required to submit FAFSA. *Faculty research:* Native American art, modern Latin American art, pre-Columbian art, architectural art, American art, medieval art, Spanish Colonial Art, Latin American Art, history of photography. *Unit head:* Dr. David Craven, Chair, 505-277-5861, Fax: 505-277-5955, E-mail: dcraven@unm.edu. *Application contact:* Kat Heatherington, Graduate Advisor, 505-277-6672, Fax: 505-277-5955, E-mail: art255@unm.edu.

The University of North Carolina at Chapel Hill, Graduate School, College of Arts and Sciences, Department of Art, Program in Art History, Chapel Hill, NC 27599. Offers MA, PhD. *Degree requirements:* For master's, one foreign language, comprehensive exam, thesis; for doctorate, one foreign language, comprehensive exam, thesis/dissertation. *Entrance requirements:* For master's and doctorate, GRE General Test, minimum GPA of 3.0.

University of North Texas, Toulouse Graduate School, College of Visual Arts and Design, Department of Art Education and Art History, Denton, TX 76203. Offers art education (MA, PhD); art history (MA); art museum education (Certificate); arts leadership (Certificate). Part-time and evening/weekend programs available. *Degree requirements:* For master's, one foreign language, comprehensive exam (for some programs), thesis (for some programs); for doctorate, comprehensive exam, thesis/dissertation. *Entrance requirements:* For master's, GRE, writing sample, statement of purpose; for doctorate, GRE, master's degree in art education, writing sample, slides, statement of purpose. Additional exam requirements/recommendations for international students: Recommended—TOEFL (minimum score 550 paper-based; 213 computer-based; 79 iBT). *Expenses:* Tuition, state resident: full-time $4298; part-time $239 per credit hour. Tuition, nonresident: full-time $10,782; part-time $549 per credit hour. Required fees: $1292; $270 per credit hour. *Financial support:* Fellowships with partial tuition reimbursements, research assistantships with partial tuition reimbursements, teaching assistantships with partial tuition reimbursements, Federal Work-Study, scholarships/grants, health care benefits, and unspecified assistantships available. Support available to part-time students. Financial award applicants required to submit FAFSA. *Faculty research:* Aesthetics, visual culture, arts leadership, British art, Latin American art, French art, Indian art, contemporary Arab art.

University of Notre Dame, Graduate School, College of Arts and Letters, Division of Humanities, Department of Art, Art History, and Design, Notre Dame, IN 46556. Offers art history (MA); design (MFA), including graphic design, industrial design; studio art (MFA), including ceramics, painting, photography, printmaking, sculpture. *Accreditation:* NASAD. *Degree requirements:* For master's, comprehensive exam (for some programs), thesis. *Entrance requirements:* For master's, GRE General Test, minimum GPA of 3.0. Additional exam requirements/recommendations for international students: Required—TOEFL (minimum score 600 paper-based; 250 computer-based; 80 iBT). Electronic applications accepted. *Faculty research:* Studio art practice in ceramics, printing, photography, printmaking and sculpture, graphic design and industrial design, digital imaging in design and photography, Renaissance and American art history, contemporary art theory and criticism.

University of Oklahoma, Weitzenhoffer Family College of Fine Arts, School of Art and Art History, Program in Art History, Norman, OK 73019. Offers art history (MA, PhD), including art of the American West (PhD), Native American art (PhD). *Students:* 9 full-time (8 women), 6 part-time (5 women); includes 3 minority (all American Indian or Alaska Native, non-Hispanic/Latino). Average age 29. 11 applicants, 45% accepted, 5 enrolled. In 2010, 6 master's awarded. Terminal master's awarded for partial completion of doctoral program. *Degree requirements:* For master's, thesis, departmental qualifying exam, reading proficiency in French/German. *Entrance requirements:* For master's, GRE General Test, minimum GPA of 3.0, 18 undergraduate hours in art history, writing sample, 3 letters of recommendation. Additional exam requirements/recommendations for international students: Required—TOEFL (minimum score 550 paper-based; 213 computer-based; 79 iBT). *Application deadline:* For fall admission, 2/1 priority date for domestic students, 2/1 for international students; for spring admission, 10/1 for domestic and international students. Applications are processed on a rolling basis. Application fee: $40 ($90 for international students). Electronic applications accepted. *Expenses:* Tuition, state resident: full-time $3893; part-time $162.20 per credit hour. Tuition, nonresident: full-time $14,167; part-time $590.30 per credit hour. Required fees: $2523; $94.60 per credit hour. Tuition and fees vary according to course load and degree level. *Financial support:* In 2010–11, 15 students received support. Career-related internships or fieldwork, institutionally sponsored loans, scholarships/grants, tuition waivers (partial), and unspecified assistantships available. Support available to part-time students. Financial award application deadline: 4/7; financial award applicants required to submit FAFSA. *Faculty research:* American West, Native American art, medieval, Renaissance and Baroque, contemporary art, nineteenth century art, medieval/Romanesque. *Unit head:* Mary Jo Watson, Director, 405-325-2691, Fax: 405-325-1668, E-mail: mjwatson@ou.edu. *Application contact:* Susan H. Caldwell, Assistant Director/Professor, 405-325-3252, Fax: 405-325-1668, E-mail: shcaldwell@ou.edu.

University of Oregon, Graduate School, School of Architecture and Allied Arts, Department of Art History, Eugene, OR 97403. Offers MA, PhD. *Degree requirements:* For master's, one foreign language, thesis or alternative; for doctorate, 2 foreign languages, thesis/dissertation. *Entrance requirements:* For master's, GRE General Test, minimum GPA of 3.0; for doctorate, minimum GPA of 3.0. Additional exam requirements/recommendations for international students: Required—TOEFL. *Faculty research:* Scytho-Siberian art, modern Chinese painting, European landscape painting, American architecture, German expressionist graphics.

University of Pennsylvania, School of Arts and Sciences, Graduate Group in the History of Art, Philadelphia, PA 19104. Offers AM, PhD. *Faculty:* 21 full-time (9 women), 6 part-time/adjunct (3 women). *Students:* 38 full-time (30 women), 2 part-time (both women); includes 2 Hispanic/Latino, 5 international. 209 applicants, 7% accepted, 7 enrolled. In 2010, 7 master's, 1 doctorate awarded. Terminal master's awarded for partial completion of doctoral program. *Degree requirements:* For master's, 2 foreign languages, thesis; for doctorate, 2 foreign languages, thesis/dissertation. *Entrance requirements:* For master's and doctorate, GRE, language background according to subfield of interest. Additional exam requirements/recommendations for international students: Required—TOEFL. *Application deadline:* For fall admission, 12/1 priority date for domestic students. Application fee: $70. Electronic applications accepted. *Expenses:* Tuition: Full-time $25,660; part-time $4758 per course. Required fees: $2152; $270 per course. Tuition and fees vary according to course load, degree level and program. *Financial support:* Fellowships, research assistantships, teaching assistantships, institutionally sponsored loans, scholarships/grants, traineeships, health care benefits, and unspecified assistantships available. Financial award application deadline: 12/15. *Unit head:* Robert Ousterhout, Graduate Chair, 215-898-3249, E-mail: ousterob@sas.upenn.edu. *Application contact:* Robert Ousterhout, Graduate Chair, 215-898-3249, E-mail: ousterob@sas.upenn.edu.

University of Pittsburgh, School of Arts and Sciences, Department of History of Art and Architecture, Pittsburgh, PA 15260. Offers MA, PhD. *Faculty:* 13 full-time (7 women). *Students:* 31 full-time (26 women); includes 5 Asian, non-Hispanic/Latino; 1 Hispanic/Latino. Average age 33. 51 applicants, 12% accepted, 5 enrolled. In 2010, 3 master's, 6 doctorates awarded. Terminal master's awarded for partial completion of doctoral program. *Degree requirements:* For master's, one foreign language, thesis; for doctorate, 2 foreign languages, comprehensive exam, thesis/dissertation. *Entrance requirements:* For doctorate, GRE General Test, 3 letters of recommendation, writing sample, foreign language questionnaire, statement of purpose. Additional exam requirements/recommendations for international students: Required—TOEFL (minimum score 550 paper-based; 213 computer-based; 80 iBT). *Application deadline:* For fall admission, 1/15 for domestic and international students. Application fee: $50. Electronic applications accepted. *Expenses:* Tuition, state resident: full-time $17,304; part-time $701 per credit. Tuition, nonresident: full-time $29,554; part-time $1210 per credit. Required fees: $740; $214 per term. Tuition and fees vary according to program. *Financial support:* In 2010–11, 29 students received support, including 16 fellowships with full tuition reimbursements available (averaging $17,972 per year), 13 teaching assistantships with full tuition reimbursements available (averaging $15,064 per year); research assistantships with full tuition reimbursements available, career-related internships or fieldwork, Federal Work-Study, scholarships/grants, health care benefits, and tuition waivers (partial) also available. Financial award application deadline: 1/15. *Faculty research:* Asian, medieval, Renaissance/Baroque, modern art and architecture, contemporary. *Unit head:* Dr. Kirk Savage, Chair, 412-648-2405, Fax: 412-648-2792, E-mail: ksa@pitt.edu. *Application contact:* Dr. Josh Ellenbogen, Director, Graduate Studies, 412-648-8530, Fax: 412-648-2792, E-mail: jme23@pitt.edu.

University of Rochester, School of Arts and Sciences, Department of Art and Art History, Rochester, NY 14627. Offers visual and cultural studies (MA, PhD). Terminal master's awarded for partial completion of doctoral program. *Degree requirements:* For master's, thesis optional; for doctorate, one foreign language, thesis/dissertation, qualifying exam. *Entrance requirements:* For master's and doctorate, GRE General Test. Additional exam requirements/recommendations for international students: Required—TOEFL.

University of St. Thomas, Graduate Studies, College of Arts and Sciences, Department of Art History, St. Paul, MN 55105-1096. Offers MA. Part-time and evening/weekend programs available. *Faculty:* 5 full-time (3 women), 4 part-time/adjunct (all women). *Students:* 9 full-time (7 women), 21 part-time (19 women); includes 1 American Indian or Alaska Native, non-Hispanic/Latino; 1 Hispanic/Latino, 1 international. Average age 29. 12 applicants, 67% accepted, 7 enrolled. In 2010, 7 master's awarded. *Degree requirements:* For master's, thesis, oral exam, reading proficiency in 1 foreign language. *Entrance requirements:* For master's, bachelor's degree in art history or related field; 3 letters of recommendation; writing sample. Additional exam requirements/recommendations for international students: Required—TOEFL. *Application deadline:* For fall admission, 3/1 for domestic and international students; for spring admission, 11/1 for domestic and international students. Application fee: $50. *Financial support:* In 2010–11, 16 students received support, including 8 fellowships (averaging $4,000 per year), 4 research assistantships (averaging $870 per year); career-related internships or fieldwork, institutionally sponsored loans, scholarships/grants, and unspecified assistantships also available. Support available to part-time students. Financial award application deadline: 4/1; financial award applicants required to submit FAFSA. *Faculty research:* Pictorial narrative and theory; feminist theory and women's artistic practice; art, ritual, and popular culture; architectural history; modernism. *Unit head:* Dr. Mark Stansbury-O'Donnell, Chair, 651-962-5560, Fax: 651-962-5861, E-mail: m9stansburyo@stthomas.edu. *Application contact:* Dr. Victoria M. Young, Director of Graduate Studies, 651-962-5640, Fax: 651-962-5861, E-mail: vmyoung@stthomas.edu.

University of South Africa, College of Human Sciences, Pretoria, South Africa. Offers adult education (M Ed); African languages (MA, PhD); African politics (MA, PhD); Afrikaans (MA, PhD); ancient history (MA, PhD); ancient Near Eastern studies (MA, PhD); anthropology (MA, PhD); applied linguistics (MA); Arabic (MA, PhD); archaeology (MA); art history (MA); Biblical archaeology (MA); Biblical studies (M Th, D Th, PhD); Christian spirituality (M Th, D Th); church history (M Th, D Th); classical studies (MA, PhD); clinical psychology (MA); communication (MA, PhD); comparative education (M Ed, Ed D); consulting psychology (D Admin, D Com, PhD); curriculum studies (M Ed, Ed D); development studies (M Admin, MA, D Admin, PhD); didactics (M Ed, Ed D); education (M Tech); education management (M Ed, Ed D); educational psychology (M Ed); English (MA); environmental education (M Ed); French (MA, PhD); German (MA, PhD); Greek (MA); guidance and counseling (M Ed); health studies (MA, PhD), including health sciences education (MA), health services management (MA), medical and surgical nursing science (critical care general) (MA), midwifery and neonatal nursing science (MA), trauma and emergency care (MA); history (MA, PhD); history of education (Ed D); inclusive education (M Ed, Ed D); information and communications technology policy and regulation (MA); information science (MA, MIS, PhD); international politics (MA, PhD); Islamic studies (MA, PhD); Italian (MA, PhD); Judaica (MA, PhD); linguistics (MA, PhD); mathematical education (M Ed); mathematics education (MA); missiology (M Th, D Th); modern Hebrew (MA, PhD); musicology (MA, MMus, D Mus, PhD); natural science education (M Ed); New Testament (M Th, D Th); Old Testament (D Th); pastoral therapy (M Th, D Th); philosophy (MA); philosophy of education (M Ed, Ed D); politics (MA, PhD); Portuguese (MA, PhD); practical theology (M Th, D Th); psychology (MA, MS, PhD); psychology of education (M Ed, Ed D); public health (MA); religious studies (MA, D Th, PhD); Romance languages (MA); Russian (MA, PhD); Semitic languages (MA, PhD); social behavior studies in HIV/AIDS (MA); social science (mental health) (MA); social science in development studies (MA); social science in psychology (MA); social science in social work (MA); social science in sociology (MA); social work (MSW, DSW, PhD); socio-education (M Ed, Ed D); sociolinguistics (MA); sociology (MA, PhD); Spanish (MA, PhD); systematic theology (M Th, D Th); TESOL (teaching English to speakers of other languages) (MA); theological ethics (M Th, D Th); theory of literature (MA, PhD); urban ministries (D Th); urban ministry (M Th).

University of South Carolina, The Graduate School, College of Arts and Sciences, Department of Art, Program in Art History, Columbia, SC 29208. Offers MA. *Accreditation:* NASAD. Part-time programs available. *Degree requirements:* For master's, one foreign language, comprehensive exam, thesis. *Entrance requirements:* For master's, GRE General Test or MAT, writing sample. Additional exam requirements/recommendations for international students: Required—TOEFL. Electronic applications accepted. *Faculty research:* History of art and architecture.

University of Southern California, Graduate School, Dana and David Dornsife College of Letters, Arts and Sciences, Department of Art History, Los Angeles, CA 90089. Offers art history (MA, PhD); visual studies (Graduate Certificate). *Faculty:* 11 full-time (7 women), 5 part-time/adjunct (2 women). *Students:* 34 full-time (27 women); includes 7 minority (6 Asian, non-Hispanic/Latino; 1 Hispanic/Latino), 4 international. 40 applicants, 10% accepted, 4 enrolled. In 2010, 6 master's, 1 doctorate, 4 other advanced degrees awarded. *Degree requirements:* For doctorate, 2 foreign languages, comprehensive exam, thesis/dissertation, 60 units. *Entrance requirements:* For doctorate, GRE. Additional exam requirements/recommendations for international students: Required—TOEFL. *Application deadline:* For fall admission, 12/1 for domestic students. Application fee: $85. *Expenses:* Tuition: Full-time $31,240; part-time $1420 per unit. Required fees: $600. One-time fee: $35 full-time. Full-time tuition and fees vary according to degree level and program. *Financial support:* In 2010–11, 31 students received support, including 10 fellowships with full tuition reimbursements available (averaging $19,000 per year), 12 teaching assistantships with full tuition reimbursements available (averaging $19,000 per year); career-related internships or fieldwork, institutionally sponsored loans, scholarships/grants, health care benefits, unspecified assistantships, and cash awards for travel and research also available. Financial award application deadline: 2/1. *Faculty research:* Ancient, medieval, Renaissance, eighteenth-nineteenth century, contemporary. *Unit head:* Dr. Carolyn Malone, Professor and Chair, 213-740-4552, Fax: 213-740-8971, E-mail: cmalone@usc.edu. *Application contact:* Jeanne Herman, Academic Advisor, 213-740-9516, Fax: 213-740-8971, E-mail: jaherman@usc.edu.

University of South Florida, Graduate School, College of The Arts, School of Art and Art History, Tampa, FL 33620-9951. Offers art history (MA); studio art (MFA). *Accreditation:* NASAD. Part-time programs available. *Faculty:* 8 full-time (4 women). *Students:* 40 full-time (22 women), 8 part-time (6 women); includes 1 Black or African American, non-Hispanic/Latino; 2 American Indian or Alaska Native, non-Hispanic/Latino; 5 Hispanic/Latino; 1 Two or more races, non-Hispanic/Latino, 3 international. Average age 31. 105 applicants, 25% accepted, 17 enrolled. In 2010, 12 master's awarded. *Degree requirements:* For master's, thesis, exhibition (MFA). *Entrance requirements:* For master's, GRE General Test (MA), minimum GPA of 3.0 in last 60 hours of coursework. *Application deadline:* For fall admission, 1/15 for domestic students, 1/2 for international students. Application fee: $30. *Financial support:* In 2010–11, 34

Art History

University of South Florida (continued)

teaching assistantships with partial tuition reimbursements (averaging $9,265 per year) were awarded; scholarships/grants, health care benefits, and unspecified assistantships also available. Support available to part-time students. Financial award application deadline: 2/15; financial award applicants required to submit FAFSA. *Faculty research:* Contemporary art and role of the artist, identity strategies, political iconography, art practice and technology, construction of race in art. Total annual research expenditures: $184,644. *Unit head:* Prof. Wallace Wilson, Director, School of Art and Art History, 813-974-2360, Fax: 813-974-9226, E-mail: wwilson2@usf.edu. *Application contact:* Gloria Ann Quigley, Academic Specialist, 813-974-9249, Fax: 813-974-9226, E-mail: gquigley@usf.edu.

The University of Texas at Austin, Graduate School, College of Fine Arts, Department of Art and Art History, Program in Art History, Austin, TX 78712-1111. Offers MA, PhD. *Accreditation:* NASAD. Part-time programs available. *Degree requirements:* For master's, one foreign language, thesis; for doctorate, 2 foreign languages, thesis/dissertation, oral and written qualifying exam. *Entrance requirements:* For master's, GRE General Test, 2 samples of written work; for doctorate, GRE General Test, minimum GPA of 3.0, 2 samples of written work. Electronic applications accepted.

The University of Texas at San Antonio, College of Liberal and Fine Arts, Department of Art and Art History, San Antonio, TX 78249-0617. Offers art (MFA); art history (MA). *Accreditation:* NASAD (one or more programs are accredited). *Faculty:* 15 full-time (7 women). *Students:* 25 full-time (16 women), 14 part-time (12 women); includes 12 minority (1 American Indian or Alaska Native, non-Hispanic/Latino; 10 Hispanic/Latino; 1 Two or more races, non-Hispanic/Latino), 2 international. Average age 30. 30 applicants, 60% accepted, 8 enrolled. In 2010, 10 master's awarded. *Degree requirements:* For master's, comprehensive exam (for some programs), thesis (for some programs). *Entrance requirements:* For master's, GRE General Test, portfolio, minimum GPA of 3.0 in last 60 hours, 3 letters of recommendation. Additional exam requirements/recommendations for international students: Required—TOEFL (minimum score 500 paper-based; 173 computer-based; 61 iBT), IELTS (minimum score 5). *Application deadline:* For fall admission, 7/1 for domestic students, 4/1 for international students; for spring admission, 11/1 for domestic students, 9/1 for international students. Applications are processed on a rolling basis. Application fee: $45 ($80 for international students). Electronic applications accepted. *Expenses:* Tuition, state resident: full-time $4172; part-time $231.75 per credit hour. Tuition, nonresident: full-time $15,332; part-time $851.75 per credit hour. *Financial support:* In 2010–11, 24 students received support, including 15 research assistantships (averaging $15,074 per year), 13 teaching assistantships (averaging $7,569 per year); career-related internships or fieldwork, scholarships/grants, tuition waivers (partial), and unspecified assistantships also available. Support available to part-time students. *Faculty research:* Artistic production in media; art history and criticism, focusing on American and Hispanic art. *Unit head:* Dr. Gregory Elliott, Department Chair, 210-458-4362, Fax: 210-458-4356, E-mail: greg.elliott@utsa.edu. *Application contact:* Veronica Ramirez, Assistant Dean of the Graduate School, 210-458-4330, Fax: 210-458-4332, E-mail: graduatestudies@utsa.edu.

The University of Texas at Tyler, College of Arts and Sciences, Department of Art and Art History, Tyler, TX 75799-0001. Offers art history (MA); interdisciplinary (MAIS); studio art (MFA). *Degree requirements:* For master's, thesis, graduate committee review. *Entrance requirements:* For master's, minimum GPA of 3.0. Additional exam requirements/recommendations for international students: Required—TOEFL (minimum score 79 computer-based). *Faculty research:* Classical myths in contemporary art, social issues in contemporary art, casting methods, Renaissance art.

University of Toronto, School of Graduate Studies, Humanities Division, Department of Art, Toronto, ON M5S 1A1, Canada. Offers art history (MA, PhD); visual studies (MVS). Part-time programs available. *Degree requirements:* For master's, 2 foreign languages, language proficiency exams; for doctorate, 2 foreign languages, comprehensive exam, thesis/dissertation. *Entrance requirements:* For master's, coursework in a foreign language, 3 letters of reference, sample research paper, minimum B+ average in senior art history and/or humanities courses; for doctorate, minimum A– average in senior art history and/or humanities courses, 2 letters of reference, sample research paper.

University of Utah, Graduate School, College of Fine Arts, Department of Art and Art History, Program in Art History, Salt Lake City, UT 84112-0380. Offers MA. Part-time programs available. *Faculty:* 6 full-time (4 women), 1 part-time/adjunct (0 women). *Students:* 7 full-time (all women), 1 (woman) part-time; includes 1 Hispanic/Latino. Average age 26. 12 applicants, 42% accepted, 3 enrolled. In 2010, 2 master's awarded. *Degree requirements:* For master's, one foreign language, comprehensive exam, thesis, thesis defense. *Entrance requirements:* For master's, curriculum vitae, academic writing sample, letters of recommendation. Additional exam requirements/recommendations for international students: Required—TOEFL (minimum score 600 paper-based; 173 computer-based). *Application deadline:* For fall admission, 1/2 priority date for domestic and international students. Application fee: $55 ($65 for international students). Electronic applications accepted. *Expenses:* Tuition, area resident: Part-time $179.19 per credit hour. Tuition, state resident: full-time $4384. Tuition, nonresident: full-time $16,684; part-time $630.67 per credit hour. Required fees: $350 per semester. Tuition and fees vary according to course load, degree level and program. *Financial support:* In 2010–11, 1 fellowship, 6 teaching assistantships with partial tuition reimbursements were awarded; research assistantships with partial tuition reimbursements, Federal Work-Study, institutionally sponsored loans, scholarships/grants, tuition waivers (partial), unspecified assistantships, and stipends also available. Financial award application deadline: 1/2; financial award applicants required to submit FAFSA. *Faculty research:* Asian art, Latin American art, Baroque art, European/American art, twentieth century/contemporary art. *Unit head:* Director, 801-581-8677, Fax: 801-585-6171. *Application contact:* Dr. Paul Monty Paret, Director of Graduate Studies, 801-581-8677, Fax: 801-585-6171, E-mail: paul.paret@utah.edu.

University of Victoria, Faculty of Graduate Studies, Faculty of Fine Arts, Department of History in Art, Victoria, BC V8W 2Y2, Canada. Offers MA, PhD. *Degree requirements:* For master's, one foreign language, thesis (for some programs), oral defense; for doctorate, 2 foreign languages, comprehensive exam, thesis/dissertation, oral defense. *Entrance requirements:* For master's, minimum B+ average in undergraduate course work; for doctorate, minimum B+ average in graduate course work. Additional exam requirements/recommendations for international students: Required—TOEFL (minimum score 575 paper-based; 233 computer-based), IELTS (minimum score 7). Electronic applications accepted. *Faculty research:* Europe, Southeast Asia, China and Islamic world, architecture of North America and the Islamic World, film.

University of Virginia, College and Graduate School of Arts and Sciences, Program in Art and Architectural History, Charlottesville, VA 22903. Offers MA, PhD. *Faculty:* 19 full-time (7 women), 3 part-time/adjunct (all women). *Students:* 54 full-time (41 women); includes 1 Hispanic/Latino; 1 Two or more races, non-Hispanic/Latino, 1 international. Average age 31. 120 applicants, 23% accepted, 10 enrolled. In 2010, 7 master's, 3 doctorates awarded. *Degree requirements:* For master's, one foreign language, comprehensive exam, thesis; for doctorate, 2 foreign languages, thesis/dissertation, oral exam. *Entrance requirements:* For master's and doctorate, GRE, 2 letters of recommendation. *Application deadline:* For fall admission, 12/7 for domestic and international students. Applications are processed on a rolling basis. Electronic applications accepted. *Financial support:* Application deadline: 12/7. *Unit head:* Howard Singerman, Chair, 434-924-6123, Fax: 434-924-3647, E-mail: artdept@virginia.edu. *Application contact:* Douglas Fordham, Director of Graduate Studies, 434-924-6130, Fax: 434-924-3647, E-mail: df2p@virginia.edu.

University of Washington, Graduate School, College of Arts and Sciences, School of Art, Division of Art History, Seattle, WA 98195. Offers MA, PhD. Terminal master's awarded for partial completion of doctoral program. *Degree requirements:* For master's, 2 foreign languages, practicum or thesis; for doctorate, 2 foreign languages, thesis/dissertation. *Entrance requirements:* For master's, GRE General Test, minimum undergraduate GPA of 3.0, undergraduate major in art history or equivalent; for doctorate, GRE General Test, MA in art history, minimum graduate GPA of 3.0. Additional exam requirements/recommendations for international students: Required—TOEFL (minimum score 580 paper-based; 237 computer-based). Electronic applications accepted. *Faculty research:* European-American (all periods), Japanese, Chinese, African, and Native American art.

University of Wisconsin–Madison, Graduate School, College of Letters and Science, Department of Art History, Madison, WI 53706-1380. Offers MA, PhD. Part-time programs available. Terminal master's awarded for partial completion of doctoral program. *Degree requirements:* For master's, one foreign language; for doctorate, 2 foreign languages, thesis/dissertation. *Entrance requirements:* For master's and doctorate, GRE. Additional exam requirements/recommendations for international students: Required—TOEFL. Electronic applications accepted. *Expenses:* Tuition, state resident: full-time $9887; part-time $617.96 per credit. Tuition, nonresident: full-time $24,054; part-time $1503.40 per credit. Required fees: $67.63 per credit. Tuition and fees vary according to reciprocity agreements. *Faculty research:* Twentieth-century, African art, Italian Renaissance, Dutch, material culture.

University of Wisconsin–Milwaukee, Graduate School, College of Letters and Sciences, Department of Art History, Milwaukee, WI 53201-0413. Offers art history (MA); art museum studies (Certificate). Part-time programs available. *Faculty:* 9 full-time (5 women). *Students:* 20 full-time (17 women), 9 part-time (7 women); includes 1 Asian, non-Hispanic/Latino; 3 Hispanic/Latino. Average age 29. 23 applicants, 61% accepted, 8 enrolled. In 2010, 6 master's awarded. *Degree requirements:* For master's, one foreign language, comprehensive exam, thesis or alternative. *Entrance requirements:* For master's, GRE. Additional exam requirements/recommendations for international students: Required—TOEFL (minimum score 550 paper-based; 79 iBT), IELTS (minimum score 6.5). *Application deadline:* For fall admission, 1/1 priority date for domestic students; for spring admission, 9/1 for domestic students. Applications are processed on a rolling basis. Application fee: $56 ($96 for international students). *Financial support:* In 2010–11, 7 teaching assistantships were awarded; fellowships, research assistantships, career-related internships or fieldwork and unspecified assistantships also available. Support available to part-time students. Financial award application deadline: 4/15; financial award applicants required to submit FAFSA. *Faculty research:* Ancient Mediterranean art through contemporary Western art, Chinese art, Pre-Columbian art, film, theory. *Unit head:* Kenneth Bendiner, Chair, 414-229-5015, Fax: 414-229-2935, E-mail: bendiner@uwm.edu. *Application contact:* Derek Counts, General Information Contact, 414-229-3466, E-mail: dbc@uwm.edu.

University of Wisconsin–Superior, Graduate Division, Department of Visual Arts, Superior, WI 54880-4500. Offers art education (MA); art history (MA); art therapy (MA); studio arts (MA). Part-time programs available. *Degree requirements:* For master's, comprehensive exam, exhibit. *Entrance requirements:* For master's, minimum GPA of 2.75, portfolio.

Virginia Commonwealth University, Graduate School, School of the Arts, Department of Art History, Richmond, VA 23284-9005. Offers architectural history (MA); art history (MA, PhD); historical studies (MA); museum studies (MA). *Accreditation:* NASAD. *Faculty:* 10 full-time (4 women). *Students:* 15 full-time (13 women), 27 part-time (24 women); includes 4 minority (1 Asian, non-Hispanic/Latino; 3 Hispanic/Latino), 1 international. 52 applicants, 48% accepted, 12 enrolled. In 2010, 9 master's, 5 doctorates awarded. *Degree requirements:* For master's, thesis; for doctorate, comprehensive exam, thesis/dissertation. *Entrance requirements:* For master's and doctorate, GRE General Test. *Application deadline:* For fall admission, 1/15 for domestic students. Application fee: $50. Electronic applications accepted. *Expenses:* Tuition, state resident: full-time $4308; part-time $479 per credit hour. Tuition, nonresident: full-time $8942; part-time $994 per credit hour. Required fees: $2000; $85 per credit hour. Tuition and fees vary according to course level, course load, degree level, campus/location and program. *Financial support:* Fellowships, teaching assistantships, career-related internships or fieldwork, Federal Work-Study, and institutionally sponsored loans available. Support available to part-time students. Financial award application deadline: 3/15; financial award applicants required to submit FAFSA. *Faculty research:* Modern, nineteenth-century, Renaissance, American, and medieval art. *Unit head:* Dr. Dina Bangdel, Director of Graduate Studies, 804-628-7027, Fax: 804-828-7468, E-mail: dbangdel@vcu.edu. *Application contact:* Dr. Dina Bangdel, Director of Graduate Studies, 804-628-7027, Fax: 804-828-7468, E-mail: dbangdel@vcu.edu.

Washington University in St. Louis, Graduate School of Arts and Sciences, Department of Art History and Archaeology, St. Louis, MO 63130-4899. Offers art history (MA, PhD); classical archaeology (MA, PhD). *Degree requirements:* For doctorate, 2 foreign languages, comprehensive exam, thesis/dissertation. *Entrance requirements:* For master's and doctorate, GRE General Test, sample of written work. Electronic applications accepted.

See Display on page 189 and Close-Up on page 231.

Wayne State University, College of Fine, Performing and Communication Arts, Department of Art and Art History, Program in Art History, Detroit, MI 48202. Offers MA. *Faculty:* 19 full-time (9 women), 2 part-time/adjunct (0 women). *Students:* 2 full-time (both women), 7 part-time (6 women); includes 1 minority (Two or more races, non-Hispanic/Latino). Average age 37. 6 applicants, 33% accepted, 1 enrolled. *Degree requirements:* For master's, one foreign language. *Entrance requirements:* Additional exam requirements/recommendations for international students: Required—TOEFL (minimum score 550 paper-based; 213 computer-based); Recommended—TWE (minimum score 6). *Application deadline:* For fall admission, 4/1 for domestic students, 6/1 for international students; for winter admission, 10/1 for international students; for spring admission, 2/1 for international students. Application fee: $30 ($50 for international students). Electronic applications accepted. *Expenses:* Tuition, state resident: full-time $7662; part-time $478.85 per credit hour. Tuition, nonresident: full-time $16,920; part-time $1057.55 per credit hour. Required fees: $571.20; $35.70 per credit hour. $188.05 per semester. Tuition and fees vary according to course load and program. *Financial support:* In 2010–11, 1 teaching assistantship (averaging $14,620 per year) was awarded. *Faculty research:* Ancient, medieval, and nineteenth and twentieth century art history; theory and criticism. *Unit head:* Dr. John Richardson, Chair, 313-577-2980, Fax: 313-577-3491, E-mail: af5343@wayne.edu. *Application contact:* Brian Madigan, Associate Professor, 313-577-2685, E-mail: bmadigan@wayne.edu.

West Virginia University, College of Creative Arts, Division of Art and Design, Morgantown, WV 26506. Offers art education (MA); art history (MA); ceramics (MFA); graphic design (MFA); painting (MFA); printmaking (MFA); sculpture (MFA); studio art (MA). *Accreditation:* NASAD. *Degree requirements:* For master's, thesis, exhibit. *Entrance requirements:* For master's, minimum GPA of 2.75, portfolio. Additional exam requirements/recommendations for international students: Required—TOEFL. *Expenses:* Contact institution. *Faculty research:* Medieval art history.

Williams College, Program in the History of Art, Williamstown, MA 01267. Offers MA. Offered jointly with Sterling and Francine Clark Art Institute. Part-time programs available. *Degree requirements:* For master's, 2 foreign languages, symposium paper and lecture. *Entrance requirements:* For master's, GRE General Test. Additional exam requirements/recommendations for international students: Required—TOEFL. Electronic applications accepted.

Yale University, Graduate School of Arts and Sciences, Department of History of Art, New Haven, CT 06520. Offers PhD. *Degree requirements:* For doctorate, 2 foreign languages, thesis/dissertation. *Entrance requirements:* For doctorate, GRE General Test.

York University, Faculty of Graduate Studies, Faculty of Fine Arts, Program in Art History, Toronto, ON M3J 1P3, Canada. Offers MA, PhD. Part-time programs available. *Degree requirements:* For master's, one foreign language, thesis or alternative. Electronic applications accepted.

Arts Administration

American University, College of Arts and Sciences, Department of Performing Arts, Washington, DC 20016-8053. Offers arts management (MA, Certificate). Part-time and evening/weekend programs available. *Faculty:* 22 full-time (9 women), 49 part-time/adjunct (20 women). *Students:* 37 full-time (28 women), 34 part-time (29 women); includes 10 minority (1 Black or African American, non-Hispanic/Latino; 4 Asian, non-Hispanic/Latino; 5 Hispanic/Latino), 4 international. Average age 28. 77 applicants, 68% accepted, 21 enrolled. In 2010, 14 master's awarded. *Degree requirements:* For master's, comprehensive exam, thesis or alternative. *Entrance requirements:* For master's, GRE, minimum GPA of 3.0; for Certificate, bachelor's degree. Additional exam requirements/recommendations for international students: Required—TOEFL. *Application deadline:* For fall admission, 2/1 priority date for domestic students; for spring admission, 10/1 priority date for domestic students. Application fee: $80. *Financial support:* Fellowships with tuition reimbursements, research assistantships with full and partial tuition reimbursements, teaching assistantships, career-related internships or fieldwork, Federal Work-Study, and institutionally sponsored loans available. Support available to part-time students. Financial award application deadline: 2/1. *Faculty research:* Choreography, history, technology. *Unit head:* Dr. Caleen Jennings, Chair, 202-885-3430, Fax: 202-885-1092, E-mail: cjennin@american.edu. *Application contact:* Kathleen Clowery, Director, Graduate Admissions, 202-885-3621, Fax: 202-885-1505.

Boston University, Metropolitan College, Program in Arts Administration, Boston, MA 02215. Offers arts administration (MS, Graduate Certificate); fundraising management (Graduate Certificate). Part-time and evening/weekend programs available. *Faculty:* 2 full-time (0 women), 10 part-time/adjunct (3 women). *Students:* 6 full-time (all women), 73 part-time (65 women); includes 5 minority (1 Black or African American, non-Hispanic/Latino; 1 Asian, non-Hispanic/Latino; 3 Hispanic/Latino), 9 international. Average age 27. 128 applicants, 59% accepted, 39 enrolled. In 2010, 35 master's awarded. *Degree requirements:* For master's, internship. *Entrance requirements:* Additional exam requirements/recommendations for international students: Required—TOEFL (minimum score 590 paper-based; 213 computer-based; 84 iBT), IELTS, TWE. *Application deadline:* For fall admission, 3/31 priority date for domestic and international students; for spring admission, 11/15 priority date for domestic and international students. Applications are processed on a rolling basis. Application fee: $70. Electronic applications accepted. *Expenses:* Tuition: Full-time $39,314; part-time $1228 per credit. Required fees: $40 per semester. *Financial support:* In 2010–11, 4 research assistantships with partial tuition reimbursements (averaging $2,500 per year) were awarded; career-related internships or fieldwork, unspecified assistantships, and office assistantships also available. Support available to part-time students. Financial award applicants required to submit FAFSA. *Faculty research:* Cultural policy, artists' rights, museum practices, audience development. *Unit head:* Prof. Daniel Ranalli, Associate Professor/Director, 617-353-4064, Fax: 617-353-1230, E-mail: artsad@bu.edu. *Application contact:* Jeannie Motherwell, Program Assistant, 617-353-4064, Fax: 617-358-1230, E-mail: jmoth@bu.edu.

Carnegie Mellon University, H. John Heinz III College, School of Public Policy and Management, Master of Arts Management Program, Pittsburgh, PA 15213-3891. Offers MAM. *Degree requirements:* For master's, internship. *Entrance requirements:* For master's, GRE or GMAT, college-level course in advanced algebra/pre-calculus; college-level courses in economics and statistics (recommended). Additional exam requirements/recommendations for international students: Required—TOEFL or IELTS. Electronic applications accepted.

Claremont Graduate University, Graduate Programs, Program in Arts Management, Claremont, CA 91711-6160. Offers MA. *Students:* 34 full-time (28 women), 4 part-time (all women); includes 13 minority (2 Black or African American, non-Hispanic/Latino; 4 Asian, non-Hispanic/Latino; 6 Hispanic/Latino; 1 Two or more races, non-Hispanic/Latino), 5 international. Average age 31. In 2010, 8 degrees awarded. *Entrance requirements:* For master's, GRE General Test. Additional exam requirements/recommendations for international students: Required—TOEFL (minimum score 550 paper-based; 213 computer-based; 80 iBT). *Application deadline:* For fall admission, 2/1 priority date for domestic students. Applications are processed on a rolling basis. Application fee: $60. Electronic applications accepted. *Expenses:* Tuition: Full-time $35,748; part-time $1554 per unit. Required fees: $215 per semester. *Financial support:* Fellowships, research assistantships, teaching assistantships, Federal Work-Study, institutionally sponsored loans, and scholarships/grants available. Support available to part-time students. Financial award application deadline: 2/15; financial award applicants required to submit FAFSA. *Unit head:* Laura Zucker, Director, 909-607-9109, Fax: 909-621-8330, E-mail: laura.zucker@cgu.edu. *Application contact:* Susan Hampson, Admissions and Academic Support, 909-607-1278, Fax: 909-607-1221, E-mail: susan.hampson@cgu.edu.

The College at Brockport, State University of New York, School of Education and Human Services, Department of Public Administration, Brockport, NY 14420-2997. Offers arts administration (AGC); nonprofit management (AGC); public administration (MPA), including general public administration, health care management, nonprofit management, public safety. *Accreditation:* NASPAA. Part-time and evening/weekend programs available. *Students:* 26 full-time (17 women), 80 part-time (64 women); includes 12 Black or African American, non-Hispanic/Latino; 2 Asian, non-Hispanic/Latino; 5 Hispanic/Latino. 48 applicants, 79% accepted, 27 enrolled. In 2010, 49 master's, 2 other advanced degrees awarded. *Degree requirements:* For master's, thesis or alternative. *Entrance requirements:* For master's, GRE or minimum GPA of 3.0, letters of recommendation, statement of objectives; current resume. Additional exam requirements/recommendations for international students: Required—TOEFL (minimum score 550 paper-based; 213 computer-based; 79 iBT). *Application deadline:* For fall admission, 3/1 priority date for domestic and international students; for spring admission, 10/1 priority date for domestic and international students. Application fee: $50. Electronic applications accepted. *Financial support:* In 2010–11, teaching assistantships with full tuition reimbursements (averaging $6,000 per year); Federal Work-Study, scholarships/grants, and unspecified assistantships also available. Support available to part-time students. Financial award application deadline: 3/15; financial award applicants required to submit FAFSA. *Faculty research:* E-government, performance management, nonprofits and policy implementation, Medicaid and disabilities. *Unit head:* Dr. Ed Downey, Chairperson, 585-395-2375, Fax: 585-395-2172, E-mail: edowney@brockport.edu. *Application contact:* Dr. Ed Downey, Chairperson, 585-395-2375, Fax: 585-395-2172, E-mail: edowney@brockport.edu.

College of Charleston, Graduate School, School of the Arts, Program in Arts Management, Charleston, SC 29424-0001. Offers MPA, Certificate. Part-time and evening/weekend programs available. *Faculty:* 1 (woman) full-time. *Students:* 3 part-time (2 women); includes 1 minority (Hispanic/Latino). Average age 25. 3 applicants, 100% accepted, 3 enrolled. In 2010, 3 other advanced degrees awarded. *Entrance requirements:* For degree, minimum GPA of 3.0, writing sample. Additional exam requirements/recommendations for international students: Required—TOEFL (minimum score 81 iBT). *Application deadline:* For fall admission, 4/1 for domestic students; for spring admission, 11/1 for domestic students. Application fee: $45. *Unit head:* Scott Peterson, Director, 843-953-8421, E-mail: petersons@cofc.edu. *Application contact:* Susan Hallatt, Director of Graduate Admissions, 843-953-5614, Fax: 843-953-1434, E-mail: hallatts@cofc.edu.

Columbia College Chicago, Graduate School, Department of Arts, Entertainment and Media Management, Chicago, IL 60605-1996. Offers arts, entertainment and media management (MA), including media management, music business management, performing arts management, visual arts management. Evening/weekend programs available. *Students:* 68 full-time (53 women), 45 part-time (33 women); includes 44 minority (29 Black or African American, non-Hispanic/Latino; 1 American Indian or Alaska Native, non-Hispanic/Latino; 5 Asian, non-Hispanic/Latino; 9 Hispanic/Latino), 8 international. Average age 28. 252 applicants, 35% accepted, 31 enrolled. In 2010, 52 master's awarded. *Degree requirements:* For master's, thesis, internship. *Entrance requirements:* For master's, self-assessment essay. Additional exam requirements/recommendations for international students: Required—TOEFL (minimum score 550 paper-based; 213 computer-based). *Application deadline:* For fall admission, 1/15 for domestic and international students. Application fee: $55. Electronic applications accepted. *Expenses:* Tuition: Full-time $16,966; part-time $684 per credit. Required fees: $520; $113 per semester. One-time fee: $150 full-time. Tuition and fees vary according to course load and program. *Financial support:* Fellowships, career-related internships or fieldwork, Federal Work-Study, and scholarships/grants available. Support available to part-time students. Financial award application deadline: 8/13; financial award applicants required to submit FAFSA. *Unit head:* Prof. Dawn Larsen, Director of Graduate Studies, 312-369-7639, E-mail: dlarsen@colum.edu. *Application contact:* Cate Lagueux, Director of Graduate Admissions, 312-369-7260, Fax: 312-369-8047, E-mail: clagueux@colum.edu.

Drexel University, Antoinette Westphal College of Media Arts and Design, Program in Arts Administration, Philadelphia, PA 19104-2875. Offers MS. *Accreditation:* NASAD. Part-time and evening/weekend programs available. *Degree requirements:* For master's, thesis, internship. *Entrance requirements:* For master's, GRE, interview, minimum GPA of 3.0, previous course work in arts and business. Additional exam requirements/recommendations for international students: Required—TOEFL. Electronic applications accepted. *Faculty research:* Evaluation of art administration structures, funding for the arts, impact of politics in the arts, computer applications.

Eastern Michigan University, Graduate School, College of Arts and Sciences, Department of Communication, Media and Theatre Arts, Program in Arts Administration, Ypsilanti, MI 48197. Offers theatre arts-arts administration (MA). Part-time and evening/weekend programs available. Postbaccalaureate distance learning degree programs offered (minimal on-campus study). *Students:* 6 full-time (5 women), 15 part-time (12 women); includes 2 minority (1 Black or African American, non-Hispanic/Latino; 1 Hispanic/Latino), 3 international. Average age 31. In 2010, 7 master's awarded. *Entrance requirements:* Additional exam requirements/recommendations for international students: Required—TOEFL. *Application deadline:* Applications are processed on a rolling basis. Application fee: $35. *Financial support:* Fellowships, research assistantships with full tuition reimbursements, teaching assistantships with full tuition reimbursements, career-related internships or fieldwork, Federal Work-Study, institutionally sponsored loans, scholarships/grants, tuition waivers (partial), and unspecified assistantships available. Support available to part-time students. Financial award applicants required to submit FAFSA. *Unit head:* Kenneth Stevens, Coordinator, 734-487-1153, Fax: 734-487-3443, E-mail: ken.stevens@emich.edu. *Application contact:* Kenneth Stevens, Coordinator, 734-487-1153, Fax: 734-487-3443, E-mail: ken.stevens@emich.edu.

Fashion Institute of Technology, School of Graduate Studies, Program in Art Market: Principles and Practices, New York, NY 10001-5992. Offers MA. *Accreditation:* NASAD. *Degree requirements:* For master's, one foreign language, thesis, internship. *Entrance requirements:* For master's, GRE General Test, previous course work in art history, 4 semesters of a foreign language. Additional exam requirements/recommendations for international students: Required—TOEFL (minimum score 550 paper-based; 213 computer-based). Electronic applications accepted.

See Display on next page and Close-Up on page 217.

Florida State University, The Graduate School, College of Music, Tallahassee, FL 32306. Offers accompanying (MM); arts administration (MA); choral conducting (MM); composition (MM, DM); ethnomusicology (MM); general music (MA); instrumental accompanying (MM); instrumental conducting (MM); jazz studies (MM); music education (MM Ed, PhD); music theory (MM, PhD); music therapy (MM); musicology (MM, PhD), including ethnomusicology (PhD), historical musicology; opera (MM); performance (MM, DM); piano pedagogy (MM); piano technology (MA); vocal accompanying (MM). *Accreditation:* NASM. *Faculty:* 88 full-time, 13 part-time/adjunct. *Students:* 406 full-time (211 women); includes 28 Black or African American, non-Hispanic/Latino; 38 Asian, non-Hispanic/Latino; 32 Hispanic/Latino. Average age 26. 525 applicants, 38% accepted, 145 enrolled. In 2010, 102 master's, 41 doctorates awarded. *Degree requirements:* For master's, comprehensive exam (for some programs), thesis (for some programs), departmental qualifying exam; for doctorate, comprehensive exam (for some programs), thesis/dissertation, departmental qualifying exam. *Entrance requirements:* For master's and doctorate, audition, GRE General Test or minimum GPA of 3.0. Additional exam requirements/recommendations for international students: Required—TOEFL (minimum score 550 paper-based; 213 computer-based). *Application deadline:* For fall admission, 7/1 for domestic students, 5/2 for international students; for spring admission, 11/3 for domestic students, 9/1 for international students. Applications are processed on a rolling basis. Application fee: $30. Electronic applications accepted. *Expenses:* Tuition, state resident: full-time $8238.24. *Financial support:* In 2010–11, 225 students received support, including 3 fellowships with full tuition reimbursements available (averaging $15,000 per year), 9 research assistantships with full tuition reimbursements available (averaging $4,000 per year), 173 teaching assistantships with full tuition reimbursements available (averaging $4,000 per year); career-related internships or fieldwork, Federal Work-Study, and tuition waivers (partial) also available. Support available to part-time students. Financial award application deadline: 2/28; financial award applicants required to submit FAFSA. *Unit head:* Dr. Don Gibson, Dean, 850-644-4361, Fax: 850-644-2033. *Application contact:* Dr. Seth Beckman, Senior Associate Dean for Academic Affairs/Director of Graduate Studies, 850-644-5848, Fax: 850-644-2033, E-mail: sbeckman@admin.fsu.edu.

George Mason University, College of Visual and Performing Arts, Program in Arts Management, Fairfax, VA 22030. Offers arts entrepreneurship (Certificate); arts management (MA); fund raising and development in the arts (Certificate); public relations and marketing in the arts (Certificate); special events management in the arts (Certificate). *Accreditation:* NASAD. *Faculty:* 1 (woman) full-time, 9 part-time/adjunct (5 women). *Students:* 50 full-time (44 women), 41 part-time (36 women); includes 4 Black or African American, non-Hispanic/Latino; 2 Asian, non-Hispanic/Latino; 4 Hispanic/Latino; 1 Two or more races, non-Hispanic/Latino, 8 international. Average age 29. 90 applicants, 61% accepted, 29 enrolled. In 2010, 38 master's awarded. *Entrance requirements:* For master's, GRE (recommended), minimum GPA of 3.0, 2 letters of recommendation, personal interview, resume, work experience. Additional exam requirements/recommendations for international students: Required—TOEFL. *Application deadline:* For fall admission, 3/1 priority date for domestic students; for spring admission, 10/1 for domestic students. Applications are processed on a rolling basis. Application fee: $100. Electronic applications accepted. *Expenses:* Tuition, state resident: full-time $8192; part-time $440 per credit hour. Tuition, nonresident: full-time $22,952; part-time $1055 per credit hour. Required fees: $2364; $99 per credit hour. *Financial support:* Application deadline: 3/1. *Faculty research:* Information technology for arts managers, special topics in arts management, directions in gallery management, arts in society, public relations/marketing strategies for art organizations. *Unit head:* William Reeder, Dean, 703-993-8624, Fax: 703-993-8883. *Application contact:* Richard Kamenitzer, Director, 703-993-9194, E-mail: rkamenit@gmu.edu.

Goucher College, Program in Arts Administration, Baltimore, MD 21204-2794. Offers MA. Part-time programs available. Postbaccalaureate distance learning degree programs offered (minimal on-campus study). *Faculty:* 16 part-time/adjunct (10 women). *Students:* 20 full-time (17 women), 7 part-time (6 women); includes 2 Black or African American, non-Hispanic/Latino, 1 international. Average age 35. In 2010, 10 master's awarded. *Degree requirements:* For master's, internship, major paper. *Entrance requirements:* For master's, 2 years of post-baccalaureate work experience. *Application deadline:* For fall admission, 3/15 for domestic students. Application fee: $50. *Expenses:* Contact institution. *Financial support:* Institutionally sponsored loans available. Financial award application deadline: 3/15. *Unit head:* Dr. Ramona Baker, Director, 410-337-6200, Fax: 410-337-6085, E-mail: ramona.baker@goucher.edu.

Arts Administration

Goucher College (continued)
Application contact: Megan Cornett, Director of Marketing and Communications, 410-337-6200, Fax: 410-337-6085, E-mail: mcornett@goucher.edu.

HEC Montreal, School of Business Administration, Diploma Programs in Administration, Program in Management of Cultural Organizations, Montréal, QC H3T 2A7, Canada. Offers Diploma. All courses are given in French. Part-time programs available. *Students:* 33 full-time (30 women), 142 part-time (113 women). 77 applicants, 78% accepted, 49 enrolled. In 2010, 68 Diplomas awarded. *Degree requirements:* For Diploma, one foreign language. *Entrance requirements:* For degree, 2 years of relevant work experience, 2 letters of recommendation. *Application deadline:* For fall admission, 4/15 for domestic and international students; for winter admission, 9/15 for domestic and international students. Application fee: $78 Canadian dollars. Electronic applications accepted. *Expenses:* Tuition, area resident: Part-time $68.93 per credit. Tuition, state resident: full-time $2481.48; part-time $188.92 per credit. Tuition, nonresident: full-time $6801; part-time $482.06 per course. International tuition: $17,354.16 full-time. Required fees: $1309.50; $30.28 per credit. $93.45 per term. Tuition and fees vary according to degree level and program. *Financial support:* Scholarships/grants available. Financial award application deadline: 9/2. *Unit head:* Silvia Ponce, Director, 514-340-6393, Fax: 514-340-6915, E-mail: silvia.ponce@hec.ca. *Application contact:* Marie Deshaies, Senior Student Advisor, 514-340-6135, Fax: 514-340-6411, E-mail: marie.deshaies@hec.ca.

Indiana University Bloomington, School of Public and Environmental Affairs, Program in Arts Administration, Bloomington, IN 47405-7000. Offers MAAA. *Unit head:* Jennifer Forney, Director of Graduate Student Services, 812-855-9485, Fax: 812-856-3665, E-mail: speampo@indiana.edu. *Application contact:* Audrey Whittaker, Admissions Assistant, 812-855-2840, E-mail: speaapps@indiana.edu.

Montclair State University, The Graduate School, School of the Arts, Department of Theatre and Dance, Montclair, NJ 07043-1624. Offers theatre (MA), including arts management, production/stage management, theatre studies. *Accreditation:* NAST. Part-time and evening/weekend programs available. *Faculty:* 15 full-time (8 women), 35 part-time/adjunct (25 women). *Students:* 10 full-time (7 women), 22 part-time (14 women); includes 2 Black or African American, non-Hispanic/Latino; 3 Hispanic/Latino. Average age 28. 22 applicants, 64% accepted, 10 enrolled. In 2010, 8 master's awarded. *Degree requirements:* For master's, comprehensive exam, thesis or alternative. *Entrance requirements:* For master's, GRE General Test, 2 letters of recommendation. Additional exam requirements/recommendations for international students: Required—TOEFL (minimum iBT score of 83) or IELTS. *Application deadline:* For fall admission, 6/1 for international students; for spring admission, 10/1 for international students. Applications are processed on a rolling basis. Application fee: $60. Electronic applications accepted. *Expenses:* Tuition, state resident: part-time $501.34 per credit. Tuition, nonresident: part-time $773.88 per credit. Required fees: $71.15 per credit. *Financial support:* In 2010–11, 3 research assistantships with full tuition reimbursements (averaging $7,000 per year) were awarded; Federal Work-Study, scholarships/grants, and unspecified assistantships also available. Support available to part-time students. Financial award application deadline: 3/1; financial award applicants required to submit FAFSA. *Unit head:* Dr. Eric Diamond, Chairperson, 973-655-4217, E-mail: peterson@mail.montclair.edu. *Application contact:* Amy Aiello, Director of Graduate Admissions and Operations, 973-655-5147, E-mail: petersonj@mail.montclair.edu.

New York University, Steinhardt School of Culture, Education, and Human Development, Department of Art and Art Professions, Program in Visual Arts Administration, New York, NY 10003. Offers for-profit sector (MA); not-for-profit sector (MA). Part-time programs available. *Faculty:* 3 full-time (2 women). *Students:* 79 full-time (73 women), 35 part-time (33 women); includes 4 Black or African American, non-Hispanic/Latino; 7 Asian, non-Hispanic/Latino; 4 Hispanic/Latino, 18 international. Average age 25. 183 applicants, 43% accepted, 59 enrolled. In 2010, 28 master's awarded. *Degree requirements:* For master's, thesis (for some programs). *Entrance requirements:* For master's, interview. Additional exam requirements/recommendations for international students: Required—TOEFL. *Application deadline:* For fall admission, 12/1

priority date for domestic and international students. Applications are processed on a rolling basis. Application fee: $75. Electronic applications accepted. *Financial support:* Career-related internships or fieldwork, Federal Work-Study, institutionally sponsored loans, scholarships/grants, and tuition waivers (partial) available. Support available to part-time students. Financial award application deadline: 2/1; financial award applicants required to submit FAFSA. *Faculty research:* Corporate philanthropy, contemporary art and culture, public art and urban development, cultural policy, arts advocacy. *Unit head:* Sandra Lang, Head, 212-998-5723, Fax: 212-995-4320, E-mail: sandra.lang@nyu.edu. *Application contact:* 212-998-5030, Fax: 212-995-4328, E-mail: steinhardt.gradadmissions@nyu.edu.

New York University, Steinhardt School of Culture, Education, and Human Development, Department of Music and Performing Arts Professions, Program in Performing Arts Administration, New York, NY 10012-1019. Offers MA. Part-time programs available. *Faculty:* 1 full-time (0 women). *Students:* 36 full-time (28 women), 15 part-time (11 women); includes 2 Black or African American, non-Hispanic/Latino; 1 Asian, non-Hispanic/Latino, 12 international. Average age 27. 147 applicants, 45% accepted, 27 enrolled. In 2010, 14 master's awarded. *Degree requirements:* For master's, thesis (for some programs). *Entrance requirements:* For master's, interview. Additional exam requirements/recommendations for international students: Required—TOEFL. *Application deadline:* For fall admission, 12/1 priority date for domestic students, 12/1 for international students. Applications are processed on a rolling basis. Application fee: $75. Electronic applications accepted. *Financial support:* Career-related internships or fieldwork, Federal Work-Study, institutionally sponsored loans, scholarships/grants, and tuition waivers (partial) available. Support available to part-time students. Financial award application deadline: 2/1; financial award applicants required to submit FAFSA. *Faculty research:* Legal dimensions of arts management, global arts management, cultural policy. *Unit head:* Prof. Brann J. Wry, Director, 212-998-5424, Fax: 212-995-4560. *Application contact:* 212-998-5030, Fax: 212-995-4328, E-mail: steinhardt.gradadmissions@nyu.edu.

New York University, Tisch School of the Arts, Program in Arts Politics, New York, NY 10012-1019. Offers MA. *Faculty:* 3 full-time (2 women), 4 part-time/adjunct (3 women). *Students:* 10 full-time (9 women), 1 (woman) part-time; includes 1 Black or African American, non-Hispanic/Latino; 3 Asian, non-Hispanic/Latino. Average age 25. 45 applicants, 58% accepted. *Degree requirements:* For master's, thesis. *Entrance requirements:* For master's, professional resume, writing sample, statement of purpose. Additional exam requirements/recommendations for international students: Required—TOEFL or IELTS. *Application deadline:* For fall admission, 1/1 for domestic and international students. Application fee: $60. *Financial support:* In 2010–11, 2 students received support. Federal Work-Study and scholarships/grants available. Financial award application deadline: 2/15; financial award applicants required to submit FAFSA. *Unit head:* Randy Martin, Director of the program, 212-992-8248. *Application contact:* Dan Sandford, Director of Graduate Admissions, 212-998-1918, Fax: 212-995-4060, E-mail: tisch.gradadmissions@nyu.edu.

The Ohio State University, Graduate School, College of Arts and Sciences, Division of Arts and Humanities, Department of Art Education, Program in Arts Policy and Administration, Columbus, OH 43210. Offers MA. *Faculty:* 14. *Students:* 10 full-time (all women), 1 part-time; includes 1 Black or African American, non-Hispanic/Latino, 2 international. Average age 25. In 2010, 7 master's awarded. *Degree requirements:* For master's, thesis. *Entrance requirements:* For master's, GRE General Test. Additional exam requirements/recommendations for international students: Required—TOEFL (minimum score 600 paper-based; 250 computer-based). *Application deadline:* For fall admission, 8/15 priority date for domestic students, 7/1 priority date for international students; for winter admission, 12/1 priority date for domestic students, 11/1 priority date for international students; for spring admission, 3/1 priority date for domestic students, 2/1 priority date for international students. Applications are processed on a rolling basis. Application fee: $40 ($50 for international students). Electronic applications accepted. *Expenses:* Tuition, state resident: full-time $10,605. Tuition, nonresident: full-time $26,535. Tuition and fees vary according to course load and program. *Financial support:* Fellowships, career-related internships or fieldwork and unspecified assistantships available.

Support available to part-time students. Financial award application deadline: 4/5; financial award applicants required to submit FAFSA. *Faculty research:* Public policy and advocacy. *Unit head:* Christine Ballengee-Morris, Graduate Studies Committee Chair, 614-292-1230, E-mail: morris.390@osu.edu. *Application contact:* 614-292-9444, Fax: 614-292-3895, E-mail: domestic.grad@osu.edu.

Pratt Institute, School of Art and Design, Program in Arts and Cultural Management, New York, NY 10011. Offers MPS. Part-time and evening/weekend programs available. *Faculty:* 1 (woman) full-time, 13 part-time/adjunct (9 women). *Students:* 49 full-time (42 women), 4 part-time (all women); includes 4 Black or African American, non-Hispanic/Latino; 4 Asian, non-Hispanic/Latino; 4 Hispanic/Latino; 1 Two or more races, non-Hispanic/Latino, 15 international. Average age 28. 118 applicants, 36% accepted, 26 enrolled. In 2010, 29 master's awarded. *Degree requirements:* For master's, thesis. *Entrance requirements:* For master's, letters of recommendation, portfolio. Additional exam requirements/recommendations for international students: Required—TOEFL (minimum score 600 paper-based; 250 computer-based; 100 iBT). *Application deadline:* For fall admission, 1/5 for domestic and international students; for spring admission, 10/1 for domestic and international students. Application fee: $50 ($90 for international students). Electronic applications accepted. *Expenses:* Tuition: Full-time $22,734; part-time $1263 per credit. Required fees: $1280. *Financial support:* Career-related internships or fieldwork, Federal Work-Study, institutionally sponsored loans, scholarships/grants, health care benefits, and unspecified assistantships available. Support available to part-time students. Financial award application deadline: 2/1; financial award applicants required to submit FAFSA. *Unit head:* Monica Shay, Director, 212-647-7560, E-mail: mshay@pratt.edu. *Application contact:* Young Hah, Director of Graduate Admissions, 718-636-3683, Fax: 718-399-4242, E-mail: yhah@pratt.edu.

Pratt Institute, School of Art and Design, Program in Design Management, New York, NY 10011. Offers MPS. Part-time programs available. *Faculty:* 2 full-time (both women), 8 part-time/adjunct (4 women). *Students:* 46 full-time (31 women), 1 (woman) part-time; includes 4 Black or African American, non-Hispanic/Latino; 6 Asian, non-Hispanic/Latino; 1 Hispanic/Latino; 1 Two or more races, non-Hispanic/Latino, 15 international. Average age 31. 102 applicants, 53% accepted, 21 enrolled. In 2010, 20 master's awarded. *Degree requirements:* For master's, thesis. *Entrance requirements:* For master's, letters of recommendation, portfolio. Additional exam requirements/recommendations for international students: Required—TOEFL (minimum score 600 paper-based; 250 computer-based; 100 iBT). *Application deadline:* For fall admission, 1/5 for domestic and international students; for spring admission, 10/1 for domestic and international students. Application fee: $50 ($90 for international students). Electronic applications accepted. *Expenses:* Tuition: Full-time $22,734; part-time $1263 per credit. Required fees: $1280. *Financial support:* Career-related internships or fieldwork, Federal Work-Study, institutionally sponsored loans, scholarships/grants, health care benefits, and unspecified assistantships available. Support available to part-time students. Financial award application deadline: 2/1; financial award applicants required to submit FAFSA. *Unit head:* Mary McBride, Chairperson, 212-647-7538, E-mail: mmcb1033@pratt.edu. *Application contact:* Young Hah, Director of Graduate Admissions, 718-636-3683, Fax: 718-399-4242, E-mail: yhah@pratt.edu.

See Display on page 92 and Close-Up on page 131.

Regis University, College for Professional Studies, School of Humanities and Social Sciences, MA Program, Denver, CO 80221-1099. Offers communication (MA); fine arts (Certificate); interdisciplinary studies (MA); mediation and conflict resolution (Certificate); psychology (MA); social justice, peace, and reconciliation (Certificate); technical communication (Certificate). Program also offered in Henderson and Las Vegas (Summerlin), NV. Part-time and evening/weekend programs available. Postbaccalaureate distance learning degree programs offered (minimal on-campus study). *Degree requirements:* For master's, thesis, research project. *Entrance requirements:* For master's, resume, recommendations. Additional exam requirements/recommendations for international students: Required—TOEFL (minimum score 213 computer-based), TWE (minimum score 5). Electronic applications accepted. *Expenses:* Contact institution. *Faculty research:* Independent/nonresidential graduate study: new methods and models, adult learning and the capstone experience, Goal Setting, behavior of Adult students, Innovative Studies for Community Colleges.

Rhode Island College, School of Graduate Studies, Faculty of Arts and Sciences, Department of Art, Providence, RI 02908-1991. Offers art education (MA, MAT); media studies (MA). *Accreditation:* NASAD (one or more programs are accredited). Part-time and evening/weekend programs available. *Faculty:* 10 full-time (4 women), 1 part-time/adjunct (0 women). *Students:* 7 full-time (4 women), 17 part-time (13 women). Average age 38. In 2010, 9 master's awarded. *Degree requirements:* For master's, thesis. *Entrance requirements:* For master's, GRE General Test, portfolio (MA), 3 letters of recommendation, interview. Additional exam requirements/recommendations for international students: Recommended—TOEFL (minimum score 550 paper-based; 213 computer-based; 79 iBT). *Application deadline:* For fall admission, 3/1 for domestic students. Applications are processed on a rolling basis. Application fee: $50. *Expenses:* Tuition, state resident: full-time $8208; part-time $342 per credit hour. Tuition, nonresident: full-time $16,080; part-time $670 per credit hour. Required fees: $554; $20 per credit. $72 per term. *Financial support:* Teaching assistantships with full tuition reimbursements, career-related internships or fieldwork, Federal Work-Study, scholarships/grants, health care benefits, and unspecified assistantships available. Support available to part-time students. Financial award application deadline: 5/15; financial award applicants required to submit FAFSA. *Unit head:* Prof. William Martin, Chair, 401-456-8054. *Application contact:* Graduate Studies, 401-456-8700.

Ryerson University, School of Graduate Studies, Program in Photographic Preservation and Collections Management, Toronto, ON M5B 2K3, Canada. Offers MA.

Saint Mary's University of Minnesota, Schools of Graduate and Professional Programs, Graduate School of Business and Technology, Arts and Cultural Management Program, Winona, MN 55987-1399. Offers MA. *Unit head:* Paula Justich, Director, 612-728-5165, Fax: 612-728-5121, E-mail: pjustich@smumn.edu. *Application contact:* Yasin Alsaidi, Director of Admissions for Graduate and Professional Programs, 612-728-5207, Fax: 612-728-5121, E-mail: yalsaidi@smumn.edu.

St. Thomas University, School of Leadership Studies, Program in Art Management, Miami Gardens, FL 33054-6459. Offers MA.

Savannah College of Art and Design, Graduate School, Program in Arts Administration, Savannah, GA 31402-3146. Offers MA. Part-time programs available. Postbaccalaureate distance learning degree programs offered (no on-campus study). *Faculty:* 4 full-time (1 woman), 1 (woman) part-time/adjunct. *Students:* 64 full-time (57 women), 50 part-time (42 women); includes 17 Black or African American, non-Hispanic/Latino; 2 Asian, non-Hispanic/Latino; 1 Two or more races, non-Hispanic/Latino, 4 international. Average age 29. In 2010, 15 master's awarded. *Degree requirements:* For master's, thesis. *Entrance requirements:* For master's, interview. Additional exam requirements/recommendations for international students: Required—TOEFL (minimum score 450 paper-based; 133 computer-based). *Application deadline:* For fall admission, 4/1 priority date for domestic and international students. Application fee: $35. *Expenses:* Tuition: Full-time $29,520; part-time $3280 per quarter. Tuition and fees vary according to campus/location. *Financial support:* Fellowships, career-related internships or fieldwork, Federal Work-Study, and scholarships/grants available. Financial award application deadline: 4/1; financial award applicants required to submit FAFSA. *Unit head:* James Marchant, Coordinator, 404-253-5481, E-mail: jmarchan@scad.edu. *Application contact:* Elizabeth Mathis, Director of Graduate Recruitment, 912-525-5965, Fax: 912-525-5985, E-mail: emathis@scad.edu.

School of the Art Institute of Chicago, Graduate Division, Program in Arts Administration and Policy, Chicago, IL 60603-3103. Offers MAAAP. *Accreditation:* NASAD. *Degree requirements:* For master's, thesis, telephone interview. *Entrance requirements:* Additional exam requirements/recommendations for international students: Required—TOEFL, IELTS. *Faculty research:* Latin American artists, activist art, community-based art.

See Close-Up on page 225.

Shenandoah University, Shenandoah Conservatory, Winchester, VA 22601-5195. Offers arts management (MS); church music (MM, Certificate); collaborative piano (MM); composition (MM); conducting (MM); music education (MME, DMA); music therapy (MMT, Certificate); pedagogy (MM, DMA); performance (MM, DMA, Artist Diploma). *Accreditation:* NASM. *Faculty:* 38 full-time (15 women), 14 part-time/adjunct (5 women). *Students:* 63 full-time (38 women), 119 part-time (76 women); includes 18 minority (7 Black or African American, non-Hispanic/Latino; 5 Asian, non-Hispanic/Latino; 5 Hispanic/Latino; 1 Two or more races, non-Hispanic/Latino), 40 international. Average age 34. 109 applicants, 75% accepted, 51 enrolled. In 2010, 29 master's, 12 doctorates, 14 other advanced degrees awarded. *Degree requirements:* For master's, comprehensive exam (for some programs), thesis (for some programs), internship (MS), recital (MM), research teaching project or thesis (MME), project (MA); for doctorate, comprehensive exam, thesis/dissertation (for some programs), dissertation or teaching project, recital; for other advanced degree, research project, recital. *Entrance requirements:* For master's, audition, minimum GPA of 2.5, writing sample, resume; for doctorate, audition, minimum GPA of 3.25, 2 letters of recommendation, writing sample, resume; for other advanced degree, bachelor's or master's degree; minimum GPA of 2.5. Additional exam requirements/recommendations for international students: Required—TOEFL (minimum score 550 paper-based; 213 computer-based; 79 iBT), IELTS (minimum score 6.5), Sakae Institute of Study Abroad (550). *Application deadline:* Applications are processed on a rolling basis. Application fee: $30. Electronic applications accepted. *Expenses:* Tuition: Full-time $17,352; part-time $723 per credit. Tuition and fees vary according to course load and program. *Financial support:* Application deadline: 3/15. *Unit head:* Dr. Michael J. Stepniak, Dean, 540-665-4600, Fax: 540-665-5402, E-mail: mstepnia@su.edu. *Application contact:* David Anthony, Dean of Admissions, 540-665-4581, Fax: 540-665-4627, E-mail: admit@su.edu.

Sotheby's Institute of Art–London, Graduate Programs, London, United Kingdom. Offers art business (MA); contemporary art (MA); contemporary design (MA); East Asian art (MA); fine and decorative art (MA); photography (MA).

Sotheby's Institute of Art–New York, Graduate Programs, New York, NY 10021. Offers American fine and decorative art (MA); art business (MA); contemporary art (MA). *Accreditation:* NASAD.

Southern Methodist University, Meadows School of the Arts, Division of Arts Administration, Dallas, TX 75275. Offers MA/MBA. *Faculty:* 3 full-time (all women), 1 (woman) part-time/adjunct. *Students:* 21 full-time (16 women); includes 1 Black or African American, non-Hispanic/Latino; 1 Asian, non-Hispanic/Latino, 1 international. Average age 26. 18 applicants, 72% accepted, 7 enrolled. *Entrance requirements:* Additional exam requirements/recommendations for international students: Required—TOEFL (minimum score 600 paper-based; 250 computer-based; 100 iBT). *Application deadline:* For fall admission, 1/15 priority date for domestic and international students. Applications are processed on a rolling basis. Application fee: $75. Electronic applications accepted. *Unit head:* Dr. P. Gregory Warden, Interim Chair, 214-768-3425, E-mail: lhilliar@smu.edu. *Application contact:* Lynette Hilliard, Assistant Director, 214-768-3425, E-mail: ihilliar@smu.edu.

Southern Utah University, College of Performing and Visual Arts, Program in Arts Administration, Cedar City, UT 84720-2498. Offers MFA. *Faculty:* 1 full-time (0 women), 3 part-time/adjunct (0 women). *Students:* 7 full-time (6 women). Average age 26. 25 applicants, 28% accepted, 7 enrolled. In 2010, 5 master's awarded. *Entrance requirements:* For master's, GRE General Test, interview, 3 letters of recommendation, resume, minimum GPA of 3.0. *Application deadline:* For fall admission, 3/31 for domestic students. Applications are processed on a rolling basis. Application fee: $50 ($65 for international students). Electronic applications accepted. *Financial support:* In 2010–11, 7 fellowships with full tuition reimbursements (averaging $8,000 per year) were awarded. *Unit head:* Shauna Mendini, Interim Dean, 435-865-8554, Fax: 435-865-8580, E-mail: mendini_s@suu.edu. *Application contact:* Matt Neves, Director, 435-586-7873, Fax: 435-865-8657, E-mail: neves@suu.edu.

Teachers College, Columbia University, Graduate Faculty of Education, Department of Arts and Humanities, Program in Arts Administration, New York, NY 10027-6696. Offers MA. *Faculty:* 2 full-time (1 woman), 8 part-time/adjunct (3 women). *Students:* 58 full-time (52 women), 15 part-time (10 women); includes 9 minority (3 Black or African American, non-Hispanic/Latino; 4 Asian, non-Hispanic/Latino; 1 Hispanic/Latino; 1 Two or more races, non-Hispanic/Latino), 22 international. Average age 28. 143 applicants, 32% accepted, 31 enrolled. In 2010, 27 master's awarded. *Degree requirements:* For master's, thesis, internship. *Entrance requirements:* For master's, GRE, approximately 3 years of related experience. Additional exam requirements/recommendations for international students: Required—TOEFL (minimum score 600 paper-based). *Application deadline:* For fall admission, 1/15 priority date for domestic students. Application fee: $65. *Expenses:* Tuition: Full-time $28,272; part-time $1178 per credit. Required fees: $756; $378 per semester. *Financial support:* Career-related internships or fieldwork, Federal Work-Study, institutionally sponsored loans, tuition waivers (partial), and unspecified assistantships available. Financial award application deadline: 2/1. *Faculty research:* Artists' career development, arts law, American culture, strategic management, international training. *Unit head:* Joan Jeffri, Director, 212-678-3268, Fax: 212-678-4048, E-mail: arad@columbia.edu. *Application contact:* Joan Jeffri, Director, 212-678-3268, Fax: 212-678-4048, E-mail: arad@columbia.edu.

Temple University, Tyler School of Art, Department of Art History, Philadelphia, PA 19122-6096. Offers MA, PhD. Part-time programs available. *Faculty:* 11 full-time (7 women). *Students:* 52 full-time (46 women), 8 part-time (all women); includes 1 Asian, non-Hispanic/Latino; 1 Hispanic/Latino, 2 international. 62 applicants, 65% accepted, 18 enrolled. In 2010, 13 master's, 1 doctorate awarded. Terminal master's awarded for partial completion of doctoral program. *Degree requirements:* For master's, 2 foreign languages, thesis, comprehensive slide exam; for doctorate, thesis/dissertation, qualifying exam. *Entrance requirements:* For master's, GRE General Test, minimum GPA of 3.0; for doctorate, MA in art history. Additional exam requirements/recommendations for international students: Required—TOEFL. *Application deadline:* For fall admission, 4/15 for domestic students, 12/15 for international students; for spring admission, 11/15 for domestic students, 8/1 for international students. Applications are processed on a rolling basis. Application fee: $50. Electronic applications accepted. *Financial support:* Fellowships, research assistantships with full tuition reimbursements, teaching assistantships with full tuition reimbursements, career-related internships or fieldwork, institutionally sponsored loans, and technical assistantships available. Financial award application deadline: 1/15. *Faculty research:* Aegean, Greek, and Roman art; early Christian art; medieval art and architecture; Renaissance and Baroque painting, sculpture, and architecture; nineteenth and twentieth century painting and sculpture. *Unit head:* Dr. Gerald Silk, Chair, 215-204-7837, Fax: 215-204-6951, E-mail: gsilk@temple.edu. *Application contact:* Dr. Gerald Silk, Chair, 215-204-7837, Fax: 215-204-6951, E-mail: gsilk@temple.edu.

Universidad del Turabo, Graduate Programs, School of Social Sciences and Humanities, Programs in Public Affairs, Program in Arts Administration, Gurabo, PR 00778-3030. Offers MPA.

The University of Akron, Graduate School, College of Creative and Professional Arts, School of Dance, Theatre, and Arts Administration, Program in Arts Administration, Akron, OH 44325. Offers MA. *Accreditation:* NASAD. *Students:* 25 full-time (21 women), 6 part-time (5 women); includes 1 Black or African American, non-Hispanic/Latino; 1 Hispanic/Latino, 5 international. Average age 29. 27 applicants, 70% accepted, 9 enrolled. In 2010, 3 master's awarded. *Degree requirements:* For master's, thesis optional. *Entrance requirements:* For master's, minimum GPA of 2.75, 300 word statement of intent summarizing student background and

Arts Administration

The University of Akron (continued)

outlining career goals. Additional exam requirements/recommendations for international students: Required—TOEFL (minimum score 550 paper-based; 213 computer-based; 79 iBT). *Application deadline:* For fall admission, 3/15 priority date for domestic and international students. Application fee: $30 ($40 for international students). Electronic applications accepted. *Expenses:* Tuition, state resident: full-time $6800; part-time $378 per credit hour. Tuition, nonresident: full-time $11,644; part-time $647 per credit hour. Required fees: $1265. One-time fee: $30 full-time. *Application contact:* Durand Pope, Coordinator, 330-972-5380, E-mail: dpope@uakron.edu.

University of Cincinnati, Graduate School, College-Conservatory of Music, Divisions of Opera, Musical Theater, Drama, and Arts Administration, Cincinnati, OH 45221. Offers arts administration (MA); directing (MFA); theater design and production (MFA); voice and opera (MM, DMA); MBA/MA. *Accreditation:* NAST (one or more programs are accredited). *Degree requirements:* For master's, final project. *Entrance requirements:* For master's, GMAT (MA), audition/interview. Additional exam requirements/recommendations for international students: Required—TOEFL (minimum score 520 paper-based; 190 computer-based). Electronic applications accepted.

University of Denver, University College, Denver, CO 80208. Offers arts and culture (MLS, Certificate), including art, literature, and culture, arts development and program management (Certificate), creative writing; environmental policy and management (MAS, Certificate), including energy and sustainability (Certificate), environmental assessment of nuclear power (Certificate), environmental health and safety (Certificate), environmental management, natural resource management (Certificate); geographic information systems (MAS, Certificate); global affairs (MLS, Certificate), including translation studies, world history and culture; healthcare leadership (MPH, Certificate), including healthcare policy, law, and ethics, medical and healthcare information technologies, strategic management of healthcare; information and communications technology (MCIS, Certificate), including database design and administration (Certificate), geographic information systems (MCIS), information security systems security (Certificate), information systems security (MCIS), project management (MCIS, MPS, Certificate), software design and administration (Certificate), software design and programming (MCIS), technology management, telecommunications technology (MCIS), Web design and development; leadership and organizations (MPS, Certificate), including human capital in organizations, philanthropic leadership, project management (MCIS, MPS, Certificate), strategic innovation and change; organizational and professional communication (MPS, Certificate), including alternative dispute resolution, organizational communication, organizational development and training, public relations and marketing; security management (MAS, Certificate), including emergency planning and response, information security (MAS), organizational security; strategic human resource management (MPS, Certificate), including global human resources (MPS), human resource management and development (MPS). Part-time and evening/weekend programs available. Postbaccalaureate distance learning degree programs offered (no on-campus study). *Faculty:* 7 full-time (2 women), 212 part-time/adjunct (83 women). *Students:* 52 full-time (19 women), 1,044 part-time (625 women); includes 196 minority (81 Black or African American, non-Hispanic/Latino; 7 American Indian or Alaska Native, non-Hispanic/Latino; 30 Asian, non-Hispanic/Latino; 66 Hispanic/Latino; 3 Native Hawaiian or other Pacific Islander, non-Hispanic/Latino; 9 Two or more races, non-Hispanic/Latino), 76 international. Average age 36. 488 applicants, 91% accepted, 339 enrolled. In 2010, 286 master's, 130 other advanced degrees awarded. *Entrance requirements:* Additional exam requirements/recommendations for international students: Required—TOEFL (minimum score 550 paper-based; 80 iBT). *Application deadline:* For fall admission, 6/22 priority date for domestic students, 6/10 priority date for international students; for winter admission, 9/15 priority date for domestic students, 9/6 priority date for international students; for spring admission, 2/3 priority date for domestic students, 12/15 priority date for international students. Applications are processed on a rolling basis. Application fee: $75. Electronic applications accepted. *Expenses:* Contact institution. *Financial support:* Applicants required to submit FAFSA. *Unit head:* Dr. James Davis, Dean, 303-871-2291, Fax: 303-871-4047, E-mail: jdavis@du.edu. *Application contact:* Information Contact, 303-871-3155, Fax: 303-871-4047, E-mail: ucolinfo@du.edu.

University of Florida, Graduate School, Warrington College of Business Administration, Hough Graduate School of Business, Programs in Business Administration, Gainesville, FL 32611. Offers accounting (MBA); arts administration (MBA); business strategy and public policy (MBA); competitive strategy (MBA); decision and information sciences (MBA); electronic commerce (MBA); finance (MBA); general business (MBA); global management (MBA); Graham-Buffett security analysis (MBA); health administration (MBA); human resources management (MBA); international studies (MBA); Latin American business (MBA); management (MBA); marketing (MBA); sports administration (MBA); JD/MBA; MBA/MS; MBA/PhD; MBA/Pharm D; MD/MBA. *Accreditation:* AACSB. Part-time and evening/weekend programs available. *Faculty:* 71 full-time (10 women). *Students:* 187 full-time (44 women), 305 part-time (83 women); includes 25 Black or African American, non-Hispanic/Latino; 2 American Indian or Alaska Native, non-Hispanic/Latino; 52 Asian, non-Hispanic/Latino; 54 Hispanic/Latino, 11 international. Average age 31. 919 applicants, 33% accepted, 225 enrolled. In 2010, 492 master's awarded. *Degree requirements:* For master's, capstone course. *Entrance requirements:* For master's, GMAT, minimum GPA of 3.0, interview. Additional exam requirements/recommendations for international students: Required—TOEFL (minimum score 550 paper-based; 213 computer-based; 80 iBT), IELTS (minimum score 6). *Application deadline:* For fall admission, 7/1 for domestic students, 1/1 for international students; for spring admission, 12/1 for domestic and international students. Applications are processed on a rolling basis. Application fee: $30. Electronic applications accepted. *Expenses:* Tuition, state resident: full-time $10,915.92. Tuition, nonresident: full-time $28,309. *Financial support:* In 2010–11, 1 student received support, including 1 teaching assistantship (averaging $20,600 per year); career-related internships or fieldwork, scholarships/grants, and unspecified assistantships also available. Support available to part-time students. Financial award applicants required to submit FAFSA. *Faculty research:* Accounting, finance, insurance, management, real estate, urban analysis marketing. *Unit head:* Prof. Alexander D. Sevilla, Assistant Dean and Director MBA Programs, 352-273-3252 Ext. 1206, E-mail: alex.sevilla@warrington.ufl.edu. *Application contact:* Prof. Kelli Gust, Associate Director of MBA Programs, 352-273-3255, Fax: 352-392-8791, E-mail: kelly.gust@ warrington.ufl.edu.

The University of Manchester, School of Arts, Histories and Cultures, Manchester, United Kingdom. Offers anthropology, media and performance (PhD); applied theatre professional (PhD); archaeology (PhD); art history and visual studies (PhD); arts management and cultural policy (PhD); classics and ancient history (PhD); composition (PhD); creative writing (PhD); drama (PhD); economic and social history (PhD); electroacoustic composition (PhD); English and American studies (PhD); history (PhD); humanitarianism and conflict response (PhD); museology (PhD); music (PhD); musicology (PhD); religions and theology (PhD).

University of New Orleans, Graduate School, College of Liberal Arts, Program in Arts Administration, New Orleans, LA 70148. Offers MA. Part-time programs available. *Degree requirements:* For master's, internship. *Entrance requirements:* For master's, GMAT, GRE General Test. Additional exam requirements/recommendations for international students: Required—TOEFL (minimum score 550 paper-based; 213 computer-based; 79 iBT). Electronic applications accepted.

The University of North Carolina at Charlotte, Graduate School, College of Arts and Sciences, Department of Political Science, Charlotte, NC 28223-0001. Offers emergency management (Certificate); non-profit management (Certificate); public administration (MPA, PhD), including arts administration (MPA), emergency management (MPA), non-profit management (MPA), public finance (MPA), urban management and policy (PhD); public finance (Certificate); public policy (PhD); urban management and policy (Certificate). *Accreditation:* NASPAA. Part-time and evening/weekend programs available. *Faculty:* 19 full-time (8 women), 3 part-time/adjunct (2 women). *Students:* 51 full-time (37 women), 75 part-time (49 women); includes 32 minority (26 Black or African American, non-Hispanic/Latino; 1 Asian, non-Hispanic/Latino; 2 Hispanic/Latino; 3 Two or more races, non-Hispanic/Latino), 11 international. Average age 29. 99 applicants, 72% accepted, 42 enrolled. In 2010, 15 master's, 5 doctorates awarded. *Degree requirements:* For master's, thesis or alternative; for doctorate, thesis/dissertation. *Entrance requirements:* For master's, GRE General Test or MAT, minimum GPA of 3.0 in undergraduate major, 2.75 overall. Additional exam requirements/recommendations for international students: Required—TOEFL (minimum score 557 paper-based; 220 computer-based; 83 iBT). *Application deadline:* For fall admission, 7/1 for domestic students, 5/1 for international students; for spring admission, 11/1 for domestic students, 10/1 for international students. Applications are processed on a rolling basis. Application fee: $55. Electronic applications accepted. *Expenses:* Tuition, state resident: full-time $3464. Tuition, nonresident: full-time $14,297. Required fees: $2094. Tuition and fees vary according to course load. *Financial support:* In 2010–11, 22 students received support, including 16 research assistantships (averaging $6,943 per year), 6 teaching assistantships (averaging $9,380 per year); career-related internships or fieldwork, Federal Work-Study, institutionally sponsored loans, scholarships/grants, unspecified assistantships, and administrative assistantship also available. Support available to part-time students. Financial award application deadline: 4/1; financial award applicants required to submit FAFSA. *Faculty research:* Terrorism, public administration, nonprofit and arts administration, educational policy, social policy. Total annual research expenditures: $242,404. *Unit head:* Dr. Theodore S. Arrington, Chair, 704-687-2571, Fax: 704-687-3497, E-mail: tarrngtn@uncc.edu. *Application contact:* Kathy B. Giddings, Director of Graduate Admissions, 704-687-5503, Fax: 704-687-3279, E-mail: gradadm@uncc.edu.

University of North Carolina School of the Arts, School of Design and Production, Winston-Salem, NC 27127-2188. Offers costume design (MFA); costume technology (MFA); performance arts management (MFA); scene design (MFA); scene painting/properties (MFA); sound design (MFA); stage automation (MFA); technical direction (MFA); wig and make-up design (MFA). *Faculty:* 19 full-time (4 women), 16 part-time/adjunct (6 women). *Students:* 73 full-time (50 women); includes 3 Black or African American, non-Hispanic/Latino; 2 American Indian or Alaska Native, non-Hispanic/Latino; 3 Asian, non-Hispanic/Latino; 2 Hispanic/Latino, 3 international. Average age 25. 86 applicants, 77% accepted, 48 enrolled. In 2010, 21 master's awarded. *Degree requirements:* For master's, thesis (for some programs), project. *Entrance requirements:* For master's, interview, portfolio. Additional exam requirements/recommendations for international students: Required—TOEFL. *Application deadline:* For fall admission, 4/1 priority date for domestic students. Applications are processed on a rolling basis. Application fee: $60 ($100 for international students). Electronic applications accepted. *Expenses:* Tuition, state resident: full-time $4946. Tuition, nonresident: full-time $17,253. Required fees: $2092. *Financial support:* In 2010–11, 2 teaching assistantships with partial tuition reimbursements (averaging $1,500 per year) were awarded; career-related internships or fieldwork, Federal Work-Study, unspecified assistantships, and Academic Common Market also available. Support available to part-time students. Financial award application deadline: 3/15; financial award applicants required to submit FAFSA. *Unit head:* Joseph A. Tilford, Dean, 336-770-3214 Ext. 103, Fax: 336-770-3213, E-mail: tilford@uncsa.edu. *Application contact:* Sheeler Lawson, Director of Admissions, 336-770-3290, Fax: 336-770-3370, E-mail: admissions@uncsa.edu.

University of Oregon, Graduate School, School of Architecture and Allied Arts, Program in Arts and Administration, Eugene, OR 97403. Offers arts management (MA, MS); media management (MA, MS). *Degree requirements:* For master's, summer internship, thesis/project. *Entrance requirements:* For master's, minimum GPA of 3.0; bachelor's degree in history, practice of visual, performing arts or other related degree. Additional exam requirements/recommendations for international students: Required—TOEFL. *Faculty research:* Museum education, arts program evaluation, community arts, information management, arts marketing.

University of Southern California, Graduate School, Roski School of Fine Arts, Art and Curatorial Practices in the Public Sphere Program, Los Angeles, CA 90089. Offers MA. *Faculty:* 3 full-time (2 women), 8 part-time/adjunct (5 women). *Students:* 22 full-time (20 women); includes 8 minority (1 Black or African American, non-Hispanic/Latino; 2 Asian, non-Hispanic/Latino; 5 Hispanic/Latino). 52 applicants, 37% accepted, 9 enrolled. In 2010, 12 master's awarded. *Degree requirements:* For master's, thesis, practicum exhibition. *Entrance requirements:* For master's, GRE, personal statement, writing sample, three letters of recommendation. Additional exam requirements/recommendations for international students: Required—TOEFL (minimum score 600 paper-based; 250 computer-based; 100 iBT). *Application deadline:* For fall admission, 2/1 priority date for domestic and international students. Applications are processed on a rolling basis. Application fee: $85. Electronic applications accepted. *Expenses:* Tuition: Full-time $31,240; part-time $1420 per unit. Required fees: $600. One-time fee: $35 full-time. Full-time tuition and fees vary according to degree level and program. *Financial support:* In 2010–11, 12 students received support, including 12 fellowships (averaging $3,500 per year); career-related internships or fieldwork, Federal Work-Study, scholarships/grants, traineeships, and faculty assistantships also available. Financial award application deadline: 2/1; financial award applicants required to submit FAFSA. *Faculty research:* Curatorial studies, exhibition histories, modern and contemporary art, public art. *Unit head:* Dr. Rhea Anastas, Interim Director, 213-743-4562, Fax: 213-743-4563. *Application contact:* Elizabeth Lovins, Program Coordinator, 213-743-8540, Fax: 213-743-4563, E-mail: lovins@usc.edu.

University of Wisconsin–Madison, Graduate School, Wisconsin School of Business, Wisconsin Full-Time MBA Program, Madison, WI 53706-1380. Offers applied security analysis (MBA); arts administration (MBA); brand and product management (MBA); corporate finance and investment banking (MBA); entrepreneurial management (MBA); marketing research (MBA); operations and technology management (MBA); real estate (MBA); risk management and insurance (MBA); strategic human resource management (MBA); strategic management in the life and engineering sciences (MBA); supply chain management (MBA). *Faculty:* 32 full-time (4 women), 17 part-time/adjunct (3 women). *Students:* 242 full-time (74 women); includes 16 Black or African American, non-Hispanic/Latino; 3 American Indian or Alaska Native, non-Hispanic/Latino; 16 Asian, non-Hispanic/Latino; 12 Hispanic/Latino, 29 international. Average age 28. 526 applicants, 32% accepted, 117 enrolled. In 2010, 106 master's awarded. *Entrance requirements:* For master's, GMAT, bachelor's or equivalent degree, 2 years of work experience, letters of recommendation. Additional exam requirements/recommendations for international students: Required—TOEFL (minimum score 600 paper-based; 250 computer-based; 100 iBT), IELTS. *Application deadline:* For fall admission, 11/4 for domestic students, 11/1 for international students; for winter admission, 2/5 for domestic and international students; for spring admission, 5/15 for domestic students, 4/5 for international students. Applications are processed on a rolling basis. Application fee: $56. Electronic applications accepted. *Expenses:* Tuition, state resident: full-time $9887; part-time $617.96 per credit. Tuition, nonresident: full-time $24,054; part-time $1503.40 per credit. Required fees: $67.63 per credit. Tuition and fees vary according to reciprocity agreements. *Financial support:* In 2010–11, 103 students received support, including 13 fellowships with full and partial tuition reimbursements available (averaging $15,000 per year), 53 research assistantships with full tuition reimbursements available (averaging $8,000 per year), 35 teaching assistantships with full tuition reimbursements available (averaging $11,000 per year); scholarships/grants, health care benefits, and unspecified assistantships also available. Financial award application deadline: 4/5; financial award applicants required to submit FAFSA. *Faculty research:* Market consequences of International Financial Reporting Standards (IFRS), inter-firm relationships and strategic partnerships, application of Bayesian statistical methods and applied probability models to understanding individuals' behaviors in the context of customer relationship management (CRM) applications, liquidity provision and the structure of financial markets, strategic management of global startups. *Unit head:* Dr. Kenneth A. Kavajecz, Associate Dean of Master's Programs, 608-265-3494, Fax: 608-265-4192, E-mail: kkavajecz@bus.wisc.edu. *Application contact:* Maria Reis, Assistant Director of MBA Marketing and Recruiting, 608-262-4000, Fax: 608-265-4192, E-mail: mreis@bus.wisc.edu.

Valparaiso University, Graduate School, Program in Arts and Entertainment Administration, Valparaiso, IN 46383. Offers MA. Part-time and evening/weekend programs available. *Students:* 1 full-time (0 women), 1 (woman) part-time; both minorities (1 Hispanic/Latino; 1 Two or more races, non-Hispanic/Latino). Average age 37. *Degree requirements:* For master's, internship or research project. *Entrance requirements:* Additional exam requirements/recommendations for international students: Required—TOEFL (minimum score 550 paper-based; 213 computer-based; 80 iBT). *Application deadline:* Applications are processed on a rolling basis. Application fee: $30 ($50 for international students). Electronic applications accepted. *Expenses:* Tuition: Full-time $9540; part-time $530 per credit hour. Required fees: $292; $95 per semester. Tuition and fees vary according to program. *Financial support:* Available to part-time students. Applicants required to submit FAFSA. *Unit head:* Dr. David L. Rowland, Dean, Graduate School and Continuing Education/Associate Provost, 219-464-5313, Fax: 219-464-5381, E-mail: david.rowland@valpo.edu. *Application contact:* Laura Groth, Coordinator of Student Services and Support, 219-464-5313, Fax: 219-464-5381, E-mail: laura.groth@valpo.edu.

Webster University, Leigh Gerdine College of Fine Arts, Department of Art, Program in Arts Management and Leadership, St. Louis, MO 63119-3194. Offers MFA. Part-time and evening/weekend programs available. *Degree requirements:* For master's, thesis. *Entrance requirements:* For master's, GRE, BA or BFA in related field, interview. *Expenses:* Tuition: Part-time $585 per credit hour. Tuition and fees vary according to degree level, campus/location and program.

Winthrop University, College of Visual and Performing Arts, Department of Art, Rock Hill, SC 29733. Offers art (MFA); art administration (MA); art education (MA). *Accreditation:* NASAD. Part-time programs available. *Degree requirements:* For master's, thesis, documented exhibit, oral exam. *Entrance requirements:* For master's, GRE General Test or MAT, PRAXIS (MA), minimum GPA of 3.0, resume, slide portfolio, teaching certificate (MA). Electronic applications accepted.

Art Therapy

Adler Graduate School, Program in Adlerian Counseling and Psychotherapy, Richfield, MN 55423. Offers art therapy (MA); clinical mental health counseling (MA); marriage and family therapy (MA); non-clinical Adlerian studies (MA); online Adlerian studies (MA); organizational wellness and transformation (MA); parent coaching (Certificate); personal and professional life coaching (Certificate); school counseling (MA). Part-time and evening/weekend programs available. *Faculty:* 11 full-time (4 women), 48 part-time/adjunct (28 women). *Students:* 442 part-time (361 women). Average age 37. *Degree requirements:* For master's, thesis or alternative, 500-700 hour internship (depending on license choice). *Entrance requirements:* For master's, minimum undergraduate GPA of 3.0, 12 credits of course work in psychology or related field. *Application deadline:* Applications are processed on a rolling basis. Application fee: $50. *Expenses:* Tuition: Part-time $455 per credit. *Financial support:* Career-related internships or fieldwork and tuition waivers available. Support available to part-time students. Financial award applicants required to submit FAFSA. *Unit head:* Dr. Dan Haugen, President, 612-861-7554 Ext. 107, Fax: 612-861-7559, E-mail: haugen@alfredadler.edu. *Application contact:* Evelyn B. Haas, Director of Student Services and Admissions, 612-861-7554 Ext. 103, Fax: 612-861-7559, E-mail: ev@alfredadler.edu.

Adler School of Professional Psychology, Programs in Psychology, Chicago, IL 60602. Offers advanced Adlerian psychotherapy (Certificate); art therapy (MA); clinical neuropsychology (Certificate); clinical psychology (Psy D); community psychology (MA); counseling and organizational psychology (MA); counseling psychology (MA); forensic psychology (MA); gerontological counseling (MA); marriage and family counseling (MA); marriage and family therapy (Certificate); organizational psychology (MA); police psychology (MA); rehabilitation counseling (MA); sport and health psychology (MA); substance abuse counseling (Certificate); Psy D/Certificate; Psy D/MACAT; Psy D/MACP; Psy D/MAMFC; Psy D/MASAC. *Accreditation:* APA. Part-time and evening/weekend programs available. Postbaccalaureate distance learning degree programs offered (minimal on-campus study). *Faculty:* 40 full-time (18 women), 61 part-time/adjunct (31 women). *Students:* 688 full-time (532 women), 142 part-time (110 women). Average age 27.Terminal master's awarded for partial completion of doctoral program. *Degree requirements:* For master's, thesis or alternative, oral exam, practicum; for doctorate, thesis/dissertation, clinical exam, internship, oral exam, practicum, written qualifying exam. *Entrance requirements:* For master's, 12 semester hours in psychology, minimum GPA of 3.0; for doctorate, 18 semester hours in psychology, minimum GPA of 3.25; for Certificate, appropriate master's or doctoral degree. Additional exam requirements/recommendations for international students: Required—TOEFL (minimum score 550 paper-based; 213 computer-based; 79 iBT). *Application deadline:* For fall admission, 2/15 priority date for domestic students, 12/1 priority date for international students. Applications are processed on a rolling basis. Application fee: $50. Electronic applications accepted. *Financial support:* Career-related internships or fieldwork, Federal Work-Study, scholarships/grants, and tuition waivers (full and partial) available. Support available to part-time students. Financial award application deadline: 5/15; financial award applicants required to submit FAFSA. *Application contact:* Michelle Brice, Director of Admissions, 312-662-4113, Fax: 312-662-4199, E-mail: admissions@adler.edu.

Albertus Magnus College, Program in Art Therapy, New Haven, CT 06511-1189. Offers MAAT. Part-time and evening/weekend programs available. *Faculty:* 7 full-time (6 women), 5 part-time/adjunct (3 women). *Students:* 17 full-time (14 women), 41 part-time (40 women); includes 8 Black or African American, non-Hispanic/Latino; 10 Hispanic/Latino. Average age 35. 22 applicants, 82% accepted, 16 enrolled. In 2010, 5 master's awarded. *Degree requirements:* For master's, thesis. *Entrance requirements:* For master's, interview, writing sample. *Application deadline:* For fall admission, 8/30 for domestic students; for spring admission, 12/30 for domestic students. Application fee: $35. *Expenses:* Tuition: Full-time $12,582; part-time $2097 per course. Required fees: $90; $25 per course. *Financial support:* Available to part-time students. Application deadline: 8/15. *Unit head:* Donna Kaiser, Director, 203-773-8903, Fax: 203-773-3117. *Application contact:* Donna Kaiser, Director, 203-773-8903, Fax: 203-773-3117.

Athabasca University, Graduate Centre for Applied Psychology, Athabasca, AB T9S 3A3, Canada. Offers art therapy (MC); career counseling (MC); counseling (Advanced Certificate); counseling psychology (MC); school counseling (MC).

Caldwell College, Graduate Studies, Program in Counseling Psychology, Caldwell, NJ 07006-6195. Offers art therapy (MA); counseling psychology (MA); school counseling (MA). Part-time and evening/weekend programs available. *Degree requirements:* For master's, comprehensive exam, practicum. *Entrance requirements:* For master's, GRE General Test, minimum GPA of 3.0. Additional exam requirements/recommendations for international students: Required—TOEFL (minimum score 580 paper-based; 237 computer-based). Electronic applications accepted.

California Institute of Integral Studies, School of Professional Psychology, San Francisco, CA 94103. Offers clinical psychology (Psy D); community mental health (MA); drama therapy (MA); expressive arts therapy (MA); integral counseling psychology (MA); integral counseling psychology-weekend (MA); somatic psychology (MA). *Accreditation:* APA. Part-time and evening/weekend programs available. *Students:* 651 full-time (476 women), 74 part-time (62 women); includes 146 minority (32 Black or African American, non-Hispanic/Latino; 1 American Indian or Alaska Native, non-Hispanic/Latino; 53 Asian, non-Hispanic/Latino; 43 Hispanic/Latino; 17 Two or more races, non-Hispanic/Latino), 52 international. Average age 37. 556 applicants, 72% accepted, 247 enrolled. In 2010, 148 master's, 27 doctorates awarded. *Degree requirements:* For doctorate, comprehensive exam, thesis/dissertation. *Entrance requirements:* For master's, minimum GPA of 3.0, letters of recommendation, writing sample; for doctorate, GRE, MA in psychology or social work with appropriate practical experience for advanced standing, or BA with a minimum GPA of 3.1; letters of recommendation; writing sample. Additional exam requirements/recommendations for international students: Required—TOEFL. *Application deadline:* For fall admission, 2/1 priority date for domestic and international students; for spring admission, 10/15 priority date for domestic and international students. Applications are processed on a rolling basis. Application fee: $65. Electronic applications accepted. *Expenses:* Tuition: Full-time $15,660; part-time $870 per semester hour. Required fees: $95 per semester. *Financial support:* Research assistantships with tuition reimbursements, teaching assistantships with tuition reimbursements, career-related internships or fieldwork, Federal Work-Study, scholarships/grants, and tuition waivers (partial) available. Support available to part-time students. Financial award application deadline: 4/15; financial award applicants required to submit FAFSA. *Faculty research:* Transpersonal psychology, somatic psychology, expressive arts therapy, drama therapy, community mental health, ecopsychology. *Application contact:* David Townes, Senior Admissions Counselor, 415-575-6152, Fax: 415-575-1268, E-mail: dtownes@ciis.edu.

California State University, Los Angeles, Graduate Studies, College of Arts and Letters, Department of Art, Los Angeles, CA 90032-8530. Offers art (MA), including art education, art history, art therapy, ceramics, metals, and textiles, design (MA, MFA), painting, sculpture, and graphic arts, photography; fine arts (MFA), including crafts, design (MA, MFA), studio arts. *Accreditation:* NASAD (one or more programs are accredited). Part-time and evening/weekend programs available. *Faculty:* 9 full-time (5 women), 3 part-time/adjunct (2 women). *Students:* 27 full-time (19 women), 33 part-time (22 women); includes 24 minority (3 Black or African American, non-Hispanic/Latino; 7 Asian, non-Hispanic/Latino; 13 Hispanic/Latino; 1 Two or more races, non-Hispanic/Latino), 9 international. Average age 36. 19 applicants, 100% accepted, 13 enrolled. In 2010, 26 master's awarded. *Degree requirements:* For master's, comprehensive exam, project or thesis. *Entrance requirements:* For master's, portfolio. Additional exam requirements/recommendations for international students: Required—TOEFL (minimum score 500 paper-based; 173 computer-based). *Application deadline:* For fall admission, 5/1 for domestic and international students. Applications are processed on a rolling basis. Application fee: $55. Electronic applications accepted. *Financial support:* Federal Work-Study available. Support available to part-time students. Financial award application deadline: 3/1. *Faculty research:* The artist and the book, conceptual art, ceramic processes, computer graphics, architectural graphics. *Unit head:* Dr. Abbas Daneshvari, Chair, 323-343-4010, Fax: 323-343-4045, E-mail: adanesh@calstatela.edu. *Application contact:* Dr. Alan Muchlinski, Dean of Graduate Studies, 323-343-3820, Fax: 323-343-5653, E-mail: amuchli@exchange.calstatela.edu.

The College of New Rochelle, Graduate School, Division of Art and Communication Studies, Program in Art Therapy, New Rochelle, NY 10805-2308. Offers art therapy (MS); art therapy/counseling (MS). Part-time and evening/weekend programs available. *Degree requirements:* For master's, thesis, practicum, fieldwork. *Entrance requirements:* For master's, 12 credits in psychology, 15 credits in studio art, portfolio. *Faculty research:* Phototherapy, assessment and evaluation, developmental stages in art, creativity and mental illness.

Concordia University, School of Graduate Studies, Faculty of Fine Arts, Department of Creative Arts Therapies, Montréal, QC H3G 1M8, Canada. Offers MA.

Drexel University, College of Nursing and Health Professions, Program in Creative Arts in Therapy, Specialization in Art Therapy, Philadelphia, PA 19104-2875. Offers MA, PMC. *Accreditation:* NASAD. *Degree requirements:* For master's, comprehensive exam, thesis. *Entrance requirements:* For master's, GRE General Test or MAT, interview, minimum GPA of 2.75, portfolio. Electronic applications accepted.

Eastern Virginia Medical School, Graduate Art Therapy and Counseling Program, Norfolk, VA 23501-1980. Offers MS. *Faculty:* 3 full-time, 1 part-time/adjunct. *Students:* 42 applicants, 74% accepted, 20 enrolled. In 2010, 13 master's awarded. *Degree requirements:* For master's, thesis, internship. *Entrance requirements:* For master's, 12 credit hours in psychology, including abnormal and developmental; 18 credit hours in studio art; face-to-face interview; portfolio (diverse media preferred). *Application deadline:* For fall admission, 1/1 priority date for domestic and international students. Application fee: $60. Electronic applications accepted. *Expenses:* Contact institution. *Financial support:* Institutionally sponsored loans available. *Faculty research:* Art therapy projective imagery assessment: a collection of children's drawings. *Unit head:* Abby Calisch, Director, 757-446-5895, Fax: 757-446-6179, E-mail: artthrpy@evms.edu. *Application contact:* Rose Mwayungu, Admissions and Enrollment Manager for Health Professions, 757-446-7153, Fax: 757-446-8915, E-mail: mwayunra@evms.edu.

Emporia State University, Graduate School, Teachers College, Department of Psychology, Art Therapy, Rehabilitation and Mental Health Counseling, Program in Art Therapy, Emporia, KS 66801-5087. Offers MS. Part-time programs available. *Students:* 14 full-time (12 women), 11 part-time (all women); includes 1 minority (Two or more races, non-Hispanic/Latino), 2 international. 13 applicants, 69% accepted, 9 enrolled. In 2010, 4 master's awarded. *Degree requirements:* For master's, comprehensive exam or thesis, internship. *Entrance requirements:* For master's, GRE General Test or MAT, graduate essay exam, appropriate bachelor's degree. Additional exam requirements/recommendations for international students: Required—TOEFL (minimum score 520 paper-based; 133 computer-based; 68 iBT). *Application deadline:* For fall admission, 6/1 for domestic students; for spring admission, 10/1 for domestic students. Applications are processed on a rolling basis. Application fee: $30 ($75 for international students). Electronic applications accepted. *Expenses:* Tuition, state resident: full-time $4382; part-time $183 per credit hour. Tuition, nonresident: full-time $13,572; part-time $566 per credit hour. Required fees: $1022; $62 per credit hour. Tuition and fees vary according to course level, course load and campus/location. *Financial support:* Career-related internships or fieldwork, Federal Work-Study, institutionally sponsored loans, health care benefits, and unspecified assistantships available. Financial award application deadline: 3/15; financial award applicants required to submit FAFSA. *Unit head:* Dr. Brian W. Schrader, Chair, 620-341-5317, E-mail: bschrade@emporia.edu. *Application contact:* Mary Sewell, Admissions Coordinator, 800-950-GRAD, Fax: 620-341-5909, E-mail: msewell@emporia.edu.

The George Washington University, Columbian College of Arts and Sciences, Program in Art Therapy, Washington, DC 20052. Offers MA. *Faculty:* 4 full-time (all women), 16 part-time/adjunct (15 women). *Students:* 56 full-time (55 women), 17 part-time (16 women); includes 15 minority (3 Black or African American, non-Hispanic/Latino; 2 American Indian or Alaska Native, non-Hispanic/Latino; 3 Asian, non-Hispanic/Latino; 5 Hispanic/Latino; 1 Native Hawaiian or other Pacific Islander, non-Hispanic/Latino; 1 Two or more races, non-Hispanic/Latino), 10 international. Average age 28. 59 applicants, 78% accepted, 33 enrolled. In 2010, 24 master's awarded. *Degree requirements:* For master's, internship, practicum paper. *Entrance requirements:* For master's, GRE General Test, interview, minimum GPA of 3.0. Additional exam requirements/recommendations for international students: Required—TOEFL (minimum score 550 paper-based; 213 computer-based; 80 iBT). *Application deadline:* For fall admission, 1/1 priority date for domestic students. Application fee: $75. *Financial support:* In 2010–11, 11 students received

Art Therapy

The George Washington University *(continued)*
support; fellowships with partial tuition reimbursements available, career-related internships or fieldwork, Federal Work-Study, institutionally sponsored loans, and tuition waivers available. *Unit head:* Heidi Bardot, Director, 202-994-4148, E-mail: hbardot@gwu.edu. *Application contact:* Information Contact, 202-994-6285, Fax: 202-994-1404, E-mail: artx@gwu.edu.

Hofstra University, School of Education, Health, and Human Services, Programs in Counseling, Hempstead, NY 11549. Offers counseling (MS Ed, PD); creative arts therapy (MA); gerontology (MS, Advanced Certificate); marriage and family therapy (MA); mental health counseling (MA); rehabilitation counseling (MS Ed, CAS, PD); rehabilitation counseling in mental health (MS Ed, CAS); school counselor-bilingual extension (Advanced Certificate). Part-time and evening/weekend programs available. *Students:* 145 full-time (132 women), 80 part-time (74 women); includes 41 minority (23 Black or African American, non-Hispanic/Latino; 5 Asian, non-Hispanic/Latino; 11 Hispanic/Latino; 1 Native Hawaiian or other Pacific Islander, non-Hispanic/Latino; 1 Two or more races, non-Hispanic/Latino), 8 international. Average age 30. 187 applicants, 63% accepted, 67 enrolled. In 2010, 79 master's, 1 other advanced degree awarded. *Degree requirements:* For master's, comprehensive exam (for some programs), thesis (for some programs), internship, practicum, student teaching, seminars. *Entrance requirements:* For master's, GRE, interview, letters of recommendation, portfolio, essay, professional experience, certification; for other advanced degree, GRE, interview, letters of recommendation, essay, professional experience, resume, master's degree. Additional exam requirements/recommendations for international students: Required—TOEFL (minimum score 550 paper-based; 213 computer-based; 80 iBT). *Application deadline:* Applications are processed on a rolling basis. Application fee: $70 ($75 for international students). Electronic applications accepted. *Expenses:* Tuition: Full-time $18,000; part-time $1000 per credit hour. Required fees: $970; $145 per term. Tuition and fees vary according to program. *Financial support:* In 2010–11, 102 students received support, including 27 fellowships with full and partial tuition reimbursements available (averaging $2,466 per year), 4 research assistantships with full and partial tuition reimbursements available (averaging $14,567 per year); career-related internships or fieldwork, Federal Work-Study, institutionally sponsored loans, scholarships/grants, tuition waivers (full and partial), unspecified assistantships, and scholarships also available. Support available to part-time students. Financial award applicants required to submit FAFSA. *Faculty research:* Bereavement, loss, and trauma counseling, creativity for non-artists. *Unit head:* Dr. Darra Pace, Chairperson, 516-463-6476, Fax: 516-463-6415, E-mail: cprdzp@hofstra.edu. *Application contact:* Carol Drummer, Dean of Graduate Admissions, 516-463-4876, Fax: 516-463-4664, E-mail: gradstudent@hofstra.edu.

Lesley University, Graduate School of Arts and Social Sciences, Division of Expressive Therapies, Cambridge, MA 02138-2790. Offers art (MA); dance (MA); expressive therapies (MA, PhD, CAGS); music (MA). Terminal master's awarded for partial completion of doctoral program. *Degree requirements:* For master's, internship, practicum; for doctorate, thesis/dissertation. *Entrance requirements:* For master's, art portfolio, performance DVD; for doctorate, GRE or MAT. Additional exam requirements/recommendations for international students: Required—TOEFL (minimum score 550 paper-based; 213 computer-based; 80 iBT).

Long Island University, C.W. Post Campus, School of Visual and Performing Arts, Department of Art, Brookville, NY 11548-1300. Offers art (MA); art education (MS); clinical art therapy (MA); fine art and design (MFA). Part-time and evening/weekend programs available. *Degree requirements:* For master's, thesis. Electronic applications accepted. *Faculty research:* Painting, sculpture, installation, computers, video.

Marylhurst University, Department of Art Therapy Counseling, Marylhurst, OR 97036-0261. Offers art therapy (PGC); art therapy counseling (MA); counseling (PGC). Part-time programs available. *Faculty:* 3 full-time (all women), 4 part-time/adjunct (all women). *Students:* 5 full-time (3 women), 25 part-time (20 women); includes 1 American Indian or Alaska Native, non-Hispanic/Latino; 1 Asian, non-Hispanic/Latino; 4 Hispanic/Latino; 1 Two or more races, non-Hispanic/Latino. Average age 34. 30 applicants, 83% accepted, 18 enrolled. In 2010, 18 master's awarded. *Degree requirements:* For master's, comprehensive exam, practica. *Entrance requirements:* For master's, MAT, minimum GPA of 3.0, course work in psychology and art, slide portfolio, letters of reference, resume, autobiography, portfolio. Additional exam requirements/recommendations for international students: Required—TOEFL (minimum score 550 paper-based; 213 computer-based; 80 iBT). *Application deadline:* For fall admission, 1/31 priority date for domestic and international students. Applications are processed on a rolling basis. Application fee: $50. Electronic applications accepted. *Expenses:* Contact institution. *Financial support:* Scholarships/grants available. Support available to part-time students. Financial award applicants required to submit FAFSA. *Faculty research:* Scientific approaches to art therapy research, child and adolescent psychotherapy, multicultural counseling. *Unit head:* Christine Turner, Chair, 503-636-8141, Fax: 503-636-9526, E-mail: cturner@marylhurst.edu. *Application contact:* Maruska Lynch, Graduate Admissions Specialist, 800-634-9982 Ext. 6322, Fax: 503-699-6320, E-mail: admissions@marylhurst.edu.

Marywood University, Academic Affairs, Insalaco College of Creative and Performing Arts, Art Department, Program in Art Therapy, Scranton, PA 18509-1598. Offers MA, Post Master's Certificate. *Accreditation:* NASAD. *Entrance requirements:* Additional exam requirements/recommendations for international students: Required—TOEFL (minimum score 550 paper-based; 213 computer-based; 79 iBT). Electronic applications accepted. *Expenses:* Tuition: Part-time $735 per credit. Required fees: $470 per semester. Tuition and fees vary according to degree level and campus/location. *Faculty research:* Perspectives of leading educators in art therapy, current trends in art education.

Mount Mary College, Graduate Programs, Program in Art Therapy, Milwaukee, WI 53222-4597. Offers MS. Evening/weekend programs available. *Degree requirements:* For master's, thesis or alternative, internship. *Entrance requirements:* For master's, minimum GPA of 2.75, portfolio. Additional exam requirements/recommendations for international students: Required—TOEFL (minimum score 500 paper-based; 173 computer-based). Electronic applications accepted. *Faculty research:* Art-based research in art therapy, consensus-group supervision, art therapy in public school programs.

Naropa University, Graduate Programs, Program in Transpersonal Counseling Psychology, Concentration in Art Therapy, Boulder, CO 80302-6697. Offers MA. *Faculty:* 2 full-time (1 woman), 6 part-time/adjunct (4 women). *Students:* 37 full-time (36 women), 11 part-time (all women); includes 6 minority (1 Black or African American, non-Hispanic/Latino; 1 American Indian or Alaska Native, non-Hispanic/Latino; 2 Hispanic/Latino; 2 Two or more races, non-Hispanic/Latino), 1 international. Average age 28. 57 applicants, 44% accepted, 16 enrolled. In 2010, 13 master's awarded. *Degree requirements:* For master's, internships, 180 direct art contact hours of studio-based work. *Entrance requirements:* For master's, portfolio (21 slides), in-person interview, course work in psychology and art, resume, letter of interest, 3 letters of recommendation. Additional exam requirements/recommendations for international students: Required—TOEFL (minimum score 600 paper-based; 250 computer-based). *Application deadline:* For fall admission, 1/15 priority date for domestic and international students. Applications are processed on a rolling basis. Application fee: $60. Electronic applications accepted. *Expenses:* Tuition: Full-time $17,820; part-time $810 per credit. Required fees: $305 per semester. Tuition and fees vary according to course load, program and reciprocity agreements. *Financial support:* In 2010–11, 28 students received support, including 4 research assistantships with partial tuition reimbursements available (averaging $2,250 per year); teaching assistantships with partial tuition reimbursements available, career-related internships or fieldwork, Federal Work-Study, scholarships/grants, health care benefits, tuition waivers (partial), and unspecified assistantships also available. Support available to part-time students. Financial award application deadline: 3/1; financial award applicants required to submit FAFSA. *Unit head:* Dr. MacAndrew Jack, Director, Graduate School of Psychology, 303-245-4752, E-mail: mjack@naropa.edu. *Application contact:* Office of Admissions, 303-546-3572, Fax: 303-546-3583, E-mail: admissions@naropa.edu.

Nazareth College of Rochester, Graduate Studies, Department of Creative Arts Therapy, Program in Art Therapy, Rochester, NY 14618-3790. Offers MS. Part-time programs available. *Entrance requirements:* For master's, minimum GPA of 3.0, portfolio review.

New York University, Steinhardt School of Culture, Education, and Human Development, Department of Art and Art Professions, Program in Art Therapy, New York, NY 10003. Offers MA. Part-time programs available. *Faculty:* 1 (woman) full-time. *Students:* 37 full-time (34 women), 9 part-time (7 women); includes 1 Black or African American, non-Hispanic/Latino; 2 Asian, non-Hispanic/Latino; 2 Hispanic/Latino, 3 international. Average age 27. 174 applicants, 21% accepted, 22 enrolled. In 2010, 18 master's awarded. *Degree requirements:* For master's, thesis (for some programs). *Entrance requirements:* For master's, interview, portfolio. Additional exam requirements/recommendations for international students: Required—TOEFL. *Application deadline:* For fall admission, 12/1 priority date for domestic and international students. Applications are processed on a rolling basis. Application fee: $75. Electronic applications accepted. *Financial support:* Career-related internships or fieldwork, Federal Work-Study, institutionally sponsored loans, scholarships/grants, and tuition waivers (partial) available. Support available to part-time students. Financial award application deadline: 2/1; financial award applicants required to submit FAFSA. *Faculty research:* Art therapy in non-clinical settings, international art therapy. *Unit head:* Prof. Ikuko Acosta, Director, 212-998-5726, Fax: 212-995-4320, E-mail: ia4@nyu.edu. *Application contact:* 212-998-5030, Fax: 212-995-4328, E-mail: steinhardt.gradadmissions@nyu.edu.

Notre Dame de Namur University, Division of Academic Affairs, College of Arts and Sciences, Department of Art Therapy Psychology, Belmont, CA 94002-1908. Offers art therapy (MA); marriage and family therapy (MA). Part-time programs available. *Faculty:* 4 full-time (3 women), 8 part-time/adjunct (7 women). *Students:* 38 full-time (all women), 74 part-time (72 women); includes 33 minority (3 Black or African American, non-Hispanic/Latino; 10 Asian, non-Hispanic/Latino; 16 Hispanic/Latino; 2 Native Hawaiian or other Pacific Islander, non-Hispanic/Latino; 2 Two or more races, non-Hispanic/Latino), 8 international. Average age 33. 82 applicants, 40% accepted, 31 enrolled. In 2010, 28 master's awarded. *Degree requirements:* For master's, thesis, oral presentation, portfolio. *Entrance requirements:* For master's, interview, minimum GPA of 2.5. Additional exam requirements/recommendations for international students: Required—TOEFL (minimum score 550 paper-based; 213 computer-based; 79 iBT). *Application deadline:* For fall admission, 8/1 priority date for domestic students; for spring admission, 12/1 priority date for domestic students. Applications are processed on a rolling basis. Application fee: $60. Electronic applications accepted. *Expenses:* Tuition: Full-time $14,220; part-time $790 per credit. Required fees: $35 per semester. Tuition and fees vary according to program. *Financial support:* Career-related internships or fieldwork available. Support available to part-time students. Financial award applicants required to submit FAFSA. *Unit head:* Dr. Richard Carolan, Chair, 650-508-3556, Fax: 650-508-3736. *Application contact:* Candace Hallmark, Associate Director of Admissions, 650-508-3600, Fax: 650-508-3426, E-mail: grad.admit@ndnu.edu.

Ottawa University, Graduate Studies-Arizona, Program in Professional Counseling, Ottawa, KS 66067-3399. Offers Christian counseling (MA); expressive arts therapy (MA); marriage and family therapy (MA); treatment of trauma, abuse and deprivation (MA). Programs offered in Mesa, Phoenix, Tempe and West Valley, AZ. Part-time and evening/weekend programs available. Postbaccalaureate distance learning degree programs offered. *Degree requirements:* For master's, comprehensive exam, thesis or alternative, field experience, practicum. *Entrance requirements:* For master's, minimum undergraduate GPA of 3.0; course work in theories of personality, abnormal psychology, and human growth and development. Additional exam requirements/recommendations for international students: Required—TOEFL (minimum score 550 paper-based; 213 computer-based).

Pratt Institute, School of Art and Design, Programs in Creative Arts Therapy, Brooklyn, NY 11205-3899. Offers art therapy and creativity development (MPS); art therapy-special education (MPS); dance/movement therapy (MS). *Accreditation:* NASAD (one or more programs are accredited). Part-time programs available. *Faculty:* 3 full-time (all women), 19 part-time/adjunct (16 women). *Students:* 103 full-time (97 women), 1 (woman) part-time; includes 4 Black or African American, non-Hispanic/Latino; 7 Asian, non-Hispanic/Latino; 8 Hispanic/Latino; 2 Two or more races, non-Hispanic/Latino, 7 international. Average age 29. 192 applicants, 34% accepted, 32 enrolled. In 2010, 41 master's awarded. *Degree requirements:* For master's, thesis. *Entrance requirements:* For master's, letters of recommendation, portfolio. Additional exam requirements/recommendations for international students: Required—TOEFL (minimum score 600 paper-based; 250 computer-based; 100 iBT). *Application deadline:* For fall admission, 1/5 for domestic and international students; for spring admission, 10/1 for domestic and international students. Applications are processed on a rolling basis. Application fee: $50 ($90 for international students). Electronic applications accepted. *Expenses:* Tuition: Full-time $22,734; part-time $1263 per credit. Required fees: $1280. *Financial support:* Career-related internships or fieldwork, Federal Work-Study, institutionally sponsored loans, scholarships/grants, health care benefits, tuition waivers (full), and unspecified assistantships available. Support available to part-time students. Financial award application deadline: 2/1; financial award applicants required to submit FAFSA. *Faculty research:* Psychology and aesthetic interaction, art therapy and AIDS, art therapy and autism, art diagnosis. *Unit head:* Jean Davis, Chairperson, 718-636-3428, E-mail: jdavis@pratt.edu. *Application contact:* Young Hah, Director of Graduate Admissions, 718-636-3683, Fax: 718-399-4242, E-mail: yhah@pratt.edu.

See Display on page 92 and Close-Up on page 131.

Prescott College, Graduate Programs, Program in Counseling and Psychology, Prescott, AZ 86301. Offers adventure-based psychotherapy (MA); counseling psychology (MA); ecopsychology (MA); ecotherapy (MA); equine-assisted mental health (MA); expressive arts therapy (MA); somatic psychology (MA); student-directed independent study (MA). Part-time programs available. Postbaccalaureate distance learning degree programs offered (minimal on-campus study). *Faculty:* 3 full-time (all women), 25 part-time/adjunct (18 women). *Students:* 71 full-time (55 women), 59 part-time (50 women); includes 16 minority (4 Black or African American, non-Hispanic/Latino; 2 American Indian or Alaska Native, non-Hispanic/Latino; 1 Asian, non-Hispanic/Latino; 3 Hispanic/Latino; 1 Native Hawaiian or other Pacific Islander, non-Hispanic/Latino; 5 Two or more races, non-Hispanic/Latino), 5 international. Average age 38. 107 applicants, 79% accepted, 54 enrolled. In 2010, 23 master's awarded. *Degree requirements:* For master's, thesis, fieldwork or internship, practicum. *Entrance requirements:* For master's, 2 letters of recommendation, resume. Additional exam requirements/recommendations for international students: Required—TOEFL (minimum score 500 paper-based; 173 computer-based). *Application deadline:* For fall admission, 4/15 priority date for domestic and international students; for spring admission, 9/15 priority date for domestic and international students. Applications are processed on a rolling basis. Application fee: $40. Electronic applications accepted. *Expenses:* Tuition: Full-time $15,600; part-time $650 per credit. Required fees: $50 per term. One-time fee: $190. Tuition and fees vary according to course load and degree level. *Financial support:* Career-related internships or fieldwork, Federal Work-Study, and scholarships/grants available. Financial award applicants required to submit FAFSA. *Unit head:* Camille Smith, Chair, 602-373-3881, Fax: 928-776-5151, E-mail: csmith@prescott.edu. *Application contact:* Kerstin Alicki, Admissions Counselor, 877-412-8705, Fax: 928-277-4695, E-mail: admissions@prescott.edu.

Saint Mary-of-the-Woods College, Program in Art Therapy, Saint Mary-of-the-Woods, IN 47876. Offers MA, Post-Master's Certificate. Part-time and evening/weekend programs available. Postbaccalaureate distance learning degree programs offered (minimal on-campus study). *Degree requirements:* For master's, thesis or project. *Entrance requirements:* For master's, minimum GPA of 2.5; for Post-Master's Certificate, 12 credit hours in abnormal and developmental psychology, 15 credit hours in studio art skills, art portfolio, interview, minimum GPA of 2.5. Electronic applications accepted.

Salve Regina University, Graduate Studies, Holistic Graduate Programs, Newport, RI 02840-4192. Offers expressive and creative arts (CAGS); holistic counseling (MA); holistic leadership (MA, CAGS); mental health (CAGS). Part-time and evening/weekend programs available.

Degree requirements: For master's, internship, project. *Entrance requirements:* For master's, GMAT, GRE General Test, or MAT. Additional exam requirements/recommendations for international students: Required—TOEFL (minimum score 600 paper-based; 250 computer-based; 100 iBT) or IELTS. Electronic applications accepted. *Expenses:* Tuition: Full-time $7740; part-time $430 per credit. Required fees: $40 per semester. Tuition and fees vary according to course level and degree level.

School of the Art Institute of Chicago, Graduate Division, Program in Art Therapy, Chicago, IL 60603-3103. Offers MAAT. Program offered jointly with Rush University. *Accreditation:* NASAD. *Degree requirements:* For master's, thesis, personal interview. *Entrance requirements:* Additional exam requirements/recommendations for international students: Required—TOEFL, IELTS. *Faculty research:* Migrane, ousider art, community-based practice.

See Close-Up on page 225.

School of Visual Arts, Graduate Programs, Art Therapy Department, New York, NY 10010-3994. Offers MPS. *Degree requirements:* For master's, thesis or 750 internship hours. *Entrance requirements:* For master's, portfolio, bachelor's degree with 12 credits in undergraduate psychology including child and abnormal psychology, 18 credits of studio art. Additional exam requirements/recommendations for international students: Required—TOEFL (minimum score 550 paper-based; 213 computer-based; 79 iBT). Electronic applications accepted.

Seton Hill University, Program in Art Therapy, Greensburg, PA 15601. Offers MA. Part-time programs available. *Faculty:* 2 full-time (both women), 6 part-time/adjunct (all women). *Students:* 39 full-time (38 women), 18 part-time (16 women). Average age 31. 58 applicants, 45% accepted, 18 enrolled. In 2010, 12 master's awarded. *Degree requirements:* For master's, thesis or alternative. *Entrance requirements:* For master's, portfolio; 12 undergraduate credits in psychology, 18 in art; minimum GPA of 3.0; experience working with people; 3 letters of recommendation; writing sample; current resume. Additional exam requirements/recommendations for international students: Required—TOEFL (minimum score 650 paper-based; 280 computer-based), IELTS (minimum score 7). *Application deadline:* For fall admission, 8/15 priority date for domestic students; for spring admission, 12/15 for domestic students. Applications are processed on a rolling basis. Application fee: $35. Electronic applications accepted. *Expenses:* Tuition: Full-time $13,050; part-time $725 per credit. Required fees: $700; $34 per credit. $50 per semester. Tuition and fees vary according to course load and program. *Financial support:* Federal Work-Study, scholarships/grants, tuition waivers (partial), and unspecified assistantships available. Support available to part-time students. Financial award application deadline: 8/15; financial award applicants required to submit FAFSA. *Faculty research:* Art therapy with the deaf, art therapy with children. *Unit head:* Nina Denninger, Director, 724-830-1047, Fax: 724-830-1294, E-mail: denninger@setonhill.edu. *Application contact:* Laurel Komarny, Program Counselor, 724-838-4209, Fax: 724-830-1891, E-mail: 1komarny@setonhill.edu.

Southern Illinois University Edwardsville, Graduate School, College of Arts and Sciences, Department of Art and Design, Program in Art Therapy Counseling, Edwardsville, IL 62026-0001. Offers MA. Part-time programs available. *Students:* 25 full-time (24 women), 6 part-time (5 women); includes 5 minority (1 Black or African American, non-Hispanic/Latino; 1 Asian, non-Hispanic/Latino; 3 Hispanic/Latino), 1 international. Average age 26. 41 applicants, 27% accepted. In 2010, 10 master's awarded. *Degree requirements:* For master's, thesis or alternative, project. *Entrance requirements:* For master's, MAT, portfolio. Additional exam requirements/recommendations for international students: Required—TOEFL (minimum score 550 paper-based; 213 computer-based; 79 iBT), IELTS (minimum score 6.5). *Application deadline:* For fall admission, 2/1 for domestic and international students. Application fee: $30. Electronic applications accepted. *Expenses:* Tuition, state resident: full-time $6012; part-time $1503 per semester. Tuition, nonresident: full-time $15,030; part-time $3758 per semester. Required fees: $1711; $675 per semester. *Financial support:* In 2010–11, fellowships (averaging $8,370 per year), research assistantships (averaging $8,064 per year), 10 teaching assistantships with full tuition reimbursements (averaging $8,064 per year) were awarded; career-related internships or fieldwork, scholarships/grants, and unspecified assistantships also available. Financial award application deadline: 3/1; financial award applicants required to submit FAFSA. *Unit head:* Dr. Patricia Klorer, Program Director, 618-650-3183, E-mail: pklorer@siue.edu. *Application contact:* Michelle Robinson, Coordinator of Graduate Recruitment, 618-650-2811, Fax: 618-650-3523, E-mail: michero@siue.edu.

Southwestern College, Program in Art Therapy/Counseling, Santa Fe, NM 87502-4788. Offers MA. Part-time and evening/weekend programs available. *Degree requirements:* For master's, internship. *Entrance requirements:* For master's, resume, slide portfolio, interview, 3

letters of reference. Additional exam requirements/recommendations for international students: Required—TOEFL.

Springfield College, Graduate Programs, Program in Art Therapy, Springfield, MA 01109-3797. Offers M Ed, MS, CAGS. Part-time programs available. *Degree requirements:* For master's, research project, final art exhibition. *Entrance requirements:* For master's, portfolio, prerequisite courses required for accreditation. Additional exam requirements/recommendations for international students: Required—TOEFL (minimum score 550 paper-based; 213 computer-based). Electronic applications accepted. *Faculty research:* Stage development in art, psychopathology of expression, art history and art therapy.

University of Maryland, College Park, Academic Affairs, College of Education, Department of Counseling and Personnel Services, College Park, MD 20742. Offers college student personnel (M Ed, MA); college student personnel administration (PhD); community counseling (CAGS); community/career counseling (M Ed, MA); counseling and personnel services (M Ed, MA, PhD), including art therapy (M Ed), college student personnel (M Ed), counseling and personnel services (PhD), counseling psychology (M Ed), mental health counseling (M Ed), school counseling (M Ed); counseling psychology (PhD); counselor education (PhD); rehabilitation counseling (M Ed, MA, AGSC); school counseling (M Ed, MA); school psychology (M Ed, MA, PhD). *Accreditation:* ACA (one or more programs are accredited); APA (one or more programs are accredited); CORE (one or more programs are accredited); NCATE. Part-time and evening/weekend programs available. Postbaccalaureate distance learning degree programs offered (no on-campus study). *Faculty:* 33 full-time (18 women), 1 (woman) part-time/adjunct. *Students:* 136 full-time (105 women), 16 part-time (11 women); includes 23 Black or African American, non-Hispanic/Latino; 19 Asian, non-Hispanic/Latino; 12 Hispanic/Latino; 5 Two or more races, non-Hispanic/Latino, 11 international. 407 applicants, 11% accepted, 25 enrolled. In 2010, 38 master's, 15 doctorates, 4 other advanced degrees awarded. *Degree requirements:* For master's, thesis (for some programs); for doctorate, thesis/dissertation. *Entrance requirements:* For master's, GRE General Test or MAT, minimum GPA of 3.0, 3 letters of recommendation; for doctorate, GRE General Test or MAT, minimum GPA of 3.5, 3 letters of recommendation. Additional exam requirements/recommendations for international students: Required—TOEFL. *Application deadline:* For fall admission, 12/15 for domestic and international students; for spring admission, 6/1 for international students. Applications are processed on a rolling basis. Application fee: $75. Electronic applications accepted. *Expenses:* Tuition, state resident: part-time $471 per credit hour. Tuition, nonresident: part-time $1016 per credit hour. Required fees: $337 per term. *Financial support:* In 2010–11, 15 fellowships with partial tuition reimbursements (averaging $11,738 per year), 3 research assistantships (averaging $17,258 per year), 83 teaching assistantships with tuition reimbursements (averaging $16,131 per year) were awarded; career-related internships or fieldwork, Federal Work-Study, and scholarships/grants also available. Support available to part-time students. Financial award applicants required to submit FAFSA. *Faculty research:* Educational psychology, counseling, health. Total annual research expenditures: $838,213. *Unit head:* Dr. Dennis Kivlighan, Chair, 301-405-2858, E-mail: dennisk@umd.edu. *Application contact:* Dean of Graduate School, 301-405-0358.

University of Wisconsin–Superior, Graduate Division, Department of Visual Arts, Superior, WI 54880-4500. Offers art education (MA); art history (MA); art therapy (MA); studio arts (MA). Part-time programs available. *Degree requirements:* For master's, comprehensive exam, exhibit. *Entrance requirements:* For master's, minimum GPA of 2.75, portfolio.

Ursuline College, School of Graduate Studies, Program in Art Therapy Counseling, Pepper Pike, OH 44124-4398. Offers MA. Part-time programs available. *Faculty:* 4 full-time (all women), 9 part-time/adjunct (8 women). *Students:* 20 full-time (19 women), 67 part-time (65 women); includes 9 minority (4 Black or African American, non-Hispanic/Latino; 1 Asian, non-Hispanic/Latino; 1 Hispanic/Latino; 3 Two or more races, non-Hispanic/Latino). Average age 32. 34 applicants, 79% accepted, 19 enrolled. In 2010, 16 master's awarded. *Degree requirements:* For master's, thesis, 700 hour internship. *Entrance requirements:* For master's, BA in psychology, social sciences, or related field; minimum undergraduate GPA of 3.0; portfolio; work experience with human service agency. Additional exam requirements/recommendations for international students: Required—TOEFL (minimum score 500 paper-based; 173 computer-based). *Application deadline:* For fall admission, 8/1 priority date for domestic students. Applications are processed on a rolling basis. Application fee: $25. *Expenses:* Tuition: Full-time $15,138; part-time $841 per credit. Required fees: $240; $120 per semester. *Financial support:* In 2010–11, 9 students received support. Federal Work-Study available. Financial award application deadline: 3/1; financial award applicants required to submit FAFSA. *Faculty research:* Art therapy used with psychiatric and geriatric populations, art therapy used in treatment of chemical dependency, family therapy, child art therapy. *Unit head:* Gale Rule-Hoffman, Director, 440-646-8138, Fax: 440-684-6088. *Application contact:* Melanie Steele, Graduate Admission Assistant, 440-646-8199, Fax: 440-684-3168, E-mail: graduateadmissions@ursuline.edu.

Decorative Arts

Bard Graduate Center: Decorative Arts, Design History, Material Culture, Graduate Studies, New York, NY 10024-3602. Offers M Phil, MA, PhD. Part-time programs available. *Degree requirements:* For master's, one foreign language, internship, qualifying paper; for doctorate, 2 foreign languages, thesis/dissertation, exams. *Entrance requirements:* For master's, GRE General Test, writing sample, 3 letters of recommendation; for doctorate, GRE General Test, master's thesis or equivalent, 3 letters of recommendation. Additional exam requirements/recommendations for international students: Required—TOEFL. *Faculty research:* English craftsmen; ancient furniture; aesthetics and politics; Art Nouveau jewelry; European sculpture; New York and American material culture; modern design history; early modern Europe; history and theory of museums; comparative medieval material culture (China, Islam, Europe); archaeology, anthropology, and material culture.

See Display on page 190 and Close-Up on page 215.

Corcoran College of Art and Design, Graduate Programs, Washington, DC 20006-4804. Offers art education (MAT); history of decorative arts (MA); interior design (MA). *Accreditation:*

NASAD. Part-time programs available. *Entrance requirements:* Additional exam requirements/recommendations for international students: Required—TOEFL.

The New School: A University, Parsons The New School for Design, Program in the History of Decorative Arts and Design, New York, NY 10011. Offers MA. Offered jointly with the Cooper-Hewitt Museum and the Smithsonian Institution. *Accreditation:* NASAD. Part-time programs available. *Degree requirements:* For master's, one foreign language, comprehensive exam or thesis project. *Entrance requirements:* For master's, sample of written work. Additional exam requirements/recommendations for international students: Required—TOEFL (minimum score 580 paper-based; 237 computer-based; 92 iBT). Electronic applications accepted.

Sotheby's Institute of Art–London, Graduate Programs, London, United Kingdom. Offers art business (MA); contemporary art (MA); contemporary design (MA); East Asian art (MA); fine and decorative art (MA); photography (MA).

Sotheby's Institute of Art–New York, Graduate Programs, New York, NY 10021. Offers American fine and decorative art (MA); art business (MA); contemporary art (MA). *Accreditation:* NASAD.

Museum Studies

Arizona State University, College of Liberal Arts and Sciences, School of Human Evolution and Social Change, Tempe, AZ 85287-2402. Offers anthropology (PhD); anthropology (archaeology) (PhD); anthropology (bioarchaeology) (PhD); anthropology (museum studies) (MA); anthropology (physical) (PhD); applied mathematics for the life and social sciences (PhD); environmental social science (PhD); environmental social science (urbanism) (PhD); global health (MA); global health (health and culture) (PhD); global health (urbanism) (PhD);

immigration studies (Graduate Certificate). *Faculty:* 52 full-time (19 women), 4 part-time/adjunct (2 women). *Students:* 127 full-time (77 women), 52 part-time (37 women); includes 43 minority (8 Black or African American, non-Hispanic/Latino; 4 American Indian or Alaska Native, non-Hispanic/Latino; 4 Asian, non-Hispanic/Latino; 26 Hispanic/Latino; 1 Two or more races, non-Hispanic/Latino), 19 international. Average age 32. 250 applicants, 24% accepted, 25 enrolled. In 2010, 8 master's, 18 doctorates, 7 other advanced degrees awarded. Terminal

Museum Studies

Arizona State University (continued)
master's awarded for partial completion of doctoral program. *Degree requirements:* For master's, thesis or alternative, interactive Program of Study (iPOS) submitted before completing 50 percent of required credit hours; for doctorate, comprehensive exam, thesis/dissertation, interactive Program of Study (iPOS) submitted before completing 50 percent of required credit hours. *Entrance requirements:* For master's and doctorate, GRE, minimum GPA of 3.0 or equivalent in last 2 years of work leading to bachelor's degree. Additional exam requirements/recommendations for international students: Required—TOEFL, IELTS, or Pearson Test of English. *Application deadline:* For fall admission, 12/15 for domestic students, 12/1 for international students. Applications are processed on a rolling basis. Application fee: $70 ($90 for international students). Electronic applications accepted. *Expenses:* Tuition, state resident: full-time $8510; part-time $608 per credit. Tuition, nonresident: full-time $16,542; part-time $919 per credit. Required fees: $339; $110 per credit. Part-time tuition and fees vary according to course load. *Financial support:* In 2010–11, 30 research assistantships with full and partial tuition reimbursements (averaging $14,993 per year), 63 teaching assistantships with full and partial tuition reimbursements (averaging $15,266 per year) were awarded; fellowships with full tuition reimbursements, career-related internships or fieldwork, Federal Work-Study, institutionally sponsored loans, scholarships/grants, and tuition waivers (full and partial) also available. Financial award application deadline: 3/1; financial award applicants required to submit FAFSA. Total annual research expenditures: $3.8 million. *Unit head:* Dr. Sander van der Leeuw, Director, 480-965-6214, E-mail: vanderle@asu.edu. *Application contact:* Graduate Admissions, 480-965-6113.

Bard College, Center for Curatorial Studies, Annandale-on-Hudson, NY 12504. Offers MA. *Degree requirements:* For master's, thesis, exhibition. *Entrance requirements:* For master's, exhibition review, 3 letters of recommendation. Additional exam requirements/recommendations for international students: Required—TOEFL (minimum score 550 paper-based). Electronic applications accepted. *Expenses:* Contact institution. *Faculty research:* Contemporary art, history of exhibition, curatorial practice.

Baylor University, Graduate School, College of Arts and Sciences, Department of Museum Studies, Waco, TX 76798. Offers MA. *Faculty:* 6 part-time/adjunct (3 women). *Students:* 21 full-time (19 women), 1 (woman) part-time; includes 3 minority (1 American Indian or Alaska Native, non-Hispanic/Latino; 2 Hispanic/Latino). 13 applicants, 85% accepted. In 2010, 9 master's awarded. *Degree requirements:* For master's, thesis or alternative. *Entrance requirements:* For master's, GRE General Test. *Application deadline:* For fall admission, 4/30 priority date for domestic students. Applications are processed on a rolling basis. Application fee: $25. Electronic applications accepted. *Financial support:* In 2010–11, 3 research assistantships with partial tuition reimbursements (averaging $7,200 per year) were awarded; career-related internships or fieldwork, Federal Work-Study, institutionally sponsored loans, tuition waivers (full and partial), and unspecified assistantships also available. Support available to part-time students. Financial award application deadline: 6/1; financial award applicants required to submit FAFSA. *Faculty research:* Paleontology/archaeology, preservation. *Unit head:* Dr. Kenneth Hafertepe, Graduate Program Director, 254-710-1233, Fax: 254-710-1173, E-mail: kenneth_hafertepe@baylor.edu. *Application contact:* Marcia Cooper, Administrative Assistant, 254-710-1233, Fax: 254-710-3870, E-mail: marcia_cooper@baylor.edu.

Boston University, Graduate School of Arts and Sciences, Department of Art History, Boston, MA 02215. Offers art history (MA, PhD); museum studies (Certificate). *Students:* 44 full-time (39 women), 9 part-time (8 women); includes 6 minority (4 Black or African American, non-Hispanic/Latino; 1 Asian, non-Hispanic/Latino; 1 Two or more races, non-Hispanic/Latino), 7 international. Average age 32. 227 applicants, 32% accepted, 14 enrolled. In 2010, 11 master's, 6 doctorates awarded. Terminal master's awarded for partial completion of doctoral program. *Degree requirements:* For master's, one foreign language, comprehensive exam, thesis; for doctorate, 2 foreign languages, comprehensive exam, thesis/dissertation. *Entrance requirements:* For master's and doctorate, GRE General Test, 3 letters of recommendation; for Certificate, GRE General Test. Additional exam requirements/recommendations for international students: Required—TOEFL (minimum score 600 paper-based; 250 computer-based). *Application deadline:* For fall admission, 1/15 for domestic and international students; for spring admission, 10/15 for domestic and international students. Application fee: $70. *Expenses:* Tuition: Full-time $39,314; part-time $1228 per credit. Required fees: $40 per semester. *Financial support:* In 2010–11, 20 students received support, including 2 fellowships (averaging $19,300 per year), 1 research assistantship (averaging $18,800 per year), 6 teaching assistantships with full tuition reimbursements available (averaging $18,800 per year); career-related internships or fieldwork, Federal Work-Study, and unspecified assistantships also available. Support available to part-time students. Financial award application deadline: 1/15; financial award applicants required to submit FAFSA. *Unit head:* Fred S. Kleiner, Chairman, 617-353-2520, Fax: 617-353-3243, E-mail: fsk@bu.edu. *Application contact:* Cheryl Crombie, Administrative Assistant, 617-353-2522, Fax: 617-353-3243, E-mail: ccrombie@bu.edu.

Brown University, Graduate School, Department of Anthropology, Providence, RI 02912. Offers anthropology (AM, PhD); museum studies (AM). *Degree requirements:* For doctorate, one foreign language, thesis/dissertation, preliminary exam.

California College of the Arts, Graduate Programs, Program in Curatorial Practice, San Francisco, CA 94107. Offers MA. *Faculty:* 2 full-time (1 woman), 10 part-time/adjunct (4 women). *Students:* 22 full-time (17 women), 2 part-time (both women); includes 2 Black or African American, non-Hispanic/Latino; 2 Hispanic/Latino, 5 international. Average age 29. 50 applicants, 56% accepted, 14 enrolled. In 2010, 11 master's awarded. *Degree requirements:* For master's, thesis, exhibit. *Entrance requirements:* For master's, appropriate bachelor's degree, portfolio, resume, letters of recommendation, transcript. Additional exam requirements/recommendations for international students: Required—TOEFL (minimum score 600 paper-based; 250 computer-based; 100 iBT). *Application deadline:* For fall admission, 1/5 for domestic and international students. Application fee: $70. Electronic applications accepted. *Expenses:* Tuition: Full-time $38,550; part-time $1285 per unit. One-time fee: $185 full-time. *Financial support:* In 2010–11, 2 fellowships (averaging $18,000 per year), teaching assistantships (averaging $2,000 per year) were awarded; career-related internships or fieldwork, Federal Work-Study, scholarships/grants, and health care benefits also available. *Unit head:* Leigh Markopoulos, Chair, 415-551-9249, E-mail: lmarkopoulos@cca.edu. *Application contact:* Heidi Geis, Assistant Director of Graduate Admissions, 415-703-9523 Ext. 9533, Fax: 415-703-9539, E-mail: hgeis@cca.edu.

California State University, Chico, Graduate School, College of Behavioral and Social Sciences, Department of Anthropology, Chico, CA 95929-0722. Offers museum studies (MA). *Students:* 22 full-time (19 women), 13 part-time (9 women); includes 1 Asian, non-Hispanic/Latino; 3 Hispanic/Latino, 1 international. Average age 29. 62 applicants, 32% accepted, 17 enrolled. In 2010, 8 master's awarded. *Degree requirements:* For master's, thesis. *Entrance requirements:* For master's, GRE General Test, 2 letters of recommendation. Additional exam requirements/recommendations for international students: Required—TOEFL (minimum score 550 paper-based; 213 computer-based; 80 iBT), IELTS (minimum score 6.5). *Application deadline:* For fall admission, 1/15 for domestic students, 3/1 for international students. Application fee: $55. Electronic applications accepted. *Financial support:* Fellowships, career-related internships or fieldwork available. *Unit head:* Dr. William Collins, Graduate Coordinator, 530-898-4953. *Application contact:* Dr. William Collins, Graduate Coordinator, 530-898-4953.

Caribbean University, Graduate School, Bayamón, PR 00960-0493. Offers administration and supervision (MA Ed); criminal justice (MA); curriculum and instruction (MA Ed, PhD), including elementary education (MA Ed), English education (MA Ed), history education (MA Ed), mathematics education (MA Ed), primary education (MA Ed), science education (MA Ed), Spanish education (MA Ed); educational technology in instructional systems (MA Ed); gerontology (MSN); human resources (MBA); museology, archiving and art history (MA Ed); neonatal pediatrics (MSN); physical education (MA Ed); special education (MA Ed). *Entrance requirements:* For master's, interview, minimum GPA of 2.5.

Case Western Reserve University, School of Graduate Studies, Department of Art History and Art, Program in Art History and Museum Studies, Cleveland, OH 44106. Offers MA, PhD. Part-time programs available. *Faculty:* 8 full-time (6 women), 12 part-time/adjunct (6 women). *Students:* 11 full-time (all women), 5 part-time (4 women), 1 international. Average age 27. 43 applicants, 42% accepted, 6 enrolled. In 2010, 7 master's awarded. *Degree requirements:* For master's, one foreign language, thesis or alternative; for doctorate, 2 foreign languages, thesis/dissertation. *Entrance requirements:* For master's, GRE General Test, 2 samples of written work; for doctorate, GRE General Test, 2 samples of written work and MA thesis. Additional exam requirements/recommendations for international students: Required—TOEFL (minimum score 550 paper-based; 213 computer-based; 79 iBT). *Application deadline:* For fall admission, 1/1 priority date for domestic students. Applications are processed on a rolling basis. Application fee: $50. Electronic applications accepted. *Financial support:* Fellowships, research assistantships, teaching assistantships, career-related internships or fieldwork available. Financial award application deadline: 2/15. *Faculty research:* Greek art and architecture, northern Baroque, Italian Renaissance and Baroque, abstract expressionism, Indian art, nineteenth century French art, American and contemporary art. *Unit head:* Catherine Scallen, Chair, 216-368-2383, Fax: 216-368-4681, E-mail: catherine.scallen@case.edu. *Application contact:* Debby Tenenbaum, Assistant, 216-368-4118, Fax: 216-368-4681, E-mail: deborah.tenenbaum@case.edu.

Christie's Education, Program in Modern Art, Connoisseurship, and the History of the Art Market, New York, NY 10036. Offers MA. *Degree requirements:* For master's, one foreign language, thesis. *Entrance requirements:* For master's, GRE, writing sample, 3 letters of recommendation. Additional exam requirements/recommendations for international students: Required—TOEFL.

City College of the City University of New York, Graduate School, College of Liberal Arts and Science, Division of the Humanities and Arts, Department of Art, Concentrations in Art History and Museum Studies, New York, NY 10031-9198. Offers art history (MA); museum studies (MA). Part-time programs available. *Degree requirements:* For master's, one foreign language, thesis. *Entrance requirements:* For master's, minimum GPA of 3.0, portfolio, art history paper. Additional exam requirements/recommendations for international students: Required—TOEFL (minimum score 577 paper-based; 90 iBT). Electronic applications accepted. *Faculty research:* Egyptian, Greek, medieval, Romanesque, and Ottoman art.

Claremont Graduate University, Graduate Programs, School of Arts and Humanities, Department of Cultural Studies, Claremont, CA 91711-6160. Offers Africana studies (Certificate); cultural studies (MA, PhD); media studies (MA, PhD); museum studies (MA). Part-time programs available. *Faculty:* 2 full-time (1 woman), 1 (woman) part-time/adjunct. *Students:* 57 full-time (36 women), 9 part-time (8 women); includes 12 Black or African American, non-Hispanic/Latino; 1 American Indian or Alaska Native, non-Hispanic/Latino; 3 Asian, non-Hispanic/Latino; 9 Hispanic/Latino; 5 Two or more races, non-Hispanic/Latino, 6 international. Average age 36. In 2010, 9 master's, 5 doctorates awarded. *Entrance requirements:* For master's and doctorate, GRE General Test. Additional exam requirements/recommendations for international students: Required—TOEFL (minimum score 550 paper-based; 213 computer-based; 80 iBT). *Application deadline:* For fall admission, 2/1 priority date for domestic students. Applications are processed on a rolling basis. Application fee: $60. Electronic applications accepted. *Expenses:* Tuition: Full-time $35,748; part-time $1554 per unit. Required fees: $215 per semester. *Financial support:* Fellowships, research assistantships, Federal Work-Study, institutionally sponsored loans, and scholarships/grants available. Support available to part-time students. Financial award application deadline: 2/15; financial award applicants required to submit FAFSA. *Unit head:* Eve Oishi, Chair, 909-607-7587, E-mail: eve.oishi@cgu.edu. *Application contact:* Susan Hampson, Admissions Coordinator, 909-607-1278, Fax: 909-607-1221, E-mail: humanities@cgu.edu.

Cleveland State University, College of Graduate Studies, College of Liberal Arts and Social Sciences, Department of History, Cleveland, OH 44115. Offers art history (MA); history (MA); museum studies (MA). Part-time and evening/weekend programs available. *Faculty:* 18 full-time (6 women), 10 part-time/adjunct (2 women). *Students:* 14 full-time (7 women), 19 part-time (12 women); includes 2 Black or African American, non-Hispanic/Latino. Average age 34. 39 applicants, 51% accepted, 14 enrolled. In 2010, 20 master's awarded. *Degree requirements:* For master's, thesis optional. *Entrance requirements:* For master's, minimum GPA of 3.0, bachelor's degree in history. Additional exam requirements/recommendations for international students: Required—TOEFL (minimum score 525 paper-based; 197 computer-based). *Application deadline:* For fall admission, 7/15 priority date for domestic students. Applications are processed on a rolling basis. Application fee: $30. Electronic applications accepted. *Expenses:* Tuition, state resident: full-time $8447; part-time $469 per credit hour. Tuition, nonresident: full-time $16,020; part-time $890 per credit hour. Required fees: $50. *Financial support:* In 2010–11, 7 students received support, including research assistantships with full tuition reimbursements available (averaging $8,600 per year); career-related internships or fieldwork and unspecified assistantships also available. *Faculty research:* African Diaspora, social history and the city, early modern Europe, local history. *Unit head:* Dr. Elizabeth A. Lehfeldt, Chairperson, 216-687-3920, Fax: 216-687-5592, E-mail: e.lehfeldt@csuohio.edu. *Application contact:* Dr. Robert S. Shelton, Graduate Director, 216-687-3927, E-mail: r.s.shelton@csuohio.edu.

Cleveland State University, College of Graduate Studies, College of Sciences and Health Professions, Department of Biological, Geological, and Environmental Sciences, Cleveland, OH 44115. Offers biology (MS); environmental science (MS); museum studies for natural historians (MS); regulatory biology (PhD); JD/MS. Part-time programs available. *Faculty:* 11 full-time (3 women), 6 part-time/adjunct (3 women). *Students:* 74 full-time (42 women), 35 part-time (19 women); includes 2 Black or African American, non-Hispanic/Latino; 2 Asian, non-Hispanic/Latino; 3 Hispanic/Latino, 41 international. Average age 30. 64 applicants, 13% accepted, 5 enrolled. In 2010, 12 master's, 2 doctorates awarded. Terminal master's awarded for partial completion of doctoral program. *Degree requirements:* For master's, comprehensive exam (for some programs), thesis (for some programs); for doctorate, comprehensive exam, thesis/dissertation. *Entrance requirements:* For master's, GRE General Test, 2 letters of recommendation; for doctorate, GRE General Test, 2 letters of recommendation; 1-2 page essay; statement of career goals and research interests. Additional exam requirements/recommendations for international students: Required—TOEFL (minimum score 525 paper-based; 197 computer-based). *Application deadline:* For fall admission, 4/1 priority date for domestic and international students; for spring admission, 12/1 priority date for domestic students. Applications are processed on a rolling basis. Application fee: $30. Electronic applications accepted. *Expenses:* Tuition, state resident: full-time $8447; part-time $469 per credit hour. Tuition, nonresident: full-time $16,020; part-time $890 per credit hour. Required fees: $50. *Financial support:* In 2010–11, 29 students received support, including research assistantships with full and partial tuition reimbursements available (averaging $16,500 per year), teaching assistantships with full and partial tuition reimbursements available (averaging $16,500 per year); institutionally sponsored loans and unspecified assistantships also available. *Faculty research:* Molecular and cell biology, immunology, urban ecology. *Unit head:* Dr. Jeffrey Dean, Chair, 216-687-2120, Fax: 216-687-6972, E-mail: j.dean@csuohio.edu. *Application contact:* Dr. Jeffrey Dean, Chair, 216-687-2120, Fax: 216-687-6972, E-mail: j.dean@csuohio.edu.

Duquesne University, Graduate School of Liberal Arts, Department of History, Pittsburgh, PA 15282-0001. Offers archival, museum, and editing studies (MA); history (MA). Part-time and evening/weekend programs available. *Faculty:* 6 full-time (1 woman), 3 part-time/adjunct (1 woman). *Students:* 38 full-time (25 women), 9 part-time (4 women). Average age 26. 52 applicants, 67% accepted, 20 enrolled. In 2010, 20 master's awarded. *Degree requirements:* For master's, comprehensive exam (for some programs), thesis optional. *Entrance requirements:* For master's, GRE General Test, writing sample. Additional exam requirements/recommendations for international students: Required—TOEFL. *Application deadline:* For fall admission, 8/15 for domestic students, 5/1 for international students; for spring admission, 11/1 priority date for domestic students. Applications are processed on a rolling basis. Electronic applications accepted. *Expenses:* Tuition: Part-time $884 per credit. Required fees: $84 per credit. Tuition and fees vary according to course load. *Financial support:* In 2010–11, 4 research assistantships with full tuition reimbursements (averaging $6,000 per year) were awarded; career-related internships or fieldwork, Federal Work-Study, scholarships/grants, tuition waivers (full and partial), and unspecified assistantships also available. Support available to part-time students. Financial award application deadline: 5/1. *Faculty research:* American studies, immigration history, local social history, applied history, Eastern European history. *Unit head:* Dr. Holly Mayer, Chair, 412-396-6470, E-mail: mayer@duq.edu. *Application contact:* Dr. Holly Mayer, Chair, 412-396-6470, E-mail: mayer@duq.edu.

Fashion Institute of Technology, School of Graduate Studies, Program in Exhibition Design, New York, NY 10001-5992. Offers MA. *Entrance requirements:* Additional exam requirements/recommendations for international students: Required—TOEFL (minimum score 550 paper-based; 213 computer-based). Electronic applications accepted.

See Display below and Close-Up on page 123.

Fashion Institute of Technology, School of Graduate Studies, Programs in Fashion and Textile Studies: History, Theory, Museum Practice, New York, NY 10001-5992. Offers MA. *Accreditation:* NASAD. *Degree requirements:* For master's, one foreign language, thesis, internship. *Entrance requirements:* For master's, GRE General Test or GRE Subject Test, previous course work in art history and chemistry, 4 semesters of a foreign language. Additional exam requirements/recommendations for international students: Required—TOEFL (minimum score 550 paper-based; 213 computer-based). Electronic applications accepted.

See Display below and Close-Up on page 219.

Florida State University, The Graduate School, College of Visual Arts, Theatre and Dance, Department of Art History, Tallahassee, FL 32306. Offers art history (MA, PhD); museum studies (Certificate). *Accreditation:* NASAD. Part-time programs available. *Faculty:* 10 full-time (5 women), 5 part-time/adjunct (3 women). *Students:* 34 full-time (26 women), 15 part-time (14 women); includes 4 minority (1 Asian, non-Hispanic/Latino; 2 Hispanic/Latino; 1 Two or more races, non-Hispanic/Latino), 1 international. Average age 32. 54 applicants, 54% accepted, 16 enrolled. In 2010, 9 master's, 4 doctorates awarded. Terminal master's awarded for partial completion of doctoral program. *Degree requirements:* For master's, one foreign language, thesis (for some programs), first-year review; for doctorate, 2 foreign languages, comprehensive exam, thesis/dissertation, first-year review. *Entrance requirements:* For master's, GRE General Test, minimum GPA of 3.0; for doctorate, GRE General Test, minimum GPA of 3.5. Additional exam requirements/recommendations for international students: Required—TOEFL. *Application deadline:* For fall admission, 1/10 for domestic students, 1/11 for international students. Application fee: $30. Electronic applications accepted. *Expenses:* Tuition, state resident: full-time $8238.24. *Financial support:* In 2010–11, 27 students received support, including 1 fellowship with full tuition reimbursement available (averaging $18,000 per year), 21 research assistantships with full tuition reimbursements available (averaging $5,000 per year), 5 teaching assistantships with full tuition reimbursements available (averaging $13,000 per year); career-related internships or fieldwork, Federal Work-Study, institutionally sponsored loans, scholarships/grants, and unspecified assistantships also available. Financial award application deadline: 1/11; financial award applicants required to submit FAFSA. *Faculty research:* Modern art and critical theory; medieval, Renaissance and Baroque art; Pre-Colombian. *Unit head:* Dr. Adam Jolles, Professor/Chair, 850-644-7066, Fax: 850-644-7065, E-mail: ajolles@fsu.edu. *Application contact:* Kathy Braun, Programs Coordinator/Graduate Student Advisor, 850-644-8207, Fax: 850-644-7065.

Florida State University, The Graduate School, College of Visual Arts, Theatre and Dance, Program in Museum Studies, Tallahassee, FL 32306. Offers Certificate. Part-time programs available. *Students:* 46 part-time (37 women); includes 3 Asian, non-Hispanic/Latino; 2 Hispanic/Latino. Average age 24. 10 applicants, 100% accepted, 10 enrolled. In 2010, 7 Certificates awarded. *Degree requirements:* For Certificate, internship. *Entrance requirements:* For degree,

GRE, graduate degree or current study towards a graduate degree. *Application deadline:* For fall admission, 8/15 priority date for domestic and international students; for spring admission, 12/15 for domestic and international students. Applications are processed on a rolling basis. Application fee: $30. *Expenses:* Tuition, state resident: full-time $8238.24. *Financial support:* Career-related internships or fieldwork available. *Unit head:* Dr. Teri R. Yoo, Academic Coordinator, 850-645-4681, Fax: 850-644-7229, E-mail: tyoo@fsu.edu. *Application contact:* Dr. Teri R. Yoo, Academic Coordinator, 850-645-4681, Fax: 850-644-7229, E-mail: tyoo@fsu.edu.

The George Washington University, Columbian College of Arts and Sciences, Department of Fine Arts and Art History, Program in Art History, Washington, DC 20052. Offers art history (MA); museum training (MA). Part-time and evening/weekend programs available. *Students:* 14 full-time (13 women), 11 part-time (all women); includes 1 Asian, non-Hispanic/Latino; 1 Hispanic/Latino. Average age 29. 64 applicants, 59% accepted. In 2010, 7 master's awarded. *Degree requirements:* For master's, one foreign language, comprehensive exam, thesis or alternative. *Entrance requirements:* For master's, GRE General Test, bachelor's degree in field, minimum GPA of 3.0. Additional exam requirements/recommendations for international students: Required—TOEFL (minimum score 550 paper-based; 213 computer-based; 80 iBT). *Application deadline:* For fall admission, 3/1 priority date for domestic students, 1/15 priority date for international students; for spring admission, 10/1 priority date for domestic students, 9/1 priority date for international students. Applications are processed on a rolling basis. Application fee: $75. Electronic applications accepted. *Financial support:* In 2010–11, 3 students received support; fellowships, teaching assistantships, career-related internships or fieldwork and Federal Work-Study available. Financial award application deadline: 1/15. *Application contact:* Information Contact, 202-994-6085, Fax: 202-994-8657, E-mail: art@gwu.edu.

The George Washington University, Columbian College of Arts and Sciences, Program in Museum Studies, Washington, DC 20052. Offers MA, Certificate. Part-time and evening/weekend programs available. *Faculty:* 4 full-time (all women), 3 part-time/adjunct (all women). *Students:* 91 full-time (82 women), 64 part-time (56 women); includes 10 Black or African American, non-Hispanic/Latino; 2 American Indian or Alaska Native, non-Hispanic/Latino; 5 Asian, non-Hispanic/Latino; 4 Hispanic/Latino, 3 international. Average age 27. 283 applicants, 54% accepted, 56 enrolled. In 2010, 43 master's, 22 other advanced degrees awarded. *Degree requirements:* For master's, comprehensive exam, internship. *Entrance requirements:* For master's, GRE General Test, minimum GPA of 3.0. Additional exam requirements/recommendations for international students: Required—TOEFL (minimum score 550 paper-based; 213 computer-based; 80 iBT). *Application deadline:* For fall admission, 2/1 priority date for domestic students, 1/15 priority date for international students; for spring admission, 10/15 priority date for domestic students, 9/1 priority date for international students. Applications are processed on a rolling basis. Application fee: $75. Electronic applications accepted. *Financial support:* In 2010–11, 15 students received support; fellowships with tuition reimbursements available, career-related internships or fieldwork, Federal Work-Study, institutionally sponsored loans, and tuition waivers available. Financial award application deadline: 1/15. *Unit head:* Kym S. Rice, Director, 202-994-0165, Fax: 202-994-7034, E-mail: kym@gwu.edu. *Application contact:* Information Contact, 202-994-7030, Fax: 202-994-7034, E-mail: mstd@gwu.edu.

Harvard University, Extension School, Cambridge, MA 02138-3722. Offers applied sciences (CAS); biotechnology (ALM); educational technologies (ALM); educational technology (CET); English for graduate and professional studies (DGP); environmental management (ALM, CEM); information technology (ALM); journalism (ALM); liberal arts (ALM); management (ALM, CM); mathematics for teaching (ALM); museum studies (ALM); premedical studies (Diploma); publication and communication (CPC). Part-time and evening/weekend programs available. *Degree requirements:* For master's, thesis. *Entrance requirements:* For master's, 3 completed graduate courses with grade of B or higher. Additional exam requirements/recommendations for international students: Required—TOEFL (minimum score 600 paper-based; 250 computer-based), TWE (minimum score 5). *Expenses:* Contact institution.

Indiana University–Purdue University Indianapolis, School of Liberal Arts, Department of Museum Studies, Indianapolis, IN 46202. Offers MS, Certificate. *Students:* 28 full-time (25

Museum Studies

Indiana University–Purdue University Indianapolis (continued)
women), 12 part-time (all women); includes 1 minority (Hispanic/Latino). Average age 27. 69 applicants, 46% accepted, 26 enrolled. In 2010, 11 master's, 4 other advanced degrees awarded. *Entrance requirements:* For master's, GRE. *Application deadline:* For fall admission, 2/1 for domestic students; for spring admission, 10/1 for domestic students. Application fee: $55 ($65 for international students). *Financial support:* In 2010–11, 1 fellowship with partial tuition reimbursement (averaging $9,000 per year), 3 teaching assistantships (averaging $9,667 per year) were awarded. Financial award application deadline: 2/1; financial award applicants required to submit FAFSA. *Unit head:* Robert W. White, Dean, School of Liberal Arts, 317-274-8448. *Application contact:* Becky Ellis, Information Contact, 317-274-1490, E-mail: museum@iupui.edu.

John F. Kennedy University, School of Education and Liberal Arts, Department of Museum Studies, Berkeley, CA 94702. Offers museum studies (MA, Certificate), including administration, collections management, public programming. Part-time programs available. *Degree requirements:* For master's, project. *Entrance requirements:* For master's, interview. Additional exam requirements/recommendations for international students: Required—TOEFL, TWE. *Faculty research:* Emerging museum philosophies, multicultural diversity issues in museums, trends in collections management and preventive conservation, effective programming techniques and application for diverse audiences.

The Johns Hopkins University, Zanvyl Krieger School of Arts and Sciences, Advanced Academic Programs, Program in Museum Studies, Baltimore, MD 21218-2699. Offers MA. Postbaccalaureate distance learning degree programs offered (minimal on-campus study). *Faculty:* 2 full-time (both women), 21 part-time/adjunct (11 women). *Students:* 4 full-time (all women), 218 part-time (190 women); includes 30 minority (7 Black or African American, non-Hispanic/Latino; 1 American Indian or Alaska Native, non-Hispanic/Latino; 7 Asian, non-Hispanic/Latino; 8 Hispanic/Latino; 1 Native Hawaiian or other Pacific Islander, non-Hispanic/Latino; 6 Two or more races, non-Hispanic/Latino), 8 international. Average age 33. 140 applicants, 47% accepted, 65 enrolled. In 2010, 9 master's awarded. Application fee: $75. *Financial support:* Scholarships/grants available. *Unit head:* Phyllis Hecht, Associate Program Chair, 202-452-1968, E-mail: phecht@jhu.edu. *Application contact:* Valana M. McMickens, Admissions Manager, 202-452-1941, Fax: 202-452-1970, E-mail: aapadmissions@jhu.edu.

Maryland Institute College of Art, Graduate Studies, Program in Curatorial Practice, Baltimore, MD 21217. Offers MFA. Part-time programs available. *Entrance requirements:* For master's, portfolio, 40 studio credits, 6 credits in art history. Additional exam requirements/recommendations for international students: Required—TOEFL (minimum score 550 paper-based; 213 computer-based; 80 iBT). *Application deadline:* For fall admission, 1/15 for domestic and international students. Application fee: $60. *Expenses:* Tuition: Full-time $34,550; part-time $1440 per credit hour. Required fees: $1140; $570 per term. *Financial support:* Application deadline: 3/1. *Unit head:* Guna Nadarajan, Associate Provost for Research and Dean of Graduate Studies, 410-225-5273, Fax: 410-225-5275, E-mail: graduate@mica.edu. *Application contact:* Scott G. Kelly, Associate Dean of Graduate Admission, 410-225-2256, Fax: 410-225-2408, E-mail: graduate@mica.edu.

Montclair State University, The Graduate School, School of the Arts, Department of Art and Design, Montclair, NJ 07043-1624. Offers art (Certificate); fine arts (MA), including museum management, studio; studio art (MFA). *Accreditation:* NASAD (one or more programs are accredited). Part-time and evening/weekend programs available. *Faculty:* 28 full-time (12 women), 91 part-time/adjunct (50 women). *Students:* 37 full-time (25 women), 30 part-time (24 women); includes 2 Black or African American, non-Hispanic/Latino; 4 Asian, non-Hispanic/Latino; 5 Hispanic/Latino; 2 Two or more races, non-Hispanic/Latino, 3 international. Average age 34. 49 applicants, 71% accepted, 18 enrolled. In 2010, 16 master's awarded. *Degree requirements:* For master's, project. *Entrance requirements:* For master's, GRE General Test or MAT (MA), portfolio, undergraduate degree in fine arts or equivalent, 2 letters of recommendation, teaching certificate (art education). Additional exam requirements/recommendations for international students: Required—TOEFL (minimum iBT score of 83) or IELTS. *Application deadline:* For fall admission, 2/1 for domestic and international students. Applications are processed on a rolling basis. Application fee: $60. Electronic applications accepted. *Expenses:* Tuition, state resident: part-time $501.34 per credit. Tuition, nonresident: part-time $773.88 per credit. Required fees: $71.15 per credit. *Financial support:* In 2010–11, 4 research assistantships with full tuition reimbursements (averaging $7,000 per year) were awarded; Federal Work-Study, scholarships/grants, and unspecified assistantships also available. Support available to part-time students. Financial award application deadline: 3/1; financial award applicants required to submit FAFSA. *Unit head:* Dr. Scott Gordley, Chairperson, 973-655-7295. *Application contact:* Amy Aiello, Director of Graduate Admissions and Operations, 973-655-5147, E-mail: graduate.school@montclair.edu.

New York University, Graduate School of Arts and Science, Program in Museum Studies, New York, NY 10012-1019. Offers museum studies (MA, Advanced Certificate), including Africana studies (MA), Hebrew and Judaic studies (MA), Latin American and Caribbean studies (MA), Near Eastern studies (MA). Part-time and evening/weekend programs available. *Students:* 61 full-time (56 women), 16 part-time (13 women); includes 1 Black or African American, non-Hispanic/Latino; 1 American Indian or Alaska Native, non-Hispanic/Latino; 6 Asian, non-Hispanic/Latino; 5 Hispanic/Latino, 14 international. Average age 26. 200 applicants, 50% accepted, 38 enrolled. In 2010, 40 master's, 3 other advanced degrees awarded. *Entrance requirements:* For degree, master's degree or PhD. Additional exam requirements/recommendations for international students: Required—TOEFL. *Application deadline:* For fall admission, 2/15 for domestic students; for spring admission, 11/1 for domestic students. Application fee: $90. *Financial support:* Application deadline: 2/15. *Faculty research:* Modern and contemporary art, history of museums and exhibitions, conservation of cultural materials, museum anthropology, ethnography. *Unit head:* Bruce Altshuler, Director, 212-998-8080, Fax: 212-995-4185, E-Mail: museum.studies@nyu.edu. *Application contact:* Tatiana Kamorina, Department Administrator, 212-998-8080, Fax: 212-995-4185, E-mail: museum.studies@nyu.edu.

San Francisco Art Institute, Graduate Program, Department of Exhibition and Museum Studies, San Francisco, CA 94133. Offers MA. *Entrance requirements:* Additional exam requirements/recommendations for international students: Required—TOEFL (minimum score 580 paper-based; 237 computer-based). Electronic applications accepted.

San Francisco State University, Division of Graduate Studies, College of Humanities, Museum Studies Program, San Francisco, CA 94132-1722. Offers MA. Part-time programs available. *Financial support:* Career-related internships or fieldwork and Federal Work-Study available. *Unit head:* Dr. Linda Ellis, Director, 415-338-1612, E-mail: ellisl@sfsu.edu. *Application contact:* Christine Fogarty, Program Coordinator, 415-405-0599, Fax: 415-338-1775, E-mail: cfog@sfsu.edu.

Seton Hall University, College of Arts and Sciences, Department of Art, Music and Design, South Orange, NJ 07079-2697. Offers museum professions (MA), including exhibition development, museum education, museum management, museum registration. Part-time and evening/weekend programs available. *Degree requirements:* For master's, thesis. *Entrance requirements:* For master's, GRE General Test, previous course work in art history. Additional exam requirements/recommendations for international students: Required—TOEFL. Electronic applications accepted. *Faculty research:* History of museums, museum education, theory of museums, nineteenth century art, African-American art, Renaissance art history, museum registration, museum ethics.

Southern Illinois University Edwardsville, Graduate School, College of Arts and Sciences, Department of Historical Studies, Program in Museum Studies, Edwardsville, IL 62026-0001. Offers Postbaccalaureate Certificate. Part-time and evening/weekend programs available. *Students:* 2 full-time (both women), 4 part-time (3 women). Average age 26. 3 applicants, 33%

accepted. In 2010, 8 Postbaccalaureate Certificates awarded. *Entrance requirements:* Additional exam requirements/recommendations for international students: Required—TOEFL (minimum score 550 paper-based; 213 computer-based; 79 iBT), IELTS (minimum score 6.5). *Application deadline:* For fall admission, 7/22 for domestic students, 6/1 for international students; for spring admission, 12/9 for domestic students, 10/1 for international students. Applications are processed on a rolling basis. Application fee: $30. Electronic applications accepted. *Expenses:* Tuition, state resident: full-time $6012; part-time $1503 per semester. Tuition, nonresident: full-time $15,030; part-time $3758 per semester. Required fees: $1711; $675 per semester. *Financial support:* In 2010–11, 1 teaching assistantship with full tuition reimbursement (averaging $8,064 per year) was awarded; fellowships with full tuition reimbursements, research assistantships with full tuition reimbursements, career-related internships or fieldwork, Federal Work-Study, institutionally sponsored loans, scholarships/grants, traineeships, and unspecified assistantships also available. Support available to part-time students. Financial award application deadline: 3/1; financial award applicants required to submit FAFSA. *Unit head:* Dr. Laura Fowler Milsk, Director, 618-650-2145, E-mail: lmilsk@siue.edu. *Application contact:* Dr. Laura Fowler Milsk, Director, 618-650-2145, E-mail: lmilsk@siue.edu.

State University of New York College at Oneonta, Graduate Education, Cooperstown Graduate Program in History Museum Studies, Cooperstown, NY 13326. Offers MA. *Students:* 29 full-time (23 women), 2 part-time (1 woman). Average age 25. 93 applicants, 34% accepted, 31 enrolled. In 2010, 16 master's awarded. *Degree requirements:* For master's, research paper or thesis. *Entrance requirements:* For master's, GRE General Test. *Application deadline:* For fall admission, 1/10 for domestic students. Application fee: $50. *Expenses:* Contact institution. *Unit head:* Dr. Gretchen Sorin, Director, 607-547-2586, Fax: 607-547-8926, E-mail: sorings@oneonta.edu. *Application contact:* Patrick J. Mente, Director of Graduate Studies, 607-436-2523, Fax: 607-436-3084, E-mail: gradstudies@oneonta.edu.

Syracuse University, College of Visual and Performing Arts, Program in Museum Studies, Syracuse, NY 13244. Offers MA. *Accreditation:* NASAD. *Students:* 23 full-time (20 women), 2 part-time (1 woman); includes 3 minority (1 Black or African American, non-Hispanic/Latino; 1 Asian, non-Hispanic/Latino; 1 Two or more races, non-Hispanic/Latino). Average age 26. 39 applicants, 79% accepted, 11 enrolled. In 2010, 15 master's awarded. *Degree requirements:* For master's, thesis or alternative. *Entrance requirements:* Additional exam requirements/recommendations for international students: Required—TOEFL (minimum score 100 iBT). *Application deadline:* For fall admission, 2/1 priority date for domestic and international students. Application fee: $75. Electronic applications accepted. *Expenses:* Tuition: Part-time $1162 per credit. *Financial support:* Fellowships with full tuition reimbursements, teaching assistantships with full and partial tuition reimbursements available. Financial award application deadline: 1/1; financial award applicants required to submit FAFSA. *Unit head:* Dr. Lucinda Havenhand, Chair, 315-443-2455, Fax: 315-443-1303, E-mail: lkhavenh@syr.edu. *Application contact:* Harriett Conti, Assistant Dean for Recruitment and Admissions, 315-443-5755, E-mail: hmconti@syr.edu.

Texas Tech University, Graduate School, Programs in Museum Science and Heritage Management, Lubbock, TX 79409. Offers heritage management (MS); museum science (MA). Part-time programs available. *Faculty:* 6 full-time (4 women). *Students:* 38 full-time (33 women), 3 part-time (all women); includes 1 Black or African American, non-Hispanic/Latino; 1 American Indian or Alaska Native, non-Hispanic/Latino; 6 Hispanic/Latino. Average age 25. 35 applicants, 74% accepted, 20 enrolled. In 2010, 18 master's awarded. *Degree requirements:* For master's, thesis. *Entrance requirements:* For master's, GRE General Test. Additional exam requirements/recommendations for international students: Required—TOEFL (minimum score 550 paper-based; 213 computer-based; 79 iBT). *Application deadline:* For fall admission, 6/1 priority date for domestic students, 1/15 priority date for international students; for spring admission, 9/1 priority date for domestic students, 6/15 priority date for international students. Applications are processed on a rolling basis. Application fee: $50 ($75 for international students). Electronic applications accepted. *Expenses:* Tuition, state resident: full-time $5495.76; part-time $228.99 per credit hour. Tuition, nonresident: full-time $12,936; part-time $538.99 per credit hour. Required fees: $2674; $36 per credit hour. $905 per semester. *Financial support:* In 2010–11, 4 students received support, including 2 research assistantships with partial tuition reimbursements available (averaging $2,393 per year); teaching assistantships with partial tuition reimbursements available. Financial award application deadline: 4/15; financial award applicants required to submit FAFSA. *Faculty research:* Lubbock Lake Landmark, regional American fine art, museum education, Southern Plains cultural and natural heritage, natural science research. Total annual research expenditures: $143,295. *Unit head:* Dr. Eileen Johnson, Chair, 806-742-2442, Fax: 806-742-1136, E-mail: eileen.johnson@ttu.edu. *Application contact:* Claudia Cory, Assistant to the Director, 806-742-2442 Ext. 222, Fax: 806-742-1136, E-mail: claudia.cory@ttu.edu.

Tufts University, Graduate School of Arts and Sciences, Graduate Certificate Programs, Museum Studies Program, Medford, MA 02155. Offers Certificate. Part-time and evening/weekend programs available. *Expenses:* Contact institution.

Université de Montréal, Faculty of Arts and Sciences, Program in Museology, Montréal, QC H3C 3J7, Canada. Offers MA. Program offered jointly with Université du Québec à Montréal. Electronic applications accepted. *Faculty research:* Museum exhibits, museum education, natural science and museums, new technologies and museums.

Université du Québec à Montréal, Graduate Programs, Program in Museology, Montréal, QC H3C 3P8, Canada. Offers MA. Part-time programs available. *Entrance requirements:* For master's, appropriate bachelor's degree or equivalent and proficiency in French.

Université Laval, Faculty of Letters, Department of History, Program in Museology, Québec, QC G1K 7P4, Canada. Offers Diploma. Part-time programs available. *Entrance requirements:* For degree, English exam (comprehension of English), knowledge of French. Electronic applications accepted.

University at Buffalo, the State University of New York, Graduate School, College of Arts and Sciences, Department of Visual Studies, Program in Art History, Buffalo, NY 14260. Offers art history (MA); critical museum studies (Certificate). Part-time programs available. *Degree requirements:* For master's, one foreign language, thesis, field exam. *Entrance requirements:* Additional exam requirements/recommendations for international students: Required—TOEFL (minimum score 79 iBT). Electronic applications accepted. *Faculty research:* Frank Lloyd Wright, non-Western art, Renaissance, Bronze Age Crete, American art.

The University of British Columbia, Faculty of Arts and Faculty of Graduate Studies, Department of Art History, Visual Art, and Theory, Vancouver, BC V6T1Z2, Canada. Offers art history (MA, PhD, Diploma); critical and curatorial studies (MA); visual art (MFA). *Degree requirements:* For master's, one foreign language, thesis, final exhibition (MFA, MA in critical and curatorial studies); for doctorate, 2 foreign languages, comprehensive exam, thesis/dissertation. *Entrance requirements:* For master's, bachelor's degree with minimum B+ average (MFA, MA in critical and curatorial studies), A- (MA in art history); for doctorate, master's degree with minimum A- average. Additional exam requirements/recommendations for international students: Required—TOEFL (minimum score 600 paper-based; 250 computer-based). Electronic applications accepted. Tuition charges are reported in Canadian dollars. *Expenses:* Tuition, area resident: Full-time $4179 Canadian dollars. International tuition: $7344 Canadian dollars full-time. *Faculty research:* Conceptual art, Asian art, indigenous North American art, post-second war art, eighteenth and nineteenth century art, curatorial, digital art.

University of California, Riverside, Graduate Division, Department of History, Riverside, CA 92521-0102. Offers archival management (MA); historic preservation (MA); history (MA, PhD); museum curatorship (MA). Part-time programs available. Terminal master's awarded for partial completion of doctoral program. *Degree requirements:* For master's, one foreign language, comprehensive exam, internship report and oral exams, or thesis; for doctorate, 2 foreign languages, thesis/dissertation, qualifying exams, teaching experience. *Entrance requirements:*

For master's, GRE General Test, minimum GPA of 3.2; for doctorate, GRE General Test, MA in history, minimum GPA of 3.2. Additional exam requirements/recommendations for international students: Required—TOEFL (minimum score 550 paper-based; 213 computer-based; 80 iBT). Electronic applications accepted. *Faculty research:* Native American history, United States, public history, Russia, Europe.

University of Central Oklahoma, College of Graduate Studies and Research, College of Liberal Arts, Department of History, Edmond, OK 73034-5209. Offers history (MA); museum studies (MA); social studies teaching (MA); Southwestern studies (MA). Part-time programs available. *Degree requirements:* For master's, thesis optional. *Entrance requirements:* Additional exam requirements/recommendations for international students: Required—TOEFL (minimum score 550 paper-based; 213 computer-based). Electronic applications accepted. *Faculty research:* China, Russia, civil war, American naval logistics.

University of Colorado Boulder, Graduate School, Museum and Field Studies Program, Boulder, CO 80309. Offers MS. *Students:* 16 full-time (15 women), 2 part-time (1 woman). Average age 29. 72 applicants, 9 enrolled. In 2010, 11 master's awarded. *Degree requirements:* For master's, comprehensive exam, thesis or alternative. *Entrance requirements:* For master's, GRE General Test, GRE Subject Test, minimum undergraduate GPA of 3.0. *Application deadline:* For fall admission, 1/15 for domestic students, 12/1 for international students. Application fee: $50 ($60 for international students). *Financial support:* In 2010–11, 1 fellowship (averaging $3,000 per year), 2 research assistantships (averaging $6,584 per year) were awarded; career-related internships or fieldwork, Federal Work-Study, institutionally sponsored loans, and tuition waivers (partial) also available. Financial award application deadline: 2/1; financial award applicants required to submit FAFSA. Total annual research expenditures: $111,794.

University of Denver, Division of Arts, Humanities and Social Sciences, Department of Anthropology, Denver, CO 80208. Offers archaeology (MA); cultural anthropology (MA); museum studies (MA). Part-time programs available. *Faculty:* 8 full-time (4 women). *Students:* 1 (woman) full-time, 17 part-time (12 women); includes 4 minority (2 Black or African American, non-Hispanic/Latino; 1 American Indian or Alaska Native, non-Hispanic/Latino; 1 Hispanic/Latino), 1 international. Average age 26. 45 applicants, 47% accepted, 8 enrolled. In 2010, 11 master's awarded. *Degree requirements:* For master's, comprehensive exam, thesis or alternative, proficiency in foreign language other than English or in quantitative methods. *Entrance requirements:* For master's, GRE General Test. Additional exam requirements/recommendations for international students: Required—TOEFL (minimum score 550 paper-based; 80 iBT). *Application deadline:* Applications are processed on a rolling basis. Application fee: $60. Electronic applications accepted. *Expenses:* Tuition: Full-time $35,604; part-time $29,670 per year. Required fees: $687 per year. Tuition and fees vary according to program. *Financial support:* In 2010–11, 12 teaching assistantships with full and partial tuition reimbursements (averaging $4,667 per year) were awarded; career-related internships or fieldwork, Federal Work-Study, institutionally sponsored loans, scholarships/grants, and unspecified assistantships also available. Support available to part-time students. Financial award application deadline: 3/15; financial award applicants required to submit FAFSA. *Faculty research:* Gender, class, race, ground-penetrating radar, archaeology. *Unit head:* Dr. Dean J. Saitta, Chair, 303-871-2680, E-mail: dsaitta@du.edu. *Application contact:* Carrie Shrader, Assistant to Chair, 303-871-2677, E-mail: anth02@du.edu.

University of Denver, Division of Arts, Humanities and Social Sciences, School of Art and Art History, Denver, CO 80208. Offers art history (MA); art history/museum studies (MA); electronic media arts and design (MFA). *Accreditation:* NASAD. Part-time programs available. *Faculty:* 13 full-time (7 women), 10 part-time/adjunct (3 women). *Students:* 14 full-time (12 women), 11 part-time (10 women); includes 2 minority (both Hispanic/Latino). Average age 29. 61 applicants, 46% accepted, 11 enrolled. In 2010, 19 master's awarded. *Degree requirements:* For master's, one foreign language, comprehensive exam, research paper. *Entrance requirements:* For master's, GRE General Test. Additional exam requirements/recommendations for international students: Required—TOEFL (minimum score 550 paper-based; 80 iBT). *Application deadline:* Applications are processed on a rolling basis. Application fee: $60. Electronic applications accepted. *Expenses:* Tuition: Full-time $35,604; part-time $29,670 per year. Required fees: $687 per year. Tuition and fees vary according to program. *Financial support:* In 2010–11, 2 teaching assistantships with full and partial tuition reimbursements (averaging $10,500 per year) were awarded; career-related internships or fieldwork, Federal Work-Study, institutionally sponsored loans, scholarships/grants, and unspecified assistantships also available. Support available to part-time students. Financial award application deadline: 3/1; financial award applicants required to submit FAFSA. *Faculty research:* Images of women in alchemical manuscripts and books, Giovanni Benedetto, Salvatore Castiglione. *Unit head:* Dr. M. E. Warlick, Director, 303-871-2371, E-mail: mwarlick@du.edu. *Application contact:* Dr. Annabeth Headrick, Graduate Admissions Coordinator, 303-871-3574, E-mail: saah-interest@du.edu.

University of Florida, Graduate School, College of Fine Arts, School of Art and Art History, Gainesville, FL 32611. Offers art (MFA), including ceramics, creative photography, drawing, electronic intermedia, graphic design, painting, printmaking, sculpture; art education (MA); art history (MA, PhD); digital arts and sciences (MA); museology (museum studies) (MA). *Accreditation:* NASAD. Postbaccalaureate distance learning degree programs offered (minimal on-campus study). *Faculty:* 29 full-time (14 women). *Students:* 107 full-time (72 women), 57 part-time (52 women); includes 6 Black or African American, non-Hispanic/Latino; 1 American Indian or Alaska Native, non-Hispanic/Latino; 5 Asian, non-Hispanic/Latino; 13 Hispanic/Latino, 14 international. Average age 31. 282 applicants, 30% accepted, 61 enrolled. In 2010, 24 master's, 3 doctorates awarded. *Degree requirements:* For master's, thesis, project or thesis (MFA); 1 foreign language (MA in art history); for doctorate, 2 foreign languages, comprehensive exam, thesis/dissertation. *Entrance requirements:* For master's, GRE General Test, portfolio (MFA), writing sample (MA), minimum GPA of 3.0; for doctorate, GRE General Test, minimum GPA of 3.0. Additional exam requirements/recommendations for international students: Required—TOEFL (minimum score 550 paper-based; 213 computer-based; 80 iBT), IELTS (minimum score 6). *Application deadline:* For fall admission, 1/1 priority date for domestic students, 1/1 for international students; for spring admission, 11/1 for domestic and international students. Applications are processed on a rolling basis. Application fee: $30. Electronic applications accepted. *Expenses:* Tuition, state resident: full-time $10,915.92. Tuition, nonresident: full-time $28,309. *Financial support:* In 2010–11, 36 students received support, including 9 fellowships, 3 research assistantships with tuition reimbursements available (averaging $12,789 per year), 24 teaching assistantships with tuition reimbursements available (averaging $10,512 per year); Federal Work-Study, institutionally sponsored loans, and unspecified assistantships also available. Financial award applicants required to submit FAFSA. *Faculty research:* Studio production, art historical studies of style context. *Unit head:* Laura Robertsoon, SR Associate in Graduate Studies, 352-846-3425, E-mail: laurar@ufl.edu. *Application contact:* Lauren G. Lake, Coordinator, 352-273-3032, Fax: 352-392-8453, E-mail: lglake@arts.ufl.edu.

University of Hawaii at Manoa, Graduate Division, College of Arts and Humanities, Department of American Studies, Program in Museum Studies, Honolulu, HI 96822. Offers Graduate Certificate. Part-time programs available. *Faculty:* 34 full-time (10 women). *Students:* 51 full-time (16 women), 16 part-time (3 women); includes 24 minority (1 American Indian or Alaska Native, non-Hispanic/Latino; 6 Asian, non-Hispanic/Latino; 1 Hispanic/Latino; 4 Native Hawaiian or other Pacific Islander, non-Hispanic/Latino; 12 Two or more races, non-Hispanic/Latino), 10 international. Average age 34. 62 applicants, 55% accepted, 15 enrolled. In 2010, 7 Graduate Certificates awarded. *Entrance requirements:* Additional exam requirements/recommendations for international students: Required—TOEFL (minimum score 600 paper-based; 250 computer-based; 100 iBT), IELTS (minimum score 7). *Application deadline:* For fall admission, 3/1 for domestic and international students; for spring admission, 9/1 for domestic and international students. Application fee: $60. *Financial support:* In 2010–11, 18 fellowships (averaging $6,775 per year), 1 research assistantship (averaging $17,496 per year), 14 teaching assistantships (averaging $15,055 per year) were awarded. *Application contact:* Karen Kosasa, Director, 808-956-8676, Fax: 808-956-4733, E-mail: kosasa@hawaii.edu.

The University of Kansas, Graduate Studies, College of Liberal Arts and Sciences, Museum Studies Program, Lawrence, KS 66045-7545. Offers MA. Part-time programs available. *Faculty:* 4 part-time/adjunct. *Students:* 20 full-time (16 women), 6 part-time (3 women); includes 3 minority (all Hispanic/Latino), 2 international. Average age 26. 43 applicants, 51% accepted, 9 enrolled. In 2010, 11 master's awarded. *Degree requirements:* For master's, comprehensive exam, 18 hours of required courses; 18 hours in academic track courses; 6 credit hours supervised internship. *Entrance requirements:* For master's, GRE, 3 letters of recommendation, resume, writing sample, statement of purpose, official transcripts. Additional exam requirements/recommendations for international students: Required—TOEFL. *Application deadline:* For fall admission, 1/1 priority date for domestic and international students; for spring admission, 8/15 priority date for domestic and international students. Applications are processed on a rolling basis. Application fee: $55 ($65 for international students). Electronic applications accepted. *Expenses:* Tuition, state resident: full-time $7092; part-time $295.50 per credit hour. Tuition, nonresident: full-time $16,590; part-time $691.25 per credit hour. Required fees: $858; $71.49 per credit hour. Tuition and fees vary according to course load, campus/location and program. *Financial support:* Research assistantships with partial tuition reimbursements, career-related internships or fieldwork and unspecified assistantships available. *Faculty research:* Museum history, museum theory, collection studies, museum anthropology, cultural studies, history, natural history, American Studies, anthropology, geology. *Unit head:* Dr. Dennis Domer, Director, 785-864-4543, E-mail: museumstudies@ku.edu. *Application contact:* Holly Shriner, Senior Administrative Associate, 785-864-4543, Fax: 785-864-0370, E-mail: hshriner@ku.edu.

University of Louisville, Graduate School, College of Arts and Sciences, Department of Fine Arts, Louisville, KY 40292. Offers art history (MA, PhD); creative art (MA); curatorial studies (MA). *Faculty:* 18 full-time (8 women), 3 part-time/adjunct (0 women). *Students:* 22 full-time (19 women), 12 part-time (10 women); includes 1 Black or African American, non-Hispanic/Latino, 2 international. Average age 34. 21 applicants, 48% accepted, 7 enrolled. In 2010, 8 master's, 1 doctorate awarded. *Degree requirements:* For master's, thesis; for doctorate, 2 foreign languages, comprehensive exam, thesis/dissertation. *Entrance requirements:* For master's and doctorate, GRE General Test. *Application deadline:* For fall admission, 1/15 for domestic and international students. Applications are processed on a rolling basis. Application fee: $50. *Expenses:* Tuition, state resident: full-time $9144; part-time $508 per credit hour. Tuition, nonresident: full-time $19,026; part-time $1057 per credit hour. Tuition and fees vary according to program and reciprocity agreements. *Financial support:* In 2010–11, 5 teaching assistantships with full tuition reimbursements (averaging $18,000 per year) were awarded. Financial award application deadline: 1/15. *Faculty research:* Art history in the periods from ancient to contemporary and various regions, 2-D and 3D Studio areas, intermedia, curatorial studies. *Unit head:* Prof. Ying Kit Chan, Chair, 502-852-6794, Fax: 502-852-6791, E-mail: chan@louisville.edu. *Application contact:* Libby Leggett, Director, Graduate Admissions, 502-852-3101, Fax: 502-852-6536, E-mail: gradadm@louisville.edu.

The University of Manchester, School of Arts, Histories and Cultures, Manchester, United Kingdom. Offers anthropology, media and performance (PhD); applied theatre professional (PhD); archaeology (PhD); art history and visual studies (PhD); arts management and cultural policy (PhD); classics and ancient history (PhD); composition (PhD); creative writing (PhD); drama (PhD); economic and social history (PhD); electroacoustic composition (PhD); English and American studies (PhD); history (PhD); humanitarianism and conflict response (PhD); museology (PhD); music (PhD); musicology (PhD); religions and theology (PhD).

University of Missouri–St. Louis, College of Arts and Sciences, Department of History, St. Louis, MO 63121. Offers history (MA); museum studies (MA, Certificate). Part-time and evening/weekend programs available. *Faculty:* 20 full-time (4 women), 4 part-time/adjunct (0 women). *Students:* 29 full-time (19 women), 44 part-time (19 women); includes 4 minority (2 Black or African American, non-Hispanic/Latino; 2 Hispanic/Latino). Average age 31. 55 applicants, 67% accepted, 23 enrolled. In 2010, 19 master's, 11 other advanced degrees awarded. *Degree requirements:* For master's, thesis (for some programs). *Entrance requirements:* For master's, writing sample and minimum GPA of 2.75 (for history), 3.2 (for museum studies). Additional exam requirements/recommendations for international students: Required—TOEFL (minimum score 550 paper-based; 213 computer-based). *Application deadline:* For fall admission, 7/1 priority date for domestic and international students; for spring admission, 12/1 priority date for domestic and international students. Applications are processed on a rolling basis. Application fee: $35 ($40 for international students). Electronic applications accepted. *Expenses:* Tuition, state resident: full-time $5522; part-time $306.80 per credit hour. Tuition, nonresident: full-time $14,253; part-time $792.10 per credit hour. Required fees: $658; $49 per credit hour. One-time fee: $12. Tuition and fees vary according to program. *Financial support:* In 2010–11, 14 research assistantships with full and partial tuition reimbursements (averaging $7,500 per year), 5 teaching assistantships with full and partial tuition reimbursements (averaging $6,060 per year) were awarded; career-related internships or fieldwork also available. Financial award applicants required to submit FAFSA. *Faculty research:* U. S., European, East Asian, Latin American, and African history. *Unit head:* Dr. Winston Hsieh, Director of Graduate Studies, 314-516-5681, Fax: 314-516-5415, E-mail: hsiehw@umsl.edu. *Application contact:* 314-516-5458, Fax: 314-516-6996, E-mail: gradadm@umsl.edu.

University of New Hampshire, Graduate School, College of Liberal Arts, Department of History, Durham, NH 03824. Offers history (MA, PhD); museum studies (MA). Part-time programs available. *Faculty:* 24 full-time (13 women). *Students:* 25 full-time (10 women), 15 part-time (8 women); includes 1 minority (Asian, non-Hispanic/Latino), 1 international. Average age 36. 94 applicants, 24% accepted, 6 enrolled. In 2010, 7 master's, 5 doctorates awarded. *Degree requirements:* For master's, thesis or alternative; for doctorate, 2 foreign languages, thesis/dissertation. *Entrance requirements:* For master's and doctorate, GRE General Test. Additional exam requirements/recommendations for international students: Required—TOEFL (minimum score 550 paper-based; 213 computer-based; 80 iBT). *Application deadline:* For fall admission, 6/1 priority date for domestic students, 4/15 for international students; for spring admission, 12/1 for domestic students. Applications are processed on a rolling basis. Application fee: $65. Electronic applications accepted. *Financial support:* In 2010–11, 16 students received support, including 16 fellowships, 1 teaching assistantship; research assistantships, career-related internships or fieldwork, Federal Work-Study, scholarships/grants, and tuition waivers (full and partial) also available. Support available to part-time students. Financial award application deadline: 2/15. *Unit head:* Dr. Jan Golinski, Chairperson, 603-862-1764. *Application contact:* Susan Kilday, Administrative Assistant, 603-862-1764, E-mail: history.grad@unh.edu.

The University of North Carolina at Greensboro, Graduate School, College of Arts and Sciences, Department of History, Greensboro, NC 27412-5001. Offers historic preservation (Certificate); history (MA); museum studies (Certificate); U.S. history (PhD). Part-time programs available. *Entrance requirements:* For master's, GRE General Test. Additional exam requirements/recommendations for international students: Required—TOEFL. Electronic applications accepted. *Faculty research:* Simultaneous discovery in science, progressive social reform, Robert Mayer.

The University of North Carolina at Greensboro, Graduate School, School of Human Environmental Sciences, Department of Interior Architecture, Greensboro, NC 27412-5001. Offers historic preservation (Certificate); interior architecture (MS); museum studies (Certificate). *Degree requirements:* For master's, thesis. *Entrance requirements:* For master's, GRE General Test or MAT, bachelor's degree in interior design, interview, portfolio. Additional exam requirements/recommendations for international students: Required—TOEFL. Electronic applications accepted.

University of North Texas, Toulouse Graduate School, College of Visual Arts and Design, Department of Art Education and Art History, Denton, TX 76203. Offers art education (MA, PhD); art history (MA); art museum education (Certificate); arts leadership (Certificate). Part-time and evening/weekend programs available. *Degree requirements:* For master's, one foreign

Museum Studies

University of North Texas *(continued)*
language, comprehensive exam (for some programs), thesis (for some programs); for doctorate, comprehensive exam, thesis/dissertation. *Entrance requirements:* For master's, GRE, writing sample, statement of purpose; for doctorate, GRE, master's degree in art education, writing sample, slides, statement of purpose. Additional exam requirements/recommendations for international students: Recommended—TOEFL (minimum score 550 paper-based; 213 computer-based; 79 iBT). *Expenses:* Tuition, state resident: full-time $4298; part-time $239 per credit hour. Tuition, nonresident: full-time $10,782; part-time $549 per credit hour. Required fees: $1292; $270 per credit hour. *Financial support:* Fellowships with partial tuition reimbursements, research assistantships with partial tuition reimbursements, teaching assistantships with partial tuition reimbursements, Federal Work-Study, scholarships/grants, health care benefits, and unspecified assistantships available. Support available to part-time students. Financial award applicants required to submit FAFSA. *Faculty research:* Aesthetics, visual culture, arts leadership, British art, Latin American art, French art, Indian art, contemporary Arab art.

University of Oklahoma, College of Liberal Studies, Norman, OK 73019. Offers human and health services administration (MA); integrated studies (MA); museum studies (MA); prevention science (MPS). Part-time programs available. Postbaccalaureate distance learning degree programs offered (no on-campus study). *Faculty:* 16 full-time (12 women), 13 part-time/adjunct (4 women). *Students:* 30 full-time (18 women), 432 part-time (221 women); includes 99 minority (31 Black or African American, non-Hispanic/Latino; 33 American Indian or Alaska Native, non-Hispanic/Latino; 4 Asian, non-Hispanic/Latino; 21 Hispanic/Latino; 10 Two or more races, non-Hispanic/Latino), 1 international. Average age 36. 159 applicants, 94% accepted, 113 enrolled. In 2010, 114 master's awarded. *Degree requirements:* For master's, minimum of 33 semester hours, including thesis, research project, internship, or comprehensive exam. *Entrance requirements:* For master's, minimum GPA of 3.0 in last 60 hours, writing sample. Additional exam requirements/recommendations for international students: Required—TOEFL (minimum score 550 paper-based; 213 computer-based; 79 iBT). *Application deadline:* For fall admission, 7/15 priority date for domestic students, 4/1 for international students; for spring admission, 12/1 for domestic students, 9/1 for international students. Applications are processed on a rolling basis. Application fee: $40 ($90 for international students). Electronic applications accepted. *Expenses:* Tuition, state resident: full-time $3893; part-time $162.20 per credit hour. Tuition, nonresident: full-time $14,167; part-time $590.30 per credit hour. Required fees: $2523; $94.60 per credit hour. Tuition and fees vary according to course load and degree level. *Financial support:* In 2010–11, 358 students received support. Career-related internships or fieldwork, institutionally sponsored loans, scholarships/grants, and tuition waivers (partial) available. Support available to part-time students. Financial award applicants required to submit FAFSA. *Faculty research:* Administrative leadership, criminal justice, museum studies, health administration, prevention science. *Unit head:* Dr. James Pappas, Dean and Vice President for University Outreach, 405-325-6361, Fax: 405-325-7196, E-mail: jpappas@ou.edu. *Application contact:* Kelly Collyar, Coordinator, Recruitment and Admissions, 800-522-4389, Fax: 405-325-7132, E-mail: clsinfo@ou.edu.

University of South Carolina, The Graduate School, College of Arts and Sciences, Department of History, Program in Public History, Columbia, SC 29208. Offers archives (MA); historic preservation (MA); museum (MA); museum management (Certificate); MLIS/MA. *Degree requirements:* For master's, one foreign language, thesis, internship. *Entrance requirements:* For master's, GRE General Test, writing sample. Additional exam requirements/recommendations for international students: Required—TOEFL. Electronic applications accepted. *Faculty research:* Museum studies, historic preservation, archives administration.

The University of the Arts, College of Art, Media and Design, Department of Museum Studies, Philadelphia, PA 19102-4944. Offers museum communication (MA); museum education (MA); museum exhibition planning and design (MFA). *Accreditation:* NASAD. *Degree requirements:* For master's, thesis, internship. *Entrance requirements:* For master's, official transcripts, three letters of recommendation, one- to two-page statement, personal interview; academic writing sample and examples of work (for museum communication); two examples of academic and professional writing (for museum education); portfolio and/or writing samples (for museum exhibition planning and design). Additional exam requirements/recommendations for international students: Required—TOEFL (minimum score 580 paper-based, 92 iBT) or IELTS (minimum score 6.5).

See Display on page 187 and Close-Up on page 229.

University of Toronto, School of Graduate Studies, Humanities Division, Department of Art, Toronto, ON M5S 1A1, Canada. Offers art history (MA, PhD); visual studies (MVS). Part-time programs available. *Degree requirements:* For master's, 2 foreign languages, language proficiency exams; for doctorate, 2 foreign languages, comprehensive exam, thesis/dissertation. *Entrance requirements:* For master's, coursework in a foreign language, 3 letters of reference, sample research paper, minimum B+ average in senior art history and/or humanities courses; for doctorate, minimum A– average in senior art history and/or humanities courses, 2 letters of reference, sample research paper.

University of Toronto, School of Graduate Studies, Humanities Division, Program in Museum Studies, Toronto, ON M5S 1A1, Canada. Offers MM St. *Expenses:* Contact institution.

University of Tulsa, Graduate School, Program in Museum Science and Management, Tulsa, OK 74104-3189. Offers anthropology (MA); general (MA); history (MA); Native American (MA). Part-time programs available. *Faculty:* 9 full-time (1 woman). *Students:* 6 full-time (all women); includes 1 minority (Black or African American, non-Hispanic/Latino). Average age 29. 14 applicants, 86% accepted, 6 enrolled. *Degree requirements:* For master's, final semester internship or independent research project. *Entrance requirements:* For master's, GRE General Test. Additional exam requirements/recommendations for international students: Required—TOEFL (minimum score 575 paper-based; 231 computer-based; 91 iBT), IELTS (minimum score 6.5). *Application deadline:* Applications are processed on a rolling basis. Application fee: $40. Electronic applications accepted. *Expenses:* Tuition: Full-time $16,902; part-time $939 per credit hour. Required fees: $1020; $4 per credit hour. Tuition and fees vary according to course load. *Financial support:* In 2010–11, 4 students received support, including 1 research assistantship with full and partial tuition reimbursement available (averaging $5,504 per year), 3 teaching assistantships with full and partial tuition reimbursements available (averaging $13,040 per year); fellowships with full and partial tuition reimbursements available, career-related internships or fieldwork, Federal Work-Study, scholarships/grants, health care benefits, tuition waivers (full and partial), and unspecified assistantships also available. Support available to part-time students. Total annual research expenditures: $12,000. *Unit head:* Dr. Bob Pickering, Senior Curator, 918-596-2706, Fax: 918-596-2770, E-mail: bob-pickering@utulsa.edu. *Application contact:* Graduate School, 918-631-2336, Fax: 918-631-2156, E-mail: grad@utulsa.edu.

University of Washington, Graduate School, Museology Graduate Program, Seattle, WA 98195. Offers MA. *Degree requirements:* For master's, thesis or alternative. *Entrance requirements:* For master's, GRE General Test, minimum GPA of 3.0. Additional exam requirements/recommendations for international students: Required—TOEFL (minimum score 580 paper-based; 237 computer-based; 92 iBT). Electronic applications accepted. *Expenses:*

Contact institution. *Faculty research:* Collection management, conservation, art history, anthropology, administration.

University of West Georgia, College of Arts and Sciences, Department of History, Carrollton, GA 30118. Offers history (MA); museum studies (Certificate); public history (Certificate). Part-time programs available. *Faculty:* 16 full-time (6 women). *Students:* 25 full-time (16 women), 15 part-time (8 women); includes 1 American Indian or Alaska Native, non-Hispanic/Latino; 2 Hispanic/Latino; 1 Two or more races, non-Hispanic/Latino. Average age 33. 16 applicants, 69% accepted, 8 enrolled. In 2010, 7 master's, 8 other advanced degrees awarded. *Degree requirements:* For master's, one foreign language, comprehensive exam, thesis or alternative. *Entrance requirements:* For master's, GRE General Test (minimum score 400 verbal, 400 quantitative, 3.5 writing), undergraduate degree in history or related social studies, minimum GPA of 2.75. *Application deadline:* For fall admission, 7/17 for domestic students; for spring admission, 11/20 for domestic students. Applications are processed on a rolling basis. Application fee: $30. Electronic applications accepted. *Expenses:* Tuition, state resident: full-time $4130; part-time $173 per semester hour. Tuition, nonresident: full-time $16,524; part-time $689 per semester hour. Required fees: $1586; $44.01 per semester hour. $397 per semester. Tuition and fees vary according to program. *Financial support:* In 2010–11, 7 students received support, including research assistantships with full tuition reimbursements available (averaging $6,000 per year); career-related internships or fieldwork, scholarships/grants, and unspecified assistantships also available. Support available to part-time students. Financial award application deadline: 7/1; financial award applicants required to submit FAFSA. *Faculty research:* Public history, United States, Russia/Soviet Union, Africa, Europe. *Unit head:* Dr. Howard Steven Goodson, Interim Chair, 678-839-6042, E-mail: hgoodson@westga.edu. *Application contact:* Dr. Charles W. Clark, Dean, 678-839-6508, E-mail: cclark@westga.edu.

University of Wisconsin–Milwaukee, Graduate School, College of Letters and Sciences, Department of Anthropology, Milwaukee, WI 53201-0413. Offers anthropology (PhD); museum studies (Certificate). *Faculty:* 18 full-time (8 women). *Students:* 65 full-time (46 women), 31 part-time (24 women); includes 3 Black or African American, non-Hispanic/Latino; 2 Hispanic/Latino, 2 international. Average age 33. 51 applicants, 78% accepted, 16 enrolled. In 2010, 15 master's, 2 doctorates awarded. *Degree requirements:* For master's, thesis or alternative; for doctorate, one foreign language, thesis/dissertation, departmental qualifying exam. *Entrance requirements:* For master's, GRE; for doctorate, GRE, minimum GPA of 3.0, master's degree. Additional exam requirements/recommendations for international students: Required—TOEFL (minimum score 550 paper-based; 79 iBT), IELTS (minimum score 6.5). *Application deadline:* For fall admission, 1/1 priority date for domestic students; for spring admission, 9/1 for domestic students. Applications are processed on a rolling basis. Application fee: $56 ($96 for international students). *Financial support:* In 2010–11, 4 fellowships, 2 research assistantships, 26 teaching assistantships were awarded; career-related internships or fieldwork, unspecified assistantships, and project assistantships also available. Support available to part-time students. Financial award application deadline: 4/15; financial award applicants required to submit FAFSA. Total annual research expenditures: $752,931. *Unit head:* Patrick Gray, Representative, 414-229-4822, Fax: 414-229-5848, E-mail: jpgray@uwm.edu. *Application contact:* General Information Contact, 414-229-4982, Fax: 414-229-6967, E-mail: gradschool@uwm.edu.

University of Wisconsin–Milwaukee, Graduate School, College of Letters and Sciences, Department of Art History, Milwaukee, WI 53201-0413. Offers art history (MA); art museum studies (Certificate). Part-time programs available. *Faculty:* 9 full-time (5 women). *Students:* 20 full-time (17 women), 9 part-time (7 women); includes 1 Asian, non-Hispanic/Latino; 3 Hispanic/Latino. Average age 29. 23 applicants, 61% accepted, 8 enrolled. In 2010, 6 master's awarded. *Degree requirements:* For master's, one foreign language, comprehensive exam, thesis or alternative. *Entrance requirements:* For master's, GRE. Additional exam requirements/recommendations for international students: Required—TOEFL (minimum score 550 paper-based; 79 iBT), IELTS (minimum score 6.5). *Application deadline:* For fall admission, 1/1 priority date for domestic students; for spring admission, 9/1 for domestic students. Applications are processed on a rolling basis. Application fee: $56 ($96 for international students). *Financial support:* In 2010–11, 7 teaching assistantships were awarded; fellowships, research assistantships, career-related internships or fieldwork and unspecified assistantships also available. Support available to part-time students. Financial award application deadline: 4/15; financial award applicants required to submit FAFSA. *Faculty research:* Ancient Mediterranean art through contemporary Western art, Chinese art, Pre-Columbian art, film, theory. *Unit head:* Kenneth Bendiner, Chair, 414-229-5015, Fax: 414-229-2935, E-mail: bendiner@uwm.edu. *Application contact:* Derek Counts, General Information Contact, 414-229-3466, E-mail: dbc@uwm.edu.

Virginia Commonwealth University, Graduate School, School of the Arts, Department of Art History, Richmond, VA 23284-9005. Offers architectural history (MA); art history (MA, PhD); historical studies (MA); museum studies (MA). *Accreditation:* NASAD. *Faculty:* 10 full-time (4 women). *Students:* 15 full-time (13 women), 27 part-time (24 women); includes 4 minority (1 Asian, non-Hispanic/Latino; 3 Hispanic/Latino), 1 international. 52 applicants, 48% accepted, 12 enrolled. In 2010, 9 master's, 5 doctorates awarded. *Degree requirements:* For master's, thesis; for doctorate, comprehensive exam, thesis/dissertation. *Entrance requirements:* For master's and doctorate, GRE General Test. *Application deadline:* For fall admission, 1/15 for domestic students. Application fee: $50. Electronic applications accepted. *Expenses:* Tuition, state resident: full-time $4308; part-time $479 per credit hour. Tuition, nonresident: full-time $8942; part-time $994 per credit hour. Required fees: $2000; $85 per credit hour. Tuition and fees vary according to course level, course load, degree level, campus/location and program. *Financial support:* Fellowships, teaching assistantships, career-related internships or fieldwork, Federal Work-Study, and institutionally sponsored loans available. Support available to part-time students. Financial award application deadline: 3/15; financial award applicants required to submit FAFSA. *Faculty research:* Modern, nineteenth-century, Renaissance, American, and medieval art. *Unit head:* Dr. Dina Bangdel, Director of Graduate Studies, 804-628-7027, Fax: 804-828-7468, E-mail: dbangdel@vcu.edu. *Application contact:* Dr. Dina Bangdel, Director of Graduate Studies, 804-628-7027, Fax: 804-828-7468, E-mail: dbangdel@vcu.edu.

Western Illinois University, School of Graduate Studies, College of Fine Arts and Communication, Program in Museum Studies, Macomb, IL 61455-1390. Offers MA, Certificate. *Accreditation:* NASAD. Part-time programs available. *Students:* 19 full-time (17 women), 12 part-time (11 women); includes 1 minority (Hispanic/Latino). Average age 31. 13 applicants, 77% accepted. In 2010, 12 master's awarded. *Entrance requirements:* For master's, minimum GPA of 3.0. Additional exam requirements/recommendations for international students: Required—TOEFL (minimum score 600 paper-based; 250 computer-based; 100 iBT). *Application deadline:* Applications are processed on a rolling basis. Application fee: $30. Electronic applications accepted. *Expenses:* Tuition, state resident: full-time $6370; part-time $265.40 per credit hour. Tuition, nonresident: full-time $12,740; part-time $530.80 per credit hour. Required fees: $75.67 per credit hour. *Financial support:* In 2010–11, 3 students received support, including 3 research assistantships with full tuition reimbursements available (averaging $7,280 per year). Financial award applicants required to submit FAFSA. *Unit head:* Ann Rowson Love, Director, 309-762-9481 Ext. 266, E-mail: a-rowsonlove@wiu.edu. *Application contact:* Evelyn Hoing, Assistant Director of Graduate Studies, 309-298-1806, Fax: 309-298-2345, E-mail: grad-office@wiu.edu.

ADELPHI UNIVERSITY

College of Arts and Sciences
Program in Fine Arts

Programs of Study

The study of art is the study of making. To make is to create, to interpret, and, finally, to understand one's own vision of the world. To study art and the history of art is to study the very essence of the self and of civilization. The Department of Art and Art History offers a program of study that leads to the Master of Arts degree in studio art. Course requirements total 36 credits. Students generally concentrate in a primary area of studio work (up to 15 credits), supplemented by one or more secondary areas of studio concentration. Concentration areas include ceramics, painting, photography, printmaking, and sculpture. Completion of degree requirements may be undertaken on a part-time basis or by attending summer sessions. Information on these options may be obtained from the department.

The department also offers course options for the Master of Arts degree in art education for those seeking New York State certification for teaching primary and secondary level. Students who successfully complete the program graduate with a Master of Arts degree from the School of Education. Students should consult with the department chair or their graduate faculty adviser to determine the necessary courses to fulfill the degree requirements.

Research Facilities

The University's primary research holdings are at Swirbul Library and include 600,000 volumes (including bound periodicals and government publications), 806,000 items in microformats, 33,000 audiovisual items, and access to over 61,000 electronic journal titles. Online access is provided to more than 221 research databases.

Opened in fall 2005, the 18,000-square-foot Fine Arts and Facilities Building greatly expands Adelphi's art studio and classroom space. The one-story building takes advantage of natural light to illuminate two painting studios, a sculpture and ceramics studio, and a printmaking studio. An outdoor courtyard contains kilns and display boxes for student artwork. The department retained its space on the third floor of Blodgett Hall, including its state-of-the-art digital graphics design studio and faculty offices.

Financial Aid

Adelphi University offers a wide variety of federal aid programs, state grants, scholarship and fellowship programs, on- and off-campus employment, and teaching and research assistantships.

Cost of Study

For the 2011–12 academic year, the tuition rate is $930 per credit. University fees range from $315 to $550 per semester.

Living and Housing Costs

The University assists single and married students in finding suitable accommodations whenever possible. The cost of living is dependent upon location and the number of rooms rented.

Location

Located in historic Garden City, New York, 45 minutes from Manhattan and 20 minutes from Queens, Adelphi's 75-acre suburban campus is known for the beauty of its landscape and architecture. The campus is a short walk from the Long Island Rail Road and is convenient to New York's major airports and several major highways. Off-campus centers are located in Manhattan, Hauppauge, and Poughkeepsie.

The University and The College

Founded in 1896, Adelphi is a fully accredited, private university with nearly 8,000 undergraduate, graduate, and returning-adult students in the arts and sciences, business, clinical psychology, education, nursing, and social work. Students come from forty-one states and from forty-eight countries. *The Princeton Review* named Adelphi University a Best College in the Northeastern Region, and *Fiske Guide to Colleges* recognized Adelphi as a "Best Buy" in higher education for the fifth year in a row. The University is one of only twenty-four private institutions in the nation to earn this recognition.

Mindful of the cultural inheritance of the past, the College of Arts and Sciences encompasses those realms of inquiry that have characterized the modern pursuit of knowledge. The faculty members of the College place a high priority on their students' intellectual development in and out of the classroom and structure programs and opportunities to foster that growth. Students analyze original research or other creative work, develop firsthand facility with creative or research methodologies, undertake collaborative work with peers and mentors, engage in serious internships, and hone communicative skills.

Applying

An applicant must have earned a baccalaureate degree from an accredited four-year college and have developed a portfolio of art work in a representative range of media. A student must submit the completed application form, the $50 application fee, official college transcripts, and two letters of recommendation. A formal portfolio presentation is required of all applicants. All portfolios are reviewed by a faculty committee, and selected applicants are invited to campus for a tour and interview. Portfolios should contain twelve to fifteen examples of recent work.

Correspondence and Information

David Hornung, Department Chair
Blodgett Hall, Room 301
College of Arts and Sciences
Adelphi University
Garden City, New York 11530
Phone: 516-877-4460
Fax: 516-877-4459
E-mail: hornung@adelphi.edu
Web site: http://academics.adelphi.edu/artsci/art/graduate/

Adelphi University

THE FACULTY

Andrea Begel, Assistant Professor, Ph.D., Columbia, 2004. Italian and Northern Renaissance art, fourteenth-century fresco painting.
Hugh Crean, Professor; Ph.D., CUNY, 1990.
Dale Flashner, Graphic Design Studio Art Director and Senior Adjunct Professor; M.A., Adelphi, 1984. Advertising design, computer graphics.
Carson Fox, Assistant Professor; M.F.A., Rutgers, 1999. Printmaking, sculpture, installation.
Geoffrey Grogan, Associate Professor; M.F.A., M.S., Pratt, 1996. Comic books, contemporary art history and theory.
Jennifer Maloney, Assistant Professor; M.F.A., CUNY, Brooklyn, 2003. Color theory and practice, painting.
Thomas McAnulty, Professor; M.F.A., Indiana, 1976. Sculpture, three-dimensional design.
Kellyann Monaghan, Associate Professor; M.F.A., CUNY, Brooklyn, 2001. Painting studio, drawing.
Maya Muratov, Assistant Professor, Ph.D., NYU, 2005. Greek and Roman art; theater culture, and popular entertainment in the ancient Mediterranean.

Adelphi's campus in historic Garden City, Long Island, New York.

A registered arboretum, Adelphi is truly a green campus.

BARD GRADUATE CENTER: DECORATIVE ARTS, DESIGN HISTORY, MATERIAL CULTURE

Programs of Study

The Bard Graduate Center (BGC) is a graduate institute affiliated with Bard College committed to the encyclopedic study of things in their historical context, drawing on methodologies and approaches from art and design history, economic history, history of technology, philosophy, anthropology, and archaeology. The project of the school is to study the cultural history of the material world.

Founded in 1993, the BGC offers M.A. and Ph.D. degrees. It is an international study and exhibition center in New York City devoted to the interdisciplinary study of the decorative arts, design history, cultural history, history and theory of museums, Renaissance and early modern studies, cultural geography, American art and culture, Asian Art, the Arts of Antiquity, eighteenth through twentieth century design and European Studies, and the material culture of New York City. Programs are designed to prepare students for careers or career advancement in museums; galleries; auction houses; government agencies; art-related education, research, publishing, and communications; and landscape and historic preservation.

There is hands-on examination of materials and objects and an extensive connection to special programs and exhibition projects with the Metropolitan Museum of Art, the New York Historical Society, the Brooklyn Museum of Art, the American Museum of Natural History, the Frick Collection, and other major cultural institutions. As part of their studies, all students undertake an internship at one of more than 250 institutions.

A semiannual interdisciplinary journal, *West 86th,* is published by the BGC and features scholarly articles about the decorative arts and their interpretation as well as book reviews. Advanced graduate students are invited to submit articles for possible publication.

Research Facilities

The Bard Graduate Center occupies a six-story town house at 18 West 86th Street and a second, newly renovated town house at 38 West 86th Street in Manhattan. The buildings' elegantly appointed rooms provide an aesthetically appropriate setting for the study of the decorative arts. Its facilities include a 40,000-volume research library; a new digital media research lab; exhibition galleries; classrooms; faculty offices; student lounges; outdoor terraces; symposium spaces; and administrative offices.

Financial Aid

The BGC offers fellowships, scholarships, and a student campus employment program. Aid is awarded on the basis of need and merit. Financial aid applications are due by January 3. About 85 percent of students receive some financial aid.

Cost of Study

The average annual tuition for incoming full-time students in the 2010–11 academic year was $25,780 for M.A. students, based on a cost of $1140 per credit. Tuition and fees for Ph.D. students averaged $30,840 for incoming full-time students in the 2010–11 academic year; they vary for subsequent years of doctoral work. Students may contact the Office of Admissions for more detailed and updated fee schedules.

Living and Housing Costs

Bard Hall, located at 410 West 58th Street, provides housing for students, faculty members, and visiting scholars. Nine residential floors offer a variety of furnished studios and one- and two-bedroom suites with kitchens and baths. Apartments are offered year-round. For the 2010–11 academic year, the cost of a studio unit was approximately $14,000, a one-bedroom unit was $16,800, and a two-bedroom unit was $13,800 per student.

Student Group

The Bard Graduate Center accepts approximately 20–25 full-time and a limited number of part-time students into the program annually. Applications are received from many countries and from across the United States. The BGC welcomes students of all ages and backgrounds as well as working professionals.

Location

The Bard Graduate Center is located on the Upper West Side of Manhattan, near Central Park. It is situated in a landmark neighborhood conveniently served by public transportation, with easy access to the innumerable museums, libraries, auction houses, and galleries of metropolitan New York.

The College and The Center

Established by Bard College in 1993, the Bard Graduate Center is one of the many "satellite" institutions that surround the 150-year-old undergraduate liberal arts college. Others include the Jerome Levy Economics Institute of Bard College, the Milton Avery Graduate School of the Arts, and the Center for Curatorial Studies in Art and Contemporary Culture. Other graduate divisions are located in Annandale, New York.

Applying

Students are admitted to the graduate programs annually for fall admission. The application deadline for admission and financial aid is January 3. Applicants to the M.A. program must have a bachelor's degree or the equivalent; applicants to the Ph.D. program are expected to have completed a master's degree in either the decorative arts or a related field. Because of the interdisciplinary nature of the program, there are no limitations on the applicant's prior field of study. Successful applicants, however, will have had some previous study, training, or work experience in the history of art, architecture, archeology, history, the decorative arts, cultural history, or material culture studies.

Applications should include scores on the General Test of the Graduate Record Examinations (GRE), three letters of recommendation, a short resume, a sample of scholarly writing, and a statement of intent describing academic and professional objectives. International candidates must submit TOEFL scores and a Certification of Finances. An interview is required. The application fee for 2010–11 was $65.

Correspondence and Information

Office of Admissions
Bard Graduate Center: Decorative Arts, Design History, Material Culture
38 West 86th Street
New York, New York 10024
Phone: 212-501-3057
Fax: 212-501-3065
E-mail: admissions@bgc.bard.edu
Web site: http://www.bgc.bard.edu

Bard Graduate Center: Decorative Arts, Design History, Material Culture

THE FACULTY AND THEIR RESEARCH

The BGC maintains a distinguished core of full-time faculty members, supplemented by eminent decorative arts scholars visiting from a broad range of national and international museums and institutions of higher learning.

The Bard Graduate Center Faculty

Susan Weber Soros, Iris Horowitz Professor in the History of the Decorative Arts and Director; Ph.D., Royal College of Art. Furniture studies.
Peter N. Miller, Professor and Chair of Academic Programs; Ph.D., Cambridge. European cultural history.
Kenneth Ames, Professor; Ph.D., Pennsylvania. Nineteenth century.
Jeffrey Collins, Professor; Ph.D., Yale. Eighteenth-century European art and culture.
Aaron Glass, Assistant Professor; Ph.D., NYU. Museum anthropology.
David Jaffee, Professor; Ph.D., Harvard. Landscape history and cultural geography.
Pat Kirkham, Professor; Ph.D., London. Eighteenth-, nineteenth-, and twentieth-century design history and gender studies.
Deborah L. Krohn, Associate Professor; Ph.D., Harvard. Early Modern material culture in southern Europe and museum studies.
François Louis, Associate Professor; Ph.D., Zurich. Art history of Tang and Song China, Chinese goldsmithing.
Michele Majer, Assistant Professor; M.A., NYU. Costume historian.
Andrew Morrall, Professor; Ph.D., Courtauld Institute of Art (England). Fourteenth- to eighteenth-century European arts.
Amy Ogata, Associate Professor; Ph.D., Princeton. Nineteenth- and twentieth-century design history.
Elizabeth Simpson, Professor; Ph.D., Pennsylvania. The arts of the ancient world.
Paul Stirton, Associate Professor; Ph.D. Courtauld Institute of Art (England). Design history.
Ittai Weinryb, Ph.D., Johns Hopkins. Medieval material culture.
Catherine Whalen, Assistant Professor; Ph.D., Yale. American material culture and twentieth-century design.

Additional Teaching Staff

Kimon Keramidas, Ph.D., CUNY.
Nina Stritzler-Levine, M.A., CUNY.

Students utilize one of the several study alcoves located at the BGC.

A professor initiates discussion in a seminar-style class, the typical classroom environment at the BGC.

FASHION INSTITUTE OF TECHNOLOGY
State University of New York

M.A. in Art Market: Principles and Practices

Programs of Study

The Fashion Institute of Technology (FIT), a State University of New York (SUNY) college of art and design, business, and technology, is home to a mix of innovative achievers, creative thinkers, and industry pioneers. FIT fosters interdisciplinary initiatives, advances research, and provides access to an international network of professionals. With selective admissions and a reputation for excellence, FIT offers its diverse student body access to world-class faculty, dynamic and relevant curricula, and a superior education at an affordable cost. It offers seven programs of graduate study. The programs in Art Market: Principles and Practices; Exhibition Design; Fashion and Textile Studies: History, Theory, Museum Practice; and Sustainable Interior Environments lead to the Master of Arts (M.A.) degree. The Illustration program leads to the Master of Fine Arts (M.F.A.) degree. The Master of Professional Studies (M.P.S.) degree programs are Cosmetics and Fragrance Marketing and Management, and Global Fashion Management.

Art Market: Principles and Practices is a 48-credit, full- or part-time M.A. program preparing students for careers in the business, collection, and exhibition of art. The curriculum includes art history, writing for the art market, gallery design and operation, business practices, computer technology for the art world, marketing, valuation and appraisal, exhibition theory, and art law and professional ethics. Students are required to complete a relevant internship and to research and write a master's qualifying paper. Graduating students must also complete a practicum in which they assemble a group show from concept to execution at a New York City gallery.

Research Facilities

The School of Graduate Studies is primarily located in the campus's Shirley Goodman Resource Center, which also houses the Gladys Marcus Library and The Museum at FIT. School of Graduate Studies facilities include conference rooms; a fully equipped conservation laboratory; a multipurpose laboratory for conservation projects and the dressing of mannequins; storage facilities for costume and textile materials; a graduate student lounge with computer and printer access; a graduate student library reading room with computers, reference materials, and copies of past classes' qualifying and thesis papers; specialized wireless classrooms; and classrooms equipped with model stands, easels, and drafting tables.

The Gladys Marcus Library houses more than 300,000 volumes of print, nonprint, and digital resources. Specialized holdings include industry reference materials, manufacturers' catalogues, original fashion sketches and scrapbooks, portfolios of plates, photographs, and sample books. The FIT Digital Library provides access to over 90 searchable online databases.

The Museum at FIT houses one of the world's most important collections of clothing and textiles and is the only museum in New York City dedicated to the art of fashion. The permanent collection encompasses more than 50,000 garments and accessories dating from the eighteenth century, with particular strength in twentieth-century fashion, as well as 30,000 textiles and 100,000 textile swatches. Each year, nearly 100,000 visitors are drawn to the museum's award-winning exhibitions and public programs.

Financial Aid

FIT directly administers its institutional grants, scholarships, and loans. Federal funding administered by the college may include Federal Perkins Loans, federally subsidized and unsubsidized Direct Loans for students, Grad PLUS loans, and the Federal Work-Study Program. Priority for institutionally administered funds is given to students enrolled and designated as full-time.

Cost of Study

Tuition for New York State residents is $4099 per semester, or $342 per credit. Out-of-state residents' tuition is $6972 per semester, or $581 per credit. Tuition and fees are subject to change at the discretion of FIT's Board of Trustees. Additional expenses—for class materials, textbooks, and travel—may apply and vary per program.

Living and Housing Costs

Residence facilities are available to graduate students. Traditional residence hall accommodations (including meal plan) cost from $5920 to $6095 per semester. Apartment-style housing options (not including meal plan) cost from $5065 to $9880 per semester.

Student Group

Enrollment in the School of Graduate Studies is approximately 200 students per academic year, allowing considerable individualized advisement. Students come to FIT from throughout the country and around the world.

Student Outcomes

Art Market: Principles and Practices graduates find employment as art gallery directors, public art program directors, art consultants for private and corporate collections, art foundation administrators, museum marketing and development directors, independent curators, auction house department heads, and artists' representatives.

Location

FIT is connected to New York City, to students, and to careers. Located in Manhattan's Chelsea neighborhood, it places students at the heart of the advertising, visual arts, marketing, fashion, business, design, and communications industries. Students gain unparalleled exposure to their field through guest lectures, field trips, internships, and sponsored competitions. The location provides access to major museums, galleries, and auction houses as well as dining, entertainment, and shopping options. The campus is near subway, bus, and commuter rail lines.

Applying

Applicants to all School of Graduate Studies programs must hold a baccalaureate degree in an appropriate major from a college or university, with a cumulative GPA of 3.0 or higher. International students from non-English-speaking countries are required to submit minimum TOEFL scores of 550 on the written test, 213 on the computer test, or 80 on the Internet test. Students applying to the Art Market: Principles and Practices program must submit GRE scores. Each major has additional, specialized prerequisites for admission; for detailed information, students should visit the School of Graduate Studies on FIT's Web site.

Domestic and international students use the same application when seeking admission. The deadline for completed applications with transcripts and supplemental materials is February 15 for the Art Market: Principles and Practices program. After the deadline date, applicants are considered on a rolling admissions basis. Candidates may apply online at www.fitnyc.edu/gradstudies.

Correspondence and Information

School of Graduate Studies
Room E315
Fashion Institute of Technology
227 West 27 Street
New York, New York 10001-5992

Phone: 212-217-4300
Fax: 212-217-4301
E-mail: gradinfo@fitnyc.edu
Web site: http://www.fitnyc.edu/gradstudies
http://www.fitnyc.edu/artmarket

Fashion Institute of Technology

THE FACULTY

The faculty members listed below constitute a partial listing. Guest lecturers are not included.

Katherine Jánszky Michaelsen, Associate Chairperson; Ph.D., Columbia.

Catherine Hannah Behrend, M.B.A., NYU; Certificate in Executive Education, INSEAD (France).
Ágnes Berecz, Ph.D., Sorbonne (Paris).
Elizabeth M. Grady, Ph.D., Northwestern.
John Lee, B.A., Vassar.
Donald McMichael, M.B.A, Duke.
Sheri L. Pasquarella, B.A., Stony Brook, SUNY.
Lucille A. Roussin, Ph.D., Columbia; J.D., Yeshiva.
Martha Schwendener, M.A., Texas at Austin.
Beth Miller Servetar, M.F.A., Bennington.
Gayle M. Skluzacek, B.A., Barat.
Courtney Strimple, M.A., Fashion Institute of Technology.
Andrew Weinstein, Ph.D., NYU.

FASHION INSTITUTE OF TECHNOLOGY
State University of New York

M.A. in Fashion and Textile Studies: History, Theory, Museum Practice

Programs of Study
The Fashion Institute of Technology (FIT), a State University of New York (SUNY) college of art and design, business, and technology, is home to a mix of innovative achievers, creative thinkers, and industry pioneers. FIT fosters interdisciplinary initiatives, advances research, and provides access to an international network of professionals. With selective admissions and a reputation for excellence, FIT offers its diverse student body access to world-class faculty, dynamic and relevant curricula, and a superior education at an affordable cost. It offers seven programs of graduate study. The programs in Art Market: Principles and Practices; Exhibition Design; Fashion and Textile Studies: History, Theory, Museum Practice; and Sustainable Interior Environments lead to the Master of Arts (M.A.) degree. The Illustration program leads to the Master of Fine Arts (M.F.A.) degree. The Master of Professional Studies (M.P.S.) degree programs are Cosmetics and Fragrance Marketing and Management, and Global Fashion Management.

The 48-credit, full- or part-time Fashion and Textile Studies: History, Theory, Museum Practice M.A. program prepares students for professional curatorial, conservation, education, and other scholarly careers that focus on historic clothing, accessories, textiles, and related materials. The curriculum incorporates conservation skills, current collections management methods, exhibition techniques, art historical methodologies, material culture studies, and gender studies and utilizes the resources of The Museum at FIT, one of the world's largest collections of clothing, textiles, and accessories. Students may elect either a conservation or curatorial emphasis; they may also select up to two independent study courses with an appropriate focus on their chosen specialization. All students are required to complete an internship in the field, write a master's qualifying paper based on original research, and take an active role in a yearlong course culminating in a professional exhibition.

Research Facilities
The School of Graduate Studies is primarily located in the campus's Shirley Goodman Resource Center, which also houses the Gladys Marcus Library and The Museum at FIT. School of Graduate Studies facilities include conference rooms; a fully equipped conservation laboratory; a multipurpose laboratory for conservation projects and the dressing of mannequins; storage facilities for costume and textile materials; a graduate student lounge with computer and printer access; a graduate student library reading room with computers, reference materials, and copies of past classes' qualifying and thesis papers; specialized wireless classrooms; and classrooms equipped with model stands, easels, and drafting tables.

The Gladys Marcus Library houses more than 300,000 volumes of print, nonprint, and digital resources. Specialized holdings include industry reference materials, manufacturers' catalogues, original fashion sketches and scrapbooks, portfolios of plates, photographs, and sample books. The FIT Digital Library provides access to over 90 searchable online databases.

The Museum at FIT houses one of the world's most important collections of clothing and textiles and is the only museum in New York City dedicated to the art of fashion. The permanent collection encompasses more than 50,000 garments and accessories dating from the eighteenth century, with particular strength in twentieth-century fashion, as well as 30,000 textiles and 100,000 textile swatches. Each year, nearly 100,000 visitors are drawn to the museum's award-winning exhibitions and public programs.

Financial Aid
FIT directly administers its institutional grants, scholarships, and loans. Federal funding administered by the college may include Federal Perkins Loans, federally subsidized and unsubsidized Direct Loans for students, Grad PLUS loans, and the Federal Work-Study Program. Priority for institutionally administered funds is given to students enrolled and designated as full-time.

Cost of Study
Tuition for New York State residents is $4099 per semester, or $342 per credit. Out-of-state residents' tuition is $6972 per semester, or $581 per credit. Tuition and fees are subject to change at the discretion of FIT's Board of Trustees. Additional expenses—for class materials, textbooks, and travel—may apply and vary per program.

Living and Housing Costs
Residence facilities are available to graduate students. Traditional residence hall accommodations (including meal plan) cost from $5920 to $6095 per semester. Apartment-style housing options (not including meal plan) cost from $5065 to $9880 per semester.

Student Group
Enrollment in the School of Graduate Studies is approximately 200 students per academic year, allowing considerable individualized advisement. Students come to FIT from throughout the country and around the world.

Student Outcomes
Graduates of the Fashion and Textile Studies: History, Theory, Museum Practice program find positions as museum curators, research specialists, collections managers and registrars, historic house directors, museum educators, independent exhibition curators, corporate curators, fashion and textile historians, costume and textile conservators, auction house department specialists and researchers, vintage clothing and textile dealers, and consultants.

Location
FIT is connected to New York City, to students, and to careers. Located in Manhattan's Chelsea neighborhood, it places students at the heart of the advertising, visual arts, marketing, fashion, business, design, and communications industries. Students gain unparalleled exposure to their field through guest lectures, field trips, internships, and sponsored competitions. The location provides access to major museums, galleries, and auction houses as well as dining, entertainment, and shopping options. The campus is near subway, bus, and commuter rail lines.

Applying
Applicants to all School of Graduate Studies programs must hold a baccalaureate degree in an appropriate major from a college or university, with a cumulative GPA of 3.0 or higher. International students from non-English-speaking countries are required to submit minimum TOEFL scores of 550 on the written test, 213 on the computer test, or 80 on the Internet test. Students applying to the Fashion and Textile Studies: History, Theory, Museum Practice program must submit GRE scores. Each major has additional, specialized prerequisites for admission; for detailed information, students should visit the School of Graduate Studies on FIT's Web site.

Domestic and international students use the same application when seeking admission. The deadline for completed applications with transcripts and supplemental materials is February 15 for the Fashion and Textile Studies: History, Theory, Museum Practice program. After the deadline date, applicants are considered on a rolling admissions basis. Candidates may apply online at www.fitnyc.edu/gradstudies.

Correspondence and Information
School of Graduate Studies
Room E315
Fashion Institute of Technology
227 West 27 Street
New York, New York 10001-5992

Phone: 212-217-4300
Fax: 212-217-4301
E-mail: gradinfo@fitnyc.edu
Web site: http://www.fitnyc.edu/gradstudies
http://www.fitnyc.edu/fashiontextilehistory

Fashion Institute of Technology

THE FACULTY

The faculty members listed below constitute a partial listing. Guest lecturers are not included.

Denyse Montegut, Associate Chairperson; Ph.D. candidate, Delaware.

June Burns Bové, M.A., NYU.
Nancy Deihl, M.A., NYU.
Judith Eisenberg, M.A., Wichita State.
Rebecca Fifield, M.A., George Washington.
Lourdes M. Font, Ph.D., NYU.
Donna Ghelerter, M.A., Fashion Institute of Technology.
Désirée Koslin, M.F.A., CUNY, City College; Ph.D., NYU.
Diane Maglio, M.A., Fashion Institute of Technology.
Elizabeth McMahon, Ph.D. candidate, Bard Graduate Center.
Sarah Scaturro, B.A., Colorado.
Rebecca Shea, M.A., Fashion Institute of Technology.
Valerie Soll, B.A., Oregon.
Denise Stone, M.A., Fashion Institute of Technology.
Tanya Wetenhall, M.A., Fashion Institute of Technology.

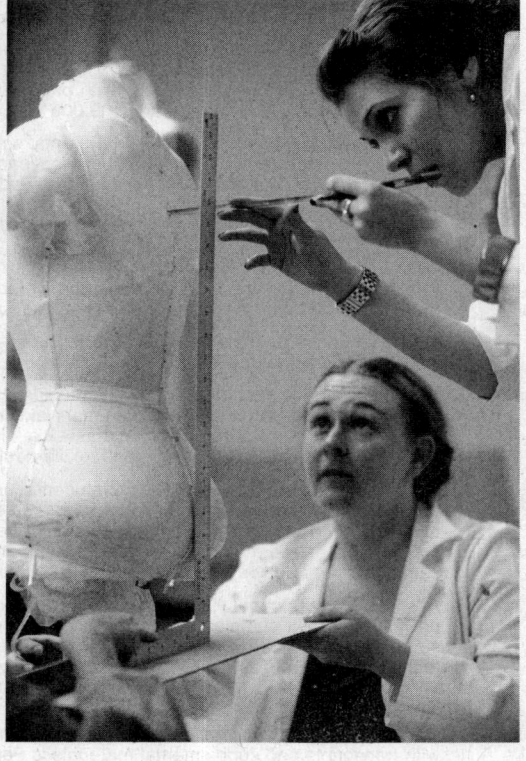

Memphis College of Art

MEMPHIS COLLEGE OF ART

Graduate Programs in Studio Practice and Art Education

Programs of Study

Memphis College of Art (MCA) is a professional center of art and design education, dedicated to preparing individuals for lives of creating, problem solving, and critical thinking. MCA is a cultural wellspring of creativity, nurturing and educating artists of all levels since 1936. Located within the 340-acre Overton Park, MCA offers state-of-the-art facilities, excellent faculty members, interdisciplinary programs, and cutting-edge exhibitions to the public and those pursuing B.F.A., M.F.A., or M.A. in art education and M.A.T. degrees.

As a studio-intensive program, the M.F.A. at Memphis College of Art offers a catalytic environment with the goal of developing artistic practices that contribute significantly to contemporary culture. The program offers the opportunity to focus on traditional studio practice, digital technologies, or an interdisciplinary course of study. Areas of study include, but are not limited to, painting, drawing, photography, printmaking, papermaking/book arts, sculpture, digital media, or an individually tailored program of interdisciplinary study. Studio practice is enhanced with course work in issues of history, theory, and criticism. The program consists of structured course work and independent studio practice, with the second year culminating in the M.F.A. thesis exhibition and written thesis document.

The Master of Arts in Art Education (M.A.Art.Ed.) program is designed for experienced, licensed educators who are ready to further develop their artistic, scholarly, and leadership capabilities in art education. The program explores new approaches to creating, teaching, and researching visual art processes.

The Master of Arts in Teaching (M.A.T.) art education program is designed for artists committed to the growth and development of others through the exchange of knowledge, but who are not yet certified as teachers. It is a full-time, two-year or 40-credit-hour program that integrates hands-on experience in teaching with studio preparation; ensuring students are informed by practice, current theory, and research. Upon completion of this program and obtaining passing scores on the required Praxis exams, graduates are eligible for K–12 certification in art in Tennessee and, by reciprocal agreement, most other states.

Research Facilities

All three graduate programs, graduate studios, and labs are located in the new Nesin Graduate School facility in downtown Memphis. The 44,000-square-foot building houses director and faculty offices, an exhibition gallery, individual studio space, model classrooms, a teacher resource center, computer labs, and a retail store. Graduate students have 24-hour studio access for the duration of their candidacy. MCA's extensive undergraduate facilities in Rust Hall are also available to graduate students, with a shuttle service for convenient transport. Rust Hall's resources include a 4,400-square-foot shop for woodworking, metalworking, mat cutting, glass cutting, and stretcher and frame construction; large metal, clay, and sculpture studios; and a separate foundry and welding area for castings and metalwork. Printmaking, papermaking, and book arts are supported with facilities for lithography, etching, serigraphy, and other print processes; letterpresses and a bindery; and a wet room equipped with beaters, a 36-square-foot vacuum table, hydraulic press, and a pulper. The photo lab includes large- and medium-format work stations, a digital imaging area with digital cameras, slide and transparency scanners, flatbed scanners, high-resolution film printers; and a lighting studio with strobe equipment, and backgrounds. There are also facilities for non-silver and alternative photo processes including digital negative printers and a large UV-exposure unit. Four fully equipped digital labs with separate sound, animation, and shooting studios support photo, animation, and video work, and a large-format digital printing lab is available for oversized archival imaging.

Financial Aid

Aid is available for the M.F.A. and M.A.T. programs through renewable scholarships for incoming students, teaching assistantships (in the third semester only), work-study, Federal Stafford Student Loans and PLUS loans, and additional merit-based scholarship opportunities for second-year students. Students interested in government-based aid are required to complete the Free Application for Federal Student Aid (FAFSA). Applicants should contact the Financial Aid Office or the Admissions Office for forms and information. Teaching professionals in the M.A. in art education and the alternative licensure programs receive a special tuition discount and are not eligible for other institutional scholarships.

Cost of Study

Tuition and fees for the M.F.A. and M.A.T. programs for the 2011–12 academic year are $25,500. This does not include the cost of materials, supplies, and books, which is estimated at $2500. The M.A.Art.Ed. and alternative licensure programs are $520 per credit hour.

Living and Housing Costs

The estimated average cost of food and housing and miscellaneous expenses for the 2011–12 school year is $12,000. There is a large variety of affordable housing available. Student residences conveniently located within walking distance of the main campus provide living space for more than 150 students. Suite-style living (single rooms with shared common areas), shared apartments for two, and several single, efficiency apartments are available. The Office of Admissions assists students in locating a place to live and in obtaining roommate referrals.

Student Group

The student body is comprised of students who have demonstrated achievement in their field. Many have pursued careers as fine artists, graphic designers, photographers, professional weavers, surface designers, interior designers, and teachers. There are nearly equal numbers of men and women. The students in the graduate program come from all regions of the United States and from several other countries.

Location

Memphis is a great place for an aspiring artist to study. Known for blues, barbecue, and Elvis, Memphis is also home to Fortune 500 companies, an NBA team, a symphony, an opera company, a theater, a number of colleges and universities, museums, art galleries, and almost 1 million residents. Annual festivals and celebrations are popular with students. The Graduate School is located in the heart of downtown across from the National Civil Rights Museum in the South Main Arts District. Rust Hall is located in a 342-acre wooded park in midtown Memphis, adjacent to the Memphis Brooks Museum of Art, the Memphis Zoo, and a nine-hole golf course.

The College and The Programs

The College, founded in 1936, is accredited by the Southern Association of Colleges and Schools Commission on Colleges (SACSCOC) and is a member of the National Association of Schools of Art and Design (NASAD). All of the College's graduate programs stress independent work toward self-defined career goals relative to the program chosen.

Applying

M.F.A. applications must be submitted by February 1 for the fall semester and November 1 for the spring semester. Graduate Education applications are accepted on a rolling basis. Application requirements include college transcripts, a portfolio with a minimum of fifteen slides (or other appropriate format), a resume, and one letter of recommendation each from a collegiate adviser or instructor and a contemporary. The applicant must also prepare a written statement of not less than 250 words describing his or her reasons for wishing to join the graduate program, life goals, and creative dreams. M.F.A. students are also asked to submit an artist statement describing the direction of their artwork. A personal interview or conference call may be required—a date and time is arranged by the Dean of Admissions after all application requirements have been met. Students are accepted for admissions in either the fall or spring semester (or summer for the graduate programs in education), based on space availability. In addition, international students must submit a minimum TOEFL score of 525 (195 on the computer-based test), certified translations of academic records, and an affidavit of support verifying ability to meet projected annual costs. Applications are available online at www.mca.edu/admissions.

Correspondence and Information

Office of Admissions, Graduate Programs
Memphis College of Art
1930 Poplar Avenue
Overton Park
Memphis, Tennessee 38104-2764
Phone: 901-272-5151
　　　　800-727-1088 (toll-free)
Fax: 901-272-5158
E-mail: info@mca.edu
Web site: http://www.mca.edu

Memphis College of Art

THE FACULTY

In addition to the regular faculty members listed below, there are guest faculty members and advisers each semester.

Nona Bolin, Professor; M.A., Memphis; M.A., Vanderbilt. Liberal studies.
Fred Burton, Professor; M.F.A., Wichita State; M.A., Kent State. Painting/drawing.
Haley Morris Cafiero, Assistant Professor; M.F.A., Arizona. Photography.
Rob Canfield, Associate Professor; Ph.D., Arizona. Liberal studies.
David Chioffi, Assistant Professor; M.A., Wesleyan. Graphic design.
Ellen Daugherty, Assistant Professor; Ph.D., Virginia. Art history.
Maritza Davila, Professor; M.F.A., Pratt. Printmaking.
Adrian Duran, Assistant Professor; Ph.D., Delaware. Art history.
Tom Lee, Associate Professor; M.F.A., Mississippi. Sculpture.
Susan Maakestad, Associate Professor; M.A., Central Washington; M.F.A., Iowa. Painting.
Remy Miller, Professor; M.F.A., Bowling Green State. Drawing.
Howard Paine, Director of M.F.A. Programs; M.F.A., Washington (St. Louis). Computer arts/design.
Joel Priddy, Assistant Professor; M.F.A., School of Visual Arts. Illustration.
Bill Price, Instructor; M.F.A., Southern Illinois. Sculpture/metals.
James Ramsey, Assistant Professor; Ph.D., Tulane. Art history.
Robert Riseling, Professor; M.A., Northern Iowa; M.F.A., Wisconsin. Painting/drawing.
Meredith Root, Assistant Professor; M.F.A., Wisconsin. Digital media.
Jennifer Sargent, Associate Professor; M.F.A., Arizona State. Surface design.
Cynthia Thompson, Associate Professor; M.F.A., Rutgers. Papermaking/book arts.
Leandra Urrutia, Assistant Professor; M.F.A., Mississippi. Sculpture.
Cathy Wilson, Director of Graduate Programs in Education; M.A.T., Ed.D., Memphis.
Jill Wissmiller, Assistant Professor; M.F.A., Northwestern. Digital media.

Memphis College of art offers students extensive gallery and studio facilities.

A student at work at Memphis College of Art.

SCAD
The University for Creative Careers®

SAVANNAH COLLEGE OF ART AND DESIGN

Graduate School

Programs of Study

Savannah College of Art and Design (SCAD) offers Master of Architecture (M.Arch.), Master of Arts (M.A.), Master of Arts in Teaching (M.A.T.), Master of Fine Arts (M.F.A.), and Master of Urban Design (M.U.D.) degrees and graduate certificates.

The M.A. program is a one-year course of study requiring 45 quarter credit hours. The M.F.A. and M.U.D. programs are two-year courses of study requiring 90 quarter credit hours. The M.A. and M.F.A. are offered in accessory design, advertising, animation, architectural history, design management, fashion, fibers, film and television, furniture design, graphic design, historic preservation, illustration, industrial design, interactive design and game development, interior design, jewelry and objects, luxury and fashion management, motion media design, painting, performing arts, photography, printmaking, production design, sculpture, sequential art, sound design, and visual effects. In addition, M.A. degrees are offered in art history, arts administration, cinema studies, design for sustainability, and illustration design. M.F.A. degrees in service design and writing are also offered. The M.A.T. program requires 60 credit hours completed in one full year of intensive study and field experience.

The professional Master of Architecture degree program is a six-year course of study requiring 180 undergraduate and 90 graduate hours for a total of 270 quarter credit hours encompassing a foundation studies curriculum, general education curriculum, major program curriculum, and electives. The M.Arch. degree is accredited by the National Architectural Accrediting Board.

Online programs, including M.A. and M.F.A. degrees and graduate certificates, are offered through SCAD eLearning.

Research Facilities

Specialized educational resources facilitate research and build knowledge. In every department and program, SCAD students work with advanced professional-level technology, equipment, and resources. For example, SCAD is a Digidesign-certified Pro School for sound design and students can become Pro Tools–certified before graduating. Sequential art students create work using Wacom Cintiq displays. Extensive details regarding the facilities, equipment, and resources available for students in the various programs can be found on the following page.

SCAD libraries are focal points for inspiration, information, study, and research. Collections vary and are targeted to the needs of each SCAD community. At each location, the library contributes to every aspect of academic and intellectual life by providing a broad range of collections and services, including access to digital images, online databases, media, course reserves, archival materials, and personalized research instruction.

Financial Aid

Scholarships and fellowships are available to eligible incoming students based on academic and/or artistic achievement and financial need. Approximately 90 percent of SCAD students receive some form of financial assistance. For more information, students should visit http://www.scad.edu/scholarships.

Cost of Study

Graduate tuition for 2011–12 is $30,960.

Living and Housing Costs

Housing fees for the 2011–12 academic year range from $7185 for dormitory style to $8835 for an apartment-style unit with a separate bedroom. The basic meal plan rate per quarter is $1490.

Student Group

The total enrollment is more than 10,000 students, of whom 16 percent are graduate students. Approximately 20 percent of the graduate students are international.

Location

The College has locations in Savannah and Atlanta, Georgia; Hong Kong; and Lacoste, France. Online programs are offered through SCAD eLearning.

In the heart of Midtown Atlanta, nearly 2,000 SCAD students thrive in the milieu of Fortune 500 companies, as well as leading fine art and design organizations and other nonprofits. SCAD Atlanta is in the center of a fast-paced, major U.S. metropolis.

Within the venerable walls of the historic former North Kowloon Magistracy building, SCAD brings prestigious U.S. art and design education and professional career preparation to Hong Kong, a sophisticated international city on the southeastern coast of China.

SCAD's flagship location in Savannah offers a unique university experience in a charming historic environment near the beautiful beaches of the coastal South.

SCAD Lacoste is a residential study-abroad location in France, offering immersion in the history and culture of Provence.

The SCAD eLearning environment encompasses an online global community, where students learn from SCAD faculty and one another, participating in critiques, meetings, and collaborative projects. Students complete undergraduate and graduate degree requirements completely online or in combination with on-site courses.

The College

The Savannah College of Art and Design exists to prepare talented students for professional creative careers, emphasizing learning through individual attention in a positively oriented university environment. The goal of the College is to nurture and cultivate the unique qualities of each student through an interesting curriculum, in an inspiring environment, under the leadership of involved professors.

SCAD is accredited by the Commission on Colleges of the Southern Association of Colleges and Schools (1866 Southern Lane, Decatur, Georgia 30033-4097; phone: 404-679-4500) to award bachelor's and master's degrees. The M.Arch. degree is accredited by the National Architectural Accrediting Board. The Master of Arts in Teaching degrees are approved by the Georgia Professional Standards Commission. SCAD is licensed by the South Carolina Commission on Higher Education. The SCAD interior design Bachelor of Fine Arts degree is accredited by the Council for Interior Design Accreditation (206 Grandville Ave., Suite 350, Grand Rapids, Michigan 49503; http://accredit-id.org).

Applying

Admission requirements for graduate applicants include a completed application for admission; nonrefundable application fee ($35 for online; $70 for paper form); a bachelor's degree or its equivalent with an official transcript/mark sheet from each college/university attended; evidence of English proficiency for applicants whose first language is not English; two recommendations; statement of purpose; portfolio, writing submission, or audition; and résumé. An interview is recommended but not required. GRE scores are recommended. Applicants to the M.A.T. must have qualifying test scores on the Georgia Assessment for the Certification of Educators, the SAT, the ACT, or the GRE.

In addition, if applicable, applicants must provide any other documents or materials required to obtain a student visa. Portfolio requirements vary; applicants should consult the Web site (www.scad.edu/portfolio) for information. SCAD accepts applications on a rolling basis. Students may enter in the fall, winter, spring, or summer. Those applying for financial aid should complete the online application and Free Application for Federal Student Aid (FAFSA). SCAD'S FAFSA code is 015022.

Correspondence and Information

SCAD Atlanta:
Admission Department
P.O. Box 77300
Atlanta, Georgia 30357-1300
For sending packages:
1600 Peachtree Street, NE
Atlanta, Georgia 30309
Phone: 404-253-2700
　　　877-722-3285 (toll-free)
E-mail: scadatl@scad.edu
Web site: http://www.scad.edu

SCAD Savannah and SCAD eLearning:
Admission Department
P.O. Box 2072
Savannah, Georgia 31402-2072
For sending packages:
22 East Lathrop Avenue
Savannah, Georgia 31415
Phone: 912-525-5100
　　　800-869-7223 (toll-free in U.S.)
E-mail: admission@scad.edu

SCAD Hong Kong:
Admission Department
P.O. Box 2072
Savannah, Georgia 31402-2072
For sending packages:
22 East Lathrop Avenue
Savannah, Georgia 31415
Phone: 852-2253-8000 (in Hong Kong)
E-mail: admission_hk@scad.edu

Savannah College of Art and Design

THE FACULTY

A complete faculty listing is available online at http://www.scad.edu/faculty.

Research Facilities and Equipment

SCAD offers students a wide array of facilities, equipment, and resources needed for the various degree programs.

Students of the building arts use the latest electronic design software including Bentley MicroStation V8, 3D Studio VIZ, SURFCAM AutoCAD, and Autodesk Maya and Revit. Fibers students work with Compu-Dobby looms, an electronic Jacquard loom, and a Mimaki textile printer. The advanced technology labs for furniture and industrial design students include computer numerically controlled equipment for rapid prototyping and production as well as a large envelope five-axis CNC router and laser cutters. Computer resources include SolidWorks and Rhino 3-D. Seven 3-D printers allow students to print ABS and polycarbonate 3-D models of their computer-generated designs.

Photography students work in both digital and film/chemistry labs equipped with Macintosh computers, Adobe CS5 software, Imacon scanners, and wide-format inkjet printers. Students can expose and process RA-4 photographic materials using a Durst Theta printer in Atlanta and an Epsilon printer in Savannah.

Jewelry and Objects students explore a wide range of technology in facilities for precision casting, finishing, enameling, laser welding, lapidary, anodizing, CAD/CAM, forming, and stone setting processes. Resources include a laser welder and microscope system, a Stratasys Dimension SST 1200 printer for ABS plastic, two Solidscape T66 wax printers, and two Roland JWX-10 milling machines. Advanced modeling tools include Sensable pens with ClayTools software. Accessory design students use specialized equipment such as men's and women's shoe lasts, a shoe-finishing machine, and cylinder industrial sewing machines. Industry-standard Lectra Romans CAD software is used for designing bags and shoes. Fashion students use industry-standard dress forms, cutting tables, professional sewing machines, and specialty finishing equipment. Digital labs offer an Infinity Plus plotter for patternmaking and a Mimaki textile printer, as well as software including Kaledo, Vision Fashion Studio, Gerber Suite, Lectra U4ia, and Virtual Fashion Pro.

Film and Digital Media students work with equipment found at major production and postproduction facilities, and use digital technology, nonlinear editing systems digital audio workstations and comprehensive labs for screenwriting, scheduling and budgeting. Production facilities and equipment include Steadicam EFP, Super Panther and Fisher dollies, chroma key/green studio, and sound stage. Students have access to high-end Avid Media Composer Nitris DX and Symphony Nitris DX editing suites. Cameras include Red One digital 4k cameras, Panavision Panaflex G2 cameras, Arriflex 416, and 35 mm Arriflex and 35 mm Moviecam.

Located adjacent to the High Museum of Art in Midtown Atlanta, the sculpture facility is one of the finest in the Southeast. Designed by architect Renzo Piano, the facility houses a comprehensive wood and metal shop, a foundry for bronze and stainless steel, and studios and support equipment, as well as exhibition space.

Performing Arts facilities in Savannah include the 1,200-seat historic Lucas Theatre for the Arts, the 1,100-seat Trustees Theater, the ninety-seat Afifi Amphitheater at the Pei Ling Chan Garden for the Arts, and the 150-seat black-box Mondanaro Theater.

SCAD galleries and exhibitions in Savannah, Atlanta, Hong Kong, and Lacoste showcase the work of students, alumni, faculty and other distinguished and emerging artists.

The SCAD Museum of Art in Savannah is an integral part of the SCAD educational experience. The museum engages in education, exhibitions, research, collection care, and programming. Among its significant collection of 4,500 objects, the museum has seventeenth- to nineteenth-century British and American works, including paintings by Van Dyck, Hogarth, and Gainsborough; prints by Hogarth, Goya, and Renoir; twentieth-century works by Picasso and de Kooning; a major African American collection with iconic works by Bearden and Lawrence; nineteenth- and twentieth-century photography; and designer costumes from the twentieth and twenty-first centuries. A planned 60,000-square-foot expansion is slated to add galleries, classrooms, and a theater to the museum complex.

SCHOOL OF THE ART INSTITUTE OF CHICAGO

Graduate Division

Programs of Study

Graduate programs at the School of the Art Institute of Chicago (SAIC) leading to the M.F.A. in Studio degree are offered in the following studio areas: art and technology studies; ceramics; designed objects; design for emerging technologies; fiber and material studies; film, video, and new media; interior architecture; painting and drawing; performance; photography; printmedia; sculpture; sound; visual communication; and writing. Other advanced degree programs offered are an M.A. in Arts Administration and Policy; an M.A. in Art Education; an M.A. in Art Therapy; an M.A. in Modern Art History, Theory, and Criticism; an M.A. in Teaching; an M.A. in Visual and Critical Studies; an M.S. in Historic Preservation; a dual-degree M.A. in Modern Art History, Theory, and Criticism/M.A. in Arts Administration and Policy; and a Graduate Certificate in Art History, Theory, and Criticism. Since 2006 SAIC has offered the Master of Architecture; the Master of Architecture, with an emphasis in interior design; and the Master of Design in Designed Objects degrees.

Postbaccalaureate certificates in fashion, studio, and writing are also offered.

Other programs offered by SAIC include a Master of Design in Fashion, Body, and Garment and a Master of Arts in New Arts Journalism.

Research Facilities

Among the facilities for research and study, in addition to the studio areas provided by individual departments, are the school library, with more than 85,000 books, periodicals, films, videos, records, CDs, and picture files; the 4,500-volume Joan Flasch Artists' Book Collection; and the Film Study Collections of 800 short and experimental films for class study. The Ryerson and Burnham libraries, the second-largest art and architecture reference libraries in the country, are housed in the Art Institute of Chicago museum and have approximately 220,000 volumes. Other resources include the Video Data Bank, with more than 600 artists' videotapes; the Gene Siskel Film Center; the Poetry Center; the Fashion Resource Center; and the Roger Brown Study Collection.

Financial Aid

Financial assistance for graduate students is available in the form of fellowships, merit and need-based scholarships, assistantships, grants, institutionally sponsored loans, Federal Perkins Loans, and Federal Work-Study Program awards. All students who wish to apply for financial assistance must file the Free Application for Federal Student Aid (FAFSA) form. All financial aid forms and instructions may be obtained through the School's Financial Aid office. Of the full-time graduate students, 83 percent are partially or completely funded.

Cost of Study

For up-to-date tuition and fees information, prospective students should visit http://www.saic.edu.

Living and Housing Costs

Estimated academic-year expenses for an independent, single student, exclusive of tuition, range from $8000 to $12,000, depending upon the housing choice a student makes. (This estimate includes room and board, transportation, supplies, and personal expenses.)

Student Group

Of a total enrollment of 2,463, there are 599 students registered in the Graduate Division. Approximately 65 percent are women, and about 18 percent are international students.

Location

The School of the Art Institute of Chicago offers the advantages of a central location in a large, culturally rich, metropolitan center. The Chicago area has a population of about 7 million and, as an urban center, offers a broad range of cultural activities, along with an efficient public transportation system and well-established, diversified neighborhoods.

The School

The Art Institute of Chicago, comprising the School and the museum, was founded under another name by a small group of artists in 1866. Their purpose was to provide an exceptional education in the studio arts in conjunction with exhibition opportunities. The small art school expanded from a rented facility to its present location in the heart of Chicago's downtown area. The School has become one of the largest independent schools of art and design in the country. Its modern facility adjoins the Art Institute of Chicago Museum, which was built for the World's Columbian Exhibition in 1893. The museum's extensive collection of masterpieces constitutes one of the finest in the world. The partnership between the museum and the School offers unlimited resources for research and study; students have extensive access to the permanent collection, the traveling exhibitions, the Prints and Drawings Room, and the Photography Study Center.

Applying

The School of the Art Institute of Chicago invites applications for admission from students of exceptional promise who have graduated from liberal arts colleges, fine arts schools, and state universities and colleges, as well as those who have completed partial M.F.A. degree programs at other schools. The Admissions Review Committee carefully reviews the portfolios and academic credentials of all applicants. Students are required to submit a portfolio of up to twenty examples of recent work, transcripts from each college previously attended, a statement of purpose, and two to three letters of recommendation. The M.F.A. (in studio areas) application deadline is January 10 for fall admission. Students interested in applying to other degree programs should visit http://www.saic.edu for application guidelines.

Correspondence and Information

Graduate Admissions
Admissions Office
School of the Art Institute of Chicago
36 South Wabash Avenue, Suite 1201
Chicago, Illinois 60603
Phone: 312-629-6100
        800-232-7242 (toll-free)
E-mail: admiss@saic.edu
Web site: http://www.saic.edu

School of the Art Institute of Chicago

THE FACULTY

ARCHITECTURE, INTERIOR ARCHITECTURE, AND DESIGNED OBJECTS
Hennie Reynders, Chair. Cynthia Coleman, Garret Eakin, Ellen Grimes, May Hawfield, Jaak Jurisson, Don Kalec, Linda Keane, Thomas Kong, Carl Ray Miller, Anders Nereim, Ben Nicholson, Helen Marie Nugent, Douglas Pancoast, Tristan Sterk.

ART AND TECHNOLOGY STUDIES
Benjamin Chang, Chair. Claudia Hart, Coordinator. Shawn Decker, Peter Gena, William Harper, Tiffany Holmes, Jason Hopkins, Eduardo Kac, John Manning, Dan Miller, Judd Morrissey, Greg Mowery.

ART EDUCATION
Karyn Sandlos, Chair and Director, Master of Arts in Teaching (MAT). Andres Hernandez, Director, Master of Arts in Art Education (MAAE). Jerome Hausman, Drea Howenstein, Rebecca Keller, Nicole Marroquinn, Angela Paterakis, Patricia Pelletier, Therese Quinn, David Rodriguez.

ART THERAPY
Catherine Moon, Chair. Danniel Anthon, Deborah Benke, Barbara Fish, William Miles, Joanne Ramseyer, Suellen Semekowski, Terri Sweig, Savneet Talwar, Randy Vick.

ARTS ADMINISTRATION AND POLICY
Nicholas Lowe, Chair. Bob Brodsky, John Corbett, Michael Dorf, Adelheid Mers, Amy Reichert, Michael Ryan, Rachel Weiss.

CERAMICS
Xavier Toubes, Chair. Thomas Laureman, William O'Brien, Patricia Rieger, Katherine Ross.

DESIGN FOR EMERGING TECHNOLOGIES
Anders Nereim, Coordinator. Benjamin Chang, Shawn Decker, Peter Gena, Linda Keane, John Manning, Carl Ray Miller, Dan Miller, Douglas Pancoast.

DESIGNED OBJECTS
Helen Maria Nugent, Coordinator. Linda Keane, Carl Ray Miller, Anders Nereim, Lisa Norton, Douglas Pancoast, Jim Termeer, Bruce Tharp.

FASHION
Andrea Reynders, Chair. Katrin Schnabl, Graduate Program Director. Sandra Michel Adams, Bambi Breakstone, Gillion Carrara, Nick Cave, Shane Gabier, Conrad Hamather, Anke Loh, Liat Smestad.

FIBER AND MATERIALS STUDIES
Anne Wilson, Chair. Amy Honchell, Graduate Coordinator. Marianne Fairbanks, Diana Guerrero-Macia, Kathryn Hixson, Joan Livingstone, Christy Matson, Ellen Rothenberg, Christine Tarkowski, Fraser Taylor.

FILM, VIDEO, AND NEW MEDIA
Gregg Bordowitz, Chair. Tatsuyuki Aoki, Jon Cates, Thomas Comerford, Sharon Couzin, Daniel Eisenberg, Shellie Fleming, Michele Mahoney, Mary Patten, John Petrakis, Anne Quirynen, Christopher Sullivan, Jim Trainor, Danielle Wilmouth.

HISTORIC PRESERVATION
Vincent L. Michael, Chair. Rolf Achilles, Craig Deller, Carol Dyson, Richard Friedman, Martha Frish, Yunxia Gao, Jean Guarino, Elaine Harrington, Donald Kalec, Charles Pipal, Anthony Rubano, Anne Sullivan, Terry Tatum, Neal Vogel, Tim Wittman, Carol Yetken.

LIBERAL ARTS
Raja Halwani, Chair. Paul Ashley, Romi Crawford, Calvin Forbes, Peter Gena, Barbara Guenther, James McManus, Karen Morris, Michael Nagelbach, Patrick Rivers, Kathryn Shaffer, Elizabeth Wright, Andrew Yang.

MODERN ART HISTORY, THEORY, AND CRITICISM
Kym Pinder, Chair. Nora Taylor, Director, Master of Arts in Modern Art History, Theory, and Criticism (MAAH). Rolf Achilles, Simon Anderson, Christine Atha, Shane Campbell, Gillion Carrara, Alan Cohen, Audrey Colby, Delinda Collier, Christopher Cutrone, Jim Elkins, Patricia Erens, David Getsy, Michael Golec, James Hugunin, Rebecca Keller, Kai Wood Mah, Deborah Mancoff, Stanley Murashige, Michael Newman, Daniel Quiles, Michael Rabe, David Raskin, Shawn Michelle Smith, Robin Stern, Charles Stuckey, Lisa Wainwright, Tim Wittman, James Yood.

NEW ARTS JOURNALISM
James Yood, Program Director. Cynthia Coleman, Margaret Hawkins, Tiffany Holmes, Michel Miner.

PAINTING AND DRAWING
Susanne Doremus, Chair. Candida Alvarez, Susanna Coffey, Dan Devening, Judith Geichman, Gaylen Gerber, Michelle Grabner, Sheridan Gustin, Philip Hanson, Richard Hull, Michiko Itatani, Susan Kraut, Marion Kryczka, José Lerma, Jim Lutes, Terry Myers, Jim Nutt, Elizabeth Ockwell, John Phillips, Frank Piatek, Scott Reeder, Tyson Reeder, Richard Rezec, Kay Rosen, Barbara Rossi, John Rozelle, Elizabeth Rupprecht, Jerry Saltz, Joanne Scott, Hazma Walker, Kevin Wolff.

PERFORMANCE
Faith Wilding, Chair. Werner Herterich, Lin Hixson, Mark Jeffery, Ginger Krebs, Trevor Martin, Roberto Sifuentes, Blair Thomas.

PHOTOGRAPHY
Barbara DeGenevieve, Chair. Daniel Bauer, Aimee Beaubien, Shannon Benine, Patty Carroll, Robert Clarke-Davis, Ken Fandell, Catherine Glass, Irena Knezevic, Alan Labb, Mayumi Lake, Jason Lazarus, Heidi Norton, Claire Pentecost, Karen Savage, Lewis Toby, Brian Ulrich.

PRINTMEDIA
Peter Power, Chair. Sally Alatalo, Jeanine Coupe-Ryding, Doug Huston, Myungah Hyon, Michael Miller, Mark Pascale, Karen Savage.

SCULPTURE
Laurie Palmer, Chair and Graduate Coordinator. José Ferreira, Preston Jackson, Mary Jane Jacob, Jin Soo Kim, Paul Martin, Adelheid Mers, Fred Nagelbach, Lisa Norton, Carolyn Ottmers, Stephen Reber, Richard Rezac, Frances Whitehead, James Zanzi.

SOUND
Shawn Decker, Chair. Nicholas Collins, John Corbett, Rob Drinkwater, Peter Gena, Eric Leonardson, Lou Mallozzi, Julia Miller, Robert Snyder, Lori Talley.

VISUAL AND CRITICAL STUDIES
Maud Lavin, Chair and Graduate Director. Gregg Bordowitz, Stanford Carpenter, James Elkins, Terri Kapsalis, Karen Morris, Patrick Rivers, Shawn Michelle Smith.

VISUAL COMMUNICATION
John Bowers, Chair. Frank DeBose, Alyson Beaton, Georgia Bockos, Gokhan Ersan, Stephen Farrell, Alysia Kaplan, B. J. Krivanek, Margaret MacNamara, Michael Miner, Jennifer Moody, Daniel Morgenthaler, Olivia Petrides, David Philmloe, Don Pollack, Catherine Ruggie-Saunders, Ann Tyler, Kimberly Viviano, Connie White.

WRITING
Sara Levine, Chair. Carol Anshaw, Rosellen Brown, Anne Calcagno, Elizabeth Cross, Mary Cross, Janet Desaulniers, Amy England, Calvin Forbes, Matthew Goulish, Joseph Grigley, James McManus, Michael Meyers, Beth Nugent, Beau O'Reilly, Elise Paschen, Bin Ramke, Jill Riddell, Ellen Rothenberg, Margaret Sloane, Leila Wilson.

SYRACUSE UNIVERSITY

College of Visual and Performing Arts

Programs of Study

Syracuse University's renowned College of Visual and Performing Arts (VPA) offers eighteen graduate programs, many nationally ranked. The College's four schools/departments include the School of Art and Design; the Department of Communication and Rhetorical Studies; the Department of Drama; and the Rose, Jules R., and Stanford S. Setnor School of Music.

Because the College recognizes the link between education, critical thinking, and cultural knowledge, each program's curriculum is designed to balance academic and intellectual rigor with extensive studio practice. Faculty advisers carefully establish the parameters of each graduate student's course of study while encouraging exploration, collaboration, and interdisciplinary study. In the studio, students are challenged to develop their own vision and identity as artists and designers and to take advantage of the many opportunities and resources available both on campus and in the greater Syracuse community.

The School of Art and Design is the first university-based degree-granting art school in the country and currently one of the most highly ranked. Faculty members are internationally recognized artists and scholars who are actively engaged in their disciplines and committed to teaching and mentoring emerging artists and designers.

The School of Art and Design offers the Master of Fine Arts (M.F.A.) degree in art photography, art video, ceramics, collaborative design, computer art, film, illustration, jewelry and metalsmithing, painting, printmaking, and sculpture; a Master of Arts (M.A) degree in museum studies; and a Master of Science (M.S.) degree in art education.

The Department of Communication and Rhetorical Studies offers a highly specialized graduate program in communication and rhetorical studies that stresses innovative thinking, theoretical and methodological diversity, and practical application. This bold, inventive approach to communication and rhetorical studies promotes the exploration of important threads in the making of good praxis, understand the importance of good scholarly work, and thrive upon the demands of excellence.

The department offers three areas of study that provide a comprehensive view of the discipline and allow students to select a path for further study should they choose to pursue a doctorate degree. Communication Theory and Research focuses on the study of human communication as symbolic interaction; Cosmopolitan Studies uses a variety of critical, feminist, postmodern, and postcolonial perspectives to examine organizing as a communication phenomenon; and Rhetorical Theory and Criticism focuses on the study of rhetoric from antiquities to contemporary theories.

The Setnor School of Music's philosophy of graduate education focuses on preparing students for lifelong careers in the world of music and music education. The school challenges each student to take his or her musicianship to the next level, with private study and collaborative music-making in small- and large-group settings. Students are also challenged to think critically about music and expand their horizons in the arts and humanities. This professionally oriented approach prepares graduate students for positions of vital importance in the music world and as music educators in public schools and universities. Each graduate student receives a high level of personal attention and commitment from Setnor's acclaimed faculty. The faculty members closely mentor the students, who can interact with them in diverse musical settings both on and off campus. Many faculty members are performing professionals, and their musical activities provide students with valuable learning opportunities such as observing rehearsals and performances.

Opportunities for musical growth and professional development abound within the intimate environment of the school and the larger setting of the University. Setnor's vibrant musical and academic community is well-suited to students with outstanding musicianship, a collegial attitude, and an inquisitive, open mind.

The Setnor School of Music offers the Master of Music (M.Mus.) degree in conducting, music composition, and performance and a Master of Science (M.S.) degree in music education. Two professional certification master's degree programs are available within the music education program for those who hold New York State initial certification in music and want to meet academic requirements for professional certification.

Research Facilities

The combined Syracuse University and Law Library collections contain more than 3.1 million volumes, 21,000 serials and periodicals, 7.3 million microforms, 34,000 databases and computer files, and 1 million items in other formats, including CDs, films, videotapes, photographs, and slides. Library resources are available from several locations and through the Internet. Additional information can be found at http://library.syr.edu/.

Financial Aid

Tuition scholarships support graduate education for students with superior qualifications and are awarded at varying levels. Graduate assistantships are instrumental in providing teaching, administrative, and research support for the University. Teaching assistantships (TAs) provide students with excellent opportunities to teach and work closely with faculty members to prepare for the professoriate. The University's nationally recognized TA program helps graduate students prepare to be successful as students, scholars, teachers, advisers, and role models. The orientation and ongoing professional development activities sponsored by the Graduate School enable teaching assistants and teaching associates to enhance their teaching skills and provide opportunities for rich, multidisciplinary conversations about teaching and graduate study.

Graduate fellowships support graduate education for those with truly outstanding qualifications and the potential to make significant contributions in their future professional or scholarly endeavors. The College nominates 2 students each year for the University Fellowship, which consists of a stipend and full tuition scholarship.

There are also a number of special scholarships and awards within the college that may be awarded to new and returning students with outstanding qualifications and the potential to make significant contributions in their future professional or scholarly endeavors.

Cost of Study

For 2011–12, tuition for graduate students is $21,708 (based on 18 credit hours per academic year at $1206 per credit hour). Billable expenses, such as fees, housing, and meals, are estimated at $13,676. Books and supplies, personal expenses, transportation, and medical insurance costs average $5966 per academic year, for an estimated total cost of attendance of $41,350.

The total amount of financial aid that students may receive for an academic year (fall and spring semesters) cannot exceed the cost of attendance. Additional details are available online at http://www.syr.edu/financialaid/costofattendance.

Living and Housing Costs

University housing for single graduate students is extremely limited; a shared apartment costs approximately $12,000 for the calendar year. Most graduate students choose to live in one of the numerous apartment complexes and rental houses available within walking distance or on the bus line. Rent is dependent on a number of factors, but ranges from approximately $400 to $1000 per month.

Student Group

The University is home to approximately 12,370 undergraduates and 5,300 graduate students who form a thriving intellectual community. VPA is the second-largest academic unit at the University, with approximately 2,100 undergraduate students and 140 graduate students.

Location

Syracuse is located in the center of New York State, approximately 250 miles from New York City. The population is 150,000 (400,000 in the greater metropolitan region). The city is accessible by air transportation through Hancock International Airport, as well as rail and bus. Cultural opportunities abound; the region is home to more than forty museums and galleries, including the Everson Museum of Art, Syracuse Stage (the Actors Equity theater affiliated with VPA's Department of Drama), the Landmark Theater, the Redhouse, and Salt City Center for the Performing Arts. The historic Armory Square district in downtown Syracuse features specialty shops, contemporary cafes, galleries, clubs, and a popular nightlife.

The University and The School

Syracuse University (SU) was founded in 1870 by the United Methodist Church, with assistance from the city of Syracuse and is one of the oldest and most comprehensive universities in the country. Privately endowed, coeducational, and nonsectarian, the University comprises eleven schools and colleges, many of them internationally renowned, with rich opportunities for interdisciplinary study. A member of the Association of American Universities and the Council of Graduate Schools, Syracuse University is considered one of the nation's major institutions of higher learning.

Applying

A complete application should include the online application, statement of purpose, three letters of academic/professional reference, and degree-bearing transcripts from all undergraduate institutions. None of the programs in the College of Visual and Performing arts require the GRE; however, the Department of Communication and Rhetorical Studies and the School of Art and Design's museum studies program will review them if they are submitted. International students must submit TOEFL or IELTS scores and must show sufficient funding for the first year of graduate study. Program-specific requirements such as portfolio, audition, and writing samples can be found at http://vpa.syr.edu/prospective-students/graduate/requirements.

Correspondence and Information

Office of Recruitment and Admissions
College of Visual and Performing Arts
Syracuse University
202 Crouse College
Syracuse, New York 13244-1010
Phone: 315-443-2769
     315-443-2543 (Graduate School Dean's office)
     315-443-4492 (Graduate application inquiries)
     315-443-1701 (Graduate awards)
E-mail: admissg@syr.edu
Web site: http://vpa.syr.edu

Syracuse University

THE FACULTY

Faculty and staff members are the driving force behind the mission, vision, and values of the College of Visual and Performing Arts. For details about faculty members, prospective students should visit http://vpa.syr.edu/directory.

Additional Facilities and Resources

Galleries

The University's Coalition of Museum and Art Centers (CMAC) offers a variety of galleries, facilities, and organizations on campus, including SUArt Galleries, Light Work, community darkrooms, the Community Folk Art Center, and the Warehouse Gallery. CMAC strives to support the creation and presentation of work by emerging, mature, and internationally recognized artists while promoting innovation and excellence; embracing diversity; and fostering creative collaborations with local, national, and international communities; and by actively supporting the acquisition, presentation, and interpretation of works of art from across a broad spectrum of visual art practices and histories. In addition there is the Special Collections Research Center and the Louise and Bernard Palitz Gallery at Lubin House, the University's New York City home. Some of the graduate programs maintain dedicated gallery space, such as the ZOID gallery in the Comstock Art Facility and XL Projects, the downtown gallery space. Off campus, students have shown work at Syracuse's Everson Museum of Art, Spark Contemporary Art Space, and in the Syracuse International Film and Video Festival.

Theater

The Department of Drama presents four to five major productions a year, while scenes, short plays, and experimental efforts are shown in the department's intimate Black Box Theatre. Syracuse Stage, a regional Equity theater, shares space with the department and presents a full season of shows each year.

Music

The Setnor School of Music hosts approximately 175 concerts each year in the Setnor Auditorium, featuring students, faculty, and guest artists and ensembles.

Lectures

In addition to the nationally and internationally known visiting artists and lecturers who come to VPA each year, many of the CMAC galleries sponsor artist talks. In addition, the University Lecture Series presents prominent speakers from the areas of architecture and design; the humanities and sciences; and public policy, management, and communications.

Computing Resources

Students have access to a broad range of computing and information technology services. Services include AirOrange, SU's wireless network, which is available in University-owned buildings both on and off campus; wired Internet connections in residence halls and libraries; high-tech, multimedia classrooms; e-mail; and public computer labs equipped with the latest software used in academic course work, including statistical analysis, database management tools, and multimedia applications. Students also have access to space on the central computing system for file storage and for creating personal Web pages. Additional computing resources for academic programs and research activities are available through the University's schools and colleges. A full range of student-computing support services is provided by SU's Information Technology and Services (ITS). Information about these services is available at http://its.syr.edu/rescom.

Career Services

Professionals in all schools collaborate through a Career Services Network to align counseling, career information, experiential learning, and recruiting services for students. The hub of the network is SU's Center for Career Services. Its resources and services encompass personalized career counseling and assessment, job search coaching, resume and cover letter critiques, interview simulations, print and online career information, and on-and off-campus recruiting coordination. More details are available at the Career Services Center's Web site, http://careerservices.syr.edu.

Lesbian, Gay, Bisexual, and Transgender (LGBT) Resource Center

The mission of the LGBT Resource Center is to provide education, advocacy, support, and safe communal space for lesbian, gay, bisexual, transgender, questioning, and straight-allied students, staff, faculty, parents, and alumni of SU. The center promotes the academic and personal growth and development of LGBT students, advocates unrestricted access to and full involvement in University life, and serves as a catalyst for the creation of a campus environment free from intolerance for all students.

THE UNIVERSITY OF THE ARTS

UNIVERSITY OF THE ARTS

Graduate Programs

Programs of Study

University of the Arts (UArts), located on the Avenue of the Arts in Center City Philadelphia, offers graduate programs in art education; art education with a concentration in educational media; book arts/printmaking; ceramics, painting, and sculpture; industrial design; jazz studies; museum communication; museum education; museum exhibition, planning, and design; music education; teaching visual arts; postbaccalaureate certificate in crafts; postbaccalaureate teaching program (nondegree); and postbaccalaureate teaching program professional semester. The graduate programs offer an impressive combination of strengths: exceptionally accomplished faculty members, a remarkably individualized and interactive learning environment, access to outstanding facilities and resources, specialized studios, and programs of study that are both highly focused and highly flexible.

In the visual arts, programs include the Master of Arts in art education, designed to develop the studio, intellectual, and professional education background for educators; the Master of Arts in Teaching visual arts, which incorporates preparation for certification to teach art in grades K–12; the Master of Fine Arts in book arts/printmaking, which builds on the University's thirty-year tradition of involvement with the book and the printed image; and the Master of Fine Arts in studio art. The M.F.A. in studio art program is designed to be completed in three years through part-time study. Also offered are the Master of Fine Arts in museum exhibition planning and design, which was developed with the support of the National Association of Museum Exhibition (NAME); the Master of Arts in museum communication; the Master of Arts in museum education; and the Master of Industrial Design.

In performance, the Master of Arts in Teaching in music education is a one-year-plus-summer program designed for students who have a bachelor's degree in music theory/composition, music history/literature, or other noneducation courses of study. The Master of Music in jazz studies is a one-year, 32-credit program. Designed as a finishing program in jazz performance, components of the program include advanced private instruction, hands-on internships and pedagogy study, and ensemble performances.

Research Facilities

Students use state-of-the-art digital-technology facilities, which include computer labs that support professional-level creative work, collaboration, and research. There is a dedicated Mac lab for graduate students and a wireless network throughout UArts buildings. In addition to multiple high-end graphics labs, the University hosts a New Media Center comprising two dual-platform digital laboratories that enable the integration of animation and 3-D modeling. Also available on campus are the Borowsky Center for Publication Arts; photography, film, and animation facilities with studios and darkrooms, video editing suites, and two Oxberry Master Series animation stands; recording studios, state-of-the-art music technology MIDI studios and editing suites, and practice rooms; a bronze foundry and plaster workshop; and crafts studios and workshops for ceramics, metals, wood, glassblowing, papermaking, and fibers. Other important facilities include the digital forge 3-D printer, a bookbindery, and stone and metal welding shops.

Financial Aid

The Free Application for Federal Student Aid (FAFSA) must be filed by applicants for financial aid. Graduate teaching assistantships are available for qualified applicants. Some teaching and technical assistantships are awarded by the University of the Arts; the amounts of these awards vary.

Cost of Study

Tuition for the 2011–12 academic year is $33,500 plus applicable technology, book supplies, and activity fees.

Living and Housing Costs

There is limited University housing for graduate students. Dining Services meal plans are available at various meal-per-week levels.

Student Group

Students come from forty states and territories and thirty countries; about 5 percent of the total enrollment of 2,500 are international students. The graduate programs enrolled 237 students in 2010–11.

Location

The University's campus spans the vibrant Avenue of the Arts from South Street to Walnut Street and is the cultural hub of Center City Philadelphia. Next door to the University's historic Hamilton Hall is the city's magnificent Kimmel Center for the Performing Arts; in adjacent blocks are the famous Academy of Music, Wilma Theater, Suzanne Roberts Theater, and the University's historic Merriam Theater, which books touring Broadway shows for the public and hosts UArts student performances. The area also has excellent museums (Philadelphia Museum of Art and Barnes Museum), galleries, music and dance facilities, superb restaurants, and retail stores. Of historic importance, but also modern and sophisticated, the city is at the same time one of the nation's major metropolitan centers and a series of small, close-knit neighborhoods with beautiful tree-lined squares. Fairmount Park, one of the country's largest public park systems, provides facilities for sports activities and picnicking. Statistics show that UArts is one of the safest campuses in the city.

The University

The University of the Arts is composed of the College of Art, Media, and Design, and the College of Performing Arts. UArts prepares students for more than a hundred professional career paths in the visual, performing, and communication arts.

The College of Art, Media, and Design is a professional community dedicated to the visual arts, design, and film. Founded in 1876 to train artists to translate the technological advances of the Industrial Revolution, it is today one of the nation's leading schools of its kind. The College of Performing Arts focuses on music, dance, acting, and musical theater. Founded in 1870 to educate musicians, it has expanded to offer demanding undergraduate programs of ballet, modern dance, and jazz dance as well as a program in theater arts.

The University of the Arts sponsors a variety of activities that include exhibitions, performances, social events, lectures, and regular gallery and museum trips to New York City and Washington, D.C.

Applying

Required application materials include the University's Application for Graduate Study, a personal statement of intent, a nonrefundable fee of $60, official college transcripts, and at least three letters of recommendation. Portfolios must be submitted by applicants to the visual arts programs. An audition is required for applicants to the music program. International students must submit a Certification of Finance and TOEFL scores in the event the student's first language is other than English.

Applications for the fall term should be submitted by January 15 for priority consideration. Applications submitted after January 15 are considered on a space-available basis. Applications for January admission (art and music education only) should be submitted by November 15. Applications for the low-residency M.F.A. in studio art should be submitted by January 1.

Correspondence and Information

Dean of Admission
University of the Arts
320 South Broad Street
Philadelphia, Pennsylvania 19102
Phone: 215-717-6049
       800-616-ARTS (toll-free)
Fax: 215-717-6045
E-mail: admissions@uarts.edu
Web site: http://www.uarts.edu

University of the Arts

THE FACULTY

Faculty members at the University of the Arts are active, working artists immersed in their craft, who bring their knowledge and access to their professional networks to their students. Because its classes have an average 10:1 student to teacher ratio, the University affords students the opportunity to work closely with faculty members every day. Noteworthy among them are Dr. Slavko Milekic, known for his groundbreaking innovations in interactive digital technology; groundbreaking Momix choreographer Brian Sanders; and Nick Jr. animator Chris McDonnell. Liberal arts professor, author, and social critic Camille Paglia is known for her dissident feminist point of view; the *New York Times* named her essay on Madonna one of the "most influential essays of the century."

WASHINGTON UNIVERSITY IN ST. LOUIS

Sam Fox School of Design & Visual Arts
Graduate School of Art
M.F.A. in Visual Arts Program

Program of Study

In response to complex, shifting global cultures, rapidly evolving technologies, and changes to the environment, the Graduate School of Art offers a two-year, critically engaged studio program that provides the framework for collaboration and both disciplinary-specific and nondisciplinary study. Upon completion of their course of study, students at the Graduate School of Art are granted the Master of Fine Arts (M.F.A.) in visual art, the terminal professional degree in studio art. The Graduate School of Art subscribes to the standards for the M.F.A. degree as set forth and accepted by the College Art Association of America (CAA) and the National Association of Schools of Art and Design (NASAD).

Today's vastly expanded context for creative work also requires artists to understand various modes of critical analysis. Throughout the program, students are encouraged to investigate the relationship between thinking and making, and to articulate the conceptual underpinnings of their work. Graduate seminars provide students opportunities to study theory through the lens of studio practice, while a robust thesis seminar supports students in their writing and in the development of their ideas. The Public Lecture Series and various fellows' programs bring nationally and internationally recognized artists, architects, historians, and critics to campus, promoting new ideas in practice, theory, and technology in art, architecture, and design. Invited speakers often come to graduate students' studios for one-on-one reviews of their work.

On a broader scale, the graduate program prepares students to understand the broad landscape of contemporary creative practices and consider ways in which they can incite progressive social change, address challenges in the environment, and assume their roles as global citizens through avenues such as public engagement opportunities and study abroad programs including the Berlin program. In furthering those objectives, the Graduate School of Art also offers collaborative research, production, and travel grants.

Research Facilities

The School maintains a full range of studio facilities that support work across media, including sculpture, painting, printmaking, fashion, photography and digital imaging, and time-based media. During the academic year, students have 24-hour access to their studios, as well as most shop areas. Other resources include the Collaborative Technology Center, the Creative Research Institute, Whitaker Media Lab, the Nancy Spirtas Kranzberg Studio for the Illustrated Book, Island Press, Des Lee Gallery, and the Kenneth and Nancy Kranzberg Art & Architecture Library. The Mildred Lane Kemper Art Museum provides students with additional opportunities for meaningful encounters with art and visual culture through curricular integration; the Teaching in the Galleries Program; and internships in curatorial, publications, and education departments. In addition, the annual M.F.A. exhibition is installed at the Kemper Art Museum.

Financial Aid

An application for financial aid will have no effect on the admission decision. Fellowship, scholarship, and assistantship awards are based primarily on artistic and academic merit. Loan assistance is awarded based on financial need. The Graduate School of Art strives to provide aid to as many fellows as possible. All students accepted for graduate admission are automatically considered for several full-tuition fellowships and scholarships, as well as partial-tuition remission art scholarships. These include the Henrietta Wahlert Scholarship for Painters and Sculptors, the Eliza McMillan Scholarship for Women, and the Graduate School of Art Fellowship Awards, which recognize and reward exceptional talent and artistic/academic performance. All scholarships are renewable for the second year. In addition, the Danforth Scholarship is awarded based on nominations from Art alumni. Two fellowship opportunities—the Mr. and Mrs. Spencer T. Olin Fellowship for Women and the Chancellor's Graduate Fellowship—require the submission of a separate application to the M.F.A. program.

Cost of Study

The tuition for M.F.A. students for the 2011–12 academic year is $33,350. Additional fees, including the cost of health service, student activity, and a graduate trip are approximately $1700 per year.

Living and Housing Costs

Approximately $885 per month should be budgeted to provide for living costs (room and board). Most students prefer to rent an apartment near the School. In addition, an average cost of $2600 may be budgeted for books and supplies.

Student Group

Students studying at the Graduate School of Art produce a wide range of work in varying media and conceptual scope. They are a critically engaged, self-directed, and tight-knit community, working in a dedicated facility with individual studios.

Location

The St. Louis area offers a variety of musical, cultural, and sports events throughout the academic year. Washington University is contiguous with the city of St. Louis and adjoins its suburbs. The Saint Louis Art Museum, located in Forest Park, has assembled one of the finest comprehensive art collections in the country. The Contemporary Art Museum St. Louis and the Pulitzer Foundation for the Arts are both located in nearby Grand Center.

The University and The School

Washington University, a medium-sized, independent university, is dedicated to challenging its faculty and students alike to seek new knowledge and greater understanding of an ever-changing, multicultural world. The University is counted among the world's leaders in teaching and research, and draws students and faculty to St. Louis from all fifty states and more than 110 nations. The University is highly regarded for its commitment to excellence in learning. Its programs, administration, facilities, resources, and activities combine to further its mission of teaching, research, and service to society.

The Sam Fox School of Design & Visual Arts is housed in a five-building complex of new and recently renovated facilities that includes the Mildred Lane Kemper Art Museum, home to one of the finest university collections of important paintings, sculptures, photographs, and installations by nineteenth-, twentieth-, and twenty-first-century American and European artists, along with significant antiquities and a large number of prints and drawings. The Sam Fox School hosts a lively series of lectures, symposia, and exhibitions, and enjoys strong collaborations with the Pulitzer Foundation for the Arts, Laumeier Sculpture Park, the Contemporary Art Museum St. Louis, Missouri Botanical Garden, and the Saint Louis Art Museum.

Applying

The online application for fall 2012 is available as of October 2011. Applications to the Graduate Art program, along with all supporting materials, are due January 5, 2012. No midyear applications are accepted. Admissions decisions are based on portfolio, academic records, statement of objectives, and references. Specific requirements include: B.F.A. degree or equivalent academic preparation, 15 to 18 credits of art history, grade point average above 3.0, and good writing skills.

Correspondence and Information

Patricia Olynyk, Director, Graduate School of Art, and Florence and Frank Bush Professor of Art
Sam Fox School of Design & Visual Arts
Washington University in St. Louis
Campus Box 1031
One Brookings Drive
St. Louis, Missouri 63130
Phone: 314-935-8423
Fax: 314-935-4862
E-mail: olynyk@samfox.wustl.edu
Web site: http://samfoxschool.wustl.edu/artarch/gradart

Washington University in St. Louis

THE FACULTY AND THEIR RESEARCH

Jamie Adams, Associate Professor, Painting and Drawing; M.F.A., Pennsylvania Academy of the Fine Arts, 2000.

Lauren Adams, Assistant Professor; Painting; M.F.A. (multimedia), Carnegie Mellon, 2007.

Lisa Bulawsky, Associate Professor of Printmaking/Drawing and Director of Island Press; M.F.A. (printmaking), Kansas, 1995.

Michael Byron, Professor and Area Coordinator, Painting; M.F.A., Nova Scotia College of Art and Design, 1981.

Carmon Colangelo, Dean of Sam Fox School of Design & Visual Arts and E. Desmond Lee Professor for Collaboration in the Arts; M.F.A. (printmaking), LSU, 1983.

Ron Fondaw, Professor and Area Coordinator, Sculpture; M.F.A., Illinois at Urbana-Champaign, 1978.

Robert Gero, Lecturer, Graduate Studies and Sculpture; Ph.D. (philosophy), New School, 2004; M.F.A. (sculpture), California State, Los Angeles, 1998.

Joan Hall, Kenneth E. Hudson Professor of Art, Sculpture; M.F.A., Nebraska–Lincoln, 1978.

Jana Harper, Senior Lecturer, Illustrated Book; M.F.A. (printmaking, book arts), Arizona State, 2001.

John Hendrix, Assistant Professor, Communication Design; M.F.A. (illustration), School of Visual Arts, 2003.

Balázs Kicsiny, Henry L. and Natalie E. Freund Visiting Artist; D.L.A., Hungarian Academy of Fine Arts, Budapest, 2008.

Irena Knezevic, Assistant Professor, Digital Imaging & Photography; M.F.A., Illinois at Chicago, 2007.

Chelsea Knight, Henry L. and Natalie E. Freund Teaching Fellow; M.F.A., Art Institute of Chicago, 2007.

Richard Krueger, Associate Professor, Digital Imaging & Photography; M.F.A. (photography and digital imaging), Notre Dame, 1991.

Arny Nadler, Associate Professor, Core 3D; M.F.A., Cranbrook Academy of Art, 1994.

Jon Navy, Senior Lecturer, Collaborative Technologies Center; M.F.A. (time arts), Art Institute of Chicago 1991.

Patricia Olynyk, Director, Graduate School of Art and Florence and Frank Bush Professor of Art; M.F.A., California College of the Arts, 1988.

Frank Oros, Associate Professor, Core; B.S. (communication arts and sciences), Western Michigan, 1975.

John Sarra, Senior Lecturer, Painting; M.F.A. (painting), Washington (St. Louis), 1997.

Buzz Spector, Dean of College & Graduate School of Art and Jane Reuter Hitzeman and Herbert F. Hitzeman Jr. Professor of Art; M.F.A., Chicago, 1978.

Denise Ward-Brown, Associate Professor, Sculpture; M.F.A., Howard, 1984.

Cheryl Wassenaar, Associate Professor, Director of Core; M.F.A., Cincinnati, 2000.

Monika Weiss, Assistant Professor, New Media; M.F.A. (drawing and painting), Academy of Fine Arts, Warsaw, 1989.

Section 4
Comparative and Interdisciplinary Arts

This section contains a directory of institutions offering graduate work in comparative and interdisciplinary arts. Additional information about programs listed in the directory but not augmented by an in-depth entry may be obtained by writing directly to the dean of a graduate school or chair of a department at the address given in the directory.

For programs offering related work, see also in this book *Applied Arts and Design, Architecture, Art and Art History,* and *Performing Arts.* In another guide in this series:

Graduate Programs in Business, Education, Health, Information Studies, Law & Social Work
See *Subject Areas (Art Education)*

CONTENTS

Comparative and Interdisciplinary Arts

Bradley University, Graduate School, Slane College of Communications and Fine Arts, Department of Art, Peoria, IL 61625-0002. Offers ceramics (MA, MFA); drawing/illustration (MA, MFA); interdisciplinary art (MA, MFA); painting (MA, MFA); photography (MA, MFA); printmaking (MA, MFA); sculpture (MA, MFA); visual communication and design (MA, MFA). *Accreditation:* NASAD. Part-time programs available. *Degree requirements:* For master's, comprehensive exam, thesis, final exhibit. *Entrance requirements:* For master's, portfolio, 2 letters of recommendation. Additional exam requirements/recommendations for international students: Required—TOEFL (minimum score 550 paper-based; 213 computer-based; 79 iBT).

Brigham Young University, Graduate Studies, College of Humanities, Department of Humanities, Classics, and Comparative Literature, Provo, UT 84602-1001. Offers comparative studies (MA). *Faculty:* 25 full-time (5 women). *Students:* 16 full-time (10 women). Average age 26. 14 applicants, 50% accepted, 7 enrolled. In 2010, 6 master's awarded. *Degree requirements:* For master's, 2 foreign languages, thesis. *Entrance requirements:* For master's, GRE, minimum GPA of 3.0 in last 60 hours. Additional exam requirements/recommendations for international students: Required—TOEFL (minimum score 580 paper-based; 85 iBT), IELTS (minimum score 7). *Application deadline:* For fall admission, 3/1 for domestic and international students. Application fee: $50. Electronic applications accepted. *Expenses:* Tuition: Full-time $5580; part-time $310 per credit hour. Tuition and fees vary according to program and student's religious affiliation. *Financial support:* In 2010–11, 16 students received support, including 39 fellowships with full and partial tuition reimbursements available (averaging $1,306 per year), 5 research assistantships (averaging $1,400 per year), 36 teaching assistantships (averaging $2,317 per year); career-related internships or fieldwork, institutionally sponsored loans, scholarships/grants, tuition waivers (full and partial), and student instructorships also available. Support available to part-time students. *Unit head:* Dr. Michael J. Call, Chair, 801-422-2550, Fax: 801-422-0305, E-mail: michael_call@byu.edu. *Application contact:* Carolyn Hone, Graduate Secretary for Humanities and Comparative Literature, 801-422-4430, Fax: 801-422-0305, E-mail: carolyn_hone@byu.edu.

Columbia College Chicago, Graduate School, Program in Interdisciplinary Arts, Chicago, IL 60605-1996. Offers interdisciplinary arts (MA); interdisciplinary book and paper arts (MFA). Part-time and evening/weekend programs available. *Students:* 43 full-time (30 women), 15 part-time (12 women); includes 3 Black or African American, non-Hispanic/Latino; 1 Asian, non-Hispanic/Latino; 2 Hispanic/Latino; 2 Two or more races, non-Hispanic/Latino, 4 international. Average age 30. 61 applicants, 85% accepted, 27 enrolled. In 2010, 24 master's awarded. *Degree requirements:* For master's, interview, minimum GPA of 3.0, portfolio, work sample. Additional exam requirements/recommendations for international students: Required—TOEFL (minimum score 550 paper-based; 213 computer-based). *Application deadline:* For fall admission, 1/14 priority date for domestic students, 1/15 priority date for international students. Applications are processed on a rolling basis. Application fee: $55. Electronic applications accepted. *Expenses:* Tuition: Full-time $16,966; part-time $684 per credit. Required fees: $520; $113 per semester. One-time fee: $150 full-time. Tuition and fees vary according to course load and program. *Financial support:* Fellowships, career-related internships or fieldwork, Federal Work-Study, and scholarships/grants available. Support available to part-time students. Financial award application deadline: 8/13; financial award applicants required to submit FAFSA. *Unit head:* Jeff Abell, Department Chair, 312-369-7270, E-mail: jabell@colum.edu. *Application contact:* Cate Lagueux, Director of Graduate Admissions, 312-369-7260, Fax: 312-369-8047, E-mail: clagueux@colum.edu.

Florida Atlantic University, Dorothy F. Schmidt College of Arts and Letters, Department of Comparative Studies, Boca Raton, FL 33431-0991. Offers PhD. Part-time programs available. *Students:* 5 full-time (4 women), 51 part-time (34 women); includes 12 minority (4 Black or African American, non-Hispanic/Latino; 1 Asian, non-Hispanic/Latino; 7 Hispanic/Latino), 3 international. Average age 40. 28 applicants, 0% accepted, 0 enrolled. In 2010, 8 doctorates awarded. *Degree requirements:* For doctorate, one foreign language, comprehensive exam, thesis/dissertation. *Entrance requirements:* For doctorate, GRE, minimum GPA of 3.5, 3 references. Additional exam requirements/recommendations for international students: Required—TOEFL. *Application deadline:* For fall admission, 2/1 priority date for domestic and international students. Applications are processed on a rolling basis. Application fee: $30. *Expenses:* Tuition, area resident: Part-time $319.96 per credit. Tuition, state resident: part-time $319.96 per credit. Tuition, nonresident: part-time $926.42 per credit. *Financial support:* Teaching assistantships with tuition reimbursements available. *Faculty research:* Arts, humanities, social sciences. *Unit head:* Dr. Emily Stockard, Interim Director, 561-297-2817, Fax: 561-297-2058, E-mail: stockard@fau.edu. *Application contact:* Dr. Emily Stockard, Interim Director, 561-297-2817, Fax: 561-297-2058, E-mail: stockard@fau.edu.

Goddard College, Graduate Division, Master of Fine Arts in Interdisciplinary Arts Program, Plainfield, VT 05667-9432. Offers MFA. Postbaccalaureate distance learning degree programs offered (minimal on-campus study). *Degree requirements:* For master's, thesis. *Entrance requirements:* For master's, relevant undergraduate degree, 3 letters of recommendation, study plan and resource list, interview, portfolio, artistic resume. Electronic applications accepted.

John F. Kennedy University, Graduate School of Holistic Studies, Department of Arts and Consciousness, Program in Transformative Arts, Pleasant Hill, CA 94523-4817. Offers MA. Part-time and evening/weekend programs available. *Degree requirements:* For master's, thesis or alternative. *Entrance requirements:* For master's, interview. Additional exam requirements/recommendations for international students: Required—TOEFL. *Expenses:* Contact institution.

Ohio University, Graduate College, College of Fine Arts, School of Interdisciplinary Arts, Athens, OH 45701-2979. Offers PhD. *Students:* 20 full-time (11 women), 6 part-time (2 women); includes 4 minority (2 Black or African American, non-Hispanic/Latino; 1 Asian, non-Hispanic/Latino; 1 Two or more races, non-Hispanic/Latino), 8 international. 1 applicant, 0% accepted, 0 enrolled. In 2010, 1 doctorate awarded. *Degree requirements:* For doctorate, 2 foreign languages, comprehensive exam, thesis/dissertation. *Entrance requirements:* For doctorate, GRE or MAT, master's degree. Additional exam requirements/recommendations for international students: Required—TOEFL (minimum score 575 paper-based; 91 iBT) or IELTS (minimum score 7). *Application deadline:* For fall admission, 1/31 priority date for domestic and international students. Application fee: $50 ($55 for international students). Electronic applications accepted. *Financial support:* In 2010–11, teaching assistantships with tuition reimbursements available (averaging $15,615 per year); Federal Work-Study and institutionally sponsored loans also available. Financial award application deadline: 1/31. *Faculty research:* Comparative studies of theater, music, and the visual arts. *Unit head:* Dr. Dora J. Wilson, Director, 740-593-9413, Fax: 740-593-0578, E-mail: wilsond@ohio.edu. *Application contact:* Brenda Llewellyn, Administrative Coordinator, 740-593-1314, E-mail: llewelb@ohio.edu.

Simon Fraser University, Graduate Studies, Faculty of Arts and Social Sciences, School for the Contemporary Arts, Burnaby, BC V5A 1S6, Canada. Offers MFA. *Degree requirements:* For master's, thesis or alternative. *Entrance requirements:* For master's, minimum GPA of 3.0. Additional exam requirements/recommendations for international students: Required—TOEFL or IELTS. *Faculty research:* Dance theory, screenplays, drawing and painting, acting, electroacoustic music.

Section 5
Film, Television, and Video

This section contains a directory of institutions offering graduate work in film, television, and video. Additional information about programs listed in the directory may be obtained by writing directly to the dean of a graduate school or chair of a department at the address given in the directory.

For programs offering related work, see also in this book *Art and Art History* and *Communication and Media*. In the other guides in this series:

Graduate Programs in Engineering & Applied Sciences
See *Telecommunications*
Graduate Programs in Business, Education, Health, Information Studies, Law & Social Work
See *Advertising and Public Relations*

CONTENTS

Program Directories

Close-Ups and Displays

Film, Television, and Video Production

Academy of Art University, Graduate Program, School of Animation and Visual Effects, San Francisco, CA 94105-3410. Offers 2D animation (MFA); 3D animation (MFA); 3D modeling (MFA); visual effects (MFA). Part-time programs available. Postbaccalaureate distance learning degree programs offered (no on-campus study). *Faculty:* 20 full-time (4 women), 90 part-time/adjunct (17 women). *Students:* 613 full-time (224 women), 340 part-time (118 women); includes 41 Black or African American, non-Hispanic/Latino; 3 American Indian or Alaska Native, non-Hispanic/Latino; 70 Asian, non-Hispanic/Latino; 47 Hispanic/Latino; 1 Native Hawaiian or other Pacific Islander, non-Hispanic/Latino, 448 international. Average age 29. 244 applicants. In 2010, 109 master's awarded. *Degree requirements:* For master's, thesis, final review. *Entrance requirements:* For master's, portfolio. *Application deadline:* For fall admission, 9/7 for domestic and international students; for spring admission, 2/2 for domestic and international students. Applications are processed on a rolling basis. Application fee: $100 ($500 for international students). Electronic applications accepted. *Expenses:* Tuition: Full-time $20,160; part-time $840 per semester hour. Required fees: $45 per semester. *Financial support:* Career-related internships or fieldwork and Federal Work-Study available. Support available to part-time students. Financial award application deadline: 8/10; financial award applicants required to submit FAFSA.

Academy of Art University, Graduate Program, School of Motion Pictures and Television, San Francisco, CA 94105-3410. Offers MFA. Part-time programs available. Postbaccalaureate distance learning degree programs offered (no on-campus study). *Faculty:* 10 full-time (3 women), 98 part-time/adjunct (33 women). *Students:* 253 full-time (105 women), 154 part-time (67 women); includes 43 Black or African American, non-Hispanic/Latino; 4 American Indian or Alaska Native, non-Hispanic/Latino; 14 Asian, non-Hispanic/Latino; 26 Hispanic/Latino; 1 Native Hawaiian or other Pacific Islander, non-Hispanic/Latino, 111 international. Average age 31. 153 applicants. In 2010, 58 master's awarded. *Degree requirements:* For master's, thesis, final review. *Entrance requirements:* For master's, portfolio. *Application deadline:* For fall admission, 9/7 for domestic and international students; for spring admission, 2/2 for domestic and international students. Applications are processed on a rolling basis. Application fee: $100 ($500 for international students). Electronic applications accepted. *Expenses:* Tuition: Full-time $20,160; part-time $840 per semester hour. Required fees: $45 per semester. *Financial support:* Career-related internships or fieldwork and Federal Work-Study available. Support available to part-time students. Financial award application deadline: 8/10; financial award applicants required to submit FAFSA. *Application contact:* 800-544-ARTS, Fax: 415-263-4130, E-mail: info@academyart.edu.

Academy of Art University, Graduate Program, School of Music Production and Sound Design for Visual Media, San Francisco, CA 94105-3410. Offers MFA. Part-time programs available. Postbaccalaureate distance learning degree programs offered (no on-campus study). *Faculty:* 1 full-time (0 women), 11 part-time/adjunct (2 women). *Students:* 26 full-time (10 women), 8 part-time (2 women); includes 1 Black or African American, non-Hispanic/Latino; 2 Asian, non-Hispanic/Latino; 2 Hispanic/Latino, 15 international. Average age 30. 19 applicants. *Degree requirements:* For master's, thesis, final review. *Application deadline:* For fall admission, 9/7 for domestic and international students; for spring admission, 2/2 for domestic and international students. Applications are processed on a rolling basis. Application fee: $100 ($500 for international students). Electronic applications accepted. *Expenses:* Tuition: Full-time $20,160; part-time $840 per semester hour. Required fees: $45 per semester. *Financial support:* Career-related internships or fieldwork and Federal Work-Study available. Support available to part-time students. Financial award application deadline: 8/10; financial award applicants required to submit FAFSA.

American Film Institute Conservatory, Graduate Program, Los Angeles, CA 90027-1657. Offers cinematography (MFA); directing (MFA); editing (MFA); producing (MFA); production design (MFA); screenwriting (MFA). *Faculty:* 13 full-time (1 woman), 65 part-time/adjunct (22 women). *Students:* 356 full-time (117 women); includes 81 minority (23 Black or African American, non-Hispanic/Latino; 1 American Indian or Alaska Native, non-Hispanic/Latino; 23 Asian, non-Hispanic/Latino; 21 Hispanic/Latino; 13 Two or more races, non-Hispanic/Latino), 89 international. Average age 26. 629 applicants, 32% accepted, 136 enrolled. In 2010, 120 master's awarded. *Degree requirements:* For master's, one foreign language, thesis. *Entrance requirements:* Additional exam requirements/recommendations for international students: Required—TOEFL (minimum score 600 paper-based; 250 computer-based; 100 iBT). *Application deadline:* For fall admission, 12/1 for domestic and international students. Applications are processed on a rolling basis. Application fee: $75. *Expenses:* Tuition: Full-time $37,112. Required fees: $2484. *Financial support:* In 2010–11, 198 students received support, including 16 teaching assistantships with partial tuition reimbursements available (averaging $3,000 per year); career-related internships or fieldwork, scholarships/grants, and unspecified assistantships also available. Financial award application deadline: 4/15; financial award applicants required to submit FAFSA. *Faculty research:* Film production, TV production. *Application contact:* Karin Tucker, Admissions Manager, 323-856-7609, Fax: 323-856-7683, E-mail: ktucker@afi.com.

American University, School of Communication, Film and Electronic Media Program, Washington, DC 20016-8001. Offers MFA. Part-time and evening/weekend programs available. *Faculty:* 14 full-time (6 women). *Students:* 47 full-time (22 women), 40 part-time (23 women), 3 international. 74 applicants, 59% accepted, 26 enrolled. In 2010, 141 master's awarded. *Degree requirements:* For master's, comprehensive exam, thesis or alternative. *Entrance requirements:* For master's, GRE General Test. Additional exam requirements/recommendations for international students: Required—TOEFL (minimum score 600 paper-based; 250 computer-based; 100 iBT), IELTS. *Application deadline:* For fall admission, 2/1 priority date for domestic and international students; for spring admission, 11/15 for domestic and international students. Applications are processed on a rolling basis. Application fee: $50. Electronic applications accepted. *Financial support:* In 2010–11, 10 students received support, including 2 fellowships with partial tuition reimbursements available (averaging $13,000 per year), 2 research assistantships with partial tuition reimbursements available (averaging $11,000 per year), 4 teaching assistantships with partial tuition reimbursements available (averaging $11,000 per year); career-related internships or fieldwork, Federal Work-Study, institutionally sponsored loans, scholarships/grants, tuition waivers (partial), and unspecified assistantships also available. Financial award application deadline: 2/1; financial award applicants required to submit FAFSA. *Faculty research:* Documentary film production, social media, media and public policy, visual literacy, new technology. *Unit head:* Prof. John Douglass, Director, Film and Media Arts Division, 202-885-2045, Fax: 202-885-2019, E-mail: jdougla@american.edu. *Application contact:* Sharmeen Ahsan-Bracciale, Graduate Admissions Office, 202-885-2040, Fax: 202-885-2019, E-mail: sharmeen@american.edu.

American University, School of Communication, Film and Video Program, Washington, DC 20016-8001. Offers MA. Part-time and evening/weekend programs available. *Faculty:* 14 full-time (6 women). *Students:* 26 full-time (12 women), 26 part-time (14 women). 64 applicants, 69% accepted, 16 enrolled. In 2010, 29 master's awarded. *Degree requirements:* For master's, comprehensive exam, thesis or alternative. *Entrance requirements:* For master's, GRE General Test. Additional exam requirements/recommendations for international students: Required—TOEFL (minimum score 660 paper-based; 250 computer-based; 100 iBT), IELTS (minimum score 7). *Application deadline:* For fall admission, 2/1 priority date for domestic and international students; for spring admission, 11/15 for domestic and international students. Applications are processed on a rolling basis. Application fee: $50. Electronic applications accepted. *Financial support:* In 2010–11, 2 research assistantships with partial tuition reimbursements (averaging $11,000 per year), 4 teaching assistantships with partial tuition reimbursements (averaging $11,000 per year) were awarded; career-related internships or fieldwork, Federal Work-Study, institutionally sponsored loans, scholarships/grants, tuition waivers (partial), and unspecified assistantships also available. Financial award application deadline: 2/1; financial award applicants required to submit FAFSA. *Faculty research:* Documentary film and video production, visual literacy, Eastern European cinema, media and public policy, social media. *Unit head:* Prof. John Douglass, Director, Film and Media Arts Division, 202-885-2045, Fax: 202-885-2019, E-mail: jdougla@american.edu. *Application contact:* Sharmeen Ahsan-Bracciale, Graduate Admissions Office, 202-885-2040, Fax: 202-885-2019, E-mail: sharmeen@american.edu.

American University, School of Communication, Weekend Programs in Communication, Washington, DC 20016-8001. Offers interactive journalism (MA); news media studies (MA); producing for film and video (MA); public communication (MA). *Accreditation:* ACEJMC. Part-time and evening/weekend programs available. *Faculty:* 5 part-time/adjunct (2 women). *Students:* 113 part-time (64 women). 105 applicants, 72% accepted, 59 enrolled. In 2010, 15 master's awarded. *Degree requirements:* For master's, comprehensive exam, thesis or alternative. *Entrance requirements:* Additional exam requirements/recommendations for international students: Required—TOEFL (minimum score 600 paper-based; 250 computer-based; 100 iBT). *Application deadline:* For fall admission, 8/1 for domestic students. Applications are processed on a rolling basis. Application fee: $50. Electronic applications accepted. *Financial support:* In 2010–11, 3 fellowships (averaging $3,500 per year) were awarded; institutionally sponsored loans also available. Financial award applicants required to submit FAFSA. *Unit head:* Prof. Rose Ann Robertson, Associate Dean, 202-885-2002, E-mail: rrobert@american.edu. *Application contact:* Sharmeen Ahsan-Bracciale, Director of Graduate Services, 202-885-2040, Fax: 202-885-2019, E-mail: sharmeen@american.edu.

Antioch University Midwest, Graduate Programs, Individualized Liberal and Professional Studies Program, Yellow Springs, OH 45387-1609. Offers liberal and professional studies (MA), including counseling, creative writing, education, film studies, liberal studies, management, modern literature, psychology, theatre, visual arts. Part-time and evening/weekend programs available. Postbaccalaureate distance learning degree programs offered (minimal on-campus study). *Faculty:* 2 full-time (1 woman), 2 part-time/adjunct (both women). *Students:* 15 full-time (11 women), 34 part-time (22 women); includes 11 minority (8 Black or African American, non-Hispanic/Latino; 3 Hispanic/Latino). Average age 40. 13 applicants, 69% accepted, 5 enrolled. In 2010, 18 master's awarded. *Degree requirements:* For master's, thesis or alternative. *Entrance requirements:* For master's, resume, goal statement, interview. *Application deadline:* For fall admission, 8/1 for domestic students; for winter admission, 12/1 for domestic students; for spring admission, 3/10 for domestic students. Applications are processed on a rolling basis. Application fee: $50. Electronic applications accepted. *Expenses:* Contact institution. *Financial support:* Federal Work-Study available. Financial award applicants required to submit FAFSA. *Unit head:* Dr. Joseph Cronin, Chair, 937-769-1894, Fax: 937-769-1807, E-mail: jcronin@antioch.edu. *Application contact:* Seth Gordon, Assistant Director of Admissions, 937-769-1800 Ext. 1825, Fax: 937-769-1804, E-mail: sgordon@antioch.edu.

Arizona State University, College of Liberal Arts and Sciences, Program in Film and Media Studies, Tempe, AZ 85287-0402. Offers American media and popular culture (MAS). Part-time and evening/weekend programs available. Postbaccalaureate distance learning degree programs offered (no on-campus study). *Faculty:* 10 full-time (3 women). *Students:* 5 full-time (all women), 12 part-time (4 women); includes 4 minority (all Hispanic/Latino). Average age 32. 20 applicants, 20% accepted, 3 enrolled. *Degree requirements:* For master's, integrated project. *Entrance requirements:* For master's, minimum GPA of 3.0 or equivalent in last 2 years of work leading to bachelor's degree. Additional exam requirements/recommendations for international students: Required—TOEFL, IELTS, or Pearson Test of English. *Application deadline:* For fall admission, 3/15 for domestic and international students; for spring admission, 10/15 for domestic and international students. Applications are processed on a rolling basis. Application fee: $70 ($90 for international students). Electronic applications accepted. *Expenses:* Contact institution. *Financial support:* In 2010–11, 1 teaching assistantship with full and partial tuition reimbursement (averaging $15,000 per year) was awarded; career-related internships or fieldwork, Federal Work-Study, institutionally sponsored loans, scholarships/grants, and tuition waivers (partial) also available. Financial award application deadline: 3/1; financial award applicants required to submit FAFSA. Total annual research expenditures: $198,441. *Unit head:* Dr. Bambi Haggins, Director, 480-965-6747, Fax: 480-965-9110, E-mail: bambi.haggins@asu.edu. *Application contact:* Graduate Admissions, 480-965-6113.

Art Center College of Design, Graduate Division, Broadcast Cinema Department, Pasadena, CA 91103. Offers MFA. *Accreditation:* NASAD. *Faculty:* 3 part-time/adjunct (0 women). *Students:* 41 full-time (7 women), 29 part-time (9 women); includes 19 minority (7 Black or African American, non-Hispanic/Latino; 5 Asian, non-Hispanic/Latino; 4 Hispanic/Latino; 2 Native Hawaiian or other Pacific Islander, non-Hispanic/Latino; 1 Two or more races, non-Hispanic/Latino), 18 international. Average age 29. 29 applicants, 83% accepted, 14 enrolled. *Application deadline:* For fall admission, 3/1 for domestic and international students; for spring admission, 10/1 for domestic and international students. Application fee: $50 ($70 for international students). *Expenses:* Tuition: Part-time $17,220 per term. *Unit head:* Robert Peterson, Chair, 626-396-2274. *Application contact:* Robert Peterson, Chair, 626-396-2274.

See Display on page 89 and Close-Up on page 119.

The Art Institute of California–San Francisco, Master of Fine Arts Program, San Francisco, CA 94102. Offers computer animation (MFA).

Bob Jones University, Graduate Programs, Greenville, SC 29614. Offers accountancy (MS); Bible (MA); Bible translation (MA); Biblical studies (Certificate); broadcast management (MS); business administration (MBA); church history (MA, PhD); church ministries (MA); church music (MM); cinema and video production (MA); counseling (MS); curriculum and instruction (Ed D); divinity (M Div); dramatic production (MA); educational leadership (MS, Ed D, Ed S); elementary education (M Ed, MAT); English (M Ed, MA, MAT); fine arts (MA); graphic design (MA); history (M Ed, MA); illustration (MA); interpretative speech (MA); mathematics (M Ed, MAT); medical missions (Certificate); ministry (MM, D Min); multi-categorical special education (M Ed, MAT); music (M Ed); New Testament interpretation (PhD); Old Testament interpretation (PhD); orchestral instrument performance (MM); organ performance (MM); pastoral studies (MA); personnel services (MS, Ed S); piano pedagogy (MM); piano performance (MM); platform arts (MA); radio and television broadcasting (MS); rhetoric and public address (MA); secondary education (M Ed); studio art (MA); teaching Bible (MA); theology (MA, PhD); voice performance (MM); youth ministries (MA); M Div/MM.

Boston University, College of Communication, Department of Film and Television, Boston, MA 02215. Offers film production (MFA); film studies (MFA); media ventures (MS); screenwriting (MFA); television production (MS); MBA/MS. Part-time programs available. *Faculty:* 13 full-time, 27 part-time/adjunct. *Students:* 80 full-time (44 women), 11 part-time (4 women); includes 12 minority (7 Black or African American, non-Hispanic/Latino; 2 Asian, non-Hispanic/Latino; 2 Hispanic/Latino; 1 Two or more races, non-Hispanic/Latino), 17 international. Average age 26. In 2010, 54 master's awarded. *Degree requirements:* For master's, thesis. *Entrance requirements:* For master's, GRE General Test, sample of written or creative work. Additional exam requirements/recommendations for international students: Required—TOEFL (minimum score 600 paper-based; 250 computer-based; 100 iBT). *Application deadline:* For fall admission, 2/1 for domestic and international students. Application fee: $70. Electronic applications accepted. *Expenses:* Tuition: Full-time $39,314; part-time $1228 per credit. Required fees: $40 per semester. *Financial support:* Teaching assistantships with partial tuition reimbursements, career-related internships or fieldwork, Federal Work-Study, institutionally sponsored loans, scholarships/grants, and unspecified assistantships available. Support available to part-time students. Financial award application deadline: 2/1; financial award applicants required to submit FAFSA. *Unit head:* Paul Schneider, Chairman, 617-353-3483, Fax: 617-353-1084, E-mail: ftvchair@bu.edu. *Application contact:* Jennifer Healey, Administrator of Graduate Services, 617-353-3481, Fax: 617-358-0399, E-mail: comgrad@bu.edu.

Film, Television, and Video Production

Bowling Green State University, Graduate College, College of Arts and Sciences, Department of Theatre and Film, Bowling Green, OH 43403. Offers MA, PhD. *Accreditation:* NAST. Part-time programs available. Terminal master's awarded for partial completion of doctoral program. *Degree requirements:* For master's, thesis or alternative; for doctorate, comprehensive exam, thesis/dissertation, 9 hour research tool. *Entrance requirements:* For master's and doctorate, GRE General Test. Additional exam requirements/recommendations for international students: Required—TOEFL. Electronic applications accepted. *Faculty research:* Theatre history, dramatic theory, cultural studies, performance studies, American theatre history.

Brigham Young University, Graduate Studies, College of Fine Arts and Communications, Department of Theatre and Media Arts, Provo, UT 84602-6404. Offers MA. MA program accepts applications in odd-numbered years only. *Accreditation:* NAST. *Faculty:* 18 full-time (6 women). *Students:* 1 full-time (0 women), 11 part-time (8 women), 1 international. Average age 31. In 2010, 4 master's awarded. *Degree requirements:* For master's, comprehensive exam, thesis, 32 hours, oral defense. *Entrance requirements:* For master's, GRE General Test, writing samples. Additional exam requirements/recommendations for international students: Required—TOEFL (minimum score 580 paper-based; 237 computer-based; 85 iBT). *Application deadline:* For fall admission, 2/1 priority date for domestic and international students. Application fee: $50. Electronic applications accepted. *Expenses:* Tuition: Full-time $5580; part-time $310 per credit hour. Tuition and fees vary according to program and student's religious affiliation. *Financial support:* In 2010–11, 12 students received support, including 4 research assistantships with partial tuition reimbursements available (averaging $3,500 per year), 12 teaching assistantships with partial tuition reimbursements available (averaging $3,500 per year); career-related internships or fieldwork, institutionally sponsored loans, scholarships/grants, health care benefits, tuition waivers (partial), unspecified assistantships, and administrative aides also available. Support available to part-time students. *Faculty research:* Media literacy, children's media, theatre historiography, performance studies, popular culture. *Unit head:* Dr. Rodger D. Sorensen, Department Chair, 801-422-8132, Fax: 801-422-0654, E-mail: rodger_sorensen@byu.edu. *Application contact:* Katie Boyer, Secretary, 801-422-6645, Fax: 801-422-0654, E-mail: tma.secretary@gmail.com.

Brooklyn College of the City University of New York, Division of Graduate Studies, Department of Television and Radio, Brooklyn, NY 11210-2889. Offers media studies (MS); television production (MFA). Part-time and evening/weekend programs available. *Students:* 14 full-time (8 women), 39 part-time (11 women); includes 16 minority (9 Black or African American, non-Hispanic/Latino; 1 Asian, non-Hispanic/Latino; 6 Hispanic/Latino), 15 international. Average age 29. 56 applicants, 71% accepted, 23 enrolled. In 2010, 23 master's awarded. *Degree requirements:* For master's, comprehensive exam. *Entrance requirements:* For master's, GRE General Test or MAT, 12 credits in television/radio with a minimum B average, 2 letters of recommendation. Additional exam requirements/recommendations for international students: Required—TOEFL (minimum score 580 paper-based; 237 computer-based; 92 iBT). *Application deadline:* For fall admission, 3/1 priority date for domestic students, 2/1 priority date for international students; for spring admission, 11/1 priority date for domestic students, 10/1 priority date for international students. Applications are processed on a rolling basis. Application fee: $125. Electronic applications accepted. *Expenses:* Tuition, state resident: full-time $7360; part-time $310 per credit hour. Tuition, nonresident: full-time $13,800; part-time $575 per credit hour. Required fees: $190 per semester. *Financial support:* Career-related internships or fieldwork, Federal Work-Study, and institutionally sponsored loans available. Support available to part-time students. Financial award application deadline: 5/1; financial award applicants required to submit FAFSA. *Faculty research:* Criticism, research methods, audience behavior, policy and regulation, program history, international television and radio. *Unit head:* Dr. Fred Wasser, Chairperson, 718-951-5555, E-mail: fwasser@brooklyn.cuny.edu. *Application contact:* Hernan Sierra, Graduate Admissions Coordinator, 718-951-4536, Fax: 718-951-4506, E-mail: grads@brooklyn.cuny.edu.

California College of the Arts, Graduate Programs, Programs in Fine Art, San Francisco, CA 94107. Offers ceramics (MFA); film/video/performance (MFA); glass (MFA); jewelry/metal arts (MFA); painting/drawing (MFA); photography (MFA); printmaking (MFA); sculpture (MFA); textiles (MFA); wood/furniture (MFA). *Accreditation:* NASAD. *Faculty:* 20 full-time (10 women), 25 part-time/adjunct (14 women). *Students:* 95 full-time (66 women), 12 part-time (9 women); includes 3 Black or African American, non-Hispanic/Latino; 1 American Indian or Alaska Native, non-Hispanic/Latino; 5 Asian, non-Hispanic/Latino; 20 Hispanic/Latino; 2 Native Hawaiian or other Pacific Islander, non-Hispanic/Latino, 7 international. Average age 30. 462 applicants, 37% accepted, 55 enrolled. In 2010, 173 master's awarded. *Degree requirements:* For master's, thesis, exhibit. *Entrance requirements:* For master's, appropriate bachelor's degree, portfolio, resume, 2 letters of recommendation, transcript. Additional exam requirements/recommendations for international students: Required—TOEFL (minimum score 600 paper-based; 250 computer-based; 100 iBT). *Application deadline:* For fall admission, 1/5 for domestic and international students. Application fee: $70. Electronic applications accepted. *Expenses:* Tuition: Full-time $38,550; part-time $1285 per unit. One-time fee: $185 full-time. *Financial support:* In 2010–11, 12 fellowships (averaging $27,000 per year), teaching assistantships (averaging $2,000 per year) were awarded; career-related internships or fieldwork, Federal Work-Study, scholarships/grants, and health care benefits also available. Financial award application deadline: 3/1; financial award applicants required to submit FAFSA. *Unit head:* Ted Purves, Chair, 415-551-9214, Fax: 415-703-9539, E-mail: tpurves@cca.edu. *Application contact:* Heidi Geis, Assistant Director of Graduate Admissions, 415-703-9523 Ext. 9533, Fax: 415-703-9539, E-mail: hgeis@cca.edu.

California Institute of the Arts, School of Film/Video, Valencia, CA 91355-2340. Offers experimental animation (MFA); film directing (MFA, Adv C); film/video (Adv C). *Entrance requirements:* For master's, portfolio. Additional exam requirements/recommendations for international students: Required—TOEFL. Electronic applications accepted. *Faculty research:* Experimental and character animation, experimental film/video, video graphics.

California State University, Fullerton, Graduate Studies, College of the Arts, Department of Theatre and Dance, Fullerton, CA 92834-9480. Offers acting (MFA); acting and directing (MA); dance (MA); directing (MFA); dramatic literature/criticism (MA); oral interpretation (MA); playwriting (MA); technical theater (MA); technical theater and design (MFA); television (MA); theatre for children (MA); theatre history (MA). *Accreditation:* NAST (one or more programs are accredited). Part-time programs available. *Students:* 17 full-time (9 women), 1 part-time (0 women); includes 2 Hispanic/Latino; 1 Two or more races, non-Hispanic/Latino. Average age 29. 11 applicants, 27% accepted, 3 enrolled. In 2010, 7 master's awarded. *Degree requirements:* For master's, oral and written exam, project or thesis. *Entrance requirements:* For master's, major in theatre or related field, audition or interview, minimum GPA of 2.5 in last 60 units of course work. Application fee: $55. *Financial support:* Career-related internships or fieldwork, Federal Work-Study, institutionally sponsored loans, and scholarships/grants available. Support available to part-time students. Financial award application deadline: 3/1; financial award applicants required to submit FAFSA. *Unit head:* Dr. Susan Hallman, Chair, 657-278-3628. *Application contact:* Admissions/Applications, 657-278-2371.

California State University, Los Angeles, Graduate Studies, College of Arts and Letters, Department of Communication Studies, Los Angeles, CA 90032-8530. Offers speech communication (MA); television, film and theatre (MFA). Part-time and evening/weekend programs available. *Faculty:* 11 full-time (5 women), 3 part-time/adjunct (2 women). *Students:* 85 full-time (52 women), 57 part-time (41 women); includes 58 minority (20 Black or African American, non-Hispanic/Latino; 7 Asian, non-Hispanic/Latino; 26 Hispanic/Latino; 5 Two or more races, non-Hispanic/Latino), 29 international. Average age 32. 93 applicants, 100% accepted, 54 enrolled. In 2010, 19 master's awarded. *Degree requirements:* For master's, comprehensive exam or thesis. *Entrance requirements:* For master's, minimum GPA of 2.75 in last 90 units of course work. Additional exam requirements/recommendations for international students: Required—TOEFL (minimum score 500 paper-based; 173 computer-based). *Application deadline:* For fall admission, 5/1 for domestic and international students. Applications are processed on a rolling basis. Application fee: $55. Electronic applications accepted. *Financial support:* Career-related internships or fieldwork and Federal Work-Study available. Support available to part-time students. Financial award application deadline: 3/1. *Faculty research:* Organizational, interpersonal, intercultural, and instructional communication; rhetorical theories. *Unit head:* Dr. Bryant Keith Alexander, Chair, 323-343-4200, Fax: 323-343-6467, E-mail: abryant@calstatela.edu. *Application contact:* Dr. Alan Muchlinski, Dean of Graduate Studies, 323-343-3820, Fax: 323-343-5653, E-mail: amuchli@exchange.calstatela.edu.

California State University, Northridge, Graduate Studies, College of Arts, Media, and Communication, Department of Cinema and Television Arts, Northridge, CA 91330. Offers screenwriting (MA). *Entrance requirements:* For master's, GRE (if cumulative undergraduate GPA less than 3.0).

Carleton University, Faculty of Graduate Studies, Faculty of Arts and Social Sciences, School for Studies in Art and Culture, Program in Film Studies, Ottawa, ON K1S 5B6, Canada. Offers MA. *Degree requirements:* For master's, thesis. *Entrance requirements:* For master's, honors degree. Additional exam requirements/recommendations for international students: Required—TOEFL.

Carnegie Mellon University, School of Computer Science and College of Fine Arts, Program in Entertainment Technology, Pittsburgh, PA 15213-3891. Offers MET.

Central Michigan University, College of Graduate Studies, College of Communication and Fine Arts, School of Broadcasting and Cinematic Arts, Mount Pleasant, MI 48859. Offers electronic media management (MA); electronic media production (MA); electronic media studies (MA); film theory and criticism (MA). Part-time programs available. *Faculty:* 11 full-time (2 women), 1 part-time/adjunct (0 women). *Students:* 15 full-time (4 women), 18 part-time (7 women); includes 2 Black or African American, non-Hispanic/Latino; 1 Asian, non-Hispanic/Latino; 1 Hispanic/Latino, 6 international. Average age 26. *Degree requirements:* For master's, thesis or alternative. *Entrance requirements:* For master's, undergraduate degree in broadcasting, film studies, or an associated discipline with minimum GPA of 2.7. *Application deadline:* For fall admission, 6/1 for international students; for spring admission, 10/1 for international students. Applications are processed on a rolling basis. Application fee: $35 ($45 for international students). Electronic applications accepted. *Expenses:* Tuition, state resident: full-time $8208; part-time $456 per credit hour. Tuition, nonresident: full-time $13,788; part-time $766 per credit hour. One-time fee: $25. *Financial support:* Fellowships with tuition reimbursements, teaching assistantships with tuition reimbursements, career-related internships or fieldwork, Federal Work-Study, unspecified assistantships, and out-of-state merit awards, non-resident graduate awards available. Financial award application deadline: 3/1. *Faculty research:* Multimedia production, film history and criticism, writing and promotions, international broadcasting and media systems, history of American broadcasting. *Unit head:* Dr. Peter B. Orlik, Chairperson, 989-774-3851, Fax: 989-774-2426, E-mail: peter.b.orlik@cmich.edu. *Application contact:* Dr. Patricia Williamson, Graduate Program Coordinator, 989-774-2561, Fax: 989-774-2426, E-mail: willi1pa@cmich.edu.

Chapman University, Graduate Studies, Dodge College of Film and Media Arts, Conservatory of Motion Pictures, Orange, CA 92866. Offers film and television producing (MFA); film production (MFA); film studies (MA); production design (MFA); screenwriting (MFA); JD/MFA; MBA/MFA. Part-time and evening/weekend programs available. *Faculty:* 34 full-time (7 women), 52 part-time/adjunct (16 women). *Students:* 230 full-time (86 women), 11 part-time (3 women); includes 8 Black or African American, non-Hispanic/Latino; 2 American Indian or Alaska Native, non-Hispanic/Latino; 7 Asian, non-Hispanic/Latino; 14 Hispanic/Latino, 40 international. Average age 27. 342 applicants, 44% accepted, 85 enrolled. In 2010, 76 master's awarded. *Degree requirements:* For master's, thesis. *Entrance requirements:* For master's, GRE General Test, minimum undergraduate GPA of 2.5, portfolio. Additional exam requirements/recommendations for international students: Required—TOEFL (minimum score 550 paper-based). *Application deadline:* For fall admission, 3/1 priority date for domestic students. Application fee: $55. Electronic applications accepted. *Expenses:* Contact institution. *Financial support:* Fellowships, Federal Work-Study and scholarships/grants available. Financial award application deadline: 6/30; financial award applicants required to submit FAFSA. *Unit head:* Joseph Slowensky, Director, 714-744-7882, E-mail: jslowens@chapman.edu. *Application contact:* Jojo Delfin, Information Contact, 714-997-6786, E-mail: delfin@chapman.edu.

Chatham University, Program in Film and Digital Technology, Pittsburgh, PA 15232-2826. Offers emerging media (MFA). Part-time and evening/weekend programs available. *Degree requirements:* For master's, thesis, capstone project. *Entrance requirements:* Additional exam requirements/recommendations for international students: Required—TOEFL (minimum score 600 paper-based; 250 computer-based; 100 iBT), IELTS (minimum score 6.5), TWE. Electronic applications accepted.

Columbia College Chicago, Graduate School, Department of Film and Video, Chicago, IL 60605-1996. Offers MFA. Part-time programs available. *Students:* 23 full-time (4 women), 25 part-time (14 women); includes 7 Black or African American, non-Hispanic/Latino; 1 American Indian or Alaska Native, non-Hispanic/Latino; 1 Asian, non-Hispanic/Latino; 4 Hispanic/Latino, 3 international. Average age 31. 97 applicants, 22% accepted, 11 enrolled. In 2010, 6 master's awarded. *Degree requirements:* For master's, thesis, film project. *Entrance requirements:* For master's, interview, minimum GPA of 3.0, portfolio or script. Additional exam requirements/recommendations for international students: Required—TOEFL (minimum score 550 paper-based; 213 computer-based). *Application deadline:* For fall admission, 1/5 for domestic and international students. Application fee: $55. Electronic applications accepted. *Expenses:* Tuition: Full-time $16,966; part-time $684 per credit. Required fees: $520; $113 per semester. One-time fee: $150 full-time. Tuition and fees vary according to course load and program. *Financial support:* Fellowships, career-related internships or fieldwork, Federal Work-Study, scholarships/grants, and unspecified assistantships available. Support available to part-time students. Financial award application deadline: 8/13; financial award applicants required to submit FAFSA. *Unit head:* Prof. Wenhwa Ts'ao, Chairperson, 312-369-6765, E-mail: wtsao@colum.edu. *Application contact:* Cate Lagueux, Senior Vice President, Office of Provost, 312-369-7260, Fax: 312-369-8047, E-mail: clagueux@colum.edu.

Columbia University, School of the Arts, Film Division, New York, NY 10027. Offers creative producing (MFA); directing (MFA); film studies (MA); screenwriting (MFA). *Degree requirements:* For master's, thesis. *Entrance requirements:* For master's, 3 letters of recommendation, writing sample, complete a scene, feature film treatment (optional visual submission). Additional exam requirements/recommendations for international students: Required—TOEFL (minimum score 600 paper-based; 250 computer-based; 100 iBT). Electronic applications accepted.

See Close-Up on page 295.

Concordia University, School of Graduate Studies, Faculty of Fine Arts, Department of Studio Arts, Montréal, QC H3G 1M8, Canada. Offers studio arts (MFA), including film production, open media, painting, photography, print media, sculpture, ceramics and fibers. *Degree requirements:* For master's, thesis or alternative. *Entrance requirements:* For master's, portfolio.

Concordia University, School of Graduate Studies, Faculty of Fine Arts, Mel Hoppenheim School of Cinema, Montréal, QC H3G 1M8, Canada. Offers film studies (MA).

DePaul University, College of Computing and Digital Media, Chicago, IL 60604. Offers animation (MA, MFA); applied technology (MS); business information technology (MS); cinema (MFA); cinema production (MS); computational finance (MS); computer and information sciences (PhD); computer game development (MS); computer graphics and motion technology (MS); computer information and network security (MS); computer science (MS); e-commerce technology (MS); human-computer interaction (MS); information systems (MS); information technology (MA); information technology project management (MS); network engineering and management (MS); predictive analytics (MS); screenwriting (MFA); software engineering (MS); JD/MA; JD/MS. Part-time and evening/weekend programs available. Postbaccalaureate distance

Film, Television, and Video Production

DePaul University (continued)
learning degree programs offered (no on-campus study). *Faculty:* 51 full-time (11 women), 50 part-time/adjunct (9 women). *Students:* 952 full-time (230 women), 927 part-time (226 women); includes 557 minority (205 Black or African American, non-Hispanic/Latino; 2 American Indian or Alaska Native, non-Hispanic/Latino; 167 Asian, non-Hispanic/Latino; 136 Hispanic/Latino; 7 Native Hawaiian or other Pacific Islander, non-Hispanic/Latino; 40 Two or more races, non-Hispanic/Latino), 292 international. Average age 31. 896 applicants, 70% accepted, 324 enrolled. In 2010, 417 master's, 6 doctorates awarded. *Degree requirements:* For master's, thesis (for some programs); for doctorate, comprehensive exam, thesis/dissertation. *Entrance requirements:* For master's, GRE or GMAT (MS in computational finance only), bachelor's degree, resume (MS in predictive analytics only), IT experience (MS in information technology project management only), portfolio review (MFA); for doctorate, GRE, master's degree in computer science. Additional exam requirements/recommendations for international students: Required—TOEFL (minimum score 550 paper-based; 213 computer-based; 80 iBT), IELTS (minimum score 6.5), Pearson Test of English (minimum score 53). *Application deadline:* For fall admission, 8/15 priority date for domestic students, 6/1 priority date for international students; for winter admission, 12/15 priority date for domestic students, 9/15 priority date for international students; for spring admission, 3/1 priority date for domestic students, 12/15 priority date for international students. Applications are processed on a rolling basis. Application fee: $25. Electronic applications accepted. *Expenses:* Contact institution. *Financial support:* In 2010–11, 102 students received support, including 4 fellowships with full tuition reimbursements available (averaging $24,435 per year), 6 research assistantships (averaging $21,100 per year), 92 teaching assistantships with full and partial tuition reimbursements available (averaging $6,904 per year); Federal Work-Study, scholarships/grants, tuition waivers (full and partial), and unspecified assistantships also available. Support available to part-time students. Financial award application deadline: 4/30; financial award applicants required to submit FAFSA. *Faculty research:* Bioinformatics, visual computing, graphics and animation, high performance and scientific computing, databases. Total annual research expenditures: $1.4 million. *Unit head:* Dr. David Miller, Dean, 312-362-8381, Fax: 312-362-5185. *Application contact:* Dr. Liz Friedman, Assistant Dean of Student Services, 312-362-8714, Fax: 312-362-5179, E-mail: efriedm2@cdm.depaul.edu.

Drexel University, Antoinette Westphal College of Media Arts and Design, Program in Television Management, Philadelphia, PA 19104-2875. Offers MS, MS/MBA.

Florida Atlantic University, Dorothy F. Schmidt College of Arts and Letters, School of Communication and Multimedia Studies, Boca Raton, FL 33431-0991. Offers communication studies (MA); film and video (Certificate); film studies (MA); multimedia journalism studies (MA). Part-time programs available. *Faculty:* 28 full-time (10 women), 14 part-time/adjunct (3 women). *Students:* 19 full-time (15 women), 15 part-time (11 women); includes 8 minority (3 Black or African American, non-Hispanic/Latino; 1 American Indian or Alaska Native, non-Hispanic/Latino; 1 Asian, non-Hispanic/Latino; 1 Hispanic/Latino; 2 Two or more races, non-Hispanic/Latino), 6 international. Average age 28. 42 applicants, 26% accepted, 8 enrolled. In 2010, 3 master's awarded. *Degree requirements:* For master's, one foreign language, comprehensive exam (for some programs), thesis (for some programs). *Entrance requirements:* For master's, GRE General Test, minimum GPA of 3.0. *Application deadline:* For fall admission, 7/1 priority date for domestic students, 4/1 for international students; for spring admission, 11/1 for domestic students, 10/1 for international students. Applications are processed on a rolling basis. Application fee: $30. Electronic applications accepted. *Expenses:* Tuition, area resident: Part-time $319.96 per credit. Tuition, state resident: part-time $319.96 per credit. Tuition, nonresident: part-time $926.42 per credit. *Financial support:* Teaching assistantships with partial tuition reimbursements, Federal Work-Study and institutionally sponsored loans available. Support available to part-time students. Financial award application deadline: 3/1. *Faculty research:* Cultural studies, gender studies, film, communication theory, journalism, new media. *Unit head:* Dr. Susan S. Reilly, Director, 561-297-1095, Fax: 561-297-2615, E-mail: sreilly@fau.edu. *Application contact:* Dr. Eric M. Freedman, Graduate Coordinator, 561-297-2534, Fax: 561-297-2615, E-mail: efreedma@fau.edu.

Florida State University, The Graduate School, College of Motion Picture Arts, Tallahassee, FL 32306-2350. Offers production (MFA); screen and play writing (MFA). *Faculty:* 13 full-time (2 women), 4 part-time/adjunct (1 woman). *Students:* 61 full-time (24 women); includes 6 Black or African American, non-Hispanic/Latino; 8 Hispanic/Latino, 6 international. Average age 27. 182 applicants, 23% accepted, 30 enrolled. In 2010, 28 master's awarded. *Degree requirements:* For master's, thesis, thesis project. *Entrance requirements:* For master's, minimum GPA of 3.0, film/video experience. Additional exam requirements/recommendations for international students: Required—TOEFL (minimum score 550 paper-based; 253 computer-based; 80 iBT). *Application deadline:* For fall admission, 12/1 for domestic and international students. Application fee: $30. *Expenses:* Tuition, state resident: full-time $8238.24. *Financial support:* In 2010–11, 22 students received support, including 1 fellowship with partial tuition reimbursement available (averaging $6,300 per year), 22 teaching assistantships with partial tuition reimbursements available (averaging $4,100 per year); Federal Work-Study and unspecified assistantships also available. Financial award application deadline: 1/1; financial award applicants required to submit FAFSA. *Faculty research:* Producing, screenwriting, directing, cinematography, editing. *Unit head:* Frank Patterson, Dean, 850-644-0453, Fax: 850-644-2626. *Application contact:* Carrie Lewis, Coordinator of Student Services, 850-644-8524, Fax: 850-644-2626, E-mail: clewis@film.fsu.edu.

Georgia State University, College of Arts and Sciences, Department of Communication, Atlanta, GA 30302-3083. Offers film/video/digital imaging (MA); human communication and social influence (MA); mass communication (MA); moving image studies (PhD); public communication (PhD). Part-time programs available. *Degree requirements:* For master's, one foreign language, thesis or alternative; for doctorate, comprehensive exam, thesis/dissertation. *Entrance requirements:* For master's and doctorate, GRE General Test. Additional exam requirements/recommendations for international students: Required—TOEFL (minimum score 80 computer-based). Electronic applications accepted. *Faculty research:* Critical/cultural studies, rhetoric studies, film/media studies, mass communications/journalism, audience studies.

Hofstra University, School of Communication, Program in Documentary Studies and Production, Hempstead, NY 11549. Offers MFA. Part-time and evening/weekend programs available. *Faculty:* 8 full-time (2 women). *Students:* 13 full-time (8 women), 7 part-time (5 women); includes 3 minority (all Asian, non-Hispanic/Latino), 4 international. Average age 30. 22 applicants, 86% accepted, 8 enrolled. *Degree requirements:* For master's, thesis, thesis project. *Entrance requirements:* For master's, 2 letters of recommendation, portfolio, interview, essay. Additional exam requirements/recommendations for international students: Required—TOEFL (minimum score 550 paper-based; 213 computer-based; 80 iBT). *Application deadline:* Applications are processed on a rolling basis. Application fee: $70 ($75 for international students). Electronic applications accepted. *Expenses:* Tuition: Full-time $18,000; part-time $1000 per credit hour. Required fees: $970; $145 per term. Tuition and fees vary according to program. *Financial support:* In 2010–11, 4 students received support, including 3 fellowships with full and partial tuition reimbursements available (averaging $2,000 per year), 1 research assistantship with full and partial tuition reimbursement available (averaging $10,529 per year); Federal Work-Study, institutionally sponsored loans, scholarships/grants, tuition waivers (full and partial), and unspecified assistantships also available. Support available to part-time students. Financial award applicants required to submit FAFSA. *Faculty research:* Cultural studies, women, urban studies, class, grassroots movements and personal documentary; documentary film aesthetics, history and theory, animation and feminism; community and citizen's media; indigenous movements in Latin America; development and globalization; sports, music, culture, experimental documentary. *Unit head:* Dr. Christine Noschese, Program Director, 516-463-7141, E-mail: avfczn@hofstra.edu. *Application contact:* Carol Drummer, Dean of Graduate Admissions, 516-463-4876, Fax: 516-463-4664, E-mail: gradstudent@hofstra.edu.

Hollins University, Graduate Programs, Program in Screenwriting and Film Studies, Roanoke, VA 24020-1603. Offers MA, MFA. Offered during summer only. Part-time programs available. *Degree requirements:* For master's, one foreign language, comprehensive exam, thesis. *Entrance requirements:* For master's, letters of recommendation, portfolio. Additional exam requirements/recommendations for international students: Required—TOEFL (minimum score 550 paper-based; 213 computer-based; 79 iBT). Electronic applications accepted. *Faculty research:* German film, women in film, censorship, minorities in film.

Howard University, School of Communications, Department of Radio, Television and Film, Washington, DC 20059-0002. Offers film (MFA). Part-time programs available. *Degree requirements:* For master's, thesis optional. *Entrance requirements:* For master's, GRE General Test, minimum GPA of 3.0.

Humboldt State University, Academic Programs, College of Arts, Humanities, and Social Sciences, Department of Theatre, Film and Dance, Arcata, CA 95521-8299. Offers theatre arts (MA, MFA), including film production (MA), production (MA), scenography (MFA). *Students:* 15 full-time (12 women), 2 part-time (1 woman); includes 1 Hispanic/Latino. Average age 36. 16 applicants, 63% accepted, 6 enrolled. In 2010, 4 master's awarded. *Degree requirements:* For master's, thesis or alternative, qualifying exam. *Entrance requirements:* For master's, minimum GPA of 2.5. Additional exam requirements/recommendations for international students: Required—TOEFL (minimum score 500 paper-based; 173 computer-based). *Application deadline:* For fall admission, 4/15 for domestic students. Applications are processed on a rolling basis. Application fee: $55. Tuition and fees vary according to program. *Financial support:* Fellowships available. Financial award application deadline: 3/1; financial award applicants required to submit FAFSA. *Faculty research:* Physical theater, design, playwriting. *Unit head:* Dr. Margaret Kelso, Chair, 707-826-5492, Fax: 707-826-5494, E-mail: margaret.kelso@humboldt.edu. *Application contact:* Dr. Jody Sekas, Coordinator, 707-826-4337, Fax: 707-826-5494, E-mail: jjs1@humboldt.edu.

Loyola Marymount University, School of Film and Television, Department of Production, Program in Production (Film and Television), Los Angeles, CA 90045-8347. Offers MFA. *Faculty:* 12 full-time (3 women), 1 part-time/adjunct (0 women). *Students:* 51 full-time (15 women), 6 part-time (1 woman); includes 6 Black or African American, non-Hispanic/Latino; 4 Asian, non-Hispanic/Latino; 3 Hispanic/Latino; 2 Two or more races, non-Hispanic/Latino, 10 international. Average age 28. 114 applicants, 58% accepted, 27 enrolled. In 2010, 18 master's awarded. *Degree requirements:* For master's, thesis, film. *Entrance requirements:* For master's, GRE General Test, creative work, 2 letters of recommendation, personal statement. Additional exam requirements/recommendations for international students: Required—TOEFL (minimum score 600 paper-based; 250 computer-based; 100 iBT). *Application deadline:* For fall admission, 2/15 for domestic students. Application fee: $50. Electronic applications accepted. *Financial support:* In 2010–11, 49 students received support, including 3 research assistantships (averaging $1,280 per year); career-related internships or fieldwork and scholarships/grants also available. Support available to part-time students. Financial award application deadline: 6/1; financial award applicants required to submit FAFSA. *Unit head:* Glenn Gebhard, Program Director, 310-338-3025, E-mail: ggebhard@lmu.edu. *Application contact:* Chake H. Kouyoumjian, Associate Dean of Graduate Admissions, 310-338-2721, Fax: 310-338-6086, E-mail: ckouyoum@lmu.edu.

Marywood University, Academic Affairs, Insalaco College of Creative and Performing Arts, Department of Communication Arts, Program in Communication Arts, Scranton, PA 18509-1598. Offers interdisciplinary (MA); media management (MA); production (MA). *Entrance requirements:* Additional exam requirements/recommendations for international students: Required—TOEFL (minimum score 550 paper-based; 213 computer-based; 79 iBT). Electronic applications accepted. *Expenses:* Tuition: Part-time $735 per credit. Required fees: $470 per semester. Tuition and fees vary according to degree level and campus/location.

Massachusetts College of Art and Design, Graduate Programs, Master of Fine Arts (MFA) Program, Boston, MA 02115-5882. Offers ceramics (MFA); design (MFA); fibers (MFA); film/video (MFA); glass (MFA); media and performing arts (MFA); metals/jewelry (MFA); painting (MFA); photography (MFA); printmaking (MFA); sculpture (MFA). *Accreditation:* NASAD. *Faculty:* 14 full-time (7 women), 16 part-time/adjunct (10 women). *Students:* 86 full-time (51 women), 9 part-time (5 women); includes 10 minority (1 Asian, non-Hispanic/Latino; 6 Hispanic/Latino; 3 Two or more races, non-Hispanic/Latino), 14 international. Average age 34. 298 applicants, 28% accepted, 41 enrolled. In 2010, 40 master's awarded. *Degree requirements:* For master's, thesis, exhibit. *Entrance requirements:* For master's, 12 units of course work in art history, portfolio, resume, letters of reference, interview. Additional exam requirements/recommendations for international students: Required—TOEFL (minimum score 563 paper-based; 223 computer-based; 85 iBT); Recommended—IELTS (minimum score 6.5). *Application deadline:* For fall admission, 1/15 for domestic and international students. Application fee: $85. Electronic applications accepted. *Expenses:* Tuition, state resident: part-time $665 per credit. Tuition, nonresident: part-time $665 per credit. *Financial support:* In 2010–11, 19 fellowships (averaging $5,000 per year), 43 research assistantships (averaging $2,000 per year), 44 teaching assistantships (averaging $2,000 per year) were awarded; career-related internships or fieldwork and Federal Work-Study also available. Support available to part-time students. Financial award application deadline: 5/1; financial award applicants required to submit FAFSA. *Unit head:* George Creamer, Dean of Graduate Programs, 617-879-7163, Fax: 617-879-7171, E-mail: creamer@massart.edu. *Application contact:* George Creamer, Dean of Graduate Programs, 617-879-7163, Fax: 617-879-7171, E-mail: creamer@massart.edu.

Miami International University of Art & Design, Program in Film, Miami, FL 33132-1418. Offers MFA. Postbaccalaureate distance learning degree programs offered. *Application contact:* Office of Graduate Admissions, 305-428-5700.

See Close-Up1 on page 129.

Minneapolis College of Art and Design, Program in Visual Studies, Minneapolis, MN 55404-4347. Offers animation (MFA); comic art (MFA); drawing (MFA); filmmaking (MFA); fine arts (MFA); furniture design (MFA); graphic design (MFA); illustration (MFA); interactive media (MFA); painting (MFA); photography (MFA); printmaking (MFA); sculpture (MFA). *Accreditation:* NASAD. Part-time programs available. *Degree requirements:* For master's, thesis, thesis exhibit. *Entrance requirements:* For master's, portfolio of visual artwork, resume, 3 letters of recommendation. Additional exam requirements/recommendations for international students: Required—TOEFL (minimum score 550 paper-based; 213 computer-based; 79 iBT). Electronic applications accepted. *Faculty research:* Visual arts: animation, comic art, drawing, filmmaking, furniture design, graphic design, illustration, interactive media, painting, photography, printmaking, sculpture.

Montana State University, College of Graduate Studies, College of Arts and Architecture, School of Film and Photography, Bozeman, MT 59717. Offers science and natural history filmmaking (MFA). Part-time programs available. *Faculty:* 15 full-time (4 women), 6 part-time/adjunct (2 women). *Students:* 28 full-time (14 women), 22 part-time (9 women); includes 5 minority (1 Black or African American, non-Hispanic/Latino; 2 Hispanic/Latino; 2 Two or more races, non-Hispanic/Latino), 3 international. Average age 30. 25 applicants, 56% accepted, 12 enrolled. In 2010, 12 master's awarded. *Degree requirements:* For master's, comprehensive exam. *Entrance requirements:* For master's, GRE General Test, minimum GPA of 3.0, resume, 3 letters of recommendation. Additional exam requirements/recommendations for international students: Required—TOEFL (minimum score 550 paper-based; 213 computer-based). *Application deadline:* For fall admission, 7/15 priority date for domestic students, 5/15 priority date for international students; for spring admission, 12/1 priority date for domestic students, 10/1 priority date for international students. Applications are processed on a rolling basis. Application fee: $30. Electronic applications accepted. *Expenses:* Tuition, state resident: full-time $5553.90. Tuition, nonresident: full-time $14,646. Required fees: $1233. *Financial support:* In 2010–11, 25 students received support, including 2 research assistantships (averaging $2,500 per year), 10 teaching assistantships (averaging $10 per year); career-related internships or fieldwork, traineeships, health care benefits, and unspecified assistantships also available. Financial award application deadline: 3/1; financial award applicants required to submit FAFSA. *Faculty research:* Science and natural history filmmaking, science communication, public outreach, new media production, environmental communication. Total annual research expenditures: $42,678. *Unit head:* Robert Arnold, Department Head, 406-994-7588, Fax: 406-994-6545, E-mail: rarnold@montana.edu. *Application contact:* Dr. Carl A. Fox, Vice Provost for Graduate Education, 406-994-4145, Fax: 406-994-7433, E-mail: gradstudy@montana.edu.

New York Film Academy, Program in Filmmaking–Hollywood, Los Angeles, CA 90068. Offers acting for film (MFA); cinematography (MFA); filmmaking (MFA); photography (MFA); producing (MFA); screenwriting (MFA). *Accreditation:* NASAD.

New York Film Academy, Program in Filmmaking–New York, New York, NY 10003. Offers acting for film (MFA); filmmaking (MFA); producing (MFA); screenwriting (MFA).

New York Film Academy, Program in Filmmaking–United Arab Emirates, Abu Dhabi, CA 90068, United Arab Emirates. Offers acting for film (MFA); filmmaking (MFA); producing (MFA); screenwriting (MFA).

New York University, Tisch School of the Arts Asia, Singapore, NY 248923, Singapore. Offers animation and digital arts (MFA); dramatic writing (MFA); film production (MFA). *Entrance requirements:* Additional exam requirements/recommendations for international students: Required—TOEFL (minimum score 610 paper-based; 250 computer-based; 105 iBT). Electronic applications accepted.

New York University, Tisch School of the Arts and Graduate School of Arts and Science, Department of Cinema Studies, Program in Moving Image Archiving and Preservation, New York, NY 10012-1019. Offers MA. *Faculty:* 2 full-time, 4 part-time/adjunct. *Students:* 16 full-time (6 women), 1 (woman) part-time; includes 1 Hispanic/Latino. Average age 28. 15 applicants, 87% accepted, 7 enrolled. In 2010, 6 master's awarded. *Degree requirements:* For master's, internship. *Entrance requirements:* For master's, GRE. Additional exam requirements/recommendations for international students: Required—TOEFL or IELTS. *Application deadline:* For fall admission, 12/1 for domestic and international students. Application fee: $60. Electronic applications accepted. *Financial support:* In 2010–11, 11 students received support, including 5 fellowships with full and partial tuition reimbursements available; tuition waivers (partial) also available. Financial award application deadline: 2/15. *Unit head:* Howard Besser, Head, 212-998-1618. *Application contact:* Dan Sandford, Director of Graduate Admissions, 212-998-1918, Fax: 212-995-4060, E-mail: tisch.gradadmissions@nyu.edu.

New York University, Tisch School of the Arts, Kanbar Institute of Film and Television, New York, NY 10012-1019. Offers MFA. *Faculty:* 19 full-time, 20 part-time/adjunct. *Students:* 111 full-time (53 women), 76 part-time (35 women); includes 23 Black or African American, non-Hispanic/Latino; 2 American Indian or Alaska Native, non-Hispanic/Latino; 36 Asian, non-Hispanic/Latino; 6 Hispanic/Latino. Average age 25. 630 applicants, 9% accepted, 37 enrolled. In 2010, 30 master's awarded. *Degree requirements:* For master's, 4 films. *Entrance requirements:* For master's, portfolio. Additional exam requirements/recommendations for international students: Required—TOEFL or IELTS. *Application deadline:* For fall admission, 12/1 for domestic and international students. Application fee: $60. Electronic applications accepted. *Financial support:* In 2010–11, 60 students received support, including 16 fellowships with full and partial tuition reimbursements available, 6 teaching assistantships with tuition reimbursements available; Federal Work-Study, institutionally sponsored loans, scholarships/grants, tuition waivers (full and partial), and unspecified assistantships also available. Financial award application deadline: 2/15; financial award applicants required to submit FAFSA. *Unit head:* John Tintori, Chair, 212-998-1780, E-mail: jt42@nyu.edu. *Application contact:* Dan Sandford, Director of Graduate Admissions, 212-998-1918, Fax: 212-995-4060, E-mail: tisch.gradadmissions@nyu.edu.

Northwestern University, The Graduate School, School of Communication, Department of Radio/Television/Film, Evanston, IL 60208. Offers MA, MFA, PhD. Admissions and degrees offered through The Graduate School. Part-time programs available. Terminal master's awarded for partial completion of doctoral program. *Degree requirements:* For master's, comprehensive exam or thesis; for doctorate, thesis/dissertation, qualifying exam. *Entrance requirements:* For master's and doctorate, GRE General Test. Additional exam requirements/recommendations for international students: Required—TOEFL. Electronic applications accepted. *Faculty research:* Art and new media, media theory and criticism, gender, media history, documentary.

Ohio University, Graduate College, College of Fine Arts, School of Film, Athens, OH 45701-2979. Offers film (MFA); film studies (MA). *Students:* 45 full-time (17 women), 8 part-time (2 women); includes 8 minority (3 Black or African American, non-Hispanic/Latino; 1 American Indian or Alaska Native, non-Hispanic/Latino; 2 Asian, non-Hispanic/Latino; 1 Hispanic/Latino; 1 Two or more races, non-Hispanic/Latino), 13 international. Average age 25. 139 applicants, 11% accepted, 10 enrolled. In 2010, 15 master's awarded. *Degree requirements:* For master's, one foreign language, thesis. *Entrance requirements:* Additional exam requirements/recommendations for international students: Required—TOEFL (minimum score 550 paper-based; 80 iBT) or IELTS (minimum score 6.5). *Application deadline:* For fall admission, 2/1 for domestic and international students. Application fee: $50 ($55 for international students). Electronic applications accepted. *Financial support:* In 2010–11, 34 students received support; research assistantships with full tuition reimbursements available, teaching assistantships with full tuition reimbursements available, institutionally sponsored loans, scholarships/grants, tuition waivers (full and partial), and unspecified assistantships available. Financial award application deadline: 2/1. *Faculty research:* Scriptwriting, sound, editing, cinematography, film theory, digital post production. *Unit head:* Steven Ross, Director, 740-593-9969, Fax: 740-593-1328, E-mail: rosss2@ohio.edu. *Application contact:* Tamra LaGraff, Administrative Associate, 740-593-1323, Fax: 740-593-1328, E-mail: lagraff@ohio.edu.

Pepperdine University, Seaver College, Humanities and Teacher Education Division, Master of Fine Arts Program in Writing for Screen and Television, Malibu, CA 90263. Offers MFA. *Students:* 6 full-time (1 woman), 14 part-time (3 women); includes 1 minority (Asian, non-Hispanic/Latino). 23 applicants, 65% accepted, 8 enrolled. *Entrance requirements:* For master's, GRE General Test, statement of purpose and intent for writing as a vocation, script writing sample, letters of recommendation. Additional exam requirements/recommendations for international students: Required—TOEFL. *Application deadline:* For fall admission, 2/1 priority date for domestic students. Application fee: $55. Electronic applications accepted. *Unit head:* Dr. Maire Mullins, Chair/Professor of English, Humanities and Teacher Education Division, 310-506-4894, E-mail: maire.mullins@pepperdine.edu. *Application contact:* Michael Truschke, Dean of Admission and Enrollment Management, 310-506-6165, Fax: 310-506-4861, E-mail: admission-seaver@pepperdine.edu.

Polytechnic Institute of NYU, Department of Electrical and Computer Engineering, Major in Image Processing, Brooklyn, NY 11201-2990. Offers Certificate. *Entrance requirements:* Additional exam requirements/recommendations for international students: Required—TOEFL (minimum score 550 paper-based; 213 computer-based; 80 iBT); Recommended—IELTS (minimum score 6.5). *Application deadline:* For fall admission, 7/31 priority date for domestic students, 4/30 priority date for international students; for spring admission, 12/31 priority date for domestic students, 10/30 priority date for international students. Applications are processed on a rolling basis. Application fee: $75. Electronic applications accepted. *Expenses:* Tuition: Full-time $21,492; part-time $1194 per credit. Required fees: $385 per semester. Tuition and fees vary according to course load. *Financial support:* Institutionally sponsored loans, scholarships/grants, and unspecified assistantships available. Support available to part-time students. *Unit head:* Dr. Jonathan Chao, Head, 718-860-3478, Fax: 718-260-3302, E-mail: chao@poly.edu. *Application contact:* JeanCarlo Bonilla, Director, Graduate Enrollment Management, 718-260-3182, Fax: 718-260-3624, E-mail: gradinfo@poly.edu.

Regent University, Graduate School, School of Communication and the Arts, Virginia Beach, VA 23464-9800. Offers acting (MFA); cinema arts/television arts (MA); communication (MA, PhD); digital media (MA); directing for cinema/television (MA, MFA); editing for cinema/television (MA); journalism (MA); producing for cinema/television (MA, MFA); script and screenwriting (MFA); theatre (MA). Part-time programs available. Postbaccalaureate distance learning degree programs offered (minimal on-campus study). *Faculty:* 29 full-time (4 women), 25 part-time/adjunct (5 women). *Students:* 93 full-time (48 women), 167 part-time (80 women); includes 45 Black or African American, non-Hispanic/Latino; 2 American Indian or Alaska Native, non-Hispanic/Latino; 3 Asian, non-Hispanic/Latino; 9 Hispanic/Latino, 11 international. Average age 32. 247 applicants, 45% accepted, 65 enrolled. In 2010, 82 master's, 17 doctorates awarded. *Degree requirements:* For master's, thesis or alternative; for doctorate, thesis/dissertation. *Entrance requirements:* For master's, GRE General Test or MAT, minimum undergraduate GPA of 3.0, writing sample, computer literacy survey, recommendation, resume, interview, audition (MFA programs); for doctorate, GRE General Test, minimum graduate GPA of 3.0, writing sample, computer literacy survey, recommendation, interview, transcripts. Additional exam requirements/recommendations for international students: Required—TOEFL (minimum score 577 paper-based; 233 computer-based). *Application deadline:* For fall admission, 3/1 priority date for domestic students; for spring admission, 10/1 priority date for domestic students. Applications are processed on a rolling basis. Application fee: $50. Electronic applications accepted. *Expenses:* Contact institution. *Financial support:* Fellowships with full and partial tuition reimbursements, career-related internships or fieldwork, scholarships/grants, tuition waivers (full and partial), and unspecified assistantships available. Support available to part-time students. Financial award application deadline: 9/1; financial award applicants required to submit FAFSA. *Faculty research:* Southern gospel music, education and entertainment, celebrities and the media, journalism and ethics, C. S. Lewis. *Unit head:* Dr. Emmanuel Ayee, Interim Dean, 757-352-4945, Fax: 757-352-4291, E-mail: eayee@regent.edu. *Application contact:* Matthew Chadwick, Director of Enrollment Support Services, 800-373-5504, Fax: 757-352-4381, E-mail: admissions@regent.edu.

Rochester Institute of Technology, Graduate Enrollment Services, College of Imaging Arts and Sciences, School of Photographic Arts and Sciences, Program in Imaging Arts, Rochester, NY 14623-5603. Offers MFA. *Accreditation:* NASAD. Part-time programs available. *Students:* 64 full-time (30 women), 32 part-time (22 women); includes 2 Black or African American, non-Hispanic/Latino; 2 Asian, non-Hispanic/Latino; 3 Hispanic/Latino; 1 Two or more races, non-Hispanic/Latino, 40 international. Average age 29. 207 applicants, 33% accepted, 35 enrolled. In 2010, 21 master's awarded. *Degree requirements:* For master's, thesis, exhibit. *Entrance requirements:* For master's, portfolio, minimum GPA of 3.0. Additional exam requirements/recommendations for international students: Required—TOEFL (minimum score 550 paper-based; 213 computer-based; 79 iBT) or IELTS (minimum score 6.5). *Application deadline:* For fall admission, 2/15 priority date for domestic and international students. Applications are processed on a rolling basis. Application fee: $50. Electronic applications accepted. *Expenses:* Tuition: Full-time $33,234; part-time $924 per credit hour. Required fees: $219. *Financial support:* In 2010–11, 45 students received support; fellowships with partial tuition reimbursements available, research assistantships with partial tuition reimbursements available, teaching assistantships with partial tuition reimbursements available, career-related internships or fieldwork, institutionally sponsored loans, scholarships/grants, tuition waivers (partial), and unspecified assistantships available. Support available to part-time students. Financial award application deadline: 8/30; financial award applicants required to submit FAFSA. *Unit head:* Angela Kelly, Graduate Program Director, 585-475-2616, Fax: 585-475-5804, E-mail: amkpph@rit.edu. *Application contact:* Diane Ellison, Assistant Vice President, Graduate Enrollment Services, 585-475-2229, Fax: 585-475-7164, E-mail: gradinfo@rit.edu.

St. Thomas University, School of Leadership Studies, Program in Electronic Media, Miami Gardens, FL 33054-6459. Offers MA.

San Diego State University, Graduate and Research Affairs, College of Professional Studies and Fine Arts, School of Theater, Television and Film, Program in Television, Film, and New Media Production, San Diego, CA 92182. Offers MA. *Entrance requirements:* For master's, GRE General Test, 3 letters of recommendation, resume, sample reel, influential book list, influential films list, hobby list. Additional exam requirements/recommendations for international students: Required—TOEFL. Electronic applications accepted. *Faculty research:* Experimental film and television programs, documentary film, television research and production.

San Francisco Art Institute, Graduate Program, Department of Film, San Francisco, CA 94133. Offers MFA, Certificate. *Accreditation:* NASAD. Part-time programs available. *Degree requirements:* For master's and Certificate, oral reviews. *Entrance requirements:* For master's and Certificate, portfolio. Additional exam requirements/recommendations for international students: Required—TOEFL (minimum score 580 paper-based; 237 computer-based). Electronic applications accepted.

San Francisco Art Institute, Graduate Program, Department of New Genres, San Francisco, CA 94133. Offers new genres (Certificate); performance/video (MFA). *Accreditation:* NASAD. Part-time programs available. *Degree requirements:* For master's and Certificate, oral reviews. *Entrance requirements:* For master's and Certificate, portfolio. Additional exam requirements/recommendations for international students: Required—TOEFL (minimum score 580 paper-based; 237 computer-based). Electronic applications accepted.

San Francisco State University, Division of Graduate Studies, College of Creative Arts, Department of Cinema, San Francisco, CA 94132-1722. Offers cinema (MFA); cinema studies (MA). *Unit head:* Martha Gorzycki, Chair, 415-338-1879. *Application contact:* Erin Persley, Assistant Graduate Programs Coordinator, 415-338-1724, E-mail: cinegrad@sfsu.edu.

San Jose State University, Graduate Studies and Research, College of Humanities and the Arts, Department of Television, Radio, Film and Theatre, San Jose, CA 95192-0001. Offers theatre arts (MA). *Accreditation:* NAST. *Degree requirements:* For master's, written exam. *Entrance requirements:* Additional exam requirements/recommendations for international students: Required—TOEFL (minimum score 570 paper-based). Electronic applications accepted.

San Jose State University, Graduate Studies and Research, College of Humanities and the Arts, School of Art and Design, San Jose, CA 95192-0001. Offers animation/illustration (MA); art history (MA); digital media arts (MFA); photography (MFA); pictorial arts (MFA); spatial arts (MFA). *Accreditation:* NASAD (one or more programs are accredited). *Entrance requirements:* For master's, GRE. Electronic applications accepted.

Savannah College of Art and Design, Graduate School, Program in Animation, Savannah, GA 31402-3146. Offers MA, MFA. Part-time programs available. *Faculty:* 21 full-time (4 women), 1 part-time/adjunct (0 women). *Students:* 112 full-time (49 women), 19 part-time (9 women); includes 6 Black or African American, non-Hispanic/Latino; 1 American Indian or Alaska Native, non-Hispanic/Latino; 2 Asian, non-Hispanic/Latino; 1 Hispanic/Latino, 47 international. Average age 26. In 2010, 34 master's awarded. *Degree requirements:* For master's, thesis, internships. *Entrance requirements:* For master's, interview, portfolio. Additional exam requirements/recommendations for international students: Required—TOEFL (minimum score 450 paper-based; 133 computer-based). *Application deadline:* For fall admission, 4/1 priority date for domestic and international students. Applications are processed on a rolling basis. Application fee: $35. Electronic applications accepted. *Expenses:* Tuition: Full-time $29,520; part-time $3280 per quarter. Tuition and fees vary according to campus/location. *Financial support:* Fellowships, career-related internships or fieldwork, Federal Work-Study, and scholarships/grants available. Financial award application deadline: 4/1; financial award applicants required to submit FAFSA. *Unit head:* Jeremy Moorshead, Chair, 912-525-8527, Fax: 912-525-8597, E-mail: jmoorshe@scad.edu. *Application contact:* Elizabeth Mathis, Director of Graduate and International Enrollment, 912-525-5965, Fax: 912-525-5985, E-mail: admission@scad.edu.

See Display on page 177 and Close-Up on page 223

Film, Television, and Video Production

Savannah College of Art and Design, Graduate School, Program in Film and Television, Savannah, GA 31402-3146. Offers MA, MFA. Part-time programs available. *Faculty:* 17 full-time (2 women), 3 part-time/adjunct (1 woman). *Students:* 95 full-time (30 women), 11 part-time (3 women); includes 10 Black or African American, non-Hispanic/Latino; 1 American Indian or Alaska Native, non-Hispanic/Latino; 1 Asian, non-Hispanic/Latino; 4 Hispanic/Latino, 22 international. Average age 27. In 2010, 31 master's awarded. *Degree requirements:* For master's, thesis, internship. *Entrance requirements:* For master's, interview, videotape. Additional exam requirements/recommendations for international students: Required—TOEFL (minimum score 450 paper-based; 133 computer-based). *Application deadline:* For fall admission, 4/1 priority date for domestic and international students. Applications are processed on a rolling basis. Application fee: $35. Electronic applications accepted. *Expenses:* Tuition: Full-time $29,520; part-time $3280 per quarter. Tuition and fees vary according to campus/location. *Financial support:* Fellowships, career-related internships or fieldwork, Federal Work-Study, and scholarships/grants available. Financial award application deadline: 4/1; financial award applicants required to submit FAFSA. *Unit head:* Christopher Auer, Chair, 912-525-6418, Fax: 912-525-6488, E-mail: cjauer@scad.edu. *Application contact:* Elizabeth Mathis, Director of Graduate Recruitment, 912-525-5965, Fax: 912-525-5985, E-mail: emathis@scad.edu.

See Display on page 177 and Close-Up on page 223

Savannah College of Art and Design, Graduate School, Program in Sound Design, Savannah, GA 31402-3146. Offers MA, MFA. Part-time programs available. *Faculty:* 7 full-time (0 women), 1 part-time/adjunct (0 women). *Students:* 15 full-time (0 women), 4 part-time (0 women); includes 3 Black or African American, non-Hispanic/Latino. Average age 27. In 2010, 9 master's awarded. *Degree requirements:* For master's, thesis, internships. *Entrance requirements:* For master's, interview, portfolio. Additional exam requirements/recommendations for international students: Required—TOEFL (minimum score 450 paper-based; 133 computer-based). *Application deadline:* For fall admission, 4/1 priority date for domestic and international students. Application fee: $35. *Expenses:* Tuition: Full-time $29,520; part-time $3280 per quarter. Tuition and fees vary according to campus/location. *Financial support:* Fellowships, career-related internships or fieldwork, Federal Work-Study, and scholarships/grants available. Financial award application deadline: 4/1; financial award applicants required to submit FAFSA. *Unit head:* David Stone, Chair, 912-525-8509, Fax: 912-525-6459, E-mail: dstone@scad.edu. *Application contact:* Elizabeth Mathis, Director of Graduate Recruitment, 912-525-5965, Fax: 912-525-5985, E-mail: emathis@scad.edu.

See Display on page 177 and Close-Up on page 223

School of the Art Institute of Chicago, Graduate Division, Department of Film, Video, and New Media, Chicago, IL 60603-3103. Offers MFA. *Accreditation:* NASAD. *Degree requirements:* For master's, thesis exhibit. *Entrance requirements:* Additional exam requirements/recommendations for international students: Required—TOEFL (minimum score 550 paper-based; 213 computer-based; 80 iBT), IELTS (minimum score 6.5). Electronic applications accepted.

See Close-Up on page 225.

School of the Art Institute of Chicago, Graduate Division, Department of Sound, Chicago, IL 60603-3103. Offers MFA. *Entrance requirements:* Additional exam requirements/recommendations for international students: Required—TOEFL, IELTS.

See Close-Up on page 225.

School of Visual Arts, Graduate Programs, Program in Photography, Video and Related Media, New York, NY 10010-3994. Offers MFA. *Accreditation:* NASAD. *Degree requirements:* For master's, final review, project or thesis. *Entrance requirements:* For master's, portfolio. Additional exam requirements/recommendations for international students: Required—TOEFL (minimum score 550 paper-based; 213 computer-based; 79 iBT). Electronic applications accepted.

Southern Methodist University, Meadows School of the Arts, Department of Cinema and Television, Dallas, TX 75275. Offers MA, MFA. *Faculty:* 9 full-time (2 women), 7 part-time/adjunct (1 woman). *Students:* 7 full-time (1 woman), 3 part-time (2 women); includes 1 Black or African American, non-Hispanic/Latino; 1 American Indian or Alaska Native, non-Hispanic/Latino; 1 Hispanic/Latino; 1 Two or more races, non-Hispanic/Latino, 1 international. Average age 36. In 2010, 7 master's awarded. *Unit head:* Sean Griffin, Chair, 214-768-4356, E-mail: spgriffi@mail.smu.edu. *Application contact:* Jean Cherry, Director of Graduate Admissions and Records, 214-768-3765, Fax: 214-768-3272, E-mail: jcherry@smu.edu.

Southern Methodist University, Meadows School of the Arts, Division of Communication Arts, Dallas, TX 75275. Offers MA. Part-time and evening/weekend programs available. *Faculty:* 19 full-time (7 women), 11 part-time/adjunct (1 woman). *Students:* 34 full-time (25 women), 3 part-time (2 women); includes 1 Black or African American, non-Hispanic/Latino; 1 American Indian or Alaska Native, non-Hispanic/Latino; 6 Hispanic/Latino; 1 Two or more races, non-Hispanic/Latino, 3 international. Average age 27. 9 applicants, 78% accepted, 4 enrolled. In 2010, 6 master's awarded. *Degree requirements:* For master's, thesis or alternative. *Entrance requirements:* For master's, GRE General Test, minimum undergraduate GPA of 3.0 in major field during last 2 years. Additional exam requirements/recommendations for international students: Required—TOEFL (minimum score 550 paper-based; 213 computer-based; 80 iBT). *Application deadline:* For fall admission, 3/1 priority date for domestic and international students. Application fee: $75. *Financial support:* In 2010–11, 7 students received support, including 7 teaching assistantships (averaging $6,500 per year); research assistantships, scholarships/grants, tuition waivers (full), and unspecified assistantships also available. Financial award application deadline: 3/15. *Faculty research:* Digital sound, new technology, film and gender study, popular film and TV genres, Asian cinema. Total annual research expenditures: $10,000. *Unit head:* Rick Worland, Chair, 214-768-3708, Fax: 214-768-2784, E-mail: rworland@smu.edu. *Application contact:* Jean Cherry, Director of Graduate Admissions and Records, 214-768-3765, Fax: 214-768-3272, E-mail: jcherry@smu.edu.

Syracuse University, College of Visual and Performing Arts, Program in Film, Syracuse, NY 13244. Offers MFA. *Students:* 11 full-time (5 women), 1 (woman) part-time; includes 2 minority (1 Asian, non-Hispanic/Latino; 1 Hispanic/Latino), 8 international. Average age 27. 51 applicants, 24% accepted, 5 enrolled. In 2010, 1 master's awarded. *Degree requirements:* For master's, thesis or alternative. *Entrance requirements:* For master's, portfolio. Additional exam requirements/recommendations for international students: Required—TOEFL (minimum score 100 iBT). *Application deadline:* For fall admission, 2/1 priority date for domestic and international students. Application fee: $75. Electronic applications accepted. *Expenses:* Tuition: Part-time $1162 per credit. *Financial support:* Fellowships with full tuition reimbursements, teaching assistantships with full and partial tuition reimbursements available. Financial award application deadline: 1/1; financial award applicants required to submit FAFSA. *Unit head:* Heath Hanlin, Chair, 315-443-1033, E-mail: hahanlin@syr.edu. *Application contact:* Harriett Conti, Assistant Dean for Recruitment and Admissions, 315-443-5755, E-mail: hmconti@syr.edu.

See Display on page 179 and Close-Up on page 227.

Syracuse University, S. I. Newhouse School of Public Communications, Program in Documentary Film and History, Syracuse, NY 13244. Offers MA. *Students:* 6 full-time (4 women), 3 part-time (0 women); includes 1 minority (Asian, non-Hispanic/Latino), 2 international. Average age 28. 16 applicants, 75% accepted, 6 enrolled. In 2010, 9 master's awarded. *Entrance requirements:* For master's, GRE General Test. Additional exam requirements/recommendations for international students: Required—TOEFL (minimum score 100 iBT). *Application deadline:* For fall admission, 2/1 priority date for domestic and international students. Application fee: $45. Electronic applications accepted. *Expenses:* Tuition: Part-time $1162 per credit. *Financial support:* Fellowships with full tuition reimbursements, research assistantships with partial tuition reimbursements, teaching assistantships with partial tuition reimbursements available. Financial award application deadline: 2/1. *Unit head:* Richard Breyer, Director, 315-443-9249. *Application contact:* Martha Coria, Graduate Records Office, 315-443-5749, Fax: 315-443-1834, E-mail: pcgrad@syr.edu.

See Display on page 179 and Close-Up on page 227.

Temple University, School of Communications and Theater, Department of Film and Media Arts, Philadelphia, PA 19122-6096. Offers MFA. Part-time programs available. *Faculty:* 16 full-time (5 women). *Students:* 45 full-time (21 women), 5 part-time (3 women); includes 3 Black or African American, non-Hispanic/Latino; 1 Hispanic/Latino; 1 Two or more races, non-Hispanic/Latino, 16 international. 87 applicants, 29% accepted, 12 enrolled. In 2010, 7 master's awarded. *Degree requirements:* For master's, comprehensive exam, project. *Entrance requirements:* For master's, GRE General Test, minimum GPA of 3.0; exhibit. Additional exam requirements/recommendations for international students: Required—TOEFL (minimum score 550 paper-based; 213 computer-based; 79 iBT). *Application deadline:* For fall admission, 1/15 for domestic students, 12/15 for international students. Application fee: $50. Electronic applications accepted. *Financial support:* Fellowships, research assistantships with partial tuition reimbursements, Federal Work-Study and institutionally sponsored loans available. Financial award application deadline: 1/15; financial award applicants required to submit FAFSA. *Faculty research:* Filmmaking and videography, documentary theory and practice, screenwriting, media culture studies, film studies. *Unit head:* Dr. Nora Alter, Chair, 215-204-3859, Fax: 215-204-5280, E-mail: film@temple.edu. *Application contact:* Dr. Nora Alter, Chair, 215-204-3859, Fax: 215-204-5280, E-mail: film@temple.edu.

Universidad Autonoma de Guadalajara, Graduate Programs, Guadalajara, Mexico. Offers administrative law and justice (LL M); advertising and corporate communications (MA); architecture (M Arch); business (MBA); computational science (MCC); education (Ed M, Ed D); English-Spanish translation (MA); entrepreneurship and management (MBA); integrated management of digital animation (MA); international business (MIB); international corporate law (LL M); internet technologies (MS); manufacturing systems (MMS); occupational health (MS); philosophy (MA, PhD); power electronics (MS); quality systems (MQS); renewable energy (MS); social evaluation of projects (MBA); strategic market research (MBA); tax law (MA); teaching mathematics (MA).

The University of Alabama, Graduate School, College of Communication and Information Sciences, Department of Telecommunication and Film, Tuscaloosa, AL 35487-0152. Offers MA. *Faculty:* 10 full-time (3 women). *Students:* 9 full-time (5 women), 4 part-time (2 women); includes 2 minority (1 Black or African American, non-Hispanic/Latino; 1 Two or more races, non-Hispanic/Latino), 3 international. Average age 28. 13 applicants, 77% accepted, 7 enrolled. In 2010, 4 master's awarded. Terminal master's awarded for partial completion of doctoral program. *Degree requirements:* For master's, comprehensive exam, thesis or alternative. *Entrance requirements:* For master's, GRE, minimum GPA of 3.0. Additional exam requirements/recommendations for international students: Required—TOEFL (minimum score 600 paper-based; 79 iBT). *Application deadline:* For fall admission, 4/15 priority date for domestic students, 1/15 priority date for international students; for spring admission, 11/1 for domestic students, 10/1 priority date for international students. Applications are processed on a rolling basis. Application fee: $50 ($60 for international students). Electronic applications accepted. *Expenses:* Tuition, state resident: full-time $7900. Tuition, nonresident: full-time $20,500. *Financial support:* In 2010–11, 6 students received support, including 2 research assistantships with tuition reimbursements available (averaging $9,825 per year), 2 teaching assistantships with tuition reimbursements available (averaging $9,825 per year); institutionally sponsored loans also available. Financial award application deadline: 2/15. *Faculty research:* Entertainment theory, news and public affairs, effects of telecommunications, management, media law and policy. *Unit head:* Dr. Gary A. Copeland, Chair, 205-348-6350, Fax: 205-348-5162, E-mail: copeland@ua.edu. *Application contact:* Dr. Shuhua Zhou, Graduate Coordinator, 205-348-8653, Fax: 205-348-5162, E-mail: szhou@bama.ua.edu.

The University of British Columbia, Faculty of Arts, Creative Writing Program, Vancouver, BC V6T 1Z1, Canada. Offers creative writing (MFA); creative writing and film (MFA); creative writing and theatre (MFA). Part-time programs available. Postbaccalaureate distance learning degree programs offered (minimal on-campus study). *Degree requirements:* For master's, thesis. *Entrance requirements:* For master's, sample of written work. Additional exam requirements/recommendations for international students: Required—TOEFL (minimum score 550 paper-based; 213 computer-based). Electronic applications accepted. *Expenses:* Contact institution. *Faculty research:* Writing of fiction; poetry, creative nonfiction, plays for stage, screen, television, radio, writing for children and translation, song lyrics and libretto, new media and graphic novel.

The University of British Columbia, Faculty of Arts and Faculty of Graduate Studies, Department of Theatre and Film, Film Program, Vancouver, BC V6T 1Z2, Canada. Offers creative writing and film production (MFA); film production (MFA, Diploma); film studies (MA). *Degree requirements:* For master's, variable foreign language requirement, comprehensive exam, thesis (MA), thesis or project (MFA). *Entrance requirements:* For master's, portfolio (MFA). Additional exam requirements/recommendations for international students: Required—TOEFL (minimum score 600 paper-based; 250 computer-based). Electronic applications accepted. Tuition charges are reported in Canadian dollars. *Expenses:* Tuition, area resident: Full-time $4179 Canadian dollars. International tuition: $7344 Canadian dollars full-time. *Faculty research:* Film theory and violence; American and European cinema; cult cinema; Irish cinema.

University of California, Los Angeles, Graduate Division, School of Theater, Film and Television, Department of Film, Television, and Digital Media, Los Angeles, CA 90034. Offers film and television (MA, MFA, PhD); MFA/MA. *Faculty:* 23 full-time (9 women). *Students:* 285 full-time (135 women); includes 92 minority (24 Black or African American, non-Hispanic/Latino; 3 American Indian or Alaska Native, non-Hispanic/Latino; 31 Asian, non-Hispanic/Latino; 29 Hispanic/Latino; 1 Native Hawaiian or other Pacific Islander, non-Hispanic/Latino; 4 Two or more races, non-Hispanic/Latino), 30 international. Average age 30. 1,290 applicants, 11% accepted, 97 enrolled. In 2010, 83 master's, 5 doctorates awarded. *Degree requirements:* For master's, comprehensive exam; for doctorate, one foreign language, thesis/dissertation, oral and written qualifying exams. *Entrance requirements:* For master's, film or TV project, animation, or script (MFA), minimum GPA of 3.0; for doctorate, GRE General Test, minimum undergraduate GPA of 3.0. Application fee: $70 ($90 for international students). Electronic applications accepted. *Financial support:* In 2010–11, 207 fellowships with full and partial tuition reimbursements, 13 research assistantships with full and partial tuition reimbursements, 113 teaching assistantships with full and partial tuition reimbursements were awarded; Federal Work-Study, institutionally sponsored loans, scholarships/grants, health care benefits, tuition waivers (full and partial), and unspecified assistantships also available. Financial award application deadline: 3/1; financial award applicants required to submit FAFSA. *Unit head:* Barbara Boyle, Chair, 310-825-7741. *Application contact:* Department Office, 310-206-8441, E-mail: filmgrad@tft.ucla.edu.

University of California, Los Angeles, Graduate Division, School of Theater, Film and Television, Interdepartmental Program in Moving Image Archive Studies, Los Angeles, CA 90095. Offers MA. *Students:* 20 full-time (14 women); includes 4 minority (3 Hispanic/Latino; 1 Two or more races, non-Hispanic/Latino), 1 international. Average age 28. 38 applicants, 37% accepted, 11 enrolled. In 2010, 10 master's awarded. Application fee: $70 ($90 for international students). Electronic applications accepted. *Financial support:* In 2010–11, 14 fellowships, 1 teaching assistantship were awarded; research assistantships, Federal Work-Study, scholarships/grants, and unspecified assistantships also available. *Unit head:* Nick Browne, Chair, 310-825-4089, E-mail: browne@ucla.edu. *Application contact:* Departmental Office, 310-206-4966, E-mail: lwatsky@tft.ucla.edu.

University of California, Santa Barbara, Graduate Division, College of Letters and Sciences, Division of Humanities and Fine Arts, Department of Film and Media Studies, Santa Barbara, CA 93106-4010. Offers film and media studies (PhD); global studies (PhD); technology and society (PhD); MA/PhD. *Faculty:* 28 full-time (15 women). *Students:* 29 full-time (16 women); includes 4 Asian, non-Hispanic/Latino; 1 Hispanic/Latino. Average age 27. 106 applicants, 9% accepted, 5 enrolled. In 2010, 1 doctorate awarded. Terminal master's awarded for partial completion of doctoral program. *Degree requirements:* For doctorate, one foreign language, comprehensive exam, thesis/dissertation. *Entrance requirements:* For doctorate, GRE. Additional exam requirements/recommendations for international students: Required—TOEFL (minimum score 600 paper-based; 100 iBT), IELTS (minimum score 7). *Application deadline:* For fall admission, 12/1 priority date for domestic and international students. Application fee: $70 ($90 for international students). Electronic applications accepted. *Financial support:* In 2010–11, 23 students received support, including 10 fellowships with full tuition reimbursements available (averaging $17,143 per year), 3 research assistantships with full and partial tuition reimbursements available (averaging $11,893 per year), 17 teaching assistantships with partial tuition reimbursements available (averaging $11,254 per year). Financial award application deadline: 12/1; financial award applicants required to submit FAFSA. *Faculty research:* Classical film theory, film and television history, historiography, cultural studies, global media, media industries, regulation and policy. *Unit head:* Prof. Lisa Parks, Chair, 805-893-2120, Fax: 805-893-8630, E-mail: parks@filmandmedia.ucsb.edu. *Application contact:* Melany J. Miners, Graduate Program Assistant, 805-893-8535, Fax: 805-893-8630, E-mail: mminers@filmandmedia.ucsb.edu.

University of Central Arkansas, Graduate School, College of Fine Arts and Communication, Program in Digital Filmmaking, Conway, AR 72035-0001. Offers MFA. *Students:* 18 full-time (6 women), 8 part-time (0 women); includes 2 minority (1 Black or African American, non-Hispanic/Latino; 1 Asian, non-Hispanic/Latino), 1 international. Average age 29. In 2010, 4 master's awarded. *Degree requirements:* For master's, thesis. *Entrance requirements:* For master's, GRE General Test, minimum GPA of 2.7. Additional exam requirements/recommendations for international students: Required—TOEFL (minimum score 550 paper-based; 213 computer-based). *Application deadline:* For fall admission, 3/1 priority date for domestic and international students; for spring admission, 10/1 priority date for domestic and international students. Applications are processed on a rolling basis. Application fee: $25 ($50 for international students). *Financial support:* Unspecified assistantships available. *Unit head:* Dr. Bruce Hutchinson, Chair, 501-450-3162, E-mail: josepha@uca.edu. *Application contact:* Susan Wood, Admissions Assistant, 501-450-3124, Fax: 501-450-5678, E-mail: swood@uca.edu.

University of Central Florida, College of Arts and Humanities, Division of Film and Digital Media, Orlando, FL 32816. Offers MFA. *Faculty:* 16 full-time (5 women), 3 part-time/adjunct (2 women). *Students:* 14 full-time (3 women), 4 part-time (0 women); includes 1 Black or African American, non-Hispanic/Latino; 2 Hispanic/Latino, 1 international. Average age 27. 21 applicants, 38% accepted, 7 enrolled. In 2010, 5 master's awarded. Application fee: $30. *Expenses:* Tuition, state resident: part-time $256.56 per credit hour. Tuition, nonresident: part-time $1011.52 per credit hour. Part-time tuition and fees vary according to program. *Financial support:* In 2010–11, 10 students received support, including 2 fellowships with partial tuition reimbursements available (averaging $5,300 per year), 9 teaching assistantships (averaging $5,500 per year). *Unit head:* Stephen Schlow, Interim Chair, 407-823-2845, Fax: 407-823-3659, E-mail: sschlow@mail.ucf.edu. *Application contact:* Stephen Schlow, Interim Chair, 407-823-2845, Fax: 407-823-3659, E-mail: sschlow@mail.ucf.edu.

The University of Iowa, Graduate College, College of Liberal Arts and Sciences, Department of Cinema and Comparative Literature, Program in Film and Video Production, Iowa City, IA 52242-1316. Offers MA, MFA. *Degree requirements:* For master's, thesis (for some programs), exam. *Entrance requirements:* For master's, GRE General Test, minimum GPA of 3.0. Additional exam requirements/recommendations for international students: Required—TOEFL (minimum score 550 paper-based; 213 computer-based; 81 iBT). Electronic applications accepted.

University of Memphis, Graduate School, College of Communication and Fine Arts, Department of Communication, Memphis, TN 38152. Offers communication (MA); communication arts (PhD); film and video production (MA). Part-time programs available. *Faculty:* 12 full-time (6 women). *Students:* 51 full-time (38 women), 49 part-time (30 women); includes 27 minority (21 Black or African American, non-Hispanic/Latino; 1 American Indian or Alaska Native, non-Hispanic/Latino; 1 Asian, non-Hispanic/Latino; 3 Hispanic/Latino; 1 Two or more races, non-Hispanic/Latino), 2 international. Average age 35. 98 applicants, 48% accepted, 16 enrolled. In 2010, 6 master's, 4 doctorates awarded. *Degree requirements:* For master's, comprehensive exam, thesis or alternative; for doctorate, comprehensive exam, thesis/dissertation. *Entrance requirements:* For master's and doctorate, GRE General Test. Additional exam requirements/recommendations for international students: Required—TOEFL (minimum score 600 paper-based; 250 computer-based). *Application deadline:* For fall admission, 2/1 for domestic and international students. Application fee: $35 ($60 for international students). *Financial support:* In 2010–11, 27 students received support; research assistantships with full tuition reimbursements available, teaching assistantships with full tuition reimbursements available, Federal Work-Study, scholarships/grants, and unspecified assistantships available. Financial award application deadline: 2/15; financial award applicants required to submit FAFSA. *Faculty research:* Rhetoric, media studies, applied communication (health communication). *Unit head:* Dr. Sandra Sarkela, Chair, 901-678-3173, Fax: 901-678-4331, E-mail: ssarkela@memphis.edu. *Application contact:* Dr. Amanda Young, Coordinator of Graduate Studies, 901-678-3612, Fax: 901-678-4331, E-mail: ajyoung@memphis.edu.

University of Miami, Graduate School, School of Communication, Coral Gables, FL 33124. Offers communication (PhD); communication studies (MA); film studies (MA, PhD); motion pictures (MFA), including production, producing, and screenwriting; print journalism (MA); public relations (MA); Spanish language journalism (MA); television broadcast journalism (MA). *Accreditation:* ACEJMC. Part-time programs available. *Degree requirements:* For master's, comprehensive exam (for some programs), thesis (for some programs); for doctorate, comprehensive exam, thesis/dissertation. *Entrance requirements:* For master's, GRE General Test; for doctorate, GRE General Test, master's thesis or scholarly research. Additional exam requirements/recommendations for international students: Required—TOEFL (minimum score 600 paper-based; 250 computer-based; 100 iBT). Electronic applications accepted. *Faculty research:* Communication studies, mass communication, international/interpersonal communication, film studies, journalism.

University of Nevada, Las Vegas, Graduate College, College of Fine Arts, Department of Film, Las Vegas, NV 89154-5015. Offers screenwriting (MFA). Part-time programs available. *Faculty:* 6 full-time (0 women), 7 part-time/adjunct (0 women). *Students:* 8 full-time (3 women); includes 4 minority (1 Black or African American, non-Hispanic/Latino; 3 Two or more races, non-Hispanic/Latino). Average age 33. 14 applicants, 14% accepted, 1 enrolled. In 2010, 1 master's awarded. *Degree requirements:* For master's, comprehensive exam, creative project. *Entrance requirements:* Additional exam requirements/recommendations for international students: Required—TOEFL (minimum score 550 paper-based; 213 computer-based), IELTS (minimum score 7). *Application deadline:* For fall admission, 1/15 priority date for domestic and international students. Applications are processed on a rolling basis. Application fee: $60 ($95 for international students). Electronic applications accepted. *Expenses:* Tuition, area resident: Part-time $239.50 per credit. Tuition, state resident: part-time $239.50 per credit. Tuition, nonresident: part-time $503 per credit. Required fees: $108 per semester. Tuition and fees vary according to course load, program and reciprocity agreements. *Financial support:* In 2010–11, 8 teaching assistantships with partial tuition reimbursements (averaging $10,000 per year) were awarded; institutionally sponsored loans, scholarships/grants, health care benefits, and unspecified assistantships also available. Financial award application deadline: 3/1. *Faculty research:* Screenwriting, playwriting, production techniques, production planning/script coordination, sustaining contacts with professional world. Total annual research expenditures: $33,395. *Unit head:* Francisco Menendez, Chair/ Professor, 702-895-4223, Fax: 702-895-4395, E-mail: francisco.menendez@unlv.edu. *Application contact:* Graduate College Admissions Evaluator, 702-895-3320, Fax: 702-895-4180, E-mail: gradcollege@unlv.edu.

University of New Orleans, Graduate School, College of Liberal Arts, Department of Film, Theatre and Communication Arts, New Orleans, LA 70148. Offers film production (MFA); theatre directing (MFA); theatre performance (MFA). *Accreditation:* NAST. *Degree requirements:* For master's, comprehensive exam, thesis. *Entrance requirements:* Additional exam requirements/recommendations for international students: Required—TOEFL (minimum score 550 paper-based; 213 computer-based; 79 iBT). Electronic applications accepted. *Faculty research:* Mass communication theory, nineteenth- and twentieth-century theater history, film criticism and history.

The University of North Carolina at Greensboro, Graduate School, College of Arts and Sciences, Department of Broadcasting and Cinema, Greensboro, NC 27412-5001. Offers film and video production (MFA).

University of North Carolina School of the Arts, School of Filmmaking, Winston-Salem, NC 27127-2188. Offers film music composition (MFA). *Faculty:* 1 full-time (0 women). *Students:* 6 full-time (1 woman); includes 1 Asian, non-Hispanic/Latino. Average age 25. 6 applicants, 33% accepted, 2 enrolled. In 2010, 3 master's awarded. *Entrance requirements:* For master's, audition, performance, portfolio, interview. Additional exam requirements/recommendations for international students: Required—TOEFL. *Application deadline:* For fall admission, 4/1 priority date for domestic students. Applications are processed on a rolling basis. Application fee: $60 ($100 for international students). *Expenses:* Tuition, state resident: full-time $4946. Tuition, nonresident: full-time $17,253. Required fees: $2092. *Financial support:* In 2010–11, fellowships (averaging $2,000 per year); career-related internships or fieldwork, Federal Work-Study, and Academic Common Market also available. Support available to part-time students. Financial award application deadline: 3/15; financial award applicants required to submit FAFSA. *Unit head:* Jordan Kerner, Dean, 336-770-1330, Fax: 336-770-1339, E-mail: kernerj@uncsa.edu. *Application contact:* Sheeler Lawson, Director of Admissions, 336-770-3290, Fax: 336-770-3370, E-mail: admissions@uncsa.edu.

University of North Texas, Toulouse Graduate School, College of Arts and Sciences, Department of Radio, Television and Film, Denton, TX 76203. Offers MA, MFA, MS. Part-time programs available. *Degree requirements:* For master's, thesis, thesis production (MFA). *Entrance requirements:* For master's, GRE General Test, writing sample, goal statement, 2 letters of recommendation (3 for MFA), portfolio (for MFA only). Additional exam requirements/recommendations for international students: Recommended—TOEFL (minimum score 550 paper-based; 213 computer-based; 79 iBT). *Application deadline:* Applications are processed on a rolling basis. Electronic applications accepted. *Expenses:* Tuition, state resident: full-time $4298; part-time $239 per credit hour. Tuition, nonresident: full-time $10,782; part-time $549 per credit hour. Required fees: $1292; $270 per credit hour. *Financial support:* Fellowships, research assistantships, teaching assistantships, career-related internships or fieldwork, Federal Work-Study, and institutionally sponsored loans available. Financial award applicants required to submit FAFSA. *Faculty research:* Media law and regulation, industry studies, film and broadcasting history, documentary production, critical and cultural studies. *Application contact:* Director of Graduate Studies, 940-565-3222, Fax: 940-369-7838, E-mail: samuel.sauls@unt.edu.

University of Oklahoma, Weitzenhoffer Family College of Fine Arts, School of Art and Art History, Program in Art, Norman, OK 73019. Offers art (MFA), including ceramics, film, painting, photography, printmaking, sculpture, video, visual communication. MA applicants admitted fall/spring; MFA applicants admitted fall only. *Students:* 17 full-time (9 women), 2 part-time (1 woman); includes 5 minority (3 American Indian or Alaska Native, non-Hispanic/Latino; 2 Native Hawaiian or other Pacific Islander, non-Hispanic/Latino), 3 international. Average age 29. 27 applicants, 41% accepted, 8 enrolled. In 2010, 3 master's awarded. *Degree requirements:* For master's, thesis (MA), exhibit (MFA), departmental qualifying exam. *Entrance requirements:* For master's, GRE General Test (MA). Additional exam requirements/recommendations for international students: Required—TOEFL (minimum score 550 paper-based; 213 computer-based; 79 iBT). *Application deadline:* For fall admission, 2/1 for domestic and international students; for spring admission, 10/1 for domestic and international students. Applications are processed on a rolling basis. Application fee: $40 ($90 for international students). Electronic applications accepted. *Expenses:* Tuition, state resident: full-time $3893; part-time $162.20 per credit hour. Tuition, nonresident: full-time $14,167; part-time $590.30 per credit hour. Required fees: $2523; $94.60 per credit hour. Tuition and fees vary according to course load and degree level. *Financial support:* Career-related internships or fieldwork, scholarships/grants, tuition waivers (full and partial), and unspecified assistantships available. Financial award application deadline: 4/7; financial award applicants required to submit FAFSA. *Faculty research:* Interactions between technology and art; propaganda banners relating to the nuclear age; investigation of the nature of structures; relationships between history, myth and culture; gestural vase forms and slabbed formed architectural vessels. *Unit head:* Mary Jo Watson, Director, 405-325-2691, Fax: 405-325-1668, E-mail: mjwatson@ou.edu. *Application contact:* Andrew Strout, Graduate Liaison, 405-325-4094, Fax: 405-325-1668, E-mail: aestrout@ou.edu.

University of Southern California, Graduate School, School of Cinematic Arts, Division of Animation and Digital Arts, Los Angeles, CA 90089. Offers MFA. *Faculty:* 9 full-time (5 women), 20 part-time/adjunct (7 women). *Students:* 44 full-time (21 women); includes 17 minority (4 Black or African American, non-Hispanic/Latino; 3 Asian, non-Hispanic/Latino; 8 Hispanic/Latino; 2 Two or more races, non-Hispanic/Latino), 9 international. In 2010, 13 master's awarded. *Degree requirements:* For master's, thesis, digital media and research documentation. *Application deadline:* For fall admission, 12/1 for domestic and international students. Electronic applications accepted. *Expenses:* Contact institution. *Financial support:* In 2010–11, 17 students received support, including 3 fellowships with partial tuition reimbursements available; career-related internships or fieldwork, scholarships/grants, and tuition waivers (partial) also available. Financial award applicants required to submit FAFSA. *Faculty research:* Character animation, visual effects, motion graphics, documentary animation, experimental animation. *Unit head:* Kathy Evelyn Smith, Chair and Associate Professor, 213-821-1348, Fax: 213-740-5869, E-mail: kates@usc.edu. *Application contact:* Daphne M. Sigismondi, Program Specialist, 213-740-3986, Fax: 213-740-5869, E-mail: dsigismondi@cinema.usc.edu.

University of Southern California, Graduate School, School of Cinematic Arts, Division of Film and Television Production, Los Angeles, CA 90089. Offers film and television production (MFA). *Faculty:* 34 full-time (8 women), 76 part-time/adjunct (13 women). *Students:* 375 full-time (117 women), 34 part-time (12 women); includes 111 minority (32 Black or African American, non-Hispanic/Latino; 2 American Indian or Alaska Native, non-Hispanic/Latino; 32 Asian, non-Hispanic/Latino; 35 Hispanic/Latino; 10 Two or more races, non-Hispanic/Latino), 65 international. In 2010, 66 master's awarded. Terminal master's awarded for partial completion of doctoral program. *Degree requirements:* For master's, advanced project. *Entrance requirements:* For master's, None. Additional exam requirements/recommendations for international students: Required—TOEFL (minimum score 600 paper-based; 250 computer-based). *Application deadline:* For fall admission, 12/1 for domestic and international students; for spring admission, 8/1 for domestic and international students. Application fee: $85. Electronic applications accepted. *Expenses:* Tuition: Full-time $31,240; part-time $1420 per unit. Required fees: $600. One-time fee: $35 full-time. Full-time tuition and fees vary according to degree level and program. *Financial support:* In 2010–11, 51 students received support, including 3 fellowships with partial tuition reimbursements available (averaging $20,000 per year), 117 teaching assistantships (averaging $3,000 per year); career-related internships or fieldwork, Federal Work-Study, institutionally sponsored loans, scholarships/grants, health care benefits, unspecified assistantships, and student assistantships also available. Support available to part-time students. Financial award application deadline: 5/3; financial award applicants required to submit FAFSA. *Faculty research:* Documentary filmmaking, narrative filmmaking, initiatives related to health issues, science foundation project, global workshops in China. Total annual research expenditures: $500,000. *Unit head:* Michael Taylor, Chair, 213-821-3113, Fax: 213-740-3395, E-mail: taylor@cinema.usc.edu. *Application contact:* Shahla Rahimzadeh, Admissions Director, 213-740-8358, Fax: 213-740-4013, E-mail: admissions@cinema.usc.edu.

University of Southern California, Graduate School, School of Cinematic Arts, The Peter Stark Producing Program, Los Angeles, CA 90089. Offers motion picture producing (MFA).

University of Southern California (continued)

Faculty: 1 full-time (0 women), 24 part-time/adjunct (6 women). *Students:* 50 full-time (23 women); includes 9 minority (3 Black or African American, non-Hispanic/Latino; 3 Asian, non-Hispanic/Latino; 2 Hispanic/Latino; 1 Two or more races, non-Hispanic/Latino), 11 international. 189 applicants, 13% accepted, 25 enrolled. In 2010, 25 master's awarded. *Degree requirements:* For master's, thesis, set curriculum, oral examination. *Entrance requirements:* For master's, GRE. Additional exam requirements/recommendations for international students: Required—TOEFL (minimum score 600 paper-based; 250 computer-based; 100 iBT), IELTS (minimum score 7). *Application deadline:* For fall admission, 12/1 for domestic and international students. Application fee: $85. Electronic applications accepted. *Expenses:* Tuition: Full-time $31,240; part-time $1420 per unit. Required fees: $600. One-time fee: $35 full-time. Full-time tuition and fees vary according to degree level and program. *Financial support:* In 2010–11, 16 students received support, including 2 teaching assistantships with partial tuition reimbursements available (averaging $6,000 per year); Federal Work-Study, institutionally sponsored loans, and scholarships/grants also available. Financial award application deadline: 3/9; financial award applicants required to submit FAFSA. *Unit head:* Richard Shepherd, Assistant Director, 213-740-3304, Fax: 213-745-6652, E-mail: rshepherd@cinema.usc.edu. *Application contact:* Richard Shepherd, Assistant Director, 213-740-3304, Fax: 213-745-6652, E-mail: rshepherd@cinema.usc.edu.

University of Southern California, Graduate School, School of Cinematic Arts, Writing for Screen and Television Division, Los Angeles, CA 90089. Offers MFA. *Faculty:* 15 full-time (3 women), 53 part-time/adjunct (11 women). *Students:* 66 full-time (34 women), 8 part-time (3 women); includes 17 minority (4 Black or African American, non-Hispanic/Latino; 3 Asian, non-Hispanic/Latino; 4 Hispanic/Latino; 6 Two or more races, non-Hispanic/Latino), 5 international. 197 applicants, 18% accepted, 32 enrolled. In 2010, 26 master's awarded. *Degree requirements:* For master's, thesis or alternative. *Entrance requirements:* For master's, GRE. Additional exam requirements/recommendations for international students: Required—TOEFL. *Application deadline:* For fall admission, 12/1 for domestic and international students. Application fee: $95. Electronic applications accepted. *Expenses:* Tuition: Full-time $31,240; part-time $1420 per unit. Required fees: $600. One-time fee: $35 full-time. Full-time tuition and fees vary according to degree level and program. *Financial support:* In 2010–11, 22 students received support, including 4 fellowships with full tuition reimbursements available (averaging $20,000 per year); Federal Work-Study, scholarships/grants, and unspecified assistantships also available. Financial award application deadline: 3/9; financial award applicants required to submit FAFSA. *Faculty research:* Dramatic storytelling, new media content and distribution, television and film character development, theory of storytelling, interactive writing. *Unit head:* Jack Epps, Chair, 213-740-3303, Fax: 213-740-8035, E-mail: kburkett@cinema.usc.edu. *Application contact:* Michael Lane, MFA Program Coordinator, 213-740-3303, E-mail: mlane@cinema.usc.edu.

The University of Texas at Arlington, Graduate School, College of Liberal Arts, Department of Art and Art History, Arlington, TX 76019. Offers film and video (MFA); glass (MFA); intermedia (MFA); visual communication (MFA). *Accreditation:* NASAD. *Faculty:* 21 full-time (7 women). *Students:* 25 full-time (10 women), 3 part-time (all women); includes 5 minority (1 Black or African American, non-Hispanic/Latino; 1 American Indian or Alaska Native, non-Hispanic/Latino; 1 Asian, non-Hispanic/Latino; 2 Hispanic/Latino), 2 international. 24 applicants, 63% accepted, 10 enrolled. In 2010, 3 master's awarded. *Degree requirements:* For master's, thesis or alternative. *Entrance requirements:* For master's, minimum GPA of 3.0, 3 letters of recommendation, portfolio, resume. Additional exam requirements/recommendations for international students: Required—TOEFL (minimum score 550 paper-based; 213 computer-based). *Application deadline:* For fall admission, 1/15 priority date for domestic and international students; for spring admission, 10/15 priority date for domestic and international students. Applications are processed on a rolling basis. Electronic applications accepted. *Expenses:* Tuition, state resident: full-time $7500. Tuition, nonresident: full-time $13,080. International tuition: $13,250 full-time. *Financial support:* In 2010–11, 4 fellowships (averaging $1,000 per year), 4 research assistantships (averaging $4,000 per year), 18 teaching assistantships (averaging $6,000 per year) were awarded; scholarships/grants and unspecified assistantships also available. Financial award applicants required to submit FAFSA. *Unit head:* Prof. Robert Hower, Chair/Professor, 817-272-2891, Fax: 817-272-2805, E-mail: hower@uta.edu. *Application contact:* Prof. Nancy Palmeri, Graduate Advisor/Associate Professor, 817-272-2891, Fax: 817-272-2805, E-mail: palmeri@uta.edu.

The University of Texas at Austin, Graduate School, College of Communication, Department of Radio-Television-Film, Austin, TX 78712-1111. Offers film and video production (MFA); radio-television-film (MA, PhD); screenwriting (MFA). *Degree requirements:* For master's, thesis (for some programs); for doctorate, thesis/dissertation. *Entrance requirements:* For master's and doctorate, GRE General Test. Electronic applications accepted. *Faculty research:* International communication, film studies, media and culture, telecommunication and new media, gender and sexuality.

University of the Sacred Heart, Graduate Programs, Department of Communication, San Juan, PR 00914-0383. Offers contemporary culture and media (MA); digital journalism (MA, Certificate); editing for media (MA, Certificate); public relations (MA, Certificate); publicity (MA, Certificate); scriptwriting (MA, Certificate). Part-time and evening/weekend programs available. *Degree requirements:* For master's, thesis.

University of Utah, Graduate School, College of Fine Arts, Division of Film Studies, Salt Lake City, UT 84112-0380. Offers MFA. *Faculty:* 7 full-time (2 women), 4 part-time/adjunct (0 women). *Students:* 23 full-time (10 women), 3 part-time (2 women); includes 1 minority (Hispanic/Latino), 1 international. Average age 33. 42 applicants, 45% accepted, 18 enrolled. In 2010, 1 master's awarded. *Degree requirements:* For master's, comprehensive exam, film or video portfolio. *Entrance requirements:* For master's, minimum GPA of 3.0. Additional exam requirements/recommendations for international students: Required—TOEFL (minimum score 500 paper-based; 173 computer-based). *Application deadline:* For fall admission, 12/31 for domestic and international students. Application fee: $55 ($65 for international students). *Expenses:* Tuition, area resident: Part-time $179.19 per credit hour. Tuition, state resident: full-time $4384. Tuition, nonresident: full-time $16,684; part-time $630.67 per credit hour. Required fees: $350 per semester. Tuition and fees vary according to course load, degree level and program. *Financial support:* In 2010–11, 9 teaching assistantships with full and partial tuition reimbursements (averaging $8,500 per year) were awarded; career-related internships or fieldwork, Federal Work-Study, institutionally sponsored loans, health care benefits, and unspecified assistantships also available. Financial award application deadline: 3/1; financial award applicants required to submit FAFSA. *Faculty research:* Film history, criticism, cultural studies, production of narrative and documentary films. Total annual research expenditures: $254,339. *Unit head:* Prof. Kevin D. Hanson, Chair, 801-581-7428, Fax: 801-585-3192, E-mail: kevin.hanson@utah.edu. *Application contact:* Prof. Connie Wilkerson, Director of Graduate Studies, 801-585-9278, Fax: 801-585-3192, E-mail: connie.wilkerson@utah.edu.

University of Victoria, Faculty of Graduate Studies, Faculty of Fine Arts, Department of Visual Arts, Victoria, BC V8W 2Y2, Canada. Offers digital multimedia (MFA); drawing (MFA); painting (MFA); photography (MFA); sculpture (MFA); video (MFA). *Degree requirements:* For master's, exhibit, oral exam. *Entrance requirements:* For master's, portfolio, BFA. Additional exam requirements/recommendations for international students: Required—TOEFL (minimum score 575 paper-based; 233 computer-based), IELTS (minimum score 7). Electronic applications accepted.

University of Wisconsin–Milwaukee, Graduate School, Peck School of the Arts, Program in Performing Arts, Milwaukee, WI 53201-0413. Offers dance (MFA); film (MFA); theatre (MFA). Part-time programs available. *Faculty:* 28 full-time (16 women). *Students:* 17 full-time (10 women), 2 part-time (0 women); includes 1 Black or African American, non-Hispanic/Latino; 2 Hispanic/Latino, 1 international. Average age 34. 31 applicants, 23% accepted, 6 enrolled. In 2010, 17 master's awarded. *Degree requirements:* For master's, variable foreign language requirement, comprehensive exam, thesis or alternative. *Entrance requirements:* For master's, audition, interview. Additional exam requirements/recommendations for international students: Required—TOEFL (minimum score 550 paper-based; 79 iBT), IELTS (minimum score 6.5). *Application deadline:* For fall admission, 1/1 priority date for domestic students; for spring admission, 9/1 for domestic students. Applications are processed on a rolling basis. Application fee: $56 ($96 for international students). Electronic applications accepted. *Financial support:* In 2010–11, 5 fellowships with full tuition reimbursements, 9 teaching assistantships with full tuition reimbursements were awarded; career-related internships or fieldwork, health care benefits, unspecified assistantships, and project assistantships also available. Support available to part-time students. Financial award application deadline: 4/15; financial award applicants required to submit FAFSA. *Unit head:* Simone Ferro, Representative, 414-229-4178, E-mail: sferro@uwm.edu. *Application contact:* General Information Contact, 414-229-4982, Fax: 414-229-6967, E-mail: gradschool@uwm.edu.

Western State College of Colorado, Program in Creative Writing, Gunnison, CO 81231. Offers mainstream genre fiction (MFA); poetry (MFA); screenwriting (MFA). Postbaccalaureate distance learning degree programs offered (minimal on-campus study). *Degree requirements:* For master's, thesis.

See Display on page 571 and Close-Up on page 575.

York University, Faculty of Graduate Studies, Faculty of Fine Arts, Program in Film, Toronto, ON M3J 1P3, Canada. Offers MA, MFA, PhD. *Degree requirements:* For master's, thesis. *Entrance requirements:* For master's, portfolio. Electronic applications accepted.

Film, Television, and Video Theory and Criticism

Boston University, College of Communication, Department of Film and Television, Boston, MA 02215. Offers film production (MFA); film studies (MFA); media ventures (MS); screenwriting (MFA); television production (MS); MBA/MS. Part-time programs available. *Faculty:* 13 full-time, 27 part-time/adjunct. *Students:* 80 full-time (44 women), 11 part-time (4 women); includes 12 minority (7 Black or African American, non-Hispanic/Latino; 2 Asian, non-Hispanic/Latino; 2 Hispanic/Latino; 1 Two or more races, non-Hispanic/Latino), 17 international. Average age 26. In 2010, 54 master's awarded. *Degree requirements:* For master's, thesis. *Entrance requirements:* For master's, GRE General Test, sample of written or creative work. Additional exam requirements/recommendations for international students: Required—TOEFL (minimum score 600 paper-based; 250 computer-based; 100 iBT). *Application deadline:* For fall admission, 2/1 for domestic and international students. Application fee: $70. Electronic applications accepted. *Expenses:* Tuition: Full-time $39,314; part-time $1228 per credit. Required fees: $40 per semester. *Financial support:* Teaching assistantships with partial tuition reimbursements, career-related internships or fieldwork, Federal Work-Study, institutionally sponsored loans, scholarships/grants, and unspecified assistantships available. Support available to part-time students. Financial award application deadline: 2/1; financial award applicants required to submit FAFSA. *Unit head:* Paul Schneider, Chairman, 617-353-3483, Fax: 617-353-1084, E-mail: ftvchair@bu.edu. *Application contact:* Jennifer Healey, Administrator of Graduate Services, 617-353-3481, Fax: 617-358-0399, E-mail: comgrad@bu.edu.

California College of the Arts, Graduate Programs, Program in Visual and Critical Studies, San Francisco, CA 94107. Offers MA. *Faculty:* 8 full-time (6 women), 5 part-time/adjunct (all women). *Students:* 21 full-time (17 women), 1 part-time (0 women). Average age 29. 221 applicants, 64% accepted. In 2010, 4 master's awarded. *Degree requirements:* For master's, thesis. *Entrance requirements:* For master's, appropriate bachelor's degree, portfolio, resume, 2 letters of recommendation, transcripts. Additional exam requirements/recommendations for international students: Required—TOEFL (minimum score 600 paper-based; 250 computer-based; 100 iBT). *Application deadline:* For fall admission, 1/5 for domestic and international students. Application fee: $70. Electronic applications accepted. *Expenses:* Tuition: Full-time $38,550; part-time $1285 per unit. One-time fee: $185 full-time. *Financial support:* In 2010–11, 2 fellowships (averaging $11,000 per year), teaching assistantships (averaging $2,000 per year) were awarded; career-related internships or fieldwork, Federal Work-Study, scholarships/grants, and health care benefits also available. Financial award application deadline: 3/2; financial award applicants required to submit FAFSA. *Unit head:* Tirza Latimer, Chair, 415-551-9250, E-mail: tlatimer@cca.edu. *Application contact:* Heidi Geis, Assistant Director of Graduate Admissions, 415-703-9523 Ext. 9533, Fax: 415-703-9539, E-mail: hgeis@cca.edu.

Central Michigan University, College of Graduate Studies, College of Communication and Fine Arts, School of Broadcasting and Cinematic Arts, Mount Pleasant, MI 48859. Offers electronic media management (MA); electronic media production (MA); electronic media studies (MA); film theory and criticism (MA). Part-time programs available. *Faculty:* 11 full-time (2 women), 1 part-time/adjunct (0 women). *Students:* 15 full-time (4 women), 18 part-time (7 women); includes 2 Black or African American, non-Hispanic/Latino; 1 Asian, non-Hispanic/Latino; 1 Hispanic/Latino, 6 international. Average age 26. *Degree requirements:* For master's, thesis or alternative. *Entrance requirements:* For master's, undergraduate degree in broadcasting, film studies, or an associated discipline with minimum GPA of 2.7. *Application deadline:* For fall admission, 6/1 for international students; for spring admission, 10/1 for international students. Applications are processed on a rolling basis. Application fee: $35 ($45 for international students). Electronic applications accepted. *Expenses:* Tuition, state resident: full-time $8208; part-time $456 per credit hour. Tuition, nonresident: full-time $13,788; part-time $766 per credit hour. One-time fee: $25. *Financial support:* Fellowships with tuition reimbursements, teaching assistantships with tuition reimbursements, career-related internships or fieldwork, Federal Work-Study, unspecified assistantships, and out-of-state merit awards, non-resident graduate awards available. Financial award application deadline: 3/1. *Faculty research:* Multimedia production, film history and criticism, writing and promotions, international broadcasting and media systems, history of American broadcasting. *Unit head:* Dr. Peter B. Orlik, Chairperson, 989-774-3851, Fax: 989-774-2426, E-mail: peter.b.orlik@cmich.edu. *Application contact:* Dr. Patricia Williamson, Graduate Program Coordinator, 989-774-2561, Fax: 989-774-2426, E-mail: willi1pa@cmich.edu.

Claremont Graduate University, Graduate Programs, School of Arts and Humanities, Department of English, Claremont, CA 91711-6160. Offers American studies (MA, PhD); critical theory (MA, PhD); early modern studies (MA, PhD); English (M Phil, MA, PhD); literary theory (PhD); literature (MA, PhD); literature and creative writing (MA); literature and film (MA); MBA/MA; MBA/PhD. Part-time programs available. *Faculty:* 2 full-time (both women), 4 part-time/adjunct (1 woman). *Students:* 88 full-time (56 women), 14 part-time (12 women); includes 1 Black or African American, non-Hispanic/Latino; 9 Asian, non-Hispanic/Latino; 7 Hispanic/Latino; 5 Two or more races, non-Hispanic/Latino, 7 international. Average age 34. In 2010, 9 master's, 10 doctorates awarded. *Entrance requirements:* For master's and doctorate, GRE General Test. Additional exam requirements/recommendations for international students: Required—TOEFL (minimum score 550 paper-based; 213 computer-based; 80 iBT). *Application deadline:* For fall admission, 2/1 priority date for domestic students. Applications are processed on a rolling basis. Application fee: $60. Electronic applications accepted. *Expenses:* Tuition: Full-time $35,748; part-time $1554 per unit. Required fees: $215 per semester. *Financial support:* Fellowships, Federal Work-Study, institutionally sponsored loans, and scholarships/grants available. Support available to part-time students. Financial award application deadline: 2/15; financial award applicants required to submit FAFSA. *Faculty research:* American, comparative, and English Renaissance literature; modernism; feminist literature and theory. *Unit head:* Elysabeth Flores Griffith, Administrative Director, 909-607-3877, E-mail: elysabeth.flores@cgu.edu. *Application contact:* Susan Hampson, Admissions Coordinator, 909-607-1278, Fax: 909-607-1221, E-mail: humanities@cgu.edu.

College of Staten Island of the City University of New York, Graduate Programs, Program in Cinema and Media Studies, Staten Island, NY 10314-6600. Offers MA. Part-time and evening/weekend programs available. *Faculty:* 6 full-time (3 women). *Students:* 1 full-time (0 women), 19 part-time (7 women); includes 2 Hispanic/Latino, 3 international. Average age 27. 26 applicants, 31% accepted, 4 enrolled. In 2010, 5 master's awarded. *Degree requirements:* For master's, comprehensive exam, original film, media or production thesis or written examination. *Entrance requirements:* For master's, 10-12 page critical writing sample on film or media topic, 3 letters of recommendation. Additional exam requirements/recommendations for international students: Required—TOEFL (minimum score 550 paper-based; 213 computer-based; 79 iBT), IELTS (minimum score 6.5). *Application deadline:* For fall admission, 4/15 priority date for domestic and international students; for spring admission, 11/15 priority date for domestic and international students. Applications are processed on a rolling basis. Application fee: $125. Electronic applications accepted. *Expenses:* Tuition, state resident: full-time $7730; part-time $325 per credit. Tuition, nonresident: full-time $14,520; part-time $605 per credit. Required fees: $378. *Financial support:* In 2010–11, 4 teaching assistantships (averaging $1,250 per year) were awarded; career-related internships or fieldwork, Federal Work-Study, and scholarships/grants also available. Support available to part-time students. Financial award applicants required to submit FAFSA. *Unit head:* Dr. Matthew Solomon, Coordinator/Associate Professor, 718-982-2548, E-mail: cinemamasters@mail.csi.cuny.edu. *Application contact:* Sasha Spence, Assistant Director of Graduate Recruitment and Admissions, 718-982-2699, Fax: 718-982-2500, E-mail: sasha.spence@csi.cuny.edu.

Concordia University, School of Graduate Studies, Faculty of Fine Arts, Mel Hoppenheim School of Cinema, Montréal, QC H3G 1M8, Canada. Offers film studies (MA).

Emory University, Laney Graduate School, Department of Film Studies, Atlanta, GA 30322-1100. Offers MA, PhD/Certificate. *Degree requirements:* For master's, comprehensive exam, thesis or alternative. *Entrance requirements:* For master's, GRE General Test, 3 letters of reference, 2 writing samples. Additional exam requirements/recommendations for international students: Required—TOEFL. Electronic applications accepted. *Expenses:* Tuition: Full-time $33,800. Required fees: $1300. *Faculty research:* International film history, film theory, film style, feminism and film, reception.

Emory University, Laney Graduate School, Department of Spanish and Portuguese, Atlanta, GA 30322-1100. Offers comparative literature (Certificate); film studies (Certificate); Spanish (PhD); women's studies (Certificate). *Degree requirements:* For doctorate, 2 foreign languages, comprehensive exam, thesis/dissertation. *Entrance requirements:* For doctorate, GRE General Test. Additional exam requirements/recommendations for international students: Required—TOEFL. Electronic applications accepted. *Expenses:* Tuition: Full-time $33,800. Required fees: $1300. *Faculty research:* Spanish literature, Spanish-American literature, literary theory, criticism, cultural studies.

Florida Atlantic University, Dorothy F. Schmidt College of Arts and Letters, School of Communication and Multimedia Studies, Boca Raton, FL 33431-0991. Offers communication studies (MA); film and video (Certificate); film studies (MA); multimedia journalism studies (MA). Part-time programs available. *Faculty:* 28 full-time (10 women), 14 part-time/adjunct (3 women). *Students:* 19 full-time (15 women), 15 part-time (11 women); includes 8 minority (3 Black or African American, non-Hispanic/Latino; 1 American Indian or Alaska Native, non-Hispanic/Latino; 1 Asian, non-Hispanic/Latino; 1 Hispanic/Latino; 2 Two or more races, non-Hispanic/Latino), 6 international. Average age 28. 42 applicants, 26% accepted, 8 enrolled. In 2010, 3 master's awarded. *Degree requirements:* For master's, one foreign language, comprehensive exam (for some programs), thesis (for some programs). *Entrance requirements:* For master's, GRE General Test, minimum GPA of 3.0. *Application deadline:* For fall admission, 7/1 priority date for domestic students, 4/1 for international students; for spring admission, 11/1 for domestic students, 10/1 for international students. Applications are processed on a rolling basis. Application fee: $30. Electronic applications accepted. *Expenses:* Tuition, area resident: Part-time $319.96 per credit. Tuition, state resident: part-time $319.96 per credit. Tuition, nonresident: part-time $926.42 per credit. *Financial support:* Teaching assistantships with partial tuition reimbursements, Federal Work-Study and institutionally sponsored loans available. Support available to part-time students. Financial award application deadline: 3/1. *Faculty research:* Cultural studies, gender studies, film, communication theory, journalism, new media. *Unit head:* Dr. Susan S. Reilly, Director, 561-297-1095, Fax: 561-297-2615, E-mail: sreilly@fau.edu. *Application contact:* Dr. Eric M. Freedman, Graduate Coordinator, 561-297-2534, Fax: 561-297-2615, E-mail: efreedma@fau.edu.

Hollins University, Graduate Programs, Program in Screenwriting and Film Studies, Roanoke, VA 24020-1603. Offers MA, MFA. Offered during summer only. Part-time programs available. *Degree requirements:* For master's, one foreign language, comprehensive exam, thesis. *Entrance requirements:* For master's, letters of recommendation, portfolio. Additional exam requirements/recommendations for international students: Required—TOEFL (minimum score 550 paper-based; 213 computer-based; 79 iBT). Electronic applications accepted. *Faculty research:* German film, women in film, censorship, minorities in film.

Indiana University Bloomington, University Graduate School, College of Arts and Sciences, Department of Communication and Culture, Bloomington, IN 47405-7000. Offers film and media studies (PhD); performance and ethnography (PhD); rhetoric and public culture (PhD). *Faculty:* 24 full-time (12 women). *Students:* 81 full-time (41 women), 3 part-time (all women); includes 10 minority (2 Black or African American, non-Hispanic/Latino; 8 Hispanic/Latino), 10 international. Average age 32. 187 applicants, 12% accepted, 11 enrolled. In 2010, 4 master's, 7 doctorates awarded. *Degree requirements:* For master's, comprehensive exam; for doctorate, one foreign language, comprehensive exam, thesis/dissertation, student teaching. *Entrance requirements:* For master's and doctorate, GRE General Test (recommended), minimum GPA of 3.0, 3 letters of recommendation, writing sample. Additional exam requirements/recommendations for international students: Required—TOEFL (minimum score 550 paper-based; 213 computer-based). *Application deadline:* For winter admission, 1/1 for domestic students, 12/1 for international students. Application fee: $55 ($65 for international students). Electronic applications accepted. *Financial support:* In 2010–11, 65 students received support, including 4 fellowships with full tuition reimbursements available (averaging $18,000 per year), 48 teaching assistantships with full tuition reimbursements available (averaging $13,257 per year). Financial award application deadline: 4/15. *Faculty research:* Rhetoric and public culture, film and media studies, performance ethnography. *Unit head:* Prof. Gregory A. Waller, Chair, 812-855-2367, Fax: 812-855-6014, E-mail: cmcl@indiana.edu. *Application contact:* Kathy P. Teige, Graduate Secretary, 812-855-6389, Fax: 812-855-6014, E-mail: kteige@indiana.edu.

New York University, Tisch School of the Arts and Graduate School of Arts and Science, Department of Cinema Studies, New York, NY 10012-1019. Offers cinema studies (MA, PhD); moving image archiving and preservation (MA). *Faculty:* 15 full-time, 9 part-time/adjunct. *Students:* 70 full-time (36 women), 2 part-time (1 woman); includes 1 Black or African American, non-Hispanic/Latino; 1 American Indian or Alaska Native, non-Hispanic/Latino; 6 Asian, non-Hispanic/Latino; 6 Hispanic/Latino. Average age 31. 233 applicants, 42% accepted, 49 enrolled. In 2010, 26 master's, 8 doctorates awarded. *Degree requirements:* For master's, comprehensive exam; for doctorate, one foreign language, thesis/dissertation, 3 comprehensive exams. *Entrance requirements:* For master's, GRE, sample of written work; for doctorate, GRE, master's degree, writing sample. Additional exam requirements/recommendations for international students: Required—TOEFL or IELTS. *Application deadline:* For fall admission, 12/1 for domestic and international students. Application fee: $60. Electronic applications accepted. *Expenses:* Contact institution. *Financial support:* In 2010–11, 59 students received support, including 45 fellowships with full and partial tuition reimbursements available, 10 research assistantships, 4 teaching assistantships; Federal Work-Study, institutionally sponsored loans, tuition waivers (full and partial), and unspecified assistantships also available. Support available to part-time students. Financial award application deadline: 2/15; financial award applicants required to submit FAFSA. *Faculty research:* History and aesthetics of American, European, and Third World cinemas; theory of film and the moving image; cultural studies; gay and lesbian media. *Unit head:* Dr. Richard Allen, Chair, 212-998-1600. *Application contact:* Dan Sandford, Director of Graduate Admissions, 212-998-1918, Fax: 212-995-4060, E-mail: tisch.gradadmissions@nyu.edu.

Ohio University, Graduate College, College of Fine Arts, School of Film, Athens, OH 45701-2979. Offers film (MFA); film studies (MA). *Students:* 45 full-time (17 women), 8 part-time (2 women); includes 8 minority (3 Black or African American, non-Hispanic/Latino; 1 American Indian or Alaska Native, non-Hispanic/Latino; 2 Asian, non-Hispanic/Latino; 1 Hispanic/Latino; 1 Two or more races, non-Hispanic/Latino), 13 international. Average age 25. 139 applicants, 11% accepted, 10 enrolled. In 2010, 15 master's awarded. *Degree requirements:* For master's, one foreign language, thesis. *Entrance requirements:* Additional exam requirements/recommendations for international students: Required—TOEFL (minimum score 550 paper-based; 80 iBT) or IELTS (minimum score 6.5). *Application deadline:* For fall admission, 2/1 for domestic and international students. Application fee: $50 ($55 for international students). Electronic applications accepted. *Financial support:* In 2010–11, 34 students received support; research assistantships with full tuition reimbursements available, teaching assistantships with full tuition reimbursements available, institutionally sponsored loans, scholarships/grants, tuition waivers (full and partial), and unspecified assistantships available. Financial award application deadline: 2/1. *Faculty research:* Scriptwriting, sound, editing, cinematography, film theory, digital post production. *Unit head:* Steven Ross, Director, 740-593-9969, Fax: 740-593-1328, E-mail: rosss2@ohio.edu. *Application contact:* Tamra LaGraff, Administrative Associate, 740-593-1323, Fax: 740-593-1328, E-mail: lagraff@ohio.edu.

San Francisco State University, Division of Graduate Studies, College of Creative Arts, Department of Cinema, San Francisco, CA 94132-1722. Offers cinema (MFA); cinema studies (MA). *Unit head:* Martha Gorzycki, Chair, 415-338-1879. *Application contact:* Erin Persley, Assistant Graduate Programs Coordinator, 415-338-1724, E-mail: cinegrad@sfsu.edu.

Savannah College of Art and Design, Graduate School, Program in Cinema Studies, Savannah, GA 31402-3146. Offers MA. Part-time programs available. *Faculty:* 2 full-time (1 woman). *Students:* 12 full-time (5 women), 2 part-time (1 woman); includes 1 Black or African American, non-Hispanic/Latino; 1 Hispanic/Latino, 1 international. Average age 26. In 2010, 2 master's awarded. *Degree requirements:* For master's, thesis. *Entrance requirements:* For master's, interview. Additional exam requirements/recommendations for international students: Required—TOEFL (minimum score 450 paper-based; 133 computer-based). *Application deadline:* For fall admission, 4/1 priority date for domestic and international students. Applications are processed on a rolling basis. Application fee: $35. Electronic applications accepted. *Expenses:* Tuition: Full-time $29,520; part-time $3280 per quarter. Tuition and fees vary according to campus/location. *Financial support:* Fellowships, career-related internships or fieldwork, Federal Work-Study, and scholarships/grants available. Financial award application deadline: 4/1; financial award applicants required to submit FAFSA. *Unit head:* Roger Rawlings, Program Coordinator, 912-525-6525, Fax: 912-525-6037, E-mail: rrawling@scad.edu. *Application contact:* Elizabeth Mathis, Director of Graduate Recruitment, 912-525-5965, Fax: 912-525-5985, E-mail: emathis@scad.edu.

Syracuse University, S. I. Newhouse School of Public Communications, Program in Documentary Film and History, Syracuse, NY 13244. Offers MA. *Students:* 6 full-time (4 women), 3 part-time (0 women); includes 1 minority (Asian, non-Hispanic/Latino), 2 international. Average age 28. 16 applicants, 75% accepted, 6 enrolled. In 2010, 9 master's awarded. *Entrance requirements:* For master's, GRE General Test. Additional exam requirements/recommendations for international students: Required—TOEFL (minimum score 100 iBT). *Application deadline:* For fall admission, 2/1 priority date for domestic and international students. Application fee: $45. Electronic applications accepted. *Expenses:* Tuition: Part-time $1162 per credit. *Financial support:* Fellowships with full tuition reimbursements, research assistantships with partial tuition reimbursements, teaching assistantships with partial tuition reimbursements available. Financial award application deadline: 2/1. *Unit head:* Richard Breyer, Director, 315-443-9249. *Application contact:* Martha Coria, Graduate Records Office, 315-443-5749, Fax: 315-443-1834, E-mail: pcgrad@syr.edu.

Université de Montréal, Faculty of Arts and Sciences, Department of Art History and Film Studies, Montréal, QC H3C 3J7, Canada. Offers art history (MA, PhD); film studies (MA, PhD). Programs offered jointly with Concordia University, Université Laval, and Université du Québec à Montréal. *Degree requirements:* For master's, thesis. Electronic applications accepted. *Faculty research:* Western art from the Middle Ages, classic and modern theory, modern and contemporary art, Canadian art.

Université Laval, Faculty of Letters, Department of Literature, Programs in Literature and Arts of the Screen and Stage, Québec, QC G1K 7P4, Canada. Offers MA, PhD. Part-time programs available. Terminal master's awarded for partial completion of doctoral program. *Degree requirements:* For master's, thesis; for doctorate, comprehensive exam, thesis/dissertation. *Entrance requirements:* For master's and doctorate, linguistics exams, knowledge of French, knowledge of a second language. Electronic applications accepted.

The University of British Columbia, Faculty of Arts and Faculty of Graduate Studies, Department of Theatre and Film, Film Program, Vancouver, BC V6T 1Z2, Canada. Offers creative writing and film production (MFA); film production (MFA, Diploma); film studies (MA). *Degree requirements:* For master's, variable foreign language requirement, comprehensive exam, thesis (MA), thesis or project (MFA). *Entrance requirements:* For master's, portfolio (MFA). Additional exam requirements/recommendations for international students: Required—TOEFL (minimum score 600 paper-based; 250 computer-based). Electronic applications accepted. Tuition charges are reported in Canadian dollars. *Expenses:* Tuition, area resident: Full-time $4179 Canadian dollars. International tuition: $7344 Canadian dollars full-time. *Faculty research:* Film theory and violence; American and European cinema; cult cinema; Irish cinema.

University of California, Santa Cruz, Division of Graduate Studies, Division of the Arts, Department of Film and Digital Media, Santa Cruz, CA 95064. Offers PhD. *Students:* 4 full-time (1 woman); includes 2 minority (both Asian, non-Hispanic/Latino). Average age 33. 61 applicants, 10% accepted, 4 enrolled. *Degree requirements:* For doctorate, one foreign language, thesis/dissertation, qualifying exams. *Entrance requirements:* For doctorate, GRE. Additional exam requirements/recommendations for international students: Required—TOEFL (minimum score 550 paper-based; 220 computer-based; 83 iBT); Recommended—IELTS (minimum score 8). *Application deadline:* For fall admission, 12/2 for domestic and international students. Application

Film, Television, and Video Theory and Criticism

University of California, Santa Cruz (continued)

fee: $70 ($90 for international students). Electronic applications accepted. *Financial support:* Fellowships, research assistantships, teaching assistantships, institutionally sponsored loans and tuition waivers available. Financial award applicants required to submit FAFSA. *Faculty research:* Integrating critical and creative practice, working across media, pursuing new modes of social and political engagement, fostering global cultural citizenship. *Unit head:* Robert Valiente-Neighbours, Graduate Program Coordinator, 831-459-4706, E-mail: fdmphd@ucsc.edu. *Application contact:* Robert Valiente-Neighbours, Graduate Program Coordinator, 831-459-4706, E-mail: fdmphd@ucsc.edu.

University of Chicago, Division of the Humanities, Committee on Cinema and Media Studies, Chicago, IL 60637-1513. Offers AM, PhD. *Degree requirements:* For master's, one foreign language, thesis; for doctorate, 2 foreign languages, thesis/dissertation.

The University of Iowa, Graduate College, College of Liberal Arts and Sciences, Department of Cinema and Comparative Literature, Program in Film Studies, Iowa City, IA 52242-1316. Offers MA, PhD. *Degree requirements:* For master's, thesis optional, exam; for doctorate, comprehensive exam, thesis/dissertation. *Entrance requirements:* For master's and doctorate, GRE General Test, minimum GPA of 3.0. Additional exam requirements/recommendations for international students: Required—TOEFL (minimum score 550 paper-based; 213 computer-based; 81 iBT). Electronic applications accepted.

The University of Kansas, Graduate Studies, College of Liberal Arts and Sciences, Department of Film and Media Studies, Lawrence, KS 66045. Offers MA, PhD. *Faculty:* 10 full-time (2 women). *Students:* 25 full-time (7 women), 2 part-time (1 woman); includes 4 minority (2 Asian, non-Hispanic/Latino; 2 Two or more races, non-Hispanic/Latino), 3 international. Average age 32. 23 applicants, 43% accepted, 7 enrolled. In 2010, 2 master's, 1 doctorate awarded. *Degree requirements:* For master's, thesis; for doctorate, one foreign language, comprehensive exam, thesis/dissertation. *Entrance requirements:* For master's, GRE General Test, minimum GPA of 3.2; for doctorate, GRE General Test, minimum GPA of 3.5; MA in film or related field. Additional exam requirements/recommendations for international students: Required—TOEFL. *Application deadline:* For fall admission, 2/15 for domestic and international students. Application fee: $55 ($65 for international students). Electronic applications accepted. *Expenses:* Tuition, state resident: full-time $7092; part-time $295.50 per credit hour. Tuition, nonresident: full-time $16,590; part-time $691.25 per credit hour. Required fees: $858; $71.49 per credit hour. Tuition and fees vary according to course load, campus/location and program. *Financial support:* Teaching assistantships with full and partial tuition reimbursements available. Financial award application deadline: 1/1; financial award applicants required to submit FAFSA. *Faculty research:* Film and media theory, film and media history, East Asian cinema, Latin American cinema, film and video production. *Unit head:* Dr. Tamara L. Falicov, Chair, 785-864-1353, Fax: 785-331-2671, E-mail: tfalicov@ku.edu. *Application contact:* Dr. Michael Baskett, Associate Professor, 785-864-1384, Fax: 785-331-2671, E-mail: eiga@ku.edu.

The University of Kansas, Graduate Studies, College of Liberal Arts and Sciences, Department of Theatre and Film, Lawrence, KS 66045. Offers theatre (MA, PhD); theatre design (MFA), including scenography. *Faculty:* 15 full-time (7 women). *Students:* 18 full-time (10 women), 1 (woman) part-time; includes 1 minority (Two or more races, non-Hispanic/Latino), 3 international. Average age 32. 14 applicants, 93% accepted, 6 enrolled. In 2010, 3 master's, 3 doctorates awarded. *Degree requirements:* For master's, thesis; for doctorate, one foreign language, comprehensive exam, thesis/dissertation. *Entrance requirements:* For master's, GRE General Test, minimum GPA of 3.2; for doctorate, GRE General Test, minimum GPA of 3.5; MA or MFA in theatre or related field. Additional exam requirements/recommendations for international students: Required—TOEFL. *Application deadline:* For fall admission, 1/1 priority date for domestic students, 1/1 for international students. Application fee: $55 ($65 for international students). Electronic applications accepted. *Expenses:* Tuition, state resident: full-time $7092; part-time $295.50 per credit hour. Tuition, nonresident: full-time $16,590; part-time $691.25 per credit hour. Required fees: $858; $71.49 per credit hour. Tuition and fees vary according to course load, campus/location and program. *Financial support:* In 2010–11, 2 research assistantships with full tuition reimbursements, 9 teaching assistantships with full and partial tuition reimbursements (averaging $12,650 per year) were awarded; fellowships with tuition reimbursements, Federal Work-Study, scholarships/grants, and unspecified assistantships also available. Financial award application deadline: 1/1. *Faculty research:* Theatre history, performance studies, scenography, theatre historiography. *Unit head:* John Staniunas, Chair, 785-864-3511, Fax: 785-864-5251, E-mail: stanj@ku.edu. *Application contact:* Dr. John Gronbeck-Tedesco, Director of Graduate Studies, 785-864-3511, Fax: 785-864-5251, E-mail: jgt@ku.edu.

University of Miami, Graduate School, School of Communication, Coral Gables, FL 33124. Offers communication (PhD); communication studies (MA); film studies (MA, PhD); motion pictures (MFA), including production, producing, and screenwriting; print journalism (MA); public relations (MA); Spanish language journalism (MA); television broadcast journalism (MA). *Accreditation:* ACEJMC. Part-time programs available. *Degree requirements:* For master's, comprehensive exam (for some programs), thesis (for some programs); for doctorate, comprehensive exam, thesis/dissertation. *Entrance requirements:* For master's, GRE General Test; for doctorate, GRE General Test, master's thesis or scholarly research. Additional exam requirements/recommendations for international students: Required—TOEFL (minimum score 600 paper-based; 250 computer-based; 100 iBT). Electronic applications accepted. *Faculty research:* Communication studies, mass communication, international/interpersonal communication, film studies, journalism.

University of Michigan, Horace H. Rackham School of Graduate Studies, College of Literature, Science, and the Arts, Department of Screen Arts and Cultures, Ann Arbor, MI 48109. Offers PhD, Certificate. *Degree requirements:* For doctorate, one foreign language, comprehensive exam, thesis/dissertation; for Certificate, 15 credit hours (3 directed study). *Entrance requirements:* For doctorate, GRE. Additional exam requirements/recommendations for international students: Required—TOEFL. Electronic applications accepted. *Expenses:* Tuition, state resident: full-time $17,784; part-time $1116 per credit hour. Tuition, nonresident: full-time $35,944; part-time $2125 per credit hour. International tuition: $35,994 full-time. Required fees: $95 per semester. Tuition and fees vary according to course load, degree level and program. *Faculty research:* Transnational cinema, classical Hollywood cinema, silent cinema, film theory, television.

University of Pittsburgh, School of Arts and Sciences, Program in Film Studies, Pittsburgh, PA 15260. Offers Certificate. *Expenses:* Tuition, state resident: full-time $17,304; part-time $701 per credit. Tuition, nonresident: full-time $29,554; part-time $1210 per credit. Required fees: $740; $214 per term. Tuition and fees vary according to program. *Unit head:* Dr. Nicole Constable, Associate Dean, Graduate Studies and Research, 412-624-6094, Fax: 412-624-6855, E-mail: constable@fcas.pitt.edu. *Application contact:* Dave R. Carmen, Administrative Secretary, 412-624-6094, Fax: 412-624-6855, E-mail: drc41@pitt.edu.

University of Southern California, Graduate School, School of Cinematic Arts, Division of Critical Studies, Los Angeles, CA 90089. Offers cinema-television (MA); cinema-television (critical studies) (PhD). *Faculty:* 16 full-time (9 women), 6 part-time/adjunct (2 women). *Students:* 87 full-time (53 women), 1 (woman) part-time; includes 24 minority (7 Black or African American, non-Hispanic/Latino; 8 Asian, non-Hispanic/Latino; 8 Hispanic/Latino; 1 Two or more races, non-Hispanic/Latino), 14 international. 299 applicants, 11% accepted, 20 enrolled. In 2010, 15 master's, 9 doctorates awarded. *Degree requirements:* For master's, comprehensive exam; for doctorate, comprehensive exam, thesis/dissertation. *Entrance requirements:* For master's and doctorate, GRE. Additional exam requirements/recommendations for international students: Required—TOEFL (minimum score 100 iBT). *Application deadline:* For fall admission, 12/1 for domestic and international students. Application fee: $85. Electronic applications accepted. *Expenses:* Tuition: Full-time $31,240; part-time $1420 per unit. Required fees: $600. One-time fee: $35 full-time. Full-time tuition and fees vary according to degree level and program. *Financial support:* In 2010–11, 84 students received support, including 10 fellowships with full tuition reimbursements available (averaging $25,000 per year), 2 research assistantships (averaging $5,000 per year), 43 teaching assistantships with full tuition reimbursements available (averaging $19,500 per year); career-related internships or fieldwork, Federal Work-Study, institutionally sponsored loans, scholarships/grants, health care benefits, and unspecified assistantships also available. Financial award application deadline: 5/2; financial award applicants required to submit FAFSA. *Faculty research:* Transnational cinema, race and cultural studies, global media, television studies, digital media, feminist studies. Total annual research expenditures: $200,000. *Unit head:* Dr. Akira Mizuta Lippit, Chair, 213-740-3334, Fax: 213-740-9471, E-mail: lippit@usc.edu. *Application contact:* Kim Greene, Program Coordinator, 213-740-7515, Fax: 213-740-9471.

University of South Florida, Graduate School, College of Arts and Sciences, Department of Humanities and Cultural Studies, Tampa, FL 33620-9951. Offers American studies (MA); film studies (MLA); humanities (MLA). Part-time and evening/weekend programs available. *Faculty:* 5 full-time (3 women). *Students:* 23 full-time (13 women), 18 part-time (12 women); includes 9 Black or African American, non-Hispanic/Latino; 4 Hispanic/Latino; 2 Two or more races, non-Hispanic/Latino, 1 international. Average age 34. 34 applicants, 47% accepted, 12 enrolled. In 2010, 9 master's awarded. *Degree requirements:* For master's, comprehensive exam, thesis. *Entrance requirements:* For master's, GRE General Test, minimum GPA of 3.0 in last 60 hours, academic writing sample. Additional exam requirements/recommendations for international students: Required—TOEFL (minimum score 550 paper-based; 213 computer-based). *Application deadline:* For fall admission, 2/15 priority date for domestic students, 1/2 for international students; for spring admission, 10/15 priority date for domestic students, 6/1 for international students. Application fee: $30. *Financial support:* Scholarships/grants available. Financial award application deadline: 4/1. *Faculty research:* American South, American autobiography, material culture, critical theory, cultural studies. *Unit head:* Daniel Belgrad, Chairperson, 813-974-9388, Fax: 813-974-9409, E-mail: dbelgrad@cas.usf.edu. *Application contact:* Maria Cizmic, Program Director, 813-974-9383, Fax: 813-974-9409, E-mail: mcizmic@cas.usf.edu.

University of Toronto, School of Graduate Studies, Humanities Division, Cinema Studies Institute, Toronto, ON M5S 1A1, Canada. Offers MA.

University of Wisconsin–Madison, Graduate School, College of Letters and Science, Department of Communication Arts, Madison, WI 53706-1380. Offers communication science (MA, PhD); film (MA, PhD); media and cultural studies (MA, PhD); rhetoric (MA, PhD). Terminal master's awarded for partial completion of doctoral program. *Degree requirements:* For master's, one foreign language, thesis (for some programs); for doctorate, one foreign language, thesis/dissertation. *Entrance requirements:* For master's and doctorate, GRE General Test, minimum GPA of 3.5. Electronic applications accepted. *Expenses:* Tuition, state resident: full-time $9887; part-time $617.96 per credit. Tuition, nonresident: full-time $24,054; part-time $1503.40 per credit. Required fees: $67.63 per credit. Tuition and fees vary according to reciprocity agreements.

Wilfrid Laurier University, Faculty of Graduate and Postdoctoral Studies, Faculty of Arts, Department of English and Film Studies, Waterloo, ON N2L 3C5, Canada. Offers gender and genre (MA, PhD); nation, diaspora, culture (PhD); textuality, media and print studies (PhD). *Faculty:* 22 full-time (14 women). *Students:* 29 full-time (16 women), 1 (woman) part-time. 71 applicants, 48% accepted, 18 enrolled. In 2010, 15 master's, 2 doctorates awarded. *Degree requirements:* For master's, thesis optional; for doctorate, thesis/dissertation. *Entrance requirements:* For master's, honours BA or the equivalent in English, minimum B+ in English courses above first year level; for doctorate, MA in English, minimum A- average in graduate work. Additional exam requirements/recommendations for international students: Recommended—TOEFL (minimum score 89 iBT). *Application deadline:* For fall admission, 2/1 priority date for domestic and international students. Application fee: $100. Electronic applications accepted. Tuition and fees charges are reported in Canadian dollars. *Expenses:* Tuition, area resident: Full-time $15,300 Canadian dollars; part-time $1200 Canadian dollars per credit. International tuition: $21,300 Canadian dollars full-time. Required fees: $650 Canadian dollars; $100 Canadian dollars per credit. Tuition and fees vary according to course load, degree level, campus/location and program. *Financial support:* In 2010–11, 44 fellowships, 44 teaching assistantships were awarded; career-related internships or fieldwork, scholarships/grants, health care benefits, and unspecified assistantships also available. *Faculty research:* Gender and genre, Canadian studies, early modern studies, postcolonial studies, nineteenth century studies. *Unit head:* Dr. Tanis MacDonald, Graduate Coordinator, 519-884-0710 Ext. 2931, Fax: 519-884-8307, E-mail: tmacdonald@wlu.ca. *Application contact:* Jennifer Williams, Graduate Admissions and Records Officer, 519-884-0710 Ext. 3536, Fax: 519-884-1020, E-mail: gradstudies@wlu.ca.

Yale University, Graduate School of Arts and Sciences, Department of East Asian Languages and Literatures, New Haven, CT 06520. Offers East Asian languages and literatures (PhD); East Asian languages and literatures and film studies (PhD). *Degree requirements:* For doctorate, 2 foreign languages, thesis/dissertation. *Entrance requirements:* For doctorate, GRE General Test.

Yale University, Graduate School of Arts and Sciences, Department of Slavic Languages and Literatures, New Haven, CT 06520. Offers medieval Slavic literature and philology (PhD); Polish literature (PhD); Russian literature (PhD); Slavic languages and literatures and film studies (PhD). *Degree requirements:* For doctorate, 3 foreign languages, thesis/dissertation. *Entrance requirements:* For doctorate, GRE General Test.

Yale University, Graduate School of Arts and Sciences, Interdisciplinary Program in Film Studies, New Haven, CT 06520. Offers PhD.

Section 6
Performing Arts

This section contains a directory of institutions offering graduate work in performing arts, followed by an in-depth entry submitted by an institution that chose to prepare a detailed program description. Additional information about programs listed in the directory but not augmented by an in-depth entry may be obtained by writing directly to the dean of a graduate school or chair of a department at the address given in the directory.

For programs offering related work, see also in this book *Area and Cultural Studies, Art and Art History, Communication and Media,* and *Film, Television, and Video.* In another guide in this series: *Graduate Programs in Business, Education, Health, Information Studies, Law & Social Work*

See *Leisure Studies and Recreation, Subject Areas (Music Education),* and *Physical Education and Kinesiology*

CONTENTS

Dance

Arizona State University, Herberger Institute for Design and the Arts, Department of Dance, Tempe, AZ 85287-0304. Offers dance (MFA); dance (interdisciplinary digital media and performance) (MFA). *Faculty:* 11 full-time (8 women). *Students:* 16 full-time (15 women), 1 (woman) part-time; includes 3 minority (1 Black or African American, non-Hispanic/Latino; 2 Two or more races, non-Hispanic/Latino), 1 international. Average age 26. 20 applicants, 55% accepted, 5 enrolled. In 2010, 5 master's awarded. *Degree requirements:* For master's, thesis optional, project, written document and oral defense, interactive Program of Study (iPOS) submitted before completing 50 percent of required credit hours. *Entrance requirements:* For master's, personal statement relating to school's core values, resume, 3 letters of recommendation from professionals in the dance field. *Application deadline:* For fall admission, 12/1 for domestic and international students. Application fee: $70 ($90 for international students). Electronic applications accepted. *Expenses:* Tuition, state resident: full-time $8510; part-time $608 per credit. Tuition, nonresident: full-time $16,542; part-time $919 per credit. Required fees: $339; $110 per credit. Part-time tuition and fees vary according to course load. *Financial support:* In 2010–11, 3 research assistantships with full and partial tuition reimbursements (averaging $9,750 per year), 10 teaching assistantships with full and partial tuition reimbursements (averaging $6,599 per year) were awarded; fellowships with full and partial tuition reimbursements, institutionally sponsored loans, scholarships/grants, and tuition waivers (full and partial) also available. Financial award application deadline: 3/1. Total annual research expenditures: $27,955. *Unit head:* Simon Dove, Director, 480-965-3428, Fax: 480-965-2247, E-mail: simon.dove@asu.edu. *Application contact:* Graduate Admissions, 480-965-6113.

Bennington College, Graduate Programs, MFA in Dance Program, Bennington, VT 05201. Offers MFA. Part-time programs available. *Faculty:* 3 full-time (2 women), 3 part-time/adjunct (2 women). *Students:* 2 full-time (0 women); includes 1 Black or African American, non-Hispanic/Latino. Average age 38. 9 applicants, 0% accepted, 0 enrolled. *Degree requirements:* For master's, performances. *Application deadline:* For fall admission, 2/1 for domestic students. Application fee: $60. *Expenses:* Tuition: Full-time $20,950; part-time $2935 per course. One-time fee: $75. Tuition and fees vary according to program. *Financial support:* In 2010–11, 2 students received support, including 2 teaching assistantships (averaging $20,950 per year); unspecified assistantships also available. Financial award application deadline: 4/1; financial award applicants required to submit FAFSA. *Faculty research:* Exploration of relationship between emergent improvisation and complex systems. *Unit head:* Terry Creach, Professor, 802-440-4536, E-mail: tcreach@bennington.edu. *Application contact:* Mary Surdam, Admissions Coordinator, 802-440-4887, Fax: 802-440-4320, E-mail: admissions@bennington.edu.

California Institute of the Arts, School of Dance, Valencia, CA 91355-2340. Offers MFA, Adv C. *Accreditation:* NASD. *Degree requirements:* For master's, thesis presentation. *Entrance requirements:* For master's, audition, video of choreography. Additional exam requirements/recommendations for international students: Required—TOEFL.

California State University, Fullerton, Graduate Studies, College of the Arts, Department of Theatre and Dance, Fullerton, CA 92834-9480. Offers acting (MFA); acting and directing (MA); dance (MA); directing (MFA); dramatic literature/criticism (MA); oral interpretation (MA); playwriting (MA); technical theater (MA); technical theater and design (MFA); television (MA); theatre for children (MA); theatre history (MA). *Accreditation:* NAST (one or more programs are accredited). Part-time programs available. *Students:* 17 full-time (9 women), 1 part-time (0 women); includes 2 Hispanic/Latino; 1 Two or more races, non-Hispanic/Latino. Average age 29. 11 applicants, 27% accepted, 3 enrolled. In 2010, 7 master's awarded. *Degree requirements:* For master's, oral and written exam, project or thesis. *Entrance requirements:* For master's, major in theatre or related field, audition or interview, minimum GPA of 2.5 in last 60 units of course work. Application fee: $55. *Financial support:* Career-related internships or fieldwork, Federal Work-Study, institutionally sponsored loans, and scholarships/grants available. Support available to part-time students. Financial award application deadline: 3/1; financial award applicants required to submit FAFSA. *Unit head:* Dr. Susan Hallman, Chair, 657-278-3628. *Application contact:* Admissions/Applications, 657-278-2371.

California State University, Long Beach, Graduate Studies, College of the Arts, Department of Dance, Long Beach, CA 90840. Offers MA, MFA. *Accreditation:* NASD. Part-time programs available. *Faculty:* 5 full-time (4 women), 3 part-time/adjunct (2 women). *Students:* 10 full-time (7 women); includes 1 Asian, non-Hispanic/Latino. Average age 28. 24 applicants, 21% accepted, 4 enrolled. In 2010, 1 master's awarded. *Degree requirements:* For master's, thesis. *Application deadline:* Applications are processed on a rolling basis. Application fee: $5. Electronic applications accepted. *Financial support:* Federal Work-Study, institutionally sponsored loans, scholarships/grants, and traineeships available. Financial award application deadline: 3/2. *Unit head:* Prof. Cyrus Parker-Jeannette, Chair, 562-985-4747, Fax: 562-985-7896, E-mail: cyparker@csulb.edu. *Application contact:* Dr. Colleen Dunagan, Graduate Advisor, 562-985-7040, Fax: 562-985-7896, E-mail: cdunagan@csulb.edu.

California State University, Sacramento, Graduate Studies, College of Arts and Letters, Department of Theatre and Dance, Sacramento, CA 95819. Offers MA. Part-time programs available. *Degree requirements:* For master's, thesis or alternative, writing proficiency exam. *Entrance requirements:* For master's, GRE General Test, BA in drama or equivalent, minimum GPA of 2.5 during previous 2 years of course work. Additional exam requirements/recommendations for international students: Required—TOEFL. Electronic applications accepted.

Case Western Reserve University, School of Graduate Studies, Department of Theater and Dance, Cleveland, OH 44106. Offers acting (MFA); contemporary dance (MFA); dance (MA); theater (MFA). *Faculty:* 8 full-time (3 women), 1 part-time/adjunct (0 women). *Students:* 14 full-time (9 women); includes 1 Black or African American, non-Hispanic/Latino; 1 Hispanic/Latino, 3 international. Average age 27. 5 applicants, 40% accepted, 2 enrolled. In 2010, 10 master's awarded. *Degree requirements:* For master's, thesis, oral presentation and defense, portfolio, thesis concert production and presentation (MFA). *Entrance requirements:* For master's, audition, interview. Additional exam requirements/recommendations for international students: Required—TOEFL (minimum score 550 paper-based; 213 computer-based; 79 iBT). *Application deadline:* For fall admission, 1/1 priority date for domestic students. Applications are processed on a rolling basis. Application fee: $50. Electronic applications accepted. *Financial support:* Fellowships, career-related internships or fieldwork and tuition waivers (full and partial) available. Financial award application deadline: 1/1. *Faculty research:* Playwriting; history of theater; participation in professional area theaters in performing, design, acting, coaching, and dance5. *Unit head:* Ron Wilson, Chairman, 216-368-6142, Fax: 216-368-5184, E-mail: ron.wilson@case.edu. *Application contact:* Scarlett Grala, Administrative Assistant, 216-368-4868, Fax: 216-368-5184, E-mail: ksg@po.cwru.edu.

The College at Brockport, State University of New York, School of the Arts, Humanities and Social Sciences, Department of Dance, Brockport, NY 14420-2997. Offers dance (MA, MFA), including choreography/performance (MA), dance education (preK-12) (MA), dance studies (MA). *Accreditation:* NASD. Part-time programs available. *Students:* 21 full-time (20 women), 3 part-time (all women); includes 1 Black or African American, non-Hispanic/Latino; 3 Asian, non-Hispanic/Latino; 1 Hispanic/Latino. 30 applicants, 63% accepted, 13 enrolled. In 2010, 6 master's awarded. *Degree requirements:* For master's, thesis or alternative. *Entrance requirements:* For master's, local writing assessment assignment, audition/interview, minimum GPA of 3.0, letters of recommendation. Additional exam requirements/recommendations for international students: Required—TOEFL (minimum score 550 paper-based; 213 computer-based; 79 iBT). *Application deadline:* For fall admission, 4/15 priority date for domestic and international students. Application fee: $50. Electronic applications accepted. *Financial support:* In 2010–11, 3 teaching assistantships with full tuition reimbursements (averaging $6,000 per year) were awarded; Federal Work-Study, scholarships/grants, and unspecified assistantships also available. Support available to part-time students. Financial award application deadline: 3/15; financial award applicants required to submit FAFSA. *Faculty research:* Choreography and performance, world dance and culture, dance process and theory, dance education, dance science and somatics. *Unit head:* Dr. Maura Keefe, Chairperson, 585-395-2153, Fax: 585-395-5134, E-mail: mkeefe@brockport.edu. *Application contact:* Dr. Maura Keefe, Graduate Program Director, 585-395-5302, Fax: 585-395-5134, E-mail: mkeefe@brockport.edu.

Florida State University, The Graduate School, College of Visual Arts, Theatre and Dance, School of Dance, Tallahassee, FL 32306-2120. Offers American dance studies (MA); dance (MFA); studio and related studies (MA). *Accreditation:* NASD. *Faculty:* 15 full-time (9 women), 3 part-time/adjunct (2 women). *Students:* 27 full-time (26 women); includes 6 minority (all Black or African American, non-Hispanic/Latino). Average age 28. 24 applicants, 58% accepted, 9 enrolled. In 2010, 14 master's awarded. *Degree requirements:* For master's, comprehensive exam (for some programs), thesis (for some programs), technical proficiency; 1 foreign language (MA in American dance studies). *Entrance requirements:* For master's, GRE General Test (MA in American dance studies), audition, writing sample, interview. Additional exam requirements/recommendations for international students: Required—TOEFL (minimum score 550 paper-based; 80 iBT). *Application deadline:* For fall admission, 6/1 priority date for domestic and international students; for spring admission, 11/1 priority date for domestic and international students. Applications are processed on a rolling basis. Application fee: $30. Electronic applications accepted. *Expenses:* Tuition, state resident: full-time $8238.24. *Financial support:* In 2010–11, 27 students received support, including 7 research assistantships with full tuition reimbursements available (averaging $5,000 per year), 20 teaching assistantships with full tuition reimbursements available (averaging $5,000 per year); fellowships with full tuition reimbursements available, scholarships/grants, health care benefits, and unspecified assistantships also available. Financial award application deadline: 6/30; financial award applicants required to submit FAFSA. *Faculty research:* Choreography, performance, dance and cultural significance, American dance history, dance technology. Total annual research expenditures: $131,959. *Unit head:* Russell Sandifer, Professor and Co-Chair, 850-644-1024, Fax: 850-644-1277, E-mail: rsandifer@fsu.edu. *Application contact:* Prof. Patricia Phillips, Co-Chair, 850-644-1024, Fax: 850-644-1277, E-mail: pphillips@fsu.edu.

George Mason University, College of Visual and Performing Arts, Program in Dance, Fairfax, VA 22030. Offers MFA. *Faculty:* 8 full-time (5 women), 8 part-time/adjunct (7 women). *Students:* 2 applicants. In 2010, 1 master's awarded. *Degree requirements:* For master's, choreographed performance. *Entrance requirements:* For master's, video of choreography or performance, resume, 3 letters of recommendation, curriculum vitae. Additional exam requirements/recommendations for international students: Required—TOEFL (minimum score 570 paper-based; 230 computer-based; 88 iBT). *Application deadline:* For fall admission, 4/1 for domestic students. Application fee: $100. Electronic applications accepted. *Expenses:* Tuition, state resident: full-time $8192; part-time $440 per credit hour. Tuition, nonresident: full-time $22,952; part-time $1055 per credit hour. Required fees: $2364; $99 per credit hour. *Financial support:* Career-related internships or fieldwork, Federal Work-Study, scholarships/grants, and unspecified assistantships available. Financial award application deadline: 3/1; financial award applicants required to submit FAFSA. *Faculty research:* Choreography, performance. *Unit head:* Elizabeth Price, Chair, 703-993-2137, E-mail: eprice@gmu.edu. *Application contact:* Karen Studd, Associate Professor, 703-993-3196, E-mail: kstudd@gmu.edu.

The George Washington University, Columbian College of Arts and Sciences, Department of Theatre and Dance, Washington, DC 20052. Offers classical acting (MFA); dance (MFA); design (MFA). Part-time and evening/weekend programs available. *Faculty:* 10 full-time (6 women), 20 part-time/adjunct (12 women). *Students:* 19 full-time (12 women), 18 part-time (10 women); includes 4 Black or African American, non-Hispanic/Latino; 1 Asian, non-Hispanic/Latino; 1 Native Hawaiian or other Pacific Islander, non-Hispanic/Latino, 3 international. Average age 34. 77 applicants, 34% accepted. In 2010, 17 master's awarded. *Degree requirements:* For master's, thesis. *Entrance requirements:* For master's, minimum GPA of 3.0, portfolio. Additional exam requirements/recommendations for international students: Required—TOEFL (minimum score 550 paper-based; 213 computer-based; 80 iBT). *Application deadline:* For fall admission, 8/1 priority date for domestic students; for spring admission, 10/1 priority date for domestic students. Applications are processed on a rolling basis. Application fee: $75. Electronic applications accepted. *Financial support:* In 2010–11, 2 students received support; fellowships with tuition reimbursements available, teaching assistantships with tuition reimbursements available, career-related internships or fieldwork, Federal Work-Study, and tuition waivers available. *Unit head:* Alan G. Wade, Interim Chair, 202-994-3664, E-mail: awade@gwu.edu. *Application contact:* Information Contact, 202-994-8072, E-mail: trdanews@gwu.edu.

Hollins University, Graduate Programs, Program in Dance, Roanoke, VA 24020-1603. Offers MFA. Part-time programs available. *Degree requirements:* For master's, thesis. *Entrance requirements:* For master's, videotape of selected works, 3 letters of recommendation, resume. Additional exam requirements/recommendations for international students: Required—TOEFL (minimum score 550 paper-based; 213 computer-based; 79 iBT). Electronic applications accepted.

Mills College, Graduate Studies, Department of Dance, Oakland, CA 94613-1000. Offers dance (MA, MFA), including choreography and performance (MA). Part-time programs available. *Faculty:* 5 full-time (4 women), 9 part-time/adjunct (7 women). *Students:* 18 full-time (16 women); includes 2 Black or African American, non-Hispanic/Latino; 2 Asian, non-Hispanic/Latino; 2 Hispanic/Latino. Average age 30. 43 applicants, 58% accepted, 18 enrolled. In 2010, 8 master's awarded. *Degree requirements:* For master's, comprehensive exam, thesis, performance. *Entrance requirements:* For master's, DVD recording of original choreography of up to two choreographic works (for MFA); writing sample with topic related to field of dance studies (for MA). Additional exam requirements/recommendations for international students: Required—TOEFL. *Application deadline:* For fall admission, 2/1 priority date for domestic students, 12/15 for international students. Applications are processed on a rolling basis. Application fee: $50. *Expenses:* Tuition: Full-time $28,280; part-time $7070 per course. Required fees: $1058; $1058 per year. Tuition and fees vary according to program. *Financial support:* In 2010–11, 18 students received support, including 18 fellowships (averaging $4,852 per year), 9 teaching assistantships with partial tuition reimbursements available (averaging $4,886 per year); scholarships/grants and unspecified assistantships also available. Financial award application deadline: 2/1; financial award applicants required to submit FAFSA. *Faculty research:* Modern techniques, movement for actors, choreography, dance criticism and analysis, dance and literature. *Unit head:* Sonya Delwaide, Head, 510-430-3258, E-mail: sdelwaid@mills.edu. *Application contact:* Jessica King, Graduate Admission Specialist, 510-430-3305, Fax: 510-430-2159, E-mail: grad-studies@mills.edu.

New York University, Steinhardt School of Culture, Education, and Human Development, Department of Music and Performing Arts Professions, Program in Dance Education, New York, NY 10012-1019. Offers dance education (Ed D, PhD); teaching dance in higher education and the professions (MA), including ABT ballet pedagogy. Part-time programs available. *Faculty:* 2 full-time (both women). *Students:* 53 full-time (51 women), 29 part-time (25 women); includes 15 Black or African American, non-Hispanic/Latino; 5 Asian, non-Hispanic/Latino; 2 Hispanic/Latino, 12 international. Average age 29. 58 applicants, 83% accepted, 38 enrolled. In 2010, 41 master's awarded. *Degree requirements:* For master's, thesis (for some programs); for doctorate, thesis/dissertation. *Entrance requirements:* For master's, audition, interview; for doctorate, GRE General Test, audition, interview. Additional exam requirements/recommendations for international students: Required—TOEFL. *Application deadline:* For fall admission, 12/15 priority date for domestic and international students; for spring admission, 11/1 for domestic and international students. Applications are processed on a rolling basis. Application fee: $75. Electronic applications accepted. *Financial support:* Career-related internships or fieldwork, Federal Work-Study, institutionally sponsored loans, and scholarships/grants available. Support available to part-time students. Financial award application deadline: 2/1; financial award applicants required to submit FAFSA. *Faculty research:* Dance cognition and creativity, technology in dance, development of teacher expertise, ballet pedagogy. *Unit head:* Dr. Susan Koff, Director, 212-998-5424, Fax: 212-995-4043, E-mail: sk120@nyu.edu. *Application contact:* 212-998-5030, Fax: 212-995-4328, E-mail: steinhardt.gradadmissions@nyu.edu.

New York University, Tisch School of the Arts, Department of Dance, New York, NY 10012-1019. Offers MFA. *Faculty:* 11 full-time, 16 part-time/adjunct. *Students:* 29 full-time (25 women), 1 part-time (0 women); includes 2 Black or African American, non-Hispanic/Latino; 3 Asian, non-Hispanic/Latino. Average age 27. 81 applicants, 31% accepted, 15 enrolled. In 2010, 13 master's awarded. *Entrance requirements:* For master's, audition. Additional exam requirements/recommendations for international students: Required—TOEFL or IELTS. *Application deadline:* For fall admission, 1/1 priority date for domestic students, 1/1 for international students. Application fee: $60. Electronic applications accepted. *Financial support:* In 2010–11, 19 fellowships with full and partial tuition reimbursements were awarded; Federal Work-Study, institutionally sponsored loans, tuition waivers (partial), and unspecified assistantships also available. Financial award application deadline: 2/15; financial award applicants required to submit FAFSA. *Unit head:* Cherylyn Lavagnino, Chair, 212-998-1980, Fax: 212-995-4644. *Application contact:* Dan Sandford, Director of Graduate Admissions, 212-998-1918, Fax: 212-995-4060, E-mail: tisch.gradadmissions@nyu.edu.

New York University, Tisch School of the Arts and Graduate School of Arts and Science, Department of Performance Studies, New York, NY 10012-1019. Offers MA, PhD. *Faculty:* 12 full-time (7 women), 4 part-time/adjunct (3 women). *Students:* 63 full-time (46 women), 1 (woman) part-time; includes 4 Black or African American, non-Hispanic/Latino; 4 Asian, non-Hispanic/Latino; 8 Hispanic/Latino. Average age 31. 198 applicants, 51% accepted, 54 enrolled. In 2010, 36 master's, 7 doctorates awarded. *Degree requirements:* For doctorate, one foreign language, comprehensive exam, thesis/dissertation, dissertation defense, qualifying exam. *Entrance requirements:* For master's, sample of written work; for doctorate, master's degree, writing sample. Additional exam requirements/recommendations for international students: Required—TOEFL or IELTS. *Application deadline:* For fall admission, 12/1 for domestic and international students. Application fee: $60. Electronic applications accepted. *Expenses:* Contact institution. *Financial support:* In 2010–11, 32 students received support, including 24 fellowships with full and partial tuition reimbursements available, 4 research assistantships, 4 teaching assistantships; Federal Work-Study, institutionally sponsored loans, tuition waivers (partial), and unspecified assistantships also available. Financial award application deadline: 2/15; financial award applicants required to submit CSS PROFILE or FAFSA. *Faculty research:* Performance theory, dance, folklore and festivals, postcolonial theory, anthropology and gender studies. *Unit head:* Jose Munoz, Chair, 212-998-1620, Fax: 212-995-4571, E-mail: performance.studies@nyu.edu. *Application contact:* Dan Sandford, Director of Graduate Admissions, 212-998-1918, Fax: 212-995-4060, E-mail: tisch.gradadmissions@nyu.edu.

Northern Illinois University, Graduate School, College of Visual and Performing Arts, School of Theatre and Dance, De Kalb, IL 60115-2854. Offers MFA. *Accreditation:* NAST. Part-time programs available. *Faculty:* 16 full-time (9 women). *Students:* 30 full-time (14 women), 2 part-time (1 woman); includes 2 Black or African American, non-Hispanic/Latino; 1 American Indian or Alaska Native, non-Hispanic/Latino; 2 Hispanic/Latino; 1 Two or more races, non-Hispanic/Latino, 1 international. Average age 26. 43 applicants, 49% accepted, 19 enrolled. In 2010, 14 master's awarded. *Degree requirements:* For master's, comprehensive exam, final project and defense. *Entrance requirements:* For master's, minimum GPA of 2.75, audition or portfolio. Additional exam requirements/recommendations for international students: Required—TOEFL (minimum score 550 paper-based; 213 computer-based). *Application deadline:* For fall admission, 4/1 priority date for domestic students, 5/1 for international students; for spring admission, 10/15 priority date for domestic students, 10/1 for international students. Applications are processed on a rolling basis. Application fee: $30. Electronic applications accepted. *Expenses:* Tuition, state resident: full-time $7200; part-time $300 per credit hour. Tuition, nonresident: full-time $14,400; part-time $600 per credit hour. Required fees: $79 per credit hour. *Financial support:* In 2010–11, 30 teaching assistantships with full tuition reimbursements were awarded; fellowships with full tuition reimbursements, research assistantships with full tuition reimbursements, career-related internships or fieldwork, Federal Work-Study, scholarships/grants, tuition waivers (full), and staff assistantships also available. Support available to part-time students. Financial award applicants required to submit FAFSA. *Faculty research:* Theatre history, choreography, performance art spectacles, storytelling, computer visualization of the ethical space. *Unit head:* Alexander Gelman, Director, 815-753-8253, Fax: 815-753-8415, E-mail: agelman@niu.edu. *Application contact:* Terrence McClellan, Information Contact, 815-753-8257, E-mail: tmcclell@niu.edu.

The Ohio State University, Graduate School, College of Arts and Sciences, Division of Arts and Humanities, Department of Dance, Columbus, OH 43210. Offers choreography (MFA); dance (MA, MFA, PhD); dance and technology (MFA); dance studies (PhD); Labanotation (MFA); lighting (MFA); performance (MFA). *Accreditation:* NASD. *Faculty:* 17. *Students:* 31 full-time (24 women), 7 part-time (5 women); includes 3 Black or African American, non-Hispanic/Latino; 1 Asian, non-Hispanic/Latino; 2 Hispanic/Latino, 4 international. Average age 30. In 2010, 9 master's awarded. *Degree requirements:* For master's, thesis optional. *Entrance requirements:* For master's, GRE General Test (MA); for doctorate, GRE General Test. Additional exam requirements/recommendations for international students: Recommended—TOEFL (minimum score 600 paper-based; 250 computer-based). *Application deadline:* For fall admission, 8/15 priority date for domestic students, 7/1 priority date for international students; for winter admission, 12/1 priority date for domestic students, 11/1 priority date for international students; for spring admission, 3/1 priority date for domestic students, 2/1 priority date for international students. Applications are processed on a rolling basis. Application fee: $40 ($50 for international students). Electronic applications accepted. *Expenses:* Tuition, state resident: full-time $10,605. Tuition, nonresident: full-time $26,535. Tuition and fees vary according to course load and program. *Financial support:* Fellowships, teaching assistantships, Federal Work-Study and institutionally sponsored loans available. Support available to part-time students. *Unit head:* Susan Van Pelt Petry, Chair, 614-292-0984, E-mail: petry.37@osu.edu. *Application contact:* 614-292-9444, Fax: 614-292-3895, E-mail: domestic.grad@osu.edu.

Oklahoma City University, Margaret E. Petree College of Performing Arts, Ann Lacy School of American Dance and Arts Management, Oklahoma City, OK 73106-1402. Offers dance (MFA). *Degree requirements:* For master's, thesis optional. *Entrance requirements:* For master's, minimum GPA of 3.0, audition. Additional exam requirements/recommendations for international students: Required—TOEFL (minimum score 600 paper-based).

Purchase College, State University of New York, Conservatory of Dance, Purchase, NY 10577-1400. Offers MFA. *Degree requirements:* For master's, performance. *Entrance requirements:* For master's, audition. Electronic applications accepted.

Sam Houston State University, College of Arts and Sciences, Department of Theatre and Dance, Huntsville, TX 77341. Offers dance (MFA). *Faculty:* 3 full-time (2 women). *Students:* 9 full-time (7 women), 2 part-time (both women). Average age 26. 4 applicants, 75% accepted, 3 enrolled. In 2010, 1 master's awarded. *Degree requirements:* For master's, thesis, project. *Entrance requirements:* For master's, GRE General Test. Additional exam requirements/recommendations for international students: Required—TOEFL (minimum score 550 paper-based; 213 computer-based; 79 iBT). *Application deadline:* For fall admission, 8/1 for domestic and international students; for spring admission, 12/1 for domestic and international students. Applications are processed on a rolling basis. Application fee: $20. *Expenses:* Tuition, state resident: full-time $1363; part-time $163 per credit hour. Tuition, nonresident: full-time $3856; part-time $473 per credit hour. *Financial support:* Teaching assistantships, career-related internships or fieldwork, Federal Work-Study, and institutionally sponsored loans available. Financial award application deadline: 5/31; financial award applicants required to submit FAFSA. *Unit head:* Penelope Hasekoester, Chair, 936-294-1330, Fax: 936-294-3898, E-mail: drm_pah@shsu.edu. *Application contact:* Penelope Hasekoester, Chair, 936-294-1330, Fax: 936-294-3898, E-mail: drm_pah@shsu.edu.

Sarah Lawrence College, Graduate Studies, Program in Dance, Bronxville, NY 10708-5999. Offers MFA. *Degree requirements:* For master's, performance. *Entrance requirements:* For master's, audition, minimum B average in undergraduate course work.

Smith College, Graduate and Special Programs, Department of Dance, Northampton, MA 01063. Offers MFA. Part-time programs available. *Faculty:* 2 full-time (1 woman), 1 (woman) part-time/adjunct. *Students:* 8 part-time (all women); includes 1 Black or African American, non-Hispanic/Latino. Average age 27. 15 applicants, 27% accepted, 4 enrolled. In 2010, 3 master's awarded. *Degree requirements:* For master's, thesis performance. *Entrance requirements:* For master's, audition. Additional exam requirements/recommendations for international students: Required—TOEFL (minimum score 590 paper-based; 243 computer-based; 97 iBT). *Application deadline:* For fall admission, 1/15 for domestic and international students. Application fee: $60. *Expenses:* Tuition: Full-time $14,520; part-time $1210 per credit. *Financial support:* In 2010–11, 8 students received support, including 8 teaching assistantships with full tuition reimbursements available (averaging $5,955 per year); institutionally sponsored loans and scholarships/grants also available. Support available to part-time students. Financial award application deadline: 1/15; financial award applicants required to submit CSS PROFILE or FAFSA. *Unit head:* Rodger Blum, Chair, 413-585-3234, E-mail: rblum@smith.edu. *Application contact:* Susan Waltner, Graduate Student Adviser, 413-585-3236, E-mail: swaltner@smith.edu.

Southern Methodist University, Meadows School of the Arts, Division of Dance, Dallas, TX 75275. Offers MFA. *Faculty:* 8 full-time (5 women), 3 part-time/adjunct (all women). *Students:* 1 (woman) part-time. Average age 48. In 2010, 4 master's awarded. *Degree requirements:* For master's, thesis or alternative, written qualifying exam. *Entrance requirements:* For master's, BA or BFA in dance, interview, professional-level experience. Additional exam requirements/recommendations for international students: Required—TOEFL (minimum score 550 paper-based; 213 computer-based; 80 iBT). *Application deadline:* For fall admission, 3/1 priority date for domestic and international students. Applications are processed on a rolling basis. Application fee: $75. *Financial support:* In 2010–11, 4 teaching assistantships (averaging $3,000 per year) were awarded; scholarships/grants and unspecified assistantships also available. Financial award application deadline: 3/1; financial award applicants required to submit FAFSA. *Faculty research:* Labanotation, dance preservation and documentation, dance history. *Unit head:* Myra Woodruff, Chair, 214-768-2718, Fax: 214-768-4540, E-mail: woodruff@smu.edu. *Application contact:* Jean Cherry, Director of Graduate Admissions and Records, 214-768-3765, Fax: 214-768-3272, E-mail: jcherry@smu.edu.

Temple University, Esther Boyer College of Music and Dance, Department of Dance, Philadelphia, PA 19122-6096. Offers Ed M, MFA, PhD. *Accreditation:* NASD. Part-time programs available. *Faculty:* 9 full-time (6 women). *Students:* 41 full-time (35 women), 3 part-time (all women); includes 4 Black or African American, non-Hispanic/Latino; 2 Asian, non-Hispanic/Latino; 4 Hispanic/Latino, 6 international. 33 applicants, 45% accepted, 11 enrolled. In 2010, 13 master's, 1 doctorate awarded. *Degree requirements:* For master's, thesis optional, professional project; for doctorate, thesis/dissertation. *Entrance requirements:* For master's and doctorate, minimum GPA of 3.0, audition/interview. Additional exam requirements/recommendations for international students: Required—TOEFL. *Application deadline:* For fall admission, 1/15 for domestic students, 12/15 for international students. Application fee: $50. Electronic applications accepted. *Financial support:* Fellowships, teaching assistantships, Federal Work-Study, scholarships/grants, and tuition waivers available. Financial award application deadline: 1/15; financial award applicants required to submit FAFSA. *Faculty research:* Cultural studies, dance education, dance technology, aesthetics. *Unit head:* Dr. Kariamu Welsh, Chair, 215-204-6286, Fax: 215-204-4347, E-mail: kariamu@temple.edu. *Application contact:* Dr. Kariamu Welsh, Chair, 215-204-6286, Fax: 215-204-4347, E-mail: kariamu@temple.edu.

Texas Tech University, Graduate School, College of Visual and Performing Arts, Fine Arts Doctoral Program, Lubbock, TX 79409. Offers arts (PhD). *Accreditation:* NAST. Part-time programs available. *Students:* 46 full-time (22 women), 32 part-time (15 women); includes 2 Black or African American, non-Hispanic/Latino; 1 American Indian or Alaska Native, non-Hispanic/Latino; 1 Asian, non-Hispanic/Latino; 5 Hispanic/Latino, 10 international. Average age 35. 36 applicants, 44% accepted, 9 enrolled. In 2010, 14 doctorates awarded. *Degree requirements:* For doctorate, comprehensive exam, thesis/dissertation. *Entrance requirements:* For doctorate, GRE General Test. Additional exam requirements/recommendations for international students: Required—TOEFL (minimum score 550 paper-based; 213 computer-based; 79 iBT). *Application deadline:* For fall admission, 6/1 priority date for domestic students, 1/15 priority date for international students; for spring admission, 9/1 priority date for domestic students, 6/15 priority date for international students. Applications are processed on a rolling basis. Application fee: $50 ($75 for international students). Electronic applications accepted. *Expenses:* Tuition, state resident: full-time $5495.76; part-time $228.99 per credit hour. Tuition, nonresident: full-time $12,936; part-time $538.99 per credit hour. Required fees: $2674; $36 per credit hour. $905 per semester. *Financial support:* Research assistantships with partial tuition reimbursements, teaching assistantships with partial tuition reimbursements available. Financial award application deadline: 4/15; financial award applicants required to submit FAFSA. *Faculty research:* Art criticism and theory, music, theatre arts; arts education; history of arts. *Unit head:* Dr. Brian D. Steele, Director, 806-742-0700, Fax: 806-742-0695, E-mail: brian.steele@ttu.edu. *Application contact:* Dr. Brian D. Steele, Director, 806-742-0700, Fax: 806-742-0695, E-mail: brian.steele@ttu.edu.

Texas Woman's University, Graduate School, College of Arts and Sciences, School of the Arts, Department of Dance, Denton, TX 76201. Offers MA, MFA, PhD. *Accreditation:* NASD. *Faculty:* 6 full-time (5 women). *Students:* 28 full-time (27 women), 20 part-time (17 women); includes 3 Black or African American, non-Hispanic/Latino; 1 Asian, non-Hispanic/Latino; 3 Hispanic/Latino, 5 international. Average age 36. 26 applicants, 54% accepted, 10 enrolled. In 2010, 5 master's, 2 doctorates awarded. *Degree requirements:* For master's, thesis (for some programs), choreography portfolio, professional paper; for doctorate, comprehensive exam, thesis/dissertation. *Entrance requirements:* For master's, audition, 3 letters of recommendation, interview, writing sample, solo performance, resume, personal essay; for doctorate, interview, 3 letters of reference, scholarly writing sample, resume, personal essay, curriculum vitae, sample syllabus for university-level course. Additional exam requirements/recommendations for international students: Required—TOEFL (minimum score 550 paper-based; 213 computer-based; 79 iBT). *Application deadline:* For fall admission, 2/1 priority date for domestic and international students. Applications are processed on a rolling basis. Application fee: $50 ($75 for international students). Electronic applications accepted. *Expenses:* Tuition, state resident: full-time $3834; part-time $213 per credit hour. Tuition, nonresident: full-time $9468; part-time $526 per credit hour. Required fees: $1247; $220 per credit hour. *Financial support:* In 2010–11, 32 students received support, including 10 research assistantships (averaging $12,942 per year), 9 teaching assistantships (averaging $12,942 per year); career-related internships or fieldwork, Federal Work-Study, institutionally sponsored loans, scholarships/grants, traineeships, health care benefits, tuition waivers (partial), and unspecified assistantships also available. Support available to part-time students. Financial award application deadline: 3/1; financial award applicants required to submit FAFSA. *Faculty research:* Performance, choreography, pedagogy, somatic practices, theorizing artistic practice. *Unit head:* Dr. Penelope Hanstein, Chair, 940-898-2085, Fax: 940-898-2098, E-mail: dance@twu.edu. *Application contact:* Dr. Samuel Wheeler, Assistant Director of Admissions, 940-898-3188, Fax: 940-898-3081, E-mail: wheelersr@twu.edu.

Tulane University, School of Liberal Arts, Department of Theatre and Dance, New Orleans, LA 70118-5669. Offers design and technical production (MFA). *Entrance requirements:* For master's, GRE General Test, minimum B average in undergraduate course work. Additional exam requirements/recommendations for international students: Required—TOEFL. Electronic applications accepted. *Faculty research:* Scene design, stage management, costume design, technical direction, lighting design.

Université du Québec à Montréal, Graduate Programs, Program in Dance, Montréal, QC H3C 3P8, Canada. Offers MA. Part-time programs available. *Degree requirements:* For master's,

Dance

Université du Québec à Montréal (continued)

thesis optional. *Entrance requirements:* For master's, appropriate bachelor's degree or equivalent and proficiency in French.

The University of Arizona, College of Fine Arts, School of Dance, Tucson, AZ 85721. Offers MFA. *Faculty:* 7 full-time (5 women). *Students:* 11 full-time (7 women), 1 part-time; includes 5 minority (2 Asian, non-Hispanic/Latino; 3 Two or more races, non-Hispanic/Latino), 1 international. Average age 33. 15 applicants, 40% accepted, 6 enrolled. In 2010, 5 master's awarded. Application fee: $75. *Expenses:* Tuition, state resident: full-time $7692. *Financial support:* In 2010–11, 10 teaching assistantships with full tuition reimbursements (averaging $16,581 per year) were awarded. *Unit head:* Jory Hancock, Interim Dean and Director, 520-626-8030, E-mail: jory@email.arizona.edu. *Application contact:* General Information, 520-621-1301, Fax: 520-621-1307, E-mail: finearts@email.arizona.edu.

University of California, Irvine, Claire Trevor School of the Arts, Department of Dance, Irvine, CA 92697. Offers MFA. *Students:* 18 full-time (16 women); includes 2 minority (1 Black or African American, non-Hispanic/Latino; 1 Hispanic/Latino), 2 international. Average age 28. 34 applicants, 35% accepted, 9 enrolled. In 2010, 10 master's awarded. *Degree requirements:* For master's, thesis. *Entrance requirements:* For master's, minimum GPA of 3.0. *Application deadline:* For fall admission, 1/15 priority date for domestic students, 1/15 for international students. Applications are processed on a rolling basis. Application fee: $80 ($100 for international students). Electronic applications accepted. *Financial support:* Fellowships, teaching assistantships, institutionally sponsored loans, traineeships, health care benefits, and unspecified assistantships available. Financial award application deadline: 3/1; financial award applicants required to submit FAFSA. *Faculty research:* Dance science, digital technology, history and theory, choreography. *Unit head:* Alan Terricciano, Chair, 949-824-5744, Fax: 949-824-4563, E-mail: aterricc@uci.edu. *Application contact:* Diane Enriquez, Department Manager, 949-824-6929, Fax: 949-824-4563, E-mail: d.enriquez@uci.edu.

University of California, Los Angeles, Graduate Division, School of the Arts and Architecture, Department of World Arts and Cultures, Los Angeles, CA 90095. Offers culture and performance (MA, PhD); dance (MFA). *Faculty:* 18 full-time (9 women). *Students:* 48 full-time (33 women); includes 21 minority (4 Black or African American, non-Hispanic/Latino; 4 Asian, non-Hispanic/Latino; 12 Hispanic/Latino; 1 Two or more races, non-Hispanic/Latino), 4 international. Average age 32. 77 applicants, 26% accepted, 16 enrolled. In 2010, 6 master's, 2 doctorates awarded. *Degree requirements:* For master's, comprehensive exam or thesis; for doctorate, one foreign language, thesis/dissertation, oral and written qualifying exams. *Entrance requirements:* For master's, minimum GPA of 3.0; for doctorate, GRE General Test, writing sample. Application fee: $70 ($90 for international students). Electronic applications accepted. *Financial support:* In 2010–11, 42 fellowships, 8 research assistantships, 24 teaching assistantships were awarded; Federal Work-Study, institutionally sponsored loans, scholarships/grants, tuition waivers (full and partial), and unspecified assistantships also available. Financial award application deadline: 3/1. *Unit head:* Angelia Leung, Head, 310-206-1336, E-mail: aleung@arts.ucla.edu. *Application contact:* Department Office, 310-825-8537, E-mail: lcblanco@arts.ucla.edu.

University of California, Riverside, Graduate Division, Department of Dance, Riverside, CA 92521. Offers critical dance studies (PhD); experimental choreography (MFA). *Faculty:* 8 full-time (7 women). *Students:* 29 full-time (27 women); includes 2 Black or African American, non-Hispanic/Latino; 2 Asian, non-Hispanic/Latino; 3 Hispanic/Latino, 6 international. Average age 36. 32 applicants, 41% accepted, 6 enrolled. In 2010, 2 master's, 4 doctorates awarded. *Degree requirements:* For doctorate, one foreign language, thesis/dissertation, qualifying exams. *Entrance requirements:* For master's, DVD of choreographed piece (MFA); for doctorate, GRE General Test, minimum GPA of 3.2, writing sample. Additional exam requirements/recommendations for international students: Required—TOEFL (minimum score 550 paper-based; 213 computer-based; 80 iBT). *Application deadline:* For fall admission, 1/5 for domestic and international students. Application fee: $80 ($100 for international students). Electronic applications accepted. *Financial support:* In 2010–11, 13 students received support, including fellowships with full tuition reimbursements available (averaging $12,000 per year), teaching assistantships with full tuition reimbursements available (averaging $15,600 per year); research assistantships with tuition reimbursements available, career-related internships or fieldwork, Federal Work-Study, institutionally sponsored loans, tuition waivers (full and partial), and unspecified assistantships also available. Financial award application deadline: 1/5; financial award applicants required to submit FAFSA. *Faculty research:* Movement analysis, cultural postcolonial gender studies of performance, theories of dance, anthropology of dance, history and reconstruction of dance. *Unit head:* Dr. Linda Tomko, Chair, 951-827-3944, Fax: 951-827-4651, E-mail: linda.tomko@ucr.edu. *Application contact:* Dr. Anthea Kraut, Graduate Adviser, 951-827-3944, Fax: 951-827-4651, E-mail: danceadvising@ucr.edu.

University of Colorado Boulder, Graduate School, College of Arts and Sciences, Department of Theatre and Dance, Boulder, CO 80309. Offers dance (MFA); theatre (MA, PhD). *Faculty:* 15 full-time (8 women). *Students:* 42 full-time (28 women), 8 part-time (5 women); includes 7 minority (4 Black or African American, non-Hispanic/Latino; 3 Hispanic/Latino), 2 international. Average age 34. 61 applicants, 14 enrolled. In 2010, 6 master's, 3 doctorates awarded. Terminal master's awarded for partial completion of doctoral program. *Degree requirements:* For master's, comprehensive exam, thesis; for doctorate, one foreign language, thesis/dissertation. *Entrance requirements:* For master's, GRE General Test (MA), audition (MFA), minimum undergraduate GPA of 2.75. *Application deadline:* For fall admission, 1/15 priority date for domestic students, 12/1 for international students. Application fee: $50 ($60 for international students). *Financial support:* In 2010–11, 16 fellowships (averaging $2,499 per year), 14 research assistantships (averaging $1,463 per year) were awarded; tuition waivers (full) also available. Financial award application deadline: 1/15. *Faculty research:* Dance: performance choreography, pedagogy administration, body therapies, multi-media forms, film/video, cultural studies, non-concert forms, music, poetry/writing/literature, kinesiology, theatre: theatre history, theory and literature, theatre production, acting, directing, dramaturgy and design.

University of Hawaii at Manoa, Graduate Division, College of Arts and Humanities, Department of Theatre and Dance, Honolulu, HI 96822. Offers dance (MA, MFA); theatre (MA, MFA, PhD). Part-time programs available. *Faculty:* 14 full-time (8 women), 7 part-time/adjunct (5 women). *Students:* 53 full-time (37 women), 9 part-time (7 women); includes 21 minority (1 Black or African American, non-Hispanic/Latino; 2 American Indian or Alaska Native, non-Hispanic/Latino; 8 Asian, non-Hispanic/Latino; 1 Hispanic/Latino; 1 Native Hawaiian or other Pacific Islander, non-Hispanic/Latino; 8 Two or more races, non-Hispanic/Latino), 7 international. Average age 33. 71 applicants, 62% accepted, 21 enrolled. In 2010, 13 master's, 1 doctorate awarded. *Degree requirements:* For master's, one foreign language, thesis optional; for doctorate, one foreign language, comprehensive exam, thesis/dissertation. *Entrance requirements:* For master's and doctorate, GRE General Test. Additional exam requirements/recommendations for international students: Required—TOEFL (minimum score 600 paper-based; 250 computer-based; 100 iBT), IELTS (minimum score 7). *Application deadline:* For fall admission, 2/1 for domestic students, 1/15 for international students; for spring admission, 9/1 for domestic students, 8/1 for international students. Application fee: $50. *Financial support:* In 2010–11, 12 students received support, including 26 fellowships, 3 research assistantships, 14 teaching assistantships; Federal Work-Study, institutionally sponsored loans, tuition waivers (full), and unspecified assistantships also available. Financial award application deadline: 2/1. *Faculty research:* Asian theatre, feminist theatre and dance, Russian theatre, Australian theatre. *Unit head:* Dennis Carroll, Chair, 808-956-2588, E-mail: carroll@hawaii.edu. *Application contact:* Dennis Carroll, Chair, 808-956-2588, E-mail: carroll@hawaii.edu.

University of Illinois at Urbana–Champaign, Graduate College, College of Fine and Applied Arts, Department of Dance, Champaign, IL 61820. Offers MFA. *Accreditation:* NASD. *Faculty:* 9 full-time (7 women). *Students:* 11 full-time (9 women), 1 (woman) part-time; includes 2 Hispanic/Latino. 32 applicants, 16% accepted, 3 enrolled. In 2010, 3 master's awarded. *Entrance requirements:* For master's, audition, minimum GPA of 3.0. Additional exam requirements/recommendations for international students: Required—TOEFL (minimum score 550 paper-based; 213 computer-based). *Application deadline:* Applications are processed on a rolling basis. Application fee: $75 ($90 for international students). Electronic applications accepted. *Financial support:* In 2010–11, 6 fellowships, 9 teaching assistantships were awarded; research assistantships, tuition waivers (full and partial) also available. *Unit head:* Jan K. Erkert, Head, 217-333-1010, Fax: 217-333-3000, E-mail: erkert@illinois.edu. *Application contact:* Jacqueline Kinsman, Assistant to the Head, 217-333-1011, Fax: 217-333-3000, E-mail: jkinsman@illinois.edu.

The University of Iowa, Graduate College, College of Liberal Arts and Sciences, Department of Dance, Iowa City, IA 52242-1316. Offers MFA. *Accreditation:* NASD. *Degree requirements:* For master's, thesis, exam. *Entrance requirements:* For master's, minimum GPA of 3.0. Additional exam requirements/recommendations for international students: Required—TOEFL (minimum score 550 paper-based; 213 computer-based; 81 iBT). Electronic applications accepted.

University of Maryland, Baltimore County, Graduate School, College of Arts, Humanities and Social Sciences, Department of Education, Program in Teaching, Baltimore, MD 21250. Offers early childhood education (MAT); elementary education (MAT); secondary education (MAT), including art, biology, chemistry, dance, earth/space science, English, foreign language, mathematics, music, physics, theatre; secondary science (MAT), including social studies. Part-time and evening/weekend programs available. *Faculty:* 24 full-time (18 women), 25 part-time/adjunct (19 women). *Students:* 59 full-time (46 women), 56 part-time (42 women); includes 1 Black or African American, non-Hispanic/Latino; 8 Asian, non-Hispanic/Latino; 3 Hispanic/Latino, 3 international. Average age 31. 88 applicants, 57% accepted, 39 enrolled. In 2010, 106 master's awarded. *Degree requirements:* For master's, comprehensive exam (for some programs), thesis (for some programs). *Entrance requirements:* For master's, PRAXIS I and II, minimum GPA of 3.0. Additional exam requirements/recommendations for international students: Required—TOEFL. *Application deadline:* For fall admission, 6/1 for domestic students; for spring admission, 11/1 for domestic students. Applications are processed on a rolling basis. Application fee: $50. Electronic applications accepted. *Financial support:* In 2010–11, 6 students received support, including research assistantships with full tuition reimbursements available (averaging $12,000 per year); career-related internships or fieldwork, Federal Work-Study, scholarships/grants, tuition waivers, and unspecified assistantships also available. Financial award application deadline: 3/1. *Faculty research:* STEM teacher education, culturally sensitive pedagogy, ESOL/bilingual education, early childhood education, language, literacy and culture. *Unit head:* Dr. Susan M. Blunck, Director, 410-455-2869, Fax: 410-455-3986, E-mail: blunck@umbc.edu. *Application contact:* Cheryl Johnson, 410-455-3388, E-mail: blackwel@umbc.edu.

University of Maryland, College Park, Academic Affairs, College of Arts and Humanities, Department of Dance, College Park, MD 20742. Offers MFA. *Students:* 9 full-time (5 women); includes 1 minority (Black or African American, non-Hispanic/Latino), 1 international. 27 applicants, 15% accepted, 4 enrolled. In 2010, 3 master's awarded. *Degree requirements:* For master's, final project. *Entrance requirements:* For master's, audition/interview, video tapes/writing sample. Additional exam requirements/recommendations for international students: Required—TOEFL. *Application deadline:* For fall admission, 2/1 for domestic and international students. Applications are processed on a rolling basis. Application fee: $75. Electronic applications accepted. *Expenses:* Tuition, state resident: part-time $471 per credit hour. Tuition, nonresident: part-time $1016 per credit hour. Required fees: $337 per term. *Financial support:* In 2010–11, 1 fellowship with full tuition reimbursement (averaging $19,000 per year), 8 teaching assistantships (averaging $19,625 per year) were awarded; research assistantships, Federal Work-Study and scholarships/grants also available. *Faculty research:* Performance and choreography. *Unit head:* Anne Warren, Associate Director of Dance, 301-405-3187, E-mail: awarren@umd.edu. *Application contact:* Dr. Charles A. Caramello, Dean of Graduate School, 301-405-0358, Fax: 301-314-9305.

University of Maryland, College Park, Academic Affairs, College of Arts and Humanities, School of Theatre, Dance and Performance Studies, College Park, MD 20742. Offers dance (MFA); performance (MFA); theatre and performance studies (MA, PhD); theatre design (MFA). *Faculty:* 25 full-time (14 women), 9 part-time/adjunct (6 women). *Students:* 58 full-time (33 women), 2 part-time (1 woman); includes 7 minority (2 Black or African American, non-Hispanic/Latino; 1 Asian, non-Hispanic/Latino; 3 Hispanic/Latino; 1 Native Hawaiian or other Pacific Islander, non-Hispanic/Latino), 4 international. 138 applicants, 26% accepted, 26 enrolled. In 2010, 9 master's, 4 doctorates awarded. *Degree requirements:* For master's, comprehensive exam, thesis optional; for doctorate, thesis/dissertation. *Entrance requirements:* For master's, GRE General Test, minimum GPA of 3.0, writing sample, portfolio (MFA), 3 letters of recommendation; for doctorate, GRE General Test, writing sample. Additional exam requirements/recommendations for international students: Required—TOEFL. *Application deadline:* For fall admission, 2/1 for domestic and international students. Applications are processed on a rolling basis. Application fee: $75. Electronic applications accepted. *Expenses:* Tuition, state resident: part-time $471 per credit hour. Tuition, nonresident: part-time $1016 per credit hour. Required fees: $337 per term. *Financial support:* In 2010–11, 3 fellowships with full tuition reimbursements (averaging $19,667 per year), 49 teaching assistantships (averaging $19,543 per year) were awarded; research assistantships, Federal Work-Study and scholarships/grants also available. Support available to part-time students. Financial award applicants required to submit FAFSA. *Faculty research:* Dance, performance, history/theory, design and production. *Unit head:* Daniel M. Wagner, Professor and Director, 301-405-6679, E-mail: dmwagner@umd.edu. *Application contact:* Dr. Charles A. Caramello, Dean of Graduate School, 301-405-0358, Fax: 301-314-9305.

University of Michigan, Horace H. Rackham School of Graduate Studies, School of Music, Theatre, and Dance, Department of Dance, Ann Arbor, MI 48109-2217. Offers modern dance performance and choreography (MFA). Offered through the Horace H. Rackham School of Graduate Studies. *Accreditation:* NASD. *Degree requirements:* For master's, thesis. *Entrance requirements:* For master's, audition. Additional exam requirements/recommendations for international students: Required—TOEFL (minimum score 600 paper-based; 250 computer-based; 100 iBT). Electronic applications accepted. *Expenses:* Tuition, state resident: full-time $17,784; part-time $1116 per credit hour. Tuition, nonresident: full-time $35,944; part-time $2125 per credit hour. International tuition: $35,994 full-time. Required fees: $95 per semester. Tuition and fees vary according to course load, degree level and program. *Faculty research:* Life forms software.

University of Minnesota, Twin Cities Campus, Graduate School, College of Liberal Arts, Department of Theatre Arts and Dance, Minneapolis, MN 55455-0213. Offers design technology (MFA); theatre arts and dance (MA, PhD). *Accreditation:* NAST (one or more programs are accredited). Terminal master's awarded for partial completion of doctoral program. *Degree requirements:* For master's, thesis (for some programs), final creative project (MFA), foreign language (MA); for doctorate, one foreign language, thesis/dissertation, oral defense, written exams. *Entrance requirements:* For master's, GRE General Test, minimum GPA of 3.0, audition or portfolio; for doctorate, GRE General Test, minimum GPA of 3.0, writing sample, 1 foreign language. Additional exam requirements/recommendations for international students: Required—TOEFL (minimum score 550 paper-based; 213 computer-based; 79 iBT). Electronic applications accepted. *Faculty research:* Theatre history, Eastern European theatre, performance studies, medieval studies.

University of New Mexico, Graduate School, College of Fine Arts, Department of Theatre and Dance, Albuquerque, NM 87131-2039. Offers dance (MFA); dance history (MA); dramatic writing (MFA); theatre education and outreach (MA). *Accreditation:* NASD; NAST. *Faculty:* 23 full-time (11 women), 15 part-time/adjunct (10 women). *Students:* 19 full-time (16 women), 4 part-time (all women); includes 9 minority (1 American Indian or Alaska Native, non-Hispanic/Latino; 2 Asian, non-Hispanic/Latino; 6 Hispanic/Latino). Average age 31. 33 applicants, 21% accepted, 7 enrolled. In 2010, 3 master's awarded. *Degree requirements:* For master's, comprehensive exam (for some programs), thesis (for some programs). *Entrance requirements:*

For master's, minimum GPA of 3.0; undergraduate major in theatre, dance or closely related field; 3 letters of recommendation; letter of intent; BA, BFA, BS, or MA in dance movement science or related field, or equivalent experience (for MFA in dance). *Application deadline:* For fall admission, 4/15 for domestic students; for spring admission, 11/10 for domestic students. Application fee: $50. Electronic applications accepted. *Expenses:* Tuition, state resident: full-time $5991; part-time $251 per credit hour. Tuition, nonresident: full-time $14,405; part-time $800.20 per credit hour. Tuition and fees vary according to course level, course load, program and reciprocity agreements. *Financial support:* In 2010–11, 20 students received support, including 1 fellowship (averaging $7,200 per year), 1 research assistantship with partial tuition reimbursement available (averaging $3,750 per year), 3 teaching assistantships with partial tuition reimbursements available (averaging $4,482 per year); Federal Work-Study, health care benefits, tuition waivers (partial), and unspecified assistantships also available. Financial award application deadline: 3/1; financial award applicants required to submit FAFSA. *Faculty research:* Theater education and outreach, choreography, dramatic writing, dance history/criticism. *Unit head:* Bill Liotta, Chair, 505-277-4332, Fax: 505-277-8921, E-mail: wliotta@unm.edu. *Application contact:* Christina Squire, Administrator II, 505-277-7362, Fax: 505-277-8921, E-mail: csquire@unm.edu.

The University of North Carolina at Charlotte, Graduate School, College of Education, Department of Middle, Secondary and K-12 Education, Charlotte, NC 28223-0001. Offers art education (MAT); curriculum and instruction (PhD); dance education (MAT); foreign language education (MAT); middle grades and secondary education (M Ed); middle grades education (MAT); music education (MAT); secondary education (MAT); teaching English as a second language (M Ed); theatre education (MAT). *Faculty:* 16 full-time (8 women), 6 part-time/adjunct (5 women). *Students:* 149 full-time (112 women), 943 part-time (735 women); includes 281 minority (189 Black or African American, non-Hispanic/Latino; 9 American Indian or Alaska Native, non-Hispanic/Latino; 23 Asian, non-Hispanic/Latino; 51 Hispanic/Latino; 9 Two or more races, non-Hispanic/Latino), 6 international. Average age 31. 224 applicants, 96% accepted, 173 enrolled. In 2010, 72 master's awarded. *Entrance requirements:* For master's, GRE or MAT. Additional exam requirements/recommendations for international students: Required—TOEFL (minimum score 557 paper-based; 220 computer-based; 83 iBT). *Application deadline:* For fall admission, 7/1 for domestic students, 5/1 for international students; for spring admission, 11/1 for domestic students, 10/1 for international students. Applications are processed on a rolling basis. Application fee: $55. Electronic applications accepted. *Expenses:* Tuition, state resident: full-time $3464. Tuition, nonresident: full-time $14,297. Required fees: $2094. Tuition and fees vary according to course load. *Financial support:* In 2010–11, 11 students received support, including 1 research assistantship (averaging $16,000 per year), 7 teaching assistantships (averaging $9,357 per year); career-related internships or fieldwork, institutionally sponsored loans, scholarships/grants, and unspecified assistantships also available. Support available to part-time students. Financial award application deadline: 4/1; financial award applicants required to submit FAFSA. Total annual research expenditures: $22,468. *Unit head:* Melba Spooner, Chair, 704-687-8704, Fax: 704-687-6430, E-mail: mcspoone@uncc.edu. *Application contact:* Kathy B. Giddings, Director of Graduate Admissions, 704-687-5503, Fax: 704-687-3279, E-mail: gradadm@uncc.edu.

The University of North Carolina at Greensboro, Graduate School, School of Health and Human Performance, Department of Dance, Greensboro, NC 27412-5001. Offers MA, MFA. *Accreditation:* NASD. *Degree requirements:* For master's, thesis. *Entrance requirements:* For master's, GRE General Test or MAT, audition or video (MFA). Additional exam requirements/recommendations for international students: Required—TOEFL. Electronic applications accepted. *Faculty research:* Consciousness-raising images, perspectives on ballet.

University of Oklahoma, Weitzenhoffer Family College of Fine Arts, School of Dance, Norman, OK 73019. Offers MFA. *Faculty:* 7 full-time (3 women). *Students:* 6 full-time (all women), 1 (woman) part-time. Average age 36. 4 applicants, 50% accepted, 1 enrolled. In 2010, 1 master's awarded. *Degree requirements:* For master's, comprehensive exam, departmental qualifying exams, solo performance or choreography of a work. *Entrance requirements:* For master's, minimum GPA of 3.0 or equivalent experience, resume, audition, interview, 3 letters of reference, video, personal choreography. Additional exam requirements/recommendations for international students: Required—TOEFL (minimum score 550 paper-based; 213 computer-based; 79 iBT). *Application deadline:* For fall admission, 6/1 for domestic students, 4/1 for international students; for spring admission, 11/1 for domestic students, 9/1 for international students. Applications are processed on a rolling basis. Application fee: $40 ($90 for international students). Electronic applications accepted. *Expenses:* Tuition, state resident: full-time $3893; part-time $162.20 per credit hour. Tuition, nonresident: full-time $14,167; part-time $590.30 per credit hour. Required fees: $2523; $94.60 per credit hour. Tuition and fees vary according to course load and degree level. *Financial support:* In 2010–11, 5 students received support, including 5 fellowships with full tuition reimbursements available (averaging $4,800 per year), 6 teaching assistantships with partial tuition reimbursements available (averaging $14,034 per year); health care benefits and unspecified assistantships also available. Support available to part-time students. Financial award application deadline: 3/15; financial award applicants required to submit FAFSA. *Faculty research:* Dance history, body science, teaching methods, choreography, performance. *Unit head:* Mary Margaret Holt, Director, 405-325-4051, Fax: 405-325-7024, E-mail: marymholt@ou.edu. *Application contact:* Jeremy Lindberg, Associate Professor, 405-325-0567, Fax: 405-325-7024, E-mail: jlindberg@ou.edu.

University of Oregon, Graduate School, School of Music, Department of Dance, Eugene, OR 97403. Offers MA, MS. *Degree requirements:* For master's, thesis or alternative. *Entrance requirements:* For master's, minimum GPA of 3.0. Additional exam requirements/recommendations for international students: Required—TOEFL. *Faculty research:* Choreography, dance history, dance pedagogy, scientific aspects of dance.

The University of Texas at Austin, Graduate School, College of Fine Arts, Department of Theatre and Dance, Austin, TX 78712-1111. Offers acting (MFA); dance (MFA); directing (MFA); drama and theatre for youth (MFA); performance as public practice (MA, MFA, PhD); playwriting (MFA); theatre technology (MFA); theatrical design (MFA). *Accreditation:* NASD. *Degree requirements:* For master's, thesis; for doctorate, variable foreign language requirement, thesis/dissertation. *Entrance requirements:* For master's and doctorate, GRE General Test.

University of Utah, Graduate School, College of Fine Arts, Department of Ballet, Salt Lake City, UT 84112. Offers MFA. *Accreditation:* NASD. *Faculty:* 4 full-time (3 women), 1 part-time/adjunct (0 women). *Students:* 11 full-time (10 women); includes 3 minority (all Asian, non-Hispanic/Latino), 1 international. Average age 27. 12 applicants, 58% accepted, 3 enrolled. In 2010, 3 master's awarded. *Degree requirements:* For master's, one foreign language, choreography projects, performance, teaching experience with written support. *Entrance requirements:* For master's, audition, videos/DVDs of teaching and choreography. Additional exam requirements/recommendations for international students: Required—TOEFL (minimum score 500 paper-based; 173 computer-based). *Application deadline:* For fall admission, 4/1 for domestic and international students; for spring admission, 10/1 for domestic and international students. Applications are processed on a rolling basis. Application fee: $55 ($65 for international students). *Expenses:* Tuition, area resident: Part-time $179.19 per credit hour. Tuition, state resident: full-time $4384. Tuition, nonresident: full-time $16,684; part-time $630.67 per credit hour. Required fees: $350 per semester. Tuition and fees vary according to course load, degree level and program. *Financial support:* In 2010–11, 1 teaching assistantship with full and partial tuition reimbursement (averaging $5,700 per year) was awarded; Federal Work-Study, institutionally sponsored loans, and scholarships/grants also available. Financial award application deadline: 3/1; financial award applicants required to submit FAFSA. *Faculty research:* Choreography, jazz, technique, fitness and dance injuries. Total annual research expenditures: $5,710. *Unit head:* Bene' C. Arnold, Interim Chair, 801-581-8231, Fax: 801-581-5442, E-mail: bene.arnold@utah.edu. *Application contact:* Richard Wacko, Associate Professor, 801-587-3742, E-mail: richard.wacko@utah.edu.

University of Utah, Graduate School, College of Fine Arts, Department of Modern Dance, Salt Lake City, UT 84112-0280. Offers MFA. *Accreditation:* NASD. *Faculty:* 11 full-time (7 women). *Students:* 21 full-time (18 women), 1 (woman) part-time; includes 1 minority (Hispanic/Latino), 4 international. Average age 28. 23 applicants, 48% accepted, 11 enrolled. In 2010, 7 master's awarded. *Degree requirements:* For master's, thesis, project, oral examination. *Entrance requirements:* For master's, audition, interview, minimum GPA of 3.0. Additional exam requirements/recommendations for international students: Required—TOEFL (minimum score 500 paper-based; 173 computer-based). *Application deadline:* For fall admission, 3/1 for domestic and international students. Applications are processed on a rolling basis. Application fee: $55 ($65 for international students). Electronic applications accepted. *Expenses:* Tuition, area resident: Part-time $179.19 per credit hour. Tuition, state resident: full-time $4384. Tuition, nonresident: full-time $16,684; part-time $630.67 per credit hour. Required fees: $350 per semester. Tuition and fees vary according to course load, degree level and program. *Financial support:* In 2010–11, 14 students received support; fellowships with full and partial tuition reimbursements available, teaching assistantships with full and partial tuition reimbursements available, Federal Work-Study, institutionally sponsored loans, scholarships/grants, health care benefits, and unspecified assistantships available. Financial award application deadline: 3/1; financial award applicants required to submit FAFSA. *Faculty research:* Choreography, teaching methods, performance, cultural studies, dance technology. Total annual research expenditures: $400. *Unit head:* Stephen Koester, Chair, 801-581-7327, Fax: 801-581-5442, E-mail: stephen.koester@utah.edu. *Application contact:* Eric Handman, Director of Graduate Studies, 801-587-9813, Fax: 801-581-5442, E-mail: eric.handman@utah.edu.

University of Washington, Graduate School, College of Arts and Sciences, Program in Dance, Seattle, WA 98195-1150. Offers MFA. *Faculty:* 5 full-time (4 women), 1 (woman) part-time/adjunct. *Students:* 7 full-time (3 women); includes 1 Black or African American, non-Hispanic/Latino; 1 Asian, non-Hispanic/Latino; 1 Hispanic/Latino. Average age 34. 16 applicants, 19% accepted, 3 enrolled. In 2010, 3 master's awarded. *Degree requirements:* For master's, performance, project. *Entrance requirements:* For master's, 8 years of professional dance experience, resume, performance DVD or VHS tape, 3 letters of reference. Additional exam requirements/recommendations for international students: Required—TOEFL. *Application deadline:* For fall admission, 10/15 priority date for domestic students, 9/15 priority date for international students. Application fee: $75. Electronic applications accepted. *Financial support:* In 2010–11, 7 students received support; teaching assistantships with full tuition reimbursements available, health care benefits available. Financial award application deadline: 10/15. *Faculty research:* Choreography, history, anatomy, ethnography, integrated dance. *Unit head:* Elizabeth Cooper, Director, 206-543-4178, Fax: 206-543-8610, E-mail: bcoop@u.washington.edu. *Application contact:* Jennifer Salk, Associate Professor, 206-543-5594, Fax: 206-543-8610, E-mail: jsalk@u.washington.edu.

University of Wisconsin–Milwaukee, Graduate School, Peck School of the Arts, Program in Performing Arts, Milwaukee, WI 53201-0413. Offers dance (MFA); film (MFA); theatre (MFA). Part-time programs available. *Faculty:* 28 full-time (16 women). *Students:* 17 full-time (10 women), 2 part-time (0 women); includes 1 Black or African American, non-Hispanic/Latino; 2 Hispanic/Latino, 1 international. Average age 34. 31 applicants, 23% accepted, 6 enrolled. In 2010, 17 master's awarded. *Degree requirements:* For master's, variable foreign language requirement, comprehensive exam, thesis or alternative. *Entrance requirements:* For master's, audition, interview. Additional exam requirements/recommendations for international students: Required—TOEFL (minimum score 550 paper-based; 79 iBT), IELTS (minimum score 6.5). *Application deadline:* For fall admission, 1/1 priority date for domestic students; for spring admission, 9/1 for domestic students. Applications are processed on a rolling basis. Application fee: $56 ($96 for international students). Electronic applications accepted. *Financial support:* In 2010–11, 5 fellowships with full tuition reimbursements, 9 teaching assistantships with full tuition reimbursements were awarded; career-related internships or fieldwork, health care benefits, unspecified assistantships, and project assistantships also available. Support available to part-time students. Financial award application deadline: 4/15; financial award applicants required to submit FAFSA. *Unit head:* Simone Ferro, Representative, 414-229-4178, E-mail: sferro@uwm.edu. *Application contact:* General Information Contact, 414-229-4982, Fax: 414-229-6967, E-mail: gradschool@uwm.edu.

York University, Faculty of Graduate Studies, Faculty of Fine Arts, Program in Dance, Toronto, ON M3J 1P3, Canada. Offers MA, MFA. *Degree requirements:* For master's, thesis or alternative. Electronic applications accepted.

Music

Academy of Art University, Graduate Program, School of Music Production and Sound Design for Visual Media, San Francisco, CA 94105-3410. Offers MFA. Part-time programs available. Postbaccalaureate distance learning degree programs offered (no on-campus study). *Faculty:* 1 full-time (0 women), 11 part-time/adjunct (2 women). *Students:* 26 full-time (10 women), 8 part-time (2 women); includes 1 Black or African American, non-Hispanic/Latino; 2 Asian, non-Hispanic/Latino; 2 Hispanic/Latino, 15 international. Average age 30. 19 applicants. *Degree requirements:* For master's, thesis, final review. *Application deadline:* For fall admission, 9/7 for domestic and international students; for spring admission, 2/2 for domestic and international students. Applications are processed on a rolling basis. Application fee: $100 ($500 for international students). Electronic applications accepted. *Expenses:* Tuition: Full-time $20,160; part-time $840 per semester hour. Required fees: $45 per semester. *Financial support:* Career-related internships or fieldwork and Federal Work-Study available. Support available to part-time students. Financial award application deadline: 8/10; financial award applicants required to submit FAFSA.

Alabama Agricultural and Mechanical University, School of Graduate Studies, School of Education, Area in Music Education, Huntsville, AL 35811. Offers music (MS); music education (M Ed). *Accreditation:* NCATE. Part-time and evening/weekend programs available. *Degree requirements:* For master's, comprehensive exam. *Entrance requirements:* For master's, GRE General Test. Additional exam requirements/recommendations for international students: Required—TOEFL (minimum score 500 paper-based; 173 computer-based; 61 iBT). Electronic applications accepted. *Faculty research:* Jazz and black music, Alabama folk music.

Alabama State University, Department of Music, Montgomery, AL 36101-0271. Offers instrumental music (M Ed); vocal/choral music (M Ed). *Accreditation:* NASM. Part-time programs available. *Degree requirements:* For master's, comprehensive exam. *Entrance requirements:* For master's, GRE General Test or MAT, graduate writing competency test. Additional exam requirements/recommendations for international students: Required—TOEFL (minimum score 500 paper-based; 173 computer-based). *Faculty research:* Computer applications.

Music

Andrews University, School of Graduate Studies, College of Arts and Sciences, Department of Music, Berrien Springs, MI 49104. Offers M Mus, MA. *Accreditation:* NASM. *Degree requirements:* For master's, variable foreign language requirement. *Entrance requirements:* For master's, GRE Subject Test, minimum undergraduate GPA of 2.6. Additional exam requirements/recommendations for international students: Required—TOEFL (minimum score 550 paper-based).

Appalachian State University, Cratis D. Williams Graduate School, Center for Appalachian Studies, Boone, NC 28608. Offers culture (MA); music (MA); sustainable development (MA). Part-time programs available. *Faculty:* 14 full-time (5 women). *Students:* 25 full-time (15 women), 5 part-time (4 women); includes 1 Hispanic/Latino. 20 applicants, 85% accepted, 12 enrolled. In 2010, 11 master's awarded. *Degree requirements:* For master's, one foreign language, comprehensive exam, thesis optional. *Entrance requirements:* For master's, GRE General Test, 3 letters of recommendation. Additional exam requirements/recommendations for international students: Required—TOEFL (minimum score 570 paper-based; 230 computer-based; 79 iBT), IELTS (minimum score 6.5). *Application deadline:* For fall admission, 7/1 for domestic students, 2/1 for international students; for spring admission, 11/1 for domestic students, 7/1 for international students. Applications are processed on a rolling basis. Application fee: $55. Electronic applications accepted. *Expenses:* Tuition, state resident: full-time $3428; part-time $428 per unit. Tuition, nonresident: full-time $14,518; part-time $1814 per unit. Required fees: $2320; $344 per unit. Tuition and fees vary according to campus/location. *Financial support:* In 2010–11, 8 research assistantships (averaging $8,000 per year) were awarded; fellowships, teaching assistantships, career-related internships or fieldwork, Federal Work-Study, scholarships/grants, and unspecified assistantships also available. Financial award application deadline: 4/1; financial award applicants required to submit FAFSA. *Faculty research:* Appalachian culture, sustainable development, Appalachian music. Total annual research expenditures: $35,275. *Unit head:* Dr. Pat Beaver, Director, 828-262-2550, E-mail: beaverpd@appstate.edu. *Application contact:* Dr. Katherine Ledford, Graduate Program Director, 828-262-4089, E-mail: ledfordke@appstate.edu.

Appalachian State University, Cratis D. Williams Graduate School, School of Music, Boone, NC 28608. Offers music education (MM); music performance (MM); music therapy (MMT). *Accreditation:* NASM. Part-time programs available. *Faculty:* 28 full-time (8 women), 2 part-time/adjunct (1 woman). *Students:* 30 full-time (20 women), 4 part-time (3 women); includes 1 minority (Hispanic/Latino). 34 applicants, 82% accepted, 21 enrolled. In 2010, 22 master's awarded. *Degree requirements:* For master's, comprehensive exam, thesis or alternative. *Entrance requirements:* For master's, GRE General Test, 3 letters of reference, audition. Additional exam requirements/recommendations for international students: Required—TOEFL (minimum score 550 paper-based; 230 computer-based; 79 iBT), IELTS (minimum score 6.5). *Application deadline:* For fall admission, 7/1 for domestic students, 2/1 for international students; for spring admission, 11/1 for domestic students, 7/1 for international students. Applications are processed on a rolling basis. Application fee: $55. Electronic applications accepted. *Expenses:* Tuition, state resident: full-time $3428; part-time $428 per unit. Tuition, nonresident: full-time $14,518; part-time $1814 per unit. Required fees: $2320; $344 per unit. Tuition and fees vary according to campus/location. *Financial support:* In 2010–11, 16 research assistantships (averaging $8,000 per year) were awarded; fellowships, teaching assistantships, career-related internships or fieldwork, Federal Work-Study, scholarships/grants, tuition waivers (partial), and unspecified assistantships also available. Financial award application deadline: 4/1; financial award applicants required to submit FAFSA. *Faculty research:* Music of the Holocaust, Celtic folk music, early nineteenth century performance practice, hypermeter and phase rhythm, world music, music and psychoneuroimmunology. Total annual research expenditures: $8,500. *Unit head:* Dr. William Pelto, Dean, 828-262-6446, E-mail: peltowl@appstate.edu. *Application contact:* Dr. Jennifer Snodgrass, Graduate Program Director, 828-262-6463, E-mail: snodgrassjs@appstate.edu.

Arizona State University, Herberger Institute for Design and the Arts, School of Music, Tempe, AZ 85287-0405. Offers composition (MM); music (conducting) (DMA); music (ethnomusicology) (MA); music (interdisciplinary digital media/performance) (DMA); music (music history and literature) (MA); music (performance) (DMA); music education (MM, PhD); music therapy (MM); performance (MM). *Accreditation:* NASM. *Faculty:* 66 full-time (21 women), 1 (woman) part-time/adjunct. *Students:* 236 full-time (133 women), 133 part-time (71 women); includes 39 minority (6 Black or African American, non-Hispanic/Latino; 17 Asian, non-Hispanic/Latino; 13 Hispanic/Latino; 3 Two or more races, non-Hispanic/Latino), 63 international. Average age 29. 406 applicants, 47% accepted, 105 enrolled. In 2010, 81 master's, 40 doctorates awarded. Terminal master's awarded for partial completion of doctoral program. *Degree requirements:* For master's, thesis (for some programs), interactive Program of Study (iPOS) submitted before completing 50 percent of required credit hours; for doctorate, comprehensive exam, thesis/dissertation, interactive Program of Study (iPOS) submitted before completing 50 percent of required credit hours. *Entrance requirements:* For master's, minimum GPA of 3.0 or equivalent in last 2 years of work leading to bachelor's degree, 3 letters of recommendation, resume; for doctorate, GRE or MAT, minimum GPA of 3.0 or equivalent in last 2 years of work leading to bachelor's degree, 3 letters of recommendation, curriculum vitae, statement of intent. Additional exam requirements/recommendations for international students: Required—TOEFL, IELTS, or Pearson Test of English. *Application deadline:* For fall admission, 12/1 for domestic and international students; for spring admission, 10/1 for domestic and international students. Applications are processed on a rolling basis. Application fee: $70 ($90 for international students). Electronic applications accepted. *Expenses:* Tuition, state resident: full-time $8510; part-time $608 per credit. Tuition, nonresident: full-time $16,542; part-time $919 per credit. Required fees: $339; $110 per credit. Part-time tuition and fees vary according to course load. *Financial support:* In 2010–11, 1 research assistantship with full and partial tuition reimbursement (averaging $4,000 per year), 74 teaching assistantships with full and partial tuition reimbursements (averaging $4,191 per year) were awarded; fellowships with full and partial tuition reimbursements, Federal Work-Study, institutionally sponsored loans, scholarships/grants, and tuition waivers (full and partial) also available. Financial award application deadline: 3/1; financial award applicants required to submit FAFSA. Total annual research expenditures: $5,914. *Unit head:* Dr. Kimberly Marshall, Director, 480-727-6222, Fax: 480-965-2659, E-mail: kimberly.marshall@asu.edu. *Application contact:* Graduate Admissions, 480-965-6113.

Arkansas State University, Graduate School, College of Fine Arts, Department of Music, Jonesboro, State University, AR 72467. Offers music education (MME, SCCT); performance (MM). *Accreditation:* NASM (one or more programs are accredited). Part-time programs available. *Faculty:* 14 full-time (3 women), 2 part-time/adjunct (both women). *Students:* 2 full-time (1 woman), 7 part-time (3 women). Average age 30. 9 applicants, 100% accepted, 6 enrolled. In 2010, 7 master's, 3 SCCTs awarded. *Degree requirements:* For master's, 2 foreign languages, comprehensive exam, thesis or alternative; for SCCT, comprehensive exam. *Entrance requirements:* For master's, GRE General Test or MAT, university entrance exam, appropriate bachelor's degree, audition, letters of recommendation, teaching experience, official transcripts, immunization records, valid teaching certificate; for SCCT, GRE General Test or MAT, interview, master's degree, official transcript, immunization records, letters of recommendation. Additional exam requirements/recommendations for international students: Required—TOEFL (minimum score 550 paper-based; 213 computer-based; 79 iBT), IELTS (minimum score 6), PTE: Pearson Test of English Academic (56). *Application deadline:* For fall admission, 7/1 for domestic and international students; for spring admission, 11/15 for domestic students, 11/14 for international students. Applications are processed on a rolling basis. Application fee: $30 ($40 for international students). Electronic applications accepted. *Expenses:* Tuition, state resident: full-time $3888; part-time $216 per credit hour. Tuition, nonresident: full-time $9918; part-time $551 per credit hour. International tuition: $8376 full-time. Required fees: $932; $49 per credit hour. $25 per term. One-time fee: $30. Tuition and fees vary according to course load and program. *Financial support:* In 2010–11, 6 students received support; teaching assistantships, career-related internships or fieldwork, scholarships/grants, and unspecified assistantships available. Financial award application deadline: 7/1; financial award applicants required to submit FAFSA. *Unit head:* Ken Hatch, Interim Chair, 870-972-2094, Fax: 870-972-3932, E-mail: khatch@astate.edu. *Application contact:* Dr. Andrew Sustich, Dean of the Graduate School, 870-972-3029, Fax: 870-972-3857, E-mail: sustich@astate.edu.

Austin Peay State University, College of Graduate Studies, College of Arts and Letters, Department of Music, Clarksville, TN 37044. Offers music education (M Mu); music performance (M Mu). *Accreditation:* NASM. Part-time programs available. *Faculty:* 12 full-time (5 women), 1 (woman) part-time/adjunct. *Students:* 21 full-time (11 women), 7 part-time (2 women); includes 6 minority (3 Black or African American, non-Hispanic/Latino; 1 Hispanic/Latino; 2 Two or more races, non-Hispanic/Latino). Average age 28. 22 applicants, 100% accepted, 10 enrolled. In 2010, 9 master's awarded. *Degree requirements:* For master's, comprehensive exam, thesis optional. *Entrance requirements:* For master's, GRE General Test, diagnostic exams, audition, bachelor's degree, 3 letters of recommendation. Additional exam requirements/recommendations for international students: Required—TOEFL (minimum score 500 paper-based; 173 computer-based). *Application deadline:* For fall admission, 7/27 priority date for domestic students; for spring admission, 12/17 priority date for domestic students. Applications are processed on a rolling basis. Application fee: $25. Electronic applications accepted. *Expenses:* Tuition, state resident: full-time $6480; part-time $324 per credit hour. Tuition, nonresident: full-time $17,960; part-time $898 per credit hour. Required fees: $1244; $61.20 per credit hour. *Financial support:* In 2010–11, research assistantships with full tuition reimbursements (averaging $5,174 per year); career-related internships or fieldwork, Federal Work-Study, institutionally sponsored loans, scholarships/grants, and unspecified assistantships also available. Support available to part-time students. Financial award application deadline: 3/1; financial award applicants required to submit FAFSA. *Unit head:* Dr. Douglas Rose, Chair, 931-221-7808, Fax: 931-221-7529, E-mail: rosed@apsu.edu. *Application contact:* Dr. Dixie Dennis, Dean, College of Graduate Studies, 931-221-7662, Fax: 931-221-7641, E-mail: dennisdi@apsu.edu.

Azusa Pacific University, School of Music, Azusa, CA 91702-7000. Offers education (M Mus); performance (M Mus). *Accreditation:* NASM. Part-time and evening/weekend programs available. *Students:* 25 full-time (7 women), 24 part-time (11 women); includes 3 Black or African American, non-Hispanic/Latino; 1 Asian, non-Hispanic/Latino; 5 Hispanic/Latino, 9 international. Average age 29. In 2010, 22 master's awarded. *Degree requirements:* For master's, recital. *Entrance requirements:* For master's, interview, audition. Additional exam requirements/recommendations for international students: Required—TOEFL (minimum score 550 paper-based). Application fee: $45 ($65 for international students). *Financial support:* In 2010–11, 7 students received support. Career-related internships or fieldwork available. Support available to part-time students. Financial award applicants required to submit FAFSA. *Unit head:* Dr. Donald Neufeld, Acting Dean, 626-812-3848, E-mail: dfunderburk@apu.edu. *Application contact:* Graduate Admissions, 626-815-5470, Fax: 626-815-3867, E-mail: dfunderburk@apu.edu.

Bard College, Conservatory of Music, The Conductors Institute, Annandale-on-Hudson, NY 12504. Offers MFA. *Entrance requirements:* For master's, resume, 3 letters of recommendation.

Bard College, Conservatory of Music, Graduate Program in Vocal Arts, Annandale-on-Hudson, NY 12504. Offers MM. *Entrance requirements:* For master's, portfolio, 3 letters of recommendation, headshot, repertoire list.

Baylor University, Graduate School, School of Music, Waco, TX 76798. Offers church music (MM); collaborative piano (MM); composition (MM); conducting (MM); music history and literature (MM); music theory (MM); performance (MM); piano pedagogy and performance (MM); M Div/MM. *Accreditation:* NASM. *Students:* 13 full-time (6 women), 38 part-time (25 women); includes 6 minority (1 Asian, non-Hispanic/Latino; 2 Hispanic/Latino; 3 Two or more races, non-Hispanic/Latino), 10 international. In 2010, 29 master's awarded. *Degree requirements:* For master's, variable foreign language requirement, thesis (for some programs). *Entrance requirements:* For master's, GRE General Test. *Application deadline:* For fall admission, 8/1 for domestic students; for spring admission, 12/1 for domestic students. Applications are processed on a rolling basis. Application fee: $25. *Financial support:* In 2010–11, 43 teaching assistantships with full tuition reimbursements (averaging $5,990 per year) were awarded; Federal Work-Study and institutionally sponsored loans also available. *Unit head:* Dr. David Music, Graduate Program Director, 254-710-2360, Fax: 254-710-1191, E-mail: david_music@baylor.edu. *Application contact:* Melinda Coates, Administrative Assistant, 254-710-2360, Fax: 254-710-3870, E-mail: melinda_coats@baylor.edu.

Belmont University, College of Visual and Performing Arts, School of Music, Nashville, TN 37212-3757. Offers church music (MM); composition (MM); music education (MM); pedagogy (MM); performance (MM). *Accreditation:* NASM. Part-time programs available. *Faculty:* 26 full-time (8 women), 12 part-time/adjunct (3 women). *Students:* 10 full-time (4 women), 43 part-time (24 women); includes 4 minority (all Black or African American, non-Hispanic/Latino), 1 international. Average age 28. 19 applicants, 89% accepted, 13 enrolled. In 2010, 16 master's awarded. *Degree requirements:* For master's, comprehensive exam, thesis (for some programs). *Entrance requirements:* For master's, placement exam, GRE or MAT, audition, interview, minimum GPA of 2.75. Additional exam requirements/recommendations for international students: Required—TOEFL (minimum score 500 paper-based; 173 computer-based). *Application deadline:* For fall admission, 5/1 priority date for domestic students, 5/1 for international students; for spring admission, 11/1 priority date for domestic students, 11/1 for international students. Applications are processed on a rolling basis. Application fee: $50. Electronic applications accepted. *Expenses:* Tuition: Part-time $1800 per course. Required fees: $295 per semester. Tuition and fees vary according to degree level and program. *Financial support:* In 2010–11, 15 fellowships (averaging $2,000 per year), 5 teaching assistantships (averaging $2,000 per year) were awarded; career-related internships or fieldwork, scholarships/grants, and unspecified assistantships also available. Financial award application deadline: 3/1; financial award applicants required to submit FAFSA. *Unit head:* Dr. Robert Gregg, Director, 615-460-8111, Fax: 615-386-0239, E-mail: greggr@mail.belmont.edu. *Application contact:* Russ Cornwall, Graduate Secretary, 615-460-8117, Fax: 615-386-0239, E-mail: cornwallr@mail.belmont.edu.

Bennington College, Graduate Programs, MFA in Music Program, Bennington, VT 05201. Offers MFA. Part-time programs available. *Faculty:* 7 full-time (2 women), 3 part-time/adjunct (1 woman). *Students:* 2 full-time (1 woman). Average age 46. 3 applicants, 33% accepted, 1 enrolled. *Degree requirements:* For master's, thesis, concert performances. *Application deadline:* For fall admission, 2/1 for domestic students. Application fee: $60. *Expenses:* Tuition: Full-time $20,950; part-time $2935 per course. One-time fee: $75. Tuition and fees vary according to program. *Financial support:* In 2010–11, 2 students received support, including 3 teaching assistantships (averaging $8,729 per year). Financial award application deadline: 4/1; financial award applicants required to submit FAFSA. *Unit head:* Allen Shawn, Director, 802-440-4525, E-mail: ashawn@bennington.edu. *Application contact:* Mary Surdam, Admissions Coordinator, 802-440-4887, Fax: 802-440-4320, E-mail: admissions@bennington.edu.

Bethesda Christian University, Graduate and Professional Programs, Anaheim, CA 92801. Offers biblical studies (MA); music (MA); theology (M Div). *Entrance requirements:* For M Div and master's, interview.

Bob Jones University, Graduate Programs, Greenville, SC 29614. Offers accountancy (MS); Bible (MA); Bible translation (MA); Biblical studies (Certificate); broadcast management (MS); business administration (MBA); church history (MA, PhD); church ministries (MA); church music (MM); cinema and video production (MA); counseling (MS); curriculum and instruction (Ed D); divinity (M Div); dramatic production (MA); educational leadership (MS, Ed D, Ed S); elementary education (M Ed, MAT); English (M Ed, MA, MAT); fine arts (MA); graphic design (MA); history (M Ed, MA); illustration (MA); interpretative speech (MA); mathematics (M Ed, MAT); medical missions (Certificate); ministry (MM, D Min); multi-categorical special education (M Ed, MAT); music (M Ed); New Testament interpretation (PhD); Old Testament interpretation (PhD); orchestral instrument performance (MM); organ performance (MM); pastoral studies (MA); personnel services (MS, Ed S); piano pedagogy (MM); piano performance (MM); platform arts (MA); radio and television broadcasting (MS); rhetoric and public address (MA); secondary education (M Ed); studio art (MA); teaching Bible (MA); theology (MA, PhD); voice performance (MM); youth ministries (MA); M Div/MM.

Boise State University, Graduate College, College of Arts and Sciences, Department of Music, Boise, ID 83725-0399. Offers music (MM); music education (MM); pedagogy (MM); performance (MM). *Accreditation:* NASM. Part-time programs available. *Degree requirements:* For master's, thesis optional. *Entrance requirements:* For master's, minimum GPA of 3.0, performance demonstration. Electronic applications accepted.

The Boston Conservatory, Graduate Division, Music Division, Boston, MA 02215. Offers music (MM, ADP, Certificate); music education (MM). Part-time programs available. *Degree requirements:* For master's, thesis (for some programs), recital; for other advanced degree, recital. *Entrance requirements:* For master's and other advanced degree, audition. Electronic applications accepted.

Boston University, College of Fine Arts, School of Music, Boston, MA 02215. Offers collaborative piano (MM, DMA); composition (MM, DMA); conducting (MM, Artist Diploma, Performance Diploma); historical performance (MM, DMA, Artist Diploma, Performance Diploma); music education (MM, DMA); music theory (MM); musicology (MM); opera performance (Certificate); performance (MM, DMA, Artist Diploma, Performance Diploma). *Accreditation:* NASM. Part-time programs available. *Faculty:* 36 full-time, 21 part-time/adjunct. *Students:* 832 full-time (486 women), 107 part-time (53 women); includes 120 minority (43 Black or African American, non-Hispanic/Latino; 6 American Indian or Alaska Native, non-Hispanic/Latino; 27 Asian, non-Hispanic/Latino; 33 Hispanic/Latino; 2 Native Hawaiian or other Pacific Islander, non-Hispanic/Latino; 9 Two or more races, non-Hispanic/Latino), 160 international. Average age 34. 1,014 applicants, 37% accepted, 121 enrolled. In 2010, 213 master's, 38 doctorates, 14 other advanced degrees awarded. *Degree requirements:* For master's, thesis; for doctorate, 2 foreign languages, thesis/dissertation. *Entrance requirements:* Additional exam requirements/recommendations for international students: Required—TOEFL. *Application deadline:* For fall admission, 1/1 priority date for domestic and international students. Application fee: $60. Electronic applications accepted. *Expenses:* Tuition: Full-time $39,314; part-time $1228 per credit. Required fees: $40 per semester. *Financial support:* Fellowships, teaching assistantships available. Financial award application deadline: 1/15. *Unit head:* Robert Dodson, Director, 617-353-8789, Fax: 617-353-7455, E-mail: rdodson@bu.edu. *Application contact:* Mark Krone, Manager, Graduate Admissions, 617-353-3350, E-mail: arts@bu.edu.

Boston University, Graduate School of Arts and Sciences, Department of Music, Boston, MA 02215. Offers composition (MA); music education (MA); music history/theory (PhD); musicology (MA, PhD). *Accreditation:* NASM. *Students:* 3 full-time (2 women), 1 part-time (0 women); includes 2 minority (1 Hispanic/Latino; 1 Two or more races, non-Hispanic/Latino). Average age 26. 19 applicants, 32% accepted, 2 enrolled. In 2010, 1 master's awarded. *Degree requirements:* For master's, 2 foreign languages, comprehensive exam, thesis; for doctorate, 2 foreign languages, comprehensive exam, thesis/dissertation. *Entrance requirements:* For master's and doctorate, GRE General Test, musical composition or research paper, 3 letters of recommendation. Additional exam requirements/recommendations for international students: Required—TOEFL (minimum score 550 paper-based; 213 computer-based). *Application deadline:* For fall admission, 3/15 for domestic and international students. Application fee: $70. Electronic applications accepted. *Expenses:* Tuition: Full-time $39,314; part-time $1228 per credit. Required fees: $40 per semester. *Financial support:* Federal Work-Study, scholarships/grants, and unspecified assistantships available. Support available to part-time students. Financial award application deadline: 1/15; financial award applicants required to submit FAFSA. *Unit head:* Jeremy Yudkin, Director, 617-353-3362, Fax: 617-353-7455, E-mail: yudkinj@bu.edu. *Application contact:* Jessica Smith, Administrative Coordinator, 617-353-6887, Fax: 617-353-7455, E-mail: smithj08@bu.edu.

Bowling Green State University, Graduate College, College of Musical Arts, Bowling Green, OH 43403. Offers composition (MM); contemporary music (DMA), including composition, performance; ethnomusicology (MM); music education (MM), including choral, comprehensive, instrumental; music history (MM); music theory (MM); performance (MM). *Accreditation:* NASM. Part-time programs available. *Degree requirements:* For master's, thesis or alternative, recitals; for doctorate, comprehensive exam, thesis/dissertation. *Entrance requirements:* For master's, GRE General Test, diagnostic placement exams in music history and theory, audition, interview. Additional exam requirements/recommendations for international students: Required—TOEFL. Electronic applications accepted. *Faculty research:* Ethnomusicology.

Brandeis University, Graduate School of Arts and Sciences, Department of Music, Waltham, MA 02454-9110. Offers composition and theory (MA, MFA, PhD); music and women's and gender studies (MA); musicology (MA, MFA, PhD). Part-time programs available. *Faculty:* 7 full-time (1 woman), 9 part-time/adjunct (4 women). *Students:* 43 full-time (18 women), 3 part-time (all women); includes 7 Black or African American, non-Hispanic/Latino; 3 Asian, non-Hispanic/Latino; 1 Hispanic/Latino, 7 international. 88 applicants, 30% accepted, 11 enrolled. In 2010, 11 master's, 2 doctorates awarded. Terminal master's awarded for partial completion of doctoral program. *Degree requirements:* For master's, one foreign language, thesis or alternative; for doctorate, 2 foreign languages, comprehensive exam, thesis/dissertation. *Entrance requirements:* For master's, GRE General Test (musicology), resume, sample of work (music composition), letters of recommendation; for doctorate, GRE General Test (musicology), resume, writing sample (musicology), letters of recommendation, sample of recording work (composition). Additional exam requirements/recommendations for international students: Required—TOEFL (minimum score 600 paper-based; 250 computer-based; 100 iBT); Recommended—IELTS (minimum score 7). *Application deadline:* For fall admission, 1/15 priority date for domestic and international students. Application fee: $75. Electronic applications accepted. *Financial support:* In 2010–11, 28 students received support, including 24 fellowships with full tuition reimbursements available (averaging $20,000 per year), 4 teaching assistantships with partial tuition reimbursements available (averaging $3,200 per year); research assistantships, scholarships/grants, health care benefits, and tuition waivers (full and partial) also available. Support available to part-time students. Financial award application deadline: 4/15; financial award applicants required to submit FAFSA. *Faculty research:* Composition, performance, theory and analysis, music history, electronic music. *Unit head:* Prof. Mary Ruth Ray, Chair, 781-736-3310, E-mail: ray@brandeis.edu. *Application contact:* Mark Kagan, Senior Academic Administrator, 781-736-3311, E-mail: kagan@brandeis.edu.

Brandon University, School of Music, Brandon, MB R7A 6A9, Canada. Offers composition (M Mus); music education (M Mus); performance and literature (M Mus), including clarinet, conducting, jazz, piano, strings. Part-time programs available. *Faculty:* 7 full-time (5 women). *Students:* 11 full-time (4 women), 1 part-time (0 women), 2 international. Average age 25. 2 applicants, 100% accepted. In 2010, 2 master's awarded. *Degree requirements:* For master's, comprehensive exam (for some programs), thesis (for some programs), 2 recitals. *Entrance requirements:* For master's, B Mus. Additional exam requirements/recommendations for international students: Required—TOEFL or IELTS. *Application deadline:* For spring admission, 5/1 priority date for domestic students. Applications are processed on a rolling basis. Application fee: $60 ($125 for international students). Electronic applications accepted. *Financial support:* In 2010–11, 4 students received support, including 1 research assistantship, 5 teaching assistantships (averaging $3,250 per year). Financial award application deadline: 5/1. *Faculty research:* Composition, evaluation and assessment, performance anxiety, philosophy of music, teacher education. *Unit head:* Dr. Michael Kim, Dean, 204-727-9633, Fax: 204-728-6839, E-mail: kimm@brandonu.ca. *Application contact:* Dr. Patrick Carrabre, Joint Chair of Graduate Music Department (Performance & Literature), 204-727-9666, Fax: 204-728-6839.

Brigham Young University, Graduate Studies, College of Fine Arts and Communications, School of Music, Provo, UT 84602-1001. Offers composition (MM); conducting (MM); music education (MA, MM); musicology (MA); performance (MM). *Accreditation:* NASM. *Faculty:* 44 full-time (8 women). *Students:* 64 full-time (46 women), 14 part-time (5 women); includes 6 Asian, non-Hispanic/Latino; 1 Hispanic/Latino. Average age 27. 75 applicants, 57% accepted, 38 enrolled. In 2010, 19 master's awarded. *Degree requirements:* For master's, comprehensive exam (for some programs), thesis (for some programs), recital, project or composition (for some programs). *Entrance requirements:* For master's, placement exam, minimum GPA of 3.0 in last 60 hours, BM. Additional exam requirements/recommendations for international students: Required—TOEFL (minimum score 580 paper-based; 237 computer-based; 85 iBT). *Application deadline:* For fall admission, 2/1 priority date for domestic students, 1/15 priority date for international students. Application fee: $50. Electronic applications accepted. *Expenses:* Tuition: Full-time $5580; part-time $310 per credit hour. Tuition and fees vary according to program and student's religious affiliation. *Financial support:* In 2010–11, 67 students received support, including 46 teaching assistantships (averaging $5,000 per year); research assistantships, career-related internships or fieldwork, institutionally sponsored loans, scholarships/grants, tuition waivers (partial), and unspecified assistantships also available. Support available to part-time students. Financial award application deadline: 2/1; financial award applicants required to submit FAFSA. *Faculty research:* Louis Armstrong, rock and roll, Balinese gamelan. *Unit head:* Prof. Kory L. Katseanes, Director, 801-422-6304, Fax: 801-422-0533, E-mail: kory_katseanes@byu.edu. *Application contact:* Dr. Thomas L. Durham, Graduate Coordinator, 801-422-3226, Fax: 801-422-0533, E-mail: thomas_durham@byu.edu.

Brooklyn College of the City University of New York, Division of Graduate Studies, Conservatory of Music, Brooklyn, NY 11210-2889. Offers composition (MM); music (DMA, PhD); music education (MA); musicology (MA); performance (MM); performance practice (MA). Part-time programs available. *Students:* 2 full-time (1 woman), 78 part-time (50 women); includes 19 minority (3 Black or African American, non-Hispanic/Latino; 4 Asian, non-Hispanic/Latino; 12 Hispanic/Latino), 14 international. Average age 29. 68 applicants, 74% accepted, 28 enrolled. In 2010, 22 master's awarded. *Degree requirements:* For master's, one foreign language, comprehensive exam, thesis. *Entrance requirements:* For master's, placement exam, 36 credits in music, audition, completed composition, writing sample. Additional exam requirements/recommendations for international students: Required—TOEFL (minimum score 550 paper-based; 213 computer-based; 79 iBT). *Application deadline:* For fall admission, 3/1 priority date for domestic students, 2/1 priority date for international students; for spring admission, 11/1 priority date for domestic students, 10/1 priority date for international students. Applications are processed on a rolling basis. Application fee: $125. Electronic applications accepted. *Expenses:* Tuition, state resident: full-time $7360; part-time $310 per credit hour. Tuition, nonresident: full-time $13,800; part-time $575 per credit hour. Required fees: $190 per semester. *Financial support:* Career-related internships or fieldwork, Federal Work-Study, institutionally sponsored loans, and scholarships/grants available. Support available to part-time students. Financial award application deadline: 5/1; financial award applicants required to submit FAFSA. *Faculty research:* American music, computer music. *Unit head:* Dr. Bruce MacIntyre, Chairperson, 718-951-5286, E-mail: brucem@brooklyn.cuny.edu. *Application contact:* Hernan Sierra, Graduate Admissions Coordinator, 718-951-4536, Fax: 718-951-4506, E-mail: grads@brooklyn.cuny.edu.

Brooklyn College of the City University of New York, Division of Graduate Studies, Program in Performance and Interactive Media Arts, Brooklyn, NY 11210-2889. Offers MFA, CAS. *Students:* 11 full-time (8 women), 17 part-time (10 women); includes 5 minority (3 Black or African American, non-Hispanic/Latino; 2 Hispanic/Latino), 3 international. Average age 32. 26 applicants, 69% accepted, 12 enrolled. In 2010, 8 master's awarded. *Entrance requirements:* For master's, 2 letters of recommendation, resume, portfolio, interview; for CAS, 2 letters of recommendation. Additional exam requirements/recommendations for international students: Required—TOEFL (minimum score 500 paper-based; 173 computer-based; 61 iBT). *Application deadline:* For fall admission, 2/15 priority date for domestic students, 2/1 priority date for international students. Applications are processed on a rolling basis. Application fee: $125. Electronic applications accepted. *Expenses:* Tuition, state resident: full-time $7360; part-time $310 per credit hour. Tuition, nonresident: full-time $13,800; part-time $575 per credit hour. Required fees: $190 per semester. *Financial support:* Application deadline: 5/1. *Unit head:* Dr. David Grubbs, Director, 718-951-4203, E-mail: dgrubbs@brooklyn.cuny.edu. *Application contact:* Hernan Sierra, Graduate Admissions Coordinator, 718-951-4536, Fax: 718-951-4506, E-mail: grads@brooklyn.cuny.edu.

Brown University, Graduate School, Department of Music, Providence, RI 02912. Offers electronic music and multimedia (PhD); ethnomusicology (PhD). *Degree requirements:* For doctorate, 2 foreign languages, comprehensive exam, thesis/dissertation, departmental qualifying exam. *Entrance requirements:* For doctorate, GRE General Test. *Faculty research:* Ethnomusicology.

Butler University, Jordan College of Fine Arts, Department of Music, Indianapolis, IN 46208-3485. Offers composition (MM); conducting (MM); music (MM); music education (MM); music history (MM); organ (MM); performance (MM). *Accreditation:* NASM. Part-time and evening/weekend programs available. *Faculty:* 19 full-time (4 women), 13 part-time/adjunct (6 women). *Students:* 23 full-time (11 women), 23 part-time (12 women), 5 international. Average age 27. 45 applicants, 69% accepted, 17 enrolled. In 2010, 16 master's awarded. *Degree requirements:* For master's, thesis (for some programs). *Entrance requirements:* For master's, GRE General Test, GRE Subject Test, audition, interview. *Application deadline:* For fall admission, 8/15 priority date for domestic students. Applications are processed on a rolling basis. Application fee: $35. Electronic applications accepted. *Expenses:* Tuition: Full-time $29,740; part-time $1250 per credit. Required fees: $818; $430 per credit. Tuition and fees vary according to program. *Financial support:* In 2010–11, 15 teaching assistantships with full tuition reimbursements (averaging $2,500 per year) were awarded; fellowships, career-related internships or fieldwork, institutionally sponsored loans, and scholarships/grants also available. Support available to part-time students. Financial award application deadline: 7/15; financial award applicants required to submit FAFSA. *Unit head:* Dr. Daniel Bolin, Head, 317-940-9988, Fax: 317-940-9658, E-mail: dbolin@butler.edu. *Application contact:* Kathy Lang, Admission Representative, 317-940-9646, Fax: 317-940-9658, E-mail: klang@butler.edu.

California Baptist University, Program in Music, Riverside, CA 92504-3206. Offers conducting (MM); music education (MM); performance (MM). *Accreditation:* NASM. Part-time programs available. *Faculty:* 5 full-time (2 women), 1 (woman) part-time/adjunct. *Students:* 14 full-time (9 women), 4 part-time (3 women); includes 5 minority (2 Black or African American, non-Hispanic/Latino; 1 Asian, non-Hispanic/Latino; 2 Hispanic/Latino), 7 international. 9 applicants, 89% accepted, 7 enrolled. In 2010, 6 master's awarded. *Degree requirements:* For master's, thesis or alternative. *Entrance requirements:* For master's, minimum undergraduate GPA of 2.75; bachelor's degree in music. Additional exam requirements/recommendations for international students: Required—TOEFL (minimum score 575 paper-based; 230 computer-based; 89 iBT). *Application deadline:* For fall admission, 8/1 priority date for domestic students, 7/1 for international students; for spring admission, 12/1 priority date for domestic students, 10/15 for international students. Applications are processed on a rolling basis. Application fee: $45. Electronic applications accepted. *Expenses:* Tuition: Full-time $8532; part-time $474 per unit. Required fees: $355 per semester. One-time fee: $45 full-time. Tuition and fees vary according to course load and program. *Financial support:* Federal Work-Study and scholarships/grants available. Support available to part-time students. Financial award applicants required to submit FAFSA. *Unit head:* Dr. Gary Bonner, Dean, School of Music, 951-343-4251, Fax: 951-343-4570, E-mail: gbonner@calbaptist.edu. *Application contact:* Gail Ronveaux, Dean of Graduate Enrollment, 951-343-5045, Fax: 951-343-5095, E-mail: graduateadmissions@calbaptist.edu.

California Institute of the Arts, School of Music, Valencia, CA 91355-2340. Offers African music (MFA, Adv C); composition (MFA, Adv C); composition/new media (MFA, Adv C); Indonesian music (MFA, Adv C); jazz (MFA, Adv C); North Indian music (MFA, Adv C); performance (MFA, Adv C); performer/composer (MFA, Adv C); voice (MFA, Adv C); world music performance (MFA). *Accreditation:* NASM. Part-time programs available. *Degree requirements:* For master's, composition or recital. *Entrance requirements:* For master's, audition or portfolio. Additional exam requirements/recommendations for international students:

Music

California Institute of the Arts (continued)

Required—TOEFL. Electronic applications accepted. *Faculty research:* Music composition and twentieth century performance practice, interactive multimedia and computer music, music cognition.

California State University, Chico, Graduate School, College of Humanities and Fine Arts, Department of Music, Chico, CA 95929-0722. Offers MA. *Students:* 2 part-time (0 women). Average age 43. In 2010, 5 master's awarded. *Degree requirements:* For master's, thesis or alternative, recital. *Entrance requirements:* For master's, GRE General Test, departmental exam, audition tape (for off-campus applicants), music scores (for composers), 2 letters of recommendation. Additional exam requirements/recommendations for international students: Required—TOEFL (minimum score 550 paper-based; 213 computer-based; 80 iBT), IELTS (minimum score 6.5). *Application deadline:* For fall admission, 3/1 priority date for domestic students, 3/1 for international students; for spring admission, 9/15 priority date for domestic students, 9/15 for international students. Applications are processed on a rolling basis. Application fee: $55. Electronic applications accepted. *Financial support:* Teaching assistantships available. *Unit head:* Dr. Warren Pinckney, Graduate Coordinator, 530-898-4795. *Application contact:* Dr. Warren Pinckney, Graduate Coordinator, 530-898-4795.

California State University, East Bay, Office of Academic Programs and Graduate Studies, College of Letters, Arts, and Social Sciences, Department of Music, Hayward, CA 94542-3000. Offers MA. *Accreditation:* NASM. Part-time programs available. *Faculty:* 6 full-time (0 women). *Students:* 14 full-time (5 women), 14 part-time (6 women); includes 2 Asian, non-Hispanic/Latino; 2 Hispanic/Latino, 5 international. Average age 36. 28 applicants, 43% accepted, 5 enrolled. In 2010, 1 master's awarded. *Degree requirements:* For master's, variable foreign language requirement, comprehensive exam, project, recital, or thesis. *Entrance requirements:* For master's, minimum GPA of 3.0 in field; audition or work sample. Additional exam requirements/recommendations for international students: Required—TOEFL (minimum score 550 paper-based; 213 computer-based). *Application deadline:* For fall admission, 6/30 for domestic and international students. Application fee: $55. Electronic applications accepted. *Financial support:* Fellowships, Federal Work-Study, institutionally sponsored loans, and scholarships/grants available. Support available to part-time students. Financial award application deadline: 3/2. *Unit head:* Dr. Rafael Hernandez, Chair, 510-885-3135, E-mail: rafael.hernandez@csueastbay.edu. *Application contact:* Dr. Donna Wiley, Interim Associate Director, 510-885-2928, Fax: 510-885-4777, E-mail: donna.wiley@csueastbay.edu.

California State University, Fresno, Division of Graduate Studies, College of Arts and Humanities, Department of Music, Fresno, CA 93740-8027. Offers music (MA); music education (MA); performance (MA). *Accreditation:* NASM. Part-time programs available. *Degree requirements:* For master's, thesis or alternative. *Entrance requirements:* For master's, GRE General Test, BA in music, minimum GPA of 3.0. Additional exam requirements/recommendations for international students: Required—TOEFL. Electronic applications accepted. *Faculty research:* Technology transfer, folk art.

California State University, Fullerton, Graduate Studies, College of the Arts, Department of Music, Fullerton, CA 92834-9480. Offers music education (MA); music history and literature (MA); performance (MM); piano pedagogy (MA); theory-composition (MM). *Accreditation:* NASM. Part-time programs available. *Students:* 19 full-time (7 women), 37 part-time (19 women); includes 3 Black or African American, non-Hispanic/Latino; 11 Asian, non-Hispanic/Latino; 5 Hispanic/Latino, 5 international. Average age 30. 67 applicants, 33% accepted, 16 enrolled. In 2010, 16 master's awarded. *Degree requirements:* For master's, comprehensive exam, project or thesis. *Entrance requirements:* For master's, audition, major in music or related field, minimum GPA of 2.5 in last 60 units of course work. Application fee: $55. *Financial support:* Career-related internships or fieldwork, Federal Work-Study, institutionally sponsored loans, and scholarships/grants available. Support available to part-time students. Financial award application deadline: 3/1; financial award applicants required to submit FAFSA. *Unit head:* Dr. Marc Dickey, Chair, 657-278-3511. *Application contact:* Admissions/Applications, 657-278-2371.

California State University, Long Beach, Graduate Studies, College of the Arts, Department of Music, Long Beach, CA 90840. Offers composition (MM); conducting-choral (MM); conducting-instrumental (MM); instrument/vocal performance (MM); jazz studies (MM); music (MA); opera performance (MM). *Accreditation:* NASM. Part-time programs available. *Faculty:* 22 full-time (6 women), 27 part-time/adjunct (10 women). *Students:* 56 full-time (31 women), 29 part-time (13 women); includes 1 Black or African American, non-Hispanic/Latino; 10 Asian, non-Hispanic/Latino; 11 Hispanic/Latino, 7 international. Average age 29. 122 applicants, 36% accepted, 32 enrolled. In 2010, 32 master's awarded. *Degree requirements:* For master's, thesis or alternative, departmental qualifying exam. *Application deadline:* For fall admission, 5/1 for domestic students; for spring admission, 12/1 for domestic students. Applications are processed on a rolling basis. Application fee: $55. Electronic applications accepted. *Financial support:* Federal Work-Study, institutionally sponsored loans, and scholarships/grants available. Financial award application deadline: 3/2. *Unit head:* John A. Carnahan, Director, 562-985-4781, Fax: 562-985-2490, E-mail: jcarnaha@csulb.edu. *Application contact:* Dr. Leland Vail, Graduate Advisor, 562-985-4399, Fax: 562-985-2490, E-mail: lvail@csulb.edu.

California State University, Los Angeles, Graduate Studies, College of Arts and Letters, Department of Music, Los Angeles, CA 90032-8530. Offers music composition (MM); music education (MA); musicology (MA); performance (MM). *Accreditation:* NASM. Part-time and evening/weekend programs available. *Faculty:* 5 full-time (1 woman), 12 part-time/adjunct (4 women). *Students:* 15 full-time (4 women), 36 part-time (13 women); includes 22 minority (3 Black or African American, non-Hispanic/Latino; 5 Asian, non-Hispanic/Latino; 13 Hispanic/Latino; 1 Two or more races, non-Hispanic/Latino), 3 international. Average age 38. 17 applicants, 94% accepted, 14 enrolled. In 2010, 38 master's awarded. *Degree requirements:* For master's, comprehensive exam, project or thesis. *Entrance requirements:* For master's, audition. Additional exam requirements/recommendations for international students: Required—TOEFL (minimum score 500 paper-based; 173 computer-based). *Application deadline:* For fall admission, 5/1 for domestic and international students. Applications are processed on a rolling basis. Application fee: $55. Electronic applications accepted. *Financial support:* Career-related internships or fieldwork and Federal Work-Study available. Support available to part-time students. Financial award application deadline: 3/1. *Faculty research:* Gregorian semiology, Baroque opera. *Unit head:* Dr. George DeGraffenreid, Chair, 323-343-4060, Fax: 323-343-4063, E-mail: gdegraf@calstatela.edu. *Application contact:* Dr. Alan Muchlinski, Dean of Graduate Studies, 323-343-3820, Fax: 323-343-5653, E-mail: amuchli@exchange.calstatela.edu.

California State University, Northridge, Graduate Studies, College of Arts, Media, and Communication, Department of Music, Northridge, CA 91330. Offers composition (MM); conducting (MM); music education (MA); performance (MM). *Accreditation:* NASM. *Degree requirements:* For master's, thesis. *Entrance requirements:* For master's, audition, GRE General Test or minimum GPA of 3.0. Additional exam requirements/recommendations for international students: Required—TOEFL. *Faculty research:* Touring program.

California State University, Sacramento, Graduate Studies, College of Arts and Letters, Department of Music, Sacramento, CA 95819. Offers MM. Part-time programs available. *Degree requirements:* For master's, thesis or alternative, writing proficiency exam. *Entrance requirements:* For master's, BA in music or equivalent, minimum GPA of 2.5 during previous 2 years of course work. Additional exam requirements/recommendations for international students: Required—TOEFL. Electronic applications accepted.

Campbellsville University, School of Music, Campbellsville, KY 42718-2799. Offers church music (MM); music (MM); music education (MM). *Accreditation:* NASM. Part-time programs available. *Degree requirements:* For master's, thesis (for some programs), paper or recital. *Entrance requirements:* For master's, GRE General Test or PRAXIS, minimum GPA of 2.75. Additional exam requirements/recommendations for international students: Required—TOEFL (minimum score 550 paper-based). Electronic applications accepted. *Expenses:* Tuition: Full-time $7110; part-time $395 per contact hour. Required fees: $250; $75 per course.

Capital University, Conservatory of Music, Columbus, OH 43209-2394. Offers music education (MM), including instrumental emphasis, Kodály emphasis. Program offered only in summer. *Accreditation:* NASM. Part-time programs available. *Degree requirements:* For master's, comprehensive exam, thesis or alternative, chamber performance exam. *Entrance requirements:* For master's, music theory exam, minimum undergraduate GPA of 3.0. Additional exam requirements/recommendations for international students: Required—TOEFL (minimum score 550 paper-based; 213 computer-based; 80 iBT). Electronic applications accepted. *Expenses:* Contact institution. *Faculty research:* Folk song research, Kodály method, performance, composition.

Cardinal Stritch University, College of Arts and Sciences, Music Department, Milwaukee, WI 53217-3985. Offers piano (MM). Part-time programs available. *Degree requirements:* For master's, comprehensive exam, recital permission audition. *Entrance requirements:* For master's, placement test in music theory and music history, 3 letters of recommendation, audition. Electronic applications accepted.

Carleton University, Faculty of Graduate Studies, Faculty of Arts and Social Sciences, School for Studies in Art and Culture, Program in Music and Culture, Ottawa, ON K1S 5B6, Canada. Offers MA.

Carnegie Mellon University, College of Fine Arts, School of Music, Pittsburgh, PA 15213-3891. Offers composition (MM); conducting (MM); instrumental performance (MM); music and technology (MS); music education (MM); vocal performance (MM). *Accreditation:* NASM. Part-time programs available. *Degree requirements:* For master's, comprehensive exam, recital. *Entrance requirements:* For master's, audition. *Faculty research:* Computer music, music history.

Case Western Reserve University, School of Graduate Studies, Department of Music, Cleveland, OH 44106. Offers early music (MA, D Mus A); music education (MA, PhD); music history (MA); musicology (PhD). *Accreditation:* NASM (one or more programs are accredited). *Faculty:* 15 full-time (5 women), 8 part-time/adjunct (5 women). *Students:* 28 full-time (16 women), 9 part-time (2 women); includes 1 Black or African American, non-Hispanic/Latino; 1 Asian, non-Hispanic/Latino, 1 international. Average age 30. 46 applicants, 30% accepted, 14 enrolled. In 2010, 7 master's, 2 doctorates awarded. *Degree requirements:* For doctorate, thesis/dissertation. *Entrance requirements:* For master's and doctorate, GRE, audition, 2 writing samples, interview. Additional exam requirements/recommendations for international students: Required—TOEFL (minimum score 550 paper-based; 213 computer-based; 79 iBT). *Application deadline:* For fall admission, 1/15 priority date for domestic students. Application fee: $50. Electronic applications accepted. *Financial support:* Fellowships, research assistantships, teaching assistantships, career-related internships or fieldwork and tuition waivers (full) available. Financial award application deadline: 1/15; financial award applicants required to submit FAFSA. *Faculty research:* Early music performance practices; sixteenth, seventeenth, and twentieth centuries; Mahler; wind ensemble direction; measurement/evaluation in music education. *Unit head:* Mary E. Davis, Chair, 216-368-2400, Fax: 216-368-6557, E-mail: info@music.case.edu. *Application contact:* Laura Stauffer, Admissions, 216-368-2400, Fax: 216-368-6557, E-mail: info@music.case.edu.

The Catholic University of America, The Benjamin T. Rome School of Music, Washington, DC 20064. Offers MA, MM, MMSM, DMA, PhD, Certificate. *Accreditation:* NASM. Part-time programs available. *Faculty:* 18 full-time (5 women), 20 part-time/adjunct (8 women). *Students:* 43 full-time (27 women), 89 part-time (49 women); includes 4 Black or African American, non-Hispanic/Latino; 10 Asian, non-Hispanic/Latino; 6 Hispanic/Latino, 26 international. Average age 34. 108 applicants, 61% accepted, 30 enrolled. In 2010, 16 master's, 14 doctorates awarded. *Degree requirements:* For master's, comprehensive exam (for some programs), thesis (for some programs); for doctorate, comprehensive exam (for some programs), thesis/dissertation (for some programs), minimum GPA of 3.0. *Entrance requirements:* For master's, theory placement test, 2 letters of recommendation, minimum undergraduate B average, BA in music, demonstration of performance proficiency; for doctorate, qualifying exam, statement of purpose, official copies of academic transcripts, 4 letters of recommendation, audition/interview. Additional exam requirements/recommendations for international students: Required—TOEFL (minimum score 580 paper-based; 237 computer-based). *Application deadline:* For fall admission, 8/1 priority date for domestic students, 7/15 for international students; for spring admission, 12/1 priority date for domestic students, 10/15 for international students. Applications are processed on a rolling basis. Application fee: $55. Electronic applications accepted. *Expenses:* Tuition: Full-time $33,580; part-time $1315 per credit hour. Required fees: $80; $40 per semester hour. One-time fee: $425. *Financial support:* Fellowships, research assistantships, teaching assistantships, Federal Work-Study, scholarships/grants, tuition waivers (full and partial), and unspecified assistantships available. Financial award application deadline: 2/1; financial award applicants required to submit FAFSA. *Faculty research:* Composition, sacred music, orchestral instruments, piano, voice, music history and theory. *Unit head:* Murry Sidlin, Dean, 202-319-5417, Fax: 202-319-6280, E-mail: cua-music@cua.edu. *Application contact:* Andrew Woodall, Director of Graduate Admissions, 202-319-5057, Fax: 202-319-6533, E-mail: cua-admissions@cua.edu.

Central Michigan University, College of Graduate Studies, College of Communication and Fine Arts, School of Music, Mount Pleasant, MI 48859. Offers conducting (MM); music composition (MM); music education (MM); music performance (MM); piano pedagogy (MM). *Accreditation:* NASM. Part-time programs available. *Faculty:* 28 full-time (10 women), 5 part-time/adjunct (2 women). *Students:* 9 full-time (3 women), 29 part-time (11 women); includes 1 Black or African American, non-Hispanic/Latino; 1 Hispanic/Latino, 3 international. Average age 29. *Degree requirements:* For master's, thesis or alternative. *Application deadline:* For fall admission, 6/1 for international students; for spring admission, 10/1 for international students. Applications are processed on a rolling basis. Application fee: $35 ($45 for international students). Electronic applications accepted. *Expenses:* Tuition, state resident: full-time $8208; part-time $456 per credit hour. Tuition, nonresident: full-time $13,788; part-time $766 per credit hour. One-time fee: $25. *Financial support:* Fellowships with tuition reimbursements, research assistantships with tuition reimbursements, teaching assistantships with tuition reimbursements, Federal Work-Study, unspecified assistantships, and out-of-state merit awards, non-resident graduate awards available. *Faculty research:* Music education, music composition, conducting, music performance, piano pedagogy. *Unit head:* Dr. Randi L'Hommedieu, Director, 989-774-3281, Fax: 989-774-3766, E-mail: randi.louis.l'hommedieu@cmich.edu. *Application contact:* Dr. Daniel L. Steele, Associate Dean and Graduate Coordinator, 989-774-1970, Fax: 989-774-3766, E-mail: steel1dl@cmich.edu.

Central Washington University, Graduate Studies and Research, College of Arts and Humanities, Department of Music, Ellensburg, WA 98926. Offers MM. *Accreditation:* NASM. *Degree requirements:* For master's, thesis or alternative. *Entrance requirements:* For master's, minimum GPA of 3.0. Additional exam requirements/recommendations for international students: Required—TOEFL (minimum score 550 paper-based; 213 computer-based; 79 iBT). Electronic applications accepted.

City College of the City University of New York, Graduate School, College of Liberal Arts and Science, Division of the Humanities and Arts, Department of Music, New York, NY 10031-9198. Offers MA. Part-time programs available. *Degree requirements:* For master's, one foreign language, thesis. *Entrance requirements:* For master's, minimum GPA of 3.0, portfolio (composition), writing samples (history and theory), audition (performance). Additional exam requirements/recommendations for international students: Required—TOEFL (minimum score 575 paper-based; 90 iBT). Electronic applications accepted. *Faculty research:* Tonal theory, American music, musicology, atonal theory, performance.

Claremont Graduate University, Graduate Programs, School of Arts and Humanities, Department of Music, Claremont, CA 91711-6160. Offers church music (MA, DCM); composition (MA, DMA); historical performance practices (MA, DMA); musicology (MA, PhD); performance (MA, DMA); MBA/PhD. Part-time programs available. *Faculty:* 3 full-time (1 woman). *Students:* 44 full-time (17 women), 2 part-time (0 women); includes 1 Black or African American, non-Hispanic/Latino; 6 Asian, non-Hispanic/Latino; 7 Hispanic/Latino, 6 international. Average age 37. In 2010, 3 master's, 8 doctorates awarded. Terminal master's awarded for partial completion of doctoral program. *Degree requirements:* For master's, one foreign language, comprehensive exam, thesis (for some programs), oral and written qualifying exams, recitals; for doctorate, 2 foreign languages, comprehensive exam, thesis/dissertation (for some programs), oral and written qualifying exams, oral defense of dissertation, recitals. *Entrance requirements:* For master's and doctorate, GRE General Test, auditions, compositions, or papers. Additional exam requirements/recommendations for international students: Required—TOEFL (minimum score 550 paper-based; 213 computer-based; 80 iBT). *Application deadline:* For fall admission, 2/1 priority date for domestic students. Applications are processed on a rolling basis. Application fee: $60. Electronic applications accepted. *Expenses:* Tuition: Full-time $35,748; part-time $1554 per unit. Required fees: $215 per semester. *Financial support:* Fellowships, research assistantships, teaching assistantships, Federal Work-Study, institutionally sponsored loans, and scholarships/grants available. Support available to part-time students. Financial award application deadline: 2/15; financial award applicants required to submit FAFSA. *Unit head:* Robert Zappulla, Chair, 909-607-9664, Fax: 909-607-3694, E-mail: robert.zappulla@cgu.edu. *Application contact:* Sylvia Quintana, Department Secretary, 909-607-3289, Fax: 909-607-1221, E-mail: sylvia.quintana@cgu.edu.

Cleveland Institute of Music, Graduate Programs, Cleveland, OH 44106-1776. Offers MM, DMA, AD, CPS. DMA and MM programs offered jointly with Case Western Reserve University. *Accreditation:* NASM (one or more programs are accredited). *Degree requirements:* For master's, comprehensive exam, recital; for doctorate, comprehensive exam, thesis/dissertation (for some programs), final projects; for other advanced degree, recital. *Entrance requirements:* For master's, theory placement tests, audition; for doctorate, diagnostic exams, theory placement test, audition; for other advanced degree, audition. Additional exam requirements/recommendations for international students: Required—TOEFL (minimum score 550 paper-based; 213 computer-based). Electronic applications accepted.

Cleveland State University, College of Graduate Studies, College of Liberal Arts and Social Sciences, Department of Music, Cleveland, OH 44115. Offers composition (MM); music education (MM); performance (MM). *Accreditation:* NASM. Part-time and evening/weekend programs available. *Faculty:* 11 full-time (4 women), 27 part-time/adjunct (5 women). *Students:* 12 full-time (5 women), 32 part-time (14 women); includes 2 Black or African American, non-Hispanic/Latino; 1 Asian, non-Hispanic/Latino; 1 Two or more races, non-Hispanic/Latino, 5 international. Average age 29. 50 applicants, 64% accepted, 22 enrolled. In 2010, 8 master's awarded. *Degree requirements:* For master's, comprehensive exam, thesis or recital. *Entrance requirements:* For master's, departmental assessment in music history, minimum undergraduate GPA of 2.75. Additional exam requirements/recommendations for international students: Required—TOEFL (minimum score 525 paper-based; 197 computer-based). *Application deadline:* For fall admission, 7/15 priority date for domestic students. Applications are processed on a rolling basis. Application fee: $30. *Expenses:* Tuition, state resident: full-time $8447; part-time $469 per credit hour. Tuition, nonresident: full-time $16,020; part-time $890 per credit hour. Required fees: $50. *Financial support:* In 2010–11, 15 students received support, including 11 research assistantships with full tuition reimbursements available (averaging $3,612 per year); tuition waivers (partial) and unspecified assistantships also available. Financial award application deadline: 3/1. *Faculty research:* Ethnomusicology, classical-Romantic music, new performance practices, electronic music, interdisciplinary studies. Total annual research expenditures: $121,000. *Unit head:* Dr. Eric E. Ziolek, Chairperson, 216-687-2301, Fax: 216-687-9279, E-mail: e.ziolek@csuohio.edu. *Application contact:* Dr. Birch Browning, Coordinator of Graduate Studies and Admission, 216-687-3768, Fax: 216-687-9279, E-mail: b.browning@csuohio.edu.

The College of Saint Rose, Graduate Studies, School of Arts and Humanities, Music Department, Program in Music, Albany, NY 12203-1419. Offers MA. *Accreditation:* NASM. *Degree requirements:* For master's, final project. *Entrance requirements:* For master's, audition, minimum undergraduate GPA of 3.0. Additional exam requirements/recommendations for international students: Required—TOEFL (minimum score 550 paper-based; 213 computer-based). Electronic applications accepted.

Colorado State University, Graduate School, College of Liberal Arts, Department of Music, Theater, and Dance, Fort Collins, CO 80523-1779. Offers music (MM). *Accreditation:* NASM. Part-time programs available. *Faculty:* 29 full-time (9 women). *Students:* 71 full-time (46 women), 79 part-time (64 women); includes 20 minority (5 Asian, non-Hispanic/Latino; 12 Hispanic/Latino; 3 Two or more races, non-Hispanic/Latino), 15 international. Average age 30. 85 applicants, 78% accepted, 48 enrolled. In 2010, 47 master's awarded. *Degree requirements:* For master's, variable foreign language requirement, comprehensive exam (for some programs), thesis (for some programs), 2 recitals, project. *Entrance requirements:* For master's, minimum GPA of 3.0, audition, bachelor's degree, letters of recommendation. Additional exam requirements/recommendations for international students: Required—TOEFL (minimum score 550 paper-based; 213 computer-based; 80 iBT). *Application deadline:* For fall admission, 2/15 priority date for domestic students; for spring admission, 11/15 priority date for domestic students. Applications are processed on a rolling basis. Application fee: $50. Electronic applications accepted. *Expenses:* Tuition, state resident: full-time $7434; part-time $413 per credit. Tuition, nonresident: full-time $19,022; part-time $1057 per credit. Required fees: $1729; $88 per credit. *Financial support:* In 2010–11, 25 students received support, including 25 teaching assistantships with full and partial tuition reimbursements available (averaging $6,850 per year); fellowships, research assistantships with partial tuition reimbursements available, career-related internships or fieldwork, Federal Work-Study, scholarships/grants, traineeships, and unspecified assistantships also available. Financial award application deadline: 3/1; financial award applicants required to submit FAFSA. *Faculty research:* Neurobiology, musicology, music literacy, music learning, music therapy. *Unit head:* Dr. Michael H. Thaut, Chair, 970-491-5529, Fax: 970-491-7541, E-mail: michael.thaut@colostate.edu. *Application contact:* Dr. William B. Davis, Graduate Coordinator, 970-491-5888, Fax: 970-491-7541, E-mail: william.davis@colostate.edu.

Columbia College Chicago, Graduate School, Program in Music Composition for the Screen, Chicago, IL 60605-1996. Offers MFA. *Students:* 24 full-time (5 women); includes 3 Black or African American, non-Hispanic/Latino; 1 Hispanic/Latino, 5 international. Average age 25. 43 applicants, 53% accepted, 12 enrolled. In 2010, 10 master's awarded. *Application deadline:* For fall admission, 1/5 for domestic and international students. *Expenses:* Tuition: Full-time $16,966; part-time $684 per credit. Required fees: $520; $113 per semester. One-time fee: $150 full-time. Tuition and fees vary according to course load and program. *Unit head:* J. Richard Dunscomb, Chair, 312-369-6272, E-mail: rdunscomb@colum.edu. *Application contact:* Cate Lagueux, Director of Graduate Admissions, 312-369-7260, Fax: 312-369-8047, E-mail: clagueux@colum.edu.

Columbia University, Graduate School of Arts and Sciences, Division of Humanities, Department of Music, New York, NY 10027. Offers M Phil, MA, DMA, PhD. *Degree requirements:* For master's, 2 foreign languages, thesis or alternative; for doctorate, variable foreign language requirement, thesis/dissertation. *Entrance requirements:* For master's and doctorate, GRE General Test, GRE Subject Test, sample of written work. Additional exam requirements/recommendations for international students: Required—TOEFL. *Faculty research:* Historical musicology, ethnomusicology, composition and theory.

Concordia University, School of Graduate Studies, Faculty of Fine Arts, Department of Music, Montréal, QC H3G 1M8, Canada. Offers advanced music performance studies (Diploma). *Degree requirements:* For Diploma, performance, 2 recitals.

Concordia University Chicago, College of Graduate and Innovative Programs, Program in Church Music, River Forest, IL 60305-1499. Offers MCM. *Accreditation:* NASM. Part-time programs available. *Degree requirements:* For master's, composition, recital, or thesis. *Entrance requirements:* For master's, minimum GPA of 2.9, audition. Additional exam requirements/recommendations for international students: Required—TOEFL (minimum score 550 paper-based; 195 computer-based). Electronic applications accepted. *Faculty research:* Twentieth-century sacred choral music, liturgical context of sacred music after the Council of Trent, dance and music of J.S. Bach.

Concordia University Chicago, College of Graduate and Innovative Programs, Program in Music, River Forest, IL 60305-1499. Offers MA. Part-time programs available. *Degree requirements:* For master's, composition, recital, or thesis. *Entrance requirements:* For master's, minimum GPA of 2.9, audition. Additional exam requirements/recommendations for international students: Required—TOEFL (minimum score 550 paper-based; 195 computer-based). Electronic applications accepted.

Concordia University Wisconsin, Graduate Programs, School of Arts and Sciences, Program in Church Music, Mequon, WI 53097-2402. Offers MCM. *Degree requirements:* For master's, comprehensive exam, thesis or alternative. *Entrance requirements:* For master's, minimum GPA of 3.0. Additional exam requirements/recommendations for international students: Required—TOEFL.

Conservatorio de Musica, Program in Musical Performance, San Juan, PR 00907. Offers guitar (Diploma); orchestral instruments (Diploma); piano (Diploma); vocal performance (Diploma). *Entrance requirements:* For degree, 3 letters of recommendation, audition, degree in music, minimum GPA of 2.5.

Converse College, Carroll McDaniel Petrie School of Music, Spartanburg, SC 29302-0006. Offers instrumental performance (M Mus); music education (M Mus); piano pedagogy (M Mus); vocal performance (M Mus). *Accreditation:* NASM. Part-time and evening/weekend programs available. *Degree requirements:* For master's, variable foreign language requirement, comprehensive exam, thesis (for some programs), recitals. *Entrance requirements:* For master's, NTE (music education), audition, 3 letters of recommendation. Additional exam requirements/recommendations for international students: Required—TOEFL. Electronic applications accepted. *Expenses:* Tuition: Part-time $365 per credit hour. *Faculty research:* Chamber music, opera, performance, composition, recording.

Cornell University, Graduate School, Graduate Fields of Arts and Sciences, Field of Music, Ithaca, NY 14853-0001. Offers composition (DMA); musicology (PhD); performance practice (DMA); theory of music (MA). *Faculty:* 18 full-time (5 women). *Students:* 35 full-time (16 women); includes 1 Black or African American, non-Hispanic/Latino; 2 Asian, non-Hispanic/Latino; 1 Hispanic/Latino, 16 international. Average age 27. 154 applicants, 7% accepted, 7 enrolled. In 2010, 4 master's, 6 doctorates awarded. *Degree requirements:* For doctorate, comprehensive exam, thesis/dissertation, 1 foreign language (DMA), 2 foreign languages (PhD). *Entrance requirements:* For doctorate, GRE General Test, 2 music papers (PhD); 2 recent scores (with recording) and 1 music paper (DMA in composition); 1 music paper, recording and audition (DMA in performance practice). Additional exam requirements/recommendations for international students: Required—TOEFL (minimum score 600 paper-based; 250 computer-based; 77 iBT). *Application deadline:* For fall admission, 1/15 for domestic students. Application fee: $80. Electronic applications accepted. *Expenses:* Tuition: Full-time $29,500. Required fees: $76. Tuition and fees vary according to degree level and program. *Financial support:* In 2010–11, 10 fellowships with full tuition reimbursements, 19 teaching assistantships with full tuition reimbursements were awarded; research assistantships with full tuition reimbursements, institutionally sponsored loans, scholarships/grants, health care benefits, tuition waivers (full and partial), and unspecified assistantships also available. Financial award applicants required to submit FAFSA. *Faculty research:* Music history, music theory, performance practice, ethnomusicology, composition. *Unit head:* Director of Graduate Studies, 607-255-9078. *Application contact:* Graduate Field Assistant, 607-255-9078, E-mail: grad_music@cornell.edu.

Curtis Institute of Music, Graduate Studies, Philadelphia, PA 19103-6107. Offers opera (MM). *Accreditation:* NASM. *Entrance requirements:* For master's, audition or performance in 2 or more principal roles or 6 major scenes.

Dalhousie University, Faculty of Arts and Social Science, Department of Musicology, Halifax, NS B3H 4R2, Canada. Offers MA. *Entrance requirements:* Additional exam requirements/recommendations for international students: Required—TOEFL, IELTS, CANTEST, CAEL, or Michigan English Language Assessment Battery. Electronic applications accepted.

Dartmouth College, Arts and Sciences Graduate Programs, Department of Music, Hanover, NH 03755. Offers electro-acoustic music (AM). *Degree requirements:* For master's, thesis or alternative. *Entrance requirements:* Additional exam requirements/recommendations for international students: Required—TOEFL. *Faculty research:* Composition and design of computer music software and related topics.

DePaul University, School of Music, Chicago, IL 60614. Offers applied music (performance) (MM, Certificate); jazz studies (MM), including composition, performance; music composition (MM); music education (MM). *Accreditation:* NASM (one or more programs are accredited). Part-time and evening/weekend programs available. *Faculty:* 11 full-time (2 women), 50 part-time/adjunct (14 women). *Students:* 50 full-time (29 women), 73 part-time (38 women); includes 5 Black or African American, non-Hispanic/Latino; 5 Asian, non-Hispanic/Latino; 5 Hispanic/Latino; 1 Two or more races, non-Hispanic/Latino, 28 international. Average age 24. 312 applicants, 31% accepted, 50 enrolled. In 2010, 40 master's, 5 Certificates awarded. *Degree requirements:* For master's, comprehensive exam, terminal project, recital (for performers); for Certificate, recital. *Entrance requirements:* For master's, bachelor's degree in music or related field, minimum GPA of 3.0, auditions (performance), scores (composition); for Certificate, master's degree in performance or related field, auditions (for performance majors). Additional exam requirements/recommendations for international students: Required—TOEFL (minimum score 550 paper-based; 213 computer-based; 80 iBT). *Application deadline:* For fall admission, 1/15 priority date for domestic and international students. Applications are processed on a rolling basis. Application fee: $40. Electronic applications accepted. *Expenses:* Contact institution. *Financial support:* In 2010–11, 4 fellowships with partial tuition reimbursements were awarded; teaching assistantships, career-related internships or fieldwork, Federal Work-Study, scholarships/grants, and tuition waivers also available. Support available to part-time students. Financial award application deadline: 1/15. *Unit head:* Dr. Donald E. Casey, Dean, 773-325-7256, E-mail: dcasey@depaul.edu. *Application contact:* Ross Beacraft, Director of Admissions, 773-325-7444, Fax: 773-325-7429, E-mail: rbeacraf@depaul.edu.

Duke University, Graduate School, Department of Music, Durham, NC 27708. Offers music composition (AM, PhD); musicology (AM, PhD); performance practice (AM, PhD). Part-time programs available. *Faculty:* 13 full-time. *Students:* 33 full-time (15 women); includes 1 Asian, non-Hispanic/Latino, 8 international. 28 applicants, 14% accepted, 2 enrolled. In 2010, 8 master's, 6 doctorates awarded. Terminal master's awarded for partial completion of doctoral program. *Degree requirements:* For master's, 2 foreign languages; for doctorate, 3 foreign languages, thesis/dissertation. *Entrance requirements:* For master's, GRE General Test, paper on musical topic (for musicology); paper and recording (for performance practice); samples of compositions (for music composition); for doctorate, GRE General Test, paper on musical topic (for musicology); samples of compositions (for music composition). Additional exam requirements/recommendations for international students: Required—TOEFL (minimum score 550 paper-based; 213 computer-based; 83 iBT), IELTS (minimum score 7). *Application deadline:* For fall admission, 12/8 priority date for domestic and international students; for spring admission, 11/1 for domestic students. Application fee: $75. Electronic applications accepted. *Financial support:* Fellowships, research assistantships, teaching assistantships, Federal Work-Study available. Financial award application deadline: 12/31. *Unit head:* Philip Rupprecht, Director of

Music

Duke University (continued)
Graduate Studies, 919-660-3308, Fax: 919-660-3301, E-mail: christy.reuss@duke.edu. *Application contact:* Elizabeth Hutton, Director of Admissions, 919-684-3913, Fax: 919-684-2277, E-mail: grad-admissions@duke.edu.

Duquesne University, Mary Pappert School of Music, Pittsburgh, PA 15282-0001. Offers music composition (MM); music education (MM); music performance (MM, AD); music technology (MM), including digital pedagogy, electronic composition, electronic performance; music theory (MM); sacred music (MM). *Accreditation:* NASM. Part-time programs available. *Faculty:* 26 full-time (10 women), 72 part-time/adjunct (16 women). *Students:* 78 full-time (40 women), 22 part-time (12 women); includes 3 Black or African American, non-Hispanic/Latino; 14 Asian, non-Hispanic/Latino; 3 Hispanic/Latino. Average age 23. 105 applicants, 66% accepted, 50 enrolled. In 2010, 40 master's awarded. *Degree requirements:* For master's, comprehensive exam, thesis (for some programs), recital (music performance); for AD, recital. *Entrance requirements:* For master's, audition, minimum undergraduate QPA of 3.0 in music, portfolio of original compositions, theoretical papers, or music education experience; for AD, audition. Additional exam requirements/recommendations for international students: Required—TOEFL (minimum score 550 paper-based; 213 computer-based; 79 iBT). *Application deadline:* For fall admission, 7/1 priority date for domestic and international students; for spring admission, 12/1 priority date for domestic and international students. Applications are processed on a rolling basis. Application fee: $50. Electronic applications accepted. *Expenses:* Contact institution. *Financial support:* In 2010–11, 57 students received support. Career-related internships or fieldwork, institutionally sponsored loans, scholarships/grants, tuition waivers (full and partial), unspecified assistantships, and assistantships ($11,938) available. Financial award application deadline: 4/1. *Faculty research:* Performance; computer-assisted instruction in music at elementary and secondary levels; electronic music; contemporary music, theory, and analysis; development of online graduate music courses. Total annual research expenditures: $104,000. *Unit head:* Dr. Edward W. Kocher, Dean, 412-396-6082, Fax: 412-396-1524, E-mail: kocher@duq.edu. *Application contact:* Peggy Eiseman, Administrative Assistant of Admissions, 412-396-5064, Fax: 412-396-5719, E-mail: eiseman@duq.edu.

East Carolina University, Graduate School, College of Fine Arts and Communication, School of Music, Greenville, NC 27858-4353. Offers music education (MM); music therapy (MM); performance (MM); theory and composition (MM). *Accreditation:* NASM. Part-time programs available. *Degree requirements:* For master's, comprehensive exam, thesis optional. *Entrance requirements:* For master's, GRE General Test or MAT. Additional exam requirements/recommendations for international students: Required—TOEFL. *Expenses:* Tuition, state resident: full-time $3130; part-time $391.25 per credit hour. Tuition, nonresident: full-time $13,817; part-time $1727.13 per credit hour. Required fees: $1916; $239.50 per credit hour. Tuition and fees vary according to campus/location and program.

Eastern Illinois University, Graduate School, College of Arts and Humanities, Department of Music, Charleston, IL 61920-3099. Offers MA. *Accreditation:* NASM. Part-time programs available. *Degree requirements:* For master's, thesis or alternative, recital.

Eastern Kentucky University, The Graduate School, College of Arts and Sciences, Department of Music, Richmond, KY 40475-3102. Offers choral conducting (MM); performance (MM); theory/composition (MM). *Accreditation:* NASM. Part-time programs available. *Degree requirements:* For master's, thesis optional. *Entrance requirements:* For master's, GRE General Test, minimum GPA of 2.5. *Faculty research:* Technology.

Eastern Michigan University, Graduate School, College of Arts and Sciences, Department of Communication, Media and Theatre Arts, Programs in Theatre Arts, Ypsilanti, MI 48197. Offers interpretation/performance studies (MA); theatre arts (MA). Part-time and evening/weekend programs available. Postbaccalaureate distance learning degree programs offered (minimal on-campus study). *Students:* 2 full-time (1 woman), 17 part-time (9 women); includes 2 minority (both Black or African American, non-Hispanic/Latino). Average age 32. 14 applicants, 93% accepted, 6 enrolled. In 2010, 6 master's awarded. *Degree requirements:* For master's, thesis or alternative. *Entrance requirements:* Additional exam requirements/recommendations for international students: Required—TOEFL. *Application deadline:* Applications are processed on a rolling basis. Application fee: $35. *Financial support:* Fellowships, research assistantships with full tuition reimbursements, teaching assistantships with full tuition reimbursements, career-related internships or fieldwork, Federal Work-Study, institutionally sponsored loans, scholarships/grants, and unspecified assistantships available. Support available to part-time students. Financial award applicants required to submit FAFSA. *Unit head:* Kenneth Stevens, Coordinator, 734-487-1153, Fax: 734-487-3443, E-mail: ken.stevens@emich.edu. *Application contact:* Kenneth Stevens, Coordinator, 734-487-1153, Fax: 734-487-3443, E-mail: ken.stevens@emich.edu.

Eastern Michigan University, Graduate School, College of Arts and Sciences, Department of Music and Dance, Ypsilanti, MI 48197. Offers music composition (MM); music education (MM); music pedagogy (MM); music performance (MM). *Accreditation:* NASM. Part-time and evening/weekend programs available. Postbaccalaureate distance learning degree programs offered (minimal on-campus study). *Faculty:* 26 full-time (10 women). *Students:* 7 full-time (5 women), 23 part-time (13 women); includes 7 minority (4 Black or African American, non-Hispanic/Latino; 1 Asian, non-Hispanic/Latino; 2 Hispanic/Latino), 6 international. Average age 30. 24 applicants, 63% accepted, 9 enrolled. In 2010, 13 master's awarded. *Entrance requirements:* Additional exam requirements/recommendations for international students: Required—TOEFL. *Application deadline:* Applications are processed on a rolling basis. Application fee: $35. *Financial support:* Fellowships, research assistantships with full tuition reimbursements, teaching assistantships with full tuition reimbursements, career-related internships or fieldwork, Federal Work-Study, institutionally sponsored loans, scholarships/grants, tuition waivers (partial), and unspecified assistantships available. Support available to part-time students. Financial award applicants required to submit FAFSA. *Unit head:* Dr. David Woike, Department Head, 734-487-4380, Fax: 734-487-6939, E-mail: dwoike@emich.edu. *Application contact:* Dr. David Pierce, Coordinator of Music Advising, 734-487-4380, Fax: 734-487-6939, E-mail: david.pierce@emich.edu.

Eastern Washington University, Graduate Studies, College of Arts and Letters, Department of Music, Cheney, WA 99004-2431. Offers composition (MA); instrumental/vocal performance (MA); music education (MA); music history and literature (MA). *Accreditation:* NASM. Part-time programs available. *Degree requirements:* For master's, comprehensive exam, thesis or alternative. *Entrance requirements:* For master's, GRE General Test, minimum GPA of 3.0.

Edinboro University of Pennsylvania, School of Education, Department of Professional Studies, Edinboro, PA 16444. Offers counseling (MA), including community counseling, elementary guidance, rehabilitation counseling, secondary guidance, student personnel services; educational leadership (M Ed), including elementary school administration, secondary school administration; educational psychology (M Ed); educational specialist school psychology (MS); elementary principal (Certificate); elementary school guidance counselor (Certificate); K-12 school administration (Certificate); letter of eligibility (Certificate); reading (M Ed); reading specialist (Certificate); school psychology (Certificate); school supervision (Certificate), including music, special education. Part-time and evening/weekend programs available. *Faculty:* 24 full-time (18 women), 9 part-time/adjunct (5 women). *Students:* 181 full-time (144 women), 736 part-time (581 women); includes 32 minority (23 Black or African American, non-Hispanic/Latino; 3 American Indian or Alaska Native, non-Hispanic/Latino; 1 Asian, non-Hispanic/Latino; 5 Hispanic/Latino. Average age 32. In 2010, 318 master's, 49 other advanced degrees awarded. *Degree requirements:* For master's, thesis or alternative, competency exam; for Certificate, thesis or alternative. *Entrance requirements:* For master's and Certificate, GRE or MAT, minimum QPA of 2.5. *Application deadline:* Applications are processed on a rolling basis. Application fee: $30. Electronic applications accepted. *Expenses:* Tuition, state resident: full-time $6966; part-time $387 per credit. Tuition, nonresident: full-time $11,146; part-time $619 per credit. Required fees: $2401.70; $96.25 per credit. *Financial support:* In 2010–11, 60

research assistantships with full and partial tuition reimbursements (averaging $4,050 per year) were awarded; career-related internships or fieldwork, Federal Work-Study, scholarships/grants, and unspecified assistantships also available. Support available to part-time students. Financial award application deadline: 2/15; financial award applicants required to submit FAFSA. *Unit head:* Dr. Salene Cowher, Program Head, Counseling, 814-732-1116, E-mail: scowher@edinboro.edu. *Application contact:* Dr. Andrew Pushchack, Program Head, Educational Leadership, 814-732-1548, E-mail: apushchack@edinboro.edu.

Emory University, Laney Graduate School, Department of Music, Atlanta, GA 30322-1100. Offers choral conducting (MM, MSM); organ performance (MM, MSM). *Degree requirements:* For master's, comprehensive exam, recital or worship service/recital. *Entrance requirements:* For master's, GRE General Test, audition, interview. Additional exam requirements/recommendations for international students: Required—TOEFL. Electronic applications accepted. *Expenses:* Tuition: Full-time $33,800. Required fees: $1300. *Faculty research:* 19th century criticism, Schenker, Bach Aria styles, contemporary passion music, Andriesson, cross-cultural research, organ performance.

Emporia State University, Graduate School, College of Liberal Arts and Sciences, Department of Music, Emporia, KS 66801-5087. Offers music education (MM), including instrumental, vocal; performance (MM). *Accreditation:* NASM. Part-time programs available. *Faculty:* 13 full-time (5 women), 4 part-time/adjunct (all women). *Students:* 7 full-time (4 women), 8 part-time (6 women); includes 1 minority (Black or African American, non-Hispanic/Latino), 6 international. 2 applicants, 100% accepted, 2 enrolled. In 2010, 1 master's awarded. *Degree requirements:* For master's, comprehensive exam or thesis. *Entrance requirements:* For master's, music qualifying exam, appropriate undergraduate degree. Additional exam requirements/recommendations for international students: Required—TOEFL (minimum score 520 paper-based; 133 computer-based; 68 iBT). *Application deadline:* For fall admission, 8/15 priority date for domestic students. Applications are processed on a rolling basis. Application fee: $30 ($75 for international students). Electronic applications accepted. *Expenses:* Tuition, state resident: full-time $4382; part-time $183 per credit hour. Tuition, nonresident: full-time $13,572; part-time $566 per credit hour. Required fees: $1022; $62 per credit hour. Tuition and fees vary according to course level, course load and campus/location. *Financial support:* In 2010–11, 1 research assistantship with full tuition reimbursement (averaging $3,530 per year), 3 teaching assistantships with full tuition reimbursements (averaging $5,883 per year) were awarded; Federal Work-Study, institutionally sponsored loans, health care benefits, and unspecified assistantships also available. Financial award application deadline: 3/15; financial award applicants required to submit FAFSA. *Unit head:* Dr. Allan D. Comstock, Chair, 620-341-5431, E-mail: acomstoc@emporia.edu. *Application contact:* Dr. Andrew Houchins, Graduate Coordinator, 620-341-6089, E-mail: ahouchin@emporia.edu.

Five Towns College, Department of Music, Dix Hills, NY 11746-6055. Offers jazz/commercial music (MM); music (DMA); music education (MM). Part-time programs available. *Faculty:* 6 full-time (2 women), 15 part-time/adjunct (4 women). *Students:* 18 full-time (5 women), 23 part-time (4 women); includes 4 minority (3 Black or African American, non-Hispanic/Latino; 1 Hispanic/Latino), 10 international. Average age 28. 20 applicants, 70% accepted, 6 enrolled. In 2010, 3 master's awarded. *Degree requirements:* For master's, thesis, exams, major composition or capstone project, recital; for doctorate, comprehensive exam, thesis/dissertation, final oral exam. *Entrance requirements:* For master's, audition, bachelor's degree in music or music education, minimum GPA of 2.75, 36 hours of course work in performance; for doctorate, master's degree in music, minimum GPA of 3.0, 3 letters of recommendation. Additional exam requirements/recommendations for international students: Required—TOEFL (minimum score 550 paper-based; 213 computer-based; 80 iBT). *Application deadline:* For fall admission, 9/1 for domestic and international students; for spring admission, 1/25 for domestic and international students. Applications are processed on a rolling basis. Application fee: $50. *Expenses:* Tuition: Full-time $13,200; part-time $550 per credit. Required fees: $300 per semester. One-time fee: $85. Tuition and fees vary according to course level, course load, degree level, program and student level. *Financial support:* Fellowships with tuition reimbursements, tuition waivers (partial) available. Financial award applicants required to submit FAFSA. *Faculty research:* Teaching methods, teaching strategies and techniques, analysis of modern music, jazz. *Unit head:* Dr. Jill Miller-Thorn, Dean of Graduate Studies, 631-656-2142, Fax: 631-656-2172, E-mail: jmillerthorn@ftc.edu. *Application contact:* Jerry Cohen, Dean of Enrollment, 631-656-2121, Fax: 631-656-2172, E-mail: jcohen@ftc.edu.

Florida Atlantic University, Dorothy F. Schmidt College of Arts and Letters, Department of Music, Boca Raton, FL 33431-0991. Offers commercial music (MA); music history/literature (MA); performance (MA). *Accreditation:* NASM. Part-time programs available. *Faculty:* 19 full-time (9 women), 26 part-time/adjunct (7 women). *Students:* 23 full-time (10 women), 8 part-time (3 women); includes 7 minority (3 Black or African American, non-Hispanic/Latino; 4 Hispanic/Latino), 9 international. Average age 35. 14 applicants, 71% accepted, 8 enrolled. In 2010, 14 master's awarded. *Degree requirements:* For master's, lecture/recital or thesis. *Entrance requirements:* For master's, audition, minimum GPA of 3.0 in last 60 hours of course work, placement evaluations in music history and theory. *Application deadline:* For fall admission, 7/1 priority date for domestic students, 2/15 for international students; for spring admission, 11/1 for domestic students, 7/15 for international students. Applications are processed on a rolling basis. Application fee: $30. *Expenses:* Tuition, area resident: Part-time $319.96 per credit. Tuition, state resident: part-time $319.96 per credit. Tuition, nonresident: part-time $926.42 per credit. *Financial support:* Fellowships with partial tuition reimbursements, teaching assistantships with partial tuition reimbursements, career-related internships or fieldwork, Federal Work-Study, and scholarships/grants available. Financial award application deadline: 5/1. *Faculty research:* Classical guitar history and literature, women composers, Mozart opera, composition, performance. *Unit head:* Dr. Heather J. Coltman, Chair, 561-297-3821, Fax: 561-297-2944, E-mail: coltman@fau.edu. *Application contact:* Dr. Heather J. Coltman, Chair, 561-297-3821, Fax: 561-297-2944, E-mail: coltman@fau.edu.

Florida International University, College of Architecture and the Arts, School of Music, Miami, FL 33199. Offers music (MM); music education (MS). Part-time and evening/weekend programs available. *Faculty:* 19 full-time (4 women), 11 part-time/adjunct (3 women). *Students:* 29 full-time (13 women), 11 part-time (3 women); includes 1 Black or African American, non-Hispanic/Latino; 1 Asian, non-Hispanic/Latino; 20 Hispanic/Latino. Average age 27. 42 applicants, 43% accepted, 18 enrolled. In 2010, 15 master's awarded. *Degree requirements:* For master's, thesis (for some programs). *Entrance requirements:* For master's, GRE (depending on program), statement of intent; 2 letters of recommendation; audition, interview and/or writing sample (depending on the area). Additional exam requirements/recommendations for international students: Required—TOEFL (minimum score 550 paper-based; 80 iBT). *Application deadline:* For fall admission, 6/1 for domestic students, 4/1 for international students; for spring admission, 10/1 for domestic students, 9/1 for international students. Applications are processed on a rolling basis. Application fee: $30. Electronic applications accepted. *Financial support:* Institutionally sponsored loans and scholarships/grants available. Financial award application deadline: 3/1; financial award applicants required to submit FAFSA. *Unit head:* Orlando Garcia, Chair, 305-348-3357, Fax: 305-348-4073, E-mail: orlando.garcia@fiu.edu. *Application contact:* Joel Galand, Graduate Program Director, 305-348-2896, Fax: 305-348-4073, E-mail: joel.galand@fiu.edu.

Florida State University, The Graduate School, College of Arts and Sciences, Department of English, Tallahassee, FL 32312. Offers creative writing (MFA); English (PhD), including creative writing, literature, rhetoric and composition; literature (MA); rhetoric and composition (MA). Part-time programs available. *Faculty:* 48 full-time (23 women), 6 part-time/adjunct (1 woman). *Students:* 150 full-time (90 women), 20 part-time (10 women); includes 15 Black or African American, non-Hispanic/Latino; 1 American Indian or Alaska Native, non-Hispanic/Latino; 5 Asian, non-Hispanic/Latino; 10 Hispanic/Latino. Average age 30. 480 applicants, 21% accepted, 58 enrolled. In 2010, 22 master's, 14 doctorates awarded. *Degree requirements:* For master's, one foreign language, thesis or alternative; for doctorate, comprehensive exam, thesis/dissertation, 27 hours of coursework, 24 hours of dissertation work. *Entrance requirements:*

For master's and doctorate, GRE General Test, GRE Subject Test (literature only), sample of written work, 3 letters of recommendation, resume. Additional exam requirements/recommendations for international students: Required—TOEFL. *Application deadline:* For fall admission, 1/1 priority date for domestic and international students. Application fee: $30. Electronic applications accepted. *Expenses:* Tuition, state resident: full-time $8238.24. *Financial support:* In 2010–11, 126 students received support, including 5 fellowships, teaching assistantships (averaging $11,375 per year); career-related internships or fieldwork, Federal Work-Study, and institutionally sponsored loans also available. Financial award application deadline: 1/1; financial award applicants required to submit FAFSA. *Faculty research:* British and Irish literature, American literature, creative writing, rhetoric and composition, multiethnic transnational literature. *Unit head:* Dr. Ralph Berry, Chairman, 850-644-4230, Fax: 850-644-0811, E-mail: rberry@fsu.edu. *Application contact:* Dr. Ralph Berry, Chairman, 850-644-4230, Fax: 850-644-0811, E-mail: rberry@fsu.edu.

Florida State University, The Graduate School, College of Music, Tallahassee, FL 32306. Offers accompanying (MM); arts administration (MA); choral conducting (MM); composition (MM, DM); ethnomusicology (MM); general music (MA); instrumental accompanying (MM); instrumental conducting (MM); jazz studies (MM); music education (MM Ed, PhD); music theory (MM, PhD); music therapy (MM); musicology (MM, PhD), including ethnomusicology (PhD), historical musicology; opera (MM); performance (MM, DM); piano pedagogy (MM); piano technology (MA); vocal accompanying (MM). *Accreditation:* NASM. *Faculty:* 88 full-time, 13 part-time/adjunct. *Students:* 406 full-time (211 women); includes 28 Black or African American, non-Hispanic/Latino; 38 Asian, non-Hispanic/Latino; 32 Hispanic/Latino. Average age 26. 525 applicants, 38% accepted, 145 enrolled. In 2010, 102 master's, 41 doctorates awarded. *Degree requirements:* For master's, comprehensive exam (for some programs), thesis (for some programs), departmental qualifying exam; for doctorate, comprehensive exam (for some programs), thesis/dissertation, departmental qualifying exam. *Entrance requirements:* For master's and doctorate, audition, GRE General Test or minimum GPA of 3.0. Additional exam requirements/recommendations for international students: Required—TOEFL (minimum score 550 paper-based; 213 computer-based). *Application deadline:* For fall admission, 7/1 for domestic students, 5/2 for international students; for spring admission, 11/3 for domestic students, 9/1 for international students. Applications are processed on a rolling basis. Application fee: $30. Electronic applications accepted. *Expenses:* Tuition, state resident: full-time $8238.24. *Financial support:* In 2010–11, 225 students received support, including 3 fellowships with full tuition reimbursements available (averaging $15,000 per year), 9 research assistantships with full tuition reimbursements available (averaging $4,000 per year), 173 teaching assistantships with full tuition reimbursements available (averaging $4,000 per year); career-related internships or fieldwork, Federal Work-Study, and tuition waivers (partial) also available. Support available to part-time students. Financial award application deadline: 2/28; financial award applicants required to submit FAFSA. *Unit head:* Dr. Don Gibson, Dean, 850-644-4361, Fax: 850-644-2033. *Application contact:* Dr. Seth Beckman, Senior Associate Dean for Academic Affairs/Director of Graduate Studies, 850-644-5848, Fax: 850-644-2033, E-mail: sbeckman@admin.fsu.edu.

Fuller Theological Seminary, Graduate School of Theology, Pasadena, CA 91182. Offers Christian leadership (MACL); evangelism (MA); family life education (MA); ministry (M Div, D Min); pastoral ministry (MA); recovery ministry (MA); theology (MAT, Th M, PhD); worship music ministry (MA); worship, theology, and the arts (MA); youth, family, and culture (MA). M Div offered jointly with Denver Conservative Baptist Seminary; D Min with Tyndale University College & Seminary. *Accreditation:* ACIPE; ATS (one or more programs are accredited). Part-time and evening/weekend programs available. *Degree requirements:* For doctorate, variable foreign language requirement, thesis/dissertation; for M Div, 2 foreign languages. *Entrance requirements:* For doctorate, GRE General Test. *Faculty research:* New Testament, Old Testament, systematic theology, history, practical theology.

Garrett-Evangelical Theological Seminary, Graduate and Professional Programs, Evanston, IL 60201-3298. Offers Bible and culture (PhD); Christian education (MA); Christian education and congregational studies (PhD); contemporary theology and culture (PhD); divinity (M Div); ethics, church, and society (MA); liturgical studies (PhD); ministry (D Min); music ministry (MA); pastoral care and counseling (MA); pastoral theology, personality, and culture (PhD); spiritual formation and evangelism (MA); theological studies (MTS); M Div/MSW. M Div/MSW offered jointly with Loyola University Chicago. *Accreditation:* ACIPE; ATS (one or more programs are accredited). Part-time programs available. *Degree requirements:* For master's, thesis (for some programs); for doctorate, thesis/dissertation. *Entrance requirements:* For doctorate, GRE (PhD). Additional exam requirements/recommendations for international students: Required—TOEFL (minimum score 560 paper-based; 230 computer-based). Electronic applications accepted.

George Mason University, College of Visual and Performing Arts, School of Music, Fairfax, VA 22030. Offers instrumental performance artist (Certificate); music (MM); music education (PhD); musical arts (DMA); piano performance artist (Certificate); vocal performance artist (Certificate). *Accreditation:* NASM. Part-time and evening/weekend programs available. *Faculty:* 20 full-time (8 women), 20 part-time/adjunct (12 women). *Students:* 19 full-time (6 women), 38 part-time (25 women); includes 1 Black or African American, non-Hispanic/Latino; 5 Asian, non-Hispanic/Latino; 3 Hispanic/Latino; 1 Two or more races, non-Hispanic/Latino. Average age 30. 65 applicants, 54% accepted, 21 enrolled. In 2010, 24 master's awarded. *Degree requirements:* For master's, recital (for all except MM in music education), summer auditions, portfolios, compositions. *Entrance requirements:* For master's, 2 letters of recommendation. Additional exam requirements/recommendations for international students: Required—TOEFL (minimum score 570 paper-based; 230 computer-based; 88 iBT). *Application deadline:* For fall admission, 4/1 priority date for domestic students; for spring admission, 11/1 priority date for domestic students. Applications are processed on a rolling basis. Application fee: $100. Electronic applications accepted. *Expenses:* Contact institution. *Financial support:* Career-related internships or fieldwork, Federal Work-Study, scholarships/grants, unspecified assistantships, and health care benefits (full-time research or teaching assistantship recipients) available. Financial award application deadline: 3/1; financial award applicants required to submit FAFSA. *Faculty research:* Single or multiple instruments, music education, composition, conducting, pedagogy. *Unit head:* James Gardner, Director, 703-993-1380, E-mail: jgviolin@gmu.edu. *Application contact:* Victoria Salmon, Graduate Studies, 703-993-4541, E-mail: vsalmon@gmu.edu.

Georgia Southern University, Jack N. Averitt College of Graduate Studies, College of Liberal Arts and Social Sciences, Department of Music, Statesboro, GA 30460. Offers MM. *Accreditation:* NASM. Part-time and evening/weekend programs available. *Students:* 11 full-time (6 women), 17 part-time (4 women); includes 7 Black or African American, non-Hispanic/Latino; 1 Hispanic/Latino, 2 international. Average age 28. 16 applicants, 88% accepted, 8 enrolled. In 2010, 5 master's awarded. *Degree requirements:* For master's, comprehensive exam, recital or final project. *Entrance requirements:* For master's, minimum GPA of 2.5, audition, letters of recommendation. Additional exam requirements/recommendations for international students: Required—TOEFL (minimum score 550 paper-based; 213 computer-based; 80 iBT). *Application deadline:* For fall admission, 3/1 priority date for domestic and international students; for spring admission, 10/1 priority date for domestic students, 10/1 for international students. Applications are processed on a rolling basis. Application fee: $50. Electronic applications accepted. *Expenses:* Tuition, state resident: full-time $6000; part-time $250 per semester hour. Tuition, nonresident: full-time $23,976; part-time $999 per semester hour. Required fees: $1644. *Financial support:* In 2010–11, 27 students received support, including research assistantships with partial tuition reimbursements available (averaging $7,200 per year), teaching assistantships with partial tuition reimbursements available (averaging $7,200 per year); Federal Work-Study, scholarships/grants, tuition waivers (partial), and unspecified assistantships also available. Support available to part-time students. Financial award application deadline: 4/15; financial award applicants required to submit FAFSA. *Faculty research:* Music history and literature, technology in music, music composition, music performance, music/education. *Unit head:* Dr. Richard E. Mercier, Chair, 912-478-5396, Fax: 912-478-1295, E-mail: rmercier@georgiasouthern.edu. *Application contact:* Dr. Charles Ziglar, Coordinator for Graduate Student Recruitment, 912-478-5635, Fax: 912-478-0740, E-mail: gradadmissions@georgiasouthern.edu.

Georgia State University, College of Arts and Sciences, School of Music, Atlanta, GA 30303. Offers M Mu. *Accreditation:* NASM. Part-time and evening/weekend programs available. *Degree requirements:* For master's, comprehensive exam, thesis (for some programs), recital, exam. *Entrance requirements:* For master's, GRE General Test or MAT (music education), GRE (composition), departmental supplemental form, audition. Additional exam requirements/recommendations for international students: Required—TOEFL. Electronic applications accepted. *Faculty research:* Teaching effectiveness assessment, computer music applications, arts/arts education policy, community music, psychology of music learning.

Graduate School and University Center of the City University of New York, Graduate Studies, Program in Music, New York, NY 10016-4039. Offers DMA, PhD. *Degree requirements:* For doctorate, 2 foreign languages, thesis/dissertation. *Entrance requirements:* For doctorate, GRE General Test. Additional exam requirements/recommendations for international students: Required—TOEFL. Electronic applications accepted.

Gratz College, Graduate Programs, Program in Jewish Music, Melrose Park, PA 19027. Offers MA, Certificate, MA/MA. Part-time programs available. *Degree requirements:* For master's, one foreign language, comprehensive exam, recital or thesis. *Entrance requirements:* For master's, audition, interview.

Hardin-Simmons University, Graduate School, School of Music and Fine Arts, Abilene, TX 79698-0001. Offers church music (MM); music education (MM); music performance (MM); theory-composition (MM). *Accreditation:* NASM. Part-time programs available. *Faculty:* 11 full-time (3 women). *Students:* 4 full-time (1 woman), 3 part-time (all women). Average age 30. 7 applicants, 57% accepted, 4 enrolled. In 2010, 6 master's awarded. *Degree requirements:* For master's, one foreign language, comprehensive exam, thesis (for some programs). *Entrance requirements:* For master's, minimum undergraduate GPA of 3.0 in major, 2.7 overall; performance; writing sample; demonstrated knowledge in chosen area. Additional exam requirements/recommendations for international students: Required—TOEFL (minimum score 550 paper-based; 213 computer-based; 75 iBT). *Application deadline:* For fall admission, 8/15 priority date for domestic students, 4/1 for international students; for spring admission, 1/5 priority date for domestic students, 9/1 for international students. Applications are processed on a rolling basis. Application fee: $50. *Expenses:* Tuition: Full-time $12,150; part-time $675 per credit hour. Required fees: $650; $110 per semester. Tuition and fees vary according to degree level. *Financial support:* In 2010–11, 3 fellowships (averaging $1,200 per year) were awarded; career-related internships or fieldwork and scholarships/grants also available. Support available to part-time students. Financial award application deadline: 6/30; financial award applicants required to submit FAFSA. *Unit head:* Dr. Lynette Chambers, Program Director, 325-670-1430, Fax: 325-670-5873, E-mail: lborman@hsutx.edu. *Application contact:* Dr. Nancy Kucinski, Dean of Graduate Studies, 325-670-1298, Fax: 325-670-1564, E-mail: gradoff@hsutx.edu.

Harvard University, Graduate School of Arts and Sciences, Department of Music, Cambridge, MA 02138. Offers composition (AM, PhD); musicology (AM); musicology and ethnomusicology (PhD); theory (AM, PhD). *Degree requirements:* For doctorate, 3 foreign languages, thesis/dissertation, composition, analytical paper. *Entrance requirements:* For master's and doctorate, GRE General Test. Additional exam requirements/recommendations for international students: Required—TOEFL. *Expenses:* Tuition: Full-time $34,976. Required fees: $1166. Full-time tuition and fees vary according to program.

Hebrew College, Program in Jewish Studies, Newton Centre, MA 02459. Offers Jewish liturgical music (Certificate); Jewish music education (Certificate); Jewish studies (MA). Part-time and evening/weekend programs available. Postbaccalaureate distance learning degree programs offered (minimal on-campus study). *Degree requirements:* For master's, one foreign language. *Entrance requirements:* For master's, GRE, interview. Additional exam requirements/recommendations for international students: Required—TOEFL.

Hebrew Union College–Jewish Institute of Religion, School of Sacred Music, New York, NY 10012-1186. Offers MSM. *Degree requirements:* For master's, one foreign language, thesis, recital. *Entrance requirements:* For master's, GRE, minimum 2 years of college-level Hebrew, bachelor's degree in music or related area, trained singing voice. Additional exam requirements/recommendations for international students: Required—TOEFL. *Expenses:* Contact institution.

Hofstra University, School of Education, Health, and Human Services, Programs in Teaching K-12, Hempstead, NY 11549. Offers bilingual education (MS Ed); bilingual extension (CAS), including education/speech language pathology, intensive teacher institute; family and consumer science (MS Ed); fine art and music education (Advanced Certificate); fine arts education (MA, MS Ed); middle childhood extension (Advanced Certificate), including grades 5-6 or 7-9; music education (MA, MS Ed); teaching languages other than English and TESOL (MS Ed); TESOL (MS Ed); wind conducting (MA). Part-time and evening/weekend programs available. *Students:* 65 full-time (55 women), 67 part-time (52 women); includes 8 Black or African American, non-Hispanic/Latino; 8 Asian, non-Hispanic/Latino; 16 Hispanic/Latino; 1 Two or more races, non-Hispanic/Latino, 1 international. Average age 30. 102 applicants, 87% accepted, 41 enrolled. In 2010, 56 master's, 24 other advanced degrees awarded. *Degree requirements:* For master's, one foreign language, thesis (for some programs), completion of electronic and Tk20 portfolios. *Entrance requirements:* For master's, 2 letters of recommendation, portfolio, teacher certification (MA), essay; for other advanced degree, 2 letters of recommendation, interview, teaching certificate, essay. Additional exam requirements/recommendations for international students: Required—TOEFL (minimum score 550 paper-based; 213 computer-based; 80 iBT). *Application deadline:* Applications are processed on a rolling basis. Application fee: $70 ($75 for international students). Electronic applications accepted. *Expenses:* Tuition: Full-time $18,000; part-time $1000 per credit hour. Required fees: $970; $145 per term. Tuition and fees vary according to program. *Financial support:* In 2010–11, 49 students received support, including 14 fellowships with full and partial tuition reimbursements available (averaging $2,750 per year), 2 research assistantships with full and partial tuition reimbursements available (averaging $9,091 per year); career-related internships or fieldwork, Federal Work-Study, institutionally sponsored loans, scholarships/grants, tuition waivers (full and partial), unspecified assistantships, and scholarships also available. Support available to part-time students. Financial award applicants required to submit FAFSA. *Faculty research:* The teacher/artist, interdisciplinary curriculum, applied linguistics, structural inequalities, creativity. *Unit head:* Dr. Esther Fusco, Chairperson, 516-463-7704, Fax: 516-463-6196, E-mail: catezf@hofstra.edu. *Application contact:* Carol Drummer, Dean of Graduate Admissions, 516-463-4876, Fax: 516-463-4664, E-mail: gradstudent@hofstra.edu.

Hollins University, Graduate Programs, Program in Liberal Studies, Roanoke, VA 24020-1603. Offers humanities (MALS); interdisciplinary studies (MALS); justice and legal studies (MALS); liberal studies (CAS); social science (MALS); visual and performing arts (MALS). Part-time and evening/weekend programs available. *Degree requirements:* For master's, thesis. *Entrance requirements:* For master's, letters of recommendation, interview. Additional exam requirements/recommendations for international students: Required—TOEFL (minimum score 550 paper-based; 213 computer-based; 79 iBT). Electronic applications accepted. *Faculty research:* Elderly blacks, film, feminist economics, US voting patterns, Wagner, diversity.

Holy Names University, Graduate Division, Department of Music, Oakland, CA 94619-1699. Offers Kodaly specialist certificate (Certificate); Kodaly summer certificate (Certificate); music education with Kodaly emphasis (MM); piano pedagogy (MM); piano pedagogy with Suzuki emphasis (MM); vocal pedagogy (MM). *Degree requirements:* For master's, comprehensive exam, recital. *Entrance requirements:* For master's, audition, minimum undergraduate GPA of 2.6 overall, 3.0 in major. Additional exam requirements/recommendations for international students: Required—TOEFL (minimum score 550 paper-based; 213 computer-based; 80 iBT).

Music

Holy Names University (continued)
Expenses: Tuition: Full-time $13,788; part-time $766 per credit. Required fees: $340; $170 per semester. *Faculty research:* Performance practice with special interest in baroque, Romantic, and twentieth-century instrumental and vocal music, choral pedagogy, Hungarian music education.

Hope International University, School of Graduate and Professional Studies, Programs in Ministry, Fullerton, CA 92831-3138. Offers Christian leadership (MCM); church music (MA); church music (Korean track) (MCM); church planting (MCM); intercultural studies (MCM); worship (MCM). Part-time and evening/weekend programs available. Postbaccalaureate distance learning degree programs offered (minimal on-campus study). *Degree requirements:* For master's, thesis (for some programs), project. *Entrance requirements:* For master's, minimum GPA of 3.0, MCM program requires an undergraduate degree in music, 2 references. Additional exam requirements/recommendations for international students: Required—TOEFL (minimum score 550 paper-based; 213 computer-based; 86 iBT); Recommended—IELTS (minimum score 6.5). Electronic applications accepted. *Expenses:* Contact institution. *Faculty research:* Church dynamics, growth methodologies.

Houghton College, Greatbatch School of Music, Houghton, NY 14744. Offers collaborative performance (MMus); composition (MMus); conducting (MMus); music (MA); performance (MMus); world music with theology and intercultural studies (MA). *Accreditation:* NASM. *Degree requirements:* For master's, comprehensive exam (for some programs), thesis (for some programs), recitals (for some programs). *Entrance requirements:* For master's, B Mus or equivalent. Additional exam requirements/recommendations for international students: Required—TOEFL (minimum score 600 paper-based; 250 computer-based). Electronic applications accepted. *Faculty research:* Bach Studies; original compositions; professional performance; contemporary women composers; music in Christian worship.

Howard University, Graduate School, Division of Fine Arts, Department of Music, Washington, DC 20059-0002. Offers applied music (MM); instrument (MM Ed); jazz studies (MM); organ (MM Ed); piano (MM Ed); voice (MM Ed). *Accreditation:* NASM. Part-time programs available. *Degree requirements:* For master's, comprehensive exam, thesis or alternative, departmental qualifying exam, recital. *Entrance requirements:* For master's, minimum GPA of 3.0, bachelor's degree in music or music education. Additional exam requirements/recommendations for international students: Required—TOEFL.

Hunter College of the City University of New York, Graduate School, School of Arts and Sciences, Department of Music, New York, NY 10021-5085. Offers music (MA); music education (MA). Part-time and evening/weekend programs available. *Faculty:* 12 full-time (3 women), 3 part-time/adjunct (2 women). *Students:* 4 full-time (3 women), 27 part-time (15 women); includes 2 Black or African American, non-Hispanic/Latino; 1 Asian, non-Hispanic/Latino; 1 Hispanic/Latino, 4 international. Average age 31. 47 applicants, 40% accepted, 12 enrolled. In 2010, 10 master's awarded. *Degree requirements:* For master's, one foreign language, thesis, composition, essay, or recital; proficiency exam. *Entrance requirements:* For master's, undergraduate major in music (minimum 24 credits) or equivalent, sample of work, research paper. Additional exam requirements/recommendations for international students: Required—TOEFL. *Application deadline:* For fall admission, 4/1 for domestic students, 2/1 for international students; for spring admission, 11/1 for domestic students, 9/1 for international students. Applications are processed on a rolling basis. Application fee: $125. *Financial support:* In 2010–11, 4 fellowships (averaging $1,000 per year) were awarded; Federal Work-Study, tuition waivers (partial), and lesson stipends also available. Support available to part-time students. Financial award application deadline: 4/15. *Faculty research:* African and African-American music, Bach, Renaissance music, early romantic music, theory of tonal music. *Unit head:* Dr. Ruth DeFord, Department Chair, 212-772-5026, Fax: 212-772-5022, E-mail: ruth.deford@hunter.cuny.edu. *Application contact:* L. Pondie Burstein, Graduate Adviser, 212-772-5152, E-mail: huntermust@aol.com.

Illinois State University, Graduate School, College of Fine Arts, School of Music, Normal, IL 61790-2200. Offers MM, MM Ed. *Accreditation:* NASM. *Degree requirements:* For master's, thesis or alternative, performance. *Entrance requirements:* For master's, minimum GPA of 3.0 in music, 2.6 overall; auditions. *Faculty research:* Concerts on the Quad summer concert series.

Indiana State University, College of Graduate and Professional Studies, College of Arts and Sciences, Department of Music, Terre Haute, IN 47809. Offers music performance (MM). *Accreditation:* NASM. *Degree requirements:* For master's, comprehensive exam, thesis, qualifying exam. Electronic applications accepted.

Indiana University Bloomington, Jacobs School of Music, Bloomington, IN 47405-7000. Offers MA, MM, MM/MLS, MME, MS, DM, DME, PhD, AD, Performance Diploma, Spec, MA/MLS. *Accreditation:* NASM (one or more programs are accredited). *Faculty:* 139 full-time (35 women), 11 part-time/adjunct (3 women). *Students:* 715 full-time (363 women), 184 part-time (94 women); includes 17 Black or African American, non-Hispanic/Latino; 2 American Indian or Alaska Native, non-Hispanic/Latino; 58 Asian, non-Hispanic/Latino; 22 Hispanic/Latino; 9 Two or more races, non-Hispanic/Latino, 237 international. Average age 28. 1,353 applicants, 28% accepted, 240 enrolled. In 2010, 134 master's, 36 doctorates, 59 other advanced degrees awarded. Terminal master's awarded for partial completion of doctoral program. *Degree requirements:* For master's, comprehensive exam (for some programs); for doctorate, comprehensive exam, thesis/dissertation. *Entrance requirements:* For master's and doctorate, GRE, audition, 3 letters of recommendation. Additional exam requirements/recommendations for international students: Required—TOEFL (minimum score 560 paper-based; 223 computer-based; 84 iBT). *Application deadline:* For fall admission, 12/1 for domestic and international students; for spring admission, 9/1 for domestic and international students. Applications are processed on a rolling basis. Application fee: $135 ($145 for international students). Electronic applications accepted. *Expenses:* Contact institution. *Financial support:* In 2010–11, 225 students received support, including 6 fellowships with full and partial tuition reimbursements available (averaging $17,000 per year), 85 teaching assistantships with full tuition reimbursements available (averaging $6,000 per year); research assistantships with tuition reimbursements available, Federal Work-Study, institutionally sponsored loans, scholarships/grants, health care benefits, tuition waivers (full and partial), and unspecified assistantships also available. Support available to part-time students. Financial award application deadline: 3/1; financial award applicants required to submit FAFSA. Total annual research expenditures: $8,300. *Unit head:* Gwyn Richards, Dean, 812-855-2435, E-mail: jln@indiana.edu. *Application contact:* Music Admissions, 812-855-7998, Fax: 812-856-6086, E-mail: musicadm@indiana.edu.

Indiana University Bloomington, University Graduate School, College of Arts and Sciences, Department of Communication and Culture, Bloomington, IN 47405-7000. Offers film and media studies (PhD); performance and ethnography (PhD); rhetoric and public culture (PhD). *Faculty:* 24 full-time (12 women). *Students:* 81 full-time (41 women), 3 part-time (all women); includes 10 minority (2 Black or African American, non-Hispanic/Latino; 8 Hispanic/Latino), 10 international. Average age 32. 187 applicants, 12% accepted, 11 enrolled. In 2010, 4 master's, 7 doctorates awarded. *Degree requirements:* For master's, comprehensive exam; for doctorate, one foreign language, comprehensive exam, thesis/dissertation, student teaching. *Entrance requirements:* For master's and doctorate, GRE General Test (recommended), minimum GPA of 3.0, 3 letters of recommendation, writing sample. Additional exam requirements/recommendations for international students: Required—TOEFL (minimum score 550 paper-based; 213 computer-based). *Application deadline:* For winter admission, 1/1 for domestic students, 12/1 for international students. Application fee: $55 ($65 for international students). Electronic applications accepted. *Financial support:* In 2010–11, 65 students received support, including 4 fellowships with full tuition reimbursements available (averaging $18,000 per year), 48 teaching assistantships with full tuition reimbursements available (averaging $13,257 per year). Financial award application deadline: 4/15. *Faculty research:* Rhetoric and public culture, film and media studies, performance ethnography. *Unit head:* Prof. Gregory A. Waller, Chair, 812-855-2367, Fax: 812-855-6014, E-mail: cmcl@indiana.edu. *Application contact:* Kathy P. Teige, Graduate Secretary, 812-855-6389, Fax: 812-855-6014, E-mail: kteige@indiana.edu.

Indiana University Bloomington, University Graduate School, College of Arts and Sciences, Department of Folklore and Ethnomusicology, Bloomington, IN 47408-3890. Offers folklore (MA, PhD), including ethnomusicology. Part-time programs available. *Faculty:* 17 full-time (7 women), 12 part-time/adjunct (7 women). *Students:* 115 full-time (72 women), 1 part-time (0 women); includes 14 minority (9 Black or African American, non-Hispanic/Latino; 5 Hispanic/Latino), 27 international. Average age 33. 72 applicants, 44% accepted, 18 enrolled. In 2010, 12 master's, 14 doctorates awarded. *Degree requirements:* For master's, one foreign language, comprehensive exam, project or thesis; for doctorate, 2 foreign languages, comprehensive exam, thesis/dissertation. *Entrance requirements:* For master's and doctorate, GRE General Test, minimum GPA of 3.0. Additional exam requirements/recommendations for international students: Required—TOEFL (minimum score 550 paper-based; 213 computer-based; 79 iBT). *Application deadline:* For fall admission, 1/15 for domestic students, 12/1 for international students. Application fee: $55 ($65 for international students). Electronic applications accepted. *Financial support:* In 2010–11, 80 students received support, including 1 fellowship with full tuition reimbursement available (averaging $15,000 per year), 16 research assistantships with full tuition reimbursements available (averaging $11,000 per year), 12 teaching assistantships with full tuition reimbursements available (averaging $11,300 per year); Federal Work-Study, scholarships/grants, health care benefits, and unspecified assistantships also available. Financial award application deadline: 3/1; financial award applicants required to submit FAFSA. *Faculty research:* Narrative, performance studies, material culture, popular culture, music. *Unit head:* Dr. John McDowell, Chair, 812-855-0390, Fax: 812-855-4008, E-mail: mcdowell@indiana.edu. *Application contact:* Michelle Melhouse, Graduate Recorder, 812-855-0389, Fax: 812-855-4008, E-mail: mmelhous@indiana.edu.

Indiana University of Pennsylvania, School of Graduate Studies and Research, College of Fine Arts, Department of Music and Music Education, Program in Music, Indiana, PA 15705-1087. Offers music education (MA); music history and literature (MA); music theory and composition (MA); performance (MA). *Accreditation:* NASM. Part-time programs available. *Faculty:* 10 full-time (2 women). *Students:* 8 full-time (3 women), 4 part-time (1 woman), 1 international. Average age 31. 18 applicants, 28% accepted, 4 enrolled. In 2010, 7 master's awarded. *Degree requirements:* For master's, thesis optional. *Entrance requirements:* For master's, 2 letters of recommendation, audition. Additional exam requirements/recommendations for international students: Required—TOEFL. *Application deadline:* For fall admission, 7/1 priority date for domestic students; for spring admission, 11/1 for domestic students. Applications are processed on a rolling basis. Application fee: $40. *Financial support:* In 2010–11, 5 research assistantships with full and partial tuition reimbursements (averaging $4,896 per year) were awarded; fellowships, Federal Work-Study also available. Support available to part-time students. Financial award application deadline: 3/15; financial award applicants required to submit FAFSA. *Unit head:* Dr. Stephanie Caulder, Head, 724-357-4408, E-mail: stephanie.caulder@iup.edu. *Application contact:* Dr. Stephanie Caulder, Head, 724-357-4408, E-mail: stephanie.caulder@iup.edu.

Indiana University–Purdue University Indianapolis, School of Engineering and Technology, School of Music, Indianapolis, IN 46202-2896. Offers music technology (MS). Part-time and evening/weekend programs available. Postbaccalaureate distance learning degree programs offered. *Students:* 11 full-time (1 woman), 35 part-time (6 women); includes 5 minority (all Black or African American, non-Hispanic/Latino), 3 international. Average age 32. 31 applicants, 71% accepted, 16 enrolled. In 2010, 18 master's awarded. *Degree requirements:* For master's, internship or final project. *Entrance requirements:* For master's, audition, minimum GPA of 3.0. Additional exam requirements/recommendations for international students: Required—TOEFL. *Application deadline:* For fall admission, 4/15 priority date for domestic students, 3/15 for international students; for spring admission, 11/15 priority date for domestic students, 11/15 for international students. Applications are processed on a rolling basis. Application fee: $55 ($65 for international students). *Financial support:* Teaching assistantships with full tuition reimbursements, Federal Work-Study, institutionally sponsored loans, and scholarships/grants available. Support available to part-time students. Financial award application deadline: 11/15. *Unit head:* G. David Peters, Director, 317-278-2594. *Application contact:* G. David Peters, Director, 317-278-2594.

Indiana University South Bend, School of the Arts, South Bend, IN 46634-7111. Offers music (MM); studio teaching (MM). Part-time programs available. *Faculty:* 1 full-time (0 women). *Students:* 14 full-time (10 women), 3 part-time (all women); includes 1 minority (Black or African American, non-Hispanic/Latino), 14 international. Average age 29. 13 applicants, 62% accepted, 6 enrolled. In 2010, 3 master's awarded. *Entrance requirements:* For master's, performance audition. *Application deadline:* For fall admission, 7/1 priority date for domestic students; for spring admission, 11/1 for domestic students. Applications are processed on a rolling basis. Application fee: $50 ($60 for international students). *Financial support:* In 2010–11, 4 fellowships (averaging $2,855 per year), 1 teaching assistantship (averaging $1,320 per year) were awarded; Federal Work-Study also available. Support available to part-time students. Financial award application deadline: 3/1; financial award applicants required to submit FAFSA. *Faculty research:* Orchestral conducting. *Unit head:* Dr. Thomas Miller, Dean, 574-520-4301, Fax: 574-520-4317, E-mail: messelst@iusb.edu. *Application contact:* Dr. Thomas Miller, Dean, 574-520-4301, Fax: 574-520-4317, E-mail: messelst@iusb.edu.

Ithaca College, Division of Graduate and Professional Studies, School of Music, Programs in Music and Music Education, Ithaca, NY 14850. Offers composition (MM); conducting (MM); music education (MM, MS); performance (MM); Suzuki pedagogy (MM). *Accreditation:* NASM. Part-time programs available. *Faculty:* 57 full-time (20 women), 2 part-time/adjunct (1 woman). *Students:* 40 full-time (18 women), 5 part-time (3 women); includes 5 minority (2 Black or African American, non-Hispanic/Latino; 1 Asian, non-Hispanic/Latino; 1 Hispanic/Latino; 1 Two or more races, non-Hispanic/Latino), 3 international. Average age 25. 135 applicants, 40% accepted, 17 enrolled. In 2010, 32 master's awarded. *Degree requirements:* For master's, comprehensive exam, thesis (for some programs). *Entrance requirements:* For master's, audition, minimum GPA of 3.0. Additional exam requirements/recommendations for international students: Required—TOEFL (minimum score 550 paper-based; 213 computer-based; 80 iBT). *Application deadline:* For fall admission, 3/1 for domestic and international students; for spring admission, 12/1 for domestic and international students. Applications are processed on a rolling basis. Application fee: $40. Electronic applications accepted. *Expenses:* Tuition: Full-time $19,890; part-time $663 per credit hour. *Financial support:* In 2010–11, 36 students received support, including 36 teaching assistantships (averaging $8,780 per year); career-related internships or fieldwork, Federal Work-Study, scholarships/grants, and unspecified assistantships also available. Support available to part-time students. Financial award application deadline: 3/1; financial award applicants required to submit CSS PROFILE or FAFSA. *Faculty research:* Musical performance and performance studies; musical composition; music theory and analysis; music education, teaching and learning; musical direction and conducting. *Unit head:* Dr. Timothy Johnson, Chairperson, Graduate Studies in Music, 607-274-3527, Fax: 607-274-1263, E-mail: gps@ithaca.edu. *Application contact:* Rob Gearhart, Dean, Graduate and Professional Studies, 607-274-3527, Fax: 607-274-1263, E-mail: gps@ithaca.edu.

Jacksonville State University, College of Graduate Studies and Continuing Education, College of Arts and Sciences, Department of Music, Jacksonville, AL 36265-1602. Offers MA. *Accreditation:* NASM. Part-time and evening/weekend programs available. *Degree requirements:* For master's, comprehensive exam, thesis (for some programs). *Entrance requirements:* For master's, GRE General Test or MAT. Electronic applications accepted.

James Madison University, The Graduate School, College of Visual and Performing Arts, School of Music, Doctor of Musical Arts Program, Harrisonburg, VA 22807. Offers DMA. Part-time programs available. *Students:* 24 full-time (9 women), 2 part-time (1 woman); includes 4 minority (1 Black or African American, non-Hispanic/Latino; 1 Asian, non-Hispanic/Latino; 2

Hispanic/Latino), 2 international. Average age 27. *Degree requirements:* For doctorate, comprehensive exam, written and oral exams. *Entrance requirements:* For doctorate, GRE General Test, written statement of future goals (professional and educational), 3 letters of recommendation, audition. Additional exam requirements/recommendations for international students: Required—TOEFL. *Application deadline:* For fall admission, 4/1 priority date for domestic students, 4/1 for international students; for spring admission, 4/1 priority date for domestic students, 4/1 for international students. Applications are processed on a rolling basis. Application fee: $55. Electronic applications accepted. *Financial support:* In 2010–11, 21 students received support. 1 graduate assistantships ($7382), 20 doctoral assistantships ($14,500) available. Financial award application deadline: 3/1; financial award applicants required to submit FAFSA. *Unit head:* Dr. Jeffrey A. Showell, Academic Unit Head, 540-568-3614, E-mail: showelja@jmu.edu. *Application contact:* Dr. Mary Jane Speare, Graduate Coordinator, 540-568-3687.

The Jewish Theological Seminary, H. L. Miller Cantorial School and College of Jewish Music, New York, NY 10027-4649. Offers MSM. *Degree requirements:* For master's, one foreign language, comprehensive exam, departmental qualifying exam, recitals. *Entrance requirements:* For master's, music aptitude test, audition, interview, 3 letters of recommendation. Additional exam requirements/recommendations for international students: Required—TOEFL. *Expenses:* Contact institution.

The Johns Hopkins University, Peabody Conservatory, Baltimore, MD 21218-2699. Offers MA, MM, DMA, AD, GPD. *Accreditation:* NASM. *Faculty:* 72 full-time (20 women), 60 part-time/adjunct (22 women). *Students:* 332 full-time (188 women), 16 part-time (11 women); includes 62 minority (15 Black or African American, non-Hispanic/Latino; 30 Asian, non-Hispanic/Latino; 12 Hispanic/Latino; 5 Two or more races, non-Hispanic/Latino), 134 international. Average age 25. 763 applicants, 53% accepted, 181 enrolled. In 2010, 100 master's, 5 doctorates, 31 other advanced degrees awarded. *Degree requirements:* For master's, thesis (for some programs), departmental qualifying exam, recital; for doctorate, 2 foreign languages, thesis/dissertation (for some programs), departmental qualifying exam, recitals; for other advanced degree, recitals. *Entrance requirements:* For master's and other advanced degree, audition; for doctorate, audition, interview. Additional exam requirements/recommendations for international students: Required—TOEFL (minimum score 550 paper-based; 213 computer-based; 79 iBT). *Application deadline:* For fall admission, 12/1 for domestic students. Application fee: $100. *Expenses:* Contact institution. *Financial support:* In 2010–11, 293 students received support, including 61 teaching assistantships (averaging $23,738 per year); Federal Work-Study, institutionally sponsored loans, scholarships/grants, and unspecified assistantships also available. Financial award application deadline: 2/1; financial award applicants required to submit FAFSA. Total annual research expenditures: $340,964. *Unit head:* Jeffrey Sharkey, Director, 410-234-4700, Fax: 410-659-8131. *Application contact:* David Lane, Director of Admissions, 800-368-2521, Fax: 410-659-8102, E-mail: admissions@peabody.jhu.edu.

The Juilliard School, Program in Music, New York, NY 10023-6588. Offers MM, DMA, Artist Diploma, Diploma. *Degree requirements:* For master's and other advanced degree, performance jury, recital; for doctorate, one foreign language, thesis/dissertation, performance jury, 3 recitals. *Entrance requirements:* For master's and other advanced degree, audition; for doctorate, audition, interview, dossier. Additional exam requirements/recommendations for international students: Required—TOEFL (minimum score 570 paper-based; 230 computer-based; 89 iBT). Electronic applications accepted.

Kansas State University, Graduate School, College of Arts and Sciences, Department of Music, Manhattan, KS 66506. Offers music education (MM); music education/band conducting (MM); music history and literature (MM); performance (MM); performance with pedagogy emphasis (MM); theory and composition (MM). *Accreditation:* NASM. Part-time programs available. *Degree requirements:* For master's, thesis optional. *Entrance requirements:* For master's, GRE, audition (in person or recording), interview (music education). Additional exam requirements/recommendations for international students: Required—TOEFL (minimum score 600 paper-based). Electronic applications accepted. *Faculty research:* Music since 1945, music by women composers, American music, opera, current performance practices.

Kent State University, College of the Arts, Hugh A. Glauser School of Music, Kent, OH 44242-0001. Offers composition (MA); conducting (MM); ethnomusicology (MA); music education (MM, PhD); musicology (MA); musicology-ethnomusicology (PhD); performance (MM); theory (MA); theory and composition (PhD). *Accreditation:* NASM. *Degree requirements:* For master's, variable foreign language requirement, comprehensive exam, 2 recitals, essay and recital, or thesis; for doctorate, variable foreign language requirement, comprehensive exam, thesis/dissertation. *Entrance requirements:* For master's, diagnostic exams in music history and theory, audition, minimum GPA of 2.75; for doctorate, diagnostic exams in music history and theory, master's thesis or scholarly paper, minimum GPA of 3.0. Additional exam requirements/recommendations for international students: Required—TOEFL. Electronic applications accepted. *Expenses:* Tuition, state resident: full-time $7866; part-time $437 per credit hour. Tuition, nonresident: full-time $14,022; part-time $779 per credit hour. *Faculty research:* Music composition, performance, teaching and history.

Lamar University, College of Graduate Studies, College of Fine Arts and Communication, Department of Music, Theatre, and Dance, Beaumont, TX 77710. Offers music education (MM Ed); music performance (MM); theatre (MS). *Accreditation:* NASM (one or more programs are accredited). *Faculty:* 9 full-time (2 women), 1 part-time/adjunct (0 women). *Students:* 6 full-time (2 women), 7 part-time (5 women); includes 2 Black or African American, non-Hispanic/Latino; 1 Hispanic/Latino. Average age 28. 9 applicants, 67% accepted, 4 enrolled. In 2010, 3 master's awarded. *Degree requirements:* For master's, comprehensive exam, thesis optional. *Entrance requirements:* For master's, GRE General Test, theory placement exams, audition. Additional exam requirements/recommendations for international students: Required—TOEFL. *Application deadline:* For fall admission, 8/1 for domestic students; for spring admission, 12/1 for domestic students. Applications are processed on a rolling basis. Application fee: $25 ($50 for international students). *Expenses:* Tuition, state resident: full-time $4160; part-time $208 per credit hour. Tuition, nonresident: full-time $10,360; part-time $518 per credit hour. *Financial support:* In 2010–11, 4 fellowships with tuition reimbursements (averaging $2,000 per year), 2 teaching assistantships were awarded; institutionally sponsored loans and tuition waivers (partial) also available. Support available to part-time students. Financial award application deadline: 4/1. *Faculty research:* Performance: ensembles and personal. *Unit head:* Dr. L. Randolph Babin, Chair, 409-880-8144, Fax: 409-880-8143, E-mail: babinlr@hal.lamar.edu. *Application contact:* Dr. Robert M. Culbertson, Adviser, 409-880-8073, Fax: 409-880-8143, E-mail: culbertsrm@hal.lamar.edu.

Lee University, Program in Music, Cleveland, TN 37320-3450. Offers church music (MCM); music education (MM); music performance (MM). *Accreditation:* NASM. Part-time programs available. *Faculty:* 17 full-time (3 women), 9 part-time/adjunct (5 women). *Students:* 17 full-time (9 women), 19 part-time (10 women); includes 1 Black or African American, non-Hispanic/Latino, 4 international. Average age 29. 15 applicants, 100% accepted, 12 enrolled. In 2010, 8 master's awarded. *Degree requirements:* For master's, variable foreign language requirement, comprehensive exam, thesis, internship. *Entrance requirements:* For master's, audition, resume, interview, minimum GPA of 2.75. Additional exam requirements/recommendations for international students: Required—TOEFL (minimum score 450 paper-based; 45 computer-based). *Application deadline:* For fall admission, 4/1 for domestic students; for spring admission, 10/1 for domestic students. Applications are processed on a rolling basis. Application fee: $25. *Expenses:* Tuition: Full-time $12,120; part-time $506 per credit hour. Required fees: $560; $305 per semester. Part-time tuition and fees vary according to course load and campus/location. *Financial support:* Teaching assistantships, career-related internships or fieldwork, Federal Work-Study, institutionally sponsored loans, and scholarships/grants available. Financial award application deadline: 3/1; financial award applicants required to submit FAFSA. *Unit head:* Dr. Jim W. Burns, Director, 423-614-8240, Fax: 423-614-8242, E-mail: gradmusic@leeuniversity.edu. *Application contact:* Vicki Glasscock, Graduate Admissions Director, 423-614-8059, E-mail: vglasscock@leeuniversity.edu.

Long Island University, C.W. Post Campus, School of Visual and Performing Arts, Department of Music, Brookville, NY 11548-1300. Offers music (MA); music education (MS). Part-time programs available. *Degree requirements:* For master's, thesis. *Entrance requirements:* For master's, GRE General Test (MA), GRE Subject Test in music, minimum undergraduate GPA of 3.0, 2 professional and/or academic letters of recommendation, current resume. Electronic applications accepted. *Faculty research:* Performance, composing, musicology, conducting, computer-based music technology.

Longy School of Music, Conservatory at Longy, Cambridge, MA 02138. Offers chamber ensemble (Artist Diploma); collaborative piano (MM, Artist Diploma, GPD); composition (MM); Dalcroze eurhythmics (MM); early music (MM, Artist Diploma, GPD); instrumental performance (MM, Artist Diploma, GPD); modern American music (MM, GPD); opera performance (MM, GPD); organ performance (MM, Artist Diploma, GPD); piano performance (MM, Artist Diploma, GPD); vocal performance (MM, Artist Diploma, GPD). *Accreditation:* NASM. Part-time programs available. *Faculty:* 98 part-time/adjunct (52 women). *Students:* 174 full-time (119 women), 28 part-time (18 women); includes 6 Black or African American, non-Hispanic/Latino; 9 Asian, non-Hispanic/Latino; 1 Hispanic/Latino, 46 international. Average age 28. 231 applicants, 74% accepted, 99 enrolled. In 2010, 42 master's, 21 GPDs awarded. *Degree requirements:* For master's, thesis (for some programs), recital; for other advanced degree, recital. *Entrance requirements:* For master's and other advanced degree, audition. Additional exam requirements/recommendations for international students: Required—TOEFL (minimum score 550 paper-based; 213 computer-based; 79 iBT). *Application deadline:* For fall admission, 12/1 priority date for domestic and international students; for spring admission, 11/1 for domestic and international students. Application fee: $100. Electronic applications accepted. *Financial support:* In 2010–11, 165 students received support, including 12 teaching assistantships (averaging $3,000 per year); scholarships/grants and unspecified assistantships also available. Financial award application deadline: 3/1; financial award applicants required to submit FAFSA. *Unit head:* Karen Zorn, President, 617-876-0956, Fax: 617-876-9326, E-mail: music@longy.edu. *Application contact:* Alex Powell, Director of Admissions and Student Services, 617-876-0956 Ext. 1521, Fax: 617-876-9326, E-mail: admissions@longy.edu.

Louisiana State University and Agricultural and Mechanical College, Graduate School, College of Music and Dramatic Arts, School of Music, Baton Rouge, LA 70803. Offers music (MM, DMA, PhD); music education (PhD). *Accreditation:* NASM. Part-time programs available. *Faculty:* 49 full-time (15 women). *Students:* 151 full-time (70 women), 32 part-time (17 women); includes 4 Black or African American, non-Hispanic/Latino; 1 American Indian or Alaska Native, non-Hispanic/Latino; 6 Asian, non-Hispanic/Latino; 7 Hispanic/Latino; 1 Two or more races, non-Hispanic/Latino, 43 international. Average age 29. 186 applicants, 52% accepted, 42 enrolled. In 2010, 43 master's, 21 doctorates awarded. Terminal master's awarded for partial completion of doctoral program. *Degree requirements:* For doctorate, thesis/dissertation (for some programs). *Entrance requirements:* For master's, minimum GPA of 3.0, audition/interview; for doctorate, GRE General Test, minimum GPA of 3.0, audition/interview. Additional exam requirements/recommendations for international students: Required—TOEFL (minimum score 550 paper-based; 213 computer-based; 79 iBT) or IELTS (minimum score 6.5). *Application deadline:* For fall admission, 3/15 priority date for domestic students, 5/15 for international students; for spring admission, 10/15 for international students. Applications are processed on a rolling basis. Application fee: $50 ($70 for international students). Electronic applications accepted. *Financial support:* In 2010–11, 149 students received support, including 5 fellowships (averaging $16,143 per year), 2 research assistantships with full and partial tuition reimbursements available (averaging $12,700 per year), 80 teaching assistantships with full and partial tuition reimbursements available (averaging $10,820 per year); Federal Work-Study, institutionally sponsored loans, scholarships/grants, health care benefits, tuition waivers (full and partial), and unspecified assistantships also available. Support available to part-time students. Financial award applicants required to submit FAFSA. *Faculty research:* Music education, music literature, formal and harmonic analysis, pedagogy, performance. Total annual research expenditures: $1,946. *Unit head:* Dr. Willis Delony, Interim Dean, 225-578-3261, Fax: 225-578-2562. *Application contact:* Dr. Lori Bade, Director of Graduate Studies, 225-578-3261, Fax: 225-578-2562, E-mail: lbade1@lsu.edu.

Loyola University New Orleans, College of Music and Fine Arts, New Orleans, LA 70118-6195. Offers music therapy (MMT); performance (MM). *Accreditation:* NASM. Part-time programs available. *Students:* 27 full-time (14 women), 3 part-time (all women); includes 7 Black or African American, non-Hispanic/Latino; 1 Hispanic/Latino, 2 international. Average age 26. 28 applicants, 71% accepted, 11 enrolled. In 2010, 1 master's awarded. *Degree requirements:* For master's, thesis, comprehensive written and oral exams. *Entrance requirements:* For master's, performance audition, appropriate bachelor's degree, minimum GPA of 3.0, letters of recommendation, resume. Additional exam requirements/recommendations for international students: Required—TOEFL (minimum score 550 paper-based; 213 computer-based). *Application deadline:* For fall admission, 8/15 priority date for domestic and international students; for spring admission, 1/1 priority date for domestic and international students. Applications are processed on a rolling basis. Application fee: $20. Electronic applications accepted. *Expenses:* Contact institution. *Financial support:* Career-related internships or fieldwork, Federal Work-Study, institutionally sponsored loans, scholarships/grants, and unspecified assistantships available. Support available to part-time students. Financial award application deadline: 5/1; financial award applicants required to submit FAFSA. *Faculty research:* Music business, music therapy, musicology, music theory, music education. *Unit head:* Donald R. Boomgaarden, Dean, 504-865-3039, Fax: 504-865-2852, E-mail: deancmfa@loyno.edu. *Application contact:* Anthony A. Decuir, Associate Dean, 504-865-3037, Fax: 504-865-2852, E-mail: decuir@loyno.edu.

Lynchburg College, Graduate Studies, School of Communications and the Arts, MA Program in Music, Lynchburg, VA 24501-3199. Offers MA. Part-time programs available. *Faculty:* 3 full-time (2 women), 4 part-time/adjunct (2 women). *Students:* 1 (woman) full-time, 4 part-time (3 women). Average age 33. 7 applicants, 86% accepted. In 2010, 1 master's awarded. *Degree requirements:* For master's, comprehensive exam, recital. *Entrance requirements:* For master's, portfolio, official transcripts, personal essay, 3 letters of recommendation. Additional exam requirements/recommendations for international students: Required—TOEFL (minimum score 530 paper-based; 197 computer-based; 71 iBT), IELTS (minimum score 6.5). *Application deadline:* For fall admission, 7/31 for domestic students, 6/1 for international students; for spring admission, 11/30 for domestic students, 10/15 for international students. Applications are processed on a rolling basis. Electronic applications accepted. *Expenses:* Tuition: Full-time $7200; part-time $400 per credit hour. Required fees: $20; $5.10 per credit hour. $15 per term. Tuition and fees vary according to degree level and program. *Financial support:* Fellowships, Federal Work-Study, scholarships/grants, health care benefits, and unspecified assistantships available. Support available to part-time students. Financial award application deadline: 7/31; financial award applicants required to submit FAFSA. *Unit head:* Dr. Jong Kim, Professor and Program Coordinator, MA in Music, 434-544-8443, E-mail: kim@lynchburg.edu. *Application contact:* Dr. Jong Kim, Professor and Program Coordinator, MA in Music, 434-544-8443, E-mail: kim@lynchburg.edu.

Lynn University, Conservatory of Music, Boca Raton, FL 33431-5598. Offers composition (MM); performance (MM); professional performance (Certificate). *Accreditation:* NASM. Part-time and evening/weekend programs available. *Degree requirements:* For Certificate, performance, recitals, orchestra, chamber music. *Entrance requirements:* For master's, resume, 2 letters of recommendation, minimum undergraduate GPA of 3.0; for Certificate, bachelor's degree in music performance or equivalent, audition. Additional exam requirements/recommendations for international students: Required—TOEFL (minimum score 550 paper-based; 213 computer-based).

Manhattan School of Music, Graduate Programs, New York, NY 10027-4698. Offers composition (MM, DMA); jazz (MM, DMA); music performance (MM, DMA); orchestral

Music

Manhattan School of Music (continued)

performance (MM). *Degree requirements:* For master's, recital; for doctorate, variable foreign language requirement, thesis/dissertation, departmental qualifying exam, recitals. *Entrance requirements:* For master's, audition, pre-screen CD, bachelor's degree; for doctorate, departmental exam, audition, interview, pre-screen CD, master's degree. Additional exam requirements/recommendations for international students: Required—TOEFL (minimum score 550 paper-based; 213 computer-based; 79 iBT). Electronic applications accepted.

Manhattan School of Music, Professional Studies Certificate Program, New York, NY 10027-4698. Offers instrumental music (CPS), including accompanying, brass, composition, guitar, orchestral performance, organ, piano, strings, voice, woodwinds; vocal music (CPS), including accompanying, brass, composition, guitar, orchestral performance, organ, piano, strings, voice, woodwinds. *Degree requirements:* For CPS, recital. *Entrance requirements:* For degree, audition, pre-screen CD. Additional exam requirements/recommendations for international students: Required—TOEFL (minimum score 550 paper-based; 213 computer-based). Electronic applications accepted.

Mansfield University of Pennsylvania, Graduate Studies, Department of Music, Mansfield, PA 16933. Offers band conducting (MA); choral conducting (MA); performance (MA). *Accreditation:* NASM. Part-time and evening/weekend programs available. *Degree requirements:* For master's, comprehensive exam, thesis optional. *Entrance requirements:* For master's, minimum GPA of 3.0, audition. Additional exam requirements/recommendations for international students: Required—TOEFL (minimum score 550 paper-based; 220 computer-based). Electronic applications accepted. *Expenses:* Tuition, state resident: full-time $6966; part-time $387 per credit hour. Tuition, nonresident: full-time $11,146; part-time $619 per credit hour. Required fees: $1456; $68 per credit hour.

Marshall University, Academic Affairs Division, College of Fine Arts, Department of Music, Huntington, WV 25755. Offers MA. *Accreditation:* NASM. Evening/weekend programs available. *Faculty:* 17 full-time (4 women), 1 (woman) part-time/adjunct. *Students:* 12 full-time (5 women), 6 part-time (3 women); includes 1 Black or African American, non-Hispanic/Latino, 3 international. Average age 29. In 2010, 6 master's awarded. *Degree requirements:* For master's, thesis optional. Application fee: $40. *Unit head:* Dr. Jeffrey Pappas, Chairperson, 304-696-3117, E-mail: pappas@marshall.edu. *Application contact:* Information Contact, 304-746-1900, Fax: 304-746-1902, E-mail: services@marshall.edu.

McGill University, Faculty of Graduate and Postdoctoral Studies, Schulich School of Music, Montréal, QC H3A 2T5, Canada. Offers composition (M Mus, D Mus, PhD); music education (MA, PhD); music technology (MA, PhD); musicology (MA, PhD); performance (M Mus); performance studies (D Mus); sound recording (M Mus, PhD); theory (MA, PhD).

Memorial University of Newfoundland, School of Graduate Studies, Interdisciplinary Program in Ethnomusicology, St. John's, NL A1C 5S7, Canada. Offers MA, PhD. *Degree requirements:* For master's, thesis optional, research paper (non-thesis option); for doctorate, one foreign language, comprehensive exam, thesis/dissertation, oral defense of thesis. *Entrance requirements:* For master's, minimum B+ average with a B Mus or humanities/social sciences degree; for doctorate, MA in ethnomusicology or a related field.

Memorial University of Newfoundland, School of Graduate Studies, School of Music, St. John's, NL A1C 5S7, Canada. Offers conducting (MMus); performance pedagogy (MMus); performing (MMus). *Entrance requirements:* For master's, diagnostic exams measuring skills and knowledge in musical literacy, B Mus with first-class standing, audition (ca. 60 min. performance). Electronic applications accepted.

Mercer University, Graduate Studies, Macon Campus, School of Music, Macon, GA 31207-0003. Offers choral conducting (MM); church music (M Div, MM); collaborative piano (MM); instrumental conducting (MM); performance (MM). Part-time programs available. *Faculty:* 2 full-time (0 women). *Students:* 16 full-time (6 women); includes 4 minority (3 Black or African American, non-Hispanic/Latino; 1 Asian, non-Hispanic/Latino). Average age 28. 5 applicants, 100% accepted, 5 enrolled. In 2010, 8 master's awarded. *Degree requirements:* For master's, comprehensive exam, recitals. *Entrance requirements:* For master's, GRE, audition. Additional exam requirements/recommendations for international students: Required—TOEFL (minimum score 550 paper-based; 213 computer-based; 80 iBT). *Application deadline:* Applications are processed on a rolling basis. Application fee: $100. Electronic applications accepted. *Expenses:* Contact institution. *Financial support:* In 2010–11, 14 students received support. Tuition waivers and unspecified assistantships available. Financial award applicants required to submit FAFSA. *Faculty research:* Philosophy of church music, performance practices of the Baroque and Classical periods, organ repertoire of the High Baroque. Total annual research expenditures: $5,000. *Unit head:* Dr. Charles David Keith, Director of Graduate Studies, 478-301-4012, Fax: 478-301-5633, E-mail: keith_cd@mercer.edu. *Application contact:* Kimberly T. Beach, Enrollment Associate, 478-301-2570, Fax: 478-301-2650, E-mail: beach_kt@mercer.edu.

Messiah College, Program in Conducting, Grantham, PA 17027. Offers choral conducting (MM); orchestral conducting (MM); wind conducting (MM). *Accreditation:* NASM. Part-time programs available. *Degree requirements:* For master's, advanced conducting project. *Application deadline:* Applications are processed on a rolling basis. Application fee: $30. Electronic applications accepted. *Financial support:* Applicants required to submit FAFSA. *Unit head:* Dr. Bradley Genevro, Program Coordinator, 717-796-1800 Ext. 2750, Fax: 717-691-2386, E-mail: bgenevro@messiah.edu. *Application contact:* Dr. Bradley Genevro, Program Coordinator, 717-796-1800 Ext. 2750, Fax: 717-691-2386, E-mail: bgenevro@messiah.edu.

Miami University, Graduate School, School of Fine Arts, Department of Music, Oxford, OH 45056. Offers music education (MM); music performance (MM). *Accreditation:* NASM. *Students:* 25 full-time (12 women), 4 part-time (3 women); includes 9 minority (4 Black or African American, non-Hispanic/Latino; 1 Asian, non-Hispanic/Latino; 4 Hispanic/Latino), 2 international. Average age 27. In 2010, 23 master's awarded. *Entrance requirements:* For master's, audition, minimum undergraduate GPA of 3.0 during previous 2 years or overall. Application fee: $50. *Expenses:* Tuition, state resident: full-time $11,616; part-time $484 per credit hour. Tuition, nonresident: full-time $25,656; part-time $1069 per credit hour. Required fees: $528. *Financial support:* Fellowships with full tuition reimbursements, research assistantships, teaching assistantships, Federal Work-Study, health care benefits, tuition waivers (full), and unspecified assistantships available. Financial award application deadline: 3/1. *Unit head:* Dr. Judith Delzell, Chair, 513-529-1428. *Application contact:* Dr. Claire Boge, Graduate Advisor, 513-529-1441, E-mail: bogecl@muohio.edu.

Michigan State University, The Graduate School, College of Music, East Lansing, MI 48824. Offers collaborative piano (M Mus); jazz studies (M Mus); music (PhD); music composition (M Mus, DMA); music conducting (M Mus, DMA); music education (M Mus); music performance (M Mus, DMA); music theory (M Mus); music therapy (M Mus); musicology (MA); piano pedagogy (M Mus). *Accreditation:* NASM. *Entrance requirements:* Additional exam requirements/recommendations for international students: Required—TOEFL. Electronic applications accepted.

Middle Tennessee State University, College of Graduate Studies, College of Liberal Arts, School of Music, Murfreesboro, TN 37132. Offers MA. *Accreditation:* NASM. Part-time and evening/weekend programs available. Postbaccalaureate distance learning degree programs offered. *Faculty:* 16 full-time (6 women), 2 part-time/adjunct (1 woman). *Students:* 9 full-time (5 women), 25 part-time (16 women); includes 2 Black or African American, non-Hispanic/Latino; 3 Asian, non-Hispanic/Latino; 2 Hispanic/Latino; 1 Two or more races, non-Hispanic/Latino. Average age 27. 26 applicants, 73% accepted, 19 enrolled. In 2010, 10 master's awarded. *Degree requirements:* For master's, one foreign language, comprehensive exam, thesis optional. *Entrance requirements:* For master's, GRE or MAT. Additional exam requirements/recommendations for international students: Required—TOEFL (minimum score 525 paper-based; 195 computer-based; 71 iBT) or IELTS (minimum score 6). *Application deadline:* For fall admission, 6/1 for domestic and international students. Applications are processed on a rolling basis. Application fee: $25 ($30 for international students). Electronic applications accepted. *Expenses:* Tuition, state resident: full-time $4632. Tuition, nonresident: full-time $11,520. *Financial support:* In 2010–11, 12 students received support. Institutionally sponsored loans available. Support available to part-time students. Financial award application deadline: 5/1; financial award applicants required to submit FAFSA. *Unit head:* Dr. George T. Riordan, Director, 615-898-2469, Fax: 615-898-5037, E-mail: griordan@mtsu.edu. *Application contact:* Dr. Michael Allen, Dean and Vice Provost for Research, 615-898-2840, Fax: 615-904-8020, E-mail: mallen@mtsu.edu.

Middle Tennessee State University, College of Graduate Studies, College of Mass Communication, Department of Recording Industry, Murfreesboro, TN 37132. Offers recording arts and technologies (MFA). Part-time and evening/weekend programs available. Postbaccalaureate distance learning degree programs offered. *Faculty:* 15 full-time (1 woman). *Students:* 13 full-time (3 women), 27 part-time (4 women); includes 6 Black or African American, non-Hispanic/Latino; 1 Hispanic/Latino. Average age 27. 35 applicants, 31% accepted, 11 enrolled. In 2010, 6 master's awarded. *Degree requirements:* For master's, comprehensive exam, thesis optional. *Entrance requirements:* For master's, GRE. Additional exam requirements/recommendations for international students: Required—TOEFL (minimum score 525 paper-based; 195 computer-based; 71 iBT) or IELTS (minimum score 6). *Application deadline:* For fall admission, 6/1 for domestic and international students. Applications are processed on a rolling basis. Application fee: $25 ($30 for international students). *Expenses:* Tuition, state resident: full-time $4632. Tuition, nonresident: full-time $11,520. *Financial support:* In 2010–11, 4 students received support. Institutionally sponsored loans available. Support available to part-time students. Financial award application deadline: 5/1. *Faculty research:* Digital audio, music production. *Unit head:* Dr. Loren Mulraine, Chair, 615-898-2578, Fax: 615-898-5682, E-mail: lmulrain@mtsu.edu. *Application contact:* Dr. Michael Allen, Dean and Vice Provost for Research, 615-898-2840, Fax: 615-904-8020, E-mail: mallen@mtsu.edu.

Midwestern Baptist Theological Seminary, Graduate and Professional Programs, Kansas City, MO 64118-4697. Offers Biblical archaeology (MA); Biblical languages (MA); Christian education (M Div, MACE); Christian foundations—lay ministry (Graduate Certificate); collegiate ministries (M Div); counseling (MA); educational ministry (D Ed Min); international church planting (M Div); ministry (M Div, D Min); North American church planting (M Div); sacred music (MCM); urban ministry (M Div); worship leadership (M Div); youth ministry (M Div). *Accreditation:* ATS. Part-time programs available. Postbaccalaureate distance learning degree programs offered (minimal on-campus study). *Degree requirements:* For doctorate, thesis/dissertation; for M Div, 2 foreign languages. *Entrance requirements:* For doctorate, MAT. Electronic applications accepted. *Faculty research:* Ministerial studies, Biblical and theological studies, missions, counseling.

Mills College, Graduate Studies, Department of Dance, Oakland, CA 94613-1000. Offers dance (MA, MFA), including choreography and performance (MA). Part-time programs available. *Faculty:* 5 full-time (4 women), 9 part-time/adjunct (7 women). *Students:* 18 full-time (16 women); includes 2 Black or African American, non-Hispanic/Latino; 2 Asian, non-Hispanic/Latino; 2 Hispanic/Latino. Average age 30. 43 applicants, 58% accepted, 18 enrolled. In 2010, 8 master's awarded. *Degree requirements:* For master's, comprehensive exam, thesis, performance. *Entrance requirements:* For master's, DVD recording of original choreography of up to two choreographic works (for MFA); writing sample with topic related to field of dance studies (for MA). Additional exam requirements/recommendations for international students: Required—TOEFL. *Application deadline:* For fall admission, 2/1 priority date for domestic students, 12/15 for international students. Applications are processed on a rolling basis. Application fee: $50. *Expenses:* Tuition: Full-time $28,280; part-time $7070 per course. Required fees: $1058; $1058 per year. Tuition and fees vary according to program. *Financial support:* In 2010–11, 18 students received support, including 18 fellowships (averaging $4,852 per year), 9 teaching assistantships with partial tuition reimbursements available (averaging $4,886 per year); scholarships/grants and unspecified assistantships also available. Financial award application deadline: 2/1; financial award applicants required to submit FAFSA. *Faculty research:* Modern techniques, movement for actors, choreography, dance criticism and analysis, dance and literature. *Unit head:* Sonya Delwaide, Head, 510-430-3258, E-mail: sdelwaid@mills.edu. *Application contact:* Jessica King, Graduate Admission Specialist, 510-430-3305, Fax: 510-430-2159, E-mail: grad-studies@mills.edu.

Mills College, Graduate Studies, Department of Music, Oakland, CA 94613-1000. Offers composition (MA); electronic music and recording media (MFA); music performance and literature (MFA). Part-time programs available. *Faculty:* 6 full-time (2 women), 5 part-time/adjunct (4 women). *Students:* 50 full-time (13 women); includes 2 Black or African American, non-Hispanic/Latino; 1 Asian, non-Hispanic/Latino; 5 Hispanic/Latino; 2 Two or more races, non-Hispanic/Latino. Average age 28. 88 applicants, 63% accepted, 23 enrolled. In 2010, 18 master's awarded. *Degree requirements:* For master's, variable foreign language requirement, thesis, performance or recital. *Entrance requirements:* For master's, portfolio or audition. Additional exam requirements/recommendations for international students: Required—TOEFL (minimum score 550 paper-based; 213 computer-based; 80 iBT), IELTS (minimum score 6). *Application deadline:* For fall admission, 1/15 priority date for domestic students, 12/15 for international students; for spring admission, 11/1 priority date for domestic students, 10/1 for international students. Applications are processed on a rolling basis. Application fee: $50. Electronic applications accepted. *Expenses:* Tuition: Full-time $28,280; part-time $7070 per course. Required fees: $1058; $1058 per year. Tuition and fees vary according to program. *Financial support:* In 2010–11, 45 students received support, including 45 fellowships (averaging $5,817 per year), 25 teaching assistantships with partial tuition reimbursements available (averaging $8,659 per year); scholarships/grants also available. Support available to part-time students. Financial award application deadline: 2/1; financial award applicants required to submit FAFSA. *Faculty research:* Electronic and computer music, twentieth century theory and performance practice, Mozart, music theory. Total annual research expenditures: $7,500. *Unit head:* Fred Frith, Chairperson, 510-430-2171, Fax: 510-430-3314, E-mail: grad-studies@mills.edu. *Application contact:* Jessica King, Graduate Admission Specialist, 510-430-3305, Fax: 510-430-2159, E-mail: grad-studies@mills.edu.

Minnesota State University Mankato, College of Graduate Studies, College of Arts and Humanities, Department of Music, Mankato, MN 56001. Offers MAT, MM. *Accreditation:* NASM. *Students:* 5 full-time (3 women), 1 part-time (0 women). *Degree requirements:* For master's, comprehensive exam, thesis or alternative. *Entrance requirements:* For master's, minimum GPA of 3.0 during previous 2 years, audition or test. Additional exam requirements/recommendations for international students: Required—TOEFL. *Application deadline:* For fall admission, 7/1 priority date for domestic students; for spring admission, 11/1 for domestic students. Applications are processed on a rolling basis. Application fee: $40. Electronic applications accepted. *Financial support:* Research assistantships with full tuition reimbursements, teaching assistantships with full tuition reimbursements, career-related internships or fieldwork, Federal Work-Study, and institutionally sponsored loans available. Support available to part-time students. Financial award application deadline: 3/15. *Unit head:* Dr. David Dickau, Graduate Coordinator, 507-389-2118. *Application contact:* 507-389-2321, E-mail: grad@mnsu.edu.

Mississippi College, Graduate School, College of Arts and Sciences, School of Christian Studies and the Arts, Department of Music, Clinton, MS 39058. Offers applied music performance (MM); conducting (MM); music education (MM); music performance: organ (MM); vocal pedagogy (MM). *Accreditation:* NASM. Part-time and evening/weekend programs available. *Degree requirements:* For master's, comprehensive exam, recital. *Entrance requirements:* For master's, GRE, minimum GPA of 2.5. Additional exam requirements/recommendations for international students: Recommended—IELTS. Electronic applications accepted.

Missouri State University, Graduate College, College of Arts and Letters, Department of Music, Springfield, MO 65897. Offers music (MM), including conducting, music education, music pedagogy, music theory and composition, performance; secondary education (MS Ed), including music. *Accreditation:* NASM. Part-time programs available. *Degree requirements:*

For master's, comprehensive exam, thesis or alternative. *Entrance requirements:* For master's, GRE, interview/audition (MM), 9-12 teaching certification (MS Ed). Additional exam requirements/recommendations for international students: Required—TOEFL (minimum score 550 paper-based; 213 computer-based; 79 iBT). Electronic applications accepted. *Expenses:* Tuition, state resident: full-time $3348; part-time $186 per credit hour. Tuition, nonresident: full-time $6696; part-time $372 per credit hour. Required fees: $238 per semester. Tuition and fees vary according to course level, course load and program. *Faculty research:* Bulgarian violin literature, Ozarks fiddle music, carillon, nineteenth century piano.

Montclair State University, The Graduate School, School of the Arts, Department of Music, Montclair, NJ 07043-1624. Offers music (AD, Certificate); music education (MA); music therapy (MA, Certificate); performance (MA, Certificate); theory/composition (MA). *Accreditation:* NASM. Part-time and evening/weekend programs available. *Faculty:* 20 full-time (7 women), 101 part-time/adjunct (46 women). *Students:* 24 full-time (11 women), 37 part-time (14 women); includes 1 Black or African American, non-Hispanic/Latino; 3 Asian, non-Hispanic/Latino; 2 Hispanic/Latino, 7 international. Average age 31. 43 applicants, 58% accepted, 21 enrolled. In 2010, 12 master's, 7 other advanced degrees awarded. *Degree requirements:* For master's, comprehensive exam, compositions, recitals, or thesis. *Entrance requirements:* For master's, GRE General Test, audition; teaching certificate (MA in music education). Additional exam requirements/recommendations for international students: Required—TOEFL (minimum score: 83 iBT) or IELTS. *Application deadline:* For fall admission, 6/1 for international students; for spring admission, 10/1 for international students. Applications are processed on a rolling basis. Application fee: $60. Electronic applications accepted. *Expenses:* Tuition, state resident: part-time $501.34 per credit. Tuition, nonresident: part-time $773.88 per credit. Required fees: $71.15 per credit. *Financial support:* In 2010–11, 3 research assistantships with full tuition reimbursements (averaging $7,000 per year) were awarded; Federal Work-Study, scholarships/grants, and unspecified assistantships also available. Support available to part-time students. Financial award application deadline: 3/1; financial award applicants required to submit FAFSA. *Unit head:* Prof. Robert Aldridge, Chairperson, 973-655-7212. *Application contact:* Amy Aiello, Director of Graduate Admissions and Operations, 973-655-5147, Fax: 973-655-7869, E-mail: graduate.school@montclair.edu.

Morehead State University, Graduate Programs, Caudill College of Arts, Humanities and Social Sciences, Department of Music, Theatre and Dance, Morehead, KY 40351. Offers music education (MM); music performance (MM). *Accreditation:* NASM. Part-time and evening/weekend programs available. *Degree requirements:* For master's, comprehensive exam, oral and written exams. *Entrance requirements:* For master's, music entrance exam, BA in music with minimum GPA of 3.0, 2.5 overall; audition. Additional exam requirements/recommendations for international students: Required—TOEFL (minimum score 550 paper-based; 173 computer-based). Electronic applications accepted. *Faculty research:* Musical instrument digital interface (MIDI) applications, tonal concepts of euphonium and baritone horn, digital synthesis, computer-assisted instruction in music, musical composition.

Morgan State University, School of Graduate Studies, College of Liberal Arts, Department of Music, Baltimore, MD 21251. Offers MA. *Accreditation:* NASM. Part-time and evening/weekend programs available. *Degree requirements:* For master's, comprehensive exam, thesis. *Entrance requirements:* Additional exam requirements/recommendations for international students: Required—TOEFL (minimum score 550 paper-based; 213 computer-based).

Murray State University, College of Humanities and Fine Arts, Program in Music, Murray, KY 42071. Offers music education (MME). *Accreditation:* NASM. Part-time programs available. *Entrance requirements:* For master's, GRE General Test or MAT. Additional exam requirements/recommendations for international students: Required—TOEFL.

New England Conservatory of Music, Graduate Program in Music, Boston, MA 02115-5000. Offers MM, DMA, Diploma. *Accreditation:* NASM (one or more programs are accredited). *Faculty:* 92 full-time (30 women), 115 part-time/adjunct (32 women). *Students:* 359 full-time (181 women), 26 part-time (14 women); includes 51 minority (4 Black or African American, non-Hispanic/Latino; 24 Asian, non-Hispanic/Latino; 12 Hispanic/Latino; 1 Native Hawaiian or other Pacific Islander, non-Hispanic/Latino; 10 Two or more races, non-Hispanic/Latino), 133 international. Average age 25. 1,622 applicants, 26% accepted, 172 enrolled. In 2010, 150 master's, 5 doctorates, 33 Diplomas awarded. *Degree requirements:* For master's, thesis (for some programs), recital; for doctorate, one foreign language, comprehensive exam, thesis/dissertation, qualifying exams, recital. *Entrance requirements:* For master's and Diploma, audition; for doctorate, music theory and musicology exam, audition. Additional exam requirements/recommendations for international students: Required—TOEFL (minimum score 550 paper-based; 213 computer-based; 79 iBT). *Application deadline:* For fall admission, 12/1 priority date for domestic and international students; for spring admission, 11/1 for domestic and international students. Applications are processed on a rolling basis. Application fee: $115. *Expenses:* Tuition: Full-time $34,500; part-time $2200 per credit hour. Required fees: $450; $450 per year. *Financial support:* In 2010–11, 347 students received support, including 339 fellowships with partial tuition reimbursements available (averaging $16,232 per year); teaching assistantships, Federal Work-Study, scholarships/grants, and tuition waivers (partial) also available. Support available to part-time students. Financial award application deadline: 12/1; financial award applicants required to submit FAFSA. *Unit head:* Tom Novak, Dean of the College, 617-585-1304, Fax: 617-585-1303, E-mail: tnovak@newenglandconservatory.edu. *Application contact:* Christina Daly, Director of Admissions, 617-585-1101, Fax: 617-585-1115, E-mail: christina.daly@newenglandconservatory.edu.

New Jersey City University, Graduate Studies and Continuing Education, William J. Maxwell College of Arts and Sciences, Department of Music, Dance and Theatre, Jersey City, NJ 07305-1597. Offers music education (MA); performance (MM). *Accreditation:* NASM. Part-time and evening/weekend programs available. *Degree requirements:* For master's, thesis optional, recital. *Entrance requirements:* For master's, GRE General Test or MAT. Additional exam requirements/recommendations for international students: Required—TOEFL.

New Mexico State University, Graduate School, College of Arts and Sciences, Department of Music, Las Cruces, NM 88003-8001. Offers conducting (MM); music education (MM); performance (MM). *Accreditation:* NASM. Part-time programs available. *Faculty:* 13 full-time (5 women), 3 part-time/adjunct (0 women). *Students:* 17 full-time (8 women), 17 part-time (5 women); includes 11 minority (all Hispanic/Latino), 11 international. Average age 30. 20 applicants, 100% accepted, 15 enrolled. In 2010, 6 master's awarded. *Degree requirements:* For master's, comprehensive exam (for some programs), thesis (for some programs), recital. *Entrance requirements:* For master's, diagnostic exam, audition, bachelor's degree or equivalent from an accredited institution. Additional exam requirements/recommendations for international students: Required—TOEFL. *Application deadline:* For fall admission, 7/1 priority date for domestic students; for spring admission, 11/1 for domestic students. Applications are processed on a rolling basis. Application fee: $30 ($50 for international students). Electronic applications accepted. *Expenses:* Contact institution. *Financial support:* In 2010–11, 13 students received support, including 9 teaching assistantships (averaging $9,009 per year); fellowships, Federal Work-Study and health care benefits also available. Support available to part-time students. Financial award application deadline: 3/1. *Faculty research:* Music education, contemporary wind band literature, performance. *Unit head:* Dr. Ken Van Winkle, Head, 575-646-2421, Fax: 575-646-8199, E-mail: kvanwink@nmsu.edu. *Application contact:* Dr. Lisa Van Winkle, Assistant Professor, 575-646-2523, Fax: 575-646-2472, E-mail: lvanwink@nmsu.edu.

New Orleans Baptist Theological Seminary, Graduate and Professional Programs, Division of Church Music Ministries, New Orleans, LA 70126-4858. Offers M Div, MMCM, DMA. *Accreditation:* NASM. Postbaccalaureate distance learning degree programs offered. *Faculty:* 4 full-time (0 women). *Students:* 32 full-time (4 women), 17 part-time (2 women); includes 3 Black or African American, non-Hispanic/Latino; 2 Hispanic/Latino, 1 international. Average age 32. 13 applicants, 77% accepted, 9 enrolled. In 2010, 4 master's awarded. *Degree requirements:* For doctorate, one foreign language, thesis/dissertation. *Entrance requirements:* For doctorate, GRE General Test. Additional exam requirements/recommendations for international students: Required—TOEFL. *Application deadline:* For fall admission, 7/20 priority date for domestic students; for spring admission, 12/20 for domestic students. Applications are processed on a rolling basis. Application fee: $25. *Expenses:* Tuition: Full-time $3040. Required fees: $160 per credit hour. $80 per semester. One-time fee: $80 full-time. Tuition and fees vary according to course load and student's religious affiliation. *Financial support:* Institutionally sponsored loans available. Support available to part-time students. *Unit head:* Dr. Greg Woodward, Chairman, 504-282-4455, E-mail: gwoodward@nobts.edu. *Application contact:* Dr. Paul E. Gregoire, Director of Admissions and Registrar, 504-282-4455 Ext. 3337, Fax: 504-286-3591, E-mail: registrar@nobts.edu.

The New School: A University, Mannes College The New School for Music, New York, NY 10024. Offers music performance and composition (MM). *Degree requirements:* For master's, recital, professional performance with graduation juries. *Entrance requirements:* For master's, audition. Additional exam requirements/recommendations for international students: Required—TOEFL. Electronic applications accepted.

New York University, Graduate School of Arts and Science, Department of Music, New York, NY 10012-1019. Offers composition and theory (MA, PhD); early music performance (Advanced Certificate); ethnomusicology (MA, PhD). *Students:* 44 full-time (19 women); includes 1 Black or African American, non-Hispanic/Latino; 1 Asian, non-Hispanic/Latino, 15 international. Average age 33. 170 applicants, 6% accepted, 5 enrolled. In 2010, 4 master's, 9 doctorates awarded. Terminal master's awarded for partial completion of doctoral program. *Degree requirements:* For master's, one foreign language, thesis (for some programs), general exam; for doctorate, 2 foreign languages, thesis/dissertation, general and special exams. *Entrance requirements:* For master's, GRE General Test, bachelor's degree in liberal arts or music; for doctorate, GRE General Test, master's degree in music; for Advanced Certificate, bachelor's degree in music. Additional exam requirements/recommendations for international students: Required—TOEFL. *Application deadline:* For fall admission, 1/4 for domestic students. Application fee: $90. *Financial support:* Fellowships with tuition reimbursements, teaching assistantships with tuition reimbursements, Federal Work-Study, institutionally sponsored loans, scholarships/grants, health care benefits, and unspecified assistantships available. Financial award application deadline: 1/4; financial award applicants required to submit FAFSA. *Faculty research:* Early music (nineteenth century), Wagner, Verdi, performance practice. *Unit head:* Michael Beckerman, Chair, 212-998-8300, Fax: 212-995-4147, E-mail: fas.music.gradadmissions@nyu.edu. *Application contact:* Elizabeth Hoffman, Director of Graduate Studies, 212-998-8300, Fax: 212-995-4147, E-mail: fas.music.gradadmissions@nuy.edu.

New York University, Steinhardt School of Culture, Education, and Human Development, Department of Music and Performing Arts Professions, Program in Music Business, New York, NY 10012-1019. Offers MA. Part-time programs available. *Faculty:* 4 full-time (2 women). *Students:* 64 full-time (30 women), 12 part-time (9 women); includes 7 Black or African American, non-Hispanic/Latino; 5 Asian, non-Hispanic/Latino; 5 Hispanic/Latino, 15 international. Average age 25. 145 applicants, 35% accepted, 38 enrolled. In 2010, 33 master's awarded. *Degree requirements:* For master's, thesis (for some programs). *Entrance requirements:* For master's, interview. Additional exam requirements/recommendations for international students: Required—TOEFL. *Application deadline:* For fall admission, 12/1 priority date for domestic and international students. Applications are processed on a rolling basis. Application fee: $75. Electronic applications accepted. *Financial support:* Career-related internships or fieldwork, Federal Work-Study, scholarships/grants, and tuition waivers (partial) available. Support available to part-time students. Financial award application deadline: 2/1; financial award applicants required to submit FAFSA. *Faculty research:* Strategic marketing, new technologies, intellectual property, entrepreneurship, globalization, music in video games. *Unit head:* Dr. Catherine Moore, Director, 212-998-5424, Fax: 212-998-4560, E-mail: catherine.moore@nyu.edu. *Application contact:* 212-998-5030, Fax: 212-995-4328, E-mail: steinhardt.gradadmissions@nyu.edu.

New York University, Steinhardt School of Culture, Education, and Human Development, Department of Music and Performing Arts Professions, Program in Music Performance and Composition, New York, NY 10012-1019. Offers instrumental performance (MM), including instrumental performance, jazz instrumental performance; music performance and composition (MA, PhD), including composition; music theory and composition (MM, PhD), including music theory and compostition (MM), scoring for film and multimedia (MM); piano performance (MM), including collaborative performance, collaborative piano, solo piano; vocal pedagogy (Advanced Certificate); vocal performance (MM), including classical voice, music theatre performance; vocal performance/vocal pedagogy (MM), including classical voice, music theatre performance; MM/Advanced Certificate. Part-time programs available. *Faculty:* 22 full-time (6 women). *Students:* 235 full-time (101 women), 63 part-time (18 women); includes 13 Black or African American, non-Hispanic/Latino; 24 Asian, non-Hispanic/Latino; 12 Hispanic/Latino, 85 international. Average age 27. 439 applicants, 52% accepted, 125 enrolled. In 2010, 104 master's, 5 doctorates, 5 other advanced degrees awarded. *Degree requirements:* For master's, thesis (for some programs); for doctorate, thesis/dissertation. *Entrance requirements:* For master's, audition; for doctorate, GRE General Test, audition, interview. Additional exam requirements/recommendations for international students: Required—TOEFL. *Application deadline:* For fall admission, 12/1 priority date for domestic and international students; for spring admission, 11/1 for domestic and international students. Applications are processed on a rolling basis. Application fee: $75. Electronic applications accepted. *Financial support:* Fellowships with full and partial tuition reimbursements, Federal Work-Study, scholarships/grants, and tuition waivers (partial) available. Support available to part-time students. Financial award application deadline: 2/1; financial award applicants required to submit FAFSA. *Faculty research:* Aesthetics, performance analysis, twentieth century music, music methodologies for arts criticism and analysis. *Application contact:* 212-998-5030, Fax: 212-995-4328, E-mail: steinhardt.gradadmissions@nyu.edu.

New York University, Steinhardt School of Culture, Education, and Human Development, Department of Music and Performing Arts Professions, Program in Music Technology, New York, NY 10012-1019. Offers MM, PhD. Part-time programs available. *Faculty:* 4 full-time (2 women). *Students:* 78 full-time (17 women), 27 part-time (6 women); includes 8 Black or African American, non-Hispanic/Latino; 9 Asian, non-Hispanic/Latino; 3 Hispanic/Latino, 29 international. Average age 27. 125 applicants, 69% accepted, 55 enrolled. In 2010, 24 master's awarded. *Degree requirements:* For master's, thesis (for some programs); for doctorate, thesis/dissertation. *Entrance requirements:* For master's, portfolio; for doctorate, essay, 3 letters of recommendation, master's degree. Additional exam requirements/recommendations for international students: Required—TOEFL. *Application deadline:* For fall admission, 12/1 priority date for domestic and international students; for spring admission, 11/1 for domestic and international students. Applications are processed on a rolling basis. Application fee: $75. Electronic applications accepted. *Financial support:* Fellowships with full and partial tuition reimbursements, research assistantships with full and partial tuition reimbursements, career-related internships or fieldwork, Federal Work-Study, institutionally sponsored loans, scholarships/grants, and tuition waivers (partial) available. Support available to part-time students. Financial award application deadline: 2/1; financial award applicants required to submit FAFSA. *Faculty research:* Pattern processing in music, computer music, acoustics, music perception, interactive music systems. *Unit head:* Dr. Kenneth J. Peacock, Director, 212-998-5424, Fax: 212-995-4043. *Application contact:* 212-998-5030, Fax: 212-995-4328, E-mail: steinhardt.gradadmissions@nyu.edu.

New York University, Tisch School of the Arts, Graduate Musical Theatre Writing Program, New York, NY 10012-1019. Offers MFA. *Faculty:* 6 full-time, 14 part-time/adjunct. *Students:* 61 full-time (27 women); includes 1 Black or African American, non-Hispanic/Latino; 5 Asian, non-Hispanic/Latino; 1 Hispanic/Latino. Average age 28. 60 applicants, 73% accepted, 30 enrolled. In 2010, 21 master's awarded. *Degree requirements:* For master's, full-length musical theatre work. *Entrance requirements:* For master's, interview, portfolio. Additional exam requirements/recommendations for international students: Required—TOEFL or IELTS.

Music

New York University (continued)

Application deadline: For fall admission, 2/1 priority date for domestic and international students. Application fee: $60. Electronic applications accepted. *Financial support:* In 2010–11, 18 students received support; fellowships with tuition reimbursements available, career-related internships or fieldwork, Federal Work-Study, tuition waivers (partial), and unspecified assistantships available. Financial award application deadline: 2/15; financial award applicants required to submit FAFSA. *Unit head:* Sarah Schlesinger, Chair, 212-998-1830, Fax: 212-995-4873, E-mail: musical.theatre@nyu.edu. *Application contact:* Dan Sandford, Director of Graduate Admissions, 212-998-1918, Fax: 212-995-4060, E-mail: tisch.gradadmissions@nyu.edu.

The Nigerian Baptist Theological Seminary, Graduate Studies, Ogbomoso, Nigeria. Offers church music (M Div, M Th, Diploma); divinity (M Div); ministry (D Min); religious education (M Div, M Th, PhD); theological studies (MATS); theology (M Th, PhD). Part-time programs available. *Degree requirements:* For master's, thesis, 2 Nigerian languages; for M Div, thesis/dissertation (for some programs), 2 biblical languages; for Diploma, thesis or alternative.

Norfolk State University, School of Graduate Studies, School of Liberal Arts, Department of Music, Norfolk, VA 23504. Offers music (MM); music education (MM); performance (MM); theory and composition (MM). *Accreditation:* NASM. Part-time programs available. *Degree requirements:* For master's, thesis or alternative. *Entrance requirements:* For master's, minimum GPA of 2.7, letters of recommendation. Additional exam requirements/recommendations for international students: Required—TOEFL.

North Carolina Central University, Division of Academic Affairs, College of Liberal Arts, Department of Music, Durham, NC 27707-3129. Offers jazz studies (MM).

North Dakota State University, College of Graduate and Interdisciplinary Studies, College of Arts, Humanities and Social Sciences, Department of Music, Fargo, ND 58108. Offers M Ed, MM, DMA. *Accreditation:* NASM. *Students:* 18 full-time (6 women), 12 part-time (6 women); includes 1 Hispanic/Latino, 2 international. In 2010, 2 master's, 5 doctorates awarded. *Degree requirements:* For master's, 2 foreign languages, comprehensive exam, thesis or alternative, recitals; for doctorate, 2 foreign languages, comprehensive exam, thesis/dissertation or alternative, recitals. *Entrance requirements:* For master's and doctorate, music history, music theory, performance audition. Additional exam requirements/recommendations for international students: Required—TOEFL (minimum score 525 paper-based; 197 computer-based; 71 iBT). *Application deadline:* Applications are processed on a rolling basis. Application fee: $45 ($60 for international students). Electronic applications accepted. *Financial support:* Fellowships with full tuition reimbursements, teaching assistantships with full tuition reimbursements, tuition waivers (partial) and unspecified assistantships available. Support available to part-time students. Financial award applicants required to submit FAFSA. *Faculty research:* Performance, conducting. *Unit head:* Dr. John Miller, Director, Division of Fine Arts, 701-231-7932, E-mail: ej.miller@ndsu.edu. *Application contact:* Dr. Jo Ann Miller, Director, Graduate Studies, 701-231-7822, E-mail: jo.miller@ndsu.edu.

Northeastern Illinois University, Graduate College, College of Arts and Sciences, Department of Music, Program in Music, Chicago, IL 60625-4699. Offers MA. *Accreditation:* NASM. Part-time and evening/weekend programs available. *Faculty:* 16 full-time (6 women), 18 part-time/adjunct (4 women). *Students:* 6 full-time (1 woman), 20 part-time (14 women); includes 7 minority (4 Asian, non-Hispanic/Latino; 2 Hispanic/Latino; 1 Two or more races, non-Hispanic/Latino). Average age 38. 15 applicants, 73% accepted. In 2010, 10 master's awarded. *Degree requirements:* For master's, comprehensive exam, thesis optional. *Entrance requirements:* For master's, departmental exam, audition, minimum GPA of 2.75. Additional exam requirements/recommendations for international students: Required—TOEFL (minimum score 550 paper-based; 213 computer-based; 79 iBT). *Application deadline:* Applications are processed on a rolling basis. Application fee: $30. Electronic applications accepted. *Financial support:* In 2010–11, 15 students received support, including 1 research assistantship with full and partial tuition reimbursement available (averaging $6,600 per year); career-related internships or fieldwork, Federal Work-Study, institutionally sponsored loans, scholarships/grants, tuition waivers (full and partial), and unspecified assistantships also available. Support available to part-time students. Financial award applicants required to submit FAFSA. *Faculty research:* World music, computers as applied instruments, vocal pedagogy, vocal interpretation, jazz repertory. *Unit head:* Dr. Shayne Cofer, Department Chair. *Application contact:* Dr. Shayne Cofer, Department Chair.

Northern Arizona University, Graduate College, College of Arts and Letters, School of Music, Flagstaff, AZ 86011. Offers choral conducting (MM); instrumental conducting (MM); instrumental performance (MM); musicology (MM); performance (Certificate); piano accompanying and chamber music (MM); Suzuki violin/viola (MM); theory or composition (MM); vocal performance (MM). *Accreditation:* NASM. *Faculty:* 41 full-time (16 women). *Students:* 29 full-time (15 women); includes 5 minority (3 Black or African American, non-Hispanic/Latino; 2 Hispanic/Latino), 1 international. Average age 30. 32 applicants, 66% accepted, 9 enrolled. In 2010, 12 master's awarded. *Degree requirements:* For master's, comprehensive exam, thesis (for some programs), departmental exams. *Entrance requirements:* For master's, bachelor's degree in music, minimum GPA of 3.0, audition. Additional exam requirements/recommendations for international students: Required—TOEFL (minimum score 550 paper-based; 213 computer-based; 80 iBT), IELTS (minimum score 7). *Application deadline:* For fall admission, 3/15 priority date for domestic and international students. Applications are processed on a rolling basis. Application fee: $65. Electronic applications accepted. *Financial support:* In 2010–11, 11 teaching assistantships with partial tuition reimbursements (averaging $9,174 per year) were awarded; Federal Work-Study, scholarships/grants, health care benefits, tuition waivers (full and partial), and unspecified assistantships also available. Financial award applicants required to submit FAFSA. *Unit head:* Dr. Todd E. Sullivan, Chair, 928-523-3731, Fax: 928-523-2562, E-mail: todd.sullivan@nau.edu. *Application contact:* Joyce Richards, Administrative Associate, 928-523-3731, Fax: 928-523-2562, E-mail: joyce.richards@nau.edu.

Northern Illinois University, Graduate School, College of Visual and Performing Arts, School of Music, De Kalb, IL 60115-2854. Offers MM, Performer's Certificate. *Accreditation:* NASM. Part-time programs available. *Faculty:* 33 full-time (3 women), 14 part-time/adjunct (3 women). *Students:* 61 full-time (30 women), 35 part-time (24 women); includes 5 Black or African American, non-Hispanic/Latino; 7 Asian, non-Hispanic/Latino; 2 Hispanic/Latino; 1 Two or more races, non-Hispanic/Latino, 21 international. Average age 28. 74 applicants, 61% accepted, 27 enrolled. In 2010, 39 master's, 20 Performer's Certificates awarded. *Degree requirements:* For master's, comprehensive exam, thesis optional, recital or project; for Performer's Certificate, recitals. *Entrance requirements:* For master's, minimum GPA of 2.75, appropriate bachelor's degree, audition, interview; for Performer's Certificate, minimum GPA of 2.75 (undergraduate), 3.2 (graduate); audition. Additional exam requirements/recommendations for international students: Required—TOEFL (minimum score 550 paper-based; 213 computer-based). *Application deadline:* For fall admission, 4/1 for domestic students, 5/1 for international students; for spring admission, 11/1 for domestic students, 10/1 for international students. Applications are processed on a rolling basis. Application fee: $30. Electronic applications accepted. *Expenses:* Tuition, state resident: full-time $7200; part-time $300 per credit hour. Tuition, nonresident: full-time $14,400; part-time $600 per credit hour. Required fees: $79 per credit hour. *Financial support:* In 2010–11, 27 teaching assistantships with full tuition reimbursements were awarded; fellowships with full tuition reimbursements, research assistantships with full tuition reimbursements, Federal Work-Study, scholarships/grants, tuition waivers (full), and staff assistantships also available. Support available to part-time students. Financial award applicants required to submit FAFSA. *Faculty research:* Impact of music on urban children and acquisition of language skills, music in seventeenth century Madrid, Finnish music and culture, jazz studies. *Unit head:* Dr. Paul Bauer, Director, 815-753-1551, Fax: 815-753-1759, E-mail: paulbauer@niu.edu. *Application contact:* Dr. Charles T. Blickhan, Graduate Coordinator, 815-753-0394, E-mail: blickhan@niu.edu.

Northern Kentucky University, Office of Graduate Programs, College of Arts and Sciences, Program in English, Highland Heights, KY 41099. Offers composition and rhetoric (Certificate); creative writing (Certificate); cultural studies (Certificate); English (MA); professional writing (Certificate). Part-time and evening/weekend programs available. *Faculty:* 11 full-time (6 women). *Students:* 8 full-time (5 women), 66 part-time (53 women); includes 6 minority (4 Black or African American, non-Hispanic/Latino; 1 Hispanic/Latino; 1 Two or more races, non-Hispanic/Latino). Average age 34. 36 applicants, 94% accepted, 32 enrolled. In 2010, 3 master's awarded. *Degree requirements:* For master's, comprehensive exam (for some programs), comprehensive exam, thesis, project, or portfolio. *Entrance requirements:* For master's, minimum GPA of 3.0, two letters of reference. Additional exam requirements/recommendations for international students: Required—TOEFL (minimum score 550 paper-based; 213 computer-based; 79 iBT); Recommended—IELTS (minimum score 6.5). *Application deadline:* For fall admission, 7/1 priority date for domestic students, 6/1 priority date for international students; for spring admission, 11/1 for domestic students, 10/1 for international students. Applications are processed on a rolling basis. Application fee: $40. Electronic applications accepted. *Expenses:* Tuition, state resident: full-time $7254; part-time $403 per credit hour. Tuition, nonresident: full-time $12,492; part-time $694 per credit hour. Tuition and fees vary according to degree level and program. *Financial support:* Unspecified assistantships available. Financial award applicants required to submit FAFSA. *Faculty research:* Composition and rhetoric, creative writing, English and American literature, professional writing, cultural studies. *Unit head:* Dr. Roxanne Kent-Drury, Coordinator, 859-572-6636, Fax: 859-572-6093, E-mail: rkdrury@nku.edu. *Application contact:* Dr. Peg Griffin, Director of Graduate Programs, 859-572-6934, Fax: 859-572-6670, E-mail: griffinp@nku.edu.

North Park University, School of Music, Chicago, IL 60625-4895. Offers vocal performance (MM). *Accreditation:* NASM.

Northwestern State University of Louisiana, Graduate Studies and Research, School of Creative and Performing Arts, Program in Music, Natchitoches, LA 71497. Offers MM. *Accreditation:* NASM. *Degree requirements:* For master's, comprehensive exam, thesis or alternative. *Entrance requirements:* For master's, GRE General Test, minimum undergraduate GPA of 2.5.

Northwestern University, The Graduate School, School of Communication, Department of Performance Studies, Evanston, IL 60208. Offers MA, PhD. Admissions and degrees offered through The Graduate School. Part-time programs available. Terminal master's awarded for partial completion of doctoral program. *Degree requirements:* For master's, recital; for doctorate, one foreign language, thesis/dissertation, recital. *Entrance requirements:* For master's and doctorate, GRE General Test. Additional exam requirements/recommendations for international students: Required—TOEFL. *Faculty research:* Adaptation/performance of literature, ethnography of performance, critical cultural studies, performance theory, intercultural performance, gender studies.

Northwestern University, Henry and Leigh Bienen School of Music, Department of Music Performance, Evanston, IL 60208. Offers collaborative arts (DM); conducting (MM, DM); jazz (MM); performance (MM), including string chamber music and orchestral literature; piano performance (MM, DM, CP); piano performance and collaborative arts (MM); piano performance and pedagogy (MM); string performance and pedagogy (MM); strings (MM, DM); strings, winds and percussion (CP); voice (MM, DM, CP); winds and percussion (MM, DM). *Accreditation:* NASM. *Degree requirements:* For master's, recital; for doctorate, comprehensive exam, thesis/dissertation, 3 recitals; for CP, 2 recitals. *Entrance requirements:* For master's, audition, preliminary tapes in voice, flute, percussion; for doctorate, written essay exam (theory and music history), audition, preliminary tapes; for CP, audition, preliminary tapes. Additional exam requirements/recommendations for international students: Required—TOEFL (minimum score 600 paper-based; 250 computer-based; 100 iBT).

Northwestern University, Henry and Leigh Bienen School of Music, Department of Music Studies, Evanston, IL 60208. Offers music composition (DM); music education (MM, PhD); music theory (MM, PhD); musicology (MM, PhD). PhD admissions and degree offered through The Graduate School. *Accreditation:* NASM. *Degree requirements:* For doctorate, comprehensive exam, thesis/dissertation. *Entrance requirements:* For master's, portfolio or research papers; for doctorate, GRE General Test (PhD), portfolio, research papers. Additional exam requirements/recommendations for international students: Required—TOEFL (minimum score 600 paper-based; 250 computer-based; 100 iBT). *Faculty research:* Music cognition, cognitive learning, aesthetic education, computer music, technology in education.

Notre Dame de Namur University, Division of Academic Affairs, College of Arts and Sciences, Department of Music, Belmont, CA 94002-1908. Offers musical performance (MFA, Certificate). Part-time programs available. *Faculty:* 2 full-time (1 woman), 8 part-time/adjunct (4 women). *Students:* 8 full-time (6 women), 5 part-time (3 women); includes 1 Asian, non-Hispanic/Latino; 1 Hispanic/Latino, 1 international. Average age 30. 6 applicants, 100% accepted, 4 enrolled. In 2010, 4 master's awarded. *Degree requirements:* For master's, exams. *Entrance requirements:* For master's, audition, appropriate bachelor's degree, minimum GPA of 2.5. Additional exam requirements/recommendations for international students: Required—TOEFL (minimum score 550 paper-based; 213 computer-based; 79 iBT). *Application deadline:* For fall admission, 8/1 priority date for domestic students; for spring admission, 12/1 priority date for domestic students. Applications are processed on a rolling basis. Application fee: $60. Electronic applications accepted. *Expenses:* Tuition: Full-time $14,220; part-time $790 per credit. Required fees: $35 per semester. Tuition and fees vary according to program. *Financial support:* Available to part-time students. Applicants required to submit FAFSA. *Unit head:* Debra Lambert, Chair, 650-580-3694. *Application contact:* Candace Hallmark, Associate Director of Admissions, 650-508-3600, Fax: 650-508-3426, E-mail: grad.admit@ndnu.edu.

Oakland University, Graduate Study and Lifelong Learning, College of Arts and Sciences, Department of Music, Rochester, MI 48309-4401. Offers music (MM); music education (PhD). *Accreditation:* NASM. *Entrance requirements:* For master's, minimum GPA of 3.0 for unconditional admission. Additional exam requirements/recommendations for international students: Required—TOEFL (minimum score 550 paper-based; 213 computer-based). Electronic applications accepted. *Expenses:* Contact institution.

Oberlin College, Conservatory of Music, Oberlin, OH 44074-1588. Offers MM, MMT, AD. *Accreditation:* NASM. *Degree requirements:* For master's, 2 recitals. *Entrance requirements:* For master's, audition. Additional exam requirements/recommendations for international students: Required—TOEFL (minimum score 550 paper-based; 213 computer-based; 79 iBT). Electronic applications accepted.

The Ohio State University, Graduate School, College of Arts and Sciences, Division of Arts and Humanities, Department of Dance, Columbus, OH 43210. Offers choreography (MFA); dance (MA, MFA, PhD); dance and technology (MFA); dance studies (PhD); Labanotation (MFA); lighting (MFA); performance (MFA). *Accreditation:* NASD. *Faculty:* 17. *Students:* 31 full-time (24 women), 7 part-time (5 women); includes 3 Black or African American, non-Hispanic/Latino; 1 Asian, non-Hispanic/Latino; 2 Hispanic/Latino, 4 international. Average age 30. In 2010, 9 master's awarded. *Degree requirements:* For master's, thesis optional. *Entrance requirements:* For master's, GRE General Test (MA); for doctorate, GRE General Test. Additional exam requirements/recommendations for international students: Recommended—TOEFL (minimum score 600 paper-based; 250 computer-based). *Application deadline:* For fall admission, 8/15 priority date for domestic students, 7/1 priority date for international students; for winter admission, 12/1 priority date for domestic students, 11/1 priority date for international students; for spring admission, 3/1 priority date for domestic students, 2/1 priority date for international students. Applications are processed on a rolling basis. Application fee: $40 ($50 for international students). Electronic applications accepted. *Expenses:* Tuition, state resident: full-time $10,605. Tuition, nonresident: full-time $26,535. Tuition and fees vary according to course load and program. *Financial support:* Fellowships, teaching assistantships, Federal Work-Study and institutionally sponsored loans available. Support available to part-time students. *Unit* *head:* Susan Van Pelt Petry, Chair, 614-292-0984, E-mail: petry.37@osu.edu. *Application contact:* 614-292-9444, Fax: 614-292-3895, E-mail: domestic.grad@osu.edu.

The Ohio State University, Graduate School, College of Arts and Sciences, Division of Arts and Humanities, School of Music, Columbus, OH 43210. Offers MA, MM, DMA, PhD. *Accreditation:* NASM. Part-time programs available. *Faculty:* 59. *Students:* 114 full-time (62 women), 59 part-time (33 women); includes 11 Black or African American, non-Hispanic/Latino; 5 Asian, non-Hispanic/Latino; 7 Hispanic/Latino, 32 international. Average age 30. In 2010, 31 master's, 29 doctorates awarded. *Degree requirements:* For master's, thesis optional; for doctorate, 2 foreign languages, thesis/dissertation. *Entrance requirements:* For master's and doctorate, GRE General Test. Additional exam requirements/recommendations for international students: Recommended—TOEFL (minimum score 600 paper-based; 250 computer-based). *Application deadline:* For fall admission, 8/15 priority date for domestic students, 7/1 priority date for international students; for winter admission, 12/1 priority date for domestic students, 11/1 priority date for international students; for spring admission, 3/1 priority date for domestic students, 2/1 priority date for international students. Applications are processed on a rolling basis. Application fee: $40 ($50 for international students). Electronic applications accepted. *Expenses:* Tuition, state resident: full-time $10,605. Tuition, nonresident: full-time $26,535. Tuition and fees vary according to course load and program. *Financial support:* Fellowships, research assistantships, teaching assistantships, Federal Work-Study, institutionally sponsored loans, and unspecified assistantships available. Support available to part-time students. *Unit head:* Richard Blatti, Interim Director, 614-292-7664, E-mail: blatti.1@osu.edu. *Application contact:* 614-292-9444, Fax: 614-292-3895, E-mail: domestic.grad@osu.edu.

Ohio University, Graduate College, College of Fine Arts, School of Music, Athens, OH 45701-2979. Offers accompanying (MM); composition (MM); conducting (MM); history/literature (MM); music education (MM); music therapy (MM); performance (MM, Certificate); performance/pedagogy (MM); theory (MM). *Accreditation:* NASM. Part-time and evening/weekend programs available. Postbaccalaureate distance learning degree programs offered (minimal on-campus study). *Students:* 42 full-time (19 women), 7 part-time (3 women); includes 6 minority (2 Black or African American, non-Hispanic/Latino; 1 Asian, non-Hispanic/Latino; 2 Hispanic/Latino; 1 Two or more races, non-Hispanic/Latino), 9 international. 65 applicants, 52% accepted, 16 enrolled. In 2010, 12 master's awarded. *Degree requirements:* For master's, comprehensive exam, thesis (for some programs), oral exam. *Entrance requirements:* For master's, audition, interview, portfolio, recordings (varies by program). Additional exam requirements/recommendations for international students: Required—TOEFL (minimum score 550 paper-based; 80 iBT) or IELTS (minimum score 6.5). *Application deadline:* For fall admission, 1/1 priority date for domestic and international students. Application fee: $50 ($55 for international students). Electronic applications accepted. *Financial support:* In 2010–11, 35 teaching assistantships with full and partial tuition reimbursements (averaging $4,500 per year) were awarded; career-related internships or fieldwork, Federal Work-Study, institutionally sponsored loans, and tuition waivers (full and partial) also available. Financial award application deadline: 1/1. *Unit head:* Dr. W. Michael Parkinson, Director, 740-593-4244, Fax: 740-593-1429, E-mail: parkinsw@ohio.edu. *Application contact:* Dr. Richard Wetzel, Graduate Chair, 740-593-1652, Fax: 740-593-1429, E-mail: wetzel@ohio.edu.

Oklahoma City University, Margaret E. Petree College of Performing Arts, Wanda L. Bass School of Music, Oklahoma City, OK 73106-1402. Offers composition (MM); conducting (MM); musical theatre (MM); opera performance (MM); performance (MM). *Accreditation:* NASM. Part-time programs available. *Degree requirements:* For master's, thesis, departmental qualifying exam, recital. *Entrance requirements:* For master's, audition, bachelor's degree in music, minimum GPA of 3.0. Additional exam requirements/recommendations for international students: Required—TOEFL.

Oklahoma State University, College of Arts and Sciences, Department of Music, Stillwater, OK 74078. Offers pedagogy and performance (MM). *Accreditation:* NASM. *Faculty:* 27 full-time (9 women), 9 part-time/adjunct (3 women). *Students:* 15 full-time (4 women), 4 part-time (0 women); includes 1 Asian, non-Hispanic/Latino, 2 international. Average age 27. 35 applicants, 63% accepted, 11 enrolled. In 2010, 7 master's awarded. *Degree requirements:* For master's, final project, oral exam. *Entrance requirements:* For master's, GRE, audition. Additional exam requirements/recommendations for international students: Required—TOEFL (minimum score 550 paper-based; 79 iBT). *Application deadline:* For fall admission, 3/1 priority date for international students; for spring admission, 8/1 priority date for international students. Applications are processed on a rolling basis. Application fee: $40 ($75 for international students). Electronic applications accepted. *Expenses:* Tuition, state resident: full-time $3716; part-time $154.85 per credit hour. Tuition, nonresident: full-time $14,892; part-time $621 per credit hour. Required fees: $2044; $85.20 per credit hour. One-time fee: $50. Tuition and fees vary according to course load and campus/location. *Financial support:* In 2010–11, 12 teaching assistantships (averaging $7,371 per year) were awarded; career-related internships or fieldwork, Federal Work-Study, scholarships/grants, health care benefits, tuition waivers (partial), and unspecified assistantships also available. Support available to part-time students. Financial award application deadline: 3/1; financial award applicants required to submit FAFSA. *Faculty research:* Discovery and presentation of music literature of other countries, transportation of ancient music literature to modern notation. *Unit head:* Dr. Brant Adams, Head, 405-744-6133, Fax: 405-744-9324. *Application contact:* Dr. Gordon Emslie, Dean, 405-744-6368, Fax: 405-744-0355, E-mail: grad-i@okstate.edu.

Penn State University Park, Graduate School, College of Arts and Architecture, School of Music, State College, University Park, PA 16802-1503. Offers M Mus, MA, MME, DMA, PhD. *Accreditation:* NASM.

Phillips Theological Seminary, Programs in Theology, Tulsa, OK 74116. Offers administration of church agencies (M Div); campus ministry (M Div); church-related social work (M Div); college and seminary teaching (M Div); global mission work (M Div); institutional chaplaincy (M Div); ministerial vocations in Christian education (M Div); ministry (D Min), including parish ministry, pastoral counseling, practices of ministry; ministry and culture (MAMC), including Christian education, congregational leadership, history and practice of Christian spirituality, theology, ethics, and culture; ministry of music (M Div); pastoral care and counseling (M Div); pastoral ministry (M Div); theological studies (MTS). *Accreditation:* ATS. Part-time programs available. Postbaccalaureate distance learning degree programs offered (minimal on-campus study). *Degree requirements:* For master's, thesis (for some programs); for doctorate, thesis/dissertation. *Entrance requirements:* For master's, minimum GPA of 2.5; for doctorate, M Div, minimum GPA of 3.0. *Faculty research:* Biblical studies, historical studies, theology and culture, practical theology, theology and film.

Pittsburg State University, Graduate School, College of Arts and Sciences, Department of Music, Pittsburg, KS 66762. Offers instrumental music education (MM); music history/music literature (MM); performance (MM), including orchestral performance, organ, piano, voice; theory and composition (MM); vocal music education (MM). *Accreditation:* NASM. *Degree requirements:* For master's, thesis or alternative.

Point Park University, Conservatory of Performing Arts, Pittsburgh, PA 15222-1984. Offers theatre arts-acting (MFA). *Faculty:* 3 full-time, 1 part-time/adjunct. *Students:* 6 full-time (3 women), 1 international. Average age 42. 6 applicants, 0% accepted, 0 enrolled. *Degree requirements:* For master's, comprehensive exam (for some programs), thesis or alternative. *Entrance requirements:* For master's, interview, undergraduate degree in related field, theatre experience. Additional exam requirements/recommendations for international students: Required—TOEFL (minimum score 550 paper-based; 79 iBT). *Application deadline:* Applications are processed on a rolling basis. Application fee: $30. Electronic applications accepted. *Expenses:* Tuition: Full-time $12,456; part-time $692 per credit. Required fees: $630; $35 per credit. *Financial support:* In 2010–11, 6 students received support, including 5 teaching assistantships with full tuition reimbursements available (averaging $6,400 per year); scholarships/grants also available. Financial award application deadline: 4/15; financial award applicants required to submit FAFSA. *Unit head:* Ronald Allan-Lindblom, Dean/Artistic Producing Director,

412-392-3454, Fax: 412-392-2424, E-mail: rlindblom@pointpark.edu. *Application contact:* Lynn C. Ribar, Associate Director, Adult and Graduate Enrollment, 412-392-3908, Fax: 412-392-6164, E-mail: lribar@pointpark.edu.

Portland State University, Graduate Studies, School of Fine and Performing Arts, Department of Music, Portland, OR 97207-0751. Offers conducting (MMC); music education (MAT, MST); performance (MMP). *Accreditation:* NASM. Part-time programs available. *Faculty:* 25 full-time (9 women), 39 part-time/adjunct (12 women). *Students:* 20 full-time (11 women), 24 part-time (15 women); includes 1 American Indian or Alaska Native, non-Hispanic/Latino; 1 Asian, non-Hispanic/Latino, 3 international. Average age 30. 19 applicants, 89% accepted, 2 enrolled. In 2010, 11 master's awarded. *Degree requirements:* For master's, variable foreign language requirement, exit exam. *Entrance requirements:* For master's, GRE General Test, departmental exam, minimum GPA of 3.0 in upper-division course work or 2.75 overall. Additional exam requirements/recommendations for international students: Required—TOEFL (minimum score 550 paper-based; 213 computer-based). *Application deadline:* For fall admission, 8/1 priority date for domestic students, 8/1 for international students; for winter admission, 11/15 for domestic students, 10/1 for international students; for spring admission, 2/1 for domestic and international students. Applications are processed on a rolling basis. Application fee: $50. *Expenses:* Tuition, state resident: full-time $8505; part-time $315 per credit. Tuition, nonresident: full-time $13,284; part-time $492 per credit. Required fees: $1482; $21 per credit. $99 per term. One-time fee: $120. Part-time tuition and fees vary according to course load and program. *Financial support:* Research assistantships with full tuition reimbursements, teaching assistantships with full tuition reimbursements, Federal Work-Study, scholarships/grants, and unspecified assistantships available. Support available to part-time students. Financial award application deadline: 3/1; financial award applicants required to submit FAFSA. *Faculty research:* Composition, music analysis, music history, jazz. *Unit head:* Bryan Johanson, Chair, 503-725-3382, Fax: 503-725-8215. *Application contact:* Bryan Johanson, Chair, 503-725-3382, Fax: 503-725-8215.

Princeton University, Graduate School, Department of Music, Princeton, NJ 08544-1019. Offers composition (PhD); musicology (PhD). *Degree requirements:* For doctorate, variable foreign language requirement, thesis/dissertation. *Entrance requirements:* For doctorate, GRE General Test, sample of written work. Additional exam requirements/recommendations for international students: Required—TOEFL (minimum score 600 paper-based; 250 computer-based). Electronic applications accepted. *Faculty research:* Computer synthesis, history of Western music, comparative musicology, theory.

Purchase College, State University of New York, Conservatory of Music, Purchase, NY 10577-1400. Offers composition (MM); instrumental performance (MM); jazz studies (MM); studio composition (MM); voice and opera studies (MM). *Degree requirements:* For master's, thesis or alternative, composition, performance. *Entrance requirements:* For master's, audition. Electronic applications accepted.

Queens College of the City University of New York, Division of Graduate Studies, Arts and Humanities Division, Aaron Copland School of Music, Flushing, NY 11367-1597. Offers MA. Part-time programs available. *Faculty:* 25 full-time (5 women). *Students:* 24 full-time (9 women), 133 part-time (45 women); includes 4 Black or African American, non-Hispanic/Latino; 2 Asian, non-Hispanic/Latino; 11 Hispanic/Latino, 75 international. 173 applicants, 49% accepted, 57 enrolled. In 2010, 65 master's awarded. *Degree requirements:* For master's, one foreign language, qualifying exams, recital. *Entrance requirements:* For master's, audition, bachelor's degree in music, minimum GPA of 3.0. Additional exam requirements/recommendations for international students: Required—TOEFL. *Application deadline:* For fall admission, 4/1 for domestic students; for spring admission, 11/1 for domestic students. Applications are processed on a rolling basis. Application fee: $125. *Financial support:* Career-related internships or fieldwork, Federal Work-Study, institutionally sponsored loans, and tuition waivers (partial) available. Support available to part-time students. Financial award application deadline: 4/1; financial award applicants required to submit FAFSA. *Unit head:* Dr. Edward Smaldone, Chair/Director, 718-997-3800, E-mail: edward_smaldone@qc.edu. *Application contact:* Mario Caruso, Director of Graduate Admissions, 718-997-5200, Fax: 718-997-5193, E-mail: graduate_admissions@qc.edu.

Radford University, College of Graduate and Professional Studies, College of Visual and Performing Arts, Department of Music, Radford, VA 24142. Offers music (MA); music education (MS); music therapy (MS). *Accreditation:* NASM. Part-time programs available. *Faculty:* 13 full-time (3 women), 7 part-time/adjunct (3 women). *Students:* 16 full-time (9 women), 2 part-time (both women); includes 1 minority (Black or African American, non-Hispanic/Latino), 1 international. Average age 28. 16 applicants, 94% accepted, 11 enrolled. In 2010, 9 master's awarded. *Degree requirements:* For master's, comprehensive exam, thesis or alternative. *Entrance requirements:* For master's, GRE, major field test in music or PRAXIS II (content knowledge), written diagnostics exams in music, minimum GPA of 2.75; 3 letters of reference. Additional exam requirements/recommendations for international students: Required—TOEFL (minimum score 550 paper-based; 213 computer-based; 79 iBT). *Application deadline:* For fall admission, 2/15 priority date for domestic students, 12/1 for international students; for spring admission, 7/1 for international students. Applications are processed on a rolling basis. Application fee: $50. Electronic applications accepted. *Expenses:* Tuition, state resident: full-time $5746; part-time $239 per credit hour. Tuition, nonresident: full-time $14,174; part-time $591 per credit hour. Required fees: $2634; $111 per credit hour. *Financial support:* In 2010–11, 13 students received support, including 4 research assistantships with partial tuition reimbursements available (averaging $8,000 per year), 8 teaching assistantships with partial tuition reimbursements available (averaging $8,700 per year); career-related internships or fieldwork, Federal Work-Study, institutionally sponsored loans, scholarships/grants, and unspecified assistantships also available. Financial award application deadline: 3/1; financial award applicants required to submit FAFSA. *Unit head:* Dr. Allen F. Wojtera, Chair, 540-831-5177, Fax: 540-831-6133, E-mail: awojtera@radford.edu. *Application contact:* Rebecca Conner, Graduate Admissions, 540-831-5431, Fax: 540-831-6061, E-mail: gradcollege@radford.edu.

Reinhardt University, Program in Music, Waleska, GA 30183-2981. Offers conducting (MM); music education (MM); piano pedagogy (MM). *Accreditation:* NASM. Part-time and evening/weekend programs available. Postbaccalaureate distance learning degree programs offered. *Faculty:* 3 full-time (1 woman), 6 part-time/adjunct (2 women). *Students:* 9 part-time (6 women). Average age 33. 11 applicants, 82% accepted, 9 enrolled. *Entrance requirements:* For master's, GRE, audition (for piano pedagogy and conducting), 2 letters of reference. Additional exam requirements/recommendations for international students: Required—TOEFL. *Application deadline:* For fall admission, 5/7 for domestic and international students. Applications are processed on a rolling basis. Application fee: $25. Electronic applications accepted. *Expenses:* Tuition: Full-time $8400; part-time $350 per credit hour. Required fees: $125 per semester. *Financial support:* Application deadline: 5/1. *Unit head:* Dr. Paula Thomas-Lee, Graduate Program Coordinator for Masters in Music, 770-720-5658, E-mail: ptl@reinhardt.edu. *Application contact:* Ray Schumacher, Admissions Counselor, 770-993-6971, Fax: 770-475-0263, E-mail: res@reinhardt.edu.

Rice University, Graduate Programs, Shepherd School of Music, Houston, TX 77251-1892. Offers composition (MM, DMA); conducting (MM); musicology (MM); performance (MM, DMA); theory (MM). *Degree requirements:* For master's, thesis (for some programs), 2 recitals; for doctorate, one foreign language, comprehensive exam, thesis/dissertation, 4 recitals. *Entrance requirements:* For master's, GRE General Test (musicology); for doctorate, GRE General Test. Additional exam requirements/recommendations for international students: Required—TOEFL (minimum score 600 paper-based; 250 computer-based; 100 iBT), IELTS (minimum score 7). *Faculty research:* Musicology, performance, theory, composition.

Rider University, Westminster Choir College, Programs in Music, Lawrenceville, NJ 08648-3001. Offers choral conducting (MM); composition (MM); organ performance (MM); piano accompanying and coaching (MM); piano pedagogy and performance (MM); piano performance (MM); sacred music (MM); vocal pedagogy and performance (MM); vocal training (MVP).

Music

Rider University (continued)
Part-time programs available. *Degree requirements:* For master's, variable foreign language requirement, departmental qualifying exam. *Entrance requirements:* For master's, audition, interview, repertoire list, 2 letters of reference, resume. Additional exam requirements/recommendations for international students: Required—TOEFL (minimum score 525 paper-based; 195 computer-based). Electronic applications accepted. *Expenses:* Tuition: Full-time $29,870; part-time $667.34 per credit. Required fees: $350; $11.60 per credit. Part-time tuition and fees vary according to program.

Roosevelt University, Graduate Division, Chicago College of Performing Arts, The Music Conservatory, Chicago, IL 60605. Offers music (MM); piano pedagogy (Diploma). *Accreditation:* NASM. Part-time and evening/weekend programs available.

Rowan University, Graduate School, College of Fine and Performing Arts, Program in Music, Glassboro, NJ 08028-1701. Offers performance (MM). *Accreditation:* NASM. Part-time and evening/weekend programs available. *Faculty:* 11 full-time (3 women), 21 part-time/adjunct (6 women). *Students:* 4 full-time (2 women), 14 part-time (9 women); includes 3 Asian, non-Hispanic/Latino; 1 Hispanic/Latino. Average age 30. 5 applicants, 60% accepted, 3 enrolled. In 2010, 2 master's awarded. *Degree requirements:* For master's, thesis (for some programs). *Entrance requirements:* For master's, GRE General Test. Additional exam requirements/recommendations for international students: Required—TOEFL. *Application deadline:* Applications are processed on a rolling basis. Application fee: $65 ($200 for international students). Electronic applications accepted. *Expenses:* Tuition, area resident: Part-time $602 per semester hour. Tuition, nonresident: part-time $602 per semester hour. Required fees: $100 per semester hour. One-time fee: $10 part-time. *Financial support:* Career-related internships or fieldwork, scholarships/grants, health care benefits, and unspecified assistantships available. Support available to part-time students. *Unit head:* Dr. Horacio Sosa, Dean, College Graduate and Continuing Education, 856-256-4747, Fax: 856-256-5638, E-mail: sosa@rowan.edu. *Application contact:* Karen Haynes, Graduate Coordinator, 856-256-4052, Fax: 856-256-4436, E-mail: haynes@rowan.edu.

Rutgers, The State University of New Jersey, Newark, Graduate School, Program in Jazz History and Research, Newark, NJ 07102. Offers MA. *Faculty:* 3 full-time (0 women). *Students:* 5 full-time (1 woman), 8 part-time (0 women); includes 2 Black or African American, non-Hispanic/Latino. 10 applicants, 60% accepted, 6 enrolled. In 2010, 8 master's awarded. *Entrance requirements:* For master's, GRE, minimum B average. Application fee: $60. Electronic applications accepted. *Expenses:* Tuition, state resident: part-time $600 per credit. Tuition, nonresident: full-time $10,694. *Financial support:* Tuition waivers (full and partial) available. *Unit head:* Dr. Lewis Porter, Director, 973-353-5119 Ext. 30, E-mail: lporter@andromeda.rutgers.edu. *Application contact:* Jason Hand, Director of Admissions, 973-353-5205, Fax: 973-353-1440.

Rutgers, The State University of New Jersey, New Brunswick, Mason Gross School of the Arts, Music Department, New Brunswick, NJ 08901. Offers collaborative piano (MM, DMA); conducting: choral (MM, DMA); conducting: instrumental (MM, DMA); conducting: orchestral (MM, DMA); jazz studies (MM); music (DMA, AD); music education (MM, DMA); music performance (MM). *Accreditation:* NASM. *Faculty:* 32 full-time (10 women), 28 part-time/adjunct (8 women). *Students:* 78 full-time (42 women), 141 part-time (81 women); includes 3 Black or African American, non-Hispanic/Latino; 23 Asian, non-Hispanic/Latino; 5 Hispanic/Latino. Average age 30. 326 applicants, 27% accepted, 58 enrolled. In 2010, 30 master's, 21 doctorates awarded. *Degree requirements:* For doctorate, one foreign language. *Entrance requirements:* For master's and doctorate, audition. Additional exam requirements/recommendations for international students: Required—TOEFL (minimum score 550 paper-based; 213 computer-based), IELTS (minimum score 7). *Application deadline:* For fall admission, 2/1 for domestic students, 11/1 for international students; for spring admission, 11/1 for domestic students, 2/1 for international students. Applications are processed on a rolling basis. Application fee: $65. Electronic applications accepted. *Expenses:* Tuition, state resident: full-time $7200; part-time $600 per credit. Tuition, nonresident: full-time $11,124; part-time $927 per credit. *Financial support:* In 2010–11, 98 students received support, including 16 fellowships with full tuition reimbursements available (averaging $6,000 per year), 13 teaching assistantships with partial tuition reimbursements available (averaging $8,860 per year); Federal Work-Study, institutionally sponsored loans, scholarships/grants, and tuition waivers also available. Support available to part-time students. Financial award application deadline: 2/1; financial award applicants required to submit FAFSA. *Faculty research:* Performance, twentieth century music, jazz, music education. *Unit head:* Dr. Richard Chrisman, Graduate Director, 732-932-9272, Fax: 732-932-1517, E-mail: chrisman@rci.rutgers.edu. *Application contact:* Lois Fromer, Senior Administrative Assistant, 732-932-9190, Fax: 732-932-1517, E-mail: fromer@rci.rutgers.edu.

St. Cloud State University, School of Graduate Studies, College of Fine Arts and Humanities, Department of Music, St. Cloud, MN 56301-4498. Offers conducting and literature (MM); music education (MM); piano pedagogy (MM). *Accreditation:* NASM. *Degree requirements:* For master's, comprehensive exam (for some programs), thesis or alternative. *Entrance requirements:* For master's, GRE General Test, minimum GPA of 2.75. Additional exam requirements/recommendations for international students: Required—Michigan English Language Assessment Battery; Recommended—TOEFL (minimum score 550 paper-based; 213 computer-based), IELTS (minimum score 6.5). Electronic applications accepted.

Saint John's University, Saint John's School of Theology and Seminary, Collegeville, MN 56321. Offers divinity (M Div); liturgical music (MA); liturgical studies (MA); pastoral ministry (MA); theology (MA), including church history, liturgy, monastic studies, scripture, spirituality, systematics; M Div/MA. *Accreditation:* ATS. Part-time programs available. Postbaccalaureate distance learning degree programs offered (no on-campus study). *Degree requirements:* For master's, one foreign language, comprehensive exam (for some programs), thesis (for some programs). *Entrance requirements:* For master's, GRE General Test or MAT. Electronic applications accepted. *Faculty research:* Religious education, biblical literature.

Saint Joseph's College, Rensselaer Program of Church Music and Liturgy, Rensselaer, IN 47978. Offers church music and liturgy (MA); pastoral liturgy and music (Diploma). Offered during summer only. Part-time programs available. *Degree requirements:* For master's, thesis, research paper, service recital. *Entrance requirements:* For master's, entrance exams in music theory, conducting, keyboard, voice, and history.

St. Vladimir's Orthodox Theological Seminary, Graduate School of Theology, Crestwood, NY 10707-1699. Offers general theological studies (MA); liturgical music (MA); religious education (MA); theology (M Div, M Th, D Min); M Div/MA. MA in general theological studies, M Div offered jointly with St. Nersess Seminary. *Accreditation:* ATS. Part-time programs available. *Degree requirements:* For master's, one foreign language, thesis, fieldwork; for doctorate, thesis/dissertation, fieldwork; for M Div, one foreign language, thesis/dissertation, fieldwork. *Entrance requirements:* For doctorate, M Div, minimum GPA of 3.0. Additional exam requirements/recommendations for international students: Required—TOEFL (minimum score 250 computer-based).

Samford University, School of the Arts, Birmingham, AL 35229. Offers church music (MM); music (MME), including instrumental, vocal choral; piano pedagogy (MM). *Accreditation:* NASM. Part-time programs available. *Faculty:* 10 full-time (4 women), 5 part-time/adjunct (1 woman). *Students:* 11 full-time (6 women), 3 part-time (1 woman), 1 international. Average age 28. 13 applicants, 77% accepted, 10 enrolled. In 2010, 7 master's awarded. *Degree requirements:* For master's, oral exams, comprehensive exam (MME). *Entrance requirements:* For master's, GRE General Test or MAT, institutional exam; PRAXIS II (for MME), minimum GPA of 3.0. Additional exam requirements/recommendations for international students: Required—TOEFL (minimum score 550 paper-based; 213 computer-based). *Application deadline:* For fall admission, 5/1 priority date for domestic students; for spring admission, 12/1 priority date for domestic students. Applications are processed on a rolling basis. Application fee: $35. *Expenses:* Tuition: Part-time $622 per credit. Required fees: $110 per semester. *Financial support:* In 2010–11, 11 students received support, including research assistantships (averaging $4,000 per year); Federal Work-Study, scholarships/grants, tuition waivers (partial), and unspecified assistantships also available. Financial award application deadline: 9/1. *Faculty research:* Hymnology, choral techniques, assessment of music learning at elementary and secondary levels, piano pedagogy, special education and inclusion, learning theories. *Unit head:* Dr. Billy J. Strickland, Associate Dean, 205-726-4363, E-mail: bjstrick@samford.edu. *Application contact:* Dr. Moya Nordlund, Director, Graduate Studies, 205-726-2651, Fax: 205-726-2165, E-mail: mlnordlu@samford.edu.

Sam Houston State University, College of Arts and Sciences, School of Music, Huntsville, TX 77341. Offers music (MM); music education (MM). *Accreditation:* NASM. Part-time programs available. *Faculty:* 14 full-time (3 women), 1 part-time/adjunct (0 women). *Students:* 9 full-time (5 women), 10 part-time (5 women); includes 1 Black or African American, non-Hispanic/Latino; 1 Asian, non-Hispanic/Latino, 2 international. Average age 34. 11 applicants, 91% accepted, 9 enrolled. In 2010, 13 master's awarded. *Degree requirements:* For master's, thesis (for some programs), departmental qualifying exam. *Entrance requirements:* For master's, GRE General Test. Additional exam requirements/recommendations for international students: Required—TOEFL (minimum score 550 paper-based; 213 computer-based; 79 iBT). *Application deadline:* For fall admission, 8/1 for domestic and international students; for spring admission, 12/1 for domestic and international students. Applications are processed on a rolling basis. Application fee: $20. *Expenses:* Tuition, state resident: full-time $1363; part-time $163 per credit hour. Tuition, nonresident: full-time $3856; part-time $473 per credit hour. *Financial support:* Teaching assistantships, Federal Work-Study and scholarships/grants available. Financial award application deadline: 5/31; financial award applicants required to submit FAFSA. *Unit head:* Dr. James Bankhead, Director, 936-294-3808, Fax: 936-294-3765, E-mail: bankhead@shsu.edu. *Application contact:* Scott Plugge, Advisor, 936-294-1393, E-mail: plugge@shsu.edu.

San Diego State University, Graduate and Research Affairs, College of Professional Studies and Fine Arts, School of Music and Dance, San Diego, CA 92182. Offers composition (acoustic and electronic) (MM); conducting (MM); ethnomusicology (MA); jazz studies (MM); musicology (MA); performance (MM); piano pedagogy (MM); theory (MA). *Degree requirements:* For master's, comprehensive exam (for some programs), thesis (for some programs). *Entrance requirements:* For master's, GRE General Test, bachelor's degree in related field, 2 letters of reference. Additional exam requirements/recommendations for international students: Required—TOEFL. Electronic applications accepted.

San Francisco Conservatory of Music, Graduate Division, San Francisco, CA 94102. Offers chamber music (MM); classical guitar (MM); composition (MM); conducting (MM); keyboards (MM); orchestral instruments (MM); voice (MM). *Accreditation:* NASM. *Degree requirements:* For master's, variable foreign language requirement, 1-2 recitals, 1-3 juried performances. *Entrance requirements:* For master's, audition, recommendations. Additional exam requirements/recommendations for international students: Required—TOEFL (minimum score 500 paper-based; 173 computer-based; 61 iBT). Electronic applications accepted.

San Francisco State University, Division of Graduate Studies, College of Creative Arts, School of Music and Dance, San Francisco, CA 94132-1722. Offers chamber music (MM); classical performance (MM); composition (MA); conducting (MM); music education (MA); music history (MA). *Accreditation:* NASM. *Unit head:* Dianthe Spencer, Director, 415-338-1431. *Application contact:* Dr. Cyrus Ginwala, Graduate Coordinator, 415-338-1431, E-mail: cginwala@sfsu.edu.

San Jose State University, Graduate Studies and Research, College of Humanities and the Arts, School of Music and Dance, San Jose, CA 95192-0001. Offers music (MA). *Accreditation:* NASM. *Degree requirements:* For master's, thesis or alternative. *Entrance requirements:* For master's, minimum GPA of 3.0 in last 60 units of undergraduate coursework; 3 letters of recommendation; audition or portfolio. Additional exam requirements/recommendations for international students: Required—TOEFL (minimum score 590 paper-based; 243 computer-based; 96 iBT). Electronic applications accepted.

Savannah College of Art and Design, Graduate School, Savannah, GA 31402-3146. Offers accessory design (MA, MFA); advertising design (MA, MFA); animation (MA, MFA); architectural history (MA, MFA); architecture (M Arch); art history (MA); arts administration (MA); broadcast design (MA, MFA); cinema studies (MA); commercial photography (MA); digital photography (MA); documentary photography (MA); fashion (MA, MFA); fibers (MA, MFA); film and television (MA, MFA); furniture design (MA, MFA); graphic design (MA, MFA); historic preservation (MA, MFA, Graduate Certificate); illustration (MA, MFA); illustration design (MA); industrial design (MA, MFA); interactive design and game development (MA, MFA, Graduate Certificate); interior design (MA, MFA); international preservation (MA); luxury and fashion management (MA, MFA); metals and jewelry (MA, MFA); painting (MA, MFA); performing arts (MFA); photography (MA, MFA); printmaking (MA, MFA); production design (MA, MFA); professional education (MAT), including art, drama; professional writing (MFA); sculpture (MA, MFA); sequential art (MA, MFA); service design (MFA); sound design (MA, MFA); urban design and development (MUD); visual effects (MA, MFA). Part-time programs available. Postbaccalaureate distance learning degree programs offered (no on-campus study). *Students:* 1,576 full-time (898 women), 407 part-time (240 women); includes 208 minority (115 Black or African American, non-Hispanic/Latino; 8 American Indian or Alaska Native, non-Hispanic/Latino; 29 Asian, non-Hispanic/Latino; 45 Hispanic/Latino; 2 Native Hawaiian or other Pacific Islander, non-Hispanic/Latino; 9 Two or more races, non-Hispanic/Latino), 435 international. Average age 28. 2,826 applicants, 36% accepted, 642 enrolled. In 2010, 534 master's, 8 other advanced degrees awarded. *Degree requirements:* For master's, thesis, internship. *Entrance requirements:* For master's, interview, 3 letters of recommendation. Additional exam requirements/recommendations for international students: Required—TOEFL (minimum score 550 paper-based; 133 computer-based). *Application deadline:* For fall admission, 4/1 priority date for domestic and international students. Applications are processed on a rolling basis. Application fee: $35. Electronic applications accepted. *Expenses:* Tuition: Full-time $29,520; part-time $3280 per quarter. Tuition and fees vary according to campus/location. *Financial support:* Fellowships, career-related internships or fieldwork, Federal Work-Study, and scholarships/grants available. Financial award application deadline: 4/1; financial award applicants required to submit FAFSA. *Unit head:* Edward Dupuy, Dean of Graduate Studies, 912-525-5838, E-mail: edupuy@scad.edu. *Application contact:* Elizabeth Mathis, Director of Graduate Recruitment, 912-525-5965, Fax: 912-525-5985, E-mail: emathis@scad.edu.

See Display on page 177 and Close-Up on page 223

School of the Art Institute of Chicago, Graduate Division, Department of Performance, Chicago, IL 60603-3103. Offers MFA. *Entrance requirements:* Additional exam requirements/recommendations for international students: Required—TOEFL, IELTS.

See Close-Up on page 225.

Seabury-Western Theological Seminary, School of Theology, Evanston, IL 60201-2976. Offers advanced theological studies (Certificate); church music and liturgy (MTS); congregational development (D Min); preaching (D Min); theological studies (MA); theology (M Div, L Th). D Min in congregational development offered in summer only; D Min in preaching offered jointly with Chicago Theological Seminary, Lutheran School of Theology at Chicago, McCormick Theological Seminary, and Northern Baptist Theological Seminary. *Accreditation:* ACIPE; ATS (one or more programs are accredited). Part-time programs available. *Degree requirements:* For master's, thesis; for doctorate, thesis/dissertation; for other advanced degree, thesis (for some programs). *Entrance requirements:* For M Div and master's, interview, sample of written work. *Faculty research:* Liturgical interpretations of baptism, trinitarian theology, congregational development, post modern biblical criticism-Matthew.

Shenandoah University, Shenandoah Conservatory, Winchester, VA 22601-5195. Offers arts management (MS); church music (MM, Certificate); collaborative piano (MM); composition (MM); conducting (MM); music education (MME, DMA); music therapy (MMT, Certificate); pedagogy (MM, DMA); performance (MM, DMA, Artist Diploma). *Accreditation:* NASM. *Faculty:* 38 full-time (15 women), 14 part-time/adjunct (5 women). *Students:* 63 full-time (38 women), 119 part-time (76 women); includes 18 minority (7 Black or African American, non-Hispanic/Latino; 5 Asian, non-Hispanic/Latino; 5 Hispanic/Latino; 1 Two or more races, non-Hispanic/Latino), 40 international. Average age 34. 109 applicants, 75% accepted, 51 enrolled. In 2010, 29 master's, 12 doctorates, 14 other advanced degrees awarded. *Degree requirements:* For master's, comprehensive exam (for some programs), thesis (for some programs), internship (MS), recital (MM), research teaching project or thesis (MME), project (MA); for doctorate, comprehensive exam, thesis/dissertation (for some programs), dissertation or teaching project, recital; for other advanced degree, research project, recital. *Entrance requirements:* For master's, audition, minimum GPA of 2.5, writing sample, resume; for doctorate, audition, minimum GPA of 3.25, 2 letters of recommendation, writing sample, resume; for other advanced degree, bachelor's or master's degree; minimum GPA of 2.5. Additional exam requirements/recommendations for international students: Required—TOEFL (minimum score 550 paper-based; 213 computer-based; 79 iBT), IELTS (minimum score 6.5), Sakae Institute of Study Abroad (550). *Application deadline:* Applications are processed on a rolling basis. Application fee: $30. Electronic applications accepted. *Expenses:* Tuition: Full-time $17,352; part-time $723 per credit. Tuition and fees vary according to course load and program. *Financial support:* Application deadline: 3/15. *Unit head:* Dr. Michael J. Stepniak, Dean, 540-665-4600, Fax: 540-665-5402, E-mail: mstepnia@su.edu. *Application contact:* David Anthony, Dean of Admissions, 540-665-4581, Fax: 540-665-4627, E-mail: admit@su.edu.

Southeastern Baptist Theological Seminary, Graduate and Professional Programs, Wake Forest, NC 27588-1889. Offers advanced biblical studies (M Div); Christian education (M Div, MACE); Christian ethics (PhD); Christian ministry (M Div); Christian planting (M Div); church music (MACM); counseling (MACO); evangelism (PhD); language (M Div); ministry (D Min); New Testament (PhD); Old Testament (PhD); philosophy (PhD); theology (Th M, PhD); women's studies (M Div). *Accreditation:* ACIPE; ATS (one or more programs are accredited). *Degree requirements:* For master's, thesis (for some programs), oral exam; for doctorate, thesis/dissertation, fieldwork; for M Div, supervised ministry. *Entrance requirements:* For master's, Cooperative English Test, minimum GPA of 2.0, M Div or equivalent (Th M); for doctorate, GRE General Test or MAT, Cooperative English Test, M Div or equivalent, 3 years of professional experience.

Southeastern Louisiana University, College of Arts, Humanities and Social Sciences, Department of Music and Dramatic Arts, Hammond, LA 70402. Offers music (M Mus), including music theory; music (M Mus), including performance. *Accreditation:* NASM. Part-time programs available. *Faculty:* 10 full-time (1 woman), 4 part-time/adjunct (3 women). *Students:* 12 full-time (7 women), 4 part-time (3 women); includes 1 minority (Black or African American, non-Hispanic/Latino), 5 international. Average age 26. 11 applicants, 45% accepted, 5 enrolled. In 2010, 5 master's awarded. *Degree requirements:* For master's, comprehensive exam, thesis (for some programs), recital (for some programs). *Entrance requirements:* For master's, bachelor's degree in music, senior recital. Additional exam requirements/recommendations for international students: Required—TOEFL (minimum score 500 paper-based; 173 computer-based; 61 iBT). *Application deadline:* For fall admission, 7/15 priority date for domestic students, 6/1 priority date for international students; for spring admission, 12/1 priority date for domestic students, 10/1 priority date for international students. Applications are processed on a rolling basis. Application fee: $20 ($30 for international students). Electronic applications accepted. *Expenses:* Tuition, state resident: full-time $3533. Tuition, nonresident: full-time $12,002. Required fees: $907. Tuition and fees vary according to degree level. *Financial support:* In 2010–11, 14 students received support, including 13 teaching assistantships (averaging $9,508 per year); career-related internships or fieldwork, Federal Work-Study, institutionally sponsored loans, scholarships/grants, and administrative assistantship also available. Support available to part-time students. Financial award application deadline: 5/1; financial award applicants required to submit FAFSA. *Faculty research:* The life and compositions of composer Elie Siegmeister, piano works of Ferde Grofe, music for wind symphony, original compositions (faculty composers), music performance (faculty performers). *Unit head:* Dr. David Evenson, Department Head, 985-549-2184, Fax: 985-549-2892, E-mail: devenson@selu.edu. *Application contact:* Sandra Meyers, Graduate Admissions Analyst, 985-549-5620, Fax: 985-549-5632, E-mail: admissions@selu.edu.

Southern Baptist Theological Seminary, School of Church Ministries, Louisville, KY 40280-0004. Offers children's and family ministry (M Div, MA); church music (M Div, MA, MCM); college ministry (M Div, MA); discipleship and family ministry (M Div, MA); family ministry (PhD); higher education (PhD); leadership (M Div, MA, PhD); ministry (D Ed Min, D Min); women's leadership (M Div, MA); worship leadership (M Div, MA); youth and family ministry (M Div, MA). Part-time programs available. Postbaccalaureate distance learning degree programs offered (minimal on-campus study). *Degree requirements:* For doctorate, thesis/dissertation; for M Div, 2 foreign languages. *Entrance requirements:* For doctorate, GRE General Test, interview, M Div or MACE. Additional exam requirements/recommendations for international students: Required—TWE. *Faculty research:* Gerontology, creative teaching methods, faith development in children, faith development in youth, transformational learning.

Southern Illinois University Carbondale, Graduate School, College of Liberal Arts, School of Music, Carbondale, IL 62901-4701. Offers composition and theory (MM); history and literature (MM); music education (MM); opera/music theater (MM); performance (MM); piano pedagogy (MM). *Accreditation:* NASM. Part-time programs available. *Degree requirements:* For master's, one foreign language, thesis or alternative. *Entrance requirements:* For master's, audition, minimum GPA of 2.7. Additional exam requirements/recommendations for international students: Required—TOEFL. *Faculty research:* Performance practices, historical research, operatic development.

Southern Illinois University Edwardsville, Graduate School, College of Arts and Sciences, Department of Music, Program in Music, Edwardsville, IL 62026-0001. Offers music education (MM); music performance (MM). Part-time programs available. *Faculty:* 15 full-time (4 women). *Students:* 6 full-time (1 woman), 23 part-time (12 women); includes 1 Black or African American, non-Hispanic/Latino; 2 Asian, non-Hispanic/Latino; 1 Hispanic/Latino. Average age 26. 22 applicants, 41% accepted. In 2010, 13 master's awarded. *Degree requirements:* For master's, one foreign language, thesis (for some programs), recital. *Entrance requirements:* Additional exam requirements/recommendations for international students: Required—TOEFL (minimum score 550 paper-based; 213 computer-based; 79 iBT), IELTS (minimum score 6.5). *Application deadline:* For fall admission, 7/22 for domestic students, 6/1 for international students; for spring admission, 12/9 for domestic students, 10/1 for international students. Applications are processed on a rolling basis. Application fee: $30. Electronic applications accepted. *Expenses:* Tuition, state resident: full-time $6012; part-time $1503 per semester. Tuition, nonresident: full-time $15,030; part-time $3758 per semester. Required fees: $1711; $675 per semester. *Financial support:* In 2010–11, 11 teaching assistantships with full tuition reimbursements (averaging $8,064 per year) were awarded; career-related internships or fieldwork, Federal Work-Study, institutionally sponsored loans, scholarships/grants, and traineeships also available. Support available to part-time students. Financial award application deadline: 3/1; financial award applicants required to submit FAFSA. *Unit head:* Dr. Audrey Tallant, Chair, 618-650-3900, E-mail: atallan@siue.edu. *Application contact:* Dr. Darryl Coan, Director, 618-650-2012, E-mail: dcoan@siue.edu.

Southern Methodist University, Meadows School of the Arts, Division of Music, Dallas, TX 75275. Offers conducting (MM); music composition (MM); music education (MM); music history (MM); music theory (MM); performance (MM); piano performance and pedagogy (MM); sacred music (MSM). *Accreditation:* NASM. Part-time programs available. *Faculty:* 33 full-time (11 women), 39 part-time/adjunct (16 women). *Students:* 23 full-time (14 women), 92 part-time (44 women); includes 9 Black or African American, non-Hispanic/Latino; 4 Asian, non-Hispanic/Latino; 6 Hispanic/Latino; 2 Native Hawaiian or other Pacific Islander, non-Hispanic/Latino, 27 international. Average age 27. 148 applicants, 54% accepted, 55 enrolled. In 2010, 44 master's, 9 Certificates awarded. *Degree requirements:* For master's, variable foreign language requirement, comprehensive exam, project, recital, or thesis. *Entrance requirements:* For master's, placement exams in music history and theory, audition; bachelor's degree in music or equivalent; minimum GPA of 3.0; research paper in history, theory, education. Additional exam requirements/recommendations for international students: Required—TOEFL (minimum score 550 paper-based; 213 computer-based; 80 iBT). *Application deadline:* For fall admission, 3/1 priority date for domestic and international students; for spring admission, 11/1 for domestic and international students. Applications are processed on a rolling basis. Application fee: $75. Electronic applications accepted. *Financial support:* In 2010–11, 77 students received support, including 70 teaching assistantships with full and partial tuition reimbursements available (averaging $4,000 per year); career-related internships or fieldwork, Federal Work-Study, scholarships/grants, tuition waivers (full and partial), and unspecified assistantships also available. Financial award application deadline: 3/1; financial award applicants required to submit FAFSA. *Faculty research:* Music perception and cognition, computer-based instruction, music medicine and therapy, theoretical and historical analysis-medieval to contemporary. *Unit head:* Dr. Sam Holland, Director, 214-768-1951, Fax: 214-768-4669, E-mail: sholland@smu.edu. *Application contact:* Joe S. Hoselton, Graduate Admissions and Records Coordinator, 214-768-3765, Fax: 214-768-3272, E-mail: hoselton@smu.edu.

Southwestern Baptist Theological Seminary, School of Church Music, Fort Worth, TX 76122-0000. Offers MACM, MAWSHP, MM, DMA, PhD, SPCM. *Accreditation:* NASM. Part-time programs available. Terminal master's awarded for partial completion of doctoral program. *Degree requirements:* For master's, comprehensive exam, thesis; for doctorate, comprehensive exam, thesis/dissertation. *Entrance requirements:* For master's, audition; for doctorate, MM or equivalent. Additional exam requirements/recommendations for international students: Required—TOEFL. Electronic applications accepted.

Southwestern College, Fifth-Year Graduate Programs, Winfield, KS 67156-2499. Offers leadership (MS); management (MBA); music (MA), including education, performance. Part-time programs available. *Faculty:* 9 full-time (1 woman), 8 part-time/adjunct (2 women). *Students:* 9 full-time (3 women), 8 part-time (3 women), 6 international. Average age 25. 10 applicants, 90% accepted, 9 enrolled. In 2010, 26 master's awarded. *Entrance requirements:* For master's, baccalaureate degree, minimum GPA of 3.0. Additional exam requirements/recommendations for international students: Required—TOEFL (minimum score 550 paper-based; 213 computer-based). *Application deadline:* For fall admission, 4/1 priority date for domestic students; for spring admission, 12/1 priority date for domestic students. Applications are processed on a rolling basis. Electronic applications accepted. *Expenses:* Tuition: Full-time $7470; part-time $415 per credit hour. Tuition and fees vary according to program. *Financial support:* In 2010–11, 6 students received support. Federal Work-Study, tuition waivers (partial), and unspecified assistantships available. Financial award application deadline: 4/1; financial award applicants required to submit FAFSA. *Unit head:* Dr. James Sheppard, Vice President for Academic Affairs, 620-229-6227, Fax: 620-229-6224, E-mail: james.sheppard@sckans.edu. *Application contact:* Marla Sexson, Director of Admissions, 800-846-1543 Ext. 6364, Fax: 620-229-6344, E-mail: marla.sexson@sckans.edu.

Southwestern Oklahoma State University, College of Arts and Sciences, Department of Music, Weatherford, OK 73096-3098. Offers music education (MM); performance (MM). *Accreditation:* NASM. Part-time programs available. *Degree requirements:* For master's, comprehensive exam, recital (music performance). *Entrance requirements:* For master's, minimum GPA of 2.5. Additional exam requirements/recommendations for international students: Required—TOEFL.

Stanford University, School of Humanities and Sciences, Department of Music, Stanford, CA 94305-9991. Offers computer-based music theory and acoustics (MA, PhD); music composition (MA, DMA); music history (MA); music, science, and technology (MA); musicology (PhD). Terminal master's awarded for partial completion of doctoral program. *Degree requirements:* For master's, variable foreign language requirement, thesis or alternative, project; for doctorate, variable foreign language requirement, thesis/dissertation (for some programs), qualifying, special area, and oral exams (PhD); composition project, lecture-demonstration exams (DMA). *Entrance requirements:* For master's and doctorate, GRE General Test, departmental theory/analysis test, samples of work. Additional exam requirements/recommendations for international students: Required—TOEFL. Electronic applications accepted. *Expenses:* Tuition: Full-time $38,700; part-time $860 per unit. One-time fee: $200 full-time.

State University of New York at Binghamton, Graduate School, School of Arts and Sciences, Department of Music, Binghamton, NY 13902-6000. Offers MA, MM. *Accreditation:* NASM. *Faculty:* 10 full-time (2 women), 28 part-time/adjunct (12 women). *Students:* 13 full-time (7 women), 2 part-time (0 women); includes 1 Black or African American, non-Hispanic/Latino; 1 Hispanic/Latino, 1 international. Average age 26. 31 applicants, 35% accepted, 8 enrolled. In 2010, 13 master's awarded. *Degree requirements:* For master's, one foreign language, thesis. *Entrance requirements:* For master's, GRE General Test, GRE Subject Test. Additional exam requirements/recommendations for international students: Required—TOEFL (minimum score 550 paper-based; 213 computer-based; 80 iBT). *Application deadline:* For fall admission, 6/15 priority date for domestic and international students; for spring admission, 10/15 priority date for domestic and international students. Applications are processed on a rolling basis. Application fee: $60. Electronic applications accepted. *Financial support:* In 2010–11, 7 students received support, including 1 fellowship with full tuition reimbursement available (averaging $9,500 per year), 6 teaching assistantships with full tuition reimbursements available (averaging $9,500 per year); career-related internships or fieldwork, Federal Work-Study, institutionally sponsored loans, scholarships/grants, health care benefits, tuition waivers (full and partial), and unspecified assistantships also available. Financial award application deadline: 2/15; financial award applicants required to submit FAFSA. *Unit head:* Dr. Timothy Perry, Chairperson, 607-777-2591, E-mail: tperry@binghamton.edu. *Application contact:* Catherine Smith, Recruiting and Admissions Coordinator, 607-777-2151, Fax: 607-777-2501, E-mail: cmsmith@binghamton.edu.

State University of New York at Fredonia, Graduate Studies, School of Music, Program in Music, Fredonia, NY 14063-1136. Offers MM. *Accreditation:* NASM. Part-time and evening/weekend programs available. *Degree requirements:* For master's, thesis optional. *Expenses:* Tuition, state resident: full-time $8370; part-time $349 per credit hour. Tuition, nonresident: full-time $13,250; part-time $552 per credit hour. Required fees: $1328; $55.15 per credit hour.

State University of New York at New Paltz, Graduate School, School of Fine and Performing Arts, Department of Music, New Paltz, NY 12561. Offers music therapy (MS). *Accreditation:* NASM. Part-time programs available. *Faculty:* 5 full-time (4 women), 3 part-time/adjunct (all women). *Students:* 21 full-time (18 women), 13 part-time (9 women); includes 3 Asian, non-Hispanic/Latino, 6 international. Average age 29. 22 applicants, 68% accepted, 14 enrolled. In 2010, 10 master's awarded. *Degree requirements:* For master's, thesis. *Entrance requirements:* For master's, audition, minimum GPA of 3.0. Additional exam requirements/recommendations for international students: Required—TOEFL (minimum score 550 paper-based; 213 computer-based; 80 iBT), IELTS (minimum score 6.5). *Application deadline:* For fall admission, 5/15 for domestic and international students; for spring admission, 11/15 for domestic and international students. Application fee: $50. Electronic applications accepted. *Expenses:* Tuition, state resident: full-time $8370; part-time $349 per credit hour. Tuition, nonresident: full-time $13,780; part-time $574 per credit hour. Required fees: $1165; $33.80 per credit hour. $175 per term. Tuition and fees vary according to program. *Financial support:* In 2010–11, 3 students received support, including 3 teaching assistantships with partial tuition reimbursements available (averaging $5,000 per year). Financial award application deadline: 8/1; financial award applicants required to submit FAFSA. *Unit head:* Dr. Carole Cowan, Chair, 845-257-2701, E-mail: cowanc@newpaltz.edu. *Application contact:* Dr. Carole Cowan, Chair, 845-257-2701, E-mail: cowanc@newpaltz.edu.

Music

State University of New York College at Potsdam, Crane School of Music, Potsdam, NY 13676. Offers music composition (MM); music education (MM); music performance (MM). *Accreditation:* NASM. Part-time programs available. *Faculty:* 25 full-time (9 women), 5 part-time/adjunct (1 woman). *Students:* 10 full-time (5 women), 11 part-time (2 women); includes 2 minority (1 Black or African American, non-Hispanic/Latino; 1 Asian, non-Hispanic/Latino). 28 applicants, 61% accepted, 13 enrolled. In 2010, 21 master's awarded. *Degree requirements:* For master's, variable foreign language requirement, thesis. *Entrance requirements:* For master's, audition, minimum GPA of 3.0. Additional exam requirements/recommendations for international students: Required—TOEFL (minimum score 550 paper-based; 213 computer-based; 80 iBT), IELTS (minimum score 6). *Application deadline:* For fall admission, 4/1 for domestic and international students; for winter admission, 10/15 for domestic and international students; for spring admission, 3/1 for domestic and international students. Applications are processed on a rolling basis. Application fee: $50. *Financial support:* In 2010–11, 2 students received support; teaching assistantships with full tuition reimbursements available, career-related internships or fieldwork, Federal Work-Study, scholarships/grants, and unspecified assistantships available. Support available to part-time students. Financial award application deadline: 3/1; financial award applicants required to submit FAFSA. *Unit head:* Dr. Michael R. Sitton, Dean, 315-267-2415, Fax: 315-267-2413, E-mail: sittonmr@potsdam.edu. *Application contact:* Karen Miller, Secretary, 315-267-3418, Fax: 315-267-2413, E-mail: millerkl@potsdam.edu.

Stephen F. Austin State University, Graduate School, College of Fine Arts, School of Music, Nacogdoches, TX 75962. Offers MA, MM. *Accreditation:* NASM (one or more programs are accredited). Part-time programs available. *Degree requirements:* For master's, comprehensive exam, thesis optional. *Entrance requirements:* For master's, GRE General Test, audition. Additional exam requirements/recommendations for international students: Required—TOEFL. *Faculty research:* Music classroom methodology, serial music, seventeenth century sacred music, vocal pedagogy, organ duet literature.

Stony Brook University, State University of New York, Graduate School, College of Arts and Sciences, Department of Music, Program in Ethnomusicology, Stony Brook, NY 11794. Offers MA, PhD. *Entrance requirements:* For master's and doctorate, GRE, 3 letters of recommendation. Additional exam requirements/recommendations for international students: Required—TOEFL. *Application deadline:* For fall admission, 1/15 for domestic students. Application fee: $100. *Expenses:* Tuition, state resident: full-time $8370; part-time $349 per credit. Tuition, nonresident: full-time $13,780; part-time $574 per credit. Required fees: $994. *Financial support:* Teaching assistantships, scholarships/grants available. *Unit head:* Judith Lochhead, Graduate Director, 631-632-7330, Fax: 631-632-7404, E-mail: judith.lochhead@stonybrook.edu. *Application contact:* Judith Lochhead, Graduate Director, 631-632-7330, Fax: 631-632-7404, E-mail: judith.lochhead@stonybrook.edu.

Stony Brook University, State University of New York, Graduate School, College of Arts and Sciences, Department of Music, Program in Music History/Theory, Stony Brook, NY 11794. Offers MA, PhD. *Students:* 44 full-time (18 women), 3 part-time (1 woman); includes 2 Black or African American, non-Hispanic/Latino; 4 Hispanic/Latino, 10 international. 94 applicants, 26% accepted, 11 enrolled. In 2010, 9 master's, 2 doctorates awarded. *Degree requirements:* For doctorate, thesis/dissertation. *Entrance requirements:* For master's and doctorate, GRE General Test. Additional exam requirements/recommendations for international students: Required—TOEFL. *Application deadline:* For fall admission, 1/15 for domestic students. Application fee: $100. Electronic applications accepted. *Expenses:* Tuition, state resident: full-time $8370; part-time $349 per credit. Tuition, nonresident: full-time $13,780; part-time $574 per credit. Required fees: $994. *Unit head:* Dr. Judy Lochhead, Chair, 631-632-7330. *Application contact:* Dr. Perry Goldstein, Director, 631-632-7330, Fax: 631-632-7404.

Stony Brook University, State University of New York, Graduate School, College of Arts and Sciences, Department of Music, Program in Music Performance, Stony Brook, NY 11794. Offers MM, DMA. *Students:* 178 full-time (102 women), 17 part-time (13 women); includes 1 Black or African American, non-Hispanic/Latino; 25 Asian, non-Hispanic/Latino; 6 Hispanic/Latino, 69 international. 398 applicants, 22% accepted, 38 enrolled. In 2010, 13 master's, 28 doctorates awarded. *Degree requirements:* For doctorate, thesis/dissertation. *Entrance requirements:* For master's and doctorate, GRE General Test. Additional exam requirements/recommendations for international students: Required—TOEFL. *Application deadline:* For fall admission, 1/15 for domestic students. Application fee: $100. *Expenses:* Tuition, state resident: full-time $8370; part-time $349 per credit. Tuition, nonresident: full-time $13,780; part-time $574 per credit. Required fees: $994. *Unit head:* Dr. Judith Lochhead, Chair, 631-632-7330. *Application contact:* Dr. Perry Goldstein, Director, 631-632-7330, Fax: 631-632-7404.

Syracuse University, College of Visual and Performing Arts, Program in Conducting, Syracuse, NY 13244. Offers M Mu. *Accreditation:* NASM. *Students:* 2 full-time (0 women). Average age 26. 6 applicants, 50% accepted, 1 enrolled. In 2010, 2 master's awarded. *Degree requirements:* For master's, thesis or alternative. *Entrance requirements:* For master's, audition, interview. Additional exam requirements/recommendations for international students: Required—TOEFL (minimum score 100 iBT). *Application deadline:* For fall admission, 2/1 priority date for domestic and international students. Application fee: $75. Electronic applications accepted. *Expenses:* Tuition: Part-time $1162 per credit. *Financial support:* Fellowships with full tuition reimbursements, teaching assistantships with full and partial tuition reimbursements, Federal Work-Study and tuition waivers (partial) available. Financial award application deadline: 1/1; financial award applicants required to submit FAFSA. *Unit head:* Dr. Bradley Ethington, Director, 315-443-5892, E-mail: bpething@syr.edu. *Application contact:* Harriett Conti, Assistant Dean for Recruitment and Admissions, 315-443-5755, E-mail: hmconti@syr.edu.

See Display on page 179 and Close-Up on page 227.

Syracuse University, College of Visual and Performing Arts, Program in Music Composition, Syracuse, NY 13244. Offers M Mus. *Students:* 4 full-time (1 woman), 1 international. Average age 26. 9 applicants, 33% accepted, 2 enrolled. In 2010, 1 master's awarded. *Degree requirements:* For master's, thesis or alternative. *Entrance requirements:* For master's, performance recording. Additional exam requirements/recommendations for international students: Required—TOEFL (minimum score 100 iBT). *Application deadline:* For fall admission, 2/1 priority date for domestic and international students. Application fee: $75. Electronic applications accepted. *Expenses:* Tuition: Part-time $1162 per credit. *Financial support:* Fellowships with full tuition reimbursements, teaching assistantships with full and partial tuition reimbursements available. Financial award application deadline: 1/1; financial award applicants required to submit FAFSA. *Unit head:* Dr. Bradley Ethington, Chair, 315-443-5893, E-mail: bpething@syr.edu. *Application contact:* Harriett Conti, Assistant Dean for Recruitment and Admissions, 315-443-5755, E-mail: hmconti@syr.edu.

See Display on page 179 and Close-Up on page 227.

Syracuse University, College of Visual and Performing Arts, Program in Organ, Syracuse, NY 13244. Offers M Mus. In 2010, 1 master's awarded. *Degree requirements:* For master's, thesis or alternative. *Entrance requirements:* For master's, audition. Additional exam requirements/recommendations for international students: Required—TOEFL (minimum score 100 iBT). *Application deadline:* For fall admission, 2/1 priority date for domestic and international students. Application fee: $75. Electronic applications accepted. *Expenses:* Tuition: Part-time $1162 per credit. *Financial support:* Fellowships with full tuition reimbursements, teaching assistantships with full and partial tuition reimbursements available. Financial award application deadline: 1/1; financial award applicants required to submit FAFSA. *Unit head:* Dr. Bradley Ethington, Chair, 315-443-5893. *Application contact:* Harriett Conti, Assistant Dean of Recruitment and Admissions, 315-443-5755, E-mail: hmconti@syr.edu.

See Display on page 179 and Close-Up on page 227.

Syracuse University, College of Visual and Performing Arts, Program in Percussion, Syracuse, NY 13244. Offers M Mus. *Degree requirements:* For master's, thesis or alternative. *Entrance requirements:* For master's, audition. Additional exam requirements/recommendations for international students: Required—TOEFL (minimum score 100 iBT). *Application deadline:* For fall admission, 2/1 priority date for domestic and international students. Application fee: $75. Electronic applications accepted. *Expenses:* Tuition: Part-time $1162 per credit. *Financial support:* Fellowships with full tuition reimbursements, teaching assistantships with full and partial tuition reimbursements available. Financial award application deadline: 1/1; financial award applicants required to submit FAFSA. *Unit head:* Dr. Bradley Ethington, Chair, 315-443-5893, E-mail: bpething@syr.edu. *Application contact:* Harriett Conti, Assistant Dean for Recruitment and Admissions, 315-443-5755, E-mail: hmconti@syr.edu.

Syracuse University, College of Visual and Performing Arts, Program in Piano, Syracuse, NY 13244. Offers M Mus. *Students:* 4 full-time (3 women), 3 international. Average age 22. 8 applicants, 38% accepted, 2 enrolled. In 2010, 2 master's awarded. *Degree requirements:* For master's, thesis or alternative. *Entrance requirements:* For master's, audition. Additional exam requirements/recommendations for international students: Required—TOEFL (minimum score 100 iBT). *Application deadline:* For fall admission, 2/1 priority date for domestic and international students. Application fee: $75. Electronic applications accepted. *Expenses:* Tuition: Part-time $1162 per credit. *Financial support:* Fellowships with full tuition reimbursements, teaching assistantships with full and partial tuition reimbursements available. Financial award application deadline: 1/1; financial award applicants required to submit FAFSA. *Unit head:* Dr. Bradley Ethington, Chair, 315-443-5893, E-mail: bpething@syr.edu. *Application contact:* Harriett Conti, Assistant Dean for Recruitment and Admissions, 315-443-5755, E-mail: hmconti@syr.edu.

See Display on page 179 and Close-Up on page 227.

Syracuse University, College of Visual and Performing Arts, Program in Strings, Syracuse, NY 13244. Offers M Mus. *Students:* 3 full-time (1 woman), 2 international. Average age 25. 5 applicants, 100% accepted, 1 enrolled. In 2010, 1 master's awarded. *Degree requirements:* For master's, thesis or alternative. *Entrance requirements:* Additional exam requirements/recommendations for international students: Required—TOEFL (minimum score 100 iBT). *Application deadline:* For fall admission, 2/1 priority date for domestic and international students. Application fee: $75. Electronic applications accepted. *Expenses:* Tuition: Part-time $1162 per credit. *Financial support:* Fellowships with full tuition reimbursements, teaching assistantships with full and partial tuition reimbursements available. Financial award application deadline: 1/1. *Unit head:* Dr. Bradley Ethington, Chair, 315-443-5893, E-mail: bpething@syr.edu. *Application contact:* Harriett Conti, Assistant Dean for Recruitment and Admissions, 315-443-5755, E-mail: hmconti@syr.edu.

See Display on page 179 and Close-Up on page 227.

Syracuse University, College of Visual and Performing Arts, Program in Voice, Syracuse, NY 13244. Offers M Mus. *Students:* 3 full-time (all women), 1 international. Average age 33. 5 applicants, 40% accepted, 0 enrolled. In 2010, 1 master's awarded. *Degree requirements:* For master's, thesis or alternative. *Entrance requirements:* For master's, audition. Additional exam requirements/recommendations for international students: Required—TOEFL (minimum score 100 iBT). *Application deadline:* For fall admission, 2/1 priority date for domestic and international students. Application fee: $75. Electronic applications accepted. *Expenses:* Tuition: Part-time $1162 per credit. *Financial support:* Fellowships with full tuition reimbursements, teaching assistantships with full and partial tuition reimbursements available. Financial award application deadline: 1/1; financial award applicants required to submit FAFSA. *Unit head:* Dr. Bradley Ethington, Chair, 315-443-5893, E-mail: bpething@syr.edu. *Application contact:* Harriett Conti, Assistant Dean for Recruitment and Admissions, 315-443-5755, E-mail: hmconti@syr.edu.

See Display on page 179 and Close-Up on page 227.

Syracuse University, College of Visual and Performing Arts, Program in Wind Instruments, Syracuse, NY 13244. Offers M Mus. *Students:* 2 full-time (1 woman), 1 international. Average age 22. 6 applicants, 50% accepted, 2 enrolled. *Degree requirements:* For master's, thesis or alternative. *Entrance requirements:* For master's, audition. Additional exam requirements/recommendations for international students: Required—TOEFL (minimum score 100 iBT). *Application deadline:* For fall admission, 2/1 priority date for domestic and international students. Application fee: $75. Electronic applications accepted. *Expenses:* Tuition: Part-time $1162 per credit. *Financial support:* Fellowships with full tuition reimbursements, teaching assistantships with full and partial tuition reimbursements available. Financial award application deadline: 1/1; financial award applicants required to submit FAFSA. *Unit head:* Dr. Bradley Ethington, Chair, 315-443-5893, E-mail: bpething@syr.edu. *Application contact:* Harriett Conti, Assistant Dean for Recruitment and Admissions, 315-443-5755, E-mail: hmconti@syr.edu.

See Display on page 179 and Close-Up on page 227.

Temple University, Esther Boyer College of Music and Dance, Department of Music, Philadelphia, PA 19122-6096. Offers MM, MMT, DMA, PhD. Part-time and evening/weekend programs available. *Faculty:* 32 full-time (10 women). *Students:* 170 full-time (102 women), 61 part-time (35 women); includes 6 Black or African American, non-Hispanic/Latino; 16 Asian, non-Hispanic/Latino; 7 Hispanic/Latino; 1 Native Hawaiian or other Pacific Islander, non-Hispanic/Latino, 46 international. 385 applicants, 36% accepted, 78 enrolled. In 2010, 48 master's, 2 doctorates awarded. *Degree requirements:* For doctorate, thesis/dissertation. *Entrance requirements:* Additional exam requirements/recommendations for international students: Required—TOEFL. *Application deadline:* For fall admission, 11/15 for international students; for spring admission, 8/1 for international students. Applications are processed on a rolling basis. Application fee: $50. Electronic applications accepted. *Financial support:* Fellowships with full and partial tuition reimbursements, research assistantships with full and partial tuition reimbursements, teaching assistantships with full and partial tuition reimbursements, career-related internships or fieldwork, Federal Work-Study, and scholarships/grants available. Financial award application deadline: 1/15; financial award applicants required to submit FAFSA. *Unit head:* Dr. Robert T. Stroker, Dean, 215-204-5527, Fax: 215-204-4957, E-mail: rstroker@temple.edu. *Application contact:* Dr. Robert T. Stroker, Dean, 215-204-5527, Fax: 215-204-4957, E-mail: rstroker@temple.edu.

Texas A&M University–Commerce, Graduate School, College of Arts and Sciences, Department of Music, Commerce, TX 75429-3011. Offers music (MA, MS); music composition (MA, MM); music education (MA, MM, MS); music literature (MA); music performance (MA, MM); music theory (MA, MM). *Accreditation:* NASM. Part-time programs available. *Degree requirements:* For master's, comprehensive exam, thesis (for some programs). *Entrance requirements:* For master's, GRE General Test. Electronic applications accepted.

Texas Christian University, AddRan College of Liberal Arts, Department of English, Fort Worth, TX 76129-0002. Offers composition (MA); English (PhD), including rhetoric and/or literature; literature (MA); rhetoric (MA); rhetoric/composition (PhD). Part-time and evening/weekend programs available. In 2010, 3 master's, 2 doctorates awarded. *Degree requirements:* For master's, one foreign language, thesis, candidacy exam; for doctorate, one foreign language, comprehensive exam, thesis/dissertation, 66 hours, diagnostic exam, qualifying exam. *Entrance requirements:* For master's and doctorate, GRE General Test, 30 hours of English; 12 hours of foreign language study. Additional exam requirements/recommendations for international students: Required—TOEFL. *Application deadline:* For fall admission, 1/31 for domestic and international students; for winter admission, 1/10 for domestic and international students; for spring admission, 10/15 for domestic and international students. Applications are processed on a rolling basis. Application fee: $50. Electronic applications accepted. *Expenses:* Tuition: Full-time $18,720; part-time $1040 per credit hour. Tuition and fees vary according to course load and program. *Financial support:* In 2010–11, 39 students received support, including 2 fellowships with full tuition reimbursements available (averaging $17,500 per year), 29 teaching assistantships with full tuition reimbursements available (averaging $15,000 per year); research assistantships with full tuition reimbursements available, tuition waivers (full) and unspecified assistantships also available. Financial award application deadline: 1/10; financial award applicants required to submit FAFSA. *Unit head:* Dr. Brad Lucas, Chairperson, 817-257-7240, E-mail: b.e.lucas2@tcu.edu. *Application contact:* Dr. Mona Narain, Associate Professor/ Director of Graduate Studies, 817-257-7284, E-mail: m.narain@tcu.edu.

Texas Christian University, College of Fine Arts, School of Music, Fort Worth, TX 76129-0002. Offers composition (DMA); conducting (M Mus, DMA); music education (MM Ed); musicology (M Mus); organ performance (M Mus); pedagogy (DMA); performance (DMA); piano (Artist Diploma); piano pedagogy (M Mus); piano performance (M Mus); string performance (M Mus); theory/composition (M Mus); vocal performance (M Mus); voice pedagogy (M Mus); wind and percussion performance (M Mus). *Accreditation:* NASM. *Students:* 47 full-time (19 women); includes 21 minority (1 Black or African American, non-Hispanic/Latino; 6 Asian, non-Hispanic/Latino; 12 Hispanic/Latino; 2 Two or more races, non-Hispanic/Latino). *Degree requirements:* For master's, one foreign language, comprehensive exam, thesis (for some programs), thesis or recital; for doctorate, one foreign language, comprehensive exam, thesis/ dissertation. *Entrance requirements:* For master's, GRE General Test (theory/composition, musicology), audition or composition/theory, letters of recommendation; for doctorate, GRE General Test, on site entrance exam, audition, interview. Additional exam requirements/ recommendations for international students: Required—TOEFL (minimum score 550 paper-based; 250 computer-based; 80 iBT), TOEFL iBT (minimum score 80; 100 for DMA). *Application deadline:* For fall admission, 1/15 for domestic and international students; for spring admission, 10/1 for domestic and international students. Application fee: $0. *Expenses:* Tuition: Full-time $18,720; part-time $1040 per credit hour. Tuition and fees vary according to course load and program. *Financial support:* Application deadline: 1/15. *Unit head:* Dr. Richard Gipson, Director, 817-257-7602. *Application contact:* Dr. Joseph Butler, Associate Dean, College of Fine Arts, 817-257-6629, E-mail: j.butler@tcu.edu.

Texas Southern University, College of Liberal Arts and Behavioral Sciences, Department of Fine Arts, Houston, TX 77004-4584. Offers fine arts (MA); music (MA). Part-time programs available. *Faculty:* 3 full-time (1 woman), 1 (woman) part-time/adjunct. *Students:* 2 full-time (0 women), 5 part-time (2 women); includes all Black or African American, non-Hispanic/Latino. Average age 42. 4 applicants, 100% accepted, 3 enrolled. *Degree requirements:* For master's, one foreign language, comprehensive exam, recital. *Entrance requirements:* For master's, GRE General Test, minimum GPA of 2.5. Additional exam requirements/recommendations for international students: Required—TOEFL. *Application deadline:* For fall admission, 7/1 for domestic and international students; for spring admission, 11/1 for domestic and international students. Applications are processed on a rolling basis. Application fee: $50 ($75 for international students). Electronic applications accepted. *Expenses:* Tuition, state resident: full-time $1875; part-time $100 per credit hour. Tuition, nonresident: full-time $6641; part-time $343 per credit hour. Tuition and fees vary according to course level, course load and degree level. *Financial support:* Fellowships, teaching assistantships, scholarships/grants and unspecified assistantships available. Support available to part-time students. Financial award application deadline: 5/1. *Faculty research:* Music theory, choral music, composition, percussion composition, ethnic musicology. *Unit head:* Dr. Dianne F. Jemison-Pollard, Chair, 713-313-7337, Fax: 713-313-1869, E-mail: jemison_dp@tsu.edu. *Application contact:* Dr. Gregory Maddox, Dean of the Graduate School, 713-313-7011 Ext. 4410, Fax: 713-639-1876, E-mail: maddox_gh@tsu.edu.

Texas State University–San Marcos, Graduate School, College of Fine Arts and Communication, School of Music, Program in Music Performance, San Marcos, TX 78666. Offers MM. *Accreditation:* NASM. Part-time programs available. *Faculty:* 18 full-time (6 women), 1 (woman) part-time/adjunct. *Students:* 43 full-time (20 women), 11 part-time (6 women); includes 1 Black or African American, non-Hispanic/Latino; 3 Asian, non-Hispanic/Latino; 14 Hispanic/Latino; 1 Two or more races, non-Hispanic/Latino, 9 international. Average age 30. 24 applicants, 71% accepted, 13 enrolled. In 2010, 19 master's awarded. *Degree requirements:* For master's, comprehensive exam. *Entrance requirements:* For master's, minimum GPA of 2.75 in last 60 hours of course work. Additional exam requirements/recommendations for international students: Required—TOEFL (minimum score 550 paper-based; 213 computer-based; 78 iBT). *Application deadline:* For fall admission, 6/15 priority date for domestic students, 6/1 for international students; for spring admission, 10/15 priority date for domestic students, 10/1 for international students. Applications are processed on a rolling basis. Application fee: $40 ($90 for international students). Electronic applications accepted. *Expenses:* Tuition, state resident: full-time $6024; part-time $251 per credit hour. Tuition, nonresident: full-time $13,536; part-time $564 per credit hour. Required fees: $1776; $50 per credit hour. $306 per semester. *Financial support:* In 2010–11, 31 students received support, including 21 teaching assistantships (averaging $1,246 per year); research assistantships, career-related internships or fieldwork, Federal Work-Study, institutionally sponsored loans, scholarships/grants, and unspecified assistantships also available. Support available to part-time students. Financial award application deadline: 4/1; financial award applicants required to submit FAFSA. *Unit head:* Dr. Kevin Mooney, Graduate Advisor, 512-245-2651, Fax: 512-245-8181, E-mail: km30@txstate.edu. *Application contact:* Dr. J. Michael Willoughby, Dean of Graduate School, 512-245-2581, Fax: 512-245-8365, E-mail: gradcollege@txstate.edu.

Texas State University–San Marcos, Graduate School, College of Liberal Arts, Department of English, Program in Rhetoric and Composition, San Marcos, TX 78666. Offers MA. Part-time programs available. *Faculty:* 5 full-time (3 women). *Students:* 12 full-time (8 women), 11 part-time (7 women); includes 6 minority (1 American Indian or Alaska Native, non-Hispanic/Latino; 4 Hispanic/Latino; 1 Two or more races, non-Hispanic/Latino). Average age 33. 15 applicants, 100% accepted, 12 enrolled. In 2010, 3 master's awarded. *Degree requirements:* For master's, comprehensive exam, thesis optional. *Entrance requirements:* For master's, minimum GPA of 3.25 in minimum of 24 hours of undergraduate English, 6 hours of a foreign language. Additional exam requirements/recommendations for international students: Required—TOEFL (minimum score 550 paper-based; 213 computer-based; 78 iBT). *Application deadline:* For fall admission, 6/15 for domestic students, 6/1 for international students; for spring admission, 10/15 for domestic students, 10/1 for international students. Applications are processed on a rolling basis. Application fee: $40 ($90 for international students). Electronic applications accepted. *Expenses:* Tuition, state resident: full-time $6024; part-time $251 per credit hour. Tuition, nonresident: full-time $13,536; part-time $564 per credit hour. Required fees: $1776; $50 per credit hour. $306 per semester. *Financial support:* In 2010–11, 12 students received support, including 4 research assistantships (averaging $5,727 per year), 4 teaching assistantships (averaging $5,385 per year); Federal Work-Study, institutionally sponsored loans, scholarships/grants, and unspecified assistantships also available. Support available to part-time students. Financial award application deadline: 4/1; financial award applicants required to submit FAFSA. *Unit head:* Dr. Rebecca Jackson, Graduate Advisor, 512-245-2163, E-mail: rj10@txstate.edu. *Application contact:* Dr. J. Michael Willoughby, Dean of Graduate School, 512-245-2581, Fax: 512-245-8365, E-mail: gradcollege@txstate.edu.

Texas Tech University, Graduate School, College of Visual and Performing Arts, Fine Arts Doctoral Program, Lubbock, TX 79409. Offers arts (PhD). *Accreditation:* NAST. Part-time programs available. *Students:* 46 full-time (22 women), 32 part-time (15 women); includes 2 Black or African American, non-Hispanic/Latino; 1 American Indian or Alaska Native, non-Hispanic/Latino; 1 Asian, non-Hispanic/Latino; 5 Hispanic/Latino, 10 international. Average age 35. 36 applicants, 44% accepted, 9 enrolled. In 2010, 14 doctorates awarded. *Degree requirements:* For doctorate, comprehensive exam, thesis/dissertation. *Entrance requirements:* For doctorate, GRE General Test. Additional exam requirements/recommendations for international students: Required—TOEFL (minimum score 550 paper-based; 213 computer-based; 79 iBT). *Application deadline:* For fall admission, 6/1 priority date for domestic students, 1/15 priority date for international students; for spring admission, 9/1 priority date for domestic students, 6/15 priority date for international students. Applications are processed on a rolling basis. Application fee: $50 ($75 for international students). Electronic applications accepted. *Expenses:* Tuition, state resident: full-time $5495.76; part-time $228.99 per credit hour. Tuition, nonresident: full-time $12,936; part-time $538.99 per credit hour. Required fees: $2674; $36 per credit hour. $905 per semester. *Financial support:* Research assistantships with partial tuition reimbursements, teaching assistantships with partial tuition reimbursements available. Financial award application deadline: 4/15; financial award applicants required to submit FAFSA. *Faculty research:* Art criticism and theory, music, theatre arts; arts education; history of arts. *Unit head:* Dr. Brian D. Steele, Director, 806-742-0700, Fax: 806-742-0695, E-mail: brian.steele@ttu.edu. *Application contact:* Dr. Brian D. Steele, Director, 806-742-0700, Fax: 806-742-0695, E-mail: brian.steele@ttu.edu.

Texas Tech University, Graduate School, College of Visual and Performing Arts, School of Music, Lubbock, TX 79409. Offers music (MM, DMA); music education (MM Ed). *Accreditation:* NASM. Part-time programs available. *Faculty:* 41 full-time (15 women), 2 part-time/adjunct (0 women). *Students:* 104 full-time (50 women), 34 part-time (14 women); includes 4 Black or African American, non-Hispanic/Latino; 1 American Indian or Alaska Native, non-Hispanic/Latino; 1 Asian, non-Hispanic/Latino; 14 Hispanic/Latino; 1 Two or more races, non-Hispanic/Latino, 33 international. Average age 29. 114 applicants, 64% accepted, 37 enrolled. In 2010, 29 master's, 14 doctorates awarded. *Degree requirements:* For master's, thesis or alternative; for doctorate, thesis/dissertation. *Entrance requirements:* For master's and doctorate, GRE General Test. Additional exam requirements/recommendations for international students: Required—TOEFL (minimum score 550 paper-based; 213 computer-based; 79 iBT). *Application deadline:* For fall admission, 6/1 priority date for domestic students, 1/15 priority date for international students; for spring admission, 6/1 priority date for domestic students, 6/15 priority date for international students. Applications are processed on a rolling basis. Application fee: $50 ($75 for international students). Electronic applications accepted. *Expenses:* Tuition, state resident: full-time $5495.76; part-time $228.99 per credit hour. Tuition, nonresident: full-time $12,936; part-time $538.99 per credit hour. Required fees: $2674; $36 per credit hour. $905 per semester. *Financial support:* In 2010–11, 82 students received support, including 1 research assistantship with partial tuition reimbursement available (averaging $4,354 per year), 45 teaching assistantships with partial tuition reimbursements available (averaging $5,346 per year). Financial award application deadline: 4/15; financial award applicants required to submit FAFSA. *Faculty research:* Strategies for music pedagogy in grades K-12, performance practice of traditional music, role of the woman piano virtuoso, vernacular music center, voice health and culture. Total annual research expenditures: $6,359. *Unit head:* Prof. William Ballenger, Director, 806-742-2270, Fax: 806-742-2294, E-mail: william.ballenger@ttu.edu. *Application contact:* Carin Wanner, Admissions and Scholarship Coordinator, 806-742-2270 Ext. 225, Fax: 806-742-2294, E-mail: melissacarin.wanner@ttu.edu.

Texas Woman's University, Graduate School, College of Arts and Sciences, School of the Arts, Department of Music and Drama, Denton, TX 76201. Offers drama (MA); music (MA). *Accreditation:* NASM. Part-time programs available. *Faculty:* 14 full-time (8 women). *Students:* 43 full-time (31 women), 42 part-time (29 women); includes 5 Black or African American, non-Hispanic/Latino; 2 Asian, non-Hispanic/Latino; 6 Hispanic/Latino, 13 international. Average age 32. 38 applicants, 89% accepted, 21 enrolled. In 2010, 12 master's awarded. *Degree requirements:* For master's, thesis optional, project recital. *Entrance requirements:* For master's, music history/theory placement exam (music only). Additional exam requirements/ recommendations for international students: Required—TOEFL (minimum score 550 paper-based; 213 computer-based; 79 iBT). *Application deadline:* For fall admission, 7/1 priority date for domestic students, 3/1 for international students; for spring admission, 12/1 priority date for domestic students, 7/1 for international students. Applications are processed on a rolling basis. Application fee: $50 ($75 for international students). Electronic applications accepted. *Expenses:* Tuition, state resident: full-time $3834; part-time $213 per credit hour. Tuition, nonresident: full-time $9468; part-time $526 per credit hour. Required fees: $1247; $220 per credit hour. *Financial support:* In 2010–11, 40 students received support, including 9 research assistantships (averaging $9,684 per year); career-related internships or fieldwork, Federal Work-Study, institutionally sponsored loans, scholarships/grants, traineeships, health care benefits, tuition waivers (partial), and unspecified assistantships also available. Support available to part-time students. Financial award application deadline: 3/1; financial award applicants required to submit FAFSA. *Faculty research:* Musical development in early childhood, little known or neglected compositions for flute (especially by women composers), relationship of visual art to piano music, pedagogical development of the singing voice, guided imagery and music. *Unit head:* Dr. James Chenevert, Chair, 940-898-2500, Fax: 940-898-2494, E-mail: music@twu.edu. *Application contact:* Dr. Samuel Wheeler, Assistant Director of Admissions, 940-898-3188, Fax: 940-898-3081, E-mail: wheelersr@twu.edu.

Towson University, Program in Music Performance and Composition, Towson, MD 21252-0001. Offers MM. *Accreditation:* NASM. Part-time and evening/weekend programs available. *Students:* 9 full-time (2 women), 8 part-time (2 women); includes 7 minority (2 Black or African American, non-Hispanic/Latino; 1 American Indian or Alaska Native, non-Hispanic/Latino; 2 Asian, non-Hispanic/Latino; 2 Hispanic/Latino), 3 international. Average age 30. In 2010, 5 master's awarded. *Degree requirements:* For master's, exam. *Entrance requirements:* For master's, audition, bachelor's degree in music or music education, minimum GPA of 3.0. *Application deadline:* Applications are processed on a rolling basis. Application fee: $50. Electronic applications accepted. *Expenses:* Tuition, state resident: part-time $324 per credit. Tuition, nonresident: part-time $681 per credit. Required fees: $95 per term. *Financial support:* Teaching assistantships, Federal Work-Study and unspecified assistantships available. Financial award application deadline: 4/1; financial award applicants required to submit FAFSA. *Unit head:* Dr. Luis Engelke, Graduate Program Director, 410-704-4664, E-mail: lengelke@towson.edu. *Application contact:* 410-704-2501, Fax: 410-704-4675, E-mail: grads@towson.edu.

Trinity Lutheran Seminary, Graduate and Professional Programs, Columbus, OH 43209-2334. Offers Christian education (MA); church music (MA); divinity (M Div); sacred theology (STM); theological studies (MTS); youth and family ministry (MA); MSN/MTS; MTS/JD. *Accreditation:* ACIPE; ATS. Part-time programs available. *Faculty:* 15 full-time (7 women), 7 part-time/adjunct (2 women). *Students:* 110 full-time (42 women), 35 part-time (19 women); includes 21 minority (15 Black or African American, non-Hispanic/Latino; 4 Asian, non-Hispanic/Latino; 2 Hispanic/Latino), 4 international. Average age 35. 71 applicants, 77% accepted, 49 enrolled. In 2010, 29 first professional degrees, 9 master's awarded. *Degree requirements:* For master's, comprehensive exam (for some programs), thesis (for some programs); for M Div, 2 foreign languages, internship. *Entrance requirements:* For master's, M Div or equivalent (STM). Additional exam requirements/recommendations for international students: Required—TOEFL (minimum score 500 paper-based; 173 computer-based; 61 iBT). *Application deadline:* For fall admission, 7/15 priority date for domestic and international students. Applications are processed on a rolling basis. Application fee: $25. *Expenses:* Tuition: Full-time $13,020; part-time $434 per semester hour. Required fees: $165 per semester. One-time fee: $150. *Financial support:* In 2010–11, 102 students received support. Career-related internships or fieldwork, Federal Work-Study, institutionally sponsored loans, and scholarships/grants available. Support available to part-time students. Financial award application deadline: 5/1; financial award applicants required to submit FAFSA. *Unit head:* Dr. James Childs, Interim Academic Dean, 614-235-4136 Ext. 4670, Fax: 614-384-4635. *Application contact:* Rev. Sheri L. Ayers, Director of Admissions, 614-235-4136 Ext. 4614, Fax: 866-610-8572, E-mail: sayers@tls.edu.

Troy University, Graduate School, College of Education, Program in Postsecondary Education, Troy, AL 36082. Offers adult education (M Ed); biology (M Ed); criminal justice (M Ed); English (M Ed); foundations of education (M Ed); general science (M Ed); higher education administration (M Ed); history (M Ed); instructional technology (M Ed); mathematics (M Ed); music industry (M Ed); physical fitness (M Ed); political science (M Ed); public administration (M Ed); social science (M Ed); teaching English (M Ed). *Accreditation:* NCATE. Part-time and evening/ weekend programs available. *Students:* 314 full-time (247 women), 153 part-time (122 women); includes 255 minority (242 Black or African American, non-Hispanic/Latino; 3 American Indian or Alaska Native, non-Hispanic/Latino; 5 Asian, non-Hispanic/Latino; 5 Hispanic/Latino). Average age 34. 223 applicants, 89% accepted. In 2010, 364 master's awarded. *Degree requirements:* For master's, comprehensive exam, thesis. *Entrance requirements:* For master's, MAT (minimum score 385), minimum GPA of 2.5. Additional exam requirements/recommendations for international students: Required—TOEFL (minimum score 523 paper-based; 193 computer-based; 70 iBT), IELTS, or ACT compass ESL (minimum Listening, Reading, and Grammar score: 270). *Application deadline:* Applications are processed on a rolling basis. Application fee: $50.

Music

Troy University (continued)
Electronic applications accepted. *Expenses:* Tuition, state resident: full-time $4428; part-time $246 per credit hour. Tuition, nonresident: full-time $8856; part-time $492 per credit hour. Required fees: $432; $24 per credit hour. $50 per term. Tuition and fees vary according to program. *Financial support:* Available to part-time students. Applicants required to submit FAFSA. *Unit head:* Dr. Andrew Creamer, Chair, 334-670-3350, Fax: 334-670-3296, E-mail: drcreamer@troy.edu. *Application contact:* Brenda K. Campbell, Director of Graduate Admissions, 334-670-3178, Fax: 334-670-3733, E-mail: bcamp@troy.edu.

Truman State University, Graduate School, School of Arts and Letters, Program in Music, Kirksville, MO 63501-4221. Offers MA. *Accreditation:* NASM. *Degree requirements:* For master's, comprehensive exam, thesis or alternative. *Entrance requirements:* For master's, GRE General Test, minimum GPA of 3.0. Additional exam requirements/recommendations for international students: Required—TOEFL (minimum score 550 paper-based; 213 computer-based). Electronic applications accepted.

Tufts University, Graduate School of Arts and Sciences, Department of Music, Medford, MA 02155. Offers ethnomusicology (MA); music history and literature (MA); music theory and composition (MA). Part-time programs available. *Degree requirements:* For master's, one foreign language, thesis. *Entrance requirements:* For master's, GRE General Test, writing sample or musical score. Additional exam requirements/recommendations for international students: Required—TOEFL (minimum score 550 paper-based; 213 computer-based; 80 iBT). Electronic applications accepted. *Expenses:* Tuition: Full-time $39,624; part-time $3962 per course. Required fees: $40 per year. Full-time tuition and fees vary according to degree level, program and student level. Part-time tuition and fees vary according to course load.

Tulane University, School of Liberal Arts, Department of Music, New Orleans, LA 70118-5669. Offers MA, MFA. *Degree requirements:* For master's, one foreign language, thesis (for some programs), recital or composition (MA). *Entrance requirements:* For master's, GRE General Test, minimum B average in undergraduate course work. Additional exam requirements/recommendations for international students: Required—TOEFL. Electronic applications accepted. *Faculty research:* New Orleans music, composition, piano, voice, music theatre, classical guitar.

Université de Montréal, Faculty of Music, Montréal, QC H3C 3J7, Canada. Offers composition (M Mus, D Mus); interpretation (M Mus, D Mus, DESS); music (MA, PhD); orchestral repertoire (DESS). *Degree requirements:* For doctorate, thesis/dissertation, general exam. Electronic applications accepted. *Faculty research:* Semiology, music in Creole areas, computer-assisted composition, Argentinean tango.

Université Laval, Faculty of Music, Programs in Music, Québec, QC G1K 7P4, Canada. Offers composition (M Mus); instrumental didactics (M Mus); interpretation (M Mus); music education (M Mus, PhD); musicology (M Mus, PhD). Terminal master's awarded for partial completion of doctoral program. *Degree requirements:* For master's, thesis (for some programs); for doctorate, comprehensive exam, thesis/dissertation. *Entrance requirements:* For master's, English exam, audition, knowledge of French; for doctorate, English exam, knowledge of French, third language. Electronic applications accepted.

University at Buffalo, the State University of New York, Graduate School, College of Arts and Sciences, Department of Music, Buffalo, NY 14260. Offers historical musicology and music theory (PhD); music composition (MA, PhD); music history (MA); music performance (MM); music theory (MA). *Faculty:* 20 full-time (4 women), 17 part-time/adjunct (3 women). *Students:* 74 full-time (27 women), 3 part-time (2 women); includes 1 Black or African American, non-Hispanic/Latino; 1 American Indian or Alaska Native, non-Hispanic/Latino; 6 Asian, non-Hispanic/Latino; 3 Hispanic/Latino, 17 international. Average age 31. 93 applicants, 43% accepted, 27 enrolled. In 2010, 10 master's, 6 doctorates awarded. Terminal master's awarded for partial completion of doctoral program. *Degree requirements:* For master's, variable foreign language requirement, comprehensive exam (for some programs), thesis optional, recitals (MM); for doctorate, variable foreign language requirement, comprehensive exam, thesis/dissertation. *Entrance requirements:* For master's, audition (MM), compositions, writing sample(s), essay, letters of recommendation; for doctorate, GRE General Test, compositions, writing sample(s), essay, letters of recommendation. Additional exam requirements/recommendations for international students: Required—TOEFL (minimum score 550 paper-based; 213 computer-based; 79 iBT). *Application deadline:* For fall admission, 1/1 priority date for domestic and international students; for spring admission, 10/1 for domestic students, 8/1 priority date for international students. Applications are processed on a rolling basis. Application fee: $75. Electronic applications accepted. *Financial support:* In 2010–11, 17 students received support, including 11 fellowships with full tuition reimbursements available (averaging $17,850 per year), 6 teaching assistantships with full tuition reimbursements available (averaging $15,850 per year); research assistantships with partial tuition reimbursements available, career-related internships or fieldwork, Federal Work-Study, institutionally sponsored loans, scholarships/grants, tuition waivers (partial), and unspecified assistantships also available. Financial award application deadline: 1/1; financial award applicants required to submit FAFSA. *Faculty research:* Music composition, music theory, historical musicology, concert performance. *Unit head:* Prof. Charles J. Smith, Chairperson, 716-645-0639, Fax: 716-645-3824, E-mail: cjsmith@buffalo.edu. *Application contact:* Karen A. Sausner, Director of Student Programs, 716-645-2758, Fax: 716-645-6196, E-mail: ksausner@buffalo.edu.

The University of Akron, Graduate School, College of Creative and Professional Arts, School of Music, Program in Composition, Akron, OH 44325. Offers MM. *Students:* 2 full-time (0 women). Average age 29. 2 applicants, 100% accepted, 1 enrolled. *Degree requirements:* For master's, comprehensive exam, thesis or project. *Entrance requirements:* For master's, theory diagnostic exam, minimum GPA of 2.75, three letters of recommendation, sample of scholarly writing, composition portfolio, interview. Additional exam requirements/recommendations for international students: Required—TOEFL (minimum score 550 paper-based; 213 computer-based; 79 iBT). *Application deadline:* Applications are processed on a rolling basis. Application fee: $30 ($40 for international students). Electronic applications accepted. *Expenses:* Tuition, state resident: full-time $6800; part-time $378 per credit hour. Tuition, nonresident: full-time $11,644; part-time $647 per credit hour. Required fees: $1265. One-time fee: $30 full-time. *Unit head:* Dr. Daniel W. McCarthy, Program Contact, 330-972-2199, E-mail: dmccarthy@uakron.edu. *Application contact:* Dr. Michele Mills, Graduate Coordinator, 330-972-5762, E-mail: mt4@uakron.edu.

The University of Akron, Graduate School, College of Creative and Professional Arts, School of Music, Program in Music History and Literature, Akron, OH 44325. Offers MM. *Students:* 3 full-time (2 women), 2 part-time (0 women); includes 1 Black or African American, non-Hispanic/Latino, 1 international. Average age 40. 4 applicants, 75% accepted, 3 enrolled. In 2010, 3 master's awarded. *Degree requirements:* For master's, comprehensive exam, thesis optional, thesis or project. *Entrance requirements:* For master's, history diagnostic exam, minimum GPA of 2.75, three letters of recommendation, sample of scholarly writing, interview. Additional exam requirements/recommendations for international students: Required—TOEFL (minimum score 550 paper-based; 213 computer-based; 79 iBT). *Application deadline:* Applications are processed on a rolling basis. Application fee: $30 ($40 for international students). Electronic applications accepted. *Expenses:* Tuition, state resident: full-time $6800; part-time $378 per credit hour. Tuition, nonresident: full-time $11,644; part-time $647 per credit hour. Required fees: $1265. One-time fee: $30 full-time. *Unit head:* Dr. Brooks Toliver, Program Contact, 330-972-5207, E-mail: brooks@uakron.edu. *Application contact:* Dr. Michele Mills, Graduate Coordinator, 330-972-5762, E-mail: mt4@uakron.edu.

The University of Akron, Graduate School, College of Creative and Professional Arts, School of Music, Program in Music Technology, Akron, OH 44325. Offers MM. *Students:* 3 full-time (0 women), 1 international. Average age 28. 2 applicants, 50% accepted, 1 enrolled. In 2010, 1 master's awarded. *Degree requirements:* For master's, comprehensive exam, thesis optional, thesis or project. *Entrance requirements:* For master's, minimum GPA of 2.75, three letters of recommendation, interview. Additional exam requirements/recommendations for international students: Required—TOEFL (minimum score 550 paper-based; 213 computer-based; 79 iBT). *Application deadline:* Applications are processed on a rolling basis. Application fee: $30 ($40 for international students). Electronic applications accepted. *Expenses:* Tuition, state resident: full-time $6800; part-time $378 per credit hour. Tuition, nonresident: full-time $11,644; part-time $647 per credit hour. Required fees: $1265. One-time fee: $30 full-time. *Unit head:* V. Douglas Hicks, Program Contact, 330-972-6356, E-mail: vhicks@uakron.edu. *Application contact:* Dr. Michele Mills, Graduate Coordinator.

The University of Akron, Graduate School, College of Creative and Professional Arts, School of Music, Program in Performance, Akron, OH 44325. Offers MM. *Students:* 41 full-time (22 women), 8 part-time (5 women); includes 3 Black or African American, non-Hispanic/Latino; 5 Hispanic/Latino, 3 international. Average age 28. 49 applicants, 80% accepted, 21 enrolled. In 2010, 23 master's awarded. *Degree requirements:* For master's, comprehensive exam. *Entrance requirements:* For master's, minimum GPA of 2.75, three letters of recommendation, audition. Additional exam requirements/recommendations for international students: Required—TOEFL (minimum score 550 paper-based; 213 computer-based; 79 iBT). *Application deadline:* Applications are processed on a rolling basis. Application fee: $30 ($40 for international students). Electronic applications accepted. *Expenses:* Tuition, state resident: full-time $6800; part-time $378 per credit hour. Tuition, nonresident: full-time $11,644; part-time $647 per credit hour. Required fees: $1265. One-time fee: $30 full-time. *Unit head:* Dr. Michelle Mills, Program Contact, 330-972-5762, E-mail: mt4@uakron.edu. *Application contact:* Dr. Michelle Mills, Program Contact, 330-972-5762, E-mail: mt4@uakron.edu.

The University of Akron, Graduate School, College of Creative and Professional Arts, School of Music, Program in Theory, Akron, OH 44325. Offers MM. *Students:* 1 (woman) full-time, 2 part-time (1 woman). Average age 30. 3 applicants, 33% accepted, 1 enrolled. *Degree requirements:* For master's, comprehensive exam, thesis or project. *Entrance requirements:* For master's, minimum GPA of 2.75, interview, three letters of recommendation. Additional exam requirements/recommendations for international students: Required—TOEFL (minimum score 550 paper-based; 213 computer-based; 79 iBT). *Application deadline:* Applications are processed on a rolling basis. Application fee: $30 ($40 for international students). Electronic applications accepted. *Expenses:* Tuition, state resident: full-time $6800; part-time $378 per credit hour. Tuition, nonresident: full-time $11,644; part-time $647 per credit hour. Required fees: $1265. One-time fee: $30 full-time. *Unit head:* Dr. Daniel W. McCarthy, Head, 330-972-2199, E-mail: dmccarthy@uakron.edu. *Application contact:* Dr. Daniel W. McCarthy, Head, 330-972-2199, E-mail: dmccarthy@uakron.edu.

The University of Alabama, Graduate School, College of Arts and Sciences, Department of English, Tuscaloosa, AL 35487. Offers composition and rhetoric (PhD); creative writing (MFA), including fiction, poetry; literature (MA, PhD); rhetoric and composition (MA); teaching English as a second language (MATESOL). *Faculty:* 31 full-time (14 women). *Students:* 64 full-time (46 women), 75 part-time (44 women); includes 15 minority (11 Black or African American, non-Hispanic/Latino; 1 Asian, non-Hispanic/Latino; 1 Hispanic/Latino; 1 Native Hawaiian or other Pacific Islander, non-Hispanic/Latino; 1 Two or more races, non-Hispanic/Latino), 7 international. Average age 28. 364 applicants, 20% accepted, 46 enrolled. In 2010, 40 master's, 7 doctorates awarded. *Degree requirements:* For master's, one foreign language, comprehensive exam, thesis (for some programs); for doctorate, 2 foreign languages, comprehensive exam, thesis/dissertation. *Entrance requirements:* For master's and doctorate, GRE, minimum GPA of 3.0, critical writing sample. Additional exam requirements/recommendations for international students: Required—TOEFL. *Application deadline:* For fall admission, 1/15 priority date for domestic students, 1/15 for international students. Application fee: $50 ($60 for international students). Electronic applications accepted. *Expenses:* Tuition, state resident: full-time $7900. Tuition, nonresident: full-time $20,500. *Financial support:* In 2010–11, 7 fellowships with full tuition reimbursements (averaging $15,000 per year), 1 research assistantship (averaging $11,708 per year), 106 teaching assistantships with full tuition reimbursements (averaging $11,708 per year) were awarded; career-related internships or fieldwork, scholarships/grants, health care benefits, and unspecified assistantships also available. Financial award application deadline: 1/15. *Faculty research:* Critical theory; modern, Renaissance, and African-American literature. *Unit head:* Dr. Catherine E. Davies, Director of Graduate Studies, 205-348-8499, E-mail: cdavies@bama.ua.edu. *Application contact:* Vernita W. James, Office Assistant II, 205-348-0766, Fax: 205-348-1388, E-mail: vwjames@bama.ua.edu.

The University of Alabama, Graduate School, College of Arts and Sciences, School of Music, Tuscaloosa, AL 35487. Offers arranging (MM); choral conducting (MM, DMA); composition (MM, DMA); music education (MA, PhD); music history (MM); performance (MM, DMA); theory (MM); wind conducting (MM, DMA). *Accreditation:* NASM. *Faculty:* 36 full-time (13 women), 1 part-time/adjunct (0 women). *Students:* 51 full-time (23 women), 39 part-time (19 women); includes 12 minority (3 Black or African American, non-Hispanic/Latino; 5 Asian, non-Hispanic/Latino; 3 Hispanic/Latino; 1 Two or more races, non-Hispanic/Latino), 12 international. Average age 31. 68 applicants, 54% accepted, 16 enrolled. In 2010, 12 master's, 5 doctorates awarded. *Degree requirements:* For master's, comprehensive exam, thesis; oral and written exams, recital; for doctorate, comprehensive exam, thesis/dissertation, oral and written exams, recital. *Entrance requirements:* For master's and doctorate, audition. Additional exam requirements/recommendations for international students: Required—TOEFL or IELTS. *Application deadline:* For fall admission, 2/1 priority date for domestic and international students; for winter admission, 2/1 for domestic students, 2/1 priority date for international students; for spring admission, 2/1 priority date for domestic and international students. Applications are processed on a rolling basis. Application fee: $50 ($60 for international students). Electronic applications accepted. *Expenses:* Tuition, state resident: full-time $7900. Tuition, nonresident: full-time $20,500. *Financial support:* In 2010–11, 22 students received support, including 1 fellowship with tuition reimbursement available (averaging $30,000 per year), 40 teaching assistantships with full and partial tuition reimbursements available (averaging $8,181 per year); Federal Work-Study, institutionally sponsored loans, and unspecified assistantships also available. Financial award application deadline: 7/14. *Faculty research:* Performance practice, musicology, theory, composition. *Unit head:* Charles G. Snead, Director, 205-348-7110, Fax: 205-348-1473, E-mail: ssnead@music.ua.edu. *Application contact:* Dr. Marvin Johnson, Director of Graduate Studies, 205-348-6604, Fax: 205-348-1473, E-mail: mjohnson@music.ua.edu.

University of Alaska Fairbanks, College of Liberal Arts, Department of Music, Fairbanks, AK 99775-5660. Offers conducting (MA); music education (MA); music history (MA); music theory/composition (MA); performance (MA). *Accreditation:* NASM. Part-time programs available. *Faculty:* 10 full-time (3 women). *Students:* 9 full-time (7 women), 4 part-time (0 women), 2 international. Average age 28. 5 applicants, 80% accepted, 2 enrolled. In 2010, 2 master's awarded. *Degree requirements:* For master's, comprehensive exam, thesis or alternative, oral exam, oral defense. *Entrance requirements:* For master's, evaluative preliminary examination in music theory and history. Additional exam requirements/recommendations for international students: Required—TOEFL (minimum score 550 paper-based; 213 computer-based; 80 iBT). *Application deadline:* For fall admission, 6/1 for domestic students, 3/1 for international students; for spring admission, 10/15 for domestic students, 9/1 for international students. Applications are processed on a rolling basis. Application fee: $60. Electronic applications accepted. *Expenses:* Tuition, state resident: full-time $5688; part-time $316 per credit. Tuition, nonresident: full-time $11,628; part-time $646 per credit. Required fees: $289 per semester. Tuition and fees vary according to course load and reciprocity agreements. *Financial support:* In 2010–11, 8 teaching assistantships with tuition reimbursements (averaging $12,407 per year) were awarded; fellowships with tuition reimbursements, Federal Work-Study, scholarships/grants, health care benefits, and unspecified assistantships also available. Support available to part-time students. Financial award application deadline: 7/1; financial award applicants required to submit FAFSA. *Faculty research:* Symphony, opera, jazz, chamber and solo performance. *Unit head:* Dr. Eduard Zilberkant, Department Chair, 907-474-7555, Fax: 907-474-6420, E-mail: uaf.music@alaska.edu. *Application contact:* Dr. Eduard Zilberkant, Department Chair, 907-474-7555, Fax: 907-474-6420, E-mail: uaf.music@alaska.edu.

University of Alberta, Faculty of Graduate Studies and Research, Department of Music, Edmonton, AB T6G 2E1, Canada. Offers applied music (M Mus); choral conducting (M Mus); composition (M Mus); music (PhD); organ and choral conductors (D Mus); piano (D Mus). *Degree requirements:* For master's, one foreign language, thesis; for doctorate, one foreign language, thesis/dissertation. *Entrance requirements:* Additional exam requirements/recommendations for international students: Required—TOEFL (minimum score 550 paper-based; 213 computer-based). Electronic applications accepted. *Faculty research:* Classical/Indian and West African music, popular music, choral conducting, theory and composition, musicology, applied music.

The University of Arizona, College of Fine Arts, School of Music, Tucson, AZ 85721. Offers composition (MM, A Mus D); conducting (MM, A Mus D); music education (MM, PhD); music theory (MM, PhD); musicology (MM); performance (MM, A Mus D). *Accreditation:* NASD (one or more programs are accredited); NASM (one or more programs are accredited). Part-time programs available. *Faculty:* 41 full-time (12 women), 1 part-time/adjunct (0 women). *Students:* 107 full-time (41 women), 83 part-time (40 women); includes 3 Black or African American, non-Hispanic/Latino; 7 Asian, non-Hispanic/Latino; 14 Hispanic/Latino; 3 Two or more races, non-Hispanic/Latino, 38 international. Average age 34. 162 applicants, 48% accepted, 50 enrolled. In 2010, 19 master's, 15 doctorates awarded. *Degree requirements:* For master's, thesis or alternative, orals; for doctorate, comprehensive exam, thesis/dissertation or alternative. *Entrance requirements:* For master's, 3 letters of recommendation; for doctorate, 3 letters of recommendation, statement of purpose. Additional exam requirements/recommendations for international students: Required—TOEFL (minimum score 550 paper-based; 213 computer-based; 79 iBT). *Application deadline:* For fall admission, 6/1 for domestic students, 12/1 for international students; for spring admission, 10/1 for domestic students, 6/1 for international students. Applications are processed on a rolling basis. Application fee: $75. Electronic applications accepted. *Expenses:* Tuition, state resident: full-time $7692. *Financial support:* In 2010–11, 64 teaching assistantships with full tuition reimbursements (averaging $16,132 per year) were awarded; career-related internships or fieldwork, institutionally sponsored loans, scholarships/grants, health care benefits, tuition waivers (full), and unspecified assistantships also available. Support available to part-time students. Financial award application deadline: 2/15; financial award applicants required to submit FAFSA. *Faculty research:* Music in general education, psychology of music learning, innovation in string music education, Zarzuela, Franz Liszt's work. Total annual research expenditures: $934. *Unit head:* Dr. Peter A. McAllister, Director, 520-621-7023, Fax: 520-621-1351, E-mail: pmcallis@email.arizona.edu. *Application contact:* Lyneen Elmore, 520-621-5929, Fax: 520-621-8118, E-mail: lyneen@u.arizona.edu.

The University of Arizona, College of Humanities, Department of English, Rhetoric, Composition and the Teaching of English Program, Tucson, AZ 85721. Offers PhD. *Students:* 38 full-time (29 women), 14 part-time (11 women); includes 11 minority (4 Asian, non-Hispanic/Latino; 5 Hispanic/Latino; 2 Two or more races, non-Hispanic/Latino). Average age 35. 41 applicants, 15% accepted, 6 enrolled. In 2010, 17 doctorates awarded. *Degree requirements:* For doctorate, one foreign language, comprehensive exam, thesis/dissertation. *Entrance requirements:* For doctorate, GRE General Test, 3 letters of recommendation, writing sample. Additional exam requirements/recommendations for international students: Required—TOEFL (minimum score 550 paper-based; 213 computer-based; 79 iBT). *Application deadline:* Applications are processed on a rolling basis. Application fee: $75. Electronic applications accepted. *Expenses:* Tuition, state resident: full-time $7692. *Unit head:* Theresa Enos, Director, 520-621-3255, Fax: 520-621-7397, E-mail: enos@u.arizona.edu. *Application contact:* Alison Miller, Program Assistant, 520-621-7213, Fax: 520-621-7397, E-mail: admiller@u.arizona.edu.

University of Arkansas, Graduate School, J. William Fulbright College of Arts and Sciences, Department of Music, Fayetteville, AR 72701-1201. Offers MM. *Accreditation:* NASM. *Students:* 20 full-time (8 women), 10 part-time (4 women); includes 3 minority (1 Black or African American, non-Hispanic/Latino; 1 American Indian or Alaska Native, non-Hispanic/Latino; 1 Hispanic/Latino), 4 international. 17 applicants, 100% accepted. In 2010, 14 master's awarded. *Entrance requirements:* For master's, GRE General Test. *Application deadline:* For fall admission, 4/1 for international students; for spring admission, 10/1 for international students. Applications are processed on a rolling basis. Application fee: $40 ($50 for international students). Electronic applications accepted. *Financial support:* In 2010–11, 5 research assistantships, 17 teaching assistantships were awarded; fellowships, career-related internships or fieldwork and Federal Work-Study also available. Support available to part-time students. Financial award application deadline: 4/1; financial award applicants required to submit FAFSA. *Unit head:* Dr. Ronda Mains, Departmental Chair, 479-575-4701, Fax: 479-575-5409, E-mail: rmains@uark.edu. *Application contact:* Dr. Stephen Gates, Graduate Coordinator, 479-575-4701, E-mail: sgates@uark.edu.

The University of British Columbia, Faculty of Arts and Faculty of Graduate Studies, School of Music, Vancouver, BC V6T 1Z2, Canada. Offers M Mus, MA, DMA, PhD. Part-time programs available. *Degree requirements:* For master's, recital (M Mus), thesis (MA); for doctorate, one foreign language, comprehensive exam, public performance or composition (DMA), dissertation (PhD). *Entrance requirements:* For master's, audition/performance (M Mus); for doctorate, audition/performance (DMA). Additional exam requirements/recommendations for international students: Required—TOEFL (minimum score 580 paper-based; 237 computer-based; 93 iBT). Electronic applications accepted. Tuition charges are reported in Canadian dollars. *Expenses:* Tuition, area resident: Full-time $4179 Canadian dollars. International tuition: $7344 Canadian dollars full-time. *Faculty research:* Performance, composition, opera, musicology, ethnomusicology, theory.

University of Calgary, Faculty of Graduate Studies, Faculty of Fine Arts, Department of Music, Calgary, AB T2N 1N4, Canada. Offers M Mus, MA, PhD. *Degree requirements:* For master's, one foreign language, thesis; for doctorate, 2 foreign languages, thesis/dissertation. *Entrance requirements:* For master's, audition (performance), 3 compositions. Additional exam requirements/recommendations for international students: Required—TOEFL. Electronic applications accepted. *Faculty research:* Musicology, theory and composition, performance and performance practice, teaching methodology, folk music collection and analyses.

University of California, Berkeley, Graduate Division, College of Letters and Science, Department of Music, Berkeley, CA 94720-1500. Offers composition (PhD); ethnomusicology (PhD); musicology (PhD). *Degree requirements:* For doctorate, 2 foreign languages, thesis/dissertation, qualifying exam. *Entrance requirements:* For doctorate, GRE General Test, minimum GPA of 3.0, examples of work, 3 letters of recommendation. Additional exam requirements/recommendations for international students: Required—TOEFL (minimum score 570 paper-based; 230 computer-based). *Faculty research:* Historical musicology, music criticism, computer music.

University of California, Davis, Graduate Studies, Program in Music, Davis, CA 95616. Offers composition (MA, PhD); conducting (MA, PhD); musicology (MA, PhD). Terminal master's awarded for partial completion of doctoral program. *Degree requirements:* For master's, one foreign language, thesis; for doctorate, 2 foreign languages, thesis/dissertation. *Entrance requirements:* For master's, minimum GPA of 3.0; for doctorate, GRE, minimum GPA of 3.0. Additional exam requirements/recommendations for international students: Required—TOEFL (minimum score 550 paper-based; 213 computer-based). Electronic applications accepted.

University of California, Davis, Graduate Studies, Program in Performance Studies, Davis, CA 95616. Offers dramatic art (PhD). *Degree requirements:* For doctorate, 2 foreign languages, thesis/dissertation. *Entrance requirements:* For doctorate, GRE, minimum GPA of 3.25. Additional exam requirements/recommendations for international students: Required—TOEFL (minimum score 550 paper-based; 213 computer-based). Electronic applications accepted.

University of California, Irvine, Claire Trevor School of the Arts, Department of Music, Irvine, CA 92697. Offers accompanying (MFA); choral conducting (MFA); composition and technology (MFA); guitar/lute performance (MFA); instrumental performance (MFA); jazz instrumental/composition (MFA); piano performance (MFA); vocal performance (MFA). *Students:* 23 full-time (7 women), 1 part-time (0 women); includes 11 minority (1 Black or African American, non-Hispanic/Latino; 1 American Indian or Alaska Native, non-Hispanic/Latino; 3 Asian, non-Hispanic/Latino; 5 Hispanic/Latino; 1 Two or more races, non-Hispanic/Latino), 2 international. Average age 28. 31 applicants, 39% accepted, 11 enrolled. In 2010, 10 master's awarded. *Degree requirements:* For master's, one foreign language, thesis. *Entrance requirements:* For master's, minimum GPA of 3.0. *Application deadline:* For fall admission, 1/15 priority date for domestic students, 1/15 for international students. Applications are processed on a rolling basis. Application fee: $80 ($100 for international students). Electronic applications accepted. *Financial support:* Fellowships, teaching assistantships, institutionally sponsored loans, traineeships, health care benefits, and unspecified assistantships available. Financial award application deadline: 3/1; financial award applicants required to submit FAFSA. *Faculty research:* Composition, instrumental and choral performance, African-American music, Italian baroque music and performance practice. *Unit head:* David L. Brodbeck, Chair, 949-824-4281, Fax: 949-824-4914, E-mail: david.brodbeck@uci.edu. *Application contact:* Sally L. Avila, Administrative Assistant, 949-824-6615, Fax: 949-824-4914, E-mail: slavila@uci.edu.

University of California, Los Angeles, Graduate Division, College of Letters and Science, Department of Musicology, Los Angeles, CA 90095. Offers MA, PhD. *Faculty:* 9 full-time (5 women). *Students:* 27 full-time (18 women); includes 1 minority (Asian, non-Hispanic/Latino), 5 international. Average age 29. 49 applicants, 12% accepted, 4 enrolled. In 2010, 1 master's, 4 doctorates awarded. Terminal master's awarded for partial completion of doctoral program. *Degree requirements:* For master's, one foreign language, thesis; for doctorate, 2 foreign languages, thesis/dissertation, oral and written qualifying exams. *Entrance requirements:* For master's, minimum GPA of 3.0, sample of written work; for doctorate, minimum undergraduate GPA of 3.0, MA or equivalent in music, sample of written work. *Application deadline:* For fall admission, 12/1 for domestic and international students. Application fee: $70 ($90 for international students). Electronic applications accepted. *Financial support:* In 2010–11, 28 fellowships with full and partial tuition reimbursements, 8 research assistantships with full and partial tuition reimbursements, 21 teaching assistantships with full and partial tuition reimbursements were awarded; Federal Work-Study, health care benefits, tuition waivers (full and partial), and unspecified assistantships also available. Financial award application deadline: 3/1; financial award applicants required to submit FAFSA. *Unit head:* Dr. Robert Fink, Chair, 310-206-7549, E-mail: rfink@humnet.ucla.edu. *Application contact:* Department Office, 310-206-5187, E-mail: bvannost@humnet.ucla.edu.

University of California, Los Angeles, Graduate Division, School of the Arts and Architecture, Department of Ethnomusicology, Los Angeles, CA 90095. Offers MA, PhD. *Faculty:* 14 full-time (4 women). *Students:* 35 full-time (18 women); includes 12 minority (2 Black or African American, non-Hispanic/Latino; 5 Asian, non-Hispanic/Latino; 5 Hispanic/Latino), 1 international. Average age 29. 76 applicants, 18% accepted, 6 enrolled. In 2010, 6 master's, 5 doctorates awarded. *Degree requirements:* For master's, one foreign language; for doctorate, 2 foreign languages, thesis/dissertation, oral and written qualifying exams. *Entrance requirements:* For master's, minimum GPA of 3.0, sample research paper, musical performance ability. *Application deadline:* For fall admission, 12/15 for domestic students. Application fee: $70 ($90 for international students). Electronic applications accepted. *Financial support:* In 2010–11, 28 fellowships, 3 research assistantships, 17 teaching assistantships were awarded; Federal Work-Study, institutionally sponsored loans, and tuition waivers (full and partial) also available. Financial award application deadline: 3/2. *Unit head:* Dr. Helen Rees, Chair, 310-206-3034, E-mail: hrees@arts.ucla.edu. *Application contact:* Sandra McKerroll, Graduate Advisor, 310-825-4769, E-mail: sandram@arts.ucla.edu.

University of California, Los Angeles, Graduate Division, School of the Arts and Architecture, Department of Music, Los Angeles, CA 90095. Offers composition (MA, PhD); performance (MM, DMA). *Faculty:* 23 full-time (2 women). *Students:* 85 full-time (44 women); includes 26 minority (5 Black or African American, non-Hispanic/Latino; 13 Asian, non-Hispanic/Latino; 8 Hispanic/Latino), 17 international. Average age 28. 269 applicants, 19% accepted, 26 enrolled. In 2010, 15 master's, 12 doctorates awarded. *Degree requirements:* For master's, one foreign language, thesis, final recital (MM), oral and written qualifying exams (MA); for doctorate, one foreign language, thesis/dissertation, oral/written qualifying exams; lecture recital (DMA); 2 foreign languages (PhD). *Entrance requirements:* For master's, departmental assessment exams, minimum GPA of 3.0, audition (MM); sample of work (MA); for doctorate, departmental assessment exams, minimum GPA of 3.0, audition (DMA); sample of work (PhD). *Application deadline:* For fall admission, 12/30 for domestic students. Application fee: $70 ($90 for international students). Electronic applications accepted. *Financial support:* In 2010–11, 69 students received support, including 65 fellowships, 32 teaching assistantships; research assistantships, Federal Work-Study, institutionally sponsored loans, and tuition waivers (full and partial) also available. Financial award application deadline: 3/2. *Unit head:* Dr. Roger Bourland, Chair, 310-825-1839, E-mail: rbourland@arts.ucla.edu. *Application contact:* Information Contact, 310-825-4769, E-mail: sandram@arts.ucla.edu.

University of California, Riverside, Graduate Division, Department of Music, Riverside, CA 92521-0102. Offers composition (PhD); ethnomusicology (MA, PhD); musicology (PhD). *Faculty:* 9 full-time (2 women). *Students:* 24 full-time (12 women); includes 3 Asian, non-Hispanic/Latino; 4 Hispanic/Latino, 2 international. Average age 28. 26 applicants, 27% accepted, 4 enrolled. In 2010, 4 master's, 1 doctorate awarded. Terminal master's awarded for partial completion of doctoral program. *Degree requirements:* For master's, one foreign language, comprehensive exam, thesis (for some programs), oral exams; for doctorate, 2 foreign languages, comprehensive exam, thesis/dissertation, written and oral qualifying examination. *Entrance requirements:* For master's and doctorate, GRE General Test, minimum GPA of 3.2. Additional exam requirements/recommendations for international students: Required—TOEFL (minimum score 550 paper-based; 213 computer-based; 80 iBT). *Application deadline:* For fall admission, 5/1 for domestic and international students. Applications are processed on a rolling basis. Application fee: $70 ($85 for international students). Electronic applications accepted. *Financial support:* In 2010–11, 3 students received support, including 3 fellowships with full and partial tuition reimbursements available (averaging $12,000 per year), 3 teaching assistantships with partial tuition reimbursements available (averaging $16,500 per year); research assistantships, career-related internships or fieldwork, Federal Work-Study, institutionally sponsored loans, health care benefits, and tuition waivers (full and partial) also available. Financial award application deadline: 4/15; financial award applicants required to submit FAFSA. *Faculty research:* Composition, ethnomusicology (especially Southeast Asian and Asian-American music), cultural musicology, gender studies, performance practice. Total annual research expenditures: $60,695. *Unit head:* Dr. Deborah Wong, Chair, 951-827-3726, Fax: 951-827-4651, E-mail: deborah.wong@ucr.edu. *Application contact:* Dr. Tim Labor, Graduate Adviser, 951-827-5703, Fax: 951-827-4651, E-mail: timlabor@ucr.edu.

University of California, San Diego, Office of Graduate Studies, Department of Music, La Jolla, CA 92093. Offers MA, DMA, PhD. *Degree requirements:* For master's, thesis; for doctorate, thesis/dissertation. Electronic applications accepted. *Faculty research:* Computer music, extended instrumental techniques, comparison of brain wave resonances with musical resonances, composition, performance.

University of California, Santa Barbara, Graduate Division, College of Letters and Sciences, Division of Humanities and Fine Arts, Department of Music, Santa Barbara, CA 93106-6070. Offers brass (MM); composition (MA, PhD); conducting (MM, DMA); ethnomusicology (MA, PhD); feminist studies (PhD); keyboard (MM, DMA); musicology (MA, PhD); piano accompanying (MM); strings (MM, DMA, PhD); theory (MA, PhD); voice (MM, DMA); woodwinds (MM); MA/PhD; MM/DMA. *Faculty:* 28 full-time (6 women), 17 part-time/adjunct (6 women). *Students:* 73 full-time (31 women); includes 5 Asian, non-Hispanic/Latino; 3 Hispanic/Latino; 1 Native Hawaiian or other Pacific Islander, non-Hispanic/Latino. Average age 28. 94 applicants, 28% accepted, 15 enrolled. In 2010, 8 master's, 2 doctorates awarded. *Degree requirements:* For master's, variable foreign language requirement, comprehensive exam (for some programs), thesis (for some programs); for doctorate, variable foreign language requirement, comprehensive exam, thesis/dissertation. *Entrance requirements:* For master's and doctorate, GRE. Additional

Music

University of California, Santa Barbara (continued)
exam requirements/recommendations for international students: Required—TOEFL (minimum score 550 paper-based; 80 iBT), IELTS (minimum score 7). *Application deadline:* For fall admission, 1/15 for domestic and international students. Application fee: $70 ($90 for international students). Electronic applications accepted. *Financial support:* In 2010–11, 66 students received support, including 50 fellowships with full and partial tuition reimbursements available (averaging $5,728 per year), 1 research assistantship with full and partial tuition reimbursement available (averaging $1,778 per year), 37 teaching assistantships with partial tuition reimbursements available (averaging $9,866 per year); career-related internships or fieldwork, Federal Work-Study, institutionally sponsored loans, health care benefits, tuition waivers (full and partial), and unspecified assistantships also available. Financial award application deadline: 1/15; financial award applicants required to submit FAFSA. *Faculty research:* Music theory, ethnomusicology, musicology, music performance, music composition. *Unit head:* Dr. Paul Berkowitz, Chair, Fax: 805-893-7194. *Application contact:* Carly Yartz, Student Affairs Officer, 805-893-4603, Fax: 805-893-7194, E-mail: cyartz@music.ucsb.edu.

University of California, Santa Cruz, Division of Graduate Studies, Division of the Arts, Department of Music, Santa Cruz, CA 95064. Offers ethnomusicology (MA); music (PhD), including cross-cultural and interdisciplinary studies; music composition (MA, DMA), including world music composition (DMA); music composition (DMA), including computer-assisted (algorithmic) composition; performance practice (MA). *Students:* 21 full-time (6 women), 4 part-time (1 woman); includes 7 minority (1 Black or African American, non-Hispanic/Latino; 4 Asian, non-Hispanic/Latino; 1 Native Hawaiian or other Pacific Islander, non-Hispanic/Latino; 1 Two or more races, non-Hispanic/Latino), 4 international. Average age 36. 33 applicants, 36% accepted, 6 enrolled. In 2010, 6 master's, 1 doctorate awarded. *Degree requirements:* For master's, one foreign language, thesis, recital; for doctorate, one foreign language, thesis/dissertation, qualifying and final examinations. *Entrance requirements:* For master's, GRE General Test, 3 letters of recommendation, writing or composition sample, 10-20 minute unedited recording; for doctorate, GRE General Test, 3 letters of recommendation, writing sample. Additional exam requirements/recommendations for international students: Required—TOEFL (minimum score 550 paper-based; 220 computer-based; 83 iBT); Recommended—IELTS (minimum score 8). *Application deadline:* For fall admission, 1/5 for domestic and international students. Application fee: $70 ($90 for international students). Electronic applications accepted. *Financial support:* Fellowships, research assistantships, teaching assistantships, institutionally sponsored loans and tuition waivers available. Financial award applicants required to submit FAFSA. *Faculty research:* Western music history, new music, composition, ethnomusicology, musicology. *Unit head:* Laura McShane, Graduate Program Coordinator, 831-459-3199, E-mail: lmcshane@ucsc.edu. *Application contact:* Laura McShane, Graduate Program Coordinator, 831-459-3199, E-mail: lmcshane@ucsc.edu.

University of Central Arkansas, Graduate School, College of Fine Arts and Communication, Department of Music, Conway, AR 72035-0001. Offers choral conducting (MM); instrumental conducting (MM); music education (MM); music theory (MM); performance (MM). *Accreditation:* NASM. Part-time programs available. *Faculty:* 12 full-time (4 women), 1 part-time/adjunct (0 women). *Students:* 13 full-time (5 women), 5 part-time (4 women); includes 3 minority (2 Black or African American, non-Hispanic/Latino; 1 American Indian or Alaska Native, non-Hispanic/Latino), 2 international. Average age 29. 13 applicants, 100% accepted, 8 enrolled. In 2010, 6 master's awarded. *Degree requirements:* For master's, comprehensive exam, thesis optional. *Entrance requirements:* For master's, GRE General Test, minimum GPA of 2.7. Additional exam requirements/recommendations for international students: Required—TOEFL (minimum score 550 paper-based; 213 computer-based). *Application deadline:* For fall admission, 3/1 priority date for domestic students; for spring admission, 10/1 priority date for domestic students. Applications are processed on a rolling basis. Application fee: $25 ($50 for international students). *Financial support:* Federal Work-Study, scholarships/grants, tuition waivers (partial), and unspecified assistantships available. Financial award application deadline: 2/15; financial award applicants required to submit FAFSA. *Unit head:* Jeffrey Jarvis, Unit Head, 501-450-3163. *Application contact:* Brenda Herring, Admissions Assistant, 501-450-5065, Fax: 501-450-5678, E-mail: bherring@uca.edu.

University of Central Florida, College of Arts and Humanities, Department of Music, Orlando, FL 32816. Offers MA. *Accreditation:* NASM; NCATE. Part-time and evening/weekend programs available. *Faculty:* 23 full-time (2 women), 17 part-time/adjunct (10 women). *Students:* 15 full-time (7 women), 19 part-time (9 women); includes 1 Black or African American, non-Hispanic/Latino; 1 American Indian or Alaska Native, non-Hispanic/Latino; 2 Asian, non-Hispanic/Latino; 4 Hispanic/Latino. Average age 34. 34 applicants, 65% accepted, 15 enrolled. In 2010, 10 master's awarded. *Entrance requirements:* For master's, GRE General Test. Additional exam requirements/recommendations for international students: Required—TOEFL. *Application deadline:* For fall admission, 7/15 for domestic students; for spring admission, 12/1 for domestic students. Application fee: $30. Electronic applications accepted. *Expenses:* Tuition, state resident: part-time $256.56 per credit hour. Tuition, nonresident: part-time $1011.52 per credit hour. Part-time tuition and fees vary according to program. *Financial support:* In 2010–11, 7 students received support, including 1 fellowship with partial tuition reimbursement available (averaging $4,000 per year), 1 research assistantship (averaging $8,000 per year), 6 teaching assistantships with partial tuition reimbursements available (averaging $10,100 per year); career-related internships or fieldwork, Federal Work-Study, institutionally sponsored loans, tuition waivers (partial), and unspecified assistantships also available. Financial award application deadline: 3/1; financial award applicants required to submit FAFSA. *Unit head:* Jeffrey Moore, Chair, 407-823-2879, Fax: 407-823-3378, E-mail: jmmoore@mail.ucf.edu. *Application contact:* Jeffrey Moore, Chair, 407-823-2879, Fax: 407-823-3378, E-mail: jmmoore@mail.ucf.edu.

University of Central Missouri, The Graduate School, College of Arts, Humanities and Social Sciences, Warrensburg, MO 64093. Offers English (MA); history (MA); mass communication (MA); music (MA); psychology (MS); speech communication (MA); teaching English as a second language (MA); theatre (MA). Part-time programs available. *Entrance requirements:* Additional exam requirements/recommendations for international students: Required—TOEFL (minimum score 550 paper-based; 79 computer-based). Electronic applications accepted.

University of Central Oklahoma, College of Graduate Studies and Research, College of Fine Arts and Design, Department of Music, Edmond, OK 73034-5209. Offers music education (MM); performance (MM). *Accreditation:* NASM. Part-time programs available. *Entrance requirements:* Additional exam requirements/recommendations for international students: Required—TOEFL (minimum score 550 paper-based; 213 computer-based). Electronic applications accepted. *Faculty research:* Opera/orchestral composition, western/world music, ethnomusicology, literature for librettos.

University of Chicago, Division of the Humanities, Department of Music, Chicago, IL 60637-1513. Offers AM, PhD. *Degree requirements:* For master's, 2 foreign languages, thesis; for doctorate, 3 foreign languages, thesis/dissertation. *Entrance requirements:* For master's and doctorate, GRE General Test. Additional exam requirements/recommendations for international students: Required—TOEFL.

University of Cincinnati, Graduate School, College-Conservatory of Music, Division of Composition, Musicology and Theory, Cincinnati, OH 45221. Offers composition (MM, DMA); music history (MM); music theory (MM, PhD); musicology (PhD). *Accreditation:* NASM. *Degree requirements:* For master's, variable foreign language requirement, comprehensive exam, thesis; for doctorate, variable foreign language requirement, comprehensive exam, thesis/dissertation. *Entrance requirements:* For master's and doctorate, GRE General Test, interview. Additional exam requirements/recommendations for international students: Required—TOEFL (minimum score 520 paper-based; 190 computer-based). Electronic applications accepted.

University of Cincinnati, Graduate School, College-Conservatory of Music, Division of Ensembles and Conducting, Cincinnati, OH 45221. Offers choral conducting (MM, DMA); orchestral conducting (MM, DMA); wind conducting (MM, DMA). *Accreditation:* NASM. *Degree requirements:* For master's, comprehensive exam, conducting performances; for doctorate, one foreign language, comprehensive exam, thesis/dissertation, conducting performances, lecture recital. *Entrance requirements:* For master's and doctorate, GRE General Test, audition, interview. Additional exam requirements/recommendations for international students: Required—TOEFL (minimum score 520 paper-based; 190 computer-based). Electronic applications accepted.

University of Cincinnati, Graduate School, College-Conservatory of Music, Division of Keyboard Studies, Cincinnati, OH 45221. Offers MM, DMA, AD. *Degree requirements:* For master's, comprehensive exam; for doctorate, one foreign language, comprehensive exam, thesis/dissertation. *Entrance requirements:* For master's and doctorate, GRE General Test, audition; for AD, audition. Additional exam requirements/recommendations for international students: Required—TOEFL (minimum score 520 paper-based; 190 computer-based). Electronic applications accepted.

University of Cincinnati, Graduate School, College-Conservatory of Music, Division of Performance Studies, Cincinnati, OH 45221. Offers performance (MM, DMA, AD). MM, DMA, and AD are available for every instrument. *Accreditation:* NASM. *Degree requirements:* For master's, comprehensive exam, recitals; for doctorate, one foreign language, comprehensive exam, thesis/dissertation, recitals; for AD, recitals. *Entrance requirements:* For master's and doctorate, GRE General Test, audition. Additional exam requirements/recommendations for international students: Required—TOEFL (minimum score 520 paper-based; 190 computer-based). Electronic applications accepted. *Faculty research:* Performance, guest teaching.

University of Cincinnati, Graduate School, College-Conservatory of Music, Divisions of Opera, Musical Theater, Drama, and Arts Administration, Cincinnati, OH 45221. Offers arts administration (MA); directing (MFA); theater design and production (MFA); voice and opera (MM, DMA); MBA/MA. *Accreditation:* NAST (one or more programs are accredited). *Degree requirements:* For master's, final project. *Entrance requirements:* For master's, GMAT (MA), audition/interview. Additional exam requirements/recommendations for international students: Required—TOEFL (minimum score 520 paper-based; 190 computer-based). Electronic applications accepted.

University of Colorado Boulder, Graduate School, College of Music, Boulder, CO 80309. Offers composition (M Mus, D Mus A); conducting (M Mus); instrumental conducting and literature (D Mus A); literature and performance of choral music (D Mus A); music education (M Mus Ed, PhD); musicology (PhD); performance (M Mus, D Mus A); performance/pedagogy (M Mus, D Mus A); theory (M Mus). *Accreditation:* NASM. *Faculty:* 56 full-time (20 women). *Students:* 202 full-time (101 women), 56 part-time (29 women); includes 3 Black or African American, non-Hispanic/Latino; 11 Asian, non-Hispanic/Latino; 13 Hispanic/Latino; 3 Two or more races, non-Hispanic/Latino, 28 international. Average age 30. 493 applicants, 83 enrolled. In 2010, 46 master's, 34 doctorates awarded. Terminal master's awarded for partial completion of doctoral program. *Degree requirements:* For master's, variable foreign language requirement, comprehensive exam, thesis or alternative, recital; for doctorate, variable foreign language requirement, thesis/dissertation. *Entrance requirements:* For master's, GRE General Test, GRE Subject Test (music literature), minimum undergraduate GPA of 2.75; for doctorate, GRE General Test, GRE Subject Test, audition, sample of research. *Application deadline:* For fall admission, 3/1 priority date for domestic students, 12/1 for international students. Applications are processed on a rolling basis. Application fee: $50 ($60 for international students). *Financial support:* In 2010–11, 88 fellowships (averaging $3,325 per year), 38 research assistantships (averaging $6,550 per year) were awarded; tuition waivers (full) also available. Financial award application deadline: 3/1. Total annual research expenditures: $8,116.

University of Colorado Denver, College of Arts and Media, Denver, CO 80217-3364. Offers recording arts (MS). Part-time and evening/weekend programs available. *Faculty:* 34 full-time (11 women), 2 part-time/adjunct (0 women). *Students:* 13 full-time (0 women), 2 part-time (0 women); includes 1 Hispanic/Latino. Average age 30. 20 applicants, 45% accepted, 8 enrolled. In 2010, 4 master's awarded. *Degree requirements:* For master's, 34 credits, thesis/portfolio. *Entrance requirements:* For master's, GRE General Test, minimum GPA of 3.0, portfolio, resume, interview, 3 letters of recommendation. Additional exam requirements/recommendations for international students: Required—TOEFL (minimum score 500 paper-based; 173 computer-based). *Application deadline:* For fall admission, 2/15 for domestic students, 1/1 for international students. Application fee: $50 ($75 for international students). Electronic applications accepted. *Expenses:* Contact institution. *Financial support:* In 2010–11, 2 students received support. Federal Work-Study and scholarships/grants available. Financial award application deadline: 4/1; financial award applicants required to submit FAFSA. *Faculty research:* Audio forensics, audio pedagogy, concert recordings, digital audio workstations, music law. Total annual research expenditures: $711,741. *Unit head:* Dr. David Dynak, Dean, 303-556-2279, Fax: 303-556-2335, E-mail: david.dynak@ucdenver.edu. *Application contact:* Clark Strickland, Assistant Dean for Programs and Resources, 303-556-2279, Fax: 303-556-2335, E-mail: clark.strickland@ucdenver.edu.

University of Connecticut, Graduate School, School of Fine Arts, Department of Music, Storrs, CT 06269. Offers conducting (M Mus, DMA); historical musicology (MA); music (Performer's Certificate); music education (M Mus, PhD); music theory (MA); music theory and history (PhD); performance (M Mus, DMA). *Accreditation:* NASM. Terminal master's awarded for partial completion of doctoral program. *Degree requirements:* For master's, comprehensive exam; for doctorate, thesis/dissertation. *Entrance requirements:* For master's, GRE General Test, GRE Subject Test, audition; for doctorate, GRE Subject Test, MAT, audition. Additional exam requirements/recommendations for international students: Required—TOEFL (minimum score 550 paper-based; 213 computer-based).

University of Delaware, College of Arts and Sciences, Department of Music, Newark, DE 19716. Offers composition (MM); music education (MM); performance (MM). *Accreditation:* NASM. Part-time programs available. *Entrance requirements:* For master's, audition. Additional exam requirements/recommendations for international students: Required—TOEFL. Electronic applications accepted. *Faculty research:* Teaching of music.

University of Denver, Division of Arts, Humanities and Social Sciences, Lamont School of Music, Denver, CO 80208. Offers choral conducting (MA); composition (MA); jazz and commercial music (Certificate); jazz studies (MM); music theory (MA); musicology (MA); orchestral conducting (MM); performance (MM); piano pedagogy (MM); Suzuki pedagogy (MA, MM), including cello (MM), violin (MA); Suzuki teaching (Certificate); wind conducting (MM). *Accreditation:* NASM. Part-time programs available. *Faculty:* 26 full-time (8 women), 41 part-time/adjunct (20 women). *Students:* 22 full-time (12 women), 43 part-time (22 women); includes 8 minority (1 Black or African American, non-Hispanic/Latino; 3 Asian, non-Hispanic/Latino; 2 Hispanic/Latino; 1 Native Hawaiian or other Pacific Islander, non-Hispanic/Latino; 1 Two or more races, non-Hispanic/Latino), 6 international. Average age 28. 97 applicants, 58% accepted, 34 enrolled. In 2010, 24 master's, 3 other advanced degrees awarded. *Degree requirements:* For master's, one foreign language, comprehensive exam (for some programs), thesis (for some programs), recital or project (for performance). *Entrance requirements:* For master's, GRE General Test. Additional exam requirements/recommendations for international students: Required—TOEFL (minimum score 550 paper-based; 80 iBT). *Application deadline:* Applications are processed on a rolling basis. Application fee: $60. Electronic applications accepted. *Expenses:* Tuition: Full-time $35,604; part-time $29,670 per year. Required fees: $687 per year. Tuition and fees vary according to program. *Financial support:* In 2010–11, 35 teaching assistantships with full and partial tuition reimbursements (averaging $6,600 per year) were awarded; career-related internships or fieldwork, Federal Work-Study, institutionally sponsored loans, scholarships/grants, and unspecified assistantships also available. Support available to part-time students. Financial award application deadline: 3/1; financial award applicants required to submit FAFSA. *Unit head:* Joseph Docksey, Director, 303-871-6986, Fax: 303-871-3118, E-mail: jdocksey@du.edu. *Application contact:* Jerrod Price, Director of Admission, 303-871-6950, Fax: 303-871-3118, E-mail: jerrod.price@du.edu.

University of Florida, Graduate School, College of Fine Arts, School of Music, Gainesville, FL 32611. Offers choral conducting (MM, PhD); composition/theory (MM, PhD); ethnomusicology (PhD); instrumental conducting (MM, PhD); music (MM, PhD); music education (MM, PhD); music history and literature (MM); musicology (PhD); performance (MM); sacred music (MM). *Accreditation:* NASM. *Faculty:* 32 full-time (9 women), 1 part-time/adjunct (0 women). *Students:* 78 full-time (39 women), 26 part-time (14 women); includes 5 Black or African American, non-Hispanic/Latino; 1 American Indian or Alaska Native, non-Hispanic/Latino; 2 Asian, non-Hispanic/Latino; 5 Hispanic/Latino, 22 international. Average age 32. 104 applicants, 49% accepted, 33 enrolled. In 2010, 24 master's, 4 doctorates awarded. *Degree requirements:* For master's, variable foreign language requirement, comprehensive exam, thesis, recital; for doctorate, thesis/dissertation. *Entrance requirements:* For master's and doctorate, GRE General Test, audition, minimum GPA of 3.0. Additional exam requirements/recommendations for international students: Required—TOEFL (minimum score 550 paper-based; 213 computer-based; 80 iBT), IELTS (minimum score 6). *Application deadline:* For fall admission, 1/1 priority date for domestic students, 1/1 for international students; for spring admission, 11/1 for domestic and international students. Applications are processed on a rolling basis. Application fee: $30. Electronic applications accepted. *Expenses:* Tuition, state resident: full-time $10,915.92. Tuition, nonresident: full-time $28,309. *Financial support:* In 2010–11, 28 students received support, including 3 fellowships with full tuition reimbursements available, 7 research assistantships with tuition reimbursements available (averaging $15,825 per year), 18 teaching assistantships with tuition reimbursements available (averaging $11,678 per year); unspecified assistantships also available. Financial award applicants required to submit FAFSA. *Unit head:* John A. Duff, Program Director, 352-273-3167 Ext. 207, E-mail: jduff@arts.ufl.edu. *Application contact:* Dr. Leslie S. Odom, Graduate Coordinator, 352-273-3172, Fax: 352-352-0461, E-mail: lodom@arts.ufl.edu.

University of Georgia, College of Arts and Sciences, Hugh Hodgson School of Music, Athens, GA 30602. Offers MA, MM, DMA, PhD. *Accreditation:* NASM. *Faculty:* 38 full-time (10 women). *Students:* 102 full-time (48 women), 36 part-time (9 women); includes 4 Black or African American, non-Hispanic/Latino; 5 Asian, non-Hispanic/Latino; 1 Hispanic/Latino; 1 Native Hawaiian or other Pacific Islander, non-Hispanic/Latino, 11 international. 162 applicants, 49% accepted, 52 enrolled. In 2010, 18 master's, 16 doctorates awarded. *Degree requirements:* For master's, variable foreign language requirement, thesis (MA); for doctorate, variable foreign language requirement, thesis/dissertation. *Entrance requirements:* For master's and doctorate, GRE General Test. *Application deadline:* For fall admission, 7/1 priority date for domestic students; for spring admission, 11/15 for domestic students. Application fee: $50. Electronic applications accepted. *Expenses:* Tuition, state resident: full-time $7200; part-time $344 per credit hour. Tuition, nonresident: full-time $21,900; part-time $944 per credit hour. Tuition and fees vary according to course load and program. *Financial support:* Fellowships, research assistantships, teaching assistantships, unspecified assistantships available. *Unit head:* Dr. Dale Monson, Director, 706-542-2776, Fax: 706-542-2773, E-mail: dmonson@uga.edu. *Application contact:* Dr. Adrian Childs, Graduate Coordinator, 206-542-2765, E-mail: apchilds@uga.edu.

University of Hartford, The Hartt School, West Hartford, CT 06117-1599. Offers choral conducting (MM Ed); composition (MM, DMA, Artist Diploma, Diploma); conducting (MM, DMA, Artist Diploma, Diploma), including choral (MM, Diploma), instrumental (MM, Diploma); early childhood education (MM Ed); instrumental conducting (MM Ed); Kodály (MM Ed); music (CAGS); music education (DMA, PhD); music history (MM); music theory (MM); pedagogy (MM Ed); performance (MM, MM Ed, DMA, Artist Diploma, Diploma); research (MM Ed); technology (MM Ed). Part-time programs available. *Degree requirements:* For master's, variable foreign language requirement, thesis (for some programs), recital; for doctorate, variable foreign language requirement, thesis/dissertation (for some programs), recital; for other advanced degree, recital. *Entrance requirements:* For master's, audition, letters of recommendation; for doctorate, proficiency exam, audition, interview, research paper; for other advanced degree, audition. Additional exam requirements/recommendations for international students: Required—TOEFL. Electronic applications accepted. *Expenses:* Contact institution.

University of Hawaii at Manoa, Graduate Division, College of Arts and Humanities, Department of Music, Honolulu, HI 96822. Offers M Mus, MA, PhD. *Accreditation:* NASM. Part-time programs available. *Students:* 6 full-time (2 women), 12 part-time (10 women); includes 9 minority (4 Asian, non-Hispanic/Latino; 2 Native Hawaiian or other Pacific Islander, non-Hispanic/Latino; 3 Two or more races, non-Hispanic/Latino), 1 international. Average age 35. 13 applicants, 69% accepted, 8 enrolled. *Degree requirements:* For master's, variable foreign language requirement, thesis optional; for doctorate, variable foreign language requirement, comprehensive exam, thesis/dissertation. *Entrance requirements:* For master's, GRE General Test, diagnostic exams in acoustics theory; for doctorate, diagnostic exams in music history and theory, GRE General Test. Additional exam requirements/recommendations for international students: Required—TOEFL (minimum score 540 paper-based; 207 computer-based; 76 iBT), IELTS (minimum score 5). *Application deadline:* For fall admission, 2/1 for domestic students, 1/15 for international students; for spring admission, 9/1 for domestic students, 8/1 for international students. Application fee: $60. *Financial support:* In 2010–11, 1 fellowship (averaging $2,000 per year), 1 research assistantship (averaging $17,495 per year), 1 teaching assistantship (averaging $14,382 per year) were awarded; Federal Work-Study and tuition waivers (full) also available. *Faculty research:* Original compositions, nineteenth century German music, Korean and Indonesian music, piano/voice performance, Pacific music. *Application contact:* Lesley Wright, Graduate Field Chairperson, 808-956-7756, Fax: 808-956-9657, E-mail: wright@hawaii.edu.

University of Houston, College of Liberal Arts and Social Sciences, Moores School of Music, Houston, TX 77204. Offers accompanying and chamber music (MM); applied music (MM); composition (MM); music education (DMA); music theory (MM); performance (DMA). *Accreditation:* NASM. Part-time programs available. *Faculty:* 25 full-time (5 women), 21 part-time/adjunct (8 women). *Students:* 110 full-time (56 women), 42 part-time (21 women); includes 26 minority (6 Black or African American, non-Hispanic/Latino; 7 Asian, non-Hispanic/Latino; 6 Hispanic/Latino; 1 Native Hawaiian or other Pacific Islander, non-Hispanic/Latino; 6 Two or more races, non-Hispanic/Latino), 32 international. Average age 29. 128 applicants, 50% accepted, 42 enrolled. In 2010, 37 master's, 5 doctorates awarded. *Degree requirements:* For master's, one foreign language, comprehensive exam, recital; for doctorate, one foreign language, comprehensive exam, thesis/dissertation. *Entrance requirements:* For master's, audition, resume, 3 letters of recommendation; for doctorate, writing sample, audition, statement of purpose, resume. Additional exam requirements/recommendations for international students: Required—TOEFL (minimum score 550 paper-based; 213 computer-based; 79 iBT), IELTS (minimum score 6.5). *Application deadline:* For fall admission, 3/1 for domestic and international students; for spring admission, 11/1 for domestic and international students. Application fee: $0 ($75 for international students). Electronic applications accepted. *Expenses:* Tuition, state resident: full-time $8592; part-time $358 per credit hour. Tuition, nonresident: full-time $16,032; part-time $668 per credit hour. Required fees: $2889. Tuition and fees vary according to course load and program. *Financial support:* In 2010–11, 3 fellowships with full tuition reimbursements (averaging $8,767 per year), 56 teaching assistantships with full tuition reimbursements (averaging $5,112 per year) were awarded; career-related internships or fieldwork, Federal Work-Study, institutionally sponsored loans, scholarships/grants, health care benefits, and unspecified assistantships also available. Support available to part-time students. Financial award application deadline: 2/1. *Faculty research:* Twentieth century music, Baroque music, history of music theory, music analysis. *Unit head:* David Ashley White, Chairperson, 713-743-3009, Fax: 713-743-3166, E-mail: dwhite@uh.edu. *Application contact:* Douglas Goldberg, Graduate Advisor, 713-743-3314, Fax: 713-743-3166, E-mail: gradmusic@uh.edu.

University of Idaho, College of Graduate Studies, College of Letters, Arts and Social Sciences, Lionel Hampton School of Music, Moscow, ID 83844-2282. Offers M Mus, MA. *Accreditation:* NASM. *Faculty:* 16 full-time, 1 part-time/adjunct. *Students:* 14 full-time, 10 part-time. Average age 31. In 2010, 8 master's awarded. *Degree requirements:* For master's, one foreign language, thesis or alternative. *Entrance requirements:* For master's, minimum GPA of 2.8. *Application deadline:* For fall admission, 8/1 for domestic students; for spring admission, 12/15 for domestic students. Applications are processed on a rolling basis. Application fee: $60. Electronic applications accepted. *Expenses:* Tuition, nonresident: part-time $580 per credit. Required fees: $306 per credit. *Financial support:* Research assistantships, teaching assistantships available. Financial award applicants required to submit FAFSA. *Unit head:* Dr. Kevin B. Woelfel, Director, 208-885-6231, E-mail: music@uidaho.edu. *Application contact:* Dr. Kevin B. Woelfel, Director, 208-885-6231, E-mail: music@uidaho.edu.

University of Illinois at Urbana–Champaign, Graduate College, College of Fine and Applied Arts, School of Music, Champaign, IL 61820. Offers music (M Mus, DMA, AD); music education (MME, Ed D, PhD); musicology (PhD). *Accreditation:* NASM. *Faculty:* 68 full-time (14 women), 8 part-time/adjunct (4 women). *Students:* 278 full-time (138 women), 90 part-time (49 women); includes 7 Black or African American, non-Hispanic/Latino; 11 Asian, non-Hispanic/Latino; 12 Hispanic/Latino; 6 Two or more races, non-Hispanic/Latino, 137 international. 573 applicants, 23% accepted, 96 enrolled. In 2010, 67 master's, 32 doctorates awarded. *Entrance requirements:* For master's and doctorate, minimum GPA of 3.0. Additional exam requirements/recommendations for international students: Required—TOEFL (minimum score 590 paper-based; 243 computer-based). *Application deadline:* Applications are processed on a rolling basis. Application fee: $75 ($90 for international students). Electronic applications accepted. *Financial support:* In 2010–11, 19 fellowships, 6 research assistantships, 112 teaching assistantships were awarded; tuition waivers (full and partial) also available. *Unit head:* Karl Kramer, Director, 217-244-2676, Fax: 217-244-4585, E-mail: kramerk@illinois.edu. *Application contact:* Jennifer Phillips, Office Manager, 217-244-8385, Fax: 217-244-4585, E-mail: jhorn@illinois.edu.

The University of Iowa, Graduate College, College of Liberal Arts and Sciences, School of Music, Iowa City, IA 52242-1316. Offers MA, MFA, DMA, PhD. *Accreditation:* NASM. *Degree requirements:* For master's, thesis (for some programs), exam; for doctorate, comprehensive exam, thesis/dissertation. *Entrance requirements:* For master's and doctorate, minimum GPA of 3.0. Additional exam requirements/recommendations for international students: Required—TOEFL (minimum score 550 paper-based; 213 computer-based; 81 iBT). Electronic applications accepted.

The University of Kansas, Graduate Studies, School of Music, Program in Music, Lawrence, KS 66045. Offers MM, DMA, PhD. *Accreditation:* NASM. *Faculty:* 41 full-time (10 women), 11 part-time/adjunct (3 women). *Students:* 129 full-time (67 women), 28 part-time (14 women); includes 18 minority (4 Black or African American, non-Hispanic/Latino; 3 Asian, non-Hispanic/Latino; 11 Hispanic/Latino), 33 international. Average age 30. 181 applicants, 51% accepted, 42 enrolled. In 2010, 20 master's, 21 doctorates awarded. *Degree requirements:* For master's, comprehensive exam (for some programs), thesis (for some programs), recitals; for doctorate, comprehensive exam, thesis/dissertation, recitals (DMA). *Entrance requirements:* For master's, KU Musicology and Music Theory diagnostic exam, minimum GPA of 3.0, audition (performance); for doctorate, GRE (PhD); KU Musicology and Music Theory diagnostic exam, minimum GPA of 3.0, audition (DMA). Additional exam requirements/recommendations for international students: Required—TOEFL (minimum score 53 paper-based; 20 computer-based; 20 iBT), TOEFL or IELTS (minimum score 6). *Application deadline:* For fall admission, 12/15 priority date for domestic and international students; for spring admission, 5/1 priority date for domestic and international students. Applications are processed on a rolling basis. Application fee: $55 ($65 for international students). Electronic applications accepted. *Expenses:* Tuition, state resident: full-time $7092; part-time $295.50 per credit hour. Tuition, nonresident: full-time $16,590; part-time $691.25 per credit hour. Required fees: $858; $71.49 per credit hour. Tuition and fees vary according to course load, campus/location and program. *Financial support:* Fellowships with full tuition reimbursements, teaching assistantships with full and partial tuition reimbursements, institutionally sponsored loans, scholarships/grants, and unspecified assistantships available. Financial award application deadline: 12/15; financial award applicants required to submit FAFSA. *Faculty research:* Musicology, music theory, church music, music composition, performance. *Unit head:* Dr. Robert Walzel, 785-864-3421, Fax: 785-864-5866, E-mail: music@ku.edu. *Application contact:* Kay Coblentz, Senior Administrative Associate, 785-864-2862, Fax: 785-864-5866, E-mail: kcoblent@ku.edu.

University of Kentucky, Graduate School, College of Fine Arts, Program in Music, Lexington, KY 40506-0032. Offers music (PhD); music composition (MM); music education (MM); music performance (MM); music theory (MA); musical arts (DMA); musicology (MA). *Accreditation:* NASM. Part-time and evening/weekend programs available. *Degree requirements:* For master's, variable foreign language requirement, comprehensive exam, thesis (for some programs); for doctorate, variable foreign language requirement, comprehensive exam, thesis/dissertation. *Entrance requirements:* For master's, GRE General Test, minimum undergraduate GPA of 2.75; for doctorate, GRE General Test, minimum undergraduate GPA of 2.75, graduate 3.0. Additional exam requirements/recommendations for international students: Required—TOEFL (minimum score 550 paper-based; 213 computer-based). Electronic applications accepted. *Faculty research:* Musicology, music theory, jazz, music education, performance and conducting.

University of Lethbridge, School of Graduate Studies, Lethbridge, AB T1K 3M4, Canada. Offers accounting (MScM); addictions counseling (M Sc); agricultural biotechnology (M Sc); agricultural studies (M Sc, MA); anthropology (MA); archaeology (MA); art (MA, MFA); biochemistry (M Sc); biological sciences (M Sc); biomolecular science (PhD); biosystems and biodiversity (PhD); Canadian studies (MA); chemistry (M Sc); computer science (M Sc); computer science and geographical information science (M Sc); counseling psychology (M Ed); dramatic arts (MA); earth, space, and physical science (PhD); economics (MA); educational leadership (M Ed); English (MA); environmental science (M Sc); evolution and behavior (PhD); exercise science (M Sc); finance (MScM); French (MA); French/German (MA); French/Spanish (MA); general education (M Ed); general management (MScM); geography (M Sc, MA); German (MA); health science (M Sc); history (MA); human resource management and labour relations (MScM); individualized multidisciplinary (M Sc, MA); information systems (MScM); international management (MScM); kinesiology (M Sc, MA); management (M Sc, MA); marketing (MScM); mathematics (M Sc); music (M Mus, MA); Native American studies (MA); neuroscience (M Sc, PhD); new media (MA); nursing (M Sc); philosophy (MA); physics (M Sc); policy and strategy (MScM); political science (MA); psychology (M Sc, MA); religious studies (MA); social sciences (MA); sociology (MA); theatre and dramatic arts (MFA); theoretical and computational science (PhD); urban and regional studies (MA); women's studies (MA). Part-time and evening/weekend programs available. *Degree requirements:* For doctorate, comprehensive exam, thesis/dissertation. *Entrance requirements:* For master's, GMAT (M Sc in management), bachelor's degree in related field, minimum GPA of 3.0 during previous 20 graded semester courses, 2 years teaching or related experience (M Ed); for doctorate, master's degree, minimum graduate GPA of 3.5. Additional exam requirements/recommendations for international students: Required—TOEFL. *Faculty research:* Movement and brain plasticity, gibberellin physiology, photosynthesis, carbon cycling, molecular properties of main-group ring components.

University of Louisiana at Lafayette, College of the Arts, School of Music, Lafayette, LA 70504. Offers conducting (MM); pedagogy (MM); vocal and instrumental performance (MM). *Accreditation:* NASM. *Degree requirements:* For master's, thesis or alternative. *Entrance requirements:* For master's, GRE General Test, minimum GPA of 2.75. Additional exam requirements/recommendations for international students: Required—TOEFL (minimum score 550 paper-based; 213 computer-based). Electronic applications accepted. *Faculty research:* Nineteenth century American music, trumpet pedagogy, fifteenth century Renaissance polyphony, Charles Ives.

University of Louisiana at Monroe, Graduate School, College of Arts and Sciences, School of Visual and Performing Arts, Program in Music, Monroe, LA 71209-0001. Offers MM. *Accreditation:* NASM. Part-time programs available. *Students:* 5 full-time (1 woman), 1 part-time (0 women). Average age 28. In 2010, 9 master's awarded. *Degree requirements:* For master's, thesis (for some programs). *Entrance requirements:* For master's, GRE, minimum GPA of 2.5. Additional exam requirements/recommendations for international students: Required—TOEFL (minimum score 500 paper-based; 173 computer-based; 61 iBT). *Application deadline:* For fall

Music

University of Louisiana at Monroe (continued)
admission, 8/24 priority date for domestic students, 7/1 for international students; for winter admission, 12/14 priority date for domestic students; for spring admission, 1/19 for domestic students, 11/1 for international students. Applications are processed on a rolling basis. Application fee: $20 ($30 for international students). Electronic applications accepted. *Expenses:* Tuition, state resident: full-time $2991; part-time $197 per credit hour. Tuition, nonresident: full-time $2991; part-time $197 per credit hour. International tuition: $10,288 full-time. *Financial support:* In 2010–11, 4 teaching assistantships with full tuition reimbursements (averaging $2,500 per year) were awarded; career-related internships or fieldwork, Federal Work-Study, and unspecified assistantships also available. Financial award application deadline: 4/1; financial award applicants required to submit FAFSA. *Unit head:* Dr. Mark R. Clark, Dean, 318-342-1569, Fax: 318-342-1599, E-mail: mclark@ulm.edu. *Application contact:* Dr. Mark R. Clark, Dean, 318-342-1569, Fax: 318-342-1599, E-mail: mclark@ulm.edu.

University of Louisville, Graduate School, School of Music, Louisville, KY 40292-0001. Offers music composition (MM); music education (MME); music history and literature (MM); music theory (MM); performance (MM). *Accreditation:* NASM. Part-time and evening/weekend programs available. *Faculty:* 33 full-time (10 women), 38 part-time/adjunct (10 women). *Students:* 57 full-time (22 women), 4 part-time (3 women); includes 1 Black or African American, non-Hispanic/Latino; 1 Asian, non-Hispanic/Latino; 2 Hispanic/Latino; 1 Two or more races, non-Hispanic/Latino, 13 international. Average age 27. 73 applicants, 70% accepted, 31 enrolled. In 2010, 28 master's awarded. *Degree requirements:* For master's, one foreign language, recital (performance), paper or thesis (music education), major composition (composition). *Entrance requirements:* For master's, GRE General Test, music history and theory entrance exams, jazz entrance exam, audition, portfolio. Additional exam requirements/recommendations for international students: Required—TOEFL (minimum score 550 paper-based; 213 computer-based; 79 iBT). *Application deadline:* For fall admission, 3/15 priority date for domestic and international students; for spring admission, 11/15 priority date for domestic and international students. Applications are processed on a rolling basis. Application fee: $50. Electronic applications accepted. *Expenses:* Tuition, state resident: full-time $9144; part-time $508 per credit hour. Tuition, nonresident: full-time $19,026; part-time $1057 per credit hour. Tuition and fees vary according to program and reciprocity agreements. *Financial support:* In 2010–11, 50 students received support, including 3 fellowships with full tuition reimbursements available (averaging $12,000 per year), 24 teaching assistantships with full tuition reimbursements available (averaging $12,000 per year); scholarships/grants, health care benefits, tuition waivers (full and partial), and unspecified assistantships also available. Financial award application deadline: 3/1; financial award applicants required to submit FAFSA. *Faculty research:* Performance, composition, music education, music therapy, music history. *Unit head:* Dr. Christopher Doane, Dean, 502-852-6907, Fax: 502-852-1874, E-mail: doane@louisville.edu. *Application contact:* Toni Robinson, Admissions Counselor, 502-852-1623, Fax: 502-852-0520, E-mail: toni.robinson@louisville.edu.

University of Maine, Graduate School, College of Liberal Arts and Sciences, Department of English, Orono, ME 04469. Offers composition and pedagogy (MA); creative (MA); gender and literature (MA); poetry and poetics (MA). Part-time and evening/weekend programs available. *Faculty:* 18 full-time (7 women), 20 part-time/adjunct (10 women). *Students:* 25 full-time (8 women), 6 part-time (5 women). Average age 28. 36 applicants, 47% accepted, 14 enrolled. In 2010, 13 degrees awarded. *Degree requirements:* For master's, one foreign language, thesis optional. *Entrance requirements:* For master's, GRE General Test, minimum GPA of 3.0. Additional exam requirements/recommendations for international students: Required—TOEFL. *Application deadline:* For fall admission, 2/1 priority date for domestic students. Applications are processed on a rolling basis. Application fee: $65. Electronic applications accepted. *Expenses:* Tuition, state resident: full-time $400. Tuition, nonresident: full-time $1050. *Financial support:* In 2010–11, 21 teaching assistantships with tuition reimbursements (averaging $12,790 per year) were awarded; Federal Work-Study and tuition waivers (full and partial) also available. Financial award application deadline: 3/1. *Faculty research:* Contemporary poetics, contemporary criticism, composition theory and pedagogy, feminist approaches to literature. *Unit head:* Dr. Naomi Jacobs, Chair, 207-581-3822, Fax: 207-581-1604. *Application contact:* Scott G. Delcourt, Associate Dean of the Graduate School, 207-581-3291, Fax: 207-581-3232, E-mail: graduate@maine.edu.

University of Maine, Graduate School, College of Liberal Arts and Sciences, School of Performing Arts, Orono, ME 04469. Offers choral conducting (MM); collaborative piano (MM); instrumental (MM); instrumental conducting (MM); vocal (MM). Part-time programs available. *Faculty:* 11 full-time (4 women), 4 part-time/adjunct (2 women). *Students:* 6 full-time (0 women), 9 part-time (2 women), 2 international. Average age 33. 2 applicants, 100% accepted, 2 enrolled. In 2010, 3 master's awarded. *Entrance requirements:* For master's, GRE General Test. Additional exam requirements/recommendations for international students: Required—TOEFL. *Application deadline:* For fall admission, 2/1 priority date for domestic students. Applications are processed on a rolling basis. Application fee: $65. Electronic applications accepted. *Expenses:* Tuition, state resident: full-time $400. Tuition, nonresident: full-time $1050. *Financial support:* In 2010–11, 4 teaching assistantships with tuition reimbursements (averaging $12,790 per year) were awarded; career-related internships or fieldwork, Federal Work-Study, institutionally sponsored loans, scholarships/grants, and tuition waivers (full and partial) also available. Support available to part-time students. Financial award application deadline: 3/1. *Unit head:* Dr. Currin Farnham, Director, 207-581-4702, Fax: 207-581-4701. *Application contact:* Scott G. Delcourt, Associate Dean of the Graduate School, 207-581-3291, Fax: 207-581-3232, E-mail: graduate@maine.edu.

The University of Manchester, School of Arts, Histories and Cultures, Manchester, United Kingdom. Offers anthropology, media and performance (PhD); applied theatre professional (PhD); archaeology (PhD); art history and visual studies (PhD); arts management and cultural policy (PhD); classics and ancient history (PhD); composition (PhD); creative writing (PhD); drama (PhD); economic and social history (PhD); electroacoustic composition (PhD); English and American studies (PhD); history (PhD); humanitarianism and conflict response (PhD); museology (PhD); music (PhD); musicology (PhD); religions and theology (PhD).

University of Manitoba, Faculty of Graduate Studies, Marcel A. Desautels Faculty of Music, Winnipeg, MB R3T 2N2, Canada. Offers M Mus.

University of Maryland, Baltimore County, Graduate School, College of Arts, Humanities and Social Sciences, Department of Music, Baltimore, MD 21250. Offers American contemporary music (Postbaccalaureate Certificate). *Faculty:* 10 full-time (5 women), 22 part-time/adjunct (11 women). *Students:* 3 full-time (1 woman); includes 1 Asian, non-Hispanic/Latino. Average age 25. 9 applicants, 56% accepted, 3 enrolled. In 2010, 5 Postbaccalaureate Certificates awarded. *Entrance requirements:* For degree, minimum GPA of 3.0, resume, reference letters, DVD of performance. *Application deadline:* For fall admission, 12/1 for domestic and international students; for winter admission, 1/30 for domestic and international students; for spring admission, 5/15 priority date for domestic students, 4/15 for international students. Applications are processed on a rolling basis. Application fee: $50. *Expenses:* Contact institution. *Financial support:* Applicants required to submit FAFSA. *Faculty research:* Music, composition, performance, music technology, contemporary music. *Unit head:* Dr. E. Michael Richards, Chair, 410-455-3064, E-mail: emrichards@umbc.edu. *Application contact:* Dr. Anna Rubin, Director, 410-455-3190, Fax: 410-455-1181, E-mail: airubin@umbc.edu.

University of Maryland, College Park, Academic Affairs, College of Arts and Humanities, School of Music, Program in Ethnomusicology, College Park, MD 20742. Offers MA. *Students:* 23 full-time (17 women), 5 part-time (4 women); includes 1 American Indian or Alaska Native, non-Hispanic/Latino; 1 Asian, non-Hispanic/Latino; 1 Hispanic/Latino, 8 international. 3 applicants, 67% accepted, 0 enrolled. In 2010, 2 master's awarded. *Degree requirements:* For master's, comprehensive exam, thesis optional, oral defense. *Entrance requirements:* Additional exam requirements/recommendations for international students: Required—TOEFL. *Application deadline:* For fall admission, 12/1 for domestic and international students; for spring admission, 6/1 for international students. Application fee: $75. *Expenses:* Tuition, state resident: part-time $471 per credit hour. Tuition, nonresident: part-time $1016 per credit hour. Required fees: $337 per term. *Financial support:* In 2010–11, 12 teaching assistantships (averaging $16,022 per year) were awarded; fellowships also available. *Unit head:* Dr. Robert Gibson, Director, 301-405-5553, Fax: 301-314-9504, E-mail: rgibson@umd.edu. *Application contact:* Dr. Charles A. Caramello, Dean of Graduate School, 301-405-0358, Fax: 301-314-9305, E-mail: ccaramel@umd.edu.

University of Maryland, College Park, Academic Affairs, College of Arts and Humanities, School of Music, Program in Music, College Park, MD 20742. Offers M Ed, MA, MM, DMA, Ed D, PhD. *Students:* 162 full-time (81 women), 47 part-time (23 women); includes 36 minority (7 Black or African American, non-Hispanic/Latino; 18 Asian, non-Hispanic/Latino; 9 Hispanic/Latino; 2 Two or more races, non-Hispanic/Latino), 31 international. 652 applicants, 20% accepted, 63 enrolled. In 2010, 54 master's, 37 doctorates awarded. *Entrance requirements:* Additional exam requirements/recommendations for international students: Required—TOEFL. *Application deadline:* For fall admission, 12/1 for domestic and international students. Application fee: $75. *Expenses:* Tuition, state resident: part-time $471 per credit hour. Tuition, nonresident: part-time $1016 per credit hour. Required fees: $337 per term. *Financial support:* In 2010–11, 4 fellowships with full and partial tuition reimbursements (averaging $14,501 per year), 103 teaching assistantships (averaging $15,886 per year) were awarded. *Unit head:* Dr. Robert Gibson, Director, 301-405-5553, Fax: 301-314-9504, E-mail: rgibson@umd.edu. *Application contact:* Dean of Graduate School, 301-405-0358, Fax: 301-314-9305.

University of Maryland, College Park, Academic Affairs, College of Arts and Humanities, School of Theatre, Dance and Performance Studies, College Park, MD 20742. Offers dance (MFA); performance (MFA); theatre and performance studies (MA, PhD); theatre design (MFA). *Faculty:* 25 full-time (14 women), 9 part-time/adjunct (6 women). *Students:* 58 full-time (33 women), 2 part-time (1 woman); includes 7 minority (2 Black or African American, non-Hispanic/Latino; 1 Asian, non-Hispanic/Latino; 3 Hispanic/Latino; 1 Native Hawaiian or other Pacific Islander, non-Hispanic/Latino), 4 international. 138 applicants, 26% accepted, 26 enrolled. In 2010, 9 master's, 4 doctorates awarded. *Degree requirements:* For master's, comprehensive exam, thesis optional; for doctorate, thesis/dissertation. *Entrance requirements:* For master's, GRE General Test, minimum GPA of 3.0, writing sample, portfolio (MFA), 3 letters of recommendation; for doctorate, GRE General Test, writing sample. Additional exam requirements/recommendations for international students: Required—TOEFL. *Application deadline:* For fall admission, 2/1 for domestic and international students. Applications are processed on a rolling basis. Application fee: $75. Electronic applications accepted. *Expenses:* Tuition, state resident: part-time $471 per credit hour. Tuition, nonresident: part-time $1016 per credit hour. Required fees: $337 per term. *Financial support:* In 2010–11, 3 fellowships with full tuition reimbursements (averaging $19,667 per year), 49 teaching assistantships (averaging $19,543 per year) were awarded; research assistantships, Federal Work-Study and scholarships/grants also available. Support available to part-time students. Financial award applicants required to submit FAFSA. *Faculty research:* Dance, performance, history/theory, design and production. *Unit head:* Daniel M. Wagner, Professor and Director, 301-405-6679, E-mail: dmwagner@umd.edu. *Application contact:* Dr. Charles A. Caramello, Dean of Graduate School, 301-405-0358, Fax: 301-314-9305.

University of Massachusetts Amherst, Graduate School, College of Humanities and Fine Arts, Department of Music and Dance, Amherst, MA 01003. Offers music (MM, PhD). *Accreditation:* NASM. Part-time programs available. *Faculty:* 17 full-time (3 women). *Students:* 60 full-time (22 women), 28 part-time (11 women); includes 7 minority (2 Black or African American, non-Hispanic/Latino; 2 Asian, non-Hispanic/Latino; 1 Hispanic/Latino; 2 Two or more races, non-Hispanic/Latino), 10 international. Average age 29. 111 applicants, 66% accepted, 41 enrolled. In 2010, 26 master's awarded. Terminal master's awarded for partial completion of doctoral program. *Degree requirements:* For master's, thesis or alternative; for doctorate, comprehensive exam, thesis/dissertation. *Entrance requirements:* For master's and doctorate, original scores, research papers, audition or tape. Additional exam requirements/recommendations for international students: Required—TOEFL (minimum score 550 paper-based; 213 computer-based; 80 iBT), IELTS (minimum score 6.5). *Application deadline:* For fall admission, 1/15 for domestic and international students; for spring admission, 10/1 for domestic and international students. Applications are processed on a rolling basis. Application fee: $50 ($65 for international students). Electronic applications accepted. *Expenses:* Tuition, state resident: full-time $2640. Required fees: $8282. One-time fee: $357 full-time. *Financial support:* In 2010–11, 16 fellowships with full tuition reimbursements (averaging $3,856 per year), 46 teaching assistantships with full tuition reimbursements (averaging $5,841 per year) were awarded; research assistantships, career-related internships or fieldwork, Federal Work-Study, scholarships/grants, traineeships, health care benefits, tuition waivers (full), and unspecified assistantships also available. Support available to part-time students. Financial award application deadline: 1/15; financial award applicants required to submit FAFSA. *Unit head:* Dr. Jeff Cox, Graduate Program Director, 413-545-0311, Fax: 413-545-2092. *Application contact:* Jean M. Ames, Supervisor of Admissions, 413-545-0722, Fax: 413-577-0010, E-mail: gradadm@grad.umass.edu.

University of Massachusetts Lowell, College of Arts and Sciences, Department of Music, Lowell, MA 01854-2881. Offers music education (MM); sound recording technology (MM). *Accreditation:* NASM. Part-time programs available. *Degree requirements:* For master's, one foreign language, thesis. *Entrance requirements:* For master's, MAT, audition. Electronic applications accepted.

University of Memphis, Graduate School, College of Communication and Fine Arts, Rudi E. Scheidt School of Music, Memphis, TN 38152. Offers applied music (M Mu, DMA); composition (M Mu, DMA); conducting (M Mu, DMA); historical musicology (PhD); jazz and studio performance (M Mu); music education (M Mu, DMA); musicology (M Mu). *Accreditation:* NASM. Part-time programs available. *Faculty:* 36 full-time (7 women), 7 part-time/adjunct (4 women). *Students:* 84 full-time (34 women), 44 part-time (21 women); includes 17 Black or African American, non-Hispanic/Latino; 2 Asian, non-Hispanic/Latino; 5 Hispanic/Latino, 24 international. Average age 32. 76 applicants, 87% accepted, 42 enrolled. In 2010, 13 master's, 10 doctorates awarded. Terminal master's awarded for partial completion of doctoral program. *Degree requirements:* For master's, comprehensive exam, thesis or alternative; for doctorate, one foreign language, comprehensive exam, thesis/dissertation, exam. *Entrance requirements:* For master's, GRE General Test or MAT, proficiency exam, audition; for doctorate, GRE General Test or MAT, proficiency exam, audition, master's degree. Additional exam requirements/recommendations for international students: Required—TOEFL. *Application deadline:* For fall admission, 8/1 for domestic students; for spring admission, 12/1 for domestic students. Applications are processed on a rolling basis. Application fee: $35 ($60 for international students). *Financial support:* In 2010–11, 73 students received support; research assistantships with full and partial tuition reimbursements available, teaching assistantships with full and partial tuition reimbursements available, Federal Work-Study, scholarships/grants, and unspecified assistantships available. Financial award application deadline: 2/15; financial award applicants required to submit FAFSA. *Faculty research:* Spanish Renaissance, twentieth century music, Project OPTIMUS, composition, musical performance, regional music, performance, performance practice, composition. *Unit head:* Dr. Patricia J. Hoy, Director, 901-678-2541, Fax: 901-678-3096, E-mail: phoy@memphis.edu. *Application contact:* Dr. John Baur, Assistant Director for Graduate Admissions, 901-678-3362, Fax: 901-678-3096, E-mail: jbaur@memphis.edu.

University of Miami, Graduate School, Frost School of Music, Department of Instrumental Performance, Coral Gables, FL 33124. Offers instrumental conducting (MM, DMA); instrumental performance (MM, DMA, AD); multiple woodwinds (MM, DMA). *Accreditation:* NASM. *Degree requirements:* For master's, thesis, recital paper, recital; for doctorate, thesis/dissertation, essay, 2 research tools, 3 recitals. *Entrance requirements:* For master's and doctorate, GRE General Test, audition. Additional exam requirements/recommendations for international students: Required—TOEFL (minimum score 550 paper-based; 213 computer-based; 59 iBT). Electronic applications accepted. *Faculty research:* Performance, conducting, composition.

University of Miami, Graduate School, Frost School of Music, Department of Keyboard Performance, Coral Gables, FL 33124. Offers accompanying and chamber music (MM, DMA); keyboard performance and pedagogy (MM, DMA); piano performance (MM, DMA, AD). *Accreditation:* NASM. *Degree requirements:* For master's, thesis, recital paper, recital; for doctorate, thesis/dissertation, essay, 2 research tools, 3 recitals. *Entrance requirements:* For master's and doctorate, GRE General Test, audition. Additional exam requirements/recommendations for international students: Required—TOEFL (minimum score 555 paper-based; 213 computer-based; 59 iBT). Electronic applications accepted.

University of Miami, Graduate School, Frost School of Music, Department of Music Media and Industry, Coral Gables, FL 33124. Offers music business and entertainment industries (MM); music engineering (MS). *Accreditation:* NASM. *Degree requirements:* For master's, thesis, internship (MM), research project (MS). *Entrance requirements:* For master's, GRE General Test. Additional exam requirements/recommendations for international students: Required—TOEFL (minimum score 550 paper-based; 213 computer-based; 59 iBT). Electronic applications accepted. *Faculty research:* Recording rights and property, digital sound design, recording industry, Internet-based music industries.

University of Miami, Graduate School, Frost School of Music, Department of Musicology, Coral Gables, FL 33124. Offers MM. *Accreditation:* NASM. *Degree requirements:* For master's, thesis. *Entrance requirements:* For master's, GRE General Test. Additional exam requirements/recommendations for international students: Required—TOEFL (minimum score 550 paper-based; 213 computer-based; 59 iBT). Electronic applications accepted.

University of Miami, Graduate School, Frost School of Music, Department of Music Theory-Composition, Coral Gables, FL 33124. Offers composition (MM, DMA); electronic music (MM); media writing and production (MM); music theory (MM). *Accreditation:* NASM. *Degree requirements:* For master's, thesis; for doctorate, thesis/dissertation, essay. *Entrance requirements:* For master's and doctorate, GRE General Test, portfolio. Additional exam requirements/recommendations for international students: Required—TOEFL (minimum score 550 paper-based; 213 computer-based; 59 iBT). Electronic applications accepted. *Faculty research:* Composition, commercial music and media music.

University of Miami, Graduate School, Frost School of Music, Department of Studio Music and Jazz, Coral Gables, FL 33124. Offers jazz composition (DMA); jazz pedagogy (MM); jazz performance (MM, DMA); studio jazz writing (MM). *Accreditation:* NASM. *Degree requirements:* For master's, thesis. *Entrance requirements:* For master's and doctorate, GRE General Test, portfolio. Additional exam requirements/recommendations for international students: Required—TOEFL (minimum score 550 paper-based; 213 computer-based; 59 iBT). Electronic applications accepted. *Faculty research:* Jazz performance, jazz conducting, jjazz composition.

University of Miami, Graduate School, Frost School of Music, Department of Vocal Performance, Coral Gables, FL 33124. Offers choral conducting (MM, DMA); vocal pedagogy (DMA); vocal performance (MM, DMA, AD). *Accreditation:* NASM. *Degree requirements:* For master's, 2 foreign languages, thesis, recital paper; for doctorate, thesis/dissertation, essay. *Entrance requirements:* For master's and doctorate, GRE General Test, audition. Additional exam requirements/recommendations for international students: Required—TOEFL (minimum score 550 paper-based; 213 computer-based; 59 iBT). Electronic applications accepted. *Faculty research:* Opera, musical theatre, performance, directing, pedagogy.

University of Michigan, Horace H. Rackham School of Graduate Studies, School of Music, Theatre, and Dance, Ann Arbor, MI 48109-2085. Offers MA, MFA, MM, A Mus D, PhD, Spec M, MBA/MM. *Accreditation:* NASM. *Entrance requirements:* For master's, audition, portfolio, interview. Additional exam requirements/recommendations for international students: Required—TOEFL (minimum score 560 paper-based; 237 computer-based). Electronic applications accepted. *Expenses:* Tuition, state resident: full-time $17,784; part-time $1116 per credit hour. Tuition, nonresident: full-time $35,944; part-time $2125 per credit hour. International tuition: $35,994 full-time. Required fees: $95 per semester. Tuition and fees vary according to course load, degree level and program.

University of Minnesota, Duluth, Graduate School, School of Fine Arts, Department of Music, Duluth, MN 55812-2496. Offers music education (MM); performance (MM). *Accreditation:* NASM. Part-time programs available. *Degree requirements:* For master's, comprehensive exam, thesis (for some programs), recital (MM in performance). *Entrance requirements:* For master's, audition, minimum GPA of 3.0, sample of written work, interview, bachelor's degree in music, video of teaching. Additional exam requirements/recommendations for international students: Required—TOEFL (minimum score 550 paper-based; 213 computer-based). *Faculty research:* Band composition, music aesthetics, learning theory, value theory, music advocacy.

University of Minnesota, Twin Cities Campus, Graduate School, College of Liberal Arts, School of Music, Minneapolis, MN 55455-0213. Offers MA, MM, DMA, PhD. *Accreditation:* NASM. *Degree requirements:* For master's, comprehensive exam, thesis (for some programs), foreign language (MA), recital (MM); for doctorate, comprehensive exam, thesis/dissertation (for some programs), 5 recitals (DMA); 2 foreign languages or computer languages, dissertation (PhD). *Entrance requirements:* For master's, GRE (MA); for doctorate, GRE (PhD). Additional exam requirements/recommendations for international students: Required—TOEFL (minimum score 550 paper-based; 213 computer-based; 79 iBT), IELTS (minimum score 6.5), TOEFL iBT also requires minimum of 21 in writing and 19 in reading. Electronic applications accepted.

University of Mississippi, Graduate School, College of Liberal Arts, Department of Music, Oxford, University, MS 38677. Offers MM, DA. *Accreditation:* NASM. *Students:* 40 full-time (13 women), 12 part-time (4 women); includes 11 Black or African American, non-Hispanic/Latino; 3 Asian, non-Hispanic/Latino; 1 Hispanic/Latino. In 2010, 9 master's, 4 doctorates awarded. *Degree requirements:* For master's, thesis (for some programs); for doctorate, thesis/dissertation. *Entrance requirements:* For master's, GRE General Test, minimum GPA of 3.0; for doctorate, GRE General Test. Additional exam requirements/recommendations for international students: Required—TOEFL. *Application deadline:* For fall admission, 4/1 for domestic students; for spring admission, 10/1 for domestic students. Applications are processed on a rolling basis. Application fee: $25. Electronic applications accepted. *Financial support:* Scholarships/grants available. Financial award application deadline: 3/1; financial award applicants required to submit FAFSA. *Unit head:* Dr. Charles Gates, Chairman, 662-915-7268, Fax: 662-915-1203, E-mail: music@olemiss.edu. *Application contact:* Dr. Christy M. Wyandt, Associate Dean, 662-915-7474, Fax: 662-915-7577, E-mail: cwyandt@olemiss.edu.

University of Missouri, Graduate School, College of Arts and Sciences, School of Music, Columbia, MO 65211. Offers MA, MM. *Accreditation:* NASM. *Degree requirements:* For master's, 3 foreign languages, thesis. *Entrance requirements:* For master's, minimum GPA of 3.0. Additional exam requirements/recommendations for international students: Required—TOEFL (minimum score 500 paper-based; 173 computer-based; 61 iBT). Electronic applications accepted.

University of Missouri–Kansas City, Conservatory of Music, Kansas City, MO 64110-2499. Offers composition (MM, DMA); conducting (MM, DMA); music (MA); music education (MME, PhD); music history and literature (MM); music theory (MM); performance (MM, DMA). PhD (interdisciplinary) offered through the School of Graduate Studies. *Accreditation:* NASM. Part-time programs available. *Faculty:* 58 full-time (25 women), 33 part-time/adjunct (13 women). *Students:* 135 full-time (59 women), 101 part-time (51 women); includes 16 minority (10 Black or African American, non-Hispanic/Latino; 3 Asian, non-Hispanic/Latino; 3 Hispanic/Latino), 56 international. Average age 29. 335 applicants, 25% accepted, 74 enrolled. In 2010, 56 master's, 20 doctorates awarded. *Degree requirements:* For master's, variable foreign language requirement, comprehensive exam, thesis (for some programs); for doctorate, variable foreign language requirement, comprehensive exam, thesis/dissertation or alternative. *Entrance requirements:* For master's, minimum GPA of 3.0 in major, auditions (for MM in performance); for doctorate, minimum graduate GPA of 3.5, auditions (for DMA in performance), portfolio of compositions.

Additional exam requirements/recommendations for international students: Required—TOEFL (minimum score 550 paper-based; 213 computer-based; 80 iBT). *Application deadline:* For fall admission, 1/15 priority date for domestic students, 1/15 for international students. Application fee: $45 ($50 for international students). *Expenses:* Tuition, state resident: full-time $5522.40; part-time $306.80 per credit hour. Tuition, nonresident: full-time $7128; part-time $792 per credit hour. Required fees: $261.15 per term. *Financial support:* In 2010–11, 56 teaching assistantships with partial tuition reimbursements (averaging $8,835 per year) were awarded; career-related internships or fieldwork, Federal Work-Study, institutionally sponsored loans, scholarships/grants, tuition waivers (partial), and unspecified assistantships also available. Support available to part-time students. Financial award application deadline: 3/1; financial award applicants required to submit FAFSA. *Faculty research:* Electro-acoustic composition, affective music responses, American music theatre, Russian choral music, music therapy and Alzheimer's. *Unit head:* Peter Witte, Dean, 816-235-2731, Fax: 816-235-5265, E-mail: wittep@umkc.edu. *Application contact:* William Everett, Associate Dean, 816-235-2857, Fax: 816-235-5264, E-mail: everettw@umkc.edu.

The University of Montana, Graduate School, School of Fine Arts, Department of Music, Missoula, MT 59812-0002. Offers music (MM), including composition/technology, music education, musical theater, performance. *Accreditation:* NASM. *Entrance requirements:* For master's, GRE General Test, GRE Subject Test, portfolio.

University of Nebraska at Omaha, Graduate Studies, College of Communication, Fine Arts and Media, Department of Music, Omaha, NE 68182. Offers MM. *Accreditation:* NASM. Part-time and evening/weekend programs available. *Faculty:* 12 full-time (3 women). *Students:* 8 full-time (4 women), 30 part-time (16 women); includes 3 minority (all Black or African American, non-Hispanic/Latino). Average age 30. 17 applicants, 65% accepted, 9 enrolled. In 2010, 6 master's awarded. *Degree requirements:* For master's, comprehensive exam, thesis (for some programs). *Entrance requirements:* For master's, departmental diagnostic exam, minimum GPA of 3.0. Additional exam requirements/recommendations for international students: Required—TOEFL (minimum score 500 paper-based; 173 computer-based; 61 iBT). *Application deadline:* For fall admission, 6/15 priority date for domestic students; for spring admission, 11/15 priority date for domestic students. Applications are processed on a rolling basis. Application fee: $45. Electronic applications accepted. *Financial support:* In 2010–11, 23 students received support; research assistantships with tuition reimbursements available, career-related internships or fieldwork, Federal Work-Study, institutionally sponsored loans, scholarships/grants, tuition waivers (partial), and unspecified assistantships available. Support available to part-time students. Financial award application deadline: 3/1; financial award applicants required to submit FAFSA. *Unit head:* Dr. Melissa Berke, Chairperson, 402-554-2251. *Application contact:* Dr. Roger Foltz, Director, Graduate Studies, 402-554-2341, Fax: 402-554-3143, E-mail: graduate@unomaha.edu.

University of Nebraska–Lincoln, Graduate College, College of Arts and Sciences, Department of English, Lincoln, NE 68588-0333. Offers composition and rhetoric (MA, PhD); creative writing (MA, PhD); literature studies (MA, PhD). *Degree requirements:* For master's, thesis optional; for doctorate, one foreign language, comprehensive exam, thesis/dissertation. *Entrance requirements:* For master's, writing sample; for doctorate, GRE General Test, writing sample. Additional exam requirements/recommendations for international students: Required—TOEFL (minimum score 600 paper-based; 250 computer-based). Electronic applications accepted. *Faculty research:* Creative writing, composition and rhetoric, women's studies, North American literature, medieval/Renaissance studies.

University of Nebraska–Lincoln, Graduate College, College of Fine and Performing Arts, School of Music, Lincoln, NE 68588. Offers composition (MM, DMA); conducting (MM, DMA); music education (MM, PhD); music history (MM); music theory (MM); performance (MM, DMA); piano pedagogy (MM); woodwind specialties (MM). *Accreditation:* NASM. *Degree requirements:* For master's, thesis optional; for doctorate, comprehensive exam, thesis/dissertation. *Entrance requirements:* For master's and doctorate, audition. Additional exam requirements/recommendations for international students: Required—TOEFL. Electronic applications accepted. *Faculty research:* Mozart, Tchaikovsky, Josquin des Prez, practice of J.S. Bach's organ works, instructional strategies in music education.

University of Nevada, Las Vegas, Graduate College, College of Fine Arts, Department of Music, Las Vegas, NV 89154-5025. Offers music (MM); musical arts (DMA). *Accreditation:* NASM. Part-time programs available. *Faculty:* 28 full-time (8 women), 19 part-time/adjunct (5 women). *Students:* 69 full-time (30 women), 35 part-time (21 women); includes 27 minority (4 Black or African American, non-Hispanic/Latino; 2 Asian, non-Hispanic/Latino; 4 Hispanic/Latino; 17 Two or more races, non-Hispanic/Latino), 15 international. Average age 31. 65 applicants, 86% accepted, 33 enrolled. In 2010, 29 master's awarded. *Degree requirements:* For master's, thesis optional, oral and/or written comprehensive exam; for doctorate, one foreign language, comprehensive exam, lecture-recital and document. *Entrance requirements:* Additional exam requirements/recommendations for international students: Required—TOEFL (minimum score 550 paper-based; 213 computer-based; 80 iBT), IELTS (minimum score 7). *Application deadline:* For fall admission, 4/1 priority date for domestic and international students; for spring admission, 11/1 priority date for domestic and international students. Applications are processed on a rolling basis. Application fee: $60 ($95 for international students). Electronic applications accepted. *Expenses:* Tuition, area resident: Part-time $239.50 per credit. Tuition, state resident: part-time $239.50 per credit. Tuition, nonresident: part-time $503 per credit. Required fees: $108 per semester. Tuition and fees vary according to course load, program and reciprocity agreements. *Financial support:* In 2010–11, 40 students received support, including 1 research assistantship with partial tuition reimbursement available (averaging $10,000 per year), 39 teaching assistantships with partial tuition reimbursements available (averaging $10,948 per year); institutionally sponsored loans, scholarships/grants, health care benefits, and unspecified assistantships also available. Financial award application deadline: 3/1. *Faculty research:* Technology in preparing future teachers, multimedia resources in teacher education, public policy in arts education, Roman music history, Wagner. *Unit head:* Dr. Jonathan Good, Chair/Professor, 702-895-3332, Fax: 702-895-4239, E-mail: janathan.good@unlv.edu. *Application contact:* Graduate College Admissions Evaluator, 702-895-3320, Fax: 702-895-4180, E-mail: gradcollege@unlv.edu.

University of Nevada, Reno, Graduate School, College of Liberal Arts, Department of Music, Reno, NV 89557. Offers MA, MM. *Accreditation:* NASM. *Degree requirements:* For master's, thesis optional. *Entrance requirements:* For master's, minimum GPA of 2.75. Additional exam requirements/recommendations for international students: Required—TOEFL (minimum score 500 paper-based; 173 computer-based; 61 iBT), IELTS (minimum score 6). Electronic applications accepted. *Expenses:* Tuition, state resident: full-time $2219; part-time $246 per credit. Tuition, nonresident: part-time $510 per credit. International tuition: $9009 full-time. Required fees: $59 per term. One-time fee: $101. Tuition and fees vary according to course load. *Faculty research:* Performance, conducting, music composition and arranging.

University of New Hampshire, Graduate School, College of Liberal Arts, Department of Music, Durham, NH 03824. Offers music education (MA); music history (MA). *Accreditation:* NASM. *Faculty:* 17 full-time (3 women). *Students:* 8 full-time (2 women), 2 part-time (0 women); includes 1 minority (Hispanic/Latino), 1 international. Average age 32. 18 applicants, 39% accepted, 1 enrolled. In 2010, 3 master's awarded. *Degree requirements:* For master's, one foreign language. *Entrance requirements:* For master's, audition. Additional exam requirements/recommendations for international students: Required—TOEFL (minimum score 550 paper-based; 213 computer-based; 80 iBT). *Application deadline:* For fall admission, 4/1 priority date for domestic students, 4/1 for international students; for spring admission, 12/1 for domestic students. Applications are processed on a rolling basis. Application fee: $65. Electronic applications accepted. *Financial support:* In 2010–11, 5 students received support, including 4 teaching assistantships; fellowships, research assistantships, career-related internships or fieldwork, Federal Work-Study, scholarships/grants, and tuition waivers (full and partial) also available. Support available to part-time students. Financial award application deadline: 2/15.

Music

University of New Hampshire (continued)
Unit head: Dr. Rob Stibler, Chairperson, 603-862-2418. *Application contact:* Alexis Zaricki, Administrative Assistant, 603-862-2418, E-mail: grad.music@unh.edu.

University of New Mexico, Graduate School, College of Fine Arts, Department of Music, Albuquerque, NM 87131-0001. Offers collaborative piano (M Mu); conducting (M Mu); music education (M Mu); music history and literature (M Mu); performance (M Mu); theory and composition (M Mu). *Accreditation:* NASM. Part-time programs available. *Faculty:* 48 full-time (16 women), 24 part-time/adjunct (11 women). *Students:* 52 full-time (20 women), 38 part-time (20 women); includes 3 Black or African American, non-Hispanic/Latino; 1 Asian, non-Hispanic/Latino; 12 Hispanic/Latino, 9 international. Average age 29. 101 applicants, 59% accepted, 36 enrolled. In 2010, 22 master's awarded. *Degree requirements:* For master's, variable foreign language requirement, comprehensive exam, thesis (for some programs), recital (for some programs). *Entrance requirements:* For master's, placement exams in music history and theory. Additional exam requirements/recommendations for international students: Required—TOEFL (minimum score 550 paper-based; 213 computer-based). *Application deadline:* For fall admission, 7/1 for domestic students, 5/1 for international students; for spring admission, 11/1 for domestic students, 10/1 for international students. Applications are processed on a rolling basis. Application fee: $50. Electronic applications accepted. *Expenses:* Tuition, state resident: full-time $5991; part-time $251 per credit hour. Tuition, nonresident: full-time $14,405; part-time $800.20 per credit hour. Tuition and fees vary according to course level, course load, program and reciprocity agreements. *Financial support:* In 2010–11, 74 students received support, including 2 research assistantships (averaging $4,062 per year), 10 teaching assistantships with full and partial tuition reimbursements available (averaging $4,761 per year); Federal Work-Study, scholarships/grants, and unspecified assistantships also available. Support available to part-time students. Financial award application deadline: 2/1; financial award applicants required to submit FAFSA. *Faculty research:* Opera, twentieth century and contemporary music, performance, conducting. Total annual research expenditures: $16,650. *Unit head:* Dr. Steven Block, Chair, 505-277-2127, Fax: 505-277-4202, E-mail: sblock@unm.edu. *Application contact:* Colleen M. Sheinberg, Graduate Coordinator, 505-277-8401, Fax: 505-277-4202, E-mail: colleens@unm.edu.

University of New Orleans, Graduate School, College of Liberal Arts, Department of Music, New Orleans, LA 70148. Offers MM. *Accreditation:* NASM. Evening/weekend programs available. *Degree requirements:* For master's, recital. *Entrance requirements:* For master's, GRE General Test, audition. Additional exam requirements/recommendations for international students: Required—TOEFL (minimum score 550 paper-based; 213 computer-based; 79 iBT). Electronic applications accepted. *Faculty research:* American jazz, Czech music, Hispanic music.

The University of North Carolina at Chapel Hill, Graduate School, College of Arts and Sciences, Department of Music, Chapel Hill, NC 27599. Offers MA, PhD. Terminal master's awarded for partial completion of doctoral program. *Degree requirements:* For master's, one foreign language, thesis, theory and keyboard exams; for doctorate, 2 foreign languages, comprehensive exam, thesis/dissertation, theory and keyboard exams. *Entrance requirements:* For master's and doctorate, GRE General Test, department diagnostic exam, minimum GPA of 3.0. Additional exam requirements/recommendations for international students: Required—TOEFL. Electronic applications accepted. *Expenses:* Contact institution. *Faculty research:* Music theory, ethnomusicology, music history.

The University of North Carolina at Greensboro, Graduate School, School of Music, Greensboro, NC 27412-5001. Offers composition (MM); education (MM); music education (PhD); performance (MM, DMA). *Accreditation:* NASM. *Degree requirements:* For master's, variable foreign language requirement, thesis (for some programs), recital; for doctorate, comprehensive exam, thesis/dissertation, diagnostic exam, recital. *Entrance requirements:* For master's, GRE General Test, NTE, audition; for doctorate, GRE General Test, GRE Subject Test (music), audition. Additional exam requirements/recommendations for international students: Required—TOEFL. Electronic applications accepted.

University of North Carolina School of the Arts, School of Filmmaking, Winston-Salem, NC 27127-2188. Offers film music composition (MFA). *Faculty:* 1 full-time (0 women). *Students:* 6 full-time (1 woman); includes 1 Asian, non-Hispanic/Latino. Average age 25. 6 applicants, 33% accepted, 2 enrolled. In 2010, 3 master's awarded. *Entrance requirements:* For master's, audition, performance, portfolio, interview. Additional exam requirements/recommendations for international students: Required—TOEFL. *Application deadline:* For fall admission, 4/1 priority date for domestic students. Applications are processed on a rolling basis. Application fee: $60 ($100 for international students). *Expenses:* Tuition, state resident: full-time $4946. Tuition, nonresident: full-time $17,253. Required fees: $2092. *Financial support:* In 2010–11, fellowships (averaging $2,000 per year); career-related internships or fieldwork, Federal Work-Study, and Academic Common Market also available. Support available to part-time students. Financial award application deadline: 3/15; financial award applicants required to submit FAFSA. *Unit head:* Jordan Kerner, Dean, 336-770-1330, Fax: 336-770-1339, E-mail: kernerj@uncsa.edu. *Application contact:* Sheeler Lawson, Director of Admissions, 336-770-3290, Fax: 336-770-3370, E-mail: admissions@uncsa.edu.

University of North Carolina School of the Arts, School of Music, Winston-Salem, NC 27127-2188. Offers music performance (MM), including chamber music performance. *Faculty:* 30 full-time (9 women), 11 part-time/adjunct (3 women). *Students:* 46 full-time (18 women); includes 6 Black or African American, non-Hispanic/Latino; 1 American Indian or Alaska Native, non-Hispanic/Latino; 1 Asian, non-Hispanic/Latino; 1 Hispanic/Latino, 3 international. Average age 25. In 2010, 20 master's awarded. *Entrance requirements:* For master's, audition (music performance), interview, original score. Additional exam requirements/recommendations for international students: Required—TOEFL. *Application deadline:* For fall admission, 4/1 priority date for domestic students. Applications are processed on a rolling basis. Application fee: $60 ($100 for international students). *Expenses:* Tuition, state resident: full-time $4946. Tuition, nonresident: full-time $17,253. Required fees: $2092. *Financial support:* In 2010–11, 8 fellowships with partial tuition reimbursements (averaging $2,000 per year), 3 teaching assistantships with partial tuition reimbursements (averaging $3,000 per year) were awarded; career-related internships or fieldwork and Federal Work-Study also available. Financial award application deadline: 3/15; financial award applicants required to submit FAFSA. *Unit head:* Dr. Wade Weast, Dean, 336-770-3251, Fax: 336-770-3248, E-mail: weastw@uncsa.edu. *Application contact:* Sheeler Lawson, Director of Admissions, 336-770-3290, Fax: 336-770-3370, E-mail: admissions@uncsa.edu.

University of North Dakota, Graduate School, College of Arts and Sciences, Department of Music, Grand Forks, ND 58202. Offers music (M Mus); music education (M Mus, DMEd). *Accreditation:* NASM. Part-time programs available. *Faculty:* 17 full-time (7 women). *Students:* 10 full-time (5 women), 11 part-time (7 women); includes 1 minority (Hispanic/Latino), 2 international. Average age 34. 11 applicants, 73% accepted, 6 enrolled. In 2010, 7 master's awarded. *Degree requirements:* For master's, comprehensive exam, thesis or alternative. *Entrance requirements:* For master's, minimum GPA of 3.0. Additional exam requirements/recommendations for international students: Required—TOEFL (minimum score 550 paper-based; 213 computer-based; 79 iBT), IELTS (minimum score 6.5). *Application deadline:* For fall admission, 8/1 priority date for domestic students, 5/1 priority date for international students; for spring admission, 12/1 priority date for domestic students, 9/1 priority date for international students. Applications are processed on a rolling basis. Application fee: $35. Electronic applications accepted. *Expenses:* Tuition, state resident: full-time $5857; part-time $306.74 per credit. Tuition, nonresident: full-time $15,666; part-time $729.77 per credit. Required fees: $53.42 per credit. Tuition and fees vary according to course load, program and reciprocity agreements. *Financial support:* In 2010–11, 7 students received support, including 7 teaching assistantships with full tuition reimbursements available (averaging $5,950 per year); fellowships with full and partial tuition reimbursements available, research assistantships with full and partial tuition reimbursements available, Federal Work-Study, institutionally sponsored loans, scholarships/grants, health care benefits, tuition waivers (full and partial), and unspecified assistantships also available. Support available to part-time students. Financial award application deadline: 3/15; financial award applicants required to submit FAFSA. *Unit head:* Dr. Michael Wittgraf, Graduate Director, 701-777-2644, Fax: 701-777-3320, E-mail: michael.wittgraf@und.edu. *Application contact:* Debbie Ford, Admissions Specialist, 701-777-0749, Fax: 701-777-3619, E-mail: debra.ford@gradschool.und.edu.

University of Northern Colorado, Graduate School, College of Performing and Visual Arts, School of Music, Greeley, CO 80639. Offers collaborative keyboard (MM); conducting (MM); instrumental performance (MM); jazz studies (MM); music conducting (DA); music education (MM, DA); music history and literature (MM, DA); music performance (DA); music theory and composition (MM, DA); vocal performance (MM). *Accreditation:* NASM; NCATE (one or more programs are accredited). Part-time programs available. *Faculty:* 31 full-time (7 women). *Students:* 90 full-time (37 women), 22 part-time (12 women); includes 14 minority (5 Black or African American, non-Hispanic/Latino; 7 Asian, non-Hispanic/Latino; 2 Hispanic/Latino), 9 international. Average age 29. 87 applicants, 68% accepted, 38 enrolled. In 2010, 22 master's, 3 doctorates awarded. *Degree requirements:* For master's, comprehensive exam, thesis or alternative; for doctorate, comprehensive exam, thesis/dissertation. *Entrance requirements:* For master's, audition; for doctorate, GRE General Test, audition, 3 letters of recommendation. *Application deadline:* Applications are processed on a rolling basis. Application fee: $50 ($60 for international students). Electronic applications accepted. *Expenses:* Tuition, state resident: full-time $6199; part-time $344 per credit hour. Tuition, nonresident: full-time $14,834; part-time $824 per credit hour. Required fees: $1091; $60.60 per credit hour. Tuition and fees vary according to course load, degree level and program. *Financial support:* In 2010–11, 45 research assistantships (averaging $4,649 per year), 22 teaching assistantships (averaging $4,219 per year) were awarded; fellowships, unspecified assistantships also available. Financial award application deadline: 3/1; financial award applicants required to submit FAFSA. *Unit head:* David Caffey, Director, 970-351-2679. *Application contact:* Linda Sisson, Graduate Student Admission Coordinator, 970-351-1807, Fax: 970-351-2371, E-mail: linda.sisson@unco.edu.

University of Northern Iowa, Graduate College, College of Humanities and Fine Arts, School of Music, Program in Music, Cedar Falls, IA 50614. Offers composition (MM); conducting (MM); music (MA); music history (MM); performance (MM), including voice, wind, percussion, keyboard or strings. *Accreditation:* NASM. *Students:* 35 full-time (27 women), 8 part-time (5 women); includes 3 minority (1 Black or African American, non-Hispanic/Latino; 1 Hispanic/Latino; 1 Two or more races, non-Hispanic/Latino), 10 international. 38 applicants, 61% accepted, 13 enrolled. In 2010, 13 master's awarded. *Degree requirements:* For master's, comprehensive exam, thesis or alternative. *Entrance requirements:* For master's, written diagnostic exam in theory, music history, expository writing skills and in the area of claimed competency, portfolio, tape recordings of compositions, in person auditions, minimum GPA of 3.0. Additional exam requirements/recommendations for international students: Required—TOEFL (minimum score 500 paper-based; 180 computer-based; 61 iBT). *Application deadline:* For fall admission, 8/1 priority date for domestic students. Applications are processed on a rolling basis. Application fee: $50 ($70 for international students). Electronic applications accepted. *Financial support:* Career-related internships or fieldwork, Federal Work-Study, and tuition waivers (full and partial) available. Support available to part-time students. Financial award application deadline: 2/1. *Unit head:* Dr. Ronald Johnson, Coordinator, 319-273-6058, Fax: 319-273-7320, E-mail: ronald.johnson@uni.edu. *Application contact:* Laurie S. Russell, Record Analyst, 319-273-2623, Fax: 319-273-2885, E-mail: laurie.russell@uni.edu.

University of North Texas, Toulouse Graduate School, College of Music, Denton, TX 76203-5017. Offers composition (MM, DMA); jazz studies (MM); music (MA); music education (MM, MME, PhD); music theory (MM, PhD); musicology (MM, PhD); performance (MM, DMA). *Accreditation:* NASM. Terminal master's awarded for partial completion of doctoral program. *Degree requirements:* For master's, one foreign language, comprehensive exam (for some programs), thesis (for some programs); for doctorate, one foreign language, comprehensive exam (for some programs), thesis/dissertation (for some programs). *Entrance requirements:* For master's and doctorate, audition, writing samples. Additional exam requirements/recommendations for international students: Recommended—TOEFL (minimum score 550 paper-based; 213 computer-based). *Application deadline:* Applications are processed on a rolling basis. Electronic applications accepted. *Expenses:* Tuition, state resident: full-time $4298; part-time $239 per credit hour. Tuition, nonresident: full-time $10,782; part-time $549 per credit hour. Required fees: $1292; $270 per credit hour. *Financial support:* Fellowships with partial tuition reimbursements, research assistantships, teaching assistantships with partial tuition reimbursements, career-related internships or fieldwork, Federal Work-Study, institutionally sponsored loans, and scholarships/grants available. Financial award application deadline: 4/1. *Faculty research:* Electro-acoustical music, intermedia, music and medicine, music performance. *Application contact:* Admissions and Scholarship Services, 940-367-7771, Fax: 940-565-2002.

University of Oklahoma, Weitzenhoffer Family College of Fine Arts, School of Music, Norman, OK 73019. Offers choral conducting (M Mus, M Mus Ed); conducting (DMA); instrumental conducting (M Mus, M Mus Ed); music composition (M Mus, DMA); music education (M Mus Ed, PhD), including choral or wind instrument conducting (PhD), general (PhD), instrumental (primary) (M Mus Ed), instrumental (secondary) (M Mus Ed), Kodaly concepts, piano pedagogy (PhD), voice pedagogy (M Mus Ed); music theory (M Mus); musicology (M Mus); organ (M Mus, DMA), including performance; piano (M Mus, DMA), including performance, performance and pedagogy; piano pedagogy (M Mus Ed); vocal/general (M Mus Ed); voice (M Mus, DMA), including performance, performance and pedagogy; wind/percussion/string (M Mus, DMA), including performance. *Accreditation:* NASM. *Faculty:* 48 full-time (12 women), 2 part-time/adjunct (1 woman). *Students:* 98 full-time (50 women), 62 part-time (35 women); includes 15 minority (4 Black or African American, non-Hispanic/Latino; 3 American Indian or Alaska Native, non-Hispanic/Latino; 4 Asian, non-Hispanic/Latino; 3 Hispanic/Latino; 1 Two or more races, non-Hispanic/Latino), 18 international. Average age 31. 126 applicants, 57% accepted, 47 enrolled. In 2010, 25 master's, 12 doctorates awarded. *Degree requirements:* For master's, variable foreign language requirement, thesis (for some programs), departmental qualifying exam, oral and preliminary exams; for doctorate, variable foreign language requirement, thesis/dissertation, departmental qualifying exam, general and oral exams. *Entrance requirements:* For master's, audition, BA in music, minimum GPA of 3.0; for doctorate, audition, minimum GPA of 3.0. Additional exam requirements/recommendations for international students: Required—TOEFL (minimum score 550 paper-based; 213 computer-based; 79 iBT). *Application deadline:* For fall admission, 6/1 priority date for domestic students, 4/1 for international students; for spring admission, 11/1 for domestic students, 9/1 for international students. Applications are processed on a rolling basis. Application fee: $40 ($90 for international students). Electronic applications accepted. *Expenses:* Tuition, state resident: full-time $3893; part-time $162.20 per credit hour. Tuition, nonresident: full-time $14,167; part-time $590.30 per credit hour. Required fees: $2523; $94.60 per credit hour. Tuition and fees vary according to course load and degree level. *Financial support:* In 2010–11, 131 students received support, including 7 fellowships with full tuition reimbursements available (averaging $5,000 per year), 17 research assistantships with partial tuition reimbursements available (averaging $11,472 per year), 73 teaching assistantships with partial tuition reimbursements available (averaging $10,107 per year); unspecified assistantships also available. Financial award application deadline: 4/7; financial award applicants required to submit FAFSA. *Faculty research:* Piano pedagogy, music education, instrumental and vocal performance, conducting, composition. Total annual research expenditures: $29,475. *Unit head:* Dr. Steven Curtis, Director, 405-325-2081, Fax: 405-325-7574, E-mail: scurtis@ou.edu. *Application contact:* Jan Russell, Office Assistant, 405-325-5393, Fax: 405-325-7574, E-mail: jrussell@ou.edu.

University of Oregon, Graduate School, School of Music, Program in Music, Eugene, OR 97403. Offers composition (M Mus, DMA, PhD); conducting (M Mus); jazz studies (M Mus); music (MA), including music history, music theory; music history (PhD); music theory (PhD); performance (M Mus, DMA); piano pedagogy (M Mus). *Entrance requirements:* For master's, minimum GPA of 3.0, audition (performance applicants), videotape or interview (conducting applicants); for doctorate, GRE General Test, minimum GPA of 3.0, audition (performance applicants), videotape or interview (conducting applicants). Additional exam requirements/recommendations for international students: Required—TOEFL.

University of Ottawa, Faculty of Graduate and Postdoctoral Studies, Faculty of Arts, Department of Music, Ottawa, ON K1N 6N5, Canada. Offers music (M Mus, MA); orchestral studies (Certificate); piano pedagogy research (Certificate). *Degree requirements:* For master's, thesis optional. *Entrance requirements:* For master's, honors degree or equivalent, minimum B+ average. Electronic applications accepted. *Faculty research:* Performance, theory, musicology.

University of Pennsylvania, School of Arts and Sciences, Graduate Group in Music, Philadelphia, PA 19104. Offers AM, PhD. *Faculty:* 12 full-time (5 women), 4 part-time/adjunct (0 women). *Students:* 37 full-time (21 women); includes 2 Black or African American, non-Hispanic/Latino; 1 Hispanic/Latino, 8 international. 129 applicants, 4% accepted, 2 enrolled. In 2010, 3 master's, 6 doctorates awarded. Terminal master's awarded for partial completion of doctoral program. *Degree requirements:* For master's, variable foreign language requirement; for doctorate, variable foreign language requirement, thesis/dissertation. *Entrance requirements:* For master's and doctorate, GRE General Test, GRE Subject Test, samples of previous work. Additional exam requirements/recommendations for international students: Required—TOEFL. *Application deadline:* For fall admission, 12/1 priority date for domestic students. Application fee: $70. Electronic applications accepted. *Expenses:* Tuition: Full-time $25,660; part-time $4758 per course. Required fees: $2152; $270 per course. Tuition and fees vary according to course load, degree level and program. *Financial support:* Institutionally sponsored loans, scholarships/grants, traineeships, health care benefits, and unspecified assistantships available. Financial award application deadline: 12/15. *Unit head:* James Primosch, Department Chair, Music, 215-898-7544, E-mail: primosch@sas.upenn.edu. *Application contact:* James Primosch, Department Chair, Music, 215-898-7544, E-mail: primosch@sas.upenn.edu.

University of Pittsburgh, School of Arts and Sciences, Department of Music, Pittsburgh, PA 15260. Offers composition and theory (MA, PhD); ethnomusicology (MA, PhD); historical musicology (MA, PhD); jazz studies (MA, PhD). Part-time programs available. *Faculty:* 10 full-time (3 women), 1 part-time/adjunct (0 women). *Students:* 42 full-time (11 women), 1 (woman) part-time; includes 2 Black or African American, non-Hispanic/Latino; 8 Asian, non-Hispanic/Latino, 6 international. Average age 28. 70 applicants, 21% accepted, 5 enrolled. In 2010, 3 master's, 2 doctorates awarded. Terminal master's awarded for partial completion of doctoral program. *Degree requirements:* For master's, comprehensive exam, thesis, 1 foreign language (historical musicology); for doctorate, one foreign language, comprehensive exam, thesis/dissertation, 2 foreign languages (historical musicology). *Entrance requirements:* For master's and doctorate, GRE General Test, samples of work, references. Additional exam requirements/recommendations for international students: Required—TOEFL (minimum score 600 paper-based; 250 computer-based). *Application deadline:* For fall admission, 1/5 for domestic and international students. Application fee: $50. Electronic applications accepted. *Expenses:* Tuition, state resident: full-time $17,304; part-time $701 per credit. Tuition, nonresident: full-time $29,554; part-time $1210 per credit. Required fees: $740; $214 per term. Tuition and fees vary according to program. *Financial support:* In 2010–11, 27 students received support, including 9 fellowships with full tuition reimbursements available (averaging $17,900 per year), 1 research assistantship with full and partial tuition reimbursement available (averaging $12,670 per year), 17 teaching assistantships with full and partial tuition reimbursements available (averaging $15,520 per year); scholarships/grants, health care benefits, tuition waivers (partial), and unspecified assistantships also available. Financial award application deadline: 1/5. *Faculty research:* Composition, ethnomusicology, historical musicology, intercultural musicology, jazz studies. Total annual research expenditures: $100,000. *Unit head:* Dr. Mathew Rosenblum, Chairman, 412-624-4126, Fax: 412-624-4186, E-mail: rosenblu@pitt.edu. *Application contact:* Dr. Bell Yung, Director of Graduate Admissions, 412-624-4124, Fax: 412-624-4186, E-mail: byun@pitt.edu.

University of Pittsburgh, School of Arts and Sciences, Department of Theatre Arts, Pittsburgh, PA 15260. Offers performance pedagogy (MFA); theatre and performance studies (MA, PhD). *Accreditation:* NAST. *Faculty:* 4 full-time (2 women). *Students:* 22 full-time (12 women); includes 1 minority (Black or African American, non-Hispanic/Latino), 1 international. Average age 30. 29 applicants, 34% accepted, 6 enrolled. In 2010, 2 master's, 3 doctorates awarded. Terminal master's awarded for partial completion of doctoral program. *Degree requirements:* For master's, comprehensive exam; for doctorate, one foreign language, comprehensive exam, thesis/dissertation, diagnostic exams. *Entrance requirements:* For master's and doctorate, GRE General Test, samples of written work. Additional exam requirements/recommendations for international students: Required—TOEFL (minimum score 550 paper-based; 213 computer-based; 80 iBT). *Application deadline:* For fall admission, 1/15 priority date for domestic and international students. Application fee: $50. Electronic applications accepted. *Expenses:* Tuition, state resident: full-time $17,304; part-time $701 per credit. Tuition, nonresident: full-time $29,554; part-time $1210 per credit. Required fees: $740; $214 per term. Tuition and fees vary according to program. *Financial support:* In 2010–11, 18 students received support, including 9 research assistantships with full and partial tuition reimbursements available (averaging $12,670 per year), 14 teaching assistantships with full and partial tuition reimbursements available (averaging $16,140 per year); career-related internships or fieldwork, Federal Work-Study, institutionally sponsored loans, scholarships/grants, health care benefits, and unspecified assistantships also available. Support available to part-time students. Financial award application deadline: 1/15; financial award applicants required to submit FAFSA. *Faculty research:* American theatre, Renaissance theatre, Asian theatre, dramatic structure, performance theory. *Unit head:* Dr. Bruce McConachie, Chairman, 412-624-6156, Fax: 412-624-6338, E-mail: bamcco@pitt.edu. *Application contact:* Connie Anne Markiw, Graduate Secretary, 412-624-6568, Fax: 412-624-6338, E-mail: cam177@pitt.edu.

University of Redlands, College of Arts and Sciences, School of Music, Redlands, CA 92373-0999. Offers MM. *Accreditation:* NASM. Part-time programs available. *Degree requirements:* For master's, comprehensive exam, thesis, 3 recitals, major conducted ensemble. *Entrance requirements:* For master's, GRE, bachelor's degree in music, minimum GPA of 2.75, audition, original scores. Additional exam requirements/recommendations for international students: Required—TOEFL (minimum score 550 paper-based). *Expenses:* Contact institution. *Faculty research:* Performance, composition.

University of Regina, Faculty of Graduate Studies and Research, Faculty of Fine Arts, Department of Music, Regina, SK S4S 0A2, Canada. Offers conducting (MMus); music theory (MA); musicology (MA). *Faculty:* 7 full-time (5 women). *Students:* 2 full-time (1 woman). 3 applicants, 33% accepted. In 2010, 1 master's awarded. *Degree requirements:* For master's, thesis (for some programs), recital, oral exam, jury examinations. *Entrance requirements:* For master's, music theory and history, B Mus or equivalent. Additional exam requirements/recommendations for international students: Required—TOEFL (minimum score 580 paper-based; 80 iBT). *Application deadline:* For fall admission, 2/15 for domestic and international students. Application fee: $100. Electronic applications accepted. Tuition and fees charges are reported in Canadian dollars. *Expenses:* Tuition, area resident: Full-time $3244.50 Canadian dollars; part-time $180.25 Canadian dollars per credit hour. International tuition: $4744.50 Canadian dollars full-time. Required fees: $494 Canadian dollars; $115.25 Canadian dollars per credit hour. $115.25 Canadian dollars per semester. Tuition and fees vary according to program. *Financial support:* Fellowships, research assistantships, teaching assistantships, scholarships/grants available. Financial award application deadline: 6/15. *Faculty research:* Renaissance, Baroque, and medieval music; music of the Classical and Romantic eras; analysis of music written since 1900; music theory; history of music theory. *Unit head:* Dr. Lynn Cavanagh, Head, 306-585-5537, Fax: 306-585-5549, E-mail: lynn.cavanagh@uregina.ca. *Application contact:* Pauline Minevich, Graduate Program Coordinator, 306-585-5507, Fax: 306-585-5549, E-mail: pauline.minevich@uregina.ca.

University of Rhode Island, Graduate School, College of Arts and Sciences, Department of Music, Kingston, RI 02881. Offers music education (MM); music performance (MM). *Accreditation:* NASM. Part-time programs available. *Faculty:* 12 full-time (5 women), 1 part-time/adjunct (0 women). *Students:* 12 full-time (2 women), 6 part-time (1 woman); includes 1 minority (Asian, non-Hispanic/Latino). In 2010, 4 master's awarded. *Entrance requirements:* For master's, 2 letters of recommendation, audition. Additional exam requirements/recommendations for international students: Required—TOEFL (minimum score 550 paper-based; 213 computer-based). *Application deadline:* For fall admission, 7/15 for domestic students, 2/1 for international students; for spring admission, 7/15 for international students. Application fee: $65. Electronic applications accepted. *Expenses:* Tuition, state resident: full-time $9588; part-time $533 per credit hour. Tuition, nonresident: full-time $22,968; part-time $1276 per credit hour. Required fees: $1282; $68 per semester. Tuition and fees vary according to program. *Financial support:* In 2010–11, 3 teaching assistantships with full and partial tuition reimbursements (averaging $6,947 per year) were awarded. Financial award application deadline: 3/15; financial award applicants required to submit FAFSA. *Unit head:* Dr. Joe Parillo, Chair, 401-874-2431, Fax: 401-874-2772, E-mail: jparillo@uri.edu. *Application contact:* Dr. Eliane Aberdam, Co-Director of Graduate Studies, 401-874-2794, Fax: 401-874-2772, E-mail: eliane@uri.edu.

University of Rochester, Eastman School of Music, Program in Ethnomusicology, Rochester, NY 14627.

University of Rochester, Eastman School of Music, Program in Music Theory Pedagogy, Rochester, NY 14627.

University of Rochester, Eastman School of Music, Programs in Music Composition, Rochester, NY 14627.

University of Rochester, Eastman School of Music, Programs in Musicology, Rochester, NY 14627.

University of Rochester, Eastman School of Music, Programs in Music Theory, Rochester, NY 14627.

University of St. Thomas, Graduate Studies, College of Arts and Sciences, Graduate Programs in Music Education, St. Paul, MN 55105-1096. Offers choral (MA); Dalcroze (MA); instrumental (MA); Kodaly (MA); Orff (MA); piano pedagogy (MA). *Accreditation:* NASM; NCATE. Part-time programs available. *Faculty:* 9 full-time (4 women), 20 part-time/adjunct (10 women). *Students:* 115 part-time (86 women); includes 3 minority (2 Black or African American, non-Hispanic/Latino; 1 Asian, non-Hispanic/Latino). Average age 30. 5 applicants, 100% accepted, 5 enrolled. In 2010, 24 master's awarded. *Degree requirements:* For master's, comprehensive exam, thesis, music history theory and diagnostic exam, piano recital (for piano pedagogy students). *Entrance requirements:* For master's, performance assessment hearing, interview. Additional exam requirements/recommendations for international students: Required—TOEFL (minimum score 550 paper-based; 80 iBT). *Application deadline:* For fall admission, 7/1 for domestic students; for winter admission, 12/1 for domestic students; for spring admission, 4/1 for domestic students. Applications are processed on a rolling basis. Application fee: $50. Electronic applications accepted. *Financial support:* In 2010–11, 8 students received support; fellowships, research assistantships, teaching assistantships, Federal Work-Study, institutionally sponsored loans, scholarships/grants, and tuition waivers (partial) available. Financial award application deadline: 4/1; financial award applicants required to submit FAFSA. *Faculty research:* Kodaly, choral conducting, piano pedagogy, Orff. *Unit head:* Dr. Doug C. Orzolek, Director, 800-328-6819 Ext. 25878, Fax: 651-962-5886, E-mail: dcorzolek@stthomas.edu. *Application contact:* Beverly H. Johnson, Program Coordinator, 800-328-6819 Ext. 25870, Fax: 651-962-5886, E-mail: bhjohnson@stthomas.edu.

University of Saskatchewan, College of Graduate Studies and Research, College of Arts and Sciences, Department of Music, Saskatoon, SK S7N 5A2, Canada. Offers M Mus, MA. *Degree requirements:* For master's, thesis. *Entrance requirements:* Additional exam requirements/recommendations for international students: Required—TOEFL (minimum score 80 iBT); Recommended—IELTS (minimum score 6.5). Electronic applications accepted.

University of South Africa, College of Human Sciences, Pretoria, South Africa. Offers adult education (M Ed); African languages (MA, PhD); African politics (MA, PhD); Afrikaans (MA, PhD); ancient history (MA, PhD); ancient Near Eastern studies (MA, PhD); anthropology (MA, PhD); applied linguistics (MA); Arabic (MA, PhD); archaeology (MA); art history (MA); Biblical archaeology (MA); Biblical studies (M Th, D Th, PhD); Christian spirituality (M Th, D Th); church history (M Th, D Th); classical studies (MA, PhD); clinical psychology (MA); communication (MA, PhD); comparative education (M Ed, Ed D); consulting psychology (D Admin, D Com, PhD); curriculum studies (M Ed, Ed D); development studies (M Admin, MA, D Admin, PhD); didactics (M Ed, Ed D); education (M Tech); education management (M Ed, Ed D); educational psychology (M Ed); English (MA); environmental education (M Ed); French (MA, PhD); German (MA, PhD); Greek (MA); guidance and counseling (M Ed); health studies (MA, PhD), including health sciences education (MA), health services management (MA), medical and surgical nursing science (critical care general) (MA), midwifery and neonatal nursing science (MA), trauma and emergency care (MA); history (MA, PhD); history of education (Ed D); inclusive education (M Ed, Ed D); information and communications technology policy and regulation (MA); information science (MA, MIS, PhD); international politics (MA, PhD); Islamic studies (MA, PhD); Italian (MA, PhD); Judaica (MA, PhD); linguistics (MA, PhD); mathematical education (M Ed); mathematics education (MA); missiology (M Th, D Th); modern Hebrew (MA, PhD); musicology (MA, MMus, D Mus, PhD); natural science education (M Ed); New Testament (M Th, D Th); Old Testament (D Th); pastoral therapy (M Th, D Th); philosophy (MA); philosophy of education (M Ed, Ed D); politics (MA, PhD); Portuguese (MA, PhD); practical theology (M Th, D Th); psychology (MA, MS, PhD); psychology of education (M Ed, Ed D); public health (MA); religious studies (MA, D Th, PhD); Romance languages (MA); Russian (MA, PhD); Semitic languages (MA, PhD); social behavior studies in HIV/AIDS (MA); social science (mental health) (MA); social science in development studies (MA); social science in psychology (MA); social science in social work (MA); social science in sociology (MA); social work (MSW, DSW, PhD); socio-education (M Ed, Ed D); sociolinguistics (MA); sociology (MA, PhD); Spanish (MA, PhD); systematic theology (M Th, D Th); TESOL (teaching English to speakers of other languages) (MA); theological ethics (M Th, D Th); theory of literature (MA, PhD); urban ministries (D Th); urban ministry (M Th).

University of South Carolina, The Graduate School, School of Music, Columbia, SC 29208. Offers composition (MM, DMA); conducting (MM, DMA); jazz studies (MM); music education (MM Ed, PhD); music history (MM); music performance (Certificate); music theory (MM); opera theater (MM); performance (MM, DMA); piano pedagogy (MM, DMA). *Accreditation:* NASM (one or more programs are accredited). Part-time programs available. *Degree requirements:* For master's, 5 foreign languages, comprehensive exam, thesis (for some programs); for doctorate, one foreign language, comprehensive exam, thesis/dissertation; for Certificate, recitals. *Entrance requirements:* For master's and doctorate, GRE General Test or MAT, music diagnostic exam. Additional exam requirements/recommendations for international students: Required—TOEFL (minimum score 570 paper-based; 230 computer-based). Electronic applications accepted. *Expenses:* Contact institution. *Faculty research:* Music skills in pre-school children, evaluation of school performing ensembles.

The University of South Dakota, Graduate School, College of Fine Arts, Department of Music, Vermillion, SD 57069-2390. Offers MM. *Accreditation:* NASM. *Degree requirements:* For master's, thesis or alternative. *Entrance requirements:* For master's, minimum GPA of 2.7, audition or performance tape. Additional exam requirements/recommendations for international students: Required—TOEFL (minimum score 550 paper-based; 213 computer-based; 79 iBT). Electronic applications accepted.

University of Southern California, Graduate School, Thornton School of Music, Los Angeles, CA 90089. Offers brass performance (MM, DMA, Graduate Certificate); choral and sacred music (MM, DMA); classical guitar (MM, DMA, Graduate Certificate); composition (MM, DMA); early music (MM, DMA); harp performance (MM, DMA, Graduate Certificate); historical musicology (PhD); jazz studies (MM, DMA, Graduate Certificate); keyboard collaborative arts

Music

University of Southern California (continued)
(MM, DMA, Graduate Certificate); music education (MM, DMA); organ performance (MM, DMA, Graduate Certificate); percussion performance (MM, DMA, Graduate Certificate); piano performance (MM, DMA, Graduate Certificate); scoring for motion pictures and television (Graduate Certificate); strings performance (MM, DMA, Graduate Certificate); studio jazz guitar (MM, DMA, Graduate Certificate); teaching music (MA); vocal arts (classical voice/ opera) (MM, DMA, Graduate Certificate); woodwind performance (MM, DMA, Graduate Certificate). *Accreditation:* NASM. Part-time and evening/weekend programs available. *Faculty:* 75 full-time (14 women), 120 part-time/adjunct (24 women). *Students:* 399 full-time (172 women), 47 part-time (31 women); includes 106 minority (9 Black or African American, non-Hispanic/Latino; 2 American Indian or Alaska Native, non-Hispanic/Latino; 53 Asian, non-Hispanic/Latino; 29 Hispanic/Latino; 1 Native Hawaiian or other Pacific Islander, non-Hispanic/Latino; 12 Two or more races, non-Hispanic/Latino), 103 international. 934 applicants, 35% accepted, 192 enrolled. In 2010, 54 master's, 2 doctorates, 96 other advanced degrees awarded. Terminal master's awarded for partial completion of doctoral program. *Degree requirements:* For master's, variable foreign language requirement, comprehensive exam (for some programs), thesis (for some programs); for doctorate, variable foreign language requirement, comprehensive exam, thesis/dissertation (for some programs). *Entrance requirements:* For master's, GRE (for MA Early Music and MM Music Education); for doctorate, GRE (for DMA). Additional exam requirements/recommendations for international students: Required—TOEFL (minimum score 560 paper-based; 220 computer-based; 83 iBT). *Application deadline:* For fall admission, 12/1 for domestic and international students; for spring admission, 10/1 for domestic and international students. Application fee: $85. Electronic applications accepted. *Expenses:* Contact institution. *Financial support:* In 2010–11, 60 teaching assistantships with full tuition reimbursements (averaging $9,600 per year) were awarded; scholarships/ grants and tuition waivers also available. Financial award application deadline: 12/1; financial award applicants required to submit FAFSA. *Faculty research:* Early Modern musical improvisation and composition, maternal sound stimulation of the premature infant, physiological characteristics of jazz guitarists, the musical experience of the very young child, electronic music. *Unit head:* P. J. Woolston, Director of Admission, 213-740-8986, E-mail: woolston@usc.edu. *Application contact:* Ligaya J. Jones, Admission Coordinator, 213-740-8986, E-mail: ljones@thornton.usc.edu.

University of Southern Maine, College of Arts and Sciences, Program in Music, Portland, ME 04104-9300. Offers MM. *Accreditation:* NASM.

University of Southern Mississippi, Graduate School, College of Arts and Letters, Department of Theatre and Dance, Hattiesburg, MS 39406-0001. Offers directing (MFA); performance (MFA); technical (MFA). *Accreditation:* NAST. Part-time programs available. *Faculty:* 8 full-time (5 women). *Students:* 21 full-time (9 women); includes 2 Black or African American, non-Hispanic/Latino; 1 Asian, non-Hispanic/Latino; 3 Hispanic/Latino; 1 Two or more races, non-Hispanic/Latino. Average age 28. 20 applicants, 40% accepted, 7 enrolled. In 2010, 7 master's awarded. *Degree requirements:* For master's, comprehensive exam, thesis or alternative, creative project. *Entrance requirements:* For master's, GRE General Test, minimum GPA of 3.0. Additional exam requirements/recommendations for international students: Required—TOEFL, IELTS. *Application deadline:* For fall admission, 3/1 priority date for domestic students, 3/1 for international students; for spring admission, 1/10 priority date for domestic and international students. Applications are processed on a rolling basis. Application fee: $50. *Financial support:* In 2010–11, 20 teaching assistantships with full tuition reimbursements (averaging $7,065 per year) were awarded; research assistantships, career-related internships or fieldwork, Federal Work-Study, institutionally sponsored loans, health care benefits, and unspecified assistantships also available. Support available to part-time students. Financial award application deadline: 3/15; financial award applicants required to submit FAFSA. *Faculty research:* Technical design, acting. *Unit head:* Louis Rackoff, Chair, 601-266-4994, Fax: 601-266-6423. *Application contact:* Louis Rackoff, Director, Graduate Studies, 601-266-4994, Fax: 601-266-6423, E-mail: graduatestudies@usm.edu.

University of Southern Mississippi, Graduate School, College of Arts and Letters, School of Music, Hattiesburg, MS 39406-0001. Offers conducting (MM); history and literature (MM); music education (MME, PhD); performance (MM); performance and pedagogy (DMA); theory and composition (MM); woodwind performance (MM). *Accreditation:* NASM. *Faculty:* 33 full-time (10 women), 2 part-time/adjunct (0 women). *Students:* 75 full-time (23 women), 42 part-time (16 women); includes 10 Black or African American, non-Hispanic/Latino; 1 Hispanic/Latino; 1 Two or more races, non-Hispanic/Latino, 19 international. Average age 32. 77 applicants, 70% accepted, 42 enrolled. In 2010, 30 master's, 3 doctorates awarded. Terminal master's awarded for partial completion of doctoral program. *Degree requirements:* For master's, comprehensive exam, thesis (for some programs); for doctorate, comprehensive exam, thesis/dissertation. *Entrance requirements:* For master's, GRE General Test, minimum GPA of 2.75 in last 60 hours; for doctorate, GRE General Test, minimum GPA of 3.5. Additional exam requirements/ recommendations for international students: Required—TOEFL, IELTS. *Application deadline:* For fall admission, 3/1 priority date for domestic students; for spring admission, 12/13 for domestic students. Applications are processed on a rolling basis. Application fee: $50. *Financial support:* In 2010–11, 1 fellowship with full tuition reimbursement (averaging $12,000 per year), 51 teaching assistantships with full tuition reimbursements (averaging $6,000 per year) were awarded; research assistantships, Federal Work-Study, institutionally sponsored loans, scholarships/grants, health care benefits, tuition waivers (partial), and unspecified assistantships also available. Financial award application deadline: 3/15; financial award applicants required to submit FAFSA. *Faculty research:* Music theory, composition, music performance. *Unit head:* Dr. Michael Miles, Director, 601-266-5543, Fax: 601-266-6427, E-mail: michael.a.miles@usm.edu. *Application contact:* Dr. Jennifer Shank, Director, Graduate Studies, 601-266-5369, Fax: 601-266-6427.

University of South Florida, Graduate School, College of The Arts, School of Music, Tampa, FL 33620-9951. Offers chamber music (MM); composition (MM); conducting (MM); electro-acoustic music (MM); jazz studies (MM), including composition, performance; music education (MA, PhD); piano pedagogy (MM); theory (MM). *Accreditation:* NASM. Part-time and evening/ weekend programs available. *Faculty:* 18 full-time (5 women). *Students:* 68 full-time (28 women), 27 part-time (11 women); includes 7 Black or African American, non-Hispanic/Latino; 4 Asian, non-Hispanic/Latino; 7 Hispanic/Latino, 9 international. Average age 30. 94 applicants, 65% accepted, 41 enrolled. In 2010, 34 master's, 3 doctorates awarded. *Degree requirements:* For master's, comprehensive exam, thesis, 30-34 credit hours; for doctorate, comprehensive exam, thesis/dissertation. *Entrance requirements:* For master's, diagnostic exam in theory and history, audition, portfolio, minimum GPA of 3.0; for doctorate, GRE, writing samples, interview, teaching video. Additional exam requirements/recommendations for international students: Required—TOEFL (minimum score 550 paper-based; 213 computer-based). *Application deadline:* For fall admission, 2/15 priority date for domestic students, 3/15 for international students; for spring admission, 10/15 for domestic students, 6/1 for international students. Application fee: $30. *Financial support:* In 2010–11, 43 teaching assistantships with tuition reimbursements (averaging $25,121 per year) were awarded; unspecified assistantships also available. Financial award application deadline: 2/15. *Faculty research:* Education, conducting, performance, history, theory. Total annual research expenditures: $17,941. *Unit head:* Wade Weast, Director, 813-974-2311, Fax: 813-974-8721, E-mail: wweast@usf.edu. *Application contact:* David Williams, Program Director, 813-974-2311, Fax: 813-974-8721, E-mail: davidw@usf.edu.

The University of Tennessee, Graduate School, College of Arts and Sciences, Department of Theatre, Knoxville, TN 37996. Offers costume design (MFA); lighting design (MFA); performance (MFA); scene design (MFA); theatre technology (MFA). *Degree requirements:* For master's, thesis or alternative. *Entrance requirements:* For master's, audition, minimum GPA of 2.7. Additional exam requirements/recommendations for international students: Required—TOEFL. Electronic applications accepted. *Expenses:* Tuition, state resident: full-time $7440; part-time $414 per credit hour. Tuition, nonresident: full-time $22,478; part-time $1250 per credit hour. Required fees: $922; $43 per credit hour. Tuition and fees vary according to program.

The University of Tennessee, Graduate School, College of Arts and Sciences, School of Music, Knoxville, TN 37996. Offers accompanying (MM); choral conducting (MM); composition (MM); instrumental conducting (MM); jazz (MM); music education (MM); music theory (MM); musicology (MM); performance (MM); piano pedagogy and literature (MM). *Accreditation:* NASM. Part-time programs available. *Degree requirements:* For master's, thesis (for some programs). *Entrance requirements:* For master's, audition, minimum GPA of 2.7. Additional exam requirements/recommendations for international students: Required—TOEFL. Electronic applications accepted. *Expenses:* Tuition, state resident: full-time $7440; part-time $414 per credit hour. Tuition, nonresident: full-time $22,478; part-time $1250 per credit hour. Required fees: $922; $43 per credit hour. Tuition and fees vary according to program.

The University of Tennessee at Chattanooga, Graduate School, College of Arts and Sciences, Department of Music, Chattanooga, TN 37403. Offers music education (MM); performance (MM). *Accreditation:* NASM. Part-time programs available. *Faculty:* 7 full-time (1 woman). *Students:* 7 full-time (3 women), 8 part-time (4 women), 1 international. Average age 30. 5 applicants, 100% accepted, 4 enrolled. In 2010, 2 master's awarded. *Degree requirements:* For master's, comprehensive exam, thesis or alternative, senior recital. *Entrance requirements:* For master's, GRE General Test or MAT, bachelor's degree in music, audition for placement. Additional exam requirements/recommendations for international students: Required—TOEFL (minimum score 550 paper-based; 213 computer-based; 79 iBT), IELTS (minimum score 6). *Application deadline:* For fall admission, 8/1 priority date for domestic students, 6/1 for international students; for spring admission, 12/1 priority date for domestic students, 10/1 for international students. Applications are processed on a rolling basis. Application fee: $35. Electronic applications accepted. *Financial support:* In 2010–11, 5 research assistantships with full and partial tuition reimbursements (averaging $5,500 per year) were awarded; Federal Work-Study, scholarships/grants, and unspecified assistantships also available. *Faculty research:* Music education, conducting, opera, vocal instruction, orchestras. *Unit head:* Dr. Lee Harris, Department Head, 423-425-4601, Fax: 423-425-4603, E-mail: lee-harris@utc.edu. *Application contact:* Dr. Jerald Ainsworth, Dean of Graduate Studies, 423-425-4478, Fax: 423-425-5223, E-mail: jerald-ainsworth@utc.edu.

The University of Texas at Arlington, Graduate School, College of Liberal Arts, Department of Music, Arlington, TX 76019. Offers education (MM); performance (MM). *Accreditation:* NASM. Part-time and evening/weekend programs available. *Faculty:* 25 full-time (9 women). *Students:* 16 full-time (6 women), 13 part-time (10 women); includes 4 minority (3 Hispanic/ Latino; 1 Two or more races, non-Hispanic/Latino), 7 international. 13 applicants, 92% accepted, 10 enrolled. In 2010, 8 master's awarded. *Degree requirements:* For master's, comprehensive exam, thesis optional. *Entrance requirements:* For master's, GRE, 3 letters of recommendation, minimum GPA of 3.0 in last 60 hours of course work. Additional exam requirements/ recommendations for international students: Required—TOEFL (minimum score 550 paper-based; 213 computer-based). *Application deadline:* For fall admission, 6/1 priority date for domestic students. Applications are processed on a rolling basis. Application fee: $35 ($50 for international students). Electronic applications accepted. *Expenses:* Tuition, state resident: full-time $7500. Tuition, nonresident: full-time $13,080. International tuition: $13,250 full-time. *Financial support:* In 2010–11, 7 teaching assistantships with partial tuition reimbursements (averaging $7,500 per year) were awarded; scholarships/grants also available. *Unit head:* Dr. John Burton, Chair, 817-272-3471, Fax: 817-272-3434. *Application contact:* Dr. Clifton Evans, Graduate Advisor, 817-272-5027, Fax: 817-272-3434, E-mail: cevans@uta.edu.

The University of Texas at Austin, Graduate School, College of Fine Arts, Butler School of Music, Austin, TX 78712-1111. Offers M Music, DMA, PhD. *Accreditation:* NASM. Part-time programs available. *Degree requirements:* For master's, one foreign language, comprehensive exam, thesis (for some programs), recital (performance or composition majors); for doctorate, one foreign language, comprehensive exam, thesis/dissertation (for some programs), recital for performance or composition majors. *Entrance requirements:* For master's, GRE General Test (unless a performance or composition major), audition (performance majors); for doctorate, GRE General Test (not required for performance or composition majors), audition (performance majors). Electronic applications accepted.

The University of Texas at El Paso, Graduate School, College of Liberal Arts, Department of Music, El Paso, TX 79968-0001. Offers music education (MM); music performance (MM). *Accreditation:* NASM. Part-time and evening/weekend programs available. *Students:* 23 (7 women); includes 1 Black or African American, non-Hispanic/Latino; 1 American Indian or Alaska Native, non-Hispanic/Latino; 11 Hispanic/Latino, 4 international. Average age 34. In 2010, 8 master's awarded. *Degree requirements:* For master's, thesis optional. *Entrance requirements:* For master's, audition, interview, letters of recommendation. Additional exam requirements/recommendations for international students: Required—TOEFL; Recommended—IELTS. *Application deadline:* For fall admission, 8/1 priority date for domestic students, 3/1 for international students; for spring admission, 11/1 priority date for domestic students, 9/1 for international students. Applications are processed on a rolling basis. Application fee: $45 ($80 for international students). Electronic applications accepted. *Financial support:* In 2010–11, research assistantships (averaging $18,625 per year), teaching assistantships with partial tuition reimbursements (averaging $14,900 per year) were awarded; fellowships with partial tuition reimbursements, institutionally sponsored loans, scholarships/grants, health care benefits, tuition waivers (partial), and unspecified assistantships also available. Support available to part-time students. Financial award application deadline: 3/15; financial award applicants required to submit FAFSA. *Unit head:* Dr. Lowell Graham, Chair, 915-747-5606, Fax: 915-747-5023, E-mail: legraham@utep.edu. *Application contact:* Dr. Patricia D. Witherspoon, Dean of the Graduate School, 915-747-5491, Fax: 915-747-5788, E-mail: withersp@utep.edu.

The University of Texas at San Antonio, College of Liberal and Fine Arts, Department of Music, San Antonio, TX 78249-0617. Offers keyboard pedagogy (Graduate Certificate); keyboard performance (Graduate Certificate); music (MM). *Accreditation:* NASM. Part-time programs available. *Faculty:* 18 full-time (8 women), 2 part-time/adjunct (1 woman). *Students:* 11 full-time (9 women), 11 part-time (3 women); includes 10 minority (1 Asian, non-Hispanic/Latino; 8 Hispanic/Latino; 1 Two or more races, non-Hispanic/Latino), 1 international. Average age 28. 16 applicants, 63% accepted, 5 enrolled. In 2010, 6 master's awarded. *Degree requirements:* For master's, one foreign language, comprehensive exam (for some programs), thesis (for some programs), recital. *Entrance requirements:* For master's, GRE, audition, 3 letters of recommendation. Additional exam requirements/recommendations for international students: Required—TOEFL (minimum score 500 paper-based; 173 computer-based; 61 iBT), IELTS (minimum score 5). *Application deadline:* For fall admission, 7/1 for domestic students, 4/1 for international students; for spring admission, 11/1 for domestic students, 9/1 for international students. Applications are processed on a rolling basis. Application fee: $45 ($80 for international students). Electronic applications accepted. *Expenses:* Tuition, state resident: full-time $4172; part-time $231.75 per credit hour. Tuition, nonresident: full-time $15,332; part-time $851.75 per credit hour. *Financial support:* In 2010–11, 9 students received support, including 8 research assistantships (averaging $8,354 per year), 3 teaching assistantships (averaging $3,990 per year); career-related internships or fieldwork, scholarships/grants, and unspecified assistantships also available. Support available to part-time students. Financial award application deadline: 3/1. *Faculty research:* Vocal singing health, rhythmic and movement therapy, implied harmonic and polyphonic structures in music, historical music of Latin America, documenting early twentieth century American choral music. Total annual research expenditures: $6,881. *Unit head:* Dr. David Frego, Department Chair, 210-458-4354, E-mail: david.frego@utsa.edu. *Application contact:* Veronica Ramirez, Assistant Dean of the Graduate School, 210-458-4330, Fax: 210-458-4332, E-mail: graduatestudies@utsa.edu.

The University of Texas–Pan American, College of Arts and Humanities, Department of Music, Edinburg, TX 78539. Offers ethnomusicology (M Mus); interdisciplinary studies (MAIS); music education (M Mus); performance (M Mus). *Accreditation:* NASM. Part-time programs available. *Degree requirements:* For master's, comprehensive exam, thesis optional, recital (performance). *Entrance requirements:* For master's, audition for performance area, bachelor's degree in music. *Faculty research:* Music history, instrumental pedagogy, vocal pedagogy, music education, ethnomusicology.

The University of the Arts, College of Performing Arts, School of Music, Program in Jazz Studies, Philadelphia, PA 19102-4944. Offers MM. *Degree requirements:* For master's, recital, thesis/project. *Entrance requirements:* For master's, audition consisting of a performance, interview and written examination to measure aural, theoretical, arranging and historical skills and knowledge; official transcripts from each undergraduate or graduate school attended; three letters of recommendation; one- to two-page statement of professional plans and goals. Additional exam requirements/recommendations for international students: Required—TOEFL (minimum score 580 paper-based, 92 iBT) or IELTS (minimum score 6.5).

See Display on page 187 and Close-Up on page 229.

University of the Pacific, Conservatory of Music, Stockton, CA 95211-0197. Offers MA, MM. *Accreditation:* NASM. *Faculty:* 4 full-time (3 women), 3 part-time/adjunct (2 women). *Students:* 17 full-time (13 women), 10 part-time (8 women); includes 3 Asian, non-Hispanic/Latino; 1 Hispanic/Latino, 4 international. Average age 28. 42 applicants, 48% accepted, 9 enrolled. In 2010, 3 master's awarded. *Entrance requirements:* For master's, GRE General Test. Additional exam requirements/recommendations for international students: Required—TOEFL (minimum score 475 paper-based; 150 computer-based). *Application deadline:* For fall admission, 3/1 priority date for domestic students; for spring admission, 10/1 priority date for domestic students. Applications are processed on a rolling basis. Application fee: $75. *Financial support:* Teaching assistantships, institutionally sponsored loans available. Support available to part-time students. Financial award application deadline: 3/1; financial award applicants required to submit FAFSA. *Unit head:* Dr. Giulio Ongaro, Dean, 209-946-2417. *Application contact:* Dr. Therese West, Chairperson, 209-946-3194.

The University of Toledo, College of Graduate Studies, College of Visual and Performing Arts, Department of Music, Toledo, OH 43606-3390. Offers music performance (MMP). *Accreditation:* NASM. *Faculty:* 7. *Students:* 8 full-time (2 women), 1 (woman) part-time; includes 1 minority (Hispanic/Latino), 2 international. Average age 31. 10 applicants, 40% accepted, 3 enrolled. In 2010, 4 master's awarded. *Degree requirements:* For master's, comprehensive exam, diagnostic theory exam. *Entrance requirements:* For master's, GRE if less than 2.7 GPA. A minimum 2.7 cumulative point-hour ratio (on a 4.0 scale) for all previous academic work. Audition required. Additional exam requirements/recommendations for international students: Required—TOEFL (minimum score 550 paper-based; 213 computer-based; 80 iBT), IELTS (minimum score 6.5). *Application deadline:* For fall admission, 1/15 priority date for domestic and international students. Applications are processed on a rolling basis. Application fee: $45 ($75 for international students). Electronic applications accepted. *Expenses:* Tuition, state resident: full-time $11,426; part-time $476 per credit hour. Tuition, nonresident: full-time $21,660; part-time $903 per credit hour. One-time fee: $62. *Financial support:* Federal Work-Study, institutionally sponsored loans, scholarships/grants, tuition waivers (full), and unspecified assistantships available. Support available to part-time students. *Unit head:* Dr. Timothy Brakel, Acting Chair, 419-530-2448, E-mail: timothy.brakel@utoledo.edu. *Application contact:* Graduate School Office, 419-530-4723, Fax: 419-530-4724, E-mail: grdsch@utnet.utoledo.edu.

University of Toronto, School of Graduate Studies, Humanities Division, Faculty of Music, Toronto, ON M5S 1A1, Canada. Offers composition (M Mus, DMA); music education (MA, PhD); musicology/theory (MA, PhD); performance (M Mus, DMA). Part-time programs available. *Degree requirements:* For master's, comprehensive exam (for some programs), oral examination (Mus M in composition), 1 foreign language (MA); for doctorate, thesis/dissertation (for some programs), recital of original works (Mus Doc), thesis (PhD). *Entrance requirements:* For master's, BM in area of specialization with minimum B average in final 2 years, original compositions (Mus M in composition); for doctorate, master's degree in area of specialization, minimum B+ average, at least 2 extended compositions (Mus Doc).

University of Trinity College, Faculty of Divinity, Toronto, ON M5S 1H8, Canada. Offers ministry (Diploma); ministry for church musicians (Diploma); theology (M Div, MA, MTS, Th M, D Min, PhD, Th D, Diploma, L Th); M Div/MA. *Accreditation:* ATS. Part-time programs available. *Faculty:* 3 full-time (1 woman), 31 part-time/adjunct (4 women). *Students:* 50 full-time (15 women), 84 part-time (39 women). Average age 45. *Degree requirements:* For master's, 2 foreign languages, thesis (for some programs); for doctorate, 3 foreign languages, comprehensive exam, thesis/dissertation; for M Div, thesis/dissertation optional; for other advanced degree, thesis (for some programs). *Entrance requirements:* For M Div, interview; for master's, 1 language (modern or ancient), interview; for doctorate, 2 languages (modern and ancient). Additional exam requirements/recommendations for international students: Required—TOEFL, TWE. *Application deadline:* For fall admission, 3/31 priority date for domestic and international students; for winter admission, 12/31 for domestic and international students; for spring admission, 4/30 priority date for domestic and international students. Applications are processed on a rolling basis. Application fee: $0. *Financial support:* Fellowships, teaching assistantships, career-related internships or fieldwork, institutionally sponsored loans, and bursaries available. Support available to part-time students. Financial award application deadline: 5/15. *Faculty research:* Interreligious dialogue, feminist theology, systematic theology, philosophy of religion, pastoral theology. *Unit head:* Dr. David Neelands, Dean, 416-978-7750, Fax: 416-978-4949, E-mail: divdean@trinity.utoronto.ca. *Application contact:* Rachel Richards, Administrative Assistant to the Dean, 416-978-2133, Fax: 416-978-4949, E-mail: divinity@trinity.utoronto.ca.

University of Utah, Graduate School, College of Fine Arts, School of Music, Salt Lake City, UT 84112. Offers M Mus, MA, DMA, PhD. *Accreditation:* NASM. *Faculty:* 30 full-time (12 women), 24 part-time/adjunct (7 women). *Students:* 81 full-time (47 women), 36 part-time (17 women); includes 12 minority (2 American Indian or Alaska Native, non-Hispanic/Latino; 3 Asian, non-Hispanic/Latino; 5 Hispanic/Latino; 1 Native Hawaiian or other Pacific Islander, non-Hispanic/Latino; 1 Two or more races, non-Hispanic/Latino), 22 international. Average age 31. 110 applicants, 50% accepted, 38 enrolled. In 2010, 36 master's, 3 doctorates awarded. *Degree requirements:* For master's, variable foreign language requirement, thesis (for some programs), 2 recitals, final oral exam; for doctorate, one foreign language, comprehensive exam (for some programs), final oral exam, 4 recitals (DMA); thesis (PhD). *Entrance requirements:* For master's and doctorate, placement exams, minimum GPA of 3.0, audition, bachelor's degree in music. Additional exam requirements/recommendations for international students: Required—TOEFL (minimum score 563 paper-based; 223 computer-based; 85 iBT). *Application deadline:* For fall admission, 2/15 for domestic students, 1/15 for international students; for spring admission, 10/1 for domestic students, 9/1 for international students. Applications are processed on a rolling basis. Application fee: $55 ($65 for international students). Electronic applications accepted. *Expenses:* Tuition, area resident: Part-time $179.19 per credit hour. Tuition, state resident: full-time $4384. Tuition, nonresident: full-time $16,684; part-time $630.67 per credit hour. Required fees: $350 per semester. Tuition and fees vary according to course load, degree level and program. *Financial support:* In 2010–11, 52 students received support, including 52 teaching assistantships with full and partial tuition reimbursements available (averaging $8,250 per year); fellowships with full and partial tuition reimbursements available, research assistantships with full and partial tuition reimbursements available, health care benefits and unspecified assistantships also available. Financial award application deadline: 2/1. *Faculty research:* Music education, conducting, musicology, composition, performance. Total annual research expenditures: $1,873. *Unit head:* Dr. Robert Baldwin, Interim Director, 801-581-6762, Fax: 801-581-5683, E-mail: robert.baldwin@music.utah.edu. *Application contact:* Jill Wilson, Academic Coordinator, 801-585-6972, Fax: 801-581-5683, E-mail: jill.wilson@utah.edu.

University of Utah, Graduate School, College of Humanities, Department of English, Salt Lake City, UT 84112. Offers American studies (PhD); British American literature (MA, PhD); creative writing (MA, MFA, PhD), including rhetoric/composition (MA, PhD); literature (PhD); rhetoric and composition (PhD). *Faculty:* 35 full-time (16 women), 1 part-time/adjunct (0 women). *Students:* 57 full-time (32 women), 19 part-time (12 women); includes 5 minority (1 Black or African American, non-Hispanic/Latino; 1 American Indian or Alaska Native, non-Hispanic/Latino; 1 Asian, non-Hispanic/Latino; 2 Two or more races, non-Hispanic/Latino), 4 international. Average age 33. 281 applicants, 11% accepted, 27 enrolled. In 2010, 13 master's, 3 doctorates awarded. Terminal master's awarded for partial completion of doctoral program. *Degree requirements:* For master's, one foreign language, comprehensive exam, thesis (for some programs), written exam; for doctorate, 2 foreign languages, comprehensive exam, thesis/dissertation, 2 standard level languages/1 advanced level language. *Entrance requirements:* For master's and doctorate, GRE General Test, minimum GPA of 3.2. Additional exam requirements/recommendations for international students: Required—TOEFL (minimum score 650 paper-based; 280 computer-based; 115 iBT); Recommended—IELTS (minimum score 9). *Application deadline:* For fall admission, 12/15 for domestic and international students. Application fee: $55 ($65 for international students). Electronic applications accepted. *Expenses:* Tuition, area resident: Part-time $179.19 per credit hour. Tuition, state resident: full-time $4384. Tuition, nonresident: full-time $16,684; part-time $630.67 per credit hour. Required fees: $350 per semester. Tuition and fees vary according to course load, degree level and program. *Financial support:* In 2010–11, 60 students received support, including 11 fellowships with full tuition reimbursements available (averaging $12,400 per year), 49 teaching assistantships with full tuition reimbursements available (averaging $12,400 per year); research assistantships, health care benefits also available. Financial award application deadline: 12/15; financial award applicants required to submit FAFSA. *Faculty research:* Poetics and modern poetry, nineteenth and twentieth century British and American literature, the American west, environmental studies, critical theory and race and gender studies, fiction. Total annual research expenditures: $32,329. *Unit head:* Prof. Vincent P. Pecora, Chair, 801-581-6168, E-mail: v.pecora@utah.edu. *Application contact:* Prof. Scott Black, Director of Graduate Studies, 801-581-5137, E-mail: scott.black@utah.edu.

University of Victoria, Faculty of Graduate Studies, Faculty of Fine Arts, School of Music, Victoria, BC V8W 2Y2, Canada. Offers composition (M Mus); musicology (MA, PhD); musicology with performance (MA); performance (M Mus). *Degree requirements:* For master's, 2 foreign languages, thesis; for doctorate, 2 foreign languages, thesis/dissertation, candidacy exam. *Entrance requirements:* For master's, theory placement test, audition or sample papers and compositions; for doctorate, audition or sample papers and compositions. Additional exam requirements/recommendations for international students: Required—TOEFL (minimum score 575 paper-based; 233 computer-based), IELTS (minimum score 7). Electronic applications accepted. *Faculty research:* Beethoven, Wagner, metrical structure in tonal music, French baroque, eighteenth century opera.

University of Virginia, College and Graduate School of Arts and Sciences, Department of Music, Charlottesville, VA 22903. Offers MA, PhD. *Faculty:* 12 full-time (3 women), 13 part-time/adjunct (5 women). *Students:* 31 full-time (11 women); includes 1 Asian, non-Hispanic/Latino; 1 Two or more races, non-Hispanic/Latino, 5 international. Average age 30. 53 applicants, 15% accepted, 7 enrolled. In 2010, 4 master's, 2 doctorates awarded. *Degree requirements:* For master's, one foreign language, article-length paper; for doctorate, one foreign language, comprehensive exam, thesis/dissertation. *Entrance requirements:* For master's and doctorate, GRE General Test, 2 writing samples or portfolio. Additional exam requirements/recommendations for international students: Required—TOEFL (minimum score 600 paper-based; 250 computer-based; 90 iBT), IELTS (minimum score 7). *Application deadline:* For fall admission, 1/1 for domestic students, 1/2 for international students. Applications are processed on a rolling basis. Application fee: $60. Electronic applications accepted. *Financial support:* Teaching assistantships available. Financial award applicants required to submit FAFSA. *Unit head:* Richard Will, Chair, 434-924-3052, Fax: 434-924-6033, E-mail: rw6w@virginia.edu. *Application contact:* Fred Maus, Director of Graduate Studies, 434-924-3052, Fax: 434-924-6033, E-mail: fem2x@virginia.edu.

University of Washington, Graduate School, College of Arts and Sciences, School of Music, Concentration in Choral Conducting, Seattle, WA 98195. Offers MM, DMA.

University of Washington, Graduate School, College of Arts and Sciences, School of Music, Concentration in Ethnomusicology, Seattle, WA 98195. Offers MA.

University of Washington, Graduate School, College of Arts and Sciences, School of Music, Concentration in Music History, Seattle, WA 98195. Offers MA, PhD.

University of Washington, Graduate School, College of Arts and Sciences, School of Music, Department of Choral Music, Seattle, WA 98195. Offers choral conducting (MM, DMA).

The University of Western Ontario, Faculty of Graduate Studies, Faculty of Arts and Humanities, Don Wright Faculty of Music, London, ON N6A 5B8, Canada. Offers music (M Mus, PhD); popular music and culture (MA). Part-time programs available. Terminal master's awarded for partial completion of doctoral program. *Degree requirements:* For master's, 2 foreign languages, thesis (for some programs), recital; for doctorate, 2 foreign languages, thesis/dissertation. *Entrance requirements:* For master's, honors degree in music; minimum A average in proposed area of concentration, B average overall; for doctorate, MA or equivalent. *Faculty research:* Systematic musicology, musicology, theory, music education.

University of West Georgia, College of Arts and Sciences, Department of Music, Carrollton, GA 30118. Offers music education (M Mus); performance (M Mus). *Accreditation:* NASM. Part-time programs available. *Faculty:* 7 full-time (3 women), 3 part-time/adjunct (2 women). *Students:* 2 full-time (0 women), 10 part-time (5 women); includes 4 Black or African American, non-Hispanic/Latino; 1 Asian, non-Hispanic/Latino. Average age 35. 5 applicants, 80% accepted, 0 enrolled. In 2010, 4 master's awarded. *Degree requirements:* For master's, comprehensive exam, thesis optional, recital (MM in performance), departmental qualifying exam. *Entrance requirements:* For master's, qualifying exam, minimum GPA of 2.5, bachelor's degree in music education or teacher certification (music education), performance evaluation. *Application deadline:* For fall admission, 7/17 for domestic students; for spring admission, 11/20 for domestic students. Applications are processed on a rolling basis. Application fee: $30. Electronic applications accepted. *Expenses:* Tuition, state resident: full-time $4130; part-time $173 per semester hour. Tuition, nonresident: full-time $16,524; part-time $689 per semester hour. Required fees: $1586; $44.01 per semester hour. $397 per semester. Tuition and fees vary according to program. *Financial support:* In 2010–11, 1 student received support, including 1 research assistantship with full tuition reimbursement available (averaging $6,000 per year); career-related internships or fieldwork, tuition waivers (full), and unspecified assistantships also available. Support available to part-time students. Financial award application deadline: 7/1; financial award applicants required to submit FAFSA. *Faculty research:* Musicology, instrumental music/music education, jazz performance, French music. *Unit head:* Dr. Kevin Hibbard, Chair, 678-839-6516, Fax: 678-839-6259, E-mail: khibbard@westga.edu. *Application contact:* Dr. Charles W. Clark, Dean, 678-839-6508, E-mail: cclark@westga.edu.

University of Wisconsin–Madison, Graduate School, College of Letters and Science, School of Music, Program in Composition, Madison, WI 53706-1380. Offers MM, DMA. *Accreditation:* NASM. *Degree requirements:* For doctorate, thesis/dissertation. *Expenses:* Tuition, state resident: full-time $9887; part-time $617.96 per credit. Tuition, nonresident: full-time $24,054; part-time $1503.40 per credit. Required fees: $67.63 per credit. Tuition and fees vary according to reciprocity agreements.

University of Wisconsin–Madison, Graduate School, College of Letters and Science, School of Music, Program in Conducting, Madison, WI 53706-1380. Offers choral (MM, DMA); instrumental (MM, DMA); orchestral (MM, DMA). *Accreditation:* NASM. *Degree requirements:* For doctorate, thesis/dissertation. *Expenses:* Tuition, state resident: full-time $9887; part-time $617.96 per credit. Tuition, nonresident: full-time $24,054; part-time $1503.40 per credit. Required fees: $67.63 per credit. Tuition and fees vary according to reciprocity agreements.

University of Wisconsin–Madison, Graduate School, College of Letters and Science, School of Music, Program in Musicology and Ethnomusicology, Madison, WI 53706-1380. Offers

Music

University of Wisconsin–Madison (continued)
ethnomusicology (MA, PhD); historical musicology (PhD); music history (MA). *Accreditation:* NASM. *Degree requirements:* For doctorate, 2 foreign languages, thesis/dissertation. *Entrance requirements:* For doctorate, GRE General Test. *Expenses:* Tuition, state resident: full-time $9887; part-time $617.96 per credit. Tuition, nonresident: full-time $24,054; part-time $1503.40 per credit. Required fees: $67.63 per credit. Tuition and fees vary according to reciprocity agreements.

University of Wisconsin–Madison, Graduate School, College of Letters and Science, School of Music, Program in Music Performance, Madison, WI 53706-1380. Offers MM, DMA. *Accreditation:* NASM. *Degree requirements:* For doctorate, one foreign language, thesis/dissertation. *Expenses:* Tuition, state resident: full-time $9887; part-time $617.96 per credit. Tuition, nonresident: full-time $24,054; part-time $1503.40 per credit. Required fees: $67.63 per credit. Tuition and fees vary according to reciprocity agreements.

University of Wisconsin–Madison, Graduate School, College of Letters and Science, School of Music, Program in Music Theory, Madison, WI 53706-1380. Offers MA, PhD. *Accreditation:* NASM. *Degree requirements:* For master's, thesis, 1 foreign language (MA); for doctorate, 2 foreign languages, thesis/dissertation. *Entrance requirements:* For master's, GRE General Test (MA); for doctorate, GRE General Test. *Expenses:* Tuition, state resident: full-time $9887; part-time $617.96 per credit. Tuition, nonresident: full-time $24,054; part-time $1503.40 per credit. Required fees: $67.63 per credit. Tuition and fees vary according to reciprocity agreements.

University of Wisconsin–Milwaukee, Graduate School, Peck School of the Arts, Department of Music, Milwaukee, WI 53201-0413. Offers chamber music performance (Certificate); music composition (MM); music education (MM); music history and literature (MM); opera and vocal arts (Certificate); string pedagogy (MM); MLIS/MM. *Accreditation:* NASM. Part-time programs available. *Faculty:* 24 full-time (7 women). *Students:* 48 full-time (26 women), 21 part-time (9 women); includes 4 Asian, non-Hispanic/Latino, 8 international. Average age 28. 64 applicants, 56% accepted, 27 enrolled. In 2010, 22 master's awarded. *Degree requirements:* For master's, variable foreign language requirement, comprehensive exam, thesis or alternative. *Entrance requirements:* For master's, GRE General Test, GRE Subject Test, audition, interview. Additional exam requirements/recommendations for international students: Required—TOEFL (minimum score 550 paper-based; 79 iBT), IELTS (minimum score 6.5). *Application deadline:* For fall admission, 1/1 priority date for domestic students; for spring admission, 9/1 for domestic students. Applications are processed on a rolling basis. Application fee: $56 ($96 for international students). Electronic applications accepted. *Expenses:* Contact institution. *Financial support:* In 2010–11, 14 teaching assistantships were awarded; fellowships, career-related internships or fieldwork, health care benefits, unspecified assistantships, and project assistantships also available. Support available to part-time students. Financial award application deadline: 4/15. *Unit head:* Gillian Rodger, Representative, 414-229-5162, Fax: 414-229-2776, E-mail: grodger@uwm.edu. *Application contact:* General Information Contact, 414-229-4982, Fax: 414-229-6967, E-mail: gradschool@uwm.edu.

University of Wyoming, College of Arts and Sciences, Department of Music, Laramie, WY 82070. Offers music education (MME); performance (MM). *Accreditation:* NASM. *Degree requirements:* For master's, comprehensive exam, thesis or alternative. *Entrance requirements:* For master's, minimum GPA of 3.0. Additional exam requirements/recommendations for international students: Required—TOEFL (minimum score 540 paper-based; 207 computer-based). Electronic applications accepted.

Valley Forge Christian College, Program in Music Technology, Phoenixville, PA 19460. Offers MM. Postbaccalaureate distance learning degree programs offered (minimal on-campus study).

Vermont College of Fine Arts, Program in Music Composition, Montpelier, VT 05602. Offers MFA. Postbaccalaureate distance learning degree programs offered (minimal on-campus study). *Expenses:* Tuition: Full-time $17,820. Required fees: $270. *Unit head:* Carol Beatty, Program Director, 866-934-8232 Ext. 8610, E-mail: carol.beatty@vermontcollege.edu. *Application contact:* Debbie New, Assistant Director of Admissions, 802-828-8636, E-mail: debbie.new@vermontcollege.edu.

Virginia Commonwealth University, Graduate School, School of the Arts, Department of Music, Richmond, VA 23284-9005. Offers education (MM). *Accreditation:* NASM. *Faculty:* 11 full-time (4 women). *Students:* 6 part-time (4 women); includes 1 minority (Asian, non-Hispanic/Latino). 1 applicant, 0% accepted, 0 enrolled. In 2010, 6 master's awarded. *Degree requirements:* For master's, departmental qualifying exam, recital. *Entrance requirements:* For master's, department examination, audition or tapes, portfolio. Additional exam requirements/recommendations for international students: Required—TOEFL (minimum score 600 paper-based; 250 computer-based; 100 iBT). *Application deadline:* For fall admission, 4/1 for domestic students. Application fee: $50. Electronic applications accepted. *Expenses:* Tuition, state resident: full-time $4308; part-time $479 per credit hour. Tuition, nonresident: full-time $8942; part-time $994 per credit hour. Required fees: $2000; $85 per credit hour. Tuition and fees vary according to course level, course load, degree level, campus/location and program. *Financial support:* Fellowships, teaching assistantships, career-related internships or fieldwork, Federal Work-Study, and institutionally sponsored loans available. Support available to part-time students. Financial award application deadline: 3/15. *Faculty research:* Composition, conducting, education, performance. *Unit head:* Darryl Harper, Interim Chair, 804-828-1166, Fax: 804-828-6469, E-mail: dharper2@vcu.edu. *Application contact:* Racquel C. Wallace, Admissions and records specialist, 804-828-1167, E-mail: wallacerc@vcu.edu.

Washington State University, Graduate School, College of Liberal Arts, School of Music and Theatre Arts, Pullman, WA 99164. Offers composition (MA); jazz (MA); music (MA); music education (MA); performance (MA). *Accreditation:* NASM. *Degree requirements:* For master's, comprehensive exam (for some programs), thesis (for some programs), oral exam. *Entrance requirements:* For master's, audition, minimum GPA of 3.0, 3 letters of recommendation, composition portfolio and recording (composition), writing sample and written philosophy (music education), writing sample (music history), in-depth audition (performance). Additional exam requirements/recommendations for international students: Required—TOEFL, IELTS. *Application deadline:* For fall admission, 1/10 priority date for domestic students, 1/10 for international students; for spring admission, 7/1 for domestic and international students. Applications are processed on a rolling basis. Application fee: $50. Electronic applications accepted. *Expenses:* Tuition, state resident: full-time $8552; part-time $443 per credit. Tuition, nonresident: full-time $21,650; part-time $1083 per credit. Required fees: $846. *Financial support:* Fellowships, research assistantships, teaching assistantships with full and partial tuition reimbursements, career-related internships or fieldwork, Federal Work-Study, institutionally sponsored loans, and tuition waivers (partial) available. Financial award application deadline: 2/15; financial award applicants required to submit FAFSA. *Unit head:* Dr. Gregory W. Yasinitsky, Director, 509-335-4244, Fax: 509-335-4245, E-mail: yasinits@wsu.edu. *Application contact:* Graduate School Admissions, 800-GRAD-WSU, Fax: 509-335-1949, E-mail: gradsch@wsu.edu.

Washington University in St. Louis, Graduate School of Arts and Sciences, Department of Music, St. Louis, MO 63130-4899. Offers MM, PhD. Terminal master's awarded for partial completion of doctoral program. *Degree requirements:* For master's, thesis or alternative; for doctorate, thesis/dissertation. *Entrance requirements:* For master's, GRE General Test, departmental exam; for doctorate, departmental exam, GRE General Test. Electronic applications accepted.

Wayne State University, College of Fine, Performing and Communication Arts, Department of Music, Detroit, MI 48202. Offers choral conducting (MM); composition (MM); music (MA, MM); music education (MM); orchestral studies (Certificate); performance (MM); theory (MM). *Accreditation:* NASM. *Faculty:* 14 full-time (4 women), 4 part-time/adjunct (0 women). *Students:* 15 full-time (3 women), 14 part-time (5 women); includes 1 minority (Black or African American, non-Hispanic/Latino), 3 international. Average age 32. 21 applicants, 71% accepted, 9 enrolled. In 2010, 14 master's awarded. *Degree requirements:* For master's, variable foreign language requirement. *Entrance requirements:* For master's, audition, interview. Additional exam requirements/recommendations for international students: Required—TOEFL (minimum score 550 paper-based; 213 computer-based); Recommended—TWE (minimum score 6). *Application deadline:* For fall admission, 4/1 for domestic students, 6/1 for international students; for winter admission, 10/1 for international students; for spring admission, 2/1 for international students. Applications are processed on a rolling basis. Application fee: $30 ($50 for international students). Electronic applications accepted. *Expenses:* Tuition, state resident: full-time $7662; part-time $478.85 per credit hour. Tuition, nonresident: full-time $16,920; part-time $1057.55 per credit hour. Required fees: $571.20; $35.70 per credit hour. $188.05 per semester. Tuition and fees vary according to course load and program. *Financial support:* In 2010–11, 12 students received support; research assistantships, teaching assistantships, career-related internships or fieldwork, Federal Work-Study, institutionally sponsored loans, and scholarships/grants available. Support available to part-time students. *Faculty research:* Teacher training, pedagogy, musicology, composition/theory, conducting/performance practice. *Unit head:* Dr. John Van Der Weg, Chair, 313-577-1800, Fax: 313-577-5420, E-mail: music.chair@wayne.edu. *Application contact:* Mary Wischusen, Graduate Director, 313-577-2612, E-mail: mary.wischusen@wayne.edu.

Webster University, Leigh Gerdine College of Fine Arts, Department of Music, St. Louis, MO 63119-3194. Offers church music (MM); composition (MM); conducting (MM); jazz studies (MM); music (MA); music education (MM); performance (MM); piano (MM). *Accreditation:* NASM. *Entrance requirements:* Additional exam requirements/recommendations for international students: Required—TOEFL. *Expenses:* Tuition: Part-time $585 per credit hour. Tuition and fees vary according to degree level, campus/location and program.

Wesleyan University, Graduate Programs, Department of Music, Middletown, CT 06459. Offers composition (MA); ethnomusicology (MA, PhD). *Faculty:* 7 full-time (2 women). *Students:* 21 full-time (11 women); includes 2 Black or African American, non-Hispanic/Latino; 1 American Indian or Alaska Native, non-Hispanic/Latino; 6 Asian, non-Hispanic/Latino; 2 Hispanic/Latino, 7 international. Average age 31. 66 applicants, 29% accepted, 8 enrolled. In 2010, 7 master's awarded. *Degree requirements:* For master's, one foreign language, thesis; for doctorate, 2 foreign languages, comprehensive exam, thesis/dissertation. *Entrance requirements:* For doctorate, MA. Additional exam requirements/recommendations for international students: Required—TOEFL. *Application deadline:* For fall admission, 1/15 for domestic and international students. Application fee: $75. Electronic applications accepted. *Expenses:* Tuition: Full-time $43,404. Required fees: $830. *Financial support:* In 2010–11, 21 students received support, including 21 teaching assistantships with full tuition reimbursements available (averaging $14,000 per year). *Faculty research:* Ethnomusicology, musicology, music theory, composition, performance. *Unit head:* Dr. Su Zheng, Director of Graduate Studies/Associate Professor, 860-685-2582, Fax: 860-685-2651, E-mail: szheng@wesleyan.edu. *Application contact:* Deborah Shore, Administrative Assistant, 860-685-2598, Fax: 860-685-2651, E-mail: dshore@wesleyan.edu.

West Chester University of Pennsylvania, Office of Graduate Studies, College of Visual and Performing Arts, Department of Applied Music, West Chester, PA 19383. Offers accompanying (MM); performance (MM); piano pedagogy (MM, Certificate). Part-time and evening/weekend programs available. *Students:* 14 full-time (7 women), 20 part-time (12 women); includes 4 minority (2 Black or African American, non-Hispanic/Latino; 2 Asian, non-Hispanic/Latino), 6 international. Average age 27. 23 applicants, 65% accepted, 8 enrolled. In 2010, 7 master's awarded. *Degree requirements:* For master's, comprehensive exam, thesis optional, recital. *Entrance requirements:* For master's and Certificate, GRE General Test, School of Music Graduate Admission Test (GAT), audition, interview. Additional exam requirements/recommendations for international students: Required—TOEFL (minimum score 550 paper-based; 213 computer-based; 80 iBT). *Application deadline:* For fall admission, 4/15 priority date for domestic students, 3/15 for international students; for spring admission, 10/15 for domestic students, 9/1 for international students. Applications are processed on a rolling basis. Application fee: $35. Electronic applications accepted. *Expenses:* Tuition, state resident: full-time $6966; part-time $387 per credit. Tuition, nonresident: full-time $11,146; part-time $619 per credit. Required fees: $1614.40; $133.24 per credit. Part-time tuition and fees vary according to campus/location. *Financial support:* Unspecified assistantships available. Support available to part-time students. Financial award application deadline: 2/15; financial award applicants required to submit FAFSA. *Unit head:* Dr. Chris Hanning, Chair, 610-436-4178, E-mail: channing@wcupa.edu. *Application contact:* Dr. J. Bryan Burton, Graduate Coordinator, 610-436-2222, E-mail: jburton@wcupa.edu.

West Chester University of Pennsylvania, Office of Graduate Studies, College of Visual and Performing Arts, Department of Music Education, West Chester, PA 19383. Offers Kodaly methodology (Certificate); music education (Teaching Certificate); music technology (Certificate); Orff-Schulwerk (Certificate); performance (MM); research (MM); technology (MM); twenty-first century music education (Certificate). *Accreditation:* NASM; NCATE. Part-time and evening/weekend programs available. *Students:* 1 (woman) full-time, 26 part-time (17 women); includes 1 minority (Black or African American, non-Hispanic/Latino). Average age 28. 27 applicants, 74% accepted, 4 enrolled. In 2010, 18 master's, 5 Certificates awarded. *Degree requirements:* For master's, comprehensive exam, thesis optional, recital. *Entrance requirements:* For master's and other advanced degree, GRE General Test, School of Music Graduate Admission Test (GAT), audition, interview. Additional exam requirements/recommendations for international students: Required—TOEFL (minimum score 550 paper-based; 213 computer-based; 80 iBT). *Application deadline:* For fall admission, 4/15 priority date for domestic students, 3/15 for international students; for spring admission, 10/15 for domestic students, 9/1 for international students. Applications are processed on a rolling basis. Application fee: $35. Electronic applications accepted. *Expenses:* Tuition, state resident: full-time $6966; part-time $387 per credit. Tuition, nonresident: full-time $11,146; part-time $619 per credit. Required fees: $1614.40; $133.24 per credit. Part-time tuition and fees vary according to campus/location. *Financial support:* Unspecified assistantships available. Support available to part-time students. Financial award application deadline: 2/15; financial award applicants required to submit FAFSA. *Faculty research:* Developing music listening skills. *Unit head:* Dr. J. Bryan Burton, Chair and Graduate Coordinator, 610-436-2222, E-mail: jburton@wcupa.edu. *Application contact:* Dr. J. Bryan Burton, Chair and Graduate Coordinator, 610-436-2222, E-mail: jburton@wcupa.edu.

West Chester University of Pennsylvania, Office of Graduate Studies, College of Visual and Performing Arts, Department of Music History and Literature, West Chester, PA 19383. Offers music history (MA). Part-time and evening/weekend programs available. *Students:* 2 full-time (1 woman), 1 (woman) part-time. Average age 23. 2 applicants, 100% accepted, 1 enrolled. In 2010, 1 master's awarded. *Degree requirements:* For master's, comprehensive exam, thesis optional. *Entrance requirements:* For master's, GRE General Test, School of Music Graduate Admission Test (GAT), audition, interview. Additional exam requirements/recommendations for international students: Required—TOEFL (minimum score 550 paper-based; 213 computer-based; 80 iBT). *Application deadline:* For fall admission, 4/15 priority date for domestic students, 3/15 for international students; for spring admission, 10/15 for domestic students, 9/1 for international students. Applications are processed on a rolling basis. Application fee: $35. Electronic applications accepted. *Expenses:* Tuition, state resident: full-time $6966; part-time $387 per credit. Tuition, nonresident: full-time $11,146; part-time $619 per credit. Required fees: $1614.40; $133.24 per credit. Part-time tuition and fees vary according to campus/location. *Financial support:* Unspecified assistantships available. Support available to part-time students. Financial award application deadline: 2/15; financial award applicants required to submit FAFSA. *Faculty research:* Musicology, eighteenth century European music. *Unit head:* Dr. Scott Balthazar, Chair, 610-436-2284, E-mail: sbalthazar@wcupa.edu. *Application contact:* Dr. J. Bryan Burton, Graduate Coordinator, 610-436-2222, E-mail: jburton@wcupa.edu.

West Chester University of Pennsylvania, Office of Graduate Studies, College of Visual and Performing Arts, Department of Music Theory and Composition, West Chester, PA 19383.

Offers music: composition (MM); music: history and literature (MM); music: theory and composition (MM). Part-time and evening/weekend programs available. *Students:* 2 full-time (0 women), 2 part-time (0 women). Average age 27. 1 applicant, 100% accepted, 0 enrolled. In 2010, 2 master's awarded. *Degree requirements:* For master's, comprehensive exam, thesis optional. *Entrance requirements:* For master's, GRE General Test, School of Music Graduate Admission Test (GAT), audition, interview. Additional exam requirements/recommendations for international students: Required—TOEFL (minimum score 550 paper-based; 213 computer-based; 80 iBT). *Application deadline:* For fall admission, 4/15 priority date for domestic students, 3/15 for international students; for spring admission, 10/15 for domestic students, 9/1 for international students. Applications are processed on a rolling basis. Application fee: $35. Electronic applications accepted. *Expenses:* Tuition, state resident: full-time $6966; part-time $387 per credit. Tuition, nonresident: full-time $11,146; part-time $619 per credit. Required fees: $1614.40; $133.24 per credit. Part-time tuition and fees vary according to campus/location. *Financial support:* Unspecified assistantships available. Support available to part-time students. Financial award application deadline: 2/15; financial award applicants required to submit FAFSA. *Unit head:* Dr. Robert Maggio, Chair, 610-436-2646. *Application contact:* Dr. J. Bryan Burton, Graduate Coordinator, 610-436-2222, E-mail: jburton@wcupa.edu.

Western Carolina University, Graduate School, College of Fine and Performing Arts, School of Music, Cullowhee, NC 28723. Offers MM. *Accreditation:* NASM. Part-time programs available. *Degree requirements:* For master's, comprehensive exam, thesis. *Entrance requirements:* For master's, GRE, music entrance exam, appropriate undergraduate degree, live audition and/or interview. Additional exam requirements/recommendations for international students: Required—TOEFL (minimum score 550 paper-based; 270 computer-based; 79 iBT). *Faculty research:* Music experiences for K-12 students, marching band, sound mixing for television, music technology, choral methods, music history.

Western Illinois University, School of Graduate Studies, College of Fine Arts and Communication, School of Music, Macomb, IL 61455-1390. Offers MM. *Accreditation:* NASM. Part-time programs available. *Students:* 25 full-time (17 women), 5 part-time (all women); includes 2 minority (1 Asian, non-Hispanic/Latino; 1 Hispanic/Latino), 6 international. Average age 27. 27 applicants, 37% accepted. In 2010, 6 master's awarded. *Degree requirements:* For master's, comprehensive exam, thesis or alternative. *Entrance requirements:* For master's, audition. Additional exam requirements/recommendations for international students: Required—TOEFL (minimum score 550 paper-based; 213 computer-based; 80 iBT). *Application deadline:* Applications are processed on a rolling basis. Application fee: $30. Electronic applications accepted. *Expenses:* Tuition, state resident: full-time $6370; part-time $265.40 per credit hour. Tuition, nonresident: full-time $12,740; part-time $530.80 per credit hour. Required fees: $75.67 per credit hour. *Financial support:* In 2010–11, 23 students received support, including 23 research assistantships with full tuition reimbursements available (averaging $7,280 per year). Financial award applicants required to submit FAFSA. *Unit head:* Dr. Bart Shanklin, Director, 309-298-1544. *Application contact:* Evelyn Hoing, Assistant Director of Graduate Studies, 309-298-1806, Fax: 309-298-2345, E-mail: grad-office@wiu.edu.

Western Michigan University, Graduate College, College of Fine Arts, School of Music, Kalamazoo, MI 49008. Offers composition (MM); conducting (MM); music (MA); music education (MM); music therapy (MM); performance (MM). *Accreditation:* NASM.

Western Oregon University, Graduate Programs, College of Liberal Arts and Sciences, Division of Creative Arts, Monmouth, OR 97361-1394. Offers contemporary music (MM). *Accreditation:* NASM. *Entrance requirements:* Additional exam requirements/recommendations for international students: Required—TOEFL (minimum score 550 paper-based; 213 computer-based; 79 iBT), IELTS (minimum score 6.5).

Western Washington University, Graduate School, College of Fine and Performing Arts, Department of Music, Bellingham, WA 98225-5996. Offers M Mus. *Accreditation:* NASM. Part-time programs available. *Degree requirements:* For master's, thesis. *Entrance requirements:* For master's, GRE General Test, department placement exams, audition, portfolio, minimum GPA of 3.0 in last 60 semester hours or last 90 quarter hours of course work. Additional exam requirements/recommendations for international students: Required—TOEFL (minimum score 567 paper-based; 227 computer-based). Electronic applications accepted. *Faculty research:* Baroque opera, historical music of the Silk Road, original composition, 20th century orchestral music, 13th century polyphony.

West Texas A&M University, College of Fine Arts and Humanities, Department of Music and Dance, Program in Music, Canyon, TX 79016-0001. Offers MA. *Accreditation:* NASM. Part-time programs available. *Degree requirements:* For master's, comprehensive exam, thesis optional. *Entrance requirements:* For master's, GRE General Test. Additional exam requirements/recommendations for international students: Required—TOEFL (minimum score 550 paper-based). Electronic applications accepted.

West Texas A&M University, College of Fine Arts and Humanities, Department of Music and Dance, Program in Performance, Canyon, TX 79016-0001. Offers MM. *Accreditation:* NASM. Part-time programs available. *Degree requirements:* For master's, comprehensive exam, thesis optional. *Entrance requirements:* For master's, GRE General Test. Additional exam requirements/recommendations for international students: Required—TOEFL (minimum score 550 paper-based). Electronic applications accepted.

West Virginia University, College of Creative Arts, Division of Music, Morgantown, WV 26506. Offers music composition (MM, DMA); music education (MM, PhD); music history (MM); music performance (MM, DMA); music theory (MM). *Accreditation:* NASM. *Degree requirements:* For master's, comprehensive exam, thesis (for some programs), recitals; for doctorate, variable foreign language requirement, comprehensive exam, thesis/dissertation, recitals (DMA). *Entrance requirements:* For master's, GRE General Test (music history), minimum GPA of 3.0, audition; for doctorate, GRE General Test (music education), minimum GPA of 3.0, audition. Additional exam requirements/recommendations for international students: Required—TOEFL. *Faculty research:* Jazz history, seventeenth century French court music, nineteenth century composition theory.

Wichita State University, Graduate School, College of Fine Arts, School of Music, Wichita, KS 67260. Offers music (MM); music education (MME). *Accreditation:* NASM. Part-time programs available. *Unit head:* Prof. Russ Widener, Director, 316-978-6435, Fax: 316-978-3625, E-mail: russ.widener@wichita.edu. *Application contact:* Dr. Mark Foley, Graduate Coordinator, 316-978-3103, E-mail: mark.foley@wichita.edu.

William Paterson University of New Jersey, College of the Arts and Communication, Wayne, NJ 07470-8420. Offers art (MFA); music (MM); professional communication (MA). *Accreditation:* NASAD. Part-time and evening/weekend programs available. *Entrance requirements:* For master's, minimum GPA of 2.75. Electronic applications accepted.

Winthrop University, College of Visual and Performing Arts, Department of Music, Rock Hill, SC 29733. Offers conducting (MM); music education (MME); performance (MM). *Accreditation:* NASM. Part-time programs available. *Degree requirements:* For master's, oral and written exams, recital (MM). *Entrance requirements:* For master's, GRE General Test, audition, minimum GPA of 3.0, 2 recitals. Electronic applications accepted.

Wright State University, School of Graduate Studies, College of Liberal Arts, Department of Music, Dayton, OH 45435. Offers music education (M Mus); performance (M Mus). *Accreditation:* NASM. Part-time programs available. *Degree requirements:* For master's, thesis or alternative, oral exam. *Entrance requirements:* For master's, theory placement test, BA in music. Additional exam requirements/recommendations for international students: Required—TOEFL. *Faculty research:* General music, current needs, role of teacher, expectations in music education.

Yale University, Graduate School of Arts and Sciences, Department of Music, New Haven, CT 06520. Offers music history (MA); music theory (MA). *Accreditation:* NASM. Terminal master's awarded for partial completion of doctoral program. *Degree requirements:* For master's, one foreign language; for doctorate, 3 foreign languages, thesis/dissertation. *Entrance requirements:* For doctorate, GRE General Test, GRE Subject Test.

Yale University, School of Music, New Haven, CT 06520. Offers MM, MMA, DMA, AD, Certificate. *Accreditation:* NASM. *Faculty:* 30 full-time (9 women), 29 part-time/adjunct (3 women). *Students:* 217 full-time (86 women); includes 5 Black or African American, non-Hispanic/Latino; 14 Asian, non-Hispanic/Latino; 2 Hispanic/Latino, 80 international. Average age 24. 1,463 applicants, 7% accepted, 98 enrolled. In 2010, 79 master's, 6 doctorates, 31 other advanced degrees awarded. Terminal master's awarded for partial completion of doctoral program. *Degree requirements:* For master's, one foreign language, thesis (for some programs), recitals; for doctorate, one foreign language, thesis/dissertation, oral and written exam, recitals; for other advanced degree, one foreign language, recitals. *Entrance requirements:* For master's and other advanced degree, departmental exams, audition; for doctorate, departmental exams in history and theory of music, audition. Additional exam requirements/recommendations for international students: Required—TOEFL (minimum score 567 paper-based; 227 computer-based; 86 iBT). *Application deadline:* For fall admission, 12/1 for domestic and international students. Application fee: $100. Electronic applications accepted. *Expenses:* Contact institution. *Financial support:* In 2010–11, 217 students received support, including 217 fellowships (averaging $31,000 per year); Federal Work-Study and scholarships/grants also available. Financial award application deadline: 5/30; financial award applicants required to submit FAFSA. *Faculty research:* Performance, composition, conducting, music history and theory. *Unit head:* Robert Blocker, Dean, 203-432-4160, Fax: 203-432-7542. *Application contact:* Suzanne M. Stringer, Registrar and Financial Aid Administrator, 203-432-1962, Fax: 203-432-7448, E-mail: suzanne.stringer@yale.edu.

York University, Faculty of Graduate Studies, Faculty of Fine Arts, Program in Ethnomusicology and Musicology, Toronto, ON M3J 1P3, Canada. Offers composition (MA); musicology and ethnomusicology (MA, PhD). Part-time programs available. *Degree requirements:* For master's, one foreign language, thesis optional; for doctorate, 2 foreign languages, comprehensive exam, thesis/dissertation. *Entrance requirements:* For master's, portfolio. Electronic applications accepted.

Youngstown State University, Graduate School, College of Fine and Performing Arts, Dana School of Music, Youngstown, OH 44555-0001. Offers jazz studies (MM); music education (MM); music history and literature (MM); music theory and composition (MM); performance (MM). *Accreditation:* NASM. Part-time and evening/weekend programs available. *Degree requirements:* For master's, one foreign language, thesis optional, final qualifying exam. *Entrance requirements:* For master's, audition; GRE General Test or minimum GPA of 2.7. Additional exam requirements/recommendations for international students: Required—TOEFL. *Faculty research:* Teaching education, use of computers, conducting.

Theater

American Conservatory Theater, Program in Acting, San Francisco, CA 94108-5800. Offers MFA, Certificate. Certificate open only to applicants with undergraduate degree from a non-accredited institution. Curriculum is the same as MFA Program in Acting. *Degree requirements:* For master's, thesis (for some programs), performance. *Entrance requirements:* For master's, audition, interview, bachelor's degree from an accredited institution, 2 confidential letters of recommendation.

Antioch University Midwest, Graduate Programs, Individualized Liberal and Professional Studies Program, Yellow Springs, OH 45387-1609. Offers liberal and professional studies (MA), including counseling, creative writing, education, film studies, liberal studies, management, modern literature, psychology, theatre, visual arts. Part-time and evening/weekend programs available. Postbaccalaureate distance learning degree programs offered (minimal on-campus study). *Faculty:* 2 full-time (1 woman), 2 part-time/adjunct (both women). *Students:* 15 full-time (11 women), 34 part-time (22 women); includes 11 minority (8 Black or African American, non-Hispanic/Latino; 3 Hispanic/Latino). Average age 40. 13 applicants, 69% accepted, 5 enrolled. In 2010, 18 master's awarded. *Degree requirements:* For master's, thesis or alternative. *Entrance requirements:* For master's, resume, goal statement, interview. *Application deadline:* For fall admission, 8/1 for domestic students; for winter admission, 12/1 for domestic students; for spring admission, 3/10 for domestic students. Applications are processed on a rolling basis. Application fee: $50. Electronic applications accepted. *Expenses:* Contact institution. *Financial support:* Federal Work-Study available. Financial award applicants required to submit FAFSA. *Unit head:* Dr. Joseph Cronin, Chair, 937-769-1894, Fax: 937-769-1807, E-mail: jcronin@antioch.edu. *Application contact:* Seth Gordon, Assistant Director of Admissions, 937-769-1800 Ext. 1825, Fax: 937-769-1804, E-mail: sgordon@antioch.edu.

Arcadia University, Graduate Studies, Department of Education, Glenside, PA 19038-3295. Offers art education (M Ed, MA Ed); biology education (MA Ed); chemistry education (MA Ed); child development (CAS); computer education (M Ed, CAS); computer education 7-12 (MA Ed); early childhood education (M Ed, CAS), including individualized (M Ed), master teacher (M Ed), research in child development (M Ed); educational leadership (M Ed, CAS); educational psychology (CAS); elementary education (M Ed, CAS); English education (MA Ed); environmental education (MA Ed, CAS); history education (MA Ed); language arts (M Ed, CAS); mathematics education (M Ed, MA Ed, CAS); music education (MA Ed); psychology (MA Ed); pupil personnel services (CAS); reading (M Ed, CAS); school library science (M Ed); science education (M Ed, CAS); secondary education (M Ed, CAS); special education (M Ed, Ed D, CAS); theater arts (MA Ed); written communication (MA Ed). *Accreditation:* NASAD. Part-time and evening/weekend programs available. Postbaccalaureate distance learning degree programs offered (minimal on-campus study). *Faculty:* 12 full-time (8 women), 38 part-time/adjunct (26 women). *Students:* 101 full-time (80 women), 667 part-time (508 women); includes 85 Black or African American, non-Hispanic/Latino; 10 Asian, non-Hispanic/Latino; 9 Hispanic/Latino; 5 Two or more races, non-Hispanic/Latino, 1 international. Average age 32. In 2010, 211 master's, 6 doctorates awarded. *Application deadline:* Applications are processed on a rolling basis. Application fee: $50. Electronic applications accepted. *Expenses:* Contact institution. *Financial support:* Career-related internships or fieldwork, tuition waivers (partial), and unspecified assistantships available. *Unit head:* Dr. Steven P. Gulkus. *Application contact:* 215-572-2925, Fax: 215-572-2126, E-mail: grad@arcadia.edu.

Arizona State University, Herberger Institute for Design and the Arts, School of Theatre and Film, Tempe, AZ 85287-2002. Offers theatre (MA, MFA); theatre (directing) (MFA); theatre (dramatic writing) (MFA); theatre (interdisciplinary digital media and performance) (MFA);

Theater

Arizona State University (continued)

theatre (performance design) (MFA); theatre (performance) (MFA); theatre (theatre and performance of the Americas) (PhD); theatre (theatre for youth) (PhD). *Faculty:* 28 full-time (12 women). *Students:* 47 full-time (28 women), 12 part-time (6 women); includes 10 minority (3 Black or African American, non-Hispanic/Latino; 1 Asian, non-Hispanic/Latino; 4 Hispanic/Latino; 2 Two or more races, non-Hispanic/Latino), 4 international. Average age 30. 52 applicants, 48% accepted, 16 enrolled. In 2010, 4 master's, 2 doctorates awarded. Terminal master's awarded for partial completion of doctoral program. *Degree requirements:* For master's, comprehensive exam (for some programs), thesis (for some programs), applied project (for some programs); interactive Program of Study (iPOS) submitted before completing 50 percent of required credit hours; for doctorate, comprehensive exam, thesis/dissertation, interactive Program of Study (iPOS) submitted before completing 50 percent of required credit hours. *Entrance requirements:* For master's, GRE or MAT, minimum GPA of 3.0 in last 2 years of work leading to bachelor's degree (depending on program); for doctorate, GRE, minimum GPA of 3.0 or equivalent in last 2 years of work leading to bachelor's degree, 3 letters of recommendation, resume, scholarly writing sample, statement of purpose. Additional exam requirements/recommendations for international students: Required—TOEFL, IELTS, or Pearson Test of English. *Application deadline:* For fall admission, 1/15 for domestic and international students. Application fee: $70 ($90 for international students). Electronic applications accepted. *Expenses:* Tuition, state resident: full-time $8510; part-time $608 per credit. Tuition, nonresident: full-time $16,542; part-time $919 per credit. Required fees: $339; $110 per credit. Part-time tuition and fees vary according to course load. *Financial support:* In 2010–11, 4 research assistantships with full and partial tuition reimbursements (averaging $9,021 per year), 38 teaching assistantships with full and partial tuition reimbursements (averaging $8,322 per year) were awarded; fellowships with full and partial tuition reimbursements, Federal Work-Study, institutionally sponsored loans, scholarships/grants, and tuition waivers (full and partial) also available. Financial award application deadline: 3/1; financial award applicants required to submit FAFSA. Total annual research expenditures: $111,392. *Unit head:* Guillermo Reyes, Interim Director, 480-965-0519, E-mail: guillermo.reyes@asu.edu. *Application contact:* Graduate Admissions, 480-965-6113.

Arkansas State University, Graduate School, College of Communications, Department of Communication Studies, Jonesboro, State University, AR 72467. Offers communication studies and theatre arts (MA); communication studies and theatre arts education (SCCT). Part-time programs available. *Faculty:* 5 full-time (2 women). *Students:* 5 full-time (2 women), 7 part-time (2 women); includes 6 minority (all Black or African American, non-Hispanic/Latino), 1 international. Average age 28. 15 applicants, 60% accepted, 8 enrolled. In 2010, 4 master's awarded. *Degree requirements:* For master's, one foreign language, comprehensive exam, thesis or alternative; for SCCT, comprehensive exam. *Entrance requirements:* For master's, GRE General Test or MAT, appropriate bachelor's degree, writing sample, letter of recommendation, official transcripts, immunization records; for SCCT, GRE or MAT, appropriate master's degree, interview, official transcript, immunization records. Additional exam requirements/recommendations for international students: Required—TOEFL (minimum score 550 paper-based; 213 computer-based; 79 iBT), IELTS (minimum score 6), PTE: Pearson Test of English Academic (56). *Application deadline:* For fall admission, 7/1 for domestic and international students; for spring admission, 11/15 for domestic students, 11/14 for international students. Applications are processed on a rolling basis. Application fee: $30 ($40 for international students). Electronic applications accepted. *Expenses:* Tuition, state resident: full-time $3888; part-time $216 per credit hour. Tuition, nonresident: full-time $9918; part-time $551 per credit hour. International tuition: $8376 full-time. Required fees: $932; $49 per credit hour. $25 per term. One-time fee: $30. Tuition and fees vary according to course load and program. *Financial support:* In 2010–11, 5 students received support; teaching assistantships, career-related internships or fieldwork, scholarships/grants, and unspecified assistantships available. Financial award application deadline: 7/1; financial award applicants required to submit FAFSA. *Unit head:* Dr. Thomas Bagland, Chair, 870-972-3091, Fax: 870-972-3856, E-mail: tbaglan@astate.edu. *Application contact:* Dr. Andrew Sustich, Dean of the Graduate School, 870-972-3029, Fax: 870-972-3857, E-mail: sustich@astate.edu.

Arkansas State University, Graduate School, College of Fine Arts, Department of Theatre, Jonesboro, State University, AR 72467. Offers communication studies and theatre arts (MA); communication studies and theatre arts education (SCCT). Part-time programs available. *Faculty:* 3 full-time (1 woman). *Students:* 2 full-time (1 woman), 2 part-time (1 woman). Average age 27. 3 applicants, 67% accepted, 2 enrolled. *Degree requirements:* For master's, one foreign language, comprehensive exam, thesis or alternative; for SCCT, comprehensive exam. *Entrance requirements:* For master's, GRE General Test or MAT, appropriate bachelor's degree, writing sample, letters of recommendation, official transcript, immunization records; for SCCT, GRE General Test or MAT, interview, master's degree, official transcript, immunization records. Additional exam requirements/recommendations for international students: Required—TOEFL (minimum score 550 paper-based; 213 computer-based; 79 iBT), IELTS (minimum score 6), PTE: Pearson Test of English Academic (56). *Application deadline:* For fall admission, 7/1 for domestic and international students; for spring admission, 11/15 for domestic students, 11/14 for international students. Applications are processed on a rolling basis. Application fee: $30 ($40 for international students). Electronic applications accepted. *Expenses:* Tuition, state resident: full-time $3888; part-time $216 per credit hour. Tuition, nonresident: full-time $9918; part-time $551 per credit hour. International tuition: $8376 full-time. Required fees: $932; $49 per credit hour. $25 per term. One-time fee: $30. Tuition and fees vary according to course load and program. *Financial support:* In 2010–11, 3 students received support; teaching assistantships, career-related internships or fieldwork, scholarships/grants, and unspecified assistantships available. Financial award application deadline: 7/1; financial award applicants required to submit FAFSA. *Unit head:* Bobby Simpson, Chair, 870-972-2037, Fax: 870-972-2830, E-mail: bsimpson@astate.edu. *Application contact:* Dr. Andrew Sustich, Dean of the Graduate School, 870-972-3029, Fax: 870-972-3857, E-mail: sustich@astate.edu.

Austin College, Program in Education, Sherman, TX 75090-4400. Offers art education (MA); elementary education (MA); middle school education (MA); music education (MA); physical education and coaching (MA); secondary education (MA); theatre education (MA). Part-time programs available. *Faculty:* 5 full-time (4 women), 1 (woman) part-time/adjunct. *Students:* 19 full-time (16 women), 2 part-time (1 woman); includes 1 minority (Hispanic/Latino). Average age 23. In 2010, 24 master's awarded. *Degree requirements:* For master's, one foreign language, thesis or alternative. *Entrance requirements:* For master's, Texas Academic Skills Program Test. *Application deadline:* For fall admission, 5/1 priority date for domestic students; for spring admission, 1/15 priority date for domestic students. Applications are processed on a rolling basis. Application fee: $35. Electronic applications accepted. *Expenses:* Tuition: Full-time $34,545. Required fees: $160. *Financial support:* Career-related internships or fieldwork, Federal Work-Study, scholarships/grants, and unspecified assistantships available. Support available to part-time students. Financial award application deadline: 4/1; financial award applicants required to submit FAFSA. *Unit head:* Dr. Barbara Sylvester, Director of Teaching Program, 903-813-2327, E-mail: bsylvester@austincollege.edu. *Application contact:* Dr. Barbara Sylvester, Director of Teaching Program, 903-813-2327, E-mail: bsylvester@austincollege.edu.

Baylor University, Graduate School, College of Arts and Sciences, Department of Theatre Arts, Waco, TX 76798. Offers directing (MFA). *Accreditation:* NAST. *Students:* 5 full-time (2 women); includes 1 minority (Two or more races, non-Hispanic/Latino). In 2010, 2 master's awarded. *Degree requirements:* For master's, thesis. *Entrance requirements:* For master's, GRE General Test. *Application deadline:* Applications are processed on a rolling basis. Application fee: $25. *Financial support:* Fellowships, teaching assistantships, Federal Work-Study and institutionally sponsored loans available. *Unit head:* Dr. DeAnna Toten Beard, Graduate Program Director, 254-710-6486, Fax: 254-710-1765, E-mail: deanna_toten_beard@baylor.edu. *Application contact:* Renee Cluke, Administrative Assistant, 254-710-1861, Fax: 254-710-1765, E-mail: renee_cluke@baylor.edu.

Bennington College, Graduate Programs, MA in Teaching Program, Bennington, VT 05201. Offers art education (MAT); early childhood (MAT); elementary education (MAT); English education (MAT); foreign language education (MAT); K-12 education (MAT); mathematics education (MAT); music education (MAT); science education (MAT); secondary education (MAT); social studies education (MAT); theater arts (MAT). *Faculty:* 3 part-time/adjunct (2 women). *Students:* 4 full-time (2 women), 1 part-time (0 women). Average age 31. 9 applicants, 56% accepted, 2 enrolled. In 2010, 7 master's awarded. *Degree requirements:* For master's, comprehensive exam, 1 year teaching practicum, professional portfolio. *Entrance requirements:* For master's, interview. *Application deadline:* For fall admission, 3/1 for domestic students. Application fee: $60. *Expenses:* Contact institution. *Financial support:* In 2010–11, 4 students received support, including 1 fellowship (averaging $7,000 per year); scholarships/grants and unspecified assistantships also available. Financial award application deadline: 4/1; financial award applicants required to submit FAFSA. *Unit head:* Carol Meyer, Director of Programs in Teacher Education, 802-440-4375, E-mail: cmeyer@bennington.edu. *Application contact:* Nancy Pearlman, Assistant Director of Programs in Teacher Education, 802-440-4710, Fax: 802-440-4383, E-mail: npearlman@bennington.edu.

Bob Jones University, Graduate Programs, Greenville, SC 29614. Offers accountancy (MS); Bible (MA); Bible translation (MA); Biblical studies (Certificate); broadcast management (MS); business administration (MBA); church history (MA, PhD); church ministries (MA); church music (MM); cinema and video production (MA); counseling (MS); curriculum and instruction (Ed D); divinity (M Div); dramatic production (MA); educational leadership (MS, Ed D, Ed S); elementary education (M Ed, MAT); English (M Ed, MA, MAT); fine arts (MA); graphic design (MA); history (M Ed, MA); illustration (MA); interpretative speech (MA); mathematics (M Ed, MAT); medical missions (Certificate); ministry (MM, D Min); multi-categorical special education (M Ed, MAT); music (M Ed); New Testament interpretation (PhD); Old Testament interpretation (PhD); orchestral instrument performance (MM); organ performance (MM); pastoral studies (MA); personnel services (MS, Ed S); piano pedagogy (MM); piano performance (MM); platform arts (MA); radio and television broadcasting (MS); rhetoric and public address (MA); secondary education (M Ed); studio art (MA); teaching Bible (MA); theology (MA, PhD); voice performance (MM); youth ministries (MA); M Div/MM.

The Boston Conservatory, Graduate Division, Theater Division, Boston, MA 02215. Offers MM. Part-time programs available. *Degree requirements:* For master's, performances. *Entrance requirements:* For master's, audition. Additional exam requirements/recommendations for international students: Required—TOEFL (minimum score 580 paper-based; 237 computer-based). Electronic applications accepted.

Boston University, College of Fine Arts, School of Theatre, Boston, MA 02215. Offers costume design (MFA); costume production (MFA); directing (MFA); lighting design (MFA); scene design (MFA); technical production (MFA, Certificate); theatre crafts (Certificate); theatre education (MFA). *Faculty:* 16 full-time, 9 part-time/adjunct. *Students:* 48 full-time (28 women), 24 part-time (21 women); includes 9 minority (3 Black or African American, non-Hispanic/Latino; 5 Hispanic/Latino; 1 Two or more races, non-Hispanic/Latino), 6 international. Average age 28. 141 applicants, 13% accepted, 5 enrolled. In 2010, 17 master's awarded. *Entrance requirements:* For master's, interview, portfolio. Additional exam requirements/recommendations for international students: Required—TOEFL. *Application deadline:* For fall admission, 2/15 priority date for domestic and international students. Application fee: $60. *Expenses:* Tuition: Full-time $39,314; part-time $1228 per credit. Required fees: $40 per semester. *Financial support:* Fellowships, teaching assistantships available. Financial award application deadline: 2/15. *Unit head:* Jim Petosa, Director, 617-353-3390. *Application contact:* Mark Krone, Manager, Graduate Admissions, 617-353-3350, E-mail: arts@bu.edu.

Bowling Green State University, Graduate College, College of Arts and Sciences, Department of Theatre and Film, Bowling Green, OH 43403. Offers MA, PhD. *Accreditation:* NAST. Part-time programs available. Terminal master's awarded for partial completion of doctoral program. *Degree requirements:* For master's, thesis or alternative; for doctorate, comprehensive exam, thesis/dissertation, 9 hour research tool. *Entrance requirements:* For master's and doctorate, GRE General Test. Additional exam requirements/recommendations for international students: Required—TOEFL. Electronic applications accepted. *Faculty research:* Theatre history, dramatic theory, cultural studies, performance studies, American theatre history.

Brandeis University, Graduate School of Arts and Sciences, Department of Theater Arts, Waltham, MA 02454-9110. Offers acting (MFA). *Faculty:* 10 full-time (6 women), 10 part-time/adjunct (4 women). *Students:* 18 full-time (9 women); includes 3 Black or African American, non-Hispanic/Latino; 1 Hispanic/Latino, 2 international. 19 applicants, 5% accepted, 0 enrolled. In 2010, 7 master's awarded. *Entrance requirements:* For master's, curriculum vitae or resume, 2 letters of recommendation, interview and audition (acting), head shot and artistic resume. Additional exam requirements/recommendations for international students: Required—TOEFL (minimum score 600 paper-based; 250 computer-based; 100 iBT); Recommended—IELTS (minimum score 7). *Application deadline:* For fall admission, 2/15 priority date for domestic students. Applications are processed on a rolling basis. Application fee: $75. Electronic applications accepted. *Financial support:* In 2010–11, 22 students received support, including 10 fellowships with full tuition reimbursements available (averaging $10,800 per year), 8 teaching assistantships with partial tuition reimbursements available (averaging $3,200 per year); research assistantships with tuition reimbursements available, career-related internships or fieldwork, institutionally sponsored loans, scholarships/grants, and tuition waivers (full and partial) also available. Financial award application deadline: 4/15; financial award applicants required to submit FAFSA. *Faculty research:* Acting, dramatic writing, dramaturgy, movement, voice and speech, theater literature. *Unit head:* Prof. Marya Lowry, Director of Graduate Studies, 781-736-3340, Fax: 781-736-3408, E-mail: theater@brandeis.edu. *Application contact:* Alicia Hyland, Academic Administrator, 781-736-3340, Fax: 781-736-3408, E-mail: theater@brandeis.edu.

Brigham Young University, Graduate Studies, College of Fine Arts and Communications, Department of Theatre and Media Arts, Provo, UT 84602-6404. Offers MA. MA program accepts applications in odd-numbered years only. *Accreditation:* NAST. *Faculty:* 18 full-time (6 women). *Students:* 1 full-time (0 women), 11 part-time (8 women), 1 international. Average age 31. In 2010, 4 master's awarded. *Degree requirements:* For master's, comprehensive exam, thesis, 32 hours, oral defense. *Entrance requirements:* For master's, GRE General Test, writing samples. Additional exam requirements/recommendations for international students: Required—TOEFL (minimum score 580 paper-based; 237 computer-based; 85 iBT). *Application deadline:* For fall admission, 2/1 priority date for domestic and international students. Application fee: $50. Electronic applications accepted. *Expenses:* Tuition: Full-time $5580; part-time $310 per credit hour. Tuition and fees vary according to program and student's religious affiliation. *Financial support:* In 2010–11, 12 students received support, including 4 research assistantships with partial tuition reimbursements available (averaging $3,500 per year), 12 teaching assistantships with partial tuition reimbursements available (averaging $3,500 per year); career-related internships or fieldwork, institutionally sponsored loans, scholarships/grants, health care benefits, tuition waivers (partial), unspecified assistantships, and administrative aides also available. Support available to part-time students. *Faculty research:* Media literacy, children's media, theatre historiography, performance studies, popular culture. *Unit head:* Dr. Rodger D. Sorensen, Department Chair, 801-422-8132, Fax: 801-422-0654, E-mail: rodger_sorensen@byu.edu. *Application contact:* Katie Boyer, Secretary, 801-422-6645, Fax: 801-422-0654, E-mail: tma.secretary@gmail.com.

Brooklyn College of the City University of New York, Division of Graduate Studies, Department of Theater, Brooklyn, NY 11210-2889. Offers acting (MFA); criticism and history (MA); design and technical production (MFA); directing (MFA); performing arts management (MFA); theater (PhD). Part-time programs available. *Students:* 45 full-time (32 women), 25 part-time (13 women); includes 7 minority (4 Black or African American, non-Hispanic/Latino; 1 Asian, non-Hispanic/Latino; 2 Hispanic/Latino), 11 international. Average age 30. 135 applicants, 28% accepted, 30 enrolled. In 2010, 35 master's awarded. *Degree requirements:* For master's, thesis, professional residency. *Entrance requirements:* For master's, audition or interview, 18 credits in theater, 2 letters of recommendation, essay. Additional exam requirements/

recommendations for international students: Required—TOEFL. *Application deadline:* For fall admission, 2/1 for domestic and international students. Application fee: $125. Electronic applications accepted. *Expenses:* Tuition, state resident: full-time $7360; part-time $310 per credit hour. Tuition, nonresident: full-time $13,800; part-time $575 per credit hour. Required fees: $190 per semester. *Financial support:* Career-related internships or fieldwork, Federal Work-Study, institutionally sponsored loans, and scholarships/grants available. Support available to part-time students. Financial award application deadline: 5/1; financial award applicants required to submit FAFSA. *Faculty research:* Multiculturalism and the arts, art education, arts collaboration. *Unit head:* Dr. Victor Marsh, Chairperson, 718-951-5666, Fax: 718-951-4606, E-mail: kmarsh@brooklyn.cuny.edu. *Application contact:* Hernan Sierra, Graduate Admissions Coordinator, 718-951-4536, Fax: 718-951-4506, E-mail: grads@brooklyn.cuny.edu.

Brown University, Graduate School, Department of Theatre Arts and Performance Studies, Providence, RI 02912. Offers acting and directing (MFA); playwriting (MFA); theatre and performance studies (PhD). *Degree requirements:* For master's, thesis or alternative. *Entrance requirements:* For master's, GRE General Test.

California Institute of the Arts, School of Theatre, Valencia, CA 91355-2340. Offers acting (MFA, Adv C); design and technology (Adv C); directing (MFA); performing arts design and technology (MFA); theater management (MFA, Adv C); writing for performance (MFA). *Accreditation:* NAST. *Degree requirements:* For master's, thesis (for some programs), faculty review, performance or portfolio. *Entrance requirements:* For master's, audition or portfolio, interview. Additional exam requirements/recommendations for international students: Required—TOEFL. Electronic applications accepted.

California State University, Fullerton, Graduate Studies, College of the Arts, Department of Theatre and Dance, Fullerton, CA 92834-9480. Offers acting (MFA); acting and directing (MA); dance (MA); directing (MFA); dramatic literature/criticism (MA); oral interpretation (MA); playwriting (MA); technical theater (MA); technical theater and design (MFA); television (MA); theatre for children (MA); theatre history (MA). *Accreditation:* NAST (one or more programs are accredited). Part-time programs available. *Students:* 17 full-time (9 women), 1 part-time (0 women); includes 2 Hispanic/Latino; 1 Two or more races, non-Hispanic/Latino. Average age 29. 11 applicants, 27% accepted, 3 enrolled. In 2010, 7 master's awarded. *Degree requirements:* For master's, oral and written exam, project or thesis. *Entrance requirements:* For master's, major in theatre or related field, audition or interview, minimum GPA of 2.5 in last 60 units of course work. Application fee: $55. *Financial support:* Career-related internships or fieldwork, Federal Work-Study, institutionally sponsored loans, and scholarships/grants available. Support available to part-time students. Financial award application deadline: 3/1; financial award applicants required to submit FAFSA. *Unit head:* Dr. Susan Hallman, Chair, 657-278-3628. *Application contact:* Admissions/Applications, 657-278-2371.

California State University, Long Beach, Graduate Studies, College of the Arts, Department of Theatre Arts, Long Beach, CA 90840. Offers acting (MFA); design (MFA); theatre management (MFA); MBA/MFA. *Accreditation:* NAST. Part-time programs available. *Faculty:* 7 full-time (4 women), 2 part-time/adjunct (0 women). *Students:* 22 full-time (14 women), 2 part-time (both women); includes 1 Asian, non-Hispanic/Latino, 7 international. Average age 31. 41 applicants, 44% accepted, 12 enrolled. In 2010, 13 master's awarded. *Degree requirements:* For master's, thesis or alternative. *Application deadline:* For fall admission, 7/1 for domestic students; for spring admission, 12/1 for domestic students. Applications are processed on a rolling basis. Application fee: $55. Electronic applications accepted. *Financial support:* Research assistantships, teaching assistantships, Federal Work-Study, institutionally sponsored loans, scholarships/grants, and traineeships available. Financial award application deadline: 3/2. *Unit head:* Dr. Joanne L. Gordon, Chair, 562-985-7891, Fax: 562-985-2263, E-mail: jgordon@csulb.edu. *Application contact:* Barbara Matthews, Graduate Advisor, 562-985-4042, Fax: 562-985-2263, E-mail: jmatthew@csulb.edu.

California State University, Los Angeles, Graduate Studies, College of Arts and Letters, Department of Communication Studies, Los Angeles, CA 90032-8530. Offers speech communication (MA); television, film and theatre (MFA). Part-time and evening/weekend programs available. *Faculty:* 11 full-time (5 women), 3 part-time/adjunct (2 women). *Students:* 85 full-time (52 women), 57 part-time (41 women); includes 58 minority (20 Black or African American, non-Hispanic/Latino; 7 Asian, non-Hispanic/Latino; 26 Hispanic/Latino; 5 Two or more races, non-Hispanic/Latino), 29 international. Average age 32. 93 applicants, 100% accepted, 54 enrolled. In 2010, 19 master's awarded. *Degree requirements:* For master's, comprehensive exam or thesis. *Entrance requirements:* For master's, minimum GPA of 2.75 in last 90 units of course work. Additional exam requirements/recommendations for international students: Required—TOEFL (minimum score 500 paper-based; 173 computer-based). *Application deadline:* For fall admission, 5/1 for domestic and international students. Applications are processed on a rolling basis. Application fee: $55. Electronic applications accepted. *Financial support:* Career-related internships or fieldwork and Federal Work-Study available. Support available to part-time students. Financial award application deadline: 3/1. *Faculty research:* Organizational, interpersonal, intercultural, and instructional communication; rhetorical theories. *Unit head:* Dr. Bryant Keith Alexander, Chair, 323-343-4200, Fax: 323-343-6467, E-mail: abryant@calstatela.edu. *Application contact:* Dr. Alan Muchlinski, Dean of Graduate Studies, 323-343-3820, Fax: 323-343-5653, E-mail: amuchli@exchange.calstatela.edu.

California State University, Los Angeles, Graduate Studies, College of Arts and Letters, Department of Theater Arts and Dance, Los Angeles, CA 90032-8530. Offers theater arts (MA). Part-time and evening/weekend programs available. *Faculty:* 5 full-time (4 women). *Students:* 9 full-time (6 women); 11 part-time (7 women); includes 6 minority (3 Asian, non-Hispanic/Latino; 2 Hispanic/Latino; 1 Two or more races, non-Hispanic/Latino), 4 international. Average age 38. 9 applicants, 100% accepted, 3 enrolled. In 2010, 6 master's awarded. *Degree requirements:* For master's, comprehensive exam, project or thesis. *Entrance requirements:* For master's, minimum GPA of 2.5, 30 units of course work in theater. Additional exam requirements/recommendations for international students: Required—TOEFL (minimum score 500 paper-based; 173 computer-based). *Application deadline:* For fall admission, 5/1 for domestic and international students. Applications are processed on a rolling basis. Application fee: $55. Electronic applications accepted. *Financial support:* Federal Work-Study available. Support available to part-time students. Financial award application deadline: 3/1. *Faculty research:* Sondheim, Taiwanese theater, Australian theater, absurdism, dramaturgy. *Unit head:* Dr. James Hatfield, Chair, 323-343-4110, Fax: 323-343-5567, E-mail: jhatfie@calstatela.edu. *Application contact:* Dr. Alan Muchlinski, Dean of Graduate Studies, 323-343-3820, Fax: 323-343-5653, E-mail: amuchli@exchange.calstatela.edu.

California State University, Northridge, Graduate Studies, College of Arts, Media, and Communication, Department of Theatre, Northridge, CA 91330. Offers MA. *Accreditation:* NAST. *Degree requirements:* For master's, thesis. *Entrance requirements:* For master's, GRE General Test or minimum GPA of 3.0. Additional exam requirements/recommendations for international students: Required—TOEFL.

California State University, Sacramento, Graduate Studies, College of Arts and Letters, Department of Theatre and Dance, Sacramento, CA 95819. Offers MA. Part-time programs available. *Degree requirements:* For master's, thesis or alternative, writing proficiency exam. *Entrance requirements:* For master's, GRE General Test, BA in drama or equivalent, minimum GPA of 2.5 during previous 2 years of course work. Additional exam requirements/recommendations for international students: Required—TOEFL. Electronic applications accepted.

California State University, Sacramento, Graduate Studies, College of Social Sciences and Interdisciplinary Studies, Liberal Arts Program, Sacramento, CA 95819. Offers French (MA); German (MA); Spanish (MA); theater arts (MA). *Degree requirements:* For master's, writing proficiency exam. *Entrance requirements:* Additional exam requirements/recommendations for international students: Required—TOEFL. Electronic applications accepted.

California State University, San Bernardino, Graduate Studies, College of Arts and Letters, Department of Theatre Arts, San Bernardino, CA 92407-2397. Offers theatre arts (MA); theatre education (MA); theatre for youth (MA). *Degree requirements:* For master's, thesis. *Entrance requirements:* For master's, writing exam.

Carnegie Mellon University, College of Fine Arts, School of Drama, Pittsburgh, PA 15213-3891. Offers design (MFA); directing (MFA); dramatic writing (MFA); production technology and management (MFA). *Degree requirements:* For master's, thesis (for some programs). *Entrance requirements:* For master's, audition, portfolio review, interview. Additional exam requirements/recommendations for international students: Required—TOEFL. *Faculty research:* Developing voice and speech compact disc.

Case Western Reserve University, School of Graduate Studies, Department of Theater and Dance, Cleveland, OH 44106. Offers acting (MFA); contemporary dance (MFA); dance (MA); theater (MFA). *Faculty:* 8 full-time (3 women), 1 part-time/adjunct (0 women). *Students:* 14 full-time (9 women); includes 1 Black or African American, non-Hispanic/Latino; 1 Hispanic/Latino, 3 international. Average age 27. 5 applicants, 40% accepted, 2 enrolled. In 2010, 10 master's awarded. *Degree requirements:* For master's, thesis, oral presentation and defense, portfolio, thesis concert production and presentation (MFA). *Entrance requirements:* For master's, audition, interview. Additional exam requirements/recommendations for international students: Required—TOEFL (minimum score 550 paper-based; 213 computer-based; 79 iBT). *Application deadline:* For fall admission, 1/1 priority date for domestic students. Applications are processed on a rolling basis. Application fee: $50. Electronic applications accepted. *Financial support:* Fellowships, career-related internships or fieldwork and tuition waivers (full and partial) available. Financial award application deadline: 1/1. *Faculty research:* Playwriting; history of theater; participation in professional area theaters in performing, design, acting, coaching, and dance5. *Unit head:* Ron Wilson, Chairman, 216-368-6142, Fax: 216-368-5184, E-mail: ron.wilson@case.edu. *Application contact:* Scarlett Grala, Administrative Assistant, 216-368-4868, Fax: 216-368-5184, E-mail: ksg@po.cwru.edu.

The Catholic University of America, School of Arts and Sciences, Department of Drama, Washington, DC 20064. Offers acting, directing, and playwriting (MFA); theatre education (MA); theatre history and criticism (MA). Part-time programs available. *Faculty:* 7 full-time (3 women), 11 part-time/adjunct (5 women). *Students:* 15 full-time (8 women), 22 part-time (16 women); includes 3 Black or African American, non-Hispanic/Latino; 1 American Indian or Alaska Native, non-Hispanic/Latino. Average age 29. 19 applicants, 74% accepted, 10 enrolled. In 2010, 5 master's awarded. *Degree requirements:* For master's, variable foreign language requirement, comprehensive exam, thesis or alternative. *Entrance requirements:* For master's, GRE General Test, statement of purpose, official copies of academic transcripts, three letters of recommendation. Additional exam requirements/recommendations for international students: Required—TOEFL (minimum score 580 paper-based; 237 computer-based). *Application deadline:* For fall admission, 8/1 priority date for domestic students, 7/15 for international students; for spring admission, 12/1 priority date for domestic students, 10/15 for international students. Applications are processed on a rolling basis. Application fee: $55. Electronic applications accepted. *Expenses:* Tuition: Full-time $33,580; part-time $1315 per credit hour. Required fees: $80; $40 per semester hour. One-time fee: $425. *Financial support:* Fellowships, research assistantships, teaching assistantships, Federal Work-Study, scholarships/grants, tuition waivers (full and partial), and unspecified assistantships available. Financial award application deadline: 2/1; financial award applicants required to submit FAFSA. *Faculty research:* Acting, directing, playwriting, costume design, Shakespearean stage history. *Unit head:* Gail Beach, Chair, 202-319-5351, Fax: 202-319-5359, E-mail: beach@cua.edu. *Application contact:* Andrew Woodall, Director of Graduate Admissions, 202-319-5057, Fax: 202-319-6533, E-mail: cua-admissions@cua.edu.

Central Washington University, Graduate Studies and Research, College of Arts and Humanities, Department of Theatre Arts, Ellensburg, WA 98926. Offers theatre production (MA); theatre studies (MA). Part-time programs available. *Degree requirements:* For master's, thesis or alternative. *Entrance requirements:* For master's, minimum GPA of 3.0. Additional exam requirements/recommendations for international students: Required—TOEFL (minimum score 550 paper-based; 213 computer-based; 79 iBT). Electronic applications accepted.

Columbia University, Graduate School of Arts and Sciences, Program in Theatre, New York, NY 10027. Offers M Phil, MA, PhD. *Degree requirements:* For master's, one foreign language, thesis, written exam; for doctorate, 2 foreign languages, thesis/dissertation. *Entrance requirements:* For master's and doctorate, GRE General Test, writing sample. Additional exam requirements/recommendations for international students: Required—TOEFL.

Columbia University, School of the Arts, Theatre Arts Division, New York, NY 10027. Offers acting (MFA); directing (MFA); dramaturgy (MFA); playwriting (MFA); stage management (MFA); theater management (MFA); JD/MFA. *Degree requirements:* For master's, thesis, 2 internships. *Entrance requirements:* For master's, 3 letters of recommendation, resume. Additional exam requirements/recommendations for international students: Required—TOEFL (minimum score 600 paper-based; 250 computer-based; 100 iBT). Electronic applications accepted.

See Close-Up on page 295.

Cornell University, Graduate School, Graduate Fields of Arts and Sciences, Field of Theatre Arts, Ithaca, NY 14853-0001. Offers drama and the theatre (PhD); theatre history (PhD); theatre theory and aesthetics (PhD). *Faculty:* 18 full-time (7 women). *Students:* 10 full-time (6 women), 5 international. Average age 31. 29 applicants, 10% accepted, 2 enrolled. In 2010, 1 doctorate awarded. *Degree requirements:* For doctorate, 2 foreign languages, comprehensive exam, thesis/dissertation. *Entrance requirements:* For doctorate, GRE General Test, sample of written work, 3 letters of recommendation. Additional exam requirements/recommendations for international students: Required—TOEFL (minimum score 600 paper-based; 250 computer-based; 77 iBT). *Application deadline:* For fall admission, 1/15 for domestic students. Application fee: $80. Electronic applications accepted. *Expenses:* Tuition: Full-time $29,500. Required fees: $76. Tuition and fees vary according to degree level and program. *Financial support:* In 2010–11, 4 fellowships with full tuition reimbursements, 6 teaching assistantships with full tuition reimbursements were awarded; research assistantships with full tuition reimbursements, institutionally sponsored loans, scholarships/grants, health care benefits, tuition waivers (full and partial), and unspecified assistantships also available. Financial award applicants required to submit FAFSA. *Faculty research:* Cultural studies and critical theory, seventeenth to twenty-first century European and American theater, theory of the performing arts, film history and theory, feminism and theater. *Unit head:* Director of Graduate Studies, 607-254-2757, Fax: 607-254-2733. *Application contact:* Graduate Field Assistant, 607-254-2757, Fax: 607-254-2733, E-mail: theatre_grad@cornell.edu.

Dell'Arte International School of Physical Theatre, MFA Program, Blue Lake, CA 95525. Offers ensemble based physical theatre (MFA). *Accreditation:* NAST. *Degree requirements:* For master's, thesis. *Entrance requirements:* For master's, undergraduate degree, audition. Electronic applications accepted. *Faculty research:* Physical theatre, international theatre, ensemble, devised.

DePaul University, The Theatre School, Chicago, IL 60614. Offers acting (MFA); arts leadership (MFA); directing (MFA). *Faculty:* 21 full-time (12 women), 21 part-time/adjunct (10 women). *Students:* 39 full-time (19 women); includes 8 Black or African American, non-Hispanic/Latino; 1 Asian, non-Hispanic/Latino; 1 Hispanic/Latino. Average age 28. 261 applicants, 8% accepted, 14 enrolled. In 2010, 14 master's awarded. *Degree requirements:* For master's, comprehensive exam, thesis. *Entrance requirements:* For master's, audition or interview. Additional exam requirements/recommendations for international students: Required—TOEFL (minimum score 550 paper-based; 213 computer-based; 80 iBT), IELTS (minimum score 6.5). *Application deadline:* For fall admission, 1/1 priority date for domestic and international students. Application fee: $25. Electronic applications accepted. *Expenses:* Contact institution. *Financial support:* In

Theater

DePaul University (continued)

2010–11, 39 students received support, including 39 fellowships (averaging $17,800 per year); career-related internships or fieldwork, Federal Work-Study, institutionally sponsored loans, and scholarships/grants also available. Financial award application deadline: 2/15; financial award applicants required to submit FAFSA. *Unit head:* John Culbert, Dean, 773-325-7954, Fax: 773-325-7920, E-mail: jculbert@depaul.edu. *Application contact:* Jason Beck, Director of Admissions, 773-325-7999, Fax: 773-325-7920, E-mail: jbeck1@depaul.edu.

Drew University, Caspersen School of Graduate Studies, Program in Education, Madison, NJ 07940-1493. Offers biology (MAT); chemistry (MAT); English (MAT); French (MAT); Italian (MAT); math (MAT); physics (MAT); social studies (MAT); Spanish (MAT); theatre arts (MAT). Part-time programs available. *Entrance requirements:* For master's, transcripts, personal statement, recommendations. Additional exam requirements/recommendations for international students: Required—TOEFL, TWE. *Expenses:* Contact institution.

Eastern Michigan University, Graduate School, College of Arts and Sciences, Department of Communication, Media and Theatre Arts, Program in Arts Administration, Ypsilanti, MI 48197. Offers theatre arts-arts administration (MA). Part-time and evening/weekend programs available. Postbaccalaureate distance learning degree programs offered (minimal on-campus study). *Students:* 6 full-time (5 women), 15 part-time (12 women); includes 2 minority (1 Black or African American, non-Hispanic/Latino; 1 Hispanic/Latino), 3 international. Average age 31. In 2010, 7 master's awarded. *Entrance requirements:* Additional exam requirements/recommendations for international students: Required—TOEFL. *Application deadline:* Applications are processed on a rolling basis. Application fee: $35. *Financial support:* Fellowships, research assistantships with full tuition reimbursements, teaching assistantships with full tuition reimbursements, career-related internships or fieldwork, Federal Work-Study, institutionally sponsored loans, scholarships/grants, tuition waivers (partial), and unspecified assistantships available. Support available to part-time students. Financial award applicants required to submit FAFSA. *Unit head:* Kenneth Stevens, Coordinator, 734-487-1153, Fax: 734-487-3443, E-mail: ken.stevens@emich.edu. *Application contact:* Kenneth Stevens, Coordinator, 734-487-1153, Fax: 734-487-3443, E-mail: ken.stevens@emich.edu.

Eastern Michigan University, Graduate School, College of Arts and Sciences, Department of Communication, Media and Theatre Arts, Program in Drama/Theatre for the Young, Ypsilanti, MI 48197. Offers MA, MFA. Part-time programs available. Postbaccalaureate distance learning degree programs offered (minimal on-campus study). *Students:* 9 full-time (7 women), 6 part-time (4 women); includes 4 minority (all Black or African American, non-Hispanic/Latino), 2 international. Average age 30. In 2010, 6 master's awarded. *Degree requirements:* For master's, thesis optional. *Entrance requirements:* Additional exam requirements/recommendations for international students: Required—TOEFL. *Application deadline:* Applications are processed on a rolling basis. Application fee: $35. *Financial support:* Fellowships, research assistantships with full tuition reimbursements, teaching assistantships with full tuition reimbursements, career-related internships or fieldwork, Federal Work-Study, institutionally sponsored loans, scholarships/grants, tuition waivers (partial), and unspecified assistantships available. Support available to part-time students. Financial award applicants required to submit FAFSA. *Unit head:* Prof. Patricia Zimmer, Coordinator, 734-487-0031, Fax: 734-487-3443, E-mail: patricia.zimmer@emich.edu. *Application contact:* Graduate Coordinator.

Eastern Michigan University, Graduate School, College of Arts and Sciences, Department of Communication, Media and Theatre Arts, Programs in Theatre Arts, Ypsilanti, MI 48197. Offers interpretation/performance studies (MA); theatre arts (MA). Part-time and evening/weekend programs available. Postbaccalaureate distance learning degree programs offered (minimal on-campus study). *Students:* 2 full-time (1 woman), 17 part-time (9 women); includes 2 minority (both Black or African American, non-Hispanic/Latino). Average age 32. 14 applicants, 93% accepted, 6 enrolled. In 2010, 6 master's awarded. *Degree requirements:* For master's, thesis or alternative. *Entrance requirements:* Additional exam requirements/recommendations for international students: Required—TOEFL. *Application deadline:* Applications are processed on a rolling basis. Application fee: $35. *Financial support:* Fellowships, research assistantships with full tuition reimbursements, teaching assistantships with full tuition reimbursements, career-related internships or fieldwork, Federal Work-Study, institutionally sponsored loans, scholarships/grants, and unspecified assistantships available. Support available to part-time students. Financial award applicants required to submit FAFSA. *Unit head:* Kenneth Stevens, Coordinator, 734-487-1153, Fax: 734-487-3443, E-mail: ken.stevens@emich.edu. *Application contact:* Kenneth Stevens, Coordinator, 734-487-1153, Fax: 734-487-3443, E-mail: ken.stevens@emich.edu.

Emerson College, Graduate Studies, School of the Arts, Department of Performing Arts, Program in Theatre Education, Boston, MA 02116-4624. Offers MA. Part-time programs available. *Entrance requirements:* For master's, GRE General Test. Additional exam requirements/recommendations for international students: Required—TOEFL (minimum score 550 paper-based; 213 computer-based; 80 iBT), IELTS (minimum score 6.5). Electronic applications accepted. *Faculty research:* Theater.

Florida Atlantic University, Dorothy F. Schmidt College of Arts and Letters, Department of Theatre and Dance, Boca Raton, FL 33431-0991. Offers acting (MFA); design and technology (MFA). *Faculty:* 10 full-time (2 women), 1 (woman) part-time/adjunct. *Students:* 21 full-time (12 women), 1 part-time (0 women); includes 3 minority (1 Black or African American, non-Hispanic/Latino; 1 Hispanic/Latino; 1 Two or more races, non-Hispanic/Latino). Average age 29. 27 applicants, 37% accepted, 7 enrolled. *Degree requirements:* For master's, thesis, production. *Entrance requirements:* For master's, GRE General Test, minimum GPA of 3.0 during last 60 hours of undergraduate course work. *Application deadline:* For fall admission, 8/15 priority date for domestic students, 8/15 for international students. Applications are processed on a rolling basis. Application fee: $30. *Expenses:* Tuition, area resident: Part-time $319.96 per credit. Tuition, state resident: part-time $319.96 per credit. Tuition, nonresident: part-time $926.42 per credit. *Financial support:* Fellowships, teaching assistantships with full tuition reimbursements, career-related internships or fieldwork, Federal Work-Study, and institutionally sponsored loans available. Support available to part-time students. Financial award application deadline: 3/31. *Faculty research:* Contemporary British theatre, Eastern European playwrights, Latin American drama. *Unit head:* Dr. Gvozden Kopani, Chair, 561-297-3815, Fax: 561-297-2180, E-mail: dkopani@fau.edu. *Application contact:* Dr. Emily Stockard, Associate Dean, 561-297-2817, Fax: 561-297-2744, E-mail: stockard@fau.edu.

Florida State University, The Graduate School, School of Theatre, Tallahassee, FL 32306. Offers acting (MFA); directing (MFA); lighting, costume, and scenic design (MFA); technical production (MFA); theater management (MFA); theatre (MA, MS, PhD). *Accreditation:* NAST. *Faculty:* 20 full-time (10 women). *Students:* 103 full-time (51 women), 9 part-time (6 women); includes 3 Black or African American, non-Hispanic/Latino; 1 Asian, non-Hispanic/Latino; 4 Hispanic/Latino. Average age 25. 139 applicants, 24% accepted, 27 enrolled. In 2010, 28 master's, 1 doctorate awarded. *Degree requirements:* For master's, one foreign language, comprehensive exam (for some programs), thesis (for some programs); for doctorate, one foreign language, comprehensive exam, thesis/dissertation. *Entrance requirements:* For master's, GRE General Test, writing sample (MA), interview and portfolio (MFA), minimum undergraduate GPA of 3.0, audition (MFA in acting). Additional exam requirements/recommendations for international students: Required—TOEFL. *Application deadline:* For fall admission, 2/15 priority date for domestic and international students. Applications are processed on a rolling basis. Application fee: $30. Electronic applications accepted. *Expenses:* Tuition, state resident: full-time $8238.24. *Financial support:* In 2010–11, 1 fellowship with full tuition reimbursement (averaging $18,000 per year), 30 research assistantships with full tuition reimbursements (averaging $8,300 per year), 57 teaching assistantships with full tuition reimbursements (averaging $8,900 per year) were awarded; career-related internships or fieldwork, Federal Work-Study, institutionally sponsored loans, scholarships/grants, health care benefits, and unspecified assistantships also available. Financial award application deadline: 1/1; financial award applicants required to submit FAFSA. *Faculty research:* Gender theatre, performance theory, computers in theatre, dramaturgy, music theatre performance. *Unit head:* Cameron Jackson, Director, 850-644-7257, Fax: 850-644-7408, E-mail: ccjackson@admin.fsu.edu. *Application contact:* Barbara Thomas, Program Assistant, 850-644-7234, Fax: 850-644-7246, E-mail: bgthomas@admin.fsu.edu.

Fontbonne University, Graduate Programs, Department of Fine Arts, St. Louis, MO 63105-3098. Offers art (MA); fine arts (MFA); theater education (MA). Part-time and evening/weekend programs available. *Faculty:* 7 full-time (2 women), 8 part-time/adjunct (7 women). *Students:* 8 full-time (2 women), 7 part-time (5 women); includes 1 Black or African American, non-Hispanic/Latino; 3 Asian, non-Hispanic/Latino. Average age 41. In 2010, 10 master's awarded. *Degree requirements:* For master's, thesis exhibit (MFA). *Entrance requirements:* For master's, minimum GPA of 3.0, portfolio. *Application deadline:* For fall admission, 8/1 priority date for domestic students. Applications are processed on a rolling basis. Application fee: $25. *Expenses:* Tuition: Full-time $11,328. Full-time tuition and fees vary according to program. *Financial support:* In 2010–11, teaching assistantships (averaging $2,500 per year). Support available to part-time students. Financial award application deadline: 4/1; financial award applicants required to submit FAFSA. *Unit head:* Catherine Connor-Talasek, Chairperson, 314-889-1431, Fax: 314-889-4545, E-mail: cconnor@fontbonne.edu. *Application contact:* Catherine Connor-Talasek, Chairperson, 314-889-1431, Fax: 314-889-4545, E-mail: cconnor@fontbonne.edu.

The George Washington University, Columbian College of Arts and Sciences, Department of Theatre and Dance, Washington, DC 20052. Offers classical acting (MFA); dance (MFA); design (MFA). Part-time and evening/weekend programs available. *Faculty:* 10 full-time (6 women), 20 part-time/adjunct (12 women). *Students:* 19 full-time (12 women), 18 part-time (10 women); includes 4 Black or African American, non-Hispanic/Latino; 1 Asian, non-Hispanic/Latino; 1 Native Hawaiian or other Pacific Islander, non-Hispanic/Latino, 3 international. Average age 34. 77 applicants, 34% accepted. In 2010, 17 master's awarded. *Degree requirements:* For master's, thesis. *Entrance requirements:* For master's, minimum GPA of 3.0, portfolio. Additional exam requirements/recommendations for international students: Required—TOEFL (minimum score 550 paper-based; 213 computer-based; 80 iBT). *Application deadline:* For fall admission, 8/1 priority date for domestic students; for spring admission, 10/1 priority date for domestic students. Applications are processed on a rolling basis. Application fee: $75. Electronic applications accepted. *Financial support:* In 2010–11, 2 students received support; fellowships with tuition reimbursements available, teaching assistantships with tuition reimbursements available, career-related internships or fieldwork, Federal Work-Study, and tuition waivers available. *Unit head:* Alan G. Wade, Interim Chair, 202-994-3664, E-mail: awade@gwu.edu. *Application contact:* Information Contact, 202-994-8072, E-mail: trdanews@gwu.edu.

Graduate School and University Center of the City University of New York, Graduate Studies, Program in Theatre, New York, NY 10016-4039. Offers PhD. *Degree requirements:* For doctorate, 2 foreign languages, thesis/dissertation. *Entrance requirements:* For doctorate, GRE General Test, writing sample. Additional exam requirements/recommendations for international students: Required—TOEFL. Electronic applications accepted.

Hollins University, Graduate Programs, Program in Playwriting, Roanoke, VA 24020-1603. Offers MFA. Part-time programs available. *Degree requirements:* For master's, comprehensive exam, thesis. *Entrance requirements:* For master's, letters of recommendation, writing samples. Additional exam requirements/recommendations for international students: Required—TOEFL (minimum score 550 paper-based; 213 computer-based; 79 iBT).

Humboldt State University, Academic Programs, College of Arts, Humanities, and Social Sciences, Department of Theatre, Film and Dance, Arcata, CA 95521-8299. Offers theatre arts (MA, MFA), including film production (MA), production (MA), scenography (MFA). *Students:* 15 full-time (12 women), 2 part-time (1 woman); includes 1 Hispanic/Latino. Average age 36. 16 applicants, 63% accepted, 6 enrolled. In 2010, 4 master's awarded. *Degree requirements:* For master's, thesis or alternative, qualifying exam. *Entrance requirements:* For master's, minimum GPA of 2.5. Additional exam requirements/recommendations for international students: Required—TOEFL (minimum score 500 paper-based; 173 computer-based). *Application deadline:* For fall admission, 4/15 for domestic students. Applications are processed on a rolling basis. Application fee: $55. Tuition and fees vary according to program. *Financial support:* Fellowships available. Financial award application deadline: 3/1; financial award applicants required to submit FAFSA. *Faculty research:* Physical theater, design, playwriting. *Unit head:* Dr. Margaret Kelso, Chair, 707-826-5492, Fax: 707-826-5494, E-mail: margaret.kelso@humboldt.edu. *Application contact:* Dr. Jody Sekas, Coordinator, 707-826-4337, Fax: 707-826-5494, E-mail: jjs1@humboldt.edu.

Hunter College of the City University of New York, Graduate School, School of Arts and Sciences, Department of Theatre, New York, NY 10021-5085. Offers playwriting (MFA); theatre (MA). Part-time and evening/weekend programs available. *Faculty:* 5 full-time (4 women), 1 part-time/adjunct (0 women). *Students:* 1 full-time (0 women), 41 part-time (27 women); includes 4 Black or African American, non-Hispanic/Latino; 3 Hispanic/Latino, 5 international. Average age 34. 18 applicants, 56% accepted, 7 enrolled. In 2010, 5 master's awarded. *Degree requirements:* For master's, comprehensive exam, thesis. *Entrance requirements:* For master's, GRE General Test. Additional exam requirements/recommendations for international students: Required—TOEFL. *Application deadline:* For fall admission, 4/1 for domestic students, 2/1 for international students; for spring admission, 11/1 for domestic students, 9/1 for international students. Application fee: $125. *Financial support:* In 2010–11, 1 fellowship (averaging $3,000 per year), 4 teaching assistantships were awarded; research assistantships, career-related internships or fieldwork, Federal Work-Study, and tuition waivers (partial) also available. Support available to part-time students. Financial award application deadline: 4/15. *Faculty research:* Modern French mimes, acting techniques, directing, New York avant-garde theater and popular entertainment, playwriting. *Unit head:* Dr. Barbara Bosch, Chairperson, 212-772-5148, Fax: 212-650-3584, E-mail: bbosch@hunter.cuny.edu. *Application contact:* Mira Felner, Graduate Advisor, 212-772-4642, E-mail: theatre@hunter.cuny.edu.

Idaho State University, Office of Graduate Studies, College of Arts and Sciences, Program in Theatre and Dance, Pocatello, ID 83209-8006. Offers theatre (MA). *Accreditation:* NAST. Part-time programs available. *Degree requirements:* For master's, comprehensive exam, thesis optional, oral and written exam. *Entrance requirements:* For master's, GRE General Test (35th percentile or above on one of the 3 sections). Additional exam requirements/recommendations for international students: Required—TOEFL (minimum score 550 paper-based; 213 computer-based; 80 iBT). Electronic applications accepted. *Faculty research:* Theatre history, technical theatre.

Illinois State University, Graduate School, College of Fine Arts, School of Theatre, Normal, IL 61790-2200. Offers MA, MFA, MS. *Accreditation:* NAST. Part-time programs available. *Degree requirements:* For master's, variable foreign language requirement, thesis or alternative. *Entrance requirements:* For master's, sample of written work, minimum GPA of 3.0 in last 60 hours of course work. *Faculty research:* Illinois Shakespeare festival.

Indiana University Bloomington, University Graduate School, College of Arts and Sciences, Department of Theatre and Drama, Bloomington, IN 47405-7000. Offers acting (MFA); design and technology (MFA); directing (MFA); literature (MA, PhD); playwriting (MFA); theatre and drama (MAT); theatre history (MA, PhD); theory (MA, PhD). *Accreditation:* NAST. *Faculty:* 20 full-time (4 women). *Students:* 45 full-time (19 women); includes 10 minority (1 Black or African American, non-Hispanic/Latino; 1 Asian, non-Hispanic/Latino; 6 Hispanic/Latino; 2 Two or more races, non-Hispanic/Latino), 6 international. Average age 29. 31 applicants, 16% accepted, 4 enrolled. In 2010, 1 master's awarded. Terminal master's awarded for partial completion of doctoral program. *Degree requirements:* For master's, one foreign language, comprehensive exam, thesis; for doctorate, 2 foreign languages, comprehensive exam, thesis/dissertation, 90 credit hours. *Entrance requirements:* For master's, audition, interview, portfolio or script analysis; for doctorate, GRE General Test. Additional exam requirements/recommendations for international students: Required—TOEFL (minimum score 550 paper-based; 213 computer-based; 80 iBT). *Application deadline:* For fall admission, 1/15 priority date for domestic students, 12/1 for international students. Application fee: $55 ($65 for international students). Electronic applications accepted. *Financial support:* In 2010–11, 8 teaching assistantships with full tuition reimbursements (averaging $12,815 per year) were awarded; fellowships with tuition reimbursements, research assistantships with tuition reimbursements, career-related internships or fieldwork, Federal Work-Study, institutionally sponsored loans, scholarships/grants, health care benefits, and unspecified assistantships also available. Financial award application deadline: 3/1. *Faculty research:* American, western European, world literature; history and theory; theatrical production, design and technology; acting; directing; playwriting. *Unit head:* Jonathan R. Michaelsen, Chairperson and Professor, 812-855-4535, Fax: 812-856-0698, E-mail: theatre@indiana.edu. *Application contact:* Barb Grinder, Administrative Secretary, 812-855-4535, Fax: 812-855-0698, E-mail: bgrinder@indiana.edu.

Kansas State University, Graduate School, College of Arts and Sciences, Department of Communication Studies, Theatre and Dance, Manhattan, KS 66505. Offers rhetoric/communication (MA); theatre (MA). *Degree requirements:* For master's, thesis or alternative. *Entrance requirements:* For master's, GRE General Test (recommended), minimum GPA of 3.0. Additional exam requirements/recommendations for international students: Required—TOEFL. Electronic applications accepted. *Faculty research:* Drama therapy, directing, costume design, scenic design, technical theatre mechanics and safety.

Kent State University, College of the Arts, School of Theatre and Dance, Kent, OH 44242-0001. Offers acting (MFA); design and technology (MFA); theatre (MA, MFA). *Accreditation:* NAST. Part-time programs available. *Degree requirements:* For master's, thesis. *Entrance requirements:* For master's, GRE General Test, minimum GPA of 2.75. Additional exam requirements/recommendations for international students: Required—TOEFL. Electronic applications accepted. *Expenses:* Tuition, state resident: full-time $7866; part-time $437 per credit hour. Tuition, nonresident: full-time $14,022; part-time $779 per credit hour. *Faculty research:* Scene design, costume design, lighting design, technical direction, musical theatre.

Lamar University, College of Graduate Studies, College of Fine Arts and Communication, Department of Music, Theatre, and Dance, Beaumont, TX 77710. Offers music education (MM Ed); music performance (MM); theatre (MS). *Accreditation:* NASM (one or more programs are accredited). *Faculty:* 9 full-time (2 women), 1 part-time/adjunct (0 women). *Students:* 6 full-time (2 women), 7 part-time (5 women); includes 2 Black or African American, non-Hispanic/Latino; 1 Hispanic/Latino. Average age 28. 9 applicants, 67% accepted, 4 enrolled. In 2010, 3 master's awarded. *Degree requirements:* For master's, comprehensive exam, thesis optional. *Entrance requirements:* For master's, GRE General Test, theory placement exams, audition. Additional exam requirements/recommendations for international students: Required—TOEFL. *Application deadline:* For fall admission, 8/1 for domestic students; for spring admission, 12/1 for domestic students. Applications are processed on a rolling basis. Application fee: $25 ($50 for international students). *Expenses:* Tuition, state resident: full-time $4160; part-time $208 per credit hour. Tuition, nonresident: full-time $10,360; part-time $518 per credit hour. *Financial support:* In 2010–11, 4 fellowships with tuition reimbursements (averaging $2,000 per year), 2 teaching assistantships were awarded; institutionally sponsored loans and tuition waivers (partial) also available. Support available to part-time students. Financial award application deadline: 4/1. *Faculty research:* Performance: ensembles and personal. *Unit head:* Dr. L. Randolph Babin, Chair, 409-880-8144, Fax: 409-880-8143, E-mail: babinlr@hal.lamar.edu. *Application contact:* Dr. Robert M. Culbertson, Adviser, 409-880-8073, Fax: 409-880-8143, E-mail: culbertsrm@hal.lamar.edu.

Lindenwood University, Graduate Programs, School of Fine and Performing Arts, St. Charles, MO 63301-1695. Offers arts management (MA); communication arts (MA); studio art (MA, MFA); theatre (MA, MFA). Part-time programs available. *Faculty:* 15 full-time (6 women), 5 part-time/adjunct (2 women). *Students:* 24 full-time (14 women), 16 part-time (12 women); includes 3 minority (all Black or African American, non-Hispanic/Latino), 3 international. Average age 30. 6 applicants, 2 enrolled. In 2010, 9 master's awarded. *Degree requirements:* For master's, thesis (for some programs). *Entrance requirements:* For master's, audition or interview, minimum GPA of 3.0, submission of portfolio, letter of recommendation. Additional exam requirements/recommendations for international students: Required—TOEFL (minimum score 550 paper-based; 213 computer-based; 80 iBT). *Application deadline:* For fall admission, 8/27 priority date for domestic and international students; for spring admission, 1/28 priority date for domestic and international students. Applications are processed on a rolling basis. Application fee: $30 ($100 for international students). Electronic applications accepted. *Expenses:* Tuition: Full-time $13,260; part-time $380 per credit hour. Required fees: $340. One-time fee: $30. Tuition and fees vary according to course level and course load. *Financial support:* In 2010–11, 10 students received support. Career-related internships or fieldwork, institutionally sponsored loans, tuition waivers (partial), and unspecified assistantships available. Financial award application deadline: 6/30; financial award applicants required to submit FAFSA. *Unit head:* Donnell Walsh, Dean of Fine Arts, 636-949-4853, Fax: 636-949-4910, E-mail: dwalsh@lindenwood.edu. *Application contact:* Brett Barger, Dean of Evening Admissions and Extension Campuses, 636-949-4934, Fax: 636-949-4109, E-mail: adultadmissions@lindenwood.edu.

Long Island University, C.W. Post Campus, School of Visual and Performing Arts, Department of Theatre, Film, Dance and Arts Management, Brookville, NY 11548-1300. Offers interactive multimedia (MA); theatre (MA). Part-time and evening/weekend programs available. *Degree requirements:* For master's, thesis. *Entrance requirements:* For master's, placement exam. Electronic applications accepted. *Faculty research:* Playwriting, intercultural dance and theatre, translation, Suzuki, set and costume design.

Louisiana State University and Agricultural and Mechanical College, Graduate School, College of Music and Dramatic Arts, Department of Theatre, Baton Rouge, LA 70803. Offers acting (MFA); directing (MFA); theatre (PhD); theatre design/technology (MFA). *Accreditation:* NAST. *Faculty:* 17 full-time (6 women). *Students:* 31 full-time (11 women), 5 part-time (4 women); includes 1 Black or African American, non-Hispanic/Latino; 1 Asian, non-Hispanic/Latino; 2 Hispanic/Latino, 2 international. Average age 34. 46 applicants, 33% accepted, 14 enrolled. In 2010, 2 master's, 1 doctorate awarded. *Degree requirements:* For master's, thesis; for doctorate, one foreign language, thesis/dissertation. *Entrance requirements:* For master's, GRE General Test, audition, minimum GPA of 3.0; for doctorate, GRE General Test, minimum GPA of 3.0. Additional exam requirements/recommendations for international students: Required—TOEFL (minimum score 550 paper-based; 213 computer-based; 79 iBT) or IELTS (minimum score 6.5). *Application deadline:* For fall admission, 1/25 priority date for domestic students, 5/15 for international students; for spring admission, 10/15 for international students. Applications are processed on a rolling basis. Application fee: $50 ($70 for international students). Electronic applications accepted. *Financial support:* In 2010–11, 33 students received support, including 3 fellowships with full and partial tuition reimbursements available (averaging $16,427 per year), 23 teaching assistantships with full and partial tuition reimbursements available (averaging $11,913 per year); research assistantships with full and partial tuition reimbursements available, Federal Work-Study, scholarships/grants, health care benefits, tuition waivers (full and partial), and unspecified assistantships also available. Support available to part-time students. Financial award application deadline: 6/15; financial award applicants required to submit FAFSA. *Faculty research:* Acting, American drama, arts administration, theatre history, dramatic theory/literature, black drama. *Unit head:* Dr. Kristin Sosnowsky, Interim Chair, 225-578-4174, Fax: 225-578-4135, E-mail: ksosno1@lsu.edu. *Application contact:* Leigh Clemons, Head, MFA in Theatre Design/Technology, 225-578-9273, E-mail: clemons@lsu.edu.

Mary Baldwin College, Graduate Studies, Program in Shakespeare and Renaissance Literature in Performance, Staunton, VA 24401-3610. Offers acting (M Litt); directing (M Litt); Shakespeare and Renaissance literature in performance (MFA); teaching (M Litt). *Entrance requirements:* For master's, GRE (M Litt).

Massachusetts College of Art and Design, Graduate Programs, Master of Fine Arts (MFA) Program, Boston, MA 02115-5882. Offers ceramics (MFA); design (MFA); fibers (MFA); film/video (MFA); glass (MFA); media and performing arts (MFA); metals/jewelry (MFA); painting (MFA); photography (MFA); printmaking (MFA); sculpture (MFA). *Accreditation:* NASAD. *Faculty:* 14 full-time (7 women), 16 part-time/adjunct (10 women). *Students:* 86 full-time (51 women), 9 part-time (5 women); includes 10 minority (1 Asian, non-Hispanic/Latino; 6 Hispanic/Latino; 3 Two or more races, non-Hispanic/Latino), 14 international. Average age 34. 298 applicants, 28% accepted, 41 enrolled. In 2010, 40 master's awarded. *Degree requirements:* For master's, thesis, exhibit. *Entrance requirements:* For master's, 12 units of course work in art history, portfolio, resume, letters of reference, interview. Additional exam requirements/recommendations for international students: Required—TOEFL (minimum score 563 paper-based; 223 computer-based; 85 iBT); Recommended—IELTS (minimum score 6.5). *Application deadline:* For fall admission, 1/15 for domestic and international students. Application fee: $85. Electronic applications accepted. *Expenses:* Tuition, state resident: part-time $665 per credit. Tuition, nonresident: part-time $665 per credit. *Financial support:* In 2010–11, 19 fellowships (averaging $5,000 per year), 43 research assistantships (averaging $2,000 per year), 44 teaching assistantships (averaging $2,000 per year) were awarded; career-related internships or fieldwork and Federal Work-Study also available. Support available to part-time students. Financial award application deadline: 5/1; financial award applicants required to submit FAFSA. *Unit head:* George Creamer, Dean of Graduate Programs, 617-879-7163, Fax: 617-879-7171, E-mail: creamer@massart.edu. *Application contact:* George Creamer, Dean of Graduate Programs, 617-879-7163, Fax: 617-879-7171, E-mail: creamer@massart.edu.

Miami University, Graduate School, School of Fine Arts, Department of Theatre, Oxford, OH 45056. Offers MA. *Accreditation:* NAST. *Students:* 8 full-time (4 women); includes 2 minority (both Black or African American, non-Hispanic/Latino), 2 international. Average age 28. In 2010, 3 master's awarded. *Entrance requirements:* For master's, minimum undergraduate GPA of 3.0 during previous 2 years or 2.75 overall. Application fee: $50. *Expenses:* Tuition, state resident: full-time $11,616; part-time $484 per credit hour. Tuition, nonresident: full-time $25,656; part-time $1069 per credit hour. Required fees: $528. *Financial support:* Fellowships with full tuition reimbursements, research assistantships, teaching assistantships, career-related internships or fieldwork, Federal Work-Study, health care benefits, tuition waivers (full), and unspecified assistantships available. Financial award application deadline: 3/1. *Unit head:* Dr. Elizabeth Mullenix, Chair, 513-529-3053, E-mail: mullener@muohio.edu. *Application contact:* Dr. Paul K. Jackson, Interim Director of Graduate Studies, 513-529-1406, E-mail: jacksopk@muohio.edu.

Michigan State University, The Graduate School, College of Arts and Letters, Department of Theatre, East Lansing, MI 48824. Offers MA, MFA. *Entrance requirements:* Additional exam requirements/recommendations for international students: Required—TOEFL. Electronic applications accepted.

Minnesota State University Mankato, College of Graduate Studies, College of Arts and Humanities, Department of Theatre and Dance, Mankato, MN 56001. Offers theatre arts (MA, MFA). *Students:* 17 full-time (7 women), 6 part-time (3 women). *Degree requirements:* For master's, one foreign language, comprehensive exam, thesis. *Entrance requirements:* For master's, minimum GPA of 3.0 during previous 2 years, 3 letters of recommendation, resume of theatre work, audition. Additional exam requirements/recommendations for international students: Required—TOEFL. *Application deadline:* For fall admission, 7/1 priority date for domestic students, 5/1 for international students; for spring admission, 11/1 for domestic students, 10/1 for international students. Applications are processed on a rolling basis. Application fee: $40. Electronic applications accepted. *Financial support:* Research assistantships with full tuition reimbursements, teaching assistantships with full tuition reimbursements, career-related internships or fieldwork, Federal Work-Study, institutionally sponsored loans, and unspecified assistantships available. Support available to part-time students. Financial award application deadline: 3/15; financial award applicants required to submit FAFSA. *Unit head:* Dr. Paul Hustoles, Chairperson, 507-389-2118. *Application contact:* 507-389-2321, E-mail: grad@mnsu.edu.

Missouri State University, Graduate College, College of Arts and Letters, Department of Theatre and Dance, Springfield, MO 65897. Offers secondary education (MS Ed), including speech and theatre; theatre (MA). *Accreditation:* NAST. Part-time programs available. *Degree requirements:* For master's, comprehensive exam, thesis or alternative. *Entrance requirements:* For master's, minimum GPA of 3.0 (MA), 9-12 teaching certification (MS Ed). Additional exam requirements/recommendations for international students: Required—TOEFL (minimum score 550 paper-based; 213 computer-based; 79 iBT). Electronic applications accepted. *Expenses:* Tuition, state resident: full-time $3348; part-time $186 per credit hour. Tuition, nonresident: full-time $6696; part-time $372 per credit hour. Required fees: $238 per semester. Tuition and fees vary according to course level, course load and program.

Montclair State University, The Graduate School, School of the Arts, Department of Theatre and Dance, Montclair, NJ 07043-1624. Offers theatre (MA), including arts management, production/stage management, theatre studies. *Accreditation:* NAST. Part-time and evening/weekend programs available. *Faculty:* 15 full-time (8 women), 35 part-time/adjunct (25 women). *Students:* 10 full-time (7 women), 22 part-time (14 women); includes 2 Black or African American, non-Hispanic/Latino; 3 Hispanic/Latino. Average age 28. 22 applicants, 64% accepted, 10 enrolled. In 2010, 8 master's awarded. *Degree requirements:* For master's, comprehensive exam, thesis or alternative. *Entrance requirements:* For master's, GRE General Test, 2 letters of recommendation. Additional exam requirements/recommendations for international students: Required—TOEFL (minimum iBT score of 83) or IELTS. *Application deadline:* For fall admission, 6/1 for international students; for spring admission, 10/1 for international students. Applications are processed on a rolling basis. Application fee: $60. Electronic applications accepted. *Expenses:* Tuition, state resident: part-time $501.34 per credit. Tuition, nonresident: part-time $773.88 per credit. Required fees: $71.15 per credit. *Financial support:* In 2010–11, 3 research assistantships with full tuition reimbursements (averaging $7,000 per year) were awarded; Federal Work-Study, scholarships/grants, and unspecified assistantships also available. Support available to part-time students. Financial award application deadline: 3/1; financial award applicants required to submit FAFSA. *Unit head:* Dr. Eric Diamond, Chairperson, 973-655-4217, E-mail: peterson@mail.montclair.edu. *Application contact:* Amy Aiello, Director of Graduate Admissions and Operations, 973-655-5147, E-mail: petersonj@mail.montclair.edu.

Naropa University, Graduate Programs, Program in Theater: Contemporary Performance, Boulder, CO 80302-6697. Offers MFA. *Faculty:* 3 full-time (2 women), 1 (woman) part-time/adjunct. *Students:* 21 full-time (10 women); includes 1 Black or African American, non-Hispanic/Latino; 3 Two or more races, non-Hispanic/Latino, 2 international. Average age 34. 46 applicants, 61% accepted, 10 enrolled. In 2010, 14 master's awarded. *Degree requirements:* For master's, culminating projects and performances. *Entrance requirements:* For master's, interview, head shot, resume, 3 letters of recommendation, letter of interest. Additional exam requirements/recommendations for international students: Required—TOEFL (minimum score 600 paper-based; 250 computer-based). *Application deadline:* For fall admission, 1/15 priority date for domestic and international students. Applications are processed on a rolling basis. Application fee: $60. Electronic applications accepted. *Expenses:* Tuition: Full-time $17,820; part-time $810 per credit. Required fees: $305 per semester. Tuition and fees vary according to course load, program and reciprocity agreements. *Financial support:* In 2010–11, 9 students received support, including 2 research assistantships with partial tuition reimbursements available (averaging $2,000 per year), 1 teaching assistantship with partial tuition reimbursement available (averaging $2,000 per year); Federal Work-Study, scholarships/grants, health care benefits, tuition waivers (partial), and unspecified assistantships also available. Support available to part-time students. Financial award application deadline: 3/1; financial award applicants required to submit FAFSA. *Unit head:* Sue Hammond West, Director, School of the Arts, 303-546-3585, E-mail: suewest@naropa.edu. *Application contact:* Donna McIntyre, Associate Director of Graduate Admissions, 303-536-3555, Fax: 303-546-3583, E-mail: donna@naropa.edu.

National Theatre Conservatory, Department of Acting, Denver, CO 80204-2157. Offers MFA, Certificate. *Entrance requirements:* For master's, audition/interview.

Theater

The New School: A University, The New School for Drama, New York, NY 10014. Offers acting (MFA); directing (MFA); playwriting (MFA). *Degree requirements:* For master's, thesis, student involvement in theatrical production and presentation. *Entrance requirements:* For master's, audition (acting), interview (directing and playwriting). Additional exam requirements/recommendations for international students: Required—TOEFL (minimum score 600 paper-based; 250 computer-based; 100 iBT). Electronic applications accepted. *Expenses:* Contact institution.

New York University, Steinhardt School of Culture, Education, and Human Development, Department of Music and Performing Arts Professions, Program in Educational Theatre, New York, NY 10012-1019. Offers dual certification: educational theatre and English 7-12 (MA); dual certification: educational theatre and social studies (MA); educational theatre (Ed D, PhD, Advanced Certificate); educational theatre for colleges and communities (MA); teaching educational theatre, all grades (MA). Part-time programs available. *Faculty:* 4 full-time (1 woman). *Students:* 89 full-time (65 women), 68 part-time (50 women); includes 14 Black or African American, non-Hispanic/Latino; 1 American Indian or Alaska Native, non-Hispanic/Latino; 8 Asian, non-Hispanic/Latino; 7 Hispanic/Latino, 6 international. Average age 30. 101 applicants, 88% accepted, 60 enrolled. In 2010, 72 master's, 3 doctorates awarded. *Degree requirements:* For master's, thesis (for some programs); for doctorate, thesis/dissertation. *Entrance requirements:* For master's, audition; for doctorate, GRE General Test, interview; for Advanced Certificate, master's degree. Additional exam requirements/recommendations for international students: Required—TOEFL. *Application deadline:* For fall admission, 12/1 priority date for domestic and international students; for spring admission, 11/1 for domestic and international students. Applications are processed on a rolling basis. Application fee: $75. Electronic applications accepted. *Financial support:* Teaching assistantships with partial tuition reimbursements, career-related internships or fieldwork, Federal Work-Study, institutionally sponsored loans, and scholarships/grants available. Support available to part-time students. Financial award application deadline: 2/1; financial award applicants required to submit FAFSA. *Faculty research:* Theatre for young audiences, drama in education, applied theatre, arts education assessment, reflective praxis. *Unit head:* Dr. Philip Taylor, Director, 212-998-5424, Fax: 212-995-4043. *Application contact:* 212-998-5030, Fax: 212-995-4328, E-mail: steinhardt.gradadmissions@nyu.edu.

New York University, Steinhardt School of Culture, Education, and Human Development, Department of Music and Performing Arts Professions, Program in Music Performance and Composition, New York, NY 10012-1019. Offers instrumental performance (MM), including instrumental performance, jazz instrumental performance; music performance and composition (MA, PhD), including composition; music theory and composition (MM, PhD), including music theory and compostition (MM), scoring for film and multimedia (MM); piano performance (MM), including collaborative performance, collaborative piano, solo piano; vocal pedagogy (Advanced Certificate); vocal performance (MM), including classical voice, music theatre performance; vocal performance/vocal pedagogy (MM), including classical voice, music theatre performance; MM/Advanced Certificate. Part-time programs available. *Faculty:* 22 full-time (6 women). *Students:* 235 full-time (101 women), 63 part-time (18 women); includes 13 Black or African American, non-Hispanic/Latino; 24 Asian, non-Hispanic/Latino; 12 Hispanic/Latino, 85 international. Average age 27. 439 applicants, 52% accepted, 125 enrolled. In 2010, 104 master's, 5 doctorates, 5 other advanced degrees awarded. *Degree requirements:* For master's, thesis (for some programs); for doctorate, thesis/dissertation. *Entrance requirements:* For master's, audition; for doctorate, GRE General Test, audition, interview. Additional exam requirements/recommendations for international students: Required—TOEFL. *Application deadline:* For fall admission, 12/1 priority date for domestic and international students; for spring admission, 11/1 for domestic and international students. Applications are processed on a rolling basis. Application fee: $75. Electronic applications accepted. *Financial support:* Fellowships with full and partial tuition reimbursements, Federal Work-Study, scholarships/grants, and tuition waivers (partial) available. Support available to part-time students. Financial award application deadline: 2/1; financial award applicants required to submit FAFSA. *Faculty research:* Aesthetics, performance analysis, twentieth century music, music methodologies for arts criticism and analysis. *Application contact:* 212-998-5030, Fax: 212-995-4328, E-mail: steinhardt.gradadmissions@nyu.edu.

New York University, Tisch School of the Arts and Graduate School of Arts and Science, Department of Performance Studies, New York, NY 10012-1019. Offers MA, PhD. *Faculty:* 12 full-time (7 women), 4 part-time/adjunct (3 women). *Students:* 63 full-time (46 women), 1 (woman) part-time; includes 4 Black or African American, non-Hispanic/Latino; 4 Asian, non-Hispanic/Latino; 8 Hispanic/Latino. Average age 31. 198 applicants, 51% accepted, 54 enrolled. In 2010, 36 master's, 7 doctorates awarded. *Degree requirements:* For doctorate, one foreign language, comprehensive exam, thesis/dissertation, dissertation defense, qualifying exam. *Entrance requirements:* For master's, sample of written work; for doctorate, master's degree, writing sample. Additional exam requirements/recommendations for international students: Required—TOEFL or IELTS. *Application deadline:* For fall admission, 12/1 for domestic and international students. Application fee: $60. Electronic applications accepted. *Expenses:* Contact institution. *Financial support:* In 2010–11, 32 students received support, including 24 fellowships with full and partial tuition reimbursements available, 4 research assistantships, 4 teaching assistantships; Federal Work-Study, institutionally sponsored loans, tuition waivers (partial), and unspecified assistantships also available. Financial award application deadline: 2/15; financial award applicants required to submit CSS PROFILE or FAFSA. *Faculty research:* Performance theory, dance, folklore and festivals, postcolonial theory, anthropology and gender studies. *Unit head:* Jose Munoz, Chair, 212-998-1620, Fax: 212-995-4571, E-mail: performance.studies@nyu.edu. *Application contact:* Dan Sandford, Director of Graduate Admissions, 212-998-1918, Fax: 212-995-4060, E-mail: tisch.gradadmissions@nyu.edu.

New York University, Tisch School of the Arts, Graduate Acting Program, New York, NY 10012-1019. Offers MFA. *Faculty:* 9 full-time (6 women), 11 part-time/adjunct (5 women). *Students:* 52 full-time (23 women); includes 8 Black or African American, non-Hispanic/Latino; 3 Asian, non-Hispanic/Latino; 1 Hispanic/Latino. Average age 26. 761 applicants, 4% accepted, 18 enrolled. In 2010, 18 master's awarded. *Entrance requirements:* For master's, audition. *Application deadline:* For fall admission, 1/1 for domestic and international students. Application fee: $60. Electronic applications accepted. *Financial support:* In 2010–11, 30 students received support, including 4 fellowships with full and partial tuition reimbursements available; Federal Work-Study, institutionally sponsored loans, scholarships/grants, tuition waivers (full and partial), and unspecified assistantships also available. Financial award application deadline: 2/15; financial award applicants required to submit FAFSA. *Unit head:* Mark Wing-Davey, Chair, 212-998-1964, Fax: 212-995-4067. *Application contact:* Dan Sandford, Director of Graduate Admissions, 212-998-1918, Fax: 212-995-4060, E-mail: tisch.gradadmissions@nyu.edu.

Northern Illinois University, Graduate School, College of Visual and Performing Arts, School of Theatre and Dance, De Kalb, IL 60115-2854. Offers MFA. *Accreditation:* NAST. Part-time programs available. *Faculty:* 16 full-time (9 women). *Students:* 30 full-time (14 women), 2 part-time (1 woman); includes 2 Black or African American, non-Hispanic/Latino; 1 American Indian or Alaska Native, non-Hispanic/Latino; 2 Hispanic/Latino; 1 Two or more races, non-Hispanic/Latino, 1 international. Average age 26. 43 applicants, 49% accepted, 19 enrolled. In 2010, 14 master's awarded. *Degree requirements:* For master's, comprehensive exam, final project and defense. *Entrance requirements:* For master's, minimum GPA of 2.75, audition or portfolio. Additional exam requirements/recommendations for international students: Required—TOEFL (minimum score 550 paper-based; 213 computer-based). *Application deadline:* For fall admission, 4/1 priority date for domestic students, 5/1 for international students; for spring admission, 10/15 priority date for domestic students, 10/1 for international students. Applications are processed on a rolling basis. Application fee: $30. Electronic applications accepted. *Expenses:* Tuition, state resident: full-time $7200; part-time $300 per credit hour. Tuition, nonresident: full-time $14,400; part-time $600 per credit hour. Required fees: $79 per credit hour. *Financial support:* In 2010–11, 30 teaching assistantships with full tuition reimbursements were awarded; fellowships with full tuition reimbursements, research assistantships with full tuition reimbursements, career-related internships or fieldwork, Federal Work-Study, scholarships/grants, tuition waivers (full), and staff assistantships also available. Support available to part-time students. Financial award applicants required to submit FAFSA. *Faculty research:* Theatre history, choreography, performance art spectacles, storytelling, computer visualization of the ethical space. *Unit head:* Alexander Gelman, Director, 815-753-8253, Fax: 815-753-8415, E-mail: agelman@niu.edu. *Application contact:* Terrence McClellan, Information Contact, 815-753-8257, E-mail: tmcclell@niu.edu.

Northwestern University, The Graduate School, School of Communication, Department of Theatre, Evanston, IL 60208. Offers directing (MFA); stage design (MFA); theatre (MA). Admissions and degrees offered through The Graduate School. *Degree requirements:* For master's, thesis (MFA). *Entrance requirements:* For master's, GRE General Test. Additional exam requirements/recommendations for international students: Required—TOEFL. *Faculty research:* Critical analysis, theory and history of theatre and drama, philosophy of dance and movement, performance in multicultural contexts, storytelling, computer design process.

Northwestern University, The Graduate School, School of Communication, Interdisciplinary PhD Program in Theatre and Drama, Evanston, IL 60208. Offers PhD. Admissions and degree offered through The Graduate School. *Degree requirements:* For doctorate, thesis/dissertation, qualifying and final oral exams. *Entrance requirements:* For doctorate, GRE General Test, sample of written work. Additional exam requirements/recommendations for international students: Required—TOEFL. Electronic applications accepted. *Faculty research:* Theory and history of theatre and drama, performance theory, performance in multicultural contexts, critical analysis drama, theatre historiography.

The Ohio State University, Graduate School, College of Arts and Sciences, Division of Arts and Humanities, Department of Theatre, Columbus, OH 43210. Offers MA, MFA, PhD. *Accreditation:* NAST. *Faculty:* 22. *Students:* 38 full-time (22 women), 15 part-time (5 women); includes 3 Black or African American, non-Hispanic/Latino; 1 Asian, non-Hispanic/Latino; 3 Hispanic/Latino, 9 international. Average age 33. In 2010, 5 master's, 2 doctorates awarded. *Degree requirements:* For master's, thesis (for some programs); for doctorate, one foreign language, thesis/dissertation. *Entrance requirements:* For master's, GRE General Test (MA); for doctorate, GRE General Test. Additional exam requirements/recommendations for international students: Recommended—TOEFL (minimum score 600 paper-based; 250 computer-based). *Application deadline:* For fall admission, 8/15 priority date for domestic students, 7/1 priority date for international students; for winter admission, 12/1 priority date for domestic students, 11/1 priority date for international students; for spring admission, 3/1 priority date for domestic students, 2/1 priority date for international students. Applications are processed on a rolling basis. Application fee: $40 ($50 for international students). Electronic applications accepted. *Expenses:* Tuition, state resident: full-time $10,605. Tuition, nonresident: full-time $26,535. Tuition and fees vary according to course load and program. *Financial support:* Fellowships, teaching assistantships, Federal Work-Study and institutionally sponsored loans available. Support available to part-time students. *Unit head:* Dan Gray, Interim Chair, 614-292-8412, E-mail: gray.215@osu.edu. *Application contact:* 614-292-9444, Fax: 614-292-3895, E-mail: domestic.grad@osu.edu.

Ohio University, Graduate College, College of Fine Arts, School of Theater, Athens, OH 45701-2979. Offers MA, MFA. *Accreditation:* NAST. *Students:* 58 full-time (31 women), 2 part-time (1 woman); includes 4 minority (3 Hispanic/Latino; 1 Two or more races, non-Hispanic/Latino), 4 international. 68 applicants, 38% accepted, 23 enrolled. In 2010, 18 master's awarded. *Degree requirements:* For master's, thesis or alternative. *Entrance requirements:* For master's, minimum GPA of 3.0. Additional exam requirements/recommendations for international students: Required—TOEFL (minimum score 550 paper-based; 80 iBT) or IELTS (minimum score 6.5). *Application deadline:* For fall admission, 3/15 priority date for domestic and international students. Application fee: $50 ($55 for international students). Electronic applications accepted. *Financial support:* Research assistantships with full and partial tuition reimbursements, career-related internships or fieldwork, Federal Work-Study, institutionally sponsored loans, scholarships/grants, tuition waivers (partial), and unspecified assistantships available. Financial award application deadline: 3/15; financial award applicants required to submit FAFSA. *Unit head:* Madeleine Scott, Interim Director, 740-593-4818, Fax: 740-593-4817, E-mail: fisherw@ohio.edu. *Application contact:* Barbara M. Fiocchi, Administrative Assistant, 740-593-4818, Fax: 740-593-4817, E-mail: fiocchi@ohio.edu.

Oklahoma City University, Margaret E. Petree College of Performing Arts, School of Theatre, Oklahoma City, OK 73106-1402. Offers costume design (MA); technical theater (MA); theater (MA); theater for young audiences (MA). Part-time programs available. *Degree requirements:* For master's, thesis or alternative. *Entrance requirements:* For master's, interview, audition, writing sample. Additional exam requirements/recommendations for international students: Required—TOEFL (minimum score 550 paper-based; 173 computer-based; 80 iBT). *Faculty research:* Translation of plays, writing plays, dramaturgical research for plays and educational outreach materials.

Oklahoma State University, College of Arts and Sciences, Department of Theatre, Stillwater, OK 74078. Offers MA. *Accreditation:* NAST. *Faculty:* 11 full-time (4 women), 1 part-time/adjunct (0 women). *Students:* 4 full-time (2 women), 2 part-time (1 woman); includes 1 Black or African American, non-Hispanic/Latino. Average age 27. 6 applicants, 50% accepted, 3 enrolled. In 2010, 1 master's awarded. *Degree requirements:* For master's, creative component or thesis. *Entrance requirements:* For master's, GRE. Additional exam requirements/recommendations for international students: Required—TOEFL (minimum score 550 paper-based; 79 iBT). *Application deadline:* For fall admission, 3/1 priority date for international students; for spring admission, 8/1 priority date for international students. Applications are processed on a rolling basis. Application fee: $40 ($75 for international students). Electronic applications accepted. *Expenses:* Tuition, state resident: full-time $3716; part-time $154.85 per credit hour. Tuition, nonresident: full-time $14,892; part-time $621 per credit hour. Required fees: $2044; $85.20 per credit hour. One-time fee: $50. Tuition and fees vary according to course load and campus/location. *Financial support:* In 2010–11, 7 teaching assistantships (averaging $10,263 per year) were awarded; career-related internships or fieldwork, Federal Work-Study, scholarships/grants, health care benefits, tuition waivers (partial), and unspecified assistantships also available. Support available to part-time students. Financial award application deadline: 3/1; financial award applicants required to submit FAFSA. *Faculty research:* Historical scene painting and scenic art, Eastern European stage design, stage direction, voice and diction for the actor, stage choreography and dance. *Unit head:* Kevin Doolen, Head, 405-744-6094, Fax: 405-744-6509. *Application contact:* Dr. Gordon Emslie, Dean, 405-744-6368, Fax: 405-744-0355, E-mail: grad-i@okstate.edu.

Pace University, Dyson College of Arts and Sciences, The Actors Studio MFA, New York, NY 10038. Offers acting (MFA); directing (MFA); playwriting (MFA). *Entrance requirements:* Additional exam requirements/recommendations for international students: Required—TOEFL.

Penn State University Park, Graduate School, College of Arts and Architecture, School of Theatre, State College, University Park, PA 16802-1503. Offers MFA. *Accreditation:* NAST.

Pittsburg State University, Graduate School, College of Arts and Sciences, Department of Communication, Pittsburg, KS 66762. Offers applied communication (MA); communication education (MA); theatre (MA). *Degree requirements:* For master's, thesis or alternative.

Point Park University, Conservatory of Performing Arts, Pittsburgh, PA 15222-1984. Offers theatre arts-acting (MFA). *Faculty:* 3 full-time, 1 part-time/adjunct. *Students:* 6 full-time (3 women), 1 international. Average age 42. 6 applicants, 0% accepted, 0 enrolled. *Degree requirements:* For master's, comprehensive exam (for some programs), thesis or alternative. *Entrance requirements:* For master's, interview, undergraduate degree in related field, theatre experience. Additional exam requirements/recommendations for international students: Required—TOEFL (minimum score 550 paper-based; 79 iBT). *Application deadline:* Applications are processed on a rolling basis. Application fee: $30. Electronic applications accepted. *Expenses:* Tuition: Full-time $12,456; part-time $692 per credit. Required fees: $630; $35 per credit. *Financial support:* In 2010–11, 6 students received support, including 5 teaching assistantships with full tuition reimbursements available (averaging $6,400 per year); scholarships/grants also available. Financial award application deadline: 4/15; financial award applicants required to submit FAFSA. *Unit head:* Ronald Allan-Lindblom, Dean/Artistic Producing Director, 412-392-3454, Fax: 412-392-2424, E-mail: rlindblom@pointpark.edu. *Application contact:* Lynn C. Ribar, Associate Director, Adult and Graduate Enrollment, 412-392-3908, Fax: 412-392-6164, E-mail: lribar@pointpark.edu.

Portland State University, Graduate Studies, School of Fine and Performing Arts, Department of Theater Arts, Portland, OR 97207-0751. Offers MA, MS, MA/MS. *Accreditation:* NAST. *Faculty:* 13 full-time (7 women), 11 part-time/adjunct (4 women). *Students:* 4 full-time (3 women), 4 part-time (3 women). Average age 37. 6 applicants, 100% accepted, 2 enrolled. In 2010, 2 master's awarded. *Degree requirements:* For master's, variable foreign language requirement, thesis or alternative. *Entrance requirements:* For master's, minimum GPA of 3.0 in upper-division course work or 2.75 overall, 24 credits in theater arts. Additional exam requirements/recommendations for international students: Required—TOEFL (minimum score 550 paper-based; 213 computer-based). *Application deadline:* For fall admission, 4/1 priority date for domestic students, 3/1 priority date for international students; for winter admission, 9/1 for domestic students; for spring admission, 11/1 for domestic students. Applications are processed on a rolling basis. Application fee: $50. *Expenses:* Tuition, state resident: full-time $8505; part-time $315 per credit. Tuition, nonresident: full-time $13,284; part-time $492 per credit. Required fees: $1482; $21 per credit. $99 per term. One-time fee: $120. Part-time tuition and fees vary according to course load and program. *Financial support:* Research assistantships, teaching assistantships with full tuition reimbursements, career-related internships or fieldwork, Federal Work-Study, and unspecified assistantships available. Support available to part-time students. Financial award application deadline: 3/1; financial award applicants required to submit FAFSA. *Faculty research:* Design, acting/directing, scene/costume technology, dramatic literature, theater history. *Unit head:* Sarah Andrews-Collier, Chair, 503-725-4612, Fax: 503-725-4624, E-mail: andrews@pdx.edu. *Application contact:* Richard Wattenberg, Coordinator, 503-725-4602, Fax: 503-725-4624, E-mail: wattenbergr@pdx.edu.

Purchase College, State University of New York, Conservatory of Theatre Arts, Purchase, NY 10577-1400. Offers theatre design/stage technology (MFA). *Degree requirements:* For master's, thesis or alternative, performance. *Entrance requirements:* For master's, BFA, interview, portfolio. Electronic applications accepted.

Purdue University, Graduate School, College of Liberal Arts, Department of Visual and Performing Arts, West Lafayette, IN 47907. Offers art and design (MA); theatre (MA, MFA). *Accreditation:* NASAD; NAST. Part-time programs available. *Degree requirements:* For master's, terminal exhibit, project, or thesis. *Entrance requirements:* Additional exam requirements/recommendations for international students: Required—TOEFL. Electronic applications accepted. *Faculty research:* Design, fine arts, photography, acting, directing, theatre technology.

Regent University, Graduate School, School of Communication and the Arts, Virginia Beach, VA 23464-9800. Offers acting (MFA); cinema arts/television arts (MA); communication (MA, PhD); digital media (MA); directing for cinema/television (MA, MFA); editing for cinema/television (MA); journalism (MA); producing for cinema/television (MA, MFA); script and screenwriting (MFA); theatre (MA). Part-time programs available. Postbaccalaureate distance learning degree programs offered (minimal on-campus study). *Faculty:* 29 full-time (4 women), 25 part-time/adjunct (5 women). *Students:* 93 full-time (48 women), 167 part-time (80 women); includes 45 Black or African American, non-Hispanic/Latino; 2 American Indian or Alaska Native, non-Hispanic/Latino; 3 Asian, non-Hispanic/Latino; 9 Hispanic/Latino, 11 international. Average age 32. 247 applicants, 45% accepted, 65 enrolled. In 2010, 82 master's, 17 doctorates awarded. *Degree requirements:* For master's, thesis or alternative; for doctorate, thesis/dissertation. *Entrance requirements:* For master's, GRE General Test or MAT, minimum undergraduate GPA of 3.0, writing sample, computer literacy survey, recommendation, resume, interview, audition (MFA programs); for doctorate, GRE General Test, minimum graduate GPA of 3.0, writing sample, computer literacy survey, recommendation, interview, transcripts. Additional exam requirements/recommendations for international students: Required—TOEFL (minimum score 577 paper-based; 233 computer-based). *Application deadline:* For fall admission, 3/1 priority date for domestic students; for spring admission, 10/1 priority date for domestic students. Applications are processed on a rolling basis. Application fee: $50. Electronic applications accepted. *Expenses:* Contact institution. *Financial support:* Fellowships with full and partial tuition reimbursements, career-related internships or fieldwork, scholarships/grants, tuition waivers (full and partial), and unspecified assistantships available. Support available to part-time students. Financial award application deadline: 9/1; financial award applicants required to submit FAFSA. *Faculty research:* Southern gospel music, education and entertainment, celebrities and the media, journalism and ethics, C. S. Lewis. *Unit head:* Dr. Emmanuel Ayee, Interim Dean, 757-352-4945, Fax: 757-352-4291, E-mail: eayee@regent.edu. *Application contact:* Matthew Chadwick, Director of Enrollment Support Services, 800-373-5504, Fax: 757-352-4381, E-mail: admissions@regent.edu.

Roosevelt University, Graduate Division, Chicago College of Performing Arts, Theatre Conservatory, Chicago, IL 60605. Offers directing and dramaturgy (MFA); musical theatre (MFA); theatre (MA, MFA); theatre-directing (MA); theatre-performance (MFA). MA is a special 3-summer program for high school teachers only. *Degree requirements:* For master's, thesis production/performance. *Entrance requirements:* For master's, audition, interview, minimum GPA of 2.5. *Faculty research:* Brecht, Shakespeare, contemporary and new work, fully mounted theatre.

Rowan University, Graduate School, College of Fine and Performing Arts, Program in Theatre, Glassboro, NJ 08028-1701. Offers theatre (MA); theatre education (MST). *Accreditation:* NAST. Part-time and evening/weekend programs available. *Faculty:* 8 full-time (3 women), 12 part-time/adjunct (6 women). *Students:* 2 full-time (1 woman). Average age 23. In 2010, 2 master's awarded. *Degree requirements:* For master's, thesis. *Entrance requirements:* For master's, GRE General Test. Additional exam requirements/recommendations for international students: Required—TOEFL. *Application deadline:* Applications are processed on a rolling basis. Application fee: $65 ($200 for international students). Electronic applications accepted. *Expenses:* Tuition, area resident: Part-time $602 per semester hour. Tuition, nonresident: part-time $602 per semester hour. Required fees: $100 per semester hour. One-time fee: $10 part-time. *Financial support:* Career-related internships or fieldwork, scholarships/grants, health care benefits, and unspecified assistantships available. Support available to part-time students. *Unit head:* Dr. Horacio Sosa, Dean, College of Graduate and Continuing Education, 856-256-4747, Fax: 856-256-5638, E-mail: sosa@rowan.edu. *Application contact:* Karen Haynes, Graduate Coordinator, 856-256-4052, Fax: 856-256-4436, E-mail: haynes@rowan.edu.

Rutgers, The State University of New Jersey, New Brunswick, Mason Gross School of the Arts, Theater Arts Department, New Brunswick, NJ 08901. Offers acting (MFA); design (MFA); directing (MFA); playwriting (MFA); stage management (MFA). *Faculty:* 13 full-time (8 women), 21 part-time/adjunct (6 women). *Students:* 67 full-time (41 women); includes 10 Black or African American, non-Hispanic/Latino; 1 Hispanic/Latino. Average age 27. 183 applicants, 17% accepted, 27 enrolled. In 2010, 22 master's awarded. *Degree requirements:* For master's, thesis (for some programs), performance project. *Entrance requirements:* For master's, audition, interview, portfolio. Additional exam requirements/recommendations for international students: Required—TOEFL (minimum score 550 paper-based; 213 computer-based), IELTS (minimum score 7). *Application deadline:* For fall admission, 3/1 for domestic and international students. Application fee: $65. Electronic applications accepted. *Expenses:* Tuition, state resident: full-time $7200; part-time $600 per credit. Tuition, nonresident: full-time $11,124; part-time $927 per credit. *Financial support:* In 2010–11, 16 fellowships (averaging $1,000 per year), 62 teaching assistantships with partial tuition reimbursements (averaging $3,700 per year) were awarded; career-related internships or fieldwork, Federal Work-Study, scholarships/grants, and health care benefits also available. Financial award application deadline: 3/1; financial award applicants required to submit FAFSA. *Faculty research:* Faculty of working professional. *Unit head:* Michael Miller, Interim Chair, 732-932-9891 Ext. 10, Fax: 732-932-1409. *Application contact:* Barbara Harwanko, Administrative Assistant, 732-932-9891 Ext. 10, Fax: 732-932-1409, E-mail: harwanko@masongross.rutgers.edu.

San Diego State University, Graduate and Research Affairs, College of Professional Studies and Fine Arts, School of Theater, Television and Film, San Diego, CA 92182. Offers television, film, and new media production (MA); theatre arts (MA, MFA). *Accreditation:* NAST. Part-time programs available. *Degree requirements:* For master's, thesis. *Entrance requirements:* For master's, GRE General Test, 3 letters of recommendation, interview. Additional exam requirements/recommendations for international students: Required—TOEFL. Electronic applications accepted.

San Francisco State University, Division of Graduate Studies, College of Creative Arts, Department of Theatre Arts, San Francisco, CA 94132-1722. Offers drama (MA); theatre arts (MFA), including design/technical production. *Accreditation:* NAST. *Unit head:* Todd Roehrmam, Chair, 415-338-1341. *Application contact:* Joel Schechter, MA Coordinator, 415-338-1331, E-mail: jschech@sfsu.edu.

San Jose State University, Graduate Studies and Research, College of Humanities and the Arts, Department of Television, Radio, Film and Theatre, San Jose, CA 95192-0001. Offers theatre arts (MA). *Accreditation:* NAST. *Degree requirements:* For master's, written exam. *Entrance requirements:* Additional exam requirements/recommendations for international students: Required—TOEFL (minimum score 570 paper-based). Electronic applications accepted.

Sarah Lawrence College, Graduate Studies, Program in Theater, Bronxville, NY 10708-5999. Offers MFA. *Degree requirements:* For master's, portfolio. *Entrance requirements:* For master's, interview, minimum B average in undergraduate course work. Additional exam requirements/recommendations for international students: Required—TOEFL (minimum score 600 paper-based).

Savannah College of Art and Design, Graduate School, Program in Production Design, Savannah, GA 31402-3146. Offers MA, MFA. Part-time programs available. *Faculty:* 4 full-time (0 women), 1 (woman) part-time/adjunct. *Students:* 9 full-time (6 women), 3 part-time (all women); includes 2 Black or African American, non-Hispanic/Latino, 3 international. Average age 28. *Degree requirements:* For master's, thesis. *Entrance requirements:* For master's, interview, portfolio. Additional exam requirements/recommendations for international students: Required—TOEFL (minimum score 450 paper-based; 133 computer-based). *Application deadline:* For fall admission, 4/1 priority date for domestic and international students. Applications are processed on a rolling basis. Application fee: $35. Electronic applications accepted. *Expenses:* Tuition: Full-time $29,520; part-time $3280 per quarter. Tuition and fees vary according to campus/location. *Financial support:* Fellowships, career-related internships or fieldwork, Federal Work-Study, and scholarships/grants available. Financial award application deadline: 4/1; financial award applicants required to submit FAFSA. *Unit head:* Robert Mond, Chair, 912-525-6947, Fax: 912-525-6935, E-mail: rmond@scad.edu. *Application contact:* Elizabeth Mathis, Director of Graduate Recruitment, 912-525-5965, Fax: 912-525-5985, E-mail: emathis@scad.edu.

Savannah College of Art and Design, Graduate School, Program in Professional Education, Savannah, GA 31402-3146. Offers art (MAT); drama (MAT). *Faculty:* 3 full-time (all women), 2 part-time/adjunct (both women). *Students:* 17 full-time (all women); includes 2 Hispanic/Latino; 1 Two or more races, non-Hispanic/Latino, 1 international. Average age 26. In 2010, 6 master's awarded. *Degree requirements:* For master's, comprehensive exam, student teaching. *Entrance requirements:* Additional exam requirements/recommendations for international students: Required—TOEFL (minimum score 450 paper-based; 133 computer-based). *Application deadline:* For fall admission, 4/1 priority date for domestic and international students. Applications are processed on a rolling basis. Application fee: $35. Electronic applications accepted. *Expenses:* Tuition: Full-time $29,520; part-time $3280 per quarter. Tuition and fees vary according to campus/location. *Financial support:* Fellowships, career-related internships or fieldwork, Federal Work-Study, and scholarships/grants available. Financial award application deadline: 4/1; financial award applicants required to submit FAFSA. *Unit head:* Audra Price, Chair, 877-722-3285, E-mail: aprice@scad.edu. *Application contact:* Elizabeth Mathis, Director of Graduate Recruitment, 912-525-5965, Fax: 912-525-5985, E-mail: emathis@scad.edu.

Smith College, Graduate and Special Programs, Department of Theatre, Northampton, MA 01063. Offers playwriting (MFA). Part-time programs available. *Faculty:* 8 full-time (6 women). *Students:* 4 full-time (1 woman); includes 1 Asian, non-Hispanic/Latino. Average age 27. 11 applicants, 36% accepted, 3 enrolled. *Degree requirements:* For master's, one foreign language, thesis. *Entrance requirements:* Additional exam requirements/recommendations for international students: Required—TOEFL (minimum score 590 paper-based; 243 computer-based; 97 iBT). *Application deadline:* For fall admission, 4/1 for domestic students, 1/15 for international students. Application fee: $60. *Expenses:* Tuition: Full-time $14,520; part-time $1210 per credit. *Financial support:* In 2010–11, 4 students received support. Institutionally sponsored loans and scholarships/grants available. Support available to part-time students. Financial award application deadline: 1/15; financial award applicants required to submit CSS PROFILE or FAFSA. *Unit head:* Leonard Berkman, Graduate Adviser, 413-585-3206, E-mail: lberkman@smith.edu. *Application contact:* Leonard Berkman, Graduate Adviser, 413-585-3206, E-mail: lberkman@smith.edu.

Southern Illinois University Carbondale, Graduate School, College of Liberal Arts, Theater Department, Carbondale, IL 62901-4701. Offers speech/theater (PhD); theater (MFA). *Accreditation:* NAST (one or more programs are accredited). Part-time programs available. *Degree requirements:* For master's, thesis; for doctorate, thesis/dissertation. *Entrance requirements:* For master's, minimum GPA of 2.7; for doctorate, minimum GPA of 3.25. Additional exam requirements/recommendations for international students: Required—TOEFL. *Faculty research:* Scenography, theater performance, theater history, dramatic criticism, theater technology, playwriting.

Southern Methodist University, Meadows School of the Arts, Division of Theatre, Dallas, TX 75275. Offers acting (MFA); design (MFA). *Accreditation:* NAST. *Faculty:* 18 full-time (7 women), 5 part-time/adjunct (3 women). *Students:* 19 full-time (10 women); includes 2 Black or African American, non-Hispanic/Latino; 1 Hispanic/Latino; 1 Native Hawaiian or other Pacific Islander, non-Hispanic/Latino. Average age 26. 24 applicants, 54% accepted, 13 enrolled. In 2010, 8 master's awarded. *Entrance requirements:* For master's, audition or interview. Additional exam requirements/recommendations for international students: Required—TOEFL (minimum score 550 paper-based; 213 computer-based; 80 iBT). *Application deadline:* For fall admission, 2/15 priority date for domestic and international students. Applications are processed on a rolling basis. Application fee: $75. Electronic applications accepted. *Financial support:* In 2010–11, 20 teaching assistantships (averaging $6,600 per year) were awarded; scholarships/grants and unspecified assistantships also available. Financial award application deadline: 3/1; financial award applicants required to submit FAFSA. *Faculty research:* European lighting techniques. *Unit head:* Cecil O'Neal, Chair, 214-768-2558, Fax: 214-768-1136, E-mail: coneal@smu.edu. *Application contact:* Joe S. Hoselton, Graduate Admissions and Records Coordinator, 214-768-3765, Fax: 214-768-3272, E-mail: hoselton@smu.edu.

Stanford University, School of Humanities and Sciences, Department of Drama, Stanford, CA 94305-9991. Offers PhD. *Degree requirements:* For doctorate, one foreign language, thesis/dissertation, qualifying exams. *Entrance requirements:* For doctorate, GRE General Test, summary of production experience. Additional exam requirements/recommendations for international students: Required—TOEFL. Electronic applications accepted. *Expenses:* Tuition: Full-time $38,700; part-time $860 per unit. One-time fee: $200 full-time.

State University of New York at Binghamton, Graduate School, School of Arts and Sciences, Department of Theater, Binghamton, NY 13902-6000. Offers MA. *Faculty:* 8 full-time (4

Theater

State University of New York at Binghamton (continued)
women), 9 part-time/adjunct (4 women). *Students:* 8 full-time (6 women), 2 part-time (1 woman), 1 international. Average age 32. 7 applicants, 71% accepted, 3 enrolled. In 2010, 5 master's awarded. *Degree requirements:* For master's, thesis. *Entrance requirements:* For master's, GRE General Test, GRE Subject Test. Additional exam requirements/recommendations for international students: Required—TOEFL (minimum score 550 paper-based; 213 computer-based; 80 iBT). *Application deadline:* For fall admission, 8/1 priority date for domestic and international students; for spring admission, 12/15 priority date for domestic and international students. Applications are processed on a rolling basis. Application fee: $60. Electronic applications accepted. *Financial support:* In 2010–11, 3 students received support. Career-related internships or fieldwork, Federal Work-Study, institutionally sponsored loans, scholarships/grants, health care benefits, and unspecified assistantships available. Financial award application deadline: 2/15; financial award applicants required to submit FAFSA. *Unit head:* Dr. John E. Vestal, Chairperson, 607-777-2360, E-mail: jvestal@binghamton.edu. *Application contact:* Catherine Smith, Recruiting and Admissions Coordinator, 607-777-2151, Fax: 607-777-2501, E-mail: cmsmith@binghamton.edu.

Stony Brook University, State University of New York, Graduate School, College of Arts and Sciences, Department of Theatre Arts, Program in Dramaturgy, Stony Brook, NY 11794. Offers MFA. *Students:* 14 full-time (12 women), 1 part-time (0 women); includes 1 American Indian or Alaska Native, non-Hispanic/Latino; 1 Asian, non-Hispanic/Latino; 2 Hispanic/Latino; 1 Two or more races, non-Hispanic/Latino. Average age 29. 10 applicants, 90% accepted, 5 enrolled. In 2010, 4 master's awarded. *Degree requirements:* For master's, one foreign language, thesis. *Entrance requirements:* For master's, GRE General Test. Additional exam requirements/recommendations for international students: Required—TOEFL. *Application deadline:* For fall admission, 1/15 for domestic students. Application fee: $100. *Expenses:* Tuition, state resident: full-time $8370; part-time $349 per credit. Tuition, nonresident: full-time $13,780; part-time $574 per credit. Required fees: $994. *Unit head:* Prof. Nick Mangano, Chair, 631-632-7300, Fax: 631-632-7258. *Application contact:* Michael Zelenak, Director of Graduate Studies, 631-632-7280.

Stony Brook University, State University of New York, Graduate School, College of Arts and Sciences, Department of Theatre Arts, Program in Theatre Arts, Stony Brook, NY 11794. Offers MA. Evening/weekend programs available. *Students:* 3 full-time (2 women). Average age 35. 4 applicants, 100% accepted, 2 enrolled. In 2010, 1 master's awarded. *Degree requirements:* For master's, one foreign language, thesis. *Entrance requirements:* For master's, GRE General Test. Additional exam requirements/recommendations for international students: Required—TOEFL. *Application deadline:* For fall admission, 1/15 for domestic students. Application fee: $100. *Expenses:* Tuition, state resident: full-time $8370; part-time $349 per credit. Tuition, nonresident: full-time $13,780; part-time $574 per credit. Required fees: $994. *Unit head:* Prof. Nick Mangano, Chair, 631-632-7300, Fax: 631-632-7258. *Application contact:* Michael Zelenak, Director of Graduate Studies, 631-632-7280.

Temple University, School of Communications and Theater, Department of Theater, Philadelphia, PA 19122-6096. Offers acting (MFA); design (MFA); directing (MFA). *Accreditation:* NAST. Part-time programs available. *Faculty:* 12 full-time (7 women). *Students:* 27 full-time (11 women), 4 part-time (2 women); includes 1 Black or African American, non-Hispanic/Latino; 1 Hispanic/Latino, 2 international. 25 applicants, 24% accepted, 6 enrolled. In 2010, 5 master's awarded. *Degree requirements:* For master's, thesis (for some programs). *Entrance requirements:* For master's, minimum GPA of 3.0; audition/interview, portfolio, or samples of written work. Additional exam requirements/recommendations for international students: Required—TOEFL (minimum score 550 paper-based; 213 computer-based; 79 iBT). *Application deadline:* For fall admission, 12/15 for international students. Application fee: $50. Electronic applications accepted. *Financial support:* Federal Work-Study and institutionally sponsored loans available. Financial award application deadline: 1/15; financial award applicants required to submit FAFSA. *Unit head:* Marie Anne Chiment, Chair, 215-204-8414, Fax: 215-204-8566, E-mail: theater@temple.edu. *Application contact:* Marie Anne Chiment, Chair, 215-204-8414, Fax: 215-204-8566, E-mail: theater@temple.edu.

Texas A&M University–Commerce, Graduate School, College of Arts and Sciences, Department of Communication and Theatre, Commerce, TX 75429-3011. Offers theatre (MA, MS). Part-time programs available. *Degree requirements:* For master's, comprehensive exam, thesis (for some programs). *Entrance requirements:* For master's, GRE General Test. Electronic applications accepted. *Faculty research:* Theater history.

Texas State University–San Marcos, Graduate School, College of Fine Arts and Communication, Department of Theatre and Dance, Program in Theatre Arts, San Marcos, TX 78666. Offers MA. Part-time and evening/weekend programs available. *Faculty:* 7 full-time (4 women). *Students:* 17 full-time (9 women), 2 part-time (both women); includes 1 Black or African American, non-Hispanic/Latino; 3 Hispanic/Latino. Average age 31. 20 applicants, 55% accepted, 8 enrolled. In 2010, 7 master's awarded. *Degree requirements:* For master's, comprehensive exam, thesis (for some programs). *Entrance requirements:* For master's, GRE General Test, minimum GPA of 2.75 in last 60 hours of course work. Additional exam requirements/recommendations for international students: Required—TOEFL (minimum score 550 paper-based; 213 computer-based; 78 iBT). *Application deadline:* For fall admission, 3/15 priority date for domestic students, 3/15 for international students. Applications are processed on a rolling basis. Application fee: $40 ($90 for international students). Electronic applications accepted. *Expenses:* Tuition, state resident: full-time $6024; part-time $251 per credit hour. Tuition, nonresident: full-time $13,536; part-time $564 per credit hour. Required fees: $1776; $50 per credit hour. $306 per semester. *Financial support:* In 2010–11, 13 students received support, including 14 teaching assistantships (averaging $1,900 per year); Federal Work-Study, institutionally sponsored loans, scholarships/grants, and unspecified assistantships also available. Support available to part-time students. Financial award application deadline: 4/1; financial award applicants required to submit FAFSA. *Faculty research:* Theatre history (especially nineteenth century American theatre), stage productions, playwriting. *Unit head:* Dr. Debra Charlton, Graduate Adviser, 512-245-1450, Fax: 512-245-8440, E-mail: dc21@txstate.edu. *Application contact:* Dr. J. Michael Willoughby, Dean of Graduate School, 512-245-2581, Fax: 512-245-8365, E-mail: gradcollege@txstate.edu.

Texas Tech University, Graduate School, College of Visual and Performing Arts, Department of Theatre and Dance, Lubbock, TX 79409. Offers theatre arts (MA, MFA). *Accreditation:* NAST. Part-time programs available. *Faculty:* 10 full-time (5 women). *Students:* 43 full-time (22 women), 22 part-time (12 women); includes 3 Black or African American, non-Hispanic/Latino; 1 Asian, non-Hispanic/Latino; 3 Hispanic/Latino; 2 Two or more races, non-Hispanic/Latino, 6 international. Average age 33. 54 applicants, 59% accepted, 17 enrolled. In 2010, 4 master's awarded. *Degree requirements:* For master's, variable foreign language requirement, thesis. *Entrance requirements:* For master's, GRE General Test. Additional exam requirements/recommendations for international students: Required—TOEFL (minimum score 550 paper-based; 213 computer-based; 79 iBT). *Application deadline:* For fall admission, 6/1 priority date for domestic students, 1/15 priority date for international students; for spring admission, 9/1 priority date for domestic students, 6/15 priority date for international students. Applications are processed on a rolling basis. Application fee: $50 ($75 for international students). Electronic applications accepted. *Expenses:* Tuition, state resident: full-time $5495.76; part-time $228.99 per credit hour. Tuition, nonresident: full-time $12,936; part-time $538.99 per credit hour. Required fees: $2674; $36 per credit hour. $905 per semester. *Financial support:* In 2010–11, 40 students received support, including 2 research assistantships with partial tuition reimbursements available (averaging $8,538 per year), 17 teaching assistantships with partial tuition reimbursements available (averaging $5,335 per year). Financial award application deadline: 4/15; financial award applicants required to submit FAFSA. *Faculty research:* New student plays program, theatre planning, dramaturgy; feminist theatre; arts administration; dance aesthetics. *Unit head:* Prof. Frederick B. Christoffel, Chair, 806-742-3601 Ext. 228, Fax: 806-742-1338, E-mail: fred.christoffel@ttu.edu. *Application contact:* Dr. James Bush, Graduate Adviser, 806-742-3601 Ext. 230, Fax: 806-742-1338, E-mail: james.bush@ttu.edu.

Texas Tech University, Graduate School, College of Visual and Performing Arts, Fine Arts Doctoral Program, Lubbock, TX 79409. Offers arts (PhD). *Accreditation:* NAST. Part-time programs available. *Students:* 46 full-time (22 women), 32 part-time (15 women); includes 2 Black or African American, non-Hispanic/Latino; 1 American Indian or Alaska Native, non-Hispanic/Latino; 1 Asian, non-Hispanic/Latino; 5 Hispanic/Latino, 10 international. Average age 35. 36 applicants, 44% accepted, 9 enrolled. In 2010, 14 doctorates awarded. *Degree requirements:* For doctorate, comprehensive exam, thesis/dissertation. *Entrance requirements:* For doctorate, GRE General Test. Additional exam requirements/recommendations for international students: Required—TOEFL (minimum score 550 paper-based; 213 computer-based; 79 iBT). *Application deadline:* For fall admission, 6/1 priority date for domestic students, 1/15 priority date for international students; for spring admission, 9/1 priority date for domestic students, 6/15 priority date for international students. Applications are processed on a rolling basis. Application fee: $50 ($75 for international students). Electronic applications accepted. *Expenses:* Tuition, state resident: full-time $5495.76; part-time $228.99 per credit hour. Tuition, nonresident: full-time $12,936; part-time $538.99 per credit hour. Required fees: $2674; $36 per credit hour. $905 per semester. *Financial support:* Research assistantships with partial tuition reimbursements, teaching assistantships with partial tuition reimbursements available. Financial award application deadline: 4/15; financial award applicants required to submit FAFSA. *Faculty research:* Art criticism and theory, music, theatre arts; arts education; history of arts. *Unit head:* Dr. Brian D. Steele, Director, 806-742-0700, Fax: 806-742-0695, E-mail: brian.steele@ttu.edu. *Application contact:* Dr. Brian D. Steele, Director, 806-742-0700, Fax: 806-742-0695, E-mail: brian.steele@ttu.edu.

Texas Woman's University, Graduate School, College of Arts and Sciences, School of the Arts, Department of Music and Drama, Denton, TX 76201. Offers drama (MA); music (MA). *Accreditation:* NASM. Part-time programs available. *Faculty:* 14 full-time (8 women). *Students:* 43 full-time (31 women), 42 part-time (29 women); includes 5 Black or African American, non-Hispanic/Latino; 2 Asian, non-Hispanic/Latino; 6 Hispanic/Latino, 13 international. Average age 32. 38 applicants, 89% accepted, 21 enrolled. In 2010, 12 master's awarded. *Degree requirements:* For master's, thesis optional, project recital. *Entrance requirements:* For master's, music history/theory placement exam (music only). Additional exam requirements/recommendations for international students: Required—TOEFL (minimum score 550 paper-based; 213 computer-based; 79 iBT). *Application deadline:* For fall admission, 7/1 priority date for domestic students, 3/1 for international students; for spring admission, 12/1 priority date for domestic students, 7/1 for international students. Applications are processed on a rolling basis. Application fee: $50 ($75 for international students). Electronic applications accepted. *Expenses:* Tuition, state resident: full-time $3834; part-time $213 per credit hour. Tuition, nonresident: full-time $9468; part-time $526 per credit hour. Required fees: $1247; $220 per credit hour. *Financial support:* In 2010–11, 40 students received support, including 9 research assistantships (averaging $9,684 per year); career-related internships or fieldwork, Federal Work-Study, institutionally sponsored loans, scholarships/grants, traineeships, health care benefits, tuition waivers (partial), and unspecified assistantships also available. Support available to part-time students. Financial award application deadline: 3/1; financial award applicants required to submit FAFSA. *Faculty research:* Musical development in early childhood, little known or neglected compositions for flute (especially by women composers), relationship of visual art to piano music, pedagogical development of the singing voice, guided imagery and music. *Unit head:* Dr. James Chenevert, Chair, 940-898-2500, Fax: 940-898-2494, E-mail: music@twu.edu. *Application contact:* Dr. Samuel Wheeler, Assistant Director of Admissions, 940-898-3188, Fax: 940-898-3081, E-mail: wheelersr@twu.edu.

Towson University, Program in Theatre, Towson, MD 21252-0001. Offers MFA. *Accreditation:* NAST. *Students:* 12 full-time (9 women), 5 part-time (4 women); includes 1 minority (Black or African American, non-Hispanic/Latino), 2 international. Average age 34. In 2010, 4 master's awarded. *Degree requirements:* For master's, thesis. *Entrance requirements:* For master's, audition or portfolio, interview, minimum GPA of 3.0. *Application deadline:* For fall admission, 3/1 for domestic students. Application fee: $50. Electronic applications accepted. *Expenses:* Tuition, state resident: part-time $324 per credit. Tuition, nonresident: part-time $681 per credit. Required fees: $95 per term. *Financial support:* In 2010–11, 1 fellowship with tuition reimbursement (averaging $10,000 per year), 1 teaching assistantship with tuition reimbursement (averaging $6,000 per year) were awarded; unspecified assistantships also available. Financial award application deadline: 4/1; financial award applicants required to submit FAFSA. *Faculty research:* Playwriting, directing, entrepreneurship in the arts, movement theatre, design, drama. *Unit head:* Stephen Nunns, Graduate Program Director, 410-704-4519, E-mail: snunns@towson.edu. *Application contact:* 410-704-2501, Fax: 410-704-4675, E-mail: grads@towson.edu.

Tufts University, Graduate School of Arts and Sciences, Department of Drama and Dance, Medford, MA 02155. Offers drama (MA); dramatic literature and criticism (PhD); theater history (PhD). Terminal master's awarded for partial completion of doctoral program. *Degree requirements:* For master's, one foreign language, thesis; for doctorate, 2 foreign languages, thesis/dissertation, oral exam, written general exam. *Entrance requirements:* For master's and doctorate, GRE General Test, writing sample. Additional exam requirements/recommendations for international students: Required—TOEFL (minimum score 600 paper-based; 250 computer-based; 80 iBT). Electronic applications accepted. *Expenses:* Tuition: Full-time $39,624; part-time $3962 per course. Required fees: $40 per year. Full-time tuition and fees vary according to degree level, program and student level. Part-time tuition and fees vary according to course load.

Tulane University, School of Liberal Arts, Department of Theatre and Dance, New Orleans, LA 70118-5669. Offers design and technical production (MFA). *Entrance requirements:* For master's, GRE General Test, minimum B average in undergraduate course work. Additional exam requirements/recommendations for international students: Required—TOEFL. Electronic applications accepted. *Faculty research:* Scene design, stage management, costume design, technical direction, lighting design.

Université de Sherbrooke, Faculty of Letters and Human Sciences, Department of Letters and Communications, Sherbrooke, QC J1K 2R1, Canada. Offers comparative Canadian literature (MA, PhD); French literature (MA, PhD); linguistics (MA); theatre (MA). *Degree requirements:* For master's, thesis or alternative; for doctorate, thesis/dissertation. *Entrance requirements:* For master's, minimum GPA of 2.8; for doctorate, minimum GPA of 3.0.

Université Laval, Faculty of Letters, Department of Literature, Programs in Literature and Arts of the Screen and Stage, Québec, QC G1K 7P4, Canada. Offers MA, PhD. Part-time programs available. Terminal master's awarded for partial completion of doctoral program. *Degree requirements:* For master's, thesis; for doctorate, comprehensive exam, thesis/dissertation. *Entrance requirements:* For master's and doctorate, linguistics exams, knowledge of French, knowledge of a second language. Electronic applications accepted.

University at Albany, State University of New York, College of Arts and Sciences, Department of Theatre, Albany, NY 12222-0001. Offers MA. *Entrance requirements:* Additional exam requirements/recommendations for international students: Required—TOEFL (minimum score 550 paper-based; 213 computer-based). Electronic applications accepted.

The University of Akron, Graduate School, College of Creative and Professional Arts, School of Dance, Theatre, and Arts Administration, Program in Theatre Arts, Akron, OH 44325. Offers MA. *Students:* 25 full-time (21 women), 10 part-time (6 women); includes 1 Black or African American, non-Hispanic/Latino; 1 Hispanic/Latino, 5 international. Average age 31. 28 applicants, 71% accepted, 10 enrolled. In 2010, 5 master's awarded. *Degree requirements:* For master's, thesis optional. *Entrance requirements:* For master's, minimum GPA of 2.75, 300-word statement of intent summarizing student background and outlining career goals. Additional exam requirements/recommendations for international students: Required—TOEFL (minimum score 550 paper-based; 213 computer-based; 79 iBT). *Application deadline:* For fall admission, 3/15 priority date for domestic and international students. Application fee: $30 ($40 for international students). Electronic applications accepted. *Expenses:* Tuition, state resident: full-time $6800; part-time $378 per credit hour. Tuition, nonresident: full-time $11,644; part-time $647 per credit hour. Required fees: $1265. One-time fee: $30 full-time. *Application contact:* James Slowiak, Coordinator, 330-972-5909, E-mail: slowiak@uakron.edu.

The University of Alabama, Graduate School, College of Arts and Sciences, Department of Theatre and Dance, Tuscaloosa, AL 35487. Offers acting (MFA); costume design (MFA); directing (MFA); scene design/technical production (MFA); stage management (MFA); theatre (MFA); theatre management/administration (MFA). *Accreditation:* NAST. *Faculty:* 10 full-time (2 women). *Students:* 37 full-time (19 women), 2 part-time (1 woman); includes 4 minority (2 Black or African American, non-Hispanic/Latino; 1 Asian, non-Hispanic/Latino; 1 Hispanic/Latino), 1 international. Average age 29. 35 applicants, 63% accepted, 15 enrolled. In 2010, 2 master's awarded. *Degree requirements:* For master's, thesis project. *Entrance requirements:* For master's, auditions and/or portfolio review. *Application deadline:* For fall admission, 4/1 for domestic students, 3/1 for international students. Applications are processed on a rolling basis. Application fee: $50 ($60 for international students). Electronic applications accepted. *Expenses:* Tuition, state resident: full-time $7900. Tuition, nonresident: full-time $20,500. *Financial support:* In 2010–11, 20 research assistantships (averaging $11,508 per year), 16 teaching assistantships (averaging $11,508 per year) were awarded; career-related internships or fieldwork, health care benefits, and unspecified assistantships also available. *Faculty research:* Acting and theatre history, directing, design practice and production, technical direction, theatre management. *Unit head:* Prof. William Teague, Chairman and Professor, 205-348-5283, Fax: 205-348-9048, E-mail: wteague@as.ua.edu. *Application contact:* Pamela McCray, Recruiting Contact, 205-348-5283, Fax: 205-348-9048, E-mail: pmccray@as.ua.edu.

University of Alberta, Faculty of Graduate Studies and Research, Department of Drama, Edmonton, AB T6G 2E1, Canada. Offers design (MFA); directing (MFA); drama (MA). *Degree requirements:* For master's, one foreign language, production thesis. *Faculty research:* Dramaturgy, history, theory and criticism, design.

The University of Arizona, College of Fine Arts, School of Theatre Arts, Tucson, AZ 85721. Offers MA, MFA. *Accreditation:* NAST. *Faculty:* 14. *Students:* 11 full-time (8 women), 2 part-time (0 women); includes 4 minority (2 Hispanic/Latino; 2 Two or more races, non-Hispanic/Latino). Average age 28. 12 applicants, 33% accepted, 2 enrolled. In 2010, 6 master's awarded. *Degree requirements:* For master's, comprehensive exam (for some programs), thesis (for some programs), production monograph. *Entrance requirements:* For master's, 3 letters of recommendation, portfolio. Additional exam requirements/recommendations for international students: Required—TOEFL (minimum score 550 paper-based; 213 computer-based; 79 iBT). *Application deadline:* For fall admission, 2/15 for domestic students, 12/1 for international students. Applications are processed on a rolling basis. Application fee: $75. Electronic applications accepted. *Expenses:* Tuition, state resident: full-time $7692. *Financial support:* In 2010–11, 11 teaching assistantships with full tuition reimbursements (averaging $16,581 per year) were awarded; career-related internships or fieldwork, Federal Work-Study, institutionally sponsored loans, scholarships/grants, health care benefits, tuition waivers (full), and unspecified assistantships also available. Financial award application deadline: 3/1; financial award applicants required to submit FAFSA. *Faculty research:* Modern and contemporary theater, cultural studies, musical theater, women and theater. *Unit head:* Jerry Dickey, Interim Director, 520-621-8740, E-mail: jdickey@email.arizona.edu. *Application contact:* Justine M. Collins, Assistant to Director of Administration, 520-621-7007, Fax: 520-621-2412, E-mail: jcollins@email.arizona.edu.

University of Arkansas, Graduate School, J. William Fulbright College of Arts and Sciences, Department of Drama, Fayetteville, AR 72701-1201. Offers MA, MFA. *Students:* 25 full-time (13 women), 1 part-time (0 women); includes 5 minority (2 Black or African American, non-Hispanic/Latino; 3 Hispanic/Latino), 2 international. 9 applicants, 11% accepted. In 2010, 6 master's awarded. *Degree requirements:* For master's, thesis optional. *Application deadline:* For fall admission, 4/1 for international students; for spring admission, 10/1 for international students. Applications are processed on a rolling basis. Application fee: $40 ($50 for international students). Electronic applications accepted. *Financial support:* In 2010–11, 24 fellowships with tuition reimbursements, 6 research assistantships, 16 teaching assistantships were awarded; career-related internships or fieldwork and Federal Work-Study also available. Support available to part-time students. Financial award application deadline: 4/1; financial award applicants required to submit FAFSA. *Unit head:* Dr. Andrew Gibbs, Department Chairperson, 479-575-2953, Fax: 479-575-7602, E-mail: dagibbs@uark.edu. *Application contact:* Dr. Andrew Gibbs, Department Chairperson, 479-575-2953, Fax: 479-575-7602, E-mail: dagibbs@uark.edu.

The University of British Columbia, Faculty of Arts, Creative Writing Program, Vancouver, BC V6T 1Z1, Canada. Offers creative writing (MFA); creative writing and film (MFA); creative writing and theatre (MFA). Part-time programs available. Postbaccalaureate distance learning degree programs offered (minimal on-campus study). *Degree requirements:* For master's, thesis. *Entrance requirements:* For master's, sample of written work. Additional exam requirements/recommendations for international students: Required—TOEFL (minimum score 550 paper-based; 213 computer-based). Electronic applications accepted. *Expenses:* Contact institution. *Faculty research:* Writing of fiction; poetry, creative nonfiction, plays for stage, screen, television, radio, writing for children and translation, song lyrics and libretto, new media and graphic novel.

The University of British Columbia, Faculty of Arts and Faculty of Graduate Studies, Department of Theatre and Film, Theatre Program, Vancouver, BC V6T 1Z2, Canada. Offers theatre (MA, PhD); theatre design (MFA); theatre directing (MFA). *Degree requirements:* For master's, variable foreign language requirement, comprehensive exam, thesis; for doctorate, 2 foreign languages, comprehensive exam, thesis/dissertation. *Entrance requirements:* For master's, portfolio (MFA); for doctorate, MA or equivalent. Additional exam requirements/recommendations for international students: Required—TOEFL score of 550 paper-based, 213 computer-based required for MFA; score of 600 paper-based, 250 computer-based required for MA and PhD programs. Tuition charges are reported in Canadian dollars. *Expenses:* Tuition, area resident: Full-time $4179 Canadian dollars. International tuition: $7344 Canadian dollars full-time. *Faculty research:* Devising theatre; Canadian theatre; multicultural and theatre arts; stage lighting and costume design.

University of Calgary, Faculty of Graduate Studies, Faculty of Fine Arts, Department of Drama, Calgary, AB T2N 1N4, Canada. Offers design and technical theatre (MFA); directing (MFA); playwriting (MFA); theatre studies (MFA). *Degree requirements:* For master's, thesis. *Entrance requirements:* For master's, bachelor's degree in drama, minimum GPA of 3.0, portfolio (design and playwriting). Additional exam requirements/recommendations for international students: Required—TOEFL. *Faculty research:* Popular theatre, collective creation, technical design, dramaturgy, directing styles.

University of California, Berkeley, Graduate Division, College of Letters and Science, Group in Performance Studies, Berkeley, CA 94720-1500. Offers PhD. *Degree requirements:* For doctorate, one foreign language, thesis/dissertation, qualifying exam. *Entrance requirements:* For doctorate, GRE General Test, sample of critical writing, 3 letters of recommendation. Additional exam requirements/recommendations for international students: Required—TOEFL. Electronic applications accepted. *Faculty research:* Postcolonial performance; gender, sexuality, and performance; political performance; dramatic literature and theory; race, ethnicity, performance.

University of California, Davis, Graduate Studies, Program in Dramatic Art, Davis, CA 95616. Offers acting (MFA); dramatic art (PhD). *Entrance requirements:* For master's, minimum GPA of 3.0, portfolio. Additional exam requirements/recommendations for international students: Required—TOEFL (minimum score 550 paper-based; 213 computer-based). Electronic applications accepted. *Faculty research:* Twentieth century performance and culture.

University of California, Davis, Graduate Studies, Program in Performance Studies, Davis, CA 95616. Offers dramatic art (PhD). *Degree requirements:* For doctorate, 2 foreign languages, thesis/dissertation. *Entrance requirements:* For doctorate, GRE, minimum GPA of 3.25. Additional exam requirements/recommendations for international students: Required—TOEFL (minimum score 550 paper-based; 213 computer-based). Electronic applications accepted.

University of California, Irvine, Claire Trevor School of the Arts, Department of Drama, Irvine, CA 92697. Offers acting (MFA); design and stage management (MFA); directing (MFA); drama (MFA); drama and theatre (PhD). *Students:* 74 full-time (44 women), 1 part-time (0 women); includes 17 minority (5 Black or African American, non-Hispanic/Latino; 2 Asian, non-Hispanic/Latino; 5 Hispanic/Latino; 5 Two or more races, non-Hispanic/Latino), 2 international. Average age 26. 292 applicants, 9% accepted, 25 enrolled. In 2010, 18 master's, 1 doctorate awarded. *Degree requirements:* For master's, comprehensive exam, thesis; for doctorate, one foreign language, thesis/dissertation. *Entrance requirements:* For master's, audition, interview, or portfolio; minimum GPA of 3.0; for doctorate, GRE, minimum GPA of 3.5, critical writing samples. *Application deadline:* For fall admission, 1/15 priority date for domestic students, 1/15 for international students. Applications are processed on a rolling basis. Application fee: $80 ($100 for international students). Electronic applications accepted. *Financial support:* Fellowships, teaching assistantships, institutionally sponsored loans, traineeships, health care benefits, and unspecified assistantships available. Financial award application deadline: 3/1; financial award applicants required to submit FAFSA. *Faculty research:* Costume, scenery, and lighting design; production; theatre history, literature, and criticism. *Unit head:* Prof. Eli Simon, Chair, 949-824-7062, E-mail: esimon@uci.edu. *Application contact:* Coleen Jayne Williamson, Office Manager, 949-824-6332, Fax: 949-824-3475, E-mail: nelsonc@uci.edu.

University of California, Los Angeles, Graduate Division, School of Theater, Film and Television, Department of Theater, Los Angeles, CA 90095. Offers theater (MA, MFA); theater and performance studies (PhD). *Accreditation:* NAST. *Faculty:* 18 full-time (7 women). *Students:* 82 full-time (41 women); includes 19 minority (8 Black or African American, non-Hispanic/Latino; 2 American Indian or Alaska Native, non-Hispanic/Latino; 3 Asian, non-Hispanic/Latino; 5 Hispanic/Latino; 1 Two or more races, non-Hispanic/Latino), 8 international. Average age 28. 291 applicants, 13% accepted, 26 enrolled. In 2010, 22 master's, 2 doctorates awarded. *Degree requirements:* For master's, comprehensive exam or thesis; for doctorate, one foreign language, thesis/dissertation, oral and written exam. *Entrance requirements:* For master's, minimum GPA of 3.0, interview, portfolio, resume, script, audition; for doctorate, GRE General Test, minimum undergraduate GPA of 3.0. Application fee: $70 ($90 for international students). Electronic applications accepted. *Financial support:* In 2010–11, 65 fellowships with full and partial tuition reimbursements, 4 research assistantships with full and partial tuition reimbursements, 50 teaching assistantships with full and partial tuition reimbursements were awarded; career-related internships or fieldwork, Federal Work-Study, institutionally sponsored loans, scholarships/grants, traineeships, health care benefits, tuition waivers (full and partial), and unspecified assistantships also available. Financial award application deadline: 3/1; financial award applicants required to submit FAFSA. *Unit head:* Michael Hackett, Chair, 310-825-7008, E-mail: mhackett@tft.ucla.edu. *Application contact:* Departmental Office, 310-825-8787, E-mail: info@tft.ucla.edu.

University of California, San Diego, Office of Graduate Studies, Department of Theatre and Dance, La Jolla, CA 92093. Offers acting (MFA); design (MFA); directing (MFA); drama and theatre (PhD); playwriting (MFA); stage management (MFA); theatre (PhD). *Degree requirements:* For master's, thesis. *Entrance requirements:* For master's, GRE General Test (directing, playwriting). Electronic applications accepted.

University of California, Santa Barbara, Graduate Division, College of Letters and Sciences, Division of Humanities and Fine Arts, Department of Theatre and Dance, Santa Barbara, CA 93106-7060. Offers theater studies (MA, PhD), including european medieval studies (PhD), feminist studies (PhD), theatre studies (PhD); MA/PhD. *Faculty:* 8 full-time (4 women). *Students:* 14 full-time (9 women); includes 2 Black or African American, non-Hispanic/Latino; 1 Hispanic/Latino. Average age 31. 22 applicants, 41% accepted, 3 enrolled. In 2010, 3 master's, 5 doctorates awarded. Terminal master's awarded for partial completion of doctoral program. *Degree requirements:* For master's, comprehensive exam, thesis; for doctorate, one foreign language, comprehensive exam, thesis/dissertation. *Entrance requirements:* For master's and doctorate, GRE. Additional exam requirements/recommendations for international students: Required—TOEFL (minimum score 550 paper-based; 80 iBT), IELTS (minimum score 7). *Application deadline:* For fall admission, 1/5 priority date for domestic and international students. Application fee: $70 ($90 for international students). Electronic applications accepted. *Financial support:* In 2010–11, 14 students received support, including 11 fellowships with full tuition reimbursements available (averaging $7,764 per year), 14 teaching assistantships with full and partial tuition reimbursements available (averaging $13,666 per year). Financial award applicants required to submit FAFSA. *Faculty research:* English and American theater and Ancient Greek; Spanish, Latin-American and Caribbean performance; Renaissance and Baroque drama, and intercultural theory; East Asian performance, gender and nationalism; Korean cultural studies, Russian literature, and Slavic folklore; history of German theater, Shakespeare, and European opera; postcolonialism, performance-based ethnography, globalism and national identity formation in Africa. *Unit head:* Prof. Simon Williams, Chairperson, 805-893-5515, Fax: 805-893-7029, E-mail: williams@theaterdance.ucsb.edu. *Application contact:* Mary Tench, Graduate Program Assistant, 805-893-3147, Fax: 805-893-7029, E-mail: mtench@theaterdance.ucsb.edu.

University of California, Santa Cruz, Division of Graduate Studies, Division of the Arts, Department of Theater Arts, Santa Cruz, CA 95064. Offers Certificate. *Students:* 9 full-time (7 women); includes 4 minority (2 Asian, non-Hispanic/Latino; 1 Hispanic/Latino; 1 Two or more races, non-Hispanic/Latino). Average age 24. 22 applicants, 55% accepted, 9 enrolled. In 2010, 8 Certificates awarded. *Entrance requirements:* Additional exam requirements/recommendations for international students: Required—TOEFL (minimum score 550 paper-based; 220 computer-based; 83 iBT); Recommended—IELTS (minimum score 8). *Application deadline:* For fall admission, 3/1 for domestic and international students. Application fee: $70 ($90 for international students). Electronic applications accepted. *Financial support:* Fellowships, research assistantships, teaching assistantships, institutionally sponsored loans and tuition waivers available. Financial award applicants required to submit FAFSA. *Unit head:* Angela Beck, Graduate Program Coordinator, 831-459-2974, E-mail: ahbeck@ucsc.edu. *Application contact:* Angela Beck, Graduate Program Coordinator, 831-459-2974, E-mail: ahbeck@ucsc.edu.

University of Central Florida, College of Arts and Humanities, Department of Theatre, Orlando, FL 32816. Offers MA, MFA. *Faculty:* 22 full-time (10 women), 6 part-time/adjunct (3 women). *Students:* 32 full-time (22 women), 20 part-time (13 women); includes 2 Black or African American, non-Hispanic/Latino, 1 international. Average age 29. 20 applicants, 30% accepted, 3 enrolled. In 2010, 15 master's awarded. Application fee: $30. Electronic applications accepted. *Expenses:* Tuition, state resident: part-time $256.56 per credit hour. Tuition, nonresident: part-time $1011.52 per credit hour. Part-time tuition and fees vary according to program. *Financial support:* In 2010–11, 21 students received support, including 4 fellowships (averaging $6,200 per year), 7 research assistantships (averaging $7,700 per year), 12 teaching assistantships (averaging $6,800 per year). *Unit head:* Dr. Christopher Niess, Interim Chair, 407-823-0876, Fax: 407-823-6446, E-mail: cneiss@mail.ucf.edu. *Application contact:* Dr. Christopher Niess, Interim Chair, 407-823-0876, Fax: 407-823-6446, E-mail: cneiss@mail.ucf.edu.

University of Central Missouri, The Graduate School, College of Arts, Humanities and Social Sciences, Warrensburg, MO 64093. Offers English (MA); history (MA); mass communication (MA); music (MA); psychology (MS); speech communication (MA); teaching English as a second language (MA); theatre (MA). Part-time programs available. *Entrance requirements:* Additional exam requirements/recommendations for international students: Required—TOEFL (minimum score 550 paper-based; 79 computer-based). Electronic applications accepted.

Theater

University of Cincinnati, Graduate School, College-Conservatory of Music, Divisions of Opera, Musical Theater, Drama, and Arts Administration, Cincinnati, OH 45221. Offers arts administration (MA); directing (MFA); theater design and production (MFA); voice and opera (MM, DMA); MBA/MA. *Accreditation:* NAST (one or more programs are accredited). *Degree requirements:* For master's, final project. *Entrance requirements:* For master's, GMAT (MA), audition/interview. Additional exam requirements/recommendations for international students: Required—TOEFL (minimum score 520 paper-based; 190 computer-based). Electronic applications accepted.

University of Colorado Boulder, Graduate School, College of Arts and Sciences, Department of Theatre and Dance, Boulder, CO 80309. Offers dance (MFA); theatre (MA, PhD). *Faculty:* 15 full-time (8 women). *Students:* 42 full-time (28 women), 8 part-time (5 women); includes 7 minority (4 Black or African American, non-Hispanic/Latino; 3 Hispanic/Latino), 2 international. Average age 34. 61 applicants, 14 enrolled. In 2010, 6 master's, 3 doctorates awarded. Terminal master's awarded for partial completion of doctoral program. *Degree requirements:* For master's, comprehensive exam, thesis; for doctorate, one foreign language, thesis/dissertation. *Entrance requirements:* For master's, GRE General Test (MA), audition (MFA), minimum undergraduate GPA of 2.75. *Application deadline:* For fall admission, 1/15 priority date for domestic students, 12/1 for international students. Application fee: $50 ($60 for international students). *Financial support:* In 2010–11, 16 fellowships (averaging $2,499 per year), 14 research assistantships (averaging $1,463 per year) were awarded; tuition waivers (full) also available. Financial award application deadline: 1/15. *Faculty research:* Dance: performance choreography, pedagogy administration, body therapies, multi-media forms, film/video, cultural studies, non-concert forms, music, poetry/writing/literature, kinesiology, theatre: theatre history, theory and literature, theatre production, acting, directing, dramaturgy and design.

University of Connecticut, Graduate School, School of Fine Arts, Department of Dramatic Arts, Storrs, CT 06269. Offers acting (MFA); costume design (MFA); lighting design (MFA); puppetry (MA, MFA); scenic design (MFA). *Degree requirements:* For master's, comprehensive exam. *Entrance requirements:* Additional exam requirements/recommendations for international students: Required—TOEFL (minimum score 550 paper-based; 213 computer-based). Electronic applications accepted.

University of Delaware, College of Arts and Sciences, Department of Theatre, Professional Theatre Training Program, Newark, DE 19716. Offers acting (MFA); stage management (MFA); technical production (MFA). Students are matriculated into program once every three years. *Entrance requirements:* For master's, audition, interview. Electronic applications accepted. *Faculty research:* Theatre training, acting, technical production, stage management.

University of Florida, Graduate School, College of Fine Arts, School of Theatre and Dance, Gainesville, FL 32611. Offers theatre (MFA). *Accreditation:* NAST. *Faculty:* 18 full-time (6 women). *Students:* 36 full-time (16 women); includes 6 Black or African American, non-Hispanic/Latino; 2 Asian, non-Hispanic/Latino; 2 Hispanic/Latino, 1 international. Average age 28. 17 applicants, 76% accepted, 13 enrolled. In 2010, 9 master's awarded. *Degree requirements:* For master's, thesis, creative project. *Entrance requirements:* For master's, GRE General Exam, audition/portfolio, bachelor's degree in theatre, interview, Minimum GPA of 3.0. Additional exam requirements/recommendations for international students: Required—TOEFL (minimum score 550 paper-based; 213 computer-based; 80 iBT), IELTS (minimum score 6). *Application deadline:* For fall admission, 1/1 priority date for domestic students, 1/1 for international students; for spring admission, 11/1 for domestic and international students. Applications are processed on a rolling basis. Application fee: $30. Electronic applications accepted. *Expenses:* Tuition, state resident: full-time $10,915.92. Tuition, nonresident: full-time $28,309. *Financial support:* In 2010–11, 30 students received support, including 4 fellowships, 5 research assistantships with tuition reimbursements available (averaging $16,242 per year), 21 teaching assistantships with tuition reimbursements available (averaging $14,372 per year); career-related internships or fieldwork, Federal Work-Study, institutionally sponsored loans, and unspecified assistantships also available. Financial award applicants required to submit FAFSA. *Faculty research:* Aesthetics of lighting design for the theater, production, history of theatre, criticism. *Unit head:* Paul F. Favini, Chair, 352-273-0501, Fax: 352-392-5114, E-mail: pfavini@arts.ufl.edu. *Application contact:* Dr. Ralf E. Remshardt, Graduate Coordinator, 352-273-0513, Fax: 352-392-5114, E-mail: drralf@ufl.edu.

University of Georgia, College of Arts and Sciences, Department of Theatre and Film Studies, Athens, GA 30602. Offers theatre (MFA, PhD). *Accreditation:* NAST. *Faculty:* 14 full-time (4 women), 1 part-time/adjunct (0 women). *Students:* 39 full-time (16 women), 6 part-time (all women); includes 2 Black or African American, non-Hispanic/Latino; 1 Asian, non-Hispanic/Latino, 3 international. Average age 23. 25 applicants, 56% accepted, 12 enrolled. In 2010, 2 master's, 1 doctorate awarded. *Degree requirements:* For master's, comprehensive exam, written report; for doctorate, one foreign language, comprehensive exam, thesis/dissertation. *Entrance requirements:* For master's and doctorate, GRE General Test. Additional exam requirements/recommendations for international students: Required—TOEFL (minimum score 550 paper-based). *Application deadline:* For fall admission, 7/1 for domestic students, 4/15 for international students; for winter admission, 11/15 for domestic students, 10/15 for international students; for spring admission, 5/1 for domestic students, 2/15 for international students. Application fee: $50. Electronic applications accepted. *Expenses:* Tuition, state resident: full-time $7200; part-time $344 per credit hour. Tuition, nonresident: full-time $21,900; part-time $944 per credit hour. Tuition and fees vary according to course load and program. *Financial support:* In 2010–11, research assistantships with full tuition reimbursements (averaging $10,089 per year), teaching assistantships with full tuition reimbursements (averaging $9,462 per year) were awarded; fellowships, health care benefits and unspecified assistantships also available. Financial award application deadline: 2/15. *Faculty research:* Digital media, African-American theatre, Indian theatre, history of animation, vaudeville and popular culture history. Total annual research expenditures: $375,984. *Unit head:* Dr. David Z. Saltz, Head, 706-542-2836, Fax: 706-542-2080, E-mail: saltz@uga.edu. *Application contact:* Dr. John Kundert-Gibbs, Graduate Coordinator, 706-542-9801, E-mail: jkundert@uga.edu.

University of Guelph, Graduate Studies, College of Arts, School of English and Theatre Studies, Program in Drama, Guelph, ON N1G 2W1, Canada. Offers MA. Part-time programs available. *Degree requirements:* For master's, thesis (for some programs). *Entrance requirements:* For master's, 2 letters of reference, 4 year honours undergraduate degree in English or drama. Additional exam requirements/recommendations for international students: Required—TOEFL. Electronic applications accepted. *Faculty research:* Canadian theatre, Renaissance, nineteenth and twentieth century drama and theatre, Shaw, theatre history, dramatic literature, performance theory.

University of Hawaii at Manoa, Graduate Division, College of Arts and Humanities, Department of Theatre and Dance, Honolulu, HI 96822. Offers dance (MA, MFA); theatre (MA, MFA, PhD). Part-time programs available. *Faculty:* 14 full-time (8 women), 7 part-time/adjunct (5 women). *Students:* 53 full-time (37 women), 9 part-time (7 women); includes 21 minority (1 Black or African American, non-Hispanic/Latino; 2 American Indian or Alaska Native, non-Hispanic/Latino; 8 Asian, non-Hispanic/Latino; 1 Hispanic/Latino; 1 Native Hawaiian or other Pacific Islander, non-Hispanic/Latino; 8 Two or more races, non-Hispanic/Latino), 7 international. Average age 33. 71 applicants, 62% accepted, 21 enrolled. In 2010, 13 master's, 1 doctorate awarded. *Degree requirements:* For master's, one foreign language, thesis optional; for doctorate, one foreign language, comprehensive exam, thesis/dissertation. *Entrance requirements:* For master's and doctorate, GRE General Test. Additional exam requirements/recommendations for international students: Required—TOEFL (minimum score 600 paper-based; 250 computer-based; 100 iBT), IELTS (minimum score 7). *Application deadline:* For fall admission, 2/1 for domestic students, 1/15 for international students; for spring admission, 9/1 for domestic students, 8/1 for international students. Application fee: $50. *Financial support:* In 2010–11, 12 students received support, including 26 fellowships, 3 research assistantships, 14 teaching assistantships; Federal Work-Study, institutionally sponsored loans, tuition waivers (full), and unspecified assistantships also available. Financial award application deadline: 2/1. *Faculty research:* Asian theatre, feminist theatre and dance, Russian theatre, Australian theatre. *Unit head:* Dennis Carroll, Chair, 808-956-2588, E-mail: carroll@hawaii.edu. *Application contact:* Dennis Carroll, Chair, 808-956-2588, E-mail: carroll@hawaii.edu.

University of Houston, College of Liberal Arts and Social Sciences, School of Theatre and Dance, Houston, TX 77204. Offers MA, MFA. Part-time programs available. *Faculty:* 7 full-time (1 woman), 5 part-time/adjunct (2 women). *Students:* 31 full-time (16 women); includes 2 Hispanic/Latino, 1 international. Average age 27. 12 applicants, 100% accepted, 12 enrolled. In 2010, 29 master's awarded. *Degree requirements:* For master's, thesis optional. *Entrance requirements:* For master's, GRE General Test, audition/interview (for MFA). *Application deadline:* For fall admission, 4/1 for domestic and international students. Application fee: $25 ($75 for international students). Electronic applications accepted. *Expenses:* Tuition, state resident: full-time $8592; part-time $358 per credit hour. Tuition, nonresident: full-time $16,032; part-time $668 per credit hour. Required fees: $2889. Tuition and fees vary according to course load and program. *Financial support:* Career-related internships or fieldwork, Federal Work-Study, institutionally sponsored loans, scholarships/grants, health care benefits, and unspecified assistantships available. Support available to part-time students. Financial award application deadline: 2/1. *Unit head:* Steven Wallace, Chairperson, 713-743-3003, Fax: 713-743-2648, E-mail: swwallace@uh.edu. *Application contact:* Jack Young, Graduate Acting & Directing, 713-743-0705, E-mail: jyoung2@mail.uh.edu.

University of Idaho, College of Graduate Studies, College of Letters, Arts and Social Sciences, Department of Theatre and Film, Moscow, ID 83844-2282. Offers theatre arts (MFA). *Faculty:* 3 full-time, 1 part-time/adjunct. *Students:* 23 full-time, 1 part-time. Average age 30. In 2010, 5 master's awarded. *Entrance requirements:* For master's, minimum GPA of 2.8. *Application deadline:* For fall admission, 8/1 for domestic students; for spring admission, 12/15 for domestic students. Applications are processed on a rolling basis. Application fee: $60. Electronic applications accepted. *Expenses:* Tuition, nonresident: part-time $580 per credit. Required fees: $306 per credit. *Financial support:* Research assistantships, teaching assistantships available. Financial award applicants required to submit FAFSA. *Unit head:* Dr. Dean Fields Panttaja, Chair, 208-885-5182, E-mail: theatre@uidaho.edu. *Application contact:* Dr. Dean Fields Panttaja, Chair, 208-885-5182, E-mail: theatre@uidaho.edu.

University of Illinois at Urbana–Champaign, Graduate College, College of Fine and Applied Arts, Department of Theatre, Champaign, IL 61820. Offers MA, MFA, PhD. *Accreditation:* NAST. *Faculty:* 14 full-time (5 women), 3 part-time/adjunct (2 women). *Students:* 60 full-time (31 women), 2 part-time (both women); includes 6 minority (2 Black or African American, non-Hispanic/Latino; 1 Asian, non-Hispanic/Latino; 1 Hispanic/Latino; 2 Two or more races, non-Hispanic/Latino), 9 international. 69 applicants, 36% accepted, 20 enrolled. In 2010, 15 master's, 2 doctorates awarded. *Entrance requirements:* For master's, minimum GPA of 3.0; audition, portfolio or writing sample; for doctorate, writing sample; master's degree, minimum GPA of 3.0. Additional exam requirements/recommendations for international students: Required—TOEFL (minimum score 550 paper-based; 213 computer-based). *Application deadline:* Applications are processed on a rolling basis. Application fee: $75 ($90 for international students). Electronic applications accepted. *Financial support:* In 2010–11, 8 fellowships, 2 research assistantships, 22 teaching assistantships were awarded; tuition waivers (full and partial) also available. *Unit head:* Brant Pope, Head, 217-333-2371, Fax: 217-244-1861, E-mail: brant@illinois.edu. *Application contact:* David Swinford, Admissions and Records Officer, 217-244-6189, Fax: 217-244-1861, E-mail: dswinfor@illinois.edu.

The University of Iowa, Graduate College, College of Liberal Arts and Sciences, Department of Theatre Arts, Iowa City, IA 52242-1316. Offers MFA. *Accreditation:* NAST. *Degree requirements:* For master's, thesis, exam. *Entrance requirements:* For master's, minimum GPA of 3.0. Additional exam requirements/recommendations for international students: Required—TOEFL (minimum score 550 paper-based; 213 computer-based; 81 iBT). Electronic applications accepted.

The University of Kansas, Graduate Studies, College of Liberal Arts and Sciences, Department of Theatre and Film, Lawrence, KS 66045. Offers theatre (MA, PhD); theatre design (MFA), including scenography. *Faculty:* 15 full-time (7 women). *Students:* 18 full-time (10 women), 1 (woman) part-time; includes 1 minority (Two or more races, non-Hispanic/Latino), 3 international. Average age 32. 14 applicants, 93% accepted, 6 enrolled. In 2010, 3 master's, 3 doctorates awarded. *Degree requirements:* For master's, thesis; for doctorate, one foreign language, comprehensive exam, thesis/dissertation. *Entrance requirements:* For master's, GRE General Test, minimum GPA of 3.2; for doctorate, GRE General Test, minimum GPA of 3.5; MA or MFA in theatre or related field. Additional exam requirements/recommendations for international students: Required—TOEFL. *Application deadline:* For fall admission, 1/1 priority date for domestic students, 1/1 for international students. Application fee: $55 ($65 for international students). Electronic applications accepted. *Expenses:* Tuition, state resident: full-time $7092; part-time $295.50 per credit hour. Tuition, nonresident: full-time $16,590; part-time $691.25 per credit hour. Required fees: $858; $71.49 per credit hour. Tuition and fees vary according to course load, campus/location and program. *Financial support:* In 2010–11, 2 research assistantships with full tuition reimbursements, 9 teaching assistantships with full and partial tuition reimbursements (averaging $12,650 per year) were awarded; fellowships with tuition reimbursements, Federal Work-Study, scholarships/grants, and unspecified assistantships also available. Financial award application deadline: 1/1. *Faculty research:* Theatre history, performance studies, scenography, theatre historiography. *Unit head:* John Staniunas, Chair, 785-864-3511, Fax: 785-864-5251, E-mail: stanj@ku.edu. *Application contact:* Dr. John Gronbeck-Tedesco, Director of Graduate Studies, 785-864-3511, Fax: 785-864-5251, E-mail: jgt@ku.edu.

University of Kentucky, Graduate School, College of Fine Arts, Program in Theatre, Lexington, KY 40506-0032. Offers MA. *Degree requirements:* For master's, comprehensive exam, thesis optional. *Entrance requirements:* For master's, GRE General Test, minimum undergraduate GPA of 2.75. Additional exam requirements/recommendations for international students: Required—TOEFL (minimum score 550 paper-based; 213 computer-based). Electronic applications accepted. *Faculty research:* Historical, critical, practical, theoretical, and experimental perspectives of acting, directing, design, performance, and dramaturgy.

University of Lethbridge, School of Graduate Studies, Lethbridge, AB T1K 3M4, Canada. Offers accounting (MScM); addictions counseling (M Sc); agricultural biotechnology (M Sc); agricultural studies (M Sc, MA); anthropology (MA); archaeology (MA); art (MA, MFA); biochemistry (M Sc); biological sciences (M Sc); biomolecular science (PhD); biosystems and biodiversity (PhD); Canadian studies (MA); chemistry (M Sc); computer science (M Sc); computer science and geographical information science (M Sc); counseling psychology (M Ed); dramatic arts (MA); earth, space, and physical science (PhD); economics (MA); educational leadership (M Ed); English (MA); environmental science (M Sc); evolution and behavior (PhD); exercise science (M Sc); finance (MScM); French (MA); French/German (MA); French/Spanish (MA); general education (M Ed); general management (MScM); geography (M Sc, MA); German (MA); health science (M Sc); history (MA); human resource management and labour relations (MScM); individualized multidisciplinary (M Sc, MA); information systems (MScM); international management (MScM); kinesiology (M Sc, MA); management (M Sc, MA); marketing (MScM); mathematics (M Sc); music (M Mus, MA); Native American studies (MA); neuroscience (M Sc, PhD); new media (MA); nursing (M Sc); philosophy (MA); physics (M Sc); policy and strategy (MScM); political science (MA); psychology (M Sc, MA); religious studies (MA); social sciences (MA); sociology (MA); theatre and dramatic arts (MFA); theoretical and computational science (PhD); urban and regional studies (MA); women's studies (MA). Part-time and evening/weekend programs available. *Degree requirements:* For doctorate, comprehensive exam, thesis/dissertation. *Entrance requirements:* For master's, GMAT (M Sc in management), bachelor's degree in related field, minimum GPA of 3.0 during previous 20 graded semester courses, 2 years teaching or related experience (M Ed); for doctorate, master's degree, minimum graduate GPA of 3.5. Additional exam requirements/recommendations for international students: Required—TOEFL. *Faculty research:* Movement and brain plasticity, gibberellin physiology, photosynthesis, carbon cycling, molecular properties of main-group ring components.

University of Louisville, Graduate School, College of Arts and Sciences, Department of Theatre Arts, Louisville, KY 40292-0001. Offers performance (MFA). *Accreditation:* NAST. Part-time programs available. *Faculty:* 6 full-time (4 women), 1 (woman) part-time/adjunct. *Students:* 14 full-time (7 women); includes 5 Black or African American, non-Hispanic/Latino; 1 Hispanic/Latino; 1 Two or more races, non-Hispanic/Latino. Average age 29. 9 applicants, 78% accepted, 5 enrolled. In 2010, 5 master's awarded. *Degree requirements:* For master's, thesis, performance project, monograph. *Entrance requirements:* For master's, GRE General Test, auditions and portfolio review. *Application deadline:* For spring admission, 4/15 priority date for domestic students. Applications are processed on a rolling basis. Application fee: $50. Electronic applications accepted. *Expenses:* Tuition, state resident: full-time $9144; part-time $508 per credit hour. Tuition, nonresident: full-time $19,026; part-time $1057 per credit hour. Tuition and fees vary according to program and reciprocity agreements. *Financial support:* In 2010–11, 12 teaching assistantships (averaging $12,000 per year) were awarded; scholarships/grants and health care benefits also available. Financial award application deadline: 3/15; financial award applicants required to submit FAFSA. *Faculty research:* Speech/dialects, especially for actors of color; African diaspora theatre; community acting and creation of new works; peace studies; African-American theatre. Total annual research expenditures: $10,000. *Unit head:* Dr. Russell Vandenbroucke, Chair, 502-852-8444, Fax: 502-852-7235, E-mail: r.vandenbrouke@louisville.edu. *Application contact:* Libby Leggett, Director, Graduate Admissions, 502-852-3101, Fax: 502-852-6536, E-mail: gradadm@louisville.edu.

The University of Manchester, School of Arts, Histories and Cultures, Manchester, United Kingdom. Offers anthropology, media and performance (PhD); applied theatre professional (PhD); archaeology (PhD); art history and visual studies (PhD); arts management and cultural policy (PhD); classics and ancient history (PhD); composition (PhD); creative writing (PhD); drama (PhD); economic and social history (PhD); electroacoustic composition (PhD); English and American studies (PhD); history (PhD); humanitarianism and conflict response (PhD); museology (PhD); music (PhD); musicology (PhD); religions and theology (PhD).

University of Maryland, Baltimore County, Graduate School, College of Arts, Humanities and Social Sciences, Department of Education, Program in Teaching, Baltimore, MD 21250. Offers early childhood education (MAT); elementary education (MAT); secondary education (MAT), including art, biology, chemistry, dance, earth/space science, English, foreign language, mathematics, music, physics, theatre; secondary science (MAT), including social studies. Part-time and evening/weekend programs available. *Faculty:* 24 full-time (18 women), 25 part-time/adjunct (19 women). *Students:* 59 full-time (46 women), 56 part-time (42 women); includes 1 Black or African American, non-Hispanic/Latino; 8 Asian, non-Hispanic/Latino; 3 Hispanic/Latino, 3 international. Average age 31. 88 applicants, 57% accepted, 39 enrolled. In 2010, 106 master's awarded. *Degree requirements:* For master's, comprehensive exam (for some programs), thesis (for some programs). *Entrance requirements:* For master's, PRAXIS I and II, minimum GPA of 3.0. Additional exam requirements/recommendations for international students: Required—TOEFL. *Application deadline:* For fall admission, 6/1 for domestic students; for spring admission, 11/1 for domestic students. Applications are processed on a rolling basis. Application fee: $50. Electronic applications accepted. *Financial support:* In 2010–11, 6 students received support, including research assistantships with full tuition reimbursements available (averaging $12,000 per year); career-related internships or fieldwork, Federal Work-Study, scholarships/grants, tuition waivers, and unspecified assistantships also available. Financial award application deadline: 3/1. *Faculty research:* STEM teacher education, culturally sensitive pedagogy, ESOL/bilingual education, early childhood education, language, literacy and culture. *Unit head:* Dr. Susan M. Blunck, Director, 410-455-2869, Fax: 410-455-3986, E-mail: blunck@umbc.edu. *Application contact:* Cheryl Johnson, 410-455-3388, E-mail: blackwel@umbc.edu.

University of Maryland, College Park, Academic Affairs, College of Arts and Humanities, School of Theatre, Dance and Performance Studies, Theatre Design Program, College Park, MD 20742. Offers MFA. *Students:* 18 full-time (9 women); includes 1 minority (Hispanic/Latino), 1 international. 29 applicants, 48% accepted, 9 enrolled. In 2010, 5 master's awarded. *Degree requirements:* For master's, comprehensive exam, thesis optional. *Entrance requirements:* For master's, GRE General Test, portfolio, writing sample, 3 letters of recommendation. Additional exam requirements/recommendations for international students: Required—TOEFL. *Application deadline:* For fall admission, 4/15 for domestic students, 2/1 for international students. Applications are processed on a rolling basis. Application fee: $75. Electronic applications accepted. *Expenses:* Tuition, state resident: part-time $471 per credit hour. Tuition, nonresident: part-time $1016 per credit hour. Required fees: $337 per term. *Financial support:* In 2010–11, 17 teaching assistantships (averaging $19,529 per year) were awarded; Federal Work-Study and scholarships/grants also available. Support available to part-time students. Financial award applicants required to submit FAFSA. *Unit head:* Daniel M. Wagner, Professor and Director, 301-405-6679, E-mail: dmwagner@umd.edu. *Application contact:* Dean of Graduate School, 301-405-0358, Fax: 301-314-9305.

University of Massachusetts Amherst, Graduate School, College of Humanities and Fine Arts, Department of Theater, Amherst, MA 01003. Offers MFA. Part-time programs available. *Faculty:* 14 full-time (6 women). *Students:* 11 full-time (7 women); includes 1 minority (Black or African American, non-Hispanic/Latino). Average age 27. *Degree requirements:* For master's, thesis. *Entrance requirements:* For master's, GRE General Test, resume of production experience, 2 critical essays or design portfolio. Additional exam requirements/recommendations for international students: Required—TOEFL (minimum score 550 paper-based; 213 computer-based; 80 iBT), IELTS (minimum score 6.5). *Application deadline:* For fall admission, 2/1 for domestic and international students. Applications are processed on a rolling basis. Application fee: $50 ($65 for international students). Electronic applications accepted. *Expenses:* Tuition, state resident: full-time $2640. Required fees: $8282. One-time fee: $357 full-time. *Financial support:* In 2010–11, 14 teaching assistantships with full tuition reimbursements (averaging $13,995 per year) were awarded; fellowships, research assistantships, career-related internships or fieldwork, Federal Work-Study, scholarships/grants, traineeships, health care benefits, tuition waivers (full), and unspecified assistantships also available. Support available to part-time students. Financial award application deadline: 2/1; financial award applicants required to submit FAFSA. *Unit head:* Dr. Milan Dragicevich, Graduate Program Director, 413-545-3490, Fax: 413-577-0025. *Application contact:* Jean M. Ames, Supervisor of Admissions, 413-545-0722, Fax: 413-577-0010, E-mail: gradadm@grad.umass.edu.

University of Memphis, Graduate School, College of Communication and Fine Arts, Department of Theatre and Dance, Memphis, TN 38152. Offers theatre (MFA). *Accreditation:* NAST. *Faculty:* 9 full-time (3 women), 2 part-time/adjunct (both women). *Students:* 16 full-time (9 women). Average age 30. 19 applicants, 42% accepted, 8 enrolled. In 2010, 5 master's awarded. *Degree requirements:* For master's, comprehensive exam, practicum. *Entrance requirements:* For master's, minimum GPA of 3.0 in major, 2.5 overall. *Application deadline:* For fall admission, 8/1 for domestic students; for spring admission, 12/1 for domestic students. Applications are processed on a rolling basis. Application fee: $35 ($60 for international students). *Financial support:* In 2010–11, 12 students received support; research assistantships with full tuition reimbursements available, teaching assistantships with full tuition reimbursements available, career-related internships or fieldwork, Federal Work-Study, institutionally sponsored loans, scholarships/grants, and unspecified assistantships available. Financial award application deadline: 2/15; financial award applicants required to submit FAFSA. *Faculty research:* Theatre design, production management, Lessac vocal training, movement styles, directing. *Unit head:* Prof. Robert A. Hetherington, Chair, 901-678-2523, Fax: 901-678-4331, E-mail: rhether@memphis.edu. *Application contact:* Prof. Robert A. Hetherington, Chair, 901-678-2523, Fax: 901-678-4331, E-mail: rhether@memphis.edu.

University of Michigan, Horace H. Rackham School of Graduate Studies, School of Music, Theatre, and Dance, Department of Theatre and Drama, Ann Arbor, MI 48109. Offers design (MFA); theatre (PhD). *Degree requirements:* For master's, thesis; for doctorate, one foreign language, thesis/dissertation, preliminary exam, qualifying exam. *Entrance requirements:* For master's, portfolio, interview, writing sample; for doctorate, GRE General Test, writing sample, interview. Additional exam requirements/recommendations for international students: Required—TOEFL (minimum score 600 paper-based; 250 computer-based; 100 iBT). Electronic applications accepted. *Expenses:* Tuition, state resident: full-time $17,784; part-time $1116 per credit hour. Tuition, nonresident: full-time $35,944; part-time $2125 per credit hour. International tuition: $35,994 full-time. Required fees: $95 per semester. Tuition and fees vary according to course load, degree level and program. *Faculty research:* Silent film, avant-garde drama, popular entertainment.

University of Minnesota, Twin Cities Campus, Graduate School, College of Liberal Arts, Department of Theatre Arts and Dance, Minneapolis, MN 55455-0213. Offers design technology (MFA); theatre arts and dance (MA, PhD). *Accreditation:* NAST (one or more programs are accredited). Terminal master's awarded for partial completion of doctoral program. *Degree requirements:* For master's, thesis (for some programs), final creative project (MFA), foreign language (MA); for doctorate, one foreign language, thesis/dissertation, oral defense, written exams. *Entrance requirements:* For master's, GRE General Test, minimum GPA of 3.0, audition or portfolio; for doctorate, GRE General Test, minimum GPA of 3.0, writing sample, 1 foreign language. Additional exam requirements/recommendations for international students: Required—TOEFL (minimum score 550 paper-based; 213 computer-based; 79 iBT). Electronic applications accepted. *Faculty research:* Theatre history, Eastern European theatre, performance studies, medieval studies.

University of Missouri, Graduate School, College of Arts and Sciences, Department of Theatre, Columbia, MO 65211. Offers MA, PhD. Part-time programs available. *Degree requirements:* For doctorate, thesis/dissertation. *Entrance requirements:* For master's, GRE General Test, minimum GPA of 3.0 overall and in last 60 hours; for doctorate, GRE General Test, minimum GPA of 3.0 overall and in last 60 hours, 3.5 in master's program. Additional exam requirements/recommendations for international students: Required—TOEFL (minimum score 650 paper-based; 280 computer-based; 114 iBT). Electronic applications accepted.

University of Missouri–Kansas City, College of Arts and Sciences, Theatre Department, Kansas City, MO 64110-2499. Offers acting (MFA); design technology (MFA); theatre (MA). *Accreditation:* NAST. *Faculty:* 16 full-time (6 women), 10 part-time/adjunct (3 women). *Students:* 58 full-time (31 women), 12 part-time (7 women); includes 12 minority (4 Black or African American, non-Hispanic/Latino; 1 American Indian or Alaska Native, non-Hispanic/Latino; 7 Hispanic/Latino), 1 international. Average age 28. 53 applicants, 42% accepted, 19 enrolled. In 2010, 28 master's awarded. *Degree requirements:* For master's, thesis. *Entrance requirements:* For master's, audition or portfolio, interview. Additional exam requirements/recommendations for international students: Required—TOEFL (minimum score 550 paper-based; 213 computer-based; 80 iBT). *Application deadline:* For fall admission, 3/1 priority date for domestic and international students; for spring admission, 11/1 priority date for domestic and international students. Applications are processed on a rolling basis. Application fee: $45 ($50 for international students). Electronic applications accepted. *Expenses:* Tuition, state resident: full-time $5522.40; part-time $306.80 per credit hour. Tuition, nonresident: full-time $7128; part-time $792 per credit hour. Required fees: $261.15 per term. *Financial support:* In 2010–11, 63 teaching assistantships with partial tuition reimbursements (averaging $9,269 per year) were awarded; career-related internships or fieldwork, Federal Work-Study, institutionally sponsored loans, and scholarships/grants also available. Financial award application deadline: 3/1; financial award applicants required to submit FAFSA. *Faculty research:* Contemporary Russian theatre, Shakespeare in performance, subtle energies in actor training, multi-channel sound, renovation of Zuni Pueblo historic Spanish mission. *Unit head:* Tom Mardikes, Chair, 816-235-2784, Fax: 816-235-6562, E-mail: mardikest@umkc.edu. *Application contact:* Cindy Stofiel, Student Affairs Representative, 816-235-6683, Fax: 816-235-6562, E-mail: stofielc@umkc.edu.

The University of Montana, Graduate School, School of Fine Arts, Department of Drama/Dance, Missoula, MT 59812-0002. Offers fine arts (MA, MFA), including acting (MFA), design/technology (MFA), directing (MFA), drama (MA), integrated arts and education (MA), media arts (MFA). *Accreditation:* NAST (one or more programs are accredited). *Degree requirements:* For master's, thesis or alternative. *Entrance requirements:* For master's, GRE General Test, audition, portfolio, production notebook.

The University of Montana, Graduate School, School of Fine Arts, Department of Music, Missoula, MT 59812-0002. Offers music (MM), including composition/technology, music education, musical theater, performance. *Accreditation:* NASM. *Entrance requirements:* For master's, GRE General Test, GRE Subject Test, portfolio.

University of Nebraska at Omaha, Graduate Studies, College of Communication, Fine Arts and Media, Department of Theatre, Omaha, NE 68182. Offers MA. Part-time programs available. *Faculty:* 6 full-time (2 women). *Students:* 9 full-time (6 women), 6 part-time (4 women); includes 1 minority (Asian, non-Hispanic/Latino), 1 international. Average age 34. 5 applicants, 80% accepted, 2 enrolled. In 2010, 2 master's awarded. *Degree requirements:* For master's, comprehensive exam, thesis (for some programs). *Entrance requirements:* For master's, GRE General Test or MAT, minimum GPA of 3.0. Additional exam requirements/recommendations for international students: Required—TOEFL (minimum score 500 paper-based; 173 computer-based; 61 iBT). *Application deadline:* For fall admission, 7/31 priority date for domestic students; for spring admission, 12/1 priority date for domestic students. Applications are processed on a rolling basis. Application fee: $45. Electronic applications accepted. *Financial support:* In 2010–11, 13 students received support; fellowships, research assistantships with tuition reimbursements available, Federal Work-Study, institutionally sponsored loans, scholarships/grants, tuition waivers (full), and unspecified assistantships available. Support available to part-time students. Financial award application deadline: 3/1; financial award applicants required to submit FAFSA. *Unit head:* D. Scott Glasser, Chairperson, 402-554-2406. *Application contact:* Dr. Cynthia Phaneuf, Student Contact, 402-554-2406.

University of Nebraska–Lincoln, Graduate College, College of Fine and Performing Arts, Johnny Carson School of Theatre and Film, Lincoln, NE 68588. Offers acting (MFA); costume (MFA); directing (MFA); stage design (MFA). *Accreditation:* NAST. *Degree requirements:* For master's, thesis. *Entrance requirements:* For master's, audition, portfolio. Additional exam requirements/recommendations for international students: Required—TOEFL (minimum score 500 paper-based; 173 computer-based). Electronic applications accepted. *Faculty research:* American theatre history, British theatre history, modern American drama, contemporary performance, Elizabethan theatre history.

University of Nevada, Las Vegas, Graduate College, College of Fine Arts, Department of Theatre, Las Vegas, NV 89154-5036. Offers theatre arts (MA, MFA). *Accreditation:* NAST. Part-time programs available. *Faculty:* 13 full-time (2 women), 4 part-time/adjunct (2 women). *Students:* 37 full-time (18 women), 8 part-time (5 women); includes 19 minority (2 Black or African American, non-Hispanic/Latino; 2 Hispanic/Latino; 15 Two or more races, non-Hispanic/Latino), 3 international. Average age 32. 65 applicants, 65% accepted, 30 enrolled. In 2010, 17 master's awarded. *Degree requirements:* For master's, thesis (for some programs), creative project, oral exam. *Entrance requirements:* Additional exam requirements/recommendations for international students: Required—TOEFL (minimum score 550 paper-based; 213 computer-based; 80 iBT), IELTS (minimum score 7). *Application deadline:* For fall admission, 8/1 priority date for domestic and international students. Applications are processed on a rolling basis. Application fee: $60 ($95 for international students). Electronic applications accepted. *Expenses:* Tuition, area resident: Part-time $239.50 per credit. Tuition, state resident: part-time $239.50 per credit. Tuition, nonresident: part-time $503 per credit. Required fees: $108 per semester. Tuition and fees vary according to course load, program and reciprocity agreements. *Financial support:* In 2010–11, 32 students received support, including 16 research assistantships with partial tuition reimbursements available (averaging $10,000 per year), 16 teaching assistantships with partial tuition reimbursements available (averaging $10,000 per year); institutionally sponsored loans, scholarships/grants, health care benefits, and unspecified assistantships also available. Financial award application deadline: 3/1. *Faculty research:* Designing scenery,

Theater

University of Nevada, Las Vegas (continued)
costumes or lighting for a production for a regional theatre; directing or stage managing for a regional theatre; serving as technical director/consultant for a regional theatre; acting for a regional theatre. *Unit head:* Brackley Frayer, Chair/Associate Professor, 702-895-3666, Fax: 702-895-0833, E-mail: brackley.frayer@unlv.edu. *Application contact:* Graduate College Admissions Evaluator, 702-895-3320, Fax: 702-895-4180, E-mail: gradcollege@unlv.edu.

University of New Mexico, Graduate School, College of Fine Arts, Department of Theatre and Dance, Albuquerque, NM 87131-2039. Offers dance (MFA); dance history (MA); dramatic writing (MFA); theatre education and outreach (MA). *Accreditation:* NASD; NAST. *Faculty:* 23 full-time (11 women), 15 part-time/adjunct (10 women). *Students:* 19 full-time (16 women), 4 part-time (all women); includes 9 minority (1 American Indian or Alaska Native, non-Hispanic/Latino; 2 Asian, non-Hispanic/Latino; 6 Hispanic/Latino). Average age 31. 33 applicants, 21% accepted, 7 enrolled. In 2010, 3 master's awarded. *Degree requirements:* For master's, comprehensive exam (for some programs), thesis (for some programs). *Entrance requirements:* For master's, minimum GPA of 3.0; undergraduate major in theatre, dance or closely related field; 3 letters of recommendation; letter of intent; BA, BFA, BS, or MA in dance movement science or related field, or equivalent experience (for MFA in dance). *Application deadline:* For fall admission, 4/15 for domestic students; for spring admission, 11/10 for domestic students. Application fee: $50. Electronic applications accepted. *Expenses:* Tuition, state resident: full-time $5991; part-time $251 per credit hour. Tuition, nonresident: full-time $14,405; part-time $800.20 per credit hour. Tuition and fees vary according to course level, course load, program and reciprocity agreements. *Financial support:* In 2010–11, 20 students received support, including 1 fellowship (averaging $7,200 per year), 1 research assistantship with partial tuition reimbursement available (averaging $3,750 per year), 3 teaching assistantships with partial tuition reimbursements available (averaging $4,482 per year); Federal Work-Study, health care benefits, tuition waivers (partial), and unspecified assistantships also available. Financial award application deadline: 3/1; financial award applicants required to submit FAFSA. *Faculty research:* Theater education and outreach, choreography, dramatic writing, dance history/criticism. *Unit head:* Bill Liotta, Chair, 505-277-4332, Fax: 505-277-8921, E-mail: wliotta@unm.edu. *Application contact:* Christina Squire, Administrator II, 505-277-7362, Fax: 505-277-8921, E-mail: csquire@unm.edu.

University of New Orleans, Graduate School, College of Liberal Arts, Department of Film, Theatre and Communication Arts, New Orleans, LA 70148. Offers film production (MFA); theatre directing (MFA); theatre performance (MFA). *Accreditation:* NAST. *Degree requirements:* For master's, comprehensive exam, thesis. *Entrance requirements:* Additional exam requirements/recommendations for international students: Required—TOEFL (minimum score 550 paper-based; 213 computer-based; 79 iBT). Electronic applications accepted. *Faculty research:* Mass communication theory, nineteenth- and twentieth-century theater history, film criticism and history.

The University of North Carolina at Chapel Hill, Graduate School, College of Arts and Sciences, Department of Dramatic Art, Chapel Hill, NC 27599. Offers acting (MFA); costume production (MFA); technical production (MFA). *Entrance requirements:* For master's, audition or portfolio.

The University of North Carolina at Charlotte, Graduate School, College of Education, Department of Middle, Secondary and K-12 Education, Charlotte, NC 28223-0001. Offers art education (MAT); curriculum and instruction (PhD); dance education (MAT); foreign language education (MAT); middle grades and secondary education (M Ed); middle grades education (MAT); music education (MAT); secondary education (MAT); teaching English as a second language (M Ed); theatre education (MAT). *Faculty:* 16 full-time (8 women), 6 part-time/adjunct (5 women). *Students:* 149 full-time (112 women), 943 part-time (735 women); includes 281 minority (189 Black or African American, non-Hispanic/Latino; 9 American Indian or Alaska Native, non-Hispanic/Latino; 23 Asian, non-Hispanic/Latino; 51 Hispanic/Latino; 9 Two or more races, non-Hispanic/Latino), 6 international. Average age 31. 224 applicants, 96% accepted, 173 enrolled. In 2010, 72 master's awarded. *Entrance requirements:* For master's, GRE or MAT. Additional exam requirements/recommendations for international students: Required—TOEFL (minimum score 557 paper-based; 220 computer-based; 83 iBT). *Application deadline:* For fall admission, 7/1 for domestic students, 5/1 for international students; for spring admission, 11/1 for domestic students, 10/1 for international students. Applications are processed on a rolling basis. Application fee: $55. Electronic applications accepted. *Expenses:* Tuition, state resident: full-time $3464. Tuition, nonresident: full-time $14,297. Required fees: $2094. Tuition and fees vary according to course load. *Financial support:* In 2010–11, 11 students received support, including 1 research assistantship (averaging $16,000 per year), 7 teaching assistantships (averaging $9,357 per year); career-related internships or fieldwork, institutionally sponsored loans, scholarships/grants, and unspecified assistantships also available. Support available to part-time students. Financial award application deadline: 4/1; financial award applicants required to submit FAFSA. Total annual research expenditures: $22,468. *Unit head:* Melba Spooner, Chair, 704-687-8704, Fax: 704-687-6430, E-mail: mcspoone@uncc.edu. *Application contact:* Kathy B. Giddings, Director of Graduate Admissions, 704-687-5503, Fax: 704-687-3279, E-mail: gradadm@uncc.edu.

The University of North Carolina at Greensboro, Graduate School, College of Arts and Sciences, Department of Theater, Greensboro, NC 27412-5001. Offers acting (MFA); design (MFA); directing (MFA); theater education (M Ed); theater for youth (MFA). *Accreditation:* NAST. *Entrance requirements:* For master's, portfolio, interviews. Electronic applications accepted.

University of North Carolina School of the Arts, School of Design and Production, Winston-Salem, NC 27127-2188. Offers costume design (MFA); costume technology (MFA); performance arts management (MFA); scene design (MFA); scene painting/properties (MFA); sound design (MFA); stage automation (MFA); technical direction (MFA); wig and make-up design (MFA). *Faculty:* 19 full-time (4 women), 16 part-time/adjunct (6 women). *Students:* 73 full-time (50 women); includes 3 Black or African American, non-Hispanic/Latino; 2 American Indian or Alaska Native, non-Hispanic/Latino; 3 Asian, non-Hispanic/Latino; 2 Hispanic/Latino, 3 international. Average age 25. 86 applicants, 77% accepted, 48 enrolled. In 2010, 21 master's awarded. *Degree requirements:* For master's, thesis (for some programs), project. *Entrance requirements:* For master's, interview, portfolio. Additional exam requirements/recommendations for international students: Required—TOEFL. *Application deadline:* For fall admission, 4/1 priority date for domestic students. Applications are processed on a rolling basis. Application fee: $60 ($100 for international students). Electronic applications accepted. *Expenses:* Tuition, state resident: full-time $4946. Tuition, nonresident: full-time $17,253. Required fees: $2092. *Financial support:* In 2010–11, 2 teaching assistantships with partial tuition reimbursements (averaging $1,500 per year) were awarded; career-related internships or fieldwork, Federal Work-Study, unspecified assistantships, and Academic Common Market also available. Support available to part-time students. Financial award application deadline: 3/15; financial award applicants required to submit FAFSA. *Unit head:* Joseph A. Tilford, Dean, 336-770-3214 Ext. 103, Fax: 336-770-3213, E-mail: tilford@uncsa.edu. *Application contact:* Sheeler Lawson, Director of Admissions, 336-770-3290, Fax: 336-770-3370, E-mail: admissions@uncsa.edu.

University of North Dakota, Graduate School, College of Arts and Sciences, Department of Theatre Arts, Grand Forks, ND 58202. Offers MA. *Accreditation:* NAST. *Faculty:* 5 full-time (3 women), 1 (woman) part-time/adjunct. *Students:* 7 full-time (1 woman), 2 part-time (both women). Average age 33. 10 applicants, 30% accepted, 3 enrolled. In 2010, 1 master's awarded. *Degree requirements:* For master's, comprehensive exam, thesis or alternative. *Entrance requirements:* For master's, minimum GPA of 3.0. Additional exam requirements/recommendations for international students: Required—TOEFL (minimum score 550 paper-based; 213 computer-based; 79 iBT), IELTS (minimum score 6.5). *Application deadline:* For fall admission, 8/1 priority date for domestic students, 5/1 priority date for international students; for spring admission, 12/1 priority date for domestic students, 9/1 priority date for international students. Applications are processed on a rolling basis. Application fee: $35. Electronic applica-

tions accepted. *Expenses:* Tuition, state resident: full-time $5857; part-time $306.74 per credit. Tuition, nonresident: full-time $15,666; part-time $729.77 per credit. Required fees: $53.42 per credit. Tuition and fees vary according to course load, program and reciprocity agreements. *Financial support:* In 2010–11, 5 students received support, including 5 teaching assistantships with full and partial tuition reimbursements available (averaging $6,508 per year); fellowships with full and partial tuition reimbursements available, research assistantships with full and partial tuition reimbursements available, Federal Work-Study, institutionally sponsored loans, scholarships/grants, and tuition waivers (full and partial) also available. Support available to part-time students. Financial award application deadline: 3/15; financial award applicants required to submit FAFSA. *Unit head:* Dr. Kathleen Mclennon, Graduate Director, 701-777-3446, Fax: 701-777-3522, E-mail: kathleenmclennon@mail.und.nodak.edu. *Application contact:* Matt Anderson, Admissions Specialist, 701-777-2947, Fax: 701-777-3619, E-mail: matthew.anderson@gradschool.und.edu.

University of Oklahoma, Weitzenhoffer Family College of Fine Arts, School of Drama, Norman, OK 73019. Offers drama (MA, MFA), including acting/directing/design (MFA), design (MFA), directing (MFA). *Accreditation:* NAST. Part-time programs available. *Faculty:* 9 full-time (4 women). *Students:* 9 full-time (4 women); includes 1 minority (Two or more races, non-Hispanic/Latino). Average age 32. 6 applicants, 33% accepted, 2 enrolled. In 2010, 5 master's awarded. *Degree requirements:* For master's, comprehensive exam, thesis (MA), departmental qualifying exam. *Entrance requirements:* For master's, BA with 36 hours in drama, auditions. Additional exam requirements/recommendations for international students: Required—TOEFL (minimum score 550 paper-based; 213 computer-based; 79 iBT). *Application deadline:* For fall admission, 3/1 for domestic and international students; for spring admission, 11/1 for domestic students, 9/1 for international students. Applications are processed on a rolling basis. Application fee: $40 ($90 for international students). Electronic applications accepted. *Expenses:* Tuition, state resident: full-time $3893; part-time $162.20 per credit hour. Tuition, nonresident: full-time $14,167; part-time $590.30 per credit hour. Required fees: $2523; $94.60 per credit hour. Tuition and fees vary according to course load and degree level. *Financial support:* In 2010–11, 1 research assistantship with partial tuition reimbursement (averaging $9,586 per year), 6 teaching assistantships with partial tuition reimbursements (averaging $9,586 per year) were awarded; Federal Work-Study also available. Financial award application deadline: 4/7; financial award applicants required to submit FAFSA. *Faculty research:* Directing, design, acting, dramaturgy, stage management, theatre pedagogy. *Unit head:* Dr. Tom Orr, Director, 405-325-4021, Fax: 405-325-0400, E-mail: thorr@ou.edu. *Application contact:* Dr. Kae Koger, Graduate Liaison, 405-325-4021, Fax: 405-325-0400, E-mail: akoger@ou.edu.

University of Oregon, Graduate School, College of Arts and Sciences, Department of Theater Arts, Eugene, OR 97403. Offers MA, MFA, MS, PhD. *Degree requirements:* For master's, variable foreign language requirement, thesis or alternative; for doctorate, variable foreign language requirement, thesis/dissertation. *Entrance requirements:* For master's and doctorate, minimum GPA of 3.0. Additional exam requirements/recommendations for international students: Required—TOEFL.

University of Ottawa, Faculty of Graduate and Postdoctoral Studies, Faculty of Arts, Department of Theatre, Ottawa, ON K1N 6N5, Canada. Offers directing for theatre (MA). Electronic applications accepted. *Faculty research:* Lamise en scéne.

University of Pittsburgh, School of Arts and Sciences, Department of Theatre Arts, Pittsburgh, PA 15260. Offers performance pedagogy (MFA); theatre and performance studies (MA, PhD). *Accreditation:* NAST. *Faculty:* 4 full-time (2 women). *Students:* 22 full-time (12 women); includes 1 minority (Black or African American, non-Hispanic/Latino), 1 international. Average age 30. 29 applicants, 34% accepted, 6 enrolled. In 2010, 2 master's, 3 doctorates awarded. Terminal master's awarded for partial completion of doctoral program. *Degree requirements:* For master's, comprehensive exam; for doctorate, one foreign language, comprehensive exam, thesis/dissertation, diagnostic exams. *Entrance requirements:* For master's and doctorate, GRE General Test, samples of written work. Additional exam requirements/recommendations for international students: Required—TOEFL (minimum score 550 paper-based; 213 computer-based; 80 iBT). *Application deadline:* For fall admission, 1/15 priority date for domestic and international students. Application fee: $50. Electronic applications accepted. *Expenses:* Tuition, state resident: full-time $17,304; part-time $701 per credit. Tuition, nonresident: full-time $29,554; part-time $1210 per credit. Required fees: $740; $214 per term. Tuition and fees vary according to program. *Financial support:* In 2010–11, 18 students received support, including 9 research assistantships with full and partial tuition reimbursements available (averaging $12,670 per year), 14 teaching assistantships with full and partial tuition reimbursements available (averaging $16,140 per year); career-related internships or fieldwork, Federal Work-Study, institutionally sponsored loans, scholarships/grants, health care benefits, and unspecified assistantships also available. Support available to part-time students. Financial award application deadline: 1/15; financial award applicants required to submit FAFSA. *Faculty research:* American theatre, Renaissance theatre, Asian theatre, dramatic structure, performance theory. *Unit head:* Dr. Bruce McConachie, Chairman, 412-624-6156, Fax: 412-624-6338, E-mail: bamcco@pitt.edu. *Application contact:* Connie Anne Markiw, Graduate Secretary, 412-624-6568, Fax: 412-624-6338, E-mail: cam177@pitt.edu.

University of Portland, College of Arts and Sciences, Department of Performing and Fine Arts, Portland, OR 97203-5798. Offers directing (MFA). Part-time and evening/weekend programs available. *Faculty:* 3 full-time (1 woman). *Students:* 5 full-time (3 women), 1 (woman) part-time; includes 1 Black or African American, non-Hispanic/Latino. Average age 36. In 2010, 5 master's awarded. *Degree requirements:* For master's, thesis optional. *Entrance requirements:* For master's, GRE General Test, minimum GPA of 3.0, resume, 3 letters of recommendation, statement of goals, official transcripts. Additional exam requirements/recommendations for international students: Required—TOEFL (minimum score 600 paper-based; 100 iBT), IELTS (minimum score 7.5). *Application deadline:* For fall admission, 7/15 priority date for domestic and international students; for spring admission, 12/15 priority date for domestic and international students. Applications are processed on a rolling basis. Application fee: $50. *Expenses:* Tuition: Part-time $940 per credit hour. Tuition and fees vary according to program. *Financial support:* Federal Work-Study, scholarships/grants, and tuition waivers (partial) available. Financial award application deadline: 3/1; financial award applicants required to submit FAFSA. *Unit head:* Dr. Kenneth Kleszynski, Head, 503-943-7294, E-mail: kkleszyn@up.edu. *Application contact:* Chris James Olinger, Administrative Assistant, 503-943-7107, Fax: 503-943-7315, E-mail: olingerc@up.edu.

University of San Diego, College of Arts and Sciences, Program in Dramatic Arts, San Diego, CA 92110-2492. Offers MFA. *Faculty:* 4 full-time (2 women). *Students:* 14 full-time (7 women); includes 1 Black or African American, non-Hispanic/Latino; 1 American Indian or Alaska Native, non-Hispanic/Latino. Average age 28. 375 applicants, 2% accepted, 7 enrolled. In 2010, 7 master's awarded. *Entrance requirements:* For master's, audition. Additional exam requirements/recommendations for international students: Required—TOEFL (minimum score 580 paper-based; 237 computer-based; 83 iBT), TWE. *Application deadline:* For fall admission, 1/4 for domestic and international students. Application fee: $55. *Expenses:* Tuition: Full-time $21,744; part-time $1208 per unit. Required fees: $224. Full-time tuition and fees vary according to course load and degree level. *Financial support:* In 2010–11, 14 students received support, including 14 fellowships with full tuition reimbursements available; career-related internships or fieldwork, Federal Work-Study, and institutionally sponsored loans also available. Financial award application deadline: 4/1; financial award applicants required to submit FAFSA. *Faculty research:* Drama, acting, instruction, voice and speech. *Unit head:* Richard Seer, Graduate Program Director, 619-260-8813, Fax: 619-231-5879. *Application contact:* Stephen Pultz, Director of Admissions and Enrollment, 619-260-4506, Fax: 619-260-6836, E-mail: admissions@sandiego.edu.

University of Saskatchewan, College of Graduate Studies and Research, College of Arts and Sciences, Department of Drama, Saskatoon, SK S7N 5A2, Canada. Offers MA. *Degree requirements:* For master's, thesis. *Entrance requirements:* Additional exam requirements/

recommendations for international students: Required—TOEFL (minimum score 80 iBT); Recommended—IELTS (minimum score 6.5). Electronic applications accepted.

University of South Carolina, The Graduate School, College of Arts and Sciences, Department of Theater and Dance, Columbia, SC 29208. Offers theater (MA, MAT, MFA). IMA and MAT offered in cooperation with the College of Education. *Accreditation:* NAST (one or more programs are accredited). *Degree requirements:* For master's, comprehensive exam, thesis. *Entrance requirements:* For master's, GRE General Test, GRE or MAT (MAT), audition, interview (for MFA degree). Additional exam requirements/recommendations for international students: Required—TOEFL. Electronic applications accepted. *Faculty research:* Computer assisted design, rhetoric of science and technology, Alexander Technique, script analysis, Lessac Method.

University of South Carolina, The Graduate School, College of Education, Department of Instruction and Teacher Education, Program in Secondary Education, Columbia, SC 29208. Offers art education (IMA, MAT); business education (IMA, MAT); English (MAT); foreign language (MAT); health education (MAT); mathematics (MAT); science (IMA, MAT); secondary (Ed D); secondary education (MT, PhD); social studies (MAT); theatre and speech (MAT). IMA and MT offered jointly with the subject areas. *Accreditation:* NCATE. *Degree requirements:* For master's, comprehensive exam, thesis (for some programs), foreign language (MA); for doctorate, one foreign language, comprehensive exam, thesis/dissertation. *Entrance requirements:* For master's, GRE General Test or MAT, teaching certificate (IMA, M Ed), interview; for doctorate, GRE General Test or MAT, interview. *Faculty research:* Middle school programs, professional development, school collaboration.

The University of South Dakota, Graduate School, College of Fine Arts, Department of Theatre, Vermillion, SD 57069-2390. Offers MA, MFA. *Accreditation:* NAST. *Degree requirements:* For master's, thesis or alternative. *Entrance requirements:* For master's, GRE (MA), minimum GPA of 2.7, portfolio. Additional exam requirements/recommendations for international students: Required—TOEFL (minimum score 550 paper-based; 213 computer-based; 79 iBT). Electronic applications accepted.

University of Southern California, Graduate School, School of Theatre, Los Angeles, CA 90089. Offers acting (MFA); applied theatre arts (MA); dramatic writing (MFA). *Faculty:* 10 full-time (3 women), 9 part-time/adjunct (6 women). *Students:* 48 full-time (26 women); includes 21 minority (7 Black or African American, non-Hispanic/Latino; 4 Asian, non-Hispanic/Latino; 5 Hispanic/Latino; 5 Two or more races, non-Hispanic/Latino), 2 international. In 2010, 13 master's awarded. *Degree requirements:* For master's, comprehensive exam. *Entrance requirements:* For master's, GRE. Additional exam requirements/recommendations for international students: Required—TOEFL. *Application deadline:* For fall admission, 1/12 for domestic and international students. Application fee: $85. Electronic applications accepted. *Expenses:* Tuition: Full-time $31,240; part-time $1420 per unit. Required fees: $600. One-time fee: $35 full-time. Tuition and fees vary according to degree level and program. *Financial support:* In 2010–11, 6 teaching assistantships with partial tuition reimbursements (averaging $34,000 per year) were awarded; scholarships/grants and tuition waivers also available. Financial award application deadline: 1/12; financial award applicants required to submit FAFSA. *Unit head:* Sergio Ramirez, Director of Academic and Student Services, 213-821-4163, Fax: 213-821-1193, E-mail: sergio.ramirez@usc.edu. *Application contact:* Sergio Ramirez, Director of Academic and Student Services, 213-821-4163, Fax: 213-821-1193, E-mail: sergio.ramirez@usc.edu.

University of Southern Mississippi, Graduate School, College of Arts and Letters, Department of Theatre and Dance, Hattiesburg, MS 39406-0001. Offers directing (MFA); performance (MFA); technical (MFA). *Accreditation:* NAST. Part-time programs available. *Faculty:* 8 full-time (5 women). *Students:* 21 full-time (9 women); includes 2 Black or African American, non-Hispanic/Latino; 1 Asian, non-Hispanic/Latino; 3 Hispanic/Latino; 1 Two or more races, non-Hispanic/Latino. Average age 28. 20 applicants, 40% accepted, 7 enrolled. In 2010, 7 master's awarded. *Degree requirements:* For master's, comprehensive exam, thesis or alternative, creative project. *Entrance requirements:* For master's, GRE General Test, minimum GPA of 3.0. Additional exam requirements/recommendations for international students: Required—TOEFL, IELTS. *Application deadline:* For fall admission, 3/1 priority date for domestic students, 3/1 for international students; for spring admission, 1/10 priority date for domestic and international students. Applications are processed on a rolling basis. Application fee: $50. *Financial support:* In 2010–11, 20 teaching assistantships with full tuition reimbursements (averaging $7,065 per year) were awarded; research assistantships, career-related internships or fieldwork, Federal Work-Study, institutionally sponsored loans, health care benefits, and unspecified assistantships also available. Support available to part-time students. Financial award application deadline: 3/15; financial award applicants required to submit FAFSA. *Faculty research:* Technical design, acting. *Unit head:* Louis Rackoff, Chair, 601-266-4994, Fax: 601-266-6423. *Application contact:* Louis Rackoff, Director, Graduate Studies, 601-266-4994, Fax: 601-266-6423, E-mail: graduatestudies@usm.edu.

The University of Tennessee, Graduate School, College of Arts and Sciences, Department of Theatre, Knoxville, TN 37996. Offers costume design (MFA); lighting design (MFA); performance (MFA); scene design (MFA); theatre technology (MFA). *Degree requirements:* For master's, thesis or alternative. *Entrance requirements:* For master's, audition, minimum GPA of 2.7. Additional exam requirements/recommendations for international students: Required—TOEFL. Electronic applications accepted. *Expenses:* Tuition, state resident: full-time $7440; part-time $414 per credit hour. Tuition, nonresident: full-time $22,478; part-time $1250 per credit hour. Required fees: $922; $43 per credit hour. Tuition and fees vary according to program.

The University of Texas at Austin, Graduate School, College of Fine Arts, Department of Theatre and Dance, Austin, TX 78712-1111. Offers acting (MFA); dance (MFA); directing (MFA); drama and theatre for youth (MFA); performance as public practice (MA, MFA, PhD); playwriting (MFA); theatre technology (MFA); theatrical design (MFA). *Accreditation:* NASD. *Degree requirements:* For master's, thesis; for doctorate, variable foreign language requirement, thesis/dissertation. *Entrance requirements:* For master's and doctorate, GRE General Test.

The University of Texas–Pan American, College of Arts and Humanities, Department of Communications, Edinburg, TX 78539. Offers communication (MA); theatre (MA). *Accreditation:* NAST. Part-time and evening/weekend programs available. *Degree requirements:* For master's, comprehensive exam, thesis or alternative. *Entrance requirements:* For master's, minimum GPA of 3.0. Additional exam requirements/recommendations for international students: Required—TOEFL. *Faculty research:* Rhetorical theory, intercultural and mass communication, American theatre, multicultural theatre and drama, television and film.

University of the Cumberlands, Graduate Programs in Education, Williamsburg, KY 40769-1372. Offers all grades (P-12) (M Ed); business and marketing (MA Ed, MAT); director of pupil personnel (Certificate); director of special education (Certificate); educational administration and supervision (Ed S); educational leadership (Ed D); elementary education (MA Ed, MAT); instructional leadership—principalship (MA Ed); instructional leadership—school principal (Certificate); middle school education (MA Ed, MAT); reading and writing (MA Ed); school counseling (MA Ed); school superintendent (Certificate); secondary education (MA Ed, MAT); special education (MAT); supervisor of instruction (Certificate); teacher leader (MA Ed). Part-time and evening/weekend programs available. Postbaccalaureate distance learning degree programs offered. *Faculty:* 33 full-time (15 women), 26 part-time/adjunct (12 women). *Students:* 1,198 full-time (818 women), 260 part-time (168 women); includes 44 Black or African American, non-Hispanic/Latino; 4 American Indian or Alaska Native, non-Hispanic/Latino; 7 Asian, non-Hispanic/Latino; 10 Hispanic/Latino, 2 international. Average age 33. In 2010, 291 master's, 97 other advanced degrees awarded. *Degree requirements:* For master's, comprehensive exam. *Application deadline:* Applications are processed on a rolling basis. Application fee: $30. Electronic applications accepted. *Expenses:* Tuition: Full-time $6984; part-time $291 per credit hour. Required fees: $50 per term. Tuition and fees vary according to course level, course load and program. *Financial support:* Unspecified assistantships available. *Unit head:* Dr. Robert Heffern, Department Chair, 800-549-2200 Ext. 4588, Fax: 606-539-4588, E-mail: robert.heffern@ucumberlands.edu. *Application contact:* Donna Stanfill, Director of Graduate Admissions, 606-539-4390.

University of Toronto, School of Graduate Studies, Humanities Division, Centre for the Study of Drama, Toronto, ON M5S 1A1, Canada. Offers MA, PhD. Part-time programs available. *Degree requirements:* For doctorate, one foreign language, thesis/dissertation, language examination, qualifying examination, oral examination. *Entrance requirements:* For master's, minimum B+ average, significant coursework in drama and related disciplines, resume, 2 letters of recommendation; for doctorate, minimum A- average, resumé, MA in drama; 2 letters of recommendation.

University of Tulsa, Graduate School, College of Arts and Sciences, School of Education, Program in Teaching Arts, Tulsa, OK 74104-3189. Offers art (MTA); biology (MTA); English (MTA); history (MTA); mathematics (MTA); theatre (MTA). Part-time programs available. *Students:* 2 part-time (both women); includes 1 minority (American Indian or Alaska Native, non-Hispanic/Latino). Average age 31. 1 applicant, 0% accepted, 0 enrolled. In 2010, 2 master's awarded. *Entrance requirements:* For master's, GRE General Test. Additional exam requirements/recommendations for international students: Required—TOEFL (minimum score 575 paper-based; 231 computer-based), IELTS (minimum score 6.5). *Application deadline:* Applications are processed on a rolling basis. Application fee: $40. Electronic applications accepted. *Expenses:* Tuition: Full-time $16,902; part-time $939 per credit hour. Required fees: $1020; $4 per credit hour. Tuition and fees vary according to course load. *Financial support:* In 2010–11, 2 students received support, including 2 fellowships with full and partial tuition reimbursements available (averaging $2,191 per year); research assistantships with full and partial tuition reimbursements available, teaching assistantships with full and partial tuition reimbursements available, Federal Work-Study, scholarships/grants, and tuition waivers (full and partial) also available. Support available to part-time students. Financial award application deadline: 2/1; financial award applicants required to submit FAFSA. *Unit head:* Dr. David Brown, Advisor, 918-631-2719, Fax: 918-631-2133, E-mail: david-brown@utulsa.edu. *Application contact:* Dr. David Brown, Advisor, 918-631-2719, Fax: 918-631-2133, E-mail: david-brown@utulsa.edu.

University of Victoria, Faculty of Graduate Studies, Faculty of Fine Arts, Department of Theatre, Victoria, BC V8W 2Y2, Canada. Offers design (MFA); directing (MFA); theatre history (MA). *Degree requirements:* For master's, thesis. *Entrance requirements:* Additional exam requirements/recommendations for international students: Required—TOEFL (minimum score 575 paper-based; 233 computer-based), IELTS (minimum score 7). Electronic applications accepted.

University of Virginia, College and Graduate School of Arts and Sciences, Department of Drama, Charlottesville, VA 22903. Offers MFA. *Faculty:* 17 full-time (8 women), 1 (woman) part-time/adjunct. *Students:* 17 full-time (9 women); includes 1 Black or African American, non-Hispanic/Latino; 1 Native Hawaiian or other Pacific Islander, non-Hispanic/Latino, 1 international. Average age 28. 1 applicant, 100% accepted, 1 enrolled. *Degree requirements:* For master's, thesis project. *Entrance requirements:* For master's, GRE General Test, resume; 3 letters of recommendation. Additional exam requirements/recommendations for international students: Required—TOEFL (minimum score 600 paper-based; 250 computer-based; 90 iBT), IELTS (minimum score 7). *Application deadline:* For fall admission, 2/20 for domestic and international students. Applications are processed on a rolling basis. Application fee: $60. Electronic applications accepted. *Financial support:* Fellowships, teaching assistantships available. Financial award applicants required to submit FAFSA. *Faculty research:* Acting, scenic design, lighting design, technical direction, costume design/technology. *Unit head:* Tom Bloom, Chair, 434-924-3326, Fax: 434-924-1447, E-mail: drama@virginia.edu. *Application contact:* Tom Bloom, Chair, 434-924-3326, Fax: 434-924-1447, E-mail: drama@virginia.edu.

University of Washington, Graduate School, College of Arts and Sciences, School of Drama, Seattle, WA 98195. Offers acting (MFA); costume design (MFA); directing (MFA); dramatic theory (PhD); lighting design (MFA); scenic design (MFA); theatre and performance history (PhD). *Degree requirements:* For master's, thesis; for doctorate, one foreign language, comprehensive exam, thesis/dissertation. *Entrance requirements:* For master's, interview, minimum GPA of 3.0, portfolio; for doctorate, GRE General Test, minimum GPA of 3.0, writing sample. Additional exam requirements/recommendations for international students: Required—TOEFL. *Faculty research:* Semiotics, Suzuki actor training, modern American theatre, ethnic American theatre.

University of Wisconsin–Madison, Graduate School, College of Letters and Science, Department of Theatre and Drama, Madison, WI 53706-1380. Offers MA, MFA, PhD. *Accreditation:* NAST. Part-time programs available. *Degree requirements:* For master's, thesis; for doctorate, thesis/dissertation. *Entrance requirements:* For master's and doctorate, GRE. Electronic applications accepted. *Expenses:* Tuition, state resident: full-time $9887; part-time $617.96 per credit. Tuition, nonresident: full-time $24,054; part-time $1503.40 per credit. Required fees: $67.63 per credit. Tuition and fees vary according to reciprocity agreements. *Faculty research:* Theories and histories of dance, theatre and performance studies; Russian theatre and dance; postmodern performance; Holocaust drama; race and representation.

University of Wisconsin–Milwaukee, Graduate School, Peck School of the Arts, Program in Performing Arts, Milwaukee, WI 53201-0413. Offers dance (MFA); film (MFA); theatre (MFA). Part-time programs available. *Faculty:* 28 full-time (16 women). *Students:* 17 full-time (10 women), 2 part-time (0 women); includes 1 Black or African American, non-Hispanic/Latino; 2 Hispanic/Latino, 1 international. Average age 34. 31 applicants, 23% accepted, 6 enrolled. In 2010, 17 master's awarded. *Degree requirements:* For master's, variable foreign language requirement, comprehensive exam, thesis or alternative. *Entrance requirements:* For master's, audition, interview. Additional exam requirements/recommendations for international students: Required—TOEFL (minimum score 550 paper-based; 79 iBT), IELTS (minimum score 6.5). *Application deadline:* For fall admission, 1/1 priority date for domestic students; for spring admission, 9/1 for domestic students. Applications are processed on a rolling basis. Application fee: $56 ($96 for international students). Electronic applications accepted. *Financial support:* In 2010–11, 5 fellowships with full tuition reimbursements, 9 teaching assistantships with full tuition reimbursements were awarded; career-related internships or fieldwork, health care benefits, unspecified assistantships, and project assistantships also available. Support available to part-time students. Financial award application deadline: 4/15; financial award applicants required to submit FAFSA. *Unit head:* Simone Ferro, Representative, 414-229-4178, E-mail: sferro@uwm.edu. *Application contact:* General Information Contact, 414-229-4982, Fax: 414-229-6967, E-mail: gradschool@uwm.edu.

University of Wisconsin–Superior, Graduate Division, Department of Communicating Arts, Superior, WI 54880-4500. Offers mass communication (MA); speech communication (MA); theater (MA). Part-time programs available. *Degree requirements:* For master's, comprehensive exam, thesis or alternative, position paper or project. *Entrance requirements:* For master's, minimum GPA of 2.75. *Faculty research:* Multimedia technology, ethics in journalism, diversity, electronic portfolio assessment.

Utah State University, School of Graduate Studies, College of Humanities, Arts and Social Sciences, Department of Theatre Arts, Logan, UT 84322. Offers advanced technical practice (MFA); design (MFA); theatre arts (MA, MFA). *Degree requirements:* For master's, variable foreign language requirement, thesis (for some programs), summer internship (MFA). *Entrance requirements:* For master's, GRE General Test or MAT, portfolio (MFA), minimum GPA of 3.0, interview, BS or 20 semester credit. Additional exam requirements/recommendations for international students: Required—TOEFL. *Faculty research:* Seventeenth and eighteenth century Spanish theatre, Greek and Roman theatre, interpretation of literature for performance.

Villanova University, Graduate School of Liberal Arts and Sciences, Department of Theatre, Villanova, PA 19085-1699. Offers MA. Part-time and evening/weekend programs available. *Faculty:* 6 full-time (1 woman), 2 part-time/adjunct (both women). *Students:* 27 full-time (18

Theater

Villanova University (continued)
women), 2 part-time (both women); includes 4 minority (2 Black or African American, non-Hispanic/Latino; 2 Hispanic/Latino). Average age 30. 21 applicants, 100% accepted, 14 enrolled. In 2010, 14 master's awarded. *Degree requirements:* For master's, comprehensive exam. *Entrance requirements:* For master's, GRE, minimum GPA of 3.0. Additional exam requirements/recommendations for international students: Required—TOEFL. *Application deadline:* For fall admission, 3/1 priority date for domestic and international students; for spring admission, 11/15 priority date for domestic and international students. Applications are processed on a rolling basis. Application fee: $50. Electronic applications accepted. *Expenses:* Tuition: Part-time $700 per credit. Part-time tuition and fees vary according to degree level and program. *Financial support:* Research assistantships, Federal Work-Study, scholarships/grants, and unspecified assistantships available. Financial award applicants required to submit FAFSA. *Unit head:* Fr. Richard Cannuli, Chairperson, 610-519-4760. *Application contact:* Dr. Adele Lindenmeyr, Dean, Graduate School of Liberal Arts and Sciences, 610-519-7093, Fax: 610-519-7096.

Virginia Commonwealth University, Graduate School, School of the Arts, Department of Theatre, Richmond, VA 23284-9005. Offers costume design (MFA); pedagogy (MFA); scene design/technical theater (MFA). *Accreditation:* NAST. *Faculty:* 9 full-time (4 women). *Students:* 40 full-time (25 women), 4 part-time (2 women); includes 8 minority (4 Black or African American, non-Hispanic/Latino; 1 Asian, non-Hispanic/Latino; 2 Hispanic/Latino; 1 Two or more races, non-Hispanic/Latino), 1 international. 47 applicants, 49% accepted, 17 enrolled. In 2010, 12 master's awarded. *Degree requirements:* For master's, thesis (for some programs). *Entrance requirements:* For master's, audition, portfolio. Additional exam requirements/recommendations for international students: Required—TOEFL (minimum score 600 paper-based; 250 computer-based; 100 iBT). *Application deadline:* For fall admission, 5/1 priority date for domestic students. Application fee: $50. Electronic applications accepted. *Expenses:* Tuition, state resident: full-time $4308; part-time $479 per credit hour. Tuition, nonresident: full-time $8942; part-time $994 per credit hour. Required fees: $2000; $85 per credit hour. Tuition and fees vary according to course level, course load, degree level, campus/location and program. *Financial support:* Fellowships, teaching assistantships, career-related internships or fieldwork, Federal Work-Study, and institutionally sponsored loans available. Support available to part-time students. Financial award application deadline: 3/15. *Faculty research:* Dramatic literature, speech. *Unit head:* David S. Leong, Chair, 804-828-1514, Fax: 804-828-6741, E-mail: dsleong@vcu.edu. *Application contact:* Dr. Noreen C. Barnes, Director of Graduate Studies, 804-827-1677, E-mail: nbarnesm@vcu.edu.

Virginia Polytechnic Institute and State University, Graduate School, College of Liberal Arts and Human Sciences, Department of Theatre and Cinema, Blacksburg, VA 24061. Offers directing and public dialogue (MFA); stage management (MFA); theatre design and technology (MFA). *Accreditation:* NAST. *Entrance requirements:* For master's, GRE, GMAT. Additional exam requirements/recommendations for international students: Required—TOEFL (minimum score 550 paper-based; 213 computer-based). Electronic applications accepted. *Expenses:* Tuition, state resident: full-time $9399; part-time $488 per credit hour. Tuition, nonresident: full-time $17,854; part-time $957.75 per credit hour. Required fees: $1534. Full-time tuition and fees vary according to program.

Wayne State University, College of Fine, Performing and Communication Arts, Department of Theatre, Detroit, MI 48202. Offers MA, MFA, PhD. *Accreditation:* NAST. *Faculty:* 15 full-time (7 women), 1 (woman) part-time/adjunct. *Students:* 44 full-time (16 women), 4 part-time (all women); includes 6 minority (4 Black or African American, non-Hispanic/Latino; 2 Two or more races, non-Hispanic/Latino), 1 international. Average age 30. 30 applicants, 67% accepted, 14 enrolled. In 2010, 16 master's, 3 doctorates awarded. *Degree requirements:* For master's, thesis (for some programs); for doctorate, one foreign language, thesis/dissertation. *Entrance requirements:* For master's, minimum GPA of 3.0, auditions, interviews; for doctorate, GRE, MA with minimum GPA of 3.3; directing experience; recommendations; scholarly paper; statement of goals. Additional exam requirements/recommendations for international students: Required—TOEFL (minimum score 550 paper-based; 213 computer-based); Recommended—TWE (minimum score 6). *Application deadline:* For fall admission, 4/1 for domestic students, 6/1 for international students; for winter admission, 10/1 for international students; for spring admission, 2/1 for international students. Application fee: $30 ($50 for international students). Electronic applications accepted. *Expenses:* Tuition, state resident: full-time $7662; part-time $478.85 per credit hour. Tuition, nonresident: full-time $16,920; part-time $1057.55 per credit hour. Required fees: $571.20; $35.70 per credit hour. $188.05 per semester. Tuition and fees vary according to course load and program. *Financial support:* In 2010–11, 1 fellowship (averaging $18,000 per year), 36 research assistantships (averaging $14,620 per year), 3 teaching assistantships (averaging $15,160 per year) were awarded. *Faculty research:* Dramatic criticism, lighting design, acting, directing, scenography. *Unit head:* Blair Anderson, Chair, 313-577-3508, Fax: 313-577-0935, E-mail: ad5298@wayne.edu. *Application contact:* James Thomas, Professor, 313-577-0789, E-mail: jthomas@wayne.edu.

Western Illinois University, School of Graduate Studies, College of Fine Arts and Communication, Department of Theatre and Dance, Macomb, IL 61455-1390. Offers acting (MFA); design (MFA); directing (MFA). *Accreditation:* NAST. Part-time programs available. *Students:* 23 full-time (11 women), 5 part-time (1 woman), 1 international. Average age 29. 36 applicants, 33% accepted. In 2010, 12 master's awarded. *Degree requirements:* For master's, comprehensive exam, thesis or alternative, creative project, written exam. *Entrance requirements:* For master's, audition or interview. Additional exam requirements/recommendations for international students: Required—TOEFL (minimum score 550 paper-based; 213 computer-based; 80 iBT). *Application deadline:* Applications are processed on a rolling basis. Application fee: $30. Electronic applications accepted. *Expenses:* Tuition, state resident: full-time $6370; part-time $265.40 per credit hour. Tuition, nonresident: full-time $12,740; part-time $530.80 per credit hour. Required fees: $75.67 per credit hour. *Financial support:* In 2010–11, 25 students received support, including 19 research assistantships with full tuition reimbursements available (averaging $7,280 per year), 6 teaching assistantships with full tuition reimbursements available (averaging $8,400 per year). Financial award applicants required to submit FAFSA. *Unit head:* Dr. David Patrick, Chairperson, 309-298-1543. *Application contact:* Evelyn Hoing, Assistant Director of Graduate Studies, 309-298-1806, Fax: 309-298-2345, E-mail: grad-office@wiu.edu.

West Virginia University, College of Creative Arts, Division of Theatre and Dance, Morgantown, WV 26506. Offers acting (MFA); theatre design/technology (MFA). *Accreditation:* NAST. Part-time programs available. *Degree requirements:* For master's, thesis, oral defense. *Entrance requirements:* For master's, minimum GPA of 3.0, audition or portfolio. Additional exam requirements/recommendations for international students: Required—TOEFL. *Faculty research:* Professional directing, consulting, design.

Yale University, School of Drama, New Haven, CT 06520. Offers MFA, DFA, Certificate, MBA/MFA. *Faculty:* 66 full-time (43 women), 43 part-time/adjunct (23 women). *Students:* 208 full-time (106 women); includes 42 minority (13 Black or African American, non-Hispanic/Latino; 2 American Indian or Alaska Native, non-Hispanic/Latino; 12 Asian, non-Hispanic/Latino; 14 Hispanic/Latino; 1 Two or more races, non-Hispanic/Latino), 27 international. Average age 27. 1,520 applicants, 4% accepted, 64 enrolled. In 2010, 69 master's, 1 doctorate awarded. *Degree requirements:* For master's, comprehensive exam (for some programs), thesis (for some programs); for doctorate, thesis/dissertation. *Entrance requirements:* For master's, GRE verbal and quantitative (for dramaturgy and dramatic criticism, stage management, theater management, and technical design and production), in-person audition (for acting); portfolio review (for design). Additional exam requirements/recommendations for international students: Required—TOEFL. *Application deadline:* For fall admission, 1/3 for domestic and international students. Application fee: $110. Electronic applications accepted. *Financial support:* In 2010–11, 193 students received support. Career-related internships or fieldwork, Federal Work-Study, institutionally sponsored loans, scholarships/grants, and health care benefits available. Financial award application deadline: 2/15; financial award applicants required to submit FAFSA. *Unit head:* Dean James Bundy, Dean/Artistic Director of Yale Repertory Theatre, 203-432-1505. *Application contact:* Maria Leveton, Registrar/Admissions Administrator, 203-432-1507, Fax: 203-432-9668.

York University, Faculty of Graduate Studies, Faculty of Fine Arts, Program in Theatre, Toronto, ON M3J 1P3, Canada. Offers MFA. *Degree requirements:* For master's, thesis. Electronic applications accepted.

York University, Faculty of Graduate Studies, Faculty of Fine Arts, Program in Theatre Studies, Toronto, ON M3J 1P3, Canada. Offers MA, PhD.

Therapies—Dance, Drama, and Music

Antioch University New England, Graduate School, Department of Applied Psychology, Program in Dance/Movement Therapy and Counseling, Keene, NH 03431-3552. Offers M Ed, MA. *Degree requirements:* For master's, thesis, internship, practicum. *Entrance requirements:* For master's, previous course work and work experience in psychology, experience in dance or movement. Additional exam requirements/recommendations for international students: Required—TOEFL (minimum score 600 paper-based; 250 computer-based). Electronic applications accepted. *Expenses:* Contact institution. *Faculty research:* Research attitudes and needs of dance/movement therapists.

Appalachian State University, Cratis D. Williams Graduate School, School of Music, Boone, NC 28608. Offers music education (MM); music performance (MM); music therapy (MMT). *Accreditation:* NASM. Part-time programs available. *Faculty:* 28 full-time (8 women), 2 part-time/adjunct (1 woman). *Students:* 30 full-time (20 women), 4 part-time (3 women); includes 1 minority (Hispanic/Latino). 34 applicants, 82% accepted, 21 enrolled. In 2010, 22 master's awarded. *Degree requirements:* For master's, comprehensive exam, thesis or alternative. *Entrance requirements:* For master's, GRE General Test, 3 letters of reference, audition. Additional exam requirements/recommendations for international students: Required—TOEFL (minimum score 550 paper-based; 230 computer-based; 79 iBT), IELTS (minimum score 6.5). *Application deadline:* For fall admission, 7/1 for domestic students, 2/1 for international students; for spring admission, 11/1 for domestic students, 7/1 for international students. Applications are processed on a rolling basis. Application fee: $55. Electronic applications accepted. *Expenses:* Tuition, state resident: full-time $3428; part-time $428 per unit. Tuition, nonresident: full-time $14,518; part-time $1814 per unit. Required fees: $2320; $344 per unit. Tuition and fees vary according to campus/location. *Financial support:* In 2010–11, 16 research assistantships (averaging $8,000 per year) were awarded; fellowships, teaching assistantships, career-related internships or fieldwork, Federal Work-Study, scholarships/grants, tuition waivers (partial), and unspecified assistantships also available. Financial award application deadline: 4/1; financial award applicants required to submit FAFSA. *Faculty research:* Music of the Holocaust, Celtic folk music, early nineteenth century performance practice, hypermeter and phase rhythm, world music, music and psychoneuroimmunology. Total annual research expenditures: $8,500. *Unit head:* Dr. William Pelto, Dean, 828-262-6446, E-mail: peltowl@appstate.edu. *Application contact:* Dr. Jennifer Snodgrass, Graduate Program Director, 828-262-6463, E-mail: snodgrassjs@appstate.edu.

Arizona State University, Herberger Institute for Design and the Arts, School of Music, Tempe, AZ 85287-0405. Offers composition (MM); music (conducting) (DMA); music (ethnomusicology) (MA); music (interdisciplinary digital media/performance) (DMA); music (music history and literature) (MA); music (performance) (DMA); music education (MM, PhD); music therapy (MM); performance (MM). *Accreditation:* NASM. *Faculty:* 66 full-time (21 women), 1 (woman) part-time/adjunct. *Students:* 236 full-time (133 women), 133 part-time (71 women); includes 39 minority (6 Black or African American, non-Hispanic/Latino; 17 Asian, non-Hispanic/Latino; 13 Hispanic/Latino; 3 Two or more races, non-Hispanic/Latino), 63 international. Average age 29. 406 applicants, 47% accepted, 105 enrolled. In 2010, 81 master's, 40 doctorates awarded. Terminal master's awarded for partial completion of doctoral program. *Degree requirements:* For master's, thesis (for some programs), interactive Program of Study (iPOS) submitted before completing 50 percent of required credit hours; for doctorate, comprehensive exam, thesis/dissertation, interactive Program of Study (iPOS) submitted before completing 50 percent of required credit hours. *Entrance requirements:* For master's, minimum GPA of 3.0 or equivalent in last 2 years of work leading to bachelor's degree, 3 letters of recommendation, resume; for doctorate, GRE or MAT, minimum GPA of 3.0 or equivalent in last 2 years of work leading to bachelor's degree, 3 letters of recommendation, curriculum vitae, statement of intent. Additional exam requirements/recommendations for international students: Required—TOEFL, IELTS, or Pearson Test of English. *Application deadline:* For fall admission, 12/1 for domestic and international students; for spring admission, 10/1 for domestic and international students. Applications are processed on a rolling basis. Application fee: $70 ($90 for international students). Electronic applications accepted. *Expenses:* Tuition, state resident: full-time $8510; part-time $608 per credit. Tuition, nonresident: full-time $16,542; part-time $919 per credit. Required fees: $339; $110 per credit. Part-time tuition and fees vary according to course load. *Financial support:* In 2010–11, 1 research assistantship with full and partial tuition reimbursement (averaging $4,000 per year), 74 teaching assistantships with full and partial tuition reimbursements (averaging $4,191 per year) were awarded; fellowships with full and partial tuition reimbursements, Federal Work-Study, institutionally sponsored loans, scholarships/grants, and tuition waivers (full and partial) also available. Financial award application deadline: 3/1; financial award applicants required to submit FAFSA. Total annual research expenditures: $5,914. *Unit head:* Dr. Kimberly Marshall, Director, 480-727-6222, Fax: 480-965-2659, E-mail: kimberly.marshall@asu.edu. *Application contact:* Graduate Admissions, 480-965-6113.

California Institute of Integral Studies, School of Professional Psychology, San Francisco, CA 94103. Offers clinical psychology (Psy D); community mental health (MA); drama therapy (MA); expressive arts therapy (MA); integral counseling psychology (MA); integral counseling psychology-weekend (MA); somatic psychology (MA). *Accreditation:* APA. Part-time and evening/weekend programs available. *Students:* 651 full-time (476 women), 74 part-time (62 women); includes 146 minority (32 Black or African American, non-Hispanic/Latino; 1 American Indian or Alaska Native, non-Hispanic/Latino; 53 Asian, non-Hispanic/Latino; 43 Hispanic/Latino; 17 Two or more races, non-Hispanic/Latino), 52 international. Average age 37. 556 applicants, 72% accepted, 247 enrolled. In 2010, 148 master's, 27 doctorates awarded. *Degree requirements:* For doctorate, comprehensive exam, thesis/dissertation. *Entrance requirements:* For master's, minimum GPA of 3.0, letters of recommendation, writing sample; for doctorate, GRE, MA in psychology or social work with appropriate practical experience for advanced standing, or BA with a minimum GPA of 3.1; letters of recommendation; writing sample. Additional exam requirements/recommendations for international students: Required—TOEFL. *Application deadline:* For fall admission, 2/1 priority date for domestic and international students;

for spring admission, 10/15 priority date for domestic and international students. Applications are processed on a rolling basis. Application fee: $65. Electronic applications accepted. *Expenses:* Tuition: Full-time $15,660; part-time $870 per semester hour. Required fees: $95 per semester. *Financial support:* Research assistantships with tuition reimbursements, teaching assistantships with tuition reimbursements, career-related internships or fieldwork, Federal Work-Study, scholarships/grants, and tuition waivers (partial) available. Support available to part-time students. Financial award application deadline: 4/15; financial award applicants required to submit FAFSA. *Faculty research:* Transpersonal psychology, somatic psychology, expressive arts therapy, drama therapy, community mental health, ecopsychology. *Application contact:* David Townes, Senior Admissions Counselor, 415-575-6152, Fax: 415-575-1268, E-mail: dtownes@ciis.edu.

Columbia College Chicago, Graduate School, Program in Dance/Movement Therapy, Chicago, IL 60605-1996. Offers MA, Certificate. Part-time programs available. *Students:* 28 full-time (all women), 23 part-time (all women); includes 12 minority (6 Black or African American, non-Hispanic/Latino; 1 American Indian or Alaska Native, non-Hispanic/Latino; 2 Asian, non-Hispanic/Latino; 2 Hispanic/Latino; 1 Two or more races, non-Hispanic/Latino), 1 international. Average age 27. 68 applicants, 37% accepted, 15 enrolled. In 2010, 15 master's awarded. *Degree requirements:* For master's, thesis, internship. *Entrance requirements:* For master's, movement assessment, interview, minimum GPA of 3.0. Additional exam requirements/recommendations for international students: Required—TOEFL (minimum score 550 paper-based; 213 computer-based). *Application deadline:* For fall admission, 1/5 for domestic and international students. Application fee: $55. *Expenses:* Tuition: Full-time $16,966; part-time $684 per credit. Required fees: $520; $113 per semester. One-time fee: $150 full-time. Tuition and fees vary according to course load and program. *Financial support:* Fellowships, career-related internships or fieldwork, Federal Work-Study, and scholarships/grants available. Support available to part-time students. Financial award application deadline: 8/13; financial award applicants required to submit FAFSA. *Unit head:* Susan Imus, Chairperson, 312-369-7097, Fax: 312-369-8054, E-mail: simus@colum.edu. *Application contact:* Cate Lagueux, Director of Graduate Admissions, 312-369-7260, Fax: 312-369-8047, E-mail: clagueux@colum.edu.

Drexel University, College of Nursing and Health Professions, Program in Creative Arts in Therapy, Specialization in Dance/Movement Therapy, Philadelphia, PA 19104-2875. Offers MA, PMC. Part-time programs available. *Degree requirements:* For master's, comprehensive exam, thesis. *Entrance requirements:* For master's, GRE General Test or MAT, audition, interview, minimum GPA of 2.75. Electronic applications accepted. *Faculty research:* Family nonverbal communication, early intervention, sexual abuse.

Drexel University, College of Nursing and Health Professions, Program in Creative Arts in Therapy, Specialization in Music Therapy, Philadelphia, PA 19104-2875. Offers MA, PMC. Part-time programs available. *Degree requirements:* For master's, comprehensive exam, thesis. *Entrance requirements:* For master's, GRE General Test or MAT, audition, interview, minimum GPA of 2.75. Electronic applications accepted. *Faculty research:* Early childhood intervention through creative art therapies, rhythm and dementia, music therapy and bulimia, assessment of adolescent suicide.

East Carolina University, Graduate School, College of Fine Arts and Communication, School of Music, Greenville, NC 27858-4353. Offers music education (MM); music therapy (MM); performance (MM); theory and composition (MM). *Accreditation:* NASM. Part-time programs available. *Degree requirements:* For master's, comprehensive exam, thesis optional. *Entrance requirements:* For master's, GRE General Test or MAT. Additional exam requirements/recommendations for international students: Required—TOEFL. *Expenses:* Tuition, state resident: full-time $3130; part-time $391.25 per credit hour. Tuition, nonresident: full-time $13,817; part-time $1727.13 per credit hour. Required fees: $1916; $239.50 per credit hour. Tuition and fees vary according to campus/location and program.

Florida State University, The Graduate School, College of Music, Tallahassee, FL 32306. Offers accompanying (MM); arts administration (MA); choral conducting (MM); composition (MM, DM); ethnomusicology (MM); general music (MA); instrumental accompanying (MM); instrumental conducting (MM); jazz studies (MM); music education (MM Ed, PhD); music theory (MM, PhD); music therapy (MM); musicology (MM, PhD), including ethnomusicology (PhD), historical musicology; opera (MM); performance (MM, DM); piano pedagogy (MM); piano technology (MA); vocal accompanying (MM). *Accreditation:* NASM. *Faculty:* 88 full-time, 13 part-time/adjunct. *Students:* 406 full-time (211 women); includes 28 Black or African American, non-Hispanic/Latino; 38 Asian, non-Hispanic/Latino; 32 Hispanic/Latino. Average age 26. 525 applicants, 38% accepted, 145 enrolled. In 2010, 102 master's, 41 doctorates awarded. *Degree requirements:* For master's, comprehensive exam (for some programs), thesis (for some programs), departmental qualifying exam; for doctorate, comprehensive exam (for some programs), thesis/dissertation, departmental qualifying exam. *Entrance requirements:* For master's and doctorate, audition, GRE General Test or minimum GPA of 3.0. Additional exam requirements/recommendations for international students: Required—TOEFL (minimum score 550 paper-based; 213 computer-based). *Application deadline:* For fall admission, 7/1 for domestic students, 5/2 for international students; for spring admission, 11/3 for domestic students, 9/1 for international students. Applications are processed on a rolling basis. Application fee: $30. Electronic applications accepted. *Expenses:* Tuition, state resident: full-time $8238.24. *Financial support:* In 2010–11, 225 students received support, including 3 fellowships with full tuition reimbursements available (averaging $15,000 per year), 9 research assistantships with full tuition reimbursements available (averaging $4,000 per year), 173 teaching assistantships with full tuition reimbursements available (averaging $4,000 per year); career-related internships or fieldwork, Federal Work-Study, and tuition waivers (partial) also available. Support available to part-time students. Financial award application deadline: 2/28; financial award applicants required to submit FAFSA. *Unit head:* Dr. Don Gibson, Dean, 850-644-4361, Fax: 850-644-2033. *Application contact:* Dr. Seth Beckman, Senior Associate Dean for Academic Affairs/Director of Graduate Studies, 850-644-5848, Fax: 850-644-2033, E-mail: sbeckman@admin.fsu.edu.

Georgia College & State University, Graduate School, College of Health Sciences, Program in Music Therapy, Milledgeville, GA 31061. Offers MMT. Part-time and evening/weekend programs available. Postbaccalaureate distance learning degree programs offered (minimal on-campus study). *Faculty:* 3 full-time (2 women). *Students:* 5 full-time (3 women), 9 part-time (8 women); includes 3 minority (1 Black or African American, non-Hispanic/Latino; 2 Asian, non-Hispanic/Latino), 2 international. Average age 27. 4 applicants, 100% accepted, 3 enrolled. *Degree requirements:* For master's, comprehensive exam, thesis or alternative. *Entrance requirements:* For master's, MAT or GRE, bachelor's degree in music therapy or equivalent, 2 letters of recommendation, Internet access. Additional exam requirements/recommendations for international students: Recommended—TOEFL (minimum score 550 paper-based; 213 computer-based; 79 iBT). *Application deadline:* For fall admission, 7/1 priority date for domestic students; for spring admission, 11/15 priority date for domestic students. Applications are processed on a rolling basis. Application fee: $40. Electronic applications accepted. *Expenses:* Tuition, state resident: full-time $4806; part-time $267 per hour. Tuition, nonresident: full-time $17,802; part-time $989 per hour. Tuition and fees vary according to course load. *Financial support:* In 2010–11, 2 research assistantships were awarded; career-related internships or fieldwork and unspecified assistantships also available. Support available to part-time students. Financial award application deadline: 3/1; financial award applicants required to submit FAFSA. *Unit head:* Dr. Chesley Mercado, Director, 478-445-2645, Fax: 478-445-2645, E-mail: chesley.mercado@gcsu.edu. *Application contact:* Dr. Chesley Mercado, Director, 478-445-2645, Fax: 478-445-2645, E-mail: chesley.mercado@gcsu.edu.

Immaculata University, College of Graduate Studies, Program in Music Therapy, Immaculata, PA 19345. Offers MA. *Accreditation:* NASM. Part-time and evening/weekend programs available. *Students:* 8 full-time (5 women), 9 part-time (all women). Average age 33. 9 applicants, 78% accepted, 7 enrolled. In 2010, 3 master's awarded. *Degree requirements:* For master's, comprehensive exam, thesis optional. *Entrance requirements:* For master's, GRE General Test or MAT, minimum GPA of 3.0. Additional exam requirements/recommendations for international students: Required—TOEFL. *Application deadline:* Applications are processed on a rolling basis. Application fee: $50. Electronic applications accepted. *Financial support:* Application deadline: 5/1. *Faculty research:* Biofeedback music laboratory, experimental music therapy, virtual arts therapies, sound beam. *Unit head:* Dr. Anthony Meadows, Chair, 610-647-4400 Ext. 3159, Fax: 610-993-8550, E-mail: babrams@immaculata.edu. *Application contact:* 610-647-4400 Ext. 3211, Fax: 610-993-8550, E-mail: graduate@immaculata.edu.

Lesley University, Graduate School of Arts and Social Sciences, Division of Expressive Therapies, Cambridge, MA 02138-2790. Offers art (MA); dance (MA); expressive therapies (MA, PhD, CAGS); music (MA). Terminal master's awarded for partial completion of doctoral program. *Degree requirements:* For master's, internship, practicum; for doctorate, thesis/dissertation. *Entrance requirements:* For master's, art portfolio, performance DVD; for doctorate, GRE or MAT. Additional exam requirements/recommendations for international students: Required—TOEFL (minimum score 550 paper-based; 213 computer-based; 80 iBT).

Loyola University New Orleans, College of Music and Fine Arts, New Orleans, LA 70118-6195. Offers music therapy (MMT); performance (MM). *Accreditation:* NASM. Part-time programs available. *Students:* 27 full-time (14 women), 3 part-time (all women); includes 7 Black or African American, non-Hispanic/Latino; 1 Hispanic/Latino, 2 international. Average age 26. 28 applicants, 71% accepted, 11 enrolled. In 2010, 1 master's awarded. *Degree requirements:* For master's, thesis, comprehensive written and oral exams. *Entrance requirements:* For master's, performance audition, appropriate bachelor's degree, minimum GPA of 3.0, letters of recommendation, resume. Additional exam requirements/recommendations for international students: Required—TOEFL (minimum score 550 paper-based; 213 computer-based). *Application deadline:* For fall admission, 8/15 priority date for domestic and international students; for spring admission, 1/1 priority date for domestic and international students. Applications are processed on a rolling basis. Application fee: $20. Electronic applications accepted. *Expenses:* Contact institution. *Financial support:* Career-related internships or fieldwork, Federal Work-Study, institutionally sponsored loans, scholarships/grants, and unspecified assistantships available. Support available to part-time students. Financial award application deadline: 5/1; financial award applicants required to submit FAFSA. *Faculty research:* Music business, music therapy, musicology, music theory, music education. *Unit head:* Donald R. Boomgaarden, Dean, 504-865-3039, Fax: 504-865-2852, E-mail: deancmfa@loyno.edu. *Application contact:* Anthony A. Decuir, Associate Dean, 504-865-3037, Fax: 504-865-2852, E-mail: decuir@loyno.edu.

Maryville University of Saint Louis, School of Health Professions, Program in Music Therapy, St. Louis, MO 63141-7299. Offers MMT. *Accreditation:* NASM. Part-time programs available. *Students:* 8 full-time (all women), 4 part-time (all women), 3 international. Average age 30. *Entrance requirements:* For master's, music audition, interview, minimum undergraduate GPA of 3.0, 3 letters of recommendation. Additional exam requirements/recommendations for international students: Required—TOEFL (minimum score 550 paper-based). *Application deadline:* Applications are processed on a rolling basis. Application fee: $40 ($60 for international students). Electronic applications accepted. *Expenses:* Tuition: Full-time $21,100; part-time $633.50 per credit hour. Required fees: $150 per semester. *Financial support:* Application deadline: 3/1. *Unit head:* Dr. Cynthia Briggs, Director, 314-529-9441, Fax: 314-529-9495, E-mail: cbriggs@maryville.edu. *Application contact:* Dr. Cynthia Briggs, Director, 314-529-9441, Fax: 314-529-9495, E-mail: cbriggs@maryville.edu.

Marywood University, Academic Affairs, Insalaco College of Creative and Performing Arts, Music, Theatre and Dance Department, Program in Music Therapy, Scranton, PA 18509-1598. Offers MMT, Certificate. *Accreditation:* NASM. *Entrance requirements:* Additional exam requirements/recommendations for international students: Required—TOEFL (minimum score 550 paper-based; 213 computer-based; 79 iBT). Electronic applications accepted. *Expenses:* Tuition: Part-time $735 per credit. Required fees: $470 per semester. Tuition and fees vary according to degree level and campus/location.

Michigan State University, The Graduate School, College of Music, East Lansing, MI 48824. Offers collaborative piano (M Mus); jazz studies (M Mus); music (PhD); music composition (M Mus, DMA); music conducting (M Mus, DMA); music education (M Mus); music performance (M Mus, DMA); music theory (M Mus); music therapy (M Mus); musicology (MA); piano pedagogy (M Mus). *Accreditation:* NASM. *Entrance requirements:* Additional exam requirements/recommendations for international students: Required—TOEFL. Electronic applications accepted.

Molloy College, Graduate Music Therapy Program, Rockville Centre, NY 11571-5002. Offers MS. *Faculty:* 2 full-time (1 woman), 2 part-time/adjunct (both women). *Students:* 13 full-time (11 women), 20 part-time (15 women); includes 2 Black or African American, non-Hispanic/Latino; 7 Asian, non-Hispanic/Latino; 2 Hispanic/Latino. Average age 32. In 2010, 1 master's awarded. *Application deadline:* Applications are processed on a rolling basis. *Application contact:* Dr. Mary O'Shaughnessy, Interim Associate Dean/Director, 516-678-5000 Ext. 6838, Fax: 516-256-2267, E-mail: moshaughnessy@molloy.edu.

Montclair State University, The Graduate School, School of the Arts, Department of Music, Montclair, NJ 07043-1624. Offers music (AD, Certificate); music education (MA); music therapy (MA, Certificate); performance (MA, Certificate); theory/composition (MA). *Accreditation:* NASM. Part-time and evening/weekend programs available. *Faculty:* 20 full-time (7 women), 101 part-time/adjunct (46 women). *Students:* 24 full-time (11 women), 37 part-time (14 women); includes 1 Black or African American, non-Hispanic/Latino; 3 Asian, non-Hispanic/Latino; 2 Hispanic/Latino, 7 international. Average age 31. 43 applicants, 58% accepted, 21 enrolled. In 2010, 12 master's, 7 other advanced degrees awarded. *Degree requirements:* For master's, comprehensive exam, compositions, recitals, or thesis. *Entrance requirements:* For master's, GRE General Test, audition; teaching certificate (MA in music education). Additional exam requirements/recommendations for international students: Required—TOEFL (minimum score: 83 iBT) or IELTS. *Application deadline:* For fall admission, 6/1 for international students; for spring admission, 10/1 for international students. Applications are processed on a rolling basis. Application fee: $60. Electronic applications accepted. *Expenses:* Tuition, state resident: part-time $501.34 per credit. Tuition, nonresident: part-time $773.88 per credit. Required fees: $71.15 per credit. *Financial support:* In 2010–11, 3 research assistantships with full tuition reimbursements (averaging $7,000 per year) were awarded; Federal Work-Study, scholarships/grants, and unspecified assistantships also available. Support available to part-time students. Financial award application deadline: 3/1; financial award applicants required to submit FAFSA. *Unit head:* Prof. Robert Aldridge, Chairperson, 973-655-7212. *Application contact:* Amy Aiello, Director of Graduate Admissions and Operations, 973-655-5147, Fax: 973-655-7869, E-mail: graduate.school@montclair.edu.

Naropa University, Graduate Programs, Program in Somatic Counseling Psychology, Concentration in Dance/Movement Therapy, Boulder, CO 80302-6697. Offers MA. Part-time programs available. *Faculty:* 2 full-time (1 woman), 13 part-time/adjunct (10 women). *Students:* 19 full-time (all women), 4 part-time (all women); includes 6 minority (1 Black or African American, non-Hispanic/Latino; 1 Hispanic/Latino; 4 Two or more races, non-Hispanic/Latino), 1 international. Average age 31. 32 applicants, 66% accepted, 7 enrolled. In 2010, 5 master's awarded. *Degree requirements:* For master's, comprehensive exam, thesis, internship, fieldwork, portfolio. *Entrance requirements:* For master's, in-person interview, course work in psychology and anatomy, experience in 3 forms of dance, resume, letter of interest, 3 letters of recommendation. Additional exam requirements/recommendations for international students: Required—TOEFL (minimum score 600 paper-based; 250 computer-based). *Application deadline:* For fall admission, 1/15 priority date for domestic and international students. Applications are processed on a rolling basis. Application fee: $60. Electronic applications accepted. *Expenses:* Tuition: Full-time $17,820; part-time $810 per credit. Required fees: $305 per semester. Tuition and fees vary according to course load, program and reciprocity agreements. *Financial support:* In 2010–11, 6 students received support; research assistantships with partial tuition reimbursements available, teaching assistantships with partial tuition reimbursements available, career-related internships or fieldwork, Federal Work-Study, scholarships/

Therapies—Dance, Drama, and Music

Naropa University (continued)

grants, health care benefits, tuition waivers (partial), and unspecified assistantships available. Support available to part-time students. Financial award application deadline: 3/1; financial award applicants required to submit FAFSA. *Unit head:* Dr. MacAndrew Jack, Director, Graduate School of Psychology, 303-245-4752, E-mail: mjack@naropa.edu. *Application contact:* Roslynn Regnery, Graduate Admissions Counselor, 303-546-3598, Fax: 303-546-3583, E-mail: rregnery@naropa.edu.

Nazareth College of Rochester, Graduate Studies, Department of Creative Arts Therapy, Program in Music Therapy, Rochester, NY 14618-3790. Offers MS. *Entrance requirements:* For master's, audition, minimum GPA of 3.0.

New York University, Steinhardt School of Culture, Education, and Human Development, Department of Music and Performing Arts Professions, Program in Drama Therapy, New York, NY 10012-1019. Offers MA. Part-time programs available. *Faculty:* 1 full-time (0 women). *Students:* 29 full-time (28 women), 10 part-time (8 women); includes 4 Black or African American, non-Hispanic/Latino; 1 American Indian or Alaska Native, non-Hispanic/Latino; 1 Asian, non-Hispanic/Latino; 2 Hispanic/Latino, 5 international. Average age 29. 70 applicants, 31% accepted, 19 enrolled. In 2010, 18 master's awarded. *Degree requirements:* For master's, thesis (for some programs). *Entrance requirements:* For master's, audition, interview. Additional exam requirements/recommendations for international students: Required—TOEFL. *Application deadline:* For fall admission, 12/15 priority date for domestic and international students; for spring admission, 11/1 for domestic and international students. Applications are processed on a rolling basis. Application fee: $75. Electronic applications accepted. *Financial support:* Career-related internships or fieldwork, Federal Work-Study, institutionally sponsored loans, scholarships/grants, and tuition waivers (partial) available. Support available to part-time students. Financial award application deadline: 2/1; financial award applicants required to submit FAFSA. *Faculty research:* Meaning of role in drama, therapy, and everyday life; clinical approaches to drama therapy; trauma effects on children. *Unit head:* Dr. Robert Landy, Director, 212-998-5424. *Application contact:* 212-998-5030, Fax: 212-995-4328, E-mail: steinhardt.gradadmissions@nyu.edu.

New York University, Steinhardt School of Culture, Education, and Human Development, Department of Music and Performing Arts Professions, Program in Music Therapy, New York, NY 10012-1019. Offers MA. Part-time programs available. *Faculty:* 1 (woman) full-time. *Students:* 27 full-time (20 women), 18 part-time (11 women); includes 2 Black or African American, non-Hispanic/Latino; 3 Asian, non-Hispanic/Latino; 2 Hispanic/Latino, 13 international. Average age 30. 81 applicants, 30% accepted, 20 enrolled. In 2010, 20 master's awarded. *Degree requirements:* For master's, thesis (for some programs). *Entrance requirements:* For master's, audition, interview. Additional exam requirements/recommendations for international students: Required—TOEFL. *Application deadline:* For fall admission, 12/1 priority date for domestic and international students. Applications are processed on a rolling basis. Application fee: $75. Electronic applications accepted. *Financial support:* Career-related internships or fieldwork, Federal Work-Study, institutionally sponsored loans, scholarships/grants, and tuition waivers (partial) available. Support available to part-time students. Financial award application deadline: 2/1; financial award applicants required to submit FAFSA. *Faculty research:* Music therapy in special education, including autism and emotional disabilities; guided imagery. *Unit head:* Prof. Barbara Hesser, Director, 212-998-5424, Fax: 212-995-4043. *Application contact:* 212-998-5030, Fax: 212-995-4328, E-mail: steinhardt.gradadmissions@nyu.edu.

Ohio University, Graduate College, College of Fine Arts, School of Music, Athens, OH 45701-2979. Offers accompanying (MM); composition (MM); conducting (MM); history/literature (MM); music education (MM); music therapy (MM); performance (MM, Certificate); performance/pedagogy (MM); theory (MM). *Accreditation:* NASM. Part-time and evening/weekend programs available. Postbaccalaureate distance learning degree programs offered (minimal on-campus study). *Students:* 42 full-time (19 women), 7 part-time (3 women); includes 6 minority (2 Black or African American, non-Hispanic/Latino; 1 Asian, non-Hispanic/Latino; 2 Hispanic/Latino; 1 Two or more races, non-Hispanic/Latino), 9 international. 65 applicants, 52% accepted, 16 enrolled. In 2010, 12 master's awarded. *Degree requirements:* For master's, comprehensive exam, thesis (for some programs), oral exam. *Entrance requirements:* For master's, audition, interview, portfolio, recordings (varies by program). Additional exam requirements/recommendations for international students: Required—TOEFL (minimum score 550 paper-based; 80 iBT) or IELTS (minimum score 6.5). *Application deadline:* For fall admission, 1/1 priority date for domestic and international students. Application fee: $50 ($55 for international students). Electronic applications accepted. *Financial support:* In 2010–11, 35 teaching assistantships with full and partial tuition reimbursements (averaging $4,500 per year) were awarded; career-related internships or fieldwork, Federal Work-Study, institutionally sponsored loans, and tuition waivers (full and partial) also available. Financial award application deadline: 1/1. *Unit head:* Dr. W. Michael Parkinson, Director, 740-593-4244, Fax: 740-593-1429, E-mail: parkinsw@ohio.edu. *Application contact:* Dr. Richard Wetzel, Graduate Chair, 740-593-1652, Fax: 740-593-1429, E-mail: wetzel@ohio.edu.

Pratt Institute, School of Art and Design, Programs in Creative Arts Therapy, Brooklyn, NY 11205-3899. Offers art therapy and creativity development (MPS); art therapy-special education (MPS); dance/movement therapy (MS). *Accreditation:* NASAD (one or more programs are accredited). Part-time programs available. *Faculty:* 3 full-time (all women), 19 part-time/adjunct (16 women). *Students:* 103 full-time (97 women), 1 (woman) part-time; includes 4 Black or African American, non-Hispanic/Latino; 7 Asian, non-Hispanic/Latino; 8 Hispanic/Latino; 2 Two or more races, non-Hispanic/Latino, 7 international. Average age 29. 192 applicants, 34% accepted, 32 enrolled. In 2010, 41 master's awarded. *Degree requirements:* For master's, thesis. *Entrance requirements:* For master's, letters of recommendation, portfolio. Additional exam requirements/recommendations for international students: Required—TOEFL (minimum score 600 paper-based; 250 computer-based; 100 iBT). *Application deadline:* For fall admission, 1/5 for domestic and international students; for spring admission, 10/1 for domestic and international students. Applications are processed on a rolling basis. Application fee: $50 ($90 for international students). Electronic applications accepted. *Expenses:* Tuition: Full-time $22,734; part-time $1263 per credit. Required fees: $1280. *Financial support:* Career-related internships or fieldwork, Federal Work-Study, institutionally sponsored loans, scholarships/grants, health care benefits, tuition waivers (full), and unspecified assistantships available. Support available to part-time students. Financial award application deadline: 2/1; financial award applicants required to submit FAFSA. *Faculty research:* Psychology and aesthetic interaction, art therapy and AIDS, art therapy and autism, art diagnosis. *Unit head:* Jean Davis, Chairperson, 718-636-3428, E-mail: jdavis@pratt.edu. *Application contact:* Young Hah, Director of Graduate Admissions, 718-636-3683, Fax: 718-399-4242, E-mail: yhah@pratt.edu.

See Display on page 92 and Close-Up on page 131.

Radford University, College of Graduate and Professional Studies, College of Visual and Performing Arts, Department of Music, Radford, VA 24142. Offers music (MA); music education (MS); music therapy (MS). *Accreditation:* NASM. Part-time programs available. *Faculty:* 13 full-time (3 women), 7 part-time/adjunct (3 women). *Students:* 16 full-time (9 women), 2 part-time (both women); includes 1 minority (Black or African American, non-Hispanic/Latino), 1 international. Average age 28. 16 applicants, 94% accepted, 11 enrolled. In 2010, 9 master's awarded. *Degree requirements:* For master's, comprehensive exam, thesis or alternative. *Entrance requirements:* For master's, GRE, major field test in music or PRAXIS II (content knowledge), written diagnostics exams in music, minimum GPA of 2.75; 3 letters of reference. Additional exam requirements/recommendations for international students: Required—TOEFL (minimum score 550 paper-based; 213 computer-based; 79 iBT). *Application deadline:* For fall admission, 2/15 priority date for domestic students, 12/1 for international students; for spring admission, 7/1 for international students. Applications are processed on a rolling basis. Application fee: $50. Electronic applications accepted. *Expenses:* Tuition, state resident: full-time $5746; part-time $239 per credit hour. Tuition, nonresident: full-time $14,174; part-time $591 per credit hour. Required fees: $2634; $111 per credit hour. *Financial support:* In 2010–11, 13 students received support, including 4 research assistantships with partial tuition reimbursements available (averaging $8,000 per year), 8 teaching assistantships with partial tuition reimbursements available (averaging $8,700 per year); career-related internships or fieldwork, Federal Work-Study, institutionally sponsored loans, scholarships/grants, and unspecified assistantships also available. Financial award application deadline: 3/1; financial award applicants required to submit FAFSA. *Unit head:* Dr. Allen F. Wojtera, Chair, 540-831-5177, Fax: 540-831-6133, E-mail: awojtera@radford.edu. *Application contact:* Rebecca Conner, Graduate Admissions, 540-831-5431, Fax: 540-831-6061, E-mail: gradcollege@radford.edu.

Saint Mary-of-the-Woods College, Program in Music Therapy, Saint Mary-of-the-Woods, IN 47876. Offers MA. *Accreditation:* NASM. Part-time programs available. Postbaccalaureate distance learning degree programs offered (minimal on-campus study). *Degree requirements:* For master's, thesis or alternative, qualifying exam, portfolio completion. *Entrance requirements:* For master's, diagnostic music exam, audition. Electronic applications accepted.

Shenandoah University, Shenandoah Conservatory, Winchester, VA 22601-5195. Offers arts management (MS); church music (MM, Certificate); collaborative piano (MM); composition (MM); conducting (MM); music education (MME, DMA); music therapy (MMT, Certificate); pedagogy (MM, DMA); performance (MM, DMA, Artist Diploma). *Accreditation:* NASM. *Faculty:* 38 full-time (15 women), 14 part-time/adjunct (5 women). *Students:* 63 full-time (38 women), 119 part-time (76 women); includes 18 minority (7 Black or African American, non-Hispanic/Latino; 5 Asian, non-Hispanic/Latino; 5 Hispanic/Latino; 1 Two or more races, non-Hispanic/Latino), 40 international. Average age 34. 109 applicants, 75% accepted, 51 enrolled. In 2010, 29 master's, 12 doctorates, 14 other advanced degrees awarded. *Degree requirements:* For master's, comprehensive exam (for some programs), thesis (for some programs), internship (MS), recital (MM), research teaching project or thesis (MME), project (MA); for doctorate, comprehensive exam, thesis/dissertation (for some programs), dissertation or teaching project, recital; for other advanced degree, research project, recital. *Entrance requirements:* For master's, audition, minimum GPA of 2.5, writing sample, resume; for doctorate, audition, minimum GPA of 3.25, 2 letters of recommendation, writing sample, resume; for other advanced degree, bachelor's or master's degree; minimum GPA of 2.5. Additional exam requirements/recommendations for international students: Required—TOEFL (minimum score 550 paper-based; 213 computer-based; 79 iBT), IELTS (minimum score 6.5), Sakae Institute of Study Abroad (550). *Application deadline:* Applications are processed on a rolling basis. Application fee: $30. Electronic applications accepted. *Expenses:* Tuition: Full-time $17,352; part-time $723 per credit. Tuition and fees vary according to course load and program. *Financial support:* Application deadline: 3/15. *Unit head:* Dr. Michael J. Stepniak, Dean, 540-665-4600, Fax: 540-665-5402, E-mail: mstepnia@su.edu. *Application contact:* David Anthony, Dean of Admissions, 540-665-4581, Fax: 540-665-4627, E-mail: admit@su.edu.

State University of New York at New Paltz, Graduate School, School of Fine and Performing Arts, Department of Music, New Paltz, NY 12561. Offers music therapy (MS). *Accreditation:* NASM. Part-time programs available. *Faculty:* 5 full-time (4 women), 3 part-time/adjunct (all women). *Students:* 21 full-time (18 women), 13 part-time (9 women); includes 3 Asian, non-Hispanic/Latino, 6 international. Average age 29. 22 applicants, 68% accepted, 14 enrolled. In 2010, 10 master's awarded. *Degree requirements:* For master's, thesis. *Entrance requirements:* For master's, audition, minimum GPA of 3.0. Additional exam requirements/recommendations for international students: Required—TOEFL (minimum score 550 paper-based; 213 computer-based; 80 iBT), IELTS (minimum score 6.5). *Application deadline:* For fall admission, 5/15 for domestic and international students; for spring admission, 11/15 for domestic and international students. Application fee: $50. Electronic applications accepted. *Expenses:* Tuition, state resident: full-time $8370; part-time $349 per credit hour. Tuition, nonresident: full-time $13,780; part-time $574 per credit hour. Required fees: $1165; $33.80 per credit hour. $175 per term. Tuition and fees vary according to program. *Financial support:* In 2010–11, 3 students received support, including 3 teaching assistantships with partial tuition reimbursements available (averaging $5,000 per year). Financial award application deadline: 8/1; financial award applicants required to submit FAFSA. *Unit head:* Dr. Carole Cowan, Chair, 845-257-2701, E-mail: cowanc@newpaltz.edu. *Application contact:* Dr. Carole Cowan, Chair, 845-257-2701, E-mail: cowanc@newpaltz.edu.

Temple University, Esther Boyer College of Music and Dance, Philadelphia, PA 19122-6096. Offers Ed M, MFA, MM, MMT, DMA, PhD. *Accreditation:* NASM. Part-time and evening/weekend programs available. *Faculty:* 41 full-time (16 women). *Students:* 211 full-time (137 women), 64 part-time (38 women); includes 10 Black or African American, non-Hispanic/Latino; 18 Asian, non-Hispanic/Latino; 11 Hispanic/Latino; 1 Native Hawaiian or other Pacific Islander, non-Hispanic/Latino, 52 international. Average age 29. 418 applicants, 36% accepted, 89 enrolled. In 2010, 61 master's, 3 doctorates awarded. *Degree requirements:* For doctorate, thesis/dissertation. *Entrance requirements:* Additional exam requirements/recommendations for international students: Required—TOEFL. *Application deadline:* For fall admission, 12/15 for international students; for spring admission, 8/1 for international students. Applications are processed on a rolling basis. Application fee: $50. Electronic applications accepted. *Financial support:* Fellowships with full and partial tuition reimbursements, research assistantships with full and partial tuition reimbursements, teaching assistantships with full and partial tuition reimbursements, career-related internships or fieldwork, Federal Work-Study, and scholarships/grants available. Financial award application deadline: 1/15; financial award applicants required to submit FAFSA. *Faculty research:* Music-learning theory, guided imagery in music, computer music synthesis, musical instrument digital interface (MIDI) applications. *Unit head:* Dr. Robert T. Stroker, Dean, 215-204-5527, Fax: 215-204-4957, E-mail: rstroker@temple.edu. *Application contact:* Dr. Robert T. Stroker, Dean, 215-204-5527, Fax: 215-204-4957, E-mail: rstroker@temple.edu.

The University of Kansas, Graduate Studies, School of Music, Program in Music Therapy, Lawrence, KS 66045. Offers MME. *Faculty:* 8 full-time, 2 part-time/adjunct. *Students:* 8 full-time (all women), 11 part-time (10 women); includes 2 minority (both Asian, non-Hispanic/Latino), 2 international. Average age 29. 19 applicants, 74% accepted, 7 enrolled. In 2010, 5 master's awarded. *Degree requirements:* For master's, comprehensive exam, thesis or alternative. *Entrance requirements:* For master's, GRE General Test, minimum undergraduate GPA of 3.0, video, reference letters, transcripts. Additional exam requirements/recommendations for international students: Required—TOEFL (minimum score 570 paper-based; 230 computer-based; 92 iBT), IELTS, Required: TOEFL minimum score 570 paper-based, 230 CBI, 92 iBT or 6.0 band scores on IELTS; Recommended—TWE. *Application deadline:* For fall admission, 2/15 priority date for domestic students, 2/15 for international students. Applications are processed on a rolling basis. Application fee: $55 ($65 for international students). Electronic applications accepted. *Expenses:* Tuition, state resident: full-time $7092; part-time $295.50 per credit hour. Tuition, nonresident: full-time $16,590; part-time $691.25 per credit hour. Required fees: $858; $71.49 per credit hour. Tuition and fees vary according to course load, campus/location and program. *Financial support:* Fellowships, research assistantships with partial tuition reimbursements, teaching assistantships with full and partial tuition reimbursements, institutionally sponsored loans, scholarships/grants, and unspecified assistantships available. Financial award application deadline: 12/15; financial award applicants required to submit FAFSA. *Faculty research:* Music therapy in health, wellness, gerontology, pediatrics, early intervention, autism and hospice; Orff music therapy; influence of music on behavior. *Unit head:* Robert Walzel, Dean, 785-864-3421, Fax: 785-864-5366, E-mail: music@ku.edu. *Application contact:* Dr. James Daugherty, Director of Graduate Studies, 785-864-9637, Fax: 785-864-9640, E-mail: jdaugher@ku.edu.

University of Miami, Graduate School, Frost School of Music, Department of Music Education and Music Therapy, Coral Gables, FL 33124. Offers music education (MM, PhD, Spec M); music therapy (MM). *Accreditation:* NASM. *Degree requirements:* For master's, thesis; for doctorate, thesis/dissertation, 2 research tools; for Spec M, thesis, research project. *Entrance requirements:* For master's and doctorate, GRE General Test. Additional exam requirements/recommendations for international students: Required—TOEFL (minimum score 550 paper-based; 213 computer-based; 59 iBT). Electronic applications accepted. *Faculty research:* Motivation, quantitative research, early childhood, instrumental music, elementary music.

University of the Pacific, Conservatory of Music, Program in Music Therapy, Stockton, CA 95211-0197. Offers MA. *Faculty:* 2 full-time (both women). *Students:* 11 full-time (9 women), 9 part-time (7 women); includes 3 Asian, non-Hispanic/Latino; 1 Hispanic/Latino, 3 international. Average age 30. 18 applicants, 44% accepted, 4 enrolled. *Degree requirements:* For master's, thesis (for some programs). *Entrance requirements:* For master's, GRE General Test. Additional exam requirements/recommendations for international students: Required—TOEFL (minimum score 475 paper-based; 150 computer-based). Application fee: $75. *Financial support:* Teaching assistantships, institutionally sponsored loans available. Support available to part-time students. Financial award application deadline: 3/1; financial award applicants required to submit FAFSA. *Unit head:* Dr. Therese West, Chairperson, 209-946-3194. *Application contact:* Dr. Therese West, Chairperson, 209-946-3194.

Western Michigan University, Graduate College, College of Fine Arts, School of Music, Kalamazoo, MI 49008. Offers composition (MM); conducting (MM); music (MA); music education (MM); music therapy (MM); performance (MM). *Accreditation:* NASM.

Wilfrid Laurier University, Faculty of Graduate and Postdoctoral Studies, Faculty of Music, Waterloo, ON N2L 3C5, Canada. Offers MMT. *Faculty:* 2 full-time (1 woman). *Students:* 13 full-time (11 women). 13 applicants, 54% accepted, 5 enrolled. In 2010, 9 master's awarded. *Entrance requirements:* For master's, 4-year honours BA in music therapy with minimum B average in final year, grade 6 RCM and grade 10 performance ability (for 1-year program); 4-year honours BA in allied area (music or psychology) with minimum B average in final year, grade 6 RCM, grade 10 performance ability (for 2-year program). Additional exam requirements/recommendations for international students: Required—TOEFL (minimum score 89 iBT). *Application deadline:* For fall admission, 4/15 priority date for domestic and international students. Application fee: $125. Electronic applications accepted. Tuition and fees charges are reported in Canadian dollars. *Expenses:* Tuition, area resident: Full-time $15,300 Canadian dollars; part-time $1200 Canadian dollars per credit. International tuition: $21,300 Canadian dollars full-time. Required fees: $650 Canadian dollars; $100 Canadian dollars per credit. Tuition and fees vary according to course load, degree level, campus/location and program. *Financial support:* In 2010–11, 9 fellowships, 9 teaching assistantships were awarded; career-related internships or fieldwork, scholarships/grants, health care benefits, and unspecified assistantships also available. *Faculty research:* Group analytic music therapy, music psychotherapy, low frequency sound wave, aesthetic music therapy. *Unit head:* Dr. Colin Lee, Graduate Coordinator, 519-884-1970 Ext. 2892, Fax: 519-747-9129, E-mail: clee@wlu.ca. *Application contact:* Jennifer Willaims, Graduate Admissions and Records Officer, 519-884-0710 Ext. 3536, Fax: 519-884-1020, E-mail: gradstudies@wlu.ca.

COLUMBIA UNIVERSITY

School of the Arts
Programs in Film, Theatre Arts, Visual Arts, and Writing

Programs of Study	The School of the Arts offers M.F.A. degrees in film (concentrations in screenwriting/directing and creative producing); theater arts (concentrations in acting, directing, dramaturgy, playwriting, stage management, and theater management and producing); visual arts (areas of study include digital media, drawing, painting, photography, printmaking, sculpture, installation, performance, and video art); and writing (concentrations in fiction, creative nonfiction, and poetry) and an M.A. degree in film studies. In addition, a Ph.D. in theater is available through the Graduate School of Arts and Sciences, and a joint J.D./M.F.A. in theater management and producing is available in conjunction with Columbia Law School. The School also offers summer programs, including master classes; workshops; and credit and noncredit courses in film, theater arts, visual arts and writing; and global programs around the world.

The School of the Arts enrolls full-time students only, except in the M.A. in film studies program, where students can attend part-time. The M.F.A. degree programs require 60 points of completed course work. Once the 60 points of course work are completed, each student completes a thesis and/or internships, often under Research Arts student status.

Prospective students should visit http://arts.columbia.edu for all specific program requirements and information.

Research Facilities

The School of the Arts is located on Columbia's Morningside campus in the vibrant Upper West Side of Manhattan, with New York City's world-renowned museums, Broadway and Off-Broadway theaters, film centers, galleries, cultural foundations, poetry houses and literary hubs all nearby. The School is also home to Miller Theatre, the LeRoy Neiman Center for Print Studies, the Columbia University Arts Initiative, and the Office of Community Outreach for the Arts. The University's twenty-two libraries and countless research centers and institutes are all also available for students.

Financial Aid

The School of the Arts and Columbia University Office of Student Financial Planning work carefully with students to arrange the financing of their degrees. Loan packages, fellowships, scholarships, and other options are available for eligible students. Students are encouraged to actively explore all options, even before acceptance into the school, to develop a plan to support the costs of graduate study.

More information is available at http://arts.columbia.edu/financing-your-degree.

Cost of Study

Tuition and fees for 2011–12 are approximately $50,000 for the year, based on full-time matriculation of 12 to 18 credits per semester.

Living and Housing Costs

The University estimates that students need about $23,000 per year to cover living expenses and housing in New York City. Students can find housing around campus in the Morningside Heights neighborhood, in surrounding Manhattan neighborhoods and boroughs, and in the greater New York area. Columbia University apartment housing consists of a limited number of apartment shares; dormitory-style rooms; and one-bedroom, studio, and family units for which priority is given to couples and families. This housing is primarily located within walking distance of campus.

Additional details are available at http://facilities.columbia.edu/housing.

Student Group

In fall 2010 the School enrolled 862 students from more than forty countries: 341 in film, 162 in theater arts, 305 in writing, and 54 in visual arts.

Location

Columbia University (including Barnard College and Teacher's College) occupies approximately eighteen square blocks in the Morningside Heights area of Manhattan. The School of the Arts is on the Morningside Campus, at 116th Street and Broadway on the Upper West Side of Manhattan

The University and The School

Columbia, founded in 1754, is comprised of three undergraduate schools, thirteen graduate and professional schools, and a school of continuing education. Additional information is available at http://arts.columbia.edu/columbia-university.

Applying

Applications are accepted for the fall semester only. The application cost for fall 2012 is $110 for the online application and $175 for the paper application. The GRE is not required for application. International students are required to take the TOEFL prior to application; the minimum score required for admission is 600 on the written test, 250 on the computer-based test, and 100 on the Internet-based test.

Deadlines and more information are available at http://arts.columbia.edu/apply.

Correspondence and Information

Office of Admissions
School of the Arts
Columbia University
305 Dodge Hall, MC 1808
2960 Broadway
New York, New York 10027
Phone: 212-854-2134
E-mail: admissions-arts@columbia.edu
Web site: http://arts.columbia.edu

Columbia University

THE FACULTY

The faculty is comprised of acclaimed and internationally renowned artists, film and theater directors, playwrights, producers, poets, writers of fiction and nonfiction, critics, and scholars.

Additional information about full-time and adjunct faculty members is available at http://arts.columbia.edu.

ACADEMIC AND PROFESSIONAL PROGRAMS IN THE HUMANITIES

Section 7
History

This section contains a directory of institutions offering graduate work in history. Additional information about programs listed in the directory may be obtained by writing directly to the dean of a graduate school or chair of a department at the address given in the directory.

For programs offering related work, see also in this book *Area and Cultural Studies, Architecture, Humanities, Political Science and International Affairs,* and *Sociology, Anthropology, and Archaeology.*

CONTENTS

Program Directories

History

Adams State College, The Graduate School, Department of History, Government and Philosophy, Alamosa, CO 81102. Offers history (MA).

American Public University System, AMU/APU Graduate Programs, Charles Town, WV 25414. Offers accounting (MBA); administration and supervision (M Ed); air warfare (MA Military Studies); asymmetrical warfare (MA Military Studies); criminal justice (MA); emergency and disaster management (MA); entrepreneurship (MBA); environmental policy and management (MS); finance (MBA); general (MBA); global business management (MBA); guidance and counseling (M Ed); history (MA); homeland security (MA); homeland security resource allocation (MBA); humanities (MA); information technology (MS); information technology management (MBA); intelligence studies (MA); international relations and conflict resolution (MA); joint warfare (MA Military Studies); land warfare (MA Military Studies); legal studies (MA); management (MA), including defense mangement, general, human resource management, organizational leadership, public administration; marketing (MBA); military history (MA); national security studies (MA); naval warfare (MA Military Studies); nonprofit management (MBA); political science (MA); psychology (MA); public administration (MA); public health (MA); security management (MA); space studies (MS); sports management (MS); strategic leadership (MA Military Studies); teaching (M Ed), including elementary, secondary social sciences; transportation and logistics management (MA). Programs offered via distance learning only. Part-time and evening/weekend programs available. Postbaccalaureate distance learning degree programs offered (no on-campus study). *Faculty:* 253 full-time (134 women), 1,208 part-time/adjunct (570 women). *Students:* 956 full-time (422 women), 8,476 part-time (2,821 women); includes 2,511 minority (1,218 Black or African American, non-Hispanic/Latino; 68 American Indian or Alaska Native, non-Hispanic/Latino; 219 Asian, non-Hispanic/Latino; 705 Hispanic/Latino; 46 Native Hawaiian or other Pacific Islander, non-Hispanic/Latino; 255 Two or more races, non-Hispanic/Latino), 107 international. Average age 35. 9,550 applicants, 100% accepted. In 2010, 1,688 master's awarded. *Degree requirements:* For master's, comprehensive exam or practicum. *Entrance requirements:* For master's, official transcript showing earned bachelor's degree from institution accredited by recognized accrediting body. Additional exam requirements/recommendations for international students: Required—TOEFL (minimum score 550 paper-based; 213 computer-based), IELTS (minimum score 6.5). *Application deadline:* Applications are processed on a rolling basis. Application fee: $0. Electronic applications accepted. *Financial support:* Applicants required to submit FAFSA. *Faculty research:* Military history, criminal justice, management performance, national security. *Unit head:* Dr. Frank McCluskey, Provost, 877-468-6268, Fax: 304-724-3780. *Application contact:* Terry Grant, Director of Enrollment Management, 877-468-6268, Fax: 304-724-3780, E-mail: info@apus.edu.

American University, College of Arts and Sciences, Department of History, Washington, DC 20016-8038. Offers MA, PhD. Part-time and evening/weekend programs available. *Faculty:* 23 full-time (13 women), 6 part-time/adjunct (3 women). *Students:* 35 full-time (18 women), 65 part-time (32 women); includes 10 minority (5 Black or African American, non-Hispanic/Latino; 3 Asian, non-Hispanic/Latino; 2 Hispanic/Latino), 5 international. Average age 31. 141 applicants, 57% accepted, 29 enrolled. In 2010, 17 master's, 2 doctorates awarded. *Degree requirements:* For master's, comprehensive exam, thesis or alternative, tools of research in foreign language, methods, history or methodology; for doctorate, thesis/dissertation, tools of research, 2 seminars, 2 colloquia. *Entrance requirements:* For master's, GRE, two letters of recommendation; for doctorate, GRE, two letters of recommendation, sample of written work. Additional exam requirements/recommendations for international students: Required—TOEFL. *Application deadline:* For fall admission, 2/1 priority date for domestic students; for spring admission, 10/1 priority date for domestic students. Application fee: $80. *Financial support:* In 2010–11, 20 students received support; fellowships, research assistantships with tuition reimbursements available, teaching assistantships with tuition reimbursements available, career-related internships or fieldwork, institutionally sponsored loans, tuition waivers (full and partial), and unspecified assistantships available. Financial award application deadline: 2/1. *Faculty research:* U. S. political and diplomatic history, modern European history, U. S. social and cultural history, recent U. S. history, early republic, modern Europe. *Unit head:* Dr. Katharina Vester, Chair, 202-885-2409, Fax: 202-885-6166, E-mail: vester@american.edu. *Application contact:* Kathleen Clowery, Director of Graduate Admissions, 202-885-3621, Fax: 202-885-1505, E-mail: clowery@american.edu.

American University of Beirut, Graduate Programs, Faculty of Arts and Sciences, Beirut, Lebanon. Offers anthropology (MA); Arabic language and literature (MA); archaeology (MA); biology (MS); chemistry (MS); computational science (MS); computer science (MS); economics (MA); education (MA); English language (MA); English literature (MA); environmental policy planning (MSES); financial economics (MAFE); geology (MS); history (MA); mathematics (MA, MS); Middle Eastern studies (MA); philosophy (MA); physics (MS); political studies (MA); psychology (MA); public administration (MA); sociology (MA); statistics (MA, MS). Part-time programs available. *Faculty:* 229 full-time (98 women), 136 part-time/adjunct (79 women). *Students:* 158 full-time (104 women), 263 part-time (171 women). Average age 25. 356 applicants, 59% accepted, 127 enrolled. In 2010, 57 master's awarded. *Degree requirements:* For master's, one foreign language, comprehensive exam, thesis (for some programs). *Entrance requirements:* For master's, GRE, letter of recommendation. Additional exam requirements/recommendations for international students: Required—TOEFL (minimum score 600 paper-based; 250 computer-based; 97 iBT), IELTS (minimum score 7). *Application deadline:* For fall admission, 4/30 for domestic and international students; for spring admission, 11/1 for domestic and international students. Application fee: $50. *Expenses:* Tuition: Full-time $12,294; part-time $683 per credit. Required fees: $499; $499 per credit. Tuition and fees vary according to course load and program. *Financial support:* In 2010–11, 33 students received support. Career-related internships or fieldwork, institutionally sponsored loans, scholarships/grants, health care benefits, and unspecified assistantships available. Financial award application deadline: 2/4; financial award applicants required to submit FAFSA. *Faculty research:* Modern and contemporary world theatre; mineralogy, petrology, and geochemistry; cell differentiation and transformation; combinatorial technologies; philosophy of action; continental philosophy; Phoenician epigraphy; nascent complex societies and urbanism; the economies of the Arab world; environmental economics; tectonophysics; host-parasite interactions; innate immunity; insect-plant interactions; history of the Ottoman archives; decentralization; transparency and corruption. Total annual research expenditures: $622,243. *Unit head:* Dr. Patrick McGreevy, Dean, 961-137-4374 Ext. 3800, Fax: 961-174-4461, E-mail: pm07@aub.edu.lb. *Application contact:* Dr. Salim Kanaan, Director, Admissions Office, 961-135-0000 Ext. 2594, Fax: 961-175-0775, E-mail: sk00@aub.edu.lb.

Andrews University, School of Graduate Studies, College of Arts and Sciences, Department of History, Berrien Springs, MI 49104. Offers MA, MAT. Part-time programs available. *Degree requirements:* For master's, variable foreign language requirement, thesis optional. *Entrance requirements:* For master's, GRE Subject Test. *Faculty research:* American intellectual history, Civil War, American church history, modern German history.

Angelo State University, College of Graduate Studies, College of Liberal and Fine Arts, Department of History, San Angelo, TX 76909. Offers MA. Part-time and evening/weekend programs available. *Faculty:* 3 full-time (0 women). *Students:* 1 (woman) full-time, 8 part-time (5 women). Average age 38. 10 applicants, 60% accepted, 6 enrolled. In 2010, 3 master's awarded. *Degree requirements:* For master's, comprehensive exam, thesis optional. *Entrance requirements:* For master's, GRE General Test, essay. Additional exam requirements/recommendations for international students: Required—TOEFL or IELTS. *Application deadline:* For fall admission, 7/15 priority date for domestic students, 6/10 for international students; for spring admission, 12/1 priority date for domestic students, 11/1 for international students. Applications are processed on a rolling basis. Application fee: $40 ($50 for international students). Electronic applications accepted. *Expenses:* Tuition, state resident: full-time $4560; part-time $152 per credit hour. Tuition, nonresident: full-time $13,860; part-time $462 per credit hour. Required fees: $2132. Tuition and fees vary according to course load. *Financial support:* In 2010–11, 4 students received support. Federal Work-Study, scholarships/grants, and unspecified assistantships available. Support available to part-time students. Financial award application deadline: 3/1. *Unit head:* Dr. Ken Heineman, Department Head, 325-942-2113, Fax: 325-942-2057, E-mail: kenneth.heineman@angelo.edu. *Application contact:* Dr. Shirley Eoff, Graduate Advisor, 325-942-2203 Ext. 2722, Fax: 325-942-2057, E-mail: shirley.eoff@angelo.edu.

Appalachian State University, Cratis D. Williams Graduate School, Department of History, Boone, NC 28608. Offers history (MA); public history (MA). Part-time programs available. Postbaccalaureate distance learning degree programs offered (no on-campus study). *Faculty:* 30 full-time (11 women), 1 part-time/adjunct (0 women). *Students:* 31 full-time (13 women), 13 part-time (6 women); includes 1 Black or African American, non-Hispanic/Latino; 1 Asian, non-Hispanic/Latino. 52 applicants, 81% accepted, 22 enrolled. In 2010, 20 master's awarded. *Degree requirements:* For master's, one foreign language, comprehensive exam, thesis (for some programs). *Entrance requirements:* For master's, GRE General Test, 3 letters of recommendation. Additional exam requirements/recommendations for international students: Required—TOEFL (minimum score 570 paper-based; 230 computer-based; 79 iBT), IELTS (minimum score 6.5). *Application deadline:* For fall admission, 7/1 for domestic students, 2/1 for international students; for spring admission, 11/1 for domestic students, 7/1 for international students. Applications are processed on a rolling basis. Application fee: $55. Electronic applications accepted. *Expenses:* Tuition, state resident: full-time $3428; part-time $428 per unit. Tuition, nonresident: full-time $14,518; part-time $1814 per unit. Required fees: $2320; $344 per unit. Tuition and fees vary according to campus/location. *Financial support:* In 2010–11, 4 research assistantships (averaging $10,000 per year), 7 teaching assistantships (averaging $8,000 per year) were awarded; fellowships, career-related internships or fieldwork, Federal Work-Study, scholarships/grants, and unspecified assistantships also available. Financial award application deadline: 4/1; financial award applicants required to submit FAFSA. *Faculty research:* Women's history, social/cultural history, U. S. history, Latin America, medieval studies. Total annual research expenditures: $298,000. *Unit head:* Dr. Lucinda McCray, Chairperson, 828-262-2282, E-mail: mccraylm@appstate.edu. *Application contact:* Dr. Lisa Holliday, Graduate Program Director, 828-262-6014, E-mail: hollidaylr@appstate.edu.

Arizona State University, College of Liberal Arts and Sciences, School of Historical, Philosophical and Religious Studies, Tempe, AZ 85287-4301. Offers East/Southeast Asian history (MA, PhD); European history (MA, PhD); Latin American studies (MA, PhD); North American history (MA, PhD); philosophy (MA, PhD); public history (MA); religious studies (MA, PhD); scholarly publishing (Graduate Certificate). Part-time programs available. *Faculty:* 70 full-time (29 women), 2 part-time/adjunct (0 women). *Students:* 125 full-time (58 women), 68 part-time (37 women); includes 21 minority (5 Black or African American, non-Hispanic/Latino; 3 American Indian or Alaska Native, non-Hispanic/Latino; 1 Asian, non-Hispanic/Latino; 11 Hispanic/Latino; 1 Two or more races, non-Hispanic/Latino), 16 international. Average age 34. 221 applicants, 51% accepted, 41 enrolled. In 2010, 24 master's, 10 doctorates, 3 other advanced degrees awarded. Terminal master's awarded for partial completion of doctoral program. *Degree requirements:* For master's, thesis or alternative, interactive Program of Study (iPOS) submitted before completing 50 percent of required credit hours; for doctorate, variable foreign language requirement, comprehensive exam, thesis/dissertation, interactive Program of Study (iPOS) submitted before completing 50 percent of required credit hours. *Entrance requirements:* For master's and doctorate, GRE, minimum GPA of 3.0 or equivalent in last 2 years of work leading to bachelor's degree. Additional exam requirements/recommendations for international students: Required—TOEFL, IELTS, or Pearson Test of English. *Application deadline:* For fall admission, 1/1 for domestic and international students. Applications are processed on a rolling basis. Application fee: $70 ($90 for international students). Electronic applications accepted. *Expenses:* Tuition, state resident: full-time $8510; part-time $608 per credit. Tuition, nonresident: full-time $16,542; part-time $919 per credit. Required fees: $339; $110 per credit. Part-time tuition and fees vary according to course load. *Financial support:* In 2010–11, 26 research assistantships with full and partial tuition reimbursements (averaging $12,900 per year), 69 teaching assistantships with full and partial tuition reimbursements (averaging $11,771 per year) were awarded; fellowships with full tuition reimbursements, career-related internships or fieldwork, institutionally sponsored loans, scholarships/grants, and tuition waivers (partial) also available. Financial award application deadline: 3/1; financial award applicants required to submit FAFSA. Total annual research expenditures: $1.3 million. *Unit head:* Mark Von Hagen, Director, 480-965-4186, E-mail: mark.vonhagen@asu.edu. *Application contact:* Graduate Admissions, 480-965-6113.

Arkansas State University, Graduate School, College of Humanities and Social Sciences, Department of History, Jonesboro, State University, AR 72467. Offers history (MA); history education (MSE, SCCT); social science education (MSE). Part-time programs available. *Faculty:* 14 full-time (7 women), 2 part-time/adjunct (both women). *Students:* 8 full-time (4 women), 25 part-time (16 women); includes 3 minority (2 Black or African American, non-Hispanic/Latino; 1 Hispanic/Latino). Average age 34. 18 applicants, 67% accepted, 7 enrolled. In 2010, 9 master's awarded. *Degree requirements:* For master's, comprehensive exam, thesis or alternative; for SCCT, comprehensive exam. *Entrance requirements:* For master's, GRE General Test or MAT, GMAT, appropriate bachelor's degree, letters of reference, official transcript, valid teaching certificate (for MSE), immunization records; for SCCT, GRE General Test or MAT, interview, master's degree, letters of reference, official transcript, immunization records. Additional exam requirements/recommendations for international students: Required—TOEFL (minimum score 550 paper-based; 213 computer-based; 79 iBT), IELTS (minimum score 6), PTE: Pearson Test of English Academic (56). *Application deadline:* For fall admission, 7/1 for domestic and international students; for spring admission, 11/15 for domestic students, 11/14 for international students. Applications are processed on a rolling basis. Application fee: $30 ($40 for international students). Electronic applications accepted. *Expenses:* Tuition, state resident: full-time $3888; part-time $216 per credit hour. Tuition, nonresident: full-time $9918; part-time $551 per credit hour. International tuition: $8376 full-time. Required fees: $932; $49 per credit hour. $25 per term. One-time fee: $30. Tuition and fees vary according to course load and program. *Financial support:* In 2010–11, 9 students received support. Career-related internships or fieldwork, scholarships/grants, and unspecified assistantships available. Financial award application deadline: 7/1; financial award applicants required to submit FAFSA. *Unit head:* Dr. Gina Hogue, Chair, 870-972-3046, Fax: 870-972-2880, E-mail: ghogue@astate.edu. *Application contact:* Dr. Andrew Sustich, Dean of the Graduate School, 870-972-3029, Fax: 870-972-3857, E-mail: sustich@astate.edu.

Arkansas Tech University, Graduate College, College of Arts and Humanities, Russellville, AR 72801. Offers communication (MLA); English (M Ed, MA); fine arts (MLA); history (MA); multi-media journalism (MA); psychology (MS); social science (MLA); Spanish (MA, MLA); teaching English as a second language (MA, MLA). Part-time programs available. *Students:* 39 full-time (23 women), 87 part-time (69 women); includes 13 minority (3 Black or African American, non-Hispanic/Latino; 1 American Indian or Alaska Native, non-Hispanic/Latino; 1 Asian, non-Hispanic/Latino; 8 Hispanic/Latino), 14 international. Average age 32. In 2010, 54 master's awarded. *Degree requirements:* For master's, comprehensive exam (for some programs), thesis (for some programs), project. *Entrance requirements:* For master's, GRE General Test or MAT. Additional exam requirements/recommendations for international students: Required—TOEFL (minimum score 550 paper-based; 213 computer-based; 79 iBT), IELTS (minimum score 6). *Application deadline:* For fall admission, 3/1 priority date for domestic students, 5/1 priority date for international students; for spring admission, 10/1 priority date for domestic and international students. Applications are processed on a rolling basis. Application fee: $0 ($50 for international students). Electronic applications accepted. *Expenses:* Tuition, state resident: full-time $4680; part-time $195 per credit hour. Tuition, nonresident: full-time $9360; part-time $390 per credit hour. Required fees: $714; $14 per credit hour. One-time fee:

$326 part-time. Tuition and fees vary according to course load. *Financial support:* In 2010–11, teaching assistantships with full tuition reimbursements (averaging $4,000 per year); research assistantships, career-related internships or fieldwork, Federal Work-Study, scholarships/grants, health care benefits, and unspecified assistantships also available. Support available to part-time students. Financial award application deadline: 4/15; financial award applicants required to submit FAFSA. *Unit head:* Dr. Micheal Tarver, Dean, 479-968-0274, Fax: 479-964-0812, E-mail: mtarver@atu.edu. *Application contact:* Dr. Mary B. Gunter, Dean of Graduate College, 479-968-0398, Fax: 479-964-0542, E-mail: graduate.school@atu.edu.

Armstrong Atlantic State University, School of Graduate Studies, Program in History, Savannah, GA 31419-1997. Offers MA. Part-time and evening/weekend programs available. *Degree requirements:* For master's, one foreign language, comprehensive exam, thesis (for some programs). *Entrance requirements:* For master's, GRE General Test, minimum GPA of 3.0, letters of recommendation, BA in history or equivalent. Additional exam requirements/recommendations for international students: Required—TOEFL (minimum score 523 paper-based; 193 computer-based). Electronic applications accepted. *Faculty research:* Public history; European, Latin American, African, and United State history.

Ashland Theological Seminary, Graduate Programs, Ashland, OH 44805. Offers biblical and theological studies (MA, MAR), including New Testament (MA), Old Testament (MA); Christian ministry (MAPT); Christian studies (Diploma); clinical counseling (MAC, MACC); historical studies (MA), including church history; ministry (D Min); pastoral ministry (M Div); theological studies (MA). *Accreditation:* ATS. Part-time programs available. *Faculty:* 23 full-time (6 women), 38 part-time/adjunct (15 women). *Students:* 464 full-time (258 women), 117 part-time (70 women); includes 240 minority (221 Black or African American, non-Hispanic/Latino; 4 American Indian or Alaska Native, non-Hispanic/Latino; 8 Asian, non-Hispanic/Latino; 7 Hispanic/Latino), 11 international. Average age 43. 89 applicants, 100% accepted, 88 enrolled. In 2010, 34 first professional degrees, 100 master's, 27 doctorates, 2 other advanced degrees awarded. *Degree requirements:* For master's, 2 foreign languages, comprehensive exam (for some programs), thesis (for some programs); for doctorate, thesis/dissertation; for M Div, 2 foreign languages, comprehensive exam (for some programs). *Entrance requirements:* For M Div, minimum GPA of 2.75; for master's, minimum undergraduate GPA of 2.75; for doctorate, M Div, minimum undergraduate GPA of 3.0. Additional exam requirements/recommendations for international students: Required—TOEFL (minimum score 500 paper-based; 173 computer-based; 65 iBT). *Application deadline:* For fall admission, 8/30 for domestic students. Applications are processed on a rolling basis. Application fee: $30. Electronic applications accepted. *Financial support:* In 2010–11, 156 students received support, including 17 teaching assistantships; research assistantships, career-related internships or fieldwork, institutionally sponsored loans, scholarships/grants, and unspecified assistantships also available. Support available to part-time students. Financial award application deadline: 5/15; financial award applicants required to submit FAFSA. *Faculty research:* Semitic languages and linguistics, rhetorical and social-scientific criticism, Anabaptist studies, inner spiritual healing, African-American clergy in film and literature. *Unit head:* Dr. John C. Shultz, President, 419-289-5160, Fax: 419-289-5969, E-mail: jshultz@ashland.edu. *Application contact:* Glenn Black, Director of Enrollment Management, 419-289-5151, Fax: 419-289-5969, E-mail: gblack@ashland.edu.

Ashland University, College of Arts and Sciences, Program in American History and Government, Ashland, OH 44805-3702. Offers MAHG. Part-time programs available. *Faculty:* 6 full-time (0 women), 36 part-time/adjunct (3 women). *Students:* 74 full-time (36 women), 65 part-time (31 women); includes 13 minority (1 Black or African American, non-Hispanic/Latino; 2 American Indian or Alaska Native, non-Hispanic/Latino; 4 Asian, non-Hispanic/Latino; 6 Hispanic/Latino). Average age 39. 91 applicants, 70% accepted, 44 enrolled. In 2010, 3 master's awarded. *Degree requirements:* For master's, capstone project or thesis. *Entrance requirements:* For master's, minimum undergraduate GPA of 2.75, 3.0 graduate. *Application deadline:* Applications are processed on a rolling basis. Application fee: $30. Electronic applications accepted. *Expenses:* Contact institution. *Financial support:* In 2010–11, 15 students received support. Application deadline: 4/15. *Faculty research:* American founding, United States Civil War, Progressive Era. *Unit head:* Dr. Peter W. Schramm, Chair, 419-289-5411, Fax: 419-289-5425, E-mail: pschramm@ashland.edu. *Application contact:* Christian A. Pascarella, Director, 419-289-5411, Fax: 419-289-5425, E-mail: cpascare@ashland.edu.

Auburn University, Graduate School, College of Liberal Arts, Department of History, Auburn University, AL 36849. Offers MA, PhD. Part-time programs available. *Faculty:* 31 full-time (10 women), 2 part-time/adjunct (0 women). *Students:* 23 full-time (6 women), 33 part-time (10 women); includes 3 Black or African American, non-Hispanic/Latino; 1 Hispanic/Latino, 1 international. Average age 34. 60 applicants, 50% accepted, 13 enrolled. In 2010, 8 master's, 9 doctorates awarded. *Degree requirements:* For master's, thesis, oral exam; for doctorate, 2 foreign languages, thesis/dissertation. *Entrance requirements:* For master's, GRE General Test; for doctorate, GRE General Test, master's degree with thesis. *Application deadline:* For fall admission, 7/7 for domestic students; for spring admission, 11/24 for domestic students. Applications are processed on a rolling basis. Application fee: $50 ($60 for international students). Electronic applications accepted. *Expenses:* Tuition, state resident: full-time $7002. Tuition, nonresident: full-time $21,898. International tuition: $22,116 full-time. Required fees: $892. Tuition and fees vary according to course load and program. *Financial support:* Teaching assistantships, Federal Work-Study available. Support available to part-time students. Financial award application deadline: 3/15; financial award applicants required to submit FAFSA. *Unit head:* David Carter, Graduate Program Officer, 334-844-6673. *Application contact:* Dr. George Flowers, Dean of the Graduate School, 334-844-2125.

Ball State University, Graduate School, College of Sciences and Humanities, Department of History, Muncie, IN 47306-1099. Offers MA. *Faculty:* 24. *Students:* 13 full-time (1 woman), 22 part-time (10 women). Average age 26. 30 applicants, 57% accepted, 12 enrolled. In 2010, 10 master's awarded. Application fee: $50. *Expenses:* Tuition, state resident: full-time $6160; part-time $299 per credit hour. Tuition, nonresident: full-time $16,020; part-time $783 per credit hour. Required fees: $2278; $95 per credit hour. *Financial support:* In 2010–11, 6 teaching assistantships with full tuition reimbursements (averaging $9,820 per year) were awarded. Financial award application deadline: 3/1. *Faculty research:* European, British, and American history. *Unit head:* Dr. Kevin Smith. *Application contact:* Dr. Kenneth Swope, Graduate Program Director, 765-285-8700, Fax: 765-285-5612, E-mail: kswope@bsu.edu.

Baylor University, Graduate School, College of Arts and Sciences, Department of History, Waco, TX 76798. Offers MA. Part-time and evening/weekend programs available. *Students:* 14 full-time (8 women); includes 2 minority (both Two or more races, non-Hispanic/Latino). In 2010, 6 master's awarded. *Degree requirements:* For master's, comprehensive exam, thesis, foreign language translation exam. *Entrance requirements:* For master's, GRE General Test, 24 semester hours in history. *Application deadline:* For fall admission, 8/1 for domestic students. Applications are processed on a rolling basis. Application fee: $25. *Financial support:* Fellowships, research assistantships, Federal Work-Study and institutionally sponsored loans available. Financial award application deadline: 4/15. *Faculty research:* U. S. women's history, naval history, Chinese missions, late nineteenth century Germany, twentieth century urban U. S. *Unit head:* Dr. Barry Hankins, Graduate Program Director, 254-710-4667, Fax: 254-710-2551, E-mail: barry_hankins@baylor.edu. *Application contact:* Linda Conlon, Administrative Assistant, 254-710-6293, Fax: 254-710-3870.

Bob Jones University, Graduate Programs, Greenville, SC 29614. Offers accountancy (MS); Bible (MA); Bible translation (MA); Biblical studies (Certificate); broadcast management (MS); business administration (MBA); church history (MA, PhD); church ministries (MA); church music (MM); cinema and video production (MA); counseling (MS); curriculum and instruction (Ed D); divinity (M Div); dramatic production (MA); educational leadership (MS, Ed D, Ed S); elementary education (M Ed, MAT); English (M Ed, MA, MAT); fine arts (MA); graphic design (MA); history (M Ed, MA); illustration (MA); interpretative speech (MA); mathematics (M Ed, MAT); medical missions (Certificate); ministry (MM, D Min); multi-categorical special education (M Ed, MAT); music (M Ed); New Testament interpretation (PhD); Old Testament interpretation (PhD); orchestral instrument performance (MM); organ performance (MM); pastoral studies (MA); personnel services (MS, Ed S); piano pedagogy (MM); piano performance (MM); platform arts (MA); radio and television broadcasting (MS); rhetoric and public address (MA); secondary education (M Ed); studio art (MA); teaching Bible (MA); theology (MA, PhD); voice performance (MM); youth ministries (MA); M Div/MM.

Boise State University, Graduate College, College of Social Sciences and Public Affairs, Department of History, Boise, ID 83725-0399. Offers MA. Part-time programs available. *Degree requirements:* For master's, thesis. *Entrance requirements:* For master's, GRE General Test, minimum GPA of 3.0. Electronic applications accepted. *Faculty research:* Public history, American social and cultural history, European history, Third World history.

Boston College, Graduate School of Arts and Sciences, Department of History, Chestnut Hill, MA 02467-3800. Offers European national studies (MA); history (MA, PhD); medieval studies (MA). Terminal master's awarded for partial completion of doctoral program. *Degree requirements:* For master's, one foreign language, comprehensive exam, thesis optional; for doctorate, 2 foreign languages, comprehensive exam, thesis/dissertation. *Entrance requirements:* For master's and doctorate, GRE General Test, writing sample. Additional exam requirements/recommendations for international students: Required—TOEFL (minimum score 600 paper-based; 250 computer-based; 100 iBT). Electronic applications accepted. *Faculty research:* Modern and early modern European, U. S., Russian, and Soviet history; European and U. S. intellectual history.

Boston University, Graduate School of Arts and Sciences, Department of History, Boston, MA 02215. Offers MA, PhD. *Students:* 77 full-time (37 women), 11 part-time (7 women); includes 13 minority (3 Black or African American, non-Hispanic/Latino; 3 Asian, non-Hispanic/Latino; 4 Hispanic/Latino; 3 Two or more races, non-Hispanic/Latino), 8 international. Average age 29. 195 applicants, 39% accepted, 10 enrolled. In 2010, 8 master's, 6 doctorates awarded. Terminal master's awarded for partial completion of doctoral program. *Degree requirements:* For master's, one foreign language; for doctorate, 2 foreign languages, comprehensive exam, thesis/dissertation. *Entrance requirements:* For master's and doctorate, GRE General Test, 2 letters of recommendation. Additional exam requirements/recommendations for international students: Required—TOEFL (minimum score 550 paper-based; 213 computer-based). *Application deadline:* For fall admission, 1/15 for domestic and international students. Application fee: $70. Electronic applications accepted. *Expenses:* Tuition: Full-time $39,314; part-time $1228 per credit. Required fees: $40 per semester. *Financial support:* In 2010–11, 28 students received support, including 4 fellowships with full tuition reimbursements available (averaging $19,300 per year), 1 research assistantship with full tuition reimbursement available (averaging $18,800 per year), 10 teaching assistantships with full tuition reimbursements available (averaging $18,800 per year); Federal Work-Study, scholarships/grants, and unspecified assistantships also available. Support available to part-time students. Financial award application deadline: 1/15; financial award applicants required to submit FAFSA. *Unit head:* Bruce Schulman, Chairman, 617-353-2550, Fax: 617-353-2556, E-mail: bjschulm@bu.edu. *Application contact:* James T. Dutton, Department Administrator, 617-353-2555, Fax: 617-353-2556, E-mail: jtdutton@bu.edu.

Boston University, School of Education, Boston, MA 02215. Offers counseling (Ed M, CAGS), including community, school, sport psychology; counseling psychology (Ed D); curriculum and teaching (Ed M, Ed D, CAGS), including early childhood (Ed D), educational media and technology (Ed D), English and language arts (Ed D), mathematics (Ed D), physical education and coaching (Ed D), science (Ed D), social studies education (Ed D), special education (Ed D); developmental studies (Ed D), including literacy and language, reading education; developmental studies in literacy and language education (Ed M, CAGS); early childhood education (Ed M, CAGS); education of the deaf (Ed M, CAGS); educational leadership and development (Ed D), including educational administration (Ed M, Ed D, CAGS), higher education administration (Ed M, Ed D, CAGS); educational media and technology (Ed M, CAGS); elementary education (Ed M); English and language arts (Ed M, CAGS); English education (MAT); health education (Ed M, CAGS); Latin and classical studies (MAT); mathematics education (Ed M, MAT, CAGS); mathematics for teaching (MMT); modern foreign language education (MAT), including French, Spanish; physical education and coaching (Ed M, CAGS); policy, planning, and administration (Ed M, CAGS), including community education leadership, educational administration (Ed M, Ed D, CAGS), higher education administration (Ed M, Ed D, CAGS); reading education (Ed M, CAGS); science education (Ed M, MAT, CAGS), including biology (MAT), chemistry (MAT), earth science (MAT), general science (MAT), physics (MAT); social studies education (Ed M, MAT, CAGS), including history (MAT), political science (MAT); special education (Ed M, Ed D, CAGS), including disability studies (Ed M), moderate disabilities (Ed M), severe disabilities (Ed M), special education administration (Ed M); teaching English as a second language (Ed M, CAGS). Part-time programs available. *Faculty:* 57 full-time, 39 part-time/adjunct. *Students:* 245 full-time (191 women), 376 part-time (274 women); includes 83 minority (14 Black or African American, non-Hispanic/Latino; 2 American Indian or Alaska Native, non-Hispanic/Latino; 28 Asian, non-Hispanic/Latino; 31 Hispanic/Latino; 2 Native Hawaiian or other Pacific Islander, non-Hispanic/Latino; 6 Two or more races, non-Hispanic/Latino), 79 international. Average age 30. 1,270 applicants, 66% accepted, 292 enrolled. In 2010, 273 master's, 15 doctorates, 7 other advanced degrees awarded. Terminal master's awarded for partial completion of doctoral program. *Degree requirements:* For master's, thesis (for some programs); for doctorate, comprehensive exam, thesis/dissertation; for CAGS, comprehensive exam. *Entrance requirements:* For master's and CAGS, GRE General Test or Miller Analogies Test (MAT); for doctorate, GRE General Test. Additional exam requirements/recommendations for international students: Required—TOEFL, IELTS. *Application deadline:* For fall admission, 1/15 priority date for domestic and international students; for spring admission, 9/15 priority date for domestic and international students. Applications are processed on a rolling basis. Application fee: $70. Electronic applications accepted. *Expenses:* Tuition: Full-time $39,314; part-time $1228 per credit. Required fees: $40 per semester. *Financial support:* In 2010–11, 276 students received support, including 31 fellowships with full tuition reimbursements available, 16 research assistantships, 26 teaching assistantships with partial tuition reimbursements available; career-related internships or fieldwork, Federal Work-Study, and scholarships/grants also available. Support available to part-time students. Financial award applicants required to submit FAFSA. *Faculty research:* Deaf studies, social emotional learning, civic engagement and education, STEM education, pre-college educational pipelines. Total annual research expenditures: $2.6 million. *Unit head:* Dr. Hardin Coleman, Dean, 617-353-3213. *Application contact:* Dana Fernandez, Director of Enrollment, 617-353-4237, Fax: 617-353-8937, E-mail: sedgrad@bu.edu.

Bowling Green State University, Graduate College, College of Arts and Sciences, Department of History, Bowling Green, OH 43403. Offers history (MA, MAT, PhD); public history (MA); MA/MA. Part-time programs available. *Degree requirements:* For master's, thesis or alternative; for doctorate, one foreign language, comprehensive exam, thesis/dissertation. *Entrance requirements:* For master's and doctorate, GRE General Test. Additional exam requirements/recommendations for international students: Required—TOEFL. Electronic applications accepted. *Faculty research:* Policy history, modern Europe, recent United States history, East Asia, Latin America.

Brandeis University, Graduate School of Arts and Sciences, Department of History, Waltham, MA 02454-9110. Offers MA, PhD. Part-time programs available. *Faculty:* 13 full-time (3 women), 4 part-time/adjunct (2 women). *Students:* 52 full-time (17 women); includes 1 Asian, non-Hispanic/Latino; 1 Hispanic/Latino, 3 international. 111 applicants, 22% accepted, 11 enrolled. In 2010, 14 master's, 3 doctorates awarded. Terminal master's awarded for partial completion of doctoral program. *Degree requirements:* For master's, one foreign language, thesis, colloquia, seminars; for doctorate, one foreign language, comprehensive exam, thesis/dissertation, colloquia, seminars. *Entrance requirements:* For master's, GRE General Test, resume, writing sample, letters of recommendation; for doctorate, GRE General Test, resume, writing sample, letter of recommendation, statement of purpose. Additional exam requirements/recommendations for international students: Required—TOEFL (minimum score 600 paper-based; 250 computer-

History

Brandeis University (continued)
based; 100 iBT); Recommended—IELTS (minimum score 7). *Application deadline:* For fall admission, 1/15 priority date for domestic students. Application fee: $75. Electronic applications accepted. *Financial support:* In 2010–11, 26 fellowships with full tuition reimbursements (averaging $20,000 per year), teaching assistantships (averaging $3,200 per year) were awarded; research assistantships, scholarships/grants, health care benefits, and tuition waivers (full and partial) also available. Support available to part-time students. Financial award application deadline: 4/15; financial award applicants required to submit FAFSA. *Faculty research:* American and European history, world history, regional and national history. *Unit head:* Dr. Mark Hulliung, Director of Graduate Studies, 781-736-2272, Fax: 781-736-2273, E-mail: historia@brandeis.edu. *Application contact:* Dona DiLorenzo, Department Administrator, 781-736-2272, Fax: 781-736-2273, E-mail: delorenz@brandeis.edu.

Brock University, Faculty of Graduate Studies, Faculty of Humanities, Program in History, St. Catharines, ON L2S 3A1, Canada. Offers MA. Part-time programs available. *Degree requirements:* For master's, thesis optional. *Entrance requirements:* For master's, honors degree in history. Additional exam requirements/recommendations for international students: Required—TOEFL (minimum score 550 paper-based; 213 computer-based; 80 iBT), IELTS (minimum score 6.5), TWE (minimum score 4). Electronic applications accepted.

Brooklyn College of the City University of New York, Division of Graduate Studies, Department of History, Brooklyn, NY 11210-2889. Offers MA, PhD. Part-time and evening/weekend programs available. *Students:* 1 (woman) full-time, 54 part-time (32 women); includes 20 minority (10 Black or African American, non-Hispanic/Latino; 6 Asian, non-Hispanic/Latino; 4 Hispanic/Latino), 1 international. Average age 30. 40 applicants, 80% accepted, 9 enrolled. In 2010, 15 master's awarded. *Degree requirements:* For master's, 30 credits. *Entrance requirements:* For master's, 12 credits in history, minimum GPA of 3.0 in major, 2 letters of recommendation. Additional exam requirements/recommendations for international students: Required—TOEFL (minimum score 650 paper-based; 280 computer-based; 114 iBT). *Application deadline:* For fall admission, 3/1 priority date for domestic students, 2/1 priority date for international students; for spring admission, 11/1 priority date for domestic students, 10/1 priority date for international students. Applications are processed on a rolling basis. Application fee: $125. Electronic applications accepted. *Expenses:* Tuition, state resident: full-time $7360; part-time $310 per credit hour. Tuition, nonresident: full-time $13,800; part-time $575 per credit hour. Required fees: $190 per semester. *Financial support:* Federal Work-Study, institutionally sponsored loans, and scholarships/grants available. Support available to part-time students. Financial award application deadline: 5/1; financial award applicants required to submit FAFSA. *Faculty research:* Modern European, U. S., medieval, women's, Asian, and Caribbean history. *Unit head:* Dr. David Troyansky, Chairperson, 718-951-5303, E-mail: troyansky@brooklyn.cuny.edu. *Application contact:* Hernan Sierra, Graduate Admissions Coordinator, 718-951-4536, Fax: 718-951-4506, E-mail: grads@brooklyn.cuny.edu.

Brown University, Graduate School, Department of History, Providence, RI 02912. Offers MA, PhD. *Degree requirements:* For master's, thesis or alternative; for doctorate, variable foreign language requirement, thesis/dissertation, preliminary exam.

Buffalo State College, State University of New York, The Graduate School, Faculty of Natural and Social Sciences, Department of History and Social Studies, Buffalo, NY 14222-1095. Offers history (MA); secondary education (MS Ed), including social studies. Part-time and evening/weekend programs available. *Degree requirements:* For master's, one foreign language, thesis (for some programs), project (MS Ed). *Entrance requirements:* For master's, minimum GPA of 2.75, 30 hours in history (MA), 36 hours in history or social sciences (MS Ed). Additional exam requirements/recommendations for international students: Required—TOEFL (minimum score 550 paper-based; 213 computer-based).

Butler University, College of Liberal Arts and Sciences, Department of History, Indianapolis, IN 46208-3485. Offers MA. Part-time programs available. *Students:* 1 full-time (0 women), 1 part-time (0 women). Average age 23. 6 applicants, 33% accepted, 0 enrolled. In 2010, 1 master's awarded. *Degree requirements:* For master's, thesis or alternative. *Entrance requirements:* For master's, GRE General Test, minimum GPA of 3.25 in undergraduate major. *Application deadline:* For fall admission, 8/15 priority date for domestic students. Applications are processed on a rolling basis. Application fee: $35. Electronic applications accepted. *Expenses:* Tuition: Full-time $29,740; part-time $1250 per credit. Required fees: $818; $430 per credit. Tuition and fees vary according to program. *Financial support:* Institutionally sponsored loans available. Support available to part-time students. Financial award applicants required to submit FAFSA. *Faculty research:* Gender issues in Africa, Indiana history, transnational migration, French Revolution. *Unit head:* Dr. Scott Swanson, Head, 317-940-9680, E-mail: sswanson@butler.edu. *Application contact:* Pamela Bender, Student Services Specialist, 317-940-8100, Fax: 317-940-8250, E-mail: pbender@butler.edu.

California Polytechnic State University, San Luis Obispo, College of Liberal Arts, Department of History, San Luis Obispo, CA 93407. Offers MA. Part-time programs available. *Faculty:* 1 full-time (0 women). *Students:* 6 full-time (2 women), 27 part-time (7 women); includes 6 minority (5 Hispanic/Latino; 1 Two or more races, non-Hispanic/Latino). Average age 30. 27 applicants, 59% accepted, 9 enrolled. In 2010, 4 master's awarded. *Degree requirements:* For master's, comprehensive exam (for some programs), thesis (for some programs). *Entrance requirements:* For master's, minimum GPA of 3.0 in last 90 quarter units of course work, writing sample. Additional exam requirements/recommendations for international students: Required—TOEFL (minimum score 550 paper-based; 213 computer-based) or IELTS (minimum score 6). *Application deadline:* For fall admission, 7/1 for domestic students, 11/30 for international students; for winter admission, 10/1 for domestic students, 6/30 for international students; for spring admission, 2/1 for domestic students. Applications are processed on a rolling basis. Application fee: $55. Electronic applications accepted. *Expenses:* Tuition, state resident: full-time $5386; part-time $3124 per year. Tuition, nonresident: full-time $11,160; part-time $248 per unit. Required fees: $2250; $614 per term. One-time fee: $2250 full-time; $1842 part-time. *Financial support:* Federal Work-Study and scholarships/grants available. Support available to part-time students. Financial award application deadline: 3/2; financial award applicants required to submit FAFSA. *Faculty research:* American history, European history, Asian history, African history, comparative world history. *Unit head:* Dr. Tom Trice, Graduate Coordinator, 805-756-2724, Fax: 805-756-5055, E-mail: ttrice@calpoly.edu. *Application contact:* Dr. Tom Trice, Graduate Coordinator, 805-756-2724, Fax: 805-756-5055, E-mail: ttrice@calpoly.edu.

California State Polytechnic University, Pomona, Academic Affairs, College of Letters, Arts, and Social Sciences, Program in History, Pomona, CA 91768-2557. Offers MA. Part-time programs available. *Students:* 1 (woman) full-time, 28 part-time (14 women); includes 8 minority (2 Black or African American, non-Hispanic/Latino; 1 Asian, non-Hispanic/Latino; 5 Hispanic/Latino). Average age 36. 17 applicants, 0% accepted, 0 enrolled. In 2010, 7 master's awarded. *Degree requirements:* For master's, comprehensive exam (for some programs), thesis (for some programs). *Application deadline:* For fall admission, 5/1 priority date for domestic students; for winter admission, 10/15 priority date for domestic students; for spring admission, 1/20 priority date for domestic students. Applications are processed on a rolling basis. Application fee: $55. Electronic applications accepted. *Expenses:* Tuition, state resident: full-time $5386; part-time $2850 per year. Tuition, nonresident: full-time $12,082; part-time $248 per credit. Required fees: $577; $248 per credit. $577 per year. Tuition and fees vary according to course load and program. *Unit head:* Dr. Mahmood Ibrahim, Graduate Coordinator, 909-869-3867, E-mail: mibrahim@csupomona.edu. *Application contact:* Scott J. Duncan, Director, Admissions, 909-869-3258, E-mail: sjduncan@csupomona.edu.

California State University, Bakersfield, Division of Graduate Studies, School of Humanities and Social Sciences, Program in History, Bakersfield, CA 93311. Offers MA. *Degree requirements:* For master's, comprehensive exam or thesis. *Entrance requirements:* For master's, 2 letters of recommendation. *Faculty research:* American, European, Latin American, and modern Chinese history.

California State University, Chico, Graduate School, College of Humanities and Fine Arts, Department of History, Chico, CA 95929-0722. Offers MA. Part-time programs available. *Students:* 11 full-time (5 women), 12 part-time (3 women); includes 1 Hispanic/Latino, 1 international. Average age 31. 15 applicants, 67% accepted, 6 enrolled. In 2010, 2 master's awarded. *Degree requirements:* For master's, thesis or alternative, oral exam. *Entrance requirements:* For master's, GRE General Test, 2 letters of recommendation, writing sample. Additional exam requirements/recommendations for international students: Required—TOEFL (minimum score 550 paper-based; 213 computer-based; 80 iBT), IELTS (minimum score 6.5). *Application deadline:* For fall admission, 3/1 priority date for domestic students, 3/1 for international students; for spring admission, 9/15 priority date for domestic students, 9/15 for international students. Applications are processed on a rolling basis. Application fee: $55. Electronic applications accepted. *Unit head:* Dr. Kate Transchel, Graduate Coordinator, 530-898-6417, E-mail: ktranschel@csuchico.edu. *Application contact:* Dr. Kate Transchel, Graduate Coordinator, 530-898-6417, E-mail: ktranschel@csuchico.edu.

California State University, East Bay, Office of Academic Programs and Graduate Studies, College of Letters, Arts, and Social Sciences, Department of History, Hayward, CA 94542-3000. Offers MA. Part-time and evening/weekend programs available. *Faculty:* 9 full-time (5 women), 2 part-time/adjunct (0 women). *Students:* 9 full-time (3 women), 29 part-time (13 women); includes 1 Asian, non-Hispanic/Latino; 2 Hispanic/Latino. Average age 39. 38 applicants, 66% accepted, 15 enrolled. In 2010, 5 master's awarded. *Degree requirements:* For master's, one foreign language, comprehensive exam, project or thesis. *Entrance requirements:* For master's, minimum GPA of 3.0 in field, 3.3 in history. Additional exam requirements/recommendations for international students: Required—TOEFL (minimum score 550 paper-based; 213 computer-based). *Application deadline:* For fall admission, 6/30 for domestic and international students. Applications are processed on a rolling basis. Application fee: $55. Electronic applications accepted. *Financial support:* Fellowships, teaching assistantships, career-related internships or fieldwork, Federal Work-Study, institutionally sponsored loans, and scholarships/grants available. Support available to part-time students. Financial award application deadline: 3/2; financial award applicants required to submit FAFSA. *Unit head:* Dr. Nancy Thompson, Chair, 510-885-3207, Fax: 510-885-4791, E-mail: nancy.thompson@csueastbay.edu. *Application contact:* Dr. Donna Wiley, Interim Associate Director, 510-885-2928, Fax: 510-885-4777, E-mail: donna.wiley@csueastbay.edu.

California State University, Fresno, Division of Graduate Studies, College of Social Sciences, Department of History, Fresno, CA 93740-8027. Offers history-teaching option (MA); history-traditional track (MA). Part-time and evening/weekend programs available. *Degree requirements:* For master's, thesis or alternative. *Entrance requirements:* For master's, GRE General Test, minimum GPA of 3.0. Additional exam requirements/recommendations for international students: Required—TOEFL. Electronic applications accepted. *Faculty research:* International education, classical art history, improving teacher quality.

California State University, Fullerton, Graduate Studies, College of Humanities and Social Sciences, Department of History, Fullerton, CA 92834-9480. Offers MA. Part-time programs available. *Students:* 17 full-time (9 women), 65 part-time (23 women); includes 2 Black or African American, non-Hispanic/Latino; 2 American Indian or Alaska Native, non-Hispanic/Latino; 6 Asian, non-Hispanic/Latino; 15 Hispanic/Latino; 2 Two or more races, non-Hispanic/Latino, 1 international. Average age 30. 80 applicants, 68% accepted, 34 enrolled. In 2010, 16 master's awarded. *Degree requirements:* For master's, comprehensive exam, project or thesis. *Entrance requirements:* For master's, undergraduate major in history or related field, minimum GPA of 3.0. Application fee: $55. *Financial support:* Career-related internships or fieldwork, Federal Work-Study, institutionally sponsored loans, and scholarships/grants available. Support available to part-time students. Financial award application deadline: 3/1; financial award applicants required to submit FAFSA. *Unit head:* Dr. William Haddad, Chair, 657-278-3474. *Application contact:* Admissions/Applications, 657-278-2371.

California State University, Long Beach, Graduate Studies, College of Liberal Arts, Department of History, Long Beach, CA 90840. Offers Africa and the Middle East (MA); ancient/medieval Europe (MA); Asia (MA); Latin America (MA); modern Europe (MA); United States (MA); world (MA). Part-time and evening/weekend programs available. *Faculty:* 12 full-time (7 women). *Students:* 18 full-time (6 women), 51 part-time (18 women); includes 3 Black or African American, non-Hispanic/Latino; 1 American Indian or Alaska Native, non-Hispanic/Latino; 3 Asian, non-Hispanic/Latino; 16 Hispanic/Latino, 1 international. Average age 30. 80 applicants, 53% accepted, 30 enrolled. In 2010, 11 master's awarded. *Degree requirements:* For master's, one foreign language, comprehensive exam or thesis. *Application deadline:* For fall admission, 3/1 for domestic students. Applications are processed on a rolling basis. Application fee: $55. Electronic applications accepted. *Financial support:* Research assistantships, Federal Work-Study, institutionally sponsored loans, and scholarships/grants available. Financial award application deadline: 3/2. *Faculty research:* All periods of European and American history, recent Asian and African history. *Unit head:* Dr. Nancy Quam-Wickham, Department Chair, 562-985-4431, Fax: 562-985-5431, E-mail: quamwick@csulb.edu. *Application contact:* Dr. Houri Berberian, Graduate Advisor, 562-985-4524, Fax: 562-985-4431, E-mail: hberber@csulb.edu.

California State University, Los Angeles, Graduate Studies, College of Natural and Social Sciences, Department of History, Los Angeles, CA 90032-8530. Offers MA. Part-time and evening/weekend programs available. *Faculty:* 4 full-time (1 woman), 2 part-time/adjunct (both women). *Students:* 17 full-time (9 women), 64 part-time (26 women); includes 37 minority (1 Black or African American, non-Hispanic/Latino; 1 American Indian or Alaska Native, non-Hispanic/Latino; 5 Asian, non-Hispanic/Latino; 28 Hispanic/Latino; 2 Two or more races, non-Hispanic/Latino), 3 international. Average age 34. 33 applicants, 100% accepted, 22 enrolled. In 2010, 17 master's awarded. *Degree requirements:* For master's, one foreign language, comprehensive exam or thesis. *Entrance requirements:* For master's, minimum GPA of 3.0, undergraduate major in history. Additional exam requirements/recommendations for international students: Required—TOEFL (minimum score 500 paper-based; 173 computer-based). *Application deadline:* For fall admission, 5/1 for domestic and international students. Applications are processed on a rolling basis. Application fee: $55. Electronic applications accepted. *Financial support:* Federal Work-Study available. Support available to part-time students. Financial award application deadline: 3/1. *Faculty research:* Ancient and modern Europe, the Middle East, Latin America, U. S. history-Bill of Rights. *Unit head:* Dr. Cheryl A. Koos, Chair, 323-343-2020, Fax: 323-343-6431, E-mail: ckoos@calstatela.edu. *Application contact:* Dr. Alan Muchlinski, Dean of Graduate Studies, 323-343-3820, Fax: 323-343-5653, E-mail: amuchli@exchange.calstatela.edu.

California State University, Northridge, Graduate Studies, College of Social and Behavioral Sciences, Department of History, Northridge, CA 91330. Offers MA. *Degree requirements:* For master's, one foreign language. *Entrance requirements:* For master's, GRE General Test or minimum GPA of 3.0, 2 letters of recommendation. Additional exam requirements/recommendations for international students: Required—TOEFL.

California State University, Stanislaus, College of Humanities and Social Sciences, Program in History (MA), Turlock, CA 95382. Offers history (MA); international relations (MA); secondary school teachers (MA). Part-time programs available. *Faculty:* 7. *Students:* 8 full-time (4 women), 17 part-time (5 women); includes 7 minority (1 Asian, non-Hispanic/Latino; 3 Hispanic/Latino; 1 Native Hawaiian or other Pacific Islander, non-Hispanic/Latino; 2 Two or more races, non-Hispanic/Latino). Average age 35. 10 applicants, 70% accepted, 5 enrolled. In 2010, 9 master's awarded. *Degree requirements:* For master's, comprehensive exam, thesis or alternative. *Entrance requirements:* For master's, GRE, minimum GPA of 3.0, personal statement. Additional exam requirements/recommendations for international students: Required—TOEFL (minimum score 575 paper-based; 233 computer-based). *Application deadline:* For fall admission, 5/1 for domestic students; for spring admission, 1/7 for domestic students. Application fee:

$55. Electronic applications accepted. Tuition and fees vary according to program. *Financial support:* Fellowships, Federal Work-Study available. Financial award application deadline: 3/1; financial award applicants required to submit FAFSA. *Faculty research:* History of Ancient Greece, history and ecology of the central valley, acculturation and gender. *Unit head:* Dr. Bret Carroll, History Department Chair, 209-667-3238, Fax: 209-667-3132, E-mail: bcarroll@csustan.edu. *Application contact:* Graduate School, 209-667-3129, Fax: 209-664-7025.

Cardinal Stritch University, College of Arts and Sciences, Department of History, Milwaukee, WI 53217-3985. Offers MA. Part-time programs available. *Degree requirements:* For master's, comprehensive exam, research project. *Entrance requirements:* For master's, minimum GPA of 3.0, 2 letters of recommendation. Electronic applications accepted.

Carleton University, Faculty of Graduate Studies, Faculty of Arts and Social Sciences, Department of History, Ottawa, ON K1S 5B6, Canada. Offers MA, PhD. *Degree requirements:* For master's, one foreign language, thesis; for doctorate, one foreign language, thesis/dissertation. *Entrance requirements:* For master's, honors degree; for doctorate, master's degree. Additional exam requirements/recommendations for international students: Required—TOEFL. *Faculty research:* Canadian, American, British, modern French, and modern Russian history; international, medieval, and European intellectual history; women's history.

Carnegie Mellon University, College of Humanities and Social Sciences, Department of History, Pittsburgh, PA 15213-3891. Offers African and African-American diaspora (PhD); culture and power (PhD); gender and the family (PhD); history (MA, MS); history and policy (MA); labor and politics (PhD); science, technology, medicine and environment (PhD). Part-time programs available. *Degree requirements:* For doctorate, oral and written comprehensive exams, dissertation defense. *Entrance requirements:* For doctorate, GRE General Test. Additional exam requirements/recommendations for international students: Required—TOEFL. Electronic applications accepted. *Faculty research:* Anthropology and history, African American history, technology/environment, cultural history analysis.

Case Western Reserve University, School of Graduate Studies, Department of History, Cleveland, OH 44106. Offers MA, PhD. Part-time programs available. *Faculty:* 16 full-time (7 women), 3 part-time/adjunct (1 woman). *Students:* 27 full-time (12 women), 6 part-time (0 women); includes 1 Black or African American, non-Hispanic/Latino; 1 Asian, non-Hispanic/Latino, 2 international. Average age 35. 24 applicants, 42% accepted, 8 enrolled. In 2010, 3 master's, 2 doctorates awarded. Terminal master's awarded for partial completion of doctoral program. *Degree requirements:* For master's, thesis; for doctorate, thesis/dissertation. *Entrance requirements:* For master's and doctorate, GRE General Test, writing sample, short essay. Additional exam requirements/recommendations for international students: Required—TOEFL (minimum score 550 paper-based; 213 computer-based). *Application deadline:* For fall admission, 1/31 for domestic students. Application fee: $50. Electronic applications accepted. *Financial support:* Fellowships, research assistantships, teaching assistantships, career-related internships or fieldwork, tuition waivers (full and partial), and unspecified assistantships available. Financial award application deadline: 1/31; financial award applicants required to submit FAFSA. *Faculty research:* American social history, social policy history, history of technology, environment, science, and medicine. *Unit head:* Jonathan Sadowsky, Chair, 216-368-2622, Fax: 216-368-4681, E-mail: jonathan.sadowsky@case.edu. *Application contact:* Marissa Ross, Department Assistant, 216-368-2380, Fax: 216-368-4681, E-mail: mar14@case.edu.

The Catholic University of America, School of Arts and Sciences, Department of History, Washington, DC 20064. Offers history (MA, PhD); religion and society in the late medieval and early modern world (MA); MA/JD; MSLS/MA. Part-time programs available. *Faculty:* 13 full-time (7 women), 2 part-time/adjunct (0 women). *Students:* 16 full-time (12 women), 27 part-time (12 women); includes 1 American Indian or Alaska Native, non-Hispanic/Latino; 1 Hispanic/Latino, 3 international. Average age 32. 51 applicants, 41% accepted, 11 enrolled. In 2010, 5 master's, 3 doctorates awarded. *Degree requirements:* For master's, one foreign language, comprehensive exam, thesis optional; for doctorate, 2 foreign languages, comprehensive exam, thesis/dissertation. *Entrance requirements:* For master's and doctorate, GRE General Test, statement of purpose, official copies of academic transcripts, three letters of recommendation, writing sample. Additional exam requirements/recommendations for international students: Required—TOEFL (minimum score 580 paper-based; 237 computer-based). *Application deadline:* For fall admission, 8/1 priority date for domestic students, 7/15 for international students; for spring admission, 12/1 priority date for domestic students, 10/15 for international students. Applications are processed on a rolling basis. Application fee: $55. Electronic applications accepted. *Expenses:* Tuition: Full-time $33,580; part-time $1315 per credit hour. Required fees: $80; $40 per semester hour. One-time fee: $425. *Financial support:* Fellowships, research assistantships, teaching assistantships, Federal Work-Study, scholarships/grants, tuition waivers (full and partial), and unspecified assistantships available. Financial award application deadline: 2/1; financial award applicants required to submit FAFSA. *Faculty research:* Modern European intellectual history, history of mathematics and sciences, Renaissance, Catholic reformation, medieval women and gender. *Unit head:* Dr. Jerry Muller, Chair, 202-319-5484, Fax: 202-319-5569, E-mail: mullerj@cua.edu. *Application contact:* Andrew Woodall, Director of Graduate Admissions, 202-319-5057, Fax: 202-319-6533, E-mail: cua-admissions@cua.edu.

Central Connecticut State University, School of Graduate Studies, School of Arts and Sciences, Department of History, New Britain, CT 06050-4010. Offers history (MA, Certificate); public history (MA); social studies (Certificate). Part-time and evening/weekend programs available. *Faculty:* 18 full-time (9 women), 23 part-time/adjunct (5 women). *Students:* 32 full-time (12 women), 35 part-time (16 women); includes 5 minority (1 Asian, non-Hispanic/Latino; 3 Hispanic/Latino; 1 Two or more races, non-Hispanic/Latino). Average age 29. 57 applicants, 61% accepted, 22 enrolled. In 2010, 12 master's, 5 other advanced degrees awarded. *Degree requirements:* For master's, comprehensive exam, thesis or alternative; for Certificate, qualifying exam. *Entrance requirements:* For master's, minimum undergraduate GPA of 3.0. Additional exam requirements/recommendations for international students: Required—TOEFL. *Application deadline:* For fall admission, 5/1 for domestic students; for spring admission, 12/1 for domestic students. Applications are processed on a rolling basis. Application fee: $50. Electronic applications accepted. *Expenses:* Tuition, area resident: Full-time $5012; part-time $470 per credit. Tuition, state resident: full-time $7518; part-time $482 per credit. Tuition, nonresident: full-time $13,962; part-time $482 per credit. Required fees: $3772. One-time fee: $62 part-time. *Financial support:* In 2010–11, 7 students received support, including 6 research assistantships; career-related internships or fieldwork, Federal Work-Study, scholarships/grants, and unspecified assistantships also available. Support available to part-time students. Financial award application deadline: 2/15; financial award applicants required to submit FAFSA. *Faculty research:* American West, African history, Eastern Europe, modern Middle East, East Asia. *Unit head:* Dr. Glenn Sunshine, Chair, 860-832-2800. *Application contact:* Dr. Glenn Sunshine, Chair, 860-832-2800.

Central European University, Graduate Studies, Department of History, Budapest, Hungary. Offers MA, PhD. *Faculty:* 10 full-time (2 women), 11 part-time/adjunct (1 woman). *Students:* 99 full-time (45 women). Average age 28. 143 applicants, 49% accepted, 43 enrolled. In 2010, 27 master's, 7 doctorates awarded. Terminal master's awarded for partial completion of doctoral program. *Degree requirements:* For master's, one foreign language, thesis; for doctorate, one foreign language, comprehensive exam, thesis/dissertation. *Entrance requirements:* For master's and doctorate, interview. Additional exam requirements/recommendations for international students: Required—TOEFL (minimum score 570 paper-based; 230 computer-based). *Application deadline:* For fall admission, 1/5 for domestic and international students. Application fee: $0. Electronic applications accepted. Tuition and fees charges are reported in euros. *Expenses:* Tuition: Full-time 11,000 euros. Required fees: 250 euros. One-time fee: 200 euros full-time. Tuition and fees vary according to degree level, program, reciprocity agreements and student level. *Financial support:* In 2010–11, 46 students received support, including 43 fellowships with full and partial tuition reimbursements available (averaging $6,000 per year); career-related internships or fieldwork, institutionally sponsored loans, scholarships/grants, and tuition waivers (full and partial) also available. *Faculty research:* Early modern intellectual history, history of ideas, contemporary historiography, comparative history of empires, symbolic geography, history of cultural and religious coexistence. *Unit head:* Dr. Lazlo Kontler, Head, 361-327-3022, Fax: 361-327-3191, E-mail: history@ceu.hu. *Application contact:* Agnes Bendik, Coordinator, 361-327-3000 Ext. 2591, Fax: 361-235-6145, E-mail: history@ceu.hu.

Central Michigan University, College of Graduate Studies, College of Humanities and Social and Behavioral Sciences, Department of History, Mount Pleasant, MI 48859. Offers European history (Graduate Certificate); history (MA, PhD); modern history (Graduate Certificate); United States history (Graduate Certificate). Part-time programs available. *Faculty:* 15 full-time (4 women). *Students:* 38 full-time (11 women), 23 part-time (8 women); includes 2 Black or African American, non-Hispanic/Latino; 1 Asian, non-Hispanic/Latino, 5 international. Average age 30. *Degree requirements:* For master's, thesis or alternative; for doctorate, comprehensive exam, thesis/dissertation. Application fee: $35 ($45 for international students). Electronic applications accepted. *Expenses:* Tuition, state resident: full-time $8208; part-time $456 per credit hour. Tuition, nonresident: full-time $13,788; part-time $766 per credit hour. One-time fee: $25. *Financial support:* Fellowships with tuition reimbursements, research assistantships with tuition reimbursements, teaching assistantships with tuition reimbursements, Federal Work-Study, unspecified assistantships, and out-of-state merit awards, non-resident graduate awards available. *Faculty research:* Colonial and revolutionary United States history, modern European history, Latin American and transatlantic history, transnational and comparative history, United States social history. *Unit head:* Dr. Mitchell K. Hall, Chairperson, 989-773-3374, Fax: 989-774-1156, E-mail: hall1mk@cmich.edu. *Application contact:* Dr. Mitchell K. Hall, Chairperson, 989-773-3374, Fax: 989-774-1156, E-mail: hall1mk@cmich.edu.

Central Washington University, Graduate Studies and Research, College of Arts and Humanities, Department of History, Ellensburg, WA 98926. Offers MA. *Degree requirements:* For master's, thesis or alternative. *Entrance requirements:* For master's, GRE General Test, minimum GPA of 3.0. Additional exam requirements/recommendations for international students: Required—TOEFL (minimum score 550 paper-based; 213 computer-based; 79 iBT). Electronic applications accepted.

Centro de Estudios Avanzados de Puerto Rico y el Caribe, Graduate Program in Puerto Rican and Caribbean Studies, Old San Juan, PR 00902-3970. Offers Puerto Rican and Caribbean history (MA, PhD); Puerto Rican and Caribbean literature (MA, PhD); Puerto Rican studies (MA). Part-time and evening/weekend programs available. *Degree requirements:* For master's, comprehensive exam, thesis; for doctorate, 2 foreign languages, comprehensive exam, thesis/dissertation. *Entrance requirements:* For master's and doctorate, interview. *Faculty research:* Literature, history, art, folklore, and culture of Puerto Rico and Caribbean countries.

Chicago State University, School of Graduate and Professional Studies, College of Arts and Sciences, Department of History, Philosophy, and Political Science, Chicago, IL 60628. Offers MA. Part-time and evening/weekend programs available. *Degree requirements:* For master's, thesis optional. *Entrance requirements:* For master's, minimum GPA of 2.75. Electronic applications accepted. *Faculty research:* Gregory the Great-use in later Middle Ages, Renaissance alchemy, Liberian wars, Waldo Frank, Sangalan oral traditions.

The Citadel, The Military College of South Carolina, Citadel Graduate College, Department of History, Charleston, SC 29409. Offers MA. Program offered jointly with The Graduate School of the College of Charleston. Part-time and evening/weekend programs available. *Faculty:* 9 full-time (4 women). *Students:* 2 full-time (0 women), 14 part-time (3 women); includes 1 Hispanic/Latino. Average age 36. In 2010, 3 master's awarded. *Degree requirements:* For master's, comprehensive exam, thesis optional. *Entrance requirements:* For master's, GRE (minimum score of 1000 and 4-6 on the writing assessment sections) or MAT (minimum score 410), minimum undergraduate GPA of 2.5 (3.0 in major); 3 letters of recommendation; evidence of ability to conduct research and present findings. Additional exam requirements/recommendations for international students: Required—TOEFL (minimum score 550 paper-based; 213 computer-based). *Application deadline:* For fall admission, 3/1 for domestic students; for spring admission, 10/1 for domestic students. Application fee: $30. Electronic applications accepted. *Expenses:* Tuition, state resident: part-time $460 per credit hour. Tuition, nonresident: part-time $756 per credit hour. Required fees: $40 per term. *Financial support:* Fellowships, health care benefits and unspecified assistantships available. Support available to part-time students. Financial award application deadline: 7/1; financial award applicants required to submit FAFSA. *Unit head:* Dr. Keith N. Knapp, Department Head, 843-953-5073, Fax: 843-953-7020, E-mail: keith.knapp@citadel.edu. *Application contact:* Dr. Katherine H. Grenier, Director of Graduate Studies, 843-953-6935, Fax: 843-953-7020, E-mail: grenierk@citadel.edu.

City College of the City University of New York, Graduate School, College of Liberal Arts and Science, Division of the Humanities and Arts, Department of History, New York, NY 10031-9198. Offers MA. Part-time programs available. *Degree requirements:* For master's, one foreign language, comprehensive exam, thesis. *Entrance requirements:* Additional exam requirements/recommendations for international students: Required—TOEFL (minimum score 600 paper-based; 100 iBT). Electronic applications accepted. *Faculty research:* Latin American, European, Asian, urban, and architectural history.

Claremont Graduate University, Graduate Programs, School of Arts and Humanities, Department of History, Claremont, CA 91711-6160. Offers Africana history (Certificate); American studies and U. S. history (MA, PhD); archival studies (MA); early modern studies (MA, PhD); European studies (MA, PhD); oral history (MA, PhD); MBA/MA; MBA/PhD. *Faculty:* 4 full-time (2 women), 1 part-time/adjunct (0 women). *Students:* 75 full-time (36 women), 2 part-time (1 woman); includes 25 minority (3 Black or African American, non-Hispanic/Latino; 1 American Indian or Alaska Native, non-Hispanic/Latino; 6 Asian, non-Hispanic/Latino; 9 Hispanic/Latino; 1 Native Hawaiian or other Pacific Islander, non-Hispanic/Latino; 5 Two or more races, non-Hispanic/Latino), 2 international. Average age 36. In 2010, 12 master's, 2 doctorates awarded. Terminal master's awarded for partial completion of doctoral program. *Entrance requirements:* For master's and doctorate, GRE General Test. Additional exam requirements/recommendations for international students: Required—TOEFL (minimum score 550 paper-based; 213 computer-based; 80 iBT). *Application deadline:* For fall admission, 2/1 priority date for domestic students. Applications are processed on a rolling basis. Application fee: $60. Electronic applications accepted. *Expenses:* Tuition: Full-time $35,748; part-time $1554 per unit. Required fees: $215 per semester. *Financial support:* Fellowships, research assistantships, Federal Work-Study, institutionally sponsored loans, and scholarships/grants available. Support available to part-time students. Financial award application deadline: 2/15; financial award applicants required to submit FAFSA. *Faculty research:* Intellectual and social history, cultural studies, gender studies, Western history, Chicano history. *Unit head:* Janet Farrell Brodie, Chair, 909-621-8880, Fax: 909-621-8609, E-mail: janet.brodie@cgu.edu. *Application contact:* Susan Hampson, Admissions Coordinator, 909-607-1278, E-mail: humanities@cgu.edu.

Clark Atlanta University, School of Arts and Sciences, Department of History, Atlanta, GA 30314. Offers MA, DAH. Part-time programs available. *Faculty:* 3 full-time (2 women). *Students:* 2 full-time (1 woman), 9 part-time (5 women); includes all Black or African American, non-Hispanic/Latino. Average age 34. 2 applicants, 100% accepted, 1 enrolled. *Degree requirements:* For master's, one foreign language, comprehensive exam, thesis; for doctorate, one foreign language, comprehensive exam, thesis/dissertation. *Entrance requirements:* For master's, GRE General Test, minimum GPA of 2.5. Additional exam requirements/recommendations for international students: Required—TOEFL (minimum score 500 paper-based; 173 computer-based; 61 iBT). *Application deadline:* For fall admission, 4/1 for domestic and international students; for spring admission, 11/1 for domestic and international students. Applications are processed on a rolling basis. Application fee: $40 ($55 for international students). Electronic applications accepted. *Expenses:* Tuition: Full-time $12,942; part-time $719 per credit hour. Required fees: $710; $355 per semester. *Financial support:* Scholarships/grants and unspecified assistantships available. Financial award application deadline: 4/30; financial award applicants required to submit FAFSA. *Faculty research:* Education for public service. *Unit head:* Dr.

History

Clark Atlanta University (continued)

Shirley Williams-Kirksey, Dean, 404-880-6774, E-mail: skirksey@cau.edu. *Application contact:* Michelle Clark-Davis, Graduate Program Admissions, 404-880-6605, E-mail: cauadmissions@cau.edu.

Clark University, Graduate School, Department of History, Worcester, MA 01610-1477. Offers American history (MA, PhD); history (MA, CAGS); Holocaust history (PhD). *Faculty:* 11 full-time (5 women). *Students:* 19 full-time (9 women), 2 part-time (0 women), 4 international. Average age 29. 57 applicants, 23% accepted, 11 enrolled. In 2010, 2 master's, 2 doctorates awarded. *Degree requirements:* For master's, thesis, oral exam; for doctorate, thesis/dissertation. *Entrance requirements:* Additional exam requirements/recommendations for international students: Required—TOEFL. *Application deadline:* For fall admission, 1/15 priority date for domestic students. Applications are processed on a rolling basis. Application fee: $50. *Expenses:* Tuition: Full-time $37,000; part-time $1156 per credit hour. Required fees: $30; $1156 per credit hour. *Financial support:* In 2010–11, fellowships with full and partial tuition reimbursements (averaging $11,850 per year), research assistantships with full and partial tuition reimbursements (averaging $11,850 per year), 4 teaching assistantships with full and partial tuition reimbursements (averaging $11,850 per year) were awarded; tuition waivers (full and partial) also available. *Faculty research:* American political history, comparative history, modern German and European history, Holocaust history, American family history. Total annual research expenditures: $15,000. *Unit head:* Dr. Amy Richter, Chair, 508-793-7288. *Application contact:* Diane Fenner, Academic Secretary, 508-793-7288, Fax: 508-793-8816, E-mail: history@clarku.edu.

Clemson University, Graduate School, College of Architecture, Arts, and Humanities, Department of History, Clemson, SC 29634. Offers MA. Part-time programs available. *Faculty:* 21 full-time (8 women), 1 (woman) part-time/adjunct. *Students:* 20 full-time (8 women), 6 part-time (2 women); includes 1 American Indian or Alaska Native, non-Hispanic/Latino; 1 Asian, non-Hispanic/Latino; 3 Hispanic/Latino. Average age 29. 26 applicants, 54% accepted, 10 enrolled. In 2010, 11 master's awarded. *Degree requirements:* For master's, one foreign language, thesis. *Entrance requirements:* For master's, GRE General Test. Additional exam requirements/recommendations for international students: Required—TOEFL. *Application deadline:* For fall admission, 2/20 for domestic and international students; for spring admission, 11/1 for domestic students, 9/15 for international students. Application fee: $70 ($80 for international students). Electronic applications accepted. *Expenses:* Tuition, state resident: full-time $6492; part-time $400 per credit hour. Tuition, nonresident: full-time $13,634; part-time $800 per credit hour. Required fees: $262 per semester. Part-time tuition and fees vary according to course load and program. *Financial support:* In 2010–11, 17 students received support, including 15 teaching assistantships with partial tuition reimbursements available (averaging $9,992 per year); research assistantships with partial tuition reimbursements available, career-related internships or fieldwork, institutionally sponsored loans, scholarships/grants, health care benefits, and unspecified assistantships also available. Support available to part-time students. Financial award application deadline: 2/15; financial award applicants required to submit FAFSA. *Faculty research:* American, European, British, and Third World history. Total annual research expenditures: $7,988. *Unit head:* Dr. Thomas Kuehn, Chair, 864-656-5361, Fax: 864-656-1015, E-mail: tjkuehn@clemson.edu. *Application contact:* Dr. Paul Anderson, Graduate Coordinator, 864-656-5362, Fax: 864-656-1015, E-mail: pcander@clemson.edu.

Cleveland State University, College of Graduate Studies, College of Liberal Arts and Social Sciences, Department of History, Cleveland, OH 44115. Offers art history (MA); history (MA); museum studies (MA). Part-time and evening/weekend programs available. *Faculty:* 18 full-time (6 women), 10 part-time/adjunct (2 women). *Students:* 14 full-time (7 women), 19 part-time (12 women); includes 2 Black or African American, non-Hispanic/Latino. Average age 34. 39 applicants, 51% accepted, 14 enrolled. In 2010, 20 master's awarded. *Degree requirements:* For master's, thesis optional. *Entrance requirements:* For master's, minimum GPA of 3.0, bachelor's degree in history. Additional exam requirements/recommendations for international students: Required—TOEFL (minimum score 525 paper-based; 197 computer-based). *Application deadline:* For fall admission, 7/15 priority date for domestic students. Applications are processed on a rolling basis. Application fee: $30. Electronic applications accepted. *Expenses:* Tuition, state resident: full-time $8447; part-time $469 per credit hour. Tuition, nonresident: full-time $16,020; part-time $890 per credit hour. Required fees: $50. *Financial support:* In 2010–11, 7 students received support, including research assistantships with full tuition reimbursements available (averaging $8,600 per year); career-related internships or fieldwork and unspecified assistantships also available. *Faculty research:* African Diaspora, social history and the city, early modern Europe, local history. *Unit head:* Dr. Elizabeth A. Lehfeldt, Chairperson, 216-687-3920, Fax: 216-687-5592, E-mail: e.lehfeldt@csuohio.edu. *Application contact:* Dr. Robert S. Shelton, Graduate Director, 216-687-3927, E-mail: r.s.shelton@csuohio.edu.

The College at Brockport, State University of New York, School of the Arts, Humanities and Social Sciences, Department of History, Brockport, NY 14420-2997. Offers history (MA), including American history, American/world history, world history. Part-time and evening/weekend programs available. *Students:* 27 full-time (12 women), 28 part-time (12 women); includes 4 minority (2 American Indian or Alaska Native, non-Hispanic/Latino; 2 Hispanic/Latino). 26 applicants, 65% accepted, 17 enrolled. In 2010, 7 master's awarded. *Degree requirements:* For master's, thesis or alternative. *Entrance requirements:* For master's, minimum GPA of 3.0, writing sample, letters of recommendation, statement of objectives. Additional exam requirements/recommendations for international students: Required—TOEFL (minimum score 550 paper-based; 213 computer-based; 79 iBT). *Application deadline:* For fall admission, 6/1 priority date for domestic and international students; for spring admission, 11/15 priority date for domestic and international students. Application fee: $50. Electronic applications accepted. *Financial support:* In 2010–11, 1 fellowship with tuition reimbursement (averaging $1,600 per year), 2 teaching assistantships with full tuition reimbursements (averaging $6,000 per year) were awarded; Federal Work-Study, scholarships/grants, and unspecified assistantships also available. Support available to part-time students. Financial award application deadline: 3/15; financial award applicants required to submit FAFSA. *Faculty research:* American history, women's history, European history, world history, cultural history. *Unit head:* Dr. Alison Parker, Chairperson, 585-395-5694, Fax: 585-395-2620, E-mail: aparker@brockport.edu. *Application contact:* Dr. Morag Martin, Graduate Director, 585-395-5690, Fax: 585-395-2620, E-mail: mmartin@brockport.edu.

College of Charleston, Graduate School, School of Humanities and Social Sciences, Program in History, Charleston, SC 29424-0001. Offers MA. Program offered jointly with The Citadel, The Military College of South Carolina. Part-time and evening/weekend programs available. *Faculty:* 24 full-time (8 women), 1 part-time/adjunct (0 women). *Students:* 16 full-time (10 women), 12 part-time (7 women); includes 5 minority (2 Black or African American, non-Hispanic/Latino; 3 Two or more races, non-Hispanic/Latino). Average age 27. 29 applicants, 45% accepted, 11 enrolled. In 2010, 13 master's awarded. *Degree requirements:* For master's, comprehensive exam, thesis optional. *Entrance requirements:* For master's, GRE General Test or MAT, writing sample. Additional exam requirements/recommendations for international students: Required—TOEFL (minimum score 81 iBT). *Application deadline:* For fall admission, 3/1 for domestic students; for spring admission, 10/15 for domestic students. Applications are processed on a rolling basis. Application fee: $45. Electronic applications accepted. *Financial support:* In 2010–11, research assistantships (averaging $12,400 per year); career-related internships or fieldwork, Federal Work-Study, scholarships/grants, and unspecified assistantships also available. Financial award application deadline: 4/1; financial award applicants required to submit FAFSA. *Faculty research:* Modern West Africa, labor history, Southern womens' education, Native Americans, the Atlantic world. *Unit head:* Dr. Jason Coy, Director, 843-953-8273, Fax: 843-953-6349, E-mail: coyj@cofc.edu. *Application contact:* Susan Hallatt, Director of Graduate Admissions, 843-953-5614, Fax: 843-953-1434, E-mail: hallatts@cofc.edu.

The College of Saint Rose, Graduate Studies, School of Arts and Humanities, Program in History/Political Science, Albany, NY 12203-1419. Offers MA. Part-time and evening/weekend programs available. *Degree requirements:* For master's, final paper/project, thesis or comprehensive exam. *Entrance requirements:* For master's, minimum undergraduate GPA of 3.0, 12 undergraduate credits in US history and/or political science. Additional exam requirements/recommendations for international students: Required—TOEFL (minimum score 550 paper-based; 213 computer-based). Electronic applications accepted.

College of Staten Island of the City University of New York, Graduate Programs, Program in History, Staten Island, NY 10314-6600. Offers MA. Part-time and evening/weekend programs available. *Faculty:* 5 full-time (3 women). *Students:* 1 (woman) full-time, 25 part-time (9 women); includes 1 Hispanic/Latino, 1 international. Average age 32. 24 applicants, 50% accepted, 10 enrolled. In 2010, 6 master's awarded. *Degree requirements:* For master's, thesis. *Entrance requirements:* For master's, minimum GPA of 3.0 overall and in undergraduate history courses, 2 academic letters of recommendation, letter explaining interest. Additional exam requirements/recommendations for international students: Required—TOEFL (minimum score 550 paper-based; 213 computer-based; 79 iBT), IELTS (minimum score 6.5). *Application deadline:* For fall admission, 5/20 for domestic and international students; for spring admission, 12/10 for domestic and international students. Applications are processed on a rolling basis. Application fee: $125. Electronic applications accepted. *Expenses:* Tuition, state resident: full-time $7730; part-time $325 per credit. Tuition, nonresident: full-time $14,520; part-time $605 per credit. Required fees: $378. *Financial support:* Career-related internships or fieldwork, Federal Work-Study, and scholarships/grants available. Support available to part-time students. Financial award applicants required to submit FAFSA. *Unit head:* Dr. Sandra Gambetti, Coordinator, 718-982-2870 Ext. 2915, Fax: 718-982-2864, E-mail: historymakers@mail.csi.cuny.edu. *Application contact:* Sasha Spence, Assistant Director of Graduate Recruitment and Admissions, 718-982-2699, Fax: 718-982-2500, E-mail: sasha.spence@csi.cuny.edu.

The College of William and Mary, Faculty of Arts and Sciences, Lyon Gardiner Tyler Department of History, Williamsburg, VA 23187-8795. Offers MA, PhD. Part-time programs available. *Faculty:* 25 full-time (11 women), 5 part-time/adjunct (1 woman). *Students:* 58 full-time (36 women); includes 2 minority (both Black or African American, non-Hispanic/Latino), 1 international. Average age 29. 158 applicants, 17% accepted, 15 enrolled. In 2010, 15 master's, 4 doctorates awarded. Terminal master's awarded for partial completion of doctoral program. *Degree requirements:* For master's, one foreign language, comprehensive exam, thesis; for doctorate, one foreign language, comprehensive exam, thesis/dissertation. *Entrance requirements:* For master's and doctorate, GRE General Test, minimum GPA of 3.0. Additional exam requirements/recommendations for international students: Required—TOEFL. *Application deadline:* For fall admission, 12/5 for domestic and international students. Application fee: $45. Electronic applications accepted. *Expenses:* Tuition, state resident: full-time $6400; part-time $345 per credit hour. Tuition, nonresident: full-time $19,720; part-time $920 per credit hour. Required fees: $4368. *Financial support:* In 2010–11, 40 students received support, including 3 fellowships with full tuition reimbursements available (averaging $18,000 per year), 14 research assistantships with full tuition reimbursements available (averaging $18,000 per year), 11 teaching assistantships with full tuition reimbursements available (averaging $18,000 per year); career-related internships or fieldwork also available. Financial award application deadline: 12/5; financial award applicants required to submit FAFSA. *Faculty research:* Early American, U. S., and comparative and transitional history. Total annual research expenditures: $155,481. *Unit head:* Dr. Leisa Meyer, Chair, 757-221-6285, Fax: 757-221-2111, E-mail: ldmeyer@wm.edu. *Application contact:* Dr. Cindy Hahamovitch, Director of Graduate Studies, 757-221-3720, Fax: 757-221-2111, E-mail: cxhaha@wm.edu.

Colorado State University, Graduate School, College of Liberal Arts, Department of History, Fort Collins, CO 80523-1776. Offers MA. Part-time programs available. *Faculty:* 17 full-time (6 women). *Students:* 26 full-time (17 women), 13 part-time (6 women); includes 3 minority (2 Hispanic/Latino; 1 Two or more races, non-Hispanic/Latino), 1 international. Average age 30. 43 applicants, 42% accepted, 15 enrolled. In 2010, 24 master's awarded. *Degree requirements:* For master's, variable foreign language requirement, comprehensive exam (for some programs), thesis (for some programs), written and oral exams. *Entrance requirements:* For master's, GRE General Test, minimum GPA of 3.0, minimum 21 credits in history, letters of recommendation. Additional exam requirements/recommendations for international students: Required—TOEFL (minimum score 550 paper-based; 213 computer-based; 80 iBT). *Application deadline:* For fall admission, 2/1 priority date for domestic and international students; for spring admission, 11/1 for domestic and international students. Application fee: $50. Electronic applications accepted. *Expenses:* Tuition, state resident: full-time $7434; part-time $413 per credit. Tuition, nonresident: full-time $19,022; part-time $1057 per credit. Required fees: $1729; $88 per credit. *Financial support:* In 2010–11, 22 students received support, including 22 teaching assistantships with tuition reimbursements available (averaging $12,020 per year); fellowships, research assistantships, career-related internships or fieldwork, Federal Work-Study, institutionally sponsored loans, scholarships/grants, traineeships, and unspecified assistantships also available. Financial award application deadline: 3/1; financial award applicants required to submit FAFSA. *Faculty research:* U. S. history, world history, gender history, European history, environmental history. Total annual research expenditures: $210,839. *Unit head:* Dr. Diane Margolf, Professor and Chair, 970-491-6334, Fax: 970-491-2941, E-mail: diane.margolf@colostate.edu. *Application contact:* Nancy Rehe, Graduate Contact, 970-491-6334, Fax: 970-491-2941, E-mail: nancy.rehe@colostate.edu.

Columbia University, Graduate School of Arts and Sciences, Division of Social Sciences, Department of History, New York, NY 10027. Offers American history (M Phil, MA, PhD); history (M Phil, MA, PhD); JD/MA; JD/PhD. Part-time programs available. *Degree requirements:* For master's, one foreign language, thesis; for doctorate, variable foreign language requirement, thesis/dissertation. *Entrance requirements:* For master's and doctorate, GRE General Test, writing sample. Additional exam requirements/recommendations for international students: Required—TOEFL.

Columbia University, Graduate School of Arts and Sciences, Program in History and Literature, 75006 Paris, NY 10027, France. Offers MA. Courses taught in English or French. *Entrance requirements:* For master's, GRE General Test, curriculum vitae, official transcripts, statement of purpose, writing sample, three letters of recommendation. Additional exam requirements/recommendations for international students: Required—TOEFL.

Concordia University, School of Graduate Studies, Faculty of Arts and Science, Department of History, Montréal, QC H3G 1M8, Canada. Offers MA, PhD. *Degree requirements:* For master's, one foreign language, thesis optional; for doctorate, one foreign language, comprehensive exam, thesis/dissertation. *Entrance requirements:* For master's, honors degree in history or equivalent. *Faculty research:* Canadian history, European social history, Canadian-American relations.

Converse College, School of Education and Graduate Studies, Program in Liberal Arts, Spartanburg, SC 29302-0006. Offers English (MLA); history (MLA); political science (MLA). *Degree requirements:* For master's, capstone paper. *Entrance requirements:* For master's, minimum GPA of 3.0, 2 recommendations. *Expenses:* Tuition: Part-time $365 per credit hour.

Cornell University, Graduate School, Graduate Fields of Arts and Sciences, Field of History, Ithaca, NY 14853-0001. Offers African history (MA, PhD); American history (MA, PhD); ancient history (MA, PhD); early modern European history (MA, PhD); English history (MA, PhD); French history (MA, PhD); German history (MA, PhD); history of science (MA, PhD); Latin American history (MA, PhD); medieval Chinese history (MA, PhD); medieval history (MA, PhD); modern Chinese history (MA, PhD); modern European history (MA, PhD); modern Japanese history (MA, PhD); premodern Islamic history (MA, PhD); premodern Japanese history (MA, PhD); Renaissance history (MA, PhD); Russian history (MA, PhD); Southeast Asian history (MA, PhD). *Faculty:* 53 full-time (15 women). *Students:* 59 full-time (30 women); includes 3 Black or African American, non-Hispanic/Latino; 2 Asian, non-Hispanic/Latino; 4 Hispanic/Latino, 22 international. Average age 30. 217 applicants, 6% accepted, 8 enrolled. In

2010, 9 master's, 5 doctorates awarded. Terminal master's awarded for partial completion of doctoral program. *Degree requirements:* For master's, thesis; for doctorate, 2 foreign languages, comprehensive exam, thesis/dissertation, 1 year of teaching experience. *Entrance requirements:* For master's and doctorate, GRE General Test, writing sample, 3 letters of recommendation. Additional exam requirements/recommendations for international students: Required—TOEFL (minimum score 550 paper-based; 213 computer-based; 77 iBT). *Application deadline:* For fall admission, 1/15 for domestic students. Application fee: $80. Electronic applications accepted. *Expenses:* Tuition: Full-time $29,500. Required fees: $76. Tuition and fees vary according to degree level and program. *Financial support:* In 2010–11, 26 fellowships with full tuition reimbursements, 27 teaching assistantships with full tuition reimbursements were awarded; research assistantships with full tuition reimbursements, institutionally sponsored loans, scholarships/grants, health care benefits, tuition waivers (full and partial), and unspecified assistantships also available. Financial award applicants required to submit FAFSA. *Unit head:* Director of Graduate Studies, 607-255-6738, Fax: 607-255-0469. *Application contact:* Graduate Field Assistant, 607-255-6738, Fax: 607-255-0469, E-mail: history_grad_info@cornell.edu.

Dalhousie University, Faculty of Arts and Social Science, Department of History, Halifax, NS B3H 4R2, Canada. Offers MA, PhD. *Entrance requirements:* Additional exam requirements/recommendations for international students: Required—TOEFL, IELTS, CANTEST, CAEL, or Michigan English Language Assessment Battery. Electronic applications accepted. *Faculty research:* African, British, Russian, Canadian and medieval history.

DePaul University, College of Liberal Arts and Sciences, Department of History, Chicago, IL 60614. Offers MA. Part-time and evening/weekend programs available. *Faculty:* 28 full-time (11 women), 7 part-time/adjunct (3 women). *Students:* 17 full-time (5 women), 17 part-time (10 women); includes 4 minority (1 Black or African American, non-Hispanic/Latino; 1 Asian, non-Hispanic/Latino; 2 Hispanic/Latino). Average age 32. 56 applicants, 70% accepted, 16 enrolled. In 2010, 6 master's awarded. *Degree requirements:* For master's, thesis optional, three core courses and nine colloquia. *Entrance requirements:* For master's, GRE General Test, bachelor's degree in social science or history, or history minor. Additional exam requirements/recommendations for international students: Required—TOEFL. *Application deadline:* 5/1 priority date for domestic and international students. Applications are processed on a rolling basis. Application fee: $40. Electronic applications accepted. *Financial support:* In 2010–11, 2 students received support, including 2 fellowships (averaging $7,000 per year); career-related internships or fieldwork, scholarships/grants, and tuition waivers (full) also available. Financial award application deadline: 5/1. *Faculty research:* U. S., Europe, Latin America, Asia, Africa. *Unit head:* Dr. Warren C. Schultz, Chairperson, 773-325-1561, Fax: 773-325-4764, E-mail: wschultz@depaul.edu. *Application contact:* Dr. Roshanna P. Sylvester, Graduate Director, 773-325-7825, Fax: 773-325-4764, E-mail: rsylvest@depaul.edu.

Drew University, Caspersen School of Graduate Studies, Program in History and Culture, Madison, NJ 07940-1493. Offers intellectual history (MA, PhD). Part-time programs available. Terminal master's awarded for partial completion of doctoral program. *Degree requirements:* For master's, thesis; for doctorate, one foreign language, comprehensive exam (for some programs), thesis/dissertation. *Entrance requirements:* For master's and doctorate, GRE, transcripts, personal statement, writing sample, recommendations. Additional exam requirements/recommendations for international students: Required—TOEFL (minimum score 585 paper-based; 240 computer-based; 95 iBT), TWE.

Duke University, Graduate School, Department of History, Durham, NC 27708. Offers history (AM, PhD); Latin American studies (PhD); JD/AM; MD/PhD. *Faculty:* 37 full-time. *Students:* 62 full-time (37 women); includes 8 Black or African American, non-Hispanic/Latino; 1 Hispanic/Latino, 7 international. 207 applicants, 14% accepted, 17 enrolled. In 2010, 4 master's, 4 doctorates awarded. *Degree requirements:* For doctorate, 2 foreign languages, thesis/dissertation. *Entrance requirements:* For doctorate, GRE General Test. Additional exam requirements/recommendations for international students: Required—TOEFL (minimum score 550 paper-based; 213 computer-based; 83 iBT), IELTS (minimum score 7). *Application deadline:* For fall admission, 12/8 priority date for domestic and international students. Application fee: $75. Electronic applications accepted. *Financial support:* Fellowships, research assistantships, teaching assistantships, Federal Work-Study available. Financial award application deadline: 12/8. *Unit head:* Peter Sigal, Director of Graduate Studies, 919-681-5746, Fax: 919-681-7670, E-mail: rmennis@duke.edu. *Application contact:* Elizabeth Hutton, Director, Graduate Admission, 919-684-3913, Fax: 919-684-2277, E-mail: grad-admissions@duke.edu.

Duquesne University, Graduate School of Liberal Arts, Department of History, Pittsburgh, PA 15282-0001. Offers archival, museum, and editing studies (MA); history (MA). Part-time and evening/weekend programs available. *Faculty:* 6 full-time (1 woman), 3 part-time/adjunct (1 woman). *Students:* 38 full-time (25 women), 9 part-time (4 women). Average age 26. 52 applicants, 67% accepted, 20 enrolled. In 2010, 20 master's awarded. *Degree requirements:* For master's, comprehensive exam (for some programs), thesis optional. *Entrance requirements:* For master's, GRE General Test, writing sample. Additional exam requirements/recommendations for international students: Required—TOEFL. *Application deadline:* For fall admission, 8/15 for domestic students, 5/1 for international students; for spring admission, 11/1 priority date for domestic students. Applications are processed on a rolling basis. Electronic applications accepted. *Expenses:* Tuition: Part-time $884 per credit. Required fees: $84 per credit. Tuition and fees vary according to course load. *Financial support:* In 2010–11, 4 research assistantships with full tuition reimbursements (averaging $6,000 per year) were awarded; career-related internships or fieldwork, Federal Work-Study, scholarships/grants, tuition waivers (full and partial), and unspecified assistantships also available. Support available to part-time students. Financial award application deadline: 5/1. *Faculty research:* American studies, immigration history, local social history, applied history, Eastern European history. *Unit head:* Dr. Holly Mayer, Chair, 412-396-6470, E-mail: mayer@duq.edu. *Application contact:* Dr. Holly Mayer, Chair, 412-396-6470, E-mail: mayer@duq.edu.

East Carolina University, Graduate School, Thomas Harriot College of Arts and Sciences, Department of History, Greenville, NC 27858-4353. Offers American history (MA); European history (MA); maritime history (MA). Part-time and evening/weekend programs available. *Degree requirements:* For master's, one foreign language, comprehensive exam, thesis. *Entrance requirements:* For master's, GRE General Test, GRE Subject Test. Additional exam requirements/recommendations for international students: Required—TOEFL. *Expenses:* Tuition, state resident: full-time $3130; part-time $391.25 per credit hour. Tuition, nonresident: full-time $13,817; part-time $1727.13 per credit hour. Required fees: $1916; $239.50 per credit hour. Tuition and fees vary according to campus/location and program.

Eastern Illinois University, Graduate School, College of Arts and Humanities, Department of History, Charleston, IL 61920-3099. Offers historical administration (MA); history (MA). Part-time programs available.

Eastern Kentucky University, The Graduate School, College of Arts and Sciences, Department of History, Richmond, KY 40475-3102. Offers MA. Part-time programs available. *Degree requirements:* For master's, comprehensive exam, thesis optional. *Entrance requirements:* For master's, GRE General Test, GRE Subject Test, minimum GPA of 2.5. *Faculty research:* Twentieth-century U.S. history, Kentucky history, British history, world history, Eastern Europe.

Eastern Michigan University, Graduate School, College of Arts and Sciences, Department of History and Philosophy, Programs in History, Ypsilanti, MI 48197. Offers history (MA); state and local history (Graduate Certificate). Part-time and evening/weekend programs available. Postbaccalaureate distance learning degree programs offered (minimal on-campus study). *Students:* 9 full-time (3 women), 66 part-time (25 women); includes 8 minority (5 Black or African American, non-Hispanic/Latino; 1 Asian, non-Hispanic/Latino; 1 Hispanic/Latino; 1 Two or more races, non-Hispanic/Latino). Average age 35. In 2010, 14 master's awarded. *Degree requirements:* For master's, thesis optional. *Entrance requirements:* Additional exam requirements/recommendations for international students: Required—TOEFL. *Application deadline:* Applications are processed on a rolling basis. Application fee: $35. *Financial support:* Fellowships, research assistantships with full tuition reimbursements, teaching assistantships with full tuition reimbursements, career-related internships or fieldwork, Federal Work-Study, institutionally sponsored loans, scholarships/grants, tuition waivers (partial), and unspecified assistantships available. Support available to part-time students. Financial award applicants required to submit FAFSA. *Application contact:* Dr. Ronald Delph, Coordinator, 734-487-0053, Fax: 734-487-6835, E-mail: rdelph@emich.edu.

Eastern Washington University, Graduate Studies, College of Social and Behavioral Sciences, Department of History, Cheney, WA 99004-2431. Offers MA. *Degree requirements:* For master's, comprehensive exam, thesis optional. *Entrance requirements:* For master's, minimum GPA of 3.0.

East Stroudsburg University of Pennsylvania, Graduate School, College of Arts and Sciences, Department of History, East Stroudsburg, PA 18301-2999. Offers M Ed, MA. Part-time and evening/weekend programs available. *Degree requirements:* For master's, comprehensive exam, thesis, thesis defense. *Entrance requirements:* For master's, Commonwealth of Pennsylvania Department of Education Certification Requirements (M Ed). Additional exam requirements/recommendations for international students: Required—TOEFL (minimum score 560 paper-based; 220 computer-based; 83 iBT).

East Tennessee State University, School of Graduate Studies, College of Arts and Sciences, Department of History, Johnson City, TN 37614. Offers MA. Part-time and evening/weekend programs available. *Faculty:* 12 full-time (2 women). *Students:* 34 full-time (18 women), 17 part-time (9 women); includes 5 minority (2 Black or African American, non-Hispanic/Latino; 1 American Indian or Alaska Native, non-Hispanic/Latino; 2 Two or more races, non-Hispanic/Latino), 1 international. Average age 34. 41 applicants, 59% accepted, 18 enrolled. In 2010, 18 master's awarded. *Degree requirements:* For master's, comprehensive exam, thesis optional. *Entrance requirements:* For master's, bachelor's degree in history, minimum GPA of 3.0. Additional exam requirements/recommendations for international students: Required—TOEFL (minimum score 550 paper-based; 213 computer-based; 79 iBT). *Application deadline:* For fall admission, 3/1 priority date for domestic students, 1/30 for international students; for spring admission, 11/1 for domestic students, 9/30 for international students. Application fee: $25 ($35 for international students). Electronic applications accepted. *Financial support:* In 2010–11, 7 teaching assistantships with full tuition reimbursements (averaging $6,000 per year) were awarded; research assistantships with full tuition reimbursements, institutionally sponsored loans and scholarships/grants also available. Financial award application deadline: 7/1; financial award applicants required to submit FAFSA. *Faculty research:* Post-World War II German occupation, biographies of Eleanor Copenhaver Anderson and Harry M. Candill, the Miss America Pageant, encyclopedia of colonialism, the new Georgia campaign in the Pacific war. *Unit head:* Dr. Ronnie M. Day, Chair, 423-439-4222, Fax: 423-439-5373, E-mail: dayr@etsu.edu. *Application contact:* Admissions and Records Clerk, 423-439-4221, Fax: 423-439-5624, E-mail: gradsch@etsu.edu.

Emory & Henry College, Graduate Programs, Emory, VA 24327-0947. Offers American history (MA Ed); organizational leadership (MOL); professional studies (M Ed); reading specialist (MA Ed). Part-time and evening/weekend programs available. *Entrance requirements:* For master's, GRE or PRAXIS I, recommendations, writing sample.

Emory University, Laney Graduate School, Department of History, Atlanta, GA 30322-1100. Offers PhD. *Degree requirements:* For doctorate, 2 foreign languages, comprehensive exam, thesis/dissertation. *Entrance requirements:* For doctorate, GRE General Test, minimum GPA of 3.0. Electronic applications accepted. *Expenses:* Tuition: Full-time $33,800. Required fees: $1300. *Faculty research:* U.S., modern Europe, early modern Europe, medieval Europe, Latin America, Africa.

Emporia State University, Graduate School, College of Liberal Arts and Sciences, Department of Social Sciences, Program in History, Emporia, KS 66801-5087. Offers American history (MA); world history (MA). Part-time programs available. *Students:* 3 full-time (2 women), 14 part-time (4 women); includes 1 minority (Black or African American, non-Hispanic/Latino). 8 applicants, 100% accepted, 6 enrolled. In 2010, 6 master's awarded. *Degree requirements:* For master's, comprehensive exam or thesis. *Entrance requirements:* For master's, 12 credit hours in history, minimum undergraduate GPA of 2.5, writing sample. Additional exam requirements/recommendations for international students: Required—TOEFL (minimum score 520 paper-based; 133 computer-based; 68 iBT). *Application deadline:* For fall admission, 8/15 priority date for domestic students. Applications are processed on a rolling basis. Application fee: $30 ($75 for international students). Electronic applications accepted. *Expenses:* Tuition, state resident: full-time $4382; part-time $183 per credit hour. Tuition, nonresident: full-time $13,572; part-time $566 per credit hour. Required fees: $1022; $62 per credit hour. Tuition and fees vary according to course level, course load and campus/location. *Financial support:* Federal Work-Study, institutionally sponsored loans, health care benefits, and unspecified assistantships available. Financial award application deadline: 3/15; financial award applicants required to submit FAFSA. *Faculty research:* Great Plains history. *Unit head:* Dr. Ellen Hansen, Chair, 620-341-5461, E-mail: ehansen@emporia.edu. *Application contact:* Dr. Deborah Gerish, Assistant Professor, 620-341-5579, E-mail: dgerish@emporia.edu.

Fairleigh Dickinson University, Metropolitan Campus, University College: Arts, Sciences, and Professional Studies, School of History, Political and International Studies, Program in History, Teaneck, NJ 07666-1914. Offers MA. *Students:* 1 full-time (0 women). Average age 23. 5 applicants, 60% accepted, 1 enrolled. *Application deadline:* Applications are processed on a rolling basis. Application fee: $40. *Application contact:* Susan Brooman, University Director of Graduate Admissions, 201-692-2554, Fax: 201-692-2560, E-mail: globaleducation@fdu.edu.

Faulkner University, Great Books Honors College, Montgomery, AL 36109-3398. Offers M Litt.

Fayetteville State University, Graduate School, Department of Geography, History and Political Science, Fayetteville, NC 28301-4298. Offers history (MA); political science (MA). Part-time and evening/weekend programs available. *Faculty:* 8 full-time (2 women). *Students:* 3 full-time (2 women), 6 part-time (3 women); includes 7 Black or African American, non-Hispanic/Latino. Average age 40. 4 applicants, 100% accepted, 4 enrolled. In 2010, 1 master's awarded. *Degree requirements:* For master's, comprehensive exam, internship. *Entrance requirements:* For master's, GRE General Test. *Application deadline:* For fall admission, 4/15 for domestic students; for spring admission, 10/15 for domestic students. Applications are processed on a rolling basis. Application fee: $35. Electronic applications accepted. *Unit head:* Dr. Adeguke Ademiluyi, Chairperson, 910-672-1137, E-mail: aademiluyi@uncfsu.edu. *Application contact:* Katrina Hoffman, Graduate Admissions Officer, 910-672-1374, Fax: 910-672-1470, E-mail: khoffma1@uncfsu.edu.

Fitchburg State University, Division of Graduate and Continuing Education, Programs in History and Teaching History (Secondary Level), Fitchburg, MA 01420-2697. Offers MA, MAT, Certificate. *Accreditation:* NCATE. Part-time and evening/weekend programs available. *Students:* 1 full-time (0 women), 35 part-time (22 women); includes 1 Hispanic/Latino. Average age 31. 9 applicants, 78% accepted, 7 enrolled. In 2010, 7 master's awarded. *Entrance requirements:* For master's, GRE General Test or MAT, appropriate bachelor's degree, letters of recommendation, resume. Additional exam requirements/recommendations for international students: Required—TOEFL (minimum score 550 paper-based; 213 computer-based; 79 iBT). *Application deadline:* Applications are processed on a rolling basis. Application fee: $25 ($50 for international students). *Expenses:* Tuition, area resident: Part-time $150 per credit. Tuition, state resident: part-time $150 per credit. Tuition, nonresident: part-time $150 per credit. Required fees: $127 per credit. *Financial support:* In 2010–11, research assistantships with partial tuition reimbursements (averaging $5,500 per year); Federal Work-Study, scholarships/grants, and unspecified assistantships also available. Support available to part-time students. Financial award application deadline: 3/1; financial award applicants required to submit FAFSA. *Unit*

History

Fitchburg State University (continued)

head: Dr. Laura Baker, Chair, 978-665-3379, Fax: 978-665-3658, E-mail: gce@fitchburgstate.edu. *Application contact:* Director of Admissions, 978-665-3144, Fax: 978-665-4540, E-mail: admissions@fitchburgstate.edu.

Florida Agricultural and Mechanical University, Division of Graduate Studies, Research, and Continuing Education, College of Arts and Sciences, Division of History and Political Sciences, Program in Applied Social Science, Tallahassee, FL 32307-3200. Offers African American history (MASS); criminal justice (MASS); economics (MASS); history (MASS); political science (MASS); public administration (MASS); public management (MASS); social work (MASS); sociology (MASS). Part-time programs available. *Degree requirements:* For master's, thesis optional. *Entrance requirements:* For master's, GRE General Test, minimum GPA of 3.0. *Faculty research:* Southern history, black history, election trends, presidential history.

Florida Atlantic University, Dorothy F. Schmidt College of Arts and Letters, Department of History, Boca Raton, FL 33431-0991. Offers environmental studies (Certificate); history (MA). Part-time programs available. *Faculty:* 20 full-time (10 women), 1 part-time/adjunct (0 women). *Students:* 19 full-time (7 women), 15 part-time (3 women); includes 3 minority (1 Black or African American, non-Hispanic/Latino; 2 Hispanic/Latino), 1 international. Average age 33. 33 applicants, 45% accepted, 12 enrolled. In 2010, 6 master's awarded. *Degree requirements:* For master's, one foreign language, thesis optional. *Entrance requirements:* For master's, GRE General Test, minimum GPA of 3.0. *Application deadline:* For fall admission, 6/1 priority date for domestic students, 2/15 for international students; for spring admission, 10/15 for domestic students, 8/15 for international students. Applications are processed on a rolling basis. Application fee: $30. Electronic applications accepted. *Expenses:* Tuition, area resident: Part-time $319.96 per credit. Tuition, state resident: part-time $319.96 per credit. Tuition, nonresident: part-time $926.42 per credit. *Financial support:* Fellowships, research assistantships, teaching assistantships with tuition reimbursements, career-related internships or fieldwork, Federal Work-Study, and tuition waivers (partial) available. Support available to part-time students. Financial award application deadline: 3/1. *Faculty research:* Twentieth century America, U. S. urban history, Florida history, history of socialism, Latin America. *Unit head:* Dr. Patricia Kollander, Chair, 561-297-3841, Fax: 561-297-2704, E-mail: kollande@fau.edu. *Application contact:* Ben Lowe, Director of Graduate Programs, 561-297-3846, Fax: 561-297-2704, E-mail: bplowe@fau.edu.

Florida Gulf Coast University, College of Arts and Sciences, Program in History, Fort Myers, FL 33965-6565. Offers MA. Part-time and evening/weekend programs available. *Faculty:* 187 full-time (78 women), 177 part-time/adjunct (70 women). *Students:* 23 full-time (9 women), 6 part-time (1 woman); includes 1 Black or African American, non-Hispanic/Latino; 2 Hispanic/Latino. Average age 37. 11 applicants, 91% accepted, 9 enrolled. In 2010, 4 master's awarded. *Entrance requirements:* Additional exam requirements/recommendations for international students: Required—TOEFL (minimum score 550 paper-based; 213 computer-based). *Application deadline:* For fall admission, 2/15 priority date for domestic students; for spring admission, 10/1 for domestic students. Applications are processed on a rolling basis. Electronic applications accepted. *Expenses:* Tuition, state resident: part-time $322.08 per credit hour. Tuition, nonresident: part-time $1117.08 per credit hour. *Unit head:* Eric Strahorn, Head, 239-590-7214, E-mail: estraho@fgcu.edu. *Application contact:* Patricia Rice, Executive Secretary, 239-590-7196, Fax: 239-590-7200, E-mail: price@fgcu.edu.

Florida International University, College of Arts and Sciences, Department of History, Miami, FL 33199. Offers Atlantic civilization (PhD); history (MA). Part-time and evening/weekend programs available. *Faculty:* 21 full-time (12 women), 6 part-time/adjunct (3 women). *Students:* 32 full-time (14 women), 68 part-time (33 women); includes 10 Black or African American, non-Hispanic/Latino; 2 American Indian or Alaska Native, non-Hispanic/Latino; 2 Asian, non-Hispanic/Latino; 45 Hispanic/Latino; 1 Native Hawaiian or other Pacific Islander, non-Hispanic/Latino, 4 international. Average age 28. 92 applicants, 46% accepted, 41 enrolled. In 2010, 11 master's, 1 doctorate awarded. *Degree requirements:* For master's, one foreign language, thesis optional; for doctorate, 2 foreign languages, comprehensive exam, thesis/dissertation. *Entrance requirements:* For master's, 12 credits of history courses (non-history majors), 2 letters of recommendation; writing sample, minimum GPA of 3.25; for doctorate, GRE General Test (minimum score of 1120), two letters of recommendation, statement of purpose, curriculum vitae, writing sample, minimum GPA of 3.25. Additional exam requirements/recommendations for international students: Required—TOEFL (minimum score 575 paper-based; 232 computer-based; 90 iBT). *Application deadline:* For fall admission, 1/15 priority date for domestic students, 1/15 for international students. Application fee: $30. Electronic applications accepted. *Financial support:* Institutionally sponsored loans, scholarships/grants, and unspecified assistantships available. Financial award application deadline: 3/1; financial award applicants required to submit FAFSA. *Faculty research:* European social history, American culture, social and labor history, Latin American culture and social history, military history, Diaspora studies. *Unit head:* Dr. Kenneth Lipartito, Chair, 305-348-2328, Fax: 305-348-3561, E-mail: kenneth.lipartito@fiu.edu. *Application contact:* Dr. Gwyn Davies, Director of Graduate Studies, 305-348-2328, Fax: 305-348-3561, E-mail: daviesg@fiu.edu.

Florida State University, The Graduate School, College of Arts and Sciences, Department of History, Tallahassee, FL 32306. Offers historical administration (MA); history (MA, PhD). Part-time programs available. *Faculty:* 27 full-time (6 women). *Students:* 88 full-time (28 women), 32 part-time (17 women); includes 6 Black or African American, non-Hispanic/Latino; 5 Hispanic/Latino, 4 international. Average age 26. 73 applicants, 60% accepted, 19 enrolled. In 2010, 11 master's, 13 doctorates awarded. *Degree requirements:* For master's, one foreign language, comprehensive exam (for some programs), thesis (for some programs), internships; for doctorate, one foreign language, comprehensive exam, thesis/dissertation. *Entrance requirements:* For master's, GRE General Test, minimum GPA of 3.3, minimum 18 hours of course work in history; for doctorate, GRE General Test, minimum GPA of 3.3 (undergraduate), 3.65 (graduate). Additional exam requirements/recommendations for international students: Required—TOEFL (minimum score 550 paper-based; 213 computer-based; 80 iBT). *Application deadline:* For fall admission, 12/1 for domestic students. Applications are processed on a rolling basis. Application fee: $30. Electronic applications accepted. *Expenses:* Tuition, state resident: full-time $8238.24. *Financial support:* In 2010–11, 81 students received support, including 2 fellowships with full tuition reimbursements available (averaging $14,700 per year), 4 research assistantships with full tuition reimbursements available (averaging $9,900 per year), 27 teaching assistantships with full tuition reimbursements available (averaging $11,550 per year); Federal Work-Study, institutionally sponsored loans, scholarships/grants, and unspecified assistantships also available. Financial award application deadline: 1/10; financial award applicants required to submit FAFSA. *Faculty research:* Southern and Caribbean studies, Napoleon and the French Revolution, modern Europe, Latin America, U. S. intellectual and cultural history. *Unit head:* Dr. Jonathan Grant, Chair, 850-644-5888, Fax: 850-644-6402, E-mail: jgrant@fsu.edu. *Application contact:* Christine Pignatiello, Academic Support Assistant, 850-644-2610, Fax: 850-644-6402, E-mail: cpignatiello@fsu.edu.

Fordham University, Graduate School of Arts and Sciences, Department of History, New York, NY 10458. Offers MA, PhD. Part-time and evening/weekend programs available. *Faculty:* 32 full-time (14 women). *Students:* 27 full-time (11 women), 40 part-time (18 women); includes 1 Black or African American, non-Hispanic/Latino; 2 Asian, non-Hispanic/Latino; 7 Hispanic/Latino, 2 international. Average age 31. 111 applicants, 48% accepted, 18 enrolled. In 2010, 3 master's, 18 doctorates awarded. Terminal master's awarded for partial completion of doctoral program. *Degree requirements:* For master's, one foreign language, thesis optional; for doctorate, 2 foreign languages, comprehensive exam, thesis/dissertation. *Entrance requirements:* For master's and doctorate, GRE General Test. Additional exam requirements/recommendations for international students: Required—TOEFL (minimum score 650 paper-based; 280 computer-based). *Application deadline:* For fall admission, 1/4 priority date for domestic students; for spring admission, 11/1 for domestic students. Application fee: $70. Electronic applications accepted. *Financial support:* In 2010–11, 23 students received support, including 2 fellowships with tuition reimbursements available (averaging $23,000 per year), 13 research assistantships with tuition reimbursements available (averaging $18,704 per year), 8 teaching assistantships with tuition reimbursements available (averaging $18,802 per year); institutionally sponsored loans, tuition waivers (full and partial), and unspecified assistantships also available. Financial award application deadline: 1/4; financial award applicants required to submit FAFSA. *Unit head:* Dr. Doran Ben-Atar, Chair, 718-817-3925, Fax: 718-817-4680. *Application contact:* Charlene Dundie, Director of Graduate Admissions, 718-817-4420, Fax: 718-817-3566, E-mail: dundie@fordham.edu.

Fort Hays State University, Graduate School, College of Arts and Sciences, Department of History, Hays, KS 67601-4099. Offers MA. *Degree requirements:* For master's, comprehensive exam, thesis or alternative. *Entrance requirements:* For master's, minimum undergraduate GPA of 3.0. Additional exam requirements/recommendations for international students: Required—TOEFL (minimum score 550 paper-based; 213 computer-based). Electronic applications accepted. *Faculty research:* Seventeenth century English legal history, Native American history, immigration history, Volga German settlement.

George Mason University, College of Humanities and Social Sciences, Department of History and Art History, Program in History, Fairfax, VA 22030. Offers MA, PhD. Evening/weekend programs available. *Faculty:* 49 full-time (19 women), 19 part-time/adjunct (10 women). *Students:* 38 full-time (17 women), 188 part-time (80 women); includes 5 Black or African American, non-Hispanic/Latino; 5 Asian, non-Hispanic/Latino; 6 Hispanic/Latino; 1 Two or more races, non-Hispanic/Latino, 1 international. Average age 36. 224 applicants, 61% accepted, 58 enrolled. In 2010, 58 master's, 2 doctorates awarded. *Degree requirements:* For master's, comprehensive exam, translation language exam; for doctorate, comprehensive exam, thesis/dissertation. *Entrance requirements:* For master's, GRE (waived for students who received their undergraduate degree 10 or more years ago or hold another graduate degree), 2 letters of recommendation; for doctorate, GRE, 3 letters of recommendation, writing sample, official transcripts. Additional exam requirements/recommendations for international students: Required—TOEFL (minimum score 570 paper-based; 230 computer-based; 88 iBT). *Application deadline:* For fall admission, 4/15 priority date for domestic students; for spring admission, 11/1 for domestic students. Applications are processed on a rolling basis. Application fee: $100. Electronic applications accepted. *Expenses:* Tuition, state resident: full-time $8192; part-time $440 per credit hour. Tuition, nonresident: full-time $22,952; part-time $1055 per credit hour. Required fees: $2364; $99 per credit hour. *Financial support:* In 2010–11, 28 students received support, including 2 fellowships with full tuition reimbursements available (averaging $18,000 per year), 14 research assistantships with full and partial tuition reimbursements available (averaging $13,635 per year), 12 teaching assistantships with full and partial tuition reimbursements available (averaging $13,443 per year); career-related internships or fieldwork, Federal Work-Study, scholarships/grants, unspecified assistantships, and health care benefits (full-time research or teaching assistantship recipients) also available. Financial award application deadline: 3/1; financial award applicants required to submit FAFSA. *Faculty research:* History and new media, American history (digital), building digital archives in the 1930's. *Unit head:* Brian Platt, Chair, 703-993-1253, E-mail: bplatt1@gmu.edu. *Application contact:* Ellen Todd, Art History Advisor, 703-993-4374, E-mail: etodd@gmu.edu.

Georgetown University, Graduate School of Arts and Sciences, Department of History, Washington, DC 20057-1305. Offers global history (MA); global, international and comparative history (MA); history (MA, PhD); MA/PhD; MS/MA. MA in global history offered jointly with history department at King's College London. *Degree requirements:* For master's, thesis (for some programs); for doctorate, 2 foreign languages, comprehensive exam, thesis/dissertation. *Entrance requirements:* For master's and doctorate, GRE General Test. Additional exam requirements/recommendations for international students: Required—TOEFL.

Georgetown University, Graduate School of Arts and Sciences, School of Continuing Studies, Washington, DC 20057. Offers American studies (MALS); Catholic studies (MALS); classical civilizations (MALS); disability studies (MPS); ethics and the professions (MALS); human resources management (MPS); humanities (MALS); individualized study (MALS); international affairs (MALS); Islam and Muslim-Christian relations (MALS); journalism (MPS); liberal studies (DLS); literature and society (MALS); medieval and early modern European studies (MALS); public relations and corporate communications (MPS); real estate (MPS); religious studies (MALS); social and public policy (MALS); sports industry management (MPS); the theory and practice of American democracy (MALS); visual culture (MALS). *Entrance requirements:* Additional exam requirements/recommendations for international students: Required—TOEFL.

The George Washington University, Columbian College of Arts and Sciences, Department of History, Washington, DC 20052. Offers MA, PhD. Part-time and evening/weekend programs available. *Faculty:* 23 full-time (11 women), 20 part-time/adjunct (6 women). *Students:* 37 full-time (11 women), 34 part-time (18 women); includes 1 Black or African American, non-Hispanic/Latino; 1 American Indian or Alaska Native, non-Hispanic/Latino; 1 Asian, non-Hispanic/Latino, 4 international. Average age 30. 205 applicants, 42% accepted, 18 enrolled. In 2010, 11 master's, 4 doctorates awarded. Terminal master's awarded for partial completion of doctoral program. *Degree requirements:* For master's, one foreign language, comprehensive exam, thesis or alternative; for doctorate, 2 foreign languages, thesis/dissertation, general exam. *Entrance requirements:* For master's and doctorate, GRE General Test, minimum GPA of 3.0. Additional exam requirements/recommendations for international students: Required—TOEFL (minimum score 550 paper-based; 213 computer-based; 80 iBT). *Application deadline:* For fall admission, 1/15 priority date for domestic and international students; for spring admission, 10/1 priority date for domestic students, 9/1 priority date for international students. Applications are processed on a rolling basis. Application fee: $75. Electronic applications accepted. *Financial support:* In 2010–11, 28 students received support; fellowships with full tuition reimbursements available, teaching assistantships with tuition reimbursements available, career-related internships or fieldwork, Federal Work-Study, and tuition waivers available. Financial award application deadline: 1/15. *Unit head:* Tyler G. Anbinder, Chair, 202-994-6470, E-mail: anbinder@gwu.edu. *Application contact:* Information Contact, 202-994-6230, Fax: 202-994-6231, E-mail: history@gwu.edu.

Georgia College & State University, Graduate School, College of Arts and Sciences, Department of History, Geography and Philosophy, Milledgeville, GA 31061. Offers history (advanced studies) (MA); history (predoctoral) (MA); public history (MA). Part-time and evening/weekend programs available. *Students:* 6 full-time (3 women), 7 part-time (4 women). Average age 30. 7 applicants, 100% accepted, 5 enrolled. In 2010, 2 master's awarded. *Degree requirements:* For master's, one foreign language, comprehensive exam (for some programs), thesis optional. *Entrance requirements:* For master's, GRE, 2 letters of reference, transcript, minimum GPA of 3.0. Additional exam requirements/recommendations for international students: Recommended—TOEFL (minimum score 550 paper-based; 213 computer-based; 79 iBT). *Application deadline:* For fall admission, 7/1 priority date for domestic students, 4/1 priority date for international students; for spring admission, 11/15 priority date for domestic students, 9/1 priority date for international students. Applications are processed on a rolling basis. Application fee: $40. Electronic applications accepted. *Expenses:* Tuition, state resident: full-time $4806; part-time $267 per hour. Tuition, nonresident: full-time $17,802; part-time $989 per hour. Tuition and fees vary according to course load. *Financial support:* In 2010–11, 7 research assistantships were awarded; unspecified assistantships also available. Support available to part-time students. Financial award applicants required to submit FAFSA. *Unit head:* Dr. John Fair, Graduate Coordinator for MA in History Program, 478-445-5215, E-mail: john.fair@gcsu.edu. *Application contact:* Dr. John Fair, Graduate Coordinator for MA in History Program, 478-445-5215, E-mail: john.fair@gcsu.edu.

Georgia Southern University, Jack N. Averitt College of Graduate Studies, College of Liberal Arts and Social Sciences, Department of History, Statesboro, GA 30460. Offers MA. Part-time programs available. *Students:* 14 full-time (3 women), 12 part-time (3 women); includes 2 Black or African American, non-Hispanic/Latino; 1 American Indian or Alaska Native, non-Hispanic/Latino. Average age 29. 7 applicants, 100% accepted, 5 enrolled. In 2010, 3 master's awarded. *Degree requirements:* For master's, one foreign language, thesis optional, terminal exams. *Entrance requirements:* For master's, GRE General Test, minimum GPA of 3.0, undergraduate major in history or equivalent, letters of reference. Additional exam requirements/recommendations for international students: Required—TOEFL (minimum score 550 paper-based; 213 computer-based; 80 iBT). *Application deadline:* For fall admission, 3/1 priority date for domestic and international students; for spring admission, 10/1 priority date for domestic students, 10/1 for international students. Applications are processed on a rolling basis. Application fee: $50. Electronic applications accepted. *Expenses:* Tuition, state resident: full-time $6000; part-time $250 per semester hour. Tuition, nonresident: full-time $23,976; part-time $999 per semester hour. Required fees: $1644. *Financial support:* In 2010–11, 21 students received support, including research assistantships with partial tuition reimbursements available (averaging $7,200 per year), teaching assistantships with partial tuition reimbursements available (averaging $7,200 per year); career-related internships or fieldwork, Federal Work-Study, scholarships/grants, tuition waivers (partial), and unspecified assistantships also available. Support available to part-time students. Financial award application deadline: 4/15; financial award applicants required to submit FAFSA. *Faculty research:* Women's/gender history, American South, military history. Total annual research expenditures: $3,000. *Unit head:* Dr. Johnathan O'Neill, Chair, 912-478-0752, Fax: 912-478-0377, E-mail: joneill@georgiasouthern.edu. *Application contact:* Dr. Charles Ziglar, Coordinator for Graduate Student Recruitment, 912-478-5635, Fax: 912-478-0740, E-mail: gradadmissions@georgiasouthern.edu.

Georgia State University, College of Arts and Sciences, Department of History, Program in History, Atlanta, GA 30302-3083. Offers MA, PhD. Part-time and evening/weekend programs available. *Degree requirements:* For master's, one foreign language, thesis, exam; for doctorate, 2 foreign languages, thesis/dissertation, exam. *Entrance requirements:* For master's, GRE General Test; for doctorate, GRE General Test, sample of written work. Additional exam requirements/recommendations for international students: Required—TOEFL. Electronic applications accepted. *Faculty research:* World, U.S. South, cultural history, public history, labor.

Graduate School and University Center of the City University of New York, Graduate Studies, Program in History, New York, NY 10016-4039. Offers PhD. *Degree requirements:* For doctorate, one foreign language, thesis/dissertation. *Entrance requirements:* For doctorate, GRE General Test, writing sample (15 pages). Additional exam requirements/recommendations for international students: Required—TOEFL. Electronic applications accepted.

Hardin-Simmons University, Graduate School, Cynthia Ann Parker College of Liberal Arts, Department of History, Abilene, TX 79698-0001. Offers MA. Part-time programs available. *Faculty:* 3 full-time (1 woman). *Students:* 2 part-time (0 women). Average age 37. 3 applicants, 33% accepted, 1 enrolled. In 2010, 1 master's awarded. *Degree requirements:* For master's, one foreign language, comprehensive exam, thesis or alternative. *Entrance requirements:* For master's, GRE, minimum undergraduate GPA of 3.0 in history, 2.7 overall; 18 upper-level hours of course work in history; letters of recommendation; resume; writing sample. Additional exam requirements/recommendations for international students: Required—TOEFL (minimum score 550 paper-based; 213 computer-based; 75 iBT). *Application deadline:* For fall admission, 8/15 priority date for domestic students, 4/1 for international students; for spring admission, 1/5 priority date for domestic students, 9/1 for international students. Applications are processed on a rolling basis. Application fee: $50. *Expenses:* Tuition: Full-time $12,150; part-time $675 per credit hour. Required fees: $650; $110 per semester. Tuition and fees vary according to degree level. *Financial support:* In 2010–11, 1 student received support; fellowships, scholarships/grants available. Support available to part-time students. Financial award application deadline: 6/30; financial award applicants required to submit FAFSA. *Faculty research:* Vietnam, diplomatic history, Texas politics, Mexico and NAFTA, classical warfare. *Unit head:* Dr. Mark Beasley, Program Director, 325-670-1279, Fax: 325-670-1526, E-mail: mbeasley@hsutx.edu. *Application contact:* Dr. Nancy Kucinski, Dean of Graduate Studies, 325-670-1298, Fax: 325-670-1564, E-mail: gradoff@hsutx.edu.

Harvard University, Graduate School of Arts and Sciences, Department of History, Cambridge, MA 02138. Offers African history (PhD); American history (PhD); ancient, medieval, early modern, and modern Europe (PhD), including Central Europe, Russia, Southeastern Europe, Western Europe; diplomatic history (PhD); East Asian history (PhD); economic and social history (PhD); intellectual history (PhD); Latin American history (PhD); Near Eastern history (PhD); oceanic history (PhD). *Degree requirements:* For doctorate, variable foreign language requirement, thesis/dissertation, oral general exam. *Entrance requirements:* For doctorate, GRE General Test, proficiency in 2 languages. Additional exam requirements/recommendations for international students: Required—TOEFL. *Expenses:* Tuition: Full-time $34,976. Required fees: $1166. Full-time tuition and fees vary according to program.

High Point University, Norcross Graduate School, High Point, NC 27262-3598. Offers business administration (MBA); educational leadership (M Ed); elementary education (M Ed); history (MA); nonprofit management (MA); secondary math (M Ed); special education (M Ed); strategic communication (MA); teaching elementary education k-6 (MAT); teaching secondary mathematics 9-12 (MAT). *Accreditation:* ACBSP; NCATE. Part-time and evening/weekend programs available. *Faculty:* 30 full-time (11 women), 5 part-time/adjunct (1 woman). *Students:* 17 full-time (10 women), 292 part-time (198 women); includes 107 minority (100 Black or African American, non-Hispanic/Latino; 1 Asian, non-Hispanic/Latino; 6 Hispanic/Latino), 19 international. 249 applicants, 69% accepted, 141 enrolled. *Degree requirements:* For master's, comprehensive exam (for some programs), thesis (for some programs). *Entrance requirements:* For master's, GMAT (MBA), GRE, MAT, minimum GPA of 3.0. Additional exam requirements/recommendations for international students: Required—TOEFL (minimum score 550 paper-based). *Application deadline:* For fall admission, 4/15 priority date for domestic and international students; for spring admission, 10/15 priority date for domestic and international students. Applications are processed on a rolling basis. Application fee: $50. Electronic applications accepted. *Expenses:* Tuition: Full-time $11,520; part-time $640 per hour. Required fees: $90; $150 per semester. Part-time tuition and fees vary according to program. *Financial support:* Federal Work-Study available. Support available to part-time students. Financial award application deadline: 3/1; financial award applicants required to submit FAFSA. *Unit head:* Tracy Collum, Associate Dean, 336-767-4840, Fax: 336-841-9024, E-mail: tcollum@highpoint.edu. *Application contact:* Tracy Collum, Associate Dean, 336-767-4840, Fax: 336-841-9024, E-mail: tcollum@highpoint.edu.

Howard University, Graduate School, Department of History, Washington, DC 20059-0002. Offers African diaspora (MA, PhD); African history (MA, PhD); Latin America and the Caribbean (MA, PhD); public history (MA); United States history (MA, PhD). Part-time programs available. Terminal master's awarded for partial completion of doctoral program. *Degree requirements:* For master's, one foreign language, thesis optional; for doctorate, 2 foreign languages, comprehensive exam, thesis/dissertation. *Entrance requirements:* For master's, GRE General Test, minimum GPA of 3.0, 3 letters of recommendation; for doctorate, GRE General Test, minimum GPA of 3.5, 3 letters of recommendation. Additional exam requirements/recommendations for international students: Required—TOEFL. Electronic applications accepted. *Faculty research:* Africa diaspora, U.S. diplomatic relations, Caribbean economic history.

Hunter College of the City University of New York, Graduate School, School of Arts and Sciences, Department of History, New York, NY 10021-5085. Offers MA. *Faculty:* 11 full-time (4 women), 1 (woman) part-time/adjunct. *Students:* 52 part-time (22 women); includes 1 Black or African American, non-Hispanic/Latino; 1 American Indian or Alaska Native, non-Hispanic/Latino; 9 Hispanic/Latino, 1 international. Average age 35. 49 applicants, 35% accepted, 9 enrolled. In 2010, 16 master's awarded. *Degree requirements:* For master's, one foreign language, comprehensive exam, thesis, essay, language exam. *Entrance requirements:* For master's, GRE General Test, minimum of 18 credits in undergraduate history or related field. Additional exam requirements/recommendations for international students: Required—TOEFL. *Application deadline:* For fall admission, 4/1 for domestic students, 2/1 for international students; for spring admission, 11/1 for domestic students, 9/1 for international students. Application fee: $125. *Financial support:* Federal Work-Study, scholarships/grants, and tuition waivers (partial)

available. Support available to part-time students. *Unit head:* Dr. Barbara Welter, Chair and Graduate Advisor, 212-772-5487, E-mail: bwelter@hunter.cuny.edu. *Application contact:* William Zlata, Director for Graduate Admissions, 212-772-4482, Fax: 212-650-3336, E-mail: admissions@hunter.cuny.edu.

Idaho State University, Office of Graduate Studies, College of Arts and Sciences, Department of History, Pocatello, ID 83209-8079. Offers historical resources management (MA). Part-time programs available. *Degree requirements:* For master's, comprehensive exam, thesis optional, internship. *Entrance requirements:* For master's, GRE, 3 letters of recommendation, minimum of 18 upper division history credits. Additional exam requirements/recommendations for international students: Required—TOEFL (minimum score 550 paper-based; 213 computer-based; 80 iBT). Electronic applications accepted. *Faculty research:* Historical geographic information systems, historical and urban geography, environmental history and environmental policy, United States political history, womens' and gender history.

Illinois State University, Graduate School, College of Arts and Sciences, Department of History, Normal, IL 61790-2200. Offers MA, MS. *Degree requirements:* For master's, thesis or alternative. *Entrance requirements:* For master's, GRE General Test, minimum GPA of 2.6 in last 60 hours of course work.

Indiana State University, College of Graduate and Professional Studies, College of Arts and Sciences, Department of History, Terre Haute, IN 47809. Offers MA, MS. Part-time and evening/weekend programs available. *Degree requirements:* For master's, comprehensive exam (for some programs), thesis or alternative. *Entrance requirements:* For master's, equivalent of minor in geography or geology. Additional exam requirements/recommendations for international students: Required—TOEFL (minimum score 550 paper-based).

Indiana University Bloomington, University Graduate School, College of Arts and Sciences, Department of History, Bloomington, IN 47405-7000. Offers MA, MAT, PhD, MA/MLS. *Faculty:* 44 full-time (12 women), 34 part-time/adjunct (15 women). *Students:* 143 full-time (76 women), 8 part-time (5 women); includes 22 minority (9 Black or African American, non-Hispanic/Latino; 4 Asian, non-Hispanic/Latino; 9 Hispanic/Latino), 18 international. Average age 31. 292 applicants, 15% accepted, 26 enrolled. In 2010, 15 master's, 6 doctorates awarded. Terminal master's awarded for partial completion of doctoral program. *Degree requirements:* For master's, one foreign language, thesis optional; for doctorate, variable foreign language requirement, comprehensive exam, thesis/dissertation. *Entrance requirements:* For master's and doctorate, GRE General Test. Additional exam requirements/recommendations for international students: Required—TOEFL. *Application deadline:* For fall admission, 12/15 for domestic students, 11/15 for international students. Application fee: $55 ($65 for international students). Electronic applications accepted. *Financial support:* In 2010–11, 34 fellowships with full tuition reimbursements (averaging $15,000 per year), 15 teaching assistantships with full tuition reimbursements (averaging $14,772 per year) were awarded; research assistantships with full tuition reimbursements, career-related internships or fieldwork, Federal Work-Study, institutionally sponsored loans, scholarships/grants, traineeships, health care benefits, and unspecified assistantships also available. *Faculty research:* Medieval and early modern Europe, Russia, Latin America, Middle East, Great Britain, United States, Africa and African Diaspora, Europe, eastern Europe. *Unit head:* Dr. Peter Guardino, Chairman, 812-855-3236, Fax: 812-855-3378, E-mail: pguardin@indiana.edu. *Application contact:* Joey Kremer, Admissions Secretary, 812-855-8233, Fax: 812-855-3378, E-mail: histadm@indiana.edu.

Indiana University of Pennsylvania, School of Graduate Studies and Research, College of Humanities and Social Sciences, Department of History, Program in History, Indiana, PA 15705-1087. Offers MA. Part-time programs available. *Faculty:* 11 full-time (5 women). *Students:* 18 full-time (9 women), 4 part-time (2 women); includes 2 minority (1 Native Hawaiian or other Pacific Islander, non-Hispanic/Latino; 1 Two or more races, non-Hispanic/Latino). Average age 26. 23 applicants, 70% accepted, 11 enrolled. In 2010, 3 master's awarded. *Degree requirements:* For master's, thesis optional. *Entrance requirements:* For master's, GRE, 2 letters of recommendation. Additional exam requirements/recommendations for international students: Required—TOEFL. *Application deadline:* For spring admission, 11/1 for domestic students. Applications are processed on a rolling basis. Application fee: $40. *Financial support:* In 2010–11, 5 research assistantships with full and partial tuition reimbursements (averaging $2,870 per year) were awarded; fellowships, Federal Work-Study also available. Support available to part-time students. Financial award application deadline: 3/15; financial award applicants required to submit FAFSA. *Unit head:* Dr. Werner Lippert, Graduate Coordinator, 724-357-2573, E-mail: werner.lippert@iup.edu. *Application contact:* Dr. Tami Whited, Graduate Coordinator, 724-357-2573, E-mail: twhited@iup.edu.

Indiana University–Purdue University Indianapolis, School of Liberal Arts, Department of History, Indianapolis, IN 46202-2896. Offers history (MA); public history (MA); MA/MLS. Part-time and evening/weekend programs available. *Faculty:* 14 full-time (6 women). *Students:* 13 full-time (9 women), 28 part-time (23 women); includes 1 minority (Black or African American, non-Hispanic/Latino), 1 international. Average age 33. 33 applicants, 48% accepted, 12 enrolled. In 2010, 19 master's awarded. *Degree requirements:* For master's, one foreign language, thesis. *Entrance requirements:* For master's, GRE General Test, minimum GPA of 3.0. *Application deadline:* For fall admission, 2/1 priority date for domestic students. Applications are processed on a rolling basis. Application fee: $55 ($65 for international students). *Financial support:* In 2010–11, 1 fellowship with full tuition reimbursement (averaging $10,000 per year), 19 teaching assistantships with full tuition reimbursements (averaging $8,612 per year) were awarded; research assistantships with full tuition reimbursements, career-related internships or fieldwork also available. *Unit head:* Robert Barrows, Chair, 317-274-2457. *Application contact:* Mary Gelzleichter, Graduate Secretary, 317-274-5840, Fax: 317-278-7800, E-mail: mgelzlei@liupui.edu.

Inter American University of Puerto Rico, Metropolitan Campus, Graduate Programs, Program in History, San Juan, PR 00919-1293. Offers American history (PhD); history (MA, PhD).

Inter American University of Puerto Rico, Metropolitan Campus, Graduate Programs, Program in History Education, San Juan, PR 00919-1293. Offers MA.

Iona College, School of Arts and Science, Program in History, New Rochelle, NY 10801-1890. Offers MA. Part-time and evening/weekend programs available. *Faculty:* 8 full-time (1 woman). *Students:* 3 full-time (2 women), 15 part-time (8 women); includes 3 minority (1 Black or African American, non-Hispanic/Latino; 2 Hispanic/Latino), 1 international. Average age 31. 10 applicants, 70% accepted, 4 enrolled. In 2010, 8 master's awarded. *Degree requirements:* For master's, one foreign language, thesis. *Entrance requirements:* For master's, undergraduate major in history or related field, minimum GPA of 3.0. Additional exam requirements/recommendations for international students: Required—TOEFL (minimum score 550 paper-based; 213 computer-based). *Application deadline:* Applications are processed on a rolling basis. Application fee: $50. Electronic applications accepted. *Expenses:* Tuition: Part-time $830 per credit. Required fees: $225 per credit. *Financial support:* Unspecified assistantships available. Financial award application deadline: 4/15; financial award applicants required to submit FAFSA. *Faculty research:* Global studies, American diplomacy, Native Americans, foreign policy, Armenian history. *Unit head:* Dr. James Carroll, Chairman, 914-633-2694, E-mail: jcarroll@iona.edu. *Application contact:* Veronica Jarek-Prinz, Director of Graduate Admissions, 914-633-2420, Fax: 914-633-2277, E-mail: vjarekprinz@iona.edu.

Iowa State University of Science and Technology, Graduate College, College of Liberal Arts and Sciences, Department of History, Ames, IA 50011. Offers agricultural history and rural studies (PhD); history (MA); history of technology and science (MA, PhD). *Faculty:* 18 full-time (5 women). *Students:* 30 full-time (8 women), 18 part-time (5 women); includes 1 Black or African American, non-Hispanic/Latino, 5 international. 31 applicants, 61% accepted, 13 enrolled. In 2010, 5 master's, 3 doctorates awarded. *Degree requirements:* For master's, thesis or alternative; for doctorate, thesis/dissertation. *Entrance requirements:* For master's and doctorate,

History

Iowa State University of Science and Technology (continued)

GRE General Test. Additional exam requirements/recommendations for international students: Required—TOEFL (minimum score 600 paper-based; 79 iBT), IELTS (minimum score 7). *Application deadline:* For fall admission, 1/15 priority date for domestic and international students. Applications are processed on a rolling basis. Application fee: $40 ($90 for international students). Electronic applications accepted. *Financial support:* In 2010–11, 1 research assistantship with full and partial tuition reimbursement (averaging $20,295 per year), 21 teaching assistantships with full and partial tuition reimbursements (averaging $9,263 per year) were awarded; scholarships/grants, health care benefits, and unspecified assistantships also available. *Unit head:* Dr. Charles Dobbs, Chair, 515-294-7266, Fax: 515-294-6390, E-mail: cdobbs@iastate.edu. *Application contact:* Dr. Pamela Riney-Kehrberg, Information Contact, 515-294-1451, Fax: 515-294-6390.

Jackson State University, Graduate School, College of Liberal Arts, Department of History and Philosophy, Jackson, MS 39217. Offers history (MA). Part-time and evening/weekend programs available. *Faculty:* 5 full-time (0 women). *Students:* 11 full-time (5 women), 20 part-time (12 women); includes 28 Black or African American, non-Hispanic/Latino. Average age 39. In 2010, 3 master's awarded. *Degree requirements:* For master's, comprehensive exam, thesis or alternative. *Entrance requirements:* For master's, GRE General Test. Additional exam requirements/recommendations for international students: Required—TOEFL (minimum score 520 paper-based; 195 computer-based; 67 iBT). *Application deadline:* For fall admission, 3/1 priority date for domestic students, 3/1 for international students; for spring admission, 10/1 for domestic and international students. Applications are processed on a rolling basis. Application fee: $25. *Expenses:* Tuition, state resident: full-time $5050; part-time $281 per credit hour. Tuition, nonresident: full-time $12,380; part-time $689 per credit hour. *Financial support:* Career-related internships or fieldwork, Federal Work-Study, scholarships/grants, and unspecified assistantships available. Support available to part-time students. Financial award application deadline: 3/1; financial award applicants required to submit FAFSA. *Unit head:* Dr. Dernoral Davis, Chair, 601-979-2191, Fax: 601-979-2192, E-mail: dernoral.davis@jsums.edu. *Application contact:* Sharlene Wilson, Director of Graduate Admissions, 601-979-2455, Fax: 601-979-4325, E-mail: sharlene.f.wilson@jsums.edu.

Jacksonville State University, College of Graduate Studies and Continuing Education, College of Arts and Sciences, Department of History, Jacksonville, AL 36265-1602. Offers MA. Part-time and evening/weekend programs available. *Degree requirements:* For master's, comprehensive exam, thesis (for some programs). *Entrance requirements:* For master's, GRE General Test or MAT. Electronic applications accepted.

James Madison University, The Graduate School, College of Arts and Letters, Department of History, Harrisonburg, VA 22807. Offers MA. Part-time programs available. *Faculty:* 15 full-time (3 women), 2 part-time/adjunct (1 woman). *Students:* 25 full-time (12 women), 8 part-time (4 women), 1 international. Average age 27. In 2010, 11 master's awarded. *Degree requirements:* For master's, one foreign language, comprehensive exam, thesis, reading exam in a language. *Entrance requirements:* For master's, GRE General Test, GRE Subject Test, 2 letters of recommendation. Additional exam requirements/recommendations for international students: Required—TOEFL. *Application deadline:* For fall admission, 1/15 for domestic students. Applications are processed on a rolling basis. Application fee: $55. Electronic applications accepted. *Financial support:* In 2010–11, 11 students received support, including 4 teaching assistantships with full tuition reimbursements available (averaging $8,664 per year); Federal Work-Study and 7 graduate assistantships ($7382) also available. Financial award application deadline: 3/1; financial award applicants required to submit FAFSA. *Unit head:* Dr. Michael J. Galgano, Academic Unit Head, 540-568-6132. *Application contact:* Lynette M. Bible, Director of Graduate Admissions, 540-568-6395, Fax: 540-568-7860, E-mail: biblelm@jmu.edu.

John Carroll University, Graduate School, Department of History, University Heights, OH 44118-4581. Offers MA. Part-time and evening/weekend programs available. *Degree requirements:* For master's, comprehensive exam, research essay or thesis. *Entrance requirements:* For master's, GRE General Test, minimum GPA of 2.5. Additional exam requirements/recommendations for international students: Required—TOEFL. Electronic applications accepted. *Faculty research:* Social history of Cleveland, early national Pennsylvania, modern Japanese journalism, Catholic Reformation.

The Johns Hopkins University, Zanvyl Krieger School of Arts and Sciences, Department of History, Baltimore, MD 21218-2699. Offers PhD. *Faculty:* 23 full-time (7 women). *Students:* 52 full-time (26 women); includes 3 minority (1 Asian, non-Hispanic/Latino; 1 Hispanic/Latino; 1 Two or more races, non-Hispanic/Latino), 18 international. Average age 29. 140 applicants, 6% accepted, 7 enrolled. In 2010, 7 doctorates awarded. *Degree requirements:* For doctorate, variable foreign language requirement, comprehensive exam, thesis/dissertation. *Entrance requirements:* For doctorate, GRE General Test. Additional exam requirements/recommendations for international students: Required—TOEFL (minimum score 600 paper-based; 250 computer-based; 100 iBT), IELTS. *Application deadline:* For fall admission, 12/15 for domestic and international students. Application fee: $75. Electronic applications accepted. *Financial support:* In 2010–11, 55 students received support; fellowships with full tuition reimbursements available, research assistantships with full tuition reimbursements available, teaching assistantships with full tuition reimbursements available, Federal Work-Study and institutionally sponsored loans available. Financial award application deadline: 4/15; financial award applicants required to submit FAFSA. *Faculty research:* American, European, Latin American, East Asian, and African history. Total annual research expenditures: $179,717. *Unit head:* Dr. William T. Rowe, Chair, 410-516-7575, Fax: 410-516-7586, E-mail: wtrowe@jhu.edu. *Application contact:* Megan B. Zeller, Senior Administrative Coordinator, 410-516-5296, Fax: 410-516-7586, E-mail: mzeller4@jhu.edu.

Kansas State University, Graduate School, College of Arts and Sciences, Department of History, Manhattan, KS 66506. Offers history (MA); security studies (MA, PhD). Part-time programs available. *Degree requirements:* For master's, thesis (for some programs); for doctorate, one foreign language, thesis/dissertation, qualifying exam. *Entrance requirements:* For master's, GRE General Test or MAT, minimum undergraduate GPA of 3.0; for doctorate, GRE General Test or MAT. Additional exam requirements/recommendations for international students: Required—TOEFL (minimum score 600 paper-based). Electronic applications accepted. *Faculty research:* Environmental history, history of Christianity, American social history, history of war and society, history of international relations and diplomacy.

Kent State University, College of Arts and Sciences, Department of History, Kent, OH 44242-0001. Offers MA, PhD. Part-time programs available. *Degree requirements:* For master's, variable foreign language requirement, thesis optional; for doctorate, variable foreign language requirement, thesis/dissertation. *Entrance requirements:* For master's, GRE General Test, GRE Subject Test, minimum GPA of 2.75; for doctorate, GRE General Test, GRE Subject Test, minimum GPA of 3.0. Additional exam requirements/recommendations for international students: Required—TOEFL. Electronic applications accepted. *Expenses:* Tuition, state resident: full-time $7866; part-time $437 per credit hour. Tuition, nonresident: full-time $14,022; part-time $779 per credit hour. *Faculty research:* African American, civil war, British empire, Latin America, public history.

Lakehead University, Graduate Studies, Department of History, Thunder Bay, ON P7B 5E1, Canada. Offers gerontology (MA); history (MA); women's studies (MA). Part-time programs available. *Degree requirements:* For master's, one foreign language, thesis. *Entrance requirements:* For master's, minimum B average. Additional exam requirements/recommendations for international students: Required—TOEFL. *Faculty research:* Canadian history, British history, Russian/German history, women's studies.

Lamar University, College of Graduate Studies, College of Arts and Sciences, Department of History, Beaumont, TX 77710. Offers MA. Part-time programs available. *Faculty:* 5 full-time (2 women). *Students:* 5 full-time (3 women), 2 part-time (1 woman). Average age 30. 6 applicants, 67% accepted, 4 enrolled. In 2010, 1 master's awarded. *Degree requirements:* For master's, comprehensive exam (for some programs), thesis (for some programs). *Entrance requirements:* For master's, GRE General Test, minimum GPA of 2.5 in last 60 hours of undergraduate course work. Additional exam requirements/recommendations for international students: Required—TOEFL. *Application deadline:* For fall admission, 8/1 for domestic students; for spring admission, 12/1 for domestic students. Applications are processed on a rolling basis. Application fee: $25 ($50 for international students). *Expenses:* Tuition, state resident: full-time $4160; part-time $208 per credit hour. Tuition, nonresident: full-time $10,360; part-time $518 per credit hour. *Financial support:* In 2010–11, fellowships (averaging $1,000 per year), teaching assistantships (averaging $2,000 per year) were awarded. Financial award application deadline: 4/1. *Faculty research:* Old South, nineteenth century reform, twentieth century U. S., religion in America's South, Renaissance/early modern Europe. *Unit head:* Dr. John Storey, Chair, 409-880-8511, Fax: 409-880-8710, E-mail: storeyjw@hal.lamar.edu. *Application contact:* Dr. Howell H. Gwin, Graduate Adviser, 409-880-8530, Fax: 409-880-8710, E-mail: gwinhh@hal.lamar.edu.

La Salle University, School of Arts and Sciences, Program in History, Philadelphia, PA 19141-1199. Offers MA. Part-time programs available.

Laurentian University, School of Graduate Studies and Research, Programme in History, Sudbury, ON P3E 2C6, Canada. Offers European history (MA); history of Northern Ontario (MA); North American history (MA). Part-time programs available. *Degree requirements:* For master's, thesis or alternative. *Entrance requirements:* For master's, honors degree with minimum second class. *Faculty research:* Franco-Ontarian history, northern Ontarian history, Canadian social history, European social history, Franco-Canadian history.

Lehigh University, College of Arts and Sciences, Department of History, Bethlehem, PA 18015. Offers American history (PhD); British history (PhD); history (MA). Part-time programs available. *Faculty:* 16 full-time (5 women). *Students:* 20 full-time (10 women), 16 part-time (2 women). Average age 32. 33 applicants, 73% accepted, 11 enrolled. In 2010, 3 master's, 2 doctorates awarded. Terminal master's awarded for partial completion of doctoral program. *Degree requirements:* For master's, thesis optional, comprehensive exam or thesis; for doctorate, comprehensive exam, thesis/dissertation. *Entrance requirements:* For master's, GRE General Test, recommendations; for doctorate, GRE General Test, recommendations, writing samples. Additional exam requirements/recommendations for international students: Required—TOEFL. *Application deadline:* For fall admission, 7/15 for domestic students; for winter admission, 1/15 priority date for domestic and international students. Applications are processed on a rolling basis. Application fee: $65. Electronic applications accepted. *Financial support:* In 2010–11, 34 students received support, including fellowships with full tuition reimbursements available (averaging $25,000 per year), research assistantships with full tuition reimbursements available (averaging $15,600 per year), 10 teaching assistantships with full tuition reimbursements available (averaging $18,400 per year); institutionally sponsored loans, scholarships/grants, tuition waivers (full and partial), and unspecified assistantships also available. Support available to part-time students. Financial award application deadline: 1/15. *Faculty research:* Colonial America, modern America, history of technology. *Unit head:* Dr. Stephen H. Cutcliffe, Chairman, 610-758-3360, Fax: 610-758-6554, E-mail: shc0@lehigh.edu. *Application contact:* Dr. Roger D. Simon, Graduate Coordinator, 610-758-3368, Fax: 610-758-6554, E-mail: rds2@lehigh.edu.

Lehman College of the City University of New York, Division of Arts and Humanities, Department of History, Bronx, NY 10468-1589. Offers MA. Part-time and evening/weekend programs available. *Degree requirements:* For master's, comprehensive exam, thesis. *Entrance requirements:* For master's, 18 undergraduate credits in history, minimum GPA of 2.7.

Lincoln University, School of Graduate Studies and Continuing Education, Jefferson City, MO 65102. Offers business administration (MBA), including accounting, entrepreneurship, management, public administration and policy; educational leadership (Ed S), including elementary leadership, secondary leadership, superintendency; guidance and counseling (M Ed), including community/agency counseling, elementary school, secondary school; history (MA); school administration and supervision (M Ed), including elementary school administration, secondary school administration, special education administration; school teaching (M Ed), including elementary school teaching, secondary school teaching; social science (MA), including history, political science, sociology; sociology (MA); sociology/criminal justice (MA). Part-time and evening/weekend programs available. *Degree requirements:* For master's and Ed S, comprehensive exam, thesis optional. *Entrance requirements:* For master's and Ed S, GRE, MAT or GMAT, minimum GPA of 2.75 in major, 2.5 overall; 3 letters of recommendation; minimum C average in English composition; personal statement of purpose. Additional exam requirements/recommendations for international students: Required—TOEFL (minimum score 500 paper-based; 173 computer-based; 61 iBT). *Faculty research:* Suicide prevention.

Long Island University, Brooklyn Campus, Richard L. Conolly College of Liberal Arts and Sciences, Program in Social Science, Brooklyn, NY 11201-8423. Offers history (MS); United Nations studies (Certificate). Part-time and evening/weekend programs available. *Entrance requirements:* For master's, 2 letters of recommendation. Additional exam requirements/recommendations for international students: Required—TOEFL (minimum score 500 paper-based; 173 computer-based). Electronic applications accepted.

Long Island University, C.W. Post Campus, College of Liberal Arts and Sciences, Department of History, Brookville, NY 11548-1300. Offers MA. Part-time and evening/weekend programs available. *Degree requirements:* For master's, comprehensive exam or thesis. *Entrance requirements:* For master's, bachelor's degree in history, minimum GPA of 3.0. Electronic applications accepted. *Faculty research:* American slavery, women's studies, military history.

Louisiana State University and Agricultural and Mechanical College, Graduate School, College of Humanities and Social Sciences, Department of History, Baton Rouge, LA 70803. Offers MA, PhD. Part-time programs available. *Faculty:* 27 full-time (9 women). *Students:* 55 full-time (21 women), 16 part-time (7 women); includes 1 American Indian or Alaska Native, non-Hispanic/Latino; 1 Asian, non-Hispanic/Latino; 1 Hispanic/Latino, 2 international. Average age 31. 106 applicants, 42% accepted, 9 enrolled. In 2010, 14 master's, 6 doctorates awarded. Terminal master's awarded for partial completion of doctoral program. *Degree requirements:* For master's, thesis (for some programs), oral exam; for doctorate, one foreign language, thesis/dissertation, comprehensive written and oral exams. *Entrance requirements:* For master's and doctorate, GRE General Test, minimum GPA of 3.0. Additional exam requirements/recommendations for international students: Required—TOEFL (minimum score 550 paper-based; 213 computer-based; 79 iBT) or IELTS (minimum score 6.5). *Application deadline:* For fall admission, 1/25 priority date for domestic students, 5/15 for international students; for spring admission, 10/15 for international students. Applications are processed on a rolling basis. Application fee: $50 ($70 for international students). Electronic applications accepted. *Financial support:* In 2010–11, 50 students received support, including 1 fellowship with full tuition reimbursement available (averaging $29,011 per year), 27 teaching assistantships with partial tuition reimbursements available (averaging $12,854 per year); research assistantships with partial tuition reimbursements available, career-related internships or fieldwork, Federal Work-Study, institutionally sponsored loans, health care benefits, and unspecified assistantships also available. Support available to part-time students. Financial award application deadline: 1/15; financial award applicants required to submit FAFSA. *Faculty research:* U. S. South, Civil War; modern Europe, British; medieval history. Total annual research expenditures: $70,696. *Unit head:* Dr. Victor Stater, Chair, 225-578-4505, Fax: 225-578-4909, E-mail: stater@lsu.edu. *Application contact:* Dr. Christine Kooi, Graduate Advisor, 225-578-4499, Fax: 225-578-4909, E-mail: ckooi1@lsu.edu.

Louisiana Tech University, Graduate School, College of Liberal Arts, Department of History, Ruston, LA 71272. Offers MA. Part-time programs available. *Degree requirements:* For master's, thesis or alternative. *Entrance requirements:* For master's, GRE General Test.

Loyola University Chicago, Graduate School, Department of History, Chicago, IL 60660. Offers history (MA, PhD); public history (MA). Part-time and evening/weekend programs available. *Faculty:* 25 full-time (9 women), 4 part-time/adjunct (3 women). *Students:* 56 full-time (27 women), 57 part-time (30 women); includes 11 minority (3 Black or African American, non-Hispanic/Latino; 1 American Indian or Alaska Native, non-Hispanic/Latino; 7 Hispanic/Latino). Average age 31. 121 applicants, 53% accepted, 26 enrolled. In 2010, 17 master's, 5 doctorates awarded. Terminal master's awarded for partial completion of doctoral program. *Degree requirements:* For master's, one foreign language, comprehensive exam, essay; for doctorate, 2 foreign languages, comprehensive exam, thesis/dissertation. *Entrance requirements:* For master's, GRE General Test, research paper; for doctorate, GRE General Test, seminar paper or master's thesis. Additional exam requirements/recommendations for international students: Required—TOEFL (minimum score 550 paper-based; 213 computer-based), IELTS. *Application deadline:* For fall admission, 5/1 for domestic students; for spring admission, 10/1 for domestic students. Applications are processed on a rolling basis. Application fee: $50. Electronic applications accepted. *Expenses:* Tuition: Full-time $14,940; part-time $830 per credit hour. Required fees: $87 per semester. Part-time tuition and fees vary according to course load and program. *Financial support:* In 2010–11, 24 students received support, including 11 fellowships with full tuition reimbursements available (averaging $14,500 per year), 13 teaching assistantships with full tuition reimbursements available (averaging $16,500 per year); research assistantships with full tuition reimbursements available, Federal Work-Study also available. Financial award application deadline: 1/1; financial award applicants required to submit FAFSA. *Faculty research:* Medieval and early modern Europe, U. S. public history, U. S. urban history, gender history, Britain and Ireland. *Unit head:* Dr. Timothy Gilfoyle, Chair, 773-508-2232, Fax: 773-508-2153, E-mail: tgilfoy@luc.edu. *Application contact:* Dr. Suzanne Kaufman, Director, Graduate Programs, 773-508-2233, Fax: 773-508-2153, E-mail: skaufma@luc.edu.

Lynchburg College, Graduate Studies, School of Humanities and Social Sciences, MA Program in History, Lynchburg, VA 24501-3199. Offers MA. Part-time and evening/weekend programs available. *Faculty:* 7 full-time (2 women). *Students:* 5 full-time (4 women), 6 part-time (3 women). Average age 33. 13 applicants, 62% accepted. In 2010, 2 master's awarded. *Degree requirements:* For master's, comprehensive exam, thesis or alternative. *Entrance requirements:* For master's, GRE, Official transcripts, personal essay, 3 letters of recommendation. Additional exam requirements/recommendations for international students: Required—TOEFL (minimum score 530 paper-based; 197 computer-based; 71 iBT), IELTS (minimum score 6.5). *Application deadline:* For fall admission, 7/31 for domestic students, 6/1 for international students; for spring admission, 11/30 for domestic students, 10/15 for international students. Applications are processed on a rolling basis. Application fee: $30. Electronic applications accepted. *Expenses:* Tuition: Full-time $7200; part-time $400 per credit hour. Required fees: $20; $5.10 per credit hour. $15 per term. Tuition and fees vary according to degree level and program. *Financial support:* Fellowships, research assistantships, Federal Work-Study, scholarships/grants, health care benefits, and unspecified assistantships available. Support available to part-time students. Financial award application deadline: 7/31; financial award applicants required to submit FAFSA. *Unit head:* Dr. Nichole Sanders, Associate Professor and Director, MA in History, 434-544-8117, E-mail: sanders.n@lynchburg.edu. *Application contact:* Dr. Nichole Sanders, Associate Professor and Director, MA in History, 434-544-8117, E-mail: sanders.n@lynchburg.edu.

Marquette University, Graduate School, College of Arts and Sciences, Department of History, Milwaukee, WI 53201-1881. Offers European history (MA, PhD); global studies (MA); United States history (MA, PhD). Part-time programs available. *Faculty:* 23 full-time (6 women), 1 part-time/adjunct (0 women). *Students:* 32 full-time (15 women), 5 part-time (2 women); includes 1 minority (Two or more races, non-Hispanic/Latino), 1 international. Average age 30. 49 applicants, 57% accepted, 13 enrolled. In 2010, 6 master's, 3 doctorates awarded. Terminal master's awarded for partial completion of doctoral program. *Degree requirements:* For master's, comprehensive exam, essay, 2 classes of research seminars (6 hours); for doctorate, one foreign language, comprehensive exam, thesis/dissertation, 2 research seminars, dissertation seminar. *Entrance requirements:* For master's, GRE General Test, official transcripts from all current and previous colleges/universities except Marquette, one-page statement of purpose, three letters of recommendation from former teachers; for doctorate, GRE General Test, official transcripts from all current and previous colleges/universities except Marquette, one-page statement of purpose, three letters of recommendation from former teachers, writing sample. Additional exam requirements/recommendations for international students: Required—TOEFL (minimum score 530 paper-based; 78 computer-based). *Application deadline:* For fall admission, 12/31 for domestic and international students. Application fee: $50. Electronic applications accepted. *Expenses:* Tuition: Full-time $16,290; part-time $905 per credit hour. Tuition and fees vary according to program. *Financial support:* In 2010–11, 3 fellowships, 7 research assistantships, 14 teaching assistantships were awarded; Federal Work-Study, institutionally sponsored loans, scholarships/grants, and tuition waivers (full and partial) also available. Support available to part-time students. Financial award application deadline: 2/15. *Faculty research:* Children's history, Soviet and post-Soviet history, modern Ireland and Britain, Japan and martial arts, American Catholicism. Total annual research expenditures: $5,905. *Unit head:* James Marten, Chair, 414-288-7901, Fax: 414-288-1578. *Application contact:* Erin Fox, Assistant Director for Recruitment, 414-288-5319, Fax: 414-288-1902, E-mail: erin.fox@marquette.edu.

Marshall University, Academic Affairs Division, College of Liberal Arts, Department of History, Huntington, WV 25755. Offers MA. *Faculty:* 13 full-time (4 women). *Students:* 14 full-time (6 women), 7 part-time (2 women). Average age 31. In 2010, 9 master's awarded. *Degree requirements:* For master's, thesis optional. Application fee: $40. *Unit head:* Dr. Dan Holbrook, Interim Chair, 304-696-2417, Fax: 304-696-2957, E-mail: holbrook@marshall.edu. *Application contact:* Graduate Admissions, 304-746-1900, Fax: 304-746-1902, E-mail: services@marshall.edu.

McGill University, Faculty of Graduate and Postdoctoral Studies, Faculty of Arts, Department of History, Montréal, QC H3A 2T5, Canada. Offers history (MA, PhD); history of medicine (MA).

McMaster University, School of Graduate Studies, Faculty of Humanities, Department of History, Hamilton, ON L8S 4M2, Canada. Offers MA, PhD. Part-time programs available. *Degree requirements:* For master's, one foreign language, thesis or alternative; for doctorate, one foreign language, comprehensive exam, thesis/dissertation. *Entrance requirements:* For master's, honors BA in history, minimum B+ average. Additional exam requirements/recommendations for international students: Required—TOEFL (minimum score 580 paper-based; 237 computer-based). *Faculty research:* Canadian, European, British, U.S. history; ancient history.

Memorial University of Newfoundland, School of Graduate Studies, Department of History, St. John's, NL A1C 5S7, Canada. Offers MA, PhD. Part-time programs available. *Degree requirements:* For master's, thesis or comprehensive exam; for doctorate, one foreign language, comprehensive exam, thesis/dissertation, oral defense of thesis. *Entrance requirements:* For master's, honors degree or equivalent; for doctorate, master's degree. Electronic applications accepted. *Faculty research:* Canadian history, maritime history, Newfoundland history, social history, labor history.

Miami University, Graduate School, College of Arts and Science, Department of History, Oxford, OH 45056. Offers MA. Part-time programs available. *Students:* 20 full-time (12 women), 1 international. Average age 27. In 2010, 6 master's awarded. *Entrance requirements:* For master's, minimum undergraduate GPA of 3.0. Additional exam requirements/recommendations for international students: Required—TOEFL. *Application deadline:* For fall admission, 1/10 for domestic and international students. Application fee: $50. Electronic applications accepted. *Expenses:* Tuition, state resident: full-time $11,616; part-time $484 per credit hour. Tuition, nonresident: full-time $25,656; part-time $1069 per credit hour. Required fees: $528. *Financial support:* Fellowships with full tuition reimbursements, research assistantships, teaching assistantships, Federal Work-Study, institutionally sponsored loans, health care benefits, tuition waivers (full), and unspecified assistantships available. Financial award application deadline: 3/1; financial award applicants required to submit FAFSA. *Unit head:* Dr. Charlotte Goldy, Department Chair, 513-529-5143, E-mail: goldycn@muohio.edu. *Application contact:* Dr. Wietse deBoer, Director of Graduate Studies, 513-529-5146, E-mail: deboerwt@muohio.edu.

Michigan State University, The Graduate School, College of Social Science, Department of History, East Lansing, MI 48824. Offers history (MA, PhD); history-secondary school teaching (MA). *Entrance requirements:* Additional exam requirements/recommendations for international students: Required—TOEFL. Electronic applications accepted.

Middle Tennessee State University, College of Graduate Studies, College of Liberal Arts, Department of History, Program in History, Murfreesboro, TN 37132. Offers MA. Part-time and evening/weekend programs available. Postbaccalaureate distance learning degree programs offered. *Students:* 5 full-time (all women), 64 part-time (40 women); includes 1 Black or African American, non-Hispanic/Latino; 2 Hispanic/Latino. 20 applicants, 80% accepted, 16 enrolled. In 2010, 16 master's awarded. *Degree requirements:* For master's, one foreign language, comprehensive exam, thesis. *Entrance requirements:* For master's, GRE. Additional exam requirements/recommendations for international students: Required—TOEFL (minimum score 525 paper-based; 195 computer-based; 71 iBT) or IELTS (minimum score 6). *Application deadline:* For fall admission, 6/1 for domestic and international students. Applications are processed on a rolling basis. Application fee: $25 ($30 for international students). *Expenses:* Tuition, state resident: full-time $4632. Tuition, nonresident: full-time $11,520. *Financial support:* Application deadline: 5/1. *Unit head:* Dr. Amy Sayward, Chair, 615-898-2569, Fax: 615-898-5881, E-mail: asayward@mtsu.edu. *Application contact:* Dr. Michael Allen, Dean and Vice Provost for Research, 615-898-2840, Fax: 615-904-8020, E-mail: mallen@mtsu.edu.

Midwestern State University, Graduate Studies, College of Humanities and Social Sciences, Department of History, Wichita Falls, TX 76308. Offers MA. Part-time programs available. *Faculty:* 4 full-time (1 woman), 1 part-time/adjunct (0 women). *Students:* 6 full-time (2 women), 16 part-time (6 women); includes 1 Hispanic/Latino. Average age 34. 15 applicants, 80% accepted, 8 enrolled. In 2010, 2 master's awarded. *Degree requirements:* For master's, one foreign language. *Entrance requirements:* For master's, GRE General Test. Additional exam requirements/recommendations for international students: Required—TOEFL (minimum score 550 paper-based; 213 computer-based). *Application deadline:* For fall admission, 7/1 priority date for domestic students, 4/1 for international students; for spring admission, 11/1 priority date for domestic students, 8/1 for international students. Applications are processed on a rolling basis. Application fee: $35 ($50 for international students). Electronic applications accepted. *Expenses:* Tuition, state resident: full-time $1620; part-time $90 per credit hour. Tuition, nonresident: full-time $2160; part-time $120 per credit hour. International tuition: $7200 full-time. *Financial support:* In 2010–11, 14 students received support; teaching assistantships with partial tuition reimbursements available, career-related internships or fieldwork, Federal Work-Study, institutionally sponsored loans, scholarships/grants, and unspecified assistantships available. Support available to part-time students. Financial award application deadline: 3/1; financial award applicants required to submit FAFSA. *Faculty research:* Early modern England, Spanish borderlands, Jacksonian era, New Deal, Texas and the Southwest. *Unit head:* Dr. Harry Hewitt, Graduate Coordinator, 940-397-4152, E-mail: harry.hewitt@mwsu.edu. *Application contact:* 800-842-1922, Fax: 940-397-4672, E-mail: admissions@mwsu.edu.

Millersville University of Pennsylvania, College of Graduate and Professional Studies, School of Humanities and Social Sciences, Department of History, Millersville, PA 17551-0302. Offers MA. Part-time and evening/weekend programs available. *Faculty:* 12 full-time (5 women), 6 part-time/adjunct (5 women). *Students:* 9 full-time (4 women), 19 part-time (6 women); includes 1 Black or African American, non-Hispanic/Latino, 1 international. Average age 33. 12 applicants, 83% accepted, 7 enrolled. In 2010, 9 master's awarded. *Degree requirements:* For master's, thesis optional. *Entrance requirements:* For master's, MAT or GRE (GRE preferred), 3 letters of recommendation. Additional exam requirements/recommendations for international students: Required—TOEFL (minimum score 500 paper-based; 183 computer-based; 65 iBT) or IELTS (minimum score 6). *Application deadline:* For fall admission, 1/15 priority date for domestic and international students; for winter admission, 10/1 priority date for domestic and international students; for spring admission, 10/1 priority date for domestic and international students. Applications are processed on a rolling basis. Application fee: $40 ($50 for international students). Electronic applications accepted. *Expenses:* Tuition, state resident: full-time $6966; part-time $387 per credit. Tuition, nonresident: full-time $11,146; part-time $619 per credit. Required fees: $1829.50; $88 per credit. One-time fee: $60 part-time. Tuition and fees vary according to course load. *Financial support:* In 2010–11, 3 students received support, including 3 research assistantships with full tuition reimbursements available (averaging $5,066 per year); institutionally sponsored loans and unspecified assistantships also available. Support available to part-time students. Financial award application deadline: 3/15; financial award applicants required to submit FAFSA. *Faculty research:* Anglo-American Puritanism, Vietnam War, colonial Caribbean, Renaissance music, Pennsylvania history. Total annual research expenditures: $46,933. *Unit head:* Dr. Francis Bremer, Chair, 717-872-3548, Fax: 717-871-2485, E-mail: francis.bremer@millersville.edu. *Application contact:* Dr. Victor S. DeSantis, Dean of Graduate and Professional Studies, 717-872-3099, Fax: 717-872-3453, E-mail: victor.desantis@millersville.edu.

Minnesota State University Mankato, College of Graduate Studies, College of Social and Behavioral Sciences, Department of History, Mankato, MN 56001. Offers history (MA, MS); social studies (MAT). *Students:* 1 full-time (0 women), 14 part-time (4 women). *Degree requirements:* For master's, one foreign language, comprehensive exam, thesis or alternative. *Entrance requirements:* For master's, minimum GPA of 3.0 during previous 2 years. Additional exam requirements/recommendations for international students: Required—TOEFL. *Application deadline:* For fall admission, 7/1 priority date for domestic students; for spring admission, 11/1 for domestic students. Applications are processed on a rolling basis. Application fee: $40. Electronic applications accepted. *Financial support:* Research assistantships, teaching assistantships with full tuition reimbursements, career-related internships or fieldwork, Federal Work-Study, institutionally sponsored loans, and unspecified assistantships available. Support available to part-time students. Financial award application deadline: 3/15. *Faculty research:* Charivaris, Lindbergh in the U. S., Dutch trade to South America in the seventeenth and eighteenth centuries. *Unit head:* Dr. Kathleen Gorman, Graduate Coordinator, 507-389-2720. *Application contact:* 507-389-2321, E-mail: grad@mnsu.edu.

Mississippi College, Graduate School, College of Arts and Sciences, School of Humanities and Social Sciences, Department of History, Political Science, Administration of Justice, and Paralegal Studies, Clinton, MS 39058. Offers administration of justice (MSS); history (M Ed, MA, MSS); paralegal studies (Certificate); political science (MSS); social sciences (M Ed, MSS). Part-time programs available. *Degree requirements:* For master's, one foreign language, comprehensive exam, thesis (for some programs). *Entrance requirements:* For master's, GRE or NTE, minimum GPA of 2.5. Additional exam requirements/recommendations for international students: Recommended—IELTS. Electronic applications accepted.

Mississippi State University, College of Arts and Sciences, Department of History, Mississippi State, MS 39762. Offers history (PhD); U. S. and European history (MA). Part-time programs available. *Faculty:* 17 full-time (6 women). *Students:* 36 full-time (15 women), 9 part-time (3 women); includes 2 minority (1 Black or African American, non-Hispanic/Latino; 1 Asian, non-Hispanic/Latino). Average age 30. 35 applicants, 74% accepted, 18 enrolled. In 2010, 10 master's, 4 doctorates awarded. *Degree requirements:* For master's, one foreign language, comprehensive exam, thesis optional; for doctorate, 2 foreign languages, thesis/dissertation, comprehensive oral and written exam. *Entrance requirements:* For master's, minimum GPA of 3.0 on last two years of undergraduate courses; for doctorate, GRE, writing sample, minimum graduate GPA of 3.0. Additional exam requirements/recommendations for

History

Mississippi State University (continued)
international students: Required—TOEFL (minimum score 475 paper-based; 153 computer-based; 53 iBT); Recommended—IELTS (minimum score 4.5). *Application deadline:* For fall admission, 4/1 for domestic students, 5/1 for international students; for spring admission, 11/1 for domestic students, 9/1 for international students. Applications are processed on a rolling basis. Application fee: $40. Electronic applications accepted. *Expenses:* Tuition, state resident: full-time $2730.50; part-time $304 per credit hour. Tuition, nonresident: full-time $6901; part-time $767 per credit hour. *Financial support:* In 2010–11, 31 teaching assistantships with full tuition reimbursements (averaging $10,977 per year) were awarded; Federal Work-Study, institutionally sponsored loans, scholarships/grants, and unspecified assistantships also available. Financial award application deadline: 4/1; financial award applicants required to submit FAFSA. *Faculty research:* U. S. political, diplomatic, military, social, and cultural history; modern Europe; Latin America; Asian history; African history. *Unit head:* Dr. Alan I. Marcus, Head, 662-325-3604, Fax: 662-325-1139, E-mail: aim10@msstate.edu. *Application contact:* Dr. Peter Messer, Associate Professor and Graduate Coordinator, 662-325-3604, Fax: 662-325-1139, E-mail: pmesser@history.msstate.edu.

Missouri State University, Graduate College, College of Humanities and Public Affairs, Department of History, Springfield, MO 65897. Offers history (MA); secondary education (MS Ed), including history, social science. Part-time programs available. *Degree requirements:* For master's, comprehensive exam, thesis or alternative. *Entrance requirements:* For master's, minimum GPA of 2.75, 24 hours of undergraduate course work in history (MA), 9-12 teaching certification (MS Ed). Additional exam requirements/recommendations for international students: Required—TOEFL (minimum score 550 paper-based; 213 computer-based; 79 iBT). Electronic applications accepted. *Expenses:* Tuition, state resident: full-time $3348; part-time $186 per credit hour. Tuition, nonresident: full-time $6696; part-time $372 per credit hour. Required fees: $238 per semester. Tuition and fees vary according to course level, course load and program. *Faculty research:* U.S. history, Native American history, Latin American history, women's history, ancient Near East.

Monmouth University, The Graduate School, Department of History, West Long Branch, NJ 07764-1898. Offers European specialization (MA); U. S. specialization (MA); world specialization (MA). Part-time and evening/weekend programs available. *Faculty:* 12 full-time (3 women). *Students:* 5 full-time (4 women), 56 part-time (28 women); includes 1 Black or African American, non-Hispanic/Latino; 1 Asian, non-Hispanic/Latino; 3 Hispanic/Latino; 1 Two or more races, non-Hispanic/Latino. Average age 36. 22 applicants, 100% accepted, 17 enrolled. In 2010, 16 master's awarded. *Degree requirements:* For master's, comprehensive exam, thesis or alternative. *Entrance requirements:* For master's, minimum GPA of 3.0 in major, 2.5 overall. Additional exam requirements/recommendations for international students: Required—TOEFL (minimum score 550 paper-based; 213 computer-based; 79 iBT), IELTS (minimum score 6) or Michigan English Language Assessment Battery (minimum score 77), Cambridge A, B, C. *Application deadline:* For fall admission, 7/15 priority date for domestic students, 6/1 for international students; for spring admission, 11/15 priority date for domestic students, 11/1 for international students. Applications are processed on a rolling basis. Application fee: $50. Electronic applications accepted. *Expenses:* Tuition: Full-time $19,572; part-time $816 per credit. Required fees: $628; $157 per semester. *Financial support:* In 2010–11, 46 students received support, including 39 fellowships (averaging $1,073 per year), 5 research assistantships (averaging $4,934 per year); career-related internships or fieldwork, scholarships/grants, and unspecified assistantships also available. Support available to part-time students. Financial award applicants required to submit FAFSA. *Faculty research:* U.S. business; labor; British, German, and French Revolutions; Soviet Union; Africa. *Unit head:* Dr. Maryann Rhett, Program Director, 732-263-5768, Fax: 732-263-5112, E-mail: mrhett@monmouth.edu. *Application contact:* Kevin Roane, Director, Office of Graduate Admission, 732-571-3452, Fax: 732-263-5123, E-mail: gradadm@monmouth.edu.

Montana State University, College of Graduate Studies, College of Letters and Science, Department of History, Bozeman, MT 59717. Offers MA, PhD. Part-time programs available. *Faculty:* 20 full-time (7 women), 5 part-time/adjunct (2 women). *Students:* 6 full-time (1 woman), 18 part-time (8 women); includes 2 minority (1 Hispanic/Latino; 1 Two or more races, non-Hispanic/Latino), 1 international. Average age 37. 16 applicants, 63% accepted, 7 enrolled. In 2010, 12 master's awarded. *Degree requirements:* For master's, comprehensive exam; for doctorate, comprehensive exam, thesis/dissertation. *Entrance requirements:* For master's, GRE General Test, transcripts, 3 letters of recommendation, writing sample, statement of interest; for doctorate, GRE General Test, MA, transcripts, 3 letters of recommendation, writing sample, statement of interest. Additional exam requirements/recommendations for international students: Required—TOEFL (minimum score 550 paper-based; 213 computer-based). *Application deadline:* For fall admission, 7/15 priority date for domestic students, 5/15 priority date for international students; for spring admission, 12/1 priority date for domestic students, 10/1 priority date for international students. Applications are processed on a rolling basis. Application fee: $30. Electronic applications accepted. *Expenses:* Tuition, state resident: full-time $5553.90. Tuition, nonresident: full-time $14,646. Required fees: $1233. *Financial support:* In 2010–11, 15 students received support, including 4 research assistantships (averaging $15,000 per year), 8 teaching assistantships with full tuition reimbursements available (averaging $13,000 per year); research grants also available. Financial award application deadline: 3/1; financial award applicants required to submit FAFSA. *Faculty research:* Science, environment, technology, American West, science and technology, environmental history, Asian studies. Total annual research expenditures: $273,428. *Unit head:* Dr. Brett Walker, Head, 406-994-4395, Fax: 406-994-6879, E-mail: bwalker@montana.edu. *Application contact:* Dr. Brett Walker, Head, 406-994-4395, Fax: 406-994-6879, E-mail: bwalker@montana.edu.

Montclair State University, The Graduate School, College of Humanities and Social Sciences, Department of History, Montclair, NJ 07043-1624. Offers history (MA); social studies (Certificate). Part-time and evening/weekend programs available. *Faculty:* 18 full-time (7 women), 19 part-time/adjunct (3 women). *Students:* 3 full-time (1 woman), 22 part-time (9 women); includes 1 Black or African American, non-Hispanic/Latino; 2 Hispanic/Latino. Average age 31. 17 applicants, 41% accepted, 5 enrolled. In 2010, 8 master's awarded. *Degree requirements:* For master's, comprehensive exam. *Entrance requirements:* For master's, GRE General Test, 2 letters of recommendation. Additional exam requirements/recommendations for international students: Required—TOEFL (minimum score: 83 iBT) or IELTS. *Application deadline:* For fall admission, 6/1 for international students; for spring admission, 11/1 for international students. Applications are processed on a rolling basis. Application fee: $60. Electronic applications accepted. *Expenses:* Tuition, state resident: part-time $501.34 per credit. Tuition, nonresident: part-time $773.88 per credit. Required fees: $71.15 per credit. *Financial support:* In 2010–11, 2 research assistantships with full tuition reimbursements (averaging $7,000 per year) were awarded; Federal Work-Study, scholarships/grants, and unspecified assistantships also available. Support available to part-time students. Financial award application deadline: 3/1. *Unit head:* Dr. Michael Whelan, Chairperson, 973-655-7848. *Application contact:* Amy Aiello, Director of Admissions and Operations, 973-655-5147, Fax: 973-655-7869, E-mail: graduate.school@montclair.edu.

Morgan State University, School of Graduate Studies, College of Liberal Arts, Department of History and Geography, Baltimore, MD 21251. Offers African-American studies (MA); history (MA, PhD). Part-time and evening/weekend programs available. *Degree requirements:* For master's, comprehensive exam, thesis; for doctorate, comprehensive exam, thesis/dissertation. *Entrance requirements:* For master's, minimum GPA of 2.5; for doctorate, GRE or MAT. Additional exam requirements/recommendations for international students: Required—TOEFL (minimum score 550 paper-based; 213 computer-based). *Faculty research:* Women's history, African diaspora history, urban history.

Murray State University, College of Humanities and Fine Arts, Program in History, Murray, KY 42071. Offers MA. Part-time programs available. *Degree requirements:* For master's, one foreign language, comprehensive exam, thesis (for some programs). *Entrance requirements:* For master's, GRE General Test. Additional exam requirements/recommendations for international students: Required—TOEFL.

National University, Academic Affairs, College of Letters and Sciences, Department of Art and Humanities, La Jolla, CA 92037-1011. Offers creative writing (MFA); English (MA); history (MA). Part-time and evening/weekend programs available. Postbaccalaureate distance learning degree programs offered (no on-campus study). *Faculty:* 17 full-time (6 women), 198 part-time/adjunct (110 women). *Students:* 198 full-time (144 women), 534 part-time (364 women); includes 99 Black or African American, non-Hispanic/Latino; 6 American Indian or Alaska Native, non-Hispanic/Latino; 10 Asian, non-Hispanic/Latino; 54 Hispanic/Latino; 14 Two or more races, non-Hispanic/Latino. Average age 38. 424 applicants, 100% accepted, 289 enrolled. In 2010, 222 master's awarded. *Degree requirements:* For master's, thesis (for some programs). *Entrance requirements:* For master's, interview, minimum GPA of 2.5. Additional exam requirements/recommendations for international students: Required—TOEFL (minimum score 550 paper-based; 213 computer-based; 79 iBT), IELTS (minimum score 6). *Application deadline:* Applications are processed on a rolling basis. Application fee: $60 ($65 for international students). Electronic applications accepted. *Expenses:* Tuition: Full-time $9450; part-time $350 per unit. Required fees: $350 per unit. One-time fee: $60. *Financial support:* Career-related internships or fieldwork, institutionally sponsored loans, scholarships/grants, and tuition waivers (partial) available. Support available to part-time students. Financial award application deadline: 6/30; financial award applicants required to submit FAFSA. *Unit head:* Dr. Janet Baker, Chair, 858-642-8472, Fax: 858-642-8715, E-mail: jbaker@nu.edu. *Application contact:* Dominick Giovanniello, Associate Regional Dean—San Diego, 800-NAT-UNIV, Fax: 858-541-7792, E-mail: dgiovann@nu.edu.

National University, Academic Affairs, College of Letters and Sciences, Department of Social Sciences, La Jolla, CA 92037-1011. Offers history (MA). Part-time and evening/weekend programs available. Postbaccalaureate distance learning degree programs offered (no on-campus study). *Faculty:* 11 full-time (4 women), 67 part-time/adjunct (29 women). *Students:* 15 full-time (5 women), 32 part-time (15 women); includes 2 Black or African American, non-Hispanic/Latino; 11 Hispanic/Latino; 1 Two or more races, non-Hispanic/Latino. Average age 33. 72 applicants, 100% accepted, 39 enrolled. *Degree requirements:* For master's, thesis (for some programs). *Entrance requirements:* For master's, interview, minimum GPA of 2.5. Additional exam requirements/recommendations for international students: Required—TOEFL (minimum score 550 paper-based; 213 computer-based; 79 iBT), IELTS (minimum score 6). *Application deadline:* Applications are processed on a rolling basis. Application fee: $60 ($65 for international students). Electronic applications accepted. *Expenses:* Tuition: Full-time $9450; part-time $350 per unit. Required fees: $350 per unit. One-time fee: $60. *Financial support:* Career-related internships or fieldwork, institutionally sponsored loans, scholarships/grants, and tuition waivers available. Support available to part-time students. Financial award application deadline: 6/30; financial award applicants required to submit FAFSA. *Unit head:* Dr. Douglas Slawson, Head, 858-642-8390, E-mail: dslawson@nu.edu. *Application contact:* Dominick Giovanniello, Associate Regional Dean—San Diego, 800-NAT-UNIV, Fax: 858-541-7792, E-mail: dgiovann@nu.edu.

Nebraska Wesleyan University, University College, Program in Historical Studies, Lincoln, NE 68504-2796. Offers MA. Part-time programs available. *Expenses:* Contact institution.

New Jersey Institute of Technology, Office of Graduate Studies, College of Science and Liberal Arts, Federated Department of History, Newark, NJ 07102. Offers MA, MAT. MA, MAT offered jointly with Rutgers, The State University of New Jersey, Newark. Part-time and evening/weekend programs available. *Faculty:* 8 full-time (2 women), 4 part-time/adjunct (1 woman). *Entrance requirements:* For master's, GRE General Test, minimum B average in undergraduate course work. Additional exam requirements/recommendations for international students: Required—TOEFL (minimum score 550 paper-based; 213 computer-based; 79 iBT). *Application deadline:* For fall admission, 6/5 priority date for domestic students; for spring admission, 10/15 for domestic students. Applications are processed on a rolling basis. Application fee: $65. Electronic applications accepted. *Expenses:* Tuition, state resident: full-time $14,724; part-time $818 per credit. Tuition, nonresident: full-time $20,304; part-time $1128 per credit. Required fees: $2272; $209 per credit. $103 per semester. One-time fee: $312 full-time; $212 part-time. *Financial support:* Fellowships with full and partial tuition reimbursements, research assistantships with full and partial tuition reimbursements, teaching assistantships with full and partial tuition reimbursements, career-related internships or fieldwork, Federal Work-Study, institutionally sponsored loans, and unspecified assistantships available. Financial award application deadline: 3/15. Total annual research expenditures: $379,761. *Unit head:* Dr. Neil M. Maher, Chair, 973-596-6348, E-mail: neil.m.maher@njit.edu. *Application contact:* Kathryn Kelly, Director of Admissions, 973-596-3300, Fax: 973-596-3461, E-mail: admissions@njit.edu.

New Mexico State University, Graduate School, College of Arts and Sciences, Department of History, Las Cruces, NM 88003-8001. Offers history (MA); public history (MA). Part-time programs available. *Faculty:* 12 full-time (3 women), 3 part-time/adjunct (0 women). *Students:* 30 full-time (18 women), 23 part-time (10 women); includes 18 minority (2 Black or African American, non-Hispanic/Latino; 2 American Indian or Alaska Native, non-Hispanic/Latino; 2 Asian, non-Hispanic/Latino; 11 Hispanic/Latino; 1 Two or more races, non-Hispanic/Latino). Average age 33. 28 applicants, 93% accepted, 16 enrolled. In 2010, 16 master's awarded. *Degree requirements:* For master's, one foreign language, comprehensive exam, thesis (for some programs). *Entrance requirements:* For master's, 12 undergraduate history credits, writing sample. Additional exam requirements/recommendations for international students: Required—TOEFL (minimum score 530 paper-based; 71 iBT). *Application deadline:* For fall admission, 7/1 priority date for domestic students; for spring admission, 11/1 for domestic students. Applications are processed on a rolling basis. Application fee: $30 ($50 for international students). Electronic applications accepted. *Expenses:* Tuition, state resident: full-time $4536; part-time $242 per credit. Tuition, nonresident: full-time $15,816; part-time $712 per credit. Required fees: $636 per term. *Financial support:* In 2010–11, 10 teaching assistantships with partial tuition reimbursements (averaging $6,280 per year) were awarded; fellowships, research assistantships with partial tuition reimbursements, career-related internships or fieldwork, Federal Work-Study, and health care benefits also available. Support available to part-time students. Financial award application deadline: 3/1. *Faculty research:* U. S. Southwestern and border history, Latin American history, U. S. women's history, European history, history of science, public history, East Asian history. *Unit head:* Dr. Jon Hunner, Head, 575-646-4601, Fax: 575-646-6096, E-mail: jhunner@nmsu.edu. *Application contact:* Dr. Andrea Orzoff, Director of Graduate Studies, 575-646-4612, Fax: 575-646-6096, E-mail: aorzoff@nmsu.edu.

The New School: A University, The New School for Social Research, Department in Historical Studies, New York, NY 10003. Offers MA, PhD. Part-time and evening/weekend programs available. Terminal master's awarded for partial completion of doctoral program. *Degree requirements:* For master's, thesis; for doctorate, comprehensive exam, thesis/dissertation, qualifying exam. *Entrance requirements:* For master's, GRE General Test; for doctorate, GRE General Test, MA. Additional exam requirements/recommendations for international students: Required—TOEFL (minimum score 600 paper-based; 250 computer-based; 100 iBT). Electronic applications accepted.

New York University, Graduate School of Arts and Science, Department of History, New York, NY 10012-1019. Offers African diaspora (PhD); African history (PhD); archival management and historical editing (Advanced Certificate); Atlantic history (PhD); French studies/history (PhD); Hebrew and Judaic studies/history (PhD); history (MA, PhD), including Europe (PhD), Latin American and the Caribbean (PhD), United States (PhD), women's history (MA); Middle Eastern history (MA); Middle Eastern studies/history (PhD); public history (Advanced Certificate); world history (MA); JD/MA; MA/Advanced Certificate. Part-time programs available. *Faculty:* 43 full-time (19 women). *Students:* 135 full-time (84 women), 42 part-time (30 women); includes 15 Black or African American, non-Hispanic/Latino; 2 Asian, non-Hispanic/Latino; 11

Hispanic/Latino, 41 international. Average age 30. 541 applicants, 21% accepted, 43 enrolled. In 2010, 28 master's, 14 doctorates, 3 other advanced degrees awarded. Terminal master's awarded for partial completion of doctoral program. *Degree requirements:* For master's, seminar paper; for doctorate, one foreign language, thesis/dissertation, oral and written exams; for Advanced Certificate, internship. *Entrance requirements:* For master's, GRE General Test, minimum GPA of 3.0, writing sample; for doctorate, GRE. Additional exam requirements/recommendations for international students: Required—TOEFL. *Application deadline:* For fall admission, 12/15 for domestic students. Application fee: $90. *Financial support:* Fellowships with tuition reimbursements, research assistantships, teaching assistantships with tuition reimbursements, career-related internships or fieldwork, Federal Work-Study, institutionally sponsored loans, scholarships/grants, health care benefits, and unspecified assistantships available. Financial award application deadline: 12/15; financial award applicants required to submit FAFSA. *Faculty research:* African, East Asian, medieval, early modern, and modern European history; U. S. history; African and African Diaspora; Latin American history; Atlantic World. *Unit head:* Joanna Waley-Cohen, Chair, 212-998-8600, Fax: 212-995-4017, E-mail: history.dept@nyu.edu. *Application contact:* Fiona Griffiths, Director of Graduate Studies, 212-998-8600, Fax: 212-995-4017, E-mail: history.dept@nyu.edu.

New York University, Graduate School of Arts and Science, Institute for the Study of the Ancient World, New York, NY 10012-1019. Offers PhD. *Students:* 5 full-time (2 women), 3 international. Average age 30. 25 applicants, 16% accepted, 2 enrolled. *Degree requirements:* For doctorate, 4 foreign languages, comprehensive exam, thesis/dissertation, fieldwork, teaching experience. *Application deadline:* For fall admission, 1/4 for domestic students. Application fee: $90. Electronic applications accepted. *Financial support:* Fellowships covering tuition, fees, and twelve-month stipend (about $33,000) available. Financial award application deadline: 1/4. *Unit head:* Dr. Roger Bagnall, Director, 212-992-7833, Fax: 212-995-4014, E-mail: isaw@nyu.edu. *Application contact:* Alexander Lawson, Director of Graduate Studies, 212-992-7833, Fax: 212-995-4014, E-mail: isaw@nyu.edu.

North Carolina Central University, Division of Academic Affairs, College of Liberal Arts, Department of History, Durham, NC 27707-3129. Offers MA. Part-time and evening/weekend programs available. *Degree requirements:* For master's, one foreign language, comprehensive exam, thesis. *Entrance requirements:* For master's, GRE, minimum GPA of 3.0 in major, 2.5 overall. Additional exam requirements/recommendations for international students: Required—TOEFL.

North Carolina State University, Graduate School, College of Humanities and Social Sciences, Department of History, Raleigh, NC 27695. Offers history (MA); public history (MA). Part-time and evening/weekend programs available. *Degree requirements:* For master's, thesis. *Entrance requirements:* For master's, GRE General Test. Electronic applications accepted. *Faculty research:* History of the United States, Europe, Asia Africa and the Middle East; history of science; intellectual, cultural, social, environmental and political history.

North Dakota State University, College of Graduate and Interdisciplinary Studies, College of Arts, Humanities and Social Sciences, Department of History, Fargo, ND 58108. Offers MA, MS, PhD. Part-time and evening/weekend programs available. *Faculty:* 9 full-time (1 woman), 2 part-time/adjunct (0 women). *Students:* 10 full-time (1 woman), 10 part-time (5 women); includes 1 Black or African American, non-Hispanic/Latino; 1 American Indian or Alaska Native, non-Hispanic/Latino; 1 Hispanic/Latino, 2 international. Average age 27. 11 applicants, 91% accepted, 10 enrolled. In 2010, 12 master's awarded. *Degree requirements:* For master's, one foreign language, comprehensive exam, thesis optional; for doctorate, 2 foreign languages, comprehensive exam, thesis/dissertation. *Entrance requirements:* For master's and doctorate, GRE General Test. Additional exam requirements/recommendations for international students: Required—TOEFL (minimum score 600 paper-based; 250 computer-based; 100 iBT). *Application deadline:* For fall admission, 2/10 priority date for domestic and international students. Applications are processed on a rolling basis. Application fee: $45 ($60 for international students). *Financial support:* In 2010–11, 9 students received support, including 1 fellowship with tuition reimbursement available (averaging $15,000 per year), 2 research assistantships with full tuition reimbursements available (averaging $9,400 per year), 4 teaching assistantships with full tuition reimbursements available (averaging $8,200 per year); career-related internships or fieldwork, Federal Work-Study, institutionally sponsored loans, and tuition waivers also available. Financial award application deadline: 3/15. *Faculty research:* Recent U. S., modern English; early modern European, North Dakota, Latin American, and Great Plains history. *Unit head:* Dr. John K. Cox, Head, 701-231-8654, Fax: 701-231-1047, E-mail: john.cox.l@ndsu.edu. *Application contact:* Dr. Jim Norris, Graduate Coordinator, 701-231-8827, Fax: 701-231-1047, E-mail: jim.norris@nodak.edu.

Northeastern Illinois University, Graduate College, College of Arts and Sciences, Department of History, Program in History, Chicago, IL 60625-4699. Offers MA. Part-time and evening/weekend programs available. *Faculty:* 11 full-time (3 women), 3 part-time/adjunct (0 women). *Students:* 2 full-time (1 woman), 26 part-time (11 women); includes 6 minority (1 Black or African American, non-Hispanic/Latino; 1 Asian, non-Hispanic/Latino; 4 Hispanic/Latino). Average age 38. 15 applicants, 67% accepted, 6 enrolled. In 2010, 5 master's awarded. *Degree requirements:* For master's, comprehensive exam, thesis optional. *Entrance requirements:* For master's, 24 undergraduate hours in history, minimum GPA of 2.75. Additional exam requirements/recommendations for international students: Required—TOEFL (minimum score 550 paper-based; 213 computer-based; 79 iBT). *Application deadline:* For fall admission, 4/1 priority date for domestic students; for spring admission, 8/15 for domestic students. Applications are processed on a rolling basis. Application fee: $3. Electronic applications accepted. *Financial support:* In 2010–11, 21 students received support, including 2 research assistantships with full and partial tuition reimbursements available (averaging $6,600 per year); career-related internships or fieldwork, Federal Work-Study, institutionally sponsored loans, scholarships/grants, tuition waivers (full and partial), and unspecified assistantships also available. Support available to part-time students. Financial award applicants required to submit FAFSA. *Faculty research:* Africa; East Asia; European medieval, early-modern, and modern history; U. S. social, cultural, and intellectual history. *Unit head:* Dr. Patrick B. Miller, Department Chair. *Application contact:* Dr. Patrick B. Miller, Department Chair.

Northeastern University, College of Social Sciences and Humanities, Department of History, Boston, MA 02115-5096. Offers history (MA); public history (MA); world history (PhD). Part-time and evening/weekend programs available. *Faculty:* 15 full-time (6 women), 2 part-time/adjunct (0 women). *Students:* 55 full-time (33 women), 4 part-time (3 women); includes 3 minority (2 Black or African American, non-Hispanic/Latino; 1 Two or more races, non-Hispanic/Latino), 1 international. 116 applicants, 40% accepted, 19 enrolled. In 2010, 11 master's awarded. Terminal master's awarded for partial completion of doctoral program. *Degree requirements:* For master's, one foreign language, thesis or alternative, project; for doctorate, thesis/dissertation. *Entrance requirements:* For master's and doctorate, GRE General Test. Additional exam requirements/recommendations for international students: Required—TOEFL. *Application deadline:* For fall admission, 2/1 for domestic students. Application fee: $50. Electronic applications accepted. *Financial support:* In 2010–11, 13 teaching assistantships with tuition reimbursements (averaging $14,035 per year) were awarded; research assistantships with tuition reimbursements, career-related internships or fieldwork, scholarships/grants, and tuition waivers (full and partial) also available. Financial award application deadline: 2/1; financial award applicants required to submit FAFSA. *Faculty research:* World history, U. S. social history. *Unit head:* Dr. Laura Frader, Chair, 617-373-2660, Fax: 617-373-2661. *Application contact:* Dr. Christina Gilmartin, Graduate Coordinator, 617-373-2660, Fax: 617-373-2661.

Northern Arizona University, Graduate College, College of Arts and Letters, Department of History, Flagstaff, AZ 86011. Offers MA, PhD. Part-time programs available. *Faculty:* 15 full-time (7 women). *Students:* 18 full-time (7 women), 10 part-time (5 women); includes 6 minority (1 Black or African American, non-Hispanic/Latino; 3 American Indian or Alaska Native, non-Hispanic/Latino; 2 Hispanic/Latino), 1 international. Average age 39. 26 applicants, 69% accepted, 10 enrolled. In 2010, 9 master's, 1 doctorate awarded. *Degree requirements:* For master's, thesis (for some programs), thesis or departmental qualifying exam; for doctorate, thesis/dissertation. *Entrance requirements:* For master's and doctorate, GRE General Test. Additional exam requirements/recommendations for international students: Required—TOEFL (minimum score 550 paper-based; 213 computer-based; 80 iBT), IELTS (minimum score 7). *Application deadline:* For fall admission, 2/15 priority date for domestic students, 2/1 priority date for international students; for spring admission, 10/1 priority date for domestic and international students. Applications are processed on a rolling basis. Application fee: $65. Electronic applications accepted. *Financial support:* In 2010–11, 8 teaching assistantships with partial tuition reimbursements (averaging $11,300 per year) were awarded; Federal Work-Study, scholarships/grants, health care benefits, tuition waivers (full and partial), and unspecified assistantships also available. Financial award applicants required to submit FAFSA. *Faculty research:* Twentieth century U. S., U. S. trans-Mississippi West, Arizona and the Southwest, women's history, U. S. intellectual history. Total annual research expenditures: $78,000. *Unit head:* Dr. Charles Connell, Chair, 928-523-8418, Fax: 928-523-1277, E-mail: charles.connell@nau.edu. *Application contact:* Beth Grimes, Administrative Associate, 928-523-4378, Fax: 928-523-1277, E-mail: beth.grimes@nau.edu.

Northern Illinois University, Graduate School, College of Liberal Arts and Sciences, Department of History, De Kalb, IL 60115-2854. Offers MA, PhD. Part-time programs available. *Faculty:* 18 full-time (8 women), 2 part-time/adjunct (0 women). *Students:* 29 full-time (9 women), 34 part-time (19 women); includes 2 Black or African American, non-Hispanic/Latino; 2 Hispanic/Latino, 3 international. Average age 35. 66 applicants, 53% accepted, 18 enrolled. In 2010, 9 master's, 2 doctorates awarded. Terminal master's awarded for partial completion of doctoral program. *Degree requirements:* For master's, variable foreign language requirement, comprehensive exam, thesis optional, research seminars; for doctorate, variable foreign language requirement, thesis/dissertation, candidacy exam, dissertation defense, research seminars. *Entrance requirements:* For master's, GRE General Test, minimum GPA of 2.75; for doctorate, GRE General Test, minimum undergraduate GPA of 2.75, graduate 3.2. Additional exam requirements/recommendations for international students: Required—TOEFL (minimum score 550 paper-based; 213 computer-based). *Application deadline:* For fall admission, 6/1 for domestic students, 5/1 for international students; for spring admission, 11/1 for domestic students, 10/1 for international students. Applications are processed on a rolling basis. Application fee: $30. Electronic applications accepted. *Expenses:* Tuition, state resident: full-time $7200; part-time $300 per credit hour. Tuition, nonresident: full-time $14,400; part-time $600 per credit hour. Required fees: $79 per credit hour. *Financial support:* In 2010–11, 18 teaching assistantships with full tuition reimbursements were awarded; fellowships with full tuition reimbursements, research assistantships with full tuition reimbursements, career-related internships or fieldwork, Federal Work-Study, scholarships/grants, tuition waivers (full), and unspecified assistantships also available. Support available to part-time students. Financial award applicants required to submit FAFSA. *Faculty research:* History of the Carolingian empire, world history of early modern Europe, modern Irish history, history of the Ming dynasty. *Unit head:* Dr. Beatrix Hoffman, Chair, 815-753-0851, Fax: 815-753-6302, E-mail: beatrix@niu.edu. *Application contact:* Dr. E. Taylor Atkins, Assistant Chair and Director of Graduate Studies, 815-753-6699, E-mail: etatkins@niu.edu.

Northwestern University, The Graduate School, Judd A. and Marjorie Weinberg College of Arts and Sciences, Department of History, Evanston, IL 60208. Offers PhD, JD/PhD. Admissions and degrees offered through The Graduate School. *Degree requirements:* For doctorate, variable foreign language requirement, thesis/dissertation, major and minor field exams. *Entrance requirements:* For doctorate, sample of written work. Additional exam requirements/recommendations for international students: Required—TOEFL. Electronic applications accepted. *Faculty research:* Medieval and early modern Europe, Africa, race and slavery, Atlantic history, gender.

Northwestern University, School of Continuing Studies, Program in Liberal Studies, Evanston, IL 60208. Offers American studies (MA); history (MA); religious and ethical studies (MA).

Northwest Missouri State University, Graduate School, College of Arts and Sciences, Department of History, Humanities, and Political Science, Maryville, MO 64468-6001. Offers history (MA); teaching history (MS Ed). Part-time programs available. *Faculty:* 13 full-time (3 women). *Students:* 12 full-time (7 women), 3 part-time (0 women); includes 1 Two or more races, non-Hispanic/Latino, 1 international. 10 applicants, 70% accepted, 5 enrolled. In 2010, 4 master's awarded. *Degree requirements:* For master's, comprehensive exam, thesis. *Entrance requirements:* For master's, GRE General Test, undergraduate major/minor in social studies/humanities, minimum undergraduate GPA of 2.5, writing sample. Additional exam requirements/recommendations for international students: Required—TOEFL (minimum score 550 paper-based; 213 computer-based). *Application deadline:* For fall admission, 7/1 for domestic and international students; for spring admission, 11/15 for domestic and international students. Applications are processed on a rolling basis. Application fee: $0 ($50 for international students). *Financial support:* In 2010–11, 2 research assistantships with full tuition reimbursements (averaging $6,000 per year) were awarded. Financial award application deadline: 4/1; financial award applicants required to submit FAFSA. *Unit head:* Dr. Michael Steiner, Chairperson, 660-562-1288. *Application contact:* Dr. Gregory Haddock, Dean of Graduate School, 660-562-1145, Fax: 660-562-1096, E-mail: gradsch@nwmissouri.edu.

Oakland University, Graduate Study and Lifelong Learning, College of Arts and Sciences, Department of History, Rochester, MI 48309-4401. Offers MA. Part-time and evening/weekend programs available. *Entrance requirements:* For master's, minimum GPA of 3.0 for unconditional admission. Additional exam requirements/recommendations for international students: Required—TOEFL (minimum score 550 paper-based; 213 computer-based). Electronic applications accepted.

The Ohio State University, Graduate School, College of Arts and Sciences, Division of Arts and Humanities, Department of History, Columbus, OH 43210. Offers MA, PhD. *Faculty:* 73. *Students:* 72 full-time (35 women), 53 part-time (18 women); includes 9 Black or African American, non-Hispanic/Latino; 1 American Indian or Alaska Native, non-Hispanic/Latino; 1 Asian, non-Hispanic/Latino; 5 Hispanic/Latino; 1 Two or more races, non-Hispanic/Latino, 15 international. Average age 30. In 2010, 17 master's, 16 doctorates awarded. *Degree requirements:* For master's, thesis optional; for doctorate, variable foreign language requirement, thesis/dissertation. *Entrance requirements:* For master's and doctorate, GRE General Test. Additional exam requirements/recommendations for international students: Required—TOEFL (minimum score 600 paper-based; 250 computer-based). *Application deadline:* For fall admission, 8/15 priority date for domestic students, 7/1 priority date for international students; for winter admission, 12/1 priority date for domestic students, 11/1 priority date for international students; for spring admission, 3/1 priority date for domestic students, 2/1 priority date for international students. Applications are processed on a rolling basis. Application fee: $40 ($50 for international students). Electronic applications accepted. *Expenses:* Tuition, state resident: full-time $10,605. Tuition, nonresident: full-time $26,535. Tuition and fees vary according to course load and program. *Financial support:* Fellowships, research assistantships, teaching assistantships, Federal Work-Study, institutionally sponsored loans, and unspecified assistantships available. Support available to part-time students. *Unit head:* Peter Hahn, Chair, 614-292-3001, E-mail: hahn.29@osu.edu. *Application contact:* 614-247-9444, Fax: 614-292-3895, E-mail: domestic.grad@osu.edu.

Ohio University, Graduate College, College of Arts and Sciences, Department of History, Athens, OH 45701-2979. Offers MA, PhD. *Students:* 43 full-time (7 women), 8 part-time (3 women); includes 1 minority (Hispanic/Latino), 8 international. 31 applicants, 48% accepted, 13 enrolled. In 2010, 8 master's, 2 doctorates awarded. *Degree requirements:* For master's, one foreign language, thesis optional; for doctorate, 2 foreign languages, comprehensive exam, thesis/dissertation. *Entrance requirements:* For master's, GRE, minimum GPA of 3.0; for doctorate, GRE, minimum GPA of 3.0, MA. Additional exam requirements/recommendations for international students: Required—TOEFL (minimum score 550 paper-based; 80 iBT) or IELTS (minimum score 6.5). *Application deadline:* For fall admission, 2/1 priority date for

History

Ohio University (continued)

domestic and international students. Application fee: $50 ($55 for international students). Electronic applications accepted. *Financial support:* Fellowships with tuition reimbursements, teaching assistantships with tuition reimbursements, Federal Work-Study and institutionally sponsored loans available. Financial award application deadline: 2/1. *Faculty research:* U. S. foreign relations, modern Europe, Latin America, southeast Asia, U. S. women. *Unit head:* Dr. Patrick Barr-Melej, Chair, 740-591-1851, Fax: 740-593-0259, E-mail: bar-mel@ohio.edu. *Application contact:* Dr. Chester Pach, Graduate Chair, 740-593-4353, Fax: 740-593-0259, E-mail: pach@ohio.edu.

Oklahoma State University, College of Arts and Sciences, Department of History, Stillwater, OK 74078. Offers MA, PhD. *Faculty:* 25 full-time (6 women), 1 part-time/adjunct (0 women). *Students:* 15 full-time (8 women), 53 part-time (20 women); includes 2 American Indian or Alaska Native, non-Hispanic/Latino; 2 Asian, non-Hispanic/Latino, 1 international. Average age 32. 52 applicants, 58% accepted, 20 enrolled. In 2010, 11 master's, 5 doctorates awarded. *Degree requirements:* For master's, thesis; for doctorate, comprehensive exam, thesis/dissertation. *Entrance requirements:* For master's and doctorate, GRE. Additional exam requirements/recommendations for international students: Required—TOEFL (minimum score 550 paper-based; 79 iBT). *Application deadline:* For fall admission, 3/1 priority date for international students; for spring admission, 8/1 priority date for international students. Applications are processed on a rolling basis. Application fee: $40 ($75 for international students). Electronic applications accepted. *Expenses:* Tuition, state resident: full-time $3716; part-time $154.85 per credit hour. Tuition, nonresident: full-time $14,892; part-time $621 per credit hour. Required fees: $2044; $85.20 per credit hour. One-time fee: $50. Tuition and fees vary according to course load and campus/location. *Financial support:* In 2010–11, 34 teaching assistantships (averaging $12,919 per year) were awarded; career-related internships or fieldwork, Federal Work-Study, scholarships/grants, health care benefits, tuition waivers (partial), and unspecified assistantships also available. Support available to part-time students. Financial award application deadline: 3/1; financial award applicants required to submit FAFSA. *Faculty research:* U. S. history, the American West, Native American history, modern European history, women's history. *Unit head:* Dr. Michael F. Logan, Head, 405-744-5678, Fax: 405-744-5400. *Application contact:* Dr. Gordon Emslie, Dean, 405-744-6368, Fax: 405-744-0355, E-mail: grad-i@okstate.edu.

Old Dominion University, College of Arts and Letters, Program in History, Norfolk, VA 23529. Offers MA. Part-time and evening/weekend programs available. *Faculty:* 16 full-time (7 women). *Students:* 22 full-time (14 women), 23 part-time (7 women); includes 3 minority (2 Hispanic/Latino; 1 Two or more races, non-Hispanic/Latino), 1 international. Average age 33. 41 applicants, 80% accepted, 20 enrolled. In 2010, 13 master's awarded. *Degree requirements:* For master's, comprehensive exam, thesis optional. *Entrance requirements:* For master's, GRE General Test, 24 credits in history with minimum GPA of 3.0. *Application deadline:* For fall admission, 6/1 for domestic students; for spring admission, 11/1 for domestic students. Applications are processed on a rolling basis. Application fee: $40. Electronic applications accepted. *Expenses:* Tuition, state resident: full-time $8592; part-time $358 per credit. Tuition, nonresident: full-time $21,672; part-time $903 per credit. Required fees: $119 per semester. One-time fee: $50. *Financial support:* In 2010–11, 1 fellowship with full tuition reimbursement (averaging $8,000 per year), 6 teaching assistantships with partial tuition reimbursements (averaging $8,000 per year) were awarded; career-related internships or fieldwork and scholarships/grants also available. Support available to part-time students. Financial award application deadline: 2/15; financial award applicants required to submit FAFSA. *Faculty research:* History: maritime, American, European, modern Asia, and Africa. *Unit head:* Dr. Ingo K. Heidbrink, Graduate Program Director, 757-683-3949, Fax: 757-683-5644, E-mail: histgpd@odu.edu. *Application contact:* Dr. Ingo K. Heidbrink, Graduate Program Director, 757-683-3949, Fax: 757-683-5644, E-mail: histgpd@odu.edu.

Oregon State University, Graduate School, College of Liberal Arts, Department of History, Corvallis, OR 97331. Offers history of science (MA, PhD).

Penn State University Park, Graduate School, College of the Liberal Arts, Department of History, State College, University Park, PA 16802-1503. Offers MA, PhD.

Pepperdine University, Seaver College, Humanities and Teacher Education Division, Malibu, CA 90263. Offers American studies (MA); history (MA); writing for screen and television (MFA). Part-time programs available. *Students:* 23 part-time (16 women); includes 1 minority (Asian, non-Hispanic/Latino). 8 applicants, 88% accepted, 7 enrolled. In 2010, 3 master's awarded. *Degree requirements:* For master's, oral and written exams. *Entrance requirements:* For master's, GRE General Test, writing sample, letters of recommendation. Additional exam requirements/recommendations for international students: Required—TOEFL. *Application deadline:* For fall admission, 2/1 priority date for domestic students. Applications are processed on a rolling basis. Application fee: $55. *Financial support:* Applicants required to submit FAFSA. *Unit head:* Dr. Maire Mullins, Chair/Professor of English, 310-506-4235, Fax: 310-506-7307, E-mail: maire.mullins@pepperdine.edu. *Application contact:* Michael Truschke, Dean of Admission and Enrollment Management, 310-506-6165, Fax: 310-506-4861, E-mail: admission-seaver@pepperdine.edu.

Pittsburg State University, Graduate School, College of Arts and Sciences, Department of History, Pittsburg, KS 66762. Offers MA. *Degree requirements:* For master's, thesis or alternative.

Pontifical Catholic University of Puerto Rico, College of Arts and Humanities, Department of History, Ponce, PR 00717-0777. Offers MA. *Entrance requirements:* For master's, GRE General Test, minimum GPA of 2.75, 2 letters of recommendation.

Portland State University, Graduate Studies, College of Liberal Arts and Sciences, Department of History, Portland, OR 97207-0751. Offers MA. Part-time programs available. *Faculty:* 21 full-time (8 women), 2 part-time/adjunct (1 woman). *Students:* 25 full-time (13 women), 28 part-time (15 women); includes 1 American Indian or Alaska Native, non-Hispanic/Latino; 1 Asian, non-Hispanic/Latino; 1 Hispanic/Latino; 1 Two or more races, non-Hispanic/Latino, 1 international. Average age 35. 53 applicants, 45% accepted, 14 enrolled. In 2010, 11 master's awarded. *Degree requirements:* For master's, one foreign language, thesis, oral and written exams. *Entrance requirements:* For master's, GRE General Test, minimum GPA of 3.5 in upper-division history courses, 2 letters of recommendation, BA/BS in history. Additional exam requirements/recommendations for international students: Required—TOEFL (minimum score 550 paper-based; 213 computer-based). *Application deadline:* For fall admission, 2/15 for domestic and international students; for winter admission, 9/1 for domestic students, 6/1 for international students; for spring admission, 11/1 for domestic and international students. Application fee: $50. *Expenses:* Tuition, state resident: full-time $8505; part-time $315 per credit. Tuition, nonresident: full-time $13,284; part-time $492 per credit. Required fees: $1482; $21 per credit. $99 per term. One-time fee: $120. Part-time tuition and fees vary according to course load and program. *Financial support:* In 2010–11, 2 research assistantships with full tuition reimbursements (averaging $11,238 per year) were awarded; teaching assistantships with full tuition reimbursements, career-related internships or fieldwork, Federal Work-Study, scholarships/grants, and unspecified assistantships also available. Support available to part-time students. Financial award application deadline: 3/1; financial award applicants required to submit FAFSA. *Faculty research:* Germany and modern Europe, early modern France and England, Mexico in the 1920's, eighteenth century France, Reformation, U. S. cultural history. Total annual research expenditures: $22,802. *Unit head:* Dr. Thomas Luckett, Chair, 503-725-3982, Fax: 503-725-3953, E-mail: luckettt@pdx.edu. *Application contact:* Dr. Richard Beyler, Graduate Coordinator, 503-725-3996, Fax: 503-725-3953, E-mail: beylerr@pdx.edu.

Princeton University, Graduate School, Department of Classics, Princeton, NJ 08544-1019. Offers classical and hellenic studies (PhD); classical philosophy (PhD); history (the ancient world) (PhD); literature and philology (PhD). *Degree requirements:* For doctorate, thesis/dissertation. *Entrance requirements:* For doctorate, GRE General Test, sample of written work. Additional exam requirements/recommendations for international students: Required—TOEFL (minimum score 600 paper-based; 250 computer-based). Electronic applications accepted.

Princeton University, Graduate School, Department of History, Princeton, NJ 08544-1019. Offers history (PhD); history of science (PhD). *Degree requirements:* For doctorate, variable foreign language requirement, comprehensive exam, thesis/dissertation. *Entrance requirements:* For doctorate, GRE General Test, sample of written work. Additional exam requirements/recommendations for international students: Required—TOEFL (minimum score 600 paper-based; 250 computer-based). Electronic applications accepted. *Faculty research:* World comparative, Europe-early modern, modern, late antique, medieval.

Providence College, Graduate Studies, Department of History, Providence, RI 02918. Offers American history (MA); European history (MA). Part-time and evening/weekend programs available. *Faculty:* 14 part-time/adjunct (3 women). *Students:* 23 full-time (7 women), 37 part-time (15 women); includes 1 minority (Black or African American, non-Hispanic/Latino). Average age 30. 14 applicants, 100% accepted. In 2010, 28 master's awarded. *Degree requirements:* For master's, comprehensive exam, thesis optional. *Entrance requirements:* Additional exam requirements/recommendations for international students: Required—TOEFL (minimum score 550 paper-based; 213 computer-based; 80 iBT). *Application deadline:* For fall admission, 8/1 priority date for domestic and international students; for spring admission, 12/31 priority date for domestic students, 12/1 priority date for international students. Applications are processed on a rolling basis. Application fee: $55. *Expenses:* Tuition: Part-time $367 per credit. Required fees: $367. *Financial support:* In 2010–11, 8 research assistantships with full tuition reimbursements (averaging $8,400 per year) were awarded; career-related internships or fieldwork, institutionally sponsored loans, and unspecified assistantships also available. Support available to part-time students. Financial award application deadline: 8/1; financial award applicants required to submit FAFSA. *Faculty research:* Modern Europe, American social and political history, modern Ireland, Rhode Island, eastern European history. *Unit head:* Dr. Paul O'Malley, Director of Graduate Programs, 401-865-2193, Fax: 401-865-1193, E-mail: pomalley@providence.edu. *Application contact:* Phyllis S. Cardullo, Senior Administrative Coordinator, 401-865-2193, Fax: 401-865-1193, E-mail: pcardull@providence.edu.

Purdue University, Graduate School, College of Liberal Arts, Department of History, West Lafayette, IN 47907. Offers MA, PhD. Part-time programs available. *Degree requirements:* For master's, thesis optional; for doctorate, 2 foreign languages, thesis/dissertation. *Entrance requirements:* For master's and doctorate, GRE General Test, sample of written work. Additional exam requirements/recommendations for international students: Required—TOEFL. Electronic applications accepted. *Faculty research:* U.S. history, early modern and modern European history, global women's history, U.S. minority history, medieval history.

Purdue University Calumet, Graduate Studies Office, School of Liberal Arts and Social Sciences, Department of History and Political Science, Hammond, IN 46323-2094. Offers history (MA). Part-time and evening/weekend programs available. *Faculty:* 5 full-time (1 woman), 2 part-time/adjunct (1 woman). *Students:* 4 full-time (3 women), 17 part-time (6 women); includes 1 Black or African American, non-Hispanic/Latino. In 2010, 3 master's awarded. *Entrance requirements:* Additional exam requirements/recommendations for international students: Required—TOEFL. Application fee: $55. *Expenses:* Tuition, state resident: full-time $6867. Tuition, nonresident: full-time $14,157. *Financial support:* In 2010–11, 1 research assistantship (averaging $1,500 per year) was awarded. Financial award application deadline: 3/1. *Faculty research:* Mid-east, German history, U. S. regional history, U. S. social history, Holocaust. *Unit head:* Dr. Saul Lerner, Graduate Advisor, 219-989-2329, E-mail: lerner@purduecal.edu. *Application contact:* Dr. Saul Lerner, Graduate Advisor, 219-989-2329, E-mail: lerner@purduecal.edu.

Queens College of the City University of New York, Division of Graduate Studies, Social Science Division, Department of History, Flushing, NY 11367-1597. Offers MA. Part-time and evening/weekend programs available. *Faculty:* 24 full-time (12 women). *Students:* 2 full-time (1 woman), 85 part-time (32 women); includes 4 Black or African American, non-Hispanic/Latino; 9 Asian, non-Hispanic/Latino; 9 Hispanic/Latino, 1 international. 70 applicants, 59% accepted, 27 enrolled. In 2010, 9 master's awarded. *Degree requirements:* For master's, one foreign language, comprehensive exam, thesis. *Entrance requirements:* For master's, minimum GPA of 3.0. Additional exam requirements/recommendations for international students: Required—TOEFL. *Application deadline:* For fall admission, 4/1 for domestic students; for spring admission, 11/1 for domestic students. Applications are processed on a rolling basis. Application fee: $125. *Financial support:* Career-related internships or fieldwork, Federal Work-Study, institutionally sponsored loans, and tuition waivers (partial) available. Support available to part-time students. Financial award application deadline: 4/1; financial award applicants required to submit FAFSA. *Faculty research:* Ancient, modern European, medieval, and American history. *Unit head:* Dr. Frank Warren, Chairperson, 718-997-5350, E-mail: frank_warren@qc.edu. *Application contact:* Dr. Jon Peterson, Graduate Adviser, 718-997-5350, E-mail: jon_peterson@qc.edu.

Rhode Island College, School of Graduate Studies, Faculty of Arts and Sciences, Department of History, Providence, RI 02908-1991. Offers MA. Part-time and evening/weekend programs available. *Faculty:* 9 full-time (2 women). *Students:* 1 (woman) full-time, 3 part-time (2 women); includes 1 minority (Two or more races, non-Hispanic/Latino). Average age 41. In 2010, 2 master's awarded. *Degree requirements:* For master's, oral exam or thesis. *Entrance requirements:* For master's, GRE General and Subject Tests, 3 letters of recommendation, interview. Additional exam requirements/recommendations for international students: Recommended—TOEFL (minimum score 550 paper-based; 213 computer-based; 79 iBT). *Application deadline:* For fall admission, 3/1 for domestic students; for spring admission, 11/1 for domestic students. Applications are processed on a rolling basis. Application fee: $50. *Expenses:* Tuition, state resident: full-time $8208; part-time $342 per credit hour. Tuition, nonresident: full-time $16,080; part-time $670 per credit hour. Required fees: $554; $20 per credit. $72 per term. *Financial support:* In 2010–11, 1 teaching assistantship with full tuition reimbursement (averaging $4,550 per year) was awarded; Federal Work-Study, scholarships/grants, health care benefits, and unspecified assistantships also available. Support available to part-time students. Financial award application deadline: 5/15; financial award applicants required to submit FAFSA. *Unit head:* Dr. Robert Cvornvek, Chair, 401-456-8039. *Application contact:* Graduate Studies, 401-456-8700.

Rice University, Graduate Programs, School of Humanities, Department of History, Houston, TX 77251-1892. Offers MA, PhD. Terminal master's awarded for partial completion of doctoral program. *Degree requirements:* For doctorate, variable foreign language requirement, comprehensive exam, thesis/dissertation, 4 semesters of coursework. *Entrance requirements:* For doctorate, GRE, writing samples, letters of recommendation, personal statement, transcripts. Additional exam requirements/recommendations for international students: Required—TOEFL (minimum score 600 paper-based; 250 computer-based; 90 iBT) or IELTS (minimum score 7). Electronic applications accepted. *Faculty research:* U. S. Southern, Caribbean, African-American, world, Latin American.

Roosevelt University, Graduate Division, College of Arts and Sciences, Department of History, Art, and Philosophy, Chicago, IL 60605. Offers history (MA). Part-time and evening/weekend programs available. *Degree requirements:* For master's, thesis or alternative. *Faculty research:* American social history, Holocaust, European history, African-American history, popular culture.

Rutgers, The State University of New Jersey, Camden, Graduate School of Arts and Sciences, Program in American and Public History, Camden, NJ 08102. Offers MA. Part-time and evening/weekend programs available. *Faculty:* 15 full-time (6 women), 3 part-time/adjunct (2 women). *Students:* 3 full-time (1 woman), 34 part-time (13 women); includes 1 American Indian or Alaska Native, non-Hispanic/Latino; 1 Hispanic/Latino. Average age 34. 32 applicants, 88% accepted, 13 enrolled. In 2010, 6 degrees awarded. *Degree requirements:* For master's, comprehensive exam, thesis optional, 30 credits. *Entrance requirements:* For master's, GRE General Test (for full-time applicants), 3 letters of recommendation; history or related undergraduate degree (preferred). Additional exam requirements/recommendations for international students: Required—TOEFL, IELTS. *Application deadline:* For fall admission, 7/1 priority date for domestic students; for spring admission, 11/15 for domestic students. Applications are processed on a rolling basis. Application fee: $65. Electronic applications accepted. *Expenses:* Tuition, state resident: full-time $4963; part-time $319 per credit. Tuition, nonresident: full-time $10,493; part-time $680 per credit. *Financial support:* In 2010–11, 4 fellowships with partial tuition reimbursements (averaging $1,550 per year) were awarded; Federal Work-Study, scholarships/grants, and tuition waivers (partial) also available. Financial award application deadline: 3/15; financial award applicants required to submit FAFSA. *Faculty research:* Women's history, military history, Afro-American history, urban history, history of technology. Total annual research expenditures: $44,250. *Unit head:* Dr. Philip Scranton, Director, 856-225-2713, Fax: 856-225-6602, E-mail: scranton@camden.rutgers.edu. *Application contact:* Leona Pellot, Graduate Secretary, 856-225-6080, Fax: 856-225-6602, E-mail: pellot@camden.rutgers.edu.

Rutgers, The State University of New Jersey, Newark, Graduate School, Program in History, Newark, NJ 07102. Offers MA, MAT. MA, MAT offered jointly with New Jersey Institute of Technology. Part-time and evening/weekend programs available. *Faculty:* 19 full-time (8 women), 10 part-time/adjunct (3 women). *Students:* 25 full-time (8 women), 62 part-time (22 women); includes 7 Black or African American, non-Hispanic/Latino; 1 Asian, non-Hispanic/Latino; 10 Hispanic/Latino. 81 applicants, 79% accepted, 30 enrolled. In 2010, 18 master's awarded. *Degree requirements:* For master's, one foreign language, comprehensive exam, thesis optional. *Entrance requirements:* For master's, GRE, minimum undergraduate B average. *Application deadline:* For fall admission, 7/1 priority date for domestic students; for spring admission, 12/1 for domestic students. Applications are processed on a rolling basis. Application fee: $60. *Expenses:* Tuition, state resident: part-time $600 per credit. Tuition, nonresident: full-time $10,694. *Financial support:* In 2010–11, 5 teaching assistantships with full and partial tuition reimbursements (averaging $23,112 per year) were awarded; career-related internships or fieldwork, Federal Work-Study, and tuition waivers (full and partial) also available. Support available to part-time students. Financial award application deadline: 3/1. *Faculty research:* Global history, American history, American diplomatic and legal history, women's history, history of technology, environment and medicine. *Unit head:* Dr. Susan Carruthers, Director, 973-353-5410 Ext. 34, Fax: 973-353-1193, E-mail: scarruth@andromeda.rutgers.edu. *Application contact:* Christina Strasburger, Department Administrator, 973-353-5410, Fax: 973-353-1193, E-mail: cstras@andromeda.rutgers.edu.

Rutgers, The State University of New Jersey, New Brunswick, Graduate School-New Brunswick, Program in History, Piscataway, NJ 08854-8097. Offers African-American history (PhD); early American history (PhD); early modern European history (PhD); east Asian history (PhD); global and comparative history (PhD); history (PhD); history of diplomacy and foreign relations (PhD); history of technology, environment and health (PhD); history of the Atlantic cultures and African diaspora (PhD); Latin American history (PhD); medieval history (PhD); modern European history (PhD); nineteenth and twentieth century American history (PhD); women's and gender history (PhD). *Degree requirements:* For doctorate, thesis/dissertation. *Entrance requirements:* For doctorate, GRE General Test, sample of written work. Electronic applications accepted. *Expenses:* Tuition, state resident: full-time $7200; part-time $600 per credit. Tuition, nonresident: full-time $11,124; part-time $927 per credit. *Faculty research:* American history, European history, Afro-American history, women's history, Latin American history.

St. Cloud State University, School of Graduate Studies, College of Social Sciences, Department of History, St. Cloud, MN 56301-4498. Offers MA, MS. Part-time programs available. *Degree requirements:* For master's, thesis or alternative. *Entrance requirements:* For master's, GRE General Test, GRE Subject Test, minimum GPA of 2.75. Additional exam requirements/recommendations for international students: Required—Michigan English Language Assessment Battery; Recommended—TOEFL (minimum score 550 paper-based; 213 computer-based), IELTS (minimum score 6.5).

St. John's University, St. John's College of Liberal Arts and Sciences, Department of History, Queens, NY 11439. Offers history (MA); modern world history (DA). Part-time and evening/weekend programs available. *Students:* 18 full-time (6 women), 34 part-time (11 women); includes 15 minority (5 Black or African American, non-Hispanic/Latino; 3 Asian, non-Hispanic/Latino; 6 Hispanic/Latino; 1 Two or more races, non-Hispanic/Latino), 7 international. Average age 35. 49 applicants, 65% accepted, 18 enrolled. In 2010, 10 master's, 6 doctorates awarded. *Degree requirements:* For master's, one foreign language, comprehensive exam, thesis optional; for doctorate, one foreign language, comprehensive exam, thesis/dissertation, internship, practicum. *Entrance requirements:* For master's, minimum GPA of 3.0; for doctorate, interview; minimum GPA of 3.5 in history, 3.0 overall; writing sample, 3 letters of recommendation, personal essay. Additional exam requirements/recommendations for international students: Required—TOEFL (minimum score 600 paper-based; 250 computer-based; 100 iBT), IELTS (minimum score 5.5). *Application deadline:* For fall admission, 5/1 priority date for domestic and international students; for spring admission, 11/1 priority date for domestic and international students. Applications are processed on a rolling basis. Application fee: $70. Electronic applications accepted. *Expenses:* Tuition: Full-time $17,100; part-time $950 per credit. Required fees: $340; $170 per semester. Tuition and fees vary according to program. *Financial support:* Fellowships, research assistantships, scholarships/grants available. Support available to part-time students. Financial award application deadline: 3/1; financial award applicants required to submit FAFSA. *Faculty research:* European economic history, history of East Asian culture, Irish history. *Unit head:* Dr. Mauricio Borrero, Chair, 718-990-6228, E-mail: borrerom@stjohns.edu. *Application contact:* Kathleen Davis, Director of Graduate Admission, 718-990-1601, Fax: 718-990-5686, E-mail: gradhelp@stjohns.edu.

Saint Louis University, Graduate Education, College of Arts and Sciences and Graduate Education, Department of History, St. Louis, MO 63103-2097. Offers MA, MA-R, PhD. Part-time programs available. *Degree requirements:* For master's, one foreign language, comprehensive exam, thesis optional, comprehensive oral exam; for doctorate, 2 foreign languages, comprehensive exam, thesis/dissertation, preliminary oral and written exams. *Entrance requirements:* For master's, GRE General Test, letters of recommendation, resume, writing sample; for doctorate, GRE General Test, letters of recommendation, resumé, writing sample, goal statement, transcripts. Additional exam requirements/recommendations for international students: Required—TOEFL (minimum score 525 paper-based; 194 computer-based). Electronic applications accepted. *Faculty research:* Medieval Europe, Crusades, Byzantine Empire, US West and Borderlands, Early Modern Europe.

Saint Mary's University, Faculty of Arts, Department of History, Halifax, NS B3H 3C3, Canada. Offers MA. Part-time programs available. *Degree requirements:* For master's, one foreign language, comprehensive exam, thesis. *Entrance requirements:* For master's, honors degree. *Expenses:* Contact institution. *Faculty research:* Atlantic Canada, British Empire, history of science, South Africa.

Salem State University, School of Graduate Studies, Program in History, Salem, MA 01970-5353. Offers MA, MAT. Part-time and evening/weekend programs available. *Students:* 7 full-time (2 women), 66 part-time (24 women); includes 1 Hispanic/Latino. Average age 33. 27 applicants, 85% accepted, 23 enrolled. In 2010, 24 master's awarded. *Entrance requirements:* For master's, GRE or MAT. Additional exam requirements/recommendations for international students: Required—TOEFL (minimum score 550 paper-based; 80 iBT) or IELTS (minimum score 5.5). *Application deadline:* For fall admission, 5/1 for domestic students; for spring admission, 10/1 for domestic students. Applications are processed on a rolling basis. Application fee: $50. *Expenses:* Tuition, state resident: full-time $2520; part-time $290 per credit hour. Tuition, nonresident: full-time $4140; part-time $380 per credit hour. Required fees: $2700. *Financial support:* Career-related internships or fieldwork, Federal Work-Study, scholarships/grants, and unspecified assistantships available. Support available to part-time students. Financial award application deadline: 5/1; financial award applicants required to submit FAFSA. *Unit head:* Bethany Jay, Program Coordinator, 978-542-6321, Fax: 978-542-7215, E-mail: bjay@salemstate.edu. *Application contact:* Dr. Lee A. Brossoit, Assistant Dean of Graduate Admissions, 978-542-6675, Fax: 978-542-7215, E-mail: lbrossoit@salemstate.edu.

Salisbury University, Graduate Division, Program in History, Salisbury, MD 21801-6837. Offers MA. Part-time programs available. *Faculty:* 8 full-time (2 women). *Students:* 5 full-time (1 woman), 11 part-time (5 women); includes 1 minority (Black or African American, non-Hispanic/Latino), 1 international. Average age 27. 4 applicants, 100% accepted, 3 enrolled. In 2010, 3 master's awarded. *Degree requirements:* For master's, comprehensive exam, thesis optional, 2 research and 3 reading seminars, final and oral exam. *Entrance requirements:* For master's, GRE General Test, minimum GPA of 3.0, 3 letters of recommendation. Additional exam requirements/recommendations for international students: Required—TOEFL (minimum score 550 paper-based; 213 computer-based; 79 iBT). *Application deadline:* For fall admission, 5/15 for domestic students; for spring admission, 10/15 for domestic students. Application fee: $45. Electronic applications accepted. *Financial support:* In 2010–11, 5 students received support. Career-related internships or fieldwork and scholarships/grants available. Support available to part-time students. Financial award applicants required to submit FAFSA. *Faculty research:* History of science and technology, U. S. foreign relations, Maryland history, African-American history, medieval history. *Unit head:* Dr. Creston S. Long, Director, 410-548-5091, Fax: 410-677-5038, E-mail: cslong@salisbury.edu. *Application contact:* Mia C. Vye, Administrative Assistant II, 410-548-4499, Fax: 410-677-5038, E-mail: mcvye@salisbury.edu.

Sam Houston State University, College of Humanities and Social Sciences, Department of History, Huntsville, TX 77341. Offers MA. Part-time and evening/weekend programs available. *Faculty:* 14 full-time (5 women). *Students:* 18 full-time (9 women), 65 part-time (18 women); includes 2 Black or African American, non-Hispanic/Latino; 5 Hispanic/Latino, 1 international. Average age 35. 49 applicants, 78% accepted, 30 enrolled. In 2010, 13 master's awarded. *Entrance requirements:* For master's, GRE General Test. Additional exam requirements/recommendations for international students: Required—TOEFL (minimum score 550 paper-based; 213 computer-based; 79 iBT). *Application deadline:* For fall admission, 8/1 for domestic students; for spring admission, 12/1 for domestic students. Application fee: $20. *Expenses:* Tuition, state resident: full-time $1363; part-time $163 per credit hour. Tuition, nonresident: full-time $3856; part-time $473 per credit hour. *Financial support:* Teaching assistantships, Federal Work-Study and institutionally sponsored loans available. Support available to part-time students. Financial award application deadline: 5/31; financial award applicants required to submit FAFSA. *Unit head:* Dr. Terry Bilhartz, Chair, 936-294-1483, Fax: 936-294-3938, E-mail: his_tdb@shsu.edu. *Application contact:* Dr. Ken Hendrickson, Advisor, 936-294-1482, E-mail: his_keh@shsu.edu.

San Diego State University, Graduate and Research Affairs, College of Arts and Letters, Department of History, San Diego, CA 92182. Offers MA. *Degree requirements:* For master's, one foreign language. *Entrance requirements:* For master's, GRE General Test, bachelor's degree in related field. Additional exam requirements/recommendations for international students: Required—TOEFL. Electronic applications accepted. *Faculty research:* Latin American history, Filipino history.

San Francisco State University, Division of Graduate Studies, College of Behavioral and Social Sciences, Department of History, San Francisco, CA 94132-1722. Offers MA. *Unit head:* Dr. Barbara Loomis, Chair, 415-338-1604, E-mail: barbaral@sfsu.edu. *Application contact:* Dr. Jarbel Rodriguez, Graduate Coordinator, 415-338-1604, E-mail: jarbel@sfsu.edu.

San Jose State University, Graduate Studies and Research, College of Social Sciences, Department of History, San Jose, CA 95192-0001. Offers history (MA); history education (MA). *Degree requirements:* For master's, comprehensive exam, thesis or alternative. *Entrance requirements:* For master's, bachelor's degree or 15 units of course work in history, minimum GPA of 3.0. Electronic applications accepted.

Sarah Lawrence College, Graduate Studies, Program in Women's History, Bronxville, NY 10708-5999. Offers MA. Part-time programs available. *Degree requirements:* For master's, thesis. *Entrance requirements:* For master's, previous course work in history, minimum B average in undergraduate course work. Additional exam requirements/recommendations for international students: Required—TOEFL (minimum score 600 paper-based).

Seton Hall University, College of Arts and Sciences, Department of History, South Orange, NJ 07079-2697. Offers history (MA), including Catholic history, European history, global history, United States history. Part-time programs available. *Degree requirements:* For master's, thesis or comprehensive exam. *Entrance requirements:* For master's, GRE. Additional exam requirements/recommendations for international students: Required—TOEFL. Electronic applications accepted. *Faculty research:* Catholic history, European history, global history, United States history, African American history.

Shippensburg University of Pennsylvania, School of Graduate Studies, College of Arts and Sciences, Department of History and Philosophy, Shippensburg, PA 17257-2299. Offers applied history (MA, Certificate). Part-time and evening/weekend programs available. *Faculty:* 8 full-time (1 woman). *Students:* 11 full-time (6 women), 19 part-time (5 women). Average age 33. 30 applicants, 60% accepted, 8 enrolled. In 2010, 20 master's awarded. *Degree requirements:* For master's, thesis optional, thesis or internship. *Entrance requirements:* For master's, interview. Additional exam requirements/recommendations for international students: Required—TOEFL (minimum score 580 paper-based; 237 computer-based); Recommended—IELTS (minimum score 6). *Application deadline:* For fall admission, 3/1 for international students; for spring admission, 7/1 for international students. Applications are processed on a rolling basis. Application fee: $30. Electronic applications accepted. *Expenses:* Tuition, state resident: full-time $6966. Tuition, nonresident: full-time $11,146. Required fees: $1802. *Financial support:* In 2010–11, 5 research assistantships with full tuition reimbursements (averaging $5,000 per year) were awarded; career-related internships or fieldwork, scholarships/grants, unspecified assistantships, and resident hall director and student payroll positions also available. Support available to part-time students. Financial award application deadline: 3/1; financial award applicants required to submit FAFSA. *Unit head:* Dr. Stephen Burg, Program Director, 717-477-1621, Fax: 717-477-4062, E-mail: sbburg@ship.edu. *Application contact:* Jeremy R. Goshorn, Associate Dean of Graduate Admissions, 717-477-1231, Fax: 717-477-4016, E-mail: jrgoshorn@ship.edu.

Shippensburg University of Pennsylvania, School of Graduate Studies, College of Education and Human Services, Department of Teacher Education, Shippensburg, PA 17257-2299. Offers curriculum and instruction (M Ed), including biology, early childhood education, elementary education, English, geography/earth science, history, mathematics, middle school education, modern languages; reading (M Ed). *Accreditation:* NCATE. Part-time and evening/weekend programs available. *Faculty:* 15 full-time (13 women), 11 part-time/adjunct (9 women). *Students:* 15 full-time (11 women), 170 part-time (158 women); includes 10 minority (7 Black or African American, non-Hispanic/Latino; 2 Hispanic/Latino; 1 Two or more races, non-Hispanic/Latino), 2 international. Average age 30. 74 applicants, 68% accepted, 31 enrolled. In 2010, 66 master's awarded. *Degree requirements:* For master's, comprehensive exam (for some programs), thesis optional, practicum or internship; capstone seminar (for some programs). *Entrance requirements:* For master's, MAT (if GPA less than 2.75), interview, 3 letters of reference, questionnaire of teaching background and future goals. Additional exam requirements/recommendations for international students: Required—TOEFL (minimum score 580 paper-based; 237 computer-based); Recommended—IELTS (minimum score 6). *Application deadline:* For fall admission, 6/1 priority date for domestic students, 3/1 for international students; for spring admission, 9/1 priority date for domestic students, 7/1 for international students. Applications are processed on a rolling basis. Application fee: $30. Electronic applications accepted. *Expenses:* Tuition, state resident: full-time $6966. Tuition, nonresident: full-time $11,146. Required fees: $1802. *Financial support:* In 2010–11, 3 research assistantships with full tuition reimbursements (averaging $5,000 per year) were awarded; career-related internships or fieldwork, scholarships/grants, unspecified assistantships, and resident hall director and student payroll positions also available. Support available to part-time students. Financial award

History

Shippensburg University of Pennsylvania *(continued)*
application deadline: 3/1; financial award applicants required to submit FAFSA. *Unit head:* Dr. Christine A. Royce, Chairperson, 717-477-1688, Fax: 717-477-4046, E-mail: caroyc@ship.edu. *Application contact:* Jeremy R. Goshorn, Associate Dean of Graduate Admissions, 717-477-1231, Fax: 717-477-4016, E-mail: jrgoshorn@ship.edu.

Simmons College, College of Arts and Sciences Graduate Studies, Program in History, Boston, MA 02115. Offers MA. Part-time programs available. *Degree requirements:* For master's, thesis optional. Electronic applications accepted. *Faculty research:* Gender history, cultural history, American history, transnational history.

Simon Fraser University, Graduate Studies, Faculty of Arts and Social Sciences, Department of History, Burnaby, BC V5A 1S6, Canada. Offers MA, PhD. *Degree requirements:* For master's, one foreign language, thesis or alternative, project; for doctorate, one foreign language, comprehensive exam, thesis/dissertation. *Entrance requirements:* For master's, minimum GPA of 3.0; for doctorate, minimum GPA of 3.5. Additional exam requirements/recommendations for international students: Required—TOEFL or IELTS. *Faculty research:* Colonialism and imperialism, Canadian history, Middle East and Islam labor, Victorian intellect.

Slippery Rock University of Pennsylvania, Graduate Studies (Recruitment), College of Education, Department of Secondary Education/Foundations of Education, Slippery Rock, PA 16057-1383. Offers educational leadership (M Ed); secondary education in English (M Ed); secondary education in history (M Ed); secondary education in math/science (M Ed). *Accreditation:* NCATE. Part-time and evening/weekend programs available. *Faculty:* 7 full-time (2 women). *Students:* 84 full-time (44 women), 16 part-time (6 women); includes 7 minority (1 Black or African American, non-Hispanic/Latino; 1 American Indian or Alaska Native, non-Hispanic/Latino; 2 Asian, non-Hispanic/Latino; 3 Hispanic/Latino), 1 international. Average age 27. 82 applicants, 72% accepted, 51 enrolled. In 2010, 41 master's awarded. *Degree requirements:* For master's, comprehensive exam, thesis (for some programs). *Entrance requirements:* For master's, GRE General Test, MAT. Additional exam requirements/recommendations for international students: Required—TOEFL (minimum score 550 paper-based; 213 computer-based; 80 iBT). *Application deadline:* For fall admission, 3/1 priority date for domestic students, 5/1 priority date for international students; for spring admission, 11/1 priority date for domestic students, 9/1 priority date for international students. Applications are processed on a rolling basis. Application fee: $25 ($30 for international students). Electronic applications accepted. *Expenses:* Tuition, state resident: full-time $6966; part-time $387 per credit. Tuition, nonresident: full-time $11,146; part-time $619 per credit. Required fees: $2388; $202 per credit. *Financial support:* Career-related internships or fieldwork, Federal Work-Study, institutionally sponsored loans, scholarships/grants, tuition waivers (partial), and unspecified assistantships available. Support available to part-time students. Financial award application deadline: 5/1; financial award applicants required to submit FAFSA. *Unit head:* Dr. Jeffrey Lehman, Graduate Coordinator, 724-738-2311, Fax: 724-738-4987, E-mail: jeffrey.lehman@sru.edu. *Application contact:* Angela Piverotto, Interim Director of Graduate Studies, 724-738-2051, Fax: 724-738-2146, E-mail: graduate.admissions@sru.edu.

Slippery Rock University of Pennsylvania, Graduate Studies (Recruitment), College of Humanities, Fine and Performing Arts, Department of History, Slippery Rock, PA 16057-1383. Offers MA. Part-time and evening/weekend programs available. *Faculty:* 5 full-time (1 woman), 1 part-time/adjunct (0 women). *Students:* 22 full-time (5 women), 8 part-time (0 women); includes 1 minority (American Indian or Alaska Native, non-Hispanic/Latino). Average age 28. 20 applicants, 75% accepted, 11 enrolled. In 2010, 13 master's awarded. *Degree requirements:* For master's, comprehensive exam, thesis (for some programs). *Entrance requirements:* For master's, GRE General Test, minimum GPA of 2.75. Additional exam requirements/recommendations for international students: Required—TOEFL (minimum score 550 paper-based; 213 computer-based; 80 iBT). *Application deadline:* For fall admission, 3/1 priority date for domestic students, 5/1 priority date for international students; for spring admission, 11/1 priority date for domestic students, 9/1 priority date for international students. Applications are processed on a rolling basis. Application fee: $25 ($30 for international students). Electronic applications accepted. *Expenses:* Tuition, state resident: full-time $6966; part-time $387 per credit. Tuition, nonresident: full-time $11,146; part-time $619 per credit. Required fees: $2388; $202 per credit. *Financial support:* Career-related internships or fieldwork, Federal Work-Study, institutionally sponsored loans, scholarships/grants, tuition waivers (partial), and unspecified assistantships available. Support available to part-time students. Financial award application deadline: 5/1; financial award applicants required to submit FAFSA. *Unit head:* Dr. Eric Tuten, Graduate Coordinator, 724-738-4913, Fax: 724-738-4762, E-mail: jeric.tuten@sru.edu. *Application contact:* Angela Piverotto, Interim Director of Graduate Studies, 724-738-2051, Fax: 724-738-2146, E-mail: graduate.admissions@sru.edu.

Smith College, Graduate and Special Programs, Department of History, Northampton, MA 01063. Offers MAT. *Faculty:* 10 full-time (5 women), 1 (woman) part-time/adjunct. *Students:* 2 full-time (1 woman). Average age 23. 3 applicants, 100% accepted, 2 enrolled. In 2010, 1 master's awarded. *Entrance requirements:* Additional exam requirements/recommendations for international students: Required—TOEFL (minimum score 590 paper-based; 243 computer-based; 97 iBT). *Application deadline:* For fall admission, 4/15 for domestic students, 1/15 for international students; for spring admission, 12/1 for domestic students. Application fee: $60. *Expenses:* Tuition: Full-time $14,520; part-time $1210 per credit. *Financial support:* In 2010–11, 2 students received support. Career-related internships or fieldwork, institutionally sponsored loans, and scholarships/grants available. Support available to part-time students. Financial award application deadline: 1/15; financial award applicants required to submit CSS PROFILE or FAFSA. *Unit head:* Serguei Glebov, Associate Professor, 413-585-3742, E-mail: sglebov@smith.edu. *Application contact:* Ruth Morgan, Administrative Assistant, 413-585-3050, Fax: 413-585-3054, E-mail: gradstdy@smith.edu.

Sonoma State University, School of Social Sciences, Department of History, Rohnert Park, BC 94928. Offers MA. Part-time programs available. *Faculty:* 3 full-time (2 women). *Students:* 11 part-time (4 women); includes 2 minority (1 Hispanic/Latino; 1 Two or more races, non-Hispanic/Latino). Average age 31. 8 applicants, 63% accepted, 1 enrolled. In 2010, 6 master's awarded. *Degree requirements:* For master's, thesis or alternative. *Entrance requirements:* For master's, GRE General Test or GRE Subject Test, minimum GPA of 3.0. Additional exam requirements/recommendations for international students: Required—TOEFL (minimum score 500 paper-based; 173 computer-based). *Application deadline:* For fall admission, 11/30 for domestic students; for spring admission, 8/31 for domestic students. Application fee: $55. *Financial support:* Fellowships, research assistantships, teaching assistantships, career-related internships or fieldwork and Federal Work-Study available. Financial award application deadline: 3/2; financial award applicants required to submit FAFSA. *Unit head:* Dr. Michelle Jolly, Chair, 707-664-2461, E-mail: michelle.jolly@sonoma.edu. *Application contact:* Kathleen Noonan, Coordinator of Graduate Studies, 707-664-2959, Fax: 707-664-4060, E-mail: kathleen.noonan@sonoma.edu.

Southeastern Louisiana University, College of Arts, Humanities and Social Sciences, Department of History and Political Science, Hammond, LA 70402. Offers history (MA). Part-time programs available. *Faculty:* 12 full-time (1 woman). *Students:* 10 full-time (3 women), 34 part-time (18 women); includes 4 minority (2 Black or African American, non-Hispanic/Latino; 1 American Indian or Alaska Native, non-Hispanic/Latino; 1 Asian, non-Hispanic/Latino). Average age 30. 27 applicants, 70% accepted, 13 enrolled. In 2010, 16 master's awarded. *Degree requirements:* For master's, comprehensive exam, thesis optional. *Entrance requirements:* For master's, GRE General Test (900 or better), 30 undergraduate credits in history, minimum GPA of 2.5. Additional exam requirements/recommendations for international students: Required—TOEFL (minimum score 500 paper-based; 173 computer-based; 61 iBT). *Application deadline:* For fall admission, 7/15 priority date for domestic students, 6/1 priority date for international students; for spring admission, 12/1 priority date for domestic students, 10/1 priority date for international students. Applications are processed on a rolling basis. Application fee: $20 ($30 for international students). Electronic applications accepted. *Expenses:*

Tuition, state resident: full-time $3533. Tuition, nonresident: full-time $12,002. Required fees: $907. Tuition and fees vary according to degree level. *Financial support:* In 2010–11, 9 students received support, including 9 teaching assistantships (averaging $9,367 per year); career-related internships or fieldwork, Federal Work-Study, and institutionally sponsored loans also available. Support available to part-time students. Financial award application deadline: 5/1; financial award applicants required to submit FAFSA. *Faculty research:* American history, British history, Southern history, public history, European history. *Unit head:* Dr. William Robison, Department Head, 985-549-2109, Fax: 985-549-2012, E-mail: wrobison@selu.edu. *Application contact:* Sandra Meyers, Graduate Admissions Analyst, 985-549-5620, Fax: 985-549-5632, E-mail: admissions@selu.edu.

Southeast Missouri State University, School of Graduate Studies, Department of History, Cape Girardeau, MO 63701-4799. Offers heritage education (Certificate); historic preservation (Certificate); history (MA); public history (MA), including heritage education, historic preservation. Part-time and evening/weekend programs available. *Faculty:* 10 full-time (2 women). *Students:* 5 full-time (all women), 9 part-time (3 women). Average age 31. 9 applicants, 100% accepted, 4 enrolled. In 2010, 5 master's awarded. *Degree requirements:* For master's, comprehensive exam (for some programs), thesis (for some programs), paper (for history); for Certificate, internship, advanced project in applied history, exam, and paper (for historic preservation). *Entrance requirements:* For master's, GRE, minimum undergraduate GPA of 2.75; 3 reference letters; writing sample; letter of intent. Additional exam requirements/recommendations for international students: Required—TOEFL (minimum score 550 paper-based; 213 computer-based; 79 iBT); Recommended—IELTS (minimum score 6). *Application deadline:* For fall admission, 8/1 for domestic students, 6/1 for international students; for spring admission, 11/21 for domestic students, 10/1 for international students. Applications are processed on a rolling basis. Application fee: $25 ($35 for international students). Electronic applications accepted. *Expenses:* Tuition, state resident: full-time $4698; part-time $261 per credit hour. Tuition, nonresident: full-time $8379; part-time $465.50 per credit hour. *Financial support:* In 2010–11, 4 students received support, including 5 teaching assistantships with full tuition reimbursements available (averaging $7,600 per year); career-related internships or fieldwork, Federal Work-Study, institutionally sponsored loans, scholarships/grants, tuition waivers (full), and unspecified assistantships also available. Financial award application deadline: 6/30; financial award applicants required to submit FAFSA. *Faculty research:* Modern America, historic preservation, world history. *Unit head:* Dr. Wayne H. Bowen, Chairperson, 573-651-2179, E-mail: wbowen@semo.edu. *Application contact:* Gail Amick, Administrative Secretary, 573-651-2049, Fax: 573-651-2001, E-mail: gamick@semo.edu.

Southern Connecticut State University, School of Graduate Studies, School of Arts and Sciences, Department of History, New Haven, CT 06515-1355. Offers MA, MS, MLS/MA. Part-time and evening/weekend programs available. *Faculty:* 19 full-time (7 women). *Students:* 28 full-time (15 women), 30 part-time (11 women); includes 2 Black or African American, non-Hispanic/Latino; 2 Two or more races, non-Hispanic/Latino. 52 applicants, 25% accepted, 10 enrolled. In 2010, 13 master's awarded. *Degree requirements:* For master's, one foreign language, thesis. *Entrance requirements:* For master's, interview, undergraduate major or minor in history. *Application deadline:* For fall admission, 7/15 priority date for domestic students. Applications are processed on a rolling basis. Application fee: $50. Electronic applications accepted. *Expenses:* Tuition, state resident: full-time $5137; part-time $518 per credit. Tuition, nonresident: part-time $542 per credit. Required fees: $4008; $55 per semester. Tuition and fees vary according to program. *Financial support:* Career-related internships or fieldwork available. Financial award application deadline: 4/15; financial award applicants required to submit FAFSA. *Unit head:* Dr. Steven Judd, Chairperson, 203-392-5605, Fax: 203-392-5670, E-mail: judds1@southernct.edu. *Application contact:* Dr. Christine Petto, Graduate Coordinator, 203-392-5612, Fax: 203-392-5670, E-mail: pettoc1@southernct.edu.

Southern Illinois University Carbondale, Graduate School, College of Liberal Arts, Department of History, Carbondale, IL 62901-4701. Offers MA, PhD. Part-time programs available. *Degree requirements:* For master's, one foreign language, research papers or thesis, written exams; for doctorate, 2 foreign languages, thesis/dissertation. *Entrance requirements:* For master's, GRE General Test, minimum GPA of 3.0; for doctorate, GRE General Test, minimum GPA of 3.25. Additional exam requirements/recommendations for international students: Required—TOEFL. *Faculty research:* American, Asian, European, and Latin American history, global history.

Southern Illinois University Edwardsville, Graduate School, College of Arts and Sciences, Department of Historical Studies, Program in History, Edwardsville, IL 62026-0001. Offers MA. Part-time and evening/weekend programs available. *Faculty:* 16 full-time (6 women). *Students:* 13 full-time (5 women), 14 part-time (7 women); includes 4 minority (3 Black or African American, non-Hispanic/Latino; 1 American Indian or Alaska Native, non-Hispanic/Latino), 1 international. Average age 26. 29 applicants, 41% accepted. In 2010, 8 master's awarded. *Degree requirements:* For master's, one foreign language, thesis (for some programs), final exam. *Entrance requirements:* For master's, GRE. Additional exam requirements/recommendations for international students: Required—TOEFL (minimum score 550 paper-based; 213 computer-based; 79 iBT), IELTS (minimum score 6.5). *Application deadline:* For fall admission, 2/28 for domestic students, 6/1 for international students; for spring admission, 10/1 for international students. Application fee: $30. Electronic applications accepted. *Expenses:* Tuition, state resident: full-time $6012; part-time $1503 per semester. Tuition, nonresident: full-time $15,030; part-time $3758 per semester. Required fees: $1711; $675 per semester. *Financial support:* In 2010–11, 1 research assistantship with full tuition reimbursement (averaging $8,064 per year), 12 teaching assistantships with full tuition reimbursements (averaging $8,064 per year) were awarded; fellowships with full tuition reimbursements, career-related internships or fieldwork, Federal Work-Study, institutionally sponsored loans, scholarships/grants, traineeships, and unspecified assistantships also available. Support available to part-time students. Financial award application deadline: 3/1; financial award applicants required to submit FAFSA. *Unit head:* Dr. Carole Frick, Director, 618-650-3237, E-mail: cfrick@siue.edu. *Application contact:* Dr. Laura Fowler, Program Director, 618-650-2145, E-mail: lmilsk@siue.edu.

Southern Methodist University, Dedman College, Clements Department of History, Dallas, TX 75275. Offers MA, PhD. Part-time programs available. *Faculty:* 24 full-time (10 women), 1 part-time/adjunct (0 women). *Students:* 8 full-time (2 women), 16 part-time (7 women); includes 1 American Indian or Alaska Native, non-Hispanic/Latino; 6 Hispanic/Latino, 1 international. Average age 31. 21 applicants, 43% accepted, 7 enrolled. In 2010, 8 master's, 3 doctorates awarded. Terminal master's awarded for partial completion of doctoral program. *Degree requirements:* For master's, one foreign language, thesis, oral exam, thesis defense; for doctorate, one foreign language, thesis/dissertation, oral exam, dissertation defense. *Entrance requirements:* For master's and doctorate, GRE General Test, minimum GPA of 3.0, 12 undergraduate hours in advanced level history, writing sample. Additional exam requirements/recommendations for international students: Required—TOEFL. *Application deadline:* For fall admission, 2/1 priority date for domestic and international students. Applications are processed on a rolling basis. Application fee: $60. Electronic applications accepted. *Financial support:* In 2010–11, 20 students received support, including 12 fellowships with full tuition reimbursements available (averaging $16,000 per year), 1 research assistantship (averaging $30,000 per year); career-related internships or fieldwork, institutionally sponsored loans, scholarships/grants, health care benefits, and tuition waivers (full and partial) also available. Financial award application deadline: 2/1; financial award applicants required to submit FAFSA. *Faculty research:* U. S. history, European history, Latin America, Africa/Middle East, China. *Unit head:* Dr. Kathleen A. Wellman, Chair, 214-768-2970, Fax: 214-768-2404, E-mail: hist@smu.edu. *Application contact:* Dr. Sherry L. Smith, Graduate Director, 214-768-1312, Fax: 214-768-2404, E-mail: hist@smu.edu.

Southern University and Agricultural and Mechanical College, Graduate School, College of Arts and Humanities, Department of History, Baton Rouge, LA 70813. Offers social sciences (MA). Part-time programs available. *Degree requirements:* For master's, thesis. *Entrance* *requirements:* For master's, GRE General Test. Additional exam requirements/recommendations for international students: Required—TOEFL (minimum score 525 paper-based; 193 computer-based).

Southwestern Assemblies of God University, Thomas F. Harrison School of Graduate Studies, Program in History, Waxahachie, TX 75165-5735. Offers MA.

Spring Hill College, Graduate Programs, Program in Liberal Arts, Mobile, AL 36608-1791. Offers fine arts (MLA); history and social science (MLA); leadership and ethics (MLA); literature (MLA). Part-time and evening/weekend programs available. *Faculty:* 5 full-time (2 women), 2 part-time/adjunct (1 woman). *Students:* 3 full-time (2 women), 31 part-time (19 women); includes 10 minority (9 Black or African American, non-Hispanic/Latino; 1 Hispanic/Latino). Average age 37. In 2010, 12 master's awarded. *Degree requirements:* For master's, capstone course, completion of program within 6 years of initial admittance. *Entrance requirements:* For master's, bachelor's degree with minimum undergraduate GPA of 3.0 or graduate/professional degree. Additional exam requirements/recommendations for international students: Required—TOEFL (minimum score 550 paper-based; 213 computer-based; 80 iBT), IELTS (minimum score 6.5), CPE or CAE (score: C), MELAB (score: 90). *Application deadline:* For fall admission, 8/1 priority date for domestic and international students; for spring admission, 12/1 priority date for domestic and international students. Applications are processed on a rolling basis. Application fee: $25 ($35 for international students). Electronic applications accepted. *Expenses:* Contact institution. *Financial support:* Applicants required to submit FAFSA. *Unit head:* Dr. Alexander R. Landi, Director, 251-380-3056, Fax: 251-460-2115, E-mail: landi@shc.edu. *Application contact:* Donna B. Tarasavage, Director of Admissions, Graduate and Continuing Studies, 251-380-3067, Fax: 251-460-2190, E-mail: dtarasavage@shc.edu.

Stanford University, School of Humanities and Sciences, Department of History, Stanford, CA 94305-9991. Offers MA, PhD. Terminal master's awarded for partial completion of doctoral program. *Degree requirements:* For doctorate, variable foreign language requirement, thesis/dissertation, oral exam. *Entrance requirements:* For master's and doctorate, GRE General Test. Additional exam requirements/recommendations for international students: Required—TOEFL. Electronic applications accepted. *Expenses:* Tuition: Full-time $38,700; part-time $860 per unit. One-time fee: $200 full-time.

State University of New York at Binghamton, Graduate School, School of Arts and Sciences, Department of History, Binghamton, NY 13902-6000. Offers MA, PhD. Part-time programs available. *Faculty:* 26 full-time (11 women), 5 part-time/adjunct (2 women). *Students:* 33 full-time (19 women), 65 part-time (38 women); includes 3 Asian, non-Hispanic/Latino; 4 Hispanic/Latino, 13 international. Average age 34. 82 applicants, 45% accepted, 20 enrolled. In 2010, 9 master's, 4 doctorates awarded. Terminal master's awarded for partial completion of doctoral program. *Degree requirements:* For master's, one foreign language, thesis or alternative, written exam; for doctorate, variable foreign language requirement, comprehensive exam, thesis/dissertation. *Entrance requirements:* For master's and doctorate, GRE General Test, GRE Subject Test. Additional exam requirements/recommendations for international students: Required—TOEFL (minimum score 550 paper-based; 213 computer-based; 80 iBT). *Application deadline:* For fall admission, 4/15 priority date for domestic and international students; for spring admission, 11/1 priority date for domestic and international students. Applications are processed on a rolling basis. Application fee: $60. Electronic applications accepted. *Financial support:* In 2010–11, 50 students received support, including 5 fellowships with full tuition reimbursements available (averaging $15,000 per year), 2 research assistantships with full tuition reimbursements available (averaging $15,000 per year), 40 teaching assistantships with full tuition reimbursements available (averaging $15,000 per year); career-related internships or fieldwork, Federal Work-Study, institutionally sponsored loans, scholarships/grants, health care benefits, tuition waivers (full), and unspecified assistantships also available. Financial award application deadline: 2/15; financial award applicants required to submit FAFSA. *Unit head:* Dr. Nancy Appelbaum, Chairperson, 607-777-4420, E-mail: nappel@binghamton.edu. *Application contact:* Catherine Smith, Recruiting and Admissions Coordinator, 607-777-2151, Fax: 607-777-2501, E-mail: cmsmith@binghamton.edu.

State University of New York at Oswego, Graduate Studies, College of Liberal Arts and Sciences, Department of History, Oswego, NY 13126. Offers MA. Part-time programs available. *Faculty:* 7 full-time (1 woman), 1 part-time/adjunct (0 women). *Students:* 3 full-time (all women), 7 part-time (2 women); includes 1 Hispanic/Latino. Average age 25. 13 applicants, 62% accepted. In 2010, 7 master's awarded. *Degree requirements:* For master's, thesis optional. *Entrance requirements:* For master's, writing sample. Additional exam requirements/recommendations for international students: Required—TOEFL (minimum score 560 paper-based; 220 computer-based). *Application deadline:* For fall admission, 4/1 for domestic students; for spring admission, 10/1 for domestic students. Applications are processed on a rolling basis. Application fee: $50. *Expenses:* Tuition, state resident: full-time $8370; part-time $349 per credit hour. Tuition, nonresident: full-time $13,780; part-time $574 per credit hour. Required fees: $853; $22.59 per credit hour. *Financial support:* In 2010–11, 4 students received support, including 1 fellowship with full tuition reimbursement available (averaging $5,100 per year), 3 teaching assistantships with full tuition reimbursements available (averaging $3,800 per year); career-related internships or fieldwork, Federal Work-Study, institutionally sponsored loans, scholarships/grants, health care benefits, and unspecified assistantships also available. Support available to part-time students. Financial award application deadline: 4/1; financial award applicants required to submit FAFSA. *Unit head:* Dr. Frank Bryne, Chair, 315-312-2170, E-mail: frank.byrne@oswego.edu. *Application contact:* Dr. Douglas Deal, Graduate Program Coordinator, 315-312-3441, E-mail: douglas.deal@oswego.edu.

State University of New York College at Cortland, Graduate Studies, School of Arts and Sciences, Department of History, Cortland, NY 13045. Offers MA, MS Ed. Part-time and evening/weekend programs available. *Degree requirements:* For master's, one foreign language, comprehensive exam (for some programs), thesis (for some programs). *Entrance requirements:* For master's, GRE General Test, GRE Subject Test. Additional exam requirements/recommendations for international students: Required—TOEFL.

Stephen F. Austin State University, Graduate School, College of Liberal Arts, Department of History, Nacogdoches, TX 75962. Offers MA. Part-time and evening/weekend programs available. *Degree requirements:* For master's, comprehensive exam. *Entrance requirements:* For master's, GRE General Test. Additional exam requirements/recommendations for international students: Required—TOEFL. *Faculty research:* U.S.-Third World foreign policy, racial attitudes of antebellum Southern whites, naval warfare in World War II, demography of East Texas, medieval sermons.

Stony Brook University, State University of New York, Graduate School, College of Arts and Sciences, Department of History, Stony Brook, NY 11794. Offers MA, PhD. Evening/weekend programs available. *Faculty:* 27 full-time (13 women), 1 (woman) part-time/adjunct. *Students:* 84 full-time (35 women), 6 part-time (3 women); includes 7 Black or African American, non-Hispanic/Latino; 2 Asian, non-Hispanic/Latino; 5 Hispanic/Latino, 21 international. Average age 33. 88 applicants, 28% accepted, 12 enrolled. In 2010, 9 master's, 6 doctorates awarded. *Degree requirements:* For doctorate, thesis/dissertation. *Entrance requirements:* For master's and doctorate, GRE General Test. Additional exam requirements/recommendations for international students: Required—TOEFL. *Application deadline:* For fall admission, 1/15 for domestic students. Application fee: $100. *Expenses:* Tuition, state resident: full-time $8370; part-time $349 per credit. Tuition, nonresident: full-time $13,780; part-time $574 per credit. Required fees: $994. *Financial support:* In 2010–11, 1 research assistantship, 41 teaching assistantships were awarded; fellowships also available. *Faculty research:* Social, cultural, and political history. Total annual research expenditures: $84,091. *Unit head:* Nancy Tomes, Chair, 631-632-7500, Fax: 631-632-7367. *Application contact:* Brooke Larson, Graduate Coordinator, 631-632-7500, Fax: 631-632-7367.

Sul Ross State University, School of Arts and Sciences, Department of Behavioral and Social Sciences, Program in History, Alpine, TX 79832. Offers MA. Part-time and evening/weekend programs available. *Degree requirements:* For master's, thesis optional. *Entrance requirements:* For master's, GRE General Test, minimum GPA of 2.5 in last 60 hours of undergraduate work. *Faculty research:* Borderland/Southwestern studies, British studies, women's history, Native American studies, local history.

Syracuse University, Maxwell School of Citizenship and Public Affairs, Program in History, Syracuse, NY 13244. Offers MA, PhD. Part-time programs available. *Students:* 42 full-time (14 women), 10 part-time (3 women); includes 4 minority (2 Black or African American, non-Hispanic/Latino; 1 Asian, non-Hispanic/Latino; 1 Two or more races, non-Hispanic/Latino), 7 international. Average age 36. 44 applicants, 23% accepted, 4 enrolled. In 2010, 7 master's, 3 doctorates awarded. Terminal master's awarded for partial completion of doctoral program. *Degree requirements:* For master's, comprehensive exam, thesis or alternative; for doctorate, 2 foreign languages, comprehensive exam, thesis/dissertation. *Entrance requirements:* For master's and doctorate, GRE General Test. Additional exam requirements/recommendations for international students: Required—TOEFL (minimum score 100 iBT). *Application deadline:* For fall admission, 2/1 priority date for domestic and international students. Application fee: $75. Electronic applications accepted. *Expenses:* Tuition: Part-time $1162 per credit. *Financial support:* Fellowships with full tuition reimbursements, research assistantships with full and partial tuition reimbursements, teaching assistantships with full and partial tuition reimbursements available. Financial award application deadline: 1/1; financial award applicants required to submit FAFSA. *Faculty research:* American, medieval, European, South East Asian, and Russian history. *Unit head:* Dr. Paul Hagenloh, Director of Graduate Studies, 315-443-2210, Fax: 315-443-5876, E-mail: phagenlo@syr.edu. *Application contact:* Pat Bohrer, Information Contact, 315-443-2210, E-mail: pabohrer@syr.edu.

Tarleton State University, College of Graduate Studies, College of Liberal and Fine Arts, Department of Social Sciences, Stephenville, TX 76402. Offers history (MA); political science (MA). Part-time and evening/weekend programs available. Postbaccalaureate distance learning degree programs offered (minimal on-campus study). *Degree requirements:* For master's, variable foreign language requirement, comprehensive exam, thesis optional. *Entrance requirements:* For master's, GRE General Test, minimum GPA of 3.0. Additional exam requirements/recommendations for international students: Required—TOEFL (minimum score 550 paper-based; 213 computer-based; 80 iBT). Electronic applications accepted.

Teachers College, Columbia University, Graduate Faculty of Education, Department of Arts and Humanities, Program in History and Education, New York, NY 10027-6696. Offers Ed M, MA, Ed D, PhD. *Faculty:* 2 full-time (1 woman), 1 (woman) part-time/adjunct. *Students:* 2 full-time (both women), 17 part-time (12 women); includes 6 minority (4 Black or African American, non-Hispanic/Latino; 1 Asian, non-Hispanic/Latino; 1 Two or more races, non-Hispanic/Latino), 1 international. Average age 38. 17 applicants, 53% accepted, 4 enrolled. In 2010, 1 doctorate awarded. *Degree requirements:* For master's, formal essay; for doctorate, 2 foreign languages, thesis/dissertation. *Entrance requirements:* For master's, GRE, sample of historical writing (Ed M); for doctorate, GRE, sample of historical writing. *Application deadline:* For fall admission, 12/15 for domestic students. Application fee: $65. *Expenses:* Tuition: Full-time $28,272; part-time $1178 per credit. Required fees: $756; $378 per semester. *Financial support:* Career-related internships or fieldwork, Federal Work-Study, institutionally sponsored loans, and tuition waivers (full and partial) available. Support available to part-time students. Financial award application deadline: 2/1. *Faculty research:* History of American education, urban areas, women, immigrants, and African-Americans. *Unit head:* Prof. Cally Waite, Program Coordinator, 212-678-4138, E-mail: cwaite@tc.edu. *Application contact:* Prof. Cally Waite, Program Coordinator, 212-678-4138, E-mail: cwaite@tc.edu.

Temple University, College of Liberal Arts, Department of History, Philadelphia, PA 19122-6096. Offers MA, PhD. Part-time and evening/weekend programs available. *Faculty:* 36 full-time (13 women). *Students:* 97 full-time (26 women), 13 part-time (2 women); includes 5 Black or African American, non-Hispanic/Latino; 1 American Indian or Alaska Native, non-Hispanic/Latino; 1 Asian, non-Hispanic/Latino; 1 Hispanic/Latino, 4 international. 220 applicants, 37% accepted, 26 enrolled. In 2010, 10 master's, 7 doctorates awarded. Terminal master's awarded for partial completion of doctoral program. *Degree requirements:* For doctorate, one foreign language, thesis/dissertation. *Entrance requirements:* For master's and doctorate, GRE General Test, minimum GPA of 3.0. Additional exam requirements/recommendations for international students: Required—TOEFL (minimum score 550 paper-based; 213 computer-based; 79 iBT). *Application deadline:* For fall admission, 1/15 priority date for domestic students, 12/15 for international students; for spring admission, 10/15 priority date for domestic students, 8/1 for international students. Application fee: $50. Electronic applications accepted. *Financial support:* Fellowships with tuition reimbursements, teaching assistantships with tuition reimbursements, career-related internships or fieldwork and tuition waivers (partial) available. Support available to part-time students. Financial award application deadline: 1/15; financial award applicants required to submit FAFSA. *Faculty research:* Third World; American military and diplomatic history; American social, cultural, and public history, European history. *Unit head:* Dr. Beth Bailey, Chair, 215-204-7461, Fax: 215-204-5891, E-mail: history@temple.edu. *Application contact:* Dr. Beth Bailey, Chair, 215-204-7461, Fax: 215-204-5891, E-mail: history@temple.edu.

Texas A&M International University, Office of Graduate Studies and Research, College of Arts and Sciences, Department of Social Sciences, Laredo, TX 78041-1900. Offers history (MA); political science (MA); public administration (MPA). *Faculty:* 8 full-time (3 women). *Students:* 4 full-time (2 women), 52 part-time (27 women); includes 1 Asian, non-Hispanic/Latino; 52 Hispanic/Latino, 1 international. Average age 30. 35 applicants, 74% accepted, 19 enrolled. In 2010, 10 master's awarded. *Degree requirements:* For master's, thesis (for some programs). *Entrance requirements:* For master's, GRE General Test. Additional exam requirements/recommendations for international students: Required—TOEFL (minimum score 550 paper-based; 213 computer-based). *Application deadline:* For fall admission, 4/30 priority date for domestic students; for spring admission, 11/30 for domestic students, 10/1 for international students. Applications are processed on a rolling basis. Application fee: $25. *Financial support:* In 2010–11, 14 students received support, including 7 research assistantships. Financial award application deadline: 11/1. *Unit head:* Dr. Mohammed Ben-Ruwin, Chair, 956-328-2632, E-mail: mbenruwin@tamiu.edu. *Application contact:* Suzanne Hansen-Alford, Director of Admissions, 956-326-3023, Fax: 956-326-3021, E-mail: graduateschool@tamiu.edu.

Texas A&M University, College of Liberal Arts, Department of History, College Station, TX 77843. Offers MA, PhD. Part-time programs available. *Faculty:* 23. *Students:* 48 full-time (14 women), 28 part-time (6 women); includes 3 Black or African American, non-Hispanic/Latino; 5 Hispanic/Latino, 4 international. Average age 32. In 2010, 4 master's, 3 doctorates awarded. Terminal master's awarded for partial completion of doctoral program. *Degree requirements:* For master's, one foreign language, thesis optional; for doctorate, 2 foreign languages, thesis/dissertation. *Entrance requirements:* For master's and doctorate, GRE General Test. Additional exam requirements/recommendations for international students: Required—TOEFL. *Application deadline:* For fall admission, 3/1 for domestic students. Application fee: $50 ($75 for international students). *Financial support:* In 2010–11, fellowships (averaging $4,000 per year); research assistantships, teaching assistantships with partial tuition reimbursements. Financial award application deadline: 2/1. *Faculty research:* Recent U. S. history, Southwest, border studies, military history, Europe. *Unit head:* Dr. Walter L. Buenger, Head, 979-845-7170, E-mail: w-buenger@tamu.edu. *Application contact:* Albert S. Broussard, Coordinator, 979-845-7151, Fax: 979-862-4314.

Texas A&M University–Commerce, Graduate School, College of Arts and Sciences, Department of History, Commerce, TX 75429-3011. Offers history (MA, MS); social sciences (M Ed, MS). Part-time programs available. *Degree requirements:* For master's, comprehensive exam, thesis (for some programs). *Entrance requirements:* For master's, GRE General Test. Electronic applications accepted. *Faculty research:* American foreign policy, colonial America, Texas politics, Medieval England.

Texas A&M University–Corpus Christi, Graduate Studies and Research, College of Liberal Arts, Corpus Christi, TX 78412-5503. Offers English (MA); history (MA); psychology (MA);

History

Texas A&M University–Corpus Christi (continued)

public administration (MPA); studio arts (MA, MFA). Part-time and evening/weekend programs available. *Degree requirements:* For master's, comprehensive exam, thesis (for some programs). *Entrance requirements:* For master's, GRE General Test. Additional exam requirements/recommendations for international students: Required—TOEFL. Electronic applications accepted.

Texas A&M University–Kingsville, College of Graduate Studies, College of Arts and Sciences, Program in History and Political Science, Kingsville, TX 78363. Offers MA, MS. Part-time and evening/weekend programs available. *Degree requirements:* For master's, comprehensive exam, thesis or alternative. *Entrance requirements:* For master's, GRE General Test. Additional exam requirements/recommendations for international students: Required—TOEFL.

Texas Christian University, AddRan College of Liberal Arts, Department of History, Fort Worth, TX 76129-0002. Offers MA, PhD. *Faculty:* 16 full-time (4 women). *Students:* 49 full-time (16 women); includes 2 Hispanic/Latino, 1 international. In 2010, 2 master's, 5 doctorates awarded. Terminal master's awarded for partial completion of doctoral program. *Degree requirements:* For master's, thesis; for doctorate, one foreign language, comprehensive exam, thesis/dissertation, qualifying exams. *Entrance requirements:* For master's and doctorate, GRE General Test. Additional exam requirements/recommendations for international students: Required—TOEFL. *Application deadline:* For fall admission, 2/1 for domestic students; for winter admission, 2/1 for domestic students; for spring admission, 2/1 for domestic students. Applications are processed on a rolling basis. Application fee: $50. *Expenses:* Tuition: Full-time $18,720; part-time $1040 per credit hour. Tuition and fees vary according to course load and program. *Financial support:* In 2010–11, fellowships with full tuition reimbursements (averaging $15,000 per year), teaching assistantships (averaging $15,000 per year) were awarded; tuition waivers and unspecified assistantships also available. Financial award application deadline: 2/1. *Unit head:* Dr. Peter Worthing, Chairperson, 817-257-5882, Fax: 817-257-5650, E-mail: p.worthing@tcu.edu. *Application contact:* Dr. Todd Kerstetter, Director of Graduate Studies, 817-257-6736, Fax: 817-257-5650, E-mail: t.kerstetter@tcu.edu.

Texas Southern University, College of Liberal Arts and Behavioral Sciences, Department of History and Geography, Houston, TX 77004-4584. Offers history (MA). Part-time and evening/weekend programs available. *Faculty:* 5 full-time (3 women). *Students:* 7 full-time (4 women), 14 part-time (4 women); includes 18 Black or African American, non-Hispanic/Latino; 1 Hispanic/Latino. Average age 37. 14 applicants, 100% accepted, 13 enrolled. In 2010, 2 master's awarded. *Degree requirements:* For master's, comprehensive exam, thesis optional. *Entrance requirements:* For master's, GRE General Test, minimum GPA of 2.5. Additional exam requirements/recommendations for international students: Required—TOEFL. *Application deadline:* For fall admission, 7/1 for domestic and international students; for spring admission, 11/1 for domestic and international students. Applications are processed on a rolling basis. Application fee: $50 ($75 for international students). Electronic applications accepted. *Expenses:* Tuition, state resident: full-time $1875; part-time $100 per credit hour. Tuition, nonresident: full-time $6641; part-time $343 per credit hour. Tuition and fees vary according to course level, course load and degree level. *Financial support:* In 2010–11, 3 teaching assistantships (averaging $3,440 per year) were awarded; scholarships/grants and unspecified assistantships also available. Support available to part-time students. Financial award application deadline: 5/1. *Faculty research:* American, Colonial, African, Asian, and African-American history. *Unit head:* Dr. Ethopia Keleta, Chair, 713-313-7324, Fax: 713-313-4236, E-mail: keleta_ex@tsu.edu. *Application contact:* Dr. Gregory Maddox, Dean of the Graduate School, 713-313-7011 Ext. 4410, Fax: 713-639-1876, E-mail: maddox_gh@tsu.edu.

Texas State University–San Marcos, Graduate School, College of Liberal Arts, Department of History, San Marcos, TX 78666. Offers M Ed, MA. Part-time programs available. *Faculty:* 16 full-time (8 women), 2 part-time/adjunct (0 women). *Students:* 33 full-time (21 women), 43 part-time (21 women); includes 11 minority (10 Hispanic/Latino; 1 Two or more races, non-Hispanic/Latino). Average age 33. 35 applicants, 94% accepted, 23 enrolled. In 2010, 22 master's awarded. *Degree requirements:* For master's, comprehensive exam, thesis (for some programs). *Entrance requirements:* For master's, GRE General Test, minimum of 24 hours of undergraduate history with minimum GPA of 3.25; 6 hours of undergraduate foreign language; 2 letters of reference; essay. Additional exam requirements/recommendations for international students: Required—TOEFL (minimum score 550 paper-based; 213 computer-based; 78 iBT). *Application deadline:* For fall admission, 6/15 priority date for domestic students, 6/1 for international students; for spring admission, 10/15 priority date for domestic students, 10/1 for international students. Applications are processed on a rolling basis. Application fee: $40 ($90 for international students). Electronic applications accepted. *Expenses:* Tuition, state resident: full-time $6024; part-time $251 per credit hour. Tuition, nonresident: full-time $13,536; part-time $564 per credit hour. Required fees: $1776; $50 per credit hour. $306 per semester. *Financial support:* In 2010–11, 25 students received support, including 1 research assistantship (averaging $4,928 per year), 28 teaching assistantships (averaging $5,097 per year); Federal Work-Study, institutionally sponsored loans, scholarships/grants, and unspecified assistantships also available. Support available to part-time students. Financial award application deadline: 4/1; financial award applicants required to submit FAFSA. *Unit head:* Dr. Mary C. Brennan, Chair, 512-245-2142, Fax: 512-245-3043, E-mail: mb18@txstate.edu. *Application contact:* Dr. Mary Brennan, Graduate Adviser, 512-245-2110, Fax: 512-245-3043, E-mail: mb18@txstate.edu.

Texas Tech University, Graduate School, College of Arts and Sciences, Department of History, Lubbock, TX 79409. Offers MA, PhD. Part-time programs available. *Faculty:* 22 full-time (6 women). *Students:* 49 full-time (17 women), 27 part-time (10 women); includes 1 Black or African American, non-Hispanic/Latino; 2 Asian, non-Hispanic/Latino; 7 Hispanic/Latino; 1 Two or more races, non-Hispanic/Latino, 4 international. Average age 32. 51 applicants, 45% accepted, 15 enrolled. In 2010, 8 master's, 3 doctorates awarded. *Degree requirements:* For master's, one foreign language, thesis or alternative; for doctorate, 2 foreign languages, thesis/dissertation. *Entrance requirements:* For master's and doctorate, GRE General Test. Additional exam requirements/recommendations for international students: Required—TOEFL (minimum score 550 paper-based; 213 computer-based; 79 iBT). *Application deadline:* For fall admission, 6/1 priority date for domestic students, 1/15 priority date for international students; for spring admission, 9/1 priority date for domestic students, 6/15 priority date for international students. Applications are processed on a rolling basis. Application fee: $50 ($75 for international students). Electronic applications accepted. *Expenses:* Tuition, state resident: full-time $5495.76; part-time $228.99 per credit hour. Tuition, nonresident: full-time $12,936; part-time $538.99 per credit hour. Required fees: $2674; $36 per credit hour. $905 per semester. *Financial support:* In 2010–11, 49 students received support, including 3 research assistantships with partial tuition reimbursements available (averaging $1,474 per year), 24 teaching assistantships with partial tuition reimbursements available (averaging $4,317 per year). Financial award application deadline: 4/15; financial award applicants required to submit FAFSA. *Faculty research:* History of United States Southwest/West, the borderlands, history of Vietnam War and United States military history, history of Hispanics/Latinos and other U. S. minorities, history of Europe. Total annual research expenditures: $27,151. *Unit head:* Dr. Randy McBee, Chair, 806-742-1004, Fax: 806-742-1060, E-mail: randy.mcbee@ttu.edu. *Application contact:* Dr. Gretchen Adams, Graduate Adviser, 806-742-3744, Fax: 806-742-1060.

Texas Woman's University, Graduate School, College of Arts and Sciences, Department of History and Government, Denton, TX 76201. Offers government (MA); history (MA). Part-time and evening/weekend programs available. *Faculty:* 10 full-time (4 women), 1 (woman) part-time/adjunct. *Students:* 7 full-time (5 women), 31 part-time (28 women); includes 4 Black or African American, non-Hispanic/Latino; 2 American Indian or Alaska Native, non-Hispanic/Latino; 1 Asian, non-Hispanic/Latino; 2 Hispanic/Latino. Average age 39. 14 applicants, 100% accepted, 10 enrolled. In 2010, 7 master's awarded. *Degree requirements:* For master's, comprehensive exam, thesis. *Entrance requirements:* For master's, minimum GPA of 3.0, written statement of purpose; 2 letters of reference. Additional exam requirements/recommendations for international students: Required—TOEFL (minimum score 550 paper-based; 213 computer-based; 79 iBT). *Application deadline:* For fall admission, 7/1 priority date

for domestic students, 3/1 for international students; for spring admission, 12/1 priority date for domestic students, 7/1 for international students. Applications are processed on a rolling basis. Application fee: $50 ($75 for international students). Electronic applications accepted. *Expenses:* Tuition, state resident: full-time $3834; part-time $213 per credit hour. Tuition, nonresident: full-time $9468; part-time $526 per credit hour. Required fees: $1247; $220 per credit hour. *Financial support:* In 2010–11, 16 students received support, including 14 research assistantships (averaging $11,520 per year), 2 teaching assistantships (averaging $11,520 per year); career-related internships or fieldwork, Federal Work-Study, institutionally sponsored loans, scholarships/grants, traineeships, health care benefits, and unspecified assistantships also available. Support available to part-time students. Financial award application deadline: 3/1; financial award applicants required to submit FAFSA. *Faculty research:* U. S. history, politics, and law; global history, politics, and law; Latin American and Caribbean history; legal studies; women in history, politics, and law. Total annual research expenditures: $505,193. *Unit head:* Dr. Mark Kessler, Chair, 940-898-2133, Fax: 940-898-2130, E-mail: historygov@twu.edu. *Application contact:* Dr. Samuel Wheeler, Assistant Director of Admissions, 940-898-3188, Fax: 940-898-3081, E-mail: wheelersr@twu.edu.

Trinity Western University, School of Graduate Studies, Program in Interdisciplinary Humanities, Langley, BC V2Y 1Y1, Canada. Offers general humanities (MAIH); specialized (MAIH), including English, history, philosophy. Part-time programs available. *Degree requirements:* For master's, thesis or alternative, 36 semester hours. *Entrance requirements:* For master's, strong undergraduate degree in humanities or English, history or philosophy. Electronic applications accepted. *Faculty research:* Literary theory, gender, medieval and early modern literature, philosophy of religion, Thomas Merton's poetics.

Troy University, Graduate School, College of Education, Program in Postsecondary Education, Troy, AL 36082. Offers adult education (M Ed); biology (M Ed); criminal justice (M Ed); English (M Ed); foundations of education (M Ed); general science (M Ed); higher education administration (M Ed); history (M Ed); instructional technology (M Ed); mathematics (M Ed); music industry (M Ed); physical fitness (M Ed); political science (M Ed); public administration (M Ed); social science (M Ed); teaching English (M Ed). *Accreditation:* NCATE. Part-time and evening/weekend programs available. *Students:* 314 full-time (247 women), 153 part-time (122 women); includes 255 minority (242 Black or African American, non-Hispanic/Latino; 3 American Indian or Alaska Native, non-Hispanic/Latino; 5 Asian, non-Hispanic/Latino; 5 Hispanic/Latino). Average age 34. 223 applicants, 89% accepted. In 2010, 364 master's awarded. *Degree requirements:* For master's, comprehensive exam, thesis. *Entrance requirements:* For master's, MAT (minimum score 385), minimum GPA of 2.5. Additional exam requirements/recommendations for international students: Required—TOEFL (minimum score 523 paper-based; 193 computer-based; 70 iBT), IELTS, or ACT compass ESL (minimum Listening, Reading, and Grammar score: 270). *Application deadline:* Applications are processed on a rolling basis. Application fee: $50. Electronic applications accepted. *Expenses:* Tuition, state resident: full-time $4428; part-time $246 per credit hour. Tuition, nonresident: full-time $8856; part-time $492 per credit hour. Required fees: $432; $24 per credit hour. $50 per term. Tuition and fees vary according to program. *Financial support:* Available to part-time students. Applicants required to submit FAFSA. *Unit head:* Dr. Andrew Creamer, Chair, 334-670-3350, Fax: 334-670-3296, E-mail: drcreamer@troy.edu. *Application contact:* Brenda K. Campbell, Director of Graduate Admissions, 334-670-3178, Fax: 334-670-3733, E-mail: bcamp@troy.edu.

Troy University, Graduate School, College of Education, Program in Secondary Education, Troy, AL 36082. Offers 5th year biology (MS); 5th year computer science (MS); 5th year history (MS); 5th year language arts (MS); 5th year mathematics (MS); 5th year social science (MS); traditional biology (MS); traditional computer science (MS); traditional history (MS); traditional language arts (MS); traditional mathematics (MS); traditional social science (MS). *Accreditation:* NCATE. Part-time and evening/weekend programs available. *Students:* 21 full-time (15 women), 23 part-time (18 women); includes 8 minority (all Black or African American, non-Hispanic/Latino). Average age 33. 12 applicants, 67% accepted. In 2010, 30 master's awarded. *Degree requirements:* For master's, comprehensive exam, thesis. *Entrance requirements:* For master's, minimum GPA of 2.5, bachelor's degree. Additional exam requirements/recommendations for international students: Required—TOEFL (minimum score 523 paper-based; 193 computer-based; 70 iBT), IELTS (minimum score 6). *Application deadline:* Applications are processed on a rolling basis. Application fee: $50. Electronic applications accepted. *Expenses:* Tuition, state resident: full-time $4428; part-time $246 per credit hour. Tuition, nonresident: full-time $8856; part-time $492 per credit hour. Required fees: $432; $24 per credit hour. $50 per term. Tuition and fees vary according to program. *Financial support:* Career-related internships or fieldwork available. Support available to part-time students. Financial award applicants required to submit FAFSA. *Unit head:* Dr. Marian Parker, Coordinator, 334-670-5661, Fax: 334-670-3548, E-mail: mjparker@troy.edu. *Application contact:* Brenda K. Campbell, Director of Graduate Admissions, 334-670-3178, Fax: 334-670-3733, E-mail: bcamp@troy.edu.

Tufts University, Graduate School of Arts and Sciences, Department of History, Medford, MA 02155. Offers MA, PhD. Terminal master's awarded for partial completion of doctoral program. *Degree requirements:* For master's, one foreign language; for doctorate, 2 foreign languages, thesis/dissertation. *Entrance requirements:* For master's and doctorate, GRE General Test, writing sample. Additional exam requirements/recommendations for international students: Required—TOEFL (minimum score 550 paper-based; 213 computer-based; 80 iBT). Electronic applications accepted. *Expenses:* Tuition: Full-time $39,624; part-time $3962 per course. Required fees: $40 per year. Full-time tuition and fees vary according to degree level, program and student level. Part-time tuition and fees vary according to course load.

Tulane University, School of Liberal Arts, Department of History, New Orleans, LA 70118-5669. Offers MA, PhD. *Degree requirements:* For master's, one foreign language, thesis; for doctorate, variable foreign language requirement, thesis/dissertation. *Entrance requirements:* For master's, GRE General Test, minimum B average in undergraduate course work; for doctorate, GRE General Test. Additional exam requirements/recommendations for international students: Required—TOEFL. Electronic applications accepted.

Union Institute & University, Master of Arts Program–Online, Montpelier, VT 05602. Offers creativity studies (MA); education (MA); health and wellness (MA); history and culture (MA); leadership, public policy, and social issues (MA); literature and writing (MA); psychology (MA). Part-time programs available. Postbaccalaureate distance learning degree programs offered (no on-campus study). *Faculty:* 2 full-time (1 woman), 18 part-time/adjunct (11 women). *Students:* 27 full-time (26 women), 119 part-time (98 women); includes 34 minority (25 Black or African American, non-Hispanic/Latino; 3 American Indian or Alaska Native, non-Hispanic/Latino; 6 Hispanic/Latino). Average age 40. In 2010, 26 master's awarded. *Degree requirements:* For master's, thesis. *Application deadline:* Applications are processed on a rolling basis. Application fee: $50. Electronic applications accepted. *Expenses:* Tuition: Full-time $16,430; part-time $685 per credit hour. Required fees: $174; $44 per term. Tuition and fees vary according to course load, degree level and program. *Financial support:* Career-related internships or fieldwork and tuition waivers available. Financial award applicants required to submit FAFSA. *Unit head:* Dr. Brian Webb, Program Director, 802-828-8777, E-mail: brian.webb@tui.edu. *Application contact:* Diane Robinson, Director of Admissions, 888-828-8575, E-mail: diane.robinson@myunion.edu.

Université de Moncton, Faculty of Arts and Social Sciences, Department of History and Geography, Moncton, NB E1A 3E9, Canada. Offers history (MA). *Degree requirements:* For master's, thesis, proficiency in English and French. *Entrance requirements:* For master's, honors degree in history, minimum GPA of 2.7. Electronic applications accepted. *Faculty research:* Economic and social history (Canada, France, Acadia), sociocultural history, women's history, labor history, history of the press.

Université de Montréal, Faculty of Arts and Sciences, Department of History, Montréal, QC H3C 3J7, Canada. Offers MA, PhD. *Degree requirements:* For master's, thesis; for doctorate, thesis/dissertation, general exam. *Entrance requirements:* For doctorate, master's degree in related field. Electronic applications accepted. *Faculty research:* Preindustrial Quebec, Quebec working class, Quebec intellectual, diffusion of scientific thought, history of medicine.

Université de Sherbrooke, Faculty of Letters and Human Sciences, Department of Human Sciences, Sherbrooke, QC J1K 2R1, Canada. Offers history (MA); philosophy (MA). *Degree requirements:* For master's, thesis. *Entrance requirements:* For master's, minimum GPA of 2.75. *Faculty research:* Political, social, and urban history; history of women.

Université du Québec à Montréal, Graduate Programs, Program in History, Montréal, QC H3C 3P8, Canada. Offers MA, PhD. Part-time programs available. *Degree requirements:* For master's, thesis; for doctorate, thesis/dissertation. *Entrance requirements:* For master's, appropriate bachelor's degree or equivalent, proficiency in French; for doctorate, appropriate master's degree or equivalent, proficiency in French.

Université Laval, Faculty of Letters, Department of History, Programs in History, Québec, QC G1K 7P4, Canada. Offers MA, PhD. Terminal master's awarded for partial completion of doctoral program. *Degree requirements:* For master's, thesis (for some programs); for doctorate, comprehensive exam, thesis/dissertation. *Entrance requirements:* For master's and doctorate, English exam (comprehension of written English), knowledge of French. Electronic applications accepted.

Université Laval, Faculty of Letters, Department of Literature, Programs in Ancient Civilization, Québec, QC G1K 7P4, Canada. Offers MA, PhD. Part-time programs available. Terminal master's awarded for partial completion of doctoral program. *Degree requirements:* For master's, thesis; for doctorate, comprehensive exam, thesis/dissertation. *Entrance requirements:* For master's and doctorate, English test (comprehension of written English), knowledge of French, knowledge of an ancient language. Electronic applications accepted.

University at Albany, State University of New York, College of Arts and Sciences, Department of History, Albany, NY 12222-0001. Offers history (MA, PhD); public history (Certificate). Part-time programs available. *Degree requirements:* For master's, variable foreign language requirement, exam, research paper or thesis; for doctorate, thesis/dissertation. *Entrance requirements:* For master's, minimum GPA of 3.0; for doctorate, GRE General Test, minimum GPA of 3.0. Additional exam requirements/recommendations for international students: Required—TOEFL (minimum score 550 paper-based; 213 computer-based). Electronic applications accepted. *Faculty research:* American history (all phases); public policy; European history (Medieval to modern); Asian, African, and Latin American history.

University at Buffalo, the State University of New York, Graduate School, College of Arts and Sciences, Department of History, Buffalo, NY 14260. Offers MA, PhD. Part-time programs available. *Faculty:* 24 full-time (11 women), 12 part-time/adjunct (4 women). *Students:* 60 full-time (25 women), 13 part-time (5 women); includes 1 Black or African American, non-Hispanic/Latino; 1 Asian, non-Hispanic/Latino; 1 Hispanic/Latino; 1 Native Hawaiian or other Pacific Islander, non-Hispanic/Latino, 1 international. Average age 29. 93 applicants, 52% accepted, 32 enrolled. In 2010, 18 master's, 5 doctorates awarded. Terminal master's awarded for partial completion of doctoral program. *Degree requirements:* For master's, project; for doctorate, variable foreign language requirement, thesis/dissertation, general exam. *Entrance requirements:* For master's and doctorate, GRE General Test. Additional exam requirements/recommendations for international students: Required—TOEFL (minimum score 79 iBT). *Application deadline:* For fall admission, 4/1 for domestic and international students; for spring admission, 10/1 priority date for domestic students, 10/1 for international students. Application fee: $75. Electronic applications accepted. *Financial support:* In 2010–11, 28 students received support, including 5 fellowships with full tuition reimbursements available (averaging $14,000 per year), 21 teaching assistantships with full tuition reimbursements available (averaging $15,000 per year); Federal Work-Study, institutionally sponsored loans, and unspecified assistantships also available. Financial award application deadline: 1/15; financial award applicants required to submit FAFSA. *Faculty research:* Early modern and modern European social, cultural and intellectual history; American social, cultural and political history; north and south Atlantic world history; Latin America; East Asian history; women's and gender history. Total annual research expenditures: $35,000. *Unit head:* Dr. James Bono, Chair, 716-645-8423, Fax: 716-645-5954, E-mail: hischaos@buffalo.edu. *Application contact:* Dr. Jason Young, Director of Graduate Studies, 716-645-8412, Fax: 716-645-8422, E-mail: ubhistor@buffalo.edu.

The University of Akron, Graduate School, Buchtel College of Arts and Sciences, Department of History, Akron, OH 44325. Offers MA, PhD. Part-time programs available. *Faculty:* 20 full-time (8 women), 33 part-time/adjunct (14 women). *Students:* 23 full-time (12 women), 20 part-time (9 women); includes 1 Black or African American, non-Hispanic/Latino; 1 American Indian or Alaska Native, non-Hispanic/Latino; 1 Asian, non-Hispanic/Latino, 1 international. Average age 33. 36 applicants, 69% accepted, 13 enrolled. In 2010, 2 master's awarded. *Degree requirements:* For master's, one foreign language, thesis optional, written exams, seminars; for doctorate, 2 foreign languages, comprehensive exam, thesis/dissertation, written exams, oral exams. *Entrance requirements:* For master's, GRE, minimum GPA of 3.0, writing sample, three letters of recommendation, letter of intent; for doctorate, GRE, minimum GPA of 3.5, three letters of recommendation, personal statement, writing sample, evidence of reading knowledge in one foreign language. Additional exam requirements/recommendations for international students: Required—TOEFL (minimum score 580 paper-based; 237 computer-based; 92 iBT). *Application deadline:* For fall admission, 2/1 for domestic and international students. Application fee: $30 ($40 for international students). *Expenses:* Tuition, state resident: full-time $6800; part-time $378 per credit hour. Tuition, nonresident: full-time $11,644; part-time $647 per credit hour. Required fees: $1265. One-time fee: $30 full-time. *Financial support:* In 2010–11, 2 research assistantships, 16 teaching assistantships with full tuition reimbursements were awarded; career-related internships or fieldwork, Federal Work-Study, and tuition waivers (partial) also available. Support available to part-time students. *Faculty research:* European, American, and world history. Total annual research expenditures: $120,262. *Unit head:* Dr. Michael Sheng, Chair, 330-972-7007, E-mail: whixson@uakron.edu. *Application contact:* Dr. Michael Graham, Graduate Director, 330-972-7007.

The University of Alabama, Graduate School, College of Arts and Sciences, Department of History, Tuscaloosa, AL 35487. Offers MA, PhD. *Faculty:* 26 full-time (8 women). *Students:* 45 full-time (14 women), 33 part-time (10 women); includes 6 minority (3 Black or African American, non-Hispanic/Latino; 3 Hispanic/Latino), 1 international. Average age 29. 74 applicants, 47% accepted, 17 enrolled. In 2010, 9 master's, 4 doctorates awarded. Terminal master's awarded for partial completion of doctoral program. *Degree requirements:* For master's, one foreign language, thesis optional, oral exam; for doctorate, 2 foreign languages, comprehensive exam, thesis/dissertation, oral exams, written exam. *Entrance requirements:* For master's and doctorate, GRE General Test. *Application deadline:* For fall admission, 5/1 for domestic students. Applications are processed on a rolling basis. Application fee: $50 ($60 for international students). *Expenses:* Tuition, state resident: full-time $7900. Tuition, nonresident: full-time $20,500. *Financial support:* In 2010–11, 29 students received support, including 6 fellowships with full tuition reimbursements available (averaging $10,000 per year), research assistantships (averaging $10,000 per year), 23 teaching assistantships with full tuition reimbursements available (averaging $10,200 per year); institutionally sponsored loans and unspecified assistantships also available. Financial award application deadline: 1/15. *Faculty research:* U. S., modern European, Latin American, military, and southern U. S. history. Total annual research expenditures: $69,673. *Unit head:* Dr. Michael Mendle, Chair, 205-348-7103. *Application contact:* Dr. Lisa Lindquist Dorr, Graduate Director, 205-348-1859, E-mail: ldorr@bama.ua.edu.

The University of Alabama at Birmingham, College of Arts and Sciences, Program in History, Birmingham, AL 35294. Offers MA. Part-time programs available. *Students:* 12 full-time (4 women), 14 part-time (7 women); includes 4 minority (1 Black or African American, non-Hispanic/Latino; 1 Hispanic/Latino; 2 Two or more races, non-Hispanic/Latino). Average age 36. 15 applicants, 73% accepted, 5 enrolled. In 2010, 107 master's awarded. *Degree requirements:* For master's, variable foreign language requirement, thesis or alternative. *Entrance requirements:* For master's, GRE General Test or MAT. *Application deadline:* Applications are processed on a rolling basis. Electronic applications accepted. *Expenses:* Tuition, state resident: full-time $5482. Tuition, nonresident: full-time $12,430. Tuition and fees vary according to program. *Financial support:* In 2010–11, 4 research assistantships, 5 teaching assistantships were awarded; institutionally sponsored loans also available. *Faculty research:* History of Europe, United States, Latin America, American South. *Unit head:* Dr. Carolyn Conley, Chair, 205-934-8691, Fax: 205-975-8360. *Application contact:* Julie Bryant, Director of Graduate Admissions, 205-934-8227, Fax: 205-934-8413, E-mail: jbryant@uab.edu.

The University of Alabama in Huntsville, School of Graduate Studies, College of Liberal Arts, Department of History, Huntsville, AL 35899. Offers MA. Part-time and evening/weekend programs available. *Faculty:* 10 full-time (3 women). *Students:* 7 full-time (1 woman), 7 part-time (3 women); includes 1 minority (Black or African American, non-Hispanic/Latino). Average age 36. 14 applicants, 50% accepted, 4 enrolled. In 2010, 4 master's awarded. *Degree requirements:* For master's, one foreign language, comprehensive exam, thesis or alternative, oral and written exams. *Entrance requirements:* For master's, GRE General Test, minimum GPA of 3.0, bachelor's degree in history or related area. Additional exam requirements/recommendations for international students: Required—TOEFL (minimum score 500 paper-based; 173 computer-based; 62 iBT). *Application deadline:* For fall admission, 7/15 for domestic students, 4/1 for international students; for spring admission, 11/30 for domestic students, 9/1 for international students. Applications are processed on a rolling basis. Application fee: $40 ($50 for international students). Electronic applications accepted. *Expenses:* Tuition, state resident: full-time $7250; part-time $407.75 per credit hour. Tuition, nonresident: full-time $17,358; part-time $970.05 per credit hour. Required fees: $246.80 per semester. Tuition and fees vary according to course load and program. *Financial support:* In 2010–11, 5 students received support, including 1 research assistantship with full tuition reimbursement available (averaging $8,460 per year); career-related internships or fieldwork, Federal Work-Study, institutionally sponsored loans, scholarships/grants, health care benefits, and unspecified assistantships also available. Support available to part-time students. Financial award application deadline: 4/1; financial award applicants required to submit FAFSA. *Faculty research:* American and European history, U. S. diplomatic history, Old South, ancient and medieval history, Latin American history. *Unit head:* Dr. Andrew Dunar, Chair, 256-824-6312, Fax: 256-824-6477, E-mail: dunara@uah.edu. *Application contact:* Kathy Biggs, Graduate Studies Admissions Manager, 256-824-6199, Fax: 256-824-6405, E-mail: deangrad@uah.edu.

University of Alaska Fairbanks, College of Liberal Arts, Department of Northern Studies, Fairbanks, AK 99775-6460. Offers environmental politics and policy (MA); Northern history (MA). Part-time programs available. *Students:* 15 full-time (9 women), 21 part-time (13 women); includes 6 minority (1 Black or African American, non-Hispanic/Latino; 2 American Indian or Alaska Native, non-Hispanic/Latino; 1 Hispanic/Latino; 2 Two or more races, non-Hispanic/Latino), 2 international. Average age 39. 14 applicants, 57% accepted, 8 enrolled. In 2010, 9 master's awarded. *Degree requirements:* For master's, comprehensive exam, thesis or alternative. *Entrance requirements:* Additional exam requirements/recommendations for international students: Required—TOEFL (minimum score 550 paper-based; 213 computer-based; 80 iBT). *Application deadline:* For fall admission, 6/1 for domestic students, 3/1 for international students; for spring admission, 10/15 for domestic students, 9/1 for international students. Applications are processed on a rolling basis. Application fee: $60. Electronic applications accepted. *Expenses:* Tuition, state resident: full-time $5688; part-time $316 per credit. Tuition, nonresident: full-time $11,628; part-time $646 per credit. Required fees: $289 per semester. Tuition and fees vary according to course load and reciprocity agreements. *Financial support:* In 2010–11, 9 teaching assistantships with tuition reimbursements (averaging $7,462 per year) were awarded; fellowships with tuition reimbursements, research assistantships with tuition reimbursements, career-related internships or fieldwork, Federal Work-Study, scholarships/grants, health care benefits, and unspecified assistantships also available. Support available to part-time students. Financial award application deadline: 1/1; financial award applicants required to submit FAFSA. *Faculty research:* Canadian history, environmental history, Native Alaskan history and art, fetal alcohol syndrome. *Unit head:* Mary Ehrlander, Director, 907-474-7126, Fax: 907-474-5817, E-mail: fynors@uaf.edu. *Application contact:* Mary Ehrlander, Director, 907-474-7126, Fax: 907-474-5817, E-mail: fynors@uaf.edu.

University of Alberta, Faculty of Graduate Studies and Research, Department of History and Classics, Edmonton, AB T6G 2E1, Canada. Offers ancient history (PhD); classical archaeology (MA, PhD); classical literature (PhD); classics (MA); history (MA, PhD). Part-time and evening/weekend programs available. *Degree requirements:* For master's, one foreign language, thesis (for some programs); for doctorate, one foreign language, thesis/dissertation. *Entrance requirements:* For master's, minimum B+ average; for doctorate, minimum A- average. Additional exam requirements/recommendations for international students: Required—TOEFL (minimum score 580 paper-based; 237 computer-based). Electronic applications accepted. *Faculty research:* Western Canada, classical archaeology, Britain, Eastern Europe, East Asia.

The University of Arizona, College of Social and Behavioral Sciences, Department of History, Tucson, AZ 85721. Offers MA, PhD. Part-time programs available. *Faculty:* 23 full-time (8 women), 5 part-time/adjunct (3 women). *Students:* 53 full-time (26 women), 21 part-time (10 women); includes 1 American Indian or Alaska Native, non-Hispanic/Latino; 9 Hispanic/Latino; 3 Two or more races, non-Hispanic/Latino, 9 international. Average age 34. 91 applicants, 14% accepted, 11 enrolled. In 2010, 7 master's, 5 doctorates awarded. Terminal master's awarded for partial completion of doctoral program. *Degree requirements:* For master's, one foreign language, comprehensive exam, thesis optional; for doctorate, 2 foreign languages, comprehensive exam, thesis/dissertation. *Entrance requirements:* For master's, GRE General Test, 3 letters of recommendation, writing sample; for doctorate, GRE General Test, 3 letters of recommendation, statement of purpose, 2 writing samples. Additional exam requirements/recommendations for international students: Required—TOEFL (minimum score 550 paper-based; 213 computer-based; 79 iBT). *Application deadline:* For fall admission, 1/15 for domestic and international students. Applications are processed on a rolling basis. Application fee: $65. Electronic applications accepted. *Expenses:* Tuition, state resident: full-time $7692. *Financial support:* In 2010–11, 38 teaching assistantships with full tuition reimbursements (averaging $18,289 per year) were awarded; research assistantships with full tuition reimbursements, career-related internships or fieldwork, Federal Work-Study, institutionally sponsored loans, scholarships/grants, health care benefits, tuition waivers (full and partial), and unspecified assistantships also available. Financial award application deadline: 2/1. *Faculty research:* Latin American history, European history, U. S. history, women's history, global/environmental history. Total annual research expenditures: $202,034. *Unit head:* Dr. Kevin Gosner, Head, 520-621-1168, Fax: 520-621-2422, E-mail: kgosner@u.arizona.edu. *Application contact:* Gina M. Wasson, Information Contact, 520-621-5860, Fax: 520-621-2422, E-mail: gmus@u.arizona.edu.

University of Arkansas, Graduate School, J. William Fulbright College of Arts and Sciences, Department of History, Fayetteville, AR 72701-1201. Offers MA, PhD. Part-time programs available. *Students:* 21 full-time (9 women), 47 part-time (14 women); includes 2 minority (1 Black or African American, non-Hispanic/Latino; 1 Asian, non-Hispanic/Latino), 6 international. 20 applicants, 95% accepted. In 2010, 11 master's, 4 doctorates awarded. *Degree requirements:* For master's, thesis optional; for doctorate, 2 foreign languages, thesis/dissertation. *Entrance requirements:* For master's, GRE General Test; for doctorate, GRE General Test, GRE Subject Test. *Application deadline:* For fall admission, 4/1 for international students; for spring admission, 10/1 for international students. Applications are processed on a rolling basis. Application fee: $40 ($50 for international students). Electronic applications accepted. *Financial support:* In 2010–11, 11 fellowships with tuition reimbursements, 6 research assistantships, 14 teaching assistantships were awarded; career-related internships or fieldwork and Federal Work-Study also available. Support available to part-time students. Financial award application deadline: 4/1; financial award applicants required to submit FAFSA. *Unit head:* Dr. Lynda Coon, Departmental Chairperson, 479-575-3001, Fax: 479-575-2775, E-mail: llcoon@uark.edu. *Application contact:* Dr. Kathryn Sloan, Graduate Coordinator, 479-575-3001, Fax: 479-575-2775, E-mail: ksloan@uark.edu.

History

The University of British Columbia, Faculty of Arts, Department of History, Vancouver, BC V6T 1Z1, Canada. Offers MA, PhD. Part-time programs available. *Faculty:* 34 full-time (11 women). *Students:* 78 full-time (32 women). Average age 24. 109 applicants, 24% accepted, 15 enrolled. In 2010, 5 master's, 2 doctorates awarded. *Degree requirements:* For master's, one foreign language, thesis, six 3-credit courses; for doctorate, one foreign language, comprehensive exam, thesis/dissertation, four or five 3-credit courses. *Entrance requirements:* For master's, four-year bachelor's degree; for doctorate, master's degree (or equivalent) in history, first-class (A) standing in graduate courses, language relevant to dissertation research. Additional exam requirements/recommendations for international students: Required—TOEFL (minimum score 570 paper-based; 230 computer-based). *Application deadline:* For fall admission, 1/8 for domestic students, 1/2 for international students. Applications are processed on a rolling basis. Application fee: $90 Canadian dollars ($150 Canadian dollars for international students). Electronic applications accepted. Tuition charges are reported in Canadian dollars. *Expenses:* Tuition, area resident: Full-time $4179 Canadian dollars. International tuition: $7344 Canadian dollars full-time. *Financial support:* In 2010–11, 17 students received support, including 24 fellowships with partial tuition reimbursements available (averaging $17,500 per year), 7 research assistantships with partial tuition reimbursements available (averaging $3,700 per year), 35 teaching assistantships with partial tuition reimbursements available (averaging $10,914 per year); scholarships/grants, tuition waivers (partial), and unspecified assistantships also available. Financial award application deadline: 9/15. *Faculty research:* Canadian, British, European, modern Chinese and Japanese history; international relations. *Unit head:* Dr. Daniel F. Vickers, Head, 604-827-3560, Fax: 604-822-6658, E-mail: dvickers@interchange.ubc.ca. *Application contact:* Dr. Alejandra Bronfman, Graduate Advisor, 604-822-5163, Fax: 604-822-6658, E-mail: bronfman@interchange.ubc.ca.

University of Calgary, Faculty of Graduate Studies, Faculty of Social Sciences, Department of History, Calgary, AB T2N 1N4, Canada. Offers MA, PhD. Part-time programs available. *Degree requirements:* For master's, one foreign language, thesis; for doctorate, one foreign language, thesis/dissertation, 3 written comprehensive exams, oral candidacy exam. *Entrance requirements:* For master's, minimum GPA of 3.4, writing sample; for doctorate, sample of written work, master's degree in history. Electronic applications accepted. *Faculty research:* Military history, Canadian history, Latin American history, gender/women's history, native history.

University of California, Berkeley, Graduate Division, College of Letters and Science, Department of History, Berkeley, CA 94720-2550. Offers PhD, MA/PhD. *Faculty:* 49 full-time (17 women). *Students:* 212 full-time (96 women); includes 3 Black or African American, non-Hispanic/Latino; 19 Asian, non-Hispanic/Latino; 13 Hispanic/Latino; 1 Native Hawaiian or other Pacific Islander, non-Hispanic/Latino; 7 Two or more races, non-Hispanic/Latino, 16 international. 396 applicants, 11% accepted, 24 enrolled. In 2010, 21 doctorates awarded. *Degree requirements:* For doctorate, variable foreign language requirement, comprehensive exam, thesis/dissertation. *Entrance requirements:* For doctorate, GRE General Test, minimum GPA of 3.0, 3 letters of recommendation, writing sample (not to exceed 10 pages), academic transcripts, 2 essays, statement of purpose, personal statement. Additional exam requirements/recommendations for international students: Required—TOEFL (minimum score 570 paper-based; 230 computer-based; 68 iBT). *Application deadline:* For fall admission, 12/1 for domestic and international students. Application fee: $70 ($90 for international students). Electronic applications accepted. *Financial support:* In 2010–11, 150 students received support, including 100 fellowships with full and partial tuition reimbursements available (averaging $9,000 per year), research assistantships with partial tuition reimbursements available (averaging $3,200 per year), 110 teaching assistantships with partial tuition reimbursements available (averaging $8,500 per year); Federal Work-Study, institutionally sponsored loans, scholarships/grants, health care benefits, tuition waivers (full and partial), and unspecified assistantships also available. Financial award application deadline: 3/1; financial award applicants required to submit FAFSA. *Faculty research:* Africa, ancient Greece and Rome, Britain, Europe (ancient Greece and Rome, medieval, early modern, late modern), Asia (China, Japan, south, southeast), Jewish, Latin America, Middle East, science, U. S. history. *Unit head:* Prof. Mary Elizabeth Berry, Chair, 510-642-3402, Fax: 510-643-5323, E-mail: histadm@berkeley.edu. *Application contact:* Barbara Hayashida, Graduate Admissions Coordinator, 510-642-2378, Fax: 510-643-5323, E-mail: histadm@berkeley.edu.

University of California, Berkeley, Graduate Division, College of Letters and Science, Group in Ancient History and Mediterranean Archaeology, Berkeley, CA 94720-1500. Offers MA, PhD. *Degree requirements:* For master's, one foreign language, exam or thesis; for doctorate, 2 foreign languages, thesis/dissertation, qualifying exam. *Entrance requirements:* For master's and doctorate, GRE General Test, minimum GPA of 3.0, 3 letters of recommendation. Additional exam requirements/recommendations for international students: Required—TOEFL (minimum score 570 paper-based; 230 computer-based), TWE.

University of California, Davis, Graduate Studies, Program in History, Davis, CA 95616. Offers MA, PhD. Terminal master's awarded for partial completion of doctoral program. *Degree requirements:* For master's, one foreign language, comprehensive exam (for some programs), thesis (for some programs); for doctorate, 2 foreign languages, thesis/dissertation. *Entrance requirements:* For master's, GRE General Test, minimum GPA of 3.0, writing sample; for doctorate, GRE General Test, master's degree, writing sample. Additional exam requirements/recommendations for international students: Required—TOEFL (minimum score 550 paper-based; 213 computer-based). Electronic applications accepted. *Faculty research:* American social, cultural, and western history; modern and early history; modern European, East Asian, and Latin American history; history of science and medicine; cross-cultural history of women.

University of California, Irvine, School of Humanities, Department of History, Irvine, CA 92697. Offers MA, PhD. *Students:* 85 full-time (47 women), 7 part-time (3 women); includes 17 minority (1 Black or African American, non-Hispanic/Latino; 6 Asian, non-Hispanic/Latino; 8 Hispanic/Latino; 2 Two or more races, non-Hispanic/Latino), 9 international. Average age 28. 104 applicants, 33% accepted, 16 enrolled. In 2010, 12 master's, 10 doctorates awarded. *Degree requirements:* For doctorate, thesis/dissertation. *Entrance requirements:* For master's and doctorate, GRE General Test, minimum GPA of 3.0. Additional exam requirements/recommendations for international students: Required—TOEFL (minimum score 550 paper-based; 213 computer-based). *Application deadline:* For fall admission, 1/2 priority date for domestic students, 1/2 for international students. Application fee: $80 ($100 for international students). Electronic applications accepted. *Financial support:* Fellowships, research assistantships with full tuition reimbursements, teaching assistantships, institutionally sponsored loans, traineeships, health care benefits, and unspecified assistantships available. Financial award application deadline: 3/1; financial award applicants required to submit FAFSA. *Faculty research:* European, U. S., Latin American, ancient, and East Asian history. *Unit head:* Prof. Jeffrey Natha Wasserstrom, Chair, 949-824-6521, Fax: 949-824-2865, E-mail: jwassers@uci.edu. *Application contact:* Alicia A. Sanchez, Graduate Program Coordinator, 949-824-5891, Fax: 949-824-2865, E-mail: carol@uci.edu.

University of California, Los Angeles, Graduate Division, College of Letters and Science, Department of History, Los Angeles, CA 90095. Offers MA, PhD, MLIS/MA. *Faculty:* 67 full-time (21 women). *Students:* 197 full-time (104 women); includes 41 minority (6 Black or African American, non-Hispanic/Latino; 3 American Indian or Alaska Native, non-Hispanic/Latino; 12 Asian, non-Hispanic/Latino; 19 Hispanic/Latino; 1 Native Hawaiian or other Pacific Islander, non-Hispanic/Latino), 23 international. Average age 32. 352 applicants, 20% accepted, 23 enrolled. In 2010, 30 master's, 21 doctorates awarded. Terminal master's awarded for partial completion of doctoral program. *Degree requirements:* For master's, one foreign language, comprehensive exam; for doctorate, variable foreign language requirement, thesis/dissertation, oral and written qualifying exams. *Entrance requirements:* For master's, GRE General Test, minimum GPA of 3.0; for doctorate, GRE General Test, minimum undergraduate GPA of 3.0. *Application deadline:* For fall admission, 12/15 for domestic and international students. Application fee: $70 ($90 for international students). Electronic applications accepted. *Financial support:* In 2010–11, 151 fellowships with full and partial tuition reimbursements, 49 research assistantships with full and partial tuition reimbursements, 122 teaching assistantships with full and partial tuition reimbursements were awarded; Federal Work-Study, institutionally sponsored loans, scholarships/grants, health care benefits, tuition waivers (full and partial), and unspecified assistantships also available. Financial award application deadline: 3/1; financial award applicants required to submit FAFSA. *Unit head:* Dr. David Myers, Chair, 310-825-1883, E-mail: myers@history.ucla.edu. *Application contact:* Department Office, 310-206-2627, E-mail: gradoffice@history.ucla.edu.

University of California, Riverside, Graduate Division, Department of History, Riverside, CA 92521-0102. Offers archival management (MA); historic preservation (MA); history (MA, PhD); museum curatorship (MA). Part-time programs available. Terminal master's awarded for partial completion of doctoral program. *Degree requirements:* For master's, one foreign language, comprehensive exam, internship report and oral exams, or thesis; for doctorate, 2 foreign languages, thesis/dissertation, qualifying exams, teaching experience. *Entrance requirements:* For master's, GRE General Test, minimum GPA of 3.2; for doctorate, GRE General Test, MA in history, minimum GPA of 3.2. Additional exam requirements/recommendations for international students: Required—TOEFL (minimum score 550 paper-based; 213 computer-based; 80 iBT). Electronic applications accepted. *Faculty research:* Native American history, United States, public history, Russia, Europe.

University of California, San Diego, Office of Graduate Studies, Department of History, La Jolla, CA 92093. Offers history (MA, PhD); Judaic studies (MA); science studies (PhD). *Degree requirements:* For doctorate, thesis/dissertation. *Entrance requirements:* For master's and doctorate, GRE General Test. Electronic applications accepted.

University of California, Santa Barbara, Graduate Division, College of Letters and Sciences, Division of Humanities and Fine Arts, Department of History, Santa Barbara, CA 93106-9410. Offers ancient Mediterranean studies (PhD); European medieval studies (PhD); feminist studies (PhD); global studies (PhD); history (PhD); public history (PhD); technology and society (PhD); MA/PhD. *Faculty:* 42 full-time (18 women), 10 part-time/adjunct (6 women). *Students:* 92 full-time (50 women); includes 1 Black or African American, non-Hispanic/Latino; 6 Asian, non-Hispanic/Latino; 11 Hispanic/Latino. Average age 34. 124 applicants, 19% accepted, 8 enrolled. In 2010, 20 doctorates awarded. *Degree requirements:* For doctorate, variable foreign language requirement, comprehensive exam, thesis/dissertation. *Entrance requirements:* For doctorate, GRE. Additional exam requirements/recommendations for international students: Required—TOEFL (minimum score 550 paper-based; 80 iBT), IELTS (minimum score 7). *Application deadline:* For fall admission, 12/5 priority date for domestic and international students. Application fee: $70 ($90 for international students). Electronic applications accepted. *Financial support:* In 2010–11, 92 students received support, including 68 fellowships with full and partial tuition reimbursements available (averaging $6,583 per year), 4 research assistantships with full and partial tuition reimbursements available (averaging $5,862 per year), 57 teaching assistantships with full and partial tuition reimbursements available (averaging $12,123 per year); tuition waivers (partial) also available. Financial award application deadline: 12/5; financial award applicants required to submit FAFSA. *Faculty research:* Europe, U. S., Latin America, Africa, Middle East, East Asia. *Unit head:* John Majewski, Chair, 805-893-2837, E-mail: majewski@history.ucrb.edu. *Application contact:* Sharon Farmer, Director of Graduate Studies, 805-893-3398, E-mail: farmer@history.ucsb.edu.

University of California, Santa Cruz, Division of Graduate Studies, Division of Humanities, Department of History, Santa Cruz, CA 95064. Offers MA, PhD. *Students:* 30 full-time (14 women), 3 part-time (1 woman); includes 2 Black or African American, non-Hispanic/Latino; 3 Asian, non-Hispanic/Latino; 5 Hispanic/Latino, 2 international. Average age 33. 51 applicants, 24% accepted, 4 enrolled. In 2010, 9 master's, 3 doctorates awarded. *Degree requirements:* For doctorate, variable foreign language requirement, comprehensive exam, thesis/dissertation, qualifying exam. *Entrance requirements:* For master's and doctorate, GRE, writing sample of up to 30 pages. Additional exam requirements/recommendations for international students: Required—TOEFL (minimum score 550 paper-based; 220 computer-based; 83 iBT); Recommended—IELTS (minimum score 8). *Application deadline:* For fall admission, 12/15 for domestic and international students. Application fee: $70 ($90 for international students). Electronic applications accepted. *Financial support:* Fellowships, research assistantships, teaching assistantships, institutionally sponsored loans and tuition waivers available. Financial award applicants required to submit FAFSA. *Faculty research:* Comparative, interdisciplinary approach to history; the Americas, Asia, the Islamic world, and Europe since 1500; society history. *Unit head:* Christine Khoo, Graduate Advisor, 831-459-2621, E-mail: ckhoo@ucsc.edu. *Application contact:* Christine Khoo, Graduate Advisor, 831-459-2621, E-mail: ckhoo@ucsc.edu.

University of Central Arkansas, Graduate School, College of Liberal Arts, Department of History, Conway, AR 72035-0001. Offers MA. Part-time programs available. *Faculty:* 15 full-time (4 women). *Students:* 6 full-time (3 women), 10 part-time (5 women); includes 2 minority (1 American Indian or Alaska Native, non-Hispanic/Latino; 1 Two or more races, non-Hispanic/Latino). Average age 32. 7 applicants, 100% accepted, 4 enrolled. In 2010, 4 master's awarded. *Degree requirements:* For master's, one foreign language, comprehensive exam, thesis optional. *Entrance requirements:* For master's, GRE General Test, minimum GPA of 2.7. Additional exam requirements/recommendations for international students: Required—TOEFL (minimum score 550 paper-based; 213 computer-based). *Application deadline:* For fall admission, 3/1 priority date for domestic students; for spring admission, 10/1 priority date for domestic students. Applications are processed on a rolling basis. Application fee: $25 ($40 for international students). *Financial support:* Federal Work-Study, scholarships/grants, and unspecified assistantships available. Financial award application deadline: 2/15; financial award applicants required to submit FAFSA. *Faculty research:* History Day, Russian culture. *Unit head:* Dr. Ken Barnes, Chairperson, 501-450-5631, Fax: 501-450-5185, E-mail: kennethb@uca.edu. *Application contact:* Susan Wood, Admissions Assistant, 501-450-3124, Fax: 501-450-5678, E-mail: swood@uca.edu.

University of Central Florida, College of Arts and Humanities, Department of History, Orlando, FL 32816. Offers MA. Part-time and evening/weekend programs available. *Faculty:* 30 full-time (14 women), 21 part-time/adjunct (8 women). *Students:* 26 full-time (7 women), 44 part-time (16 women); includes 2 Black or African American, non-Hispanic/Latino; 1 Asian, non-Hispanic/Latino; 7 Hispanic/Latino. Average age 29. 40 applicants, 68% accepted, 17 enrolled. In 2010, 10 master's awarded. *Degree requirements:* For master's, thesis, written exam. *Entrance requirements:* For master's, GRE General Test, minimum GPA of 3.0 in last 60 hours. Additional exam requirements/recommendations for international students: Required—TOEFL. *Application deadline:* For fall admission, 7/15 for domestic students; for spring admission, 12/1 for domestic students. Electronic applications accepted. *Expenses:* Tuition, state resident: part-time $256.56 per credit hour. Tuition, nonresident: part-time $1011.52 per credit hour. Part-time tuition and fees vary according to program. *Financial support:* In 2010–11, 14 students received support, including 4 fellowships with partial tuition reimbursements available (averaging $5,300 per year), 2 research assistantships with partial tuition reimbursements available (averaging $4,900 per year), 11 teaching assistantships with partial tuition reimbursements available (averaging $5,100 per year); career-related internships or fieldwork, Federal Work-Study, institutionally sponsored loans, tuition waivers (partial), and unspecified assistantships also available. Financial award application deadline: 3/1; financial award applicants required to submit FAFSA. *Unit head:* Dr. Rosalind Beiler, Chair, 407-823-6467, E-mail: beiler@mail.ucf.edu. *Application contact:* Dr. Rosalind Beiler, Chair, 407-823-6467, E-mail: beiler@mail.ucf.edu.

University of Central Missouri, The Graduate School, College of Arts, Humanities and Social Sciences, Warrensburg, MO 64093. Offers English (MA); history (MA); mass communication (MA); music (MA); psychology (MS); speech communication (MA); teaching English as a second language (MA); theatre (MA). Part-time programs available. *Entrance requirements:* Additional exam requirements/recommendations for international students: Required—TOEFL (minimum score 550 paper-based; 79 computer-based). Electronic applications accepted.

University of Central Oklahoma, College of Graduate Studies and Research, College of Liberal Arts, Department of History, Edmond, OK 73034-5209. Offers history (MA); museum studies (MA); social studies teaching (MA); Southwestern studies (MA). Part-time programs available. *Degree requirements:* For master's, thesis optional. *Entrance requirements:* Additional exam requirements/recommendations for international students: Required—TOEFL (minimum score 550 paper-based; 213 computer-based). Electronic applications accepted. *Faculty research:* China, Russia, civil war, American naval logistics.

University of Chicago, Division of Social Sciences, Department of History, Chicago, IL 60637-1513. Offers PhD. *Degree requirements:* For doctorate, variable foreign language requirement, thesis/dissertation, oral exams in 3 fields. *Entrance requirements:* For doctorate, GRE General Test. Additional exam requirements/recommendations for international students: Required—TOEFL, IELTS (minimum score 7). Electronic applications accepted.

University of Cincinnati, Graduate School, McMicken College of Arts and Sciences, Department of History, Cincinnati, OH 45221. Offers MA, PhD. Terminal master's awarded for partial completion of doctoral program. *Degree requirements:* For master's, comprehensive exam, thesis optional; for doctorate, comprehensive exam, thesis/dissertation. *Entrance requirements:* For master's, GRE General Test, BA in history; for doctorate, GRE General Test, MA in history. Additional exam requirements/recommendations for international students: Required—TOEFL (minimum score 600 paper-based). Electronic applications accepted. *Faculty research:* US cultural and social history, women's history, US and British intellectual history, modern Europe.

University of Colorado at Colorado Springs, College of Letters, Arts and Sciences, Department of History, Colorado Springs, CO 80933-7150. Offers MA. Part-time and evening/weekend programs available. *Faculty:* 7 full-time (3 women), 3 part-time/adjunct (2 women). *Students:* 29 full-time (14 women), 12 part-time (5 women); includes 2 Hispanic/Latino. Average age 33. 12 applicants, 92% accepted, 9 enrolled. In 2010, 11 master's awarded. *Degree requirements:* For master's, portfolio of 3-4 research projects, oral exam. *Entrance requirements:* For master's, minimum GPA of 2.75, writing sample. *Application deadline:* For fall admission, 3/1 for domestic students; for spring admission, 10/15 for domestic students. Applications are processed on a rolling basis. Application fee: $60 ($75 for international students). *Expenses:* Tuition, state resident: full-time $7916. Tuition, nonresident: full-time $16,610. Tuition and fees vary according to course load, degree level, program, reciprocity agreements and student level. *Financial support:* Teaching assistantships, Federal Work-Study and scholarships/grants available. Support available to part-time students. Financial award application deadline: 3/1; financial award applicants required to submit FAFSA. *Faculty research:* U. S. to 1865, Latin America, India, medieval and modern Europe. *Unit head:* Dr. Robert E. Sackett, Chair, 719-255-4079, Fax: 719-255-4068, E-mail: rsackett@uccs.edu. *Application contact:* Debbie Scott, Administrative Assistant, 719-255-4069, Fax: 719-255-4068, E-mail: dscott@uccs.edu.

University of Colorado Boulder, Graduate School, College of Arts and Sciences, Department of History, Boulder, CO 80309. Offers MA, PhD. *Faculty:* 33 full-time (13 women). *Students:* 50 full-time (19 women), 14 part-time (7 women); includes 6 minority (1 Black or African American, non-Hispanic/Latino; 1 American Indian or Alaska Native, non-Hispanic/Latino; 1 Asian, non-Hispanic/Latino; 3 Hispanic/Latino), 2 international. Average age 34. 113 applicants, 13 enrolled. In 2010, 7 master's, 5 doctorates awarded. Terminal master's awarded for partial completion of doctoral program. *Degree requirements:* For master's, comprehensive exam, thesis optional; for doctorate, one foreign language, thesis/dissertation. *Entrance requirements:* For master's, GRE General Test, minimum undergraduate GPA of 2.75; for doctorate, GRE General Test. *Application deadline:* For fall admission, 1/1 priority date for domestic students, 1/1 for international students. Application fee: $50 ($60 for international students). *Financial support:* In 2010–11, 14 fellowships (averaging $12,686 per year), 24 research assistantships (averaging $9,141 per year) were awarded; tuition waivers (full) also available. *Faculty research:* History of the American West; early American history; history of women and gender; American political, social and intellectual history; early modern and modern European social history. Total annual research expenditures: $93,419.

University of Colorado Denver, College of Liberal Arts and Sciences, Department of History, Denver, CO 80217. Offers European history (MA); global history (MA); public history (MA); U. S. history (MA). Part-time and evening/weekend programs available. *Faculty:* 12 full-time (6 women), 2 part-time/adjunct (1 woman). *Students:* 29 full-time (17 women), 30 part-time (12 women); includes 1 Black or African American, non-Hispanic/Latino; 1 American Indian or Alaska Native, non-Hispanic/Latino; 3 Hispanic/Latino. Average age 36. 25 applicants, 60% accepted, 10 enrolled. In 2010, 17 master's awarded. *Degree requirements:* For master's, comprehensive exam, thesis optional, 36 semester hours (12 courses). *Entrance requirements:* For master's, GRE General Test, writing sample, minimum GPA of 3.25, letters of recommendation. Additional exam requirements/recommendations for international students: Required—TOEFL (minimum score 525 paper-based; 197 computer-based). *Application deadline:* For fall admission, 4/1 for domestic students; for spring admission, 10/1 for domestic students. Applications are processed on a rolling basis. Application fee: $50 ($75 for international students). Electronic applications accepted. *Expenses:* Tuition, state resident: full-time $7332; part-time $355 per credit hour. Tuition, nonresident: full-time $18,990; part-time $1055 per credit hour. Required fees: $998. Tuition and fees vary according to course level, course load, degree level, campus/location, program, reciprocity agreements and student level. *Financial support:* Research assistantships, teaching assistantships, Federal Work-Study available. Financial award application deadline: 4/1; financial award applicants required to submit FAFSA. *Faculty research:* Uses of pre-modern Islamic heritage in modern India; relationship between liberal understandings of democracy, crime, and police discretion; relationships between gender, class, health, and welfare in nineteenth and early twentieth century England; U. S. business cultures and their influences on marketing and personnel practices; intersection of business and political ideologies; social and environmental history of the Rocky Mountain West. *Unit head:* Dr. Marjorie Levine-Clark, Associate Professor and Chair, 303-556-2896. *Application contact:* Tabitha Fitzpatrick, Program Assistant, 303-556-4830, E-mail: tabitha.fitzpatrick@ucdenver.edu.

University of Connecticut, Graduate School, College of Liberal Arts and Sciences, Department of History, Storrs, CT 06269. Offers MA, PhD. Terminal master's awarded for partial completion of doctoral program. *Degree requirements:* For master's, comprehensive exam; for doctorate, thesis/dissertation. *Entrance requirements:* For master's and doctorate, GRE General Test, GRE Subject Test. Additional exam requirements/recommendations for international students: Required—TOEFL (minimum score 550 paper-based; 213 computer-based). Electronic applications accepted.

University of Delaware, College of Arts and Sciences, Department of History, Hagley Program in the History of Technology and Industrialization, Newark, DE 19716. Offers MA, PhD. *Degree requirements:* For master's, thesis optional; for doctorate, comprehensive exam, thesis/dissertation. *Entrance requirements:* For master's and doctorate, interview. Electronic applications accepted.

University of Denver, University College, Denver, CO 80208. Offers arts and culture (MLS, Certificate), including art, literature, and culture, arts development and program management (Certificate), creative writing; environmental policy and management (MAS, Certificate), including energy and sustainability (Certificate), environmental assessment of nuclear power (Certificate), environmental health and safety (Certificate), environmental management, natural resource management (Certificate); geographic information systems (MAS, Certificate); global affairs (MLS, Certificate), including translation studies, world history and culture; healthcare leadership (MPH, Certificate), including healthcare policy, law, and ethics, medical and healthcare information technologies, strategic management of healthcare; information and communications technology (MCIS, Certificate), including database design and administration (Certificate), geographic information systems (MCIS), information security systems security (Certificate), information systems security (MCIS), project management (MCIS, MPS, Certificate), software design and administration (Certificate), software design and programming (MCIS), technology management, telecommunications technology (MCIS), Web design and development; leadership and organizations (MPS, Certificate), including human capital in organizations, philanthropic leadership, project management (MCIS, MPS, Certificate), strategic innovation and change; organizational and professional communication (MPS, Certificate), including alternative dispute resolution, organizational communication, organizational development and training, public relations and marketing; security management (MAS, Certificate), including emergency planning and response, information security (MAS), organizational security; strategic human resource management (MPS, Certificate), including global human resources (MPS), human resource management and development (MPS). Part-time and evening/weekend programs available. Postbaccalaureate distance learning degree programs offered (no on-campus study). *Faculty:* 7 full-time (2 women), 212 part-time/adjunct (83 women). *Students:* 52 full-time (19 women), 1,044 part-time (625 women); includes 196 minority (81 Black or African American, non-Hispanic/Latino; 7 American Indian or Alaska Native, non-Hispanic/Latino; 30 Asian, non-Hispanic/Latino; 66 Hispanic/Latino; 3 Native Hawaiian or other Pacific Islander, non-Hispanic/Latino; 9 Two or more races, non-Hispanic/Latino), 76 international. Average age 36. 488 applicants, 91% accepted, 339 enrolled. In 2010, 286 master's, 130 other advanced degrees awarded. *Entrance requirements:* Additional exam requirements/recommendations for international students: Required—TOEFL (minimum score 550 paper-based; 80 iBT). *Application deadline:* For fall admission, 6/22 priority date for domestic students, 6/10 priority date for international students; for winter admission, 9/15 priority date for domestic students, 9/6 priority date for international students; for spring admission, 2/3 priority date for domestic students, 12/15 priority date for international students. Applications are processed on a rolling basis. Application fee: $75. Electronic applications accepted. *Expenses:* Contact institution. *Financial support:* Applicants required to submit FAFSA. *Unit head:* Dr. James Davis, Dean, 303-871-2291, Fax: 303-871-4047, E-mail: jdavis@du.edu. *Application contact:* Information Contact, 303-871-3155, Fax: 303-871-4047, E-mail: ucolinfo@du.edu.

University of Florida, Graduate School, College of Liberal Arts and Sciences, Department of History, Gainesville, FL 32611. Offers African history (MA, PhD); American history (MA, PhD); European history (MA, PhD); Latin American history (MA, PhD); JD/MA; JD/PhD. Part-time programs available. *Faculty:* 31 full-time (10 women), 5 part-time/adjunct (4 women). *Students:* 81 full-time (33 women), 17 part-time (8 women); includes 3 Black or African American, non-Hispanic/Latino; 2 American Indian or Alaska Native, non-Hispanic/Latino; 2 Asian, non-Hispanic/Latino; 1 Hispanic/Latino, 12 international. Average age 30. 150 applicants, 29% accepted, 21 enrolled. In 2010, 19 master's, 8 doctorates awarded. Terminal master's awarded for partial completion of doctoral program. *Degree requirements:* For master's, variable foreign language requirement, thesis optional, 30 credit hours; for doctorate, variable foreign language requirement, comprehensive exam, thesis/dissertation, 90 credit hours. *Entrance requirements:* For master's and doctorate, GRE General Test, minimum GPA of 3.0. Additional exam requirements/recommendations for international students: Required—TOEFL (minimum score 550 paper-based; 213 computer-based; 80 iBT), IELTS (minimum score 6). *Application deadline:* For fall admission, 1/1 priority date for domestic students, 1/1 for international students. Applications are processed on a rolling basis. Application fee: $30. Electronic applications accepted. *Expenses:* Tuition, state resident: full-time $10,915.92. Tuition, nonresident: full-time $28,309. *Financial support:* In 2010–11, 70 students received support, including 30 fellowships, 13 research assistantships (averaging $16,665 per year), 27 teaching assistantships (averaging $16,733 per year); career-related internships or fieldwork and unspecified assistantships also available. Financial award application deadline: 1/15; financial award applicants required to submit FAFSA. *Faculty research:* Latin America and Caribbean history, nineteenth-century U. S. history, medieval Europe history, African history and Atlantic world history. *Unit head:* Dr. Ida L. Altman, Chair, 352-392-9634, E-mail: ialtman@ufl.edu. *Application contact:* Nina Caputo, Graduate Coordinator, 352-273-3379, Fax: 352-392-6927, E-mail: ncaputo@ufl.edu.

University of Georgia, College of Arts and Sciences, Department of History, Athens, GA 30602. Offers MA, PhD. *Faculty:* 31 full-time (9 women). *Students:* 46 full-time (18 women), 16 part-time (8 women); includes 5 Black or African American, non-Hispanic/Latino; 1 American Indian or Alaska Native, non-Hispanic/Latino, 5 international. 148 applicants, 18% accepted, 13 enrolled. In 2010, 7 master's, 8 doctorates awarded. *Degree requirements:* For master's, one foreign language, thesis; for doctorate, one foreign language, thesis/dissertation. *Entrance requirements:* For master's and doctorate, GRE General Test. *Application deadline:* For fall admission, 7/1 priority date for domestic students; for spring admission, 11/15 for domestic students. Application fee: $50. Electronic applications accepted. *Expenses:* Tuition, state resident: full-time $7200; part-time $344 per credit hour. Tuition, nonresident: full-time $21,900; part-time $944 per credit hour. Tuition and fees vary according to course load and program. *Financial support:* Fellowships, research assistantships, teaching assistantships, unspecified assistantships available. *Unit head:* Dr. John Morrow, Head, 706-542-2510, E-mail: jmorrow@uga.edu. *Application contact:* Dr. Benjamin G. Ehlers, Graduate Coordinator, 706-542-2537, Fax: 706-542-4367, E-mail: hiscoord@uga.edu.

University of Guelph, Graduate Studies, College of Arts, Department of History, Guelph, ON N1G 2W1, Canada. Offers MA, PhD. MA, PhD offered jointly with University of Waterloo, Wilfrid Laurier University. Part-time programs available. *Degree requirements:* For master's, one foreign language, thesis (for some programs); for doctorate, one foreign language, thesis/dissertation, 3 qualifying fields. *Entrance requirements:* For master's, minimum B+ average during previous 2 years of course work; for doctorate, minimum A- average in MA. Additional exam requirements/recommendations for international students: Required—TOEFL (minimum score 550 paper-based; 219 computer-based). Electronic applications accepted. *Faculty research:* Gender and family, Scottish history, rural and urban community studies, eighteenth century England, Canadian legal and social history, modern Europe.

University of Hawaii at Manoa, Graduate Division, College of Arts and Humanities, Department of History, Honolulu, HI 96822. Offers MA, PhD. Part-time programs available. *Faculty:* 34 full-time (10 women). *Students:* 51 full-time (16 women), 16 part-time (3 women); includes 24 minority (1 American Indian or Alaska Native, non-Hispanic/Latino; 6 Asian, non-Hispanic/Latino; 1 Hispanic/Latino; 4 Native Hawaiian or other Pacific Islander, non-Hispanic/Latino; 12 Two or more races, non-Hispanic/Latino), 10 international. Average age 34. 62 applicants, 55% accepted, 15 enrolled. In 2010, 5 master's, 1 doctorate awarded. *Degree requirements:* For master's, 2 foreign languages, thesis optional; for doctorate, 2 foreign languages, comprehensive exam, thesis/dissertation. *Entrance requirements:* For master's, GRE, minimum GPA of 3.0, writing sample; for doctorate, GRE, MA, sample of written work. Additional exam requirements/recommendations for international students: Required—TOEFL (minimum score 580 paper-based; 237 computer-based; 92 iBT), IELTS (minimum score 5). *Application deadline:* For fall admission, 1/1 for domestic and international students. Application fee: $60. *Financial support:* In 2010–11, 18 fellowships (averaging $6,775 per year), 1 research assistantship (averaging $17,495 per year), 14 teaching assistantships (averaging $15,055 per year) were awarded; scholarships/grants and tuition waivers (full) also available. Financial award application deadline: 2/1. *Faculty research:* Asian, Pacific, world, American and European history. Total annual research expenditures: $100,914. *Application contact:* James Kraft, Graduate Chair, 808-956-8358, Fax: 808-956-9600, E-mail: gradhist@hawaii.edu.

University of Houston, College of Liberal Arts and Social Sciences, Department of History, Houston, TX 77204. Offers MA, PhD. Part-time programs available. *Faculty:* 24 full-time (10 women), 3 part-time/adjunct (2 women). *Students:* 63 full-time (31 women), 30 part-time (19 women); includes 3 Black or African American, non-Hispanic/Latino; 1 American Indian or Alaska Native, non-Hispanic/Latino; 1 Asian, non-Hispanic/Latino; 17 Hispanic/Latino; 3 Two or more races, non-Hispanic/Latino, 1 international. Average age 33. 65 applicants, 58% accepted, 22 enrolled. In 2010, 10 master's, 10 doctorates awarded. Terminal master's awarded for partial completion of doctoral program. *Degree requirements:* For master's, one foreign language, thesis (for some programs); for doctorate, one foreign language, comprehensive exam, thesis/dissertation. *Entrance requirements:* For master's, GRE General Test, minimum GPA of 3.3; for doctorate, GRE General Test, minimum GPA of 3.67. Additional exam requirements/recommendations for international students: Required—TOEFL. *Application deadline:* For fall admission, 1/15 for domestic students; for spring admission, 11/1 for domestic students. Application fee: $75 for international students. Electronic applications accepted. *Expenses:* Tuition, state resident: full-time $8592; part-time $358 per credit hour. Tuition,

History

University of Houston (continued)

nonresident: full-time $16,032; part-time $668 per credit hour. Required fees: $2889. Tuition and fees vary according to course load and program. *Financial support:* In 2010–11, 2 fellowships with full tuition reimbursements (averaging $2,000 per year), 4 research assistantships with full tuition reimbursements (averaging $10,416 per year), 15 teaching assistantships with full tuition reimbursements (averaging $9,584 per year) were awarded; career-related internships or fieldwork, Federal Work-Study, institutionally sponsored loans, scholarships/grants, health care benefits, and unspecified assistantships also available. Support available to part-time students. Financial award application deadline: 2/1. *Faculty research:* U. S., Latin American, European, social, and women's history. *Unit head:* Dr. John Hart, Chairperson, 713-743-3008, Fax: 713-743-3216, E-mail: jhart@uh.edu. *Application contact:* Dr. John Hart, Chairperson, 713-743-3008, Fax: 713-743-3216, E-mail: jhart@uh.edu.

University of Houston–Clear Lake, School of Human Sciences and Humanities, Programs in Humanities and Fine Arts, Houston, TX 77058-1098. Offers history (MA); humanities (MA); literature (MA). Part-time and evening/weekend programs available. Postbaccalaureate distance learning degree programs offered (minimal on-campus study). *Degree requirements:* For master's, thesis or alternative. *Entrance requirements:* For master's, GRE General Test. Additional exam requirements/recommendations for international students: Required—TOEFL (minimum score 550 paper-based; 213 computer-based). *Faculty research:* Digital media studies, Latin American history, labor history, Chaucer evolution versus creationism debate.

University of Idaho, College of Graduate Studies, College of Letters, Arts and Social Sciences, Department of History, Moscow, ID 83844-2282. Offers MA, PhD. *Faculty:* 6 full-time, 1 part-time/adjunct. *Students:* 7 full-time, 8 part-time. Average age 40. In 2010, 3 master's awarded. *Degree requirements:* For doctorate, thesis/dissertation. *Entrance requirements:* For master's, minimum GPA of 2.8; for doctorate, minimum undergraduate GPA of 2.8, 3.0 graduate. *Application deadline:* For fall admission, 8/1 for domestic students; for spring admission, 12/15 for domestic students. Applications are processed on a rolling basis. Application fee: $60. Electronic applications accepted. *Expenses:* Tuition, nonresident: part-time $580 per credit. Required fees: $306 per credit. *Financial support:* Research assistantships, teaching assistantships available. Financial award applicants required to submit FAFSA. *Unit head:* Dr. Richard Spence, Chair, 208-885-6253, E-mail: history@uidaho.edu. *Application contact:* Dr. Richard Spence, Chair, 208-885-6253, E-mail: history@uidaho.edu.

University of Illinois at Chicago, Graduate College, College of Liberal Arts and Sciences, Department of History, Chicago, IL 60607-7128. Offers MA, MAT, PhD. Part-time and evening/weekend programs available. *Degree requirements:* For master's, one foreign language, comprehensive exam; for doctorate, 2 foreign languages, comprehensive exam, thesis/dissertation. *Entrance requirements:* For master's and doctorate, GRE General Test, previous course work in a foreign language, minimum GPA of 3.0. Additional exam requirements/recommendations for international students: Required—TOEFL. Electronic applications accepted. *Faculty research:* American urban and immigration history, early modern European history, Eastern European history.

University of Illinois at Springfield, Graduate Programs, College of Liberal Arts and Sciences, Program in History, Springfield, IL 62703-5407. Offers MA. Part-time and evening/weekend programs available. *Degree requirements:* For master's, thesis, internship, or historiography. *Entrance requirements:* For master's, BA in history or related field, minimum undergraduate GPA of 3.0, writing sample. Additional exam requirements/recommendations for international students: Required—TOEFL (minimum score 500 paper-based; 176 computer-based; 61 iBT). Electronic applications accepted. *Expenses:* Tuition, state resident: full-time $6774; part-time $282.25 per credit hour. Tuition, nonresident: full-time $15,078; part-time $628.25 per credit hour. Required fees: $15.25 per credit hour. $492 per term.

University of Illinois at Urbana–Champaign, Graduate College, College of Liberal Arts and Sciences, Department of History, Champaign, IL 61820. Offers MA, PhD. *Faculty:* 38 full-time (14 women). *Students:* 91 full-time (46 women), 21 part-time (10 women); includes 23 minority (11 Black or African American, non-Hispanic/Latino; 3 Asian, non-Hispanic/Latino; 5 Hispanic/Latino; 4 Two or more races, non-Hispanic/Latino), 18 international. 217 applicants, 6% accepted, 7 enrolled. In 2010, 13 master's, 15 doctorates awarded. *Entrance requirements:* For master's, GRE General Test, minimum GPA of 3.25; writing sample; for doctorate, GRE, minimum GPA of 3.5; writing sample. Additional exam requirements/recommendations for international students: Required—TOEFL (minimum score 600 paper-based; 250 computer-based). *Application deadline:* Applications are processed on a rolling basis. Application fee: $75 ($90 for international students). Electronic applications accepted. *Financial support:* In 2010–11, 54 fellowships, 15 research assistantships, 45 teaching assistantships were awarded; tuition waivers (full and partial) also available. *Unit head:* Antoinette Burton, Chair, 217-244-2075, Fax: 217-333-2297, E-mail: aburton@illinois.edu. *Application contact:* Elaine B. Sampson, Office Manager, 217-244-2591, Fax: 217-333-2297, E-mail: esampson@illinois.edu.

University of Indianapolis, Graduate Programs, College of Arts and Sciences, Department of History and Political Science, Indianapolis, IN 46227-3697. Offers history (MA); international relations (MA). Part-time and evening/weekend programs available. *Faculty:* 5 full-time (2 women). *Students:* 5 full-time (1 woman), 25 part-time (15 women); includes 3 minority (2 Black or African American, non-Hispanic/Latino; 1 Hispanic/Latino), 3 international. Average age 29. In 2010, 7 master's awarded. *Degree requirements:* For master's, thesis optional. *Entrance requirements:* For master's, GRE Subject Test, minimum GPA of 3.0, 3 letters of recommendation. Additional exam requirements/recommendations for international students: Required—TOEFL (minimum score 550 paper-based; 213 computer-based). *Application deadline:* Applications are processed on a rolling basis. Application fee: $30. Electronic applications accepted. Tuition and fees vary according to course load, degree level and program. *Financial support:* Federal Work-Study, scholarships/grants, and tuition waivers (full and partial) available. Support available to part-time students. Financial award application deadline: 5/1; financial award applicants required to submit FAFSA. *Unit head:* Dr. Lawrence Sondhaus, Chairperson, 317-788-2196, Fax: 317-788-3480, E-mail: sondhaus@uindy.edu. *Application contact:* Dr. Lawrence Sondhaus, Chairperson, 317-788-2196, Fax: 317-788-3480, E-mail: sondhaus@uindy.edu.

The University of Iowa, Graduate College, College of Liberal Arts and Sciences, Department of History, Iowa City, IA 52242-1316. Offers MA, PhD. *Degree requirements:* For master's, thesis optional, exam; for doctorate, comprehensive exam, thesis/dissertation. *Entrance requirements:* For master's and doctorate, GRE General Test, minimum GPA of 3.0. Additional exam requirements/recommendations for international students: Required—TOEFL (minimum score 550 paper-based; 213 computer-based; 81 iBT). Electronic applications accepted.

The University of Kansas, Graduate Studies, College of Liberal Arts and Sciences, Department of History, Lawrence, KS 66045. Offers MA, PhD. Part-time programs available. *Students:* 77 full-time (25 women), 14 part-time (3 women); includes 9 minority (2 American Indian or Alaska Native, non-Hispanic/Latino; 2 Asian, non-Hispanic/Latino; 5 Hispanic/Latino), 4 international. Average age 35. 99 applicants, 30% accepted, 15 enrolled. In 2010, 9 master's, 8 doctorates awarded. *Degree requirements:* For master's, variable foreign language requirement, 2 professional quality papers; for doctorate, variable foreign language requirement, comprehensive exam, thesis/dissertation. *Entrance requirements:* For master's and doctorate, GRE General Test, minimum GPA of 3.0. Additional exam requirements/recommendations for international students: Required—TOEFL. *Application deadline:* For fall admission, 12/1 for domestic students, 11/1 for international students. Application fee: $55 ($65 for international students). Electronic applications accepted. *Expenses:* Tuition, state resident: full-time $7092; part-time $295.50 per credit hour. Tuition, nonresident: full-time $16,590; part-time $691.25 per credit hour. Required fees: $858; $71.49 per credit hour. Tuition and fees vary according to course load, campus/location and program. *Financial support:* In 2010–11, 6 fellowships with full tuition reimbursements, 31 teaching assistantships with full tuition reimbursements were awarded; research assistantships with full and partial tuition reimbursements, unspecified assistantships also available. Financial award application deadline: 12/1. *Faculty research:* Environment, military, early modern, East Asia, Russia/East Europe. *Unit head:* Dr. Paul Kelton, Chair, 785-864-9441, Fax: 785-864-5046, E-mail: pkelton@ku.edu. *Application contact:* Graduate Program Administrator, Fax: 785-864-5046.

University of Kentucky, Graduate School, College of Arts and Sciences, Program in History, Lexington, KY 40506-0032. Offers MA, PhD. Part-time programs available. *Degree requirements:* For master's, one foreign language, comprehensive exam, thesis optional; for doctorate, variable foreign language requirement, comprehensive exam, thesis/dissertation. *Entrance requirements:* For master's, GRE General Test, minimum undergraduate GPA of 2.75; for doctorate, GRE General Test, minimum graduate GPA of 3.0. Additional exam requirements/recommendations for international students: Required—TOEFL (minimum score 550 paper-based; 213 computer-based). Electronic applications accepted. *Faculty research:* English, British, European history; U.S. social, political and diplomatic history; U.S. early national history; U.S. Southern history; Native American and African-American history.

University of Lethbridge, School of Graduate Studies, Lethbridge, AB T1K 3M4, Canada. Offers accounting (MScM); addictions counseling (M Sc); agricultural biotechnology (M Sc); agricultural studies (M Sc, MA); anthropology (MA); archaeology (MA); art (MA, MFA); biochemistry (M Sc); biological sciences (M Sc); biomolecular science (PhD); biosystems and biodiversity (PhD); Canadian studies (MA); chemistry (M Sc); computer science (M Sc); computer science and geographical information science (M Sc); counseling psychology (M Ed); dramatic arts (MA); earth, space, and physical science (PhD); economics (MA); educational leadership (M Ed); English (MA); environmental science (M Sc); evolution and behavior (PhD); exercise science (M Sc); finance (MScM); French (MA); French/German (MA); French/Spanish (MA); general education (M Ed); general management (MScM); geography (M Sc, MA); German (MA); health science (M Sc); history (MA); human resource management and labour relations (MScM); individualized multidisciplinary (M Sc, MA); information systems (MScM); international management (MScM); kinesiology (M Sc, MA); management (M Sc, MA); marketing (MScM); mathematics (M Sc); music (M Mus, MA); Native American studies (MA); neuroscience (M Sc, PhD); new media (MA); nursing (M Sc); philosophy (MA); physics (M Sc); policy and strategy (MScM); political science (MA); psychology (M Sc, MA); religious studies (MA); social sciences (MA); sociology (MA); theatre and dramatic arts (MFA); theoretical and computational science (PhD); urban and regional studies (MA); women's studies (MA). Part-time and evening/weekend programs available. *Degree requirements:* For doctorate, comprehensive exam, thesis/dissertation. *Entrance requirements:* For master's, GMAT (M Sc in management), bachelor's degree in related field, minimum GPA of 3.0 during previous 20 graded semester courses, 2 years teaching or related experience (M Ed); for doctorate, master's degree, minimum graduate GPA of 3.5. Additional exam requirements/recommendations for international students: Required—TOEFL. *Faculty research:* Movement and brain plasticity, gibberellin physiology, photosynthesis, carbon cycling, molecular properties of main-group ring components.

University of Louisiana at Lafayette, College of Liberal Arts, Department of History and Geography, Lafayette, LA 70504. Offers history (MA). Part-time programs available. *Degree requirements:* For master's, one foreign language, thesis or alternative. *Entrance requirements:* For master's, GRE General Test, minimum GPA of 2.75. Additional exam requirements/recommendations for international students: Required—TOEFL (minimum score 550 paper-based; 213 computer-based). Electronic applications accepted.

University of Louisiana at Monroe, Graduate School, College of Arts and Sciences, Department of History, Monroe, LA 71209-0001. Offers MA. Part-time and evening/weekend programs available. *Faculty:* 8 full-time (2 women). *Students:* 11 full-time (4 women), 4 part-time (2 women); includes 1 Black or African American, non-Hispanic/Latino. Average age 37. In 2010, 8 master's awarded. *Degree requirements:* For master's, thesis (for some programs). *Entrance requirements:* For master's, GRE General Test, minimum undergraduate GPA of 2.5. Additional exam requirements/recommendations for international students: Required—TOEFL (minimum score 500 paper-based; 173 computer-based; 61 iBT). *Application deadline:* For fall admission, 8/24 priority date for domestic students, 7/1 for international students; for winter admission, 12/14 priority date for domestic students; for spring admission, 1/19 for domestic students, 11/1 for international students. Applications are processed on a rolling basis. Application fee: $20 ($30 for international students). Electronic applications accepted. *Expenses:* Tuition, state resident: full-time $2991; part-time $197 per credit hour. Tuition, nonresident: full-time $2991; part-time $197 per credit hour. International tuition: $10,288 full-time. *Financial support:* In 2010–11, 7 research assistantships with full tuition reimbursements (averaging $3,200 per year) were awarded; career-related internships or fieldwork, Federal Work-Study, and unspecified assistantships also available. Financial award application deadline: 4/1; financial award applicants required to submit FAFSA. *Faculty research:* Early Louisiana settlements, Soviet history, Louisiana *Tigers* in Civil War, Anglo-American relations, U. S./east European relations. *Unit head:* Dr. Ralph W. Brown, Department Head, 318-342-1402, E-mail: rbrown@ulm.edu. *Application contact:* Dr. Ralph W. Brown, Department Head, 318-342-1402, E-mail: rbrown@ulm.edu.

University of Louisville, Graduate School, College of Arts and Sciences, Department of History, Louisville, KY 40292-0001. Offers history (MA); public history (Certificate). Part-time and evening/weekend programs available. *Faculty:* 17 full-time (4 women). *Students:* 17 full-time (6 women), 12 part-time (3 women); includes 1 Black or African American, non-Hispanic/Latino; 1 American Indian or Alaska Native, non-Hispanic/Latino. Average age 29. 22 applicants, 68% accepted, 9 enrolled. In 2010, 6 master's awarded. *Degree requirements:* For master's, variable foreign language requirement, comprehensive exam (for some programs), thesis (for some programs). *Entrance requirements:* For master's, GRE General Test. Additional exam requirements/recommendations for international students: Required—TOEFL. *Application deadline:* For fall admission, 5/15 for domestic students, 5/1 for international students; for spring admission, 12/1 for domestic students, 11/1 for international students. Applications are processed on a rolling basis. Application fee: $50. Electronic applications accepted. *Expenses:* Tuition, state resident: full-time $9144; part-time $508 per credit hour. Tuition, nonresident: full-time $19,026; part-time $1057 per credit hour. Tuition and fees vary according to program and reciprocity agreements. *Financial support:* In 2010–11, 2 students received support, including 2 teaching assistantships (averaging $12,000 per year). Financial award applicants required to submit FAFSA. *Faculty research:* United States, British Empire, twentieth century women's history, Latin America, African diaspora. *Unit head:* Dr. Tracy Elaine K'Meyer, Chair, 502-852-6817, Fax: 502-852-0770, E-mail: tracyk@louisville.edu. *Application contact:* Libby Leggett, Director, Graduate Admissions, 502-852-3101, Fax: 502-852-6536, E-mail: gradadm@louisville.edu.

University of Maine, Graduate School, College of Liberal Arts and Sciences, Department of History, Orono, ME 04469. Offers American studies (MA, PhD); Canadian studies (MA, PhD); East Asian (MA); environmental (MA); European (MA); technology (MA). *Faculty:* 11 full-time (1 woman), 2 part-time/adjunct (1 woman). *Students:* 24 full-time (8 women), 35 part-time (13 women); includes 4 minority (2 American Indian or Alaska Native, non-Hispanic/Latino; 2 Hispanic/Latino). Average age 38. 43 applicants, 40% accepted, 15 enrolled. In 2010, 5 master's, 3 doctorates awarded. Terminal master's awarded for partial completion of doctoral program. *Degree requirements:* For master's, variable foreign language requirement, thesis optional; for doctorate, one foreign language, thesis/dissertation. *Entrance requirements:* For master's and doctorate, GRE General Test. Additional exam requirements/recommendations for international students: Required—TOEFL. *Application deadline:* For fall admission, 2/1 priority date for domestic students. Applications are processed on a rolling basis. Application fee: $65. Electronic applications accepted. *Expenses:* Tuition, state resident: full-time $400. Tuition, nonresident: full-time $1050. *Financial support:* In 2010–11, 9 teaching assistantships with tuition reimbursements (averaging $12,790 per year) were awarded; career-related internships or fieldwork, Federal Work-Study, and tuition waivers (full and partial) also available. Support available to part-time students. Financial award application deadline: 3/1. *Faculty research:* Canadian labor and working classes; American social, cultural, and urban history. *Unit head:* Dr. Nathan Godfried, Chair, 207-581-1923, Fax: 207-581-1817. *Application contact:*

Scott G. Delcourt, Associate Dean of the Graduate School, 207-581-3291, Fax: 207-581-3232, E-mail: graduate@maine.edu.

The University of Manchester, School of Arts, Histories and Cultures, Manchester, United Kingdom. Offers anthropology, media and performance (PhD); applied theatre professional (PhD); archaeology (PhD); art history and visual studies (PhD); arts management and cultural policy (PhD); classics and ancient history (PhD); composition (PhD); creative writing (PhD); drama (PhD); economic and social history (PhD); electroacoustic composition (PhD); English and American studies (PhD); history (PhD); humanitarianism and conflict response (PhD); museology (PhD); music (PhD); musicology (PhD); religions and theology (PhD).

University of Manitoba, Faculty of Graduate Studies, Faculty of Arts, Department of History, Winnipeg, MB R3T 2N2, Canada. Offers archival studies (MA); history (MA, PhD). MA offered jointly with The University of Winnipeg. *Degree requirements:* For master's, thesis; for doctorate, one foreign language, thesis/dissertation.

University of Maryland, Baltimore County, Graduate School, College of Arts, Humanities and Social Sciences, Department of History, Baltimore, MD 21250. Offers historical studies (MA). Part-time and evening/weekend programs available. *Faculty:* 16 full-time (10 women), 9 part-time/adjunct (1 woman). *Students:* 23 full-time (15 women), 42 part-time (25 women); includes 5 Black or African American, non-Hispanic/Latino; 6 Asian, non-Hispanic/Latino; 1 Hispanic/Latino. Average age 33. 38 applicants, 61% accepted, 15 enrolled. In 2010, 11 master's awarded. *Degree requirements:* For master's, thesis. *Entrance requirements:* For master's, GRE General Test, minimum GPA of 3.0. Additional exam requirements/recommendations for international students: Required—TOEFL. *Application deadline:* For fall admission, 3/10 priority date for domestic students, 1/1 for international students; for spring admission, 11/1 priority date for domestic students, 5/1 for international students. Application fee: $50. Electronic applications accepted. *Financial support:* In 2010–11, 11 students received support, including 1 research assistantship with full tuition reimbursement available (averaging $11,324 per year), 9 teaching assistantships with full and partial tuition reimbursements available (averaging $11,324 per year); career-related internships or fieldwork, health care benefits, tuition waivers (partial), and unspecified assistantships also available. Financial award application deadline: 3/10; financial award applicants required to submit FAFSA. *Faculty research:* Archival administration, historical editing, U. S. history, European history, Asian History. Total annual research expenditures: $50,000. *Unit head:* Dr. Anne Sarah Rubin, Graduate Program Directory, 410-455-1661, Fax: 410-455-1045, E-mail: arubin@umbc.edu. *Application contact:* Carla S. Ison, Administrative Assistant, 410-455-2049, Fax: 410-455-1045, E-mail: ison@umbc.edu.

University of Maryland, College Park, Academic Affairs, College of Arts and Humanities, Department of History, College Park, MD 20742. Offers MA, PhD. *Faculty:* 66 full-time (28 women), 7 part-time/adjunct (4 women). *Students:* 99 full-time (30 women), 23 part-time (8 women); includes 13 minority (6 Black or African American, non-Hispanic/Latino; 2 Asian, non-Hispanic/Latino; 4 Hispanic/Latino; 1 Two or more races, non-Hispanic/Latino), 8 international. 259 applicants, 22% accepted, 19 enrolled. In 2010, 17 master's, 9 doctorates awarded. *Degree requirements:* For master's, comprehensive exam, thesis optional; for doctorate, one foreign language, thesis/dissertation, oral and written exams. *Entrance requirements:* For master's, GRE General Test, minimum GPA of 3.25, writing sample, 3 letters of recommendation; for doctorate, GRE General Test, minimum GPA of 3.5. Additional exam requirements/recommendations for international students: Required—TOEFL. *Application deadline:* For fall admission, 12/15 for domestic and international students. Applications are processed on a rolling basis. Application fee: $75. Electronic applications accepted. *Expenses:* Tuition, state resident: part-time $471 per credit hour. Tuition, nonresident: part-time $1016 per credit hour. Required fees: $337 per term. *Financial support:* In 2010–11, 6 fellowships with full and partial tuition reimbursements (averaging $16,199 per year), 9 research assistantships (averaging $16,933 per year), 50 teaching assistantships (averaging $16,881 per year) were awarded; career-related internships or fieldwork, Federal Work-Study, and scholarships/grants also available. Support available to part-time students. Financial award applicants required to submit FAFSA. *Faculty research:* Ancient, British, East Asian, Latin American, and diplomatic history; papers of Samuel Gompers; Freedman and Southern Society; Caesarea excavations; Folger Institute. Total annual research expenditures: $428,726. *Unit head:* Dr. Richard N. Price, Chair, 301-405-4260, Fax: 301-314-9652, E-mail: rnp@umd.edu. *Application contact:* Director, Graduate Admissions and Records, 301-405-0376, Fax: 301-314-9305.

University of Maryland, College Park, Academic Affairs, Program in History, Library, and Information Services, College Park, MD 20742. Offers MA/MLS. *Students:* 16 full-time (13 women), 4 part-time (all women); includes 1 minority (Hispanic/Latino). 51 applicants, 39% accepted, 11 enrolled. *Entrance requirements:* Additional exam requirements/recommendations for international students: Required—TOEFL. *Application deadline:* For fall admission, 12/15 for domestic and international students. Applications are processed on a rolling basis. Application fee: $75. Electronic applications accepted. *Expenses:* Tuition, state resident: part-time $471 per credit hour. Tuition, nonresident: part-time $1016 per credit hour. Required fees: $337 per term. *Financial support:* In 2010–11, 6 teaching assistantships (averaging $16,773 per year) were awarded; fellowships, research assistantships also available. Financial award applicants required to submit FAFSA. *Unit head:* Dr. Diane Barlow, Associate Dean, 301-405-2042, Fax: 301-314-9145, E-mail: dbarlow@umd.edu. *Application contact:* Dr. Charles A. Caramello, Dean of Graduate School, 301-405-0358, Fax: 301-314-9305.

University of Massachusetts Amherst, Graduate School, College of Humanities and Fine Arts, Department of History, Amherst, MA 01003. Offers ancient history (MA); British Empire history (MA); European (medieval and modern) history (MA, PhD); Islamic history (MA); Latin American history (MA, PhD); modern global history (MA); public history (MA); science and technology history (MA); U. S. history (MA, PhD). Part-time programs available. *Faculty:* 38 full-time (17 women). *Students:* 38 full-time (20 women), 29 part-time (16 women); includes 6 minority (1 Black or African American, non-Hispanic/Latino; 1 American Indian or Alaska Native, non-Hispanic/Latino; 1 Asian, non-Hispanic/Latino; 3 Hispanic/Latino), 3 international. Average age 32. 165 applicants, 32% accepted, 22 enrolled. In 2010, 10 master's, 6 doctorates awarded. Terminal master's awarded for partial completion of doctoral program. *Degree requirements:* For master's, one foreign language, thesis or alternative; for doctorate, one foreign language, comprehensive exam, thesis/dissertation. *Entrance requirements:* For master's and doctorate, GRE General Test, writing sample. Additional exam requirements/recommendations for international students: Required—TOEFL (minimum score 550 paper-based; 213 computer-based; 80 iBT), IELTS (minimum score 6.5). *Application deadline:* For fall admission, 1/2 for domestic and international students. Applications are processed on a rolling basis. Application fee: $50 ($65 for international students). Electronic applications accepted. *Expenses:* Tuition, state resident: full-time $2640. Required fees: $8282. One-time fee: $357 full-time. *Financial support:* In 2010–11, 1 fellowship with full tuition reimbursement (averaging $14,661 per year), 4 research assistantships with full tuition reimbursements (averaging $4,089 per year), 39 teaching assistantships with full tuition reimbursements (averaging $12,153 per year) were awarded; career-related internships or fieldwork, Federal Work-Study, scholarships/grants, traineeships, health care benefits, tuition waivers (full), and unspecified assistantships also available. Support available to part-time students. Financial award application deadline: 1/2; financial award applicants required to submit FAFSA. *Faculty research:* Ancient and medieval history; global and comparative history; public history; history of science, technology, medicine and the environment; history of women, gender, sexuality and family. *Unit head:* Dr. Marla Miller, Graduate Program Director, 413-545-6791, Fax: 413-545-6137. *Application contact:* Jean M. Ames, Supervisor of Admissions, 413-545-0722, Fax: 413-577-0010, E-mail: gradadm@grad.umass.edu.

University of Massachusetts Boston, Office of Graduate Studies, College of Liberal Arts, Program in History, Boston, MA 02125-3393. Offers archival methods (MA); historical archaeology (MA); history (MA). Part-time and evening/weekend programs available. *Degree requirements:* For master's, thesis, oral exam. *Entrance requirements:* For master's, minimum GPA of 2.75. *Faculty research:* European intellectual history, American labor and social history in 19th century, colonial American Revolution, Afro-American Cold War.

University of Memphis, Graduate School, College of Arts and Sciences, Department of History, Memphis, TN 38152. Offers ancient Egyptian history (MA, PhD). Postbaccalaureate distance learning degree programs offered (no on-campus study). *Faculty:* 22 full-time (6 women), 3 part-time/adjunct (0 women). *Students:* 53 full-time (31 women), 59 part-time (30 women); includes 17 Black or African American, non-Hispanic/Latino; 4 Two or more races, non-Hispanic/Latino, 2 international. Average age 36. 50 applicants, 90% accepted, 15 enrolled. In 2010, 10 master's, 7 doctorates awarded. *Degree requirements:* For master's, comprehensive exam, thesis optional; for doctorate, one foreign language, comprehensive exam, thesis/dissertation, 60 credits plus 12 dissertation credits, 2 research seminars. *Entrance requirements:* For master's, GRE General Test or MAT, 18 undergraduate hours of course work in history with minimum GPA of 3.0, 2 letters of recommendation, writing sample; for doctorate, GRE General Test, GRE Subject Test, MA in history or related field, three letters of recommendation, writing sample, statement of purpose. Additional exam requirements/recommendations for international students: Required—TOEFL. *Application deadline:* For fall admission, 1/15 for domestic students; for spring admission, 9/15 for domestic students. Applications are processed on a rolling basis. Application fee: $35 ($60 for international students). Electronic applications accepted. *Financial support:* In 2010–11, 54 students received support; research assistantships with full tuition reimbursements available, teaching assistantships with full tuition reimbursements available, career-related internships or fieldwork, Federal Work-Study, scholarships/grants, and unspecified assistantships available. Financial award application deadline: 2/15; financial award applicants required to submit FAFSA. *Faculty research:* African/African-American history; U. S. history; ancient Egyptian history; modern European history; women, gender, and family studies. *Unit head:* Dr. Janann Sherman, Chairman, 901-678-2515, Fax: 901-678-2720, E-mail: sherman@memphis.edu. *Application contact:* Dr. James M. Blythe, Coordinator of Graduate Studies, 901-678-3381, Fax: 901-678-2720, E-mail: jmblythe@memphis.edu.

University of Miami, Graduate School, College of Arts and Sciences, Department of History, Coral Gables, FL 33124. Offers MA, PhD. Part-time programs available. Terminal master's awarded for partial completion of doctoral program. *Degree requirements:* For master's, one foreign language, comprehensive exam, thesis optional; for doctorate, one foreign language, comprehensive exam, thesis/dissertation. *Entrance requirements:* For master's and doctorate, GRE General Test, GRE Subject Test. Additional exam requirements/recommendations for international students: Required—TOEFL (minimum score 550 paper-based; 213 computer-based; 59 iBT). Electronic applications accepted. *Faculty research:* Latin American, European, U.S., and public history.

University of Michigan, Horace H. Rackham School of Graduate Studies, College of Literature, Science, and the Arts, Department of History, Ann Arbor, MI 48109. Offers PhD. *Degree requirements:* For doctorate, 2 foreign languages, thesis/dissertation, oral defense of dissertation, preliminary exam. *Entrance requirements:* For doctorate, GRE General Test, writing sample. Additional exam requirements/recommendations for international students: Required—TOEFL. Electronic applications accepted. *Expenses:* Tuition, state resident: full-time $17,784; part-time $1116 per credit hour. Tuition, nonresident: full-time $35,944; part-time $2125 per credit hour. International tuition: $35,994 full-time. Required fees: $95 per semester. Tuition and fees vary according to course load, degree level and program. *Faculty research:* Europe, Latin America, Africa, Asia, Middle East/Near East, United States, world/global, science/medicine/technology, and topical/thematic history.

University of Michigan, Horace H. Rackham School of Graduate Studies, College of Literature, Science, and the Arts, Department of Women's Studies, Ann Arbor, MI 48109. Offers English and women's studies (PhD); history and women's studies (PhD); lesbian, gay, bisexual, transgender, queer (LGBTQ) studies (Certificate); psychology and women's studies (PhD); sociology and women's studies (PhD); women's studies (Certificate). *Faculty:* 77 full-time (71 women). *Students:* 71 full-time (63 women); includes 6 Black or African American, non-Hispanic/Latino; 11 Asian, non-Hispanic/Latino; 7 Hispanic/Latino; 4 Two or more races, non-Hispanic/Latino. Average age 30. 101 applicants, 10% accepted, 9 enrolled. In 2010, 5 doctorates, 8 other advanced degrees awarded. *Degree requirements:* For doctorate, variable foreign language requirement, comprehensive exam (for some programs), thesis/dissertation. *Entrance requirements:* For doctorate, GRE General Test, previous undergraduate course work in women's studies; for Certificate, GRE General Test, previous course work in women's studies. Additional exam requirements/recommendations for international students: Required—TOEFL. *Application deadline:* For fall admission, 12/1 for domestic and international students. Application fee: $65 ($75 for international students). Electronic applications accepted. *Expenses:* Tuition, state resident: full-time $17,784; part-time $1116 per credit hour. Tuition, nonresident: full-time $35,944; part-time $2125 per credit hour. International tuition: $35,994 full-time. Required fees: $95 per semester. Tuition and fees vary according to course load, degree level and program. *Financial support:* In 2010–11, 39 students received support, including 21 fellowships with full tuition reimbursements available (averaging $16,800 per year), 18 teaching assistantships with full tuition reimbursements available (averaging $17,270 per year); career-related internships or fieldwork, institutionally sponsored loans, scholarships/grants, traineeships, health care benefits, and unspecified assistantships also available. *Faculty research:* Gender issues, LGBTQ studies, sexuality, women and science, global feminism. *Unit head:* Elizabeth R. Cole, Chair, Department of Women's Studies, Professor of Women's Studies, Professor of Afroamerican and African Studies, Professor of Psychology, 734-763-2047, Fax: 734-647-4943, E-mail: wsdgradInquiry@umich.edu. *Application contact:* Aimee Germain, Graduate Program Coordinator, 734-763-2047, Fax: 734-647-4943, E-mail: wsdgradinquiry@umich.edu.

University of Michigan, Horace H. Rackham School of Graduate Studies, College of Literature, Science, and the Arts, Doctoral Program in Anthropology and History, Ann Arbor, MI 48109. Offers PhD. *Degree requirements:* For doctorate, 2 foreign languages, thesis/dissertation, oral defense of dissertation, preliminary exam. *Entrance requirements:* For doctorate, GRE General Test, writing sample. Additional exam requirements/recommendations for international students: Required—TOEFL. Electronic applications accepted. *Expenses:* Tuition, state resident: full-time $17,784; part-time $1116 per credit hour. Tuition, nonresident: full-time $35,944; part-time $2125 per credit hour. International tuition: $35,994 full-time. Required fees: $95 per semester. Tuition and fees vary according to course load, degree level and program. *Faculty research:* Historical anthropology.

University of Michigan, Horace H. Rackham School of Graduate Studies, College of Literature, Science, and the Arts, Interdepartmental Program in Greek and Roman History, Ann Arbor, MI 48109. Offers PhD, Certificate. *Faculty:* 8 full-time (2 women), 13 part-time/adjunct (6 women). *Students:* 13 full-time (6 women), 2 international. Average age 27. 25 applicants, 8% accepted, 2 enrolled. *Degree requirements:* For doctorate, 4 foreign languages, comprehensive exam, thesis/dissertation, oral defense of dissertation, dissertation prospectus, preliminary exams. *Entrance requirements:* For doctorate, GRE, minimum of 2 years each of classical Greek and Latin. Additional exam requirements/recommendations for international students: Required—TOEFL (minimum score 560 paper-based; 220 computer-based). *Application deadline:* For fall admission, 12/15 for domestic and international students. Application fee: $65 ($75 for international students). Electronic applications accepted. *Expenses:* Tuition, state resident: full-time $17,784; part-time $1116 per credit hour. Tuition, nonresident: full-time $35,944; part-time $2125 per credit hour. International tuition: $35,994 full-time. Required fees: $95 per semester. Tuition and fees vary according to course load, degree level and program. *Financial support:* In 2010–11, 10 students received support, including 4 fellowships with full tuition reimbursements available (averaging $16,800 per year), 8 teaching assistantships with full tuition reimbursements available (averaging $16,694 per year); career-related internships or fieldwork, Federal Work-Study, institutionally sponsored loans, scholarships/grants, traineeships, health care benefits, tuition waivers (full), and unspecified assistantships also available. Financial award application deadline: 3/15. *Faculty research:* Greek history, Roman history. *Unit head:*

History

University of Michigan (continued)
Prof. Sara Forsdyke, Professor, 734-936-6098, Fax: 734-763-4959, E-mail: forsdyke@umich.edu. *Application contact:* Michelle M. Biggs, Graduate Coordinator, 734-647-2330, Fax: 734-763-4959, E-mail: mbiggs@umich.edu.

University of Minnesota, Twin Cities Campus, Graduate School, College of Liberal Arts, Department of Classical and Near Eastern Studies, Minneapolis, MN 55455-0213. Offers ancient and medieval art and archaeology (MA, PhD); classics (MA, PhD); Greek (MA, PhD); Latin (MA, PhD); religions in antiquity (MA). Part-time programs available. Terminal master's awarded for partial completion of doctoral program. *Degree requirements:* For master's, 2 foreign languages, comprehensive exam, thesis or alternative; for doctorate, variable foreign language requirement, comprehensive exam, thesis/dissertation. *Entrance requirements:* For master's and doctorate, GRE, 3 letters of recommendation, writing sample, copies of transcripts, personal statement. Additional exam requirements/recommendations for international students: Required—TOEFL. Electronic applications accepted. *Faculty research:* Greek and Latin literature, religions in antiquity, ancient Near East.

University of Minnesota, Twin Cities Campus, Graduate School, College of Liberal Arts, Department of History, Minneapolis, MN 55455-0213. Offers MA, PhD. *Degree requirements:* For master's, one foreign language, comprehensive exam, thesis or alternative; for doctorate, 2 foreign languages, comprehensive exam, thesis/dissertation. *Entrance requirements:* For doctorate, GRE General Test, writing sample, letters of recommendation. Additional exam requirements/recommendations for international students: Required—TOEFL (minimum score 550 paper-based; 213 computer-based). Electronic applications accepted. *Faculty research:* Early and modern United States; medieval, early modern and modern Europe; Africa; East and South Asia; Latin America.

University of Mississippi, Graduate School, College of Liberal Arts, Department of History, Oxford, University, MS 38677. Offers MA, PhD. *Students:* 49 full-time (19 women), 11 part-time (6 women); includes 7 Black or African American, non-Hispanic/Latino; 1 Hispanic/Latino. In 2010, 4 master's, 6 doctorates awarded. *Degree requirements:* For doctorate, thesis/dissertation. *Entrance requirements:* For master's, GRE General Test, GRE Subject Test, minimum GPA of 3.0; for doctorate, GRE General Test, GRE Subject Test. Additional exam requirements/recommendations for international students: Required—TOEFL. *Application deadline:* For fall admission, 1/15 for domestic students; for spring admission, 11/1 for domestic students. Applications are processed on a rolling basis. Application fee: $25. Electronic applications accepted. *Financial support:* Scholarships/grants available. Financial award application deadline: 3/1; financial award applicants required to submit FAFSA. *Unit head:* Dr. Joseph P. Ward, Chair, 662-915-7148, Fax: 662-915-7033, E-mail: history@olemiss.edu. *Application contact:* Dr. Joseph P. Ward, Chair, 662-915-7148, Fax: 662-915-7033, E-mail: history@olemiss.edu.

University of Missouri, Graduate School, College of Arts and Sciences, Department of History, Columbia, MO 65211. Offers MA, PhD. *Faculty:* 16 full-time (5 women), 2 part-time/adjunct (0 women). *Students:* 47 full-time (15 women), 5 part-time (2 women); includes 3 minority (all Black or African American, non-Hispanic/Latino). Average age 32. 62 applicants, 18% accepted, 9 enrolled. In 2010, 7 master's, 2 doctorates awarded. *Degree requirements:* For master's, thesis; for doctorate, 2 foreign languages, comprehensive exam, thesis/dissertation. *Entrance requirements:* For master's, GRE General Test, minimum GPA of 3.0 in last 60 hours, 3.3 in undergraduate history courses; at least 18 hours in history; BA or BS; for doctorate, GRE General Test, minimum GPA of 3.0; MA in history (strongly preferred); master's thesis or research seminar paper. Additional exam requirements/recommendations for international students: Required—TOEFL (minimum score 500 paper-based; 173 computer-based; 61 iBT). *Application deadline:* For fall admission, 1/14 priority date for domestic students. Applications are processed on a rolling basis. Application fee: $45 ($60 for international students). Electronic applications accepted. *Financial support:* In 2010–11, 6 fellowships with full tuition reimbursements, 1 research assistantship with full tuition reimbursement, 28 teaching assistantships with full tuition reimbursements were awarded; institutionally sponsored loans, health care benefits, and unspecified assistantships also available. *Faculty research:* U. S. history, African-American history, Ancient history, Latin American history, Asian history. *Unit head:* Dr. Russell Zguta, Department Chair, 573-882-9458, E-mail: zgutar@missouri.edu. *Application contact:* Nancy Taube, Graduate Studies Administrator, 573-882-9461, E-mail: tauben@missouri.edu.

University of Missouri–Kansas City, College of Arts and Sciences, Department of History, Kansas City, MO 64110-2499. Offers MA, PhD. PhD (interdisciplinary) offered through the School of Graduate Studies. Part-time programs available. *Faculty:* 17 full-time (8 women), 3 part-time/adjunct (1 woman). *Students:* 9 full-time (4 women), 25 part-time (15 women); includes 3 minority (1 Black or African American, non-Hispanic/Latino; 1 Asian, non-Hispanic/Latino; 1 Hispanic/Latino). Average age 35. 35 applicants, 49% accepted, 13 enrolled. In 2010, 4 master's awarded. *Degree requirements:* For master's, thesis optional; for doctorate, one foreign language, thesis/dissertation. *Entrance requirements:* For master's, GRE General Test, minimum GPA of 3.0, 2 writing samples, 3 letters of recommendation; for doctorate, GRE General Test. Additional exam requirements/recommendations for international students: Required—TOEFL (minimum score 550 paper-based; 213 computer-based; 80 iBT). *Application deadline:* For fall admission, 3/15 for domestic and international students; for spring admission, 10/1 priority date for domestic students, 10/1 for international students. Applications are processed on a rolling basis. Application fee: $45 ($50 for international students). Electronic applications accepted. *Expenses:* Tuition, state resident: full-time $5522.40; part-time $306.80 per credit hour. Tuition, nonresident: full-time $7128; part-time $792 per credit hour. Required fees: $261.15 per term. *Financial support:* In 2010–11, 10 teaching assistantships with partial tuition reimbursements (averaging $11,022 per year) were awarded; career-related internships or fieldwork, Federal Work-Study, institutionally sponsored loans, and tuition waivers (full and partial) also available. Support available to part-time students. Financial award application deadline: 3/1; financial award applicants required to submit FAFSA. *Faculty research:* U. S. history, Europe, women and gender, religious studies, history of science. *Unit head:* Dr. Gary Ebersole, Chair, 816-235-1631, Fax: 816-235-5723, E-mail: ebersoleg@umkc.edu. *Application contact:* Dr. Andrew Bergerson, Principal Graduate Advisor, 816-235-1631, Fax: 816-235-5723, E-mail: bergersona@umkc.edu.

The University of Montana, Graduate School, College of Arts and Sciences, Department of History, Missoula, MT 59812-0002. Offers MA, PhD. *Degree requirements:* For master's, thesis or additional course work/professional paper. *Entrance requirements:* For master's, GRE General Test. Additional exam requirements/recommendations for international students: Required—TOEFL.

University of Nebraska at Kearney, College of Graduate Study, College of Natural and Social Sciences, Department of History, Kearney, NE 68849-0001. Offers history (MA). Part-time and evening/weekend programs available. *Degree requirements:* For master's, thesis optional. *Entrance requirements:* For master's, GRE General Test, writing sample. Additional exam requirements/recommendations for international students: Required—TOEFL (minimum score 550 paper-based; 213 computer-based). Electronic applications accepted. *Faculty research:* Military history, labor history/labor and the law, state formation and nationalism, American intellectual history, Civil War and Reconstruction.

University of Nebraska at Omaha, Graduate Studies, College of Arts and Sciences, Department of History, Omaha, NE 68182. Offers MA. Part-time and evening/weekend programs available. *Faculty:* 13 full-time (4 women). *Students:* 4 full-time (1 woman), 53 part-time (25 women); includes 1 minority (American Indian or Alaska Native, non-Hispanic/Latino). Average age 31. 14 applicants, 79% accepted, 8 enrolled. In 2010, 12 master's awarded. *Degree requirements:* For master's, comprehensive exam, thesis (for some programs). *Entrance requirements:* For master's, minimum GPA of 3.0, 21 hours of course work in history, 2 letters of recommendation. Additional exam requirements/recommendations for international students: Required—TOEFL (minimum score 500 paper-based; 173 computer-based; 61 iBT). *Application deadline:* For fall admission, 7/1 priority date for domestic students; for spring admission, 12/1 priority date for domestic students. Applications are processed on a rolling basis. Application fee: $45. Electronic applications accepted. *Financial support:* In 2010–11, 33 students received support; fellowships, research assistantships with tuition reimbursements available, teaching assistantships with tuition reimbursements available, Federal Work-Study, institutionally sponsored loans, scholarships/grants, tuition waivers (partial), and unspecified assistantships available. Support available to part-time students. Financial award application deadline: 3/1; financial award applicants required to submit FAFSA. *Unit head:* Dr. Sharon Wood, Chairperson, 402-554-2593. *Application contact:* Dr. John Grigg, Student Contact, 402-554-2593.

University of Nebraska–Lincoln, Graduate College, College of Arts and Sciences, Department of History, Lincoln, NE 68588. Offers MA, PhD. *Degree requirements:* For master's, thesis optional; for doctorate, one foreign language, comprehensive exam, thesis/dissertation. *Entrance requirements:* For master's and doctorate, GRE General Test, GRE Subject Test, writing sample. Additional exam requirements/recommendations for international students: Required—TOEFL (minimum score 575 paper-based; 233 computer-based). Electronic applications accepted. *Faculty research:* Military history, indigenous peoples, German history, American history (American West society and culture).

University of Nevada, Las Vegas, Graduate College, College of Liberal Arts, Department of History, Las Vegas, NV 89154-5020. Offers MA, PhD. Part-time programs available. *Faculty:* 25 full-time (8 women). *Students:* 27 full-time (14 women), 40 part-time (21 women); includes 23 minority (3 Hispanic/Latino; 1 Native Hawaiian or other Pacific Islander, non-Hispanic/Latino; 19 Two or more races, non-Hispanic/Latino), 3 international. Average age 38. 59 applicants, 46% accepted, 14 enrolled. In 2010, 11 master's, 4 doctorates awarded. *Degree requirements:* For master's, one foreign language, comprehensive exam (for some programs), thesis (for some programs); for doctorate, 2 foreign languages, comprehensive exam, thesis/dissertation. *Entrance requirements:* For master's, minimum overall GPA of 3.0, 3.3 in history courses; for doctorate, GRE General Test, minimum overall GPA of 3.0, 3.3 in history courses. Additional exam requirements/recommendations for international students: Required—TOEFL (minimum score 550 paper-based; 213 computer-based; 80 iBT), IELTS (minimum score 7). *Application deadline:* For fall admission, 6/1 priority date for domestic and international students; for spring admission, 11/1 priority date for domestic and international students. Applications are processed on a rolling basis. Application fee: $60 ($95 for international students). Electronic applications accepted. *Expenses:* Tuition, area resident: Part-time $239.50 per credit. Tuition, state resident: part-time $239.50 per credit. Tuition, nonresident: part-time $503 per credit. Required fees: $108 per semester. Tuition and fees vary according to course load, program and reciprocity agreements. *Financial support:* In 2010–11, 24 students received support, including 1 fellowship with full tuition reimbursement available (averaging $20,000 per year), 23 teaching assistantships with partial tuition reimbursements available (averaging $11,739 per year); institutionally sponsored loans, scholarships/grants, health care benefits, and unspecified assistantships also available. Financial award application deadline: 3/1. *Faculty research:* The Western United States, American cultural and intellectual, European cultural and intellectual, American race and gender, global religion. Total annual research expenditures: $68,915. *Unit head:* Dr. David Wrobel, Chair/Professor, 702-895-0810, Fax: 702-895-1782, E-mail: david.wrobel@unlv.edu. *Application contact:* Graduate College Admissions Evaluator, 702-895-3320, Fax: 702-895-4180, E-mail: gradcollege@unlv.edu.

University of Nevada, Reno, Graduate School, College of Liberal Arts, Department of History, Reno, NV 89557. Offers MA, PhD. Terminal master's awarded for partial completion of doctoral program. *Degree requirements:* For master's, thesis optional; for doctorate, one foreign language, thesis/dissertation. *Entrance requirements:* For master's, GRE General Test, minimum GPA of 2.75; for doctorate, GRE General Test, minimum GPA of 3.0. Additional exam requirements/recommendations for international students: Required—TOEFL (minimum score 500 paper-based; 173 computer-based; 61 iBT), IELTS (minimum score 6). Electronic applications accepted. *Expenses:* Tuition, state resident: full-time $2219; part-time $246 per credit. Tuition, nonresident: part-time $510 per credit. International tuition: $9009 full-time. Required fees: $59 per term. One-time fee: $101. Tuition and fees vary according to course load. *Faculty research:* History of medicine, science, environmental history, western America, social/cultural history.

University of New Brunswick Fredericton, School of Graduate Studies, Faculty of Arts, Department of History, Fredericton, NB E3B 5A3, Canada. Offers MA, PhD. Part-time programs available. *Faculty:* 15 full-time (5 women), 3 part-time/adjunct (1 woman). *Students:* 47 full-time (17 women), 11 part-time (6 women). In 2010, 9 master's, 7 doctorates awarded. *Degree requirements:* For master's, thesis; for doctorate, thesis/dissertation. *Entrance requirements:* For master's, minimum GPA of 3.0, resume, writing sample and/or statement of research interests, honours degree in history or equivalent; for doctorate, minimum GPA of 3.0, statement of research interests, writing sample, master's degree in history. Additional exam requirements/recommendations for international students: Required—TOEFL. *Application deadline:* For fall admission, 3/1 priority date for domestic students. Applications are processed on a rolling basis. Application fee: $50 Canadian dollars. *Expenses:* Tuition, area resident: Full-time $3708; part-time $927 per term. International tuition: $6300 full-time. Required fees: $50 per term. *Financial support:* In 2010–11, 25 research assistantships, 22 teaching assistantships were awarded; fellowships, scholarships/grants also available. *Faculty research:* Canadian/military international/colonial American/early modern history. *Unit head:* Dr. Sean Kennedy, Director of Graduate Studies, 506-447-3415, Fax: 506-453-5068, E-mail: skennedy@unb.ca. *Application contact:* Elizabeth Adshade, Graduate Secretary, 506-458-7471, Fax: 506-453-5068, E-mail: eliz@unb.ca.

University of New Hampshire, Graduate School, College of Liberal Arts, Department of History, Durham, NH 03824. Offers history (MA, PhD); museum studies (MA). Part-time programs available. *Faculty:* 24 full-time (13 women). *Students:* 25 full-time (10 women), 15 part-time (8 women); includes 1 minority (Asian, non-Hispanic/Latino), 1 international. Average age 36. 94 applicants, 24% accepted, 6 enrolled. In 2010, 7 master's, 5 doctorates awarded. *Degree requirements:* For master's, thesis or alternative; for doctorate, 2 foreign languages, thesis/dissertation. *Entrance requirements:* For master's and doctorate, GRE General Test. Additional exam requirements/recommendations for international students: Required—TOEFL (minimum score 550 paper-based; 213 computer-based; 80 iBT). *Application deadline:* For fall admission, 6/1 priority date for domestic students, 4/15 for international students; for spring admission, 12/1 for domestic students. Applications are processed on a rolling basis. Application fee: $65. Electronic applications accepted. *Financial support:* In 2010–11, 16 students received support, including 16 fellowships, 1 teaching assistantship; research assistantships, career-related internships or fieldwork, Federal Work-Study, scholarships/grants, and tuition waivers (full and partial) also available. Support available to part-time students. Financial award application deadline: 2/15. *Unit head:* Dr. Jan Golinski, Chairperson, 603-862-1764. *Application contact:* Susan Kilday, Administrative Assistant, 603-862-1764, E-mail: history.grad@unh.edu.

University of New Mexico, Graduate School, College of Arts and Sciences, Department of History, Albuquerque, NM 87131-2039. Offers MA, PhD. Part-time programs available. *Faculty:* 26 full-time (14 women), 9 part-time/adjunct (4 women). *Students:* 66 full-time (22 women), 43 part-time (21 women); includes 6 American Indian or Alaska Native, non-Hispanic/Latino; 15 Hispanic/Latino, 2 international. Average age 36. 87 applicants, 48% accepted, 17 enrolled. In 2010, 7 master's, 5 doctorates awarded. Terminal master's awarded for partial completion of doctoral program. *Degree requirements:* For master's, one foreign language, comprehensive exam, thesis optional; for doctorate, one foreign language, comprehensive exam, thesis/dissertation. *Entrance requirements:* For master's, GRE, BA in history or equivalent; for doctorate, MA in history or equivalent. Additional exam requirements/recommendations for international students: Required—TOEFL. *Application deadline:* For fall admission, 1/15 for domestic students; for spring admission, 10/15 for domestic students. Application fee: $50. Electronic applications accepted. *Expenses:* Tuition, state resident: full-time $5991; part-time $251 per credit hour. Tuition, nonresident: full-time $14,405; part-time $800.20 per credit hour.

Tuition and fees vary according to course level, course load, program and reciprocity agreements. *Financial support:* In 2010–11, 81 students received support, including 14 fellowships (averaging $8,282 per year), 25 research assistantships (averaging $7,555 per year), 10 teaching assistantships with full tuition reimbursements available (averaging $8,390 per year); institutionally sponsored loans, scholarships/grants, and health care benefits also available. Financial award application deadline: 1/15; financial award applicants required to submit FAFSA. *Faculty research:* American Western history, Asian history, environmental history, European history, frontiers and borderlands, gender and sexuality, Latin American history, politics and economy, race and ethnicity, religion, United States history, war and society. *Unit head:* Dr. Charlie Steen, Chair, 505-277-2451, Fax: 505-277-6023, E-mail: csteen@unm.edu. *Application contact:* Yolanda Martinez, Department Administrator, 505-277-2451, Fax: 505-277-6023, E-mail: history@unm.edu.

University of New Orleans, Graduate School, College of Liberal Arts, Department of History, New Orleans, LA 70148. Offers history (MA). *Degree requirements:* For master's, one foreign language, thesis (for some programs). *Entrance requirements:* For master's, GRE General Test. Additional exam requirements/recommendations for international students: Required—TOEFL (minimum score 550 paper-based; 213 computer-based; 79 iBT). Electronic applications accepted. *Faculty research:* Recent U.S. political, military, urban, regional, and legal history.

University of North Alabama, College of Arts and Sciences, Department of History and Political Science, Florence, AL 35632-0001. Offers MA. *Faculty:* 1 full-time (0 women), 7 part-time/adjunct (1 woman). *Students:* 8 full-time (1 woman), 10 part-time (5 women). Average age 36. In 2010, 4 master's awarded. *Expenses:* Tuition, state resident: full-time $5472; part-time $228 per credit hour. Tuition, nonresident: full-time $10,944; part-time $456 per credit hour. Required fees: $986. Tuition and fees vary according to course load. *Unit head:* Dr. Christopher Maynard, Chair, 256-765-4306, E-mail: camaynard@una.edu. *Application contact:* Kim Mauldin, Director of Admissions, 256-765-4608, Fax: 256-765-4960, E-mail: komauldin@una.edu.

The University of North Carolina at Chapel Hill, Graduate School, College of Arts and Sciences, Department of History, Chapel Hill, NC 27599. Offers MA, PhD. Terminal master's awarded for partial completion of doctoral program. *Degree requirements:* For master's, one foreign language, thesis, oral thesis defense; for doctorate, 2 foreign languages, comprehensive exam, thesis/dissertation, oral dissertation defense. *Entrance requirements:* For master's and doctorate, GRE General Test, minimum GPA of 3.0. Electronic applications accepted.

The University of North Carolina at Charlotte, Graduate School, College of Arts and Sciences, Department of History, Charlotte, NC 28223-0001. Offers MA. Part-time and evening/weekend programs available. *Faculty:* 21 full-time (7 women). *Students:* 21 full-time (10 women), 33 part-time (15 women); includes 9 minority (6 Black or African American, non-Hispanic/Latino; 2 American Indian or Alaska Native, non-Hispanic/Latino; 1 Hispanic/Latino). Average age 30. 38 applicants, 71% accepted, 15 enrolled. In 2010, 11 master's awarded. *Degree requirements:* For master's, thesis or comprehensive exam. *Entrance requirements:* For master's, GRE General Test, minimum GPA of 3.0 in undergraduate major, 2.75 overall. Additional exam requirements/recommendations for international students: Required—TOEFL (minimum score 557 paper-based; 220 computer-based; 83 iBT). *Application deadline:* For fall admission, 7/1 for domestic students, 5/1 for international students; for spring admission, 11/1 for domestic students, 10/1 for international students. Applications are processed on a rolling basis. Application fee: $55. Electronic applications accepted. *Expenses:* Tuition, state resident: full-time $3464. Tuition, nonresident: full-time $14,297. Required fees: $2094. Tuition and fees vary according to course load. *Financial support:* In 2010–11, 12 students received support, including 12 teaching assistantships (averaging $8,667 per year); career-related internships or fieldwork, Federal Work-Study, institutionally sponsored loans, scholarships/grants, and unspecified assistantships also available. Support available to part-time students. Financial award application deadline: 4/1; financial award applicants required to submit FAFSA. *Faculty research:* Southern United States history; Latin American history; race and gender history; urban history; history of science, medicine, technology. Total annual research expenditures: $2,972. *Unit head:* Dr. Jurgen Buchenau, Chair, 704-687-4646, Fax: 704-687-3218, E-mail: jbuchenau@uncc.edu. *Application contact:* Kathy B. Giddings, Director of Graduate Admissions, 704-687-5530, Fax: 704-687-3279, E-mail: gradadm@uncc.edu.

The University of North Carolina at Greensboro, Graduate School, College of Arts and Sciences, Department of History, Greensboro, NC 27412-5001. Offers historic preservation (Certificate); history (MA); museum studies (Certificate); U.S. history (PhD). Part-time programs available. *Entrance requirements:* For master's, GRE General Test. Additional exam requirements/recommendations for international students: Required—TOEFL. Electronic applications accepted. *Faculty research:* Simultaneous discovery in science, progressive social reform, Robert Mayer.

The University of North Carolina Wilmington, College of Arts and Sciences, Department of History, Wilmington, NC 28403-3297. Offers MA. Part-time programs available. *Faculty:* 20 full-time (8 women). *Students:* 22 full-time (12 women), 24 part-time (16 women); includes 1 Black or African American, non-Hispanic/Latino. Average age 29. 23 applicants, 65% accepted, 10 enrolled. In 2010, 9 master's awarded. *Degree requirements:* For master's, comprehensive exam, thesis. *Entrance requirements:* For master's, GRE General Test, minimum B average in undergraduate major. Additional exam requirements/recommendations for international students: Required—TOEFL (minimum score 550 paper-based; 217 computer-based; 79 iBT), IELTS (minimum score 6.5). *Application deadline:* For fall admission, 6/1 for domestic students. Applications are processed on a rolling basis. Application fee: $60. *Financial support:* In 2010–11, 14 teaching assistantships with full and partial tuition reimbursements (averaging $9,500 per year) were awarded; career-related internships or fieldwork and Federal Work-Study also available. Support available to part-time students. Financial award application deadline: 3/15. *Unit head:* Dr. Paul Townend, Chair, 910-962-3307, Fax: 910-962-7011, E-mail: townendp@uncw.edu. *Application contact:* Dr. David La Vere, Graduate Coordinator, 910-962-3315, E-mail: lavered@uncw.edu.

University of North Dakota, Graduate School, College of Arts and Sciences, Department of History, Grand Forks, ND 58202. Offers MA, DA, PhD. Part-time programs available. *Faculty:* 11 full-time (4 women), 7 part-time/adjunct (2 women). *Students:* 18 full-time (9 women), 17 part-time (8 women); includes 2 minority (both American Indian or Alaska Native, non-Hispanic/Latino), 1 international. Average age 32. 18 applicants, 56% accepted, 9 enrolled. In 2010, 4 master's, 1 doctorate awarded. *Degree requirements:* For master's, comprehensive exam (for some programs), thesis (for some programs), final exam; for doctorate, comprehensive exam, thesis/dissertation, final exam. *Entrance requirements:* For master's, minimum GPA of 3.0; for doctorate, minimum GPA of 3.5. Additional exam requirements/recommendations for international students: Required—TOEFL (minimum score 550 paper-based; 213 computer-based; 79 iBT), IELTS (minimum score 6.5). *Application deadline:* For fall admission, 8/1 priority date for domestic students, 5/1 priority date for international students; for spring admission, 12/1 priority date for domestic students, 9/1 priority date for international students. Applications are processed on a rolling basis. Application fee: $35. Electronic applications accepted. *Expenses:* Tuition, state resident: full-time $5857; part-time $306.74 per credit. Tuition, nonresident: full-time $15,666; part-time $729.77 per credit. Required fees: $53.42 per credit. Tuition and fees vary according to course load, program and reciprocity agreements. *Financial support:* In 2010–11, 19 students received support, including 18 teaching assistantships with full and partial tuition reimbursements available (averaging $6,626 per year); fellowships with full and partial tuition reimbursements available, research assistantships with full and partial tuition reimbursements available, career-related internships or fieldwork, Federal Work-Study, institutionally sponsored loans, scholarships/grants, health care benefits, tuition waivers (full and partial), and unspecified assistantships also available. Support available to part-time students. Financial award application deadline: 3/15; financial award applicants required to submit FAFSA. *Faculty research:* U. S. history, Latin America, Russia, modern Europe, women studies. *Unit head:* Dr. Hans P. Broedel, Graduate Director, 701-777-2693, Fax: 701-777-4636, E-mail: history_und@mail.und.nodak.edu. *Application contact:* Matt Anderson, Admissions Specialist, 701-777-2947, Fax: 701-777-3619, E-mail: matthew.anderson@gradschool.und.edu.

University of Northern British Columbia, Office of Graduate Studies, Prince George, BC V2N 4Z9, Canada. Offers business administration (Diploma); community health science (M Sc); disability management (MA); education (M Ed); first nations studies (MA); gender studies (MA); history (MA); interdisciplinary studies (MA); international studies (MA); mathematical, computer and physical sciences (M Sc); natural resources and environmental studies (M Sc, MA, MNRES, PhD); political science (MA); psychology (M Sc, PhD); social work (MSW). Part-time and evening/weekend programs available. Postbaccalaureate distance learning degree programs offered (no on-campus study). *Degree requirements:* For master's, thesis; for doctorate, thesis/dissertation. *Entrance requirements:* For master's, GRE, minimum B average in undergraduate course work; for doctorate, candidacy exam, minimum A average in graduate course work.

University of Northern Colorado, Graduate School, College of Humanities and Social Sciences, Program in History, Greeley, CO 80639. Offers MA. Part-time programs available. *Faculty:* 6 full-time (2 women). *Students:* 3 full-time (0 women), 13 part-time (6 women); includes 1 minority (Hispanic/Latino). Average age 33. 10 applicants, 60% accepted, 3 enrolled. In 2010, 2 master's awarded. *Degree requirements:* For master's, comprehensive exam, thesis or alternative. *Entrance requirements:* For master's, GRE, 3 letters of recommendation. *Application deadline:* Applications are processed on a rolling basis. Application fee: $50 ($60 for international students). Electronic applications accepted. *Expenses:* Tuition, state resident: full-time $6199; part-time $344 per credit hour. Tuition, nonresident: full-time $14,834; part-time $824 per credit hour. Required fees: $1091; $60.60 per credit hour. Tuition and fees vary according to course load, degree level and program. *Financial support:* In 2010–11, 2 teaching assistantships (averaging $8,547 per year) were awarded. Financial award application deadline: 3/1; financial award applicants required to submit FAFSA. *Unit head:* Dr. Michael Welsh, Program Coordinator, 970-351-2905, Fax: 970-351-2199. *Application contact:* Linda Sisson, Graduate Student Admission Coordinator, 970-351-1807, Fax: 970-351-2371, E-mail: linda.sisson@unco.edu.

University of Northern Colorado, Graduate School, College of Humanities and Social Sciences, School of History, Philosophy and Political Science, Greeley, CO 80639. Offers history (MA). Part-time programs available. *Faculty:* 6 full-time (2 women). *Students:* 3 full-time (0 women), 13 part-time (6 women); includes 1 minority (Hispanic/Latino). Average age 33. 10 applicants, 60% accepted, 3 enrolled. In 2010, 2 master's awarded. *Degree requirements:* For master's, comprehensive exam, thesis or alternative. *Entrance requirements:* For master's, GRE, 3 letters of reference. *Application deadline:* Applications are processed on a rolling basis. Application fee: $50 ($60 for international students). Electronic applications accepted. *Expenses:* Tuition, state resident: full-time $6199; part-time $344 per credit hour. Tuition, nonresident: full-time $14,834; part-time $824 per credit hour. Required fees: $1091; $60.60 per credit hour. Tuition and fees vary according to course load, degree level and program. *Financial support:* In 2010–11, 2 teaching assistantships (averaging $8,547 per year) were awarded; fellowships, research assistantships, unspecified assistantships also available. Financial award application deadline: 3/1; financial award applicants required to submit FAFSA. *Unit head:* Dr. Barry Rothaus, Director, 970-351-2905, Fax: 970-351-2199. *Application contact:* Linda Sisson, Graduate Student Admission Coordinator, 970-351-1807, Fax: 970-351-2371, E-mail: linda.sisson@unco.edu.

University of Northern Iowa, Graduate College, College of Social and Behavioral Sciences, Department of History, Cedar Falls, IA 50614. Offers history (MA); public history (MA). Part-time programs available. *Students:* 14 full-time (6 women), 12 part-time (5 women); includes 3 minority (1 American Indian or Alaska Native, non-Hispanic/Latino; 1 Asian, non-Hispanic/Latino; 1 Hispanic/Latino). 22 applicants, 59% accepted, 6 enrolled. In 2010, 5 master's awarded. *Degree requirements:* For master's, comprehensive exam (for some programs), thesis or alternative. *Entrance requirements:* For master's, minimum GPA of 3.2. Additional exam requirements/recommendations for international students: Required—TOEFL (minimum score 500 paper-based; 180 computer-based; 61 iBT). *Application deadline:* For fall admission, 8/1 priority date for domestic students. Applications are processed on a rolling basis. Application fee: $50 ($70 for international students). Electronic applications accepted. *Financial support:* Career-related internships or fieldwork, Federal Work-Study, scholarships/grants, and tuition waivers (full and partial) available. Support available to part-time students. Financial award application deadline: 2/1. *Unit head:* Dr. Robert Martin, Head, 319-273-2097, Fax: 319-273-5846, E-mail: robert.martin@uni.edu. *Application contact:* Laurie S. Russell, Record Analyst, 319-273-2623, Fax: 319-273-2885, E-mail: laurie.russell@uni.edu.

University of North Florida, College of Arts and Sciences, Department of History, Jacksonville, FL 32224. Offers European history (MA); U. S. history (MA). Part-time programs available. *Faculty:* 14 full-time (5 women). *Students:* 17 full-time (9 women), 24 part-time (15 women); includes 1 American Indian or Alaska Native, non-Hispanic/Latino; 1 Asian, non-Hispanic/Latino; 2 Hispanic/Latino. Average age 35. 19 applicants, 74% accepted, 12 enrolled. In 2010, 12 master's awarded. *Degree requirements:* For master's, comprehensive exam (for some programs), thesis optional. *Entrance requirements:* For master's, GRE General Test, 3 letters of recommendation, minimum GPA of 3.0 in last 60 hours of course work. Additional exam requirements/recommendations for international students: Required—TOEFL (minimum score 500 paper-based; 173 computer-based; 61 iBT). *Application deadline:* For fall admission, 7/1 priority date for domestic students, 5/1 for international students; for spring admission, 11/1 priority date for domestic students, 10/1 for international students. Applications are processed on a rolling basis. Application fee: $30. Electronic applications accepted. *Expenses:* Tuition, state resident: full-time $7646.40; part-time $318.60 per credit hour. Tuition, nonresident: full-time $23,502; part-time $979.24 per credit hour. Required fees: $1208.88; $50.37 per credit hour. Tuition and fees vary according to course load and program. *Financial support:* In 2010–11, 12 students received support, including 10 teaching assistantships (averaging $4,868 per year); career-related internships or fieldwork, Federal Work-Study, scholarships/grants, tuition waivers (partial), and unspecified assistantships also available. Financial award application deadline: 4/1; financial award applicants required to submit FAFSA. *Unit head:* Dr. Dale Clifford, 904-620-2886, Fax: 904-620-1018, E-mail: clifford@unf.edu. *Application contact:* Lillith Richardson, Assistant Director, The Graduate School, 904-620-1360, Fax: 904-620-1362, E-mail: graduateschool@unf.edu.

University of North Texas, Toulouse Graduate School, College of Arts and Sciences, Department of History, Denton, TX 76203. Offers MA, MS, PhD. Part-time programs available. Terminal master's awarded for partial completion of doctoral program. *Degree requirements:* For master's, one foreign language, comprehensive exam, thesis or alternative; for doctorate, 2 foreign languages, comprehensive exam, thesis/dissertation. *Entrance requirements:* For master's and doctorate, GRE General Test. Additional exam requirements/recommendations for international students: Recommended—TOEFL (minimum score 550 paper-based; 213 computer-based). *Expenses:* Tuition, state resident: full-time $4298; part-time $239 per credit hour. Tuition, nonresident: full-time $10,782; part-time $549 per credit hour. Required fees: $1292; $270 per credit hour. *Financial support:* Fellowships with tuition reimbursements, teaching assistantships, career-related internships or fieldwork, Federal Work-Study, and institutionally sponsored loans available. Financial award application deadline: 2/15. *Faculty research:* U. S. local, Texas, women's, European and military history. *Application contact:* Undergraduate and Graduate Advisor, 940-565-4208, Fax: 940-369-8838, E-mail: krj@unt.edu.

University of Notre Dame, Graduate School, College of Arts and Letters, Division of Humanities, Department of History, Notre Dame, IN 46556. Offers MA, PhD. *Degree requirements:* For doctorate, one foreign language, thesis/dissertation, candidacy exam. *Entrance requirements:* For doctorate, GRE General Test. Additional exam requirements/recommendations for international students: Required—TOEFL (minimum score 600 paper-based; 250 computer-based;

History

University of Notre Dame (continued)

80 iBT). Electronic applications accepted. *Faculty research:* U. S., modern European and medieval history; history of European and U. S. religions; U. S. and European intellectual and cultural history; history of Central Europe.

University of Oklahoma, College of Arts and Sciences, Department of History, Norman, OK 73019. Offers MA, PhD. Part-time and evening/weekend programs available. *Faculty:* 36 full-time (9 women), 2 part-time/adjunct (0 women). *Students:* 34 full-time (12 women), 18 part-time (7 women); includes 6 minority (1 American Indian or Alaska Native, non-Hispanic/Latino; 2 Asian, non-Hispanic/Latino; 2 Hispanic/Latino; 1 Two or more races, non-Hispanic/Latino). Average age 33. 46 applicants, 33% accepted, 8 enrolled. In 2010, 8 master's, 7 doctorates awarded. Terminal master's awarded for partial completion of doctoral program. *Degree requirements:* For master's, one foreign language, thesis or alternative, oral and written exams; for doctorate, 2 foreign languages, thesis/dissertation, oral and written exams. *Entrance requirements:* For master's, GRE General Test, BA with 20 hours in history; for doctorate, GRE General Test. Additional exam requirements/recommendations for international students: Required—TOEFL (minimum score 550 paper-based; 213 computer-based; 79 iBT). *Application deadline:* For fall admission, 4/1 for domestic and international students; for spring admission, 11/1 for domestic students, 9/1 for international students. Applications are processed on a rolling basis. Application fee: $40 ($90 for international students). Electronic applications accepted. *Expenses:* Tuition, state resident: full-time $3893; part-time $162.20 per credit hour. Tuition, nonresident: full-time $14,167; part-time $590.30 per credit hour. Required fees: $2523; $94.60 per credit hour. Tuition and fees vary according to course load and degree level. *Financial support:* In 2010–11, 46 students received support, including 6 fellowships with full tuition reimbursements available (averaging $5,000 per year), 4 research assistantships with partial tuition reimbursements available (averaging $12,228 per year), 27 teaching assistantships with partial tuition reimbursements available (averaging $14,284 per year); health care benefits and unspecified assistantships also available. Financial award application deadline: 1/31. *Faculty research:* Environmental, Western, Latin American and Native American history. *Unit head:* Dr. Robert L. Griswold, Chair, 405-325-6002, Fax: 405-325-4503, E-mail: rgriswold@ou.edu. *Application contact:* Dr. Terry Rugeley, Professor, 405-625-6002, Fax: 405-325-4503, E-mail: trugeley@ou.edu.

University of Oregon, Graduate School, College of Arts and Sciences, Department of History, Eugene, OR 97403. Offers MA, PhD. *Degree requirements:* For master's, one foreign language, thesis or alternative, written exam; for doctorate, 2 foreign languages, thesis/dissertation, oral and written exams. *Entrance requirements:* For master's and doctorate, GRE General Test, minimum GPA of 3.0. Additional exam requirements/recommendations for international students: Required—TOEFL. *Faculty research:* U.S., European, East and Southeast Asian, Latin American, and ancient history.

University of Ottawa, Faculty of Graduate and Postdoctoral Studies, Faculty of Arts, Department of History, Ottawa, ON K1N 6N5, Canada. Offers MA, PhD. *Degree requirements:* For master's, 2 foreign languages, thesis or alternative; for doctorate, 2 foreign languages, thesis/dissertation, oral exam. *Entrance requirements:* For master's, honors degree or equivalent, minimum B average; for doctorate, master's degree, minimum B+ average. Electronic applications accepted. *Faculty research:* Canadian history.

University of Pennsylvania, School of Arts and Sciences, Graduate Group in Ancient History, Philadelphia, PA 19104. Offers AM, PhD. *Faculty:* 26 full-time (10 women), 6 part-time/adjunct (0 women). *Students:* 12 full-time (3 women); includes 1 Asian, non-Hispanic/Latino. 38 applicants, 5% accepted, 1 enrolled. In 2010, 2 master's, 5 doctorates awarded. *Degree requirements:* For doctorate, 4 foreign languages, thesis/dissertation. *Application deadline:* For fall admission, 12/1 priority date for domestic students. Application fee: $70. Electronic applications accepted. *Expenses:* Tuition: Full-time $25,660; part-time $4758 per course. Required fees: $2152; $270 per course. Tuition and fees vary according to course load, degree level and program. *Financial support:* Institutionally sponsored loans, scholarships/grants, traineeships, health care benefits, and unspecified assistantships available. Financial award application deadline: 12/15. *Unit head:* Cynthia Damon, Graduate Chair in Ancient History, 215-573-0250, E-mail: cdamon@sas.upenn.edu. *Application contact:* Cynthia Damon, Graduate Chair in Ancient History, 215-573-0250, E-mail: cdamon@sas.upenn.edu.

University of Pennsylvania, School of Arts and Sciences, Graduate Group in History, Philadelphia, PA 19104. Offers AM, PhD. *Faculty:* 64 full-time (29 women), 10 part-time/adjunct (2 women). *Students:* 97 full-time (50 women), 10 part-time (3 women); includes 9 Black or African American, non-Hispanic/Latino; 1 Asian, non-Hispanic/Latino; 2 Hispanic/Latino, 21 international. 433 applicants, 6% accepted, 15 enrolled. In 2010, 12 master's, 15 doctorates awarded. Terminal master's awarded for partial completion of doctoral program. *Degree requirements:* For master's, thesis; for doctorate, one foreign language, thesis/dissertation. *Entrance requirements:* For master's and doctorate, GRE General Test. Additional exam requirements/recommendations for international students: Required—TOEFL. *Application deadline:* For fall admission, 12/1 priority date for domestic students. Application fee: $70. Electronic applications accepted. *Expenses:* Tuition: Full-time $25,660; part-time $4758 per course. Required fees: $2152; $270 per course. Tuition and fees vary according to course load, degree level and program. *Financial support:* Institutionally sponsored loans, scholarships/grants, traineeships, health care benefits, and unspecified assistantships available. Financial award application deadline: 12/15. *Unit head:* Kathy Peiss, Department Chair, History, 215-898-2746, E-mail: peiss@sas.upenn.edu. *Application contact:* Kathy Peiss, Department Chair, History, 215-898-2746, E-mail: peiss@sas.upenn.edu.

University of Pittsburgh, School of Arts and Sciences, Department of History, Pittsburgh, PA 15260. Offers MA, PhD. *Faculty:* 24 full-time (6 women), 10 part-time/adjunct (2 women). *Students:* 38 full-time (17 women); includes 2 Asian, non-Hispanic/Latino; 7 Hispanic/Latino; 1 Two or more races, non-Hispanic/Latino. 109 applicants, 15% accepted, 8 enrolled. In 2010, 4 master's, 2 doctorates awarded. Terminal master's awarded for partial completion of doctoral program. *Degree requirements:* For master's, one foreign language, oral exam, 1 seminar paper; for doctorate, 2 foreign languages, comprehensive exam, thesis/dissertation. *Entrance requirements:* For master's and doctorate, GRE General Test. Additional exam requirements/recommendations for international students: Required—TOEFL (minimum score 88 computer-based). *Application deadline:* For fall admission, 1/15 for domestic and international students. Application fee: $50. Electronic applications accepted. *Expenses:* Tuition, state resident: full-time $17,304; part-time $701 per credit. Tuition, nonresident: full-time $29,554; part-time $1210 per credit. Required fees: $740; $214 per term. Tuition and fees vary according to program. *Financial support:* In 2010–11, 5 fellowships with tuition reimbursements (averaging $14,000 per year), 24 teaching assistantships with tuition reimbursements (averaging $14,777 per year) were awarded; Federal Work-Study, scholarships/grants, and tuition waivers (full and partial) also available. Financial award application deadline: 1/15. *Faculty research:* Western Europe, Latin America, Russia, Eastern Europe, U. S., East Asia. *Unit head:* Dr. George Reid Andrews, Chairman, 412-648-7452, Fax: 412-648-9074. *Application contact:* Molly Estes, Graduate Secretary, 412-648-7454, Fax: 412-648-9074, E-mail: wid2@pitt.edu.

University of Puerto Rico, Río Piedras, College of Humanities, Department of History, San Juan, PR 00931-3300. Offers Caribbean history (PhD); history (MA); Puerto Rican history (PhD). Part-time programs available. *Degree requirements:* For master's, one foreign language, comprehensive exam, thesis; for doctorate, one foreign language, comprehensive exam, thesis/dissertation. *Entrance requirements:* For master's, PAEG or GRE, interview, minimum GPA of 3.0, 2 letters of recommendation; for doctorate, PAEG or GRE, interview, master's degree, minimum GPA of 3.0, 2 letters of recommendation.

University of Regina, Faculty of Graduate Studies and Research, Faculty of Arts, Department of History, Regina, SK S4S 0A2, Canada. Offers MA. Part-time programs available. *Faculty:* 13 full-time (4 women), 2 part-time/adjunct (both women). *Students:* 3 full-time (2 women). 3 applicants, 100% accepted. In 2010, 2 master's awarded. *Degree requirements:* For master's, thesis. *Entrance requirements:* Additional exam requirements/recommendations for international students: Required—TOEFL (minimum score 580 paper-based; 80 iBT). *Application deadline:* Applications are processed on a rolling basis. Application fee: $100. Electronic applications accepted. Tuition and fees charges are reported in Canadian dollars. *Expenses:* Tuition, area resident: Full-time $3244.50 Canadian dollars; part-time $180.25 Canadian dollars per credit hour. International tuition: $4744.50 Canadian dollars full-time. Required fees: $494 Canadian dollars; $115.25 Canadian dollars per credit hour. $115.25 Canadian dollars per semester. Tuition and fees vary according to program. *Financial support:* In 2010–11, 2 fellowships (averaging $18,000 per year), 5 teaching assistantships (averaging $6,759 per year) were awarded; research assistantships, scholarships/grants also available. Financial award application deadline: 6/15. *Faculty research:* Canadian, European, Asian, British, and the Americas history. *Unit head:* Dr. Ian Germani, Head, 306-585-4213, Fax: 306-585-4827, E-mail: ian.germani@uregina.ca. *Application contact:* Dr. Philip Charrier, Graduate Program Coordinator, 306-585-4215, Fax: 306-585-4827, E-mail: philip.charrier@uregina.ca.

University of Rhode Island, Graduate School, College of Arts and Sciences, Department of History, Kingston, RI 02881. Offers MA, MA/PhD, MLIS/MA. Part-time programs available. *Faculty:* 13 full-time (9 women), 3 part-time/adjunct (0 women). *Students:* 8 full-time (5 women), 7 part-time (2 women); includes 1 minority (Two or more races, non-Hispanic/Latino). In 2010, 4 master's awarded. *Degree requirements:* For master's, comprehensive exam (for some programs), thesis optional. *Entrance requirements:* For master's, GRE, 2 letters of recommendation. Additional exam requirements/recommendations for international students: Required—TOEFL (minimum score 550 paper-based; 213 computer-based). *Application deadline:* For fall admission, 7/15 for domestic students, 2/1 for international students; for spring admission, 11/15 for domestic students, 7/15 for international students. Application fee: $65. Electronic applications accepted. *Expenses:* Tuition, state resident: full-time $9588; part-time $533 per credit hour. Tuition, nonresident: full-time $22,968; part-time $1276 per credit hour. Required fees: $1282; $68 per semester. Tuition and fees vary according to program. *Financial support:* In 2010–11, 3 teaching assistantships with full tuition reimbursements (averaging $13,894 per year) were awarded. Financial award application deadline: 2/1; financial award applicants required to submit FAFSA. Total annual research expenditures: $33,094. *Unit head:* Dr. Marie J. Schwartz, Chair, 401-874-4090, Fax: 401-874-2595, E-mail: schwartz@uri.edu. *Application contact:* Dr. Evelyn Sterne, Director of Graduate Studies, 401-874-4074, Fax: 401-874-2595, E-mail: sterne@mail.uri.edu.

University of Rochester, School of Arts and Sciences, Department of History, Rochester, NY 14627. Offers MA, PhD. Terminal master's awarded for partial completion of doctoral program. *Degree requirements:* For master's, one foreign language, thesis or alternative; for doctorate, 2 foreign languages, thesis/dissertation, comprehensive oral exam, qualifying exam. *Entrance requirements:* For master's and doctorate, GRE General Test, sample of written work. Additional exam requirements/recommendations for international students: Required—TOEFL.

University of San Diego, College of Arts and Sciences, Department of History, San Diego, CA 92110-2492. Offers MA. Part-time and evening/weekend programs available. *Faculty:* 3 full-time (1 woman), 1 part-time/adjunct (0 women). *Students:* 9 full-time (4 women), 22 part-time (10 women); includes 1 Black or African American, non-Hispanic/Latino; 1 Asian, non-Hispanic/Latino; 2 Hispanic/Latino. Average age 31. 26 applicants, 85% accepted, 10 enrolled. In 2010, 5 master's awarded. *Degree requirements:* For master's, thesis. *Entrance requirements:* For master's, GRE General Test, minimum GPA of 3.0. Additional exam requirements/recommendations for international students: Required—TOEFL (minimum score 580 paper-based; 237 computer-based; 83 iBT), TWE. *Application deadline:* For fall admission, 8/31 for domestic and international students; for spring admission, 11/15 for domestic and international students. Applications are processed on a rolling basis. Application fee: $45. Electronic applications accepted. *Expenses:* Tuition: Full-time $21,744; part-time $1208 per unit. Required fees: $224. Full-time tuition and fees vary according to course load and degree level. *Financial support:* In 2010–11, 16 students received support. Career-related internships or fieldwork, Federal Work-Study, institutionally sponsored loans, and unspecified assistantships available. Support available to part-time students. Financial award application deadline: 4/1; financial award applicants required to submit FAFSA. *Faculty research:* History of the American West, history of California, history of Mexico and Latin America, public history, environmental history. *Unit head:* Dr. Michael Gonzalez, Graduate Program Director, 619-260-4756, Fax: 619-260-2272, E-mail: michaelg@sandiego.edu. *Application contact:* Stephen Pultz, Director of Admissions and Enrollment, 619-260-4506, Fax: 619-260-6836, E-mail: admissions@sandiego.edu.

University of Saskatchewan, College of Graduate Studies and Research, College of Arts and Sciences, Department of History, Saskatoon, SK S7N 5A2, Canada. Offers MA, PhD. Part-time programs available. *Degree requirements:* For master's, thesis; for doctorate, comprehensive exam (for some programs), thesis/dissertation. *Entrance requirements:* Additional exam requirements/recommendations for international students: Required—TOEFL (minimum score 80 iBT); Recommended—IELTS (minimum score 6.5). Electronic applications accepted.

The University of Scranton, College of Graduate and Continuing Education, Department of History, Scranton, PA 18510. Offers MA. Part-time and evening/weekend programs available. *Faculty:* 11 full-time (2 women). *Students:* 4 full-time (2 women), 4 part-time (1 woman). Average age 31. In 2010, 5 master's awarded. *Degree requirements:* For master's, comprehensive exam, thesis (for some programs), capstone experience. *Entrance requirements:* For master's, minimum GPA of 2.75. Additional exam requirements/recommendations for international students: Required—TOEFL (minimum score 500 paper-based; 173 computer-based), IELTS (minimum score 5.5). *Application deadline:* Applications are processed on a rolling basis. Application fee: $0. *Financial support:* In 2010–11, 1 student received support, including 1 teaching assistantship with full tuition reimbursement available (averaging $6,600 per year); fellowships, career-related internships or fieldwork, Federal Work-Study, and unspecified assistantships also available. Support available to part-time students. Financial award application deadline: 3/1. *Faculty research:* American, European, Latin American, Russian, and Chinese history. *Unit head:* Dr. Robert W. Shaffern, Director, 570-941-4360, Fax: 570-941-7625. *Application contact:* Joseph M. Roback, Director of Admissions, 570-941-4385, Fax: 570-941-5928, E-mail: robackj2@scranton.edu.

University of South Africa, College of Human Sciences, Pretoria, South Africa. Offers adult education (M Ed); African languages (MA, PhD); African politics (MA, PhD); Afrikaans (MA, PhD); ancient history (MA, PhD); ancient Near Eastern studies (MA, PhD); anthropology (MA, PhD); applied linguistics (MA); Arabic (MA, PhD); archaeology (MA); art history (MA); Biblical archaeology (MA); Biblical studies (M Th, D Th, PhD); Christian spirituality (M Th, D Th); church history (M Th, D Th); classical studies (MA, PhD); clinical psychology (MA); communication (MA, PhD); comparative education (M Ed, Ed D); consulting psychology (D Admin, D Com, PhD); curriculum studies (M Ed, Ed D); development studies (M Admin, MA, D Admin, PhD); didactics (M Ed, Ed D); education (M Tech); education management (M Ed, Ed D); educational psychology (M Ed); English (MA); environmental education (M Ed); French (MA, PhD); German (MA, PhD); Greek (MA); guidance and counseling (M Ed); health studies (MA, PhD), including health sciences education (MA), health services management (MA), medical and surgical nursing science (critical care general) (MA), midwifery and neonatal nursing science (MA), trauma and emergency care (MA); history (MA, PhD); history of education (Ed D); inclusive education (M Ed, Ed D); information and communications technology policy and regulation (MA); information science (MA, MIS, PhD); international politics (MA, PhD); Islamic studies (MA, PhD); Italian (MA, PhD); Judaica (MA, PhD); linguistics (MA, PhD); mathematical education (M Ed); mathematics education (MA); missiology (M Th, D Th); modern Hebrew (MA, PhD); musicology (MA, MMus, D Mus, PhD); natural science education (M Ed); New Testament (M Th, D Th); Old Testament (D Th); pastoral therapy (M Th, D Th); philosophy (MA); philosophy of education (M Ed, Ed D); politics (MA, PhD); Portuguese (MA, PhD); practical theology (M Th, D Th); psychology (MA, MS, PhD); psychology of education (M Ed, Ed D); public health (MA); religious studies (MA, D Th, PhD); Romance languages (MA); Russian (MA, PhD); Semitic languages (MA, PhD); social behavior studies in HIV/AIDS (MA);

social science (mental health) (MA); social science in development studies (MA); social science in psychology (MA); social science in social work (MA); social science in sociology (MA); social work (MSW, DSW, PhD); socio-education (M Ed, Ed D); sociolinguistics (MA); sociology (MA, PhD); Spanish (MA, PhD); systematic theology (M Th, D Th); TESOL (teaching English to speakers of other languages) (MA); theological ethics (M Th, D Th); theory of literature (MA, PhD); urban ministries (D Th); urban ministry (M Th).

University of South Alabama, Graduate School, College of Arts and Sciences, Department of History, Mobile, AL 36688. Offers MA. Part-time and evening/weekend programs available. *Faculty:* 13 full-time (5 women). *Students:* 14 full-time (7 women), 9 part-time (3 women); includes 3 minority (all Black or African American, non-Hispanic/Latino), 1 international. 17 applicants, 35% accepted, 4 enrolled. In 2010, 7 master's awarded. *Degree requirements:* For master's, one foreign language, comprehensive exam, thesis optional, 33 credit hours of graduate course work with minimum of 21 each at 500 level and in 2 distinct fields. *Entrance requirements:* For master's, GRE General Test, GRE Subject Test, 21 hours of course work in history, minimum GPA of 3.0. Additional exam requirements/recommendations for international students: Required—TOEFL. *Application deadline:* For fall admission, 8/1 priority date for domestic students, 6/15 priority date for international students; for spring admission, 12/15 priority date for domestic students, 11/1 priority date for international students. Applications are processed on a rolling basis. Application fee: $35. *Expenses:* Tuition, state resident: part-time $300 per credit hour. Tuition, nonresident: part-time $600 per credit hour. Required fees: $150 per semester. *Financial support:* Fellowships, research assistantships available. Support available to part-time students. Financial award application deadline: 4/1. *Unit head:* Dr. Clarence Mohr, Chair, 251-460-6210. *Application contact:* Dr. Martha Brazy, Graduate Coordinator, 251-460-6210.

University of South Carolina, The Graduate School, College of Arts and Sciences, Department of History, Columbia, SC 29208. Offers history (MA, PhD); public history (MA, Certificate), including archives (MA), historic preservation (MA), museum (MA), museum management (Certificate); MLIS/MA. IMA and MAT offered in cooperation with the College of Education. Part-time programs available. Terminal master's awarded for partial completion of doctoral program. *Degree requirements:* For master's, one foreign language, thesis; for doctorate, one foreign language, thesis/dissertation. *Entrance requirements:* For master's and doctorate, GRE General Test. Additional exam requirements/recommendations for international students: Required—TOEFL. Electronic applications accepted. *Faculty research:* U.S. history; European history; Latin American history; history of science and technology.

The University of South Dakota, Graduate School, College of Arts and Sciences, Department of History, Vermillion, SD 57069-2390. Offers MA, JD/MA. Part-time programs available. *Degree requirements:* For master's, thesis (for some programs). *Entrance requirements:* For master's, GRE General Test, minimum GPA of 2.7. Additional exam requirements/recommendations for international students: Required—TOEFL (minimum score 550 paper-based; 213 computer-based; 79 iBT). Electronic applications accepted.

University of Southern California, Graduate School, Dana and David Dornsife College of Letters, Arts and Sciences, Department of History, Los Angeles, CA 90089. Offers MA, PhD. *Faculty:* 28 full-time (15 women). *Students:* 57 full-time (31 women), 1 (woman) part-time; includes 14 minority (1 Black or African American, non-Hispanic/Latino; 2 Asian, non-Hispanic/Latino; 10 Hispanic/Latino; 1 Two or more races, non-Hispanic/Latino), 7 international. 115 applicants, 14% accepted, 6 enrolled. In 2010, 10 master's, 8 doctorates awarded. Terminal master's awarded for partial completion of doctoral program. *Degree requirements:* For master's, variable foreign language requirement, comprehensive exam (for some programs), thesis (for some programs), 28 semester units of acceptable coursework; for doctorate, 2 foreign languages, comprehensive exam, thesis/dissertation, 60 semester units of acceptable coursework. *Entrance requirements:* For master's, [no direct admission to master's program]; for doctorate, GRE General Test. *Application deadline:* For fall admission, 12/1 for domestic and international students. Application fee: $85. Electronic applications accepted. *Expenses:* Tuition: Full-time $31,240; part-time $1420 per unit. Required fees: $600. One-time fee: $35 full-time. Full-time tuition and fees vary according to degree level and program. *Financial support:* In 2010–11, 56 students received support, including 25 fellowships with full tuition reimbursements available (averaging $21,000 per year), 8 research assistantships with full tuition reimbursements available (averaging $19,800 per year), 23 teaching assistantships with full tuition reimbursements available (averaging $19,800 per year); scholarships/grants, health care benefits, and unspecified assistantships also available. Financial award application deadline: 12/1. *Faculty research:* U. S. North American and Latin American history, California and Western American history (including Borderlands), European history from the early Middle Ages to present, East Asian (Chinese, Japanese, Korean) history, early modern Atlantic world/world history. *Unit head:* Dr. Peter C. Mancall, Chair, 213-740-1657, Fax: 213-740-6999, E-mail: mancall@usc.edu. *Application contact:* Dr. Joseph A. Styles, Student Advisor, 213-740-1659, Fax: 213-740-6999, E-mail: styles@usc.edu.

University of Southern Mississippi, Graduate School, College of Arts and Letters, Department of History, Hattiesburg, MS 39406-0001. Offers MA, MS, PhD. Part-time programs available. *Faculty:* 18 full-time (6 women). *Students:* 30 full-time (9 women), 22 part-time (6 women), 1 international. Average age 33. 41 applicants, 44% accepted, 10 enrolled. In 2010, 9 master's, 2 doctorates awarded. *Degree requirements:* For master's, one foreign language, comprehensive exam, thesis (for some programs); for doctorate, 2 foreign languages, comprehensive exam, thesis/dissertation. *Entrance requirements:* For master's, GRE General Test, minimum GPA of 3.0 in field of study, 2.75 in last 2 years; for doctorate, GRE General Test, minimum GPA of 3.5. Additional exam requirements/recommendations for international students: Required—TOEFL, IELTS. *Application deadline:* For fall admission, 3/1 priority date for domestic students, 3/1 for international students. Applications are processed on a rolling basis. Application fee: $50. *Financial support:* In 2010–11, 1 fellowship with full tuition reimbursement (averaging $12,000 per year), 1 research assistantship with full tuition reimbursement (averaging $12,000 per year), 20 teaching assistantships with full tuition reimbursements (averaging $9,000 per year) were awarded; Federal Work-Study, institutionally sponsored loans, scholarships/grants, health care benefits, and unspecified assistantships also available. Financial award application deadline: 3/15; financial award applicants required to submit FAFSA. *Faculty research:* Civil War, civil rights, modern European history, war history. *Unit head:* Dr. Phyllis Jestice, Chair, 601-266-4333, Fax: 601-266-4334. *Application contact:* Dr. Kyle Zelner, Director of Graduate Studies, 601-266-4333, Fax: 601-266-4334, E-mail: graduatestudies@usm.edu.

University of South Florida, Graduate School, College of Arts and Sciences, Department of History, Tampa, FL 33620-9951. Offers MA, PhD. Part-time and evening/weekend programs available. *Faculty:* 11 full-time (4 women). *Students:* 23 full-time (10 women), 21 part-time (11 women); includes 2 Hispanic/Latino. Average age 35. 47 applicants, 43% accepted, 12 enrolled. In 2010, 18 master's awarded. *Degree requirements:* For master's, one foreign language, comprehensive exam, thesis optional; for doctorate, variable foreign language requirement, comprehensive exam, thesis/dissertation. *Entrance requirements:* For master's, GRE General Test (minimum score 500 verbal, 500 quantitative, 4.5 writing), minimum GPA of 3.0, 2 letters of recommendation, writing sample; for doctorate, GRE General Test (minimum score 500 verbal, 500 quantitative, 4.5 writing), minimum GPA of 3.0, MA in history or directly related field, writing sample, foreign language proficiency. Additional exam requirements/recommendations for international students: Required—TOEFL (minimum score 550 paper-based; 213 computer-based). *Application deadline:* For fall admission, 1/15 priority date for domestic students, 1/15 for international students. Applications are processed on a rolling basis. Application fee: $30. Electronic applications accepted. *Financial support:* In 2010–11, 16 teaching assistantships with tuition reimbursements (averaging $15,000 per year) were awarded; unspecified assistantships also available. Financial award application deadline: 1/15. *Faculty research:* U. S. history, European history, Latin American history, medieval history, ancient history. Total annual research expenditures: $192,884. *Unit head:* Dr. Fraser Ottanelli, Chairperson, 813-974-6209, Fax: 813-974-6228, E-mail: ottanelli@usf.edu. *Application contact:* Barbara Berglund, Program Director, 813-974-6225, Fax: 813-974-6228, E-mail: bberglun@usf.edu.

The University of Tennessee, Graduate School, College of Arts and Sciences, Department of History, Knoxville, TN 37996. Offers American history (PhD); European history (PhD); history (MA). Part-time programs available. *Degree requirements:* For master's, thesis or alternative; for doctorate, one foreign language, thesis/dissertation. *Entrance requirements:* For master's and doctorate, GRE General Test, minimum GPA of 2.7. Additional exam requirements/recommendations for international students: Required—TOEFL. Electronic applications accepted. *Expenses:* Tuition, state resident: full-time $7440; part-time $414 per credit hour. Tuition, nonresident: full-time $22,478; part-time $1250 per credit hour. Required fees: $922; $43 per credit hour. Tuition and fees vary according to program.

The University of Texas at Arlington, Graduate School, College of Liberal Arts, Department of History, Arlington, TX 76019. Offers history (MA); transatlantic history (PhD). Part-time and evening/weekend programs available. *Faculty:* 20 full-time (5 women), 3 part-time/adjunct (0 women). *Students:* 35 full-time (15 women), 77 part-time (35 women); includes 19 minority (3 Black or African American, non-Hispanic/Latino; 1 American Indian or Alaska Native, non-Hispanic/Latino; 2 Asian, non-Hispanic/Latino; 10 Hispanic/Latino; 3 Two or more races, non-Hispanic/Latino), 3 international. 45 applicants, 80% accepted, 28 enrolled. In 2010, 24 master's, 3 doctorates awarded. *Degree requirements:* For master's, one foreign language, comprehensive exam (for some programs), thesis (for some programs); for doctorate, one foreign language, comprehensive exam, thesis/dissertation. *Entrance requirements:* For master's, GRE General Test, minimum GPA of 3.0 in last 60 hours, 3 letters of recommendation; for doctorate, GRE General Test, minimum graduate GPA of 3.5, 3 letters of recommendation, academic writing sample. Additional exam requirements/recommendations for international students: Required—TOEFL (minimum score 550 paper-based; 213 computer-based). *Application deadline:* For fall admission, 6/15 for domestic students. Applications are processed on a rolling basis. Application fee: $35 ($50 for international students). Electronic applications accepted. *Expenses:* Tuition, state resident: full-time $7500. Tuition, nonresident: full-time $13,080. International tuition: $13,250 full-time. *Financial support:* In 2010–11, 56 fellowships with full tuition reimbursements (averaging $2,000 per year), 2 research assistantships (averaging $10,000 per year), 19 teaching assistantships (averaging $12,000 per year) were awarded; career-related internships or fieldwork, scholarships/grants, and 5-6 full-tuition fellowships, conference travel support also available. Financial award application deadline: 5/1; financial award applicants required to submit FAFSA. *Unit head:* Dr. Marvin Dulaney, Chair, 817-272-2861, Fax: 817-272-2852, E-mail: history@uta.edu. *Application contact:* Dr. John Garrigus, Graduate Advisor, 817-272-2861, Fax: 817-272-2852, E-mail: garrigus@uta.edu.

The University of Texas at Austin, Graduate School, College of Liberal Arts, Department of History, Austin, TX 78712-1111. Offers MA, PhD. *Degree requirements:* For doctorate, thesis/dissertation. *Entrance requirements:* For master's and doctorate, GRE General Test. Electronic applications accepted. *Faculty research:* U.S., Latin American, European, African, Asian, and Middle Eastern history.

The University of Texas at Brownsville, Graduate Studies, College of Liberal Arts, Department of History, Brownsville, TX 78520-4991. Offers MAIS. Part-time and evening/weekend programs available. *Degree requirements:* For master's, comprehensive exam, thesis optional. *Entrance requirements:* For master's, GRE General Test. Additional exam requirements/recommendations for international students: Required—TOEFL.

The University of Texas at Dallas, School of Arts and Humanities, Program in Humanities, Richardson, TX 75080. Offers aesthetic studies (MA, MAT, PhD); history (MA); history of ideas (MA, MAT, PhD); humanities (MA, PhD); Latin American studies (MA); studies in literature (MA, MAT, PhD). *Faculty:* 44 full-time (14 women). *Students:* 161 full-time (95 women), 178 part-time (104 women); includes 71 minority (22 Black or African American, non-Hispanic/Latino; 4 American Indian or Alaska Native, non-Hispanic/Latino; 16 Asian, non-Hispanic/Latino; 24 Hispanic/Latino; 5 Two or more races, non-Hispanic/Latino), 22 international. Average age 38. 156 applicants, 70% accepted, 79 enrolled. In 2010, 46 master's, 20 doctorates awarded. *Degree requirements:* For master's, one foreign language, portfolio, thesis, or capstone project; for doctorate, one foreign language, thesis/dissertation. *Entrance requirements:* For master's, minimum GPA of 3.3 in upper-level coursework in field; for doctorate, doctoral field examinations, minimum GPA of 3.3 in upper-level coursework in field. Additional exam requirements/recommendations for international students: Required—TOEFL (minimum score 550 paper-based; 215 computer-based). *Application deadline:* For fall admission, 7/15 for domestic students, 5/1 priority date for international students; for spring admission, 11/15 for domestic students, 9/1 priority date for international students. Applications are processed on a rolling basis. Application fee: $50 ($100 for international students). Electronic applications accepted. *Expenses:* Tuition, state resident: full-time $10,248; part-time $569 per credit hour. Tuition, nonresident: full-time $18,544; part-time $1030 per credit hour. Tuition and fees vary according to course load. *Financial support:* In 2010–11, 151 students received support, including 5 research assistantships with partial tuition reimbursements available (averaging $10,905 per year), 82 teaching assistantships with partial tuition reimbursements available (averaging $10,156 per year); career-related internships or fieldwork, Federal Work-Study, institutionally sponsored loans, scholarships/grants, and unspecified assistantships also available. Support available to part-time students. Financial award application deadline: 4/30; financial award applicants required to submit FAFSA. *Faculty research:* Holocaust studies, U. S. /Mexico studies, translation studies, art history research, Chinese studies. *Unit head:* Dr. Michael Wilson, Associate Dean for Graduate Education, 972-883-2080, E-mail: mwilson@utdallas.edu. *Application contact:* Dr. Michael Wilson, Associate Dean of Graduate Studies, 972-883-2756, Fax: 972-883-2989, E-mail: mwilson@utdallas.edu.

The University of Texas at El Paso, Graduate School, College of Liberal Arts, Department of History, El Paso, TX 79968-0001. Offers border history (MA); borderlands history (PhD); history (MA). Part-time and evening/weekend programs available. *Students:* 70 (35 women); includes 3 Black or African American, non-Hispanic/Latino; 1 Asian, non-Hispanic/Latino; 46 Hispanic/Latino, 2 international. Average age 34. In 2010, 7 master's, 1 doctorate awarded. *Degree requirements:* For master's, thesis optional; for doctorate, thesis/dissertation. *Entrance requirements:* For master's, GRE, minimum GPA of 3.0, writing sample, letters of recommendation; for doctorate, GRE, statement of purpose, writing sample, letters of recommendation. Additional exam requirements/recommendations for international students: Required—TOEFL; Recommended—IELTS. *Application deadline:* For fall admission, 8/1 for domestic students, 3/1 for international students; for spring admission, 12/15 priority date for domestic students, 9/1 for international students. Applications are processed on a rolling basis. Application fee: $45 ($80 for international students). Electronic applications accepted. *Financial support:* In 2010–11, research assistantships with partial tuition reimbursements (averaging $21,125 per year), teaching assistantships with partial tuition reimbursements (averaging $16,900 per year) were awarded; fellowships with partial tuition reimbursements, institutionally sponsored loans, scholarships/grants, health care benefits, tuition waivers (partial), and unspecified assistantships also available. Support available to part-time students. Financial award application deadline: 3/15; financial award applicants required to submit FAFSA. *Unit head:* Dr. Paul Edison, Chair, 915-747-5508, Fax: 915-747-5948, E-mail: pedison@utep.edu. *Application contact:* Dr. Patricia D. Witherspoon, Dean of the Graduate School, 915-747-5491, Fax: 915-747-5788, E-mail: withersp@utep.edu.

The University of Texas at San Antonio, College of Liberal and Fine Arts, Department of History, San Antonio, TX 78249-0617. Offers MA. Part-time and evening/weekend programs available. *Faculty:* 13 full-time (4 women). *Students:* 29 full-time (12 women), 72 part-time (31 women); includes 41 minority (3 Asian, non-Hispanic/Latino; 37 Hispanic/Latino; 1 Two or more races, non-Hispanic/Latino). Average age 34. 47 applicants, 74% accepted, 30 enrolled. In 2010, 20 master's awarded. *Degree requirements:* For master's, comprehensive exam (for some programs), thesis (for some programs). *Entrance requirements:* For master's, GRE, minimum GPA of 3.0 in last 60 hours. Additional exam requirements/recommendations for international students: Required—TOEFL (minimum score 500 paper-based; 173 computer-based; 61 iBT), IELTS (minimum score 5). *Application deadline:* For fall admission, 7/1 for domestic students, 4/1 for international students; for spring admission, 11/1 for domestic

History

The University of Texas at San Antonio (continued)
students, 9/1 for international students. Applications are processed on a rolling basis. Application fee: $45 ($80 for international students). Electronic applications accepted. *Expenses:* Tuition, state resident: full-time $4172; part-time $231.75 per credit hour. Tuition, nonresident: full-time $15,332; part-time $851.75 per credit hour. *Financial support:* In 2010–11, 35 students received support, including 12 research assistantships (averaging $7,598 per year); career-related internships or fieldwork, scholarships/grants, tuition waivers, and unspecified assistantships also available. Total annual research expenditures: $7,537. *Unit head:* Dr. Gregg Michel, Department Chair, 210-458-4033, Fax: 210-458-4796, E-mail: history@utsa.edu. *Application contact:* Veronica Ramirez, Assistant Dean of the Graduate School, 210-458-4330, Fax: 210-458-4332, E-mail: graduatestudies@utsa.edu.

The University of Texas at Tyler, College of Arts and Sciences, Department of History, Tyler, TX 75799-0001. Offers history (MA). Part-time and evening/weekend programs available. *Degree requirements:* For master's, one foreign language, comprehensive exam, thesis optional. *Entrance requirements:* For master's, GRE General Test, minimum GPA of 3.0. Additional exam requirements/recommendations for international students: Required—TOEFL (minimum score 79 computer-based). Electronic applications accepted. *Faculty research:* Early and modern U.S. history, early modern and modern European history.

The University of Texas of the Permian Basin, Office of Graduate Studies, College of Arts and Sciences, Department of History, Odessa, TX 79762-0001. Offers MA. Part-time and evening/weekend programs available. *Degree requirements:* For master's, comprehensive exam (for some programs), thesis (for some programs). *Entrance requirements:* For master's, GRE General Test. Additional exam requirements/recommendations for international students: Required—TOEFL (minimum score 550 paper-based; 213 computer-based).

The University of Texas–Pan American, College of Arts and Humanities, Department of History, Edinburg, TX 78539. Offers MA, MAIS. Part-time and evening/weekend programs available. *Degree requirements:* For master's, comprehensive exam, thesis or alternative. *Entrance requirements:* For master's, GRE General Test, minimum GPA of 3.0. *Faculty research:* Texas-Mexican legacy, modern America, Southwest, labor, modern Europe.

The University of Toledo, College of Graduate Studies, College of Language, Literature and Social Sciences, Department of History, Toledo, OH 43606-3390. Offers MA, PhD. Part-time programs available. *Faculty:* 14. *Students:* 18 full-time (11 women), 6 part-time (3 women); includes 2 minority (1 Black or African American, non-Hispanic/Latino; 1 Hispanic/Latino). Average age 29. 22 applicants, 41% accepted, 2 enrolled. In 2010, 2 master's, 2 doctorates awarded. *Degree requirements:* For master's, thesis or comprehensive exam; for doctorate, thesis/dissertation, oral and written exams. *Entrance requirements:* For master's and doctorate, GRE General Test, minimum cumulative point-hour ratio of 2.7 for all previous academic work, three letters of recommendation. Additional exam requirements/recommendations for international students: Required—TOEFL (minimum score 550 paper-based; 213 computer-based; 80 iBT), IELTS (minimum score 6.5). *Application deadline:* For fall admission, 1/15 priority date for domestic and international students. Applications are processed on a rolling basis. Application fee: $45 ($75 for international students). Electronic applications accepted. *Expenses:* Tuition, state resident: full-time $11,426; part-time $476 per credit hour. Tuition, nonresident: full-time $21,660; part-time $903 per credit hour. One-time fee: $62. *Financial support:* Teaching assistantships with full tuition reimbursements, Federal Work-Study, institutionally sponsored loans, scholarships/grants, tuition waivers (full), and unspecified assistantships available. *Faculty research:* U. S. diplomatic history, U. S. history, urban history, public history, European history. *Unit head:* Dr. William O'Neal, Interim Chair, 419-530-2242, E-mail: william.oneal@utoledo.edu. *Application contact:* Graduate School Office, 419-530-4723, Fax: 419-530-4724, E-mail: grdsch@utnet.utoledo.edu.

University of Toronto, School of Graduate Studies, Humanities Division, Department of History, Toronto, ON M5S 1A1, Canada. Offers MA, PhD. Part-time programs available. *Degree requirements:* For master's, one foreign language, thesis or research essay, French language exam; for doctorate, comprehensive exam, thesis/dissertation, oral examination/thesis defense. *Entrance requirements:* For master's, minimum B+ average or GPA of 3.3, 6 full academic year history courses; for doctorate, MA in history, minimum A– average or GPA of 3.7.

University of Tulsa, Graduate School, College of Arts and Sciences, Department of History, Tulsa, OK 74104-3189. Offers MA, MTA, JD/MA. Part-time programs available. *Faculty:* 8 full-time (2 women), 2 part-time/adjunct (1 woman). *Students:* 7 full-time (1 woman), 3 part-time (1 woman); includes 2 minority (both American Indian or Alaska Native, non-Hispanic/Latino). Average age 28. 4 applicants, 75% accepted, 3 enrolled. In 2010, 4 master's awarded. *Degree requirements:* For master's, one foreign language, comprehensive exam or oral defense of thesis. *Entrance requirements:* For master's, GRE General Test, writing sample. Additional exam requirements/recommendations for international students: Required—TOEFL (minimum score 575 paper-based; 231 computer-based; 91 iBT), IELTS (minimum score 6.5). *Application deadline:* Applications are processed on a rolling basis. Application fee: $40. Electronic applications accepted. *Expenses:* Tuition: Full-time $16,902; part-time $939 per credit hour. Required fees: $1020; $4 per credit hour. Tuition and fees vary according to course load. *Financial support:* In 2010–11, 7 students received support, including 2 fellowships with full and partial tuition reimbursements available (averaging $14,000 per year), 6 teaching assistantships with full and partial tuition reimbursements available (averaging $11,942 per year); Federal Work-Study, scholarships/grants, health care benefits, tuition waivers (full and partial), and unspecified assistantships also available. Support available to part-time students. Financial award application deadline: 2/1; financial award applicants required to submit FAFSA. *Faculty research:* United States history, modern European history, comparative history. *Unit head:* Dr. Thomas Buoye, Chairperson, 918-631-2825, Fax: 918-631-2057, E-mail: thomas-buoye@utulsa.edu. *Application contact:* Dr. Christine Ruane, Adviser, 918-631-3814, Fax: 918-631-2057, E-mail: christine-ruane@utulsa.edu.

University of Tulsa, Graduate School, College of Arts and Sciences, School of Education, Program in Teaching Arts, Tulsa, OK 74104-3189. Offers art (MTA); biology (MTA); English (MTA); history (MTA); mathematics (MTA); theatre (MTA). Part-time programs available. *Students:* 2 part-time (both women); includes 1 minority (American Indian or Alaska Native, non-Hispanic/Latino). Average age 31. 1 applicant, 0% accepted, 0 enrolled. In 2010, 2 master's awarded. *Entrance requirements:* For master's, GRE General Test. Additional exam requirements/recommendations for international students: Required—TOEFL (minimum score 575 paper-based; 231 computer-based), IELTS (minimum score 6.5). *Application deadline:* Applications are processed on a rolling basis. Application fee: $40. Electronic applications accepted. *Expenses:* Tuition: Full-time $16,902; part-time $939 per credit hour. Required fees: $1020; $4 per credit hour. Tuition and fees vary according to course load. *Financial support:* In 2010–11, 2 students received support, including 2 fellowships with full and partial tuition reimbursements available (averaging $2,191 per year); research assistantships with full and partial tuition reimbursements available, teaching assistantships with full and partial tuition reimbursements available, Federal Work-Study, scholarships/grants, and tuition waivers (full and partial) also available. Support available to part-time students. Financial award application deadline: 2/1; financial award applicants required to submit FAFSA. *Unit head:* Dr. David Brown, Advisor, 918-631-2719, Fax: 918-631-2133, E-mail: david-brown@utulsa.edu. *Application contact:* Dr. David Brown, Advisor, 918-631-2719, Fax: 918-631-2133, E-mail: david-brown@utulsa.edu.

University of Tulsa, Graduate School, Program in Museum Science and Management, Tulsa, OK 74104-3189. Offers anthropology (MA); general (MA); history (MA); Native American (MA). Part-time programs available. *Faculty:* 9 full-time (1 woman). *Students:* 6 full-time (all women); includes 1 minority (Black or African American, non-Hispanic/Latino). Average age 29. 14 applicants, 86% accepted, 6 enrolled. *Degree requirements:* For master's, final semester internship or independent research project. *Entrance requirements:* For master's, GRE General Test. Additional exam requirements/recommendations for international students: Required—TOEFL (minimum score 575 paper-based; 231 computer-based; 91 iBT), IELTS (minimum score 6.5). *Application deadline:* Applications are processed on a rolling basis. Application fee: $40. Electronic applications accepted. *Expenses:* Tuition: Full-time $16,902; part-time $939 per credit hour. Required fees: $1020; $4 per credit hour. Tuition and fees vary according to course load. *Financial support:* In 2010–11, 4 students received support, including 1 research assistantship with full and partial tuition reimbursement available (averaging $5,504 per year), 3 teaching assistantships with full and partial tuition reimbursements available (averaging $13,040 per year); fellowships with full and partial tuition reimbursements available, career-related internships or fieldwork, Federal Work-Study, scholarships/grants, health care benefits, tuition waivers (full and partial), and unspecified assistantships also available. Support available to part-time students. Total annual research expenditures: $12,000. *Unit head:* Dr. Bob Pickering, Senior Curator, 918-596-2706, Fax: 918-596-2770, E-mail: bob-pickering@utulsa.edu. *Application contact:* Graduate School, 918-631-2336, Fax: 918-631-2156, E-mail: grad@utulsa.edu.

University of Utah, Graduate School, College of Humanities, Department of History, Salt Lake City, UT 84112. Offers MA, MS, PhD. Part-time and evening/weekend programs available. *Faculty:* 25 full-time (7 women), 1 part-time/adjunct (0 women). *Students:* 27 full-time (14 women), 43 part-time (21 women); includes 5 minority (2 Asian, non-Hispanic/Latino; 2 Hispanic/Latino; 1 Native Hawaiian or other Pacific Islander, non-Hispanic/Latino), 3 international. Average age 35. 89 applicants, 43% accepted, 16 enrolled. In 2010, 7 master's, 4 doctorates awarded. Terminal master's awarded for partial completion of doctoral program. *Degree requirements:* For master's, one foreign language, comprehensive exam (for some programs), thesis (for some programs); for doctorate, 2 foreign languages, comprehensive exam, thesis/dissertation. *Entrance requirements:* For master's, GRE General Test, minimum GPA of 3.2; for doctorate, GRE General Test, minimum graduate GPA of 3.6. Additional exam requirements/recommendations for international students: Required—TOEFL (minimum score 500 paper-based; 173 computer-based). *Application deadline:* For fall admission, 1/15 for domestic and international students. Application fee: $55 ($65 for international students). Electronic applications accepted. *Expenses:* Tuition, area resident: Part-time $179.19 per credit hour. Tuition, state resident: full-time $4384. Tuition, nonresident: full-time $16,684; part-time $630.67 per credit hour. Required fees: $350 per semester. Tuition and fees vary according to course load, degree level and program. *Financial support:* In 2010–11, 13 students received support, including 3 fellowships (averaging $12,000 per year), 14 teaching assistantships with full tuition reimbursements available (averaging $11,000 per year); career-related internships or fieldwork also available. Financial award application deadline: 1/15; financial award applicants required to submit FAFSA. *Faculty research:* U. S. history, European history, Asian history, Middle East, Latin America. Total annual research expenditures: $11,866. *Unit head:* Prof. James Lehning, Chair, 801-581-5685, Fax: 801-585-0580, E-mail: jim.lehning@utah.edu. *Application contact:* Karleton Munn, Graduate Secretary, 801-581-6121, Fax: 801-585-0580, E-mail: karleton.munn@utah.edu.

University of Utah, Graduate School, College of Humanities, Program in Middle East Studies, Salt Lake City, UT 84112. Offers anthropology (MA); Arabic (MA, PhD); Arabic and linguistics (MA, PhD); Hebrew (MA); history (MA, PhD); Persian (MA, PhD); political science (MA, PhD); Turkish (MA). *Students:* 20 full-time (10 women), 15 part-time (5 women), 8 international. Average age 33. 28 applicants, 29% accepted, 3 enrolled. In 2010, 3 master's awarded. Terminal master's awarded for partial completion of doctoral program. *Degree requirements:* For master's, 2 foreign languages, comprehensive exam, thesis optional; for doctorate, 3 foreign languages, comprehensive exam, thesis/dissertation. *Entrance requirements:* For master's, GRE General Test, minimum GPA of 3.2; for doctorate, GRE General Test, MA in Middle East studies or equivalent, minimum GPA of 3.2. Additional exam requirements/recommendations for international students: Required—TOEFL (minimum score 580 paper-based; 237 computer-based; 92 iBT). *Application deadline:* For fall admission, 1/15 priority date for domestic and international students. Application fee: $55 ($65 for international students). Electronic applications accepted. *Expenses:* Tuition, area resident: Part-time $179.19 per credit hour. Tuition, state resident: full-time $4384. Tuition, nonresident: full-time $16,684; part-time $630.67 per credit hour. Required fees: $350 per semester. Tuition and fees vary according to course load, degree level and program. *Financial support:* In 2010–11, 17 students received support, including 11 fellowships with full tuition reimbursements available (averaging $14,000 per year), 6 teaching assistantships with full tuition reimbursements available (averaging $12,000 per year); unspecified assistantships also available. Financial award application deadline: 1/15. *Faculty research:* Arabic linguistics; Islamic studies; Middle Eastern history; political science; Judaic studies; anthropology; Arabic, Persian, Hebrew, and Turkish language and literature. *Application contact:* Peter von Sivers, Director of Graduate Studies, 801-581-8073, Fax: 801-581-6183, E-mail: peter.vonsivers@utah.edu.

University of Vermont, Graduate College, College of Arts and Sciences, Department of History, Burlington, VT 05405. Offers MA. *Students:* 21 (8 women); includes 1 American Indian or Alaska Native, non-Hispanic/Latino. 28 applicants, 64% accepted, 9 enrolled. In 2010, 6 master's awarded. *Degree requirements:* For master's, thesis. *Entrance requirements:* For master's, GRE General Test, sample project. Additional exam requirements/recommendations for international students: Required—TOEFL (minimum score 550 paper-based; 213 computer-based; 80 iBT). *Application deadline:* For fall admission, 5/1 priority date for domestic students. Applications are processed on a rolling basis. Application fee: $40. Electronic applications accepted. *Expenses:* Tuition, state resident: part-time $537 per credit hour. Tuition, nonresident: part-time $1355 per credit hour. *Financial support:* Fellowships, research assistantships, teaching assistantships, career-related internships or fieldwork available. Financial award application deadline: 3/1. *Faculty research:* American, European, and Asian history. *Unit head:* Dr. Steven Zdatny, Chair, 802-656-3180. *Application contact:* Dr. Paul Deslandes, Coordinator, 802-656-3180.

University of Victoria, Faculty of Graduate Studies, Faculty of Humanities, Department of History, Victoria, BC V8W 2Y2, Canada. Offers MA, PhD. Part-time programs available. *Degree requirements:* For master's, one foreign language, thesis; for doctorate, one foreign language, comprehensive exam, thesis/dissertation. *Entrance requirements:* Additional exam requirements/recommendations for international students: Required—TOEFL (minimum score 600 paper-based; 250 computer-based), TWE. Electronic applications accepted. *Faculty research:* Canadian social history, Canadian gender history, Canadian native history, Canadian military history, British Columbian history, Western history, medieval history, world history.

University of Virginia, College and Graduate School of Arts and Sciences, Department of History, Charlottesville, VA 22903. Offers MA, PhD, JD/MA. *Faculty:* 38 full-time (6 women), 1 part-time/adjunct (0 women). *Students:* 117 full-time (43 women); includes 1 Black or African American, non-Hispanic/Latino; 1 Asian, non-Hispanic/Latino; 3 Hispanic/Latino; 1 Two or more races, non-Hispanic/Latino, 13 international. Average age 29. 233 applicants, 22% accepted, 20 enrolled. In 2010, 16 master's, 10 doctorates awarded. *Degree requirements:* For master's, one foreign language, essay; for doctorate, variable foreign language requirement, comprehensive exam, thesis/dissertation. *Entrance requirements:* For master's and doctorate, GRE General Test, 2 or more letters of recommendation. Additional exam requirements/recommendations for international students: Required—TOEFL (minimum score 600 paper-based; 250 computer-based; 90 iBT), IELTS (minimum score 7). *Application deadline:* For fall admission, 12/1 for domestic and international students. Applications are processed on a rolling basis. Application fee: $60. Electronic applications accepted. *Financial support:* Fellowships, teaching assistantships available. Financial award application deadline: 12/1; financial award applicants required to submit FAFSA. *Unit head:* Brian Owensby, Chair, 434-924-7146, Fax: 434-924-7891, E-mail: history@virginia.edu. *Application contact:* Philip Zelikow, Director of Graduate Admissions, 434-924-6382, Fax: 434-924-7891, E-mail: zelikow@virginia.edu.

University of Washington, Graduate School, College of Arts and Sciences, Department of History, Seattle, WA 98195. Offers MA, PhD. Part-time programs available. *Degree requirements:* For master's, one foreign language, comprehensive exam, thesis optional; for doctorate, one foreign language, comprehensive exam, thesis/dissertation. *Entrance requirements:* For master's and doctorate, GRE, minimum GPA of 3.0. Additional exam requirements/recommendations for international students: Required—TOEFL. Electronic applications accepted. *Faculty research:* U.S., Asia, Europe, comparative history.

University of Waterloo, Graduate Studies, Faculty of Arts, Department of Classical Studies, Waterloo, ON N2L 3G1, Canada. Offers ancient Mediterranean cultures (MA). *Degree requirements:* For master's, one foreign language. *Faculty research:* Ancient history, philosophy, anthropology, religion, culture.

University of Waterloo, Graduate Studies, Faculty of Arts, Department of History, Waterloo, ON N2L 3G1, Canada. Offers MA, PhD. PhD offered jointly with University of Guelph, Wilfrid Laurier University. Part-time and evening/weekend programs available. *Degree requirements:* For master's, one foreign language, thesis optional; for doctorate, one foreign language, thesis/dissertation. *Entrance requirements:* For master's, honors degree, minimum B+ average, resume; for doctorate, master's degree, minimum A average, resume, writing sample. Additional exam requirements/recommendations for international students: Required—TOEFL, TWE. Electronic applications accepted. *Faculty research:* Canadian, British, international, modern, European, and U.S. history; women's history; imperialism and slavery.

The University of Western Ontario, Faculty of Graduate Studies, Social Sciences Division, Department of History, London, ON N6A 5B8, Canada. Offers MA, PhD. Part-time programs available. *Degree requirements:* For master's, one foreign language, thesis (for some programs); for doctorate, one foreign language, thesis/dissertation. *Entrance requirements:* For master's, minimum B+ average on last 10 senior courses; for doctorate, minimum A- average on MA or last year honors degree. Additional exam requirements/recommendations for international students: Required—TOEFL. *Faculty research:* Canadian, U.S., Britain, Modern Europe, British Empire and Commonwealth Latin America.

University of West Florida, College of Arts and Sciences: Arts, Department of History, Pensacola, FL 32514-5750. Offers history (MA); military history (MA); public history (MA). Part-time and evening/weekend programs available. *Faculty:* 8 full-time (2 women). *Students:* 10 full-time (7 women), 33 part-time (19 women); includes 1 Black or African American, non-Hispanic/Latino; 1 Asian, non-Hispanic/Latino; 2 Hispanic/Latino. Average age 30. 25 applicants, 52% accepted, 11 enrolled. In 2010, 10 master's awarded. *Degree requirements:* For master's, thesis or alternative. *Entrance requirements:* For master's, GRE General Test, minimum GPA of 3.0, minimum 15 hours of upper-level history courses. Additional exam requirements/recommendations for international students: Required—TOEFL (minimum score 550 paper-based; 213 computer-based). *Application deadline:* For fall admission, 6/1 for domestic students, 5/15 for international students; for spring admission, 10/1 for domestic and international students. Applications are processed on a rolling basis. Application fee: $30. *Expenses:* Tuition, state resident: full-time $4982; part-time $208 per credit hour. Tuition, nonresident: full-time $20,059; part-time $836 per credit hour. Required fees: $1365; $57 per credit hour. *Financial support:* In 2010–11, 20 fellowships with partial tuition reimbursements (averaging $377 per year), 13 research assistantships with partial tuition reimbursements (averaging $3,280 per year) were awarded; unspecified assistantships also available. Financial award application deadline: 4/15; financial award applicants required to submit FAFSA. *Unit head:* Dr. John J. Clune, Chairperson, 850-474-2680. *Application contact:* Terry McCray, Assistant Director of Graduate Admissions, 850-473-7718, Fax: 850-473-7714, E-mail: gradadmissions@uwf.edu.

University of West Georgia, College of Arts and Sciences, Department of History, Carrollton, GA 30118. Offers history (MA); museum studies (Certificate); public history (Certificate). Part-time programs available. *Faculty:* 16 full-time (6 women). *Students:* 25 full-time (16 women), 15 part-time (8 women); includes 1 American Indian or Alaska Native, non-Hispanic/Latino; 2 Hispanic/Latino; 1 Two or more races, non-Hispanic/Latino. Average age 33. 16 applicants, 69% accepted, 8 enrolled. In 2010, 7 master's, 8 other advanced degrees awarded. *Degree requirements:* For master's, one foreign language, comprehensive exam, thesis or alternative. *Entrance requirements:* For master's, GRE General Test (minimum score 400 verbal, 400 quantitative, 3.5 writing), undergraduate degree in history or related social studies, minimum GPA of 2.75. *Application deadline:* For fall admission, 7/17 for domestic students; for spring admission, 11/20 for domestic students. Applications are processed on a rolling basis. Application fee: $30. Electronic applications accepted. *Expenses:* Tuition, state resident: full-time $4130; part-time $173 per semester hour. Tuition, nonresident: full-time $16,524; part-time $689 per semester hour. Required fees: $1586; $44.01 per semester hour. $397 per semester. Tuition and fees vary according to program. *Financial support:* In 2010–11, 7 students received support, including research assistantships with full tuition reimbursements available (averaging $6,000 per year); career-related internships or fieldwork, scholarships/grants, and unspecified assistantships also available. Support available to part-time students. Financial award application deadline: 7/1; financial award applicants required to submit FAFSA. *Faculty research:* Public history, United States, Russia/Soviet Union, Africa, Europe. *Unit head:* Dr. Howard Steven Goodson, Interim Chair, 678-839-6042, E-mail: hgoodson@westga.edu. *Application contact:* Dr. Charles W. Clark, Dean, 678-839-6508, E-mail: cclark@westga.edu.

University of Windsor, Faculty of Graduate Studies, Faculty of Arts and Social Sciences, Department of History, Windsor, ON N9B 3P4, Canada. Offers MA. Part-time programs available. *Degree requirements:* For master's, thesis (for some programs). *Entrance requirements:* For master's, minimum B average. Additional exam requirements/recommendations for international students: Required—TOEFL (minimum score 600 paper-based; 250 computer-based). Electronic applications accepted. *Faculty research:* Gender history, social-history questions about class gender and national identity, divorce in France: 1792-1816, gender and sexuality in Western Europe during the high and later Middle Ages, U.S.-Canadian comparisons in women's history.

The University of Winnipeg, Graduate Studies, Department of History, Winnipeg, MB R3B 2E9, Canada. Offers MA. Program offered jointly with University of Manitoba. Part-time and evening/weekend programs available. *Degree requirements:* For master's, one foreign language, comprehensive exam or thesis. *Faculty research:* Canadian social history, European diplomacy, Indian history, colonial America, medieval history.

University of Wisconsin–Eau Claire, College of Arts and Sciences, Department of History, Eau Claire, WI 54702-4004. Offers public history (MA). Part-time programs available. *Faculty:* 12 full-time (7 women). *Students:* 14 full-time (4 women), 16 part-time (1 woman); includes 3 minority (1 American Indian or Alaska Native, non-Hispanic/Latino; 2 Hispanic/Latino). Average age 31. 17 applicants, 100% accepted, 10 enrolled. In 2010, 8 master's awarded. *Degree requirements:* For master's, comprehensive exam, thesis optional, oral and written exams. *Entrance requirements:* For master's, minimum GPA of 3.15 during last 2 years, 3.3 in history, or 3.0 overall; research paper; bachelor's degree with minimum of 24 credits in history. Additional exam requirements/recommendations for international students: Required—TOEFL (minimum score 550 paper-based; 213 computer-based; 79 iBT); Recommended—IELTS (minimum score 7). *Application deadline:* For fall admission, 3/1 priority date for domestic and international students. Applications are processed on a rolling basis. Application fee: $56. *Expenses:* Tuition, state resident: full-time $7001; part-time $389 per credit. Tuition, nonresident: full-time $16,771; part-time $932 per credit. Required fees: $1057; $58.49 per credit. *Financial support:* In 2010–11, 14 students received support, including 5 fellowships (averaging $1,784 per year); Federal Work-Study and unspecified assistantships also available. Financial award application deadline: 3/1; financial award applicants required to submit FAFSA. *Unit head:* Dr. Kate Lang, Chair, 715-836-5501, Fax: 715-836-3540, E-mail: langkh@uwec.edu. *Application contact:* Dr. Jane Pederson, Director, 715-836-5900, E-mail: pedersjm@uwec.edu.

University of Wisconsin–Madison, Graduate School, College of Letters and Science, Department of History, Madison, WI 53706-1380. Offers African history (MA, PhD); Central Asian history (MA, PhD); comparative world history (MA, PhD); East Asian history (MA, PhD); European history (MA, PhD); gender and women's history (MA, PhD); Latin American and Caribbean history (MA, PhD); Middle Eastern history (MA, PhD); South Asian history (MA, PhD); Southeast Asian history (MA, PhD); United States history (MA, PhD). Terminal master's awarded for partial completion of doctoral program. *Degree requirements:* For master's, thesis (for some programs); for doctorate, variable foreign language requirement, thesis/dissertation. *Entrance requirements:* For master's and doctorate, GRE General Test. Additional exam requirements/recommendations for international students: Required—Michigan English Language Assessment Battery or TOEFL. Electronic applications accepted. *Expenses:* Tuition, state resident: full-time $9887; part-time $617.96 per credit. Tuition, nonresident: full-time $24,054; part-time $1503.40 per credit. Required fees: $67.63 per credit. Tuition and fees vary according to reciprocity agreements. *Faculty research:* American, African, European, Asian, Latin American, and Middle Eastern history.

University of Wisconsin–Milwaukee, Graduate School, College of Letters and Sciences, Department of History, Milwaukee, WI 53201-0413. Offers global history (PhD); history (MA); modern studies (PhD); urban history (PhD). Part-time programs available. *Faculty:* 34 full-time (16 women). *Students:* 29 full-time (12 women), 46 part-time (19 women); includes 1 Black or African American, non-Hispanic/Latino; 2 Hispanic/Latino, 2 international. Average age 32. 80 applicants, 60% accepted, 19 enrolled. In 2010, 25 master's, 1 doctorate awarded. *Degree requirements:* For master's, comprehensive exam, thesis or alternative; for doctorate, thesis/dissertation. *Entrance requirements:* For master's and doctorate, GRE General Test. Additional exam requirements/recommendations for international students: Required—TOEFL (minimum score 550 paper-based; 79 iBT), IELTS (minimum score 6.5). *Application deadline:* For fall admission, 1/1 priority date for domestic students; for spring admission, 9/1 for domestic students. Applications are processed on a rolling basis. Application fee: $56 ($96 for international students). Electronic applications accepted. *Financial support:* In 2010–11, 23 teaching assistantships were awarded; career-related internships or fieldwork and unspecified assistantships also available. Support available to part-time students. Financial award application deadline: 4/15; financial award applicants required to submit FAFSA. Total annual research expenditures: $9,560. *Unit head:* Aims McGuinness, Representative, 414-229-4361, Fax: 414-229-2435, E-mail: smia@uwm.edu. *Application contact:* General Information Contact, 414-229-4982, Fax: 414-229-6967, E-mail: gradschool@uwm.edu.

University of Wisconsin–Stevens Point, College of Letters and Science, Department of History, Stevens Point, WI 54481-3897. Offers MST. *Degree requirements:* For master's, thesis or alternative.

University of Wyoming, College of Arts and Sciences, Department of History, Laramie, WY 82070. Offers MA, MAT. Part-time programs available. *Degree requirements:* For master's, one foreign language, thesis (for some programs). *Entrance requirements:* For master's, GRE General Test, minimum GPA of 3.0, 12 semester hours of undergraduate course work in history. Additional exam requirements/recommendations for international students: Required—TOEFL. Electronic applications accepted. *Faculty research:* American West, Native American history, nineteenth and twentieth century U.S. history, European history, Asian studies.

Utah State University, School of Graduate Studies, College of Humanities, Arts and Social Sciences, Department of History, Logan, UT 84322. Offers MA, MS. Part-time and evening/weekend programs available. *Degree requirements:* For master's, one foreign language, thesis. *Entrance requirements:* For master's, GRE General Test, minimum GPA of 3.0. Additional exam requirements/recommendations for international students: Required—TOEFL. Electronic applications accepted. *Faculty research:* U.S. race and ethnicity, early modern and modern Europe, environmental history, western regional history.

Valdosta State University, Department of History, Valdosta, GA 31698. Offers MA. Part-time programs available. *Faculty:* 11 full-time (3 women). *Students:* 7 full-time (2 women), 10 part-time (4 women). Average age 22. 11 applicants, 73% accepted, 8 enrolled. In 2010, 1 master's awarded. *Degree requirements:* For master's, one foreign language, thesis optional, comprehensive written and/or oral exams. *Entrance requirements:* For master's, GRE General Test, minimum GPA of 2.5. Additional exam requirements/recommendations for international students: Required—TOEFL (minimum score 523 paper-based; 193 computer-based). *Application deadline:* For fall admission, 5/15 for domestic and international students; for spring admission, 11/15 for domestic and international students. Applications are processed on a rolling basis. Application fee: $35. Electronic applications accepted. *Expenses:* Tuition, state resident: full-time $5256; part-time $197 per credit hour. Tuition, nonresident: full-time $14,490; part-time $710 per credit hour. Required fees: $855 per semester. Tuition and fees vary according to course load and campus/location. *Financial support:* In 2010–11, 5 students received support, including 5 research assistantships with full tuition reimbursements available (averaging $3,652 per year); scholarships/grants and unspecified assistantships also available. Support available to part-time students. Financial award application deadline: 7/1; financial award applicants required to submit FAFSA. *Faculty research:* Georgia history, U. S. history, Napoleonic France, American diplomatic history, English history. *Unit head:* Dr. Paul Riggs, Head, 229-333-5947, Fax: 229-249-4865. *Application contact:* Misty Lamb, Admissions Specialist, 229-333-5694, Fax: 229-245-3853, E-mail: mllamb@valdosta.edu.

Valparaiso University, Graduate School, Programs in Liberal Studies, Concentration in History, Valparaiso, IN 46383. Offers MALS, Post-Master's Certificate, JD/MALS. Part-time and evening/weekend programs available. *Students:* 10 full-time (6 women), 1 (woman) part-time. Average age 28. In 2010, 4 master's awarded. *Entrance requirements:* For master's, minimum GPA of 3.0. Additional exam requirements/recommendations for international students: Required—TOEFL (minimum score 550 paper-based; 213 computer-based; 80 iBT). *Application deadline:* Applications are processed on a rolling basis. Application fee: $30 ($50 for international students). Electronic applications accepted. *Expenses:* Tuition: Full-time $9540; part-time $530 per credit hour. Required fees: $292; $95 per semester. Tuition and fees vary according to program. *Financial support:* Available to part-time students. Applicants required to submit FAFSA. *Faculty research:* Regional Chinese history, British history, Martin Luther, Latin American history, African history. *Unit head:* Dr. David L. Rowland, Dean, Graduate School and Continuing Education/Associate Provost, 219-464-5313, Fax: 219-464-5381, E-mail: david.rowland@valpo.edu. *Application contact:* Laura Groth, Coordinator of Student Services and Support, 219-464-5313, Fax: 219-464-5381, E-mail: laura.groth@valpo.edu.

Vanderbilt University, Graduate School, Department of History, Nashville, TN 37240-1001. Offers MA, MAT, PhD. *Faculty:* 37 full-time (10 women). *Students:* 46 full-time (30 women), 3 part-time (1 woman); includes 4 Black or African American, non-Hispanic/Latino; 1 American Indian or Alaska Native, non-Hispanic/Latino; 1 Asian, non-Hispanic/Latino; 4 Hispanic/Latino; 1 Two or more races, non-Hispanic/Latino. Average age 31. 255 applicants, 6% accepted, 10 enrolled. In 2010, 5 master's, 7 doctorates awarded. Terminal master's awarded for partial completion of doctoral program. *Degree requirements:* For doctorate, one foreign language, comprehensive exam, thesis/dissertation, final and qualifying exams. *Entrance requirements:* For doctorate, GRE General Test, sample of written work (recommended). Additional exam requirements/recommendations for international students: Required—TOEFL (minimum score 570 paper-based; 230 computer-based; 88 iBT). *Application deadline:* For fall admission, 1/15 for domestic and international students. Application fee: $0. Electronic applications accepted. *Financial support:* Fellowships with full tuition reimbursements, teaching assistantships with full tuition reimbursements, Federal Work-Study, institutionally sponsored loans, scholarships/grants, and health care benefits available. Financial award application deadline: 1/15; financial award applicants required to submit CSS PROFILE or FAFSA. *Faculty research:* Southern American history, recent U. S. history, intellectual and cultural history, European history, Latin American history. *Unit head:* Dr. Elizabeth Lunback, Chair, 615-322-2575, Fax: 615-343-6002, E-mail: elizabeth.lunbeck@vanderbilt.edu. *Application contact:* Dr. Matthew Ramsey, Director of Graduate Studies, 615-322-0096, Fax: 615-343-6002, E-mail: matthew.ramsey@vanderbilt.edu.

Villanova University, Graduate School of Liberal Arts and Sciences, Department of History, Villanova, PA 19085-1699. Offers MA. Part-time and evening/weekend programs available. *Faculty:* 10 full-time (4 women), 2 part-time/adjunct (both women). *Students:* 63 full-time (25

History

Villanova University (continued)
women), 25 part-time (12 women); includes 3 minority (1 Hispanic/Latino; 2 Two or more races, non-Hispanic/Latino), 1 international. Average age 29. 65 applicants, 82% accepted, 33 enrolled. In 2010, 27 master's awarded. *Degree requirements:* For master's, comprehensive exam, thesis optional. *Entrance requirements:* For master's, GRE General Test, minimum GPA of 3.0. Additional exam requirements/recommendations for international students: Required—TOEFL. *Application deadline:* For fall admission, 3/1 priority date for domestic and international students; for spring admission, 11/15 priority date for domestic and international students. Applications are processed on a rolling basis. Application fee: $50. Electronic applications accepted. *Expenses:* Tuition: Part-time $700 per credit. Part-time tuition and fees vary according to degree level and program. *Financial support:* Research assistantships, Federal Work-Study and scholarships/grants available. Financial award applicants required to submit FAFSA. *Unit head:* Dr. Marc Gallicchio, Chairperson, 610-519-4660. *Application contact:* Dr. Adele Lindenmeyr, Dean, Graduate School of Liberal Arts and Sciences, 610-519-7093, Fax: 610-519-7096.

Virginia Commonwealth University, Graduate School, College of Humanities and Sciences, Department of History, Richmond, VA 23284-9005. Offers MA. Part-time programs available. *Students:* 20 full-time (9 women), 15 part-time (6 women); includes 4 minority (1 Black or African American, non-Hispanic/Latino; 1 Hispanic/Latino; 2 Two or more races, non-Hispanic/Latino). 26 applicants, 50% accepted, 9 enrolled. In 2010, 12 master's awarded. *Degree requirements:* For master's, thesis optional. *Entrance requirements:* For master's, GRE General Test, 30 undergraduate credits in history. Additional exam requirements/recommendations for international students: Required—TOEFL (minimum score 600 paper-based; 250 computer-based; 100 iBT); Recommended—IELTS (minimum score 6.5). *Application deadline:* For fall admission, 7/1 for domestic students; for spring admission, 12/1 for domestic students. Application fee: $50. Electronic applications accepted. *Expenses:* Tuition, state resident: full-time $4308; part-time $479 per credit hour. Tuition, nonresident: full-time $8942; part-time $994 per credit hour. Required fees: $2000; $85 per credit hour. Tuition and fees vary according to course level, course load, degree level, campus/location and program. *Financial support:* Research assistantships, teaching assistantships, Federal Work-Study, institutionally sponsored loans, and tuition waivers (full and partial) available. Support available to part-time students. Financial award applicants required to submit FAFSA. *Faculty research:* United States history, history of the South, urban history, African American history, colonial American history, the Civil War, twentieth-century American history, European history, trans-Atlantic history. *Unit head:* Dr. Bernard Moitt, Chair, 804-828-9755, Fax: 804-828-7085, E-mail: bmoitt@vcu.edu. *Application contact:* Dr. Timothy N. Thurber, Director of Graduate Studies, 804-828-4760, Fax: 804-828-7085, E-mail: tnthurber@vcu.edu.

Virginia Commonwealth University, Graduate School, School of the Arts, Department of Art History, Richmond, VA 23284-9005. Offers architectural history (MA); art history (MA, PhD); historical studies (MA); museum studies (MA). *Accreditation:* NASAD. *Faculty:* 10 full-time (4 women). *Students:* 15 full-time (13 women), 27 part-time (24 women); includes 4 minority (1 Asian, non-Hispanic/Latino; 3 Hispanic/Latino), 1 international. 52 applicants, 48% accepted, 12 enrolled. In 2010, 9 master's, 5 doctorates awarded. *Degree requirements:* For master's, thesis; for doctorate, comprehensive exam, thesis/dissertation. *Entrance requirements:* For master's and doctorate, GRE General Test. *Application deadline:* For fall admission, 1/15 for domestic students. Application fee: $50. Electronic applications accepted. *Expenses:* Tuition, state resident: full-time $4308; part-time $479 per credit hour. Tuition, nonresident: full-time $8942; part-time $994 per credit hour. Required fees: $2000; $85 per credit hour. Tuition and fees vary according to course level, course load, degree level, campus/location and program. *Financial support:* Fellowships, teaching assistantships, career-related internships or fieldwork, Federal Work-Study, and institutionally sponsored loans available. Support available to part-time students. Financial award application deadline: 3/15; financial award applicants required to submit FAFSA. *Faculty research:* Modern, nineteenth-century, Renaissance, American, and medieval art. *Unit head:* Dr. Dina Bangdel, Director of Graduate Studies, 804-628-7027, Fax: 804-828-7468, E-mail: dbangdel@vcu.edu. *Application contact:* Dr. Dina Bangdel, Director of Graduate Studies, 804-628-7027, Fax: 804-828-7468, E-mail: dbangdel@vcu.edu.

Virginia Polytechnic Institute and State University, Graduate School, College of Liberal Arts and Human Sciences, Department of History, Blacksburg, VA 24061. Offers MA. *Faculty:* 24 full-time (5 women). *Students:* 13 full-time (5 women), 2 part-time (1 woman). Average age 27. 22 applicants, 45% accepted, 5 enrolled. In 2010, 11 master's awarded. *Degree requirements:* For master's, comprehensive exam (for some programs), thesis (for some programs). *Entrance requirements:* For master's, GRE. Additional exam requirements/recommendations for international students: Required—TOEFL (minimum score 550 paper-based; 213 computer-based). *Application deadline:* For fall admission, 7/1 for domestic and international students; for spring admission, 12/1 for domestic and international students. Applications are processed on a rolling basis. Application fee: $65. Electronic applications accepted. *Expenses:* Tuition, state resident: full-time $9399; part-time $488 per credit hour. Tuition, nonresident: full-time $17,854; part-time $957.75 per credit hour. Required fees: $1534. Full-time tuition and fees vary according to program. *Financial support:* In 2010–11, 1 fellowship with full tuition reimbursement (averaging $20,000 per year), 13 teaching assistantships with full tuition reimbursements (averaging $12,383 per year) were awarded; career-related internships or fieldwork, Federal Work-Study, scholarships/grants, health care benefits, and unspecified assistantships also available. Financial award application deadline: 1/15. *Faculty research:* History of the U. S.; race, class and gender; European area studies; history of science and technology. Total annual research expenditures: $134,516. *Unit head:* Dr. Mark V. Barrow, UNIT HEAD, 540-231-5331, Fax: 540-231-8724, E-mail: mabarro2@vt.edu. *Application contact:* Amy Nelson, Contact, 540-231-8369, Fax: 540-231-8724, E-mail: anelson@vt.edu.

Virginia State University, School of Graduate Studies, Research, and Outreach, School of Liberal Arts and Education, Department of History, Petersburg, VA 23806-0001. Offers MA. *Degree requirements:* For master's, one foreign language, thesis (for some programs). *Entrance requirements:* For master's, GRE General Test, minimum GPA of 2.5. *Expenses:* Tuition, state resident: full-time $5576; part-time $335 per credit hour. Tuition, nonresident: full-time $13,402; part-time $670 per credit hour.

Washington College, Graduate Programs, Department of History, Chestertown, MD 21620-1197. Offers MA. Part-time and evening/weekend programs available. *Expenses:* Tuition: Part-time $1125 per course. Required fees: $100 per course.

Washington State University, Graduate School, College of Liberal Arts, Department of History, Pullman, WA 99164. Offers early and modern European history (MA, PhD); environmental history (MA, PhD); Latin American history (MA, PhD); modern East Asia history (MA, PhD); public history (MA, PhD); U. S. history (MA, PhD); women's history (MA, PhD); world history (MA, PhD). Part-time programs available. *Faculty:* 25. *Students:* 38 full-time (22 women), 10 part-time (4 women); includes 1 American Indian or Alaska Native, non-Hispanic/Latino; 2 Hispanic/Latino, 2 international. Average age 33. 57 applicants, 47% accepted, 10 enrolled. In 2010, 10 master's, 2 doctorates awarded. *Degree requirements:* For master's, comprehensive exam (for some programs), thesis, oral exam; for doctorate, one foreign language, comprehensive exam, thesis/dissertation, oral and written exam. *Entrance requirements:* For master's and doctorate, GRE General Test, official transcripts from all universities attended; three letters of recommendation; statement of purpose; writing sample; Preferred Fields of Study form; Language Background form. Additional exam requirements/recommendations for international students: Required—TOEFL (minimum score 550 paper-based), IELTS. *Application deadline:* For fall admission, 1/10 for domestic and international students; for spring admission, 7/1 for domestic and international students. Applications are processed on a rolling basis. Application fee: $50. Electronic applications accepted. *Expenses:* Tuition, state resident: full-time $8552; part-time $443 per credit. Tuition, nonresident: full-time $21,650; part-time $1083 per credit. Required fees: $846. *Financial support:* In 2010–11, 1 fellowship with partial tuition reimbursement (averaging $3,000 per year), research assistantships with full and partial tuition reimbursements (averaging $13,917 per year), 28 teaching assistantships with full and partial tuition reimbursements (averaging $13,056 per year) were awarded; career-related internships or fieldwork, Federal Work-Study, institutionally sponsored loans, scholarships/grants, and health care benefits also available. Financial award application deadline: 2/15; financial award applicants required to submit FAFSA. *Faculty research:* Public, world, environmental, women's and U. S. history. *Unit head:* Dr. Raymond Sun, Chair, 509-335-5139, Fax: 509-335-4171, E-mail: pietz@wsu.edu. *Application contact:* Graduate Studies Director, 509-335-4030, Fax: 509-335-4171, E-mail: kale@wsu.edu.

Washington State University, Graduate School, College of Liberal Arts, Program in American Studies, Pullman, WA 99164. Offers ethnic studies (MA, PhD); feminist studies (MA, PhD); history (MA, PhD); literature (MA, PhD). Part-time programs available. *Faculty:* 35. *Students:* 23 full-time (14 women), 4 part-time (2 women); includes 5 Black or African American, non-Hispanic/Latino; 4 American Indian or Alaska Native, non-Hispanic/Latino; 4 Asian, non-Hispanic/Latino; 4 Hispanic/Latino, 2 international. Average age 35. 55 applicants, 7% accepted, 3 enrolled. In 2010, 1 master's, 3 doctorates awarded. *Degree requirements:* For master's, one foreign language, comprehensive exam (for some programs), thesis optional, oral exam; for doctorate, one foreign language, comprehensive exam (for some programs), thesis/dissertation, oral exam. *Entrance requirements:* For master's and doctorate, GRE General Test, official college transcripts sent directly from each institution attended, 3-5 page statement of purpose describing areas of interest, minimum GPA of 3.0, writing sample, 3 letters of recommendation. Additional exam requirements/recommendations for international students: Required—TOEFL, IELTS. *Application deadline:* For fall admission, 1/10 priority date for domestic and international students; for spring admission, 7/1 priority date for domestic and international students. Applications are processed on a rolling basis. Application fee: $50. *Expenses:* Tuition, state resident: full-time $8552; part-time $443 per credit. Tuition, nonresident: full-time $21,650; part-time $1083 per credit. Required fees: $846. *Financial support:* In 2010–11, 1 fellowship (averaging $6,950 per year), 3 research assistantships with full and partial tuition reimbursements (averaging $14,634 per year), 17 teaching assistantships with full and partial tuition reimbursements (averaging $13,383 per year) were awarded; career-related internships or fieldwork, Federal Work-Study, institutionally sponsored loans, health care benefits, tuition waivers (partial), and teaching associateships also available. Financial award application deadline: 2/15; financial award applicants required to submit FAFSA. *Faculty research:* The American West in multicultural perspective; nineteenth century historical, literary, and cultural studies; comparative American ethnic literatures and cultures; American cultures and the environment; American rhetoric. *Unit head:* Dr. Rory J. Ong, Director, 509-335-1560, E-mail: rjong@mail.wsu.edu. *Application contact:* Graduate School Admissions, 800-GRADWSU, Fax: 509-335-1949, E-mail: gradsch@wsu.edu.

Washington State University Vancouver, Graduate Programs, Program in History, Vancouver, WA 98686. Offers MA. Part-time programs available. *Faculty:* 7. *Students:* 4 full-time (2 women), 2 part-time (1 woman); includes 1 American Indian or Alaska Native, non-Hispanic/Latino, 1 international. In 2010, 1 master's awarded. *Degree requirements:* For master's, comprehensive exam (for some programs), thesis. *Entrance requirements:* For master's, GRE, minimum GPA of 3.0, writing sample, language background form, preferred field of study form, 3 letters of recommendation. Additional exam requirements/recommendations for international students: Required—TOEFL (minimum score 550 paper-based; 213 computer-based). *Application deadline:* For fall admission, 1/10 priority date for domestic students, 1/10 for international students; for spring admission, 7/1 priority date for domestic students, 7/1 for international students. Application fee: $50. *Financial support:* In 2010–11, research assistantships (averaging $14,634 per year), teaching assistantships with full and partial tuition reimbursements (averaging $13,383 per year) were awarded; career-related internships or fieldwork, Federal Work-Study, and unspecified assistantships also available. Financial award application deadline: 2/15. *Faculty research:* Immigration, gender, slavery, labor, public history. *Unit head:* Dr. Sue Peabody, Associate Chair, 360-546-9647, E-mail: speabody@vancouver.wsu.edu. *Application contact:* Marie Loudermilk, Program Coordinator, 360-546-9640, E-mail: loudermilk@vancouver.wsu.edu.

Washington University in St. Louis, Graduate School of Arts and Sciences, Department of History, St. Louis, MO 63130-4899. Offers American history (MA, PhD); Asian history (MA, PhD); British history (MA, PhD); European history (MA, PhD); Latin American history (MA, PhD); Middle Eastern history (MA, PhD). Terminal master's awarded for partial completion of doctoral program. *Degree requirements:* For master's, one foreign language, thesis (for some programs); for doctorate, 2 foreign languages, thesis/dissertation. *Entrance requirements:* For master's and doctorate, GRE General Test. Electronic applications accepted.

Wayne State University, College of Liberal Arts and Sciences, Department of History, Detroit, MI 48202. Offers MA, PhD, JD/MA. Evening/weekend programs available. *Faculty:* 36 full-time (16 women), 6 part-time/adjunct (4 women). *Students:* 25 full-time (9 women), 24 part-time (7 women); includes 2 minority (both Black or African American, non-Hispanic/Latino), 1 international. Average age 40. 29 applicants, 48% accepted, 10 enrolled. In 2010, 14 master's, 3 doctorates awarded. *Degree requirements:* For doctorate, 2 foreign languages, thesis/dissertation, qualifying exam in 4 fields of history. *Entrance requirements:* For master's, GRE General Test, GRE Subject Test, minimum GPA of 3.0 in history, 2.75 overall; for doctorate, GRE General Test, GRE Subject Test, minimum GPA of 3.0. Additional exam requirements/recommendations for international students: Required—TOEFL (minimum score 550 paper-based; 213 computer-based); Recommended—TWE (minimum score 6). *Application deadline:* For fall admission, 7/1 priority date for domestic students, 6/1 for international students; for winter admission, 10/1 for international students; for spring admission, 2/1 for international students. Applications are processed on a rolling basis. Application fee: $30 ($50 for international students). Electronic applications accepted. *Expenses:* Tuition, state resident: full-time $7662; part-time $478.85 per credit hour. Tuition, nonresident: full-time $16,920; part-time $1057.55 per credit hour. Required fees: $571.20; $35.70 per credit hour. $188.05 per semester. Tuition and fees vary according to course load and program. *Financial support:* In 2010–11, 3 fellowships with tuition reimbursements (averaging $15,409 per year), 5 teaching assistantships with tuition reimbursements (averaging $15,181 per year) were awarded; research assistantships, institutionally sponsored loans also available. Support available to part-time students. Financial award application deadline: 3/1. *Faculty research:* Labor and social history, citizenship and governance, modern U. S. history, early modern and modern European history, African-American history. *Unit head:* Dr. Marc Kruman, Chair, 313-577-2525, Fax: 313-577-6987, E-mail: aa1277@wayne.edu. *Application contact:* Mel Small, Graduate Director, 313-577-6138, E-mail: m.small@wayne.edu.

West Chester University of Pennsylvania, Office of Graduate Studies, College of Arts and Sciences, Department of History, West Chester, PA 19383. Offers history (M Ed, MA); holocaust and genocide studies (MA, Certificate). Part-time and evening/weekend programs available. *Students:* 9 full-time (7 women), 34 part-time (19 women); includes 3 minority (2 Asian, non-Hispanic/Latino; 1 Hispanic/Latino). Average age 30. 30 applicants, 57% accepted, 9 enrolled. In 2010, 18 master's awarded. *Degree requirements:* For master's, comprehensive exam (for some programs), thesis optional. *Entrance requirements:* For master's, statement of professional goals, writing sample, minimum GPA of 3.0 in history, three letters of recommendation. Additional exam requirements/recommendations for international students: Required—TOEFL (minimum score 550 paper-based; 213 computer-based; 80 iBT). *Application deadline:* For fall admission, 4/15 priority date for domestic students, 3/15 for international students; for spring admission, 10/15 for domestic students, 9/1 for international students. Applications are processed on a rolling basis. Application fee: $35. Electronic applications accepted. *Expenses:* Tuition, state resident: full-time $6966; part-time $387 per credit. Tuition, nonresident: full-time $11,146; part-time $619 per credit. Required fees: $1614.40; $133.24 per credit. Part-time tuition and fees vary according to campus/location. *Financial support:* Unspecified assistantships available. Support available to part-time students. Financial award application deadline: 2/15; financial award applicants required to submit FAFSA. *Faculty research:* Oral histories, siege of Leningrad. *Unit head:* Dr. Wayne Hanley, Chair, 610-436-

2201, E-mail: whanley@wcupa.edu. *Application contact:* Dr. Jonathan Friedman, Graduate Coordinator of Holocaust and Genocide Studies, 610-436-2972, E-mail: jfriedman@wcupa.edu.

Western Carolina University, Graduate School, College of Arts and Sciences, Department of History, Cullowhee, NC 28723. Offers MA. Part-time and evening/weekend programs available. *Degree requirements:* For master's, one foreign language, comprehensive exam, thesis or alternative. *Entrance requirements:* For master's, GRE General Test, appropriate undergraduate degree, 3 letters of recommendation. Additional exam requirements/recommendations for international students: Required—TOEFL (minimum score 550 paper-based; 270 computer-based; 79 iBT). *Faculty research:* Social and economic history of the American South, Islamic world history, German history, social and political protest, medieval social history.

Western Connecticut State University, Division of Graduate Studies and External Programs, School of Arts and Sciences, Department of History, Danbury, CT 06810-6885. Offers MA. Part-time programs available. *Students:* 8 full-time (4 women), 21 part-time (5 women); includes 1 minority (Hispanic/Latino). Average age 42. In 2010, 4 master's awarded. *Degree requirements:* For master's, thesis or research project, completion of program in 6 years. *Entrance requirements:* For master's, minimum GPA of 2.5. Additional exam requirements/recommendations for international students: Recommended—TOEFL (minimum score 550 paper-based; 213 computer-based; 79 iBT), IELTS (minimum score 6). *Application deadline:* For fall admission, 8/5 priority date for domestic students; for spring admission, 1/5 priority date for domestic students. Applications are processed on a rolling basis. Application fee: $50. *Expenses:* Tuition, state resident: full-time $5012; part-time $417 per credit hour. Tuition, nonresident: full-time $13,962; part-time $423 per credit hour. Required fees: $3886. Full-time tuition and fees vary according to course load, degree level and program. *Financial support:* Application deadline: 5/1. *Unit head:* Dr. Michael Nolan, Assistant Professor, 203-837-8483, Fax: 203-837-8525, E-mail: nolanm@wcsu.edu. *Application contact:* Chris Shankle, Associate Director of Graduate Studies, 203-837-9005, Fax: 203-837-8326, E-mail: shanklec@wcsu.edu.

Western Illinois University, School of Graduate Studies, College of Arts and Sciences, Department of History, Macomb, IL 61455-1390. Offers MA. Part-time programs available. *Students:* 17 full-time (6 women), 11 part-time (4 women); includes 1 minority (Asian, non-Hispanic/Latino), 1 international. Average age 27. 18 applicants, 67% accepted. In 2010, 17 master's awarded. *Degree requirements:* For master's, thesis or alternative. *Entrance requirements:* Additional exam requirements/recommendations for international students: Required—TOEFL (minimum score 550 paper-based; 213 computer-based; 80 iBT). *Application deadline:* Applications are processed on a rolling basis. Application fee: $30. Electronic applications accepted. *Expenses:* Tuition, state resident: full-time $6370; part-time $265.40 per credit hour. Tuition, nonresident: full-time $12,740; part-time $530.80 per credit hour. Required fees: $75.67 per credit hour. *Financial support:* In 2010–11, 9 students received support, including 9 research assistantships with full tuition reimbursements available (averaging $7,280 per year). Financial award applicants required to submit FAFSA. *Unit head:* Dr. Virginia Boynton, Chairperson, 309-298-1053. *Application contact:* Evelyn Hoing, Assistant Director of Graduate Studies, 309-298-1806, Fax: 309-298-2345, E-mail: grad-office@wiu.edu.

Western Kentucky University, Graduate Studies, Potter College of Arts and Letters, Department of History, Bowling Green, KY 42101. Offers MA, MA Ed. Part-time and evening/weekend programs available. Postbaccalaureate distance learning degree programs offered. *Degree requirements:* For master's, comprehensive exam, thesis optional, final exam. *Entrance requirements:* For master's, GRE General Test, minimum GPA of 2.75. Additional exam requirements/recommendations for international students: Required—TOEFL (minimum score 555 paper-based; 213 computer-based; 79 iBT). *Faculty research:* U.S.A, Europe, China, India, Latin America.

Western Michigan University, Graduate College, College of Arts and Sciences, Department of History, Kalamazoo, MI 49008. Offers MA, PhD. *Degree requirements:* For master's, thesis optional, oral exams; for doctorate, thesis/dissertation, oral exam. *Entrance requirements:* For doctorate, GRE General Test.

Western Washington University, Graduate School, College of Humanities and Social Sciences, Department of History, Bellingham, WA 98225-5996. Offers MA. Part-time programs available. *Degree requirements:* For master's, one foreign language, comprehensive exam, thesis (for some programs). *Entrance requirements:* For master's, GRE General Test, minimum GPA of 3.0 in last 60 semester hours or last 90 quarter hours. Additional exam requirements/recommendations for international students: Required—TOEFL (minimum score 567 paper-based; 227 computer-based). Electronic applications accepted.

Westfield State University, Division of Graduate and Continuing Education, Department of History, Westfield, MA 01086. Offers M Ed. Part-time and evening/weekend programs available. *Degree requirements:* For master's, thesis. *Entrance requirements:* For master's, GRE General Test or MAT, minimum undergraduate GPA of 2.7.

West Texas A&M University, College of Education and Social Sciences, Department of History and Political Science, Program in History, Canyon, TX 79016-0001. Offers MA. Part-time and evening/weekend programs available. *Degree requirements:* For master's, comprehensive exam, thesis optional. *Entrance requirements:* For master's, GRE General Test. Additional exam requirements/recommendations for international students: Required—TOEFL (minimum score 550 paper-based). Electronic applications accepted. *Faculty research:* John B. Stetson Jr. (an American businessman in Warsaw), creation of kokugo in late Meiji Japan, canon law on cyberspace, Russian and American frontiers, Texas women of two cultures.

West Virginia University, Eberly College of Arts and Sciences, Department of History, Morgantown, WV 26506. Offers African history (MA, PhD); African-American history (MA, PhD); American history (MA, PhD); Appalachian/regional history (MA, PhD); East Asian history (MA, PhD); European history (MA, PhD); history of science and technology (MA, PhD); Latin American history (MA). Part-time programs available. *Degree requirements:* For master's, one foreign language, thesis (for some programs), oral exam, thesis defense; for doctorate, one foreign language, comprehensive exam, thesis/dissertation, dissertation defense. *Entrance requirements:* For master's, GRE General Test, minimum GPA of 3.0; for doctorate, GRE General Test. Additional exam requirements/recommendations for international students: Required—TOEFL (minimum score 550 paper-based), IELTS (minimum score 6.5). Electronic applications accepted. *Faculty research:* U.S., Appalachia, modern Europe, Africa, colonial and post-colonial societies.

Wichita State University, Graduate School, Fairmount College of Liberal Arts and Sciences, Department of History, Wichita, KS 67260. Offers MA. Part-time programs available. *Unit head:* Dr. Robert Owens, Chair, 316-978-3150, Fax: 316-978-3473, E-mail: robert.owens@wichita.edu. *Application contact:* Dr. John Dreifort, Graduate Coordinator, 316-978-3150, Fax: 316-978-3473, E-mail: john.dreifort@wichita.edu.

Wilfrid Laurier University, Faculty of Graduate and Postdoctoral Studies, Faculty of Arts, Department of History, Waterloo, ON N2L 3C5, Canada. Offers MA, PhD. Part-time programs available. *Faculty:* 22 full-time (5 women). *Students:* 35 full-time (20 women), 5 part-time (1 woman), 3 international. 166 applicants, 18% accepted, 18 enrolled. In 2010, 12 master's, 1 doctorate awarded. *Degree requirements:* For master's, thesis optional; for doctorate, thesis/dissertation. *Entrance requirements:* For master's, honors BA or the equivalent in history; minimum B+ average in undergraduate course work, exclusive of first year level courses; for doctorate, MA in history, minimum A- average. Additional exam requirements/recommendations for international students: Required—TOEFL (minimum score 89 iBT). *Application deadline:* For fall admission, 2/1 priority date for domestic and international students. Application fee: $100. Electronic applications accepted. Tuition and fees charges are reported in Canadian dollars. *Expenses:* Tuition, area resident: Full-time $15,300 Canadian dollars; part-time $1200 Canadian dollars per credit. International tuition: $21,300 Canadian dollars full-time. Required fees: $650 Canadian dollars; $100 Canadian dollars per credit. Tuition and fees vary according to course load, degree level, campus/location and program. *Financial support:* In 2010–11, 50 fellowships, 50 teaching assistantships were awarded; career-related internships or fieldwork, scholarships/grants, health care benefits, and unspecified assistantships also available. *Faculty research:* Canadian, early modern European, modern European, Scottish, race, class, imperialism, slavery, British, urban and rural, science/medicine/technology, gender/women's/family, international, United States. *Unit head:* Dr. Susan Neylan, Graduate Coordinator, 519-884-0710 Ext. 3595, Fax: 519-746-3655, E-mail: sneylan@wlu.ca. *Application contact:* Jennifer Williams, Graduate Admission and Records Officer, 519-884-0710 Ext. 3536, Fax: 519-884-1020, E-mail: gradstudies@wlu.ca.

William Paterson University of New Jersey, College of Humanities and Social Sciences, Wayne, NJ 07470-8420. Offers clinical and counseling psychology (MA); English (MA); history (MA); public policy and international affairs (MA); sociology (MA). Part-time and evening/weekend programs available. Electronic applications accepted.

Winthrop University, College of Arts and Sciences, Department of History, Rock Hill, SC 29733. Offers MA. Part-time programs available. *Degree requirements:* For master's, one foreign language, thesis optional. *Entrance requirements:* For master's, GRE General Test or PRAXIS, 24 hours of history at the undergraduate level. Electronic applications accepted.

Worcester State University, Graduate Studies, Program in History, Worcester, MA 01602-2597. Offers MA. Part-time programs available. *Faculty:* 3 full-time (2 women), 1 part-time/adjunct (0 women). *Students:* 1 full-time (0 women), 13 part-time (5 women); includes 1 Black or African American, non-Hispanic/Latino. Average age 39. 10 applicants, 90% accepted, 4 enrolled. In 2010, 11 master's awarded. *Degree requirements:* For master's, comprehensive exam (for some programs), thesis optional. *Entrance requirements:* For master's, GRE General Test or MAT, 18 undergraduate credits in history, including U. S. history and Western civilizations. Additional exam requirements/recommendations for international students: Required—TOEFL (minimum score 500 paper-based; 61 iBT). *Application deadline:* Applications are processed on a rolling basis. Application fee: $40. Electronic applications accepted. *Expenses:* Tuition, state resident: full-time $2700; part-time $150 per credit. Tuition, nonresident: full-time $2700; part-time $150 per credit. Required fees: $2016; $112 per credit. *Financial support:* In 2010–11, 1 student received support, including 1 research assistantship with full tuition reimbursement available (averaging $4,800 per year); career-related internships or fieldwork, scholarships/grants, and unspecified assistantships also available. Financial award application deadline: 3/1; financial award applicants required to submit FAFSA. *Faculty research:* Labor history, Middle East politics, American-Russian relations, American-East Asian relations. *Unit head:* Dr. Charlotte Haller, Coordinator, 508-929-8046, Fax: 508-929-8155, E-mail: challer1@worcester.edu. *Application contact:* Sara Grady, Assistant Dean of Graduate and Continuing Education, 508-929-8787, Fax: 508-929-8100, E-mail: sara.grady@worcester.edu.

Wright State University, School of Graduate Studies, College of Liberal Arts, Department of History, Dayton, OH 45435. Offers MA. *Degree requirements:* For master's, thesis optional. *Entrance requirements:* For master's, GRE General Test, minimum GPA of 3.0 in history, 2.7 overall. Additional exam requirements/recommendations for international students: Required—TOEFL. *Faculty research:* U.S. religions; women's, Southern, European, and archival history.

Yale University, Graduate School of Arts and Sciences, Department of History, New Haven, CT 06520. Offers history (M Phil, MA, PhD); history of science and medicine (MA, PhD). Terminal master's awarded for partial completion of doctoral program. *Degree requirements:* For master's, one foreign language; for doctorate, 2 foreign languages, thesis/dissertation. *Entrance requirements:* For doctorate, GRE General Test.

York University, Faculty of Graduate Studies, Faculty of Arts, Program in History, Toronto, ON M3J 1P3, Canada. Offers MA, PhD. Part-time programs available. *Degree requirements:* For master's, thesis or alternative; for doctorate, one foreign language, comprehensive exam, thesis/dissertation, qualifying exam. Electronic applications accepted.

Youngstown State University, Graduate School, College of Liberal Arts and Social Sciences, Department of History, Youngstown, OH 44555-0001. Offers MA. Part-time programs available. *Degree requirements:* For master's, thesis optional, oral and written exams. *Entrance requirements:* For master's, minimum GPA of 2.75. Additional exam requirements/recommendations for international students: Required—TOEFL. *Faculty research:* Holocaust, Marxism, nineteenth- and twentieth-century United States, historic preservation, revolutionary France.

History of Medicine

McGill University, Faculty of Graduate and Postdoctoral Studies, Faculty of Arts, Department of History, Montréal, QC H3A 2T5, Canada. Offers history (MA, PhD); history of medicine (MA).

McGill University, Faculty of Graduate and Postdoctoral Studies, Faculty of Medicine, Department of Social Studies in Medicine, Montréal, QC H3A 2T5, Canada. Offers medical anthropology (MA, PhD); medical history (MA, PhD); medical sociology (MA, PhD).

Rutgers, The State University of New Jersey, New Brunswick, Graduate School-New Brunswick, Program in History, Piscataway, NJ 08854-8097. Offers African-American history (PhD); early American history (PhD); early modern European history (PhD); east Asian history (PhD); global and comparative history (PhD); history (PhD); history of diplomacy and foreign relations (PhD); history of technology, environment and health (PhD); history of the Atlantic cultures and African diaspora (PhD); Latin American history (PhD); medieval history (PhD); modern European history (PhD); nineteenth and twentieth century American history (PhD); women's and gender history (PhD). *Degree requirements:* For doctorate, thesis/dissertation. *Entrance requirements:* For doctorate, GRE General Test, sample of written work. Electronic applications accepted. *Expenses:* Tuition, state resident: full-time $7200; part-time $600 per credit. Tuition, nonresident: full-time $11,124; part-time $927 per credit. *Faculty research:* American history, European history, Afro-American history, women's history, Latin American history.

The University of Manchester, Faculty of Life Sciences, Manchester, United Kingdom. Offers adaptive organismal biology (M Phil, PhD); animal biology (M Phil, PhD); biochemistry (M Phil, PhD); bioinformatics (M Phil, PhD); biomolecular sciences (M Phil, PhD); biotechnology (M Phil, PhD); cell biology (M Phil, PhD); cell matrix research (M Phil, PhD); channels and transporters (M Phil, PhD); developmental biology (M Phil, PhD); Egyptology (M Phil, PhD); environmental biology (M Phil, PhD); evolutionary biology (M Phil, PhD); gene expression (M Phil, PhD);

History of Medicine

The University of Manchester (continued)
genetics (M Phil, PhD); history of science, technology and medicine (M Phil, PhD); immunology (M Phil, PhD); integrative neurobiology and behavior (M Phil, PhD); membrane trafficking (M Phil, PhD); microbiology (M Phil, PhD); molecular and cellular neuroscience (M Phil, PhD); molecular biology (M Phil, PhD); molecular cancer studies (M Phil, PhD); neuroscience (M Phil, PhD); ophthalmology (M Phil, PhD); optometry (M Phil, PhD); organelle function (M Phil, PhD); pharmacology (M Phil, PhD); physiology (M Phil, PhD); plant sciences (M Phil, PhD); stem cell research (M Phil, PhD); structural biology (M Phil, PhD); systems neuroscience (M Phil, PhD); toxicology (M Phil, PhD).

University of Minnesota, Twin Cities Campus, Graduate School, Program in the History of Science, Technology and Medicine, Minneapolis, MN 55455-0213. Offers MA, PhD. Part-time programs available. *Degree requirements:* For master's, one foreign language, thesis or alternative; for doctorate, 2 foreign languages, thesis/dissertation. *Entrance requirements:* For master's and doctorate, GRE General Test. *Faculty research:* History of infectious diseases, history of public health, history of evolutionary biology, history of infertility, women in science.

Yale University, Graduate School of Arts and Sciences, Department of History, Program in the History of Science and Medicine, New Haven, CT 06520. Offers MS, PhD. *Degree requirements:* For doctorate, 2 foreign languages, thesis/dissertation. *Entrance requirements:* For doctorate, GRE General Test.

History of Science and Technology

Arizona State University, Graduate College, Program in Human and Social Dimensions of Science and Technology, Tempe, AZ 85287-5603. Offers PhD. *Faculty:* 43 full-time (13 women). *Students:* 9 full-time (5 women), 3 part-time (2 women); includes 2 minority (1 Asian, non-Hispanic/Latino; 1 Hispanic/Latino), 1 international. Average age 38. 21 applicants, 29% accepted, 2 enrolled. *Degree requirements:* For doctorate, comprehensive exam, thesis/ dissertation, interactive Program of Study (iPOS) submitted before completing 50 percent of required credit hours. *Entrance requirements:* For doctorate, GRE, minimum GPA of 3.0 in the last 2 years of work leading to the bachelor's degree, 3 letters of recommendation, statement of research interests and goals, curriculum vitae or resume, completed academic record form, 10-25 page writing sample. Additional exam requirements/recommendations for international students: Required—TOEFL (minimum score 550 paper-based; 213 computer-based; 80 iBT), IELTS (minimum score 6.5). *Application deadline:* For fall admission, 12/15 for domestic and international students. Application fee: $70 ($90 for international students). Electronic applications accepted. *Expenses:* Tuition, state resident: full-time $8510; part-time $608 per credit. Tuition, nonresident: full-time $16,542; part-time $919 per credit. Required fees: $339; $110 per credit. Part-time tuition and fees vary according to course load. *Financial support:* In 2010–11, 4 research assistantships with full and partial tuition reimbursements (averaging $17,355 per year), 2 teaching assistantships with full and partial tuition reimbursements (averaging $15,500 per year) were awarded; fellowships with full and partial tuition reimbursements, institutionally sponsored loans, scholarships/grants, and tuition waivers (full and partial) also available. Financial award application deadline: 3/1; financial award applicants required to submit FAFSA. *Unit head:* Dr. Clark A. Miller, Chair, 480-965-1778, E-mail: hsd@asu.edu. *Application contact:* Graduate Admissions, 480-965-6113, Fax: 480-965-5158.

Carnegie Mellon University, College of Humanities and Social Sciences, Department of History, Pittsburgh, PA 15213-3891. Offers African and African-American diaspora (PhD); culture and power (PhD); gender and the family (PhD); history (MA, MS); history and policy (MA); labor and politics (PhD); science, technology, medicine and environment (PhD). Part-time programs available. *Degree requirements:* For doctorate, oral and written comprehensive exams, dissertation defense. *Entrance requirements:* For doctorate, GRE General Test. Additional exam requirements/recommendations for international students: Required—TOEFL. Electronic applications accepted. *Faculty research:* Anthropology and history, African American history, technology/environment, cultural history analysis.

Cornell University, Graduate School, Graduate Fields of Arts and Sciences, Field of History, Ithaca, NY 14853-0001. Offers African history (MA, PhD); American history (MA, PhD); ancient history (MA, PhD); early modern European history (MA, PhD); English history (MA, PhD); French history (MA, PhD); German history (MA, PhD); history of science (MA, PhD); Latin American history (MA, PhD); medieval Chinese history (MA, PhD); medieval history (MA, PhD); modern Chinese history (MA, PhD); modern European history (MA, PhD); modern Japanese history (MA, PhD); premodern Islamic history (MA, PhD); premodern Japanese history (MA, PhD); Renaissance history (MA, PhD); Russian history (MA, PhD); Southeast Asian history (MA, PhD). *Faculty:* 53 full-time (15 women). *Students:* 59 full-time (30 women); includes 3 Black or African American, non-Hispanic/Latino; 2 Asian, non-Hispanic/Latino; 4 Hispanic/Latino, 22 international. Average age 30. 217 applicants, 6% accepted, 8 enrolled. In 2010, 9 master's, 5 doctorates awarded. Terminal master's awarded for partial completion of doctoral program. *Degree requirements:* For master's, thesis; for doctorate, 2 foreign languages, comprehensive exam, thesis/dissertation, 1 year of teaching experience. *Entrance requirements:* For master's and doctorate, GRE General Test, writing sample, 3 letters of recommendation. Additional exam requirements/recommendations for international students: Required—TOEFL (minimum score 550 paper-based; 213 computer-based; 77 iBT). *Application deadline:* For fall admission, 1/15 for domestic students. Application fee: $80. Electronic applications accepted. *Expenses:* Tuition: Full-time $29,500. Required fees: $76. Tuition and fees vary according to degree level and program. *Financial support:* In 2010–11, 26 fellowships with full tuition reimbursements, 27 teaching assistantships with full tuition reimbursements were awarded; research assistantships with full tuition reimbursements, institutionally sponsored loans, scholarships/grants, health care benefits, tuition waivers (full and partial), and unspecified assistantships also available. Financial award applicants required to submit FAFSA. *Unit head:* Director of Graduate Studies, 607-255-6738, Fax: 607-255-0469. *Application contact:* Graduate Field Assistant, 607-255-6738, Fax: 607-255-0469, E-mail: history_grad_info@cornell.edu.

Cornell University, Graduate School, Graduate Fields of Arts and Sciences, Field of Science and Technology Studies, Ithaca, NY 14853-0001. Offers history and philosophy of science and technology (MA, PhD); social studies of science and technology (MA, PhD). *Faculty:* 20 full-time (10 women). *Students:* 24 full-time (15 women); includes 2 Black or African American, non-Hispanic/Latino; 4 Asian, non-Hispanic/Latino, 7 international. Average age 29. 60 applicants, 15% accepted, 5 enrolled. In 2010, 4 master's awarded. Terminal master's awarded for partial completion of doctoral program. *Degree requirements:* For master's, one foreign language, thesis; for doctorate, one foreign language, comprehensive exam, thesis/dissertation. *Entrance requirements:* For master's and doctorate, GRE General Test, writing sample, 3 letters of recommendation. Additional exam requirements/recommendations for international students: Required—TOEFL (minimum score 550 paper-based; 213 computer-based; 77 iBT). *Application deadline:* For fall admission, 1/10 for domestic students. Application fee: $80. Electronic applications accepted. *Expenses:* Tuition: Full-time $29,500. Required fees: $76. Tuition and fees vary according to degree level and program. *Financial support:* In 2010–11, 10 fellowships with full tuition reimbursements, 1 research assistantship with full tuition reimbursement, 10 teaching assistantships with full tuition reimbursements were awarded; institutionally sponsored loans, scholarships/grants, health care benefits, tuition waivers (full and partial), and unspecified assistantships also available. Financial award applicants required to submit FAFSA. *Faculty research:* History, philosophy, sociology, politics, and policy of science and technology; gender, legal order, environment, and communication. *Unit head:* Director of Graduate Studies, 607-255-6234. *Application contact:* Graduate Field Assistant, 607-255-6234, E-mail: stsgradfield@cornell.edu.

Drexel University, College of Arts and Sciences, Department of History and Politics, Philadelphia, PA 19104-2875. Offers science, technology and society (MS). Part-time programs available. *Entrance requirements:* For master's, GRE. Additional exam requirements/ recommendations for international students: Required—TOEFL. Electronic applications accepted.

Georgia Institute of Technology, Graduate Studies and Research, Ivan Allen College of Policy and International Affairs, School of History, Technology, and Society, Atlanta, GA 30332-0001. Offers history and sociology of technology and science (MS, PhD). Terminal master's awarded for partial completion of doctoral program. *Degree requirements:* For master's, research paper; for doctorate, one foreign language, comprehensive exam, thesis/dissertation. *Entrance requirements:* Additional exam requirements/recommendations for international students: Required—TOEFL. Electronic applications accepted. *Faculty research:* Industrialization, labor history, modern Europe, social history, sociology of science.

Harvard University, Graduate School of Arts and Sciences, Department of the History of Science, Cambridge, MA 02138. Offers AM, PhD. Terminal master's awarded for partial completion of doctoral program. *Degree requirements:* For master's, one foreign language; for doctorate, 2 foreign languages, thesis/dissertation. *Entrance requirements:* For master's and doctorate, GRE General Test. Additional exam requirements/recommendations for international students: Required—TOEFL. *Expenses:* Tuition: Full-time $34,976. Required fees: $1166. Full-time tuition and fees vary according to program.

Indiana University Bloomington, University Graduate School, College of Arts and Sciences, Department of History and Philosophy of Science, Bloomington, IN 47405-7000. Offers MA, PhD, MLS/MA. Part-time programs available. *Faculty:* 9 full-time (2 women). *Students:* 31 full-time (5 women), 5 part-time (1 woman); includes 2 minority (both Hispanic/Latino), 7 international. Average age 33. 41 applicants, 76% accepted, 6 enrolled. In 2010, 5 master's, 3 doctorates awarded. Terminal master's awarded for partial completion of doctoral program. *Degree requirements:* For master's, one foreign language, thesis optional; for doctorate, 2 foreign languages, thesis/dissertation. *Entrance requirements:* For master's and doctorate, GRE General Test. Additional exam requirements/recommendations for international students: Required—TOEFL. *Application deadline:* For fall admission, 1/15 priority date for domestic students, 12/15 for international students. Application fee: $55 ($65 for international students). Electronic applications accepted. *Financial support:* In 2010–11, 2 fellowships with full tuition reimbursements (averaging $15,000 per year), 4 research assistantships with full tuition reimbursements (averaging $12,628 per year), 11 teaching assistantships with full tuition reimbursements (averaging $11,838 per year) were awarded; institutionally sponsored loans, scholarships/grants, health care benefits, and unspecified assistantships also available. Financial award application deadline: 3/1; financial award applicants required to submit FAFSA. *Faculty research:* History of scientific ideas, instruments, and institutions; foundations of physics; history of philosophy of science; history and philosophy of biology; early modern science and medicine. *Unit head:* Domenico Bertoloni Meli, Chair, 812-855-8746, E-mail: dbmeli@indiana.edu. *Application contact:* Peggy Roberts, Graduate Secretary, 812-855-3622, Fax: 812-855-3631, E-mail: hpscdept@indiana.edu.

Iowa State University of Science and Technology, Graduate College, College of Liberal Arts and Sciences, Department of History, Ames, IA 50011. Offers agricultural history and rural studies (PhD); history (MA); history of technology and science (MA, PhD). *Faculty:* 18 full-time (5 women). *Students:* 30 full-time (8 women), 18 part-time (5 women); includes 1 Black or African American, non-Hispanic/Latino, 5 international. 31 applicants, 61% accepted, 13 enrolled. In 2010, 5 master's, 3 doctorates awarded. *Degree requirements:* For master's, thesis or alternative; for doctorate, thesis/dissertation. *Entrance requirements:* For master's and doctorate, GRE General Test. Additional exam requirements/recommendations for international students: Required—TOEFL (minimum score 600 paper-based; 79 iBT), IELTS (minimum score 7). *Application deadline:* For fall admission, 1/15 priority date for domestic and international students. Applications are processed on a rolling basis. Application fee: $40 ($90 for international students). Electronic applications accepted. *Financial support:* In 2010–11, 1 research assistantship with full and partial tuition reimbursement (averaging $20,295 per year), 21 teaching assistantships with full and partial tuition reimbursements (averaging $9,263 per year) were awarded; scholarships/grants, health care benefits, and unspecified assistantships also available. *Unit head:* Dr. Charles Dobbs, Chair, 515-294-7266, Fax: 515-294-6390, E-mail: cdobbs@iastate.edu. *Application contact:* Dr. Pamela Riney-Kehrberg, Information Contact, 515-294-1451, Fax: 515-294-6390.

The Johns Hopkins University, Zanvyl Krieger School of Arts and Sciences, Department of the History of Science and Technology, Baltimore, MD 21218-2699. Offers MA, PhD. *Faculty:* 6 full-time (3 women), 9 part-time/adjunct (3 women). *Students:* 9 full-time (4 women), 1 part-time (0 women), 3 international. Average age 28. 23 applicants, 9% accepted, 1 enrolled. Terminal master's awarded for partial completion of doctoral program. *Degree requirements:* For master's, one foreign language, thesis; for doctorate, 2 foreign languages, thesis/ dissertation. *Entrance requirements:* For doctorate, GRE General Test. Additional exam requirements/recommendations for international students: Required—TOEFL (minimum score 600 paper-based; 250 computer-based; 100 iBT), IELTS. *Application deadline:* For fall admission, 1/15 for domestic and international students. Applications are processed on a rolling basis. Application fee: $75. Electronic applications accepted. *Financial support:* In 2010–11, 7 students received support, including 3 fellowships with full tuition reimbursements available (averaging $18,500 per year), 4 teaching assistantships with full tuition reimbursements available (averaging $18,500 per year); career-related internships or fieldwork, Federal Work-Study, institutionally sponsored loans, and health care benefits also available. Financial award application deadline: 1/31; financial award applicants required to submit FAFSA. *Faculty research:* History of physical and biological sciences, history of technology, history of medicine (sixteenth-twentieth centuries), environmental science (nineteenth-twentieth century). Total annual research expenditures: $45,236. *Unit head:* Dr. Sharon Kingsland, Chair, 410-516-7505, Fax: 410-516-7502, E-mail: sharon@jhu.edu. *Application contact:* Danielle Stout, Academic Program Coordinator, 410-516-7501, Fax: 410-516-7502, E-mail: danielle@jhu.edu.

Massachusetts Institute of Technology, School of Humanities, Arts, and Social Sciences, Program in Science, Technology, and Society, Cambridge, MA 02139. Offers history, anthropology, and science, technology and society (PhD). *Faculty:* 13 full-time (5 women). *Students:* 28 full-time (17 women); includes 4 minority (1 Black or African American, non-Hispanic/Latino; 1 American Indian or Alaska Native, non-Hispanic/Latino; 1 Asian, non-Hispanic/Latino; 1 Two or more races, non-Hispanic/Latino), 7 international. Average age 30. 146 applicants, 6% accepted, 5 enrolled. In 2010, 1 doctorate awarded. *Degree requirements:* For doctorate, comprehensive exam, thesis/dissertation. *Entrance requirements:* For doctorate, GRE General Test. Additional exam requirements/recommendations for international students: Required—TOEFL (minimum score 577 paper-based; 233 computer-based; 90 iBT), IELTS (minimum score 7). *Application deadline:* For fall admission, 1/1 for domestic and international students. Application fee: $75. Electronic applications accepted. *Expenses:* Tuition: Full-time

$38,940; part-time $605 per unit. Required fees: $272. *Financial support:* In 2010–11, 25 students received support, including 19 fellowships with tuition reimbursements available (averaging $31,612 per year), 1 research assistantship (averaging $30,697 per year), 6 teaching assistantships with tuition reimbursements available (averaging $31,405 per year); Federal Work-Study, institutionally sponsored loans, scholarships/grants, traineeships, health care benefits, and unspecified assistantships also available. *Faculty research:* History of science; history of technology; sociology of science and technology; anthropology of science and technology; science, technology, and society; aeronautics and astronautics; humans and automation. Total annual research expenditures: $472,000. *Unit head:* Prof. David A. Mindell, Director, 617-253-4062, Fax: 617-258-8118, E-mail: stsprogram@mit.edu. *Application contact:* Karen Gardner, Academic Administrator, 617-253-9759, Fax: 617-258-8118, E-mail: hasts@mit.edu.

Oregon State University, Graduate School, College of Liberal Arts, Department of History, Corvallis, OR 97331. Offers history of science (MA, PhD).

Polytechnic Institute of NYU, Department of Humanities and Social Sciences, Major in History of Science, Brooklyn, NY 11201-2990. Offers MS. Part-time and evening/weekend programs available. *Degree requirements:* For master's, comprehensive exam (for some programs), thesis (for some programs). *Entrance requirements:* Additional exam requirements/recommendations for international students: Required—TOEFL (minimum score 550 paper-based; 213 computer-based; 80 iBT); Recommended—IELTS (minimum score 6.5). *Application deadline:* For fall admission, 7/31 priority date for domestic students, 4/30 priority date for international students; for spring admission, 12/31 priority date for domestic students, 11/30 priority date for international students. Applications are processed on a rolling basis. Application fee: $75. Electronic applications accepted. *Expenses:* Tuition: Full-time $21,492; part-time $1194 per credit. Required fees: $385 per semester. Tuition and fees vary according to course load. *Financial support:* Institutionally sponsored loans, scholarships/grants, and unspecified assistantships available. Support available to part-time students. *Unit head:* Prof. Teresa Feroli, Head, 718-260-3422, E-mail: tferoli@poly.edu. *Application contact:* JeanCarlo Bonilla, Director of Graduate Enrollment Management, 718-260-3182, Fax: 718-260-3624, E-mail: gradinfo@poly.edu.

Princeton University, Graduate School, Department of History, Program in History of Science, Princeton, NJ 08544-1019. Offers PhD. *Degree requirements:* For doctorate, 2 foreign languages, thesis/dissertation. *Entrance requirements:* For doctorate, GRE General Test, sample of written work, 3 letters of recommendation. Additional exam requirements/recommendations for international students: Required—TOEFL (minimum score 600 paper-based; 250 computer-based). Electronic applications accepted. *Faculty research:* Early modern science, history of modern life sciences, history of physical sciences, history of modern technology, science and medicine in European expansion and colonialism.

Rensselaer Polytechnic Institute, Graduate School, School of Humanities, Arts, and Social Sciences, Program in Science and Technology Studies, Troy, NY 12180-3590. Offers design studies (MS, PhD); policy studies (MS, PhD); science studies (MS, PhD); sustainability studies (MS, PhD); technology studies (MS, PhD). *Faculty:* 15 full-time (5 women). *Students:* 20 full-time (5 women), 4 part-time (2 women); includes 2 Black or African American, non-Hispanic/Latino; 1 Asian, non-Hispanic/Latino, 4 international. Average age 27. 19 applicants, 42% accepted, 5 enrolled. In 2010, 2 master's, 1 doctorate awarded. Terminal master's awarded for partial completion of doctoral program. *Degree requirements:* For master's, thesis (for some programs); for doctorate, comprehensive exam, thesis/dissertation. *Entrance requirements:* For master's and doctorate, GRE General Test. Additional exam requirements/recommendations for international students: Required—TOEFL (minimum score 600 paper-based; 250 computer-based). *Application deadline:* For fall admission, 1/15 priority date for domestic students, 1/15 for international students. Applications are processed on a rolling basis. Application fee: $75. Electronic applications accepted. *Expenses:* Tuition: Full-time $39,600; part-time $1650 per credit. Required fees: $1896. *Financial support:* In 2010–11, 22 students received support, including 6 fellowships with tuition reimbursements available (averaging $19,800 per year), 2 research assistantships with full tuition reimbursements available (averaging $19,800 per year), 11 teaching assistantships with full tuition reimbursements available (averaging $19,800 per year); career-related internships or fieldwork, institutionally sponsored loans, and tuition waivers (partial) also available. Financial award application deadline: 1/15. *Faculty research:* Communities and technology, social dimensions of IT and biotechnology, ethics and policy, design. Total annual research expenditures: $75,000. *Unit head:* Dr. Sharon Anderson-Gold, Chair, 518-276-8837, Fax: 518-276-2659, E-mail: anders@rpi.edu. *Application contact:* Dr. Edward J. Woodhouse, Director of Graduate Studies, 518-276-8506, Fax: 518-276-2659, E-mail: woodhouse@rpi.edu.

Rutgers, The State University of New Jersey, New Brunswick, Graduate School-New Brunswick, Program in History, Piscataway, NJ 08854-8097. Offers African-American history (PhD); early American history (PhD); early modern European history (PhD); east Asian history (PhD); global and comparative history (PhD); history (PhD); history of diplomacy and foreign relations (PhD); history of technology, environment and health (PhD); history of the Atlantic cultures and African diaspora (PhD); Latin American history (PhD); medieval history (PhD); modern European history (PhD); nineteenth and twentieth century American history (PhD); women's and gender history (PhD). *Degree requirements:* For doctorate, thesis/dissertation. *Entrance requirements:* For doctorate, GRE General Test, sample of written work. Electronic applications accepted. *Expenses:* Tuition, state resident: full-time $7200; part-time $600 per credit. Tuition, nonresident: full-time $11,124; part-time $927 per credit. *Faculty research:* American history, European history, Afro-American history, women's history, Latin American history.

University of California, Berkeley, Graduate Division, College of Letters and Science, Group in Logic and the Methodology of Science, Berkeley, CA 94720-1500. Offers PhD. *Degree requirements:* For doctorate, qualifying exam, oral defense of dissertation. *Entrance requirements:* For doctorate, GRE General Test, minimum GPA of 3.5, 3 letters of recommendation. *Faculty research:* Set theory, recursion theory, theoretical computer science, philosophy of mathematics, philosophy of language.

University of California, San Diego, Office of Graduate Studies, Department of History, La Jolla, CA 92093. Offers history (MA, PhD); Judaic studies (MA); science studies (PhD). *Degree requirements:* For doctorate, thesis/dissertation. *Entrance requirements:* For master's and doctorate, GRE General Test. Electronic applications accepted.

University of California, San Francisco, Graduate Division, Department of History of Health Sciences, San Francisco, CA 94143. Offers MA, PhD, MD/PhD. Terminal master's awarded for partial completion of doctoral program. *Degree requirements:* For master's, 2 foreign languages, thesis; for doctorate, 2 foreign languages, thesis/dissertation. *Entrance requirements:* For master's and doctorate, GRE General Test.

University of Delaware, College of Arts and Sciences, Department of History, Hagley Program in the History of Technology and Industrialization, Newark, DE 19716. Offers MA, PhD. *Degree requirements:* For master's, thesis optional; for doctorate, comprehensive exam, thesis/dissertation. *Entrance requirements:* For master's and doctorate, interview. Electronic applications accepted.

University of Maine, Graduate School, College of Liberal Arts and Sciences, Department of History, Orono, ME 04469. Offers American studies (MA, PhD); Canadian studies (MA, PhD); East Asian (MA); environmental (MA); European (MA); technology (MA). *Faculty:* 11 full-time (1 woman), 2 part-time/adjunct (1 woman). *Students:* 24 full-time (8 women), 35 part-time (13 women); includes 4 minority (2 American Indian or Alaska Native, non-Hispanic/Latino; 2 Hispanic/Latino). Average age 38. 43 applicants, 40% accepted, 15 enrolled. In 2010, 5 master's, 3 doctorates awarded. Terminal master's awarded for partial completion of doctoral program. *Degree requirements:* For master's, variable foreign language requirement, thesis optional; for doctorate, one foreign language, thesis/dissertation. *Entrance requirements:* For master's and doctorate, GRE General Test. Additional exam requirements/recommendations for international students: Required—TOEFL. *Application deadline:* For fall admission, 2/1 priority date for domestic students. Applications are processed on a rolling basis. Application fee: $65. Electronic applications accepted. *Expenses:* Tuition, state resident: full-time $400. Tuition, nonresident: full-time $1050. *Financial support:* In 2010–11, 9 teaching assistantships with tuition reimbursements (averaging $12,790 per year) were awarded; career-related internships or fieldwork, Federal Work-Study, and tuition waivers (full and partial) also available. Support available to part-time students. Financial award application deadline: 3/1. *Faculty research:* Canadian labor and working classes; American social, cultural, and urban history. *Unit head:* Dr. Nathan Godfried, Chair, 207-581-1923, Fax: 207-581-1817. *Application contact:* Scott G. Delcourt, Associate Dean of the Graduate School, 207-581-3291, Fax: 207-581-3232, E-mail: graduate@maine.edu.

The University of Manchester, Faculty of Life Sciences, Manchester, United Kingdom. Offers adaptive organismal biology (M Phil, PhD); animal biology (M Phil, PhD); biochemistry (M Phil, PhD); bioinformatics (M Phil, PhD); biomolecular sciences (M Phil, PhD); biotechnology (M Phil, PhD); cell biology (M Phil, PhD); cell matrix research (M Phil, PhD); channels and transporters (M Phil, PhD); developmental biology (M Phil, PhD); Egyptology (M Phil, PhD); environmental biology (M Phil, PhD); evolutionary biology (M Phil, PhD); gene expression (M Phil, PhD); genetics (M Phil, PhD); history of science, technology and medicine (M Phil, PhD); immunology (M Phil, PhD); integrative neurobiology and behavior (M Phil, PhD); membrane trafficking (M Phil, PhD); microbiology (M Phil, PhD); molecular and cellular neuroscience (M Phil, PhD); molecular biology (M Phil, PhD); molecular cancer studies (M Phil, PhD); neuroscience (M Phil, PhD); ophthalmology (M Phil, PhD); optometry (M Phil, PhD); organelle function (M Phil, PhD); pharmacology (M Phil, PhD); physiology (M Phil, PhD); plant sciences (M Phil, PhD); stem cell research (M Phil, PhD); structural biology (M Phil, PhD); systems neuroscience (M Phil, PhD); toxicology (M Phil, PhD).

University of Massachusetts Amherst, Graduate School, College of Humanities and Fine Arts, Department of History, Amherst, MA 01003. Offers ancient history (MA); British Empire history (MA); European (medieval and modern) history (MA, PhD); Islamic history (MA); Latin American history (MA, PhD); modern global history (MA); public history (MA); science and technology history (MA); U. S. history (MA, PhD). Part-time programs available. *Faculty:* 38 full-time (17 women). *Students:* 38 full-time (20 women), 29 part-time (16 women); includes 6 minority (1 Black or African American, non-Hispanic/Latino; 1 American Indian or Alaska Native, non-Hispanic/Latino; 1 Asian, non-Hispanic/Latino; 3 Hispanic/Latino), 3 international. Average age 32. 165 applicants, 32% accepted, 22 enrolled. In 2010, 10 master's, 6 doctorates awarded. Terminal master's awarded for partial completion of doctoral program. *Degree requirements:* For master's, one foreign language, thesis or alternative; for doctorate, one foreign language, comprehensive exam, thesis/dissertation. *Entrance requirements:* For master's and doctorate, GRE General Test, writing sample. Additional exam requirements/recommendations for international students: Required—TOEFL (minimum score 550 paper-based; 213 computer-based; 80 iBT), IELTS (minimum score 6.5). *Application deadline:* For fall admission, 1/2 for domestic and international students. Applications are processed on a rolling basis. Application fee: $50 ($65 for international students). Electronic applications accepted. *Expenses:* Tuition, state resident: full-time $2640. Required fees: $8282. One-time fee: $357 full-time. *Financial support:* In 2010–11, 1 fellowship with full tuition reimbursement (averaging $14,661 per year), 4 research assistantships with full tuition reimbursements (averaging $4,089 per year), 39 teaching assistantships with full tuition reimbursements (averaging $12,153 per year) were awarded; career-related internships or fieldwork, Federal Work-Study, scholarships/grants, traineeships, health care benefits, tuition waivers (full), and unspecified assistantships also available. Support available to part-time students. Financial award application deadline: 1/2; financial award applicants required to submit FAFSA. *Faculty research:* Ancient and medieval history; global and comparative history; public history; history of science, technology, medicine and the environment; history of women, gender, sexuality and family. *Unit head:* Dr. Marla Miller, Graduate Program Director, 413-545-6791, Fax: 413-545-6137. *Application contact:* Jean M. Ames, Supervisor of Admissions, 413-545-0722, Fax: 413-577-0010, E-mail: gradadm@grad.umass.edu.

University of Minnesota, Twin Cities Campus, Institute of Technology, Program in History of Science and Technology, Minneapolis, MN 55455-0213. Offers MA, PhD. Terminal master's awarded for partial completion of doctoral program. *Degree requirements:* For master's, one foreign language; for doctorate, 2 foreign languages, thesis/dissertation. *Entrance requirements:* For master's and doctorate, GRE General Test. *Faculty research:* History of physics, biology, and technology.

University of Notre Dame, Graduate School, College of Arts and Letters, Division of Humanities, Program in History and Philosophy of Science, Notre Dame, IN 46556. Offers history and philosophy of science (MA, PhD); theology and science (PhD). *Degree requirements:* For doctorate, 2 foreign languages, comprehensive exam, thesis/dissertation, candidacy exam. *Entrance requirements:* For doctorate, GRE General Test. Additional exam requirements/recommendations for international students: Required—TOEFL (minimum score 600 paper-based; 250 computer-based; 80 iBT). Electronic applications accepted. *Faculty research:* Philosophy of physics, science and ethics, history and philosophy of biology, history of medicine and technology, history and philosophy of economics.

University of Oklahoma, College of Arts and Sciences, Department of History of Science, Norman, OK 73019. Offers MA, PhD. *Faculty:* 11 full-time (4 women). *Students:* 11 full-time (6 women), 6 part-time (3 women); includes 1 minority (Hispanic/Latino). Average age 31. 15 applicants, 53% accepted, 2 enrolled. In 2010, 4 master's, 1 doctorate awarded. Terminal master's awarded for partial completion of doctoral program. *Degree requirements:* For master's, one foreign language, thesis (for some programs); for doctorate, 2 foreign languages, thesis/dissertation. *Entrance requirements:* For master's, GRE, minimum GPA of 3.0 in last 60 hours, 3 letters of reference, writing sample; for doctorate, GRE. Additional exam requirements/recommendations for international students: Required—TOEFL (minimum score 550 paper-based; 213 computer-based; 79 iBT). *Application deadline:* For fall admission, 1/15 priority date for domestic students, 4/1 for international students; for spring admission, 11/1 for domestic students, 9/1 for international students. Application fee: $40 ($90 for international students). Electronic applications accepted. *Expenses:* Tuition, state resident: full-time $3893; part-time $162.20 per credit hour. Tuition, nonresident: full-time $14,167; part-time $590.30 per credit hour. Required fees: $2523; $94.60 per credit hour. Tuition and fees vary according to course load and degree level. *Financial support:* In 2010–11, 17 students received support, including 2 fellowships with full tuition reimbursements available (averaging $5,000 per year), 4 research assistantships with partial tuition reimbursements available (averaging $15,351 per year), 6 teaching assistantships with partial tuition reimbursements available (averaging $14,391 per year); Federal Work-Study, institutionally sponsored loans, scholarships/grants, traineeships, health care benefits, and unspecified assistantships also available. Financial award applicants required to submit FAFSA. *Faculty research:* Premodern science; biological and the social sciences in the Modern World; science and religion; history of technology; science, the public, and popular culture in the modern era; history of medicine and biomedical science. Total annual research expenditures: $54,118. *Unit head:* Steven J. Livesey, Professor and Department Chair, 405-325-2213, Fax: 405-325-2363, E-mail: slivesey@ou.edu. *Application contact:* Stella Graves Stuart, Graduate Recruitment Specialist, 405-325-2213, Fax: 405-325-2363, E-mail: slgstuart@ou.edu.

University of Pennsylvania, School of Arts and Sciences, Graduate Group in the History and Sociology of Science, Philadelphia, PA 19104. Offers AM, PhD. *Faculty:* 36 full-time (14 women), 7 part-time/adjunct (2 women). *Students:* 25 full-time (18 women), 1 part-time (0 women); includes 1 Asian, non-Hispanic/Latino, 3 international. 48 applicants, 15% accepted, 4 enrolled. In 2010, 2 master's, 7 doctorates awarded. *Degree requirements:* For master's, thesis or alternative; for doctorate, 2 foreign languages, thesis/dissertation. *Entrance requirements:* For master's and doctorate, GRE General Test. Additional exam requirements/

History of Science and Technology

University of Pennsylvania (continued)
recommendations for international students: Required—TOEFL. *Application deadline:* For fall admission, 12/1 priority date for domestic students. Application fee: $70. Electronic applications accepted. *Expenses:* Tuition: Full-time $25,660; part-time $4758 per course. Required fees: $2152; $270 per course. Tuition and fees vary according to course load, degree level and program. *Financial support:* Fellowships, research assistantships, teaching assistantships, institutionally sponsored loans, scholarships/grants, traineeships, health care benefits, and unspecified assistantships available. Financial award application deadline: 12/15. *Unit head:* Robert A. Aronowitz, Graduate Chair, 215-898-5621, E-mail: aronowit@wharton.upenn.edu. *Application contact:* Robert A. Aronowitz, Graduate Chair, 215-898-5621, E-mail: aronowit@wharton.upenn.edu.

University of Pittsburgh, School of Arts and Sciences, Department of History and Philosophy of Science, Pittsburgh, PA 15260. Offers MA, PhD. *Faculty:* 8 full-time (1 woman), 1 part-time/adjunct (0 women). *Students:* 30 full-time (9 women), 1 part-time (0 women); includes 5 Asian, non-Hispanic/Latino, 5 international. Average age 29. 63 applicants, 11% accepted, 3 enrolled. In 2010, 1 doctorate awarded. Terminal master's awarded for partial completion of doctoral program. *Degree requirements:* For master's, one foreign language, comprehensive exam; for doctorate, 2 foreign languages, comprehensive exam, thesis/dissertation. *Entrance requirements:* For master's and doctorate, GRE General Test. Additional exam requirements/recommendations for international students: Required—TOEFL (minimum score 550 paper-based; 213 computer-based). *Application deadline:* For fall admission, 1/10 for domestic and international students. Application fee: $50. Electronic applications accepted. *Expenses:* Tuition, state resident: full-time $17,304; part-time $701 per credit. Tuition, nonresident: full-time $29,554; part-time $1210 per credit. Required fees: $740; $214 per term. Tuition and fees vary according to program. *Financial support:* In 2010–11, 25 students received support, including 14 fellowships with full tuition reimbursements available, 11 teaching assistantships with full tuition reimbursements available; health care benefits also available. Financial award application deadline: 1/10. *Faculty research:* History and philosophy of biology, psychology, neuroscience; history and philosophy of physics; early modern science; rhetoric of science; philosophy of social science. *Unit head:* Dr. Sandra Mitchell, Chairman, 412-624-5896, Fax: 412-624-6825, E-mail: smitchel@pitt.edu. *Application contact:* Joann McIntyre, Graduate Admissions Secretary, 412-624-5896, Fax: 412-624-6825, E-mail: vanna@pitt.edu.

University of Toronto, School of Graduate Studies, Humanities Division, Institute for the History and Philosophy of Science and Technology, Toronto, ON M5S 1A1, Canada. Offers MA, PhD. Part-time programs available. *Degree requirements:* For master's, one foreign language, thesis optional, reading ability in French or German; for doctorate, 2 foreign languages, thesis/dissertation, reading knowledge examinations, thesis defense. *Entrance requirements:* For master's, 2 letters of reference; for doctorate, 2 letters of reference, MA in history and philosophy of science and technology, minimum A– average. Additional exam requirements/recommendations for international students: Required—TOEFL (minimum score 580 paper-based; 237 computer-based), TWE (minimum score 5).

University of Wisconsin–Madison, Graduate School, College of Letters and Science, Department of History of Science, Madison, WI 53706-1380. Offers history of medicine (MA); history of science (MA, PhD). Terminal master's awarded for partial completion of doctoral program. *Degree requirements:* For master's, thesis; for doctorate, 2 foreign languages, thesis/dissertation. *Entrance requirements:* For master's and doctorate, GRE General Test. Electronic applications accepted. *Expenses:* Tuition, state resident: full-time $9887; part-time $617.96 per credit. Tuition, nonresident: full-time $24,054; part-time $1503.40 per credit. Required fees: $67.63 per credit. Tuition and fees vary according to reciprocity agreements. *Faculty research:* History of biology, physical sciences, technology, medicine.

Virginia Polytechnic Institute and State University, Graduate School, College of Liberal Arts and Human Sciences, Program in Science and Technology Studies, Blacksburg, VA 24061. Offers history of science and technology (Certificate); philosophy of science and technology (Certificate); politics and policy studies of science and technology (Certificate); science and technology studies (MS, PhD, Certificate); social and cultural studies of science and technology (Certificate). *Faculty:* 11 full-time (6 women). *Students:* 27 full-time (15 women), 29 part-time (11 women); includes 3 Black or African American, non-Hispanic/Latino; 1 Asian, non-Hispanic/Latino, 6 international. Average age 41. 22 applicants, 36% accepted, 4 enrolled. In 2010, 5 master's, 5 doctorates awarded. *Degree requirements:* For master's, comprehensive exam (for some programs), thesis (for some programs); for doctorate, comprehensive exam (for some programs), thesis/dissertation (for some programs). *Entrance requirements:* For master's and doctorate, GRE. Additional exam requirements/recommendations for international students: Required—TOEFL (minimum score 550 paper-based; 213 computer-based). *Application deadline:* For fall admission, 7/1 for domestic and international students; for spring admission, 12/1 for domestic and international students. Applications are processed on a rolling basis. Application fee: $65. Electronic applications accepted. *Expenses:* Tuition, state resident: full-time $9399; part-time $488 per credit hour. Tuition, nonresident: full-time $17,854; part-time $957.75 per credit hour. Required fees: $1534. Full-time tuition and fees vary according to program. *Financial support:* In 2010–11, 1 fellowship with full tuition reimbursement (averaging $1,824 per year), 11 teaching assistantships with full tuition reimbursements (averaging $12,053 per year) were awarded; career-related internships or fieldwork, Federal Work-Study, scholarships/grants, health care benefits, and unspecified assistantships also available. Financial award application deadline: 1/15. Total annual research expenditures: $87,162. *Unit head:* Dr. Skip R. Furman, UNIT HEAD, 540-231-8966, Fax: 540-231-7013, E-mail: furman@vt.edu. *Application contact:* Crystal Harrell, Contact, 540-231-7615, Fax: 540-231-7013, E-mail: crystalharrell@vt.edu.

West Virginia University, Eberly College of Arts and Sciences, Department of History, Morgantown, WV 26506. Offers African history (MA, PhD); African-American history (MA, PhD); American history (MA, PhD); Appalachian/regional history (MA, PhD); East Asian history (MA, PhD); European history (MA, PhD); history of science and technology (MA, PhD); Latin American history (MA). Part-time programs available. *Degree requirements:* For master's, one foreign language, thesis (for some programs), oral exam, thesis defense; for doctorate, one foreign language, comprehensive exam, thesis/dissertation, dissertation defense. *Entrance requirements:* For master's, GRE General Test, minimum GPA of 3.0; for doctorate, GRE General Test. Additional exam requirements/recommendations for international students: Required—TOEFL (minimum score 550 paper-based), IELTS (minimum score 6.5). Electronic applications accepted. *Faculty research:* U.S., Appalachia, modern Europe, Africa, colonial and post-colonial societies.

Yale University, Graduate School of Arts and Sciences, Department of History, Program in the History of Science and Medicine, New Haven, CT 06520. Offers MS, PhD. *Degree requirements:* For doctorate, 2 foreign languages, thesis/dissertation. *Entrance requirements:* For doctorate, GRE General Test.

Medieval and Renaissance Studies

Arizona State University, College of Liberal Arts and Sciences, Department of English, Tempe, AZ 85287-0302. Offers applied linguistics (PhD); creative writing (MFA); English (MA, PhD), including comparative literature (MA), linguistics (MA), literature, rhetoric and composition (MA), rhetoric/composition and linguistics (PhD); linguistics (Graduate Certificate); teaching English to speakers of other languages (MTESOL). *Faculty:* 138 full-time (86 women). *Students:* 183 full-time (115 women), 98 part-time (73 women); includes 35 minority (6 Black or African American, non-Hispanic/Latino; 5 American Indian or Alaska Native, non-Hispanic/Latino; 10 Asian, non-Hispanic/Latino; 13 Hispanic/Latino; 1 Two or more races, non-Hispanic/Latino), 34 international. Average age 33. 597 applicants, 31% accepted, 88 enrolled. In 2010, 52 master's, 11 doctorates awarded. Terminal master's awarded for partial completion of doctoral program. *Degree requirements:* For master's, variable foreign language requirement, comprehensive exam (for some programs), thesis (for some programs), interactive Program of Study (iPOS) submitted before completing 50 percent of required credit hours; for doctorate, variable foreign language requirement, comprehensive exam, thesis/dissertation, interactive Program of Study (iPOS) submitted before completing 50 percent of required credit hours. *Entrance requirements:* For master's and doctorate, GRE, minimum GPA of 3.0 or equivalent in last 2 years of work leading to bachelor's degree. Additional exam requirements/recommendations for international students: Required—TOEFL, IELTS, or Pearson Test of English. *Application deadline:* For fall admission, 1/15 priority date for domestic students, 9/15 priority date for international students. Applications are processed on a rolling basis. Application fee: $70 ($90 for international students). Electronic applications accepted. *Expenses:* Tuition, state resident: full-time $8510; part-time $608 per credit. Tuition, nonresident: full-time $16,542; part-time $919 per credit. Required fees: $339; $110 per credit. Part-time tuition and fees vary according to course load. *Financial support:* In 2010–11, 12 research assistantships with tuition reimbursements (averaging $10,337 per year), 111 teaching assistantships with full and partial tuition reimbursements (averaging $13,799 per year) were awarded; fellowships with full tuition reimbursements, career-related internships or fieldwork, Federal Work-Study, institutionally sponsored loans, scholarships/grants, and tuition waivers (full and partial) also available. Financial award application deadline: 3/1; financial award applicants required to submit FAFSA. Total annual research expenditures: $734,687. *Unit head:* Dr. Maureen Goggin, Associate Chair, 480-965-1804, E-mail: maureen.goggin@asu.edu. *Application contact:* Graduate Admissions, 480-965-6113.

California State University, Long Beach, Graduate Studies, College of Liberal Arts, Department of History, Long Beach, CA 90840. Offers Africa and the Middle East (MA); ancient/medieval Europe (MA); Asia (MA); Latin America (MA); modern Europe (MA); United States (MA); world (MA). Part-time and evening/weekend programs available. *Faculty:* 12 full-time (7 women). *Students:* 18 full-time (6 women), 51 part-time (18 women); includes 3 Black or African American, non-Hispanic/Latino; 1 American Indian or Alaska Native, non-Hispanic/Latino; 3 Asian, non-Hispanic/Latino; 16 Hispanic/Latino, 1 international. Average age 30. 80 applicants, 53% accepted, 30 enrolled. In 2010, 11 master's awarded. *Degree requirements:* For master's, one foreign language, comprehensive exam or thesis. *Application deadline:* For fall admission, 3/1 for domestic students. Applications are processed on a rolling basis. Application fee: $55. Electronic applications accepted. *Financial support:* Research assistantships, Federal Work-Study, institutionally sponsored loans, and scholarships/grants available. Financial award application deadline: 3/2. *Faculty research:* All periods of European and American history, recent Asian and African history. *Unit head:* Dr. Nancy Quam-Wickham, Department Chair, 562-985-4431, Fax: 562-985-5431, E-mail: quamwick@csulb.edu. *Application contact:* Dr. Houri Berberian, Graduate Advisor, 562-985-4524, Fax: 562-985-4431, E-mail: hberber@csulb.edu.

The Catholic University of America, School of Arts and Sciences, Department of History, Washington, DC 20064. Offers history (MA, PhD); religion and society in the late medieval and early modern world (MA); MA/JD; MSLS/MA. Part-time programs available. *Faculty:* 13 full-time (7 women), 2 part-time/adjunct (0 women). *Students:* 16 full-time (12 women), 27 part-time (12 women); includes 1 American Indian or Alaska Native, non-Hispanic/Latino; 1 Hispanic/Latino, 3 international. Average age 32. 51 applicants, 41% accepted, 11 enrolled. In 2010, 5 master's, 3 doctorates awarded. *Degree requirements:* For master's, one foreign language, comprehensive exam, thesis optional; for doctorate, 2 foreign languages, comprehensive exam, thesis/dissertation. *Entrance requirements:* For master's and doctorate, GRE General Test, statement of purpose, official copies of academic transcripts, three letters of recommendation, writing sample. Additional exam requirements/recommendations for international students: Required—TOEFL (minimum score 580 paper-based; 237 computer-based). *Application deadline:* For fall admission, 8/1 priority date for domestic students, 7/15 for international students; for spring admission, 12/1 priority date for domestic students, 10/15 for international students. Applications are processed on a rolling basis. Application fee: $55. Electronic applications accepted. *Expenses:* Tuition: Full-time $33,580; part-time $1315 per credit hour. Required fees: $80; $40 per semester hour. One-time fee: $425. *Financial support:* Fellowships, research assistantships, teaching assistantships, Federal Work-Study, scholarships/grants, tuition waivers (full and partial), and unspecified assistantships available. Financial award application deadline: 2/1; financial award applicants required to submit FAFSA. *Faculty research:* Modern European intellectual history, history of mathematics and sciences, Renaissance, Catholic reformation, medieval women and gender. *Unit head:* Dr. Jerry Muller, Chair, 202-319-5484, Fax: 202-319-5569, E-mail: mullerj@cua.edu. *Application contact:* Andrew Woodall, Director of Graduate Admissions, 202-319-5057, Fax: 202-319-6533, E-mail: cua-admissions@cua.edu.

The Catholic University of America, School of Arts and Sciences, Program in Medieval and Byzantine Studies, Washington, DC 20064. Offers MA, PhD, Certificate. Part-time programs available. *Students:* 5 full-time (0 women), 7 part-time (2 women). Average age 32. 27 applicants, 59% accepted, 5 enrolled. In 2010, 3 master's awarded. *Degree requirements:* For master's, one foreign language, comprehensive exam, thesis or alternative; for doctorate, 2 foreign languages, comprehensive exam, thesis/dissertation. *Entrance requirements:* For master's and doctorate, GRE General Test, statement of purpose, official copies of academic transcripts, three letters of recommendation. Additional exam requirements/recommendations for international students: Required—TOEFL (minimum score 580 paper-based; 237 computer-based). *Application deadline:* For fall admission, 8/1 priority date for domestic students, 7/15 for international students; for spring admission, 12/1 priority date for domestic students, 10/15 for international students. Applications are processed on a rolling basis. Application fee: $55. Electronic applications accepted. *Expenses:* Tuition: Full-time $33,580; part-time $1315 per credit hour. Required fees: $80; $40 per semester hour. One-time fee: $425. *Financial support:* Fellowships, research assistantships, teaching assistantships, Federal Work-Study, scholarships/grants, tuition waivers (full and partial), and unspecified assistantships available. Financial award application deadline: 2/1; financial award applicants required to submit FAFSA. *Faculty research:* Franciscan and medieval theology, history and medieval theology, medieval institutional history, medieval political theology, early medieval history. *Unit head:* Dr. Lilla Kop??r, Director, 202-319-5794, Fax: 202-319-6609, E-mail: kopar@cua.edu. *Application contact:* Andrew Woodall, Director of Graduate Admissions, 202-319-5057, Fax: 202-319-6533, E-mail: cua-admissions@cua.edu.

Central European University, Graduate Studies, School of Social Sciences and Humanities, Budapest, Hungary. Offers economics (MA, PhD); gender studies (MA, PhD); international relations and European studies (MA, PhD); mathematics and its applications (MS, PhD); medieval studies (MA, PhD); nationalism studies (MA, PhD); philosophy (MA, PhD); political science (MA, PhD); public policy (MA, PhD); sociology and social anthropology (MA, PhD). *Faculty:* 90 full-time (29 women), 13 part-time/adjunct (7 women). *Students:* 732 full-time (404 women). Average age 28. 3,639 applicants, 22% accepted, 416 enrolled. In 2010, 278 master's, 16 doctorates awarded. Terminal master's awarded for partial completion of doctoral program. *Degree requirements:* For master's, one foreign language, thesis; for doctorate, one foreign language, comprehensive exam, thesis/dissertation. *Entrance requirements:* For master's, interview; for doctorate, GRE, CEU subject test, interview. Additional exam requirements/recommendations for international students: Required—TOEFL (minimum score 570 paper-based; 230 computer-based); Recommended—IELTS (minimum score 6.5). *Application deadline:* For fall admission, 1/15 priority date for domestic and international students. Application fee: $0. Electronic applications accepted. Tuition and fees charges are reported in euros. *Expenses:* Tuition: Full-time 11,000 euros. Required fees: 250 euros. One-time fee: 200 euros full-time. Tuition and fees vary according to degree level, program, reciprocity agreements and student level. *Financial support:* In 2010–11, 402 students received support, including 416 fellowships with full and partial tuition reimbursements available (averaging $6,200 per year); career-related internships or fieldwork, institutionally sponsored loans, and scholarships/grants also available. Financial award application deadline: 1/5. *Faculty research:* Civil society, fiscal decentralization, party politics, political philosophy (especially liberalism, theory of democracy). Total annual research expenditures: $35,000. *Unit head:* Dr. Katalin Farkas, Provost/Academic Pro Rector, 361-327-3000 Ext. 2227, E-mail: farkask@ceu.hu. *Application contact:* Zsuzsanna Jaszberenyi, Admissions Officer, 361-327-3009, Fax: 361-327-3211, E-mail: admissions@ceu.hu.

Columbia University, Graduate School of Arts and Sciences, Program in Liberal Studies, New York, NY 10027. Offers American studies (MA); East Asian studies (MA); human rights studies (MA); Islamic culture studies (MA); Jewish studies (MA); medieval studies (MA); modern European studies (MA); South Asian studies (MA). Part-time and evening/weekend programs available. *Degree requirements:* For master's, thesis.

Cornell University, Graduate School, Graduate Fields of Arts and Sciences, Field of Archaeology, Ithaca, NY 14853-0001. Offers environmental archaeology (MA); historical archaeology (MA); Latin American archaeology (MA); medieval archaeology (MA); Mediterranean and Near Eastern archaeology (MA); Stone Age archaeology (MA). *Faculty:* 18 full-time (5 women). *Students:* 8 full-time (7 women); includes 1 Hispanic/Latino. Average age 24. 23 applicants, 30% accepted, 3 enrolled. *Degree requirements:* For master's, one foreign language, thesis. *Entrance requirements:* For master's, GRE General Test, 3 letters of recommendation, sample of written work. Additional exam requirements/recommendations for international students: Required—TOEFL (minimum score 550 paper-based; 213 computer-based; 77 iBT). *Application deadline:* For fall admission, 1/15 for domestic students. Application fee: $80. Electronic applications accepted. *Expenses:* Tuition: Full-time $29,500. Required fees: $76. Tuition and fees vary according to degree level and program. *Financial support:* In 2010–11, 1 fellowship with full tuition reimbursement, 3 teaching assistantships with full tuition reimbursements were awarded; research assistantships with full tuition reimbursements, institutionally sponsored loans, scholarships/grants, health care benefits, tuition waivers (full and partial), and unspecified assistantships also available. Financial award applicants required to submit FAFSA. *Faculty research:* Anatolia, Lydia, Sardis, classical and Hellenistic Greece; science in archaeology; North American Indians; Stone Age Africa; Mayan trade. *Unit head:* Director of Graduate Studies, 607-255-6768, E-mail: blj7@cornell.edu. *Application contact:* Graduate Field Assistant, 607-255-6768, E-mail: dsd6@cornell.edu.

Cornell University, Graduate School, Graduate Fields of Arts and Sciences, Field of English Language and Literature, Ithaca, NY 14853-0001. Offers African-American literature (PhD); American literature after 1865 (PhD); American literature to 1865 (PhD); American studies (PhD); colonial and postcolonial literature (PhD); creative writing (MFA); cultural studies (PhD); dramatic literature (PhD); English poetry (PhD); English Renaissance to 1660 (PhD); lesbian, bisexual, and gay literature studies (PhD); literary criticism and theory (PhD); nineteenth century (PhD); Old and Middle English (PhD); prose fiction (PhD); Restoration and eighteenth century (PhD); twentieth century (PhD); women's literature (PhD); MFA/PhD. *Faculty:* 56 full-time (29 women). *Students:* 100 full-time (56 women); includes 5 Black or African American, non-Hispanic/Latino; 3 American Indian or Alaska Native, non-Hispanic/Latino; 10 Asian, non-Hispanic/Latino; 8 Hispanic/Latino, 12 international. Average age 27. 1,091 applicants, 4% accepted, 21 enrolled. In 2010, 25 master's, 12 doctorates awarded. Terminal master's awarded for partial completion of doctoral program. *Degree requirements:* For master's, one foreign language, thesis; for doctorate, one foreign language, comprehensive exam, thesis/dissertation, teaching experience. *Entrance requirements:* For master's, GRE General Test, 3 letters of recommendation, creative writing sample; for doctorate, GRE General Test, GRE Subject Test (English), 3 letters of recommendation, writing sample. Additional exam requirements/recommendations for international students: Required—TOEFL (minimum score 600 paper-based; 250 computer-based; 77 iBT). *Application deadline:* For fall admission, 1/10 for domestic students. Application fee: $80. Electronic applications accepted. *Expenses:* Tuition: Full-time $29,500. Required fees: $76. Tuition and fees vary according to degree level and program. *Financial support:* In 2010–11, 32 fellowships with full tuition reimbursements, 60 teaching assistantships with full tuition reimbursements were awarded; research assistantships with full tuition reimbursements, institutionally sponsored loans, scholarships/grants, health care benefits, tuition waivers (full and partial), and unspecified assistantships also available. Financial award applicants required to submit FAFSA. *Faculty research:* English and American literature, women's writing, ethnic and post-colonial literature, critical theory, medievalism. *Unit head:* Director of Graduate Studies, 607-255-7989, Fax: 607-255-6661. *Application contact:* Graduate Field Assistant, 607-255-7989, Fax: 607-255-6661, E-mail: english_grad@cornell.edu.

Cornell University, Graduate School, Graduate Fields of Arts and Sciences, Field of History, Ithaca, NY 14853-0001. Offers African history (MA, PhD); American history (MA, PhD); ancient history (MA, PhD); early modern European history (MA, PhD); English history (MA, PhD); French history (MA, PhD); German history (MA, PhD); history of science (MA, PhD); Latin American history (MA, PhD); medieval Chinese history (MA, PhD); medieval history (MA, PhD); modern Chinese history (MA, PhD); modern European history (MA, PhD); modern Japanese history (MA, PhD); premodern Islamic history (MA, PhD); premodern Japanese history (MA, PhD); Renaissance history (MA, PhD); Russian history (MA, PhD); Southeast Asian history (MA, PhD). *Faculty:* 53 full-time (15 women). *Students:* 59 full-time (30 women); includes 3 Black or African American, non-Hispanic/Latino; 2 Asian, non-Hispanic/Latino; 4 Hispanic/Latino, 22 international. Average age 30. 217 applicants, 6% accepted, 8 enrolled. In 2010, 9 master's, 5 doctorates awarded. Terminal master's awarded for partial completion of doctoral program. *Degree requirements:* For master's, thesis; for doctorate, 2 foreign languages, comprehensive exam, thesis/dissertation, 1 year of teaching experience. *Entrance requirements:* For master's and doctorate, GRE General Test, writing sample, 3 letters of recommendation. Additional exam requirements/recommendations for international students: Required—TOEFL (minimum score 550 paper-based; 213 computer-based; 77 iBT). *Application deadline:* For fall admission, 1/15 for domestic students. Application fee: $80. Electronic applications accepted. *Expenses:* Tuition: Full-time $29,500. Required fees: $76. Tuition and fees vary according to degree level and program. *Financial support:* In 2010–11, 26 fellowships with full tuition reimbursements, 27 teaching assistantships with full tuition reimbursements were awarded; research assistantships with full tuition reimbursements, institutionally sponsored loans, scholarships/grants, health care benefits, tuition waivers (full and partial), and unspecified assistantships also available. Financial award applicants required to submit FAFSA. *Unit head:* Director of Graduate Studies, 607-255-6738, Fax: 607-255-0469. *Application contact:* Graduate Field Assistant, 607-255-6738, Fax: 607-255-0469, E-mail: history_grad_info@cornell.edu.

Cornell University, Graduate School, Graduate Fields of Arts and Sciences, Field of History of Art, Archaeology and Visual Studies, Ithaca, NY 14853. Offers American art (PhD); ancient art and archaeology (PhD); Asian art (PhD); Baroque art (PhD); medieval art (PhD); modern art (PhD); Renaissance art (PhD); Southeast Asian art (PhD); theory and criticism (PhD). *Faculty:* 24 full-time (15 women). *Students:* 21 full-time (19 women); includes 1 Black or African American, non-Hispanic/Latino; 2 American Indian or Alaska Native, non-Hispanic/Latino; 1 Hispanic/Latino, 7 international. Average age 31. 71 applicants, 7% accepted, 5 enrolled. In 2010, 2 doctorates awarded. *Degree requirements:* For doctorate, one foreign language, comprehensive exam, thesis/dissertation, general exams in 3 areas. *Entrance requirements:* For doctorate, GRE General Test, sample of written work, 3 letters of recommendation. Additional exam requirements/recommendations for international students: Required—TOEFL (minimum score 550 paper-based; 213 computer-based; 77 iBT). *Application deadline:* For fall admission, 1/15 for domestic students. Application fee: $80. Electronic applications accepted. *Expenses:* Tuition: Full-time $29,500. Required fees: $76. Tuition and fees vary according to degree level and program. *Financial support:* In 2010–11, 8 fellowships with full tuition reimbursements, 11 teaching assistantships with full tuition reimbursements were awarded; research assistantships with full tuition reimbursements, institutionally sponsored loans, scholarships/grants, health care benefits, tuition waivers (full and partial), and unspecified assistantships also available. Financial award applicants required to submit FAFSA. *Unit head:* Director of Graduate Studies, 607-255-4905, Fax: 607-255-0566, E-mail: art_history@cornell.edu. *Application contact:* Graduate Field Assistant, 607-255-4905, Fax: 607-255-0566, E-mail: art_history@cornell.edu.

Cornell University, Graduate School, Graduate Fields of Arts and Sciences, Field of Medieval Studies, Ithaca, NY 14853-0001. Offers medieval archaeology (PhD); medieval art (PhD); medieval history (PhD); medieval literature (PhD); medieval music (PhD); medieval philology and linguistics (PhD); medieval philosophy (PhD). *Faculty:* 32 full-time (9 women). *Students:* 14 full-time (9 women); includes 1 Asian, non-Hispanic/Latino, 2 international. Average age 26. 46 applicants, 9% accepted, 4 enrolled. In 2010, 3 doctorates awarded. *Degree requirements:* For doctorate, 3 foreign languages, comprehensive exam, thesis/dissertation, teaching experience. *Entrance requirements:* For doctorate, GRE General Test, 3 letters of recommendation, proficiency in Latin (recommended), 20 page writing sample on a Medieval topic. Additional exam requirements/recommendations for international students: Required—TOEFL (minimum score 600 paper-based; 250 computer-based; 77 iBT). *Application deadline:* For fall admission, 1/15 for domestic students. Application fee: $80. Electronic applications accepted. *Expenses:* Tuition: Full-time $29,500. Required fees: $76. Tuition and fees vary according to degree level and program. *Financial support:* In 2010–11, 5 fellowships with full tuition reimbursements, 9 teaching assistantships with full tuition reimbursements were awarded; research assistantships with full tuition reimbursements, institutionally sponsored loans, scholarships/grants, health care benefits, tuition waivers (full and partial), and unspecified assistantships also available. Financial award applicants required to submit FAFSA. *Faculty research:* Interdisciplinary study of medieval culture, languages, literatures, history, archaeology. *Unit head:* Director of Graduate Studies, 607-255-8545. *Application contact:* Graduate Field Assistant, 607-255-8545, E-mail: medievalst@cornell.edu.

Fordham University, Graduate School of Arts and Sciences, Center for Medieval Studies, New York, NY 10458. Offers MA, Certificate. Part-time and evening/weekend programs available. *Students:* 12 full-time (4 women), 11 part-time (9 women); includes 1 Asian, non-Hispanic/Latino. Average age 28. 34 applicants, 59% accepted, 9 enrolled. In 2010, 5 master's awarded. *Degree requirements:* For master's, thesis. *Entrance requirements:* For master's, GRE General Test. Additional exam requirements/recommendations for international students: Required—TOEFL (minimum score 650 paper-based; 280 computer-based). *Application deadline:* For fall admission, 1/4 priority date for domestic students; for spring admission, 11/1 for domestic students. Application fee: $70. Electronic applications accepted. *Financial support:* In 2010–11, 4 students received support, including 4 research assistantships with tuition reimbursements available (averaging $17,915 per year); institutionally sponsored loans, tuition waivers (full and partial), and unspecified assistantships also available. Financial award application deadline: 1/4; financial award applicants required to submit FAFSA. *Faculty research:* Medieval literature, history, philosophy, theology, and fine arts; Anglo-Norman. Total annual research expenditures: $77,440. *Unit head:* Dr. Maryanne Kowaleski, Director, 718-817-4655, E-mail: kowaleski@fordham.edu. *Application contact:* Charlene Dundie, Director of Graduate Admissions, 718-817-4420, Fax: 718-817-3566, E-mail: dundie@fordham.edu.

Georgetown University, Graduate School of Arts and Sciences, School of Continuing Studies, Washington, DC 20057. Offers American studies (MALS); Catholic studies (MALS); classical civilizations (MALS); disability studies (MPS); ethics and the professions (MALS); human resources management (MPS); humanities (MALS); individualized study (MALS); international affairs (MALS); Islam and Muslim-Christian relations (MALS); journalism (MPS); liberal studies (DLS); literature and society (MALS); medieval and early modern European studies (MALS); public relations and corporate communications (MPS); real estate (MPS); religious studies (MALS); social and public policy (MALS); sports industry management (MPS); the theory and practice of American democracy (MALS); visual culture (MALS). *Entrance requirements:* Additional exam requirements/recommendations for international students: Required—TOEFL.

Graduate School and University Center of the City University of New York, Graduate Studies, Interdisciplinary Studies, New York, NY 10016-4039. Offers language in social context (PhD); medieval studies (PhD); public policy (MA, PhD); urban studies (MA, PhD); women's studies (MA, PhD). Terminal master's awarded for partial completion of doctoral program. *Degree requirements:* For master's, thesis; for doctorate, comprehensive exam, thesis/dissertation. *Entrance requirements:* For master's and doctorate, GRE General Test.

Harvard University, Graduate School of Arts and Sciences, Department of English and American Literature and Language, Cambridge, MA 02138. Offers critical theory (PhD); eighteenth-century literature (PhD); literature: nineteenth-century to the present (PhD); medieval literature and language (PhD); modern British and American literature (PhD); Renaissance literature (PhD). Terminal master's awarded for partial completion of doctoral program. *Degree requirements:* For doctorate, 2 foreign languages, thesis/dissertation, oral exam. *Entrance requirements:* For doctorate, GRE General Test, GRE Subject Test, writing sample. Additional exam requirements/recommendations for international students: Required—TOEFL. *Expenses:* Tuition: Full-time $34,976. Required fees: $1166. Full-time tuition and fees vary according to program. *Faculty research:* Old and Middle English language and literature, drama, creative writing, transition to Romanticism, history and theory of criticism.

Indiana University Bloomington, University Graduate School, College of Arts and Sciences, Department of Germanic Studies, Bloomington, IN 47405-7000. Offers German philology and linguistics (PhD); German studies (MA, PhD), including German (MA), German literature and culture (MA), German literature and linguistics (MA); medieval German studies (PhD); teaching German (MAT). *Faculty:* 13 full-time (4 women), 6 part-time/adjunct (2 women). *Students:* 35 full-time (19 women), 2 part-time (1 woman); includes 1 Black or African American, non-Hispanic/Latino; 1 Hispanic/Latino, 8 international. Average age 31. 34 applicants, 41% accepted, 5 enrolled. In 2010, 6 master's, 3 doctorates awarded. Terminal master's awarded for partial completion of doctoral program. *Degree requirements:* For master's, one foreign language, project; for doctorate, one foreign language, comprehensive exam, thesis/dissertation. *Entrance requirements:* For master's, GRE General Test, BA in German or equivalent; for doctorate, GRE General Test, MA in German or equivalent. Additional exam requirements/recommendations for international students: Required—TOEFL. *Application deadline:* For fall admission, 1/15 priority date for domestic students, 12/15 for international students; for spring admission, 9/1 priority date for domestic students, 9/1 for international students. Applications are processed on a rolling basis. Application fee: $55 ($65 for international students). *Financial support:* In 2010–11, 7 fellowships with full and partial tuition reimbursements (averaging $16,000 per year), 17 teaching assistantships with full tuition reimbursements (averaging $13,455 per year) were awarded; research assistantships, Federal Work-Study, institutionally sponsored loans, scholarships/grants, and unspecified assistantships also available. Support available to part-time students. Financial award application deadline: 1/15; financial award applicants required to submit FAFSA. *Faculty research:* German and other European literature: medieval to modern/postmodern, German and culture studies, Germanic philology, literary theory, literature and the other arts. *Unit head:* William Rasch, Department Chairman, 812-855-7947, Fax: 812-855-8292, E-mail: wrasch@indiana.edu. *Application contact:* Michelle Dunbar, Graduate Secretary, 812-855-7947, E-mail: midunbar@indiana.edu.

Medieval and Renaissance Studies

Rutgers, The State University of New Jersey, New Brunswick, Graduate School-New Brunswick, Program in History, Piscataway, NJ 08854-8097. Offers African-American history (PhD); early American history (PhD); early modern European history (PhD); east Asian history (PhD); global and comparative history (PhD); history (PhD); history of diplomacy and foreign relations (PhD); history of technology, environment and health (PhD); history of the Atlantic cultures and African diaspora (PhD); Latin American history (PhD); medieval history (PhD); modern European history (PhD); nineteenth and twentieth century American history (PhD); women's and gender history (PhD). *Degree requirements:* For doctorate, thesis/dissertation. *Entrance requirements:* For doctorate, GRE General Test, sample of written work. Electronic applications accepted. *Expenses:* Tuition, state resident: full-time $7200; part-time $600 per credit. Tuition, nonresident: full-time $11,124; part-time $927 per credit. *Faculty research:* American history, European history, Afro-American history, women's history, Latin American history.

Southern Methodist University, Dedman College, Program in Medieval Studies, Dallas, TX 75275. Offers MA. Part-time programs available. *Students:* 2 part-time (1 woman). Average age 34. *Degree requirements:* For master's, 2 foreign languages, thesis. *Entrance requirements:* For master's, GRE General Test, minimum GPA of 3.0. *Application deadline:* Applications are processed on a rolling basis. Application fee: $60. Electronic applications accepted. *Financial support:* Federal Work-Study and institutionally sponsored loans available. *Faculty research:* Byzantine culture, medieval Europe, Arthurian literature, Chaucer, Romance. *Unit head:* Dr. Bonnie Wheeler, Director, 214-768-2949, Fax: 214-768-1234, E-mail: bwheeler@smu.edu. *Application contact:* Barbara Phillips, Assistant Dean, 214-768-4202, Fax: 214-768-4235, E-mail: bphillips@smu.edu.

University of California, Santa Barbara, Graduate Division, College of Letters and Sciences, Division of Humanities and Fine Arts, Department of English, Santa Barbara, CA 93106-3170. Offers English (PhD); European medieval studies (PhD); feminist studies (PhD); global studies (PhD); technology and society (PhD); MA/PhD. *Faculty:* 26 full-time (13 women), 17 part-time/adjunct (12 women). *Students:* 68 full-time (37 women); includes 2 Black or African American, non-Hispanic/Latino; 5 Asian, non-Hispanic/Latino; 2 Hispanic/Latino. Average age 30. 173 applicants, 12% accepted, 8 enrolled. In 2010, 4 doctorates awarded. Terminal master's awarded for partial completion of doctoral program. *Degree requirements:* For doctorate, one foreign language, comprehensive exam, thesis/dissertation. *Entrance requirements:* For doctorate, GRE General Test, GRE Subject Test (English). Additional exam requirements/recommendations for international students: Required—TOEFL (minimum score 550 paper-based; 80 iBT), IELTS (minimum score 7). *Application deadline:* For fall admission, 12/15 priority date for domestic and international students. Application fee: $70 ($90 for international students). Electronic applications accepted. *Financial support:* In 2010–11, 68 students received support, including 38 fellowships with full and partial tuition reimbursements available (averaging $9,204 per year), 3 research assistantships with full and partial tuition reimbursements available (averaging $10,512 per year), 50 teaching assistantships with full and partial tuition reimbursements available (averaging $13,031 per year); career-related internships or fieldwork and tuition waivers (full and partial) also available. Financial award application deadline: 12/15; financial award applicants required to submit FAFSA. *Faculty research:* Medieval, Romantic, and Victorian studies; gender studies and feminist theory; literature and the mind; American literature; literature and new media/information culture. Total annual research expenditures: $25,000. *Unit head:* Prof. Ken Hiltner, Graduate Program Chair, 805-564-2304, Fax: 805-893-7492, E-mail: hiltner@english.ucsb.edu. *Application contact:* Mary Rae Staton, Graduate Program Staff Advisor, 805-893-2639, Fax: 805-893-7492, E-mail: staton@hfa.ucsb.edu.

University of California, Santa Barbara, Graduate Division, College of Letters and Sciences, Division of Humanities and Fine Arts, Department of History, Santa Barbara, CA 93106-9410. Offers ancient Mediterranean studies (PhD); European medieval studies (PhD); feminist studies (PhD); global studies (PhD); history (PhD); public history (PhD); technology and society (PhD); MA/PhD. *Faculty:* 42 full-time (18 women), 10 part-time/adjunct (6 women). *Students:* 92 full-time (50 women); includes 1 Black or African American, non-Hispanic/Latino; 6 Asian, non-Hispanic/Latino; 11 Hispanic/Latino. Average age 34. 124 applicants, 19% accepted, 8 enrolled. In 2010, 20 doctorates awarded. *Degree requirements:* For doctorate, variable foreign language requirement, comprehensive exam, thesis/dissertation. *Entrance requirements:* For doctorate, GRE. Additional exam requirements/recommendations for international students: Required—TOEFL (minimum score 550 paper-based; 80 iBT), IELTS (minimum score 7). *Application deadline:* For fall admission, 12/5 priority date for domestic and international students. Application fee: $70 ($90 for international students). Electronic applications accepted. *Financial support:* In 2010–11, 92 students received support, including 68 fellowships with full and partial tuition reimbursements available (averaging $6,583 per year), 4 research assistantships with full and partial tuition reimbursements available (averaging $5,862 per year), 57 teaching assistantships with full and partial tuition reimbursements available (averaging $12,123 per year); tuition waivers (partial) also available. Financial award application deadline: 12/5; financial award applicants required to submit FAFSA. *Faculty research:* Europe, U. S., Latin America, Africa, Middle East, East Asia. *Unit head:* John Majewski, Chair, 805-893-2837, E-mail: majewski@history.ucrb.edu. *Application contact:* Sharon Farmer, Director of Graduate Studies, 805-893-3398, E-mail: farmer@history.ucsb.edu.

University of California, Santa Barbara, Graduate Division, College of Letters and Sciences, Division of Humanities and Fine Arts, Department of History of Art and Architecture, Santa Barbara, CA 93106-2014. Offers art history (PhD), including art history, European medieval studies, feminist studies; MA/PhD. *Faculty:* 18 full-time (8 women), 6 part-time/adjunct (2 women). *Students:* 45 full-time (40 women); includes 7 Asian, non-Hispanic/Latino; 4 Hispanic/Latino. Average age 32. 93 applicants, 11% accepted, 8 enrolled. In 2010, 3 doctorates awarded. Terminal master's awarded for partial completion of doctoral program. *Degree requirements:* For doctorate, 2 foreign languages, comprehensive exam, thesis/dissertation. *Entrance requirements:* For doctorate, GRE. Additional exam requirements/recommendations for international students: Required—TOEFL (minimum score 550 paper-based; 80 iBT), IELTS (minimum score 7). *Application deadline:* For fall admission, 12/15 priority date for domestic and international students. Application fee: $70 ($90 for international students). Electronic applications accepted. *Financial support:* In 2010–11, 31 students received support, including 24 fellowships with full tuition reimbursements available (averaging $9,585 per year), 1 research assistantship with full and partial tuition reimbursement available (averaging $15,896 per year), 21 teaching assistantships with partial tuition reimbursements available (averaging $11,884 per year); career-related internships or fieldwork, institutionally sponsored loans, and tuition waivers (full and partial) also available. Financial award application deadline: 12/15; financial award applicants required to submit FAFSA. *Faculty research:* History of architecture, Renaissance-Italian, Baroque, American. Total annual research expenditures: $72,000. *Unit head:* Prof. Ulrich Keller, Chair, 805-893-8710, Fax: 805-893-7117, E-mail: ukeller@arthisory.ucsb.edu. *Application contact:* Graduate Program Administrator, 805-893-2454, Fax: 805-893-7117, E-mail: lfredrickson@hfa.ucsb.edu.

University of California, Santa Barbara, Graduate Division, College of Letters and Sciences, Division of Humanities and Fine Arts, Department of Religious Studies, Santa Barbara, CA 93106-3130. Offers ancient Mediterranean studies (PhD); European medieval studies (PhD); feminist studies (PhD); global studies (PhD); religious studies (MA, PhD); translation studies (PhD); MA/PhD. *Faculty:* 19 full-time (9 women), 8 part-time/adjunct (3 women). *Students:* 79 full-time (29 women); includes 2 Black or African American, non-Hispanic/Latino; 1 American Indian or Alaska Native, non-Hispanic/Latino; 9 Asian, non-Hispanic/Latino; 5 Hispanic/Latino. Average age 31. 139 applicants, 22% accepted, 10 enrolled. In 2010, 11 master's, 10 doctorates awarded. *Degree requirements:* For master's, one foreign language, comprehensive exam (for some programs), thesis (for some programs), colloquium; for doctorate, one foreign language, thesis/dissertation, methodology, colloquium. *Entrance requirements:* For master's and doctorate, GRE General Test. Additional exam requirements/recommendations for international students: Required—TOEFL (minimum score 550 paper-based; 80 iBT), IELTS (minimum score 7). *Application deadline:* For fall admission, 12/1 for domestic and international students. Application fee: $70 ($90 for international students). Electronic applications accepted. *Financial support:* In 2010–11, 64 students received support, including 31 fellowships with full tuition reimbursements available (averaging $12,351 per year), 4 research assistantships with full and partial tuition reimbursements available (averaging $4,147 per year), 37 teaching assistantships with partial tuition reimbursements available (averaging $9,573 per year); career-related internships or fieldwork, scholarships/grants, tuition waivers (full and partial), and associateships also available. Financial award application deadline: 12/1; financial award applicants required to submit FAFSA. *Faculty research:* Area studies; religious traditions; theory and method in the study of religion; religion, culture, and politics; spirituality and religious experience. *Unit head:* Prof. Jose I. Cabezon, Professor and Chair, 805-893-3564, Fax: 805-893-7671, E-mail: jcabezon@religion.ucsb.edu. *Application contact:* Sally J. Lombrozo, Graduate Program Assistant, 805-893-2744, Fax: 805-893-7671, E-mail: lombrozo@hfa.ucsb.edu.

University of California, Santa Barbara, Graduate Division, College of Letters and Sciences, Division of Humanities and Fine Arts, Department of Spanish and Portuguese, Santa Barbara, CA 93106-4150. Offers Hispanic languages and literature (PhD), including European medieval studies, feminist studies, Hispanic linguistics, Hispanic literature, Luso-Brazilian literature; Hispanic linguistics (MA); Luso-Brazilian literature (MA); Spanish or Spanish-American literature (MA); MA/PhD. Spanish Language Institute available during summer session. *Faculty:* 16 full-time (7 women). *Students:* 32 full-time (22 women); includes 1 Black or African American, non-Hispanic/Latino; 1 Asian, non-Hispanic/Latino; 9 Hispanic/Latino. Average age 32. 34 applicants, 26% accepted, 5 enrolled. In 2010, 3 master's, 3 doctorates awarded. Terminal master's awarded for partial completion of doctoral program. *Degree requirements:* For master's, 2 foreign languages, comprehensive exam (for some programs), thesis optional; for doctorate, 3 foreign languages, comprehensive exam, thesis/dissertation. *Entrance requirements:* For master's and doctorate, GRE. Additional exam requirements/recommendations for international students: Required—TOEFL (minimum score 550 paper-based; 80 iBT), IELTS (minimum score 7). *Application deadline:* For fall admission, 12/15 for domestic and international students. Application fee: $70 ($90 for international students). Electronic applications accepted. *Financial support:* In 2010–11, 32 students received support, including 12 fellowships with full and partial tuition reimbursements available (averaging $10,016 per year), 27 teaching assistantships with full and partial tuition reimbursements available (averaging $14,583 per year); career-related internships or fieldwork, Federal Work-Study, tuition waivers (full and partial), and unspecified assistantships also available. Financial award application deadline: 12/15; financial award applicants required to submit FAFSA. *Faculty research:* Nineteenth century Spanish and Portuguese literature, Spanish and Spanish American literature, nineteenth and twentieth century Portuguese and Brazilian literatures, Hispanic linguistics, Catalan language and culture. *Unit head:* Prof. Francisco A. Lomeli, Chair, 805-893-5715, Fax: 805-893-8341, E-mail: lomeli@spanport.ucsb.edu. *Application contact:* Ashley Bradbury, Graduate Program Assistant, 805-893-2131, Fax: 805-893-8341, E-mail: ashley@hfa.ucsb.edu.

University of California, Santa Barbara, Graduate Division, College of Letters and Sciences, Division of Humanities and Fine Arts, Department of Theatre and Dance, Santa Barbara, CA 93106-7060. Offers theater studies (MA, PhD), including european medieval studies (PhD), feminist studies (PhD), theatre studies (PhD); MA/PhD. *Faculty:* 8 full-time (4 women). *Students:* 14 full-time (9 women); includes 2 Black or African American, non-Hispanic/Latino; 1 Hispanic/Latino. Average age 31. 22 applicants, 41% accepted, 3 enrolled. In 2010, 3 master's, 5 doctorates awarded. Terminal master's awarded for partial completion of doctoral program. *Degree requirements:* For master's, comprehensive exam, thesis; for doctorate, one foreign language, comprehensive exam, thesis/dissertation. *Entrance requirements:* For master's and doctorate, GRE. Additional exam requirements/recommendations for international students: Required—TOEFL (minimum score 550 paper-based; 80 iBT), IELTS (minimum score 7). *Application deadline:* For fall admission, 1/5 priority date for domestic and international students. Application fee: $70 ($90 for international students). Electronic applications accepted. *Financial support:* In 2010–11, 14 students received support, including 11 fellowships with full tuition reimbursements available (averaging $7,764 per year), 14 teaching assistantships with full and partial tuition reimbursements available (averaging $13,666 per year). Financial award applicants required to submit FAFSA. *Faculty research:* English and American theater and Ancient Greek; Spanish, Latin-American and Caribbean performance; Renaissance and Baroque drama, and intercultural theory; East Asian performance, gender and nationalism; Korean cultural studies, Russian literature, and Slavic folklore; history of German theater, Shakespeare, and European opera; postcolonialism, performance-based ethnography, globalism and national identity formation in Africa. *Unit head:* Prof. Simon Williams, Chairperson, 805-893-5515, Fax: 805-893-7029, E-mail: williams@theaterdance.ucsb.edu. *Application contact:* Mary Tench, Graduate Program Assistant, 805-893-3147, Fax: 805-893-7029, E-mail: mtench@theaterdance.ucsb.edu.

University of Connecticut, Graduate School, College of Liberal Arts and Sciences, Field of Medieval Studies, Storrs, CT 06269. Offers MA, PhD. Terminal master's awarded for partial completion of doctoral program. *Degree requirements:* For master's, comprehensive exam; for doctorate, 3 foreign languages, thesis/dissertation. *Entrance requirements:* For master's and doctorate, GRE General Test, GRE Subject Test. Additional exam requirements/recommendations for international students: Required—TOEFL (minimum score 550 paper-based; 213 computer-based). Electronic applications accepted.

University of Guelph, Graduate Studies, College of Arts, School of English and Theatre Studies, Joint Program in Literary Studies/Theatre Studies in English, Guelph, ON N1G 2W1, Canada. Offers PhD. Part-time programs available. *Degree requirements:* For doctorate, one foreign language, comprehensive exam, thesis/dissertation. *Entrance requirements:* For doctorate, MA, 3 letters of reference, writing samples, resume, minimum A- average in graduate course work. Additional exam requirements/recommendations for international students: Required—TOEFL. Electronic applications accepted. *Faculty research:* Canadian studies, Early Modern studies, Postcolonial studies, studies in gender and genre, 19th Century studies.

University of Michigan, Horace H. Rackham School of Graduate Studies, College of Literature, Science, and the Arts, Program in Medieval and Early Modern Studies, Ann Arbor, MI 48109. Offers Certificate. Interdisciplinary program offered through Departments of History, English Language and Literature, History of Art, Romance Languages and Literatures, and Near Eastern Studies. *Entrance requirements:* For degree, acceptance by Horace H. Rackham School of Graduate Studies, minimum A- average grade. *Expenses:* Tuition, state resident: full-time $17,784; part-time $1116 per credit hour. Tuition, nonresident: full-time $35,944; part-time $2125 per credit hour. International tuition: $35,994 full-time. Required fees: $95 per semester. Tuition and fees vary according to course load, degree level and program.

University of Minnesota, Twin Cities Campus, Graduate School, College of Liberal Arts, Department of German, Scandinavian, and Dutch, Minneapolis, MN 55455-0213. Offers Germanic studies: German and Scandinavian studies track (PhD); Germanic studies: German track (MA, PhD); Germanic studies: Germanic medieval studies track (MA, PhD); Germanic studies: Scandinavian studies track (MA); Germanic studies: teaching track (MA). Part-time programs available. Terminal master's awarded for partial completion of doctoral program. *Degree requirements:* For doctorate, 2 foreign languages, thesis/dissertation. *Entrance requirements:* For master's, GRE General Test, BA in German, Scandinavian, or equivalent; for doctorate, GRE General Test, MA in German, Scandinavian, or equivalent. Additional exam requirements/recommendations for international students: Required—TOEFL (minimum score 550 paper-based; 213 computer-based; 79 iBT). Electronic applications accepted. *Faculty research:* Cultural studies, literary theory, feminist criticism, film, Germanic philology.

University of Notre Dame, Graduate School, College of Arts and Letters, Division of Humanities, Medieval Institute, Notre Dame, IN 46556. Offers MMS, PhD. Terminal master's awarded for partial completion of doctoral program. *Degree requirements:* For master's, 3 foreign languages, comprehensive exam; for doctorate, 3 foreign languages, thesis/dissertation, candidacy exam. *Entrance requirements:* For master's and doctorate, GRE General Test. Additional exam requirements/recommendations for international students: Required—TOEFL (minimum score

600 paper-based; 250 computer-based; 80 iBT). Electronic applications accepted. *Faculty research:* Medieval history, vernacular literatures, theology, philosophy, Ambrosiana manuscripts and drawings.

University of Pittsburgh, School of Arts and Sciences, Program in Medieval and Renaissance Studies, Pittsburgh, PA 15260. Offers Certificate. Part-time programs available. *Faculty:* 36 full-time (12 women). *Students:* 14 full-time (8 women); includes 1 Black or African American, non-Hispanic/Latino; 1 Hispanic/Latino. Average age 31. 1 applicant, 100% accepted, 1 enrolled. In 2010, 2 Certificates awarded. *Degree requirements:* For Certificate, thesis. *Entrance requirements:* For degree, minimum GPA of 3.0. *Application deadline:* Applications are processed on a rolling basis. *Expenses:* Tuition, state resident: full-time $17,304; part-time $701 per credit. Tuition, nonresident: full-time $29,554; part-time $1210 per credit. Required fees: $740; $214 per term. Tuition and fees vary according to program. *Unit head:* Dr. Nicole Constable, Associate Dean, Graduate Studies and Research, 412-624-6094, Fax: 412-624-6855, E-mail: constable@fcas.pitt.edu. *Application contact:* Matthew Carulli, Program Administrator, 412-624-5220, Fax: 412-624-6263, E-mail: mdc24@pitt.edu.

University of Toronto, School of Graduate Studies, Humanities Division, Centre for Medieval Studies, Toronto, ON M5S 1A1, Canada. Offers MA, PhD. Part-time programs available. *Degree requirements:* For master's, one foreign language, 4 courses or 3 courses and a thesis; for doctorate, 3 foreign languages, thesis/dissertation, proficiency in Latin, German and French. *Entrance requirements:* For master's, letters of reference, minimum B+ average, course work in the medieval period; for doctorate, letters of reference, passing score on MA Latin examination. Additional exam requirements/recommendations for international students: Required—TOEFL (minimum score 580 paper-based; 237 computer-based), TWE (minimum score 5).

Western Michigan University, Graduate College, College of Arts and Sciences, Department of Medieval Studies, Kalamazoo, MI 49008. Offers MA. *Degree requirements:* For master's, one foreign language, thesis optional, oral exam.

Yale University, Graduate School of Arts and Sciences, Interdisciplinary Program in Medieval Studies, New Haven, CT 06520. Offers M Phil, PhD. *Entrance requirements:* For doctorate, GRE General Test.

Yale University, Graduate School of Arts and Sciences, Program in Renaissance Studies, New Haven, CT 06520. Offers PhD. *Degree requirements:* For doctorate, 3 foreign languages. *Entrance requirements:* For doctorate, GRE General Test.

Public History

Appalachian State University, Cratis D. Williams Graduate School, Department of History, Boone, NC 28608. Offers history (MA); public history (MA). Part-time programs available. Postbaccalaureate distance learning degree programs offered (no on-campus study). *Faculty:* 30 full-time (11 women), 1 part-time/adjunct (0 women). *Students:* 31 full-time (13 women), 13 part-time (6 women); includes 1 Black or African American, non-Hispanic/Latino; 1 Asian, non-Hispanic/Latino. 52 applicants, 81% accepted, 22 enrolled. In 2010, 20 master's awarded. *Degree requirements:* For master's, one foreign language, comprehensive exam, thesis (for some programs). *Entrance requirements:* For master's, GRE General Test, 3 letters of recommendation. Additional exam requirements/recommendations for international students: Required—TOEFL (minimum score 570 paper-based; 230 computer-based; 79 iBT), IELTS (minimum score 6.5). *Application deadline:* For fall admission, 7/1 for domestic students, 2/1 for international students; for spring admission, 11/1 for domestic students, 7/1 for international students. Applications are processed on a rolling basis. Application fee: $55. Electronic applications accepted. *Expenses:* Tuition, state resident: full-time $3428; part-time $428 per unit. Tuition, nonresident: full-time $14,518; part-time $1814 per unit. Required fees: $2320; $344 per unit. Tuition and fees vary according to campus/location. *Financial support:* In 2010–11, 4 research assistantships (averaging $10,000 per year), 7 teaching assistantships (averaging $8,000 per year) were awarded; fellowships, career-related internships or fieldwork, Federal Work-Study, scholarships/grants, and unspecified assistantships also available. Financial award application deadline: 4/1; financial award applicants required to submit FAFSA. *Faculty research:* Women's history, social/cultural history, U. S. history, Latin America, medieval studies. Total annual research expenditures: $298,000. *Unit head:* Dr. Lucinda McCray, Chairperson, 828-262-2282, E-mail: mccraylm@appstate.edu. *Application contact:* Dr. Lisa Holliday, Graduate Program Director, 828-262-6014, E-mail: hollidaylr@appstate.edu.

Arizona State University, College of Liberal Arts and Sciences, School of Historical, Philosophical and Religious Studies, Tempe, AZ 85287-4301. Offers East/Southeast Asian history (MA, PhD); European history (MA, PhD); Latin American studies (MA, PhD); North American history (MA, PhD); philosophy (MA, PhD); public history (MA); religious studies (MA, PhD); scholarly publishing (Graduate Certificate). Part-time programs available. *Faculty:* 70 full-time (29 women), 2 part-time/adjunct (0 women). *Students:* 125 full-time (58 women), 68 part-time (37 women); includes 21 minority (5 Black or African American, non-Hispanic/Latino; 3 American Indian or Alaska Native, non-Hispanic/Latino; 1 Asian, non-Hispanic/Latino; 11 Hispanic/Latino; 1 Two or more races, non-Hispanic/Latino), 16 international. Average age 34. 221 applicants, 51% accepted, 41 enrolled. In 2010, 24 master's, 10 doctorates, 3 other advanced degrees awarded. Terminal master's awarded for partial completion of doctoral program. *Degree requirements:* For master's, thesis or alternative, interactive Program of Study (iPOS) submitted before completing 50 percent of required credit hours; for doctorate, variable foreign language requirement, comprehensive exam, thesis/dissertation, interactive Program of Study (iPOS) submitted before completing 50 percent of required credit hours. *Entrance requirements:* For master's and doctorate, GRE, minimum GPA of 3.0 or equivalent in last 2 years of work leading to bachelor's degree. Additional exam requirements/recommendations for international students: Required—TOEFL, IELTS, or Pearson Test of English. *Application deadline:* For fall admission, 1/1 for domestic and international students. Applications are processed on a rolling basis. Application fee: $70 ($90 for international students). Electronic applications accepted. *Expenses:* Tuition, state resident: full-time $8510; part-time $608 per credit. Tuition, nonresident: full-time $16,542; part-time $919 per credit. Required fees: $339; $110 per credit. Part-time tuition and fees vary according to course load. *Financial support:* In 2010–11, 26 research assistantships with full and partial tuition reimbursements (averaging $12,900 per year), 69 teaching assistantships with full and partial tuition reimbursements (averaging $11,771 per year) were awarded; fellowships with full tuition reimbursements, career-related internships or fieldwork, institutionally sponsored loans, scholarships/grants, and tuition waivers (partial) also available. Financial award application deadline: 3/1; financial award applicants required to submit FAFSA. Total annual research expenditures: $1.3 million. *Unit head:* Mark Von Hagen, Director, 480-965-4186, E-mail: mark.vonhagen@asu.edu. *Application contact:* Graduate Admissions, 480-965-6113.

California State University, Sacramento, Graduate Studies, College of Arts and Letters, Department of History, Sacramento, CA 95819. Offers public history (MA). Part-time programs available. *Degree requirements:* For master's, thesis or alternative, writing proficiency exam. *Entrance requirements:* For master's, GRE General Test, minimum GPA of 3.25 in history, 3.0 overall during previous 2 years; BA in history or equivalent. Additional exam requirements/recommendations for international students: Required—TOEFL. Electronic applications accepted.

Eastern Illinois University, Graduate School, College of Arts and Humanities, Department of History, Charleston, IL 61920-3099. Offers historical administration (MA); history (MA). Part-time programs available.

Florida State University, The Graduate School, College of Arts and Sciences, Department of History, Tallahassee, FL 32306. Offers historical administration (MA); history (MA, PhD). Part-time programs available. *Faculty:* 27 full-time (6 women). *Students:* 88 full-time (28 women), 32 part-time (17 women); includes 6 Black or African American, non-Hispanic/Latino; 5 Hispanic/Latino, 4 international. Average age 26. 73 applicants, 60% accepted, 19 enrolled. In 2010, 11 master's, 13 doctorates awarded. *Degree requirements:* For master's, one foreign language, comprehensive exam (for some programs), thesis (for some programs), internships; for doctorate, one foreign language, comprehensive exam, thesis/dissertation. *Entrance requirements:* For master's, GRE General Test, minimum GPA of 3.3, minimum 18 hours of course work in history; for doctorate, GRE General Test, minimum GPA of 3.3 (undergraduate), 3.65 (graduate). Additional exam requirements/recommendations for international students: Required—TOEFL (minimum score 550 paper-based; 213 computer-based; 80 iBT). *Application deadline:* For fall admission, 12/1 for domestic students. Applications are processed on a rolling basis. Application fee: $30. Electronic applications accepted. *Expenses:* Tuition, state resident: full-time $8238.24. *Financial support:* In 2010–11, 81 students received support, including 2 fellowships with full tuition reimbursements available (averaging $14,700 per year), 4 research assistantships with full tuition reimbursements available (averaging $9,900 per year), 27 teaching assistantships with full tuition reimbursements available (averaging $11,550 per year); Federal Work-Study, institutionally sponsored loans, scholarships/grants, and unspecified assistantships also available. Financial award application deadline: 1/10; financial award applicants required to submit FAFSA. *Faculty research:* Southern and Caribbean studies, Napoleon and the French Revolution, modern Europe, Latin America, U. S. intellectual and cultural history. *Unit head:* Dr. Jonathan Grant, Chair, 850-644-5888, Fax: 850-644-6402, E-mail: jgrant@fsu.edu. *Application contact:* Christine Pignatiello, Academic Support Assistant, 850-644-2610, Fax: 850-644-6402, E-mail: cpignatiello@fsu.edu.

Georgia College & State University, Graduate School, College of Arts and Sciences, Department of History, Geography and Philosophy, Milledgeville, GA 31061. Offers history (advanced studies) (MA); history (predoctoral) (MA); public history (MA). Part-time and evening/weekend programs available. *Students:* 6 full-time (3 women), 7 part-time (4 women). Average age 30. 7 applicants, 100% accepted, 5 enrolled. In 2010, 2 master's awarded. *Degree requirements:* For master's, one foreign language, comprehensive exam (for some programs), thesis optional. *Entrance requirements:* For master's, GRE, 2 letters of reference, transcript, minimum GPA of 3.0. Additional exam requirements/recommendations for international students: Recommended—TOEFL (minimum score 550 paper-based; 213 computer-based; 79 iBT). *Application deadline:* For fall admission, 7/1 priority date for domestic students, 4/1 priority date for international students; for spring admission, 11/15 priority date for domestic students, 9/1 priority date for international students. Applications are processed on a rolling basis. Application fee: $40. Electronic applications accepted. *Expenses:* Tuition, state resident: full-time $4806; part-time $267 per hour. Tuition, nonresident: full-time $17,802; part-time $989 per hour. Tuition and fees vary according to course load. *Financial support:* In 2010–11, 7 research assistantships were awarded; unspecified assistantships also available. Support available to part-time students. Financial award applicants required to submit FAFSA. *Unit head:* Dr. John Fair, Graduate Coordinator for MA in History Program, 478-445-5215, E-mail: john.fair@gcsu.edu. *Application contact:* Dr. John Fair, Graduate Coordinator for MA in History Program, 478-445-5215, E-mail: john.fair@gcsu.edu.

Indiana University–Purdue University Indianapolis, School of Liberal Arts, Department of History, Indianapolis, IN 46202-2896. Offers history (MA); public history (MA); MA/MLS. Part-time and evening/weekend programs available. *Faculty:* 14 full-time (6 women). *Students:* 13 full-time (9 women), 28 part-time (23 women); includes 1 minority (Black or African American, non-Hispanic/Latino), 1 international. Average age 33. 33 applicants, 48% accepted, 12 enrolled. In 2010, 19 master's awarded. *Degree requirements:* For master's, one foreign language, thesis. *Entrance requirements:* For master's, GRE General Test, minimum GPA of 3.0. *Application deadline:* For fall admission, 2/1 priority date for domestic students. Applications are processed on a rolling basis. Application fee: $55 ($65 for international students). *Financial support:* In 2010–11, 1 fellowship with full tuition reimbursement (averaging $10,000 per year), 19 teaching assistantships with full tuition reimbursements (averaging $8,612 per year) were awarded; research assistantships with full tuition reimbursements, career-related internships or fieldwork also available. *Unit head:* Robert Barrows, Chair, 317-274-2457. *Application contact:* Mary Gelzleichter, Graduate Secretary, 317-274-5840, Fax: 317-278-7800, E-mail: mgelzlei@iupui.edu.

Loyola University Chicago, Graduate School, Department of History, Chicago, IL 60660. Offers history (MA, PhD); public history (MA). Part-time and evening/weekend programs available. *Faculty:* 25 full-time (9 women), 4 part-time/adjunct (3 women). *Students:* 56 full-time (27 women), 57 part-time (30 women); includes 11 minority (3 Black or African American, non-Hispanic/Latino; 1 American Indian or Alaska Native, non-Hispanic/Latino; 7 Hispanic/Latino). Average age 31. 121 applicants, 53% accepted, 26 enrolled. In 2010, 17 master's, 5 doctorates awarded. Terminal master's awarded for partial completion of doctoral program. *Degree requirements:* For master's, one foreign language, comprehensive exam, essay; for doctorate, 2 foreign languages, comprehensive exam, thesis/dissertation. *Entrance requirements:* For master's, GRE General Test, research paper; for doctorate, GRE General Test, seminar paper or master's thesis. Additional exam requirements/recommendations for international students: Required—TOEFL (minimum score 550 paper-based; 213 computer-based), IELTS. *Application deadline:* For fall admission, 5/1 for domestic students; for spring admission, 10/1 for domestic students. Applications are processed on a rolling basis. Application fee: $50. Electronic applications accepted. *Expenses:* Tuition: Full-time $14,940; part-time $830 per credit hour. Required fees: $87 per semester. Part-time tuition and fees vary according to course load and program. *Financial support:* In 2010–11, 24 students received support, including 11 fellowships with full tuition reimbursements available (averaging $14,500 per year), 13 teaching assistantships with full tuition reimbursements available (averaging $16,500 per year); research assistantships with full tuition reimbursements available, Federal Work-Study also available. Financial award application deadline: 1/1; financial award applicants required to submit FAFSA. *Faculty research:* Medieval and early modern Europe, U. S. public history, U. S. urban history, gender history, Britain and Ireland. *Unit head:* Dr. Timothy Gilfoyle, Chair, 773-508-2232, Fax: 773-508-2153, E-mail: tgilfoy@luc.edu. *Application contact:* Dr. Suzanne Kaufman, Director, Graduate Programs, 773-508-2233, Fax: 773-508-2153, E-mail: skaufma@luc.edu.

Middle Tennessee State University, College of Graduate Studies, College of Liberal Arts, Department of History, Program in Public History, Murfreesboro, TN 37132. Offers MA, PhD. Part-time and evening/weekend programs available. Postbaccalaureate distance learning degree programs offered. *Students:* 1 (woman) full-time, 17 part-time (11 women); includes 1 Black or African American, non-Hispanic/Latino. 35 applicants, 69% accepted. In 2010, 8 doctorates awarded. *Degree requirements:* For master's, one foreign language, comprehensive exam, thesis; for doctorate, comprehensive exam, thesis/dissertation. *Entrance requirements:* For master's and doctorate, GRE. Additional exam requirements/recommendations for inter-

Public History

Middle Tennessee State University (continued)
national students: Required—TOEFL (minimum score 525 paper-based; 195 computer-based; 71 iBT) or IELTS (minimum score 6). *Application deadline:* For fall admission, 6/1 for domestic and international students. Applications are processed on a rolling basis. Application fee: $25 ($30 for international students). *Expenses:* Tuition, state resident: full-time $4632. Tuition, nonresident: full-time $11,520. *Financial support:* Application deadline: 5/1. *Unit head:* Dr. Amy Sayward, Chair, 615-898-2569, Fax: 615-898-5881, E-mail: asayward@mtsu.edu. *Application contact:* Dr. Michael Allen, Dean and Vice Provost for Research, 615-898-2840, Fax: 615-904-8020, E-mail: mallen@mtsu.edu.

New York University, Graduate School of Arts and Science, Department of History, New York, NY 10012-1019. Offers African diaspora (PhD); African history (PhD); archival management and historical editing (Advanced Certificate); Atlantic history (PhD); French studies/history (PhD); Hebrew and Judaic studies/history (PhD); history (MA, PhD), including Europe (PhD), Latin American and the Caribbean (PhD), United States (PhD), women's history (MA); Middle Eastern history (MA); Middle Eastern studies/history (PhD); public history (Advanced Certificate); world history (MA); JD/MA; MA/Advanced Certificate. Part-time programs available. *Faculty:* 43 full-time (19 women). *Students:* 135 full-time (84 women), 42 part-time (30 women); includes 15 Black or African American, non-Hispanic/Latino; 2 Asian, non-Hispanic/Latino; 11 Hispanic/Latino, 41 international. Average age 30. 541 applicants, 21% accepted, 43 enrolled. In 2010, 28 master's, 14 doctorates, 3 other advanced degrees awarded. Terminal master's awarded for partial completion of doctoral program. *Degree requirements:* For master's, seminar paper; for doctorate, one foreign language, thesis/dissertation, oral and written exams; for Advanced Certificate, internship. *Entrance requirements:* For master's, GRE General Test, minimum GPA of 3.0, writing sample; for doctorate, GRE. Additional exam requirements/recommendations for international students: Required—TOEFL. *Application deadline:* For fall admission, 12/15 for domestic students. Application fee: $90. *Financial support:* Fellowships with tuition reimbursements, research assistantships, teaching assistantships with tuition reimbursements, career-related internships or fieldwork, Federal Work-Study, institutionally sponsored loans, scholarships/grants, health care benefits, and unspecified assistantships available. Financial award application deadline: 12/15; financial award applicants required to submit FAFSA. *Faculty research:* African, East Asian, medieval, early modern, and modern European history; U. S. history; African and African Diaspora; Latin American history; Atlantic World. *Unit head:* Joanna Waley-Cohen, Chair, 212-998-8600, Fax: 212-995-4017, E-mail: history.dept@nyu.edu. *Application contact:* Fiona Griffiths, Director of Graduate Studies, 212-998-8600, Fax: 212-995-4017, E-mail: history.dept@nyu.edu.

North Carolina State University, Graduate School, College of Humanities and Social Sciences, Department of History, Program in Public History, Raleigh, NC 27695. Offers MA. *Degree requirements:* For master's, thesis optional. *Entrance requirements:* For master's, GRE General Test. Electronic applications accepted.

Northeastern University, College of Social Sciences and Humanities, Department of History, Boston, MA 02115-5096. Offers history (MA); public history (MA); world history (PhD). Part-time and evening/weekend programs available. *Faculty:* 15 full-time (6 women), 2 part-time/adjunct (0 women). *Students:* 55 full-time (33 women), 4 part-time (3 women); includes 3 minority (2 Black or African American, non-Hispanic/Latino; 1 Two or more races, non-Hispanic/Latino), 1 international. 116 applicants, 40% accepted, 19 enrolled. In 2010, 11 master's awarded. Terminal master's awarded for partial completion of doctoral program. *Degree requirements:* For master's, one foreign language, thesis or alternative, project; for doctorate, thesis/dissertation. *Entrance requirements:* For master's and doctorate, GRE General Test. Additional exam requirements/recommendations for international students: Required—TOEFL. *Application deadline:* For fall admission, 2/1 for domestic students. Application fee: $50. Electronic applications accepted. *Financial support:* In 2010–11, 13 teaching assistantships with tuition reimbursements (averaging $14,035 per year) were awarded; research assistantships with tuition reimbursements, career-related internships or fieldwork, scholarships/grants, and tuition waivers (full and partial) also available. Financial award application deadline: 2/1; financial award applicants required to submit FAFSA. *Faculty research:* World history, U. S. social history. *Unit head:* Dr. Laura Frader, Chair, 617-373-2660, Fax: 617-373-2661. *Application contact:* Dr. Christina Gilmartin, Graduate Coordinator, 617-373-2660, Fax: 617-373-2661.

Northern Kentucky University, Office of Graduate Programs, College of Arts and Sciences, Program in Public History, Highland Heights, KY 41099. Offers MA, Certificate. Part-time programs available. *Faculty:* 2 full-time (1 woman). *Students:* 17 full-time (8 women), 20 part-time (11 women); includes 2 minority (1 Black or African American, non-Hispanic/Latino; 1 Hispanic/Latino). Average age 33. 25 applicants, 72% accepted, 15 enrolled. *Degree requirements:* For master's, comprehensive exam. *Entrance requirements:* For master's, bachelor's degree in history or related field from regionally-accredited institution with minimum undergraduate GPA of 2.5; official transcripts for all undergraduate and graduate work; 2 letters of reference. Additional exam requirements/recommendations for international students: Required—TOEFL (minimum score 550 paper-based; 213 computer-based; 79 iBT); Recommended—IELTS (minimum score 6.5). *Application deadline:* For fall admission, 8/1 priority date for domestic students, 6/1 priority date for international students; for spring admission, 12/1 priority date for domestic students, 10/1 priority date for international students. Applications are processed on a rolling basis. Application fee: $40. Electronic applications accepted. *Expenses:* Tuition, state resident: full-time $7254; part-time $403 per credit hour. Tuition, nonresident: full-time $12,492; part-time $694 per credit hour. Tuition and fees vary according to degree level and program. *Financial support:* Applicants required to submit FAFSA. *Faculty research:* Local and regional history, oral history, Appalachian history, Gilded Age and Progressive Eras. *Unit head:* Dr. Rebecca Bailey, Director, 859-572-5176, E-mail: publichistory@nku.edu. *Application contact:* Dr. Rebecca Bailey, Director of Graduate Programs, 859-572-5176, E-mail: baileyr4@nku.edu.

Rutgers, The State University of New Jersey, Camden, Graduate School of Arts and Sciences, Program in American and Public History, Camden, NJ 08102. Offers MA. Part-time and evening/weekend programs available. *Faculty:* 15 full-time (6 women), 3 part-time/adjunct (2 women). *Students:* 3 full-time (1 woman), 34 part-time (13 women); includes 1 American Indian or Alaska Native, non-Hispanic/Latino; 1 Hispanic/Latino. Average age 34. 32 applicants, 88% accepted, 13 enrolled. In 2010, 6 degrees awarded. *Degree requirements:* For master's, comprehensive exam, thesis optional, 30 credits. *Entrance requirements:* For master's, GRE General Test (for full-time applicants), 3 letters of recommendation; history or related undergraduate degree (preferred). Additional exam requirements/recommendations for international students: Required—TOEFL, IELTS. *Application deadline:* For fall admission, 7/1 priority date for domestic students; for spring admission, 11/15 for domestic students. Applications are processed on a rolling basis. Application fee: $65. Electronic applications accepted. *Expenses:* Tuition, state resident: full-time $4963; part-time $319 per credit. Tuition, nonresident: full-time $10,493; part-time $680 per credit. *Financial support:* In 2010–11, 4 fellowships with partial tuition reimbursements (averaging $1,550 per year) were awarded; Federal Work-Study, scholarships/grants, and tuition waivers (partial) also available. Financial award application deadline: 3/15; financial award applicants required to submit FAFSA. *Faculty research:* Women's history, military history, Afro-American history, urban history, history of technology. Total annual research expenditures: $44,250. *Unit head:* Dr. Philip Scranton, Director, 856-225-2713, Fax: 856-225-6602, E-mail: scranton@camden.rutgers.edu. *Application contact:* Leona Pellot, Graduate Secretary, 856-225-6080, Fax: 856-225-6602, E-mail: pellot@camden.rutgers.edu.

Shippensburg University of Pennsylvania, School of Graduate Studies, College of Arts and Sciences, Department of History and Philosophy, Shippensburg, PA 17257-2299. Offers applied history (MA, Certificate). Part-time and evening/weekend programs available. *Faculty:* 8 full-time (1 woman). *Students:* 11 full-time (6 women), 19 part-time (5 women). Average age 33. 30 applicants, 60% accepted, 8 enrolled. In 2010, 20 master's awarded. *Degree requirements:* For master's, thesis optional, thesis or internship. *Entrance requirements:* For master's, interview. Additional exam requirements/recommendations for international students: Required—TOEFL (minimum score 580 paper-based; 237 computer-based); Recommended—IELTS (minimum score 6). *Application deadline:* For fall admission, 3/1 for international students; for spring admission, 7/1 for international students. Applications are processed on a rolling basis. Application fee: $30. Electronic applications accepted. *Expenses:* Tuition, state resident: full-time $6966. Tuition, nonresident: full-time $11,146. Required fees: $1802. *Financial support:* In 2010–11, 5 research assistantships with full tuition reimbursements (averaging $5,000 per year) were awarded; career-related internships or fieldwork, scholarships/grants, unspecified assistantships, and resident hall director and student payroll positions also available. Support available to part-time students. Financial award application deadline: 3/1; financial award applicants required to submit FAFSA. *Unit head:* Dr. Stephen Burg, Program Director, 717-477-1621, Fax: 717-477-4062, E-mail: sbburg@ship.edu. *Application contact:* Jeremy R. Goshorn, Associate Dean of Graduate Admissions, 717-477-1231, Fax: 717-477-4016, E-mail: jrgoshorn@ship.edu.

Shippensburg University of Pennsylvania, School of Graduate Studies, College of Arts and Sciences, Department of Sociology and Anthropology, Shippensburg, PA 17257-2299. Offers organizational development and leadership (MS), including business, communications, education, environmental management, higher education, historical administration, individual and organizational development, public organizations, social structures and organizations. Part-time and evening/weekend programs available. *Faculty:* 3 full-time (all women). *Students:* 18 full-time (13 women), 46 part-time (33 women); includes 11 minority (6 Black or African American, non-Hispanic/Latino; 3 Asian, non-Hispanic/Latino; 2 Two or more races, non-Hispanic/Latino), 2 international. Average age 32. 56 applicants, 55% accepted, 20 enrolled. In 2010, 28 master's awarded. *Degree requirements:* For master's, capstone experience including internship. *Entrance requirements:* For master's, interview (if GPA less than 2.75), resume, personal goals statement. Additional exam requirements/recommendations for international students: Required—TOEFL (minimum score 580 paper-based; 237 computer-based); Recommended—IELTS (minimum score 6). *Application deadline:* For fall admission, 3/1 for international students; for spring admission, 7/1 for international students. Applications are processed on a rolling basis. Application fee: $30. Electronic applications accepted. *Expenses:* Tuition, state resident: full-time $6966. Tuition, nonresident: full-time $11,146. Required fees: $1802. *Financial support:* In 2010–11, 8 research assistantships with full tuition reimbursements (averaging $5,000 per year) were awarded; career-related internships or fieldwork, scholarships/grants, unspecified assistantships, and resident hall director and student payroll positions also available. Support available to part-time students. Financial award applicants required to submit FAFSA. *Unit head:* Dr. Barbara Denison, Chairperson, 717-477-1735, Fax: 717-477-4011, E-mail: bjdeni@ship.edu. *Application contact:* Jeremy R. Goshorn, Associate Dean of Graduate Admissions, 717-477-1231, Fax: 717-477-4016, E-mail: jrgoshorn@ship.edu.

Simmons College, Graduate School of Library and Information Science and College of Arts and Sciences Graduate Studies, Program in History and Archives Management, Boston, MA 02115. Offers Certificate, MS/MA. Part-time and evening/weekend programs available. *Entrance requirements:* Additional exam requirements/recommendations for international students: Required—TOEFL (minimum score 550 paper-based; 213 computer-based; 79 iBT). Electronic applications accepted. *Expenses:* Contact institution. *Faculty research:* Library leadership, archives and preservation, organization, information use and users.

Sonoma State University, School of Social Sciences, Program in Cultural Resources Management, Rohnert Park, CA 94928. Offers MA. Part-time programs available. *Faculty:* 6 full-time (5 women). *Students:* 1 full-time (0 women), 21 part-time (14 women); includes 4 minority (2 Hispanic/Latino; 1 Native Hawaiian or other Pacific Islander, non-Hispanic/Latino; 1 Two or more races, non-Hispanic/Latino). Average age 31. 13 applicants, 54% accepted, 3 enrolled. In 2010, 8 master's awarded. *Degree requirements:* For master's, thesis. *Entrance requirements:* For master's, minimum GPA of 3.0. Additional exam requirements/recommendations for international students: Required—TOEFL (minimum score 500 paper-based; 173 computer-based). *Application deadline:* For fall admission, 1/31 for domestic students. Application fee: $55. *Financial support:* Career-related internships or fieldwork, scholarships/grants, traineeships, and unspecified assistantships available. Financial award application deadline: 3/2; financial award applicants required to submit FAFSA. *Unit head:* Dr. Karin Jaffe, Chair, Anthropology Department, 707-664-2944, Fax: 707-664-2505, E-mail: jkarin.jaffe@sonoma.edu. *Application contact:* Margaret Purser, Coordinator, 707-664-3164, Fax: 707-664-2505, E-mail: purser@sonoma.edu.

Southeast Missouri State University, School of Graduate Studies, Department of History, Cape Girardeau, MO 63701-4799. Offers heritage education (Certificate); historic preservation (Certificate); history (MA); public history (MA), including heritage education, historic preservation. Part-time and evening/weekend programs available. *Faculty:* 10 full-time (2 women). *Students:* 5 full-time (all women), 9 part-time (3 women). Average age 31. 9 applicants, 100% accepted, 4 enrolled. In 2010, 5 master's awarded. *Degree requirements:* For master's, comprehensive exam (for some programs), thesis (for some programs), paper (for history); for Certificate, internship, advanced project in applied history, exam, and paper (for historic preservation). *Entrance requirements:* For master's, GRE, minimum undergraduate GPA of 2.75; 3 reference letters; writing sample; letter of intent. Additional exam requirements/recommendations for international students: Required—TOEFL (minimum score 550 paper-based; 213 computer-based; 79 iBT); Recommended—IELTS (minimum score 6). *Application deadline:* For fall admission, 8/1 for domestic students, 6/1 for international students; for spring admission, 11/21 for domestic students, 10/1 for international students. Applications are processed on a rolling basis. Application fee: $25 ($35 for international students). Electronic applications accepted. *Expenses:* Tuition, state resident: full-time $4698; part-time $261 per credit hour. Tuition, nonresident: full-time $8379; part-time $465.50 per credit hour. *Financial support:* In 2010–11, 4 students received support, including 5 teaching assistantships with full tuition reimbursements available (averaging $7,600 per year); career-related internships or fieldwork, Federal Work-Study, institutionally sponsored loans, scholarships/grants, tuition waivers (full), and unspecified assistantships also available. Financial award application deadline: 6/30; financial award applicants required to submit FAFSA. *Faculty research:* Modern America, historic preservation, world history. *Unit head:* Dr. Wayne H. Bowen, Chairperson, 573-651-2179, E-mail: wbowen@semo.edu. *Application contact:* Gail Amick, Administrative Secretary, 573-651-2049, Fax: 573-651-2001, E-mail: gamick@semo.edu.

University at Albany, State University of New York, College of Arts and Sciences, Department of History, Albany, NY 12222-0001. Offers history (MA, PhD); public history (Certificate). Part-time programs available. *Degree requirements:* For master's, variable foreign language requirement, exam, research paper or thesis; for doctorate, thesis/dissertation. *Entrance requirements:* For master's, minimum GPA of 3.0; for doctorate, GRE General Test, minimum GPA of 3.0. Additional exam requirements/recommendations for international students: Required—TOEFL (minimum score 550 paper-based; 213 computer-based). Electronic applications accepted. *Faculty research:* American history (all phases); public policy; European history (Medieval to modern); Asian, African, and Latin American history.

University of Arkansas at Little Rock, Graduate School, College of Arts, Humanities, and Social Science, Department of History, Little Rock, AR 72204-1099. Offers public history (MA). Part-time programs available. *Degree requirements:* For master's, oral exam. *Entrance requirements:* For master's, GRE General Test, minimum GPA of 3.25 in history, 2.7 overall; 18 hours of art history. *Faculty research:* Historic preservation and restoration, museum studies, archives.

University of Colorado Denver, College of Liberal Arts and Sciences, Department of History, Denver, CO 80217. Offers European history (MA); global history (MA); public history (MA); U. S. history (MA). Part-time and evening/weekend programs available. *Faculty:* 12 full-time (6 women), 2 part-time/adjunct (1 woman). *Students:* 29 full-time (17 women), 30 part-time (12 women); includes 1 Black or African American, non-Hispanic/Latino; 1 American Indian or Alaska Native, non-Hispanic/Latino; 3 Hispanic/Latino. Average age 36. 25 applicants, 60%

accepted, 10 enrolled. In 2010, 17 master's awarded. *Degree requirements:* For master's, comprehensive exam, thesis optional, 36 semester hours (12 courses). *Entrance requirements:* For master's, GRE General Test, writing sample, minimum GPA of 3.25, letters of recommendation. Additional exam requirements/recommendations for international students: Required—TOEFL (minimum score 525 paper-based; 197 computer-based). *Application deadline:* For fall admission, 4/1 for domestic students; for spring admission, 10/1 for domestic students. Applications are processed on a rolling basis. Application fee: $50 ($75 for international students). Electronic applications accepted. *Expenses:* Tuition, state resident: full-time $7332; part-time $355 per credit hour. Tuition, nonresident: full-time $18,990; part-time $1055 per credit hour. Required fees: $998. Tuition and fees vary according to course level, course load, degree level, campus/location, program, reciprocity agreements and student level. *Financial support:* Research assistantships, teaching assistantships, Federal Work-Study available. Financial award application deadline: 4/1; financial award applicants required to submit FAFSA. *Faculty research:* Uses of pre-modern Islamic heritage in modern India; relationship between liberal understandings of democracy, crime, and police discretion; relationships between gender, class, health, and welfare in nineteenth and early twentieth century England; U. S. business cultures and their influences on marketing and personnel practices; intersection of business and political ideologies; social and environmental history of the Rocky Mountain West. *Unit head:* Dr. Marjorie Levine-Clark, Associate Professor and Chair, 303-556-2896. *Application contact:* Tabitha Fitzpatrick, Program Assistant, 303-556-4830, E-mail: tabitha.fitzpatrick@ucdenver.edu.

University of Illinois at Springfield, Graduate Programs, College of Liberal Arts and Sciences, Program in History, Springfield, IL 62703-5407. Offers MA. Part-time and evening/weekend programs available. *Degree requirements:* For master's, thesis, internship, or historiography. *Entrance requirements:* For master's, BA in history or related field, minimum undergraduate GPA of 3.0, writing sample. Additional exam requirements/recommendations for international students: Required—TOEFL (minimum score 500 paper-based; 176 computer-based; 61 iBT). Electronic applications accepted. *Expenses:* Tuition, state resident: full-time $6774; part-time $282.25 per credit hour. Tuition, nonresident: full-time $15,078; part-time $628.25 per credit hour. Required fees: $15.25 per credit hour. $492 per term.

University of Louisville, Graduate School, College of Arts and Sciences, Department of History, Louisville, KY 40292-0001. Offers history (MA); public history (Certificate). Part-time and evening/weekend programs available. *Faculty:* 17 full-time (4 women). *Students:* 17 full-time (6 women), 12 part-time (3 women); includes 1 Black or African American, non-Hispanic/Latino; 1 American Indian or Alaska Native, non-Hispanic/Latino. Average age 29. 22 applicants, 68% accepted, 9 enrolled. In 2010, 6 master's awarded. *Degree requirements:* For master's, variable foreign language requirement, comprehensive exam (for some programs), thesis (for some programs). *Entrance requirements:* For master's, GRE General Test. Additional exam requirements/recommendations for international students: Required—TOEFL. *Application deadline:* For fall admission, 5/15 for domestic students, 5/1 for international students; for spring admission, 12/1 for domestic students, 11/1 for international students. Applications are processed on a rolling basis. Application fee: $50. Electronic applications accepted. *Expenses:* Tuition, state resident: full-time $9144; part-time $508 per credit hour. Tuition, nonresident: full-time $19,026; part-time $1057 per credit hour. Tuition and fees vary according to program and reciprocity agreements. *Financial support:* In 2010–11, 2 students received support, including 2 teaching assistantships (averaging $12,000 per year). Financial award applicants required to submit FAFSA. *Faculty research:* United States, British Empire, twentieth century women's history, Latin America, African diaspora. *Unit head:* Dr. Tracy Elaine K'Meyer, Chair, 502-852-6817, Fax: 502-852-0770, E-mail: tracyk@louisville.edu. *Application contact:* Libby Leggett, Director, Graduate Admissions, 502-852-3101, Fax: 502-852-6536, E-mail: gradadm@louisville.edu.

University of Maryland, Baltimore County, Graduate School, College of Arts, Humanities and Social Sciences, Department of Public Policy, Program in Public Policy, Baltimore, MD 21250. Offers economics (PhD); education (MPP, PhD); evaluation (MPP); health (MPP, PhD); management (MPP, PhD); policy history (PhD); urban (MPP, PhD). Part-time and evening/weekend programs available. *Faculty:* 10 full-time (3 women), 2 part-time/adjunct (0 women). *Students:* 62 full-time (37 women), 94 part-time (54 women); includes 39 minority (25 Black or African American, non-Hispanic/Latino; 6 Asian, non-Hispanic/Latino; 2 Hispanic/Latino; 1 Native Hawaiian or other Pacific Islander, non-Hispanic/Latino; 5 Two or more races, non-Hispanic/Latino), 10 international. Average age 36. 102 applicants, 65% accepted, 28 enrolled. In 2010, 20 master's, 8 doctorates awarded. Terminal master's awarded for partial completion of doctoral program. *Degree requirements:* For master's, thesis optional, public analysis paper, internship for pre-service; for doctorate, comprehensive exam, thesis/dissertation, comprehensive and field qualifying exams. *Entrance requirements:* For master's, GRE General Test, 3 academic letters of reference, transcripts, resume; for doctorate, GRE General Test, 3 academic letters of reference, transcripts, resume, research paper. Additional exam requirements/recommendations for international students: Required—TOEFL (minimum score 550 paper-based; 213 computer-based; 80 iBT). *Application deadline:* For fall admission, 1/15 priority date for domestic students, 1/1 priority date for international students; for spring admission, 11/1 priority date for domestic students, 5/1 priority date for international students. Applications are processed on a rolling basis. Application fee: $50. Electronic applications accepted. *Financial support:* In 2010–11, 26 students received support, including fellowships (averaging $3,000 per year), 21 research assistantships with full tuition reimbursements available (averaging $17,400 per year); career-related internships or fieldwork, Federal Work-Study, scholarships/grants, health care benefits, and unspecified assistantships also available. Support available to part-time students. Financial award application deadline: 1/15; financial award applicants required to submit FAFSA. *Faculty research:* Health policy, education policy, urban policy, public management, evaluation and analytical methods. *Unit head:* Dr. Donald Norris, Chair, 410-455-1455, E-mail: norris@umbc.edu. *Application contact:* Sally F. Helms, Administrator of Academic Affairs, 410-455-3202, Fax: 410-455-1172, E-mail: gradposi@umbc.edu.

University of Massachusetts Amherst, Graduate School, College of Humanities and Fine Arts, Department of History, Amherst, MA 01003. Offers ancient history (MA); British Empire history (MA); European (medieval and modern) history (MA, PhD); Islamic history (MA); Latin American history (MA, PhD); modern global history (MA); public history (MA); science and technology history (MA); U. S. history (MA, PhD). Part-time programs available. *Faculty:* 38 full-time (17 women). *Students:* 38 full-time (20 women), 29 part-time (16 women); includes 6 minority (1 Black or African American, non-Hispanic/Latino; 1 American Indian or Alaska Native, non-Hispanic/Latino; 1 Asian, non-Hispanic/Latino; 3 Hispanic/Latino), 3 international. Average age 32. 165 applicants, 32% accepted, 22 enrolled. In 2010, 10 master's, 6 doctorates awarded. Terminal master's awarded for partial completion of doctoral program. *Degree requirements:* For master's, one foreign language, thesis or alternative; for doctorate, one foreign language, comprehensive exam, thesis/dissertation. *Entrance requirements:* For master's and doctorate, GRE General Test, writing sample. Additional exam requirements/recommendations for international students: Required—TOEFL (minimum score 550 paper-based; 213 computer-based; 80 iBT), IELTS (minimum score 6.5). *Application deadline:* For fall admission, 1/2 for domestic and international students. Applications are processed on a rolling basis. Application fee: $50 ($65 for international students). Electronic applications accepted. *Expenses:* Tuition, state resident: full-time $2640. Required fees: $8282. One-time fee: $357 full-time. *Financial support:* In 2010–11, 1 fellowship with full tuition reimbursement (averaging $14,661 per year), 4 research assistantships with full tuition reimbursements (averaging $4,089 per year), 39 teaching assistantships with full tuition reimbursements (averaging $12,153 per year) were awarded; career-related internships or fieldwork, Federal Work-Study, scholarships/grants, traineeships, health care benefits, tuition waivers (full), and unspecified assistantships also available. Support available to part-time students. Financial award application deadline: 1/2; financial award applicants required to submit FAFSA. *Faculty research:* Ancient and medieval history; global and comparative history; public history; history of science, technology, medicine and the environment; history of women, gender, sexuality

and family. *Unit head:* Dr. Marla Miller, Graduate Program Director, 413-545-6791, Fax: 413-545-6137. *Application contact:* Jean M. Ames, Supervisor of Admissions, 413-545-0722, Fax: 413-577-0010, E-mail: gradadm@grad.umass.edu.

University of Northern Iowa, Graduate College, College of Social and Behavioral Sciences, Department of History, Cedar Falls, IA 50614. Offers history (MA); public history (MA). Part-time programs available. *Students:* 14 full-time (6 women), 12 part-time (5 women); includes 3 minority (1 American Indian or Alaska Native, non-Hispanic/Latino; 1 Asian, non-Hispanic/Latino; 1 Hispanic/Latino). 22 applicants, 59% accepted, 6 enrolled. In 2010, 5 master's awarded. *Degree requirements:* For master's, comprehensive exam (for some programs), thesis or alternative. *Entrance requirements:* For master's, minimum GPA of 3.2. Additional exam requirements/recommendations for international students: Required—TOEFL (minimum score 500 paper-based; 180 computer-based; 61 iBT). *Application deadline:* For fall admission, 8/1 priority date for domestic students. Applications are processed on a rolling basis. Application fee: $50 ($70 for international students). Electronic applications accepted. *Financial support:* Career-related internships or fieldwork, Federal Work-Study, scholarships/grants, and tuition waivers (full and partial) available. Support available to part-time students. Financial award application deadline: 2/1. *Unit head:* Dr. Robert Martin, Head, 319-273-2097, Fax: 319-273-5846, E-mail: robert.martin@uni.edu. *Application contact:* Laurie S. Russell, Record Analyst, 319-273-2623, Fax: 319-273-2885, E-mail: laurie.russell@uni.edu.

University of South Carolina, The Graduate School, College of Arts and Sciences, Department of History, Program in Public History, Columbia, SC 29208. Offers archives (MA); historic preservation (MA); museum (MA); museum management (Certificate); MLIS/MA. *Degree requirements:* For master's, one foreign language, thesis, internship. *Entrance requirements:* For master's, GRE General Test, writing sample. Additional exam requirements/recommendations for international students: Required—TOEFL. Electronic applications accepted. *Faculty research:* Museum studies, historic preservation, archives administration.

The University of Texas at Austin, Graduate School, College of Liberal Arts, Department of Anthropology, Program in Folklore and Public Culture, Austin, TX 78712-1111. Offers MA, PhD. Part-time programs available. Terminal master's awarded for partial completion of doctoral program. *Degree requirements:* For master's, one foreign language, thesis, report; for doctorate, one foreign language, thesis/dissertation. *Entrance requirements:* For master's and doctorate, GRE General Test. Electronic applications accepted. *Faculty research:* Expressive culture, gender, genre, folklore and culture of British Isles, ethnography of speaking.

University of West Florida, College of Arts and Sciences: Arts, Department of History, Pensacola, FL 32514-5750. Offers history (MA); military history (MA); public history (MA). Part-time and evening/weekend programs available. *Faculty:* 8 full-time (2 women). *Students:* 10 full-time (7 women), 33 part-time (19 women); includes 1 Black or African American, non-Hispanic/Latino; 1 Asian, non-Hispanic/Latino; 2 Hispanic/Latino. Average age 30. 25 applicants, 52% accepted, 11 enrolled. In 2010, 10 master's awarded. *Degree requirements:* For master's, thesis or alternative. *Entrance requirements:* For master's, GRE General Test, minimum GPA of 3.0, minimum 15 hours of upper-level history courses. Additional exam requirements/recommendations for international students: Required—TOEFL (minimum score 550 paper-based; 213 computer-based). *Application deadline:* For fall admission, 6/1 for domestic students, 5/15 for international students; for spring admission, 10/1 for domestic and international students. Applications are processed on a rolling basis. Application fee: $30. *Expenses:* Tuition, state resident: full-time $4982; part-time $208 per credit hour. Tuition, nonresident: full-time $20,059; part-time $836 per credit hour. Required fees: $1365; $57 per credit hour. *Financial support:* In 2010–11, 20 fellowships with partial tuition reimbursements (averaging $377 per year), 13 research assistantships with partial tuition reimbursements (averaging $3,280 per year) were awarded; unspecified assistantships also available. Financial award application deadline: 4/15; financial award applicants required to submit FAFSA. *Unit head:* Dr. John J. Clune, Chairperson, 850-474-2680. *Application contact:* Terry McCray, Assistant Director of Graduate Admissions, 850-473-7718, Fax: 850-473-7714, E-mail: gradadmissions@uwf.edu.

University of West Georgia, College of Arts and Sciences, Department of History, Carrollton, GA 30118. Offers history (MA); museum studies (Certificate); public history (Certificate). Part-time programs available. *Faculty:* 16 full-time (6 women). *Students:* 25 full-time (16 women), 15 part-time (8 women); includes 1 American Indian or Alaska Native, non-Hispanic/Latino; 2 Hispanic/Latino; 1 Two or more races, non-Hispanic/Latino. Average age 33. 16 applicants, 69% accepted, 8 enrolled. In 2010, 7 master's, 8 other advanced degrees awarded. *Degree requirements:* For master's, one foreign language, comprehensive exam, thesis or alternative. *Entrance requirements:* For master's, GRE General Test (minimum score 400 verbal, 400 quantitative, 3.5 writing), undergraduate degree in history or related social studies, minimum GPA of 2.75. *Application deadline:* For fall admission, 7/17 for domestic students; for spring admission, 11/20 for domestic students. Applications are processed on a rolling basis. Application fee: $30. Electronic applications accepted. *Expenses:* Tuition, state resident: full-time $4130; part-time $173 per semester hour. Tuition, nonresident: full-time $16,524; part-time $689 per semester hour. Required fees: $1586; $44.01 per semester hour. $397 per semester. Tuition and fees vary according to program. *Financial support:* In 2010–11, 7 students received support, including research assistantships with full tuition reimbursements available (averaging $6,000 per year); career-related internships or fieldwork, scholarships/grants, and unspecified assistantships also available. Support available to part-time students. Financial award application deadline: 7/1; financial award applicants required to submit FAFSA. *Faculty research:* Public history, United States, Russia/Soviet Union, Africa, Europe. *Unit head:* Dr. Howard Steven Goodson, Interim Chair, 678-839-6042, E-mail: hgoodson@westga.edu. *Application contact:* Dr. Charles W. Clark, Dean, 678-839-6508, E-mail: cclark@westga.edu.

Washington State University, Graduate School, College of Liberal Arts, Department of History, Pullman, WA 99164. Offers early and modern European history (MA, PhD); environmental history (MA, PhD); Latin American history (MA, PhD); modern East Asia history (MA, PhD); public history (MA, PhD); U. S. history (MA, PhD); women's history (MA, PhD); world history (MA, PhD). Part-time programs available. *Faculty:* 25. *Students:* 38 full-time (22 women), 10 part-time (4 women); includes 1 American Indian or Alaska Native, non-Hispanic/Latino; 2 Hispanic/Latino, 2 international. Average age 33. 57 applicants, 47% accepted, 10 enrolled. In 2010, 10 master's, 2 doctorates awarded. *Degree requirements:* For master's, comprehensive exam (for some programs), thesis, oral exam; for doctorate, one foreign language, comprehensive exam, thesis/dissertation, oral and written exam. *Entrance requirements:* For master's and doctorate, GRE General Test, official transcripts from all universities attended; three letters of recommendation; statement of purpose; writing sample; Preferred Fields of Study form; Language Background form. Additional exam requirements/recommendations for international students: Required—TOEFL (minimum score 550 paper-based), IELTS. *Application deadline:* For fall admission, 1/10 for domestic and international students; for spring admission, 7/1 for domestic and international students. Applications are processed on a rolling basis. Application fee: $50. Electronic applications accepted. *Expenses:* Tuition, state resident: full-time $8552; part-time $443 per credit. Tuition, nonresident: full-time $21,650; part-time $1083 per credit. Required fees: $846. *Financial support:* In 2010–11, 1 fellowship with partial tuition reimbursement (averaging $3,000 per year), research assistantships with full and partial tuition reimbursements (averaging $13,917 per year), 28 teaching assistantships with full and partial tuition reimbursements (averaging $13,056 per year) were awarded; career-related internships or fieldwork, Federal Work-Study, institutionally sponsored loans, scholarships/grants, and health care benefits also available. Financial award application deadline: 2/15; financial award applicants required to submit FAFSA. *Faculty research:* Public, world, environmental, women's and U. S. history. *Unit head:* Dr. Raymond Sun, Chair, 509-335-5139, Fax: 509-335-4171, E-mail: pietz@wsu.edu. *Application contact:* Graduate Studies Director, 509-335-4030, Fax: 509-335-4171, E-mail: kale@wsu.edu.

Section 8
Humanities

This section contains a directory of institutions offering graduate work in humanities, followed by an in-depth entry submitted by an institution that chose to prepare a detailed program description. Additional information about programs listed in the directory but not augmented by an in-depth entry may be obtained by writing directly to the dean of a graduate school or chair of a department at the address given in the directory.

For programs offering related work, see also in this book *Area and Cultural Studies, Geography, Interdisciplinary Studies, Philosophy, Political Science, and International Affairs, Religious Studies,* and *Sociology, Anthropology, and Archaeology.* In another guide in this series:

Graduate Programs in Engineering & Applied Sciences
See *Management of Engineering and Technology*

CONTENTS

Program Directories

Close-Up and Display

Humanities

American Public University System, AMU/APU Graduate Programs, Charles Town, WV 25414. Offers accounting (MBA); administration and supervision (M Ed); air warfare (MA Military Studies); asymmetrical warfare (MA Military Studies); criminal justice (MA); emergency and disaster management (MA); entrepreneurship (MBA); environmental policy and management (MS); finance (MBA); general (MBA); global business management (MBA); guidance and counseling (M Ed); history (MA); homeland security (MA); homeland security resource allocation (MBA); humanities (MA); information technology (MS); information technology management (MBA); intelligence studies (MA); international relations and conflict resolution (MA); joint warfare (MA Military Studies); land warfare (MA Military Studies); legal studies (MA); management (MA), including defense mangement, general, human resource management, organizational leadership, public administration; marketing (MBA); military history (MA); national security studies (MA); naval warfare (MA Military Studies); nonprofit management (MBA); political science (MA); psychology (MA); public administration (MA); public health (MA); security management (MA); space studies (MS); sports management (MS); strategic leadership (MA Military Studies); teaching (M Ed), including elementary, secondary social sciences; transportation and logistics management (MA). Programs offered via distance learning only. Part-time and evening/weekend programs available. Postbaccalaureate distance learning degree programs offered (no on-campus study). *Faculty:* 253 full-time (134 women), 1,208 part-time/adjunct (570 women). *Students:* 956 full-time (422 women), 8,476 part-time (2,821 women); includes 2,511 minority (1,218 Black or African American, non-Hispanic/Latino; 68 American Indian or Alaska Native, non-Hispanic/Latino; 219 Asian, non-Hispanic/Latino; 705 Hispanic/Latino; 46 Native Hawaiian or other Pacific Islander, non-Hispanic/Latino; 255 Two or more races, non-Hispanic/Latino), 107 international. Average age 35. 9,550 applicants, 100% accepted. In 2010, 1,688 master's awarded. *Degree requirements:* For master's, comprehensive exam or practicum. *Entrance requirements:* For master's, official transcript showing earned bachelor's degree from institution accredited by recognized accrediting body. Additional exam requirements/recommendations for international students: Required—TOEFL (minimum score 550 paper-based; 213 computer-based), IELTS (minimum score 6.5). *Application deadline:* Applications are processed on a rolling basis. Application fee: $0. Electronic applications accepted. *Financial support:* Applicants required to submit FAFSA. *Faculty research:* Military history, criminal justice, management performance, national security. *Unit head:* Dr. Frank McCluskey, Provost, 877-468-6268, Fax: 304-724-3780. *Application contact:* Terry Grant, Director of Enrollment Management, 877-468-6268, Fax: 304-724-3780, E-mail: info@apus.edu.

Arcadia University, Graduate Studies, Program in Humanities, Glenside, PA 19038-3295. Offers fine arts, theater, and music (MAH); history, philosophy, and religion (MAH); literature and language (MAH). Part-time programs available. *Faculty:* 15 full-time (3 women). *Students:* 5 full-time (4 women), 16 part-time (12 women); includes 2 minority (1 Black or African American, non-Hispanic/Latino; 1 Two or more races, non-Hispanic/Latino), 1 international. Average age 41. In 2010, 10 master's awarded. *Degree requirements:* For master's, thesis or alternative. *Application deadline:* Applications are processed on a rolling basis. Application fee: $50. *Expenses:* Contact institution. *Financial support:* Unspecified assistantships available. *Unit head:* Dr. Richard Wertime, Coordinator, 215-572-2963. *Application contact:* 215-572-2925, Fax: 215-572-2126, E-mail: grad@arcadia.edu.

Brigham Young University, Graduate Studies, College of Humanities, Department of Humanities, Classics, and Comparative Literature, Provo, UT 84602-1001. Offers comparative studies (MA). *Faculty:* 25 full-time (5 women). *Students:* 16 full-time (10 women). Average age 26. 14 applicants, 50% accepted, 7 enrolled. In 2010, 6 master's awarded. *Degree requirements:* For master's, 2 foreign languages, thesis. *Entrance requirements:* For master's, GRE, minimum GPA of 3.0 in last 60 hours. Additional exam requirements/recommendations for international students: Required—TOEFL (minimum score 580 paper-based; 85 iBT), IELTS (minimum score 7). *Application deadline:* For fall admission, 3/1 for domestic and international students. Application fee: $50. Electronic applications accepted. *Expenses:* Tuition: Full-time $5580; part-time $310 per credit hour. Tuition and fees vary according to program and student's religious affiliation. *Financial support:* In 2010–11, 16 students received support, including 39 fellowships with full and partial tuition reimbursements available (averaging $1,306 per year), 5 research assistantships (averaging $1,400 per year), 36 teaching assistantships (averaging $2,317 per year); career-related internships or fieldwork, institutionally sponsored loans, scholarships/grants, tuition waivers (full and partial), and student instructorships also available. Support available to part-time students. *Unit head:* Dr. Michael J. Call, Chair, 801-422-2550, Fax: 801-422-0305, E-mail: michael_call@byu.edu. *Application contact:* Carolyn Hone, Graduate Secretary for Humanities and Comparative Literature, 801-422-4430, Fax: 801-422-0305, E-mail: carolyn_hone@byu.edu.

California Institute of Integral Studies, School of Consciousness and Transformation, San Francisco, CA 94103. Offers creative inquiry/interdisciplinary arts (MFA); cultural anthropology and social transformation (MA); East-West psychology (MA, PhD); integrative health studies (MA); philosophy and religion (MA, PhD), including Asian and comparative studies, philosophy, cosmology, and consciousness, women's spirituality; social and cultural anthropology (PhD); transformative leadership (MA); transformative studies (PhD); writing and consciousness (MFA). Part-time and evening/weekend programs available. Postbaccalaureate distance learning degree programs offered (minimal on-campus study). *Students:* 455 full-time (315 women), 133 part-time (90 women); includes 47 Black or African American, non-Hispanic/Latino; 3 American Indian or Alaska Native, non-Hispanic/Latino; 21 Asian, non-Hispanic/Latino; 41 Hispanic/Latino, 40 international. Average age 37. 265 applicants, 91% accepted, 163 enrolled. In 2010, 64 master's, 22 doctorates awarded. Terminal master's awarded for partial completion of doctoral program. *Degree requirements:* For master's, thesis optional; for doctorate, comprehensive exam, thesis/dissertation, 1 foreign language (Asian comparative studies). *Entrance requirements:* For master's, minimum GPA of 3.0, letters of recommendation, writing sample; for doctorate, master's degree, minimum GPA of 3.0, letters of recommendation, writing sample. Additional exam requirements/recommendations for international students: Required—TOEFL. *Application deadline:* For fall admission, 2/1 priority date for domestic and international students; for spring admission, 10/15 priority date for domestic and international students. Applications are processed on a rolling basis. Application fee: $65. Electronic applications accepted. *Expenses:* Tuition: Full-time $15,660; part-time $870 per semester hour. Required fees: $95 per semester. *Financial support:* In 2010–11, 255 students received support; research assistantships, teaching assistantships, career-related internships or fieldwork, Federal Work-Study, scholarships/grants, and tuition waivers (partial) available. Support available to part-time students. Financial award application deadline: 4/15; financial award applicants required to submit FAFSA. *Faculty research:* Ecology and sustainablility, philosophy and religion, East-West psychology, integrative health, social and cultural anthropology, transformative leadership. *Application contact:* Allyson Werner, Associate Director of Admissions, 415-575-6155, Fax: 415-575-1268.

California State University, Dominguez Hills, College of Arts and Humanities, Program in Arts and Humanities, Carson, CA 90747-0001. Offers MA. Part-time and evening/weekend programs available. *Faculty:* 14 full-time (8 women), 5 part-time/adjunct (2 women). *Students:* 2 full-time (1 woman), 33 part-time (23 women); includes 9 Black or African American, non-Hispanic/Latino; 3 Asian, non-Hispanic/Latino; 5 Hispanic/Latino; 2 Two or more races, non-Hispanic/Latino, 1 international. Average age 41. 18 applicants, 94% accepted, 11 enrolled. In 2010, 6 master's awarded. *Degree requirements:* For master's, thesis or alternative. *Entrance requirements:* For master's, minimum GPA of 3.0. *Application deadline:* For fall admission, 6/1 for domestic students. Applications are processed on a rolling basis. Application fee: $55. *Financial support:* Institutionally sponsored loans available. Support available to part-time students. Financial award application deadline: 8/1. *Faculty research:* African American music, postmodernism, cities of antiquity, Faust, African studies. *Unit head:* Dr. Lorna Fitzsimmons, Coordinator, 310-243-3036, E-mail: lfitzsimmons@csudh.edu. *Application contact:* Brandy McLelland, Interim Director, Student Information Services, 310-243-3645, E-mail: bmclelland@csudh.edu.

California State University, Dominguez Hills, College of Extended and International Education, Humanities External Degree Program, Carson, CA 90747-0001. Offers MA. Part-time and evening/weekend programs available. Postbaccalaureate distance learning degree programs offered. *Faculty:* 8 full-time (4 women), 34 part-time/adjunct (13 women). *Students:* 5 full-time (1 woman), 334 part-time (182 women); includes 7 Black or African American, non-Hispanic/Latino; 2 American Indian or Alaska Native, non-Hispanic/Latino; 10 Asian, non-Hispanic/Latino; 24 Hispanic/Latino; 1 Native Hawaiian or other Pacific Islander, non-Hispanic/Latino. Average age 43. 74 applicants, 84% accepted, 44 enrolled. In 2010, 64 master's awarded. *Degree requirements:* For master's, thesis, advancement to candidacy essays. *Entrance requirements:* Additional exam requirements/recommendations for international students: Required—TOEFL. *Application deadline:* For fall admission, 6/1 for domestic and international students; for winter admission, 10/1 for domestic students, 11/1 for international students; for spring admission, 3/1 for domestic and international students. Application fee: $55. Electronic applications accepted. *Expenses:* Contact institution. *Financial support:* Applicants required to submit FAFSA. *Faculty research:* Nineteenth and twentieth century literature, Arab history, Greek philosophy, ancient history, East Asian, Soviet cultural history, Native American history and culture, feminist studies. *Unit head:* Dr. Patricia Cherin, Coordinator, 310-243-3191, Fax: 310-516-4399, E-mail: huxonline@csudh.edu. *Application contact:* Lisa Ayers, Program Assistant, 310-243-3190, Fax: 310-516-4399, E-mail: layers@csudh.edu.

See Display on next page and Close-Up on page 353.

California State University, East Bay, Office of Academic Programs and Graduate Studies, College of Education and Allied Studies, Department of Kinesiology, Hayward, CA 94542-3000. Offers exercise physiology (MS); humanities/cultural studies (MS); professional perspectives (MS); skill acquisition/sport psychology (MS). *Faculty:* 6 full-time (3 women). *Students:* 17 full-time (12 women), 14 part-time (6 women); includes 15 minority (3 Black or African American, non-Hispanic/Latino; 1 American Indian or Alaska Native, non-Hispanic/Latino; 5 Asian, non-Hispanic/Latino; 5 Hispanic/Latino; 1 Two or more races, non-Hispanic/Latino). Average age 31. 31 applicants, 74% accepted, 10 enrolled. In 2010, 16 master's awarded. *Degree requirements:* For master's, exam or thesis. *Entrance requirements:* For master's, BA in kinesiology or related discipline, minimum major course work GPA of 3.0. Additional exam requirements/recommendations for international students: Required—TOEFL (minimum score 550 paper-based; 213 computer-based). *Application deadline:* For fall admission, 6/30 for domestic and international students. Applications are processed on a rolling basis. Application fee: $55. Electronic applications accepted. *Financial support:* Fellowships, Federal Work-Study, institutionally sponsored loans, and scholarships/grants available. Support available to part-time students. Financial award application deadline: 3/2; financial award applicants required to submit FAFSA. *Unit head:* Dr. Penny McCullagh, Chair, 510-885-3061, Fax: 510-885-2423, E-mail: penny.mccullagh@csueastbay.edu. *Application contact:* Dr. Donna Wiley, Interim Associate Director, 510-885-2928, Fax: 510-885-4777, E-mail: donna.wiley@csueastbay.edu.

Carlow University, Humanities Division, Pittsburgh, PA 15213-3165. Offers creative writing (MFA), including fiction, nonfiction, poetry. Part-time and evening/weekend programs available. Postbaccalaureate distance learning degree programs offered (minimal on-campus study). *Students:* 34 part-time (31 women); includes 3 Black or African American, non-Hispanic/Latino. Average age 41. 1 applicant, 100% accepted, 1 enrolled. In 2010, 11 master's awarded. *Degree requirements:* For master's, thesis or alternative. *Entrance requirements:* For master's, minimum GPA of 3.0, resume, writing samples, 2 letters of recommendation. Additional exam requirements/recommendations for international students: Required—TOEFL (minimum score 550 paper-based; 213 computer-based). *Application deadline:* For fall admission, 6/15 priority date for domestic and international students; for spring admission, 11/15 priority date for domestic and international students. Applications are processed on a rolling basis. Application fee: $20. *Expenses:* Tuition: Full-time $9900; part-time $660 per credit. Tuition and fees vary according to course load, degree level and program. *Financial support:* Career-related internships or fieldwork, Federal Work-Study, and scholarships/grants available. Support available to part-time students. Financial award application deadline: 4/1; financial award applicants required to submit FAFSA. *Unit head:* Dr. Ellie Wymard, Director of MFA Program, 412-578-6597, Fax: 412-578-8706, E-mail: wymardex@carlow.edu. *Application contact:* Jo Danhires, Administrative Assistant of Admissions, 412-578-6059, Fax: 412-578-6321, E-mail: gradstudies@carlow.edu.

Central European University, Graduate Studies, School of Social Sciences and Humanities, Budapest, Hungary. Offers economics (MA, PhD); gender studies (MA, PhD); international relations and European studies (MA, PhD); mathematics and its applications (MS, PhD); medieval studies (MA, PhD); nationalism studies (MA, PhD); philosophy (MA, PhD); political science (MA, PhD); public policy (MA, PhD); sociology and social anthropology (MA, PhD). *Faculty:* 90 full-time (29 women), 13 part-time/adjunct (7 women). *Students:* 732 full-time (404 women). Average age 28. 3,639 applicants, 22% accepted, 416 enrolled. In 2010, 278 master's, 16 doctorates awarded. Terminal master's awarded for partial completion of doctoral program. *Degree requirements:* For master's, one foreign language, thesis; for doctorate, one foreign language, comprehensive exam, thesis/dissertation. *Entrance requirements:* For master's, interview; for doctorate, GRE, CEU subject test, interview. Additional exam requirements/recommendations for international students: Required—TOEFL (minimum score 570 paper-based; 230 computer-based); Recommended—IELTS (minimum score 6.5). *Application deadline:* For fall admission, 1/15 priority date for domestic and international students. Application fee: $0. Electronic applications accepted. Tuition and fees charges are reported in euros. *Expenses:* Tuition: Full-time 11,000 euros. Required fees: 250 euros. One-time fee: 200 euros full-time. Tuition and fees vary according to degree level, program, reciprocity agreements and student level. *Financial support:* In 2010–11, 402 students received support, including 416 fellowships with full and partial tuition reimbursements available (averaging $6,200 per year); career-related internships or fieldwork, institutionally sponsored loans, and scholarships/grants also available. Financial award application deadline: 1/5. *Faculty research:* Civil society, fiscal decentralization, party politics, political philosophy (especially liberalism, theory of democracy). Total annual research expenditures: $35,000. *Unit head:* Dr. Katalin Farkas, Provost/Academic Pro Rector, 361-327-3000 Ext. 2227, E-mail: farkask@ceu.hu. *Application contact:* Zsuzsanna Jaszberenyi, Admissions Officer, 361-327-3009, Fax: 361-327-3211, E-mail: admissions@ceu.hu.

Central Michigan University, College of Graduate Studies, College of Humanities and Social and Behavioral Sciences, Program in Humanities, Mount Pleasant, MI 48859. Offers humanities (MA), including contemporary issues in the humanities: race, class, and gender, images and ideas of self, Native American issues in modern culture, popular culture studies, the rise of industrial society. Part-time and evening/weekend programs available. *Students:* 2 full-time (both women), 10 part-time (6 women); includes 1 American Indian or Alaska Native, non-Hispanic/Latino; 2 Hispanic/Latino. Average age 37. *Degree requirements:* For master's, thesis or alternative. *Application deadline:* For fall admission, 6/1 for international students; for spring admission, 10/1 for international students. Applications are processed on a rolling basis. Application fee: $35 ($45 for international students). Electronic applications accepted. *Expenses:* Tuition, state resident: full-time $8208; part-time $456 per credit hour. Tuition, nonresident: full-time $13,788; part-time $766 per credit hour. One-time fee: $25. *Financial support:* Fellowships with tuition reimbursements, Federal Work-Study, unspecified assistantships, and out-of-state merit awards, non-resident graduate awards available. *Faculty research:* Rise of industrial society; images and ideas of self; contemporary issues of race, class, and gender; popular culture; Native American issues in modern culture. *Unit head:* Dr. Susan A. Schiller, Director, 989-774-3681, Fax: 989-774-7106, E-mail: schil1sa@cmich.edu. *Application contact:*

Judith L. Prince, Director of Graduate Student Services, 989-774-1059, Fax: 989-774-1857, E-mail: judith.l.prince@cmich.edu.

Claremont Graduate University, Graduate Programs, School of Arts and Humanities, Claremont, CA 91711-6160. Offers M Phil, MA, MFA, DCM, DMA, PhD, Certificate, MA/PhD, MBA/MA, MBA/PhD. Part-time programs available. *Faculty:* 19 full-time (9 women), 6 part-time/adjunct (2 women). *Students:* 361 full-time (194 women), 31 part-time (22 women); includes 116 minority (21 Black or African American, non-Hispanic/Latino; 2 American Indian or Alaska Native, non-Hispanic/Latino; 33 Asian, non-Hispanic/Latino; 42 Hispanic/Latino; 1 Native Hawaiian or other Pacific Islander, non-Hispanic/Latino; 17 Two or more races, non-Hispanic/Latino), 25 international. Average age 35. In 2010, 78 master's, 26 doctorates, 3 other advanced degrees awarded. *Degree requirements:* For doctorate, 2 foreign languages, comprehensive exam, thesis/dissertation, oral and written qualifying exams, oral defense of dissertation, recitals. *Entrance requirements:* For master's and doctorate, GRE General Test. Additional exam requirements/recommendations for international students: Required—TOEFL (minimum score 550 paper-based; 213 computer-based; 80 iBT). *Application deadline:* For fall admission, 2/1 priority date for domestic students. Applications are processed on a rolling basis. Application fee: $60. Electronic applications accepted. *Expenses:* Tuition: Full-time $35,748; part-time $1554 per unit. Required fees: $215 per semester. *Financial support:* Fellowships, research assistantships, teaching assistantships, Federal Work-Study, institutionally sponsored loans, and scholarships/grants available. Support available to part-time students. Financial award application deadline: 2/15; financial award applicants required to submit FAFSA. *Unit head:* Lisa Flores Griffith, Administrative Director, 909-607-3877, Fax: 909-607-3877, E-mail: elysabeth.flores@cgu.edu. *Application contact:* Susan Hampson, Admissions and Academic Support, 909-607-1278, Fax: 909-607-1221, E-mail: susan.hampson@cgu.edu.

Clemson University, Graduate School, Program in International Family and Community Studies, Clemson, SC 29634. Offers PhD. *Faculty:* 6 full-time (2 women), 8 part-time/adjunct. *Students:* 12 full-time (11 women), 5 part-time (4 women); includes 2 Black or African American, non-Hispanic/Latino; 1 Asian, non-Hispanic/Latino, 5 international. Average age 36. 20 applicants, 20% accepted, 4 enrolled. In 2010, 2 doctorates awarded. *Degree requirements:* For doctorate, thesis/dissertation. *Entrance requirements:* For doctorate, GRE General Test. Additional exam requirements/recommendations for international students: Required—TOEFL. *Application deadline:* Applications are processed on a rolling basis. Application fee: $70 ($80 for international students). Electronic applications accepted. *Expenses:* Contact institution. *Financial support:* In 2010–11, 12 students received support, including 1 fellowship with full and partial tuition reimbursement available (averaging $4,000 per year), 17 research assistantships with partial tuition reimbursements available (averaging $13,914 per year); career-related internships or fieldwork, institutionally sponsored loans, scholarships/grants, health care benefits, and unspecified assistantships also available. Support available to part-time students. *Unit head:* Dr. Gary B. Melton, Director, 864-656-6271. *Application contact:* Information Contact, 864-656-3195, E-mail: gradapp@clemson.edu.

College of the Humanities and Sciences, Harrison Middleton University, Graduate Program, Tempe, AZ 85282. Offers education (MA, Ed D); humanities (MA); imaginative literature (MA); interdisciplinary studies (DA); jurisprudence (MA); natural science (MA); philosophy and religion (MA); social science (MA). Part-time and evening/weekend programs available. Post-baccalaureate distance learning degree programs offered (no on-campus study). *Faculty:* 17 full-time (7 women), 14 part-time/adjunct (6 women). *Students:* 52 full-time (20 women). In 2010, 4 master's awarded. *Degree requirements:* For master's and doctorate, capstone project. *Entrance requirements:* For doctorate, 3 academic letters of reference, interview. *Application deadline:* Applications are processed on a rolling basis. Application fee: $50. Electronic applications accepted. *Expenses:* Tuition: Part-time $300 per credit hour. One-time fee: $350 part-time. *Faculty research:* Japanese animation, educational leadership, war art, John Muir's wilderness. *Application contact:* Deborah Deacon, Dean of Graduate Studies, 877-248-6724, Fax: 800-762-1622, E-mail: ddeacon@hmu.edu.

The Colorado College, Department of Education, Experienced Teacher Program, Colorado Springs, CO 80903-3294. Offers arts and humanities (MAT); liberal arts (MAT); Southwest studies (MAT). Programs offered during summer only. Part-time programs available. *Degree requirements:* For master's, thesis, oral exam, 50-page paper. *Expenses:* Contact institution.

Concordia University, School of Graduate Studies, Faculty of Arts and Science, Program in Humanities, Montréal, QC H3G 1M8, Canada. Offers PhD. *Degree requirements:* For doctorate, one foreign language, comprehensive exam, thesis/dissertation.

Dominican University of California, Graduate Programs, School of Arts, Humanities and Social Sciences, Program in Humanities, San Rafael, CA 94901-2298. Offers MA. Part-time programs available. *Faculty:* 7 full-time (3 women), 3 part-time/adjunct (1 woman). *Students:* 10 full-time (6 women), 35 part-time (26 women); includes 7 minority (2 Black or African American, non-Hispanic/Latino; 1 Asian, non-Hispanic/Latino; 3 Hispanic/Latino; 1 Two or more races, non-Hispanic/Latino), 2 international. Average age 42. 38 applicants, 71% accepted, 20 enrolled. In 2010, 9 master's awarded. *Degree requirements:* For master's, thesis or alternative. *Entrance requirements:* For master's, minimum GPA of 3.0, interview. Additional exam requirements/recommendations for international students: Required—TOEFL (minimum score 550 paper-based; 213 computer-based; 80 iBT), IELTS (minimum score 7). *Application deadline:* For fall admission, 6/15 priority date for domestic and international students; for spring admission, 11/15 priority date for domestic and international students. Applications are processed on a rolling basis. Application fee: $40. Electronic applications accepted. *Financial support:* In 2010–11, 16 students received support; fellowships, scholarships/grants available. Support available to part-time students. Financial award application deadline: 3/2; financial award applicants required to submit FAFSA. *Unit head:* Dr. Martin Anderson, Chair, 415-482-3582, Fax: 415-257-0120, E-mail: martin.anderson@dominican.edu. *Application contact:* Moriah Dunning, Director, 415-485-3246, Fax: 415-485-3214, E-mail: moriah.dunning@dominican.edu.

Drew University, Caspersen School of Graduate Studies, Program in Medical Humanities, Madison, NJ 07940-1493. Offers MMH, DMH, CMH. Part-time and evening/weekend programs available. *Degree requirements:* For master's, thesis; for doctorate, thesis/dissertation. *Entrance requirements:* For master's and doctorate, transcripts, writing sample, personal statement, recommendations. Additional exam requirements/recommendations for international students: Required—TOEFL (minimum score 585 paper-based; 240 computer-based; 95 iBT), TWE (minimum score 4). *Expenses:* Contact institution. *Faculty research:* Biomedical ethics, medical narrative, history of medicine, medicine and the arts.

Duke University, Graduate School, Program in Humanities, Durham, NC 27708. Offers AM, JD/AM. Part-time programs available. *Students:* 11 full-time (5 women); includes 2 Black or African American, non-Hispanic/Latino, 1 international. 22 applicants, 68% accepted, 6 enrolled. In 2010, 5 master's awarded. *Entrance requirements:* For master's, GRE General Test. Additional exam requirements/recommendations for international students: Required—TOEFL (minimum score 550 paper-based; 213 computer-based; 83 iBT), IELTS (minimum score 7). *Application deadline:* For fall admission, 1/30 priority date for domestic and international students; for spring admission, 10/15 priority date for domestic and international students. Application fee: $75. Electronic applications accepted. *Unit head:* Dr. David Bell, Director, 919-681-3252, Fax: 919-684-2277, E-mail: jgw1@duke.edu. *Application contact:* Elizabeth Hutton, Director of Admissions, 919-684-3913, Fax: 919-684-2277, E-mail: grad-admissions@duke.edu.

Georgetown University, Graduate School of Arts and Sciences, School of Continuing Studies, Washington, DC 20057. Offers American studies (MALS); Catholic studies (MALS); classical civilizations (MALS); disability studies (MPS); ethics and the professions (MALS); human resources management (MPS); humanities (MALS); individualized study (MALS); international affairs (MALS); Islam and Muslim-Christian relations (MALS); journalism (MPS); liberal studies (DLS); literature and society (MALS); medieval and early modern European studies (MALS); public relations and corporate communications (MPS); real estate (MPS); religious studies (MALS); social and public policy (MALS); sports industry management (MPS); the theory and practice of American democracy (MALS); visual culture (MALS). *Entrance requirements:* Additional exam requirements/recommendations for international students: Required—TOEFL.

Humanities

Hofstra University, School of Education, Health, and Human Services, Programs in Learning and Teaching, Hempstead, NY 11549. Offers learning and teaching (Ed D), including applied linguistics, art education, arts and humanities, early childhood education, English education, human development, math education, math, science, and technology, multicultural education, physical education, science education, social studies education, special education. Part-time and evening/weekend programs available. *Students:* 2 full-time (both women), 26 part-time (21 women); includes 2 Black or African American, non-Hispanic/Latino, 1 international. Average age 36. 26 applicants, 38% accepted, 9 enrolled. *Degree requirements:* For doctorate, comprehensive exam, thesis/dissertation. *Entrance requirements:* For doctorate, GRE, 3 letters of recommendation, essay, interview, 2 years full-time teaching. Additional exam requirements/recommendations for international students: Required—TOEFL (minimum score 550 paper-based; 213 computer-based; 80 iBT). *Application deadline:* Applications are processed on a rolling basis. Application fee: $70 ($75 for international students). Electronic applications accepted. *Expenses:* Tuition: Full-time $18,000; part-time $1000 per credit hour. Required fees: $970; $145 per term. Tuition and fees vary according to program. *Financial support:* In 2010–11, 27 students received support, including 22 fellowships with full and partial tuition reimbursements available (averaging $5,468 per year); research assistantships with full and partial tuition reimbursements available, Federal Work-Study, institutionally sponsored loans, scholarships/grants, tuition waivers (full and partial), and scholarships also available. Support available to part-time students. Financial award applicants required to submit FAFSA. *Faculty research:* Critical thinking, professional development, teacher quality, quantitative research. *Unit head:* Dr. Esther Fusco, Chairperson, 516-463-7704, Fax: 516-463-6196, E-mail: catajs@hofstra.edu. *Application contact:* Carol Drummer, Dean of Graduate Admissions, 516-463-4876, Fax: 516-463-4664, E-mail: gradstudent@hofstra.edu.

Hollins University, Graduate Programs, Program in Liberal Studies, Roanoke, VA 24020-1603. Offers humanities (MALS); interdisciplinary studies (MALS); justice and legal studies (MALS); liberal studies (CAS); social science (MALS); visual and performing arts (MALS). Part-time and evening/weekend programs available. *Degree requirements:* For master's, thesis. *Entrance requirements:* For master's, letters of recommendation, interview. Additional exam requirements/recommendations for international students: Required—TOEFL (minimum score 550 paper-based; 213 computer-based; 79 iBT). Electronic applications accepted. *Faculty research:* Elderly blacks, film, feminist economics, US voting patterns, Wagner, diversity.

Hood College, Graduate School, Program in Humanities, Frederick, MD 21701-8575. Offers MA. Part-time and evening/weekend programs available. *Faculty:* 5 full-time (all women), 2 part-time/adjunct (1 woman). *Students:* 3 full-time (2 women), 32 part-time (24 women); includes 1 Hispanic/Latino; 1 Two or more races, non-Hispanic/Latino. Average age 34. 16 applicants, 88% accepted, 9 enrolled. In 2010, 9 master's awarded. *Degree requirements:* For master's, capstone/research project. *Entrance requirements:* For master's, minimum GPA of 2.75. Additional exam requirements/recommendations for international students: Required—TOEFL (minimum score 575 paper-based; 231 computer-based; 89 iBT). *Application deadline:* For fall admission, 7/15 for domestic and international students; for spring admission, 12/15 for domestic and international students. Applications are processed on a rolling basis. Application fee: $35. Electronic applications accepted. *Expenses:* Tuition: Full-time $6480; part-time $360 per credit. Required fees: $100; $50 per term. *Financial support:* Applicants required to submit FAFSA. *Unit head:* Dr. Amy Gottfried, Director, 301-696-3744, E-mail: gottfried@hood.edu. *Application contact:* Dr. Allen P. Flora, Dean of Graduate School, 301-696-3811, Fax: 301-696-3597, E-mail: gofurther@hood.edu.

Instituto Tecnologico de Santo Domingo, Graduate School, Area of Humanities and Social Sciences, Santo Domingo, Dominican Republic. Offers accounting (Certificate); adult education (Certificate); applied linguistics (MA); economics (MA); education (M Ed); educational psychology (MA, Certificate); gender and development (MA, Certificate); humanistic studies (MA); international marketing management (Certificate); international relations in the Caribbean basin (Certificate); intervention systems in family therapy (MA); linguistic and literary communication (Certificate); pedagogical support (MA); social science education (M Ed); sustainable human development (MA); terminal illness and death psychology (Certificate); youth and adult education (M Ed).

Instituto Tecnológico y de Estudios Superiores de Monterrey, Campus Central de Veracruz, Graduate Programs, Córdoba, Mexico. Offers administration (MA); administration of information technologies (MTI); computer sciences (MCC); education (MEE); educational institution administration (MAD); educational technology (MTE); electronic commerce (MCE); finance (MAF); humanistic studies (MEH); international business for Latin America (MNL); marketing (MMT); science (MCP); technology management (MTT). Part-time and evening/weekend programs available. Postbaccalaureate distance learning degree programs offered (minimal on-campus study). *Degree requirements:* For master's, thesis (for some programs). *Entrance requirements:* For master's, PAEP College Board. Electronic applications accepted.

Instituto Tecnológico y de Estudios Superiores de Monterrey, Campus Ciudad de México, Virtual University Division, Ciudad de Mexico, Mexico. Offers administration of information technologies (MA); computer sciences (MA); education (MA, PhD); educational technology (MA); environmental engineering (MA); environmental systems (MA); humanistic studies (MA); industrial engineering (MA); international business for Latin America (MA); quality systems (MA); quality systems and productivity (MA). Part-time and evening/weekend programs available. Postbaccalaureate distance learning degree programs offered (minimal on-campus study). *Entrance requirements:* For master's and doctorate, Instituto entrance exam. Additional exam requirements/recommendations for international students: Required—TOEFL.

Instituto Tecnológico y de Estudios Superiores de Monterrey, Campus Ciudad Juárez, Program in Humanistic Studies, Ciudad Juárez, Mexico. Offers MEH.

Instituto Tecnológico y de Estudios Superiores de Monterrey, Campus Estado de México, Professional and Graduate Division, Estado de Mexico, Mexico. Offers administration of information technologies (MITA); architecture (M Arch); business administration (GMBA, MBA); computer sciences (MCS, PhD); education (M Ed); educational institution administration (MAD); educational technology and innovation (PhD); electronic commerce (MEC); environmental systems (MS); finance (MAF); humanistic studies (MHS); information sciences and knowledge management (MISKM); information systems (MS); manufacturing systems (MS); marketing (MEM); quality systems and productivity (MS); science and materials engineering (PhD); telecommunications management (MTM). Part-time programs available. Postbaccalaureate distance learning degree programs offered (minimal on-campus study). *Degree requirements:* For master's, one foreign language, thesis (for some programs); for doctorate, one foreign language, thesis/dissertation. *Entrance requirements:* For master's, E-PAEP 500, interview; for doctorate, E-PAEP 500, research proposal. Additional exam requirements/recommendations for international students: Required—TOEFL (minimum score 550 paper-based). *Faculty research:* Surface treatments by plasmas, mechanical properties, robotics, graphical computing, mechatronics security protocols.

Instituto Tecnológico y de Estudios Superiores de Monterrey, Campus Irapuato, Graduate Programs, Irapuato, Mexico. Offers administration (MBA); administration of information technology (MAIT); administration of telecommunications (MAT); architecture (M Arch); computer science (MCS); education (M Ed); educational administration (MEA); educational innovation and technology (DEIT); educational technology (MET); electronic commerce (MBA); environmental administration and planning (MEAP); environmental systems (MES); finances (MBA); humanistic studies (MHS); international management for Latin American executives (MIMLAE); library and information science (MLIS); manufacturing quality management (MMQM); marketing research (MBA).

John Carroll University, Graduate School, Program in Humanities, University Heights, OH 44118-4581. Offers MA. Part-time and evening/weekend programs available. *Degree requirements:* For master's, thesis optional, comprehensive research essay. *Entrance*

requirements: For master's, minimum GPA of 2.75, interview. Electronic applications accepted. *Faculty research:* Modern French history, modern American Catholic history.

Laura and Alvin Siegal College of Judaic Studies, Graduate Programs, Beachwood, OH 44122-7116. Offers humanities (MA), including Holocaust studies; religious education (MAJS), including Jewish education, Judaic studies. Part-time and evening/weekend programs available. Postbaccalaureate distance learning degree programs offered (no on-campus study). *Degree requirements:* For master's, one foreign language, thesis. *Entrance requirements:* For master's, interview.

Laurentian University, School of Graduate Studies and Research, Programme in Humanities: Interpretation and Values, Sudbury, ON P3E 2C6, Canada. Offers MA. Part-time programs available. *Faculty research:* Modern Canadian literature; aboriginal languages and cultures; relation between ethics, religion, and the arts; narrative conventions; Renaissance drama and Reformation literature, Biblical and philosophical hermeneutics.

Marshall University, Academic Affairs Division, College of Liberal Arts, Program in Humanities, Huntington, WV 25755. Offers MA. Part-time and evening/weekend programs available. *Faculty:* 1 full-time (0 women), 3 part-time/adjunct (0 women). *Students:* 6 full-time (3 women), 12 part-time (8 women); includes 1 Black or African American, non-Hispanic/Latino; 1 American Indian or Alaska Native, non-Hispanic/Latino; 1 Hispanic/Latino. Average age 38. In 2010, 8 master's awarded. *Degree requirements:* For master's, thesis, comprehensive assessment. *Entrance requirements:* For master's, GRE General Test, MAT, bachelor's degree in humanities, minimum undergraduate GPA of 3.0. Application fee: $40. *Financial support:* Applicants required to submit FAFSA. *Unit head:* Dr. Luke Eric Lassiter, Chairperson, 304-746-1923, E-mail: lassiter@marshall.edu. *Application contact:* Information Contact, 304-746-1900, Fax: 304-746-1902, E-mail: services@marshall.edu.

Marymount University, School of Arts and Sciences, Program in Humanities, Arlington, VA 22207-4299. Offers MA. Part-time and evening/weekend programs available. *Degree requirements:* For master's, thesis or alternative. *Entrance requirements:* For master's, minimum GPA of 3.0; undergraduate major or minor in art history, English, history, or philosophy; 2 letters of recommendation; interview; writing sample; essay. Additional exam requirements/recommendations for international students: Required—TOEFL (minimum score 600 paper-based; 250 computer-based; 96 iBT), IELTS (minimum score 6.5). Electronic applications accepted.

Memorial University of Newfoundland, School of Graduate Studies, Interdisciplinary Programs in Humanities, St. John's, NL A1C 5S7, Canada. Offers M Phil. *Degree requirements:* For master's, comprehensive exam, journal. *Entrance requirements:* For master's, honors bachelor's degree. Electronic applications accepted. *Faculty research:* Western language, philosophy, literature, and history.

Mount St. Mary's College, Graduate Division, Program in Humanities, Los Angeles, CA 90049-1599. Offers MA. *Entrance requirements:* For master's, minimum GPA of 3.0. Additional exam requirements/recommendations for international students: Required—TOEFL (minimum score 550 paper-based).

National University, Academic Affairs, College of Letters and Sciences, Department of Art and Humanities, La Jolla, CA 92037-1011. Offers creative writing (MFA); English (MA); history (MA). Part-time and evening/weekend programs available. Postbaccalaureate distance learning degree programs offered (no on-campus study). *Faculty:* 17 full-time (6 women), 198 part-time/adjunct (110 women). *Students:* 198 full-time (144 women), 534 part-time (364 women); includes 99 Black or African American, non-Hispanic/Latino; 6 American Indian or Alaska Native, non-Hispanic/Latino; 10 Asian, non-Hispanic/Latino; 54 Hispanic/Latino; 14 Two or more races, non-Hispanic/Latino. Average age 38. 424 applicants, 100% accepted, 289 enrolled. In 2010, 222 master's awarded. *Degree requirements:* For master's, thesis (for some programs). *Entrance requirements:* For master's, interview, minimum GPA of 2.5. Additional exam requirements/recommendations for international students: Required—TOEFL (minimum score 550 paper-based; 213 computer-based; 79 iBT), IELTS (minimum score 6). *Application deadline:* Applications are processed on a rolling basis. Application fee: $60 ($65 for international students). Electronic applications accepted. *Expenses:* Tuition: Full-time $9450; part-time $350 per unit. Required fees: $350 per unit. One-time fee: $60. *Financial support:* Career-related internships or fieldwork, institutionally sponsored loans, scholarships/grants, and tuition waivers (partial) available. Support available to part-time students. Financial award application deadline: 6/30; financial award applicants required to submit FAFSA. *Unit head:* Dr. Janet Baker, Chair, 858-642-8472, Fax: 858-642-8715, E-mail: jbaker@nu.edu. *Application contact:* Dominick Giovanniello, Associate Regional Dean—San Diego, 800-NAT-UNIV, Fax: 858-541-7792, E-mail: dgiovann@nu.edu.

New York University, Graduate School of Arts and Science, Draper Interdisciplinary Program in Humanities and Social Thought, New York, NY 10012-1019. Offers humanities and social thought (MA); religion (Advanced Certificate); social theory (Advanced Certificate). Part-time programs available. *Faculty:* 6 full-time (3 women). *Students:* 115 full-time (69 women), 118 part-time (76 women); includes 12 Black or African American, non-Hispanic/Latino; 9 Asian, non-Hispanic/Latino; 18 Hispanic/Latino, 19 international. Average age 28. 415 applicants, 51% accepted, 97 enrolled. In 2010, 69 master's awarded. *Degree requirements:* For master's, thesis, comprehensive exam or essay. *Entrance requirements:* For degree, master's degree. Additional exam requirements/recommendations for international students: Required—TOEFL. *Application deadline:* For fall admission, 7/1 for domestic students; for spring admission, 12/1 for domestic students. Applications are processed on a rolling basis. Application fee: $90. *Financial support:* Teaching assistantships with tuition reimbursements, Federal Work-Study, institutionally sponsored loans, and tuition waivers (partial) available. Financial award application deadline: 7/1; financial award applicants required to submit FAFSA. *Faculty research:* Art world, gender politics, global histories, literary cultures, the city. *Unit head:* Robin Nagle, Director, 212-998-8070, Fax: 212-995-4691, E-mail: draper.program@nyu.edu. *Application contact:* Robert Dimit, Associate Director, 212-998-8070, Fax: 212-995-4691, E-mail: draper.program@nyu.edu.

Nova Southeastern University, Graduate School of Humanities and Social Sciences, Department of Multi-Disciplinary Studies, Fort Lauderdale, FL 33314-7796. Offers college student affairs (MS); college student personnel administration (Certificate); cross-disciplinary studies (MA); national security affairs (MS); qualitative methods (Certificate). Part-time programs available. Postbaccalaureate distance learning degree programs offered (minimal on-campus study). *Faculty:* 1 (woman) full-time, 52 part-time/adjunct (30 women). *Students:* 50 full-time (34 women), 65 part-time (52 women); includes 34 Black or African American, non-Hispanic/Latino; 3 Asian, non-Hispanic/Latino; 25 Hispanic/Latino; 1 Two or more races, non-Hispanic/Latino, 6 international. Average age 32. 76 applicants, 66% accepted, 40 enrolled. In 2010, 27 master's awarded. *Degree requirements:* For master's, comprehensive exam, thesis optional, portfolio. *Entrance requirements:* For master's, interview, minimum GPA of 3.0. Additional exam requirements/recommendations for international students: Required—TOEFL. *Application deadline:* For fall admission, 7/1 priority date for domestic and international students; for winter admission, 11/1 priority date for domestic and international students; for spring admission, 3/1 priority date for domestic and international students. Applications are processed on a rolling basis. Application fee: $50. Electronic applications accepted. *Financial support:* In 2010–11, 1 research assistantship (averaging $15,000 per year) was awarded; career-related internships or fieldwork, Federal Work-Study, institutionally sponsored loans, and scholarships/grants also available. Financial award applicants required to submit CSS PROFILE. *Unit head:* Dr. Judith McKay, Chair, 954-262-3060, Fax: 954-262-3893, E-mail: mckayj@nsu.nova.edu. *Application contact:* Marcia Arango, Student Recruitment Coordinator, 954-262-3006, Fax: 954-262-3968, E-mail: marango@nsu.nova.edu.

Old Dominion University, College of Arts and Letters, Program in Humanities, Norfolk, VA 23529. Offers MA. Part-time and evening/weekend programs available. *Faculty:* 1 full-time (0 women). *Students:* 11 full-time (5 women), 14 part-time (9 women); includes 5 minority (3 Black or African American, non-Hispanic/Latino; 2 Two or more races, non-Hispanic/Latino), 2 international. Average age 37. 27 applicants, 96% accepted. In 2010, 10 master's awarded. *Degree requirements:* For master's, thesis optional, project. *Entrance requirements:* For master's, GRE General Test, minimum GPA of 3.0. *Application deadline:* For fall admission, 7/1 for domestic students; for spring admission, 10/1 for domestic students. Applications are processed on a rolling basis. Application fee: $40. Electronic applications accepted. *Expenses:* Tuition, state resident: full-time $8592; part-time $358 per credit. Tuition, nonresident: full-time $21,672; part-time $903 per credit. Required fees: $119 per semester. One-time fee: $50. *Financial support:* In 2010–11, 3 students received support, including 4 research assistantships (averaging $5,000 per year); career-related internships or fieldwork, scholarships/grants, and unspecified assistantships also available. Financial award application deadline: 2/15; financial award applicants required to submit FAFSA. *Faculty research:* Media studies, communications, cultural studies, gender studies, American literature. *Unit head:* Dr. Jeffrey P. Jones, Graduate Program Director, 757-683-3719, Fax: 757-683-6191, E-mail: humgpd@odu.edu. *Application contact:* Dr. Robert Wojtowicz, Associate Dean, 757-683-6077, Fax: 757-683-5746, E-mail: rwojtowi@odu.edu.

Penn State Harrisburg, Graduate School, School of Humanities, Middletown, PA 17057-4898. Offers American studies (MA). Evening/weekend programs available. *Unit head:* Dr. Kathryn Robinson, Director, 717-948-6470, E-mail: kdr12@psu.edu. *Application contact:* Robert Coffman, Director of Admissions, 717-948-6250, Fax: 717-948-6325, E-mail: ric1@psu.edu.

Pepperdine University, Seaver College, Humanities and Teacher Education Division, Malibu, CA 90263. Offers American studies (MA); history (MA); writing for screen and television (MFA). Part-time programs available. *Students:* 23 part-time (16 women); includes 1 minority (Asian, non-Hispanic/Latino). 8 applicants, 88% accepted, 7 enrolled. In 2010, 3 master's awarded. *Degree requirements:* For master's, oral and written exams. *Entrance requirements:* For master's, GRE General Test, writing sample, letters of recommendation. Additional exam requirements/recommendations for international students: Required—TOEFL. *Application deadline:* For fall admission, 2/1 priority date for domestic students. Applications are processed on a rolling basis. Application fee: $55. *Financial support:* Applicants required to submit FAFSA. *Unit head:* Dr. Maire Mullins, Chair/Professor of English, 310-506-4235, Fax: 310-506-7307, E-mail: maire.mullins@pepperdine.edu. *Application contact:* Michael Truschke, Dean of Admission and Enrollment Management, 310-506-6165, Fax: 310-506-4861, E-mail: admission-seaver@pepperdine.edu.

Polytechnic Institute of NYU, Department of Humanities and Social Sciences, Brooklyn, NY 11201-2990. Offers environment—behavior studies (Graduate Certificate); environment-behavior studies (MS); history of science (MS); integrated digital media (MS, Graduate Certificate); technical writing and specialized journalism (MS). Part-time and evening/weekend programs available. *Faculty:* 5 full-time (2 women), 6 part-time/adjunct (3 women). *Students:* 31 full-time (15 women), 4 part-time (3 women); includes 4 Black or African American, non-Hispanic/Latino; 1 American Indian or Alaska Native, non-Hispanic/Latino; 1 Asian, non-Hispanic/Latino, 19 international. Average age 28. 37 applicants, 68% accepted, 15 enrolled. In 2010, 22 master's awarded. *Degree requirements:* For master's, comprehensive exam (for some programs), thesis (for some programs). *Entrance requirements:* Additional exam requirements/recommendations for international students: Required—TOEFL (minimum score 550 paper-based; 213 computer-based; 80 iBT); Recommended—IELTS (minimum score 6.5). *Application deadline:* For fall admission, 7/31 priority date for domestic students, 4/30 priority date for international students; for spring admission, 12/31 priority date for domestic students, 11/30 priority date for international students. Applications are processed on a rolling basis. Application fee: $75. Electronic applications accepted. *Expenses:* Tuition: Full-time $21,492; part-time $1194 per credit. Required fees: $385 per semester. Tuition and fees vary according to course load. *Financial support:* Fellowships, research assistantships, teaching assistantships, career-related internships or fieldwork, institutionally sponsored loans, scholarships/grants, and unspecified assistantships available. Support available to part-time students. Financial award applicants required to submit FAFSA. *Faculty research:* Trade magazine journalism, technical writing, financial reporting, medical and science reporting, industrial advertising and public relations. Total annual research expenditures: $146,549. *Unit head:* Prof. Kristen Day, Head, 718-260-3999, E-mail: kday@poly.edu. *Application contact:* JeanCarlo Bonilla, Director, Graduate Enrollment Management, 718-260-3182, Fax: 718-260-3624, E-mail: gradinfo@poly.edu.

Prescott College, Graduate Programs, Program in Humanities, Prescott, AZ 86301. Offers humanities (MA); student-directed independent study (MA). Part-time programs available. Postbaccalaureate distance learning degree programs offered (minimal on-campus study). *Faculty:* 44 part-time/adjunct (29 women). *Students:* 15 full-time (11 women), 36 part-time (25 women); includes 10 minority (6 Black or African American, non-Hispanic/Latino; 2 Hispanic/Latino; 2 Two or more races, non-Hispanic/Latino), 1 international. Average age 40. 36 applicants, 67% accepted, 16 enrolled. In 2010, 11 master's awarded. *Degree requirements:* For master's, thesis, fieldwork or internship, practicum. *Entrance requirements:* For master's, 2 letters of recommendation, resume. Additional exam requirements/recommendations for international students: Required—TOEFL (minimum score 500 paper-based; 173 computer-based). *Application deadline:* For fall admission, 4/15 priority date for domestic and international students; for spring admission, 9/15 priority date for domestic and international students. Applications are processed on a rolling basis. Application fee: $40. Electronic applications accepted. *Expenses:* Tuition: Full-time $15,600; part-time $650 per credit. Required fees: $50 per term. One-time fee: $190. Tuition and fees vary according to course load and degree level. *Financial support:* Career-related internships or fieldwork, Federal Work-Study, and scholarships/grants available. Financial award applicants required to submit FAFSA. *Unit head:* Dr. Randall Amster, Chair, 928-350-2238, Fax: 928-776-5151, E-mail: ramster@prescott.edu. *Application contact:* Kerstin Alicki, Admissions Counselor, 877-412-8705, Fax: 928-277-4695, E-mail: admissions@prescott.edu.

St. Edward's University, New College, Program in Liberal Arts, Austin, TX 78704. Offers global issues (MLA); humanities (MLA); liberal arts (Certificate); social sciences (MLA). Part-time and evening/weekend programs available. *Students:* 6 full-time (5 women), 80 part-time (54 women); includes 28 minority (6 Black or African American, non-Hispanic/Latino; 2 Asian, non-Hispanic/Latino; 19 Hispanic/Latino; 1 Two or more races, non-Hispanic/Latino), 1 international. Average age 34. 47 applicants, 68% accepted, 24 enrolled. In 2010, 29 master's awarded. *Degree requirements:* For master's, minimum of 24 resident hours. *Entrance requirements:* For master's, minimum GPA of 2.75 in last 60 hours of course work, interview. Additional exam requirements/recommendations for international students: Required—TOEFL (minimum score 550 paper-based; 213 computer-based; 79 iBT) or IELTS (minimum score 6). *Application deadline:* For fall admission, 7/1 for domestic and international students; for spring admission, 11/1 for domestic and international students. Applications are processed on a rolling basis. Application fee: $45 ($50 for international students). Electronic applications accepted. *Expenses:* Tuition: Full-time $16,200; part-time $900 per credit hour. Required fees: $50 per trimester. Full-time tuition and fees vary according to course load and program. *Financial support:* In 2010–11, 2 students received support. Scholarships/grants available. *Unit head:* Dr. H. Ramsey Fowler, Director, 512-448-8648, Fax: 512-448-8492, E-mail: ramseyf@stewards.edu. *Application contact:* Carrie Martin, Graduate Admission Coordinator, 512-233-1694, Fax: 512-428-1032, E-mail: carriem@stedwards.edu.

Salve Regina University, Graduate Studies, Program in Humanities, Newport, RI 02840-4192. Offers MA, PhD, CAGS. Part-time and evening/weekend programs available. Postbaccalaureate distance learning degree programs offered (no on-campus study). *Degree requirements:* For master's, thesis optional; for doctorate, one foreign language, comprehensive exam, thesis/dissertation. *Entrance requirements:* For master's, GMAT, GRE General Test, or MAT; for doctorate, GRE General Test. Additional exam requirements/recommendations for international students: Required—TOEFL (minimum score 600 paper-based; 250 computer-based; 100 iBT) or IELTS. Electronic applications accepted. *Expenses:* Tuition: Full-time $7740; part-time $430 per credit. Required fees: $40 per semester. Tuition and fees vary according to course level and degree level.

Sam Houston State University, College of Humanities and Social Sciences, Huntsville, TX 77341. Offers English and foreign languages (MA), including English; family and consumer sciences (MS), including dietetics, family and consumer sciences; history (MA); political science (MA, MPA), including political science (MA), public administration (MPA); psychology and philosophy (MA, PhD), including clinical psychology (PhD), psychology (MA); sociology (MA); speech communication (MA). *Faculty:* 60 full-time (30 women), 1 part-time/adjunct (0 women). *Students:* 123 full-time (92 women), 169 part-time (97 women); includes 12 Black or African American, non-Hispanic/Latino; 3 Asian, non-Hispanic/Latino; 16 Hispanic/Latino, 10 international. Average age 30. 216 applicants, 56% accepted, 96 enrolled. In 2010, 67 master's, 4 doctorates awarded. *Entrance requirements:* For master's, GRE General Test. Additional exam requirements/recommendations for international students: Required—TOEFL (minimum score 550 paper-based; 213 computer-based; 79 iBT). *Application deadline:* For fall admission, 8/1 for domestic students; for spring admission, 12/1 for domestic students. Application fee: $20. *Expenses:* Tuition, state resident: full-time $1363; part-time $163 per credit hour. Tuition, nonresident: full-time $3856; part-time $473 per credit hour. *Unit head:* Dr. John deCastro, Dean, 936-294-2200, Fax: 936-294-2207, E-mail: jmd018@shsu.edu. *Application contact:* Dr. Kandi Tayebi, Dean of Graduate Studies and Associate Vice President for Academic Affairs, 936-294-1971, Fax: 936-294-1271, E-mail: graduate@shsu.edu.

San Francisco State University, Division of Graduate Studies, College of Humanities, Department of Humanities, San Francisco, CA 94132-1722. Offers MA. Part-time and evening/weekend programs available. *Unit head:* Dr. Saul Steier, Chair, 415-338-1830. *Application contact:* Dr. Mary Scott, Graduate Coordinator, 415-338-7425, E-mail: mscott@sfsu.edu.

Stanford University, School of Humanities and Sciences, Department of Humanities, Stanford, CA 94305-9991. Offers MA. *Degree requirements:* For master's, one foreign language, thesis. *Entrance requirements:* For master's, GRE General Test. Additional exam requirements/recommendations for international students: Required—TOEFL. Electronic applications accepted. *Expenses:* Tuition: Full-time $38,700; part-time $860 per unit. One-time fee: $200 full-time.

Texas Tech University, Graduate School, College of Arts and Sciences, Department of Classical and Modern Languages and Literatures, Lubbock, TX 79409. Offers applied linguistics (MA); classics (MA); German (MA); Romance language (MA); Romance languages-French (MA); Romance languages-Spanish (MA); Spanish (PhD); MBA/MA. Part-time programs available. *Faculty:* 28 full-time (12 women), 1 part-time/adjunct (0 women). *Students:* 86 full-time (51 women), 21 part-time (12 women); includes 1 Black or African American, non-Hispanic/Latino; 18 Hispanic/Latino, 49 international. Average age 30. 72 applicants, 65% accepted, 33 enrolled. In 2010, 32 master's, 5 doctorates awarded. *Degree requirements:* For master's, comprehensive exam, thesis or alternative; for doctorate, comprehensive exam, thesis/dissertation. *Entrance requirements:* For master's and doctorate, GRE General Test. Additional exam requirements/recommendations for international students: Required—TOEFL (minimum score 550 paper-based; 213 computer-based; 79 iBT). *Application deadline:* For fall admission, 6/1 priority date for domestic students, 1/15 priority date for international students; for spring admission, 9/1 priority date for domestic students, 6/15 priority date for international students. Applications are processed on a rolling basis. Application fee: $50 ($75 for international students). Electronic applications accepted. *Expenses:* Tuition, state resident: full-time $5495.76; part-time $228.99 per credit hour. Tuition, nonresident: full-time $12,936; part-time $538.99 per credit hour. Required fees: $2674; $36 per credit hour. $905 per semester. *Financial support:* In 2010–11, 80 students received support, including 2 research assistantships with partial tuition reimbursements available (averaging $9,907 per year), 35 teaching assistantships with partial tuition reimbursements available (averaging $6,303 per year). Financial award application deadline: 4/15; financial award applicants required to submit FAFSA. *Faculty research:* Literature, comparative literature, linguistics, culture, pedagogy. Total annual research expenditures: $52,504. *Unit head:* Dr. Laura Jean Beard, Interim Chair and Professor, 806-742-4355, Fax: 806-742-3306, E-mail: laura.beard@ttu.edu. *Application contact:* Liz Hildebrand, Senior Advisor, 806-742-4055, Fax: 806-742-3306, E-mail: liz.hildebrand@ttu.edu.

Tiffin University, Program in Humanities, Tiffin, OH 44883-2161. Offers MH. Part-time and evening/weekend programs available. Postbaccalaureate distance learning degree programs offered (no on-campus study). *Faculty:* 6 full-time (3 women), 6 part-time/adjunct (4 women). *Students:* 20 full-time (13 women), 111 part-time (87 women). 112 applicants, 79% accepted, 34 enrolled. In 2010, 340 master's awarded. *Entrance requirements:* For master's, work experience. Additional exam requirements/recommendations for international students: Required—TOEFL (minimum score 550 paper-based; 213 computer-based). *Application deadline:* For fall admission, 9/1 for domestic students; for spring admission, 1/9 for domestic students. Application fee: $0. *Unit head:* Miriam Fankhauser, Dean of Arts and Sciences, 419-448-3426, Fax: 419-443-5002, E-mail: mfankhau@tiffin.edu. *Application contact:* Kristi Krintzline, Director of Graduate Admissions, 800-968-6446 Ext. 3445, Fax: 419-443-5002, E-mail: krintzlineka@tiffin.edu.

Towson University, Program in Humanities, Towson, MD 21252-0001. Offers MA. Part-time and evening/weekend programs available. *Students:* 3 full-time (2 women), 13 part-time (8 women); includes 5 minority (3 Black or African American, non-Hispanic/Latino; 1 American Indian or Alaska Native, non-Hispanic/Latino; 1 Two or more races, non-Hispanic/Latino). Average age 26. In 2010, 4 master's awarded. *Degree requirements:* For master's, thesis or alternative. *Entrance requirements:* For master's, 2 letters of recommendation, minimum GPA of 3.0, research paper. Additional exam requirements/recommendations for international students: Required—TOEFL. *Application deadline:* Applications are processed on a rolling basis. Application fee: $50. Electronic applications accepted. *Expenses:* Tuition, state resident: part-time $324 per credit. Tuition, nonresident: part-time $681 per credit. Required fees: $95 per term. *Financial support:* Application deadline: 4/1. *Unit head:* Lana Portolano, Graduate Program Director, 410-704-3770, E-mail: ghahn@towson.edu. *Application contact:* 410-704-2501, Fax: 410-704-4675, E-mail: grads@towson.edu.

Trinity Western University, School of Graduate Studies, Program in Interdisciplinary Humanities, Langley, BC V2Y 1Y1, Canada. Offers general humanities (MAIH); specialized (MAIH), including English, history, philosophy. Part-time programs available. *Degree requirements:* For master's, thesis or alternative, 36 semester hours. *Entrance requirements:* For master's, strong undergraduate degree in humanities or English, history or philosophy. Electronic applications accepted. *Faculty research:* Literary theory, gender, medieval and early modern literature, philosophy of religion, Thomas Merton's poetics.

Union Institute & University, PhD Program in Interdisciplinary Studies, Cincinnati, OH 45206-1925. Offers ethical and creative leadership (PhD), including Martin Luther King studies; humanities and culture (PhD), including Martin Luther King studies; public policy and social change (PhD), including Martin Luther King studies. Program requires participation in brief on-campus residencies twice each year (January and July). Postbaccalaureate distance learning degree programs offered (minimal on-campus study). *Faculty:* 4 full-time (1 woman), 14 part-time/adjunct (9 women). *Students:* 103 full-time (60 women), 3 part-time (1 woman); includes 42 minority (40 Black or African American, non-Hispanic/Latino; 1 American Indian or Alaska Native, non-Hispanic/Latino; 1 Hispanic/Latino). Average age 46. In 2010, 2 doctorates awarded. *Degree requirements:* For doctorate, comprehensive exam, thesis/dissertation. *Entrance requirements:* For doctorate, master's degree, letters of recommendation, interview. *Application deadline:* Applications are processed on a rolling basis. Application fee: $50. *Expenses:* Tuition: Full-time $16,430; part-time $685 per credit hour. Required fees: $174; $44 per term. Tuition and fees vary according to course load, degree level and program. *Financial support:* Federal Work-Study, scholarships/grants, and tuition waivers (partial) available. Financial award application deadline: 5/1; financial award applicants required to submit FAFSA. *Faculty research:* Social responsibility, ethical leadership, Martin Luther King studies. *Unit head:* Dr. Larry Preston, Dean, 513-861-6400 Ext. 1151, E-mail: larry.preston@myunion.edu. *Application contact:* Michelle Flick, Admissions Counselor, 800-486-3116 Ext. 1225.

Humanities

United Theological Seminary of the Twin Cities, Graduate Programs, New Brighton, MN 55112-2598. Offers advanced theological studies (Diploma); justice and peace studies (M Div, MA); leadership toward racial justice (M Div, MA, Certificate); Methodist studies (M Div, MA, Certificate); ministry (D Min); ministry renewal and professional development (Certificate); pastoral care and counseling (M Div, MA, MARL); religion and theology (MA); theological and religious studies (Certificate); theology and the arts (M Div, MA); urban ministry (M Div, MA, MARL); women's studies: religion, theology and ministry (M Div, MA). *Accreditation:* ACIPE; ATS. Part-time and evening/weekend programs available. *Faculty:* 8 full-time (5 women), 28 part-time/adjunct (16 women). *Students:* 57 full-time (41 women), 94 part-time (61 women); includes 6 minority (5 Black or African American, non-Hispanic/Latino; 1 Hispanic/Latino), 1 international. Average age 47. 49 applicants, 98% accepted, 41 enrolled. In 2010, 10 first professional degrees, 6 master's, 4 doctorates, 2 other advanced degrees awarded. *Degree requirements:* For master's, thesis; for doctorate, comprehensive exam, thesis/dissertation; for M Div, integrative notebook, spiritual chronicle. *Entrance requirements:* For M Div and master's, minimum GPA of 2.75; strong analytical, reflective thinking and writing skills; vocational and academic goals compatible with those of Seminary; for doctorate, M Div or equivalent, minimum GPA of 3.0, 3 years experience in professional ministry; for other advanced degree, BA or equivalent life experience; strong analytical, reflective thinking and writing skills (Certificate); proficiency in English language, previous study of theology at a theological school, recommendation of student's denomination (Diploma). Additional exam requirements/recommendations for international students: Required—TOEFL (minimum score 550 paper-based). *Application deadline:* For fall admission, 7/1 priority date for domestic students, 11/1 priority date for international students; for winter admission, 11/1 priority date for domestic students; for spring admission, 11/15 priority date for domestic students. Applications are processed on a rolling basis. Application fee: $50. *Expenses:* Tuition: Full-time $13,014; part-time $482 per credit hour. One-time fee: $170. Tuition and fees vary according to course load, degree level and program. *Financial support:* In 2010–11, 120 students received support. Career-related internships or fieldwork, institutionally sponsored loans, and scholarships/grants available. Support available to part-time students. Financial award application deadline: 5/1; financial award applicants required to submit FAFSA. *Unit head:* Prof. Susan K. Ebbers, Dean of the Seminary, 651-255-6143 Ext. 108, Fax: 651-633-4315, E-mail: sebbers@unitedseminary.edu. *Application contact:* Rev. Glen Herrington-Hall, Director of Admissions, 651-255-6107 Ext. 107, Fax: 651-633-4315, E-mail: gherrington-hall@unitedseminary.edu.

University of California, Santa Cruz, Division of Graduate Studies, Division of Humanities, Program in the History of Consciousness, Santa Cruz, CA 95064. Offers PhD. *Students:* 29 full-time (13 women), 1 part-time (0 women); includes 8 minority (2 Black or African American, non-Hispanic/Latino; 3 Asian, non-Hispanic/Latino; 3 Hispanic/Latino), 2 international. Average age 32. In 2010, 8 doctorates awarded. *Degree requirements:* For doctorate, one foreign language, thesis/dissertation, qualifying exam. *Entrance requirements:* For doctorate, GRE General Test. Additional exam requirements/recommendations for international students: Required—TOEFL (minimum score 550 paper-based; 220 computer-based; 83 iBT); Recommended—IELTS (minimum score 8). *Application deadline:* For fall admission, 12/10 for domestic and international students. Application fee: $70 ($90 for international students). Electronic applications accepted. *Financial support:* Fellowships, teaching assistantships, institutionally sponsored loans and tuition waivers available. Financial award applicants required to submit FAFSA. *Faculty research:* Interdisciplinary humanities and social sciences, political theory, cultural theory, feminist studies, literary theory. *Unit head:* Anne Spalliero, Graduate Program Coordinator, 831-459-1478, E-mail: amspa@ucsc.edu. *Application contact:* Anne Spalliero, Graduate Program Coordinator, 831-459-1478, E-mail: amspa@ucsc.edu.

University of Chicago, Division of the Humanities, Master of Arts Program in the Humanities, Chicago, IL 60637-1513. Offers MA. MAPH students take courses from faculty members of all departments at University of Chicago. Part-time programs available. *Degree requirements:* For master's, thesis. *Entrance requirements:* For master's, GRE General Test. Additional exam requirements/recommendations for international students: Required—TOEFL (minimum score 600 paper-based; 260 computer-based). Electronic applications accepted.

University of Colorado Denver, College of Liberal Arts and Sciences, Program in Humanities, Denver, CO 80217-3364. Offers community health science (MSS); humanities (MH); international studies (MSS); social science (MSS); society and the environment (MSS); women's and gender studies (MSS). Part-time and evening/weekend programs available. *Students:* 53 full-time (39 women), 35 part-time (22 women); includes 4 Black or African American, non-Hispanic/Latino; 1 American Indian or Alaska Native, non-Hispanic/Latino; 3 Asian, non-Hispanic/Latino; 7 Hispanic/Latino, 1 international. Average age 33. 41 applicants, 54% accepted, 19 enrolled. In 2010, 29 master's awarded. *Degree requirements:* For master's, thesis or alternative, 36 credit hours, project or thesis. *Entrance requirements:* For master's, writing sample, statement of purpose/letter of intent. Additional exam requirements/recommendations for international students: Required—TOEFL (minimum score 525 paper-based). *Application deadline:* For fall admission, 5/15 priority date for domestic students; for spring admission, 10/15 priority date for domestic students. Application fee: $50 ($75 for international students). Electronic applications accepted. *Expenses:* Tuition, state resident: full-time $7332; part-time $355 per credit hour. Tuition, nonresident: full-time $18,990; part-time $1055 per credit hour. Required fees: $998. Tuition and fees vary according to course level, course load, degree level, campus/location, program, reciprocity agreements and student level. *Financial support:* Federal Work-Study and scholarships/grants available. Financial award application deadline: 4/1; financial award applicants required to submit FAFSA. *Faculty research:* Women and gender in the classical Mediterranean, communication theory and democracy, relationship between psychology and philosophy. *Unit head:* Myra Bookman, Associate Director of Humanities and Social Science, 303-556-2496, Fax: 303-556-8100, E-mail: myra.bookman@ucdenver.edu. *Application contact:* Catherine Osmundson, Program Assistant, 303-556-2305, E-mail: catherine.osmundson@ucdenver.edu.

University of Dallas, Braniff Graduate School of Liberal Arts, Program in Humanities, Irving, TX 75062-4736. Offers M Hum, MA. Part-time programs available. *Degree requirements:* For master's, one foreign language, comprehensive exam, thesis (for some programs). *Entrance requirements:* For master's, GRE General Test. Additional exam requirements/recommendations for international students: Required—TOEFL. *Expenses:* Tuition: Full-time $7500; part-time $720 per credit hour. Required fees: $500; $60 per credit hour. $300 per semester. One-time fee: $150. Tuition and fees vary according to program and student level. *Faculty research:* Classical epic poetry, scholastic poetry, Renaissance drama, nineteenth and twentieth century Continental philosophy.

University of Houston–Clear Lake, School of Human Sciences and Humanities, Programs in Humanities and Fine Arts, Houston, TX 77058-1098. Offers history (MA); humanities (MA); literature (MA). Part-time and evening/weekend programs available. Postbaccalaureate distance learning degree programs offered (minimal on-campus study). *Degree requirements:* For master's, thesis or alternative. *Entrance requirements:* For master's, GRE General Test. Additional exam requirements/recommendations for international students: Required—TOEFL (minimum score 550 paper-based; 213 computer-based). *Faculty research:* Digital media studies, Latin American history, labor history, Chaucer evolution versus creationism debate.

University of Louisville, Graduate School, College of Arts and Sciences, Department of Humanities, Louisville, KY 40292-0001. Offers MA, PhD, MA/JD, MA/MBA. *Faculty:* 14 full-time (9 women). *Students:* 33 full-time (23 women), 41 part-time (22 women); includes 2 Black or African American, non-Hispanic/Latino; 4 Asian, non-Hispanic/Latino; 1 Hispanic/Latino; 3 Two or more races, non-Hispanic/Latino. Average age 38. 33 applicants, 64% accepted, 15 enrolled. In 2010, 5 master's, 6 doctorates awarded. *Degree requirements:* For master's, one foreign language, comprehensive exam (for some programs), thesis (for some programs), directed study culminating project; for doctorate, 2 foreign languages, comprehensive exam, thesis/dissertation, internship. *Entrance requirements:* For master's, GRE General Test, letters of recommendation, transcripts; for doctorate, GRE General Test, letters of recommendation, transcripts, writing sample. *Application deadline:* For fall admission, 1/15 priority date for domestic and international students. Application fee: $50. Electronic applications accepted. *Expenses:* Tuition, state resident: full-time $9144; part-time $508 per credit hour. Tuition, nonresident: full-time $19,026; part-time $1057 per credit hour. Tuition and fees vary according to program and reciprocity agreements. *Financial support:* Fellowships, teaching assistantships, institutionally sponsored loans, scholarships/grants, and tuition waivers available. *Faculty research:* Studies in culture, aesthetics and creativity, religious studies, linguistics. *Unit head:* Prof. Elaine O. Wise, Chair, Division of Humanities, 502-852-7149, Fax: 502-852-0078, E-mail: elaine.wise@louisville.edu. *Application contact:* Libby Leggett, Director, Graduate Admissions, 502-852-3101, Fax: 502-852-6536, E-mail: gradadm@louisville.edu.

University of South Florida, Graduate School, College of Arts and Sciences, Department of Humanities and Cultural Studies, Tampa, FL 33620-9951. Offers American studies (MA); film studies (MLA); humanities (MLA). Part-time and evening/weekend programs available. *Faculty:* 5 full-time (3 women). *Students:* 23 full-time (13 women), 18 part-time (12 women); includes 9 Black or African American, non-Hispanic/Latino; 4 Hispanic/Latino; 2 Two or more races, non-Hispanic/Latino, 1 international. Average age 34. 34 applicants, 47% accepted, 12 enrolled. In 2010, 9 master's awarded. *Degree requirements:* For master's, comprehensive exam, thesis. *Entrance requirements:* For master's, GRE General Test, minimum GPA of 3.0 in last 60 hours, academic writing sample. Additional exam requirements/recommendations for international students: Required—TOEFL (minimum score 550 paper-based; 213 computer-based). *Application deadline:* For fall admission, 2/15 priority date for domestic students, 1/2 for international students; for spring admission, 10/15 priority date for domestic students, 6/1 for international students. Application fee: $30. *Financial support:* Scholarships/grants available. Financial award application deadline: 4/1. *Faculty research:* American South, American autobiography, material culture, critical theory, cultural studies. *Unit head:* Daniel Belgrad, Chairperson, 813-974-9388, Fax: 813-974-9409, E-mail: dbelgrad@cas.usf.edu. *Application contact:* Maria Cizmic, Program Director, 813-974-9383, Fax: 813-974-9409, E-mail: mcizmic@cas.usf.edu.

The University of Texas at Dallas, School of Arts and Humanities, Program in Humanities, Richardson, TX 75080. Offers aesthetic studies (MA, MAT, PhD); history (MA); history of ideas (MA, MAT, PhD); humanities (MA, PhD); Latin American studies (MA); studies in literature (MA, MAT, PhD). *Faculty:* 44 full-time (14 women). *Students:* 161 full-time (95 women), 178 part-time (104 women); includes 71 minority (22 Black or African American, non-Hispanic/Latino; 4 American Indian or Alaska Native, non-Hispanic/Latino; 16 Asian, non-Hispanic/Latino; 24 Hispanic/Latino; 5 Two or more races, non-Hispanic/Latino), 22 international. Average age 38. 156 applicants, 70% accepted, 79 enrolled. In 2010, 46 master's, 20 doctorates awarded. *Degree requirements:* For master's, one foreign language, portfolio, thesis, or capstone project; for doctorate, one foreign language, thesis/dissertation. *Entrance requirements:* For master's, minimum GPA of 3.3 in upper-level coursework in field; for doctorate, doctoral field examinations, minimum GPA of 3.3 in upper-level coursework in field. Additional exam requirements/recommendations for international students: Required—TOEFL (minimum score 550 paper-based; 215 computer-based). *Application deadline:* For fall admission, 7/15 for domestic students, 5/1 priority date for international students; for spring admission, 11/15 for domestic students, 9/1 priority date for international students. Applications are processed on a rolling basis. Application fee: $50 ($100 for international students). Electronic applications accepted. *Expenses:* Tuition, state resident: full-time $10,248; part-time $569 per credit hour. Tuition, nonresident: full-time $18,544; part-time $1030 per credit hour. Tuition and fees vary according to course load. *Financial support:* In 2010–11, 151 students received support, including 5 research assistantships with partial tuition reimbursements available (averaging $10,905 per year), 82 teaching assistantships with partial tuition reimbursements available (averaging $10,156 per year); career-related internships or fieldwork, Federal Work-Study, institutionally sponsored loans, scholarships/grants, and unspecified assistantships also available. Support available to part-time students. Financial award application deadline: 4/30; financial award applicants required to submit FAFSA. *Faculty research:* Holocaust studies, U. S. /Mexico studies, translation studies, art history research, Chinese studies. *Unit head:* Dr. Michael Wilson, Associate Dean for Graduate Education, 972-883-2080, E-mail: mwilson@utdallas.edu. *Application contact:* Dr. Michael Wilson, Associate Dean of Graduate Studies, 972-883-2756, Fax: 972-883-2989, E-mail: mwilson@utdallas.edu.

The University of Texas Medical Branch, Graduate School of Biomedical Sciences, Program in Medical Humanities, Galveston, TX 77555. Offers MA, PhD. *Degree requirements:* For master's, thesis; for doctorate, thesis/dissertation. *Entrance requirements:* For master's and doctorate, GRE General Test, writing sample. Additional exam requirements/recommendations for international students: Required—TOEFL (minimum score 550 paper-based; 213 computer-based). Electronic applications accepted.

University of Utah, Graduate School, College of Humanities, Environmental Humanities Graduate Program, Salt Lake City, UT 84112-1107. Offers MA, MS. *Faculty:* 9 full-time (5 women), 4 part-time/adjunct (2 women). *Students:* 23 full-time (12 women), 7 part-time (3 women); includes 1 minority (Hispanic/Latino), 1 international. Average age 31. 19 applicants, 68% accepted, 9 enrolled. In 2010, 3 master's awarded. *Degree requirements:* For master's, one foreign language, comprehensive exam (for some programs), thesis (for some programs), thesis, project, or comprehensive exams. *Entrance requirements:* For master's, GRE, minimum undergraduate GPA of 3.0; undergraduate degree. Additional exam requirements/recommendations for international students: Required—TOEFL (minimum score 500 paper-based; 173 computer-based; 61 iBT). *Application deadline:* For fall admission, 4/1 for domestic and international students; for spring admission, 11/1 for domestic and international students. Applications are processed on a rolling basis. Application fee: $55 ($65 for international students). *Expenses:* Tuition, area resident: Part-time $179.19 per credit hour. Tuition, state resident: full-time $4384. Tuition, nonresident: full-time $16,684; part-time $630.67 per credit hour. Required fees: $350 per semester. Tuition and fees vary according to course load, degree level and program. *Financial support:* In 2010–11, 12 students received support, including 12 fellowships with full tuition reimbursements available (averaging $13,000 per year); health care benefits also available. Financial award application deadline: 2/1. *Faculty research:* Environmental writing, history/philosophy of science, environmental rhetoric and communication, the nuclear American West, American environmental history, urban environmentalism. Total annual research expenditures: $1,000. *Unit head:* Dr. Robert D. Newman, Dean and Associate Vice President of Interdisciplinary Studies, 801-581-6214, Fax: 801-585-5190, E-mail: robert.newman@utah.edu. *Application contact:* Dr. Stephen Tatum, Director, 801-581-4035, Fax: 801-585-5190, E-mail: stephen.tatum@english.utah.edu.

Villanova University, Graduate School of Liberal Arts and Sciences, Department of Humanities and Augustinian Tradition, Villanova, PA 19085-1699. Offers MA. Part-time and evening/weekend programs available. *Faculty:* 1 full-time (0 women), 2 part-time/adjunct (0 women). *Students:* 8 full-time (3 women), 4 part-time (2 women); includes 2 Asian, non-Hispanic/Latino. Average age 30. 11 applicants, 91% accepted, 6 enrolled. In 2010, 7 master's awarded. *Degree requirements:* For master's, comprehensive exam. *Entrance requirements:* For master's, GRE, statement of objectives. Additional exam requirements/recommendations for international students: Required—TOEFL. *Application deadline:* For fall admission, 3/1 priority date for domestic and international students; for spring admission, 11/15 priority date for domestic and international students. Applications are processed on a rolling basis. Electronic applications accepted. *Expenses:* Tuition: Part-time $700 per credit. Part-time tuition and fees vary according to degree level and program. *Financial support:* Research assistantships, Federal Work-Study available. Financial award applicants required to submit FAFSA. *Unit head:* Dr. Kevin Hughes. *Application contact:* Dr. Adele Lindenmeyr, Dean, Graduate School of Liberal Arts and Sciences, 610-519-7093, Fax: 610-519-7096.

Virginia Commonwealth University, Graduate School, College of Humanities and Sciences, Richmond, VA 23284-9005. Offers MA, MFA, MPA, MS, MURP, PhD, CASR, CCJA, CPM, CURP, Certificate, Graduate Certificate, JD/MURP, MSW/Certificate. Part-time and evening/weekend programs available. *Students:* 775 full-time (449 women), 1,057 part-time (654 women); includes 445 minority (249 Black or African American, non-Hispanic/Latino; 6 American

Indian or Alaska Native, non-Hispanic/Latino; 88 Asian, non-Hispanic/Latino; 53 Hispanic/Latino; 3 Native Hawaiian or other Pacific Islander, non-Hispanic/Latino; 46 Two or more races, non-Hispanic/Latino), 117 international. 1,486 applicants, 40% accepted, 214 enrolled. In 2010, 352 master's, 39 doctorates, 84 other advanced degrees awarded. *Entrance requirements:* For master's and doctorate, Varies by program. Additional exam requirements/recommendations for international students: Required—Either TOEFL (minimum score: paper-based 600, computer-based 250) or IELTS (6.5). Application fee: $50. Electronic applications accepted. *Expenses:* Tuition, state resident: full-time $4308; part-time $479 per credit hour. Tuition, nonresident: full-time $8942; part-time $994 per credit hour. Required fees: $2000; $85 per credit hour. Tuition and fees vary according to course level, course load, degree level, campus/location and program. *Financial support:* Fellowships, research assistantships, teaching assistantships, career-related internships or fieldwork, Federal Work-Study, institutionally sponsored loans, scholarships/grants, and tuition waivers (full and partial) available. Support available to part-time students. Financial award applicants required to submit FAFSA. *Unit head:* Dr. Fred M. Hawkridge, Interim Dean, 804-828-1674, E-mail: fmhawkri@vcu.edu. *Application contact:* Dr. Fred M. Hawkridge, Interim Dean, 804-828-1674, E-mail: fmhawkri@vcu.edu.

Virginia Polytechnic Institute and State University, Graduate School, College of Liberal Arts and Human Sciences, Alliance for Social, Political, Ethical, and Cultural Thought, Blacksburg, VA 24061. Offers PhD, Certificate. *Expenses:* Tuition, state resident: full-time $9399; part-time $488 per credit hour. Tuition, nonresident: full-time $17,854; part-time $957.75 per credit hour. Required fees: $1534. Full-time tuition and fees vary according to program.

Wright State University, School of Graduate Studies, College of Liberal Arts, Interdisciplinary Program in Humanities, Dayton, OH 45435. Offers M Hum. *Degree requirements:* For master's, thesis or alternative. *Entrance requirements:* Additional exam requirements/recommendations for international students: Required—TOEFL.

York University, Faculty of Graduate Studies, Faculty of Arts, Program in Humanities, Toronto, ON M3J 1P3, Canada. Offers MA, PhD. Part-time programs available. *Degree requirements:* For master's, thesis or alternative; for doctorate, comprehensive exam, thesis/dissertation. *Entrance requirements:* Additional exam requirements/recommendations for international students: Required—TOEFL (minimum score 600 paper-based; 250 computer-based). Electronic applications accepted.

Liberal Studies

Abilene Christian University, Graduate School, Interdisciplinary Program in the Liberal Arts, Abilene, TX 79699-9100. Offers MLA. Part-time programs available. *Students:* 1 full-time (0 women), 3 part-time (1 woman). 2 applicants, 50% accepted, 1 enrolled. In 2010, 2 master's awarded. *Degree requirements:* For master's, comprehensive exam, thesis or alternative. *Entrance requirements:* For master's, GRE General Test, MAT. Additional exam requirements/recommendations for international students: Required—TOEFL (minimum score 550 paper-based; 213 computer-based). *Application deadline:* For fall admission, 4/1 priority date for domestic students; for spring admission, 11/1 for domestic students. Applications are processed on a rolling basis. Application fee: $40. Electronic applications accepted. *Expenses:* Tuition: Full-time $12,906; part-time $717 per hour. Required fees: $1250; $61.50 per unit. *Financial support:* In 2010–11, 1 student received support. Federal Work-Study available. Support available to part-time students. Financial award application deadline: 4/1; financial award applicants required to submit FAFSA. *Unit head:* Dr. David Merrell, Graduate Adviser, 325-674-2035, Fax: 325-674-6844, E-mail: merrelld@acu.edu. *Application contact:* David Pittman, Graduate Admissions Counselor, 325-674-2656, Fax: 325-674-6717, E-mail: gradinfo@acu.edu.

Alaska Pacific University, Graduate Programs, Liberal Studies Department, Anchorage, AK 99508-4672. Offers self-designed study (MA).

Albertus Magnus College, Master of Arts in Liberal Studies Program, New Haven, CT 06511-1189. Offers MALS. Part-time and evening/weekend programs available. *Faculty:* 5 full-time (3 women), 4 part-time/adjunct (2 women). *Students:* 25 part-time (21 women); includes 2 Black or African American, non-Hispanic/Latino; 2 Hispanic/Latino. Average age 39. 8 applicants, 88% accepted, 6 enrolled. In 2010, 3 master's awarded. *Degree requirements:* For master's, thesis. *Entrance requirements:* For master's, interview, writing sample. *Application deadline:* For fall admission, 8/31 priority date for domestic students; for spring admission, 1/10 for domestic students. Applications are processed on a rolling basis. Application fee: $25. *Expenses:* Tuition: Full-time $12,582; part-time $2097 per course. Required fees: $90; $25 per course. *Financial support:* Available to part-time students. Application deadline: 8/15. *Unit head:* Dr. Paul Robichaud, Director, 203-773-8556, Fax: 203-773-3117, E-mail: probichaud@albertus.edu.

Alvernia University, Graduate Studies, Program in Liberal Studies, Reading, PA 19607-1799. Offers MALS. Part-time and evening/weekend programs available. *Degree requirements:* For master's, thesis optional. *Entrance requirements:* For master's, MAT or GRE (alumni excluded). Electronic applications accepted.

Antioch University Midwest, Graduate Programs, Individualized Liberal and Professional Studies Program, Yellow Springs, OH 45387-1609. Offers liberal and professional studies (MA), including counseling, creative writing, education, film studies, liberal studies, management, modern literature, psychology, theatre, visual arts. Part-time and evening/weekend programs available. Postbaccalaureate distance learning degree programs offered (minimal on-campus study). *Faculty:* 2 full-time (1 woman), 2 part-time/adjunct (both women). *Students:* 15 full-time (11 women), 34 part-time (22 women); includes 11 minority (8 Black or African American, non-Hispanic/Latino; 3 Hispanic/Latino). Average age 40. 13 applicants, 69% accepted, 5 enrolled. In 2010, 18 master's awarded. *Degree requirements:* For master's, thesis or alternative. *Entrance requirements:* For master's, resume, goal statement, interview. *Application deadline:* For fall admission, 8/1 for domestic students; for winter admission, 12/1 for domestic students; for spring admission, 3/10 for domestic students. Applications are processed on a rolling basis. Application fee: $50. Electronic applications accepted. *Expenses:* Contact institution. *Financial support:* Federal Work-Study available. Financial award applicants required to submit FAFSA. *Unit head:* Dr. Joseph Cronin, Chair, 937-769-1894, Fax: 937-769-1807, E-mail: jcronin@antioch.edu. *Application contact:* Seth Gordon, Assistant Director of Admissions, 937-769-1800 Ext. 1825, Fax: 937-769-1804, E-mail: sgordon@antioch.edu.

Arizona State University, College of Liberal Arts and Sciences, Program in Liberal Studies, Tempe, AZ 85287-6505. Offers liberal studies (MLS); liberal studies (film and media studies) (MLS). Part-time and evening/weekend programs available. *Students:* 25 full-time (15 women), 32 part-time (23 women); includes 19 minority (7 Black or African American, non-Hispanic/Latino; 3 American Indian or Alaska Native, non-Hispanic/Latino; 1 Asian, non-Hispanic/Latino; 7 Hispanic/Latino; 1 Two or more races, non-Hispanic/Latino), 3 international. Average age 35. 30 applicants, 83% accepted, 16 enrolled. In 2010, 22 master's awarded. *Degree requirements:* For master's, thesis or alternative, integrated/capstone project, interactive Program of Study (iPOS) submitted before completing 50 percent of required credit hours. *Entrance requirements:* For master's, minimum GPA of 3.0 or equivalent in last 2 years of work leading to bachelor's degree, resume or biographical statement, personal letter expressing liberal studies concentration interest, official college transcripts, 2 letters of recommendation, interview with program director (recommended). Additional exam requirements/recommendations for international students: Required—TOEFL, IELTS, or Pearson Test of English. *Application deadline:* For fall admission, 7/15 for domestic and international students; for spring admission, 12/15 for domestic and international students. Application fee: $70 ($90 for international students). Electronic applications accepted. *Expenses:* Contact institution. *Financial support:* Institutionally sponsored loans available. Financial award application deadline: 3/1; financial award applicants required to submit FAFSA. *Unit head:* Paul Morris, Program Director, 480-727-0819, E-mail: paulmorris@asu.edu. *Application contact:* Graduate Admissions, 480-965-6113.

Armstrong Atlantic State University, School of Graduate Studies, Program in Liberal and Professional Studies, Savannah, GA 31419-1997. Offers MALPS. Part-time programs available. *Degree requirements:* For master's, comprehensive exam, project. *Entrance requirements:* For master's, GRE, minimum GPA of 2.5, letters of recommendation. Additional exam requirements/recommendations for international students: Required—TOEFL (minimum score 523 paper-based; 193 computer-based).

Auburn University Montgomery, School of Liberal Arts, Montgomery, AL 36124-4023. Offers MLA. Part-time and evening/weekend programs available. *Degree requirements:* For master's, thesis. *Entrance requirements:* For master's, GRE or MAT. Electronic applications accepted.

Baker University, School of Professional and Graduate Studies, Program in Liberal Arts, Baldwin City, KS 66006-0065. Offers MLA. Program also offered in Overland Park, KS. Part-time and evening/weekend programs available. *Students:* 17 full-time (12 women), 63 part-time (42 women); includes 9 Black or African American, non-Hispanic/Latino; 1 American Indian or Alaska Native, non-Hispanic/Latino; 1 Asian, non-Hispanic/Latino; 4 Hispanic/Latino; 1 Two or more races, non-Hispanic/Latino. Average age 35. In 2010, 40 master's awarded. *Degree requirements:* For master's, portfolio of learning. *Entrance requirements:* Additional exam requirements/recommendations for international students: Required—TOEFL (minimum score 600 paper-based; 250 computer-based; 100 iBT). *Application deadline:* Applications are processed on a rolling basis. Application fee: $20. *Financial support:* Applicants required to submit FAFSA. *Unit head:* Dr. Peggy Harris, Vice President and Dean, 785-594-8492, Fax: 785-594-8363, E-mail: peggy.harris@bakeru.edu. *Application contact:* Dr. Peggy Harris, Vice President and Dean, 785-594-8492, Fax: 785-594-8363, E-mail: peggy.harris@bakeru.edu.

Barry University, School of Arts and Sciences, Interdisciplinary Program, Miami Shores, FL 33161-6695. Offers MA.

Bradley University, Graduate School, College of Liberal Arts and Sciences, Program in Liberal Studies, Peoria, IL 61625-0002. Offers MLS. Part-time and evening/weekend programs available. *Degree requirements:* For master's, comprehensive exam, colloquium. *Entrance requirements:* For master's, 2 letters of recommendation. Additional exam requirements/recommendations for international students: Required—TOEFL (minimum score 550 paper-based; 213 computer-based; 79 iBT). *Expenses:* Contact institution.

Brooklyn College of the City University of New York, Division of Graduate Studies, Liberal Studies Program, Brooklyn, NY 11210-2889. Offers MA. Part-time programs available. *Students:* 2 part-time (1 woman); includes 1 minority (Black or African American, non-Hispanic/Latino). Average age 38. In 2010, 3 master's awarded. *Degree requirements:* For master's, thesis or alternative, final project. *Entrance requirements:* For master's, interview, 2 letters of recommendation, essay. Additional exam requirements/recommendations for international students: Required—TOEFL. *Application deadline:* For fall admission, 3/1 priority date for domestic students, 2/1 priority date for international students; for spring admission, 11/1 priority date for domestic students, 10/1 priority date for international students. Applications are processed on a rolling basis. Application fee: $125. Electronic applications accepted. *Expenses:* Tuition, state resident: full-time $7360; part-time $310 per credit hour. Tuition, nonresident: full-time $13,800; part-time $575 per credit hour. Required fees: $190 per semester. *Financial support:* Federal Work-Study, institutionally sponsored loans, and scholarships/grants available. Support available to part-time students. Financial award application deadline: 5/1; financial award applicants required to submit FAFSA. *Faculty research:* Language acquisition, Judaic biography, ecocriticism. *Unit head:* Dr. Philip Gallagher, Director, 718-951-5252, E-mail: philipg@brooklyn.cuny.edu. *Application contact:* Hernan Sierra, Graduate Admissions Coordinator, 718-951-4536, Fax: 718-951-4506, E-mail: grads@brooklyn.cuny.edu.

Brooklyn College of the City University of New York, Division of Graduate Studies, School of Education, Program in Childhood Education, Brooklyn, NY 11210-2889. Offers bilingual education (MS Ed); liberal arts (MS Ed); mathematics (MS Ed); science/environmental education (MS Ed). Part-time and evening/weekend programs available. *Students:* 12 full-time (all women), 207 part-time (185 women); includes 97 minority (59 Black or African American, non-Hispanic/Latino; 3 American Indian or Alaska Native, non-Hispanic/Latino; 15 Asian, non-Hispanic/Latino; 20 Hispanic/Latino), 6 international. Average age 31. 99 applicants, 93% accepted, 46 enrolled. In 2010, 125 master's awarded. *Entrance requirements:* For master's, LAST, interview, previous course work in education, writing sample, resume, 2 letters of recommendation. Additional exam requirements/recommendations for international students: Required—TOEFL (minimum score 500 paper-based; 173 computer-based; 61 iBT). *Application deadline:* For fall admission, 3/1 priority date for domestic students, 2/1 priority date for international students; for spring admission, 11/1 priority date for domestic students, 10/1 priority date for international students. Applications are processed on a rolling basis. Application fee: $125. Electronic applications accepted. *Expenses:* Tuition, state resident: full-time $7360; part-time $310 per credit hour. Tuition, nonresident: full-time $13,800; part-time $575 per credit hour. Required fees: $190 per semester. *Financial support:* Career-related internships or fieldwork, Federal Work-Study, institutionally sponsored loans, and scholarships/grants available. Support available to part-time students. Financial award application deadline: 5/1; financial award applicants required to submit FAFSA. *Faculty research:* Emotional intelligence, multiculturalism, arts immersion, the Holocaust. *Unit head:* Dr. Wayne Reed, Program Head, 718-951-5214, E-mail: wreed@brooklyn.cuny.edu. *Application contact:* Hernan Sierra, Graduate Admissions Coordinator, 718-951-4536, Fax: 718-951-4506, E-mail: grads@brooklyn.cuny.edu.

California State University, Sacramento, Graduate Studies, College of Social Sciences and Interdisciplinary Studies, Liberal Arts Program, Sacramento, CA 95819. Offers French (MA); German (MA); Spanish (MA); theater arts (MA). *Degree requirements:* For master's, writing proficiency exam. *Entrance requirements:* Additional exam requirements/recommendations for international students: Required—TOEFL. Electronic applications accepted.

Cardinal Stritch University, College of Arts and Sciences, Milwaukee, WI 53217-3985. Offers MA, MM, MS. Part-time and evening/weekend programs available. *Degree requirements:* For master's, thesis.

Clark University, Graduate School, College of Professional and Continuing Education, Program in Liberal Studies, Worcester, MA 01610-1477. Offers MALA. Part-time and evening/weekend programs available. *Students:* 1 (woman) part-time. Average age 28. In 2010, 2 master's awarded. *Degree requirements:* For master's, thesis optional. *Application deadline:* Applications are processed on a rolling basis. Application fee: $50. Electronic applications accepted. *Expenses:* Tuition: Full-time $37,000; part-time $1156 per credit hour. Required fees: $30; $1156 per credit hour. *Financial support:* Career-related internships or fieldwork available. Support available to part-time students. *Unit head:* Max E. Hess, Director of Graduate Studies,

Liberal Studies

Clark University (continued)
508-793-7217, Fax: 508-793-7232. *Application contact:* Julia Parent, Director of Marketing, Communications, and Admissions, 508-793-7217, Fax: 508-793-7232, E-mail: jparent@clarku.edu.

Clayton State University, School of Graduate Studies, Program in Liberal Studies, Morrow, GA 30260-0285. Offers MALS. Part-time programs available. *Degree requirements:* For master's, thesis optional. *Entrance requirements:* For master's, GRE. Additional exam requirements/recommendations for international students: Required—TOEFL (minimum score 550 paper-based; 213 computer-based; 80 iBT). Electronic applications accepted. *Expenses:* Contact institution.

The College at Brockport, State University of New York, Office of the Vice Provost, Program in Liberal Studies, Brockport, NY 14420-2997. Offers MA. Part-time programs available. *Students:* 10 full-time (6 women), 13 part-time (7 women); includes 2 Black or African American, non-Hispanic/Latino; 2 American Indian or Alaska Native, non-Hispanic/Latino; 1 Asian, non-Hispanic/Latino; 1 Hispanic/Latino. 14 applicants, 79% accepted, 10 enrolled. In 2010, 14 master's awarded. *Degree requirements:* For master's, portfolio. *Entrance requirements:* For master's, minimum GPA of 3.0, letters of recommendation. Additional exam requirements/recommendations for international students: Required—TOEFL (minimum score 550 paper-based; 213 computer-based; 79 iBT). *Application deadline:* For fall admission, 6/15 priority date for domestic and international students; for spring admission, 10/15 priority date for domestic and international students. Application fee: $50. Electronic applications accepted. *Financial support:* Federal Work-Study, scholarships/grants, and unspecified assistantships available. Support available to part-time students. Financial award application deadline: 3/15; financial award applicants required to submit FAFSA. *Unit head:* Dr. Kalathur Rajasethupathy, Director, 585-395-2262, Fax: 585-395-2172, E-mail: kraja@brockport.edu. *Application contact:* Dr. Kalathur Rajasethupathy, Director, 585-395-2262, Fax: 585-395-2172, E-mail: kraja@brockport.edu.

College of Notre Dame of Maryland, Graduate Studies, Program in Liberal Studies, Baltimore, MD 21210-2476. Offers MA. Part-time and evening/weekend programs available. *Degree requirements:* For master's, thesis or alternative. *Entrance requirements:* For master's, minimum GPA of 3.0. Additional exam requirements/recommendations for international students: Required—TOEFL (minimum score 500 paper-based; 173 computer-based; 61 iBT). Electronic applications accepted.

College of Staten Island of the City University of New York, Graduate Programs, Program in Liberal Studies, Staten Island, NY 10314-6600. Offers MA. Evening/weekend programs available. *Faculty:* 3 full-time (0 women), 1 part-time/adjunct (0 women). *Students:* 44 part-time (27 women); includes 8 minority (4 Black or African American, non-Hispanic/Latino; 2 Asian, non-Hispanic/Latino; 2 Hispanic/Latino), 1 international. Average age 36. 34 applicants, 59% accepted, 15 enrolled. In 2010, 6 master's awarded. *Degree requirements:* For master's, thesis. *Entrance requirements:* For master's, minimum undergraduate GPA of 3.0, interview. Additional exam requirements/recommendations for international students: Required—TOEFL (minimum score 550 paper-based; 213 computer-based; 79 iBT), IELTS (minimum score 6.5). *Application deadline:* For fall admission, 6/1 for domestic and international students. Applications are processed on a rolling basis. Application fee: $125. Electronic applications accepted. *Expenses:* Tuition, state resident: full-time $7730; part-time $325 per credit. Tuition, nonresident: full-time $14,520; part-time $605 per credit. Required fees: $378. *Financial support:* Fellowships, research assistantships, teaching assistantships, career-related internships or fieldwork, Federal Work-Study, and scholarships/grants available. Support available to part-time students. Financial award applicants required to submit FAFSA. Total annual research expenditures: $168,000. *Unit head:* Dr. David Traboulay, Coordinator, 718-982-2877, E-mail: mals@mail.csi.cuny.edu. *Application contact:* Sasha Spence, Assistant Director of Graduate Recruitment and Admissions, 718-982-2699, Fax: 718-982-2500, E-mail: sasha.spence@csi.cuny.edu.

The Colorado College, Department of Education, Experienced Teacher Program, Colorado Springs, CO 80903-3294. Offers arts and humanities (MAT); liberal arts (MAT); Southwest studies (MAT). Programs offered during summer only. Part-time programs available. *Degree requirements:* For master's, thesis, oral exam, 50-page paper. *Expenses:* Contact institution.

Columbia University, Graduate School of Arts and Sciences, Program in Liberal Studies, New York, NY 10027. Offers American studies (MA); East Asian studies (MA); human rights studies (MA); Islamic culture studies (MA); Jewish studies (MA); medieval studies (MA); modern European studies (MA); South Asian studies (MA). Part-time and evening/weekend programs available. *Degree requirements:* For master's, thesis.

Concordia University Chicago, College of Graduate and Innovative Programs, Program in Liberal Studies, River Forest, IL 60305-1499. Offers MA. *Entrance requirements:* Additional exam requirements/recommendations for international students: Required—TOEFL (minimum score 550 paper-based; 195 computer-based). Electronic applications accepted.

Converse College, School of Education and Graduate Studies, Program in Liberal Arts, Spartanburg, SC 29302-0006. Offers English (MLA); history (MLA); political science (MLA). *Degree requirements:* For master's, capstone paper. *Entrance requirements:* For master's, minimum GPA of 3.0, 2 recommendations. *Expenses:* Tuition: Part-time $365 per credit hour.

Creighton University, Graduate School, College of Arts and Sciences, Program in Liberal Studies, Omaha, NE 68178-0001. Offers MLS. Part-time and evening/weekend programs available. *Faculty:* 16 full-time (4 women). *Students:* 2 full-time (1 woman), 20 part-time (14 women); includes 3 minority (all Black or African American, non-Hispanic/Latino), 1 international. Average age 34. 6 applicants, 67% accepted, 4 enrolled. In 2010, 3 master's awarded. *Degree requirements:* For master's, thesis optional. *Entrance requirements:* For master's, 3 letters of recommendation. Additional exam requirements/recommendations for international students: Required—TOEFL (minimum score 550 paper-based; 213 computer-based; 80 iBT). *Application deadline:* For fall admission, 3/1 priority date for domestic and international students; for winter admission, 12/1 priority date for domestic students, 7/1 priority date for international students; for spring admission, 4/1 priority date for domestic students, 10/1 priority date for international students. Applications are processed on a rolling basis. Application fee: $50. Electronic applications accepted. *Expenses:* Tuition: Full-time $12,168; part-time $676 per credit hour. Required fees: $131 per semester. Tuition and fees vary according to program. *Financial support:* Available to part-time students. Applicants required to submit FAFSA. *Unit head:* Dr. Richard White, Professor of Philosophy, 402-280-2642, E-mail: rwhite@creighton.edu. *Application contact:* Taunya Plater, Senior Program Coordinator, 402-280-2870, Fax: 402-280-2899, E-mail: taunyaplater@creighton.edu.

Dallas Baptist University, College of Adult Education, Liberal Arts Program, Dallas, TX 75211-9299. Offers arts (MLA); Christian ministry (MLA); English (MLA); English as a second language (MLA); fine arts (MLA); history (MLA); missions (MLA); political science (MLA). Part-time and evening/weekend programs available. *Entrance requirements:* For master's, minimum GPA of 3.0. Additional exam requirements/recommendations for international students: Required—TOEFL. Electronic applications accepted. *Expenses:* Tuition: Full-time $11,394; part-time $633 per credit hour. *Faculty research:* Milton and seventeenth-century Puritans, inter-Biblical years, nineteenth-century literature, Latin American and Texas history.

Dartmouth College, Arts and Sciences Graduate Programs, Program in Liberal Studies, Hanover, NH 03755. Offers MALS. Part-time programs available. *Degree requirements:* For master's, thesis. *Entrance requirements:* Additional exam requirements/recommendations for international students: Required—TOEFL.

Dowling College, Programs in Arts and Sciences, Oakdale, NY 11769-1999. Offers integrated math and science (MS); liberal studies (MA). Part-time and evening/weekend programs available. *Faculty:* 6 full-time (1 woman). *Students:* 3 full-time (2 women), 9 part-time (6 women); includes 1 minority (Asian, non-Hispanic/Latino). Average age 33. 14 applicants, 79% accepted, 6 enrolled. In 2010, 1 master's awarded. *Degree requirements:* For master's, comprehensive exam, thesis. *Entrance requirements:* For master's, minimum undergraduate GPA of 3.0, 2 letters of recommendation. Additional exam requirements/recommendations for international students: Required—TOEFL (minimum score 550 paper-based). *Application deadline:* For fall admission, 9/1 priority date for domestic students; for winter admission, 1/1 priority date for domestic students; for spring admission, 2/1 priority date for domestic students. Applications are processed on a rolling basis. Application fee: $50. Electronic applications accepted. *Expenses:* Tuition: Part-time $884 per credit hour. Part-time tuition and fees vary according to degree level and campus/location. *Financial support:* Federal Work-Study available. Support available to part-time students. Financial award application deadline: 6/30; financial award applicants required to submit FAFSA. *Unit head:* Dr. Paul Abramson, Dean, 631-244-3162, Fax: 631-244-1035, E-mail: abramsop@dowling.edu. *Application contact:* Ronnie S. Macdonald, Assistant Vice President for Enrollment Services/Dean of Admissions, 631-244-3357, Fax: 631-244-1059, E-mail: macdonar@dowling.edu.

Duke University, Graduate School, Program in Liberal Studies, Durham, NC 27708. Offers AM. Part-time and evening/weekend programs available. *Degree requirements:* For master's, thesis or alternative, final project. *Entrance requirements:* For master's, interview. Additional exam requirements/recommendations for international students: Required—IELTS (preferred) or TOEFL. Electronic applications accepted.

Duquesne University, School of Leadership and Professional Advancement, Pittsburgh, PA 15282-0001. Offers leadership (MS), including business ethics, community leadership, global leadership, information technology, leadership, liberal studies, professional administration, sports leadership. Part-time and evening/weekend programs available. Postbaccalaureate distance learning degree programs offered (no on-campus study). *Faculty:* 1 full-time (0 women), 70 part-time/adjunct (35 women). *Students:* 275 full-time, 171 part-time; includes 20 Black or African American, non-Hispanic/Latino; 1 American Indian or Alaska Native, non-Hispanic/Latino; 6 Asian, non-Hispanic/Latino; 3 Hispanic/Latino. Average age 31. 161 applicants, 73% accepted, 103 enrolled. In 2010, 108 master's awarded. *Degree requirements:* For master's, capstone course. *Entrance requirements:* For master's, professional work experience, 500-word essay. Additional exam requirements/recommendations for international students: Required—TOEFL. *Application deadline:* Applications are processed on a rolling basis. Application fee: $0. Electronic applications accepted. *Expenses:* Tuition: Part-time $884 per credit. Required fees: $84 per credit. Tuition and fees vary according to course load. *Financial support:* Applicants required to submit FAFSA. *Unit head:* Dr. Dorothy Bassett, Dean, 412-396-2141, Fax: 412-396-4711, E-mail: bassettd@duq.edu. *Application contact:* Marianne Leister, Director of Student Services, 412-396-4933, Fax: 412-396-5072, E-mail: leister@duq.edu.

East Tennessee State University, School of Graduate Studies, Division of Cross-Disciplinary Studies, Johnson City, TN 37614. Offers archival studies (MALS); strategic leadership (MPS); training and development (MPS). Part-time programs available. Postbaccalaureate distance learning degree programs offered (no on-campus study). *Faculty:* 2 full-time (1 woman). *Students:* 14 full-time (9 women), 61 part-time (51 women); includes 11 minority (5 Black or African American, non-Hispanic/Latino; 1 American Indian or Alaska Native, non-Hispanic/Latino; 3 Hispanic/Latino; 2 Two or more races, non-Hispanic/Latino). Average age 42. 47 applicants, 66% accepted, 25 enrolled. In 2010, 14 master's, 2 other advanced degrees awarded. *Degree requirements:* For master's, comprehensive exam, professional project. *Entrance requirements:* For master's, GRE General Test, minimum GPA of 2.75, professional portfolio. Additional exam requirements/recommendations for international students: Required—TOEFL (minimum score 550 paper-based; 213 computer-based; 79 iBT). *Application deadline:* For fall admission, 6/1 for domestic students, 4/30 for international students; for spring admission, 11/1 for domestic students, 9/30 for international students. Application fee: $25 ($35 for international students). Electronic applications accepted. *Financial support:* In 2010–11, 2 research assistantships with full tuition reimbursements (averaging $5,500 per year) were awarded; teaching assistantships with full tuition reimbursements, institutionally sponsored loans, scholarships/grants, and unspecified assistantships also available. Financial award application deadline: 7/1; financial award applicants required to submit FAFSA. *Unit head:* Dr. Rick E. Osborn, Associate Dean, 423-439-4223, Fax: 423-439-7091, E-mail: osbornr@etsu.edu. *Application contact:* Admissions and Records Clerk, 423-439-4221, Fax: 423-439-5624, E-mail: gradsch@etsu.edu.

Excelsior College, School of Liberal Arts, Albany, NY 12203-5159. Offers liberal studies (MA). Part-time and evening/weekend programs available. Postbaccalaureate distance learning degree programs offered (no on-campus study). *Degree requirements:* For master's, thesis or alternative. Electronic applications accepted.

Faulkner University, Alabama Christian College of Arts and Sciences, Department of Humanities, Montgomery, AL 36109-3398. Offers liberal arts (MLA).

Florida Atlantic University, Dorothy F. Schmidt College of Arts and Letters, Program in Liberal Studies, Boca Raton, FL 33431-0991. Offers MA. *Students:* 8 part-time (4 women); includes 2 minority (1 Black or African American, non-Hispanic/Latino; 1 Hispanic/Latino). Average age 40. 2 applicants, 0% accepted, 0 enrolled. *Degree requirements:* For master's, thesis or alternative. *Entrance requirements:* For master's, GRE General Test. *Application deadline:* For fall admission, 2/1 priority date for domestic students, 2/1 for international students; for spring admission, 10/1 for domestic and international students. Applications are processed on a rolling basis. Application fee: $30. *Expenses:* Tuition, area resident: Part-time $319.96 per credit. Tuition, state resident: part-time $319.96 per credit. Tuition, nonresident: part-time $926.42 per credit. *Unit head:* Dr. Clevis Headley, Director, 561-297-3920, E-mail: headley@fau.edu. *Application contact:* Dr. Emily Stockard, Associate Dean, 561-297-2817, Fax: 561-297-2744, E-mail: stockard@fau.edu.

Florida International University, College of Arts and Sciences, Program in Liberal Studies, Miami, FL 33199. Offers MA. Part-time and evening/weekend programs available. *Students:* 2 full-time (1 woman), 12 part-time (9 women); includes 1 Black or African American, non-Hispanic/Latino; 2 Asian, non-Hispanic/Latino; 8 Hispanic/Latino. Average age 29. 25 applicants, 32% accepted, 5 enrolled. In 2010, 2 master's awarded. *Degree requirements:* For master's, thesis optional. *Entrance requirements:* For master's, minimum GPA of 3.0, 2-3 letters of recommendation, writing sample, curriculum vitae. Additional exam requirements/recommendations for international students: Required—TOEFL (minimum score 550 paper-based; 80 iBT). *Application deadline:* For fall admission, 6/1 for domestic students, 4/1 for international students; for spring admission, 10/1 for domestic students, 9/1 for international students. Applications are processed on a rolling basis. Application fee: $30. Electronic applications accepted. *Financial support:* Institutionally sponsored loans and scholarships/grants available. Financial award application deadline: 3/1; financial award applicants required to submit FAFSA. *Unit head:* Dr. Leonard Keller, Chair, 305-348-2865, Fax: 305-348-7201, E-mail: leonard.keller@fiu.edu. *Application contact:* Dr. Kiriake Xerohemona, Graduate Program Director, 305-348-2185, Fax: 305-348-7201, E-mail: xerohemo@fiu.edu.

Fordham University, Graduate School of Arts and Sciences, Program in Humanities and Sciences, New York, NY 10458. Offers MA. Part-time and evening/weekend programs available. *Students:* 3 full-time (2 women), 18 part-time (11 women); includes 2 Black or African American, non-Hispanic/Latino; 1 American Indian or Alaska Native, non-Hispanic/Latino; 1 Hispanic/Latino, 1 international. Average age 26. 17 applicants, 88% accepted, 8 enrolled. In 2010, 10 master's awarded. *Degree requirements:* For master's, final paper. *Entrance requirements:* Additional exam requirements/recommendations for international students: Required—TOEFL (minimum score 650 paper-based; 280 computer-based). *Application deadline:* For fall admission, 1/4 priority date for domestic students; for spring admission, 11/1 for domestic students. Application fee: $70. Electronic applications accepted. *Financial support:* In 2010–11, 1 student received support, including 1 research assistantship (averaging $18,400 per year); institutionally sponsored loans and tuition waivers (full and partial) also available. Financial award application deadline: 1/4; financial award applicants required to submit FAFSA. *Unit head:* Dr. Hugo

Benavides, Director, 718-817-4407, E-mail: benavides@fordham.edu. *Application contact:* Charlene Dundie, Director of Graduate Admissions, 718-817-4420, Fax: 718-817-3566, E-mail: dundie@fordham.edu.

Fort Hays State University, Graduate School, College of Arts and Sciences, Center for Interdisciplinary Studies, Hays, KS 67601-4099. Offers liberal studies (MLS). Postbaccalaureate distance learning degree programs offered (minimal on-campus study). *Degree requirements:* For master's, comprehensive exam, thesis or alternative. *Entrance requirements:* Additional exam requirements/recommendations for international students: Required—TOEFL (minimum score 550 paper-based; 213 computer-based). Electronic applications accepted.

Georgetown University, Graduate School of Arts and Sciences, School of Continuing Studies, Washington, DC 20057. Offers American studies (MALS); Catholic studies (MALS); classical civilizations (MALS); disability studies (MPS); ethics and the professions (MALS); human resources management (MPS); humanities (MALS); individualized study (MALS); international affairs (MALS); Islam and Muslim-Christian relations (MALS); journalism (MPS); liberal studies (DLS); literature and society (MALS); medieval and early modern European studies (MALS); public relations and corporate communications (MPS); real estate (MPS); religious studies (MALS); social and public policy (MALS); sports industry management (MPS); the theory and practice of American democracy (MALS); visual culture (MALS). *Entrance requirements:* Additional exam requirements/recommendations for international students: Required—TOEFL.

Graduate School and University Center of the City University of New York, Graduate Studies, Program in Liberal Studies, New York, NY 10016-4039. Offers MA. *Degree requirements:* For master's, thesis. *Entrance requirements:* For master's, GRE General Test. Additional exam requirements/recommendations for international students: Required—TOEFL. Electronic applications accepted.

Hamline University, Graduate School of Liberal Studies, St. Paul, MN 55104-1284. Offers liberal studies (MALS, CALS); writing (MFA); writing for children and young adults (MFA). Part-time and evening/weekend programs available. Postbaccalaureate distance learning degree programs offered (minimal on-campus study). *Faculty:* 6 full-time (4 women), 7 part-time/adjunct (5 women). *Students:* 94 full-time (76 women), 119 part-time (85 women); includes 8 minority (6 Black or African American, non-Hispanic/Latino; 1 American Indian or Alaska Native, non-Hispanic/Latino; 1 Hispanic/Latino), 1 international. Average age 37. 73 applicants, 70% accepted, 30 enrolled. In 2010, 60 master's awarded. *Degree requirements:* For master's, thesis. *Entrance requirements:* For master's, official transcripts, 20-page writing sample (MFA), letters of recommendation. *Application deadline:* For fall admission, 1/5 for domestic and international students; for spring admission, 9/1 for domestic and international students. Applications are processed on a rolling basis. Application fee: $0. Electronic applications accepted. *Expenses:* Contact institution. *Financial support:* Federal Work-Study and scholarships/grants available. Support available to part-time students. Financial award applicants required to submit FAFSA. *Unit head:* Mary Rockcastle, Dean, 651-523-2047, Fax: 651-523-2490, E-mail: mrockcastle@gw.hamline.edu. *Application contact:* Rae A. Lenway, Director, Graduate Recruitment and Admission, 651-523-2900, Fax: 651-523-3058, E-mail: rlenway01@gw.hamline.edu.

Harvard University, Extension School, Cambridge, MA 02138-3722. Offers applied sciences (CAS); biotechnology (ALM); educational technologies (ALM); educational technology (CET); English for graduate and professional studies (DGP); environmental management (ALM, CEM); information technology (ALM); journalism (ALM); liberal arts (ALM); management (ALM, CM); mathematics for teaching (ALM); museum studies (ALM); premedical studies (Diploma); publication and communication (CPC). Part-time and evening/weekend programs available. *Degree requirements:* For master's, thesis. *Entrance requirements:* For master's, 3 completed graduate courses with grade of B or higher. Additional exam requirements/recommendations for international students: Required—TOEFL (minimum score 600 paper-based; 250 computer-based), TWE (minimum score 5). *Expenses:* Contact institution.

Henderson State University, Graduate Studies, Ellis College of Arts and Sciences, Arkadelphia, AR 71999-0001. Offers MLA. Part-time programs available. *Entrance requirements:* For master's, minimum GPA of 2.7, interview. Additional exam requirements/recommendations for international students: Required—TOEFL (minimum score 550 paper-based; 213 computer-based); Recommended—IELTS (minimum score 6). Electronic applications accepted. *Expenses:* Tuition, state resident: full-time $3978; part-time $221 per credit hour. Tuition, nonresident: full-time $7956; part-time $442 per credit hour. Tuition and fees vary according to course load.

Hollins University, Graduate Programs, Program in Liberal Studies, Roanoke, VA 24020-1603. Offers humanities (MALS); interdisciplinary studies (MALS); justice and legal studies (MALS); liberal studies (CAS); social science (MALS); visual and performing arts (MALS). Part-time and evening/weekend programs available. *Degree requirements:* For master's, thesis. *Entrance requirements:* For master's, letters of recommendation, interview. Additional exam requirements/recommendations for international students: Required—TOEFL (minimum score 550 paper-based; 213 computer-based; 79 iBT). Electronic applications accepted. *Faculty research:* Elderly blacks, film, feminist economics, US voting patterns, Wagner, diversity.

Houston Baptist University, College of Arts and Humanities, Program in Liberal Arts, Houston, TX 77074-3298. Offers MLA. Part-time and evening/weekend programs available. *Entrance requirements:* For master's, interview, minimum GPA of 2.5, writing sample. Additional exam requirements/recommendations for international students: Required—TOEFL (minimum score 550 paper-based; 213 computer-based).

Indiana University Kokomo, School of Arts and Sciences, Kokomo, IN 46904-9003. Offers liberal studies (MALS). *Faculty:* 32 full-time (10 women). *Students:* 20 part-time (13 women); includes 2 Hispanic/Latino. Average age 44. 3 applicants, 100% accepted, 3 enrolled. In 2010, 3 master's awarded. *Degree requirements:* For master's, thesis. *Entrance requirements:* For master's, minimum GPA of 3.0. Additional exam requirements/recommendations for international students: Required—TOEFL. *Application deadline:* For fall admission, 4/15 priority date for domestic students; for spring admission, 10/15 priority date for domestic students. Applications are processed on a rolling basis. Application fee: $40 ($50 for international students). *Faculty research:* Bibliography and textual studies, comparative literature, current global issues/political science. *Unit head:* Dr. Susan Sciame-Giesecke, Dean, 765-455-9258, Fax: 765-455-9566, E-mail: sgieseck@iuk.edu. *Application contact:* Dr. Susan Sciame-Giesecke, Dean, 765-455-9258, Fax: 765-455-9566, E-mail: sgieseck@iuk.edu.

Indiana University–Purdue University Fort Wayne, College of Arts and Sciences, Program in Liberal Studies, Fort Wayne, IN 46805-1499. Offers MLS. Part-time programs available. *Students:* 4 full-time (all women), 29 part-time (18 women); includes 5 minority (3 Black or African American, non-Hispanic/Latino; 1 Asian, non-Hispanic/Latino; 1 Two or more races, non-Hispanic/Latino). Average age 39. 14 applicants, 86% accepted, 9 enrolled. In 2010, 6 master's awarded. *Entrance requirements:* For master's, minimum GPA of 3.0, major or minor in related area, three letters of recommendation. Additional exam requirements/recommendations for international students: Required—TOEFL (minimum score 550 paper-based; 213 computer-based; 77 iBT). *Application deadline:* For fall admission, 8/1 for domestic students; for spring admission, 12/1 for domestic students. Applications are processed on a rolling basis. Application fee: $50. *Expenses:* Tuition, state resident: full-time $4824; part-time $268 per credit. Tuition, nonresident: full-time $11,625; part-time $646 per credit. Required fees: $555; $30.85 per credit. Tuition and fees vary according to course load. *Financial support:* Scholarships/grants available. Support available to part-time students. Financial award application deadline: 3/1; financial award applicants required to submit FAFSA. *Unit head:* Dr. Michael E. Kaufmann, Director, 260-481-6760, Fax: 260-481-6985, E-mail: kaufmann@ipfw.edu. *Application contact:* Dr. Michael E. Kaufmann, Director, 260-481-6760, Fax: 260-481-6985, E-mail: kaufmann@ipfw.edu.

Indiana University–Purdue University Indianapolis, School of Liberal Arts, Indianapolis, IN 46202-2896. Offers MA, MS, XMA, PhD, Certificate, JD/MA, MA/MA, MA/MLS, MD/MA. *Students:* 126 full-time (86 women), 164 part-time (116 women); includes 35 minority (19 Black or African American, non-Hispanic/Latino; 1 American Indian or Alaska Native, non-Hispanic/Latino; 6 Asian, non-Hispanic/Latino; 7 Hispanic/Latino; 2 Two or more races, non-Hispanic/Latino), 26 international. Average age 33. 227 applicants, 55% accepted, 92 enrolled. In 2010, 126 master's, 7 other advanced degrees awarded. Application fee: $55 ($65 for international students). *Unit head:* Robert W. White, Dean, School of Liberal Arts, 317-274-8448. *Application contact:* Director of Research and Graduate Programs, 317-274-8305.

Indiana University South Bend, College of Liberal Arts and Sciences, South Bend, IN 46634-7111. Offers applied mathematics and computer science (MS); applied psychology (MA); English (MA); liberal studies (MLS). Part-time and evening/weekend programs available. *Faculty:* 79 full-time (33 women). *Students:* 34 full-time (18 women), 100 part-time (69 women); includes 23 minority (15 Black or African American, non-Hispanic/Latino; 2 American Indian or Alaska Native, non-Hispanic/Latino; 3 Asian, non-Hispanic/Latino; 2 Hispanic/Latino; 1 Two or more races, non-Hispanic/Latino), 16 international. Average age 37. 44 applicants, 84% accepted, 27 enrolled. In 2010, 21 master's awarded. *Degree requirements:* For master's, thesis (for some programs). *Entrance requirements:* For master's, minimum GPA of 3.0. Additional exam requirements/recommendations for international students: Required—TOEFL. *Application deadline:* For fall admission, 7/31 priority date for domestic students, 7/1 priority date for international students; for spring admission, 3/31 priority date for domestic students, 11/1 priority date for international students. Applications are processed on a rolling basis. Application fee: $50 ($60 for international students). *Financial support:* In 2010–11, 5 students received support, including 5 teaching assistantships; Federal Work-Study also available. Support available to part-time students. *Faculty research:* Artificial intelligence, bioinformatics, English language and literature, creative writing, computer networks. Total annual research expenditures: $127,000. *Unit head:* Dr. Lynn R. Williams, Dean, 574-520-4322, Fax: 574-520-4528, E-mail: lwilliam@iusb.edu. *Application contact:* Dr. Lynn R. Williams, Dean, 574-520-4322, Fax: 574-520-4528, E-mail: lwilliam@iusb.edu.

Indiana University Southeast, Program in Liberal Studies, New Albany, IN 47150-6405. Offers MLS. *Students:* 2 full-time (0 women), 37 part-time (23 women); includes 5 Black or African American, non-Hispanic/Latino; 1 Two or more races, non-Hispanic/Latino. Average age 42. 11 applicants, 73% accepted, 6 enrolled. In 2010, 4 master's awarded. *Degree requirements:* For master's, thesis or alternative. *Entrance requirements:* For master's, 3 letters of recommendation. *Unit head:* Dr. Sandra S. French, Director, 812-941-2393, E-mail: sfrench@ius.edu. *Application contact:* Debra Voyles, Administrative Assistant, 812-941-2604, E-mail: davoyles@ius.edu.

Jacksonville State University, College of Graduate Studies and Continuing Education, College of Arts and Sciences, Department of Liberal Studies, Jacksonville, AL 36265-1602. Offers MA. Part-time and evening/weekend programs available. *Degree requirements:* For master's, comprehensive exam, thesis (for some programs). Electronic applications accepted.

The Johns Hopkins University, Zanvyl Krieger School of Arts and Sciences, Advanced Academic Programs, Program in Liberal Arts, Baltimore, MD 21218-2699. Offers MA, Certificate. Part-time and evening/weekend programs available. *Faculty:* 1 (woman) full-time, 9 part-time/adjunct (3 women). *Students:* 2 full-time (0 women), 96 part-time (68 women); includes 20 minority (13 Black or African American, non-Hispanic/Latino; 3 Asian, non-Hispanic/Latino; 2 Hispanic/Latino; 2 Two or more races, non-Hispanic/Latino), 3 international. Average age 38. 38 applicants, 53% accepted, 16 enrolled. In 2010, 21 master's awarded. *Degree requirements:* For master's, thesis. *Entrance requirements:* Additional exam requirements/recommendations for international students: Required—TOEFL (minimum score 250 computer-based; 100 iBT). *Application deadline:* For fall admission, 5/31 priority date for domestic students, 4/30 priority date for international students; for spring admission, 10/31 priority date for domestic and international students. Applications are processed on a rolling basis. Application fee: $75. Electronic applications accepted. *Financial support:* Applicants required to submit FAFSA. *Unit head:* Dr. Melissa Hilbish, Associate Program Chair, 410-516-4640, E-mail: mhilbish@jhu.edu. *Application contact:* Valana M. McMickens, Admissions Manager, 202-452-1941, Fax: 202-452-1970, E-mail: aapadmissions@jhu.edu.

Kean University, College of Visual and Performing Arts, Program in Liberal Studies, Union, NJ 07083. Offers MA. Part-time and evening/weekend programs available. *Students:* 3 full-time (all women), 13 part-time (12 women); includes 3 Black or African American, non-Hispanic/Latino; 2 Asian, non-Hispanic/Latino; 2 Hispanic/Latino; 1 Two or more races, non-Hispanic/Latino, 1 international. Average age 40. 6 applicants, 100% accepted, 5 enrolled. In 2010, 5 master's awarded. *Degree requirements:* For master's, comprehensive exam. *Entrance requirements:* For master's, minimum GPA of 3.0, 3 letters of recommendation, interview, transcripts, autobiographical narrative. *Application deadline:* For fall admission, 6/1 for domestic students; for spring admission, 11/1 for domestic students. Application fee: $75 ($150 for international students). Electronic applications accepted. *Expenses:* Tuition, state resident: full-time $10,872; part-time $500 per credit. Tuition, nonresident: full-time $14,736; part-time $614 per credit. Required fees: $2740.80; $125 per credit. Part-time tuition and fees vary according to course load and degree level. *Financial support:* In 2010–11, 1 research assistantship with full tuition reimbursement (averaging $3,263 per year) was awarded; unspecified assistantships also available. Financial award applicants required to submit FAFSA. *Unit head:* Dr. C. Koros, Program Coordinator, 908-737-0388, E-mail: mals@kean.edu. *Application contact:* Steven Koch, Pre-Admissions Coordinator, 908-737-5924, Fax: 908-737-5925, E-mail: skoch@kean.edu.

Kent State University, College of Arts and Sciences, Program in Liberal Studies, Kent, OH 44242-0001. Offers MLS. Part-time programs available. *Degree requirements:* For master's, thesis. *Entrance requirements:* For master's, minimum GPA of 2.75. Electronic applications accepted. *Expenses:* Tuition, state resident: full-time $7866; part-time $437 per credit hour. Tuition, nonresident: full-time $14,022; part-time $779 per credit hour.

Lake Forest College, Graduate Program in Liberal Studies, Lake Forest, IL 60045. Offers MLS. Part-time and evening/weekend programs available. *Faculty:* 16 full-time (7 women). *Students:* 4 full-time (2 women), 41 part-time (22 women), 2 international. Average age 42. 26 applicants, 58% accepted, 12 enrolled. In 2010, 8 master's awarded. *Degree requirements:* For master's, thesis optional. *Entrance requirements:* For master's, interview. Additional exam requirements/recommendations for international students: Required—TOEFL (minimum score 550 paper-based). *Application deadline:* For fall admission, 7/1 priority date for domestic students, 6/1 priority date for international students; for winter admission, 12/15 priority date for domestic students, 10/1 priority date for international students. Applications are processed on a rolling basis. Application fee: $20. *Expenses:* Contact institution. *Financial support:* In 2010–11, 9 students received support. Partial tuition waivers for full-time teachers available. Financial award application deadline: 7/1. *Faculty research:* Latin American film, the European Left, solid state chemistry, cast iron architecture, concepts of education in nineteenth-century America. *Unit head:* Prof. D. L. LeMahieu, Director, 847-735-5133, Fax: 847-735-6291, E-mail: lemahieu@lakeforest.edu. *Application contact:* Prof. Carol Gayle, Associate Director, 847-735-5083, Fax: 847-735-6291, E-mail: gayle@lakeforest.edu.

Lock Haven University of Pennsylvania, Department of Liberal Arts, Lock Haven, PA 17745-2390. Offers MLA. *Degree requirements:* For master's, thesis. *Entrance requirements:* For master's, minimum undergraduate GPA of 3.0. Additional exam requirements/recommendations for international students: Required—TOEFL. Electronic applications accepted. *Expenses:* Tuition, state resident: full-time $9073; part-time $599.26 per credit. Tuition, nonresident: full-time $13,400; part-time $894.81 per credit. Tuition and fees vary according to program.

Louisiana State University and Agricultural and Mechanical College, Graduate School, College of Humanities and Social Sciences, Interdepartmental Program in the Liberal Arts, Baton Rouge, LA 70803. Offers MALA. Part-time and evening/weekend programs available. *Students:* 10 full-time (2 women), 13 part-time (2 women); includes 2 Black or African American,

Liberal Studies

Louisiana State University and Agricultural and Mechanical College (continued)
non-Hispanic/Latino. Average age 36. 14 applicants, 71% accepted, 1 enrolled. In 2010, 10 master's awarded. *Degree requirements:* For master's, project or thesis. *Entrance requirements:* For master's, GRE General Test, minimum GPA of 3.0. Additional exam requirements/recommendations for international students: Required—TOEFL (minimum score 550 paper-based; 213 computer-based; 79 iBT) or IELTS (minimum score 6.5). *Application deadline:* For fall admission, 1/25 priority date for domestic students, 5/15 for international students; for spring admission, 10/15 for international students. Applications are processed on a rolling basis. Application fee: $50 ($70 for international students). Electronic applications accepted. *Financial support:* Fellowships with full tuition reimbursements, research assistantships with partial tuition reimbursements, teaching assistantships with partial tuition reimbursements, Federal Work-Study and health care benefits available. Financial award applicants required to submit FAFSA. *Unit head:* Dr. William Clark, Director, 225-578-3183, Fax: 225-578-6447. *Application contact:* Dr. Robin Roberts, Associate Dean, 225-578-8273, Fax: 225-587-6447, E-mail: rrobert@lsu.edu.

Louisiana State University in Shreveport, College of Liberal Arts, Program in Liberal Arts, Shreveport, LA 71115-2399. Offers MA. Part-time and evening/weekend programs available. *Students:* 13 full-time (8 women), 43 part-time (28 women); includes 14 minority (11 Black or African American, non-Hispanic/Latino; 1 American Indian or Alaska Native, non-Hispanic/Latino; 2 Hispanic/Latino), 1 international. Average age 37. 22 applicants, 100% accepted, 15 enrolled. In 2010, 12 master's awarded. *Degree requirements:* For master's, comprehensive exam, thesis or alternative. *Entrance requirements:* For master's, interview, minimum GPA of 3.0 during final 2 years of course work, statement of purpose. Additional exam requirements/recommendations for international students: Required—TOEFL (minimum score 500 paper-based; 173 computer-based; 61 iBT). *Application deadline:* For fall admission, 6/30 for domestic and international students; for spring admission, 11/30 for domestic and international students. Applications are processed on a rolling basis. Application fee: $10 ($20 for international students). *Expenses:* Tuition, state resident: full-time $3272; part-time $181.80 per credit hour. Tuition, nonresident: full-time $7902; part-time $471.19 per credit hour. Required fees: $850; $47 per credit hour. *Financial support:* In 2010–11, 3 students received support, including 3 research assistantships with partial tuition reimbursements available (averaging $30,000 per year). *Unit head:* Dr. Helen Taylor, Program Director, 318-797-5211, Fax: 318-797-5358, E-mail: helen.taylor@lsus.edu. *Application contact:* Yvonne Yarbrough, Secretary, Graduate Studies, 318-797-5247, Fax: 318-798-4120, E-mail: yyarbrou@lsus.edu.

Loyola University Maryland, Graduate Programs, Loyola College of Arts and Sciences, Program in Liberal Studies, Baltimore, MD 21210-2699. Offers MMS. Part-time and evening/weekend programs available. *Entrance requirements:* For master's, GRE General Test, GRE Subject Test (recommended). Additional exam requirements/recommendations for international students: Required—TOEFL (minimum score 550 paper-based; 213 computer-based).

Madonna University, Program in Liberal Studies, Livonia, MI 48150-1173. Offers MALS.

Manhattanville College, Graduate Programs, Humanities and Social Sciences Programs, Program in Liberal Studies, Purchase, NY 10577-2132. Offers MA. Part-time and evening/weekend programs available. *Students:* 1 (woman) full-time, 7 part-time (5 women); includes 1 Black or African American, non-Hispanic/Latino. In 2010, 4 master's awarded. *Degree requirements:* For master's, thesis. *Entrance requirements:* For master's, interview, 2 letters of recommendation. Additional exam requirements/recommendations for international students: Required—TOEFL. *Application deadline:* Applications are processed on a rolling basis. Application fee: $75. *Expenses:* Tuition: Full-time $16,110; part-time $895 per credit. Required fees: $50 per semester. *Financial support:* Career-related internships or fieldwork, Federal Work-Study, institutionally sponsored loans, and unspecified assistantships available. Financial award applicants required to submit FAFSA. *Unit head:* Donald Richards, Interim Dean, School of Graduate and Professional Studies, 914-323-5469, Fax: 914-694-3488, E-mail: gps@mville.edu. *Application contact:* Office of Admissions for Graduate and Professional Studies, 914-323-5418, E-mail: gps@mville.edu.

McDaniel College, Graduate and Professional Studies, Program in Liberal Studies, Westminster, MD 21157-4390. Offers MLA. Part-time and evening/weekend programs available. *Degree requirements:* For master's, final project. *Entrance requirements:* For master's, letters of reference (3). Additional exam requirements/recommendations for international students: Required—TOEFL (minimum score 213 computer-based).

Metropolitan State University, College of Arts and Sciences, St. Paul, MN 55106-5000. Offers computer science (MS); liberal studies (MA); technical communication (MS). Part-time and evening/weekend programs available. *Students:* 38 full-time (16 women), 72 part-time (49 women); includes 4 Black or African American, non-Hispanic/Latino; 8 Asian, non-Hispanic/Latino; 3 Hispanic/Latino, 13 international. Average age 38. In 2010, 22 master's awarded. *Entrance requirements:* For master's, minimum GPA of 2.75, resume. Additional exam requirements/recommendations for international students: Required—TOEFL (minimum score 550 paper-based; 213 computer-based). *Application deadline:* For fall admission, 8/1 priority date for domestic students, 3/15 for international students; for winter admission, 10/15 for international students; for spring admission, 12/1 priority date for domestic students, 3/15 for international students. Applications are processed on a rolling basis. Application fee: $20. Electronic applications accepted. *Expenses:* Tuition, state resident: full-time $5827; part-time $291 per credit hour. Tuition, nonresident: full-time $11,654; part-time $583 per credit hour. Required fees: $10 per credit hour. Tuition and fees vary according to degree level. *Financial support:* Research assistantships available. Financial award applicants required to submit FAFSA. *Unit head:* Dr. Becky Omdahl, Dean, 651-793-1443, Fax: 651-793-1446, E-mail: becky.omdahl@metrostate.edu. *Application contact:* Lucille Maghrak, Graduate Studies Coordinator, 651-793-1932, E-mail: lucille.maghrak@metrostate.edu.

Minnesota State University Moorhead, Graduate Studies, College of Arts and Humanities, Program in Liberal Studies, Moorhead, MN 56563-0002. Offers MLA. Part-time and evening/weekend programs available. *Degree requirements:* For master's, thesis, final oral exam. *Entrance requirements:* For master's, minimum GPA of 2.75. Additional exam requirements/recommendations for international students: Required—TOEFL (minimum score 570 paper-based; 230 computer-based). Electronic applications accepted.

Mississippi College, Graduate School, Program in Liberal Studies, Clinton, MS 39058. Offers MLS. Part-time programs available. *Degree requirements:* For master's, comprehensive exam, thesis optional. *Entrance requirements:* For master's, GRE, minimum GPA of 2.5. Additional exam requirements/recommendations for international students: Recommended—IELTS.

Monmouth University, The Graduate School, Program in Liberal Arts, West Long Branch, NJ 07764-1898. Offers MA. Part-time and evening/weekend programs available. *Faculty:* 2 full-time (1 woman), 1 (woman) part-time/adjunct. *Students:* 5 full-time (0 women), 9 part-time (8 women); includes 2 Black or African American, non-Hispanic/Latino. Average age 35. 7 applicants, 100% accepted, 5 enrolled. *Degree requirements:* For master's, thesis or alternative, project. *Entrance requirements:* For master's, minimum GPA of 3.0 in major, 2.5 overall. Additional exam requirements/recommendations for international students: Required—TOEFL (minimum score 550 paper-based; 213 computer-based; 79 iBT), IELTS (minimum score 5) or Michigan English Language Assessment Battery (minimum score 77), Cambridge A, B, C. *Application deadline:* For fall admission, 7/15 priority date for domestic students, 6/1 for international students; for spring admission, 11/15 priority date for domestic students, 11/1 for international students. Applications are processed on a rolling basis. Application fee: $50. Electronic applications accepted. *Expenses:* Tuition: Full-time $19,572; part-time $816 per credit. Required fees: $628; $157 per semester. *Financial support:* In 2010–11, 3 students received support, including 3 fellowships (averaging $667 per year); research assistantships,

career-related internships or fieldwork, scholarships/grants, and unspecified assistantships also available. Support available to part-time students. Financial award applicants required to submit FAFSA. *Faculty research:* Labor history, war and society, technology, historical archeology, art and society. *Unit head:* Dr. Aaron Ansell, Director, 732-263-5451, Fax: 732-263-5192, E-mail: aansell@monmouth.edu. *Application contact:* Kevin Roane, Director, Office of Graduate Admission, 732-571-3452, Fax: 732-263-5123, E-mail: gradadm@monmouth.edu.

Nazareth College of Rochester, Graduate Studies, Department of Liberal Studies, Rochester, NY 14618-3790. Offers MA. *Entrance requirements:* For master's, minimum GPA of 3.0.

The New School: A University, The New School for Social Research, Department in Liberal Studies, New York, NY 10003. Offers MA. Part-time and evening/weekend programs available. *Degree requirements:* For master's, thesis. *Entrance requirements:* For master's, GRE General Test. Additional exam requirements/recommendations for international students: Required—TOEFL (minimum score 600 paper-based; 250 computer-based; 100 iBT). Electronic applications accepted.

North Carolina State University, Graduate School, College of Humanities and Social Sciences, Program in Liberal Studies, Raleigh, NC 27695. Offers MA. Part-time and evening/weekend programs available. *Degree requirements:* For master's, thesis optional. Electronic applications accepted. *Faculty research:* Humanities, social sciences, sciences.

North Central College, Graduate and Continuing Education Programs, Program in Liberal Studies, Naperville, IL 60566-7063. Offers MALS. Part-time and evening/weekend programs available. *Faculty:* 6 full-time (2 women), 4 part-time/adjunct (0 women). *Students:* 5 full-time (all women), 7 part-time (5 women). Average age 32. In 2010, 7 master's awarded. *Degree requirements:* For master's, thesis optional, project. *Entrance requirements:* For master's, interview. Additional exam requirements/recommendations for international students: Required—TOEFL (minimum score 577 paper-based; 233 computer-based; 90 iBT). *Application deadline:* For fall admission, 8/15 for domestic students; for winter admission, 12/1 for domestic students; for spring admission, 2/1 for domestic students. Applications are processed on a rolling basis. Application fee: $25. *Expenses:* Contact institution. *Financial support:* Scholarships/grants available. Support available to part-time students. *Unit head:* Dr. Richard Guzman, Program Coordinator, 630-637-5285. *Application contact:* Wendy Kulpinski, Director and Graduate and Continuing Education Admissions, 630-637-5808, Fax: 630-637-5844, E-mail: wekulpinski@noctrl.edu.

Northern Arizona University, Graduate College, College of Social and Behavioral Sciences, Program in Sustainable Communities, Flagstaff, AZ 86011. Offers MA. Part-time programs available. *Faculty:* 1 (woman) full-time. *Students:* 43 full-time (29 women), 18 part-time (15 women); includes 8 minority (3 American Indian or Alaska Native, non-Hispanic/Latino; 1 Asian, non-Hispanic/Latino; 4 Hispanic/Latino). Average age 40. 38 applicants, 66% accepted, 19 enrolled. In 2010, 11 master's awarded. *Degree requirements:* For master's, thesis. *Entrance requirements:* For master's, minimum GPA of 3.0. Additional exam requirements/recommendations for international students: Required—TOEFL (minimum score 550 paper-based; 213 computer-based; 80 iBT), IELTS (minimum score 7). *Application deadline:* For fall admission, 3/15 priority date for domestic and international students. Applications are processed on a rolling basis. Application fee: $65. Electronic applications accepted. *Financial support:* Federal Work-Study, scholarships/grants, health care benefits, tuition waivers (full and partial), and unspecified assistantships available. Support available to part-time students. Financial award applicants required to submit FAFSA. *Unit head:* Dr. Luis Fernandez, Director, 928-523-2382, Fax: 928-523-2020, E-mail: luis.fernandez@nau.edu. *Application contact:* Tamara Ramirez, Program Coordinator, 928-523-0499, Fax: 928-523-2020, E-mail: sustainable.communities@nau.edu.

Northern Kentucky University, Office of Graduate Programs, College of Arts and Sciences, Program in Integrative Studies, Highland Heights, KY 41099. Offers civic engagement (Certificate); integrative studies (MA). Part-time and evening/weekend programs available. Postbaccalaureate distance learning degree programs offered (no on-campus study). *Students:* 9 full-time (4 women), 36 part-time (27 women); includes 8 minority (6 Black or African American, non-Hispanic/Latino; 1 American Indian or Alaska Native, non-Hispanic/Latino; 1 Asian, non-Hispanic/Latino), 2 international. Average age 36. 35 applicants, 60% accepted, 15 enrolled. In 2010, 16 master's awarded. *Degree requirements:* For master's, thesis optional, capstone. *Entrance requirements:* For master's, minimum GPA of 3.0, resume, 2 letters of recommendation, 1 letter of intent. Additional exam requirements/recommendations for international students: Required—TOEFL (minimum score 550 paper-based; 213 computer-based; 79 iBT); Recommended—IELTS (minimum score 6.5). *Application deadline:* For fall admission, 8/1 for domestic students, 6/1 for international students; for spring admission, 12/1 for domestic students, 10/1 for international students. Applications are processed on a rolling basis. Application fee: $40. Electronic applications accepted. *Expenses:* Tuition, state resident: full-time $7254; part-time $403 per credit hour. Tuition, nonresident: full-time $12,492; part-time $694 per credit hour. Tuition and fees vary according to degree level and program. *Financial support:* Unspecified assistantships available. Financial award applicants required to submit FAFSA. *Faculty research:* Medieval literature, general education and assessment. *Unit head:* Dr. Bill Attenweiler, Director, 859-572-5831, E-mail: attenweilerb@nku.edu. *Application contact:* Dr. Peg Griffin, Director of Graduate Programs, 859-572-6934, Fax: 859-572-6670, E-mail: griffinp@nku.edu.

Northwestern University, The Graduate School, Interdepartmental Programs, Interdisciplinary Program in Liberal Studies, Evanston, IL 60208. Offers MA. Admissions and degree offered through The Graduate School. Part-time and evening/weekend programs available. *Degree requirements:* For master's, thesis. *Entrance requirements:* For master's, writing sample. Additional exam requirements/recommendations for international students: Required—TOEFL. *Faculty research:* Urban and social history, literary criticism and comparative literature, women's studies, media and film criticism, philosophy.

Northwestern University, School of Continuing Studies, Program in Liberal Studies, Evanston, IL 60208. Offers American studies (MA); history (MA); religious and ethical studies (MA).

Oakland University, Graduate Study and Lifelong Learning, College of Arts and Sciences, Program in Liberal Studies, Rochester, MI 48309-4401. Offers MA. *Entrance requirements:* For master's, minimum GPA of 3.0 for unconditional admission. Additional exam requirements/recommendations for international students: Required—TOEFL (minimum score 550 paper-based; 213 computer-based). Electronic applications accepted.

Occidental College, Graduate Studies, Department of Education, Program in Elementary Education, Los Angeles, CA 90041-3314. Offers liberal studies (MAT). Part-time programs available. *Degree requirements:* For master's, comprehensive exam, graduate synthesis paper. *Entrance requirements:* For master's, GRE General Test, minimum GPA of 3.0. Additional exam requirements/recommendations for international students: Required—TOEFL (minimum score 625 paper-based; 263 computer-based). *Expenses:* Contact institution.

Ohio Dominican University, Graduate Programs, Program in Liberal Studies, Columbus, OH 43219-2099. Offers MA. Part-time and evening/weekend programs available. *Students:* 5 full-time (3 women), 16 part-time (11 women); includes 4 minority (3 Black or African American, non-Hispanic/Latino; 1 Hispanic/Latino). Average age 37. In 2010, 4 master's awarded. *Degree requirements:* For master's, comprehensive exam or thesis. *Entrance requirements:* For master's, minimum undergraduate GPA of 3.0, 3 letters of recommendation. Additional exam requirements/recommendations for international students: Required—TOEFL (minimum score 550 paper-based; 213 computer-based), IELTS (minimum score 6.5). *Application deadline:* For fall admission, 7/15 priority date for domestic students, 7/18 priority date for international students; for spring admission, 12/18 priority date for domestic and international students. Applications are processed on a rolling basis. Application fee: $25. *Expenses:* Tuition: Part-time $485 per credit hour. *Financial support:* Applicants required to submit FAFSA. *Unit head:* Dr. Ronald Carstens, Director, 614-251-4663, E-mail: carstenr@ohiodominican.edu. *Application contact:*

Jill M. Westerfeld, Assistant Director Graduate Admissions, 614-251-4725, Fax: 614-251-6654, E-mail: westerfj@ohiodominican.edu.

Oklahoma City University, Petree College of Arts and Sciences, Program in Liberal Arts, Oklahoma City, OK 73106-1402. Offers art (MLA); general studies (MLA); leadership/management (MLA); literature (MLA); mass communications (MLA); philosophy (MLA); writing (MLA). Part-time and evening/weekend programs available. *Degree requirements:* For master's, comprehensive exam, thesis optional. *Entrance requirements:* Additional exam requirements/recommendations for international students: Required—TOEFL (minimum score 550 paper-based).

Queens College of the City University of New York, Division of Graduate Studies, Social Science Division, Program in Liberal Studies, Flushing, NY 11367-1597. Offers MALS. Part-time and evening/weekend programs available. *Faculty:* 4 full-time (0 women). *Students:* 23 part-time (13 women); includes 7 Black or African American, non-Hispanic/Latino; 3 Hispanic/Latino. 23 applicants, 48% accepted, 7 enrolled. *Degree requirements:* For master's, thesis. *Entrance requirements:* For master's, minimum GPA of 3.0. Additional exam requirements/recommendations for international students: Required—TOEFL. *Application deadline:* For fall admission, 4/1 for domestic students; for spring admission, 11/1 for domestic students. Applications are processed on a rolling basis. Application fee: $125. *Financial support:* Career-related internships or fieldwork, Federal Work-Study, institutionally sponsored loans, and tuition waivers (partial) available. Support available to part-time students. Financial award application deadline: 4/1; financial award applicants required to submit FAFSA. *Unit head:* Dr. Nick Jordan, Graduate Adviser, 718-997-5350. *Application contact:* Mario Caruso, Director of Graduate Admissions, 718-997-5200, Fax: 718-997-5193, E-mail: graduate_admissions@qc.edu.

Ramapo College of New Jersey, Master of Arts in Liberal Studies Program, Mahwah, NJ 07430. Offers MALS. Part-time and evening/weekend programs available. *Faculty:* 5 part-time/adjunct (4 women). *Students:* 29 part-time (16 women); includes 7 minority (4 Black or African American, non-Hispanic/Latino; 3 Hispanic/Latino). Average age 40. 5 applicants, 100% accepted, 4 enrolled. In 2010, 7 master's awarded. *Degree requirements:* For master's, thesis. *Entrance requirements:* For master's, minimum undergraduate GPA of 3.0, 2 letters of recommendation. Additional exam requirements/recommendations for international students: Required—TOEFL (minimum score 550 paper-based; 213 computer-based; 90 iBT). *Application deadline:* For fall admission, 9/1 priority date for domestic and international students; for spring admission, 1/30 priority date for domestic and international students. Applications are processed on a rolling basis. Application fee: $60. Electronic applications accepted. *Expenses:* Tuition, state resident: part-time $525.30 per credit. Tuition, nonresident: part-time $675.20 per credit. Required fees: $107.70 per credit. *Financial support:* Tuition waivers (full) available. Financial award applicants required to submit FAFSA. *Faculty research:* History of science, women's studies, Native American studies, theology, genocide studies. *Unit head:* Dr. Anthony T. Padovano, Director, 201-684-7430, Fax: 201-684-7973, E-mail: apadovan@ramapo.edu. *Application contact:* Melissa C. Kupfer, MALS Secretary, 201-684-7709, Fax: 201-684-7973, E-mail: mkupfer@ramapo.edu.

Reed College, Graduate Program in Liberal Studies, Portland, OR 97202-8199. Offers MALS. Part-time and evening/weekend programs available. *Faculty:* 14 part-time/adjunct (6 women). *Students:* 36 part-time (20 women); includes 2 Asian, non-Hispanic/Latino; 1 Hispanic/Latino. Average age 40. 12 applicants, 58% accepted, 4 enrolled. In 2010, 5 master's awarded. *Degree requirements:* For master's, thesis, oral defense of thesis. *Entrance requirements:* For master's, interview, letters of recommendation. *Application deadline:* For fall admission, 7/1 priority date for domestic students; for spring admission, 12/1 priority date for domestic students. Applications are processed on a rolling basis. Application fee: $60. *Expenses:* Tuition: Part-time $3710 per unit. Part-time tuition and fees vary according to course load. *Financial support:* In 2010–11, 7 students received support. Scholarships/grants, health care benefits, and institutional scholarship available. Support available to part-time students. Financial award application deadline: 5/1; financial award applicants required to submit CSS PROFILE or FAFSA. *Unit head:* Barbara A. Amen, Director, Graduate Studies, 503-777-7259, Fax: 503-517-7345, E-mail: bamen@reed.edu. *Application contact:* Barbara A. Amen, Director, Graduate Studies, 503-777-7259, Fax: 503-517-7345, E-mail: bamen@reed.edu.

Rice University, Graduate Programs, Susanne M. Glasscock School of Continuing Studies, Houston, TX 77251-1892. Offers MLS. Part-time and evening/weekend programs available. *Degree requirements:* For master's, thesis or alternative, capstone paper/project. *Entrance requirements:* For master's, bachelor's degree from accredited institution; minimum GPA of 3.0; two letters of recommendation; personal statement; 3 writing samples; current resume. Additional exam requirements/recommendations for international students: Required—TOEFL (minimum score 600 paper-based; 250 computer-based; 90 iBT). *Expenses:* Contact institution.

Rollins College, Hamilton Holt School, Program in Liberal Studies, Winter Park, FL 32789. Offers MLS. Part-time and evening/weekend programs available. *Faculty:* 10 full-time (5 women), 4 part-time/adjunct (3 women). *Students:* 4 full-time (2 women), 80 part-time (56 women); includes 13 minority (3 Black or African American, non-Hispanic/Latino; 2 Asian, non-Hispanic/Latino; 8 Hispanic/Latino), 2 international. Average age 39. 58 applicants, 81% accepted, 25 enrolled. In 2010, 18 master's awarded. *Degree requirements:* For master's, thesis. *Entrance requirements:* For master's, interview. Additional exam requirements/recommendations for international students: Required—TOEFL (minimum score 550 paper-based; 213 computer-based; 80 iBT). *Application deadline:* For fall admission, 4/1 for domestic students; for spring admission, 12/1 for domestic students. Application fee: $50. *Expenses:* Contact institution. *Financial support:* In 2010–11, 31 students received support. Career-related internships or fieldwork, scholarships/grants, and unspecified assistantships available. Support available to part-time students. Financial award applicants required to submit FAFSA. *Unit head:* Dr. Patricia Lancaster, Director, 407-646-2237, Fax: 407-646-2363. *Application contact:* Christian Ricaurte, Coordinator of Records and Registration, 407-646-2653, Fax: 407-646-1551, E-mail: cricaurte@rollins.edu.

Rutgers, The State University of New Jersey, Camden, Graduate School of Arts and Sciences, Program in Liberal Studies, Camden, NJ 08102. Offers MALS. Part-time and evening/weekend programs available. *Faculty:* 41 full-time (15 women), 2 part-time/adjunct (both women). *Students:* 5 full-time (1 woman), 32 part-time (21 women); includes 8 Black or African American, non-Hispanic/Latino; 2 Hispanic/Latino. Average age 33. 47 applicants, 72% accepted, 16 enrolled. In 2010, 4 master's awarded. *Degree requirements:* For master's, thesis, 30 credits. *Entrance requirements:* For master's, 2 letters of recommendation, writing sample, statement of personal, professional and academic goals. Additional exam requirements/recommendations for international students: Required—TOEFL, IELTS. *Application deadline:* For fall admission, 3/1 priority date for domestic students; for spring admission, 12/1 priority date for domestic students. Applications are processed on a rolling basis. Application fee: $65. Electronic applications accepted. *Expenses:* Tuition, state resident: full-time $4963; part-time $319 per credit. Tuition, nonresident: full-time $10,493; part-time $680 per credit. *Financial support:* In 2010–11, 27 students received support, including 9 fellowships with partial tuition reimbursements available (averaging $555 per year); Federal Work-Study, scholarships/grants, and tuition waivers (partial) also available. Financial award application deadline: 3/15; financial award applicants required to submit FAFSA. *Faculty research:* Psychology, English, history, philosophy, religion. *Unit head:* Dr. Stuart Charme, Director, 856-225-6700, Fax: 856-225-6602, E-mail: scharme@camden.rutgers.edu. *Application contact:* 856-225-6700, E-mail: gradlibs@camden.rutgers.edu.

St. Edward's University, New College, Program in Liberal Arts, Austin, TX 78704. Offers global issues (MLA); humanities (MLA); liberal arts (Certificate); social sciences (MLA). Part-time and evening/weekend programs available. *Students:* 6 full-time (5 women), 80 part-time (54 women); includes 28 minority (6 Black or African American, non-Hispanic/Latino; 2 Asian, non-Hispanic/Latino; 19 Hispanic/Latino; 1 Two or more races, non-Hispanic/Latino), 1 international. Average age 34. 47 applicants, 68% accepted, 24 enrolled. In 2010, 29 master's awarded. *Degree requirements:* For master's, minimum of 24 resident hours. *Entrance*

requirements: For master's, minimum GPA of 2.75 in last 60 hours of course work, interview. Additional exam requirements/recommendations for international students: Required—TOEFL (minimum score 550 paper-based; 213 computer-based; 79 iBT) or IELTS (minimum score 6). *Application deadline:* For fall admission, 7/1 for domestic and international students; for spring admission, 11/1 for domestic and international students. Applications are processed on a rolling basis. Application fee: $45 ($50 for international students). Electronic applications accepted. *Expenses:* Tuition: Full-time $16,200; part-time $900 per credit hour. Required fees: $50 per trimester. Full-time tuition and fees vary according to course load and program. *Financial support:* In 2010–11, 2 students received support. Scholarships/grants available. *Unit head:* Dr. H. Ramsey Fowler, Director, 512-448-8648, Fax: 512-448-8492, E-mail: ramseyf@stewards.edu. *Application contact:* Carrie Martin, Graduate Admission Coordinator, 512-233-1694, Fax: 512-428-1032, E-mail: carriem@stedwards.edu.

St. Edward's University, School of Education, Program in Teaching, Austin, TX 78704. Offers curriculum leadership (Certificate); instructional technology (Certificate); mediation (Certificate); mentoring and supervision (Certificate); special education (Certificate); sports management (Certificate); teaching (MA), including conflict resolution, initial teacher certification, liberal arts, special education, sports management, teacher leadership. Part-time and evening/weekend programs available. *Students:* 7 full-time (6 women), 38 part-time (28 women); includes 13 minority (2 Black or African American, non-Hispanic/Latino; 10 Hispanic/Latino; 1 Two or more races, non-Hispanic/Latino). Average age 29. 25 applicants, 80% accepted, 17 enrolled. In 2010, 14 master's awarded. *Degree requirements:* For master's, minimum of 24 resident hours. *Entrance requirements:* For master's, GRE General Test, minimum GPA of 3.0 in last 60 hours or 2.75 overall. Additional exam requirements/recommendations for international students: Required—TOEFL (minimum score 550 paper-based; 213 computer-based; 79 iBT) or IELTS (minimum score 6). *Application deadline:* For fall admission, 7/1 for domestic and international students; for spring admission, 11/1 for domestic and international students. Applications are processed on a rolling basis. Application fee: $45 ($50 for international students). Electronic applications accepted. *Expenses:* Tuition: Full-time $16,200; part-time $900 per credit hour. Required fees: $50 per trimester. Full-time tuition and fees vary according to course load and program. *Financial support:* In 2010–11, 4 students received support. Scholarships/grants available. *Faculty research:* Assessment, school change and improvement, program change, curriculum evaluation in schools. *Unit head:* Dr. David Hollier, Director, 512-448-8666, Fax: 512-428-1372, E-mail: davidrh@stedwards.edu. *Application contact:* Carrie Martin, Graduate Admission Coordinator, 512-233-1694, Fax: 512-428-1032, E-mail: carriem@stedwards.edu.

St. John's College, Graduate Institute in Liberal Education, Annapolis, MD 21404. Offers liberal arts (MALA). Evening/weekend programs available. *Degree requirements:* For master's, thesis optional. *Entrance requirements:* Additional exam requirements/recommendations for international students: Required—TOEFL (minimum score 650 paper-based; 250 computer-based; 112 iBT), TWE (minimum score 5).

St. John's College, Graduate Institute in Liberal Education, Program in Liberal Arts, Santa Fe, NM 87505. Offers MA. Evening/weekend programs available. *Entrance requirements:* For master's, 2 letters of recommendation. Additional exam requirements/recommendations for international students: Required—TOEFL, TWE.

St. John's University, St. John's College of Liberal Arts and Sciences, Program in Liberal Studies, Queens, NY 11439. Offers MA. Part-time and evening/weekend programs available. *Students:* 3 full-time (1 woman), 11 part-time (9 women); includes 6 minority (3 Black or African American, non-Hispanic/Latino; 3 Hispanic/Latino), 1 international. Average age 38. 18 applicants, 67% accepted, 6 enrolled. In 2010, 23 master's awarded. *Degree requirements:* For master's, capstone project. *Entrance requirements:* For master's, minimum GPA of 3.0, personal essay, 2 letters of recommendation, 6 credit hours in area of concentration. Additional exam requirements/recommendations for international students: Required—TOEFL (minimum score 600 paper-based; 250 computer-based; 100 iBT), IELTS (minimum score 5.5). *Application deadline:* For fall admission, 5/1 priority date for domestic and international students; for spring admission, 11/1 priority date for domestic and international students. Applications are processed on a rolling basis. Application fee: $70. Electronic applications accepted. *Expenses:* Tuition: Full-time $17,100; part-time $950 per credit. Required fees: $340; $170 per semester. Tuition and fees vary according to program. *Financial support:* Career-related internships or fieldwork and scholarships/grants available. Support available to part-time students. *Unit head:* Fr. Jean-Pierre Ruiz, Director, 718-990-6467, E-mail: ruizj@stjohns.edu. *Application contact:* Kathleen Davis, Director of Graduate Admission, 718-990-1601, Fax: 718-990-5686, E-mail: gradhelp@stjohns.edu.

St. Norbert College, Program in Liberal Studies, De Pere, WI 54115-2099. Offers MA. Part-time programs available. *Faculty:* 5 part-time/adjunct (1 woman). *Students:* 21 part-time (12 women); includes 1 American Indian or Alaska Native, non-Hispanic/Latino; 2 Hispanic/Latino. Average age 33. 5 applicants, 100% accepted, 5 enrolled. *Degree requirements:* For master's, thesis. *Application deadline:* Applications are processed on a rolling basis. Application fee: $50. Electronic applications accepted. *Expenses:* Tuition: Part-time $390 per credit hour. *Unit head:* Dr. Howard Ebert, Director, 920-403-3956, Fax: 920-403-4086, E-mail: howard.ebert@snc.edu. *Application contact:* Program Coordinator, 920-403-3155, Fax: 920-403-4086, E-mail: deette.radant@snc.edu.

San Diego State University, Graduate and Research Affairs, College of Arts and Letters, Program in Liberal Arts and Sciences, San Diego, CA 92182. Offers MA. Part-time and evening/weekend programs available. *Degree requirements:* For master's, thesis. *Entrance requirements:* For master's, GRE General Test. Additional exam requirements/recommendations for international students: Required—TOEFL. Electronic applications accepted.

Simon Fraser University, Graduate Studies, Faculty of Arts and Social Sciences, Program in Liberal Studies, Burnaby, BC V5A 1S6, Canada. Offers MALS. Part-time and evening/weekend programs available. *Degree requirements:* For master's, thesis or alternative. *Entrance requirements:* For master's, minimum GPA of 3.0. Additional exam requirements/recommendations for international students: Required—TOEFL or IELTS. *Faculty research:* Humanities, psychology, history, women's studies, English.

Skidmore College, Liberal Studies Program, Saratoga Springs, NY 12866. Offers MA. Part-time programs available. Postbaccalaureate distance learning degree programs offered (minimal on-campus study). *Degree requirements:* For master's, thesis. Electronic applications accepted.

Southern Methodist University, Annette Caldwell Simmons School of Education and Human Development, Program in Liberal Studies, Dallas, TX 75275. Offers MLS. *Faculty:* 15 part-time/adjunct (8 women). *Students:* 11 full-time (5 women), 204 part-time (150 women); includes 25 Black or African American, non-Hispanic/Latino; 3 American Indian or Alaska Native, non-Hispanic/Latino; 6 Asian, non-Hispanic/Latino; 15 Hispanic/Latino, 3 international. Average age 41. *Unit head:* Dr. David J. Chard, Dean, 214-768-7587, Fax: 214-768-1797. *Application contact:* Associate Vice President for Research and Dean of Graduate Studies.

Spring Hill College, Graduate Programs, Program in Liberal Arts, Mobile, AL 36608-1791. Offers fine arts (MLA); history and social science (MLA); leadership and ethics (MLA); literature (MLA). Part-time and evening/weekend programs available. *Faculty:* 5 full-time (2 women), 2 part-time/adjunct (1 woman). *Students:* 3 full-time (2 women), 31 part-time (19 women); includes 10 minority (9 Black or African American, non-Hispanic/Latino; 1 Hispanic/Latino). Average age 37. In 2010, 12 master's awarded. *Degree requirements:* For master's, capstone course, completion of program within 6 years of initial admittance. *Entrance requirements:* For master's, bachelor's degree with minimum undergraduate GPA of 3.0 or graduate/professional degree. Additional exam requirements/recommendations for international students: Required—TOEFL (minimum score 550 paper-based; 213 computer-based; 80 iBT), IELTS (minimum score 6.5), CPE or CAE (score: C), MELAB (score: 90). *Application deadline:* For fall admission, 8/1 priority date for domestic and international students; for spring admission, 12/1 priority date for domestic and international students. Applications are processed on a rolling basis. Application

Liberal Studies

Spring Hill College (continued)
fee: $25 ($35 for international students). Electronic applications accepted. *Expenses:* Contact institution. *Financial support:* Applicants required to submit FAFSA. *Unit head:* Dr. Alexander R. Landi, Director, 251-380-3056, Fax: 251-460-2115, E-mail: landi@shc.edu. *Application contact:* Donna B. Tarasavage, Director of Admissions, Graduate and Continuing Studies, 251-380-3067, Fax: 251-460-2190, E-mail: dtarasavage@shc.edu.

State University of New York at Plattsburgh, School of Business and Economics, Program in Liberal Studies, Plattsburgh, NY 12901-2681. Offers MA. Part-time and evening/weekend programs available. *Degree requirements:* For master's, thesis. *Entrance requirements:* For master's, GRE, GMAT, or MAT. Additional exam requirements/recommendations for international students: Required—TOEFL (minimum score 550 paper-based; 213 computer-based; 79 iBT).

State University of New York Empire State College, Graduate Studies, Program in Liberal Studies, Saratoga Springs, NY 12866-4391. Offers MA. Part-time and evening/weekend programs available. Postbaccalaureate distance learning degree programs offered (minimal on-campus study). *Degree requirements:* For master's, thesis. *Entrance requirements:* Additional exam requirements/recommendations for international students: Required—TOEFL (minimum score 600 paper-based; 250 computer-based). Electronic applications accepted.

Stony Brook University, State University of New York, School of Professional Development, Stony Brook, NY 11794. Offers biology-grade 7-12 (MAT); chemistry-grade 7-12 (MAT); coaching (Graduate Certificate); coaching online (Graduate Certificate); computer integrated engineering (Graduate Certificate); earth science-grade 7-12 (MAT); educational computing (Graduate Certificate); educational leadership (Advanced Certificate); English-grade 7-12 (MAT); environmental management (Graduate Certificate); environmental/occupational health and safety (Graduate Certificate); French-grade 7-12 (MAT); German-grade 7-12 (MAT); human resource management (Graduate Certificate); human resource management online (Graduate Certificate); information systems management (Graduate Certificate); Italian-grade 7-12 (MAT); liberal studies (MA); liberal studies online (MAT); mathematics-grade 7-12 (MAT); operation research (Graduate Certificate); physics-grade 7-12 (MAT); professional studies online (MPS); school administration and supervision (Graduate Certificate); school building leadership (Graduate Certificate); school district administration (Graduate Certificate); school district business leadership (Advanced Certificate); school district leadership (Graduate Certificate); social science and the professions (MPS), including environmental waste management, human resource management; social studies-grade 7-12 (MAT); Spanish-grade 7-12 (MAT); waste management (Graduate Certificate). Part-time and evening/weekend programs available. Postbaccalaureate distance learning degree programs offered. *Faculty:* 25 full-time (10 women), 105 part-time/adjunct (40 women). *Students:* 360 full-time (228 women), 1,097 part-time (729 women); includes 180 minority (65 Black or African American, non-Hispanic/Latino; 2 American Indian or Alaska Native, non-Hispanic/Latino; 30 Asian, non-Hispanic/Latino; 81 Hispanic/Latino; 1 Native Hawaiian or other Pacific Islander, non-Hispanic/Latino; 1 Two or more races, non-Hispanic/Latino), 10 international. Average age 28. In 2010, 505 master's, 187 other advanced degrees awarded. *Degree requirements:* For master's, one foreign language, thesis or alternative. *Application deadline:* Applications are processed on a rolling basis. Application fee: $100. *Expenses:* Tuition, state resident: full-time $8370; part-time $349 per credit. Tuition, nonresident: full-time $13,780; part-time $574 per credit. Required fees: $994. *Financial support:* In 2010–11, 1 teaching assistantship was awarded; fellowships, research assistantships, career-related internships or fieldwork also available. Support available to part-time students. *Unit head:* Dr. Paul J. Edelson, Dean, 631-632-7052, Fax: 631-632-9046, E-mail: paul.edelson@stonybrook.edu. *Application contact:* Dr. Paul J. Edelson, Dean, 631-632-7052, Fax: 631-632-9046, E-mail: paul.edelson@stonybrook.edu.

Tarleton State University, College of Graduate Studies, Program in Liberal Studies, Stephenville, TX 76402. Offers MS. Part-time and evening/weekend programs available. *Entrance requirements:* Additional exam requirements/recommendations for international students: Required—TOEFL (minimum score 550 paper-based; 213 computer-based; 80 iBT). Electronic applications accepted.

Temple University, College of Liberal Arts, Program in Liberal Arts, Philadelphia, PA 19122-6096. Offers MLA. Part-time and evening/weekend programs available. *Students:* 7 full-time (5 women), 39 part-time (23 women); includes 13 Black or African American, non-Hispanic/Latino; 1 American Indian or Alaska Native, non-Hispanic/Latino; 4 Hispanic/Latino. 35 applicants, 63% accepted, 15 enrolled. In 2010, 7 master's awarded. *Degree requirements:* For master's, thesis, qualifying paper. *Entrance requirements:* Additional exam requirements/recommendations for international students: Required—TOEFL (minimum score 550 paper-based; 213 computer-based; 79 iBT). *Application deadline:* For fall admission, 7/15 for domestic students, 12/15 for international students; for spring admission, 11/15 for domestic students, 8/1 for international students. Applications are processed on a rolling basis. Application fee: $50. Electronic applications accepted. *Financial support:* Career-related internships or fieldwork, Federal Work-Study, and institutionally sponsored loans available. *Unit head:* Dr. Jayne K. Drake, Director, 215-204-1644, Fax: 215-204-9611, E-mail: mla@temple.edu. *Application contact:* Dr. Jayne K. Drake, Director, 215-204-1644, Fax: 215-204-9611, E-mail: mla@temple.edu.

Texas Christian University, Graduate Studies, Fort Worth, TX 76129-0002. Offers MLA. Part-time and evening/weekend programs available. Postbaccalaureate distance learning degree programs offered (no on-campus study). *Entrance requirements:* Additional exam requirements/recommendations for international students: Required—TOEFL (minimum score 550 paper-based; 213 computer-based; 80 iBT). *Application deadline:* For fall admission, 8/1 for domestic students; for spring admission, 1/1 for domestic students. Applications are processed on a rolling basis. Application fee: $50. *Expenses:* Tuition: Full-time $18,720; part-time $1040 per credit hour. Tuition and fees vary according to course load and program. *Financial support:* Applicants required to submit FAFSA. *Unit head:* Dr. Bonnie Melhart, Associate Provost for Academic Affairs, 817-257-7104, E-mail: b.melhart@tcu.edu. *Application contact:* Anita Unger, Graduate Program Coordinator, 817-257-7515, E-mail: a.unger@tcu.edu.

Thomas Edison State College, Heavin School of Arts and Sciences, Program in Liberal Studies, Trenton, NJ 08608-1176. Offers MALS. Part-time programs available. Postbaccalaureate distance learning degree programs offered (no on-campus study). *Students:* 87 part-time (60 women); includes 22 Black or African American, non-Hispanic/Latino; 1 American Indian or Alaska Native, non-Hispanic/Latino; 4 Asian, non-Hispanic/Latino; 5 Hispanic/Latino, 1 international. Average age 42. In 2010, 16 master's awarded. *Degree requirements:* For master's, final project. *Entrance requirements:* For master's, bachelor's degree from a regionally-accredited college or university; minimum 2 letters of recommendation; 3-5 years of related working experience; current resume. Additional exam requirements/recommendations for international students: Required—TOEFL (minimum score 550 paper-based; 213 computer-based; 79 iBT). *Application deadline:* For fall admission, 8/15 priority date for domestic and international students; for winter admission, 11/15 priority date for domestic and international students; for spring admission, 2/15 priority date for domestic and international students. Applications are processed on a rolling basis. Application fee: $75. Electronic applications accepted. *Financial support:* Applicants required to submit FAFSA. *Unit head:* Dr. Susan Davenport, Dean, Heavin School of Arts and Sciences, 609-984-1130, Fax: 609-984-0740, E-mail: info@tesc.edu. *Application contact:* David Hoftiezer, Director of Admissions, 888-442-8372, Fax: 609-984-8447, E-mail: admissions@tesc.edu.

Towson University, Program in Professional Studies, Towson, MD 21252-0001. Offers MA. Part-time and evening/weekend programs available. *Students:* 18 full-time (11 women), 32 part-time (22 women); includes 12 minority (11 Black or African American, non-Hispanic/Latino; 1 Hispanic/Latino), 1 international. Average age 32. In 2010, 10 master's awarded. *Degree requirements:* For master's, thesis optional, exam. *Entrance requirements:* For master's, minimum GPA of 3.0. *Application deadline:* Applications are processed on a rolling basis. Application fee: $50. Electronic applications accepted. *Expenses:* Tuition, state resident: part-time $324 per credit. Tuition, nonresident: part-time $681 per credit. Required fees: $95 per term. *Financial support:* Federal Work-Study and unspecified assistantships available. Financial award application deadline: 4/1; financial award applicants required to submit FAFSA. *Faculty research:* History, World War II, counseling, marriage and family, human development. *Unit head:* Dr. James Smith, Graduate Program Director, 410-704-4620, E-mail: jmsmith@towson.edu. *Application contact:* 410-704-2501, Fax: 410-704-4678, E-mail: grads@towson.edu.

Tulane University, Program in Liberal Arts, New Orleans, LA 70118-5669. Offers MLA. Part-time programs available. *Degree requirements:* For master's, thesis. *Entrance requirements:* For master's, GRE General Test, minimum B average in undergraduate course work. Additional exam requirements/recommendations for international students: Required—TOEFL.

University at Albany, State University of New York, College of Arts and Sciences, Liberal Studies Program, Albany, NY 12222-0001. Offers MA. *Entrance requirements:* Additional exam requirements/recommendations for international students: Required—TOEFL (minimum score 550 paper-based; 213 computer-based). Electronic applications accepted.

University of Arkansas at Little Rock, Graduate School, College of Arts, Humanities, and Social Science, Department of Philosophy and Liberal Studies, Little Rock, AR 72204-1099. Offers MALS. *Entrance requirements:* For master's, GRE.

University of Delaware, College of Arts and Sciences, Program in Liberal Studies, Newark, DE 19716. Offers MALS. Part-time and evening/weekend programs available. *Degree requirements:* For master's, thesis. Electronic applications accepted. *Faculty research:* British Raj, medical and scientific ethics, Jewish-American novelists, intellectual freedom.

University of Detroit Mercy, College of Liberal Arts and Education, Program in Liberal Studies, Detroit, MI 48221. Offers MALS. Part-time programs available.

University of Maine, Graduate School, Program in Liberal Studies, Orono, ME 04469. Offers Maine studies (MA); new media (MA); peace studies (MA). Part-time and evening/weekend programs available. *Students:* 2 full-time (both women), 19 part-time (13 women); includes 2 American Indian or Alaska Native, non-Hispanic/Latino, 1 international. Average age 47. 5 applicants, 40% accepted, 2 enrolled. In 2010, 6 master's awarded. *Degree requirements:* For master's, project. *Entrance requirements:* Additional exam requirements/recommendations for international students: Required—TOEFL. *Application deadline:* For fall admission, 4/1 for domestic students; for spring admission, 11/1 for domestic students. Applications are processed on a rolling basis. Application fee: $65. Electronic applications accepted. *Expenses:* Tuition, state resident: full-time $400. Tuition, nonresident: full-time $1050. *Financial support:* Federal Work-Study and institutionally sponsored loans available. Financial award application deadline: 3/1. *Unit head:* Amaranta Ruiz-Nelson, Coordinator, 207-581-3222, Fax: 207-581-3232, E-mail: graduate@maine.edu. *Application contact:* Amaranta Ruiz-Nelson, Coordinator, 207-581-3222, Fax: 207-581-3232, E-mail: graduate@maine.edu.

University of Memphis, Graduate School, University College, Memphis, TN 38152. Offers liberal studies (MALS); merchandising and consumer science (MS), including consumer science and education; strategic leadership (MPS). Part-time and evening/weekend programs available. *Faculty:* 3 full-time (2 women), 3 part-time/adjunct (1 woman). *Students:* 30 full-time (19 women), 122 part-time (93 women); includes 88 Black or African American, non-Hispanic/Latino; 1 American Indian or Alaska Native, non-Hispanic/Latino; 1 Asian, non-Hispanic/Latino; 1 Hispanic/Latino, 1 international. Average age 40. 89 applicants, 74% accepted, 8 enrolled. In 2010, 41 master's awarded. *Degree requirements:* For master's, comprehensive exam, thesis (for some programs). *Entrance requirements:* For master's, MAT, GRE General Test (MS), interview (MALS). Additional exam requirements/recommendations for international students: Required—TOEFL (minimum score 550 paper-based; 210 computer-based). *Application deadline:* For fall admission, 7/1 for domestic students, 5/1 for international students; for spring admission, 11/1 for domestic students, 9/15 for international students. Applications are processed on a rolling basis. Application fee: $35 ($60 for international students). Electronic applications accepted. *Financial support:* In 2010–11, 123 students received support; research assistantships with full tuition reimbursements available, teaching assistantships with tuition reimbursements available, Federal Work-Study, scholarships/grants, and unspecified assistantships available. Financial award application deadline: 2/15; financial award applicants required to submit FAFSA. *Faculty research:* Media ethics, history of psychiatry, public relations. *Unit head:* Dr. Dan Lattimore, Dean, 901-678-2991. *Application contact:* Dr. Herbert McCree, Coordinator of Graduate Studies, 901-678-4171, Fax: 901-678-3363, E-mail: hmccree@memphis.edu.

University of Miami, Graduate School, College of Arts and Sciences, Program in Liberal Studies, Coral Gables, FL 33124. Offers MALS. Part-time and evening/weekend programs available. *Degree requirements:* For master's, thesis or alternative. *Entrance requirements:* For master's, minimum GPA of 3.0. Additional exam requirements/recommendations for international students: Required—TOEFL. Electronic applications accepted. *Expenses:* Contact institution.

University of Michigan–Dearborn, College of Arts, Sciences, and Letters, Master of Arts in Liberal Studies Program, Dearborn, MI 48128. Offers MA. Part-time and evening/weekend programs available. *Faculty:* 14 full-time (7 women). *Students:* 1 (woman) full-time, 16 part-time (8 women); includes 3 minority (1 Asian, non-Hispanic/Latino; 1 Native Hawaiian or other Pacific Islander, non-Hispanic/Latino; 1 Two or more races, non-Hispanic/Latino). Average age 42. 13 applicants, 54% accepted, 7 enrolled. In 2010, 9 master's awarded. *Degree requirements:* For master's, thesis or alternative, capstone course. *Entrance requirements:* For master's, minimum GPA of 3.0, writing sample, interview. Additional exam requirements/recommendations for international students: Required—TOEFL (minimum score 560 paper-based; 220 computer-based). *Application deadline:* For fall admission, 8/1 priority date for domestic students, 4/1 for international students; for winter admission, 12/1 priority date for domestic students, 11/1 for international students; for spring admission, 4/1 for domestic students, 3/1 for international students. Applications are processed on a rolling basis. Application fee: $60 ($75 for international students). *Financial support:* Scholarships/grants available. Support available to part-time students. Financial award application deadline: 4/1; financial award applicants required to submit FAFSA. *Faculty research:* History of science studies, consciousness, memory studies, early American history, environmental studies. *Unit head:* Dr. Erik Bond, Director, 313-593-5168, Fax: 313-583-6700, E-mail: erikbond@umd.umich.edu. *Application contact:* Carol Ligienza, Coordinator, CASL Graduate Programs, 313-593-1183, Fax: 313-583-6700, E-mail: caslgrad@umd.umich.edu.

University of Minnesota, Duluth, Graduate School, College of Liberal Arts, Department of Sociology/Anthropology, Liberal Studies Program, Duluth, MN 55812-2496. Offers MLS. Part-time and evening/weekend programs available. *Faculty research:* Nature of knowledge, cultural studies, language, literature, sociology.

University of New Hampshire, Graduate School, College of Liberal Arts, Program in Liberal Studies, Durham, NH 03824. Offers MALS. *Faculty:* 5 full-time (3 women). *Students:* 5 full-time (3 women), 19 part-time (8 women); includes 2 minority (1 Asian, non-Hispanic/Latino; 1 Hispanic/Latino). Average age 40. 12 applicants, 67% accepted, 5 enrolled. In 2010, 4 master's awarded. *Entrance requirements:* Additional exam requirements/recommendations for international students: Required—TOEFL (minimum score 550 paper-based; 213 computer-based; 80 iBT). *Application deadline:* For fall admission, 6/1 for domestic students, 4/1 for international students; for spring admission, 12/1 for domestic students. Applications are processed on a rolling basis. Application fee: $65. Electronic applications accepted. *Financial support:* Fellowships, research assistantships, teaching assistantships available. Financial award application deadline: 2/15. *Unit head:* Dr. Warren Brown, Chairperson, 603-862-3225, E-mail: liberal.studies@unh.edu. *Application contact:* Janis Marshall, 603-862-7150, E-mail: liberal.studies@unh.edu.

The University of North Carolina at Asheville, Graduate Studies, Asheville, NC 28804-3299. Offers MLA. Part-time and evening/weekend programs available. *Faculty:* 8 full-time (5 women), 5 part-time/adjunct (2 women). *Students:* 45 part-time (27 women); includes 1 Asian, non-Hispanic/Latino; 2 Two or more races, non-Hispanic/Latino. Average age 43. 29 applicants, 97% accepted, 15 enrolled. In 2010, 8 master's awarded. *Degree requirements:* For master's, thesis. *Application deadline:* For fall admission, 4/15 for domestic students; for spring admission, 11/15 for domestic students. Applications are processed on a rolling basis. Application fee: $50. *Expenses:* Tuition, state resident: full-time $3110. Tuition, nonresident: full-time $15,706. Required fees: $2097. *Financial support:* Federal Work-Study and institutionally sponsored loans available. Support available to part-time students. Financial award application deadline: 5/1; financial award applicants required to submit FAFSA.

The University of North Carolina at Charlotte, Graduate School, College of Arts and Sciences, Program in Interdisciplinary Studies, Charlotte, NC 28223-0001. Offers gerontology (MA, Certificate); Latin American studies (MA); liberal studies (MA); women's studies (Certificate). *Faculty:* 2 full-time (1 woman), 2 part-time/adjunct (both women). *Students:* 15 full-time (14 women), 53 part-time (39 women); includes 20 minority (11 Black or African American, non-Hispanic/Latino; 8 Hispanic/Latino; 1 Two or more races, non-Hispanic/Latino), 5 international. Average age 30. 24 applicants, 96% accepted, 15 enrolled. In 2010, 16 master's awarded. *Degree requirements:* For master's, thesis optional, comprehensive exam or project. *Entrance requirements:* For master's, GRE General Test or MAT, minimum GPA of 3.0 during previous 2 years, 2.75 overall. Additional exam requirements/recommendations for international students: Required—TOEFL (minimum score 557 paper-based; 220 computer-based; 83 iBT). *Application deadline:* For fall admission, 7/1 for domestic students, 5/1 for international students; for spring admission, 11/1 for domestic students, 10/1 for international students. Applications are processed on a rolling basis. Application fee: $55. Electronic applications accepted. *Expenses:* Tuition, state resident: full-time $3464. Tuition, nonresident: full-time $14,297. Required fees: $2094. Tuition and fees vary according to course load. *Financial support:* In 2010–11, 7 students received support, including 2 research assistantships (averaging $3,025 per year), 5 teaching assistantships (averaging $7,950 per year); career-related internships or fieldwork, institutionally sponsored loans, scholarships/grants, and unspecified assistantships also available. Support available to part-time students. Financial award application deadline: 4/1; financial award applicants required to submit FAFSA. *Unit head:* Dr. Paula Eckard, Interim Director, 704-687-4309, Fax: 704-687-4347, E-mail: pgeckard@uncc.edu. *Application contact:* Kathy B. Giddings, Director of Graduate Admissions, 704-687-5503, Fax: 704-687-3279, E-mail: gradadm@uncc.edu.

The University of North Carolina at Greensboro, Graduate School, Program in Liberal Studies, Greensboro, NC 27412-5001. Offers MALS. Electronic applications accepted.

The University of North Carolina Wilmington, College of Arts and Sciences, Interdisciplinary Program in Liberal Studies, Wilmington, NC 28403-3297. Offers MA. Part-time programs available. *Students:* 11 full-time (7 women), 55 part-time (41 women); includes 13 minority (5 Black or African American, non-Hispanic/Latino; 2 American Indian or Alaska Native, non-Hispanic/Latino; 5 Hispanic/Latino; 1 Two or more races, non-Hispanic/Latino). Average age 39. 24 applicants, 75% accepted, 18 enrolled. In 2010, 19 master's awarded. *Degree requirements:* For master's, comprehensive exam, thesis or alternative, final project. *Entrance requirements:* For master's, minimum GPA of 3.0, writing sample. Additional exam requirements/recommendations for international students: Required—TOEFL (minimum score 550 paper-based; 217 computer-based; 79 iBT), IELTS (minimum score 6.5). *Application deadline:* For fall admission, 3/15 for domestic students. Application fee: $60. *Financial support:* In 2010–11, 3 teaching assistantships (averaging $9,500 per year) were awarded. Financial award application deadline: 3/15. *Unit head:* Dr. Herb Berg, Director, 910-962-3299, E-mail: bergh@uncw.edu. *Application contact:* Dr. Herb Berg, Dean, Graduate School, 910-962-3299, E-mail: bergh@uncw.edu.

University of Oklahoma, College of Liberal Studies, Norman, OK 73019. Offers human and health services administration (MA); integrated studies (MA); museum studies (MA); prevention science (MPS). Part-time programs available. Postbaccalaureate distance learning degree programs offered (no on-campus study). *Faculty:* 16 full-time (12 women), 13 part-time/adjunct (4 women). *Students:* 30 full-time (18 women), 432 part-time (221 women); includes 99 minority (31 Black or African American, non-Hispanic/Latino; 33 American Indian or Alaska Native, non-Hispanic/Latino; 4 Asian, non-Hispanic/Latino; 21 Hispanic/Latino; 10 Two or more races, non-Hispanic/Latino), 1 international. Average age 36. 159 applicants, 94% accepted, 113 enrolled. In 2010, 114 master's awarded. *Degree requirements:* For master's, minimum of 33 semester hours, including thesis, research project, internship, or comprehensive exam. *Entrance requirements:* For master's, minimum GPA of 3.0 in last 60 hours, writing sample. Additional exam requirements/recommendations for international students: Required—TOEFL (minimum score 550 paper-based; 213 computer-based; 79 iBT). *Application deadline:* For fall admission, 7/15 priority date for domestic students, 4/1 for international students; for spring admission, 12/1 for domestic students, 9/1 for international students. Applications are processed on a rolling basis. Application fee: $40 ($90 for international students). Electronic applications accepted. *Expenses:* Tuition, state resident: full-time $3893; part-time $162.20 per credit hour. Tuition, nonresident: full-time $14,167; part-time $590.30 per credit hour. Required fees: $2523; $94.60 per credit hour. Tuition and fees vary according to course load and degree level. *Financial support:* In 2010–11, 358 students received support. Career-related internships or fieldwork, institutionally sponsored loans, scholarships/grants, and tuition waivers (partial) available. Support available to part-time students. Financial award applicants required to submit FAFSA. *Faculty research:* Administrative leadership, criminal justice, museum studies, health administration, prevention science. *Unit head:* Dr. James Pappas, Dean and Vice President for University Outreach, 405-325-6361, Fax: 405-325-7196, E-mail: jpappas@ou.edu. *Application contact:* Kelly Collyar, Coordinator, Recruitment and Admissions, 800-522-4389, Fax: 405-325-7132, E-mail: clsinfo@ou.edu.

University of Pennsylvania, School of Arts and Sciences, College of Liberal and Professional Studies, Philadelphia, PA 19104. Offers environmental studies (MES); individualized study (MLA). *Students:* 97 full-time (63 women), 256 part-time (165 women); includes 15 Black or African American, non-Hispanic/Latino; 1 American Indian or Alaska Native, non-Hispanic/Latino; 16 Asian, non-Hispanic/Latino; 15 Hispanic/Latino, 33 international. 600 applicants, 46% accepted, 213 enrolled. In 2010, 151 master's awarded. *Application deadline:* For fall admission, 12/1 priority date for domestic students. Application fee: $70. Electronic applications accepted. *Expenses:* Tuition: Full-time $25,660; part-time $4758 per course. Required fees: $2152; $270 per course. Tuition and fees vary according to course load, degree level and program. *Unit head:* Dr. Kristine Billmyer, Associate Dean and Director, College of Liberal and Professional Studies, 215-898-8681, E-mail: gdasdmis@sas.upenn.edu. *Application contact:* Patricia Rea, Coordinator for Admissions, 215-573-5816, Fax: 215-573-8068, E-mail: gdasadmis@sas.upenn.edu.

University of St. Thomas, Program in Liberal Arts, Houston, TX 77006-4696. Offers MLA. Part-time and evening/weekend programs available. *Faculty:* 34 full-time (14 women), 15 part-time/adjunct (7 women). *Students:* 47 full-time (30 women), 122 part-time (84 women); includes 61 minority (22 Black or African American, non-Hispanic/Latino; 1 American Indian or Alaska Native, non-Hispanic/Latino; 8 Asian, non-Hispanic/Latino; 26 Hispanic/Latino; 1 Native Hawaiian or other Pacific Islander, non-Hispanic/Latino; 3 Two or more races, non-Hispanic/Latino), 16 international. Average age 34. 63 applicants, 94% accepted, 49 enrolled. In 2010, 30 master's awarded. *Degree requirements:* For master's, thesis optional, capstone, minimum cumulative GPA of 3.0. *Entrance requirements:* For master's, 4 year undergraduate degree with minimum GPA of 2.5, essay, 2 letters of recommendation, interview. Additional exam requirements/recommendations for international students: Required—TOEFL (minimum score 250 computer-based; 100 iBT), ELS exam (level 112). *Application deadline:* Applications are processed on a rolling basis. Application fee: $35. Electronic applications accepted. *Expenses:* Tuition: Full-time $15,696; part-time $872 per credit hour. Required fees: $236; $83 per term. One-time fee: $100. Tuition and fees vary according to course load, campus/location and program. *Financial support:* In 2010–11, 19 students received support. Federal Work-Study, scholarships/grants, and state work-study, institutional employment available. Support available to part-time students. Financial award application deadline: 4/15; financial award applicants required to submit FAFSA. *Unit head:* Dr. Ravi Srinivas, Dean, 713-525-6951, Fax: 713-525-6924, E-mail: mla@stthom.edu. *Application contact:* Kate Henderson, Program Assistant, 713-525-6951, Fax: 713-525-6924, E-mail: mla@stthom.edu.

University of Southern Indiana, Graduate Studies, College of Liberal Arts, Program in Liberal Studies, Evansville, IN 47712-3590. Offers MA. Part-time and evening/weekend programs available. *Faculty:* 3 full-time (0 women). *Students:* 6 full-time (0 women), 25 part-time (18 women); includes 2 Black or African American, non-Hispanic/Latino; 1 Asian, non-Hispanic/Latino, 2 international. Average age 35. 6 applicants, 100% accepted, 6 enrolled. In 2010, 14 master's awarded. *Entrance requirements:* For master's, minimum GPA of 2.5, resume, interview. Additional exam requirements/recommendations for international students: Required—TOEFL (minimum score 550 paper-based; 213 computer-based; 79 iBT), IELTS (minimum score 6). *Application deadline:* For fall admission, 8/15 priority date for domestic students, 3/1 priority date for international students. Applications are processed on a rolling basis. Application fee: $25. Electronic applications accepted. *Expenses:* Tuition, state resident: full-time $4823; part-time $267.95 per credit hour. Tuition, nonresident: full-time $9515; part-time $528.62 per credit hour. Required fees: $220; $22.75 per term. Tuition and fees vary according to course load and reciprocity agreements. *Financial support:* In 2010–11, 8 students received support. Federal Work-Study, scholarships/grants, tuition waivers (full and partial), and unspecified assistantships available. Financial award application deadline: 3/1; financial award applicants required to submit FAFSA. *Unit head:* Dr. Thomas M. Rivers, Director, 812-464-1753, E-mail: trivers@usi.edu. *Application contact:* Dr. Thomas M. Rivers, Director, 812-464-1753, E-mail: trivers@usi.edu.

The University of Texas at El Paso, Graduate School, College of Liberal Arts, Interdisciplinary Program in Liberal Arts, El Paso, TX 79968-0001. Offers MAIS. Part-time and evening/weekend programs available. *Students:* 12 (5 women); includes 5 Hispanic/Latino, 4 international. Average age 34. In 2010, 5 master's awarded. *Entrance requirements:* For master's, GRE, minimum GPA of 3.0, letters of recommendation. Additional exam requirements/recommendations for international students: Required—TOEFL; Recommended—IELTS. *Application deadline:* For fall admission, 8/1 priority date for domestic students, 3/1 for international students; for spring admission, 11/1 priority date for domestic students, 9/1 for international students. Applications are processed on a rolling basis. Application fee: $45 ($80 for international students). Electronic applications accepted. *Financial support:* In 2010–11, research assistantships with tuition reimbursements (averaging $18,625 per year), teaching assistantships with partial tuition reimbursements (averaging $14,900 per year) were awarded; fellowships with partial tuition reimbursements, institutionally sponsored loans, scholarships/grants, health care benefits, tuition waivers (partial), and unspecified assistantships also available. Support available to part-time students. Financial award application deadline: 3/15; financial award applicants required to submit FAFSA. *Unit head:* Dr. Ronald Weber, Director, 915-747-7073, E-mail: rweber@utep.edu. *Application contact:* Dr. Patricia D. Witherspoon, Dean of the Graduate School, 915-747-5491, Fax: 915-747-5788, E-mail: withersp@utep.edu.

The University of Toledo, College of Graduate Studies, College of Language, Literature and Social Sciences, Master of Liberal Studies Program, Toledo, OH 43606-3390. Offers MLS. Part-time and evening/weekend programs available. *Students:* 13 full-time (7 women), 60 part-time (43 women); includes 26 minority (23 Black or African American, non-Hispanic/Latino; 1 American Indian or Alaska Native, non-Hispanic/Latino; 1 Asian, non-Hispanic/Latino; 1 Two or more races, non-Hispanic/Latino), 1 international. Average age 38. 35 applicants, 77% accepted, 25 enrolled. In 2010, 6 master's awarded. *Degree requirements:* For master's, thesis. *Entrance requirements:* For master's, GRE if cumulative GPA is less than 3.0. A minimum 2.7 cumulative point-hour ratio (on a 4.0 scale) for all previous academic work. Three Letters of Recommendation, a statement of purpose, and transcripts from all prior institutions attended. Additional exam requirements/recommendations for international students: Required—TOEFL (minimum score 550 paper-based; 213 computer-based; 80 iBT), IELTS (minimum score 6.5). *Application deadline:* For fall admission, 1/15 priority date for domestic and international students. Applications are processed on a rolling basis. Application fee: $45 ($75 for international students). Electronic applications accepted. *Expenses:* Tuition, state resident: full-time $11,426; part-time $476 per credit hour. Tuition, nonresident: full-time $21,660; part-time $903 per credit hour. One-time fee: $62. *Financial support:* Teaching assistantships with full tuition reimbursements, Federal Work-Study, institutionally sponsored loans, scholarships/grants, tuition waivers (full and partial), and unspecified assistantships available. Support available to part-time students. Financial award applicants required to submit FAFSA. *Unit head:* Dr. Lawrence Anderson-Huang, Chair, 419-530-7257, E-mail: lawrence.anderson@utoledo.edu. *Application contact:* Graduate School Office, 419-530-4723, Fax: 419-530-4724, E-mail: gradsch@utnet.utoledo.edu.

University of Wisconsin–Milwaukee, Graduate School, College of Letters and Sciences, Interdepartmental Program in Liberal Studies, Milwaukee, WI 53201-0413. Offers MLS. *Faculty:* 10 full-time (3 women). *Students:* 7 full-time (1 woman), 23 part-time (13 women); includes 2 Black or African American, non-Hispanic/Latino; 1 American Indian or Alaska Native, non-Hispanic/Latino; 1 Hispanic/Latino. Average age 40. 15 applicants, 87% accepted, 10 enrolled. In 2010, 12 master's awarded. *Entrance requirements:* For master's, interview, bachelor's degree. Additional exam requirements/recommendations for international students: Required—TOEFL (minimum score 600 paper-based; 79 iBT), IELTS (minimum score 7). *Application deadline:* Applications are processed on a rolling basis. Application fee: $56 ($96 for international students). Electronic applications accepted. *Financial support:* Fellowships, research assistantships, teaching assistantships, health care benefits, unspecified assistantships, and project assistantships available. Financial award applicants required to submit FAFSA. *Unit head:* Jeffrey R. Hayes, Representative, 414-229-5963, E-mail: jhayes@uwm.edu. *Application contact:* General Information Contact, 414-229-4982, Fax: 414-229-6967, E-mail: gradschool@uwm.edu.

Ursuline College, School of Graduate Studies, Program in Liberal Studies, Pepper Pike, OH 44124-4398. Offers MALS. *Students:* 1 (woman) full-time, 9 part-time (all women); includes 5 minority (all Black or African American, non-Hispanic/Latino). Average age 32. 8 applicants, 88% accepted, 6 enrolled. *Degree requirements:* For master's, thesis. *Entrance requirements:* For master's, minimum undergraduate GPA of 3.0. Additional exam requirements/recommendations for international students: Required—TOEFL (minimum score 500 paper-based; 173 computer-based). *Application deadline:* For fall admission, 8/1 priority date for domestic students. Applications are processed on a rolling basis. Application fee: $25. Electronic applications accepted. *Expenses:* Tuition: Full-time $15,138; part-time $841 per credit. Required fees: $240; $120 per semester. *Financial support:* Federal Work-Study available. Financial award application deadline: 3/1; financial award applicants required to submit FAFSA. *Unit head:* Dr. Tim Kinsella, Director, 440-646-8389, Fax: 440-684-6088, E-mail: tkinsell@ursuline.edu. *Application contact:* Melanie Steele, Graduate Admission Assistant, 440-646-8119, Fax: 440-684-6138, E-mail: graduateadmissions@ursuline.edu.

Utica College, Liberal Studies Program, Utica, NY 13502-4892. Offers MS. Part-time and evening/weekend programs available. *Faculty:* 19 full-time (8 women). *Students:* 18 part-time (14 women); includes 1 Black or African American, non-Hispanic/Latino; 1 Asian, non-Hispanic/Latino. Average age 28. In 2010, 5 master's awarded. *Degree requirements:* For master's, comprehensive exam or thesis. *Entrance requirements:* For master's, GRE, minimum GPA of 3.0. Additional exam requirements/recommendations for international students: Required—TOEFL (minimum score 525 paper-based; 195 computer-based). *Application deadline:* Applications are processed on a rolling basis. Application fee: $50. Electronic applications accepted. *Expenses:* Contact institution. *Financial support:* Career-related internships or fieldwork, scholarships/grants, tuition waivers (partial), and unspecified assistantships available. Support available to part-time students. Financial award application deadline: 3/15; financial award applicants required to submit FAFSA. *Unit head:* Prof. Polly Smith, Coordinator, 315-792-3124,

Liberal Studies

Utica College (continued)
E-mail: laaronson@utica.edu. *Application contact:* John D. Rowe, Director of Graduate Admissions, 315-792-3824, Fax: 315-792-3003, E-mail: jrowe@utica.edu.

Valparaiso University, Graduate School, Programs in Liberal Studies, Concentration in Human Behavior and Society, Valparaiso, IN 46383. Offers MALS, Post-Master's Certificate, JD/MALS. Part-time and evening/weekend programs available. *Students:* 3 full-time (2 women), 4 part-time (3 women); includes 1 minority (Hispanic/Latino), 2 international. Average age 30. In 2010, 4 master's, 1 other advanced degree awarded. *Entrance requirements:* For master's, minimum GPA of 3.0. Additional exam requirements/recommendations for international students: Required—TOEFL (minimum score 550 paper-based; 213 computer-based; 80 iBT). *Application deadline:* Applications are processed on a rolling basis. Application fee: $30 ($50 for international students). Electronic applications accepted. *Expenses:* Tuition: Full-time $9540; part-time $530 per credit hour. Required fees: $292; $95 per semester. Tuition and fees vary according to program. *Financial support:* Available to part-time students. Applicants required to submit FAFSA. *Unit head:* Dr. David L. Rowland, Dean, Graduate School and Continuing Education/Associate Provost, 219-464-5313, Fax: 219-464-5381, E-mail: david.rowland@valpo.edu. *Application contact:* Laura Groth, Coordinator of Student Services and Support, 219-464-5313, Fax: 219-464-5381, E-mail: laura.groth@valpo.edu.

Valparaiso University, Graduate School, Programs in Liberal Studies, Individualized Study Program, Valparaiso, IN 46383. Offers MALS, JD/MALS. Part-time and evening/weekend programs available. *Students:* 3 full-time (all women), 8 part-time (4 women); includes 1 minority (Hispanic/Latino), 2 international. Average age 32. In 2010, 5 master's awarded. *Entrance requirements:* For master's, minimum GPA of 3.0. Additional exam requirements/recommendations for international students: Required—TOEFL (minimum score 550 paper-based; 213 computer-based; 80 iBT). *Application deadline:* Applications are processed on a rolling basis. Application fee: $30 ($50 for international students). Electronic applications accepted. *Expenses:* Tuition: Full-time $9540; part-time $530 per credit hour. Required fees: $292; $95 per semester. Tuition and fees vary according to program. *Financial support:* Available to part-time students. Applicants required to submit FAFSA. *Unit head:* Dr. David L. Rowland, Dean, Graduate School and Continuing Education/Associate Provost, 219-464-5313, Fax: 219-464-5381, E-mail: david.rowland@valpo.edu. *Application contact:* Laura Groth, Coordinator of Student Services and Support, 219-464-5313, Fax: 219-464-5381, E-mail: laura.groth@valpo.edu.

Vanderbilt University, Graduate School, Program in Liberal Arts and Science, Nashville, TN 37240-1001. Offers MLAS. Part-time programs available. *Students:* 62 part-time (41 women); includes 3 Black or African American, non-Hispanic/Latino; 1 Hispanic/Latino. Average age 45. 21 applicants, 90% accepted, 15 enrolled. In 2010, 17 master's awarded. *Degree requirements:* For master's, thesis optional. *Entrance requirements:* For master's, GRE General Test. *Application deadline:* For fall admission, 1/15 priority date for domestic students, 1/15 for international students; for spring admission, 11/15 for domestic and international students. Applications are processed on a rolling basis. Application fee: $0. *Financial support:* Institutionally sponsored loans and tuition waivers (partial) available. *Unit head:* Martin Rapisarda, Associate Dean and Director, 615-936-5964, Fax: 615-343-8453, E-mail: martin.rapisarda@vanderbilt.edu. *Application contact:* Walter B. Bieschke, Program Coordinator for Graduate Admissions, 615-322-0236, Fax: 615-343-6687, E-mail: vandygrad@vanderbilt.edu.

Villanova University, Graduate School of Liberal Arts and Sciences, Program in Liberal Studies, Villanova, PA 19085. Offers American studies (Certificate); ancient worlds (Certificate); great books (Certificate); interdisciplinary studies (Post-Master's Certificate); liberal studies (MA); peace and justice studies (Certificate). Part-time and evening/weekend programs available. *Faculty:* 24 full-time. In 2010, 2 master's awarded. *Degree requirements:* For master's, comprehensive exam. *Entrance requirements:* For master's, bachelor's degree from institution accredited by one of the regional accrediting agencies with minimum undergraduate GPA of 3.0; transcripts; two letters of recommendation; two essays. Additional exam requirements/recommendations for international students: Required—TOEFL. *Application deadline:* For fall admission, 3/1 priority date for domestic and international students; for spring admission, 11/15 priority date for domestic and international students. Applications are processed on a rolling basis. Application fee: $50. Electronic applications accepted. *Expenses:* Tuition: Part-time $700 per credit. Part-time tuition and fees vary according to degree level and program. *Financial support:* Research assistantships, Federal Work-Study available. Financial award applicants required to submit FAFSA. *Unit head:* Dr. Marylu Hill, Director, Villanova Center for Liberal Education, 610-519-6936, E-mail: marylu.hill@villanova.edu. *Application contact:* Dr. Adele Lindenmeyr, Dean, Graduate School of Liberal Arts and Sciences, 610-519-7093, Fax: 610-519-7096.

Virginia Polytechnic Institute and State University, Graduate School, College of Liberal Arts and Human Sciences, Department of Religion and Culture, Blacksburg, VA 24061. Offers liberal arts (Certificate); religious studies (Certificate). *Expenses:* Tuition, state resident: full-time $9399; part-time $488 per credit hour. Tuition, nonresident: full-time $17,854; part-time $957.75 per credit hour. Required fees: $1534. Full-time tuition and fees vary according to program.

Virginia Polytechnic Institute and State University, VT Online, Blacksburg, VA 24061. Offers aerospace engineering (MS); business information systems (Graduate Certificate); career and technical education (MS); computer engineering (M Eng, MS); decision support systems (Graduate Certificate); eLearning leadership (MA); electrical engineering (M Eng, MS); engineering administration (MEA); environmental politics and policy (Graduate Certificate); foundations of political analysis (Graduate Certificate); health product risk management (Graduate Certificate); information policy and society (Graduate Certificate); information security (Graduate Certificate); instructional technology (MA); liberal arts (Graduate Certificate); life sciences: health product risk management (MS); natural resources (MNR, Graduate Certificate); networking (Graduate Certificate); nonprofit and nongovernmental organization management (Graduate Certificate); ocean engineering (MS); political science (MA); security studies (Graduate Certificate); software development (Graduate Certificate). *Expenses:* Tuition, state resident: full-time $9399; part-time $488 per credit hour. Tuition, nonresident: full-time $17,854; part-time $957.75 per credit hour. Required fees: $1534. Full-time tuition and fees vary according to program.

Wake Forest University, Graduate School of Arts and Sciences, Liberal Studies Program, Winston-Salem, NC 27109. Offers MALS. Part-time programs available. *Degree requirements:* For master's, thesis. *Entrance requirements:* Additional exam requirements/recommendations for international students: Required—TOEFL (minimum score 213 computer-based; 79 iBT). Electronic applications accepted.

Washburn University, College of Arts and Sciences, Program in Liberal Studies, Topeka, KS 66621. Offers MLS. Part-time and evening/weekend programs available. *Students:* 4 full-time (1 woman), 14 part-time (12 women). Average age 41. *Degree requirements:* For master's, thesis, 15 seminar hours. *Entrance requirements:* For master's, minimum GPA of 3.0. Additional exam requirements/recommendations for international students: Recommended—TOEFL (minimum score 550 paper-based; 80 iBT). *Application deadline:* For fall admission, 3/1 priority date for domestic students; for spring admission, 10/1 priority date for domestic students. Applications are processed on a rolling basis. Electronic applications accepted. *Expenses:* Tuition, state resident: full-time $5130; part-time $285 per credit hour. Tuition, nonresident: full-time $10,476; part-time $582 per credit hour. Required fees: $86; $43 per semester. Tuition and fees vary according to program. *Financial support:* Career-related internships or fieldwork, Federal Work-Study, and scholarships/grants available. Support available to part-time students. Financial award applicants required to submit FAFSA. *Faculty research:* European architecture/history, British cultural studies movement, American military strategy/history. *Unit head:* Dr. Bruce Mactavish, Associate Dean, College of Arts & Sciences, 785-670-1636, Fax: 785-670-1297, E-mail: bruce.mactavish@washburn.edu. *Application contact:* Dr. Bruce Mactavish, Associate Dean, College of Arts & Sciences, 785-670-1636, Fax: 785-670-1297, E-mail: bruce.mactavish@washburn.edu.

Wesleyan University, Graduate Liberal Studies Program, Middletown, CT 06459. Offers MALS, CAS. Part-time and evening/weekend programs available. *Degree requirements:* For master's, thesis optional; for CAS, thesis. *Entrance requirements:* For master's, essay, undergraduate transcripts, two letters of recommendation. Additional exam requirements/recommendations for international students: Required—TOEFL. *Application deadline:* For fall admission, 6/20 for domestic students; for spring admission, 11/7 for domestic students. Applications are processed on a rolling basis. Application fee: $100. *Expenses:* Contact institution. *Financial support:* Scholarships/grants available. Support available to part-time students. *Faculty research:* Interdisciplinary studies. *Unit head:* Sheryl Culotta, Director, 860-685-3008, Fax: 860-685-2901, E-mail: sculotta@wesleyan.edu. *Application contact:* Jennifer M. Curran, Assistant Director, Admissions and Outreach, 860-685-3338, Fax: 860-685-2901, E-mail: jcurran@wesleyan.edu.

Western Illinois University, School of Graduate Studies, College of Arts and Sciences, Program in Liberal Arts and Sciences, Macomb, IL 61455-1390. Offers MLAS. Part-time programs available. *Students:* 18 full-time (12 women), 18 part-time (15 women); includes 12 minority (8 Black or African American, non-Hispanic/Latino; 1 American Indian or Alaska Native, non-Hispanic/Latino; 3 Hispanic/Latino). Average age 34. 8 applicants, 100% accepted. In 2010, 1 master's awarded. *Degree requirements:* For master's, thesis or alternative. *Entrance requirements:* Additional exam requirements/recommendations for international students: Required—TOEFL (minimum score 550 paper-based; 213 computer-based; 80 iBT). *Application deadline:* Applications are processed on a rolling basis. Application fee: $30. Electronic applications accepted. *Expenses:* Tuition, state resident: full-time $6370; part-time $265.40 per credit hour. Tuition, nonresident: full-time $12,740; part-time $530.80 per credit hour. Required fees: $75.67 per credit hour. *Financial support:* In 2010–11, research assistantships with full tuition reimbursements (averaging $7,280 per year). Financial award applicants required to submit FAFSA. *Unit head:* Dr. Althea Alton, Program Director, 309-298-3025. *Application contact:* Evelyn Hoing, Assistant Director of Graduate Studies, 309-298-1806, Fax: 309-298-2345, E-mail: grad-office@wiu.edu.

West Virginia University, Eberly College of Arts and Sciences, Interdisciplinary Program in Liberal Studies, Morgantown, WV 26506. Offers MALS. Part-time programs available. *Degree requirements:* For master's, thesis or alternative. *Entrance requirements:* For master's, GRE General Test, minimum GPA of 3.0. Additional exam requirements/recommendations for international students: Required—TOEFL.

Wichita State University, Graduate School, Fairmount College of Liberal Arts and Sciences, Interdisciplinary Program in Liberal Studies, Wichita, KS 67260. Offers MA. Part-time programs available. *Unit head:* Dr. David Soles, Graduate Coordinator, 316-978-3125, E-mail: david.soles@wichita.edu. *Application contact:* Dr. David Soles, Graduate Coordinator, 316-978-3125, E-mail: david.soles@wichita.edu.

Widener University, College of Arts and Sciences, Program in Liberal Studies, Chester, PA 19013-5792. Offers MA. Part-time and evening/weekend programs available. *Faculty:* 4 full-time (1 woman). *Students:* 12 part-time (8 women); includes 3 Black or African American, non-Hispanic/Latino. Average age 40. 3 applicants, 100% accepted. In 2010, 2 master's awarded. *Degree requirements:* For master's, thesis, project. *Entrance requirements:* For master's, interview, minimum undergraduate GPA of 3.0. *Application deadline:* Applications are processed on a rolling basis. Application fee: $25 ($300 for international students). *Expenses:* Contact institution. *Financial support:* Federal Work-Study and tuition waivers (full and partial) available. Financial award application deadline: 5/1. *Faculty research:* Contemporary analytical metaphysics, popular culture, British art, American literature, folklore. *Unit head:* Dr. Kenneth Skinner, Director, 610-499-4287, Fax: 610-499-4605, E-mail: kenneth.a.skinner@widener.edu. *Application contact:* Dr. Kenneth Skinner, Director, 610-499-4287, Fax: 610-499-4605, E-mail: kenneth.a.skinner@widener.edu.

Winthrop University, College of Arts and Sciences, Program in Liberal Arts, Rock Hill, SC 29733. Offers MLA. Part-time programs available. *Entrance requirements:* For master's, interview, minimum GPA of 3.0. Electronic applications accepted.

CALIFORNIA STATE UNIVERSITY, DOMINGUEZ HILLS

Humanities External Degree Program

Programs of Study

Since its inception in 1974 as a correspondence program, the Humanities External Degree program (HUX) has been dedicated to providing advanced study in the humanities to learners across the globe via distance learning. Using an interdisciplinary approach, this Master of Arts in Humanities program combines the best elements of traditional, in-depth study of a particular discipline—history, literature, philosophy, music, or art—with a broader, contemporary focus on interrelating effects and influences among these disciplines. With guidance from faculty experts, participants may adapt research and writing to their interests and goals.

HUX graduates recognize the personal and practical benefits of advanced interdisciplinary study of the humanities and arts. Skills and understanding achieved through the HUX curriculum prepare the graduate for thinking clearly about complex ideas, expressing concepts effectively, and solving problems.

"The way this program is structured is almost revolutionary," said David Marks, a 2011 HUX graduate. "It's structured but still allows students to creatively explore their fields of study and be independent. The program is ahead of its time."

Research Facilities

The HUX program offers a fully accredited degree with no classroom attendance. The master's degree is earned by completing courses predesigned and packaged by California State University, Dominguez Hills (CSUDH) humanities professors and by students designing and completing their own faculty-guided independent studies. While the program now includes a computer-based course instruction option for some courses, the program is available to students worldwide regardless of Internet access or computer skills—regular mail service is all that is required. HUX faculty and staff are highly qualified and care about their students.

The HUX program has been a leader in distance education at the M.A. level since its inception in 1974, functioning as a university without walls. The last 35 years have brought many improvements, including the addition of online technologies. But HUX maintains a commitment to provide a graduate education in the humanities to anyone who meets its basic academic requirements, regardless of their computer experience.

Financial Aid

Financial assistance is available through federal student loans, grants, and work-study opportunities. The University offers a limited number of fellowships and scholarships. Students should visit the Financial Aid Web site at http://www.csudh.edu/fin_aid/default.htm for more information. Support is also available for students to present their work at professional meetings; details can be found on the Graduate Studies Web site at http://www.csudh.edu/graduatestudies/.

Cost of Study

Course fees are $233 per trimester unit. Course fees are the same for both resident and nonresident students.

Living and Housing Costs

Because this is a distance learning program, there are no living and housing costs associated with the program; students maintain their current living arrangements.

Student Group

HUX students hail from all fifty states and more than sixty countries. Participants in the program tend to have outstanding academic records; HUX students have won or placed in the CSUDH master's thesis/project competition for ten years running and regularly compete for regional honors.

HUX graduates excel in many fields. Among them are teachers and professors, business leaders, military officers, filmmakers, radio and television news anchors, and authors of books and screenplays.

Location

California State University, Dominguez Hills, in the suburban city of Carson, is a diverse, comprehensive public university that primarily serves the greater Los Angeles metropolitan area. It is located on the historic Rancho San Pedro, the oldest Spanish land grant in the Los Angeles area. The land was in the Dominguez family from 1784 until its public acquisition to establish a university in 1960.

Carson sits just a few miles from the beaches, the Long Beach Aquarium, the L.A. County Museum of Art, the Getty Center, and Disneyland.

The University

CSUDH is one of twenty-three campuses in the California State University system, part of the largest system of public higher education in the world. It has a multicultural community that is committed to excellence and educating a student population of unprecedented diversity for leadership roles. University programs enable students to develop intellectually, personally, and professionally as they apply knowledge and hands-on expertise to real-world situations. The HUX program is part of the College of Extended and International Education, which extends the resources of the university to the communities it serves.

Applying

Students who want to enroll in the HUX program must have a Bachelor of Arts or Bachelor of Science degree from a regionally accredited university or college; however, the degree does not have to be in the humanities. They must have earned a 3.0 GPA in the last 60 semester units (90 quarter units) attempted, excluding lower-division work completed after obtaining the bachelor's degree. Students with a GPA between 2.5 and 3.0 can be admitted conditionally.

Applicants must submit a completed HUX application, either online (CSU Mentor at http://www.csumentor.edu) or with a paper application requested from the HUX office. Other materials required for admission review are the application fee (payable through CSU Mentor); an essay, submitted to the HUX office (huxonline@csudh.edu); and two unopened official transcripts from each college or university previously attended sent to the HUX office at the following address: Coordinator (Application Materials), Humanities Master of Arts External Program (HUX), California State University, Dominguez Hills, 1000 East Victoria Street SAC2-2126, Carson, California 90747, USA.

For official admission to the HUX program, all materials required must be in the HUX office by March 1 for the summer trimester, June 1 for the fall trimester, and November 1 for the spring trimester.

All graduate and postbaccalaureate applicants from outside the United States, regardless of citizenship, whose preparatory education was principally in a language other than English must demonstrate competence in English. Those who do not have a bachelor's degree from a postsecondary institution where English is the principal language of instruction must receive a minimum score of 550 on the Test of English as a Foreign Language (TOEFL). Students who attended institutions outside the U.S. must have earned an undergraduate degree which has equivalency to a four-year degree program in an accredited U.S. institution.

Correspondence and Information

Humanities Master of Arts External Program
California State University, Dominguez Hills
1000 East Victoria Street
SAC2-2126
Carson, California 90747
Phone: 310-243-3190
E-mail: huxonline@csudh.edu
Web site: http://www.csudh.edu/hux

California State University, Dominguez Hills

THE FACULTY AND THEIR RESEARCH

The following is a partial listing of instructors who work most frequently with the HUX program and the area in which they teach. Many are full-time faculty members in on-campus departments; the talents of part-time and emeritus instructors are also utilized. Their years of experience and expertise, teaching both on campus and through the humanities special sessions degree program, make them an invaluable source of knowledge.

Iset Anuakan, History; Ph.D., Berkeley.
Kimberly Bohman-Kalaja, Literature; Ph.D., Princeton.
David W. Bradfield, Music; M.Mus., North Texas State.
Anita Chang, Music; D.M.A., Texas at Austin.
Patricia H. Cherin, English; Ph.D., USC.
David A. Churchman, History; Ed.D., UCLA.
Marie Connors, English; M.F.A. (creative writing/poetry), California, Irvine.
William L. Cumiford, Philosophy; Ph.D., Texas Tech.
Miguel Dominguez, Foreign Language and Literature; Ph.D., UCLA.
Myrna Donahoe, History; Ph.D., California, Irvine.
Kirstin L. Ellsworth, Art; Ph.D., Indiana Bloomington.
Bryan Feuer, History; Ph.D., UCLA.
Kate Gale, Literature; Ph.D., Claremont.
Patricia B. Gamon, Art; Ph.D., Stanford.
Daniel Greenspan, Philosophy; Ph.D., Villanova.
Judson Grenier, History; Ph.D., UCLA.
William M. Hagan, Philosophy; S.T.D., Georgetown.
Arthur L. Harshman, Art; Ph.D., Chicago.
Gilah Y. Hirsch, Art; M.F.A., UCLA.
Howard R. Holter, History; Ph.D., Wisconsin.
Fumiko Hosokawa, History; Ph.D., UCLA.
James S. Jeffers, History; Ph.D., California, Irvine.
Kathryn Kendzora, English; Ph.D., California, Irvine.
Kenneth Lee, Religion; Ph.D., Columbia.
Donald F. Lewis, Philosophy; Ph.D., Southern Illinois.
Ben Mijuskovic, Philosophy; Ph.D., California, San Diego.
Christopher Monty, History; Ph.D., UCLA.
Joanna Nachef, Music; D.M.A., USC.
Linda Pomerantz-Zhang, History; Ph.D., UCLA.
Abe C. Ravitz, English; Ph.D., NYU.
Hamoud Salhi, Political Science; Ph.D., USC.
Porfirio Sanchez, Foreign Language and Literature; Ph.D., UCLA.
Jacqueline Shannon, Music; D.M.A., Washington (Seattle).
Lyle E. Smith, English; Ph.D., Harvard.
S. Glen White, Art; M.F.A., Otis Art Institute of Los Angeles.
Joanne Zitelli, English; Ph.D., California, Irvine.

Section 9
Language and Literature

This section contains a directory of institutions offering graduate work in language and literature. Additional information about programs listed in the directory may be obtained by writing directly to the dean of a graduate school or chair of a department at the address given in the directory.

For programs offering related work, see also in this book *Area and Cultural Studies, Communication and Media, Political Science and International Affairs,* and *Sociology, Anthropology, and Archaeology.* In another guide in this series:

Graduate Programs in Business, Education, Health, Information Studies, Law & Social Work

See *Special Focus* and *Subject Areas*

CONTENTS

Program Directories

Close-Up and Display

Asian Languages

Columbia University, Graduate School of Arts and Sciences, Division of Humanities, Department of East Asian Languages and Cultures, New York, NY 10027. Offers East Asian languages and cultures (M Phil, MA, PhD); Oriental studies (M Phil, MA, PhD). *Degree requirements:* For master's, one foreign language, comprehensive exam, thesis; for doctorate, 2 foreign languages, thesis/dissertation. *Entrance requirements:* For master's and doctorate, GRE General Test. Additional exam requirements/recommendations for international students: Required—TOEFL.

Columbia University, Graduate School of Arts and Sciences, Division of Humanities, Department of Middle East Languages and Cultures, New York, NY 10027. Offers Hebrew language and literature (M Phil, MA, PhD); Middle Eastern languages and cultures (M Phil, MA, PhD); South Asian languages and cultures (M Phil, MA, PhD). Part-time programs available. *Degree requirements:* For master's, thesis, oral and written exams; for doctorate, 3 foreign languages, thesis/dissertation. *Entrance requirements:* For master's and doctorate, GRE General Test. Additional exam requirements/recommendations for international students: Required—TOEFL. *Faculty research:* Indo-Iranian, Turkish, central Asian, and Armenian studies; Arabic and ancient Semitics.

Cornell University, Graduate School, Graduate Fields of Arts and Sciences, Field of East Asian Literature, Ithaca, NY 14853-0001. Offers Asian religions (MA, PhD); Chinese linguistics (MA, PhD); Chinese philology (MA, PhD); classical Chinese literature (MA, PhD); classical Japanese literature (MA, PhD); Japanese linguistics (MA, PhD); Korean literature (MA, PhD); modern Chinese literature (MA, PhD); modern Japanese literature (MA, PhD). *Faculty:* 15 full-time (7 women). *Students:* 19 full-time (9 women); includes 1 Black or African American, non-Hispanic/Latino; 3 Asian, non-Hispanic/Latino, 10 international. Average age 30. 37 applicants, 19% accepted, 6 enrolled. In 2010, 2 master's, 4 doctorates awarded. *Degree requirements:* For master's, 2 foreign languages, thesis, teaching experience; for doctorate, 2 foreign languages, comprehensive exam, thesis/dissertation, teaching experience. *Entrance requirements:* For master's, GRE General Test, 3 years of study in Chinese, Japanese, Korean, or Vietnamese; 3 letters of recommendation; academic writing sample; for doctorate, GRE General Test, 3 years of study in Chinese, Japanese, Korean, or Vietnamese, 3 letters of recommendation, academic writing sample. Additional exam requirements/recommendations for international students: Required—TOEFL (minimum score 600 paper-based; 250 computer-based; 77 iBT). *Application deadline:* For fall admission, 1/10 priority date for domestic students. Application fee: $80. Electronic applications accepted. *Expenses:* Tuition: Full-time $29,500. Required fees: $76. Tuition and fees vary according to degree level and program. *Financial support:* In 2010–11, 13 fellowships with full tuition reimbursements, 6 teaching assistantships with full tuition reimbursements were awarded; research assistantships with full tuition reimbursements, institutionally sponsored loans, scholarships/grants, health care benefits, tuition waivers (full and partial), and unspecified assistantships also available. Financial award applicants required to submit FAFSA. *Faculty research:* Vietnamese literature; Chinese literature, drama, and film; Japanese theater and literature; popular culture in East Asia; Korean literature; Asian linguistics. *Unit head:* Director of Graduate Studies, 607-255-9099. *Application contact:* Graduate Field Assistant, 607-255-9099, E-mail: east_asian_lit@cornell.edu.

Cornell University, Graduate School, Graduate Fields of Arts and Sciences, Field of Linguistics, Ithaca, NY 14853-0001. Offers applied linguistics (MA, PhD); East Asian linguistics (MA, PhD); English linguistics (MA, PhD); general linguistics (MA, PhD); Germanic linguistics (MA, PhD); Indo-European linguistics (MA, PhD); phonetics (MA, PhD); phonological theory (MA, PhD); Romance linguistics (MA, PhD); second language acquisition (MA, PhD); semantics (MA, PhD); Slavic linguistics (MA, PhD); sociolinguistics (MA, PhD); South Asian linguistics (MA, PhD); Southeast Asian linguistics (MA, PhD); syntactic theory (MA, PhD). *Faculty:* 15 full-time (7 women). *Students:* 34 full-time (18 women); includes 3 Hispanic/Latino, 15 international. Average age 28. 111 applicants, 12% accepted, 8 enrolled. In 2010, 2 master's, 6 doctorates awarded. Terminal master's awarded for partial completion of doctoral program. *Degree requirements:* For master's, one foreign language, thesis; for doctorate, one foreign language, comprehensive exam, thesis/dissertation. *Entrance requirements:* For master's and doctorate, GRE General Test, 2 letters of recommendation. Additional exam requirements/recommendations for international students: Required—TOEFL (minimum score 600 paper-based; 250 computer-based; 77 iBT). *Application deadline:* For fall admission, 1/15 for domestic students. Application fee: $80. Electronic applications accepted. *Expenses:* Tuition: Full-time $29,500. Required fees: $76. Tuition and fees vary according to degree level and program. *Financial support:* In 2010–11, 17 fellowships with full tuition reimbursements, 1 research assistantship with full tuition reimbursement, 15 teaching assistantships with full tuition reimbursements were awarded; institutionally sponsored loans, scholarships/grants, health care benefits, tuition waivers (full and partial), and unspecified assistantships also available. Financial award applicants required to submit FAFSA. *Faculty research:* Phonology and phonetics, syntax and semantics, historical linguistics, philosophy of language, language acquisition. *Unit head:* Director of Graduate Studies, 607-255-1105. *Application contact:* Graduate Field Assistant, 607-255-1105, E-mail: lingfield@cornell.edu.

Harvard University, Graduate School of Arts and Sciences, Department of East Asian Languages and Civilizations, Cambridge, MA 02138. Offers Chinese (PhD); Japanese (PhD); Korean (PhD); Mongolian (PhD); Vietnamese (PhD). Terminal master's awarded for partial completion of doctoral program. *Degree requirements:* For doctorate, 3 foreign languages, thesis/dissertation, general exams. *Entrance requirements:* For doctorate, GRE General Test. Additional exam requirements/recommendations for international students: Required—TOEFL. *Expenses:* Tuition: Full-time $34,976. Required fees: $1166. Full-time tuition and fees vary according to program. *Faculty research:* Central Asian literature, religion, and premodern history.

Harvard University, Graduate School of Arts and Sciences, Department of Sanskrit and Indian Studies, Cambridge, MA 02138. Offers Indian philosophy (AM, PhD); Pali (AM, PhD); Sanskrit (AM, PhD); Tibetan (AM, PhD); Urdu (AM, PhD). Terminal master's awarded for partial completion of doctoral program. *Degree requirements:* For master's, 3 foreign languages; for doctorate, 3 foreign languages, thesis/dissertation. *Entrance requirements:* For master's, GRE General Test; for doctorate, GRE General Test, proficiency in French and German. Additional exam requirements/recommendations for international students: Required—TOEFL. *Expenses:* Tuition: Full-time $34,976. Required fees: $1166. Full-time tuition and fees vary according to program.

Indiana University Bloomington, University Graduate School, College of Arts and Sciences, Department of East Asian Languages and Cultures, Bloomington, IN 47408. Offers Chinese (MA, PhD); Chinese language pedagogy (MA); East Asian studies (MA); Japanese (MA, PhD); Japanese language pedagogy (MA). Part-time programs available. *Faculty:* 15 full-time (7 women), 15 part-time/adjunct (7 women). *Students:* 28 full-time (18 women), 11 part-time (6 women); includes 2 Black or African American, non-Hispanic/Latino, 11 international. Average age 29. 100 applicants, 38% accepted, 18 enrolled. In 2010, 9 master's, 1 doctorate awarded. *Degree requirements:* For master's, one foreign language, thesis; for doctorate, 2 foreign languages, comprehensive exam, thesis/dissertation. *Entrance requirements:* Additional exam requirements/recommendations for international students: Required—TOEFL (minimum score 93 iBT). *Application deadline:* For fall admission, 1/15 for domestic students, 12/1 for international students. Application fee: $55 ($65 for international students). Electronic applications accepted. *Financial support:* In 2010–11, 21 students received support, including 5 fellowships with full tuition reimbursements available (averaging $15,500 per year), 18 teaching assistantships with full tuition reimbursements available (averaging $11,633 per year). Financial award application deadline: 3/1. *Faculty research:* Postwar/postmodern Japanese fiction, modern Chinese film and literature, classical Chinese literature and philosophy, Chinese and Japanese linguistics and pedagogy, East Asian politics and economics, Chinese and Japanese history, Korean language. *Unit head:* Michael Robinson, Chair, 812-855-0856, Fax: 812-855-6402, E-mail: robime@indiana.edu. *Application contact:* Natsuko Tsujimura, Director of Graduate Studies, 812-855-5884, Fax: 812-855-6402, E-mail: tsujimur@indiana.edu.

Naropa University, Graduate Programs, Program in Indo-Tibetan Buddhism with Language, Boulder, CO 80302-6697. Offers MA. *Faculty:* 6 full-time (2 women), 10 part-time/adjunct (5 women). *Students:* 15 full-time (1 woman), 4 part-time (0 women); includes 1 American Indian or Alaska Native, non-Hispanic/Latino; 1 Asian, non-Hispanic/Latino; 1 Hispanic/Latino, 1 international. Average age 32. 19 applicants, 84% accepted, 8 enrolled. In 2010, 5 master's awarded. *Degree requirements:* For master's, comprehensive exam, thesis. *Entrance requirements:* For master's, writing sample, interview (by phone or in-person), resume, letter of interest, 3 letters of recommendation. Additional exam requirements/recommendations for international students: Required—TOEFL (minimum score 600 paper-based; 250 computer-based). *Application deadline:* For fall admission, 1/15 priority date for domestic and international students. Applications are processed on a rolling basis. Application fee: $60. Electronic applications accepted. *Expenses:* Tuition: Full-time $17,820; part-time $810 per credit. Required fees: $305 per semester. Tuition and fees vary according to course load, program and reciprocity agreements. *Financial support:* In 2010–11, 11 students received support, including 5 research assistantships with partial tuition reimbursements available (averaging $3,000 per year), 2 teaching assistantships with partial tuition reimbursements available (averaging $3,000 per year); career-related internships or fieldwork, Federal Work-Study, scholarships/grants, health care benefits, tuition waivers (partial), and unspecified assistantships also available. Support available to part-time students. Financial award application deadline: 3/1; financial award applicants required to submit FAFSA. *Unit head:* Roger Dorris, Co-Chair, 303-546-0937. *Application contact:* Donna McIntyre, Assistant Director of Admissions, 303-546-3555, Fax: 303-546-3583, E-mail: donna@naropa.edu.

The Ohio State University, Graduate School, College of Arts and Sciences, Division of Arts and Humanities, Department of East Asian Languages and Literatures, Columbus, OH 43210. Offers Chinese (MA, PhD); Japanese (MA, PhD). *Faculty:* 22. *Students:* 59 full-time (29 women), 10 part-time (5 women); includes 6 Asian, non-Hispanic/Latino; 1 Hispanic/Latino; 1 Two or more races, non-Hispanic/Latino, 26 international. Average age 27. In 2010, 15 master's, 2 doctorates awarded. *Degree requirements:* For master's, thesis optional; for doctorate, thesis/dissertation. *Entrance requirements:* Additional exam requirements/recommendations for international students: Required—TOEFL (minimum score 577 paper-based; 233 computer-based). *Application deadline:* For fall admission, 8/15 priority date for domestic students, 7/1 priority date for international students; for winter admission, 12/1 priority date for domestic students, 11/1 priority date for international students; for spring admission, 3/1 priority date for domestic students, 2/1 priority date for international students. Applications are processed on a rolling basis. Application fee: $40 ($50 for international students). Electronic applications accepted. *Expenses:* Tuition, state resident: full-time $10,605. Tuition, nonresident: full-time $26,535. Tuition and fees vary according to course load and program. *Financial support:* Fellowships, research assistantships, teaching assistantships, Federal Work-Study, institutionally sponsored loans, and unspecified assistantships available. Support available to part-time students. *Unit head:* Mari Noda, Chair, 614-688-5737, E-mail: noda.1@osu.edu. *Application contact:* Graduate Admissions, 614-292-9444, Fax: 614-292-3895, E-mail: domestic.grad@osu.edu.

St. John's College, Graduate Institute in Liberal Education, Program in Eastern Classics, Santa Fe, NM 87505. Offers MA. Part-time and evening/weekend programs available. *Entrance requirements:* For master's, 2 letters of recommendation. Additional exam requirements/recommendations for international students: Required—TOEFL, TWE. *Expenses:* Contact institution.

Seton Hall University, College of Arts and Sciences, Department of Asian Studies, South Orange, NJ 07079-2697. Offers Asian languages (MA); Asian studies (MA); teaching Chinese language and culture (MA). Part-time and evening/weekend programs available. *Degree requirements:* For master's, thesis optional. *Entrance requirements:* For master's, strong background in Asian studies or related discipline. Additional exam requirements/recommendations for international students: Required—TOEFL. Electronic applications accepted. *Faculty research:* Modern Chinese history, contemporary Chinese politics, ancient Chinese history, Hinduism, Asian business, Japanese history.

University of California, Berkeley, Graduate Division, College of Letters and Science, Department of South and Southeast Asian Studies, Berkeley, CA 94720-1500. Offers Hindi (MA, PhD); Indonesian (MA, PhD); Sanskrit (MA, PhD); Tamil (MA, PhD). Terminal master's awarded for partial completion of doctoral program. *Degree requirements:* For master's, 2 foreign languages, thesis; for doctorate, 2 foreign languages, thesis/dissertation, oral qualifying exam. *Entrance requirements:* For master's and doctorate, GRE General Test, minimum GPA of 3.0, 3 letters of recommendation. Electronic applications accepted.

University of California, Irvine, School of Humanities, Department of East Asian Languages and Literatures, Irvine, CA 92697. Offers Chinese (MA, PhD); East Asian languages and literatures (MA, PhD); Japanese (MA, PhD). *Students:* 13 full-time (11 women), 1 (woman) part-time, 11 international. Average age 28. 35 applicants, 20% accepted, 4 enrolled. In 2010, 5 doctorates awarded. *Degree requirements:* For doctorate, thesis/dissertation. *Entrance requirements:* For master's, GRE, minimum GPA of 3.0; for doctorate, GRE General Test, minimum GPA of 3.0. Additional exam requirements/recommendations for international students: Required—TOEFL (minimum score 550 paper-based; 213 computer-based). *Application deadline:* For fall admission, 1/15 priority date for domestic students, 1/15 for international students. Application fee: $80 ($100 for international students). Electronic applications accepted. *Financial support:* Fellowships with tuition reimbursements, research assistantships with full tuition reimbursements, teaching assistantships with partial tuition reimbursements, institutionally sponsored loans, traineeships, health care benefits, and unspecified assistantships available. Financial award application deadline: 3/1; financial award applicants required to submit FAFSA. *Faculty research:* Chinese, Japanese, and Korean literature and culture; language and textual analysis; historical, social, and cultural dimensions of literary study. *Unit head:* Prof. Martin W. Huang, Chair, 949-824-2802, Fax: 949-824-3248, E-mail: mwhuang@uci.edu. *Application contact:* Mindy Han, Management Services Officer, 949-824-2165, Fax: 949-824-3248, E-mail: mindyhan@uci.edu.

University of California, Los Angeles, Graduate Division, College of Letters and Science, Department of Asian Languages and Cultures, Los Angeles, CA 90095. Offers MA, PhD. *Faculty:* 24 full-time (5 women). *Students:* 52 full-time (29 women); includes 13 minority (all Asian, non-Hispanic/Latino), 20 international. Average age 33. 62 applicants, 24% accepted, 8 enrolled. In 2010, 2 master's, 6 doctorates awarded. Terminal master's awarded for partial completion of doctoral program. *Degree requirements:* For master's, one foreign language, comprehensive exam or thesis; for doctorate, 2 foreign languages, thesis/dissertation, oral and written qualifying exams. *Entrance requirements:* For master's, GRE General Test, minimum GPA of 3.0, sample of written work; for doctorate, GRE General Test, minimum undergraduate GPA of 3.0, sample of research writing or thesis in English. Additional exam requirements/recommendations for international students: Required—TOEFL. *Application deadline:* For fall admission, 12/1 for domestic and international students. Application fee: $70 ($90 for international students). Electronic applications accepted. *Financial support:* In 2010–11, 36 fellowships with full and partial tuition reimbursements, 25 research assistantships with full and partial tuition reimbursements, 27 teaching assistantships with full and partial tuition reimbursements were awarded; Federal Work-Study, institutionally sponsored loans, scholarships/grants, health care benefits, tuition waivers (full and partial), and unspecified assistantships also available. Financial award application deadline: 3/1; financial award applicants required to submit FAFSA. *Unit head:* Dr. David Schaberg, Chair, 310-206-8235, E-mail: schaberg@humnet.ucla.edu. *Application contact:* Department Office, 310-267-4008, E-mail: shanshan@humnet.ucla.edu.

University of California, Santa Barbara, Graduate Division, College of Letters and Sciences, Division of Humanities and Fine Arts, Department of East Asian Languages and Cultural Studies, Santa Barbara, CA 93106-7075. Offers East Asian language and cultural studies (MA, PhD); translation studies (PhD). *Faculty:* 14 full-time, 7 part-time/adjunct. *Students:* 13 full-time (8 women). Average age 27. 76 applicants, 28% accepted, 6 enrolled. In 2010, 2 master's awarded. *Degree requirements:* For master's, one foreign language, thesis or alternative; for doctorate, 2 foreign languages, thesis/dissertation. *Entrance requirements:* For master's and doctorate, GRE, 3 letters of recommendation, statement of purpose, personal achievements/contributions statement, resume/curriculum vitae, transcripts for post-secondary institutions attended. Additional exam requirements/recommendations for international students: Required—TOEFL (minimum score 550 paper-based; 213 computer-based; 80 iBT) or IELTS (minimum score 7). *Application deadline:* For fall admission, 4/1 for domestic and international students. Application fee: $70 ($90 for international students). Electronic applications accepted. *Financial support:* In 2010–11, 13 students received support, including 5 fellowships with full and partial tuition reimbursements available (averaging $11,651 per year), 13 teaching assistantships with partial tuition reimbursements available (averaging $8,745 per year); Federal Work-Study, institutionally sponsored loans, scholarships/grants, health care benefits, and unspecified assistantships also available. Financial award application deadline: 12/15; financial award applicants required to submit FAFSA. *Faculty research:* Chinese literature, Chinese film, Japanese society, Japanese literature, East Asian cultural studies. *Unit head:* Dr. William Powell, Chair, 805-893-4455, Fax: 805-893-3011, E-mail: bpowell@religion.ucsb.edu. *Application contact:* Sally Lombrozo, Graduate Program Assistant, 805-893-2744, Fax: 805-893-7671, E-mail: lombrozo@hfa.ucsb.edu.

University of California, Santa Barbara, Graduate Division, College of Letters and Sciences, Division of Humanities and Fine Arts, Program in Comparative Literature, Santa Barbara, CA 93106-4130. Offers comparative literature (PhD); East Asian literatures (PhD); feminist studies (PhD); French (PhD); global studies (PhD); translation studies (PhD); MA/PhD. *Faculty:* 63 full-time (31 women). *Students:* 21 full-time (14 women); includes 3 Asian, non-Hispanic/Latino; 2 Hispanic/Latino. Average age 31. 41 applicants, 12% accepted, 2 enrolled. In 2010, 1 doctorate awarded. *Degree requirements:* For doctorate, 2 foreign languages, comprehensive exam, thesis/dissertation. *Entrance requirements:* For doctorate, GRE. Additional exam requirements/recommendations for international students: Required—TOEFL (minimum score 550 paper-based; 80 iBT), IELTS (minimum score 7). *Application deadline:* For fall admission, 12/15 for domestic and international students. Application fee: $70 ($90 for international students). Electronic applications accepted. *Financial support:* In 2010–11, 19 students received support, including 14 fellowships with full and partial tuition reimbursements available (averaging $16,232 per year), 12 teaching assistantships with partial tuition reimbursements available (averaging $12,826 per year); research assistantships, Federal Work-Study, institutionally sponsored loans, scholarships/grants, health care benefits, and tuition waivers (full and partial) also available. Financial award application deadline: 12/15; financial award applicants required to submit FAFSA. *Faculty research:* Comparative literary studies in global context, critical theory, translation studies, mediatechnological studies, trauma studies. *Unit head:* Prof. Susan Derwin, Chair, 805-893-4399, Fax: 805-893-8341, E-mail: derwin@gss.ucsb.edu. *Application contact:* Ashley Bradbury, Graduate Program Assistant, 805-893-2131, Fax: 805-893-8341, E-mail: ashley@hfa.ucsb.edu.

University of Chicago, Division of the Humanities, Department of East Asian Languages and Civilizations, Chicago, IL 60637-1513. Offers AM, PhD. Terminal master's awarded for partial completion of doctoral program. *Degree requirements:* For master's, one foreign language, thesis; for doctorate, 2 foreign languages, thesis/dissertation. *Entrance requirements:* For master's and doctorate, GRE General Test. Additional exam requirements/recommendations for international students: Required—TOEFL.

University of Chicago, Division of the Humanities, Department of South Asian Languages and Civilizations, Chicago, IL 60637-1513. Offers South Asian languages and civilizations (AM, PhD), including Bengali (PhD); Hindi (PhD); Sanskrit (PhD); Tamil (PhD); Urdu (PhD). Terminal master's awarded for partial completion of doctoral program. *Degree requirements:* For master's, one foreign language, thesis; for doctorate, 2 foreign languages, thesis/dissertation. *Entrance requirements:* For master's and doctorate, GRE General Test. Additional exam requirements/recommendations for international students: Required—TOEFL.

University of Hawaii at Manoa, Graduate Division, College of Languages, Linguistics and Literature, Department of East Asian Languages and Literatures, Program in Korean, Honolulu, HI 96822. Offers MA, PhD. Part-time programs available. *Students:* 32 full-time (20 women), 12 part-time (5 women); includes 20 minority (1 Black or African American, non-Hispanic/Latino; 18 Asian, non-Hispanic/Latino; 1 Two or more races, non-Hispanic/Latino), 17 international. Average age 31. 34 applicants, 59% accepted, 15 enrolled. In 2010, 15 master's awarded. *Degree requirements:* For master's, 2 foreign languages, thesis optional; for doctorate, 2 foreign languages, comprehensive exam, thesis/dissertation. *Entrance requirements:* For master's and doctorate, GRE General Test. Additional exam requirements/recommendations for international students: Required—TOEFL (minimum score 560 paper-based; 220 computer-based; 83 iBT), IELTS (minimum score 5). *Application deadline:* For fall admission, 2/1 for domestic and international students; for spring admission, 9/1 for domestic and international students. Application fee: $60. *Financial support:* In 2010–11, 15 fellowships (averaging $3,953 per year), 6 teaching assistantships (averaging $14,862 per year) were awarded; research assistantships. Total annual research expenditures: $1.6 million. *Application contact:* Joel Cohn, Graduate Chair, 808-956-2069, Fax: 808-956-9515, E-mail: cohn@hawaii.edu.

University of Illinois at Urbana–Champaign, Graduate College, College of Liberal Arts and Sciences, School of Literatures, Cultures and Linguistics, Department of East Asian Languages and Cultures, Champaign, IL 61820. Offers Asian studies (MA); East Asian languages and cultures (PhD). *Faculty:* 16 full-time (6 women). *Students:* 31 full-time (19 women), 11 part-time (10 women); includes 1 American Indian or Alaska Native, non-Hispanic/Latino; 5 Asian, non-Hispanic/Latino, 25 international. 87 applicants, 16% accepted, 8 enrolled. In 2010, 7 master's, 5 doctorates awarded. *Entrance requirements:* For master's, GRE General Test, minimum GPA of 3.0; writing sample; for doctorate, GRE, minimum GPA of 3.0; writing sample. Additional exam requirements/recommendations for international students: Required—TOEFL (minimum score 103 iBT). *Application deadline:* Applications are processed on a rolling basis. Application fee: $75 ($90 for international students). Electronic applications accepted. *Financial support:* In 2010–11, 9 fellowships, 5 research assistantships, 26 teaching assistantships were awarded; tuition waivers (full and partial) also available. *Unit head:* Brian D. Ruppert, Head, 217-244-4012, Fax: 217-244-2223, E-mail: ruppert@illinois.edu. *Application contact:* Lynn Stanke, Office Support Specialist, 217-333-6269, Fax: 217-244-3050, E-mail: stanke@illinois.edu.

The University of Kansas, Graduate Studies, College of Liberal Arts and Sciences, Department of East Asian Languages and Cultures, Lawrence, KS 66045. Offers MA, MBA/MA. Part-time programs available. *Faculty:* 7. *Students:* 13 full-time (6 women), 5 part-time (all women); includes 6 minority (1 Black or African American, non-Hispanic/Latino; 1 American Indian or Alaska Native, non-Hispanic/Latino; 3 Asian, non-Hispanic/Latino; 1 Two or more races, non-Hispanic/Latino), 3 international. Average age 30. 13 applicants, 46% accepted, 3 enrolled. In 2010, 1 master's awarded. *Degree requirements:* For master's, one foreign language, thesis. *Entrance requirements:* For master's, GRE, 3 letters of recommendation, writing sample. Additional exam requirements/recommendations for international students: Required—TOEFL. *Application deadline:* For fall admission, 5/1 priority date for domestic students, 5/1 for international students; for spring admission, 12/1 priority date for domestic students, 12/1 for international students. Applications are processed on a rolling basis. Application fee: $55 ($65 for international students). Electronic applications accepted. *Expenses:* Tuition, state resident: full-time $7092; part-time $295.50 per credit hour. Tuition, nonresident: full-time $16,590; part-time $691.25 per credit hour. Required fees: $858; $71.49 per credit hour. Tuition and fees vary according to course load, campus/location and program. *Financial support:* Fellowships, teaching assistantships with full and partial tuition reimbursements, unspecified assistant-

ships available. Financial award application deadline: 2/1. *Faculty research:* Gender relations in literature, ancient Chinese law, visual culture of modern Japan, Japanese language pedagogy, Chinese paleography, Korean shamanism, folklore, traditional Chinese and Japanese literature, Chinese linguistics and language pedagogy. *Unit head:* Margaret Childs, Chair, 785-864-3100, E-mail: mgchilds@ku.edu. *Application contact:* Jennifer Newlin, Administrative Specialist, 785-864-3100, Fax: 785-864-4298, E-mail: ealc@ku.edu.

University of Michigan, Horace H. Rackham School of Graduate Studies, College of Literature, Science, and the Arts, Department of Asian Languages and Cultures, Ann Arbor, MI 48104. Offers MA, PhD. Students cannot apply directly to a terminal masters degree in this program. Masters are only awarded to PhD program students for partial completion of the degree. Terminal master's awarded for partial completion of doctoral program. *Degree requirements:* For master's, variable foreign language requirement, thesis; for doctorate, 2 foreign languages, thesis/dissertation, oral defense of dissertation, preliminary exam. *Entrance requirements:* For master's and doctorate, GRE General Test. Additional exam requirements/recommendations for international students: Required—TOEFL (minimum score 600 paper-based; 250 computer-based; 106 iBT). Electronic applications accepted. *Expenses:* Tuition, state resident: full-time $17,784; part-time $1116 per credit hour. Tuition, nonresident: full-time $35,944; part-time $2125 per credit hour. International tuition: $35,994 full-time. Required fees: $95 per semester. Tuition and fees vary according to course load, degree level and program. *Faculty research:* Literature, linguistics, religion, music, cinema.

University of Minnesota, Twin Cities Campus, Graduate School, College of Liberal Arts, Department of Asian Languages and Literatures, Minneapolis, MN 55455-0213. Offers Asian literatures, cultures, and media (PhD). *Degree requirements:* For doctorate, comprehensive exam, thesis/dissertation. *Entrance requirements:* For doctorate, GRE, 3 letters of recommendation. Additional exam requirements/recommendations for international students: Required—TOEFL (minimum score 550 paper-based; 213 computer-based), IELTS (minimum score 6.5). Electronic applications accepted. *Faculty research:* Gender studies, post-colonial theory, poetics and poetic theory, film studies, post modernist thought.

University of Oregon, Graduate School, College of Arts and Sciences, Department of East Asian Languages and Literature, Eugene, OR 97403. Offers Chinese (MA, PhD); Japanese (MA, PhD). *Entrance requirements:* Additional exam requirements/recommendations for international students: Required—TOEFL. *Faculty research:* Linguistics, pedagogy.

University of Southern California, Graduate School, Dana and David Dornsife College of Letters, Arts and Sciences, Department of East Asian Languages and Cultures, Los Angeles, CA 90089. Offers classical Chinese literature (MA, PhD); classical Japanese literature (MA, PhD); linguistics (MA, PhD); modern Chinese literature (MA, PhD); modern Japanese literature (MA, PhD); modern Korean literature (MA, PhD). *Faculty:* 14 full-time (7 women). *Students:* 19 full-time (14 women), 1 (woman) part-time; includes 5 minority (1 Black or African American, non-Hispanic/Latino; 4 Asian, non-Hispanic/Latino), 10 international. 37 applicants, 16% accepted, 6 enrolled. In 2010, 5 master's, 1 doctorate awarded. *Degree requirements:* For master's, thesis; for doctorate, 2 foreign languages, comprehensive exam, thesis/dissertation. *Entrance requirements:* For master's and doctorate, GRE, BA in relevant field. Additional exam requirements/recommendations for international students: Required—TOEFL. *Application deadline:* For fall admission, 12/1 priority date for domestic and international students. Application fee: $85. Electronic applications accepted. *Expenses:* Tuition: Full-time $31,240; part-time $1420 per unit. Required fees: $600. One-time fee: $35 full-time. Full-time tuition and fees vary according to degree level and program. *Financial support:* In 2010–11, 25 students received support, including 4 fellowships with full tuition reimbursements available (averaging $30,000 per year), 25 teaching assistantships with partial tuition reimbursements available (averaging $19,800 per year); scholarships/grants, health care benefits, and unspecified assistantships also available. Financial award application deadline: 12/1. *Faculty research:* Gender, visual studies, multimedia, ecocriticism, second language acquisition. *Unit head:* Dominic Cheung, Chair, 213-740-3708, Fax: 213-740-9295, E-mail: dcheung@usc.edu. *Application contact:* Sherall R. Preyer, Administrative Coordinator, 213-740-3709, Fax: 213-740-9295, E-mail: preyer@college.usc.edu.

University of Southern California, Graduate School, Dana and David Dornsife College of Letters, Arts and Sciences, Department of Linguistics, Los Angeles, CA 90089. Offers East Asian linguistics (PhD); Hispanic linguistics (PhD); linguistics (PhD); Slavic linguistics (PhD). *Faculty:* 15 full-time (10 women), 5 part-time/adjunct (3 women). *Students:* 40 full-time (26 women), 2 part-time (1 woman); includes 7 minority (5 Asian, non-Hispanic/Latino; 1 Hispanic/Latino; 1 Two or more races, non-Hispanic/Latino), 23 international. 76 applicants, 24% accepted, 7 enrolled. In 2010, 1 doctorate awarded. *Degree requirements:* For doctorate, comprehensive exam, thesis/dissertation. *Entrance requirements:* For doctorate, GRE. Additional exam requirements/recommendations for international students: Required—TOEFL (minimum score 100 iBT). *Application deadline:* For fall admission, 12/1 priority date for domestic and international students. Application fee: $85. Electronic applications accepted. *Expenses:* Tuition: Full-time $31,240; part-time $1420 per unit. Required fees: $600. One-time fee: $35 full-time. Full-time tuition and fees vary according to degree level and program. *Financial support:* In 2010–11, 37 students received support, including 12 fellowships with full tuition reimbursements available (averaging $20,000 per year), 3 research assistantships with full tuition reimbursements available (averaging $19,250 per year), 22 teaching assistantships with full tuition reimbursements available (averaging $19,250 per year); scholarships/grants, health care benefits, and unspecified assistantships also available. *Faculty research:* Syntax, phonology, phonetics, semantics, sociolinguistics, psycholinguistics. *Unit head:* Dr. James Higginbotham, Chair, 213-740-2986, Fax: 213-740-9306, E-mail: higgy@usc.edu. *Application contact:* Joyce Perez, Student Services Advisor, 213-740-3891, Fax: 213-740-9306, E-mail: jpperez@usc.edu.

The University of Texas at Austin, Graduate School, College of Liberal Arts, Department of Asian Studies, Austin, TX 78712-1111. Offers Asian cultures and languages (MA, PhD); Asian studies (MA). Part-time programs available. *Degree requirements:* For master's, thesis; for doctorate, 3 foreign languages, thesis/dissertation. *Entrance requirements:* For master's and doctorate, GRE General Test. Electronic applications accepted. *Faculty research:* Modern Taiwanese fiction, modern Japanese literature, religious studies in South Asia during classical period.

University of Washington, Graduate School, College of Arts and Sciences, Department of Asian Languages and Literature, Seattle, WA 98195. Offers Buddhist studies (MA, PhD); Chinese language and literature (MA, PhD); Japanese language and literature (MA, PhD); Korean language and literature (MA, PhD); South Asian language and literature (MA, PhD). *Degree requirements:* For master's, 2 foreign languages, general exam, thesis or 2 research papers; for doctorate, 3 foreign languages, thesis/dissertation, general exam. *Entrance requirements:* For master's, GRE, minimum GPA of 3.0; for doctorate, GRE, master's degree in related field, minimum GPA of 3.0. Additional exam requirements/recommendations for international students: Required—TOEFL. Electronic applications accepted. *Faculty research:* Textual, linguistic, philological, and literary study of languages and literatures of Asia.

University of Wisconsin–Madison, Graduate School, College of Letters and Science, Department of Languages and Cultures of Asia, Madison, WI 53706-1380. Offers civilizations and cultures (PhD); languages and cultures of Asia (MA); languages and literatures (PhD); religions of Asia (PhD). Part-time programs available. Terminal master's awarded for partial completion of doctoral program. *Degree requirements:* For master's, one foreign language, thesis or alternative; for doctorate, 2 foreign languages, thesis/dissertation. *Entrance requirements:* For master's, minimum GPA of 3.0; for doctorate, minimum GPA of 3.25, master's degree. Electronic applications accepted. *Expenses:* Tuition, state resident: full-time $9887; part-time $617.96 per credit. Tuition, nonresident: full-time $24,054; part-time $1503.40 per credit. Required fees: $67.63 per credit. Tuition and fees vary according to reciprocity agreements. *Faculty research:* Literature, folklore, religion.

Asian Languages

Washington University in St. Louis, Graduate School of Arts and Sciences, Department of Asian and Near Eastern Languages and Literatures, St. Louis, MO 63130-4899. Offers Chinese (MA); Chinese and comparative literature (PhD); Japanese (MA); Japanese and comparative literature (PhD). Terminal master's awarded for partial completion of doctoral program. *Degree requirements:* For master's, thesis optional; for doctorate, thesis/dissertation. *Entrance requirements:* For master's and doctorate, GRE General Test. Electronic applications accepted.

Washington University in St. Louis, Graduate School of Arts and Sciences, Program in East Asian Studies, St. Louis, MO 63130-4899. Offers East Asian studies (MA); JD/MA. PhD offered through specific departments. *Entrance requirements:* For master's, GRE General Test. Electronic applications accepted.

Yale University, Graduate School of Arts and Sciences, Department of East Asian Languages and Literatures, New Haven, CT 06520. Offers East Asian languages and literatures (PhD); East Asian languages and literatures and film studies (PhD). *Degree requirements:* For doctorate, 2 foreign languages, thesis/dissertation. *Entrance requirements:* For doctorate, GRE General Test.

Celtic Languages

Harvard University, Graduate School of Arts and Sciences, Department of Celtic Languages and Literatures, Cambridge, MA 02138. Offers Irish (PhD); Welsh (PhD). *Degree requirements:* For doctorate, thesis/dissertation, proficiency in 2 Celtic languages; reading knowledge of French, German, and Latin. *Entrance requirements:* For doctorate, GRE General Test. Additional exam requirements/recommendations for international students: Required—TOEFL. *Expenses:* Tuition: Full-time $34,976. Required fees: $1166. Full-time tuition and fees vary according to program.

Chinese

Arizona State University, College of Liberal Arts and Sciences, School of International Letters and Cultures, Program in Chinese, Tempe, AZ 85287-0202. Offers Asian languages and civilizations: Chinese (MA); Chinese (PhD). Part-time and evening/weekend programs available. *Faculty:* 10 full-time (5 women). *Students:* 14 full-time (9 women), 4 part-time (3 women); includes 4 minority (3 Asian, non-Hispanic/Latino; 1 Hispanic/Latino), 7 international. Average age 30. 25 applicants, 68% accepted, 10 enrolled.Terminal master's awarded for partial completion of doctoral program. *Degree requirements:* For master's, thesis, oral defense, interactive Program of Study (iPOS) submitted no later than beginning of third semester of study; for doctorate, comprehensive exam, thesis/dissertation, interactive Program of Study (iPOS) submitted before completing 50 percent of required credit hours. *Entrance requirements:* For master's, GRE, minimum GPA of 3.0 in the last two years of work leading to the bachelor's degree, BA in Chinese studies (preferred), personal statement, writing sample, 3 letters of recommendation; for doctorate, GRE, minimum GPA of 3.5 in the last two years of work leading to the bachelor's degree, completion of 3 years of modern Chinese and 1 year of classical Chinese, personal statement, writing sample, 3 letters of recommendation. Additional exam requirements/recommendations for international students: Required—TOEFL (minimum score 550 paper-based; 213 computer-based; 83 iBT), IELTS (minimum score 6.5). *Application deadline:* For fall admission, 12/15 for domestic and international students. Application fee: $70 ($90 for international students). Electronic applications accepted. *Expenses:* Tuition, state resident: full-time $8510; part-time $608 per credit. Tuition, nonresident: full-time $16,542; part-time $919 per credit. Required fees: $339; $110 per credit. Part-time tuition and fees vary according to course load. *Financial support:* In 2010–11, 5 research assistantships with full and partial tuition reimbursements (averaging $14,400 per year), 6 teaching assistantships with full and partial tuition reimbursements (averaging $13,750 per year) were awarded; fellowships with full and partial tuition reimbursements, institutionally sponsored loans, scholarships/grants, and tuition waivers (partial) also available. Financial award application deadline: 3/1; financial award applicants required to submit FAFSA. *Unit head:* Joe Cutter, Director, School of International Letters and Cultures, 480-965-3762, E-mail: joe.cutter@asu.edu. *Application contact:* Graduate Admissions, 480-965-6113.

Cornell University, Graduate School, Graduate Fields of Arts and Sciences, Field of East Asian Literature, Ithaca, NY 14853-0001. Offers Asian religions (MA, PhD); Chinese linguistics (MA, PhD); Chinese philology (MA, PhD); classical Chinese literature (MA, PhD); classical Japanese literature (MA, PhD); Japanese linguistics (MA, PhD); Korean literature (MA, PhD); modern Chinese literature (MA, PhD); modern Japanese literature (MA, PhD). *Faculty:* 15 full-time (7 women). *Students:* 19 full-time (9 women); includes 1 Black or African American, non-Hispanic/Latino; 3 Asian, non-Hispanic/Latino, 10 international. Average age 30. 37 applicants, 19% accepted, 6 enrolled. In 2010, 2 master's, 4 doctorates awarded. *Degree requirements:* For master's, 2 foreign languages, thesis, teaching experience; for doctorate, 2 foreign languages, comprehensive exam, thesis/dissertation, teaching experience. *Entrance requirements:* For master's, GRE General Test, 3 years of study in Chinese, Japanese, Korean, or Vietnamese; 3 letters of recommendation; academic writing sample; for doctorate, GRE General Test, 3 years of study in Chinese, Japanese, Korean, or Vietnamese, 3 letters of recommendation, academic writing sample. Additional exam requirements/recommendations for international students: Required—TOEFL (minimum score 600 paper-based; 250 computer-based; 77 iBT). *Application deadline:* For fall admission, 1/10 priority date for domestic students. Application fee: $80. Electronic applications accepted. *Expenses:* Tuition: Full-time $29,500. Required fees: $76. Tuition and fees vary according to degree level and program. *Financial support:* In 2010–11, 13 fellowships with full tuition reimbursements, 6 teaching assistantships with full tuition reimbursements were awarded; research assistantships with full tuition reimbursements, institutionally sponsored loans, scholarships/grants, health care benefits, tuition waivers (full and partial), and unspecified assistantships also available. Financial award applicants required to submit FAFSA. *Faculty research:* Vietnamese literature; Chinese literature, drama, and film; Japanese theater and literature; popular culture in East Asia; Korean literature; Asian linguistics. *Unit head:* Director of Graduate Studies, 607-255-9099. *Application contact:* Graduate Field Assistant, 607-255-9099, E-mail: east_asian_lit@cornell.edu.

Harvard University, Graduate School of Arts and Sciences, Department of East Asian Languages and Civilizations, Cambridge, MA 02138. Offers Chinese (PhD); Japanese (PhD); Korean (PhD); Mongolian (PhD); Vietnamese (PhD). Terminal master's awarded for partial completion of doctoral program. *Degree requirements:* For doctorate, 3 foreign languages, thesis/dissertation, general exams. *Entrance requirements:* For doctorate, GRE General Test. Additional exam requirements/recommendations for international students: Required—TOEFL. *Expenses:* Tuition: Full-time $34,976. Required fees: $1166. Full-time tuition and fees vary according to program. *Faculty research:* Central Asian literature, religion, and premodern history.

Indiana University Bloomington, University Graduate School, College of Arts and Sciences, Department of East Asian Languages and Cultures, Bloomington, IN 47408. Offers Chinese (MA, PhD); Chinese language pedagogy (MA); East Asian studies (MA); Japanese (MA, PhD); Japanese language pedagogy (MA). Part-time programs available. *Faculty:* 15 full-time (7 women), 15 part-time/adjunct (7 women). *Students:* 28 full-time (18 women), 11 part-time (6 women); includes 2 Black or African American, non-Hispanic/Latino, 11 international. Average age 29. 100 applicants, 38% accepted, 18 enrolled. In 2010, 9 master's, 1 doctorate awarded. *Degree requirements:* For master's, one foreign language, thesis; for doctorate, 2 foreign languages, comprehensive exam, thesis/dissertation. *Entrance requirements:* Additional exam requirements/recommendations for international students: Required—TOEFL (minimum score 93 iBT). *Application deadline:* For fall admission, 1/15 for domestic students, 12/1 for international students. Application fee: $55 ($65 for international students). Electronic applications accepted. *Financial support:* In 2010–11, 21 students received support, including 5 fellowships with full tuition reimbursements available (averaging $15,500 per year), 18 teaching assistantships with full tuition reimbursements available (averaging $11,633 per year). Financial award application deadline: 3/1. *Faculty research:* Postwar/postmodern Japanese fiction, modern Chinese film and literature, classical Chinese literature and philosophy, Chinese and Japanese linguistics and pedagogy, East Asian politics and economics, Chinese and Japanese history, Korean language. *Unit head:* Michael Robinson, Chair, 812-855-0856, Fax: 812-855-6402, E-mail: robime@indiana.edu. *Application contact:* Natsuko Tsujimura, Director of Graduate Studies, 812-855-5884, Fax: 812-855-6402, E-mail: tsujimur@indiana.edu.

Middlebury College, Language Schools, Chinese School, Middlebury, VT 05753-6002. Offers MA. *Faculty:* 4 full-time (3 women). *Students:* 29 full-time (23 women); includes 21 minority (all Asian, non-Hispanic/Latino). Average age 34. 49 applicants, 82% accepted, 29 enrolled. In 2010, 8 master's awarded. *Degree requirements:* For master's, one foreign language, teaching practicum. *Entrance requirements:* For master's, Placement test, 3 letters of recommendation, writing sample, curriculum vitae. Additional exam requirements/recommendations for international students: Required—TOEFL (minimum score 600 paper-based; 250 computer-based; 100 iBT). *Application deadline:* Applications are processed on a rolling basis. Application fee: $65. Electronic applications accepted. *Financial support:* In 2010–11, 2 fellowships with full tuition reimbursements (averaging $7,000 per year) were awarded; scholarships/grants also available. Financial award applicants required to submit FAFSA. *Unit head:* Dr. Jianhua Bai, Director, 802-443-5520, Fax: 802-443-2075, E-mail: jbai@middlebury.edu. *Application contact:* Anna Sun, Coordinator, 802-443-5520, Fax: 802-443-2075, E-mail: sun@middlebury.edu.

The Ohio State University, Graduate School, College of Arts and Sciences, Division of Arts and Humanities, Department of East Asian Languages and Literatures, Columbus, OH 43210. Offers Chinese (MA, PhD); Japanese (MA, PhD). *Faculty:* 22. *Students:* 59 full-time (29 women), 10 part-time (5 women); includes 6 Asian, non-Hispanic/Latino; 1 Hispanic/Latino; 1 Two or more races, non-Hispanic/Latino, 26 international. Average age 27. In 2010, 15 master's, 2 doctorates awarded. *Degree requirements:* For master's, thesis optional; for doctorate, thesis/dissertation. *Entrance requirements:* Additional exam requirements/recommendations for international students: Required—TOEFL (minimum score 577 paper-based; 233 computer-based). *Application deadline:* For fall admission, 8/15 priority date for domestic students, 7/1 priority date for international students; for winter admission, 12/1 priority date for domestic students, 11/1 priority date for international students; for spring admission, 3/1 priority date for domestic students, 2/1 priority date for international students. Applications are processed on a rolling basis. Application fee: $40 ($50 for international students). Electronic applications accepted. *Expenses:* Tuition, state resident: full-time $10,605. Tuition, nonresident: full-time $26,535. Tuition and fees vary according to course load and program. *Financial support:* Fellowships, research assistantships, teaching assistantships, Federal Work-Study, institutionally sponsored loans, and unspecified assistantships available. Support available to part-time students. *Unit head:* Mari Noda, Chair, 614-688-5737, E-mail: noda.1@osu.edu. *Application contact:* Graduate Admissions, 614-292-9444, Fax: 614-292-3895, E-mail: domestic.grad@osu.edu.

San Francisco State University, Division of Graduate Studies, College of Humanities, Department of Foreign Languages and Literatures, Program in Chinese, San Francisco, CA 94132-1722. Offers MA. *Application deadline:* Applications are processed on a rolling basis. *Unit head:* Charles Egan, Program Coordinator, 415-338-1421, E-mail: wenchao@sfsu.edu. *Application contact:* Chris Wen-Chao Li, Graduate Advisor, 415-338-1034.

Seton Hall University, College of Arts and Sciences, Department of Asian Studies, South Orange, NJ 07079-2697. Offers Asian languages (MA); Asian studies (MA); teaching Chinese language and culture (MA). Part-time and evening/weekend programs available. *Degree requirements:* For master's, thesis optional. *Entrance requirements:* For master's, strong background in Asian studies or related discipline. Additional exam requirements/recommendations for international students: Required—TOEFL. Electronic applications accepted. *Faculty research:* Modern Chinese history, contemporary Chinese politics, ancient Chinese history, Hinduism, Asian business, Japanese history.

Stanford University, School of Humanities and Sciences, Department of Asian Languages, Stanford, CA 94305-9991. Offers Chinese (MA, PhD); Japanese (MA, PhD). Terminal master's awarded for partial completion of doctoral program. *Degree requirements:* For master's, one foreign language, thesis or an annotated translation of a literary or historical text; for doctorate, 2 foreign languages, thesis/dissertation, field exams. *Entrance requirements:* For master's and doctorate, GRE General Test. Additional exam requirements/recommendations for international students: Required—TOEFL. Electronic applications accepted. *Expenses:* Tuition: Full-time $38,700; part-time $860 per unit. One-time fee: $200 full-time.

Union Graduate College, School of Education, Schenectady, NY 12308-3107. Offers biology (MAT, MS); chemistry (MAT); Chinese (MAT); earth science (MAT); English (MAT); French (MAT); general science (MAT); German (MAT); Greek (MAT); languages (MAT); Latin (MAT); mathematics (MAT); mathematics and technology (MS); mentoring and teacher leadership (AC); middle childhood extension (AC); national board certificate and teacher leadership (AC); physical science (MS); physics (MAT); social studies (MAT); Spanish (MAT). *Accreditation:* Teacher Education Accreditation Council. *Faculty:* 3 full-time (1 woman), 23 part-time/adjunct (8 women). *Students:* 50 full-time (37 women), 23 part-time (19 women); includes 4 minority (3 Asian, non-Hispanic/Latino; 1 Hispanic/Latino), 1 international. Average age 32. 70 applicants,

86% accepted, 48 enrolled. In 2010, 47 master's, 18 other advanced degrees awarded. *Degree requirements:* For master's, thesis or project. *Entrance requirements:* For master's, minimum GPA of 3.0, letters of recommendation. Additional exam requirements/recommendations for international students: Required—TOEFL (minimum score 550 paper-based; 213 computer-based). *Application deadline:* Applications are processed on a rolling basis. Application fee: $60. Electronic applications accepted. *Expenses:* Contact institution. *Financial support:* Career-related internships or fieldwork, Federal Work-Study, scholarships/grants, health care benefits, and tuition waivers (partial) available. Support available to part-time students. Financial award applicants required to submit FAFSA. *Faculty research:* Transformative learning, science education, National Board Certification, teacher leadership, teacher quality. *Unit head:* Dr. Patrick Allen, Dean, 518-631-9870, Fax: 518-631-9901. *Application contact:* Christine Angley, Assistant, 518-631-9871, Fax: 518-631-9903, E-mail: angleyc@uniongraduatecollege.edu.

University of Alberta, Faculty of Graduate Studies and Research, Department of East Asian Studies, Edmonton, AB T6G 2E1, Canada. Offers Chinese literature (MA); East Asian interdisciplinary studies (MA); Japanese literature (MA). Part-time programs available. *Degree requirements:* For master's, one foreign language, thesis. *Entrance requirements:* Additional exam requirements/recommendations for international students: Required—TOEFL. Electronic applications accepted. *Faculty research:* Classical Chinese poetry and poetics, Chinese philosophy, modern/contemporary Chinese literature, modern Japanese literature and culture, Japanese women's writing.

University of California, Berkeley, Graduate Division, College of Letters and Science, Department of East Asian Languages and Cultures, Berkeley, CA 94720-1500. Offers Chinese language (PhD); Japanese language (PhD). *Degree requirements:* For doctorate, one foreign language, thesis/dissertation, oral qualifying exam. *Entrance requirements:* For doctorate, GRE General Test, minimum GPA of 3.0, MA thesis, 3 letters of recommendation. Electronic applications accepted. *Faculty research:* Chinese and Japanese modern and classical texts, prose, and poetry; Chinese and Japanese linguistics.

University of California, Irvine, School of Humanities, Department of East Asian Languages and Literatures, Irvine, CA 92697. Offers Chinese (MA, PhD); East Asian languages and literatures (MA, PhD); Japanese (MA, PhD). *Students:* 13 full-time (11 women), 1 (woman) part-time, 11 international. Average age 28. 35 applicants, 20% accepted, 4 enrolled. In 2010, 5 doctorates awarded. *Degree requirements:* For doctorate, thesis/dissertation. *Entrance requirements:* For master's, GRE, minimum GPA of 3.0; for doctorate, GRE General Test, minimum GPA of 3.0. Additional exam requirements/recommendations for international students: Required—TOEFL (minimum score 550 paper-based; 213 computer-based). *Application deadline:* For fall admission, 1/15 priority date for domestic students, 1/15 for international students. Application fee: $80 ($100 for international students). Electronic applications accepted. *Financial support:* Fellowships with tuition reimbursements, research assistantships with full tuition reimbursements, teaching assistantships with partial tuition reimbursements, institutionally sponsored loans, traineeships, health care benefits, and unspecified assistantships available. Financial award application deadline: 3/1; financial award applicants required to submit FAFSA. *Faculty research:* Chinese, Japanese, and Korean literature and culture; language and textual analysis; historical, social, and cultural dimensions of literary study. *Unit head:* Prof. Martin W. Huang, Chair, 949-824-2802, Fax: 949-824-3248, E-mail: mwhuang@uci.edu. *Application contact:* Mindy Han, Management Services Officer, 949-824-2165, Fax: 949-824-3248, E-mail: mindyhan@uci.edu.

University of Colorado Boulder, Graduate School, College of Arts and Sciences, Department of Asian Languages and Civilizations, Boulder, CO 80309. Offers Chinese (MA, PhD); Japanese (MA, PhD). Part-time programs available. *Faculty:* 12 full-time (6 women). *Students:* 26 full-time (12 women), 4 part-time (3 women); includes 6 minority (1 Black or African American, non-Hispanic/Latino; 4 Asian, non-Hispanic/Latino; 1 Hispanic/Latino), 7 international. Average age 26. 37 applicants, 13 enrolled. In 2010, 18 master's awarded. *Degree requirements:* For master's, comprehensive exam. *Entrance requirements:* For master's, BA in Chinese or Japanese, minimum undergraduate GPA of 3.0. Additional exam requirements/recommendations for international students: Required—TOEFL. *Application deadline:* For fall admission, 1/1 priority date for domestic students, 12/1 for international students; for spring admission, 10/1 for domestic students, 9/1 for international students. Applications are processed on a rolling basis. Application fee: $50 ($60 for international students). *Financial support:* In 2010–11, 7 fellowships (averaging $13,865 per year), 10 research assistantships (averaging $6,596 per year) were awarded; career-related internships or fieldwork and Federal Work-Study also available. Financial award application deadline: 2/1. *Faculty research:* Chinese and Japanese modern and classical literature, religions, linguistics, language pedagogy, pre-modern and contemporary fiction, sociolinguistics. Total annual research expenditures: $757,691.

University of Delaware, College of Arts and Sciences, Department of Foreign Languages and Literatures, Newark, DE 19716. Offers foreign languages and literatures (MA), including French, German, Spanish; foreign languages pedagogy (MA), including French, German, Spanish; technical Chinese translation (MA). *Degree requirements:* For master's, one foreign language, comprehensive exam, thesis optional. *Entrance requirements:* For master's, GRE General Test, letters of recommendation, writing sample. Additional exam requirements/recommendations for international students: Required—TOEFL. Electronic applications accepted. *Faculty research:* Medieval to Modern French and Spanish literature, Twentieth Century German, French, Spanish literature by women, computer-assisted instruction.

University of Hawaii at Manoa, Graduate Division, College of Languages, Linguistics and Literature, Department of East Asian Languages and Literatures, Program in Chinese, Honolulu, HI 96822. Offers MA, PhD. Part-time programs available. *Faculty:* 11 full-time (4 women). *Students:* 3 full-time (0 women), 12 part-time (1 woman); includes 1 Asian, non-Hispanic/Latino, 9 international. Average age 33. 35 applicants, 60% accepted, 9 enrolled. In 2010, 3 master's, 4 doctorates awarded. *Degree requirements:* For master's, 2 foreign languages, thesis optional; for doctorate, 2 foreign languages, comprehensive exam, thesis/dissertation. *Entrance requirements:* For master's and doctorate, GRE General Test. Additional exam requirements/recommendations for international students: Required—TOEFL (minimum score 560 paper-based; 220 computer-based; 83 iBT), IELTS (minimum score 5). *Application deadline:* For fall admission, 2/1 for domestic and international students; for spring admission, 9/1 for domestic and international students. Application fee: $50. *Financial support:* In 2010–11, 5 fellowships (averaging $8,424 per year), 4 teaching assistantships (averaging $14,814 per year) were awarded. *Application contact:* Joel Cohn, Graduate Chair, 808-956-2069, Fax: 808-956-9515, E-mail: cohn@hawaii.edu.

University of Hawaii at Manoa, Graduate Division, School of Pacific and Asian Studies, Program in Asian Studies, Concentration in Chinese Studies, Honolulu, HI 96822. Offers Graduate Certificate. Part-time programs available. *Students:* Average age 32. In 2010, 3 Graduate Certificates awarded. *Degree requirements:* For Graduate Certificate, one foreign language. *Entrance requirements:* For degree, GRE. Additional exam requirements/recommendations for international students: Required—TOEFL (minimum score 560 paper-based; 220 computer-based; 83 iBT), IELTS (minimum score 5). Application fee: $60. Total annual research expenditures: $187,500. *Application contact:* Dr. Frederick Lau, Graduate Field Chairperson, 808-956-2177, Fax: 808-956-2682, E-mail: fredlau@hawaii.edu.

The University of Manchester, School of Languages, Linguistics and Cultures, Manchester, United Kingdom. Offers Arab world studies (PhD); Chinese studies (M Phil, PhD); East Asian studies (M Phil, PhD); English language (PhD); French studies (M Phil, PhD); German studies (M Phil, PhD); interpreting studies (PhD); Italian studies (M Phil, PhD); Japanese studies (M Phil, PhD); Latin American cultural studies (M Phil, PhD); linguistics (M Phil, PhD); Middle Eastern studies (M Phil, PhD); Polish studies (M Phil, PhD); Portuguese studies (M Phil, PhD); Russian studies (M Phil, PhD); Spanish studies (M Phil, PhD); translation and intercultural studies (M Phil, PhD).

University of Massachusetts Amherst, Graduate School, College of Humanities and Fine Arts, Department of Languages, Literatures, and Cultures, Programs in Asian Languages and Literatures, Amherst, MA 01003. Offers Chinese (MA); Japanese (MA). Part-time programs available. *Faculty:* 13 full-time (6 women). *Students:* 17 full-time (12 women), 9 part-time (7 women); includes 4 minority (1 Black or African American, non-Hispanic/Latino; 3 Asian, non-Hispanic/Latino), 12 international. Average age 28. 30 applicants, 80% accepted, 12 enrolled. In 2010, 10 master's awarded. *Degree requirements:* For master's, thesis, general exam. *Entrance requirements:* For master's, GRE General Test. Additional exam requirements/recommendations for international students: Required—TOEFL (minimum score 550 paper-based; 213 computer-based; 80 iBT), IELTS (minimum score 6.5). *Application deadline:* For fall admission, 2/1 for domestic and international students. Applications are processed on a rolling basis. Application fee: $50 ($65 for international students). Electronic applications accepted. *Expenses:* Tuition, state resident: full-time $2640. Required fees: $8282. One-time fee: $357 full-time. *Financial support:* In 2010–11, 21 teaching assistantships with full tuition reimbursements (averaging $8,116 per year) were awarded; fellowships, research assistantships, career-related internships or fieldwork, Federal Work-Study, scholarships/grants, traineeships, health care benefits, tuition waivers (full), and unspecified assistantships also available. Support available to part-time students. Financial award application deadline: 2/1; financial award applicants required to submit FAFSA. *Unit head:* Dr. Amanda C. Seaman, Department Head/Chair, 413-545-0886, Fax: 413-545-4975. *Application contact:* Jean M. Ames, Supervisor of Admissions, 413-545-0722, Fax: 413-577-0100, E-mail: gradadm@grad.umass.edu.

University of Oregon, Graduate School, College of Arts and Sciences, Department of East Asian Languages and Literature, Eugene, OR 97403. Offers Chinese (MA, PhD); Japanese (MA, PhD). *Entrance requirements:* Additional exam requirements/recommendations for international students: Required—TOEFL. *Faculty research:* Linguistics, pedagogy.

University of Washington, Graduate School, College of Arts and Sciences, Department of Asian Languages and Literature, Seattle, WA 98195. Offers Buddhist studies (MA, PhD); Chinese language and literature (MA, PhD); Japanese language and literature (MA, PhD); Korean language and literature (MA, PhD); South Asian language and literature (MA, PhD). *Degree requirements:* For master's, 2 foreign languages, general exam, thesis or 2 research papers; for doctorate, 3 foreign languages, thesis/dissertation, general exam. *Entrance requirements:* For master's, GRE, minimum GPA of 3.0; for doctorate, GRE, master's degree in related field, minimum GPA of 3.0. Additional exam requirements/recommendations for international students: Required—TOEFL. Electronic applications accepted. *Faculty research:* Textual, linguistic, philological, and literary study of languages and literatures of Asia.

University of Wisconsin–Madison, Graduate School, College of Letters and Science, Department of East Asian Languages and Literature, Program in Chinese Literature, Madison, WI 53706-1380. Offers MA, PhD. Part-time programs available. Terminal master's awarded for partial completion of doctoral program. *Degree requirements:* For master's, one foreign language, seminars, written exam; for doctorate, 3 foreign languages, thesis/dissertation, seminars, preliminary exams, oral exam. *Entrance requirements:* For master's, bachelor's degree or equivalent in Chinese; for doctorate, master's degree or equivalent in Chinese. Electronic applications accepted. *Expenses:* Tuition, state resident: full-time $9887; part-time $617.96 per credit. Tuition, nonresident: full-time $24,054; part-time $1503.40 per credit. Required fees: $67.63 per credit. Tuition and fees vary according to reciprocity agreements. *Faculty research:* Chinese historical and modern linguistics, classical Chinese literary and cultural history, modern Chinese literary and cultural history, Chinese paleography.

Washington University in St. Louis, Graduate School of Arts and Sciences, Department of Asian and Near Eastern Languages and Literatures, St. Louis, MO 63130-4899. Offers Chinese (MA); Chinese and comparative literature (PhD); Japanese (MA); Japanese and comparative literature (PhD). Terminal master's awarded for partial completion of doctoral program. *Degree requirements:* For master's, thesis optional; for doctorate, thesis/dissertation. *Entrance requirements:* For master's and doctorate, GRE General Test. Electronic applications accepted.

Classics

Asbury University, School of Graduate and Professional Studies, Wilmore, KY 40390-1198. Offers biology: alternative certificate (MA Ed); chemistry: alternative certificate (MA Ed); English (MA Ed); English as a second language (MA Ed); ESL (MA Ed); French (MA Ed); Latin: alternative certificate (MA Ed); mathematics: alternative certificate (MA Ed); reading/writing endorsement (MA Ed); social studies (MA Ed); social work (MSW), including child and family services; Spanish (MA Ed); special education (MA Ed); special education: alternative certificate (MA Ed); teacher as leader endorsement (MA Ed). *Accreditation:* NCATE. Part-time programs available. *Degree requirements:* For master's, action research project, portfolio. *Entrance requirements:* For master's, PRAXIS/NTE, minimum GPA of 2.75, letters of recommendation. Additional exam requirements/recommendations for international students: Required—TOEFL (minimum score 550 paper-based). Electronic applications accepted.

Bethel Seminary, Graduate and Professional Programs, St. Paul, MN 55112-6998. Offers Anglican studies (Certificate); applied ministry (MA, Certificate); biblical studies (Certificate); children's and family ministry (MACFM); Christian education (MACE); Christian thought (MACT); community ministry leadership (MA, Certificate); global and contextual studies (MA); Greek and Hebrew language track (M Div); Greek language track (M Div); Hebrew language track (M Div); lay ministry (Certificate); marriage and family therapy (MAMFT, Certificate); men's ministry leadership (Certificate); ministry (D Min); ministry leadership (Certificate); spiritual formation (Certificate); theological studies (MATS, Certificate); transformational leadership (MATL, Certificate); young life youth ministry (Certificate). *Accreditation:* ACIPE; ATS (one or more programs are accredited). Part-time and evening/weekend programs available. Post-baccalaureate distance learning degree programs offered (minimal on-campus study). *Faculty:* 26 full-time (3 women), 74 part-time/adjunct (29 women). *Students:* 729 full-time (275 women), 274 part-time (118 women); includes 75 minority (34 Black or African American, non-Hispanic/Latino; 1 American Indian or Alaska Native, non-Hispanic/Latino; 12 Asian, non-Hispanic/Latino; 16 Hispanic/Latino; 1 Native Hawaiian or other Pacific Islander, non-Hispanic/Latino; 11 Two or more races, non-Hispanic/Latino), 16 international. Average age 38. 525 applicants, 76% accepted, 265 enrolled. In 2010, 149 master's, 13 doctorates awarded. *Degree requirements:* For master's, variable foreign language requirement, thesis (for some programs); for doctorate, thesis/dissertation; for M Div, one foreign language. *Entrance requirements:* For M Div and master's, letters of reference, transcripts, personal statement; for doctorate, M Div, letters of reference, organizational support. Additional exam requirements/recommendations for international students: Required—TOEFL (minimum score 550 paper-based; 213 computer-based; 87 iBT). *Application deadline:* For fall admission, 8/1 priority date for domestic students,

Classics

Bethel Seminary (continued)
3/1 for international students; for winter admission, 12/1 priority date for domestic students; for spring admission, 3/1 priority date for domestic students. Applications are processed on a rolling basis. Application fee: $20. Electronic applications accepted. *Financial support:* In 2010–11, 655 students received support, including 18 teaching assistantships; career-related internships or fieldwork, Federal Work-Study, scholarships/grants, and tuition waivers (full) also available. Financial award application deadline: 7/15; financial award applicants required to submit FAFSA. *Faculty research:* Nature of theology, ethics, Biblical commentaries, nature of God, science and theology. *Unit head:* Dr. David Ridder, Vice President and Dean, 651-638-6553. *Application contact:* Joseph V. Dworak, Director of Admissions, 651-638-6288, Fax: 651-638-6002, E-mail: j-dworak@bethel.edu.

Boston College, Graduate School of Arts and Sciences, Department of Classics, Chestnut Hill, MA 02467-3800. Offers classics (MA); Greek (MA); Latin (MA). Part-time programs available. *Degree requirements:* For master's, one foreign language, thesis optional. *Entrance requirements:* Additional exam requirements/recommendations for international students: Required—TOEFL (minimum score 600 paper-based; 250 computer-based; 100 iBT). *Faculty research:* Classical philology, ancient history, modern Greek.

Boston University, Graduate School of Arts and Sciences, Department of Classical Studies, Boston, MA 02215. Offers MA, PhD, MA/PhD. *Faculty:* 14 full-time (6 women), 1 (woman) part-time/adjunct. *Students:* 19 full-time (10 women), 4 part-time (1 woman). Average age 28. 50 applicants, 26% accepted, 3 enrolled. In 2010, 1 master's awarded. Terminal master's awarded for partial completion of doctoral program. *Degree requirements:* For master's, one foreign language, comprehensive exam; for doctorate, 2 foreign languages, comprehensive exam, thesis/dissertation. *Entrance requirements:* For master's, GRE General Test, 3 letters of recommendation, scholarly writing sample; for doctorate, GRE General Test, 3 letters of recommendation, scholarly writing sample, personal statement. Additional exam requirements/recommendations for international students: Required—TOEFL (minimum score 550 paper-based; 213 computer-based; 84 iBT). *Application deadline:* For fall admission, 1/15 for domestic and international students; for spring admission, 10/15 for domestic and international students. Application fee: $70. Electronic applications accepted. *Expenses:* Tuition: Full-time $39,314; part-time $1228 per credit. Required fees: $40 per semester. *Financial support:* In 2010–11, 16 students received support, including 1 fellowship with full tuition reimbursement available (averaging $19,300 per year), 1 research assistantship with full tuition reimbursement available (averaging $10,000 per year), 10 teaching assistantships with full tuition reimbursements available (averaging $18,800 per year); career-related internships or fieldwork, Federal Work-Study, institutionally sponsored loans, health care benefits, and first-year scholarships also available. Support available to part-time students. Financial award application deadline: 1/15; financial award applicants required to submit FAFSA. *Faculty research:* Homer and Hesiod, tragedy and comedy, classical tradition, fifth century Athenian history, empire literature and history. *Unit head:* Dr. Loren J. Samons, Chairman, 617-353-2427, Fax: 617-353-1610, E-mail: ljs@bu.edu. *Application contact:* Stacy Fox, Department Administrator, 617-353-2426, Fax: 617-353-1610, E-mail: sfox@bu.edu.

Boston University, School of Education, Boston, MA 02215. Offers counseling (Ed M, CAGS), including community, school, sport psychology; counseling psychology (Ed D); curriculum and teaching (Ed M, Ed D, CAGS), including early childhood (Ed D), educational media and technology (Ed D), English and language arts (Ed D), mathematics (Ed D), physical education and coaching (Ed D), science (Ed D), social studies education (Ed D), special education (Ed D); developmental studies (Ed D), including literacy and language, reading education; developmental studies in literacy and language education (Ed M, CAGS); early childhood education (Ed M, CAGS); education of the deaf (Ed M, CAGS); educational leadership and development (Ed D), including educational administration (Ed M, Ed D, CAGS), higher education administration (Ed M, Ed D, CAGS); educational media and technology (Ed M, CAGS); elementary education (Ed M); English and language arts (Ed M, CAGS); English education (MAT); health education (Ed M, CAGS); Latin and classical studies (MAT); mathematics education (Ed M, MAT, CAGS); mathematics for teaching (MMT); modern foreign language education (MAT), including French, Spanish; physical education and coaching (Ed M, CAGS); policy, planning, and administration (Ed M, CAGS), including community education leadership, educational administration (Ed M, Ed D, CAGS), higher education administration (Ed M, Ed D, CAGS); reading education (Ed M, CAGS); science education (Ed M, MAT, CAGS), including biology (MAT), chemistry (MAT), earth science (MAT), general science (MAT), physics (MAT); social studies education (Ed M, MAT, CAGS), including history (MAT), political science (MAT); special education (Ed M, Ed D, CAGS), including disability studies (Ed M), moderate disabilities (Ed M), severe disabilities (Ed M), special education administration (Ed M); teaching English as a second language (Ed M, CAGS). Part-time programs available. *Faculty:* 57 full-time, 39 part-time/adjunct. *Students:* 245 full-time (191 women), 376 part-time (274 women); includes 83 minority (14 Black or African American, non-Hispanic/Latino; 2 American Indian or Alaska Native, non-Hispanic/Latino; 28 Asian, non-Hispanic/Latino; 31 Hispanic/Latino; 2 Native Hawaiian or other Pacific Islander, non-Hispanic/Latino; 6 Two or more races, non-Hispanic/Latino), 79 international. Average age 30. 1,270 applicants, 66% accepted, 292 enrolled. In 2010, 273 master's, 15 doctorates, 7 other advanced degrees awarded. Terminal master's awarded for partial completion of doctoral program. *Degree requirements:* For master's, thesis (for some programs); for doctorate, comprehensive exam, thesis/dissertation; for CAGS, comprehensive exam. *Entrance requirements:* For master's and CAGS, GRE General Test or Miller Analogies Test (MAT); for doctorate, GRE General Test. Additional exam requirements/recommendations for international students: Required—TOEFL, IELTS. *Application deadline:* For fall admission, 1/15 priority date for domestic and international students; for spring admission, 9/15 priority date for domestic and international students. Applications are processed on a rolling basis. Application fee: $70. Electronic applications accepted. *Expenses:* Tuition: Full-time $39,314; part-time $1228 per credit. Required fees: $40 per semester. *Financial support:* In 2010–11, 276 students received support, including 31 fellowships with full tuition reimbursements available, 16 research assistantships, 26 teaching assistantships with partial tuition reimbursements available; career-related internships or fieldwork, Federal Work-Study, and scholarships/grants also available. Support available to part-time students. Financial award applicants required to submit FAFSA. *Faculty research:* Deaf studies, social emotional learning, civic engagement and education, STEM education, pre-college educational pipelines. Total annual research expenditures: $2.6 million. *Unit head:* Dr. Hardin Coleman, Dean, 617-353-3213. *Application contact:* Dana Fernandez, Director of Enrollment, 617-353-4237, Fax: 617-353-8937, E-mail: sedgrad@bu.edu.

Brandeis University, Graduate School of Arts and Sciences, Department of Classical Studies, Waltham, MA 02454-9110. Offers ancient Greek and Roman studies (MA, Graduate Certificate). Part-time programs available. *Faculty:* 4 full-time (3 women). *Students:* 10 full-time (6 women), 4 part-time (all women); includes 1 American Indian or Alaska Native, non-Hispanic/Latino, 1 international. 22 applicants, 82% accepted, 10 enrolled. *Degree requirements:* For master's, variable foreign language requirement, thesis. *Entrance requirements:* For master's and Graduate Certificate, 2 recommendation letters, curriculum vitae or resume, statement of purpose, official transcript(s). Additional exam requirements/recommendations for international students: Required—TOEFL (minimum score 600 paper-based; 250 computer-based; 100 iBT); Recommended—IELTS (minimum score 7). *Application deadline:* Applications are processed on a rolling basis. Application fee: $75. Electronic applications accepted. *Financial support:* In 2010–11, 1 student received support, including 1 teaching assistantship with partial tuition reimbursement available (averaging $3,200 per year); scholarships/grants also available. Support available to part-time students. Financial award application deadline: 4/15; financial award applicants required to submit FAFSA. *Faculty research:* Roman and Greek art and archaeology, Latin and Greek language and literature, mythology, classical religion, Roman and Greek history. *Unit head:* Dr. Ann Olga Koloski-Ostrow, Chair, Graduate Certificate Program, 781-736-2183, E-mail: aoko@brandeis.edu. *Application contact:* Heidi McAllister, Department Administrator, 781-736-2180, Fax: 781-736-2184, E-mail: hmcallister@brandeis.edu.

Brock University, Faculty of Graduate Studies, Faculty of Humanities, Program in Classics, St. Catharines, ON L2S 3A1, Canada. Offers MA. Part-time programs available. *Degree requirements:* For master's, one foreign language, major research paper or thesis. *Entrance requirements:* For master's, honors degree, 3 letters of reference, written work (no more than 20 pages). Additional exam requirements/recommendations for international students: Required—TOEFL (minimum score 550 paper-based; 213 computer-based; 80 iBT), IELTS (minimum score 6.5), TWE (minimum score 4). Electronic applications accepted.

Brown University, Graduate School, Department of Classics, Providence, RI 02912. Offers MA, PhD. *Degree requirements:* For master's, one foreign language, thesis; for doctorate, 2 foreign languages, thesis/dissertation. *Entrance requirements:* For master's and doctorate, GRE General Test. *Faculty research:* Philology, archaeology, Sanskrit.

Bryn Mawr College, Graduate School of Arts and Sciences, Department of Greek, Latin, and Classical Studies, Bryn Mawr, PA 19010-2899. Offers MA, PhD. Part-time programs available. *Faculty:* 5. *Students:* 16 full-time (10 women), 3 part-time (all women); includes 1 Asian, non-Hispanic/Latino. Average age 28. 25 applicants, 24% accepted, 3 enrolled. In 2010, 1 master's awarded. *Degree requirements:* For master's, 2 foreign languages, thesis; for doctorate, 3 foreign languages, comprehensive exam, thesis/dissertation. *Entrance requirements:* For master's and doctorate, GRE General Test. Additional exam requirements/recommendations for international students: Required—TOEFL (minimum score 600 paper-based; 250 computer-based). *Application deadline:* For fall admission, 1/3 for domestic and international students. Application fee: $50. *Financial support:* In 2010–11, 9 fellowships with full tuition reimbursements (averaging $15,444 per year), 2 teaching assistantships with partial tuition reimbursements (averaging $7,000 per year) were awarded; Federal Work-Study, scholarships/grants, and tuition waivers (full and partial) also available. Support available to part-time students. Financial award application deadline: 1/3. *Unit head:* Dr. Russell Scott, Chairman, 610-526-5034, E-mail: dscott@brynmawr.edu. *Application contact:* Teri Lobo, Secretary, 610-526-5074, Fax: 610-526-5076, E-mail: lrmiller@brynmawr.edu.

See Display on page 1299 and Close-Up on page 1329.

The Catholic University of America, School of Arts and Sciences, Department of Greek and Latin, Washington, DC 20064. Offers Greek (Certificate); Greek and Latin (MA, PhD, Certificate); Latin (MA, Certificate). Part-time programs available. *Faculty:* 5 full-time (1 woman), 1 part-time/adjunct (0 women). *Students:* 8 full-time (3 women), 12 part-time (4 women); includes 2 Asian, non-Hispanic/Latino. Average age 37. 17 applicants, 71% accepted, 7 enrolled. In 2010, 2 master's, 2 other advanced degrees awarded. *Degree requirements:* For master's, one foreign language, comprehensive exam; for doctorate, 2 foreign languages, comprehensive exam, thesis/dissertation. *Entrance requirements:* For master's and doctorate, GRE General Test, statement of purpose, official copies of academic transcripts, three letters of recommendation; for Certificate, bachelor's degree. Additional exam requirements/recommendations for international students: Required—TOEFL (minimum score 580 paper-based; 237 computer-based). *Application deadline:* For fall admission, 8/1 priority date for domestic students, 7/15 for international students; for spring admission, 12/1 priority date for domestic students, 10/15 for international students. Applications are processed on a rolling basis. Application fee: $55. Electronic applications accepted. *Expenses:* Tuition: Full-time $33,580; part-time $1315 per credit hour. Required fees: $80; $40 per semester hour. One-time fee: $425. *Financial support:* Fellowships, research assistantships, teaching assistantships, Federal Work-Study, scholarships/grants, tuition waivers (full and partial), and unspecified assistantships available. Financial award application deadline: 2/1; financial award applicants required to submit FAFSA. *Faculty research:* Greek and Latin history and literature; classical, late antique and patristic history and literature. *Unit head:* Dr. William E. Klingshirn, Chair, 202-319-5216, Fax: 202-319-5297, E-mail: klingshirn@cua.edu. *Application contact:* Andrew Woodall, Director of Graduate Admissions, 202-319-5057, Fax: 202-319-6533, E-mail: cua-admissions@cua.edu.

Columbia University, Graduate School of Arts and Sciences, Division of Humanities, Department of Classics, New York, NY 10027. Offers M Phil, MA, PhD. *Degree requirements:* For master's, one foreign language, seminar paper; for doctorate, 3 foreign languages, thesis/dissertation. *Entrance requirements:* For master's, GRE General Test, reading knowledge of Greek or Latin; for doctorate, GRE General Test, reading knowledge of Greek and Latin. Additional exam requirements/recommendations for international students: Required—TOEFL. *Faculty research:* Greek and Latin literature, ancient philosophy.

Cornell University, Graduate School, Graduate Fields of Arts and Sciences, Field of Classics, Ithaca, NY 14853-0001. Offers ancient history (PhD); ancient philosophy (PhD); classical archaeology (PhD); classical myth (PhD); classical rhetoric (PhD); Greek and Latin language and linguistics (PhD); Greek language and literature (PhD); Indo-European linguistics (PhD); Latin language and literature (PhD); medieval and Renaissance Latin literature (PhD). *Faculty:* 26 full-time (5 women). *Students:* 15 full-time (5 women), 4 international. Average age 26. 58 applicants, 14% accepted, 4 enrolled. In 2010, 5 doctorates awarded. *Degree requirements:* For doctorate, 2 foreign languages, comprehensive exam, thesis/dissertation. *Entrance requirements:* For doctorate, GRE General Test, 3 letters of recommendation, sample of written work. Additional exam requirements/recommendations for international students: Required—TOEFL (minimum score 550 paper-based; 213 computer-based; 77 iBT). *Application deadline:* For fall admission, 1/15 for domestic students. Application fee: $80. Electronic applications accepted. *Expenses:* Tuition: Full-time $29,500. Required fees: $76. Tuition and fees vary according to degree level and program. *Financial support:* In 2010–11, 6 fellowships with full tuition reimbursements, 8 teaching assistantships with full tuition reimbursements were awarded; research assistantships with full tuition reimbursements, institutionally sponsored loans, scholarships/grants, health care benefits, tuition waivers (full and partial), and unspecified assistantships also available. Financial award applicants required to submit FAFSA. *Faculty research:* Greek and Roman literature, ancient philosophy, Greek and Roman archaeology, ancient history, Indo-European linguistics. *Unit head:* Director of Graduate Studies, 607-255-3354. *Application contact:* Graduate Field Assistant, 607-255-3354, E-mail: classics@cornell.edu.

Dalhousie University, Faculty of Arts and Social Science, Department of Classics, Halifax, NS B3H 4R2, Canada. Offers MA, PhD. *Entrance requirements:* Additional exam requirements/recommendations for international students: Required—TOEFL, IELTS, CANTEST, CAEL, or Michigan English Language Assessment Battery. Electronic applications accepted.

Duke University, Graduate School, Department of Classical Studies, Durham, NC 27708-0586. Offers PhD. *Faculty:* 10 full-time. *Students:* 16 full-time (4 women); includes 1 Asian, non-Hispanic/Latino, 2 international. 27 applicants, 15% accepted, 2 enrolled. In 2010, 1 doctorate awarded. *Degree requirements:* For doctorate, 2 foreign languages, thesis/dissertation. *Entrance requirements:* For doctorate, GRE General Test. Additional exam requirements/recommendations for international students: Required—TOEFL (minimum score 550 paper-based; 213 computer-based; 83 iBT), IELTS (minimum score 7). *Application deadline:* For fall admission, 12/8 priority date for domestic and international students. Application fee: $75. Electronic applications accepted. *Financial support:* Teaching assistantships, Federal Work-Study available. Financial award application deadline: 12/31. *Faculty research:* Greek Bronze Age; classical and Roman archaeology; Pompeii and Hadrian; epigraphy, papyrology, and Latin paleography. *Unit head:* Jennifer Cllare Woods, Director of Graduate Studies, 919-681-4292, Fax: 919-681-4262, E-mail: cathy.puckett@duke.edu. *Application contact:* Elizabeth Hutton, Director of Admissions, 919-684-3913, Fax: 919-684-2277, E-mail: grad-admissions@duke.edu.

Florida State University, The Graduate School, College of Arts and Sciences, Department of Classics, Tallahassee, FL 32306-1510. Offers classical archaeology (MA); classical civilization (MA); classics (MA, PhD), including archaeology (PhD), literature and languages (PhD); Greek (MA); Greek and Latin (MA); Latin (MA). Part-time programs available. *Faculty:* 13 full-time (3 women), 1 (woman) part-time/adjunct. *Students:* 43 full-time (22 women); includes 2 Asian, non-Hispanic/Latino; 1 Hispanic/Latino. Average age 24. 54 applicants, 41% accepted, 10 enrolled. In 2010, 15 master's awarded. Terminal master's awarded for partial completion of doctoral program. *Degree requirements:* For master's, 2 foreign languages, comprehensive exam (for some programs), thesis (for some programs); for doctorate, 4 foreign languages, comprehensive exam, thesis/dissertation. *Entrance requirements:* For master's, GRE General Test, minimum GPA of 3.0; for doctorate, GRE General Test, minimum GPA of 3.5. Additional exam requirements/recommendations for international students: Required—TOEFL. *Application deadline:* For fall admission, 1/15 priority date for domestic students, 2/15 for international students. Applications are processed on a rolling basis. Application fee: $30. Electronic applications accepted. *Expenses:* Tuition, state resident: full-time $8238.24. *Financial support:* In 2010–11, 43 students received support, including 4 fellowships with full tuition reimbursements available (averaging $18,000 per year), 2 research assistantships with full tuition reimbursements available (averaging $10,000 per year), 28 teaching assistantships with full tuition reimbursements available (averaging $10,000 per year); Federal Work-Study, institutionally sponsored loans, and tuition waivers (full and partial) also available. Support available to part-time students. Financial award application deadline: 1/15; financial award applicants required to submit FAFSA. *Faculty research:* Greek and Latin literature, classical archaeology, mythology, ancient history, religion. Total annual research expenditures: $100,000. *Unit head:* Dr. John M. Marincola, Chairman, 850-644-0304, Fax: 850-644-4073, E-mail: jmarincola@fsu.edu. *Application contact:* Dr. Allen Romano, Admissions Director, 850-644-0305, Fax: 850-644-4073, E-mail: aromano@fsu.edu.

Fordham University, Graduate School of Arts and Sciences, Department of Classical Languages and Literatures, New York, NY 10458. Offers classical Greek and Latin literature (MA); classics (PhD). Part-time and evening/weekend programs available. *Faculty:* 7 full-time (1 woman). *Students:* 12 full-time (4 women), 6 part-time (2 women); includes 1 minority (Hispanic/Latino), 2 international. Average age 29. 16 applicants, 50% accepted, 2 enrolled. In 2010, 1 master's awarded. Terminal master's awarded for partial completion of doctoral program. *Degree requirements:* For master's, one foreign language, comprehensive exam; for doctorate, 2 foreign languages, comprehensive exam, thesis/dissertation. *Entrance requirements:* For master's and doctorate, GRE General Test. Additional exam requirements/recommendations for international students: Required—TOEFL (minimum score 650 paper-based; 280 computer-based). *Application deadline:* For fall admission, 1/4 priority date for domestic students; for spring admission, 11/1 for domestic students. Application fee: $70. Electronic applications accepted. *Financial support:* In 2010–11, 11 students received support, including 1 fellowship with tuition reimbursement available (averaging $21,800 per year), 4 research assistantships with tuition reimbursements available (averaging $18,400 per year), 6 teaching assistantships with tuition reimbursements available (averaging $20,666 per year); Federal Work-Study, institutionally sponsored loans, scholarships/grants, tuition waivers (full and partial), and unspecified assistantships also available. Support available to part-time students. Financial award application deadline: 1/4; financial award applicants required to submit FAFSA. *Unit head:* Dr. Robert Penella, Chair, 718-817-3132, Fax: 718-817-3134, E-mail: penella@fordham.edu. *Application contact:* Charlene Dundie, Director of Graduate Admissions, 718-817-4420, Fax: 718-817-3566, E-mail: dundie@fordham.edu.

Graduate School and University Center of the City University of New York, Graduate Studies, Program in Classics, New York, NY 10016-4039. Offers MA, PhD. *Degree requirements:* For master's, 2 foreign languages, thesis; for doctorate, 2 foreign languages, thesis/dissertation. *Entrance requirements:* For master's and doctorate, GRE General Test. Additional exam requirements/recommendations for international students: Required—TOEFL. Electronic applications accepted.

Graduate School and University Center of the City University of New York, Graduate Studies, Program in Comparative Literature, New York, NY 10016-4039. Offers comparative literature (MA, PhD), including classics (PhD), German (PhD), Italian (PhD). PhD offered jointly with New York University. Terminal master's awarded for partial completion of doctoral program. *Degree requirements:* For master's, 2 foreign languages, comprehensive exam, thesis; for doctorate, 3 foreign languages, comprehensive exam, thesis/dissertation. *Entrance requirements:* For master's and doctorate, GRE General Test. Additional exam requirements/recommendations for international students: Required—TOEFL. Electronic applications accepted.

Harvard University, Graduate School of Arts and Sciences, Department of the Classics, Cambridge, MA 02138. Offers Byzantine Greek (PhD); classical archaeology (PhD); classical philology (PhD); classical philosophy (PhD); medieval Latin (PhD). *Degree requirements:* For doctorate, 4 foreign languages, thesis/dissertation, preliminary and special exams. *Entrance requirements:* For doctorate, GRE General Test. Additional exam requirements/recommendations for international students: Required—TOEFL. *Expenses:* Tuition: Full-time $34,976. Required fees: $1166. Full-time tuition and fees vary according to program.

Heritage Christian University, Graduate Programs, Florence, AL 35630. Offers counseling (MM); Greek (MA); ministry (MM); New Testament (MA). *Degree requirements:* For master's, practicum (MM), major research paper (MA). *Entrance requirements:* For master's, MAT or GRE, bachelor's degree in Bible from an accredited college or university, minimum GPA of 2.75, 3 letters of recommendation.

Hunter College of the City University of New York, Graduate School, School of Arts and Sciences, Department of Classical and Oriental Studies, Program in Teaching Latin, New York, NY 10021-5085. Offers MA. Part-time and evening/weekend programs available. *Faculty:* 2 full-time (1 woman). *Students:* 1 (woman) full-time, 17 part-time (9 women); includes 1 Black or African American, non-Hispanic/Latino; 3 Hispanic/Latino. Average age 27. 7 applicants, 86% accepted, 1 enrolled. In 2010, 6 master's awarded. *Degree requirements:* For master's, one foreign language, comprehensive exam. *Entrance requirements:* For master's, undergraduate major in Latin or equivalent with a minimum GPA of 3.0, 2.8 overall; interview, 2 letters of recommendation. Additional exam requirements/recommendations for international students: Required—TOEFL. *Application deadline:* For fall admission, 4/28 for domestic students; for spring admission, 11/21 for domestic students. Application fee: $125. *Financial support:* Federal Work-Study, scholarships/grants, and tuition waivers (partial) available. Support available to part-time students. Financial award application deadline: 4/15. *Faculty research:* Late antique religion and social history, women in antiquity, Horace and lyric poetry, Roman comedy, Latin prose. *Unit head:* Dr. Ronnie Aucona, Director, 212-772-4960, E-mail: rancona@hunter.cuny.edu. *Application contact:* William Zlata, Director of Admissions, 212-772-4482, E-mail: admissions@hunter.cuny.edu.

Indiana University Bloomington, University Graduate School; College of Arts and Sciences, Department of Classical Studies, Bloomington, IN 47405. Offers MA, MAT, PhD. Part-time programs available. *Faculty:* 5 full-time (3 women). *Students:* 28 full-time (12 women), 1 (woman) part-time; includes 1 minority (Two or more races, non-Hispanic/Latino), 1 international. Average age 28. 36 applicants, 31% accepted, 11 enrolled. In 2010, 4 master's, 4 doctorates awarded. *Degree requirements:* For master's, 2 foreign languages, comprehensive exam; for doctorate, 3 foreign languages, thesis/dissertation. *Entrance requirements:* For master's and doctorate, GRE, minimum GPA of 3.0. Additional exam requirements/recommendations for international students: Required—TOEFL. *Application deadline:* For fall admission, 1/15 priority date for domestic students, 12/15 for international students; for spring admission, 9/1 priority date for domestic students, 9/1 for international students. Applications are processed on a rolling basis. Application fee: $55 ($65 for international students). *Financial support:* In 2010–11, 10 students received support, including 1 fellowship with full tuition reimbursement available (averaging $15,000 per year), 9 teaching assistantships with full tuition reimbursements available (averaging $11,343 per year); Federal Work-Study also available. *Faculty research:* Roman literature (particularly Empire and late Latin), Greek drama, Homer, history of ideas, papyrology. *Unit head:* Prof. Matthew Christ, Chair, 812-855-6651. *Application contact:* Yvette Rollins, Graduate Secretary, 812-855-6651, E-mail: rollinsy@indiana.edu.

The Johns Hopkins University, Zanvyl Krieger School of Arts and Sciences, Department of Classics, Baltimore, MD 21218-2699. Offers PhD. *Faculty:* 5 full-time (2 women), 1 part-time/adjunct (0 women). *Students:* 17 full-time (9 women); includes 2 minority (both Hispanic/Latino), 6 international. Average age 29. 26 applicants, 19% accepted, 3 enrolled. In 2010, 1

doctorate awarded. Terminal master's awarded for partial completion of doctoral program. *Degree requirements:* For doctorate, 4 foreign languages, thesis/dissertation. *Entrance requirements:* For doctorate, GRE General Test. Additional exam requirements/recommendations for international students: Required—TOEFL (minimum score 600 paper-based; 250 computer-based), IELTS (minimum score 7). *Application deadline:* For fall admission, 1/15 for domestic and international students. Application fee: $75. Electronic applications accepted. *Financial support:* In 2010–11, 16 students received support, including 8 fellowships with full tuition reimbursements available (averaging $17,500 per year), 1 research assistantship with full tuition reimbursement available (averaging $17,500 per year), 7 teaching assistantships with full tuition reimbursements available (averaging $17,500 per year); career-related internships or fieldwork, institutionally sponsored loans, scholarships/grants, and health care benefits also available. Financial award application deadline: 1/15. *Faculty research:* Greek culture and mythology, classical sculpture, Early Imperial Roman society. *Unit head:* Dr. Matthew Roller, Professor and Chair, 410-516-5095, Fax: 410-516-4848, E-mail: mroller@jhu.edu. *Application contact:* Ginnie Miller, Admissions Coordinator, 410-516-7556, Fax: 410-516-4848, E-mail: gmiller@jhu.edu.

Kent State University, College of Arts and Sciences, Department of Modern and Classical Language Studies, Kent, OH 44242-0001. Offers French literature (MA); French, Spanish, German and Latin pedagogy (MA); German literature (MA); Spanish literature (MA); translation (MA), including French, German, Japanese, Russian, Spanish; translation studies (PhD). Part-time and evening/weekend programs available. *Degree requirements:* For master's, one foreign language, comprehensive exam (for some programs), thesis (for some programs); for doctorate, comprehensive exam, thesis/dissertation (for some programs). *Entrance requirements:* For master's, minimum GPA of 3.0, writing sample, audio tape or CD; for doctorate, 3 recommendations. Additional exam requirements/recommendations for international students: Required—TOEFL (minimum score 197 computer-based). Electronic applications accepted. *Expenses:* Tuition, state resident: full-time $7866; part-time $437 per credit hour. Tuition, nonresident: full-time $14,022; part-time $779 per credit hour. *Faculty research:* Literature, pedagogy, applied linguistics, translation studies.

Marshall University, Academic Affairs Division, College of Liberal Arts, Program in Latin, Huntington, WV 25755. Offers MA. *Students:* 4 full-time (2 women). Average age 23. *Unit head:* Caroline Perkins, Chair, 304-696-6749, E-mail: classical-studies@marshall.edu. *Application contact:* Information Contact, 304-746-1900, Fax: 304-746-1902, E-mail: services@marshall.edu.

McMaster University, School of Graduate Studies, Faculty of Humanities, Department of Classics, Hamilton, ON L8S 4M2, Canada. Offers MA, PhD. *Degree requirements:* For master's, one foreign language, thesis or alternative; for doctorate, 2 foreign languages, comprehensive exam, thesis/dissertation. *Entrance requirements:* For master's, honors degree, minimum B+ average. Additional exam requirements/recommendations for international students: Required—TOEFL (minimum score 580 paper-based; 237 computer-based). *Faculty research:* Ancient history, art and archaeology, Latin language and literature, Greek language and literature.

Memorial University of Newfoundland, School of Graduate Studies, Department of Classics, St. John's, NL A1C 5S7, Canada. Offers MA. Part-time programs available. *Degree requirements:* For master's, one foreign language, thesis, language exam, translation exam, research essay. *Entrance requirements:* For master's, honors degree in related field, course work in Greek and Latin. Electronic applications accepted. *Faculty research:* Ancient history, historiography, literature, drama, philosophy, paleography, epigraphy, and textual criticism.

New York University, Graduate School of Arts and Science, Department of Classics, New York, NY 10012-1019. Offers classics (MA, PhD); poetics and theory (Advanced Certificate). Part-time programs available. *Faculty:* 11 full-time (3 women). *Students:* 19 full-time (7 women), 1 (woman) part-time; includes 2 Asian, non-Hispanic/Latino; 1 Hispanic/Latino, 2 international. Average age 30. 67 applicants, 7% accepted, 2 enrolled. In 2010, 2 doctorates awarded. *Degree requirements:* For master's, 4 foreign languages, exam or specialized project; for doctorate, 4 foreign languages, thesis/dissertation, exams. *Entrance requirements:* For master's, GRE General Test, knowledge of Greek and Latin history and literature, proficiency in Greek and Latin translation; for doctorate, GRE General Test. Additional exam requirements/recommendations for international students: Required—TOEFL. *Application deadline:* For fall admission, 1/4 priority date for domestic students. Application fee: $90. *Financial support:* Fellowships with tuition reimbursements, teaching assistantships with tuition reimbursements, Federal Work-Study, institutionally sponsored loans, scholarships/grants, health care benefits, and unspecified assistantships available. Financial award application deadline: 1/4; financial award applicants required to submit FAFSA. *Faculty research:* Greek and Latin literature, Greek and Roman history, epigraphy, Greek and Roman philosophy, classical archeology. *Unit head:* David Levene, Chair, 212-998-8590, Fax: 212-995-4209, E-mail: gsas.classic@nyu.edu. *Application contact:* David Sider, Director of Graduate Studies, 212-998-8590, Fax: 212-995-4209, E-mail: gsas.classics@nyu.edu.

The Ohio State University, Graduate School, College of Arts and Sciences, Division of Arts and Humanities, Programs in Greek and Latin, Columbus, OH 43210. Offers ancient Greek (MA); Greek studies (MA, PhD); Latin studies (MA, PhD); modern Greek (MA, PhD). *Faculty:* 17. *Students:* 23 full-time (8 women), 5 part-time (0 women); includes 1 Black or African American, non-Hispanic/Latino; 1 Asian, non-Hispanic/Latino; 1 Hispanic/Latino. Average age 27. In 2010, 6 master's, 4 doctorates awarded. *Degree requirements:* For master's, 2 foreign languages; for doctorate, 2 foreign languages, thesis/dissertation. *Entrance requirements:* For master's and doctorate, GRE General Test. Additional exam requirements/recommendations for international students: Required—TOEFL (minimum score 600 paper-based; 250 computer-based). *Application deadline:* For fall admission, 8/15 priority date for domestic students, 7/1 priority date for international students; for winter admission, 12/1 priority date for domestic students, 11/1 priority date for international students; for spring admission, 3/1 priority date for domestic students, 2/1 priority date for international students. Applications are processed on a rolling basis. Application fee: $40 ($50 for international students). Electronic applications accepted. *Expenses:* Tuition, state resident: full-time $10,605. Tuition, nonresident: full-time $26,535. Tuition and fees vary according to course load and program. *Financial support:* Fellowships, teaching assistantships, Federal Work-Study and institutionally sponsored loans available. Support available to part-time students. *Unit head:* Fritz Graf, Chair, 614-292-7810, E-mail: graf.65@osu.edu. *Application contact:* 614-292-9444, Fax: 614-292-3895, E-mail: domestic.grad@osu.edu.

Princeton University, Graduate School, Department of Classics, Princeton, NJ 08544-1019. Offers classical and hellenic studies (PhD); classical philosophy (PhD); history (the ancient world) (PhD); literature and philology (PhD). *Degree requirements:* For doctorate, thesis/dissertation. *Entrance requirements:* For doctorate, GRE General Test, sample of written work. Additional exam requirements/recommendations for international students: Required—TOEFL (minimum score 600 paper-based; 250 computer-based). Electronic applications accepted.

Queen's University at Kingston, School of Graduate Studies and Research, Faculty of Arts and Sciences, Department of Classics, Kingston, ON K7L 3N6, Canada. Offers classics, Greek, Latin (MA). Part-time programs available. *Degree requirements:* For master's, one foreign language, thesis (for some programs). *Entrance requirements:* For master's, 3 years of Latin, 2 years of Greek. Additional exam requirements/recommendations for international students: Required—TOEFL. Electronic applications accepted. *Faculty research:* Greek and Latin literature, Greek and Roman history, ancient philosophy, Greek archaeology.

Rutgers, The State University of New Jersey, New Brunswick, Graduate School-New Brunswick, Department of Classics, Piscataway, NJ 08854-8097. Offers classics (MA, MAT, PhD); interdisciplinary classical studies and ancient history (MA, PhD). Part-time and evening/weekend programs available. Terminal master's awarded for partial completion of doctoral program. *Degree requirements:* For master's, 3 foreign languages, comprehensive exam, thesis or alternative; for doctorate, 3 foreign languages, comprehensive exam, thesis/

Classics

Rutgers, The State University of New Jersey, New Brunswick (continued)
dissertation. *Entrance requirements:* For master's and doctorate, GRE General Test. *Expenses:* Tuition, state resident: full-time $7200; part-time $600 per credit. Tuition, nonresident: full-time $11,124; part-time $927 per credit. *Faculty research:* Greek and Latin literature, Greek and Roman social and political history, mythology, religion, ancient philosophy.

San Francisco State University, Division of Graduate Studies, College of Humanities, Department of Classics, San Francisco, CA 94132-1722. Offers MA. Part-time programs available. *Application deadline:* Applications are processed on a rolling basis. *Unit head:* Dr. David Leitao, Chair, 415-338-2068, E-mail: dleitao@sfsu.edu. *Application contact:* Dr. David Smith, Graduate Coordinator, 415-338-2068, E-mail: dgsmith@sfsu.edu.

Stanford University, School of Humanities and Sciences, Department of Classics, Stanford, CA 94305-9991. Offers MA, PhD. *Degree requirements:* For master's, 2 foreign languages, thesis or alternative; for doctorate, 4 foreign languages, thesis/dissertation, general exams. *Entrance requirements:* For master's and doctorate, GRE General Test. Additional exam requirements/recommendations for international students: Required—TOEFL. Electronic applications accepted. *Expenses:* Tuition: Full-time $38,700; part-time $860 per unit. One-time fee: $200 full-time.

Texas Tech University, Graduate School, College of Arts and Sciences, Department of Classical and Modern Languages and Literatures, MA in Classics Program, Lubbock, TX 79409. Offers MA. *Students:* 8 full-time (4 women), 1 part-time (0 women), 1 international. Average age 26. 10 applicants, 70% accepted, 5 enrolled. In 2010, 6 master's awarded. *Degree requirements:* For master's, 2 foreign languages, comprehensive exam, thesis optional. *Entrance requirements:* For master's, GRE General Test. Additional exam requirements/recommendations for international students: Required—TOEFL (minimum score 550 paper-based; 213 computer-based; 79 iBT). *Application deadline:* For fall admission, 6/1 priority date for domestic students, 1/15 priority date for international students; for spring admission, 9/1 priority date for domestic students, 6/15 priority date for international students. Applications are processed on a rolling basis. Application fee: $50 ($75 for international students). Electronic applications accepted. *Expenses:* Tuition, state resident: full-time $5495.76; part-time $228.99 per credit hour. Tuition, nonresident: full-time $12,936; part-time $538.99 per credit hour. Required fees: $2674; $36 per credit hour. $905 per semester. *Financial support:* Application deadline: 4/15. *Faculty research:* Greek and Latin language, literature and criticism, archaeology, gender and sexuality, topography and identity. *Unit head:* Dr. David H. J. Larmour, Professor and Graduate Advisor, 806-742-3145 Ext. 260, Fax: 806-742-3306, E-mail: david.larmour@ttu.edu. *Application contact:* Liz Hildebrand, Senior Advisor, 806-742-4055, Fax: 806-742-3306, E-mail: liz.hildebrand@ttu.edu.

Tufts University, Graduate School of Arts and Sciences, Department of Classics, Medford, MA 02155. Offers classical archaeology (MA); classics (MA). Part-time programs available. *Degree requirements:* For master's, 2 foreign languages, comprehensive exam, thesis or alternative. *Entrance requirements:* For master's, GRE General Test, writing sample. Additional exam requirements/recommendations for international students: Required—TOEFL (minimum score 550 paper-based; 213 computer-based; 80 iBT). Electronic applications accepted. *Expenses:* Tuition: Full-time $39,624; part-time $3962 per course. Required fees: $40 per year. Full-time tuition and fees vary according to degree level, program and student level. Part-time tuition and fees vary according to course load.

Tulane University, School of Liberal Arts, Department of Classical Studies, New Orleans, LA 70118-5669. Offers MA. *Degree requirements:* For master's, 2 foreign languages, thesis or alternative. *Entrance requirements:* For master's, GRE General Test, minimum B average in undergraduate course work. Additional exam requirements/recommendations for international students: Required—TOEFL. Electronic applications accepted.

Union Graduate College, School of Education, Schenectady, NY 12308-3107. Offers biology (MAT, MS); chemistry (MAT); Chinese (MAT); earth science (MAT); English (MAT); French (MAT); general science (MAT); German (MAT); Greek (MAT); languages (MAT); Latin (MAT); mathematics (MAT); mathematics and technology (MS); mentoring and teacher leadership (AC); middle childhood extension (AC); national board certificate and teacher leadership (AC); physical science (MS); physics (MAT); social studies (MAT); Spanish (MAT). *Accreditation:* Teacher Education Accreditation Council. *Faculty:* 3 full-time (1 woman), 23 part-time/adjunct (8 women). *Students:* 50 full-time (37 women), 23 part-time (19 women); includes 4 minority (3 Asian, non-Hispanic/Latino; 1 Hispanic/Latino), 1 international. Average age 32. 70 applicants, 86% accepted, 48 enrolled. In 2010, 47 master's, 18 other advanced degrees awarded. *Degree requirements:* For master's, thesis or project. *Entrance requirements:* For master's, minimum GPA of 3.0, letters of recommendation. Additional exam requirements/recommendations for international students: Required—TOEFL (minimum score 550 paper-based; 213 computer-based). *Application deadline:* Applications are processed on a rolling basis. Application fee: $60. Electronic applications accepted. *Expenses:* Contact institution. *Financial support:* Career-related internships or fieldwork, Federal Work-Study, scholarships/grants, health care benefits, and tuition waivers (partial) available. Support available to part-time students. Financial award applicants required to submit FAFSA. *Faculty research:* Transformative learning, science education, National Board Certification, teacher leadership, teacher quality. *Unit head:* Dr. Patrick Allen, Dean, 518-631-9870, Fax: 518-631-9901. *Application contact:* Christine Angley, Assistant, 518-631-9871, Fax: 518-631-9903, E-mail: angleyc@uniongraduatecollege.edu.

Université de Montréal, Faculty of Arts and Sciences, Program in Classical Studies, Montréal, QC H3C 3J7, Canada. Offers MA. Electronic applications accepted.

University at Buffalo, the State University of New York, Graduate School, College of Arts and Sciences, Department of Classics, Buffalo, NY 14261. Offers MA, PhD. *Faculty:* 11 full-time (2 women), 1 (woman) part-time/adjunct. *Students:* 32 full-time (12 women), 2 part-time (1 woman), 5 international. Average age 28. 41 applicants, 20% accepted, 5 enrolled. In 2010, 4 master's, 1 doctorate awarded. Terminal master's awarded for partial completion of doctoral program. *Degree requirements:* For master's, 3 foreign languages, project; for doctorate, 4 foreign languages, comprehensive exam, thesis/dissertation, general and 2 special exams. *Entrance requirements:* For master's and doctorate, GRE General Test. Additional exam requirements/recommendations for international students: Required—TOEFL. *Application deadline:* For fall admission, 1/15 priority date for domestic and international students. Application fee: $75. Electronic applications accepted. *Expenses:* Contact institution. *Financial support:* In 2010–11, 18 students received support, including 14 fellowships with full tuition reimbursements available (averaging $4,700 per year), 18 teaching assistantships with full tuition reimbursements available (averaging $13,560 per year); Federal Work-Study, institutionally sponsored loans, and unspecified assistantships also available. Financial award application deadline: 1/15. *Faculty research:* Greek and Latin literature, historiography, and epigraphy; Greek archaeology, mythology, and ancient philosophy; ancient and Roman religion and women's studies. Total annual research expenditures: $37,616. *Unit head:* Dr. Carolyn Higbie, Chairman, 716-645-0455, Fax: 716-645-2225, E-mail: chigbie@buffalo.edu. *Application contact:* Dr. Neil Coffee, Director of Graduate Studies, 716-645-0452, Fax: 716-645-2225, E-mail: ncoffee@buffalo.edu.

University at Buffalo, the State University of New York, Graduate School, Graduate School of Education, Department of Learning and Instruction, Buffalo, NY 14260. Offers biology education (Ed M, Certificate); chemistry education (Ed M, Certificate); childhood education (Ed M); childhood education with bilingual extension (Ed M); early childhood education (Ed M); earth science education (Ed M, Certificate); educational technology and new literacies (Certificate); elementary education (Ed D, PhD); English education (Ed M, PhD, Certificate); English for speakers of other languages (Ed M); foreign and second language education (PhD); French education (Ed M, Certificate); general education (Ed M); German education (Ed M, Certificate); gifted education (online) (Certificate); Latin education (Ed M, Certificate); literary specialist (Ed M); mathematics education (Ed M, PhD, Certificate); music education (Ed M, Certificate); physics education (Ed M, Certificate); reading education (PhD); science and the public (online) (Ed M); science education (PhD); social studies education (Ed M, Certificate); Spanish education (Ed M, Certificate); special education (PhD); teaching and leading for diversity (Certificate); teaching English to speakers of other languages (Ed M). Part-time and evening/weekend programs available. Postbaccalaureate distance learning degree programs offered (no on-campus study). *Faculty:* 32 full-time (22 women), 53 part-time/adjunct (43 women). *Students:* 343 full-time (237 women), 340 part-time (261 women); includes 17 Black or African American, non-Hispanic/Latino; 3 American Indian or Alaska Native, non-Hispanic/Latino; 13 Asian, non-Hispanic/Latino; 13 Hispanic/Latino, 76 international. Average age 29. 587 applicants, 75% accepted, 281 enrolled. In 2010, 212 master's, 16 doctorates, 37 other advanced degrees awarded. *Degree requirements:* For master's, comprehensive exam; for doctorate, thesis/dissertation, research analysis exam, research experience component. *Entrance requirements:* For doctorate, GRE General Test or MAT, interview, writing sample, letters of recommendation. Additional exam requirements/recommendations for international students: Required—TOEFL (minimum score 600 paper-based; 96 iBT). *Application deadline:* For fall admission, 2/1 priority date for domestic and international students; for spring admission, 11/15 priority date for domestic students, 10/1 for international students. Applications are processed on a rolling basis. Application fee: $50. Electronic applications accepted. *Financial support:* In 2010–11, 21 fellowships with full tuition reimbursements (averaging $9,000 per year), 42 research assistantships with full tuition reimbursements (averaging $10,589 per year) were awarded; teaching assistantships with full tuition reimbursements, career-related internships or fieldwork, Federal Work-Study, institutionally sponsored loans, scholarships/grants, tuition waivers (partial), and unspecified assistantships also available. Financial award application deadline: 2/28; financial award applicants required to submit FAFSA. *Faculty research:* Science assessment, foreign language teaching and learning, early learning, new literacies, gender and education. *Unit head:* Dr. Jim Collins, Chair, 716-645-2455, Fax: 716-645-3161, E-mail: jcollins@buffalo.edu. *Application contact:* Cathy Dimino, Admissions Assistant, 716-645-2110, Fax: 716-645-7937, E-mail: cadimino@buffalo.edu.

University of Alberta, Faculty of Graduate Studies and Research, Department of History and Classics, Edmonton, AB T6G 2E1, Canada. Offers ancient history (PhD); classical archaeology (MA, PhD); classical literature (PhD); classics (MA); history (MA, PhD). Part-time and evening/weekend programs available. *Degree requirements:* For master's, one foreign language, thesis (for some programs); for doctorate, one foreign language, thesis/dissertation. *Entrance requirements:* For master's, minimum B+ average; for doctorate, minimum A- average. Additional exam requirements/recommendations for international students: Required—TOEFL (minimum score 580 paper-based; 237 computer-based). Electronic applications accepted. *Faculty research:* Western Canada, classical archaeology, Britain, Eastern Europe, East Asia.

The University of Arizona, College of Humanities, Department of Classics, Tucson, AZ 85721. Offers MA. Part-time programs available. *Faculty:* 4 full-time (2 women). *Students:* 25 full-time (9 women), 6 part-time (2 women); includes 1 Hispanic/Latino; 3 Two or more races, non-Hispanic/Latino. Average age 29. 47 applicants, 60% accepted, 12 enrolled. In 2010, 12 master's awarded. *Degree requirements:* For master's, one foreign language, comprehensive exam, thesis. *Entrance requirements:* For master's, GRE General Test (minimum combined score of 1000 verbal and quantitative), 2 letters of recommendation. Additional exam requirements/recommendations for international students: Required—TOEFL (minimum score 550 paper-based; 213 computer-based; 79 iBT). *Application deadline:* For fall admission, 2/15 for domestic students, 1/15 for international students. Applications are processed on a rolling basis. Application fee: $75. Electronic applications accepted. *Expenses:* Tuition, state resident: full-time $7692. *Financial support:* In 2010–11, 26 teaching assistantships with full tuition reimbursements (averaging $17,831 per year) were awarded; research assistantships with full tuition reimbursements, career-related internships or fieldwork, Federal Work-Study, institutionally sponsored loans, scholarships/grants, health care benefits, tuition waivers (full), and unspecified assistantships also available. Support available to part-time students. Financial award application deadline: 4/15. *Faculty research:* Greek and Roman archaeology, ancient Greek, modern Greek, Latin, Greek and Roman religion, women in antiquity. Total annual research expenditures: $9,645. *Unit head:* Dr. Mary Voyatzis, Head, 520-621-3446, Fax: 520-621-3678, E-mail: mev@u.arizona.edu. *Application contact:* LeeAnn Landphair, Graduate Secretary, 520-621-1396, Fax: 520-621-3678, E-mail: landphai@email.arizona.edu.

The University of British Columbia, Faculty of Arts and Faculty of Graduate Studies, Department of Classical, Near Eastern and Religious Studies, Programmes in Classics, Vancouver, BC V6T 1Z1, Canada. Offers ancient culture, religion, and ethnicity (MA); classical and near eastern archaeology (MA); classics (MA, PhD). Part-time programs available. *Degree requirements:* For master's, 2 foreign languages, thesis or comprehensive exam; for doctorate, 2 foreign languages, comprehensive exam, thesis/dissertation. *Entrance requirements:* For doctorate, MA. Additional exam requirements/recommendations for international students: Required—TOEFL (minimum score 600 paper-based; 250 computer-based), IELTS (minimum score 7.5). Electronic applications accepted. Tuition charges are reported in Canadian dollars. *Expenses:* Tuition, area resident: Full-time $4179 Canadian dollars. International tuition: $7344 Canadian dollars full-time. *Faculty research:* Classical archaeology, ancient historians, late antiquity, ancient prose fiction, epigraphy.

University of Calgary, Faculty of Graduate Studies, Faculty of Arts, Department of Greek and Roman Studies, Calgary, AB T2N 1N4, Canada. Offers MA, PhD. Part-time programs available. *Degree requirements:* For master's, one foreign language; for doctorate, 2 foreign languages, comprehensive exam, thesis/dissertation. *Entrance requirements:* For master's, BA in classics or related field, knowledge of Latin and/or Greek, minimum GPA of 3.7; for doctorate, MA in classics or related field, knowledge of Latin and Greek, GPA 3.7. Additional exam requirements/recommendations for international students: Required—TOEFL. Electronic applications accepted. *Faculty research:* Greek literature, Latin literature, Greek history, Roman history, classical archaeology.

University of California, Berkeley, Graduate Division, College of Letters and Science, Department of Classics, Berkeley, CA 94720-1500. Offers classical archaeology (MA, PhD); classics (MA, PhD); Greek (MA); Latin (MA). Terminal master's awarded for partial completion of doctoral program. *Degree requirements:* For master's, one foreign language, exams; for doctorate, 2 foreign languages, thesis/dissertation, qualifying exam. *Entrance requirements:* For master's and doctorate, GRE General Test, minimum GPA of 3.0, 3 letters of recommendation. Additional exam requirements/recommendations for international students: Required—TOEFL (minimum score 570 paper-based; 230 computer-based), TWE. *Faculty research:* Greek and Latin literature, textual criticism, history, archaeology and philosophy.

University of California, Irvine, School of Humanities, Department of Classics, Irvine, CA 92697. Offers MA, PhD. *Students:* 13 full-time (5 women); includes 2 minority (both Hispanic/Latino). Average age 28. 13 applicants, 69% accepted, 2 enrolled. In 2010, 2 doctorates awarded. Terminal master's awarded for partial completion of doctoral program. *Degree requirements:* For master's, one foreign language, thesis or alternative; for doctorate, 2 foreign languages, thesis/dissertation. *Entrance requirements:* For master's and doctorate, GRE General Test, minimum GPA of 3.0. Additional exam requirements/recommendations for international students: Required—TOEFL (minimum score 550 paper-based; 213 computer-based). *Application deadline:* For fall admission, 1/15 priority date for domestic students, 1/15 for international students. Applications are processed on a rolling basis. Application fee: $80 ($100 for international students). Electronic applications accepted. *Financial support:* Fellowships, research assistantships with full tuition reimbursements, teaching assistantships, institutionally sponsored loans, traineeships, health care benefits, and unspecified assistantships available. Financial award application deadline: 3/1; financial award applicants required to submit FAFSA. *Faculty research:* Greek literature, computer application to Greek literature, Latin literature. *Unit head:* Paul Andrew Zissos, Chair, 949-824-6584, Fax: 949-824-1966, E-mail: pzissos@uci.edu. *Application contact:* Isabel Rios, Graduate Program Administrator, 949-824-6735, Fax: 949-824-1966, E-mail: irios@uci.edu.

University of California, Los Angeles, Graduate Division, College of Letters and Science, Department of Classics, Los Angeles, CA 90095. Offers classics (MA, PhD); Greek (MA); Latin (MA). *Faculty:* 15 full-time (7 women). *Students:* 24 full-time (8 women). Average age 29. 48 applicants, 15% accepted, 5 enrolled. In 2010, 3 master's, 3 doctorates awarded. *Degree requirements:* For master's, 2 foreign languages, comprehensive exam; for doctorate, 2 foreign languages, thesis/dissertation, oral and written qualifying exams. *Entrance requirements:* For master's, GRE General Test, minimum GPA of 3.0, sample of written work; for doctorate, GRE General Test, minimum undergraduate GPA of 3.0, sample of written work, MA in classics. *Application deadline:* For fall admission, 12/15 for domestic and international students. Application fee: $70 ($90 for international students). Electronic applications accepted. *Financial support:* In 2010–11, 24 fellowships with full and partial tuition reimbursements, 3 research assistantships with full and partial tuition reimbursements, 16 teaching assistantships with full and partial tuition reimbursements were awarded; Federal Work-Study, institutionally sponsored loans, scholarships/grants, health care benefits, tuition waivers (full and partial), and unspecified assistantships also available. Financial award application deadline: 3/1; financial award applicants required to submit FAFSA. *Faculty research:* Homeric studies, archaeology, ancient comedy, ancient philosophy, Augustan poetry. *Unit head:* Dr. David Blank, Chair, 310-206-8562, E-mail: blank@humnet.ucla.edu. *Application contact:* Department Office, 310-206-1590, E-mail: dabugheida@humnet.ucla.edu.

University of California, Riverside, Graduate Division, Tri-Campus Program in Classics, Riverside, CA 92521-0102. Offers PhD. Program offered jointly with University of California, Irvine and University of California, San Diego. *Degree requirements:* For doctorate, 3 foreign languages, comprehensive exam, thesis/dissertation. *Entrance requirements:* For doctorate, GRE, MA in classics. Additional exam requirements/recommendations for international students: Required—TOEFL (minimum score 550 paper-based; 213 computer-based; 80 iBT). Electronic applications accepted. *Faculty research:* Rhetoric, Greek and Latin drama, Hellenistic poetry, Anglo-Latin literature, Greek and Latin prose.

University of California, Santa Barbara, Graduate Division, College of Letters and Sciences, Division of Humanities and Fine Arts, Department of Classics, Santa Barbara, CA 93106-2014. Offers ancient history (MA, PhD); classics (MA, PhD); literature and theory (PhD); literature and theory (MA/PhD); MA/PhD. *Faculty:* 9 full-time (4 women). *Students:* 10 full-time (4 women). Average age 28. 20 applicants, 40% accepted, 2 enrolled. In 2010, 2 master's awarded. Terminal master's awarded for partial completion of doctoral program. *Degree requirements:* For master's, 3 foreign languages, comprehensive exam; for doctorate, 4 foreign languages, comprehensive exam, thesis/dissertation. *Entrance requirements:* For master's and doctorate, GRE. Additional exam requirements/recommendations for international students: Required—TOEFL (minimum score 550 paper-based; 80 iBT), IELTS (minimum score 7). *Application deadline:* For fall admission, 12/8 priority date for domestic and international students; for winter admission, 11/1 for domestic and international students; for spring admission, 2/1 for domestic and international students. Applications are processed on a rolling basis. Application fee: $70 ($90 for international students). Electronic applications accepted. *Financial support:* In 2010–11, 9 students received support, including 7 fellowships with full tuition reimbursements available (averaging $6,013 per year), 10 teaching assistantships with partial tuition reimbursements available (averaging $11,923 per year); tuition waivers (partial) also available. Financial award application deadline: 12/5; financial award applicants required to submit FAFSA. *Faculty research:* Literary theory and cultural history, gender studies, Greek and Latin literature, Greek and Roman history, Greek and Roman drama and performance. Total annual research expenditures: $35,000. *Unit head:* Prof. Francis Dunn, Chair/Professor, 805-893-3007, Fax: 805-893-7671, E-mail: fdunn@classics.ucsb.edu. *Application contact:* Prof. Helen Morales, Graduate Advisor/Associate Professor, 805-893-3551, Fax: 805-893-7671, E-mail: hmorales@classics.ucsb.edu.

University of Chicago, Division of the Humanities, Department of Classics, Chicago, IL 60637-1513. Offers ancient philosophy (AM, PhD); classical archaeology (AM, PhD); classical languages and literatures (AM, PhD). Terminal master's awarded for partial completion of doctoral program. *Degree requirements:* For master's, one foreign language, thesis; for doctorate, 2 foreign languages, thesis/dissertation. *Entrance requirements:* For master's and doctorate, GRE General Test. Additional exam requirements/recommendations for international students: Required—TOEFL.

University of Cincinnati, Graduate School, McMicken College of Arts and Sciences, Department of Classics, Cincinnati, OH 45221. Offers MA, PhD. Part-time programs available. Terminal master's awarded for partial completion of doctoral program. *Degree requirements:* For master's, comprehensive exam (for some programs), thesis (for some programs); for doctorate, 2 foreign languages, comprehensive exam, thesis/dissertation. *Entrance requirements:* For master's and doctorate, GRE. Additional exam requirements/recommendations for international students: Required—TOEFL. Electronic applications accepted. *Faculty research:* Archaeology (bronze age and classical), philosophy (Greek and Latin), ancient history (Greek and Roman).

University of Colorado Boulder, Graduate School, College of Arts and Sciences, Department of Classics, Boulder, CO 80309. Offers MA, PhD. Part-time programs available. *Faculty:* 12 full-time (5 women). *Students:* 34 full-time (20 women); includes 1 minority (Hispanic/Latino). Average age 26. 79 applicants, 14 enrolled. In 2010, 9 master's, 1 doctorate awarded. Terminal master's awarded for partial completion of doctoral program. *Degree requirements:* For master's, one foreign language, comprehensive exam, thesis or alternative, oral exam; for doctorate, 4 foreign languages, comprehensive exam, thesis/dissertation. *Entrance requirements:* For master's, minimum undergraduate GPA of 2.75; for doctorate, master's degree in classics or related field. *Application deadline:* For fall admission, 4/10 priority date for domestic students, 4/10 for international students; for spring admission, 11/1 for domestic students, 10/1 for international students. Applications are processed on a rolling basis. Application fee: $50 ($60 for international students). *Financial support:* In 2010–11, 6 fellowships with full tuition reimbursements (averaging $19,552 per year), 6 research assistantships (averaging $10,328 per year) were awarded; Federal Work-Study, scholarships/grants, tuition waivers (full), and unspecified assistantships also available. Financial award application deadline: 2/1. *Faculty research:* Roman and Greek history, Roman and Greek art and architecture, comparative literature, Greek philosophy, textual criticism, Greek and Latin poetry, Greek and Latin prose. Total annual research expenditures: $40,000.

University of Florida, Graduate School, College of Liberal Arts and Sciences, Department of Classics, Gainesville, FL 32611. Offers classical studies (MA, PhD); Latin (MA, MAT, ML). Part-time programs available. Postbaccalaureate distance learning degree programs offered. *Faculty:* 8 full-time (4 women). *Students:* 23 full-time (7 women), 12 part-time (5 women); includes 3 Asian, non-Hispanic/Latino, 2 international. Average age 32. 26 applicants, 46% accepted, 5 enrolled. In 2010, 1 master's, 2 doctorates awarded. *Degree requirements:* For master's, one foreign language, thesis (for some programs); for doctorate, 2 foreign languages, comprehensive exam, thesis/dissertation. *Entrance requirements:* For master's, GRE General Test, minimum GPA of 3.0; for doctorate, GRE General Test, minimum GPA of 3.25 in graduate work, 3.0 in undergraduate work; MA in classical studies or equivalent. Additional exam requirements/recommendations for international students: Required—TOEFL (minimum score 550 paper-based; 213 computer-based; 80 iBT), IELTS (minimum score 6). *Application deadline:* For fall admission, 2/15 priority date for domestic students. Applications are processed on a rolling basis. Application fee: $30. Electronic applications accepted. *Expenses:* Tuition, state resident: full-time $10,915.92. Tuition, nonresident: full-time $28,309. *Financial support:* In 2010–11, 26 students received support, including 7 fellowships, 1 research assistantship (averaging $19,999 per year), 18 teaching assistantships with full tuition reimbursements available (averaging $18,143 per year); unspecified assistantships also available. Financial award applicants required to submit FAFSA. *Faculty research:* Modern Greek language, literature, culture, medicine, religion, histiography, poetry, law, society, philosophy; history of science, linguistics, classic art and architecture, Roman historiography, and gender studies. *Unit head:* Dr. Victoria E. Pagan, Chair, 352-273-3696 Ext. 262, Fax: 352-846-0297, E-mail: vepagan@ufl.edu. *Application contact:* Dr. Mary Ann Eaverly, Graduate Coordinator, 352-392-2075, Fax: 352-846-0297, E-mail: eaverly@ufl.edu.

University of Georgia, College of Arts and Sciences, Department of Classics, Athens, GA 30602. Offers classical languages (MA); Greek (MA); Latin (MA). *Faculty:* 10 full-time (3 women). *Students:* 14 full-time (6 women), 5 part-time (3 women). 37 applicants, 65% accepted, 7 enrolled. In 2010, 10 master's awarded. *Degree requirements:* For master's, one foreign language, thesis. *Entrance requirements:* For master's, GRE General Test. *Application deadline:* For fall admission, 7/1 priority date for domestic students; for spring admission, 11/15 for domestic students. Application fee: $50. Electronic applications accepted. *Expenses:* Tuition, state resident: full-time $7200; part-time $344 per credit hour. Tuition, nonresident: full-time $21,900; part-time $944 per credit hour. Tuition and fees vary according to course load and program. *Financial support:* Fellowships, research assistantships, teaching assistantships, unspecified assistantships available. *Unit head:* Dr. Naomi Norman, Head, 706-542-2187, E-mail: nnorman@uga.edu. *Application contact:* Dr. Erika T. Hermancwicz, Graduate Coordinator, 706-542-7466, Fax: 706-542-8503, E-mail: erikat@uga.edu.

University of Illinois at Urbana–Champaign, Graduate College, College of Liberal Arts and Sciences, School of Literatures, Cultures and Linguistics, Department of the Classics, Champaign, IL 61820. Offers classical philology (PhD); classics (MA); teaching of Latin (MA). *Faculty:* 8 full-time (4 women), 1 part-time/adjunct (0 women). *Students:* 12 full-time (5 women), 4 part-time (2 women); includes 1 Asian, non-Hispanic/Latino; 3 Hispanic/Latino; 1 Two or more races, non-Hispanic/Latino. 23 applicants, 35% accepted, 4 enrolled. In 2010, 6 master's awarded. *Entrance requirements:* For master's, GRE, minimum GPA of 3.0; for doctorate, GRE, writing sample; minimum GPA of 3.0. Additional exam requirements/recommendations for international students: Required—TOEFL (minimum score 79 iBT). *Application deadline:* Applications are processed on a rolling basis. Application fee: $75 ($90 for international students). Electronic applications accepted. *Financial support:* In 2010–11, 7 fellowships, 13 teaching assistantships were awarded; research assistantships, tuition waivers (full and partial) also available. *Faculty research:* Greek and Latin language, papyrology, epigraphy, classical archaeology. *Unit head:* David Sansone, Head, 217-333-7573, Fax: 217-244-8430, E-mail: dsansone@illinois.edu. *Application contact:* Lynn Stanke, Office Support Specialist, 217-333-6269, Fax: 217-244-3050, E-mail: stanke@illinois.edu.

The University of Iowa, Graduate College, College of Liberal Arts and Sciences, Department of Classics, Iowa City, IA 52242-1316. Offers MA, PhD. *Degree requirements:* For master's, exam; for doctorate, comprehensive exam, thesis/dissertation. *Entrance requirements:* For master's and doctorate, GRE General Test, minimum GPA of 3.0. Additional exam requirements/recommendations for international students: Required—TOEFL (minimum score 550 paper-based; 213 computer-based; 81 iBT). Electronic applications accepted.

The University of Kansas, Graduate Studies, College of Liberal Arts and Sciences, Department of Classics, Lawrence, KS 66045. Offers MA. Part-time programs available. *Faculty:* 8 full-time (3 women), 3 part-time/adjunct (2 women). *Students:* 10 full-time (8 women), 2 part-time (both women); includes 2 minority (1 Hispanic/Latino; 1 Two or more races, non-Hispanic/Latino). Average age 26. 24 applicants, 29% accepted, 4 enrolled. In 2010, 3 master's awarded. *Degree requirements:* For master's, 3 foreign languages, comprehensive exam, thesis optional. *Entrance requirements:* For master's, GRE (recommended), 15 junior/senior hours of course work in Latin and/or Greek (recommended). Additional exam requirements/recommendations for international students: Required—TOEFL. *Application deadline:* For fall admission, 11/1 priority date for domestic students, 2/1 priority date for international students; for spring admission, 1/15 priority date for domestic students, 10/1 priority date for international students. Applications are processed on a rolling basis. Application fee: $55 ($65 for international students). Electronic applications accepted. *Expenses:* Tuition, state resident: full-time $7092; part-time $295.50 per credit hour. Tuition, nonresident: full-time $16,590; part-time $691.25 per credit hour. Required fees: $858; $71.49 per credit hour. Tuition and fees vary according to course load, campus/location and program. *Financial support:* In 2010–11, 12 students received support, including 1 fellowship with full tuition reimbursement available (averaging $4,000 per year), 12 teaching assistantships with full and partial tuition reimbursements available; career-related internships or fieldwork, Federal Work-Study, scholarships/grants, traineeships, and unspecified assistantships also available. Support available to part-time students. Financial award application deadline: 1/15; financial award applicants required to submit FAFSA. *Faculty research:* Greek and Roman literature, Greek cultural history, Roman cultural history, translation theory, sex and gender. *Unit head:* Prof. Pamela Gordon, Chair, 785-864-3153, Fax: 785-864-5566, E-mail: pgordon@ku.edu. *Application contact:* Anthony Corbeill, Graduate Director, 785-864-2393, Fax: 785-864-5566, E-mail: corbeill@ku.edu.

University of Kentucky, Graduate School, College of Arts and Sciences, Program in Modern and Classical Languages and Literatures, Lexington, KY 40506-0032. Offers classics (MA). Part-time programs available. *Degree requirements:* For master's, one foreign language, comprehensive exam, thesis optional. *Entrance requirements:* For master's, GRE General Test, minimum undergraduate GPA of 2.75. Additional exam requirements/recommendations for international students: Required—TOEFL (minimum score 550 paper-based; 213 computer-based). Electronic applications accepted. *Faculty research:* Erasmus, Renaissance Latin, Greek and Roman epic, Greek biography, early Christian literature, classical philosophy.

The University of Manchester, School of Arts, Histories and Cultures, Manchester, United Kingdom. Offers anthropology, media and performance (PhD); applied theatre professional (PhD); archaeology (PhD); art history and visual studies (PhD); arts management and cultural policy (PhD); classics and ancient history (PhD); composition (PhD); creative writing (PhD); drama (PhD); economic and social history (PhD); electroacoustic composition (PhD); English and American studies (PhD); history (PhD); humanitarianism and conflict response (PhD); museology (PhD); music (PhD); musicology (PhD); religions and theology (PhD).

University of Manitoba, Faculty of Graduate Studies, Faculty of Arts, Department of Classics, Winnipeg, MB R3T 2N2, Canada. Offers MA. *Degree requirements:* For master's, thesis.

University of Maryland, College Park, Academic Affairs, College of Arts and Humanities, Department of Classics, College Park, MD 20742. Offers MA. *Faculty:* 6 full-time (3 women), 3 part-time/adjunct (1 woman). *Students:* 5 full-time (1 woman), 2 part-time (both women); includes 1 Hispanic/Latino. 11 applicants, 27% accepted, 3 enrolled. In 2010, 4 master's awarded. *Degree requirements:* For master's, 2 foreign languages, thesis or alternative. *Entrance requirements:* For master's, writing sample, 3 letters of recommendation. Additional exam requirements/recommendations for international students: Required—TOEFL. *Application deadline:* For fall admission, 8/15 for domestic students, 2/1 for international students; for spring admission, 11/15 for domestic students, 6/1 for international students. Applications are processed on a rolling basis. Application fee: $75. Electronic applications accepted. *Expenses:* Tuition, state resident: part-time $471 per credit hour. Tuition, nonresident: part-time $1016 per credit hour. Required fees: $337 per term. *Financial support:* In 2010–11, 5 teaching assistantships with tuition reimbursements (averaging $15,700 per year) were awarded; fellowships with full tuition reimbursements, Federal Work-Study and scholarships/grants also available. Support available to part-time students. Financial award applicants required to submit FAFSA. *Faculty research:* Latin, Greek, and Roman culture. *Unit head:* Dr. Hugh Lee, Chair, 301-405-2014, Fax: 301-314-9084, E-mail: hlee6@umd.edu. *Application contact:* Dean of Graduate School, 301-405-0376, Fax: 301-314-9305.

University of Massachusetts Amherst, Graduate School, College of Humanities and Fine Arts, Department of Classics, Amherst, MA 01003. Offers Latin and classical humanities (MAT). Part-time programs available. *Faculty:* 9 full-time (4 women). *Students:* 12 full-time (7 women); includes 1 minority (Hispanic/Latino). Average age 24. 23 applicants, 26% accepted, 6 enrolled. In 2010, 4 master's awarded. *Degree requirements:* For master's, thesis or alternative. *Entrance requirements:* For master's, GRE General Test. Additional exam requirements/recommendations for international students: Required—TOEFL (minimum score 550 paper-based; 213 computer-based; 80 iBT), IELTS (minimum score 6.5). *Application deadline:* For

Classics

University of Massachusetts Amherst (continued)
fall admission, 2/1 for domestic and international students. Applications are processed on a rolling basis. Application fee: $50 ($65 for international students). Electronic applications accepted. *Expenses:* Tuition, state resident: full-time $2640. Required fees: $8282. One-time fee: $357 full-time. *Financial support:* In 2010–11, 1 research assistantship (averaging $6,250 per year), 11 teaching assistantships with full tuition reimbursements (averaging $14,661 per year) were awarded; fellowships, career-related internships or fieldwork, Federal Work-Study, scholarships/grants, traineeships, health care benefits, tuition waivers (full), and unspecified assistantships also available. Support available to part-time students. Financial award application deadline: 2/1; financial award applicants required to submit FAFSA. *Unit head:* Dr. Teresa Ramsby, Graduate Program Director, 413-545-0512, Fax: 413-545-6995. *Application contact:* Jean M. Ames, Supervisor of Admissions, 413-545-0722, Fax: 413-577-0100, E-mail: gradadm@grad.umass.edu.

University of Michigan, Horace H. Rackham School of Graduate Studies, College of Literature, Science, and the Arts, Department of Classical Studies, Ann Arbor, MI 48109. Offers classical studies (PhD); teaching Latin (MAT). *Faculty:* 21 full-time (9 women), 6 part-time/adjunct (4 women). *Students:* 29 full-time (19 women); includes 2 Asian, non-Hispanic/Latino; 1 Hispanic/Latino, 1 international. Average age 26. 90 applicants, 7% accepted, 4 enrolled. In 2010, 7 master's, 1 doctorate awarded. Terminal master's awarded for partial completion of doctoral program. *Degree requirements:* For master's, one foreign language, comprehensive exam; for doctorate, 4 foreign languages, thesis/dissertation, oral defense of dissertation, preliminary exams. *Entrance requirements:* For master's, GRE General Test; for doctorate, GRE General Test, minimum of 3 years of college-level Latin and 2 years of college-level Greek. Additional exam requirements/recommendations for international students: Required—TOEFL (minimum score 560 paper-based; 220 computer-based). *Application deadline:* For fall admission, 1/5 for domestic and international students. Application fee: $65 ($75 for international students). Electronic applications accepted. *Expenses:* Tuition, state resident: full-time $17,784; part-time $1116 per credit hour. Tuition, nonresident: full-time $35,944; part-time $2125 per credit hour. International tuition: $35,994 full-time. Required fees: $95 per semester. Tuition and fees vary according to course load, degree level and program. *Financial support:* In 2010–11, 26 students received support, including 4 fellowships with full tuition reimbursements available (averaging $18,000 per year), 1 research assistantship (averaging $1 per year), 16 teaching assistantships with full tuition reimbursements available (averaging $16,694 per year); career-related internships or fieldwork, Federal Work-Study, institutionally sponsored loans, scholarships/grants, traineeships, health care benefits, tuition waivers (full), and unspecified assistantships also available. Financial award application deadline: 3/15. *Faculty research:* Greek and Latin literature, ancient history, papyrology, archaeology. *Unit head:* Prof. Ruth Scodel, Chair, 734-764-0360, Fax: 734-763-4959, E-mail: classics@umich.edu. *Application contact:* Michelle M. Biggs, Graduate Coordinator, 734-647-2330, Fax: 734-763-4959, E-mail: mbiggs@umich.edu.

University of Michigan, Horace H. Rackham School of Graduate Studies, College of Literature, Science, and the Arts, Interdepartmental Program in Greek and Roman History, Ann Arbor, MI 48109. Offers PhD, Certificate. *Faculty:* 8 full-time (2 women), 13 part-time/adjunct (6 women). *Students:* 13 full-time (6 women), 2 international. Average age 27. 25 applicants, 8% accepted, 2 enrolled. *Degree requirements:* For doctorate, 4 foreign languages, comprehensive exam, thesis/dissertation, oral defense of dissertation, dissertation prospectus, preliminary exams. *Entrance requirements:* For doctorate, GRE, minimum of 2 years each of classical Greek and Latin. Additional exam requirements/recommendations for international students: Required—TOEFL (minimum score 560 paper-based; 220 computer-based). *Application deadline:* For fall admission, 12/15 for domestic and international students. Application fee: $65 ($75 for international students). Electronic applications accepted. *Expenses:* Tuition, state resident: full-time $17,784; part-time $1116 per credit hour. Tuition, nonresident: full-time $35,944; part-time $2125 per credit hour. International tuition: $35,994 full-time. Required fees: $95 per semester. Tuition and fees vary according to course load, degree level and program. *Financial support:* In 2010–11, 10 students received support, including 4 fellowships with full tuition reimbursements available (averaging $16,800 per year), 8 teaching assistantships with full tuition reimbursements available (averaging $16,694 per year); career-related internships or fieldwork, Federal Work-Study, institutionally sponsored loans, scholarships/grants, traineeships, health care benefits, tuition waivers (full), and unspecified assistantships also available. Financial award application deadline: 3/15. *Faculty research:* Greek history, Roman history. *Unit head:* Prof. Sara Forsdyke, Professor, 734-936-6098, Fax: 734-763-4959, E-mail: forsdyke@umich.edu. *Application contact:* Michelle M. Biggs, Graduate Coordinator, 734-647-2330, Fax: 734-763-4959, E-mail: mbiggs@umich.edu.

University of Minnesota, Twin Cities Campus, Graduate School, College of Liberal Arts, Department of Classical and Near Eastern Studies, Minneapolis, MN 55455-0213. Offers ancient and medieval art and archaeology (MA, PhD); classics (MA, PhD); Greek (MA, PhD); Latin (MA, PhD); religions in antiquity (MA). Part-time programs available. Terminal master's awarded for partial completion of doctoral program. *Degree requirements:* For master's, 2 foreign languages, comprehensive exam, thesis or alternative; for doctorate, variable foreign language requirement, comprehensive exam, thesis/dissertation. *Entrance requirements:* For master's and doctorate, GRE, 3 letters of recommendation, writing sample, copies of transcripts, personal statement. Additional exam requirements/recommendations for international students: Required—TOEFL. Electronic applications accepted. *Faculty research:* Greek and Latin literature, religions in antiquity, ancient Near East.

University of Missouri, Graduate School, College of Arts and Sciences, Department of Classical Studies, Columbia, MO 65211. Offers classical languages (MA, PhD); classical studies (MA, PhD). *Faculty:* 9 full-time (2 women), 3 part-time/adjunct (1 woman). *Students:* 21 full-time (12 women); includes 2 minority (both Black or African American, non-Hispanic/Latino), 2 international. Average age 30. 30 applicants, 7% accepted, 2 enrolled. In 2010, 4 master's awarded. Terminal master's awarded for partial completion of doctoral program. *Degree requirements:* For master's, one foreign language; for doctorate, 2 foreign languages, comprehensive exam, thesis/dissertation. *Entrance requirements:* For master's, GRE General Test, minimum GPA of 3.0 during last 2 years; BA from accredited college/university; reading knowledge of Greek and/or Latin; for doctorate, GRE General Test, minimum GPA of 3.0; MA with major in Greek, Latin or classics or equivalent of minimum 21 hours of graduate work; reading knowledge of Greek, Latin, German, and French (or Italian). Additional exam requirements/recommendations for international students: Required—TOEFL (minimum score 500 paper-based; 173 computer-based; 61 iBT), IELTS (minimum score 5.5). *Application deadline:* For fall admission, 4/1 priority date for domestic students; for winter admission, 11/1 for domestic students. Applications are processed on a rolling basis. Application fee: $45 ($60 for international students). Electronic applications accepted. *Financial support:* In 2010–11, 4 fellowships with full tuition reimbursements, 1 research assistantship with full tuition reimbursement, 10 teaching assistantships with full tuition reimbursements were awarded; institutionally sponsored loans, traineeships, and health care benefits also available. *Faculty research:* Studies in the oral tradition, ancient Mediterranean religion, archaeology of the Ancient World, ancient political culture, late antiquity, rhetoric, the Classical Tradition. *Unit head:* Dr. Dennis Trout, Department Chair, 573-884-8593, E-mail: troutd@missouri.edu. *Application contact:* Debbie Strodtman, Administrative Assistant, 573-882-0679, E-mail: strodtmand@missouri.edu.

University of Nebraska–Lincoln, Graduate College, College of Arts and Sciences, Department of Classics and Religious Studies, Lincoln, NE 68588. Offers MA. *Degree requirements:* For master's, thesis optional. *Entrance requirements:* For master's, GRE. Additional exam requirements/recommendations for international students: Required—TOEFL (minimum score 550 paper-based; 213 computer-based). Electronic applications accepted. *Faculty research:* Greek and Latin poetry and prose, Greek and Latin linguistics, patristics, gnosticism, religion of late antiquity.

University of New Brunswick Fredericton, School of Graduate Studies, Faculty of Arts, Department of Classics and Ancient History, Fredericton, NB E3B 5A3, Canada. Offers classics (MA). Part-time programs available. *Faculty:* 4 full-time (1 woman), 5 part-time/adjunct (1 woman). *Students:* 5 full-time (2 women), 3 part-time (2 women). *Degree requirements:* For master's, thesis. *Entrance requirements:* For master's, minimum GPA of 3.0, minimum of 18 credit hours or equivalent in either Greek or Latin. Additional exam requirements/recommendations for international students: Required—TOEFL, TWE. *Application deadline:* 1/31 for domestic and international students. Applications are processed on a rolling basis. Application fee: $50 Canadian dollars. *Expenses:* Tuition, area resident: Full-time $3708; part-time $927 per term. International tuition: $6300 full-time. Required fees: $50 per term. *Financial support:* Teaching assistantships available. Financial award application deadline: 1/31. *Faculty research:* Roman history, silver-age Latin poetry, stamped roof tiles, Plato, early Christianity, Greek and Roman archaeology, late Antiquity and Byzantium. *Unit head:* Prof. William Kerr, Director of Graduate Studies, 506-458-7507, Fax: 506-447-3072, E-mail: wkerr@unb.ca. *Application contact:* Susan Miller, Graduate Secretary, 506-453-4762, Fax: 506-447-3072, E-mail: smiller@unb.ca.

The University of North Carolina at Chapel Hill, Graduate School, College of Arts and Sciences, Department of Classics, Chapel Hill, NC 27599. Offers classical archaeology (MA, PhD); classics (MA, PhD). Terminal master's awarded for partial completion of doctoral program. *Degree requirements:* For master's, one foreign language, comprehensive exam, thesis; for doctorate, 2 foreign languages, comprehensive exam, thesis/dissertation. *Entrance requirements:* For master's and doctorate, GRE General Test, minimum GPA of 3.0. Electronic applications accepted.

The University of North Carolina at Greensboro, Graduate School, College of Arts and Sciences, Department of Classical Studies, Greensboro, NC 27412-5001. Offers Latin (M Ed). *Entrance requirements:* For master's, GRE General Test, MAT, or PRAXIS. Additional exam requirements/recommendations for international students: Required—TOEFL. Electronic applications accepted.

University of Oregon, Graduate School, College of Arts and Sciences, Department of Classics, Eugene, OR 97403. Offers classical civilization (MA); classics (MA), including Greek, Latin; Greek (MA); Latin (MA). Part-time programs available. *Degree requirements:* For master's, 2 foreign languages, thesis or alternative. *Entrance requirements:* For master's, GRE General Test, minimum GPA of 3.0. Additional exam requirements/recommendations for international students: Required—TOEFL. *Faculty research:* Roman religion, Greek philosophy, archaeology, Greek and Roman literature.

University of Ottawa, Faculty of Graduate and Postdoctoral Studies, Faculty of Arts, Department of Classics and Religious Studies, Ottawa, ON K1N 6N5, Canada. Offers classical studies (MA); religious studies (PhD). *Degree requirements:* For master's, comprehensive exam, thesis or alternative; for doctorate, comprehensive exam, thesis/dissertation. *Entrance requirements:* For master's, honors degree or equivalent, minimum B average; for doctorate, master's degree, minimum B+ average. Electronic applications accepted. *Faculty research:* Religions in Canada, including Amerindian and Inuit religions; religion and culture; late antiquity.

University of Pennsylvania, School of Arts and Sciences, Graduate Group in Classical Studies, Philadelphia, PA 19104. Offers AM, PhD. *Faculty:* 17 full-time (7 women), 4 part-time/adjunct (0 women). *Students:* 23 full-time (13 women), 2 part-time (0 women); includes 1 Hispanic/Latino, 1 international. 77 applicants, 8% accepted, 4 enrolled. In 2010, 1 master's, 2 doctorates awarded. Terminal master's awarded for partial completion of doctoral program. *Degree requirements:* For master's, 3 foreign languages, thesis or alternative; for doctorate, 4 foreign languages, thesis/dissertation. *Entrance requirements:* For master's and doctorate, GRE General Test, undergraduate course work in classical language and history. Additional exam requirements/recommendations for international students: Required—TOEFL. *Application deadline:* For fall admission, 12/1 priority date for domestic students. Application fee: $70. Electronic applications accepted. *Expenses:* Tuition: Full-time $25,660; part-time $4758 per course. Required fees: $2152; $270 per course. Tuition and fees vary according to course load, degree level and program. *Financial support:* Institutionally sponsored loans, scholarships/grants, traineeships, health care benefits, and unspecified assistantships available. Financial award application deadline: 12/15. *Unit head:* Emily Wilson, Graduate Group Chair, 215-898-7425, E-mail: emilyw@sas.upenn.edu. *Application contact:* Ernestine Williams, Graduate Coordinator, 215-573-0250, E-mail: ernestin@sas.upenn.edu.

University of Pittsburgh, School of Arts and Sciences, Department of Classics, Pittsburgh, PA 15260. Offers MA, PhD. *Faculty:* 7 full-time (1 woman), 3 part-time/adjunct (0 women). *Students:* 9 full-time (1 woman), 1 international. Average age 31. 16 applicants, 38% accepted, 1 enrolled.Terminal master's awarded for partial completion of doctoral program. *Degree requirements:* For master's, one foreign language, comprehensive exam, thesis optional; for doctorate, 2 foreign languages, comprehensive exam, thesis/dissertation. *Entrance requirements:* For master's and doctorate, GRE General Test, advanced reading knowledge of Greek and Latin. Additional exam requirements/recommendations for international students: Required—TOEFL. *Application deadline:* For fall admission, 1/16 for domestic and international students. Application fee: $50. Electronic applications accepted. *Expenses:* Tuition, state resident: full-time $17,304; part-time $701 per credit. Tuition, nonresident: full-time $29,554; part-time $1210 per credit. Required fees: $740; $214 per term. Tuition and fees vary according to program. *Financial support:* In 2010–11, 6 students received support, including 2 fellowships with full tuition reimbursements available (averaging $18,350 per year), 6 teaching assistantships with full tuition reimbursements available (averaging $16,140 per year); Federal Work-Study and health care benefits also available. Financial award application deadline: 1/15. *Faculty research:* Greek and Roman poetry, Greek drama, Greek and Roman historiography, Greek societal organization. *Unit head:* Dr. D. Mark Possanza, Chairman, 412-624-4486, Fax: 412-624-4419, E-mail: possanza@pitt.edu. *Application contact:* Dr. Andrew M. Miller, Graduate Adviser, 412-624-4485, Fax: 412-624-4419, E-mail: amm2@pitt.edu.

University of South Africa, College of Human Sciences, Pretoria, South Africa. Offers adult education (M Ed); African languages (MA, PhD); African politics (MA, PhD); Afrikaans (MA, PhD); ancient history (MA, PhD); ancient Near Eastern studies (MA, PhD); anthropology (MA, PhD); applied linguistics (MA); Arabic (MA, PhD); archaeology (MA); art history (MA); Biblical archaeology (MA); Biblical studies (M Th, D Th, PhD); Christian spirituality (M Th, D Th); church history (M Th, D Th); classical studies (MA, PhD); clinical psychology (MA); communication (MA, PhD); comparative education (M Ed, Ed D); consulting psychology (D Admin, D Com, PhD); curriculum studies (M Ed, Ed D); development studies (M Admin, MA, D Admin, PhD); didactics (M Ed, Ed D); education (M Tech); education management (M Ed, Ed D); educational psychology (M Ed); English (MA); environmental education (M Ed); French (MA, PhD); German (MA, PhD); Greek (MA); guidance and counseling (M Ed); health studies (MA, PhD), including health sciences education (MA), health services management (MA), medical and surgical nursing science (critical care general) (MA), midwifery and neonatal nursing science (MA), trauma and emergency care (MA); history (MA, PhD); history of education (Ed D); inclusive education (M Ed, Ed D); information and communications technology policy and regulation (MA); information science (MA, MIS, PhD); international politics (MA, PhD); Islamic studies (MA, PhD); Italian (MA, PhD); Judaica (MA, PhD); linguistics (MA, PhD); mathematical education (M Ed); mathematics education (MA); missiology (M Th, D Th); modern Hebrew (MA, PhD); musicology (MA, MMus, D Mus, PhD); natural science education (M Ed); New Testament (M Th, D Th); Old Testament (D Th); pastoral therapy (M Th, D Th); philosophy (MA); philosophy of education (M Ed, Ed D); politics (MA, PhD); Portuguese (MA, PhD); practical theology (M Th, D Th); psychology (MA, MS, PhD); psychology of education (M Ed, Ed D); public health (MA); religious studies (MA, D Th, PhD); Romance languages (MA); Russian (MA, PhD); Semitic languages (MA, PhD); social behavior studies in HIV/AIDS (MA); social science (mental health) (MA); social science in development studies (MA); social science in psychology (MA); social science in social work (MA); social science in sociology (MA); social work (MSW, DSW, PhD); socio-education (M Ed, Ed D); sociolinguistics (MA); sociology (MA, PhD); Spanish (MA, PhD); systematic theology (M Th, D Th); TESOL (teaching

English to speakers of other languages) (MA); theological ethics (M Th, D Th); theory of literature (MA, PhD); urban ministries (D Th); urban ministry (M Th).

University of Southern California, Graduate School, Dana and David Dornsife College of Letters, Arts and Sciences, Department of Classics, Los Angeles, CA 90089. Offers MA, PhD. *Faculty:* 10 full-time (3 women), 1 (woman) part-time/adjunct. *Students:* 24 full-time (10 women); includes 3 minority (1 American Indian or Alaska Native, non-Hispanic/Latino; 1 Asian, non-Hispanic/Latino; 1 Hispanic/Latino), 6 international. 17 applicants, 29% accepted, 4 enrolled. In 2010, 3 master's, 1 doctorate awarded. Terminal master's awarded for partial completion of doctoral program. *Degree requirements:* For master's, 2 foreign languages, comprehensive exam, thesis or alternative, Greek and Latin; for doctorate, 2 foreign languages, comprehensive exam, thesis/dissertation, Greek and Latin. *Entrance requirements:* Additional exam requirements/recommendations for international students: Required—TOEFL. *Application deadline:* For fall admission, 1/15 priority date for domestic and international students. Applications are processed on a rolling basis. Application fee: $85. Electronic applications accepted. *Expenses:* Tuition: Full-time $31,240; part-time $1420 per unit. Required fees: $600. One-time fee: $35 full-time. Full-time tuition and fees vary according to degree level and program. *Financial support:* In 2010–11, 23 students received support, including 6 fellowships with full tuition reimbursements available (averaging $22,000 per year), 17 teaching assistantships with full tuition reimbursements available (averaging $19,700 per year); health care benefits and unspecified assistantships also available. *Faculty research:* Roman literature, Roman history, Greek tragedy, ancient rhetoric and oratory, Greek philosophy. *Unit head:* Prof. Thomas Habinek, Professor, 213-821-5303, Fax: 213-740-7360, E-mail: habinek@usc.edu. *Application contact:* Christine Shaw, 213-740-3677, Fax: 213-740-7360, E-mail: shawc@usc.edu.

University of South Florida, Graduate School, College of Arts and Sciences, World Languages Department, Tampa, FL 33620-9951. Offers classics: Latin/Greek (MA); French (MA); linguistics (MA); linguistics: ESL (MA); Spanish (MA). Part-time and evening/weekend programs available. *Faculty:* 10 full-time (6 women). *Students:* 38 full-time (28 women), 25 part-time (17 women); includes 3 Black or African American, non-Hispanic/Latino; 2 American Indian or Alaska Native, non-Hispanic/Latino; 3 Asian, non-Hispanic/Latino; 18 Hispanic/Latino; 1 Two or more races, non-Hispanic/Latino, 6 international. Average age 35. 65 applicants, 48% accepted, 23 enrolled. In 2010, 23 master's awarded. *Degree requirements:* For master's, comprehensive exam, thesis. *Entrance requirements:* For master's, GRE General Test, minimum GPA of 3.0 in last 60 hours. Additional exam requirements/recommendations for international students: Required—TOEFL (minimum score 600 paper-based; 250 computer-based). *Application deadline:* For fall admission, 2/15 for domestic students, 1/2 for international students; for spring admission, 10/15 for domestic students, 6/1 for international students. Application fee: $30. Electronic applications accepted. *Financial support:* In 2010–11, 31 teaching assistantships with tuition reimbursements (averaging $9,272 per year) were awarded; tuition waivers (partial) and unspecified assistantships also available. Financial award application deadline: 6/30. *Faculty research:* Second language writing, academic literacy. Total annual research expenditures: $116,653. *Unit head:* Dr. Victor Peppard, Chairperson, 813-974-2012, Fax: 813-974-1718, E-mail: peppard@.cas.usf.edu. *Application contact:* Dr. Victor Peppard, Chairperson, 813-974-2012, Fax: 813-974-1718, E-mail: peppard@.cas.usf.edu.

The University of Texas at Austin, Graduate School, College of Liberal Arts, Department of Classics, Austin, TX 78712-1111. Offers MA, PhD. *Degree requirements:* For master's, 2 foreign languages, comprehensive exam, thesis; for doctorate, 4 foreign languages, comprehensive exam, thesis/dissertation. *Entrance requirements:* For master's, GRE General Test, proficiency in classics; for doctorate, GRE General Test, master's degree in classics. Electronic applications accepted.

University of Toronto, School of Graduate Studies, Humanities Division, Department of Classics, Toronto, ON M5S 1A1, Canada. Offers MA, PhD. Part-time programs available. *Degree requirements:* For master's, qualifying examinations, sight translation exams in Greek and Latin; for doctorate, thesis/dissertation, qualifying examinations, sight translation exams in Greek and Latin. *Entrance requirements:* For master's, minimum B+ average in final year of an undergraduate program in classics, 3–4 years of course work in Greek and Latin; for doctorate, minimum B+ average with at least one A–; MA in classics.

University of Vermont, Graduate College, College of Arts and Sciences, Department of Classics, Burlington, VT 05405. Offers Greek (MA); Greek and Latin (MAT); Latin (MA). *Students:* 6 (3 women); includes 1 Hispanic/Latino. 10 applicants, 80% accepted, 2 enrolled. In 2010, 2 master's awarded. *Degree requirements:* For master's, one foreign language, thesis. *Entrance requirements:* For master's, GRE General Test. Additional exam requirements/recommendations for international students: Required—TOEFL (minimum score 550 paper-based; 213 computer-based; 80 iBT). *Application deadline:* For fall admission, 4/1 priority date for domestic students. Applications are processed on a rolling basis. Application fee: $40. Electronic applications accepted. *Expenses:* Tuition, state resident: part-time $537 per credit hour. Tuition, nonresident: part-time $1355 per credit hour. *Financial support:* Fellowships, teaching assistantships available. Financial award application deadline: 3/1. *Faculty research:* Early Greek literature. *Unit head:* Dr. Mark Usher, Chair, 802-656-3210. *Application contact:* Jacques Bailly, Coordinator, 802-656-3210.

University of Victoria, Faculty of Graduate Studies, Faculty of Humanities, Department of Greek and Roman Studies, Victoria, BC V8W 2Y2, Canada. Offers MA, PhD. PhD offered by special arrangement. Part-time programs available. *Degree requirements:* For master's, 3 foreign languages, thesis. *Entrance requirements:* For master's, knowledge of Greek and Latin. Additional exam requirements/recommendations for international students: Required—TOEFL (minimum score 575 paper-based; 233 computer-based), IELTS (minimum score 7). Electronic applications accepted. *Faculty research:* Roman social history, Roman archaeology and technology, Roman literature, Greek literature, Homer and tragedy, Greek historiography.

University of Virginia, College and Graduate School of Arts and Sciences, Department of Classics, Charlottesville, VA 22903. Offers MA, PhD. *Faculty:* 8 full-time (3 women). *Students:* 21 full-time (9 women); includes 1 Asian, non-Hispanic/Latino; 1 Hispanic/Latino, 1 international. Average age 29. 67 applicants, 12% accepted, 5 enrolled. In 2010, 4 master's, 2 doctorates awarded. *Degree requirements:* For master's, one foreign language, comprehensive exam, thesis, oral exam; for doctorate, 2 foreign languages, comprehensive exam, thesis/dissertation, oral exam. *Entrance requirements:* For master's and doctorate, GRE General Test, 2 letters of recommendation. Additional exam requirements/recommendations for international students: Required—TOEFL (minimum score 600 paper-based; 250 computer-based; 90 iBT), IELTS (minimum score 7). *Application deadline:* Applications are processed on a rolling basis. Application fee: $60. Electronic applications accepted. *Financial support:* Fellowships, teaching assistantships, unspecified assistantships available. Financial award application deadline: 1/3; financial award applicants required to submit FAFSA. *Unit head:* John Miller, Chair, 434-924-3008, Fax: 434-924-3062, E-mail: classics@virginia.edu. *Application contact:* John Dillery, Director of Graduate Admissions, 434-924-3008, E-mail: ajw6n@virginia.edu.

University of Washington, Graduate School, College of Arts and Sciences, Department of Classics, Seattle, WA 98195. Offers MA, PhD. Part-time programs available. *Faculty:* 10 full-time (6 women). *Students:* 21 full-time (16 women), 2 part-time (0 women); includes 2 Asian, non-Hispanic/Latino; 3 Hispanic/Latino, 3 international. Average age 30. 75 applicants, 24% accepted, 3 enrolled. In 2010, 5 master's, 4 doctorates awarded. Terminal master's awarded for partial completion of doctoral program. *Degree requirements:* For master's, one foreign language, thesis or alternative; for doctorate, 2 foreign languages, comprehensive exam, thesis/dissertation. *Entrance requirements:* For master's, GRE, bachelor's degree in classics, Greek, or Latin; minimum GPA of 3.0; for doctorate, GRE, minimum GPA of 3.0. Additional exam requirements/recommendations for international students: Required—TOEFL (minimum score 92 iBT). *Application deadline:* For fall admission, 1/5 for domestic students. Application fee: $50. Electronic applications accepted. *Financial support:* In 2010–11, 20 students received support, including 4 fellowships with full tuition reimbursements available (averaging $13,725 per year), 1 research assistantship with full tuition reimbursement available (averaging $13,725 per year), 15 teaching assistantships with full tuition reimbursements available (averaging $13,725 per year); Federal Work-Study, institutionally sponsored loans, and tuition waivers (partial) also available. Financial award application deadline: 3/1; financial award applicants required to submit FAFSA. *Faculty research:* Greek and Latin poetry, Greek and Roman cultural institutions, Greek and Latin historiography, Greek tragedy. *Unit head:* Prof. Alain M. Gowing, Chair, 206-543-2266, Fax: 206-543-2267, E-mail: alain@u.washington.edu. *Application contact:* Catherine Connors, Graduate Program Coordinator, 206-543-2266, Fax: 206-543-2267, E-mail: cconnors@u.washington.edu.

University of Washington, Graduate School, College of Arts and Sciences, Department of Philosophy, Seattle, WA 98195. Offers classics and philosophy (PhD); philosophy (MA, PhD). Terminal master's awarded for partial completion of doctoral program. *Degree requirements:* For master's, 3 papers; for doctorate, thesis/dissertation, general exam. *Entrance requirements:* For master's and doctorate, GRE, minimum GPA of 3.0. Additional exam requirements/recommendations for international students: Required—TOEFL. *Faculty research:* History and philosophy of science, epistemology, Aristotle's metaphysics, ethics and politics, causation in modern philosophy.

The University of Western Ontario, Faculty of Graduate Studies, Faculty of Arts and Humanities, Department of Classical Studies, London, ON N6A 5B8, Canada. Offers MA. Part-time programs available. *Degree requirements:* For master's, one foreign language. *Entrance requirements:* For master's, honors degree, minimum B+ average. Additional exam requirements/recommendations for international students: Required—TOEFL. *Faculty research:* Greek literature, Roman history and law, ancient sport, Byzantine literature, Bronze Age archaeology.

University of Wisconsin–Madison, Graduate School, College of Letters and Science, Department of Classics, Madison, WI 53706-1380. Offers classics (MA, PhD); Greek (MA); Latin (MA). Part-time programs available. Terminal master's awarded for partial completion of doctoral program. *Degree requirements:* For master's, 3 foreign languages, oral and written exams; for doctorate, 4 foreign languages, thesis/dissertation, written exams. *Entrance requirements:* For master's, GRE; for doctorate, master's degree. Electronic applications accepted. *Expenses:* Tuition, state resident: full-time $9887; part-time $617.96 per credit. Tuition, nonresident: full-time $24,054; part-time $1503.40 per credit. Required fees: $67.63 per credit. Tuition and fees vary according to reciprocity agreements. *Faculty research:* Greek tragedy, Latin elegy, historiography, Homer, Greek lyric poetry.

University of Wisconsin–Milwaukee, Graduate School, College of Letters and Sciences, Interdepartmental Program in Foreign Language and Literature, Milwaukee, WI 53201-0413. Offers classics and Hebrew studies (MAFLL); comparative literature (MAFLL); French and Italian (MAFLL); German (MAFLL); Slavic studies (MAFLL); translation (Certificate). Part-time programs available. *Faculty:* 29 full-time (14 women). *Students:* 35 full-time (27 women), 29 part-time (20 women); includes 1 Hispanic/Latino. Average age 40. 30 applicants, 67% accepted, 19 enrolled. In 2010, 24 master's awarded. *Degree requirements:* For master's, 2 foreign languages, thesis or alternative. *Entrance requirements:* Additional exam requirements/recommendations for international students: Required—TOEFL (minimum score 550 paper-based; 79 iBT), IELTS (minimum score 6.5). *Application deadline:* For fall admission, 1/1 priority date for domestic students; for spring admission, 9/1 for domestic students. Applications are processed on a rolling basis. Application fee: $56 ($96 for international students). Electronic applications accepted. *Financial support:* In 2010–11, 1 fellowship, 2 research assistantships, 26 teaching assistantships were awarded; career-related internships or fieldwork, health care benefits, unspecified assistantships, and project assistantships also available. Support available to part-time students. Financial award application deadline: 4/15; financial award applicants required to submit FAFSA. Total annual research expenditures: $304,210. *Unit head:* Gabrielle Verdier, Representative, 414-229-3346, Fax: 414-229-2741, E-mail: verdier@uwm.edu. *Application contact:* General Information Contact, 414-229-4982, Fax: 414-229-6967, E-mail: gradschool@uwm.edu.

Vanderbilt University, Graduate School, Department of Classical Studies, Nashville, TN 37240-1001. Offers classics (MA); Latin (MAT). *Faculty:* 8 full-time (4 women). *Students:* 7 full-time (4 women). Average age 24. 59 applicants, 12% accepted, 4 enrolled. In 2010, 4 master's awarded. *Degree requirements:* For master's, 2 foreign languages, thesis. *Entrance requirements:* For master's, GRE General Test. Additional exam requirements/recommendations for international students: Required—TOEFL (minimum score 570 paper-based; 230 computer-based; 88 iBT). *Application deadline:* For fall admission, 1/15 for domestic and international students. Application fee: $0. Electronic applications accepted. *Financial support:* Fellowships with full and partial tuition reimbursements, teaching assistantships with full and partial tuition reimbursements, Federal Work-Study, institutionally sponsored loans, scholarships/grants, and health care benefits available. Financial award application deadline: 1/15; financial award applicants required to submit CSS PROFILE or FAFSA. *Faculty research:* Greek and Latin literature and language, Greek and Roman history, classical archaeology, philosophy, religion. *Unit head:* Barbara Tsakirgis, Chair, 615-322-2516, Fax: 615-343-7261, E-mail: barbara.tsakirgis@vanderbilt.edu. *Application contact:* Dr. Joseph Rife, Director of Graduate Studies, 615-322-2516, Fax: 615-343-7261, E-mail: joseph.rife@vanderbilt.edu.

Washington University in St. Louis, Graduate School of Arts and Sciences, Department of Classics, St. Louis, MO 63130-4899. Offers MA. *Degree requirements:* For master's, thesis or alternative. *Entrance requirements:* For master's, GRE General Test. Electronic applications accepted.

Wayne State University, College of Liberal Arts and Sciences, Department of Classical and Modern Languages, Literatures, and Cultures, Program in Classics, Greek, and Latin, Detroit, MI 48202. Offers MA. *Faculty:* 27 full-time (13 women). *Students:* 14 full-time (10 women), 22 part-time (17 women); includes 13 minority (5 Black or African American, non-Hispanic/Latino; 3 Asian, non-Hispanic/Latino; 5 Hispanic/Latino). Average age 35. 15 applicants, 87% accepted, 10 enrolled. In 2010, 3 master's awarded. *Degree requirements:* For master's, thesis optional. *Entrance requirements:* For master's, GRE, bachelor's degree in Latin, Greek, or classics; letters of recommendation; writing sample. Additional exam requirements/recommendations for international students: Required—TOEFL (minimum score 550 paper-based; 213 computer-based); Recommended—TWE (minimum score 6). *Application deadline:* For fall admission, 7/1 priority date for domestic students, 6/1 for international students; for winter admission, 10/1 for international students; for spring admission, 2/1 for international students. Applications are processed on a rolling basis. Application fee: $30 ($50 for international students). Electronic applications accepted. *Expenses:* Tuition, state resident: full-time $7662; part-time $478.85 per credit hour. Tuition, nonresident: full-time $16,920; part-time $1057.55 per credit hour. Required fees: $571.20; $35.70 per credit hour. $188.05 per semester. Tuition and fees vary according to course load and program. *Financial support:* In 2010–11, 6 teaching assistantships (averaging $14,620 per year) were awarded. *Unit head:* Kathleen McNamee, Chair, 313-577-3032, Fax: 313-577-3266, E-mail: aa2046@wayne.edu. *Application contact:* Joel Itzkowitz, Associate Professor, 313-577-6591, E-mail: jitzkowitz@wayne.edu.

Wayne State University, College of Liberal Arts and Sciences, Program in Language Learning, Detroit, MI 48202. Offers Arabic (MA); French (MA); German (MA); Italian (MA); Latin (MA); Spanish (MA). *Faculty:* 1 full-time (0 women), 1 (woman) part-time/adjunct. *Students:* 1 (woman) full-time, 12 part-time (11 women), 1 international. Average age 32. 4 applicants, 100% accepted, 3 enrolled. In 2010, 2 master's awarded. *Expenses:* Tuition, state resident: full-time $7662; part-time $478.85 per credit hour. Tuition, nonresident: full-time $16,920; part-time $1057.55 per credit hour. Required fees: $571.20; $35.70 per credit hour. $188.05 per semester. Tuition and fees vary according to course load and program. *Financial support:* In 2010–11, 1 teaching assistantship (averaging $14,620 per year) was awarded. *Unit head:* Robert Thomas, Dean, 313-577-2519, Fax: 313-577-8971, E-mail: aa0817@wayne.edu. *Application contact:* Janet Hankin, Professor, 313-577-0841, E-mail: janet.hankin@wayne.edu.

Classics

Wilfrid Laurier University, Faculty of Graduate and Postdoctoral Studies, Faculty of Arts, Department of Archaeology and Classical Studies, Waterloo, ON N2L 3C5, Canada. Offers MA. *Faculty:* 15 full-time (6 women), 3 part-time/adjunct (1 woman). *Students:* 6 full-time (3 women). 14 applicants, 36% accepted, 2 enrolled. *Degree requirements:* For master's, thesis optional. *Entrance requirements:* For master's, minimum B+ average in last two undergraduate years (exclusive of first year level courses in those years). Additional exam requirements/recommendations for international students: Required—TOEFL (minimum score 89 iBT). *Application deadline:* For fall admission, 2/1 priority date for domestic students, 1/1 priority date for international students. Application fee: $100. Electronic applications accepted. Tuition and fees charges are reported in Canadian dollars. *Expenses:* Tuition, area resident: Full-time $15,300 Canadian dollars; part-time $1200 Canadian dollars per credit. International tuition: $21,300 Canadian dollars full-time. Required fees: $650 Canadian dollars; $100 Canadian dollars per credit. Tuition and fees vary according to course load, degree level, campus/location and program. *Financial support:* In 2010–11, 5 fellowships, 5 teaching assistantships were awarded; career-related internships or fieldwork, scholarships/grants, health care benefits, and unspecified assistantships also available. *Faculty research:* History, languages, civilizations, archaeology. *Unit head:* Dr. Gerald Schaus, Graduate Officer, 519-884-0710 Ext. 3302, Fax: 519-883-0991, E-mail: gschaus@wlu.ca. *Application contact:* Jennifer Williams, Graduate Admissions and Records Officer, 519-884-0710 Ext. 3536, Fax: 519-884-1020, E-mail: gradstudies@wlu.ca.

Yale University, Graduate School of Arts and Sciences, Department of Classics, New Haven, CT 06520. Offers M Phil, MA, PhD. *Degree requirements:* For doctorate, 2 foreign languages, thesis/dissertation. *Entrance requirements:* For doctorate, GRE General Test.

Comparative Literature

American University, College of Arts and Sciences, Department of Literature, Washington, DC 20016-8047. Offers creative writing (MFA); literature (MA). Part-time and evening/weekend programs available. *Faculty:* 43 full-time (25 women), 22 part-time/adjunct (14 women). *Students:* 51 full-time (33 women), 36 part-time (21 women); includes 12 minority (10 Black or African American, non-Hispanic/Latino; 2 Hispanic/Latino), 5 international. Average age 29. 212 applicants, 59% accepted, 27 enrolled. In 2010, 21 master's awarded. *Degree requirements:* For master's, comprehensive exam. *Entrance requirements:* For master's, GRE, writing sample, minimum GPA of 3.0, 2 letters of recommendation. Additional exam requirements/recommendations for international students: Required—TOEFL. *Application deadline:* For fall admission, 2/1 for domestic students. Application fee: $80. *Financial support:* Fellowships, research assistantships, teaching assistantships, career-related internships or fieldwork, Federal Work-Study, institutionally sponsored loans, and tuition waivers (full and partial) available. Support available to part-time students. Financial award application deadline: 2/1. *Faculty research:* British, American, Irish, Russian, and Third World literature; cinema studies; literary theory; feminist criticism. *Unit head:* Dr. Keith Leonard, Chair, 202-885-2998, Fax: 202-885-2938, E-mail: jloesbe@american.edu. *Application contact:* Kathleen Clowery, Director of Graduate Admissions, 202-885-3621, Fax: 202-885-1505.

The American University in Cairo, School of Humanities and Social Sciences, Department of English and Comparative Literature, Cairo, Egypt. Offers MA. Part-time programs available. *Degree requirements:* For master's, thesis, proficiency in French or German. *Entrance requirements:* Additional exam requirements/recommendations for international students: Required—English entrance exam and/or TOEFL.

Antioch University Midwest, Graduate Programs, Individualized Liberal and Professional Studies Program, Yellow Springs, OH 45387-1609. Offers liberal and professional studies (MA), including counseling, creative writing, education, film studies, liberal studies, management, modern literature, psychology, theatre, visual arts. Part-time and evening/weekend programs available. Postbaccalaureate distance learning degree programs offered (minimal on-campus study). *Faculty:* 2 full-time (1 woman), 2 part-time/adjunct (both women). *Students:* 15 full-time (11 women), 34 part-time (22 women); includes 11 minority (8 Black or African American, non-Hispanic/Latino; 3 Hispanic/Latino). Average age 40. 13 applicants, 69% accepted, 5 enrolled. In 2010, 18 master's awarded. *Degree requirements:* For master's, thesis or alternative. *Entrance requirements:* For master's, resume, goal statement, interview. *Application deadline:* For fall admission, 8/1 for domestic students; for winter admission, 12/1 for domestic students; for spring admission, 3/10 for domestic students. Applications are processed on a rolling basis. Application fee: $50. Electronic applications accepted. *Expenses:* Contact institution. *Financial support:* Federal Work-Study available. Financial award applicants required to submit FAFSA. *Unit head:* Dr. Joseph Cronin, Chair, 937-769-1894, Fax: 937-769-1807, E-mail: jcronin@antioch.edu. *Application contact:* Seth Gordon, Assistant Director of Admissions, 937-769-1800 Ext. 1825, Fax: 937-769-1804, E-mail: sgordon@antioch.edu.

Arizona State University, College of Liberal Arts and Sciences, Department of English, Tempe, AZ 85287-0302. Offers applied linguistics (PhD); creative writing (MFA); English (MA, PhD), including comparative literature (MA), linguistics (MA), literature, rhetoric and composition (MA), rhetoric/composition and linguistics (PhD); linguistics (Graduate Certificate); teaching English to speakers of other languages (MTESOL). *Faculty:* 138 full-time (86 women). *Students:* 183 full-time (115 women), 98 part-time (73 women); includes 35 minority (6 Black or African American, non-Hispanic/Latino; 5 American Indian or Alaska Native, non-Hispanic/Latino; 10 Asian, non-Hispanic/Latino; 13 Hispanic/Latino; 1 Two or more races, non-Hispanic/Latino), 34 international. Average age 33. 597 applicants, 31% accepted, 88 enrolled. In 2010, 52 master's, 11 doctorates awarded. Terminal master's awarded for partial completion of doctoral program. *Degree requirements:* For master's, variable foreign language requirement, comprehensive exam (for some programs), thesis (for some programs), interactive Program of Study (iPOS) submitted before completing 50 percent of required credit hours; for doctorate, variable foreign language requirement, comprehensive exam, thesis/dissertation, interactive Program of Study (iPOS) submitted before completing 50 percent of required credit hours. *Entrance requirements:* For master's and doctorate, GRE, minimum GPA of 3.0 or equivalent in last 2 years of work leading to bachelor's degree. Additional exam requirements/recommendations for international students: Required—TOEFL, IELTS, or Pearson Test of English. *Application deadline:* For fall admission, 1/15 priority date for domestic students, 9/15 priority date for international students. Applications are processed on a rolling basis. Application fee: $70 ($90 for international students). Electronic applications accepted. *Expenses:* Tuition, state resident: full-time $8510; part-time $608 per credit. Tuition, nonresident: full-time $16,542; part-time $919 per credit. Required fees: $339; $110 per credit. Part-time tuition and fees vary according to course load. *Financial support:* In 2010–11, 12 research assistantships with tuition reimbursements (averaging $10,337 per year), 111 teaching assistantships with full and partial tuition reimbursements (averaging $13,799 per year) were awarded; fellowships with full tuition reimbursements, career-related internships or fieldwork, Federal Work-Study, institutionally sponsored loans, scholarships/grants, and tuition waivers (full and partial) also available. Financial award application deadline: 3/1; financial award applicants required to submit FAFSA. Total annual research expenditures: $734,687. *Unit head:* Dr. Maureen Goggin, Associate Chair, 480-965-1804, E-mail: maureen.goggin@asu.edu. *Application contact:* Graduate Admissions, 480-965-6113.

Brigham Young University, Graduate Studies, College of Humanities, Department of Humanities, Classics, and Comparative Literature, Provo, UT 84602-1001. Offers comparative studies (MA). *Faculty:* 25 full-time (5 women). *Students:* 16 full-time (10 women). Average age 26. 14 applicants, 50% accepted, 7 enrolled. In 2010, 6 master's awarded. *Degree requirements:* For master's, 2 foreign languages, thesis. *Entrance requirements:* For master's, GRE, minimum GPA of 3.0 in last 60 hours. Additional exam requirements/recommendations for international students: Required—TOEFL (minimum score 580 paper-based; 85 iBT), IELTS (minimum score 7). *Application deadline:* For fall admission, 3/1 for domestic and international students. Application fee: $50. Electronic applications accepted. *Expenses:* Tuition: Full-time $5580; part-time $310 per credit hour. Tuition and fees vary according to program and student's religious affiliation. *Financial support:* In 2010–11, 16 students received support, including 39 fellowships with full and partial tuition reimbursements available (averaging $1,306 per year), 5 research assistantships (averaging $1,400 per year), 36 teaching assistantships (averaging $2,317 per year); career-related internships or fieldwork, institutionally sponsored loans, scholarships/grants, tuition waivers (full and partial), and student instructorships also available. Support available to part-time students. *Unit head:* Dr. Michael J. Call, Chair, 801-422-2550, Fax: 801-422-0305, E-mail: michael_call@byu.edu. *Application contact:* Carolyn Hone, Graduate Secretary for Humanities and Comparative Literature, 801-422-4430, Fax: 801-422-0305, E-mail: carolyn_hone@byu.edu.

Brock University, Faculty of Graduate Studies, Faculty of Humanities, Program in Studies in Comparative Literatures and Arts, St. Catharines, ON L2S 3A1, Canada. Offers MA. *Degree requirements:* For master's, thesis optional. *Entrance requirements:* For master's, honors degree. Additional exam requirements/recommendations for international students: Required—TOEFL (minimum score 550 paper-based; 213 computer-based; 80 iBT), IELTS (minimum score 6.5), TWE (minimum score 4). Electronic applications accepted.

Brown University, Graduate School, Department of Comparative Literature, Providence, RI 02912. Offers PhD. *Degree requirements:* For doctorate, 2 foreign languages, thesis/dissertation, preliminary exam. *Entrance requirements:* For doctorate, GRE General Test, GRE Subject Test.

California State University, Fullerton, Graduate Studies, College of Humanities and Social Sciences, Department of English and Comparative Literature, Fullerton, CA 92834-9480. Offers comparative literature (MA); English (MA). Part-time programs available. *Students:* 32 full-time (23 women), 44 part-time (30 women); includes 2 Black or African American, non-Hispanic/Latino; 5 Asian, non-Hispanic/Latino; 12 Hispanic/Latino; 3 Two or more races, non-Hispanic/Latino, 1 international. Average age 28. 88 applicants, 51% accepted, 31 enrolled. In 2010, 40 master's awarded. *Degree requirements:* For master's, comprehensive exam, thesis or alternative. *Entrance requirements:* For master's, minimum GPA of 3.0 in major, 2.5 in last 60 hours. Application fee: $55. *Financial support:* Career-related internships or fieldwork, Federal Work-Study, institutionally sponsored loans, and scholarships/grants available. Support available to part-time students. Financial award application deadline: 3/1; financial award applicants required to submit FAFSA. *Unit head:* Dr. Joseph Sawicki, Chair, 657-278-3163. *Application contact:* Admissions/Applications, 657-278-2371.

California State University, Northridge, Graduate Studies, College of Humanities, Department of English, Northridge, CA 91330. Offers creative writing (MA); literature (MA); rhetoric and composition theory (MA). Part-time and evening/weekend programs available. *Degree requirements:* For master's, thesis or alternative. *Entrance requirements:* For master's, writing proficiency test, GRE General Test or minimum GPA of 3.0. Additional exam requirements/recommendations for international students: Required—TOEFL. *Faculty research:* Reading improvement, professional writing, Dickens, Shaw, English as a second language.

Carleton University, Faculty of Graduate Studies, Faculty of Arts and Social Sciences, School for Languages, Literatures, and Comparative Literary Studies, Ottawa, ON K1S 5B6, Canada. Offers cultural mediations (PhD). *Entrance requirements:* Additional exam requirements/recommendations for international students: Required—TOEFL. *Faculty research:* Literary history, theory of literature, cross-cultural studies, modernism/postmodernism, comparative Canadian literature.

Carnegie Mellon University, College of Humanities and Social Sciences, Department of English, Pittsburgh, PA 15213-3891. Offers communication planning and design (M Des); literary and cultural studies (MA, PhD); professional writing (MAPW), including editing and publishing, policy and non-profit communication, public and media relations / corporate communications, science or healthcare communication, technical writing, writing for new media, writing for print media; rhetoric (MA, PhD). Part-time programs available. Terminal master's awarded for partial completion of doctoral program. *Degree requirements:* For doctorate, 2 foreign languages, comprehensive exam, thesis/dissertation. *Entrance requirements:* For master's and doctorate, GRE General Test. Additional exam requirements/recommendations for international students: Required—TOEFL, TWE. *Faculty research:* Cognitive processes in discourse with emphasis on writing, testing, and evaluation.

Case Western Reserve University, School of Graduate Studies, Department of Modern Languages and Literatures and Department of English, Program in World Literature, Cleveland, OH 44106. Offers MA. *Faculty:* 17 full-time (12 women), 11 part-time/adjunct (8 women). *Students:* 1 (woman) part-time. 1 applicant, 0% accepted, 0 enrolled. *Degree requirements:* For master's, 2 foreign languages, written exam. *Entrance requirements:* For master's, GRE General Test, sample of written work. Additional exam requirements/recommendations for international students: Required—TOEFL (minimum score 550 paper-based; 213 computer-based; 79 iBT). *Application deadline:* For fall admission, 3/1 for domestic students. Applications are processed on a rolling basis. Application fee: $50. Electronic applications accepted. *Financial support:* Fellowships, career-related internships or fieldwork, institutionally sponsored loans, and tuition waivers (partial) available. Financial award application deadline: 3/1; financial award applicants required to submit FAFSA. *Faculty research:* Literary theory, literary translation, Romanticism. *Unit head:* Prof. Antonio Candau, Department Chair, 216-368-8976, Fax: 216-368-2216, E-mail: antonio.candau@case.edu. *Application contact:* Prof. Marie Landers, Director, Graduate Studies (French), 216-368-3071, Fax: 216-368-2216, E-mail: marie.landers@case.edu.

Claremont Graduate University, Graduate Programs, School of Arts and Humanities, Department of English, Claremont, CA 91711-6160. Offers American studies (MA, PhD); critical theory (MA, PhD); early modern studies (MA, PhD); English (M Phil, MA, PhD); literary theory (PhD); literature (MA, PhD); literature and creative writing (MA); literature and film (MA); MBA/MA; MBA/PhD. Part-time programs available. *Faculty:* 2 full-time (both women), 4 part-time/adjunct (1 woman). *Students:* 88 full-time (56 women), 14 part-time (12 women); includes 1 Black or African American, non-Hispanic/Latino; 9 Asian, non-Hispanic/Latino; 7 Hispanic/Latino; 5 Two or more races, non-Hispanic/Latino, 7 international. Average age 34. In 2010, 9 master's, 10 doctorates awarded. *Entrance requirements:* For master's and doctorate, GRE General Test. Additional exam requirements/recommendations for international students: Required—TOEFL (minimum score 550 paper-based; 213 computer-based; 80 iBT). *Application deadline:* For fall admission, 2/1 priority date for domestic students. Applications are processed on a rolling basis. Application fee: $60. Electronic applications accepted. *Expenses:* Tuition: Full-time $35,748; part-time $1554 per unit. Required fees: $215 per semester. *Financial support:* Fellowships, Federal Work-Study, institutionally sponsored loans, and scholarships/

grants available. Support available to part-time students. Financial award application deadline: 2/15; financial award applicants required to submit FAFSA. *Faculty research:* American, comparative, and English Renaissance literature; modernism; feminist literature and theory. *Unit head:* Elysabeth Flores Griffith, Administrative Director, 909-607-3877, E-mail: elysabeth.flores@cgu.edu. *Application contact:* Susan Hampson, Admissions Coordinator, 909-607-1278, Fax: 909-607-1221, E-mail: humanities@cgu.edu.

College of the Humanities and Sciences, Harrison Middleton University, Graduate Program, Tempe, AZ 85282. Offers education (MA, Ed D); humanities (MA); imaginative literature (MA); interdisciplinary studies (DA); jurisprudence (MA); natural science (MA); philosophy and religion (MA); social science (MA). Part-time and evening/weekend programs available. Post-baccalaureate distance learning degree programs offered (no on-campus study). *Faculty:* 17 full-time (7 women), 14 part-time/adjunct (6 women). *Students:* 52 full-time (20 women). In 2010, 4 master's awarded. *Degree requirements:* For master's and doctorate, capstone project. *Entrance requirements:* For doctorate, 3 academic letters of reference, interview. *Application deadline:* Applications are processed on a rolling basis. Application fee: $50. Electronic applications accepted. *Expenses:* Tuition: Part-time $300 per credit hour. One-time fee: $350 part-time. *Faculty research:* Japanese animation, educational leadership, war art, John Muir's wilderness. *Application contact:* Deborah Deacon, Dean of Graduate Studies, 877-248-6724, Fax: 800-762-1622, E-mail: ddeacon@hmu.edu.

Columbia University, Graduate School of Arts and Sciences, Division of Humanities, Department of English and Comparative Literature, New York, NY 10027. Offers comparative literature (M Phil, MA, PhD); English literature (M Phil, MA, PhD); literature-writing (M Phil, MA, PhD). Part-time programs available. *Degree requirements:* For master's, one foreign language, comprehensive exam, seminar papers; for doctorate, thesis/dissertation. *Entrance requirements:* For master's and doctorate, GRE General Test. Additional exam requirements/recommendations for international students: Required—TOEFL. *Faculty research:* Medieval through modern literature, drama, literary criticism.

Cornell University, Graduate School, Graduate Fields of Arts and Sciences, Field of Comparative Literature, Ithaca, NY 14853-0001. Offers PhD. *Faculty:* 42 full-time (17 women). *Students:* 27 full-time (19 women); includes 3 Asian, non-Hispanic/Latino; 1 Hispanic/Latino, 9 international. Average age 29. 123 applicants, 4% accepted, 5 enrolled. In 2010, 7 doctorates awarded. *Degree requirements:* For doctorate, 2 foreign languages, comprehensive exam, thesis/dissertation, teaching experience. *Entrance requirements:* For doctorate, GRE General Test, proficiency in 2 foreign literatures, writing sample, 3 letters of recommendation. Additional exam requirements/recommendations for international students: Required—TOEFL (minimum score 550 paper-based; 213 computer-based; 77 iBT). *Application deadline:* For fall admission, 1/10 for domestic students. Application fee: $80. Electronic applications accepted. *Expenses:* Tuition: Full-time $29,500. Required fees: $76. Tuition and fees vary according to degree level and program. *Financial support:* In 2010–11, 11 fellowships with full tuition reimbursements, 12 teaching assistantships with full tuition reimbursements were awarded; research assistantships with full tuition reimbursements, institutionally sponsored loans, health care benefits, and tuition waivers (full and partial) also available. Financial award applicants required to submit FAFSA. *Faculty research:* Critical theory, European studies, Latin American studies, Asian studies. *Unit head:* Director of Graduate Studies, 607-255-4155. *Application contact:* Graduate Field Assistant, 607-255-4155, E-mail: complit@cornell.edu.

Dartmouth College, Arts and Sciences Graduate Programs, Comparative Literature Program, Hanover, NH 03755. Offers AM. *Degree requirements:* For master's, final paper, oral exams. *Entrance requirements:* For master's, proficiency in 2 languages. Additional exam requirements/recommendations for international students: Required—TOEFL. Electronic applications accepted.

Duke University, Graduate School, Program in Literature, Durham, NC 27708. Offers PhD, JD/MA. *Faculty:* 24 full-time. *Students:* 39 full-time (23 women); includes 1 Asian, non-Hispanic/Latino; 5 Hispanic/Latino, 10 international. 163 applicants, 4% accepted, 5 enrolled. In 2010, 9 doctorates awarded. *Degree requirements:* For doctorate, 2 foreign languages, thesis/dissertation. *Entrance requirements:* For doctorate, GRE General Test, writing sample. Additional exam requirements/recommendations for international students: Required—TOEFL (minimum score 550 paper-based; 213 computer-based; 83 iBT), IELTS (minimum score 7). *Application deadline:* For fall admission, 12/8 priority date for domestic and international students. Application fee: $75. *Financial support:* Fellowships, research assistantships, teaching assistantships, Federal Work-Study available. Financial award application deadline: 12/8. *Unit head:* Katherine Hayles, Director of Graduate Studies, 919-684-4233, Fax: 919-684-3598, E-mail: johns194@duke.edu. *Application contact:* Elizabeth Hutton, Director of Admissions, 919-684-3913, E-mail: grad-admissions@duke.edu.

Emory University, Laney Graduate School, Department of Comparative Literature, Atlanta, GA 30322-1100. Offers comparative literature (PhD); English (Certificate); French (Certificate); Middle Eastern studies (PhD); philosophy (Certificate); psychoanalytic studies (PhD); religion (PhD); Spanish (Certificate); women studies (Certificate). *Degree requirements:* For doctorate, 2 foreign languages, comprehensive exam, thesis/dissertation. *Entrance requirements:* For doctorate, GRE General Test, minimum GPA of 3.0. Additional exam requirements/recommendations for international students: Required—TOEFL. Electronic applications accepted. *Expenses:* Tuition: Full-time $33,800. Required fees: $1300. *Faculty research:* Literary theory, psychoanalysis trauma and testimony, literature and religion, literature and technology, literature and philosophy, politics and global culture, literature and aesthetics.

Emory University, Laney Graduate School, Department of Spanish and Portuguese, Atlanta, GA 30322-1100. Offers comparative literature (Certificate); film studies (Certificate); Spanish (PhD); women's studies (Certificate). *Degree requirements:* For doctorate, 2 foreign languages, comprehensive exam, thesis/dissertation. *Entrance requirements:* For doctorate, GRE General Test. Additional exam requirements/recommendations for international students: Required—TOEFL. Electronic applications accepted. *Expenses:* Tuition: Full-time $33,800. Required fees: $1300. *Faculty research:* Spanish literature, Spanish-American literature, literary theory, criticism, cultural studies.

Fairleigh Dickinson University, Metropolitan Campus, University College: Arts, Sciences, and Professional Studies, Department of English, Philosophy, and Humanities, Program in English and Literature, Teaneck, NJ 07666-1914. Offers MA. *Students:* 2 part-time (both women). Average age 24. In 2010, 4 master's awarded. Application fee: $40. *Application contact:* Susan Brooman, University Director of Graduate Admissions, 201-692-2554, Fax: 201-692-2560, E-mail: globaleducation@fdu.edu.

Florida Atlantic University, Dorothy F. Schmidt College of Arts and Letters, Department of Languages, Linguistics, and Comparative Literature, Boca Raton, FL 33431-0991. Offers comparative literature (MA); French (MA); linguistics (MA); Spanish (MA). Part-time programs available. *Faculty:* 30 full-time (24 women), 5 part-time/adjunct (all women). *Students:* 30 full-time (22 women), 19 part-time (15 women); includes 24 minority (4 Black or African American, non-Hispanic/Latino; 20 Hispanic/Latino), 6 international. Average age 34. 42 applicants, 57% accepted, 20 enrolled. In 2010, 5 master's awarded. *Degree requirements:* For master's, one foreign language, comprehensive exam, thesis optional. *Entrance requirements:* For master's, GRE General Test, minimum GPA of 3.0. *Application deadline:* For fall admission, 7/1 priority date for domestic students, 2/15 for international students; for spring admission, 11/1 for domestic students, 7/15 for international students. Applications are processed on a rolling basis. Application fee: $30. *Expenses:* Tuition, area resident: Part-time $319.96 per credit. Tuition, state resident: part-time $319.96 per credit. Tuition, nonresident: part-time $926.42 per credit. *Financial support:* Fellowships, research assistantships, teaching assistantships with partial tuition reimbursements, Federal Work-Study and tuition waivers (partial) available. Support available to part-time students. Financial award application deadline: 4/1. *Faculty research:* Modern European studies, modern Latin America, medieval Europe. *Unit head:* Dr. Michael Horswell, Chair, 561-297-3860, Fax: 561-297-2756, E-mail: horswell@fau.edu. *Application contact:* Dr. Emily Stockard, Associate Dean, 561-297-2817, Fax: 561-297-2744, E-mail: stockard@fau.edu.

Georgetown University, Graduate School of Arts and Sciences, School of Continuing Studies, Washington, DC 20057. Offers American studies (MALS); Catholic studies (MALS); classical civilizations (MALS); disability studies (MPS); ethics and the professions (MALS); human resources management (MPS); humanities (MALS); individualized study (MALS); international affairs (MALS); Islam and Muslim-Christian relations (MALS); journalism (MPS); liberal studies (DLS); literature and society (MALS); medieval and early modern European studies (MALS); public relations and corporate communications (MPS); real estate (MPS); religious studies (MALS); social and public policy (MALS); sports industry management (MPS); the theory and practice of American democracy (MALS); visual culture (MALS). *Entrance requirements:* Additional exam requirements/recommendations for international students: Required—TOEFL.

Graduate School and University Center of the City University of New York, Graduate Studies, Program in Comparative Literature, New York, NY 10016-4039. Offers comparative literature (MA, PhD), including classics (PhD), German (PhD), Italian (PhD). PhD offered jointly with New York University. Terminal master's awarded for partial completion of doctoral program. *Degree requirements:* For master's, 2 foreign languages, comprehensive exam, thesis; for doctorate, 3 foreign languages, comprehensive exam, thesis/dissertation. *Entrance requirements:* For master's and doctorate, GRE General Test. Additional exam requirements/recommendations for international students: Required—TOEFL. Electronic applications accepted.

Harvard University, Graduate School of Arts and Sciences, Department of Comparative Literature, Cambridge, MA 02138. Offers comparative literature (PhD); oral literature (PhD). *Degree requirements:* For doctorate, 4 foreign languages, thesis/dissertation, written and oral exams. *Entrance requirements:* For doctorate, GRE General Test, GRE Subject Test (recommended), sample of written work. Additional exam requirements/recommendations for international students: Required—TOEFL. *Expenses:* Tuition: Full-time $34,976. Required fees: $1166. Full-time tuition and fees vary according to program.

Hofstra University, College of Liberal Arts and Sciences, Programs in Forensic and Applied Linguistics, Hempstead, NY 11549. Offers applied linguistics (TESOL) (MA); linguistics (MA), including forensic linguistics. Part-time programs available. *Faculty:* 13 full-time (6 women), 1 part-time/adjunct (0 women). *Students:* 8 full-time (5 women), 2 part-time (both women), 3 international. Average age 32. 17 applicants, 76% accepted, 6 enrolled. *Degree requirements:* For master's, thesis, 36 credits; capstone. *Entrance requirements:* For master's, Bachelor's degree in related area; Interview; 2 letters of recommendation. Additional exam requirements/recommendations for international students: Required—TOEFL (minimum score 550 paper-based; 213 computer-based; 80 iBT). *Application deadline:* Applications are processed on a rolling basis. Application fee: $70 ($75 for international students). Electronic applications accepted. *Expenses:* Tuition: Full-time $18,000; part-time $1000 per credit hour. Required fees: $970; $145 per term. Tuition and fees vary according to program. *Financial support:* In 2010–11, 7 students received support; fellowships with full and partial tuition reimbursements available, research assistantships with full and partial tuition reimbursements available, Federal Work-Study, institutionally sponsored loans, scholarships/grants, tuition waivers (full and partial), and unspecified assistantships available. Support available to part-time students. Financial award applicants required to submit FAFSA. *Faculty research:* Application of linguistics to forensic data, interrogation techniques and invalid confessions, authorship analysis, forensic linguistically-enhanced threat assessment, second language acquisition, second language writing. *Unit head:* Dr. George L. Greaney, Director, 516-463-5651, E-mail: cllglg@hofstra.edu. *Application contact:* Carol Drummer, Dean of Graduate Admissions, 516-463-4876, Fax: 516-463-4664, E-mail: gradstudent@hofstra.edu.

Indiana State University, College of Graduate and Professional Studies, College of Arts and Sciences, Department of English, Terre Haute, IN 47809. Offers English teaching (MA); history (MA); literature (MA). Part-time and evening/weekend programs available. *Degree requirements:* For master's, one foreign language, thesis optional. *Entrance requirements:* For master's, minimum GPA of 2.75 in all English courses above freshman level. Additional exam requirements/recommendations for international students: Required—TOEFL (minimum score 550 paper-based). Electronic applications accepted.

Indiana University Bloomington, University Graduate School, College of Arts and Sciences, Department of Comparative Literature, Bloomington, IN 47405. Offers MA, MAT, PhD. Part-time programs available. *Faculty:* 13 full-time (5 women), 24 part-time/adjunct (12 women). *Students:* 41 full-time (29 women); includes 5 minority (1 Black or African American, non-Hispanic/Latino; 1 American Indian or Alaska Native, non-Hispanic/Latino; 2 Asian, non-Hispanic/Latino; 1 Hispanic/Latino), 13 international. Average age 31. 69 applicants, 29% accepted, 9 enrolled. In 2010, 4 master's, 2 doctorates awarded. *Degree requirements:* For master's, 2 foreign languages, comprehensive exam (for some programs), thesis (for some programs); for doctorate, 3 foreign languages, comprehensive exam, thesis/dissertation. *Entrance requirements:* For master's, GRE, proficiency in 1 foreign language, writing sample; for doctorate, GRE, proficiency in 2 foreign languages, writing sample. Additional exam requirements/recommendations for international students: Required—TOEFL (minimum score 550 paper-based; 213 computer-based; 79 iBT). *Application deadline:* For fall admission, 1/15 priority date for domestic students, 12/15 priority date for international students. Application fee: $55 ($65 for international students). Electronic applications accepted. *Financial support:* In 2010–11, 20 students received support, including 3 fellowships with full tuition reimbursements available (averaging $15,000 per year), 2 research assistantships with partial tuition reimbursements available (averaging $8,000 per year), 15 teaching assistantships with full tuition reimbursements available (averaging $11,600 per year); Federal Work-Study and unspecified assistantships also available. Financial award application deadline: 1/15. *Faculty research:* Literary theory, translation, African studies, medieval studies, comparative arts, East-West literary relations. *Unit head:* Bill Johnston, Chairperson, 812-855-8432, Fax: 812-855-2688, E-mail: billj@indiana.edu. *Application contact:* Mary Huskey, Student Services Assistant, 812-855-9602, Fax: 812-855-2688, E-mail: mphuskey@indiana.edu.

The Johns Hopkins University, Zanvyl Krieger School of Arts and Sciences, Humanities Center, Baltimore, MD 21218-2699. Offers PhD. Part-time programs available. *Faculty:* 7 full-time (4 women). *Students:* 11 full-time (5 women); includes 2 minority (1 Hispanic/Latino; 1 Two or more races, non-Hispanic/Latino), 3 international. Average age 28. 52 applicants, 2% accepted, 1 enrolled. In 2010, 1 doctorate awarded. *Degree requirements:* For doctorate, 2 foreign languages, thesis/dissertation. *Entrance requirements:* For doctorate, GRE General Test, samples of written work. Additional exam requirements/recommendations for international students: Required—TOEFL, IELTS. *Application deadline:* For fall admission, 12/1 for domestic and international students. Application fee: $75. Electronic applications accepted. *Financial support:* In 2010–11, 14 students received support, including 7 fellowships with full tuition reimbursements available (averaging $17,500 per year), 6 teaching assistantships with full tuition reimbursements available (averaging $17,500 per year); Federal Work-Study, institutionally sponsored loans, tuition waivers (full), and unspecified assistantships also available. Financial award application deadline: 12/1. *Unit head:* Prof. Hent de Vries, Chair, 410-516-0474, Fax: 410-516-4897, E-mail: hentdevries@jhu.edu. *Application contact:* Marva Philip, Administrator, 410-516-7619, Fax: 410-516-4897, E-mail: mphilip@jhu.edu.

Kent State University, College of Arts and Sciences, Department of English, Kent, OH 44242-0001. Offers comparative literature (MA); creative writing (MFA); English (PhD); English for teachers (MA); literature and writing (MA); rhetoric and composition (PhD); teaching English as a second language (MA). MFA program offered jointly with Cleveland State University, The University of Akron, and Youngstown State University. Part-time programs available. Terminal master's awarded for partial completion of doctoral program. *Degree requirements:* For master's, one foreign language, thesis optional; for doctorate, one foreign language, thesis/dissertation, qualifying exams. *Entrance requirements:* For master's and doctorate, GRE General Test, writing sample, letters of recommendation. Additional exam requirements/recommendations for international students: Required—TOEFL (minimum score 600 paper-

Comparative Literature

Kent State University (continued)
based). Electronic applications accepted. *Expenses:* Tuition, state resident: full-time $7866; part-time $437 per credit hour. Tuition, nonresident: full-time $14,022; part-time $779 per credit hour. *Faculty research:* British and American literature, textual editing, rhetoric and composition, cultural studies, linguistic and critical theories.

Long Island University, Brooklyn Campus, Richard L. Conolly College of Liberal Arts and Sciences, Department of English, Brooklyn, NY 11201-8423. Offers creative writing (MFA); literature (MA); professional writing (MA); writing and rhetoric (MA). Part-time and evening/weekend programs available. *Degree requirements:* For master's, thesis or alternative. *Entrance requirements:* For master's, 2 letters of recommendation (at least 1 from a former professor or teacher). Additional exam requirements/recommendations for international students: Required—TOEFL (minimum score 550 paper-based; 173 computer-based). Electronic applications accepted.

Louisiana State University and Agricultural and Mechanical College, Graduate School, College of Humanities and Social Sciences, Interdepartmental Program in Comparative Literature, Baton Rouge, LA 70803. Offers MA, PhD. *Students:* 8 full-time (4 women), 2 part-time (0 women); includes 2 Hispanic/Latino, 2 international. Average age 36. 1 applicant, 100% accepted, 0 enrolled. In 2010, 2 doctorates awarded. Terminal master's awarded for partial completion of doctoral program. *Degree requirements:* For master's, 2 foreign languages, thesis optional; for doctorate, 2 foreign languages, thesis/dissertation. *Entrance requirements:* For master's and doctorate, GRE General Test, minimum GPA of 3.0. Additional exam requirements/recommendations for international students: Required—TOEFL (minimum score 550 paper-based; 213 computer-based; 79 iBT). *Application deadline:* For fall admission, 7/1 priority date for domestic students, 5/15 for international students; for spring admission, 10/15 for international students. Applications are processed on a rolling basis. Application fee: $25. Electronic applications accepted. *Financial support:* In 2010–11, 8 teaching assistantships with full and partial tuition reimbursements (averaging $13,062 per year) were awarded; fellowships with full tuition reimbursements, research assistantships with full and partial tuition reimbursements, health care benefits and unspecified assistantships also available. Financial award application deadline: 3/15; financial award applicants required to submit FAFSA. *Faculty research:* World literature, Islamic studies, Dante, Foucault. *Unit head:* Dr. Adelaide Russo, Director, 225-578-5172, Fax: 225-578-6670, E-mail: frruss@lsu.edu. *Application contact:* Dr. Adelaide Russo, Director, 225-578-5172, Fax: 225-578-6670, E-mail: frruss@lsu.edu.

New York University, Graduate School of Arts and Science, Department of Comparative Literature, New York, NY 10012-1019. Offers MA, PhD. Part-time programs available. *Faculty:* 15 full-time (4 women). *Students:* 40 full-time (24 women), 10 part-time (7 women); includes 7 Hispanic/Latino, 20 international. Average age 30. 187 applicants, 6% accepted, 8 enrolled. In 2010, 7 master's, 2 doctorates awarded. *Degree requirements:* For master's, 2 foreign languages, thesis; for doctorate, 3 foreign languages, thesis/dissertation. *Entrance requirements:* For master's and doctorate, GRE General Test. Additional exam requirements/recommendations for international students: Required—TOEFL. *Application deadline:* For fall admission, 12/15 for domestic students. Application fee: $90. *Financial support:* Fellowships with tuition reimbursements, teaching assistantships with tuition reimbursements, Federal Work-Study, institutionally sponsored loans, scholarships/grants, health care benefits, and unspecified assistantships available. Financial award application deadline: 12/15; financial award applicants required to submit FAFSA. *Faculty research:* European and non-European literature and culture, comparative poetics, cultural studies, colonial and post-colonial literature and theory, philosophical issues and literary theory. *Unit head:* Jacques Lezra, Chair, 212-998-8790, Fax: 212-995-4377, E-mail: complit.info@nyu.edu. *Application contact:* Kristin J. Ross, Director of Graduate Studies, 212-998-8790, Fax: 212-995-4377, E-mail: complit.info@nyu.edu.

Northwestern University, The Graduate School, Interdepartmental Programs, Program in Literature, Evanston, IL 60208. Offers MA. Part-time programs available. *Degree requirements:* For master's, thesis. *Entrance requirements:* For master's, writing sample. Additional exam requirements/recommendations for international students: Required—TOEFL. *Faculty research:* Sociology of literature, creative writing, women writers, modernism and post-modernism.

Northwestern University, The Graduate School, Judd A. and Marjorie Weinberg College of Arts and Sciences, Department of French and Italian, Evanston, IL 60208. Offers eighteenth-century studies (Certificate); French (PhD); French and comparative literature (PhD); Italian studies (Certificate). Admissions and degrees offered through The Graduate School. *Degree requirements:* For doctorate, one foreign language, thesis/dissertation, written and oral exams. *Entrance requirements:* For doctorate, GRE, writing sample, cassette recording. Additional exam requirements/recommendations for international students: Required—TOEFL. *Faculty research:* Francophone studies, 18th century contemporary theory.

Northwestern University, The Graduate School, Judd A. and Marjorie Weinberg College of Arts and Sciences, Program in Comparative Literary Studies, Evanston, IL 60208. Offers PhD. Admissions and degrees offered through The Graduate School. Part-time programs available. *Degree requirements:* For doctorate, 2 foreign languages, thesis/dissertation, preliminary exams. *Entrance requirements:* For doctorate, GRE General Test, sample of written work. Additional exam requirements/recommendations for international students: Required—TOEFL. *Faculty research:* The novel, modernism, post-colonial literature and theory, literature and the arts, Middle Ages and Renaissance, literature and philosophy.

Northwestern University, School of Continuing Studies, Program in Literature, Evanston, IL 60208. Offers American literature (MA); British literature (MA); comparative and world literature (MA).

Oklahoma City University, Petree College of Arts and Sciences, Program in Liberal Arts, Oklahoma City, OK 73106-1402. Offers art (MLA); general studies (MLA); leadership/management (MLA); literature (MLA); mass communications (MLA); philosophy (MLA); writing (MLA). Part-time and evening/weekend programs available. *Degree requirements:* For master's, comprehensive exam, thesis optional. *Entrance requirements:* Additional exam requirements/recommendations for international students: Required—TOEFL (minimum score 550 paper-based).

Princeton University, Graduate School, Department of Comparative Literature, Princeton, NJ 08544-1019. Offers PhD. *Degree requirements:* For doctorate, variable foreign language requirement, thesis/dissertation. *Entrance requirements:* For doctorate, GRE General Test, GRE Subject Test, sample of written work. Additional exam requirements/recommendations for international students: Required—TOEFL (minimum score 600 paper-based; 250 computer-based). Electronic applications accepted.

Purdue University, Graduate School, College of Liberal Arts, Program in Comparative Literature, West Lafayette, IN 47907. Offers MA, PhD. Part-time programs available. *Degree requirements:* For master's, one foreign language; for doctorate, 2 foreign languages, thesis/dissertation. *Entrance requirements:* For master's, GRE General Test, writing sample; for doctorate, GRE General Test. Additional exam requirements/recommendations for international students: Required—TOEFL. Electronic applications accepted. *Faculty research:* Theory and criticism, philosophy and aesthetics, East Asian literature, postcolonial literature, classics.

Rutgers, The State University of New Jersey, New Brunswick, Graduate School-New Brunswick, Program in Comparative Literature, Piscataway, NJ 08854-8097. Offers MA, PhD. Part-time programs available. Terminal master's awarded for partial completion of doctoral program. *Degree requirements:* For master's, comprehensive exam; for doctorate, 3 foreign languages, thesis/dissertation, written and oral exams. *Entrance requirements:* For doctorate, GRE General Test, GRE Subject Test (recommended). Additional exam requirements/recommendations for international students: Required—TOEFL. Electronic applications accepted. *Expenses:* Tuition, state resident: full-time $7200; part-time $600 per credit. Tuition, nonresident: full-time $11,124; part-time $927 per credit. *Faculty research:* Genres and periods, modern literary theory, psychoanalytic approaches to literature, literature and gender, cultural studies.

San Francisco State University, Division of Graduate Studies, College of Humanities, Department of Comparative and World Literature, San Francisco, CA 94132-1722. Offers comparative literature (MA). Part-time programs available. *Degree requirements:* For master's, one foreign language. *Application deadline:* Applications are processed on a rolling basis. *Unit head:* Dr. David Leitao, Chair, 415-338-2068, E-mail: dleitao@sfsu.edu. *Application contact:* Dr. Shirin Khanmohamadi, Graduate Coordinator, 415-338-2068, E-mail: shirin1@sfsu.edu.

San Jose State University, Graduate Studies and Research, College of Humanities and the Arts, Department of English and Comparative Literature, San Jose, CA 95192-0001. Offers English (MFA); English literature (MA). *Degree requirements:* For master's, one foreign language, thesis or alternative. *Entrance requirements:* For master's, GRE. Additional exam requirements/recommendations for international students: Required—TOEFL. Electronic applications accepted.

Stanford University, School of Humanities and Sciences, Department of Comparative Literature, Stanford, CA 94305-9991. Offers PhD. *Degree requirements:* For doctorate, 3 foreign languages, thesis/dissertation, qualification procedures. *Entrance requirements:* For doctorate, GRE General Test, GRE Subject Test. Additional exam requirements/recommendations for international students: Required—TOEFL. Electronic applications accepted. *Expenses:* Tuition: Full-time $38,700; part-time $860 per unit. One-time fee: $200 full-time.

Stanford University, School of Humanities and Sciences, Program in Modern Thought and Literature, Stanford, CA 94305-9991. Offers PhD. *Degree requirements:* For doctorate, 2 foreign languages, thesis/dissertation, qualifying paper, oral exam. *Entrance requirements:* For doctorate, GRE General Test. Additional exam requirements/recommendations for international students: Required—TOEFL. Electronic applications accepted. *Expenses:* Tuition: Full-time $38,700; part-time $860 per unit. One-time fee: $200 full-time.

State University of New York at Binghamton, Graduate School, School of Arts and Sciences, Department of Comparative Literature, Binghamton, NY 13902-6000. Offers MA, PhD. Part-time programs available. *Faculty:* 7 full-time (5 women), 7 part-time/adjunct (4 women). *Students:* 23 full-time (14 women), 35 part-time (21 women); includes 1 Black or African American, non-Hispanic/Latino; 2 Asian, non-Hispanic/Latino; 3 Hispanic/Latino, 27 international. Average age 33. 36 applicants, 58% accepted, 8 enrolled. In 2010, 3 master's, 6 doctorates awarded. Terminal master's awarded for partial completion of doctoral program. *Degree requirements:* For master's, 2 foreign languages, thesis or alternative, written exam; for doctorate, 3 foreign languages, comprehensive exam, thesis/dissertation. *Entrance requirements:* For master's and doctorate, GRE General Test, GRE Subject Test. Additional exam requirements/recommendations for international students: Required—TOEFL (minimum score 550 paper-based; 213 computer-based; 80 iBT). *Application deadline:* For fall admission, 2/1 priority date for domestic and international students; for spring admission, 10/15 priority date for domestic and international students. Applications are processed on a rolling basis. Application fee: $60. Electronic applications accepted. *Financial support:* In 2010–11, 21 students received support, including 1 fellowship with full tuition reimbursement available (averaging $14,500 per year), 17 teaching assistantships with full tuition reimbursements available (averaging $14,500 per year); career-related internships or fieldwork, Federal Work-Study, institutionally sponsored loans, scholarships/grants, health care benefits, tuition waivers (full and partial), and unspecified assistantships also available. Financial award application deadline: 2/15; financial award applicants required to submit FAFSA. *Unit head:* Dr. Gisela Brinker-Gabler, Chairperson, 607-777-2890, E-mail: gbrinker@binghamton.edu. *Application contact:* Catherine Smith, Recruiting and Admissions Coordinator, 607-777-2151, Fax: 607-777-2501, E-mail: cmsmith@binghamton.edu.

Stony Brook University, State University of New York, Graduate School, College of Arts and Sciences, Department of Comparative Literary and Cultural Studies, Stony Brook, NY 11794. Offers comparative literature (MA, PhD); cultural studies (PhD). Evening/weekend programs available. *Faculty:* 7 full-time (1 woman), 1 part-time/adjunct (0 women). *Students:* 29 full-time (18 women), 3 part-time (all women); includes 2 Asian, non-Hispanic/Latino, 13 international. Average age 30. 98 applicants, 31% accepted, 7 enrolled. In 2010, 5 master's, 3 doctorates awarded. Terminal master's awarded for partial completion of doctoral program. *Degree requirements:* For master's, 2 foreign languages, exam; for doctorate, 3 foreign languages, comprehensive exam, thesis/dissertation. *Entrance requirements:* For master's and doctorate, GRE General Test, minimum GPA of 3.5 in major, 3.0 overall. Additional exam requirements/recommendations for international students: Required—TOEFL. *Application deadline:* For fall admission, 1/15 for domestic students. Application fee: $100. *Expenses:* Tuition, state resident: full-time $8370; part-time $349 per credit. Tuition, nonresident: full-time $13,780; part-time $574 per credit. Required fees: $994. *Financial support:* In 2010–11, 12 teaching assistantships were awarded; fellowships, research assistantships also available. *Faculty research:* Literary theory, interdisciplinary studies, literary history. *Unit head:* Prof. Krin Gabbard, Chairman, 631-632-7456. *Application contact:* Dr. Kent Marks, Assistant Dean, Admissions and Records, 631-632-4723, Fax: 631-632-7243, E-mail: kmarks@notes.cc.sunysb.edu.

Université de Montréal, Faculty of Arts and Sciences, Department of Comparative Literature, Montréal, QC H3C 3J7, Canada. Offers comparative literature (MA); literature (PhD). *Degree requirements:* For master's, 2 foreign languages, thesis; for doctorate, 3 foreign languages, thesis/dissertation, general exam. *Entrance requirements:* For doctorate, MA with minimum B+ average. Electronic applications accepted.

Université de Sherbrooke, Faculty of Letters and Human Sciences, Department of Letters and Communications, Sherbrooke, QC J1K 2R1, Canada. Offers comparative Canadian literature (MA, PhD); French literature (MA, PhD); linguistics (MA); theatre (MA). *Degree requirements:* For master's, thesis or alternative; for doctorate, thesis/dissertation. *Entrance requirements:* For master's, minimum GPA of 2.8; for doctorate, minimum GPA of 3.0.

Université du Québec à Chicoutimi, Graduate Programs, Program in Literary Studies, Chicoutimi, QC G7H 2B1, Canada. Offers MA. Program offered jointly with Université du Québec à Rimouski and Université du Québec à Trois-Rivières. Part-time programs available. *Degree requirements:* For master's, thesis optional. *Entrance requirements:* For master's, appropriate bachelor's degree, proficiency in French.

Université du Québec à Montréal, Graduate Programs, Program in Literary Studies, Montréal, QC H3C 3P8, Canada. Offers MA, PhD. Part-time programs available. *Degree requirements:* For master's, thesis; for doctorate, thesis/dissertation. *Entrance requirements:* For master's, appropriate bachelor's degree or equivalent, proficiency in French; for doctorate, appropriate master's degree or equivalent, proficiency in French.

Université du Québec à Montréal, Graduate Programs, Program in Semiology, Montréal, QC H3C 3P8, Canada. Offers PhD. Part-time programs available. *Degree requirements:* For doctorate, thesis/dissertation. *Entrance requirements:* For doctorate, appropriate master's degree or equivalent, proficiency in French.

Université du Québec à Rimouski, Graduate Programs, Program in Literary Studies, Rimouski, QC G5L 3A1, Canada. Offers MA, PhD. Programs offered jointly with Université du Québec à Chicoutimi and Université du Québec à Trois-Rivières. Part-time programs available. *Degree requirements:* For master's, thesis or alternative. *Entrance requirements:* For master's, appropriate bachelor's degree, proficiency in French.

Université du Québec à Trois-Rivières, Graduate Programs, Program in Literary Studies, Trois-Rivières, QC G9A 5H7, Canada. Offers MA. Program offered jointly with Université du Québec à Chicoutimi and Université du Québec à Rimouski. Part-time programs available. *Degree requirements:* For master's, thesis optional. *Entrance requirements:* For master's, appropriate bachelor's degree, proficiency in French.

Université Laval, Faculty of Letters, Department of Literature, Programs in Literary Studies, Québec, QC G1K 7P4, Canada. Offers MA, PhD. Part-time programs available. Terminal master's awarded for partial completion of doctoral program. *Degree requirements:* For master's, thesis; for doctorate, comprehensive exam, thesis/dissertation. *Entrance requirements:* For master's and doctorate, linguistics exams, knowledge of French, knowledge of a second language. Electronic applications accepted.

University at Buffalo, the State University of New York, Graduate School, College of Arts and Sciences, Department of Comparative Literature, Buffalo, NY 14260. Offers MA, PhD. Part-time programs available. *Faculty:* 8 full-time (2 women). *Students:* 35 full-time (20 women); includes 1 Black or African American, non-Hispanic/Latino; 2 Asian, non-Hispanic/Latino; 2 Hispanic/Latino. Average age 25. 45 applicants, 67% accepted, 13 enrolled. In 2010, 8 master's, 4 doctorates awarded. Terminal master's awarded for partial completion of doctoral program. *Degree requirements:* For master's, one foreign language, exam or thesis; for doctorate, 2 foreign languages, comprehensive exam, thesis/dissertation. *Entrance requirements:* For master's and doctorate, GRE General Test, writing sample, 3 letters of recommendation. Additional exam requirements/recommendations for international students: Required—TOEFL (minimum score 550 paper-based; 213 computer-based; 79 iBT). *Application deadline:* For fall admission, 1/15 for domestic and international students. Application fee: $75. Electronic applications accepted. *Financial support:* In 2010–11, 17 students received support, including 5 fellowships with full tuition reimbursements available (averaging $4,150 per year), 17 teaching assistantships with full tuition reimbursements available (averaging $13,600 per year); Federal Work-Study, institutionally sponsored loans, health care benefits, and unspecified assistantships also available. Financial award application deadline: 1/15; financial award applicants required to submit FAFSA. *Faculty research:* Theory; interaction between literature and philosophy; European, Francophone, African, American, and South American literature; postmodernism; postcolonialism. *Unit head:* Dr. David Johnson, Chair, 716-645-0854, Fax: 716-645-5979, E-mail: dj@buffalo.edu. *Application contact:* Dr. Krzysztof Ziarek, Director of Graduate Studies, 716-645-0858, Fax: 716-645-5979, E-mail: kziarek@buffalo.edu.

University of Arkansas, Graduate School, Interdisciplinary Program in Comparative Literature and Cultural Studies, Fayetteville, AR 72701-1201. Offers MA, PhD. *Degree requirements:* For doctorate, 2 foreign languages, comprehensive exam, thesis/dissertation optional. *Entrance requirements:* For doctorate, GRE General Test, official transcripts of all undergraduate and graduate work, three letters of recommendation, writing sample, statement of purpose. Additional exam requirements/recommendations for international students: Required—TOEFL (minimum paper-based score 550, computer-based 213, iBT 80) or IELTS (6.5). Application fee: $40 ($50 for international students). *Financial support:* Fellowships, research assistantships, teaching assistantships, Federal Work-Study and institutionally sponsored loans available. *Faculty research:* Literary and cultural theory, cultural studies, postcolonial theory, gender studies, world literature. *Unit head:* Prof. M. Keith Booker, Director, 479-575-2951, Fax: 479-575-6795, E-mail: kbooker@uark.edu. *Application contact:* Graduate Admissions, 479-575-6246, Fax: 479-575-5908, E-mail: gradinfo@uark.edu.

University of California, Berkeley, Graduate Division, College of Letters and Science, Department of Comparative Literature, Berkeley, CA 94720-1500. Offers PhD. *Degree requirements:* For doctorate, 3 foreign languages, thesis/dissertation, qualifying exam. *Entrance requirements:* For doctorate, GRE General Test, fluency in 1 foreign language (2 preferred), minimum GPA of 3.0, writing sample, 3 letters of recommendation.

University of California, Davis, Graduate Studies, Graduate Group in Comparative Literature, Davis, CA 95616. Offers PhD. *Degree requirements:* For doctorate, 3 foreign languages, thesis/dissertation. *Entrance requirements:* For doctorate, GRE General Test, minimum GPA of 3.0. Additional exam requirements/recommendations for international students: Required—TOEFL (minimum score 550 paper-based; 213 computer-based). Electronic applications accepted. *Faculty research:* Literary criticism, literary theory, gender history and literature, genre.

University of California, Irvine, School of Humanities, Department of English and Comparative Literature, Program in Comparative Literature, Irvine, CA 92697. Offers MA, PhD. *Students:* 46 full-time (26 women); includes 13 minority (1 American Indian or Alaska Native, non-Hispanic/Latino; 9 Asian, non-Hispanic/Latino; 2 Hispanic/Latino; 1 Two or more races, non-Hispanic/Latino), 2 international. Average age 28. 71 applicants, 17% accepted, 6 enrolled. In 2010, 6 master's, 5 doctorates awarded. *Degree requirements:* For master's, one foreign language; for doctorate, 2 foreign languages, thesis/dissertation. *Entrance requirements:* For doctorate, GRE General Test, minimum GPA of 3.5, sample of written work, 3 letters of recommendation. Additional exam requirements/recommendations for international students: Required—TOEFL (minimum score 550 paper-based; 213 computer-based). *Application deadline:* For fall admission, 12/15 for domestic and international students. Application fee: $80 ($100 for international students). Electronic applications accepted. *Financial support:* Fellowships with full tuition reimbursements, research assistantships with full tuition reimbursements, teaching assistantships with partial tuition reimbursements, institutionally sponsored loans and tuition waivers (partial) available. Financial award application deadline: 3/1; financial award applicants required to submit FAFSA. *Faculty research:* Critical theory, feminist studies, Asian-American studies. *Unit head:* Prof. Susan Carole Jarratt, Chair, 949-824-6406, Fax: 949-824-6416, E-mail: sjarratt@uci.edu. *Application contact:* Bindya Shankar Baliga, Graduate Coordinator, 949-824-6718, E-mail: bbaliga@uci.edu.

University of California, Los Angeles, Graduate Division, College of Letters and Science, Department of Comparative Literature, Los Angeles, CA 90095. Offers MA, PhD. *Faculty:* 10 full-time (5 women). *Students:* 42 full-time (24 women); includes 13 minority (11 Asian, non-Hispanic/Latino; 2 Hispanic/Latino), 5 international. Average age 29. 64 applicants, 11% accepted, 4 enrolled. In 2010, 3 master's, 7 doctorates awarded. Terminal master's awarded for partial completion of doctoral program. *Degree requirements:* For master's, 2 foreign languages, comprehensive exam; for doctorate, 2 foreign languages, thesis/dissertation, oral and written qualifying exams. *Entrance requirements:* For master's, GRE General Test, sample of written work, previous course work in literature, minimum GPA of 3.4 in upper-division course work; for doctorate, GRE General Test, sample of written work, MA in comparative literature. *Application deadline:* For fall admission, 12/1 for domestic and international students. Application fee: $70 ($90 for international students). Electronic applications accepted. *Financial support:* In 2010–11, 38 fellowships with full and partial tuition reimbursements, 13 research assistantships with full and partial tuition reimbursements, 29 teaching assistantships with full and partial tuition reimbursements were awarded; Federal Work-Study, institutionally sponsored loans, scholarships/grants, health care benefits, tuition waivers (full and partial), and unspecified assistantships also available. Financial award application deadline: 3/1; financial award applicants required to submit FAFSA. *Unit head:* Dr. Efrain Kristal, Chair, 310-206-0552, E-mail: kristal@ucla.edu. *Application contact:* Department Office, 310-825-7650, E-mail: manderson@humnet.ucla.edu.

University of California, Riverside, Graduate Division, Department of Comparative Literature and Foreign Languages, Riverside, CA 92521-0102. Offers comparative literature (MA, PhD). Terminal master's awarded for partial completion of doctoral program. *Degree requirements:* For master's, 3 foreign languages, comprehensive exam; for doctorate, 3 foreign languages, thesis/dissertation, qualifying exams. *Entrance requirements:* For master's and doctorate, GRE General Test, minimum GPA of 3.2. Additional exam requirements/recommendations for international students: Required—TOEFL (minimum score 550 paper-based; 213 computer-based; 80 iBT). Electronic applications accepted. *Faculty research:* French and German Enlightenment, modern drama and theatre, contemporary critical theory, East-West comparative studies, science fiction and fantasy.

University of California, San Diego, Office of Graduate Studies, Department of Literature, Program in Comparative Literature, La Jolla, CA 92093. Offers MA, PhD. *Degree requirements:* For master's, thesis; for doctorate, thesis/dissertation. *Entrance requirements:* For master's and doctorate, GRE General Test, GRE Subject Test. Electronic applications accepted. *Faculty research:* Problems of theory and method, relationship of the humanities to the social sciences.

University of California, Santa Barbara, Graduate Division, College of Letters and Sciences, Division of Humanities and Fine Arts, Program in Comparative Literature, Santa Barbara, CA 93106-4130. Offers comparative literature (PhD); East Asian literatures (PhD); feminist studies (PhD); French (PhD); global studies (PhD); translation studies (PhD); MA/PhD. *Faculty:* 63 full-time (31 women). *Students:* 21 full-time (14 women); includes 3 Asian, non-Hispanic/Latino; 2 Hispanic/Latino. Average age 31. 41 applicants, 12% accepted, 2 enrolled. In 2010, 1 doctorate awarded. *Degree requirements:* For doctorate, 2 foreign languages, comprehensive exam, thesis/dissertation. *Entrance requirements:* For doctorate, GRE. Additional exam requirements/recommendations for international students: Required—TOEFL (minimum score 550 paper-based; 80 iBT), IELTS (minimum score 7). *Application deadline:* For fall admission, 12/15 for domestic and international students. Application fee: $70 ($90 for international students). Electronic applications accepted. *Financial support:* In 2010–11, 19 students received support, including 14 fellowships with full and partial tuition reimbursements available (averaging $16,232 per year), 12 teaching assistantships with partial tuition reimbursements available (averaging $12,826 per year); research assistantships, Federal Work-Study, institutionally sponsored loans, scholarships/grants, health care benefits, and tuition waivers (full and partial) also available. Financial award application deadline: 12/15; financial award applicants required to submit FAFSA. *Faculty research:* Comparative literary studies in global context, critical theory, translation studies, mediatechnological studies, trauma studies. *Unit head:* Prof. Susan Derwin, Chair, 805-893-4399, Fax: 805-893-8341, E-mail: derwin@gss.ucsb.edu. *Application contact:* Ashley Bradbury, Graduate Program Assistant, 805-893-2131, Fax: 805-893-8341, E-mail: ashley@hfa.ucsb.edu.

University of California, Santa Cruz, Division of Graduate Studies, Division of Humanities, Department of Literature, Santa Cruz, CA 95064. Offers MA, PhD. *Students:* 65 full-time (42 women), 4 part-time (2 women); includes 1 Black or African American, non-Hispanic/Latino; 7 Asian, non-Hispanic/Latino; 2 Hispanic/Latino, 1 international. Average age 31. 183 applicants, 14% accepted, 8 enrolled. In 2010, 3 master's, 4 doctorates awarded. Terminal master's awarded for partial completion of doctoral program. *Degree requirements:* For master's, thesis; for doctorate, one foreign language, thesis/dissertation, qualifying exam. *Entrance requirements:* For master's, GRE General Test, writing sample, minimum GPA of 3.5; for doctorate, GRE General Test, minimum GPA of 3.5, writing sample. Additional exam requirements/recommendations for international students: Required—TOEFL (minimum score 550 paper-based; 220 computer-based; 83 iBT); Recommended—IELTS (minimum score 8). *Application deadline:* For fall admission, 12/1 for domestic and international students. Application fee: $70 ($90 for international students). Electronic applications accepted. *Financial support:* Fellowships, teaching assistantships, institutionally sponsored loans and tuition waivers available. Financial award applicants required to submit FAFSA. *Faculty research:* Technologies of narrative; trans/post/emergent nationalisms; poetics, poetry, and experimental writing; materialism and material culture; critical theories. *Unit head:* Emily Gregg, Graduate Program Coordinator, 831-459-4126, E-mail: egregg@ucsc.edu. *Application contact:* Emily Gregg, Graduate Program Coordinator, 831-459-4126, E-mail: egregg@ucsc.edu.

University of Chicago, Division of the Humanities, Department of Comparative Literature, Chicago, IL 60637-1513. Offers AM, PhD. Terminal master's awarded for partial completion of doctoral program. *Degree requirements:* For master's, 2 foreign languages, thesis; for doctorate, 3 foreign languages, thesis/dissertation. *Entrance requirements:* For master's and doctorate, GRE General Test.

University of Colorado Boulder, Graduate School, College of Arts and Sciences, Department of Comparative Literature and Humanities, Boulder, CO 80309. Offers MA, PhD. *Faculty:* 2 full-time (0 women). *Students:* 21 full-time (11 women), 4 part-time (3 women); includes 1 minority (Asian, non-Hispanic/Latino), 4 international. Average age 34. 31 applicants, 4 enrolled. In 2010, 7 master's, 2 doctorates awarded. Terminal master's awarded for partial completion of doctoral program. *Degree requirements:* For master's, 2 foreign languages, comprehensive exam, thesis or alternative; for doctorate, 3 foreign languages, comprehensive exam, thesis/dissertation. *Entrance requirements:* For master's, GRE General Test, minimum undergraduate GPA of 2.75; for doctorate, GRE General Test, MA in related field. *Application deadline:* For fall admission, 1/1 priority date for domestic students, 12/1 for international students. Applications are processed on a rolling basis. Application fee: $50 ($60 for international students). *Financial support:* In 2010–11, 2 fellowships (averaging $23,964 per year), 3 research assistantships (averaging $15,284 per year) were awarded; tuition waivers (full) also available. Financial award application deadline: 1/1. *Faculty research:* Enlightenment to modern literature; literary theory and history; philosophy and literature; popular culture studies; reception, translation and interpretation; gender and sexual orientation; nationalism. Total annual research expenditures: $23,115.

University of Connecticut, Graduate School, College of Liberal Arts and Sciences, Department of Modern and Classical Languages, Field of Comparative Literature and Cultural Studies, Storrs, CT 06269. Offers MA, PhD. Terminal master's awarded for partial completion of doctoral program. *Degree requirements:* For master's, comprehensive exam; for doctorate, thesis/dissertation. *Entrance requirements:* For master's and doctorate, GRE General Test, GRE Subject Test. Additional exam requirements/recommendations for international students: Required—TOEFL (minimum score 550 paper-based; 213 computer-based). Electronic applications accepted.

University of Dallas, Braniff Graduate School of Liberal Arts, Institute of Philosophic Studies, Program in Literature, Irving, TX 75062-4736. Offers PhD. *Degree requirements:* For doctorate, 2 foreign languages, comprehensive exam, thesis/dissertation, qualifying exams. *Entrance requirements:* For doctorate, GRE General Test. Additional exam requirements/recommendations for international students: Required—TOEFL. *Expenses:* Tuition: Full-time $7500; part-time $720 per credit hour. Required fees: $500; $60 per credit hour. $300 per semester. One-time fee: $150. Tuition and fees vary according to program and student level. *Faculty research:* Medieval studies, modern literature, Renaissance, Shakespeare.

University of Georgia, College of Arts and Sciences, Department of Comparative Literature, Athens, GA 30602. Offers MA, PhD. *Faculty:* 10 full-time (3 women). *Students:* 25 full-time (16 women), 5 part-time (4 women), 8 international. 29 applicants, 52% accepted, 5 enrolled. In 2010, 6 master's, 1 doctorate awarded. *Degree requirements:* For master's, 2 foreign languages, thesis; for doctorate, one foreign language, thesis/dissertation. *Entrance requirements:* For master's and doctorate, GRE General Test. *Application deadline:* For fall admission, 7/1 priority date for domestic students; for spring admission, 11/15 for domestic students. Application fee: $50. Electronic applications accepted. *Expenses:* Tuition, state resident: full-time $7200; part-time $344 per credit hour. Tuition, nonresident: full-time $21,900; part-time $944 per credit hour. Tuition and fees vary according to course load and program. *Financial support:* Fellowships, research assistantships, teaching assistantships, unspecified assistantships available. *Unit head:* Dr. James H. McGregor, Department Co-Head, 706-542-0420, E-mail: mcgregor@uga.edu. *Application contact:* Dr. Thomas Cerbu, Graduate Coordinator, 706-542-2263, Fax: 706-542-2155, E-mail: tcerbu@uga.edu.

University of Guelph, Graduate Studies, College of Arts, School of English and Theatre Studies, Joint Program in Literary Studies/Theatre Studies in English, Guelph, ON N1G 2W1, Canada. Offers PhD. Part-time programs available. *Degree requirements:* For doctorate, one foreign language, comprehensive exam, thesis/dissertation. *Entrance requirements:* For doctorate, MA, 3 letters of reference, writing samples, resume, minimum A- average in graduate course work. Additional exam requirements/recommendations for international students: Required—TOEFL. Electronic applications accepted. *Faculty research:* Canadian studies, Early Modern studies, Postcolonial studies, studies in gender and genre, 19th Century studies.

University of Houston, College of Liberal Arts and Social Sciences, Department of Modern and Classical Languages, Houston, TX 77204. Offers world cultures and literatures (MA).

Comparative Literature

University of Houston (continued)
Faculty: 11 full-time (6 women), 4 part-time/adjunct (all women). *Students:* 1 (woman) part-time. Average age 29. 7 applicants, 29% accepted, 1 enrolled. *Degree requirements:* For master's, one foreign language, thesis optional. *Entrance requirements:* For master's, GRE General Test, minimum GPA of 3.0 in last 60 hours of course work. Additional exam requirements/recommendations for international students: Required—TOEFL (minimum score 500 paper-based). *Application deadline:* For fall admission, 4/15 for domestic and international students; for spring admission, 11/1 for domestic and international students. Applications are processed on a rolling basis. Electronic applications accepted. *Expenses:* Tuition, state resident: full-time $8592; part-time $358 per credit hour. Tuition, nonresident: full-time $16,032; part-time $668 per credit hour. Required fees: $2889. Tuition and fees vary according to course load and program. *Financial support:* In 2010–11, 2 teaching assistantships with full tuition reimbursements (averaging $9,060 per year) were awarded; career-related internships or fieldwork, Federal Work-Study, institutionally sponsored loans, scholarships/grants, health care benefits, and unspecified assistantships also available. Support available to part-time students. Financial award applicants required to submit FAFSA. *Unit head:* Dr. Hildegard Glass, Chairperson, 713-743-8350, Fax: 713-743-2693, E-mail: hfglass@uh.edu. *Application contact:* Alessandro Carrera, 713-743-3069, E-mail: alessandro.carrera@mail.uh.edu.

University of Illinois at Urbana–Champaign, Graduate College, College of Liberal Arts and Sciences, School of Literatures, Cultures and Linguistics, Program in Comparative and World Literature, Champaign, IL 61820. Offers comparative literature (MA, PhD). *Faculty:* 6 full-time (5 women), 1 (woman) part-time/adjunct. *Students:* 19 full-time (13 women), 1 (woman) part-time; includes 1 Asian, non-Hispanic/Latino; 1 Hispanic/Latino, 8 international. 32 applicants, 16% accepted, 2 enrolled. In 2010, 5 master's, 3 doctorates awarded. *Entrance requirements:* For master's, minimum GPA of 3.0; writing sample. Additional exam requirements/recommendations for international students: Required—TOEFL (minimum score 105 iBT). *Application deadline:* Applications are processed on a rolling basis. Application fee: $75 ($90 for international students). Electronic applications accepted. *Financial support:* In 2010–11, 6 fellowships, 1 research assistantship, 13 teaching assistantships were awarded; tuition waivers (full and partial) also available. *Unit head:* Jean-Phillipe R. Mathy, Director, 217-244-2727, Fax: 217-244-4019, E-mail: jmathy@illinois.edu. *Application contact:* Lynn Stanke, Office Support Specialist, 217-333-6269, Fax: 217-244-4019, E-mail: stanke@illinois.edu.

The University of Iowa, Graduate College, College of Liberal Arts and Sciences, Department of Cinema and Comparative Literature, Program in Comparative Literature, Iowa City, IA 52242-1316. Offers MA, PhD. *Degree requirements:* For master's, thesis optional, exam; for doctorate, comprehensive exam, thesis/dissertation. *Entrance requirements:* For master's and doctorate, GRE General Test, minimum GPA of 3.0. Additional exam requirements/recommendations for international students: Required—TOEFL (minimum score 520 paper-based; 213 computer-based; 81 iBT). Electronic applications accepted.

The University of Iowa, Graduate College, College of Liberal Arts and Sciences, Department of Cinema and Comparative Literature, Program in Comparative Literature Translation, Iowa City, IA 52242-1316. Offers MFA. *Degree requirements:* For master's, thesis, exam. *Entrance requirements:* For master's, GRE General Test, minimum GPA of 3.0. Additional exam requirements/recommendations for international students: Required—TOEFL (minimum score 550 paper-based; 213 computer-based; 81 iBT). Electronic applications accepted.

University of Maryland, College Park, Academic Affairs, College of Arts and Humanities, Department of English, Program in Comparative Literature, College Park, MD 20742. Offers MA, PhD. *Students:* 9 full-time (6 women), 2 international. 18 applicants, 0% accepted, 0 enrolled. In 2010, 1 doctorate awarded. *Degree requirements:* For master's, thesis, oral defense; for doctorate, 3 foreign languages, thesis/dissertation, comprehensive exams in 4 areas. *Entrance requirements:* For master's, GRE General Test, minimum GPA of 3.0, foreign language, writing sample, 3 letters of recommendation; for doctorate, GRE General Test, minimum GPA of 3.0, foreign language, writing sample. Additional exam requirements/recommendations for international students: Required—TOEFL. *Application deadline:* For fall admission, 1/15 for domestic and international students. Applications are processed on a rolling basis. Application fee: $75. Electronic applications accepted. *Expenses:* Tuition, state resident: part-time $471 per credit hour. Tuition, nonresident: part-time $1016 per credit hour. Required fees: $337 per term. *Financial support:* In 2010–11, 1 fellowship with partial tuition reimbursement (averaging $13,000 per year), 5 teaching assistantships (averaging $18,021 per year) were awarded; research assistantships, career-related internships or fieldwork, Federal Work-Study, and scholarships/grants also available. Support available to part-time students. Financial award applicants required to submit FAFSA. *Faculty research:* Renaissance studies, drama, modern literature, postcolonial studies, feminist scholarship. *Unit head:* Kent Cartwright, Chair of English Department, 301-405-3807, E-mail: kcartwri@umd.edu. *Application contact:* Dean of Graduate School, 301-405-0376, Fax: 301-314-9305.

University of Massachusetts Amherst, Graduate School, College of Humanities and Fine Arts, Department of Languages, Literatures, and Cultures, Program in Comparative Literature, Amherst, MA 01003. Offers MA, PhD. Part-time programs available. *Faculty:* 13 full-time (4 women). *Students:* 42 full-time (23 women), 1 (woman) part-time; includes 9 minority (8 Hispanic/Latino; 1 Two or more races, non-Hispanic/Latino), 15 international. Average age 32. 84 applicants, 27% accepted, 10 enrolled. In 2010, 4 master's awarded. Terminal master's awarded for partial completion of doctoral program. *Degree requirements:* For master's, thesis or alternative; for doctorate, comprehensive exam, thesis/dissertation. *Entrance requirements:* For master's and doctorate, GRE General Test, writing sample. Additional exam requirements/recommendations for international students: Required—TOEFL (minimum score 550 paper-based; 213 computer-based; 80 iBT), IELTS (minimum score 6.5). *Application deadline:* For fall admission, 2/1 for domestic and international students. Applications are processed on a rolling basis. Application fee: $50 ($65 for international students). Electronic applications accepted. *Expenses:* Tuition, state resident: full-time $2640. Required fees: $8282. One-time fee: $357 full-time. *Financial support:* In 2010–11, 1 research assistantship with full tuition reimbursement (averaging $7,331 per year), 20 teaching assistantships with full tuition reimbursements (averaging $13,562 per year) were awarded; fellowships, career-related internships or fieldwork, Federal Work-Study, scholarships/grants, traineeships, health care benefits, tuition waivers (full), and unspecified assistantships also available. Support available to part-time students. Financial award application deadline: 2/1; financial award applicants required to submit FAFSA. *Unit head:* Dr. William Moebius, Department Head/Chair, 413-545-0929, Fax: 413-545-0908. *Application contact:* Jean M. Ames, Supervisor of Admissions, 413-545-0722, Fax: 413-577-0100, E-mail: gradadm@grad.umass.edu.

University of Memphis, Graduate School, College of Arts and Sciences, Department of English, Memphis, TN 38152. Offers African-American literature (Graduate Certificate); applied linguistics (PhD); composition studies (PhD); creative writing (MFA); English as a second language (MA); linguistics (MA); literary and cultural studies (PhD), including African-American literature; literature (MA); professional writing (MA, PhD); teaching English as a second language (Graduate Certificate). Part-time and evening/weekend programs available. Post-baccalaureate distance learning degree programs offered (no on-campus study). *Faculty:* 31 full-time (15 women), 2 part-time/adjunct (both women). *Students:* 108 full-time (70 women), 107 part-time (69 women); includes 15 minority (2 Black or African American, non-Hispanic/Latino; 2 Asian, non-Hispanic/Latino; 6 Hispanic/Latino; 5 Two or more races, non-Hispanic/Latino), 8 international. Average age 34. 128 applicants, 71% accepted, 29 enrolled. In 2010, 38 master's, 4 doctorates, 21 other advanced degrees awarded. Terminal master's awarded for partial completion of doctoral program. *Degree requirements:* For master's, one foreign language, comprehensive exam, thesis optional; for doctorate, 2 foreign languages, comprehensive exam, thesis/dissertation. *Entrance requirements:* For master's and doctorate, GRE. Additional exam requirements/recommendations for international students: Required—TOEFL. *Application deadline:* For fall admission, 7/1 for domestic students; for spring admission, 10/15 for domestic students. Applications are processed on a rolling basis. Application fee: $35 ($60 for international students). Electronic applications accepted. *Financial support:* In 2010–11, 123 students received support; research assistantships with full tuition reimbursements available, teaching assistantships with full tuition reimbursements available, Federal Work-Study, scholarships/grants, and unspecified assistantships available. Financial award application deadline: 2/15; financial award applicants required to submit FAFSA. *Faculty research:* Applied linguistics, British and American literature, professional writing, composition studies. *Unit head:* Dr. Verner D. Mitchell, Chair, 901-678-3099, Fax: 901-678-2226, E-mail: vdmtchll@memphis.edu. *Application contact:* Dr. Verner D. Mitchell, Director, Graduate Studies, 901-678-3099, Fax: 901-678-2226, E-mail: vdmtchll@memphis.edu.

University of Michigan, Horace H. Rackham School of Graduate Studies, College of Literature, Science, and the Arts, Department of Comparative Literature, Ann Arbor, MI 48109. Offers PhD. *Faculty:* 21 full-time (12 women). *Students:* 41 full-time (21 women); includes 2 Asian, non-Hispanic/Latino; 3 Hispanic/Latino, 15 international. Average age 31. 66 applicants, 14% accepted, 5 enrolled. In 2010, 6 doctorates awarded. *Degree requirements:* For doctorate, 2 foreign languages, thesis/dissertation, preliminary exam, topics paper, prospectus, oral defense of dissertation. *Entrance requirements:* For doctorate, GRE General Test. Additional exam requirements/recommendations for international students: Required—TOEFL (minimum score 560 paper-based; 220 computer-based; 84 iBT), Michigan English Language Assessment Battery, or IELTS (minimum score 6.5). *Application deadline:* For fall admission, 12/31 for domestic and international students. Application fee: $65 ($75 for international students). Electronic applications accepted. *Expenses:* Tuition, state resident: full-time $17,784; part-time $1116 per credit hour. Tuition, nonresident: full-time $35,944; part-time $2125 per credit hour. International tuition: $35,994 full-time. Required fees: $95 per semester. Tuition and fees vary according to course load, degree level and program. *Financial support:* In 2010–11, 40 students received support, including 11 fellowships with full tuition reimbursements available (averaging $33,879 per year), 21 teaching assistantships with full tuition reimbursements available (averaging $35,149 per year); research assistantships, career-related internships or fieldwork, Federal Work-Study, institutionally sponsored loans, scholarships/grants, health care benefits, and unspecified assistantships also available. Support available to part-time students. Financial award application deadline: 4/15. *Faculty research:* Postcolonial theory, cultural studies, ideology of aesthetics, translation studies, comparative poetics. *Unit head:* Yopie Prins, Chair, 734-763-2351, Fax: 734-764-8503, E-mail: yprins@umich.edu. *Application contact:* Nancy E. W. Harris, Student Services Coordinator, 734-647-4894, Fax: 734-764-8503, E-mail: nwh@umich.edu.

University of Minnesota, Twin Cities Campus, Graduate School, College of Liberal Arts, Department of Cultural Studies and Comparative Literature, Program in Comparative Literature, Minneapolis, MN 55455-0213. Offers PhD. *Degree requirements:* For doctorate, 3 foreign languages, comprehensive exam, thesis/dissertation. *Entrance requirements:* For doctorate, GRE General Test, sample of written work. Additional exam requirements/recommendations for international students: Required—TOEFL. *Faculty research:* Literary theory, emergent literatures, popular culture, postcolonial literature, gender and sexuality.

University of Missouri, Graduate School, College of Arts and Sciences, Department of Romance Languages and Literature, Columbia, MO 65211. Offers French (MA, PhD); literature (MA); Spanish (MA, PhD); teaching (MA). Terminal master's awarded for partial completion of doctoral program. *Degree requirements:* For master's, one foreign language; for doctorate, 4 foreign languages, comprehensive exam, thesis/dissertation. *Entrance requirements:* For master's, GRE General Test, minimum GPA of 3.0 in field of major; bachelor's degree; for doctorate, GRE General Test, minimum GPA of 3.0 in field of major; master's degree. Additional exam requirements/recommendations for international students: Required—TOEFL (minimum score 500 paper-based; 173 computer-based; 61 iBT). Electronic applications accepted.

University of Nebraska–Lincoln, Graduate College, College of Arts and Sciences, Department of English, Lincoln, NE 68588-0333. Offers composition and rhetoric (MA, PhD); creative writing (MA, PhD); literature studies (MA, PhD). *Degree requirements:* For master's, thesis optional; for doctorate, one foreign language, comprehensive exam, thesis/dissertation. *Entrance requirements:* For master's, writing sample; for doctorate, GRE General Test, writing sample. Additional exam requirements/recommendations for international students: Required—TOEFL (minimum score 600 paper-based; 250 computer-based). Electronic applications accepted. *Faculty research:* Creative writing, composition and rhetoric, women's studies, North American literature, medieval/Renaissance studies.

University of New Hampshire, Graduate School, College of Liberal Arts, Department of English, Durham, NH 03824. Offers English (MFA, PhD); English education (MST); language and linguistics (MA); literature (MA); writing (MA). Part-time programs available. *Faculty:* 35 full-time (18 women). *Students:* 60 full-time (33 women), 68 part-time (45 women); includes 5 minority (1 Black or African American, non-Hispanic/Latino; 1 Hispanic/Latino; 3 Two or more races, non-Hispanic/Latino), 5 international. Average age 33. 291 applicants, 47% accepted, 50 enrolled. In 2010, 39 master's, 6 doctorates awarded. *Degree requirements:* For master's, one foreign language; for doctorate, 2 foreign languages, thesis/dissertation. *Entrance requirements:* For master's, GRE General Test, sample of written work; for doctorate, GRE General Test, GRE Subject Test, sample of written work. Additional exam requirements/recommendations for international students: Required—TOEFL (minimum score 550 paper-based; 213 computer-based; 80 iBT). *Application deadline:* For fall admission, 6/1 priority date for domestic students, 2/15 for international students; for spring admission, 12/1 for domestic students. Applications are processed on a rolling basis. Application fee: $65. Electronic applications accepted. *Financial support:* In 2010–11, 63 students received support, including 1 fellowship, 46 teaching assistantships; research assistantships, career-related internships or fieldwork, Federal Work-Study, scholarships/grants, and tuition waivers (full and partial) also available. Support available to part-time students. Financial award application deadline: 2/15. *Unit head:* Dr. Andrew Merton, Chairperson, 603-862-3963. *Application contact:* Jamie Auger, Administrative Assistant, 603-862-3963, E-mail: engl.grad@unh.edu.

University of New Mexico, Graduate School, College of Arts and Sciences, Department of Foreign Languages and Literature, Albuquerque, NM 87131-2039. Offers comparative literature and cultural studies (MA); French (MA); French studies (PhD); German studies (MA). Part-time programs available. *Faculty:* 18 full-time (12 women), 29 part-time/adjunct (19 women). *Students:* 25 full-time (16 women), 6 part-time (4 women); includes 2 Hispanic/Latino, 8 international. Average age 32. 20 applicants, 70% accepted, 9 enrolled. In 2010, 7 master's, 1 doctorate awarded. *Degree requirements:* For master's, one foreign language, thesis optional; for doctorate, 2 foreign languages, thesis/dissertation. *Entrance requirements:* Additional exam requirements/recommendations for international students: Required—TOEFL. *Application deadline:* For fall admission, 2/1 priority date for domestic students; for spring admission, 10/1 priority date for domestic students. Application fee: $50. Electronic applications accepted. *Expenses:* Tuition, state resident: full-time $5991; part-time $251 per credit hour. Tuition, nonresident: full-time $14,405; part-time $800.20 per credit hour. Tuition and fees vary according to course level, course load, program and reciprocity agreements. *Financial support:* In 2010–11, 28 students received support, including 1 research assistantship (averaging $4,730 per year), 23 teaching assistantships with tuition reimbursements available (averaging $10,300 per year); Federal Work-Study, health care benefits, and unspecified assistantships also available. Financial award application deadline: 3/1; financial award applicants required to submit FAFSA. *Faculty research:* German, Russian, Italian, Japanese, French, comparative literature, culture studies, classics. Total annual research expenditures: $4,750. *Unit head:* Dr. Natasha Kolchevska, Chair, 505-277-4771, Fax: 505-277-3599, E-mail: nakol@unm.edu. *Application contact:* Jean Aragon, Application and Graduation Advisor, 505-277-4471, Fax: 505-277-3599, E-mail: peaslee@unm.edu.

University of Notre Dame, Graduate School, College of Arts and Letters, Division of Humanities, PhD Program in Literature, Notre Dame, IN 46556. Offers PhD. *Degree requirements:* For doctorate, 3 foreign languages, thesis/dissertation, candidacy exam. *Entrance requirements:* For doctorate, GRE General Test. Additional exam requirements/recommendations for international students: Required—TOEFL (minimum score 600 paper-based; 250 computer-based; 80 iBT). Electronic applications accepted. *Faculty research:* Interdisciplinary study of literature from a transitional and intercultural perspective; classics, East Asian, French, German, Irish, Italian, Iberian and Latin American (Portuguese, Spanish).

University of Oregon, Graduate School, College of Arts and Sciences, Program in Comparative Literature, Eugene, OR 97403. Offers MA, PhD. Part-time programs available. Terminal master's awarded for partial completion of doctoral program. *Degree requirements:* For master's, 2 foreign languages, field exam; for doctorate, 2 foreign languages, thesis/dissertation, field exam. *Entrance requirements:* For master's, previous course work in English and literature, proficiency in 3 foreign languages, writing sample; for doctorate, previous course work in English and literature, proficiency in 2 foreign languages, writing sample. Additional exam requirements/recommendations for international students: Required—TOEFL. *Faculty research:* Critical theory, historical periods, interdisciplinary approach, Feminist studies.

University of Pennsylvania, School of Arts and Sciences, Graduate Group in Comparative Literature and Literary Theory, Philadelphia, PA 19104. Offers comparative literature (AM, PhD); literary theory (AM, PhD). *Faculty:* 58 full-time (23 women), 4 part-time/adjunct (1 woman). *Students:* 29 full-time (18 women); includes 1 Asian, non-Hispanic/Latino; 1 Hispanic/Latino, 7 international. 135 applicants, 2% accepted, 3 enrolled. In 2010, 1 master's, 5 doctorates awarded. *Degree requirements:* For master's, one foreign language, thesis; for doctorate, variable foreign language requirement, thesis/dissertation. *Entrance requirements:* For master's, GRE General Test, proficiency in 1 foreign language; for doctorate, GRE General Test, master's degree in a literature field, proficiency in 1 foreign language. Additional exam requirements/recommendations for international students: Required—TOEFL. *Application deadline:* For fall admission, 12/1 priority date for domestic students. Application fee: $70. Electronic applications accepted. *Expenses:* Tuition: Full-time $25,660; part-time $4758 per course. Required fees: $2152; $270 per course. Tuition and fees vary according to course load, degree level and program. *Financial support:* Institutionally sponsored loans, scholarships/grants, traineeships, health care benefits, and unspecified assistantships available. Financial award application deadline: 12/15. *Unit head:* Kevin Platt, Graduate Chair, 215-908-1685, E-mail: kmfplatt@sas.upenn.edu. *Application contact:* JoAnn Dubil, Program Coordinator, 215-898-6836, E-mail: jdubil@sas.upenn.edu.

University of Puerto Rico, Río Piedras, College of Humanities, Department of Comparative Literature, San Juan, PR 00931-3300. Offers MA. Part-time programs available. *Degree requirements:* For master's, comprehensive exam, thesis. *Entrance requirements:* For master's, EXADEP, interview, minimum GPA of 3.0, letter of recommendation.

University of Rochester, School of Arts and Sciences, Department of English, Program in Comparative Literature, Rochester, NY 14627.

University of South Carolina, The Graduate School, College of Arts and Sciences, Department of Languages, Literatures, and Cultures, Columbia, SC 29208. Offers comparative literature (MA, PhD); foreign languages (MAT), including French, German, Spanish; French (MA); German (MA); Spanish (MA). MAT offered in cooperation with the College of Education. Part-time programs available. *Degree requirements:* For master's, one foreign language, comprehensive exam, thesis optional; for doctorate, 2 foreign languages, comprehensive exam, thesis/dissertation. *Entrance requirements:* For master's and doctorate, GRE General Test, writing sample. Additional exam requirements/recommendations for international students: Required—TOEFL (minimum score 230 computer-based; 75 iBT). Electronic applications accepted. *Faculty research:* Modern literature, linguistics, literature and culture, medieval literature, literary theory.

University of Southern California, Graduate School, Dana and David Dornsife College of Letters, Arts and Sciences, Comparative Studies in Literature and Culture Doctoral Program, Los Angeles, CA 90089. Offers comparative literature (PhD); comparative media and culture (PhD); Spanish and Latin American studies (PhD). *Faculty:* 16 full-time (7 women). *Students:* 27 full-time (17 women), 1 part-time (0 women); includes 6 minority (2 Black or African American, non-Hispanic/Latino; 2 Asian, non-Hispanic/Latino; 2 Hispanic/Latino), 6 international. In 2010, 1 doctorate awarded. *Median time to degree:* Of those who began their doctoral program in fall 2002, 50% received their degree in 8 years or less. *Degree requirements:* For doctorate, 2 foreign languages, comprehensive exam, thesis/dissertation. *Entrance requirements:* For doctorate, GRE, competence in language other than English (highly recommended). Additional exam requirements/recommendations for international students: Required—TOEFL. *Application deadline:* For fall admission, 12/1 priority date for domestic and international students. Application fee: $85. Electronic applications accepted. *Expenses:* Tuition: Full-time $31,240; part-time $1420 per unit. Required fees: $600. One-time fee: $35 full-time. Full-time tuition and fees vary according to degree level and program. *Financial support:* In 2010–11, 25 students received support, including 8 fellowships with full tuition reimbursements available (averaging $51,000 per year), 17 teaching assistantships with full tuition reimbursements available (averaging $51,000 per year). Financial award applicants required to submit FAFSA. *Faculty research:* Literary theory, Japanese film and contemporary fiction, Francophone literature and cinema, Latin American and Caribbean literature, Spanish literature and film, nineteenth and twentieth century British and American literature. *Unit head:* Prof. Peggy Kamuf, Director of Comparative Studies in Literature and Culture Doctoral Program, 213-740-0101, Fax: 213-740-8058, E-mail: kamuf@usc.edu. *Application contact:* Katherine Guevarra, Administrative Assistant, 213-740-0102, Fax: 213-740-0858, E-mail: kguevarr@usc.edu.

The University of Texas at Austin, Graduate School, College of Liberal Arts, Program in Comparative Literature, Austin, TX 78712-1111. Offers MA, PhD. *Degree requirements:* For master's, 2 foreign languages, report or thesis; for doctorate, 3 foreign languages, thesis/dissertation. *Entrance requirements:* For master's and doctorate, GRE General Test. Electronic applications accepted.

The University of Texas at Dallas, School of Arts and Humanities, Program in Humanities, Richardson, TX 75080. Offers aesthetic studies (MA, MAT, PhD); history (MA); history of ideas (MA, MAT, PhD); humanities (MA, PhD); Latin American studies (MA); studies in literature (MA, MAT, PhD). *Faculty:* 44 full-time (14 women). *Students:* 161 full-time (95 women), 178 part-time (104 women); includes 71 minority (22 Black or African American, non-Hispanic/Latino; 4 American Indian or Alaska Native, non-Hispanic/Latino; 16 Asian, non-Hispanic/Latino; 24 Hispanic/Latino; 5 Two or more races, non-Hispanic/Latino), 22 international. Average age 38. 156 applicants, 70% accepted, 79 enrolled. In 2010, 46 master's, 20 doctorates awarded. *Degree requirements:* For master's, one foreign language, portfolio, thesis, or capstone project; for doctorate, one foreign language, thesis/dissertation. *Entrance requirements:* For master's, minimum GPA of 3.3 in upper-level coursework in field; for doctorate, doctoral field examinations, minimum GPA of 3.3 in upper-level coursework in field. Additional exam requirements/recommendations for international students: Required—TOEFL (minimum score 550 paper-based; 215 computer-based). *Application deadline:* For fall admission, 7/15 for domestic students, 5/1 priority date for international students; for spring admission, 11/15 for domestic students, 9/1 priority date for international students. Applications are processed on a rolling basis. Application fee: $50 ($100 for international students). Electronic applications accepted. *Expenses:* Tuition, state resident: full-time $10,248; part-time $569 per credit hour. Tuition, nonresident: full-time $18,544; part-time $1030 per credit hour. Tuition and fees vary according to course load. *Financial support:* In 2010–11, 151 students received support, including 5 research assistantships with partial tuition reimbursements available (averaging $10,905 per year), 82 teaching assistantships with partial tuition reimbursements available (averaging $10,156 per year); career-related internships or fieldwork, Federal Work-Study, institutionally sponsored loans, scholarships/grants, and unspecified assistantships also available. Support available to part-time students. Financial award application deadline: 4/30; financial award applicants required to submit FAFSA. *Faculty research:* Holocaust studies, U. S. /Mexico studies, translation studies, art history research, Chinese studies. *Unit head:* Dr. Michael Wilson, Associate Dean for Graduate Education, 972-883-2080, E-mail: mwilson@utdallas.edu. *Application contact:* Dr. Michael Wilson, Associate Dean of Graduate Studies, 972-883-2756, Fax: 972-883-2989, E-mail: mwilson@utdallas.edu.

University of Toronto, School of Graduate Studies, Humanities Division, Centre for Comparative Literature, Toronto, ON M5S 1A1, Canada. Offers MA, PhD. Part-time programs available. *Degree requirements:* For doctorate, thesis/dissertation. *Entrance requirements:* For master's, 2 letters of recommendation, sample of work (short essay on a literary topic preferred), resume; for doctorate, 2 letters of recommendation, sample of work (short essay on a literary topic preferred), resumé.

University of Utah, Graduate School, College of Humanities, Department of Languages and Literature, Salt Lake City, UT 84112. Offers comparative literary and cultural studies (MA, PhD); French (MA, MALP); German (MA, MALP, PhD); Spanish (MA, MALP, PhD); world languages with secondary teaching licensure (MA). *Faculty:* 36 full-time (21 women). *Students:* 35 full-time (24 women), 9 part-time (7 women); includes 7 minority (1 American Indian or Alaska Native, non-Hispanic/Latino; 2 Asian, non-Hispanic/Latino; 4 Hispanic/Latino), 8 international. Average age 34. 58 applicants, 57% accepted, 24 enrolled. In 2010, 17 master's, 2 doctorates awarded. Terminal master's awarded for partial completion of doctoral program. *Degree requirements:* For master's, 2 foreign languages, comprehensive exam (for some programs), thesis (for some programs), standard proficiency in 2 languages other than English; for doctorate, 3 foreign languages, comprehensive exam, thesis/dissertation, standard proficiency in 2 languages other than English and language of study, advanced proficiency in 1 language other than English and language of study. *Entrance requirements:* For master's, GRE, bachelor's degree or strong undergraduate record in target languages, minimum GPA of 3.0; for doctorate, GRE, MA, advanced proficiency in a target language. Additional exam requirements/recommendations for international students: Required—TOEFL (minimum score 500 paper-based; 173 computer-based). *Application deadline:* For fall admission, 1/15 priority date for domestic students, 12/15 priority date for international students. Application fee: $55 ($65 for international students). Electronic applications accepted. *Expenses:* Tuition, area resident: Part-time $179.19 per credit hour. Tuition, state resident: full-time $4384. Tuition, nonresident: full-time $16,684; part-time $630.67 per credit hour. Required fees: $350 per semester. Tuition and fees vary according to course load, degree level and program. *Financial support:* In 2010–11, 24 students received support, including 2 fellowships, 22 teaching assistantships with full and partial tuition reimbursements available (averaging $11,500 per year); health care benefits also available. Financial award application deadline: 1/15; financial award applicants required to submit FAFSA. *Faculty research:* Literary study, literary theory, linguistics, cultural studies, comparative studies. Total annual research expenditures: $53,399. *Unit head:* Dr. Karin Baumgartner, Director of Graduate Studies, 801-585-3001, Fax: 801-581-7581, E-mail: karin.baumgartner@hum.utah.edu. *Application contact:* Virginia Ellinwood, Academic Advisor, 801-585-9437, Fax: 801-581-7581, E-mail: v.ellinwood@utah.edu.

University of Washington, Graduate School, College of Arts and Sciences, Department of Comparative Literature, Seattle, WA 98195. Offers MA, PhD. Part-time programs available. Terminal master's awarded for partial completion of doctoral program. *Degree requirements:* For master's, 2 foreign languages, thesis optional; for doctorate, 3 foreign languages, thesis/dissertation. *Entrance requirements:* For master's, GRE General Test, BA in comparative literature or equivalent, minimum GPA of 3.0, proficiency in 1 foreign language; for doctorate, GRE General Test, MA in comparative literature or equivalent, minimum GPA of 3.0, proficiency in 2 foreign languages. Additional exam requirements/recommendations for international students: Required—TOEFL. Electronic applications accepted. *Faculty research:* Literature and culture from classical antiquity to twentieth-century, literary theory and criticism.

The University of Western Ontario, Faculty of Graduate Studies, Faculty of Arts and Humanities, Department of Comparative Literature, London, ON N6A 5B8, Canada. Offers comparative literature (MA, PhD); Spanish (MA). Part-time programs available. *Degree requirements:* For master's, 2 foreign languages, thesis (for some programs). *Entrance requirements:* For master's, honors degree in Spanish or equivalent, minimum B average. Additional exam requirements/recommendations for international students: Required—TOEFL, TOEFL (comparative literature). *Faculty research:* Spanish golden age, Latin-American, romance, medieval, film.

University of Wisconsin–Madison, Graduate School, College of Letters and Science, Department of Comparative Literature, Madison, WI 53706-1380. Offers MA, PhD. Part-time programs available. Terminal master's awarded for partial completion of doctoral program. *Degree requirements:* For master's, one foreign language, second-year exam; for doctorate, 3 foreign languages, thesis/dissertation, 3 preliminary exams. *Entrance requirements:* For master's, GRE General Test, writing sample; for doctorate, GRE General Test. Electronic applications accepted. *Expenses:* Tuition, state resident: full-time $9887; part-time $617.96 per credit. Tuition, nonresident: full-time $24,054; part-time $1503.40 per credit. Required fees: $67.63 per credit. Tuition and fees vary according to reciprocity agreements. *Faculty research:* Literary theory, cultural criticism, classics through early modern literature, postmodernity, gender studies.

University of Wisconsin–Madison, Graduate School, College of Letters and Science, Department of East Asian Languages and Literature, Program in Chinese Literature, Madison, WI 53706-1380. Offers MA, PhD. Part-time programs available. Terminal master's awarded for partial completion of doctoral program. *Degree requirements:* For master's, one foreign language, seminars, written exam; for doctorate, 3 foreign languages, thesis/dissertation, seminars, preliminary exams, oral exam. *Entrance requirements:* For master's, bachelor's degree or equivalent in Chinese; for doctorate, master's degree or equivalent in Chinese. Electronic applications accepted. *Expenses:* Tuition, state resident: full-time $9887; part-time $617.96 per credit. Tuition, nonresident: full-time $24,054; part-time $1503.40 per credit. Required fees: $67.63 per credit. Tuition and fees vary according to reciprocity agreements. *Faculty research:* Chinese historical and modern linguistics, classical Chinese literary and cultural history, modern Chinese literary and cultural history, Chinese paleography.

University of Wisconsin–Madison, Graduate School, College of Letters and Science, Department of Scandinavian Studies, Madison, WI 53706-1380. Offers area studies (MA); folklore (PhD); literature (MA, PhD); philology (PhD). Part-time programs available. *Degree requirements:* For master's, 2 foreign languages, exam; for doctorate, thesis/dissertation, exam. *Entrance requirements:* For master's, minimum GPA of 3.25; for doctorate, minimum GPA of 3.5. Electronic applications accepted. *Expenses:* Tuition, state resident: full-time $9887; part-time $617.96 per credit. Tuition, nonresident: full-time $24,054; part-time $1503.40 per credit. Required fees: $67.63 per credit. Tuition and fees vary according to reciprocity agreements. *Faculty research:* Historical fiction, Icelandic poetry, nineteenth-century literature, theater, gender studies, folklore.

University of Wisconsin–Milwaukee, Graduate School, College of Letters and Sciences, Department of English, Milwaukee, WI 53201-0413. Offers creative writing (PhD); English (MA); international technical communication (Certificate); linguistics (PhD); professional writing (PhD); professional writing and communication (Certificate); rhetoric and composition (PhD); MLIS/MA. *Faculty:* 40 full-time (19 women). *Students:* 106 full-time (62 women), 65 part-time (45 women); includes 4 Black or African American, non-Hispanic/Latino; 5 Asian, non-Hispanic/Latino, 17 international. Average age 34. 208 applicants, 54% accepted, 29 enrolled. In 2010, 19 master's, 14 doctorates awarded. *Degree requirements:* For master's, thesis or alternative; for doctorate, one foreign language, thesis/dissertation. *Entrance requirements:* For master's, GRE General Test, GRE Subject Test; for doctorate, GRE. Additional exam requirements/recommendations for international students: Required—TOEFL (minimum score 550 paper-based; 79 iBT), IELTS (minimum score 6.5). *Application deadline:* For fall admission, 1/1 priority date for domestic students; for spring admission, 9/1 for domestic students. Applications are processed on a rolling basis. Application fee: $56 ($96 for international students). Electronic applications accepted. *Financial support:* In 2010–11, 4 fellowships, 1 research assistantship, 84 teaching assistantships were awarded; career-related internships or fieldwork, unspecified assistantships, and project assistantships also available. Support available to part-time students. Financial award application deadline: 4/15; financial award applicants

Comparative Literature

University of Wisconsin–Milwaukee (continued)
required to submit FAFSA. Total annual research expenditures: $36,259. *Unit head:* Tasha Oren, Representative, 414-229-6625, Fax: 414-229-2643, E-mail: tgoren@uwm.edu. *Application contact:* General Information Contact, 414-229-4982, Fax: 414-229-6967, E-mail: gradschool@uwm.edu.

University of Wisconsin–Milwaukee, Graduate School, College of Letters and Sciences, Interdepartmental Program in Foreign Language and Literature, Milwaukee, WI 53201-0413. Offers classics and Hebrew studies (MAFLL); comparative literature (MAFLL); French and Italian (MAFLL); German (MAFLL); Slavic studies (MAFLL); translation (Certificate). Part-time programs available. *Faculty:* 29 full-time (14 women). *Students:* 35 full-time (27 women), 29 part-time (20 women); includes 1 Hispanic/Latino. Average age 40. 30 applicants, 67% accepted, 19 enrolled. In 2010, 24 master's awarded. *Degree requirements:* For master's, 2 foreign languages, thesis or alternative. *Entrance requirements:* Additional exam requirements/recommendations for international students: Required—TOEFL (minimum score 550 paper-based; 79 iBT), IELTS (minimum score 6.5). *Application deadline:* For fall admission, 1/1 priority date for domestic students; for spring admission, 9/1 for domestic students. Applications are processed on a rolling basis. Application fee: $56 ($96 for international students). Electronic applications accepted. *Financial support:* In 2010–11, 1 fellowship, 2 research assistantships, 26 teaching assistantships were awarded; career-related internships or fieldwork, health care benefits, unspecified assistantships, and project assistantships also available. Support available to part-time students. Financial award application deadline: 4/15; financial award applicants required to submit FAFSA. Total annual research expenditures: $304,210. *Unit head:* Gabrielle Verdier, Representative, 414-229-3346, Fax: 414-229-2741, E-mail: verdier@uwm.edu. *Application contact:* General Information Contact, 414-229-4982, Fax: 414-229-6967, E-mail: gradschool@uwm.edu.

Washington University in St. Louis, Graduate School of Arts and Sciences, Department of Asian and Near Eastern Languages and Literatures, St. Louis, MO 63130-4899. Offers Chinese (MA); Chinese and comparative literature (PhD); Japanese (MA); Japanese and comparative literature (PhD). Terminal master's awarded for partial completion of doctoral program. *Degree requirements:* For master's, thesis optional; for doctorate, thesis/dissertation. *Entrance requirements:* For master's and doctorate, GRE General Test. Electronic applications accepted.

Washington University in St. Louis, Graduate School of Arts and Sciences, Program in Comparative Literature, St. Louis, MO 63130-4899. Offers MA, PhD. Terminal master's awarded for partial completion of doctoral program. *Degree requirements:* For master's, thesis or alternative; for doctorate, thesis/dissertation. *Entrance requirements:* For master's and doctorate, GRE General Test. Electronic applications accepted.

Wayne State University, College of Liberal Arts and Sciences, Department of English, Program in Comparative Literature, Detroit, MI 48202. Offers MA. *Students:* 1 (woman) full-time. Average age 39. 1 applicant, 0% accepted. *Degree requirements:* For master's, one foreign language, essay or thesis. *Entrance requirements:* For master's, GRE General Test, minimum GPA of 3.25 in English, 3.0 overall. Additional exam requirements/recommendations for international students: Required—TOEFL (minimum score 550 paper-based; 213 computer-based); Recommended—TWE (minimum score 6). *Application deadline:* For fall admission, 7/1 for domestic students, 6/1 for international students; for winter admission, 10/1 for international students; for spring admission, 2/1 for international students. Application fee: $30 ($50 for international students). Electronic applications accepted. *Expenses:* Tuition, state resident: full-time $7662; part-time $478.85 per credit hour. Tuition, nonresident: full-time $16,920; part-time $1057.55 per credit hour. Required fees: $571.20; $35.70 per credit hour. $188.05 per semester. Tuition and fees vary according to course load and program. *Financial support:* Application deadline: 3/1. *Unit head:* Dr. Richard Grusin, Chair, 313-577-7692, Fax: 313-577-8618, E-mail: aj4671@wayne.edu. *Application contact:* Ross Pudaloff, Graduate Director, 313-577-7699, E-mail: r.pudaloff@wayne.edu.

Western Kentucky University, Graduate Studies, Potter College of Arts and Letters, Department of English, Bowling Green, KY 42101. Offers education (MA); English (MA Ed); literature (MA), including American literature, British literature, literary theory, women writers, world literature; teaching English as a second language (MA); writing (MA). Part-time and evening/weekend programs available. *Degree requirements:* For master's, comprehensive exam, thesis optional, final exam. *Entrance requirements:* For master's, GRE General Test, minimum GPA of 2.75. Additional exam requirements/recommendations for international students: Required—TOEFL (minimum score 555 paper-based; 213 computer-based; 79 iBT). *Faculty research:* Improving writing, linking teacher knowledge and performance, Victorian women writers, Kentucky women writers, Kentucky poets.

Yale University, Graduate School of Arts and Sciences, Department of Comparative Literature, New Haven, CT 06520. Offers PhD. *Degree requirements:* For doctorate, 2 foreign languages, thesis/dissertation. *Entrance requirements:* For doctorate, GRE General Test.

English

Abilene Christian University, Graduate School, College of Arts and Sciences, Department of English, Abilene, TX 79699-9100. Offers composition/rhetoric (MA); literature (MA); writing (MA). Part-time programs available. *Faculty:* 16 part-time/adjunct (7 women). *Students:* 15 full-time (8 women); includes 1 Two or more races, non-Hispanic/Latino, 1 international. 18 applicants, 72% accepted, 6 enrolled. In 2010, 5 master's awarded. *Degree requirements:* For master's, one foreign language, comprehensive exam (for some programs), thesis (for some programs). *Entrance requirements:* For master's, GRE General Test. Additional exam requirements/recommendations for international students: Required—TOEFL (minimum score 550 paper-based; 213 computer-based). *Application deadline:* For fall admission, 4/1 priority date for domestic students; for spring admission, 11/1 for domestic students. Applications are processed on a rolling basis. Application fee: $40. Electronic applications accepted. *Expenses:* Tuition: Full-time $12,906; part-time $717 per hour. Required fees: $1250; $61.50 per unit. *Financial support:* In 2010–11, 14 students received support; teaching assistantships, Federal Work-Study available. Support available to part-time students. Financial award application deadline: 4/1; financial award applicants required to submit FAFSA. *Faculty research:* Feminism, Shakespearean dimensions of new literature, poetic consciousness, deconstruction myths. *Unit head:* Dr. Dana McMichael, Graduate Adviser, 325-674-2083, Fax: 325-674-2408, E-mail: dana.mcmichael@acu.edu. *Application contact:* David Pittman, Graduate Admissions Counselor, 325-674-2656, Fax: 325-674-6717, E-mail: gradinfo@acu.edu.

Acadia University, Faculty of Arts, Department of English, Wolfville, NS B4P 2R6, Canada. Offers MA. *Faculty:* 17 full-time (7 women). *Students:* 3 full-time (1 woman), 3 part-time (2 women). Average age 25. 11 applicants, 45% accepted, 3 enrolled. In 2010, 5 master's awarded. *Degree requirements:* For master's, thesis. *Entrance requirements:* For master's, honors degree in English, minimum A- average. Additional exam requirements/recommendations for international students: Required—TOEFL (minimum score 630 paper-based; 267 computer-based; 93 iBT), IELTS (minimum score 6.5). *Application deadline:* For fall admission, 2/1 priority date for domestic and international students; for spring admission, 3/30 for domestic students. Applications are processed on a rolling basis. Application fee: $50. *Financial support:* Fellowships, teaching assistantships, scholarships/grants and unspecified assistantships available. Financial award application deadline: 2/1. *Faculty research:* Renaissance, Canadian, medieval, Victorian, and Romantic literature. *Unit head:* Dr. Patricia Rigg, Chair, 902-585-1503, Fax: 902-585-1070, E-mail: patricia.rigg@acadiau.ca. *Application contact:* Christine Reed, Secretary, 902-585-1502, Fax: 902-585-1070, E-mail: christine.reed@acadiau.ca.

The American University in Cairo, School of Humanities and Social Sciences, Department of English and Comparative Literature, Cairo, Egypt. Offers MA. Part-time programs available. *Degree requirements:* For master's, thesis, proficiency in French or German. *Entrance requirements:* Additional exam requirements/recommendations for international students: Required—English entrance exam and/or TOEFL.

American University of Beirut, Graduate Programs, Faculty of Arts and Sciences, Beirut, Lebanon. Offers anthropology (MA); Arabic language and literature (MA); archaeology (MA); biology (MS); chemistry (MS); computational science (MS); computer science (MS); economics (MA); education (MA); English language (MA); English literature (MA); environmental policy planning (MSES); financial economics (MAFE); geology (MS); history (MA); mathematics (MA, MS); Middle Eastern studies (MA); philosophy (MA); physics (MS); political studies (MA); psychology (MA); public administration (MA); sociology (MA); statistics (MA, MS). Part-time programs available. *Faculty:* 229 full-time (98 women), 136 part-time/adjunct (79 women). *Students:* 158 full-time (104 women), 263 part-time (171 women). Average age 25. 356 applicants, 59% accepted, 127 enrolled. In 2010, 57 master's awarded. *Degree requirements:* For master's, one foreign language, comprehensive exam, thesis (for some programs). *Entrance requirements:* For master's, GRE, letter of recommendation. Additional exam requirements/recommendations for international students: Required—TOEFL (minimum score 600 paper-based; 250 computer-based; 97 iBT), IELTS (minimum score 7). *Application deadline:* For fall admission, 4/30 for domestic and international students; for spring admission, 11/1 for domestic and international students. Application fee: $50. *Expenses:* Tuition: Full-time $12,294; part-time $683 per credit. Required fees: $499; $499 per credit. Tuition and fees vary according to course load and program. *Financial support:* In 2010–11, 33 students received support. Career-related internships or fieldwork, institutionally sponsored loans, scholarships/grants, health care benefits, and unspecified assistantships available. Financial award application deadline: 2/4; financial award applicants required to submit FAFSA. *Faculty research:* Modern and contemporary world theatre; mineralogy, petrology, and geochemistry; cell differentiation and transformation; combinatorial technologies; philosophy of action; continental philosophy; Phoenician epigraphy; nascent complex societies and urbanism; the economies of the Arab world; environmental economics; tectonophysics; host-parasite interactions; innate immunity; insect-plant interactions; history of the Ottoman archives; decentralization; transparency and corruption. Total annual research expenditures: $622,243. *Unit head:* Dr. Patrick McGreevy, Dean, 961-137-4374 Ext. 3800, Fax: 961-174-4461, E-mail: pm07@aub.edu.lb. *Application contact:* Dr. Salim Kanaan, Director, Admissions Office, 961-135-0000 Ext. 2594, Fax: 961-175-0775, E-mail: sk00@aub.edu.lb.

Andrews University, School of Graduate Studies, College of Arts and Sciences, Department of English, Berrien Springs, MI 49104. Offers MA, MAT. Part-time programs available. *Degree requirements:* For master's, one foreign language, thesis optional. *Entrance requirements:* For master's, GRE Subject Test. Additional exam requirements/recommendations for international students: Required—TOEFL (minimum score 550 paper-based). *Faculty research:* Christianity and literature, Victorian literature, social linguistics, rhetoric, American literature.

Angelo State University, College of Graduate Studies, College of Liberal and Fine Arts, Department of English, San Angelo, TX 76909. Offers MA. Part-time and evening/weekend programs available. *Faculty:* 5 full-time (2 women). *Students:* 6 full-time (3 women), 11 part-time (6 women); includes 1 Black or African American, non-Hispanic/Latino. Average age 26. 4 applicants, 50% accepted, 2 enrolled. In 2010, 9 master's awarded. *Degree requirements:* For master's, comprehensive exam. *Entrance requirements:* For master's, essay. Additional exam requirements/recommendations for international students: Required—TOEFL or IELTS. *Application deadline:* For fall admission, 7/15 priority date for domestic students, 6/10 for international students; for spring admission, 12/1 priority date for domestic students, 11/1 for international students. Applications are processed on a rolling basis. Application fee: $40 ($50 for international students). Electronic applications accepted. *Expenses:* Tuition, state resident: full-time $4560; part-time $152 per credit hour. Tuition, nonresident: full-time $13,860; part-time $462 per credit hour. Required fees: $2132. Tuition and fees vary according to course load. *Financial support:* In 2010–11, 9 students received support, including 4 teaching assistantships (averaging $10,251 per year); Federal Work-Study, scholarships/grants, and unspecified assistantships also available. Support available to part-time students. Financial award application deadline: 3/1; financial award applicants required to submit FAFSA. *Unit head:* Dr. Laurence E. Musgrove, Department Head, 325-942-2273 Ext. 231, Fax: 325-942-2208, E-mail: lmusgrove@angelo.edu. *Application contact:* Dr. Mary Ellen Hartje, Graduate Advisor, 325-942-2269 Ext. 230, Fax: 325-942-2208, E-mail: me.hartje@angelo.edu.

Appalachian State University, Cratis D. Williams Graduate School, Department of English, Boone, NC 28608. Offers English (MA); English education (MA). Part-time programs available. Postbaccalaureate distance learning degree programs offered (no on-campus study). *Faculty:* 36 full-time (20 women), 2 part-time/adjunct (both women). *Students:* 18 full-time (13 women), 3 part-time (2 women); includes 1 Two or more races, non-Hispanic/Latino. 21 applicants, 95% accepted, 7 enrolled. In 2010, 12 master's awarded. *Degree requirements:* For master's, one foreign language, comprehensive exam, thesis (for some programs). *Entrance requirements:* For master's, GRE General Test, 3 letters of recommendation. Additional exam requirements/recommendations for international students: Required—TOEFL (minimum score 570 paper-based; 230 computer-based; 79 iBT), IELTS (minimum score 6.5). *Application deadline:* For fall admission, 7/1 for domestic students, 2/1 for international students; for spring admission, 11/1 for domestic students, 7/1 for international students. Applications are processed on a rolling basis. Application fee: $55. Electronic applications accepted. *Expenses:* Tuition, state resident: full-time $3428; part-time $428 per unit. Tuition, nonresident: full-time $14,518; part-time $1814 per unit. Required fees: $2320; $344 per unit. Tuition and fees vary according to campus/location. *Financial support:* In 2010–11, 10 research assistantships (averaging $8,000 per year), 12 teaching assistantships (averaging $8,000 per year) were awarded; fellowships, career-related internships or fieldwork, Federal Work-Study, scholarships/grants, and unspecified assistantships also available. Financial award application deadline: 4/1; financial award applicants required to submit FAFSA. *Faculty research:* Contemporary Irish literature, Romantic psychology, cultural practices of everyday life, Gullah linguistics, Renaissance women's writing. Total annual research expenditures: $1,000. *Unit head:* Dr. James Ivory, Chair, 828-262-3098, E-mail: ivoryjm@appstate.edu. *Application contact:* Dr. Colin Ramsey, Graduate Program Director, 828-262-7390, E-mail: ramseyct@appstate.edu.

Arcadia University, Graduate Studies, Department of English, Glenside, PA 19038-3295. Offers MAE. Part-time and evening/weekend programs available. *Faculty:* 8 full-time (3 women), 2 part-time/adjunct (both women). *Students:* 30 full-time (24 women), 54 part-time (39 women); includes 9 minority (8 Black or African American, non-Hispanic/Latino; 1 Asian, non-Hispanic/Latino). Average age 30. In 2010, 27 master's awarded. *Degree requirements:* For master's, thesis optional. *Application deadline:* Applications are processed on a rolling basis. Application fee: $50. *Expenses:* Contact institution. *Financial support:* Teaching assistantships, unspecified assistantships available. *Unit head:* Dr. Joanne Weiner, Chair, 215-572-2105. *Application contact:* 215-572-2925, Fax: 215-572-2126, E-mail: grad@arcadia.edu.

Arizona State University, College of Liberal Arts and Sciences, Department of English, Tempe, AZ 85287-0302. Offers applied linguistics (PhD); creative writing (MFA); English (MA, PhD), including comparative literature (MA), linguistics (MA), literature, rhetoric and composition (MA), rhetoric/composition and linguistics (PhD); linguistics (Graduate Certificate); teaching English to speakers of other languages (MTESOL). *Faculty:* 138 full-time (86 women). *Students:* 183 full-time (115 women), 98 part-time (73 women); includes 35 minority (6 Black or African American, non-Hispanic/Latino; 5 American Indian or Alaska Native, non-Hispanic/Latino; 10 Asian, non-Hispanic/Latino; 13 Hispanic/Latino; 1 Two or more races, non-Hispanic/Latino), 34 international. Average age 33. 597 applicants, 31% accepted, 88 enrolled. In 2010, 52 master's, 11 doctorates awarded. Terminal master's awarded for partial completion of doctoral program. *Degree requirements:* For master's, variable foreign language requirement, comprehensive exam (for some programs), thesis (for some programs), interactive Program of Study (iPOS) submitted before completing 50 percent of required credit hours; for doctorate, variable foreign language requirement, comprehensive exam, thesis/dissertation, interactive Program of Study (iPOS) submitted before completing 50 percent of required credit hours. *Entrance requirements:* For master's and doctorate, GRE, minimum GPA of 3.0 or equivalent in last 2 years of work leading to bachelor's degree. Additional exam requirements/recommendations for international students: Required—TOEFL, IELTS, or Pearson Test of English. *Application deadline:* For fall admission, 1/15 priority date for domestic students, 9/15 priority date for international students. Applications are processed on a rolling basis. Application fee: $70 ($90 for international students). Electronic applications accepted. *Expenses:* Tuition, state resident: full-time $8510; part-time $608 per credit. Tuition, nonresident: full-time $16,542; part-time $919 per credit. Required fees: $339; $110 per credit. Part-time tuition and fees vary according to course load. *Financial support:* In 2010–11, 12 research assistantships with tuition reimbursements (averaging $10,337 per year), 111 teaching assistantships with full and partial tuition reimbursements (averaging $13,799 per year) were awarded; fellowships with full tuition reimbursements, career-related internships or fieldwork, Federal Work-Study, institutionally sponsored loans, scholarships/grants, and tuition waivers (full and partial) also available. Financial award application deadline: 3/1; financial award applicants required to submit FAFSA. Total annual research expenditures: $734,687. *Unit head:* Dr. Maureen Goggin, Associate Chair, 480-965-1804, E-mail: maureen.goggin@asu.edu. *Application contact:* Graduate Admissions, 480-965-6113.

Arkansas State University, Graduate School, College of Humanities and Social Sciences, Department of English and Philosophy, Jonesboro, State University, AR 72467. Offers English (MA); English education (MSE, SCCT). Part-time programs available. *Faculty:* 14 full-time (4 women). *Students:* 17 full-time (13 women), 17 part-time (10 women); includes 4 minority (3 Black or African American, non-Hispanic/Latino; 1 American Indian or Alaska Native, non-Hispanic/Latino), 5 international. Average age 27. 21 applicants, 90% accepted, 12 enrolled. In 2010, 8 master's awarded. *Degree requirements:* For master's, variable foreign language requirement, comprehensive exam, thesis or alternative; for SCCT, comprehensive exam. *Entrance requirements:* For master's, GRE General Test or MAT, preliminary exam, appropriate bachelor's degree, official transcript, valid teaching certificate (for MSE), immunization records; for SCCT, GRE General Test or MAT, interview, master's degree, official transcript, immunization records. Additional exam requirements/recommendations for international students: Required—TOEFL (minimum score 550 paper-based; 213 computer-based; 79 iBT), IELTS (minimum score 6), PTE: Pearson Test of English Academic (56). *Application deadline:* Applications are processed on a rolling basis. Application fee: $30 ($40 for international students). Electronic applications accepted. *Expenses:* Tuition, state resident: full-time $3888; part-time $216 per credit hour. Tuition, nonresident: full-time $9918; part-time $551 per credit hour. International tuition: $8376 full-time. Required fees: $932; $49 per credit hour. $25 per term. One-time fee: $30. Tuition and fees vary according to course load and program. *Financial support:* In 2010–11, 14 students received support; teaching assistantships, career-related internships or fieldwork, scholarships/grants, and unspecified assistantships available. Financial award application deadline: 7/1; financial award applicants required to submit FAFSA. *Unit head:* Dr. Jerry Ball, Interim Chair, 870-972-3043, Fax: 870-972-3045, E-mail: jball@astate.edu. *Application contact:* Dr. Andrew Sustich, Dean of the Graduate School, 870-972-3029, Fax: 870-972-3857, E-mail: sustich@astate.edu.

Arkansas Tech University, Graduate College, College of Arts and Humanities, Russellville, AR 72801. Offers communication (MLA); English (M Ed, MA); fine arts (MLA); history (MA); multi-media journalism (MA); psychology (MS); social science (MLA); Spanish (MA, MLA); teaching English as a second language (MA, MLA). Part-time programs available. *Students:* 39 full-time (23 women), 87 part-time (69 women); includes 13 minority (3 Black or African American, non-Hispanic/Latino; 1 American Indian or Alaska Native, non-Hispanic/Latino; 1 Asian, non-Hispanic/Latino; 8 Hispanic/Latino), 14 international. Average age 32. In 2010, 54 master's awarded. *Degree requirements:* For master's, comprehensive exam (for some programs), thesis (for some programs), project. *Entrance requirements:* For master's, GRE General Test or MAT. Additional exam requirements/recommendations for international students: Required—TOEFL (minimum score 550 paper-based; 213 computer-based; 79 iBT), IELTS (minimum score 6). *Application deadline:* For fall admission, 3/1 priority date for domestic students, 5/1 priority date for international students; for spring admission, 10/1 priority date for domestic and international students. Applications are processed on a rolling basis. Application fee: $0 ($50 for international students). Electronic applications accepted. *Expenses:* Tuition, state resident: full-time $4680; part-time $195 per credit hour. Tuition, nonresident: full-time $9360; part-time $390 per credit hour. Required fees: $714; $14 per credit hour. One-time fee: $326 part-time. Tuition and fees vary according to course load. *Financial support:* In 2010–11, teaching assistantships with full tuition reimbursements (averaging $4,000 per year); research assistantships, career-related internships or fieldwork, Federal Work-Study, scholarships/grants, health care benefits, and unspecified assistantships also available. Support available to part-time students. Financial award application deadline: 4/15; financial award applicants required to submit FAFSA. *Unit head:* Dr. Micheal Tarver, Dean, 479-968-0274, Fax: 479-964-0812, E-mail: mtarver@atu.edu. *Application contact:* Dr. Mary B. Gunter, Dean of Graduate College, 479-968-0398, Fax: 479-964-0542, E-mail: graduate.school@atu.edu.

Asbury University, School of Graduate and Professional Studies, Wilmore, KY 40390-1198. Offers biology: alternative certificate (MA Ed); chemistry: alternative certificate (MA Ed); English (MA Ed); English as a second language (MA Ed); ESL (MA Ed); French (MA Ed); Latin: alternative certificate (MA Ed); mathematics: alternative certificate (MA Ed); reading/writing endorsement (MA Ed); social studies (MA Ed); social work (MSW), including child and family services; Spanish (MA Ed); special education (MA Ed); special education: alternative certificate (MA Ed); teacher as leader endorsement (MA Ed). *Accreditation:* NCATE. Part-time programs available. *Degree requirements:* For master's, action research project, portfolio. *Entrance requirements:* For master's, PRAXIS/NTE, minimum GPA of 2.75, letters of recommendation. Additional exam requirements/recommendations for international students: Required—TOEFL (minimum score 550 paper-based). Electronic applications accepted.

Auburn University, Graduate School, College of Liberal Arts, Department of English, Auburn University, AL 36849. Offers MA, MTPC, PhD. Part-time programs available. *Faculty:* 56 full-time (30 women), 18 part-time/adjunct (10 women). *Students:* 18 full-time (14 women), 53 part-time (37 women); includes 3 Black or African American, non-Hispanic/Latino, 1 international. Average age 29. 58 applicants, 52% accepted, 20 enrolled. In 2010, 23 master's, 4 doctorates awarded. *Degree requirements:* For master's, one foreign language, thesis optional, written exam; for doctorate, 2 foreign languages, thesis/dissertation, oral and written exams. *Entrance requirements:* For master's, GRE General Test, sample of written work; for doctorate, GRE General Test, GRE Subject Test, sample of written work. *Application deadline:* For fall admission, 7/7 for domestic students; for spring admission, 11/24 for domestic students. Applications are processed on a rolling basis. Application fee: $50 ($60 for international students). Electronic applications accepted. *Expenses:* Tuition, state resident: full-time $7002. Tuition, nonresident: full-time $21,898. International tuition: $22,116 full-time. Required fees: $892. Tuition and fees vary according to course load and program. *Financial support:* Fellowships, teaching assistantships, Federal Work-Study available. Support available to part-time students. Financial award application deadline: 3/15; financial award applicants required to submit FAFSA. *Faculty research:* English literature, American literature, linguistics, rhetoric and composition, literary theory. *Unit head:* Dr. George W. Crandell, Head, 334-844-9079. *Application contact:* Dr. George Flowers, Dean of the Graduate School, 334-844-2125.

Austin Peay State University, College of Graduate Studies, College of Arts and Letters, Department of Languages and Literature, Clarksville, TN 37044. Offers English (MA). Part-time programs available. Postbaccalaureate distance learning degree programs offered (minimal on-campus study). *Faculty:* 10 full-time (6 women). *Students:* 18 full-time (13 women), 18 part-time (10 women); includes 5 minority (3 Black or African American, non-Hispanic/Latino; 2 Two or more races, non-Hispanic/Latino), 1 international. Average age 33. 24 applicants, 96% accepted, 16 enrolled. In 2010, 8 master's awarded. *Degree requirements:* For master's, comprehensive exam, thesis optional. *Entrance requirements:* For master's, GRE General Test, 3 letters of recommendation. Additional exam requirements/recommendations for international students: Required—TOEFL (minimum score 500 paper-based; 173 computer-based). *Application deadline:* For fall admission, 7/27 priority date for domestic students; for spring admission, 12/17 priority date for domestic students. Applications are processed on a rolling basis. Application fee: $25. Electronic applications accepted. *Expenses:* Tuition, state resident: full-time $6480; part-time $324 per credit hour. Tuition, nonresident: full-time $17,960; part-time $898 per credit hour. Required fees: $1244; $61.20 per credit hour. *Financial support:* In 2010–11, research assistantships with full tuition reimbursements (averaging $5,174 per year); career-related internships or fieldwork, Federal Work-Study, institutionally sponsored loans, scholarships/grants, and unspecified assistantships also available. Support available to part-time students. Financial award application deadline: 3/1; financial award applicants required to submit FAFSA. *Faculty research:* English literature, creative writing, American literature, linguistics. *Unit head:* Dr. David Guest, Professor/Chair, 931-221-7891, Fax: 931-221-7219, E-mail: mcnabbw@apsu.edu. *Application contact:* Dr. Dixie Dennis, Dean, College of Graduate Studies, 931-221-7662, Fax: 931-221-7641, E-mail: dennisdi@apsu.edu.

Ball State University, Graduate School, College of Sciences and Humanities, Department of English, Muncie, IN 47306-1099. Offers English (MA, PhD), including composition, creative writing (MA), general (MA), literature; linguistics (MA, PhD), including applied linguistics (PhD), linguistics (MA); linguistics and teaching English to speakers of other languages (MA); teaching English to speakers of other languages (MA). *Faculty:* 38. *Students:* 44 full-time (23 women), 67 part-time (42 women); includes 5 minority (1 American Indian or Alaska Native, non-Hispanic/Latino; 2 Hispanic/Latino; 2 Two or more races, non-Hispanic/Latino), 23 international. Average age 27. 160 applicants, 32% accepted, 24 enrolled. In 2010, 18 master's, 5 doctorates awarded. *Degree requirements:* For doctorate, variable foreign language requirement, thesis/dissertation. *Entrance requirements:* For master's, GRE General Test, writing sample; for doctorate, GRE General Test, GRE Subject Test, minimum graduate GPA of 3.2, writing sample. Application fee: $25 ($35 for international students). *Expenses:* Tuition, state resident: full-time $6160; part-time $299 per credit hour. Tuition, nonresident: full-time $16,020; part-time $783 per credit hour. Required fees: $2278; $95 per credit hour. *Financial support:* In 2010–11, 48 teaching assistantships with full tuition reimbursements (averaging $15,324 per year) were awarded; fellowships, career-related internships or fieldwork and unspecified assistantships also available. Financial award application deadline: 3/1. *Faculty research:* American literature; literary editing; medieval, Renaissance, and eighteenth century British literature; rhetoric. *Unit head:* Dr. Elizabeth Riddle, Chairperson, 765-285-8535, Fax: 765-285-3765. *Application contact:* Dr. Jill Christman.

Baylor University, Graduate School, College of Arts and Sciences, Department of English, Waco, TX 76798. Offers MA, PhD. Part-time programs available. *Faculty:* 19 full-time (6 women). *Students:* 28 full-time (20 women), 42 part-time (23 women); includes 1 American Indian or Alaska Native, non-Hispanic/Latino; 1 Hispanic/Latino; 4 Two or more races, non-Hispanic/Latino, 2 international. 25 applicants, 88% accepted. In 2010, 6 master's, 6 doctorates awarded. *Degree requirements:* For master's, one foreign language, thesis; for doctorate, 2 foreign languages, thesis/dissertation. *Entrance requirements:* For master's, GRE General Test, 18 hours of upper-level course work in English; for doctorate, GRE General Test. *Application deadline:* For fall admission, 3/15 priority date for domestic students. Applications are processed on a rolling basis. Application fee: $25. Electronic applications accepted. *Financial support:* In 2010–11, 10 research assistantships, 28 teaching assistantships were awarded; fellowships, Federal Work-Study, institutionally sponsored loans, and laboratory assistantships also available. *Faculty research:* Nineteenth century British literature, Renaissance studies, American studies, medieval studies, rhetoric and composition. Total annual research expenditures: $48,400. *Unit head:* Dr. Jay Losey, Graduate Program Director, 254-710-1768, Fax: 254-710-3894, E-mail: jay_losey@baylor.edu. *Application contact:* Lois Avey, Administrative Assistant, 254-710-1768, Fax: 254-710-3870, E-mail: lois_avey@baylor.edu.

Belmont University, College of Arts and Sciences, Department of English, Nashville, TN 37212-3757. Offers literature (MA); writing (MA). Part-time and evening/weekend programs available. *Faculty:* 16 full-time (12 women). *Students:* 4 full-time (2 women), 38 part-time (29 women); includes 4 minority (all Black or African American, non-Hispanic/Latino). Average age 30. 15 applicants, 80% accepted, 12 enrolled. In 2010, 10 master's awarded. *Degree requirements:* For master's, one foreign language, comprehensive exam (for some programs), thesis optional. *Entrance requirements:* For master's, GRE, letters of recommendation, writing sample, transcripts, statement of purpose. Additional exam requirements/recommendations for international students: Required—TOEFL. *Application deadline:* For fall admission, 8/1 for domestic and international students; for spring admission, 12/1 for domestic and international students. Applications are processed on a rolling basis. Application fee: $50. Electronic applications accepted. *Expenses:* Contact institution. *Financial support:* In 2010–11, 20 students received support. Federal Work-Study and scholarships/grants available. Financial award application deadline: 8/1; financial award applicants required to submit FAFSA. *Faculty research:* Gender, creative writing, Shakespeare, popular culture, world literature. *Unit head:* Dr. Annette M. Sisson, Director of Graduate Program, 615-460-6803, Fax: 615-460-5720, E-mail: annette.sisson@belmont.edu. *Application contact:* Dr. Annette M. Sisson, Director of Graduate Program, 615-460-6803, Fax: 615-460-5720, E-mail: annette.sisson@belmont.edu.

Bemidji State University, School of Graduate Studies, Bemidji, MN 56601-2699. Offers biology (MS); counseling psychology (MS); education (M Ed, MS); English (MA, MS); environmental studies (MS); mathematics (MS); mathematics (elementary and middle level education) (MS); special education (M Sp Ed, MS). Part-time programs available. Postbaccalaureate distance learning degree programs offered (no on-campus study). *Faculty:* 142 full-time (61 women), 37 part-time/adjunct (22 women). *Students:* 82 full-time (51 women), 350 part-time (210 women); includes 21 minority (6 Black or African American, non-Hispanic/Latino; 3 American Indian or Alaska Native, non-Hispanic/Latino; 6 Asian, non-Hispanic/Latino; 6 Hispanic/Latino), 8 international. Average age 35. 491 applicants, 93% accepted, 307 enrolled. In 2010, 97 master's awarded. *Degree requirements:* For master's, comprehensive exam, thesis (for some programs). *Entrance requirements:* For master's, GRE, letters of recommendation, letters of interest. Additional exam requirements/recommendations for international students: Required—TOEFL (minimum score 550 paper-based; 213 computer-based; 80 iBT). *Application deadline:* Applications are processed on a rolling basis. Application fee: $20. Electronic applications accepted. *Expenses:* Tuition, state resident: full-time $6605; part-time $330 per credit. Tuition, nonresident: full-time $6605; part-time $330 per credit. Required fees: $107.97 per credit. *Financial support:* In 2010–11, 110 students received support, including 40 research assistantships with partial tuition reimbursements available (averaging $7,196 per year), 40 teaching assistantships with partial tuition reimbursements available (averaging $7,196 per year); career-related internships or fieldwork, Federal Work-Study, scholarships/grants, health care benefits, and unspecified assistantships also available. Support available to part-time students. Financial award application deadline: 4/15; financial award applicants required to submit FAFSA. *Unit head:* Dr. Patricia Rogers, Dean, 218-755-2027, Fax: 218-755-2258,

English

Bemidji State University (continued)
E-mail: progers@bemidjistate.edu. *Application contact:* Joan Miller, Senior Office and Administrative Specialist, 218-755-2027, Fax: 218-755-2258, E-mail: jmiller@bemidjistate.edu.

Bennington College, Graduate Programs, The Bennington Writing Seminars, Bennington, VT 05201. Offers creative writing (MFA). Postbaccalaureate distance learning degree programs offered (minimal on-campus study). *Faculty:* 17 full-time (7 women), 3 part-time/adjunct (2 women). *Students:* 105 full-time (77 women); includes 2 Black or African American, non-Hispanic/Latino; 1 American Indian or Alaska Native, non-Hispanic/Latino; 6 Asian, non-Hispanic/Latino; 4 Hispanic/Latino. Average age 41. 155 applicants, 41% accepted, 29 enrolled. In 2010, 53 master's awarded. *Degree requirements:* For master's, thesis, collection of essays or poems, or collection of short stories and/or a novel. *Entrance requirements:* For master's, manuscript. *Application deadline:* For fall admission, 3/1 for domestic students; for spring admission, 9/1 for domestic students. Application fee: $60. *Expenses:* Contact institution. *Financial support:* In 2010–11, 10 students received support. Scholarships/grants available. Financial award application deadline: 4/1; financial award applicants required to submit FAFSA. *Unit head:* Sven Birkerts, Director, 802-440-4452, Fax: 802-440-4453, E-mail: writing@bennington.edu. *Application contact:* Victoria Clausi, Associate Director, 802-440-4454, Fax: 802-440-4453, E-mail: writing@bennington.edu.

Bob Jones University, Graduate Programs, Greenville, SC 29614. Offers accountancy (MS); Bible (MA); Bible translation (MA); Biblical studies (Certificate); broadcast management (MS); business administration (MBA); church history (MA, PhD); church ministries (MA); church music (MM); cinema and video production (MA); counseling (MS); curriculum and instruction (Ed D); divinity (M Div); dramatic production (MA); educational leadership (MS, Ed D, Ed S); elementary education (M Ed, MAT); English (M Ed, MA, MAT); fine arts (MA); graphic design (MA); history (M Ed, MA); illustration (MA); interpretative speech (MA); mathematics (M Ed, MAT); medical missions (Certificate); ministry (MM, D Min); multi-categorical special education (M Ed, MAT); music (M Ed); New Testament interpretation (PhD); Old Testament interpretation (PhD); orchestral instrument performance (MM); organ performance (MM); pastoral studies (MA); personnel services (MS, Ed S); piano pedagogy (MM); piano performance (MM); platform arts (MA); radio and television broadcasting (MS); rhetoric and public address (MA); secondary education (M Ed); studio art (MA); teaching Bible (MA); theology (MA, PhD); voice performance (MM); youth ministries (MA); M Div/MM.

Boise State University, Graduate College, College of Arts and Sciences, Department of English, Program in English, Boise, ID 83725-0399. Offers MA. Part-time programs available. *Degree requirements:* For master's, thesis. *Entrance requirements:* For master's, GRE General Test, minimum GPA of 3.0. Electronic applications accepted.

Boston College, Graduate School of Arts and Sciences, Department of English, Chestnut Hill, MA 02467-3800. Offers MA, PhD. *Degree requirements:* For master's, one foreign language, thesis optional; for doctorate, 2 foreign languages, thesis/dissertation. *Entrance requirements:* For master's and doctorate, GRE General Test, GRE Subject Test. Additional exam requirements/recommendations for international students: Required—TOEFL (minimum score 600 paper-based; 250 computer-based; 100 iBT). Electronic applications accepted. *Faculty research:* English and American literature, critical theory.

Boston University, Graduate School of Arts and Sciences, Department of English, Boston, MA 02215. Offers creative writing (MA); English (MA, PhD). *Students:* 54 full-time (33 women), 7 part-time (4 women); includes 1 minority (Asian, non-Hispanic/Latino), 1 international. Average age 28. 278 applicants, 7% accepted, 15 enrolled. In 2010, 15 master's, 7 doctorates awarded. Terminal master's awarded for partial completion of doctoral program. *Degree requirements:* For master's, one foreign language, thesis; for doctorate, 2 foreign languages, comprehensive exam, thesis/dissertation, qualifying/oral exam. *Entrance requirements:* For master's and doctorate, GRE General Test, GRE Subject Test, sample of written work, 2 letters of recommendation. Additional exam requirements/recommendations for international students: Required—TOEFL (minimum score 550 paper-based; 213 computer-based). *Application deadline:* For fall admission, 1/1 for domestic and international students. Application fee: $70. Electronic applications accepted. *Expenses:* Tuition: Full-time $39,314; part-time $1228 per credit. Required fees: $40 per semester. *Financial support:* In 2010–11, 36 students received support, including 2 fellowships with full tuition reimbursements available (averaging $19,300 per year), 25 teaching assistantships with partial tuition reimbursements available (averaging $18,800 per year); Federal Work-Study, scholarships/grants, and unspecified assistantships also available. Financial award application deadline: 1/15; financial award applicants required to submit FAFSA. *Unit head:* William C. Carroll, Interim Chairman, 617-353-2509, Fax: 617-353-3653, E-mail: wcarroll@bu.edu. *Application contact:* Amanda Trainor, Administrative Assistant, 617-353-2509, Fax: 617-353-3653, E-mail: hlane@bu.edu.

Boston University, School of Education, Boston, MA 02215. Offers counseling (Ed M, CAGS), including community, school, sport psychology; counseling psychology (Ed D); curriculum and teaching (Ed M, Ed D, CAGS), including early childhood (Ed D), educational media and technology (Ed D), English and language arts (Ed D), mathematics (Ed D), physical education and coaching (Ed D), science (Ed D), social studies education (Ed D), special education (Ed D); developmental studies (Ed D), including literacy and language, reading education; developmental studies in literacy and language education (Ed M, CAGS); early childhood education (Ed M, CAGS); education of the deaf (Ed M, CAGS); educational leadership and development (Ed D), including educational administration (Ed M, Ed D, CAGS), higher education administration (Ed M, Ed D, CAGS); educational media and technology (Ed M, CAGS); elementary education (Ed M); English and language arts (Ed M, CAGS); English education (MAT); health education (Ed M, CAGS); Latin and classical studies (MAT); mathematics education (Ed M, MAT, CAGS); mathematics for teaching (MMT); modern foreign language education (MAT), including French, Spanish; physical education and coaching (Ed M, CAGS); policy, planning, and administration (Ed M, CAGS), including community education leadership, educational administration (Ed M, Ed D, CAGS), higher education administration (Ed M, Ed D, CAGS); reading education (Ed M, CAGS); science education (Ed M, MAT, CAGS), including biology (MAT), chemistry (MAT), earth science (MAT), general science (MAT), physics (MAT); social studies education (Ed M, MAT, CAGS), including history (MAT), political science (MAT); special education (Ed M, Ed D, CAGS), including disability studies (Ed M), moderate disabilities (Ed M), severe disabilities (Ed M), special education administration (Ed M); teaching English as a second language (Ed M, CAGS). Part-time programs available. *Faculty:* 57 full-time, 39 part-time/adjunct. *Students:* 245 full-time (191 women), 376 part-time (274 women); includes 83 minority (14 Black or African American, non-Hispanic/Latino; 2 American Indian or Alaska Native, non-Hispanic/Latino; 28 Asian, non-Hispanic/Latino; 31 Hispanic/Latino; 2 Native Hawaiian or other Pacific Islander, non-Hispanic/Latino; 6 Two or more races, non-Hispanic/Latino), 79 international. Average age 30. 1,270 applicants, 66% accepted, 292 enrolled. In 2010, 273 master's, 15 doctorates, 7 other advanced degrees awarded. Terminal master's awarded for partial completion of doctoral program. *Degree requirements:* For master's, thesis (for some programs); for doctorate, comprehensive exam, thesis/dissertation; for CAGS, comprehensive exam. *Entrance requirements:* For master's and CAGS, GRE General Test or Miller Analogies Test (MAT); for doctorate, GRE General Test. Additional exam requirements/recommendations for international students: Required—TOEFL, IELTS. *Application deadline:* For fall admission, 1/15 priority date for domestic and international students; for spring admission, 9/15 priority date for domestic and international students. Applications are processed on a rolling basis. Application fee: $70. Electronic applications accepted. *Expenses:* Tuition: Full-time $39,314; part-time $1228 per credit. Required fees: $40 per semester. *Financial support:* In 2010–11, 276 students received support, including 31 fellowships with full tuition reimbursements available, 16 research assistantships, 26 teaching assistantships with partial tuition reimbursements available; career-related internships or fieldwork, Federal Work-Study, and scholarships/grants also available. Support available to part-time students. Financial award applicants required to submit FAFSA. *Faculty research:* Deaf studies, social emotional learning, civic engagement and education, STEM education, pre-college educational pipelines. Total annual research expenditures: $2.6 million. *Unit head:* Dr. Hardin Coleman, Dean, 617-353-3213. *Application contact:* Dana Fernandez, Director of Enrollment, 617-353-4237, Fax: 617-353-8937, E-mail: sedgrad@bu.edu.

Bowie State University, Graduate Programs, Program in English, Bowie, MD 20715-9465. Offers MA. Part-time and evening/weekend programs available. *Entrance requirements:* For master's, minimum GPA of 2.5, English degree. Electronic applications accepted. *Expenses:* Tuition, state resident: full-time $4080; part-time $340 per credit. Tuition, nonresident: full-time $7752; part-time $646 per credit. Required fees: $2128; $340 per credit.

Bowling Green State University, Graduate College, College of Arts and Sciences, Department of English, Program in English, Bowling Green, OH 43403. Offers English (MA, PhD); literature (MA); rhetoric and writing (PhD); scientific and technical communication (MA). Part-time programs available. *Degree requirements:* For master's, thesis or alternative; for doctorate, comprehensive exam, thesis/dissertation, foreign language or proficiency in Old English. *Entrance requirements:* For master's and doctorate, GRE General Test. Additional exam requirements/recommendations for international students: Required—TOEFL. Electronic applications accepted. *Faculty research:* Postmodern literary theory, rhetorical theory, ethnic American literature, literature and culture, composition pedagogy.

Bradley University, Graduate School, College of Liberal Arts and Sciences, Department of English, Peoria, IL 61625-0002. Offers MA. Part-time programs available. *Degree requirements:* For master's, comprehensive exam. *Entrance requirements:* For master's, writing sample, 2 letters of recommendation. Additional exam requirements/recommendations for international students: Required—TOEFL (minimum score 550 paper-based; 213 computer-based; 79 iBT).

Brandeis University, Graduate School of Arts and Sciences, Department of English, Waltham, MA 02454-9110. Offers English (MA, PhD); English and women's and gender studies (MA). Part-time programs available. *Faculty:* 16 full-time (9 women), 8 part-time/adjunct (5 women). *Students:* 54 full-time (29 women), 1 (woman) part-time; includes 1 Asian, non-Hispanic/Latino; 2 Hispanic/Latino, 5 international. 177 applicants, 16% accepted, 10 enrolled. In 2010, 8 master's, 5 doctorates awarded. *Degree requirements:* For master's, one foreign language, thesis, symposium; for doctorate, 2 foreign languages, thesis/dissertation, field exam, symposium presentation, prospectus defense. *Entrance requirements:* For master's, GRE General Test, resume, sample of work, letters of recommendation; for doctorate, GRE General Test, GRE Subject Test, resume, sample of work, letters of recommendation. Additional exam requirements/recommendations for international students: Required—TOEFL (minimum score 600 paper-based; 250 computer-based; 100 iBT); Recommended—IELTS (minimum score 7). *Application deadline:* For fall admission, 1/5 for domestic and international students. Application fee: $75. Electronic applications accepted. *Financial support:* In 2010–11, 27 fellowships with full tuition reimbursements (averaging $20,000 per year), 4 teaching assistantships with partial tuition reimbursements (averaging $3,200 per year) were awarded; research assistantships with full tuition reimbursements, scholarships/grants, health care benefits, and tuition waivers (full and partial) also available. Financial award application deadline: 4/15; financial award applicants required to submit FAFSA. *Faculty research:* Feminist and gender theory, American literature, Anglophone literature, early modern literature, modernism. *Unit head:* Dr. Michael Gilmore, Director of Graduate Studies, 781-736-2130, Fax: 781-736-2179, E-mail: chaucer@brandeis.edu. *Application contact:* Lisa Pannella, Department Administrator, 781-736-2130, Fax: 781-736-2179, E-mail: pannella@brandeis.edu.

Bridgewater State University, School of Graduate Studies, School of Arts and Sciences, Department of English, Bridgewater, MA 02325-0001. Offers MA, MAT. Part-time and evening/weekend programs available. *Degree requirements:* For master's, one foreign language, comprehensive exam, thesis optional. *Entrance requirements:* For master's, GRE General Test.

Brigham Young University, Graduate Studies, College of Humanities, Department of English, Provo, UT 84602-1001. Offers creative writing (MFA); literature (MA); rhetoric/composition (MA). *Faculty:* 50 full-time (16 women). *Students:* 63 full-time (44 women), 5 part-time (2 women); includes 1 Hispanic/Latino. Average age 24. 103 applicants, 34% accepted, 31 enrolled. In 2010, 30 master's awarded. *Degree requirements:* For master's, thesis. *Entrance requirements:* For master's, GRE General Test, creative portfolio (for MFA). Additional exam requirements/recommendations for international students: Required—TOEFL. *Application deadline:* For fall admission, 1/15 for domestic and international students. Application fee: $50. Electronic applications accepted. *Expenses:* Tuition: Full-time $5580; part-time $310 per credit hour. Tuition and fees vary according to program and student's religious affiliation. *Financial support:* In 2010–11, 79 students received support, including 10 research assistantships (averaging $3,000 per year), 62 teaching assistantships (averaging $6,000 per year); career-related internships or fieldwork, institutionally sponsored loans, scholarships/grants, and tuition waivers (partial) also available. Support available to part-time students. Financial award application deadline: 3/15. *Faculty research:* English literature, American literature, rhetoric, creative writing. *Unit head:* Prof. Ed Cutler, Head, 801-422-3581, Fax: 801-422-0221, E-mail: ed_cutler@byu.edu. *Application contact:* Lou Ann C. Crisler, Graduate Secretary, 801-422-8673, Fax: 801-422-0221, E-mail: louann_crisler@byu.edu.

Brock University, Faculty of Graduate Studies, Faculty of Humanities, Program in English, St. Catharines, ON L2S 3A1, Canada. Offers MA. Part-time programs available. *Degree requirements:* For master's, thesis optional. *Entrance requirements:* For master's, honours in English. Additional exam requirements/recommendations for international students: Required—TOEFL (minimum score 550 paper-based; 213 computer-based; 80 iBT), IELTS (minimum score 6.5), TWE (minimum score 4). Electronic applications accepted. *Faculty research:* Literary theory, Canadian literature, Milton and 17th century American literature, 19th century American literature, British Romantic literature and culture.

Brooklyn College of the City University of New York, Division of Graduate Studies, Department of English, Brooklyn, NY 11210-2889. Offers creative writing (MFA), including fiction, playwriting, poetry; English (MA, PhD). Part-time and evening/weekend programs available. *Students:* 16 full-time (11 women), 181 part-time (111 women); includes 50 minority (24 Black or African American, non-Hispanic/Latino; 13 Asian, non-Hispanic/Latino; 13 Hispanic/Latino), 9 international. Average age 29. 673 applicants, 20% accepted, 72 enrolled. In 2010, 64 master's awarded. *Degree requirements:* For master's, one foreign language, comprehensive exam (for some programs), thesis (for some programs). *Entrance requirements:* For master's, advanced undergraduate courses in English, 2 letters of recommendation, writing sample, statement of purpose. Additional exam requirements/recommendations for international students: Required—TOEFL. *Application deadline:* For fall admission, 3/1 priority date for domestic students, 2/1 priority date for international students; for spring admission, 11/15 priority date for domestic students, 10/15 priority date for international students. Applications are processed on a rolling basis. Application fee: $125. Electronic applications accepted. *Expenses:* Tuition, state resident: full-time $7360; part-time $310 per credit hour. Tuition, nonresident: full-time $13,800; part-time $575 per credit hour. Required fees: $190 per semester. *Financial support:* Federal Work-Study, institutionally sponsored loans, and scholarships/grants available. Support available to part-time students. Financial award application deadline: 5/1; financial award applicants required to submit FAFSA. *Faculty research:* Cultural studies, medieval literature, Virginia Woolf. *Unit head:* Dr. Ellen Tremper, Chairperson, 718-951-5195, E-mail: etremper@brooklyn.cuny.edu. *Application contact:* Hernan Sierra, Graduate Admissions Coordinator, 718-951-4536, Fax: 718-951-4506, E-mail: grads@brooklyn.cuny.edu.

Brown University, Graduate School, Department of English, Program in Literatures and Cultures in English, Providence, RI 02912. Offers MA, PhD. *Degree requirements:* For doctorate, variable foreign language requirement, thesis/dissertation. *Entrance requirements:* For master's and doctorate, GRE General Test, GRE Subject Test.

Bucknell University, Graduate Studies, College of Arts and Sciences, Department of English, Lewisburg, PA 17837. Offers MA. Part-time programs available. *Degree requirements:* For master's, one foreign language, thesis. *Entrance requirements:* For master's, GRE General Test, GRE Subject Test, minimum GPA of 2.8. Additional exam requirements/recommendations for international students: Required—TOEFL. *Expenses:* Tuition: Full-time $36,992; part-time $4624 per course.

Buffalo State College, State University of New York, The Graduate School, Faculty of Arts and Humanities, Department of English, Buffalo, NY 14222-1095. Offers English (MA); secondary education (MS Ed), including English. Part-time and evening/weekend programs available. *Degree requirements:* For master's, thesis or project, 1 foreign language (MS Ed). *Entrance requirements:* For master's, minimum GPA of 2.75, 36 hours in English, New York teaching certificate (MS Ed). Additional exam requirements/recommendations for international students: Required—TOEFL (minimum score 550 paper-based; 213 computer-based).

Butler University, College of Liberal Arts and Sciences, Department of English, Indianapolis, IN 46208-3485. Offers MA. Part-time and evening/weekend programs available. *Faculty:* 6 full-time (3 women). *Students:* 3 full-time (1 woman), 47 part-time (29 women); includes 3 minority (1 Black or African American, non-Hispanic/Latino; 1 Asian, non-Hispanic/Latino; 1 Two or more races, non-Hispanic/Latino), 3 international. Average age 38. 49 applicants, 59% accepted, 17 enrolled. In 2010, 2 master's awarded. *Entrance requirements:* For master's, GRE General Test, GRE Subject Test. *Application deadline:* For fall admission, 8/15 priority date for domestic students. Applications are processed on a rolling basis. Application fee: $35. Electronic applications accepted. *Expenses:* Tuition: Full-time $29,740; part-time $1250 per credit. Required fees: $818; $430 per credit. Tuition and fees vary according to program. *Financial support:* Applicants required to submit FAFSA. *Faculty research:* Modern poetry, ethnic literature, liberal education, Chaucer, ethics. *Unit head:* Dr. Hilene Flanzbaum, Head, 317-940-9860, E-mail: hflanzba@butler.edu. *Application contact:* Pamela Bender, Student Services Specialist, 317-940-8100, Fax: 317-940-8250, E-mail: pbender@butler.edu.

California Baptist University, Program in English, Riverside, CA 92504-3206. Offers English pedagogy (MA); literature (MA); teaching English as a second language (TESOL) (MA). Part-time programs available. *Faculty:* 4 full-time (3 women). *Students:* 7 full-time (5 women), 20 part-time (17 women); includes 1 Hispanic/Latino, 5 international. 11 applicants, 82% accepted, 6 enrolled. In 2010, 8 master's awarded. *Degree requirements:* For master's, thesis (for some programs). *Entrance requirements:* For master's, minimum undergraduate GPA of 2.75, 18 semester hours of course work in English beyond freshman level. Additional exam requirements/recommendations for international students: Required—TOEFL (minimum score 575 paper-based; 230 computer-based; 89 iBT). *Application deadline:* For fall admission, 8/1 priority date for domestic students, 7/1 for international students; for spring admission, 12/1 priority date for domestic students, 10/15 for international students. Applications are processed on a rolling basis. Application fee: $45. Electronic applications accepted. *Expenses:* Tuition: Full-time $8532; part-time $474 per unit. Required fees: $355 per semester. One-time fee: $45 full-time. Tuition and fees vary according to course load and program. *Financial support:* Federal Work-Study and scholarships/grants available. Support available to part-time students. Financial award applicants required to submit FAFSA. *Unit head:* Dr. Jennifer Newton, Director, 951-343-4276, Fax: 951-343-4661, E-mail: jnewton@calbaptist.edu. *Application contact:* Gail Ronveaux, Dean of Graduate Enrollment, 951-343-5045, Fax: 951-343-5095, E-mail: graduateadmissions@calbaptist.edu.

California Polytechnic State University, San Luis Obispo, College of Liberal Arts, Department of English, San Luis Obispo, CA 93407. Offers MA. Part-time programs available. *Faculty:* 2 full-time (0 women). *Students:* 17 full-time (13 women), 24 part-time (17 women); includes 9 minority (1 Black or African American, non-Hispanic/Latino; 1 Asian, non-Hispanic/Latino; 3 Hispanic/Latino; 4 Two or more races, non-Hispanic/Latino). Average age 29. 51 applicants, 59% accepted, 19 enrolled. In 2010, 9 master's awarded. *Degree requirements:* For master's, one foreign language, comprehensive exam. *Entrance requirements:* For master's, minimum GPA of 3.0 in last 90 quarter units of course work, writing sample. Additional exam requirements/recommendations for international students: Required—TOEFL (minimum score 550 paper-based; 213 computer-based) or IELTS (minimum score 6). *Application deadline:* For fall admission, 7/1 for domestic students, 11/30 for international students; for winter admission, 11/1 for domestic students, 6/30 for international students; for spring admission, 2/1 for domestic students. Applications are processed on a rolling basis. Application fee: $55. *Expenses:* Tuition, state resident: full-time $5386; part-time $3124 per year. Tuition, nonresident: full-time $11,160; part-time $248 per unit. Required fees: $2250; $614 per term. One-time fee: $2250 full-time; $1842 part-time. *Financial support:* Teaching assistantships, career-related internships or fieldwork, Federal Work-Study, institutionally sponsored loans, and tutorships, writing laboratory assistantships available. Support available to part-time students. Financial award application deadline: 3/2; financial award applicants required to submit FAFSA. *Faculty research:* Feminist literary criticism, modern British novel, literary theory, Shakespeare, Victorian literature. *Unit head:* Dr. Paul Marchbanks, Graduate Coordinator, 805-756-2159, Fax: 805-756-6374, E-mail: pmarchba@calpoly.edu. *Application contact:* Dr. Paul Marchbanks, Graduate Coordinator, 805-756-2159, Fax: 805-756-6374, E-mail: pmarchba@calpoly.edu.

California State Polytechnic University, Pomona, Academic Affairs, College of Letters, Arts, and Social Sciences, Program in English, Pomona, CA 91768-2557. Offers MA. Part-time programs available. *Students:* 22 full-time (13 women), 69 part-time (50 women); includes 49 minority (4 Black or African American, non-Hispanic/Latino; 1 American Indian or Alaska Native, non-Hispanic/Latino; 13 Asian, non-Hispanic/Latino; 27 Hispanic/Latino; 2 Native Hawaiian or other Pacific Islander, non-Hispanic/Latino; 2 Two or more races, non-Hispanic/Latino). Average age 31. 62 applicants, 87% accepted, 31 enrolled. In 2010, 23 master's awarded. *Degree requirements:* For master's, one foreign language, thesis or alternative. *Application deadline:* For fall admission, 5/1 priority date for domestic students; for winter admission, 10/15 priority date for domestic students; for spring admission, 1/20 priority date for domestic students. Applications are processed on a rolling basis. Application fee: $55. Electronic applications accepted. *Expenses:* Tuition, state resident: full-time $5386; part-time $2850 per year. Tuition, nonresident: full-time $12,082; part-time $248 per credit. Required fees: $577; $248 per credit. $577 per year. Tuition and fees vary according to course load and program. *Financial support:* In 2010–11, 2 fellowships were awarded; Federal Work-Study and institutionally sponsored loans also available. Support available to part-time students. Financial award application deadline: 3/2; financial award applicants required to submit FAFSA. *Unit head:* Dr. Karen A. Russikoff, Graduate Coordinator, 909-869-3836, E-mail: krussikoff@csupomona.edu. *Application contact:* Scott J. Duncan, Director, Admissions, 909-869-3258, Fax: 909-869-4529, E-mail: sjduncan@csupomona.edu.

California State University, Bakersfield, Division of Graduate Studies, School of Humanities and Social Sciences, Program in English, Bakersfield, CA 93311. Offers MA. *Degree requirements:* For master's, comprehensive exam or thesis. *Entrance requirements:* For master's, GRE General Test, GRE Subject Test (literature), minimum GPA of 2.5 for last 90 quarter units. Additional exam requirements/recommendations for international students: Required—TOEFL (minimum score 550 paper-based; 213 computer-based).

California State University, Chico, Graduate School, College of Humanities and Fine Arts, Department of English, Program in English, Chico, CA 95929-0722. Offers MA. *Students:* 16 full-time (13 women), 16 part-time (8 women); includes 1 American Indian or Alaska Native, non-Hispanic/Latino; 5 Hispanic/Latino. Average age 34. 19 applicants, 74% accepted, 10 enrolled. In 2010, 7 master's awarded. *Degree requirements:* For master's, thesis. *Entrance requirements:* For master's, GRE General Test, 2 letters of recommendation, writing sample. Additional exam requirements/recommendations for international students: Required—TOEFL (minimum score 550 paper-based; 213 computer-based; 80 iBT), IELTS (minimum score 6.5). *Application deadline:* For fall admission, 3/1 for domestic and international students; for spring admission, 9/15 for domestic and international students. Application fee: $55. *Unit head:* Dr. Rob Davidson, Graduate Coordinator, 530-898-6457. *Application contact:* Dr. Rob Davidson, Graduate Coordinator, 530-898-6457.

California State University, Dominguez Hills, College of Arts and Humanities, Department of English, Carson, CA 90747-0001. Offers English (MA); rhetoric and composition (Certificate); teaching English as a second language (Certificate). Part-time and evening/weekend programs available. *Faculty:* 13 full-time (5 women). *Students:* 16 full-time (9 women), 67 part-time (42 women); includes 13 Black or African American, non-Hispanic/Latino; 5 Asian, non-Hispanic/Latino; 20 Hispanic/Latino; 1 Two or more races, non-Hispanic/Latino, 3 international. Average age 38. 64 applicants, 86% accepted, 24 enrolled. In 2010, 17 master's awarded. *Degree requirements:* For master's, comprehensive exam (for some programs), thesis or alternative. *Entrance requirements:* For master's, minimum GPA of 3.0 in last 60 units. Additional exam requirements/recommendations for international students: Required—TOEFL (minimum score 550 paper-based; 213 computer-based). *Application deadline:* Applications are processed on a rolling basis. Application fee: $55. Electronic applications accepted. *Faculty research:* Gender studies, transnationalism, discourse analysis, visual culture, Shakespeare. *Unit head:* Dr. Helen Oesterheld, Chair, 310-243-3322, E-mail: hoesterheld@csudh.edu. *Application contact:* 310-243-3600.

California State University, East Bay, Office of Academic Programs and Graduate Studies, College of Letters, Arts, and Social Sciences, Department of English, Hayward, CA 94542-3000. Offers MA. Part-time programs available. *Faculty:* 12 full-time (8 women), 1 (woman) part-time/adjunct. *Students:* 7 full-time (6 women), 56 part-time (42 women); includes 4 Black or African American, non-Hispanic/Latino; 1 American Indian or Alaska Native, non-Hispanic/Latino; 10 Asian, non-Hispanic/Latino; 5 Hispanic/Latino, 7 international. Average age 36. 63 applicants, 63% accepted, 21 enrolled. In 2010, 35 master's awarded. *Degree requirements:* For master's, one foreign language, comprehensive exam, thesis optional. *Entrance requirements:* For master's, minimum GPA of 3.0 in field. Additional exam requirements/recommendations for international students: Required—TOEFL (minimum score 550 paper-based; 213 computer-based). *Application deadline:* For fall admission, 6/30 for domestic and international students; for winter admission, 10/31 for domestic students; for spring admission, 11/30 for domestic students. Applications are processed on a rolling basis. Application fee: $55. Electronic applications accepted. *Financial support:* Fellowships, teaching assistantships, career-related internships or fieldwork, Federal Work-Study, institutionally sponsored loans, and scholarships/grants available. Support available to part-time students. Financial award application deadline: 3/2; financial award applicants required to submit FAFSA. *Unit head:* Dr. Dennis Chester, Chair, 510-885-3151, Fax: 510-885-4797, E-mail: dennis.chester@csueastbay.edu. *Application contact:* Dr. Donna Wiley, Interim Associate Director, 510-885-2928, Fax: 510-885-4777, E-mail: donna.wiley@csueastbay.edu.

California State University, Fresno, Division of Graduate Studies, College of Arts and Humanities, Department of English, Fresno, CA 93740-8027. Offers composition theory (MA); creative writing (MFA); literature (MA). Part-time and evening/weekend programs available. *Degree requirements:* For master's, one foreign language, thesis. *Entrance requirements:* For master's, GRE General Test, minimum GPA of 3.0, writing sample. Additional exam requirements/recommendations for international students: Required—TOEFL. Electronic applications accepted. *Faculty research:* American literature, Renaissance literature, foreign literature.

California State University, Fullerton, Graduate Studies, College of Humanities and Social Sciences, Department of English and Comparative Literature, Fullerton, CA 92834-9480. Offers comparative literature (MA); English (MA). Part-time programs available. *Students:* 32 full-time (23 women), 44 part-time (30 women); includes 2 Black or African American, non-Hispanic/Latino; 5 Asian, non-Hispanic/Latino; 12 Hispanic/Latino; 3 Two or more races, non-Hispanic/Latino, 1 international. Average age 28. 88 applicants, 51% accepted, 31 enrolled. In 2010, 40 master's awarded. *Degree requirements:* For master's, comprehensive exam, thesis or alternative. *Entrance requirements:* For master's, minimum GPA of 3.0 in major, 2.5 in last 60 hours. Application fee: $55. *Financial support:* Career-related internships or fieldwork, Federal Work-Study, institutionally sponsored loans, and scholarships/grants available. Support available to part-time students. Financial award application deadline: 3/1; financial award applicants required to submit FAFSA. *Unit head:* Dr. Joseph Sawicki, Chair, 657-278-3163. *Application contact:* Admissions/Applications, 657-278-2371.

California State University, Long Beach, Graduate Studies, College of Liberal Arts, Department of English, Long Beach, CA 90840. Offers creative writing (MFA); English (MA). Part-time programs available. *Faculty:* 24 full-time (10 women), 4 part-time/adjunct (2 women). *Students:* 67 full-time (49 women), 97 part-time (68 women); includes 3 Black or African American, non-Hispanic/Latino; 4 American Indian or Alaska Native, non-Hispanic/Latino; 13 Asian, non-Hispanic/Latino; 23 Hispanic/Latino, 2 international. Average age 30. 222 applicants, 41% accepted, 57 enrolled. In 2010, 45 master's awarded. *Degree requirements:* For master's, one foreign language, comprehensive exam or thesis. *Entrance requirements:* For master's, GRE Subject Test, minimum GPA of 3.0 in English. *Application deadline:* For fall admission, 5/1 for domestic students. Applications are processed on a rolling basis. Application fee: $55. Electronic applications accepted. *Financial support:* Federal Work-Study, institutionally sponsored loans, and scholarships/grants available. Financial award application deadline: 3/2. *Faculty research:* English and American literature, literary theory, linguistics, rhetoric and composition. *Unit head:* Dr. Eileen S. Klink, Chair, 562-985-4223, Fax: 562-985-2369, E-mail: eklink@csulb.edu. *Application contact:* Dr. Beth Lau, Graduate Adviser, 562-985-4252, Fax: 562-985-4223, E-mail: blau@csulb.edu.

California State University, Los Angeles, Graduate Studies, College of Arts and Letters, Department of English, Los Angeles, CA 90032-8530. Offers MA. Part-time and evening/weekend programs available. *Faculty:* 5 full-time (3 women), 2 part-time/adjunct (0 women). *Students:* 22 full-time (13 women), 43 part-time (20 women); includes 19 minority (1 Black or African American, non-Hispanic/Latino; 3 Asian, non-Hispanic/Latino; 14 Hispanic/Latino; 1 Two or more races, non-Hispanic/Latino), 4 international. Average age 36. 31 applicants, 100% accepted, 15 enrolled. In 2010, 36 master's awarded. *Degree requirements:* For master's, comprehensive exam or thesis. *Entrance requirements:* Additional exam requirements/recommendations for international students: Required—TOEFL (minimum score 500 paper-based; 173 computer-based). *Application deadline:* For fall admission, 5/1 for international students. Applications are processed on a rolling basis. Application fee: $55. Electronic applications accepted. *Financial support:* Federal Work-Study available. Support available to part-time students. Financial award application deadline: 3/1. *Faculty research:* English and American literature, linguistics, composition. *Unit head:* Dr. Ruben Quintero, Chair, 323-343-4140, Fax: 323-343-6470, E-mail: rquinte@calstatela.edu. *Application contact:* Dr. Alan Muchlinski, Dean of Graduate Studies, 323-343-3820, Fax: 323-343-5653, E-mail: amuchli@exchange.calstatela.edu.

California State University, Northridge, Graduate Studies, College of Humanities, Department of English, Northridge, CA 91330. Offers creative writing (MA); literature (MA); rhetoric and composition theory (MA). Part-time and evening/weekend programs available. *Degree requirements:* For master's, thesis or alternative. *Entrance requirements:* For master's, writing proficiency test, GRE General Test or minimum GPA of 3.0. Additional exam requirements/recommendations for international students: Required—TOEFL. *Faculty research:* Reading improvement, professional writing, Dickens, Shaw, English as a second language.

California State University, Sacramento, Graduate Studies, College of Arts and Letters, Department of English, Sacramento, CA 95819. Offers creative writing (MA); teaching English to speakers of other languages (MA). Part-time programs available. *Degree requirements:* For master's, thesis, project, or comprehensive exam; writing proficiency exam. *Entrance requirements:* For master's, portfolio (creative writing); minimum GPA of 3.0 in English, 2.75 overall during previous 2 years. Additional exam requirements/recommendations for international students: Required—TOEFL. Electronic applications accepted. *Faculty research:* Teaching composition, remedial writing.

California State University, San Bernardino, Graduate Studies, College of Arts and Letters, Department of English, San Bernardino, CA 92407-2397. Offers creative writing (MFA); English composition (MA). Part-time and evening/weekend programs available. *Degree requirements:*

English

California State University, San Bernardino (continued)

For master's, one foreign language, thesis. *Entrance requirements:* For master's, BA in English or linguistics, minimum GPA of 3.0. Additional exam requirements/recommendations for international students: Required—TOEFL. *Faculty research:* Composition and literary theory, theatrical theory, creative writing, relationship between evaluating writing and teaching composition.

California State University, San Marcos, College of Arts and Sciences, Program in Literature and Writing Studies, San Marcos, CA 92096-0001. Offers MA. Part-time and evening/weekend programs available. *Degree requirements:* For master's, one foreign language, thesis. *Entrance requirements:* For master's, GRE General Test, minimum GPA of 3.0, writing sample. *Faculty research:* Postcolonialism, feminism rhetoric, cultural studies, creative writing, critical theory.

California State University, Stanislaus, College of Humanities and Social Sciences, Program in English (MA), Turlock, CA 95382. Offers literature (Certificate); rhetoric and teaching writing (MA); teaching English to speakers of other languages (MA). Part-time programs available. *Faculty:* 21. *Students:* 10 full-time (7 women), 42 part-time (30 women); includes 19 minority (3 Black or African American, non-Hispanic/Latino; 1 Asian, non-Hispanic/Latino; 10 Hispanic/Latino; 1 Native Hawaiian or other Pacific Islander, non-Hispanic/Latino; 4 Two or more races, non-Hispanic/Latino), 1 international. Average age 35. 28 applicants, 68% accepted, 15 enrolled. In 2010, 19 master's awarded. *Degree requirements:* For master's, comprehensive exam, thesis or alternative. *Entrance requirements:* For master's, GRE, minimum GPA of 3.0, 2 letters of reference, personal statement. Additional exam requirements/recommendations for international students: Required—TOEFL (minimum score 575 paper-based; 233 computer-based), TWE (minimum score 4). *Application deadline:* For fall admission, 5/1 for domestic students; for spring admission, 9/15 for domestic students. Application fee: $55. Electronic applications accepted. Tuition and fees vary according to program. *Financial support:* Fellowships, research assistantships, teaching assistantships, career-related internships or fieldwork and Federal Work-Study available. Financial award application deadline: 3/1; financial award applicants required to submit FAFSA. *Faculty research:* Transnational literacies, Renaissance and medieval literature, abolition writings and slave narratives, qualitative writing. *Unit head:* Dr. Scott Davis, English Department Chair, 209-667-3361, Fax: 209-667-3720, E-mail: english@csustan.edu. *Application contact:* Graduate School, 209-667-3129, Fax: 209-664-7025, E-mail: graduate_school@csustan.edu.

Carleton University, Faculty of Graduate Studies, Faculty of Arts and Social Sciences, Department of English Language and Literature, Ottawa, ON K1S 5B6, Canada. Offers MA, PhD. *Degree requirements:* For master's, thesis optional. *Entrance requirements:* For master's, honors degree. Additional exam requirements/recommendations for international students: Required—TOEFL. *Faculty research:* British, Canadian, American, and Commonwealth literatures; English language and writing; literary criticism; social and historical context of literature.

Carnegie Mellon University, College of Humanities and Social Sciences, Department of English, Pittsburgh, PA 15213-3891. Offers communication planning and design (M Des); literary and cultural studies (MA, PhD); professional writing (MAPW), including editing and publishing, policy and non-profit communication, public and media relations / corporate communications, science or healthcare communication, technical writing, writing for new media, writing for print media; rhetoric (MA, PhD). Part-time programs available. Terminal master's awarded for partial completion of doctoral program. *Degree requirements:* For doctorate, 2 foreign languages, comprehensive exam, thesis/dissertation. *Entrance requirements:* For master's and doctorate, GRE General Test. Additional exam requirements/recommendations for international students: Required—TOEFL, TWE. *Faculty research:* Cognitive processes in discourse with emphasis on writing, testing, and evaluation.

Case Western Reserve University, School of Graduate Studies, Department of English, Cleveland, OH 44106. Offers MA, PhD. Part-time programs available. *Faculty:* 22 full-time (11 women). *Students:* 17 full-time (10 women), 15 part-time (11 women); includes 1 Black or African American, non-Hispanic/Latino, 2 international. Average age 32. 70 applicants, 20% accepted, 11 enrolled. In 2010, 4 master's, 7 doctorates awarded. *Degree requirements:* For master's, one foreign language, comprehensive exam, thesis or alternative, written exam; for doctorate, one foreign language, thesis/dissertation, oral and written exams. *Entrance requirements:* For master's and doctorate, GRE General Test, sample of written work. Additional exam requirements/recommendations for international students: Required—TOEFL (minimum score 550 paper-based; 213 computer-based; 79 iBT). *Application deadline:* For fall admission, 2/1 priority date for domestic students; for spring admission, 1/2 for domestic students. Applications are processed on a rolling basis. Application fee: $50. Electronic applications accepted. *Financial support:* Fellowships, research assistantships, teaching assistantships, Federal Work-Study, institutionally sponsored loans, and tuition waivers (partial) available. Financial award application deadline: 2/1; financial award applicants required to submit FAFSA. *Faculty research:* Sixteenth- to twentieth-century English literature, rhetorical and critical theory, women's studies, genre studies, Renaissance, America modernism, authorship. *Unit head:* Mary Grimm, Chair, 216-368-2355, Fax: 216-368-4681, E-mail: mary.grimm@case.edu. *Application contact:* Christopher Flint, Associate Professor and Graduate Director, 216-368-2362, Fax: 216-368-4367, E-mail: christopher.flint@case.edu.

The Catholic University of America, School of Arts and Sciences, Department of English Language and Literature, Washington, DC 20064. Offers English language and literature (MA, PhD); rhetoric (Certificate); MSLS/MA. Part-time programs available. *Faculty:* 12 full-time (5 women), 2 part-time/adjunct (0 women). *Students:* 17 full-time (14 women), 42 part-time (28 women), 2 international. Average age 29. 66 applicants, 41% accepted, 12 enrolled. In 2010, 8 master's, 3 doctorates awarded. *Degree requirements:* For master's, one foreign language, comprehensive exam; for doctorate, 2 foreign languages, comprehensive exam, thesis/dissertation. *Entrance requirements:* For master's and doctorate, GRE General Test, statement of purpose, official copies of academic transcripts, three letters of recommendation, writing sample. Additional exam requirements/recommendations for international students: Required—TOEFL (minimum score 580 paper-based; 237 computer-based). *Application deadline:* For fall admission, 8/1 priority date for domestic students, 7/15 for international students; for spring admission, 12/1 priority date for domestic students, 10/15 for international students. Applications are processed on a rolling basis. Application fee: $55. Electronic applications accepted. *Expenses:* Tuition: Full-time $33,580; part-time $1315 per credit hour. Required fees: $80; $40 per semester hour. One-time fee: $425. *Financial support:* Fellowships, research assistantships, teaching assistantships, Federal Work-Study, scholarships/grants, tuition waivers (full and partial), and unspecified assistantships available. Financial award application deadline: 2/1; financial award applicants required to submit FAFSA. *Faculty research:* Medieval literature, theory and history of rhetoric, Renaissance literature, religion and literature, English and American drama. *Unit head:* Dr. Ernest Suarez, Chair, 202-319-5488, Fax: 202-319-4188, E-mail: suarez@cua.edu. *Application contact:* Andrew Woodall, Director of Graduate Admissions, 202-319-5057, Fax: 202-319-6533, E-mail: cua-admissions@cua.edu.

Central Connecticut State University, School of Graduate Studies, School of Arts and Sciences, Department of English, Program in English, New Britain, CT 06050-4010. Offers MA, Certificate. Part-time and evening/weekend programs available. *Students:* 16 full-time (10 women), 29 part-time (16 women); includes 4 minority (3 Black or African American, non-Hispanic/Latino; 1 Two or more races, non-Hispanic/Latino). Average age 34. 30 applicants, 63% accepted, 12 enrolled. In 2010, 7 master's, 5 other advanced degrees awarded. *Degree requirements:* For master's, comprehensive exam, thesis or alternative; for Certificate, qualifying exam. *Entrance requirements:* For master's, minimum undergraduate GPA of 3.0. Additional exam requirements/recommendations for international students: Required—TOEFL. *Application deadline:* For fall admission, 7/1 for domestic students; for spring admission, 12/1 for domestic students. Applications are processed on a rolling basis. Application fee: $50. Electronic applications accepted. *Expenses:* Tuition, area resident: Full-time $5012; part-time $470 per credit. Tuition, state resident: full-time $7518; part-time $482 per credit. Tuition, nonresident: full-time $13,962; part-time $482 per credit. Required fees: $3772. One-time fee: $62 part-time.

Central Michigan University, College of Graduate Studies, College of Humanities and Social and Behavioral Sciences, Department of English Language and Literature, Mount Pleasant, MI 48859. Offers English composition and communication (MA); English language and literature (MA), including children's and young adult literature, creative writing, general concentration; teaching English to speakers of other languages (MA). Part-time and evening/weekend programs available. *Faculty:* 16 full-time (10 women). *Students:* 23 full-time (15 women), 61 part-time (38 women); includes 1 American Indian or Alaska Native, non-Hispanic/Latino; 1 Hispanic/Latino, 16 international. Average age 32. *Degree requirements:* For master's, thesis or alternative. *Application deadline:* For fall admission, 6/1 for international students; for spring admission, 10/1 for international students. Applications are processed on a rolling basis. Application fee: $35 ($45 for international students). Electronic applications accepted. *Expenses:* Tuition, state resident: full-time $8208; part-time $456 per credit hour. Tuition, nonresident: full-time $13,788; part-time $766 per credit hour. One-time fee: $25. *Financial support:* Fellowships with tuition reimbursements, research assistantships with tuition reimbursements, teaching assistantships with tuition reimbursements, career-related internships or fieldwork, Federal Work-Study, unspecified assistantships, and out-of-state merit awards, non-resident graduate awards available. *Faculty research:* Composition theory, science fiction history and bibliography, children's and young adult literature, nineteenth-century American literature, applied linguistics. *Unit head:* Dr. William H. Wandless, Chairperson, 989-774-3171, Fax: 989-774-1271, E-mail: wandl1wh@cmich.edu. *Application contact:* Dr. Jeffrey A. Weinstock, Coordinator, Graduate Studies in English, 989-774-3101, Fax: 989-774-1271, E-mail: weins1ja@cmich.edu.

Central Washington University, Graduate Studies and Research, College of Arts and Humanities, Department of English, Ellensburg, WA 98926. Offers English (MA); teaching English as a second language (MA). Part-time programs available. *Degree requirements:* For master's, thesis or alternative. *Entrance requirements:* For master's, GRE General Test, minimum GPA of 3.0, writing sample. Additional exam requirements/recommendations for international students: Required—TOEFL (minimum score 550 paper-based; 213 computer-based; 79 iBT). Electronic applications accepted.

Chapman University, Graduate Studies, Wilkinson College of Humanities and Social Sciences, Department of English, Orange, CA 92866. Offers creative writing (MFA); English (MA). Part-time and evening/weekend programs available. *Faculty:* 22 full-time (11 women), 20 part-time/adjunct (6 women). *Students:* 32 full-time (18 women), 29 part-time (21 women); includes 12 minority (4 Black or African American, non-Hispanic/Latino; 1 Asian, non-Hispanic/Latino; 5 Hispanic/Latino; 2 Two or more races, non-Hispanic/Latino). Average age 33. 53 applicants, 70% accepted, 19 enrolled. In 2010, 26 master's awarded. *Degree requirements:* For master's, comprehensive exam (for some programs), thesis (for some programs). *Entrance requirements:* For master's, GRE or MAT, minimum undergraduate GPA of 2.5. Additional exam requirements/recommendations for international students: Required—TOEFL (minimum score 550 paper-based; 213 computer-based; 80 iBT). *Application deadline:* For fall admission, 5/1 priority date for domestic students; for winter admission, 11/1 priority date for domestic students. Applications are processed on a rolling basis. Application fee: $60. Electronic applications accepted. *Expenses:* Contact institution. *Financial support:* Fellowships, Federal Work-Study and scholarships/grants available. Financial award applicants required to submit FAFSA. *Unit head:* Dr. Mark Axelrod, Director of Graduate Programs, 714-997-6586, E-mail: axelrod@chapman.edu. *Application contact:* Priscilla Garcia Powers, Graduate Admission Counselor, 714-997-6711, E-mail: pgarcia@chapman.edu.

Chicago State University, School of Graduate and Professional Studies, College of Arts and Sciences, Department of English, Chicago, IL 60628. Offers creative writing (MFA); English (MA). *Degree requirements:* For master's, comprehensive exam. *Entrance requirements:* For master's, minimum GPA of 2.75.

The Citadel, The Military College of South Carolina, Citadel Graduate College, Department of English, Charleston, SC 29409. Offers MA. Part-time and evening/weekend programs available. *Faculty:* 5 full-time (1 woman). *Students:* 1 (woman) full-time, 4 part-time (3 women), 1 international. Average age 27. In 2010, 2 master's awarded. *Degree requirements:* For master's, one foreign language, comprehensive exam, thesis optional. *Entrance requirements:* For master's, GRE (minimum score 1400, 4 writing) or MAT (minimum score 403), minimum undergraduate GPA of 2.5 (3.0 in major); 2 letters of recommendation from former professors or recent supervisors; writing sample showing ability to perform literary analysis and to conduct research. Additional exam requirements/recommendations for international students: Required—TOEFL (minimum score 550 paper-based; 213 computer-based). *Application deadline:* Applications are processed on a rolling basis. Application fee: $30. Electronic applications accepted. *Expenses:* Tuition, state resident: part-time $460 per credit hour. Tuition, nonresident: part-time $756 per credit hour. Required fees: $40 per term. *Financial support:* Research assistantships, career-related internships or fieldwork, health care benefits, and unspecified assistantships available. Support available to part-time students. Financial award application deadline: 7/1; financial award applicants required to submit FAFSA. *Faculty research:* Renaissance literature; eighteenth and nineteenth century British literature; eighteenth, nineteenth, and twentieth century American literature. *Unit head:* Dr. David G. Allen, Department Head, 843-953-5134, Fax: 843-953-1881, E-mail: david.allen@citadel.edu. *Application contact:* Dr. James M. Hutchisson, Graduate Coordinator, 843-953-5139, Fax: 843-953-1881, E-mail: jim.hutchisson@citadel.edu.

City College of the City University of New York, Graduate School, College of Liberal Arts and Science, Division of the Humanities and Arts, Department of English, Program in English and American Literature, New York, NY 10031-9198. Offers MA. *Degree requirements:* For master's, one foreign language, comprehensive exam, thesis. *Entrance requirements:* For master's, minimum GPA of 3.0. Additional exam requirements/recommendations for international students: Required—TOEFL (minimum score 600 paper-based; 100 iBT). Electronic applications accepted.

Claremont Graduate University, Graduate Programs, School of Arts and Humanities, Department of English, Claremont, CA 91711-6160. Offers American studies (MA, PhD); critical theory (MA, PhD); early modern studies (MA, PhD); English (M Phil, MA, PhD); literary theory (PhD); literature (MA, PhD); literature and creative writing (MA); literature and film (MA); MBA/MA; MBA/PhD. Part-time programs available. *Faculty:* 2 full-time (both women), 4 part-time/adjunct (1 woman). *Students:* 88 full-time (56 women), 14 part-time (12 women); includes 1 Black or African American, non-Hispanic/Latino; 9 Asian, non-Hispanic/Latino; 7 Hispanic/Latino; 5 Two or more races, non-Hispanic/Latino, 7 international. Average age 34. In 2010, 9 master's, 10 doctorates awarded. *Entrance requirements:* For master's and doctorate, GRE General Test. Additional exam requirements/recommendations for international students: Required—TOEFL (minimum score 550 paper-based; 213 computer-based; 80 iBT). *Application deadline:* For fall admission, 2/1 priority date for domestic students. Applications are processed on a rolling basis. Application fee: $60. Electronic applications accepted. *Expenses:* Tuition: Full-time $35,748; part-time $1554 per unit. Required fees: $215 per semester. *Financial support:* Fellowships, Federal Work-Study, institutionally sponsored loans, and scholarships/grants available. Support available to part-time students. Financial award application deadline: 2/15; financial award applicants required to submit FAFSA. *Faculty research:* American, comparative, and English Renaissance literature; modernism; feminist literature and theory. *Unit head:* Elysabeth Flores Griffith, Administrative Director, 909-607-3877, E-mail: elysabeth.flores@cgu.edu. *Application contact:* Susan Hampson, Admissions Coordinator, 909-607-1278, Fax: 909-607-1221, E-mail: humanities@cgu.edu.

Clarion University of Pennsylvania, Office of Research and Graduate Studies, College of Arts and Sciences, Department of English, Clarion, PA 16214. Offers MA. *Degree requirements:* For master's, thesis optional. *Entrance requirements:* For master's, GRE General Test, minimum QPA of 2.75. Additional exam requirements/recommendations for international students:

Required—TOEFL (minimum score 550 paper-based; 213 computer-based; 80 iBT). Electronic applications accepted.

Clark Atlanta University, School of Arts and Sciences, Department of English, Atlanta, GA 30314. Offers MA, DAH. Part-time programs available. *Faculty:* 5 full-time (3 women). *Students:* 3 full-time (all women), 18 part-time (14 women); includes all Black or African American, non-Hispanic/Latino. Average age 33. 6 applicants, 100% accepted, 3 enrolled. In 2010, 1 master's awarded. *Degree requirements:* For master's, one foreign language, comprehensive exam, thesis; for doctorate, 2 foreign languages, comprehensive exam, thesis/dissertation. *Entrance requirements:* For master's, GRE General Test, minimum GPA of 2.5. Additional exam requirements/recommendations for international students: Required—TOEFL (minimum score 500 paper-based; 173 computer-based; 61 iBT). *Application deadline:* For fall admission, 4/1 for domestic and international students; for spring admission, 11/1 for domestic and international students. Applications are processed on a rolling basis. Application fee: $40 ($55 for international students). *Expenses:* Tuition: Full-time $12,942; part-time $719 per credit hour. Required fees: $710; $355 per semester. *Financial support:* Career-related internships or fieldwork, Federal Work-Study, scholarships/grants, and unspecified assistantships available. Support available to part-time students. Financial award application deadline: 4/30; financial award applicants required to submit FAFSA. *Unit head:* Dr. Alma Vineyard, Chairperson, 404-880-6067, E-mail: avineyard@cau.edu. *Application contact:* Michelle Clark-Davis, Graduate Program Admissions, 404-880-6605, E-mail: cauadmissions@cau.edu.

Clark University, Graduate School, Department of English, Worcester, MA 01610-1477. Offers MA. Part-time programs available. *Faculty:* 10 full-time (7 women), 4 part-time/adjunct (3 women). *Students:* 11 full-time (5 women), 2 part-time (0 women), 6 international. Average age 29. 23 applicants, 78% accepted, 11 enrolled. In 2010, 12 master's awarded. *Degree requirements:* For master's, thesis, oral exam. *Entrance requirements:* For master's, GRE Subject Test. Additional exam requirements/recommendations for international students: Required—TOEFL. *Application deadline:* For fall admission, 2/1 priority date for domestic students. Applications are processed on a rolling basis. Application fee: $50. *Expenses:* Tuition: Full-time $37,000; part-time $1156 per credit hour. Required fees: $30; $1156 per credit hour. *Financial support:* In 2010–11, research assistantships with full and partial tuition reimbursements (averaging $10,300 per year), 4 teaching assistantships with full and partial tuition reimbursements (averaging $10,300 per year) were awarded; fellowships, career-related internships or fieldwork and tuition waivers (partial) also available. Support available to part-time students. Financial award application deadline: 2/15. *Faculty research:* Writings of James Fenimore Cooper, Renaissance literature, American literature, medieval literature, Victorian literature. *Unit head:* Dr. Jay Elliott, Chair, 508-793-7142. *Application contact:* Terri Rutkiewicz, Academic Secretary, 508-793-7142, Fax: 508-793-8892, E-mail: engma@clarku.edu.

Clemson University, Graduate School, College of Architecture, Arts, and Humanities, Department of English, Program in English, Clemson, SC 29634. Offers MA. Part-time and evening/weekend programs available. *Students:* 21 full-time (13 women), 11 part-time (8 women); includes 3 Black or African American, non-Hispanic/Latino; 1 Hispanic/Latino. Average age 27. 37 applicants, 49% accepted, 10 enrolled. In 2010, 20 master's awarded. *Degree requirements:* For master's, one foreign language, thesis. *Entrance requirements:* For master's, GRE, 2 letters of recommendation, writing sample (at least 8-10 pages), statement of purpose, transcripts for all undergraduate work. Additional exam requirements/recommendations for international students: Required—TOEFL. *Application deadline:* For fall admission, 2/1 for domestic and international students. Application fee: $70 ($80 for international students). Electronic applications accepted. *Expenses:* Tuition, state resident: full-time $6492; part-time $400 per credit hour. Tuition, nonresident: full-time $13,634; part-time $800 per credit hour. Required fees: $262 per semester. Part-time tuition and fees vary according to course load and program. *Financial support:* In 2010–11, 20 students received support, including 1 fellowship with full and partial tuition reimbursement available (averaging $4,800 per year), 13 teaching assistantships with partial tuition reimbursements available (averaging $13,001 per year); research assistantships with partial tuition reimbursements available, institutionally sponsored loans, scholarships/grants, and unspecified assistantships also available. Financial award application deadline: 2/1. *Faculty research:* Literary studies, textual studies, cultural studies, critical theory, new media. *Unit head:* Barton Palmer, Interim Chair, 864-656-3151, Fax: 864-656-1345, E-mail: ppalmer@clemson.edu. *Application contact:* Dr. Catherine Paul, Graduate Program Contact, 864-656-3543, Fax: 864-656-1345, E-mail: cpaul@clemson.edu.

Clemson University, Graduate School, College of Health, Education, and Human Development, Eugene T. Moore School of Education, Program in Early Childhood Education, Clemson, SC 29634. Offers early childhood education (M Ed); elementary education (M Ed); secondary English (M Ed); secondary math (M Ed); secondary science (M Ed); secondary social studies (M Ed). Part-time and evening/weekend programs available. In 2010, 3 master's awarded. *Degree requirements:* For master's, comprehensive exam. *Entrance requirements:* For master's, GRE, valid teaching certificate. Additional exam requirements/recommendations for international students: Required—TOEFL; Recommended—IELTS. *Application deadline:* Applications are processed on a rolling basis. Application fee: $70 ($80 for international students). Electronic applications accepted. *Expenses:* Contact institution. *Financial support:* Institutionally sponsored loans, health care benefits, and unspecified assistantships available. Financial award application deadline: 3/1; financial award applicants required to submit FAFSA. *Faculty research:* Elementary education, mathematics education, social studies education, English education, science education. *Unit head:* Dr. Michael J. Padilla, Director/ Associate Dean, 864-656-4444, Fax: 864-656-0311, E-mail: padilla@clemson.edu. *Application contact:* Dr. David Fleming, Graduate Programs Coordinator, 864-656-1881, Fax: 864-656-0311, E-mail: dflemin@clemson.edu.

Cleveland State University, College of Graduate Studies, College of Liberal Arts and Social Sciences, Department of English, Cleveland, OH 44115. Offers creative writing (MFA); English (MA). Part-time and evening/weekend programs available. *Faculty:* 8 full-time (2 women), 5 part-time/adjunct (1 woman). *Students:* 14 full-time (9 women), 64 part-time (43 women); includes 15 Black or African American, non-Hispanic/Latino; 1 Asian, non-Hispanic/Latino; 1 Hispanic/Latino, 2 international. Average age 34. 59 applicants, 61% accepted, 16 enrolled. In 2010, 17 master's awarded. *Degree requirements:* For master's, comprehensive exam, thesis. *Entrance requirements:* For master's, minimum GPA of 2.75, undergraduate concentration in English, writing sample, portfolio. Additional exam requirements/recommendations for international students: Required—TOEFL (525 paper-based; 197 computer-based) or IELTS (6 paper-based). *Application deadline:* For fall admission, 7/15 priority date for domestic students, 5/15 for international students; for spring admission, 12/15 for domestic students, 11/1 for international students. Applications are processed on a rolling basis. Application fee: $30. Electronic applications accepted. *Expenses:* Tuition, state resident: full-time $8447; part-time $469 per credit hour. Tuition, nonresident: full-time $16,020; part-time $890 per credit hour. Required fees: $50. *Financial support:* In 2010–11, 20 students received support, including 1 fellowship (averaging $1,000 per year), 5 research assistantships with full and partial tuition reimbursements available (averaging $3,480 per year), 7 teaching assistantships with full and partial tuition reimbursements available (averaging $3,480 per year); Federal Work-Study, institutionally sponsored loans, tuition waivers (full and partial), and unspecified assistantships also available. Support available to part-time students. Financial award application deadline: 2/15. *Faculty research:* Literary history and criticism, linguistics, literature. Total annual research expenditures: $5,000. *Unit head:* Dr. David M. Larson, Chairperson, 216-687-3951, Fax: 216-687-6943, E-mail: d.larson@csuohio.edu. *Application contact:* Dr. Jennifer M. Jeffers, Graduate Director, 216-687-3975, Fax: 216-687-6943, E-mail: j.m.jeffers53@csuohio.edu.

The College at Brockport, State University of New York, School of the Arts, Humanities and Social Sciences, Department of English, Brockport, NY 14420-2997. Offers English (MA), including creative writing, literature. Part-time programs available. *Students:* 20 full-time (14 women), 31 part-time (18 women). 25 applicants, 44% accepted, 10 enrolled. In 2010, 15 master's awarded. *Degree requirements:* For master's, thesis. *Entrance requirements:* For master's, minimum GPA of 3.0, letters of recommendation, writing sample. Additional exam requirements/recommendations for international students: Required—TOEFL (minimum score 550 paper-based; 213 computer-based; 79 iBT). *Application deadline:* For fall admission, 4/15 priority date for domestic and international students; for spring admission, 11/15 priority date for domestic and international students. Application fee: $50. Electronic applications accepted. *Financial support:* In 2010–11, 3 teaching assistantships with full tuition reimbursements (averaging $6,000 per year) were awarded; Federal Work-Study, scholarships/grants, and unspecified assistantships also available. Support available to part-time students. Financial award application deadline: 3/15; financial award applicants required to submit FAFSA. *Faculty research:* British and American literature, creative writing, film studies, children's literature, ancient and modern world literature. *Unit head:* Dr. J. Roger Kurtz, Chairperson, 585-395-2503, Fax: 585-395-2391, E-mail: rkurtz@brockport.edu. *Application contact:* Dr. Miriam Burstein, Graduate Program Director, 585-395-5827, Fax: 585-395-2391, E-mail: mburstei@brockport.edu.

College of Charleston, Graduate School, School of Humanities and Social Sciences, Program in English, Charleston, SC 29424-0001. Offers MA. Program offered jointly with The Citadel, The Military College of South Carolina. Part-time and evening/weekend programs available. *Faculty:* 34 full-time (20 women). *Students:* 18 full-time (13 women), 7 part-time (5 women). Average age 29. 25 applicants, 56% accepted, 12 enrolled. In 2010, 15 master's awarded. *Degree requirements:* For master's, one foreign language, comprehensive exam, thesis optional. *Entrance requirements:* For master's, GRE General Test or MAT, minimum GPA of 2.5 overall, 3.0 in major; 2 letters of recommendation; writing sample. Additional exam requirements/recommendations for international students: Required—TOEFL (minimum score 81 iBT). *Application deadline:* For fall admission, 5/1 for domestic students; for spring admission, 11/1 for domestic students. Application fee: $45. Electronic applications accepted. *Financial support:* In 2010–11, 5 research assistantships (averaging $12,400 per year) were awarded; fellowships, scholarships/grants and unspecified assistantships also available. Financial award application deadline: 4/1; financial award applicants required to submit FAFSA. *Unit head:* Dr. Susan Farrell, Director, 843-953-5664, Fax: 843-953-3180, E-mail: farrells@cofc.edu. *Application contact:* Susan Hallatt, Director of Graduate Admissions, 843-953-5614, Fax: 843-953-1434, E-mail: hallatts@cofc.edu.

The College of New Jersey, Graduate Division, School of Culture and Society, Department of English, Program in English, Ewing, NJ 08628. Offers MA. Part-time programs available. *Students:* 6 full-time (all women), 32 part-time (24 women); includes 3 minority (1 Black or African American, non-Hispanic/Latino; 2 Hispanic/Latino). 38 applicants, 55% accepted, 11 enrolled. In 2010, 5 master's awarded. *Degree requirements:* For master's, comprehensive exam. *Entrance requirements:* For master's, GRE, minimum GPA of 3.0 in field or 2.75 overall. Additional exam requirements/recommendations for international students: Required—TOEFL. *Application deadline:* For fall admission, 2/1 priority date for domestic students; for spring admission, 10/1 priority date for domestic students. Application fee: $70. Electronic applications accepted. *Financial support:* Tuition waivers (partial) and unspecified assistantships available. Financial award application deadline: 5/1; financial award applicants required to submit FAFSA. *Unit head:* Dr. Michele Lise Tarter, Coordinator. *Application contact:* Susan L. Hydro, Assistant Dean, Office of Graduate Studies, 609-771-2300, Fax: 609-637-5105, E-mail: graduate@tcnj.edu.

The College of Saint Rose, Graduate Studies, School of Arts and Humanities, Department of English, Albany, NY 12203-1419. Offers MA. Part-time and evening/weekend programs available. *Degree requirements:* For master's, thesis optional, advanced project. *Entrance requirements:* For master's, 24 credits in English, minimum undergraduate GPA of 3.2, writing sample. Additional exam requirements/recommendations for international students: Required—TOEFL (minimum score 550 paper-based; 213 computer-based). Electronic applications accepted.

College of Staten Island of the City University of New York, Graduate Programs, Program in English, Staten Island, NY 10314-6600. Offers MA. Part-time and evening/weekend programs available. *Faculty:* 4 full-time (3 women), 2 part-time/adjunct (both women). *Students:* 5 full-time (3 women), 31 part-time (24 women); includes 1 Black or African American, non-Hispanic/Latino; 1 Asian, non-Hispanic/Latino; 1 Hispanic/Latino, 1 international. Average age 31. 23 applicants, 65% accepted, 11 enrolled. In 2010, 8 master's awarded. *Degree requirements:* For master's, comprehensive exam, 3-hour written exam, 2 papers. *Entrance requirements:* For master's, 32 undergraduate credits in English, minimum GPA of 3.0. Additional exam requirements/recommendations for international students: Required—TOEFL (minimum score 550 paper-based; 213 computer-based; 79 iBT), IELTS (minimum score 6.5). *Application deadline:* For fall admission, 7/15 for domestic and international students; for spring admission, 12/15 for domestic and international students. Applications are processed on a rolling basis. Application fee: $125. Electronic applications accepted. *Expenses:* Tuition, state resident: full-time $7730; part-time $325 per credit. Tuition, nonresident: full-time $14,520; part-time $605 per credit. Required fees: $378. *Financial support:* In 2010–11, 1 student received support. Career-related internships or fieldwork, Federal Work-Study, and scholarships/grants available. Support available to part-time students. Financial award applicants required to submit FAFSA. *Unit head:* Dr. Maryann Feola, Coordinator, 718-982-3666, Fax: 718-982-3643, E-mail: englishmasters@mail.csi.cuny.edu. *Application contact:* Sasha Spence, Assistant Director of Graduate Recruitment Admissions, 718-982-2699, Fax: 718-982-2500, E-mail: sasha.spence@csi.cuny.edu.

Colorado State University, Graduate School, College of Liberal Arts, Department of English, Fort Collins, CO 80523-1773. Offers creative writing (MFA); English (MA). Part-time programs available. *Faculty:* 30 full-time (19 women), 1 part-time/adjunct (0 women). *Students:* 101 full-time (60 women), 46 part-time (32 women); includes 11 minority (1 American Indian or Alaska Native, non-Hispanic/Latino; 4 Asian, non-Hispanic/Latino; 5 Hispanic/Latino; 1 Two or more races, non-Hispanic/Latino), 15 international. Average age 30. 362 applicants, 26% accepted, 53 enrolled. In 2010, 48 master's awarded. *Degree requirements:* For master's, variable foreign language requirement, thesis (for some programs), exams. *Entrance requirements:* For master's, GRE, writing sample, BA/BS with minimum GPA of 3.0, letters of recommendation. Additional exam requirements/recommendations for international students: Required—TOEFL (minimum score 550 paper-based; 213 computer-based; 80 iBT). *Application deadline:* For fall admission, 4/1 priority date for domestic students; for spring admission, 9/1 priority date for domestic students. Applications are processed on a rolling basis. Application fee: $50. Electronic applications accepted. *Expenses:* Tuition, state resident: full-time $7434; part-time $413 per credit. Tuition, nonresident: full-time $19,022; part-time $1057 per credit. Required fees: $1729; $88 per credit. *Financial support:* In 2010–11, 40 students received support, including 40 teaching assistantships with full tuition reimbursements available (averaging $12,377 per year); fellowships, research assistantships, career-related internships or fieldwork, Federal Work-Study, institutionally sponsored loans, scholarships/grants, traineeships, and unspecified assistantships also available. Support available to part-time students. Financial award application deadline: 5/1; financial award applicants required to submit FAFSA. *Faculty research:* Computers and writing, environmental writing, cultural studies, new historicism, performance and identity. Total annual research expenditures: $58,341. *Unit head:* Dr. Bruce Ronda, Chair, 970-491-6428, Fax: 970-491-5601, E-mail: bruce.ronda@colostate.edu. *Application contact:* Marnie Leonard, Administrative Assistant, 970-491-2403, Fax: 970-491-7541, E-mail: marnie.leonard@colostate.edu.

Columbia University, Graduate School of Arts and Sciences, Division of Humanities, Department of English and Comparative Literature, New York, NY 10027. Offers comparative literature (M Phil, MA, PhD); English literature (M Phil, MA, PhD); literature-writing (M Phil, MA, PhD). Part-time programs available. *Degree requirements:* For master's, one foreign language, comprehensive exam, seminar papers; for doctorate, thesis/dissertation. *Entrance requirements:* For master's and doctorate, GRE General Test. Additional exam requirements/recommendations for international students: Required—TOEFL. *Faculty research:* Medieval through modern literature, drama, literary criticism.

Columbia University, Graduate School of Arts and Sciences, Program in History and Literature, 75006 Paris, NY 10027, France. Offers MA. Courses taught in English or French. *Entrance*

English

Columbia University (continued)

requirements: For master's, GRE General Test, curriculum vitae, official transcripts, statement of purpose, writing sample, three letters of recommendation. Additional exam requirements/recommendations for international students: Required—TOEFL.

Concordia University, School of Graduate Studies, Faculty of Arts and Science, Department of English, Program in English, Montréal, QC H3G 1M8, Canada. Offers MA. *Degree requirements:* For master's, one foreign language, thesis optional. *Entrance requirements:* For master's, honors degree in English, minimum GPA of 3.3 in English literature.

Converse College, School of Education and Graduate Studies, Program in Liberal Arts, Spartanburg, SC 29302-0006. Offers English (MLA); history (MLA); political science (MLA). *Degree requirements:* For master's, capstone paper. *Entrance requirements:* For master's, minimum GPA of 3.0, 2 recommendations. *Expenses:* Tuition: Part-time $365 per credit hour.

Cornell University, Graduate School, Graduate Fields of Arts and Sciences, Field of English Language and Literature, Ithaca, NY 14853-0001. Offers African-American literature (PhD); American literature after 1865 (PhD); American literature to 1865 (PhD); American studies (PhD); colonial and postcolonial literature (PhD); creative writing (MFA); cultural studies (PhD); dramatic literature (PhD); English poetry (PhD); English Renaissance to 1660 (PhD); lesbian, bisexual, and gay literature studies (PhD); literary criticism and theory (PhD); nineteenth century (PhD); Old and Middle English (PhD); prose fiction (PhD); Restoration and eighteenth century (PhD); twentieth century (PhD); women's literature (PhD); MFA/PhD. *Faculty:* 56 full-time (29 women). *Students:* 100 full-time (56 women); includes 5 Black or African American, non-Hispanic/Latino; 3 American Indian or Alaska Native, non-Hispanic/Latino; 10 Asian, non-Hispanic/Latino; 8 Hispanic/Latino, 12 international. Average age 27. 1,091 applicants, 4% accepted, 21 enrolled. In 2010, 25 master's, 12 doctorates awarded. Terminal master's awarded for partial completion of doctoral program. *Degree requirements:* For master's, one foreign language, thesis; for doctorate, one foreign language, comprehensive exam, thesis/dissertation, teaching experience. *Entrance requirements:* For master's, GRE General Test, 3 letters of recommendation, creative writing sample; for doctorate, GRE General Test, GRE Subject Test (English), 3 letters of recommendation, writing sample. Additional exam requirements/recommendations for international students: Required—TOEFL (minimum score 600 paper-based; 250 computer-based; 77 iBT). *Application deadline:* For fall admission, 1/10 for domestic students. Application fee: $80. Electronic applications accepted. *Expenses:* Tuition: Full-time $29,500. Required fees: $76. Tuition and fees vary according to degree level and program. *Financial support:* In 2010–11, 32 fellowships with full tuition reimbursements, 60 teaching assistantships with full tuition reimbursements were awarded; research assistantships with full tuition reimbursements, institutionally sponsored loans, scholarships/grants, health care benefits, tuition waivers (full and partial), and unspecified assistantships also available. Financial award applicants required to submit FAFSA. *Faculty research:* English and American literature, women's writing, ethnic and post-colonial literature, critical theory, medievalism. *Unit head:* Director of Graduate Studies, 607-255-7989, Fax: 607-255-6661. *Application contact:* Graduate Field Assistant, 607-255-7989, Fax: 607-255-6661, E-mail: english_grad@cornell.edu.

Cornell University, Graduate School, Graduate Fields of Arts and Sciences, Field of Linguistics, Ithaca, NY 14853-0001. Offers applied linguistics (MA, PhD); East Asian linguistics (MA, PhD); English linguistics (MA, PhD); general linguistics (MA, PhD); Germanic linguistics (MA, PhD); Indo-European linguistics (MA, PhD); phonetics (MA, PhD); phonological theory (MA, PhD); Romance linguistics (MA, PhD); second language acquisition (MA, PhD); semantics (MA, PhD); Slavic linguistics (MA, PhD); sociolinguistics (MA, PhD); South Asian linguistics (MA, PhD); Southeast Asian linguistics (MA, PhD); syntactic theory (MA, PhD). *Faculty:* 15 full-time (7 women). *Students:* 34 full-time (18 women); includes 3 Hispanic/Latino, 15 international. Average age 28. 111 applicants, 12% accepted, 8 enrolled. In 2010, 2 master's, 6 doctorates awarded. Terminal master's awarded for partial completion of doctoral program. *Degree requirements:* For master's, one foreign language, thesis; for doctorate, one foreign language, comprehensive exam, thesis/dissertation. *Entrance requirements:* For master's and doctorate, GRE General Test, 2 letters of recommendation. Additional exam requirements/recommendations for international students: Required—TOEFL (minimum score 600 paper-based; 250 computer-based; 77 iBT). *Application deadline:* For fall admission, 1/15 for domestic students. Application fee: $80. Electronic applications accepted. *Expenses:* Tuition: Full-time $29,500. Required fees: $76. Tuition and fees vary according to degree level and program. *Financial support:* In 2010–11, 17 fellowships with full tuition reimbursements, 1 research assistantship with full tuition reimbursement, 15 teaching assistantships with full tuition reimbursements were awarded; institutionally sponsored loans, scholarships/grants, health care benefits, tuition waivers (full and partial), and unspecified assistantships also available. Financial award applicants required to submit FAFSA. *Faculty research:* Phonology and phonetics, syntax and semantics, historical linguistics, philosophy of language, language acquisition. *Unit head:* Director of Graduate Studies, 607-255-1105. *Application contact:* Graduate Field Assistant, 607-255-1105, E-mail: lingfield@cornell.edu.

Creighton University, Graduate School, College of Arts and Sciences, Department of English, Omaha, NE 68178-0001. Offers creative writing (MA). Part-time programs available. *Faculty:* 16 full-time (8 women). *Students:* 11 full-time (6 women), 3 part-time (1 woman); includes 1 minority (Hispanic/Latino), 3 international. Average age 26. 13 applicants, 85% accepted, 2 enrolled. In 2010, 2 master's awarded. *Degree requirements:* For master's, thesis optional. *Entrance requirements:* For master's, GRE, 10-15 page writing sample, 3 letters of recommendation. Additional exam requirements/recommendations for international students: Required—TOEFL (minimum score 550 paper-based; 213 computer-based; 80 iBT). *Application deadline:* For fall admission, 3/15 priority date for domestic and international students. Application fee: $50. Electronic applications accepted. *Expenses:* Tuition: Full-time $12,168; part-time $676 per credit hour. Required fees: $131 per semester. Tuition and fees vary according to program. *Financial support:* In 2010–11, 5 fellowships with full and partial tuition reimbursements (averaging $10,698 per year) were awarded; tuition waivers (partial) and unspecified assistantships also available. Financial award applicants required to submit FAFSA. *Unit head:* Dr. Brent Spencer, Director, 402-280-2292, E-mail: brentspencer@creighton.edu. *Application contact:* Taunya Plater, Senior Program Coordinator, 402-280-2870, Fax: 402-280-2899, E-mail: taunyaplater@creighton.edu.

Dalhousie University, Faculty of Arts and Social Science, Department of English, Halifax, NS B3H 4R2, Canada. Offers MA, PhD. *Entrance requirements:* Additional exam requirements/recommendations for international students: Required—TOEFL, IELTS, CANTEST, CAEL, or Michigan English Language Assessment Battery. Electronic applications accepted. *Faculty research:* Victorian, Canadian, Renaissance, eighteenth century, and modern literature.

DePaul University, College of Liberal Arts and Sciences, Department of English, Chicago, IL 60614. Offers English (MA); writing and publishing (MA). Part-time and evening/weekend programs available. *Faculty:* 29 full-time (12 women). *Students:* 132 full-time (93 women), 63 part-time (47 women); includes 33 minority (13 Black or African American, non-Hispanic/Latino; 6 Asian, non-Hispanic/Latino; 10 Hispanic/Latino; 4 Two or more races, non-Hispanic/Latino), 3 international. Average age 27. 95 applicants, 56% accepted. In 2010, 100 master's awarded. *Degree requirements:* For master's, written exam. *Entrance requirements:* Additional exam requirements/recommendations for international students: Required—TOEFL. *Application deadline:* For fall admission, 7/1 priority date for domestic students; for winter admission, 10/1 priority date for domestic students; for spring admission, 2/1 priority date for domestic students. Applications are processed on a rolling basis. Application fee: $40. Electronic applications accepted. *Financial support:* In 2010–11, 2 research assistantships with full tuition reimbursements, 7 teaching assistantships with full tuition reimbursements (averaging $7,500 per year) were awarded; fellowships with partial tuition reimbursements, career-related internships or fieldwork, institutionally sponsored loans, scholarships/grants, tuition waivers (partial), and unspecified assistantships also available. Support available to part-time students. Financial award application deadline: 4/1. *Faculty research:* Rhetoric and composition, technical writing, creative writing, linguistics, literacy theory. *Unit head:* Dr. Janet Hickey, Chairperson, 773-325-4635, E-mail: jhicke11@depaul.edu. *Application contact:* Dr. Lesley Kordecki, Director, 773-325-1786, Fax: 773-325-8607, E-mail: lkordeck@depaul.edu.

Drew University, Caspersen School of Graduate Studies, Program in Education, Madison, NJ 07940-1493. Offers biology (MAT); chemistry (MAT); English (MAT); French (MAT); Italian (MAT); math (MAT); physics (MAT); social studies (MAT); Spanish (MAT); theatre arts (MAT). Part-time programs available. *Entrance requirements:* For master's, transcripts, personal statement, recommendations. Additional exam requirements/recommendations for international students: Required—TOEFL, TWE. *Expenses:* Contact institution.

Duke University, Graduate School, Department of English, Durham, NC 27708. Offers PhD, JD/AM. *Faculty:* 30 full-time. *Students:* 61 full-time (33 women); includes 5 Black or African American, non-Hispanic/Latino; 1 American Indian or Alaska Native, non-Hispanic/Latino; 2 Asian, non-Hispanic/Latino; 3 Hispanic/Latino, 8 international. 384 applicants, 5% accepted, 11 enrolled. In 2010, 21 doctorates awarded. *Degree requirements:* For doctorate, 2 foreign languages, thesis/dissertation. *Entrance requirements:* For doctorate, GRE General Test, writing sample. Additional exam requirements/recommendations for international students: Required—TOEFL (minimum score 550 paper-based; 213 computer-based; 83 iBT), IELTS (minimum score 7). *Application deadline:* For fall admission, 12/8 priority date for domestic and international students. Application fee: $75. Electronic applications accepted. *Financial support:* Fellowships, research assistantships, teaching assistantships, Federal Work-Study available. Financial award application deadline: 12/8. *Unit head:* Kathy Psomiades, Director of Graduate Studies, 919-684-5538, Fax: 919-684-4871, E-mail: maryscot.mullins@duke.edu. *Application contact:* Elizabeth Hutton, Director, Graduate Admissions, 919-684-3913, Fax: 919-684-2277, E-mail: grad-admissions@duke.edu.

Duquesne University, Graduate School of Liberal Arts, Program in English, Pittsburgh, PA 15282-0001. Offers MA, PhD. Part-time and evening/weekend programs available. *Faculty:* 17 full-time (10 women), 29 part-time/adjunct (17 women). *Students:* 69 full-time (52 women), 6 part-time (4 women), 2 international. Average age 25. 92 applicants, 52% accepted, 22 enrolled. In 2010, 14 master's, 9 doctorates awarded. *Degree requirements:* For master's, comprehensive exam, thesis or alternative; for doctorate, 2 foreign languages, comprehensive exam, thesis/dissertation. *Entrance requirements:* For master's and doctorate, GRE General Test, bachelor's degree in English, writing sample. Additional exam requirements/recommendations for international students: Required—TOEFL. *Application deadline:* For fall admission, 2/1 priority date for domestic and international students. Applications are processed on a rolling basis. Electronic applications accepted. *Expenses:* Tuition: Part-time $884 per credit. Required fees: $84 per credit. Tuition and fees vary according to course load. *Financial support:* In 2010–11, 22 teaching assistantships with full tuition reimbursements (averaging $15,000 per year) were awarded; research assistantships, Federal Work-Study, scholarships/grants, tuition waivers (partial), and unspecified assistantships also available. Support available to part-time students. Financial award application deadline: 5/1. *Unit head:* Dr. Magali Michael, Chair, 412-396-6420. *Application contact:* Dr. Susan Howard, Director of Graduate Studies, 412-396-6420.

East Carolina University, Graduate School, Thomas Harriot College of Arts and Sciences, Department of English, Greenville, NC 27858-4353. Offers MA. Part-time and evening/weekend programs available. *Degree requirements:* For master's, one foreign language, comprehensive exam, thesis optional. *Entrance requirements:* For master's, GRE General Test, MAT (MA Ed). Additional exam requirements/recommendations for international students: Required—TOEFL. *Expenses:* Tuition, state resident: full-time $3130; part-time $391.25 per credit hour. Tuition, nonresident: full-time $13,817; part-time $1727.13 per credit hour. Required fees: $1916; $239.50 per credit hour. Tuition and fees vary according to campus/location and program.

Eastern Illinois University, Graduate School, College of Arts and Humanities, Department of English, Charleston, IL 61920-3099. Offers MA. Part-time programs available. *Entrance requirements:* For master's, GRE General Test.

Eastern Kentucky University, The Graduate School, College of Arts and Sciences, Department of English and Theatre, Richmond, KY 40475-3102. Offers creative writing (MFA); English (MA). Part-time and evening/weekend programs available. *Degree requirements:* For master's, thesis optional. *Entrance requirements:* For master's, GRE General Test, minimum GPA of 2.5, minor in English with 3.0 GPA. *Faculty research:* Old English, Victorian studies, women's studies, rhetoric, popular culture, novel studies.

Eastern Michigan University, Graduate School, College of Arts and Sciences, Department of English Language and Literature, Program in Children's Literature, Ypsilanti, MI 48197. Offers MA. Part-time and evening/weekend programs available. Postbaccalaureate distance learning degree programs offered (minimal on-campus study). *Students:* 3 full-time (2 women), 12 part-time (10 women), 2 international. Average age 32. In 2010, 18 master's awarded. *Entrance requirements:* Additional exam requirements/recommendations for international students: Required—TOEFL. *Application deadline:* Applications are processed on a rolling basis. Application fee: $35. *Financial support:* Fellowships, research assistantships with full tuition reimbursements, teaching assistantships with full tuition reimbursements, tuition waivers (partial) available. Financial award applicants required to submit FAFSA. *Application contact:* Dr. Annette Wannamaker, Program Advisor, 734-487-0148, Fax: 734-483-9744, E-mail: awannamak@emich.edu.

Eastern Michigan University, Graduate School, College of Arts and Sciences, Department of English Language and Literature, Program in English Linguistics, Ypsilanti, MI 48197. Offers MA. Part-time and evening/weekend programs available. Postbaccalaureate distance learning degree programs offered (minimal on-campus study). *Students:* 14 full-time (7 women), 11 part-time (7 women); includes 3 minority (1 Black or African American, non-Hispanic/Latino; 2 Asian, non-Hispanic/Latino), 10 international. Average age 27. In 2010, 5 master's awarded. *Degree requirements:* For master's, thesis (for some programs). *Entrance requirements:* Additional exam requirements/recommendations for international students: Required—TOEFL. *Application deadline:* Applications are processed on a rolling basis. Application fee: $35. *Financial support:* Fellowships with tuition reimbursements, research assistantships with full tuition reimbursements, teaching assistantships with full tuition reimbursements, career-related internships or fieldwork, Federal Work-Study, institutionally sponsored loans, scholarships/grants, tuition waivers (partial), and unspecified assistantships available. Support available to part-time students. Financial award applicants required to submit FAFSA. *Application contact:* Dr. Veronica Grondona, Program Advisor, 734-487-0145, Fax: 734-483-9744, E-mail: vgrondona@emich.edu.

Eastern Michigan University, Graduate School, College of Arts and Sciences, Department of English Language and Literature, Program in Literature, Ypsilanti, MI 48197. Offers MA, Graduate Certificate. Part-time and evening/weekend programs available. Postbaccalaureate distance learning degree programs offered (minimal on-campus study). *Students:* 11 full-time (3 women), 28 part-time (16 women); includes 3 minority (1 Black or African American, non-Hispanic/Latino; 1 Asian, non-Hispanic/Latino; 1 Two or more races, non-Hispanic/Latino), 1 international. Average age 27. In 2010, 19 master's awarded. *Entrance requirements:* Additional exam requirements/recommendations for international students: Required—TOEFL. *Application deadline:* Applications are processed on a rolling basis. Application fee: $35. *Financial support:* Fellowships, research assistantships with full tuition reimbursements, teaching assistantships with full tuition reimbursements, career-related internships or fieldwork, Federal Work-Study, institutionally sponsored loans, scholarships/grants, tuition waivers (partial), and unspecified assistantships available. Support available to part-time students. Financial award applicants required to submit FAFSA. *Application contact:* Dr. Andrea Kaston-Tange, Program Coordinator, 734-487-2296, Fax: 734-483-9744, E-mail: akaston@emich.edu.

Eastern New Mexico University, Graduate School, College of Liberal Arts and Sciences, Department of Languages and Literature, Portales, NM 88130. Offers English (MA), including English, literatures and cultures of migration. Part-time programs available. *Faculty:* 7 full-time (5 women). *Students:* 6 full-time (3 women), 8 part-time (7 women); includes 4 minority (1 Black or African American, non-Hispanic/Latino; 3 Hispanic/Latino). Average age 31. 8 applicants, 63% accepted, 5 enrolled. In 2010, 4 master's awarded. *Degree requirements:* For master's, one foreign language, thesis, oral and written comprehensive exams. *Entrance requirements:* For master's, minimum GPA of 3.0, foreign language proficiency, interview. Additional exam requirements/recommendations for international students: Required—TOEFL (minimum score 550 paper-based; 213 computer-based; 79 iBT), IELTS (minimum score 6). *Application deadline:* For fall admission, 7/20 priority date for domestic students, 6/20 priority date for international students; for spring admission, 12/15 priority date for domestic students, 11/15 priority date for international students. Applications are processed on a rolling basis. Application fee: $10. Electronic applications accepted. *Expenses:* Tuition, state resident: full-time $3210; part-time $130 per credit hour. Tuition, nonresident: full-time $8652; part-time $360.50 per credit hour. Required fees: $1212; $50.50 per credit hour. Tuition and fees vary according to course load. *Financial support:* In 2010–11, 10 research assistantships with partial tuition reimbursements (averaging $8,500 per year) were awarded; tuition waivers (partial) and unspecified assistantships also available. Support available to part-time students. Financial award applicants required to submit FAFSA. *Unit head:* Dr. Linda Sumption, Graduate Coordinator, 575-562-2136, Fax: 575-562-2142, E-mail: linda.sumption@emnu.edu. *Application contact:* Sharon Johnson, Department Secretary, 575-562-2423, Fax: 575-562-2142, E-mail: sharon.johnson@enmu.edu.

Eastern Washington University, Graduate Studies, College of Arts and Letters, Department of English, Cheney, WA 99004-2431. Offers literature (MA); rhetoric, composition, and technical communication (MA); teaching English as a second language (MA). *Degree requirements:* For master's, comprehensive exam, thesis or alternative. *Entrance requirements:* For master's, GRE General Test, minimum GPA of 3.0.

East Tennessee State University, School of Graduate Studies, College of Arts and Sciences, Department of Languages and Literature, Johnson City, TN 37614. Offers MA, Certificate. Part-time and evening/weekend programs available. *Faculty:* 19 full-time (9 women). *Students:* 13 full-time (7 women), 3 part-time (all women), 1 international. Average age 27. 25 applicants, 36% accepted, 7 enrolled. In 2010, 10 master's awarded. *Degree requirements:* For master's, comprehensive exam, thesis optional. *Entrance requirements:* For master's, GRE General Test, minimum undergraduate GPA of 3.0 in English, writing samples. Additional exam requirements/recommendations for international students: Required—TOEFL (minimum score 550 paper-based; 213 computer-based; 79 iBT). *Application deadline:* For fall admission, 6/1 priority date for domestic students, 4/30 for international students; for spring admission, 11/1 priority date for domestic students, 9/30 for international students. Application fee: $25 ($35 for international students). Electronic applications accepted. *Financial support:* In 2010–11, 3 research assistantships with full tuition reimbursements (averaging $5,000 per year), 12 teaching assistantships with full tuition reimbursements (averaging $5,000 per year) were awarded; career-related internships or fieldwork, institutionally sponsored loans, scholarships/grants, and unspecified assistantships also available. Financial award application deadline: 7/1; financial award applicants required to submit FAFSA. *Faculty research:* Appalachian studies, women's studies, sports images in religion, British and American literature. *Unit head:* Dr. Judith B. Slagle, Chair, 423-439-4339, Fax: 423-439-7193, E-mail: slagle@etsu.edu. *Application contact:* Admissions and Records Clerk, 423-439-4221, Fax: 423-439-5624, E-mail: gradsch@etsu.edu.

Elmhurst College, Graduate Programs, Program in English Studies, Elmhurst, IL 60126-3296. Offers MA. Part-time and evening/weekend programs available. *Faculty:* 2 full-time (1 woman). *Students:* 15 part-time (13 women); includes 4 minority (2 Black or African American, non-Hispanic/Latino; 2 Asian, non-Hispanic/Latino). Average age 26. 11 applicants, 36% accepted, 2 enrolled. In 2010, 10 master's awarded. *Degree requirements:* For master's, thesis optional. *Entrance requirements:* For master's, 3 recommendations, resume, statement of purpose. Additional exam requirements/recommendations for international students: Required—TOEFL (minimum score 550 paper-based; 213 computer-based). *Application deadline:* Applications are processed on a rolling basis. Application fee: $0. Electronic applications accepted. *Expenses:* Contact institution. *Financial support:* In 2010–11, 2 students received support. Federal Work-Study and scholarships/grants available. Support available to part-time students. Financial award application deadline: 6/1; financial award applicants required to submit FAFSA. *Unit head:* Elizabeth D. Kuebler, Director of Adult and Graduate Admission, 630-617-3300, Fax: 630-617-5501, E-mail: sal@elmhurst.edu. *Application contact:* Elizabeth D. Kuebler, Director of Adult and Graduate Admission, 630-617-3300, Fax: 630-617-5501, E-mail: sal@elmhurst.edu.

Emory University, Laney Graduate School, Department of Comparative Literature, Atlanta, GA 30322-1100. Offers comparative literature (PhD); English (Certificate); French (Certificate); Middle Eastern studies (PhD); philosophy (Certificate); psychoanalytic studies (PhD); religion (PhD); Spanish (Certificate); women studies (Certificate). *Degree requirements:* For doctorate, 2 foreign languages, comprehensive exam, thesis/dissertation. *Entrance requirements:* For doctorate, GRE General Test, minimum GPA of 3.0. Additional exam requirements/recommendations for international students: Required—TOEFL. Electronic applications accepted. *Expenses:* Tuition: Full-time $33,800. Required fees: $1300. *Faculty research:* Literary theory, psychoanalysis trauma and testimony, literature and religion, literature and technology, literature and philosophy, politics and global culture, literature and aesthetics.

Emory University, Laney Graduate School, Department of English, Atlanta, GA 30322-1100. Offers PhD. *Degree requirements:* For doctorate, one foreign language, comprehensive exam, thesis/dissertation. *Entrance requirements:* For doctorate, GRE General Test, minimum GPA of 3.0. Additional exam requirements/recommendations for international students: Required—TOEFL. Electronic applications accepted. *Expenses:* Tuition: Full-time $33,800. Required fees: $1300. *Faculty research:* American literature, renaissance literature, twentieth century poetry, Irish literature, cultural studies.

Emporia State University, Graduate School, College of Liberal Arts and Sciences, Department of English, Modern Languages and Journalism, Emporia, KS 66801-5087. Offers English (MA); teaching English to speakers of other languages (MA). Part-time programs available. *Faculty:* 28 full-time (16 women), 3 part-time/adjunct (2 women). *Students:* 10 full-time (5 women), 34 part-time (23 women); includes 6 minority (1 American Indian or Alaska Native, non-Hispanic/Latino; 1 Asian, non-Hispanic/Latino; 2 Hispanic/Latino; 2 Two or more races, non-Hispanic/Latino), 4 international. 13 applicants, 77% accepted, 6 enrolled. In 2010, 20 master's awarded. *Degree requirements:* For master's, comprehensive exam or thesis. *Entrance requirements:* For master's, appropriate undergraduate degree, writing sample. Additional exam requirements/recommendations for international students: Required—TOEFL (minimum score 520 paper-based; 133 computer-based; 68 iBT). *Application deadline:* For fall admission, 8/15 priority date for domestic students. Applications are processed on a rolling basis. Application fee: $30 ($75 for international students). Electronic applications accepted. *Expenses:* Tuition, state resident: full-time $4382; part-time $183 per credit hour. Tuition, nonresident: full-time $13,572; part-time $566 per credit hour. Required fees: $1022; $62 per credit hour. Tuition and fees vary according to course level, course load and campus/location. *Financial support:* In 2010–11, 11 teaching assistantships with full tuition reimbursements (averaging $7,579 per year) were awarded; Federal Work-Study, institutionally sponsored loans, health care benefits, and unspecified assistantships also available. Financial award application deadline: 3/15; financial award applicants required to submit FAFSA. *Unit head:* Dr. Marie Miller, Interim Chair, 620-341-5216, E-mail: mmiller@emporia.edu. *Application contact:* Dr. Mel Storm, Graduate Coordinator, 620-341-5563, E-mail: mstorm@emporia.edu.

Fairleigh Dickinson University, Metropolitan Campus, University College: Arts, Sciences, and Professional Studies, Department of English, Philosophy, and Humanities, Program in English and Literature, Teaneck, NJ 07666-1914. Offers MA. *Students:* 2 part-time (both women). Average age 24. In 2010, 4 master's awarded. Application fee: $40. *Application contact:* Susan Brooman, University Director of Graduate Admissions, 201-692-2554, Fax: 201-692-2560, E-mail: globaleducation@fdu.edu.

Fayetteville State University, Graduate School, Program in English, Fayetteville, NC 28301-4298. Offers MA. Part-time and evening/weekend programs available. *Faculty:* 14 full-time (9 women). *Students:* 1 (woman) full-time, 3 part-time (2 women); includes 1 minority (Black or African American, non-Hispanic/Latino). Average age 29. In 2010, 3 master's awarded. *Degree requirements:* For master's, comprehensive exam, thesis, internship. *Entrance requirements:* For master's, GRE General Test. *Application deadline:* For fall admission, 4/15 for domestic students; for spring admission, 10/15 for domestic students. Applications are processed on a rolling basis. Application fee: $35. Electronic applications accepted. *Faculty research:* Online film culture; literature and pre-Raphaelite, Symbolist, and Surrealist painting; aesthetics of African-American gospel music; power of sheltered instruction. Total annual research expenditures: $19,000. *Unit head:* Dr. Edward McShane, Chairperson, 910-672-1416, E-mail: emcshane@uncsfu.edu. *Application contact:* Katrina Hoffman, Graduate Admission Officer, 910-672-1374, Fax: 910-672-1470, E-mail: khoffma1@uncfsu.edu.

Fitchburg State University, Division of Graduate and Continuing Education, Programs in English and Teaching English (Secondary Level), Fitchburg, MA 01420-2697. Offers MA, MAT, Certificate. *Accreditation:* NCATE. Part-time and evening/weekend programs available. *Students:* 1 full-time (0 women), 28 part-time (19 women). Average age 33. 12 applicants, 100% accepted, 7 enrolled. In 2010, 10 master's awarded. *Entrance requirements:* For master's, GRE General Test or MAT, letters of recommendation, resume. Additional exam requirements/recommendations for international students: Required—TOEFL (minimum score 550 paper-based; 213 computer-based; 79 iBT). *Application deadline:* Applications are processed on a rolling basis. Application fee: $25 ($50 for international students). *Expenses:* Tuition, area resident: Part-time $150 per credit. Tuition, state resident: part-time $150 per credit. Tuition, nonresident: part-time $150 per credit. Required fees: $127 per credit. *Financial support:* In 2010–11, research assistantships with partial tuition reimbursements (averaging $5,500 per year), Federal Work-Study, scholarships/grants, and unspecified assistantships also available. Support available to part-time students. Financial award application deadline: 3/1; financial award applicants required to submit FAFSA. *Unit head:* Dr. Chola Chisunka, Chair, 978-665-3445, Fax: 978-665-3658, E-mail: gce@fitchburgstate.edu. *Application contact:* Director of Admissions, 978-665-3144, Fax: 978-665-4540, E-mail: admissions@fitchburgstate.edu.

Florida Atlantic University, Dorothy F. Schmidt College of Arts and Letters, Department of English, Boca Raton, FL 33431-0991. Offers British and American literature (MA); creative nonfiction (MFA); creative writing (MA); fiction (MFA); multicultural literatures and literacies (MA); poetry (MFA); science fiction and fantasy (MA); teaching English (MAT). Part-time programs available. *Faculty:* 59 full-time (32 women), 3 part-time/adjunct (2 women). *Students:* 33 full-time (17 women), 25 part-time (18 women); includes 14 minority (2 Black or African American, non-Hispanic/Latino; 1 Asian, non-Hispanic/Latino; 11 Hispanic/Latino). Average age 30. 60 applicants, 47% accepted, 20 enrolled. In 2010, 20 master's awarded. *Degree requirements:* For master's, one foreign language, thesis. *Entrance requirements:* For master's, GRE General Test, minimum GPA of 3.0, writing samples, 2 letters of recommendation. *Application deadline:* For fall admission, 3/1 for domestic students, 2/15 for international students; for spring admission, 11/1 for domestic students, 7/15 for international students. Applications are processed on a rolling basis. Application fee: $30. Electronic applications accepted. *Expenses:* Tuition, area resident: Part-time $319.96 per credit. Tuition, state resident: part-time $319.96 per credit. Tuition, nonresident: part-time $926.42 per credit. *Financial support:* Fellowships, teaching assistantships with partial tuition reimbursements, Federal Work-Study and tuition waivers available. Support available to part-time students. Financial award application deadline: 3/1. *Faculty research:* African-American writers, critical theory, British-American, Asian-American. *Unit head:* Dr. Wenying Xu, Chair, 561-297-2065, Fax: 561-297-3807, E-mail: wxu@fau.edu. *Application contact:* Dr. Andrew Furman, Director of Graduate Studies, 561-297-3835, Fax: 561-297-3807, E-mail: afurman@fau.edu.

Florida Gulf Coast University, College of Arts and Sciences, Program in English, Fort Myers, FL 33965-6565. Offers MA. *Faculty:* 187 full-time (78 women), 177 part-time/adjunct (70 women). *Students:* 11 full-time (5 women), 15 part-time (10 women); includes 1 Black or African American, non-Hispanic/Latino; 3 Hispanic/Latino. Average age 30. 34 applicants, 62% accepted, 17 enrolled. In 2010, 8 master's awarded. *Entrance requirements:* For master's, GRE General Test, minimum GPA of 3.0. Additional exam requirements/recommendations for international students: Required—TOEFL (minimum score 550 paper-based; 213 computer-based). *Application deadline:* For fall admission, 2/15 for domestic students. Application fee: $30. *Expenses:* Tuition, state resident: part-time $322.08 per credit hour. Tuition, nonresident: part-time $1117.08 per credit hour. *Unit head:* Joe Wisdom, Chair, 239-590-7157, E-mail: jwisdom@fgcu.edu. *Application contact:* Patricia Rice, Executive Secretary, 239-590-7196, Fax: 239-590-7200, E-mail: price@fgcu.edu.

Florida International University, College of Arts and Sciences, Department of English, Program in English, Miami, FL 33199. Offers literature (MA). Part-time and evening/weekend programs available. *Students:* 10 full-time (8 women), 23 part-time (15 women); includes 1 Black or African American, non-Hispanic/Latino; 1 Asian, non-Hispanic/Latino; 21 Hispanic/Latino. Average age 28. 25 applicants, 44% accepted, 11 enrolled. In 2010, 11 master's awarded. *Degree requirements:* For master's, thesis. *Entrance requirements:* For master's, GRE General Test, minimum GPA of 3.0, letters of recommendation, letter of intent. Additional exam requirements/recommendations for international students: Required—TOEFL (minimum score 550 paper-based; 80 iBT). *Application deadline:* For fall admission, 2/1 for domestic and international students; for spring admission, 10/1 for domestic students, 9/1 for international students. Application fee: $30. Electronic applications accepted. *Financial support:* Institutionally sponsored loans and scholarships/grants available. Financial award application deadline: 3/1; financial award applicants required to submit FAFSA. *Unit head:* Dr. James Sutton, Chair, English Department, 305-348-2874, Fax: 305-348-3878, E-mail: james.sutton@fiu.edu. *Application contact:* Dr. Asher Milbauer, Director of Graduate Studies in Literature, 305-348-2259, Fax: 305-348-3878, E-mail: milbauer@fiu.edu.

Florida State University, The Graduate School, College of Arts and Sciences, Department of English, Tallahassee, FL 32312. Offers creative writing (MFA); English (PhD), including creative writing, literature, rhetoric and composition; literature (MA); rhetoric and composition (MA). Part-time programs available. *Faculty:* 48 full-time (23 women), 6 part-time/adjunct (1 woman). *Students:* 150 full-time (90 women), 20 part-time (10 women); includes 15 Black or African American, non-Hispanic/Latino; 1 American Indian or Alaska Native, non-Hispanic/Latino; 5 Asian, non-Hispanic/Latino; 10 Hispanic/Latino. Average age 30. 480 applicants, 21% accepted, 58 enrolled. In 2010, 22 master's, 14 doctorates awarded. *Degree requirements:* For master's, one foreign language, thesis or alternative; for doctorate, comprehensive exam, thesis/dissertation, 27 hours of coursework, 24 hours of dissertation work. *Entrance requirements:* For master's and doctorate, GRE General Test, GRE Subject Test (literature only), sample of written work, 3 letters of recommendation, resume. Additional exam requirements/recommendations for international students: Required—TOEFL. *Application deadline:* For fall admission, 1/1 priority date for domestic and international students. Application fee: $30. Electronic applications accepted. *Expenses:* Tuition, state resident: full-time $8238.24. *Financial support:* In 2010–11, 126 students received support, including 5 fellowships, teaching assistantships (averaging $11,375 per year); career-related internships or fieldwork, Federal Work-Study, and institutionally sponsored loans also available. Financial award application deadline: 1/1; financial award applicants required to submit FAFSA. *Faculty research:* British and Irish literature, American literature, creative writing, rhetoric and composition, multiethnic transnational literature. *Unit head:* Dr. Ralph Berry, Chairman, 850-644-4230, Fax: 850-644-0811, E-mail: rberry@fsu.edu. *Application contact:* Dr. Ralph Berry, Chairman, 850-644-4230, Fax: 850-644-0811, E-mail: rberry@fsu.edu.

English

Fordham University, Graduate School of Arts and Sciences, Department of English Language and Literature, New York, NY 10458. Offers MA, PhD. Part-time and evening/weekend programs available. *Faculty:* 37 full-time (23 women). *Students:* 75 full-time (56 women), 84 part-time (53 women); includes 3 Black or African American, non-Hispanic/Latino; 7 Hispanic/Latino, 5 international. Average age 30. 216 applicants, 36% accepted, 30 enrolled. In 2010, 10 master's, 9 doctorates awarded. Terminal master's awarded for partial completion of doctoral program. *Degree requirements:* For master's, one foreign language, comprehensive exam, thesis optional; for doctorate, 2 foreign languages, comprehensive exam, thesis/dissertation. *Entrance requirements:* For master's, GRE General Test; for doctorate, GRE General Test, GRE Subject Test. Additional exam requirements/recommendations for international students: Required—TOEFL (minimum score 650 paper-based; 280 computer-based). *Application deadline:* For fall admission, 1/4 priority date for domestic students; for spring admission, 11/1 for domestic students. Application fee: $70. Electronic applications accepted. *Financial support:* In 2010–11, 63 students received support, including 2 fellowships with tuition reimbursements available (averaging $21,900 per year), 27 research assistantships with tuition reimbursements available (averaging $18,461 per year), 34 teaching assistantships with tuition reimbursements available (averaging $14,917 per year); institutionally sponsored loans, tuition waivers (full and partial), and unspecified assistantships also available. Financial award application deadline: 1/4; financial award applicants required to submit FAFSA. *Faculty research:* Nineteenth-century British and American literature, Shakespeare and early modern drama, Aesthetic theory, Old Norse, poetics of race and gender, Anglo-Norman. Total annual research expenditures: $22,000. *Unit head:* Dr. Nicola Pitchford, Chair, 718-817-4007, Fax: 718-817-4010, E-mail: pitchford@fordham.edu. *Application contact:* Charlene Dundie, Director of Graduate Admissions, 718-817-4420, Fax: 718-817-3566, E-mail: dundie@fordham.edu.

Fort Hays State University, Graduate School, College of Arts and Sciences, Department of English, Hays, KS 67601-4099. Offers MA. *Degree requirements:* For master's, comprehensive exam, thesis or alternative. *Entrance requirements:* Additional exam requirements/recommendations for international students: Required—TOEFL (minimum score 550 paper-based; 213 computer-based). Electronic applications accepted. *Faculty research:* Eisenhower and Hansen papers, Celtic literature and culture, poetry of Robert Frost.

Gannon University, School of Graduate Studies, College of Humanities, Education, and Social Sciences, School of Humanities, Program in English, Erie, PA 16541-0001. Offers MA. Part-time and evening/weekend programs available. *Students:* 7 full-time (6 women), 9 part-time (6 women), 2 international. Average age 29. 24 applicants, 67% accepted, 0 enrolled. In 2010, 8 master's awarded. *Degree requirements:* For master's, thesis. *Entrance requirements:* For master's, GRE, interview. Additional exam requirements/recommendations for international students: Required—TOEFL (minimum score 79 iBT). *Application deadline:* Applications are processed on a rolling basis. Application fee: $25. Electronic applications accepted. *Expenses:* Tuition: Full-time $14,670; part-time $815 per credit. Required fees: $430; $18 per credit. Tuition and fees vary according to class time, course load, degree level, campus/location and program. *Financial support:* In 2010–11, 5 teaching assistantships (averaging $6,300 per year) were awarded; career-related internships or fieldwork, scholarships/grants, and unspecified assistantships also available. Financial award application deadline: 7/1; financial award applicants required to submit FAFSA. *Unit head:* Dr. Penelope Smith, Director, 814-871-7748, E-mail: smith006@gannon.edu. *Application contact:* Kara Morgan, Assistant Director of Graduate Admissions, 814-871-5831, Fax: 814-871-5827, E-mail: graduate@gannon.edu.

Gardner-Webb University, Graduate School, Department of English, Boiling Springs, NC 28017. Offers English (MA); English education (MA). Part-time and evening/weekend programs available. *Faculty:* 2 full-time (both women), 1 (woman) part-time/adjunct. *Students:* 14 part-time (10 women); includes 4 Black or African American, non-Hispanic/Latino. Average age 31. 4 applicants, 100% accepted, 4 enrolled. In 2010, 1 master's awarded. *Degree requirements:* For master's, comprehensive exam. *Entrance requirements:* For master's, GRE General Test, MAT, or NTE; PRAXIS, minimum GPA of 2.5. *Application deadline:* For fall admission, 8/1 priority date for domestic students. Applications are processed on a rolling basis. Application fee: $40. Electronic applications accepted. *Expenses:* Tuition: Part-time $325 per credit hour. *Financial support:* Unspecified assistantships available. *Unit head:* Dr. June Hobbs, Chair, 704-406-4412, Fax: 704-406-3921, E-mail: jhobbs@gardner-webb.edu. *Application contact:* Office of Graduate Admisisons, 877-498-4723, Fax: 704-406-3895, E-mail: gradinfo@gardner-webb.edu.

George Mason University, College of Humanities and Social Sciences, Department of English, Fairfax, VA 22030. Offers creative writing (MFA); English (MA); folklore studies (Certificate); linguistics (PhD); professional writing and rhetoric (Certificate); teaching English as a second language (Certificate). *Faculty:* 82 full-time (45 women), 35 part-time/adjunct (22 women). *Students:* 69 full-time (45 women), 208 part-time (153 women); includes 13 Black or African American, non-Hispanic/Latino; 3 American Indian or Alaska Native, non-Hispanic/Latino; 20 Asian, non-Hispanic/Latino; 6 Hispanic/Latino; 4 Two or more races, non-Hispanic/Latino, 10 international. Average age 31. 391 applicants, 56% accepted, 96 enrolled. In 2010, 116 master's, 11 other advanced degrees awarded. *Degree requirements:* For master's, thesis (for some programs), proficiency in a foreign language by course work or translation test. *Entrance requirements:* For master's, 30 credits in graduate English courses, minimum undergraduate GPA of 3.0, 2 letters of recommendation. Additional exam requirements/recommendations for international students: Required—TOEFL (minimum score 570 paper-based; 230 computer-based; 88 iBT). *Application deadline:* For fall admission, 3/15 priority date for domestic students; for spring admission, 10/15 for domestic students. Application fee: $100. Electronic applications accepted. *Expenses:* Tuition, state resident: full-time $8192; part-time $440 per credit hour. Tuition, nonresident: full-time $22,952; part-time $1055 per credit hour. Required fees: $2364; $99 per credit hour. *Financial support:* In 2010–11, 50 students received support, including 2 fellowships with full tuition reimbursements available (averaging $18,000 per year), 5 research assistantships with full and partial tuition reimbursements available (averaging $11,251 per year), 44 teaching assistantships with full and partial tuition reimbursements available (averaging $11,009 per year); Federal Work-Study, scholarships/grants, unspecified assistantships, and health care benefits (full-time research or teaching assistantship recipients) also available. Financial award application deadline: 3/1; financial award applicants required to submit FAFSA. *Faculty research:* Literature, professional writing and editing, writing of fiction or poetry. Total annual research expenditures: $1.2 million. *Unit head:* Robert Matz, Chair, 703-993-1170, E-mail: rmatz@gmu.edu. *Application contact:* Denise Albanese, Graduate Director, 703-993-1175, E-mail: dalbanes@gmu.edu.

Georgetown University, Graduate School of Arts and Sciences, Department of English, Washington, DC 20057. Offers British and American literature (MA). *Degree requirements:* For master's, thesis or alternative, independent study, oral exam. *Entrance requirements:* For master's, GRE General Test. Additional exam requirements/recommendations for international students: Required—TOEFL.

The George Washington University, Columbian College of Arts and Sciences, Department of English, Washington, DC 20052. Offers MA, PhD. Part-time and evening/weekend programs available. *Faculty:* 32 full-time (14 women), 17 part-time/adjunct (10 women). *Students:* 22 full-time (12 women), 24 part-time (19 women); includes 2 Black or African American, non-Hispanic/Latino; 2 Asian, non-Hispanic/Latino; 1 Hispanic/Latino, 2 international. Average age 29. 123 applicants, 26% accepted, 12 enrolled. In 2010, 11 master's, 5 doctorates awarded. Terminal master's awarded for partial completion of doctoral program. *Degree requirements:* For master's, one foreign language, comprehensive exam, thesis or alternative; for doctorate, 2 foreign languages, thesis/dissertation, general exam. *Entrance requirements:* For master's and doctorate, GRE General Test, GRE Subject Test, minimum GPA of 3.0, writing sample. Additional exam requirements/recommendations for international students: Required—TOEFL (minimum score 550 paper-based; 213 computer-based; 80 iBT). *Application deadline:* For fall admission, 1/15 priority date for domestic and international students; for spring admission, 10/1 priority date for domestic students, 9/1 priority date for international students. Applications are processed on a rolling basis. Application fee: $75. Electronic applications accepted. *Financial support:* In 2010–11, 18 students received support; fellowships with tuition reimbursements available, teaching assistantships with tuition reimbursements available, Federal Work-Study available. Financial award application deadline: 1/15. *Unit head:* Jeffrey Jerome Cohen, Chair, 202-994-6180, E-mail: jjcohen@gwu.edu. *Application contact:* Jeffrey Jerome Cohen, Chair, 202-994-6180, E-mail: jjcohen@gwu.edu.

Georgia College & State University, Graduate School, College of Arts and Sciences, Department of English and Rhetoric, Program in English, Milledgeville, GA 31061. Offers MA. Part-time and evening/weekend programs available. *Students:* 6 full-time (4 women), 10 part-time (6 women); includes 1 minority (Black or African American, non-Hispanic/Latino). Average age 27. 10 applicants, 70% accepted, 3 enrolled. *Degree requirements:* For master's, one foreign language, comprehensive exam, thesis optional. *Entrance requirements:* For master's, GRE (minimum score 550 verbal, 4.5 analytical), undergraduate major in English, minimum GPA of 3.0, 2 letters of recommendation. Additional exam requirements/recommendations for international students: Recommended—TOEFL (minimum score 550 paper-based; 213 computer-based; 79 iBT). *Application deadline:* For fall admission, 7/1 priority date for domestic students, 4/1 priority date for international students; for spring admission, 11/15 priority date for domestic students, 9/1 priority date for international students. Applications are processed on a rolling basis. Application fee: $40. Electronic applications accepted. *Expenses:* Tuition, state resident: full-time $4806; part-time $267 per hour. Tuition, nonresident: full-time $17,802; part-time $989 per hour. Tuition and fees vary according to course load. *Financial support:* In 2010–11, 5 research assistantships with full tuition reimbursements were awarded; unspecified assistantships also available. Financial award applicants required to submit FAFSA. *Unit head:* Dr. Elaine Whitaker, Chair, Department of English and Rhetoric, 478-445-4581, E-mail: elaine.whitaker@gcsu.edu. *Application contact:* Dr. Elaine Whitaker, Chair, Department of English and Rhetoric, 478-445-4581, E-mail: elaine.whitaker@gcsu.edu.

Georgia Southern University, Jack N. Averitt College of Graduate Studies, College of Liberal Arts and Social Sciences, Department of Literature and Philosophy, Statesboro, GA 30460. Offers English (MA). Part-time programs available. *Students:* 12 full-time (7 women), 7 part-time (5 women); includes 2 Two or more races, non-Hispanic/Latino, 1 international. Average age 26. 9 applicants, 89% accepted, 6 enrolled. In 2010, 11 master's awarded. *Degree requirements:* For master's, one foreign language, thesis optional, terminal exams. *Entrance requirements:* For master's, GRE General Test, minimum GPA of 3.0, letters of reference. Additional exam requirements/recommendations for international students: Required—TOEFL (minimum score 550 paper-based; 213 computer-based; 80 iBT). *Application deadline:* For fall admission, 3/1 priority date for domestic and international students; for spring admission, 10/1 priority date for domestic students, 10/1 for international students. Applications are processed on a rolling basis. Application fee: $50. Electronic applications accepted. *Expenses:* Tuition, state resident: full-time $6000; part-time $250 per semester hour. Tuition, nonresident: full-time $23,976; part-time $999 per semester hour. Required fees: $1644. *Financial support:* In 2010–11, 16 students received support, including research assistantships with partial tuition reimbursements available (averaging $7,200 per year), teaching assistantships with partial tuition reimbursements available (averaging $7,200 per year); career-related internships or fieldwork, Federal Work-Study, scholarships/grants, tuition waivers (partial), and unspecified assistantships also available. Support available to part-time students. Financial award application deadline: 4/15; financial award applicants required to submit FAFSA. *Faculty research:* Memory and language in James Joyce and Samuel Beckett; bibliography of American short-story writer Andre Dubus II; biography of Indian novelist Bharati Mukherjee; children's poetry, post-modern childhood, poetry of Randall Jarrell and Gwendolyn Brooks; message of the Hebrew Prophets, the Genesis narratives literary Gothic; writings of eighteenth and nineteenth century British nonconformist poets, diarists, pamphleteers, and letter writers. Total annual research expenditures: $33,600. *Unit head:* David Dudley, Chair, 912-478-5471, Fax: 912-478-0653, E-mail: dldudley@georgiasouthern.edu. *Application contact:* Dr. Charles Ziglar, Coordinator for Graduate Student Recruitment, 912-478-5635, Fax: 912-478-0740, E-mail: gradadmissions@georgiasouthern.edu.

Georgia State University, College of Arts and Sciences, Department of English, Atlanta, GA 30302-3083. Offers creative writing (MA, MFA, PhD), including fiction/poetry; English (MA, PhD); fiction (MFA); literary studies (MA, PhD); poetry (MFA); rhetoric and composition (MA, PhD). Part-time and evening/weekend programs available. *Degree requirements:* For master's, variable foreign language requirement, thesis; for doctorate, one foreign language, comprehensive exam, thesis/dissertation, second exam. *Entrance requirements:* For master's and doctorate, GRE General Test. Additional exam requirements/recommendations for international students: Required—TOEFL (minimum score 0 paper-based; 0 computer-based). Electronic applications accepted. *Faculty research:* Literature, theory, culture, rhetoric/composition, professional/technical writing.

Governors State University, College of Arts and Sciences, Program in English, University Park, IL 60466-0975. Offers MA. Part-time and evening/weekend programs available. *Degree requirements:* For master's, thesis or alternative. *Entrance requirements:* For master's, bachelor's degree in related field. *Expenses:* Tuition, state resident: full-time $5400; part-time $225 per credit hour. Tuition, nonresident: full-time $16,200; part-time $675 per credit hour. Required fees: $1358; $46 per credit hour. $126 per term. Tuition and fees vary according to degree level and program.

Graduate School and University Center of the City University of New York, Graduate Studies, Program in English, New York, NY 10016-4039. Offers PhD. *Degree requirements:* For doctorate, 2 foreign languages, thesis/dissertation. *Entrance requirements:* For doctorate, GRE General Test, GRE Subject Test, writing sample, curriculum vitae. Additional exam requirements/recommendations for international students: Required—TOEFL. Electronic applications accepted.

Grambling State University, School of Graduate Studies and Research, College of Education, Department of Educational Leadership, Grambling, LA 71245. Offers curriculum and instruction (Ed D); developmental education (MS, Ed D), including curriculum and instruction: reading (Ed D), English (MS), guidance and counseling (MS), higher education administration (Ed D), instructional systems and technology (Ed D), mathematics (MS), reading (MS), science (MS), student development and personnel services (Ed D); educational leadership (MS, Ed D). Part-time and evening/weekend programs available. *Degree requirements:* For master's, comprehensive exam, thesis (for some programs); for doctorate, comprehensive exam, thesis/dissertation. *Entrance requirements:* For master's, GRE, minimum GPA of 2.5 on last degree; for doctorate, GRE (minimum 1000, 500 on Verbal), master's degree, minimum GPA of 3.0 on last degree. Additional exam requirements/recommendations for international students: Required—TOEFL (minimum score 500 paper-based; 173 computer-based; 61 iBT). Electronic applications accepted.

Grand Valley State University, College of Liberal Arts and Sciences, English Department, Allendale, MI 49401-9403. Offers MA. *Entrance requirements:* Additional exam requirements/recommendations for international students: Required—TOEFL. *Faculty research:* Literary history, philosophy and literature, feminist issues in literature.

Hardin-Simmons University, Graduate School, Cynthia Ann Parker College of Liberal Arts, Department of English, Abilene, TX 79698-0001. Offers MA. Part-time programs available. *Faculty:* 5 full-time (2 women), 1 part-time/adjunct (0 women). *Students:* 2 full-time (1 woman), 3 part-time (all women), 1 international. Average age 27. 7 applicants, 29% accepted, 1 enrolled. In 2010, 2 master's awarded. *Degree requirements:* For master's, one foreign language, comprehensive exam, thesis or alternative. *Entrance requirements:* For master's, minimum undergraduate GPA of 3.0 in English, 2.7 overall; writing sample; letters of recommendation; interview. Additional exam requirements/recommendations for international students: Required—TOEFL (minimum score 550 paper-based; 213 computer-based; 75 iBT). *Application deadline:* For fall admission, 8/15 priority date for domestic students, 4/1 for international students; for spring admission, 1/5 priority date for domestic students, 9/1 for international students. Applications are processed on a rolling basis. Application fee: $50. *Expenses:* Tuition: Full-time $12,150; part-time $675 per credit hour. Required fees: $650; $110 per semester. Tuition and fees vary according to degree level. *Financial support:* In 2010–11, 5 students received support; fellowships, scholarships/grants available. Support available to part-time students. Financial award application deadline: 6/30; financial award applicants required to submit FAFSA. *Faculty research:* Milton, Tennyson, American Romantic period, Derek Walcott, women's literature. *Unit head:* Dr. Laura Pogue, Program Director, 325-670-1366, Fax: 325-670-5859, E-mail: lpogue@hsutx.edu. *Application contact:* Dr. Nancy Kucinski, Dean of Graduate Studies, 325-670-1298, Fax: 325-670-1564, E-mail: gradoff@hsutx.edu.

Harvard University, Extension School, Cambridge, MA 02138-3722. Offers applied sciences (CAS); biotechnology (ALM); educational technologies (ALM); educational technology (CET); English for graduate and professional studies (DGP); environmental management (ALM, CEM); information technology (ALM); journalism (ALM); liberal arts (ALM); management (ALM, CM); mathematics for teaching (ALM); museum studies (ALM); premedical studies (Diploma); publication and communication (CPC). Part-time and evening/weekend programs available. *Degree requirements:* For master's, thesis. *Entrance requirements:* For master's, 3 completed graduate courses with grade of B or higher. Additional exam requirements/recommendations for international students: Required—TOEFL (minimum score 600 paper-based; 250 computer-based), TWE (minimum score 5). *Expenses:* Contact institution.

Harvard University, Graduate School of Arts and Sciences, Department of English and American Literature and Language, Cambridge, MA 02138. Offers critical theory (PhD); eighteenth-century literature (PhD); literature: nineteenth-century to the present (PhD); medieval literature and language (PhD); modern British and American literature (PhD); Renaissance literature (PhD). Terminal master's awarded for partial completion of doctoral program. *Degree requirements:* For doctorate, 2 foreign languages, thesis/dissertation, oral exam. *Entrance requirements:* For doctorate, GRE General Test, GRE Subject Test, writing sample. Additional exam requirements/recommendations for international students: Required—TOEFL. *Expenses:* Tuition: Full-time $34,976. Required fees: $1166. Full-time tuition and fees vary according to program. *Faculty research:* Old and Middle English language and literature, drama, creative writing, transition to Romanticism, history and theory of criticism.

Heritage University, Graduate Programs in Education, Program in Professional Studies, Toppenish, WA 98948-9599. Offers bilingual education/ESL (M Ed); biology (M Ed); English and literature (M Ed); reading/literacy (M Ed); special education (M Ed). Part-time and evening/weekend programs available. *Degree requirements:* For master's, comprehensive exam (for some programs), thesis (for some programs).

Hofstra University, College of Liberal Arts and Sciences, Department of English, Hempstead, NY 11549. Offers creative writing (MFA); English literature (MA). Part-time programs available. *Faculty:* 13 full-time (6 women), 1 part-time/adjunct (0 women). *Students:* 16 full-time (13 women), 15 part-time (12 women); includes 4 minority (2 Black or African American, non-Hispanic/Latino; 2 Hispanic/Latino). Average age 29. 33 applicants, 85% accepted, 8 enrolled. In 2010, 10 master's awarded. *Degree requirements:* For master's, thesis optional. *Entrance requirements:* For master's, Writing sample; Minimum GPA of 3.0 in literature courses. Additional exam requirements/recommendations for international students: Required—TOEFL (minimum score 550 paper-based; 213 computer-based; 80 iBT). *Application deadline:* Applications are processed on a rolling basis. Application fee: $70 ($75 for international students): Electronic applications accepted. *Expenses:* Tuition: Full-time $18,000; part-time $1000 per credit hour. Required fees: $970; $145 per term. Tuition and fees vary according to program. *Financial support:* In 2010–11, 10 students received support, including 2 fellowships with full and partial tuition reimbursements available (averaging $3,375 per year); research assistantships with full and partial tuition reimbursements available, Federal Work-Study, institutionally sponsored loans, scholarships/grants, and tuition waivers (full and partial) also available. Support available to part-time students. Financial award applicants required to submit FAFSA. *Faculty research:* Herman Melville, disability studies, early American literature, queer theory, trauma theory, critical theory, twentieth century popular culture, Jane Austen, Toni Morrison, John Milton, William Shakespeare, British Modernism, Renaissance studies, the long eighteenth century, Victorian literature. *Unit head:* Dr. Joseph A. Fichtelberg, Chairperson, 516-463-5455, Fax: 516-463-6395, E-mail: engjaf@hofstra.edu. *Application contact:* Carol Drummer, Dean of Graduate Admissions, 516-463-4876, Fax: 516-463-4664, E-mail: gradstudent@hofstra.edu.

Hollins University, Graduate Programs, Program in Children's Literature, Roanoke, VA 24020-1603. Offers MA, MFA. Offered during summer only. Part-time programs available. *Degree requirements:* For master's, one foreign language, comprehensive exam, thesis. *Entrance requirements:* For master's, letters of recommendation, portfolio. Additional exam requirements/recommendations for international students: Required—TOEFL (minimum score 550 paper-based; 213 computer-based; 79 iBT). Electronic applications accepted. *Faculty research:* Fantasy, children's film, young adult fiction, gender studies, mythology and folk tales, children's poetry, picture books.

Howard University, Graduate School, Department of English, Washington, DC 20059-0002. Offers MA, PhD. Part-time programs available. *Degree requirements:* For master's, one foreign language, comprehensive exam, thesis; for doctorate, 2 foreign languages, comprehensive exam, thesis/dissertation, qualifying exam. *Entrance requirements:* For master's, GRE General Test, minimum GPA of 3.0; for doctorate, GRE General Test.

Humboldt State University, Academic Programs, College of Arts, Humanities, and Social Sciences, Department of English, Arcata, CA 95521-8299. Offers English (MA), including international program, literature, teaching of writing. *Students:* 22 full-time (13 women), 4 part-time (2 women); includes 4 minority (1 American Indian or Alaska Native, non-Hispanic/Latino; 1 Asian, non-Hispanic/Latino; 1 Hispanic/Latino; 1 Two or more races, non-Hispanic/Latino). Average age 32. 30 applicants, 47% accepted, 10 enrolled. In 2010, 13 master's awarded. *Degree requirements:* For master's, variable foreign language requirement, thesis or alternative, qualifying exam. *Entrance requirements:* For master's, GRE, minimum GPA of 3.0, 3 letters of recommendation, sample of writing. Additional exam requirements/recommendations for international students: Required—TOEFL (minimum score 500 paper-based; 173 computer-based). *Application deadline:* For fall admission, 3/1 for domestic students; for spring admission, 11/1 for domestic students. Applications are processed on a rolling basis. Application fee: $55. Tuition and fees vary according to program. *Financial support:* Teaching assistantships, career-related internships or fieldwork, Federal Work-Study, and institutionally sponsored loans available. Financial award application deadline: 3/1; financial award applicants required to submit FAFSA. *Faculty research:* Teaching of writing, literature. *Unit head:* Dr. Susan Bennett, Chair, 707-826-3758, Fax: 707-826-5939, E-mail: sgb1@humboldt.edu. *Application contact:* Dr. Mary Ann Creadon, Graduate Coordinator, 707-826-3758, Fax: 707-826-5939, E-mail: maryann.creadon@humboldt.edu.

Hunter College of the City University of New York, Graduate School, School of Arts and Sciences, Department of English, Program in British and American Literature, New York, NY 10021-5085. Offers MA. Part-time and evening/weekend programs available. *Faculty:* 24 full-time (14 women), 1 part-time/adjunct (0 women). *Students:* 2 full-time (1 woman), 81 part-time (56 women); includes 6 Black or African American, non-Hispanic/Latino; 4 Asian, non-Hispanic/Latino; 7 Hispanic/Latino, 3 international. Average age 32. 81 applicants, 52% accepted, 22 enrolled. In 2010, 15 master's awarded. *Degree requirements:* For master's, one foreign language, comprehensive exam, thesis, essay. *Entrance requirements:* For master's, GRE General Test, minimum 18 credits of course work in English, excluding journalism and writing. Additional exam requirements/recommendations for international students: Required—TOEFL. *Application deadline:* For fall admission, 4/1 for domestic students, 2/1 for international students; for spring admission, 11/1 for domestic students, 9/1 for international students. Application fee: $125. *Financial support:* Federal Work-Study and tuition waivers (partial) available. Support available to part-time students. Financial award application deadline: 4/15. *Unit head:* Dr. Chri na Alfar, Associate Professor, 212-772-5187, E-mail: calfar@hunter.cuny.edu. *Application contact:* David Carlson, Education Adviser, 212-772-5074, E-mail: dcarlson@hunter.cuny.edu.

Idaho State University, Office of Graduate Studies, College of Arts and Sciences, Department of English, Pocatello, ID 83209-8056. Offers English (MA, DA); English and the teaching of English (PhD); TESOL (Post-Master's Certificate). Part-time programs available. *Degree requirements:* For master's, one foreign language, comprehensive exam, thesis optional; for doctorate, one foreign language, comprehensive exam, thesis/dissertation, 2 papers, 2 teaching internships; for Post-Master's Certificate, 6 credits of elective linguistics, practicum. *Entrance requirements:* For master's, GRE General Test (minimum 50th percentile verbal), general literature exam, minimum GPA of 3.0, 3 letters of recommendation, 5-page writing sample; for doctorate, GRE General Test, GRE Subject Test, minimum GPA of 3.5, writing examples, 3 letters of recommendation, master's degree in English; for Post-Master's Certificate, GRE (minimum 35th percentile on verbal section), bachelor's degree, minimum undergraduate GPA of 3.0 in last 2 years, 3 letters of recommendation, knowledge of second language. Additional exam requirements/recommendations for international students: Required—TOEFL (minimum score 550 paper-based; 213 computer-based; 80 iBT). Electronic applications accepted. *Faculty research:* American literature, Renaissance literature, composition and rhetoric, Intermountain West studies, ethics.

Illinois State University, Graduate School, College of Arts and Sciences, Department of English, Program in English, Normal, IL 61790-2200. Offers English (MA, MS); English studies (PhD). *Degree requirements:* For doctorate, thesis/dissertation, 2 terms of residency. *Entrance requirements:* For master's, GRE General Test, minimum GPA of 3.0 in last 60 hours; for doctorate, GRE General Test.

Indiana State University, College of Graduate and Professional Studies, College of Arts and Sciences, Department of English, Terre Haute, IN 47809. Offers English teaching (MA); history (MA); literature (MA). Part-time and evening/weekend programs available. *Degree requirements:* For master's, one foreign language, thesis optional. *Entrance requirements:* For master's, minimum GPA of 2.75 in all English courses above freshman level. Additional exam requirements/recommendations for international students: Required—TOEFL (minimum score 550 paper-based). Electronic applications accepted.

Indiana University Bloomington, University Graduate School, College of Arts and Sciences, Department of English, Bloomington, IN 47405. Offers composition, literacy, and culture (PhD); creative writing (MA, MFA), including fiction, poetry; language (MA); literature (MA, PhD); writing (MA). Part-time programs available. *Faculty:* 51 full-time (23 women). *Students:* 219 full-time (144 women), 6 part-time (4 women); includes 29 minority (6 Black or African American, non-Hispanic/Latino; 11 Asian, non-Hispanic/Latino; 8 Hispanic/Latino; 4 Two or more races, non-Hispanic/Latino), 8 international. Average age 30. 677 applicants, 8% accepted, 26 enrolled. In 2010, 31 master's, 16 doctorates awarded. Terminal master's awarded for partial completion of doctoral program. *Degree requirements:* For master's, 30-36 credit hours plus one language proficiency (for MA); 60 credit hours plus thesis (for MFA); for doctorate, one foreign language, thesis/dissertation, qualifying exam, 90 credit hours. *Entrance requirements:* For master's, GRE General Test, GRE Subject Test (for all but MFA and MA in creative writing), minimum GPA of 3.5; for doctorate, GRE General Test, GRE Subject Test, minimum GPA of 3.7. Additional exam requirements/recommendations for international students: Required—TOEFL. *Application deadline:* For fall admission, 1/2 priority date for domestic students, 12/15 for international students. Application fee: $55 ($65 for international students). Electronic applications accepted. *Financial support:* In 2010–11, 8 fellowships with full and partial tuition reimbursements (averaging $15,000 per year), 96 teaching assistantships with full tuition reimbursements (averaging $15,142 per year) were awarded; research assistantships with partial tuition reimbursements, career-related internships or fieldwork and health care benefits also available. Financial award application deadline: 2/1. *Unit head:* Jonathan Elmer, Chair, 812-855-8225, Fax: 812-855-9535, E-mail: elmerj@indiana.edu. *Application contact:* Patricia Ingham, Director of Graduate Studies, 812-855-1543, Fax: 812-855-9535, E-mail: pingham@indiana.edu.

Indiana University of Pennsylvania, School of Graduate Studies and Research, College of Humanities and Social Sciences, Department of English, Program in Composition and Teaching English to Speakers of Other Languages, Indiana, PA 15705-1087. Offers composition and teaching English to speakers of other languages (PhD); teaching English (MAT); teaching English to speakers of other languages (MA). *Faculty:* 30 full-time (12 women). *Students:* 27 full-time (17 women), 135 part-time (86 women); includes 10 minority (3 Black or African American, non-Hispanic/Latino; 5 Asian, non-Hispanic/Latino; 2 Hispanic/Latino), 40 international. Average age 39. 152 applicants, 26% accepted, 17 enrolled. In 2010, 19 doctorates awarded. *Degree requirements:* For master's, thesis optional; for doctorate, one foreign language, comprehensive exam, thesis/dissertation. *Entrance requirements:* For master's and doctorate, 2 letters of recommendation. Additional exam requirements/recommendations for international students: Required—TOEFL. *Application deadline:* For fall admission, 7/1 priority date for domestic students; for spring admission, 11/1 for domestic students. Applications are processed on a rolling basis. Application fee: $40. *Financial support:* In 2010–11, 1 fellowship (averaging $1,000 per year), 21 research assistantships with full and partial tuition reimbursements (averaging $5,716 per year), 10 teaching assistantships with partial tuition reimbursements (averaging $12,936 per year) were awarded. Financial award application deadline: 3/15; financial award applicants required to submit FAFSA. *Unit head:* Dr. Ben Rafoth, Graduate Coordinator, 724-357-2272. *Application contact:* Dr. Ben Rafoth, Graduate Coordinator, 724-357-2272.

Indiana University of Pennsylvania, School of Graduate Studies and Research, College of Humanities and Social Sciences, Department of English, Program in Literature and Criticism, Indiana, PA 15705-1087. Offers generalist (MA); literature (MA); literature and criticism (PhD). *Faculty:* 30 full-time (12 women). *Students:* 24 full-time (13 women), 102 part-time (55 women); includes 13 minority (8 Black or African American, non-Hispanic/Latino; 1 American Indian or Alaska Native, non-Hispanic/Latino; 1 Asian, non-Hispanic/Latino; 3 Hispanic/Latino), 30 international. Average age 36. 78 applicants, 54% accepted, 17 enrolled. In 2010, 15 doctorates awarded. *Degree requirements:* For master's, thesis optional; for doctorate, one foreign language, comprehensive exam, thesis/dissertation. *Entrance requirements:* For master's and doctorate, 2 letters of recommendation. Additional exam requirements/recommendations for international students: Required—TOEFL. *Application deadline:* For fall admission, 7/1 priority date for domestic students; for spring admission, 11/1 for domestic students. Applications are processed on a rolling basis. Application fee: $40. *Financial support:* In 2010–11, 7 fellowships (averaging $1,071 per year), 9 research assistantships with full and partial tuition reimbursements (averaging $6,776 per year), 11 teaching assistantships with partial tuition reimbursements (averaging $12,445 per year) were awarded. Financial award application deadline: 3/15; financial award applicants required to submit FAFSA. *Unit head:* Dr. David Downing, Graduate Coordinator, 724-357-3963, E-mail: david.downing@iup.edu. *Application contact:* Dr. David Downing, Graduate Coordinator, 724-357-3963, E-mail: david.downing@iup.edu.

Indiana University–Purdue University Fort Wayne, College of Arts and Sciences, Department of English and Linguistics, Fort Wayne, IN 46805-1499. Offers English (MA, MAT); TENL (teaching English as a new language) (Certificate). Part-time programs available. *Faculty:* 30 full-time (16 women). *Students:* 8 full-time (4 women), 29 part-time (18 women); includes 2 minority (1 Asian, non-Hispanic/Latino; 1 Hispanic/Latino). Average age 35. 15 applicants, 93% accepted, 14 enrolled. In 2010, 11 master's, 4 other advanced degrees awarded. *Degree requirements:* For master's, one foreign language, thesis (for some programs), teaching certificate (MAT). *Entrance requirements:* For master's, GRE General Test, minimum GPA of 3.0, major or minor in English, 3 letters of recommendation; for Certificate, bachelor's degree with minimum GPA of 2.5. Additional exam requirements/recommendations for international students: Required—TOEFL (minimum score 600 paper-based; 260 computer-based; 77 iBT). *Application deadline:* For fall admission, 8/1 for domestic students; for spring admission, 10/15 for domestic students. Applications are processed on a rolling basis. Application fee: $50. *Expenses:* Tuition, state resident: full-time $4824; part-time $268 per credit. Tuition, nonresident:

English

Indiana University–Purdue University Fort Wayne (continued)
full-time $11,625; part-time $646 per credit. Required fees: $555; $30.85 per credit. Tuition and fees vary according to course load. *Financial support:* In 2010–11, 12 teaching assistantships with partial tuition reimbursements (averaging $12,740 per year) were awarded; career-related internships or fieldwork, scholarships/grants, and unspecified assistantships also available. Support available to part-time students. Financial award application deadline: 3/1; financial award applicants required to submit FAFSA. *Faculty research:* Shakespeare, influence in creative writing, work ethic. Total annual research expenditures: $58,767. *Unit head:* Dr. Hardin Aasand, Chair and Professor, 260-481-6750, Fax: 260-481-6985, E-mail: aasandh@ipfw.edu. *Application contact:* Dr. Michael Stapleton, Graduate Program Director, 260-481-6772, Fax: 260-481-6985, E-mail: stapletm@ipfw.edu.

Indiana University–Purdue University Indianapolis, School of Liberal Arts, Department of English, Indianapolis, IN 46202-2896. Offers English (MA); teaching English (MA). *Faculty:* 20 full-time (8 women). *Students:* 22 full-time (19 women), 20 part-time (13 women); includes 4 minority (2 Black or African American, non-Hispanic/Latino; 1 Hispanic/Latino; 1 Two or more races, non-Hispanic/Latino). Average age 32. 29 applicants, 72% accepted, 14 enrolled. In 2010, 22 master's awarded. *Entrance requirements:* For master's, GRE. Application fee: $55 ($65 for international students). *Financial support:* In 2010–11, 2 fellowships (averaging $10,000 per year), 12 teaching assistantships (averaging $7,103 per year) were awarded; research assistantships, career-related internships or fieldwork also available. *Unit head:* Susanmarie Harrington, Chair, 317-274-1153. *Application contact:* Susanmarie Harrington, Chair, 317-274-1153.

Indiana University South Bend, College of Liberal Arts and Sciences, South Bend, IN 46634-7111. Offers applied mathematics and computer science (MS); applied psychology (MA); English (MA); liberal studies (MLS). Part-time and evening/weekend programs available. *Faculty:* 79 full-time (33 women). *Students:* 34 full-time (18 women), 100 part-time (69 women); includes 23 minority (15 Black or African American, non-Hispanic/Latino; 2 American Indian or Alaska Native, non-Hispanic/Latino; 3 Asian, non-Hispanic/Latino; 2 Hispanic/Latino; 1 Two or more races, non-Hispanic/Latino), 16 international. Average age 37. 44 applicants, 84% accepted, 27 enrolled. In 2010, 21 master's awarded. *Degree requirements:* For master's, thesis (for some programs). *Entrance requirements:* For master's, minimum GPA of 3.0. Additional exam requirements/recommendations for international students: Required—TOEFL. *Application deadline:* For fall admission, 7/31 priority date for domestic students, 7/1 priority date for international students; for spring admission, 3/31 priority date for domestic students, 11/1 priority date for international students. Applications are processed on a rolling basis. Application fee: $50 ($60 for international students). *Financial support:* In 2010–11, 5 students received support, including 5 teaching assistantships; Federal Work-Study also available. Support available to part-time students. *Faculty research:* Artificial intelligence, bioinformatics, English language and literature, creative writing, computer networks. Total annual research expenditures: $127,000. *Unit head:* Dr. Lynn R. Williams, Dean, 574-520-4322, Fax: 574-520-4528, E-mail: lwilliam@iusb.edu. *Application contact:* Dr. Lynn R. Williams, Dean, 574-520-4322, Fax: 574-520-4528, E-mail: lwilliam@iusb.edu.

Inter American University of Puerto Rico, Metropolitan Campus, Graduate Programs, Program in English, San Juan, PR 00919-1293. Offers MA.

Iona College, School of Arts and Science, Department of English, New Rochelle, NY 10801-1890. Offers MA. Part-time and evening/weekend programs available. *Faculty:* 11 full-time (6 women). *Students:* 4 full-time (3 women), 9 part-time (4 women); includes 2 minority (both Black or African American, non-Hispanic/Latino). Average age 33. 6 applicants, 100% accepted, 2 enrolled. In 2010, 7 master's awarded. *Degree requirements:* For master's, one foreign language, thesis or alternative. *Entrance requirements:* For master's, minimum GPA of 3.0. Additional exam requirements/recommendations for international students: Required—TOEFL (minimum score 550 paper-based; 213 computer-based). *Application deadline:* Applications are processed on a rolling basis. Application fee: $50. Electronic applications accepted. *Expenses:* Tuition: Part-time $830 per credit. Required fees: $225 per credit. *Financial support:* Tuition waivers (partial) and unspecified assistantships available. Support available to part-time students. Financial award application deadline: 4/15; financial award applicants required to submit FAFSA. *Faculty research:* Victorian fiction, women's studies, nineteenth century American literature, Irish literature, Shakespeare. *Unit head:* Dr. Laura Shea, Chair, 914-637-2723, E-mail: lshea@iona.edu. *Application contact:* Veronica Jarek-Prinz, Director of Graduate Admissions, 914-633-2420, Fax: 914-633-2277, E-mail: vjarekprinz@iona.edu.

Iowa State University of Science and Technology, Graduate College, College of Liberal Arts and Sciences, Department of English, Ames, IA 50011. Offers creative writing (MFA); English (MA); rhetoric and professional communication (PhD). *Faculty:* 46 full-time (21 women), 9 part-time/adjunct (8 women). *Students:* 118 full-time (77 women), 45 part-time (32 women); includes 2 Black or African American, non-Hispanic/Latino; 1 Asian, non-Hispanic/Latino; 6 Hispanic/Latino, 36 international. 135 applicants, 56% accepted, 48 enrolled. In 2010, 27 master's, 5 doctorates awarded. *Degree requirements:* For master's, thesis or alternative; for doctorate, thesis/dissertation. *Entrance requirements:* For master's, GRE General Test, sample of written work, resume, portfolio in creative writing; for doctorate, GRE General Test, sample of written work, resume. Additional exam requirements/recommendations for international students: Required—TOEFL (minimum score 600 paper-based; 100 iBT), IELTS (minimum score 7). *Application deadline:* For fall admission, 1/5 priority date for domestic and international students. Application fee: $40 ($90 for international students). Electronic applications accepted. *Financial support:* In 2010–11, 7 research assistantships with full and partial tuition reimbursements (averaging $10,211 per year), 86 teaching assistantships with full and partial tuition reimbursements (averaging $13,238 per year) were awarded; fellowships, scholarships/grants, health care benefits, and unspecified assistantships also available. *Faculty research:* Creative writing, literature, rhetoric, composition and professional communication, teaching English as a second language, applied linguistics. *Unit head:* Dr. Charles Kostelnick, Chair, 515-294-2477, Fax: 515-294-2125, E-mail: englgrad@iastate.edu. *Application contact:* Dr. Constance Post, Director of Graduate Education, 515-294-3175, E-mail: englgrad@iastate.edu.

Jackson State University, Graduate School, College of Liberal Arts, Department of English and Modern Foreign Languages, Jackson, MS 39217. Offers English (MA); teaching English (MAT). Part-time and evening/weekend programs available. *Faculty:* 8 full-time (7 women). *Students:* 10 full-time (7 women), 25 part-time (21 women); includes 31 Black or African American, non-Hispanic/Latino; 1 Asian, non-Hispanic/Latino. Average age 31. In 2010, 7 master's awarded. *Degree requirements:* For master's, comprehensive exam, thesis or alternative. *Entrance requirements:* For master's, GRE General Test. Additional exam requirements/recommendations for international students: Required—TOEFL (minimum score 520 paper-based; 195 computer-based; 67 iBT). *Application deadline:* For fall admission, 3/1 priority date for domestic students, 3/1 for international students; for spring admission, 10/1 for domestic and international students. Applications are processed on a rolling basis. Application fee: $25. *Expenses:* Tuition, state resident: full-time $5050; part-time $281 per credit hour. Tuition, nonresident: full-time $12,380; part-time $689 per credit hour. *Financial support:* Career-related internships or fieldwork, Federal Work-Study, scholarships/grants, and unspecified assistantships available. Support available to part-time students. Financial award application deadline: 3/1; financial award applicants required to submit FAFSA. *Unit head:* Dr. Jean D. Chamberlain, Chair, 601-978-2111, Fax: 601-974-5942, E-mail: jean.d.chamberlain@jsums.edu. *Application contact:* Sharlene Wilson, Director of Graduate Admissions, 601-979-2455, Fax: 601-979-4325, E-mail: sharlene.f.wilson@jsums.edu.

Jacksonville State University, College of Graduate Studies and Continuing Education, College of Arts and Sciences, Department of English, Jacksonville, AL 36265-1602. Offers MA. Part-time and evening/weekend programs available. *Degree requirements:* For master's, comprehensive exam, thesis (for some programs). *Entrance requirements:* For master's, GRE General Test or MAT. Electronic applications accepted.

James Madison University, The Graduate School, College of Arts and Letters, Department of English, Harrisonburg, VA 22807. Offers MA. Part-time programs available. *Faculty:* 7 full-time (5 women). *Students:* 13 full-time (4 women), 5 part-time (4 women); includes 1 minority (Black or African American, non-Hispanic/Latino). Average age 27. In 2010, 7 master's awarded. *Degree requirements:* For master's, one foreign language, thesis, reading exam in languages, formal exam based on required reading list. *Entrance requirements:* For master's, GRE General Test, GRE Subject Test, 2 letters of recommendation, writing sample. Additional exam requirements/recommendations for international students: Required—TOEFL. *Application deadline:* For fall admission, 2/10 priority date for domestic students. Applications are processed on a rolling basis. Application fee: $55. Electronic applications accepted. *Financial support:* In 2010–11, 8 students received support, including 7 teaching assistantships with full tuition reimbursements available (averaging $8,664 per year); Federal Work-Study and 1 graduate assistantships ($7382) also available. Financial award application deadline: 3/1; financial award applicants required to submit FAFSA. *Unit head:* Dr. Mark L. Parker, Academic Unit Head, 540-568-6797. *Application contact:* Lynette M. Bible, Director of Graduate Admissions, 540-568-6395, Fax: 540-568-7860, E-mail: biblelm@jmu.edu.

John Carroll University, Graduate School, Department of English, University Heights, OH 44118-4581. Offers MA. Part-time and evening/weekend programs available. *Degree requirements:* For master's, comprehensive exam, research essay or thesis. *Entrance requirements:* For master's, GRE General Test, GRE Subject Test, minimum GPA of 3.0, writing sample. Additional exam requirements/recommendations for international students: Required—TOEFL. Electronic applications accepted. *Faculty research:* Post-colonial literature, African-American literature, Renaissance poetry, Anglo-Saxon literature, American literature.

The Johns Hopkins University, Zanvyl Krieger School of Arts and Sciences, Department of English, Baltimore, MD 21218-2699. Offers English and American literature (PhD). *Faculty:* 9 full-time (3 women). *Students:* 30 full-time (14 women), 1 (woman) part-time, 3 international. Average age 28. 130 applicants, 5% accepted, 7 enrolled. In 2010, 3 doctorates awarded. *Degree requirements:* For doctorate, 2 foreign languages, comprehensive exam, thesis/dissertation, 10 seminars, 2 oral exams. *Entrance requirements:* Additional exam requirements/recommendations for international students: Required—TOEFL (minimum score 600 paper-based; 250 computer-based; 100 iBT), IELTS. *Application deadline:* For fall admission, 12/10 priority date for domestic and international students. Application fee: $75. Electronic applications accepted. *Financial support:* In 2010–11, 30 students received support, including 12 fellowships with full tuition reimbursements available (averaging $18,000 per year), 16 teaching assistantships with full tuition reimbursements available (averaging $18,000 per year); research assistantships, Federal Work-Study, institutionally sponsored loans, and unspecified assistantships also available. Financial award application deadline: 4/15; financial award applicants required to submit FAFSA. *Faculty research:* Nineteenth century British, eighteenth century, Renaissance, American, cultural studies. Total annual research expenditures: $1,859. *Unit head:* Dr. Douglas Mao, Chair, 410-516-7335, Fax: 410-516-4757, E-mail: dougmao@jhu.edu. *Application contact:* Nicole Goode, Admissions Coordinator, 410-516-4311, Fax: 410-516-4757, E-mail: ngoode@jhu.edu.

Kansas State University, Graduate School, College of Arts and Sciences, Department of English, Manhattan, KS 66506. Offers MA. Part-time programs available. *Degree requirements:* For master's, one foreign language, thesis optional. *Entrance requirements:* For master's, GRE, minimum B average in English. Additional exam requirements/recommendations for international students: Required—TOEFL. Electronic applications accepted. *Faculty research:* Cultural studies, children's literature, American literature, rhetorical and composition theory, British literature.

Kent State University, College of Arts and Sciences, Department of English, Kent, OH 44242-0001. Offers comparative literature (MA); creative writing (MFA); English (PhD); English for teachers (MA); literature and writing (MA); rhetoric and composition (PhD); teaching English as a second language (MA). MFA program offered jointly with Cleveland State University, The University of Akron, and Youngstown State University. Part-time programs available. Terminal master's awarded for partial completion of doctoral program. *Degree requirements:* For master's, one foreign language, thesis optional; for doctorate, one foreign language, thesis/dissertation, qualifying exams. *Entrance requirements:* For master's and doctorate, GRE General Test, writing sample, letters of recommendation. Additional exam requirements/recommendations for international students: Required—TOEFL (minimum score 600 paper-based). Electronic applications accepted. *Expenses:* Tuition, state resident: full-time $7866; part-time $437 per credit hour. Tuition, nonresident: full-time $14,022; part-time $779 per credit hour. *Faculty research:* British and American literature, textual editing, rhetoric and composition, cultural studies, linguistic and critical theories.

Kutztown University of Pennsylvania, College of Liberal Arts and Sciences, Program in English, Kutztown, PA 19530-0730. Offers MA. Part-time and evening/weekend programs available. *Faculty:* 6 full-time (2 women). *Students:* 5 full-time (4 women), 14 part-time (13 women); includes 2 minority (1 Hispanic/Latino; 1 Two or more races, non-Hispanic/Latino). Average age 33. 20 applicants, 70% accepted, 5 enrolled. In 2010, 7 master's awarded. *Degree requirements:* For master's, one foreign language, comprehensive exam, thesis optional. *Entrance requirements:* For master's, GRE General Test. Additional exam requirements/recommendations for international students: Required—TOEFL (minimum score 550 paper-based; 79 iBT). *Application deadline:* For fall admission, 8/15 priority date for domestic and international students; for spring admission, 12/15 priority date for domestic and international students. Applications are processed on a rolling basis. Application fee: $35. Electronic applications accepted. *Expenses:* Tuition, state resident: full-time $6966; part-time $387 per credit. Tuition, nonresident: full-time $11,146; part-time $619 per credit hour. Required fees: $1499; $54 per credit. $68 per year. *Financial support:* Career-related internships or fieldwork, Federal Work-Study, scholarships/grants, and unspecified assistantships available. Financial award application deadline: 3/1; financial award applicants required to submit FAFSA. *Faculty research:* Women science fiction writers, Joyce Cary, myth and symbol, folklore, Victorian revision modes. *Unit head:* Dr. Janice Chernekoff, Chairperson, 610-683-4353, Fax: 610-683-4355, E-mail: cherneko@kutztown.edu. *Application contact:* Kelly D. Burr, Associate Director, Graduate Admissions, 610-683-4200, Fax: 610-683-1393, E-mail: graduate@kutztown.edu.

Lakehead University, Graduate Studies, Faculty of Social Sciences and Humanities, Department of English, Thunder Bay, ON P7B 5E1, Canada. Offers English (MA); women's studies (MA). Part-time and evening/weekend programs available. *Degree requirements:* For master's, one foreign language, thesis optional. *Entrance requirements:* For master's, minimum B average. Additional exam requirements/recommendations for international students: Required—TOEFL. *Faculty research:* Rhetoric and literary studies, children's literature, nineteenth- and twentieth-century American literature, modern literature, women's studies.

Lamar University, College of Graduate Studies, College of Arts and Sciences, Department of English and Foreign Languages, Beaumont, TX 77710. Offers English (MA). Part-time and evening/weekend programs available. *Faculty:* 9 full-time (4 women), 1 part-time/adjunct (0 women). *Students:* 7 full-time (5 women), 15 part-time (11 women); includes 1 Asian, non-Hispanic/Latino; 1 Hispanic/Latino. Average age 31. 10 applicants, 80% accepted, 7 enrolled. In 2010, 8 master's awarded. *Degree requirements:* For master's, one foreign language, thesis optional, practicum. *Entrance requirements:* For master's, GRE General Test, minimum GPA of 2.5 in last 60 hours of undergraduate course work. Additional exam requirements/recommendations for international students: Required—TOEFL. *Application deadline:* For fall admission, 8/1 for domestic students; for spring admission, 12/1 for domestic students. Applications are processed on a rolling basis. Application fee: $25 ($50 for international students). *Expenses:* Tuition, state resident: full-time $4160; part-time $208 per credit hour. Tuition, nonresident: full-time $10,360; part-time $518 per credit hour. *Financial support:* In 2010–11, 6 students received support, including 4 teaching assistantships (averaging $8,000 per year); career-related internships or fieldwork, Federal Work-Study, and institutionally sponsored loans also available. Support available to part-time students. Financial award application deadline: 4/1. *Faculty research:* British, Renaissance, nineteenth century, and American literature; creative writing; modern literature; African-American literature. *Unit head:* Dr. Joe E. Nordgren, Chair, 409-880-8558, Fax: 409-880-8591, E-mail: nordgrenje@hal.lamar.edu. *Application contact:* Dr. James W. Westgate, Assistant Dean, 409-880-7978, E-mail: westgate@hal.lamar.edu.

La Sierra University, College of Arts and Sciences, Department of English and Communication, Riverside, CA 92515. Offers communication (MA), including public relations/advertising, theory emphasis; English (MA), including literary emphasis, writing emphasis. Part-time programs available. *Degree requirements:* For master's, one foreign language. *Entrance requirements:* For master's, GRE General Test.

Lehigh University, College of Arts and Sciences, Department of English, Bethlehem, PA 18015. Offers MA, PhD. *Faculty:* 16 full-time (8 women). *Students:* 38 full-time (21 women), 9 part-time (7 women); includes 1 minority (Asian, non-Hispanic/Latino), 1 international. Average age 33. 42 applicants, 26% accepted, 8 enrolled. In 2010, 4 master's, 4 doctorates awarded. Terminal master's awarded for partial completion of doctoral program. *Degree requirements:* For master's, thesis; for doctorate, one foreign language, comprehensive exam, thesis/dissertation. *Entrance requirements:* For master's, GRE Subject Test (literature), GRE General Test, minimum GPA of 3.0 in undergraduate English courses; for doctorate, GRE Subject Test (literature), GRE General Test, minimum GPA of 3.5 in MA coursework. Additional exam requirements/recommendations for international students: Required—TOEFL (minimum score 620 paper-based; 96 iBT). *Application deadline:* For fall admission, 1/2 priority date for domestic and international students. Application fee: $65. Electronic applications accepted. *Financial support:* In 2010–11, 3 students received support, including 3 fellowships with full tuition reimbursements available (averaging $22,000 per year), 32 teaching assistantships with full tuition reimbursements available (averaging $16,900 per year); scholarships/grants and tuition waivers (full and partial) also available. Support available to part-time students. Financial award application deadline: 1/2. *Faculty research:* British and American literature, literature and social justice, Transatlantic study, rhetoric and composition. Total annual research expenditures: $12,221. *Unit head:* Dr. Scott P. Gordon, Chairperson, 610-758-3311, Fax: 610-758-6616, E-mail: spg4@lehigh.edu. *Application contact:* Dr. Dawn Keetley, Director of Graduate Studies, 610-758-5926, Fax: 610-758-6616, E-mail: dek7@lehigh.edu.

Lehman College of the City University of New York, Division of Arts and Humanities, Department of English, Bronx, NY 10468-1589. Offers MA. *Degree requirements:* For master's, thesis. *Entrance requirements:* For master's, GRE, 18 upper-level credits in U. S. or English literature.

Long Island University, Brooklyn Campus, Richard L. Conolly College of Liberal Arts and Sciences, Department of English, Brooklyn, NY 11201-8423. Offers creative writing (MFA); literature (MA); professional writing (MA); writing and rhetoric (MA). Part-time and evening/weekend programs available. *Degree requirements:* For master's, thesis or alternative. *Entrance requirements:* For master's, 2 letters of recommendation (at least 1 from a former professor or teacher). Additional exam requirements/recommendations for international students: Required—TOEFL (minimum score 550 paper-based; 173 computer-based). Electronic applications accepted.

Long Island University, C.W. Post Campus, College of Liberal Arts and Sciences, Department of English, Brookville, NY 11548-1300. Offers English (MA); English for adolescence education (MS). Part-time and evening/weekend programs available. *Degree requirements:* For master's, comprehensive exam (for some programs), thesis (for some programs). *Entrance requirements:* For master's, minimum GPA of 3.5 in major, 3.0 overall; 21 credits of English. Electronic applications accepted. *Faculty research:* English Renaissance, Sinclair Lewis: The Early Years, puppetry archives, Irish-American Experiences: literature of memory, Henry James's anxiety of Poe's influence.

Longwood University, Office of Graduate Studies, Department of English and Modern Languages, Farmville, VA 23909. Offers 6-12 initial teaching/licensure (MA); creative writing (MA); English education and writing (MA); literature (MA). Part-time programs available. *Degree requirements:* For master's, comprehensive exam (for some programs), thesis (for some programs). *Entrance requirements:* For master's, minimum GPA of 2.75. Additional exam requirements/recommendations for international students: Required—TOEFL (minimum score 550 paper-based; 213 computer-based).

Louisiana State University and Agricultural and Mechanical College, Graduate School, College of Humanities and Social Sciences, Department of English, Baton Rouge, LA 70803. Offers creative writing (MFA); English (MA, PhD). Part-time programs available. *Faculty:* 49 full-time (21 women), 1 (woman) part-time/adjunct. *Students:* 77 full-time (44 women), 9 part-time (4 women); includes 2 Black or African American, non-Hispanic/Latino; 1 Asian, non-Hispanic/Latino; 3 Hispanic/Latino; 2 Two or more races, non-Hispanic/Latino, 5 international. Average age 31. 302 applicants, 10% accepted, 19 enrolled. In 2010, 10 master's, 7 doctorates awarded. Terminal master's awarded for partial completion of doctoral program. *Degree requirements:* For master's, comprehensive exam; for doctorate, one foreign language, comprehensive exam, thesis/dissertation. *Entrance requirements:* For master's, GRE General Test, minimum GPA of 3.0; for doctorate, GRE General Test, GRE Subject Test, minimum GPA of 3.0. Additional exam requirements/recommendations for international students: Required—TOEFL (minimum score 550 paper-based; 213 computer-based; 79 iBT) or IELTS (minimum score 6.5). *Application deadline:* For fall admission, 5/15 priority date for domestic students, 5/15 for international students; for spring admission, 10/15 priority date for domestic students, 10/15 for international students. Applications are processed on a rolling basis. Application fee: $50 ($70 for international students). Electronic applications accepted. *Financial support:* In 2010–11, 80 students received support, including 1 fellowship with full tuition reimbursement available (averaging $13,435 per year), 5 research assistantships with partial tuition reimbursements available (averaging $17,000 per year), 70 teaching assistantships with partial tuition reimbursements available (averaging $16,764 per year); career-related internships or fieldwork, Federal Work-Study, traineeships, and health care benefits also available. Financial award application deadline: 2/1; financial award applicants required to submit FAFSA. *Faculty research:* American literature, British literature, cultural studies, rhetoric and composition, folklore. Total annual research expenditures: $214,726. *Unit head:* Dr. Richard Morland, Chair, 225-578-0812, Fax: 225-578-2214, E-mail: english@lsu.edu. *Application contact:* Dr. Sharon Weltman, Director of Graduate Studies, 225-578-0812, Fax: 225-578-4129, E-mail: egs@lsu.edu.

Louisiana Tech University, Graduate School, College of Liberal Arts, Department of English, Ruston, LA 71272. Offers MA. Part-time programs available. *Degree requirements:* For master's, thesis or alternative. *Entrance requirements:* For master's, GRE General Test.

Loyola Marymount University, College of Liberal Arts, Department of English, Program in English, Los Angeles, CA 90045-2659. Offers MA. *Faculty:* 28 full-time (14 women). *Students:* 24 full-time (19 women), 8 part-time (6 women); includes 3 Black or African American, non-Hispanic/Latino; 7 Hispanic/Latino; 1 Two or more races, non-Hispanic/Latino. Average age 31. 40 applicants, 53% accepted, 15 enrolled. In 2010, 14 master's awarded. *Degree requirements:* For master's, comprehensive exam. *Entrance requirements:* For master's, GRE, 2 letters of recommendation, 2-page statement of ambition, writing sample (10-15 pages). Additional exam requirements/recommendations for international students: Required—TOEFL (minimum score 600 paper-based; 250 computer-based; 100 iBT). *Application deadline:* For fall admission, 4/1 for domestic students. Application fee: $50. *Financial support:* In 2010–11, 25 students received support, including 8 research assistantships (averaging $1,290 per year), 9 teaching assistantships (averaging $20,500 per year); scholarships/grants and unspecified assistantships also available. Support available to part-time students. Financial award application deadline: 6/1; financial award applicants required to submit FAFSA. *Unit head:* Dr. Paul Harris, Chair, 310-338-4452, E-mail: pharris@lmu.edu. *Application contact:* Dr. Stephen Shepherd, Graduate Director, 310-568-6225, E-mail: sshephe1@lmu.edu.

Loyola University Chicago, Graduate School, Department of English, Chicago, IL 60660. Offers MA, PhD. Part-time and evening/weekend programs available. *Faculty:* 26 full-time (10 women), 1 part-time/adjunct (0 women). *Students:* 40 full-time (24 women), 7 part-time (5 women); includes 7 minority (3 Black or African American, non-Hispanic/Latino; 3 Hispanic/Latino; 1 Two or more races, non-Hispanic/Latino). Average age 28. 127 applicants, 27% accepted, 15 enrolled. In 2010, 9 master's, 6 doctorates awarded. Terminal master's awarded for partial completion of doctoral program. *Degree requirements:* For master's, comprehensive exam, thesis or alternative; for doctorate, one foreign language, comprehensive exam, thesis/dissertation. *Entrance requirements:* For master's, GRE General Test; for doctorate, GRE General Test, GRE Subject Test. Additional exam requirements/recommendations for international students: Required—TOEFL, IELTS. *Application deadline:* For fall admission, 6/1 for domestic students. Applications are processed on a rolling basis. Application fee: $50. Electronic applications accepted. *Expenses:* Tuition: Full-time $14,940; part-time $830 per credit hour. Required fees: $87 per semester. Part-time tuition and fees vary according to course load and program. *Financial support:* In 2010–11, 26 students received support, including 5 fellowships with full tuition reimbursements available (averaging $16,000 per year), research assistantships with full tuition reimbursements available (averaging $10,000 per year), 21 teaching assistantships with full tuition reimbursements available (averaging $16,500 per year); Federal Work-Study, institutionally sponsored loans, tuition waivers (partial), and unspecified assistantships also available. Support available to part-time students. Financial award application deadline: 1/15; financial award applicants required to submit FAFSA. *Faculty research:* Medieval and Renaissance studies, Romantic period, literary history and theory, American studies, modernism and postmodernism. *Unit head:* Dr. Pamela Caughie, Graduate Program Director, 773-508-2241, Fax: 773-508-8696, E-mail: pcaughi@luc.edu. *Application contact:* Stephen Heintz, Administrative Assistant to the Graduate Program, 773-508-2241, Fax: 773-508-8696, E-mail: sheintz@luc.edu.

Lynchburg College, Graduate Studies, School of Humanities and Social Sciences, MA Program in English, Lynchburg, VA 24501-3199. Offers MA. Part-time and evening/weekend programs available. *Faculty:* 7 full-time (5 women). *Students:* 5 full-time (4 women), 6 part-time (4 women); includes 3 minority (2 Black or African American, non-Hispanic/Latino; 1 American Indian or Alaska Native, non-Hispanic/Latino). Average age 32. 13 applicants, 54% accepted. In 2010, 7 master's awarded. *Degree requirements:* For master's, thesis. *Entrance requirements:* For master's, GRE, official transcripts, personal essay, 3 letters of recommendation. Additional exam requirements/recommendations for international students: Required—TOEFL (minimum score 530 paper-based; 197 computer-based; 71 iBT), IELTS (minimum score 6.5). *Application deadline:* For fall admission, 7/31 for domestic students, 6/1 for international students; for spring admission, 11/30 for domestic students, 10/15 for international students. Applications are processed on a rolling basis. Application fee: $30. Electronic applications accepted. *Expenses:* Tuition: Full-time $7200; part-time $400 per credit hour. Required fees: $20; $5.10 per credit hour. $15 per term. Tuition and fees vary according to degree level and program. *Financial support:* Fellowships, research assistantships, Federal Work-Study, scholarships/grants, health care benefits, and unspecified assistantships available. Support available to part-time students. Financial award application deadline: 7/31; financial award applicants required to submit FAFSA. *Unit head:* Dr. Casey Clabough, Associate Professor and Chair, Department of English, 434-544-8732, E-mail: clabough@lynchburg.edu. *Application contact:* Dr. Casey Clabough, Associate Professor and Chair, Department of English, 434-544-8732, E-mail: clabough@lynchburg.edu.

Marquette University, Graduate School, College of Arts and Sciences, Department of English, Milwaukee, WI 53201-1881. Offers American literature (PhD); British and American literature (MA); British literature (PhD). Part-time programs available. *Faculty:* 31 full-time (16 women), 21 part-time/adjunct (14 women). *Students:* 45 full-time (27 women), 22 part-time (10 women); includes 1 Asian, non-Hispanic/Latino; 2 Hispanic/Latino. Average age 30. 81 applicants, 59% accepted, 15 enrolled. In 2010, 4 master's awarded. *Degree requirements:* For master's, comprehensive exam, thesis or alternative; for doctorate, one foreign language, thesis/dissertation, qualifying exam. *Entrance requirements:* For master's and doctorate, GRE General Test, GRE Subject Test, official transcripts from all current and previous colleges/universities except Marquette, three letters of recommendation, statement of purpose, one or two writing samples. Additional exam requirements/recommendations for international students: Required—TOEFL (minimum score 530 paper-based; 78 computer-based). *Application deadline:* Applications are processed on a rolling basis. Application fee: $50. Electronic applications accepted. *Expenses:* Tuition: Full-time $16,290; part-time $905 per credit hour. Tuition and fees vary according to program. *Financial support:* In 2010–11, 2 fellowships, 6 research assistantships, 50 teaching assistantships were awarded; Federal Work-Study, institutionally sponsored loans, scholarships/grants, and tuition waivers (full and partial) also available. Support available to part-time students. Financial award application deadline: 2/15. *Faculty research:* Discourse analysis, American literature, British literature, textual criticism, literary history. Total annual research expenditures: $6,515. *Unit head:* Dr. Krista Ratcliffe, Chair, 414-288-7179, Fax: 414-288-1578. *Application contact:* Dr. John Curran, Director of Graduate Studies, 414-288-3462.

Marshall University, Academic Affairs Division, College of Liberal Arts, Department of English, Huntington, WV 25755. Offers MA. *Faculty:* 24 full-time (13 women). *Students:* 40 full-time (21 women), 11 part-time (7 women), 13 international. Average age 28. In 2010, 18 master's awarded. *Degree requirements:* For master's, one foreign language, thesis optional. *Entrance requirements:* For master's, GRE General Test. Application fee: $40. *Unit head:* Dr. Jane Hill, Interim Chairperson, 304-696-6638, E-mail: hillj@marshall.edu. *Application contact:* Dr. Katharine Rodier, Information Contact, 304-696-3128, Fax: 304-746-1902, E-mail: rodier@marshall.edu.

Mary Baldwin College, Graduate Studies, Program in Shakespeare and Renaissance Literature in Performance, Staunton, VA 24401-3610. Offers acting (M Litt); directing (M Litt); Shakespeare and Renaissance literature in performance (MFA); teaching (M Litt). *Entrance requirements:* For master's, GRE (M Litt).

Marygrove College, Graduate Division, Program in English, Detroit, MI 48221-2599. Offers MA.

Marymount University, School of Arts and Sciences, Program in Literature and Languages, Arlington, VA 22207-4299. Offers MA. Part-time and evening/weekend programs available. *Degree requirements:* For master's, thesis or alternative. *Entrance requirements:* For master's, 2 letters of recommendation, interview, minimum undergraduate GPA of 3.0 with major in English or other humanities discipline, writing sample. Additional exam requirements/recommendations for international students: Required—TOEFL (minimum score 600 paper-based; 250 computer-based; 96 iBT), IELTS (minimum score 6.5). Electronic applications accepted.

McGill University, Faculty of Graduate and Postdoctoral Studies, Faculty of Arts, Department of English, Montréal, QC H3A 2T5, Canada. Offers MA, PhD. Electronic applications accepted.

McMaster University, School of Graduate Studies, Faculty of Humanities, Department of English and Cultural Studies, Hamilton, ON L8S 4M2, Canada. Offers cultural studies and critical theory (MA); English (MA, PhD). Part-time programs available. *Degree requirements:* For master's, one foreign language, thesis; for doctorate, one foreign language, comprehensive exam, thesis/dissertation. *Entrance requirements:* For master's, honors degree, minimum B+ average in at least 6 full courses of English beyond year 1; for doctorate, MA; minimum A- average in two of three courses. Additional exam requirements/recommendations for international students: Required—TOEFL (minimum score 580 paper-based; 237 computer-based). *Faculty research:* Literary theory, feminist theory, literature of migration, Bakhting globalization.

McNeese State University, Doré School of Graduate Studies, College of Liberal Arts, Department of English and Foreign Languages, Program in English, Lake Charles, LA 70609. Offers MA. Evening/weekend programs available. *Faculty:* 14 full-time (9 women). *Students:* 6

English

McNeese State University *(continued)*
full-time (3 women), 9 part-time (7 women); includes 2 minority (1 Black or African American, non-Hispanic/Latino; 1 Hispanic/Latino) In 2010, 12 master's awarded. *Degree requirements:* For master's, one foreign language, thesis or alternative. *Entrance requirements:* For master's, GRE. *Application deadline:* For fall admission, 5/15 priority date for domestic and international students; for spring admission, 10/15 priority date for domestic and international students. Applications are processed on a rolling basis. Application fee: $20 ($30 for international students). Tuition and fees vary according to course load. *Financial support:* Teaching assistantships available. Financial award application deadline: 5/1. *Faculty research:* Textual criticism, seventeenth century literature, American women writers, Romanticism and the origins of diplomacy. *Unit head:* Dr. Jacob D. Blevins, Head, 337-475-5325, Fax: 337-475-5327, E-mail: jblevins@mcneese.edu. *Application contact:* Dr. George F. Mead, Interim Dean of Dore School of Graduate Studies, 337-475-5396, Fax: 337-475-5397, E-mail: admissions@mcneese.edu.

Memorial University of Newfoundland, School of Graduate Studies, Department of English Language and Literature, St. John's, NL A1C 5S7, Canada. Offers MA, PhD. *Degree requirements:* For master's, thesis optional; for doctorate, one foreign language, comprehensive exam, thesis/dissertation, oral thesis defense, minimum 3 semesters of full-time study. *Entrance requirements:* For master's, honors degree. Electronic applications accepted. *Faculty research:* American, British, Canadian, and Anglo-Irish literature; Newfoundland literature.

Mercy College, School of Liberal Arts, Program in English Literature, Dobbs Ferry, NY 10522-1189. Offers MA. Part-time and evening/weekend programs available. Postbaccalaureate distance learning degree programs offered (no on-campus study). *Students:* 6 full-time (all women), 62 part-time (54 women); includes 9 Black or African American, non-Hispanic/Latino; 4 Hispanic/Latino; 2 Two or more races, non-Hispanic/Latino. Average age 36. 48 applicants, 48% accepted, 16 enrolled. In 2010, 13 master's awarded. *Degree requirements:* For master's, comprehensive exam, thesis. *Entrance requirements:* For master's, 2 letters of reference; BA/BS in English with minimum GPA of 3.0, in related subject area with minor in English literature, or in another discipline demonstrating the potential to succeed in a graduate program. Additional exam requirements/recommendations for international students: Required—TOEFL (minimum score 600 paper-based; 250 computer-based; 100 iBT), IELTS (minimum score 8). *Application deadline:* For fall admission, 8/1 for international students. Applications are processed on a rolling basis. Application fee: $40. Electronic applications accepted. *Expenses:* Tuition: Full-time $13,572; part-time $754 per credit hour. Required fees: $130 per term. *Financial support:* Career-related internships or fieldwork, Federal Work-Study, scholarships/grants, and unspecified assistantships available. Support available to part-time students. Financial award applicants required to submit FAFSA. *Faculty research:* Medieval literature, poetic forms, American literature, African literature. *Unit head:* Dr. Joel N. Feimer, Program Director, 914-245-6100 Ext. 2235, E-mail: jfeimer@mercy.edu. *Application contact:* Allison Gurdineer, Senior Associate Director of Recruitment, 914-674-7601, E-mail: agurdineer@mercy.edu.

Miami University, Graduate School, College of Arts and Science, Department of English, Oxford, OH 45056. Offers MA, MAT, MTSC, PhD. Part-time programs available. *Students:* 86 full-time (48 women), 84 part-time (74 women); includes 11 minority (5 Black or African American, non-Hispanic/Latino; 3 Asian, non-Hispanic/Latino; 2 Hispanic/Latino; 1 Two or more races, non-Hispanic/Latino), 5 international. Average age 31. In 2010, 55 master's, 5 doctorates awarded. *Entrance requirements:* For master's, minimum undergraduate GPA of 3.0 during previous 2 years or 2.75 overall; for doctorate, minimum GPA of 2.75 (undergraduate), 3.0 (graduate). Additional exam requirements/recommendations for international students: Required—TOEFL. *Application deadline:* For fall admission, 1/15 for domestic and international students. Application fee: $50. *Expenses:* Tuition, state resident: full-time $11,616; part-time $484 per credit hour. Tuition, nonresident: full-time $25,656; part-time $1069 per credit hour. Required fees: $528. *Financial support:* Fellowships with full tuition reimbursements, research assistantships with full tuition reimbursements, teaching assistantships with full tuition reimbursements, Federal Work-Study, institutionally sponsored loans, tuition waivers (full), and unspecified assistantships available. Financial award application deadline: 3/1; financial award applicants required to submit FAFSA. *Unit head:* Dr. J. Kerry Powell, Chair, 513-529-5221, Fax: 513-529-1392, E-mail: english@muohio.edu. *Application contact:* Dr. Cynthia Lewiecki-Wilson, Director of Graduate Studies, 513-529-5221, E-mail: lewiecc@muohio.edu.

Michigan State University, The Graduate School, College of Arts and Letters, Department of English, East Lansing, MI 48824. Offers English (PhD); literature in English (MA). *Entrance requirements:* For master's, GRE General Test, minimum GPA of 3.25, 2 years of foreign language or American Sign Language study, 3 letters of recommendation; for doctorate, GRE General Test, master's degree in English, 2 years of foreign language study, 3 letters of recommendation. Additional exam requirements/recommendations for international students: Required—TOEFL. Electronic applications accepted.

Middlebury College, Bread Loaf School of English, Middlebury, VT 05753. Offers M Litt, MA. Offered during summer only. *Entrance requirements:* For master's, 2 letters of recommendation; statement of purpose; official transcripts (both undergraduate and graduate); 10-page writing sample. Electronic applications accepted.

Middle Tennessee State University, College of Graduate Studies, College of Liberal Arts, Department of English, Murfreesboro, TN 37132. Offers MA, PhD. Part-time and evening/weekend programs available. Postbaccalaureate distance learning degree programs offered. *Faculty:* 42 full-time (24 women). *Students:* 1 (woman) full-time, 99 part-time (66 women); includes 3 Black or African American, non-Hispanic/Latino; 2 Asian, non-Hispanic/Latino; 3 Hispanic/Latino; 4 Two or more races, non-Hispanic/Latino. Average age 34. 52 applicants, 81% accepted, 42 enrolled. In 2010, 6 master's, 2 doctorates awarded. *Degree requirements:* For master's, one foreign language, comprehensive exam, thesis optional; for doctorate, one foreign language, comprehensive exam, thesis/dissertation. *Entrance requirements:* For master's and doctorate, GRE. Additional exam requirements/recommendations for international students: Required—TOEFL (minimum score 525 paper-based; 195 computer-based; 71 iBT) or IELTS (minimum score 6). *Application deadline:* For fall admission, 6/1 for domestic and international students. Applications are processed on a rolling basis. Application fee: $25 ($30 for international students). Electronic applications accepted. *Expenses:* Tuition, state resident: full-time $4632. Tuition, nonresident: full-time $11,520. *Financial support:* In 2010-11, 40 students received support. Career-related internships or fieldwork and institutionally sponsored loans available. Support available to part-time students. Financial award application deadline: 5/1; financial award applicants required to submit FAFSA. *Unit head:* Dr. Tom Strawman, Chair, 615-898-2573, Fax: 615-898-5098, E-mail: strawman@mtsu.edu. *Application contact:* Dr. Michael Allen, Dean and Vice Provost for Research, 615-898-2840, Fax: 615-904-8020, E-mail: mallen@mtsu.edu.

Midwestern State University, Graduate Studies, College of Humanities and Social Sciences, Department of English, Wichita Falls, TX 76308. Offers MA. Part-time and evening/weekend programs available. *Faculty:* 5 full-time (0 women). *Students:* 7 full-time (5 women), 18 part-time (15 women); includes 1 Black or African American, non-Hispanic/Latino; 1 American Indian or Alaska Native, non-Hispanic/Latino; 1 Hispanic/Latino, 1 international. Average age 32. 8 applicants, 75% accepted, 4 enrolled. In 2010, 6 master's awarded. *Degree requirements:* For master's, one foreign language, thesis optional. *Entrance requirements:* For master's, GRE General Test, MAT or GMAT. Additional exam requirements/recommendations for international students: Required—TOEFL (minimum score 550 paper-based; 213 computer-based). *Application deadline:* For fall admission, 7/1 priority date for domestic students, 4/1 for international students; for spring admission, 11/1 priority date for domestic students, 8/1 for international students. Applications are processed on a rolling basis. Application fee: $35 ($50 for international students). Electronic applications accepted. *Expenses:* Tuition, state resident: full-time $1620; part-time $90 per credit hour. Tuition, nonresident: full-time $2160; part-time $120 per credit hour. International tuition: $7200 full-time. *Financial support:* In 2010-11, 11 students received support, including 7 teaching assistantships with partial tuition reimburse-

ments available (averaging $9,406 per year); career-related internships or fieldwork, Federal Work-Study, institutionally sponsored loans, scholarships/grants, tuition waivers (partial), and unspecified assistantships also available. Support available to part-time students. Financial award application deadline: 3/1; financial award applicants required to submit FAFSA. *Faculty research:* Mythology, Shakespeare, Oscar Hahn, origins of language, modern American literature. *Unit head:* Dr. Robert Johnson, Graduate Coordinator, 940-397-4300, Fax: 940-397-4931, E-mail: robert.johnson@mwsu.edu. *Application contact:* 800-842-1922, Fax: 940-397-4672, E-mail: admissions@mwsu.edu.

Millersville University of Pennsylvania, College of Graduate and Professional Studies, School of Humanities and Social Sciences, Department of English, Millersville, PA 17551-0302. Offers English (MA); English education (M Ed). Part-time programs available. *Faculty:* 24 full-time (13 women), 12 part-time/adjunct (8 women). *Students:* 18 full-time (11 women), 28 part-time (18 women); includes 1 Asian, non-Hispanic/Latino; 1 Hispanic/Latino. Average age 27. 17 applicants, 100% accepted, 12 enrolled. In 2010, 14 master's awarded. *Degree requirements:* For master's, one foreign language, thesis optional. *Entrance requirements:* For master's, GRE or MAT, 3 letters of recommendation. Additional exam requirements/recommendations for international students: Required—TOEFL (minimum score 500 paper-based; 183 computer-based; 65 iBT) or IELTS (minimum score 6). *Application deadline:* For fall admission, 1/15 priority date for domestic and international students; for winter admission, 10/1 priority date for domestic and international students; for spring admission, 10/1 priority date for domestic and international students. Applications are processed on a rolling basis. Application fee: $40 ($50 for international students). Electronic applications accepted. *Expenses:* Tuition, state resident: full-time $6966; part-time $387 per credit. Tuition, nonresident: full-time $11,146; part-time $619 per credit. Required fees: $1829.50; $88 per credit. One-time fee: $60 part-time. Tuition and fees vary according to course load. *Financial support:* In 2010-11, 7 students received support, including 7 research assistantships with full and partial tuition reimbursements available (averaging $4,875 per year); institutionally sponsored loans and unspecified assistantships also available. Support available to part-time students. Financial award application deadline: 3/15; financial award applicants required to submit FAFSA. *Faculty research:* Comparative literatures, writing studies, linguistics, film studies, curriculum and instruction/educational pedagogy. *Unit head:* Dr. Beverly Schneller, Chair, 717-871-2342, Fax: 717-871-2446, E-mail: beverly.schneller@millersville.edu. *Application contact:* Dr. Victor S. DeSantis, Dean of Graduate and Professional Studies, 717-872-3099, Fax: 717-872-3453, E-mail: victor.desantis@millersville.edu.

Mills College, Graduate Studies, Department of English, Oakland, CA 94613-1000. Offers book art and creative writing (MFA); creative writing, poetry (MFA); creative writing, prose (MFA); English and American literature (MA). Part-time programs available. *Faculty:* 14 full-time (11 women), 15 part-time/adjunct (12 women). *Students:* 94 full-time (81 women), 2 part-time (both women); includes 8 Black or African American, non-Hispanic/Latino; 4 Asian, non-Hispanic/Latino; 7 Hispanic/Latino; 1 Native Hawaiian or other Pacific Islander, non-Hispanic/Latino; 1 Two or more races, non-Hispanic/Latino. Average age 31. 155 applicants, 88% accepted, 48 enrolled. In 2010, 63 master's awarded. *Degree requirements:* For master's, comprehensive exam, thesis. *Entrance requirements:* For master's, manuscript, writing sample. Additional exam requirements/recommendations for international students: Required—TOEFL (minimum score 600 paper-based; 250 computer-based; 100 iBT), IELTS (minimum score 7). *Application deadline:* For fall admission, 12/15 priority date for domestic students, 12/15 for international students. Applications are processed on a rolling basis. Application fee: $50. Electronic applications accepted. *Expenses:* Tuition: Full-time $28,280; part-time $7070 per course. Required fees: $1058; $1058 per year. Tuition and fees vary according to program. *Financial support:* In 2010-11, 120 fellowships (averaging $5,723 per year), 37 teaching assistantships with partial tuition reimbursements (averaging $3,081 per year) were awarded; scholarships/grants also available. Support available to part-time students. Financial award application deadline: 2/1; financial award applicants required to submit FAFSA. *Faculty research:* Creative writing, African-American literature, Victorian women writers, theories of sexuality, Shakespeare. *Unit head:* Dr. Cynthia Scheinberg, Chair, 510-430-2213, E-mail: cyns@mills.edu. *Application contact:* Jessica King, Graduate Admission Specialist, 510-430-3305, Fax: 510-430-2159, E-mail: grad-studies@mills.edu.

Minnesota State University Mankato, College of Graduate Studies, College of Arts and Humanities, Department of English, Mankato, MN 56001. Offers creative writing (MFA); English (MAT); English studies (MA); teaching English as a second language (MA, Certificate); technical communication (MA, Certificate). Part-time programs available. *Students:* 46 full-time (28 women), 147 part-time (97 women). *Degree requirements:* For master's, one foreign language, comprehensive exam, thesis or alternative. *Entrance requirements:* For master's, minimum GPA of 3.0 during previous 2 years, writing sample (MFA). Additional exam requirements/recommendations for international students: Required—TOEFL (minimum score 500 paper-based; 61 iBT). *Application deadline:* For fall admission, 7/1 for domestic students, 5/1 for international students. Applications are processed on a rolling basis. Application fee: $40. Electronic applications accepted. *Financial support:* Research assistantships with full tuition reimbursements, teaching assistantships with full tuition reimbursements, career-related internships or fieldwork, Federal Work-Study, and unspecified assistantships available. Financial award application deadline: 3/15; financial award applicants required to submit FAFSA. *Faculty research:* Keats and Christianity. *Unit head:* Dr. John Banschbach, Chairperson, 507-389-2117. *Application contact:* 507-389-2321, E-mail: grad@mnsu.edu.

Mississippi College, Graduate School, College of Arts and Sciences, School of Humanities and Social Sciences, Department of English, Clinton, MS 39058. Offers M Ed, MA. Part-time and evening/weekend programs available. *Degree requirements:* For master's, one foreign language, comprehensive exam, thesis or alternative. *Entrance requirements:* For master's, GRE or NTE, minimum GPA of 2.5. Additional exam requirements/recommendations for international students: Recommended—IELTS. Electronic applications accepted.

Mississippi State University, College of Arts and Sciences, Department of English, Mississippi State, MS 39762. Offers MA. Part-time programs available. *Faculty:* 19 full-time (9 women). *Students:* 33 full-time (27 women), 3 part-time (2 women); includes 5 minority (3 Black or African American, non-Hispanic/Latino; 2 Two or more races, non-Hispanic/Latino), 1 international. Average age 25. 25 applicants, 84% accepted, 14 enrolled. In 2010, 11 master's awarded. *Degree requirements:* For master's, thesis optional, comprehensive oral or written exam. *Entrance requirements:* For master's, GRE General Test, minimum GPA of 2.75 on last two years of undergraduate courses. Additional exam requirements/recommendations for international students: Required—TOEFL (minimum score 475 paper-based; 153 computer-based; 53 iBT); Recommended—IELTS (minimum score 4.5). *Application deadline:* For fall admission, 7/1 for domestic students, 5/1 for international students; for spring admission, 11/1 for domestic students, 9/1 for international students. Applications are processed on a rolling basis. Application fee: $40. Electronic applications accepted. *Expenses:* Tuition, state resident: full-time $2730.50; part-time $304 per credit hour. Tuition, nonresident: full-time $6901; part-time $767 per credit hour. *Financial support:* In 2010-11, 22 teaching assistantships (averaging $9,218 per year) were awarded; Federal Work-Study, institutionally sponsored loans, scholarships/grants, and unspecified assistantships also available. Financial award application deadline: 4/1; financial award applicants required to submit FAFSA. *Faculty research:* Literary criticism, linguistics, textual editing, editing *Mississippi Quarterly*, Southern literature. *Unit head:* Dr. Richard Raymond, Department Head, 662-325-3606, Fax: 662-325-3645, E-mail: rr165@msstate.edu. *Application contact:* Dr. Laura Dodds, Associate Professor/Director of Graduate Studies, 662-325-3644, Fax: 662-325-3645, E-mail: ld214@msstate.edu.

Missouri State University, Graduate College, College of Arts and Letters, Department of English, Springfield, MO 65897. Offers English and writing (MA); secondary education (MS Ed), including English. Part-time and evening/weekend programs available. *Degree requirements:* For master's, one foreign language, comprehensive exam, thesis or alternative. *Entrance requirements:* For master's, GRE (MA), minimum GPA of 3.0 (MA), 9-12 teacher certification (MS Ed). Additional exam requirements/recommendations for international students: Required—

TOEFL (minimum score 550 paper-based; 213 computer-based; 79 iBT). Electronic applications accepted. *Expenses:* Tuition, state resident: full-time $3348; part-time $186 per credit hour. Tuition, nonresident: full-time $6696; part-time $372 per credit hour. Required fees: $238 per semester. Tuition and fees vary according to course level, course load and program. *Faculty research:* Renaissance literature, William Blake, autobiography, Georgian theatre, TESOL.

Monmouth University, The Graduate School, Department of English, West Long Branch, NJ 07764-1898. Offers creative writing (MA); New Jersey studies (MA); rhetoric and writing (MA). Part-time and evening/weekend programs available. *Faculty:* 12 full-time (8 women). *Students:* 9 full-time (7 women), 30 part-time (21 women); includes 1 Black or African American, non-Hispanic/Latino; 1 Asian, non-Hispanic/Latino; 1 Hispanic/Latino. Average age 32. 30 applicants, 93% accepted, 14 enrolled. In 2010, 9 master's awarded. *Degree requirements:* For master's, comprehensive exam (for some programs), thesis (for some programs). *Entrance requirements:* For master's, minimum overall GPA of 2.75, at least 15 credits in literary studies. Additional exam requirements/recommendations for international students: Required—TOEFL (minimum score 550 paper-based; 213 computer-based; 79 iBT), IELTS (minimum score 5), Michigan English Language Assessment Battery (minimum score 77), Cambridge A, B, C. *Application deadline:* For fall admission, 7/15 for domestic students, 6/1 for international students; for spring admission, 11/15 for domestic students, 11/1 for international students. Application fee: $50. *Expenses:* Tuition: Full-time $19,572; part-time $816 per credit. Required fees: $628; $157 per semester. *Financial support:* In 2010–11, 28 students received support, including 28 fellowships (averaging $1,689 per year), 5 research assistantships (averaging $4,502 per year); career-related internships or fieldwork, scholarships/grants, and unspecified assistantships also available. Support available to part-time students. Financial award applicants required to submit FAFSA. *Faculty research:* Renaissance and medieval literature, nineteenth century American literature, eighteenth century British literature and women's studies, Old English and Middle English, African diaspora and African post-colonial literature. *Unit head:* Dr. Hiede Estes, Program Director, 732-571-7547, E-mail: hestes@monmouth.edu. *Application contact:* Kevin Roane, Director, Office of Graduate Admission, 732-571-3452, Fax: 732-263-5123, E-mail: gradadm@monmouth.edu.

Montana State University, College of Graduate Studies, College of Letters and Science, Department of English, Bozeman, MT 59717. Offers MA. Part-time programs available. *Faculty:* 15 full-time (4 women), 16 part-time/adjunct (4 women). *Students:* 6 full-time (3 women), 12 part-time (10 women); includes 1 minority (Two or more races, non-Hispanic/Latino). Average age 30. 19 applicants, 74% accepted, 7 enrolled. In 2010, 10 master's awarded. *Degree requirements:* For master's, comprehensive exam. *Entrance requirements:* For master's, GRE General Test, minimum GPA of 3.0, 3 recommendations. Additional exam requirements/recommendations for international students: Required—TOEFL (minimum score 550 paper-based; 213 computer-based). *Application deadline:* For fall admission, 7/15 priority date for domestic students, 5/15 for international students; for spring admission, 12/1 priority date for domestic students, 10/1 for international students. Applications are processed on a rolling basis. Application fee: $30. Electronic applications accepted. *Expenses:* Tuition, state resident: full-time $5553.90. Tuition, nonresident: full-time $14,646. Required fees: $1233. *Financial support:* In 2010–11, 6 students received support, including 6 teaching assistantships with full tuition reimbursements available (averaging $9,500 per year). Financial award application deadline: 3/1; financial award applicants required to submit FAFSA. *Faculty research:* Writing studies, writing in the disciplines, contemporary literature, Renaissance, Shakespeare, American studies, global studies, urban studies, Victorian literature, popular culture gender and sexuality studies, pedagogy, queer theory, English education, literacy education, literary theory. Total annual research expenditures: $45,104. *Unit head:* Dr. Linda Karell, Head, 406-994-3768, Fax: 406-994-2422, E-mail: lkarell@english.montana.edu. *Application contact:* Dr. Carl A. Fox, Vice Provost for Graduate Education, 406-994-4145, Fax: 406-994-7433, E-mail: gradstudy@montana.edu.

Montclair State University, The Graduate School, College of Humanities and Social Sciences, Department of English, Montclair, NJ 07043-1624. Offers elementary school specialization: language arts/literature 5-9 (Certificate); English (MA); teaching writing (Certificate). Part-time and evening/weekend programs available. *Faculty:* 45 full-time (29 women), 55 part-time/adjunct (39 women). *Students:* 16 full-time (11 women), 60 part-time (48 women); includes 1 Asian, non-Hispanic/Latino; 3 Hispanic/Latino, 1 international. Average age 34. 34 applicants, 68% accepted, 18 enrolled. In 2010, 11 master's, 2 other advanced degrees awarded. *Degree requirements:* For master's, thesis. *Entrance requirements:* For master's, GRE General Test, 2 letters of recommendation. Additional exam requirements/recommendations for international students: Required—TOEFL (minimum score: 83 iBT) or IELTS. *Application deadline:* For fall admission, 6/1 for international students; for spring admission, 10/1 for international students. Applications are processed on a rolling basis. Application fee: $60. Electronic applications accepted. *Expenses:* Tuition, state resident: part-time $501.34 per credit. Tuition, nonresident: part-time $773.88 per credit. Required fees: $71.15 per credit. *Financial support:* In 2010–11, 8 research assistantships with full tuition reimbursements (averaging $7,000 per year) were awarded; Federal Work-Study, scholarships/grants, and unspecified assistantships also available. Support available to part-time students. Financial award application deadline: 3/1; financial award applicants required to submit FAFSA. *Faculty research:* Modernism, Shakespeare, Victorian poetry, contemporary European film, nineteenth century American literature. *Unit head:* Dr. Dan Bronson, Chairperson, 973-655-4274. *Application contact:* Amy Aiello, Director of Graduate Admissions and Operations, 973-655-5147, Fax: 973-655-7869, E-mail: graduate.school@montclair.edu.

Morehead State University, Graduate Programs, Caudill College of Arts, Humanities and Social Sciences, Department of English, Morehead, KY 40351. Offers English (MA). Part-time and evening/weekend programs available. *Degree requirements:* For master's, comprehensive exam, thesis optional. *Entrance requirements:* For master's, GRE General Test, minimum GPA of 3.0 in English; undergraduate major or minor in English. Additional exam requirements/recommendations for international students: Required—TOEFL (minimum score 500 paper-based; 173 computer-based). Electronic applications accepted. *Faculty research:* Nineteenth and twentieth century American literature, linguistics, Victorian literature, modern British literature, creative writing.

Morgan State University, School of Graduate Studies, College of Liberal Arts, Department of English, Baltimore, MD 21251. Offers MA, PhD. Part-time programs available. *Degree requirements:* For master's, comprehensive exam, thesis; for doctorate, comprehensive exam, thesis/dissertation. *Entrance requirements:* For master's, GRE, minimum GPA of 2.5; for doctorate, GRE. Additional exam requirements/recommendations for international students: Required—TOEFL (minimum score 550 paper-based; 213 computer-based). *Faculty research:* African and African-American studies, nineteenth century American literature, rhetoric, women's studies, children's literature.

Mount Mary College, Graduate Programs, Program in English, Milwaukee, WI 53222-4597. Offers MA. Evening/weekend programs available. *Degree requirements:* For master's, comprehensive exam, thesis or alternative. *Entrance requirements:* For master's, minimum GPA of 2.75. Additional exam requirements/recommendations for international students: Required—TOEFL (minimum score 500 paper-based; 173 computer-based). Electronic applications accepted.

Murray State University, College of Humanities and Fine Arts, Department of English and Philosophy, Program in English, Murray, KY 42071. Offers MA. Part-time programs available. *Degree requirements:* For master's, comprehensive exam, thesis (for some programs).

National University, Academic Affairs, College of Letters and Sciences, Department of Art and Humanities, La Jolla, CA 92037-1011. Offers creative writing (MFA); English (MA); history (MA). Part-time and evening/weekend programs available. Postbaccalaureate distance learning degree programs offered (no on-campus study). *Faculty:* 17 full-time (6 women), 198 part-time/adjunct (110 women). *Students:* 198 full-time (144 women), 534 part-time (364 women); includes 99 Black or African American, non-Hispanic/Latino; 6 American Indian or Alaska Native, non-Hispanic/Latino; 10 Asian, non-Hispanic/Latino; 54 Hispanic/Latino; 14 Two or more races, non-Hispanic/Latino. Average age 38. 424 applicants, 100% accepted, 289 enrolled. In 2010, 222 master's awarded. *Degree requirements:* For master's, thesis (for some programs). *Entrance requirements:* For master's, interview, minimum GPA of 2.5. Additional exam requirements/recommendations for international students: Required—TOEFL (minimum score 550 paper-based; 213 computer-based; 79 iBT), IELTS (minimum score 6). *Application deadline:* Applications are processed on a rolling basis. Application fee: $60 ($65 for international students). Electronic applications accepted. *Expenses:* Tuition: Full-time $9450; part-time $350 per unit. Required fees: $350 per unit. One-time fee: $60. *Financial support:* Career-related internships or fieldwork, institutionally sponsored loans, scholarships/grants, and tuition waivers (partial) available. Support available to part-time students. Financial award application deadline: 6/30; financial award applicants required to submit FAFSA. *Unit head:* Dr. Janet Baker, Chair, 858-642-8472, Fax: 858-642-8715, E-mail: jbaker@nu.edu. *Application contact:* Dominick Giovanniello, Associate Regional Dean—San Diego, 800-NAT-UNIV, Fax: 858-541-7792, E-mail: dgiovann@nu.edu.

New Mexico Highlands University, Graduate Studies, College of Arts and Sciences, Department of Humanities, Las Vegas, NM 87701. Offers English (MA), including creative writing, language, rhetoric and composition, literature. *Faculty:* 8 full-time (5 women). *Students:* 13 full-time (5 women), 2 part-time (both women); includes 1 Hispanic/Latino; 2 Two or more races, non-Hispanic/Latino. Average age 36. 10 applicants, 100% accepted, 7 enrolled. In 2010, 4 master's awarded. *Degree requirements:* For master's, comprehensive exam, thesis. *Entrance requirements:* For master's, minimum undergraduate GPA of 3.0. Additional exam requirements/recommendations for international students: Required—TOEFL (minimum score 540 paper-based; 207 computer-based). *Application deadline:* For fall admission, 8/1 priority date for domestic students. Applications are processed on a rolling basis. Application fee: $15. *Expenses:* Tuition, state resident: full-time $2544. Required fees: $624; $132 per credit hour. *Financial support:* In 2010–11, 11 students received support. Career-related internships or fieldwork, Federal Work-Study, institutionally sponsored loans, scholarships/grants, tuition waivers (full and partial), and unspecified assistantships available. Support available to part-time students. Financial award application deadline: 3/1; financial award applicants required to submit FAFSA. *Faculty research:* Twentieth century literature, life path writing in homeless shelters, native American philosophy, medieval intellectual and cultural history, creating pedagogical tools for teaching law. *Unit head:* Dr. Barbara Risch, Department Head, 505-454-3451, E-mail: barbararisch@nmhu.edu. *Application contact:* Diane Trujillo, Administrative Assistant, Graduate Studies, 505-454-3266, Fax: 505-426-2117, E-mail: dtrujillo@nmhu.edu.

New Mexico State University, Graduate School, College of Arts and Sciences, Department of English, Las Cruces, NM 88003-8001. Offers creative writing (MFA); English (MA); rhetoric and professional communication (PhD). Part-time programs available. *Faculty:* 22 full-time (13 women), 1 (woman) part-time/adjunct. *Students:* 71 full-time (39 women), 31 part-time (17 women); includes 22 minority (5 Black or African American, non-Hispanic/Latino; 2 Asian, non-Hispanic/Latino; 14 Hispanic/Latino; 1 Two or more races, non-Hispanic/Latino), 4 international. Average age 32. 109 applicants, 58% accepted, 27 enrolled. In 2010, 30 master's, 2 doctorates awarded. *Degree requirements:* For master's, one foreign language, thesis (for some programs); for doctorate, comprehensive exam, thesis/dissertation, internship. *Entrance requirements:* For master's and doctorate, sample of written work. Additional exam requirements/recommendations for international students: Required—TOEFL (minimum score 550 paper-based; 79 iBT), IELTS (minimum score 6.5). *Application deadline:* For fall admission, 2/1 for domestic and international students. Application fee: $30 ($50 for international students). Electronic applications accepted. *Expenses:* Tuition, state resident: full-time $4536; part-time $242 per credit. Tuition, nonresident: full-time $15,816; part-time $712 per credit. Required fees: $636 per term. *Financial support:* In 2010–11, 3 research assistantships (averaging $6,817 per year), 49 teaching assistantships (averaging $15,105 per year) were awarded; fellowships, career-related internships or fieldwork, Federal Work-Study, institutionally sponsored loans, scholarships/grants, health care benefits, and unspecified assistantships also available. Financial award application deadline: 2/1; financial award applicants required to submit FAFSA. *Faculty research:* Composition research, history and theory of rhetoric, technical/professional communication, creative writing, English and American literature. *Unit head:* Dr. Monica F. Torres, Head, 575-646-2319, Fax: 575-646-7725, E-mail: mftorres@nmsu.edu. *Application contact:* Dr. Elizabeth Schirmer, Director of Graduate Studies, 575-646-1733, E-mail: eschirme@nmsu.edu.

New York University, Graduate School of Arts and Science, Department of English, Program in English and American Literature, New York, NY 10012-1019. Offers MA, PhD. *Students:* 139 full-time (94 women), 12 part-time (9 women); includes 4 Black or African American, non-Hispanic/Latino; 1 American Indian or Alaska Native, non-Hispanic/Latino; 10 Asian, non-Hispanic/Latino; 9 Hispanic/Latino, 20 international. Average age 28. 630 applicants, 27% accepted, 59 enrolled. In 2010, 30 master's, 11 doctorates awarded. *Degree requirements:* For master's, one foreign language, thesis or alternative, qualifying exams, special project; for doctorate, one foreign language, thesis/dissertation. *Entrance requirements:* For master's, GRE General Test. Additional exam requirements/recommendations for international students: Required—TOEFL. *Application deadline:* For fall admission, 12/15 for domestic students. Application fee: $90. *Financial support:* Fellowships with tuition reimbursements, teaching assistantships with tuition reimbursements, Federal Work-Study, institutionally sponsored loans, scholarships/grants, health care benefits, and unspecified assistantships available. Financial award application deadline: 12/15; financial award applicants required to submit FAFSA. *Unit head:* Gabriell Starr-Harpole, Chair, 212-998-8800, Fax: 212-995-4019, E-mail: gsas.english.admissions@nyu.edu. *Application contact:* Thomas Augst, Director of Graduate Studies, 212-998-8800, Fax: 212-995-4019, E-mail: gsas.english.admissions@nyu.edu.

New York University, Steinhardt School of Culture, Education, and Human Development, Department of Teaching and Learning, Program in English Education, New York, NY 10012-1019. Offers secondary and college (PhD), including applied linguistics, comparative education, curriculum, literature and reading, media education; teachers of English 7-12 (MA); teachers of English language and literature in college (Advanced Certificate). *Accreditation:* Teacher Education Accreditation Council. Part-time programs available. *Faculty:* 4 full-time (3 women). *Students:* 43 full-time (35 women), 22 part-time (19 women); includes 5 Black or African American, non-Hispanic/Latino; 3 Asian, non-Hispanic/Latino; 2 Hispanic/Latino, 2 international. Average age 30. 95 applicants, 71% accepted, 14 enrolled. In 2010, 25 master's, 1 doctorate, 1 other advanced degree awarded. *Degree requirements:* For master's, thesis (for some programs); for doctorate, thesis/dissertation. *Entrance requirements:* For doctorate, GRE General Test, interview; for Advanced Certificate, master's degree. Additional exam requirements/recommendations for international students: Required—TOEFL. *Application deadline:* For fall admission, 12/1 priority date for domestic and international students; for spring admission, 11/1 for domestic and international students. Applications are processed on a rolling basis. Application fee: $75. Electronic applications accepted. *Financial support:* Fellowships with full and partial tuition reimbursements, teaching assistantships with full and partial tuition reimbursements, career-related internships or fieldwork, Federal Work-Study, institutionally sponsored loans, scholarships/grants, tuition waivers (partial), and unspecified assistantships available. Support available to part-time students. Financial award application deadline: 2/1; financial award applicants required to submit FAFSA. *Faculty research:* Making meaning of literature, teaching of literature, urban adolescent literacy and equity, literacy development and globalization, digital media and literacy. *Unit head:* Director, 212-998-5460, Fax: 212-995-4049. *Application contact:* 212-998-5030, Fax: 212-995-4328, E-mail: steinhardt.gradadmissions@nyu.edu.

North Carolina Agricultural and Technical State University, Graduate School, College of Arts and Sciences, Department of English, Greensboro, NC 27411. Offers English (MA); English and Afro-American literature (MA); English education (MS). Part-time and evening/weekend programs available. *Degree requirements:* For master's, comprehensive exam, qualifying exam. *Entrance requirements:* For master's, GRE General Test, minimum GPA of 3.0.

English

North Carolina Central University, Division of Academic Affairs, College of Liberal Arts, Department of English and Mass Communication, Durham, NC 27707-3129. Offers English (MA). Part-time and evening/weekend programs available. *Degree requirements:* For master's, one foreign language, comprehensive exam, thesis. *Entrance requirements:* For master's, GRE, minimum GPA of 3.0 in major, 2.5 overall. Additional exam requirements/recommendations for international students: Required—TOEFL. *Faculty research:* Victorian literature, African-American literature, women's studies, literature and film, twentieth-century literature.

North Carolina State University, Graduate School, College of Humanities and Social Sciences, Department of English, Program in English, Raleigh, NC 27695. Offers MA. *Degree requirements:* For master's, thesis. *Entrance requirements:* For master's, GRE General Test. Electronic applications accepted. *Faculty research:* Creative writing, linguistics, rhetoric and composition, rhetoric and technical communication, film studies.

North Dakota State University, College of Graduate and Interdisciplinary Studies, College of Arts, Humanities and Social Sciences, Department of English, Fargo, ND 58108. Offers MA, MS. Part-time programs available. *Faculty:* 12 full-time (6 women), 1 part-time/adjunct (0 women). *Students:* 19 full-time (12 women), 19 part-time (14 women), 2 international. Average age 31. 33 applicants, 61% accepted, 14 enrolled. In 2010, 11 master's awarded. *Degree requirements:* For master's, one foreign language, thesis. *Entrance requirements:* Additional exam requirements/recommendations for international students: Required—TOEFL (minimum score 600 paper-based; 250 computer-based; 100 iBT), IELTS (minimum score 7). *Application deadline:* For fall admission, 4/1 priority date for domestic students; for spring admission, 12/15 priority date for domestic students. Applications are processed on a rolling basis. Application fee: $45 ($60 for international students). Electronic applications accepted. *Financial support:* In 2010–11, 3 fellowships with full tuition reimbursements (averaging $12,150 per year), 1 research assistantship (averaging $3,000 per year), 18 teaching assistantships with full tuition reimbursements (averaging $8,100 per year) were awarded; Federal Work-Study, institutionally sponsored loans, and scholarships/grants also available. Support available to part-time students. Financial award application deadline: 5/1. *Faculty research:* American and English literature, women's studies, language attitudes, composition practices, computers and composition. *Unit head:* Dr. Dale Sullivan, Head, 701-231-7143, Fax: 701-231-1047, E-mail: dale.sullivan@ndsu.edu. *Application contact:* Dr. Dale Sullivan, Head, 701-231-7143, Fax: 701-231-1047, E-mail: dale.sullivan@ndsu.edu.

Northeastern Illinois University, Graduate College, College of Arts and Sciences, Department of English, Programs in English, Chicago, IL 60625-4699. Offers composition/writing (MA); literature (MA). Part-time and evening/weekend programs available. *Faculty:* 14 full-time (4 women). *Students:* 9 full-time (8 women), 32 part-time (21 women); includes 6 minority (1 Asian, non-Hispanic/Latino; 5 Hispanic/Latino). Average age 40. 25 applicants, 44% accepted. In 2010, 7 master's awarded. *Degree requirements:* For master's, comprehensive exam, thesis optional. *Entrance requirements:* For master's, 30 hours of undergraduate course work in literature and composition (literature), BA in English or approval (composition/writing), minimum GPA of 2.75. Additional exam requirements/recommendations for international students: Required—TOEFL (minimum score 550 paper-based; 213 computer-based; 79 iBT). *Application deadline:* Applications are processed on a rolling basis. Application fee: $30. Electronic applications accepted. *Financial support:* In 2010–11, 13 students received support, including 3 research assistantships with full tuition reimbursements available (averaging $6,600 per year); career-related internships or fieldwork, Federal Work-Study, institutionally sponsored loans, scholarships/grants, tuition waivers (full and partial), and unspecified assistantships also available. Support available to part-time students. Financial award applicants required to submit FAFSA. *Faculty research:* Arthurian literature, Southern American literature, rhetoric and theories of authorship. *Unit head:* Dr. Timothy R. Libretti, Graduate Adviser, 773-442-5820, Fax: 773-442-5490, E-mail: t-libretti@neiu.edu. *Application contact:* Dr. Timothy R. Libretti, Graduate Adviser, 773-442-5820, Fax: 773-442-5490, E-mail: t-libretti@neiu.edu.

Northeastern State University, Graduate College, College of Liberal Arts, Department of Languages and Literature, Tahlequah, OK 74464-2399. Offers English (MA), including literature, rhetoric/composition. *Students:* 22 full-time (16 women), 40 part-time (29 women); includes 13 minority (2 Black or African American, non-Hispanic/Latino; 9 American Indian or Alaska Native, non-Hispanic/Latino; 1 Asian, non-Hispanic/Latino; 1 Hispanic/Latino), 2 international. In 2010, 14 master's awarded. *Degree requirements:* For master's, thesis. *Entrance requirements:* For master's, GRE or MAT, minimum GPA of 2.5. Additional exam requirements/recommendations for international students: Required—TOEFL (minimum score 213 computer-based). *Application deadline:* For fall admission, 6/1 priority date for domestic students. Applications are processed on a rolling basis. Application fee: $0 ($25 for international students). Electronic applications accepted. *Expenses:* Tuition, state resident: part-time $144 per credit hour. Tuition, nonresident: part-time $384.05 per credit hour. Required fees: $34.90 per credit hour. Tuition and fees vary according to program. *Financial support:* Application deadline: 3/1. *Unit head:* Dr. Jacqueline Wilcox, Chair, 918-456-5511 Ext. 3609, E-mail: wilcoxj@nsuok.edu. *Application contact:* Margie Railey, Administrative Assistant, 918-456-5511 Ext. 2093, Fax: 918-458-2061, E-mail: railey@nsouk.edu.

Northeastern University, College of Social Sciences and Humanities, Department of English, Boston, MA 02115-5096. Offers MA, PhD. Part-time and evening/weekend programs available. *Faculty:* 33 full-time (22 women), 28 part-time/adjunct (22 women). *Students:* 67 full-time (46 women), 1 (woman) part-time; includes 5 minority (3 Asian, non-Hispanic/Latino; 2 Hispanic/Latino), 6 international. 123 applicants, 30% accepted, 13 enrolled. In 2010, 6 master's, 3 doctorates awarded. *Degree requirements:* For master's, one foreign language, comprehensive exam, qualifying exams; for doctorate, 2 foreign languages, comprehensive exam, thesis/dissertation, qualifying exams. *Entrance requirements:* For master's and doctorate, GRE General Test, GRE Subject Test, sample of written work. Additional exam requirements/recommendations for international students: Required—TOEFL. *Application deadline:* For fall admission, 2/1 priority date for domestic and international students. Applications are processed on a rolling basis. Application fee: $50. Electronic applications accepted. *Financial support:* In 2010–11, 30 teaching assistantships with tuition reimbursements (averaging $15,550 per year) were awarded; fellowships with tuition reimbursements, research assistantships with tuition reimbursements, career-related internships or fieldwork, tuition waivers (full and partial), and unspecified assistantships also available. Financial award application deadline: 3/1; financial award applicants required to submit FAFSA. *Faculty research:* Literature, creative writing, composition studies, linguistics. *Unit head:* Dr. Elizabeth Dillon, Graduate Coordinator, 617-373-3692, Fax: 617-373-2509, E-mail: gradenglish@neu.edu. *Application contact:* Jo-Anne Dickinson, Admissions Contact, 617-373-5990, Fax: 617-373-7281, E-mail: gsas@neu.edu.

Northern Arizona University, Graduate College, College of Arts and Letters, Department of English, Flagstaff, AZ 86011. Offers applied linguistics (PhD); English (MA), including creative writing, general English studies, literacy, technology and professional writing, literature, secondary English education; professional writing (Certificate); teaching English as a second language (MA, Certificate). Part-time programs available. *Faculty:* 42 full-time (30 women). *Students:* 107 full-time (70 women), 100 part-time (77 women); includes 39 minority (9 Black or African American, non-Hispanic/Latino; 4 American Indian or Alaska Native, non-Hispanic/Latino; 3 Asian, non-Hispanic/Latino; 15 Hispanic/Latino; 8 Two or more races, non-Hispanic/Latino), 27 international. Average age 31. 238 applicants, 68% accepted, 90 enrolled. In 2010, 84 master's, 2 doctorates, 20 other advanced degrees awarded. *Degree requirements:* For master's, comprehensive exam (for some programs), thesis (for some programs), departmental qualifying exam; for doctorate, comprehensive exam, thesis/dissertation, departmental qualifying exam. *Entrance requirements:* For master's, minimum GPA of 3.0 or GRE; for doctorate, GRE General Test. Additional exam requirements/recommendations for international students: Required—TOEFL (minimum score 550 paper-based; 213 computer-based; 80 iBT), IELTS (minimum score 7), TOEFL (600 paper, 250 computer, 100 iBT for PhD; 570 paper, 237 computer, 89 iBT for MA). *Application deadline:* For fall admission, 4/15 priority date for domestic students, 2/15 priority date for international students; for spring admission, 11/15 priority date for domestic and international students. Applications are processed on a rolling basis. Application fee: $65. Electronic applications accepted. *Financial support:* In 2010–11, 72 teaching assistantships with partial tuition reimbursements (averaging $11,623 per year) were awarded; Federal Work-Study, scholarships/grants, health care benefits, tuition waivers (full and partial), and unspecified assistantships also available. Financial award applicants required to submit FAFSA. *Unit head:* Dr. J. Allen Woodman, Chair, 928-523-5651, Fax: 928-523-7074, E-mail: allen.woodman@nau.edu. *Application contact:* Giovanina Bucci, Secretary, 928-523-4911, Fax: 928-523-7074, E-mail: giovanina.bucci@nau.edu.

Northern Illinois University, Graduate School, College of Liberal Arts and Sciences, Department of English, De Kalb, IL 60115-2854. Offers MA, PhD. Part-time programs available. *Faculty:* 32 full-time (13 women), 2 part-time/adjunct (both women). *Students:* 73 full-time (46 women), 68 part-time (42 women); includes 2 Black or African American, non-Hispanic/Latino; 6 Hispanic/Latino; 1 Two or more races, non-Hispanic/Latino, 5 international. Average age 32. 113 applicants, 42% accepted, 32 enrolled. In 2010, 32 master's, 4 doctorates awarded. Terminal master's awarded for partial completion of doctoral program. *Degree requirements:* For master's, variable foreign language requirement, comprehensive exam, thesis optional; for doctorate, variable foreign language requirement, thesis/dissertation, candidacy exam, dissertation defense. *Entrance requirements:* For master's, GRE General Test, minimum GPA of 2.75; for doctorate, GRE General Test, minimum GPA of 2.75 (undergraduate), 3.2 (graduate). Additional exam requirements/recommendations for international students: Required—TOEFL (minimum score 550 paper-based; 213 computer-based). *Application deadline:* For fall admission, 6/1 for domestic students, 5/1 for international students; for spring admission, 11/1 for domestic students, 10/1 for international students. Applications are processed on a rolling basis. Application fee: $30. Electronic applications accepted. *Expenses:* Tuition, state resident: full-time $7200; part-time $300 per credit hour. Tuition, nonresident: full-time $14,400; part-time $600 per credit hour. Required fees: $79 per credit hour. *Financial support:* In 2010–11, 61 teaching assistantships with full tuition reimbursements were awarded; fellowships with full tuition reimbursements, research assistantships with full tuition reimbursements, career-related internships or fieldwork, Federal Work-Study, scholarships/grants, tuition waivers (full), and unspecified assistantships also available. Support available to part-time students. Financial award applicants required to submit FAFSA. *Faculty research:* Nineteenth century English literature, linguistic programs, portfolio assembly, Mideast literature, old English folklore. *Unit head:* Dr. Phillip Eubanks, Chair, 815-753-0615, Fax: 815-753-0606, E-mail: eubanks@niu.edu. *Application contact:* Dr. Jeffrey Johnson, Director, Graduate Studies, 815-753-6602, E-mail: jsjohnson@niu.edu.

Northern Kentucky University, Office of Graduate Programs, College of Arts and Sciences, Program in English, Highland Heights, KY 41099. Offers composition and rhetoric (Certificate); creative writing (Certificate); cultural studies (Certificate); English (MA); professional writing (Certificate). Part-time and evening/weekend programs available. *Faculty:* 11 full-time (6 women). *Students:* 8 full-time (5 women), 66 part-time (53 women); includes 6 minority (4 Black or African American, non-Hispanic/Latino; 1 Hispanic/Latino; 1 Two or more races, non-Hispanic/Latino). Average age 34. 36 applicants, 94% accepted, 32 enrolled. In 2010, 3 master's awarded. *Degree requirements:* For master's, comprehensive exam (for some programs), comprehensive exam, thesis, project, or portfolio. *Entrance requirements:* For master's, minimum GPA of 3.0, two letters of reference. Additional exam requirements/recommendations for international students: Required—TOEFL (minimum score 550 paper-based; 213 computer-based; 79 iBT); Recommended—IELTS (minimum score 6.5). *Application deadline:* For fall admission, 7/1 priority date for domestic students, 6/1 priority date for international students; for spring admission, 11/1 for domestic students, 10/1 for international students. Applications are processed on a rolling basis. Application fee: $40. Electronic applications accepted. *Expenses:* Tuition, state resident: full-time $7254; part-time $403 per credit hour. Tuition, nonresident: full-time $12,492; part-time $694 per credit hour. Tuition and fees vary according to degree level and program. *Financial support:* Unspecified assistantships available. Financial award applicants required to submit FAFSA. *Faculty research:* Composition and rhetoric, creative writing, English and American literature, professional writing, cultural studies. *Unit head:* Dr. Roxanne Kent-Drury, Coordinator, 859-572-6636, Fax: 859-572-6093, E-mail: rkdrury@nku.edu. *Application contact:* Dr. Peg Griffin, Director of Graduate Programs, 859-572-6934, Fax: 859-572-6670, E-mail: griffinp@nku.edu.

Northern Michigan University, College of Graduate Studies, College of Arts and Sciences, Department of English, Marquette, MI 49855-5301. Offers creative writing (MFA); literature (MA); pedagogy (MA); writing (MA). Part-time programs available. *Degree requirements:* For master's, thesis or alternative. *Entrance requirements:* For master's, minimum GPA of 2.75.

Northwestern State University of Louisiana, Graduate Studies and Research, Department of Language and Communication, Natchitoches, LA 71497. Offers English (MA). *Degree requirements:* For master's, one foreign language, comprehensive exam, thesis or alternative. *Entrance requirements:* For master's, GRE General Test, minimum undergraduate GPA of 2.5.

Northwestern University, The Graduate School, Judd A. and Marjorie Weinberg College of Arts and Sciences, Department of English, Evanston, IL 60208. Offers MA, PhD. Admissions and degrees offered through The Graduate School. Terminal master's awarded for partial completion of doctoral program. *Degree requirements:* For master's, thesis; for doctorate, one foreign language, thesis/dissertation, oral and written qualifying exam. *Entrance requirements:* For master's and doctorate, GRE General Test, sample of written work. Additional exam requirements/recommendations for international students: Required—TOEFL. Electronic applications accepted. *Faculty research:* Renaissance literature, theatre and drama, American literature, modern European contemporary literature, poetry, cultural history.

Northwestern University, School of Continuing Studies, Program in Literature, Evanston, IL 60208. Offers American literature (MA); British literature (MA); comparative and world literature (MA).

Northwest Missouri State University, Graduate School, College of Arts and Sciences, Department of English, Maryville, MO 64468-6001. Offers English (MA); English with speech emphasis (MA); teaching English (option 1) (MS Ed); teaching English with speech emphasis (MS Ed). Part-time programs available. *Faculty:* 10 full-time (4 women). *Students:* 9 full-time (3 women); includes 1 Two or more races, non-Hispanic/Latino. 8 applicants, 63% accepted, 4 enrolled. In 2010, 4 master's awarded. *Degree requirements:* For master's, comprehensive exam, thesis optional. *Entrance requirements:* For master's, GRE General Test, minimum undergraduate GPA of 2.5, writing sample. Additional exam requirements/recommendations for international students: Required—TOEFL (minimum score 550 paper-based; 213 computer-based). *Application deadline:* For fall admission, 7/1 for domestic and international students; for spring admission, 11/15 for domestic and international students. Applications are processed on a rolling basis. Application fee: $0 ($50 for international students). *Financial support:* In 2010–11, 5 teaching assistantships with full tuition reimbursements (averaging $6,000 per year) were awarded. Financial award application deadline: 4/1; financial award applicants required to submit FAFSA. *Unit head:* Dr. Michael Hobbs, Chairperson, 660-562-1285. *Application contact:* Dr. Gregory Haddock, Dean of Graduate School, 660-562-1145, Fax: 660-562-1096, E-mail: gradsch@nwmissouri.edu.

Notre Dame de Namur University, Division of Academic Affairs, College of Arts and Sciences, Department of English, Belmont, CA 94002-1908. Offers English (MA); teaching English to speakers of other languages (Certificate). Part-time and evening/weekend programs available. *Faculty:* 5 full-time (2 women), 5 part-time/adjunct (3 women). *Students:* 4 full-time (3 women), 20 part-time (15 women); includes 1 Hispanic/Latino. Average age 28. 6 applicants, 100% accepted, 4 enrolled. In 2010, 6 master's awarded. *Degree requirements:* For master's, thesis optional, exam. *Entrance requirements:* For master's, minimum GPA of 2.5, writing sample. Additional exam requirements/recommendations for international students: Required—TOEFL (minimum score 550 paper-based; 213 computer-based; 79 iBT). *Application deadline:* For fall admission, 8/1 priority date for domestic students; for spring admission, 12/1 priority date for domestic students. Applications are processed on a rolling basis. Application fee: $50 ($500 for international students). Electronic applications accepted. *Expenses:* Tuition: Full-time $14,220;

part-time $790 per credit. Required fees: $35 per semester. Tuition and fees vary according to program. *Financial support:* Career-related internships or fieldwork available. Support available to part-time students. Financial award applicants required to submit FAFSA. *Unit head:* Jacqueline Berger, Director, 650-508-3730. *Application contact:* Candace Hallmark, Associate Director of Admissions, 650-508-3600, Fax: 650-508-3426, E-mail: grad.admit@ndnu.edu.

Oakland University, Graduate Study and Lifelong Learning, College of Arts and Sciences, Department of English, Rochester, MI 48309-4401. Offers MA. Part-time and evening/weekend programs available. *Entrance requirements:* For master's, minimum GPA of 3.0 for unconditional admission. Additional exam requirements/recommendations for international students: Required—TOEFL (minimum score 550 paper-based; 213 computer-based). Electronic applications accepted.

The Ohio State University, Graduate School, College of Arts and Sciences, Division of Arts and Humanities, Department of English, Columbus, OH 43210. Offers MA, MFA, PhD. *Faculty:* 100. *Students:* 120 full-time (74 women), 59 part-time (38 women); includes 31 minority (6 Black or African American, non-Hispanic/Latino; 4 Asian, non-Hispanic/Latino; 16 Hispanic/Latino; 1 Native Hawaiian or other Pacific Islander, non-Hispanic/Latino; 4 Two or more races, non-Hispanic/Latino), 9 international. Average age 30. In 2010, 36 master's, 6 doctorates awarded. *Degree requirements:* For master's, one foreign language, thesis or written exam; for doctorate, one foreign language, thesis/dissertation. *Entrance requirements:* For master's and doctorate, GRE General Test. Additional exam requirements/recommendations for international students: Required—TOEFL (minimum score 600 paper-based; 250 computer-based). *Application deadline:* For fall admission, 8/15 priority date for domestic students, 7/1 priority date for international students; for winter admission, 12/1 priority date for domestic students, 11/1 priority date for international students; for spring admission, 3/1 priority date for domestic students, 2/1 priority date for international students. Applications are processed on a rolling basis. Application fee: $40 ($50 for international students). Electronic applications accepted. *Expenses:* Tuition, state resident: full-time $10,605. Tuition, nonresident: full-time $26,535. Tuition and fees vary according to course load and program. *Financial support:* Fellowships, research assistantships, teaching assistantships, Federal Work-Study, institutionally sponsored loans, and unspecified assistantships available. Support available to part-time students. *Unit head:* Richard Dutton, Chair, 614-292-7661, E-mail: dutton.42@osu.edu. *Application contact:* Graduate Admissions, 614-292-9444, Fax: 614-292-3895, E-mail: domestic.grad@osu.edu.

Ohio University, Graduate College, College of Arts and Sciences, Department of English Language and Literature, Athens, OH 45701-2979. Offers MA, PhD. Part-time programs available. *Students:* 68 full-time (38 women), 3 part-time (2 women); includes 5 minority (1 Black or African American, non-Hispanic/Latino; 1 American Indian or Alaska Native, non-Hispanic/Latino; 2 Hispanic/Latino; 1 Two or more races, non-Hispanic/Latino), 10 international. 88 applicants, 22% accepted, 18 enrolled. In 2010, 16 master's, 8 doctorates awarded. *Degree requirements:* For master's, one foreign language, thesis or alternative; for doctorate, one foreign language, comprehensive exam, thesis/dissertation, oral exam, public lecture. *Entrance requirements:* For master's, GRE General Test, minimum GPA of 3.0, writing sample; for doctorate, GRE General Test, minimum GPA of 3.0, master's degree in English, writing sample. Additional exam requirements/recommendations for international students: Required—TOEFL (minimum score 550 paper-based; 80 iBT) or IELTS (minimum score 6.5). *Application deadline:* For fall admission, 1/15 for domestic and international students. Application fee: $50 ($55 for international students). Electronic applications accepted. *Financial support:* Teaching assistantships with full tuition reimbursements, Federal Work-Study, institutionally sponsored loans, and unspecified assistantships available. Financial award application deadline: 1/15. *Faculty research:* Environmental literature, post-colonial studies, print culture, film in popular culture, computers in pedagogy. Total annual research expenditures: $54,676. *Unit head:* Dr. Marsha Dutton, Department Chair, 740-597-2752, Fax: 740-593-2832, E-mail: dutton@ohio.edu. *Application contact:* Dr. Marsha Dutton, Department Chair, 740-597-2752, Fax: 740-593-2832, E-mail: dutton@ohio.edu.

Oklahoma State University, College of Arts and Sciences, Department of English, Stillwater, OK 74078. Offers creative writing (MFA); English (MA, PhD). *Faculty:* 52 full-time (31 women), 3 part-time/adjunct (all women). *Students:* 10 full-time (7 women), 145 part-time (71 women); includes 1 Black or African American, non-Hispanic/Latino; 8 American Indian or Alaska Native, non-Hispanic/Latino; 2 Asian, non-Hispanic/Latino; 5 Hispanic/Latino, 20 international. Average age 32. 148 applicants, 34% accepted, 32 enrolled. In 2010, 21 master's, 4 doctorates awarded. *Degree requirements:* For master's, comprehensive exam, thesis; for doctorate, comprehensive exam, thesis/dissertation. *Entrance requirements:* For master's, GRE General Test, minimum GPA of 3.0, writing sample; for doctorate, GRE General Test, minimum GPA of 3.5, writing sample. Additional exam requirements/recommendations for international students: Required—TOEFL (minimum score 550 paper-based; 79 iBT). *Application deadline:* For fall admission, 3/1 priority date for international students; for spring admission, 8/1 priority date for international students. Applications are processed on a rolling basis. Application fee: $40 ($75 for international students). Electronic applications accepted. *Expenses:* Tuition, state resident: full-time $3716; part-time $154.85 per credit hour. Tuition, nonresident: full-time $14,892; part-time $621 per credit hour. Required fees: $2044; $85.20 per credit hour. One-time fee: $50. Tuition and fees vary according to course load and campus/location. *Financial support:* In 2010–11, 2 research assistantships (averaging $12,960 per year), 107 teaching assistantships (averaging $14,625 per year) were awarded; career-related internships or fieldwork, Federal Work-Study, scholarships/grants, health care benefits, tuition waivers (partial), and unspecified assistantships also available. Support available to part-time students. Financial award application deadline: 3/1; financial award applicants required to submit FAFSA. *Faculty research:* American and British novels, poetry, and autobiography; Native American languages and literature; institutional history of American film, history, and adaptations; rhetoric and theories of human communication; learning strategies of second language learners. *Unit head:* Dr. Carol Moder, Head, 405-744-9474, Fax: 405-744-6326. *Application contact:* Dr. Gordon Emslie, Dean, 405-744-6368, Fax: 405-744-0355, E-mail: grad-i@okstate.edu.

Old Dominion University, College of Arts and Letters, Doctoral Program in English, Norfolk, VA 23529. Offers PhD. Part-time and evening/weekend programs available. Postbaccalaureate distance learning degree programs offered (minimal on-campus study). *Faculty:* 20 full-time (11 women), 1 (woman) part-time/adjunct. *Students:* 24 full-time (19 women), 25 part-time (19 women); includes 8 minority (5 Black or African American, non-Hispanic/Latino; 1 Hispanic/Latino; 2 Two or more races, non-Hispanic/Latino), 1 international. Average age 36. 52 applicants, 23% accepted, 11 enrolled. In 2010, 2 doctorates awarded. *Degree requirements:* For doctorate, comprehensive exam, thesis/dissertation, research competency in foreign language, statistics, or new media. *Entrance requirements:* For doctorate, GRE General Test, MA in English or related field with minimum GPA of 3.5, writing sample, resume, goals statement, letter of recommendation. Additional exam requirements/recommendations for international students: Required—TOEFL. *Application deadline:* For fall admission, 2/15 for domestic students. Application fee: $40. Electronic applications accepted. *Expenses:* Tuition, state resident: full-time $8592; part-time $358 per credit. Tuition, nonresident: full-time $21,672; part-time $903 per credit. Required fees: $119 per semester. One-time fee: $50. *Financial support:* In 2010–11, 12 students received support, including 3 fellowships with full tuition reimbursements available (averaging $15,000 per year), 1 research assistantship with full tuition reimbursement available (averaging $15,000 per year), 8 teaching assistantships with full tuition reimbursements available (averaging $15,000 per year); career-related internships or fieldwork, scholarships/grants, and unspecified assistantships also available. Support available to part-time students. Financial award application deadline: 2/15; financial award applicants required to submit FAFSA. *Faculty research:* New media studies, rhetorical history and theory, digital studies, writing studies, professional writing and document design, linguistics, textual studies, literary studies. *Unit head:* Dr. Joyce Neff, Graduate Program Director, 757-683-6875, Fax: 757-683-3241, E-mail: jneff@odu.edu. *Application contact:* Dr. Robert Wojtowicz, Associate Dean, 757-683-6077, Fax: 757-683-5746, E-mail: rwojtowi@odu.edu.

Old Dominion University, College of Arts and Letters, Master of Arts in English Program, Norfolk, VA 23529. Offers MA. Part-time and evening/weekend programs available. Postbaccalaureate distance learning degree programs offered (minimal on-campus study). *Faculty:* 17 full-time (8 women). *Students:* 24 full-time (15 women), 29 part-time (22 women); includes 12 minority (7 Black or African American, non-Hispanic/Latino; 1 American Indian or Alaska Native, non-Hispanic/Latino; 2 Hispanic/Latino; 1 Native Hawaiian or other Pacific Islander, non-Hispanic/Latino; 1 Two or more races, non-Hispanic/Latino), 2 international. Average age 31. 56 applicants, 66% accepted, 30 enrolled. In 2010, 26 master's awarded. *Degree requirements:* For master's, comprehensive exam, thesis optional. *Entrance requirements:* For master's, GRE General Test, 24 hours in English, sample of written work. Additional exam requirements/recommendations for international students: Required—TOEFL. *Application deadline:* For fall admission, 6/1 priority date for domestic students, 4/13 priority date for international students; for winter admission, 11/1 priority date for domestic students, 10/1 priority date for international students; for spring admission, 3/1 priority date for domestic students, 2/1 for international students. Applications are processed on a rolling basis. Application fee: $40. Electronic applications accepted. *Expenses:* Tuition, state resident: full-time $8592; part-time $358 per credit. Tuition, nonresident: full-time $21,672; part-time $903 per credit. Required fees: $119 per semester. One-time fee: $50. *Financial support:* In 2010–11, 3 fellowships with tuition reimbursements (averaging $15,000 per year), 2 research assistantships (averaging $1,500 per year), 6 teaching assistantships (averaging $1,500 per year) were awarded; career-related internships or fieldwork, scholarships/grants, and unspecified assistantships also available. Support available to part-time students. Financial award application deadline: 2/15; financial award applicants required to submit FAFSA. *Faculty research:* Literary theory, composition theory, professional writing, rhetoric, British and American literature. Total annual research expenditures: $3,451. *Unit head:* Dr. Joseph P. Cosco, Graduate Program Director, 757-683-5473, E-mail: jcosco@odu.edu. *Application contact:* Dr. Joseph P. Cosco, Graduate Program Director, 757-683-5473, E-mail: jcosco@odu.edu.

Old Dominion University, Darden College of Education, Programs in Secondary Education, Norfolk, VA 23529. Offers biology (MS Ed); chemistry (MS Ed); English (MS Ed); instructional technology (MS Ed); library science (MS Ed); secondary education (MS Ed). *Accreditation:* NCATE. Part-time and evening/weekend programs available. Postbaccalaureate distance learning degree programs offered (minimal on-campus study). *Faculty:* 20 full-time (16 women). *Students:* 80 full-time (46 women), 101 part-time (61 women); includes 37 minority (22 Black or African American, non-Hispanic/Latino; 2 Asian, non-Hispanic/Latino; 6 Hispanic/Latino; 1 Native Hawaiian or other Pacific Islander, non-Hispanic/Latino; 6 Two or more races, non-Hispanic/Latino). Average age 32. 67 applicants, 79% accepted, 53 enrolled. In 2010, 105 master's awarded. *Degree requirements:* For master's, comprehensive exam, thesis. *Entrance requirements:* For master's, GRE General Test or MAT, PRAXIS I (for licensure), minimum GPA of 2.8, teaching certificate. Additional exam requirements/recommendations for international students: Required—TOEFL. *Application deadline:* For fall admission, 6/1 for domestic and international students; for winter admission, 11/1 for domestic and international students; for spring admission, 3/1 for domestic and international students. Applications are processed on a rolling basis. Application fee: $50. Electronic applications accepted. *Expenses:* Tuition, state resident: full-time $8592; part-time $358 per credit. Tuition, nonresident: full-time $21,672; part-time $903 per credit. Required fees: $119 per semester. One-time fee: $50. *Financial support:* In 2010–11, 56 students received support, including fellowships (averaging $15,000 per year), 2 research assistantships with tuition reimbursements available (averaging $9,000 per year), 3 teaching assistantships with tuition reimbursements available (averaging $12,500 per year); career-related internships or fieldwork, Federal Work-Study, institutionally sponsored loans, scholarships/grants, and tuition waivers (partial) also available. Support available to part-time students. Financial award application deadline: 2/15; financial award applicants required to submit FAFSA. *Faculty research:* Use of technology, writing project for teachers, geography teaching, reading. *Unit head:* Dr. Robert Lucking, Graduate Program Director, 757-683-5545, Fax: 757-683-5862, E-mail: rlucking@odu.edu. *Application contact:* Dr. Robert Lucking, Graduate Program Director, 757-683-5545, Fax: 757-683-5862, E-mail: rlucking@odu.edu.

Oregon State University, Graduate School, College of Liberal Arts, Department of English, Corvallis, OR 97331. Offers MA, MAIS, MFA. *Degree requirements:* For master's, one foreign language, thesis. *Entrance requirements:* For master's, minimum GPA of 3.0 in last 90 hours of course work. Additional exam requirements/recommendations for international students: Required—TOEFL. *Faculty research:* Composition and rhetoric, American literature theory, American renaissance, gender studies, English drama.

Our Lady of the Lake University of San Antonio, College of Arts and Sciences, Program in English, San Antonio, TX 78207-4689. Offers communication arts (MA); English and literature (MA); English education (MA); writing (MA). Program offered jointly with University of the Incarnate Word, St. Mary's University. Part-time and evening/weekend programs available. *Students:* 6 full-time (5 women), 18 part-time (14 women); includes 17 minority (1 Black or African American, non-Hispanic/Latino; 1 American Indian or Alaska Native, non-Hispanic/Latino; 15 Hispanic/Latino). Average age 35. In 2010, 8 master's awarded. *Degree requirements:* For master's, comprehensive exam, thesis optional. *Entrance requirements:* For master's, GRE General Test or MAT, minimum GPA of 3.0 in last 60 hours, 2.5 overall. Additional exam requirements/recommendations for international students: Required—TOEFL. *Application deadline:* Applications are processed on a rolling basis. Application fee: $25 ($50 for international students). Electronic applications accepted. *Expenses:* Tuition: Full-time $13,500; part-time $750 per contact hour. Required fees: $330. Tuition and fees vary according to course level, degree level and campus/location. *Financial support:* Research assistantships, teaching assistantships, career-related internships or fieldwork, Federal Work-Study, institutionally sponsored loans, and tuition waivers (partial) available. Financial award application deadline: 4/15. *Faculty research:* Writing theory and research, contemporary Southern literature, popular culture, poetry, literature of the Southwest. *Unit head:* Dr. Michael Lueker, Chair, 210-434-6711 Ext. 2242, E-mail: luekm@lake.ollusa.edu. *Application contact:* 210-434-6711, Fax: 210-431-4036, E-mail: gradadm@lake.ollusa.edu.

Penn State University Park, Graduate School, College of the Liberal Arts, Department of English, State College, University Park, PA 16802-1503. Offers MA, MFA, PhD.

Pittsburg State University, Graduate School, College of Arts and Sciences, Department of English, Pittsburg, KS 66762. Offers MA. *Degree requirements:* For master's, thesis or alternative. *Faculty research:* American fiction, American poetry, British fiction, British poetry, composition theory.

Portland State University, Graduate Studies, College of Liberal Arts and Sciences, Department of English, Portland, OR 97207-0751. Offers MA, MA/MS. Part-time and evening/weekend programs available. *Faculty:* 40 full-time (19 women), 47 part-time/adjunct (28 women). *Students:* 116 full-time (90 women), 101 part-time (67 women); includes 1 Black or African American, non-Hispanic/Latino; 1 American Indian or Alaska Native, non-Hispanic/Latino; 6 Asian, non-Hispanic/Latino; 5 Hispanic/Latino; 3 Two or more races, non-Hispanic/Latino, 5 international. Average age 31. 299 applicants, 43% accepted, 72 enrolled. In 2010, 74 master's awarded. *Degree requirements:* For master's, one foreign language, comprehensive exam (for some programs), thesis (for some programs), oral and written exams. *Entrance requirements:* For master's, minimum GPA of 3.25 in upper-division course work and English courses or 2.75 overall, 3 letters of recommendation. Additional exam requirements/recommendations for international students: Required—TOEFL (minimum score 600 paper-based). *Application deadline:* For fall admission, 1/18 for domestic students, 1/15 for international students; for winter admission, 9/1 for domestic and international students; for spring admission, 11/1 for domestic and international students. Application fee: $50. *Expenses:* Tuition, state resident: full-time $8505; part-time $315 per credit. Tuition, nonresident: full-time $13,284; part-time $492 per credit. Required fees: $1482; $21 per credit. $99 per term. One-time fee: $120. Part-time tuition and fees vary according to course load and program. *Financial support:* In 2010–11, 17 teaching assistantships with full tuition reimbursements (averaging $6,661 per

English

Portland State University (continued)

year) were awarded; research assistantships, career-related internships or fieldwork, Federal Work-Study, scholarships/grants, and unspecified assistantships also available. Support available to part-time students. Financial award application deadline: 3/1; financial award applicants required to submit FAFSA. *Faculty research:* American literature and cultural studies, medieval and British literature, writing prose fiction and poetry, rhetoric and composition, women's literature. Total annual research expenditures: $48,095. *Unit head:* Dr. Jennifer Ruth, Interim Chair, 503-725-4944, Fax: 503-725-3561, E-mail: ruthj@pdx.edu. *Application contact:* Nixie Stark, Program Administrator, 503-725-3521, Fax: 503-725-3561, E-mail: starkn@pdx.edu.

Prairie View A&M University, College of Arts and Sciences, Department of Languages and Communication, Prairie View, TX 77446-0519. Offers English (MA). Part-time programs available. *Faculty:* 3 full-time (2 women). *Students:* 4 full-time (3 women), 6 part-time (5 women); includes 4 Black or African American, non-Hispanic/Latino. Average age 30. 2 applicants, 100% accepted, 2 enrolled. In 2010, 1 master's awarded. *Degree requirements:* For master's, comprehensive exam, thesis, exit exam. *Entrance requirements:* For master's, GRE General Test, bachelor's degree in English or equivalent. Additional exam requirements/recommendations for international students: Required—TOEFL. *Application deadline:* For fall admission, 7/1 for domestic students, 6/1 for international students; for winter admission, 4/1 for domestic students, 10/1 for international students; for spring admission, 3/1 for domestic students, 2/1 for international students. Application fee: $50. *Expenses:* Tuition, state resident: full-time $3586.14; part-time $119.06 per credit hour. Tuition, nonresident: part-time $511.23 per credit hour. *Financial support:* In 2010–11, 2 students received support, including 2 teaching assistantships (averaging $12,000 per year); career-related internships or fieldwork, Federal Work-Study, institutionally sponsored loans, and tuition waivers (full and partial) also available. Support available to part-time students. Financial award application deadline: 4/1; financial award applicants required to submit FAFSA. *Faculty research:* Composition, rhetoric, technical writing, literature, communication, pedagogy in general and for literature, online teaching. *Unit head:* Dr. Dejun Liu, Head, 936-261-3731, Fax: 936-261-3209, E-mail: deliu@pvamu.edu. *Application contact:* Dr. Dejun Liu, Head, 936-261-3731, Fax: 936-261-3209, E-mail: deliu@pvamu.edu.

Princeton University, Graduate School, Department of English, Princeton, NJ 08544-1019. Offers PhD. *Degree requirements:* For doctorate, 2 foreign languages, thesis/dissertation. *Entrance requirements:* For doctorate, GRE General Test, GRE Subject Test, sample of written work. Additional exam requirements/recommendations for international students: Required—TOEFL (minimum score 600 paper-based; 250 computer-based). Electronic applications accepted.

Purdue University, Graduate School, College of Liberal Arts, Department of English, West Lafayette, IN 47907. Offers creative writing (MFA); literature (MA, PhD), including linguistics, literature and philosophy (PhD), rhetoric and composition, theory and cultural studies (PhD). Part-time programs available. *Degree requirements:* For master's, one foreign language; for doctorate, one foreign language, thesis/dissertation. *Entrance requirements:* For master's and doctorate, GRE General Test, sample of written work. Additional exam requirements/recommendations for international students: Required—TOEFL. Electronic applications accepted. *Faculty research:* Cultural studies, postmodern narrative, contemporary women writers, composition theory, slave narratives.

Purdue University Calumet, Graduate Studies Office, School of Liberal Arts and Social Sciences, Department of English and Philosophy, Hammond, IN 46323-2094. Offers English (MA). Part-time and evening/weekend programs available. Postbaccalaureate distance learning degree programs offered (minimal on-campus study). *Faculty:* 18 full-time (7 women). *Students:* 5 full-time (all women), 32 part-time (24 women); includes 2 Black or African American, non-Hispanic/Latino. Average age 35. 10 applicants, 100% accepted, 8 enrolled. In 2010, 1 master's awarded. *Degree requirements:* For master's, comprehensive exam, thesis optional. *Entrance requirements:* Additional exam requirements/recommendations for international students: Required—TOEFL. *Application deadline:* For fall admission, 7/31 priority date for domestic students. Applications are processed on a rolling basis. Application fee: $55. Electronic applications accepted. *Expenses:* Tuition, state resident: full-time $6867. Tuition, nonresident: full-time $14,157. *Financial support:* In 2010–11, 16 students received support, including teaching assistantships with partial tuition reimbursements available (averaging $8,400 per year). Financial award application deadline: 3/1. *Faculty research:* English literature, American literature, critical theory, women's studies, historical philosophy. *Unit head:* Dr. Daniel J. Punday, Head, 219-989-2686, E-mail: punday@purduecal.edu.

Queens College of the City University of New York, Division of Graduate Studies, Arts and Humanities Division, Department of English, Flushing, NY 11367-1597. Offers creative writing (MA); English language and literature (MA). Part-time and evening/weekend programs available. *Faculty:* 53 full-time (25 women). *Students:* 5 full-time (all women), 125 part-time (88 women); includes 16 Black or African American, non-Hispanic/Latino; 9 Asian, non-Hispanic/Latino; 14 Hispanic/Latino, 2 international. 158 applicants, 38% accepted, 38 enrolled. In 2010, 32 master's awarded. *Degree requirements:* For master's, one foreign language, thesis (for some programs), oral exam (English language and literature). *Entrance requirements:* For master's, manuscript (creative writing), minimum GPA of 3.0. Additional exam requirements/recommendations for international students: Required—TOEFL. *Application deadline:* For fall admission, 4/1 for domestic students; for spring admission, 11/1 for domestic students. Applications are processed on a rolling basis. Application fee: $125. *Financial support:* Career-related internships or fieldwork, Federal Work-Study, institutionally sponsored loans, and tuition waivers (partial) available. Support available to part-time students. Financial award application deadline: 4/1; financial award applicants required to submit FAFSA. *Unit head:* Dr. Nancy Comley, Chairperson, 718-997-4600, E-mail: nancy_comley@qc.edu. *Application contact:* Dr. Talia Schaffer, Graduate Adviser, 718-997-4600, E-mail: talia_schaffer@qc.edu.

Queen's University at Kingston, School of Graduate Studies and Research, Faculty of Arts and Sciences, Department of English Language and Literature, Kingston, ON K7L 3N6, Canada. Offers MA, PhD. *Degree requirements:* For master's, one foreign language, thesis optional; for doctorate, 2 foreign languages, comprehensive exam, thesis/dissertation. *Entrance requirements:* For master's, B.A.H. upper 2nd class standing, 10 full courses in English; for doctorate, M.A. upper 2nd class standing. Additional exam requirements/recommendations for international students: Required—TOEFL, TWE. *Faculty research:* Renaissance, 18th century, post colonial, Canadian, 19th century.

Radford University, College of Graduate and Professional Studies, College of Humanities and Behavioral Sciences, Department of English, Radford, VA 24142. Offers MA, MS. Part-time programs available. *Faculty:* 22 full-time (11 women), 3 part-time/adjunct (2 women). *Students:* 33 full-time (24 women), 2 part-time (both women); includes 1 Black or African American, non-Hispanic/Latino; 2 Hispanic/Latino. Average age 27. 40 applicants, 90% accepted, 15 enrolled. In 2010, 13 master's awarded. *Degree requirements:* For master's, comprehensive exam, thesis (for some programs). *Entrance requirements:* For master's, GRE, minimum GPA of 2.75; 2 letters of reference; sample of expository writing. Additional exam requirements/recommendations for international students: Required—TOEFL (minimum score 550 paper-based; 213 computer-based; 79 iBT). *Application deadline:* For fall admission, 2/15 for domestic students, 12/1 for international students; for spring admission, 7/1 for international students. Applications are processed on a rolling basis. Application fee: $50. Electronic applications accepted. *Expenses:* Tuition, state resident: full-time $5746; part-time $239 per credit hour. Tuition, nonresident: full-time $14,174; part-time $591 per credit hour. Required fees: $2634; $111 per credit hour. *Financial support:* In 2010–11, 25 students received support, including 3 research assistantships with partial tuition reimbursements available (averaging $8,000 per year), 20 teaching assistantships with partial tuition reimbursements available (averaging $8,700 per year); career-related internships or fieldwork, Federal Work-Study, institutionally sponsored loans, scholarships/grants, and unspecified assistantships also available. Financial award application deadline: 3/1; financial award applicants required to submit FAFSA. *Unit head:* Dr. Rosemary F. Guruswamy, Chair, 540-831-5285, Fax: 540-831-6800, E-mail: rguruswa@radford.edu. *Application contact:* Rebecca Conner, Graduate Admissions, 540-831-5431, Fax: 540-831-6061, E-mail: gradcollege@radford.edu.

Rhode Island College, School of Graduate Studies, Faculty of Arts and Sciences, Department of English, Providence, RI 02908-1991. Offers creative writing (MA, CGS); English (MA); literature (CGS). Part-time and evening/weekend programs available. *Faculty:* 11 full-time (4 women). *Students:* 1 (woman) full-time, 14 part-time (7 women). Average age 34. In 2010, 12 master's awarded. *Degree requirements:* For master's, thesis (for some programs). *Entrance requirements:* For master's, GRE General Test, 3 letters of recommendation, interview. Additional exam requirements/recommendations for international students: Recommended—TOEFL (minimum score 550 paper-based; 213 computer-based; 79 iBT). *Application deadline:* For fall admission, 3/1 for domestic students; for spring admission, 11/1 for domestic students. Applications are processed on a rolling basis. Application fee: $50. *Expenses:* Tuition, state resident: full-time $8208; part-time $342 per credit hour. Tuition, nonresident: full-time $16,080; part-time $670 per credit hour. Required fees: $554; $20 per credit. $72 per term. *Financial support:* In 2010–11, 1 teaching assistantship with full tuition reimbursement (averaging $4,550 per year) was awarded; career-related internships or fieldwork, Federal Work-Study, scholarships/grants, health care benefits, and unspecified assistantships also available. Support available to part-time students. Financial award application deadline: 5/15; financial award applicants required to submit FAFSA. *Unit head:* Dr. Maureen Reddy, Chair, 401-456-8028. *Application contact:* Graduate Studies, 401-456-8700.

Rice University, Graduate Programs, School of Humanities, Department of English, Houston, TX 77251-1892. Offers MA, PhD. Terminal master's awarded for partial completion of doctoral program. *Degree requirements:* For master's, comprehensive exam, thesis (for some programs); for doctorate, comprehensive exam, thesis/dissertation. *Entrance requirements:* For master's and doctorate, GRE General Test, minimum GPA of 3.0. Additional exam requirements/recommendations for international students: Required—TOEFL (minimum score 600 paper-based; 250 computer-based; 90 iBT). Electronic applications accepted. *Faculty research:* Traditional periods and genres (excluding Old English), literary criticism and theory, Victorian literature, feminist literature, Renaissance literature, American literature, African-American literature.

Rivier College, School of Graduate Studies, Department of English, Nashua, NH 03060. Offers English (MAT); writing and literature (MA). Part-time and evening/weekend programs available. *Faculty:* 3 full-time (1 woman). *Students:* 6 full-time (all women), 17 part-time (13 women). Average age 31. 14 applicants, 14% accepted, 1 enrolled. In 2010, 13 master's awarded. *Degree requirements:* For master's, comprehensive exam (for some programs). *Entrance requirements:* For master's, GRE Subject Test. *Application deadline:* Applications are processed on a rolling basis. Application fee: $25. *Expenses:* Tuition: Part-time $456 per credit. *Financial support:* Available to part-time students. Application deadline: 2/1. *Unit head:* Dr. Brad Stull, Chairman, 603-897-8238, E-mail: bstull@rivier.edu. *Application contact:* Mathew Kittredge, Director of Graduate Admissions, 603-897-8229, Fax: 603-897-8810, E-mail: mkittredge@rivier.edu.

Roosevelt University, Graduate Division, College of Arts and Sciences, Department of Literature and Languages, Program in English, Chicago, IL 60605. Offers MA. Part-time and evening/weekend programs available. *Degree requirements:* For master's, one foreign language, thesis or alternative. *Faculty research:* Eighteenth-century Victorian literature and culture, creative writing, eighteenth through twentieth century literature, American literature and culture.

Rosemont College, Schools of Graduate and Professional Studies, Program in English and Publishing and English Literature, Rosemont, PA 19010-1699. Offers English and publishing (MA); English literature (MA). Part-time programs available. *Degree requirements:* For master's, comprehensive exam (for some programs), thesis. *Entrance requirements:* For master's, 3 letters of recommendation. Additional exam requirements/recommendations for international students: Required—TOEFL. Electronic applications accepted. *Expenses:* Tuition: Full-time $11,700; part-time $650 per credit.

Rutgers, The State University of New Jersey, Camden, Graduate School of Arts and Sciences, Program in English, Camden, NJ 08102. Offers MA. Part-time and evening/weekend programs available. *Faculty:* 17 full-time (7 women). *Students:* 17 full-time (12 women), 38 part-time (23 women); includes 1 Black or African American, non-Hispanic/Latino; 1 Asian, non-Hispanic/Latino; 1 Hispanic/Latino. Average age 30. 51 applicants, 88% accepted, 19 enrolled. In 2010, 18 master's awarded. *Degree requirements:* For master's, comprehensive exam, thesis optional, 30 credits. *Entrance requirements:* For master's, GRE General Test, 3 letters of recommendation, writing sample, statement of personal, professional, and academic goals. Additional exam requirements/recommendations for international students: Required—TOEFL, IELTS. *Application deadline:* For fall admission, 3/1 priority date for domestic students; for spring admission, 12/1 priority date for domestic students. Applications are processed on a rolling basis. Application fee: $65. Electronic applications accepted. *Expenses:* Tuition, state resident: full-time $4963; part-time $319 per credit. Tuition, nonresident: full-time $10,493; part-time $680 per credit. *Financial support:* In 2010–11, 30 students received support, including 1 fellowship with partial tuition reimbursement available (averaging $790 per year), 4 teaching assistantships with full tuition reimbursements available (averaging $26,000 per year); Federal Work-Study, institutionally sponsored loans, scholarships/grants, and tuition waivers (partial) also available. Support available to part-time students. Financial award application deadline: 3/15; financial award applicants required to submit FAFSA. *Faculty research:* British literature; American literature; women's studies; literary, poetic, and rhetorical theory; creative writing. Total annual research expenditures: $15,000. *Unit head:* Dr. Carol Singley, Director, 856-225-6121, Fax: 856-225-6602, E-mail: gradeng@camden.rutgers.edu. *Application contact:* Dr. Carol Singley, Director, 856-225-6121, Fax: 856-225-6602, E-mail: gradeng@camden.rutgers.edu.

Rutgers, The State University of New Jersey, Newark, Graduate School, Program in English, Newark, NJ 07102. Offers MA. Part-time and evening/weekend programs available. *Faculty:* 19 full-time (8 women). *Students:* 19 full-time (16 women), 39 part-time (23 women); includes 9 Black or African American, non-Hispanic/Latino; 3 Asian, non-Hispanic/Latino; 1 Hispanic/Latino. 80 applicants, 74% accepted, 24 enrolled. In 2010, 24 master's awarded. *Degree requirements:* For master's, one foreign language, comprehensive exam, thesis optional. *Entrance requirements:* For master's, GRE, minimum undergraduate B average. *Application deadline:* For fall admission, 7/15 for domestic students; for spring admission, 12/1 for domestic students. Application fee: $60. Electronic applications accepted. *Expenses:* Tuition, state resident: part-time $600 per credit. Tuition, nonresident: full-time $10,694. *Financial support:* In 2010–11, 1 fellowship with full tuition reimbursement (averaging $15,000 per year) was awarded; Federal Work-Study, institutionally sponsored loans, and tuition waivers (full and partial) also available. Support available to part-time students. Financial award application deadline: 3/1. *Faculty research:* British and American literature, cultural studies, literary theory, minority literatures. *Unit head:* Dr. Janet Larson, Director, 973-353-5405 Ext. 529, Fax: 973-353-1450, E-mail: jlarson@andromeda.rutgers.edu. *Application contact:* Jason Hand, Director of Admissions, 973-353-5205, Fax: 973-353-1440.

Rutgers, The State University of New Jersey, New Brunswick, Graduate School-New Brunswick, Program of Literatures in English, Piscataway, NJ 08854-8097. Offers PhD. *Degree requirements:* For doctorate, one foreign language, thesis/dissertation, qualifying exam. *Entrance requirements:* For doctorate, GRE General Test, GRE Subject Test, writing sample, 3 letters of recommendation. Additional exam requirements/recommendations for international students: Required—TOEFL. Electronic applications accepted. *Expenses:* Tuition, state resident: full-time $7200; part-time $600 per credit. Tuition, nonresident: full-time $11,124; part-time $927 per credit. *Faculty research:* Medieval literature; Renaissance; African American literature; 18th century British literature; feminism, gender, and sexuality; postcolonial studies.

St. Bonaventure University, School of Graduate Studies, Department of English, St. Bonaventure, NY 14778-2284. Offers MA. Part-time programs available. *Faculty:* 5 full-time (1 woman), 1 (woman) part-time/adjunct. *Students:* 11 full-time (7 women), 1 (woman) part-time; includes 1 minority (American Indian or Alaska Native, non-Hispanic/Latino). Average age 25. 10 applicants, 90% accepted, 6 enrolled. In 2010, 12 master's awarded. *Degree requirements:* For master's, one foreign language, thesis optional, oral comprehensive examination. *Entrance requirements:* For master's, GRE General Test, bachelor's degree; demonstrated competence in reading Latin, French, German or Spanish; recommendation letters; minimum of 24 hours of undergraduate English courses. Additional exam requirements/recommendations for international students: Required—TOEFL (minimum score 550 paper-based; 213 computer-based). *Application deadline:* For fall admission, 3/15 priority date for domestic students, 2/1 priority date for international students; for spring admission, 10/15 priority date for domestic students, 7/1 priority date for international students. Applications are processed on a rolling basis. Application fee: $30. Electronic applications accepted. *Expenses:* Tuition: Part-time $670 per credit hour. *Financial support:* Research assistantships, Federal Work-Study, scholarships/grants, health care benefits, and unspecified assistantships available. Support available to part-time students. Financial award application deadline: 4/15; financial award applicants required to submit FAFSA. *Unit head:* Dr. Kaplan Harris, Program Director, 716-375-2489, E-mail: kharris@sbu.edu. *Application contact:* Bruce Campbell, Director of Graduate Admissions, 716-375-2429, E-mail: gradsch@sbu.edu.

St. Cloud State University, School of Graduate Studies, College of Fine Arts and Humanities, Department of English, St. Cloud, MN 56301-4498. Offers English (MA, MS); teaching English as a second language (MA). Part-time programs available. *Degree requirements:* For master's, thesis or alternative. *Entrance requirements:* For master's, GRE General Test, minimum GPA of 2.75. Additional exam requirements/recommendations for international students: Required—Michigan English Language Assessment Battery; Recommended—TOEFL (minimum score 550 paper-based; 213 computer-based), IELTS (minimum score 6.5). Electronic applications accepted.

St. John's University, St. John's College of Liberal Arts and Sciences, Department of English, Queens, NY 11439. Offers MA, DA. Part-time and evening/weekend programs available. *Students:* 35 full-time (20 women), 46 part-time (29 women); includes 13 minority (3 Black or African American, non-Hispanic/Latino; 5 Asian, non-Hispanic/Latino; 4 Hispanic/Latino; 1 Native Hawaiian or other Pacific Islander, non-Hispanic/Latino), 4 international. Average age 33. 47 applicants, 57% accepted, 23 enrolled. In 2010, 15 master's, 3 doctorates awarded. *Degree requirements:* For master's, thesis optional, capstone; for doctorate, one foreign language, comprehensive exam, thesis/dissertation, residency. *Entrance requirements:* For master's, GRE General Test, GRE Subject Test, minimum GPA of 3.0, 2 letters of recommendation; for doctorate, GRE General Test, GRE Subject Test, interview; minimum GPA of 3.5 in literature, 3.0 overall; writing sample, 3 letters of recommendation, essay. Additional exam requirements/recommendations for international students: Required—TOEFL (minimum score 600 paper-based; 250 computer-based; 100 iBT), IELTS (minimum score 5.5). *Application deadline:* For fall admission, 5/1 priority date for domestic and international students; for spring admission, 11/1 priority date for domestic and international students. Applications are processed on a rolling basis. Application fee: $70. Electronic applications accepted. *Expenses:* Tuition: Full-time $17,100; part-time $950 per credit. Required fees: $340; $170 per semester. Tuition and fees vary according to program. *Financial support:* Fellowships, research assistantships, scholarships/grants available. Support available to part-time students. Financial award application deadline: 3/1; financial award applicants required to submit FAFSA. *Faculty research:* Modern comparative drama, literary theories and criticism, nineteenth and early twentieth century American literature, Chaucer, Elizabethan drama. *Unit head:* Dr. Stephen Sicari, Chair, 718-990-6390, E-mail: sicaris@stjohns.edu. *Application contact:* Kathleen Davis, Director of Graduate Admission, 718-990-1601, Fax: 718-990-5686, E-mail: gradhelp@stjohns.edu.

Saint Louis University, Graduate Education, College of Arts and Sciences and Graduate Education, Department of English, St. Louis, MO 63103-2097. Offers MA, MA-R, PhD. Part-time programs available. *Degree requirements:* For master's, one foreign language, comprehensive exam, thesis optional, comprehensive oral exam; for doctorate, 2 foreign languages, comprehensive exam, thesis/dissertation, preliminary oral and written exams. *Entrance requirements:* For master's, GRE General Test, GRE Subject Test, letters of recommendation, resume, writing sample, interview; for doctorate, GRE General Test, GRE Subject Test, letters of recommendation, resumé, writing sample, interview, goal statement, writing sample. Additional exam requirements/recommendations for international students: Required—TOEFL (minimum score 550 paper-based; 213 computer-based). *Faculty research:* English literature, American literature, post-colonial literature, composition, literary theory.

Saint Louis University–Madrid Campus, Graduate Programs, Master of Arts in English Program, Madrid, Spain. Offers MA. Students at the Madrid Campus may also earn a degree from the Universidad Autonoma de Madrid. Part-time programs available. *Degree requirements:* For master's, one foreign language, comprehensive exam, thesis optional. *Entrance requirements:* For master's, GRE General Test, GRE Subject Test, transcripts, 3 letters of recommendation, writing sample, personal statement, curriculum vitae. Additional exam requirements/recommendations for international students: Required—TOEFL (minimum score 550 paper-based; 80 computer-based; 80 iBT). *Faculty research:* English, Irish and American literature; literary theory; translation; linguistics.

St. Mary's University, Graduate School, Department of English and Communication Studies, Program in English Literature and Language, San Antonio, TX 78228-8507. Offers MA. Part-time programs available. *Degree requirements:* For master's, comprehensive exam. *Entrance requirements:* For master's, GRE. Additional exam requirements/recommendations for international students: Required—TOEFL (minimum score 550 paper-based; 213 computer-based; 80 iBT). Electronic applications accepted.

Saint Xavier University, Graduate Studies, School of Arts and Sciences, Department of English, Chicago, IL 60655-3105. Offers English (CAS); literary studies (MA); teaching of writing (MA); writing pedagogy (CAS). Part-time and evening/weekend programs available. *Entrance requirements:* For master's, MAT or GRE, minimum GPA of 3.0.

Salem State University, School of Graduate Studies, Program in English, Salem, MA 01970-5353. Offers English (MA, MAT, MA/MAT); MA/MAT. Part-time and evening/weekend programs available. *Students:* 17 full-time (11 women), 56 part-time (34 women); includes 2 Black or African American, non-Hispanic/Latino; 2 Asian, non-Hispanic/Latino; 1 Hispanic/Latino; 1 Two or more races, non-Hispanic/Latino. Average age 34. 14 applicants, 86% accepted, 12 enrolled. In 2010, 25 master's awarded. *Entrance requirements:* For master's, GRE or MAT. Additional exam requirements/recommendations for international students: Required—TOEFL (minimum score 550 paper-based; 80 iBT) or IELTS (minimum score 5.5). *Application deadline:* For fall admission, 5/1 for domestic students; for spring admission, 10/1 for domestic students. Applications are processed on a rolling basis. Application fee: $50. *Expenses:* Tuition, state resident: full-time $2520; part-time $290 per credit hour. Tuition, nonresident: full-time $4140; part-time $380 per credit hour. Required fees: $2700. *Financial support:* Career-related internships or fieldwork, Federal Work-Study, scholarships/grants, and unspecified assistantships available. Support available to part-time students. Financial award application deadline: 5/1; financial award applicants required to submit FAFSA. *Unit head:* Lisa Mulman, Coordinator, 978-542-6321, E-mail: lmulman@salemstate.edu. *Application contact:* Dr. Lee A. Brossoit, Assistant Dean of Graduate Admissions, 978-542-6673, Fax: 978-542-7215, E-mail: lbrossoit@salemstate.edu.

Salisbury University, Graduate Division, Program in English, Salisbury, MD 21801-6837. Offers composition, language and rhetoric (MA); literature (MA); teaching English to speakers of other languages (MA). Part-time and evening/weekend programs available. *Faculty:* 11 full-time (6 women). *Students:* 14 full-time (12 women), 17 part-time (10 women); includes 2 minority (both Two or more races, non-Hispanic/Latino). Average age 27. 31 applicants, 52% accepted, 2 enrolled. In 2010, 19 master's awarded. *Degree requirements:* For master's,

comprehensive exam (for some programs), thesis optional. *Entrance requirements:* For master's, GRE General Test, MAT or PRAXIS, minimum GPA of 3.0, 2 letters of recommendation. Additional exam requirements/recommendations for international students: Required—TOEFL (minimum score 550 paper-based; 213 computer-based; 79 iBT). *Application deadline:* For fall admission, 8/1 for domestic students; for spring admission, 1/1 for domestic students. Applications are processed on a rolling basis. Application fee: $45. Electronic applications accepted. *Financial support:* In 2010–11, 9 students received support, including 14 teaching assistantships with full tuition reimbursements available; career-related internships or fieldwork and scholarships/grants also available. Support available to part-time students. Financial award applicants required to submit FAFSA. *Faculty research:* Shakespeare, Keats, J. D. Salinger, Samuel Johnson, post-colonial theory. *Unit head:* Dr. John D. Kalb, Director, 410-543-6049, Fax: 410-548-2142, E-mail: jdkalb@salisbury.edu. *Application contact:* Dr. John D. Kalb, Director, 410-543-6049, Fax: 410-548-2142, E-mail: jdkalb@salisbury.edu.

Sam Houston State University, College of Humanities and Social Sciences, Department of English and Foreign Languages, Huntsville, TX 77341. Offers English (MA). Part-time and evening/weekend programs available. *Faculty:* 9 full-time (4 women). *Students:* 10 full-time (3 women), 34 part-time (25 women); includes 2 Hispanic/Latino. Average age 31. 14 applicants, 86% accepted, 10 enrolled. In 2010, 13 master's awarded. *Degree requirements:* For master's, comprehensive exam, thesis optional. *Entrance requirements:* For master's, GRE General Test. Additional exam requirements/recommendations for international students: Required—TOEFL (minimum score 550 paper-based; 213 computer-based; 79 iBT). *Application deadline:* For fall admission, 8/1 for domestic students; for spring admission, 12/31 for domestic students. Applications are processed on a rolling basis. Application fee: $20. *Expenses:* Tuition, state resident: full-time $1363; part-time $163 per credit hour. Tuition, nonresident: full-time $3856; part-time $473 per credit hour. *Financial support:* Teaching assistantships, Federal Work-Study and institutionally sponsored loans available. Support available to part-time students. Financial award application deadline: 5/31; financial award applicants required to submit FAFSA. *Unit head:* Dr. Helena Halmari, Chair, 936-294-1404, Fax: 936-294-1408, E-mail: eng_shh@shsu.edu. *Application contact:* Dr. Paul Child, Advisor, 936-294-1412, E-mail: eng_pwc@shsu.edu.

San Diego State University, Graduate and Research Affairs, College of Arts and Letters, Department of English and Comparative Literature, San Diego, CA 92182. Offers creative writing (MFA); English (MA). *Degree requirements:* For master's, one foreign language, comprehensive exam (for some programs), thesis (for some programs). *Entrance requirements:* For master's, GRE General Test, minimum GPA of 2.85, writing sample, 3 letters of recommendation. Additional exam requirements/recommendations for international students: Required—TOEFL. Electronic applications accepted.

San Francisco State University, Division of Graduate Studies, College of Humanities, Department of English Language and Literature, Program in Composition, San Francisco, CA 94132-1722. Offers MA. Part-time programs available. *Degree requirements:* For master's, comprehensive exam. *Entrance requirements:* Additional exam requirements/recommendations for international students: Required—TOEFL, TWE. *Application deadline:* Applications are processed on a rolling basis. *Unit head:* Dr. Bruce Avery, Chair, 415-338-2264, E-mail: english@fsu.edu. *Application contact:* Dr. Jennifer Trainor, Graduate Coordinator, 415-338-2264, E-mail: jtrainor@sfsu.edu.

San Francisco State University, Division of Graduate Studies, College of Humanities, Department of English Language and Literature, Program in Literature, San Francisco, CA 94132-1722. Offers MA. Part-time programs available. *Application deadline:* Applications are processed on a rolling basis. *Unit head:* Dr. Bruce Avery, Chair, 415-338-2264, E-mail: english@sfsu.edu. *Application contact:* Julie Paulson, Graduate Coordinator, 415-338-2264, E-mail: jpaulson@sfsu.edu.

San Jose State University, Graduate Studies and Research, College of Humanities and the Arts, Department of English and Comparative Literature, San Jose, CA 95192-0001. Offers English (MFA); English literature (MA). *Degree requirements:* For master's, one foreign language, thesis or alternative. *Entrance requirements:* For master's, GRE. Additional exam requirements/recommendations for international students: Required—TOEFL. Electronic applications accepted.

Seton Hall University, College of Arts and Sciences, Department of English, South Orange, NJ 07079-2697. Offers English (MA), including literature, writing. Part-time and evening/weekend programs available. *Degree requirements:* For master's, one foreign language, comprehensive exam, thesis. *Entrance requirements:* For master's, GRE, minimum of 21 undergraduate credits in English. Additional exam requirements/recommendations for international students: Required—TOEFL. Electronic applications accepted. *Faculty research:* The essay, modern poetry, the novel, medieval poetry, Renaissance drama.

Sewanee: The University of the South, Sewanee School of Letters, Sewanee, TN 37383-1000. Offers American and English literature (MA); creative writing (MFA). Programs offered only during the summer. Part-time programs available. *Degree requirements:* For master's, thesis (for some programs). *Entrance requirements:* For master's, writing sample, 2 letters of recommendation. Electronic applications accepted. *Expenses:* Contact institution.

Simmons College, College of Arts and Sciences Graduate Studies, Program in Children's Literature, Boston, MA 02115. Offers children's literature (MA); writing for children (MFA); MA/MFA; MAT/MA. Part-time programs available. *Entrance requirements:* For master's, writing portfolio (for MFA). Additional exam requirements/recommendations for international students: Required—TOEFL (minimum score 600 paper-based; 250 computer-based; 100 iBT). Electronic applications accepted. *Expenses:* Contact institution. *Faculty research:* Reception theory, narratology, material culture.

Simmons College, College of Arts and Sciences Graduate Studies, Program in English, Boston, MA 02115. Offers MA, MAT/MA. Part-time programs available. *Degree requirements:* For master's, one foreign language, thesis optional. *Entrance requirements:* For master's, analytical writing sample. Additional exam requirements/recommendations for international students: Required—TOEFL (minimum score 600 paper-based; 250 computer-based; 100 iBT). Electronic applications accepted. *Expenses:* Contact institution. *Faculty research:* Women in literature, native American literature, early American women's poetry.

Simon Fraser University, Graduate Studies, Faculty of Arts and Social Sciences, Department of English, Burnaby, BC V5A 1S6, Canada. Offers MA, PhD. Part-time programs available. *Degree requirements:* For master's, one foreign language, thesis or alternative; for doctorate, one foreign language, thesis/dissertation, field exams. *Entrance requirements:* For master's, minimum GPA of 3.0; for doctorate, minimum GPA of 3.5. Additional exam requirements/recommendations for international students: Required—TOEFL or IELTS. *Faculty research:* Literary criticism, literature and psychoanalysis, Renaissance drama and poetry, Shakespeare, Canadian and American literature.

Sonoma State University, Department of English, Rohnert Park, CA 94928. Offers American literature (MA); creative writing (MA); English literature (MA); world literature (MA). Part-time and evening/weekend programs available. *Faculty:* 6 full-time (4 women), 1 part-time/adjunct (0 women). *Students:* 24 full-time (16 women), 17 part-time (11 women); includes 4 minority (all Two or more races, non-Hispanic/Latino), 1 international. Average age 31. 27 applicants, 78% accepted, 9 enrolled. In 2010, 7 master's awarded. *Degree requirements:* For master's, one foreign language, thesis or alternative. *Entrance requirements:* For master's, minimum GPA of 2.5. Additional exam requirements/recommendations for international students: Required—TOEFL (minimum score 500 paper-based; 173 computer-based). *Application deadline:* For fall admission, 11/30 priority date for domestic students. Application fee: $55. *Financial support:* Teaching assistantships, career-related internships or fieldwork and Federal Work-Study available. Financial award application deadline: 3/2; financial award applicants required to submit FAFSA. *Unit head:* Dr. Thaine Stearns, Chair of Graduate Studies, 707-

English

Sonoma State University (continued)
661-2882, E-mail: thaine.stearns@sonoma.edu. *Application contact:* Dr. Sherril Jaffe, 707-664-2508, E-mail: sherril.jaffe@sonoma.edu.

South Dakota State University, Graduate School, College of Arts and Science, Department of English, Brookings, SD 57007. Offers MA. Part-time programs available. *Degree requirements:* For master's, comprehensive exam (for some programs), thesis (for some programs), oral and written exams. *Entrance requirements:* For master's, minimum GPA of 2.75. Additional exam requirements/recommendations for international students: Required—TOEFL (minimum score 600 paper-based; 250 computer-based; 100 iBT). *Faculty research:* English and American literature topics, regional literature (Midwestern), women's literature, Lakota literature and culture, rhetoric and writing.

Southeastern Louisiana University, College of Arts, Humanities and Social Sciences, Department of English, Hammond, LA 70402. Offers creative writing (MA); language and theory (MA); professional writing (MA). Part-time and evening/weekend programs available. *Faculty:* 14 full-time (7 women), 1 (woman) part-time/adjunct. *Students:* 23 full-time (13 women), 36 part-time (25 women); includes 3 minority (2 Black or African American, non-Hispanic/Latino; 1 Native Hawaiian or other Pacific Islander, non-Hispanic/Latino). Average age 29. 25 applicants, 72% accepted, 13 enrolled. In 2010, 5 master's awarded. *Degree requirements:* For master's, one foreign language, comprehensive exam, thesis (for some programs). *Entrance requirements:* For master's, GRE General Test (850 or better), 24 undergraduate credit hours in English, minimum GPA of 2.5. Additional exam requirements/recommendations for international students: Required—TOEFL (minimum score 500 paper-based; 173 computer-based; 61 iBT). *Application deadline:* For fall admission, 7/15 priority date for domestic students, 6/1 priority date for international students; for spring admission, 12/1 priority date for domestic students, 10/1 priority date for international students. Applications are processed on a rolling basis. Application fee: $20 ($30 for international students). Electronic applications accepted. *Expenses:* Tuition, state resident: full-time $3533. Tuition, nonresident: full-time $12,002. Required fees: $907. Tuition and fees vary according to degree level. *Financial support:* In 2010–11, 15 students received support, including 2 fellowships (averaging $11,700 per year), 7 research assistantships (averaging $9,300 per year); career-related internships or fieldwork, Federal Work-Study, institutionally sponsored loans, scholarships/grants, and administrative assistantship, professional assistantships also available. Support available to part-time students. Financial award application deadline: 5/1; financial award applicants required to submit FAFSA. *Faculty research:* Composition/rhetoric, professional and technical writing, film and performance studies, literary criticism, creative writing. *Unit head:* Dr. David Hanson, Department Head, 985-549-2100, Fax: 985-549-5021, E-mail: dhanson@selu.edu. *Application contact:* Sandra Meyers, Graduate Admissions Analyst, 985-549-5620, Fax: 985-549-5632, E-mail: admissions@selu.edu.

Southeast Missouri State University, School of Graduate Studies, Department of English, Cape Girardeau, MO 63701-4799. Offers English (MA); teaching English to speakers of other languages (MA). Part-time and evening/weekend programs available. Postbaccalaureate distance learning degree programs offered (no on-campus study). *Faculty:* 16 full-time (9 women). *Students:* 31 full-time (23 women), 44 part-time (35 women); includes 8 minority (5 Black or African American, non-Hispanic/Latino; 2 American Indian or Alaska Native, non-Hispanic/Latino; 1 Asian, non-Hispanic/Latino), 8 international. Average age 32. 46 applicants, 91% accepted, 22 enrolled. In 2010, 22 master's awarded. *Degree requirements:* For master's, comprehensive exam (for some programs), thesis (for some programs), scholarly paper. *Entrance requirements:* For master's, minimum undergraduate GPA of 2.5, 24 undergraduate credit hours in field (for English); teaching certificate, minimum undergraduate GPA of 2.75 or master's degree (for TESOL). Additional exam requirements/recommendations for international students: Required—TOEFL (minimum score 550 paper-based; 213 computer-based; 79 iBT); Recommended—IELTS (minimum score 6). *Application deadline:* For fall admission, 8/1 for domestic students, 6/1 for international students; for spring admission, 11/21 for domestic students, 10/1 for international students. Applications are processed on a rolling basis. Application fee: $25 ($35 for international students). Electronic applications accepted. *Expenses:* Tuition, state resident: full-time $4698; part-time $261 per credit hour. Tuition, nonresident: full-time $8379; part-time $465.50 per credit hour. *Financial support:* In 2010–11, 21 students received support, including 15 teaching assistantships with full tuition reimbursements available (averaging $7,600 per year); career-related internships or fieldwork, Federal Work-Study, institutionally sponsored loans, scholarships/grants, tuition waivers (full), and unspecified assistantships also available. Financial award application deadline: 6/30; financial award applicants required to submit FAFSA. *Faculty research:* Literature, writing, linguistics, education, TESOL. *Unit head:* Dr. Carol Scates, Chairperson and Graduate Program Coordinator, 573-651-2156, E-mail: cscates@semo.edu. *Application contact:* Gail Amick, Administrative Secretary, 573-651-2049, Fax: 573-651-2001, E-mail: gamick@semo.edu.

Southern Connecticut State University, School of Graduate Studies, School of Arts and Sciences, Department of English, New Haven, CT 06515-1355. Offers MA, MS, MLS/MS. Part-time and evening/weekend programs available. *Faculty:* 38 full-time (22 women). *Students:* 52 full-time (37 women), 45 part-time (31 women); includes 7 Black or African American, non-Hispanic/Latino; 1 Two or more races, non-Hispanic/Latino. 67 applicants, 30% accepted, 17 enrolled. In 2010, 16 master's awarded. *Degree requirements:* For master's, one foreign language, thesis or alternative. *Entrance requirements:* For master's, interview. *Application deadline:* For fall admission, 5/1 priority date for domestic students; for spring admission, 12/1 priority date for domestic students. Applications are processed on a rolling basis. Application fee: $50. Electronic applications accepted. *Expenses:* Tuition, state resident: full-time $5137; part-time $518 per credit. Tuition, nonresident: part-time $542 per credit. Required fees: $4008; $55 per semester. Tuition and fees vary according to program. *Financial support:* In 2010–11, teaching assistantships (averaging $4,800 per year). Financial award application deadline: 4/15; financial award applicants required to submit FAFSA. *Unit head:* Dr. Michael Shea, Chairperson, 203-392-6741, Fax: 203-392-6731, E-mail: sheam1@southernct.edu. *Application contact:* Dr. Ken Florey, Coordinator, 203-392-6733, Fax: 203-392-6731, E-mail: floreyk1@southernct.edu.

Southern Illinois University Carbondale, Graduate School, College of Liberal Arts, Department of English, Carbondale, IL 62901-4701. Offers composition (MA, PhD), including composition, literature, rhetoric; creative writing (MFA). *Degree requirements:* For master's, one foreign language, thesis; for doctorate, 2 foreign languages, thesis/dissertation. *Entrance requirements:* For master's, GRE General Test, GRE Subject Test, minimum GPA of 2.7; for doctorate, GRE General Test, GRE Subject Test, minimum GPA of 3.25. Additional exam requirements/recommendations for international students: Required—TOEFL. *Faculty research:* British literature, English literature, modern Continental literature, literary criticism and theory, film studies, Irish studies.

Southern Illinois University Edwardsville, Graduate School, College of Arts and Sciences, Department of English Language and Literature, Program in American and English Literature, Edwardsville, IL 62026-0001. Offers MA, Postbaccalaureate Certificate. Part-time programs available. *Students:* 7 full-time (4 women), 17 part-time (13 women); includes 3 minority (2 Black or African American, non-Hispanic/Latino; 1 Hispanic/Latino). Average age 26. In 2010, 8 master's awarded. *Degree requirements:* For master's, one foreign language, thesis (for some programs), written papers, oral examination. *Entrance requirements:* Additional exam requirements/recommendations for international students: Required—TOEFL (minimum score 550 paper-based; 213 computer-based; 79 iBT), IELTS (minimum score 6.5). *Application deadline:* For fall admission, 7/22 for domestic students, 6/1 for international students; for spring admission, 12/9 for domestic students, 10/1 for international students. Applications are processed on a rolling basis. Application fee: $30. Electronic applications accepted. *Expenses:* Tuition, state resident: full-time $6012; part-time $1503 per semester. Tuition, nonresident: full-time $15,030; part-time $3758 per semester. Required fees: $1711; $675 per semester. *Financial support:* Fellowships with full tuition reimbursements, research assistantships with full tuition reimbursements, teaching assistantships with full tuition reimbursements, Federal Work-Study, institutionally sponsored loans, scholarships/grants, and unspecified assistantships available. Support available to part-time students. Financial award application deadline: 3/1; financial award applicants required to submit FAFSA. *Unit head:* Dr. Joel Hardman, Director, 618-650-5978, E-mail: jhardma@siue.edu. *Application contact:* Dr. Joel Hardman, Director, 618-650-5978, E-mail: jhardma@siue.edu.

Southern Methodist University, Dedman College, Department of English, Dallas, TX 75275. Offers MA, PhD. *Faculty:* 41 full-time (22 women), 18 part-time/adjunct (13 women). *Students:* 15 full-time (10 women), 9 part-time (4 women); includes 1 Black or African American, non-Hispanic/Latino. Average age 28. 63 applicants, 16% accepted, 6 enrolled. In 2010, 3 master's awarded. Terminal master's awarded for partial completion of doctoral program. *Degree requirements:* For master's, one foreign language, comprehensive exam, thesis optional, oral exam; for doctorate, one foreign language, comprehensive exam, thesis/dissertation. *Entrance requirements:* For master's, GRE General Test, minimum GPA of 3.0; for doctorate, GRE General Test, minimum GPA of 3.5, BA in English or other appropriate field. Additional exam requirements/recommendations for international students: Required—TOEFL (minimum score 550 paper-based). *Application deadline:* For fall admission, 1/15 priority date for domestic and international students. Application fee: $75. Electronic applications accepted. *Financial support:* In 2010–11, 12 students received support, including 12 fellowships with full tuition reimbursements available (averaging $24,800 per year); health care benefits and tuition waivers (full) also available. Financial award application deadline: 1/15. *Faculty research:* British/American literature, critical theory, medieval studies, gender studies, book history. *Unit head:* Prof. Nina Schwartz, Chair, 214-768-2946, Fax: 214-768-1234, E-mail: nschwart@smu.edu. *Application contact:* Prof. Darryl Dickson-Carr, Director of Graduate Studies, 214-768-4689, Fax: 214-768-1234, E-mail: dcarr@smu.edu.

Spring Hill College, Graduate Programs, Program in Liberal Arts, Mobile, AL 36608-1791. Offers fine arts (MLA); history and social science (MLA); leadership and ethics (MLA); literature (MLA). Part-time and evening/weekend programs available. *Faculty:* 5 full-time (2 women), 2 part-time/adjunct (1 woman). *Students:* 3 full-time (2 women), 31 part-time (19 women); includes 10 minority (9 Black or African American, non-Hispanic/Latino; 1 Hispanic/Latino). Average age 37. In 2010, 12 master's awarded. *Degree requirements:* For master's, capstone course, completion of program within 6 years of initial admittance. *Entrance requirements:* For master's, bachelor's degree with minimum undergraduate GPA of 3.0 or graduate/professional degree. Additional exam requirements/recommendations for international students: Required—TOEFL (minimum score 550 paper-based; 213 computer-based; 80 iBT), IELTS (minimum score 6.5), CPE or CAE (score: C), MELAB (score: 90). *Application deadline:* For fall admission, 8/1 priority date for domestic and international students; for spring admission, 12/1 priority date for domestic and international students. Applications are processed on a rolling basis. Application fee: $25 ($35 for international students). Electronic applications accepted. *Expenses:* Contact institution. *Financial support:* Applicants required to submit FAFSA. *Unit head:* Dr. Alexander R. Landi, Director, 251-380-3056, Fax: 251-460-2115, E-mail: landi@shc.edu. *Application contact:* Donna B. Tarasavage, Director of Admissions, Graduate and Continuing Studies, 251-380-3067, Fax: 251-460-2190, E-mail: dtarasavage@shc.edu.

Stanford University, School of Humanities and Sciences, Department of English, Stanford, CA 94305-9991. Offers MA, PhD. Terminal master's awarded for partial completion of doctoral program. *Degree requirements:* For master's, one foreign language, thesis (for some programs); for doctorate, 2 foreign languages, thesis/dissertation, oral exam. *Entrance requirements:* For master's and doctorate, GRE General Test, GRE Subject Test. Additional exam requirements/recommendations for international students: Required—TOEFL. Electronic applications accepted. *Expenses:* Tuition: Full-time $38,700; part-time $860 per unit. One-time fee: $200 full-time.

State University of New York at Binghamton, Graduate School, School of Arts and Sciences, Department of English, Binghamton, NY 13902-6000. Offers MA, PhD. Part-time programs available. *Faculty:* 28 full-time (16 women), 17 part-time/adjunct (6 women). *Students:* 57 full-time (38 women), 48 part-time (26 women); includes 3 Black or African American, non-Hispanic/Latino; 2 American Indian or Alaska Native, non-Hispanic/Latino; 3 Asian, non-Hispanic/Latino; 10 Hispanic/Latino, 5 international. Average age 32. 131 applicants, 31% accepted, 16 enrolled. In 2010, 16 master's, 13 doctorates awarded. Terminal master's awarded for partial completion of doctoral program. *Degree requirements:* For master's, thesis (for some programs), written exam; for doctorate, one foreign language, comprehensive exam, thesis/dissertation. *Entrance requirements:* For master's and doctorate, GRE General Test, GRE Subject Test, critical writing sample. Additional exam requirements/recommendations for international students: Required—TOEFL (minimum score 550 paper-based; 213 computer-based; 80 iBT). *Application deadline:* For fall admission, 2/15 priority date for domestic and international students; for spring admission, 11/15 priority date for domestic and international students. Applications are processed on a rolling basis. Application fee: $60. Electronic applications accepted. *Financial support:* In 2010–11, 39 students received support, including 8 fellowships with full tuition reimbursements available (averaging $15,000 per year), 33 teaching assistantships with full tuition reimbursements available (averaging $15,000 per year); career-related internships or fieldwork, Federal Work-Study, institutionally sponsored loans, scholarships/grants, health care benefits, tuition waivers (full and partial), and unspecified assistantships also available. Financial award application deadline: 2/15; financial award applicants required to submit FAFSA. *Unit head:* Dr. Robert Micklus, Chairperson, 607-777-2422, E-mail: rmicklus@binghamton.edu. *Application contact:* Catherine Smith, Recruiting and Admissions Coordinator, 607-777-2151, Fax: 607-777-2501, E-mail: cmsmith@binghamton.edu.

State University of New York at Fredonia, Graduate Studies, Department of English, Fredonia, NY 14063-1136. Offers MA, MS Ed. Part-time and evening/weekend programs available. *Degree requirements:* For master's, thesis optional. *Expenses:* Tuition, state resident: full-time $8370; part-time $349 per credit hour. Tuition, nonresident: full-time $13,250; part-time $552 per credit hour. Required fees: $1328; $55.15 per credit hour.

State University of New York at New Paltz, Graduate School, School of Liberal Arts and Sciences, Department of English, New Paltz, NY 12561. Offers MA. Part-time and evening/weekend programs available. *Faculty:* 12 full-time (5 women). *Students:* 8 full-time (5 women), 40 part-time (25 women); includes 1 Black or African American, non-Hispanic/Latino; 1 Asian, non-Hispanic/Latino; 4 Hispanic/Latino. Average age 27. 28 applicants, 75% accepted, 17 enrolled. In 2010, 24 master's awarded. *Degree requirements:* For master's, comprehensive exam, thesis (for some programs), foreign language proficiency exam. *Entrance requirements:* For master's, minimum GPA of 3.0, 10-15 page writing sample. Additional exam requirements/recommendations for international students: Required—TOEFL (minimum score 563 paper-based; 85 iBT), IELTS (minimum score 7). *Application deadline:* For fall admission, 5/15 priority date for domestic students, 5/15 for international students; for spring admission, 11/15 for domestic and international students. Application fee: $50. Electronic applications accepted. *Expenses:* Tuition, state resident: full-time $8370; part-time $349 per credit hour. Tuition, nonresident: full-time $13,780; part-time $574 per credit hour. Required fees: $1165; $33.80 per credit hour. $175 per term. Tuition and fees vary according to program. *Financial support:* In 2010–11, 20 students received support, including 2 research assistantships with partial tuition reimbursements available (averaging $5,000 per year), 17 teaching assistantships with partial tuition reimbursements available (averaging $5,000 per year); career-related internships or fieldwork, Federal Work-Study, institutionally sponsored loans, and tuition waivers (full) also available. Financial award application deadline: 8/1; financial award applicants required to submit FAFSA. *Faculty research:* Twentieth century British literature, Hemingway and modernism, British modernist fiction, Faulkner and the Southern Renaissance, revisionary approaches to early twentieth century literature. *Unit head:* Dr. Thomas Olsen, Chair, 845-257-2723, E-mail: olsent@newpaltz.edu. *Application contact:* Dr. Daniel Kempton, Coordinator, 845-257-2728, E-mail: kemptond@newpaltz.edu.

State University of New York at Oswego, Graduate Studies, College of Liberal Arts and Sciences, Department of English, Oswego, NY 13126. Offers MA. Part-time programs available.

Faculty: 10 full-time (1 woman), 3 part-time/adjunct (2 women). *Students:* 11 full-time (5 women), 12 part-time (7 women). Average age 27. 17 applicants, 100% accepted. In 2010, 5 master's awarded. *Degree requirements:* For master's, thesis optional. *Entrance requirements:* Additional exam requirements/recommendations for international students: Required—TOEFL (minimum score 560 paper-based; 220 computer-based). *Application deadline:* For fall admission, 4/1 for domestic students; for spring admission, 10/1 for domestic students. Applications are processed on a rolling basis. Application fee: $50. *Expenses:* Tuition, state resident: full-time $8370; part-time $349 per credit hour. Tuition, nonresident: full-time $13,780; part-time $574 per credit hour. Required fees: $853; $22.59 per credit hour. *Financial support:* In 2010–11, 1 student received support, including 1 teaching assistantship with partial tuition reimbursement available (averaging $3,800 per year); fellowships with full tuition reimbursements available, career-related internships or fieldwork, Federal Work-Study, institutionally sponsored loans, scholarships/grants, health care benefits, and unspecified assistantships also available. Support available to part-time students. Financial award application deadline: 4/1; financial award applicants required to submit FAFSA. *Unit head:* Dr. Bennet Schaber, Chair, 315-312-2150. *Application contact:* Dr. Patrick Murphy, Graduate Program Coordinator, 315-312-2616.

State University of New York College at Cortland, Graduate Studies, School of Arts and Sciences, Department of English, Cortland, NY 13045. Offers MA, MAT, MS Ed. Part-time and evening/weekend programs available. *Degree requirements:* For master's, one foreign language, comprehensive exam, thesis (for some programs). *Entrance requirements:* For master's, GRE General Test.

State University of New York College at Potsdam, School of Arts and Sciences, Department of English and Communication, Potsdam, NY 13676. Offers English and communication (MA). Part-time and evening/weekend programs available. *Faculty:* 5 full-time (3 women). *Students:* 1 full-time (0 women), 14 part-time (9 women); includes 4 minority (3 Black or African American, non-Hispanic/Latino; 1 American Indian or Alaska Native, non-Hispanic/Latino). 6 applicants, 100% accepted, 5 enrolled. In 2010, 2 master's awarded. *Degree requirements:* For master's, one foreign language, thesis or alternative. *Entrance requirements:* For master's, minimum GPA of 3.0 in last 60 hours of undergraduate course work. Additional exam requirements/recommendations for international students: Required—TOEFL (minimum score 550 paper-based; 213 computer-based; 80 iBT), IELTS (minimum score 6). *Application deadline:* For fall admission, 4/1 for domestic students, 4/1 priority date for international students; for winter admission, 3/1 for domestic and international students; for spring admission, 10/15 for domestic students, 10/15 priority date for international students. Applications are processed on a rolling basis. Application fee: $50. *Financial support:* In 2010–11, 2 students received support; teaching assistantships with full tuition reimbursements available, Federal Work-Study and unspecified assistantships available. Support available to part-time students. Financial award application deadline: 3/1; financial award applicants required to submit FAFSA. *Unit head:* Dr. Sharmain van Blommestein, Director of Graduate Studies, 315-267-3158, Fax: 315-267-3256, E-mail: vanblos@potsdam.edu. *Application contact:* Peter Cutler, Graduate Admissions Counselor, 315-267-3154, Fax: 315-267-4802, E-mail: cutlerpj@potsdam.edu.

State University of New York College at Potsdam, School of Education and Professional Studies, Program in Secondary Education, Potsdam, NY 13676. Offers English (MST); mathematics (with grades 5-6 extension) (MST); science (MST), including biology, chemistry, earth science, physics; Social Studies (with grades 5-6 extension) (MST). *Accreditation:* NCATE. *Faculty:* 9 full-time (3 women), 3 part-time/adjunct (2 women). *Students:* 50 full-time (20 women), 1 part-time (0 women); includes 1 minority (Hispanic/Latino), 4 international. 46 applicants, 80% accepted, 35 enrolled. In 2010, 49 master's awarded. *Degree requirements:* For master's, thesis optional, culminating experience. *Entrance requirements:* For master's, minimum GPA of 2.75 in last 60 hours of course work (3.0 for English program). Additional exam requirements/recommendations for international students: Required—TOEFL (minimum score 550 paper-based; 213 computer-based; 80 iBT), IELTS (minimum score 6). *Application deadline:* For spring admission, 3/1 for domestic and international students. Applications are processed on a rolling basis. Application fee: $50. *Financial support:* Fellowships, teaching assistantships, career-related internships or fieldwork, Federal Work-Study, scholarships/grants, and unspecified assistantships available. Support available to part-time students. Financial award application deadline: 3/1; financial award applicants required to submit FAFSA. *Unit head:* Donald C. Straight, Chairperson, 315-267-2553, Fax: 315-267-4802, E-mail: straigdc@potsdam.edu. *Application contact:* Peter Cutler, Graduate Admissions Counselor, 315-267-3154, Fax: 315-267-4802, E-mail: cutlerpj@potsdam.edu.

Stephen F. Austin State University, Graduate School, College of Liberal Arts, Department of English and Philosophy, Nacogdoches, TX 75962. Offers English (MA). *Degree requirements:* For master's, comprehensive exam. *Entrance requirements:* For master's, GRE General Test. Additional exam requirements/recommendations for international students: Required—TOEFL. *Faculty research:* Creative writing, Latin American literature, modern American literature, modern British literature, literature for children.

Stetson University, College of Arts and Sciences, Division of Humanities, Department of English, DeLand, FL 32723. Offers MA. *Students:* 12 part-time (9 women). Average age 27. In 2010, 2 master's awarded. *Degree requirements:* For master's, thesis. *Entrance requirements:* For master's, GRE General Test. *Application deadline:* For fall admission, 3/1 priority date for domestic students; for spring admission, 11/1 for domestic students. Applications are processed on a rolling basis. Application fee: $25. *Unit head:* Dr. Joel Davis, Director, 386-822-7720. *Application contact:* Diana Belian, Office of Graduate Studies, 386-822-7075, Fax: 386-822-7388, E-mail: dbelian@stetson.edu.

Stony Brook University, State University of New York, Graduate School, College of Arts and Sciences, Department of Comparative Literary and Cultural Studies, Stony Brook, NY 11794. Offers comparative literature (MA, PhD); cultural studies (PhD). Evening/weekend programs available. *Faculty:* 7 full-time (1 woman), 1 part-time/adjunct (0 women). *Students:* 29 full-time (18 women), 3 part-time (all women); includes 2 Asian, non-Hispanic/Latino, 13 international. Average age 30. 98 applicants, 31% accepted, 7 enrolled. In 2010, 5 master's, 3 doctorates awarded. Terminal master's awarded for partial completion of doctoral program. *Degree requirements:* For master's, 2 foreign languages, exam; for doctorate, 3 foreign languages, comprehensive exam, thesis/dissertation. *Entrance requirements:* For master's and doctorate, GRE General Test, minimum GPA of 3.5 in major, 3.0 overall. Additional exam requirements/recommendations for international students: Required—TOEFL. *Application deadline:* For fall admission, 1/15 for domestic students. Application fee: $100. *Expenses:* Tuition, state resident: full-time $8370; part-time $349 per credit. Tuition, nonresident: full-time $13,780; part-time $574 per credit. Required fees: $994. *Financial support:* In 2010–11, 12 teaching assistantships were awarded; fellowships, research assistantships also available. *Faculty research:* Literary theory, interdisciplinary studies, literary history. *Unit head:* Prof. Krin Gabbard, Chairman, 631-632-7456. *Application contact:* Dr. Kent Marks, Assistant Dean, Admissions and Records, 631-632-4723, Fax: 631-632-7243, E-mail: kmarks@notes.cc.sunysb.edu.

Stony Brook University, State University of New York, Graduate School, College of Arts and Sciences, Department of English, Stony Brook, NY 11794. Offers composition studies (Certificate); English (MA, PhD); English education (MAT). MAT offered through the School of Professional Development. Evening/weekend programs available. *Faculty:* 26 full-time (11 women), 2 part-time/adjunct (1 woman). *Students:* 80 full-time (50 women), 26 part-time (19 women); includes 3 Black or African American, non-Hispanic/Latino; 1 American Indian or Alaska Native, non-Hispanic/Latino; 5 Asian, non-Hispanic/Latino; 2 Hispanic/Latino, 3 international. Average age 32. 175 applicants, 23% accepted, 14 enrolled. In 2010, 9 master's, 4 doctorates, 3 other advanced degrees awarded. Terminal master's awarded for partial completion of doctoral program. *Degree requirements:* For doctorate, thesis/dissertation. *Entrance requirements:* For master's and doctorate, GRE General Test. Additional exam requirements/recommendations for international students: Required—TOEFL. *Application deadline:* For fall admission, 1/15 for domestic students. Application fee: $100. *Expenses:* Tuition, state resident: full-time $8370; part-time $349 per credit. Tuition, nonresident: full-time $13,780; part-time $574 per credit. Required fees: $994. *Financial support:* In 2010–11, 1 research assistantship, 38 teaching assistantships were awarded; fellowships also available. *Faculty research:* American literature, British literature, literary critical theory, rhetoric and composition theory, women's studies. *Unit head:* Dr. Stephen Spector, Chair, 631-632-7420, Fax: 631-632-7568. *Application contact:* Dr. Helen M. Cooper, Director, 631-632-7784, Fax: 631-632-7568, E-mail: hcooper@notes.cc.sunysb.edu.

Sul Ross State University, School of Arts and Sciences, Department of Languages and Literature, Alpine, TX 79832. Offers English (MA). Part-time and evening/weekend programs available. *Degree requirements:* For master's, thesis optional. *Entrance requirements:* For master's, GRE General Test, minimum GPA of 2.5 in last 60 hours of undergraduate work. *Faculty research:* Narrative theory, feminist literary criticism, autobiography studies, multiculturalism, biblical narrative.

Syracuse University, College of Arts and Sciences, Programs in English, Syracuse, NY 13244. Offers MA, PhD. Part-time programs available. *Students:* 28 full-time (15 women), 2 part-time (1 woman), 6 international. Average age 28. 136 applicants, 20% accepted, 9 enrolled. In 2010, 5 master's, 1 doctorate awarded. *Entrance requirements:* For master's and doctorate, GRE General Test. Additional exam requirements/recommendations for international students: Required—TOEFL (minimum score 100 iBT). *Application deadline:* For fall admission, 1/10 priority date for domestic and international students. Application fee: $75. Electronic applications accepted. *Expenses:* Tuition: Part-time $1162 per credit. *Financial support:* Fellowships with full tuition reimbursements, teaching assistantships with full and partial tuition reimbursements available. Financial award application deadline: 1/1; financial award applicants required to submit FAFSA. *Unit head:* Dr. Susan Edmunds, Director of Graduate Studies, 315-443-2174, E-mail: sledmund@syr.edu. *Application contact:* Terri Zollo, Information Contact, 315-443-2174, E-mail: tazollo@syr.edu.

Tarleton State University, College of Graduate Studies, College of Liberal and Fine Arts, Department of English and Languages, Stephenville, TX 76402. Offers English (MA). Part-time and evening/weekend programs available. *Degree requirements:* For master's, comprehensive exam, thesis (for some programs). *Entrance requirements:* For master's, GRE General Test, minimum GPA of 3.0. Additional exam requirements/recommendations for international students: Required—TOEFL (minimum score 550 paper-based; 213 computer-based; 80 iBT). Electronic applications accepted.

Temple University, College of Liberal Arts, Department of English, Philadelphia, PA 19122-6096. Offers creative writing (MA, MFA); English (MA, PhD). Part-time programs available. *Faculty:* 30 full-time (15 women). *Students:* 90 full-time (50 women), 10 part-time (3 women); includes 5 Black or African American, non-Hispanic/Latino; 2 Asian, non-Hispanic/Latino; 3 Two or more races, non-Hispanic/Latino, 2 international. 218 applicants, 50% accepted, 31 enrolled. In 2010, 14 master's, 11 doctorates awarded. *Degree requirements:* For doctorate, 2 foreign languages, thesis/dissertation. *Entrance requirements:* For master's and doctorate, GRE General Test, minimum GPA of 3.0. Additional exam requirements/recommendations for international students: Required—TOEFL (minimum score 550 paper-based; 213 computer-based; 79 iBT). *Application deadline:* For fall admission, 1/15 for domestic students, 12/15 for international students. Application fee: $50. Electronic applications accepted. *Financial support:* Fellowships, teaching assistantships, Federal Work-Study available. Financial award application deadline: 1/15; financial award applicants required to submit FAFSA. *Faculty research:* Renaissance, Victorian, Modern British, and American literature; critical theory; composition. *Unit head:* Dr. Shannon Miller, Chair, 215-204-1756, Fax: 215-204-9620, E-mail: smiller@temple.edu. *Application contact:* Dr. Shannon Miller, Chair, 215-204-1756, Fax: 215-204-9620, E-mail: smiller@temple.edu.

Tennessee State University, The School of Graduate Studies and Research, College of Arts and Sciences, Department of Languages, Literature, and Philosophy, Nashville, TN 37209-1561. Offers English (MA). *Degree requirements:* For master's, thesis optional. *Entrance requirements:* For master's, GRE General Test or MAT. Electronic applications accepted. *Faculty research:* American literature, British literature, Anglo/Saxon literature, cultural/women's studies.

Tennessee Technological University, Graduate School, College of Arts and Sciences, Department of English, Cookeville, TN 38505. Offers MA. Part-time programs available. *Faculty:* 23 full-time (8 women). *Students:* 6 full-time (3 women), 9 part-time (6 women). Average age 28. 11 applicants, 73% accepted, 6 enrolled. In 2010, 3 master's awarded. *Degree requirements:* For master's, comprehensive exam, thesis or alternative. *Entrance requirements:* For master's, GRE General Test. Additional exam requirements/recommendations for international students: Required—TOEFL (minimum score 550 paper-based; 79 iBT), IELTS (minimum score 5.5). *Application deadline:* For fall admission, 8/1 for domestic students, 5/1 for international students; for spring admission, 11/1 for domestic students, 10/1 for international students. Application fee: $25 ($30 for international students). Electronic applications accepted. *Expenses:* Tuition, state resident: full-time $7934; part-time $388 per credit hour. Tuition, nonresident: full-time $19,758; part-time $962 per credit hour. *Financial support:* In 2010–11, research assistantships (averaging $4,000 per year), 9 teaching assistantships (averaging $6,750 per year) were awarded; fellowships also available. Financial award application deadline: 4/1. *Unit head:* Dr. Homer Kemp, Interim Chairperson, 931-372-3343, Fax: 931-372-6142. *Application contact:* Shelia K. Kendrick, Coordinator of Graduate Admissions, 931-372-3808, Fax: 931-372-3497, E-mail: skendrick@tntech.edu.

Texas A&M International University, Office of Graduate Studies and Research, College of Arts and Sciences, Department of Language and Literature, Laredo, TX 78041-1900. Offers English (MA); Hispanic studies (PhD); Spanish (MA). *Faculty:* 6 full-time (3 women). *Students:* 4 full-time (3 women), 34 part-time (22 women); includes 34 Hispanic/Latino, 1 international. Average age 33. 13 applicants, 77% accepted, 8 enrolled. In 2010, 15 master's awarded. *Entrance requirements:* For master's, GRE General Test. Additional exam requirements/recommendations for international students: Required—TOEFL (minimum score 550 paper-based; 213 computer-based). *Application deadline:* For fall admission, 4/30 priority date for domestic students; for spring admission, 11/30 for domestic students. Applications are processed on a rolling basis. Application fee: $25. *Financial support:* In 2010–11, 12 students received support, including 3 fellowships, 4 research assistantships, 2 teaching assistantships. Financial award application deadline: 11/1. *Unit head:* Dr. Manuel Broncano, Chair, 956-326-2470, E-mail: manuel.broncano@tamiu.edu. *Application contact:* Suzanne Hansen-Alford, Director of Graduate Recruiting, 956-326-3023, Fax: 956-326-3021, E-mail: enroll@tamiu.edu.

Texas A&M University, College of Liberal Arts, Department of English, College Station, TX 77843. Offers MA, PhD. *Faculty:* 34. *Students:* 81 full-time (52 women), 20 part-time (12 women); includes 1 Black or African American, non-Hispanic/Latino; 1 American Indian or Alaska Native, non-Hispanic/Latino; 2 Asian, non-Hispanic/Latino; 9 Hispanic/Latino, 23 international. Average age 24. In 2010, 9 master's, 17 doctorates awarded. Terminal master's awarded for partial completion of doctoral program. *Degree requirements:* For master's, one foreign language, thesis optional; for doctorate, 2 foreign languages, thesis/dissertation. *Entrance requirements:* For master's and doctorate, GRE General Test, sample of written work. Additional exam requirements/recommendations for international students: Required—TOEFL. *Application deadline:* For fall admission, 2/1 priority date for domestic and international students; for spring admission, 10/1 priority date for domestic and international students. Applications are processed on a rolling basis. Application fee: $50 ($75 for international students). Electronic applications accepted. *Financial support:* In 2010–11, fellowships with partial tuition reimbursements (averaging $10,000 per year), research assistantships with partial tuition reimbursements (averaging $12,000 per year), teaching assistantships with partial tuition reimbursements (averaging $12,000 per year) were awarded; career-related internships or fieldwork, Federal Work-Study, institutionally sponsored loans, scholarships/grants, and unspecified assistantships also available. Financial award application deadline: 4/1. *Faculty research:* American, Renaissance, medieval, textual, discourse studies. *Unit head:* Dr. Jimmie Killingworth, Head,

English

Texas A&M University (continued)
979-845-3890, E-mail: killingworth@tamu.edu. *Application contact:* Dr. Sally Robinson, Director of Graduate Studies, 979-845-8355, Fax: 979-862-2292, E-mail: sallyr@tamu.edu.

Texas A&M University–Commerce, Graduate School, College of Arts and Sciences, Department of Literature and Languages, Commerce, TX 75429-3011. Offers college teaching of English (PhD); English (MA, MS); Spanish (MA). Part-time programs available. Terminal master's awarded for partial completion of doctoral program. *Degree requirements:* For master's, comprehensive exam, thesis (for some programs); for doctorate, one foreign language, thesis/dissertation, departmental qualifying exam. *Entrance requirements:* For master's and doctorate, GRE General Test. Electronic applications accepted. *Faculty research:* Latino literature, American film studies, ethnographic research, Willa Carter.

Texas A&M University–Corpus Christi, Graduate Studies and Research, College of Liberal Arts, Program in English, Corpus Christi, TX 78412-5503. Offers MA. Part-time and evening/weekend programs available. *Degree requirements:* For master's, comprehensive exam, thesis (for some programs). *Entrance requirements:* For master's, GRE General Test. Additional exam requirements/recommendations for international students: Required—TOEFL. Electronic applications accepted.

Texas A&M University–Kingsville, College of Graduate Studies, College of Arts and Sciences, Department of Language and Literature, Kingsville, TX 78363. Offers English (MA, MS); Spanish (MA). Part-time and evening/weekend programs available. *Degree requirements:* For master's, comprehensive exam, thesis or alternative. *Entrance requirements:* For master's, GRE General Test, minimum GPA of 3.0. Additional exam requirements/recommendations for international students: Required—TOEFL. *Faculty research:* Linguistics, culture, Spanish American literature, Spanish peninsular literature, American literature.

Texas A&M University–San Antonio, School of Arts and Sciences, San Antonio, TX 78224. Offers English (MA). Part-time and evening/weekend programs available. *Faculty:* 2 full-time (both women), 1 (woman) part-time/adjunct. *Students:* 10 full-time (9 women), 2 part-time (1 woman); includes 1 Black or African American, non-Hispanic/Latino; 7 Hispanic/Latino. Average age 32. 5 applicants, 100% accepted, 5 enrolled. *Degree requirements:* For master's, comprehensive exam, thesis. *Entrance requirements:* For master's, GRE. Additional exam requirements/recommendations for international students: Required—TOEFL (minimum score 550 paper-based; 213 computer-based; 80 iBT), IELTS (minimum score 6). *Application deadline:* For fall admission, 8/15 for domestic students, 6/1 priority date for international students; for spring admission, 12/15 for domestic students, 10/1 priority date for international students. Applications are processed on a rolling basis. Application fee: $35 ($50 for international students). Electronic applications accepted. *Expenses:* Tuition, state resident: full-time $2899; part-time $161 per credit hour. Tuition, nonresident: full-time $8479; part-time $471 per credit hour. Required fees: $1056; $61 per credit hour. $368 per semester. *Financial support:* Application deadline: 3/31. *Faculty research:* 20th-century British women's literature, 20th-century American literature, visual studies, children's literature, multi-ethnic literatures. *Unit head:* Dr. William Bush, Head, 210-932-6276, E-mail: william.bush@tamusa.tamus.edu. *Application contact:* Melissa A. Villanueva, Graduate Admissions Specialist, 210-931-6200, E-mail: melissa.villanueva@tamus.tamus.edu.

Texas A&M University–Texarkana, Graduate Studies and Research, College of Education and Liberal Arts, Texarkana, TX 75505-5518. Offers adult education (MS); curriculum and instruction (M Ed); education (MS); educational administration (M Ed); English (MA); instructional technology (MS); interdisciplinary studies (MA, MS); special education (MS). Part-time and evening/weekend programs available. *Degree requirements:* For master's, comprehensive exam (for some programs), thesis optional. *Entrance requirements:* For master's, minimum GPA of 2.5 on last 60 hours of bachelor's degree. Additional exam requirements/recommendations for international students: Required—TOEFL. Electronic applications accepted.

Texas Christian University, AddRan College of Liberal Arts, Department of English, Fort Worth, TX 76129-0002. Offers composition (MA); English (PhD), including rhetoric and/or literature; literature (MA); rhetoric (MA); rhetoric/composition (PhD). Part-time and evening/weekend programs available. In 2010, 3 master's, 2 doctorates awarded. *Degree requirements:* For master's, one foreign language, thesis, candidacy exam; for doctorate, one foreign language, comprehensive exam, thesis/dissertation, 66 hours, diagnostic exam, qualifying exam. *Entrance requirements:* For master's and doctorate, GRE General Test, 30 hours of English; 12 hours of foreign language study. Additional exam requirements/recommendations for international students: Required—TOEFL. *Application deadline:* For fall admission, 1/31 for domestic and international students; for winter admission, 1/10 for domestic and international students; for spring admission, 10/15 for domestic and international students. Applications are processed on a rolling basis. Application fee: $50. Electronic applications accepted. *Expenses:* Tuition: Full-time $18,720; part-time $1040 per credit hour. Tuition and fees vary according to course load and program. *Financial support:* In 2010–11, 39 students received support, including 2 fellowships with full tuition reimbursements available (averaging $17,500 per year), 29 teaching assistantships with full tuition reimbursements available (averaging $15,000 per year); research assistantships with full tuition reimbursements available, tuition waivers (full) and unspecified assistantships also available. Financial award application deadline: 1/10; financial award applicants required to submit FAFSA. *Unit head:* Dr. Brad Lucas, Chairperson, 817-257-7240, E-mail: b.e.lucas2@tcu.edu. *Application contact:* Dr. Mona Narain, Associate Professor/Director of Graduate Studies, 817-257-7284, E-mail: m.narain@tcu.edu.

Texas Southern University, College of Liberal Arts and Behavioral Sciences, Department of English, Houston, TX 77004-4584. Offers MA. Part-time programs available. *Faculty:* 9 full-time (6 women), 1 part-time/adjunct (0 women). *Students:* 9 full-time (7 women), 5 part-time (3 women); includes 13 Black or African American, non-Hispanic/Latino; 1 Asian, non-Hispanic/Latino. Average age 35. 7 applicants, 86% accepted, 5 enrolled. In 2010, 1 master's awarded. *Degree requirements:* For master's, one foreign language, comprehensive exam, thesis. *Entrance requirements:* For master's, GRE General Test, minimum GPA of 2.5. Additional exam requirements/recommendations for international students: Required—TOEFL. *Application deadline:* For fall admission, 7/1 priority date for domestic students, 7/1 for international students; for spring admission, 11/1 for domestic and international students. Applications are processed on a rolling basis. Application fee: $50 ($75 for international students). Electronic applications accepted. *Expenses:* Tuition, state resident: full-time $1875; part-time $100 per credit hour. Tuition, nonresident: full-time $6641; part-time $343 per credit hour. Tuition and fees vary according to course level, course load and degree level. *Financial support:* In 2010–11, 3 teaching assistantships (averaging $5,120 per year) were awarded; fellowships, scholarships/grants and unspecified assistantships also available. Support available to part-time students. Financial award application deadline: 5/1. *Faculty research:* Linguistics, teaching of English, African-American literature, African literature, developmental English. *Unit head:* Dr. Rhonda Saldivar, Chair, 713-313-7536, Fax: 713-313-7538, E-mail: saldivar_rx@tsu.edu. *Application contact:* Dr. Gregory Maddox, Dean of the Graduate School, 713-313-7011 Ext. 4410, Fax: 713-639-1876, E-mail: maddox_gh@tsu.edu.

Texas State University–San Marcos, Graduate School, College of Liberal Arts, Department of English, Program in Literature, San Marcos, TX 78666. Offers MA. Part-time and evening/weekend programs available. *Faculty:* 36 full-time (18 women). *Students:* 26 full-time (17 women), 53 part-time (38 women); includes 22 minority (4 Black or African American, non-Hispanic/Latino; 1 American Indian or Alaska Native, non-Hispanic/Latino; 1 Asian, non-Hispanic/Latino; 15 Hispanic/Latino; 1 Two or more races, non-Hispanic/Latino). Average age 31. 41 applicants, 90% accepted, 24 enrolled. In 2010, 17 master's awarded. *Degree requirements:* For master's, comprehensive exam, thesis optional. *Entrance requirements:* For master's, minimum GPA of 2.75 in last 60 hours, 24 undergraduate hours of course work in English (12 advanced) with minimum GPA of 3.25, 6 hours of course work in foreign language. Additional exam requirements/recommendations for international students: Required—TOEFL (minimum score 550 paper-based; 213 computer-based; 78 iBT). *Application deadline:* For fall admission,

6/15 priority date for domestic students, 6/1 for international students; for spring admission, 10/15 priority date for domestic students, 10/1 for international students. Applications are processed on a rolling basis. Application fee: $40 ($90 for international students). Electronic applications accepted. *Expenses:* Tuition, state resident: full-time $6024; part-time $251 per credit hour. Tuition, nonresident: full-time $13,536; part-time $564 per credit hour. Required fees: $1776; $50 per credit hour. $306 per semester. *Financial support:* In 2010–11, 29 students received support, including 4 research assistantships (averaging $5,609 per year), 14 teaching assistantships (averaging $5,568 per year); Federal Work-Study and institutionally sponsored loans also available. Support available to part-time students. Financial award application deadline: 4/1; financial award applicants required to submit FAFSA. *Unit head:* Dr. Paul Cohen, Acting Graduate Adviser, 512-245-2163, Fax: 512-245-8546, E-mail: pc06@txstate.edu. *Application contact:* Dr. J. Michael Willoughby, Dean of Graduate School, 512-245-2581, Fax: 512-245-8365, E-mail: gradcollege@txstate.edu.

Texas Tech University, Graduate School, College of Arts and Sciences, Department of English, Lubbock, TX 79409. Offers English (MA, PhD); technical communication (MA); technical communication and rhetoric (PhD). Part-time programs available. *Faculty:* 38 full-time (16 women), 1 (woman) part-time/adjunct. *Students:* 106 full-time (62 women), 89 part-time (55 women); includes 4 Black or African American, non-Hispanic/Latino; 2 American Indian or Alaska Native, non-Hispanic/Latino; 7 Asian, non-Hispanic/Latino; 4 Hispanic/Latino, 18 international. Average age 34. 242 applicants, 21% accepted, 34 enrolled. In 2010, 25 master's, 11 doctorates awarded. *Degree requirements:* For master's, one foreign language, thesis (for some programs); for doctorate, one foreign language, thesis/dissertation (for some programs). *Entrance requirements:* For master's and doctorate, GRE General Test. Additional exam requirements/recommendations for international students: Required—TOEFL (minimum score 550 paper-based; 213 computer-based; 79 iBT). *Application deadline:* For fall admission, 6/1 priority date for domestic students, 1/15 priority date for international students; for spring admission, 9/1 priority date for domestic students, 6/15 priority date for international students. Applications are processed on a rolling basis. Application fee: $50 ($75 for international students). Electronic applications accepted. *Expenses:* Tuition, state resident: full-time $5495.76; part-time $228.99 per credit hour. Tuition, nonresident: full-time $12,936; part-time $538.99 per credit hour. Required fees: $2674; $36 per credit hour. $905 per semester. *Financial support:* In 2010–11, 110 students received support, including 10 research assistantships with partial tuition reimbursements available (averaging $8,815 per year), 48 teaching assistantships with partial tuition reimbursements available (averaging $6,362 per year). Financial award application deadline: 4/15; financial award applicants required to submit FAFSA. *Faculty research:* Computers and writing, technical communication and rhetoric, creative writing, nineteenth century studies, literature of social justice and the environment. *Unit head:* Dr. Sam Dragga, Chair, 806-742-2501, Fax: 806-742-0989, E-mail: sam.dragga@ttu.edu. *Application contact:* Dr. Brian McFadden, Director of Graduate Studies, 806-742-2501, Fax: 806-742-0989, E-mail: english.gradadvisor@ttu.edu.

Texas Woman's University, Graduate School, College of Arts and Sciences, Department of English, Speech, and Foreign Languages, Denton, TX 76201. Offers English (MA); rhetoric (PhD). Part-time programs available. *Faculty:* 13 full-time (7 women), 6 part-time/adjunct (0 women). *Students:* 11 full-time (8 women), 58 part-time (51 women); includes 5 Black or African American, non-Hispanic/Latino; 2 American Indian or Alaska Native, non-Hispanic/Latino; 4 Asian, non-Hispanic/Latino; 4 Hispanic/Latino, 1 international. Average age 37. 19 applicants, 68% accepted, 12 enrolled. In 2010, 7 master's, 5 doctorates awarded. *Degree requirements:* For master's, comprehensive exam, thesis; for doctorate, comprehensive exam, thesis/dissertation. *Entrance requirements:* For master's, GRE General Test (preferred minimum score 500 verbal, 350 quantitative), 3 letters of reference, interview (for graduate assistants), minimum GPA of 3.0 on previous upper division and graduate work; for doctorate, GRE General Test (preferred minimum score 500 verbal, 350 quantitative), writing sample, 3 letters of reference, interview (for graduate assistants), minimum GPA of 3.0 on previous upper-division and graduate work. Additional exam requirements/recommendations for international students: Recommended—TOEFL (minimum score 600 paper-based; 250 computer-based; 100 iBT). *Application deadline:* For fall admission, 7/1 priority date for domestic students, 3/1 for international students; for spring admission, 12/1 priority date for domestic students, 7/1 for international students. Applications are processed on a rolling basis. Application fee: $50 ($75 for international students). Electronic applications accepted. *Expenses:* Tuition, state resident: full-time $3834; part-time $213 per credit hour. Tuition, nonresident: full-time $9468; part-time $526 per credit hour. Required fees: $1247; $220 per credit hour. *Financial support:* In 2010–11, 16 students received support, including 6 research assistantships (averaging $12,942 per year), 15 teaching assistantships (averaging $12,942 per year); career-related internships or fieldwork, Federal Work-Study, institutionally sponsored loans, scholarships/grants, traineeships, health care benefits, and unspecified assistantships also available. Support available to part-time students. Financial award application deadline: 3/1; financial award applicants required to submit FAFSA. *Faculty research:* British and American literature, rhetoric: historical and applied, composition studies and technology, literary theory and criticism, women's literature and feminist rhetoric. *Unit head:* Dr. Genevieve West, Chair, 940-898-2324, Fax: 940-898-2297, E-mail: engspfl@twu.edu. *Application contact:* Dr. Samuel Wheeler, Assistant Director of Admissions, 940-898-3188, Fax: 940-898-3081, E-mail: wheelersr@twu.edu.

Trinity College, Graduate Programs, Department of English, Hartford, CT 06106-3100. Offers MA. Part-time and evening/weekend programs available. *Degree requirements:* For master's, thesis. *Entrance requirements:* For master's, minimum GPA of 3.0.

Trinity Western University, School of Graduate Studies, Program in Interdisciplinary Humanities, Langley, BC V2Y 1Y1, Canada. Offers general humanities (MAIH); specialized (MAIH), including English, history, philosophy. Part-time programs available. *Degree requirements:* For master's, thesis or alternative, 36 semester hours. *Entrance requirements:* For master's, strong undergraduate degree in humanities or English, history or philosophy. Electronic applications accepted. *Faculty research:* Literary theory, gender, medieval and early modern literature, philosophy of religion, Thomas Merton's poetics.

Truman State University, Graduate School, School of Arts and Letters, Program in English, Kirksville, MO 63501-4221. Offers MA. *Degree requirements:* For master's, thesis. *Entrance requirements:* For master's, GRE General Test, minimum GPA of 3.0. Additional exam requirements/recommendations for international students: Required—TOEFL (minimum score 550 paper-based; 213 computer-based). Electronic applications accepted.

Tufts University, Graduate School of Arts and Sciences, Department of English, Medford, MA 02155. Offers MA, PhD. Terminal master's awarded for partial completion of doctoral program. *Degree requirements:* For master's, one foreign language, thesis; for doctorate, 2 foreign languages, thesis/dissertation. *Entrance requirements:* For master's and doctorate, GRE General Test, GRE Subject Test, writing sample. Additional exam requirements/recommendations for international students: Required—TOEFL (minimum score 550 paper-based; 213 computer-based; 80 iBT). Electronic applications accepted. *Expenses:* Tuition: Full-time $39,624; part-time $3962 per course. Required fees: $40 per year. Full-time tuition and fees vary according to degree level, program and student level. Part-time tuition and fees vary according to course load.

Tulane University, School of Liberal Arts, Department of English, New Orleans, LA 70118-5669. Offers MA, PhD. *Degree requirements:* For master's, one foreign language, thesis or alternative; for doctorate, 2 foreign languages, thesis/dissertation. *Entrance requirements:* For master's, GRE General Test, minimum B average in undergraduate course work; for doctorate, GRE General Test. Additional exam requirements/recommendations for international students: Required—TOEFL. Electronic applications accepted.

Universidad de las Américas–Puebla, Division of Graduate Studies, School of Humanities, Program in Literature, Puebla, Mexico. Offers MA. Part-time and evening/weekend programs available. *Degree requirements:* For master's, one foreign language, thesis. *Entrance*

requirements: Additional exam requirements/recommendations for international students: Required—TOEFL. *Faculty research:* Women in literature, Mexican and Hispanic literature.

Université de Montréal, Faculty of Arts and Sciences, Department of English Studies, Montréal, QC H3C 3J7, Canada. Offers MA, PhD. *Degree requirements:* For doctorate, thesis/dissertation, general exam. *Entrance requirements:* For master's, BA in English with minimum B+ average; for doctorate, MA in English with minimum B+ average. Electronic applications accepted. *Faculty research:* British, Canadian, and American literature.

Université Laval, Faculty of Letters, Department of Literature, Programs in Ancient Civilization, Québec, QC G1K 7P4, Canada. Offers MA, PhD. Part-time programs available. Terminal master's awarded for partial completion of doctoral program. *Degree requirements:* For master's, thesis; for doctorate, comprehensive exam, thesis/dissertation. *Entrance requirements:* For master's and doctorate, English test (comprehension of written English), knowledge of French, knowledge of an ancient language. Electronic applications accepted.

Université Laval, Faculty of Letters, Department of Literature, Programs in English Literatures, Québec, QC G1K 7P4, Canada. Offers MA, PhD. Part-time programs available. Terminal master's awarded for partial completion of doctoral program. *Degree requirements:* For master's, thesis (for some programs); for doctorate, comprehensive exam, thesis/dissertation. *Entrance requirements:* For master's, French exam, knowledge of English; for doctorate, French exam, knowledge of English, knowledge of a third language. Electronic applications accepted.

University at Albany, State University of New York, College of Arts and Sciences, Department of English, Albany, NY 12222-0001. Offers MA, PhD. *Degree requirements:* For master's, one foreign language; for doctorate, one foreign language, comprehensive exam, thesis/dissertation, residency. *Entrance requirements:* For master's and doctorate, GRE General Test, GRE Subject Test. Additional exam requirements/recommendations for international students: Required—TOEFL (minimum score 550 paper-based; 213 computer-based). Electronic applications accepted. *Faculty research:* Women playwrights; critical literary theory; poetry and poetics; media history, writing and reporting; creative non-fiction.

University at Buffalo, the State University of New York, Graduate School, College of Arts and Sciences, Department of English, Buffalo, NY 14260. Offers MA, PhD. Part-time programs available. Terminal master's awarded for partial completion of doctoral program. *Degree requirements:* For master's, thesis or alternative; for doctorate, thesis/dissertation, departmental qualifying exam. *Entrance requirements:* For master's and doctorate, GRE General Test, sample of written work. Additional exam requirements/recommendations for international students: Required—TOEFL (minimum score 79 iBT). Electronic applications accepted. *Faculty research:* Psychoanalysis, early modern British literature, poetics, nineteenth century American literature.

The University of Akron, Graduate School, Buchtel College of Arts and Sciences, Department of English, Akron, OH 44325. Offers composition (MA); creative writing (MFA); literature (MA). Part-time programs available. *Faculty:* 28 full-time (14 women), 71 part-time/adjunct (47 women). *Students:* 42 full-time (18 women), 39 part-time (24 women); includes 6 Black or African American, non-Hispanic/Latino. Average age 32. 51 applicants, 90% accepted, 22 enrolled. In 2010, 27 master's awarded. *Degree requirements:* For master's, thesis optional. *Entrance requirements:* For master's, BA in English, minimum GPA of 2.75, writing portfolio, statement of purpose. Additional exam requirements/recommendations for international students: Required—TOEFL (minimum score 580 paper-based; 237 computer-based; 92 iBT). *Application deadline:* Applications are processed on a rolling basis. Application fee: $30 ($40 for international students). Electronic applications accepted. *Expenses:* Tuition, state resident: full-time $6800; part-time $378 per credit hour. Tuition, nonresident: full-time $11,644; part-time $647 per credit hour. Required fees: $1265. One-time fee: $30 full-time. *Financial support:* In 2010–11, 1 research assistantship with full tuition reimbursement, 25 teaching assistantships with full tuition reimbursements were awarded. *Faculty research:* British and American literary studies, literary theory, creative writing, applied linguistics. Total annual research expenditures: $51,119. *Unit head:* Dr. Michael Schuldiner, Chair, 330-972-8556, E-mail: schuldi@uakron.edu. *Application contact:* Dr. Hillary Nunn, Director of Graduate Studies, 330-972-7601, E-mail: nunn@uakron.edu.

The University of Alabama, Graduate School, College of Arts and Sciences, Department of English, Tuscaloosa, AL 35487. Offers composition and rhetoric (PhD); creative writing (MFA), including fiction, poetry; literature (MA, PhD); rhetoric and composition (MA); teaching English as a second language (MATESOL). *Faculty:* 31 full-time (14 women). *Students:* 64 full-time (46 women), 75 part-time (44 women); includes 15 minority (11 Black or African American, non-Hispanic/Latino; 1 Asian, non-Hispanic/Latino; 1 Hispanic/Latino; 1 Native Hawaiian or other Pacific Islander, non-Hispanic/Latino; 1 Two or more races, non-Hispanic/Latino), 7 international. Average age 28. 364 applicants, 20% accepted, 46 enrolled. In 2010, 40 master's, 7 doctorates awarded. *Degree requirements:* For master's, one foreign language, comprehensive exam, thesis (for some programs); for doctorate, 2 foreign languages, comprehensive exam, thesis/dissertation. *Entrance requirements:* For master's and doctorate, GRE, minimum GPA of 3.0, critical writing sample. Additional exam requirements/recommendations for international students: Required—TOEFL. *Application deadline:* For fall admission, 1/15 priority date for domestic students, 1/15 for international students. Application fee: $50 ($60 for international students). Electronic applications accepted. *Expenses:* Tuition, state resident: full-time $7900. Tuition, nonresident: full-time $20,500. *Financial support:* In 2010–11, 7 fellowships with full tuition reimbursements (averaging $15,000 per year), 1 research assistantship (averaging $11,708 per year), 106 teaching assistantships with full tuition reimbursements (averaging $11,708 per year) were awarded; career-related internships or fieldwork, scholarships/grants, health care benefits, and unspecified assistantships also available. Financial award application deadline: 1/15. *Faculty research:* Critical theory; modern, Renaissance, and African-American literature. *Unit head:* Dr. Catherine E. Davies, Director of Graduate Studies, 205-348-8499, E-mail: cdavies@bama.ua.edu. *Application contact:* Vernita W. James, Office Assistant II, 205-348-0766, Fax: 205-348-1388, E-mail: vwjames@bama.ua.edu.

The University of Alabama at Birmingham, College of Arts and Sciences, Program in English, Birmingham, AL 35294. Offers MA. *Students:* 18 full-time (12 women), 27 part-time (18 women); includes 8 minority (7 Black or African American, non-Hispanic/Latino; 1 Hispanic/Latino), 1 international. Average age 30. 20 applicants, 90% accepted, 14 enrolled. In 2010, 10 master's awarded. *Degree requirements:* For master's, one foreign language, comprehensive exam, thesis optional. *Entrance requirements:* For master's, GRE General Test or MAT, minimum GPA of 2.75. *Application deadline:* Applications are processed on a rolling basis. Electronic applications accepted. *Expenses:* Tuition, state resident: full-time $5482. Tuition, nonresident: full-time $12,430. Tuition and fees vary according to program. *Financial support:* Teaching assistantships, career-related internships or fieldwork available. *Unit head:* Dr. Peter J. Bellis, Chair, 205-934-4083, Fax: 205-975-6610. *Application contact:* Julie Bryant, Director of Graduate Admissions, 205-934-8227, Fax: 205-934-8413, E-mail: jbryant@uab.edu.

The University of Alabama in Huntsville, School of Graduate Studies, College of Liberal Arts, Department of English, Huntsville, AL 35899. Offers English (MA); teaching of English to speakers of other languages (Certificate); technical communications (Certificate). Part-time and evening/weekend programs available. *Faculty:* 13 full-time (9 women). *Students:* 16 full-time (12 women), 39 part-time (30 women); includes 15 minority (12 Black or African American, non-Hispanic/Latino; 1 American Indian or Alaska Native, non-Hispanic/Latino; 2 Hispanic/Latino). Average age 32. 34 applicants, 85% accepted, 18 enrolled. In 2010, 17 master's, 2 other advanced degrees awarded. *Degree requirements:* For master's, one foreign language, comprehensive exam, thesis or alternative, oral and written exams. *Entrance requirements:* For master's and Certificate, GRE General Test, minimum GPA of 3.0. Additional exam requirements/recommendations for international students: Required—TOEFL (minimum score 500 paper-based; 173 computer-based; 62 iBT). *Application deadline:* For fall admission, 7/15 for domestic students, 4/1 for international students; for spring admission, 11/30 for domestic students, 9/1 for international students. Applications are processed on a rolling basis. Application fee: $40 ($50 for international students). Electronic applications accepted. *Expenses:* Tuition, state resident: full-time $7250; part-time $407.75 per credit hour. Tuition, nonresident: full-time $17,358; part-time $970.05 per credit hour. Required fees: $246.80 per semester. Tuition and fees vary according to course load and program. *Financial support:* In 2010–11, 9 students received support, including 5 teaching assistantships with full and partial tuition reimbursements available (averaging $8,460 per year); career-related internships or fieldwork, Federal Work-Study, institutionally sponsored loans, scholarships/grants, health care benefits, tuition waivers, and unspecified assistantships also available. Support available to part-time students. Financial award application deadline: 4/1; financial award applicants required to submit FAFSA. *Faculty research:* American and British literature, linguistics, technical writing, women's studies, rhetoric. Total annual research expenditures: $26,119. *Unit head:* Dr. Dan Schenker, Chair, 256-824-6320, Fax: 256-824-6949, E-mail: schenkd@uah.edu. *Application contact:* Kathy Biggs, Graduate Studies Admissions Manager, 256-824-6199, Fax: 256-824-6405, E-mail: deangrad@uah.edu.

University of Alaska Anchorage, College of Arts and Sciences, Department of English, Anchorage, AK 99508. Offers MA. Part-time programs available. *Degree requirements:* For master's, comprehensive exam, thesis or alternative. *Entrance requirements:* For master's, GRE General Test, GRE Subject Test, portfolio, minimum GPA of 3.5, writing sample. Additional exam requirements/recommendations for international students: Required—TOEFL (minimum score 550 paper-based; 213 computer-based). *Faculty research:* The rhetoric of essays, American and American Indian literature, linguistics, Shakespeare, literature of war.

University of Alaska Fairbanks, College of Liberal Arts, Department of English, Fairbanks, AK 99775-5720. Offers creative writing (MFA); literature (MA); MA/MFA. Part-time programs available. *Faculty:* 16 full-time (7 women). *Students:* 28 full-time (13 women), 13 part-time (9 women); includes 8 minority (1 American Indian or Alaska Native, non-Hispanic/Latino; 3 Asian, non-Hispanic/Latino; 1 Hispanic/Latino; 3 Two or more races, non-Hispanic/Latino). Average age 31. 50 applicants, 44% accepted, 14 enrolled. In 2010, 19 master's awarded. *Degree requirements:* For master's, comprehensive exam, thesis or alternative, oral exams, oral defense. *Entrance requirements:* For master's, GRE General Test, academic writing sample. Additional exam requirements/recommendations for international students: Required—TOEFL (minimum score 550 paper-based; 213 computer-based; 80 iBT). *Application deadline:* For fall admission, 6/1 for domestic students, 3/1 for international students; for spring admission, 10/15 for domestic students, 9/1 for international students. Applications are processed on a rolling basis. Application fee: $60. Electronic applications accepted. *Expenses:* Tuition, state resident: full-time $5688; part-time $316 per credit. Tuition, nonresident: full-time $11,628; part-time $646 per credit. Required fees: $289 per semester. Tuition and fees vary according to course load and reciprocity agreements. *Financial support:* In 2010–11, 23 teaching assistantships with tuition reimbursements (averaging $11,643 per year) were awarded; fellowships with tuition reimbursements, research assistantships with tuition reimbursements, Federal Work-Study, scholarships/grants, health care benefits, and unspecified assistantships also available. Support available to part-time students. Financial award application deadline: 7/1; financial award applicants required to submit FAFSA. *Faculty research:* Traditional Alaskan native literature, British literature, pedagogy, American literature, rhetoric/composition history. *Unit head:* Richard Carr, Department Chair, 907-474-7193, Fax: 907-474-5247, E-mail: faengl@uaf.edu. *Application contact:* Richard Carr, Department Chair, 907-474-7193, Fax: 907-474-5247, E-mail: faengl@uaf.edu.

University of Alberta, Faculty of Graduate Studies and Research, Department of English and Film Studies, Edmonton, AB T6G 2E1, Canada. Offers English (MA, PhD). Part-time and evening/weekend programs available. *Degree requirements:* For master's, one foreign language, thesis optional; for doctorate, 2 foreign languages, thesis/dissertation. *Entrance requirements:* For master's, honors BA or equivalent; for doctorate, honors BA and MA. Additional exam requirements/recommendations for international students: Required—TOEFL (minimum score 600 paper-based). Electronic applications accepted. *Faculty research:* Women's writing, postcolonial theory, Victorian literature, Renaissance literature, Canadian literature.

The University of Arizona, College of Humanities, Department of English, Tucson, AZ 85721. Offers creative writing (MFA); English (MA, PhD); English language/linguistics (MA), including ESL; rhetoric, composition and the teaching of English (MA, PhD). Part-time programs available. *Faculty:* 45 full-time (16 women), 3 part-time/adjunct (1 woman). *Students:* 116 full-time (80 women), 60 part-time (35 women); includes 35 minority (1 American Indian or Alaska Native, non-Hispanic/Latino; 4 Asian, non-Hispanic/Latino; 16 Hispanic/Latino; 14 Two or more races, non-Hispanic/Latino), 8 international. Average age 34. 482 applicants, 21% accepted, 53 enrolled. In 2010, 41 master's, 25 doctorates awarded. Terminal master's awarded for partial completion of doctoral program. *Degree requirements:* For master's, one foreign language, comprehensive exam; for doctorate, one foreign language, comprehensive exam, thesis/dissertation, preliminary and qualifying exams. *Entrance requirements:* For master's, GRE General Test, GRE Subject Test, bachelor's degree in English, minimum major GPA of 3.5, writing sample; for doctorate, GRE General Test, GRE Subject Test (literature), bachelor's degree in English, minimum major GPA of 3.5, statement of purpose, writing sample. Additional exam requirements/recommendations for international students: Required—TOEFL (minimum score 550 paper-based; 213 computer-based; 79 iBT). *Application deadline:* For fall admission, 1/9 for domestic students, 12/10 for international students. Applications are processed on a rolling basis. Application fee: $75. Electronic applications accepted. *Expenses:* Tuition, state resident: full-time $7692. *Financial support:* In 2010–11, 1 research assistantship with full tuition reimbursement (averaging $20,122 per year), 133 teaching assistantships with full tuition reimbursements (averaging $19,914 per year) were awarded; career-related internships or fieldwork, scholarships/grants, health care benefits, tuition waivers (full and partial), and unspecified assistantships also available. *Faculty research:* Literature, women's studies, Southwestern literature, feminist theory. Total annual research expenditures: $129,807. *Unit head:* Dr. Jun Liu, Department Head, 520-621-3287, E-mail: junliu@email.arizona.edu. *Application contact:* Marcia Marma, Graduate Secretary, 520-621-1358, Fax: 520-621-7397, E-mail: mmarma@u.arizona.edu.

University of Arkansas, Graduate School, J. William Fulbright College of Arts and Sciences, Department of English, Program in English, Fayetteville, AR 72701-1201. Offers MA, PhD. *Students:* 26 full-time (19 women), 55 part-time (34 women); includes 5 minority (1 Black or African American, non-Hispanic/Latino; 2 American Indian or Alaska Native, non-Hispanic/Latino; 2 Hispanic/Latino), 7 international. 52 applicants, 90% accepted. In 2010, 6 master's, 4 doctorates awarded. *Degree requirements:* For master's, thesis; for doctorate, thesis/dissertation. *Entrance requirements:* For master's, GRE General Test; for doctorate, GRE General Test, GRE Subject Test. *Application deadline:* For fall admission, 4/1 for international students; for spring admission, 10/1 for international students. Applications are processed on a rolling basis. Application fee: $40 ($50 for international students). Electronic applications accepted. *Financial support:* In 2010–11, 28 fellowships with tuition reimbursements, 44 teaching assistantships were awarded; research assistantships, career-related internships or fieldwork and Federal Work-Study also available. Support available to part-time students. Financial award application deadline: 4/1; financial award applicants required to submit FAFSA. *Faculty research:* Creative writing, seventeenth century literature, twentieth century literature, American literature. *Unit head:* Dr. Joseph Candido, Department Chairperson, 479-575-4301, Fax: 479-575-5919, E-mail: candido@uark.edu. *Application contact:* Dr. Dorothy Stephens, Graduate Coordinator, 479-575-4301, E-mail: dstephen@uark.edu.

The University of British Columbia, Faculty of Arts and Faculty of Graduate Studies, Department of English, Vancouver, BC V6T 1Z1, Canada. Offers MA, PhD. *Degree requirements:* For master's, thesis or alternative; for doctorate, one foreign language, comprehensive exam, thesis/dissertation. *Entrance requirements:* For doctorate, MA. Additional exam requirements/recommendations for international students: Required—TOEFL (minimum score 615 paper-based; 258 computer-based; 104 iBT), IELTS (minimum score 8). Electronic applications accepted. Tuition charges are reported in Canadian dollars. *Expenses:* Tuition, area resident: Full-time $4179 Canadian dollars. International tuition: $7344 Canadian dollars full-time. *Faculty*

English

The University of British Columbia (continued)
research: English, American, Canadian, and Commonwealth post-colonial literature; English language; rhetoric.

The University of British Columbia, Faculty of Arts, School of Library, Archival and Information Studies, Master of Arts Program in Children's Literature, Vancouver, BC V6T 1Z1, Canada. Offers MA. Part-time programs available. *Degree requirements:* For master's, thesis. *Entrance requirements:* For master's, minimum GPA of 3.3 in undergraduate upper-division courses. Additional exam requirements/recommendations for international students: Required—TOEFL (minimum score 600 paper-based; 250 computer-based; 100 iBT). Electronic applications accepted. Tuition charges are reported in Canadian dollars. *Expenses:* Tuition, area resident: Full-time $4179 Canadian dollars. International tuition: $7344 Canadian dollars full-time. *Faculty research:* Children's and young adult literature; children's and young adult public library services; Canadian children's and young adult literature; publishing for youth.

University of Calgary, Faculty of Graduate Studies, Faculty of Arts, Department of English, Calgary, AB T2N 1N4, Canada. Offers MA, PhD. Part-time programs available. *Degree requirements:* For master's, one foreign language, comprehensive exam (for some programs), thesis; for doctorate, one foreign language, thesis/dissertation, candidacy exam. *Entrance requirements:* Additional exam requirements/recommendations for international students: Required—TOEFL (minimum score 600 paper-based; 250 computer-based). Electronic applications accepted. *Faculty research:* Various national and period literatures, creative writing, literary theory, gender and women's studies, postcolonial literatures.

University of California, Berkeley, Graduate Division, College of Letters and Science, Department of English, Berkeley, CA 94720-1500. Offers PhD. *Degree requirements:* For doctorate, 2 foreign languages, thesis/dissertation, qualifying exam. *Entrance requirements:* For doctorate, GRE General Test, GRE Subject Test, minimum GPA of 3.0, writing sample, 3 letters of recommendation.

University of California, Davis, Graduate Studies, Program in English, Davis, CA 95616. Offers creative writing (MA); English (MA, PhD). Terminal master's awarded for partial completion of doctoral program. *Degree requirements:* For master's, one foreign language, thesis optional; for doctorate, 2 foreign languages, thesis/dissertation. *Entrance requirements:* For master's and doctorate, GRE General Test, GRE Subject Test, minimum GPA of 3.0, writing sample. Additional exam requirements/recommendations for international students: Required—TOEFL (minimum score 550 paper-based; 213 computer-based). Electronic applications accepted. *Faculty research:* Feminist theory, ethnic literature, literary theory, history of literature, literature of nature.

University of California, Irvine, School of Humanities, Department of English and Comparative Literature, Program in English, Irvine, CA 92697. Offers English (MA); English and American literature (PhD). *Students:* 73 full-time (33 women), 2 part-time (1 woman); includes 15 minority (1 Black or African American, non-Hispanic/Latino; 8 Asian, non-Hispanic/Latino; 6 Hispanic/Latino), 1 international. Average age 28. 164 applicants, 12% accepted, 10 enrolled. In 2010, 26 master's, 13 doctorates awarded. Terminal master's awarded for partial completion of doctoral program. *Degree requirements:* For master's, one foreign language, comprehensive exam; for doctorate, 2 foreign languages, comprehensive exam, thesis/dissertation. *Entrance requirements:* For doctorate, GRE General Test, GRE Subject Test, minimum GPA of 3.5, sample of written work, 3 letters of recommendation. Additional exam requirements/recommendations for international students: Required—TOEFL (minimum score 550 paper-based; 213 computer-based). *Application deadline:* For fall admission, 12/1 for domestic and international students. Application fee: $80 ($100 for international students). Electronic applications accepted. *Financial support:* In 2010–11, 75 students received support; fellowships with full tuition reimbursements available, research assistantships, teaching assistantships with partial tuition reimbursements available, institutionally sponsored loans, health care benefits, tuition waivers (full and partial), and unspecified assistantships available. Financial award application deadline: 3/1; financial award applicants required to submit FAFSA. *Faculty research:* Critical theory, literary history, cultural studies. *Unit head:* Andrzej J. Warminski, Acting Chair, 949-824-5954, Fax: 949-824-2916, E-mail: ajwarmin@uci.edu. *Application contact:* Jennifer Jean Day, Graduate Program Administrator, 949-824-5323, Fax: 949-824-2916, E-mail: dayj@uci.edu.

University of California, Los Angeles, Graduate Division, College of Letters and Science, Department of English, Los Angeles, CA 90095. Offers MA, PhD. *Faculty:* 51 full-time (21 women). *Students:* 97 full-time (63 women); includes 22 minority (5 Black or African American, non-Hispanic/Latino; 8 Asian, non-Hispanic/Latino; 8 Hispanic/Latino; 1 Two or more races, non-Hispanic/Latino), 2 international. Average age 29. 309 applicants, 12% accepted, 14 enrolled. In 2010, 10 master's, 8 doctorates awarded. Terminal master's awarded for partial completion of doctoral program. *Degree requirements:* For master's, comprehensive exam or thesis; for doctorate, 2 foreign languages, thesis/dissertation, oral and written qualifying exams. *Entrance requirements:* For master's, GRE General Test, GRE Subject Test (literature), minimum GPA of 3.0, sample of written work; for doctorate, GRE General Test, GRE Subject Test (literature), minimum GPA of 3.5 (undergraduate), 3.7 (graduate), sample of written work. *Application deadline:* For fall admission, 12/15 for domestic and international students. Application fee: $70 ($90 for international students). Electronic applications accepted. *Financial support:* In 2010–11, 67 fellowships with full and partial tuition reimbursements, 29 research assistantships with full and partial tuition reimbursements, 78 teaching assistantships with full and partial tuition reimbursements were awarded; Federal Work-Study, institutionally sponsored loans, scholarships/grants, health care benefits, tuition waivers (full and partial), and unspecified assistantships also available. Financial award application deadline: 3/1; financial award applicants required to submit FAFSA. *Unit head:* Dr. Ali Behdad, Chair, 310-825-4173, E-mail: behdad@humnet.ucla.edu. *Application contact:* Departmental Office, 310-825-1223, E-mail: graduate@english.ucla.edu.

University of California, Riverside, Graduate Division, Department of English, Riverside, CA 92521-0102. Offers MA, PhD. *Faculty:* 27 full-time (15 women). *Students:* 82 full-time (48 women); includes 3 Black or African American, non-Hispanic/Latino; 1 American Indian or Alaska Native, non-Hispanic/Latino; 5 Asian, non-Hispanic/Latino; 10 Hispanic/Latino, 3 international. Average age 31. In 2010, 9 master's, 10 doctorates awarded. *Degree requirements:* For master's, one foreign language, comprehensive exam; for doctorate, 2 foreign languages, thesis/dissertation, qualifying exams. *Entrance requirements:* For master's and doctorate, GRE General Test, minimum GPA of 3.5. Additional exam requirements/recommendations for international students: Required—TOEFL (minimum score 550 paper-based; 213 computer-based; 80 iBT). *Application deadline:* For fall admission, 3/31 for domestic students, 2/1 priority date for international students. Applications are processed on a rolling basis. Application fee: $60 ($75 for international students). Electronic applications accepted. *Financial support:* In 2010–11, fellowships with full and partial tuition reimbursements (averaging $12,000 per year), teaching assistantships with full and partial tuition reimbursements (averaging $16,500 per year) were awarded; research assistantships with tuition reimbursements, career-related internships or fieldwork, Federal Work-Study, institutionally sponsored loans, and tuition waivers (full and partial) also available. Financial award application deadline: 12/10; financial award applicants required to submit FAFSA. *Faculty research:* Critical theory, cultural and film studies, lesbian and gay studies, minority and feminist discourses, rhetoric and composition. *Unit head:* Prof. Deborah Willis, Chair, 951-827-1458, Fax: 951-827-3967, E-mail: deborah.willis@ucr.edu. *Application contact:* Tina M. Feldmann, Graduate Program Assistant, 951-827-1454, Fax: 951-827-3967, E-mail: english@ucr.edu.

University of California, San Diego, Office of Graduate Studies, Department of Literature, Program in Literatures in English, La Jolla, CA 92093. Offers MA. *Degree requirements:* For master's, thesis. *Entrance requirements:* For master's, GRE General Test, GRE Subject Test. Electronic applications accepted.

University of California, Santa Barbara, Graduate Division, College of Letters and Sciences, Division of Humanities and Fine Arts, Department of English, Santa Barbara, CA 93106-3170. Offers English (PhD); European medieval studies (PhD); feminist studies (PhD); global studies (PhD); technology and society (PhD); MA/PhD. *Faculty:* 26 full-time (13 women), 17 part-time/adjunct (12 women). *Students:* 68 full-time (37 women); includes 2 Black or African American, non-Hispanic/Latino; 5 Asian, non-Hispanic/Latino; 2 Hispanic/Latino. Average age 30. 173 applicants, 12% accepted, 8 enrolled. In 2010, 4 doctorates awarded. Terminal master's awarded for partial completion of doctoral program. *Degree requirements:* For doctorate, one foreign language, comprehensive exam, thesis/dissertation. *Entrance requirements:* For doctorate, GRE General Test, GRE Subject Test (English). Additional exam requirements/recommendations for international students: Required—TOEFL (minimum score 550 paper-based; 80 iBT), IELTS (minimum score 7). *Application deadline:* For fall admission, 12/15 priority date for domestic and international students. Application fee: $70 ($90 for international students). Electronic applications accepted. *Financial support:* In 2010–11, 68 students received support, including 38 fellowships with full and partial tuition reimbursements available (averaging $9,204 per year), 3 research assistantships with full and partial tuition reimbursements available (averaging $10,512 per year), 50 teaching assistantships with full and partial tuition reimbursements available (averaging $13,031 per year); career-related internships or fieldwork and tuition waivers (full and partial) also available. Financial award application deadline: 12/15; financial award applicants required to submit FAFSA. *Faculty research:* Medieval, Romantic, and Victorian studies; gender studies and feminist theory; literature and the mind; American literature; literature and new media/information culture. Total annual research expenditures: $25,000. *Unit head:* Prof. Ken Hiltner, Graduate Program Chair, 805-564-2304, Fax: 805-893-7492, E-mail: hiltner@english.ucsb.edu. *Application contact:* Mary Rae Staton, Graduate Program Staff Advisor, 805-893-2639, Fax: 805-893-7492, E-mail: staton@hfa.ucsb.edu.

University of California, Santa Cruz, Division of Graduate Studies, Division of Humanities, Department of Literature, Santa Cruz, CA 95064. Offers MA, PhD. *Students:* 65 full-time (42 women), 4 part-time (2 women); includes 1 Black or African American, non-Hispanic/Latino; 7 Asian, non-Hispanic/Latino; 2 Hispanic/Latino, 1 international. Average age 31. 183 applicants, 14% accepted, 8 enrolled. In 2010, 3 master's, 4 doctorates awarded. Terminal master's awarded for partial completion of doctoral program. *Degree requirements:* For master's, thesis; for doctorate, one foreign language, thesis/dissertation, qualifying exam. *Entrance requirements:* For master's, GRE General Test, writing sample, minimum GPA of 3.5; for doctorate, GRE General Test, minimum GPA of 3.5, writing sample. Additional exam requirements/recommendations for international students: Required—TOEFL (minimum score 550 paper-based; 220 computer-based; 83 iBT); Recommended—IELTS (minimum score 8). *Application deadline:* For fall admission, 12/1 for domestic and international students. Application fee: $70 ($90 for international students). Electronic applications accepted. *Financial support:* Fellowships, teaching assistantships, institutionally sponsored loans and tuition waivers available. Financial award applicants required to submit FAFSA. *Faculty research:* Technologies of narrative; trans/post/emergent nationalisms; poetics, poetry, and experimental writing; materialism and material culture; critical theories. *Unit head:* Emily Gregg, Graduate Program Coordinator, 831-459-4126, E-mail: egregg@ucsc.edu. *Application contact:* Emily Gregg, Graduate Program Coordinator, 831-459-4126, E-mail: egregg@ucsc.edu.

University of Central Arkansas, Graduate School, College of Liberal Arts, Department of English, Conway, AR 72035-0001. Offers MA. Part-time programs available. *Faculty:* 17 full-time (2 women). *Students:* 12 full-time (8 women), 8 part-time (5 women); includes 1 minority (Black or African American, non-Hispanic/Latino). Average age 29. 14 applicants, 93% accepted, 13 enrolled. In 2010, 5 master's awarded. *Degree requirements:* For master's, comprehensive exam, thesis optional. *Entrance requirements:* For master's, GRE General Test, minimum GPA of 2.7. Additional exam requirements/recommendations for international students: Required—TOEFL (minimum score 550 paper-based; 213 computer-based). *Application deadline:* For fall admission, 3/1 priority date for domestic and international students; for spring admission, 10/1 priority date for domestic and international students. Applications are processed on a rolling basis. Application fee: $25 ($50 for international students). *Financial support:* Federal Work-Study, scholarships/grants, and unspecified assistantships available. Financial award application deadline: 2/15; financial award applicants required to submit FAFSA. *Faculty research:* Writing project. *Unit head:* Dr. Jay Ruud, Chairperson, 501-450-5100, Fax: 501-450-5102, E-mail: jruud@uca.edu. *Application contact:* Susan Wood, Admissions Assistant, 501-450-3124, Fax: 501-450-5678, E-mail: swood@uca.edu.

University of Central Florida, College of Arts and Humanities, Department of English, Program in English, Orlando, FL 32816. Offers creative writing (MFA); English (MA); professional writing (Certificate). *Students:* 49 full-time (25 women), 51 part-time (33 women); includes 7 Black or African American, non-Hispanic/Latino; 1 Asian, non-Hispanic/Latino; 4 Hispanic/Latino; 2 Two or more races, non-Hispanic/Latino. Average age 30. 103 applicants, 55% accepted, 42 enrolled. In 2010, 16 master's, 14 other advanced degrees awarded. Application fee: $30. Electronic applications accepted. *Expenses:* Tuition, state resident: part-time $256.56 per credit hour. Tuition, nonresident: part-time $1011.52 per credit hour. Part-time tuition and fees vary according to program. *Financial support:* In 2010–11, 30 students received support, including 6 fellowships with partial tuition reimbursements available (averaging $9,200 per year), 8 research assistantships with partial tuition reimbursements available (averaging $6,200 per year), 24 teaching assistantships with partial tuition reimbursements available (averaging $6,700 per year).

University of Central Missouri, The Graduate School, College of Arts, Humanities and Social Sciences, Warrensburg, MO 64093. Offers English (MA); history (MA); mass communication (MA); music (MA); psychology (MS); speech communication (MA); teaching English as a second language (MA); theatre (MA). Part-time programs available. *Entrance requirements:* Additional exam requirements/recommendations for international students: Required—TOEFL (minimum score 550 paper-based; 79 computer-based). Electronic applications accepted.

University of Central Oklahoma, College of Graduate Studies and Research, College of Liberal Arts, Department of English, Edmond, OK 73034-5209. Offers composition skills (MA); contemporary literature (MA); creative writing (MA); teaching English as a second language (MA); traditional studies (MA). Part-time programs available. *Degree requirements:* For master's, one foreign language. *Entrance requirements:* For master's, 24 hours of course work in English language and literature. Additional exam requirements/recommendations for international students: Required—TOEFL (minimum score 550 paper-based; 213 computer-based). Electronic applications accepted. *Faculty research:* John Milton, Harriet Beecher Stowe.

University of Chicago, Division of the Humanities, Department of English Language and Literature, Chicago, IL 60637-1513. Offers AM, PhD. *Degree requirements:* For master's, one foreign language, thesis; for doctorate, 2 foreign languages, thesis/dissertation. *Entrance requirements:* For master's and doctorate, GRE General Test, GRE Subject Test (English). Additional exam requirements/recommendations for international students: Required—TOEFL.

University of Cincinnati, Graduate School, McMicken College of Arts and Sciences, Department of English, Cincinnati, OH 45221. Offers MA, MAT, PhD. Part-time programs available. Terminal master's awarded for partial completion of doctoral program. *Degree requirements:* For master's, one foreign language, thesis (for some programs); for doctorate, 2 foreign languages, thesis/dissertation. *Entrance requirements:* For master's, GRE General Test, letters of recommendation (3), writing samples; for doctorate, GRE General Test, GRE Subject Test, letters of recommendation (3), writing samples. Additional exam requirements/recommendations for international students: Required—TOEFL. Electronic applications accepted. *Faculty research:* Literature/theory, creative writing, composition, professional writing/editing, linguistics.

University of Colorado Boulder, Graduate School, College of Arts and Sciences, Department of English, Boulder, CO 80309. Offers literature (MA, PhD), including creative writing (MA). Part-time programs available. *Faculty:* 45 full-time (25 women). *Students:* 113 full-time (64 women), 10 part-time (8 women); includes 12 minority (4 Black or African American, non-

Hispanic/Latino; 1 American Indian or Alaska Native, non-Hispanic/Latino; 3 Asian, non-Hispanic/Latino; 4 Hispanic/Latino), 1 international. Average age 31. 405 applicants, 39 enrolled. In 2010, 27 master's, 8 doctorates awarded. *Degree requirements:* For master's, one foreign language, comprehensive exam, thesis or alternative; for doctorate, 2 foreign languages, comprehensive exam, thesis/dissertation. *Entrance requirements:* For master's, GRE General Test, GRE Subject Test, minimum undergraduate GPA of 3.0; for doctorate, GRE General Test, GRE Subject Test. *Application deadline:* For fall admission, 1/1 for domestic students, 12/1 for international students. Application fee: $50 ($60 for international students). *Financial support:* In 2010–11, 22 fellowships (averaging $3,976 per year), 42 research assistantships (averaging $11,068 per year) were awarded; Federal Work-Study and tuition waivers (full) also available. Financial award application deadline: 1/1; financial award applicants required to submit FAFSA. *Faculty research:* Creative writing, literature, language, critical theory. Total annual research expenditures: $1.7 million.

University of Colorado Boulder, Graduate School, College of Arts and Sciences, Department of Spanish and Portuguese, Boulder, CO 80309. Offers Hispanic linguistics (MA); medieval/early modern Hispanic literatures (PhD); Spanish and Spanish American literatures (MA, PhD). Part-time programs available. *Faculty:* 15 full-time (6 women). *Students:* 48 full-time (30 women), 1 (woman) part-time; includes 9 minority (all Hispanic/Latino), 18 international. Average age 32. 52 applicants, 15 enrolled. In 2010, 10 master's, 2 doctorates awarded. Terminal master's awarded for partial completion of doctoral program. *Degree requirements:* For master's, one foreign language, comprehensive exam, thesis or alternative; for doctorate, 2 foreign languages, thesis/dissertation. *Entrance requirements:* For master's, minimum undergraduate GPA of 2.75. *Application deadline:* For fall admission, 12/15 priority date for domestic students, 12/15 for international students. Applications are processed on a rolling basis. Application fee: $50 ($60 for international students). *Financial support:* In 2010–11, 7 fellowships with full tuition reimbursements (averaging $3,436 per year), 19 research assistantships (averaging $12,128 per year) were awarded; tuition waivers (full) also available. Financial award application deadline: 12/15. *Faculty research:* Spanish peninsular and Spanish-American literatures; Hispanic linguistics; medieval, Golden Age, eighteenth and nineteenth century literatures.

University of Colorado Denver, College of Liberal Arts and Sciences, Department of English, Denver, CO 80217. Offers applied linguistics (MA); literature (MA); rhetoric and teaching of writing (MA). Part-time and evening/weekend programs available. *Faculty:* 23 full-time (13 women). *Students:* 45 full-time (27 women), 22 part-time (15 women); includes 3 Hispanic/Latino, 3 international. Average age 30. 39 applicants, 77% accepted, 18 enrolled. In 2010, 18 master's awarded. *Degree requirements:* For master's, variable foreign language requirement, comprehensive exam (for some programs), thesis (for some programs), minimum of 33 credit hours (for literature), 30 (for rhetoric and teaching of writing and applied linguistics). *Entrance requirements:* For master's, GRE General Test, minimum GPA of 3.0, critical writing sample, letters of recommendation, completion of 24 semester hours in English courses (at least 16 at the upper-division). *Application deadline:* For fall admission, 4/1 for domestic students; for spring admission, 10/1 for domestic students. Application fee: $50 ($75 for international students). Electronic applications accepted. *Expenses:* Tuition, state resident: full-time $7332; part-time $355 per credit hour. Tuition, nonresident: full-time $18,990; part-time $1055 per credit hour. Required fees: $998. Tuition and fees vary according to course level, course load, degree level, campus/location, program, reciprocity agreements and student level. *Financial support:* Fellowships, teaching assistantships, Federal Work-Study, scholarships/grants, and unspecified assistantships available. Financial award application deadline: 4/1; financial award applicants required to submit FAFSA. *Faculty research:* Literature, rhetoric, teaching of writing, applied linguistics. *Unit head:* Prof. Nancy Ciccone, Chair, 303-556-8395, Fax: 303-556-2959, E-mail: nancy.ciccone@ucdenver.edu. *Application contact:* English Department, 303-556-2584, Fax: 303-556-2959.

University of Connecticut, Graduate School, College of Liberal Arts and Sciences, Department of English, Storrs, CT 06269. Offers MA, PhD. Terminal master's awarded for partial completion of doctoral program. *Degree requirements:* For master's, comprehensive exam; for doctorate, thesis/dissertation. *Entrance requirements:* For master's and doctorate, GRE General Test, GRE Subject Test. Additional exam requirements/recommendations for international students: Required—TOEFL (minimum score 550 paper-based; 213 computer-based). Electronic applications accepted.

University of Dallas, Braniff Graduate School of Liberal Arts, Department of English, Irving, TX 75062-4736. Offers English literature (MA, MENG). Part-time programs available. *Degree requirements:* For master's, one foreign language. *Entrance requirements:* For master's, GRE General Test. *Expenses:* Tuition: Full-time $7500; part-time $720 per credit hour. Required fees: $500; $60 per credit hour. $300 per semester. One-time fee: $150. Tuition and fees vary according to program and student level. *Faculty research:* Modern literature, Renaissance, Shakespeare, medieval studies.

University of Dayton, Graduate School, College of Arts and Sciences, Department of English, Dayton, OH 45469-1300. Offers MA. Part-time and evening/weekend programs available. *Faculty:* 18 full-time (7 women). *Students:* 25 full-time (16 women), 13 part-time (12 women); includes 3 minority (2 Black or African American, non-Hispanic/Latino; 1 Hispanic/Latino), 1 international. Average age 31. 29 applicants, 90% accepted, 6 enrolled. In 2010, 14 master's awarded. *Degree requirements:* For master's, thesis optional. *Entrance requirements:* For master's, minimum GPA of 3.0, 24 upper level credit hours of course work in English. Additional exam requirements/recommendations for international students: Required—TOEFL (minimum score 550 paper-based; 213 computer-based; 80 iBT). *Application deadline:* For fall admission, 4/4 priority date for domestic students, 3/1 priority date for international students; for winter admission, 7/1 priority date for international students; for spring admission, 1/1 priority date for international students. Applications are processed on a rolling basis. Application fee: $0 ($50 for international students). Electronic applications accepted. *Expenses:* Tuition: Full-time $7800; part-time $650 per credit hour. *Financial support:* In 2010–11, 12 teaching assistantships with full tuition reimbursements (averaging $10,026 per year) were awarded; institutionally sponsored loans, health care benefits, and unspecified assistantships also available. Financial award applicants required to submit FAFSA. *Faculty research:* Religion and literature, rhetoric and composition, teaching literature and writing and creative writing. Total annual research expenditures: $6,000. *Unit head:* Dr. Sheila Hughes, Chair, 937-229-3434, Fax: 937-229-3563, E-mail: sheila.hughes@notes.udayton.edu. *Application contact:* Alexander Popovski, Associate Director of Graduate and International Admissions, 937-229-2357, Fax: 937-229-4729, E-mail: alex.popovski@notes.udayton.edu.

University of Delaware, College of Arts and Sciences, Department of English, Newark, DE 19716. Offers English and American literature (MA, PhD); MA/PhD. Terminal master's awarded for partial completion of doctoral program. *Degree requirements:* For master's, one foreign language, thesis optional; for doctorate, 2 foreign languages, comprehensive exam, thesis/dissertation, specialty exam. *Entrance requirements:* For master's and doctorate, GRE General Test, GRE Subject Test. Additional exam requirements/recommendations for international students: Required—TOEFL (minimum score 550 paper-based; 213 computer-based). Electronic applications accepted. *Faculty research:* Significant strengths in American literature and culture, material cultural studies, Renaissance studies, archival studies.

University of Denver, Division of Arts, Humanities and Social Sciences, Department of English, Denver, CO 80208. Offers creative writing (PhD); literary studies (MA, PhD); rhetoric and theory (PhD). Part-time programs available. *Faculty:* 18 full-time (7 women), 1 (woman) part-time/adjunct. *Students:* 32 full-time (17 women), 10 part-time (9 women), 1 international. Average age 32. 195 applicants, 11% accepted, 18 enrolled. In 2010, 3 master's, 6 doctorates awarded. *Degree requirements:* For master's, one foreign language, comprehensive exam, thesis; for doctorate, 2 foreign languages, comprehensive exam, thesis/dissertation. *Entrance requirements:* For master's and doctorate, GRE General Test, GRE Subject Test. Additional exam requirements/recommendations for international students: Required—TOEFL (minimum score 570 paper-based; 88 iBT). *Application deadline:* Applications are processed on a rolling basis. Application fee: $60. Electronic applications accepted. *Expenses:* Tuition: Full-time $35,604; part-time $29,670 per year. Required fees: $687 per year. Tuition and fees vary according to program. *Financial support:* In 2010–11, 31 teaching assistantships with full and partial tuition reimbursements (averaging $16,910 per year) were awarded; Federal Work-Study, institutionally sponsored loans, scholarships/grants, and unspecified assistantships also available. Support available to part-time students. Financial award application deadline: 3/1; financial award applicants required to submit FAFSA. *Faculty research:* Cultural studies, creative nonfiction, eighteenth century colonial literature, multicultural literature, Cervantes. *Unit head:* Dr. Clark Davis, Chair, 303-871-2900, Fax: 303-871-2853, E-mail: cldavis@du.edu. *Application contact:* Niki Herrera, Graduate Student Services Assistant, 303-871-4313, Fax: 303-871-2853, E-mail: niki.herrera@du.edu.

University of Florida, Graduate School, College of Liberal Arts and Sciences, Department of English, Gainesville, FL 32611. Offers creative writing (MFA); English (MA, PhD). *Faculty:* 42 full-time (15 women), 4 part-time/adjunct (3 women). *Students:* 148 full-time (75 women), 10 part-time (5 women); includes 8 Black or African American, non-Hispanic/Latino; 5 Asian, non-Hispanic/Latino; 20 Hispanic/Latino, 12 international. Average age 28. 366 applicants, 11% accepted, 23 enrolled. In 2010, 18 master's, 23 doctorates awarded. *Degree requirements:* For master's, one foreign language, comprehensive exam, thesis or alternative; for doctorate, one foreign language, comprehensive exam, thesis/dissertation. *Entrance requirements:* For master's and doctorate, GRE General Test, minimum GPA of 3.0. Additional exam requirements/recommendations for international students: Required—TOEFL (minimum score 550 paper-based; 213 computer-based; 80 iBT), IELTS (minimum score 6). *Application deadline:* For spring admission, 1/1 for domestic and international students. Application fee: $30. Electronic applications accepted. *Expenses:* Tuition, state resident: full-time $10,915.92. Tuition, nonresident: full-time $28,309. *Financial support:* In 2010–11, 179 students received support, including 52 fellowships with tuition reimbursements available, 30 research assistantships with tuition reimbursements available (averaging $8,003 per year), 97 teaching assistantships with tuition reimbursements available (averaging $14,593 per year); unspecified assistantships also available. Financial award application deadline: 1/15; financial award applicants required to submit FAFSA. *Faculty research:* Modern global literatures in English, film and media studies, cultural studies and critical theory, American literature, English literature. *Unit head:* Dr. Kenneth Kidd, Chair, 352-392-6650 Ext. 302, Fax: 352-392-0860, E-mail: kbkidd@ufl.edu. *Application contact:* Dr. Phillip Wegner, Graduate Coordinator, 352-392-6650 Ext. 261, Fax: 352-392-0860, E-mail: pwegner@english.ufl.edu.

University of Georgia, College of Arts and Sciences, Department of English, Athens, GA 30602. Offers creative writing (MFA, PhD); English (MA, MAT, PhD). *Faculty:* 37 full-time (16 women), 1 part-time/adjunct (0 women). *Students:* 70 full-time (38 women), 18 part-time (10 women); includes 7 Black or African American, non-Hispanic/Latino; 1 Asian, non-Hispanic/Latino, 1 international. 280 applicants, 12% accepted, 14 enrolled. In 2010, 11 master's, 14 doctorates awarded. *Degree requirements:* For master's, one foreign language, thesis (MA); for doctorate, 2 foreign languages, thesis/dissertation. *Entrance requirements:* For master's and doctorate, GRE General Test. Additional exam requirements/recommendations for international students: Required—TWE. *Application deadline:* For fall admission, 7/1 priority date for domestic students; for spring admission, 11/15 for domestic students. Application fee: $50. Electronic applications accepted. *Expenses:* Tuition, state resident: full-time $7200; part-time $344 per credit hour. Tuition, nonresident: full-time $21,900; part-time $944 per credit hour. Tuition and fees vary according to course load and program. *Financial support:* Fellowships, research assistantships, teaching assistantships, unspecified assistantships available. *Unit head:* Dr. Doug Anderson, Head, 706-543-2248, Fax: 706-542-2181, E-mail: anderson@uga.edu. *Application contact:* Dr. Adam Parkes, Graduate Coordinator, 706-542-3100, E-mail: aparkes@uga.edu.

University of Guam, Office of Graduate Studies, College of Liberal Arts and Social Sciences, Department of English, Mangilao, GU 96923. Offers MA. *Entrance requirements:* For master's, GRE. Additional exam requirements/recommendations for international students: Required—TOEFL.

University of Guelph, Graduate Studies, College of Arts, School of English and Theatre Studies, Program in English, Guelph, ON N1G 2W1, Canada. Offers MA. Part-time programs available. *Degree requirements:* For master's, thesis (for some programs). *Entrance requirements:* For master's, letters of reference, 4-year honours undergraduate degree in English or drama. Additional exam requirements/recommendations for international students: Required—TOEFL. Electronic applications accepted. *Faculty research:* Post-colonial literature, Canadian literature, children's literature, Scottish literature, American literature, cultural studies.

University of Hawaii at Manoa, Graduate Division, College of Languages, Linguistics and Literature, Department of English, Honolulu, HI 96822. Offers MA, PhD. Part-time programs available. *Faculty:* 54 full-time (22 women). *Students:* 68 full-time (50 women), 27 part-time (19 women); includes 47 minority (2 Black or African American, non-Hispanic/Latino; 20 Asian, non-Hispanic/Latino; 4 Hispanic/Latino; 9 Native Hawaiian or other Pacific Islander, non-Hispanic/Latino; 12 Two or more races, non-Hispanic/Latino), 14 international. Average age 34. 110 applicants, 25% accepted, 23 enrolled. In 2010, 20 master's, 9 doctorates awarded. *Degree requirements:* For master's, 2 foreign languages, thesis optional; for doctorate, 2 foreign languages, comprehensive exam, thesis/dissertation. *Entrance requirements:* For master's, GRE General Test; for doctorate, GRE General Test, GRE Subject Test. Additional exam requirements/recommendations for international students: Required—TOEFL (minimum score 600 paper-based; 250 computer-based; 100 iBT), IELTS (minimum score 7). Application fee: $60. *Financial support:* In 2010–11, 16 fellowships (averaging $6,065 per year), 4 research assistantships (averaging $17,672 per year), 34 teaching assistantships (averaging $12,758 per year) were awarded; tuition waivers (full) also available. Financial award application deadline: 3/1. *Faculty research:* British and American literature, creative writing, cultural studies, rhetoric and composition. Total annual research expenditures: $54,000. *Application contact:* Laura Lyons, Graduate Chair, 808-956-8956, Fax: 808-956-3083, E-mail: lelyons@hawaii.edu.

University of Houston–Clear Lake, School of Human Sciences and Humanities, Programs in Humanities and Fine Arts, Houston, TX 77058-1098. Offers history (MA); humanities (MA); literature (MA). Part-time and evening/weekend programs available. Postbaccalaureate distance learning degree programs offered (minimal on-campus study). *Degree requirements:* For master's, thesis or alternative. *Entrance requirements:* For master's, GRE General Test. Additional exam requirements/recommendations for international students: Required—TOEFL (minimum score 550 paper-based; 213 computer-based). *Faculty research:* Digital media studies, Latin American history, labor history, Chaucer evolution versus creationism debate.

University of Houston–Downtown, College of Humanities and Social Sciences, Department of English, Houston, TX 77002. Offers professional writing and technical communication (MS). Part-time and evening/weekend programs available. *Faculty:* 9 full-time (4 women). *Students:* 4 full-time (all women), 17 part-time (12 women); includes 4 Black or African American, non-Hispanic/Latino; 1 Asian, non-Hispanic/Latino; 2 Hispanic/Latino, 1 international. Average age 35. 6 applicants, 83% accepted, 4 enrolled. In 2010, 7 master's awarded. *Degree requirements:* For master's, thesis optional, graduation portfolio with oral defense. *Entrance requirements:* For master's, GRE (including Analytical Writing section), personal application statement, resume, writing sample, 3 letters of recommendation. Additional exam requirements/recommendations for international students: Required—TOEFL (minimum score 600 paper-based; 250 computer-based; 86 iBT). *Application deadline:* For fall admission, 3/15 for domestic and international students; for spring admission, 11/15 for domestic and international students. Application fee: $35 ($60 for international students). Electronic applications accepted. *Expenses:* Tuition, state resident: full-time $4280; part-time $183 per credit hour. Tuition, nonresident: full-time $9230; part-time $458 per credit hour. Required fees: $390 per term. *Financial support:* Applicants required to submit FAFSA. *Faculty research:* Environmental rhetoric, instructional design, usability, assessment, presentation slides. *Unit head:* Dr. Robert Jarrett, Chair, 713-221-8013, Fax: 713-226-5205, E-mail: jarrettr@uhd.edu. *Application contact:* Dr.

English

University of Houston–Downtown (continued)
Michelle Moosally, Coordinator of MS in Professional Writing and Technical Communication and Professor, Department of English, 713-221-8013, Fax: 713-226-5205, E-mail: mspwtc@uhd.edu.

University of Idaho, College of Graduate Studies, College of Letters, Arts and Social Sciences, Department of English, Program in English, Moscow, ID 83844-2282. Offers MA, MAT. *Students:* 18 full-time, 4 part-time. Average age 30. In 2010, 3 master's awarded. *Entrance requirements:* For master's, minimum GPA of 2.8. *Application deadline:* For fall admission, 8/1 for domestic students; for spring admission, 12/15 for domestic students. Applications are processed on a rolling basis. Application fee: $60. Electronic applications accepted. *Expenses:* Tuition, nonresident: part-time $580 per credit. Required fees: $306 per credit. *Financial support:* Research assistantships, teaching assistantships available. Financial award applicants required to submit FAFSA. *Unit head:* Dr. Gary Williams, Chair, 208-883-6156. *Application contact:* Dr. Gary Williams, Chair, 208-883-6156.

University of Illinois at Chicago, Graduate College, College of Liberal Arts and Sciences, Department of English, Chicago, IL 60607-7128. Offers English (MA, PhD), including creative writing (PhD), English education (MA), English studies, writing (MA); linguistics (MA), including teaching English to speakers of other languages/applied linguistics. Part-time and evening/weekend programs available. *Degree requirements:* For doctorate, variable foreign language requirement, thesis/dissertation, written and oral exams. *Entrance requirements:* For master's, GRE General Test, GRE Subject Test; for doctorate, GRE General Test, GRE Subject Test, minimum GPA of 2.0. Additional exam requirements/recommendations for international students: Required—TOEFL. Electronic applications accepted. *Faculty research:* Literary history and theory.

University of Illinois at Springfield, Graduate Programs, College of Liberal Arts and Sciences, Program in English, Springfield, IL 62703-5407. Offers MA. Part-time and evening/weekend programs available. *Degree requirements:* For master's, comprehensive exam, thesis, or project. *Entrance requirements:* For master's, GRE General Test, analytical writing sample, two letters of recommendation. Additional exam requirements/recommendations for international students: Required—TOEFL (minimum score 500 paper-based; 176 computer-based; 61 iBT). Electronic applications accepted. *Expenses:* Tuition, state resident: full-time $6774; part-time $282.25 per credit hour. Tuition, nonresident: full-time $15,078; part-time $628.25 per credit hour. Required fees: $15.25 per credit hour. $492 per term.

University of Illinois at Urbana–Champaign, Graduate College, College of Liberal Arts and Sciences, Department of English, Champaign, IL 61820. Offers creative writing (MFA); English (MA, PhD). *Faculty:* 49 full-time (22 women), 1 (woman) part-time/adjunct. *Students:* 72 full-time (49 women), 71 part-time (49 women); includes 3 Black or African American, non-Hispanic/Latino; 9 Asian, non-Hispanic/Latino; 12 Hispanic/Latino, 12 international. 412 applicants, 8% accepted, 12 enrolled. In 2010, 20 master's, 14 doctorates awarded. *Entrance requirements:* For master's, GRE General Test, GRE Subject Test, minimum GPA of 3.0; writing sample. Additional exam requirements/recommendations for international students: Required—TOEFL (minimum score 550 paper-based; 213 computer-based). *Application deadline:* Applications are processed on a rolling basis. Application fee: $75 ($90 for international students). Electronic applications accepted. *Financial support:* In 2010–11, 42 fellowships, 31 research assistantships, 113 teaching assistantships were awarded; tuition waivers (full and partial) also available. *Faculty research:* English and American literature, cultural studies and critical theory. *Unit head:* Curtis Perry, Head, 217-333-2391, Fax: 217-333-4321, E-mail: cperry@illinois.edu. *Application contact:* Stephanie J. Shockey, Office Support Specialist, 217-333-3646, Fax: 217-333-4321, E-mail: shockey@illinois.edu.

University of Indianapolis, Graduate Programs, College of Arts and Sciences, Department of English Language and Literature, Indianapolis, IN 46227-3697. Offers English (MA). Part-time and evening/weekend programs available. *Faculty:* 4 full-time (3 women), 1 (woman) part-time/adjunct. *Students:* 5 full-time (3 women), 16 part-time (12 women); includes 2 Black or African American, non-Hispanic/Latino, 2 international. Average age 35. In 2010, 5 master's awarded. *Entrance requirements:* For master's, GRE Subject Test, minimum GPA of 2.5. Additional exam requirements/recommendations for international students: Required—TOEFL (minimum score 550 paper-based; 213 computer-based). *Application deadline:* Applications are processed on a rolling basis. Application fee: $30. Electronic applications accepted. Tuition and fees vary according to course load, degree level and program. *Financial support:* Federal Work-Study, scholarships/grants, and tuition waivers (full and partial) available. Support available to part-time students. Financial award application deadline: 5/1; financial award applicants required to submit FAFSA. *Unit head:* Dr. William R. Dynes, Chair, 317-788-2072, Fax: 317-788-3480. *Application contact:* Dr. William R. Dynes, Chair, 317-788-2072, Fax: 317-788-3480.

The University of Iowa, Graduate College, College of Liberal Arts and Sciences, Department of English, Iowa City, IA 52242-1316. Offers English (PhD); literary criticism (PhD); literary history (PhD); literary studies (MA); nonfiction writing (MFA); rhetorical theory and stylistics (PhD); writer's workshop (MFA); JD/PhD. *Degree requirements:* For master's, thesis (for some programs), exam; for doctorate, comprehensive exam, thesis/dissertation. *Entrance requirements:* For master's and doctorate, GRE General Test, minimum GPA of 3.0. Additional exam requirements/recommendations for international students: Required—TOEFL (minimum score 640 paper-based; 273 computer-based; 111 iBT). Electronic applications accepted.

The University of Kansas, Graduate Studies, College of Liberal Arts and Sciences, Department of English, Lawrence, KS 66045. Offers creative writing (MFA); English (MA, PhD). Part-time programs available. *Faculty:* 39 full-time (18 women). *Students:* 93 full-time (63 women), 12 part-time (6 women); includes 16 minority (7 Black or African American, non-Hispanic/Latino; 1 American Indian or Alaska Native, non-Hispanic/Latino; 6 Hispanic/Latino; 2 Two or more races, non-Hispanic/Latino), 4 international. Average age 32. 173 applicants, 21% accepted, 21 enrolled. In 2010, 12 master's, 6 doctorates awarded. *Degree requirements:* For master's, one foreign language, comprehensive exam (for some programs), thesis or alternative; for doctorate, 2 foreign languages, comprehensive exam, thesis/dissertation. *Entrance requirements:* For master's and doctorate, GRE General Test, minimum GPA of 3.3. Additional exam requirements/recommendations for international students: Required—TOEFL. *Application deadline:* For fall admission, 12/31 for domestic and international students. Application fee: $55 ($65 for international students). Electronic applications accepted. *Expenses:* Tuition, state resident: full-time $7092; part-time $295.50 per credit hour. Tuition, nonresident: full-time $16,590; part-time $691.25 per credit hour. Required fees: $858; $71.49 per credit hour. Tuition and fees vary according to course load, campus/location and program. *Financial support:* Fellowships with full tuition reimbursements, research assistantships with full and partial tuition reimbursements, teaching assistantships with full and partial tuition reimbursements, unspecified assistantships available. Financial award application deadline: 12/31. *Faculty research:* African-American literature, twentieth century American literature, Renaissance literature, creative writing. *Unit head:* Marta Caminero-Santangelo, Chair, 785-864-4520, E-mail: camsan@ku.edu. *Application contact:* Joseph Harrington, Director of Graduate Studies, 785-864-4520, E-mail: jharring@ku.edu.

University of Kentucky, Graduate School, College of Arts and Sciences, Program in English, Lexington, KY 40506-0032. Offers MA, PhD. *Degree requirements:* For master's, one foreign language, comprehensive exam, thesis optional; for doctorate, one foreign language, comprehensive exam, thesis/dissertation. *Entrance requirements:* For master's, GRE General Test, minimum undergraduate GPA of 2.75; for doctorate, GRE General Test, minimum graduate GPA of 3.0. Additional exam requirements/recommendations for international students: Required—TOEFL (minimum score 550 paper-based; 213 computer-based). Electronic applications accepted.

University of Lethbridge, School of Graduate Studies, Lethbridge, AB T1K 3M4, Canada. Offers accounting (MScM); addictions counseling (M Sc); agricultural biotechnology (M Sc); agricultural studies (M Sc, MA); anthropology (MA); archaeology (MA); art (MA, MFA); biochemistry (M Sc); biological sciences (M Sc); biomolecular science (PhD); biosystems and biodiversity (PhD); Canadian studies (MA); chemistry (M Sc); computer science (M Sc); computer science and geographical information science (M Sc); counseling psychology (M Ed); dramatic arts (MA); earth, space, and physical science (PhD); economics (MA); educational leadership (M Ed); English (MA); environmental science (M Sc); evolution and behavior (PhD); exercise science (M Sc); finance (MScM); French (MA); French/German (MA); French/Spanish (MA); general education (M Ed); general management (MScM); geography (M Sc, MA); German (MA); health science (M Sc); history (MA); human resource management and labour relations (MScM); individualized multidisciplinary (M Sc, MA); information systems (MScM); international management (MScM); kinesiology (M Sc, MA); management (M Sc, MA); marketing (MScM); mathematics (M Sc); music (M Mus, MA); Native American studies (MA); neuroscience (M Sc, PhD); new media (MA); nursing (M Sc); philosophy (MA); physics (M Sc); policy and strategy (MScM); political science (MA); psychology (M Sc, MA); religious studies (MA); social sciences (MA); sociology (MA); theatre and dramatic arts (MFA); theoretical and computational science (PhD); urban and regional studies (MA); women's studies (MA). Part-time and evening/weekend programs available. *Degree requirements:* For doctorate, comprehensive exam, thesis/dissertation. *Entrance requirements:* For master's, GMAT (M Sc in management), bachelor's degree in related field, minimum GPA of 3.0 during previous 20 graded semester courses, 2 years teaching or related experience (M Ed); for doctorate, master's degree, minimum graduate GPA of 3.5. Additional exam requirements/recommendations for international students: Required—TOEFL. *Faculty research:* Movement and brain plasticity, gibberellin physiology, photosynthesis, carbon cycling, molecular properties of main-group ring components.

University of Louisiana at Lafayette, College of Liberal Arts, Department of English, Lafayette, LA 70504. Offers British and American literature (MA), including creative writing, folklore, rhetoric; creative writing (PhD); literature (PhD); rhetoric (PhD). Part-time programs available. Terminal master's awarded for partial completion of doctoral program. *Degree requirements:* For master's, one foreign language, thesis or alternative; for doctorate, 2 foreign languages, comprehensive exam, thesis/dissertation. *Entrance requirements:* For master's, GRE General Test, minimum GPA of 2.75; for doctorate, GRE General Test, minimum GPA of 3.0. Additional exam requirements/recommendations for international students: Required—TOEFL (minimum score 550 paper-based; 213 computer-based). Electronic applications accepted. *Faculty research:* Composition theory, Southern literature, medieval literature.

University of Louisiana at Monroe, Graduate School, College of Arts and Sciences, Department of English, Monroe, LA 71209-0001. Offers MA. Part-time and evening/weekend programs available. *Faculty:* 13 full-time (9 women). *Students:* 11 full-time (9 women), 7 part-time (5 women); includes 2 Black or African American, non-Hispanic/Latino. Average age 28. In 2010, 4 master's awarded. *Degree requirements:* For master's, one foreign language, thesis (for some programs). *Entrance requirements:* For master's, GRE General Test (minimum score 900 verbal and quantitative), minimum GPA of 3.0. Additional exam requirements/recommendations for international students: Required—TOEFL (minimum score 500 paper-based; 173 computer-based; 61 iBT) or Michigan English Language Assessment Battery. *Application deadline:* For fall admission, 8/24 priority date for domestic students, 7/1 for international students; for winter admission, 12/14 priority date for domestic students; for spring admission, 1/19 for domestic students, 11/1 for international students. Applications are processed on a rolling basis. Application fee: $20 ($30 for international students). Electronic applications accepted. *Expenses:* Tuition, state resident: full-time $2991; part-time $197 per credit hour. Tuition, nonresident: full-time $2991; part-time $197 per credit hour. International tuition: $10,288 full-time. *Financial support:* In 2010–11, 9 teaching assistantships with full tuition reimbursements (averaging $3,000 per year) were awarded; career-related internships or fieldwork, Federal Work-Study, institutionally sponsored loans, and unspecified assistantships also available. Financial award application deadline: 4/1; financial award applicants required to submit FAFSA. *Faculty research:* Creative writing, American literature, British literature, multicultural literature, literary theory. *Unit head:* Dr. Fleming J. McClelland, Interim Head, 318-342-1485, Fax: 318-342-1491, E-mail: mcclelland@ulm.edu. *Application contact:* Dr. Julia Guernsey-Shaw, Information Contact, 318-342-1496, E-mail: shaw@ulm.edu.

University of Louisville, Graduate School, College of Arts and Sciences, Department of English, Louisville, KY 40292. Offers English (MA), including creative writing, literature, rhetoric and composition (MA, PhD); English rhetoric and composition (PhD), including rhetoric and composition (MA, PhD). Part-time programs available. *Faculty:* 40 full-time (22 women). *Students:* 78 full-time (41 women), 25 part-time (12 women); includes 3 Black or African American, non-Hispanic/Latino; 1 American Indian or Alaska Native, non-Hispanic/Latino; 2 Asian, non-Hispanic/Latino; 2 Hispanic/Latino, 7 international. Average age 30. 97 applicants, 64% accepted, 38 enrolled. In 2010, 21 master's, 8 doctorates awarded. *Degree requirements:* For master's, one foreign language, thesis or culminating project; for doctorate, 2 foreign languages, comprehensive exam, thesis/dissertation. *Entrance requirements:* For master's, GRE General Test, 2 academic letters of recommendation; for doctorate, GRE General Test, 15-20 page critical writing sample, 1000-word statement of professional goals, 3 academic letters of recommendation, transcripts of all college work. Additional exam requirements/recommendations for international students: Required—TOEFL (minimum score 600 paper-based; 210 computer-based; 100 iBT). *Application deadline:* For fall admission, 8/1 for domestic students, 1/5 for international students; for spring admission, 12/1 for domestic students. Applications are processed on a rolling basis. Application fee: $50. Electronic applications accepted. *Expenses:* Tuition, state resident: full-time $9144; part-time $508 per credit hour. Tuition, nonresident: full-time $19,026; part-time $1057 per credit hour. Tuition and fees vary according to program and reciprocity agreements. *Financial support:* In 2010–11, 49 students received support, including 9 fellowships with full tuition reimbursements available, 40 teaching assistantships with full tuition reimbursements available; health care benefits and unspecified assistantships also available. Financial award application deadline: 1/5. *Faculty research:* American and English literatures and cultures, rhetoric and composition, critical theory and cultural studies, creative writing. Total annual research expenditures: $278,898. *Unit head:* Dr. Susan Griffin, Chair, 502-852-6801, Fax: 502-852-4182, E-mail: smgriff01@louisville.edu. *Application contact:* Libby Leggett, Director, Graduate Admissions, 502-852-3101, Fax: 502-852-6536, E-mail: gradadm@louisville.edu.

University of Maine, Graduate School, College of Liberal Arts and Sciences, Department of English, Orono, ME 04469. Offers composition and pedagogy (MA); creative (MA); gender and literature (MA); poetry and poetics (MA). Part-time and evening/weekend programs available. *Faculty:* 18 full-time (7 women), 20 part-time/adjunct (10 women). *Students:* 25 full-time (8 women), 6 part-time (5 women). Average age 28. 36 applicants, 47% accepted, 14 enrolled. In 2010, 13 degrees awarded. *Degree requirements:* For master's, one foreign language, thesis optional. *Entrance requirements:* For master's, GRE General Test, minimum GPA of 3.0. Additional exam requirements/recommendations for international students: Required—TOEFL. *Application deadline:* For fall admission, 2/1 priority date for domestic students. Applications are processed on a rolling basis. Application fee: $65. Electronic applications accepted. *Expenses:* Tuition, state resident: full-time $400. Tuition, nonresident: full-time $1050. *Financial support:* In 2010–11, 21 teaching assistantships with tuition reimbursements (averaging $12,790 per year) were awarded; Federal Work-Study and tuition waivers (full and partial) also available. Financial award application deadline: 3/1. *Faculty research:* Contemporary poetics, contemporary criticism, composition theory and pedagogy, feminist approaches to literature. *Unit head:* Dr. Naomi Jacobs, Chair, 207-581-3822, Fax: 207-581-1604. *Application contact:* Scott G. Delcourt, Associate Dean of the Graduate School, 207-581-3291, Fax: 207-581-3232, E-mail: graduate@maine.edu.

The University of Manchester, School of Arts, Histories and Cultures, Manchester, United Kingdom. Offers anthropology, media and performance (PhD); applied theatre professional (PhD); archaeology (PhD); art history and visual studies (PhD); arts management and cultural policy (PhD); classics and ancient history (PhD); composition (PhD); creative writing (PhD); drama (PhD); economic and social history (PhD); electroacoustic composition (PhD); English and American studies (PhD); history (PhD); humanitarianism and conflict response (PhD); museology (PhD); music (PhD); musicology (PhD); religions and theology (PhD).

University of Manitoba, Faculty of Graduate Studies, Faculty of Arts, Department of English, Film, and Theatre, Winnipeg, MB R3T 2N2, Canada. Offers English (MA, PhD). *Degree requirements:* For master's, one foreign language, thesis; for doctorate, one foreign language, thesis/dissertation.

University of Maryland, College Park, Academic Affairs, College of Arts and Humanities, Department of English, Program in English Language and Literature, College Park, MD 20742. Offers MA, PhD. *Students:* 113 full-time (75 women), 8 part-time (6 women); includes 17 minority (10 Black or African American, non-Hispanic/Latino; 1 Asian, non-Hispanic/Latino; 3 Hispanic/Latino; 3 Two or more races, non-Hispanic/Latino), 3 international. 217 applicants, 12% accepted, 15 enrolled. In 2010, 24 master's, 16 doctorates awarded. *Degree requirements:* For master's, thesis optional; for doctorate, one foreign language, thesis/dissertation, oral and written exams. *Entrance requirements:* For master's, GRE General Test, minimum GPA of 3.5, writing sample, 3 letters of recommendation; for doctorate, GRE General Test, minimum GPA of 3.7, writing sample. Additional exam requirements/recommendations for international students: Required—TOEFL. *Application deadline:* For fall admission, 12/1 for domestic students, 12/8 for international students. Applications are processed on a rolling basis. Application fee: $75. Electronic applications accepted. *Expenses:* Tuition, state resident: part-time $471 per credit hour. Tuition, nonresident: part-time $1016 per credit hour. Required fees: $337 per term. *Financial support:* In 2010–11, 15 fellowships with full and partial tuition reimbursements (averaging $10,649 per year), 2 research assistantships (averaging $20,498 per year), 63 teaching assistantships (averaging $17,080 per year) were awarded. Financial award applicants required to submit FAFSA. *Unit head:* Kent Cartwright, Chair, 301-405-3807, Fax: 301-314-7539, E-mail: kcartwri@umd.edu. *Application contact:* Dean of Graduate School, 301-405-0376, Fax: 301-314-9305.

University of Massachusetts Amherst, Graduate School, College of Humanities and Fine Arts, Department of English, Amherst, MA 01003. Offers creative writing (MFA); English and American literature (MA, PhD). Part-time programs available. *Faculty:* 46 full-time (22 women). *Students:* 98 full-time (55 women), 95 part-time (63 women); includes 27 minority (6 Black or African American, non-Hispanic/Latino; 1 American Indian or Alaska Native, non-Hispanic/Latino; 8 Asian, non-Hispanic/Latino; 10 Hispanic/Latino; 2 Two or more races, non-Hispanic/Latino), 7 international. Average age 31. 623 applicants, 13% accepted, 38 enrolled. In 2010, 33 master's, 7 doctorates awarded. Terminal master's awarded for partial completion of doctoral program. *Degree requirements:* For master's, one foreign language, thesis optional; for doctorate, one foreign language, comprehensive exam, thesis/dissertation. *Entrance requirements:* For master's, GRE General Test, GRE Subject Test (MA), writing sample (MFA); for doctorate, GRE General Test, GRE Subject Test. Additional exam requirements/recommendations for international students: Required—TOEFL (minimum score 550 paper-based; 213 computer-based; 80 iBT), IELTS (minimum score 6.5). *Application deadline:* For fall admission, 12/1 for domestic and international students. Applications are processed on a rolling basis. Application fee: $50 ($65 for international students). Electronic applications accepted. *Expenses:* Tuition, state resident: full-time $2640. Required fees: $8282. One-time fee: $357 full-time. *Financial support:* In 2010–11, 3 fellowships with full tuition reimbursements (averaging $5,839 per year), 8 research assistantships with full tuition reimbursements (averaging $8,705 per year), 51 teaching assistantships with full tuition reimbursements (averaging $9,896 per year) were awarded; career-related internships or fieldwork, Federal Work-Study, scholarships/grants, traineeships, health care benefits, tuition waivers (full), and unspecified assistantships also available. Support available to part-time students. Financial award application deadline: 12/1; financial award applicants required to submit FAFSA. *Unit head:* Dr. Joseph F. Bartolomeo, Department Head, 413-545-2575, Fax: 413-545-3880. *Application contact:* Jean M. Ames, Supervisor of Admissions, 413-545-0722, Fax: 413-577-0010, E-mail: gradadm@grad.umass.edu.

University of Massachusetts Boston, Office of Graduate Studies, College of Liberal Arts, Program in English, Boston, MA 02125-3393. Offers MA. Part-time and evening/weekend programs available. *Degree requirements:* For master's, one foreign language, final project. *Entrance requirements:* For master's, minimum GPA of 2.75. *Faculty research:* Working class literature, women writers, British fiction, composition theory, modern American literature.

University of Memphis, Graduate School, College of Arts and Sciences, Department of English, Memphis, TN 38152. Offers African-American literature (Graduate Certificate); applied linguistics (PhD); composition studies (PhD); creative writing (MFA); English as a second language (MA); linguistics (MA); literary and cultural studies (PhD), including African-American literature; literature (MA); professional writing (MA, PhD); teaching English as a second language (Graduate Certificate). Part-time and evening/weekend programs available. Post-baccalaureate distance learning degree programs offered (no on-campus study). *Faculty:* 31 full-time (15 women), 2 part-time/adjunct (both women). *Students:* 108 full-time (70 women), 107 part-time (69 women); includes 15 minority (2 Black or African American, non-Hispanic/Latino; 2 Asian, non-Hispanic/Latino; 6 Hispanic/Latino; 5 Two or more races, non-Hispanic/Latino), 8 international. Average age 34. 128 applicants, 71% accepted, 29 enrolled. In 2010, 38 master's, 4 doctorates, 21 other advanced degrees awarded. Terminal master's awarded for partial completion of doctoral program. *Degree requirements:* For master's, one foreign language, comprehensive exam, thesis optional; for doctorate, 2 foreign languages, comprehensive exam, thesis/dissertation. *Entrance requirements:* For master's and doctorate, GRE. Additional exam requirements/recommendations for international students: Required—TOEFL. *Application deadline:* For fall admission, 7/1 for domestic students; for spring admission, 10/15 for domestic students. Applications are processed on a rolling basis. Application fee: $35 ($60 for international students). Electronic applications accepted. *Financial support:* In 2010–11, 123 students received support; research assistantships with full tuition reimbursements available, teaching assistantships with full tuition reimbursements available, Federal Work-Study, scholarships/grants, and unspecified assistantships available. Financial award application deadline: 2/15; financial award applicants required to submit FAFSA. *Faculty research:* Applied linguistics, British and American literature, professional writing, composition studies. *Unit head:* Dr. Verner D. Mitchell, Chair, 901-678-3099, Fax: 901-678-2226, E-mail: vdmtchll@memphis.edu. *Application contact:* Dr. Verner D. Mitchell, Director, Graduate Studies, 901-678-3099, Fax: 901-678-2226, E-mail: vdmtchll@memphis.edu.

University of Miami, Graduate School, College of Arts and Sciences, Department of English, Coral Gables, FL 33124. Offers creative writing (MFA); English (MA, PhD). Part-time programs available. Terminal master's awarded for partial completion of doctoral program. *Degree requirements:* For master's, one foreign language, thesis optional; for doctorate, one foreign language, thesis/dissertation. *Entrance requirements:* For master's and doctorate, GRE General Test. Electronic applications accepted. *Faculty research:* Anglo-Irish literature, feminist criticism and theory, Caribbean literature, early modern literature and culture, postcolonial and ethnic studies.

University of Michigan, Horace H. Rackham School of Graduate Studies, College of Literature, Science, and the Arts, Department of English Language and Literature, Ann Arbor, MI 48109. Offers creative writing (MFA); English and education (PhD); English and women's studies (PhD); English language and literature (PhD). *Faculty:* 51 full-time (30 women). *Students:* 73 full-time (45 women); includes 5 minority (1 Black or African American, non-Hispanic/Latino; 4 Asian, non-Hispanic/Latino), 7 international. 339 applicants, 8% accepted, 12 enrolled. In 2010, 18 doctorates awarded. *Degree requirements:* For doctorate, 2 foreign languages, comprehensive exam, thesis/dissertation, oral defense of dissertation, preliminary exam. *Entrance requirements:* For doctorate, GRE General Test, writing sample. Additional exam requirements/recommendations for international students: Required—TOEFL (minimum score 620 paper-based; 260 computer-based; 106 iBT). *Application deadline:* For fall admission, 12/15 for domestic and international students. Application fee: $65 ($75 for international students). Electronic applications accepted. *Expenses:* Tuition, state resident: full-time $17,784; part-time $1116 per credit hour. Tuition, nonresident: full-time $35,944; part-time $2125 per credit hour. International tuition: $35,994 full-time. Required fees: $95 per semester. Tuition and fees vary according to course load, degree level and program. *Financial support:* Fellowships with full tuition reimbursements, teaching assistantships with full tuition reimbursements, health care benefits and summer funding available. *Faculty research:* Post colonialism, modernism, early modern, American, British. *Unit head:* Dr. Michael Awkward, Graduate Chair, 734-763-2267. *Application contact:* Graduate Admissions Office, 734-936-2274, Fax: 734-763-3128, E-mail: grad.eng.admis@um.cc.umich.edu.

University of Michigan, Horace H. Rackham School of Graduate Studies, College of Literature, Science, and the Arts, Department of Women's Studies, Ann Arbor, MI 48109. Offers English and women's studies (PhD); history and women's studies (PhD); lesbian, gay, bisexual, transgender, queer (LGBTQ) studies (Certificate); psychology and women's studies (PhD); sociology and women's studies (PhD); women's studies (Certificate). *Faculty:* 77 full-time (71 women). *Students:* 71 full-time (63 women); includes 6 Black or African American, non-Hispanic/Latino; 11 Asian, non-Hispanic/Latino; 7 Hispanic/Latino; 4 Two or more races, non-Hispanic/Latino. Average age 30. 101 applicants, 10% accepted, 9 enrolled. In 2010, 5 doctorates, 8 other advanced degrees awarded. *Degree requirements:* For doctorate, variable foreign language requirement, comprehensive exam (for some programs), thesis/dissertation. *Entrance requirements:* For doctorate, GRE General Test, previous undergraduate course work in women's studies; for Certificate, GRE General Test, previous course work in women's studies. Additional exam requirements/recommendations for international students: Required—TOEFL. *Application deadline:* For fall admission, 12/1 for domestic and international students. Application fee: $65 ($75 for international students). Electronic applications accepted. *Expenses:* Tuition, state resident: full-time $17,784; part-time $1116 per credit hour. Tuition, nonresident: full-time $35,944; part-time $2125 per credit hour. International tuition: $35,994 full-time. Required fees: $95 per semester. Tuition and fees vary according to course load, degree level and program. *Financial support:* In 2010–11, 39 students received support, including 21 fellowships with full tuition reimbursements available (averaging $16,800 per year), 18 teaching assistantships with full tuition reimbursements available (averaging $17,270 per year); career-related internships or fieldwork, institutionally sponsored loans, scholarships/grants, traineeships, health care benefits, and unspecified assistantships also available. *Faculty research:* Gender issues, LGBTQ studies, sexuality, women and science, global feminism. *Unit head:* Elizabeth R. Cole, Chair, Department of Women's Studies, Professor of Women's Studies, Professor of Afroamerican and African Studies, Professor of Psychology, 734-763-2047, Fax: 734-647-4943, E-mail: wsdgradInquiry@umich.edu. *Application contact:* Aimee Germain, Graduate Program Coordinator, 734-763-2047, Fax: 734-647-4943, E-mail: wsdgradinquiry@umich.edu.

University of Michigan–Flint, College of Arts and Sciences, Program in English, Flint, MI 48502-1950. Offers MA. Part-time programs available. *Entrance requirements:* Additional exam requirements/recommendations for international students: Required—TOEFL (minimum score 550 paper-based; 220 computer-based), IELTS (minimum score 6.5). *Expenses:* Contact institution.

University of Minnesota, Duluth, Graduate School, College of Liberal Arts, Department of English, Duluth, MN 55812-2496. Offers MA. Part-time programs available. *Degree requirements:* For master's, one foreign language, comprehensive exam, 2 extended papers or projects. *Entrance requirements:* For master's, GRE General Test, minimum GPA of 3.0. Additional exam requirements/recommendations for international students: Required—TOEFL (minimum score 213 computer-based). *Faculty research:* British cultural studies, Irish literature, American studies, linguistics, information design.

University of Minnesota, Twin Cities Campus, Graduate School, College of Liberal Arts, Department of English, Minneapolis, MN 55455-0213. Offers MA, MFA, PhD. Terminal master's awarded for partial completion of doctoral program. *Degree requirements:* For master's, one foreign language, thesis or alternative; for doctorate, 2 foreign languages, thesis/dissertation. *Entrance requirements:* For master's and doctorate, GRE General Test. Additional exam requirements/recommendations for international students: Required—TOEFL (minimum score 620 paper-based; 96 iBT). Electronic applications accepted. *Faculty research:* British and American literature, medieval and early modern literature, postcolonial literature, feminist studies in literature, creative writing, cultural studies.

University of Mississippi, Graduate School, College of Liberal Arts, Department of English, Oxford, University, MS 38677. Offers MA, MFA, PhD. *Students:* 73 full-time (38 women), 7 part-time (5 women); includes 3 Black or African American, non-Hispanic/Latino; 2 Hispanic/Latino; 3 Two or more races, non-Hispanic/Latino. In 2010, 4 master's, 8 doctorates awarded. *Degree requirements:* For master's, one foreign language, thesis; for doctorate, 2 foreign languages, thesis/dissertation. *Entrance requirements:* For master's, GRE General Test, minimum GPA of 3.0; for doctorate, GRE General Test. Additional exam requirements/recommendations for international students: Required—TOEFL. *Application deadline:* For fall admission, 2/1 for domestic students; for spring admission, 10/1 for domestic students. Applications are processed on a rolling basis. Application fee: $25. *Financial support:* Scholarships/grants available. Financial award application deadline: 3/1; financial award applicants required to submit FAFSA. *Unit head:* Dr. Ivo Kamps, Chairman, 662-915-7439, Fax: 662-915-5787, E-mail: engl@olemiss.edu. *Application contact:* Dr. Christy M. Wyandt, Associate Dean, 662-915-7474, Fax: 662-915-7577, E-mail: cwyandt@olemiss.edu.

University of Missouri, Graduate School, College of Arts and Sciences, Department of English, Columbia, MO 65211. Offers MA, PhD. *Faculty:* 58 full-time (36 women), 14 part-time/adjunct (7 women). *Students:* 81 full-time (46 women), 23 part-time (10 women); includes 14 minority (7 Black or African American, non-Hispanic/Latino; 1 American Indian or Alaska Native, non-Hispanic/Latino; 2 Asian, non-Hispanic/Latino; 4 Hispanic/Latino), 8 international. Average age 32. 181 applicants, 9% accepted, 15 enrolled. In 2010, 9 master's, 9 doctorates awarded. Terminal master's awarded for partial completion of doctoral program. *Degree requirements:* For doctorate, 2 foreign languages, comprehensive exam, thesis/dissertation. *Entrance requirements:* For master's, GRE General Test, minimum GPA of 3.0; for doctorate, GRE General Test, minimum GPA of 3.0; MA in English or equivalent. Additional exam requirements/recommendations for international students: Required—TOEFL (minimum score 500 paper-based; 173 computer-based; 61 iBT). *Application deadline:* For fall admission, 1/15 priority date for domestic students. Applications are processed on a rolling basis. Application fee: $45 ($60 for international students). Electronic applications accepted. *Financial support:* In 2010–11, 42 fellowships with full tuition reimbursements, 3 research assistantships with full tuition reimbursements, 47 teaching assistantships with full tuition reimbursements were awarded; institutionally sponsored loans, health care benefits, and unspecified assistantships also available. *Unit head:* Dr. Pat Okker, Department Chair, 573-882-6066, E-mail: okkerp@missouri.edu. *Application contact:* Vickie Thorp, Secretary Sr, 573-882-4676, E-mail: thorpv@missouri.edu.

University of Missouri–Kansas City, College of Arts and Sciences, Department of English Language and Literature, Kansas City, MO 64110-2499. Offers creative writing and media arts (MFA); English (MA, PhD). PhD (interdisciplinary) offered through the School of Graduate Studies. Part-time and evening/weekend programs available. *Faculty:* 22 full-time (15 women), 21 part-time/adjunct (10 women). *Students:* 11 full-time (7 women), 47 part-time (23 women); includes 6 minority (5 Black or African American, non-Hispanic/Latino; 1 Asian, non-Hispanic/Latino). Average age 30. 75 applicants, 40% accepted, 22 enrolled. In 2010, 11 master's awarded. *Degree requirements:* For master's, one foreign language; for doctorate, 2 foreign languages, comprehensive exam, thesis/dissertation. *Entrance requirements:* For master's, GRE General Test, 3 letters of recommendation. Additional exam requirements/recommendations for international students: Required—TOEFL (minimum score 550 paper-based; 213 computer-based; 80 iBT). *Application deadline:* For fall admission, 1/15 for domestic students, 1/15 priority date for international students. Applications are processed on a rolling basis. Application fee: $45 ($50 for international students). Electronic applications accepted. *Expenses:* Tuition,

English

University of Missouri–Kansas City (continued)

state resident: full-time $5522.40; part-time $306.80 per credit hour. Tuition, nonresident: full-time $7128; part-time $792 per credit hour. Required fees: $261.15 per term. *Financial support:* In 2010–11, 12 teaching assistantships (averaging $13,358 per year) were awarded; career-related internships or fieldwork, Federal Work-Study, and institutionally sponsored loans also available. Support available to part-time students. Financial award application deadline: 3/1; financial award applicants required to submit FAFSA. *Faculty research:* Creative writing: poetry and prose, computational linguistics, rhetoric and composition, African-American and British literature, print culture. Total annual research expenditures: $13,729. *Unit head:* Dr. Jeff Rydberg-Cox, Co-Chair, 816-235-2560, Fax: 816-235-1308, E-mail: rydbergcoxj@umkc.edu. *Application contact:* Dr. Laurie Ellinghausen, Director of Graduate Studies, 816-235-6032, E-mail: ellinghausenl@umkc.edu.

University of Missouri–St. Louis, College of Arts and Sciences, Department of English, St. Louis, MO 63121. Offers American literature (MA); creative writing (MFA); English literature (MA); linguistics (MA); teaching of writing (Certificate). Part-time and evening/weekend programs available. *Faculty:* 19 full-time (9 women), 2 part-time/adjunct (1 woman). *Students:* 25 full-time (12 women), 95 part-time (62 women); includes 13 minority (6 Black or African American, non-Hispanic/Latino; 2 American Indian or Alaska Native, non-Hispanic/Latino; 3 Asian, non-Hispanic/Latino; 1 Hispanic/Latino; 1 Two or more races, non-Hispanic/Latino), 1 international. Average age 30. 103 applicants, 41% accepted, 24 enrolled. In 2010, 241 master's, 5 other advanced degrees awarded. *Degree requirements:* For master's, thesis optional. *Entrance requirements:* For master's, two letters of recommendation; writing sample (MFA). Additional exam requirements/recommendations for international students: Required—TOEFL (minimum score 550 paper-based; 213 computer-based). *Application deadline:* For fall admission, 7/1 priority date for domestic and international students; for spring admission, 12/1 priority date for domestic and international students. Applications are processed on a rolling basis. Application fee: $35 ($40 for international students). Electronic applications accepted. *Expenses:* Tuition, state resident: full-time $5522; part-time $306.80 per credit hour. Tuition, nonresident: full-time $14,253; part-time $792.10 per credit hour. Required fees: $658; $49 per credit hour. One-time fee: $12. Tuition and fees vary according to program. *Financial support:* In 2010–11, 6 research assistantships with full and partial tuition reimbursements (averaging $5,666 per year), 10 teaching assistantships with full and partial tuition reimbursements (averaging $9,000 per year) were awarded. Financial award applicants required to submit FAFSA. *Faculty research:* Victorian literature, Shakespeare and Renaissance literature, eighteenth century literature, composition theory. *Unit head:* Dr. Frank Grady, Director of Graduate Studies, 314-516-5541, Fax: 314-516-5781, E-mail: fgrady@umsl.edu. *Application contact:* 314-516-5458, Fax: 314-516-5310, E-mail: gradadm@umsl.edu.

The University of Montana, Graduate School, College of Arts and Sciences, Department of English, Program in Literature, Missoula, MT 59812-0002. Offers MA. *Degree requirements:* For master's, thesis optional. *Entrance requirements:* For master's, GRE General Test, sample of written work. Additional exam requirements/recommendations for international students: Required—TOEFL. *Faculty research:* Literary history, cultural studies, criticism and theory, Western studies.

University of Montevallo, College of Arts and Sciences, Department of English, Montevallo, AL 35115. Offers English literature (MA). Part-time programs available. *Students:* 3 full-time (1 woman), 9 part-time (7 women); includes 2 minority (1 Black or African American, non-Hispanic/Latino; 1 Hispanic/Latino). In 2010, 6 master's awarded. *Degree requirements:* For master's, comprehensive exam, thesis optional. *Entrance requirements:* For master's, GRE General Test, MAT, minimum undergraduate GPA of 2.75 in last 60 hours or 2.5 overall, bachelor's degree in English or equivalent. Additional exam requirements/recommendations for international students: Required—TOEFL (minimum score 550 paper-based; 213 computer-based). *Application deadline:* For fall admission, 7/15 for domestic students; for spring admission, 11/15 for domestic students. Application fee: $25. *Expenses:* Tuition, state resident: full-time $6264; part-time $261 per credit hour. Tuition, nonresident: full-time $12,528; part-time $502 per credit hour. Required fees: $251 per semester. *Financial support:* Federal Work-Study, scholarships/grants, and unspecified assistantships available. *Unit head:* Dr. Jim Murphy, Chair, 205-665-6420, E-mail: murphyj@montevallo.edu. *Application contact:* Dr. Jim Murphy, Chair, 205-665-6420, E-mail: murphyj@montevallo.edu.

University of Nebraska at Kearney, College of Graduate Study, College of Fine Arts and Humanities, Department of English, Kearney, NE 68849-0001. Offers creative writing (MA); literature (MA). Part-time and evening/weekend programs available. *Degree requirements:* For master's, thesis optional. *Entrance requirements:* For master's, GRE General Test. Additional exam requirements/recommendations for international students: Required—TOEFL (minimum score 550 paper-based; 213 computer-based). Electronic applications accepted. *Faculty research:* Narrative theory, popular culture, western and plains literature, women's studies, media studies.

University of Nebraska at Omaha, Graduate Studies, College of Arts and Sciences, Department of English, Omaha, NE 68182. Offers advanced writing (Certificate); English (MA); teaching English to speakers of other languages (Certificate); technical communication (Certificate). Part-time and evening/weekend programs available. *Faculty:* 16 full-time (8 women). *Students:* 22 full-time (9 women), 58 part-time (44 women); includes 3 minority (1 Asian, non-Hispanic/Latino; 2 Two or more races, non-Hispanic/Latino), 2 international. Average age 32. 48 applicants, 79% accepted, 27 enrolled. In 2010, 17 master's, 15 other advanced degrees awarded. *Degree requirements:* For master's, comprehensive exam, thesis (for some programs). *Entrance requirements:* For master's, minimum GPA of 3.0, 3 letters of recommendation, writing sample. Additional exam requirements/recommendations for international students: Required—TOEFL (minimum score 600 paper-based; 250 computer-based; 100 iBT). *Application deadline:* For fall admission, 8/1 priority date for domestic students; for spring admission, 12/1 priority date for domestic students. Applications are processed on a rolling basis. Application fee: $45. Electronic applications accepted. *Financial support:* In 2010–11, 46 students received support; fellowships, teaching assistantships with tuition reimbursements available, Federal Work-Study, institutionally sponsored loans, scholarships/grants, tuition waivers (partial), and unspecified assistantships available. Support available to part-time students. Financial award application deadline: 3/1; financial award applicants required to submit FAFSA. *Unit head:* Dr. Robert Darcy, Chairperson, 402-554-3636. *Application contact:* Dr. Tracy Bridgeford, Student Contact, 402-554-3636.

University of Nebraska–Lincoln, Graduate College, College of Arts and Sciences, Department of English, Lincoln, NE 68588-0333. Offers composition and rhetoric (MA, PhD); creative writing (MA, PhD); literature studies (MA, PhD). *Degree requirements:* For master's, thesis optional; for doctorate, one foreign language, comprehensive exam, thesis/dissertation. *Entrance requirements:* For master's, writing sample; for doctorate, GRE General Test, writing sample. Additional exam requirements/recommendations for international students: Required—TOEFL (minimum score 600 paper-based; 250 computer-based). Electronic applications accepted. *Faculty research:* Creative writing, composition and rhetoric, women's studies, North American literature, medieval/Renaissance studies.

University of Nevada, Las Vegas, Graduate College, College of Liberal Arts, Department of English, Las Vegas, NV 89154-5011. Offers creative writing (MFA); English (MA, PhD). Part-time programs available. *Faculty:* 32 full-time (12 women), 5 part-time/adjunct (0 women). *Students:* 67 full-time (34 women), 26 part-time (14 women); includes 35 minority (1 Black or African American, non-Hispanic/Latino; 7 Hispanic/Latino; 1 Native Hawaiian or other Pacific Islander, non-Hispanic/Latino; 26 Two or more races, non-Hispanic/Latino), 4 international. Average age 33. 202 applicants, 13% accepted, 25 enrolled. In 2010, 16 master's, 4 doctorates awarded. *Degree requirements:* For master's, one foreign language, comprehensive exam, thesis (for some programs); for doctorate, 2 foreign languages, comprehensive exam, thesis/dissertation. *Entrance requirements:* For master's, GRE General Test (verbal); for doctorate, GRE General Test (verbal), GRE Subject Test. Additional exam requirements/recommendations for international students: Required—TOEFL (minimum score 550 paper-based; 213 computer-based; 80 iBT), IELTS (minimum score 7). *Application deadline:* For fall admission, 2/15 priority date for domestic and international students; for spring admission, 11/1 priority date for domestic and international students. Applications are processed on a rolling basis. Application fee: $60 ($95 for international students). Electronic applications accepted. *Expenses:* Tuition, area resident: Part-time $239.50 per credit. Tuition, state resident: part-time $239.50 per credit. Tuition, nonresident: part-time $503 per credit. Required fees: $108 per semester. Tuition and fees vary according to course load, program and reciprocity agreements. *Financial support:* In 2010–11, 68 students received support, including 1 fellowship with full tuition reimbursement available (averaging $14,000 per year), 12 research assistantships with partial tuition reimbursements available (averaging $13,782 per year), 55 teaching assistantships with partial tuition reimbursements available (averaging $11,127 per year); institutionally sponsored loans, scholarships/grants, health care benefits, and unspecified assistantships also available. Financial award application deadline: 3/1. *Faculty research:* Professional and technical writing, Renaissance literature, modern American and British literature, writing of novels and poetry, eighteenth- and nineteenth-century British literature. *Unit head:* Dr. Richard Harp, Chair/ Professor, 702-895-0919, Fax: 702-895-4801, E-mail: richard.harp@unlv.edu. *Application contact:* Graduate College Admissions Evaluator, 702-895-3320, Fax: 702-895-4180, E-mail: gradcollege@unlv.edu.

University of Nevada, Reno, Graduate School, College of Liberal Arts, Department of English, Reno, NV 89557. Offers MA, MATE, PhD. Terminal master's awarded for partial completion of doctoral program. *Degree requirements:* For master's, variable foreign language requirement, thesis optional; for doctorate, variable foreign language requirement, thesis/dissertation. *Entrance requirements:* For master's, GRE General Test, minimum GPA of 2.75; for doctorate, GRE General Test, minimum GPA of 3.0. Additional exam requirements/recommendations for international students: Required—TOEFL (minimum score 500 paper-based; 173 computer-based; 61 iBT), IELTS (minimum score 6). Electronic applications accepted. *Expenses:* Tuition, state resident: full-time $2219; part-time $246 per credit. Tuition, nonresident: part-time $510 per credit. International tuition: $9009 full-time. Required fees: $59 per term. One-time fee: $101. Tuition and fees vary according to course load. *Faculty research:* Translating Persian/Iraqi literature, Shakespearean literature, modern American literature, composition and rhetoric.

University of New Brunswick Fredericton, School of Graduate Studies, Faculty of Arts, Department of English, Fredericton, NB E3B 5A3, Canada. Offers MA, PhD. Part-time programs available. *Faculty:* 17 full-time (6 women), 1 (woman) part-time/adjunct. *Students:* 46 full-time (22 women), 4 part-time (1 woman). Average age 25. 62 applicants, 53% accepted, 15 enrolled. In 2010, 10 master's, 5 doctorates awarded. *Degree requirements:* For master's, thesis, 18 credit hours; for doctorate, one foreign language, comprehensive exam, thesis/dissertation. *Entrance requirements:* For master's, BA with minimum GPA of 3.6, honors English (preferred); for doctorate, minimum GPA of 3.7; MA in English. Additional exam requirements/recommendations for international students: Required—TOEFL (minimum score 550 paper-based), TWE (minimum score 4). *Application deadline:* Applications are processed on a rolling basis. Application fee: $50 Canadian dollars. *Expenses:* Tuition, area resident: Full-time $3708; part-time $927 per term. International tuition: $6300 full-time. Required fees: $50 per term. *Financial support:* In 2010–11, 16 research assistantships with full tuition reimbursements (averaging $10,750 per year), 3 teaching assistantships with full tuition reimbursements (averaging $4,000 per year) were awarded; health care benefits also available. Financial award application deadline: 1/31. *Faculty research:* Creative writing, Canadian literature, post-Colonial literature, early Modern literature, scholarly editing and textual studies, American literature, British literature. *Unit head:* Dr. Edith Snook, Director of Graduate Studies, 506-458-7397, Fax: 506-453-5069, E-mail: esnook@unb.ca. *Application contact:* Theresa Keenan, Graduate Secretary, 506-451-6809, Fax: 506-453-5069, E-mail: tkeenan@unb.ca.

University of New Hampshire, Graduate School, College of Liberal Arts, Department of English, Durham, NH 03824. Offers English (MFA, PhD); English education (MST); language and linguistics (MA); literature (MA); writing (MA). Part-time programs available. *Faculty:* 35 full-time (18 women). *Students:* 60 full-time (33 women), 68 part-time (45 women); includes 5 minority (1 Black or African American, non-Hispanic/Latino; 1 Hispanic/Latino; 3 Two or more races, non-Hispanic/Latino), 5 international. Average age 33. 291 applicants, 47% accepted, 50 enrolled. In 2010, 39 master's, 6 doctorates awarded. *Degree requirements:* For master's, one foreign language; for doctorate, 2 foreign languages, thesis/dissertation. *Entrance requirements:* For master's, GRE General Test, sample of written work; for doctorate, GRE General Test, GRE Subject Test, sample of written work. Additional exam requirements/recommendations for international students: Required—TOEFL (minimum score 550 paper-based; 213 computer-based; 80 iBT). *Application deadline:* For fall admission, 6/1 priority date for domestic students, 2/15 for international students; for spring admission, 12/1 for domestic students. Applications are processed on a rolling basis. Application fee: $65. Electronic applications accepted. *Financial support:* In 2010–11, 63 students received support, including 1 fellowship, 46 teaching assistantships; research assistantships, career-related internships or fieldwork, Federal Work-Study, scholarships/grants, and tuition waivers (full and partial) also available. Support available to part-time students. Financial award application deadline: 2/15. *Unit head:* Dr. Andrew Merton, Chairperson, 603-862-3963. *Application contact:* Jamie Auger, Administrative Assistant, 603-862-3963, E-mail: engl.grad@unh.edu.

University of New Mexico, Graduate School, College of Arts and Sciences, Department of English, Program in English, Albuquerque, NM 87131-2039. Offers MA, PhD. *Students:* 64 full-time (44 women), 16 part-time (9 women); includes 11 minority (1 Black or African American, non-Hispanic/Latino; 1 American Indian or Alaska Native, non-Hispanic/Latino; 8 Hispanic/Latino; 1 Two or more races, non-Hispanic/Latino), 2 international. Average age 34. 72 applicants, 50% accepted, 22 enrolled. In 2010, 6 master's, 3 doctorates awarded. *Degree requirements:* For master's, one foreign language, comprehensive exam (for some programs), thesis (for some programs), portfolio; for doctorate, 2 foreign languages, comprehensive exam, thesis/dissertation. *Entrance requirements:* For master's, GRE General Test; for doctorate, GRE General Test, GRE Subject Test (literature). *Application deadline:* For fall admission, 1/15 for domestic and international students. Application fee: $50. Electronic applications accepted. *Expenses:* Tuition, state resident: full-time $5991; part-time $251 per credit hour. Tuition, nonresident: full-time $14,405; part-time $800.20 per credit hour. Tuition and fees vary according to course level, course load, program and reciprocity agreements. *Financial support:* In 2010–11, 65 students received support, including 2 research assistantships (averaging $2,600 per year), 52 teaching assistantships with full tuition reimbursements available (averaging $14,216 per year); health care benefits also available. *Faculty research:* American literature, Native American literature, Chicano literature, British and Irish literature, rhetoric and writing. *Unit head:* Dr. Gail Turley Houston, Chair, 505-277-6347, Fax: 505-277-0021, E-mail: ghouston@unm.edu. *Application contact:* N. Ezra Meier, Graduate Advisor, 505-277-4437, Fax: 505-277-0021, E-mail: nezra@unm.edu.

University of New Orleans, Graduate School, College of Liberal Arts, Department of English, Program in English, New Orleans, LA 70148. Offers MA. Part-time and evening/weekend programs available. *Degree requirements:* For master's, one foreign language, thesis (for some programs). *Entrance requirements:* For master's, GRE General Test. Additional exam requirements/recommendations for international students: Required—TOEFL (minimum score 550 paper-based; 213 computer-based; 79 iBT). Electronic applications accepted.

University of North Alabama, College of Arts and Sciences, Department of English, Florence, AL 35632-0001. Offers MAEN. Part-time and evening/weekend programs available. *Faculty:* 1 full-time (0 women), 9 part-time/adjunct (5 women). *Students:* 7 full-time (5 women), 16 part-time (14 women), 4 international. Average age 29. In 2010, 6 master's awarded. *Application deadline:* For fall admission, 7/1 priority date for domestic students; for spring admission, 12/1 for domestic students. Applications are processed on a rolling basis. Application fee: $25. Electronic applications accepted. *Expenses:* Tuition, state resident: full-time $5472; part-time $228 per credit hour. Tuition, nonresident: full-time $10,944; part-time $456 per credit hour. Required fees: $986. Tuition and fees vary according to course load. *Unit head:* Dr. Ronald

Smith, Chair, 256-765-4238, Fax: 256-765-4239, E-mail: resmith@una.edu. *Application contact:* Kim Mauldin, Director of Admissions, 256-765-4608, Fax: 256-765-4960, E-mail: komauldin@una.edu.

The University of North Carolina at Chapel Hill, Graduate School, College of Arts and Sciences, Department of English, Chapel Hill, NC 27599. Offers MA, PhD. *Faculty:* 51 full-time (20 women), 12 part-time/adjunct (9 women). *Students:* 147 full-time (95 women); includes 16 minority (7 Black or African American, non-Hispanic/Latino; 1 American Indian or Alaska Native, non-Hispanic/Latino; 4 Asian, non-Hispanic/Latino; 4 Hispanic/Latino), 1 international. 333 applicants, 14% accepted, 24 enrolled. In 2010, 17 master's, 12 doctorates awarded. *Degree requirements:* For master's, one foreign language, comprehensive exam, thesis; for doctorate, 2 foreign languages, comprehensive exam, thesis/dissertation. *Entrance requirements:* For master's and doctorate, GRE General Test, GRE Subject Test, minimum GPA of 3.0 for last 2 undergraduate years, writing sample. Additional exam requirements/recommendations for international students: Required—TOEFL. *Application deadline:* For fall admission, 1/1 priority date for domestic students. Application fee: $60. Electronic applications accepted. *Financial support:* In 2010–11, 19 fellowships (averaging $12,368 per year), 5 research assistantships with full tuition reimbursements (averaging $7,000 per year), 123 teaching assistantships with full tuition reimbursements (averaging $15,000 per year) were awarded; Federal Work-Study, institutionally sponsored loans, scholarships/grants, and unspecified assistantships also available. Financial award application deadline: 3/1. *Faculty research:* African-American, Southern, period, genre, critical theory/culture studies. *Unit head:* Dr. James P. Thompson, Chairman, 919-962-6872, Fax: 919-962-3520. *Application contact:* Ramona C. Kelly, Administrative Assistant, Graduate Studies, 919-962-1454, Fax: 919-962-3520.

The University of North Carolina at Charlotte, Graduate School, College of Arts and Sciences, Department of English, Charlotte, NC 28223-0001. Offers English (MA); English education (MA); technical/professional writing (Certificate). Part-time and evening/weekend programs available. *Faculty:* 34 full-time (19 women), 1 part-time/adjunct (0 women). *Students:* 45 full-time (30 women), 76 part-time (55 women); includes 20 minority (13 Black or African American, non-Hispanic/Latino; 6 Asian, non-Hispanic/Latino; 1 Two or more races, non-Hispanic/Latino), 2 international. Average age 29. 46 applicants, 89% accepted, 31 enrolled. In 2010, 28 master's awarded. *Degree requirements:* For master's, comprehensive exam, thesis optional. *Entrance requirements:* For master's, GRE General Test, minimum undergraduate GPA of 3.0 in major, 2.75 overall. Additional exam requirements/recommendations for international students: Required—TOEFL (minimum score 557 paper-based; 220 computer-based; 83 iBT). *Application deadline:* For fall admission, 7/15 for domestic students, 5/1 for international students; for spring admission, 11/15 for domestic students, 10/1 for international students. Applications are processed on a rolling basis. Application fee: $55. Electronic applications accepted. *Expenses:* Tuition, state resident: full-time $3464. Tuition, nonresident: full-time $14,297. Required fees: $2094. Tuition and fees vary according to course load. *Financial support:* In 2010–11, 16 students received support, including 16 teaching assistantships (averaging $7,625 per year); career-related internships or fieldwork, institutionally sponsored loans, scholarships/grants, and unspecified assistantships also available. Support available to part-time students. Financial award application deadline: 4/1; financial award applicants required to submit FAFSA. *Faculty research:* English as a second language (ESL), composition theory and pedagogy, children's literature, technical and professional writing, English for specific purposes (ESP). Total annual research expenditures: $190,607. *Unit head:* Dr. Malin Pereira, Chair, 704-687-2299, Fax: 704-687-3961, E-mail: mpereira@uncc.edu. *Application contact:* Kathy B. Giddings, Director of Graduate Admissions, 704-687-5503, Fax: 704-687-3279, E-mail: gradadm@uncc.edu.

The University of North Carolina at Greensboro, Graduate School, College of Arts and Sciences, Department of English, Program in English, Greensboro, NC 27412-5001. Offers American literature (PhD); English (M Ed, MA); English literature (PhD); rhetoric and composition (PhD). *Degree requirements:* For master's, comprehensive exam, thesis or alternative; for doctorate, variable foreign language requirement, thesis/dissertation, preliminary exam. *Entrance requirements:* For master's, GRE General Test, GRE Subject Test, minimum GPA of 3.0; for doctorate, GRE General Test, GRE Subject Test, critical writing sample, minimum GPA of 3.0. Additional exam requirements/recommendations for international students: Required—TOEFL. Electronic applications accepted.

The University of North Carolina Wilmington, College of Arts and Sciences, Department of English, Wilmington, NC 28403-3297. Offers MA. *Faculty:* 23 full-time (13 women). *Students:* 13 full-time (10 women), 13 part-time (7 women); includes 1 Black or African American, non-Hispanic/Latino; 1 Asian, non-Hispanic/Latino; 1 Hispanic/Latino. Average age 30. 25 applicants, 68% accepted, 14 enrolled. In 2010, 13 master's awarded. *Degree requirements:* For master's, comprehensive exam, thesis. *Entrance requirements:* For master's, GRE General Test, minimum B average in undergraduate major. Additional exam requirements/recommendations for international students: Required—TOEFL (minimum score 550 paper-based; 217 computer-based; 79 iBT), IELTS (minimum score 6.5). *Application deadline:* For fall admission, 3/1 for domestic students. Applications are processed on a rolling basis. Application fee: $60. *Financial support:* In 2010–11, 9 teaching assistantships with full and partial tuition reimbursements (averaging $9,500 per year) were awarded; career-related internships or fieldwork and Federal Work-Study also available. Support available to part-time students. Financial award application deadline: 3/15. *Unit head:* Dr. Keith Newlin, Chair, 910-962-3615, Fax: 910-962-7186, E-mail: newlink@uncw.edu. *Application contact:* Dr. Meghan Sweeney, Graduate Coordinator, 910-962-7548, Fax: 910-962-7186, E-mail: sweeneym@uncw.edu.

University of North Dakota, Graduate School, College of Arts and Sciences, Department of English, Grand Forks, ND 58202. Offers MA, PhD. *Faculty:* 20 full-time (15 women), 1 part-time/adjunct (0 women). *Students:* 35 full-time (23 women), 20 part-time (14 women); includes 4 minority (2 American Indian or Alaska Native, non-Hispanic/Latino; 2 Hispanic/Latino), 1 international. Average age 33. 38 applicants, 34% accepted, 12 enrolled. In 2010, 3 master's, 3 doctorates awarded. *Degree requirements:* For master's, one foreign language, comprehensive exam, thesis or alternative; for doctorate, one foreign language, comprehensive exam, thesis/dissertation. *Entrance requirements:* For master's and doctorate, GRE General Test, minimum GPA of 3.0. Additional exam requirements/recommendations for international students: Required—TOEFL (minimum score 550 paper-based; 213 computer-based; 79 iBT), IELTS (minimum score 6.5). *Application deadline:* For fall admission, 2/1 for domestic and international students. Application fee: $35. Electronic applications accepted. *Expenses:* Tuition, state resident: full-time $5857; part-time $306.74 per credit. Tuition, nonresident: full-time $15,666; part-time $729.77 per credit. Required fees: $53.42 per credit. Tuition and fees vary according to course load, program and reciprocity agreements. *Financial support:* In 2010–11, 33 students received support, including 1 research assistantship with full and partial tuition reimbursement available (averaging $5,379 per year), 31 teaching assistantships with full and partial tuition reimbursements available (averaging $9,575 per year); fellowships with full and partial tuition reimbursements available, Federal Work-Study, institutionally sponsored loans, scholarships/grants, health care benefits, tuition waivers (full and partial), and unspecified assistantships also available. Support available to part-time students. Financial award application deadline: 3/15; financial award applicants required to submit FAFSA. *Faculty research:* Creative writing, rhetorical theory, cinema, American literature, European literature. Total annual research expenditures: $200,074. *Unit head:* Dr. Christopher Nelson, Graduate Director, 701-777-2762, Fax: 701-777-2373, E-mail: chris.nelson@und.edu. *Application contact:* Matt Anderson, Admissions Specialist, 701-777-2947, Fax: 701-777-3619, E-mail: matthew.anderson@gradschool.und.edu.

University of Northern Colorado, Graduate School, College of Humanities and Social Sciences, School of English Language and Literature, Program in English, Greeley, CO 80639. Offers MA. Part-time programs available. *Faculty:* 9 full-time (4 women). *Students:* 16 full-time (11 women), 13 part-time (9 women); includes 1 Black or African American, non-Hispanic/Latino; 1 Hispanic/Latino, 1 international. Average age 29. 20 applicants, 75% accepted, 13

enrolled. In 2010, 9 master's awarded. *Degree requirements:* For master's, comprehensive exam. *Entrance requirements:* For master's, GRE General Test, 2 letters of recommendation. *Application deadline:* Applications are processed on a rolling basis. Application fee: $50 ($60 for international students). Electronic applications accepted. *Expenses:* Tuition, state resident: full-time $6199; part-time $344 per credit hour. Tuition, nonresident: full-time $14,834; part-time $824 per credit hour. Required fees: $1091; $60.60 per credit hour. Tuition and fees vary according to course load, degree level and program. *Financial support:* In 2010–11, 6 research assistantships (averaging $5,009 per year), 16 teaching assistantships (averaging $9,169 per year) were awarded; unspecified assistantships also available. Financial award application deadline: 3/1; financial award applicants required to submit FAFSA. *Unit head:* Dr. Marcus Embry, Program Coordinator, 970-351-2971, Fax: 970-351-3378. *Application contact:* Linda Sisson, Graduate Student Admission Coordinator, 970-351-1807, Fax: 970-351-2371, E-mail: linda.sisson@unco.edu.

University of Northern Iowa, Graduate College, College of Humanities and Fine Arts, Department of English Language and Literature, Cedar Falls, IA 50614. Offers creative writing (MA); English (MA); literature (MA); teaching English in secondary schools (TESS) (MA), including middle/junior high and senior high; teaching English to speakers of other languages (MA). Part-time and evening/weekend programs available. *Students:* 32 full-time (22 women), 43 part-time (39 women); includes 7 minority (3 Black or African American, non-Hispanic/Latino; 2 Asian, non-Hispanic/Latino; 1 Hispanic/Latino; 1 Two or more races, non-Hispanic/Latino), 7 international. 53 applicants, 57% accepted, 21 enrolled. In 2010, 21 master's awarded. *Degree requirements:* For master's, one foreign language, comprehensive exam, thesis or alternative, portfolio. *Entrance requirements:* For master's, minimum GPA of 3.0. Additional exam requirements/recommendations for international students: Required—TOEFL (minimum score 600 paper-based; 250 computer-based; 100 iBT). *Application deadline:* For fall admission, 8/1 priority date for domestic students. Applications are processed on a rolling basis. Application fee: $50 ($70 for international students). Electronic applications accepted. *Financial support:* Career-related internships or fieldwork, Federal Work-Study, scholarships/grants, and tuition waivers (full and partial) available. Support available to part-time students. Financial award application deadline: 2/1. *Unit head:* Dr. Jeffrey S. Copeland, Head, 319-273-3855, Fax: 319-273-5807, E-mail: jeffrey.copeland@uni.edu. *Application contact:* Laurie S. Russell, Record Analyst, 319-273-2623, Fax: 319-273-2885, E-mail: laurie.russell@uni.edu.

University of North Florida, College of Arts and Sciences, Department of English, Jacksonville, FL 32224. Offers MA. Part-time and evening/weekend programs available. *Faculty:* 18 full-time (8 women). *Students:* 11 full-time (6 women), 31 part-time (20 women); includes 1 American Indian or Alaska Native, non-Hispanic/Latino; 1 Asian, non-Hispanic/Latino; 1 Two or more races, non-Hispanic/Latino. Average age 30. 22 applicants, 36% accepted, 4 enrolled. In 2010, 12 master's awarded. *Degree requirements:* For master's, comprehensive exam, thesis optional. *Entrance requirements:* For master's, GRE General Test, minimum GPA of 3.0 in last 60 hours, writing sample. Additional exam requirements/recommendations for international students: Required—TOEFL (minimum score 500 paper-based; 173 computer-based; 61 iBT). *Application deadline:* For fall admission, 7/1 priority date for domestic students, 5/1 for international students; for spring admission, 11/1 priority date for domestic students, 10/1 for international students. Applications are processed on a rolling basis. Application fee: $30. Electronic applications accepted. *Expenses:* Tuition, state resident: full-time $7646.40; part-time $318.60 per credit hour. Tuition, nonresident: full-time $23,502; part-time $979.24 per credit hour. Required fees: $1208.88; $50.37 per credit hour. Tuition and fees vary according to course load and program. *Financial support:* In 2010–11, 7 students received support; research assistantships, teaching assistantships, Federal Work-Study and scholarships/grants available. Financial award application deadline: 4/1; financial award applicants required to submit FAFSA. *Faculty research:* Genre, period, and individual author studies in British, American, and world literature; literary criticism and theory—psychological, new historical and cultural, deconstructive, feminist, narrative, mythic; film and popular culture; online poetry publishing. *Unit head:* Dr. Samuel A. Kimball, Chair, 904-620-2273, Fax: 904-620-3940, E-mail: skimball@unf.edu. *Application contact:* Lillith Richardson, Assistant Director, The Graduate School, 904-620-1360, Fax: 904-620-1362, E-mail: graduateschool@unf.edu.

University of North Texas, Toulouse Graduate School, College of Arts and Sciences, Department of English, Denton, TX 76203. Offers creative writing (MA); English (MA, PhD). Terminal master's awarded for partial completion of doctoral program. *Degree requirements:* For master's, one foreign language, comprehensive exam, thesis optional; for doctorate, one foreign language, comprehensive exam, thesis/dissertation. *Entrance requirements:* For master's, GRE General Test, minimum GPA of 3.0, personal statement, current curriculum vitae/resume, writing sample (for creative writing program); for doctorate, GRE General Test, minimum GPA of 3.5, 3 letters of recommendation, personal statement, writing sample. Additional exam requirements/recommendations for international students: Recommended—TOEFL (minimum score 550 paper-based; 213 computer-based; 79 iBT). *Expenses:* Tuition, state resident: full-time $4298; part-time $239 per credit hour. Tuition, nonresident: full-time $10,782; part-time $549 per credit hour. Required fees: $1292; $270 per credit hour. *Financial support:* Fellowships with full tuition reimbursements, teaching assistantships with partial tuition reimbursements, career-related internships or fieldwork, Federal Work-Study, institutionally sponsored loans, scholarships/grants, health care benefits, and unspecified assistantships available. Financial award application deadline: 4/1; financial award applicants required to submit FAFSA. *Faculty research:* Creative writing, British and American literature, composition and rhetoric. *Application contact:* Chair of Graduate Studies, 940-565-2114, Fax: 940-565-4355.

University of Notre Dame, Graduate School, College of Arts and Letters, Division of Humanities, Department of English, Notre Dame, IN 46556. Offers creative writing (MFA); English (MA, PhD). *Degree requirements:* For doctorate, one foreign language, thesis/dissertation, candidacy exam. *Entrance requirements:* For master's, GRE General Test, minimum GPA of 3.0; for doctorate, GRE General Test, GRE Subject Test, minimum GPA of 3.0. Additional exam requirements/recommendations for international students: Required—TOEFL (minimum score 600 paper-based; 250 computer-based; 80 iBT). Electronic applications accepted. *Faculty research:* Early modern studies (medieval/Renaissance), modern British studies (eighteenth-twentieth centuries), American Studies, literature and philosophy, Irish studies.

University of Oklahoma, College of Arts and Sciences, Department of English, Norman, OK 73019. Offers English (MA, PhD), including composition/rhetoric/literacy studies, creative writing (MA), literary studies. Part-time programs available. *Faculty:* 34 full-time (15 women). *Students:* 61 full-time (36 women), 6 part-time (5 women); includes 11 minority (1 Black or African American, non-Hispanic/Latino; 8 American Indian or Alaska Native, non-Hispanic/Latino; 2 Hispanic/Latino), 4 international. Average age 31. 56 applicants, 55% accepted, 21 enrolled. In 2010, 4 master's, 3 doctorates awarded. *Degree requirements:* For master's, one foreign language, thesis or alternative, qualifying exam; for doctorate, 2 foreign languages, comprehensive exam, thesis/dissertation, qualifying exam. *Entrance requirements:* For master's, GRE General Test, minimum GPA of 3.0, BA with 27 hours of course work in English or 15 hours of upper-level courses; for doctorate, GRE General Test, GRE Subject Test (English literature), minimum graduate GPA of 3.5. Additional exam requirements/recommendations for international students: Required—TOEFL (minimum score 550 paper-based; 213 computer-based; 79 iBT). *Application deadline:* For fall admission, 4/1 priority date for domestic students, 4/1 for international students; for spring admission, 11/1 for domestic students, 9/1 for international students. Applications are processed on a rolling basis. Application fee: $40 ($90 for international students). Electronic applications accepted. *Expenses:* Tuition, state resident: full-time $3893; part-time $162.20 per credit hour. Tuition, nonresident: full-time $14,167; part-time $590.30 per credit hour. Required fees: $2523; $94.60 per credit hour. Tuition and fees vary according to course load and degree level. *Financial support:* In 2010–11, 1 fellowship with full tuition reimbursement (averaging $2,500 per year), 3 research assistantships with partial tuition reimbursements (averaging $12,765 per year), 58 teaching assistantships with partial tuition reimbursements (averaging $12,462 per year) were awarded; scholarships/grants, health care benefits, and unspecified assistantships also available. Financial award applicants required to submit FAFSA. *Faculty research:* Literary theory, cultural studies, Native

English

University of Oklahoma (continued)

American studies, composition and rhetoric, British and American literature. *Unit head:* David Mair, Chair, 405-325-4661, Fax: 405-325-0831, E-mail: dmair@ou.edu. *Application contact:* Zara Cougher, Graduate Secretary, 405-325-0489, Fax: 405-325-0831, E-mail: scougher@ou.edu.

University of Oregon, Graduate School, College of Arts and Sciences, Department of English, Eugene, OR 97403. Offers MA, PhD. Terminal master's awarded for partial completion of doctoral program. *Degree requirements:* For master's, one foreign language; for doctorate, 2 foreign languages, thesis/dissertation. *Entrance requirements:* For master's, GRE General Test; for doctorate, GRE Subject Test (English literature), minimum GPA of 3.5. Additional exam requirements/recommendations for international students: Required—TOEFL. *Faculty research:* Old and Middle English, women writers, critical theory, literature and the environment, rhetoric and composition.

University of Ottawa, Faculty of Graduate and Postdoctoral Studies, Faculty of Arts, Department of English, Ottawa, ON K1N 6N5, Canada. Offers MA, PhD. Part-time and evening/weekend programs available. *Degree requirements:* For master's, one foreign language, thesis optional; for doctorate, 2 foreign languages, comprehensive exam, thesis/dissertation. *Entrance requirements:* For master's, honors degree or equivalent, minimum B average; for doctorate, master's degree, minimum B+ average. Electronic applications accepted. *Faculty research:* Anglo-Saxon and medieval literature.

University of Pennsylvania, School of Arts and Sciences, Graduate Group in English, Philadelphia, PA 19104. Offers AM, PhD. *Faculty:* 39 full-time (17 women), 6 part-time/adjunct (2 women). *Students:* 75 full-time (54 women), 5 part-time (2 women); includes 5 Black or African American, non-Hispanic/Latino; 5 Asian, non-Hispanic/Latino; 1 Hispanic/Latino, 8 international. 734 applicants, 1% accepted, 6 enrolled. In 2010, 13 master's, 10 doctorates awarded. Terminal master's awarded for partial completion of doctoral program. *Degree requirements:* For master's, one foreign language; for doctorate, 2 foreign languages, thesis/dissertation, oral and written qualifying exams. *Entrance requirements:* For master's, GRE General Test, GRE Subject Test, sample of written work; for doctorate, GRE General Test, GRE Subject Test. Additional exam requirements/recommendations for international students: Required—TOEFL. *Application deadline:* For fall admission, 12/1 priority date for domestic students. Application fee: $70. Electronic applications accepted. *Expenses:* Tuition: Full-time $25,660; part-time $4758 per course. Required fees: $2152; $270 per course. Tuition and fees vary according to course load, degree level and program. *Financial support:* Fellowships, teaching assistantships, institutionally sponsored loans, scholarships/grants, traineeships, health care benefits, and unspecified assistantships available. Financial award application deadline: 12/15. *Faculty research:* Renaissance literature and intellectual theory, feminist studies, literary theory. *Unit head:* Nancy Bentley, Department Chair, English, 215-898-7340, E-mail: nbentley@english.upenn.edu. *Application contact:* Nancy Bentley, Department Chair, English, 215-898-7340, E-mail: nbentley@english.upenn.edu.

University of Pittsburgh, School of Arts and Sciences, Department of English, Pittsburgh, PA 15260. Offers cultural and critical studies (PhD); English (MA); writing (MFA). Part-time programs available. *Faculty:* 51 full-time (26 women), 1 (woman) part-time/adjunct. *Students:* 117 full-time (79 women), 28 part-time (21 women); includes 15 minority (1 Black or African American, non-Hispanic/Latino; 5 Asian, non-Hispanic/Latino; 4 Hispanic/Latino; 5 Two or more races, non-Hispanic/Latino), 10 international. Average age 29. 344 applicants, 16% accepted, 17 enrolled. In 2010, 22 master's, 10 doctorates awarded. *Degree requirements:* For master's, one foreign language; for doctorate, 2 foreign languages, comprehensive exam, thesis/dissertation. *Entrance requirements:* For master's and doctorate, GRE General Test, writing sample. Additional exam requirements/recommendations for international students: Required—TOEFL (minimum score 550 paper-based; 213 computer-based; 80 iBT). *Application deadline:* For fall admission, 12/10 for domestic and international students. Application fee: $50. Electronic applications accepted. *Expenses:* Tuition, state resident: full-time $17,304; part-time $701 per credit. Tuition, nonresident: full-time $29,554; part-time $1210 per credit. Required fees: $740; $214 per term. Tuition and fees vary according to program. *Financial support:* In 2010–11, 100 students received support, including 22 fellowships with full tuition reimbursements available (averaging $17,822 per year), 5 research assistantships with full and partial tuition reimbursements available (averaging $12,300 per year), 70 teaching assistantships with full tuition reimbursements available (averaging $15,065 per year); Federal Work-Study, tuition waivers (full and partial), and unspecified assistantships also available. Financial award application deadline: 12/12. *Faculty research:* Cultural studies, literary history and theory, film, composition. *Unit head:* Dr. H. David Brumble, Chair, 412-624-6509, Fax: 412-624-6639, E-mail: brumble@pitt.edu. *Application contact:* Duane Walsh, Graduate Administrator, 412-624-6549, Fax: 412-624-6639, E-mail: engrad@pitt.edu.

University of Puerto Rico, Mayagüez Campus, Graduate Studies, College of Arts and Sciences, Department of English, Mayagüez, PR 00681-9000. Offers English education (MA). Part-time programs available. *Students:* 40 full-time (29 women), 13 part-time (9 women); includes 51 Hispanic/Latino, 2 international. 8 applicants, 63% accepted, 4 enrolled. In 2010, 8 master's awarded. *Degree requirements:* For master's, comprehensive exam, thesis optional. *Entrance requirements:* For master's, course work in linguistics or language, American literature, British literature, and structure/grammar or syntax. Additional exam requirements/recommendations for international students: Required—TOEFL (minimum score 550 paper-based; 213 computer-based). *Application deadline:* For fall admission, 2/15 for domestic and international students; for spring admission, 9/15 for domestic and international students. Applications are processed on a rolling basis. Application fee: $25. *Expenses:* Tuition, state resident: full-time $1188. Tuition, nonresident: full-time $1188. International tuition: $6126 full-time. Tuition and fees vary according to course level and course load. *Financial support:* In 2010–11, 26 students received support, including fellowships (averaging $12,000 per year), 3 research assistantships (averaging $15,000 per year), 23 teaching assistantships (averaging $8,500 per year); Federal Work-Study and institutionally sponsored loans also available. *Faculty research:* Teaching English as a second language, linguistics, American literature, British literature. *Unit head:* Dr. Kevin Carroll, Director, 787-265-3847, Fax: 787-265-3847, E-mail: kevin.carroll@upr.edu. *Application contact:* Dr. Kevin Carroll, Director, 787-265-3847, Fax: 787-265-3847, E-mail: kevin.carroll@upr.edu.

University of Puerto Rico, Río Piedras, College of Humanities, Department of English, San Juan, PR 00931-3300. Offers Caribbean linguistics (PhD); Caribbean literature (PhD); English (MA). Part-time programs available. *Degree requirements:* For master's, one foreign language, comprehensive exam, thesis; for doctorate, residency. *Entrance requirements:* For master's, PAEG or GRE, interview, minimum GPA of 3.0, 2 letters of recommendation; for doctorate, PAEG or GRE, minimum GPA of 3.0, 3 letters of recommendation, interview.

University of Regina, Faculty of Graduate Studies and Research, Faculty of Arts, Department of English, Regina, SK S4S 0A2, Canada. Offers MA. Part-time programs available. *Faculty:* 18 full-time (10 women), 2 part-time/adjunct (1 woman). *Students:* 4 full-time (all women), 8 part-time (4 women). 13 applicants, 46% accepted. In 2010, 5 master's awarded. *Degree requirements:* For master's, thesis (for some programs). *Entrance requirements:* For master's, writing sample. Additional exam requirements/recommendations for international students: Required—TOEFL (minimum score 580 paper-based; 80 iBT). Application fee: $100. Electronic applications accepted. Tuition and fees charges are reported in Canadian dollars. *Expenses:* Tuition, area resident: Full-time $3244.50 Canadian dollars; part-time $180.25 Canadian dollars per credit hour. International tuition: $4744.50 Canadian dollars full-time. Required fees: $494 Canadian dollars; $115.25 Canadian dollars per credit hour. $115.25 Canadian dollars per semester. Tuition and fees vary according to program. *Financial support:* In 2010–11, 2 fellowships (averaging $18,000 per year), 1 teaching assistantship (averaging $6,759 per year) were awarded; scholarships/grants also available. Financial award application deadline: 6/15. *Faculty research:* British, American, and Canadian literature; sixteenth, eighteenth, nineteenth, and twentieth century literature; literary theory. *Unit head:* Dr. Dorothy Lane, Head, 306-585-4465, Fax: 306-585-5429, E-mail: dorothy.lane@uregina.ca. *Application contact:* Dr. Alex MacDonald, Graduate Program Coordinator, 306-359-1223, Fax: 306-585-5429, E-mail: alex.macdonald@uregina.ca.

University of Rhode Island, Graduate School, College of Arts and Sciences, Department of English, Kingston, RI 02881. Offers MA, PhD, MLIS/MA. Part-time programs available. *Faculty:* 20 full-time (12 women). *Students:* 46 full-time (32 women), 24 part-time (16 women); includes 4 minority (1 Black or African American, non-Hispanic/Latino; 1 American Indian or Alaska Native, non-Hispanic/Latino; 1 Asian, non-Hispanic/Latino; 1 Hispanic/Latino), 4 international. In 2010, 5 master's, 12 doctorates awarded. *Degree requirements:* For master's, comprehensive exam (for some programs), thesis optional; for doctorate, comprehensive exam, thesis/dissertation. *Entrance requirements:* For master's, 3 letters of recommendation, writing sample; for doctorate, GRE, 3 letters of recommendation, writing sample. Additional exam requirements/recommendations for international students: Required—TOEFL (minimum score 550 paper-based; 213 computer-based; 91 iBT). *Application deadline:* For fall admission, 1/15 for domestic and international students. Application fee: $65. Electronic applications accepted. *Expenses:* Tuition, state resident: full-time $9588; part-time $533 per credit hour. Tuition, nonresident: full-time $22,968; part-time $1276 per credit hour. Required fees: $1282; $68 per semester. Tuition and fees vary according to program. *Financial support:* In 2010–11, 27 teaching assistantships with full tuition reimbursements (averaging $14,211 per year) were awarded. Financial award application deadline: 1/15; financial award applicants required to submit FAFSA. *Unit head:* Dr. Ryan S. Trimm, Chair, 401-874-5444, Fax: 401-874-2580, E-mail: engchair@gmail.com. *Application contact:* Dr. Naomi Mandel, Director of Graduate Studies, 401-874-4011, Fax: 401-874-2580, E-mail: enggraddir@gmail.com.

University of Rochester, School of Arts and Sciences, Department of English, Programs in English, Rochester, NY 14627.

University of St. Thomas, Graduate Studies, College of Arts and Sciences, Graduate Program in English, St. Paul, MN 55105-1096. Offers MA. Part-time and evening/weekend programs available. *Faculty:* 27 full-time (14 women). *Students:* 4 full-time (all women), 48 part-time (36 women); includes 1 Black or African American, non-Hispanic/Latino; 1 Asian, non-Hispanic/Latino; 1 Hispanic/Latino, 1 international. Average age 27. 33 applicants, 85% accepted, 19 enrolled. In 2010, 16 master's awarded. *Degree requirements:* For master's, essay. *Entrance requirements:* For master's, minimum GPA of 3.0, previous course work in literature, sample of written work. Additional exam requirements/recommendations for international students: Required—TOEFL. *Application deadline:* For fall admission, 3/1 for domestic students; for spring admission, 10/1 for domestic students. Application fee: $50. *Expenses:* Contact institution. *Financial support:* Fellowships with full and partial tuition reimbursements, research assistantships, teaching assistantships with tuition reimbursements, institutionally sponsored loans, scholarships/grants, and traineeships available. Support available to part-time students. Financial award application deadline: 4/1; financial award applicants required to submit FAFSA. *Faculty research:* Multicultural literature, literature and theory, regional writers. *Unit head:* Dr. Catherine A. Craft-Fairchild, Director, 651-962-5614, Fax: 651-962-5623, E-mail: cacraftfaire@stthomas.edu. *Application contact:* Joyce M. Poley, Coordinator, 651-962-5628, Fax: 651-962-5623, E-mail: gradenglish@stthomas.edu.

University of Saskatchewan, College of Graduate Studies and Research, College of Arts and Sciences, Department of English, Saskatoon, SK S7N 5A2, Canada. Offers MA, PhD. *Degree requirements:* For master's, one foreign language, thesis; for doctorate, one foreign language, comprehensive exam (for some programs), thesis/dissertation. *Entrance requirements:* Additional exam requirements/recommendations for international students: Required—TOEFL (minimum score 80 iBT); Recommended—IELTS (minimum score 6.5). Electronic applications accepted.

University of South Africa, College of Human Sciences, Pretoria, South Africa. Offers adult education (M Ed); African languages (MA, PhD); African politics (MA, PhD); Afrikaans (MA, PhD); ancient history (MA, PhD); ancient Near Eastern studies (MA, PhD); anthropology (MA, PhD); applied linguistics (MA); Arabic (MA, PhD); archaeology (MA); art history (MA); Biblical archaeology (MA); Biblical studies (M Th, D Th, PhD); Christian spirituality (M Th, D Th); church history (M Th, D Th); classical studies (MA, PhD); clinical psychology (MA); communication (MA, PhD); comparative education (M Ed, Ed D); consulting psychology (D Admin, D Com, PhD); curriculum studies (M Ed, Ed D); development studies (M Admin, MA, D Admin, PhD); didactics (M Ed, Ed D); education (M Tech); education management (M Ed, Ed D); educational psychology (M Ed); English (MA); environmental education (M Ed); French (MA, PhD); German (MA, PhD); Greek (MA); guidance and counseling (M Ed); health studies (MA, PhD), including health sciences education (MA), health services management (MA), medical and surgical nursing science (critical care general) (MA), midwifery and neonatal nursing science (MA), trauma and emergency care (MA); history (MA, PhD); history of education (Ed D); inclusive education (M Ed, Ed D); information and communications technology policy and regulation (MA); information science (MA, MIS, PhD); international politics (MA, PhD); Islamic studies (MA, PhD); Italian (MA, PhD); Judaica (MA, PhD); linguistics (MA, PhD); mathematical education (M Ed); mathematics education (MA); missiology (M Th, D Th); modern Hebrew (MA, PhD); musicology (MA, MMus, D Mus, PhD); natural science education (M Ed); New Testament (M Th, D Th); Old Testament (D Th); pastoral therapy (M Th, D Th); philosophy (MA); philosophy of education (M Ed, Ed D); politics (MA, PhD); Portuguese (MA, PhD); practical theology (M Th, D Th); psychology (MA, MS, PhD); psychology of education (M Ed, Ed D); public health (MA); religious studies (MA, D Th, PhD); Romance languages (MA); Russian (MA, PhD); Semitic languages (MA, PhD); social behavior studies in HIV/AIDS (MA); social science (mental health) (MA); social science in development studies (MA); social science in psychology (MA); social science in social work (MA); social science in sociology (MA); social work (MSW, DSW, PhD); socio-education (M Ed, Ed D); sociolinguistics (MA); sociology (MA, PhD); Spanish (MA, PhD); systematic theology (M Th, D Th); TESOL (teaching English to speakers of other languages) (MA); theological ethics (M Th, D Th); theory of literature (MA, PhD); urban ministries (D Th); urban ministry (M Th).

University of South Alabama, Graduate School, College of Arts and Sciences, Department of English, Mobile, AL 36688-0002. Offers MA. Part-time and evening/weekend programs available. *Faculty:* 14 full-time (5 women). *Students:* 29 full-time (23 women), 8 part-time (6 women); includes 2 minority (1 Black or African American, non-Hispanic/Latino; 1 American Indian or Alaska Native, non-Hispanic/Latino). 29 applicants, 55% accepted, 14 enrolled. In 2010, 13 master's awarded. *Degree requirements:* For master's, one foreign language, comprehensive exam, thesis optional. *Entrance requirements:* For master's, GRE General Test, BA in English or 30 hours of course work in English, minimum GPA of 3.0. Additional exam requirements/recommendations for international students: Required—TOEFL (minimum score 535 paper-based). *Application deadline:* For fall admission, 7/15 priority date for domestic students, 5/15 priority date for international students; for spring admission, 12/1 priority date for domestic students, 11/1 priority date for international students. Applications are processed on a rolling basis. Application fee: $35. *Expenses:* Tuition, state resident: part-time $300 per credit hour. Tuition, nonresident: part-time $600 per credit hour. Required fees: $150 per semester. *Financial support:* Research assistantships available. Support available to part-time students. Financial award application deadline: 4/1. *Unit head:* Dr. Patrick Cesarini, Interim Chair, 251-460-6146. *Application contact:* Dr. Ellen Harrington, Graduate Coordinator, 251-460-6146.

University of South Carolina, The Graduate School, College of Arts and Sciences, Department of English Language and Literature, Columbia, SC 29208. Offers creative writing (MFA); English (MA, PhD); English education (MAT); MLIS/MA. MAT offered in cooperation with the College of Education. Part-time programs available. *Degree requirements:* For master's, one foreign language, comprehensive exam, thesis; for doctorate, 2 foreign languages, comprehensive exam, thesis/dissertation. *Entrance requirements:* For master's, GRE General Test (MFA), GRE Subject Test (MA, MAT), sample of written work; for doctorate, GRE General Test, GRE Subject Test, sample of written work. Additional exam requirements/recommendations for international students: Required—TOEFL. Electronic applications accepted. *Faculty research:* American literature, British literature, composition and rhetoric, linguistics, speech communication.

The University of South Dakota, Graduate School, College of Arts and Sciences, Department of English, Vermillion, SD 57069-2390. Offers MA, PhD. *Degree requirements:* For master's, comprehensive exam (for some programs), thesis (for some programs); for doctorate, comprehensive exam, thesis/dissertation. *Entrance requirements:* For master's, minimum GPA of 3.0, writing sample; for doctorate, GRE, minimum GPA of 3.0, writing sample. Additional exam requirements/recommendations for international students: Required—TOEFL (minimum score 620 paper-based; 260 computer-based; 105 iBT). Electronic applications accepted.

University of Southern California, Graduate School, Dana and David Dornsife College of Letters, Arts and Sciences, Department of English, Los Angeles, CA 90089. Offers English (MA, PhD); literature and creative writing (PhD). *Faculty:* 37 full-time (18 women), 12 part-time/adjunct (5 women). *Students:* 98 full-time (57 women), 1 part-time (0 women); includes 22 minority (1 Black or African American, non-Hispanic/Latino; 1 American Indian or Alaska Native, non-Hispanic/Latino; 3 Asian, non-Hispanic/Latino; 14 Hispanic/Latino; 3 Two or more races, non-Hispanic/Latino), 8 international. In 2010, 5 master's, 21 doctorates awarded. Terminal master's awarded for partial completion of doctoral program. *Degree requirements:* For doctorate, one foreign language, comprehensive exam, thesis/dissertation. *Entrance requirements:* For doctorate, GRE General Test, GRE Subject Test (English literature). Additional exam requirements/recommendations for international students: Required—TOEFL. *Application deadline:* For fall admission, 12/1 for domestic and international students. Application fee: $85. Electronic applications accepted. *Expenses:* Tuition: Full-time $31,240; part-time $1420 per unit. Required fees: $600. One-time fee: $35 full-time. Full-time tuition and fees vary according to degree level and program. *Financial support:* In 2010–11, 54 students received support, including 12 fellowships with full tuition reimbursements available (averaging $25,500 per year), 2 research assistantships with full tuition reimbursements available (averaging $19,250 per year), 32 teaching assistantships with full tuition reimbursements available (averaging $19,800 per year); scholarships/grants, health care benefits, tuition waivers, and unspecified assistantships also available. *Faculty research:* Creative writing and literature; early modern studies; gender and sexuality; narrative studies; poetry and poetics; media, film, and popular culture; studies in race and minority literature. *Unit head:* Prof. Margaret Russett, Chair, 213-740-3727, Fax: 213-741-0377, E-mail: russett@usc.edu. *Application contact:* Flora Ruiz, Graduate Coordinator of Student Affairs, 213-740-3728, Fax: 213-741-0377, E-mail: fruiz@usc.edu.

University of Southern Mississippi, Graduate School, College of Arts and Letters, Department of English, Hattiesburg, MS 39406-0001. Offers creative writing (MA, PhD); English literature (MA, PhD). *Faculty:* 26 full-time (13 women), 1 part-time/adjunct (0 women). *Students:* 56 full-time (27 women), 20 part-time (15 women); includes 2 Black or African American, non-Hispanic/Latino; 3 Hispanic/Latino; 3 Two or more races, non-Hispanic/Latino, 4 international. Average age 33. 81 applicants, 59% accepted, 20 enrolled. In 2010, 11 master's, 8 doctorates awarded. *Degree requirements:* For master's, one foreign language, comprehensive exam, thesis; for doctorate, 2 foreign languages, comprehensive exam, thesis/dissertation. *Entrance requirements:* For master's, GRE General Test, minimum GPA of 3.0 in field of study, 2.75 in last 2 years; for doctorate, GRE General Test, minimum GPA of 3.5. Additional exam requirements/recommendations for international students: Required—TOEFL, IELTS. *Application deadline:* For fall admission, 3/15 priority date for domestic students, 3/15 for international students. Application fee: $50. Electronic applications accepted. *Financial support:* In 2010–11, 1 fellowship (averaging $14,000 per year), 2 research assistantships with full tuition reimbursements (averaging $10,000 per year), 44 teaching assistantships with full tuition reimbursements (averaging $10,000 per year) were awarded; Federal Work-Study, institutionally sponsored loans, scholarships/grants, and unspecified assistantships also available. Financial award application deadline: 3/15; financial award applicants required to submit FAFSA. *Faculty research:* English and American literature, critical theory and cultural studies, creative writing. *Unit head:* Dr. Eric Tribunella, Chair, 601-266-4319, Fax: 601-266-5757. *Application contact:* Dr. Monika Gehlawalk Lares, Graduate Coordinator, 601-266-4320, Fax: 601-266-5757.

University of South Florida, Graduate School, College of Arts and Sciences, Department of English, Tampa, FL 33620-9951. Offers MA, MFA, PhD. Part-time and evening/weekend programs available. *Faculty:* 13 full-time (8 women). *Students:* 74 full-time (48 women), 38 part-time (27 women); includes 1 Black or African American, non-Hispanic/Latino; 1 Asian, non-Hispanic/Latino; 8 Hispanic/Latino; 1 Two or more races, non-Hispanic/Latino, 2 international. Average age 35. 124 applicants, 40% accepted, 34 enrolled. In 2010, 25 master's, 13 doctorates awarded. *Degree requirements:* For master's, comprehensive exam, thesis (for some programs); for doctorate, comprehensive exam, thesis/dissertation. *Entrance requirements:* For master's, GRE General Test, minimum GPA of 3.5; for doctorate, GRE General Test, minimum GPA of 3.7. Additional exam requirements/recommendations for international students: Required—TOEFL (minimum score 550 paper-based; 213 computer-based). *Application deadline:* For fall admission, 2/1 for domestic students, 1/2 for international students. Applications are processed on a rolling basis. Application fee: $30. Electronic applications accepted. *Financial support:* In 2010–11, 76 teaching assistantships with tuition reimbursements (averaging $14,078 per year) were awarded; unspecified assistantships also available. Financial award application deadline: 6/30; financial award applicants required to submit FAFSA. *Faculty research:* British and American literature, rhetoric and composition. Total annual research expenditures: $53,025. *Unit head:* Hunt Hawkins, Chairperson, 813-974-9420, Fax: 813-974-2270, E-mail: hhawkins@cas.usf.edu. *Application contact:* Dr. Laura Runge, Director, 813-974-9469, Fax: 813-974-2270, E-mail: runge@chuma.cas.usf.edu.

The University of Tennessee, Graduate School, College of Arts and Sciences, Department of English, Knoxville, TN 37996. Offers MA, PhD. Part-time programs available. *Degree requirements:* For master's, one foreign language, thesis or alternative; for doctorate, one foreign language, thesis/dissertation. *Entrance requirements:* For master's, GRE General Test, minimum GPA of 2.7; for doctorate, GRE General Test, GRE Subject Test, minimum GPA of 2.7. Additional exam requirements/recommendations for international students: Required—TOEFL. Electronic applications accepted. *Expenses:* Tuition, state resident: full-time $7440; part-time $414 per credit hour. Tuition, nonresident: full-time $22,478; part-time $1250 per credit hour. Required fees: $922; $43 per credit hour. Tuition and fees vary according to program.

The University of Tennessee at Chattanooga, Graduate School, College of Arts and Sciences, Department of English, Chattanooga, TN 37403. Offers creative writing (MA); literary study (MA); rhetoric and writing (MA, Graduate Certificate). Part-time and evening/weekend programs available. *Faculty:* 12 full-time (7 women). *Students:* 19 full-time (13 women), 26 part-time (15 women); includes 1 minority (Two or more races, non-Hispanic/Latino), 1 international. Average age 29. 33 applicants, 88% accepted, 23 enrolled. In 2010, 20 master's awarded. *Degree requirements:* For master's, one foreign language, comprehensive exam, thesis. *Entrance requirements:* For master's, GRE General Test or GRE Subject Test (literature), minimum GPA of 3.0 in English. Additional exam requirements/recommendations for international students: Required—TOEFL (minimum score 550 paper-based; 213 computer-based; 79 iBT), IELTS (minimum score 6). *Application deadline:* For fall admission, 8/1 priority date for domestic students, 6/1 for international students; for spring admission, 12/1 priority date for domestic students, 10/1 for international students. Applications are processed on a rolling basis. Application fee: $35. Electronic applications accepted. *Financial support:* In 2010–11, 6 research assistantships with full and partial tuition reimbursements (averaging $5,500 per year) were awarded; career-related internships or fieldwork, scholarships/grants, and unspecified assistantships also available. Support available to part-time students. *Faculty research:* Technical writing, African-American literature, Milton, creative writing and poetry, American modernism and gender theory. Total annual research expenditures: $74,953. *Unit head:* Dr. Verbie Prevost, Head, 423-425-4238, Fax: 423-785-2282, E-mail: verbie-prevost@utc.edu. *Application contact:* Dr. Jerald Ainsworth, Dean of Graduate Studies, 423-425-4478, Fax: 423-425-5223, E-mail: jerald-ainsworth@utc.edu.

The University of Texas at Arlington, Graduate School, College of Liberal Arts, Department of English, Arlington, TX 76019. Offers English (MA); literature (PhD). Part-time and evening/weekend programs available. *Faculty:* 20 full-time (10 women). *Students:* 19 full-time (10 women), 98 part-time (63 women); includes 21 minority (8 Black or African American, non-Hispanic/Latino; 2 Asian, non-Hispanic/Latino; 9 Hispanic/Latino; 2 Two or more races, non-Hispanic/Latino), 3 international. 43 applicants, 86% accepted, 19 enrolled. In 2010, 6 master's, 5 doctorates awarded. *Degree requirements:* For master's, thesis or comprehensive exam; for doctorate, one foreign language, comprehensive exam, thesis/dissertation. *Entrance requirements:* For master's, GRE General Test, minimum 5-page writing sample, minimum GPA of 3.0, 3 letters of recommendation; for doctorate, GRE General Test, minimum graduate GPA of 3.5, writing sample, 3 letters of recommendation. Additional exam requirements/recommendations for international students: Required—TOEFL (minimum score 550 paper-based; 213 computer-based). *Application deadline:* For fall admission, 6/15 for domestic students. Applications are processed on a rolling basis. Application fee: $35 ($50 for international students). *Expenses:* Tuition, state resident: full-time $7500. Tuition, nonresident: full-time $13,080. International tuition: $13,250 full-time. *Financial support:* In 2010–11, 4 fellowships (averaging $2,000 per year) were awarded; scholarships/grants also available. Financial award application deadline: 5/1; financial award applicants required to submit FAFSA. *Faculty research:* Rhetoric composition, American literature, British literature, cultural studies, women's studies. *Unit head:* Dr. Wendy Faris, Chair, 817-272-2692, Fax: 817-272-2718, E-mail: wbfaris@uta.edu. *Application contact:* Dr. Tim Morris, Associate Chair for Graduate Studies, 817-272-2739, E-mail: morris@uta.edu.

The University of Texas at Austin, Graduate School, College of Liberal Arts, Department of English, Austin, TX 78712-1111. Offers creative writing (MA); English (MA, PhD). Part-time programs available. Terminal master's awarded for partial completion of doctoral program. *Degree requirements:* For master's, 2 foreign languages; for doctorate, variable foreign language requirement. *Entrance requirements:* For master's and doctorate, GRE General Test. Electronic applications accepted.

The University of Texas at Brownsville, Graduate Studies, College of Liberal Arts, Department of English, Brownsville, TX 78520-4991. Offers English (MA); interdisciplinary studies (MAIS). Part-time and evening/weekend programs available. *Degree requirements:* For master's, comprehensive exam or thesis. *Entrance requirements:* For master's, GRE General Test. Additional exam requirements/recommendations for international students: Required—TOEFL. *Faculty research:* Sandra Cisneros, Nathaniel Hawthorne, Rodolfo Araya, Isabel Allende, linguistics.

The University of Texas at Dallas, School of Arts and Humanities, Program in Humanities, Richardson, TX 75080. Offers aesthetic studies (MA, MAT, PhD); history (MA); history of ideas (MA, MAT, PhD); humanities (MA, PhD); Latin American studies (MA); studies in literature (MA, MAT, PhD). *Faculty:* 44 full-time (14 women). *Students:* 161 full-time (95 women), 178 part-time (104 women); includes 71 minority (22 Black or African American, non-Hispanic/Latino; 4 American Indian or Alaska Native, non-Hispanic/Latino; 16 Asian, non-Hispanic/Latino; 24 Hispanic/Latino; 5 Two or more races, non-Hispanic/Latino), 22 international. Average age 38. 156 applicants, 70% accepted, 79 enrolled. In 2010, 46 master's, 20 doctorates awarded. *Degree requirements:* For master's, one foreign language, portfolio, thesis, or capstone project; for doctorate, one foreign language, thesis/dissertation. *Entrance requirements:* For master's, minimum GPA of 3.3 in upper-level coursework in field; for doctorate, doctoral field examinations, minimum GPA of 3.3 in upper-level coursework in field. Additional exam requirements/recommendations for international students: Required—TOEFL (minimum score 550 paper-based; 215 computer-based). *Application deadline:* For fall admission, 7/15 for domestic students, 5/1 priority date for international students; for spring admission, 11/15 for domestic students, 9/1 priority date for international students. Applications are processed on a rolling basis. Application fee: $50 ($100 for international students). Electronic applications accepted. *Expenses:* Tuition, state resident: full-time $10,248; part-time $569 per credit hour. Tuition, nonresident: full-time $18,544; part-time $1030 per credit hour. Tuition and fees vary according to course load. *Financial support:* In 2010–11, 151 students received support, including 5 research assistantships with partial tuition reimbursements available (averaging $10,905 per year), 82 teaching assistantships with partial tuition reimbursements available (averaging $10,156 per year); career-related internships or fieldwork, Federal Work-Study, institutionally sponsored loans, scholarships/grants, and unspecified assistantships also available. Support available to part-time students. Financial award application deadline: 4/30; financial award applicants required to submit FAFSA. *Faculty research:* Holocaust studies, U. S. /Mexico studies, translation studies, art history research, Chinese studies. *Unit head:* Dr. Michael Wilson, Associate Dean for Graduate Education, 972-883-2080, E-mail: mwilson@utdallas.edu. *Application contact:* Dr. Michael Wilson, Associate Dean of Graduate Studies, 972-883-2756, Fax: 972-883-2989, E-mail: mwilson@utdallas.edu.

The University of Texas at El Paso, Graduate School, College of Liberal Arts, Department of English, El Paso, TX 79968-0001. Offers bilingual professional writing (Certificate); English and American literature (MA); rhetoric and composition (PhD); rhetoric and writing studies (MA); teaching English (MAT). Part-time and evening/weekend programs available. *Students:* 68 (47 women); includes 1 Black or African American, non-Hispanic/Latino; 1 Asian, non-Hispanic/Latino; 36 Hispanic/Latino, 2 international. Average age 34. In 2010, 18 master's awarded. *Degree requirements:* For master's, thesis optional. *Entrance requirements:* For master's, GRE General Test, minimum GPA of 3.0. Additional exam requirements/recommendations for international students: Required—TOEFL. *Application deadline:* For fall admission, 7/1 priority date for domestic students, 3/1 for international students; for spring admission, 11/1 priority date for domestic students, 9/1 for international students. Applications are processed on a rolling basis. Application fee: $15 ($65 for international students). Electronic applications accepted. *Financial support:* In 2010–11, research assistantships with partial tuition reimbursements (averaging $20,555 per year), teaching assistantships with partial tuition reimbursements (averaging $16,444 per year) were awarded; Federal Work-Study, institutionally sponsored loans, scholarships/grants, and tuition waivers (partial) also available. Financial award application deadline: 3/15; financial award applicants required to submit FAFSA. *Faculty research:* Literature, creative writing, literary theory. *Unit head:* Evelyn Posey, Chair, 915-747-5731. *Application contact:* Dr. Charles H. Ambler, Dean of the Graduate School, 915-747-5491 Ext. 7886, Fax: 915-747-5788, E-mail: cambler@utep.edu.

The University of Texas at San Antonio, College of Liberal and Fine Arts, Department of English, Classics and Philosophy, San Antonio, TX 78249-0617. Offers English (MA, PhD). Part-time and evening/weekend programs available. *Faculty:* 17 full-time (12 women). *Students:* 37 full-time (28 women), 49 part-time (34 women); includes 42 minority (2 Black or African American, non-Hispanic/Latino; 1 Asian, non-Hispanic/Latino; 36 Hispanic/Latino; 1 Native Hawaiian or other Pacific Islander, non-Hispanic/Latino; 2 Two or more races, non-Hispanic/Latino), 2 international. Average age 32. 56 applicants, 57% accepted, 18 enrolled. In 2010, 11 master's, 4 doctorates awarded. *Degree requirements:* For master's, comprehensive exam (for some programs), thesis (for some programs); for doctorate, comprehensive exam, thesis/dissertation. *Entrance requirements:* For master's, GRE General Test, minimum GPA of 3.3 on all upper division English courses; for doctorate, GRE General Test. Additional exam requirements/recommendations for international students: Required—TOEFL (minimum score 500 paper-based; 173 computer-based; 61 iBT), IELTS (minimum score 5). *Application deadline:* For fall admission, 7/1 for domestic students, 4/1 for international students; for spring admission, 11/1 for domestic students, 9/1 for international students. Applications are processed on a rolling basis. Application fee: $45 ($80 for international students). Electronic applications accepted. *Expenses:* Tuition, state resident: full-time $4172; part-time $231.75 per credit hour. Tuition, nonresident: full-time $15,332; part-time $851.75 per credit hour. *Financial support:* In 2010–11, 22 students received support, including 25 research assistantships (averaging $12,206 per year), 8 teaching assistantships (averaging $5,500 per year); career-related internships or fieldwork, institutionally sponsored loans, scholarships/grants, and unspecified assistantships also available. Support available to part-time students. *Faculty research:* History of English, principles of linguistics. Total annual research expenditures: $32,801. *Unit head:* Dr. Bridget Drinka, Department Chair, 210-458-4374, Fax: 210-458-5366, E-mail: bridget.drinka@utsa.edu.

English

The University of Texas at San Antonio (continued)
Application contact: Veronica Ramirez, Assistant Dean of the Graduate School, 210-458-4330, Fax: 210-458-4332, E-mail: graduatestudies@utsa.edu.

The University of Texas at Tyler, College of Arts and Sciences, Department of Literature and Languages, Tyler, TX 75799-0001. Offers English (MA); interdisciplinary studies (MAIS). Part-time and evening/weekend programs available. *Degree requirements:* For master's, one foreign language, comprehensive exam, thesis optional. *Entrance requirements:* For master's, GRE General Test, minimum GPA of 3.0; four semesters or the equivalent of one foreign language. Additional exam requirements/recommendations for international students: Required—TOEFL (minimum score 79 computer-based). Electronic applications accepted. *Faculty research:* Medieval and Tudor drama, Shakespeare, British Romanticism, British and Irish modernism, American realism, Greek drama, nineteenth century American literature.

The University of Texas of the Permian Basin, Office of Graduate Studies, College of Arts and Sciences, Department of Literature and Languages, Program in English, Odessa, TX 79762-0001. Offers MA. Part-time and evening/weekend programs available. *Degree requirements:* For master's, comprehensive exam (for some programs), thesis (for some programs). *Entrance requirements:* For master's, GRE General Test. Additional exam requirements/recommendations for international students: Required—TOEFL (minimum score 550 paper-based; 213 computer-based).

The University of Texas–Pan American, College of Arts and Humanities, Department of English, Edinburg, TX 78539. Offers English (MA, MAIS); English as a second language (MA). Part-time and evening/weekend programs available. *Degree requirements:* For master's, comprehensive exam, thesis optional. *Entrance requirements:* For master's, GRE General Test, minimum GPA of 3.0. *Faculty research:* Oral vs. literary culture, Borderland literature, Mexican-American literature, topics in British and American literature, discourse analysis.

University of the District of Columbia, College of Arts and Sciences, Department of English, Program in English Composition and Rhetoric, Washington, DC 20008-1175. Offers MA. *Degree requirements:* For master's, comprehensive exam. *Entrance requirements:* For master's, writing proficiency exam. *Expenses:* Tuition, state resident: full-time $7580; part-time $421 per credit. Tuition, nonresident: full-time $14,580; part-time $810 per credit. Required fees: $620; $30 per credit. One-time fee: $100 part-time.

The University of Toledo, College of Graduate Studies, College of Language, Literature and Social Sciences, Department of English, Toledo, OH 43606-3390. Offers English as a second language (MA); literature (MA); teaching of writing (Certificate). Part-time programs available. *Faculty:* 15. *Students:* 37 full-time (23 women), 12 part-time (10 women); includes 3 minority (all Black or African American, non-Hispanic/Latino), 6 international. Average age 29. 45 applicants, 73% accepted, 26 enrolled. In 2010, 19 master's, 1 other advanced degree awarded. *Degree requirements:* For master's, thesis. *Entrance requirements:* For master's, GRE if GPA is less than 3.0 for domestic students and GRE and TOEFL required for foreign students. A minimum 2.7 cumulative point-hour ratio (on a 4.0 scale) for all previous academic work. Three Letters of Recommendation, transcripts from all prior institutions attended. A critical essay for review by admissions committee. Additional exam requirements/recommendations for international students: Required—TOEFL (minimum score 550 paper-based; 213 computer-based; 80 iBT), IELTS (minimum score 6.5). *Application deadline:* For fall admission, 1/15 priority date for domestic students, 1/5 priority date for international students. Applications are processed on a rolling basis. Application fee: $45 ($75 for international students). Electronic applications accepted. *Expenses:* Tuition, state resident: full-time $11,426; part-time $476 per credit hour. Tuition, nonresident: full-time $21,660; part-time $903 per credit hour. One-time fee: $62. *Financial support:* Teaching assistantships with full tuition reimbursements, Federal Work-Study, institutionally sponsored loans, scholarships/grants, tuition waivers (full), and unspecified assistantships available. Support available to part-time students. *Faculty research:* Literary criticism, linguistics, creative writing, folklore and cultural studies. *Unit head:* Dr. Sara Lundquist, Chair, 419-530-2506, Fax: 419-530-2590, E-mail: sara.lundquist@utoledo.edu. *Application contact:* Graduate School Office, 419-530-4723, Fax: 419-530-4724, E-mail: grdsch@utoledo.edu.

University of Toronto, School of Graduate Studies, Humanities Division, Department of English, Toronto, ON M5S 1A1, Canada. Offers MA, PhD. Part-time programs available. *Degree requirements:* For master's, thesis optional; for doctorate, 2 foreign languages, thesis/dissertation. *Entrance requirements:* For master's, minimum B+ average, 2 letters of reference, portfolio (creative writing program); for doctorate, minimum A– average, 2 letters of reference, writing sample.

University of Tulsa, Graduate School, College of Arts and Sciences, Department of English Language and Literature, Tulsa, OK 74104-3189. Offers MA, MTA, PhD, JD/MA. Part-time and evening/weekend programs available. *Faculty:* 11 full-time (4 women), 1 (woman) part-time/adjunct. *Students:* 38 full-time (27 women), 10 part-time (5 women), 6 international. Average age 30. 39 applicants, 56% accepted, 6 enrolled. In 2010, 4 master's, 4 doctorates awarded. Terminal master's awarded for partial completion of doctoral program. *Degree requirements:* For master's, independent research project; for doctorate, one foreign language, comprehensive exam, thesis/dissertation. *Entrance requirements:* For master's and doctorate, GRE General Test, writing sample, list of language proficiencies. Additional exam requirements/recommendations for international students: Required—TOEFL (minimum score 575 paper-based; 231 computer-based; 91 iBT), IELTS (minimum score 6.5). *Application deadline:* For fall admission, 1/15 priority date for domestic students. Applications are processed on a rolling basis. Application fee: $40. Electronic applications accepted. *Expenses:* Tuition: Full-time $16,902; part-time $939 per credit hour. Required fees: $1020; $4 per credit hour. Tuition and fees vary according to course load. *Financial support:* In 2010–11, 47 students received support, including 14 fellowships with full and partial tuition reimbursements available (averaging $4,693 per year), 2 research assistantships with full and partial tuition reimbursements available (averaging $4,500 per year), 36 teaching assistantships with full and partial tuition reimbursements available (averaging $12,162 per year); career-related internships or fieldwork, Federal Work-Study, scholarships/grants, health care benefits, tuition waivers (full and partial), and unspecified assistantships also available. Support available to part-time students. Financial award application deadline: 1/15; financial award applicants required to submit FAFSA. *Faculty research:* Twentieth century literature; modern and contemporary British, Irish, and American literatures; Victorian literature; American studies; cultural and gender studies; African American literature; women's literature. Total annual research expenditures: $158,760. *Unit head:* Dr. Lars Engle, Chairperson, 918-631-2807, Fax: 918-631-3033, E-mail: lars-engle@utulsa.edu. *Application contact:* Dr. Laura Stevens, Advisor, 918-631-2859, Fax: 918-631-3033, E-mail: laura-stevens@utulsa.edu.

University of Tulsa, Graduate School, College of Arts and Sciences, School of Education, Program in Teaching Arts, Tulsa, OK 74104-3189. Offers art (MTA); biology (MTA); English (MTA); history (MTA); mathematics (MTA); theatre (MTA). Part-time programs available. *Students:* 2 part-time (both women); includes 1 minority (American Indian or Alaska Native, non-Hispanic/Latino). Average age 31. 1 applicant, 0% accepted, 0 enrolled. In 2010, 2 master's awarded. *Entrance requirements:* For master's, GRE General Test. Additional exam requirements/recommendations for international students: Required—TOEFL (minimum score 575 paper-based; 231 computer-based), IELTS (minimum score 6.5). *Application deadline:* Applications are processed on a rolling basis. Application fee: $40. Electronic applications accepted. *Expenses:* Tuition: Full-time $16,902; part-time $939 per credit hour. Required fees: $1020; $4 per credit hour. Tuition and fees vary according to course load. *Financial support:* In 2010–11, 2 students received support, including 2 fellowships with full and partial tuition reimbursements available (averaging $2,191 per year); research assistantships with full and partial tuition reimbursements available, teaching assistantships with full and partial tuition reimbursements available, Federal Work-Study, scholarships/grants, and tuition waivers (full and partial) also available. Support available to part-time students. Financial award application deadline: 2/1;

financial award applicants required to submit FAFSA. *Unit head:* Dr. David Brown, Advisor, 918-631-2719, Fax: 918-631-2133, E-mail: david-brown@utulsa.edu. *Application contact:* Dr. David Brown, Advisor, 918-631-2719, Fax: 918-631-2133, E-mail: david-brown@utulsa.edu.

University of Utah, Graduate School, College of Humanities, Department of English, Salt Lake City, UT 84112. Offers American studies (PhD); British American literature (MA, PhD); creative writing (MA, MFA, PhD), including rhetoric/composition (MA, PhD); literature (PhD); rhetoric and composition (PhD). *Faculty:* 35 full-time (16 women), 1 part-time/adjunct (0 women). *Students:* 57 full-time (32 women), 19 part-time (12 women); includes 5 minority (1 Black or African American, non-Hispanic/Latino; 1 American Indian or Alaska Native, non-Hispanic/Latino; 1 Asian, non-Hispanic/Latino; 2 Two or more races, non-Hispanic/Latino), 4 international. Average age 33. 281 applicants, 11% accepted, 27 enrolled. In 2010, 13 master's, 3 doctorates awarded. Terminal master's awarded for partial completion of doctoral program. *Degree requirements:* For master's, one foreign language, comprehensive exam, thesis (for some programs), written exam; for doctorate, 2 foreign languages, comprehensive exam, thesis/dissertation, 2 standard level languages/1 advanced level language. *Entrance requirements:* For master's and doctorate, GRE General Test, minimum GPA of 3.2. Additional exam requirements/recommendations for international students: Required—TOEFL (minimum score 650 paper-based; 280 computer-based; 115 iBT); Recommended—IELTS (minimum score 9). *Application deadline:* For fall admission, 12/15 for domestic and international students. Application fee: $55 ($65 for international students). Electronic applications accepted. *Expenses:* Tuition, area resident: Part-time $179.19 per credit hour. Tuition, state resident: full-time $4384. Tuition, nonresident: full-time $16,684; part-time $630.67 per credit hour. Required fees: $350 per semester. Tuition and fees vary according to course load, degree level and program. *Financial support:* In 2010–11, 60 students received support, including 11 fellowships with full tuition reimbursements available (averaging $12,400 per year), 49 teaching assistantships with full tuition reimbursements available (averaging $12,400 per year); research assistantships, health care benefits also available. Financial award application deadline: 12/15; financial award applicants required to submit FAFSA. *Faculty research:* Poetics and modern poetry, nineteenth and twentieth century British and American literature, the American west, environmental studies, critical theory and race and gender studies, fiction. Total annual research expenditures: $32,329. *Unit head:* Prof. Vincent P. Pecora, Chair, 801-581-6168, E-mail: v.pecora@utah.edu. *Application contact:* Prof. Scott Black, Director of Graduate Studies, 801-581-5137, E-mail: scott.black@utah.edu.

University of Vermont, Graduate College, College of Arts and Sciences, Department of English, Burlington, VT 05405. Offers MA. *Students:* 29 (14 women); includes 1 American Indian or Alaska Native, non-Hispanic/Latino; 1 Asian, non-Hispanic/Latino. 58 applicants, 91% accepted, 10 enrolled. In 2010, 12 master's awarded. *Degree requirements:* For master's, one foreign language, thesis. *Entrance requirements:* For master's, GRE General Test, writing sample. Additional exam requirements/recommendations for international students: Required—TOEFL (minimum score 550 paper-based; 213 computer-based; 80 iBT). *Application deadline:* For fall admission, 2/15 priority date for domestic students. Applications are processed on a rolling basis. Application fee: $40. Electronic applications accepted. *Expenses:* Tuition, state resident: part-time $537 per credit hour. Tuition, nonresident: part-time $1355 per credit hour. *Financial support:* Fellowships, teaching assistantships available. Financial award application deadline: 3/1. *Unit head:* Dr. LoKangaka Losambe, Chair, 802-656-3056. *Application contact:* Dr. Todd McGowan, Coordinator, 802-656-3056.

University of Victoria, Faculty of Graduate Studies, Faculty of Humanities, Department of English, Victoria, BC V8W 2Y2, Canada. Offers MA, PhD. Part-time programs available. *Degree requirements:* For master's, one foreign language, thesis (for some programs); for doctorate, 2 foreign languages, comprehensive exam, thesis/dissertation, candidacy exam. *Entrance requirements:* For master's, minimum A– average in last 2 years of undergraduate course work, writing sample, resume; for doctorate, minimum A– average in graduate course work, writing sample, resumé. Additional exam requirements/recommendations for international students: Required—TOEFL (minimum score 630 paper-based; 267 computer-based). Electronic applications accepted. *Faculty research:* Critical theory, nineteenth century literature, postcolonialism/multiculturalism, medieval and Renaissance literature, cultural theory.

University of Virginia, College and Graduate School of Arts and Sciences, Department of English Language and Literature, Program in English, Charlottesville, VA 22903. Offers MA, PhD, JD/MA. *Faculty:* 46 full-time (18 women), 1 part-time/adjunct (0 women). *Students:* 150 full-time (95 women), 1 (woman) part-time; includes 6 Black or African American, non-Hispanic/Latino; 5 Asian, non-Hispanic/Latino; 5 Hispanic/Latino, 3 international. Average age 28. 473 applicants, 14% accepted, 43 enrolled. In 2010, 25 master's, 11 doctorates awarded. *Degree requirements:* For master's, one foreign language, oral exam or thesis; for doctorate, 2 foreign languages, comprehensive exam, thesis/dissertation. *Entrance requirements:* For master's, GRE General Test, GRE Subject Test, 3 letters of recommendation, 2 writing samples; for doctorate, GRE General Test, GRE Subject Test, 3 letters of recommendation, 2 writing samples. Additional exam requirements/recommendations for international students: Required—TOEFL (minimum score 600 paper-based; 250 computer-based; 90 iBT), IELTS (minimum score 7). *Application deadline:* For fall admission, 1/1 for domestic students, 1/2 for international students. Applications are processed on a rolling basis. Application fee: $60. Electronic applications accepted. *Financial support:* Fellowships, teaching assistantships available. Financial award applicants required to submit FAFSA. *Unit head:* Cynthia Wall, Chair, 434-924-7105, Fax: 434-924-1478, E-mail: wall@virginia.edu. *Application contact:* Gordon Braden, Director of Graduate Admissions, 434-924-7105, Fax: 434-924-1478, E-mail: gmb5s@virginia.edu.

University of Virginia, Curry School of Education, Department of Curriculum, Instruction, and Special Education, Program in Curriculum and Instruction, Charlottesville, VA 22903. Offers curriculum and instruction (M Ed, Ed S); elementary (M Ed, Ed D); English (M Ed, Ed D); foreign language (M Ed); mathematics (M Ed, Ed D); reading (M Ed, Ed D, Ed S); science (Ed D); social studies (M Ed). *Students:* 21 full-time (14 women), 29 part-time (26 women); includes 1 Black or African American, non-Hispanic/Latino; 1 Asian, non-Hispanic/Latino; 3 Hispanic/Latino; 1 Two or more races, non-Hispanic/Latino, 1 international. Average age 34. 105 applicants, 46% accepted, 37 enrolled. In 2010, 145 master's, 2 doctorates, 23 other advanced degrees awarded. *Degree requirements:* For master's, comprehensive exam (for some programs); for doctorate, comprehensive exam, thesis/dissertation; for Ed S, comprehensive exam. *Entrance requirements:* For master's, doctorate, and Ed S, GRE General Test, 2 letters of recommendation. Additional exam requirements/recommendations for international students: Required—TOEFL (minimum score 600 paper-based; 250 computer-based; 90 iBT), IELTS (minimum score 7). *Application deadline:* Applications are processed on a rolling basis. Application fee: $60. Electronic applications accepted. *Financial support:* Fellowships with tuition reimbursements, research assistantships with tuition reimbursements, teaching assistantships with tuition reimbursements available. Financial award application deadline: 1/5; financial award applicants required to submit FAFSA.

University of Washington, Graduate School, College of Arts and Sciences, Department of English, Seattle, WA 98195. Offers creative writing (MFA); English as a second language (MAT); English literature and language (MA, MAT, PhD). Part-time programs available. Terminal master's awarded for partial completion of doctoral program. *Degree requirements:* For master's, one foreign language, thesis (for some programs); for doctorate, one foreign language, thesis/dissertation. *Entrance requirements:* For master's, GRE General Test, GRE Subject Test (MA and MAT in English), minimum GPA of 3.0; for doctorate, GRE General Test, GRE Subject Test. Additional exam requirements/recommendations for international students: Required—TOEFL. Electronic applications accepted. *Faculty research:* English and American literature, critical theory, creative writing, language theory.

University of Waterloo, Graduate Studies, Faculty of Arts, Department of English, Language and Literature, Waterloo, ON N2L 3G1, Canada. Offers English language and literature (PhD); literary studies (MA); rhetoric and communication design (MA). Part-time programs available. *Degree requirements:* For master's, one foreign language, thesis optional; for doctorate, 2 foreign languages, thesis/dissertation. *Entrance requirements:* For master's, honors degree, minimum B+ average; for doctorate, master's degree, minimum A- average. Additional exam requirements/recommendations for international students: Required—TOEFL, TWE. Electronic applications accepted. *Faculty research:* Shakespeare, American literature, rhetoric, Romantics, moderns.

The University of Western Ontario, Faculty of Graduate Studies, Faculty of Arts and Humanities, Department of English, London, ON N6A 5B8, Canada. Offers Canadian literature (MA); English (PhD); English literature (MA). *Degree requirements:* For master's, one foreign language, thesis or alternative; for doctorate, 2 foreign languages, thesis/dissertation, qualifying exam. *Entrance requirements:* For master's, minimum A average in appropriate field; for doctorate, MA or equivalent, minimum A average. Additional exam requirements/recommendations for international students: Required—TOEFL (minimum score 630 paper-based; 267 computer-based). *Faculty research:* Renaissance, nineteenth-century, modern, and postcolonial literature.

University of West Florida, College of Arts and Sciences: Arts, Department of English and Foreign Languages, Pensacola, FL 32514-5750. Offers creative writing (MA); literature (MA). Part-time and evening/weekend programs available. *Faculty:* 7 full-time (3 women). *Students:* 13 full-time (9 women), 33 part-time (19 women); includes 2 Black or African American, non-Hispanic/Latino; 2 American Indian or Alaska Native, non-Hispanic/Latino; 2 Hispanic/Latino. Average age 33. 20 applicants, 55% accepted, 7 enrolled. In 2010, 7 master's awarded. *Degree requirements:* For master's, thesis. *Entrance requirements:* For master's, GRE General Test, minimum GPA of 3.0. Additional exam requirements/recommendations for international students: Required—TOEFL (minimum score 550 paper-based; 213 computer-based). *Application deadline:* For fall admission, 6/1 for domestic students, 5/15 for international students; for spring admission, 10/1 for domestic and international students. Applications are processed on a rolling basis. Application fee: $30. *Expenses:* Tuition, state resident: full-time $4982; part-time $208 per credit hour. Tuition, nonresident: full-time $20,059; part-time $836 per credit hour. Required fees: $1365; $57 per credit hour. *Financial support:* In 2010–11, 6 fellowships with partial tuition reimbursements (averaging $924 per year), 24 research assistantships with partial tuition reimbursements (averaging $3,280 per year), 18 teaching assistantships with partial tuition reimbursements (averaging $5,571 per year) were awarded; unspecified assistantships also available. Financial award application deadline: 4/15; financial award applicants required to submit FAFSA. *Faculty research:* Faulkner, Shakespeare, American humor, women's studies, poetry. *Unit head:* Dr. Bob Yeager, Chairperson, 850-474-2923. *Application contact:* Terry McCray, Assistant Director of Graduate Admissions, 850-473-7718, Fax: 850-473-7714, E-mail: gradadmissions@uwf.edu.

University of West Georgia, College of Arts and Sciences, Department of English and Philosophy, Carrollton, GA 30118. Offers English (MA). Part-time and evening/weekend programs available. *Faculty:* 20 full-time (11 women). *Students:* 3 full-time (0 women), 28 part-time (16 women); includes 2 Black or African American, non-Hispanic/Latino; 1 American Indian or Alaska Native, non-Hispanic/Latino. Average age 29. 12 applicants, 92% accepted, 1 enrolled. In 2010, 4 master's awarded. *Degree requirements:* For master's, one foreign language, comprehensive exam, thesis optional. *Entrance requirements:* For master's, GRE General Test, NTE, undergraduate degree in English, minimum GPA of 3.2. *Application deadline:* For fall admission, 7/17 for domestic students; for spring admission, 11/20 for domestic students. Application fee: $30. Electronic applications accepted. *Expenses:* Tuition, state resident: full-time $4130; part-time $173 per semester hour. Tuition, nonresident: full-time $16,524; part-time $689 per semester hour. Required fees: $1586; $44.01 per semester hour. $397 per semester. Tuition and fees vary according to program. *Financial support:* In 2010–11, 10 students received support, including 10 research assistantships with full tuition reimbursements available (averaging $4,000 per year); career-related internships or fieldwork and unspecified assistantships also available. Support available to part-time students. Financial award application deadline: 7/1; financial award applicants required to submit FAFSA. *Unit head:* Dr. Randy Hendricks, Chair, 678-839-6512, Fax: 678-839-4849, E-mail: rhendricl@westga.edu. *Application contact:* Dr. Charles W. Clark, Dean, 678-839-6508, E-mail: cclark@westga.edu.

University of Windsor, Faculty of Graduate Studies, Faculty of Arts and Social Sciences, Department of English Language, Literature and Creative Writing, Windsor, ON N9B 3P4, Canada. Offers English: creative writing and language and literature (MA); English: language and literature (MA). Part-time programs available. *Degree requirements:* For master's, thesis. *Entrance requirements:* For master's, minimum B average, portfolio. Additional exam requirements/recommendations for international students: Required—TOEFL (minimum score 600 paper-based; 250 computer-based). Electronic applications accepted. *Faculty research:* Use of gender-related terms in popular culture; international and Aboriginal literatures: expression of cultural identity; critical analysis of authors: Pope, Munroe, Lady Morgan, Orwell, Thomas; the 'feminine" voice in literature and contemporary culture.

University of Wisconsin–Eau Claire, College of Arts and Sciences, Program in English, Eau Claire, WI 54702-4004. Offers literature and textual interpretation (MA); writing (MA). Part-time programs available. *Faculty:* 24 full-time (16 women). *Students:* 8 full-time (3 women), 11 part-time (10 women); includes 2 minority (1 Hispanic/Latino; 1 Two or more races, non-Hispanic/Latino). Average age 31. 15 applicants, 80% accepted, 8 enrolled. In 2010, 6 master's awarded. *Degree requirements:* For master's, thesis, oral defense with thesis. *Entrance requirements:* For master's, minimum GPA of 3.25 in English, 3.0 overall; bachelor's degree with minimum of 24 credits in English. Additional exam requirements/recommendations for international students: Required—TOEFL (minimum score 550 paper-based; 213 computer-based; 79 iBT); Recommended—IELTS (minimum score 7). *Application deadline:* For fall admission, 7/1 priority date for domestic students, 6/1 priority date for international students; for spring admission, 12/1 priority date for domestic students, 11/1 priority date for international students. Applications are processed on a rolling basis. Application fee: $56. *Expenses:* Tuition, state resident: full-time $7001; part-time $389 per credit. Tuition, nonresident: full-time $16,771; part-time $932 per credit. Required fees: $1057; $58.49 per credit. *Financial support:* In 2010–11, 13 students received support, including 3 fellowships (averaging $2,013 per year); Federal Work-Study and unspecified assistantships also available. Financial award application deadline: 3/1; financial award applicants required to submit FAFSA. *Unit head:* Dr. Jack Bushnell, Chair, 715-836-2639, Fax: 715-836-5996, E-mail: bushnejp@uwec.edu. *Application contact:* Dr. Jennifer Shaddock, Director, 715-836-5476, E-mail: shaddoj@uwec.edu.

University of Wisconsin–Madison, Graduate School, College of Letters and Science, Department of English, Madison, WI 53706-1380. Offers applied English linguistics (MA); composition and rhetoric (PhD); creative writing (MFA); English language and linguistics (PhD); literary studies (MA, PhD). *Degree requirements:* For doctorate, thesis/dissertation. *Expenses:* Tuition, state resident: full-time $9887; part-time $617.96 per credit. Tuition, nonresident: full-time $24,054; part-time $1503.40 per credit. Required fees: $67.63 per credit. Tuition and fees vary according to reciprocity agreements.

University of Wisconsin–Milwaukee, Graduate School, College of Letters and Sciences, Department of English, Milwaukee, WI 53201-0413. Offers creative writing (PhD); English (MA); international technical communication (Certificate); linguistics (PhD); professional writing (PhD); professional writing and communication (Certificate); rhetoric and composition (PhD); MLIS/MA. *Faculty:* 40 full-time (19 women). *Students:* 106 full-time (62 women), 65 part-time (45 women); includes 4 Black or African American, non-Hispanic/Latino; 5 Asian, non-Hispanic/Latino, 17 international. Average age 34. 208 applicants, 54% accepted, 29 enrolled. In 2010, 19 master's, 14 doctorates awarded. *Degree requirements:* For master's, thesis or alternative; for doctorate, one foreign language, thesis/dissertation. *Entrance requirements:* For master's, GRE General Test, GRE Subject Test; for doctorate, GRE. Additional exam requirements/recommendations for international students: Required—TOEFL (minimum score 550 paper-based; 79 iBT), IELTS (minimum score 6.5). *Application deadline:* For fall admission, 1/1 priority date for domestic students; for spring admission, 9/1 for domestic students. Applications are processed on a rolling basis. Application fee: $56 ($96 for international students). Electronic applications accepted. *Financial support:* In 2010–11, 4 fellowships, 1 research assistantship, 84 teaching assistantships were awarded; career-related internships or fieldwork, unspecified assistantships, and project assistantships also available. Support available to part-time students. Financial award application deadline: 4/15; financial award applicants required to submit FAFSA. Total annual research expenditures: $36,259. *Unit head:* Tasha Oren, Representative, 414-229-6625, Fax: 414-229-2643, E-mail: tgoren@uwm.edu. *Application contact:* General Information Contact, 414-229-4982, Fax: 414-229-6967, E-mail: gradschool@uwm.edu.

University of Wisconsin–Oshkosh, The Office of Graduate Studies, College of Letters and Science, Department of English, Oshkosh, WI 54901. Offers MA. Part-time programs available. *Degree requirements:* For master's, thesis or alternative. *Entrance requirements:* For master's, GRE. Additional exam requirements/recommendations for international students: Required—TOEFL (minimum score 550 paper-based; 213 computer-based; 79 iBT). Electronic applications accepted.

University of Wisconsin–Stevens Point, College of Letters and Science, Department of English, Stevens Point, WI 54481-3897. Offers MST. *Degree requirements:* For master's, thesis or alternative.

University of Wyoming, College of Arts and Sciences, Department of English, Laramie, WY 82070. Offers creative writing (MFA); English (MA). Part-time programs available. *Degree requirements:* For master's, thesis or alternative, internship. *Entrance requirements:* For master's, GRE General Test, minimum GPA of 3.0. Electronic applications accepted. *Faculty research:* Literature and theory, creative writing, English as a second language, ethnic and women's studies, composition.

Utah State University, School of Graduate Studies, College of Humanities, Arts and Social Sciences, Department of English, Logan, UT 84322. Offers American studies (MA, MS), including folklore, western American literature and culture; English (MA, MS), including literature and writing, technical writing. Part-time and evening/weekend programs available. *Degree requirements:* For master's, thesis or alternative. *Entrance requirements:* For master's, GRE General Test or MAT, minimum GPA of 3.0, recommendation letters, writing samples. Additional exam requirements/recommendations for international students: Required—TOEFL. *Faculty research:* Scottish enlightenment, material culture, composition theory, creative nonfiction, literary criticism.

Valdosta State University, Department of English, Valdosta, GA 31698. Offers MA. Part-time programs available. *Faculty:* 19 full-time (9 women). *Students:* 6 full-time (all women), 21 part-time (18 women); includes 1 Black or African American, non-Hispanic/Latino; 1 Asian, non-Hispanic/Latino; 3 Two or more races, non-Hispanic/Latino. Average age 25. 8 applicants, 88% accepted, 7 enrolled. In 2010, 4 master's awarded. *Degree requirements:* For master's, one foreign language, thesis, comprehensive written and/or oral exams. *Entrance requirements:* For master's, GRE General Test, minimum GPA of 3.0. Additional exam requirements/recommendations for international students: Required—TOEFL (minimum score 523 paper-based; 193 computer-based). *Application deadline:* For fall admission, 7/1 for domestic and international students; for spring admission, 11/1 for domestic and international students. Applications are processed on a rolling basis. Application fee: $35. Electronic applications accepted. *Expenses:* Tuition, state resident: full-time $5256; part-time $197 per credit hour. Tuition, nonresident: full-time $14,490; part-time $710 per credit hour. Required fees: $855 per semester. Tuition and fees vary according to course load and campus/location. *Financial support:* In 2010–11, 13 students received support, including 6 research assistantships with full tuition reimbursements available (averaging $4,000 per year), 7 teaching assistantships with full tuition reimbursements available (averaging $8,000 per year); institutionally sponsored loans, scholarships/grants, and unspecified assistantships also available. Support available to part-time students. Financial award application deadline: 7/1; financial award applicants required to submit FAFSA. *Faculty research:* American literature. *Unit head:* Dr. Mark Smith, Head, 229-333-5946, E-mail: marksmit@valdosta.edu. *Application contact:* Misty Lamb, Admissions Specialist, 229-333-5694, Fax: 229-245-3853, E-mail: mllamb@valdosta.edu.

Valparaiso University, Graduate School, Programs in Liberal Studies, Concentration in English, Valparaiso, IN 46383. Offers MALS, Post-Master's Certificate, JD/MALS. Part-time and evening/weekend programs available. *Students:* 2 full-time (1 woman), 7 part-time (4 women). Average age 37. In 2010, 2 master's awarded. *Entrance requirements:* For master's, minimum GPA of 3.0. Additional exam requirements/recommendations for international students: Required—TOEFL (minimum score 550 paper-based; 213 computer-based; 80 iBT). *Application deadline:* Applications are processed on a rolling basis. Application fee: $30 ($50 for international students). Electronic applications accepted. *Expenses:* Tuition: Full-time $9540; part-time $530 per credit hour. Required fees: $292; $95 per semester. Tuition and fees vary according to program. *Financial support:* Available to part-time students. Applicants required to submit FAFSA. *Unit head:* Dr. David L. Rowland, Dean, Graduate School and Continuing Education/Associate Provost, 219-464-5313, Fax: 219-464-5381, E-mail: david.rowland@valpo.edu. *Application contact:* Laura Groth, Coordinator of Student Services and Support, 219-464-5313, Fax: 219-464-5381, E-mail: laura.groth@valpo.edu.

Vanderbilt University, Graduate School, Department of English, Nashville, TN 37240-1001. Offers MA, MAT, PhD. *Faculty:* 33 full-time (17 women). *Students:* 35 full-time (24 women), 1 (woman) part-time; includes 5 Black or African American, non-Hispanic/Latino; 3 Asian, non-Hispanic/Latino; 1 Hispanic/Latino; 2 Two or more races, non-Hispanic/Latino. Average age 29. 523 applicants, 2% accepted, 8 enrolled. In 2010, 7 master's, 8 doctorates awarded. *Degree requirements:* For master's, thesis; for doctorate, one foreign language, comprehensive exam, thesis/dissertation, final and qualifying exams. *Entrance requirements:* For master's and doctorate, GRE General Test, sample of written work. Additional exam requirements/recommendations for international students: Required—TOEFL (minimum score 570 paper-based; 230 computer-based; 88 iBT). *Application deadline:* For fall admission, 1/15 for domestic and international students. Application fee: $0. Electronic applications accepted. *Financial support:* Fellowships with full and partial tuition reimbursements, research assistantships with full and partial tuition reimbursements, teaching assistantships with full tuition reimbursements, Federal Work-Study, institutionally sponsored loans, scholarships/grants, and health care benefits available. Financial award application deadline: 1/15; financial award applicants required to submit CSS PROFILE or FAFSA. *Faculty research:* British, American, and Anglophone literature, film, cultural studies, and literary theory. *Unit head:* Dr. Jay Clayton, Chair, 615-322-2542, Fax: 615-343-8028, E-mail: jay.clayton@vanderbilt.edu. *Application contact:* Dr. Dana Nelson, Director of Graduate Studies, 615-343-3185, Fax: 615-343-8028, E-mail: dana.d.nelson@vanderbilt.edu.

Villanova University, Graduate School of Liberal Arts and Sciences, Department of English, Villanova, PA 19085-1699. Offers MA. Part-time and evening/weekend programs available. *Faculty:* 7 full-time (5 women). *Students:* 33 full-time (22 women), 19 part-time (12 women); includes 8 minority (3 Asian, non-Hispanic/Latino; 3 Hispanic/Latino; 2 Two or more races, non-Hispanic/Latino). Average age 28. 53 applicants, 58% accepted, 10 enrolled. In 2010, 22 master's awarded. *Degree requirements:* For master's, comprehensive exam, thesis optional. *Entrance requirements:* For master's, GRE General Test, GRE Subject Test, minimum GPA of 3.0, writing sample. Additional exam requirements/recommendations for international students: Required—TOEFL. *Application deadline:* For fall admission, 3/1 priority date for domestic and international students; for spring admission, 11/15 priority date for domestic and international students. Applications are processed on a rolling basis. Application fee: $50. Electronic applications accepted. *Expenses:* Tuition: Part-time $700 per credit. Part-time tuition and fees vary according to degree level and program. *Financial support:* Research assistantships, Federal Work-Study, scholarships/grants, and unspecified assistantships available. Financial award applicants required to submit FAFSA. *Unit head:* Dr. Evan Radcliffe, Chairperson, 610-519-4630. *Application contact:* Dr. Adele Lindenmeyr, Dean, Graduate School of Liberal Arts and Sciences, 610-519-7093, Fax: 610-519-7096.

English

Virginia Commonwealth University, Graduate School, College of Humanities and Sciences, Department of English, Program in English, Richmond, VA 23284-9005. Offers literature (MA); writing and rhetoric (MA). Part-time programs available. *Students:* 30 full-time (16 women), 28 part-time (18 women); includes 10 minority (5 Black or African American, non-Hispanic/Latino; 1 American Indian or Alaska Native, non-Hispanic/Latino; 1 Asian, non-Hispanic/Latino; 2 Hispanic/Latino; 1 Two or more races, non-Hispanic/Latino), 1 international. 39 applicants, 69% accepted, 15 enrolled. In 2010, 16 master's awarded. *Entrance requirements:* For master's, GRE General Test. Additional exam requirements/recommendations for international students: Required—TWE, Either TOEFL (minimum score: paper-based 600, computer-based 250) or IELTS (6.5). *Application deadline:* For fall admission, 3/1 for domestic students; for spring admission, 11/15 for domestic students. Applications are processed on a rolling basis. Application fee: $50. Electronic applications accepted. *Expenses:* Tuition, state resident: full-time $4308; part-time $479 per credit hour. Tuition, nonresident: full-time $8942; part-time $994 per credit hour. Required fees: $2000; $85 per credit hour. Tuition and fees vary according to course level, course load, degree level, campus/location and program. *Financial support:* Federal Work-Study, institutionally sponsored loans, and tuition waivers (full and partial) available. Support available to part-time students. Financial award applicants required to submit FAFSA. *Faculty research:* Literature, writing, rhetoric. *Unit head:* Dr. Katherine C. Bassard, Program Director, 804-828-1329, E-mail: kcbassar@vcu.edu. *Application contact:* Thom N. Didato, Director, 804-828-1329, E-mail: tndidato@vcu.edu.

Virginia Polytechnic Institute and State University, Graduate School, College of Liberal Arts and Human Sciences, Department of English, Blacksburg, VA 24061. Offers creative writing (MFA); English (MA); rhetoric and writing (PhD). *Entrance requirements:* Additional exam requirements/recommendations for international students: Required—TOEFL. Electronic applications accepted. *Expenses:* Tuition, state resident: full-time $9399; part-time $488 per credit hour. Tuition, nonresident: full-time $17,854; part-time $957.75 per credit hour. Required fees: $1534. Full-time tuition and fees vary according to program. *Faculty research:* Critical theory, feminist criticism, textual editing, literary histor.

Virginia State University, School of Graduate Studies, Research, and Outreach, School of Liberal Arts and Education, Department of Languages and Literature, Petersburg, VA 23806-0001. Offers English (MA). Part-time and evening/weekend programs available. *Degree requirements:* For master's, one foreign language, thesis (for some programs). *Entrance requirements:* For master's, GRE General Test. *Expenses:* Tuition, state resident: full-time $5576; part-time $335 per credit hour. Tuition, nonresident: full-time $13,402; part-time $670 per credit hour. *Faculty research:* Writing and learning instruction, high-risk students, twentieth-century literature.

Wake Forest University, Graduate School of Arts and Sciences, Department of English, Winston-Salem, NC 27109. Offers MA. Part-time programs available. *Degree requirements:* For master's, one foreign language, thesis. *Entrance requirements:* For master's, GRE General Test, writing sample. Additional exam requirements/recommendations for international students: Required—TOEFL (minimum score 213 computer-based; 79 iBT). Electronic applications accepted. *Faculty research:* Modern and contemporary poetry, feminist criticism and theory, Irish literature, British Commonwealth literature, medieval poetry.

Washington College, Graduate Programs, Department of English, Chestertown, MD 21620-1197. Offers MA. Part-time and evening/weekend programs available. *Expenses:* Tuition: Part-time $1125 per course. Required fees: $100 per course.

Washington State University, Graduate School, College of Liberal Arts, Department of English, Pullman, WA 99164. Offers composition (MA); English (MA, PhD); teaching of English (MA). *Faculty:* 32. *Students:* 48 full-time (26 women), 5 part-time (4 women); includes 4 Black or African American, non-Hispanic/Latino; 3 American Indian or Alaska Native, non-Hispanic/Latino, 4 international. Average age 32. 105 applicants, 26% accepted, 10 enrolled. In 2010, 11 master's, 6 doctorates awarded. *Degree requirements:* For master's, one foreign language, comprehensive exam (for some programs), thesis (for some programs), oral exam; for doctorate, 2 foreign languages, comprehensive exam, thesis/dissertation, oral exam, written exam. *Entrance requirements:* For master's and doctorate, GRE General Test, GRE Subject Test, official transcripts; writing sample (approximately 10 pages); three letters of recommendation; statement of purpose (approximately 500 words); undergraduate major in English or other appropriate discipline. Additional exam requirements/recommendations for international students: Required—TOEFL, IELTS. *Application deadline:* For fall admission, 1/10 priority date for domestic students, 1/10 for international students. Applications are processed on a rolling basis. Application fee: $50. *Expenses:* Tuition, state resident: full-time $8552; part-time $443 per credit. Tuition, nonresident: full-time $21,650; part-time $1083 per credit. Required fees: $846. *Financial support:* In 2010–11, 48 students received support, including 1 fellowship (averaging $2,000 per year), 2 research assistantships with full and partial tuition reimbursements available (averaging $13,917 per year), 44 teaching assistantships with full and partial tuition reimbursements available (averaging $13,056 per year); career-related internships or fieldwork, Federal Work-Study, institutionally sponsored loans, scholarships/grants, health care benefits, and tuition waivers (partial) also available. Financial award application deadline: 2/10; financial award applicants required to submit FAFSA. *Faculty research:* Nationalism and gender in the American West, slavery and exploitation in nineteenth century Britain, photography and the color line, D. H. Lawrence and Mexico, social movement cultures and the arts. Total annual research expenditures: $5,000. *Unit head:* Dr. William Hamlin, Director, 509-335-7398, Fax: 509-335-2582, E-mail: whamlin@wsu.edu. *Application contact:* Graduate School Admissions, 800-GRADWSU, Fax: 509-335-1949, E-mail: gradsch@wsu.edu.

Washington State University, Graduate School, College of Liberal Arts, Program in American Studies, Pullman, WA 99164. Offers ethnic studies (MA, PhD); feminist studies (MA, PhD); history (MA, PhD); literature (MA, PhD). Part-time programs available. *Faculty:* 35. *Students:* 23 full-time (14 women), 4 part-time (2 women); includes 5 Black or African American, non-Hispanic/Latino; 4 American Indian or Alaska Native, non-Hispanic/Latino; 4 Asian, non-Hispanic/Latino; 4 Hispanic/Latino, 2 international. Average age 35. 55 applicants, 7% accepted, 3 enrolled. In 2010, 1 master's, 3 doctorates awarded. *Degree requirements:* For master's, one foreign language, comprehensive exam (for some programs), thesis optional, oral exam; for doctorate, one foreign language, comprehensive exam (for some programs), thesis/dissertation, oral exam. *Entrance requirements:* For master's and doctorate, GRE General Test, official college transcripts sent directly from each institution attended, 3-5 page statement of purpose describing areas of interest, minimum GPA of 3.0, writing sample, 3 letters of recommendation. Additional exam requirements/recommendations for international students: Required—TOEFL, IELTS. *Application deadline:* For fall admission, 1/10 priority date for domestic and international students; for spring admission, 7/1 priority date for domestic and international students. Applications are processed on a rolling basis. Application fee: $50. *Expenses:* Tuition, state resident: full-time $8552; part-time $443 per credit. Tuition, nonresident: full-time $21,650; part-time $1083 per credit. Required fees: $846. *Financial support:* In 2010–11, 1 fellowship (averaging $6,950 per year), 3 research assistantships with full and partial tuition reimbursements (averaging $14,634 per year), 17 teaching assistantships with full and partial tuition reimbursements (averaging $13,383 per year) were awarded; career-related internships or fieldwork, Federal Work-Study, institutionally sponsored loans, health care benefits, tuition waivers (partial), and teaching associateships also available. Financial award application deadline: 2/15; financial award applicants required to submit FAFSA. *Faculty research:* The American West in multicultural perspective; nineteenth century historical, literary, and cultural studies; comparative American ethnic literatures and cultures; American cultures and the environment; American rhetoric. *Unit head:* Dr. Rory J. Ong, Director, 509-335-1560, E-mail: rjong@mail.wsu.edu. *Application contact:* Graduate School Admissions, 800-GRADWSU, Fax: 509-335-1949, E-mail: gradsch@wsu.edu.

Washington University in St. Louis, Graduate School of Arts and Sciences, Department of English and American Literature, St. Louis, MO 63130-4899. Offers English and American literature (MA, PhD); writing (MFAW). Terminal master's awarded for partial completion of doctoral program. *Degree requirements:* For master's, thesis or written exam; for doctorate, 2 foreign languages, thesis/dissertation. *Entrance requirements:* For master's and doctorate, GRE General Test, sample of written work. Electronic applications accepted.

Wayne State University, College of Liberal Arts and Sciences, Department of English, Detroit, MI 48202. Offers comparative literature (MA); English (MA, PhD). *Faculty:* 26 full-time (14 women), 1 part-time/adjunct (0 women). *Students:* 94 full-time (54 women), 35 part-time (23 women); includes 13 minority (8 Black or African American, non-Hispanic/Latino; 3 Asian, non-Hispanic/Latino; 2 Hispanic/Latino), 9 international. Average age 34. 81 applicants, 43% accepted, 20 enrolled. In 2010, 8 master's, 9 doctorates awarded. *Degree requirements:* For master's, one foreign language, essay or thesis; for doctorate, one foreign language, thesis/dissertation. *Entrance requirements:* For master's, GRE General Test, minimum GPA of 3.25 in English, 3.0 overall; references; for doctorate, GRE General Test, GRE Subject Test, statement of purpose, references, sample essay. Additional exam requirements/recommendations for international students: Required—TOEFL (minimum score 550 paper-based; 213 computer-based); Recommended—TWE (minimum score 6). *Application deadline:* For fall admission, 6/1 for international students; for winter admission, 10/1 for international students; for spring admission, 2/1 for international students. Applications are processed on a rolling basis. Application fee: $30 ($50 for international students). Electronic applications accepted. *Expenses:* Tuition, state resident: full-time $7662; part-time $478.85 per credit hour. Tuition, nonresident: full-time $16,920; part-time $1057.55 per credit hour. Required fees: $571.20; $35.70 per credit hour. $188.05 per semester. Tuition and fees vary according to course load and program. *Financial support:* In 2010–11, 8 fellowships (averaging $15,320 per year), 30 teaching assistantships (averaging $14,658 per year) were awarded; research assistantships, career-related internships or fieldwork, institutionally sponsored loans, and tuition waivers (full and partial) also available. Support available to part-time students. Financial award application deadline: 3/1. *Faculty research:* English and American literature, cultural studies, composition, linguistics, film. *Unit head:* Dr. Richard Grusin, Chair, 313-577-7692, Fax: 313-577-8618, E-mail: aj4671@wayne.edu. *Application contact:* Ross Pudaloff, Graduate Director, 313-577-7699, E-mail: r.pudaloff@wayne.edu.

Weber State University, College of Arts and Humanities, Program in English, Ogden, UT 84408-1001. Offers MENG. Part-time and evening/weekend programs available. *Degree requirements:* For master's, one foreign language, additional course hours, thesis or research project. *Entrance requirements:* For master's, MAT or GRE, 3 letters of recommendation. *Faculty research:* Victoria literature, Middle East women writers, Irish literature (Seamus Heanes).

West Chester University of Pennsylvania, Office of Graduate Studies, College of Arts and Sciences, Department of English, West Chester, PA 19383. Offers English (MA, Teaching Certificate); TESL (MA, Certificate). Part-time and evening/weekend programs available. *Students:* 28 full-time (19 women), 67 part-time (50 women); includes 7 minority (6 Black or African American, non-Hispanic/Latino; 1 Hispanic/Latino), 1 international. Average age 30. 82 applicants, 88% accepted, 25 enrolled. In 2010, 31 master's awarded. *Degree requirements:* For master's, thesis optional, capstone experience (for English). *Entrance requirements:* For master's, minimum GPA of 2.8 and writing sample; two letters of recommendation, completed application with goals statement, and official transcripts (for English); three letters of recommendation and interview (for TESL); for other advanced degree, goals statement (for Certificate). Additional exam requirements/recommendations for international students: Required—TOEFL (minimum score 550 paper-based; 213 computer-based; 80 iBT). *Application deadline:* For fall admission, 4/15 priority date for domestic students, 3/15 for international students; for spring admission, 10/15 for domestic students, 9/1 for international students. Applications are processed on a rolling basis. Application fee: $35. Electronic applications accepted. *Expenses:* Tuition, state resident: full-time $6966; part-time $387 per credit. Tuition, nonresident: full-time $11,146; part-time $619 per credit. Required fees: $1614.40; $133.24 per credit. Part-time tuition and fees vary according to campus/location. *Financial support:* Unspecified assistantships available. Support available to part-time students. Financial award application deadline: 2/15; financial award applicants required to submit FAFSA. *Faculty research:* Critical theory, cultural studies, literature, composition, rhetoric, second language acquisition and teaching, second language writing, phonology, language teacher development. *Unit head:* Dr. Anne Herzog, Chair, 610-436-2822, E-mail: aherzog@wcupa.edu. *Application contact:* Dr. Carolyn Sorisio, Graduate Coordinator, 610-436-2745, E-mail: kfitts@wcupa.edu.

Western Carolina University, Graduate School, College of Arts and Sciences, Department of English, Cullowhee, NC 28723. Offers English (MA); teaching English as a second language or foreign language (MA). Part-time and evening/weekend programs available. *Degree requirements:* For master's, one foreign language, comprehensive exam, thesis (for some programs). *Entrance requirements:* For master's, GRE General Test, appropriate undergraduate degree, writing sample, 3 letters of recommendation. Additional exam requirements/recommendations for international students: Required—TOEFL (minimum score 550 paper-based; 270 computer-based; 79 iBT). *Faculty research:* TESOL, language assessment, applied linguistics, poetry, folk and fairy tales, post World War II British literature, Appalachian and southern literature.

Western Connecticut State University, Division of Graduate Studies and External Programs, School of Arts and Sciences, Department of English, Danbury, CT 06810-6885. Offers English (MA); literature option (MA); TESOL option (MA); writing option (MA). Part-time programs available. *Students:* 4 full-time (2 women), 23 part-time (18 women); includes 3 minority (2 Hispanic/Latino; 1 Two or more races, non-Hispanic/Latino). Average age 41. In 2010, 9 master's awarded. *Degree requirements:* For master's, thesis (writing option), completion of program in 6 years. *Entrance requirements:* For master's, minimum GPA of 2.5, writing sample. Additional exam requirements/recommendations for international students: Recommended—TOEFL (minimum score 550 paper-based; 213 computer-based; 79 iBT), IELTS (minimum score 6). *Application deadline:* For fall admission, 8/5 priority date for domestic students; for spring admission, 1/5 priority date for domestic students. Applications are processed on a rolling basis. Application fee: $50. *Expenses:* Tuition, state resident: full-time $5012; part-time $417 per credit hour. Tuition, nonresident: full-time $13,962; part-time $423 per credit hour. Required fees: $3886. Full-time tuition and fees vary according to course load, degree level and program. *Financial support:* Application deadline: 5/1. *Unit head:* Dr. Shouhua Qi, Co-Coordinator, 203-837-9048, Fax: 203-837-8525, E-mail: qis@wcsu.edu. *Application contact:* Chris Shankle, Associate Director of Graduate Studies, 203-837-9005, Fax: 203-837-8326, E-mail: shanklec@wcsu.edu.

Western Illinois University, School of Graduate Studies, College of Arts and Sciences, Department of English and Journalism, Macomb, IL 61455-1390. Offers English (MA); literary studies (Certificate); professional writing (Certificate); teaching writing (Certificate). Part-time programs available. *Students:* 13 full-time (11 women), 27 part-time (20 women); includes 4 minority (1 Black or African American, non-Hispanic/Latino; 2 Hispanic/Latino; 1 Two or more races, non-Hispanic/Latino), 3 international. Average age 28. 21 applicants, 86% accepted. In 2010, 15 master's, 3 other advanced degrees awarded. *Degree requirements:* For master's, thesis or alternative. *Entrance requirements:* Additional exam requirements/recommendations for international students: Required—TOEFL (minimum score 575 paper-based; 230 computer-based; 88 iBT). *Application deadline:* Applications are processed on a rolling basis. Application fee: $30. Electronic applications accepted. *Expenses:* Tuition, state resident: full-time $6370; part-time $265.40 per credit hour. Tuition, nonresident: full-time $12,740; part-time $530.80 per credit hour. Required fees: $75.67 per credit hour. *Financial support:* In 2010–11, 16 students received support, including 8 research assistantships with full tuition reimbursements available (averaging $7,280 per year), 8 teaching assistantships with full tuition reimbursements available (averaging $8,400 per year). Financial award applicants required to submit FAFSA. *Unit head:* Dr. Mark Mossman, Chairperson, 309-298-1103. *Application contact:* Evelyn Hoing, Assistant Director of Graduate Studies, 309-298-1806, Fax: 309-298-2345, E-mail: grad-office@wiu.edu.

Western Kentucky University, Graduate Studies, Potter College of Arts and Letters, Department of English, Bowling Green, KY 42101. Offers education (MA); English (MA Ed); literature (MA), including American literature, British literature, literary theory, women writers, world literature; teaching English as a second language (MA); writing (MA). Part-time and evening/weekend programs available. *Degree requirements:* For master's, comprehensive exam, thesis optional, final exam. *Entrance requirements:* For master's, GRE General Test, minimum GPA of 2.75. Additional exam requirements/recommendations for international students: Required—TOEFL (minimum score 555 paper-based; 213 computer-based; 79 iBT). *Faculty research:* Improving writing, linking teacher knowledge and performance, Victorian women writers, Kentucky women writers, Kentucky poets.

Western Michigan University, Graduate College, College of Arts and Sciences, Department of English, Kalamazoo, MI 49008. Offers creative writing (MFA, PhD); English (MA, PhD); English education (MA, PhD). *Degree requirements:* For master's, oral exams; for doctorate, one foreign language, thesis/dissertation, oral exam, written exams. *Entrance requirements:* For master's and doctorate, GRE General Test, GRE Subject Test.

Western Washington University, Graduate School, College of Humanities and Social Sciences, Department of English, Bellingham, WA 98225-5996. Offers MA. Part-time programs available. *Degree requirements:* For master's, one foreign language, comprehensive exam, thesis (for some programs). *Entrance requirements:* For master's, GRE General Test, writing sample, minimum GPA of 3.0 in last 60 semester hours or last 90 quarter hours of course work. Additional exam requirements/recommendations for international students: Required—TOEFL (minimum score 567 paper-based; 227 computer-based). Electronic applications accepted. *Faculty research:* Literature and technology, film, composition and rhetoric, technical writing, critical and cultural theory.

Westfield State University, Division of Graduate and Continuing Education, Department of English, Westfield; MA 01086. Offers MA. Part-time and evening/weekend programs available. *Degree requirements:* For master's, one foreign language, thesis. *Entrance requirements:* For master's, GRE General Test, MAT, minimum undergraduate GPA of 2.7, undergraduate course work in English.

West Texas A&M University, College of Fine Arts and Humanities, Department of English and Modern Languages, Canyon, TX 79016-0001. Offers English (MA). Part-time and evening/weekend programs available. *Degree requirements:* For master's, comprehensive exam, thesis optional. *Entrance requirements:* For master's, GRE General Test. Additional exam requirements/recommendations for international students: Required—TOEFL (minimum score 550 paper-based). Electronic applications accepted. *Faculty research:* Medieval studies, composition theory, literary criticism, Evelyn Scott, transformation of literacy in computer mediated communication.

West Virginia University, Eberly College of Arts and Sciences, Department of English, Morgantown, WV 26506. Offers creative writing (MFA); English (MA, PhD); literary/cultural studies (MA, PhD); writing (MA). Part-time and evening/weekend programs available. *Degree requirements:* For master's, one foreign language, thesis optional; for doctorate, one foreign language, thesis/dissertation, preliminary exam. *Entrance requirements:* For master's, GRE General Test, minimum GPA of 3.0; for doctorate, GRE General Test, GRE Subject Test, minimum GPA of 3.0. Additional exam requirements/recommendations for international students: Required—TOEFL. Electronic applications accepted. *Faculty research:* American studies, gender studies, media studies, cultural studies.

Wichita State University, Graduate School, Fairmount College of Liberal Arts and Sciences, Department of English, Wichita, KS 67260. Offers creative writing (MFA); English (MA). Part-time and evening/weekend programs available. *Entrance requirements:* For master's, writing sample (MFA). *Unit head:* Dr. Donald Wineke, Chair, 316-978-3130, Fax: 316-978-3548, E-mail: donald.wineke@wichita.edu. *Application contact:* Dr. Donald Wineke, Chair, 316-978-3130, Fax: 316-978-3548, E-mail: donald.wineke@wichita.edu.

Wilfrid Laurier University, Faculty of Graduate and Postdoctoral Studies, Faculty of Arts, Department of English and Film Studies, Waterloo, ON N2L 3C5, Canada. Offers gender and genre (MA, PhD); nation, diaspora, culture (PhD); textuality, media and print studies (PhD). *Faculty:* 22 full-time (14 women). *Students:* 29 full-time (16 women), 1 (woman) part-time. 71 applicants, 48% accepted, 18 enrolled. In 2010, 15 master's, 2 doctorates awarded. *Degree requirements:* For master's, thesis optional; for doctorate, thesis/dissertation. *Entrance requirements:* For master's, honours BA or the equivalent in English, minimum B+ in English courses above first year level; for doctorate, MA in English, minimum A- average in graduate work. Additional exam requirements/recommendations for international students: Recommended—TOEFL (minimum score 89 iBT). *Application deadline:* For fall admission, 2/1 priority date for domestic and international students. Application fee: $100. Electronic applications accepted. Tuition and fees charges are reported in Canadian dollars. *Expenses:* Tuition, area resident: Full-time $15,300 Canadian dollars; part-time $1200 Canadian dollars per credit. International tuition: $21,300 Canadian dollars full-time. Required fees: $650 Canadian dollars; $100 Canadian dollars per credit. Tuition and fees vary according to course load, degree level, campus/

location and program. *Financial support:* In 2010–11, 44 fellowships, 44 teaching assistantships were awarded; career-related internships or fieldwork, scholarships/grants, health care benefits, and unspecified assistantships also available. *Faculty research:* Gender and genre, Canadian studies, early modern studies, postcolonial studies, nineteenth century studies. *Unit head:* Dr. Tanis MacDonald, Graduate Coordinator, 519-884-0710 Ext. 2931, Fax: 519-884-8307, E-mail: tmacdonald@wlu.ca. *Application contact:* Jennifer Williams, Graduate Admissions and Records Officer, 519-884-0710 Ext. 3536, Fax: 519-884-1020, E-mail: gradstudies@wlu.ca.

William Paterson University of New Jersey, College of Humanities and Social Sciences, Wayne, NJ 07470-8420. Offers clinical and counseling psychology (MA); English (MA); history (MA); public policy and international affairs (MA); sociology (MA). Part-time and evening/weekend programs available. Electronic applications accepted.

Winona State University, College of Liberal Arts, Department of English, Winona, MN 55987. Offers MA, MS. Part-time programs available. *Students:* 20 full-time (11 women), 8 part-time (5 women); includes 1 minority (Asian, non-Hispanic/Latino), 9 international. Average age 30. In 2010, 6 master's awarded. *Degree requirements:* For master's, thesis or alternative. *Application deadline:* For fall admission, 7/26 priority date for domestic students; for spring admission, 12/8 for domestic students. Applications are processed on a rolling basis. Application fee: $20. *Financial support:* Teaching assistantships with partial tuition reimbursements, career-related internships or fieldwork, Federal Work-Study, and unspecified assistantships available. Support available to part-time students. Financial award applicants required to submit FAFSA. *Unit head:* Dr. Ruth Forsythe, Chairperson, 507-457-5429, E-mail: rforsythe@winona.edu. *Application contact:* Patricia Cichosz, Office Manager, Graduate Studies, 507-457-5038, E-mail: pcichosz@winona.edu.

Winthrop University, College of Arts and Sciences, Department of English, Rock Hill, SC 29733. Offers MA. Part-time and evening/weekend programs available. *Degree requirements:* For master's, one foreign language, thesis optional. *Entrance requirements:* For master's, GRE General Test, MAT or PRAXIS, 24 undergraduate hours of course work in English. Electronic applications accepted.

Wright State University, School of Graduate Studies, College of Liberal Arts, Department of English Language and Literatures, Dayton, OH 45435. Offers composition and rhetoric (MA); English (MA); literature (MA); teaching English to speakers of other languages (MA). *Degree requirements:* For master's, thesis optional, portfolio. *Entrance requirements:* For master's, 20 hours in upper-level English. Additional exam requirements/recommendations for international students: Required—TOEFL. *Faculty research:* American literature, world literature in English, applied linguistics, writing theory and pedagogy.

Xavier University, College of Arts and Sciences, Department of English, Cincinnati, OH 45207. Offers MA. Part-time and evening/weekend programs available. *Faculty:* 3 full-time (1 woman). *Students:* 7 full-time (4 women), 11 part-time (10 women), 1 international. Average age 29. 22 applicants, 73% accepted, 7 enrolled. In 2010, 7 master's awarded. *Degree requirements:* For master's, one foreign language, comprehensive exam, thesis optional. *Entrance requirements:* For master's, GRE, 2 letters of recommendation, writing sample, minimum GPA of 3.2. Additional exam requirements/recommendations for international students: Required—TOEFL (minimum score 550 paper-based; 213 computer-based; 79 iBT). *Application deadline:* Applications are processed on a rolling basis. Application fee: $35. Electronic applications accepted. *Expenses:* Tuition: Part-time $718 per credit hour. Tuition and fees vary according to degree level, campus/location and program. *Financial support:* In 2010–11, 6 students received support. Applicants required to submit FAFSA. *Faculty research:* British literature, American literature, linguistics, literary theory, composition studies. *Unit head:* Dr. Stephen Yandell, Chair, 513-745-3598, Fax: 513-745-3065, E-mail: yandell@xavier.edu. *Application contact:* Dr. Stephen Yandell, Chair, 513-745-3598, Fax: 513-745-3065, E-mail: yandell@xavier.edu.

Yale University, Graduate School of Arts and Sciences, Department of English Language and Literature, New Haven, CT 06520. Offers MA, PhD. Terminal master's awarded for partial completion of doctoral program. *Degree requirements:* For master's, 2 foreign languages; for doctorate, 3 foreign languages, thesis/dissertation. *Entrance requirements:* For master's and doctorate, GRE General Test, GRE Subject Test.

York University, Faculty of Graduate Studies, Faculty of Arts, Program in English, Toronto, ON M3J 1P3, Canada. Offers MA, PhD. Part-time programs available. *Degree requirements:* For master's, thesis or alternative; for doctorate, one foreign language, comprehensive exam, thesis/dissertation. Electronic applications accepted.

Youngstown State University, Graduate School, College of Liberal Arts and Social Sciences, Department of English, Youngstown, OH 44555-0001. Offers MA. Part-time programs available. *Degree requirements:* For master's, portfolio. *Entrance requirements:* For master's, bachelor's degree in English, minimum GPA of 2.7. Additional exam requirements/recommendations for international students: Required—TOEFL. *Faculty research:* Technical communications, multicultural literacy, children's literature, women's literature, film study, linguistics.

French

American University, College of Arts and Sciences, Department of Language and Foreign Studies, Washington, DC 20016-8045. Offers French (Certificate), including translation; Russian (Certificate), including translation; Spanish: Latin American studies (MA, Certificate), including Spanish: Latin American studies (MA), translation (Certificate); teaching English to speakers of other languages (MA, Certificate). Part-time and evening/weekend programs available. *Faculty:* 41 full-time (29 women), 43 part-time/adjunct (34 women). *Students:* 22 full-time (17 women), 39 part-time (31 women); includes 8 minority (1 Black or African American, non-Hispanic/Latino; 3 Asian, non-Hispanic/Latino; 3 Hispanic/Latino; 1 Native Hawaiian or other Pacific Islander, non-Hispanic/Latino), 6 international. Average age 34. 64 applicants, 64% accepted, 14 enrolled. In 2010, 24 master's, 28 other advanced degrees awarded. *Degree requirements:* For master's, one foreign language, comprehensive exam, thesis or alternative, portfolio, research; for Certificate, minimum 15 credit hours related coursework. *Entrance requirements:* For master's, GRE, writing sample; for Certificate, bachelor's degree. Additional exam requirements/recommendations for international students: Required—TOEFL. *Application deadline:* For fall admission, 2/1 for domestic students; for spring admission, 10/1 for domestic students. Application fee: $80. *Financial support:* Fellowships, career-related internships or fieldwork, Federal Work-Study, institutionally sponsored loans, and tuition waivers (partial) available. Financial award application deadline: 2/1. *Unit head:* Olga Rojer, Chair, 202-885-2139, Fax: 202-885-1076, E-mail: orojer@american.edu. *Application contact:* Kathleen Clowery, Director of Graduate Admissions, 202-885-3621, Fax: 202-885-1505, E-mail: clowery@american.edu.

Arizona State University, College of Liberal Arts and Sciences, School of International Letters and Cultures, Program in French, Tempe, AZ 85287-0202. Offers French (linguistics) (MA); French (literature) (MA). Part-time and evening/weekend programs available. *Faculty:* 10 full-time (6 women). *Students:* 9 full-time (6 women), 1 (woman) part-time; includes 2 minority (1 Black or African American, non-Hispanic/Latino; 1 Asian, non-Hispanic/Latino). Average age 33. 5 applicants, 80% accepted, 2 enrolled. In 2010, 5 master's awarded. *Degree requirements:* For master's, thesis or applied project, interactive Program of Study (iPOS)

submitted no later than beginning of third semester of study or before completing 50 percent of coursework towards completion of degree. *Entrance requirements:* For master's, GRE, minimum GPA of 3.25 in the last two years of work leading to the bachelor's degree in French major, personal statement, writing sample (preferably written in French), 3 letters of recommendation. Additional exam requirements/recommendations for international students: Required—TOEFL (minimum score 550 paper-based; 213 computer-based; 83 iBT), IELTS (minimum score 6.5). *Application deadline:* For fall admission, 1/31 for domestic students. Applications are processed on a rolling basis. Application fee: $70 ($90 for international students). Electronic applications accepted. *Expenses:* Tuition, state resident: full-time $8510; part-time $608 per credit. Tuition, nonresident: full-time $16,542; part-time $919 per credit. Required fees: $339; $110 per credit. Part-time tuition and fees vary according to course load. *Financial support:* In 2010–11, 10 teaching assistantships with full and partial tuition reimbursements (averaging $13,500 per year) were awarded; fellowships with full and partial tuition reimbursements, research assistantships with full and partial tuition reimbursements, institutionally sponsored loans, scholarships/grants, and tuition waivers (partial) also available. Financial award application deadline: 3/1; financial award applicants required to submit FAFSA. *Unit head:* Dr. Frederic Canovas, Director, 480-965-3382, E-mail: frederic.canovas@asu.edu. *Application contact:* Graduate Admissions, 480-965-6113.

Asbury University, School of Graduate and Professional Studies, Wilmore, KY 40390-1198. Offers biology: alternative certificate (MA Ed); chemistry: alternative certificate (MA Ed); English (MA Ed); English as a second language (MA Ed); ESL (MA Ed); French (MA Ed); Latin: alternative certificate (MA Ed); mathematics: alternative certificate (MA Ed); reading/writing endorsement (MA Ed); social studies (MA Ed); social work (MSW), including child and family services; Spanish (MA Ed); special education (MA Ed); special education: alternative certificate (MA Ed); teacher as leader endorsement (MA Ed). *Accreditation:* NCATE. Part-time programs available. *Degree requirements:* For master's, action research project, portfolio. *Entrance requirements:* For master's, PRAXIS/NTE, minimum GPA of 2.75, letters of recommendation.

French

Asbury University (continued)

Additional exam requirements/recommendations for international students: Required—TOEFL (minimum score 550 paper-based). Electronic applications accepted.

Bennington College, Graduate Programs, MA in Teaching a Second Language Program, Bennington, VT 05201. Offers education (MATSL); foreign language education (MATSL); French (MATSL); Spanish (MATSL). Part-time programs available. *Faculty:* 3 full-time (2 women), 6 part-time/adjunct (5 women). *Students:* 21 part-time (19 women); includes 4 Hispanic/Latino. Average age 36. 10 applicants, 90% accepted, 9 enrolled. In 2010, 11 master's awarded. *Degree requirements:* For master's, one foreign language, 2 major projects and presentations. *Entrance requirements:* For master's, Oral Proficiency Interview (OPI). Additional exam requirements/recommendations for international students: Required—TOEFL (minimum score 577 paper-based; 233 computer-based; 91 iBT). *Application deadline:* For spring admission, 4/1 priority date for domestic and international students. Applications are processed on a rolling basis. Application fee: $60. *Expenses:* Contact institution. *Financial support:* In 2010–11, 2 students received support. Scholarships/grants available. Financial award application deadline: 4/1; financial award applicants required to submit FAFSA. *Faculty research:* Acquisition, evaluation, assessment, conceptual teaching and learning, content-driven communication, applied linguistics. *Unit head:* Carol Meyer, Director, 802-440-4375, E-mail: cmeyer@bennington.edu. *Application contact:* Nancy Pearlman, Assistant Director, 802-440-4710, E-mail: matsl@bennington.edu.

Boston College, Graduate School of Arts and Sciences, Department of Romance Languages and Literatures, Chestnut Hill, MA 02467-3800. Offers French (MA, PhD); Italian (MA); medieval language (PhD); Spanish (MA, PhD). Part-time programs available. Terminal master's awarded for partial completion of doctoral program. *Degree requirements:* For master's, one foreign language; for doctorate, 2 foreign languages, thesis/dissertation. *Entrance requirements:* Additional exam requirements/recommendations for international students: Required—TOEFL (minimum score 600 paper-based; 250 computer-based; 100 iBT). Electronic applications accepted. *Faculty research:* Spanish-American literature, philology, medieval French romance and troubadour/trouvere lyrics, Golden Age Peninsular literature, secondary language acquisition and pedagogy.

Boston University, Graduate School of Arts and Sciences, Department of Romance Studies, Boston, MA 02215. Offers French language and literature (MA, PhD); Hispanic language and literatures (MA, PhD). *Students:* 43 full-time (37 women), 4 part-time (all women); includes 7 minority (6 Hispanic/Latino; 1 Two or more races, non-Hispanic/Latino), 13 international. Average age 31. 50 applicants, 58% accepted, 12 enrolled. In 2010, 8 master's, 3 doctorates awarded. Terminal master's awarded for partial completion of doctoral program. *Degree requirements:* For master's, one foreign language, comprehensive exam; for doctorate, 2 foreign languages, comprehensive exam, thesis/dissertation. *Entrance requirements:* For master's and doctorate, GRE General Test, sample of written work, 3 letters of recommendation. Additional exam requirements/recommendations for international students: Required—TOEFL (minimum score 550 paper-based; 213 computer-based). *Application deadline:* For fall admission, 4/15 for domestic and international students. Application fee: $70. Electronic applications accepted. *Expenses:* Tuition: Full-time $39,314; part-time $1228 per credit. Required fees: $40 per semester. *Financial support:* In 2010–11, 47 students received support, including 2 fellowships with full tuition reimbursements available (averaging $19,300 per year), 35 teaching assistantships with full tuition reimbursements available (averaging $18,800 per year); research assistantships, Federal Work-Study and scholarships/grants also available. Support available to part-time students. Financial award application deadline: 1/15; financial award applicants required to submit FAFSA. *Unit head:* James Iffland, Chairman, 617-353-6225, Fax: 617-353-6246, E-mail: lffland@bu.edu. *Application contact:* Deanna Wong, Administrative Assistant, 617-353-2641, Fax: 617-353-6246, E-mail: dswong@bu.edu.

Boston University, School of Education, Boston, MA 02215. Offers counseling (Ed M, CAGS), including community, school, sport psychology; counseling psychology (Ed D); curriculum and teaching (Ed M, Ed D, CAGS), including early childhood (Ed D), educational media and technology (Ed D), English and language arts (Ed D), mathematics (Ed D), physical education and coaching (Ed D), science (Ed D), social studies education (Ed D), special education (Ed D); developmental studies (Ed D), including literacy and language, reading education; developmental studies in literacy and language education (Ed M, CAGS); early childhood education (Ed M, CAGS); education of the deaf (Ed M, CAGS); educational leadership and development (Ed D), including educational administration (Ed M, Ed D, CAGS), higher education administration (Ed M, Ed D, CAGS); educational media and technology (Ed M, CAGS); elementary education (Ed M); English and language arts (Ed M, CAGS); English education (MAT); health education (Ed M, CAGS); Latin and classical studies (MAT); mathematics education (Ed M, MAT, CAGS); mathematics for teaching (MMT); modern foreign language education (MAT), including French, Spanish; physical education and coaching (Ed M, CAGS); policy, planning, and administration (Ed M, CAGS), including community education leadership, educational administration (Ed M, Ed D, CAGS), higher education administration (Ed M, Ed D, CAGS); reading education (Ed M, CAGS); science education (Ed M, MAT, CAGS), including biology (MAT), chemistry (MAT), earth science (MAT), general science (MAT), physics (MAT); social studies education (Ed M, MAT, CAGS), including history (MAT), political science (MAT); special education (Ed M, Ed D, CAGS), including disability studies (Ed M), moderate disabilities (Ed M), severe disabilities (Ed M), special education administration (Ed M); teaching English as a second language (Ed M, CAGS). Part-time programs available. *Faculty:* 57 full-time, 39 part-time/adjunct. *Students:* 245 full-time (191 women), 376 part-time (274 women); includes 83 minority (14 Black or African American, non-Hispanic/Latino; 2 American Indian or Alaska Native, non-Hispanic/Latino; 28 Asian, non-Hispanic/Latino; 31 Hispanic/Latino; 2 Native Hawaiian or other Pacific Islander, non-Hispanic/Latino; 6 Two or more races, non-Hispanic/Latino), 79 international. Average age 30. 1,270 applicants, 66% accepted, 292 enrolled. In 2010, 273 master's, 15 doctorates, 7 other advanced degrees awarded. Terminal master's awarded for partial completion of doctoral program. *Degree requirements:* For master's, thesis (for some programs); for doctorate, comprehensive exam, thesis/dissertation; for CAGS, comprehensive exam. *Entrance requirements:* For master's and CAGS, GRE General Test or Miller Analogies Test (MAT); for doctorate, GRE General Test. Additional exam requirements/recommendations for international students: Required—TOEFL, IELTS. *Application deadline:* For fall admission, 1/15 priority date for domestic and international students; for spring admission, 9/15 priority date for domestic and international students. Applications are processed on a rolling basis. Application fee: $70. Electronic applications accepted. *Expenses:* Tuition: Full-time $39,314; part-time $1228 per credit. Required fees: $40 per semester. *Financial support:* In 2010–11, 276 students received support, including 31 fellowships with full tuition reimbursements available, 16 research assistantships, 26 teaching assistantships with partial tuition reimbursements available; career-related internships or fieldwork, Federal Work-Study, and scholarships/grants also available. Support available to part-time students. Financial award applicants required to submit FAFSA. *Faculty research:* Deaf studies, social emotional learning, civic engagement and education, STEM education, pre-college educational pipelines. Total annual research expenditures: $2.6 million. *Unit head:* Dr. Hardin Coleman, Dean, 617-353-3213. *Application contact:* Dana Fernandez, Director of Enrollment, 617-353-4237, Fax: 617-353-8937, E-mail: sedgrad@bu.edu.

Bowling Green State University, Graduate College, College of Arts and Sciences, Department of Romance and Classical Studies, Program in French, Bowling Green, OH 43403. Offers French (MA); French education (MAT). Part-time programs available. *Degree requirements:* For master's, one foreign language, thesis or alternative. *Entrance requirements:* For master's, GRE General Test. Additional exam requirements/recommendations for international students: Required—TOEFL. Electronic applications accepted. *Faculty research:* Francophone literature, French cinema, business French, nineteenth and twentieth century literature.

Brigham Young University, Graduate Studies, College of Humanities, Department of French and Italian, Provo, UT 84602. Offers French studies (MA). *Faculty:* 11 full-time (1 woman). *Students:* 7 full-time (4 women), 3 part-time (2 women). Average age 28. 6 applicants, 67% accepted, 4 enrolled. In 2010, 5 master's awarded. *Degree requirements:* For master's, one foreign language, thesis. *Entrance requirements:* For master's, GRE General Test, BA in French. Additional exam requirements/recommendations for international students: Required—TOEFL. *Application deadline:* For fall admission, 2/28 for domestic and international students. Application fee: $50. Electronic applications accepted. *Expenses:* Tuition: Full-time $5580; part-time $310 per credit hour. Tuition and fees vary according to program and student's religious affiliation. *Financial support:* In 2010–11, 9 students received support, including 7 teaching assistantships (averaging $8,480 per year); research assistantships, career-related internships or fieldwork, institutionally sponsored loans, scholarships/grants, and tuition waivers (full and partial) also available. Support available to part-time students. *Faculty research:* Francophone studies, medieval literature, Provencal literature, existentialism, second language acquisition. *Unit head:* Dr. Corry L. Cropper, Department Chair, 801-422-4484, Fax: 801-422-0260, E-mail: corrycropper@gmail.com. *Application contact:* Dr. Anca M. Sprenger, Graduate Coordinator, 801-422-2306, Fax: 801-422-0260, E-mail: anca_sprenger@byu.edu.

Brooklyn College of the City University of New York, Division of Graduate Studies, Department of Modern Languages and Literature, Brooklyn, NY 11210-2889. Offers French (MA); modern languages and literature (PhD); Spanish (MA). *Students:* 1 (woman) full-time, 26 part-time (18 women); includes 18 minority (8 Black or African American, non-Hispanic/Latino; 10 Hispanic/Latino), 2 international. Average age 41. 14 applicants, 100% accepted, 11 enrolled. In 2010, 8 master's awarded. *Degree requirements:* For master's, comprehensive exam or research paper. *Entrance requirements:* For master's, 18 credits in advanced courses in Spanish, 2 letters of recommendation. Additional exam requirements/recommendations for international students: Required—TOEFL (minimum score 500 paper-based; 173 computer-based; 61 iBT). *Application deadline:* For fall admission, 8/15 for domestic students, 6/15 priority date for international students; for spring admission, 1/15 for domestic students, 12/15 priority date for international students. Applications are processed on a rolling basis. Application fee: $125. Electronic applications accepted. *Expenses:* Tuition, state resident: full-time $7360; part-time $310 per credit hour. Tuition, nonresident: full-time $13,800; part-time $575 per credit hour. Required fees: $190 per semester. *Financial support:* Federal Work-Study, institutionally sponsored loans, and scholarships/grants available. Support available to part-time students. Financial award application deadline: 5/1; financial award applicants required to submit FAFSA. *Faculty research:* Latin American contemporary novel, Caribbean female contemporary literature, nineteenth and twentieth century Spanish novel, twentieth century Mexican poetry. *Unit head:* Dr. Luigi Bonafinni, Chairperson, 718-951-5451, E-mail: luigi@brooklyn.cuny.edu. *Application contact:* Hernan Sierra, Graduate Admissions Coordinator, 718-951-4536, Fax: 718-951-4506, E-mail: grads@brooklyn.cuny.edu.

Brown University, Graduate School, Department of French Studies, Providence, RI 02912. Offers PhD, MA/PhD. *Degree requirements:* For doctorate, variable foreign language requirement, thesis/dissertation, preliminary exam.

Bryn Mawr College, Graduate School of Arts and Sciences, Department of French, Bryn Mawr, PA 19010-2899. Offers MA, PhD. Part-time programs available. *Faculty:* 3. *Students:* 5 full-time (4 women), 3 part-time (all women); includes 1 Black or African American, non-Hispanic/Latino; 1 Asian, non-Hispanic/Latino; 1 Two or more races, non-Hispanic/Latino, 1 international. 25 applicants, 76% accepted, 6 enrolled. In 2010, 2 master's awarded. *Degree requirements:* For master's, one foreign language, thesis. *Entrance requirements:* For master's, GRE General Test. Additional exam requirements/recommendations for international students: Required—TOEFL (minimum score 600 paper-based; 250 computer-based). *Application deadline:* For fall admission, 1/3 for domestic and international students. Application fee: $50. *Financial support:* In 2010–11, 1 teaching assistantship with partial tuition reimbursement (averaging $14,000 per year) was awarded; fellowships with full tuition reimbursements, scholarships/grants, tuition waivers, and tuition awards also available. Support available to part-time students. Financial award application deadline: 1/3. *Unit head:* Dr. Pim Higginson, Chair, 610-526-5388. *Application contact:* Teri Lobo, Secretary, 610-526-5074, Fax: 610-526-5076, E-mail: lrmiller@brynmawr.edu.

California State University, Fullerton, Graduate Studies, College of Humanities and Social Sciences, Department of Modern Languages and Literatures, Fullerton, CA 92834-9480. Offers French (MA); German (MA); Spanish (MA); teaching English to speakers of other languages (MS). Part-time programs available. *Students:* 44 full-time (32 women), 46 part-time (32 women); includes 18 Asian, non-Hispanic/Latino; 29 Hispanic/Latino; 1 Two or more races, non-Hispanic/Latino, 18 international. Average age 32. 126 applicants, 56% accepted, 41 enrolled. In 2010, 35 master's awarded. *Degree requirements:* For master's, comprehensive exam, thesis or alternative. *Entrance requirements:* For master's, minimum GPA of 2.5 in last 60 hours of course work, undergraduate major in a language. Application fee: $55. *Financial support:* Career-related internships or fieldwork, Federal Work-Study, institutionally sponsored loans, and scholarships/grants available. Support available to part-time students. Financial award application deadline: 3/1; financial award applicants required to submit FAFSA. *Unit head:* Dr. Janet Eyring, Chair, 657-278-3534. *Application contact:* Admissions/Applications, 657-278-2371.

California State University, Long Beach, Graduate Studies, College of Liberal Arts, Department of Romance, German, and Russian Languages and Literature, Program in French and Francophone Studies, Long Beach, CA 90840. Offers MA. Part-time programs available. *Students:* 10 full-time (5 women), 6 part-time (5 women); includes 1 Black or African American, non-Hispanic/Latino; 4 Asian, non-Hispanic/Latino; 3 Hispanic/Latino, 1 international. Average age 39. 12 applicants, 67% accepted, 8 enrolled. In 2010, 2 master's awarded. *Degree requirements:* For master's, one foreign language, comprehensive exam, thesis optional. *Entrance requirements:* For master's, BA in French. *Application deadline:* For fall admission, 7/1 for domestic students. Applications are processed on a rolling basis. Application fee: $55. Electronic applications accepted. *Financial support:* Federal Work-Study, institutionally sponsored loans, and scholarships/grants available. Financial award application deadline: 3/2. *Faculty research:* Eighteenth century encyclopedism, development of the novel, Chanson de Roland. *Unit head:* Dr. Clorinda Donato, Graduate Advisor, 562-985-4318, Fax: 562-985-4259, E-mail: cdonato@csulb.edu. *Application contact:* Dr. Clorinda Donato, Graduate Advisor, 562-985-4318, Fax: 562-985-4259, E-mail: cdonato@csulb.edu.

California State University, Los Angeles, Graduate Studies, College of Arts and Letters, Department of Modern Languages and Literatures, Los Angeles, CA 90032-8530. Offers French (MA); Spanish (MA). Part-time and evening/weekend programs available. *Faculty:* 4 full-time (all women), 2 part-time/adjunct (1 woman). *Students:* 14 full-time (10 women), 24 part-time (15 women); includes 26 minority (all Hispanic/Latino), 3 international. Average age 37. 17 applicants, 59% accepted, 10 enrolled. In 2010, 10 master's awarded. *Degree requirements:* For master's, comprehensive exam. *Entrance requirements:* Additional exam requirements/recommendations for international students: Required—TOEFL (minimum score 500 paper-based; 173 computer-based). *Application deadline:* For fall admission, 5/1 for domestic and international students. Applications are processed on a rolling basis. Application fee: $55. Electronic applications accepted. *Financial support:* Federal Work-Study available. Support available to part-time students. Financial award application deadline: 3/1. *Faculty research:* French literature, language teaching and methodology, Spanish poetry, Spanish-American fiction and poetry. *Unit head:* Dr. Sachiko Matsunaga, Chair, 323-343-4230, Fax: 323-343-4234, E-mail: smatsun@calstatela.edu. *Application contact:* Dr. Alan Muchlinski, Dean of Graduate Studies, 323-343-3820, Fax: 323-343-5653, E-mail: amuchli@exchange.calstatela.edu.

California State University, Sacramento, Graduate Studies, College of Social Sciences and Interdisciplinary Studies, Liberal Arts Program, Sacramento, CA 95819. Offers French (MA); German (MA); Spanish (MA); theater arts (MA). *Degree requirements:* For master's, writing proficiency exam. *Entrance requirements:* Additional exam requirements/recommendations for international students: Required—TOEFL. Electronic applications accepted.

Carleton University, Faculty of Graduate Studies, Faculty of Arts and Social Sciences, Department of French, Ottawa, ON K1S 5B6, Canada. Offers MA. *Degree requirements:* For master's, thesis optional. *Entrance requirements:* For master's, honors degree. *Faculty research:* French, French Canadian and Acadian literatures and linguistics, Francophone studies, rhetorical studies.

Case Western Reserve University, School of Graduate Studies, Department of Modern Languages and Literatures, Program in French, Cleveland, OH 44106. Offers MA. Part-time programs available. *Faculty:* 5 full-time (4 women), 2 part-time/adjunct (1 woman). *Students:* 1 (woman) full-time. 2 applicants, 100% accepted, 0 enrolled.Terminal master's awarded for partial completion of doctoral program. *Degree requirements:* For master's, one foreign language, comprehensive exam, thesis or alternative. *Entrance requirements:* For master's, GRE General Test, writing sample. Additional exam requirements/recommendations for international students: Required—TOEFL (minimum score 550 paper-based; 213 computer-based; 79 iBT). *Application deadline:* For fall admission, 3/1 priority date for domestic students. Applications are processed on a rolling basis. Application fee: $50. Electronic applications accepted. *Financial support:* Fellowships, institutionally sponsored loans and tuition waivers (full) available. Financial award application deadline: 3/1; financial award applicants required to submit FAFSA. *Faculty research:* Eighteenth- and nineteenth-century literature (novel, poetry, drama), literary theory, women's studies, cultural criticism. *Application contact:* Marie Lathers, Director, Graduate Studies (French), 216-368-3071, Fax: 216-368-2216, E-mail: mhl5@case.edu.

Central Connecticut State University, School of Graduate Studies, School of Arts and Sciences, Department of Modern Languages, Program in Modern Language, New Britain, CT 06050-4010. Offers French (MA, Certificate); German (Certificate); Italian (Certificate); modern language (MA); Spanish language and Hispanic culture (MA). Part-time and evening/weekend programs available. *Students:* 8 full-time (6 women), 32 part-time (28 women); includes 15 minority (all Hispanic/Latino), 1 international. Average age 38. 22 applicants, 95% accepted, 10 enrolled. In 2010, 17 master's awarded. *Degree requirements:* For master's, one foreign language, comprehensive exam, thesis or alternative; for Certificate, qualifying exam. *Entrance requirements:* For master's, minimum undergraduate GPA of 2.7, 24 credits of undergraduate courses in either Italian or Spanish. Additional exam requirements/recommendations for international students: Required—TOEFL. *Application deadline:* For fall admission, 7/1 for domestic students; for spring admission, 12/1 for domestic students. Applications are processed on a rolling basis. Application fee: $50. Electronic applications accepted. *Expenses:* Tuition, area resident: Full-time $5012; part-time $470 per credit. Tuition, state resident: full-time $7518; part-time $482 per credit. Tuition, nonresident: full-time $13,962; part-time $482 per credit. Required fees: $3772. One-time fee: $62 part-time. *Faculty research:* Twentieth century French theater, seventeenth century French literature, French Middle Ages.

Cleveland State University, College of Graduate Studies, College of Liberal Arts and Social Sciences, Department of Modern Languages, Cleveland, OH 44115. Offers French (M Ed); Spanish (M Ed, MA), including language and linguistics (MA), Latin American studies (MA), peninsular studies (MA), Spanish (MA). Part-time and evening/weekend programs available. *Faculty:* 12 full-time (9 women). *Students:* 7 full-time (4 women), 9 part-time (7 women); includes 1 Black or African American, non-Hispanic/Latino; 1 Asian, non-Hispanic/Latino; 3 Hispanic/Latino; 1 Two or more races, non-Hispanic/Latino, 2 international. Average age 37. 11 applicants, 100% accepted, 8 enrolled. In 2010, 9 master's awarded. *Degree requirements:* For master's, one foreign language, comprehensive exam, thesis optional, study abroad. *Entrance requirements:* For master's, undergraduate major in Spanish or equivalent, essay in Spanish, writing sample. Additional exam requirements/recommendations for international students: Required—TOEFL (minimum score 525 paper-based; 197 computer-based). *Application deadline:* For fall admission, 7/25 priority date for domestic students; for spring admission, 12/15 priority date for domestic students. Applications are processed on a rolling basis. Application fee: $30. Electronic applications accepted. *Expenses:* Tuition, state resident: full-time $8447; part-time $469 per credit hour. Tuition, nonresident: full-time $16,020; part-time $890 per credit hour. Required fees: $50. *Financial support:* In 2010–11, 6 students received support, including 6 teaching assistantships with full tuition reimbursements available (averaging $7,030 per year); Federal Work-Study also available. *Faculty research:* Second language acquisition, sociolinguistics, contemporary Spanish novel, Arabic diaspora in Latin America, border literature. *Unit head:* Dr. Tama L. Engelking, Chairperson, 216-523-7175, Fax: 216-687-4650, E-mail: t.engelking@csuohio.edu. *Application contact:* Dr. Antonio Medina-Rivera, Graduate Director, 216-523-7168, Fax: 216-687-4650, E-mail: a.medinarivera@csuohio.edu.

Columbia University, Graduate School of Arts and Sciences, Division of Humanities, Department of French and Romance Philology, New York, NY 10027. Offers French and Romance philology (M Phil, PhD); Romance languages (MA). Part-time programs available. *Degree requirements:* For master's, one foreign language, thesis, written exam; for doctorate, 2 foreign languages, thesis/dissertation. *Entrance requirements:* For master's and doctorate, GRE General Test, knowledge of Latin, writing sample. Additional exam requirements/recommendations for international students: Required—TOEFL. *Faculty research:* Theory of literature, literary semiotics, poetics.

Columbia University, Graduate School of Arts and Sciences, Program in French Cultural Studies, New York, NY 10027. Offers MA. Program offered in Paris, France. *Expenses:* Contact institution.

Concordia University, School of Graduate Studies, Faculty of Arts and Science, Department of Études Françaises, Montréal, QC H3G 1M8, Canada. Offers écriture (Certificate); anglais-français en langue et techniques de localisation (Certificate); littératures francophones et résonances médiatiques (MA); traductologie (MA); translation (Diploma). *Degree requirements:* For other advanced degree, one foreign language.

Cornell University, Graduate School, Graduate Fields of Arts and Sciences, Field of Romance Studies, Ithaca, NY 14853-0001. Offers French linguistics (PhD); French literature (PhD); Hispanic literature (PhD); Italian linguistics (PhD); Italian literature (PhD); Romance linguistics (PhD); Spanish linguistics (PhD). *Faculty:* 30 full-time (13 women). *Students:* 56 full-time (27 women); includes 11 Hispanic/Latino, 23 international. Average age 28. 95 applicants, 22% accepted, 10 enrolled. In 2010, 5 doctorates awarded. *Degree requirements:* For doctorate, 2 foreign languages, comprehensive exam, thesis/dissertation. *Entrance requirements:* For doctorate, GRE General Test, sample of written work, 3 letters of recommendation. Additional exam requirements/recommendations for international students: Required—TOEFL (minimum score 550 paper-based; 213 computer-based; 77 iBT). *Application deadline:* For fall admission, 1/15 for domestic students. Application fee: $80. Electronic applications accepted. *Expenses:* Tuition: Full-time $29,500. Required fees: $76. Tuition and fees vary according to degree level and program. *Financial support:* In 2010–11, 18 fellowships with full tuition reimbursements, 34 teaching assistantships with full tuition reimbursements were awarded; research assistantships with full tuition reimbursements, institutionally sponsored loans, scholarships/grants, health care benefits, tuition waivers (full and partial), and unspecified assistantships also available. Financial award applicants required to submit FAFSA. *Faculty research:* Literary theory, Hispanic studies, French studies, gender studies. *Unit head:* Director of Graduate Studies, 607-255-8222. *Application contact:* Graduate Field Assistant, 607-255-4246, E-mail: romance_studies@cornell.edu.

Dalhousie University, Faculty of Arts and Social Science, Department of French, Halifax, NS B3H 4R2, Canada. Offers MA, PhD. *Entrance requirements:* Additional exam requirements/recommendations for international students: Required—TOEFL, IELTS, CANTEST, CAEL, or Michigan English Language Assessment Battery. Electronic applications accepted. *Faculty research:* Literature, linguistics, French civilization, French and Francophone literature of all periods, translation and cultural studies.

Drew University, Caspersen School of Graduate Studies, Program in Education, Madison, NJ 07940-1493. Offers biology (MAT); chemistry (MAT); English (MAT); French (MAT); Italian (MAT); math (MAT); physics (MAT); social studies (MAT); Spanish (MAT); theatre arts (MAT). Part-time programs available. *Entrance requirements:* For master's, transcripts, personal statement, recommendations. Additional exam requirements/recommendations for international students: Required—TOEFL, TWE. *Expenses:* Contact institution.

Duke University, Graduate School, Department of Romance Studies, Durham, NC 27708. Offers French (PhD); Spanish (PhD); JD/AM. *Faculty:* 26 full-time. *Students:* 43 full-time (29 women); includes 2 Black or African American, non-Hispanic/Latino; 6 Hispanic/Latino, 15 international. 49 applicants, 20% accepted, 8 enrolled. In 2010, 6 doctorates awarded. *Degree requirements:* For doctorate, 2 foreign languages, thesis/dissertation. *Entrance requirements:* For doctorate, GRE General Test. Additional exam requirements/recommendations for international students: Required—TOEFL (minimum score 550 paper-based; 213 computer-based; 83 iBT), IELTS (minimum score 7). *Application deadline:* For fall admission, 12/8 priority date for domestic and international students. Application fee: $75. Electronic applications accepted. *Financial support:* Fellowships, research assistantships, teaching assistantships, Federal Work-Study available. Financial award application deadline: 12/8. *Unit head:* Esther Gabara, Director of Graduate Studies, 919-660-3114, Fax: 919-684-4029, E-mail: denise@duke.edu. *Application contact:* Elizabeth Hutton, Director of Admissions, 919-684-3913, Fax: 919-684-2277, E-mail: elizabeth.hutton@duke.edu.

Eastern Michigan University, Graduate School, College of Arts and Sciences, Department of World Languages, Programs in Foreign Languages, Ypsilanti, MI 48197. Offers French (MA); German (MA); German for business (Graduate Certificate); Hispanic language and cultures (Graduate Certificate); Japanese business practices (Graduate Certificate); Spanish (MA). Part-time and evening/weekend programs available. Postbaccalaureate distance learning degree programs offered (minimal on-campus study). *Students:* 1 (woman) full-time, 12 part-time (11 women); includes 5 minority (1 Black or African American, non-Hispanic/Latino; 1 Asian, non-Hispanic/Latino; 3 Hispanic/Latino), 1 international. Average age 44. In 2010, 8 master's awarded. *Degree requirements:* For master's, one foreign language, thesis optional. *Entrance requirements:* Additional exam requirements/recommendations for international students: Required—TOEFL. *Application deadline:* Applications are processed on a rolling basis. Application fee: $35. *Financial support:* Fellowships, research assistantships with full tuition reimbursements, teaching assistantships with full tuition reimbursements, career-related internships or fieldwork, Federal Work-Study, institutionally sponsored loans, scholarships/grants, tuition waivers (partial), and unspecified assistantships available. Support available to part-time students. Financial award applicants required to submit FAFSA. *Application contact:* Dr. Genevieve Peden, Program Advisor, 734-487-1498, Fax: 734-487-3411, E-mail: gpeden@emich.edu.

Emory University, Laney Graduate School, Department of Comparative Literature, Atlanta, GA 30322-1100. Offers comparative literature (PhD); English (Certificate); French (Certificate); Middle Eastern studies (PhD); philosophy (Certificate); psychoanalytic studies (PhD); religion (PhD); Spanish (Certificate); women studies (Certificate). *Degree requirements:* For doctorate, 2 foreign languages, comprehensive exam, thesis/dissertation. *Entrance requirements:* For doctorate, GRE General Test, minimum GPA of 3.0. Additional exam requirements/recommendations for international students: Required—TOEFL. Electronic applications accepted. *Expenses:* Tuition: Full-time $33,800. Required fees: $1300. *Faculty research:* Literary theory, psychoanalysis trauma and testimony, literature and religion, literature and technology, literature and philosophy, politics and global culture, literature and aesthetics.

Emory University, Laney Graduate School, Department of French and Italian, Atlanta, GA 30322-1100. Offers French (PhD); French and educational studies (PhD). *Degree requirements:* For doctorate, one foreign language, comprehensive exam, thesis/dissertation. *Entrance requirements:* For doctorate, GRE General Test. Electronic applications accepted. *Expenses:* Tuition: Full-time $33,800. Required fees: $1300. *Faculty research:* French literature through multidisciplinary critical approaches, second language acquisition theory.

Florida Atlantic University, Dorothy F. Schmidt College of Arts and Letters, Department of Languages, Linguistics, and Comparative Literature, Boca Raton, FL 33431-0991. Offers comparative literature (MA); French (MA); linguistics (MA); Spanish (MA). Part-time programs available. *Faculty:* 30 full-time (24 women), 5 part-time/adjunct (all women). *Students:* 30 full-time (22 women), 19 part-time (15 women); includes 24 minority (4 Black or African American, non-Hispanic/Latino; 20 Hispanic/Latino), 6 international. Average age 34. 42 applicants, 57% accepted, 20 enrolled. In 2010, 5 master's awarded. *Degree requirements:* For master's, one foreign language, comprehensive exam, thesis optional. *Entrance requirements:* For master's, GRE General Test, minimum GPA of 3.0. *Application deadline:* For fall admission, 7/1 priority date for domestic students, 2/15 for international students; for spring admission, 11/1 for domestic students, 7/15 for international students. Applications are processed on a rolling basis. Application fee: $30. *Expenses:* Tuition, area resident: Part-time $319.96 per credit. Tuition, state resident: part-time $319.96 per credit. Tuition, nonresident: part-time $926.42 per credit. *Financial support:* Fellowships, research assistantships, teaching assistantships with partial tuition reimbursements, Federal Work-Study and tuition waivers (partial) available. Support available to part-time students. Financial award application deadline: 4/1. *Faculty research:* Modern European studies, modern Latin America, medieval Europe. *Unit head:* Dr. Michael Horswell, Chair, 561-297-3860, Fax: 561-297-2756, E-mail: horswell@fau.edu. *Application contact:* Dr. Emily Stockard, Associate Dean, 561-297-2817, Fax: 561-297-2744, E-mail: stockard@fau.edu.

Florida State University, The Graduate School, College of Arts and Sciences, Department of Modern Languages, Program in French, Tallahassee, FL 32306. Offers MA, PhD. *Faculty:* 9 full-time (4 women). *Students:* 21 full-time (20 women), 2 part-time (1 woman); includes 2 Black or African American, non-Hispanic/Latino; 2 Asian, non-Hispanic/Latino. Average age 25. 22 applicants, 64% accepted, 12 enrolled. In 2010, 1 master's awarded. Terminal master's awarded for partial completion of doctoral program. *Degree requirements:* For master's, thesis optional; for doctorate, thesis/dissertation, reading knowledge of French and 2 other languages. *Entrance requirements:* For master's and doctorate, GRE General Test, minimum GPA of 3.0. Additional exam requirements/recommendations for international students: Required—TOEFL (minimum score 550 paper-based; 213 computer-based). *Application deadline:* For fall admission, 2/1 for domestic and international students. Applications are processed on a rolling basis. Application fee: $30. Electronic applications accepted. *Expenses:* Tuition, state resident: full-time $8238.24. *Financial support:* In 2010–11, 1 fellowship with partial tuition reimbursement (averaging $16,500 per year), research assistantships with partial tuition reimbursements (averaging $9,500 per year), 17 teaching assistantships with partial tuition reimbursements (averaging $11,100 per year) were awarded. Financial award application deadline: 1/15; financial award applicants required to submit FAFSA. *Faculty research:* Twentieth century European novel, Renaissance and Middle Ages literature, second language acquisition. *Application contact:* Wendy E. Pigott, Graduate Academic Coordinator, 850-644-8397, Fax: 850-644-0524, E-mail: wpigott@fsu.edu.

Georgia State University, College of Arts and Sciences, Department of Modern and Classical Languages, Program in French, Atlanta, GA 30302-3083. Offers MA. Part-time and evening/weekend programs available. *Degree requirements:* For master's, one foreign language, thesis or alternative, general exam. *Entrance requirements:* For master's, GRE General Test. Additional exam requirements/recommendations for international students: Required—TOEFL. Electronic applications accepted. *Faculty research:* French literature of the sixteenth-, eighteenth-, nineteenth-, and twentieth-centuries.

Georgia State University, College of Arts and Sciences, Department of Modern and Classical Languages, Program in Translation and Interpretation, Atlanta, GA 30302-3083. Offers French (Certificate); German (Certificate); Spanish (Certificate). Electronic applications accepted.

Graduate School and University Center of the City University of New York, Graduate Studies, Program in French, New York, NY 10016-4039. Offers PhD. *Degree requirements:* For doctorate, 2 foreign languages, thesis/dissertation. *Entrance requirements:* For doctorate,

French

Graduate School and University Center of the City University of New York (continued)

GRE General Test. Additional exam requirements/recommendations for international students: Required—TOEFL. Electronic applications accepted.

Harvard University, Graduate School of Arts and Sciences, Department of Romance Languages and Literatures, Cambridge, MA 02138. Offers French (AM, PhD); Italian (AM, PhD); Portuguese (AM, PhD); Spanish (AM, PhD). Terminal master's awarded for partial completion of doctoral program. *Degree requirements:* For master's, 2 foreign languages; for doctorate, 2 foreign languages, thesis/dissertation. *Entrance requirements:* For master's and doctorate, GRE General Test, sample of written work. Additional exam requirements/recommendations for international students: Required—TOEFL. *Expenses:* Tuition: Full-time $34,976. Required fees: $1166. Full-time tuition and fees vary according to program.

Hofstra University, School of Education, Health, and Human Services, Programs in Teaching—Secondary Education, Hempstead, NY 11549. Offers business education (MS Ed); English education (MA, MS Ed); foreign language and TESOL (MS Ed); foreign language education (MA, MS Ed), including French, German, Russian, Spanish; mathematics education (MA, MS Ed); science education (MA, MS Ed), including biology, chemistry, earth science, geology, physics; secondary education (Advanced Certificate); social studies education (MA, MS Ed). Part-time and evening/weekend programs available. Postbaccalaureate distance learning degree programs offered (minimal on-campus study). *Students:* 114 full-time (74 women), 61 part-time (36 women); includes 7 Black or African American, non-Hispanic/Latino; 1 American Indian or Alaska Native, non-Hispanic/Latino; 8 Asian, non-Hispanic/Latino; 10 Hispanic/Latino; 1 Native Hawaiian or other Pacific Islander, non-Hispanic/Latino. Average age 27. 153 applicants, 90% accepted, 59 enrolled. In 2010, 102 master's, 11 other advanced degrees awarded. *Degree requirements:* For master's, one foreign language, comprehensive exam (for some programs), thesis (for some programs), exit project, electronic portfolio, student teaching, fieldwork, curriculum project; for Advanced Certificate, 3 foreign languages, comprehensive exam (for some programs), thesis project. *Entrance requirements:* For master's, 2 letters of recommendation, teacher certification (MA), essay; for Advanced Certificate, 2 letters of recommendation, essay, interview and/or portfolio. Additional exam requirements/recommendations for international students: Required—TOEFL (minimum score 550 paper-based; 213 computer-based; 80 iBT). *Application deadline:* Applications are processed on a rolling basis. Application fee: $70 ($75 for international students). Electronic applications accepted. *Expenses:* Tuition: Full-time $18,000; part-time $1000 per credit hour. Required fees: $970; $145 per term. Tuition and fees vary according to program. *Financial support:* In 2010–11, 108 students received support, including 14 fellowships with full and partial tuition reimbursements available (averaging $3,943 per year), 1 research assistantship with full and partial tuition reimbursement available (averaging $6,574 per year); career-related internships or fieldwork, Federal Work-Study, institutionally sponsored loans, scholarships/grants, tuition waivers (full and partial), unspecified assistantships, and scholarships also available. Support available to part-time students. Financial award applicants required to submit FAFSA. *Faculty research:* Appropriate content and pedagogy in secondary school disciplines, adolescent development, secondary school organization, alternative secondary school programs. *Unit head:* Dr. Esther Fusco, Chairperson, 516-463-7704, Fax: 516-463-6196, E-mail: catezf@hofstra.edu. *Application contact:* Carol Drummer, Dean of Graduate Admissions, 516-463-4876, Fax: 516-463-4664, E-mail: gradstudent@hofstra.edu.

Howard University, Graduate School, Department of Modern Languages and Literatures, Washington, DC 20059-0002. Offers French (MA); Spanish (MA). Part-time programs available. *Degree requirements:* For master's, one foreign language, comprehensive exam, thesis. *Entrance requirements:* For master's, GRE General Test, writing samples in English and French or Spanish. *Faculty research:* African literature in French, Spanish linguistics, Spanish Peninsular literature, Spanish sociolinguistics.

Hunter College of the City University of New York, Graduate School, School of Arts and Sciences, Department of Romance Languages, Program in French, New York, NY 10021-5085. Offers French (MA); French education (MA). Part-time and evening/weekend programs available. *Faculty:* 8 full-time (4 women). *Students:* 7 part-time (5 women); includes 1 Black or African American, non-Hispanic/Latino; 1 Hispanic/Latino. Average age 31. 8 applicants, 75% accepted, 2 enrolled. In 2010, 2 master's awarded. *Degree requirements:* For master's, 2 foreign languages, comprehensive exam, thesis optional. *Entrance requirements:* For master's, GRE General Test, GRE Subject Test, ability to read, speak, and write French; interview. Additional exam requirements/recommendations for international students: Required—TOEFL. *Application deadline:* For fall admission, 4/1 for domestic students, 2/1 for international students; for spring admission, 11/1 for domestic students, 9/1 for international students. Application fee: $125. *Financial support:* Fellowships, Federal Work-Study, scholarships/grants, and tuition waivers (partial) available. Support available to part-time students. Financial award application deadline: 4/15. *Faculty research:* Contemporary French theater, Villiers-dell Isle-Adam, Voltaire, medieval folklore, fin-de-siécle. *Unit head:* Prof. Marlene Barloum, Graduate Advisor, 212-650-3511, E-mail: mbarloum@hunter.cuny.edu. *Application contact:* William Zlata, Director for Graduate Admissions, 212-772-4482, Fax: 212-650-3336, E-mail: admissions@hunter.cuny.edu.

Illinois State University, Graduate School, College of Arts and Sciences, Department of Foreign Languages, Literatures and Cultures, Normal, IL 61790-2200. Offers French (MA); French and German (MA); French and Spanish (MA); German (MA); German and Spanish (MA); Spanish (MA). *Degree requirements:* For master's, variable foreign language requirement, comprehensive exam, 1 term of residency. *Entrance requirements:* For master's, GRE General Test, minimum GPA of 2.8 in last 60 hours of course work.

Indiana University Bloomington, University Graduate School, College of Arts and Sciences, Department of French and Italian, Bloomington, IN 47405-7000. Offers French (MA, PhD), including French instruction (MA), French linguistics, French literature; Italian (MA, PhD). Part-time programs available. *Faculty:* 19 full-time (7 women). *Students:* 69 full-time (43 women), 5 part-time (2 women); includes 2 minority (1 American Indian or Alaska Native, non-Hispanic/Latino; 1 Hispanic/Latino), 23 international. Average age 30. 73 applicants, 67% accepted, 14 enrolled. In 2010, 14 master's, 6 doctorates awarded. Terminal master's awarded for partial completion of doctoral program. *Degree requirements:* For master's, one foreign language, comprehensive exam, thesis optional; for doctorate, 2 foreign languages, comprehensive exam, thesis/dissertation. *Entrance requirements:* For master's and doctorate, GRE General Test. Additional exam requirements/recommendations for international students: Required—TOEFL (minimum score 550 paper-based; 213 computer-based; 79 iBT). *Application deadline:* For fall admission, 1/15 priority date for domestic students, 12/1 priority date for international students; for spring admission, 9/1 priority date for domestic and international students. Application fee: $55 ($65 for international students). Electronic applications accepted. *Financial support:* In 2010–11, 2 fellowships with partial tuition reimbursements (averaging $14,000 per year), 4 research assistantships with partial tuition reimbursements (averaging $13,913 per year), 20 teaching assistantships with partial tuition reimbursements (averaging $12,944 per year) were awarded. Financial award application deadline: 1/15. *Faculty research:* All periods of French and Italian literature and various areas of French linguistics, including the novel and political theory, literature and fine arts, literary theory, postcolonialism, French-Creole studies, French literature of Africa and its Diaspora, humanism, medieval folklore and mythology, humor in medieval and Renaissance literature, cinema Old Occitan and Old French, emigration, second language acquisition, syntax, sociolinguistics, phonology, lexicography. *Unit head:* Prof. Emanuel Mickel, Interim Chairman, 812-855-5458, Fax: 812-855-8877, E-mail: fritchr@indiana.edu. *Application contact:* Jocelyn Karlan, Secretary, 812-855-1088, Fax: 812-855-8877, E-mail: fritgs@indiana.edu.

The Johns Hopkins University, Zanvyl Krieger School of Arts and Sciences, Department of German and Romance Languages and Literatures, Baltimore, MD 21218-2699. Offers French (PhD); German (PhD); Italian (PhD); romance languages (PhD); Spanish (PhD). *Faculty:* 31 full-time (20 women), 1 part-time/adjunct (0 women). *Students:* 52 full-time (31 women); includes 7 minority (6 Hispanic/Latino; 1 Two or more races, non-Hispanic/Latino), 20 international. Average age 30. 51 applicants, 37% accepted, 19 enrolled. In 2010, 6 doctorates awarded. *Degree requirements:* For doctorate, 2 foreign languages, thesis/dissertation. *Entrance requirements:* For doctorate, GRE General Test. Additional exam requirements/recommendations for international students: Required—TOEFL (minimum score 600 paper-based; 250 computer-based; 100 iBT), IELTS. *Application deadline:* For fall admission, 12/30 for domestic and international students. Application fee: $75. Electronic applications accepted. *Financial support:* In 2010–11, 40 fellowships with full tuition reimbursements (averaging $17,000 per year), 2 research assistantships with full tuition reimbursements (averaging $17,000 per year), 19 teaching assistantships with full tuition reimbursements (averaging $17,000 per year) were awarded; institutionally sponsored loans also available. *Faculty research:* Nineteenth century French prose and poetry, genetic theory and criticism; twentieth century Latin American literature and film; medieval and Renaissance Italian literature; gender and queer theory in German literature; the ideology of Baroque and Neobaroque aesthetics. *Unit head:* Dr. William Egginton, Chair, 410-516-7510, Fax: 410-516-5358, E-mail: egginton@jhu.edu. *Application contact:* Rebecca Swisdak, Graduate Administrative Coordinator, 410-516-7227, Fax: 410-516-5358, E-mail: rswisdak@jhu.edu.

Kansas State University, Graduate School, College of Arts and Sciences, Department of Modern Languages, Manhattan, KS 66506. Offers French (MA); German (MA); Spanish (MA). Part-time and evening/weekend programs available. Postbaccalaureate distance learning degree programs offered (minimal on-campus study). *Degree requirements:* For master's, thesis optional. *Entrance requirements:* For master's, teaching certificate. Additional exam requirements/recommendations for international students: Required—TOEFL (minimum score 560 paper-based). Electronic applications accepted. *Faculty research:* Second language acquisitions; Chicano literature; Francophone literature; cultural studies; German, French, Spanish, and Spanish-American literature from the Middle Ages to the modern era.

Kent State University, College of Arts and Sciences, Department of Modern and Classical Language Studies, Kent, OH 44242-0001. Offers French literature (MA); French, Spanish, German and Latin pedagogy (MA); German literature (MA); Spanish literature (MA); translation (MA), including French, German, Japanese, Russian, Spanish; translation studies (PhD). Part-time and evening/weekend programs available. *Degree requirements:* For master's, one foreign language, comprehensive exam (for some programs), thesis (for some programs); for doctorate, comprehensive exam, thesis/dissertation (for some programs). *Entrance requirements:* For master's, minimum GPA of 3.0, writing sample, audio tape or CD; for doctorate, 3 recommendations. Additional exam requirements/recommendations for international students: Required—TOEFL (minimum score 197 computer-based). Electronic applications accepted. *Expenses:* Tuition, state resident: full-time $7866; part-time $437 per credit hour. Tuition, nonresident: full-time $14,022; part-time $779 per credit hour. *Faculty research:* Literature, pedagogy, applied linguistics, translation studies.

Louisiana State University and Agricultural and Mechanical College, Graduate School, College of Humanities and Social Sciences, Department of French Studies, Baton Rouge, LA 70803. Offers French literature and linguistics (MA, PhD). *Faculty:* 15 full-time (6 women). *Students:* 23 full-time (14 women), 5 part-time (3 women); includes 2 Hispanic/Latino, 7 international. Average age 30. 13 applicants, 54% accepted, 5 enrolled. In 2010, 5 master's, 2 doctorates awarded. Terminal master's awarded for partial completion of doctoral program. *Degree requirements:* For master's, thesis optional; for doctorate, 2 foreign languages, thesis/dissertation. *Entrance requirements:* For master's and doctorate, GRE General Test, minimum GPA of 3.0. Additional exam requirements/recommendations for international students: Required—TOEFL (minimum score 550 paper-based; 213 computer-based; 79 iBT) or IELTS (minimum score 6.5). *Application deadline:* For fall admission, 1/25 priority date for domestic students, 5/15 for international students; for spring admission, 10/15 for international students. Applications are processed on a rolling basis. Application fee: $50 ($70 for international students). Electronic applications accepted. *Financial support:* In 2010–11, 24 students received support, including 1 fellowship with full tuition reimbursement available (averaging $13,108 per year), 2 research assistantships with partial tuition reimbursements available (averaging $19,500 per year), 18 teaching assistantships with partial tuition reimbursements available (averaging $16,667 per year); career-related internships or fieldwork, Federal Work-Study, institutionally sponsored loans, health care benefits, tuition waivers (full), and unspecified assistantships also available. Support available to part-time students. Financial award application deadline: 7/1; financial award applicants required to submit FAFSA. *Faculty research:* French literature of all periods, modern critical theory, linguistics, cinema, Francophonia. Total annual research expenditures: $39,804. *Unit head:* Dr. Greg Stone, Chair, 225-578-6627, Fax: 225-578-6628, E-mail: stone@lsu.edu. *Application contact:* Dr. Alexandre Lupin, Adviser, 225-578-6627, Fax: 225-578-6628, E-mail: frleup@lsu.edu.

McGill University, Faculty of Graduate and Postdoctoral Studies, Faculty of Arts, Department of French Language and Literature, Montréal, QC H3A 2T5, Canada. Offers MA, PhD.

McMaster University, School of Graduate Studies, Faculty of Humanities, Department of French, Hamilton, ON L8S 4M2, Canada. Offers MA. Part-time and evening/weekend programs available. *Degree requirements:* For master's, thesis or alternative. *Entrance requirements:* For master's, honors degree in French, minimum B+ average. Additional exam requirements/recommendations for international students: Required—TOEFL (minimum score 580 paper-based; 237 computer-based). *Faculty research:* Medieval literature, eighteenth- and nineteenth-century literature, twentieth-century French and Francophone literature, linguistics.

Memorial University of Newfoundland, School of Graduate Studies, Department of French and Spanish, St. John's, NL A1C 5S7, Canada. Offers French studies (MA). Part-time programs available. *Degree requirements:* For master's, one foreign language, thesis. *Entrance requirements:* For master's, honors degree (minimum 2nd class standing). Electronic applications accepted. *Faculty research:* French and French-Canadian literature, literary theory, linguistics, philosophy, translation, Francophone culture.

Miami University, Graduate School, College of Arts and Science, Department of French and Italian, Oxford, OH 45056. Offers French (MA). Part-time programs available. *Students:* 6 full-time (3 women), 3 international. Average age 24. In 2010, 7 master's awarded. *Entrance requirements:* For master's, GRE General Test (recommended), minimum undergraduate GPA of 3.0 during previous 2 years or 2.75 overall. Additional exam requirements/recommendations for international students: Required—TOEFL. Application fee: $50. *Expenses:* Tuition, state resident: full-time $11,616; part-time $484 per credit hour. Tuition, nonresident: full-time $25,656; part-time $1069 per credit hour. Required fees: $528. *Financial support:* Fellowships with full tuition reimbursements, research assistantships, teaching assistantships, Federal Work-Study, health care benefits, tuition waivers (full), and unspecified assistantships available. Financial award application deadline: 3/1; financial award applicants required to submit FAFSA. *Unit head:* Dr. Jonathan Strauss, Chair, 513-529-7508, E-mail: strausja@muohio.edu. *Application contact:* Dr. Elisabeth Hodges, Graduate Director, 513-529-5809, E-mail: hodgesed@muohio.edu.

Michigan State University, The Graduate School, College of Arts and Letters, Department of French, Classics, and Italian, East Lansing, MI 48824. Offers French (MA); French language and literature (PhD). *Entrance requirements:* Additional exam requirements/recommendations for international students: Required—TOEFL. Electronic applications accepted.

Middlebury College, Language Schools, French School, Middlebury, VT 05753-6002. Offers MA, DML. *Faculty:* 17 full-time (7 women). *Students:* 95 full-time (70 women); includes 5 Black or African American, non-Hispanic/Latino; 5 Asian, non-Hispanic/Latino; 8 Hispanic/Latino. Average age 30. 191 applicants, 75% accepted. In 2010, 32 master's, 2 doctorates awarded. *Degree requirements:* For master's, one foreign language; for doctorate, 2 foreign languages, comprehensive exam, thesis/dissertation, residence abroad, teaching experience. *Entrance requirements:* For master's, placement test, 3 letters of recommendation, writing sample; for doctorate, 1st and 2nd language placement exam, 3 letters of recommendation, writing sample. *Application deadline:* Applications are processed on a rolling basis. Application fee: $65. Electronic applications accepted. *Financial support:* Scholarships/grants available. Financial award applicants required to submit FAFSA. *Unit head:* Dr. Aline Germain-Rutherford, Director, 802-443-5526, Fax: 802-443-2075. *Application contact:* Sheila Schwaneflugel, Coordinator, 802-443-5526, Fax: 802-443-2075, E-mail: keim@middlebury.edu.

Millersville University of Pennsylvania, College of Graduate and Professional Studies, School of Humanities and Social Sciences, Department of Foreign Languages, Program in French, Millersville, PA 17551-0302. Offers M Ed, MA. Part-time programs available. *Faculty:* 8 full-time (4 women), 4 part-time/adjunct (1 woman). *Students:* 1 full-time (0 women), 1 (woman) part-time. Average age 41. 1 applicant, 100% accepted, 1 enrolled. In 2010, 1 master's awarded. *Degree requirements:* For master's, comprehensive exam, thesis optional. *Entrance requirements:* For master's, 3 letters of recommendation. Additional exam requirements/recommendations for international students: Required—TOEFL (minimum score 500 paper-based; 183 computer-based; 65 iBT) or IELTS (minimum score 6). *Application deadline:* For fall admission, 1/15 priority date for domestic and international students; for winter admission, 10/1 priority date for domestic and international students; for spring admission, 10/1 priority date for domestic and international students. Applications are processed on a rolling basis. Application fee: $40 ($50 for international students). Electronic applications accepted. *Expenses:* Tuition, state resident: full-time $6966; part-time $387 per credit. Tuition, nonresident: full-time $11,146; part-time $619 per credit. Required fees: $1829.50; $88 per credit. One-time fee: $60 part-time. Tuition and fees vary according to course load. *Financial support:* Research assistantships, institutionally sponsored loans and unspecified assistantships available. Support available to part-time students. Financial award application deadline: 3/15; financial award applicants required to submit FAFSA. *Unit head:* Dr. Christine M. Gaudry-Hudson, Coordinator of Foreign Language Graduate Program, 717-872-3663, E-mail: christine.gaudry-hudson@millersville.edu. *Application contact:* Dr. Victor S. DeSantis, Dean of Graduate Studies, 717-872-3099, Fax: 717-872-3453, E-mail: victor.desantis@millersville.edu.

Minnesota State University Mankato, College of Graduate Studies, College of Arts and Humanities, Department of Modern Languages, Program in French, Mankato, MN 56001. Offers MAT, MS. *Students:* 1 (woman) full-time, 1 (woman) part-time. *Degree requirements:* For master's, one foreign language, comprehensive exam, thesis or alternative. *Entrance requirements:* For master's, minimum GPA of 3.0 during previous 2 years. Additional exam requirements/recommendations for international students: Required—TOEFL. *Application deadline:* For fall admission, 7/1 priority date for domestic students; for spring admission, 11/1 for domestic students. Applications are processed on a rolling basis. Application fee: $40. Electronic applications accepted. *Financial support:* Research assistantships, teaching assistantships with full tuition reimbursements, unspecified assistantships available. Financial award application deadline: 3/15; financial award applicants required to submit FAFSA. *Unit head:* Dr. Evan Bibbee, Graduate Coordinator, 507-389-6250. *Application contact:* 507-389-2321, E-mail: grad@mnsu.edu.

Mississippi State University, College of Arts and Sciences, Department of Foreign Languages, Mississippi State, MS 39762. Offers foreign language (MA), including French, German, Spanish. Part-time programs available. *Faculty:* 8 full-time (3 women). *Students:* 10 full-time (8 women), 2 part-time (both women); includes 3 minority (1 Black or African American, non-Hispanic/Latino; 2 Hispanic/Latino), 1 international. Average age 29. 8 applicants, 75% accepted, 4 enrolled. In 2010, 7 master's awarded. *Degree requirements:* For master's, one foreign language, thesis optional, comprehensive oral or written exam. *Entrance requirements:* For master's, minimum GPA of 2.75 on last two years of undergraduate courses. Additional exam requirements/recommendations for international students: Required—TOEFL (minimum score 525 paper-based). *Application deadline:* For fall admission, 7/1 for domestic students, 5/1 for international students; for spring admission, 11/1 for domestic students, 9/1 for international students. Applications are processed on a rolling basis. Application fee: $40. Electronic applications accepted. *Expenses:* Tuition, state resident: full-time $2730.50; part-time $304 per credit hour. Tuition, nonresident: full-time $6901; part-time $767 per credit hour. *Financial support:* In 2010–11, 10 teaching assistantships with full tuition reimbursements (averaging $8,768 per year) were awarded; Federal Work-Study, institutionally sponsored loans, and unspecified assistantships also available. Financial award application deadline: 4/1; financial award applicants required to submit FAFSA. *Faculty research:* French, German, Spanish literature from medieval era to present; gender and cultural studies in French; Spanish-American literature; foreign language methodology; linguistics. *Unit head:* Dr. Jack Jordan, Professor/Head, 662-325-3480, Fax: 662-325-8209, E-mail: jordan@ra.msstate.edu. *Application contact:* Dr. Edward T. Potter, Assistant Professor/Graduate Coordinator, 662-325-2399, Fax: 662-325-8209, E-mail: ep75@.msstate.edu.

Montclair State University, The Graduate School, College of Education and Human Services, Department of Curriculum and Teaching, Montclair, NJ 07043-1624. Offers education (M Ed); educational technology (M Ed); learning disabilities teacher consultant (Certificate); teaching (MAT), including art, biological science, early childhood education (P-3), earth science, elementary education (K-8), English, French, health and physical education, health education, home economics, mathematics, music, physical education, physical science, social studies, Spanish, teacher of ESL, teacher of students with disabilities. Part-time and evening/weekend programs available. *Faculty:* 18 full-time (12 women), 37 part-time/adjunct (26 women). *Students:* 183 full-time (105 women), 176 part-time (136 women); includes 20 Black or African American, non-Hispanic/Latino; 7 Asian, non-Hispanic/Latino; 15 Hispanic/Latino; 2 Two or more races, non-Hispanic/Latino, 6 international. Average age 30. 123 applicants, 56% accepted, 55 enrolled. In 2010, 133 master's, 1 other advanced degree awarded. *Degree requirements:* For master's, comprehensive exam, field experience. *Entrance requirements:* For master's, GRE, 2 letters of recommendation. Additional exam requirements/recommendations for international students: Required—TOEFL (minimum iBT score of 83) or IELTS. *Application deadline:* For fall admission, 2/15 for domestic and international students; for spring admission, 9/15 for domestic and international students. Applications are processed on a rolling basis. Application fee: $60. Electronic applications accepted. *Expenses:* Tuition, state resident: part-time $501.34 per credit. Tuition, nonresident: part-time $773.88 per credit. Required fees: $71.15 per credit. *Financial support:* In 2010–11, 8 research assistantships with full tuition reimbursements (averaging $7,000 per year) were awarded; Federal Work-Study, scholarships/grants, and unspecified assistantships also available. Support available to part-time students. Financial award application deadline: 3/1; financial award applicants required to submit FAFSA. *Faculty research:* Technology in the service of democratic education, case pedagogy in teacher preparation, public education in the United States, school reform: secondary science education, role of teacher learning as an agency of school reform. Total annual research expenditures: $11,313. *Unit head:* Dr. David Schwarzer, Chairperson, 973-655-5187. *Application contact:* Amy Aiello, Director of Graduate Admissions and Operations, 973-655-5147, Fax: 973-655-7869, E-mail: graduate.school@montclair.edu.

Montclair State University, The Graduate School, College of Humanities and Social Sciences, Department of Modern Languages and Literatures, Montclair, NJ 07043-1624. Offers French (MA, Certificate), including French literature (MA), French studies (MA). Part-time and evening/weekend programs available. *Faculty:* 8 full-time (5 women), 22 part-time/adjunct (15 women). *Students:* 2 full-time (1 woman), 16 part-time (9 women); includes 6 Black or African American, non-Hispanic/Latino, 1 international. Average age 45. 5 applicants, 100% accepted, 2 enrolled. In 2010, 3 master's awarded. *Degree requirements:* For master's, comprehensive exam, thesis optional. *Entrance requirements:* For master's, GRE General Test, 24 credits of undergraduate course work in French, 2 letters of recommendation. Additional exam requirements/recommendations for international students: Required—TOEFL (minimum score 83 iBT) or IELTS. *Application deadline:* For fall admission, 6/1 for international students; for spring admission, 11/1 for international students. Applications are processed on a rolling basis. Application fee: $60. Electronic applications accepted. *Expenses:* Tuition, state resident: part-time $501.34 per credit. Tuition, nonresident: part-time $773.88 per credit. Required fees: $71.15 per credit. *Financial support:* In 2010–11, 1 research assistantship with full tuition reimbursement (averaging $7,000 per year) was awarded; Federal Work-Study, scholarships/grants, and unspecified assistantships also available. Support available to part-time students. Financial award application deadline: 3/1; financial award applicants required to submit FAFSA. *Faculty research:* Literary criticism, African and post-colonial studies, neuro-psychoanalysis; aesthetics, second language acquisition. *Unit head:* Dr. Lois Oppenheim, Chairperson, 973-655-4283. *Application contact:* Amy Aiello, Director of Graduate Admissions and Operations, 973-655-5147, Fax: 973-655-7869, E-mail: graduate.school@montclair.edu.

New York University, Graduate School of Arts and Science, Center for French Civilization and Culture, Department of French, New York, NY 10012-1019. Offers French (PhD); French language and civilization (MA); French literature (MA); Romance languages and literatures (MA). Part-time programs available. *Faculty:* 18 full-time (7 women), 2 part-time/adjunct (both women). *Students:* 66 full-time (42 women), 7 part-time (4 women); includes 4 Asian, non-Hispanic/Latino; 3 Hispanic/Latino, 19 international. Average age 29. 73 applicants, 51% accepted, 20 enrolled. In 2010, 11 master's, 4 doctorates awarded. Terminal master's awarded for partial completion of doctoral program. *Degree requirements:* For master's, one foreign language, thesis (for some programs); for doctorate, one foreign language, thesis/dissertation. *Entrance requirements:* For master's and doctorate, GRE General Test, proficiency in French. Additional exam requirements/recommendations for international students: Required—TOEFL. *Application deadline:* For fall admission, 1/4 for domestic students; for spring admission, 11/1 for domestic students. Application fee: $90. *Financial support:* Fellowships with tuition reimbursements, teaching assistantships with tuition reimbursements, Federal Work-Study, institutionally sponsored loans, scholarships/grants, traineeships, health care benefits, unspecified assistantships, and instructorships available. Financial award application deadline: 1/4; financial award applicants required to submit FAFSA. *Faculty research:* French and Francophone literature, literary theory, and history; rhetoric and poetics; cultural history; theater and cinema. *Unit head:* Judith Miller, Chair, 212-998-8700, Fax: 212-995-3539, E-mail: french.grad@nyu.edu. *Application contact:* Brett Underhill, Graduate Secretary, 212-998-8700, Fax: 212-995-3539, E-mail: french.grad@nyu.edu.

New York University, Graduate School of Arts and Science, Center for French Civilization and Culture, Institute of French Studies, New York, NY 10012-1019. Offers French civilization (PhD); French studies (MA, PhD, Advanced Certificate); French studies and anthropology (PhD); French studies and history (PhD); French studies and journalism (MA); French studies and sociology (PhD); JD/MA; MBA/MA. Part-time programs available. *Students:* 40 full-time (34 women), 6 part-time (4 women); includes 2 Black or African American, non-Hispanic/Latino; 1 Asian, non-Hispanic/Latino; 2 Hispanic/Latino, 7 international. Average age 30. 50 applicants, 72% accepted, 16 enrolled. In 2010, 13 master's, 2 doctorates awarded. Terminal master's awarded for partial completion of doctoral program. *Degree requirements:* For master's, one foreign language, comprehensive exam; for doctorate, one foreign language, thesis/dissertation, qualifying exam. *Entrance requirements:* For master's and doctorate, GRE General Test, knowledge of French. Additional exam requirements/recommendations for international students: Required—TOEFL. *Application deadline:* For fall admission, 1/4 for domestic students. Application fee: $90. *Financial support:* Fellowships with tuition reimbursements, teaching assistantships with tuition reimbursements, Federal Work-Study, institutionally sponsored loans, scholarships/grants, health care benefits, and unspecified assistantships available. Financial award application deadline: 1/4; financial award applicants required to submit FAFSA. *Faculty research:* Contemporary French society, politics, economy, and culture; French history since 1789; French cultural studies, French colonialism and the post-colonial world; France and the European community. *Unit head:* Edward Berenson, Director, 212-988-8740, Fax: 212-995-4142, E-mail: institute.french@nyu.edu. *Application contact:* Herrick Chapman, Director of Graduate Studies, 212-988-8740, Fax: 212-995-4142, E-mail: institute.french@nyu.edu.

New York University, NYU in Paris, Paris, NY 10012-1019, France. Offers teaching French as a foreign language (MA).

North Carolina State University, Graduate School, College of Humanities and Social Sciences, Department of Foreign Languages and Literatures, Program in French Language and Literature, Raleigh, NC 27695. Offers MA. *Degree requirements:* For master's, thesis optional. *Entrance requirements:* For master's, fluency in French. Electronic applications accepted. *Faculty research:* 19th-century visual culture, translation, cinema, modern theater, linguistics.

Northern Illinois University, Graduate School, College of Liberal Arts and Sciences, Department of Foreign Languages and Literatures, De Kalb, IL 60115-2854. Offers French (MA); Spanish (MA). Part-time programs available. *Faculty:* 25 full-time (11 women). *Students:* 25 part-time (19 women); includes 1 Black or African American, non-Hispanic/Latino; 9 Hispanic/Latino, 1 international. Average age 31. 10 applicants, 60% accepted, 4 enrolled. In 2010, 4 master's awarded. *Degree requirements:* For master's, one foreign language, comprehensive exam, thesis or alternative, language proficiency exam. *Entrance requirements:* For master's, GRE General Test, interview, minimum GPA of 2.75, undergraduate major in French or Spanish. Additional exam requirements/recommendations for international students: Required—TOEFL (minimum score 550 paper-based; 213 computer-based). *Application deadline:* For fall admission, 6/1 for domestic students, 5/1 for international students; for spring admission, 11/1 for domestic students, 10/1 for international students. Applications are processed on a rolling basis. Application fee: $30. Electronic applications accepted. *Expenses:* Tuition, state resident: full-time $7200; part-time $300 per credit hour. Tuition, nonresident: full-time $14,400; part-time $600 per credit hour. Required fees: $79 per credit hour. *Financial support:* In 2010–11, 14 teaching assistantships with full tuition reimbursements were awarded; fellowships with full tuition reimbursements, research assistantships with full tuition reimbursements, career-related internships or fieldwork, Federal Work-Study, scholarships/grants, tuition waivers (full), and unspecified assistantships also available. Support available to part-time students. Financial award applicants required to submit FAFSA. *Faculty research:* Francophone women writers, prosodies of French and Italian, early Spanish drama, business German, history of Burmese literature. *Unit head:* Anne Birbeck, Chair, 815-753-1259, Fax: 815-753-5989, E-mail: annie@niu.edu. *Application contact:* Graduate School Office, 815-753-0395, E-mail: gradsch@niu.edu.

Northwestern University, The Graduate School, Judd A. and Marjorie Weinberg College of Arts and Sciences, Department of French and Italian, Evanston, IL 60208. Offers eighteenth-century studies (Certificate); French (PhD); French and comparative literature (PhD); Italian studies (Certificate). Admissions and degrees offered through The Graduate School. *Degree requirements:* For doctorate, one foreign language, thesis/dissertation, written and oral exams. *Entrance requirements:* For doctorate, GRE, writing sample, cassette recording. Additional exam requirements/recommendations for international students: Required—TOEFL. *Faculty research:* Francophone studies, 18th century contemporary theory.

The Ohio State University, Graduate School, College of Arts and Sciences, Division of Arts and Humanities, Department of French and Italian, Columbus, OH 43210. Offers French (MA, PhD); Italian (MA). *Faculty:* 20. *Students:* 24 full-time (15 women), 10 part-time (7 women), 8 international. Average age 33. In 2010, 6 master's, 1 doctorate awarded. *Degree requirements:* For master's, variable foreign language requirement, thesis optional; for doctorate, variable foreign language requirement, thesis/dissertation. *Entrance requirements:* For master's and doctorate, GRE General Test. Additional exam requirements/recommendations for international students: Required—TOEFL. *Application deadline:* For fall admission, 8/15 priority date for domestic students, 7/1 priority date for international students; for winter admission, 12/1 priority date for domestic students, 11/1 priority date for international students; for spring admission, 3/1 priority date for domestic students, 2/1 priority date for international students. Applications are processed on a rolling basis. Application fee: $40 ($50 for international students). Electronic applications accepted. *Expenses:* Tuition, state resident: full-time $10,605. Tuition, nonresident: full-time $26,535. Tuition and fees vary according to course load and program. *Financial support:* Fellowships, research assistantships, teaching assistantships, Federal Work-Study, institutionally sponsored loans, and unspecified assistantships available. Support available to part-time students. *Faculty research:* Italian and Romance linguistics. *Unit head:* Diane W. Birckbichler, Graduate Studies Committee Chair, 614-292-4361, E-mail:

French

The Ohio State University (continued)
birckbichler.1@osu.edu. *Application contact:* 614-292-9444, Fax: 614-292-3895, E-mail: domestic.grad@osu.edu.

Ohio University, Graduate College, College of Arts and Sciences, Department of Modern Languages, Athens, OH 45701-2979. Offers French (MA); Spanish (MA). Part-time programs available. *Students:* 27 full-time (24 women), 2 part-time (both women); includes 4 minority (2 Black or African American, non-Hispanic/Latino; 1 Hispanic/Latino; 1 Two or more races, non-Hispanic/Latino), 3 international. 26 applicants, 73% accepted, 15 enrolled. In 2010, 12 master's awarded. *Degree requirements:* For master's, 2 foreign languages, comprehensive exam, thesis optional. *Entrance requirements:* For master's, oral and written samples. Additional exam requirements/recommendations for international students: Required—TOEFL (minimum score 550 paper-based; 80 iBT) or IELTS (minimum score 6.5). *Application deadline:* For fall admission, 1/15 priority date for domestic and international students. Application fee: $50 ($55 for international students). Electronic applications accepted. *Financial support:* In 2010–11, teaching assistantships with tuition reimbursements (averaging $10,300 per year); Federal Work-Study, institutionally sponsored loans, and tuition waivers (partial) also available. Financial award application deadline: 1/15. *Faculty research:* French and Spanish language and literature. *Unit head:* Dr. Betsy Partyka, Chair, 740-593-2765, Fax: 740-593-0729, E-mail: partyka@ohio.edu. *Application contact:* Dr. David Burton, Graduate Chair, 740-593-2762, Fax: 740-593-0729, E-mail: burtond@ohio.edu.

Penn State University Park, Graduate School, College of the Liberal Arts, School of Languages and Literatures, Department of French and Francophone Studies, State College, University Park, PA 16802-1503. Offers MA, PhD.

Portland State University, Graduate Studies, College of Liberal Arts and Sciences, Department of World Languages and Literatures, Portland, OR 97207-0751. Offers foreign literature and language (MA); French (MA); German (MA); Japanese (MA); Spanish (MA). Part-time programs available. *Faculty:* 45 full-time (30 women), 38 part-time/adjunct (29 women). *Students:* 30 full-time (21 women), 10 part-time (7 women); includes 6 minority (2 Asian, non-Hispanic/Latino; 4 Hispanic/Latino), 11 international. Average age 31. 26 applicants, 69% accepted, 15 enrolled. In 2010, 24 master's awarded. *Degree requirements:* For master's, one foreign language, thesis (for some programs). *Entrance requirements:* Additional exam requirements/recommendations for international students: Required—TOEFL (minimum score 550 paper-based; 213 computer-based). *Application deadline:* For fall admission, 4/1 for domestic students, 3/1 for international students; for winter admission, 9/1 for domestic students, 7/1 for international students; for spring admission, 11/1 for domestic and international students. Applications are processed on a rolling basis. Application fee: $50. *Expenses:* Tuition, state resident: full-time $8505; part-time $315 per credit. Tuition, nonresident: full-time $13,284; part-time $492 per credit. Required fees: $1482; $21 per credit. $99 per term. One-time fee: $120. Part-time tuition and fees vary according to course load and program. *Financial support:* In 2010–11, 6 teaching assistantships with full tuition reimbursements (averaging $9,359 per year) were awarded; research assistantships with full tuition reimbursements, Federal Work-Study, scholarships/grants, and unspecified assistantships also available. Support available to part-time students. Financial award application deadline: 3/1; financial award applicants required to submit FAFSA. *Faculty research:* Foreign language pedagogy, applied and social linguistics, literary history and criticism. *Unit head:* Dr. Jennifer Perlmutter, Chair, 503-725-8783, Fax: 503-725-5276, E-mail: jrp@pdx.edu. *Application contact:* Michael Anthony, Graduate Admissions Coordinator, 503-725-3243, E-mail: manthony@pdx.edu.

Princeton University, Graduate School, Department of French and Italian, Princeton, NJ 08544-1019. Offers French language and literature (PhD). *Degree requirements:* For doctorate, variable foreign language requirement, thesis/dissertation. *Entrance requirements:* For doctorate, GRE General Test, sample of written work. Additional exam requirements/recommendations for international students: Required—TOEFL (minimum score 600 paper-based; 250 computer-based). Electronic applications accepted.

Purdue University, Graduate School, College of Liberal Arts, Department of Foreign Languages and Literatures, West Lafayette, IN 47907. Offers French (MA, MAT, PhD), including French (MA, PhD), French education (MAT); German (MA, MAT, PhD), including German (MA, PhD), German education (MAT); Spanish (MA, MAT, PhD), including Spanish (MA, PhD), Spanish education (MAT). Terminal master's awarded for partial completion of doctoral program. *Degree requirements:* For master's, one foreign language; for doctorate, 2 foreign languages, thesis/dissertation. *Entrance requirements:* For master's, GRE, sample recording of English and language of study; for doctorate, GRE, writing sample, sample recording of English and language of study. Additional exam requirements/recommendations for international students: Required—TOEFL. Electronic applications accepted. *Faculty research:* Linguistics, semiotics, literary criticism, pedagogy.

Queens College of the City University of New York, Division of Graduate Studies, Arts and Humanities Division, Department of European Languages and Literatures, Program in French, Flushing, NY 11367-1597. Offers MA. Part-time and evening/weekend programs available. *Faculty:* 5 full-time (1 woman). *Students:* 3 part-time (all women). 5 applicants, 20% accepted, 1 enrolled. In 2010, 3 master's awarded. *Degree requirements:* For master's, 2 foreign languages, comprehensive exam, thesis or alternative. *Entrance requirements:* For master's, minimum GPA of 3.0. Additional exam requirements/recommendations for international students: Required—TOEFL. *Application deadline:* For fall admission, 4/1 for domestic students; for spring admission, 11/1 for domestic students. Applications are processed on a rolling basis. Application fee: $125. *Financial support:* Career-related internships or fieldwork, Federal Work-Study, institutionally sponsored loans, and tuition waivers (partial) available. Support available to part-time students. Financial award application deadline: 4/1; financial award applicants required to submit FAFSA. *Unit head:* Dr. Joseph Sungolowsky, Graduate Adviser, 718-997-5980. *Application contact:* Mario Caruso, Director of Graduate Admissions, 718-997-5200, Fax: 718-997-5193, E-mail: graduate_admissions@qc.edu.

Queen's University at Kingston, School of Graduate Studies and Research, Faculty of Arts and Sciences, Department of French Studies, Kingston, ON K7L 3N6, Canada. Offers MA, PhD. Part-time programs available. *Degree requirements:* For master's, thesis or 4 credits and oral exam; for doctorate, one foreign language, comprehensive exam, thesis/dissertation. *Entrance requirements:* For master's, minimum B+ average; for doctorate, minimum 80% average. Additional exam requirements/recommendations for international students: Required—TOEFL (minimum score 550 paper-based; 213 computer-based). Electronic applications accepted. *Faculty research:* Reception of Quebec literature in English Canada, autobiography and postcolonialism, irony in women's writing, critical editions of renaissance authors, aspectual systems and grammatical categories.

Rider University, Department of Graduate Education, Leadership and Counseling, Teacher Certification Program, Lawrenceville, NJ 08648-3001. Offers business education (Certificate); elementary education (Certificate); English as a second language (Certificate); English education (Certificate); mathematics education (Certificate); preschool to grade 3 (Certificate); science education (Certificate); social studies education (Certificate); world languages (Certificate), including French, German, Spanish. Part-time programs available. *Degree requirements:* For Certificate, internship, professional portfolio. *Entrance requirements:* For degree, PRAXIS, resume. Additional exam requirements/recommendations for international students: Required—TOEFL (minimum score 550 paper-based; 213 computer-based). Electronic applications accepted. *Expenses:* Tuition: Full-time $29,870; part-time $667.34 per credit. Required fees: $350; $11.60 per credit. Part-time tuition and fees vary according to program. *Faculty research:* Conceptual foundations for optimal development of creativity; creative theory, cognitive processes in mathematics learning, teacher collaboration.

Rutgers, The State University of New Jersey, New Brunswick, Graduate School-New Brunswick, Program in French, Piscataway, NJ 08854-8097. Offers French (MA, PhD); French studies (MAT). Part-time and evening/weekend programs available. Terminal master's awarded for partial completion of doctoral program. *Degree requirements:* For master's, one foreign language, written and oral exams (MA); for doctorate, 3 foreign languages, thesis/dissertation, qualifying exam. *Entrance requirements:* For master's and doctorate, GRE General Test. *Expenses:* Tuition, state resident: full-time $7200; part-time $600 per credit. Tuition, nonresident: full-time $11,124; part-time $927 per credit. *Faculty research:* Literatures in French, literary history and theory, rhetoric and poetics.

Saint Louis University, Graduate Education, College of Arts and Sciences and Graduate Education, Department of Modern and Classical Languages, St. Louis, MO 63103-2097. Offers French (MA); Spanish (MA). Part-time programs available. *Degree requirements:* For master's, one foreign language, comprehensive exam, thesis/dissertation (Spanish). *Entrance requirements:* For master's, GRE General Test or MAT, letters of recommendation, resume, interview. Additional exam requirements/recommendations for international students: Required—TOEFL (minimum score 525 paper-based; 194 computer-based). Electronic applications accepted. *Faculty research:* Culture studies, literature studies, foreign language acquisition.

San Francisco State University, Division of Graduate Studies, College of Humanities, Department of Foreign Languages and Literatures, Program in French, San Francisco, CA 94132-1722. Offers MA. *Application deadline:* Applications are processed on a rolling basis. *Unit head:* Dr. Marie-Paule Laden, Program Coordinator, 415-338-7449, E-mail: mpladen@sfsu.edu. *Application contact:* Dr. Delphine Perret, Graduate Coordinator, 415-338-6061, E-mail: dperret@sfsu.edu.

San Jose State University, Graduate Studies and Research, College of Humanities and the Arts, Department of Foreign Languages, Program in French, San Jose, CA 95192-0001. Offers MA. *Degree requirements:* For master's, 2 foreign languages, thesis or comprehensive written and oral exam. *Entrance requirements:* Additional exam requirements/recommendations for international students: Required—TOEFL (minimum score 580 paper-based). Electronic applications accepted.

Simon Fraser University, Graduate Studies, Faculty of Arts and Social Sciences, Department of French, Burnaby, BC V5A 1S6, Canada. Offers MA. *Degree requirements:* For master's, one foreign language, thesis or alternative. *Entrance requirements:* For master's, minimum GPA of 3.0. Additional exam requirements/recommendations for international students: Required—TOEFL or IELTS. *Faculty research:* French linguistics, Creole linguistics, French literature of the Middle Ages and Ancient Régime, modern and contemporary French literature, French Canadian language and literature.

Smith College, Graduate and Special Programs, Department of French Language and Literature, Northampton, MA 01063. Offers MAT. Part-time programs available. *Faculty:* 9 full-time (7 women). *Students:* 1 applicant, 100% accepted, 0 enrolled. *Degree requirements:* For master's, one foreign language. *Entrance requirements:* Additional exam requirements/recommendations for international students: Required—TOEFL (minimum score 590 paper-based; 243 computer-based; 97 iBT). *Application deadline:* For fall admission, 4/1 for domestic students, 1/15 for international students; for spring admission, 12/1 for domestic students. Application fee: $60. *Expenses:* Tuition: Full-time $14,520; part-time $1210 per credit. *Financial support:* Career-related internships or fieldwork, institutionally sponsored loans, and scholarships/grants available. Support available to part-time students. Financial award application deadline: 1/15; financial award applicants required to submit CSS PROFILE or FAFSA. *Unit head:* Mary Ellen Birkett, Chair, 413-585-3351, E-mail: mbirkett@smith.edu. *Application contact:* Ruth Morgan, Administrative Assistant, 413-585-3050, Fax: 413-585-3054, E-mail: gradstdy@smith.edu.

Stanford University, School of Humanities and Sciences, Department of French and Italian, Stanford, CA 94305-9991. Offers French (MA, PhD); Italian (MA, PhD). Terminal master's awarded for partial completion of doctoral program. *Degree requirements:* For master's, one foreign language, written exam; for doctorate, 2 foreign languages, thesis/dissertation, oral exam. *Entrance requirements:* For master's and doctorate, GRE General Test. Additional exam requirements/recommendations for international students: Required—TOEFL. Electronic applications accepted. *Expenses:* Tuition: Full-time $38,700; part-time $860 per unit. One-time fee: $200 full-time.

State University of New York at Binghamton, Graduate School, School of Arts and Sciences, Department of Romance Languages and Literatures, Program in French, Binghamton, NY 13902-6000. Offers MA. *Students:* 1 (woman) part-time. Average age 25. 1 applicant, 0% accepted, 0 enrolled. *Degree requirements:* For master's, one foreign language, comprehensive exam, thesis or alternative. *Entrance requirements:* For master's, GRE General Test, GRE Subject Test. Additional exam requirements/recommendations for international students: Required—TOEFL (minimum score 550 paper-based; 213 computer-based; 80 iBT). *Application deadline:* For fall admission, 2/15 priority date for domestic and international students; for spring admission, 11/15 priority date for domestic and international students. Applications are processed on a rolling basis. Application fee: $60. Electronic applications accepted. *Financial support:* Fellowships, research assistantships, teaching assistantships, career-related internships or fieldwork, Federal Work-Study, institutionally sponsored loans, and unspecified assistantships available. Support available to part-time students. Financial award application deadline: 2/15. *Unit head:* Dr. Antonio Sobejano-Moran, Chairperson, 607-777-4635, E-mail: antobianco@msn.com. *Application contact:* Catherine Smith, Recruiting and Admissions Coordinator, 607-777-2151, Fax: 607-777-2501, E-mail: cmsmith@binghamton.edu.

State University of New York at New Paltz, Graduate School, School of Education, Department of Secondary Education, New Paltz, NY 12561. Offers adolescence education: biology (MAT, MS Ed); adolescence education: chemistry (MAT, MS Ed); adolescence education: earth science (MAT, MS Ed); adolescence education: English (MAT, MS Ed); adolescence education: French (MAT, MS Ed); adolescence education: social studies (MAT, MS Ed); adolescence education: Spanish (MAT, MS Ed); second language education (MS Ed). *Accreditation:* NCATE. Part-time and evening/weekend programs available. *Faculty:* 7 full-time (5 women), 7 part-time/adjunct (5 women). *Students:* 84 full-time (49 women), 78 part-time (52 women); includes 1 Black or African American, non-Hispanic/Latino; 4 Asian, non-Hispanic/Latino; 20 Hispanic/Latino; 2 Two or more races, non-Hispanic/Latino, 1 international. Average age 30. 122 applicants, 75% accepted, 68 enrolled. In 2010, 88 master's awarded. *Degree requirements:* For master's, comprehensive exam (for some programs), portfolio. *Entrance requirements:* For master's, minimum GPA of 3.0, New York state teaching certificate (MS Ed). Additional exam requirements/recommendations for international students: Required—TOEFL (minimum score 550 paper-based; 213 computer-based; 80 iBT), IELTS (minimum score 6.5). *Application deadline:* For fall admission, 3/1 priority date for domestic students, 3/1 for international students; for spring admission, 10/1 priority date for domestic students, 10/1 for international students. Application fee: $50. Electronic applications accepted. *Expenses:* Tuition, state resident: full-time $8370; part-time $349 per credit hour. Tuition, nonresident: full-time $13,780; part-time $574 per credit hour. Required fees: $1165; $33.80 per credit hour. $175 per term. Tuition and fees vary according to program. *Financial support:* In 2010–11, 13 students received support, including 5 fellowships (averaging $5,000 per year), 3 research assistantships with partial tuition reimbursements available (averaging $5,000 per year); Federal Work-Study, institutionally sponsored loans, and tuition waivers (full) also available. Financial award application deadline: 8/1; financial award applicants required to submit FAFSA. *Unit head:* Dr. Devon Duhaney, Chair, 845-257-2850, E-mail: duhaneyd@newpaltz.edu. *Application contact:* Caroline Murphy, Graduate Admissions Advisor, 845-257-3285, Fax: 845-257-3284, E-mail: gradschool@newpaltz.edu.

Stony Brook University, State University of New York, Graduate School, College of Arts and Sciences, Department of European Languages, Literatures, and Cultures, Program in French, Stony Brook, NY 11794. Offers Romance languages (MA). Evening/weekend programs available. *Students:* 3 part-time (2 women). In 2010, 2 master's awarded. *Degree requirements:* For master's, one foreign language. *Entrance requirements:* For master's, GRE General Test. Additional exam requirements/recommendations for international students: Required—TOEFL.

Application deadline: For fall admission, 1/15 for domestic students. Application fee: $100. *Expenses:* Tuition, state resident: full-time $8370; part-time $349 per credit. Tuition, nonresident: full-time $13,780; part-time $574 per credit. Required fees: $994. *Unit head:* Prosper Sanou, Coordinator, 631-632-7440, E-mail: prosper.sanou@stonybrook.edu. *Application contact:* Dr. Peter Carravetta, Director of Graduate Studies, 631-632-7440, Fax: 631-632-9612.

Syracuse University, College of Arts and Sciences, Program in French and Francophone Studies, Syracuse, NY 13244. Offers MA. Part-time programs available. *Students:* 6 full-time (5 women), 1 (woman) part-time, 3 international. Average age 25. 6 applicants, 100% accepted, 3 enrolled. In 2010, 3 master's awarded. *Degree requirements:* For master's, comprehensive exam (for some programs), thesis or alternative. *Entrance requirements:* For master's, GRE General Test. Additional exam requirements/recommendations for international students: Required—TOEFL (minimum score 100 iBT). *Application deadline:* For fall admission, 1/10 priority date for domestic and international students. Application fee: $75. Electronic applications accepted. *Expenses:* Tuition: Part-time $1162 per credit. *Financial support:* Fellowships with full tuition reimbursements, teaching assistantships with full tuition reimbursements, tuition waivers available. Financial award application deadline: 1/1; financial award applicants required to submit FAFSA. *Unit head:* Dr. Jean Jonassaint, Graduate Director, 315-443-5906, E-mail: jjonassa@syr.edu. *Application contact:* Karen Ames, Information Contact, 315-443-3022, E-mail: koames@syr.edu.

Texas Tech University, Graduate School, College of Arts and Sciences, Department of Classical and Modern Languages and Literatures, Program in Romance Languages-French, Lubbock, TX 79409. Offers MA. *Students:* 22 full-time (12 women), 3 part-time (all women); includes 1 Black or African American, non-Hispanic/Latino; 5 Hispanic/Latino, 13 international. Average age 28. 19 applicants, 58% accepted, 9 enrolled. In 2010, 3 master's awarded. *Entrance requirements:* For master's, GRE General Test. Additional exam requirements/recommendations for international students: Required—TOEFL (minimum score 550 paper-based; 213 computer-based; 79 iBT). *Application deadline:* For fall admission, 6/1 priority date for domestic students, 1/15 priority date for international students; for spring admission, 9/1 priority date for domestic students, 6/15 priority date for international students. Applications are processed on a rolling basis. Application fee: $50 ($75 for international students). Electronic applications accepted. *Expenses:* Tuition, state resident: full-time $5495.76; part-time $228.99 per credit hour. Tuition, nonresident: full-time $12,936; part-time $538.99 per credit hour. Required fees: $2674; $36 per credit hour. $905 per semester. *Financial support:* Application deadline: 4/15. *Faculty research:* French and Francophone literature, French cinema, French and Francophone culture, business French. *Unit head:* Dr. Diane Wood, Professor and Graduate Advisor of French, 806-742-3145 Ext. 258, Fax: 806-742-3306, E-mail: diane.wood@ttu.edu. *Application contact:* Liz Hildebrand, Senior Advisor, 806-742-4055, Fax: 806-742-3306, E-mail: liz.hildebrand@ttu.edu.

Tufts University, Graduate School of Arts and Sciences, Program in French, Medford, MA 02155. Offers MA. Part-time programs available. *Degree requirements:* For master's, one foreign language. *Entrance requirements:* For master's, GRE General Test, writing sample. Additional exam requirements/recommendations for international students: Required—TOEFL (minimum score 550 paper-based; 213 computer-based; 80 iBT). Electronic applications accepted. *Expenses:* Tuition: Full-time $39,624; part-time $3962 per course. Required fees: $40 per year. Full-time tuition and fees vary according to degree level, program and student level. Part-time tuition and fees vary according to course load.

Tulane University, School of Liberal Arts, Department of French and Italian, New Orleans, LA 70118-5669. Offers French (MA, PhD). *Degree requirements:* For master's, one foreign language, thesis or alternative; for doctorate, 2 foreign languages, thesis/dissertation. *Entrance requirements:* For master's, GRE General Test, minimum B average in undergraduate course work; for doctorate, GRE General Test. Additional exam requirements/recommendations for international students: Required—TOEFL. Electronic applications accepted.

Université de Moncton, Faculty of Arts and Social Sciences, Department of French Studies, Moncton, NB E1A 3E9, Canada. Offers MA, PhD. Part-time programs available. Terminal master's awarded for partial completion of doctoral program. *Degree requirements:* For master's, thesis, proficiency in French; for doctorate, thesis/dissertation, proficiency in French. *Entrance requirements:* For master's, honors degree in French; for doctorate, MA in French. Electronic applications accepted. *Faculty research:* Language, linguistics, literature, ethnology, Acadian studies.

Université de Montréal, Faculty of Arts and Sciences, Department of French Literature, Montréal, QC H3C 3J7, Canada. Offers MA, PhD. *Degree requirements:* For master's, one foreign language, thesis; for doctorate, one foreign language, thesis/dissertation, general exam. Electronic applications accepted. *Faculty research:* Literary history, literary genres, critical edition, creative writing, Quebecois literature.

Université de Sherbrooke, Faculty of Letters and Human Sciences, Department of Letters and Communications, Sherbrooke, QC J1K 2R1, Canada. Offers comparative Canadian literature (MA, PhD); French literature (MA, PhD); linguistics (MA); theatre (MA). *Degree requirements:* For master's, thesis or alternative; for doctorate, thesis/dissertation. *Entrance requirements:* For master's, minimum GPA of 2.8; for doctorate, minimum GPA of 3.0.

Université du Québec à Chicoutimi, Graduate Programs, Program in Didactics of French-Mother Tongue, Chicoutimi, QC G7H 2B1, Canada. Offers Diploma. Part-time programs available. *Entrance requirements:* For degree, appropriate bachelor's degree, proficiency in French.

University at Albany, State University of New York, College of Arts and Sciences, Department of Languages, Literatures, and Cultures, Program in French, Albany, NY 12222-0001. Offers MA, PhD. *Degree requirements:* For master's, one foreign language; for doctorate, thesis/dissertation.

University at Buffalo, the State University of New York, Graduate School, College of Arts and Sciences, Department of Romance Languages and Literatures, Buffalo, NY 14260. Offers French (MA, PhD); Spanish (MA, PhD). Part-time programs available. *Faculty:* 15 full-time (9 women), 7 part-time/adjunct (6 women). *Students:* 28 full-time (22 women), 11 part-time (9 women); includes 1 Asian, non-Hispanic/Latino; 12 Two or more races, non-Hispanic/Latino. Average age 31. 16 applicants, 75% accepted, 6 enrolled. In 2010, 3 master's, 4 doctorates awarded. Terminal master's awarded for partial completion of doctoral program. *Degree requirements:* For master's, one foreign language, comprehensive exam, thesis; for doctorate, 2 foreign languages, comprehensive exam, thesis/dissertation. *Entrance requirements:* For master's and doctorate, GRE. Additional exam requirements/recommendations for international students: Required—TOEFL (minimum score 550 paper-based; 213 computer-based; 79 iBT). *Application deadline:* For fall admission, 1/15 priority date for domestic and international students. Applications are processed on a rolling basis. Application fee: $75. Electronic applications accepted. *Financial support:* In 2010–11, 26 students received support, including fellowships with full tuition reimbursements available (averaging $6,000 per year), teaching assistantships with full tuition reimbursements available (averaging $13,415 per year); Federal Work-Study, institutionally sponsored loans, and health care benefits also available. Financial award application deadline: 2/28; financial award applicants required to submit FAFSA. *Faculty research:* Romance linguistics, cultural studies, literary studies, literature and philosophy. *Unit head:* Dr. David Castillo, Chair, 716-645-0869, Fax: 716-645-5981, E-mail: dc63@buffalo.edu. *Application contact:* Dr. Justin Read, Director of Graduate Studies, 716-645-0878, Fax: 716-645-5981, E-mail: jread2@buffalo.edu.

University at Buffalo, the State University of New York, Graduate School, Graduate School of Education, Department of Learning and Instruction, Buffalo, NY 14260. Offers biology education (Ed M, Certificate); chemistry education (Ed M, Certificate); childhood education (Ed M); childhood education with bilingual extension (Ed M); early childhood education (Ed M); earth science education (Ed M, Certificate); educational technology and new literacies (Certificate); elementary education (Ed D, PhD); English education (Ed M, PhD, Certificate); English for speakers of other languages (Ed M); foreign and second language education (PhD); French education (Ed M, Certificate); general education (Ed M); German education (Ed M, Certificate); gifted education (online) (Certificate); Latin education (Ed M, Certificate); literary specialist (Ed M); mathematics education (Ed M, PhD, Certificate); music education (Ed M, Certificate); physics education (Ed M, Certificate); reading education (PhD); science and the public (online) (Ed M); science education (PhD); social studies education (Ed M, Certificate); Spanish education (Ed M, Certificate); special education (PhD); teaching and leading for diversity (Certificate); teaching English to speakers of other languages (Ed M). Part-time and evening/weekend programs available. Postbaccalaureate distance learning degree programs offered (no on-campus study). *Faculty:* 32 full-time (22 women), 53 part-time/adjunct (43 women). *Students:* 343 full-time (237 women), 340 part-time (261 women); includes 17 Black or African American, non-Hispanic/Latino; 3 American Indian or Alaska Native, non-Hispanic/Latino; 13 Asian, non-Hispanic/Latino; 13 Hispanic/Latino, 76 international. Average age 29. 587 applicants, 75% accepted, 281 enrolled. In 2010, 212 master's, 16 doctorates, 37 other advanced degrees awarded. *Degree requirements:* For master's, comprehensive exam; for doctorate, thesis/dissertation, research analysis exam, research experience component. *Entrance requirements:* For doctorate, GRE General Test or MAT, interview, writing sample, letters of recommendation. Additional exam requirements/recommendations for international students: Required—TOEFL (minimum score 600 paper-based; 96 iBT). *Application deadline:* For fall admission, 2/1 priority date for domestic and international students; for spring admission, 11/15 priority date for domestic students, 10/1 for international students. Applications are processed on a rolling basis. Application fee: $50. Electronic applications accepted. *Financial support:* In 2010–11, 21 fellowships with full tuition reimbursements (averaging $9,000 per year), 42 research assistantships with full tuition reimbursements (averaging $10,589 per year) were awarded; teaching assistantships with full tuition reimbursements, career-related internships or fieldwork, Federal Work-Study, institutionally sponsored loans, scholarships/grants, tuition waivers (partial), and unspecified assistantships also available. Financial award application deadline: 2/28; financial award applicants required to submit FAFSA. *Faculty research:* Science assessment, foreign language teaching and learning, early learning, new literacies, gender and education. *Unit head:* Dr. Jim Collins, Chair, 716-645-2455, Fax: 716-645-3161, E-mail: jcollins@buffalo.edu. *Application contact:* Cathy Dimino, Admissions Assistant, 716-645-2110, Fax: 716-645-7937, E-mail: cadimino@buffalo.edu.

The University of Alabama, Graduate School, College of Arts and Sciences, Department of Modern Languages and Classics, Tuscaloosa, AL 35487. Offers French (MA, PhD); French and Spanish (PhD); German (MA); Romance languages (MA, PhD); Spanish (MA, PhD). Part-time programs available. *Faculty:* 25 full-time (12 women). *Students:* 50 full-time (33 women), 31 part-time (19 women); includes 11 minority (2 Black or African American, non-Hispanic/Latino; 8 Hispanic/Latino; 1 Two or more races, non-Hispanic/Latino), 19 international. Average age 31. 24 applicants, 83% accepted, 11 enrolled. In 2010, 17 master's, 1 doctorate awarded. *Degree requirements:* For master's, comprehensive exam, thesis optional; for doctorate, one foreign language, thesis/dissertation, preliminary exam. *Entrance requirements:* For master's and doctorate, minimum GPA of 3.0, writing sample. Additional exam requirements/recommendations for international students: Required—TOEFL or IELTS. *Application deadline:* For fall admission, 7/6 priority date for domestic students, 1/15 priority date for international students; for spring admission, 12/5 priority date for domestic students, 6/1 priority date for international students. Applications are processed on a rolling basis. Application fee: $50 ($60 for international students). Electronic applications accepted. *Expenses:* Tuition, state resident: full-time $7900. Tuition, nonresident: full-time $20,500. *Financial support:* In 2010–11, 7 students received support, including 1 fellowship, research assistantships with full tuition reimbursements available (averaging $10,291 per year), 6 teaching assistantships with full tuition reimbursements available (averaging $10,291 per year); career-related internships or fieldwork, Federal Work-Study, institutionally sponsored loans, and scholarships/grants also available. Financial award application deadline: 7/14. *Faculty research:* Non-English literature, linguistics, culture, film. *Unit head:* Dr. Michael Picone, Chair and Professor, 205-348-5054, Fax: 205-348-2042, E-mail: mpicone@bama.ua.edu. *Application contact:* Dr. K. Barbara Fischer, Graduate Director and Associate Professor, 205-348-8465, Fax: 205-348-2042, E-mail: bfischer@bama.ua.edu.

University of Alberta, Faculty of Graduate Studies and Research, Department of Modern Languages and Cultural Studies, Edmonton, AB T6G 2E1, Canada. Offers applied linguistics (Germanic, Romance, Slavic) (MA); French language, literatures and linguistics (PhD); French language, literatures, and linguistics (MA); Germanic languages, literatures and linguistics (PhD); Germanic languages, literatures, and linguistics (MA); Italian studies (MA); Slavic languages and literatures (Russian, Ukrainian) (MA, PhD); Slavic linguistics (Russian, Ukrainian) (MA, PhD); Spanish and Latin American studies (MA, PhD); Ukrainian folklore (MA, PhD). Part-time programs available. *Degree requirements:* For master's, one foreign language, thesis; for doctorate, 2 foreign languages, comprehensive exam, thesis/dissertation. *Entrance requirements:* For master's and doctorate, 1 language other than English. Additional exam requirements/recommendations for international students: Required—Michigan English Language Assessment Battery or TOEFL (minimum score 550 paper-based; 213 computer-based). Electronic applications accepted. *Faculty research:* Russian/Ukrainian studies; German studies; contemporary Latin American, French and Francophone studies; Italian studies.

The University of Arizona, College of Humanities, Department of French and Italian, Tucson, AZ 85721. Offers French (MA). Part-time programs available. *Faculty:* 14 full-time (10 women). *Students:* 4 full-time (2 women), 6 part-time (4 women); includes 3 Black or African American, non-Hispanic/Latino, 3 international. Average age 37. 7 applicants, 29% accepted, 2 enrolled. In 2010, 1 master's awarded. *Entrance requirements:* For master's, 3 letters of reference, writing sample in French, audio recording. Additional exam requirements/recommendations for international students: Required—TOEFL (minimum score 550 paper-based; 213 computer-based; 79 iBT). *Application deadline:* For fall admission, 12/15 for domestic and international students. Applications are processed on a rolling basis. Application fee: $75. Electronic applications accepted. *Expenses:* Tuition, state resident: full-time $7692. *Financial support:* In 2010–11, 1 research assistantship (averaging $22,074 per year), 13 teaching assistantships with full tuition reimbursements (averaging $20,182 per year) were awarded; Federal Work-Study, institutionally sponsored loans, scholarships/grants, health care benefits, tuition waivers (partial), and unspecified assistantships also available. *Faculty research:* French literature (history, criticism, and theory), Francophone literature and culture, second language acquisition and teaching. *Unit head:* Dr. Irene d'Almeda, Department Head, 520-621-7349, Fax: 520-626-8022, E-mail: dalmedia@email.arizona.edu. *Application contact:* Dava Jondall, Graduate Secretary, 520-621-5345, Fax: 520-626-8022, E-mail: roman@email.arizona.edu.

University of Arkansas, Graduate School, J. William Fulbright College of Arts and Sciences, Department of World Languages, Literature and Cultures, Program in French, Fayetteville, AR 72701-1201. Offers MA. *Students:* 7 full-time (5 women), 1 (woman) part-time; includes 1 minority (Hispanic/Latino), 1 international. 4 applicants, 100% accepted. In 2010, 4 master's awarded. *Degree requirements:* For master's, variable foreign language requirement. *Application deadline:* For fall admission, 4/1 for international students; for spring admission, 10/1 for international students. Applications are processed on a rolling basis. Application fee: $40 ($50 for international students). Electronic applications accepted. *Financial support:* In 2010–11, 7 teaching assistantships were awarded; fellowships, research assistantships, career-related internships or fieldwork and Federal Work-Study also available. Support available to part-time students. Financial award application deadline: 4/1; financial award applicants required to submit FAFSA. *Unit head:* Dr. Joan Turner, Departmental Chair, 479-575-2951, Fax: 479-575-6795, E-mail: joant@uark.edu. *Application contact:* Dr. Nancy Arenberg, Graduate Coordinator, 479-575-2951, Fax: 479-575-6795, E-mail: arenberg@uark.edu.

The University of British Columbia, Faculty of Arts and Faculty of Graduate Studies, Department of French, Hispanic and Italian Studies, Vancouver, BC V6T 1Z1, Canada. Offers French (MA, PhD); Hispanic studies (MA, PhD). Part-time programs available. *Degree requirements:* For master's, thesis optional; for doctorate, 2 foreign languages, comprehensive

French

The University of British Columbia (continued)
exam, thesis/dissertation. *Entrance requirements:* For doctorate, MA. Additional exam requirements/recommendations for international students: Required—TOEFL (minimum score 550 paper-based; 213 computer-based; 80 iBT). Electronic applications accepted. Tuition charges are reported in Canadian dollars. *Expenses:* Tuition, area resident: Full-time $4179 Canadian dollars. International tuition: $7344 Canadian dollars full-time. *Faculty research:* Medieval and Renaissance literature, modern literature, romance philology and linguistics, cultural studies, women's literature.

University of California, Berkeley, Graduate Division, College of Letters and Science, Department of French, Berkeley, CA 94720-1500. Offers PhD. *Degree requirements:* For doctorate, one foreign language, thesis/dissertation, qualifying exam. *Entrance requirements:* For doctorate, minimum GPA of 3.0, 3 letters of recommendation.

University of California, Berkeley, Graduate Division, College of Letters and Science, Group in Romance Languages and Literature, Berkeley, CA 94720-1500. Offers French (PhD); Italian (PhD); Spanish (PhD). *Degree requirements:* For doctorate, thesis/dissertation, qualifying exam. *Entrance requirements:* For doctorate, GRE General Test, minimum GPA of 3.0, 3 letters of recommendation. Additional exam requirements/recommendations for international students: Required—TOEFL (minimum score 570 paper-based; 230 computer-based).

University of California, Davis, Graduate Studies, Program in French, Davis, CA 95616. Offers PhD. Part-time programs available. *Degree requirements:* For doctorate, thesis/dissertation. *Entrance requirements:* For doctorate, GRE General Test, minimum GPA of 3.0. Additional exam requirements/recommendations for international students: Required—TOEFL (minimum score 550 paper-based; 213 computer-based). Electronic applications accepted. *Faculty research:* Art and art criticism, Francophone literature, travel narrative, colonial and postcolonial studies and romance linguistics.

University of California, Irvine, School of Humanities, Department of French and Italian, Irvine, CA 92697. Offers French (MA, PhD). *Students:* 7 full-time (5 women), 1 international. Average age 28. 6 applicants, 50% accepted, 0 enrolled. In 2010, 1 master's awarded. *Degree requirements:* For doctorate, thesis/dissertation. *Entrance requirements:* For master's and doctorate, GRE General Test, minimum GPA of 3.0. Additional exam requirements/recommendations for international students: Required—TOEFL (minimum score 550 paper-based; 213 computer-based). *Application deadline:* For fall admission, 1/15 for domestic and international students. Applications are processed on a rolling basis. Application fee: $80 ($100 for international students). Electronic applications accepted. *Financial support:* Fellowships, research assistantships with full tuition reimbursements, teaching assistantships, institutionally sponsored loans, traineeships, health care benefits, and unspecified assistantships available. Financial award application deadline: 3/1; financial award applicants required to submit FAFSA. *Faculty research:* Montaigne, psychoanalysis, feminism and the problem of repression, aesthetics of nationalism and the limits of culture. *Unit head:* Prof. Ellen S. Burt, Chair, 949-824-4940, Fax: 949-824-1031, E-mail: esburt@uci.edu. *Application contact:* June DeTurk, Graduate Program Coordinator, 949-824-8793, Fax: 949-824-2803, E-mail: jdeturk@uci.edu.

University of California, Los Angeles, Graduate Division, College of Letters and Science, Department of French and Francophone Studies, Los Angeles, CA 90034. Offers MA, PhD. *Faculty:* 13 full-time (7 women). *Students:* 22 full-time (17 women); includes 2 minority (1 Asian, non-Hispanic/Latino; 1 Hispanic/Latino), 2 international. Average age 30. 16 applicants, 50% accepted, 2 enrolled. In 2010, 1 master's, 1 doctorate awarded. Terminal master's awarded for partial completion of doctoral program. *Degree requirements:* For master's, one foreign language, comprehensive exam; for doctorate, 2 foreign languages, thesis/dissertation, oral and written qualifying exams. *Entrance requirements:* For master's, GRE General Test, minimum GPA of 3.0, sample of written work in French; for doctorate, GRE General Test, MA in French or equivalent; minimum undergraduate GPA of 3.0; sample of written work in French. *Application deadline:* For fall admission, 12/15 for domestic and international students. Application fee: $70 ($90 for international students). Electronic applications accepted. *Financial support:* In 2010–11, 24 fellowships with full and partial tuition reimbursements, 5 research assistantships with full and partial tuition reimbursements, 19 teaching assistantships with full and partial tuition reimbursements were awarded; Federal Work-Study, institutionally sponsored loans, health care benefits, tuition waivers (full and partial), and unspecified assistantships also available. Financial award applicants required to submit FAFSA. *Unit head:* Dr. Dominic Thomas, Chair, 310-794-8923, E-mail: dominict@humnet.ucla.edu. *Application contact:* Department Office, 310-825-1147, E-mail: allen@humnet.ucla.edu.

University of California, San Diego, Office of Graduate Studies, Department of Literature, Program in French Literature, La Jolla, CA 92093. Offers MA. *Degree requirements:* For master's, thesis. *Entrance requirements:* For master's, GRE General Test, GRE Subject Test. Electronic applications accepted.

University of California, Santa Barbara, Graduate Division, College of Letters and Sciences, Division of Humanities and Fine Arts, Program in Comparative Literature, Santa Barbara, CA 93106-4130. Offers comparative literature (PhD); East Asian literatures (PhD); feminist studies (PhD); French (PhD); global studies (PhD); translation studies (PhD); MA/PhD. *Faculty:* 63 full-time (31 women). *Students:* 21 full-time (14 women); includes 3 Asian, non-Hispanic/Latino; 2 Hispanic/Latino. Average age 31. 41 applicants, 12% accepted, 2 enrolled. In 2010, 1 doctorate awarded. *Degree requirements:* For doctorate, 2 foreign languages, comprehensive exam, thesis/dissertation. *Entrance requirements:* For doctorate, GRE. Additional exam requirements/recommendations for international students: Required—TOEFL (minimum score 550 paper-based; 80 iBT), IELTS (minimum score 7). *Application deadline:* For fall admission, 12/15 for domestic and international students. Application fee: $70 ($90 for international students). Electronic applications accepted. *Financial support:* In 2010–11, 19 students received support, including 14 fellowships with full and partial tuition reimbursements available (averaging $16,232 per year), 12 teaching assistantships with partial tuition reimbursements available (averaging $12,826 per year); research assistantships, Federal Work-Study, institutionally sponsored loans, scholarships/grants, health care benefits, and tuition waivers (full and partial) also available. Financial award application deadline: 12/15; financial award applicants required to submit FAFSA. *Faculty research:* Comparative literary studies in global context, critical theory, translation studies, mediatechnological studies, trauma studies. *Unit head:* Prof. Susan Derwin, Chair, 805-893-4399, Fax: 805-893-8341, E-mail: derwin@gss.ucsb.edu. *Application contact:* Ashley Bradbury, Graduate Program Assistant, 805-893-2131, Fax: 805-893-8341, E-mail: ashley@hfa.ucsb.edu.

University of Chicago, Division of the Humanities, Department of Romance Languages and Literatures, Chicago, IL 60637-1513. Offers French (AM, PhD); Italian (AM, PhD); Spanish (AM, PhD). Terminal master's awarded for partial completion of doctoral program. *Degree requirements:* For master's, 2 foreign languages, thesis; for doctorate, 3 foreign languages, thesis/dissertation. *Entrance requirements:* For master's and doctorate, GRE General Test, GRE Subject Test. Additional exam requirements/recommendations for international students: Required—TOEFL.

University of Cincinnati, Graduate School, McMicken College of Arts and Sciences, Department of Romance Languages and Literature, Program in French, Cincinnati, OH 45221. Offers MA, PhD. Terminal master's awarded for partial completion of doctoral program. *Degree requirements:* For master's, thesis optional; for doctorate, 2 foreign languages, thesis/dissertation. *Entrance requirements:* For master's, minimum GPA of 3.0. Electronic applications accepted.

University of Colorado Boulder, Graduate School, College of Arts and Sciences, Department of French and Italian, Boulder, CO 80309. Offers French (MA, PhD). *Faculty:* 11 full-time (6 women). *Students:* 22 full-time (14 women), 1 (woman) part-time; includes 1 minority (Asian, non-Hispanic/Latino), 6 international. Average age 34. 13 applicants, 5 enrolled. In 2010, 2 master's, 5 doctorates awarded. Terminal master's awarded for partial completion of doctoral

program. *Degree requirements:* For master's, 2 foreign languages, comprehensive exam, thesis or alternative; for doctorate, 3 foreign languages, thesis/dissertation. *Entrance requirements:* For master's, GRE General Test, minimum undergraduate GPA of 3.0; for doctorate, GRE General Test. *Application deadline:* For fall admission, 2/1 priority date for domestic students, 1/1 for international students. Applications are processed on a rolling basis. Application fee: $50 ($60 for international students). *Financial support:* In 2010–11, 3 fellowships (averaging $1,709 per year), 20 research assistantships (averaging $13,790 per year) were awarded; tuition waivers (full) also available. Financial award application deadline: 2/1. *Faculty research:* All periods of French literature from the Middle Ages to the present (including Francophone literature, cultural studies and literary theory). Total annual research expenditures: $26,854.

University of Connecticut, Graduate School, College of Liberal Arts and Sciences, Department of Modern and Classical Languages, Field of French, Storrs, CT 06269. Offers MA, PhD. Terminal master's awarded for partial completion of doctoral program. *Degree requirements:* For master's, comprehensive exam; for doctorate, thesis/dissertation. *Entrance requirements:* For master's and doctorate, GRE General Test, GRE Subject Test. Additional exam requirements/recommendations for international students: Required—TOEFL (minimum score 550 paper-based; 213 computer-based). Electronic applications accepted.

University of Delaware, College of Arts and Sciences, Department of Foreign Languages and Literatures, Newark, DE 19716. Offers foreign languages and literatures (MA), including French, German, Spanish; foreign languages pedagogy (MA), including French, German, Spanish; technical Chinese translation (MA). *Degree requirements:* For master's, one foreign language, comprehensive exam, thesis optional. *Entrance requirements:* For master's, GRE General Test, letters of recommendation, writing sample. Additional exam requirements/recommendations for international students: Required—TOEFL. Electronic applications accepted. *Faculty research:* Medieval to Modern French and Spanish literature, Twentieth Century German, French, Spanish literature by women, computer-assisted instruction.

University of Florida, Graduate School, College of Liberal Arts and Sciences, Department of Languages, Literatures and Culture, Gainesville, FL 32611. Offers MA, PhD. *Students:* 34 full-time (24 women), 15 part-time (10 women); includes 1 Black or African American, non-Hispanic/Latino; 12 Hispanic/Latino, 18 international. Average age 36. 11 applicants, 55% accepted, 5 enrolled. In 2010, 1 master's, 7 doctorates awarded. *Degree requirements:* For master's, comprehensive exam, thesis optional; for doctorate, one foreign language, comprehensive exam, thesis/dissertation. *Entrance requirements:* For master's and doctorate, GRE General Test, minimum GPA of 3.0. Additional exam requirements/recommendations for international students: Required—TOEFL (minimum score 550 paper-based; 213 computer-based; 80 iBT), IELTS (minimum score 6). *Application deadline:* For fall admission, 6/1 priority date for domestic students. Applications are processed on a rolling basis. Application fee: $30. Electronic applications accepted. *Expenses:* Tuition, state resident: full-time $10,915.92. Tuition, nonresident: full-time $28,309. *Financial support:* In 2010–11, 42 students received support, including 9 fellowships, 3 research assistantships (averaging $16,869 per year), 30 teaching assistantships (averaging $16,345 per year); associateships also available. Financial award applicants required to submit FAFSA. *Faculty research:* Medieval epic, romance, and allegory; Renaissance and Baroque poetry; the eighteenth century novel; nineteenth century prose, poetry, and poetics; twentieth century novel, theater, and poetry; the literatures of the francophone world; French and francophone film; the literatures in Breton and Occitan; criticism and critical theory; applied linguistics; the history of French; phonology; sociolinguistics; the structure of French; French and Haitian Creole linguistics. *Unit head:* Dr. David A. Pharies, Chair, 352-392-2264, Fax: 352-392-5679, E-mail: pharies@ufl.edu. *Application contact:* Brigitte Weltman-Aron, Graduate Coordinator, 352-392-9766, E-mail: bwelman@ufl.edu.

University of Georgia, College of Arts and Sciences, Department of Romance Languages, Program in French, Athens, GA 30602. Offers MA. *Students:* 4 full-time (all women), 2 part-time (1 woman); includes 1 Black or African American, non-Hispanic/Latino. 8 applicants, 63% accepted, 4 enrolled. In 2010, 2 master's awarded. *Degree requirements:* For master's, one foreign language, thesis (MA). *Entrance requirements:* For master's, GRE General Test. *Application deadline:* For fall admission, 7/1 priority date for domestic students; for spring admission, 11/15 for domestic students. Application fee: $50. Electronic applications accepted. *Expenses:* Tuition, state resident: full-time $7200; part-time $344 per credit hour. Tuition, nonresident: full-time $21,900; part-time $944 per credit hour. Tuition and fees vary according to course load and program. *Financial support:* Fellowships, research assistantships, teaching assistantships, unspecified assistantships available. *Unit head:* Dr. Nina Hellerstein, Department Head, 706-542-3122, E-mail: hellerst@uga.edu. *Application contact:* Dr. Catherine M. Jones, Graduate Coordinator, 706-542-3159, Fax: 706-542-2272, E-mail: cmjones@uga.edu.

University of Guelph, Graduate Studies, College of Arts, School of Languages and Literatures, Guelph, ON N1G 2W1, Canada. Offers European studies (MA); French studies (MA). *Entrance requirements:* For master's, honours BA or equivalent. Electronic applications accepted. *Faculty research:* Sociolinguistics, poetics and politics of literature, language acquisition.

University of Hawaii at Manoa, Graduate Division, College of Languages, Linguistics and Literature, Department of Languages and Literatures of Europe and the Americas, Program in French, Honolulu, HI 96822. Offers MA. Part-time programs available. *Students:* 12 full-time (10 women), 3 part-time (all women); includes 9 minority (1 American Indian or Alaska Native, non-Hispanic/Latino; 4 Asian, non-Hispanic/Latino; 1 Hispanic/Latino; 1 Native Hawaiian or other Pacific Islander, non-Hispanic/Latino; 2 Two or more races, non-Hispanic/Latino). Average age 34. 13 applicants, 69% accepted, 8 enrolled. In 2010, 3 master's awarded. *Degree requirements:* For master's, one foreign language, thesis optional. *Entrance requirements:* Additional exam requirements/recommendations for international students: Required—TOEFL (minimum score 580 paper-based; 237 computer-based; 92 iBT), IELTS (minimum score 5). *Application deadline:* For fall admission, 3/1 for domestic students, 2/1 for international students; for spring admission, 9/1 for domestic students, 8/15 for international students. Application fee: $60. *Financial support:* In 2010–11, 1 fellowship (averaging $3,750 per year), 10 teaching assistantships (averaging $14,382 per year) were awarded. *Application contact:* Robert Ball, Information Contact, 808-956-4715, Fax: 808-956-9536, E-mail: rball@hawaii.edu.

University of Illinois at Chicago, Graduate College, College of Liberal Arts and Sciences, Department of Spanish, French, Italian and Portuguese, Program in French, Chicago, IL 60607-7128. Offers MA. Part-time programs available. *Degree requirements:* For master's, one foreign language, thesis optional, exam. *Entrance requirements:* For master's, minimum GPA of 2.75. Additional exam requirements/recommendations for international students: Required—TOEFL. Electronic applications accepted. *Faculty research:* French civilization, feminist theory, French theater, sociology of literature, narrative theory.

University of Illinois at Urbana–Champaign, Graduate College, College of Liberal Arts and Sciences, School of Literatures, Cultures and Linguistics, Department of French, Champaign, IL 61820. Offers MA, PhD. *Faculty:* 12 full-time (5 women). *Students:* 20 full-time (14 women), 12 part-time (9 women); includes 2 minority (both Black or African American, non-Hispanic/Latino), 6 international. 44 applicants, 41% accepted, 9 enrolled. In 2010, 6 master's, 4 doctorates awarded. *Entrance requirements:* For master's, GRE, minimum GPA of 3.0, 2 writing samples in French; for doctorate, GRE, minimum GPA of 3.5, 2 writing samples in French. Additional exam requirements/recommendations for international students: Required—TOEFL (minimum score 550 paper-based; 213 computer-based; 79 iBT) or IELTS (minimum score 6.5). *Application deadline:* Applications are processed on a rolling basis. Application fee: $75 ($90 for international students). Electronic applications accepted. *Financial support:* In 2010–11, 6 fellowships, 2 research assistantships, 28 teaching assistantships were awarded; tuition waivers (full and partial) also available. *Unit head:* Karen L. Fresco, Head, 217-244-2716, Fax: 217-244-2223, E-mail: kfresco@illinois.edu. *Application contact:* Lynn Stanke, Office Support Specialist, 217-333-6269, Fax: 217-244-3050, E-mail: stanke@illinois.edu.

The University of Iowa, Graduate College, College of Liberal Arts and Sciences, Department of French and Italian, Iowa City, IA 52242-1316. Offers French (MA, PhD). *Degree requirements:* For master's, thesis optional, exam; for doctorate, comprehensive exam, thesis/dissertation. *Entrance requirements:* For master's and doctorate, GRE General Test, minimum GPA of 3.0. Additional exam requirements/recommendations for international students: Required—TOEFL (minimum score 550 paper-based; 213 computer-based; 81 iBT). Electronic applications accepted.

The University of Kansas, Graduate Studies, College of Liberal Arts and Sciences, Department of French and Italian, Lawrence, KS 66045-7590. Offers French (MA, PhD). Part-time programs available. *Faculty:* 11 full-time (6 women), 2 part-time/adjunct (0 women). *Students:* 22 full-time (17 women), 1 (woman) part-time, 3 international. Average age 33. 13 applicants, 69% accepted, 6 enrolled. In 2010, 2 master's, 2 doctorates awarded. *Degree requirements:* For master's, one foreign language, comprehensive exam, thesis optional; for doctorate, one foreign language, comprehensive exam, thesis/dissertation. *Entrance requirements:* For master's and doctorate, GRE. Additional exam requirements/recommendations for international students: Required—TOEFL, IELTS. *Application deadline:* For fall admission, 2/15 priority date for domestic students, 1/15 priority date for international students. Applications are processed on a rolling basis. Application fee: $55 ($65 for international students). Electronic applications accepted. *Expenses:* Tuition, state resident: full-time $7092; part-time $295.50 per credit hour. Tuition, nonresident: full-time $16,590; part-time $691.25 per credit hour. Required fees: $858; $71.49 per credit hour. Tuition and fees vary according to course load, campus/location and program. *Financial support:* Fellowships, teaching assistantships with full tuition reimbursements, unspecified assistantships available. Financial award applicants required to submit FAFSA. *Faculty research:* French literature and cultural studies; Francophone literature, film. *Unit head:* Caroline Jewers, Chair, 785-864-4056, Fax: 785-864-5179, E-mail: cjewers@ku.edu. *Application contact:* Paul Scott, Associate Professor, 785-864-9042, E-mail: pascott@ku.edu.

University of Kentucky, Graduate School, College of Arts and Sciences, Program in French, Lexington, KY 40506-0032. Offers MA. *Degree requirements:* For master's, one foreign language, comprehensive exam. *Entrance requirements:* For master's, GRE General Test, minimum undergraduate GPA of 2.75. Additional exam requirements/recommendations for international students: Required—TOEFL (minimum score 550 paper-based; 213 computer-based). Electronic applications accepted. *Faculty research:* The fables of Marie DeFrance, Rabelais and reading; the family romance in eighteenth century narrative; women of Dada and surrealism; postcolonialism; postmodernism.

University of Lethbridge, School of Graduate Studies, Lethbridge, AB T1K 3M4, Canada. Offers accounting (MScM); addictions counseling (M Sc); agricultural biotechnology (M Sc); agricultural studies (M Sc, MA); anthropology (MA); archaeology (MA); art (MA, MFA); biochemistry (M Sc); biological sciences (M Sc); biomolecular science (PhD); biosystems and biodiversity (PhD); Canadian studies (MA); chemistry (M Sc); computer science (M Sc); computer science and geographical information science (M Sc); counseling psychology (M Ed); dramatic arts (MA); earth, space, and physical science (PhD); economics (MA); educational leadership (M Ed); English (MA); environmental science (M Sc); evolution and behavior (PhD); exercise science (M Sc); finance (MScM); French (MA); French/German (MA); French/Spanish (MA); general education (M Ed); general management (MScM); geography (M Sc, MA); German (MA); health science (M Sc); history (MA); human resource management and labour relations (MScM); individualized multidisciplinary (M Sc, MA); information systems (MScM); international management (MScM); kinesiology (M Sc, MA); management (M Sc, MA); marketing (MScM); mathematics (M Sc); music (M Mus, MA); Native American studies (MA); neuroscience (M Sc, PhD); new media (MA); nursing (M Sc); philosophy (MA); physics (M Sc); policy and strategy (MScM); political science (MA); psychology (M Sc, MA); religious studies (MA); social sciences (MA); sociology (MA); theatre and dramatic arts (MFA); theoretical and computational science (PhD); urban and regional studies (MA); women's studies (MA). Part-time and evening/weekend programs available. *Degree requirements:* For doctorate, comprehensive exam, thesis/dissertation. *Entrance requirements:* For master's, GMAT (M Sc in management), bachelor's degree in related field, minimum GPA of 3.0 during previous 20 graded semester courses, 2 years teaching or related experience (M Ed); for doctorate, master's degree, minimum graduate GPA of 3.5. Additional exam requirements/recommendations for international students: Required—TOEFL. *Faculty research:* Movement and brain plasticity, gibberellin physiology, photosynthesis, carbon cycling, molecular properties of main-group ring components.

University of Louisiana at Lafayette, College of Liberal Arts, Department of Modern Languages, Program in Francophone Studies, Lafayette, LA 70504. Offers PhD. *Degree requirements:* For doctorate, 2 foreign languages, comprehensive exam, thesis/dissertation. *Entrance requirements:* For doctorate, GRE General Test, minimum GPA of 2.75. Additional exam requirements/recommendations for international students: Required—TOEFL (minimum score 550 paper-based; 213 computer-based). Electronic applications accepted. *Faculty research:* Louisiana folklore, eighteenth century French literature, contemporary criticism.

University of Louisiana at Lafayette, College of Liberal Arts, Department of Modern Languages, Program in French, Lafayette, LA 70504. Offers MA. Part-time programs available. *Degree requirements:* For master's, 2 foreign languages, thesis or alternative. *Entrance requirements:* For master's, GRE General Test, minimum GPA of 2.75. Additional exam requirements/recommendations for international students: Required—TOEFL (minimum score 550 paper-based; 213 computer-based). Electronic applications accepted. *Faculty research:* Louisiana studies, nineteenth century French literature, Francophone studies.

University of Louisville, Graduate School, College of Arts and Sciences, Department of Classical and Modern Languages, Louisville, KY 40292-0001. Offers French (MA); Spanish (MA). Part-time and evening/weekend programs available. *Faculty:* 22 full-time (13 women), 1 (woman) part-time/adjunct. *Students:* 11 full-time (8 women), 14 part-time (8 women); includes 2 Black or African American, non-Hispanic/Latino; 5 Hispanic/Latino, 1 international. Average age 31. 17 applicants, 76% accepted, 10 enrolled. In 2010, 18 master's awarded. *Degree requirements:* For master's, one foreign language, thesis optional. *Entrance requirements:* For master's, GRE General Test: Recommended, but not required. Additional exam requirements/recommendations for international students: Required—TOEFL (minimum score 550 paper-based; 79 computer-based). *Application deadline:* Applications are processed on a rolling basis. Application fee: $50. Electronic applications accepted. *Expenses:* Tuition, state resident: full-time $9144; part-time $508 per credit hour. Tuition, nonresident: full-time $19,026; part-time $1057 per credit hour. Tuition and fees vary according to program and reciprocity agreements. *Financial support:* In 2010–11, 9 students received support, including 8 teaching assistantships with full tuition reimbursements available (averaging $12,000 per year); fellowships, institutionally sponsored loans, scholarships/grants, health care benefits, and unspecified assistantships also available. Financial award applicants required to submit FAFSA. *Faculty research:* Hispanic cultural studies, sociolinguistics, translation, contemporary France, medieval literature. *Unit head:* Dr. Augustus A. Mastri, Chair, 502-852-0403, Fax: 502-852-8885, E-mail: mastri@louisville.edu. *Application contact:* Libby Leggett, Director, Graduate Admissions, 502-852-3101, Fax: 502-852-6536, E-mail: gradadm@louisville.edu.

University of Maine, Graduate School, College of Liberal Arts and Sciences, Department of Modern Languages and Classics, Orono, ME 04469. Offers French (MA, MAT); North American French (MA). Part-time programs available. *Faculty:* 6 full-time (4 women), 6 part-time/adjunct (5 women). *Students:* 3 full-time (2 women), 1 (woman) part-time. Average age 29. 5 applicants, 60% accepted, 2 enrolled. In 2010, 3 degrees awarded. *Degree requirements:* For master's, one foreign language, thesis (for some programs). *Entrance requirements:* For master's, GRE General Test. Additional exam requirements/recommendations for international students: Required—TOEFL. *Application deadline:* For fall admission, 2/1 priority date for domestic students. Applications are processed on a rolling basis. Application fee: $65. Electronic applications accepted. *Expenses:* Tuition, state resident: full-time $400. Tuition, nonresident: full-time $1050. *Financial support:* In 2010–11, 3 teaching assistantships with tuition reimbursements (averaging $12,790 per year) were awarded; Federal Work-Study, tuition waivers (full and partial), and instructorships also available. Financial award application deadline: 3/1. *Faculty research:* Narratology, poetics, Quebec literature, theater, women's studies. *Unit head:* Dr. Jane Smith, Chair, 207-581-2079, Fax: 207-581-1832. *Application contact:* Scott G. Delcourt, Associate Dean of the Graduate School, 207-581-3291, Fax: 207-581-3232, E-mail: graduate@maine.edu.

The University of Manchester, School of Languages, Linguistics and Cultures, Manchester, United Kingdom. Offers Arab world studies (PhD); Chinese studies (M Phil, PhD); East Asian studies (M Phil, PhD); English language (PhD); French studies (M Phil, PhD); German studies (M Phil, PhD); interpreting studies (PhD); Italian studies (M Phil, PhD); Japanese studies (M Phil, PhD); Latin American cultural studies (M Phil, PhD); linguistics (M Phil, PhD); Middle Eastern studies (M Phil, PhD); Polish studies (M Phil, PhD); Portuguese studies (M Phil, PhD); Russian studies (M Phil, PhD); Spanish studies (M Phil, PhD); translation and intercultural studies (M Phil, PhD).

University of Manitoba, Faculty of Graduate Studies, Faculty of Arts, Department of French, Spanish and Italian, Winnipeg, MB R3T 2N2, Canada. Offers French (MA, PhD). *Degree requirements:* For master's, one foreign language, thesis; for doctorate, 2 foreign languages, thesis/dissertation.

University of Maryland, College Park, Academic Affairs, College of Arts and Humanities, School of Languages, Literature, and Cultures, Modern French Studies Program, College Park, MD 20742. Offers PhD. *Students:* 15 full-time (all women), 2 part-time (1 woman); includes 3 minority (1 Black or African American, non-Hispanic/Latino; 2 Asian, non-Hispanic/Latino), 7 international. 13 applicants, 23% accepted, 2 enrolled. In 2010, 2 doctorates awarded. *Entrance requirements:* Additional exam requirements/recommendations for international students: Required—TOEFL. *Application deadline:* For fall admission, 1/15 for domestic and international students; for spring admission, 6/1 for international students. Application fee: $75. *Expenses:* Tuition, state resident: part-time $471 per credit hour. Tuition, nonresident: part-time $1016 per credit hour. Required fees: $337 per term. *Financial support:* In 2010–11, 2 fellowships with partial tuition reimbursements (averaging $7,750 per year), 9 teaching assistantships (averaging $19,160 per year) were awarded. *Unit head:* Carol A. Mossman, Director, 301-405-4025, Fax: 301-314-9928, E-mail: cmossman@umd.edu. *Application contact:* Dr. Charles A. Caramello, Dean of Graduate School, 301-405-0358, Fax: 301-314-9305, E-mail: ccaramel@umd.edu.

University of Maryland, College Park, Academic Affairs, College of Arts and Humanities, School of Languages, Literature, and Cultures, Program in French Language and Literature, College Park, MD 20742. Offers MA. *Students:* 5 full-time (all women), 2 part-time (both women), 1 international. 17 applicants, 29% accepted, 2 enrolled. In 2010, 8 master's awarded. *Degree requirements:* For master's, one foreign language, comprehensive exam, thesis or alternative. *Entrance requirements:* For master's, GRE General Test, GRE Subject Test, minimum GPA of 3.0, 3 letters of recommendation. Additional exam requirements/recommendations for international students: Required—TOEFL. *Application deadline:* For fall admission, 1/15 for domestic and international students; for spring admission, 6/1 for international students. Applications are processed on a rolling basis. Application fee: $75. Electronic applications accepted. *Expenses:* Tuition, state resident: part-time $471 per credit hour. Tuition, nonresident: part-time $1016 per credit hour. Required fees: $337 per term. *Financial support:* In 2010–11, 1 fellowship with partial tuition reimbursement (averaging $7,500 per year), 4 teaching assistantships (averaging $19,500 per year) were awarded; Federal Work-Study also available. Support available to part-time students. Financial award applicants required to submit FAFSA. *Unit head:* Carol A. Mossman, Director, School of Languages, Literatures and Cultures, 301-405-6464, Fax: 301-314-9928, E-mail: cmossman@umd.edu. *Application contact:* Dr. Charles A. Caramello, Dean of Graduate School, 301-405-0358, Fax: 301-314-9305, E-mail: ccaramel@umd.edu.

University of Massachusetts Amherst, Graduate School, College of Humanities and Fine Arts, Department of Languages, Literatures, and Cultures, Program in French and Francophone Studies, Amherst, MA 01003. Offers French (MA, MAT). Part-time programs available. *Faculty:* 6 full-time (3 women). *Students:* 8 full-time (5 women), 2 part-time (both women), 1 international. Average age 26. 18 applicants, 78% accepted, 6 enrolled. In 2010, 7 master's awarded. *Degree requirements:* For master's, thesis or alternative. *Entrance requirements:* For master's, GRE General Test. Additional exam requirements/recommendations for international students: Required—TOEFL (minimum score 550 paper-based; 213 computer-based; 80 iBT), IELTS (minimum score 6.5). *Application deadline:* For fall admission, 2/1 for domestic and international students; for spring admission, 10/1 for domestic and international students. Applications are processed on a rolling basis. Application fee: $50 ($65 for international students). Electronic applications accepted. *Expenses:* Tuition, state resident: full-time $2640. Required fees: $8282. One-time fee: $357 full-time. *Financial support:* In 2010–11, 16 teaching assistantships with full tuition reimbursements (averaging $12,523 per year) were awarded; fellowships, research assistantships, career-related internships or fieldwork, Federal Work-Study, scholarships/grants, traineeships, health care benefits, tuition waivers (full), and unspecified assistantships also available. Support available to part-time students. Financial award application deadline: 2/1; financial award applicants required to submit FAFSA. *Unit head:* Dr. Luke P. Bouvier, Graduate Program Director, 413-545-2314, Fax: 412-545-4778. *Application contact:* Jean M. Ames, Supervisor of Admissions, 413-545-0722, Fax: 413-577-0100, E-mail: gradadm@grad.umass.edu.

University of Memphis, Graduate School, College of Arts and Sciences, Department of Foreign Languages and Literatures, Memphis, TN 38152. Offers French (MA); Spanish (MA). Part-time programs available. *Faculty:* 12 full-time (5 women), 1 part-time/adjunct (0 women). *Students:* 14 full-time (11 women), 58 part-time (57 women); includes 5 minority (3 Black or African American, non-Hispanic/Latino; 2 Hispanic/Latino), 4 international. Average age 34. 12 applicants, 92% accepted, 5 enrolled. In 2010, 7 master's awarded. *Degree requirements:* For master's, 2 foreign languages, comprehensive exam. *Entrance requirements:* For master's, GRE, interview in language of concentration. Additional exam requirements/recommendations for international students: Required—TOEFL (minimum score 79 iBT). *Application deadline:* For fall admission, 5/15 for domestic students, 4/5 for international students; for spring admission, 11/30 for domestic students, 10/5 for international students. Applications are processed on a rolling basis. Application fee: $35 ($60 for international students). Electronic applications accepted. *Financial support:* In 2010–11, 11 students received support; research assistantships with full tuition reimbursements available, teaching assistantships with full tuition reimbursements available, Federal Work-Study, scholarships/grants, and unspecified assistantships available. Financial award application deadline: 2/15; financial award applicants required to submit FAFSA. *Faculty research:* Latin American studies, Brazilian culture and literature, modernity and postmodernity, Hispanic studies, French studies, French and Hispanic culture and literature, Hispanic linguistics, applied linguistics. *Unit head:* Dr. Ralph Albanese, Professor and Chair, 901-678-2507, E-mail: ralbanes@memphis.edu. *Application contact:* Dr. Fernando Burgos, Professor and Coordinator of Graduate Studies, 901-678-3158, E-mail: fburgos@memphis.edu.

University of Miami, Graduate School, College of Arts and Sciences, Department of Modern Languages and Literatures, Coral Gables, FL 33124. Offers romance studies (PhD), including French, Spanish. *Degree requirements:* For doctorate, 2 foreign languages, thesis/dissertation, area exam, qualifying exam. *Entrance requirements:* For doctorate, 1 writing sample in English and 1 writing sample in French or Spanish, minimum GPA of 3.0, oral interview, letters of recommendation. Additional exam requirements/recommendations for international students: Required—TOEFL (minimum score 550 paper-based; 213 computer-based; 59 iBT). Electronic applications accepted. *Faculty research:* Transatlantic studies, Caribbean studies, comparative literature, gender theory, cultural studies.

University of Michigan, Horace H. Rackham School of Graduate Studies, College of Literature, Science, and the Arts, Department of Romance Languages and Literatures, Program in

French

University of Michigan (continued)

French, Ann Arbor, MI 48109. Offers PhD. *Faculty:* 8 full-time (4 women). *Students:* 11 full-time (6 women); includes 2 Black or African American, non-Hispanic/Latino. Average age 27. 25 applicants, 24% accepted, 2 enrolled. In 2010, 2 doctorates awarded. *Degree requirements:* For doctorate, 2 foreign languages, thesis/dissertation, oral defense of dissertation, preliminary exams. *Entrance requirements:* For doctorate, GRE General Test. Additional exam requirements/recommendations for international students: Required—TOEFL or Michigan English Language Assessment Battery. *Application deadline:* For fall admission, 1/1 for domestic and international students. Application fee: $65 ($75 for international students). Electronic applications accepted. *Expenses:* Tuition, state resident: full-time $17,784; part-time $1116 per credit hour. Tuition, nonresident: full-time $35,944; part-time $2125 per credit hour. International tuition: $35,994 full-time. Required fees: $95 per semester. Tuition and fees vary according to course load, degree level and program. *Financial support:* In 2010–11, 4 fellowships with full tuition reimbursements (averaging $20,000 per year), 13 teaching assistantships with full tuition reimbursements (averaging $20,000 per year) were awarded; institutionally sponsored loans, scholarships/grants, and unspecified assistantships also available. Financial award application deadline: 1/1. *Faculty research:* Comparative Romance studies, medieval and early modern studies, postcolonial and minority literatures, culture and materiality, reflection on the nature and function of scholarship. *Unit head:* Dr. Cristina Moreiras-Menor, Chair, 734-764-5344, Fax: 734-764-8163. *Application contact:* Annette Herbert, Graduate Assistant, 734-764-8164, Fax: 734-764-8163, E-mail: rll-admissions@umich.edu.

University of Minnesota, Twin Cities Campus, Graduate School, College of Liberal Arts, Department of French and Italian, Minneapolis, MN 55455-0213. Offers French (MA, PhD). Part-time programs available. *Degree requirements:* For master's, one foreign language, comprehensive exam, thesis optional; for doctorate, one foreign language, thesis/dissertation, individualized exam on topic areas. *Entrance requirements:* For master's and doctorate, GRE, minimum GPA of 3.25 (recommended). Additional exam requirements/recommendations for international students: Required—TOEFL (minimum score 550 paper-based; 213 computer-based). Electronic applications accepted. *Faculty research:* Francophone literature, cultural studies, feminism, critical theory, medieval studies.

University of Mississippi, Graduate School, College of Liberal Arts, Department of Modern Languages, Oxford, University, MS 38677. Offers French (MA); German (MA); Spanish (MA). *Students:* 39 full-time (28 women), 19 part-time (17 women); includes 8 Black or African American, non-Hispanic/Latino; 1 American Indian or Alaska Native, non-Hispanic/Latino; 7 Asian, non-Hispanic/Latino; 10 Hispanic/Latino; 1 Two or more races, non-Hispanic/Latino. In 2010, 17 master's awarded. *Degree requirements:* For master's, thesis (for some programs). *Entrance requirements:* For master's, GRE General Test, minimum GPA of 3.0. Additional exam requirements/recommendations for international students: Required—TOEFL. *Application deadline:* For fall admission, 2/1 for domestic students; for spring admission, 10/1 for domestic students. Applications are processed on a rolling basis. Application fee: $25. Electronic applications accepted. *Financial support:* Scholarships/grants available. Financial award application deadline: 3/1; financial award applicants required to submit FAFSA. *Unit head:* Dr. Donald L. Dyer, Chair, 662-915-7298, Fax: 662-915-1086, E-mail: mlangs@olemiss.edu. *Application contact:* Dr. Christy M. Wyandt, Associate Dean, 662-915-7474, Fax: 662-915-7577, E-mail: cwyandt@olemiss.edu.

University of Missouri, Graduate School, College of Arts and Sciences, Department of Romance Languages and Literature, Program in French, Columbia, MO 65211. Offers MA, PhD. *Degree requirements:* For master's, one foreign language; for doctorate, 4 foreign languages, thesis/dissertation. *Entrance requirements:* For master's and doctorate, GRE General Test, minimum GPA of 3.0. Additional exam requirements/recommendations for international students: Required—TOEFL (minimum score 500 paper-based; 173 computer-based; 61 iBT).

The University of Montana, Graduate School, College of Arts and Sciences, Department of Modern and Classical Languages and Literatures, Missoula, MT 59812-0002. Offers French (MA); German (MA); Spanish (MA). *Degree requirements:* For master's, one foreign language. *Entrance requirements:* For master's, GRE General Test. Additional exam requirements/recommendations for international students: Required—TOEFL.

University of Nebraska–Lincoln, Graduate College, College of Arts and Sciences, Department of Modern Languages and Literatures, Lincoln, NE 68588. Offers French (MA, PhD); German (MA, PhD); Spanish (MA, PhD). *Degree requirements:* For master's, thesis optional; for doctorate, comprehensive exam, thesis/dissertation. *Entrance requirements:* For master's and doctorate, writing sample in target language. Additional exam requirements/recommendations for international students: Required—TOEFL (minimum score 550 paper-based; 213 computer-based). Electronic applications accepted. *Faculty research:* French, German, and Spanish language, literature, and culture.

University of Nevada, Reno, Graduate School, College of Liberal Arts, Department of Foreign Languages and Literatures, Reno, NV 89557. Offers French (MA); German (MA); Spanish (MA). *Degree requirements:* For master's, one foreign language, thesis optional. *Entrance requirements:* For master's, GRE General Test, minimum GPA of 2.75. Additional exam requirements/recommendations for international students: Required—TOEFL (minimum score 500 paper-based; 173 computer-based; 61 iBT), IELTS (minimum score 6). *Expenses:* Tuition, state resident: full-time $2219; part-time $246 per credit. Tuition, nonresident: part-time $510 per credit. International tuition: $9009 full-time. Required fees: $59 per term. One-time fee: $101. Tuition and fees vary according to course load. *Faculty research:* Thirteenth century mysticism, contemporary Spanish and Latin American poetry and theater, French interrelation between narration and photography, exile literature and Holocaust.

University of New Mexico, Graduate School, College of Arts and Sciences, Department of Foreign Languages and Literature, Albuquerque, NM 87131-2039. Offers comparative literature and cultural studies (MA); French (MA); French studies (PhD); German studies (MA). Part-time programs available. *Faculty:* 18 full-time (12 women), 29 part-time/adjunct (19 women). *Students:* 25 full-time (16 women), 6 part-time (4 women); includes 2 Hispanic/Latino, 8 international. Average age 32. 20 applicants, 70% accepted, 9 enrolled. In 2010, 7 master's, 1 doctorate awarded. *Degree requirements:* For master's, one foreign language, thesis optional; for doctorate, 2 foreign languages, thesis/dissertation. *Entrance requirements:* Additional exam requirements/recommendations for international students: Required—TOEFL. *Application deadline:* For fall admission, 2/1 priority date for domestic students; for spring admission, 10/1 priority date for domestic students. Application fee: $50. Electronic applications accepted. *Expenses:* Tuition, state resident: full-time $5991; part-time $251 per credit hour. Tuition, nonresident: full-time $14,405; part-time $800.20 per credit hour. Tuition and fees vary according to course level, course load, program and reciprocity agreements. *Financial support:* In 2010–11, 28 students received support, including 1 research assistantship (averaging $4,730 per year), 23 teaching assistantships with tuition reimbursements available (averaging $10,300 per year); Federal Work-Study, health care benefits, and unspecified assistantships also available. Financial award application deadline: 3/1; financial award applicants required to submit FAFSA. *Faculty research:* German, Russian, Italian, Japanese, French, comparative literature, culture studies, classics. Total annual research expenditures: $4,750. *Unit head:* Dr. Natasha Kolchevska, Chair, 505-277-4771, Fax: 505-277-3599, E-mail: nakol@unm.edu. *Application contact:* Jean Aragon, Application and Graduation Advisor, 505-277-4471, Fax: 505-277-3599, E-mail: peaslee@unm.edu.

The University of North Carolina at Chapel Hill, Graduate School, College of Arts and Sciences, Department of Romance Languages, Chapel Hill, NC 27599. Offers French (MA, PhD); Italian (MA, PhD); Portuguese (MA, PhD); Romance languages (MA, PhD); Romance philology (MA, PhD); Spanish (MA, PhD). *Degree requirements:* For master's, one foreign language, comprehensive exam, thesis; for doctorate, 2 foreign languages, comprehensive exam, thesis/dissertation. *Entrance requirements:* For master's and doctorate, GRE General Test, minimum GPA of 3.0. Additional exam requirements/recommendations for international students: Required—TOEFL (minimum score 550 paper-based; 213 computer-based). Electronic applications accepted.

The University of North Carolina at Greensboro, Graduate School, College of Arts and Sciences, Department of Romance Languages, Program in French, Greensboro, NC 27412-5001. Offers MA. *Degree requirements:* For master's, one foreign language, comprehensive exam, thesis or alternative. *Entrance requirements:* For master's, GRE General Test, 3-5 minute tape demonstrating foreign language proficiency, composition in French, sample paper in English. Additional exam requirements/recommendations for international students: Required—TOEFL. Electronic applications accepted.

University of Northern Iowa, Graduate College, College of Humanities and Fine Arts, Department of Modern Languages, Program in French, Cedar Falls, IA 50614. Offers French (MA); teaching English to speakers of other languages/French (MA). Part-time and evening/weekend programs available. *Students:* 4 full-time (all women), 3 part-time (all women); includes 2 minority (1 Asian, non-Hispanic/Latino; 1 Hispanic/Latino), 2 international. 9 applicants, 44% accepted, 3 enrolled. In 2010, 2 master's awarded. *Degree requirements:* For master's, one foreign language, comprehensive exam, thesis or alternative. *Entrance requirements:* For master's, minimum GPA of 3.0, valid teaching license, documentation of successful teaching experience. Additional exam requirements/recommendations for international students: Required—TOEFL (minimum score 600 paper-based; 250 computer-based; 100 iBT). *Application deadline:* For fall admission, 8/1 priority date for domestic students. Applications are processed on a rolling basis. Application fee: $50 ($70 for international students). Electronic applications accepted. *Financial support:* Career-related internships or fieldwork, Federal Work-Study, and tuition waivers (full and partial) available. Support available to part-time students. Financial award application deadline: 2/1. *Unit head:* Dr. Anne Lair, Coordinator, 319-273-2183, Fax: 319-273-2848, E-mail: anne.lair@uni.edu. *Application contact:* Laurie S. Russell, Record Analyst, 319-273-2623, Fax: 319-273-2885, E-mail: laurie.russell@uni.edu.

University of North Texas, Toulouse Graduate School, College of Arts and Sciences, Department of Foreign Languages and Literatures, Denton, TX 76203. Offers French (MA); Spanish (MA). Part-time programs available. *Degree requirements:* For master's, 2 foreign languages, comprehensive exam, thesis optional. *Entrance requirements:* For master's, GRE General Test, minimum undergraduate GPA of 3.0, curriculum vitae, 250-word essay in French or Spanish, 12 advanced credits in French or Spanish. Additional exam requirements/recommendations for international students: Recommended—TOEFL (minimum score 550 paper-based; 213 computer-based; 79 iBT). *Expenses:* Tuition, state resident: full-time $4298; part-time $239 per credit hour. Tuition, nonresident: full-time $10,782; part-time $549 per credit hour. Required fees: $1292; $270 per credit hour. *Financial support:* Fellowships, teaching assistantships, career-related internships or fieldwork, Federal Work-Study, and institutionally sponsored loans available. Financial award application deadline: 4/1; financial award applicants required to submit FAFSA. *Faculty research:* Literature of Austria, France, Germany, Latin America, Spain; culture/civilization; applied linguistics. *Unit head:* Chair. *Application contact:* Chair.

University of Notre Dame, Graduate School, College of Arts and Letters, Division of Humanities, Department of Romance Languages and Literatures, Notre Dame, IN 46556. Offers French and Francophone studies (MA); Iberian and Latin American studies (MA); Italian studies (MA); Romance literatures (MA). *Degree requirements:* For master's, 2 foreign languages, comprehensive exam, thesis optional. *Entrance requirements:* For master's, GRE General Test, BA in target language. Additional exam requirements/recommendations for international students: Required—TOEFL (minimum score 600 paper-based; 250 computer-based; 80 iBT). Electronic applications accepted. *Faculty research:* Literature of discovery and exploration, modern literature, literary criticism, medieval literature, feminist critical theory.

University of Oklahoma, College of Arts and Sciences, Department of Modern Languages, Program in French, Norman, OK 73019. Offers MA, PhD, MBA/MA. Part-time programs available. *Students:* 9 full-time (8 women), 3 part-time (2 women); includes 1 minority (Black or African American, non-Hispanic/Latino), 3 international. Average age 29. 5 applicants, 60% accepted, 3 enrolled. In 2010, 4 master's awarded. *Degree requirements:* For master's, 2 foreign languages, comprehensive exam, thesis optional, departmental qualifying exam; for doctorate, 3 foreign languages, comprehensive exam, thesis/dissertation, departmental qualifying exam. *Entrance requirements:* For master's, BA in French or equivalent, minimum GPA of 3.0 in last 60 hours, 3 letters of recommendation. Additional exam requirements/recommendations for international students: Required—TOEFL (minimum score 550 paper-based; 213 computer-based; 79 iBT). *Application deadline:* For fall admission, 2/1 priority date for domestic students, 2/1 for international students; for spring admission, 10/1 for domestic students, 9/1 for international students. Applications are processed on a rolling basis. Application fee: $40 ($90 for international students). Electronic applications accepted. *Expenses:* Tuition, state resident: full-time $3893; part-time $162.20 per credit hour. Tuition, nonresident: full-time $14,167; part-time $590.30 per credit hour. Required fees: $2523; $94.60 per credit hour. Tuition and fees vary according to course load and degree level. *Financial support:* Scholarships/grants, health care benefits, and unspecified assistantships available. Financial award applicants required to submit FAFSA. *Faculty research:* French and Francophone literature and cultural studies, history of medicine, critical theory, food and culture, European culture and identity. *Unit head:* Dr. Pamela Genova, Chair, 405-325-6181, Fax: 405-325-0103, E-mail: genova@ou.edu. *Application contact:* Dr. Logan E. Whalen, Graduate Liaison, 405-325-5088, Fax: 405-325-0103, E-mail: mlllgradinfo@ou.edu.

University of Oregon, Graduate School, College of Arts and Sciences, Department of Romance Languages, Program in French, Eugene, OR 97403. Offers MA. Part-time programs available. *Degree requirements:* For master's, one foreign language. *Entrance requirements:* For master's, GRE General Test, minimum GPA of 3.0. Additional exam requirements/recommendations for international students: Required—TOEFL.

University of Ottawa, Faculty of Graduate and Postdoctoral Studies, Faculty of Arts, Department of Lettres Françaises, Ottawa, ON K1N 6N5, Canada. Offers MA, PhD. *Degree requirements:* For master's, thesis or alternative; for doctorate, thesis/dissertation, oral exam. *Entrance requirements:* For master's, honors degree or equivalent, minimum B average; for doctorate, master's degree, minimum B+ average. Electronic applications accepted. *Faculty research:* Littérature française, du Moyen-Âge á nos jours; littérature québécoise, des origines au XXe siecle; création littéraire.

University of Pennsylvania, School of Arts and Sciences, Graduate Group in Romance Languages, Philadelphia, PA 19104. Offers French (AM, PhD); Italian (AM, PhD); Spanish (AM, PhD). *Faculty:* 58 full-time (23 women), 4 part-time/adjunct (1 woman). *Students:* 61 full-time (34 women), 2 part-time (both women); includes 1 American Indian or Alaska Native, non-Hispanic/Latino; 12 Hispanic/Latino, 19 international. 114 applicants, 15% accepted, 11 enrolled. In 2010, 11 master's, 6 doctorates awarded. Terminal master's awarded for partial completion of doctoral program. *Degree requirements:* For master's, one foreign language, thesis or alternative; for doctorate, 2 foreign languages, thesis/dissertation. *Entrance requirements:* For master's and doctorate, GRE General Test. Additional exam requirements/recommendations for international students: Required—TOEFL. *Application deadline:* For fall admission, 12/1 priority date for domestic students. Application fee: $70. Electronic applications accepted. *Expenses:* Tuition: Full-time $25,660; part-time $4758 per course. Required fees: $2152; $270 per course. Tuition and fees vary according to course load, degree level and program. *Financial support:* In 2010–11, 23 fellowships, 2 research assistantships, 39 teaching assistantships were awarded; institutionally sponsored loans, scholarships/grants, traineeships, health care benefits, and unspecified assistantships also available. Financial award application deadline: 12/15. *Faculty research:* Literary theory and criticism, cultural studies, history of Romance literatures, gender studies. *Application contact:* Graduate Coordinator, 215-898-7429.

University of Pittsburgh, School of Arts and Sciences, Department of French and Italian, Program in French, Pittsburgh, PA 15260. Offers MA, PhD. Part-time programs available. *Faculty:* 6 full-time (3 women). *Students:* 20 full-time (11 women), 5 international. Average age 31. 18 applicants, 39% accepted, 3 enrolled. In 2010, 6 master's, 1 doctorate awarded. Terminal master's awarded for partial completion of doctoral program. *Degree requirements:* For master's, one foreign language, comprehensive exam, seminar paper; for doctorate, one foreign language, comprehensive exam, thesis/dissertation, dissertation defense. *Entrance requirements:* For master's, GRE General Test, phone interview, 2 writing samples (French and English); for doctorate, GRE General Test, phone interview, 2 writing samples (French and English), personal essay. Additional exam requirements/recommendations for international students: Required—TOEFL (minimum score 550 paper-based; 213 computer-based; 80 iBT). *Application deadline:* For fall admission, 1/10 priority date for domestic and international students. Application fee: $50. Electronic applications accepted. *Expenses:* Tuition, state resident: full-time $17,304; part-time $701 per credit. Tuition, nonresident: full-time $29,554; part-time $1210 per credit. Required fees: $740; $214 per term. Tuition and fees vary according to program. *Financial support:* In 2010–11, 16 students received support, including 3 fellowships with full tuition reimbursements available (averaging $18,546 per year), 13 teaching assistantships with full tuition reimbursements available (averaging $15,520 per year); career-related internships or fieldwork, Federal Work-Study, institutionally sponsored loans, scholarships/grants, traineeships, health care benefits, tuition waivers (partial), unspecified assistantships, and summer research stipends, summer teaching, teaching on study abroad program also available. Support available to part-time students. Financial award application deadline: 1/10; financial award applicants required to submit FAFSA. *Faculty research:* Literature and politics, constructs of the French nation, literary and cultural theory, French linguistics, gender and sexuality, French film, French and Francophone literature and culture of all periods. Total annual research expenditures: $34,000. *Unit head:* Dr. Renate Blumenfeld-Kosinski, Chair, 412-624-6224, Fax: 412-624-6263, E-mail: rbk7580@aol.com. *Application contact:* Matthew Carulli, Graduate Secretary, 412-624-5220, Fax: 412-624-6263, E-mail: mdc24@pitt.edu.

University of Regina, Faculty of Graduate Studies and Research, Faculty of Arts, Department of French, Regina, SK S4S 0A2, Canada. Offers MA. *Faculty:* 3 full-time (0 women). *Students:* 1 (woman) part-time. 3 applicants, 67% accepted. *Degree requirements:* For master's, thesis, seminar presentation. *Entrance requirements:* Additional exam requirements/recommendations for international students: Required—TOEFL (minimum score 580 paper-based; 80 iBT). *Application deadline:* Applications are processed on a rolling basis. Application fee: $100. Electronic applications accepted. Tuition and fees charges are reported in Canadian dollars. *Expenses:* Tuition, area resident: Full-time $3244.50 Canadian dollars; part-time $180.25 Canadian dollars per credit hour. International tuition: $4744.50 Canadian dollars full-time. Required fees: $494 Canadian dollars; $115.25 Canadian dollars per credit hour. $115.25 Canadian dollars per semester. Tuition and fees vary according to program. *Financial support:* Fellowships, research assistantships, teaching assistantships, scholarships/grants available. Financial award application deadline: 6/15. *Faculty research:* French literature, French linguistics, rhetoric, translation and terminology, lexicography. *Unit head:* Dr. Emmanuel Aito, Head, 306-585-4323, Fax: 306-585-4827, E-mail: emmanuel.aito@uregina.ca.

University of Rochester, School of Arts and Sciences, Department of Modern Languages and Cultures, Program in French, Rochester, NY 14627.

University of Saskatchewan, College of Graduate Studies and Research, College of Arts and Sciences, Department of Languages and Linguistics, Saskatoon, SK S7N 5A2, Canada. Offers MA. *Degree requirements:* For master's, 2 foreign languages, thesis. *Entrance requirements:* Additional exam requirements/recommendations for international students: Required—TOEFL (minimum score 80 iBT); Recommended—IELTS (minimum score 6.5). Electronic applications accepted.

University of South Africa, College of Human Sciences, Pretoria, South Africa. Offers adult education (M Ed); African languages (MA, PhD); African politics (MA, PhD); Afrikaans (MA, PhD); ancient history (MA, PhD); ancient Near Eastern studies (MA, PhD); anthropology (MA, PhD); applied linguistics (MA); Arabic (MA, PhD); archaeology (MA); art history (MA); Biblical archaeology (MA); Biblical studies (M Th, D Th, PhD); Christian spirituality (M Th, D Th); church history (M Th, D Th); classical studies (MA, PhD); clinical psychology (MA); communication (MA, PhD); comparative education (M Ed, Ed D); consulting psychology (D Admin, D Com, PhD); curriculum studies (M Ed, Ed D); development studies (M Admin, MA, D Admin, PhD); didactics (M Ed, Ed D); education (M Tech); education management (M Ed, Ed D); educational psychology (M Ed); English (MA); environmental education (M Ed); French (MA, PhD); German (MA, PhD); Greek (MA); guidance and counseling (M Ed); health studies (MA, PhD), including health sciences education (MA), health services management (MA), medical and surgical nursing science (critical care general) (MA), midwifery and neonatal nursing science (MA), trauma and emergency care (MA); history (MA, PhD); history of education (Ed D); inclusive education (M Ed, Ed D); information and communications technology policy and regulation (MA); information science (MA, MIS, PhD); international politics (MA, PhD); Islamic studies (MA, PhD); Italian (MA, PhD); Judaica (MA, PhD); linguistics (MA, PhD); mathematical education (M Ed); mathematics education (MA); missiology (M Th, D Th); modern Hebrew (MA, PhD); musicology (MA, MMus, D Mus, PhD); natural science education (M Ed); New Testament (M Th, D Th); Old Testament (D Th); pastoral therapy (M Th, D Th); philosophy (MA); philosophy of education (M Ed, Ed D); politics (MA, PhD); Portuguese (MA, PhD); practical theology (M Th, D Th); psychology (MA, MS, PhD); psychology of education (M Ed, Ed D); public health (MA); religious studies (MA, D Th, PhD); Romance languages (MA); Russian (MA, PhD); Semitic languages (MA, PhD); social behavior studies in HIV/AIDS (MA); social science (mental health) (MA); social science in development studies (MA); social science in psychology (MA); social science in social work (MA); social science in sociology (MA); social work (MSW, DSW, PhD); socio-education (M Ed, Ed D); sociolinguistics (MA); sociology (MA, PhD); Spanish (MA, PhD); systematic theology (M Th, D Th); TESOL (teaching English to speakers of other languages) (MA); theological ethics (M Th, D Th); theory of literature (MA, PhD); urban ministries (D Th); urban ministry (M Th).

University of South Carolina, The Graduate School, College of Arts and Sciences, Department of Languages, Literatures, and Cultures, Columbia, SC 29208. Offers comparative literature (MA, PhD); foreign languages (MAT), including French, German, Spanish; French (MA); German (MA); Spanish (MA). MAT offered in cooperation with the College of Education. Part-time programs available. *Degree requirements:* For master's, one foreign language, comprehensive exam, thesis optional; for doctorate, 2 foreign languages, comprehensive exam, thesis/dissertation. *Entrance requirements:* For master's and doctorate, GRE General Test, writing sample. Additional exam requirements/recommendations for international students: Required—TOEFL (minimum score 230 computer-based; 75 iBT). Electronic applications accepted. *Faculty research:* Modern literature, linguistics, literature and culture, medieval literature, literary theory.

University of South Florida, Graduate School, College of Arts and Sciences, World Languages Department, Tampa, FL 33620-9951. Offers classics: Latin/Greek (MA); French (MA); linguistics (MA); linguistics: ESL (MA); Spanish (MA). Part-time and evening/weekend programs available. *Faculty:* 10 full-time (6 women). *Students:* 38 full-time (28 women), 25 part-time (17 women); includes 3 Black or African American, non-Hispanic/Latino; 2 American Indian or Alaska Native, non-Hispanic/Latino; 3 Asian, non-Hispanic/Latino; 18 Hispanic/Latino; 1 Two or more races, non-Hispanic/Latino, 6 international. Average age 35. 65 applicants, 48% accepted, 23 enrolled. In 2010, 23 master's awarded. *Degree requirements:* For master's, comprehensive exam, thesis. *Entrance requirements:* For master's, GRE General Test, minimum GPA of 3.0 in last 60 hours. Additional exam requirements/recommendations for international students: Required—TOEFL (minimum score 600 paper-based; 250 computer-based). *Application deadline:* For fall admission, 2/15 for domestic students, 1/2 for international students; for spring admission, 10/15 for domestic students, 6/1 for international students. Application fee: $30. Electronic applications accepted. *Financial support:* In 2010–11, 31 teaching assistantships with tuition reimbursements (averaging $9,272 per year) were awarded; tuition waivers (partial) and unspecified assistantships also available. Financial award application deadline: 6/30. *Faculty research:* Second language writing, academic literacy. Total annual research expenditures: $116,653. *Unit head:* Dr. Victor Peppard, Chairperson, 813-974-2012, Fax: 813-974-1718, E-mail: peppard@.cas.usf.edu. *Application contact:* Dr. Victor Peppard, Chairperson, 813-974-2012, Fax: 813-974-1718, E-mail: peppard@.cas.usf.edu.

The University of Tennessee, Graduate School, College of Arts and Sciences, Department of Modern Foreign Languages and Literatures, Program in French, Knoxville, TN 37996. Offers MA. *Degree requirements:* For master's, one foreign language, thesis or alternative. *Entrance requirements:* For master's, minimum GPA of 2.7. Additional exam requirements/recommendations for international students: Required—TOEFL. Electronic applications accepted. *Expenses:* Tuition, state resident: full-time $7440; part-time $414 per credit hour. Tuition, nonresident: full-time $22,478; part-time $1250 per credit hour. Required fees: $922; $43 per credit hour. Tuition and fees vary according to program.

The University of Tennessee, Graduate School, College of Arts and Sciences, Department of Modern Foreign Languages and Literatures, Program in Modern Foreign Languages, Knoxville, TN 37996. Offers applied linguistics (PhD); French (PhD); German (PhD); Italian (PhD); Portuguese (PhD); Russian (PhD); Spanish (PhD). *Degree requirements:* For doctorate, 2 foreign languages, thesis/dissertation. *Entrance requirements:* For doctorate, minimum GPA of 2.7. Additional exam requirements/recommendations for international students: Required—TOEFL. Electronic applications accepted. *Expenses:* Tuition, state resident: full-time $7440; part-time $414 per credit hour. Tuition, nonresident: full-time $22,478; part-time $1250 per credit hour. Required fees: $922; $43 per credit hour. Tuition and fees vary according to program.

The University of Texas at Arlington, Graduate School, College of Liberal Arts, Department of Modern Languages, Arlington, TX 76019. Offers French (MA); Spanish (MA). Part-time and evening/weekend programs available. *Faculty:* 8 full-time (5 women), 1 (woman) part-time/adjunct. *Students:* 18 full-time (9 women), 23 part-time (16 women); includes 20 minority (6 Black or African American, non-Hispanic/Latino; 1 Asian, non-Hispanic/Latino; 11 Hispanic/Latino; 1 Native Hawaiian or other Pacific Islander, non-Hispanic/Latino; 1 Two or more races, non-Hispanic/Latino), 2 international. 14 applicants, 100% accepted, 11 enrolled. In 2010, 6 master's awarded. *Degree requirements:* For master's, 2 foreign languages, comprehensive exam, thesis optional. *Entrance requirements:* For master's, GRE General Test, minimum GPA of 3.0, 3 letters of recommendation. Additional exam requirements/recommendations for international students: Required—TOEFL (minimum score 550 paper-based; 213 computer-based). *Application deadline:* For fall admission, 6/15 for domestic students. Applications are processed on a rolling basis. Application fee: $35 ($50 for international students). *Expenses:* Tuition, state resident: full-time $7500. Tuition, nonresident: full-time $13,080. International tuition: $13,250 full-time. *Financial support:* In 2010–11, 4 fellowships with full tuition reimbursements, 14 teaching assistantships (averaging $12,000 per year) were awarded; research assistantships. Financial award application deadline: 6/1; financial award applicants required to submit FAFSA. *Unit head:* Dr. Antoinette Sol, Chair, 817-272-3161, Fax: 817-272-5408, E-mail: amsol@uta.edu. *Application contact:* Dr. Ignacio Ruiz-Perez, Graduate Advisor, 817-272-3161, Fax: 817-272-5408, E-mail: iruiz@uta.edu.

The University of Texas at Austin, Graduate School, College of Liberal Arts, Department of French and Italian, Austin, TX 78712-1111. Offers French (MA, PhD); French linguistics (MA, PhD); Italian studies (MA, PhD); Romance linguistics (MA, PhD). Part-time programs available. *Degree requirements:* For master's, one foreign language, thesis; for doctorate, 2 foreign languages, thesis/dissertation. *Entrance requirements:* For master's, GRE General Test, minimum GPA of 3.0, bachelor's degree in French or equivalent; for doctorate, GRE General Test, minimum GPA of 3.0, master's degree in French. Additional exam requirements/recommendations for international students: Required—TOEFL. Electronic applications accepted. *Faculty research:* Nineteenth-century Italian literature, Italian Renaissance, twentieth-century French literature, Francophone literature, fifteenth-century literature and culture.

The University of Toledo, College of Graduate Studies, College of Language, Literature and Social Sciences, Department of Foreign Languages, Toledo, OH 43606-3390. Offers French (MA); German (MA); Spanish (MA). Part-time programs available. *Faculty:* 6. *Students:* 2 full-time (both women), 3 part-time (2 women); includes 1 minority (Hispanic/Latino). Average age 35. 8 applicants, 25% accepted, 2 enrolled. In 2010, 2 master's awarded. *Degree requirements:* For master's, one foreign language, comprehensive exam, comprehensive reading exam in 1 additional foreign language. *Entrance requirements:* For master's, A minimum 2.7 cumulative point-hour ratio (on a 4.0 scale) for all previous academic work. Additional exam requirements/recommendations for international students: Required—TOEFL (minimum score 550 paper-based; 213 computer-based; 80 iBT), IELTS (minimum score 6.5). *Application deadline:* For fall admission, 1/15 priority date for domestic and international students. Applications are processed on a rolling basis. Application fee: $45 ($75 for international students). Electronic applications accepted. *Expenses:* Tuition, state resident: full-time $11,426; part-time $476 per credit hour. Tuition, nonresident: full-time $21,660; part-time $903 per credit hour. One-time fee: $62. *Financial support:* Teaching assistantships with full tuition reimbursements, Federal Work-Study, institutionally sponsored loans, scholarships/grants, tuition waivers (full), and unspecified assistantships available. Support available to part-time students. *Unit head:* Dr. Ruth Hottell, Chair, 419-530-4651, E-mail: ruth.hottell@utoledo.edu. *Application contact:* Graduate School Office, 419-530-4723, Fax: 419-530-4724, E-mail: grdsch@utnet.utoledo.edu.

University of Toronto, School of Graduate Studies, Humanities Division, Department of French, Toronto, ON M5S 1A1, Canada. Offers French language and literature (MA, PhD). Part-time programs available. *Degree requirements:* For master's, research essay; for doctorate, one foreign language, thesis/dissertation, field exam. *Entrance requirements:* For master's, 2 letters of reference, writing sample, minimum B+ average overall and in French, undergraduate major in French; for doctorate, 7 courses in French language and literature, minimum A-average, writing sample.

University of Utah, Graduate School, College of Humanities, Department of Languages and Literature, Salt Lake City, UT 84112. Offers comparative literary and cultural studies (MA, PhD); French (MA, MALP); German (MA, MALP, PhD); Spanish (MA, MALP, PhD); world languages with secondary teaching licensure (MA). *Faculty:* 36 full-time (21 women). *Students:* 35 full-time (24 women), 9 part-time (7 women); includes 7 minority (1 American Indian or Alaska Native, non-Hispanic/Latino; 2 Asian, non-Hispanic/Latino; 4 Hispanic/Latino), 8 international. Average age 34. 58 applicants, 57% accepted, 24 enrolled. In 2010, 17 master's, 2 doctorates awarded. Terminal master's awarded for partial completion of doctoral program. *Degree requirements:* For master's, 2 foreign languages, comprehensive exam (for some programs), thesis (for some programs), standard proficiency in 2 languages other than English; for doctorate, 3 foreign languages, comprehensive exam, thesis/dissertation, standard proficiency in 2 languages other than English and language of study, advanced proficiency in 1 language other than English and language of study. *Entrance requirements:* For master's, GRE, bachelor's degree or strong undergraduate record in target languages, minimum GPA of 3.0; for doctorate, GRE, MA, advanced proficiency in a target language. Additional exam requirements/recommendations for international students: Required—TOEFL (minimum score 500 paper-based; 173 computer-based). *Application deadline:* For fall admission, 1/15 priority date for domestic students, 12/15 priority date for international students. Application fee: $55 ($65 for international students). Electronic applications accepted. *Expenses:* Tuition, area resident: Part-time $179.19 per credit hour. Tuition, state resident: full-time $4384. Tuition, nonresident: full-time $16,684; part-time $630.67 per credit hour. Required fees: $350 per semester. Tuition and fees vary according to course load, degree level and program. *Financial support:* In 2010–11, 24 students received support, including 2 fellowships, 22 teaching assistantships with full and partial tuition reimbursements available (averaging $11,500 per year); health care benefits also available. Financial award application deadline: 1/15; financial award applicants required to submit FAFSA. *Faculty research:* Literary study, literary theory, linguistics, cultural studies, comparative studies. Total annual research expenditures: $53,399. *Unit head:* Dr.

French

University of Utah (continued)
Karin Baumgartner, Director of Graduate Studies, 801-585-3001, Fax: 801-581-7581, E-mail: karin.baumgartner@hum.utah.edu. *Application contact:* Virginia Ellinwood, Academic Advisor, 801-585-9437, Fax: 801-581-7581, E-mail: v.ellinwood@utah.edu.

University of Vermont, Graduate College, College of Arts and Sciences, Department of Romance Languages, Burlington, VT 05405. Offers French (MA). *Students:* 2 (1 woman). In 2010, 1 master's awarded. *Degree requirements:* For master's, one foreign language. *Entrance requirements:* For master's, GRE General Test. Additional exam requirements/recommendations for international students: Required—TOEFL (minimum score 550 paper-based; 213 computer-based; 80 iBT). *Application deadline:* For fall admission, 8/1 priority date for domestic students. Applications are processed on a rolling basis. Application fee: $40. Electronic applications accepted. *Expenses:* Tuition, state resident: part-time $537 per credit hour. Tuition, nonresident: part-time $1355 per credit hour. *Financial support:* Fellowships, teaching assistantships available. Financial award application deadline: 3/1. *Faculty research:* French, French-Canadian, and French-African literature. *Unit head:* Dr. G. Nunley, Chairperson, 802-656-3196. *Application contact:* Dr. Gretchen VanSlyke, Coordinator, 802-656-3196.

University of Victoria, Faculty of Graduate Studies, Faculty of Humanities, Department of French, Victoria, BC V8W 2Y2, Canada. Offers literature (MA); teaching emphasis (MA). Part-time and evening/weekend programs available. *Degree requirements:* For master's, 2 foreign languages, thesis optional. *Entrance requirements:* For master's, BA in French. Additional exam requirements/recommendations for international students: Required—TOEFL (minimum score 575 paper-based; 233 computer-based), IELTS (minimum score 7). Electronic applications accepted. *Faculty research:* French-Canadian literature, stylistics, comparative literature, Francophone literature.

University of Virginia, College and Graduate School of Arts and Sciences, Department of French, Charlottesville, VA 22903. Offers MA, PhD. *Faculty:* 14 full-time (10 women), 1 (woman) part-time/adjunct. *Students:* 31 full-time (22 women), 2 part-time (both women); includes 1 Asian, non-Hispanic/Latino, 3 international. Average age 29. 29 applicants, 31% accepted, 4 enrolled. In 2010, 3 master's, 5 doctorates awarded. *Degree requirements:* For master's, one foreign language, comprehensive exam; for doctorate, one foreign language, comprehensive exam, thesis/dissertation. *Entrance requirements:* For master's and doctorate, GRE General Test, minimum GPA of 3.0 in major and overall; 2 letters of recommendation; writing sample. Additional exam requirements/recommendations for international students: Required—TOEFL (minimum score 600 paper-based; 250 computer-based; 90 iBT), IELTS (minimum score 7). *Application deadline:* For fall admission, 12/1 for domestic and international students. Applications are processed on a rolling basis. Application fee: $60. Electronic applications accepted. *Financial support:* Fellowships, teaching assistantships available. Financial award applicants required to submit FAFSA. *Unit head:* Cheryl Krueger, 434-924-7158, Fax: 434-924-7157, E-mail: cherylkrueger@virginia.edu. *Application contact:* Claire Lyu, Director of Graduate Studies, 434-924-7158, Fax: 434-924-7157, E-mail: cl9t@virginia.edu.

University of Washington, Graduate School, College of Arts and Sciences, Department of Romance Languages and Literature, Division of French and Italian Studies, Seattle, WA 98195. Offers French (MA, PhD); Italian (MA). Terminal master's awarded for partial completion of doctoral program. *Degree requirements:* For master's, 2 foreign languages, exam; for doctorate, 3 foreign languages, thesis/dissertation, exam. *Entrance requirements:* For master's and doctorate, GRE General Test, minimum GPA of 3.0. Additional exam requirements/recommendations for international students: Required—TOEFL. Electronic applications accepted. *Faculty research:* Interdisciplinary studies, literary theory and criticism, film, major periods of French and Italian literature, Francophonie.

University of Waterloo, Graduate Studies, Faculty of Arts, Department of French Studies, Waterloo, ON N2L 3G1, Canada. Offers French (MA, PhD). Part-time programs available. *Entrance requirements:* For master's, honors degree, minimum B average, course work and assignments in French, resume. Additional exam requirements/recommendations for international students: Required—TOEFL, TWE. Electronic applications accepted. *Faculty research:* French and Quebec literature: Middle Ages through twentieth century, phonology of Acadian dialect, computerized scholarly editions of medieval and Renaissance texts.

The University of Western Ontario, Faculty of Graduate Studies, Faculty of Arts and Humanities, Department of French, London, ON N6A 5B8, Canada. Offers Canadian literature (MA); French (MA, PhD). MA (Canadian literature) offered in cooperation with Department of English. *Degree requirements:* For master's, thesis or alternative; for doctorate, one foreign language, thesis/dissertation. *Entrance requirements:* For master's, minimum B average, honors degree, 2 years of teaching experience (MAT); for doctorate, MA or equivalent, minimum B average in French. Additional exam requirements/recommendations for international students: Required—TOEFL. Electronic applications accepted.

University of West Georgia, College of Education, Department of Curriculum and Instruction, Carrollton, GA 30118. Offers art education (M Ed); art teacher education (Ed S); biology—secondary education (M Ed); biology/secondary education (Ed S); business education (M Ed, Ed S); chemistry/secondary education (Ed S); economics/secondary teacher education (Ed S); education administration and supervision (M Ed); educational leadership (M Ed, Ed S); English teacher education (M Ed, Ed S); French language teacher education (M Ed, Ed S); history teacher education (Ed S); mathematics teacher education (M Ed, Ed S); middle grades education (M Ed, Ed S); physical education teaching and coaching (M Ed); physics/secondary education (Ed S); school improvement (Ed S); science teacher education (M Ed, Ed S); secondary education (M Ed); social science—secondary education (M Ed); social science teacher education (M Ed); Spanish language teacher education (M Ed, Ed S); Spanish MAT (M Ed); sports management (M Ed). Part-time and evening/weekend programs available. *Faculty:* 18 full-time (15 women), 7 part-time/adjunct (6 women). *Students:* 104 full-time (68 women), 254 part-time (169 women); includes 89 Black or African American, non-Hispanic/Latino; 4 Asian, non-Hispanic/Latino; 3 Hispanic/Latino; 6 Two or more races, non-Hispanic/Latino, 1 international. Average age 37. 94 applicants, 67% accepted, 21 enrolled. In 2010, 86 master's, 55 other advanced degrees awarded. *Degree requirements:* For master's, comprehensive exam; for Ed S, research project. *Entrance requirements:* For master's, minimum GPA of 2.7; for Ed S, master's degree, minimum graduate GPA of 2.7. *Application deadline:* For fall admission, 7/17 for domestic students; for spring admission, 11/20 for domestic students. Applications are processed on a rolling basis. Application fee: $30. Electronic applications accepted. *Expenses:* Tuition, state resident: full-time $4130; part-time $173 per semester hour. Tuition, nonresident: full-time $16,524; part-time $689 per semester hour. Required fees: $1586; $44.01 per semester hour. $397 per semester. Tuition and fees vary according to program. *Financial support:* In 2010–11, 5 research assistantships with full tuition reimbursements (averaging $3,000 per year) were awarded; career-related internships or fieldwork and scholarships/grants also available. Support available to part-time students. Financial award applicants required to submit FAFSA. *Unit head:* Dr. Frank Butts, Chair, 678-839-6530, Fax: 678-839-6195, E-mail: fbutts@westga.edu. *Application contact:* Dr. Frank Butts, Chair, 678-839-6530, Fax: 678-839-6195, E-mail: fbutts@westga.edu.

University of Wisconsin–Madison, Graduate School, College of Letters and Science, Department of French and Italian, Program in French, Madison, WI 53706-1380. Offers MA, PhD. Part-time programs available. *Degree requirements:* For master's, one foreign language; for doctorate, one foreign language, thesis/dissertation. *Entrance requirements:* For master's and doctorate, GRE. Electronic applications accepted. *Expenses:* Tuition, state resident: full-time $9887; part-time $617.96 per credit. Tuition, nonresident: full-time $24,054; part-time $1503.40 per credit. Required fees: $67.63 per credit. Tuition and fees vary according to reciprocity agreements. *Faculty research:* Francophone literature; French literature, culture, linguistics, and language pedagogy.

University of Wisconsin–Madison, Graduate School, College of Letters and Science, Department of French and Italian, Program in French Studies, Madison, WI 53706-1380. Offers MFS, Certificate. Part-time programs available. *Degree requirements:* For master's, one foreign language, thesis, internship; for Certificate, one foreign language, internship. *Entrance requirements:* For master's, GRE. Electronic applications accepted. *Expenses:* Tuition, state resident: full-time $9887; part-time $617.96 per credit. Tuition, nonresident: full-time $24,054; part-time $1503.40 per credit. Required fees: $67.63 per credit. Tuition and fees vary according to reciprocity agreements. *Faculty research:* International development, European citizenship, French and business, foreign language education, agricultural economics.

University of Wisconsin–Milwaukee, Graduate School, College of Letters and Sciences, Interdepartmental Program in Foreign Language and Literature, Milwaukee, WI 53201-0413. Offers classics and Hebrew studies (MAFLL); comparative literature (MAFLL); French and Italian (MAFLL); German (MAFLL); Slavic studies (MAFLL); translation (Certificate). Part-time programs available. *Faculty:* 29 full-time (14 women). *Students:* 35 full-time (27 women), 29 part-time (20 women); includes 1 Hispanic/Latino. Average age 40. 30 applicants, 67% accepted, 19 enrolled. In 2010, 24 master's awarded. *Degree requirements:* For master's, 2 foreign languages, thesis or alternative. *Entrance requirements:* Additional exam requirements/recommendations for international students: Required—TOEFL (minimum score 550 paper-based; 79 iBT), IELTS (minimum score 6.5). *Application deadline:* For fall admission, 1/1 priority date for domestic students; for spring admission, 9/1 for domestic students. Applications are processed on a rolling basis. Application fee: $56 ($96 for international students). Electronic applications accepted. *Financial support:* In 2010–11, 1 fellowship, 2 research assistantships, 26 teaching assistantships were awarded; career-related internships or fieldwork, health care benefits, unspecified assistantships, and project assistantships also available. Support available to part-time students. Financial award application deadline: 4/15; financial award applicants required to submit FAFSA. Total annual research expenditures: $304,210. *Unit head:* Gabrielle Verdier, Representative, 414-229-3346, Fax: 414-229-2741, E-mail: verdier@uwm.edu. *Application contact:* General Information Contact, 414-229-4982, Fax: 414-229-6967, E-mail: gradschool@uwm.edu.

University of Wyoming, College of Arts and Sciences, Department of Modern and Classical Languages, Program in French, Laramie, WY 82070. Offers MA. Part-time programs available. *Degree requirements:* For master's, one foreign language, thesis or alternative. *Entrance requirements:* For master's, GRE General Test, minimum GPA of 3.0. *Faculty research:* Poetry, Asian literature, medieval literature, nineteenth- and twentieth century literature.

Vanderbilt University, Graduate School, Department of French and Italian, Nashville, TN 37240-1001. Offers French (MA, MAT, PhD). *Faculty:* 11 full-time (5 women). *Students:* 13 full-time (8 women); includes 1 Hispanic/Latino. Average age 30. 58 applicants, 10% accepted, 3 enrolled. In 2010, 2 master's, 1 doctorate awarded. Terminal master's awarded for partial completion of doctoral program. *Degree requirements:* For master's, one foreign language, comprehensive exam; for doctorate, 2 foreign languages, comprehensive exam, thesis/dissertation, final and qualifying exams. *Entrance requirements:* For master's and doctorate, GRE General Test. Additional exam requirements/recommendations for international students: Required—TOEFL (minimum score 570 paper-based; 230 computer-based; 88 iBT). *Application deadline:* For fall admission, 1/15 for domestic and international students. Application fee: $0. Electronic applications accepted. *Financial support:* Fellowships with full and partial tuition reimbursements, teaching assistantships with full and partial tuition reimbursements, career-related internships or fieldwork, Federal Work-Study, institutionally sponsored loans, scholarships/grants, and health care benefits available. Financial award application deadline: 1/15; financial award applicants required to submit CSS PROFILE or FAFSA. *Faculty research:* Baudelaire, Rabelais, voyage literature, postcolonial literature, medieval epic. *Unit head:* Dr. Lynn Ramey, Chair, 615-322-6900, E-mail: lynn.ramey@vanderbilt.edu. *Application contact:* Robert Barsky, Director of Graduate Studies, 615-322-6900, Fax: 615-343-6909, E-mail: robert.barsky@vanderbilt.edu.

Washington University in St. Louis, Graduate School of Arts and Sciences, Department of Romance Languages and Literatures, Program in French, St. Louis, MO 63130-4899. Offers MA, PhD. Terminal master's awarded for partial completion of doctoral program. *Degree requirements:* For master's, thesis or alternative; for doctorate, thesis/dissertation. *Entrance requirements:* For master's and doctorate, GRE General Test. Electronic applications accepted.

Wayne State University, College of Liberal Arts and Sciences, Department of Classical and Modern Languages, Literatures, and Cultures, Program in Modern Languages, Detroit, MI 48202. Offers French (PhD); German (PhD); Spanish (PhD). *Faculty:* 27 full-time (13 women). *Students:* 15 full-time (14 women), 7 part-time (5 women); includes 7 minority (all Hispanic/Latino), 3 international. Average age 41. 3 applicants, 67% accepted, 2 enrolled. In 2010, 1 doctorate awarded. *Expenses:* Tuition, state resident: full-time $7662; part-time $478.85 per credit hour. Tuition, nonresident: full-time $16,920; part-time $1057.55 per credit hour. Required fees: $571.20; $35.70 per credit hour. $188.05 per semester. Tuition and fees vary according to course load and program. *Financial support:* In 2010–11, 2 fellowships (averaging $14,113 per year), 7 teaching assistantships (averaging $14,620 per year) were awarded. *Unit head:* Dr. Michael Giordano, Graduate Director, 313-577-3051, Fax: 313-577-6243, E-mail: m.j.giordano@wayne.edu. *Application contact:* Janet Hankin, Professor, 313-577-0841, E-mail: janet.hankin@wayne.edu.

Wayne State University, College of Liberal Arts and Sciences, Program in Language Learning, Detroit, MI 48202. Offers Arabic (MA); French (MA); German (MA); Italian (MA); Latin (MA); Spanish (MA). *Faculty:* 1 full-time (0 women), 1 (woman) part-time/adjunct. *Students:* 1 (woman) full-time, 12 part-time (11 women), 1 international. Average age 32. 4 applicants, 100% accepted, 3 enrolled. In 2010, 2 master's awarded. *Expenses:* Tuition, state resident: full-time $7662; part-time $478.85 per credit hour. Tuition, nonresident: full-time $16,920; part-time $1057.55 per credit hour. Required fees: $571.20; $35.70 per credit hour. $188.05 per semester. Tuition and fees vary according to course load and program. *Financial support:* In 2010–11, 1 teaching assistantship (averaging $14,620 per year) was awarded. *Unit head:* Robert Thomas, Dean, 313-577-2519, Fax: 313-577-8971, E-mail: aa0817@wayne.edu. *Application contact:* Janet Hankin, Professor, 313-577-0841, E-mail: janet.hankin@wayne.edu.

West Chester University of Pennsylvania, Office of Graduate Studies, College of Arts and Sciences, Department of Languages and Cultures, West Chester, PA 19383. Offers French (M Ed, MA, Teaching Certificate); Spanish (M Ed, MA, Teaching Certificate). Part-time and evening/weekend programs available. *Students:* 6 full-time (5 women), 13 part-time (10 women); includes 3 minority (2 Asian, non-Hispanic/Latino; 1 Hispanic/Latino). Average age 33. 16 applicants, 88% accepted, 6 enrolled. In 2010, 6 master's awarded. *Degree requirements:* For master's, one foreign language, thesis optional, exit exam, capstone project. *Entrance requirements:* For master's, placement test. Additional exam requirements/recommendations for international students: Required—TOEFL (minimum score 550 paper-based; 213 computer-based; 80 iBT). *Application deadline:* For fall admission, 4/15 priority date for domestic students, 3/15 for international students; for spring admission, 10/15 for domestic students, 9/1 for international students. Applications are processed on a rolling basis. Application fee: $35. Electronic applications accepted. *Expenses:* Tuition, state resident: full-time $6966; part-time $387 per credit. Tuition, nonresident: full-time $11,146; part-time $619 per credit. Required fees: $1614.40; $133.24 per credit. Part-time tuition and fees vary according to campus/location. *Financial support:* Unspecified assistantships available. Support available to part-time students. Financial award application deadline: 2/15; financial award applicants required to submit FAFSA. *Faculty research:* Implementation of world languages curriculum framework. *Unit head:* Dr. Jerome Williams, Chair, 610-436-2700, Fax: 610-436-3048, E-mail: jwilliams2@wcupa.edu. *Application contact:* Dr. Rebecca Pauly, Graduate Coordinator, 610-436-2382, E-mail: rpauly@wcupa.edu.

Western Kentucky University, Graduate Studies, Potter College of Arts and Letters, Department of Modern Languages, Bowling Green, KY 42101. Offers French (MA Ed); German (MA Ed); Spanish (MA Ed).

West Virginia University, Eberly College of Arts and Sciences, Department of Foreign Languages, Morgantown, WV 26506. Offers French (MA); linguistics (MA); Spanish (MA); teaching English to speakers of other languages (MA). Part-time programs available. *Degree requirements:* For master's, one foreign language, comprehensive exam (for some programs), thesis optional. *Entrance requirements:* For master's, minimum GPA of 3.0. Electronic applications accepted. *Faculty research:* French, German, and Spanish literature; foreign language pedagogy; English as a second language; cultural studies; linguistics.

Yale University, Graduate School of Arts and Sciences, Department of French, New Haven, CT 06520. Offers M Phil, MA, PhD. *Degree requirements:* For doctorate, 3 foreign languages, thesis/dissertation. *Entrance requirements:* For doctorate, GRE General Test.

York University, Faculty of Graduate Studies, Glendon College, Program in French Studies, Toronto, ON M3J 1P3, Canada. Offers MA. *Degree requirements:* For master's, thesis or alternative. Electronic applications accepted.

German

Arizona State University, College of Liberal Arts and Sciences, School of International Letters and Cultures, Program in German, Tempe, AZ 85287-0202. Offers German (comparative literature) (MA); German (language and culture) (MA); German (literature) (MA). *Faculty:* 5 full-time (2 women). *Students:* 7 full-time (5 women), 1 part-time (0 women); includes 2 minority (1 Asian, non-Hispanic/Latino; 1 Hispanic/Latino). Average age 32. 5 applicants, 80% accepted, 1 enrolled. In 2010, 2 master's awarded. *Degree requirements:* For master's, thesis, applied pedagogical project, or paper portfolio consisting of 2 seminar papers; interactive Program of Study (iPOS) submitted no later than beginning of third semester of study or before completing 50 percent of coursework. *Entrance requirements:* For master's, minimum GPA of 3.0 in the last two years of work leading to the bachelor's degree, personal statement, writing sample (preferably written in German), 3 letters of recommendation. Additional exam requirements/recommendations for international students: Required—TOEFL (minimum score 550 paper-based; 213 computer-based; 83 iBT), IELTS (minimum score 6.5). *Application deadline:* For fall admission, 2/1 priority date for domestic and international students. Applications are processed on a rolling basis. Application fee: $70 ($90 for international students). Electronic applications accepted. *Expenses:* Tuition, state resident: full-time $8510; part-time $608 per credit. Tuition, nonresident: full-time $16,542; part-time $919 per credit. Required fees: $339; $110 per credit. Part-time tuition and fees vary according to course load. *Financial support:* In 2010–11, 5 teaching assistantships with full and partial tuition reimbursements (averaging $13,500 per year) were awarded; fellowships with full and partial tuition reimbursements, research assistantships with full and partial tuition reimbursements, institutionally sponsored loans, scholarships/grants, and tuition waivers (partial) also available. Financial award application deadline: 3/1; financial award applicants required to submit FAFSA. *Unit head:* Dr. Peter Horwath, Coordinator, 480-965-6382, E-mail: peter.horwath@asu.edu. *Application contact:* Graduate Admissions, 480-965-6113.

Bowling Green State University, Graduate College, College of Arts and Sciences, Department of German, Russian, and East Asian Languages, Bowling Green, OH 43403. Offers German (MA, MAT); MA/MA. Part-time programs available. *Degree requirements:* For master's, one foreign language, thesis or alternative. *Entrance requirements:* For master's, GRE General Test. Additional exam requirements/recommendations for international students: Required—TOEFL. Electronic applications accepted.

Brown University, Graduate School, Department of German Studies, Providence, RI 02912. Offers PhD, MA/PhD. *Degree requirements:* For doctorate, 2 foreign languages, thesis/dissertation, preliminary exam. *Entrance requirements:* For doctorate, GRE General Test.

California State University, Fullerton, Graduate Studies, College of Humanities and Social Sciences, Department of Modern Languages and Literatures, Fullerton, CA 92834-9480. Offers French (MA); German (MA); Spanish (MA); teaching English to speakers of other languages (MS). Part-time programs available. *Students:* 44 full-time (32 women), 46 part-time (32 women); includes 18 Asian, non-Hispanic/Latino; 29 Hispanic/Latino; 1 Two or more races, non-Hispanic/Latino, 18 international. Average age 32. 126 applicants, 56% accepted, 41 enrolled. In 2010, 35 master's awarded. *Degree requirements:* For master's, comprehensive exam, thesis or alternative. *Entrance requirements:* For master's, minimum GPA of 2.5 in last 60 hours of course work, undergraduate major in a language. Application fee: $55. *Financial support:* Career-related internships or fieldwork, Federal Work-Study, institutionally sponsored loans, and scholarships/grants available. Support available to part-time students. Financial award application deadline: 3/1; financial award applicants required to submit FAFSA. *Unit head:* Dr. Janet Eyring, Chair, 657-278-3534. *Application contact:* Admissions/Applications, 657-278-2371.

California State University, Long Beach, Graduate Studies, College of Liberal Arts, Department of Romance, German, and Russian Languages and Literature, Program in German, Long Beach, CA 90840. Offers MA. Part-time programs available. *Students:* 12 full-time (5 women), 6 part-time (all women); includes 1 Black or African American, non-Hispanic/Latino; 1 Asian, non-Hispanic/Latino, 3 international. Average age 32. 8 applicants, 100% accepted, 6 enrolled. In 2010, 2 master's awarded. *Degree requirements:* For master's, one foreign language, comprehensive exam or thesis. *Application deadline:* For fall admission, 7/1 for domestic students. Applications are processed on a rolling basis. Application fee: $55. Electronic applications accepted. *Financial support:* Federal Work-Study, institutionally sponsored loans, and scholarships/grants available. Financial award application deadline: 3/2. *Faculty research:* Contemporary German society, Baroque, Goethe, Wagner. *Unit head:* Dr. Lisa Vollendorf, Chair, 562-985-4318, Fax: 562-985-4259, E-mail: lvollend@csulb.edu. *Application contact:* Dr. Jeffrey High, Graduate Advisor, 562-985-5381, Fax: 562-985-2463, E-mail: jhigh@csulb.edu.

California State University, Sacramento, Graduate Studies, College of Social Sciences and Interdisciplinary Studies, Liberal Arts Program, Sacramento, CA 95819. Offers French (MA); German (MA); Spanish (MA); theater arts (MA). *Degree requirements:* For master's, writing proficiency exam. *Entrance requirements:* Additional exam requirements/recommendations for international students: Required—TOEFL. Electronic applications accepted.

Central Connecticut State University, School of Graduate Studies, School of Arts and Sciences, Department of Modern Languages, Program in Modern Language, New Britain, CT 06050-4010. Offers French (MA, Certificate); German (Certificate); Italian (Certificate); modern language (MA); Spanish language and Hispanic culture (MA). Part-time and evening/weekend programs available. *Students:* 8 full-time (6 women), 32 part-time (28 women); includes 15 minority (all Hispanic/Latino), 1 international. Average age 38. 22 applicants, 95% accepted, 10 enrolled. In 2010, 17 master's awarded. *Degree requirements:* For master's, one foreign language, comprehensive exam, thesis or alternative; for Certificate, qualifying exam. *Entrance requirements:* For master's, minimum undergraduate GPA of 2.7, 24 credits of undergraduate courses in either Italian or Spanish. Additional exam requirements/recommendations for international students: Required—TOEFL. *Application deadline:* For fall admission, 7/1 for domestic students; for spring admission, 12/1 for domestic students. Applications are processed on a rolling basis. Application fee: $50. Electronic applications accepted. *Expenses:* Tuition, area resident: Full-time $5012; part-time $470 per credit. Tuition, state resident: full-time $7518; part-time $482 per credit. Tuition, nonresident: full-time $13,962; part-time $482 per credit. Required fees: $3772. One-time fee: $62 part-time. *Faculty research:* Twentieth century French theater, seventeenth century French literature, French Middle Ages.

Columbia University, Graduate School of Arts and Sciences, Division of Humanities, Department of Germanic Languages, New York, NY 10027. Offers M Phil, MA, PhD. Part-time programs available. *Degree requirements:* For master's, one foreign language, written exam; for doctorate, 2 foreign languages, thesis/dissertation. *Entrance requirements:* For master's and doctorate, GRE General Test, GRE Subject Test, sample of written work. Additional exam

requirements/recommendations for international students: Required—TOEFL. *Faculty research:* German language and literature, comparative literature.

Cornell University, Graduate School, Graduate Fields of Arts and Sciences, Field of Germanic Studies, Ithaca, NY 14853-0001. Offers German area studies (MA, PhD); German intellectual history (MA, PhD); Germanic linguistics (MA, PhD); Germanic literature (MA, PhD); old Norse (MA, PhD). *Faculty:* 15 full-time (7 women). *Students:* 18 full-time (11 women); includes 1 American Indian or Alaska Native, non-Hispanic/Latino, 11 international. Average age 28. 32 applicants, 28% accepted, 6 enrolled. In 2010, 5 master's, 2 doctorates awarded. Terminal master's awarded for partial completion of doctoral program. *Degree requirements:* For master's, one foreign language, thesis; for doctorate, 2 foreign languages, comprehensive exam, thesis/ dissertation. *Entrance requirements:* For master's and doctorate, GRE General Test, fluency in German, writing sample, 2 letters of recommendation. Additional exam requirements/ recommendations for international students: Required—TOEFL (minimum score 550 paper-based; 213 computer-based; 77 iBT). *Application deadline:* For fall admission, 1/15 for domestic students. Application fee: $80. Electronic applications accepted. *Expenses:* Tuition: Full-time $29,500. Required fees: $76. Tuition and fees vary according to degree level and program. *Financial support:* In 2010–11, 7 fellowships with full tuition reimbursements, 9 teaching assistantships with full tuition reimbursements were awarded; research assistantships with full tuition reimbursements, institutionally sponsored loans, scholarships/grants, health care benefits, tuition waivers (full and partial), and unspecified assistantships also available. Financial award applicants required to submit FAFSA. *Faculty research:* Women's studies, minority literature, literature and intellectual history, theater and film studies, Continental philosophy. *Unit head:* Director of Graduate Studies, 607-255-4047. *Application contact:* Graduate Field Assistant, 607-255-4047, E-mail: germanic_studies@cornell.edu.

Cornell University, Graduate School, Graduate Fields of Arts and Sciences, Field of Linguistics, Ithaca, NY 14853-0001. Offers applied linguistics (MA, PhD); East Asian linguistics (MA, PhD); English linguistics (MA, PhD); general linguistics (MA, PhD); Germanic linguistics (MA, PhD); Indo-European linguistics (MA, PhD); phonetics (MA, PhD); phonological theory (MA, PhD); Romance linguistics (MA, PhD); second language acquisition (MA, PhD); semantics (MA, PhD); Slavic linguistics (MA, PhD); sociolinguistics (MA, PhD); South Asian linguistics (MA, PhD); Southeast Asian linguistics (MA, PhD); syntactic theory (MA, PhD). *Faculty:* 15 full-time (7 women). *Students:* 34 full-time (18 women); includes 3 Hispanic/Latino, 15 international. Average age 28. 111 applicants, 12% accepted, 8 enrolled. In 2010, 2 master's, 6 doctorates awarded. Terminal master's awarded for partial completion of doctoral program. *Degree requirements:* For master's, one foreign language, thesis; for doctorate, one foreign language, comprehensive exam, thesis/dissertation. *Entrance requirements:* For master's and doctorate, GRE General Test, 2 letters of recommendation. Additional exam requirements/recommendations for international students: Required—TOEFL (minimum score 600 paper-based; 250 computer-based; 77 iBT). *Application deadline:* For fall admission, 1/15 for domestic students. Application fee: $80. Electronic applications accepted. *Expenses:* Tuition: Full-time $29,500. Required fees: $76. Tuition and fees vary according to degree level and program. *Financial support:* In 2010–11, 17 fellowships with full tuition reimbursements, 1 research assistantship with full tuition reimbursement, 15 teaching assistantships with full tuition reimbursements were awarded; institutionally sponsored loans, scholarships/grants, health care benefits, tuition waivers (full and partial), and unspecified assistantships also available. Financial award applicants required to submit FAFSA. *Faculty research:* Phonology and phonetics, syntax and semantics, historical linguistics, philosophy of language, language acquisition. *Unit head:* Director of Graduate Studies, 607-255-1105. *Application contact:* Graduate Field Assistant, 607-255-1105, E-mail: lingfield@cornell.edu.

Dalhousie University, Faculty of Arts and Social Science, Department of German, Halifax, NS B3H 4R2, Canada. Offers MA. *Entrance requirements:* Additional exam requirements/ recommendations for international students: Required—TOEFL, IELTS, CANTEST, CAEL, or Michigan English Language Assessment Battery. Electronic applications accepted. *Faculty research:* Baroque age in Germany, literature and philosophy of German idealism, twentieth century German culture, aesthetics, reception of the Islamic Orient, reception of Greek and Roman antiquity, realism and ornament.

Duke University, Graduate School, Interdisciplinary Program in German Studies, Durham, NC 27708-0256. Offers PhD. Program offered jointly with University of North Carolina Chapel Hill. Part-time programs available. *Faculty:* 16 full-time. *Students:* 7 full-time (6 women); includes 1 Black or African American, non-Hispanic/Latino, 3 international. 26 applicants, 42% accepted, 5 enrolled. *Degree requirements:* For doctorate, thesis/dissertation. *Entrance requirements:* For doctorate, GRE General Test, writing sample. Additional exam requirements/ recommendations for international students: Required—TOEFL (minimum score 550 paper-based; 213 computer-based; 83 iBT), IELTS (minimum score 7). *Application deadline:* For fall admission, 12/15 priority date for domestic and international students. Application fee: $75. Electronic applications accepted. *Financial support:* Fellowships, research assistantships, teaching assistantships, Federal Work-Study available. Financial award application deadline: 12/15. *Unit head:* Thomas Pfau, Director of Graduate Studies, 919-660-3104, Fax: 919-660-3076, E-mail: sarah.gray@duke.edu. *Application contact:* Elizabeth Hutton, Director of Admissions, 919-684-3913, Fax: 919-684-2277, E-mail: grad-admissions@duke.edu.

Eastern Michigan University, Graduate School, College of Arts and Sciences, Department of World Languages, Programs in Foreign Languages, Ypsilanti, MI 48197. Offers French (MA); German (MA); German for business (Graduate Certificate); Hispanic language and cultures (Graduate Certificate); Japanese business practices (Graduate Certificate); Spanish (MA). Part-time and evening/weekend programs available. Postbaccalaureate distance learning degree programs offered (minimal on-campus study). *Students:* 1 (woman) full-time, 12 part-time (11 women); includes 5 minority (1 Black or African American, non-Hispanic/Latino; 1 Asian, non-Hispanic/Latino; 3 Hispanic/Latino), 1 international. Average age 44. In 2010, 8 master's awarded. *Degree requirements:* For master's, one foreign language, thesis optional. *Entrance requirements:* Additional exam requirements/recommendations for international students: Required—TOEFL. *Application deadline:* Applications are processed on a rolling basis. Application fee: $35. *Financial support:* Fellowships, research assistantships with full tuition reimbursements, teaching assistantships with full tuition reimbursements, career-related internships or fieldwork, Federal Work-Study, institutionally sponsored loans, scholarships/grants, tuition waivers (partial), and unspecified assistantships available. Support available to part-time students. Financial award applicants required to submit FAFSA. *Application contact:* Dr. Genevieve Peden, Program Advisor, 734-487-1498, Fax: 734-487-3411, E-mail: gpeden@emich.edu.

Florida State University, The Graduate School, College of Arts and Sciences, Department of Modern Languages, Program in German, Tallahassee, FL 32306. Offers MA. *Faculty:* 2

German

Florida State University *(continued)*
full-time (1 woman), 2 part-time/adjunct (1 woman). *Students:* 5 full-time (2 women), 1 (woman) part-time. Average age 25. 2 applicants, 100% accepted, 2 enrolled. In 2010, 2 master's awarded. *Degree requirements:* For master's, thesis optional. *Entrance requirements:* For master's, GRE General Test, minimum GPA of 3.0. Additional exam requirements/recommendations for international students: Required—TOEFL (minimum score 550 paper-based; 213 computer-based). *Application deadline:* For fall admission, 2/15 for domestic and international students. Electronic applications accepted. *Expenses:* Tuition, state resident: full-time $8238.24. *Financial support:* In 2010–11, 4 students received support, including research assistantships (averaging $12,000 per year), 5 teaching assistantships with partial tuition reimbursements available (averaging $11,100 per year). Financial award application deadline: 2/1; financial award applicants required to submit FAFSA. *Unit head:* Dr. Christian Weber, Divisional Coordinator, 850-644-8194, Fax: 850-644-0524, E-mail: eweber@fsu.edu. *Application contact:* Wendy E. Pigott, Graduate Academic Coordinator, 850-644-8397, Fax: 850-644-0524, E-mail: wpigott@fsu.edu.

Georgetown University, Graduate School of Arts and Sciences, BMW Center for German and European Studies, Washington, DC 20057. Offers MA, MA/JD, MA/PhD. *Degree requirements:* For master's, 2 foreign languages, comprehensive exam. *Entrance requirements:* For master's, GRE General Test. Additional exam requirements/recommendations for international students: Required—TOEFL. *Faculty research:* Trans-Atlantic relations, European Union, German and European Studies.

Georgetown University, Graduate School of Arts and Sciences, Department of German, Washington, DC 20057. Offers MA, MS, PhD, MA/PhD. *Degree requirements:* For master's, 2 foreign languages, research project; for doctorate, 3 foreign languages, thesis/dissertation. *Entrance requirements:* For master's, GRE General Test. Additional exam requirements/recommendations for international students: Required—TOEFL.

Georgia State University, College of Arts and Sciences, Department of Modern and Classical Languages, Program in German, Atlanta, GA 30302-3083. Offers MA. Evening/weekend programs available. *Degree requirements:* For master's, one foreign language, thesis or alternative, general exam. *Entrance requirements:* For master's, GRE General Test. Additional exam requirements/recommendations for international students: Required—TOEFL. Electronic applications accepted. *Faculty research:* Medieval and twentieth-century German literature.

Georgia State University, College of Arts and Sciences, Department of Modern and Classical Languages, Program in Translation and Interpretation, Atlanta, GA 30302-3083. Offers French (Certificate); German (Certificate); Spanish (Certificate). Electronic applications accepted.

Graduate School and University Center of the City University of New York, Graduate Studies, Program in Comparative Literature, New York, NY 10016-4039. Offers comparative literature (MA, PhD), including classics (PhD), German (PhD), Italian (PhD). PhD offered jointly with New York University. Terminal master's awarded for partial completion of doctoral program. *Degree requirements:* For master's, 2 foreign languages, comprehensive exam, thesis; for doctorate, 3 foreign languages, comprehensive exam, thesis/dissertation. *Entrance requirements:* For master's and doctorate, GRE General Test. Additional exam requirements/recommendations for international students: Required—TOEFL. Electronic applications accepted.

Graduate School and University Center of the City University of New York, Graduate Studies, Program in Germanic Languages and Literatures, New York, NY 10016-4039. Offers MA, PhD. *Degree requirements:* For master's, one foreign language, thesis; for doctorate, 2 foreign languages, thesis/dissertation. *Entrance requirements:* For master's and doctorate, GRE General Test.

Harvard University, Graduate School of Arts and Sciences, Department of Germanic Languages and Literatures, Cambridge, MA 02138. Offers German (PhD); Scandinavian (PhD). Terminal master's awarded for partial completion of doctoral program. *Degree requirements:* For doctorate, 2 foreign languages, thesis/dissertation, exams. *Entrance requirements:* For doctorate, GRE General Test, German writing sample. Additional exam requirements/recommendations for international students: Required—TOEFL. *Expenses:* Tuition: Full-time $34,976. Required fees: $1166. Full-time tuition and fees vary according to program.

Hofstra University, School of Education, Health, and Human Services, Programs in Teaching—Secondary Education, Hempstead, NY 11549. Offers business education (MS Ed); English education (MA, MS Ed); foreign language and TESOL (MS Ed); foreign language education (MA, MS Ed), including French, German, Russian, Spanish; mathematics education (MA, MS Ed); science education (MA, MS Ed), including biology, chemistry, earth science, geology, physics; secondary education (Advanced Certificate); social studies education (MA, MS Ed). Part-time and evening/weekend programs available. Postbaccalaureate distance learning degree programs offered (minimal on-campus study). *Students:* 114 full-time (74 women), 61 part-time (36 women); includes 7 Black or African American, non-Hispanic/Latino; 1 American Indian or Alaska Native, non-Hispanic/Latino; 8 Asian, non-Hispanic/Latino; 10 Hispanic/Latino; 1 Native Hawaiian or other Pacific Islander, non-Hispanic/Latino. Average age 27. 153 applicants, 90% accepted, 59 enrolled. In 2010, 102 master's, 11 other advanced degrees awarded. *Degree requirements:* For master's, one foreign language, comprehensive exam (for some programs), thesis (for some programs), exit project, electronic portfolio, student teaching, fieldwork, curriculum project; for Advanced Certificate, 3 foreign languages, comprehensive exam (for some programs), thesis project. *Entrance requirements:* For master's, 2 letters of recommendation, teacher certification (MA), essay; for Advanced Certificate, 2 letters of recommendation, essay, interview and/or portfolio. Additional exam requirements/recommendations for international students: Required—TOEFL (minimum score 550 paper-based; 213 computer-based; 80 iBT). *Application deadline:* Applications are processed on a rolling basis. Application fee: $70 ($75 for international students). Electronic applications accepted. *Expenses:* Tuition: Full-time $18,000; part-time $1000 per credit hour. Required fees: $970; $145 per term. Tuition and fees vary according to program. *Financial support:* In 2010–11, 108 students received support, including 14 fellowships with full and partial tuition reimbursements available (averaging $3,943 per year), 1 research assistantship with full and partial tuition reimbursement available (averaging $6,574 per year); career-related internships or fieldwork, Federal Work-Study, institutionally sponsored loans, scholarships/grants, tuition waivers (full and partial), unspecified assistantships, and scholarships also available. Support available to part-time students. Financial award applicants required to submit FAFSA. *Faculty research:* Appropriate content and pedagogy in secondary school disciplines, adolescent development, secondary school organization, alternative secondary school programs. *Unit head:* Dr. Esther Fusco, Chairperson, 516-463-7704, Fax: 516-463-6196, E-mail: catezf@hofstra.edu. *Application contact:* Carol Drummer, Dean of Graduate Admissions, 516-463-4876, Fax: 516-463-4664, E-mail: gradstudent@hofstra.edu.

Illinois State University, Graduate School, College of Arts and Sciences, Department of Foreign Languages, Literatures and Cultures, Normal, IL 61790-2200. Offers French (MA); French and German (MA); French and Spanish (MA); German (MA); German and Spanish (MA); Spanish (MA). *Degree requirements:* For master's, variable foreign language requirement, comprehensive exam, 1 term of residency. *Entrance requirements:* For master's, GRE General Test, minimum GPA of 2.8 in last 60 hours of course work.

Indiana University Bloomington, University Graduate School, College of Arts and Sciences, Department of Germanic Studies, Bloomington, IN 47405-7000. Offers German philology and linguistics (PhD); German studies (MA, PhD), including German (MA), German literature and culture (MA), German literature and linguistics (MA); medieval German studies (PhD); teaching German (MAT). *Faculty:* 13 full-time (4 women), 6 part-time/adjunct (2 women). *Students:* 35 full-time (19 women), 2 part-time (1 woman); includes 1 Black or African American, non-Hispanic/Latino; 1 Hispanic/Latino, 8 international. Average age 31. 34 applicants, 41% accepted, 5 enrolled. In 2010, 6 master's, 3 doctorates awarded. Terminal master's awarded for partial completion of doctoral program. *Degree requirements:* For master's, one foreign language,

project; for doctorate, one foreign language, comprehensive exam, thesis/dissertation. *Entrance requirements:* For master's, GRE General Test, BA in German or equivalent; for doctorate, GRE General Test, MA in German or equivalent. Additional exam requirements/recommendations for international students: Required—TOEFL. *Application deadline:* For fall admission, 1/15 priority date for domestic students, 12/15 for international students; for spring admission, 9/1 priority date for domestic students, 9/1 for international students. Applications are processed on a rolling basis. Application fee: $55 ($65 for international students). *Financial support:* In 2010–11, 7 fellowships with full and partial tuition reimbursements (averaging $16,000 per year), 17 teaching assistantships with full tuition reimbursements (averaging $13,455 per year) were awarded; research assistantships, Federal Work-Study, institutionally sponsored loans, scholarships/grants, and unspecified assistantships also available. Support available to part-time students. Financial award application deadline: 1/15; financial award applicants required to submit FAFSA. *Faculty research:* German and other European literature: medieval to modern/postmodern, German and culture studies, Germanic philology, literary theory, literature and the other arts. *Unit head:* William Rasch, Department Chairman, 812-855-7947, Fax: 812-855-8292, E-mail: wrasch@indiana.edu. *Application contact:* Michelle Dunbar, Graduate Secretary, 812-855-7947, E-mail: midunbar@indiana.edu.

The Johns Hopkins University, Zanvyl Krieger School of Arts and Sciences, Department of German and Romance Languages and Literatures, Baltimore, MD 21218-2699. Offers French (PhD); German (PhD); Italian (PhD); romance languages (PhD); Spanish (PhD). *Faculty:* 31 full-time (20 women), 1 part-time/adjunct (0 women). *Students:* 52 full-time (31 women); includes 7 minority (6 Hispanic/Latino; 1 Two or more races, non-Hispanic/Latino), 20 international. Average age 30. 51 applicants, 37% accepted, 19 enrolled. In 2010, 6 doctorates awarded. *Degree requirements:* For doctorate, 2 foreign languages, thesis/dissertation. *Entrance requirements:* For doctorate, GRE General Test. Additional exam requirements/recommendations for international students: Required—TOEFL (minimum score 600 paper-based; 250 computer-based; 100 iBT), IELTS. *Application deadline:* For fall admission, 12/30 for domestic and international students. Application fee: $75. Electronic applications accepted. *Financial support:* In 2010–11, 40 fellowships with full tuition reimbursements (averaging $17,000 per year), 2 research assistantships with full tuition reimbursements (averaging $17,000 per year), 19 teaching assistantships with full tuition reimbursements (averaging $17,000 per year) were awarded; institutionally sponsored loans also available. *Faculty research:* Nineteenth century French prose and poetry, genetic theory and criticism; twentieth century Latin American literature and film; medieval and Renaissance Italian literature; gender and queer theory in German literature; the ideology of Baroque and Neobaroque aesthetics. *Unit head:* Dr. William Egginton, Chair, 410-516-7510, Fax: 410-516-5358, E-mail: egginton@jhu.edu. *Application contact:* Rebecca Swisdak, Graduate Administrative Coordinator, 410-516-7227, Fax: 410-516-5358, E-mail: rswisdak@jhu.edu.

Kansas State University, Graduate School, College of Arts and Sciences, Department of Modern Languages, Manhattan, KS 66506. Offers French (MA); German (MA); Spanish (MA). Part-time and evening/weekend programs available. Postbaccalaureate distance learning degree programs offered (minimal on-campus study). *Degree requirements:* For master's, thesis optional. *Entrance requirements:* For master's, teaching certificate. Additional exam requirements/recommendations for international students: Required—TOEFL (minimum score 560 paper-based). Electronic applications accepted. *Faculty research:* Second language acquisitions; Chicano literature; Francophone literature; cultural studies; German, French, Spanish, and Spanish-American literature from the Middle Ages to the modern era.

Kent State University, College of Arts and Sciences, Department of Modern and Classical Language Studies, Kent, OH 44242-0001. Offers French literature (MA); French, Spanish, German and Latin pedagogy (MA); German literature (MA); Spanish literature (MA); translation (MA), including French, German, Japanese, Russian, Spanish; translation studies (PhD). Part-time and evening/weekend programs available. *Degree requirements:* For master's, one foreign language, comprehensive exam (for some programs), thesis (for some programs); for doctorate, comprehensive exam, thesis/dissertation (for some programs). *Entrance requirements:* For master's, minimum GPA of 3.0, writing sample, audio tape or CD; for doctorate, 3 recommendations. Additional exam requirements/recommendations for international students: Required—TOEFL (minimum score 197 computer-based). Electronic applications accepted. *Expenses:* Tuition, state resident: full-time $7866; part-time $437 per credit hour. Tuition, nonresident: full-time $14,022; part-time $779 per credit hour. *Faculty research:* Literature, pedagogy, applied linguistics, translation studies.

McGill University, Faculty of Graduate and Postdoctoral Studies, Faculty of Arts, Department of German Studies, Montréal, QC H3A 2T5, Canada. Offers MA, PhD.

Memorial University of Newfoundland, School of Graduate Studies, Department of German and Russian, St. John's, NL A1C 5S7, Canada. Offers German language and literature (M Phil, MA). Part-time programs available. *Degree requirements:* For master's, one foreign language, thesis (for some programs), comprehensive exam (M Phil). *Entrance requirements:* For master's, honors degree (minimum 2nd class standing). Electronic applications accepted. *Faculty research:* German literature from the Middle Ages to the twentieth century, German studies.

Michigan State University, The Graduate School, College of Arts and Letters, Department of Linguistics and Germanic, Slavic, Asian, and African Languages, East Lansing, MI 48824. Offers German studies (MA, PhD); linguistics (MA, PhD); teaching English to speakers of other languages (MA). Part-time and evening/weekend programs available. *Entrance requirements:* For master's, GRE General Test, minimum GPA of 3.2 in last 2 undergraduate years, 2 years of college-level foreign language, 3 letters of recommendation, portfolio (German studies); for doctorate, GRE General Test, minimum graduate GPA of 3.5, 3 letters of recommendation, master's degree or sufficient graduate course work in linguistics or language of study, master's thesis or major research paper. Additional exam requirements/recommendations for international students: Required—TOEFL. Electronic applications accepted.

Middlebury College, Language Schools, German School, Middlebury, VT 05753-6002. Offers MA, DML. *Faculty:* 6 full-time (4 women). *Students:* 24 full-time (11 women); includes 1 minority (Hispanic/Latino). Average age 29. 38 applicants, 82% accepted, 24 enrolled. In 2010, 9 master's, 1 doctorate awarded. *Degree requirements:* For master's, one foreign language; for doctorate, 2 foreign languages, comprehensive exam, thesis/dissertation, residence abroad, teaching experience. *Entrance requirements:* For master's, placement exam, 3 letters of recommendation; for doctorate, 1st and 2nd language placement exam, 3 letters of recommendation, writing sample. *Application deadline:* Applications are processed on a rolling basis. Application fee: $65. Electronic applications accepted. *Financial support:* Scholarships/grants available. Financial award applicants required to submit FAFSA. *Unit head:* Dr. Doris Kirchner, Director, 802-443-5203, Fax: 802-443-2075, E-mail: dkirchner@middlebury.edu. *Application contact:* Christina Ellison, Coordinator, 802-443-5203, Fax: 802-443-2075, E-mail: ccartwri@middlebury.edu.

Millersville University of Pennsylvania, College of Graduate and Professional Studies, School of Humanities and Social Sciences, Department of Foreign Languages, Program in German, Millersville, PA 17551-0302. Offers M Ed, MA. Part-time programs available. *Faculty:* 8 full-time (4 women), 4 part-time/adjunct (1 woman). In 2010, 2 master's awarded. *Degree requirements:* For master's, comprehensive exam, thesis optional. *Entrance requirements:* For master's, ACTFL (OPI and WPT), 3 letters of recommendation. Additional exam requirements/recommendations for international students: Required—TOEFL (minimum score 500 paper-based; 183 computer-based; 65 iBT) or IELTS (minimum score 6). *Application deadline:* For fall admission, 1/15 priority date for domestic and international students; for winter admission, 10/1 priority date for domestic and international students; for spring admission, 10/1 priority date for domestic and international students. Applications are processed on a rolling basis. Application fee: $40 ($50 for international students). Electronic applications accepted. *Expenses:* Tuition, state resident: full-time $6966; part-time $387 per credit. Tuition, nonresident: full-time $11,146; part-time $619 per credit. Required fees: $1829.50; $88 per credit. One-time fee: $60 part-time. Tuition and fees vary according to course load. *Financial support:* Research assistant-ships, institutionally sponsored loans and unspecified assistantships available. Support available to part-time students. Financial award application deadline: 3/15; financial award applicants required to submit FAFSA. *Unit head:* Dr. Christine M. Gaudry-Hudson, Coordinator of Foreign Language Graduate Program, 717-872-3663, E-mail: christine.gaudry-hudson@millersville.edu. *Application contact:* Dr. Victor S. DeSantis, Dean of Graduate and Professional Studies, 717-872-3099, Fax: 717-872-3453, E-mail: victor.desantis@millersville.edu.

Mississippi State University, College of Arts and Sciences, Department of Foreign Languages, Mississippi State, MS 39762. Offers foreign language (MA), including French, German, Spanish. Part-time programs available. *Faculty:* 8 full-time (3 women). *Students:* 10 full-time (8 women), 2 part-time (both women); includes 3 minority (1 Black or African American, non-Hispanic/Latino; 2 Hispanic/Latino), 1 international. Average age 29. 8 applicants, 75% accepted, 4 enrolled. In 2010, 7 master's awarded. *Degree requirements:* For master's, one foreign language, thesis optional, comprehensive oral or written exam. *Entrance requirements:* For master's, minimum GPA of 2.75 on last two years of undergraduate courses. Additional exam requirements/recommendations for international students: Required—TOEFL (minimum score 525 paper-based). *Application deadline:* For fall admission, 7/1 for domestic students, 5/1 for international students; for spring admission, 11/1 for domestic students, 9/1 for international students. Applications are processed on a rolling basis. Application fee: $40. Electronic applications accepted. *Expenses:* Tuition, state resident: full-time $2730.50; part-time $304 per credit hour. Tuition, nonresident: full-time $6901; part-time $767 per credit hour. *Financial support:* In 2010–11, 10 teaching assistantships with full tuition reimbursements (averaging $8,768 per year) were awarded; Federal Work-Study, institutionally sponsored loans, and unspecified assistantships also available. Financial award application deadline: 4/1; financial award applicants required to submit FAFSA. *Faculty research:* French, German, Spanish literature from medieval era to present; gender and cultural studies in French; Spanish-American literature; foreign language methodology; linguistics. *Unit head:* Dr. Jack Jordan, Professor/Head, 662-325-3480, Fax: 662-325-8209, E-mail: jordan@ra.msstate.edu. *Application contact:* Dr. Edward T. Potter, Assistant Professor/Graduate Coordinator, 662-325-2399, Fax: 662-325-8209, E-mail: ep75@.msstate.edu.

New York University, Graduate School of Arts and Science, Department of German, New York, NY 10012-1019. Offers German studies and critical thought (MA, PhD). Part-time programs available. *Faculty:* 8 full-time (5 women), 5 part-time/adjunct (0 women). *Students:* 21 full-time (10 women), 2 part-time (0 women), 12 international. Average age 32. 24 applicants, 21% accepted, 3 enrolled. In 2010, 4 doctorates awarded. Terminal master's awarded for partial completion of doctoral program. *Degree requirements:* For master's, one foreign language, thesis; for doctorate, 2 foreign languages, thesis/dissertation. *Entrance requirements:* For master's, GRE Subject Test; for doctorate, GRE Subject Test, sample of written work. Additional exam requirements/recommendations for international students: Required—TOEFL. *Application deadline:* For fall admission, 1/4 priority date for domestic students. Application fee: $90. *Financial support:* Fellowships with tuition reimbursements, teaching assistantships with tuition reimbursements, Federal Work-Study, institutionally sponsored loans, scholarships/grants, health care benefits, and unspecified assistantships available. Financial award application deadline: 1/4; financial award applicants required to submit FAFSA. *Faculty research:* Eighteenth to twentieth century literature, culture and critical thought, film and visual culture, philosophy, critical theory. *Unit head:* Paul Fleming, Chair, 212-998-8650, Fax: 212-995-4823, E-mail: german.dept@nyu.edu. *Application contact:* Lindsay O'Connor, Department Administrator, 212-998-8650, Fax: 212-995-4823, E-mail: german.dept@nyu.edu.

Northwestern University, The Graduate School, Judd A. and Marjorie Weinberg College of Arts and Sciences, Program in German Literature and Critical Thought, Evanston, IL 60208. Offers PhD. Admissions and degrees offered through The Graduate School. *Degree requirements:* For doctorate, one foreign language, thesis/dissertation. *Entrance requirements:* For doctorate, GRE General Test. Additional exam requirements/recommendations for international students: Required—TOEFL. Electronic applications accepted. *Faculty research:* Eighteenth through twentieth century German literature, comparative literature, theory, philosophy, language pedagogy.

The Ohio State University, Graduate School, College of Arts and Sciences, Division of Arts and Humanities, Department of Germanic Languages and Literatures, Columbus, OH 43210. Offers MA, PhD. *Faculty:* 16. *Students:* 16 full-time (12 women), 9 part-time (5 women), 7 international. Average age 28. In 2010, 5 master's, 1 doctorate awarded. *Degree requirements:* For master's, one foreign language, thesis optional; for doctorate, 2 foreign languages, thesis/dissertation. *Entrance requirements:* For master's and doctorate, GRE General Test. Additional exam requirements/recommendations for international students: Required—TOEFL (minimum score 600 paper-based; 250 computer-based). *Application deadline:* For fall admission, 8/15 priority date for domestic students, 7/1 priority date for international students; for winter admission, 12/1 priority date for domestic students, 11/1 priority date for international students; for spring admission, 3/1 priority date for domestic students, 2/1 priority date for international students. Applications are processed on a rolling basis. Application fee: $40 ($50 for international students). Electronic applications accepted. *Expenses:* Tuition, state resident: full-time $10,605. Tuition, nonresident: full-time $26,535. Tuition and fees vary according to course load and program. *Financial support:* Fellowships, research assistantships, teaching assistantships, Federal Work-Study and institutionally sponsored loans available. Support available to part-time students. *Faculty research:* German literature, Germanic philology, linguistics. *Unit head:* Anna A. Grotans, Chair, 614-688-4163, E-mail: grotans.1@osu.edu. *Application contact:* 614-292-9444, Fax: 614-292-3895, E-mail: domestic.grad@osu.edu.

Penn State University Park, Graduate School, College of the Liberal Arts, School of Languages and Literatures, Department of Germanic and Slavic Languages and Literatures, State College, University Park, PA 16802-1503. Offers German (MA, PhD). *Faculty research:* Literature, literary theory, culture, language pedagogy.

Portland State University, Graduate Studies, College of Liberal Arts and Sciences, Department of World Languages and Literatures, Portland, OR 97207-0751. Offers foreign literature and language (MA); French (MA); German (MA); Japanese (MA); Spanish (MA). Part-time programs available. *Faculty:* 45 full-time (30 women), 38 part-time/adjunct (29 women). *Students:* 30 full-time (21 women), 10 part-time (7 women); includes 6 minority (2 Asian, non-Hispanic/Latino; 4 Hispanic/Latino), 11 international. Average age 31. 26 applicants, 69% accepted, 15 enrolled. In 2010, 24 master's awarded. *Degree requirements:* For master's, one foreign language, thesis (for some programs). *Entrance requirements:* Additional exam requirements/recommendations for international students: Required—TOEFL (minimum score 550 paper-based; 213 computer-based). *Application deadline:* For fall admission, 4/1 for domestic students, 3/1 for international students; for winter admission, 9/1 for domestic students, 7/1 for international students; for spring admission, 11/1 for domestic and international students. Applications are processed on a rolling basis. Application fee: $50. *Expenses:* Tuition, state resident: full-time $8505; part-time $315 per credit. Tuition, nonresident: full-time $13,284; part-time $492 per credit. Required fees: $1482; $21 per credit. $99 per term. One-time fee: $120. Part-time tuition and fees vary according to course load and program. *Financial support:* In 2010–11, 6 teaching assistantships with full tuition reimbursements (averaging $9,359 per year) were awarded; research assistantships with full tuition reimbursements, Federal Work-Study, scholarships/grants, and unspecified assistantships also available. Support available to part-time students. Financial award application deadline: 3/1; financial award applicants required to submit FAFSA. *Faculty research:* Foreign language pedagogy, applied and social linguistics, literary history and criticism. *Unit head:* Dr. Jennifer Perlmutter, Chair, 503-725-8783, Fax: 503-725-5276, E-mail: jrp@pdx.edu. *Application contact:* Michael Anthony, Graduate Admissions Coordinator, 503-725-3243, E-mail: manthony@pdx.edu.

Princeton University, Graduate School, Department of German, Princeton, NJ 08544-1019. Offers PhD. *Degree requirements:* For doctorate, 2 foreign languages, thesis/dissertation. *Entrance requirements:* For doctorate, GRE General Test. Additional exam requirements/recommendations for international students: Required—TOEFL (minimum score 600 paper-based; 250 computer-based). Electronic applications accepted.

Purdue University, Graduate School, College of Liberal Arts, Department of Foreign Languages and Literatures, West Lafayette, IN 47907. Offers French (MA, MAT, PhD), including French (MA, PhD), French education (MAT); German (MA, MAT, PhD), including German (MA, PhD), German education (MAT); Spanish (MA, MAT, PhD), including Spanish (MA, PhD), Spanish education (MAT). Terminal master's awarded for partial completion of doctoral program. *Degree requirements:* For master's, one foreign language; for doctorate, 2 foreign languages, thesis/dissertation. *Entrance requirements:* For master's, GRE, sample recording of English and language of study; for doctorate, GRE, writing sample, sample recording of English and language of study. Additional exam requirements/recommendations for international students: Required—TOEFL. Electronic applications accepted. *Faculty research:* Linguistics, semiotics, literary criticism, pedagogy.

Queen's University at Kingston, School of Graduate Studies and Research, Faculty of Arts and Sciences, Department of German Language and Literature, Kingston, ON K7L 3N6, Canada. Offers MA, PhD. Part-time programs available. *Degree requirements:* For master's, thesis optional; for doctorate, one foreign language, comprehensive exam, thesis/dissertation. *Entrance requirements:* For master's, 7 German courses, honors bachelor's degree in German; for doctorate, MA or equivalent in German. Additional exam requirements/recommendations for international students: Required—TOEFL. Electronic applications accepted. *Faculty research:* Goethe and Weimar classicism, Romanticism, nineteenth- and twentieth-century German literature.

Rider University, Department of Graduate Education, Leadership and Counseling, Teacher Certification Program, Lawrenceville, NJ 08648-3001. Offers business education (Certificate); elementary education (Certificate); English as a second language (Certificate); English education (Certificate); mathematics education (Certificate); preschool to grade 3 (Certificate); science education (Certificate); social studies education (Certificate); world languages (Certificate), including French, German, Spanish. Part-time programs available. *Degree requirements:* For Certificate, internship, professional portfolio. *Entrance requirements:* For degree, PRAXIS, resume. Additional exam requirements/recommendations for international students: Required—TOEFL (minimum score 550 paper-based; 213 computer-based). Electronic applications accepted. *Expenses:* Tuition: Full-time $29,870; part-time $667.34 per credit. Required fees: $350; $11.60 per credit. Part-time tuition and fees vary according to program. *Faculty research:* Conceptual foundations for optimal development of creativity; creative theory, cognitive processes in mathematics learning, teacher collaboration.

Rutgers, The State University of New Jersey, New Brunswick, Graduate School-New Brunswick, Program in German, Piscataway, NJ 08854-8097. Offers German (MAT, PhD); German literature (MA, PhD). Part-time and evening/weekend programs available. Terminal master's awarded for partial completion of doctoral program. *Degree requirements:* For master's, one foreign language, comprehensive exam, thesis or alternative; for doctorate, 2 foreign languages, comprehensive exam, thesis/dissertation. *Entrance requirements:* For master's and doctorate, GRE General Test. Additional exam requirements/recommendations for international students: Required—TOEFL. Electronic applications accepted. *Expenses:* Tuition, state resident: full-time $7200; part-time $600 per credit. Tuition, nonresident: full-time $11,124; part-time $927 per credit. *Faculty research:* Literature and ideology; early German novella; narrative structures, mythology, psychology, and realist literature; German-American cultural history; literary theory and aesthetics; German film.

San Francisco State University, Division of Graduate Studies, College of Humanities, Department of Foreign Languages and Literatures, Program in German, San Francisco, CA 94132-1722. Offers MA. *Application deadline:* Applications are processed on a rolling basis. *Unit head:* Dr. Ilona Vandergriff, Program Coordinator, 415-338-7422, E-mail: vdgriff@sfsu.edu. *Application contact:* Dr. Ilona Vandergriff, Program Coordinator, 415-338-7422, E-mail: vdgriff@sfsu.edu.

Stanford University, School of Humanities and Sciences, Department of German Studies, Stanford, CA 94305-9991. Offers MA, PhD. *Degree requirements:* For master's, one foreign language, oral exam; for doctorate, 2 foreign languages, thesis/dissertation, oral exam, qualifying paper and exam. *Entrance requirements:* For master's and doctorate, GRE General Test. Additional exam requirements/recommendations for international students: Required—TOEFL. Electronic applications accepted. *Expenses:* Tuition: Full-time $38,700; part-time $860 per unit. One-time fee: $200 full-time.

Texas Tech University, Graduate School, College of Arts and Sciences, Department of Classical and Modern Languages and Literatures, Program in German, Lubbock, TX 79409. Offers MA. *Students:* 6 full-time (4 women), 3 part-time (1 woman), 3 international. Average age 29. 8 applicants, 63% accepted, 5 enrolled. In 2010, 1 master's awarded. *Entrance requirements:* For master's, GRE General Test. Additional exam requirements/recommendations for international students: Required—TOEFL (minimum score 550 paper-based; 213 computer-based; 79 iBT). *Application deadline:* For fall admission, 6/1 priority date for domestic students, 1/15 priority date for international students; for spring admission, 9/1 priority date for domestic students, 6/15 priority date for international students. Applications are processed on a rolling basis. Application fee: $50 ($75 for international students). Electronic applications accepted. *Expenses:* Tuition, state resident: full-time $5495.76; part-time $228.99 per credit hour. Tuition, nonresident: full-time $12,936; part-time $538.99 per credit hour. Required fees: $2674; $36 per credit hour. $905 per semester. *Financial support:* Application deadline: 4/15. *Faculty research:* Contemporary German literature, Goethe, business German, German culture, foreign language reading. *Unit head:* Dr. Charles A. Grair, Advisor/Associate Professor, 806-742-3145 Ext. 275, Fax: 806-742-3306, E-mail: charles.grair@ttu.edu. *Application contact:* Liz Hildebrand, Senior Advisor, 806-742-4055, Fax: 806-742-3306, E-mail: liz.hildebrand@ttu.edu.

Tufts University, Graduate School of Arts and Sciences, Department of Russian and German, Medford, MA 02155. Offers German (MA). Part-time programs available. *Degree requirements:* For master's, one foreign language, oral and written exam. *Entrance requirements:* Additional exam requirements/recommendations for international students: Required—TOEFL (minimum score 550 paper-based; 213 computer-based; 80 iBT). Electronic applications accepted. *Expenses:* Tuition: Full-time $39,624; part-time $3962 per course. Required fees: $40 per year. Full-time tuition and fees vary according to degree level, program and student level. Part-time tuition and fees vary according to course load.

Université de Montréal, Faculty of Arts and Sciences, Department of Literatures and Modern Languages, Program in German Studies, Montréal, QC H3C 3J7, Canada. Offers MA. *Degree requirements:* For master's, 2 foreign languages, thesis. Electronic applications accepted.

University at Buffalo, the State University of New York, Graduate School, Graduate School of Education, Department of Learning and Instruction, Buffalo, NY 14260. Offers biology education (Ed M, Certificate); chemistry education (Ed M, Certificate); childhood education (Ed M); childhood education with bilingual extension (Ed M); early childhood education (Ed M); earth science education (Ed M, Certificate); educational technology and new literacies (Certificate); elementary education (Ed D, PhD); English education (Ed M, PhD, Certificate); English for speakers of other languages (Ed M); foreign and second language education (PhD); French education (Ed M, Certificate); general education (Ed M); German education (Ed M, Certificate); gifted education (online) (Certificate); Latin education (Ed M, Certificate); literary specialist (Ed M); mathematics education (Ed M, PhD, Certificate); music education (Ed M, Certificate); physics education (Ed M, Certificate); reading education (PhD); science and the public (online) (Ed M); science education (PhD); social studies education (Ed M, Certificate); Spanish education (Ed M, Certificate); special education (PhD); teaching and leading for diversity (Certificate); teaching English to speakers of other languages (Ed M). Part-time and evening/weekend programs available. Postbaccalaureate distance learning degree programs offered (no on-campus study). *Faculty:* 32 full-time (22 women), 53 part-time/adjunct

German

University at Buffalo, the State University of New York (continued)
(43 women). *Students:* 343 full-time (237 women), 340 part-time (261 women); includes 17 Black or African American, non-Hispanic/Latino; 3 American Indian or Alaska Native, non-Hispanic/Latino; 13 Asian, non-Hispanic/Latino; 13 Hispanic/Latino, 76 international. Average age 29. 587 applicants, 75% accepted, 281 enrolled. In 2010, 212 master's, 16 doctorates, 37 other advanced degrees awarded. *Degree requirements:* For master's, comprehensive exam; for doctorate, thesis/dissertation, research analysis exam, research experience component. *Entrance requirements:* For doctorate, GRE General Test or MAT, interview, writing sample, letters of recommendation. Additional exam requirements/recommendations for international students: Required—TOEFL (minimum score 600 paper-based; 96 iBT). *Application deadline:* For fall admission, 2/1 priority date for domestic and international students; for spring admission, 11/15 priority date for domestic students, 10/1 for international students. Applications are processed on a rolling basis. Application fee: $50. Electronic applications accepted. *Financial support:* In 2010–11, 21 fellowships with full tuition reimbursements (averaging $9,000 per year), 42 research assistantships with full tuition reimbursements (averaging $10,589 per year) were awarded; teaching assistantships with full tuition reimbursements, career-related internships or fieldwork, Federal Work-Study, institutionally sponsored loans, scholarships/grants, tuition waivers (partial), and unspecified assistantships also available. Financial award application deadline: 2/28; financial award applicants required to submit FAFSA. *Faculty research:* Science assessment, foreign language teaching and learning, early learning, new literacies, gender and education. *Unit head:* Dr. Jim Collins, Chair, 716-645-2455, Fax: 716-645-3161, E-mail: jcollins@buffalo.edu. *Application contact:* Cathy Dimino, Admissions Assistant, 716-645-2110, Fax: 716-645-7937, E-mail: cadimino@buffalo.edu.

The University of Alabama, Graduate School, College of Arts and Sciences, Department of Modern Languages and Classics, Tuscaloosa, AL 35487. Offers French (MA, PhD); French and Spanish (PhD); German (MA); Romance languages (MA, PhD); Spanish (MA, PhD). Part-time programs available. *Faculty:* 25 full-time (12 women). *Students:* 50 full-time (33 women), 31 part-time (19 women); includes 11 minority (2 Black or African American, non-Hispanic/Latino; 8 Hispanic/Latino; 1 Two or more races, non-Hispanic/Latino), 19 international. Average age 31. 24 applicants, 83% accepted, 11 enrolled. In 2010, 17 master's, 1 doctorate awarded. *Degree requirements:* For master's, comprehensive exam, thesis optional; for doctorate, one foreign language, thesis/dissertation, preliminary exam. *Entrance requirements:* For master's and doctorate, minimum GPA of 3.0, writing sample. Additional exam requirements/recommendations for international students: Required—TOEFL or IELTS. *Application deadline:* For fall admission, 7/6 priority date for domestic students, 1/15 priority date for international students; for spring admission, 12/5 priority date for domestic students, 6/1 priority date for international students. Applications are processed on a rolling basis. Application fee: $50 ($60 for international students). Electronic applications accepted. *Expenses:* Tuition, state resident: full-time $7900. Tuition, nonresident: full-time $20,500. *Financial support:* In 2010–11, 7 students received support, including 1 fellowship, research assistantships with full tuition reimbursements available (averaging $10,291 per year), 6 teaching assistantships with full tuition reimbursements available (averaging $10,291 per year); career-related internships or fieldwork, Federal Work-Study, institutionally sponsored loans, and scholarships/grants also available. Financial award application deadline: 7/14. *Faculty research:* Non-English literature, linguistics, culture, film. *Unit head:* Dr. Michael Picone, Chair and Professor, 205-348-5054, Fax: 205-348-2042, E-mail: mpicone@bama.ua.edu. *Application contact:* Dr. K. Barbara Fischer, Graduate Director and Associate Professor, 205-348-8465, Fax: 205-348-2042, E-mail: bfischer@bama.ua.edu.

University of Alberta, Faculty of Graduate Studies and Research, Department of Modern Languages and Cultural Studies, Edmonton, AB T6G 2E1, Canada. Offers applied linguistics (Germanic, Romance, Slavic) (MA); French language, literatures and linguistics (PhD); French language, literatures, and linguistics (MA); Germanic languages, literatures and linguistics (PhD); Germanic languages, literatures, and linguistics (MA); Italian studies (MA); Slavic languages and literatures (Russian, Ukrainian) (MA, PhD); Slavic linguistics (Russian, Ukrainian) (MA, PhD); Spanish and Latin American studies (MA, PhD); Ukrainian folklore (MA, PhD). Part-time programs available. *Degree requirements:* For master's, one foreign language, thesis; for doctorate, 2 foreign languages, comprehensive exam, thesis/dissertation. *Entrance requirements:* For master's and doctorate, 1 language other than English. Additional exam requirements/recommendations for international students: Required—Michigan English Language Assessment Battery or TOEFL (minimum score 550 paper-based; 213 computer-based). Electronic applications accepted. *Faculty research:* Russian/Ukrainian studies; German studies; contemporary Latin American, French and Francophone studies; Italian studies.

The University of Arizona, College of Humanities, Department of German Studies, Tucson, AZ 85721. Offers German (MA). *Faculty:* 6 full-time (1 woman). *Students:* 13 full-time (8 women), 3 part-time (2 women); includes 1 minority (Two or more races, non-Hispanic/Latino), 6 international. Average age 29. 10 applicants, 70% accepted, 5 enrolled. In 2010, 1 master's awarded. *Degree requirements:* For master's, one foreign language, comprehensive exam, oral exam. *Entrance requirements:* For master's, minimum major GPA of 3.3, 3 letters of recommendation, audio sample, curriculum vitae. Additional exam requirements/recommendations for international students: Required—TOEFL (minimum score 550 paper-based; 213 computer-based; 79 iBT). *Application deadline:* For fall admission, 2/1 for domestic students, 12/1 for international students; for spring admission, 10/1 for domestic students, 6/1 for international students. Applications are processed on a rolling basis. Application fee: $75. Electronic applications accepted. *Expenses:* Tuition, state resident: full-time $7692. *Financial support:* In 2010–11, 17 teaching assistantships with full tuition reimbursements (averaging $19,182 per year) were awarded; Federal Work-Study, institutionally sponsored loans, scholarships/grants, health care benefits, tuition waivers (partial), and unspecified assistantships also available. Financial award application deadline: 3/1. *Faculty research:* Literature, language, and foreign language pedagogy; computer-assisted text analysis. *Unit head:* Dr. Mary Wildner-Bassett, Head, 520-621-1799, Fax: 520-626-8268, E-mail: wildnerb@u.arizona.edu. *Application contact:* Susanna Ruiz, Information Contact, 520-626-8123, Fax: 520-626-8268, E-mail: ruizs@u.arizona.edu.

University of Arkansas, Graduate School, J. William Fulbright College of Arts and Sciences, Department of World Languages, Literature and Cultures, Program in German, Fayetteville, AR 72701-1201. Offers MA. *Students:* 4 full-time (2 women). 4 applicants, 100% accepted. In 2010, 3 master's awarded. *Degree requirements:* For master's, variable foreign language requirement. *Application deadline:* For fall admission, 4/1 for international students; for spring admission, 10/1 for international students. Applications are processed on a rolling basis. Application fee: $40 ($50 for international students). Electronic applications accepted. *Financial support:* In 2010–11, 4 teaching assistantships were awarded; fellowships, research assistantships, career-related internships or fieldwork and Federal Work-Study also available. Support available to part-time students. Financial award application deadline: 4/1; financial award applicants required to submit FAFSA. *Unit head:* Dr. Joan Turner, Graduate Coordinator, 479-575-2951, Fax: 479-575-6795, E-mail: joant@uark.edu. *Application contact:* Dr. Jennifer Hoyer, Graduate Coordinator, 479-575-5938, E-mail: jhoyer@uark.edu.

The University of British Columbia, Faculty of Arts and Faculty of Graduate Studies, Department of Central, Eastern and Northern European Studies, Vancouver, BC V6T2Z1, Canada. Offers Germanic studies (MA, PhD). Part-time programs available. *Degree requirements:* For master's, one foreign language, thesis optional, exam; for doctorate, comprehensive exam, thesis/dissertation. *Entrance requirements:* For master's, BA in German; for doctorate, MA in German. Additional exam requirements/recommendations for international students: Required—TOEFL (minimum score 550 paper-based; 213 computer-based). Electronic applications accepted. Tuition charges are reported in Canadian dollars. *Expenses:* Tuition, area resident: Full-time $4179 Canadian dollars. International tuition: $7344 Canadian dollars full-time. *Faculty research:* Second language acquisition, media theory, performance theory, gender studies, cultural studies.

University of Calgary, Faculty of Graduate Studies, Faculty of Arts, Department of Germanic, Slavic and East Asian Studies, Calgary, AB T2N 1N4, Canada. Offers German (MA). Part-time programs available. *Degree requirements:* For master's, one foreign language, thesis. *Entrance requirements:* Additional exam requirements/recommendations for international students: Required—TOEFL. Electronic applications accepted. *Faculty research:* German language and linguistics, second language acquisition, medieval and early modern literature and culture, twentieth century German literature.

University of California, Berkeley, Graduate Division, College of Letters and Science, Department of German, Berkeley, CA 94720-1500. Offers PhD. *Degree requirements:* For doctorate, 2 foreign languages, thesis/dissertation, qualifying exam. *Entrance requirements:* For doctorate, GRE General Test, minimum GPA of 3.0, writing sample, 3 letters of recommendation. Electronic applications accepted. *Faculty research:* German literature/culture, film, Germanic linguistics, second-language acquisition.

University of California, Davis, Graduate Studies, Program in German, Davis, CA 95616. Offers MA, PhD. Terminal master's awarded for partial completion of doctoral program. *Degree requirements:* For master's, comprehensive exam (for some programs), thesis (for some programs); for doctorate, thesis/dissertation. *Entrance requirements:* For master's, GRE; for doctorate, GRE, master's degree or equivalent. Additional exam requirements/recommendations for international students: Required—TOEFL (minimum score 550 paper-based; 213 computer-based). Electronic applications accepted. *Faculty research:* Sixteenth to twentieth century medieval literature, critical theory, women's studies.

University of California, Irvine, School of Humanities, Department of German, Irvine, CA 92697. Offers MA, PhD. *Students:* 9 full-time (4 women); includes 1 minority (Two or more races, non-Hispanic/Latino). Average age 28. 7 applicants, 86% accepted, 3 enrolled. In 2010, 2 doctorates awarded. *Degree requirements:* For doctorate, thesis/dissertation. *Entrance requirements:* For master's and doctorate, GRE General Test, minimum GPA of 3.0. Additional exam requirements/recommendations for international students: Required—TOEFL (minimum score 550 paper-based; 213 computer-based). *Application deadline:* For fall admission, 1/15 priority date for domestic students, 1/15 for international students. Applications are processed on a rolling basis. Application fee: $70 ($90 for international students). Electronic applications accepted. *Financial support:* Fellowships, teaching assistantships with partial tuition reimbursements, institutionally sponsored loans, traineeships, health care benefits, and unspecified assistantships available. Financial award application deadline: 3/1; financial award applicants required to submit FAFSA. *Faculty research:* Goethe yearbook, fin de siecle theory, Thomas Mann. *Unit head:* Gail K. Hart, Chair, 949-824-6406, Fax: 949-824-6416, E-mail: gkhart@uci.edu. *Application contact:* Bindya Shankar Baliga, Graduate Coordinator, 949-824-7968, E-mail: bbaliga@uci.edu.

University of California, Los Angeles, Graduate Division, College of Letters and Science, Department of Germanic Languages, Program in Germanic Languages, Los Angeles, CA 90095. Offers MA, PhD. *Students:* 15 full-time (8 women); includes 3 minority (2 Asian, non-Hispanic/Latino; 1 Hispanic/Latino), 3 international. Average age 32. 10 applicants, 70% accepted, 4 enrolled. In 2010, 1 master's, 4 doctorates awarded. Terminal master's awarded for partial completion of doctoral program. *Degree requirements:* For master's, one foreign language, comprehensive exam or thesis; for doctorate, 2 foreign languages, oral and written qualifying exams. *Entrance requirements:* For master's, GRE General Test, BA in German, minimum GPA of 3.0, sample of written work; for doctorate, GRE General Test, minimum undergraduate GPA of 3.0, MA in German or equivalent, sample of written work. *Application deadline:* For fall admission, 12/15 for domestic and international students. Application fee: $70 ($90 for international students). Electronic applications accepted. *Financial support:* In 2010–11, 15 fellowships with full and partial tuition reimbursements, 4 research assistantships with full and partial tuition reimbursements, 10 teaching assistantships with full and partial tuition reimbursements were awarded; Federal Work-Study, health care benefits, tuition waivers (full and partial), and unspecified assistantships also available. Financial award applicants required to submit FAFSA. *Unit head:* Dr. James A. Schultz, Chair, 310-825-5194, E-mail: jschultz@humnet.ucla.edu. *Application contact:* Departmental Office, 310-825-3955, E-mail: allen@humnet.ucla.edu.

University of California, San Diego, Office of Graduate Studies, Department of Literature, Program in German Literature, La Jolla, CA 92093. Offers MA. *Degree requirements:* For master's, thesis. *Entrance requirements:* For master's, GRE General Test, GRE Subject Test. Electronic applications accepted.

University of Chicago, Division of the Humanities, Department of Germanic Languages and Literatures, Chicago, IL 60637-1513. Offers AM, PhD. Terminal master's awarded for partial completion of doctoral program. *Degree requirements:* For master's, one foreign language, thesis; for doctorate, 2 foreign languages, thesis/dissertation. *Entrance requirements:* For master's and doctorate, GRE General Test. Additional exam requirements/recommendations for international students: Required—TOEFL.

University of Cincinnati, Graduate School, McMicken College of Arts and Sciences, Department of German Studies, Cincinnati, OH 45221. Offers MA, PhD. Part-time programs available. Terminal master's awarded for partial completion of doctoral program. *Degree requirements:* For master's, one foreign language, thesis or alternative; for doctorate, 3 foreign languages, thesis/dissertation. *Entrance requirements:* For master's, GRE General Test; for doctorate, GRE General Test, MA in German or equivalent. Additional exam requirements/recommendations for international students: Required—TOEFL (minimum score 560 paper-based). Electronic applications accepted. *Faculty research:* German literary culture, language and linguistics, medieval and early modern, German-Jewish literature, 20th and 21st century German literature and film.

University of Colorado Boulder, Graduate School, College of Arts and Sciences, Department of Germanic and Slavic Languages and Literature, Boulder, CO 80309. Offers German (MA). Part-time programs available. *Faculty:* 12 full-time (4 women). *Students:* 12 full-time (7 women); includes 1 minority (Black or African American, non-Hispanic/Latino), 3 international. Average age 26. 11 applicants, 7 enrolled. In 2010, 10 master's awarded. *Degree requirements:* For master's, 2 foreign languages, comprehensive exam, thesis or alternative. *Entrance requirements:* For master's, minimum undergraduate GPA of 2.75. *Application deadline:* For fall admission, 2/1 priority date for domestic students, 12/1 for international students; for spring admission, 9/15 for domestic and international students. Application fee: $50 ($60 for international students). *Financial support:* In 2010–11, 3 fellowships (averaging $11,333 per year), 2 research assistantships (averaging $7,752 per year) were awarded; Federal Work-Study, institutionally sponsored loans, and scholarships/grants also available. Financial award application deadline: 2/1. *Faculty research:* Eighteenth, nineteenth, and twentieth century literature, culture and thought; intellectual history; film; philosophy; social and political theory; German, Scandinavian and comparative literature.

University of Connecticut, Graduate School, College of Liberal Arts and Sciences, Department of Modern and Classical Languages, Field of German, Storrs, CT 06269. Offers MA, PhD. Terminal master's awarded for partial completion of doctoral program. *Degree requirements:* For master's, comprehensive exam; for doctorate, thesis/dissertation. *Entrance requirements:* For master's and doctorate, GRE General Test. Additional exam requirements/recommendations for international students: Required—TOEFL (minimum score 550 paper-based; 213 computer-based). Electronic applications accepted.

University of Delaware, College of Arts and Sciences, Department of Foreign Languages and Literatures, Newark, DE 19716. Offers foreign languages and literatures (MA), including French, German, Spanish; foreign languages pedagogy (MA), including French, German, Spanish; technical Chinese translation (MA). *Degree requirements:* For master's, one foreign language, comprehensive exam, thesis optional. *Entrance requirements:* For master's, GRE General Test, letters of recommendation, writing sample. Additional exam requirements/

recommendations for international students: Required—TOEFL. Electronic applications accepted. *Faculty research:* Medieval to Modern French and Spanish literature, Twentieth Century German, French, Spanish literature by women, computer-assisted instruction.

University of Florida, Graduate School, College of Liberal Arts and Sciences, Department of Languages, Literatures, and Cultures, Department of Germanic and Slavic Studies, Gainesville, FL 32611. Offers German (MA, PhD). *Faculty:* 6 full-time (3 women). *Students:* 7 full-time (6 women), 1 part-time (0 women), 5 international. Average age 29. 6 applicants, 83% accepted, 3 enrolled. In 2010, 1 master's awarded. *Degree requirements:* For master's, thesis or alternative; for doctorate, comprehensive exam, thesis/dissertation. *Entrance requirements:* For master's and doctorate, GRE General Test, score at least 1000, minimum GPA of 3.0. Additional exam requirements/recommendations for international students: Required—TOEFL (minimum score 550 paper-based; 213 computer-based; 80 iBT), IELTS (minimum score 6). *Application deadline:* For fall admission, 6/1 priority date for domestic students. Applications are processed on a rolling basis. Application fee: $30. Electronic applications accepted. *Expenses:* Tuition, state resident: full-time $10,915.92. Tuition, nonresident: full-time $28,309. *Financial support:* In 2010–11, 7 students received support, including 7 teaching assistantships (averaging $14,040 per year); fellowships, research assistantships also available. Financial award applicants required to submit FAFSA. *Faculty research:* Literature and language, medieval and Early Modern studies, cultural studies, film and media. *Unit head:* Dr. Mary Watt, Chair, 352-392-2422, Fax: 352-392-1443, E-mail: marywatt@ufl.edu. *Application contact:* Dr. Will Hasty, Graduate Coordinator, 352-273-3780, Fax: 352-392-1443, E-mail: hasty@ufl.edu.

University of Georgia, College of Arts and Sciences, Department of Germanic and Slavic Studies, Athens, GA 30602. Offers German (MA). *Faculty:* 7 full-time (3 women). *Students:* 9 full-time (8 women), 6 international. 9 applicants, 100% accepted, 5 enrolled. In 2010, 4 master's awarded. *Degree requirements:* For master's, one foreign language, thesis. *Entrance requirements:* For master's, GRE General Test. *Application deadline:* For fall admission, 7/1 priority date for domestic students; for spring admission, 11/15 for domestic students. Application fee: $50. Electronic applications accepted. *Expenses:* Tuition, state resident: full-time $7200; part-time $344 per credit hour. Tuition, nonresident: full-time $21,900; part-time $944 per credit hour. Tuition and fees vary according to course load and program. *Financial support:* Fellowships, research assistantships, teaching assistantships, unspecified assistantships available. *Unit head:* Dr. Martin H. Kagel, Head, 706-542-2445, Fax: 706-583-0349, E-mail: mkagel@uga.edu. *Application contact:* Dr. Alexander Sager, Graduate Advisor, 706-542-6211, Fax: 706-542-2459, E-mail: asager@uga.edu.

University of Illinois at Chicago, Graduate College, College of Liberal Arts and Sciences, Department of Germanic Studies, Chicago, IL 60607-7128. Offers MA, PhD. PhD offered jointly with University of Illinois at Urbana–Champaign. Part-time programs available. Terminal master's awarded for partial completion of doctoral program. *Degree requirements:* For master's, thesis optional, exam; for doctorate, 2 foreign languages, thesis/dissertation. *Entrance requirements:* For master's and doctorate, GRE General Test, minimum GPA of 2.75. Additional exam requirements/recommendations for international students: Required—TOEFL. Electronic applications accepted. *Faculty research:* German literature.

University of Illinois at Urbana–Champaign, Graduate College, College of Liberal Arts and Sciences, School of Literatures, Cultures and Linguistics, Department of Germanic Languages and Literatures, Champaign, IL 61820. Offers German (MA, PhD). *Faculty:* 8 full-time (7 women). *Students:* 15 full-time (9 women), 3 part-time (1 woman); includes 1 minority (Asian, non-Hispanic/Latino), 4 international. 19 applicants, 42% accepted, 7 enrolled. In 2010, 2 master's, 2 doctorates awarded. *Entrance requirements:* For master's and doctorate, minimum GPA of 3.0; writing sample. Additional exam requirements/recommendations for international students: Required—TOEFL (minimum score 79 iBT). *Application deadline:* Applications are processed on a rolling basis. Application fee: $75 ($90 for international students). Electronic applications accepted. *Financial support:* In 2010–11, 6 fellowships, 1 research assistantship, 14 teaching assistantships were awarded; tuition waivers (full and partial) also available. *Unit head:* Mara Wade, Head, 217-333-9383, Fax: 217-244-2223, E-mail: mwade@illinois.edu. *Application contact:* Lynn Stanke, Office Support Specialist, 217-333-6269, Fax: 217-244-3050, E-mail: stanke@illinois.edu.

The University of Iowa, Graduate College, College of Liberal Arts and Sciences, Department of German, Iowa City, IA 52242-1316. Offers MA, PhD. *Degree requirements:* For master's, thesis optional, exam; for doctorate, comprehensive exam, thesis/dissertation. *Entrance requirements:* For master's and doctorate, GRE General Test, minimum GPA of 3.0. Additional exam requirements/recommendations for international students: Required—TOEFL (minimum score 600 paper-based; 250 computer-based; 100 iBT). Electronic applications accepted.

The University of Kansas, Graduate Studies, College of Liberal Arts and Sciences, Department of Germanic Languages and Literatures, Lawrence, KS 66045. Offers German (MA, PhD). Part-time programs available. *Faculty:* 6 full-time (3 women). *Students:* 20 full-time (13 women); includes 1 minority (Asian, non-Hispanic/Latino), 3 international. Average age 31. 11 applicants, 82% accepted, 6 enrolled. In 2010, 2 master's, 3 doctorates awarded. *Degree requirements:* For master's, one foreign language, comprehensive exam, thesis optional, final oral exam; for doctorate, 2 foreign languages, comprehensive exam, thesis/dissertation, final oral exam. *Entrance requirements:* For master's, GRE, undergraduate major in German or equivalent; for doctorate, GRE, MA in German. Additional exam requirements/recommendations for international students: Required—TOEFL. *Application deadline:* For fall admission, 1/15 priority date for domestic and international students. Applications are processed on a rolling basis. Application fee: $55 ($65 for international students). Electronic applications accepted. *Expenses:* Tuition, state resident: full-time $7092; part-time $295.50 per credit hour. Tuition, nonresident: full-time $16,590; part-time $691.25 per credit hour. Required fees: $858; $71.49 per credit hour. Tuition and fees vary according to course load, campus/location and program. *Financial support:* Fellowships, research assistantships with full tuition reimbursements, teaching assistantships with full tuition reimbursements, Federal Work-Study, institutionally sponsored loans, and unspecified assistantships available. Support available to part-time students. Financial award application deadline: 1/30; financial award applicants required to submit FAFSA. *Faculty research:* Humanism, eighteenth to twentieth century literature, Germanic linguistics, German-American studies, German applied linguistics, German philology. *Unit head:* William Keel, Chair, 785-864-4803, Fax: 785-864-4298, E-mail: wkeel@ku.edu. *Application contact:* Leonie Marx, Graduate Director, 785-864-4803, Fax: 785-864-4298, E-mail: marx@ku.edu.

University of Kentucky, Graduate School, College of Arts and Sciences, Program in German, Lexington, KY 40506-0032. Offers MA. *Degree requirements:* For master's, one foreign language, comprehensive exam, thesis optional. *Entrance requirements:* For master's, GRE General Test, minimum undergraduate GPA of 2.75. Additional exam requirements/recommendations for international students: Required—TOEFL (minimum score 550 paper-based; 213 computer-based). Electronic applications accepted. *Faculty research:* Medieval studies, literature from Enlightenment to present, literary theory, intellectual history, gender studies.

University of Lethbridge, School of Graduate Studies, Lethbridge, AB T1K 3M4, Canada. Offers accounting (MScM); addictions counseling (M Sc); agricultural biotechnology (M Sc); agricultural studies (M Sc, MA); anthropology (MA); archaeology (MA); art (MA, MFA); biochemistry (M Sc); biological sciences (M Sc); biomolecular science (PhD); biosystems and biodiversity (PhD); Canadian studies (MA); chemistry (M Sc); computer science (M Sc); computer science and geographical information science (M Sc); counseling psychology (M Ed); dramatic arts (MA); earth, space, and physical science (PhD); economics (MA); educational leadership (M Ed); English (MA); environmental science (M Sc); evolution and behavior (PhD); exercise science (M Sc); finance (MScM); French (MA); French/German (MA); French/Spanish (MA); general education (M Ed); general management (MScM); geography (M Sc, MA); German (MA); health science (M Sc); history (MA); human resource management and labour relations (MScM); individualized multidisciplinary (M Sc, MA); information systems (MScM); international management (MScM); kinesiology (M Sc, MA); management (M Sc, MA); marketing (MScM); mathematics (M Sc); music (M Mus, MA); Native American studies (MA); neuroscience (M Sc, PhD); new media (MA); nursing (M Sc); philosophy (MA); physics (M Sc); policy and strategy (MScM); political science (MA); psychology (M Sc, MA); religious studies (MA); social sciences (MA); sociology (MA); theatre and dramatic arts (MFA); theoretical and computational science (PhD); urban and regional studies (MA); women's studies (MA). Part-time and evening/weekend programs available. *Degree requirements:* For doctorate, comprehensive exam, thesis/dissertation. *Entrance requirements:* For master's, GMAT (M Sc in management), bachelor's degree in related field, minimum GPA of 3.0 during previous 20 graded semester courses, 2 years teaching or related experience (M Ed); for doctorate, master's degree, minimum graduate GPA of 3.5. Additional exam requirements/recommendations for international students: Required—TOEFL. *Faculty research:* Movement and brain plasticity, gibberellin physiology, photosynthesis, carbon cycling, molecular properties of main-group ring components.

The University of Manchester, School of Languages, Linguistics and Cultures, Manchester, United Kingdom. Offers Arab world studies (PhD); Chinese studies (M Phil, PhD); East Asian studies (M Phil, PhD); English language (PhD); French studies (M Phil, PhD); German studies (M Phil, PhD); interpreting studies (PhD); Italian studies (M Phil, PhD); Japanese studies (M Phil, PhD); Latin American cultural studies (M Phil, PhD); linguistics (M Phil, PhD); Middle Eastern studies (M Phil, PhD); Polish studies (M Phil, PhD); Portuguese studies (M Phil, PhD); Russian studies (M Phil, PhD); Spanish studies (M Phil, PhD); translation and intercultural studies (M Phil, PhD).

University of Manitoba, Faculty of Graduate Studies, Faculty of Arts, Department of German and Slavic Studies, Winnipeg, MB R3T 2N2, Canada. Offers German language and literature (MA); Slavic languages and literatures (MA). *Degree requirements:* For master's, one foreign language, thesis or alternative.

University of Maryland, College Park, Academic Affairs, College of Arts and Humanities, School of Languages, Literature, and Cultures, Department of Germanic Studies, College Park, MD 20742. Offers Germanic language and literature (MA, PhD). *Students:* 12 full-time (11 women), 1 part-time (0 women), 6 international. 8 applicants, 25% accepted, 1 enrolled. In 2010, 1 master's, 1 doctorate awarded. *Degree requirements:* For master's, one foreign language, thesis optional, exams; for doctorate, 2 foreign languages, comprehensive exam, thesis/dissertation, reading exam, oral defense. *Entrance requirements:* For master's, GRE General Test, writing sample, 3 letters of recommendation; for doctorate, GRE General Test, MA in German or related discipline. Additional exam requirements/recommendations for international students: Required—TOEFL. *Application deadline:* For fall admission, 1/15 for domestic and international students; for spring admission, 10/15 for domestic students, 6/1 for international students. Applications are processed on a rolling basis. Application fee: $75. Electronic applications accepted. *Expenses:* Tuition, state resident: part-time $471 per credit hour. Tuition, nonresident: part-time $1016 per credit hour. Required fees: $337 per term. *Financial support:* In 2010–11, 8 teaching assistantships (averaging $16,810 per year) were awarded; fellowships, career-related internships or fieldwork, Federal Work-Study, and scholarships/grants also available. Support available to part-time students. Financial award applicants required to submit FAFSA. *Faculty research:* Language pedagogy, Germanic philology, medieval culture. *Unit head:* Carol A. Mossman, Director, School of Languages, Literatures and Cultures, 301-405-4025, Fax: 301-314-9928, E-mail: cmossman@umd.edu. *Application contact:* Dr. Charles A. Caramello, Dean of Graduate School, 301-405-0358, Fax: 301-314-9305, E-mail: ccaramel@umd.edu.

University of Massachusetts Amherst, Graduate School, College of Humanities and Fine Arts, Department of Languages, Literatures, and Cultures, Programs in German and Scandinavian Studies, Amherst, MA 01003. Offers MA, PhD. Part-time programs available. *Faculty:* 8 full-time (3 women). *Students:* 9 full-time (6 women), 8 part-time (6 women); includes 2 minority (1 Asian, non-Hispanic/Latino; 1 Hispanic/Latino), 2 international. Average age 33. 16 applicants, 56% accepted, 3 enrolled. In 2010, 6 master's, 1 doctorate awarded. Terminal master's awarded for partial completion of doctoral program. *Degree requirements:* For master's, thesis or alternative; for doctorate, one foreign language, comprehensive exam, thesis/dissertation. *Entrance requirements:* For master's and doctorate, writing sample in English and German. Additional exam requirements/recommendations for international students: Required—TOEFL (minimum score 550 paper-based; 213 computer-based; 80 iBT), IELTS (minimum score 6.5). *Application deadline:* For fall admission, 2/1 for domestic and international students; for spring admission, 10/1 for domestic and international students. Applications are processed on a rolling basis. Application fee: $50 ($65 for international students). Electronic applications accepted. *Expenses:* Tuition, state resident: full-time $2640. Required fees: $8282. One-time fee: $357 full-time. *Financial support:* In 2010–11, 1 research assistantship with full tuition reimbursement (averaging $14,661 per year), 13 teaching assistantships with full tuition reimbursements (averaging $10,099 per year) were awarded; fellowships, career-related internships or fieldwork, Federal Work-Study, scholarships/grants, traineeships, health care benefits, tuition waivers (full), and unspecified assistantships also available. Support available to part-time students. Financial award application deadline: 2/1; financial award applicants required to submit FAFSA. *Unit head:* Dr. Andrew Donson, Graduate Program Director, 413-545-6686, Fax: 413-545-6695. *Application contact:* Jean M. Ames, Supervisor of Admissions, 413-545-0722, Fax: 413-577-0010, E-mail: gradadm@grad.umass.edu.

University of Michigan, Horace H. Rackham School of Graduate Studies, College of Literature, Science, and the Arts, Department of Germanic Languages and Literatures, Ann Arbor, MI 48109. Offers German (AM, PhD). *Degree requirements:* For doctorate, one foreign language, comprehensive exam, thesis/dissertation, oral defense of dissertation, preliminary exam. *Entrance requirements:* For doctorate, GRE General Test. Additional exam requirements/recommendations for international students: Required—TOEFL (minimum score 560 paper-based; 220 computer-based). Electronic applications accepted. *Expenses:* Tuition, state resident: full-time $17,784; part-time $1116 per credit hour. Tuition, nonresident: full-time $35,944; part-time $2125 per credit hour. International tuition: $35,994 full-time. Required fees: $95 per semester. Tuition and fees vary according to course load, degree level and program. *Faculty research:* German history, German literature, literary theory, film, political and social theory.

University of Minnesota, Twin Cities Campus, Graduate School, College of Liberal Arts, Department of German, Scandinavian, and Dutch, Minneapolis, MN 55455-0213. Offers Germanic studies: German and Scandinavian studies track (PhD); Germanic studies: German track (MA, PhD); Germanic studies: Germanic medieval studies track (MA, PhD); Germanic studies: Scandinavian studies track (MA); Germanic studies: teaching track (MA). Part-time programs available. Terminal master's awarded for partial completion of doctoral program. *Degree requirements:* For doctorate, 2 foreign languages, thesis/dissertation. *Entrance requirements:* For master's, GRE General Test, BA in German, Scandinavian, or equivalent; for doctorate, GRE General Test, MA in German, Scandinavian, or equivalent. Additional exam requirements/recommendations for international students: Required—TOEFL (minimum score 550 paper-based; 213 computer-based; 79 iBT). Electronic applications accepted. *Faculty research:* Cultural studies, literary theory, feminist criticism, film, Germanic philology.

University of Mississippi, Graduate School, College of Liberal Arts, Department of Modern Languages, Oxford, University, MS 38677. Offers French (MA); German (MA); Spanish (MA). *Students:* 39 full-time (28 women), 19 part-time (17 women); includes 8 Black or African American, non-Hispanic/Latino; 1 American Indian or Alaska Native, non-Hispanic/Latino; 7 Asian, non-Hispanic/Latino; 10 Hispanic/Latino; 1 Two or more races, non-Hispanic/Latino. In 2010, 17 master's awarded. *Degree requirements:* For master's, thesis (for some programs). *Entrance requirements:* For master's, GRE General Test, minimum GPA of 3.0. Additional exam requirements/recommendations for international students: Required—TOEFL. *Application deadline:* For fall admission, 2/1 for domestic students; for spring admission, 10/1 for domestic students. Applications are processed on a rolling basis. Application fee: $25. Electronic applications accepted. *Financial support:* Scholarships/grants available. Financial award application deadline: 3/1; financial award applicants required to submit FAFSA. *Unit head:* Dr. Donald L. Dyer, Chair, 662-915-7298, Fax: 662-915-1086, E-mail: mlangs@olemiss.edu. *Application*

German

University of Mississippi (continued)
contact: Dr. Christy M. Wyandt, Associate Dean, 662-915-7474, Fax: 662-915-7577, E-mail: cwyandt@olemiss.edu.

University of Missouri, Graduate School, College of Arts and Sciences, Department of German and Russian Studies, Columbia, MO 65211. Offers German (MA). *Faculty:* 16 full-time (7 women), 3 part-time/adjunct (1 woman). *Students:* 15 full-time (10 women), 5 part-time (2 women), 7 international. Average age 25. 12 applicants, 100% accepted, 10 enrolled. In 2010, 6 master's awarded. *Entrance requirements:* For master's, GRE General Test, minimum GPA of 3.0. Additional exam requirements/recommendations for international students: Required—TOEFL (minimum score 500 paper-based; 173 computer-based; 61 iBT). *Application deadline:* For fall admission, 3/1 priority date for domestic students. Applications are processed on a rolling basis. Application fee: $45 ($60 for international students). Electronic applications accepted. *Financial support:* In 2010–11, 18 teaching assistantships with full tuition reimbursements were awarded; institutionally sponsored loans, health care benefits, and unspecified assistantships also available. *Faculty research:* German and of Russian cultural studies, including literature, film, media studies, philosophy, and the history of science. *Unit head:* Dr. Timothy Langen, Department Chair, 573-882-6167, E-mail: langent@missouri.edu. *Application contact:* Jennifer Arnold, Administrative Associate, 573-882-4328, E-mail: arnoldj@missouri.edu.

The University of Montana, Graduate School, College of Arts and Sciences, Department of Modern and Classical Languages and Literatures, Missoula, MT 59812-0002. Offers French (MA); German (MA); Spanish (MA). *Degree requirements:* For master's, one foreign language. *Entrance requirements:* For master's, GRE General Test. Additional exam requirements/recommendations for international students: Required—TOEFL.

University of Nebraska–Lincoln, Graduate College, College of Arts and Sciences, Department of Modern Languages and Literatures, Lincoln, NE 68588. Offers French (MA, PhD); German (MA, PhD); Spanish (MA, PhD). *Degree requirements:* For master's, thesis optional; for doctorate, comprehensive exam, thesis/dissertation. *Entrance requirements:* For master's and doctorate, writing sample in target language. Additional exam requirements/recommendations for international students: Required—TOEFL (minimum score 550 paper-based; 213 computer-based). Electronic applications accepted. *Faculty research:* French, German, and Spanish language, literature, and culture.

University of Nevada, Reno, Graduate School, College of Liberal Arts, Department of Foreign Languages and Literatures, Reno, NV 89557. Offers French (MA); German (MA); Spanish (MA). *Degree requirements:* For master's, one foreign language, thesis optional. *Entrance requirements:* For master's, GRE General Test, minimum GPA of 2.75. Additional exam requirements/recommendations for international students: Required—TOEFL (minimum score 500 paper-based; 173 computer-based; 61 iBT), IELTS (minimum score 6). *Expenses:* Tuition, state resident: full-time $2219; part-time $246 per credit. Tuition, nonresident: part-time $510 per credit. International tuition: $9009 full-time. Required fees: $59 per term. One-time fee: $101. Tuition and fees vary according to course load. *Faculty research:* Thirteenth century mysticism, contemporary Spanish and Latin American poetry and theater, French interrelation between narration and photography, exile literature and Holocaust.

University of New Mexico, Graduate School, College of Arts and Sciences, Department of Foreign Languages and Literature, Albuquerque, NM 87131-2039. Offers comparative literature and cultural studies (MA); French (MA); French studies (PhD); German studies (MA). Part-time programs available. *Faculty:* 18 full-time (12 women), 29 part-time/adjunct (19 women). *Students:* 25 full-time (16 women), 6 part-time (4 women); includes 2 Hispanic/Latino, 8 international. Average age 32. 20 applicants, 70% accepted, 9 enrolled. In 2010, 7 master's, 1 doctorate awarded. *Degree requirements:* For master's, one foreign language, thesis optional; for doctorate, 2 foreign languages, thesis/dissertation. *Entrance requirements:* Additional exam requirements/recommendations for international students: Required—TOEFL. *Application deadline:* For fall admission, 2/1 priority date for domestic students; for spring admission, 10/1 priority date for domestic students. Application fee: $50. Electronic applications accepted. *Expenses:* Tuition, state resident: full-time $5991; part-time $251 per credit hour. Tuition, nonresident: full-time $14,405; part-time $800.20 per credit hour. Tuition and fees vary according to course level, course load, program and reciprocity agreements. *Financial support:* In 2010–11, 28 students received support, including 1 research assistantship (averaging $4,730 per year), 23 teaching assistantships with tuition reimbursements available (averaging $10,300 per year); Federal Work-Study, health care benefits, and unspecified assistantships also available. Financial award application deadline: 3/1; financial award applicants required to submit FAFSA. *Faculty research:* German, Russian, Italian, Japanese, French, comparative literature, culture studies, classics. Total annual research expenditures: $4,750. *Unit head:* Dr. Natasha Kolchevska, Chair, 505-277-4771, Fax: 505-277-3599, E-mail: nakol@unm.edu. *Application contact:* Jean Aragon, Application and Graduation Advisor, 505-277-4471, Fax: 505-277-3599, E-mail: peaslee@unm.edu.

The University of North Carolina at Chapel Hill, Graduate School, College of Arts and Sciences, Department of Germanic Languages, Chapel Hill, NC 27599. Offers literature and linguistics (MA, PhD). Part-time programs available. Terminal master's awarded for partial completion of doctoral program. *Degree requirements:* For master's, comprehensive exam, thesis; for doctorate, one foreign language, comprehensive exam, thesis/dissertation. *Entrance requirements:* For master's and doctorate, GRE General Test, minimum GPA of 3.0. *Faculty research:* Gender and sexuality, literature and politics, German and Jewish culture, medieval through modern literature, Germanic linguistics.

University of Northern Iowa, Graduate College, College of Humanities and Fine Arts, Department of Modern Languages, Program in German, Cedar Falls, IA 50614. Offers German (MA); teaching English to speakers of other languages/German (MA). Part-time and evening/weekend programs available. *Students:* 5 full-time (all women), 2 international. 4 applicants, 50% accepted, 1 enrolled. In 2010, 2 master's awarded. *Degree requirements:* For master's, one foreign language, comprehensive exam, thesis or alternative. *Entrance requirements:* For master's, minimum GPA of 3.0, valid teaching license, documentation of successful teaching experience. Additional exam requirements/recommendations for international students: Required—TOEFL (minimum score 600 paper-based; 250 computer-based; 100 iBT). *Application deadline:* For fall admission, 8/1 priority date for domestic students. Applications are processed on a rolling basis. Application fee: $50 ($70 for international students). *Financial support:* Career-related internships or fieldwork, Federal Work-Study, and tuition waivers (full and partial) available. Support available to part-time students. Financial award application deadline: 2/1. *Unit head:* Dr. Siegrun Wildner, Coordinator, 319-273-7131, Fax: 319-273-2848, E-mail: siegrun.wildner@uni.edu. *Application contact:* Laurie S. Russell, Record Analyst, 319-273-2623, Fax: 319-273-2885, E-mail: laurie.russell@uni.edu.

University of Oklahoma, College of Arts and Sciences, Department of Modern Languages, Program in German, Norman, OK 73019. Offers MA, MBA/MA. Part-time programs available. *Students:* 6 full-time (4 women). Average age 29. 3 applicants, 67% accepted, 2 enrolled. In 2010, 3 master's awarded. *Degree requirements:* For master's, 2 foreign languages, comprehensive exam, thesis optional, departmental qualifying exam. *Entrance requirements:* For master's, BA with 25 hours in German or equivalent, minimum GPA of 3.0 in last 60 hours, 3 letters of recommendation. Additional exam requirements/recommendations for international students: Required—TOEFL (minimum score 550 paper-based; 213 computer-based; 79 iBT). *Application deadline:* For fall admission, 2/1 priority date for domestic students, 2/1 for international students; for spring admission, 10/1 for domestic students, 9/1 for international students. Applications are processed on a rolling basis. Application fee: $40 ($90 for international students). Electronic applications accepted. *Expenses:* Tuition, state resident: full-time $3893; part-time $162.20 per credit hour. Tuition, nonresident: full-time $14,167; part-time $590.30 per credit hour. Required fees: $2523; $94.60 per credit hour. Tuition and fees vary according to course load and degree level. *Financial support:* In 2010–11, 5 students received support. Scholarships/grants, health care benefits, and unspecified assistantships available. Financial award applicants required to submit FAFSA. *Faculty research:* Film studies, German literature and culture studies, fin-de-siècle Austria, Arthurian romance, the Goethe era. *Unit head:* Dr. Pamela Genova, Chair, 405-325-6181, Fax: 405-325-0103, E-mail: genova@ou.edu. *Application contact:* Dr. Logan E. Whalen, Graduate Liaison, 405-325-5088, Fax: 405-325-0103, E-mail: mlllgradinfo@ou.edu.

University of Oregon, Graduate School, College of Arts and Sciences, Department of Germanic Languages and Literatures, Eugene, OR 97403. Offers MA, PhD. *Degree requirements:* For master's, 2 foreign languages, thesis or alternative; for doctorate, 3 foreign languages, thesis/dissertation. *Entrance requirements:* For master's and doctorate, minimum GPA of 3.0. Additional exam requirements/recommendations for international students: Required—TOEFL. *Faculty research:* Medieval language and literature, eighteenth to twentieth century literature and philosophy, literary theory, feminist literature and theory, psychoanalysis and literature.

University of Pennsylvania, School of Arts and Sciences, Graduate Group in Germanic Languages, Philadelphia, PA 19104. Offers AM, PhD. *Faculty:* 18 full-time (7 women), 8 part-time/adjunct (1 woman). *Students:* 11 full-time (8 women), 2 part-time (1 woman). 19 applicants, 32% accepted, 1 enrolled. In 2010, 3 master's, 3 doctorates awarded. Terminal master's awarded for partial completion of doctoral program. *Degree requirements:* For master's, one foreign language, thesis or alternative; for doctorate, one foreign language, comprehensive exam, thesis/dissertation. *Entrance requirements:* For master's and doctorate, GRE General Test. *Application deadline:* For fall admission, 12/1 priority date for domestic students. Application fee: $70. *Expenses:* Tuition: Full-time $25,660; part-time $4758 per course. Required fees: $2152; $270 per course. Tuition and fees vary according to course load, degree level and program. *Financial support:* Fellowships, teaching assistantships, institutionally sponsored loans, scholarships/grants, traineeships, health care benefits, and unspecified assistantships available. Financial award application deadline: 12/15. *Unit head:* Catriona MacLeod, Department Chair, German Languages and Literatures. *Application contact:* Catriona MacLeod, Department Chair, German Languages and Literatures.

University of Pittsburgh, School of Arts and Sciences, Department of German, Pittsburgh, PA 15260. Offers MA, PhD. Part-time programs available. *Faculty:* 7 full-time (4 women), 2 part-time/adjunct (0 women). *Students:* 8 full-time (6 women), 1 (woman) part-time; includes 1 Hispanic/Latino. Average age 32. 4 applicants, 75% accepted, 2 enrolled. In 2010, 3 master's awarded. Terminal master's awarded for partial completion of doctoral program. *Degree requirements:* For master's, one foreign language, comprehensive exam (for some programs), thesis; for doctorate, one foreign language, comprehensive exam, thesis/dissertation. *Entrance requirements:* For master's, bachelor's degree in German, minimum GPA of 3.0 or equivalent; for doctorate, MA. Additional exam requirements/recommendations for international students: Required—TOEFL. *Application deadline:* For spring admission, 1/5 priority date for domestic and international students. Application fee: $50. Electronic applications accepted. *Expenses:* Tuition, state resident: full-time $17,304; part-time $701 per credit. Tuition, nonresident: full-time $29,554; part-time $1210 per credit. Required fees: $740; $214 per term. Tuition and fees vary according to program. *Financial support:* In 2010–11, 7 students received support, including fellowships with tuition reimbursements available (averaging $16,140 per year), teaching assistantships with tuition reimbursements available (averaging $15,520 per year); scholarships/grants and health care benefits also available. Financial award application deadline: 1/15. *Faculty research:* Age of Goethe, German film, postwar culture, German-Jewish culture, literature and philosophy. *Unit head:* Dr. John B. Lyon, Chair, 412-624-5839, Fax: 412-624-6318, E-mail: jblyon@pitt.edu. *Application contact:* Dr. Randall Halle, Graduate Director, 412-628-2614, Fax: 412-624-6318, E-mail: rhalle@pitt.edu.

University of Rochester, School of Arts and Sciences, Department of Modern Languages and Cultures, Program in German, Rochester, NY 14627.

University of Saskatchewan, College of Graduate Studies and Research, College of Arts and Sciences, Department of Languages and Linguistics, Saskatoon, SK S7N 5A2, Canada. Offers MA. *Degree requirements:* For master's, 2 foreign languages, thesis. *Entrance requirements:* Additional exam requirements/recommendations for international students: Required—TOEFL (minimum score 80 iBT); Recommended—IELTS (minimum score 6.5). Electronic applications accepted.

University of South Africa, College of Human Sciences, Pretoria, South Africa. Offers adult education (M Ed); African languages (MA, PhD); African politics (MA, PhD); Afrikaans (MA, PhD); ancient history (MA, PhD); ancient Near Eastern studies (MA, PhD); anthropology (MA, PhD); applied linguistics (MA); Arabic (MA, PhD); archaeology (MA); art history (MA); Biblical archaeology (MA); Biblical studies (M Th, D Th, PhD); Christian spirituality (M Th, D Th); church history (M Th, D Th); classical studies (MA, PhD); clinical psychology (MA); communication (MA, PhD); comparative education (M Ed, Ed D); consulting psychology (D Admin, D Com, PhD); curriculum studies (M Ed, Ed D); development studies (M Admin, MA, D Admin, PhD); didactics (M Ed, Ed D); education (M Tech); education management (M Ed, Ed D); educational psychology (M Ed); English (MA); environmental education (M Ed); French (MA, PhD); German (MA, PhD); Greek (MA); guidance and counseling (M Ed); health studies (MA, PhD), including health sciences education (MA), health services management (MA), medical and surgical nursing science (critical care general) (MA), midwifery and neonatal nursing science (MA), trauma and emergency care (MA); history (MA, PhD); history of education (Ed D); inclusive education (M Ed, Ed D); information and communications technology policy and regulation (MA); information science (MA, MIS, PhD); international politics (MA, PhD); Islamic studies (MA, PhD); Italian (MA, PhD); Judaica (MA, PhD); linguistics (MA, PhD); mathematical education (M Ed); mathematics education (MA); missiology (M Th, D Th); modern Hebrew (MA, PhD); musicology (MA, MMus, D Mus, PhD); natural science education (M Ed); New Testament (M Th, D Th); Old Testament (D Th); pastoral therapy (M Th, D Th); philosophy (MA); philosophy of education (M Ed, Ed D); politics (MA, PhD); Portuguese (MA, PhD); practical theology (M Th, D Th); psychology (MA, MS, PhD); psychology of education (M Ed, Ed D); public health (MA); religious studies (MA, D Th, PhD); Romance languages (MA); Russian (MA, PhD); Semitic languages (MA, PhD); social behavior studies in HIV/AIDS (MA); social science (mental health) (MA); social science in development studies (MA); social science in psychology (MA); social science in social work (MA); social science in sociology (MA); social work (MSW, DSW, PhD); socio-education (M Ed, Ed D); sociolinguistics (MA); sociology (MA, PhD); Spanish (MA, PhD); systematic theology (M Th, D Th); TESOL (teaching English to speakers of other languages) (MA); theological ethics (M Th, D Th); theory of literature (MA, PhD); urban ministries (D Th); urban ministry (M Th).

University of South Carolina, The Graduate School, College of Arts and Sciences, Department of Languages, Literatures, and Cultures, Columbia, SC 29208. Offers comparative literature (MA, PhD); foreign languages (MAT), including French, German, Spanish; French (MA); German (MA); Spanish (MA). MAT offered in cooperation with the College of Education. Part-time programs available. *Degree requirements:* For master's, one foreign language, comprehensive exam, thesis optional; for doctorate, 2 foreign languages, comprehensive exam, thesis/dissertation. *Entrance requirements:* For master's and doctorate, GRE General Test, writing sample. Additional exam requirements/recommendations for international students: Required—TOEFL (minimum score 230 computer-based; 75 iBT). Electronic applications accepted. *Faculty research:* Modern literature, linguistics, literature and culture, medieval literature, literary theory.

The University of Tennessee, Graduate School, College of Arts and Sciences, Department of Modern Foreign Languages and Literatures, Program in German, Knoxville, TN 37996. Offers MA. Part-time programs available. *Degree requirements:* For master's, one foreign language, thesis or alternative. *Entrance requirements:* For master's, minimum GPA of 2.7. Additional exam requirements/recommendations for international students: Required—TOEFL. Electronic applications accepted. *Expenses:* Tuition, state resident: full-time $7440; part-time $414 per credit hour. Tuition, nonresident: full-time $22,478; part-time $1250 per credit hour. Required fees: $922; $43 per credit hour. Tuition and fees vary according to program.

The University of Tennessee, Graduate School, College of Arts and Sciences, Department of Modern Foreign Languages and Literatures, Program in Modern Foreign Languages, Knoxville, TN 37996. Offers applied linguistics (PhD); French (PhD); German (PhD); Italian (PhD); Portuguese (PhD); Russian (PhD); Spanish (PhD). *Degree requirements:* For doctorate, 2 foreign languages, thesis/dissertation. *Entrance requirements:* For doctorate, minimum GPA of 2.7. Additional exam requirements/recommendations for international students: Required—TOEFL. Electronic applications accepted. *Expenses:* Tuition, state resident: full-time $7440; part-time $414 per credit hour. Tuition, nonresident: full-time $22,478; part-time $1250 per credit hour. Required fees: $922; $43 per credit hour. Tuition and fees vary according to program.

The University of Texas at Austin, Graduate School, College of Liberal Arts, Department of Germanic Studies, Austin, TX 78712-1111. Offers MA, PhD. *Degree requirements:* For master's, one foreign language, thesis or alternative; for doctorate, 2 foreign languages, thesis/dissertation. *Entrance requirements:* For master's and doctorate, GRE General Test. *Faculty research:* Germanic languages and culture (German, Austrian, Swiss, Dutch, Danish, Norwegian, Swedish, Yiddish), language pedagogy and linguistics.

The University of Toledo, College of Graduate Studies, College of Language, Literature and Social Sciences, Department of Foreign Languages, Toledo, OH 43606-3390. Offers French (MA); German (MA); Spanish (MA). Part-time programs available. *Faculty:* 6. *Students:* 2 full-time (both women), 3 part-time (2 women); includes 1 minority (Hispanic/Latino). Average age 35. 8 applicants, 25% accepted, 2 enrolled. In 2010, 2 master's awarded. *Degree requirements:* For master's, one foreign language, comprehensive exam, comprehensive reading exam in 1 additional foreign language. *Entrance requirements:* For master's, A minimum 2.7 cumulative point-hour ratio (on a 4.0 scale) for all previous academic work. Additional exam requirements/recommendations for international students: Required—TOEFL (minimum score 550 paper-based; 213 computer-based; 80 iBT), IELTS (minimum score 6.5). *Application deadline:* For fall admission, 1/15 priority date for domestic and international students. Applications are processed on a rolling basis. Application fee: $45 ($75 for international students). Electronic applications accepted. *Expenses:* Tuition, state resident: full-time $11,426; part-time $476 per credit hour. Tuition, nonresident: full-time $21,660; part-time $903 per credit hour. One-time fee: $62. *Financial support:* Teaching assistantships with full tuition reimbursements, Federal Work-Study, institutionally sponsored loans, scholarships/grants, tuition waivers (full), and unspecified assistantships available. Support available to part-time students. *Unit head:* Dr. Ruth Hottell, Chair, 419-530-4651, E-mail: ruth.hottell@utoledo.edu. *Application contact:* Graduate School Office, 419-530-4723, Fax: 419-530-4724, E-mail: grdsch@utnet.utoledo.edu.

University of Toronto, School of Graduate Studies, Humanities Division, Department of Germanic Languages and Literatures, Toronto, ON M5S 1A1, Canada. Offers MA, PhD. Part-time programs available. *Degree requirements:* For master's, thesis optional, German language competence exam; for doctorate, thesis/dissertation, qualifying exam, thesis defense. *Entrance requirements:* For master's, 7 two-semester courses in German language and literature, 3 letters of recommendation; for doctorate, MA in German, minimum A– average, 3 letters of recommendation, writing sample, resumé.

University of Utah, Graduate School, College of Humanities, Department of Languages and Literature, Salt Lake City, UT 84112. Offers comparative literary and cultural studies (MA, PhD); French (MA, MALP); German (MA, MALP, PhD); Spanish (MA, MALP, PhD); world languages with secondary teaching licensure (MA). *Faculty:* 36 full-time (21 women). *Students:* 35 full-time (24 women), 9 part-time (7 women); includes 7 minority (1 American Indian or Alaska Native, non-Hispanic/Latino; 2 Asian, non-Hispanic/Latino; 4 Hispanic/Latino), 8 international. Average age 34. 58 applicants, 57% accepted, 24 enrolled. In 2010, 17 master's, 2 doctorates awarded. Terminal master's awarded for partial completion of doctoral program. *Degree requirements:* For master's, 2 foreign languages, comprehensive exam (for some programs), thesis (for some programs), standard proficiency in 2 languages other than English; for doctorate, 3 foreign languages, comprehensive exam, thesis/dissertation, standard proficiency in 2 languages other than English and language of study, advanced proficiency in 1 language other than English and language of study. *Entrance requirements:* For master's, GRE, bachelor's degree or strong undergraduate record in target languages, minimum GPA of 3.0; for doctorate, GRE, MA, advanced proficiency in a target language. Additional exam requirements/recommendations for international students: Required—TOEFL (minimum score 500 paper-based; 173 computer-based). *Application deadline:* For fall admission, 1/15 priority date for domestic students, 12/15 priority date for international students. Application fee: $55 ($65 for international students). Electronic applications accepted. *Expenses:* Tuition, area resident: Part-time $179.19 per credit hour. Tuition, state resident: full-time $4384. Tuition, nonresident: full-time $16,684; part-time $630.67 per credit hour. Required fees: $350 per semester. Tuition and fees vary according to course load, degree level and program. *Financial support:* In 2010–11, 24 students received support, including 2 fellowships, 22 teaching assistantships with full and partial tuition reimbursements available (averaging $11,500 per year); health care benefits also available. Financial award application deadline: 1/15; financial award applicants required to submit FAFSA. *Faculty research:* Literary study, literary theory, linguistics, cultural studies, comparative studies. Total annual research expenditures: $53,399. *Unit head:* Dr. Karin Baumgartner, Director of Graduate Studies, 801-585-3001, Fax: 801-581-7581, E-mail: karin.baumgartner@hum.utah.edu. *Application contact:* Virginia Ellinwood, Academic Advisor, 801-585-9437, Fax: 801-581-7581, E-mail: v.ellinwood@utah.edu.

University of Vermont, Graduate College, College of Arts and Sciences, Department of German and Russian, Burlington, VT 05405. Offers German (MA). *Students:* 2 (1 woman). 1 applicant, 100% accepted, 0 enrolled. *Degree requirements:* For master's, one foreign language, thesis. *Entrance requirements:* For master's, GRE General Test. Additional exam requirements/recommendations for international students: Required—TOEFL (minimum score 550 paper-based; 213 computer-based; 80 iBT). *Application deadline:* For fall admission, 4/1 priority date for domestic students. Applications are processed on a rolling basis. Application fee: $40. Electronic applications accepted. *Expenses:* Tuition, state resident: part-time $537 per credit hour. Tuition, nonresident: part-time $1355 per credit hour. *Financial support:* Fellowships, teaching assistantships available. Financial award application deadline: 3/1. *Faculty research:* Medieval, eighteenth, and nineteenth century literature; folklore. *Unit head:* Dr. W. Mieder, Chairperson, 802-656-3430. *Application contact:* Dr. D. Scrase, Coordinator, 802-656-3430.

University of Victoria, Faculty of Graduate Studies, Faculty of Humanities, Department of Germanic and Slavic Studies, Victoria, BC V8W 2Y2, Canada. Offers German studies (MA). Part-time programs available. *Degree requirements:* For master's, 2 foreign languages, oral defense of thesis. *Entrance requirements:* For master's, BA in German, minimum B+ average in undergraduate course work. Additional exam requirements/recommendations for international students: Required—TOEFL (minimum score 575 paper-based; 233 computer-based), IELTS (minimum score 7). Electronic applications accepted. *Faculty research:* Nineteenth and twentieth century German literature, literature and music, language acquisition, eighteenth and twentieth century drama and theater, military history.

University of Virginia, College and Graduate School of Arts and Sciences, Department of Germanic Languages and Literatures, Charlottesville, VA 22903. Offers German (MA, PhD). *Faculty:* 9 full-time (5 women), 2 part-time/adjunct (1 woman). *Students:* 10 full-time (3 women), 1 (woman) part-time, 4 international. Average age 28. 14 applicants, 36% accepted, 2 enrolled. In 2010, 1 master's, 3 doctorates awarded. *Degree requirements:* For master's, one foreign language, comprehensive exam, thesis; for doctorate, one foreign language, comprehensive exam, thesis/dissertation. *Entrance requirements:* For master's, GRE General Test, 3 letters of recommendation, critical writing sample; for doctorate, GRE General Test, 3 letters of recommendation; critical writing sample. Additional exam requirements/recommendations for international students: Required—TOEFL (minimum score 600 paper-based; 250 computer-based; 90 iBT), IELTS (minimum score 7). *Application deadline:* For fall admission, 1/15 for domestic and international students. Applications are processed on a rolling basis. Application fee: $60. Electronic applications accepted. *Financial support:* Applicants required to submit FAFSA. *Unit head:* Volker Kaiser, Chair, 434-924-3530, Fax: 434-924-6700, E-mail: germandepartment@virginia.edu. *Application contact:* Chad Wellmon, Director of Graduate Admissions, 434-924-7067, Fax: 434-924-6700, E-mail: bkb@virginia.edu.

University of Washington, Graduate School, College of Arts and Sciences, Department of Germanics, Seattle, WA 98195. Offers MA, PhD. Part-time programs available. Terminal master's awarded for partial completion of doctoral program. *Degree requirements:* For master's, one foreign language, 2 research papers; for doctorate, 2 foreign languages, thesis/dissertation, 3 research papers. *Entrance requirements:* For master's and doctorate, GRE, minimum GPA of 3.0. Additional exam requirements/recommendations for international students: Required—TOEFL. Electronic applications accepted. *Faculty research:* Modern German literature, Germanic linguistics and philology, language pedagogy, literary theory, cinema studies.

University of Waterloo, Graduate Studies, Faculty of Arts, Department of Germanic and Slavic Studies, Waterloo, ON N2L 3G1, Canada. Offers German (MA, PhD); Russian (MA). Part-time and evening/weekend programs available. *Degree requirements:* For master's, one foreign language, thesis optional; for doctorate, 2 foreign languages, comprehensive exam, thesis/dissertation. *Entrance requirements:* For master's, honors degree, minimum B average; for doctorate, master's degree, minimum B average. Additional exam requirements/recommendations for international students: Required—TOEFL, TWE. Electronic applications accepted. *Faculty research:* Medieval theatre; history and literature; German and Russian literary relations; seventeenth, eighteenth, nineteenth, and twentieth century German literature.

University of Wisconsin–Madison, Graduate School, College of Letters and Science, Department of German, Madison, WI 53706-1380. Offers MA, PhD. Part-time programs available. Terminal master's awarded for partial completion of doctoral program. *Degree requirements:* For master's, one foreign language, comprehensive exam, thesis optional; for doctorate, 2 foreign languages, comprehensive exam, thesis/dissertation. *Entrance requirements:* For master's and doctorate, GRE. Electronic applications accepted. *Expenses:* Tuition, state resident: full-time $9887; part-time $617.96 per credit. Tuition, nonresident: full-time $24,054; part-time $1503.40 per credit. Required fees: $67.63 per credit. Tuition and fees vary according to reciprocity agreements. *Faculty research:* Literature, culture/linguistics, film, Dutch.

University of Wisconsin–Milwaukee, Graduate School, College of Letters and Sciences, Interdepartmental Program in Foreign Language and Literature, Milwaukee, WI 53201-0413. Offers classics and Hebrew studies (MAFLL); comparative literature (MAFLL); French and Italian (MAFLL); German (MAFLL); Slavic studies (MAFLL); translation (Certificate). Part-time programs available. *Faculty:* 29 full-time (14 women). *Students:* 35 full-time (27 women), 29 part-time (20 women); includes 1 Hispanic/Latino. Average age 40. 30 applicants, 67% accepted, 19 enrolled. In 2010, 24 master's awarded. *Degree requirements:* For master's, 2 foreign languages, thesis or alternative. *Entrance requirements:* Additional exam requirements/recommendations for international students: Required—TOEFL (minimum score 550 paper-based; 79 iBT), IELTS (minimum score 6.5). *Application deadline:* For fall admission, 1/1 priority date for domestic students; for spring admission, 9/1 for domestic students. Applications are processed on a rolling basis. Application fee: $56 ($96 for international students). Electronic applications accepted. *Financial support:* In 2010–11, 1 fellowship, 2 research assistantships, 26 teaching assistantships were awarded; career-related internships or fieldwork, health care benefits, unspecified assistantships, and project assistantships also available. Support available to part-time students. Financial award application deadline: 4/15; financial award applicants required to submit FAFSA. Total annual research expenditures: $304,210. *Unit head:* Gabrielle Verdier, Representative, 414-229-3346, Fax: 414-229-2741, E-mail: verdier@uwm.edu. *Application contact:* General Information Contact, 414-229-4982, Fax: 414-229-6967, E-mail: gradschool@uwm.edu.

University of Wyoming, College of Arts and Sciences, Department of Modern and Classical Languages, Program in German, Laramie, WY 82070. Offers MA. Part-time programs available. *Degree requirements:* For master's, one foreign language, thesis or alternative. *Entrance requirements:* For master's, GRE General Test, minimum GPA of 3.0. *Faculty research:* East German literature, German literature, theatre, poetry.

Vanderbilt University, Graduate School, Department of Germanic and Slavic Languages, Nashville, TN 37240-1001. Offers German (MA, MAT, PhD). *Faculty:* 7 full-time (2 women). *Students:* 19 full-time (15 women), 1 (woman) part-time; includes 2 Hispanic/Latino. Average age 31. 27 applicants, 26% accepted, 4 enrolled. In 2010, 1 master's, 2 doctorates awarded. Terminal master's awarded for partial completion of doctoral program. *Degree requirements:* For master's, one foreign language, comprehensive exam; for doctorate, 2 foreign languages, comprehensive exam, thesis/dissertation, qualifying and final exams. *Entrance requirements:* For master's and doctorate, GRE General Test, sample of written work. Additional exam requirements/recommendations for international students: Required—TOEFL (minimum score 570 paper-based; 230 computer-based; 88 iBT). *Application deadline:* For fall admission, 1/15 for domestic and international students. Application fee: $0. Electronic applications accepted. *Financial support:* Fellowships with full and partial tuition reimbursements, teaching assistantships with full and partial tuition reimbursements, career-related internships or fieldwork, Federal Work-Study, institutionally sponsored loans, scholarships/grants, and health care benefits available. Financial award application deadline: 1/15; financial award applicants required to submit CSS PROFILE or FAFSA. *Faculty research:* 1750 to present, Middle Ages, Baroque, language pedagogy, linguistics. *Unit head:* Barbara Hahn, Acting Chair, 615-322-2611, Fax: 615-343-7258, E-mail: barbara.hahn@vanderbilt.edu. *Application contact:* Meike Werner, Director of Graduate Studies, 615-322-2611, Fax: 615-343-7258, E-mail: meike.werner@vanderbilt.edu.

Washington University in St. Louis, Graduate School of Arts and Sciences, Department of Germanic Languages and Literature, St. Louis, MO 63130-4899. Offers MA, PhD. Terminal master's awarded for partial completion of doctoral program. *Degree requirements:* For master's, thesis optional; for doctorate, thesis/dissertation. *Entrance requirements:* For master's and doctorate, GRE General Test, sample of written work. Electronic applications accepted.

Wayne State University, College of Liberal Arts and Sciences, Department of Classical and Modern Languages, Literatures, and Cultures, Program in German and Slavic Studies, Detroit, MI 48202. Offers German (MA); language learning (MA); modern languages (PhD); Russian (MA). *Faculty:* 27 full-time (13 women). *Students:* 2 full-time (1 woman), 2 part-time (both women). Average age 29. 4 applicants, 50% accepted, 1 enrolled. In 2010, 1 master's awarded. *Degree requirements:* For master's, one foreign language, thesis or alternative; for doctorate, 2 foreign languages, thesis/dissertation. *Entrance requirements:* For master's and doctorate, minimum GPA of 3.0. Additional exam requirements/recommendations for international students: Required—TOEFL (minimum score 550 paper-based; 213 computer-based); Recommended—TWE (minimum score 6). *Application deadline:* For fall admission, 7/1 for domestic students, 6/1 for international students; for winter admission, 10/1 for international students; for spring admission, 2/1 for international students. Applications are processed on a rolling basis. Application fee: $30 ($50 for international students). Electronic applications accepted. *Expenses:* Tuition, state resident: full-time $7662; part-time $478.85 per credit hour. Tuition, nonresident: full-time $16,920; part-time $1057.55 per credit hour. Required fees: $571.20; $35.70 per credit hour. $188.05 per semester. Tuition and fees vary according to course load and program. *Financial support:* In 2010–11, 1 teaching assistantship with tuition reimbursement (averaging $14,620 per year) was awarded; fellowships, research assistantships, scholarships/grants and tuition waivers (full and partial) also available. Support available to part-time students. *Faculty research:* Exile and Holocaust, minority literature, gender studies, fairytale studies, sociolinguistics. *Application contact:* Janet Hankin, Professor, 313-577-0841, E-mail: janet.hankin@wayne.edu.

Wayne State University, College of Liberal Arts and Sciences, Department of Classical and Modern Languages, Literatures, and Cultures, Program in Modern Languages, Detroit, MI 48202. Offers French (PhD); German (PhD); Spanish (PhD). *Faculty:* 27 full-time (13 women). *Students:* 15 full-time (14 women), 7 part-time (5 women); includes 7 minority (all Hispanic/Latino), 3 international. Average age 41. 3 applicants, 67% accepted, 2 enrolled. In 2010, 1

German

Wayne State University (continued)
doctorate awarded. *Expenses:* Tuition, state resident: full-time $7662; part-time $478.85 per credit hour. Tuition, nonresident: full-time $16,920; part-time $1057.55 per credit hour. Required fees: $571.20; $35.70 per credit hour. $188.05 per semester. Tuition and fees vary according to course load and program. *Financial support:* In 2010–11, 2 fellowships (averaging $14,113 per year), 7 teaching assistantships (averaging $14,620 per year) were awarded. *Unit head:* Dr. Michael Giordano, Graduate Director, 313-577-3051, Fax: 313-577-6243, E-mail: m.j.giordano@wayne.edu. *Application contact:* Janet Hankin, Professor, 313-577-0841, E-mail: janet.hankin@wayne.edu.

Wayne State University, College of Liberal Arts and Sciences, Program in Language Learning, Detroit, MI 48202. Offers Arabic (MA); French (MA); German (MA); Italian (MA); Latin (MA); Spanish (MA). *Faculty:* 1 full-time (0 women), 1 (woman) part-time/adjunct. *Students:* 1 (woman) full-time, 12 part-time (11 women), 1 international. Average age 32. 4 applicants, 100% accepted, 3 enrolled. In 2010, 2 master's awarded. *Expenses:* Tuition, state resident: full-time $7662; part-time $478.85 per credit hour. Tuition, nonresident: full-time $16,920; part-time $1057.55 per credit hour. Required fees: $571.20; $35.70 per credit hour. $188.05 per semester. Tuition and fees vary according to course load and program. *Financial support:* In 2010–11, 1 teaching assistantship (averaging $14,620 per year) was awarded. *Unit head:* Robert Thomas, Dean, 313-577-2519, Fax: 313-577-8971, E-mail: aa0817@wayne.edu. *Application contact:* Janet Hankin, Professor, 313-577-0841, E-mail: janet.hankin@wayne.edu.

Western Kentucky University, Graduate Studies, Potter College of Arts and Letters, Department of Modern Languages, Bowling Green, KY 42101. Offers French (MA Ed); German (MA Ed); Spanish (MA Ed).

Yale University, Graduate School of Arts and Sciences, Department of German, New Haven, CT 06520. Offers PhD. Terminal master's awarded for partial completion of doctoral program. *Degree requirements:* For doctorate, 3 foreign languages, thesis/dissertation. *Entrance requirements:* For doctorate, GRE General Test.

Hispanic and Latin American Languages

Boston University, Graduate School of Arts and Sciences, Department of Romance Studies, Boston, MA 02215. Offers French language and literature (MA, PhD); Hispanic language and literatures (MA, PhD). *Students:* 43 full-time (37 women), 4 part-time (all women); includes 7 minority (6 Hispanic/Latino; 1 Two or more races, non-Hispanic/Latino), 13 international. Average age 31. 50 applicants, 58% accepted, 12 enrolled. In 2010, 8 master's, 3 doctorates awarded. Terminal master's awarded for partial completion of doctoral program. *Degree requirements:* For master's, one foreign language, comprehensive exam; for doctorate, 2 foreign languages, comprehensive exam, thesis/dissertation. *Entrance requirements:* For master's and doctorate, GRE General Test, sample of written work, 3 letters of recommendation. Additional exam requirements/recommendations for international students: Required—TOEFL (minimum score 550 paper-based; 213 computer-based). *Application deadline:* For fall admission, 4/15 for domestic and international students. Application fee: $70. Electronic applications accepted. *Expenses:* Tuition: Full-time $39,314; part-time $1228 per credit. Required fees: $40 per semester. *Financial support:* In 2010–11, 47 students received support, including 2 fellowships with full tuition reimbursements available (averaging $19,300 per year), 35 teaching assistantships with full tuition reimbursements available (averaging $18,800 per year); research assistantships, Federal Work-Study and scholarships/grants also available. Support available to part-time students. Financial award application deadline: 1/15; financial award applicants required to submit FAFSA. *Unit head:* James Iffland, Chairman, 617-353-6225, Fax: 617-353-6246, E-mail: Iffland@bu.edu. *Application contact:* Deanna Wong, Administrative Assistant, 617-353-2641, Fax: 617-353-6246, E-mail: dswong@bu.edu.

Brigham Young University, Graduate Studies, College of Humanities, Department of Spanish and Portuguese, Provo, UT 84602. Offers Hispanic literature (MA); Portuguese linguistics (MA); Portuguese literature (MA); Spanish linguistics (MA); Spanish teaching (MA). Part-time programs available. *Faculty:* 32 full-time (5 women). *Students:* 15 full-time (6 women), 25 part-time (12 women); includes 9 Hispanic/Latino; 1 Native Hawaiian or other Pacific Islander, non-Hispanic/Latino. Average age 30. 23 applicants, 65% accepted, 12 enrolled. In 2010, 11 master's awarded. *Degree requirements:* For master's, one foreign language, comprehensive exam, thesis, 1 semester of teaching. *Entrance requirements:* For master's, minimum GPA of 3.5 in Spanish or Portuguese, 3.3 overall. Additional exam requirements/recommendations for international students: Required—TOEFL (minimum score 580 paper-based; 237 computer-based). *Application deadline:* For fall admission, 2/1 for domestic and international students. Application fee: $50. Electronic applications accepted. *Expenses:* Tuition: Full-time $5580; part-time $310 per credit hour. Tuition and fees vary according to program and student's religious affiliation. *Financial support:* In 2010–11, 39 students received support, including 46 teaching assistantships with partial tuition reimbursements available (averaging $10,470 per year); institutionally sponsored loans, scholarships/grants, tuition waivers (partial), and unspecified assistantships also available. Support available to part-time students. Financial award application deadline: 7/1. *Faculty research:* Mexican prose; Latin American theater, literature, phonetics, and phonology; pedagogy; classical Portuguese literature; Peninsular prose and theater. *Unit head:* Dr. Alvin F. Sherman, Chair, 801-422-3107, Fax: 801-422-0628, E-mail: alvin_sherman@byu.edu. *Application contact:* Jasmine S. Talbot, Graduate Secretary, 801-422-2196, Fax: 801-422-0628, E-mail: jasmine_talbot@byu.edu.

Central Connecticut State University, School of Graduate Studies, School of Arts and Sciences, Department of Modern Languages, Program in Modern Language, New Britain, CT 06050-4010. Offers French (MA, Certificate); German (Certificate); Italian (Certificate); modern language (MA); Spanish language and Hispanic culture (MA). Part-time and evening/weekend programs available. *Students:* 8 full-time (6 women), 32 part-time (28 women); includes 15 minority (all Hispanic/Latino), 1 international. Average age 38. 22 applicants, 95% accepted, 10 enrolled. In 2010, 17 master's awarded. *Degree requirements:* For master's, one foreign language, comprehensive exam, thesis or alternative; for Certificate, qualifying exam. *Entrance requirements:* For master's, minimum undergraduate GPA of 2.7, 24 credits of undergraduate courses in either Italian or Spanish. Additional exam requirements/recommendations for international students: Required—TOEFL. *Application deadline:* For fall admission, 7/1 for domestic students; for spring admission, 12/1 for domestic students. Applications are processed on a rolling basis. Application fee: $50. Electronic applications accepted. *Expenses:* Tuition, area resident: Full-time $5012; part-time $470 per credit. Tuition, state resident: full-time $7518; part-time $482 per credit. Tuition, nonresident: full-time $13,962; part-time $482 per credit. Required fees: $3772. One-time fee: $62 part-time. *Faculty research:* Twentieth century French theater, seventeenth century French literature, French Middle Ages.

Cornell University, Graduate School, Graduate Fields of Arts and Sciences, Field of Romance Studies, Ithaca, NY 14853-0001. Offers French linguistics (PhD); French literature (PhD); Hispanic literature (PhD); Italian linguistics (PhD); Italian literature (PhD); Romance linguistics (PhD); Spanish linguistics (PhD). *Faculty:* 30 full-time (13 women). *Students:* 56 full-time (27 women); includes 11 Hispanic/Latino, 23 international. Average age 28. 95 applicants, 22% accepted, 10 enrolled. In 2010, 5 doctorates awarded. *Degree requirements:* For doctorate, 2 foreign languages, comprehensive exam, thesis/dissertation. *Entrance requirements:* For doctorate, GRE General Test, sample of written work, 3 letters of recommendation. Additional exam requirements/recommendations for international students: Required—TOEFL (minimum score 550 paper-based; 213 computer-based; 77 iBT). *Application deadline:* For fall admission, 1/15 for domestic students. Application fee: $80. Electronic applications accepted. *Expenses:* Tuition: Full-time $29,500. Required fees: $76. Tuition and fees vary according to degree level and program. *Financial support:* In 2010–11, 18 fellowships with full tuition reimbursements, 34 teaching assistantships with full tuition reimbursements were awarded; research assistantships with full tuition reimbursements, institutionally sponsored loans, scholarships/grants, health care benefits, tuition waivers (full and partial), and unspecified assistantships also available. Financial award applicants required to submit FAFSA. *Faculty research:* Literary theory, Hispanic studies, French studies, gender studies. *Unit head:* Director of Graduate Studies, 607-255-8222. *Application contact:* Graduate Field Assistant, 607-255-4246, E-mail: romance_studies@cornell.edu.

Eastern Michigan University, Graduate School, College of Arts and Sciences, Department of World Languages, Programs in Foreign Languages, Ypsilanti, MI 48197. Offers French (MA); German (MA); German for business (Graduate Certificate); Hispanic language and cultures (Graduate Certificate); Japanese business practices (Graduate Certificate); Spanish (MA). Part-time and evening/weekend programs available. Postbaccalaureate distance learning degree programs offered (minimal on-campus study). *Students:* 1 (woman) full-time, 12 part-time (11 women); includes 5 minority (1 Black or African American, non-Hispanic/Latino; 1 Asian, non-Hispanic/Latino; 3 Hispanic/Latino), 1 international. Average age 44. In 2010, 8 master's awarded. *Degree requirements:* For master's, one foreign language, thesis optional. *Entrance requirements:* Additional exam requirements/recommendations for international students: Required—TOEFL. *Application deadline:* Applications are processed on a rolling basis. Application fee: $35. *Financial support:* Fellowships, research assistantships with full tuition reimbursements, teaching assistantships with full tuition reimbursements, career-related internships or fieldwork, Federal Work-Study, institutionally sponsored loans, scholarships/grants, tuition waivers (partial), and unspecified assistantships available. Support available to part-time students. Financial award applicants required to submit FAFSA. *Application contact:* Dr. Genevieve Peden, Program Advisor, 734-487-1498, Fax: 734-487-3411, E-mail: gpeden@emich.edu.

Graduate School and University Center of the City University of New York, Graduate Studies, Program in Hispanic and Luso-Brazilian Literatures and Languages, New York, NY 10016-4039. Offers PhD. *Degree requirements:* For doctorate, 2 foreign languages, thesis/dissertation. *Entrance requirements:* For doctorate, GRE General Test. Additional exam requirements/recommendations for international students: Required—TOEFL. Electronic applications accepted.

Indiana University Bloomington, University Graduate School, College of Arts and Sciences, Department of Spanish and Portuguese, Bloomington, IN 47405-7000. Offers Portuguese (MA, PhD); Spanish (MA, PhD), including Hispanic linguistics, literatures in Spanish. *Faculty:* 23 full-time (13 women). *Students:* 87 full-time (48 women); includes 24 minority (1 Black or African American, non-Hispanic/Latino; 1 Asian, non-Hispanic/Latino; 19 Hispanic/Latino; 2 Native Hawaiian or other Pacific Islander, non-Hispanic/Latino; 1 Two or more races, non-Hispanic/Latino), 8 international. Average age 31. 75 applicants, 45% accepted, 18 enrolled. In 2010, 8 master's, 5 doctorates awarded. *Degree requirements:* For master's, one foreign language, comprehensive exam, thesis (optional for Portuguese); for doctorate, 2 foreign languages, comprehensive exam, thesis/dissertation. *Entrance requirements:* For master's, GRE General Test, bachelor's degree in Portuguese or Spanish, minimum GPA of 3.25; for doctorate, GRE General Test, master's degree in Portuguese or Spanish, minimum GPA of 3.25. Additional exam requirements/recommendations for international students: Required—TOEFL (minimum score 213 computer-based; 79 iBT). *Application deadline:* For fall admission, 1/15 priority date for domestic students, 12/15 priority date for international students. Application fee: $55 ($65 for international students). *Financial support:* In 2010–11, 2 fellowships with full tuition reimbursements (averaging $14,790 per year), 50 teaching assistantships with full tuition reimbursements (averaging $14,790 per year) were awarded; research assistantships, scholarships/grants, health care benefits, and unspecified assistantships also available. Financial award application deadline: 1/15. *Faculty research:* Spanish-American literature, Spanish peninsular literature, Hispanic linguistics, Luso-Brazilian studies, Catalan studies. *Unit head:* Catherine Larson, Chair, 812-855-8498, E-mail: larson@indiana.edu. *Application contact:* Patrick Dove, Director of Graduate Studies, 812-855-9194, E-mail: pdove@indiana.edu.

Michigan State University, The Graduate School, College of Arts and Letters, Department of Spanish and Portuguese, East Lansing, MI 48824. Offers applied Spanish linguistics (MA); Hispanic cultural studies (PhD); Hispanic literatures (MA). *Entrance requirements:* Additional exam requirements/recommendations for international students: Required—TOEFL. Electronic applications accepted.

Queens College of the City University of New York, Division of Graduate Studies, Arts and Humanities Division, Department of Hispanic Languages and Literatures, Flushing, NY 11367-1597. Offers Spanish (MA). Part-time and evening/weekend programs available. *Faculty:* 10 full-time (6 women). *Students:* 1 (woman) full-time, 20 part-time (13 women); includes 1 Black or African American, non-Hispanic/Latino; 17 Hispanic/Latino, 2 international. 25 applicants, 36% accepted, 5 enrolled. In 2010, 4 master's awarded. *Degree requirements:* For master's, 2 foreign languages, comprehensive exam, thesis or alternative. *Entrance requirements:* For master's, minimum GPA of 3.0. Additional exam requirements/recommendations for international students: Required—TOEFL. *Application deadline:* For fall admission, 4/1 for domestic students; for spring admission, 11/1 for domestic students. Applications are processed on a rolling basis. Application fee: $125. *Financial support:* Career-related internships or fieldwork, Federal Work-Study, institutionally sponsored loans, and tuition waivers (partial) available. Support available to part-time students. Financial award application deadline: 4/1; financial award applicants required to submit FAFSA. *Unit head:* Dr. Jose Martinez-Torrejon. *Application contact:* Mario Caruso, Director of Graduate Admissions, 718-997-5200, Fax: 718-997-5193, E-mail: graduate_admissions@qc.edu.

Stony Brook University, State University of New York, Graduate School, College of Arts and Sciences, Department of Hispanic Languages and Literature, Stony Brook, NY 11794. Offers MA, PhD. Evening/weekend programs available. *Faculty:* 12 full-time (7 women), 1 (woman) part-time/adjunct. *Students:* 40 full-time (28 women), 12 part-time (9 women); includes 1 Black or African American, non-Hispanic/Latino; 20 Hispanic/Latino, 20 international. Average age 33. 41 applicants, 44% accepted, 8 enrolled. In 2010, 4 master's, 6 doctorates awarded. *Degree requirements:* For master's, one foreign language, thesis or alternative; for doctorate, 2 foreign languages, thesis/dissertation. *Entrance requirements:* For master's, GRE General Test, BA in Spanish; for doctorate, GRE General Test, MA in Spanish. Additional exam requirements/recommendations for international students: Required—TOEFL. *Application deadline:* For fall admission, 1/15 for domestic students. Application fee: $100. *Expenses:* Contact institution. *Financial support:* In 2010–11, 24 teaching assistantships were awarded; fellowships, research assistantships, tuition waivers and unspecified assistantships also available. *Faculty research:* Spanish language and literature. Total annual research expenditures: $4,469. *Unit head:* Dr. Victoriano Roncero-Lopez, Chair, 631-632-9669, E-mail: roncero@oponline.net.

Application contact: Dr. Kathleen Vernon, Director of Graduate Studies, 631-632-9668, Fax: 631-632-9724, E-mail: kvernon@notes.cc.sunysb.edu.

Université de Montréal, Faculty of Arts and Sciences, Department of Literatures and Modern Languages, Montréal, QC H3C 3J7, Canada. Offers German literature (PhD); German studies (MA); Hispanic literature (PhD); Hispanic studies (MA). Terminal master's awarded for partial completion of doctoral program. *Degree requirements:* For master's, 2 foreign languages, thesis; for doctorate, 2 foreign languages, thesis/dissertation, general exam. Electronic applications accepted.

University of California, Berkeley, Graduate Division, College of Letters and Science, Department of Hispanic Languages and Literature, Berkeley, CA 94720-1500. Offers PhD. *Degree requirements:* For doctorate, thesis/dissertation, qualifying exam. *Entrance requirements:* For doctorate, GRE General Test, minimum GPA of 3.0, 3 letters of recommendation. Additional exam requirements/recommendations for international students: Required—TOEFL (minimum score 570 paper-based; 230 computer-based).

University of California, Los Angeles, Graduate Division, College of Letters and Science, Department of Spanish and Portuguese, Program in Hispanic Languages and Literature, Los Angeles, CA 90095. Offers PhD. *Students:* 44 full-time (30 women); includes 21 minority (2 Black or African American, non-Hispanic/Latino; 1 Asian, non-Hispanic/Latino; 18 Hispanic/Latino), 5 international. Average age 31. 27 applicants, 26% accepted, 5 enrolled. In 2010, 9 doctorates awarded. *Degree requirements:* For doctorate, 2 foreign languages, thesis/dissertation, oral and written exams. *Entrance requirements:* For doctorate, GRE General Test, minimum undergraduate GPA of 3.0, sample of written work (recommended), master's degree. *Application deadline:* For fall admission, 12/31 for domestic and international students. Application fee: $70 ($90 for international students). Electronic applications accepted. *Financial support:* In 2010–11, 39 fellowships with full and partial tuition reimbursements, 5 research assistantships with full and partial tuition reimbursements, 34 teaching assistantships with full and partial tuition reimbursements were awarded; Federal Work-Study, scholarships/grants, health care benefits, tuition waivers (full and partial), and unspecified assistantships also available. Financial award applicants required to submit FAFSA. *Unit head:* Dr. Maarten Van Delden, Chair, 310-825-1220, E-mail: mvandelden@humnet.ucla.edu. *Application contact:* Department Office, 310-825-1036, E-mail: peinado@humnet.ucla.edu.

University of California, Santa Barbara, Graduate Division, College of Letters and Sciences, Division of Humanities and Fine Arts, Department of Spanish and Portuguese, Santa Barbara, CA 93106-4150. Offers Hispanic languages and literature (PhD), including European medieval studies, feminist studies, Hispanic linguistics, Hispanic literature, Luso-Brazilian literature; Hispanic linguistics (MA); Luso-Brazilian literature (MA); Spanish or Spanish-American literature (MA); MA/PhD. Spanish Language Institute available during summer session. *Faculty:* 16 full-time (7 women). *Students:* 32 full-time (22 women); includes 1 Black or African American, non-Hispanic/Latino; 1 Asian, non-Hispanic/Latino; 9 Hispanic/Latino. Average age 32. 34 applicants, 26% accepted, 5 enrolled. In 2010, 3 master's, 3 doctorates awarded. Terminal master's awarded for partial completion of doctoral program. *Degree requirements:* For master's, 2 foreign languages, comprehensive exam (for some programs), thesis optional; for doctorate, 3 foreign languages, comprehensive exam, thesis/dissertation. *Entrance requirements:* For master's and doctorate, GRE. Additional exam requirements/recommendations for international students: Required—TOEFL (minimum score 550 paper-based; 80 iBT), IELTS (minimum score 7). *Application deadline:* For fall admission, 12/15 for domestic and international students. Application fee: $70 ($90 for international students). Electronic applications accepted. *Financial support:* In 2010–11, 32 students received support, including 12 fellowships with full and partial tuition reimbursements available (averaging $10,016 per year), 27 teaching assistantships with full and partial tuition reimbursements available (averaging $14,583 per year); career-related internships or fieldwork, Federal Work-Study, tuition waivers (full and partial), and unspecified assistantships also available. Financial award application deadline: 12/15; financial award applicants required to submit FAFSA. *Faculty research:* Nineteenth century Spanish and Portuguese literature, Spanish and Spanish American literature, nineteenth and twentieth century Portuguese and Brazilian literatures, Hispanic linguistics, Catalan language and culture. *Unit head:* Prof. Francisco A. Lomeli, Chair, 805-893-5715, Fax: 805-893-8341, E-mail: lomeli@spanport.ucsb.edu. *Application contact:* Ashley Bradbury, Graduate Program Assistant, 805-893-2131, Fax: 805-893-8341, E-mail: ashley@hfa.ucsb.edu.

University of Colorado Boulder, Graduate School, College of Arts and Sciences, Department of Spanish and Portuguese, Boulder, CO 80309. Offers Hispanic linguistics (MA); medieval/early modern Hispanic literatures (PhD); Spanish and Spanish American literatures (MA, PhD). Part-time programs available. *Faculty:* 15 full-time (6 women). *Students:* 48 full-time (30 women), 1 (woman) part-time; includes 9 minority (all Hispanic/Latino), 18 international. Average age 32. 52 applicants, 15 enrolled. In 2010, 10 master's, 2 doctorates awarded. Terminal master's awarded for partial completion of doctoral program. *Degree requirements:* For master's, one foreign language, comprehensive exam, thesis or alternative; for doctorate, 2 foreign languages, thesis/dissertation. *Entrance requirements:* For master's, minimum undergraduate GPA of 2.75. *Application deadline:* For fall admission, 12/15 priority date for domestic students, 12/15 for international students. Applications are processed on a rolling basis. Application fee: $50 ($60 for international students). *Financial support:* In 2010–11, 7 fellowships with full tuition reimbursements (averaging $3,436 per year), 19 research assistantships (averaging $12,128 per year) were awarded; tuition waivers (full) also available. Financial award application deadline: 12/15. *Faculty research:* Spanish peninsular and Spanish-American literatures; Hispanic linguistics; medieval, Golden Age, eighteenth and nineteenth century literatures.

University of Illinois at Chicago, Graduate College, College of Liberal Arts and Sciences, Department of Spanish, French, Italian and Portuguese, Program in Hispanic Studies, Chicago, IL 60607-7128. Offers Hispanic linguistics (MA, PhD); Hispanic literary and cultural studies (MA, PhD). Part-time programs available. Terminal master's awarded for partial completion of doctoral program. *Degree requirements:* For master's, one foreign language, departmental qualifying exam. *Entrance requirements:* For master's, GRE General Test, minimum GPA of 2.75, undergraduate major in Spanish. Additional exam requirements/recommendations for international students: Required—TOEFL. Electronic applications accepted.

University of Massachusetts Amherst, Graduate School, College of Humanities and Fine Arts, Department of Languages, Literatures, and Cultures, Programs in Hispanic Literatures, Cultures and Linguistics, Amherst, MA 01003. Offers Hispanic literatures, cultures and linguistics (MA, PhD); teaching Spanish (MAT). Part-time programs available. *Faculty:* 13 full-time (6 women). *Students:* 25 full-time (19 women), 29 part-time (16 women); includes 17 minority (1 Asian, non-Hispanic/Latino; 16 Hispanic/Latino), 19 international. Average age 35. 42 applicants, 60% accepted, 14 enrolled. In 2010, 9 master's, 3 doctorates awarded. Terminal master's awarded for partial completion of doctoral program. *Degree requirements:* For master's, one foreign language, thesis or alternative; for doctorate, 2 foreign languages, comprehensive exam, thesis/dissertation. *Entrance requirements:* For master's and doctorate, GRE General Test, sample academic term paper. Additional exam requirements/recommendations for international students: Required—TOEFL (minimum score 550 paper-based; 213 computer-based; 80 iBT), IELTS (minimum score 6.5). *Application deadline:* For fall admission, 2/1 for domestic and international students. Applications are processed on a rolling basis. Application fee: $50 ($65 for international students). Electronic applications accepted. *Expenses:* Tuition, state resident: full-time $2640. Required fees: $8282. One-time fee: $357 full-time. *Financial support:* In 2010–11, 32 teaching assistantships with full tuition reimbursements (averaging $15,272 per year) were awarded; fellowships, research assistantships, career-related internships or fieldwork, Federal Work-Study, scholarships/grants, traineeships, health care benefits, tuition waivers (full), and unspecified assistantships also available. Support available to part-time students. Financial award application deadline: 2/1; financial award applicants required to submit FAFSA. *Unit head:* Dr. Frank C. Fagundes, Graduate Program Director, 413-545-0544, Fax: 413-545-3178. *Application contact:* Jean M. Ames, Supervisor of Admissions, 413-545-0722, Fax: 413-577-0010, E-mail: gradadm@grad.umass.edu.

University of Minnesota, Twin Cities Campus, Graduate School, College of Liberal Arts, Department of Spanish and Portuguese Studies, Minneapolis, MN 55455-0213. Offers Hispanic and Lusophone literatures, cultures and linguistics (PhD); Hispanic linguistics (MA); Hispanic literature (MA); Lusophone literature (MA). *Degree requirements:* For master's, 2 foreign languages, comprehensive exam, thesis or alternative; for doctorate, 2 foreign languages, comprehensive exam, thesis/dissertation. *Entrance requirements:* For master's and doctorate, GRE General Test, samples of written work, 3 letters of recommendation, voice sample, statement of purpose. Additional exam requirements/recommendations for international students: Required—TOEFL (minimum score 550 paper-based; 213 computer-based; 79 iBT). Electronic applications accepted. *Faculty research:* Sociohistorical approaches to literature and culture, feminist studies, literary theory, ideologies and literature, pragmatics and sociolinguistics.

The University of North Carolina at Greensboro, Graduate School, College of Arts and Sciences, Department of Romance Languages, Program in Spanish, Greensboro, NC 27412-5001. Offers advanced Spanish language and Hispanic cultural studies (Certificate); Spanish (MA). *Degree requirements:* For master's, one foreign language, comprehensive exam, thesis or alternative. *Entrance requirements:* For master's, GRE General Test, 3-5 minute tape demonstrating foreign language proficiency, composition in Spanish, sample paper in English. Additional exam requirements/recommendations for international students: Required—TOEFL. Electronic applications accepted.

University of Pittsburgh, School of Arts and Sciences, Department of Hispanic Languages and Literatures, Pittsburgh, PA 15260. Offers MA, PhD. Part-time programs available. *Faculty:* 10 full-time (2 women). *Students:* 39 full-time (23 women), 2 part-time (both women); includes 2 Black or African American, non-Hispanic/Latino; 1 Asian, non-Hispanic/Latino; 7 Hispanic/Latino, 24 international. Average age 32. 82 applicants, 34% accepted, 8 enrolled. In 2010, 6 master's, 9 doctorates awarded. Terminal master's awarded for partial completion of doctoral program. *Degree requirements:* For master's, one foreign language, comprehensive exam (for some programs), thesis or alternative, research paper; for doctorate, 2 foreign languages, comprehensive exam, thesis/dissertation. *Entrance requirements:* Additional exam requirements/recommendations for international students: Required—TOEFL (minimum score 550 paper-based; 80 iBT). *Application deadline:* For fall admission, 1/15 priority date for domestic and international students. Application fee: $50. Electronic applications accepted. *Expenses:* Tuition, state resident: full-time $17,304; part-time $701 per credit. Tuition, nonresident: full-time $29,554; part-time $1210 per credit. Required fees: $740; $214 per term. Tuition and fees vary according to program. *Financial support:* In 2010–11, 33 students received support, including 7 fellowships with full tuition reimbursements available (averaging $18,000 per year), 24 teaching assistantships with full tuition reimbursements available (averaging $15,500 per year); scholarships/grants, health care benefits, and tuition waivers (partial) also available. Financial award application deadline: 1/15. *Faculty research:* Latin American, Luso-Brazilian, and peninsular literature; cultural theory; cultural studies; race, ethnicity, and post-colonial studies; gender and sexuality studies; environment and literature; social conflict and violence. *Unit head:* Dr. Juan Duchesne-Winter, Chair, 412-624-5226, Fax: 412-624-8505, E-mail: duchesne@pitt.edu. *Application contact:* Dr. Daniel Balderston, Director of Graduate Studies, 412-628-0279, Fax: 412-624-8505, E-mail: dbalder@pitt.edu.

The University of Texas at Austin, Graduate School, College of Liberal Arts, Department of Spanish and Portuguese, Austin, TX 78712-1111. Offers Hispanic linguistics (MA, PhD); Hispanic literature (MA, PhD); Luso-Brazilian literature (MA, PhD). *Degree requirements:* For master's, 2 foreign languages, thesis or alternative; for doctorate, 3 foreign languages, thesis/dissertation. *Entrance requirements:* For master's and doctorate, GRE General Test. Electronic applications accepted.

University of Washington, Graduate School, College of Arts and Sciences, Department of Romance Languages and Literature, Division of Spanish and Portuguese Studies, Seattle, WA 98195. Offers Hispanic literary and cultural studies (MA). *Degree requirements:* For master's, 2 foreign languages, thesis optional, exam. *Entrance requirements:* For master's, GRE General Test, minimum GPA of 3.0. Additional exam requirements/recommendations for international students: Required—TOEFL. Electronic applications accepted. *Faculty research:* Medieval through modern Spanish literature and film, Latin American literature, poetry and essay, pan-Hispanic ballad, Hispanic cultural studies, second language acquisition and applied linguistics.

Italian

Boston College, Graduate School of Arts and Sciences, Department of Romance Languages and Literatures, Chestnut Hill, MA 02467-3800. Offers French (MA, PhD); Italian (MA); medieval language (PhD); Spanish (MA, PhD). Part-time programs available. Terminal master's awarded for partial completion of doctoral program. *Degree requirements:* For master's, one foreign language; for doctorate, 2 foreign languages, thesis/dissertation. *Entrance requirements:* Additional exam requirements/recommendations for international students: Required—TOEFL (minimum score 600 paper-based; 250 computer-based; 100 iBT). Electronic applications accepted. *Faculty research:* Spanish-American literature, philology, medieval French romance and troubadour/trouvere lyrics, Golden Age Peninsular literature, secondary language acquisition and pedagogy.

Brown University, Graduate School, Department of Italian Studies, Providence, RI 02912. Offers PhD, MA/PhD. Terminal master's awarded for partial completion of doctoral program. *Degree requirements:* For doctorate, 2 foreign languages, thesis/dissertation, preliminary exam.

Central Connecticut State University, School of Graduate Studies, School of Arts and Sciences, Department of Modern Languages, Program in Modern Language, New Britain, CT 06050-4010. Offers French (MA, Certificate); German (Certificate); Italian (Certificate); modern language (MA); Spanish language and Hispanic culture (MA). Part-time and evening/weekend programs available. *Students:* 8 full-time (6 women), 32 part-time (28 women); includes 15 minority (all Hispanic/Latino), 1 international. Average age 38. 22 applicants, 95% accepted, 10 enrolled. In 2010, 17 master's awarded. *Degree requirements:* For master's, one foreign language, comprehensive exam, thesis or alternative; for Certificate, qualifying exam. *Entrance requirements:* For master's, minimum undergraduate GPA of 2.7, 24 credits of undergraduate courses in either Italian or Spanish. Additional exam requirements/recommendations for international students: Required—TOEFL. *Application deadline:* For fall admission, 7/1 for domestic students; for spring admission, 12/1 for domestic students. Applications are processed on a rolling basis. Application fee: $50. Electronic applications accepted. *Expenses:* Tuition, area resident: Full-time $5012; part-time $470 per credit. Tuition, state resident: full-time $7518;

Italian

Central Connecticut State University (continued)
part-time $482 per credit. Tuition, nonresident: full-time $13,962; part-time $482 per credit. Required fees: $3772. One-time fee: $62 part-time. *Faculty research:* Twentieth century French theater, seventeenth century French literature, French Middle Ages.

Columbia University, Graduate School of Arts and Sciences, Division of Humanities, Department of Italian, New York, NY 10027. Offers M Phil, MA, PhD. Part-time programs available. *Degree requirements:* For master's, one foreign language, oral and written exams; for doctorate, 2 foreign languages, thesis/dissertation. *Entrance requirements:* For master's and doctorate, GRE General Test, writing sample. Additional exam requirements/recommendations for international students: Required—TOEFL. *Faculty research:* Medieval and Renaissance Italian literature; Italian poetry, prose, and theater; modern and contemporary Italian literature.

Cornell University, Graduate School, Graduate Fields of Arts and Sciences, Field of Romance Studies, Ithaca, NY 14853-0001. Offers French linguistics (PhD); French literature (PhD); Hispanic literature (PhD); Italian linguistics (PhD); Italian literature (PhD); Romance linguistics (PhD); Spanish linguistics (PhD). *Faculty:* 30 full-time (13 women). *Students:* 56 full-time (27 women); includes 11 Hispanic/Latino, 23 international. Average age 28. 95 applicants, 22% accepted, 10 enrolled. In 2010, 5 doctorates awarded. *Degree requirements:* For doctorate, 2 foreign languages, comprehensive exam, thesis/dissertation. *Entrance requirements:* For doctorate, GRE General Test, sample of written work, 3 letters of recommendation. Additional exam requirements/recommendations for international students: Required—TOEFL (minimum score 550 paper-based; 213 computer-based; 77 iBT). *Application deadline:* For fall admission, 1/15 for domestic students. Application fee: $80. Electronic applications accepted. *Expenses:* Tuition: Full-time $29,500. Required fees: $76. Tuition and fees vary according to degree level and program. *Financial support:* In 2010–11, 18 fellowships with full tuition reimbursements, 34 teaching assistantships with full tuition reimbursements were awarded; research assistantships with full tuition reimbursements, institutionally sponsored loans, scholarships/grants, health care benefits, tuition waivers (full and partial), and unspecified assistantships also available. Financial award applicants required to submit FAFSA. *Faculty research:* Literary theory, Hispanic studies, French studies, gender studies. *Unit head:* Director of Graduate Studies, 607-255-8222. *Application contact:* Graduate Field Assistant, 607-255-4246, E-mail: romance_studies@cornell.edu.

Drew University, Caspersen School of Graduate Studies, Program in Education, Madison, NJ 07940-1493. Offers biology (MAT); chemistry (MAT); English (MAT); French (MAT); Italian (MAT); math (MAT); physics (MAT); social studies (MAT); Spanish (MAT); theatre arts (MAT). Part-time programs available. *Entrance requirements:* For master's, transcripts, personal statement, recommendations. Additional exam requirements/recommendations for international students: Required—TOEFL, TWE. *Expenses:* Contact institution.

Florida State University, The Graduate School, College of Arts and Sciences, Department of Modern Languages, Program in Italian Studies, Tallahassee, FL 32306. Offers MA. *Faculty:* 6 full-time (2 women), 1 part-time/adjunct (0 women). *Students:* 10 full-time (7 women); includes 1 Hispanic/Latino. Average age 24. 8 applicants, 75% accepted, 5 enrolled. In 2010, 4 master's awarded. *Entrance requirements:* For master's, GRE General Test, minimum GPA of 3.0. Additional exam requirements/recommendations for international students: Required—TOEFL (minimum score 550 paper-based; 213 computer-based). *Application deadline:* For fall admission, 2/15 for domestic and international students. Applications are processed on a rolling basis. Application fee: $30. Electronic applications accepted. *Expenses:* Tuition, state resident: full-time $8238.24. *Financial support:* In 2010–11, 10 teaching assistantships with partial tuition reimbursements (averaging $11,100 per year) were awarded. Financial award application deadline: 2/15. *Unit head:* Dr. Mark Pietralunga, Coordinator, 850-644-8392, Fax: 850-644-0524, E-mail: mpietral@fsu.edu. *Application contact:* Wendy E. Pigott, Graduate Academic Coordinator, 850-644-8397, Fax: 850-644-0524, E-mail: wpigott@fsu.edu.

Graduate School and University Center of the City University of New York, Graduate Studies, Program in Comparative Literature, New York, NY 10016-4039. Offers comparative literature (MA, PhD), including classics (PhD), German (PhD), Italian (PhD). PhD offered jointly with New York University. Terminal master's awarded for partial completion of doctoral program. *Degree requirements:* For master's, 2 foreign languages, comprehensive exam, thesis; for doctorate, 3 foreign languages, comprehensive exam, thesis/dissertation. *Entrance requirements:* For master's and doctorate, GRE General Test. Additional exam requirements/recommendations for international students: Required—TOEFL. Electronic applications accepted.

Harvard University, Graduate School of Arts and Sciences, Department of Romance Languages and Literatures, Cambridge, MA 02138. Offers French (AM, PhD); Italian (AM, PhD); Portuguese (AM, PhD); Spanish (AM, PhD). Terminal master's awarded for partial completion of doctoral program. *Degree requirements:* For master's, 2 foreign languages; for doctorate, 2 foreign languages, thesis/dissertation. *Entrance requirements:* For master's and doctorate, GRE General Test, sample of written work. Additional exam requirements/recommendations for international students: Required—TOEFL. *Expenses:* Tuition: Full-time $34,976. Required fees: $1166. Full-time tuition and fees vary according to program.

Hunter College of the City University of New York, Graduate School, School of Arts and Sciences, Department of Romance Languages, Program in Italian, New York, NY 10021-5085. Offers Italian (MA); Italian education (MA). *Faculty:* 8 full-time (4 women). *Students:* 5 part-time (2 women), 1 international. Average age 31. 6 applicants, 33% accepted, 1 enrolled. In 2010, 5 master's awarded. *Degree requirements:* For master's, 2 foreign languages, comprehensive exam, thesis optional. *Entrance requirements:* For master's, GRE General Test, GRE Subject Test, ability to read, speak, and write Italian; interview. Additional exam requirements/recommendations for international students: Required—TOEFL. *Application deadline:* For fall admission, 4/1 for domestic students, 2/1 for international students; for spring admission, 11/1 for domestic students, 9/1 for international students. Application fee: $125. *Financial support:* Federal Work-Study, scholarships/grants, and tuition waivers (partial) available. Support available to part-time students. Financial award application deadline: 4/15. *Faculty research:* Dante, Middle Ages, Renaissance, contemporary Italian novel and poetry, late Renaissance and Baroque. *Unit head:* Dr. Paolo Fasoli, Graduate Co-Adviser, 212-772-5129, Fax: 212-772-5094, E-mail: pfasoli@hunter.cuny.edu. *Application contact:* William Zlata, Director for Graduate Admissions, 212-772-4482, Fax: 212-650-3336, E-mail: admissions@hunter.cuny.edu.

Indiana University Bloomington, University Graduate School, College of Arts and Sciences, Department of French and Italian, Bloomington, IN 47405-7000. Offers French (MA, PhD), including French instruction (MA), French linguistics, French literature; Italian (MA, PhD). Part-time programs available. *Faculty:* 19 full-time (7 women). *Students:* 69 full-time (43 women), 5 part-time (2 women); includes 2 minority (1 American Indian or Alaska Native, non-Hispanic/Latino; 1 Hispanic/Latino), 23 international. Average age 30. 73 applicants, 67% accepted, 14 enrolled. In 2010, 14 master's, 6 doctorates awarded. Terminal master's awarded for partial completion of doctoral program. *Degree requirements:* For master's, one foreign language, comprehensive exam, thesis optional; for doctorate, 2 foreign languages, comprehensive exam, thesis/dissertation. *Entrance requirements:* For master's and doctorate, GRE General Test. Additional exam requirements/recommendations for international students: Required—TOEFL (minimum score 550 paper-based; 213 computer-based; 79 iBT). *Application deadline:* For fall admission, 1/15 priority date for domestic students, 12/1 priority date for international students; for spring admission, 9/1 priority date for domestic and international students. Application fee: $55 ($65 for international students). Electronic applications accepted. *Financial support:* In 2010–11, 2 fellowships with partial tuition reimbursements (averaging $14,000 per year), 4 research assistantships with partial tuition reimbursements (averaging $13,913 per year), 20 teaching assistantships with partial tuition reimbursements (averaging $12,944 per year) were awarded. Financial award application deadline: 1/15. *Faculty research:* All periods of French and Italian literature and various areas of French linguistics, including the novel and political theory, literature and fine arts, literary theory, postcolonialism, French-Creole studies, French literature of Africa and its Diaspora, humanism, medieval folklore and mythology, humor in medieval and Renaissance literature, cinema Old Occitan and Old French, emigration, second language acquisition, syntax, sociolinguistics, phonology, lexicography. *Unit head:* Prof. Emanuel Mickel, Interim Chairman, 812-855-5458, Fax: 812-855-8877, E-mail: fritchr@indiana.edu. *Application contact:* Jocelyn Karlan, Secretary, 812-855-1088, Fax: 812-855-8877, E-mail: fritgs@indiana.edu.

Iona College, School of Arts and Science, Program in Foreign Languages, New Rochelle, NY 10801-1890. Offers Italian (MA); Spanish (MA). Part-time and evening/weekend programs available. *Faculty:* 4 full-time (1 woman), 1 (woman) part-time/adjunct. *Students:* 8 part-time (all women); includes 2 minority (both Hispanic/Latino). Average age 32. 5 applicants, 80% accepted, 3 enrolled. In 2010, 4 master's awarded. *Degree requirements:* For master's, thesis or alternative. *Entrance requirements:* For master's, minimum GPA of 3.0. Additional exam requirements/recommendations for international students: Required—TOEFL (minimum score 550 paper-based; 213 computer-based). *Application deadline:* Applications are processed on a rolling basis. Application fee: $50. Electronic applications accepted. *Expenses:* Tuition: Part-time $830 per credit. Required fees: $225 per credit. *Financial support:* Unspecified assistantships available. Support available to part-time students. Financial award application deadline: 4/15; financial award applicants required to submit FAFSA. *Faculty research:* Contemporary Spanish literature, linguistics, language acquisition, female Hispanic literature, Latina authors. *Unit head:* Dr. Victoria E. Ketz, Chair, 914-637-2738, E-mail: vketz@iona.edu. *Application contact:* Veronica Jarek-Prinz, Director of Graduate Admissions, 914-633-2420, Fax: 914-633-2277, E-mail: vjarekprinz@iona.edu.

The Johns Hopkins University, Zanvyl Krieger School of Arts and Sciences, Department of German and Romance Languages and Literatures, Baltimore, MD 21218-2699. Offers French (PhD); German (PhD); Italian (PhD); romance languages (PhD); Spanish (PhD). *Faculty:* 31 full-time (20 women), 1 part-time/adjunct (0 women). *Students:* 52 full-time (31 women); includes 7 minority (6 Hispanic/Latino; 1 Two or more races, non-Hispanic/Latino), 20 international. Average age 30. 51 applicants, 37% accepted, 19 enrolled. In 2010, 6 doctorates awarded. *Degree requirements:* For doctorate, 2 foreign languages, thesis/dissertation. *Entrance requirements:* For doctorate, GRE General Test. Additional exam requirements/recommendations for international students: Required—TOEFL (minimum score 600 paper-based; 250 computer-based; 100 iBT), IELTS. *Application deadline:* For fall admission, 12/30 for domestic and international students. Application fee: $75. Electronic applications accepted. *Financial support:* In 2010–11, 40 fellowships with full tuition reimbursements (averaging $17,000 per year), 2 research assistantships with full tuition reimbursements (averaging $17,000 per year), 19 teaching assistantships with full tuition reimbursements (averaging $17,000 per year) were awarded; institutionally sponsored loans also available. *Faculty research:* Nineteenth century French prose and poetry, genetic theory and criticism; twentieth century Latin American literature and film; medieval and Renaissance Italian literature; gender and queer theory in German literature; the ideology of Baroque and Neobaroque aesthetics. *Unit head:* Dr. William Egginton, Chair, 410-516-7510, Fax: 410-516-5358, E-mail: egginton@jhu.edu. *Application contact:* Rebecca Swisdak, Graduate Administrative Coordinator, 410-516-7227, Fax: 410-516-5358, E-mail: rswisdak@jhu.edu.

McGill University, Faculty of Graduate and Postdoctoral Studies, Faculty of Arts, Department of Italian Studies, Montréal, QC H3A 2T5, Canada. Offers MA, PhD.

Middlebury College, Language Schools, Italian School, Middlebury, VT 05753-6002. Offers MA, DML. *Faculty:* 14 full-time (4 women). *Students:* 62 full-time (44 women); includes 5 minority (all Hispanic/Latino). Average age 29. 106 applicants, 89% accepted, 62 enrolled. In 2010, 29 master's, 2 doctorates awarded. *Degree requirements:* For master's, one foreign language; for doctorate, 2 foreign languages, comprehensive exam, thesis/dissertation, residence abroad, teaching experience. *Entrance requirements:* For master's, placement exam, 3 letters of recommendation, writing sample; for doctorate, 1st and 2nd language placement exams, 3 letters of recommendation, writing sample. *Application deadline:* Applications are processed on a rolling basis. Application fee: $65. Electronic applications accepted. *Financial support:* Scholarships/grants available. Financial award applicants required to submit FAFSA. *Unit head:* Dr. Antonio Vitti, Director, 802-443-5727, Fax: 802-443-2075, E-mail: acvitti@middlebury.edu. *Application contact:* Kara Gennarelli, Coordinator, 802-443-5727, Fax: 802-443-2075, E-mail: kgennar@middlebury.edu.

Montclair State University, The Graduate School, College of Humanities and Social Sciences, Department of Spanish and Italian, Montclair, NJ 07043-1624. Offers Italian (Certificate); Spanish (MA, Certificate); translation and interpretation in Spanish (Certificate). Part-time and evening/weekend programs available. *Faculty:* 21 full-time (13 women), 25 part-time/adjunct (16 women). *Students:* 4 full-time (3 women), 20 part-time (17 women); includes 1 American Indian or Alaska Native, non-Hispanic/Latino; 11 Hispanic/Latino. Average age 33. 10 applicants, 90% accepted, 6 enrolled. In 2010, 7 master's awarded. *Degree requirements:* For master's, comprehensive exam, thesis or alternative. *Entrance requirements:* For master's, GRE General Test, 2 letters of recommendation. Additional exam requirements/recommendations for international students: Required—TOEFL (minimum iBT score of 83) or IELTS. *Application deadline:* For fall admission, 6/1 for international students; for spring admission, 11/1 for international students. Applications are processed on a rolling basis. Application fee: $60. Electronic applications accepted. *Expenses:* Tuition, state resident: part-time $501.34 per credit. Tuition, nonresident: part-time $773.88 per credit. Required fees: $71.15 per credit. *Financial support:* In 2010–11, 1 research assistantship with full tuition reimbursement (averaging $7,000 per year) was awarded; Federal Work-Study, scholarships/grants, and unspecified assistantships also available. Support available to part-time students. Financial award application deadline: 3/1; financial award applicants required to submit FAFSA. *Unit head:* Dr. Linda Gould Levine, Chairperson, 973-655-7506. *Application contact:* Amy Aiello, Director of Graduate Admissions and Operations, 973-655-5147, Fax: 973-655-7869, E-mail: graduate.school@montclair.edu.

New York University, Graduate School of Arts and Science, Department of Italian Studies, New York, NY 10012-1019. Offers Italian (MA, PhD); Italian studies (MA). Part-time programs available. *Faculty:* 6 full-time (3 women). *Students:* 36 full-time (22 women), 2 part-time (both women); includes 2 Hispanic/Latino, 15 international. Average age 29. 50 applicants, 48% accepted, 13 enrolled. In 2010, 12 master's, 3 doctorates awarded. Terminal master's awarded for partial completion of doctoral program. *Degree requirements:* For master's, one foreign language, thesis; for doctorate, 3 foreign languages, thesis/dissertation. *Entrance requirements:* For master's, GRE General Test, sample of written work; for doctorate, GRE General Test. Additional exam requirements/recommendations for international students: Required—TOEFL. *Application deadline:* For fall admission, 1/4 priority date for domestic students. Application fee: $90. *Financial support:* Fellowships with tuition reimbursements, teaching assistantships with tuition reimbursements, Federal Work-Study, institutionally sponsored loans, scholarships/grants, and unspecified assistantships available. Financial award application deadline: 1/4; financial award applicants required to submit FAFSA. *Faculty research:* Dante, early modern literature, fascism and culture, contemporary literature, feminist theory. *Unit head:* Ruth Ben-Ghiat, Chairman, 212-998-8730, Fax: 212-995-4012, E-mail: italian.dept@nyu.edu. *Application contact:* Maria Luisa Ardizzone, Director of Graduate Studies, 212-998-8730, Fax: 212-995-4012, E-mail: italian.dept@nyu.edu.

Northwestern University, The Graduate School, Judd A. and Marjorie Weinberg College of Arts and Sciences, Department of French and Italian, Evanston, IL 60208. Offers eighteenth-century studies (Certificate); French (PhD); French and comparative literature (PhD); Italian studies (Certificate). Admissions and degrees offered through The Graduate School. *Degree requirements:* For doctorate, one foreign language, thesis/dissertation, written and oral exams. *Entrance requirements:* For doctorate, GRE, writing sample, cassette recording. Additional exam requirements/recommendations for international students: Required—TOEFL. *Faculty research:* Francophone studies, 18th century contemporary theory.

The Ohio State University, Graduate School, College of Arts and Sciences, Division of Arts and Humanities, Department of French and Italian, Columbus, OH 43210. Offers French (MA,

PhD); Italian (MA). *Faculty:* 20. *Students:* 24 full-time (15 women), 10 part-time (7 women), 8 international. Average age 33. In 2010, 6 master's, 1 doctorate awarded. *Degree requirements:* For master's, variable foreign language requirement, thesis optional; for doctorate, variable foreign language requirement, thesis/dissertation. *Entrance requirements:* For master's and doctorate, GRE General Test. Additional exam requirements/recommendations for international students: Required—TOEFL. *Application deadline:* For fall admission, 8/15 priority date for domestic students, 7/1 priority date for international students; for winter admission, 12/1 priority date for domestic students, 11/1 priority date for international students; for spring admission, 3/1 priority date for domestic students, 2/1 priority date for international students. Applications are processed on a rolling basis. Application fee $40 ($50 for international students). Electronic applications accepted. *Expenses:* Tuition, state resident: full-time $10,605. Tuition, nonresident: full-time $26,535. Tuition and fees vary according to course load and program. *Financial support:* Fellowships, research assistantships, teaching assistantships, Federal Work-Study, institutionally sponsored loans, and unspecified assistantships available. Support available to part-time students. *Faculty research:* Italian and Romance linguistics. *Unit head:* Diane W. Birckbichler, Graduate Studies Committee Chair, 614-292-4361, E-mail: birckbichler.1@osu.edu. *Application contact:* 614-292-9444, Fax: 614-292-3895, E-mail: domestic.grad@osu.edu.

Queens College of the City University of New York, Division of Graduate Studies, Arts and Humanities Division, Department of European Languages and Literatures, Program in Italian, Flushing, NY 11367-1597. Offers MA. Part-time and evening/weekend programs available. *Faculty:* 8 full-time (4 women). *Students:* 7 part-time (5 women). 5 applicants, 60% accepted, 1 enrolled. In 2010, 1 master's awarded. *Degree requirements:* For master's, 2 foreign languages, comprehensive exam, thesis or alternative. *Entrance requirements:* For master's, minimum GPA of 3.0. Additional exam requirements/recommendations for international students: Required—TOEFL. *Application deadline:* For fall admission, 4/1 for domestic students; for spring admission, 11/1 for domestic students. Applications are processed on a rolling basis. Application fee: $125. *Financial support:* Career-related internships or fieldwork, Federal Work-Study, institutionally sponsored loans, and tuition waivers (partial) available. Support available to part-time students. Financial award application deadline: 4/1; financial award applicants required to submit FAFSA. *Application contact:* Mario Caruso, Director of Graduate Admissions, 718-997-5200, Fax: 718-997-5193, E-mail: graduate_admissions@qc.edu.

Rutgers, The State University of New Jersey, New Brunswick, Graduate School-New Brunswick, Program in Italian, Piscataway, NJ 08854-8097. Offers Italian (MA, PhD); Italian literature and literary criticism (MA); language, literature and culture (MAT). Part-time and evening/weekend programs available. Terminal master's awarded for partial completion of doctoral program. *Degree requirements:* For master's, one foreign language, comprehensive exam (for some programs), thesis optional; for doctorate, 2 foreign languages, thesis/dissertation, qualifying exam. *Entrance requirements:* For master's and doctorate, GRE General Test. Additional exam requirements/recommendations for international students: Required—TOEFL. *Expenses:* Tuition, state resident: full-time $7200; part-time $600 per credit. Tuition, nonresident: full-time $11,124; part-time $927 per credit. *Faculty research:* Literature.

San Francisco State University, Division of Graduate Studies, College of Humanities, Department of Foreign Languages and Literatures, Program in Italian, San Francisco, CA 94132-1722. Offers MA. *Application deadline:* Applications are processed on a rolling basis. *Unit head:* Elisabetta Nelsen, Chair, 415-338-7413, E-mail: enelsen@sfsu.edu. *Application contact:* Christopher Concolino, Graduate Coordinator, 415-338-3161, E-mail: foreign@sfsu.edu.

Stanford University, School of Humanities and Sciences, Department of French and Italian, Stanford, CA 94305-9991. Offers French (MA, PhD); Italian (MA, PhD). Terminal master's awarded for partial completion of doctoral program. *Degree requirements:* For master's, one foreign language, written exam; for doctorate, 2 foreign languages, thesis/dissertation, oral exam. *Entrance requirements:* For master's and doctorate, GRE General Test. Additional exam requirements/recommendations for international students: Required—TOEFL. Electronic applications accepted. *Expenses:* Tuition: Full-time $38,700; part-time $860 per unit. One-time fee: $200 full-time.

State University of New York at Binghamton, Graduate School, School of Arts and Sciences, Department of Romance Languages and Literatures, Program in Italian, Binghamton, NY 13902-6000. Offers MA. *Students:* 1 (woman) full-time, 1 part-time (0 women). Average age 38. 1 applicant, 100% accepted, 0 enrolled. In 2010, 3 master's awarded. *Degree requirements:* For master's, one foreign language, comprehensive exam, thesis or alternative. *Entrance requirements:* For master's, GRE General Test, GRE Subject Test. Additional exam requirements/recommendations for international students: Required—TOEFL (minimum score 550 paper-based; 213 computer-based; 80 iBT). *Application deadline:* For fall admission, 2/15 priority date for domestic and international students; for spring admission, 11/15 priority date for domestic and international students. Applications are processed on a rolling basis. Application fee: $60. Electronic applications accepted. *Financial support:* Fellowships, research assistantships, teaching assistantships, career-related internships or fieldwork, Federal Work-Study, institutionally sponsored loans, scholarships/grants, health care benefits, and unspecified assistantships available. Financial award application deadline: 2/15; financial award applicants required to submit FAFSA. *Unit head:* Dr. Antonio Sobejano-Moran, Chairperson, 607-777-4635, E-mail: antobianco@msn.com. *Application contact:* Catherine Smith, Recruiting and Admissions Coordinator, 607-777-2151, Fax: 607-777-2501, E-mail: cmsmith@binghamton.edu.

Stony Brook University, State University of New York, Graduate School, College of Arts and Sciences, Department of European Languages, Literatures, and Cultures, Program in Italian, Stony Brook, NY 11794. Offers MA. Evening/weekend programs available. *Students:* 5 full-time (3 women), 10 part-time (7 women). In 2010, 4 master's awarded. *Degree requirements:* For master's, one foreign language. *Entrance requirements:* For master's, GRE General Test. Additional exam requirements/recommendations for international students: Required—TOEFL. *Application deadline:* For fall admission, 1/15 for domestic students. Application fee: $100. *Expenses:* Tuition, state resident: full-time $8370; part-time $349 per credit. Tuition, nonresident: full-time $13,780; part-time $574 per credit. Required fees: $994. *Unit head:* Charles Franco, Coordinator, 631-632-1494, E-mail: charles.franco@stonybrook.edu. *Application contact:* Director of Graduate Studies, 631-632-7438, Fax: 631-632-9612.

University at Albany, State University of New York, College of Arts and Sciences, Department of Languages, Literatures, and Cultures, Program in Italian, Albany, NY 12222-0001. Offers MA.

University of Alberta, Faculty of Graduate Studies and Research, Department of Modern Languages and Cultural Studies, Edmonton, AB T6G 2E1, Canada. Offers applied linguistics (Germanic, Romance, Slavic) (MA); French language, literatures and linguistics (PhD); French language, literatures, and linguistics (MA); Germanic languages, literatures and linguistics (PhD); Germanic languages, literatures, and linguistics (MA); Italian studies (MA); Slavic languages and literatures (Russian, Ukrainian) (MA, PhD); Slavic linguistics (Russian, Ukrainian) (MA, PhD); Spanish and Latin American studies (MA, PhD); Ukrainian folklore (MA, PhD). Part-time programs available. *Degree requirements:* For master's, one foreign language, thesis; for doctorate, 2 foreign languages, comprehensive exam, thesis/dissertation. *Entrance requirements:* For master's and doctorate, 1 language other than English. Additional exam requirements/recommendations for international students: Required—Michigan English Language Assessment Battery or TOEFL (minimum score 550 paper-based; 213 computer-based). Electronic applications accepted. *Faculty research:* Russian/Ukrainian studies; German studies; contemporary Latin American, French and Francophone studies; Italian studies.

University of California, Berkeley, Graduate Division, College of Letters and Science, Department of Italian Studies, Berkeley, CA 94720-1500. Offers PhD. *Degree requirements:* For doctorate, one foreign language, thesis/dissertation, oral and written qualifying exams. *Entrance requirements:* For doctorate, GRE General Test, minimum GPA of 3.0, 3 letters of

recommendation. Additional exam requirements/recommendations for international students: Required—TOEFL (minimum score 570 paper-based; 230 computer-based). *Faculty research:* Literature and culture of Italy in Middle Ages and the Renaissance, literature and culture of Italy in nineteenth and twentieth centuries, Italian film studies, interdisciplinary cultural studies.

University of California, Berkeley, Graduate Division, College of Letters and Science, Group in Romance Languages and Literature, Berkeley, CA 94720-1500. Offers French (PhD); Italian (PhD); Spanish (PhD). *Degree requirements:* For doctorate, thesis/dissertation, qualifying exam. *Entrance requirements:* For doctorate, GRE General Test, minimum GPA of 3.0, 3 letters of recommendation. Additional exam requirements/recommendations for international students: Required—TOEFL (minimum score 570 paper-based; 230 computer-based).

University of California, Los Angeles, Graduate Division, College of Letters and Science, Department of Italian, Los Angeles, CA 90095. Offers MA, PhD. *Faculty:* 6 full-time (1 woman). *Students:* 18 full-time (14 women); includes 3 minority (all Hispanic/Latino), 2 international. Average age 30. 20 applicants, 40% accepted, 4 enrolled. In 2010, 1 master's, 6 doctorates awarded. Terminal master's awarded for partial completion of doctoral program. *Degree requirements:* For master's, one foreign language, comprehensive exam or thesis; for doctorate, 2 foreign languages, thesis/dissertation, oral and written qualifying exams. *Entrance requirements:* For master's, GRE General Test, minimum GPA of 3.0, sample of written work; for doctorate, GRE General Test, minimum undergraduate GPA of 3.0, sample of written work; statement of purpose. *Application deadline:* For fall admission, 12/15 for domestic and international students. Application fee: $70 ($90 for international students). Electronic applications accepted. *Financial support:* In 2010–11, 20 fellowships with full and partial tuition reimbursements, 4 research assistantships with full and partial tuition reimbursements, 13 teaching assistantships with full and partial tuition reimbursements were awarded; Federal Work-Study, institutionally sponsored loans, health care benefits, tuition waivers (full and partial), and unspecified assistantships also available. Financial award application deadline: 3/1. *Unit head:* Dr. Dominic Thomas, Chair, 310-794-8923. *Application contact:* Departmental Office, 310-825-1147, E-mail: allen@humnet.ucla.edu.

University of Chicago, Division of the Humanities, Department of Romance Languages and Literatures, Chicago, IL 60637-1513. Offers French (AM, PhD); Italian (AM, PhD); Spanish (AM, PhD). Terminal master's awarded for partial completion of doctoral program. *Degree requirements:* For master's, 2 foreign languages, thesis; for doctorate, 3 foreign languages, thesis/dissertation. *Entrance requirements:* For master's and doctorate, GRE General Test, GRE Subject Test. Additional exam requirements/recommendations for international students: Required—TOEFL.

University of Connecticut, Graduate School, College of Liberal Arts and Sciences, Department of Modern and Classical Languages, Field of Italian, Storrs, CT 06269. Offers MA, PhD. Terminal master's awarded for partial completion of doctoral program. *Degree requirements:* For master's, comprehensive exam; for doctorate, thesis/dissertation. *Entrance requirements:* For master's, GRE General Test. Additional exam requirements/recommendations for international students: Required—TOEFL (minimum score 550 paper-based; 213 computer-based). Electronic applications accepted.

University of Illinois at Urbana–Champaign, Graduate College, College of Liberal Arts and Sciences, School of Literatures, Cultures and Linguistics, Department of Spanish, Italian and Portuguese, Champaign, IL 61820. Offers Italian (MA, PhD); Portuguese (MA, PhD); Spanish (MA, PhD). *Faculty:* 17 full-time (10 women). *Students:* 39 full-time (29 women), 2 part-time (both women); includes 14 minority (all Hispanic/Latino), 16 international. 52 applicants, 23% accepted, 3 enrolled. In 2010, 12 master's, 6 doctorates awarded. *Entrance requirements:* For master's, GRE General Test, minimum GPA of 3.0; writing sample; for doctorate, GRE, minimum GPA of 3.0; writing sample. Additional exam requirements/recommendations for international students: Required—TOEFL (minimum score 88 iBT). *Application deadline:* Applications are processed on a rolling basis. Application fee: $75 ($90 for international students). Electronic applications accepted. *Financial support:* In 2010–11, 7 fellowships, 2 research assistantships, 39 teaching assistantships were awarded; tuition waivers (full and partial) also available. *Unit head:* Diane Musumeci, Head, 217-333-3390, Fax: 217-244-8430, E-mail: musumeci@illinois.edu. *Application contact:* Lynn Stanke, Office Support Specialist, 217-333-6269, Fax: 217-244-3050, E-mail: stanke@illinois.edu.

The University of Manchester, School of Languages, Linguistics and Cultures, Manchester, United Kingdom. Offers Arab world studies (PhD); Chinese studies (M Phil, PhD); East Asian studies (M Phil, PhD); English language (PhD); French studies (M Phil, PhD); German studies (M Phil, PhD); interpreting studies (PhD); Italian studies (M Phil, PhD); Japanese studies (M Phil, PhD); Latin American cultural studies (M Phil, PhD); linguistics (M Phil, PhD); Middle Eastern studies (M Phil, PhD); Polish studies (M Phil, PhD); Portuguese studies (M Phil, PhD); Russian studies (M Phil, PhD); Spanish studies (M Phil, PhD); translation and intercultural studies (M Phil, PhD).

University of Massachusetts Amherst, Graduate School, College of Humanities and Fine Arts, Department of Languages, Literatures, and Cultures, Program in Italian Studies, Amherst, MA 01003. Offers MAT. Part-time programs available. *Faculty:* 3 full-time (1 woman). *Students:* 4 full-time (3 women), 1 part-time (0 women), 2 international. Average age 28. 5 applicants, 80% accepted, 1 enrolled. In 2010, 1 master's awarded. *Degree requirements:* For master's, thesis or alternative. *Entrance requirements:* For master's, GRE General Test. Additional exam requirements/recommendations for international students: Required—TOEFL (minimum score 550 paper-based; 213 computer-based; 80 iBT), IELTS (minimum score 6.5). *Application deadline:* For fall admission, 2/1 for domestic and international students; for spring admission, 9/1 for domestic students, 10/1 for international students. Applications are processed on a rolling basis. Application fee: $50 ($65 for international students). Electronic applications accepted. *Expenses:* Tuition, state resident: full-time $2640. Required fees: $8282. One-time fee: $357 full-time. *Financial support:* Career-related internships or fieldwork, Federal Work-Study, scholarships/grants, traineeships, health care benefits, tuition waivers (full), and unspecified assistantships available. Support available to part-time students. Financial award application deadline: 2/1; financial award applicants required to submit FAFSA. *Unit head:* Dr. Roberto Ludovico, Graduate Program Director, 413-545-2314, Fax: 413-545-4778. *Application contact:* Jean M. Ames, Supervisor of Admissions, 413-545-0722, Fax: 413-577-0010, E-mail: gradadm@grad.umass.edu.

University of Michigan, Horace H. Rackham School of Graduate Studies, College of Literature, Science, and the Arts, Department of Romance Languages and Literatures, Program in Italian, Ann Arbor, MI 48109. Offers PhD. *Faculty:* 4 full-time (2 women), 1 part-time/adjunct (0 women). *Students:* 5 full-time (3 women). Average age 25. 7 applicants, 43% accepted, 3 enrolled. In 2010, 2 doctorates awarded. *Degree requirements:* For doctorate, 2 foreign languages, thesis/dissertation, oral defense of dissertation, preliminary exams. *Entrance requirements:* For doctorate, GRE General Test. Additional exam requirements/recommendations for international students: Required—TOEFL or Michigan English Language Assessment Battery. *Application deadline:* For fall admission, 1/1 for domestic and international students. Application fee: $65 ($75 for international students). Electronic applications accepted. *Expenses:* Tuition, state resident: full-time $17,784; part-time $1116 per credit hour. Tuition, nonresident: full-time $35,944; part-time $2125 per credit hour. International tuition: $35,994 full-time. Required fees: $95 per semester. Tuition and fees vary according to course load, degree level and program. *Financial support:* Fellowships with full tuition reimbursements, teaching assistantships with full tuition reimbursements, institutionally sponsored loans, scholarships/grants, and unspecified assistantships available. Financial award application deadline: 1/1. *Faculty research:* Cinema, transnational visual culture, nineteenth-twentieth century Italian literature, medieval and Renaissance, medieval Mediterranean literature. *Unit head:* Dr. Cristina Moreiras-Menor, Chair, 734-764-5344, Fax: 734-764-8163. *Application contact:* Annette Herbert, Graduate Assistant, 734-764-8164, Fax: 734-764-8163, E-mail: rll-admissions@umich.edu.

Italian

The University of North Carolina at Chapel Hill, Graduate School, College of Arts and Sciences, Department of Romance Languages, Chapel Hill, NC 27599. Offers French (MA, PhD); Italian (MA, PhD); Portuguese (MA, PhD); Romance languages (MA, PhD); Romance philology (MA, PhD); Spanish (MA, PhD). *Degree requirements:* For master's, one foreign language, comprehensive exam, thesis; for doctorate, 2 foreign languages, comprehensive exam, thesis/dissertation. *Entrance requirements:* For master's and doctorate, GRE General Test, minimum GPA of 3.0. Additional exam requirements/recommendations for international students: Required—TOEFL (minimum score 550 paper-based; 213 computer-based). Electronic applications accepted.

University of Notre Dame, Graduate School, College of Arts and Letters, Division of Humanities, Department of Romance Languages and Literatures, Notre Dame, IN 46556. Offers French and Francophone studies (MA); Iberian and Latin American studies (MA); Italian studies (MA); Romance literatures (MA). *Degree requirements:* For master's, 2 foreign languages, comprehensive exam, thesis optional. *Entrance requirements:* For master's, GRE General Test, BA in target language. Additional exam requirements/recommendations for international students: Required—TOEFL (minimum score 600 paper-based; 250 computer-based; 80 iBT). Electronic applications accepted. *Faculty research:* Literature of discovery and exploration, modern literature, literary criticism, medieval literature, feminist critical theory.

University of Oregon, Graduate School, College of Arts and Sciences, Department of Romance Languages, Program in Italian, Eugene, OR 97403. Offers MA. Part-time programs available. *Degree requirements:* For master's, variable foreign language requirement. *Entrance requirements:* For master's, GRE General Test, minimum GPA of 3.0. Additional exam requirements/recommendations for international students: Required—TOEFL.

University of Pennsylvania, School of Arts and Sciences, Graduate Group in Romance Languages, Philadelphia, PA 19104. Offers French (AM, PhD); Italian (AM, PhD); Spanish (AM, PhD). *Faculty:* 58 full-time (23 women), 4 part-time/adjunct (1 woman). *Students:* 61 full-time (34 women), 2 part-time (both women); includes 1 American Indian or Alaska Native, non-Hispanic/Latino; 12 Hispanic/Latino, 19 international. 114 applicants, 15% accepted, 11 enrolled. In 2010, 11 master's, 6 doctorates awarded. Terminal master's awarded for partial completion of doctoral program. *Degree requirements:* For master's, one foreign language, thesis or alternative; for doctorate, 2 foreign languages, thesis/dissertation. *Entrance requirements:* For master's and doctorate, GRE General Test. Additional exam requirements/recommendations for international students: Required—TOEFL. *Application deadline:* For fall admission, 12/1 priority date for domestic students. Application fee: $70. Electronic applications accepted. *Expenses:* Tuition: Full-time $25,660; part-time $4758 per course. Required fees: $2152; $270 per course. Tuition and fees vary according to course load, degree level and program. *Financial support:* In 2010–11, 23 fellowships, 2 research assistantships, 39 teaching assistantships were awarded; institutionally sponsored loans, scholarships/grants, traineeships, health care benefits, and unspecified assistantships also available. Financial award application deadline: 12/15. *Faculty research:* Literary theory and criticism, cultural studies, history of Romance literatures, gender studies. *Application contact:* Graduate Coordinator, 215-898-7429.

University of Pittsburgh, School of Arts and Sciences, Department of French and Italian, Program in Italian, Pittsburgh, PA 15260. Offers MA. Part-time programs available. *Faculty:* 3 full-time (2 women). *Students:* 5 full-time (all women); includes 1 Hispanic/Latino. Average age 23. 9 applicants, 89% accepted, 4 enrolled. In 2010, 4 master's awarded. *Degree requirements:* For master's, one foreign language, comprehensive exam, seminar paper. *Entrance requirements:* For master's, minimum GPA of 3.0, writing sample. Additional exam requirements/recommendations for international students: Required—TOEFL (minimum score 550 paper-based; 213 computer-based; 80 iBT). *Application deadline:* For fall admission, 2/1 priority date for domestic students, 2/1 for international students. Application fee: $50. *Expenses:* Tuition, state resident: full-time $17,304; part-time $701 per credit. Tuition, nonresident: full-time $29,554; part-time $1210 per credit. Required fees: $740; $214 per term. Tuition and fees vary according to program. *Financial support:* In 2010–11, 4 students received support, including 4 teaching assistantships with full tuition reimbursements available (averaging $15,520 per year); institutionally sponsored loans, scholarships/grants, health care benefits, and tuition waivers (partial) also available. Support available to part-time students. Financial award application deadline: 2/1; financial award applicants required to submit FAFSA. *Faculty research:* Dante and his reception, humanism and Renaissance studies, seventeenth and eighteenth century Italian literature and culture, Italian theater, Holocaust literature and film, images of Southern Italy in European literature. *Unit head:* Dr. Renate Blumenfeld-Kosinski, Chair, 412-624-6224, Fax: 412-624-6263, E-mail: rbk7580@aol.com. *Application contact:* Matthew Carulli, Graduate Secretary, 412-624-5220, Fax: 412-624-6263, E-mail: mdc24@pitt.edu.

University of South Africa, College of Human Sciences, Pretoria, South Africa. Offers adult education (M Ed); African languages (MA, PhD); African politics (MA, PhD); Afrikaans (MA, PhD); ancient history (MA, PhD); ancient Near Eastern studies (MA, PhD); anthropology (MA, PhD); applied linguistics (MA); Arabic (MA, PhD); archaeology (MA); art history (MA); Biblical archaeology (MA); Biblical studies (M Th, D Th, PhD); Christian spirituality (M Th, D Th); church history (M Th, D Th); classical studies (MA, PhD); clinical psychology (MA); communication (MA, PhD); comparative education (M Ed, Ed D); consulting psychology (D Admin, D Com, PhD); curriculum studies (M Ed, Ed D); development studies (M Admin, MA, D Admin, PhD); didactics (M Ed, Ed D); education (M Tech); education management (M Ed, Ed D); educational psychology (M Ed); English (MA); environmental education (M Ed); French (MA, PhD); German (MA, PhD); Greek (MA); guidance and counseling (M Ed); health studies (MA, PhD), including health sciences education (MA), health services management (MA), medical and surgical nursing science (critical care general) (MA), midwifery and neonatal nursing science (MA), trauma and emergency care (MA); history (MA, PhD); history of education (Ed D); inclusive education (M Ed, Ed D); information and communications technology policy and regulation (MA); information science (MA, MIS, PhD); international politics (MA, PhD); Islamic studies (MA, PhD); Italian (MA, PhD); Judaica (MA, PhD); linguistics (MA, PhD); mathematical education (M Ed); mathematics education (MA); missiology (M Th, D Th); modern Hebrew (MA, PhD); musicology (MA, MMus, D Mus, PhD); natural science education (M Ed); New Testament (M Th, D Th); Old Testament (D Th); pastoral therapy (M Th, D Th); philosophy (MA); philosophy of education (M Ed, Ed D); politics (MA, PhD); Portuguese (MA, PhD); practical theology (M Th, D Th); psychology (MA, MS, PhD); psychology of education (M Ed, Ed D); public health (MA); religious studies (MA, D Th, PhD); Romance languages (MA); Russian (MA, PhD); Semitic languages (MA, PhD); social behavior studies in HIV/AIDS (MA); social science (mental health) (MA); social science in development studies (MA); social science in psychology (MA); social science in social work (MA); social science in sociology (MA); social work (MSW, DSW, PhD); socio-education (M Ed, Ed D); sociolinguistics (MA); sociology (MA, PhD); Spanish (MA, PhD); systematic theology (M Th, D Th); TESOL (teaching English to speakers of other languages) (MA); theological ethics (M Th, D Th); theory of literature (MA, PhD); urban ministries (D Th); urban ministry (M Th).

The University of Tennessee, Graduate School, College of Arts and Sciences, Department of Modern Foreign Languages and Literatures, Program in Modern Foreign Languages, Knoxville, TN 37996. Offers applied linguistics (PhD); French (PhD); German (PhD); Italian (PhD); Portuguese (PhD); Russian (PhD); Spanish (PhD). *Degree requirements:* For doctorate, 2 foreign languages, thesis/dissertation. *Entrance requirements:* For doctorate, minimum GPA of 2.7. Additional exam requirements/recommendations for international students: Required—TOEFL. Electronic applications accepted. *Expenses:* Tuition, state resident: full-time $7440; part-time $414 per credit hour. Tuition, nonresident: full-time $22,478; part-time $1250 per credit hour. Required fees: $922; $43 per credit hour. Tuition and fees vary according to program.

The University of Texas at Austin, Graduate School, College of Liberal Arts, Department of French and Italian, Austin, TX 78712-1111. Offers French (MA, PhD); French linguistics (MA, PhD); Italian studies (MA, PhD); Romance linguistics (MA, PhD). Part-time programs available. *Degree requirements:* For master's, one foreign language, thesis; for doctorate, 2 foreign languages, thesis/dissertation. *Entrance requirements:* For master's, GRE General Test, minimum GPA of 3.0, bachelor's degree in French or equivalent; for doctorate, GRE General Test, minimum GPA of 3.0, master's degree in French. Additional exam requirements/recommendations for international students: Required—TOEFL. Electronic applications accepted. *Faculty research:* Nineteenth-century Italian literature, Italian Renaissance, twentieth-century French literature, Francophone literature, fifteenth-century literature and culture.

University of Toronto, School of Graduate Studies, Humanities Division, Department of Italian Studies, Toronto, ON M5S 1A1, Canada. Offers MA, PhD. Part-time programs available. *Degree requirements:* For doctorate, 2 foreign languages, comprehensive exam, thesis/dissertation, oral defense, language exam(s). *Entrance requirements:* For master's, minimum B average in last 2 years in Italian; minimum B average in final year, overall; 2 letters of recommendation; for doctorate, MA in Italian, minimum A– average.

University of Victoria, Faculty of Graduate Studies, Faculty of Humanities, Department of Hispanic and Italian Studies, Victoria, BC V8W 2Y2, Canada. Offers Hispanic and Italian studies (MA); Hispanic studies (MA). *Degree requirements:* For master's, one foreign language, comprehensive exam, thesis (for some programs). *Entrance requirements:* For master's, undergraduate major in Hispanic studies, minimum B+ average. Additional exam requirements/recommendations for international students: Required—TOEFL (minimum score 575 paper-based; 233 computer-based), IELTS (minimum score 7). Electronic applications accepted. *Faculty research:* Medieval/Renaissance Spanish and Italian literature, Golden Age literature, Latin American literature.

University of Virginia, College and Graduate School of Arts and Sciences, Department of Spanish, Italian and Portuguese, Program in Italian, Charlottesville, VA 22903. Offers MA. *Students:* 6 full-time (5 women), 1 (woman) part-time, 5 international. Average age 27. 6 applicants, 67% accepted, 4 enrolled. In 2010, 5 master's awarded. *Degree requirements:* For master's, one foreign language, comprehensive exam, thesis. *Entrance requirements:* For master's, GRE General Test, BA in Italian, 2 letters of recommendation. Additional exam requirements/recommendations for international students: Required—TOEFL (minimum score 600 paper-based; 250 computer-based; 90 iBT), IELTS (minimum score 7). *Application deadline:* For fall admission, 12/1 for domestic and international students. Applications are processed on a rolling basis. Application fee: $60. Electronic applications accepted. *Financial support:* Teaching assistantships available. Financial award applicants required to submit FAFSA. *Unit head:* Deborah Parker, Chair, 434-924-7159, Fax: 434-924-7160, E-mail: sipinfo@virginia.edu. *Application contact:* Enrico Cesaretti, Director of Graduate Studies, 434-924-7159, Fax: 434-924-7160, E-mail: sipinfo@virginia.edu.

University of Washington, Graduate School, College of Arts and Sciences, Department of Romance Languages and Literature, Division of French and Italian Studies, Seattle, WA 98195. Offers French (MA, PhD); Italian (MA). Terminal master's awarded for partial completion of doctoral program. *Degree requirements:* For master's, 2 foreign languages, exam; for doctorate, 3 foreign languages, thesis/dissertation, exam. *Entrance requirements:* For master's and doctorate, GRE General Test, minimum GPA of 3.0. Additional exam requirements/recommendations for international students: Required—TOEFL. Electronic applications accepted. *Faculty research:* Interdisciplinary studies, literary theory and criticism, film, major periods of French and Italian literature, Francophonie.

University of Wisconsin–Madison, Graduate School, College of Letters and Science, Department of French and Italian, Program in Italian, Madison, WI 53706-1380. Offers MA, PhD. Part-time programs available. *Degree requirements:* For master's, one foreign language; for doctorate, 2 foreign languages, thesis/dissertation. *Entrance requirements:* For master's and doctorate, GRE. Electronic applications accepted. *Expenses:* Tuition, state resident: full-time $9887; part-time $617.96 per credit. Tuition, nonresident: full-time $24,054; part-time $1503.40 per credit. Required fees: $67.63 per credit. Tuition and fees vary according to reciprocity agreements. *Faculty research:* Italian literature, culture, linguistics, cinema, and language.

University of Wisconsin–Milwaukee, Graduate School, College of Letters and Sciences, Interdepartmental Program in Foreign Language and Literature, Milwaukee, WI 53201-0413. Offers classics and Hebrew studies (MAFLL); comparative literature (MAFLL); French and Italian (MAFLL); German (MAFLL); Slavic studies (MAFLL); translation (Certificate). Part-time programs available. *Faculty:* 29 full-time (14 women). *Students:* 35 full-time (27 women), 29 part-time (20 women); includes 1 Hispanic/Latino. Average age 40. 30 applicants, 67% accepted, 19 enrolled. In 2010, 24 master's awarded. *Degree requirements:* For master's, 2 foreign languages, thesis or alternative. *Entrance requirements:* Additional exam requirements/recommendations for international students: Required—TOEFL (minimum score 550 paper-based; 79 iBT), IELTS (minimum score 6.5). *Application deadline:* For fall admission, 1/1 priority date for domestic students; for spring admission, 9/1 for domestic students. Applications are processed on a rolling basis. Application fee: $56 ($96 for international students). Electronic applications accepted. *Financial support:* In 2010–11, 1 fellowship, 2 research assistantships, 26 teaching assistantships were awarded; career-related internships or fieldwork, health care benefits, unspecified assistantships, and project assistantships also available. Support available to part-time students. Financial award application deadline: 4/15; financial award applicants required to submit FAFSA. Total annual research expenditures: $304,210. *Unit head:* Gabrielle Verdier, Representative, 414-229-3346, Fax: 414-229-2741, E-mail: verdier@uwm.edu. *Application contact:* General Information Contact, 414-229-4982, Fax: 414-229-6967, E-mail: gradschool@uwm.edu.

Wayne State University, College of Liberal Arts and Sciences, Program in Language Learning, Detroit, MI 48202. Offers Arabic (MA); French (MA); German (MA); Italian (MA); Latin (MA); Spanish (MA). *Faculty:* 1 full-time (0 women), 1 (woman) part-time/adjunct. *Students:* 1 (woman) full-time, 12 part-time (11 women), 1 international. Average age 32. 4 applicants, 100% accepted, 3 enrolled. In 2010, 2 master's awarded. *Expenses:* Tuition, state resident: full-time $7662; part-time $478.85 per credit hour. Tuition, nonresident: full-time $16,920; part-time $1057.55 per credit hour. Required fees: $571.20; $35.70 per credit hour. $188.05 per semester. Tuition and fees vary according to course load and program. *Financial support:* In 2010–11, 1 teaching assistantship (averaging $14,620 per year) was awarded. *Unit head:* Robert Thomas, Dean, 313-577-2519, Fax: 313-577-8971, E-mail: aa0817@wayne.edu. *Application contact:* Janet Hankin, Professor, 313-577-0841, E-mail: janet.hankin@wayne.edu.

Yale University, Graduate School of Arts and Sciences, Department of Italian Language and Literature, New Haven, CT 06520. Offers PhD. *Degree requirements:* For doctorate, 3 foreign languages, thesis/dissertation. *Entrance requirements:* For doctorate, GRE General Test.

Japanese

Arizona State University, College of Liberal Arts and Sciences, School of International Letters and Cultures, Program in Japanese, Tempe, AZ 85287-0202. Offers Asian languages and civilizations: Japanese (MA). Part-time and evening/weekend programs available. *Faculty:* 5 full-time (3 women). *Students:* 3 full-time (1 woman), 1 (woman) part-time, 1 international. Average age 27. 6 applicants, 33% accepted, 2 enrolled. In 2010, 2 master's awarded. *Degree requirements:* For master's, thesis, oral defense, interactive Program of Study (iPOS) submitted no later than beginning of third semester of study. *Entrance requirements:* For master's, minimum GPA of 3.25 in the last two years of work leading to the bachelor's degree; BA in Japanese or at least 5 semesters of modern Japanese (preferred); personal statement; writing sample; 3 letters of recommendation. Additional exam requirements/recommendations for international students: Required—TOEFL (minimum score 550 paper-based; 213 computer-based; 83 iBT), IELTS (minimum score 6.5). *Application deadline:* For fall admission, 1/31 for domestic students. Applications are processed on a rolling basis. Application fee: $70 ($90 for international students). Electronic applications accepted. *Expenses:* Tuition, state resident: full-time $8510; part-time $608 per credit. Tuition, nonresident: full-time $16,542; part-time $919 per credit. Required fees: $339; $110 per credit. Part-time tuition and fees vary according to course load. *Financial support:* In 2010–11, 1 teaching assistantship with full and partial tuition reimbursement (averaging $13,500 per year) was awarded; institutionally sponsored loans, scholarships/grants, and tuition waivers (partial) also available. Financial award application deadline: 3/1. *Unit head:* Dr. Anthony Chambers, Director, 480-965-0517, E-mail: anthony.chambers@asu.edu. *Application contact:* Graduate Admissions, 480-965-6113.

Cornell University, Graduate School, Graduate Fields of Arts and Sciences, Field of East Asian Literature, Ithaca, NY 14853-0001. Offers Asian religions (MA, PhD); Chinese linguistics (MA, PhD); Chinese philology (MA, PhD); classical Chinese literature (MA, PhD); classical Japanese literature (MA, PhD); Japanese linguistics (MA, PhD); Korean literature (MA, PhD); modern Chinese literature (MA, PhD); modern Japanese literature (MA, PhD). *Faculty:* 15 full-time (7 women). *Students:* 19 full-time (9 women); includes 1 Black or African American, non-Hispanic/Latino; 3 Asian, non-Hispanic/Latino, 10 international. Average age 30. 37 applicants, 19% accepted, 6 enrolled. In 2010, 2 master's, 4 doctorates awarded. *Degree requirements:* For master's, 2 foreign languages, thesis, teaching experience; for doctorate, 2 foreign languages, comprehensive exam, thesis/dissertation, teaching experience. *Entrance requirements:* For master's, GRE General Test, 3 years of study in Chinese, Japanese, Korean, or Vietnamese; 3 letters of recommendation; academic writing sample; for doctorate, GRE General Test, 3 years of study in Chinese, Japanese, Korean, or Vietnamese, 3 letters of recommendation, academic writing sample. Additional exam requirements/recommendations for international students: Required—TOEFL (minimum score 600 paper-based; 250 computer-based; 77 iBT). *Application deadline:* For fall admission, 1/10 priority date for domestic students. Application fee: $80. Electronic applications accepted. *Expenses:* Tuition: Full-time $29,500. Required fees: $76. Tuition and fees vary according to degree level and program. *Financial support:* In 2010–11, 13 fellowships with full tuition reimbursements, 6 teaching assistantships with full tuition reimbursements were awarded; research assistantships with full tuition reimbursements, institutionally sponsored loans, scholarships/grants, health care benefits, tuition waivers (full and partial), and unspecified assistantships also available. Financial award applicants required to submit FAFSA. *Faculty research:* Vietnamese literature; Chinese literature, drama, and film; Japanese theater and literature; popular culture in East Asia; Korean literature; Asian linguistics. *Unit head:* Director of Graduate Studies, 607-255-9099. *Application contact:* Graduate Field Assistant, 607-255-9099, E-mail: east_asian_lit@cornell.edu.

Eastern Michigan University, Graduate School, College of Arts and Sciences, Department of World Languages, Programs in Foreign Languages, Ypsilanti, MI 48197. Offers French (MA); German (MA); German for business (Graduate Certificate); Hispanic language and cultures (Graduate Certificate); Japanese business practices (Graduate Certificate); Spanish (MA). Part-time and evening/weekend programs available. Postbaccalaureate distance learning degree programs offered (minimal on-campus study). *Students:* 1 (woman) full-time, 12 part-time (11 women); includes 5 minority (1 Black or African American, non-Hispanic/Latino; 1 Asian, non-Hispanic/Latino; 3 Hispanic/Latino), 1 international. Average age 44. In 2010, 8 master's awarded. *Degree requirements:* For master's, one foreign language, thesis optional. *Entrance requirements:* Additional exam requirements/recommendations for international students: Required—TOEFL. *Application deadline:* Applications are processed on a rolling basis. Application fee: $35. *Financial support:* Fellowships, research assistantships with full tuition reimbursements, teaching assistantships with full tuition reimbursements, career-related internships or fieldwork, Federal Work-Study, institutionally sponsored loans, scholarships/grants, tuition waivers (partial), and unspecified assistantships available. Support available to part-time students. Financial award applicants required to submit FAFSA. *Application contact:* Dr. Genevieve Peden, Program Advisor, 734-487-1498, Fax: 734-487-3411, E-mail: gpeden@emich.edu.

Harvard University, Graduate School of Arts and Sciences, Department of East Asian Languages and Civilizations, Cambridge, MA 02138. Offers Chinese (PhD); Japanese (PhD); Korean (PhD); Mongolian (PhD); Vietnamese (PhD). Terminal master's awarded for partial completion of doctoral program. *Degree requirements:* For doctorate, 3 foreign languages, thesis/dissertation, general exams. *Entrance requirements:* For doctorate, GRE General Test. Additional exam requirements/recommendations for international students: Required—TOEFL. *Expenses:* Tuition: Full-time $34,976. Required fees: $1166. Full-time tuition and fees vary according to program. *Faculty research:* Central Asian literature, religion, and premodern history.

Indiana University Bloomington, University Graduate School, College of Arts and Sciences, Department of East Asian Languages and Cultures, Bloomington, IN 47408. Offers Chinese (MA, PhD); Chinese language pedagogy (MA); East Asian studies (MA); Japanese (MA, PhD); Japanese language pedagogy (MA). Part-time programs available. *Faculty:* 15 full-time (7 women), 15 part-time/adjunct (7 women). *Students:* 28 full-time (18 women), 11 part-time (6 women); includes 2 Black or African American, non-Hispanic/Latino, 11 international. Average age 29. 100 applicants, 38% accepted, 18 enrolled. In 2010, 9 master's, 1 doctorate awarded. *Degree requirements:* For master's, one foreign language, thesis; for doctorate, 2 foreign languages, comprehensive exam, thesis/dissertation. *Entrance requirements:* Additional exam requirements/recommendations for international students: Required—TOEFL (minimum score 93 iBT). *Application deadline:* For fall admission, 1/15 for domestic students, 12/1 for international students. Application fee: $55 ($65 for international students). Electronic applications accepted. *Financial support:* In 2010–11, 21 students received support, including 5 fellowships with full tuition reimbursements available (averaging $15,500 per year), 18 teaching assistantships with full tuition reimbursements available (averaging $11,633 per year). Financial award application deadline: 3/1. *Faculty research:* Postwar/postmodern Japanese fiction, modern Chinese film and literature, classical Chinese literature and philosophy, Chinese and Japanese linguistics and pedagogy, East Asian politics and economics, Chinese and Japanese history, Korean language. *Unit head:* Michael Robinson, Chair, 812-855-0856, Fax: 812-855-6402, E-mail: robime@indiana.edu. *Application contact:* Natsuko Tsujimura, Director of Graduate Studies, 812-855-5884, Fax: 812-855-6402, E-mail: tsujimur@indiana.edu.

Kent State University, College of Arts and Sciences, Department of Modern and Classical Language Studies, Kent, OH 44242-0001. Offers French literature (MA); French, Spanish, German and Latin pedagogy (MA); German literature (MA); Spanish literature (MA); translation (MA), including French, German, Japanese, Russian, Spanish; translation studies (PhD). Part-time and evening/weekend programs available. *Degree requirements:* For master's, one foreign language, comprehensive exam (for some programs), thesis (for some programs); for doctorate, comprehensive exam, thesis/dissertation (for some programs). *Entrance requirements:* For master's, minimum GPA of 3.0, writing sample, audio tape or CD; for doctorate, 3 recommendations. Additional exam requirements/recommendations for international students: Required—TOEFL (minimum score 197 computer-based). Electronic applications accepted. *Expenses:* Tuition, state resident: full-time $7866; part-time $437 per credit hour. Tuition, nonresident: full-time $14,022; part-time $779 per credit hour. *Faculty research:* Literature, pedagogy, applied linguistics, translation studies.

The Ohio State University, Graduate School, College of Arts and Sciences, Division of Arts and Humanities, Department of East Asian Languages and Literatures, Columbus, OH 43210. Offers Chinese (MA, PhD); Japanese (MA, PhD). *Faculty:* 22. *Students:* 59 full-time (29 women), 10 part-time (5 women); includes 6 Asian, non-Hispanic/Latino; 1 Hispanic/Latino; 1 Two or more races, non-Hispanic/Latino, 26 international. Average age 27. In 2010, 15 master's, 2 doctorates awarded. *Degree requirements:* For master's, thesis optional; for doctorate, thesis/dissertation. *Entrance requirements:* Additional exam requirements/recommendations for international students: Required—TOEFL (minimum score 577 paper-based; 233 computer-based). *Application deadline:* For fall admission, 8/15 priority date for domestic students, 7/1 priority date for international students; for winter admission, 12/1 priority date for domestic students, 11/1 priority date for international students; for spring admission, 3/1 priority date for domestic students, 2/1 priority date for international students. Applications are processed on a rolling basis. Application fee: $40 ($50 for international students). Electronic applications accepted. *Expenses:* Tuition, state resident: full-time $10,605. Tuition, nonresident: full-time $26,535. Tuition and fees vary according to course load and program. *Financial support:* Fellowships, research assistantships, teaching assistantships, Federal Work-Study, institutionally sponsored loans, and unspecified assistantships available. Support available to part-time students. *Unit head:* Mari Noda, Chair, 614-688-5737, E-mail: noda.1@osu.edu. *Application contact:* Graduate Admissions, 614-292-9444, Fax: 614-292-3895, E-mail: domestic.grad@osu.edu.

Portland State University, Graduate Studies, College of Liberal Arts and Sciences, Department of World Languages and Literatures, Portland, OR 97207-0751. Offers foreign literature and language (MA); French (MA); German (MA); Japanese (MA); Spanish (MA). Part-time programs available. *Faculty:* 45 full-time (30 women), 38 part-time/adjunct (29 women). *Students:* 30 full-time (21 women), 10 part-time (7 women); includes 6 minority (2 Asian, non-Hispanic/Latino; 4 Hispanic/Latino), 11 international. Average age 31. 26 applicants, 69% accepted, 15 enrolled. In 2010, 24 master's awarded. *Degree requirements:* For master's, one foreign language, thesis (for some programs). *Entrance requirements:* Additional exam requirements/recommendations for international students: Required—TOEFL (minimum score 550 paper-based; 213 computer-based). *Application deadline:* For fall admission, 4/1 for domestic students, 3/1 for international students; for winter admission, 9/1 for domestic students, 7/1 for international students; for spring admission, 11/1 for domestic and international students. Applications are processed on a rolling basis. Application fee: $50. *Expenses:* Tuition, state resident: full-time $8505; part-time $315 per credit. Tuition, nonresident: full-time $13,284; part-time $492 per credit. Required fees: $1482; $21 per credit. $99 per term. One-time fee: $120. Part-time tuition and fees vary according to course load and program. *Financial support:* In 2010–11, 6 teaching assistantships with full tuition reimbursements (averaging $9,359 per year) were awarded; research assistantships with full tuition reimbursements, Federal Work-Study, scholarships/grants, and unspecified assistantships also available. Support available to part-time students. Financial award application deadline: 3/1; financial award applicants required to submit FAFSA. *Faculty research:* Foreign language pedagogy, applied and social linguistics, literary history and criticism. *Unit head:* Dr. Jennifer Perlmutter, Chair, 503-725-8783, Fax: 503-725-5276, E-mail: jrp@pdx.edu. *Application contact:* Michael Anthony, Graduate Admissions Coordinator, 503-725-3243, E-mail: manthony@pdx.edu.

San Francisco State University, Division of Graduate Studies, College of Humanities, Department of Foreign Languages and Literatures, Program in Japanese, San Francisco, CA 94132-1722. Offers MA. *Application deadline:* Applications are processed on a rolling basis. *Unit head:* Dr. Makiko Asano, Program Coordinator, 415-338-1131, E-mail: masano@sfsu.edu. *Application contact:* Midori McKeon, Graduate Advisor, 415-338-1346, E-mail: mmckeon@sfsu.edu.

Soka University of America, Graduate School, Aliso Viejo, CA 92656. Offers teaching Japanese as a foreign language (Certificate). Evening/weekend programs available. *Entrance requirements:* For degree, bachelor's degree with minimum GPA of 3.0, proficiency in Japanese. Additional exam requirements/recommendations for international students: Required—TOEFL (minimum score 600 paper-based; 100 iBT).

Stanford University, School of Humanities and Sciences, Department of Asian Languages, Stanford, CA 94305-9991. Offers Chinese (MA, PhD); Japanese (MA, PhD). Terminal master's awarded for partial completion of doctoral program. *Degree requirements:* For master's, one foreign language, thesis or an annotated translation of a literary or historical text; for doctorate, 2 foreign languages, thesis/dissertation, field exams. *Entrance requirements:* For master's and doctorate, GRE General Test. Additional exam requirements/recommendations for international students: Required—TOEFL. Electronic applications accepted. *Expenses:* Tuition: Full-time $38,700; part-time $860 per unit. One-time fee: $200 full-time.

University of Alberta, Faculty of Graduate Studies and Research, Department of East Asian Studies, Edmonton, AB T6G 2E1, Canada. Offers Chinese literature (MA); East Asian interdisciplinary studies (MA); Japanese literature (MA). Part-time programs available. *Degree requirements:* For master's, one foreign language, thesis. *Entrance requirements:* Additional exam requirements/recommendations for international students: Required—TOEFL. Electronic applications accepted. *Faculty research:* Classical Chinese poetry and poetics, Chinese philosophy, modern/contemporary Chinese literature, modern Japanese literature and culture, Japanese women's writing.

University of California, Berkeley, Graduate Division, College of Letters and Science, Department of East Asian Languages and Cultures, Berkeley, CA 94720-1500. Offers Chinese language (PhD); Japanese language (PhD). *Degree requirements:* For doctorate, one foreign language, thesis/dissertation, oral qualifying exam. *Entrance requirements:* For doctorate, GRE General Test, minimum GPA of 3.0, MA thesis, 3 letters of recommendation. Electronic applications accepted. *Faculty research:* Chinese and Japanese modern and classical texts, prose, and poetry; Chinese and Japanese linguistics.

University of California, Irvine, School of Humanities, Department of East Asian Languages and Literatures, Irvine, CA 92697. Offers Chinese (MA, PhD); East Asian languages and literatures (MA, PhD); Japanese (MA, PhD). *Students:* 13 full-time (11 women), 1 (woman) part-time, 11 international. Average age 28. 35 applicants, 20% accepted, 4 enrolled. In 2010, 5 doctorates awarded. *Degree requirements:* For doctorate, thesis/dissertation. *Entrance requirements:* For master's, GRE, minimum GPA of 3.0; for doctorate, GRE General Test, minimum GPA of 3.0. Additional exam requirements/recommendations for international students: Required—TOEFL (minimum score 550 paper-based; 213 computer-based). *Application deadline:* For fall admission, 1/15 priority date for domestic students, 1/15 for international students. Application fee: $80 ($100 for international students). Electronic applications accepted. *Financial support:* Fellowships with tuition reimbursements, research assistantships with full tuition reimbursements, teaching assistantships with partial tuition reimbursements, institutionally sponsored loans, traineeships, health care benefits, and unspecified assistantships available. Financial award application deadline: 3/1; financial award applicants required to submit FAFSA. *Faculty research:* Chinese, Japanese, and Korean literature and culture; language and textual analysis; historical, social, and cultural dimensions of literary study. *Unit head:* Prof. Martin W. Huang, Chair, 949-824-2802, Fax: 949-824-3248, E-mail: mwhuang@uci.edu. *Application contact:* Mindy Han, Management Services Officer, 949-824-2165, Fax: 949-824-3248, E-mail: mindyhan@uci.edu.

University of Colorado Boulder, Graduate School, College of Arts and Sciences, Department of Asian Languages and Civilizations, Boulder, CO 80309. Offers Chinese (MA, PhD); Japanese

Japanese

University of Colorado Boulder (continued)
(MA, PhD). Part-time programs available. *Faculty:* 12 full-time (6 women). *Students:* 26 full-time (12 women), 4 part-time (3 women); includes 6 minority (1 Black or African American, non-Hispanic/Latino; 4 Asian, non-Hispanic/Latino; 1 Hispanic/Latino), 7 international. Average age 26. 37 applicants, 13 enrolled. In 2010, 18 master's awarded. *Degree requirements:* For master's, comprehensive exam. *Entrance requirements:* For master's, BA in Chinese or Japanese, minimum undergraduate GPA of 3.0. Additional exam requirements/recommendations for international students: Required—TOEFL. *Application deadline:* For fall admission, 1/1 priority date for domestic students, 12/1 for international students; for spring admission, 10/1 for domestic students, 9/1 for international students. Applications are processed on a rolling basis. Application fee: $50 ($60 for international students). *Financial support:* In 2010–11, 7 fellowships (averaging $13,865 per year), 10 research assistantships (averaging $6,596 per year) were awarded; career-related internships or fieldwork and Federal Work-Study also available. Financial award application deadline: 2/1. *Faculty research:* Chinese and Japanese modern and classical literature, religions, linguistics, language pedagogy, pre-modern and contemporary fiction, sociolinguistics. Total annual research expenditures: $757,691.

University of Hawaii at Manoa, Graduate Division, College of Languages, Linguistics and Literature, Department of East Asian Languages and Literatures, Program in Japanese, Honolulu, HI 96822. Offers MA, PhD. Part-time programs available. *Faculty:* 14 full-time (9 women). *Students:* 30 full-time (18 women), 4 part-time (2 women); includes 1 Black or African American, non-Hispanic/Latino; 5 Asian, non-Hispanic/Latino; 3 Two or more races, non-Hispanic/Latino, 14 international. Average age 32. 34 applicants, 41% accepted, 7 enrolled. In 2010, 9 master's, 4 doctorates awarded. *Degree requirements:* For master's, 2 foreign languages, thesis optional; for doctorate, 2 foreign languages, comprehensive exam, thesis/dissertation. *Entrance requirements:* For master's and doctorate, GRE General Test. Additional exam requirements/recommendations for international students: Required—TOEFL (minimum score 560 paper-based; 220 computer-based; 83 iBT), IELTS (minimum score 5). *Application deadline:* For fall admission, 2/1 for domestic and international students; for spring admission, 9/1 for domestic and international students. Application fee: $60. *Financial support:* In 2010–11, 6 fellowships (averaging $6,397 per year), 1 research assistantship (averaging $17,496 per year), 9 teaching assistantships (averaging $14,894 per year) were awarded. Total annual research expenditures: $5,000. *Application contact:* Joel Cohn, Graduate Chair, 808-956-2069, Fax: 808-956-9515, E-mail: cohn@hawaii.edu.

University of Hawaii at Manoa, Graduate Division, School of Pacific and Asian Studies, Program in Asian Studies, Concentration in Japanese Studies, Honolulu, HI 96822. Offers Graduate Certificate. Part-time programs available. *Students:* 1 full-time (0 women), 1 (woman) part-time. Average age 32. In 2010, 6 Graduate Certificates awarded. *Degree requirements:* For Graduate Certificate, one foreign language. *Entrance requirements:* For degree, GRE. Additional exam requirements/recommendations for international students: Required—TOEFL (minimum score 560 paper-based; 220 computer-based; 83 iBT), IELTS (minimum score 5). Application fee: $60. Total annual research expenditures: $649,000. *Application contact:* Robert Huey, Director, 808-956-2664, Fax: 808-956-2666, E-mail: huey@hawaii.edu.

The University of Manchester, School of Languages, Linguistics and Cultures, Manchester, United Kingdom. Offers Arab world studies (PhD); Chinese studies (M Phil, PhD); East Asian studies (M Phil, PhD); English language (PhD); French studies (M Phil, PhD); German studies (M Phil, PhD); interpreting studies (PhD); Italian studies (M Phil, PhD); Japanese studies (M Phil, PhD); Latin American cultural studies (M Phil, PhD); linguistics (M Phil, PhD); Middle Eastern studies (M Phil, PhD); Polish studies (M Phil, PhD); Portuguese studies (M Phil, PhD); Russian studies (M Phil, PhD); Spanish studies (M Phil, PhD); translation and intercultural studies (M Phil, PhD).

University of Massachusetts Amherst, Graduate School, College of Humanities and Fine Arts, Department of Languages, Literatures, and Cultures, Programs in Asian Languages and Literatures, Amherst, MA 01003. Offers Chinese (MA); Japanese (MA). Part-time programs available. *Faculty:* 13 full-time (6 women). *Students:* 17 full-time (12 women), 9 part-time (7 women); includes 4 minority (1 Black or African American, non-Hispanic/Latino; 3 Asian, non-Hispanic/Latino), 12 international. Average age 28. 30 applicants, 80% accepted, 12 enrolled. In 2010, 10 master's awarded. *Degree requirements:* For master's, thesis, general exam. *Entrance requirements:* For master's, GRE General Test. Additional exam requirements/recommendations for international students: Required—TOEFL (minimum score 550 paper-based; 213 computer-based; 80 iBT), IELTS (minimum score 6.5). *Application deadline:* For fall admission, 2/1 for domestic and international students. Applications are processed on a rolling basis. Application fee: $50 ($65 for international students). Electronic applications accepted. *Expenses:* Tuition, state resident: full-time $2640. Required fees: $8282. One-time fee: $357 full-time. *Financial support:* In 2010–11, 21 teaching assistantships with full tuition reimbursements (averaging $8,116 per year) were awarded; fellowships, research assistantships, career-related internships or fieldwork, Federal Work-Study, scholarships/grants, traineeships, health care benefits, tuition waivers (full), and unspecified assistantships also available. Support available to part-time students. Financial award application deadline: 2/1; financial award applicants required to submit FAFSA. *Unit head:* Dr. Amanda C. Seaman, Department Head/Chair, 413-545-0886, Fax: 413-545-4975. *Application contact:* Jean M. Ames, Supervisor of Admissions, 413-545-0722, Fax: 413-577-0100, E-mail: gradadm@grad.umass.edu.

University of Oregon, Graduate School, College of Arts and Sciences, Department of East Asian Languages and Literature, Eugene, OR 97403. Offers Chinese (MA, PhD); Japanese (MA, PhD). *Entrance requirements:* Additional exam requirements/recommendations for international students: Required—TOEFL. *Faculty research:* Linguistics, pedagogy.

University of Washington, Graduate School, College of Arts and Sciences, Department of Asian Languages and Literature, Seattle, WA 98195. Offers Buddhist studies (MA, PhD); Chinese language and literature (MA, PhD); Japanese language and literature (MA, PhD); Korean language and literature (MA, PhD); South Asian language and literature (MA, PhD). *Degree requirements:* For master's, 2 foreign languages, general exam, thesis or 2 research papers; for doctorate, 3 foreign languages, thesis/dissertation, general exam. *Entrance requirements:* For master's, GRE, minimum GPA of 3.0; for doctorate, GRE, master's degree in related field, minimum GPA of 3.0. Additional exam requirements/recommendations for international students: Required—TOEFL. Electronic applications accepted. *Faculty research:* Textual, linguistic, philological, and literary study of languages and literatures of Asia.

University of Washington, Graduate School, College of Engineering, Department of Human Centered Design and Engineering, Seattle, WA 98195-2315. Offers global technology and communication (MS, PhD); human centered design and engineering (MS, PhD); inter-engineering technical Japanese (MSE); technical communication (MS, PhD), including global technology and communication (MS), technical communication, user centered design; user centered design (MS, PhD). Part-time and evening/weekend programs available. Post-baccalaureate distance learning degree programs offered (no on-campus study). *Faculty:* 16 full-time (11 women), 8 part-time/adjunct (6 women). *Students:* 41 full-time (28 women), 99 part-time (49 women); includes 4 Black or African American, non-Hispanic/Latino; 15 Asian, non-Hispanic/Latino; 9 Hispanic/Latino, 6 international. Average age 34. 184 applicants, 54% accepted, 61 enrolled. In 2010, 32 master's, 3 doctorates awarded. *Degree requirements:* For master's, thesis or alternative; for doctorate, comprehensive exam, thesis/dissertation, preliminary, general, and final exams. *Entrance requirements:* For master's and doctorate, GRE General Test, minimum GPA of 3.0, transcripts, 3 letters of recommendation, curriculum vitae, personal statement of objectives. Additional exam requirements/recommendations for international students: Required—TOEFL (minimum score 600 paper-based; 237 computer-based; 92 iBT). *Application deadline:* For fall admission, 12/21 for domestic students, 11/15 priority date for international students. Applications are processed on a rolling basis. Application fee: $75. Electronic applications accepted. *Financial support:* In 2010–11, 1 student received support, including 1 fellowship with full tuition reimbursement available (averaging $22,500 per year), 14 research assistantships with full tuition reimbursements available (averaging $14,751 per year), 16 teaching assistantships with full tuition reimbursements available (averaging $13,725 per year); career-related internships or fieldwork, institutionally sponsored loans, and tuition waivers (full) also available. Financial award application deadline: 2/28; financial award applicants required to submit FAFSA. *Faculty research:* Human/computer interaction, communication design, user interface design and usability, new media design, comprehension processes. Total annual research expenditures: $1.5 million. *Unit head:* Dr. Jan Spyridakis, Professor and Chair, 206-685-1557, Fax: 206-543-8858, E-mail: jansp@u.washington.edu. *Application contact:* Gian Bruno, Academic Counselor, 206-543-1798, Fax: 206-543-8858, E-mail: gbruno@u.washington.edu.

University of Wisconsin–Madison, Graduate School, College of Letters and Science, Department of East Asian Languages and Literature, Program in Japanese Linguistics, Madison, WI 53706-1380. Offers MA, PhD. Part-time programs available. Terminal master's awarded for partial completion of doctoral program. *Degree requirements:* For master's, one foreign language, seminars, written exam; for doctorate, 3 foreign languages, thesis/dissertation, seminars, preliminary exams, oral exam. *Entrance requirements:* For master's, GRE General Test, bachelor's degree or equivalent in Japanese; for doctorate, GRE General Test, master's degree or equivalent in Japanese. Electronic applications accepted. *Expenses:* Tuition, state resident: full-time $9887; part-time $617.96 per credit. Tuition, nonresident: full-time $24,054; part-time $1503.40 per credit. Required fees: $67.63 per credit. Tuition and fees vary according to reciprocity agreements. *Faculty research:* Modern and historical Japanese linguistics, modern Japanese fiction and poetry, classical Japanese literature, language pedagogy.

Washington University in St. Louis, Graduate School of Arts and Sciences, Department of Asian and Near Eastern Languages and Literatures, St. Louis, MO 63130-4899. Offers Chinese (MA); Chinese and comparative literature (PhD); Japanese (MA); Japanese and comparative literature (PhD). Terminal master's awarded for partial completion of doctoral program. *Degree requirements:* For master's, thesis optional; for doctorate, thesis/dissertation. *Entrance requirements:* For master's and doctorate, GRE General Test. Electronic applications accepted.

Near and Middle Eastern Languages

The American University in Cairo, School of Humanities and Social Sciences, Department of Arabic and Islamic Civilizations, Cairo, Egypt. Offers Arab language and literature (MA); Islamic art and architecture (MA); Islamic studies (Diploma); Middle East studies (MA, Diploma); Middle Eastern history (MA). Part-time programs available. *Degree requirements:* For master's, thesis optional, proficiency in French or German. *Entrance requirements:* Additional exam requirements/recommendations for international students: Required—English entrance exam and/or TOEFL. Electronic applications accepted. *Faculty research:* History of early Islam, Ayubbid, and Mamluk periods; nineteenth- and twentieth-century Middle East Islamic jurisprudence; contemporary Arabic literary criticism.

American University of Beirut, Graduate Programs, Faculty of Arts and Sciences, Beirut, Lebanon. Offers anthropology (MA); Arabic language and literature (MA); archaeology (MA); biology (MS); chemistry (MS); computational science (MS); computer science (MS); economics (MA); education (MA); English language (MA); English literature (MA); environmental policy planning (MSES); financial economics (MAFE); geology (MS); history (MA); mathematics (MA, MS); Middle Eastern studies (MA); philosophy (MA); physics (MS); political studies (MA); psychology (MA); public administration (MA); sociology (MA); statistics (MA, MS). Part-time programs available. *Faculty:* 229 full-time (98 women), 136 part-time/adjunct (79 women). *Students:* 158 full-time (104 women), 263 part-time (171 women). Average age 25. 356 applicants, 59% accepted, 127 enrolled. In 2010, 57 master's awarded. *Degree requirements:* For master's, one foreign language, comprehensive exam, thesis (for some programs). *Entrance requirements:* For master's, GRE, letter of recommendation. Additional exam requirements/recommendations for international students: Required—TOEFL (minimum score 600 paper-based; 250 computer-based; 97 iBT), IELTS (minimum score 7). *Application deadline:* For fall admission, 4/30 for domestic and international students; for spring admission, 11/1 for domestic and international students. Application fee: $50. *Expenses:* Tuition: Full-time $12,294; part-time $683 per credit. Required fees: $499; $499 per credit. Tuition and fees vary according to course load and program. *Financial support:* In 2010–11, 33 students received support. Career-related internships or fieldwork, institutionally sponsored loans, scholarships/grants, health care benefits, and unspecified assistantships available. Financial award application deadline: 2/4; financial award applicants required to submit FAFSA. *Faculty research:* Modern and contemporary world theatre; mineralogy, petrology, and geochemistry; cell differentiation and transformation; combinatorial technologies; philosophy of action; continental philosophy; Phoenician epigraphy; nascent complex societies and urbanism; the economies of the Arab world; environmental economics; tectonophysics; host-parasite interactions; innate immunity; insect-plant interactions; history of the Ottoman archives; decentralization; transparency and corruption. Total annual research expenditures: $622,243. *Unit head:* Dr. Patrick McGreevy, Dean, 961-137-4374 Ext. 3800, Fax: 961-174-4461, E-mail: pm07@aub.edu.lb. *Application contact:* Dr. Salim Kanaan, Director, Admissions Office, 961-135-0000 Ext. 2594, Fax: 961-175-0775, E-mail: sk00@aub.edu.lb.

Bethel Seminary, Graduate and Professional Programs, St. Paul, MN 55112-6998. Offers Anglican studies (Certificate); applied ministry (MA, Certificate); biblical studies (Certificate); children's and family ministry (MACFM); Christian education (MACE); Christian thought (MACT); community ministry leadership (MA, Certificate); global and contextual studies (MA); Greek and Hebrew language track (M Div); Greek language track (M Div); Hebrew language track (M Div); lay ministry (Certificate); marriage and family therapy (MAMFT, Certificate); men's ministry leadership (Certificate); ministry (D Min); ministry leadership (Certificate); spiritual formation (Certificate); theological studies (MATS, Certificate); transformational leadership (MATL, Certificate); young life youth ministry (Certificate). *Accreditation:* ACIPE; ATS (one or more programs are accredited). Part-time and evening/weekend programs available. Post-baccalaureate distance learning degree programs offered (minimal on-campus study). *Faculty:* 26 full-time (3 women), 74 part-time/adjunct (29 women). *Students:* 729 full-time (275 women), 274 part-time (118 women); includes 75 minority (34 Black or African American, non-Hispanic/Latino; 1 American Indian or Alaska Native, non-Hispanic/Latino; 12 Asian, non-Hispanic/Latino; 16 Hispanic/Latino; 1 Native Hawaiian or other Pacific Islander, non-Hispanic/Latino; 11 Two or more races, non-Hispanic/Latino), 16 international. Average age 38. 525 applicants, 76% accepted, 265 enrolled. In 2010, 149 master's, 13 doctorates awarded. *Degree requirements:* For master's, variable foreign language requirement, thesis (for some programs); for doctorate, thesis/dissertation; for M Div, one foreign language. *Entrance requirements:* For

M Div and master's, letters of reference, transcripts, personal statement; for doctorate, M Div, letters of reference, organizational support. Additional exam requirements/recommendations for international students: Required—TOEFL (minimum score 550 paper-based; 213 computer-based; 87 iBT). *Application deadline:* For fall admission, 8/1 priority date for domestic students, 3/1 for international students; for winter admission, 12/1 priority date for domestic students; for spring admission, 3/1 priority date for domestic students. Applications are processed on a rolling basis. Application fee: $20. Electronic applications accepted. *Financial support:* In 2010–11, 655 students received support, including 18 teaching assistantships; career-related internships or fieldwork, Federal Work-Study, scholarships/grants, and tuition waivers (full) also available. Financial award application deadline: 7/15; financial award applicants required to submit FAFSA. *Faculty research:* Nature of theology, ethics, Biblical commentaries, nature of God, science and theology. *Unit head:* Dr. David Ridder, Vice President and Dean, 651-638-6553. *Application contact:* Joseph V. Dworak, Director of Admissions, 651-638-6288, Fax: 651-638-6002, E-mail: j-dworak@bethel.edu.

Brandeis University, Graduate School of Arts and Sciences, Department of Near Eastern and Judaic Studies, Waltham, MA 02454-9110. Offers Near Eastern and Judaic studies (MA, PhD); Near Eastern and Judaic studies and sociology (PhD); Near Eastern and Judaic studies and women's and gender studies (MA); teaching of Hebrew (MAT). Part-time programs available. *Faculty:* 23 full-time (11 women), 7 part-time/adjunct (3 women). *Students:* 64 full-time (29 women); includes 2 Hispanic/Latino, 6 international. 123 applicants, 50% accepted, 18 enrolled. In 2010, 10 master's, 2 doctorates awarded. Terminal master's awarded for partial completion of doctoral program. *Degree requirements:* For master's, one foreign language, comprehensive exam, thesis or alternative; for doctorate, 3 foreign languages, comprehensive exam, thesis/dissertation. *Entrance requirements:* For master's and doctorate, GRE General Test (recommended), letters of recommendation, transcripts, statement of purpose. Additional exam requirements/recommendations for international students: Required—TOEFL (minimum score 600 paper-based; 250 computer-based; 100 iBT); Recommended—IELTS (minimum score 7). *Application deadline:* For fall admission, 1/15 priority date for domestic and international students. Applications are processed on a rolling basis. Application fee: $75. Electronic applications accepted. *Financial support:* In 2010–11, 17 students received support, including 14 fellowships with full tuition reimbursements available (averaging $20,000 per year); research assistantships with full and partial tuition reimbursements available, teaching assistantships, scholarships/grants, health care benefits, and tuition waivers (full and partial) also available. Support available to part-time students. Financial award application deadline: 4/15; financial award applicants required to submit FAFSA. *Faculty research:* Ancient Near East and Bible, philosophy, history, modern Middle East, Islamic studies. *Unit head:* Dr. Sylvia Fishman, Chair, 781-736-2950, Fax: 781-736-2070, E-mail: fishman@brandeis.edu. *Application contact:* Joanne Arnish, Department Administrator, 781-736-2950, Fax: 781-736-2070, E-mail: arnish@brandeis.edu.

The Catholic University of America, School of Arts and Sciences, Department of Semitic and Egyptian Languages and Literatures, Washington, DC 20064. Offers Ancient Near East (Biblical Hebrew/Aramaic) (MA, PhD); Arabic (PhD); Christian Near East (Biblical Hebrew/Aramaic) (MA); Coptic (MA, PhD); Syriac (MA). Part-time programs available. *Faculty:* 3 full-time (0 women), 3 part-time/adjunct (1 woman). *Students:* 13 full-time (3 women), 15 part-time (6 women); includes 2 Black or African American, non-Hispanic/Latino; 1 Asian, non-Hispanic/Latino, 3 international. Average age 36. 18 applicants, 78% accepted, 5 enrolled. In 2010, 4 master's, 2 doctorates awarded. *Degree requirements:* For master's, one foreign language, comprehensive exam; for doctorate, 2 foreign languages, comprehensive exam, thesis/dissertation. *Entrance requirements:* For master's and doctorate, GRE General Test, statement of purpose, official copies of academic transcripts, three letters of recommendation. Additional exam requirements/recommendations for international students: Required—TOEFL (minimum score 580 paper-based; 237 computer-based). *Application deadline:* For fall admission, 8/1 priority date for domestic students, 7/15 for international students; for spring admission, 12/1 priority date for domestic students, 10/15 for international students. Applications are processed on a rolling basis. Application fee: $55. Electronic applications accepted. *Expenses:* Tuition: Full-time $33,580; part-time $1315 per credit hour. Required fees: $80; $40 per semester hour. One-time fee: $425. *Financial support:* Fellowships, research assistantships, teaching assistantships, Federal Work-Study, scholarships/grants, tuition waivers (full and partial), and unspecified assistantships available. Financial award application deadline: 2/1; financial award applicants required to submit FAFSA. *Faculty research:* Christian history and literature of the Near East, Biblical Hebrew, Arabic Christianity, Coptic, Syriac. *Unit head:* Dr. Edward M. Cook, Chair, 202-319-5083, Fax: 202-319-4735, E-mail: cooke@cua.edu. *Application contact:* Andrew Woodall, Director of Graduate Admissions, 202-319-5057, Fax: 202-319-6533, E-mail: cua-admissions@cua.edu.

Columbia University, Graduate School of Arts and Sciences, Division of Humanities, Department of Middle East Languages and Cultures, New York, NY 10027. Offers Hebrew language and literature (M Phil, MA, PhD); Middle Eastern languages and cultures (M Phil, MA, PhD); South Asian languages and cultures (M Phil, MA, PhD). Part-time programs available. *Degree requirements:* For master's, thesis, oral and written exams; for doctorate, 3 foreign languages, thesis/dissertation. *Entrance requirements:* For master's and doctorate, GRE General Test. Additional exam requirements/recommendations for international students: Required—TOEFL. *Faculty research:* Indo-Iranian, Turkish, central Asian, and Armenian studies; Arabic and ancient Semitics.

Georgetown University, Graduate School of Arts and Sciences, Department of Arabic and Islamic Studies, Washington, DC 20057. Offers Arabic area studies (PhD); Islamic studies (MA, PhD); linguistics (MA, PhD). *Degree requirements:* For master's, comprehensive exam, research project; for doctorate, one foreign language, comprehensive exam, thesis/dissertation. *Entrance requirements:* Additional exam requirements/recommendations for international students: Required—TOEFL.

Harvard University, Graduate School of Arts and Sciences, Department of Near Eastern Languages and Civilizations, Cambridge, MA 02138. Offers Akkadian and Sumerian (AM, PhD); Arabic (AM, PhD); Armenian (AM, PhD); biblical history (AM, PhD); Hebrew (AM, PhD); Indo-Muslim culture (AM, PhD); Iranian (AM, PhD); Jewish history and literature (AM, PhD); Persian (AM, PhD); Semitic philology (AM, PhD); Syro-Palestinian archaeology (AM, PhD); Turkish (AM, PhD). *Degree requirements:* For doctorate, variable foreign language requirement, thesis/dissertation, general exams. *Entrance requirements:* For master's, GRE General Test; for doctorate, GRE General Test, proficiency in a Near Eastern language. Additional exam requirements/recommendations for international students: Required—TOEFL. *Expenses:* Tuition: Full-time $34,976. Required fees: $1166. Full-time tuition and fees vary according to program.

Hebrew Union College–Jewish Institute of Religion, School of Graduate Studies, Program in Hebrew Letters, New York, NY 10012-1186. Offers DHL. *Degree requirements:* For doctorate, one foreign language, thesis/dissertation. *Entrance requirements:* For doctorate, GRE. Additional exam requirements/recommendations for international students: Required—TOEFL. *Expenses:* Contact institution. *Faculty research:* Philosophy and theology, Bible, Hebrew, pastoral care, history and Rabbinics.

Indiana University Bloomington, University Graduate School, College of Arts and Sciences, Department of Near Eastern Languages and Cultures, Bloomington, IN 47405-7000. Offers MA, PhD. Part-time programs available. *Faculty:* 5 full-time (2 women). *Students:* 44 full-time (17 women), 2 part-time (0 women); includes 1 minority (Hispanic/Latino), 25 international. Average age 33. 57 applicants, 54% accepted, 13 enrolled. In 2010, 6 master's, 2 doctorates awarded. Terminal master's awarded for partial completion of doctoral program. *Degree requirements:* For master's, 2 foreign languages, thesis or alternative; for doctorate, 3 foreign languages, thesis/dissertation. *Entrance requirements:* For master's and doctorate, GRE General Test. Additional exam requirements/recommendations for international students: Required—TOEFL. *Application deadline:* For fall admission, 1/15 priority date for domestic students, 12/15 for international students; for spring admission, 9/1 priority date for domestic students, 9/1 for international students. Applications are processed on a rolling basis. Application fee: $55 ($65 for international students). *Financial support:* In 2010–11, 3 fellowships with full and partial tuition reimbursements (averaging $15,000 per year), 1 research assistantship with full and partial tuition reimbursement (averaging $15,900 per year), 10 teaching assistantships with full and partial tuition reimbursements (averaging $14,170 per year) were awarded; Federal Work-Study, institutionally sponsored loans, tuition waivers (full and partial), and unspecified assistantships also available. Financial award application deadline: 3/1; financial award applicants required to submit FAFSA. *Faculty research:* Classical and modern Arabic literature and linguistics, Biblical and modern Hebrew studies, Persian language and literature, Islamic civilization, Iranian history and language. *Unit head:* Dr. Nazif Shahrani, Chair, 812-855-4858. *Application contact:* Elaine Wright, Administrative Secretary, 812-855-5993.

The Ohio State University, Graduate School, College of Arts and Sciences, Division of Arts and Humanities, Department of Near Eastern Languages and Cultures, Columbus, OH 43210. Offers MA, PhD. *Faculty:* 19. *Students:* 21 full-time (6 women), 2 part-time (0 women); includes 1 Black or African American, non-Hispanic/Latino; 1 Asian, non-Hispanic/Latino, 2 international. Average age 28. In 2010, 4 master's awarded. *Degree requirements:* For master's, thesis optional. *Entrance requirements:* For master's and doctorate, GRE General Test. Additional exam requirements/recommendations for international students: Required—TOEFL (minimum score 600 paper-based; 250 computer-based). *Application deadline:* For fall admission, 8/15 priority date for domestic students, 7/1 priority date for international students; for winter admission, 12/1 priority date for domestic students, 11/1 priority date for international students; for spring admission, 3/1 priority date for domestic students, 2/1 priority date for international students. Applications are processed on a rolling basis. Application fee: $40 ($50 for international students). Electronic applications accepted. *Expenses:* Tuition, state resident: full-time $10,605. Tuition, nonresident: full-time $26,535. Tuition and fees vary according to course load and program. *Financial support:* Fellowships, research assistantships, teaching assistantships, Federal Work-Study and institutionally sponsored loans available. Support available to part-time students. *Unit head:* Richard Davis, Chair, 614-292-5643, E-mail: davis.77@osu.edu. *Application contact:* 614-292-9444, Fax: 614-292-3895, E-mail: domestic.grad@osu.edu.

Oral Roberts University, School of Theology and Missions, Tulsa, OK 74171. Offers biblical literature (MA), including advanced languages, Judaic-Christian studies; Christian counseling (MA), including marriage and family therapy; divinity (M Div); missions (MA); practical theology (MA); theological/historical studies (MA); theology (D Min). Part-time programs available. Postbaccalaureate distance learning degree programs offered (minimal on-campus study). *Degree requirements:* For master's, thesis (for some programs), practicum/internship; for doctorate, thesis/dissertation, applied research project; for M Div, one foreign language, field experience. *Entrance requirements:* For M Div and master's, GRE General Test or MAT, minimum GPA of 2.5; for doctorate, M Div, minimum GPA of 3.0, 3 years of full-time ministry experience. Additional exam requirements/recommendations for international students: Required—TOEFL (minimum score 550 paper-based; 213 computer-based; 79 iBT). Electronic applications accepted.

University of California, Los Angeles, Graduate Division, College of Letters and Science, Department of Near Eastern Languages and Cultures, Los Angeles, CA 90034. Offers MA, PhD. *Faculty:* 18 full-time (5 women). *Students:* 41 full-time (21 women); includes 3 minority (1 Black or African American, non-Hispanic/Latino; 1 Hispanic/Latino; 1 Two or more races, non-Hispanic/Latino), 2 international. Average age 29. 58 applicants, 24% accepted, 4 enrolled. In 2010, 5 master's, 2 doctorates awarded. *Degree requirements:* For master's, one foreign language, comprehensive exam; for doctorate, 2 foreign languages, thesis/dissertation, oral and written qualifying exams. *Entrance requirements:* For master's and doctorate, GRE General Test, minimum GPA of 3.25, sample of written work (recommended). Additional exam requirements/recommendations for international students: Required—TOEFL. *Application deadline:* For fall admission, 12/1 for domestic and international students. Application fee: $70 ($90 for international students). Electronic applications accepted. *Financial support:* In 2010–11, 25 fellowships with full and partial tuition reimbursements, 18 research assistantships with full and partial tuition reimbursements, 27 teaching assistantships with full and partial tuition reimbursements were awarded; Federal Work-Study, institutionally sponsored loans, scholarships/grants, health care benefits, tuition waivers (full and partial), and unspecified assistantships also available. Financial award application deadline: 3/1; financial award applicants required to submit FAFSA. *Unit head:* Dr. William M. Schniedewind, Chair, 310-206-2405, E-mail: williams@humnet.ucla.edu. *Application contact:* Departmental Office, 310-825-4165, E-mail: nreast@humnet.ucla.edu.

University of Chicago, Division of the Humanities, Department of Near Eastern Languages and Civilizations, Chicago, IL 60637-1513. Offers AM, PhD. Terminal master's awarded for partial completion of doctoral program. *Degree requirements:* For master's, one foreign language, comprehensive exam, thesis; for doctorate, 2 foreign languages, comprehensive exam, thesis/dissertation. *Entrance requirements:* For master's and doctorate, GRE General Test. Additional exam requirements/recommendations for international students: Required—TOEFL.

The University of Manchester, School of Languages, Linguistics and Cultures, Manchester, United Kingdom. Offers Arab world studies (PhD); Chinese studies (M Phil, PhD); East Asian studies (M Phil, PhD); English language (PhD); French studies (M Phil, PhD); German studies (M Phil, PhD); interpreting studies (PhD); Italian studies (M Phil, PhD); Japanese studies (M Phil, PhD); Latin American cultural studies (M Phil, PhD); linguistics (M Phil, PhD); Middle Eastern studies (M Phil, PhD); Polish studies (M Phil, PhD); Portuguese studies (M Phil, PhD); Russian studies (M Phil, PhD); Spanish studies (M Phil, PhD); translation and intercultural studies (M Phil, PhD).

University of Maryland, College Park, Academic Affairs, College of Arts and Humanities, The Arabic Flagship Program, College Park, MD 20742. Offers MPS, Graduate Certificate. *Students:* 16 full-time (8 women), 5 part-time (1 woman); includes 3 minority (2 Black or African American, non-Hispanic/Latino; 1 Asian, non-Hispanic/Latino). 83 applicants, 10% accepted, 4 enrolled. *Entrance requirements:* For master's and Graduate Certificate, Arabic Language Skills Test, Reading and Listening Proficiency Test, Speaking Proficiency Test, transcripts, minimum GPA of 3.0. *Application deadline:* For fall admission, 1/15 for domestic and international students. Application fee: $75. *Expenses:* Tuition, state resident: part-time $471 per credit hour. Tuition, nonresident: part-time $1016 per credit hour. Required fees: $337 per term. *Financial support:* In 2010–11, 3 fellowships with partial tuition reimbursements (averaging $10,000 per year) were awarded. *Unit head:* Ridha Krizi, Graduate Flagship Program Coordinator, 301-405-7492, E-mail: rkrizi@umd.edu. *Application contact:* Dean of Graduate School, 301-405-0358, Fax: 301-314-9305.

University of Maryland, College Park, Academic Affairs, College of Arts and Humanities, The Persian Flagship Program, College Park, MD 20742. Offers MPS, Graduate Certificate. *Students:* 11 full-time (7 women), 1 part-time (0 women); includes 1 minority (Asian, non-Hispanic/Latino). 27 applicants, 70% accepted, 11 enrolled. In 2010, 8 master's awarded. *Entrance requirements:* For master's and Graduate Certificate, Persian Language Proficiency Test, minimum GPA of 3.0. *Application deadline:* For fall admission, 1/15 for domestic and international students. Applications are processed on a rolling basis. Application fee: $75. Electronic applications accepted. *Expenses:* Tuition, state resident: part-time $471 per credit hour. Tuition, nonresident: part-time $1016 per credit hour. Required fees: $337 per term. *Financial support:* In 2010–11, 4 fellowships with partial tuition reimbursements (averaging $9,500 per year) were awarded. *Unit head:* Dr. Ahmad Karimi-Hakkak, Professor and Director of the Center for Persian Studies, 301-405-3147, E-mail: karimi@umd.edu. *Application contact:* Dean of Graduate School, 301-405-0358, Fax: 301-314-9305.

University of Michigan, Horace H. Rackham School of Graduate Studies, College of Literature, Science, and the Arts, Department of Near Eastern Studies, Ann Arbor, MI 48109. Offers ancient Near Eastern studies (AM, PhD); Arabic for professional purposes (AM); Arabic language and literature (AM, PhD); Armenian studies (AM, PhD); Christianity in late antiquity

Near and Middle Eastern Languages

University of Michigan (continued)
(AM, PhD); Egyptology (AM, PhD); Hebrew Bible and ancient Israel (AM, PhD); Hebrew literature (AM, PhD); Islamic studies (AM, PhD); Jewish cultural studies (AM, PhD); Jewish mysticism (AM, PhD); Persian and Iranian studies (AM, PhD); Rabbinic literature (AM, PhD); Second Temple Judaism (AM, PhD); teaching of Arabic as a foreign language (AM); Turkish studies (AM, PhD). Part-time programs available. Terminal master's awarded for partial completion of doctoral program. *Degree requirements:* For master's, 2 foreign languages; for doctorate, 4 foreign languages, comprehensive exam, thesis/dissertation. *Entrance requirements:* For master's, GRE General Test; for doctorate, GRE General Test, master's degree. Additional exam requirements/recommendations for international students: Required—TOEFL (minimum score 560 paper-based; 220 computer-based; 84 iBT). Electronic applications accepted. *Expenses:* Tuition, state resident: full-time $17,784; part-time $1116 per credit hour. Tuition, nonresident: full-time $35,944; part-time $2125 per credit hour. International tuition: $35,994 full-time. Required fees: $95 per semester. Tuition and fees vary according to course load, degree level and program. *Faculty research:* Middle and Near Eastern literatures, languages, cultures from ancient times to the present.

University of South Africa, College of Human Sciences, Pretoria, South Africa. Offers adult education (M Ed); African languages (MA, PhD); African politics (MA, PhD); Afrikaans (MA, PhD); ancient history (MA, PhD); ancient Near Eastern studies (MA, PhD); anthropology (MA, PhD); applied linguistics (MA); Arabic (MA, PhD); archaeology (MA); art history (MA); Biblical archaeology (MA); Biblical studies (M Th, D Th, PhD); Christian spirituality (M Th, D Th); church history (M Th, D Th); classical studies (MA, PhD); clinical psychology (MA); communication (MA, PhD); comparative education (M Ed, Ed D); consulting psychology (D Admin, D Com, PhD); curriculum studies (M Ed, Ed D); development studies (M Admin, MA, D Admin, PhD); didactics (M Ed, Ed D); education (M Tech); education management (M Ed, Ed D); educational psychology (M Ed); English (MA); environmental education (M Ed); French (MA, PhD); German (MA, PhD); Greek (MA); guidance and counseling (M Ed); health studies (MA, PhD), including health sciences education (MA), health services management (MA), medical and surgical nursing science (critical care general) (MA), midwifery and neonatal nursing science (MA), trauma and emergency care (MA); history (MA, PhD); history of education (Ed D); inclusive education (M Ed, Ed D); information and communications technology policy and regulation (MA); information science (MA, MIS, PhD); international politics (MA, PhD); Islamic studies (MA, PhD); Italian (MA, PhD); Judaica (MA, PhD); linguistics (MA, PhD); mathematical education (M Ed); mathematics education (MA); missiology (M Th, D Th); modern Hebrew (MA, PhD); musicology (MA, MMus, D Mus, PhD); natural science education (M Ed); New Testament (M Th, D Th); Old Testament (D Th); pastoral therapy (M Th, D Th); philosophy (MA); philosophy of education (M Ed, Ed D); politics (MA, PhD); Portuguese (MA, PhD); practical theology (M Th, D Th); psychology (MA, MS, PhD); psychology of education (M Ed, Ed D); public health (MA); religious studies (MA, D Th, PhD); Romance languages (MA); Russian (MA, PhD); Semitic languages (MA, PhD); social behavior studies in HIV/AIDS (MA); social science (mental health) (MA); social science in development studies (MA); social science in psychology (MA); social science in social work (MA); social science in sociology (MA); social work (MSW, DSW, PhD); socio-education (M Ed, Ed D); sociolinguistics (MA); sociology (MA, PhD); Spanish (MA, PhD); systematic theology (M Th, D Th); TESOL (teaching English to speakers of other languages) (MA); theological ethics (M Th, D Th); theory of literature (MA, PhD); urban ministries (D Th); urban ministry (M Th).

The University of Texas at Austin, Graduate School, College of Liberal Arts, Department of Middle Eastern Studies, Austin, TX 78712-1111. Offers Arabic (MA, PhD); Hebrew (MA). *Degree requirements:* For master's, one foreign language, comprehensive exam, thesis; for doctorate, 2 foreign languages, comprehensive exam, thesis/dissertation. *Entrance requirements:* For master's and doctorate, GRE General Test. Additional exam requirements/recommendations for international students: Required—TOEFL. Electronic applications accepted. *Faculty research:*

Islamic studies, Persian language and literature, Hebrew language, Jewish studies, Arabic literature and language.

University of Utah, Graduate School, College of Humanities, Program in Middle East Studies, Salt Lake City, UT 84112. Offers anthropology (MA); Arabic (MA, PhD); Arabic and linguistics (MA, PhD); Hebrew (MA); history (MA, PhD); Persian (MA, PhD); political science (MA, PhD); Turkish (MA). *Students:* 20 full-time (10 women), 15 part-time (5 women), 8 international. Average age 33. 28 applicants, 29% accepted, 3 enrolled. In 2010, 3 master's awarded. Terminal master's awarded for partial completion of doctoral program. *Degree requirements:* For master's, 2 foreign languages, comprehensive exam, thesis optional; for doctorate, 3 foreign languages, comprehensive exam, thesis/dissertation. *Entrance requirements:* For master's, GRE General Test, minimum GPA of 3.2; for doctorate, GRE General Test, MA in Middle East studies or equivalent, minimum GPA of 3.2. Additional exam requirements/ recommendations for international students: Required—TOEFL (minimum score 580 paper-based; 237 computer-based; 92 iBT). *Application deadline:* For fall admission, 1/15 priority date for domestic and international students. Application fee: $55 ($65 for international students). Electronic applications accepted. *Expenses:* Tuition, area resident: Part-time $179.19 per credit hour. Tuition, state resident: full-time $4384. Tuition, nonresident: full-time $16,684; part-time $630.67 per credit hour. Required fees: $350 per semester. Tuition and fees vary according to course load, degree level and program. *Financial support:* In 2010–11, 17 students received support, including 11 fellowships with full tuition reimbursements available (averaging $14,000 per year), 6 teaching assistantships with full tuition reimbursements available (averaging $12,000 per year); unspecified assistantships also available. Financial award application deadline: 1/15. *Faculty research:* Arabic linguistics; Islamic studies; Middle Eastern history; political science; Judaic studies; anthropology; Arabic, Persian, Hebrew, and Turkish language and literature. *Application contact:* Peter von Sivers, Director of Graduate Studies, 801-581-8073, Fax: 801-581-6183, E-mail: peter.vonsivers@utah.edu.

University of Wisconsin–Madison, Graduate School, College of Letters and Science, Department of Hebrew and Semitic Studies, Madison, WI 53706-1380. Offers MA, PhD. Terminal master's awarded for partial completion of doctoral program. *Degree requirements:* For master's, 2 foreign languages; for doctorate, thesis/dissertation. *Entrance requirements:* For master's and doctorate, GRE. Electronic applications accepted. *Expenses:* Tuition, state resident: full-time $9887; part-time $617.96 per credit. Tuition, nonresident: full-time $24,054; part-time $1503.40 per credit. Required fees: $67.63 per credit. Tuition and fees vary according to reciprocity agreements. *Faculty research:* Biblical language and literature, Northwest Semitic languages.

Wayne State University, College of Liberal Arts and Sciences, Program in Language Learning, Detroit, MI 48202. Offers Arabic (MA); French (MA); German (MA); Italian (MA); Latin (MA); Spanish (MA). *Faculty:* 1 full-time (0 women), 1 (woman) part-time/adjunct. *Students:* 1 (woman) full-time, 12 part-time (11 women), 1 international. Average age 32. 4 applicants, 100% accepted, 3 enrolled. In 2010, 2 master's awarded. *Expenses:* Tuition, state resident: full-time $7662; part-time $478.85 per credit hour. Tuition, nonresident: full-time $16,920; part-time $1057.55 per credit hour. Required fees: $571.20; $35.70 per credit hour. $188.05 per semester. Tuition and fees vary according to course load and program. *Financial support:* In 2010–11, 1 teaching assistantship (averaging $14,620 per year) was awarded. *Unit head:* Robert Thomas, Dean, 313-577-2519, Fax: 313-577-8971, E-mail: aa0817@wayne.edu. *Application contact:* Janet Hankin, Professor, 313-577-0841, E-mail: janet.hankin@wayne.edu.

Yale University, Graduate School of Arts and Sciences, Department of Near Eastern Languages and Civilizations, New Haven, CT 06520. Offers Arabic and Islamic studies (MA, PhD); archaeology of the ancient Near East (MA, PhD); Assyriology (MA, PhD); Egyptology (MA, PhD); Graeco-Arabic studies (MA, PhD); Northwest Semitic, Bible, comparative Semitics (MA, PhD). *Degree requirements:* For doctorate, 2 foreign languages, thesis/dissertation. *Entrance requirements:* For doctorate, GRE General Test.

Portuguese

Brigham Young University, Graduate Studies, College of Humanities, Department of Spanish and Portuguese, Provo, UT 84602. Offers Hispanic literature (MA); Portuguese linguistics (MA); Portuguese literature (MA); Spanish linguistics (MA); Spanish teaching (MA). Part-time programs available. *Faculty:* 32 full-time (5 women). *Students:* 15 full-time (6 women), 25 part-time (12 women); includes 9 Hispanic/Latino; 1 Native Hawaiian or other Pacific Islander, non-Hispanic/Latino. Average age 30. 23 applicants, 65% accepted, 12 enrolled. In 2010, 11 master's awarded. *Degree requirements:* For master's, one foreign language, comprehensive exam, thesis, 1 semester of teaching. *Entrance requirements:* For master's, minimum GPA of 3.5 in Spanish or Portuguese, 3.3 overall. Additional exam requirements/recommendations for international students: Required—TOEFL (minimum score 580 paper-based; 237 computer-based). *Application deadline:* For fall admission, 2/1 for domestic and international students. Application fee: $50. Electronic applications accepted. *Expenses:* Tuition: Full-time $5580; part-time $310 per credit hour. Tuition and fees vary according to program and student's religious affiliation. *Financial support:* In 2010–11, 39 students received support, including 46 teaching assistantships with partial tuition reimbursements available (averaging $10,470 per year); institutionally sponsored loans, scholarships/grants, tuition waivers (partial), and unspecified assistantships also available. Support available to part-time students. Financial award application deadline: 7/1. *Faculty research:* Mexican prose; Latin American theater, literature, phonetics, and phonology; pedagogy; classical Portuguese literature; Peninsular prose and theater. *Unit head:* Dr. Alvin F. Sherman, Chair, 801-422-3107, Fax: 801-422-0628, E-mail: alvin_sherman@byu.edu. *Application contact:* Jasmine S. Talbot, Graduate Secretary, 801-422-2196, Fax: 801-422-0628, E-mail: jasmine_talbot@byu.edu.

Emory University, Laney Graduate School, Department of Spanish and Portuguese, Atlanta, GA 30322-1100. Offers comparative literature (Certificate); film studies (Certificate); Spanish (PhD); women's studies (Certificate). *Degree requirements:* For doctorate, 2 foreign languages, comprehensive exam, thesis/dissertation. *Entrance requirements:* For doctorate, GRE General Test. Additional exam requirements/recommendations for international students: Required—TOEFL. Electronic applications accepted. *Expenses:* Tuition: Full-time $33,800. Required fees: $1300. *Faculty research:* Spanish literature, Spanish-American literature, literary theory, criticism, cultural studies.

Harvard University, Graduate School of Arts and Sciences, Department of Romance Languages and Literatures, Cambridge, MA 02138. Offers French (AM, PhD); Italian (AM, PhD); Portuguese (AM, PhD); Spanish (AM, PhD). Terminal master's awarded for partial completion of doctoral program. *Degree requirements:* For master's, 2 foreign languages; for doctorate, 2 foreign languages, thesis/dissertation. *Entrance requirements:* For master's and doctorate, GRE General Test, sample of written work. Additional exam requirements/recommendations for international students: Required—TOEFL. *Expenses:* Tuition: Full-time $34,976. Required fees: $1166. Full-time tuition and fees vary according to program.

Indiana University Bloomington, University Graduate School, College of Arts and Sciences, Department of Spanish and Portuguese, Bloomington, IN 47405-7000. Offers Portuguese (MA, PhD); Spanish (MA, PhD), including Hispanic linguistics, literatures in Spanish. *Faculty:* 23 full-time (13 women). *Students:* 87 full-time (48 women); includes 24 minority (1 Black or African American, non-Hispanic/Latino; 1 Asian, non-Hispanic/Latino; 19 Hispanic/Latino; 2 Native Hawaiian or other Pacific Islander, non-Hispanic/Latino; 1 Two or more races, non-Hispanic/Latino), 8 international. Average age 31. 75 applicants, 45% accepted, 18 enrolled. In 2010, 8 master's, 5 doctorates awarded. *Degree requirements:* For master's, one foreign language, comprehensive exam, thesis (optional for Portuguese); for doctorate, 2 foreign languages, comprehensive exam, thesis/dissertation. *Entrance requirements:* For master's, GRE General Test, bachelor's degree in Portuguese or Spanish, minimum GPA of 3.25; for doctorate, GRE General Test, master's degree in Portuguese or Spanish, minimum GPA of 3.25. Additional exam requirements/recommendations for international students: Required—TOEFL (minimum score 213 computer-based; 79 iBT). *Application deadline:* For fall admission, 1/15 priority date for domestic students, 12/15 priority date for international students. Application fee: $55 ($65 for international students). *Financial support:* In 2010–11, 2 fellowships with full tuition reimbursements (averaging $14,790 per year), 50 teaching assistantships with full tuition reimbursements (averaging $14,790 per year) were awarded; research assistantships, scholarships/grants, health care benefits, and unspecified assistantships also available. Financial award application deadline: 1/15. *Faculty research:* Spanish-American literature, Spanish peninsular literature, Hispanic linguistics, Luso-Brazilian studies, Catalan studies. *Unit head:* Catherine Larson, Chair, 812-855-8498, E-mail: larson@indiana.edu. *Application contact:* Patrick Dove, Director of Graduate Studies, 812-855-9194, E-mail: pdove@indiana.edu.

Michigan State University, The Graduate School, College of Arts and Letters, Department of Spanish and Portuguese, East Lansing, MI 48824. Offers applied Spanish linguistics (MA); Hispanic cultural studies (PhD); Hispanic literatures (MA). *Entrance requirements:* Additional exam requirements/recommendations for international students: Required—TOEFL. Electronic applications accepted.

New York University, Graduate School of Arts and Science, Department of Spanish and Portuguese Languages and Literatures, New York, NY 10012-1019. Offers Portuguese (MA, PhD); Spanish (PhD); Spanish and Latin American literatures and cultures (MA); Spanish language and translation (MA). Part-time programs available. *Students:* 99 full-time (55 women), 12 part-time (9 women); includes 3 Black or African American, non-Hispanic/Latino; 4 Asian, non-Hispanic/Latino; 30 Hispanic/Latino, 48 international. Average age 31. 189 applicants, 42% accepted, 48 enrolled. In 2010, 39 master's, 4 doctorates awarded. *Degree requirements:* For master's, 2 foreign languages, thesis; for doctorate, 2 foreign languages, thesis/dissertation. *Entrance requirements:* For master's, GRE General Test; for doctorate, GRE General Test, master's degree. Additional exam requirements/recommendations for international students: Required—TOEFL. *Application deadline:* For fall admission, 1/4 priority date for domestic students. Application fee: $90. *Financial support:* Fellowships with tuition reimbursements, teaching assistantships with tuition reimbursements, career-related internships or fieldwork, Federal Work-Study, institutionally sponsored loans, scholarships/grants, health care benefits, and unspecified assistantships available. Financial award application deadline: 1/4; financial award applicants required to submit FAFSA. *Faculty research:* Gender and sexuality, transatlantic studies, literacy and cultural theories, colonial and post colonial studies, autobiography and modern subjectivities. *Unit head:* Jo Labanyi, Acting Chair, 212-998-8770, Fax: 212-995-4149, E-mail: spanish.portuguese.info@nyu.edu. *Application contact:* Gabriel Giorgi, Director of Graduate Studies, 212-998-8770, Fax: 212-995-4149, E-mail: spanish.portuguese.info@nyu.edu.

The Ohio State University, Graduate School, College of Arts and Sciences, Division of Arts and Humanities, Department of Spanish and Portuguese, Columbus, OH 43210. Offers MA, PhD. *Faculty:* 22. *Students:* 57 full-time (37 women), 10 part-time (6 women); includes 1 Black or African American, non-Hispanic/Latino; 1 Asian, non-Hispanic/Latino; 10 Hispanic/Latino, 18 international. Average age 31. In 2010, 9 master's, 13 doctorates awarded. *Degree requirements:* For master's, thesis optional; for doctorate, thesis/dissertation. *Entrance requirements:* For master's and doctorate, GRE General Test. Additional exam requirements/recommendations for international students: Required—TOEFL (minimum score 600 paper-based; 250 computer-based). *Application deadline:* For fall admission, 8/15 priority date for domestic students, 7/1 priority date for international students; for winter admission, 12/1 priority date for domestic students, 11/1 priority date for international students; for spring admission, 3/1 priority date for domestic students, 2/1 priority date for international students. Applications are processed on a rolling basis. Application fee: $40 ($50 for international students). Electronic applications accepted. *Expenses:* Tuition, state resident: full-time $10,605. Tuition, nonresident: full-time $26,535. Tuition and fees vary according to course load and program. *Financial support:* Fellowships, research assistantships, teaching assistantships, Federal Work-Study, institutionally sponsored loans, and unspecified assistantships available. Support available to part-time students. *Unit head:* Fernando Unzueta, Chair, 614-292-4958, E-mail: unzueta.1@osu.edu. *Application contact:* 614-292-9444, Fax: 614-292-3895, E-mail: domestic.grad@osu.edu.

Princeton University, Graduate School, Department of Spanish and Portuguese Languages and Cultures, Princeton, NJ 08544-1019. Offers PhD. *Degree requirements:* For doctorate, variable foreign language requirement, thesis/dissertation. *Entrance requirements:* For doctorate, GRE General Test, sample of written work. Additional exam requirements/recommendations for international students: Required—TOEFL (minimum score 600 paper-based; 250 computer-based). Electronic applications accepted.

Tulane University, School of Liberal Arts, Department of Spanish and Portuguese, New Orleans, LA 70118-5669. Offers Portuguese (MA); Spanish (MA); Spanish and Portuguese (PhD). *Degree requirements:* For master's, 2 foreign languages; for doctorate, 2 foreign languages, thesis/dissertation. *Entrance requirements:* For master's, GRE General Test, minimum B average in undergraduate course work; for doctorate, GRE General Test. Additional exam requirements/recommendations for international students: Required—TOEFL. Electronic applications accepted.

University of California, Los Angeles, Graduate Division, College of Letters and Science, Department of Spanish and Portuguese, Program in Portuguese, Los Angeles, CA 90095. Offers MA. *Degree requirements:* For master's, one foreign language, comprehensive exam or thesis. *Entrance requirements:* For master's, GRE General Test, minimum GPA of 3.0, sample of written work (recommended). *Application deadline:* For fall admission, 12/31 for domestic and international students. Application fee: $70 ($90 for international students). Electronic applications accepted. *Financial support:* Fellowships with full and partial tuition reimbursements, research assistantships with full and partial tuition reimbursements, teaching assistantships with full and partial tuition reimbursements, Federal Work-Study, scholarships/grants, health care benefits, tuition waivers (full and partial), and unspecified assistantships available. Financial award applicants required to submit FAFSA. *Unit head:* Dr. Maarten Van Delden, Chair, 310-825-1220, E-mail: mvandelden@humnet.ucla.edu. *Application contact:* Department Office, 310-825-1036, E-mail: peinado@humnet.ucla.edu.

University of California, Santa Barbara, Graduate Division, College of Letters and Sciences, Division of Humanities and Fine Arts, Department of Spanish and Portuguese, Santa Barbara, CA 93106-4150. Offers Hispanic languages and literature (PhD), including European medieval studies, feminist studies, Hispanic linguistics, Hispanic literature, Luso-Brazilian literature; Hispanic linguistics (MA); Luso-Brazilian literature (MA); Spanish or Spanish-American literature (MA); MA/PhD. Spanish Language Institute available during summer session. *Faculty:* 16 full-time (7 women). *Students:* 32 full-time (22 women); includes 1 Black or African American, non-Hispanic/Latino; 1 Asian, non-Hispanic/Latino; 9 Hispanic/Latino. Average age 32. 34 applicants, 26% accepted, 5 enrolled. In 2010, 3 master's, 3 doctorates awarded. Terminal master's awarded for partial completion of doctoral program. *Degree requirements:* For master's, 2 foreign languages, comprehensive exam (for some programs), thesis optional; for doctorate, 3 foreign languages, comprehensive exam, thesis/dissertation. *Entrance requirements:* For master's and doctorate, GRE. Additional exam requirements/recommendations for international students: Required—TOEFL (minimum score 550 paper-based; 80 iBT), IELTS (minimum score 7). *Application deadline:* For fall admission, 12/15 for domestic and international students. Application fee: $70 ($90 for international students). Electronic applications accepted. *Financial support:* In 2010–11, 32 students received support, including 12 fellowships with full and partial tuition reimbursements available (averaging $10,016 per year), 27 teaching assistantships with full and partial tuition reimbursements available (averaging $14,583 per year); career-related internships or fieldwork, Federal Work-Study, tuition waivers (full and partial), and unspecified assistantships also available. Financial award application deadline: 12/15; financial award applicants required to submit FAFSA. *Faculty research:* Nineteenth century Spanish and Portuguese literature, Spanish and Spanish American literature, nineteenth and twentieth century Portuguese and Brazilian literatures, Hispanic linguistics, Catalan language and culture. *Unit head:* Prof. Francisco A. Lomeli, Chair, 805-893-5715, Fax: 805-893-8341, E-mail: lomeli@spanport.ucsb.edu. *Application contact:* Ashley Bradbury, Graduate Program Assistant, 805-893-2131, Fax: 805-893-8341, E-mail: ashley@hfa.ucsb.edu.

University of Illinois at Urbana–Champaign, Graduate College, College of Liberal Arts and Sciences, School of Literatures, Cultures and Linguistics, Department of Spanish, Italian and Portuguese, Champaign, IL 61820. Offers Italian (MA, PhD); Portuguese (MA, PhD); Spanish (MA, PhD). *Faculty:* 17 full-time (10 women). *Students:* 39 full-time (29 women), 2 part-time (both women); includes 14 minority (all Hispanic/Latino), 16 international. 52 applicants, 23% accepted, 3 enrolled. In 2010, 12 master's, 6 doctorates awarded. *Entrance requirements:* For master's, GRE General Test, minimum GPA of 3.0; writing sample; for doctorate, GRE, minimum GPA of 3.0; writing sample. Additional exam requirements/recommendations for international students: Required—TOEFL (minimum score 88 iBT). *Application deadline:* Applications are processed on a rolling basis. Application fee: $75 ($90 for international students). Electronic applications accepted. *Financial support:* In 2010–11, 7 fellowships, 2 research assistantships, 39 teaching assistantships were awarded; tuition waivers (full and partial) also available. *Unit head:* Diane Musumeci, Head, 217-333-3390, Fax: 217-244-8430, E-mail: musumeci@illinois.edu. *Application contact:* Lynn Stanke, Office Support Specialist, 217-333-6269, Fax: 217-244-3050, E-mail: stanke@illinois.edu.

University of Maryland, College Park, Academic Affairs, College of Arts and Humanities, School of Languages, Literature, and Cultures, Department of Spanish and Portuguese, College Park, MD 20742. Offers MA, PhD. *Students:* 33 full-time (25 women), 2 part-time (1 woman); includes 6 Hispanic/Latino, 16 international. 35 applicants, 46% accepted, 5 enrolled. In 2010, 4 master's, 3 doctorates awarded. *Degree requirements:* For master's, comprehensive exam, thesis optional, scholarly paper; for doctorate, 2 foreign languages, thesis/dissertation. *Entrance requirements:* For master's, minimum GPA of 3.0, interview, sample research paper, minimum of 12 credits in upper-level literature, 3 letters of recommendation; for doctorate, minimum GPA of 3.0, interview, sample research paper, minimum of 12 credits in upper-level literature. Additional exam requirements/recommendations for international students: Required—TOEFL. *Application deadline:* For fall admission, 1/7 for domestic and international students; for spring admission, 6/1 for international students. Applications are processed on a rolling basis. Application fee: $75. Electronic applications accepted. *Expenses:* Tuition, state resident: part-time $471 per credit hour. Tuition, nonresident: part-time $1016 per credit hour. Required fees: $337 per term. *Financial support:* In 2010–11, 7 fellowships with partial tuition reimbursements (averaging $9,891 per year), 17 teaching assistantships (averaging $19,772 per year) were awarded; Federal Work-Study also available. Support available to part-time students. Financial award applicants required to submit FAFSA. *Unit head:* Carol A. Mossman, Director, School of Languages, Literatures, and Cultures, 301-405-4025, Fax: 301-314-9928, E-mail: cmossman@umd.edu. *Application contact:* Dr. Charles A. Caramello, Dean of Graduate School, 301-405-0358, Fax: 301-314-9305, E-mail: ccaramel@umd.edu.

University of Massachusetts Amherst, Graduate School, College of Humanities and Fine Arts, Department of Languages, Literatures, and Cultures, Programs in Hispanic Literatures, Cultures and Linguistics, Amherst, MA 01003. Offers Hispanic literatures, cultures and linguistics (MA, PhD); teaching Spanish (MAT). Part-time programs available. *Faculty:* 13 full-time (6 women). *Students:* 25 full-time (19 women), 29 part-time (16 women); includes 17 minority (1 Asian, non-Hispanic/Latino; 16 Hispanic/Latino), 19 international. Average age 35. 42 applicants, 60% accepted, 14 enrolled. In 2010, 9 master's, 3 doctorates awarded. Terminal master's awarded for partial completion of doctoral program. *Degree requirements:* For master's, one foreign language, thesis or alternative; for doctorate, 2 foreign languages, comprehensive exam, thesis/dissertation. *Entrance requirements:* For master's and doctorate, GRE General Test, sample academic term paper. Additional exam requirements/recommendations for international students: Required—TOEFL (minimum score 550 paper-based; 213 computer-based; 80 iBT), IELTS (minimum score 6.5). *Application deadline:* For fall admission, 2/1 for domestic and international students. Applications are processed on a rolling basis. Application fee: $50 ($65 for international students). Electronic applications accepted. *Expenses:* Tuition, state resident: full-time $2640. Required fees: $8282. One-time fee: $357 full-time. *Financial support:* In 2010–11, 32 teaching assistantships with full tuition reimbursements (averaging $15,272 per year) were awarded; fellowships, research assistantships, career-related internships or fieldwork, Federal Work-Study, scholarships/grants, traineeships, health care benefits, tuition waivers (full), and unspecified assistantships also available. Support available to part-time students. Financial award application deadline: 2/1; financial award applicants required to submit FAFSA. *Unit head:* Dr. Frank C. Fagundes, Graduate Program Director, 413-545-0544, Fax: 413-545-3178. *Application contact:* Jean M. Ames, Supervisor of Admissions, 413-545-0722, Fax: 413-577-0010, E-mail: gradadm@grad.umass.edu.

University of Massachusetts Dartmouth, Graduate School, College of Arts and Sciences, Department of Portuguese, North Dartmouth, MA 02747-2300. Offers Luso-Afro-Brazilian studies (PhD); Portuguese (MA). Part-time programs available. *Faculty:* 6 full-time (2 women), 1 part-time/adjunct (0 women). *Students:* 12 full-time (9 women), 13 part-time (7 women); includes 5 minority (1 Black or African American, non-Hispanic/Latino; 4 Hispanic/Latino), 5 international. Average age 35. 18 applicants, 83% accepted, 9 enrolled. In 2010, 5 master's awarded. *Degree requirements:* For master's, comprehensive exam (for some programs). *Entrance requirements:* For master's, GRE (recommended), 10 page writing sample; for doctorate, GRE. Additional exam requirements/recommendations for international students: Required—TOEFL (minimum score 500 paper-based). *Application deadline:* For fall admission, 4/20 priority date for domestic students, 2/20 priority date for international students; for spring admission, 11/15 priority date for domestic students, 9/15 priority date for international students. Applications are processed on a rolling basis. Application fee: $40 ($60 for international students). Electronic applications accepted. *Expenses:* Tuition, state resident: full-time $2071; part-time $86 per credit. Tuition, nonresident: full-time $8099; part-time $337 per credit. Required fees: $9446; $394 per credit. One-time fee: $75. Part-time tuition and fees vary according to class time, course load, degree level and reciprocity agreements. *Financial support:* In 2010–11, 2 research assistantships with full tuition reimbursements (averaging $18,558 per year), 8 teaching assistantships with full tuition reimbursements (averaging $15,000 per year) were awarded. Financial award application deadline: 3/1; financial award applicants required to submit FAFSA. *Faculty research:* Translation studies, ethnicity and migration, literature in Luso-Afro-Brazilian studies, anaphoric direct objects in Portuguese. *Unit head:* Victor J. Mendes, Director, Graduate Studies, 508-999-8338, Fax: 508-999-9272, E-mail: vmendes@umassd.edu. *Application contact:* Elan Turcotte-Shamski, Graduate Admissions Officer, 508-999-8604, Fax: 508-999-8183, E-mail: graduate@umassd.edu.

University of Minnesota, Twin Cities Campus, Graduate School, College of Liberal Arts, Department of Spanish and Portuguese Studies, Minneapolis, MN 55455-0213. Offers Hispanic and Lusophone literatures, cultures and linguistics (PhD); Hispanic linguistics (MA); Hispanic literature (MA); Lusophone literature (MA). *Degree requirements:* For master's, 2 foreign languages, comprehensive exam, thesis or alternative; for doctorate, 2 foreign languages, comprehensive exam, thesis/dissertation. *Entrance requirements:* For master's and doctorate, GRE General Test, samples of written work, 3 letters of recommendation, voice sample, statement of purpose. Additional exam requirements/recommendations for international students: Required—TOEFL (minimum score 550 paper-based; 213 computer-based; 79 iBT). Electronic applications accepted. *Faculty research:* Sociohistorical approaches to literature and culture, feminist studies, literary theory, ideologies and literature, pragmatics and sociolinguistics.

University of New Mexico, Graduate School, College of Arts and Sciences, Department of Spanish and Portuguese, Albuquerque, NM 87131-2039. Offers Portuguese (MA); Spanish (MA); Spanish and Portuguese (PhD). Part-time programs available. *Faculty:* 24 full-time (14 women), 60 part-time/adjunct (39 women). *Students:* 51 full-time (35 women), 9 part-time (8 women); includes 1 Black or African American, non-Hispanic/Latino; 36 Hispanic/Latino, 12 international. Average age 34. 45 applicants, 53% accepted, 14 enrolled. In 2010, 9 master's, 1 doctorate awarded. *Degree requirements:* For master's, one foreign language, comprehensive exam, thesis optional; for doctorate, one foreign language, comprehensive exam, thesis/dissertation. *Entrance requirements:* For master's, Versant test for Teaching assistantship, BA in Spanish or Portuguese, 3 letters of recommendation, letter of intent; for doctorate, GRE, Versant test for Teaching assistantship, 3 letters of recommendation, letter of intent, sample research paper. Additional exam requirements/recommendations for international students: Required—TOEFL (minimum score 550 paper-based; 213 computer-based). *Application deadline:* For fall admission, 1/15 priority date for domestic students; for spring admission, 11/15 for domestic students. Applications are processed on a rolling basis. Application fee: $50. Electronic applications accepted. *Expenses:* Tuition, state resident: full-time $5991; part-time $251 per credit hour. Tuition, nonresident: full-time $14,405; part-time $800.20 per credit hour. Tuition and fees vary according to course level, course load, program and reciprocity agreements. *Financial support:* In 2010–11, 53 students received support, including 2 fellowships (averaging $9,350 per year), 3 research assistantships (averaging $5,067 per year), 45 teaching assistantships with full tuition reimbursements available (averaging $12,773 per year); Federal Work-Study, institutionally sponsored loans, scholarships/grants, health care benefits, and unspecified assistantships also available. Support available to part-time students. Financial award application deadline: 3/1; financial award applicants required to submit FAFSA. *Faculty research:* Languages and literatures from the Iberian Peninsula, Latin America and the American Southwest. *Unit head:* Dr. Enrique Lamadrid, Chair, 505-277-5907, Fax: 505-277-3885, E-mail: lamadrid@unm.edu. *Application contact:* Martha Hurd, Graduate Administration Assistant, 505-277-2974, E-mail: marthah@unm.edu.

The University of North Carolina at Chapel Hill, Graduate School, College of Arts and Sciences, Department of Romance Languages, Chapel Hill, NC 27599. Offers French (MA, PhD); Italian (MA, PhD); Portuguese (MA, PhD); Romance languages (MA, PhD); Romance philology (MA, PhD); Spanish (MA, PhD). *Degree requirements:* For master's, one foreign language, comprehensive exam, thesis; for doctorate, 2 foreign languages, comprehensive exam, thesis/dissertation. *Entrance requirements:* For master's and doctorate, GRE General Test, minimum GPA of 3.0. Additional exam requirements/recommendations for international students: Required—TOEFL (minimum score 550 paper-based; 213 computer-based). Electronic applications accepted.

University of South Africa, College of Human Sciences, Pretoria, South Africa. Offers adult education (M Ed); African languages (MA, PhD); African politics (MA, PhD); Afrikaans (MA, PhD); ancient history (MA, PhD); ancient Near Eastern studies (MA, PhD); anthropology (MA, PhD); applied linguistics (MA); Arabic (MA, PhD); archaeology (MA); art history (MA); Biblical archaeology (MA); Biblical studies (M Th, D Th, PhD); Christian spirituality (M Th, D Th); church history (M Th, D Th); classical studies (MA, PhD); clinical psychology (MA); communication (MA, PhD); comparative education (M Ed, Ed D); consulting psychology (D Admin, D Com, PhD); curriculum studies (M Ed, Ed D); development studies (M Admin, MA, D Admin,

Portuguese

University of South Africa (continued)
PhD); didactics (M Ed, Ed D); education (M Tech); education management (M Ed, Ed D); educational psychology (M Ed); English (MA); environmental education (M Ed); French (MA, PhD); German (MA, PhD); Greek (MA); guidance and counseling (M Ed); health studies (MA, PhD), including health sciences education (MA), health services management (MA), medical and surgical nursing science (critical care general) (MA), midwifery and neonatal nursing science (MA), trauma and emergency care (MA); history (MA, PhD); history of education (Ed D); inclusive education (M Ed, Ed D); information and communications technology policy and regulation (MA); information science (MA, MIS, PhD); international politics (MA, PhD); Islamic studies (MA, PhD); Italian (MA, PhD); Judaica (MA, PhD); linguistics (MA, PhD); mathematical education (M Ed); mathematics education (MA); missiology (M Th, D Th); modern Hebrew (MA, PhD); musicology (MA, MMus, D Mus, PhD); natural science education (M Ed); New Testament (M Th, D Th); Old Testament (D Th); pastoral therapy (M Th, D Th); philosophy (MA); philosophy of education (M Ed, Ed D); politics (MA, PhD); Portuguese (MA, PhD); practical theology (M Th, D Th); psychology (MA, MS, PhD); psychology of education (M Ed, Ed D); public health (MA); religious studies (MA, D Th, PhD); Romance languages (MA); Russian (MA, PhD); Semitic languages (MA, PhD); social behavior studies in HIV/AIDS (MA); social science (mental health) (MA); social science in development studies (MA); social science in psychology (MA); social science in social work (MA); social science in sociology (MA); social work (MSW, DSW, PhD); socio-education (M Ed, Ed D); sociolinguistics (MA); sociology (MA, PhD); Spanish (MA, PhD); systematic theology (M Th, D Th); TESOL (teaching English to speakers of other languages) (MA); theological ethics (M Th, D Th); theory of literature (MA, PhD); urban ministries (D Th); urban ministry (M Th).

The University of Tennessee, Graduate School, College of Arts and Sciences, Department of Modern Foreign Languages and Literatures, Program in Modern Foreign Languages, Knoxville, TN 37996. Offers applied linguistics (PhD); French (PhD); German (PhD); Italian (PhD); Portuguese (PhD); Russian (PhD); Spanish (PhD). *Degree requirements:* For doctorate, 2 foreign languages, thesis/dissertation. *Entrance requirements:* For doctorate, minimum GPA of 2.7. Additional exam requirements/recommendations for international students: Required—TOEFL. Electronic applications accepted. *Expenses:* Tuition, state resident: full-time $7440; part-time $414 per credit hour. Tuition, nonresident: full-time $22,478; part-time $1250 per credit hour. Required fees: $922; $43 per credit hour. Tuition and fees vary according to program.

The University of Texas at Austin, Graduate School, College of Liberal Arts, Department of Spanish and Portuguese, Austin, TX 78712-1111. Offers Hispanic linguistics (MA, PhD); Hispanic literature (MA, PhD); Luso-Brazilian literature (MA, PhD). *Degree requirements:* For master's, 2 foreign languages, thesis or alternative; for doctorate, 3 foreign languages, thesis/dissertation. *Entrance requirements:* For master's and doctorate, GRE General Test. Electronic applications accepted.

University of Toronto, School of Graduate Studies, Humanities Division, Department of Spanish and Portuguese, Toronto, ON M5S 1A1, Canada. Offers MA, PhD. Part-time programs available. *Degree requirements:* For doctorate, thesis/dissertation. *Entrance requirements:* For master's, minimum B average in final year, 2 letters of reference; for doctorate, minimum A– average, 2 letters of reference, writing sample. Additional exam requirements/recommendations for international students: Required—TOEFL, Michigan English Language Assessment Battery, IELTS or COPE.

University of Washington, Graduate School, College of Arts and Sciences, Department of Romance Languages and Literature, Division of Spanish and Portuguese Studies, Seattle, WA 98195. Offers Hispanic literary and cultural studies (MA). *Degree requirements:* For master's, 2 foreign languages, thesis optional, exam. *Entrance requirements:* For master's, GRE General Test, minimum GPA of 3.0. Additional exam requirements/recommendations for international students: Required—TOEFL. Electronic applications accepted. *Faculty research:* Medieval through modern Spanish literature and film, Latin American literature, poetry and essay, pan-Hispanic ballad, Hispanic cultural studies, second language acquisition and applied linguistics.

University of Wisconsin–Madison, Graduate School, College of Letters and Science, Department of Spanish and Portuguese, Program in Portuguese, Madison, WI 53706-1380. Offers MA, PhD. *Degree requirements:* For master's, one foreign language; for doctorate, 2 foreign languages, thesis/dissertation. *Entrance requirements:* For master's, GRE (recommended), minimum GPA of 3.25 in Spanish or Portuguese; for doctorate, GRE (recommended), minimum graduate GPA of 3.4. Additional exam requirements/recommendations for international students: Required—TOEFL. Electronic applications accepted. *Expenses:* Tuition, state resident: full-time $9887; part-time $617.96 per credit. Tuition, nonresident: full-time $24,054; part-time $1503.40 per credit. Required fees: $67.63 per credit. Tuition and fees vary according to reciprocity agreements. *Faculty research:* Portuguese and Brazilian literature.

Vanderbilt University, Graduate School, Department of Spanish and Portuguese, Nashville, TN 37240-1001. Offers Portuguese (MA); Spanish (MA, MAT, PhD); Spanish and Portuguese (PhD). *Faculty:* 14 full-time (6 women). *Students:* 27 full-time (14 women); includes 1 Black or African American, non-Hispanic/Latino; 3 Hispanic/Latino. Average age 31. 56 applicants, 13% accepted, 5 enrolled. In 2010, 8 master's, 5 doctorates awarded. *Degree requirements:* For master's, one foreign language, thesis; for doctorate, 2 foreign languages, thesis/dissertation, final and qualifying exams. *Entrance requirements:* For master's, GRE General Test; for doctorate, GRE General Test, writing sample in Spanish. Additional exam requirements/recommendations for international students: Required—TOEFL (minimum score 570 paper-based; 230 computer-based; 88 iBT). *Application deadline:* For fall admission, 1/15 for domestic and international students. Application fee: $0. Electronic applications accepted. *Financial support:* Fellowships with full and partial tuition reimbursements, teaching assistantships with full tuition reimbursements, Federal Work-Study, institutionally sponsored loans, and health care benefits available. Financial award application deadline: 1/15; financial award applicants required to submit CSS PROFILE or FAFSA. *Faculty research:* Spanish, Portuguese, and Latin American literatures; foreign language pedagogy; Renaissance and Baroque poetry; nineteenth century Spanish novel. *Unit head:* Dr. Cathy L. Jrade, Chair, 615-322-6930, Fax: 615-343-7260, E-mail: cathy.l.jrade@vanderbilt.edu. *Application contact:* Dr. Christina Karageorgou-Bastea, Director of Graduate Studies, 615-343-4087, Fax: 615-343-7260, E-mail: christina.karageorgou@vanderbilt.edu.

Yale University, Graduate School of Arts and Sciences, Department of Spanish and Portuguese, New Haven, CT 06520. Offers Latin American literature (PhD); Luso-Brazilian and Spanish/Spanish American literatures (PhD); Spanish peninsular literature (PhD). Terminal master's awarded for partial completion of doctoral program. *Degree requirements:* For doctorate, 3 foreign languages, thesis/dissertation. *Entrance requirements:* For doctorate, GRE General Test.

Romance Languages

Appalachian State University, Cratis D. Williams Graduate School, Department of Foreign Languages and Literatures, Boone, NC 28608. Offers romance languages (MA), including Spanish or French teaching. Part-time programs available. Postbaccalaureate distance learning degree programs offered (no on-campus study). *Faculty:* 7 full-time (3 women). *Students:* 16 part-time (14 women); includes 1 Two or more races, non-Hispanic/Latino. 8 applicants, 100% accepted, 8 enrolled. In 2010, 6 master's awarded. *Degree requirements:* For master's, one foreign language, comprehensive exam, thesis optional. *Entrance requirements:* For master's, GRE General Test, 3 letters of recommendation. Additional exam requirements/recommendations for international students: Required—TOEFL (minimum score 570 paper-based; 230 computer-based; 79 iBT) or IELTS (minimum score 6.5). *Application deadline:* For fall admission, 7/1 for domestic students, 2/1 for international students; for spring admission, 11/1 for domestic students, 7/1 for international students. Applications are processed on a rolling basis. Application fee: $55. Electronic applications accepted. *Expenses:* Tuition, state resident: full-time $3428; part-time $428 per unit. Tuition, nonresident: full-time $14,518; part-time $1814 per unit. Required fees: $2320; $344 per unit. Tuition and fees vary according to campus/location. *Financial support:* In 2010–11, 1 research assistantship (averaging $7,000 per year) was awarded; fellowships, teaching assistantships, career-related internships or fieldwork and unspecified assistantships also available. Financial award application deadline: 4/1; financial award applicants required to submit FAFSA. *Faculty research:* French and Spanish literature, Latin American culture, teaching foreign languages. *Unit head:* Dr. James Fogelquist, Chairperson, 828-262-3096, Fax: 828-262-3095, E-mail: fogelquistjd@appstate.edu. *Application contact:* Dr. Beverly Moser, Graduate Coordinator, 828-262-2929, E-mail: moserba@appstate.edu.

Boston University, Graduate School of Arts and Sciences, Department of Romance Studies, Boston, MA 02215. Offers French language and literature (MA, PhD); Hispanic language and literatures (MA, PhD). *Students:* 43 full-time (37 women), 4 part-time (all women); includes 7 minority (6 Hispanic/Latino; 1 Two or more races, non-Hispanic/Latino), 13 international. Average age 31. 50 applicants, 58% accepted, 12 enrolled. In 2010, 8 master's, 3 doctorates awarded. Terminal master's awarded for partial completion of doctoral program. *Degree requirements:* For master's, one foreign language, comprehensive exam; for doctorate, 2 foreign languages, comprehensive exam, thesis/dissertation. *Entrance requirements:* For master's and doctorate, GRE General Test, sample of written work, 3 letters of recommendation. Additional exam requirements/recommendations for international students: Required—TOEFL (minimum score 550 paper-based; 213 computer-based). *Application deadline:* For fall admission, 4/15 for domestic and international students. Application fee: $70. Electronic applications accepted. *Expenses:* Tuition: Full-time $39,314; part-time $1228 per credit. Required fees: $40 per semester. *Financial support:* In 2010–11, 47 students received support, including 2 fellowships with full tuition reimbursements available (averaging $19,300 per year), 35 teaching assistantships with full tuition reimbursements available (averaging $18,800 per year); research assistantships, Federal Work-Study and scholarships/grants also available. Support available to part-time students. Financial award application deadline: 1/15; financial award applicants required to submit FAFSA. *Unit head:* James Iffland, Chairman, 617-353-6225, Fax: 617-353-6246, E-mail: Iffland@bu.edu. *Application contact:* Deanna Wong, Administrative Assistant, 617-353-2641, Fax: 617-353-6246, E-mail: dswong@bu.edu.

Clark Atlanta University, School of Arts and Sciences, Department of Foreign Languages, Atlanta, GA 30314. Offers Romance languages (MA, DAH). Part-time programs available. *Faculty:* 2 full-time (0 women). *Students:* 2 full-time (both women); includes both Black or African American, non-Hispanic/Latino. Average age 36. 1 applicant, 100% accepted, 1 enrolled. *Degree requirements:* For master's, one foreign language, thesis; for doctorate, 2 foreign languages, comprehensive exam, thesis/dissertation. *Entrance requirements:* For master's, GRE General Test, minimum GPA of 2.5. Additional exam requirements/recommendations for international students: Required—TOEFL (minimum score 500 paper-based; 173 computer-based; 61 iBT). *Application deadline:* For fall admission, 4/1 for domestic and international students; for spring admission, 11/1 for domestic and international students. Applications are processed on a rolling basis. Application fee: $40 ($55 for international students). *Expenses:* Tuition: Full-time $12,942; part-time $719 per credit hour. Required fees: $710; $355 per semester. *Financial support:* Scholarships/grants and unspecified assistantships available. Financial award application deadline: 4/30; financial award applicants required to submit FAFSA. *Unit head:* Dr. Laurent Monye, Chairperson, 404-880-8547, E-mail: lmonye@cau.edu. *Application contact:* Michelle Clark-Davis, Graduate Program Admissions, 404-880-6605, E-mail: cauadmissions@cau.edu.

Columbia University, Graduate School of Arts and Sciences, Division of Humanities, Department of French and Romance Philology, New York, NY 10027. Offers French and Romance philology (M Phil, PhD); Romance languages (MA). Part-time programs available. *Degree requirements:* For master's, one foreign language, thesis, written exam; for doctorate, 2 foreign languages, thesis/dissertation. *Entrance requirements:* For master's and doctorate, GRE General Test, knowledge of Latin, writing sample. Additional exam requirements/recommendations for international students: Required—TOEFL. *Faculty research:* Theory of literature, literary semiotics, poetics.

Cornell University, Graduate School, Graduate Fields of Arts and Sciences, Field of Linguistics, Ithaca, NY 14853-0001. Offers applied linguistics (MA, PhD); East Asian linguistics (MA, PhD); English linguistics (MA, PhD); general linguistics (MA, PhD); Germanic linguistics (MA, PhD); Indo-European linguistics (MA, PhD); phonetics (MA, PhD); phonological theory (MA, PhD); Romance linguistics (MA, PhD); second language acquisition (MA, PhD); semantics (MA, PhD); Slavic linguistics (MA, PhD); sociolinguistics (MA, PhD); South Asian linguistics (MA, PhD); Southeast Asian linguistics (MA, PhD); syntactic theory (MA, PhD). *Faculty:* 15 full-time (7 women). *Students:* 34 full-time (18 women); includes 3 Hispanic/Latino, 15 international. Average age 28. 111 applicants, 12% accepted, 8 enrolled. In 2010, 2 master's, 6 doctorates awarded. Terminal master's awarded for partial completion of doctoral program. *Degree requirements:* For master's, one foreign language, thesis; for doctorate, one foreign language, comprehensive exam, thesis/dissertation. *Entrance requirements:* For master's and doctorate, GRE General Test, 2 letters of recommendation. Additional exam requirements/recommendations for international students: Required—TOEFL (minimum score 600 paper-based; 250 computer-based; 77 iBT). *Application deadline:* For fall admission, 1/15 for domestic students. Application fee: $80. Electronic applications accepted. *Expenses:* Tuition: Full-time $29,500. Required fees: $76. Tuition and fees vary according to degree level and program. *Financial support:* In 2010–11, 17 fellowships with full tuition reimbursements, 1 research assistantship with full tuition reimbursement, 15 teaching assistantships with full tuition reimbursements were awarded; institutionally sponsored loans, scholarships/grants, health care benefits, tuition waivers (full and partial), and unspecified assistantships also available. Financial award applicants required to submit FAFSA. *Faculty research:* Phonology and phonetics, syntax and semantics, historical linguistics, philosophy of language, language acquisition. *Unit head:* Director of Graduate Studies, 607-255-1105. *Application contact:* Graduate Field Assistant, 607-255-1105, E-mail: lingfield@cornell.edu.

Cornell University, Graduate School, Graduate Fields of Arts and Sciences, Field of Romance Studies, Ithaca, NY 14853-0001. Offers French linguistics (PhD); French literature (PhD); Hispanic literature (PhD); Italian linguistics (PhD); Italian literature (PhD); Romance linguistics (PhD); Spanish linguistics (PhD). *Faculty:* 30 full-time (13 women). *Students:* 56 full-time (27 women); includes 11 Hispanic/Latino, 23 international. Average age 28. 95 applicants, 22% accepted, 10 enrolled. In 2010, 5 doctorates awarded. *Degree requirements:* For doctorate, 2 foreign languages, comprehensive exam, thesis/dissertation. *Entrance requirements:* For doctorate, GRE General Test, sample of written work, 3 letters of recommendation. Additional exam requirements/recommendations for international students: Required—TOEFL (minimum score 550 paper-based; 213 computer-based; 77 iBT). *Application deadline:* For fall admission, 1/15 for domestic students. Application fee: $80. Electronic applications accepted. *Expenses:* Tuition: Full-time $29,500. Required fees: $76. Tuition and fees vary according to degree level and program. *Financial support:* In 2010–11, 18 fellowships with full tuition reimbursements, 34 teaching assistantships with full tuition reimbursements were awarded; research assistantships with full tuition reimbursements, institutionally sponsored loans, scholarships/grants, health care benefits, tuition waivers (full and partial), and unspecified assistantships also available. Financial award applicants required to submit FAFSA. *Faculty research:* Literary theory, Hispanic studies, French studies, gender studies. *Unit head:* Director of Graduate Studies, 607-255-8222. *Application contact:* Graduate Field Assistant, 607-255-4246, E-mail: romance_studies@cornell.edu.

Hunter College of the City University of New York, Graduate School, School of Arts and Sciences, Department of Romance Languages, New York, NY 10021-5085. Offers French (MA), including French, French education; Italian (MA), including Italian, Italian education; Spanish (MA), including Spanish, Spanish education. Part-time and evening/weekend programs available. *Faculty:* 8 full-time (4 women). *Students:* 25 part-time (19 women); includes 1 Black or African American, non-Hispanic/Latino; 10 Hispanic/Latino, 2 international. Average age 32. 24 applicants, 33% accepted, 7 enrolled. In 2010, 11 master's awarded. *Degree requirements:* For master's, 2 foreign languages, comprehensive exam, thesis optional. *Entrance requirements:* For master's, GRE General Test, GRE Subject Test, interview, proficiency in chosen language. Additional exam requirements/recommendations for international students: Required—TOEFL. *Application deadline:* For fall admission, 4/1 for domestic students, 2/1 for international students; for spring admission, 11/1 for domestic students, 9/1 for international students. Application fee: $125. *Financial support:* Fellowships, Federal Work-Study, scholarships/grants, and tuition waivers (partial) available. Support available to part-time students. Financial award application deadline: 4/15. *Unit head:* Dr. Giuseppe Carlo DiScipio, Chair, 212-772-5108, Fax: 212-772-5094, E-mail: gdiscipi@hunter.cuny.edu. *Application contact:* William Zlata, Director for Graduate Admissions, 212-772-4482, Fax: 212-650-3336, E-mail: admissions@hunter.cuny.edu.

The Johns Hopkins University, Zanvyl Krieger School of Arts and Sciences, Department of German and Romance Languages and Literatures, Baltimore, MD 21218-2699. Offers French (PhD); German (PhD); Italian (PhD); romance languages (PhD); Spanish (PhD). *Faculty:* 31 full-time (20 women), 1 part-time/adjunct (0 women). *Students:* 52 full-time (31 women); includes 7 minority (6 Hispanic/Latino; 1 Two or more races, non-Hispanic/Latino), 20 international. Average age 30. 51 applicants, 37% accepted, 19 enrolled. In 2010, 6 doctorates awarded. *Degree requirements:* For doctorate, 2 foreign languages, thesis/dissertation. *Entrance requirements:* For doctorate, GRE General Test. Additional exam requirements/recommendations for international students: Required—TOEFL (minimum score 600 paper-based; 250 computer-based; 100 iBT), IELTS. *Application deadline:* For fall admission, 12/30 for domestic and international students. Application fee: $75. Electronic applications accepted. *Financial support:* In 2010–11, 40 fellowships with full tuition reimbursements (averaging $17,000 per year), 2 research assistantships with full tuition reimbursements (averaging $17,000 per year), 19 teaching assistantships with full tuition reimbursements (averaging $17,000 per year) were awarded; institutionally sponsored loans also available. *Faculty research:* Nineteenth century French prose and poetry, genetic theory and criticism; twentieth-century Latin American literature and film; medieval and Renaissance Italian literature; gender and queer theory in German literature; the ideology of Baroque and Neobaroque aesthetics. *Unit head:* Dr. William Egginton, Chair, 410-516-7510, Fax: 410-516-5358, E-mail: egginton@jhu.edu. *Application contact:* Rebecca Swisdak, Graduate Administrative Coordinator, 410-516-7227, Fax: 410-516-5358, E-mail: rswisdak@jhu.edu.

Michigan State University, The Graduate School, College of Arts and Letters, Department of French, Classics, and Italian, East Lansing, MI 48824. Offers French (MA); French language and literature (PhD). *Entrance requirements:* Additional exam requirements/recommendations for international students: Required—TOEFL. Electronic applications accepted.

New York University, Graduate School of Arts and Science, Center for French Civilization and Culture, Department of French, New York, NY 10012-1019. Offers French (PhD); French language and civilization (MA); French literature (MA); Romance languages and literatures (MA). Part-time programs available. *Faculty:* 18 full-time (7 women), 2 part-time/adjunct (both women). *Students:* 66 full-time (42 women), 7 part-time (4 women); includes 4 Asian, non-Hispanic/Latino; 3 Hispanic/Latino, 19 international. Average age 29. 73 applicants, 51% accepted, 20 enrolled. In 2010, 11 master's, 4 doctorates awarded. Terminal master's awarded for partial completion of doctoral program. *Degree requirements:* For master's, one foreign language, thesis (for some programs); for doctorate, one foreign language, thesis/dissertation. *Entrance requirements:* For master's and doctorate, GRE General Test, proficiency in French. Additional exam requirements/recommendations for international students: Required—TOEFL. *Application deadline:* For fall admission, 1/4 for domestic students; for spring admission, 11/1 for domestic students. Application fee: $90. *Financial support:* Fellowships with tuition reimbursements, teaching assistantships with tuition reimbursements, Federal Work-Study, institutionally sponsored loans, scholarships/grants, traineeships, health care benefits, unspecified assistantships, and instructorships available. Financial award application deadline: 1/4; financial award applicants required to submit FAFSA. *Faculty research:* French and Francophone literature, literary theory, and history; rhetoric and poetics; cultural history; theater and cinema. *Unit head:* Judith Miller, Chair, 212-998-8700, Fax: 212-995-3539, E-mail: french.grad@nyu.edu. *Application contact:* Brett Underhill, Graduate Secretary, 212-998-8700, Fax: 212-995-3539, E-mail: french.grad@nyu.edu.

New York University, Graduate School of Arts and Science, Department of Spanish and Portuguese Languages and Literatures, New York, NY 10012-1019. Offers Portuguese (MA, PhD); Spanish (PhD); Spanish and Latin American literatures and cultures (MA); Spanish language and translation (MA). Part-time programs available. *Students:* 99 full-time (55 women), 12 part-time (9 women); includes 3 Black or African American, non-Hispanic/Latino; 4 Asian, non-Hispanic/Latino; 30 Hispanic/Latino, 48 international. Average age 31. 189 applicants, 42% accepted, 48 enrolled. In 2010, 39 master's, 4 doctorates awarded. *Degree requirements:* For master's, 2 foreign languages, thesis; for doctorate, 2 foreign languages, thesis/dissertation. *Entrance requirements:* For master's, GRE General Test; for doctorate, GRE General Test, master's degree. Additional exam requirements/recommendations for international students: Required—TOEFL. *Application deadline:* For fall admission, 1/4 priority date for domestic students. Application fee: $90. *Financial support:* Fellowships with tuition reimbursements, teaching assistantships with tuition reimbursements, career-related internships or fieldwork, Federal Work-Study, institutionally sponsored loans, scholarships/grants, health care benefits, and unspecified assistantships available. Financial award application deadline: 1/4; financial award applicants required to submit FAFSA. *Faculty research:* Gender and sexuality, transatlantic studies, literacy and cultural theories, colonial and post colonial studies, autobiography and modern subjectivities. *Unit head:* Jo Labanyi, Acting Chair, 212-998-8770, Fax: 212-995-4149, E-mail: spanish.portuguese.info@nyu.edu. *Application contact:* Gabriel Giorgi, Director of Graduate Studies, 212-998-8770, Fax: 212-995-4149, E-mail: spanish.portuguese.info@nyu.edu.

Northern Illinois University, Graduate School, College of Liberal Arts and Sciences, Department of Foreign Languages and Literatures, De Kalb, IL 60115-2854. Offers French (MA); Spanish (MA). Part-time programs available. *Faculty:* 25 full-time (11 women). *Students:* 25 part-time (19 women); includes 1 Black or African American, non-Hispanic/Latino; 9 Hispanic/Latino, 1 international. Average age 31. 10 applicants, 60% accepted, 4 enrolled. In 2010, 4 master's awarded. *Degree requirements:* For master's, one foreign language, comprehensive exam, thesis or alternative, language proficiency exam. *Entrance requirements:* For master's, GRE General Test, interview, minimum GPA of 2.75, undergraduate major in French or Spanish. Additional exam requirements/recommendations for international students: Required—TOEFL (minimum score 550 paper-based; 213 computer-based). *Application deadline:* For fall admission, 6/1 for domestic students, 5/1 for international students; for spring admission, 11/1 for domestic students, 10/1 for international students. Applications are processed on a rolling basis. Application fee: $30. Electronic applications accepted. *Expenses:* Tuition, state resident: full-time $7200; part-time $300 per credit hour. Tuition, nonresident: full-time $14,400; part-time $600 per credit hour. Required fees: $79 per credit hour. *Financial support:* In 2010–11, 14 teaching assistantships with full tuition reimbursements were awarded; fellowships with full tuition reimbursements, research assistantships with full tuition reimbursements, career-related internships or fieldwork, Federal Work-Study, scholarships/grants, tuition waivers (full), and unspecified assistantships also available. Support available to part-time students. Financial award applicants required to submit FAFSA. *Faculty research:* Francophone women writers, prosodies of French and Italian, early Spanish drama, business German, history of Burmese literature. *Unit head:* Anne Birbeck, Chair, 815-753-1259, Fax: 815-753-5989, E-mail: annie@niu.edu. *Application contact:* Graduate School Office, 815-753-0395, E-mail: gradsch@niu.edu.

Queens College of the City University of New York, Division of Graduate Studies, Arts and Humanities Division, Department of European Languages and Literatures, Flushing, NY 11367-1597. Offers French (MA); Italian (MA). Part-time and evening/weekend programs available. *Faculty:* 13 full-time (5 women). *Students:* 10 part-time (8 women). 10 applicants, 40% accepted, 2 enrolled. In 2010, 4 master's awarded. *Degree requirements:* For master's, 2 foreign languages, comprehensive exam, thesis or alternative. *Entrance requirements:* For master's, minimum GPA of 3.0. Additional exam requirements/recommendations for international students: Required—TOEFL. *Application deadline:* For fall admission, 4/1 for domestic students; for spring admission, 11/1 for domestic students. Applications are processed on a rolling basis. Application fee: $125. *Financial support:* Career-related internships or fieldwork, Federal Work-Study, institutionally sponsored loans, and tuition waivers (partial) available. Support available to part-time students. Financial award application deadline: 4/1; financial award applicants required to submit FAFSA. *Unit head:* Dr. Royal Brown, Chairperson, 718-997-5980, E-mail: royal_brown@qc.edu. *Application contact:* Mario Caruso, Director of Graduate Admissions, 718-997-5200, Fax: 718-997-5193, E-mail: graduate_admissions@qc.edu.

San Diego State University, Graduate and Research Affairs, College of Arts and Letters, Department of European Studies, San Diego, CA 92182. Offers MA. *Degree requirements:* For master's, one foreign language. *Entrance requirements:* For master's, GRE General Test. Additional exam requirements/recommendations for international students: Required—TOEFL. Electronic applications accepted.

Stony Brook University, State University of New York, Graduate School, College of Arts and Sciences, Department of European Languages, Literatures, and Cultures, Program in French, Stony Brook, NY 11794. Offers Romance languages (MA). Evening/weekend programs available. *Students:* 3 part-time (2 women). In 2010, 2 master's awarded. *Degree requirements:* For master's, one foreign language. *Entrance requirements:* For master's, GRE General Test. Additional exam requirements/recommendations for international students: Required—TOEFL. *Application deadline:* For fall admission, 1/15 for domestic students. Application fee: $100. *Expenses:* Tuition, state resident: full-time $8370; part-time $349 per credit. Tuition, nonresident: full-time $13,780; part-time $574 per credit. Required fees: $994. *Unit head:* Prosper Sanou, Coordinator, 631-632-7440, E-mail: prosper.sanou@stonybrook.edu. *Application contact:* Dr. Peter Carravetta, Director of Graduate Studies, 631-632-7440, Fax: 631-632-9612.

Texas Tech University, Graduate School, College of Arts and Sciences, Department of Classical and Modern Languages and Literatures, Lubbock, TX 79409. Offers applied linguistics (MA); classics (MA); German (MA); Romance language (MA); Romance languages-French (MA); Romance languages-Spanish (MA); Spanish (PhD); MBA/MA. Part-time programs available. *Faculty:* 28 full-time (12 women), 1 part-time/adjunct (0 women). *Students:* 86 full-time (51 women), 21 part-time (12 women); includes 1 Black or African American, non-Hispanic/Latino; 18 Hispanic/Latino, 49 international. Average age 30. 72 applicants, 65% accepted, 33 enrolled. In 2010, 32 master's, 5 doctorates awarded. *Degree requirements:* For master's, comprehensive exam, thesis or alternative; for doctorate, comprehensive exam, thesis/dissertation. *Entrance requirements:* For master's and doctorate, GRE General Test. Additional exam requirements/recommendations for international students: Required—TOEFL (minimum score 550 paper-based; 213 computer-based; 79 iBT). *Application deadline:* For fall admission, 6/1 priority date for domestic students, 1/15 priority date for international students; for spring admission, 9/1 priority date for domestic students, 6/15 priority date for international students. Applications are processed on a rolling basis. Application fee: $50 ($75 for international students). Electronic applications accepted. *Expenses:* Tuition, state resident: full-time $5495.76; part-time $228.99 per credit hour. Tuition, nonresident: full-time $12,936; part-time $538.99 per credit hour. Required fees: $2674; $36 per credit hour. $905 per semester. *Financial support:* In 2010–11, 80 students received support, including 2 research assistantships with partial tuition reimbursements available (averaging $9,907 per year), 35 teaching assistantships with partial tuition reimbursements available (averaging $6,303 per year). Financial award application deadline: 4/15; financial award applicants required to submit FAFSA. *Faculty research:* Literature, comparative literature, linguistics, culture, pedagogy. Total annual research expenditures: $52,504. *Unit head:* Dr. Laura Jean Beard, Interim Chair and Professor, 806-742-4355, Fax: 806-742-3306, E-mail: laura.beard@ttu.edu. *Application contact:* Liz Hildebrand, Senior Advisor, 806-742-4055, Fax: 806-742-3306, E-mail: liz.hildebrand@ttu.edu.

University at Buffalo, the State University of New York, Graduate School, College of Arts and Sciences, Department of Romance Languages and Literatures, Buffalo, NY 14260. Offers French (MA, PhD); Spanish (MA, PhD). Part-time programs available. *Faculty:* 15 full-time (9 women), 7 part-time/adjunct (6 women). *Students:* 28 full-time (22 women), 11 part-time (9 women); includes 1 Asian, non-Hispanic/Latino; 12 Two or more races, non-Hispanic/Latino. Average age 31. 16 applicants, 75% accepted, 6 enrolled. In 2010, 3 master's, 4 doctorates awarded. Terminal master's awarded for partial completion of doctoral program. *Degree requirements:* For master's, one foreign language, comprehensive exam, thesis; for doctorate, 2 foreign languages, comprehensive exam, thesis/dissertation. *Entrance requirements:* For master's and doctorate, GRE. Additional exam requirements/recommendations for international students: Required—TOEFL (minimum score 550 paper-based; 213 computer-based; 79 iBT). *Application deadline:* For fall admission, 1/15 priority date for domestic and international students. Applications are processed on a rolling basis. Application fee: $75. Electronic applications accepted. *Financial support:* In 2010–11, 26 students received support, including fellowships with full tuition reimbursements available (averaging $6,000 per year), teaching assistantships with full tuition reimbursements available (averaging $13,415 per year); Federal Work-Study, institutionally sponsored loans, and health care benefits also available. Financial award application deadline: 2/28; financial award applicants required to submit FAFSA. *Faculty research:* Romance linguistics, cultural studies, literary studies, literature and philosophy. *Unit head:* Dr. David Castillo, Chair, 716-645-0869, Fax: 716-645-5981, E-mail: dc63@buffalo.edu. *Application contact:* Dr. Justin Read, Director of Graduate Studies, 716-645-0878, Fax: 716-645-5981, E-mail: jread2@buffalo.edu.

The University of Alabama, Graduate School, College of Arts and Sciences, Department of Modern Languages and Classics, Tuscaloosa, AL 35487. Offers French (MA, PhD); French and Spanish (PhD); German (MA); Romance languages (MA, PhD); Spanish (MA, PhD). Part-time programs available. *Faculty:* 25 full-time (12 women). *Students:* 50 full-time (33 women), 31 part-time (19 women); includes 11 minority (2 Black or African American, non-Hispanic/Latino; 8 Hispanic/Latino; 1 Two or more races, non-Hispanic/Latino), 19 international. Average age 31. 24 applicants, 83% accepted, 11 enrolled. In 2010, 17 master's, 1 doctorate awarded. *Degree requirements:* For master's, comprehensive exam, thesis optional; for doctorate, one foreign language, thesis/dissertation, preliminary exam. *Entrance requirements:* For master's and doctorate, minimum GPA of 3.0, writing sample. Additional exam requirements/recommendations for international students: Required—TOEFL or IELTS. *Application deadline:* For fall admission, 7/6 priority date for domestic students, 1/15 priority date for international students; for spring admission, 12/5 priority date for domestic students, 6/1 priority date for international students. Applications are processed on a rolling basis. Application fee: $50 ($60

Romance Languages

The University of Alabama (continued)

for international students). Electronic applications accepted. *Expenses:* Tuition, state resident: full-time $7900. Tuition, nonresident: full-time $20,500. *Financial support:* In 2010–11, 7 students received support, including 1 fellowship, research assistantships with full tuition reimbursements available (averaging $10,291 per year), 6 teaching assistantships with full tuition reimbursements available (averaging $10,291 per year); career-related internships or fieldwork, Federal Work-Study, institutionally sponsored loans, and scholarships/grants also available. Financial award application deadline: 7/14. *Faculty research:* Non-English literature, linguistics, culture, film. *Unit head:* Dr. Michael Picone, Chair and Professor, 205-348-5054, Fax: 205-348-2042, E-mail: mpicone@bama.ua.edu. *Application contact:* Dr. K. Barbara Fischer, Graduate Director and Associate Professor, 205-348-8465, Fax: 205-348-2042, E-mail: bfischer@bama.ua.edu.

University of California, Berkeley, Graduate Division, College of Letters and Science, Group in Romance Languages and Literature, Berkeley, CA 94720-1500. Offers French (PhD); Italian (PhD); Spanish (PhD). *Degree requirements:* For doctorate, thesis/dissertation, qualifying exam. *Entrance requirements:* For doctorate, GRE General Test, minimum GPA of 3.0, 3 letters of recommendation. Additional exam requirements/recommendations for international students: Required—TOEFL (minimum score 570 paper-based; 230 computer-based).

University of Chicago, Division of the Humanities, Department of Romance Languages and Literatures, Chicago, IL 60637-1513. Offers French (AM, PhD); Italian (AM, PhD); Spanish (AM, PhD). Terminal master's awarded for partial completion of doctoral program. *Degree requirements:* For master's, 2 foreign languages, thesis; for doctorate, 3 foreign languages, thesis/dissertation. *Entrance requirements:* For master's and doctorate, GRE General Test, GRE Subject Test. Additional exam requirements/recommendations for international students: Required—TOEFL.

University of Cincinnati, Graduate School, McMicken College of Arts and Sciences, Department of Romance Languages and Literature, Cincinnati, OH 45221. Offers French (MA, PhD); Romance languages and literatures (PhD); Spanish (MA, PhD). Terminal master's awarded for partial completion of doctoral program. *Degree requirements:* For master's, 2 foreign languages, comprehensive exam, thesis optional; for doctorate, 3 foreign languages, comprehensive exam, thesis/dissertation. *Entrance requirements:* For master's, minimum GPA of 3.0; for doctorate, MA or equivalent in French or Spanish language and literature. Additional exam requirements/recommendations for international students: Required—TOEFL (minimum score 520 paper-based; 190 computer-based). Electronic applications accepted. *Faculty research:* Teaching methods in Spanish, Spanish theater, Old French, Francophone studies, poetry.

University of Georgia, College of Arts and Sciences, Department of Romance Languages, Program in Romance Languages, Athens, GA 30602. Offers MA, PhD. *Faculty:* 28 full-time (15 women). *Students:* 56 full-time (35 women), 16 part-time (12 women); includes 4 Black or African American, non-Hispanic/Latino; 1 American Indian or Alaska Native, non-Hispanic/Latino; 8 Hispanic/Latino; 1 Two or more races, non-Hispanic/Latino, 14 international. 61 applicants, 66% accepted, 26 enrolled. In 2010, 12 master's, 7 doctorates awarded. *Degree requirements:* For master's, one foreign language, thesis (MA); for doctorate, one foreign language, thesis/dissertation. *Entrance requirements:* For master's and doctorate, GRE General Test. *Application deadline:* For fall admission, 7/1 priority date for domestic students; for spring admission, 11/15 for domestic students. Application fee: $50. Electronic applications accepted. *Expenses:* Tuition, state resident: full-time $7200; part-time $344 per credit hour. Tuition, nonresident: full-time $21,900; part-time $944 per credit hour. Tuition and fees vary according to course load and program. *Financial support:* Fellowships, research assistantships, teaching assistantships, unspecified assistantships available. *Unit head:* Dr. Nina Hellerstein, Department Head, 706-542-3122, E-mail: hellerst@uga.edu. *Application contact:* Dr. Catherine M. Jones, Graduate Coordinator, 706-542-3159, Fax: 706-542-2272, E-mail: cmjones@uga.edu.

University of Miami, Graduate School, College of Arts and Sciences, Department of Modern Languages and Literatures, Coral Gables, FL 33124. Offers romance studies (PhD), including French, Spanish. *Degree requirements:* For doctorate, 2 foreign languages, thesis/dissertation, area exam, qualifying exam. *Entrance requirements:* For doctorate, 1 writing sample in English and 1 writing sample in French or Spanish, minimum GPA of 3.0, oral interview, letters of recommendation. Additional exam requirements/recommendations for international students: Required—TOEFL (minimum score 550 paper-based; 213 computer-based; 59 iBT). Electronic applications accepted. *Faculty research:* Transatlantic studies, Caribbean studies, comparative literature, gender theory, cultural studies.

University of Michigan, Horace H. Rackham School of Graduate Studies, College of Literature, Science, and the Arts, Department of Linguistics, Ann Arbor, MI 48109. Offers linguistics (PhD); linguistics and Romance languages and literatures (PhD). *Faculty:* 16 full-time (7 women), 2 part-time/adjunct (both women). *Students:* 25 full-time (11 women); includes 1 Black or African American, non-Hispanic/Latino; 3 Asian, non-Hispanic/Latino, 9 international. Average age 30. 100 applicants, 9% accepted, 4 enrolled. In 2010, 5 doctorates awarded. *Degree requirements:* For doctorate, 2 foreign languages, thesis/dissertation, oral defense of dissertation. *Entrance requirements:* For doctorate, GRE General Test. Additional exam requirements/recommendations for international students: Required—Michigan English Language Assessment Battery; Recommended—TOEFL (minimum score 620 paper-based; 260 computer-based; 95 iBT). *Application deadline:* For fall admission, 12/7 for domestic students, 12/8 for international students. Application fee: $65 ($75 for international students). Electronic applications accepted. *Expenses:* Tuition, state resident: full-time $17,784; part-time $1116 per credit hour. Tuition, nonresident: full-time $35,944; part-time $2125 per credit hour. International tuition: $35,994 full-time. Required fees: $95 per semester. Tuition and fees vary according to course load, degree level and program. *Financial support:* In 2010–11, 23 students received support, including 13 fellowships with full tuition reimbursements available (averaging $16,800 per year), 2 research assistantships with full tuition reimbursements available (averaging $17,270 per year), 12 teaching assistantships with full tuition reimbursements available (averaging $17,270 per year); health care benefits and tuition waivers (full) also available. Financial award application deadline: 12/8. *Faculty research:* Broad-based approach to linguistics as a cognitive and social science including theoretical, experimental and computational approaches. Total annual research expenditures: $140,405. *Unit head:* Prof. Sarah Thomason, Professor/Chair, 734-764-0353, Fax: 734-936-3406, E-mail: linguistics@umich.edu. *Application contact:* Sylvia Suttor, Senior Student Services Assistant, 734-936-3403, Fax: 734-936-3406, E-mail: linggradadmissions@umich.edu.

University of Michigan, Horace H. Rackham School of Graduate Studies, College of Literature, Science, and the Arts, Department of Romance Languages and Literatures, Ann Arbor, MI 48109. Offers French (PhD); Italian (PhD); Romance linguistics (PhD); Spanish (PhD). *Faculty:* 28 full-time (13 women), 2 part-time/adjunct (1 woman). *Students:* 47 full-time (24 women); includes 27 Hispanic/Latino. Average age 27. 89 applicants, 20% accepted, 8 enrolled. In 2010, 5 doctorates awarded. *Degree requirements:* For doctorate, 2 foreign languages, thesis/dissertation, oral defense of dissertation, preliminary exams. *Entrance requirements:* For doctorate, GRE General Test. Additional exam requirements/recommendations for international students: Required—TOEFL or Michigan English Language Assessment Battery. *Application deadline:* For fall admission, 1/1 for domestic and international students. Application fee: $65 ($75 for international students). Electronic applications accepted. *Expenses:* Tuition, state resident: full-time $17,784; part-time $1116 per credit hour. Tuition, nonresident: full-time $35,944; part-time $2125 per credit hour. International tuition: $35,994 full-time. Required fees: $95 per semester. Tuition and fees vary according to course load, degree level and program. *Financial support:* In 2010–11, 1 teaching assistantship with full tuition reimbursement was awarded; fellowships with full tuition reimbursements, institutionally sponsored loans, scholarships/grants, and unspecified assistantships also available. Financial award application deadline: 1/1. *Faculty research:* Comparative Romance studies, medieval and early modern studies, postcolonial and minority literatures, culture and materiality, reflection on the nature and function of scholarship. *Unit head:* Dr. Cristina Moreiras-Menor, Chair, 734-764-5344, Fax: 734-764-8163. *Application contact:* Annette Herbert, Graduate Assistant, 734-764-8164, Fax: 734-764-8163, E-mail: rll-admissions@umich.edu.

University of Missouri, Graduate School, College of Arts and Sciences, Department of Romance Languages and Literature, Columbia, MO 65211. Offers French (MA, PhD); literature (MA); Spanish (MA, PhD); teaching (MA). Terminal master's awarded for partial completion of doctoral program. *Degree requirements:* For master's, one foreign language; for doctorate, 4 foreign languages, comprehensive exam, thesis/dissertation. *Entrance requirements:* For master's, GRE General Test, minimum GPA of 3.0 in field of major; bachelor's degree; for doctorate, GRE General Test, minimum GPA of 3.0 in field of major; master's degree. Additional exam requirements/recommendations for international students: Required—TOEFL (minimum score 500 paper-based; 173 computer-based; 61 iBT). Electronic applications accepted.

University of Missouri–Kansas City, College of Arts and Sciences, Department of Foreign Languages and Literatures, Kansas City, MO 64110-2499. Offers Romance languages and literatures (MA). Part-time programs available. *Faculty:* 11 full-time (5 women), 18 part-time/adjunct (14 women). *Students:* 5 full-time (all women), 24 part-time (18 women); includes 8 minority (2 Black or African American, non-Hispanic/Latino; 1 Asian, non-Hispanic/Latino; 4 Hispanic/Latino; 1 Two or more races, non-Hispanic/Latino). Average age 35. 10 applicants, 80% accepted, 8 enrolled. In 2010, 8 master's awarded. *Degree requirements:* For master's, 2 foreign languages. *Entrance requirements:* For master's, GRE General Test, minimum GPA of 2.75, 2 letters of recommendation. Additional exam requirements/recommendations for international students: Required—TOEFL (minimum score 550 paper-based; 213 computer-based; 80 iBT). *Application deadline:* For fall admission, 4/1 priority date for domestic and international students; for spring admission, 11/1 priority date for domestic and international students. Applications are processed on a rolling basis. Application fee: $45 ($50 for international students). Electronic applications accepted. *Expenses:* Tuition, state resident: full-time $5522.40; part-time $306.80 per credit hour. Tuition, nonresident: full-time $7128; part-time $792 per credit hour. Required fees: $261.15 per term. *Financial support:* In 2010–11, 1 teaching assistantship (averaging $6,300 per year) was awarded; Federal Work-Study, institutionally sponsored loans, and tuition waivers (full and partial) also available. Support available to part-time students. Financial award application deadline: 3/1; financial award applicants required to submit FAFSA. *Faculty research:* Literary analyses; psychology and literature; narrative techniques, poetic structure, and style; literature, politics, and society (especially in Latin America). *Unit head:* Dr. Kathy Krause, Chair, 816-235-1340, Fax: 816-235-1312, E-mail: krausek@umkc.edu. *Application contact:* Dr. Nacer Khelouz, Graduate Advisor/Assistant Professor, 816-235-1311, Fax: 816-235-1312, E-mail: admit@umkc.edu.

University of New Orleans, Graduate School, College of Liberal Arts, Department of Foreign Languages, New Orleans, LA 70148. Offers MA. Part-time and evening/weekend programs available. *Degree requirements:* For master's, one foreign language, thesis optional. *Entrance requirements:* For master's, GRE General Test, minimum B average. Additional exam requirements/recommendations for international students: Required—TOEFL (minimum score 550 paper-based; 213 computer-based; 79 iBT). Electronic applications accepted. *Faculty research:* Translation studies, Michelet, Scève, Spanish canzoniero, theories of representation.

The University of North Carolina at Chapel Hill, Graduate School, College of Arts and Sciences, Department of Romance Languages, Chapel Hill, NC 27599. Offers French (MA, PhD); Italian (MA, PhD); Portuguese (MA, PhD); Romance languages (MA, PhD); Romance philology (MA, PhD); Spanish (MA, PhD). *Degree requirements:* For master's, one foreign language, comprehensive exam, thesis; for doctorate, 2 foreign languages, comprehensive exam, thesis/dissertation. *Entrance requirements:* For master's and doctorate, GRE General Test, minimum GPA of 3.0. Additional exam requirements/recommendations for international students: Required—TOEFL (minimum score 550 paper-based; 213 computer-based). Electronic applications accepted.

University of Notre Dame, Graduate School, College of Arts and Letters, Division of Humanities, Department of Romance Languages and Literatures, Notre Dame, IN 46556. Offers French and Francophone studies (MA); Iberian and Latin American studies (MA); Italian studies (MA); Romance literatures (MA). *Degree requirements:* For master's, 2 foreign languages, comprehensive exam, thesis optional. *Entrance requirements:* For master's, GRE General Test, BA in target language. Additional exam requirements/recommendations for international students: Required—TOEFL (minimum score 600 paper-based; 250 computer-based; 80 iBT). Electronic applications accepted. *Faculty research:* Literature of discovery and exploration, modern literature, literary criticism, medieval literature, feminist critical theory.

University of Oregon, Graduate School, College of Arts and Sciences, Department of Romance Languages, Program in Romance Languages, Eugene, OR 97403. Offers MA, PhD. Part-time programs available. *Degree requirements:* For master's, 2 foreign languages; for doctorate, 2 foreign languages, thesis/dissertation. *Entrance requirements:* For master's and doctorate, GRE General Test, minimum GPA of 3.0. Additional exam requirements/recommendations for international students: Required—TOEFL.

University of Pennsylvania, School of Arts and Sciences, Graduate Group in Romance Languages, Philadelphia, PA 19104. Offers French (AM, PhD); Italian (AM, PhD); Spanish (AM, PhD). *Faculty:* 58 full-time (23 women), 4 part-time/adjunct (1 woman). *Students:* 61 full-time (34 women), 2 part-time (both women); includes 1 American Indian or Alaska Native, non-Hispanic/Latino; 12 Hispanic/Latino, 19 international. 114 applicants, 15% accepted, 11 enrolled. In 2010, 11 master's, 6 doctorates awarded. Terminal master's awarded for partial completion of doctoral program. *Degree requirements:* For master's, one foreign language, thesis or alternative; for doctorate, 2 foreign languages, thesis/dissertation. *Entrance requirements:* For master's and doctorate, GRE General Test. Additional exam requirements/recommendations for international students: Required—TOEFL. *Application deadline:* For fall admission, 12/1 priority date for domestic students. Application fee: $70. Electronic applications accepted. *Expenses:* Tuition: Full-time $25,660; part-time $4758 per course. Required fees: $2152; $270 per course. Tuition and fees vary according to course load, degree level and program. *Financial support:* In 2010–11, 23 fellowships, 2 research assistantships, 39 teaching assistantships were awarded; institutionally sponsored loans, scholarships/grants, traineeships, health care benefits, and unspecified assistantships also available. Financial award application deadline: 12/15. *Faculty research:* Literary theory and criticism, cultural studies, history of Romance literatures, gender studies. *Application contact:* Graduate Coordinator, 215-898-7429.

University of Rochester, School of Arts and Sciences, Department of Modern Languages and Cultures, Rochester, NY 14627.

University of South Africa, College of Human Sciences, Pretoria, South Africa. Offers adult education (M Ed); African languages (MA, PhD); African politics (MA, PhD); Afrikaans (MA, PhD); ancient history (MA, PhD); ancient Near Eastern studies (MA, PhD); anthropology (MA, PhD); applied linguistics (MA); Arabic (MA, PhD); archaeology (MA); art history (MA); Biblical archaeology (MA); Biblical studies (M Th, D Th, PhD); Christian spirituality (M Th, D Th); church history (M Th, D Th); classical studies (MA, PhD); clinical psychology (MA); communication (MA, PhD); comparative education (M Ed, Ed D); consulting psychology (D Admin, D Com, PhD); curriculum studies (M Ed, Ed D); development studies (M Admin, MA, D Admin, PhD); didactics (M Ed, Ed D); education (M Tech); education management (M Ed, Ed D); educational psychology (M Ed); English (MA); environmental education (M Ed); French (MA, PhD); German (MA, PhD); Greek (MA); guidance and counseling (M Ed); health studies (MA, PhD), including health sciences education (MA), health services management (MA), medical and surgical nursing science (critical care general) (MA), midwifery and neonatal nursing science (MA), trauma and emergency care (MA); history (MA, PhD); history of education (Ed D); inclusive education (M Ed, Ed D); information and communications technology policy and regulation (MA); information science (MA, MIS, PhD); international politics (MA, PhD); Islamic studies (MA, PhD); Italian (MA, PhD); Judaica (MA, PhD); linguistics (MA, PhD); mathematical education (M Ed); mathematics education (MA); missiology (M Th, D Th); modern

Hebrew (MA, PhD); musicology (MA, MMus, D Mus, PhD); natural science education (M Ed); New Testament (M Th, D Th); Old Testament (D Th); pastoral therapy (M Th, D Th); philosophy (MA); philosophy of education (M Ed, Ed D); politics (MA, PhD); Portuguese (MA, PhD); practical theology (M Th, D Th); psychology (MA, MS, PhD); psychology of education (M Ed, Ed D); public health (MA); religious studies (MA, D Th, PhD); Romance languages (MA); Russian (MA, PhD); Semitic languages (MA, PhD); social behavior studies in HIV/AIDS (MA); social science (mental health) (MA); social science in development studies (MA); social science in psychology (MA); social science in social work (MA); social science in sociology (MA); social work (MSW, DSW, PhD); socio-education (M Ed, Ed D); sociolinguistics (MA); sociology (MA, PhD); Spanish (MA, PhD); systematic theology (M Th, D Th); TESOL (teaching English to speakers of other languages) (MA); theological ethics (M Th, D Th); theory of literature (MA, PhD); urban ministries (D Th); urban ministry (M Th).

The University of Texas at Austin, Graduate School, College of Liberal Arts, Department of French and Italian, Austin, TX 78712-1111. Offers French (MA, PhD); French linguistics (MA, PhD); Italian studies (MA, PhD); Romance linguistics (MA, PhD). Part-time programs available. *Degree requirements:* For master's, one foreign language, thesis; for doctorate, 2 foreign languages, thesis/dissertation. *Entrance requirements:* For master's, GRE General Test, minimum GPA of 3.0, bachelor's degree in French or equivalent; for doctorate, GRE General Test, minimum GPA of 3.0, master's degree in French. Additional exam requirements/recommendations for international students: Required—TOEFL. Electronic applications accepted. *Faculty research:* Nineteenth-century Italian literature, Italian Renaissance, twentieth-century French literature, Francophone literature, fifteenth-century literature and culture.

University of Virginia, College and Graduate School of Arts and Sciences, Department of Spanish, Italian and Portuguese, Charlottesville, VA 22903. Offers Italian (MA); Spanish (MA, PhD). *Faculty:* 19 full-time (8 women). *Students:* 46 full-time (34 women), 5 part-time (3 women); includes 1 Asian, non-Hispanic/Latino; 6 Hispanic/Latino; 1 Two or more races,

non-Hispanic/Latino, 8 international. Average age 27. 56 applicants, 25% accepted, 12 enrolled. In 2010, 20 master's, 6 doctorates awarded. *Degree requirements:* For master's, comprehensive exam, thesis; for doctorate, one foreign language, comprehensive exam, thesis/dissertation. *Entrance requirements:* For master's and doctorate, GRE General Test, GRE Subject Test, 2 letters of recommendation. Additional exam requirements/recommendations for international students: Required—TOEFL (minimum score 600 paper-based; 250 computer-based; 90 iBT), IELTS (minimum score 7). *Application deadline:* For fall admission, 12/1 for domestic and international students. Applications are processed on a rolling basis. Application fee: $60. Electronic applications accepted. *Financial support:* Fellowships, teaching assistantships available. Financial award applicants required to submit FAFSA. *Unit head:* Deorah Parker, Chair, 434-924-7159, Fax: 434-924-7160, E-mail: sipinfo@virginia.edu. *Application contact:* Deorah Parker, Chair, 434-924-7159, Fax: 434-924-7160, E-mail: sipinfo@virginia.edu.

University of Washington, Graduate School, College of Arts and Sciences, Department of Romance Languages and Literature, Seattle, WA 98195. Offers French and Italian studies (MA, PhD), including French, Italian (MA); Spanish and Portuguese (MA), including Hispanic literary and cultural studies. Terminal master's awarded for partial completion of doctoral program. *Degree requirements:* For master's, 2 foreign languages, thesis optional; exam; for doctorate, 3 foreign languages, thesis/dissertation, exams. *Entrance requirements:* For master's and doctorate, GRE General Test, minimum GPA of 3.0. Additional exam requirements/recommendations for international students: Required—TOEFL. Electronic applications accepted.

Washington University in St. Louis, Graduate School of Arts and Sciences, Department of Romance Languages and Literatures, St. Louis, MO 63130-4899. Offers French (MA, PhD); Spanish (MA, PhD). Terminal master's awarded for partial completion of doctoral program. *Degree requirements:* For master's, thesis or alternative; for doctorate, thesis/dissertation. *Entrance requirements:* For master's and doctorate, GRE General Test. Electronic applications accepted.

Russian

American University, College of Arts and Sciences, Department of Language and Foreign Studies, Washington, DC 20016-8045. Offers French (Certificate), including translation; Russian (Certificate), including translation; Spanish: Latin American studies (MA, Certificate), including Spanish: Latin American studies (MA), translation (Certificate); teaching English to speakers of other languages (MA, Certificate). Part-time and evening/weekend programs available. *Faculty:* 41 full-time (29 women), 43 part-time/adjunct (34 women). *Students:* 22 full-time (17 women), 39 part-time (31 women); includes 8 minority (1 Black or African American, non-Hispanic/Latino; 3 Asian, non-Hispanic/Latino; 3 Hispanic/Latino; 1 Native Hawaiian or other Pacific Islander, non-Hispanic/Latino), 6 international. Average age 34. 64 applicants, 64% accepted, 14 enrolled. In 2010, 24 master's, 28 other advanced degrees awarded. *Degree requirements:* For master's, one foreign language, comprehensive exam, thesis or alternative, portfolio, research; for Certificate, minimum 15 credit hours related coursework. *Entrance requirements:* For master's, GRE, writing sample; for Certificate, bachelor's degree. Additional exam requirements/recommendations for international students: Required—TOEFL. *Application deadline:* For fall admission, 2/1 for domestic students; for spring admission, 10/1 for domestic students. Application fee: $80. *Financial support:* Fellowships, career-related internships or fieldwork, Federal Work-Study, institutionally sponsored loans, and tuition waivers (partial) available. Financial award application deadline: 2/1. *Unit head:* Olga Rojer, Chair, 202-885-2139, Fax: 202-885-1076, E-mail: orojer@american.edu. *Application contact:* Kathleen Clowery, Director of Graduate Admissions, 202-885-3621, Fax: 202-885-1505, E-mail: clowery@american.edu.

Boston College, Graduate School of Arts and Sciences, Department of Slavic and Eastern Languages, Program in Russian and Slavic Languages and Literature, Chestnut Hill, MA 02467-3800. Offers MA, MA/JD, MBA/MA. Part-time programs available. *Degree requirements:* For master's, 3 foreign languages, comprehensive exam, thesis or alternative. *Entrance requirements:* Additional exam requirements/recommendations for international students: Required—TOEFL (minimum score 600 paper-based; 250 computer-based; 100 iBT). Electronic applications accepted. *Faculty research:* Structural analysis of language, poetry and semiotic systems.

Brown University, Graduate School, Department of Slavic Languages, Providence, RI 02912. Offers Russian language and literature (AM); Slavic languages (AM); Slavic studies (PhD). *Degree requirements:* For master's, one foreign language; for doctorate, 2 foreign languages, thesis/dissertation, preliminary exam.

Columbia University, Graduate School of Arts and Sciences, Division of Humanities, Department of Slavic Languages, New York, NY 10027. Offers Russian literature (M Phil, MA, PhD); Slavic languages (M Phil, MA, PhD). *Degree requirements:* For master's, one foreign language, thesis; for doctorate, 2 foreign languages, thesis/dissertation. *Entrance requirements:* For master's and doctorate, GRE General Test. Additional exam requirements/recommendations for international students: Required—TOEFL. *Faculty research:* Polish, Serbo-Croatian, Czechoslovakian, medieval and modern Russian literature.

Harvard University, Graduate School of Arts and Sciences, Department of Slavic Languages and Literatures, Cambridge, MA 02138. Offers Polish (PhD); Russian (PhD); Serbo-Croatian (PhD); Slavic philology (PhD); Ukrainian (PhD). *Degree requirements:* For doctorate, 4 foreign languages, thesis/dissertation. *Entrance requirements:* For doctorate, GRE General Test, writing sample. Additional exam requirements/recommendations for international students: Required—TOEFL. *Expenses:* Tuition: Full-time $34,976. Required fees: $1166. Full-time tuition and fees vary according to program.

Hofstra University, School of Education, Health, and Human Services, Programs in Teaching—Secondary Education, Hempstead, NY 11549. Offers business education (MS Ed); English education (MA, MS Ed); foreign language and TESOL (MS Ed); foreign language education (MA, MS Ed), including French, German, Russian, Spanish; mathematics education (MA, MS Ed); science education (MA, MS Ed), including biology, chemistry, earth science, geology, physics; secondary education (Advanced Certificate); social studies education (MA, MS Ed). Part-time and evening/weekend programs available. Postbaccalaureate distance learning degree programs offered (minimal on-campus study). *Students:* 114 full-time (74 women), 61 part-time (36 women); includes 7 Black or African American, non-Hispanic/Latino; 1 American Indian or Alaska Native, non-Hispanic/Latino; 8 Asian, non-Hispanic/Latino; 10 Hispanic/Latino; 1 Native Hawaiian or other Pacific Islander, non-Hispanic/Latino. Average age 27. 153 applicants, 90% accepted, 59 enrolled. In 2010, 102 master's, 11 other advanced degrees awarded. *Degree requirements:* For master's, one foreign language, comprehensive exam (for some programs), thesis (for some programs), exit project, electronic portfolio, student teaching, fieldwork, curriculum project; for Advanced Certificate, 3 foreign languages, comprehensive exam (for some programs), thesis project. *Entrance requirements:* For master's, 2 letters of recommendation, teacher certification (MA), essay; for Advanced Certificate, 2 letters of recommendation, essay, interview and/or portfolio. Additional exam requirements/recommendations for international students: Required—TOEFL (minimum score 550 paper-based; 213 computer-based; 80 iBT). *Application deadline:* Applications are processed on a rolling basis. Application fee: $70 ($75 for international students). Electronic applications accepted. *Expenses:* Tuition: Full-time $18,000; part-time $1000 per credit hour. Required fees: $970; $145 per term. Tuition

and fees vary according to program. *Financial support:* In 2010–11, 108 students received support, including 14 fellowships with full and partial tuition reimbursements available (averaging $3,943 per year), 1 research assistantship with full and partial tuition reimbursement available (averaging $6,574 per year); career-related internships or fieldwork, Federal Work-Study, institutionally sponsored loans, scholarships/grants, tuition waivers (full and partial), unspecified assistantships, and scholarships also available. Support available to part-time students. Financial award applicants required to submit FAFSA. *Faculty research:* Appropriate content and pedagogy in secondary school disciplines, adolescent development, secondary school organization, alternative secondary school programs. *Unit head:* Dr. Esther Fusco, Chairperson, 516-463-7704, Fax: 516-463-6196, E-mail: catezf@hofstra.edu. *Application contact:* Carol Drummer, Dean of Graduate Admissions, 516-463-4876, Fax: 516-463-4664, E-mail: gradstudent@hofstra.edu.

Kent State University, College of Arts and Sciences, Department of Modern and Classical Language Studies, Kent, OH 44242-0001. Offers French literature (MA); French, Spanish, German and Latin pedagogy (MA); German literature (MA); Spanish literature (MA); translation (MA), including French, German, Japanese, Russian, Spanish; translation studies (PhD). Part-time and evening/weekend programs available. *Degree requirements:* For master's, one foreign language, comprehensive exam (for some programs), thesis (for some programs); for doctorate, comprehensive exam, thesis/dissertation (for some programs). *Entrance requirements:* For master's, minimum GPA of 3.0, writing sample, audio tape or CD; for doctorate, 3 recommendations. Additional exam requirements/recommendations for international students: Required—TOEFL (minimum score 197 computer-based). Electronic applications accepted. *Expenses:* Tuition, state resident: full-time $7866; part-time $437 per credit hour. Tuition, nonresident: full-time $14,022; part-time $779 per credit hour. *Faculty research:* Literature, pedagogy, applied linguistics, translation studies.

McGill University, Faculty of Graduate and Postdoctoral Studies, Faculty of Arts, Department of Russian and Slavic Studies, Montréal, QC H3A 2T5, Canada. Offers Russian literature (MA, PhD).

Middlebury College, Language Schools, Russian School, Middlebury, VT 05753-6002. Offers MA, DML. *Faculty:* 6 full-time (4 women). *Students:* 9 full-time (4 women). Average age 33. 49 applicants, 49% accepted. In 2010, 2 master's awarded. *Degree requirements:* For master's, one foreign language; for doctorate, 2 foreign languages, comprehensive exam, thesis/dissertation. *Entrance requirements:* For master's, placement exam, 3 letters of recommendation, writing sample; for doctorate, 1st and 2nd language exams, 3 letters of recommendation, writing sample. *Application deadline:* Applications are processed on a rolling basis. Application fee: $65. Electronic applications accepted. *Financial support:* In 2010–11, 2 fellowships (averaging $7,000 per year) were awarded; scholarships/grants also available. Financial award applicants required to submit FAFSA. *Unit head:* Dr. Jason Merrill, Director, 802-443-5230, Fax: 802-443-2075, E-mail: jmerrill@middlebury.edu. *Application contact:* John Stokes, Coordinator, 802-443-5230, Fax: 802-443-2075, E-mail: jstokes@middlebury.edu.

New York University, Graduate School of Arts and Science, Department of Russian and Slavic Studies, New York, NY 10012-1019. Offers Russian literature (MA); Slavic literature (MA). Part-time programs available. *Faculty:* 8 full-time (3 women). *Students:* 7 full-time (5 women), 7 part-time (2 women), 1 international. Average age 28. 16 applicants, 81% accepted, 6 enrolled. In 2010, 9 master's awarded. *Degree requirements:* For master's, one foreign language, comprehensive exam, thesis. *Entrance requirements:* For master's, GRE General Test, minimum 3 years of undergraduate Russian or equivalent. Additional exam requirements/recommendations for international students: Required—TOEFL. *Application deadline:* For fall admission, 4/15 for domestic students; for spring admission, 11/1 for domestic students. Application fee: $90. *Financial support:* Career-related internships or fieldwork, Federal Work-Study, and institutionally sponsored loans available. Financial award application deadline: 4/15; financial award applicants required to submit FAFSA. *Faculty research:* Modern Russian literature and art, contemporary Russian and East European literature, literary theory, Slavic linguistics, Russian journalism. *Unit head:* Yanni Kotsonis, Chair, 212-998-8670, Fax: 212-995-4604, E-mail: gsas.russian.and.slavic@nyu.edu. *Application contact:* Eliot Borenstein, Director of Graduate Studies, 212-998-8670, Fax: 212-995-4604, E-mail: gsas.russian.and.slavic@nyu.edu.

The Ohio State University, Graduate School, College of Arts and Sciences, Division of Arts and Humanities, Department of Slavic and East European Languages and Literatures, Columbus, OH 43210. Offers linguistics (MA); literature (MA); Russian literature (PhD); Slavic linguistics (PhD). *Faculty:* 13. *Students:* 21 full-time (12 women), 8 part-time (4 women); includes 1 Asian, non-Hispanic/Latino, 4 international. Average age 31. In 2010, 2 master's, 3 doctorates awarded. *Degree requirements:* For master's, variable foreign language requirement, thesis optional; for doctorate, variable foreign language requirement, thesis/dissertation. *Entrance requirements:* For master's and doctorate, GRE General Test. Additional exam requirements/recommendations for international students: Required—TOEFL (minimum score 600 paper-based; 250 computer-based). *Application deadline:* For fall admission, 8/15 priority date for domestic students, 7/1 priority date for international students; for winter admission, 12/1 priority date for domestic students, 11/1 priority date for international students; for spring

Russian

The Ohio State University (continued)
admission, 3/1 priority date for domestic students, 2/1 priority date for international students. Applications are processed on a rolling basis. Application fee: $40 ($50 for international students). Electronic applications accepted. *Expenses:* Tuition, state resident: full-time $10,605. Tuition, nonresident: full-time $26,535. Tuition and fees vary according to course load and program. *Financial support:* Fellowships, research assistantships, teaching assistantships, Federal Work-Study and institutionally sponsored loans available. Support available to part-time students. *Faculty research:* Polish literature. *Unit head:* Helena Goscilo, Chair, 614-247-1790, E-mail: goscilo.1@osu.edu. *Application contact:* 614-292-9444, Fax: 614-292-3895, E-mail: domestic.grad@osu.edu.

Princeton University, Graduate School, Department of Slavic Languages and Literatures, Princeton, NJ 08544-1019. Offers Russian and Slavic linguistics (PhD); Russian literature (PhD). *Degree requirements:* For doctorate, variable foreign language requirement, thesis/dissertation. *Entrance requirements:* For doctorate, GRE General Test. Additional exam requirements/recommendations for international students: Required—TOEFL (minimum score 600 paper-based; 250 computer-based). Electronic applications accepted.

Stanford University, School of Humanities and Sciences, Department of Slavic Languages and Literatures, Stanford, CA 94305-9991. Offers Russian (MA); Slavic languages and literatures (PhD). Terminal master's awarded for partial completion of doctoral program. *Degree requirements:* For master's, one foreign language, thesis or alternative; for doctorate, 3 foreign languages, thesis/dissertation. *Entrance requirements:* For master's and doctorate, GRE General Test. Additional exam requirements/recommendations for international students: Required—TOEFL. Electronic applications accepted. *Expenses:* Tuition: Full-time $38,700; part-time $860 per unit. One-time fee: $200 full-time.

University at Albany, State University of New York, College of Arts and Sciences, Department of Languages, Literatures, and Cultures, Program in Russian, Albany, NY 12222-0001. Offers Russian (MA); Russian translation (Certificate). *Faculty research:* Translation, phonology and morphology of modern Russian.

The University of Arizona, College of Humanities, Department of Russian and Slavic Studies, Tucson, AZ 85721. Offers Russian (MA). Part-time programs available. *Faculty:* 6 full-time (2 women). *Students:* 7 full-time (5 women), 5 part-time (3 women); includes 3 minority (1 Black or African American, non-Hispanic/Latino; 1 Hispanic/Latino; 1 Two or more races, non-Hispanic/Latino), 1 international. Average age 27. 15 applicants, 73% accepted, 7 enrolled. In 2010, 6 master's awarded. *Degree requirements:* For master's, one foreign language, comprehensive exam (for some programs), thesis (for some programs). *Entrance requirements:* For master's, 3 letters of recommendation, audio sample. Additional exam requirements/recommendations for international students: Required—TOEFL (minimum score 550 paper-based; 213 computer-based; 79 iBT). *Application deadline:* For fall admission, 4/1 for domestic students, 12/1 for international students; for spring admission, 10/1 for domestic students, 6/1 for international students. Applications are processed on a rolling basis. Application fee: $75. Electronic applications accepted. *Expenses:* Tuition, state resident: full-time $7692. *Financial support:* In 2010–11, 10 teaching assistantships with full tuition reimbursements (averaging $13,989 per year) were awarded; Federal Work-Study, scholarships/grants, health care benefits, tuition waivers (full), and unspecified assistantships also available. *Faculty research:* Russian literature, language/pedagogy, linguistics, Russian culture. *Unit head:* Dr. Teresa Polowy, Department Head, 520-621-7341, Fax: 520-626-4007, E-mail: tpolowy@email.arizona.edu. *Application contact:* Judi Greil, Graduate Coordinator, 520-621-3702, Fax: 520-626-4007, E-mail: greilj@u.arizona.edu.

University of California, Berkeley, Graduate Division, College of Letters and Science, Department of Slavic Languages and Literatures, Berkeley, CA 94720-1500. Offers Czech (PhD), including Czech linguistics, Czech literature; Polish (PhD), including Polish linguistics, Polish literature; Russian (PhD), including Russian linguistics, Russian literature; Serbo-Croatian (PhD), including Serbo-Croatian linguistics, Serbo-Croatian literature. Terminal master's awarded for partial completion of doctoral program. *Degree requirements:* For doctorate, thesis/dissertation, oral and written exams. *Entrance requirements:* For doctorate, GRE General Test, minimum GPA of 3.0, 3 letters of recommendation. Additional exam requirements/recommendations for international students: Required—TOEFL (minimum score 570 paper-based; 230 computer-based). Electronic applications accepted.

The University of Manchester, School of Languages, Linguistics and Cultures, Manchester, United Kingdom. Offers Arab world studies (PhD); Chinese studies (M Phil, PhD); East Asian studies (M Phil, PhD); English language (PhD); French studies (M Phil, PhD); German studies (M Phil, PhD); interpreting studies (PhD); Italian studies (M Phil, PhD); Japanese studies (M Phil, PhD); Latin American cultural studies (M Phil, PhD); linguistics (M Phil, PhD); Middle Eastern studies (M Phil, PhD); Polish studies (M Phil, PhD); Portuguese studies (M Phil, PhD); Russian studies (M Phil, PhD); Spanish studies (M Phil, PhD); translation and intercultural studies (M Phil, PhD).

University of Michigan, Horace H. Rackham School of Graduate Studies, College of Literature, Science, and the Arts, Department of Slavic Languages and Literatures, Ann Arbor, MI 48109-1275. Offers Russian (AM); Slavic languages and literatures (PhD). Terminal master's awarded for partial completion of doctoral program. *Degree requirements:* For master's, 2 foreign languages, comprehensive exam; for doctorate, 3 foreign languages, comprehensive exam, thesis/dissertation, oral defense of dissertation, preliminary exam. *Entrance requirements:* For master's, GRE General Test, 3rd-year foreign language proficiency; for doctorate, GRE General Test. Additional exam requirements/recommendations for international students: Required—TOEFL (minimum score 560 paper-based; 220 computer-based). Electronic applications accepted. *Expenses:* Tuition, state resident: full-time $17,784; part-time $1116 per credit hour. Tuition, nonresident: full-time $35,944; part-time $2125 per credit hour. International tuition: $35,994 full-time. Required fees: $95 per semester. Tuition and fees vary according to course load, degree level and program. *Faculty research:* Russian literature (all periods), Polish literature, South Slavic literatures, Czech literature, Ukrainian literature.

The University of North Carolina at Chapel Hill, Graduate School, College of Arts and Sciences, Department of Slavic Languages and Literatures, Chapel Hill, NC 27599. Offers Polish literature (PhD); Russian and east Euorpean studies (MA); Russian literature (MA, PhD); Serbo-Croatian literature (PhD); Slavic linguistics (MA, PhD). Part-time programs available. Terminal master's awarded for partial completion of doctoral program. *Degree requirements:* For master's, 2 foreign languages, comprehensive exam, thesis; for doctorate, 4 foreign languages, comprehensive exam, thesis/dissertation. *Entrance requirements:* For master's and doctorate, GRE General Test, minimum GPA of 3.0. Electronic applications accepted. *Faculty research:* Russian cultural studies, literary translation, sociolinguistics, cognitive linguistics, émigré literature.

University of Oregon, Graduate School, College of Arts and Sciences, Program in Russian and East European Studies, Eugene, OR 97403. Offers MA. Part-time programs available. *Degree requirements:* For master's, 2 foreign languages, thesis. *Entrance requirements:* For master's, GRE General Test (recommended), minimum GPA of 3.0. Additional exam requirements/recommendations for international students: Required—TOEFL. *Faculty research:* L. N. Tolstoy's middle years, Russian folklore in eighteenth century contexts, Bulgarian syntax, medieval Bulgarian texts, contemporary Russian culture film.

University of South Africa, College of Human Sciences, Pretoria, South Africa. Offers adult education (M Ed); African languages (MA, PhD); African politics (MA, PhD); Afrikaans (MA, PhD); ancient history (MA, PhD); ancient Near Eastern studies (MA, PhD); anthropology (MA, PhD); applied linguistics (MA); Arabic (MA, PhD); archaeology (MA); art history (MA); Biblical archaeology (MA); Biblical studies (M Th, D Th, PhD); Christian spirituality (M Th, D Th); church history (M Th, D Th); classical studies (MA, PhD); clinical psychology (MA); communication (MA, PhD); comparative education (M Ed, Ed D); consulting psychology (D Admin, D Com, PhD); curriculum studies (M Ed, Ed D); development studies (M Admin, MA, D Admin, PhD); didactics (M Ed, Ed D); education (M Tech); education management (M Ed, Ed D); educational psychology (M Ed); English (MA); environmental education (M Ed); French (MA, PhD); German (MA, PhD); Greek (MA); guidance and counseling (M Ed); health studies (MA, PhD), including health sciences education (MA), health services management (MA), medical and surgical nursing science (critical care general) (MA), midwifery and neonatal nursing science (MA), trauma and emergency care (MA); history (MA, PhD); history of education (Ed D); inclusive education (M Ed, Ed D); information and communications technology policy and regulation (MA); information science (MA, MIS, PhD); international politics (MA, PhD); Islamic studies (MA, PhD); Italian (MA, PhD); Judaica (MA, PhD); linguistics (MA, PhD); mathematical education (M Ed); mathematics education (MA); missiology (M Th, D Th); modern Hebrew (MA, PhD); musicology (MA, MMus, D Mus, PhD); natural science education (M Ed); New Testament (M Th, D Th); Old Testament (D Th); pastoral therapy (M Th, D Th); philosophy (MA); philosophy of education (M Ed, Ed D); politics (MA, PhD); Portuguese (MA, PhD); practical theology (M Th, D Th); psychology (MA, MS, PhD); psychology of education (M Ed, Ed D); public health (MA); religious studies (MA, D Th, PhD); Romance languages (MA); Russian (MA, PhD); Semitic languages (MA, PhD); social behavior studies in HIV/AIDS (MA); social science (mental health) (MA); social science in development studies (MA); social science in psychology (MA); social science in social work (MA); social science in sociology (MA); social work (MSW, DSW, PhD); socio-education (M Ed, Ed D); sociolinguistics (MA); sociology (MA, PhD); Spanish (MA, PhD); systematic theology (M Th, D Th); TESOL (teaching English to speakers of other languages) (MA); theological ethics (M Th, D Th); theory of literature (MA, PhD); urban ministries (D Th); urban ministry (M Th).

The University of Tennessee, Graduate School, College of Arts and Sciences, Department of Modern Foreign Languages and Literatures, Program in Modern Foreign Languages, Knoxville, TN 37996. Offers applied linguistics (PhD); French (PhD); German (PhD); Italian (PhD); Portuguese (PhD); Russian (PhD); Spanish (PhD). *Degree requirements:* For doctorate, 2 foreign languages, thesis/dissertation. *Entrance requirements:* For doctorate, minimum GPA of 2.7. Additional exam requirements/recommendations for international students: Required—TOEFL. Electronic applications accepted. *Expenses:* Tuition, state resident: full-time $7440; part-time $414 per credit hour. Tuition, nonresident: full-time $22,478; part-time $1250 per credit hour. Required fees: $922; $43 per credit hour. Tuition and fees vary according to program.

University of Washington, Graduate School, College of Arts and Sciences, Department of Slavic Languages and Literatures, Seattle, WA 98195. Offers Russian literature (MA, PhD); Slavic linguistics (MA, PhD). *Degree requirements:* For master's, 2 foreign languages, thesis optional; for doctorate, 3 foreign languages, thesis/dissertation. *Entrance requirements:* For master's and doctorate, GRE General Test, minimum GPA of 3.0. Additional exam requirements/recommendations for international students: Required—TOEFL. Electronic applications accepted. *Faculty research:* Modern and medieval East European languages and literatures, comparative literature, Russian folk literature, Slavic literary theory and criticism, computerized morphology of Russian.

University of Waterloo, Graduate Studies, Faculty of Arts, Department of Germanic and Slavic Studies, Waterloo, ON N2L 3G1, Canada. Offers German (MA, PhD); Russian (MA). Part-time and evening/weekend programs available. *Degree requirements:* For master's, one foreign language, thesis optional; for doctorate, 2 foreign languages, comprehensive exam, thesis/dissertation. *Entrance requirements:* For master's, honors degree, minimum B average; for doctorate, master's degree, minimum B average. Additional exam requirements/recommendations for international students: Required—TOEFL, TWE. Electronic applications accepted. *Faculty research:* Medieval theatre; history and literature; German and Russian literary relations; seventeenth, eighteenth, nineteenth, and twentieth century German literature.

Wayne State University, College of Liberal Arts and Sciences, Department of Classical and Modern Languages, Literatures, and Cultures, Program in German and Slavic Studies, Detroit, MI 48202. Offers German (MA); language learning (MA); modern languages (PhD); Russian (MA). *Faculty:* 27 full-time (13 women). *Students:* 2 full-time (1 woman), 2 part-time (both women). Average age 29. 4 applicants, 50% accepted, 1 enrolled. In 2010, 1 master's awarded. *Degree requirements:* For master's, one foreign language, thesis or alternative; for doctorate, 2 foreign languages, thesis/dissertation. *Entrance requirements:* For master's and doctorate, minimum GPA of 3.0. Additional exam requirements/recommendations for international students: Required—TOEFL (minimum score 550 paper-based; 213 computer-based); Recommended—TWE (minimum score 6). *Application deadline:* For fall admission, 7/1 for domestic students, 6/1 for international students; for winter admission, 10/1 for international students; for spring admission, 2/1 for international students. Applications are processed on a rolling basis. Application fee: $30 ($50 for international students). Electronic applications accepted. *Expenses:* Tuition, state resident: full-time $7662; part-time $478.85 per credit hour. Tuition, nonresident: full-time $16,920; part-time $1057.55 per credit hour. Required fees: $571.20; $35.70 per credit hour. $188.05 per semester. Tuition and fees vary according to course load and program. *Financial support:* In 2010–11, 1 teaching assistantship with tuition reimbursement (averaging $14,620 per year) was awarded; fellowships, research assistantships, scholarships/grants and tuition waivers (full and partial) also available. Support available to part-time students. *Faculty research:* Exile and Holocaust, minority literature, gender studies, fairytale studies, sociolinguistics. *Application contact:* Janet Hankin, Professor, 313-577-0841, E-mail: janet.hankin@wayne.edu.

Yale University, Graduate School of Arts and Sciences, Department of Slavic Languages and Literatures, New Haven, CT 06520. Offers medieval Slavic literature and philology (PhD); Polish literature (PhD); Russian literature (PhD); Slavic languages and literatures and film studies (PhD). *Degree requirements:* For doctorate, 3 foreign languages, thesis/dissertation. *Entrance requirements:* For doctorate, GRE General Test.

Scandinavian Languages

Cornell University, Graduate School, Graduate Fields of Arts and Sciences, Field of Germanic Studies, Ithaca, NY 14853-0001. Offers German area studies (MA, PhD); German intellectual history (MA, PhD); Germanic linguistics (MA, PhD); Germanic literature (MA, PhD); old Norse (MA, PhD). *Faculty:* 15 full-time (7 women). *Students:* 18 full-time (11 women); includes 1 American Indian or Alaska Native, non-Hispanic/Latino, 11 international. Average age 28. 32 applicants, 28% accepted, 6 enrolled. In 2010, 5 master's, 2 doctorates awarded. Terminal master's awarded for partial completion of doctoral program. *Degree requirements:* For master's, one foreign language, thesis; for doctorate, 2 foreign languages, comprehensive exam, thesis/dissertation. *Entrance requirements:* For master's and doctorate, GRE General Test, fluency in German, writing sample, 2 letters of recommendation. Additional exam requirements/recommendations for international students: Required—TOEFL (minimum score 550 paper-based; 213 computer-based; 77 iBT). *Application deadline:* For fall admission, 1/15 for domestic students. Application fee: $80. Electronic applications accepted. *Expenses:* Tuition: Full-time $29,500. Required fees: $76. Tuition and fees vary according to degree level and program. *Financial support:* In 2010–11, 7 fellowships with full tuition reimbursements, 9 teaching assistantships with full tuition reimbursements were awarded; research assistantships with full tuition reimbursements, institutionally sponsored loans, scholarships/grants, health care benefits, tuition waivers (full and partial), and unspecified assistantships also available. Financial award applicants required to submit FAFSA. *Faculty research:* Women's studies, minority literature, literature and intellectual history, theater and film studies, Continental philosophy. *Unit head:* Director of Graduate Studies, 607-255-4047. *Application contact:* Graduate Field Assistant, 607-255-4047, E-mail: germanic_studies@cornell.edu.

Harvard University, Graduate School of Arts and Sciences, Department of Germanic Languages and Literatures, Cambridge, MA 02138. Offers German (PhD); Scandinavian (PhD). Terminal master's awarded for partial completion of doctoral program. *Degree requirements:* For doctorate, 2 foreign languages, thesis/dissertation, exams. *Entrance requirements:* For doctorate, GRE General Test, German writing sample. Additional exam requirements/recommendations for international students: Required—TOEFL. *Expenses:* Tuition: Full-time $34,976. Required fees: $1166. Full-time tuition and fees vary according to program.

University of California, Berkeley, Graduate Division, College of Letters and Science, Department of Scandinavian Languages and Literatures, Berkeley, CA 94720-1500. Offers PhD. *Degree requirements:* For doctorate, 2 foreign languages, thesis/dissertation, 3 field papers, qualifying exam. *Entrance requirements:* For doctorate, GRE General Test, minimum GPA of 3.0, MA in Scandinavian language or equivalent, 3 letters of recommendation. Additional exam requirements/recommendations for international students: Required—TOEFL (minimum score 570 paper-based; 230 computer-based). *Faculty research:* Modern literatures, old Norse language and literatures, folklore, film.

University of California, Los Angeles, Graduate Division, College of Letters and Science, Department of Germanic Languages, Program in Scandinavian, Los Angeles, CA 90095. Offers MA. *Students:* 2 full-time (1 woman). Average age 36. 2 applicants, 50% accepted, 1 enrolled. In 2010, 1 master's awarded. *Degree requirements:* For master's, one foreign language, comprehensive exam. *Entrance requirements:* For master's, GRE General Test, sample of written work. *Application deadline:* For fall admission, 12/15 for domestic and international students. Application fee: $70 ($90 for international students). Electronic applications accepted. *Financial support:* In 2010–11, 1 fellowship with full and partial tuition reimbursement, 1 teaching assistantship with full and partial tuition reimbursement were awarded; research assistantships with full and partial tuition reimbursements, Federal Work-Study, institutionally sponsored loans, and health care benefits also available. Financial award application deadline: 3/1; financial award applicants required to submit FAFSA. *Unit head:* Dr. Timothy Tangherlini, Vice Chair, 310-825-7611, E-mail: tango@humnet.ucla.edu. *Application contact:* Department Office, 310-825-6828, E-mail: allen@humnet.ucla.edu.

University of Massachusetts Amherst, Graduate School, College of Humanities and Fine Arts, Department of Languages, Literatures, and Cultures, Programs in German and Scandinavian Studies, Amherst, MA 01003. Offers MA, PhD. Part-time programs available. *Faculty:* 8 full-time (3 women). *Students:* 9 full-time (6 women), 8 part-time (6 women); includes 2 minority (1 Asian, non-Hispanic/Latino; 1 Hispanic/Latino), 2 international. Average age 33. 16 applicants, 56% accepted, 3 enrolled. In 2010, 6 master's, 1 doctorate awarded. Terminal master's awarded for partial completion of doctoral program. *Degree requirements:* For master's, thesis or alternative; for doctorate, one foreign language, comprehensive exam, thesis/dissertation. *Entrance requirements:* For master's and doctorate, writing sample in English and German. Additional exam requirements/recommendations for international students: Required—TOEFL (minimum score 550 paper-based; 213 computer-based; 80 iBT), IELTS (minimum score 6.5). *Application deadline:* For fall admission, 2/1 for domestic and international students; for spring admission, 10/1 for domestic and international students. Applications are processed on a rolling basis. Application fee: $50 ($65 for international students). Electronic applications accepted. *Expenses:* Tuition, state resident: full-time $2640. Required fees: $8282. One-time fee: $357 full-time. *Financial support:* In 2010–11, 1 research assistantship with full tuition reimbursement (averaging $14,661 per year), 13 teaching assistantships with full tuition reimbursements (averaging $10,099 per year) were awarded; fellowships, career-related internships or fieldwork, Federal Work-Study, scholarships/grants, traineeships, health care benefits, tuition waivers (full), and unspecified assistantships also available. Support available to part-time students. Financial award application deadline: 2/1; financial award applicants required to submit FAFSA. *Unit head:* Dr. Andrew Donson, Graduate Program Director, 413-545-6686, Fax: 413-545-6695. *Application contact:* Jean M. Ames, Supervisor of Admissions, 413-545-0722, Fax: 413-577-0010, E-mail: gradadm@grad.umass.edu.

University of Minnesota, Twin Cities Campus, Graduate School, College of Liberal Arts, Department of German, Scandinavian, and Dutch, Minneapolis, MN 55455-0213. Offers Germanic studies: German and Scandinavian studies track (PhD); Germanic studies: German track (MA, PhD); Germanic studies: Germanic medieval studies track (MA, PhD); Germanic studies: Scandinavian studies track (MA); Germanic studies: teaching track (MA). Part-time programs available. Terminal master's awarded for partial completion of doctoral program. *Degree requirements:* For doctorate, 2 foreign languages, thesis/dissertation. *Entrance requirements:* For master's, GRE General Test, BA in German, Scandinavian, or equivalent; for doctorate, GRE General Test, MA in German, Scandinavian, or equivalent. Additional exam requirements/recommendations for international students: Required—TOEFL (minimum score 550 paper-based; 213 computer-based; 79 iBT). Electronic applications accepted. *Faculty research:* Cultural studies, literary theory, feminist criticism, film, Germanic philology.

University of Washington, Graduate School, College of Arts and Sciences, Department of Scandinavian Studies, Seattle, WA 98195. Offers MA, PhD. *Degree requirements:* For master's, one foreign language, comprehensive exam, thesis optional; for doctorate, 2 foreign languages, comprehensive exam, thesis/dissertation. *Entrance requirements:* For master's, GRE, BA in Scandinavian or equivalent, minimum GPA of 3.0; for doctorate, GRE, master's degree, minimum GPA of 3.0. Additional exam requirements/recommendations for international students: Required—TOEFL. *Faculty research:* Scandinavian folklore, history, and politics; medieval to modern Scandinavian literature; Scandinavian fiction, poetry, drama, literary history, and theory.

University of Wisconsin–Madison, Graduate School, College of Letters and Science, Department of Scandinavian Studies, Madison, WI 53706-1380. Offers area studies (MA); folklore (PhD); literature (MA, PhD); philology (PhD). Part-time programs available. *Degree requirements:* For master's, 2 foreign languages, exam; for doctorate, thesis/dissertation, exam. *Entrance requirements:* For master's, minimum GPA of 3.25; for doctorate, minimum GPA of 3.5. Electronic applications accepted. *Expenses:* Tuition, state resident: full-time $9887; part-time $617.96 per credit. Tuition, nonresident: full-time $24,054; part-time $1503.40 per credit. Required fees: $67.63 per credit. Tuition and fees vary according to reciprocity agreements. *Faculty research:* Historical fiction, Icelandic poetry, nineteenth-century literature, theater, gender studies, folklore.

Slavic Languages

Boston College, Graduate School of Arts and Sciences, Department of Slavic and Eastern Languages, Program in Russian and Slavic Languages and Literature, Chestnut Hill, MA 02467-3800. Offers MA, MA/JD, MBA/MA. Part-time programs available. *Degree requirements:* For master's, 3 foreign languages, comprehensive exam, thesis or alternative. *Entrance requirements:* Additional exam requirements/recommendations for international students: Required—TOEFL (minimum score 600 paper-based; 250 computer-based; 100 iBT). Electronic applications accepted. *Faculty research:* Structural analysis of language, poetry and semiotic systems.

Brown University, Graduate School, Department of Slavic Languages, Providence, RI 02912. Offers Russian language and literature (AM); Slavic languages (AM); Slavic studies (PhD). *Degree requirements:* For master's, one foreign language; for doctorate, 2 foreign languages, thesis/dissertation, preliminary exam.

Columbia University, Graduate School of Arts and Sciences, Division of Humanities, Department of Slavic Languages, New York, NY 10027. Offers Russian literature (M Phil, MA, PhD); Slavic languages (M Phil, MA, PhD). *Degree requirements:* For master's, one foreign language, thesis; for doctorate, 2 foreign languages, thesis/dissertation. *Entrance requirements:* For master's and doctorate, GRE General Test. Additional exam requirements/recommendations for international students: Required—TOEFL. *Faculty research:* Polish, Serbo-Croatian, Czechoslovakian, medieval and modern Russian literature.

Cornell University, Graduate School, Graduate Fields of Arts and Sciences, Field of Linguistics, Ithaca, NY 14853-0001. Offers applied linguistics (MA, PhD); East Asian linguistics (MA, PhD); English linguistics (MA, PhD); general linguistics (MA, PhD); Germanic linguistics (MA, PhD); Indo-European linguistics (MA, PhD); phonetics (MA, PhD); phonological theory (MA, PhD); Romance linguistics (MA, PhD); second language acquisition (MA, PhD); semantics (MA, PhD); Slavic linguistics (MA, PhD); sociolinguistics (MA, PhD); South Asian linguistics (MA, PhD); Southeast Asian linguistics (MA, PhD); syntactic theory (MA, PhD). *Faculty:* 15 full-time (7 women). *Students:* 34 full-time (18 women); includes 3 Hispanic/Latino, 15 international. Average age 28. 111 applicants, 12% accepted, 8 enrolled. In 2010, 2 master's, 6 doctorates awarded. Terminal master's awarded for partial completion of doctoral program. *Degree requirements:* For master's, one foreign language, thesis; for doctorate, one foreign language, comprehensive exam, thesis/dissertation. *Entrance requirements:* For master's and doctorate, GRE General Test, 2 letters of recommendation. Additional exam requirements/recommendations for international students: Required—TOEFL (minimum score 600 paper-based; 250 computer-based; 77 iBT). *Application deadline:* For fall admission, 1/15 for domestic students. Application fee: $80. Electronic applications accepted. *Expenses:* Tuition: Full-time $29,500. Required fees: $76. Tuition and fees vary according to degree level and program. *Financial support:* In 2010–11, 17 fellowships with full tuition reimbursements, 1 research assistantship with full tuition reimbursement, 15 teaching assistantships with full tuition reimbursements were awarded; institutionally sponsored loans, scholarships/grants, health care benefits, tuition waivers (full and partial), and unspecified assistantships also available. Financial award applicants required to submit FAFSA. *Faculty research:* Phonology and phonetics, syntax and semantics, historical linguistics, philosophy of language, language acquisition. *Unit head:* Director of Graduate Studies, 607-255-1105. *Application contact:* Graduate Field Assistant, 607-255-1105, E-mail: lingfield@cornell.edu.

Duke University, Graduate School, Department of Slavic and Eurasian Studies, Durham, NC 27708. Offers AM, Certificate. Part-time programs available. *Faculty:* 7 full-time. *Students:* 3 full-time (2 women). 6 applicants, 67% accepted, 2 enrolled. *Entrance requirements:* For master's, GRE General Test, writing sample. Additional exam requirements/recommendations for international students: Required—TOEFL (minimum score 550 paper-based; 213 computer-based; 83 iBT), IELTS (minimum score 7). *Application deadline:* For fall admission, 1/30 priority date for domestic and international students. Application fee: $75. Electronic applications accepted. *Financial support:* Application deadline: 1/30. *Unit head:* Jehanne Gheith, Director of Graduate Studies, 919-660-3140, Fax: 919-660-3141, E-mail: bhayes@duke.edu. *Application contact:* Elizabeth Hutton, Director of Admissions, 919-684-3913, Fax: 919-684-2277, E-mail: grad-admissions@duke.edu.

Florida State University, The Graduate School, College of Arts and Sciences, Department of Modern Languages, Program in Slavic Languages/Russian, Tallahassee, FL 32306. Offers Slavic languages and literatures (MA). *Faculty:* 3 full-time (2 women). *Students:* 3 full-time (all women), 1 part-time (0 women); includes 1 Asian, non-Hispanic/Latino. Average age 24. 4 applicants, 50% accepted, 1 enrolled. In 2010, 1 master's awarded. *Degree requirements:* For master's, thesis optional. *Entrance requirements:* For master's, GRE General Test, minimum GPA of 3.0. Additional exam requirements/recommendations for international students: Required—TOEFL (minimum score 550 paper-based; 213 computer-based). *Application deadline:* For fall admission, 2/15 for domestic and international students. Applications are processed on a rolling basis. Application fee: $30. Electronic applications accepted. *Expenses:* Tuition, state resident: full-time $8238.24. *Financial support:* In 2010–11, 3 students received support, including 4 teaching assistantships with partial tuition reimbursements available (averaging $11,100 per year); fellowships, institutionally sponsored loans also available. Financial award application deadline: 2/1; financial award applicants required to submit FAFSA. *Faculty research:* Contemporary literature, emigré literature, Old Russian word formation, political rhetoric, structure of modern Russian. Total annual research expenditures: $4,500. *Unit head:* Dr. Robert Romanchuk, Divisional Coordinator, 850-644-8198, Fax: 850-644-0524, E-mail: rromanch@fsu.edu. *Application contact:* Wendy E. Pigott, Graduate Academic Coordinator, 850-644-8397, Fax: 850-644-0524, E-mail: wpigott@fsu.edu.

Harvard University, Graduate School of Arts and Sciences, Department of Slavic Languages and Literatures, Cambridge, MA 02138. Offers Polish (PhD); Russian (PhD); Serbo-Croatian (PhD); Slavic philology (PhD); Ukrainian (PhD). *Degree requirements:* For doctorate, 4 foreign languages, thesis/dissertation. *Entrance requirements:* For doctorate, GRE General Test, writing sample. Additional exam requirements/recommendations for international students: Required—TOEFL. *Expenses:* Tuition: Full-time $34,976. Required fees: $1166. Full-time tuition and fees vary according to program.

Slavic Languages

Indiana University Bloomington, University Graduate School, College of Arts and Sciences, Department of Slavic Languages and Literatures, Bloomington, IN 47405. Offers MA, MAT, PhD. Part-time programs available. *Faculty:* 8 full-time (3 women). *Students:* 15 full-time (11 women), 3 international. Average age 29. 16 applicants, 19% accepted, 3 enrolled. In 2010, 1 master's, 1 doctorate awarded. Terminal master's awarded for partial completion of doctoral program. *Degree requirements:* For master's, variable foreign language requirement; for doctorate, variable foreign language requirement, comprehensive exam, thesis/dissertation. *Entrance requirements:* For master's, GRE General Test. Additional exam requirements/recommendations for international students: Required—TOEFL. *Application deadline:* Applications are processed on a rolling basis. Application fee: $55 ($65 for international students). *Financial support:* In 2010–11, 4 fellowships with full tuition reimbursements (averaging $14,250 per year), 3 teaching assistantships with full tuition reimbursements (averaging $11,450 per year) were awarded; research assistantships with full tuition reimbursements. Financial award application deadline: 2/1. *Faculty research:* Russian stress, Slavic accentology and morphophonemics, Eastern European literature, Bible translation. *Unit head:* Dr. Steven Franks, Chair, 812-855-9906, E-mail: feldstei@indiana.edu. *Application contact:* Tricia Wall, Summer Program and Student Services Assistant, 812-855-2608, Fax: 812-855-2107.

New York University, Graduate School of Arts and Science, Department of Russian and Slavic Studies, New York, NY 10012-1019. Offers Russian literature (MA); Slavic literature (MA). Part-time programs available. *Faculty:* 8 full-time (3 women). *Students:* 7 full-time (5 women), 7 part-time (2 women), 1 international. Average age 28. 16 applicants, 81% accepted, 6 enrolled. In 2010, 9 master's awarded. *Degree requirements:* For master's, one foreign language, comprehensive exam, thesis. *Entrance requirements:* For master's, GRE General Test, minimum 3 years of undergraduate Russian or equivalent. Additional exam requirements/recommendations for international students: Required—TOEFL. *Application deadline:* For fall admission, 4/15 for domestic students; for spring admission, 11/1 for domestic students. Application fee: $90. *Financial support:* Career-related internships or fieldwork, Federal Work-Study, and institutionally sponsored loans available. Financial award application deadline: 4/15; financial award applicants required to submit FAFSA. *Faculty research:* Modern Russian literature and art, contemporary Russian and East European literature, literary theory, Slavic linguistics, Russian journalism. *Unit head:* Yanni Kotsonis, Chair, 212-998-8670, Fax: 212-995-4604, E-mail: gsas.russian.and.slavic@nyu.edu. *Application contact:* Eliot Borenstein, Director of Graduate Studies, 212-998-8670, Fax: 212-995-4604, E-mail: gsas.russian.and.slavic@nyu.edu.

Northwestern University, The Graduate School, Judd A. and Marjorie Weinberg College of Arts and Sciences, Department of Slavic Languages and Literature, Evanston, IL 60208. Offers PhD. Admissions and degrees offered through The Graduate School. Part-time programs available. *Degree requirements:* For doctorate, 3 foreign languages, thesis/dissertation. *Entrance requirements:* For doctorate, GRE General Test. Additional exam requirements/recommendations for international students: Required—TOEFL. *Faculty research:* Russian poetry and prose, nineteenth- through twentieth-centuries, translation and Russian culture, Russian intellectual history, Slavic literature and nationalism, Polish poetry.

The Ohio State University, Graduate School, College of Arts and Sciences, Division of Arts and Humanities, Department of Slavic and East European Languages and Literatures, Columbus, OH 43210. Offers linguistics (MA); literature (MA); Russian literature (PhD); Slavic linguistics (PhD). *Faculty:* 13. *Students:* 21 full-time (12 women), 8 part-time (4 women); includes 1 Asian, non-Hispanic/Latino, 4 international. Average age 31. In 2010, 2 master's, 3 doctorates awarded. *Degree requirements:* For master's, variable foreign language requirement, thesis optional; for doctorate, variable foreign language requirement, thesis/dissertation. *Entrance requirements:* For master's and doctorate, GRE General Test. Additional exam requirements/recommendations for international students: Required—TOEFL (minimum score 600 paper-based; 250 computer-based). *Application deadline:* For fall admission, 8/15 priority date for domestic students, 7/1 priority date for international students; for winter admission, 12/1 priority date for domestic students, 11/1 priority date for international students; for spring admission, 3/1 priority date for domestic students, 2/1 priority date for international students. Applications are processed on a rolling basis. Application fee: $40 ($50 for international students). Electronic applications accepted. *Expenses:* Tuition, state resident: full-time $10,605. Tuition, nonresident: full-time $26,535. Tuition and fees vary according to course load and program. *Financial support:* Fellowships, research assistantships, teaching assistantships, Federal Work-Study and institutionally sponsored loans available. Support available to part-time students. *Faculty research:* Polish literature. *Unit head:* Helena Goscilo, Chair, 614-247-1790, E-mail: goscilo.1@osu.edu. *Application contact:* 614-292-9444, Fax: 614-292-3895, E-mail: domestic.grad@osu.edu.

Princeton University, Graduate School, Department of Slavic Languages and Literatures, Princeton, NJ 08544-1019. Offers Russian and Slavic linguistics (PhD); Russian literature (PhD). *Degree requirements:* For doctorate, variable foreign language requirement, thesis/dissertation. *Entrance requirements:* For doctorate, GRE General Test. Additional exam requirements/recommendations for international students: Required—TOEFL (minimum score 600 paper-based; 250 computer-based). Electronic applications accepted.

Stanford University, School of Humanities and Sciences, Department of Slavic Languages and Literatures, Stanford, CA 94305-9991. Offers Russian (MA); Slavic languages and literatures (PhD). Terminal master's awarded for partial completion of doctoral program. *Degree requirements:* For master's, one foreign language, thesis or alternative; for doctorate, 3 foreign languages, thesis/dissertation. *Entrance requirements:* For master's and doctorate, GRE General Test. Additional exam requirements/recommendations for international students: Required—TOEFL. Electronic applications accepted. *Expenses:* Tuition: Full-time $38,700; part-time $860 per unit. One-time fee: $200 full-time.

University of Alberta, Faculty of Graduate Studies and Research, Department of Modern Languages and Cultural Studies, Edmonton, AB T6G 2E1, Canada. Offers applied linguistics (Germanic, Romance, Slavic) (MA); French language, literatures and linguistics (PhD); French language, literatures, and linguistics (MA); Germanic languages, literatures and linguistics (PhD); Germanic languages, literatures, and linguistics (MA); Italian studies (MA); Slavic languages and literatures (Russian, Ukrainian) (MA, PhD); Slavic linguistics (Russian, Ukrainian) (MA, PhD); Spanish and Latin American studies (MA, PhD); Ukrainian folklore (MA, PhD). Part-time programs available. *Degree requirements:* For master's, one foreign language, thesis; for doctorate, 2 foreign languages, comprehensive exam, thesis/dissertation. *Entrance requirements:* For master's and doctorate, 1 language other than English. Additional exam requirements/recommendations for international students: Required—Michigan English Language Assessment Battery or TOEFL (minimum score 550 paper-based; 213 computer-based). Electronic applications accepted. *Faculty research:* Russian/Ukrainian studies; German studies; contemporary Latin American, French and Francophone studies; Italian studies.

University of California, Berkeley, Graduate Division, College of Letters and Science, Department of Slavic Languages and Literatures, Berkeley, CA 94720-1500. Offers Czech (PhD), including Czech linguistics, Czech literature; Polish (PhD), including Polish linguistics, Polish literature; Russian (PhD), including Russian linguistics, Russian literature; Serbo-Croatian (PhD), including Serbo-Croatian linguistics, Serbo-Croatian literature. Terminal master's awarded for partial completion of doctoral program. *Degree requirements:* For doctorate, thesis/dissertation, oral and written exams. *Entrance requirements:* For doctorate, GRE General Test, minimum GPA of 3.0, 3 letters of recommendation. Additional exam requirements/recommendations for international students: Required—TOEFL (minimum score 570 paper-based; 230 computer-based). Electronic applications accepted.

University of California, Los Angeles, Graduate Division, College of Letters and Science, Department of Slavic Languages and Literatures, Los Angeles, CA 90095. Offers MA, PhD. *Faculty:* 9 full-time (3 women). *Students:* 11 full-time (7 women); includes 1 minority (Hispanic/Latino). Average age 29. 11 applicants, 36% accepted, 2 enrolled. In 2010, 3 master's, 1 doctorate awarded. Terminal master's awarded for partial completion of doctoral program. *Degree requirements:* For master's, 2 foreign languages, comprehensive exam; for doctorate, 2 foreign languages, thesis/dissertation, oral and written qualifying exams. *Entrance requirements:* For master's, GRE General Test, minimum GPA of 3.0, sample of written work; for doctorate, GRE General Test, minimum undergraduate GPA of 3.0, proficiency in French and German, sample of written work. *Application deadline:* For fall admission, 1/15 for domestic and international students. Application fee: $70 ($90 for international students). Electronic applications accepted. *Financial support:* In 2010–11, 10 fellowships with full and partial tuition reimbursements, 2 research assistantships with full and partial tuition reimbursements, 7 teaching assistantships with full and partial tuition reimbursements were awarded; Federal Work-Study, institutionally sponsored loans, scholarships/grants, health care benefits, tuition waivers (full and partial), and unspecified assistantships also available. Financial award application deadline: 3/1; financial award applicants required to submit FAFSA. *Unit head:* Dr. Ronald Vroon, Chair, 310-825-8724, E-mail: vroon@humnet.ucla.edu. *Application contact:* Department Office, 310-825-3856, E-mail: slavic@humnet.ucla.edu.

University of Chicago, Division of the Humanities, Department of Slavic Languages and Literatures, Chicago, IL 60637-1513. Offers AM, PhD. Terminal master's awarded for partial completion of doctoral program. *Degree requirements:* For master's, one foreign language; for doctorate, 2 foreign languages, thesis/dissertation. *Entrance requirements:* For master's and doctorate, GRE General Test. Additional exam requirements/recommendations for international students: Required—TOEFL.

University of Illinois at Urbana–Champaign, Graduate College, College of Liberal Arts and Sciences, School of Literatures, Cultures and Linguistics, Department of Slavic Languages and Literatures, Champaign, IL 61820. Offers MA, PhD. *Faculty:* 5 full-time (1 woman). *Students:* 13 full-time (11 women), 1 (woman) part-time; includes 2 minority (1 Black or African American, non-Hispanic/Latino; 1 Asian, non-Hispanic/Latino), 6 international. 16 applicants, 31% accepted, 2 enrolled. In 2010, 2 master's awarded. *Entrance requirements:* For master's and doctorate, GRE, minimum GPA of 3.0; writing sample. Additional exam requirements/recommendations for international students: Required—TOEFL (minimum score 79 iBT). *Application deadline:* Applications are processed on a rolling basis. Application fee: $75 ($90 for international students). Electronic applications accepted. *Financial support:* In 2010–11, 8 fellowships, 2 research assistantships, 9 teaching assistantships were awarded; tuition waivers (full and partial) also available. *Unit head:* Lilya Kaganovsky, Co-Acting Head, 217-333-6157, Fax: 217-333-7310, E-mail: lilya@illinois.edu. *Application contact:* Lynn Stanke, Office Support Specialist, 217-333-6269, Fax: 217-244-3050, E-mail: stanke@illinois.edu.

The University of Kansas, Graduate Studies, College of Liberal Arts and Sciences, Department of Slavic Languages and Literatures, Lawrence, KS 66045. Offers MA, PhD. Part-time programs available. *Faculty:* 7 full-time (4 women), 1 part-time/adjunct (0 women). *Students:* 12 full-time (7 women), 1 (woman) part-time, 2 international. Average age 31. 10 applicants, 80% accepted, 3 enrolled. In 2010, 3 master's awarded. Terminal master's awarded for partial completion of doctoral program. *Degree requirements:* For master's, one foreign language, comprehensive exam, thesis or alternative; for doctorate, 3 foreign languages, comprehensive exam, thesis/dissertation, 2nd Slavic language. *Entrance requirements:* For master's, GRE, BA in Slavic languages and literatures or the equivalent; for doctorate, GRE, MA in Slavic languages and literatures. Additional exam requirements/recommendations for international students: Required—TOEFL. *Application deadline:* For winter admission, 1/31 priority date for domestic and international students. Applications are processed on a rolling basis. Application fee: $55 ($65 for international students). Electronic applications accepted. *Expenses:* Tuition, state resident: full-time $7092; part-time $295.50 per credit hour. Tuition, nonresident: full-time $16,590; part-time $691.25 per credit hour. Required fees: $858; $71.49 per credit hour. Tuition and fees vary according to course load, campus/location and program. *Financial support:* Fellowships with tuition reimbursements, teaching assistantships with full and partial tuition reimbursements, Federal Work-Study, institutionally sponsored loans, scholarships/grants, and unspecified assistantships available. Financial award application deadline: 1/31. *Faculty research:* Russian and south Slavic linguistics, Polish and Russian literature, folklore, Russian intellectual history, Slavic culture. *Unit head:* Prof. Marc L. Greenberg, Chair, 785-864-3313, Fax: 785-864-4298, E-mail: mlg@ku.edu. *Application contact:* Prof. Maria Carlson, Graduate Director, 785-864-3313, Fax: 785-864-4298, E-mail: mcarlson@ku.edu.

The University of Manchester, School of Languages, Linguistics and Cultures, Manchester, United Kingdom. Offers Arab world studies (PhD); Chinese studies (M Phil, PhD); East Asian studies (M Phil, PhD); English language (PhD); French studies (M Phil, PhD); German studies (M Phil, PhD); interpreting studies (PhD); Italian studies (M Phil, PhD); Japanese studies (M Phil, PhD); Latin American cultural studies (M Phil, PhD); linguistics (M Phil, PhD); Middle Eastern studies (M Phil, PhD); Polish studies (M Phil, PhD); Portuguese studies (M Phil, PhD); Russian studies (M Phil, PhD); Spanish studies (M Phil, PhD); translation and intercultural studies (M Phil, PhD).

University of Manitoba, Faculty of Graduate Studies, Faculty of Arts, Department of German and Slavic Studies, Winnipeg, MB R3T 2N2, Canada. Offers German language and literature (MA); Slavic languages and literatures (MA). *Degree requirements:* For master's, one foreign language, thesis or alternative.

University of Michigan, Horace H. Rackham School of Graduate Studies, College of Literature, Science, and the Arts, Department of Slavic Languages and Literatures, Ann Arbor, MI 48109-1275. Offers Russian (AM); Slavic languages and literatures (PhD). Terminal master's awarded for partial completion of doctoral program. *Degree requirements:* For master's, 2 foreign languages, comprehensive exam; for doctorate, 3 foreign languages, comprehensive exam, thesis/dissertation, oral defense of dissertation, preliminary exam. *Entrance requirements:* For master's, GRE General Test, 3rd-year foreign language proficiency; for doctorate, GRE General Test. Additional exam requirements/recommendations for international students: Required—TOEFL (minimum score 560 paper-based; 220 computer-based). Electronic applications accepted. *Expenses:* Tuition, state resident: full-time $17,784; part-time $1116 per credit hour. Tuition, nonresident: full-time $35,944; part-time $2125 per credit hour. International tuition: $35,994 full-time. Required fees: $95 per semester. Tuition and fees vary according to course load, degree level and program. *Faculty research:* Russian literature (all periods), Polish literature, South Slavic literatures, Czech literature, Ukrainian literature.

The University of North Carolina at Chapel Hill, Graduate School, College of Arts and Sciences, Department of Slavic Languages and Literatures, Chapel Hill, NC 27599. Offers Polish literature (PhD); Russian and east Euorpean studies (MA); Russian literature (MA, PhD); Serbo-Croatian literature (PhD); Slavic linguistics (MA, PhD). Part-time programs available. Terminal master's awarded for partial completion of doctoral program. *Degree requirements:* For master's, 2 foreign languages, comprehensive exam, thesis; for doctorate, 4 foreign languages, comprehensive exam, thesis/dissertation. *Entrance requirements:* For master's and doctorate, GRE General Test, minimum GPA of 3.0. Electronic applications accepted. *Faculty research:* Russian cultural studies, literary translation, sociolinguistics, cognitive linguistics, émigré literature.

University of Pittsburgh, School of Arts and Sciences, Department of Slavic Languages and Literatures, Pittsburgh, PA 15260. Offers MA, PhD. Part-time programs available. *Faculty:* 6 full-time (2 women), 1 part-time/adjunct (0 women). *Students:* 10 full-time (8 women), 2 international. Average age 28. 15 applicants, 33% accepted, 1 enrolled. In 2010, 2 master's, 2 doctorates awarded. Terminal master's awarded for partial completion of doctoral program. *Degree requirements:* For master's, 2 foreign languages, comprehensive exam; for doctorate, 3 foreign languages, comprehensive exam, thesis/dissertation. *Entrance requirements:* For master's and doctorate, GRE General Test. Additional exam requirements/recommendations for international students: Required—TOEFL. *Application deadline:* For fall admission, 1/15 priority date for domestic and international students. Application fee: $40. Electronic applications accepted. *Expenses:* Tuition, state resident: full-time $17,304; part-time $701 per credit. Tuition, nonresident: full-time $29,554; part-time $1210 per credit. Required fees: $740; $214 per term. Tuition and fees vary according to program. *Financial support:* In 2010–11, 10 students received support, including 5 fellowships with full tuition reimbursements available (averaging $18,500 per year), 6 teaching assistantships with full tuition reimbursements available (averaging $15,520 per year); Federal Work-Study, scholarships/grants, and traineeships also available. Support available to part-time students. Financial award application deadline: 1/15. *Faculty research:* Contemporary Russian literature and culture, Russian cinema. *Unit head:* Prof. David J. Birnbaum, Chair, 412-624-5906, Fax: 412-624-9714, E-mail: djbpitt@pitt.edu. *Application contact:* Christine Metil, Administrator, 412-624-5906, Fax: 412-624-9714, E-mail: metil@pitt.edu.

University of Southern California, Graduate School, Dana and David Dornsife College of Letters, Arts and Sciences, Department of Linguistics, Los Angeles, CA 90089. Offers East Asian linguistics (PhD); Hispanic linguistics (PhD); linguistics (PhD); Slavic linguistics (PhD). *Faculty:* 15 full-time (10 women), 5 part-time/adjunct (3 women). *Students:* 40 full-time (26 women), 2 part-time (1 woman); includes 7 minority (5 Asian, non-Hispanic/Latino; 1 Hispanic/Latino; 1 Two or more races, non-Hispanic/Latino), 23 international. 76 applicants, 24% accepted, 7 enrolled. In 2010, 1 doctorate awarded. *Degree requirements:* For doctorate, comprehensive exam, thesis/dissertation. *Entrance requirements:* For doctorate, GRE. Additional exam requirements/recommendations for international students: Required—TOEFL (minimum score 100 iBT). *Application deadline:* For fall admission, 12/1 priority date for domestic and international students. Application fee: $85. Electronic applications accepted. *Expenses:* Tuition: Full-time $31,240; part-time $1420 per unit. Required fees: $600. One-time fee: $35 full-time. Full-time tuition and fees vary according to degree level and program. *Financial support:* In 2010–11, 37 students received support, including 12 fellowships with full tuition reimbursements available (averaging $20,000 per year), 3 research assistantships with full tuition reimbursements available (averaging $19,250 per year), 22 teaching assistantships with full tuition reimbursements available (averaging $19,250 per year); scholarships/grants, health care benefits, and unspecified assistantships also available. *Faculty research:* Syntax, phonology, phonetics, semantics, sociolinguistics, psycholinguistics. *Unit head:* Dr. James Higginbotham, Chair, 213-740-2986, Fax: 213-740-9306, E-mail: higgy@usc.edu. *Application contact:* Joyce Perez, Student Services Advisor, 213-740-3891, Fax: 213-740-9306, E-mail: jpperez@usc.edu.

University of Southern California, Graduate School, Dana and David Dornsife College of Letters, Arts and Sciences, Department of Slavic Languages and Literatures, Los Angeles, CA 90089. Offers MA, PhD. *Faculty:* 7 full-time (2 women). *Students:* 10 full-time (8 women); includes 1 minority (Hispanic/Latino), 4 international. 9 applicants, 11% accepted, 1 enrolled. In 2010, 4 master's, 2 doctorates awarded. *Degree requirements:* For master's, one foreign language, comprehensive exam, thesis or alternative, 30 units; for doctorate, 3 foreign languages, comprehensive exam, thesis/dissertation, 60 units. *Entrance requirements:* For doctorate, GRE, BA in Russian literature or equivalent. Additional exam requirements/recommendations for international students: Required—TOEFL. *Application deadline:* For fall admission, 12/1 priority date for domestic and international students. Applications are processed on a rolling basis. Application fee: $85. Electronic applications accepted. *Expenses:* Tuition: Full-time $31,240; part-time $1420 per unit. Required fees: $600. One-time fee: $35 full-time. Full-time tuition and fees vary according to degree level and program. *Financial support:* In 2010–11, 9 students received support, including 1 fellowship with full tuition reimbursement available (averaging $21,000 per year), teaching assistantships with full tuition reimbursements available (averaging $18,900 per year); scholarships/grants, health care benefits, and unspecified assistantships also available. Financial award application deadline: 12/1. *Faculty research:* Russian avant-garde art, intertextuality in Russian literature, eighteenth century Russian culture, Russian poetry, Russian music history, twentieth century Russian literature. *Unit head:* Dr. Thomas J. Seifrid, Professor, 213-740-2735, Fax: 213-740-8550, E-mail: seifrid@usc.edu. *Application contact:* Susan Kechekian, Administrative Assistant, 213-740-2735, Fax: 213-740-8550, E-mail: susan@usc.edu.

The University of Texas at Austin, Graduate School, College of Liberal Arts, Department of Slavic and Eurasian Studies, Austin, TX 78712-1111. Offers Slavic languages (MA, PhD). *Degree requirements:* For master's, 2 foreign languages, thesis; for doctorate, 3 foreign languages, thesis/dissertation. *Entrance requirements:* For master's and doctorate, GRE General Test. Electronic applications accepted. *Faculty research:* Slavic linguistics; applied linguistics; Russian, Czech, and Slavic literature and culture.

University of Toronto, School of Graduate Studies, Humanities Division, Department of Slavic Languages and Literatures, Toronto, ON M5S 1A1, Canada. Offers MA, PhD. Part-time programs available. *Degree requirements:* For doctorate, comprehensive exam, thesis/dissertation. *Entrance requirements:* For master's, BA in related area; minimum A– average in Slavic courses taken in final year, writing sample, 2 letters of recommendation; for doctorate, MA in Slavic languages and literatures, minimum A– average, writing sample, 2 letters of recommendation.

University of Virginia, College and Graduate School of Arts and Sciences, Department of Slavic Languages and Literatures, Charlottesville, VA 22903. Offers MA, PhD. *Faculty:* 8 full-time (4 women). *Students:* 13 full-time (8 women), 4 international. Average age 28. 14 applicants, 43% accepted, 5 enrolled. In 2010, 4 master's, 2 doctorates awarded. *Degree requirements:* For master's, one foreign language, comprehensive exam, thesis (for some programs); for doctorate, one foreign language, comprehensive exam, thesis/dissertation. *Entrance requirements:* For master's, GRE General Test, 2 letters of recommendation, writing sample in English; for doctorate, GRE General Test, 2 letters of recommendation; writing sample in English. Additional exam requirements/recommendations for international students: Required—TOEFL (minimum score 600 paper-based; 250 computer-based; 90 iBT), IELTS (minimum score 7). *Application deadline:* Applications are processed on a rolling basis. Application fee: $60. Electronic applications accepted. *Financial support:* Teaching assistantships available. Financial award application deadline: 1/15; financial award applicants required to submit FAFSA. *Unit head:* Julian W. Connolly, Chair, 434-924-3548, Fax: 434-982-2744, E-mail: slavic@virginia.edu. *Application contact:* Karen Ryan, Director of Graduate Studies, 434-924-3548, Fax: 434-982-2744, E-mail: klr8p@virginia.edu.

University of Washington, Graduate School, College of Arts and Sciences, Department of Slavic Languages and Literatures, Seattle, WA 98195. Offers Russian literature (MA, PhD); Slavic linguistics (MA, PhD). *Degree requirements:* For master's, 2 foreign languages, thesis optional; for doctorate, 3 foreign languages, thesis/dissertation. *Entrance requirements:* For master's and doctorate, GRE General Test, minimum GPA of 3.0. Additional exam requirements/recommendations for international students: Required—TOEFL. Electronic applications accepted. *Faculty research:* Modern and medieval East European languages and literatures, comparative literature, Russian folk literature, Slavic literary theory and criticism, computerized morphology of Russian.

University of Wisconsin–Madison, Graduate School, College of Letters and Science, Department of Slavic Languages and Literature, Madison, WI 53706-1380. Offers MA, PhD. Part-time programs available. Terminal master's awarded for partial completion of doctoral program. *Degree requirements:* For doctorate, thesis/dissertation. *Entrance requirements:* For master's and doctorate, GRE General Test. Additional exam requirements/recommendations for international students: Required—TOEFL. Electronic applications accepted. *Expenses:* Tuition, state resident: full-time $9887; part-time $617.96 per credit. Tuition, nonresident: full-time $24,054; part-time $1503.40 per credit. Required fees: $67.63 per credit. Tuition and fees vary according to reciprocity agreements. *Faculty research:* Polish literature, linguistics, South Slavic literature, second language acquisition, nineteenth and twentieth-century Russian literature.

University of Wisconsin–Milwaukee, Graduate School, College of Letters and Sciences, Interdepartmental Program in Foreign Language and Literature, Milwaukee, WI 53201-0413. Offers classics and Hebrew studies (MAFLL); comparative literature (MAFLL); French and Italian (MAFLL); German (MAFLL); Slavic studies (MAFLL); translation (Certificate). Part-time programs available. *Faculty:* 29 full-time (14 women). *Students:* 35 full-time (27 women), 29 part-time (20 women); includes 1 Hispanic/Latino. Average age 40. 30 applicants, 67% accepted, 19 enrolled. In 2010, 24 master's awarded. *Degree requirements:* For master's, 2 foreign languages, thesis or alternative. *Entrance requirements:* Additional exam requirements/recommendations for international students: Required—TOEFL (minimum score 550 paper-based; 79 iBT), IELTS (minimum score 6.5). *Application deadline:* For fall admission, 1/1 priority date for domestic students; for spring admission, 9/1 for domestic students. Applications are processed on a rolling basis. Application fee: $56 ($96 for international students). Electronic applications accepted. *Financial support:* In 2010–11, 1 fellowship, 2 research assistantships, 26 teaching assistantships were awarded; career-related internships or fieldwork, health care benefits, unspecified assistantships, and project assistantships also available. Support available to part-time students. Financial award application deadline: 4/15; financial award applicants required to submit FAFSA. Total annual research expenditures: $304,210. *Unit head:* Gabrielle Verdier, Representative, 414-229-3346, Fax: 414-229-2741, E-mail: verdier@uwm.edu. *Application contact:* General Information Contact, 414-229-4982, Fax: 414-229-6967, E-mail: gradschool@uwm.edu.

Yale University, Graduate School of Arts and Sciences, Department of Slavic Languages and Literatures, New Haven, CT 06520. Offers medieval Slavic literature and philology (PhD); Polish literature (PhD); Russian literature (PhD); Slavic languages and literatures and film studies (PhD). *Degree requirements:* For doctorate, 3 foreign languages, thesis/dissertation. *Entrance requirements:* For doctorate, GRE General Test.

Spanish

American University, College of Arts and Sciences, Department of Language and Foreign Studies, Washington, DC 20016-8045. Offers French (Certificate), including translation; Russian (Certificate), including translation; Spanish: Latin American studies (MA, Certificate), including Spanish: Latin American studies (MA), translation (Certificate); teaching English to speakers of other languages (MA, Certificate). Part-time and evening/weekend programs available. *Faculty:* 41 full-time (29 women), 43 part-time/adjunct (34 women). *Students:* 22 full-time (17 women), 39 part-time (31 women); includes 8 minority (1 Black or African American, non-Hispanic/Latino; 3 Asian, non-Hispanic/Latino; 3 Hispanic/Latino; 1 Native Hawaiian or other Pacific Islander, non-Hispanic/Latino), 6 international. Average age 34. 64 applicants, 64% accepted, 14 enrolled. In 2010, 24 master's, 28 other advanced degrees awarded. *Degree requirements:* For master's, one foreign language, comprehensive exam, thesis or alternative, portfolio, research; for Certificate, minimum 15 credit hours related coursework. *Entrance requirements:* For master's, GRE, writing sample; for Certificate, bachelor's degree. Additional exam requirements/recommendations for international students: Required—TOEFL. *Application deadline:* For fall admission, 2/1 for domestic students; for spring admission, 10/1 for domestic students. Application fee: $80. *Financial support:* Fellowships, career-related internships or fieldwork, Federal Work-Study, institutionally sponsored loans, and tuition waivers (partial) available. Financial award application deadline: 2/1. *Unit head:* Olga Rojer, Chair, 202-885-2139, Fax: 202-885-1076, E-mail: orojer@american.edu. *Application contact:* Kathleen Clowery, Director of Graduate Admissions, 202-885-3621, Fax: 202-885-1505, E-mail: clowery@american.edu.

Arizona State University, College of Liberal Arts and Sciences, School of International Letters and Cultures, Program in Spanish, Tempe, AZ 85287-0202. Offers Spanish (cultural studies) (PhD); Spanish (linguistics) (MA), including second language acquisition/applied linguistics, sociolinguistics; Spanish (literature and culture) (MA); Spanish (literature) (PhD). Part-time programs available. *Faculty:* 11 full-time (4 women). *Students:* 53 full-time (34 women), 17 part-time (11 women); includes 35 minority (1 Black or African American, non-Hispanic/Latino; 2 Asian, non-Hispanic/Latino; 31 Hispanic/Latino; 1 Two or more races, non-Hispanic/Latino), 12 international. Average age 34. 49 applicants, 61% accepted, 19 enrolled. In 2010, 7 master's, 3 doctorates awarded. Terminal master's awarded for partial completion of doctoral program. *Degree requirements:* For master's, thesis, oral defense; written comprehensive exam (literature and culture); portfolio review (linguistics); interactive Program of Study (iPOS) submitted before completing 50 percent of required credit hours; for doctorate, comprehensive exam, thesis/dissertation, interactive Program of Study (iPOS) submitted before completing 50 percent of required credit hours. *Entrance requirements:* For master's, GRE (recommended), BA in Spanish or close equivalent from accredited institution with minimum GPA of 3.5, 3 letters of recommendation, personal statement, academic writing sample; for doctorate, GRE (recommended), MA in Spanish or equivalent from accredited institution with minimum GPA of 3.75, 3 letters of recommendation, personal statement, academic writing sample. Additional exam requirements/recommendations for international students: Required—TOEFL (minimum score 550 paper-based; 213 computer-based; 83 iBT), IELTS (minimum score 6.5). *Application deadline:* For fall admission, 1/1 for domestic and international students. Application fee: $70 ($90 for international students). Electronic applications accepted. *Expenses:* Tuition, state resident: full-time $8510; part-time $608 per credit. Tuition, nonresident: full-time $16,542; part-time $919 per credit. Required fees: $339; $110 per credit. Part-time tuition and fees vary according to course load. *Financial support:* In 2010–11, 1 research assistantship with full and partial tuition reimbursement (averaging $20,000 per year), 54 teaching assistantships with full and partial tuition reimbursements (averaging $14,235 per year) were awarded; fellowships with full and partial tuition reimbursements, institutionally sponsored loans, scholarships/grants, and tuition waivers (partial) also available. Financial award application deadline: 3/1; financial award applicants required to submit FAFSA. *Unit head:* Dr. Emil Volek, Director, 480-965-7211, E-mail: emil.volek@asu.edu. *Application contact:* Graduate Admissions, 480-965-6113.

Arkansas Tech University, Graduate College, College of Arts and Humanities, Russellville, AR 72801. Offers communication (MLA); English (M Ed, MA); fine arts (MLA); history (MA); multi-media journalism (MA); psychology (MS); social science (MLA); Spanish (MA, MLA); teaching English as a second language (MA, MLA). Part-time programs available. *Students:* 39 full-time (23 women), 87 part-time (69 women); includes 13 minority (3 Black or African American, non-Hispanic/Latino; 1 American Indian or Alaska Native, non-Hispanic/Latino; 1 Asian, non-Hispanic/Latino; 8 Hispanic/Latino), 14 international. Average age 32. In 2010, 54 master's awarded. *Degree requirements:* For master's, comprehensive exam (for some programs), thesis (for some programs), project. *Entrance requirements:* For master's, GRE General Test or MAT. Additional exam requirements/recommendations for international students: Required—TOEFL (minimum score 550 paper-based; 213 computer-based; 79 iBT), IELTS (minimum score 6). *Application deadline:* For fall admission, 3/1 priority date for domestic students, 5/1 priority date for international students; for spring admission, 10/1 priority date for domestic and international students. Applications are processed on a rolling basis. Application fee: $0 ($50 for international students). Electronic applications accepted. *Expenses:* Tuition,

Spanish

Arkansas Tech University (continued)
state resident: full-time $4680; part-time $195 per credit hour. Tuition, nonresident: full-time $9360; part-time $390 per credit hour. Required fees: $714; $14 per credit hour. One-time fee: $326 part-time. Tuition and fees vary according to course load. *Financial support:* In 2010–11, teaching assistantships with full tuition reimbursements (averaging $4,000 per year); research assistantships, career-related internships or fieldwork, Federal Work-Study, scholarships/grants, health care benefits, and unspecified assistantships also available. Support available to part-time students. Financial award application deadline: 4/15; financial award applicants required to submit FAFSA. *Unit head:* Dr. Micheal Tarver, Dean, 479-968-0274, Fax: 479-964-0812, E-mail: mtarver@atu.edu. *Application contact:* Dr. Mary B. Gunter, Dean of Graduate College, 479-968-0398, Fax: 479-964-0542, E-mail: graduate.school@atu.edu.

Asbury University, School of Graduate and Professional Studies, Wilmore, KY 40390-1198. Offers biology: alternative certificate (MA Ed); chemistry: alternative certificate (MA Ed); English (MA Ed); English as a second language (MA Ed); ESL (MA Ed); French (MA Ed); Latin: alternative certificate (MA Ed); mathematics: alternative certificate (MA Ed); reading/writing endorsement (MA Ed); social studies (MA Ed); social work (MSW), including child and family services; Spanish (MA Ed); special education (MA Ed); special education: alternative certificate (MA Ed); teacher as leader endorsement (MA Ed). *Accreditation:* NCATE. Part-time programs available. *Degree requirements:* For master's, action research project, portfolio. *Entrance requirements:* For master's, PRAXIS/NTE, minimum GPA of 2.75, letters of recommendation. Additional exam requirements/recommendations for international students: Required—TOEFL (minimum score 550 paper-based). Electronic applications accepted.

Auburn University, Graduate School, College of Liberal Arts, Department of Foreign Languages and Literatures, Auburn University, AL 36849. Offers Spanish (MA, MHS). Part-time programs available. *Faculty:* 32 full-time (20 women), 8 part-time/adjunct (6 women). *Students:* 14 full-time (9 women), 16 part-time (14 women); includes 1 Black or African American, non-Hispanic/Latino; 1 Asian, non-Hispanic/Latino; 4 Hispanic/Latino, 1 international. Average age 28. 13 applicants, 100% accepted, 13 enrolled. In 2010, 10 master's awarded. *Degree requirements:* For master's, one foreign language, comprehensive exam, thesis (for some programs). *Entrance requirements:* For master's, GRE General Test. *Application deadline:* For fall admission, 7/7 for domestic students; for spring admission, 11/24 for domestic students. Applications are processed on a rolling basis. Application fee: $50 ($60 for international students). Electronic applications accepted. *Expenses:* Tuition, state resident: full-time $7002. Tuition, nonresident: full-time $21,898. International tuition: $22,116 full-time. Required fees: $892. Tuition and fees vary according to course load and program. *Financial support:* Fellowships, teaching assistantships, Federal Work-Study available. Support available to part-time students. Financial award application deadline: 3/15; financial award applicants required to submit FAFSA. *Unit head:* Dr. Robert G. Weigel, Chair, 334-844-6350, Fax: 334-844-6378. *Application contact:* Dr. George Flowers, Dean of the Graduate School, 334-844-2125.

Baylor University, Graduate School, College of Arts and Sciences, Department of Modern Foreign Languages, Waco, TX 76798. Offers Spanish (MA). *Students:* 12 full-time (9 women); includes 3 minority (1 Asian, non-Hispanic/Latino; 2 Hispanic/Latino). In 2010, 3 master's awarded. *Entrance requirements:* For master's, GRE General Test. *Application deadline:* Applications are processed on a rolling basis. Application fee: $25. *Unit head:* Dr. Baudelio Garza, Graduate Program Director, 254-710-3711, Fax: 254-710-3799, E-mail: baudelio_garza@baylor.edu. *Application contact:* Ann Westbrook, Administrative Assistant, 254-710-6027, Fax: 254-710-3870, E-mail: ann_westbrook@baylor.edu.

Bennington College, Graduate Programs, MA in Teaching a Second Language Program, Bennington, VT 05201. Offers education (MATSL); foreign language education (MATSL); French (MATSL); Spanish (MATSL). Part-time programs available. *Faculty:* 3 full-time (2 women), 6 part-time/adjunct (5 women). *Students:* 21 part-time (19 women); includes 4 Hispanic/Latino. Average age 36. 10 applicants, 90% accepted, 9 enrolled. In 2010, 11 master's awarded. *Degree requirements:* For master's, one foreign language, 2 major projects and presentations. *Entrance requirements:* For master's, Oral Proficiency Interview (OPI). Additional exam requirements/recommendations for international students: Required—TOEFL (minimum score 577 paper-based; 233 computer-based; 91 iBT). *Application deadline:* For spring admission, 4/1 priority date for domestic and international students. Applications are processed on a rolling basis. Application fee: $60. *Expenses:* Contact institution. *Financial support:* In 2010–11, 2 students received support. Scholarships/grants available. Financial award application deadline: 4/1; financial award applicants required to submit FAFSA. *Faculty research:* Acquisition, evaluation, assessment, conceptual teaching and learning, content-driven communication, applied linguistics. *Unit head:* Carol Meyer, Director, 802-440-4375, E-mail: cmeyer@bennington.edu. *Application contact:* Nancy Pearlman, Assistant Director, 802-440-4710, E-mail: matsl@bennington.edu.

Boston College, Graduate School of Arts and Sciences, Department of Romance Languages and Literatures, Chestnut Hill, MA 02467-3800. Offers French (MA, PhD); Italian (MA); medieval language (PhD); Spanish (MA, PhD). Part-time programs available. Terminal master's awarded for partial completion of doctoral program. *Degree requirements:* For master's, one foreign language; for doctorate, 2 foreign languages, thesis/dissertation. *Entrance requirements:* Additional exam requirements/recommendations for international students: Required—TOEFL (minimum score 600 paper-based; 250 computer-based; 100 iBT). Electronic applications accepted. *Faculty research:* Spanish-American literature, philology, medieval French romance and troubadour/trouvere lyrics, Golden Age Peninsular literature, secondary language acquisition and pedagogy.

Boston University, School of Education, Boston, MA 02215. Offers counseling (Ed M, CAGS), including community, school, sport psychology; counseling psychology (Ed D); curriculum and teaching (Ed M, Ed D, CAGS), including early childhood (Ed D), educational media and technology (Ed D), English and language arts (Ed D), mathematics (Ed D), physical education and coaching (Ed D), science (Ed D), social studies education (Ed D), special education (Ed D); developmental studies (Ed D), including literacy and language, reading education; developmental studies in literacy and language education (Ed M, CAGS); early childhood education (Ed M, CAGS); education of the deaf (Ed M, CAGS); educational leadership and development (Ed D), including educational administration (Ed M, Ed D, CAGS), higher education administration (Ed M, Ed D, CAGS); educational media and technology (Ed M, CAGS); elementary education (Ed M); English and language arts (Ed M, CAGS); English education (MAT); health education (Ed M, CAGS); Latin and classical studies (MAT); mathematics education (Ed M, MAT, CAGS); mathematics for teaching (MMT); modern foreign language education (MAT), including French, Spanish; physical education and coaching (Ed M, CAGS); policy, planning, and administration (Ed M, CAGS), including community education leadership, educational administration (Ed M, Ed D, CAGS), higher education administration (Ed M, Ed D, CAGS); reading education (Ed M, CAGS); science education (Ed M, MAT, CAGS), including biology (MAT), chemistry (MAT), earth science (MAT), general science (MAT), physics (MAT); social studies education (Ed M, MAT, CAGS), including history (MAT), political science (MAT); special education (Ed M, Ed D, CAGS), including disability studies (Ed M), moderate disabilities (Ed M), severe disabilities (Ed M), special education administration (Ed M); teaching English as a second language (Ed M, CAGS). Part-time programs available. *Faculty:* 57 full-time, 39 part-time/adjunct. *Students:* 245 full-time (191 women), 376 part-time (274 women); includes 83 minority (14 Black or African American, non-Hispanic/Latino; 2 American Indian or Alaska Native, non-Hispanic/Latino; 28 Asian, non-Hispanic/Latino; 31 Hispanic/Latino; 2 Native Hawaiian or other Pacific Islander, non-Hispanic/Latino; 6 Two or more races, non-Hispanic/Latino), 79 international. Average age 30. 1,270 applicants, 66% accepted, 292 enrolled. In 2010, 273 master's, 15 doctorates, 7 other advanced degrees awarded. Terminal master's awarded for partial completion of doctoral program. *Degree requirements:* For master's, thesis (for some programs); for doctorate, comprehensive exam, thesis/dissertation; for CAGS, comprehensive exam. *Entrance requirements:* For master's and CAGS, GRE General Test or Miller Analogies Test (MAT); for doctorate, GRE General Test. Additional exam requirements/recommendations for international students: Required—TOEFL, IELTS. *Application deadline:* For fall admission, 1/15 priority date for domestic and international students; for spring admission, 9/15 priority date for domestic and international students. Applications are processed on a rolling basis. Application fee: $70. Electronic applications accepted. *Expenses:* Tuition: Full-time $39,314; part-time $1228 per credit. Required fees: $40 per semester. *Financial support:* In 2010–11, 276 students received support, including 31 fellowships with full tuition reimbursements available, 16 research assistantships, 26 teaching assistantships with partial tuition reimbursements available; career-related internships or fieldwork, Federal Work-Study, and scholarships/grants also available. Support available to part-time students. Financial award applicants required to submit FAFSA. *Faculty research:* Deaf studies, social emotional learning, civic engagement and education, STEM education, pre-college educational pipelines. Total annual research expenditures: $2.6 million. *Unit head:* Dr. Hardin Coleman, Dean, 617-353-3213. *Application contact:* Dana Fernandez, Director of Enrollment, 617-353-4237, Fax: 617-353-8937, E-mail: sedgrad@bu.edu.

Bowling Green State University, Graduate College, College of Arts and Sciences, Department of Romance and Classical Studies, Program in Spanish, Bowling Green, OH 43403. Offers Spanish (MA); Spanish education (MAT). Part-time programs available. *Degree requirements:* For master's, one foreign language, thesis or alternative. *Entrance requirements:* For master's, GRE General Test. Additional exam requirements/recommendations for international students: Required—TOEFL. Electronic applications accepted. *Faculty research:* U.S. Latino literature and culture, Latin American film and popular culture, applied linguistics, Spanish popular culture.

Brigham Young University, Graduate Studies, College of Humanities, Department of Spanish and Portuguese, Provo, UT 84602. Offers Hispanic literature (MA); Portuguese linguistics (MA); Portuguese literature (MA); Spanish linguistics (MA); Spanish teaching (MA). Part-time programs available. *Faculty:* 32 full-time (5 women). *Students:* 15 full-time (6 women), 25 part-time (12 women); includes 9 Hispanic/Latino; 1 Native Hawaiian or other Pacific Islander, non-Hispanic/Latino. Average age 30. 23 applicants, 65% accepted, 12 enrolled. In 2010, 11 master's awarded. *Degree requirements:* For master's, one foreign language, comprehensive exam, thesis, 1 semester of teaching. *Entrance requirements:* For master's, minimum GPA of 3.5 in Spanish or Portuguese, 3.3 overall. Additional exam requirements/recommendations for international students: Required—TOEFL (minimum score 580 paper-based; 237 computer-based). *Application deadline:* For fall admission, 2/1 for domestic and international students. Application fee: $50. Electronic applications accepted. *Expenses:* Tuition: Full-time $5580; part-time $310 per credit hour. Tuition and fees vary according to program and student's religious affiliation. *Financial support:* In 2010–11, 39 students received support, including 46 teaching assistantships with partial tuition reimbursements available (averaging $10,470 per year); institutionally sponsored loans, scholarships/grants, tuition waivers (partial), and unspecified assistantships also available. Support available to part-time students. Financial award application deadline: 7/1. *Faculty research:* Mexican prose; Latin American theater, literature, phonetics, and phonology; pedagogy; classical Portuguese literature; Peninsular prose and theater. *Unit head:* Dr. Alvin F. Sherman, Chair, 801-422-3107, Fax: 801-422-0628, E-mail: alvin_sherman@byu.edu. *Application contact:* Jasmine S. Talbot, Graduate Secretary, 801-422-2196, Fax: 801-422-0628, E-mail: jasmine_talbot@byu.edu.

Brooklyn College of the City University of New York, Division of Graduate Studies, Department of Modern Languages and Literature, Brooklyn, NY 11210-2889. Offers French (MA); modern languages and literature (PhD); Spanish (MA). *Students:* 1 (woman) full-time, 26 part-time (18 women); includes 18 minority (8 Black or African American, non-Hispanic/Latino; 10 Hispanic/Latino), 2 international. Average age 41. 14 applicants, 100% accepted, 11 enrolled. In 2010, 8 master's awarded. *Degree requirements:* For master's, comprehensive exam or research paper. *Entrance requirements:* For master's, 18 credits in advanced courses in Spanish, 2 letters of recommendation. Additional exam requirements/recommendations for international students: Required—TOEFL (minimum score 500 paper-based; 173 computer-based; 61 iBT). *Application deadline:* For fall admission, 8/15 for domestic students, 6/15 priority date for international students; for spring admission, 1/15 for domestic students, 12/15 priority date for international students. Applications are processed on a rolling basis. Application fee: $125. Electronic applications accepted. *Expenses:* Tuition, state resident: full-time $7360; part-time $310 per credit hour. Tuition, nonresident: full-time $13,800; part-time $575 per credit hour. Required fees: $190 per semester. *Financial support:* Federal Work-Study, institutionally sponsored loans, and scholarships/grants available. Support available to part-time students. Financial award application deadline: 5/1; financial award applicants required to submit FAFSA. *Faculty research:* Latin American contemporary novel, Caribbean female contemporary literature, nineteenth and twentieth century Spanish novel, twentieth century Mexican poetry. *Unit head:* Dr. Luigi Bonafinni, Chairperson, 718-951-5451, E-mail: luigi@brooklyn.cuny.edu. *Application contact:* Hernan Sierra, Graduate Admissions Coordinator, 718-951-4536, Fax: 718-951-4506, E-mail: grads@brooklyn.cuny.edu.

California State University, Bakersfield, Division of Graduate Studies, School of Humanities and Social Sciences, Program in Spanish, Bakersfield, CA 93311. Offers MA. *Degree requirements:* For master's, capstone course.

California State University, Fresno, Division of Graduate Studies, College of Arts and Humanities, Department of Modern and Classical Languages and Literatures, Fresno, CA 93740-8027. Offers Spanish (MA). Part-time programs available. *Degree requirements:* For master's, one foreign language, thesis or alternative. *Entrance requirements:* For master's, GRE General Test, BA in Spanish, minimum GPA of 3.0. Additional exam requirements/recommendations for international students: Required—TOEFL. Electronic applications accepted.

California State University, Fullerton, Graduate Studies, College of Humanities and Social Sciences, Department of Modern Languages and Literatures, Fullerton, CA 92834-9480. Offers French (MA); German (MA); Spanish (MA); teaching English to speakers of other languages (MS). Part-time programs available. *Students:* 44 full-time (32 women), 46 part-time (32 women); includes 18 Asian, non-Hispanic/Latino; 29 Hispanic/Latino; 1 Two or more races, non-Hispanic/Latino, 18 international. Average age 32. 126 applicants, 56% accepted, 41 enrolled. In 2010, 35 master's awarded. *Degree requirements:* For master's, comprehensive exam, thesis or alternative. *Entrance requirements:* For master's, minimum GPA of 2.5 in last 60 hours of course work, undergraduate major in a language. Application fee: $55. *Financial support:* Career-related internships or fieldwork, Federal Work-Study, institutionally sponsored loans, and scholarships/grants available. Support available to part-time students. Financial award application deadline: 3/1; financial award applicants required to submit FAFSA. *Unit head:* Dr. Janet Eyring, Chair, 657-278-3534. *Application contact:* Admissions/Applications, 657-278-2371.

California State University, Long Beach, Graduate Studies, College of Liberal Arts, Department of Romance, German, and Russian Languages and Literature, Program in Spanish, Long Beach, CA 90840. Offers MA. Part-time programs available. *Students:* 18 full-time (10 women), 25 part-time (18 women); includes 4 American Indian or Alaska Native, non-Hispanic/Latino; 26 Hispanic/Latino, 2 international. Average age 32. 35 applicants, 54% accepted, 13 enrolled. In 2010, 11 master's awarded. *Degree requirements:* For master's, one foreign language, thesis or alternative, research paper. *Entrance requirements:* For master's, BA in Spanish. *Application deadline:* For fall admission, 7/1 for domestic students. Applications are processed on a rolling basis. Application fee: $55. Electronic applications accepted. *Financial support:* Federal Work-Study, institutionally sponsored loans, and scholarships/grants available. Financial award application deadline: 3/2. *Faculty research:* Literary translation, literature and politics, women writers, Latin American poetry, Latin American theatre. *Unit head:* Dr. Lisa Vollendorf, Chair, 562-985-4318, Fax: 562-985-4259, E-mail: lvollend@csulb.edu. *Application contact:* Dr. Bonnie Gasior, Program Director, 562-985-4318, Fax: 562-985-4259, E-mail: bgasior@csulb.edu.

California State University, Los Angeles, Graduate Studies, College of Arts and Letters, Department of Modern Languages and Literatures, Los Angeles, CA 90032-8530. Offers

French (MA); Spanish (MA). Part-time and evening/weekend programs available. *Faculty:* 4 full-time (all women), 2 part-time/adjunct (1 woman). *Students:* 14 full-time (10 women), 24 part-time (15 women); includes 26 minority (all Hispanic/Latino), 3 international. Average age 37. 17 applicants, 59% accepted, 10 enrolled. In 2010, 10 master's awarded. *Degree requirements:* For master's, comprehensive exam. *Entrance requirements:* Additional exam requirements/recommendations for international students: Required—TOEFL (minimum score 500 paper-based; 173 computer-based). *Application deadline:* For fall admission, 5/1 for domestic and international students. Applications are processed on a rolling basis. Application fee: $55. Electronic applications accepted. *Financial support:* Federal Work-Study available. Support available to part-time students. Financial award application deadline: 3/1. *Faculty research:* French literature, language teaching and methodology, Spanish poetry, Spanish-American fiction and poetry. *Unit head:* Dr. Sachiko Matsunaga, Chair, 323-343-4230, Fax: 323-343-4234, E-mail: smatsun@calstatela.edu. *Application contact:* Dr. Alan Muchlinski, Dean of Graduate Studies, 323-343-3820, Fax: 323-343-5653, E-mail: amuchli@exchange.calstatela.edu.

California State University, Northridge, Graduate Studies, College of Humanities, Department of Modern and Classical Languages and Literatures, Northridge, CA 91330. Offers Spanish (MA). Part-time and evening/weekend programs available. *Degree requirements:* For master's, one foreign language. *Entrance requirements:* For master's, GRE General Test or minimum GPA of 3.0. Additional exam requirements/recommendations for international students: Required—TOEFL.

California State University, Sacramento, Graduate Studies, College of Social Sciences and Interdisciplinary Studies, Liberal Arts Program, Sacramento, CA 95819. Offers French (MA); German (MA); Spanish (MA); theater arts (MA). *Degree requirements:* For master's, writing proficiency exam. *Entrance requirements:* Additional exam requirements/recommendations for international students: Required—TOEFL. Electronic applications accepted.

California State University, San Bernardino, Graduate Studies, College of Arts and Letters, Department of World Languages and Literatures, San Bernardino, CA 92407-2397. Offers Spanish (MA). Part-time and evening/weekend programs available. *Degree requirements:* For master's, comprehensive exam, advancement to candidacy.

California State University, San Marcos, College of Arts and Sciences, Program in World Languages, San Marcos, CA 92096-0001. Offers Spanish (MA). Part-time and evening/weekend programs available. *Degree requirements:* For master's, 2 foreign languages, exam. *Entrance requirements:* For master's, GRE General Test, minimum GPA of 2.5, minimum GPA of 3.0 in upper division Spanish courses. Electronic applications accepted. *Faculty research:* Applied linguistics, golden age Spanish literature, Latin American literature, poetry, Chicano studies.

The Catholic University of America, School of Arts and Sciences, Department of Modern Languages and Literatures, Washington, DC 20064. Offers Spanish (MA, PhD). Part-time programs available. *Faculty:* 19 full-time (13 women), 10 part-time/adjunct (7 women). *Students:* 1 full-time (0 women), 15 part-time (12 women); includes 6 Hispanic/Latino, 3 international. Average age 35. 18 applicants, 56% accepted, 5 enrolled. In 2010, 4 master's, 3 doctorates awarded. *Degree requirements:* For master's, comprehensive exam; for doctorate, one foreign language, comprehensive exam, thesis/dissertation, final oral exam. *Entrance requirements:* For master's and doctorate, GRE General Test, statement of purpose, official copies of academic transcripts, three letters of recommendation. Additional exam requirements/recommendations for international students: Required—TOEFL (minimum score 580 paper-based; 237 computer-based). *Application deadline:* For fall admission, 8/1 priority date for domestic students, 7/15 for international students; for spring admission, 12/1 priority date for domestic students, 10/15 for international students. Applications are processed on a rolling basis. Application fee: $55. Electronic applications accepted. *Expenses:* Tuition: Full-time $33,580; part-time $1315 per credit hour. Required fees: $80; $40 per semester hour. One-time fee: $425. *Financial support:* Fellowships, research assistantships, teaching assistantships, Federal Work-Study, scholarships/grants, tuition waivers (full and partial), and unspecified assistantships available. Financial award application deadline: 2/1; financial award applicants required to submit FAFSA. *Faculty research:* Arthurian literature and medieval lyric, eighteenth-twentieth century Spanish literature, Latin American literature, German literature, seventeenth century French literature. *Unit head:* Dr. Lourdes M. Alvarez, Chair, 202-319-5240, Fax: 202-319-6077, E-mail: alvarezl@cua.edu. *Application contact:* Andrew Woodall, Director of Graduate Admissions, 202-319-5057, Fax: 202-319-6533, E-mail: cua-admissions@cua.edu.

Central Connecticut State University, School of Graduate Studies, School of Arts and Sciences, Department of Modern Languages, Program in Modern Language, New Britain, CT 06050-4010. Offers French (MA, Certificate); German (Certificate); Italian (Certificate); modern language (MA); Spanish language and Hispanic culture (MA). Part-time and evening/weekend programs available. *Students:* 8 full-time (6 women), 32 part-time (28 women); includes 15 minority (all Hispanic/Latino), 1 international. Average age 38. 22 applicants, 95% accepted, 10 enrolled. In 2010, 17 master's awarded. *Degree requirements:* For master's, one foreign language, comprehensive exam, thesis or alternative; for Certificate, qualifying exam. *Entrance requirements:* For master's, minimum undergraduate GPA of 2.7, 24 credits of undergraduate courses in either Italian or Spanish. Additional exam requirements/recommendations for international students: Required—TOEFL. *Application deadline:* For fall admission, 7/1 for domestic students; for spring admission, 12/1 for domestic students. Applications are processed on a rolling basis. Application fee: $50. Electronic applications accepted. *Expenses:* Tuition, area resident: Full-time $5012; part-time $470 per credit. Tuition, state resident: full-time $7518; part-time $482 per credit. Tuition, nonresident: full-time $13,962; part-time $482 per credit. Required fees: $3772. One-time fee: $62 part-time. *Faculty research:* Twentieth century French theater, seventeenth century French literature, French Middle Ages.

Central Connecticut State University, School of Graduate Studies, School of Arts and Sciences, Department of Modern Languages, Program in Spanish, New Britain, CT 06050-4010. Offers MS, Certificate. Part-time and evening/weekend programs available. *Students:* 2 full-time (both women), 4 part-time (all women); includes 1 minority (Hispanic/Latino). Average age 39. 6 applicants, 50% accepted, 1 enrolled. In 2010, 2 master's, 1 other advanced degree awarded. *Degree requirements:* For master's, one foreign language, comprehensive exam, thesis or alternative; for Certificate, qualifying exam. *Entrance requirements:* For master's, minimum undergraduate GPA of 2.7, 24 credits of undergraduate courses in either Italian or Spanish. Additional exam requirements/recommendations for international students: Required—TOEFL. *Application deadline:* For fall admission, 7/1 for domestic students; for spring admission, 12/1 for domestic students. Applications are processed on a rolling basis. Application fee: $50. Electronic applications accepted. *Expenses:* Tuition, area resident: Full-time $5012; part-time $470 per credit. Tuition, state resident: full-time $7518; part-time $482 per credit. Tuition, nonresident: full-time $13,962; part-time $482 per credit. Required fees: $3772. One-time fee: $62 part-time. *Faculty research:* Linguistics, nineteenth to twentieth century Spanish literature, Spanish Golden Age prose/drama.

Central Michigan University, College of Graduate Studies, College of Humanities and Social and Behavioral Sciences, Department of Foreign Languages, Literatures, and Cultures, Mount Pleasant, MI 48859. Offers Spanish (MA). Part-time programs available. *Faculty:* 6 full-time (5 women). *Students:* 14 part-time (10 women); includes 1 Hispanic/Latino. Average age 28. *Degree requirements:* For master's, thesis or alternative. *Application deadline:* For fall admission, 6/1 for international students; for spring admission, 10/1 for international students. Applications are processed on a rolling basis. Application fee: $35 ($45 for international students). Electronic applications accepted. *Expenses:* Tuition, state resident: full-time $8208; part-time $456 per credit hour. Tuition, nonresident: full-time $13,788; part-time $766 per credit hour. One-time fee: $25. *Financial support:* Fellowships with tuition reimbursements, unspecified assistantships and out-of-state merit awards, non-resident graduate awards available. *Unit head:* Dr. Susan Knight, Chairperson, 989-774-3786, Fax: 989-774-2323, E-mail: knigh1sm@umich.edu. *Application contact:* Dr. Krzysztof A. Kulawik, Graduate Program Coordinator, 989-774-3536, Fax: 989-774-2323, E-mail: kulaw1ka@cmich.edu.

City College of the City University of New York, Graduate School, College of Liberal Arts and Science, Division of the Humanities and Arts, Department of Foreign Languages, New York, NY 10031-9198. Offers Spanish (MA). *Degree requirements:* For master's, one foreign language, comprehensive exam, thesis or alternative. *Entrance requirements:* For master's, minimum GPA of 3.0. Additional exam requirements/recommendations for international students: Required—TOEFL (minimum score 500 paper-based; 61 iBT). Electronic applications accepted.

Cleveland State University, College of Graduate Studies, College of Liberal Arts and Social Sciences, Department of Modern Languages, Cleveland, OH 44115. Offers French (M Ed); Spanish (M Ed, MA), including language and linguistics (MA), Latin American studies (MA), peninsular studies (MA), Spanish (MA). Part-time and evening/weekend programs available. *Faculty:* 12 full-time (9 women). *Students:* 7 full-time (4 women), 9 part-time (7 women); includes 1 Black or African American, non-Hispanic/Latino; 1 Asian, non-Hispanic/Latino; 3 Hispanic/Latino; 1 Two or more races, non-Hispanic/Latino, 2 international. Average age 37. 11 applicants, 100% accepted, 8 enrolled. In 2010, 9 master's awarded. *Degree requirements:* For master's, one foreign language, comprehensive exam, thesis optional, study abroad. *Entrance requirements:* For master's, undergraduate major in Spanish or equivalent, essay in Spanish, writing sample. Additional exam requirements/recommendations for international students: Required—TOEFL (minimum score 525 paper-based; 197 computer-based). *Application deadline:* For fall admission, 7/25 priority date for domestic students; for spring admission, 12/15 priority date for domestic students. Applications are processed on a rolling basis. Application fee: $30. Electronic applications accepted. *Expenses:* Tuition, state resident: full-time $8447; part-time $469 per credit hour. Tuition, nonresident: full-time $16,020; part-time $890 per credit hour. Required fees: $50. *Financial support:* In 2010–11, 6 students received support, including 6 teaching assistantships with full tuition reimbursements available (averaging $7,030 per year); Federal Work-Study also available. *Faculty research:* Second language acquisition, sociolinguistics, contemporary Spanish novel, Arabic diaspora in Latin America, border literature. *Unit head:* Dr. Tama L. Engelking, Chairperson, 216-523-7175, Fax: 216-687-4650, E-mail: t.engelking@csuohio.edu. *Application contact:* Dr. Antonio Medina-Rivera, Graduate Director, 216-523-7168, Fax: 216-687-4650, E-mail: a.medinarivera@csuohio.edu.

Columbia University, Graduate School of Arts and Sciences, Division of Humanities, Department of Spanish and Portuguese, New York, NY 10027. Offers M Phil, MA, PhD. Part-time programs available. *Degree requirements:* For master's, one foreign language, written exam; for doctorate, 3 foreign languages, thesis/dissertation. *Entrance requirements:* For master's and doctorate, GRE General Test, GRE Subject Test, sample of written work. Additional exam requirements/recommendations for international students: Required—TOEFL. *Faculty research:* Literary theory and criticism, Spain's Golden Age: sixteenth- and seventeenth-centuries, contemporary Spanish American literature.

Cornell University, Graduate School, Graduate Fields of Arts and Sciences, Field of Romance Studies, Ithaca, NY 14853-0001. Offers French linguistics (PhD); French literature (PhD); Hispanic literature (PhD); Italian linguistics (PhD); Italian literature (PhD); Romance linguistics (PhD); Spanish linguistics (PhD). *Faculty:* 30 full-time (13 women). *Students:* 56 full-time (27 women); includes 11 Hispanic/Latino, 23 international. Average age 28. 95 applicants, 22% accepted, 10 enrolled. In 2010, 5 doctorates awarded. *Degree requirements:* For doctorate, 2 foreign languages, comprehensive exam, thesis/dissertation. *Entrance requirements:* For doctorate, GRE General Test, sample of written work, 3 letters of recommendation. Additional exam requirements/recommendations for international students: Required—TOEFL (minimum score 550 paper-based; 213 computer-based; 77 iBT). *Application deadline:* For fall admission, 1/15 for domestic students. Application fee: $80. Electronic applications accepted. *Expenses:* Tuition: Full-time $29,500. Required fees: $76. Tuition and fees vary according to degree level and program. *Financial support:* In 2010–11, 18 fellowships with full tuition reimbursements, 34 teaching assistantships with full tuition reimbursements were awarded; research assistantships with full tuition reimbursements, institutionally sponsored loans, scholarships/grants, health care benefits, tuition waivers (full and partial), and unspecified assistantships also available. Financial award applicants required to submit FAFSA. *Faculty research:* Literary theory, Hispanic studies, French studies, gender studies. *Unit head:* Director of Graduate Studies, 607-255-8222. *Application contact:* Graduate Field Assistant, 607-255-4246, E-mail: romance_studies@cornell.edu.

Drew University, Caspersen School of Graduate Studies, Program in Education, Madison, NJ 07940-1493. Offers biology (MAT); chemistry (MAT); English (MAT); French (MAT); Italian (MAT); math (MAT); physics (MAT); social studies (MAT); Spanish (MAT); theatre arts (MAT). Part-time programs available. *Entrance requirements:* For master's, transcripts, personal statement, recommendations. Additional exam requirements/recommendations for international students: Required—TOEFL, TWE. *Expenses:* Contact institution.

Duke University, Graduate School, Department of Romance Studies, Durham, NC 27708. Offers French (PhD); Spanish (PhD); JD/AM. *Faculty:* 26 full-time. *Students:* 43 full-time (29 women); includes 2 Black or African American, non-Hispanic/Latino; 6 Hispanic/Latino, 15 international. 49 applicants, 20% accepted, 8 enrolled. In 2010, 6 doctorates awarded. *Degree requirements:* For doctorate, 2 foreign languages, thesis/dissertation. *Entrance requirements:* For doctorate, GRE General Test. Additional exam requirements/recommendations for international students: Required—TOEFL (minimum score 550 paper-based; 213 computer-based; 83 iBT), IELTS (minimum score 7). *Application deadline:* For fall admission, 12/8 priority date for domestic and international students. Application fee: $75. Electronic applications accepted. *Financial support:* Fellowships, research assistantships, teaching assistantships, Federal Work-Study available. Financial award application deadline: 12/8. *Unit head:* Esther Gabara, Director of Graduate Studies, 919-660-3114, Fax: 919-684-4029, E-mail: denise@duke.edu. *Application contact:* Elizabeth Hutton, Director of Admissions, 919-684-3913, Fax: 919-684-2277, E-mail: elizabeth.hutton@duke.edu.

Eastern Michigan University, Graduate School, College of Arts and Sciences, Department of World Languages, Programs in Foreign Languages, Ypsilanti, MI 48197. Offers French (MA); German (MA); German for business (Graduate Certificate); Hispanic language and cultures (Graduate Certificate); Japanese business practices (Graduate Certificate); Spanish (MA). Part-time and evening/weekend programs available. Postbaccalaureate distance learning degree programs offered (minimal on-campus study). *Students:* 1 (woman) full-time, 12 part-time (11 women); includes 5 minority (1 Black or African American, non-Hispanic/Latino; 1 Asian, non-Hispanic/Latino; 3 Hispanic/Latino), 1 international. Average age 44. In 2010, 8 master's awarded. *Degree requirements:* For master's, one foreign language, thesis optional. *Entrance requirements:* Additional exam requirements/recommendations for international students: Required—TOEFL. *Application deadline:* Applications are processed on a rolling basis. Application fee: $35. *Financial support:* Fellowships, research assistantships with full tuition reimbursements, teaching assistantships with full tuition reimbursements, career-related internships or fieldwork, Federal Work-Study, institutionally sponsored loans, scholarships/grants, tuition waivers (partial), and unspecified assistantships available. Support available to part-time students. Financial award applicants required to submit FAFSA. *Application contact:* Dr. Genevieve Peden, Program Advisor, 734-487-1498, Fax: 734-487-3411, E-mail: gpeden@emich.edu.

Emory University, Laney Graduate School, Department of Comparative Literature, Atlanta, GA 30322-1100. Offers comparative literature (PhD); English (Certificate); French (Certificate); Middle Eastern studies (PhD); philosophy (Certificate); psychoanalytic studies (PhD); religion (PhD); Spanish (Certificate); women studies (Certificate). *Degree requirements:* For doctorate, 2 foreign languages, comprehensive exam, thesis/dissertation. *Entrance requirements:* For doctorate, GRE General Test, minimum GPA of 3.0. Additional exam requirements/recommendations for international students: Required—TOEFL. Electronic applications accepted. *Expenses:* Tuition: Full-time $33,800. Required fees: $1300. *Faculty research:* Literary theory,

Spanish

Emory University (continued)
psychoanalysis trauma and testimony, literature and religion, literature and technology, literature and philosophy, politics and global culture, literature and aesthetics.

Emory University, Laney Graduate School, Department of Spanish and Portuguese, Atlanta, GA 30322-1100. Offers comparative literature (Certificate); film studies (Certificate); Spanish (PhD); women's studies (Certificate). *Degree requirements:* For doctorate, 2 foreign languages, comprehensive exam, thesis/dissertation. *Entrance requirements:* For doctorate, GRE General Test. Additional exam requirements/recommendations for international students: Required—TOEFL. Electronic applications accepted. *Expenses:* Tuition: Full-time $33,800. Required fees: $1300. *Faculty research:* Spanish literature, Spanish-American literature, literary theory, criticism, cultural studies.

Florida Atlantic University, Dorothy F. Schmidt College of Arts and Letters, Department of Languages, Linguistics, and Comparative Literature, Boca Raton, FL 33431-0991. Offers comparative literature (MA); French (MA); linguistics (MA); Spanish (MA). Part-time programs available. *Faculty:* 30 full-time (24 women), 5 part-time/adjunct (all women). *Students:* 30 full-time (22 women), 19 part-time (15 women); includes 24 minority (4 Black or African American, non-Hispanic/Latino; 20 Hispanic/Latino), 6 international. Average age 34. 42 applicants, 57% accepted, 20 enrolled. In 2010, 5 master's awarded. *Degree requirements:* For master's, one foreign language, comprehensive exam, thesis optional. *Entrance requirements:* For master's, GRE General Test, minimum GPA of 3.0. *Application deadline:* For fall admission, 7/1 priority date for domestic students, 2/15 for international students; for spring admission, 11/1 for domestic students, 7/15 for international students. Applications are processed on a rolling basis. Application fee: $30. *Expenses:* Tuition, area resident: Part-time $319.96 per credit. Tuition, state resident: part-time $319.96 per credit. Tuition, nonresident: part-time $926.42 per credit. *Financial support:* Fellowships, research assistantships, teaching assistantships with partial tuition reimbursements, Federal Work-Study and tuition waivers (partial) available. Support available to part-time students. Financial award application deadline: 4/1. *Faculty research:* Modern European studies, modern Latin America, medieval Europe. *Unit head:* Dr. Michael Horswell, Chair, 561-297-3860, Fax: 561-297-2756, E-mail: horswell@fau.edu. *Application contact:* Dr. Emily Stockard, Associate Dean, 561-297-2817, Fax: 561-297-2744, E-mail: stockard@fau.edu.

Florida International University, College of Arts and Sciences, Department of Modern Languages, Miami, FL 33199. Offers Spanish (MA, PhD). Ph D is fall admission only. Part-time and evening/weekend programs available. *Faculty:* 22 full-time (15 women), 22 part-time/adjunct (17 women). *Students:* 19 full-time (14 women), 33 part-time (26 women); includes 1 Asian, non-Hispanic/Latino; 47 Hispanic/Latino, 1 international. Average age 37. 37 applicants, 22% accepted, 8 enrolled. In 2010, 12 master's, 3 doctorates awarded. *Degree requirements:* For master's, 2 foreign languages, comprehensive exam, thesis or 6 elective credits; for doctorate, 3 foreign languages, comprehensive exam, thesis/dissertation. *Entrance requirements:* For master's, minimum GPA of 3.0, resume, writing sample in Spanish (6-7 pages minimum), 2 letters of recommendation; for doctorate, GRE General Test (minimum score of 1120) or EXADEP (minimum score of 500), minimum GPA of 3.0, letter of intent, resume, writing sample in Spanish (15 pages minimum), 2 letters of recommendation. Additional exam requirements/recommendations for international students: Required—TOEFL (minimum score 550 paper-based; 80 iBT). *Application deadline:* For fall admission, 3/15 for domestic and international students. Application fee: $30. Electronic applications accepted. *Financial support:* Institutionally sponsored loans, scholarships/grants, and health care benefits available. Financial award application deadline: 3/1; financial award applicants required to submit FAFSA. *Faculty research:* Peninsular Spanish literature, Spanish-American literature, cultural studies, film studies, bilingualism. *Unit head:* Dr. Pascale Becel, Chair, 305-348-2851, Fax: 305-348-1085, E-mail: modlang@fiu.edu. *Application contact:* Nanett Rojas, Assistant Director of Graduate Admissions, 305-348-7442, Fax: 305-348-7441, E-mail: gradadm@fiu.edu.

Florida State University, The Graduate School, College of Arts and Sciences, Department of Modern Languages, Program in Spanish, Tallahassee, FL 32306. Offers MA, PhD. *Faculty:* 12 full-time (6 women), 1 part-time/adjunct (0 women). *Students:* 40 full-time (29 women), 4 part-time (2 women); includes 2 Black or African American, non-Hispanic/Latino; 1 American Indian or Alaska Native, non-Hispanic/Latino; 13 Hispanic/Latino. Average age 25. 32 applicants, 56% accepted, 11 enrolled. In 2010, 5 master's, 3 doctorates awarded. Terminal master's awarded for partial completion of doctoral program. *Degree requirements:* For master's, thesis optional; for doctorate, 2 foreign languages, thesis/dissertation. *Entrance requirements:* For master's and doctorate, GRE General Test, minimum GPA of 3.0. Additional exam requirements/recommendations for international students: Required—TOEFL (minimum score 550 paper-based; 213 computer-based). *Application deadline:* For fall admission, 2/15 for domestic and international students. Applications are processed on a rolling basis. Application fee: $30. Electronic applications accepted. *Expenses:* Tuition, state resident: full-time $8238.24. *Financial support:* In 2010–11, fellowships with partial tuition reimbursements (averaging $14,000 per year), research assistantships with partial tuition reimbursements (averaging $12,000 per year), 40 teaching assistantships with partial tuition reimbursements (averaging $11,200 per year) were awarded. Financial award application deadline: 2/1; financial award applicants required to submit FAFSA. *Faculty research:* Latin American theater, Hispanic literature of the United States, twentieth century Latin American poetry, Spanish-American colonial. *Unit head:* Dr. Gretchen Sunderman, Divisional Coordinator and Professor, 850-644-8186, Fax: 850-644-0524, E-mail: gsunderman@fsu.edu. *Application contact:* Wendy E. Pigott, Graduate Academic Coordinator, 850-644-8397, Fax: 850-644-0524, E-mail: wpigott@fsu.edu.

Framingham State University, Division of Graduate and Continuing Education, Program in Spanish, Framingham, MA 01701-9101. Offers M Ed.

Georgetown University, Graduate School of Arts and Sciences, Department of Spanish and Portuguese, Washington, DC 20057. Offers Spanish (MS, PhD), including Hispanic literature, Spanish linguistics, Spanish literature; MS/PhD. *Degree requirements:* For master's, one foreign language, research project; for doctorate, 3 foreign languages, thesis/dissertation. *Entrance requirements:* Additional exam requirements/recommendations for international students: Required—TOEFL.

Georgia Southern University, Jack N. Averitt College of Graduate Studies, College of Education, Department of Teaching and Learning, Program in Spanish Education, Statesboro, GA 30460. Offers MAT. *Accreditation:* NCATE. Part-time and evening/weekend programs available. *Students:* 4 full-time (2 women), 2 part-time (both women); includes 1 Black or African American, non-Hispanic/Latino. Average age 31. 1 applicant, 100% accepted, 1 enrolled. In 2010, 1 master's awarded. *Degree requirements:* For master's, portfolio, transition point assessments, exit assessment. *Entrance requirements:* For master's, GRE General Test or MAT; GACE Basic Skills and Content Assessments, minimum cumulative GPA of 2.5. Additional exam requirements/recommendations for international students: Required—TOEFL (minimum score 550 paper-based; 213 computer-based; 80 iBT). *Application deadline:* For fall admission, 3/1 for domestic students, 3/1 priority date for international students; for spring admission, 10/1 priority date for domestic students, 10/1 for international students. Applications are processed on a rolling basis. Application fee: $50. Electronic applications accepted. *Expenses:* Tuition, state resident: full-time $6000; part-time $250 per semester hour. Tuition, nonresident: full-time $23,976; part-time $999 per semester hour. Required fees: $1644. *Financial support:* In 2010–11, 6 students received support, including research assistantships with partial tuition reimbursements available (averaging $7,200 per year), teaching assistantships with partial tuition reimbursements available (averaging $7,200 per year); Federal Work-Study, scholarships/grants, tuition waivers (partial), and unspecified assistantships also available. Support available to part-time students. Financial award application deadline: 4/15; financial award applicants required to submit FAFSA. *Unit head:* Dr. Ronnie Sheppard, Department Chair, 912-478-5203, Fax: 912-478-0026, E-mail: sheppard@georgiasouthern.edu. *Application contact:* Dr. Charles Ziglar, Coordinator for Graduate Student Recruitment, 912-478-5635, Fax: 912-478-0740, E-mail: gradadmissions@georgiasouthern.edu.

Georgia Southern University, Jack N. Averitt College of Graduate Studies, College of Liberal Arts and Social Sciences, Department of Foreign Languages, Statesboro, GA 30460. Offers Spanish (MA). Part-time and evening/weekend programs available. *Students:* 11 full-time (6 women), 3 part-time (1 woman); includes 1 Black or African American, non-Hispanic/Latino; 2 Hispanic/Latino, 1 international. Average age 28. 8 applicants, 100% accepted, 4 enrolled. In 2010, 3 master's awarded. *Degree requirements:* For master's, one foreign language, thesis optional. *Entrance requirements:* For master's, GRE, minimum GPA of 3.0, letters of reference. Additional exam requirements/recommendations for international students: Required—TOEFL (minimum score 550 paper-based; 213 computer-based; 80 iBT). *Application deadline:* For fall admission, 3/1 priority date for domestic and international students; for spring admission, 10/1 priority date for domestic students, 10/1 for international students. Applications are processed on a rolling basis. Application fee: $50. Electronic applications accepted. *Expenses:* Tuition, state resident: full-time $6000; part-time $250 per semester hour. Tuition, nonresident: full-time $23,976; part-time $999 per semester hour. Required fees: $1644. *Financial support:* In 2010–11, 14 students received support, including research assistantships with partial tuition reimbursements available (averaging $7,200 per year), teaching assistantships with partial tuition reimbursements available (averaging $7,200 per year); career-related internships or fieldwork, Federal Work-Study, scholarships/grants, tuition waivers (partial), and unspecified assistantships also available. Support available to part-time students. Financial award application deadline: 4/15; financial award applicants required to submit FAFSA. *Unit head:* Dr. Eric Kartchner, Chair, 912-478-5281, Fax: 912-478-0652, E-mail: forlangs@georgiasouthern.edu. *Application contact:* Dr. Charles Ziglar, Coordinator for Graduate Student Recruitment, 912-478-5635, Fax: 912-478-0740, E-mail: gradadmissions@georgiasouthern.edu.

Georgia State University, College of Arts and Sciences, Department of Modern and Classical Languages, Program in Spanish, Atlanta, GA 30302-3083. Offers MA. Evening/weekend programs available. *Degree requirements:* For master's, one foreign language, thesis or alternative, general exam. *Entrance requirements:* For master's, GRE General Test. Additional exam requirements/recommendations for international students: Required—TOEFL. Electronic applications accepted. *Faculty research:* Spanish and Latin-American literature.

Georgia State University, College of Arts and Sciences, Department of Modern and Classical Languages, Program in Translation and Interpretation, Atlanta, GA 30302-3083. Offers French (Certificate); German (Certificate); Spanish (Certificate). Electronic applications accepted.

Harvard University, Graduate School of Arts and Sciences, Department of Romance Languages and Literatures, Cambridge, MA 02138. Offers French (AM, PhD); Italian (AM, PhD); Portuguese (AM, PhD); Spanish (AM, PhD). Terminal master's awarded for partial completion of doctoral program. *Degree requirements:* For master's, 2 foreign languages; for doctorate, 2 foreign languages, thesis/dissertation. *Entrance requirements:* For master's and doctorate, GRE General Test, sample of written work. Additional exam requirements/recommendations for international students: Required—TOEFL. *Expenses:* Tuition: Full-time $34,976. Required fees: $1166. Full-time tuition and fees vary according to program.

Hofstra University, School of Education, Health, and Human Services, Programs in Teaching—Secondary Education, Hempstead, NY 11549. Offers business education (MS Ed); English education (MA, MS Ed); foreign language and TESOL (MS Ed); foreign language education (MA, MS Ed), including French, German, Russian, Spanish; mathematics education (MA, MS Ed); science education (MA, MS Ed), including biology, chemistry, earth science, geology, physics; secondary education (Advanced Certificate); social studies education (MA, MS Ed). Part-time and evening/weekend programs available. Postbaccalaureate distance learning degree programs offered (minimal on-campus study). *Students:* 114 full-time (74 women), 61 part-time (36 women); includes 7 Black or African American, non-Hispanic/Latino; 1 American Indian or Alaska Native, non-Hispanic/Latino; 8 Asian, non-Hispanic/Latino; 10 Hispanic/Latino; 1 Native Hawaiian or other Pacific Islander, non-Hispanic/Latino. Average age 27. 153 applicants, 90% accepted, 59 enrolled. In 2010, 102 master's, 11 other advanced degrees awarded. *Degree requirements:* For master's, one foreign language, comprehensive exam (for some programs), thesis (for some programs), exit project, electronic portfolio, student teaching, fieldwork, curriculum project; for Advanced Certificate, 3 foreign languages, comprehensive exam (for some programs), thesis project. *Entrance requirements:* For master's, 2 letters of recommendation, teacher certification (MA), essay; for Advanced Certificate, 2 letters of recommendation, essay, interview and/or portfolio. Additional exam requirements/recommendations for international students: Required—TOEFL (minimum score 550 paper-based; 213 computer-based; 80 iBT). *Application deadline:* Applications are processed on a rolling basis. Application fee: $70 ($75 for international students). Electronic applications accepted. *Expenses:* Tuition: Full-time $18,000; part-time $1000 per credit hour. Required fees: $970; $145 per term. Tuition and fees vary according to program. *Financial support:* In 2010–11, 108 students received support, including 14 fellowships with full and partial tuition reimbursements available (averaging $3,943 per year), 1 research assistantship with full and partial tuition reimbursement available (averaging $6,574 per year); career-related internships or fieldwork, Federal Work-Study, institutionally sponsored loans, scholarships/grants, tuition waivers (full and partial), unspecified assistantships, and scholarships also available. Support available to part-time students. Financial award applicants required to submit FAFSA. *Faculty research:* Appropriate content and pedagogy in secondary school disciplines, adolescent development, secondary school organization, alternative secondary school programs. *Unit head:* Dr. Esther Fusco, Chairperson, 516-463-7704, Fax: 516-463-6196, E-mail: catezf@hofstra.edu. *Application contact:* Carol Drummer, Dean of Graduate Admissions, 516-463-4876, Fax: 516-463-4664, E-mail: gradstudent@hofstra.edu.

Howard University, Graduate School, Department of Modern Languages and Literatures, Washington, DC 20059-0002. Offers French (MA); Spanish (MA). Part-time programs available. *Degree requirements:* For master's, one foreign language, comprehensive exam, thesis. *Entrance requirements:* For master's, GRE General Test, writing samples in English and French or Spanish. *Faculty research:* African literature in French, Spanish linguistics, Spanish Peninsular literature, Spanish sociolinguistics.

Hunter College of the City University of New York, Graduate School, School of Arts and Sciences, Department of Romance Languages, Program in Spanish, New York, NY 10021-5085. Offers Spanish (MA); Spanish education (MA). Part-time and evening/weekend programs available. *Faculty:* 8 full-time (4 women). *Students:* 13 part-time (12 women); includes 9 Hispanic/Latino, 1 international. Average age 34. 10 applicants, 60% accepted, 4 enrolled. In 2010, 4 master's awarded. *Degree requirements:* For master's, 2 foreign languages, comprehensive exam, thesis optional. *Entrance requirements:* For master's, GRE General Test, GRE Subject Test, ability to read, speak, and write Spanish; interview. Additional exam requirements/recommendations for international students: Required—TOEFL. *Application deadline:* For fall admission, 4/1 for domestic students, 2/1 for international students; for spring admission, 11/1 for domestic students, 9/1 for international students. Application fee: $125. *Financial support:* Federal Work-Study and tuition waivers (partial) available. Support available to part-time students. Financial award application deadline: 4/15. *Faculty research:* Galician studies, contemporary Spanish poetry, Lope de Vega, comparative Hispanic literatures, contemporary Hispanic poetry. *Unit head:* Dr. James O. Pellier, Graduate Advisor, 212-772-5625, E-mail: jpellice@hunter.cuny.edu. *Application contact:* William Zlata, Director for Graduate Admissions, 212-772-4482, Fax: 212-650-3336, E-mail: admissions@hunter.cuny.edu.

Illinois State University, Graduate School, College of Arts and Sciences, Department of Foreign Languages, Literatures and Cultures, Normal, IL 61790-2200. Offers French (MA); French and German (MA); French and Spanish (MA); German (MA); German and Spanish (MA); Spanish (MA). *Degree requirements:* For master's, variable foreign language requirement, comprehensive exam, 1 term of residency. *Entrance requirements:* For master's, GRE General Test, minimum GPA of 2.8 in last 60 hours of course work.

Indiana University Bloomington, University Graduate School, College of Arts and Sciences, Department of Spanish and Portuguese, Bloomington, IN 47405-7000. Offers Portuguese (MA, PhD); Spanish (MA, PhD), including Hispanic linguistics, literatures in Spanish. *Faculty:*

23 full-time (13 women). *Students:* 87 full-time (48 women); includes 24 minority (1 Black or African American, non-Hispanic/Latino; 1 Asian, non-Hispanic/Latino; 19 Hispanic/Latino; 2 Native Hawaiian or other Pacific Islander, non-Hispanic/Latino; 1 Two or more races, non-Hispanic/Latino), 8 international. Average age 31. 75 applicants, 45% accepted, 18 enrolled. In 2010, 8 master's, 5 doctorates awarded. *Degree requirements:* For master's, one foreign language, comprehensive exam, thesis (optional for Portuguese); for doctorate, 2 foreign languages, comprehensive exam, thesis/dissertation. *Entrance requirements:* For master's, GRE General Test, bachelor's degree in Portuguese or Spanish, minimum GPA of 3.25; for doctorate, GRE General Test, master's degree in Portuguese or Spanish, minimum GPA of 3.25. Additional exam requirements/recommendations for international students: Required—TOEFL (minimum score 213 computer-based; 79 iBT). *Application deadline:* For fall admission, 1/15 priority date for domestic students, 12/15 priority date for international students. Application fee: $55 ($65 for international students). *Financial support:* In 2010–11, 2 fellowships with full tuition reimbursements (averaging $14,790 per year), 50 teaching assistantships with full tuition reimbursements (averaging $14,790 per year) were awarded; research assistantships, scholarships/grants, health care benefits, and unspecified assistantships also available. Financial award application deadline: 1/15. *Faculty research:* Spanish-American literature, Spanish peninsular literature, Hispanic linguistics, Luso-Brazilian studies, Catalan studies. *Unit head:* Catherine Larson, Chair, 812-855-8498, E-mail: larson@indiana.edu. *Application contact:* Patrick Dove, Director of Graduate Studies, 812-855-9194, E-mail: pdove@indiana.edu.

Inter American University of Puerto Rico, Metropolitan Campus, Graduate Programs, Program in Spanish, San Juan, PR 00919-1293. Offers MA. Part-time and evening/weekend programs available. *Degree requirements:* For master's, one foreign language, comprehensive exam. *Entrance requirements:* For master's, GRE or EXADEP, interview, minimum GPA of 2.5, 6 credits each of Spanish literature and Hispanic-American literature. Electronic applications accepted.

Inter American University of Puerto Rico, Metropolitan Campus, Graduate Programs, Program in Spanish Education, San Juan, PR 00919-1293. Offers MA.

Inter American University of Puerto Rico, Ponce Campus, Graduate School, Mercedita, PR 00715-1602. Offers accounting (MBA); biology (M Ed); chemistry (M Ed); criminal justice (MA); elementary education (M Ed); English as a Second Language (M Ed); finance (MBA); history (M Ed); human resources (MBA); marketing (MBA); mathematics (M Ed); Spanish (M Ed). *Entrance requirements:* For master's, minimum GPA of 2.5.

Iona College, School of Arts and Science, Program in Foreign Languages, New Rochelle, NY 10801-1890. Offers Italian (MA); Spanish (MA). Part-time and evening/weekend programs available. *Faculty:* 4 full-time (1 woman), 1 (woman) part-time/adjunct. *Students:* 8 part-time (all women); includes 2 minority (both Hispanic/Latino). Average age 32. 5 applicants, 80% accepted, 3 enrolled. In 2010, 4 master's awarded. *Degree requirements:* For master's, thesis or alternative. *Entrance requirements:* For master's, minimum GPA of 3.0. Additional exam requirements/recommendations for international students: Required—TOEFL (minimum score 550 paper-based; 213 computer-based). *Application deadline:* Applications are processed on a rolling basis. Application fee: $50. Electronic applications accepted. *Expenses:* Tuition: Part-time $830 per credit. Required fees: $225 per credit. *Financial support:* Unspecified assistantships available. Support available to part-time students. Financial award application deadline: 4/15; financial award applicants required to submit FAFSA. *Faculty research:* Contemporary Spanish literature, linguistics, language acquisition, female Hispanic literature, Latina authors. *Unit head:* Dr. Victoria E. Ketz, Chair, 914-637-2738, E-mail: vketz@iona.edu. *Application contact:* Veronica Jarek-Prinz, Director of Graduate Admissions, 914-633-2420, Fax: 914-633-2277, E-mail: vjarekprinz@iona.edu.

The Johns Hopkins University, Zanvyl Krieger School of Arts and Sciences, Department of German and Romance Languages and Literatures, Baltimore, MD 21218-2699. Offers French (PhD); German (PhD); Italian (PhD); romance languages (PhD); Spanish (PhD). *Faculty:* 31 full-time (20 women), 1 part-time/adjunct (0 women). *Students:* 52 full-time (31 women); includes 7 minority (6 Hispanic/Latino; 1 Two or more races, non-Hispanic/Latino), 20 international. Average age 30. 51 applicants, 37% accepted, 19 enrolled. In 2010, 6 doctorates awarded. *Degree requirements:* For doctorate, 2 foreign languages, thesis/dissertation. *Entrance requirements:* For doctorate, GRE General Test. Additional exam requirements/recommendations for international students: Required—TOEFL (minimum score 600 paper-based; 250 computer-based; 100 iBT), IELTS. *Application deadline:* For fall admission, 12/30 for domestic and international students. Application fee: $75. Electronic applications accepted. *Financial support:* In 2010–11, 40 fellowships with full tuition reimbursements (averaging $17,000 per year), 2 research assistantships with full tuition reimbursements (averaging $17,000 per year), 19 teaching assistantships with full tuition reimbursements (averaging $17,000 per year) were awarded; institutionally sponsored loans also available. *Faculty research:* Nineteenth century French prose and poetry, genetic theory and criticism; twentieth century Latin American literature and film; medieval and Renaissance Italian literature; gender and queer theory in German literature; the ideology of Baroque and Neobaroque aesthetics. *Unit head:* Dr. William Egginton, Chair, 410-516-7510, Fax: 410-516-5358, E-mail: egginton@jhu.edu. *Application contact:* Rebecca Swisdak, Graduate Administrative Coordinator, 410-516-7227, Fax: 410-516-5358, E-mail: rswisdak@jhu.edu.

Kansas State University, Graduate School, College of Arts and Sciences, Department of Modern Languages, Manhattan, KS 66506. Offers French (MA); German (MA); Spanish (MA). Part-time and evening/weekend programs available. Postbaccalaureate distance learning degree programs offered (minimal on-campus study). *Degree requirements:* For master's, thesis optional. *Entrance requirements:* For master's, teaching certificate. Additional exam requirements/recommendations for international students: Required—TOEFL (minimum score 560 paper-based). Electronic applications accepted. *Faculty research:* Second language acquisitions; Chicano literature; Francophone literature; cultural studies; German, French, Spanish, and Spanish-American literature from the Middle Ages to the modern era.

Kean University, College of Education, Program in Instruction and Curriculum, Union, NJ 07083. Offers bilingual (MA); classroom instruction (MA); mathematics/science/computer education (MA); teaching (MA); teaching English as a second language (MA); teaching physics (MA); world languages (Spanish) (MA). *Accreditation:* NCATE. Part-time and evening/weekend programs available. *Faculty:* 16 full-time (7 women). *Students:* 101 full-time (58 women), 136 part-time (106 women); includes 27 Black or African American, non-Hispanic/Latino; 11 Asian, non-Hispanic/Latino; 60 Hispanic/Latino; 1 Two or more races, non-Hispanic/Latino, 4 international. Average age 33. 123 applicants, 98% accepted, 96 enrolled. In 2010, 70 master's awarded. *Degree requirements:* For master's, comprehensive exam, two-semester advanced seminar. *Entrance requirements:* For master's, GRE General Test or MAT, PRAXIS, minimum GPA of 3.0, 2 letters of recommendation, interview, teacher certification (for some programs), transcripts. *Application deadline:* For fall admission, 6/1 for domestic students; for spring admission, 11/1 for domestic students. Application fee: $75 ($150 for international students). Electronic applications accepted. *Expenses:* Tuition, state resident: full-time $10,872; part-time $500 per credit. Tuition, nonresident: full-time $14,736; part-time $614 per credit. Required fees: $2740.80; $125 per credit. Part-time tuition and fees vary according to course load and degree level. *Financial support:* In 2010–11, 4 research assistantships with full tuition reimbursements (averaging $3,263 per year) were awarded; unspecified assistantships also available. Financial award applicants required to submit FAFSA. *Unit head:* Dr. Thomas Walsh, Program Coordinator, 908-737-4296, E-mail: tpwalsh@kean.edu. *Application contact:* Ann-Marie Kay, Assistant Director for Graduate Admissions, 908-737-5922, Fax: 908-737-5925, E-mail: akay@kean.edu.

Kent State University, College of Arts and Sciences, Department of Modern and Classical Language Studies, Kent, OH 44242-0001. Offers French literature (MA); French, Spanish, German and Latin pedagogy (MA); German literature (MA); Spanish literature (MA); translation (MA), including French, German, Japanese, Russian, Spanish; translation studies (PhD). Part-time and evening/weekend programs available. *Degree requirements:* For master's, one foreign language, comprehensive exam (for some programs), thesis (for some programs); for doctorate, comprehensive exam, thesis/dissertation (for some programs). *Entrance requirements:* For master's, minimum GPA of 3.0, writing sample, audio tape or CD; for doctorate, 3 recommendations. Additional exam requirements/recommendations for international students: Required—TOEFL (minimum score 197 computer-based). Electronic applications accepted. *Expenses:* Tuition, state resident: full-time $7866; part-time $437 per credit hour. Tuition, nonresident: full-time $14,022; part-time $779 per credit hour. *Faculty research:* Literature, pedagogy, applied linguistics, translation studies.

Lehman College of the City University of New York, Division of Arts and Humanities, Department of Languages and Literatures, Bronx, NY 10468-1589. Offers Spanish (MA). Part-time and evening/weekend programs available. *Degree requirements:* For master's, one foreign language.

Long Island University, C.W. Post Campus, College of Liberal Arts and Sciences, Department of Foreign Languages, Brookville, NY 11548-1300. Offers Spanish (MA); Spanish education (MS). Part-time programs available. *Degree requirements:* For master's, 2 foreign languages, comprehensive exam, thesis or alternative. *Entrance requirements:* For master's, 24 credits of undergraduate course work in Spanish. Electronic applications accepted. *Faculty research:* Making of a superhero, dialogue in the 19th century novel, nicknames, Menendez Pidal and Spanish School of Philology, women writers of Latin America.

Loyola University Chicago, Graduate School, Department of Modern Languages and Literatures, Chicago, IL 60660. Offers Spanish (MA). Part-time and evening/weekend programs available. *Faculty:* 6 full-time (4 women), 1 part-time/adjunct (0 women). *Students:* 13 full-time (9 women), 8 part-time (7 women); includes 5 minority (all Hispanic/Latino), 2 international. Average age 32. 15 applicants, 87% accepted, 7 enrolled. In 2010, 8 master's awarded. *Degree requirements:* For master's, 2 foreign languages, comprehensive exam, thesis or alternative. *Entrance requirements:* Additional exam requirements/recommendations for international students: Required—TOEFL. *Application deadline:* For fall admission, 2/10 for domestic students; for spring admission, 12/1 for domestic students. Application fee: $50. *Expenses:* Tuition: Full-time $14,940; part-time $830 per credit hour. Required fees: $87 per semester. Part-time tuition and fees vary according to course load and program. *Financial support:* In 2010–11, 6 students received support, including 3 teaching assistantships with full tuition reimbursements available (averaging $16,000 per year); unspecified assistantships also available. Financial award applicants required to submit FAFSA. *Faculty research:* Linguistics, Latin American contemporary narrative, Latin American culture and civilization, Hispanic women's studies, twentieth century peninsular writing, Golden Age, Don Quixote. *Unit head:* Dr. Wiley Feinstein, Chair, 773-508-2868, Fax: 773-508-2893, E-mail: wfeinst@luc.edu. *Application contact:* Dr. Olympia B. Gonzalez, Graduate Program Director, 773-508-2872, E-mail: ogonzal@luc.edu.

Marquette University, Graduate School, College of Arts and Sciences, Department of Foreign Languages and Literatures, Milwaukee, WI 53201-1881. Offers Spanish (MA). Part-time programs available. *Faculty:* 38 full-time (26 women), 4 part-time/adjunct (3 women). *Students:* 8 full-time (5 women), 5 part-time (all women); includes 4 minority (all Hispanic/Latino), 2 international. Average age 32. 11 applicants, 64% accepted, 2 enrolled. In 2010, 2 master's awarded. *Degree requirements:* For master's, one foreign language, comprehensive exam. *Entrance requirements:* For master's, official transcripts from all current and previous colleges/universities except Marquette, three letters of recommendation, tape recording of foreign speaking voice. Additional exam requirements/recommendations for international students: Required—TOEFL (minimum score 530 paper-based; 78 computer-based). *Application deadline:* For fall admission, 12/15 for domestic and international students. Application fee: $50. Electronic applications accepted. *Expenses:* Tuition: Full-time $16,290; part-time $905 per credit hour. Tuition and fees vary according to program. *Financial support:* In 2010–11, 8 teaching assistantships were awarded; research assistantships, Federal Work-Study, institutionally sponsored loans, scholarships/grants, and tuition waivers (full and partial) also available. Support available to part-time students. Financial award application deadline: 2/15. *Faculty research:* Latin American literature, Afro-Hispanic Literature, descriptive Spanish linguistics, Inter-American studies, foreign language education. *Unit head:* Dr. John Pustejovsky, Chair, 414-288-7063, Fax: 414-288-1578. *Application contact:* Dr. Armando Gonzales-Percz, Director of Graduate Studies, 414-288-7268, Fax: 414-288-1578.

Marshall University, Academic Affairs Division, College of Liberal Arts, Program in Spanish, Huntington, WV 25755. Offers MA. *Students:* 1 (woman) part-time. Average age 30. *Unit head:* Dr. Maria Carmen Riddel, Department Chair, 304-696-2742, E-mail: riddelm@marshall.edu. *Application contact:* Graduate Admissions, 304-746-1900, Fax: 304-746-1902, E-mail: services@marshall.edu.

Michigan State University, The Graduate School, College of Arts and Letters, Department of Spanish and Portuguese, East Lansing, MI 48824. Offers applied Spanish linguistics (MA); Hispanic cultural studies (PhD); Hispanic literatures (MA). *Entrance requirements:* Additional exam requirements/recommendations for international students: Required—TOEFL. Electronic applications accepted.

Middlebury College, Language Schools, Spanish School, Middlebury, VT 05753-6002. Offers MA, DML. *Faculty:* 26 full-time (10 women). *Students:* 175 full-time (129 women); includes 4 Black or African American, non-Hispanic/Latino; 1 American Indian or Alaska Native, non-Hispanic/Latino; 1 Asian, non-Hispanic/Latino; 44 Hispanic/Latino. Average age 30. 276 applicants, 84% accepted, 175 enrolled. In 2010, 57 master's awarded. *Degree requirements:* For master's, one foreign language; for doctorate, 2 foreign languages, comprehensive exam, thesis/dissertation, residence abroad, teaching experience. *Entrance requirements:* For master's and doctorate, placement exam, 3 letters of recommendation, writing sample. *Application deadline:* Applications are processed on a rolling basis. Application fee: $65. Electronic applications accepted. *Financial support:* Scholarships/grants available. Financial award applicants required to submit FAFSA. *Unit head:* Dr. Jacobo Sefami, Director, 802-443-5539, Fax: 802-443-2075, E-mail: jsefami@middlebury.edu. *Application contact:* Audrey LaRock, Coordinator, 802-443-5539, Fax: 802-443-2075, E-mail: larock@middlebury.edu.

Millersville University of Pennsylvania, College of Graduate and Professional Studies, School of Humanities and Social Sciences, Department of Foreign Languages, Program in Spanish, Millersville, PA 17551-0302. Offers M Ed, MA. Part-time programs available. *Faculty:* 8 full-time (4 women), 4 part-time/adjunct (1 woman). *Students:* 1 (woman) full-time, 6 part-time (5 women); includes 1 Hispanic/Latino. Average age 26. 2 applicants, 100% accepted, 1 enrolled. In 2010, 1 master's awarded. *Degree requirements:* For master's, comprehensive exam, thesis optional. *Entrance requirements:* For master's, ACTFL (OPI and WPT), writing sample, 3 letters of recommendation. Additional exam requirements/recommendations for international students: Required—TOEFL (minimum score 500 paper-based; 183 computer-based; 65 iBT) or IELTS (minimum score 6). *Application deadline:* For fall admission, 1/15 priority date for domestic and international students; for winter admission, 10/1 priority date for domestic and international students; for spring admission, 10/1 priority date for domestic and international students. Applications are processed on a rolling basis. Application fee: $40 ($50 for international students). Electronic applications accepted. *Expenses:* Tuition, state resident: full-time $6966; part-time $387 per credit. Tuition, nonresident: full-time $11,146; part-time $619 per credit. Required fees: $1829.50; $88 per credit. One-time fee: $60 part-time. Tuition and fees vary according to course load. *Financial support:* In 2010–11, 2 students received support, including 2 research assistantships with full tuition reimbursements available (averaging $5,000 per year); institutionally sponsored loans and unspecified assistantships also available. Support available to part-time students. Financial award application deadline: 3/15; financial award applicants required to submit FAFSA. *Unit head:* Dr. Christine M. Gaudry-Hudson, Coordinator of Foreign Language Graduate Program, 717-872-3663, E-mail: christine.gaudry-hudson@millersville.edu. *Application contact:* Dr. Victor S. DeSantis, Dean of Graduate and Professional Studies, 717-872-3099, Fax: 717-872-3453, E-mail: victor.desantis@millersville.edu.

Spanish

Minnesota State University Mankato, College of Graduate Studies, College of Arts and Humanities, Department of Modern Languages, Program in Spanish, Mankato, MN 56001. Offers MAT, MS. *Students:* 5 full-time (3 women), 12 part-time (4 women). *Degree requirements:* For master's, one foreign language, comprehensive exam, thesis. *Entrance requirements:* For master's, minimum GPA of 3.0 during previous 2 years. *Application deadline:* For fall admission, 7/1 priority date for domestic students; for spring admission, 11/1 for domestic students. Applications are processed on a rolling basis. Application fee: $40. Electronic applications accepted. *Financial support:* Research assistantships with full tuition reimbursements, teaching assistantships with full tuition reimbursements, career-related internships or fieldwork, Federal Work-Study, institutionally sponsored loans, and unspecified assistantships available. Support available to part-time students. Financial award application deadline: 3/15. *Unit head:* Dr. Kimberly Contag, Graduate Coordinator, 507-389-2116. *Application contact:* 507-389-2321, E-mail: grad@mnsu.edu.

Mississippi State University, College of Arts and Sciences, Department of Foreign Languages, Mississippi State, MS 39762. Offers foreign language (MA), including French, German, Spanish. Part-time programs available. *Faculty:* 8 full-time (3 women). *Students:* 10 full-time (8 women), 2 part-time (both women); includes 3 minority (1 Black or African American, non-Hispanic/Latino; 2 Hispanic/Latino), 1 international. Average age 29. 8 applicants, 75% accepted, 4 enrolled. In 2010, 7 master's awarded. *Degree requirements:* For master's, one foreign language, thesis optional, comprehensive oral or written exam. *Entrance requirements:* For master's, minimum GPA of 2.75 on last two years of undergraduate courses. Additional exam requirements/recommendations for international students: Required—TOEFL (minimum score 525 paper-based). *Application deadline:* For fall admission, 7/1 for domestic students, 5/1 for international students; for spring admission, 11/1 for domestic students, 9/1 for international students. Applications are processed on a rolling basis. Application fee: $40. Electronic applications accepted. *Expenses:* Tuition, state resident: full-time $2730.50; part-time $304 per credit hour. Tuition, nonresident: full-time $6901; part-time $767 per credit hour. *Financial support:* In 2010–11, 10 teaching assistantships with full tuition reimbursements (averaging $8,768 per year) were awarded; Federal Work-Study, institutionally sponsored loans, and unspecified assistantships also available. Financial award application deadline: 4/1; financial award applicants required to submit FAFSA. *Faculty research:* French, German, Spanish literature from medieval era to present; gender and cultural studies in French; Spanish-American literature; foreign language methodology; linguistics. *Unit head:* Dr. Jack Jordan, Professor/Head, 662-325-3480, Fax: 662-325-8209, E-mail: jordan@ra.msstate.edu. *Application contact:* Dr. Edward T. Potter, Assistant Professor/Graduate Coordinator, 662-325-2399, Fax: 662-325-8209, E-mail: ep75@.msstate.edu.

Missouri State University, Graduate College, College of Arts and Letters, Department of Modern and Classical Languages, Springfield, MO 65897. Offers secondary education (MS Ed), including Spanish. Part-time programs available. *Entrance requirements:* For master's, grades 9-12 teaching certification. Additional exam requirements/recommendations for international students: Required—TOEFL (minimum score 550 paper-based; 213 computer-based; 79 iBT), IELTS (minimum score 6). Electronic applications accepted. *Expenses:* Tuition, state resident: full-time $3348; part-time $186 per credit hour. Tuition, nonresident: full-time $6696; part-time $372 per credit hour. Required fees: $238 per semester. Tuition and fees vary according to course level, course load and program.

Montclair State University, The Graduate School, College of Education and Human Services, Department of Curriculum and Teaching, Montclair, NJ 07043-1624. Offers education (M Ed); educational technology (M Ed); learning disabilities teacher consultant (Certificate); teaching (MAT), including art, biological science, early childhood education (P-3), earth science, elementary education (K-8), English, French, health and physical education, health education, home economics, mathematics, music, physical education, physical science, social studies, Spanish, teacher of ESL, teacher of students with disabilities. Part-time and evening/weekend programs available. *Faculty:* 18 full-time (12 women), 37 part-time/adjunct (26 women). *Students:* 183 full-time (105 women), 176 part-time (136 women); includes 20 Black or African American, non-Hispanic/Latino; 7 Asian, non-Hispanic/Latino; 15 Hispanic/Latino; 2 Two or more races, non-Hispanic/Latino, 6 international. Average age 30. 123 applicants, 56% accepted, 55 enrolled. In 2010, 133 master's, 1 other advanced degree awarded. *Degree requirements:* For master's, comprehensive exam, field experience. *Entrance requirements:* For master's, GRE, 2 letters of recommendation. Additional exam requirements/recommendations for international students: Required—TOEFL (minimum iBT score of 83) or IELTS. *Application deadline:* For fall admission, 2/15 for domestic and international students; for spring admission, 9/15 for domestic and international students. Applications are processed on a rolling basis. Application fee: $60. Electronic applications accepted. *Expenses:* Tuition, state resident: part-time $501.34 per credit. Tuition, nonresident: part-time $773.88 per credit. Required fees: $71.15 per credit. *Financial support:* In 2010–11, 8 research assistantships with full tuition reimbursements (averaging $7,000 per year) were awarded; Federal Work-Study, scholarships/grants, and unspecified assistantships also available. Support available to part-time students. Financial award application deadline: 3/1; financial award applicants required to submit FAFSA. *Faculty research:* Technology in the service of democratic education, case pedagogy in teacher preparation, public education in the United States, school reform: secondary science education, role of teacher learning as an agency of school reform. Total annual research expenditures: $11,313. *Unit head:* Dr. David Schwarzer, Chairperson, 973-655-5187. *Application contact:* Amy Aiello, Director of Graduate Admissions and Operations, 973-655-5147, Fax: 973-655-7869, E-mail: graduate.school@montclair.edu.

Montclair State University, The Graduate School, College of Humanities and Social Sciences, Department of Spanish and Italian, Montclair, NJ 07043-1624. Offers Italian (Certificate); Spanish (MA, Certificate); translation and interpretation in Spanish (Certificate). Part-time and evening/weekend programs available. *Faculty:* 21 full-time (13 women), 25 part-time/adjunct (16 women). *Students:* 4 full-time (3 women), 20 part-time (17 women); includes 1 American Indian or Alaska Native, non-Hispanic/Latino; 11 Hispanic/Latino. Average age 33. 10 applicants, 90% accepted, 6 enrolled. In 2010, 7 master's awarded. *Degree requirements:* For master's, comprehensive exam, thesis or alternative. *Entrance requirements:* For master's, GRE General Test, 2 letters of recommendation. Additional exam requirements/recommendations for international students: Required—TOEFL (minimum iBT score of 83) or IELTS. *Application deadline:* For fall admission, 6/1 for international students; for spring admission, 11/1 for international students. Applications are processed on a rolling basis. Application fee: $60. Electronic applications accepted. *Expenses:* Tuition, state resident: part-time $501.34 per credit. Tuition, nonresident: part-time $773.88 per credit. Required fees: $71.15 per credit. *Financial support:* In 2010–11, 1 research assistantship with full tuition reimbursement (averaging $7,000 per year) was awarded; Federal Work-Study, scholarships/grants, and unspecified assistantships also available. Support available to part-time students. Financial award application deadline: 3/1; financial award applicants required to submit FAFSA. *Unit head:* Dr. Linda Gould Levine, Chairperson, 973-655-7506. *Application contact:* Amy Aiello, Director of Graduate Admissions and Operations, 973-655-5147, Fax: 973-655-7869, E-mail: graduate.school@montclair.edu.

New Mexico State University, Graduate School, College of Arts and Sciences, Department of Languages and Linguistics, Las Cruces, NM 88003-8001. Offers Spanish (MA). Part-time programs available. *Faculty:* 11 full-time (4 women). *Students:* 18 full-time (12 women), 30 part-time (16 women); includes 30 minority (1 Black or African American, non-Hispanic/Latino; 29 Hispanic/Latino), 10 international. Average age 37. 104 applicants, 95% accepted, 47 enrolled. In 2010, 11 master's awarded. *Degree requirements:* For master's, one foreign language, comprehensive exam, thesis optional, oral and written exams. *Entrance requirements:* For master's, sample of written work in Spanish, cassette tape in Spanish, 3 letters of reference. *Application deadline:* For fall admission, 2/15 for domestic students; for spring admission, 10/15 for domestic students. Applications are processed on a rolling basis. Application fee: $30 ($50 for international students). Electronic applications accepted. *Expenses:* Tuition, state resident: full-time $4536; part-time $242 per credit. Tuition, nonresident: full-time $15,816; part-time $712 per credit. Required fees: $636 per term. *Financial support:* In 2010–11, 14 teaching assistantships (averaging $7,900 per year) were awarded; research assistantships,

Federal Work-Study, institutionally sponsored loans, scholarships/grants, health care benefits, and unspecified assistantships also available. Support available to part-time students. Financial award application deadline: 3/1. *Faculty research:* Spanish-American literature, U. S. Hispanic and Chicano literature and border culture, Hispanic linguistics, French and German literature and linguistics. *Unit head:* Dr. Richard Rundell, Head, 575-646-3408, Fax: 575-646-7876, E-mail: rrundell@nmsu.edu. *Application contact:* Dr. Richard Rundell, Head, 575-646-3408, Fax: 575-646-7876, E-mail: rrundell@nmsu.edu.

New York University, Graduate School of Arts and Science, Department of Spanish and Portuguese Languages and Literatures, New York, NY 10012-1019. Offers Portuguese (MA, PhD); Spanish (PhD); Spanish and Latin American literatures and cultures (MA); Spanish language and translation (MA). Part-time programs available. *Students:* 99 full-time (55 women), 12 part-time (9 women); includes 3 Black or African American, non-Hispanic/Latino; 4 Asian, non-Hispanic/Latino; 30 Hispanic/Latino, 48 international. Average age 31. 189 applicants, 42% accepted, 48 enrolled. In 2010, 39 master's, 4 doctorates awarded. *Degree requirements:* For master's, 2 foreign languages, thesis; for doctorate, 2 foreign languages, thesis/dissertation. *Entrance requirements:* For master's, GRE General Test; for doctorate, GRE General Test, master's degree. Additional exam requirements/recommendations for international students: Required—TOEFL. *Application deadline:* For fall admission, 1/4 priority date for domestic students. Application fee: $90. *Financial support:* Fellowships with tuition reimbursements, teaching assistantships with tuition reimbursements, career-related internships or fieldwork, Federal Work-Study, institutionally sponsored loans, scholarships/grants, health care benefits, and unspecified assistantships available. Financial award application deadline: 1/4; financial award applicants required to submit FAFSA. *Faculty research:* Gender and sexuality, transatlantic studies, literacy and cultural theories, colonial and post colonial studies, autobiography and modern subjectivities. *Unit head:* Jo Labanyi, Acting Chair, 212-998-8770, Fax: 212-995-4149, E-mail: spanish.portuguese.info@nyu.edu. *Application contact:* Gabriel Giorgi, Director of Graduate Studies, 212-998-8770, Fax: 212-995-4149, E-mail: spanish.portuguese.info@nyu.edu.

New York University, NYU in Madrid, Madrid, NY 10012-1019, Spain. Offers creative writing in Spanish (MFA); Spanish (PhD); Spanish and Latin American literatures and cultures (MA); Spanish language and translation (MA).

North Carolina State University, Graduate School, College of Humanities and Social Sciences, Department of Foreign Languages and Literatures, Program in Spanish Language and Literature, Raleigh, NC 27695. Offers MA. *Degree requirements:* For master's, thesis optional. *Entrance requirements:* For master's, fluency in Spanish. Electronic applications accepted. *Faculty research:* Applied linguistics, technology-assisted language instruction, Latin-American literature and culture, 20th and 21st Century Spanish narrative and film, children's literature.

Northern Arizona University, Graduate College, College of Arts and Letters, Department of Modern Languages, Flagstaff, AZ 86011. Offers Spanish teaching (MAT); Spanish teaching/Spanish education (MAT). Part-time programs available. *Faculty:* 24 full-time (18 women). *Students:* 13 full-time (9 women), 3 part-time (all women); includes 5 minority (all Hispanic/Latino), 2 international. Average age 30. 10 applicants, 60% accepted, 5 enrolled. In 2010, 5 master's awarded. *Degree requirements:* For master's, comprehensive exam, thesis optional. *Entrance requirements:* For master's, bachelor's degree in Spanish (coupled with preparation in general or foreign language education courses) or Spanish secondary education, or degree/experience in related field (e.g., bilingual education); minimum GPA of 3.0 or equivalent. Additional exam requirements/recommendations for international students: Required—TOEFL (minimum score 550 paper-based; 213 computer-based; 80 iBT), IELTS (minimum score 7). *Application deadline:* For fall admission, 4/21 priority date for domestic and international students; for spring admission, 10/21 priority date for domestic students. Applications are processed on a rolling basis. Application fee: $65. Electronic applications accepted. *Financial support:* In 2010–11, 13 teaching assistantships with partial tuition reimbursements (averaging $11,300 per year) were awarded; Federal Work-Study, scholarships/grants, health care benefits, tuition waivers (full and partial), and unspecified assistantships also available. Financial award applicants required to submit FAFSA. *Unit head:* Dr. Joseph Collentine, Chair, 928-523-5334, Fax: 928-523-0963, E-mail: j.collentine@nau.edu. *Application contact:* Alexandria McConocha, Administrative Associate, 928-523-2361, Fax: 928-523-0963, E-mail: alexandria.mcconocha@nau.edu.

Northern Illinois University, Graduate School, College of Liberal Arts and Sciences, Department of Foreign Languages and Literatures, De Kalb, IL 60115-2854. Offers French (MA); Spanish (MA). Part-time programs available. *Faculty:* 25 full-time (11 women). *Students:* 25 part-time (19 women); includes 1 Black or African American, non-Hispanic/Latino; 9 Hispanic/Latino, 1 international. Average age 31. 10 applicants, 60% accepted, 4 enrolled. In 2010, 4 master's awarded. *Degree requirements:* For master's, one foreign language, comprehensive exam, thesis or alternative, language proficiency exam. *Entrance requirements:* For master's, GRE General Test, interview, minimum GPA of 2.75, undergraduate major in French or Spanish. Additional exam requirements/recommendations for international students: Required—TOEFL (minimum score 550 paper-based; 213 computer-based). *Application deadline:* For fall admission, 6/1 for domestic students, 5/1 for international students; for spring admission, 11/1 for domestic students, 10/1 for international students. Applications are processed on a rolling basis. Application fee: $30. Electronic applications accepted. *Expenses:* Tuition, state resident: full-time $7200; part-time $300 per credit hour. Tuition, nonresident: full-time $14,400; part-time $600 per credit hour. Required fees: $79 per credit hour. *Financial support:* In 2010–11, 14 teaching assistantships with full tuition reimbursements were awarded; fellowships with full tuition reimbursements, research assistantships with full tuition reimbursements, career-related internships or fieldwork, Federal Work-Study, scholarships/grants, tuition waivers (full), and unspecified assistantships also available. Support available to part-time students. Financial award applicants required to submit FAFSA. *Faculty research:* Francophone women writers, prosodies of French and Italian, early Spanish drama, business German, history of Burmese literature. *Unit head:* Anne Birbeck, Chair, 815-753-1259, Fax: 815-753-5989, E-mail: annie@niu.edu. *Application contact:* Graduate School Office, 815-753-0395, E-mail: gradsch@niu.edu.

Nova Southeastern University, Fischler School of Education and Human Services, Graduate Teacher Education Program, Fort Lauderdale, FL 33314-7796. Offers athletic administration (MS); brain research (MS, Ed S); charter school education/leadership (MS); cognitive and behavioral disabilities (MS); computer science education (Ed S); computer science education (K-12) (MS); curriculum and teaching (Ed S); curriculum, instruction and technology (MS); curriculum, instruction, management and administration (Ed S); early childhood education (MS); early literacy and reading (Ed S); early literacy education (MS); education technology (MS); educational leadership (administration K-12) (MS, Ed S); educational media (Ed S); educational media (K-12) (MS); elementary education (MS, Ed S, including ESOL endorsement (MS); English education (MS, Ed S); environmental education (MS); exceptional student education (MS), including ESOL endorsement; gifted education (MS, Ed S); interdisciplinary arts education (MS); management and administration of educational programs (MS); mathematics (MS); mathematics education (Ed S); multicultural early intervention (MS); pre-kindergarten/primary (MS); preschool education (MS); reading (MS); reading and TESOL (MS); reading education (Ed S); science (MS); science education (Ed S); secondary education (MS); social studies (MS, Ed S); Spanish language (MS); special education and reading (MS); teaching and learning (MA, MS), including curriculum and instruction (MA), elementary mathematics (MA), elementary reading (MA), K-12 technology integration (MA); teaching English to speakers of other languages (MS, Ed S); technology management and administration (Ed S); urban studies education (MS). Part-time and evening/weekend programs available. Postbaccalaureate distance learning degree programs offered (minimal on-campus study). *Faculty:* 142 full-time (84 women), 612 part-time/adjunct (410 women). *Students:* 196 full-time (175 women), 1,304 part-time (1,128 women); includes 471 Black or African American, non-Hispanic/Latino; 5 American Indian or Alaska Native, non-Hispanic/Latino; 18 Asian, non-Hispanic/Latino; 100 Hispanic/Latino. Average age 37. 1,420 applicants, 62% accepted, 661 enrolled. In 2010, 836 other advanced degrees awarded. *Degree requirements:* For master's and Ed S, practicum, internship, certification/licensure exams. *Entrance requirements:* For master's, MAT, GRE, CLAST, CBEST, PRAXIS I, General Knowledge Test, minimum GPA of 2.5; for Ed S, MAT or GRE, master's degree, teaching certificate, minimum GPA of 3.0. Additional exam requirements/recommendations for international students: Recommended— TOEFL (minimum score 550 paper-based; 213 computer-based; 80 iBT), IELTS (minimum score 6). *Application deadline:* Applications are processed on a rolling basis. Application fee: $50. Electronic applications accepted. *Financial support:* Federal Work-Study available. Support available to part-time students. Financial award application deadline: 4/15; financial award applicants required to submit FAFSA. *Faculty research:* School effectiveness, critical thinking, leadership skills acquisition, child education, multicultural education. *Unit head:* Dr. H. Wells Singleton, Dean, 800-986-3223 Ext. 28730, Fax: 954-262-3894, E-mail: singlew@nova.edu. *Application contact:* Lenny Jacobskind, Director of School-Wide Recruiting, 800-986-3223 Ext. 28538, Fax: 954-262-2914, E-mail: lenny@nova.edu.

The Ohio State University, Graduate School, College of Arts and Sciences, Division of Arts and Humanities, Department of Spanish and Portuguese, Columbus, OH 43210. Offers MA, PhD. *Faculty:* 22. *Students:* 57 full-time (37 women), 10 part-time (6 women); includes 1 Black or African American, non-Hispanic/Latino; 1 Asian, non-Hispanic/Latino; 10 Hispanic/Latino, 18 international. Average age 31. In 2010, 9 master's, 13 doctorates awarded. *Degree requirements:* For master's, thesis optional; for doctorate, thesis/dissertation. *Entrance requirements:* For master's and doctorate, GRE General Test. Additional exam requirements/recommendations for international students: Required—TOEFL (minimum score 600 paper-based; 250 computer-based). *Application deadline:* For fall admission, 8/15 priority date for domestic students, 7/1 priority date for international students; for winter admission, 12/1 priority date for domestic students, 11/1 priority date for international students; for spring admission, 3/1 priority date for domestic students, 2/1 priority date for international students. Applications are processed on a rolling basis. Application fee: $40 ($50 for international students). Electronic applications accepted. *Expenses:* Tuition, state resident: full-time $10,605. Tuition, nonresident: full-time $26,535. Tuition and fees vary according to course load and program. *Financial support:* Fellowships, research assistantships, teaching assistantships, Federal Work-Study, institutionally sponsored loans, and unspecified assistantships available. Support available to part-time students. *Unit head:* Fernando Unzueta, Chair, 614-292-4958, E-mail: unzueta.1@osu.edu. *Application contact:* 614-292-9444, Fax: 614-292-3895, E-mail: domestic.grad@osu.edu.

Ohio University, Graduate College, College of Arts and Sciences, Department of Modern Languages, Athens, OH 45701-2979. Offers French (MA); Spanish (MA). Part-time programs available. *Students:* 27 full-time (24 women), 2 part-time (both women); includes 4 minority (2 Black or African American, non-Hispanic/Latino; 1 Hispanic/Latino; 1 Two or more races, non-Hispanic/Latino), 3 international. 26 applicants, 73% accepted, 15 enrolled. In 2010, 12 master's awarded. *Degree requirements:* For master's, 2 foreign languages, comprehensive exam, thesis optional. *Entrance requirements:* For master's, oral and written samples. Additional exam requirements/recommendations for international students: Required—TOEFL (minimum score 550 paper-based; 80 iBT) or IELTS (minimum score 6.5). *Application deadline:* For fall admission, 1/15 priority date for domestic and international students. Application fee: $50 ($55 for international students). Electronic applications accepted. *Financial support:* In 2010–11, teaching assistantships with tuition reimbursements (averaging $10,300 per year); Federal Work-Study, institutionally sponsored loans, and tuition waivers (partial) also available. Financial award application deadline: 1/15. *Faculty research:* French and Spanish language and literature. *Unit head:* Dr. Betsy Partyka, Chair, 740-593-2765, Fax: 740-593-0729, E-mail: partyka@ohio.edu. *Application contact:* Dr. David Burton, Graduate Chair, 740-593-2762, Fax: 740-593-0729, E-mail: burtond@ohio.edu.

Penn State University Park, Graduate School, College of the Liberal Arts, School of Languages and Literatures, Department of Spanish, Italian, and Portuguese, State College, University Park, PA 16802-1503. Offers MA, PhD. *Unit head:* Dr. William R. Blue, Interim Head, 814-865-4252, Fax: 814-863-7944, E-mail: wrb10@psu.edu. *Application contact:* Carol Toscano, Information Contact, 814-865-1016, E-mail: clt4@psu.edu.

Pontifical Catholic University of Puerto Rico, College of Arts and Humanities, Department of Hispanic Studies, Ponce, PR 00717-0777. Offers grammar and writing (Professional Certificate); Hispanic studies (MA). Part-time and evening/weekend programs available. *Degree requirements:* For master's, variable foreign language requirement, comprehensive exam, thesis or alternative. *Entrance requirements:* For master's, GRE General Test, 2 letters of recommendation, interview, minimum GPA of 2.75. Electronic applications accepted.

Portland State University, Graduate Studies, College of Liberal Arts and Sciences, Department of World Languages and Literatures, Portland, OR 97207-0751. Offers foreign literature and language (MA); French (MA); German (MA); Japanese (MA); Spanish (MA). Part-time programs available. *Faculty:* 45 full-time (30 women), 38 part-time/adjunct (29 women). *Students:* 30 full-time (21 women), 10 part-time (7 women); includes 6 minority (2 Asian, non-Hispanic/Latino; 4 Hispanic/Latino), 11 international. Average age 31. 26 applicants, 69% accepted, 15 enrolled. In 2010, 24 master's awarded. *Degree requirements:* For master's, one foreign language, thesis (for some programs). *Entrance requirements:* Additional exam requirements/recommendations for international students: Required—TOEFL (minimum score 550 paper-based; 213 computer-based). *Application deadline:* For fall admission, 4/1 for domestic students, 3/1 for international students; for winter admission, 9/1 for domestic students, 7/1 for international students; for spring admission, 11/1 for domestic and international students. Applications are processed on a rolling basis. Application fee: $50. *Expenses:* Tuition, state resident: full-time $8505; part-time $315 per credit. Tuition, nonresident: full-time $13,284; part-time $492 per credit. Required fees: $1482; $21 per credit. $99 per term. One-time fee: $120. Part-time tuition and fees vary according to course load and program. *Financial support:* In 2010–11, 6 teaching assistantships with full tuition reimbursements (averaging $9,359 per year) were awarded; research assistantships with full tuition reimbursements, Federal Work-Study, scholarships/grants, and unspecified assistantships also available. Support available to part-time students. Financial award application deadline: 3/1; financial award applicants required to submit FAFSA. *Faculty research:* Foreign language pedagogy, applied and social linguistics, literary history and criticism. *Unit head:* Dr. Jennifer Perlmutter, Chair, 503-725-8783, Fax: 503-725-5276, E-mail: jrp@pdx.edu. *Application contact:* Michael Anthony, Graduate Admissions Coordinator, 503-725-3243, E-mail: manthony@pdx.edu.

Princeton University, Graduate School, Department of Spanish and Portuguese Languages and Cultures, Princeton, NJ 08544-1019. Offers PhD. *Degree requirements:* For doctorate, variable foreign language requirement, thesis/dissertation. *Entrance requirements:* For doctorate, GRE General Test, sample of written work. Additional exam requirements/recommendations for international students: Required—TOEFL (minimum score 600 paper-based; 250 computer-based). Electronic applications accepted.

Purdue University, Graduate School, College of Liberal Arts, Department of Foreign Languages and Literatures, West Lafayette, IN 47907. Offers French (MA, MAT, PhD), including French (MA, PhD), French education (MAT); German (MA, MAT, PhD), including German (MA, PhD), German education (MAT); Spanish (MA, MAT, PhD), including Spanish (MA, PhD), Spanish education (MAT). Terminal master's awarded for partial completion of doctoral program. *Degree requirements:* For master's, one foreign language; for doctorate, 2 foreign languages, thesis/dissertation. *Entrance requirements:* For master's, GRE, sample recording of English and language of study; for doctorate, GRE, writing sample, sample recording of English and language of study. Additional exam requirements/recommendations for international students: Required—TOEFL. Electronic applications accepted. *Faculty research:* Linguistics, semiotics, literary criticism, pedagogy.

Queens College of the City University of New York, Division of Graduate Studies, Arts and Humanities Division, Department of Hispanic Languages and Literatures, Program in Spanish, Flushing, NY 11367-1597. Offers MA. Part-time and evening/weekend programs available. *Faculty:* 10 full-time (6 women). *Students:* 1 (woman) full-time, 20 part-time (13 women); includes 1 Black or African American, non-Hispanic/Latino; 17 Hispanic/Latino, 2 international. 25 applicants, 36% accepted, 5 enrolled. In 2010, 4 master's awarded. *Degree requirements:* For master's, 2 foreign languages, comprehensive exam, thesis or alternative. *Entrance requirements:* For master's, minimum GPA of 3.0. Additional exam requirements/recommendations for international students: Required—TOEFL. *Application deadline:* For fall admission, 4/1 for domestic students; for spring admission, 11/1 for domestic students. Applications are processed on a rolling basis. Application fee: $125. *Financial support:* Career-related internships or fieldwork, Federal Work-Study, institutionally sponsored loans, and tuition waivers (partial) available. Support available to part-time students. Financial award application deadline: 4/1; financial award applicants required to submit FAFSA. *Unit head:* Dr. Irma Llorens, Graduate Adviser, 718-997-5649. *Application contact:* Mario Caruso, Director of Graduate Admissions, 718-997-5200, Fax: 718-997-5193, E-mail: graduate_admissions@qc.edu.

Queen's University at Kingston, School of Graduate Studies and Research, Faculty of Arts and Sciences, Department of Spanish and Italian, Kingston, ON K7L 3N6, Canada. Offers Spanish language and literature (MA). Part-time programs available. *Degree requirements:* For master's, one foreign language, thesis. *Entrance requirements:* Additional exam requirements/recommendations for international students: Required—TOEFL. Electronic applications accepted. *Faculty research:* Golden Age, nineteenth- and twentieth-century Peninsular novel, literary theory, colonial Latin America, nineteenth-and-twentieth century Latin America.

Rider University, Department of Graduate Education, Leadership and Counseling, Teacher Certification Program, Lawrenceville, NJ 08648-3001. Offers business education (Certificate); elementary education (Certificate); English as a second language (Certificate); English education (Certificate); mathematics education (Certificate); preschool to grade 3 (Certificate); science education (Certificate); social studies education (Certificate); world languages (Certificate), including French, German, Spanish. Part-time programs available. *Degree requirements:* For Certificate, internship, professional portfolio. *Entrance requirements:* For degree, PRAXIS, resume. Additional exam requirements/recommendations for international students: Required—TOEFL (minimum score 550 paper-based; 213 computer-based). Electronic applications accepted. *Expenses:* Tuition: Full-time $29,870; part-time $667.34 per credit. Required fees: $350; $11.60 per credit. Part-time tuition and fees vary according to program. *Faculty research:* Conceptual foundations for optimal development of creativity; creative theory, cognitive processes in mathematics learning, teacher collaboration.

Roosevelt University, Graduate Division, College of Arts and Sciences, Department of Literature and Languages, Program in Spanish, Chicago, IL 60605. Offers MA. Part-time and evening/weekend programs available. *Degree requirements:* For master's, variable foreign language requirement, thesis or alternative. *Entrance requirements:* For master's, BA in Spanish or the equivalent. *Faculty research:* Latin American narrative, feminism, Hispanic cultures, twentieth century Hispanic literature, Latino studies.

Rutgers, The State University of New Jersey, New Brunswick, Graduate School-New Brunswick, Program in Spanish, Piscataway, NJ 08854-8097. Offers bilingualism and second language acquisition (MA, PhD); Spanish (MA, MAT, PhD); Spanish literature (MA, PhD); translation (MA). Part-time programs available. *Degree requirements:* For master's, comprehensive exam (for some programs), thesis (for some programs); for doctorate, 2 foreign languages, comprehensive exam, thesis/dissertation. *Entrance requirements:* For master's and doctorate, GRE General Test. Additional exam requirements/recommendations for international students: Required—TOEFL. Electronic applications accepted. *Expenses:* Tuition, state resident: full-time $7200; part-time $600 per credit. Tuition, nonresident: full-time $11,124; part-time $927 per credit. *Faculty research:* Hispanic literature, Luso-Brazilian literature, Spanish linguistics, Spanish translation.

St. John's University, St. John's College of Liberal Arts and Sciences, Department of Languages and Literatures, Queens, NY 11439. Offers Spanish (MA). Part-time and evening/weekend programs available. *Students:* 10 full-time (6 women), 5 part-time (all women); includes 13 minority (all Hispanic/Latino). Average age 32. 13 applicants, 54% accepted, 6 enrolled. In 2010, 2 master's awarded. *Degree requirements:* For master's, comprehensive exam, thesis optional. *Entrance requirements:* For master's, 24 credits of undergraduate course work in languages (18 credits in Spanish), minimum GPA of 3.0. Additional exam requirements/recommendations for international students: Required—TOEFL (minimum score 600 paper-based; 250 computer-based; 100 iBT), IELTS (minimum score 5.5). *Application deadline:* For fall admission, 5/1 priority date for domestic and international students; for spring admission, 11/1 priority date for domestic and international students. Applications are processed on a rolling basis. Application fee: $70. Electronic applications accepted. *Expenses:* Tuition: Full-time $17,100; part-time $950 per credit. Required fees: $340; $170 per semester. Tuition and fees vary according to program. *Financial support:* Research assistantships, scholarships/grants available. Support available to part-time students. Financial award application deadline: 3/1; financial award applicants required to submit FAFSA. *Faculty research:* Paleography; early North American Spanish literature; medieval, Renaissance and Golden Century Spanish literature; journal and book editions. *Unit head:* Dr. Herbert Pierson, Chair, 718-990-5211, E-mail: piersonh@stjohns.edu. *Application contact:* Kathleen Davis, Director of Graduate Admission, 718-990-1601, Fax: 718-990-5686, E-mail: gradhelp@stjohns.edu.

Saint Louis University, Graduate Education, College of Arts and Sciences and Graduate Education, Department of Modern and Classical Languages, St. Louis, MO 63103-2097. Offers French (MA); Spanish (MA). Part-time programs available. *Degree requirements:* For master's, one foreign language, comprehensive exam, thesis/dissertation (Spanish). *Entrance requirements:* For master's, GRE General Test or MAT, letters of recommendation, resume, interview. Additional exam requirements/recommendations for international students: Required—TOEFL (minimum score 525 paper-based; 194 computer-based). Electronic applications accepted. *Faculty research:* Culture studies, literature studies, foreign language acquisition.

Saint Louis University–Madrid Campus, Graduate Programs, Master of Arts in Spanish Program, Madrid, Spain. Offers Spanish language and literature (MA). Part-time programs available. *Degree requirements:* For master's, one foreign language, comprehensive exam, thesis optional. *Entrance requirements:* For master's, GRE General Test or MAT, 3 letters of recommendation, curriculum vitae, writing sample, interview. *Faculty research:* Spanish and Latin American literature, linguistics, cultural studies, gender studies.

Salem State University, School of Graduate Studies, Program in Spanish, Salem, MA 01970-5353. Offers MAT. Part-time and evening/weekend programs available. *Students:* 27 part-time (20 women); includes 1 Black or African American, non-Hispanic/Latino; 4 Hispanic/Latino. Average age 34. 7 applicants, 100% accepted, 7 enrolled. In 2010, 14 master's awarded. *Entrance requirements:* For master's, GRE or MAT. Additional exam requirements/recommendations for international students: Required—TOEFL (minimum score 550 paper-based; 80 iBT) or IELTS (minimum score 5.5). *Application deadline:* For fall admission, 5/1 for domestic students; for spring admission, 10/1 for domestic students. Applications are processed on a rolling basis. Application fee: $50. *Expenses:* Tuition, state resident: full-time $2520; part-time $290 per credit hour. Tuition, nonresident: full-time $4140; part-time $380 per credit hour. Required fees: $2700. *Financial support:* Career-related internships or fieldwork, Federal Work-Study, scholarships/grants, and unspecified assistantships available. Support available to part-time students. Financial award application deadline: 5/1; financial award applicants required to submit FAFSA. *Unit head:* Kristine Doll, Program Coordinator, 978-542-6321, E-mail: kdoll@salemstate.edu. *Application contact:* Dr. Lee A. Brossoit, Assistant Dean of Graduate Admissions, 978-542-6675, Fax: 978-542-7215, E-mail: lbrossoit@salemstate.edu.

San Diego State University, Graduate and Research Affairs, College of Arts and Letters, Department of Spanish and Portuguese Languages and Literatures, San Diego, CA 92182. Offers Spanish (MA). *Degree requirements:* For master's, one foreign language. *Entrance requirements:* For master's, GRE General Test, 3 letters of reference. Additional exam requirements/recommendations for international students: Required—TOEFL. Electronic applications accepted. *Faculty research:* New strategies for teaching foreign languages.

Spanish

San Francisco State University, Division of Graduate Studies, College of Humanities, Department of Foreign Languages and Literatures, Program in Spanish, San Francisco, CA 94132-1722. Offers MA. Part-time programs available. *Application deadline:* Applications are processed on a rolling basis. Electronic applications accepted. *Financial support:* Unspecified assistantships available. *Unit head:* Michael Hammer, Program Coordinator, 415-338-1421, E-mail: mhammer@sfsu.edu. *Application contact:* Dr. Paola Cortes-Rocca, Graduate Coordinator, 415-338-1421, E-mail: pcortes@sfsu.edu.

San Jose State University, Graduate Studies and Research, College of Humanities and the Arts, Department of Foreign Languages, Program in Spanish, San Jose, CA 95192-0001. Offers MA. *Degree requirements:* For master's, 2 foreign languages, thesis or comprehensive exam. Electronic applications accepted.

Simmons College, College of Arts and Sciences Graduate Studies, Program in Spanish, Boston, MA 02115. Offers MA, MAT/MA. Part-time programs available. *Degree requirements:* For master's, one foreign language, thesis optional. *Entrance requirements:* For master's, analytical writing samples in Spanish. Additional exam requirements/recommendations for international students: Required—TOEFL (minimum score 600 paper-based; 250 computer-based; 100 iBT). Electronic applications accepted. *Faculty research:* Medieval and Golden Age Spanish literature, the changing roles of Latinos in the U. S., Latin-American women's fiction, post-dictatorship narratives in the Southern Cone.

Stanford University, School of Humanities and Sciences, Department of Spanish and Portuguese, Stanford, CA 94305-9991. Offers Spanish (MA, PhD). Terminal master's awarded for partial completion of doctoral program. *Degree requirements:* For master's, 2 foreign languages; for doctorate, 3 foreign languages, thesis/dissertation, oral exam. *Entrance requirements:* For master's and doctorate, GRE General Test. Additional exam requirements/recommendations for international students: Required—TOEFL. Electronic applications accepted. *Expenses:* Tuition: Full-time $38,700; part-time $860 per unit. One-time fee: $200 full-time.

State University of New York at Binghamton, Graduate School, School of Arts and Sciences, Department of Romance Languages and Literatures, Program in Spanish, Binghamton, NY 13902-6000. Offers Spanish (MA); translation (Certificate). *Students:* 2 full-time (0 women), 4 part-time (all women); includes 1 Hispanic/Latino, 1 international. Average age 30. 6 applicants, 83% accepted, 4 enrolled. In 2010, 2 master's awarded. *Degree requirements:* For master's, one foreign language, comprehensive exam, thesis or alternative. *Entrance requirements:* For master's, GRE General Test, GRE Subject Test. Additional exam requirements/recommendations for international students: Required—TOEFL (minimum score 550 paper-based; 213 computer-based; 80 iBT). *Application deadline:* For fall admission, 2/15 priority date for domestic and international students; for spring admission, 11/15 priority date for domestic and international students. Applications are processed on a rolling basis. Application fee: $60. Electronic applications accepted. *Financial support:* In 2010–11, 1 student received support, including 1 teaching assistantship with full tuition reimbursement available (averaging $9,500 per year); career-related internships or fieldwork, Federal Work-Study, institutionally sponsored loans, scholarships/grants, health care benefits, and unspecified assistantships also available. Financial award application deadline: 2/15; financial award applicants required to submit FAFSA. *Unit head:* Dr. Antonio Sobejano-Moran, Chairperson, 607-777-4635, E-mail: antobianco@msn.com. *Application contact:* Catherine Smith, Recruiting and Admissions Coordinator, 607-777-2151, Fax: 607-777-2501, E-mail: cmsmith@binghamton.edu.

State University of New York at New Paltz, Graduate School, School of Education, Department of Secondary Education, New Paltz, NY 12561. Offers adolescence education: biology (MAT, MS Ed); adolescence education: chemistry (MAT, MS Ed); adolescence education: earth science (MAT, MS Ed); adolescence education: English (MAT, MS Ed); adolescence education: French (MAT, MS Ed); adolescence education: social studies (MAT, MS Ed); adolescence education: Spanish (MAT, MS Ed); second language education (MS Ed). *Accreditation:* NCATE. Part-time and evening/weekend programs available. *Faculty:* 7 full-time (5 women), 7 part-time/adjunct (5 women). *Students:* 84 full-time (49 women), 78 part-time (52 women); includes 1 Black or African American, non-Hispanic/Latino; 4 Asian, non-Hispanic/Latino; 20 Hispanic/Latino; 2 Two or more races, non-Hispanic/Latino; 1 international. Average age 30. 122 applicants, 75% accepted, 68 enrolled. In 2010, 88 master's awarded. *Degree requirements:* For master's, comprehensive exam (for some programs), portfolio. *Entrance requirements:* For master's, minimum GPA of 3.0, New York state teaching certificate (MS Ed). Additional exam requirements/recommendations for international students: Required—TOEFL (minimum score 550 paper-based; 213 computer-based; 80 iBT), IELTS (minimum score 6.5). *Application deadline:* For fall admission, 3/1 priority date for domestic students, 3/1 for international students; for spring admission, 10/1 priority date for domestic students, 10/1 for international students. Application fee: $50. Electronic applications accepted. *Expenses:* Tuition, state resident: full-time $8370; part-time $349 per credit hour. Tuition, nonresident: full-time $13,780; part-time $574 per credit hour. Required fees: $1165; $33.80 per credit hour. $175 per term. Tuition and fees vary according to program. *Financial support:* In 2010–11, 13 students received support, including 5 fellowships (averaging $5,000 per year), 3 research assistantships with partial tuition reimbursements available (averaging $5,000 per year); Federal Work-Study, institutionally sponsored loans, and tuition waivers (full) also available. Financial award application deadline: 8/1; financial award applicants required to submit FAFSA. *Unit head:* Dr. Devon Duhaney, Chair, 845-257-2850, E-mail: duhaneyd@newpaltz.edu. *Application contact:* Caroline Murphy, Graduate Admissions Advisor, 845-257-3285, Fax: 845-257-3284, E-mail: gradschool@newpaltz.edu.

Syracuse University, College of Arts and Sciences, Program in Spanish Language, Literature and Culture, Syracuse, NY 13244. Offers MA. Part-time programs available. *Students:* 9 full-time (all women); includes 1 minority (Hispanic/Latino), 3 international. Average age 28. 10 applicants, 90% accepted, 6 enrolled. In 2010, 5 master's awarded. *Degree requirements:* For master's, comprehensive exam (for some programs), thesis or alternative. *Entrance requirements:* For master's, GRE General Test. Additional exam requirements/recommendations for international students: Required—TOEFL (minimum score 100 iBT). *Application deadline:* For fall admission, 2/1 priority date for domestic and international students. Application fee: $75. Electronic applications accepted. *Expenses:* Tuition: Part-time $1162 per credit. *Financial support:* Fellowships with full tuition reimbursements, teaching assistantships with full tuition reimbursements, tuition waivers (partial) available. Financial award application deadline: 1/1; financial award applicants required to submit FAFSA. *Unit head:* Dr. Gail Bulman, Department Chair, 315-443-5385, Fax: 315-443-5376, E-mail: gabulman@syr.edu. *Application contact:* Karen Ames, Information Contact, 315-443-3022, E-mail: koames@syr.edu.

Temple University, College of Liberal Arts, Department of Spanish and Portuguese, Philadelphia, PA 19122-6096. Offers Spanish (MA, PhD). Part-time and evening/weekend programs available. *Faculty:* 10 full-time (3 women). *Students:* 38 full-time (25 women), 7 part-time (all women); includes 1 Black or African American, non-Hispanic/Latino; 1 American Indian or Alaska Native, non-Hispanic/Latino; 15 Hispanic/Latino, 5 international. 23 applicants, 61% accepted, 7 enrolled. In 2010, 8 master's, 2 doctorates awarded. Terminal master's awarded for partial completion of doctoral program. *Degree requirements:* For master's, one foreign language; for doctorate, 2 foreign languages, thesis/dissertation. *Entrance requirements:* For master's and doctorate, GRE General Test, minimum GPA of 3.0. Additional exam requirements/recommendations for international students: Required—TOEFL (minimum score 550 paper-based; 213 computer-based; 79 iBT). *Application deadline:* For fall admission, 1/15 for domestic students, 12/15 for international students; for spring admission, 10/15 for domestic students, 8/1 for international students. Applications are processed on a rolling basis. Application fee: $50. Electronic applications accepted. *Financial support:* Fellowships, teaching assistantships with full tuition reimbursements, scholarships/grants available. Financial award application deadline: 1/15; financial award applicants required to submit FAFSA. *Faculty research:* Spanish-American literature, Spanish Peninsular literature, Hispanic linguistics. *Unit head:* Dr. Luis T. Gonzales del Valle, Chair, 215-204-8285, Fax: 215-204-2652. *Application contact:* Dr. Luis T. Gonzales del Valle, Chair, 215-204-8285, Fax: 215-204-2652.

Texas A&M International University, Office of Graduate Studies and Research, College of Arts and Sciences, Department of Language and Literature, Laredo, TX 78041-1900. Offers English (MA); Hispanic studies (PhD); Spanish (MA). *Faculty:* 6 full-time (3 women). *Students:* 4 full-time (3 women), 34 part-time (22 women); includes 34 Hispanic/Latino, 1 international. Average age 33. 13 applicants, 77% accepted, 8 enrolled. In 2010, 15 master's awarded. *Entrance requirements:* For master's, GRE General Test. Additional exam requirements/recommendations for international students: Required—TOEFL (minimum score 550 paper-based; 213 computer-based). *Application deadline:* For fall admission, 4/30 priority date for domestic students; for spring admission, 11/30 for domestic students. Applications are processed on a rolling basis. Application fee: $25. *Financial support:* In 2010–11, 12 students received support, including 3 fellowships, 4 research assistantships, 2 teaching assistantships. Financial award application deadline: 11/1. *Unit head:* Dr. Manuel Broncano, Chair, 956-326-2470, E-mail: manuel.broncano@tamiu.edu. *Application contact:* Suzanne Hansen-Alford, Director of Graduate Recruiting, 956-326-3023, Fax: 956-326-3021, E-mail: enroll@tamiu.edu.

Texas A&M University, College of Liberal Arts, Department of Hispanic Studies, College Station, TX 77843. Offers MA, PhD. *Faculty:* 11. *Students:* 28 full-time (11 women), 15 part-time (12 women); includes 21 Hispanic/Latino, 8 international. In 2010, 6 master's, 3 doctorates awarded. *Unit head:* Dr. Alberto Moreiras, Head, 979-845-2195, E-mail: moreiras@tamu.edu. *Application contact:* Eduardo Urbina, Director of Graduate Studies, 979-845-0464, E-mail: e-urbina@tamu.edu.

Texas A&M University–Commerce, Graduate School, College of Arts and Sciences, Department of Literature and Languages, Commerce, TX 75429-3011. Offers college teaching of English (PhD); English (MA, MS); Spanish (MA). Part-time programs available. Terminal master's awarded for partial completion of doctoral program. *Degree requirements:* For master's, comprehensive exam, thesis (for some programs); for doctorate, one foreign language, thesis/dissertation, departmental qualifying exam. *Entrance requirements:* For master's and doctorate, GRE General Test. Electronic applications accepted. *Faculty research:* Latino literature, American film studies, ethnographic research, Willa Carter.

Texas A&M University–Kingsville, College of Graduate Studies, College of Arts and Sciences, Department of Language and Literature, Kingsville, TX 78363. Offers English (MA, MS); Spanish (MA). Part-time and evening/weekend programs available. *Degree requirements:* For master's, comprehensive exam, thesis or alternative. *Entrance requirements:* For master's, GRE General Test, minimum GPA of 3.0. Additional exam requirements/recommendations for international students: Required—TOEFL. *Faculty research:* Linguistics, culture, Spanish American literature, Spanish peninsular literature, American literature.

Texas State University–San Marcos, Graduate School, College of Liberal Arts, Department of Modern Languages, Program in Spanish, San Marcos, TX 78666. Offers MA. Part-time and evening/weekend programs available. *Faculty:* 8 full-time (5 women). *Students:* 20 full-time (13 women), 22 part-time (15 women); includes 29 minority (1 Black or African American, non-Hispanic/Latino; 1 Asian, non-Hispanic/Latino; 27 Hispanic/Latino), 2 international. Average age 31. 20 applicants, 95% accepted, 16 enrolled. In 2010, 8 master's awarded. *Degree requirements:* For master's, one foreign language, comprehensive exam, internship (MAT), thesis (MA). *Entrance requirements:* For master's, minimum GPA of 3.0 in last 12 undergraduate hours of advanced Spanish with 6 hours in literature. Additional exam requirements/recommendations for international students: Required—TOEFL (minimum score 550 paper-based; 213 computer-based; 78 iBT). *Application deadline:* For fall admission, 6/15 priority date for domestic students, 6/1 for international students; for spring admission, 10/15 priority date for domestic students, 10/1 for international students. Applications are processed on a rolling basis. Application fee: $40 ($90 for international students). Electronic applications accepted. *Expenses:* Tuition, state resident: full-time $6024; part-time $251 per credit hour. Tuition, nonresident: full-time $13,536; part-time $564 per credit hour. Required fees: $1776; $50 per credit hour. $306 per semester. *Financial support:* In 2010–11, 20 students received support, including 10 teaching assistantships (averaging $5,684 per year); research assistantships, career-related internships or fieldwork, Federal Work-Study, and institutionally sponsored loans also available. Support available to part-time students. Financial award application deadline: 4/1; financial award applicants required to submit FAFSA. *Faculty research:* Hispanic literature, linguistics, literary theory, computer-assisted language instruction, Hispanic philology. *Unit head:* Dr. Catherine Jaffe, Advisor, 512-245-2360, Fax: 512-245-8298, E-mail: cj10@txstate.edu. *Application contact:* Dr. J. Michael Willoughby, Dean of Graduate School, 512-245-2581, Fax: 512-245-8365, E-mail: gradcollege@txstate.edu.

Texas Tech University, Graduate School, College of Arts and Sciences, Department of Classical and Modern Languages and Literatures, Program in Romance Languages-Spanish, Lubbock, TX 79409. Offers MA. Part-time programs available. *Students:* 4 full-time (all women), 1 (woman) part-time; includes 2 Hispanic/Latino. Average age 25. In 2010, 5 master's awarded. *Degree requirements:* For master's, one foreign language, thesis optional. *Entrance requirements:* For master's, GRE General Test. Additional exam requirements/recommendations for international students: Required—TOEFL (minimum score 550 paper-based; 213 computer-based; 79 iBT). *Application deadline:* For fall admission, 6/1 priority date for domestic students, 1/15 priority date for international students; for spring admission, 9/1 priority date for domestic students, 6/15 priority date for international students. Applications are processed on a rolling basis. Application fee: $50 ($75 for international students). Electronic applications accepted. *Expenses:* Tuition, state resident: full-time $5495.76; part-time $228.99 per credit hour. Tuition, nonresident: full-time $12,936; part-time $538.99 per credit hour. Required fees: $2674; $36 per credit hour. $905 per semester. *Financial support:* Application deadline: 4/15. *Faculty research:* Peninsular literature, Latin-American literature, Portuguese language and literature, Spanish linguistics. *Unit head:* Dr. Jorge Zamora, Professor and Graduate Advisor of Spanish, 806-742-3145 Ext. 281, Fax: 806-742-3306, E-mail: jorge.zamora@ttu.edu. *Application contact:* Dr. Carmen Pereira-Muro, Graduate Admissions Officer, 806-742-3145, E-mail: carmen.pereira@ttu.edu.

Texas Tech University, Graduate School, College of Arts and Sciences, Department of Classical and Modern Languages and Literatures, Program in Spanish, Lubbock, TX 79409. Offers PhD. Part-time programs available. *Students:* 25 full-time (13 women), 10 part-time (6 women); includes 10 Hispanic/Latino, 17 international. Average age 35. 16 applicants, 81% accepted, 7 enrolled. In 2010, 5 doctorates awarded. *Degree requirements:* For doctorate, one foreign language, comprehensive exam, thesis/dissertation. *Entrance requirements:* For doctorate, GRE General Test. Additional exam requirements/recommendations for international students: Required—TOEFL (minimum score 550 paper-based; 213 computer-based; 79 iBT). *Application deadline:* For fall admission, 6/1 priority date for domestic students, 1/15 priority date for international students; for spring admission, 9/1 priority date for domestic students, 6/15 priority date for international students. Applications are processed on a rolling basis. Application fee: $50 ($75 for international students). Electronic applications accepted. *Expenses:* Tuition, state resident: full-time $5495.76; part-time $228.99 per credit hour. Tuition, nonresident: full-time $12,936; part-time $538.99 per credit hour. Required fees: $2674; $36 per credit hour. $905 per semester. *Financial support:* Application deadline: 4/15. *Unit head:* Dr. Jorge Zamora, Professor/Advisor, 806-742-3145 Ext. 243, Fax: 806-742-3306, E-mail: jorge.zamora@ttu.edu. *Application contact:* Dr. Carmen Pereira-Muro, Graduate Admissions Officer, 806-742-4055, Fax: 806-742-3306, E-mail: liz.hildebrand@ttu.edu.

Tulane University, School of Liberal Arts, Department of Spanish and Portuguese, New Orleans, LA 70118-5669. Offers Portuguese (MA); Spanish (MA); Spanish and Portuguese (PhD). *Degree requirements:* For master's, 2 foreign languages; for doctorate, 2 foreign languages, thesis/dissertation. *Entrance requirements:* For master's, GRE General Test, minimum B average in undergraduate course work; for doctorate, GRE General Test. Additional exam requirements/recommendations for international students: Required—TOEFL. Electronic applications accepted.

Universidad Autonoma de Guadalajara, Graduate Programs, Guadalajara, Mexico. Offers administrative law and justice (LL M); advertising and corporate communications (MA);

architecture (M Arch); business (MBA); computational science (MCC); education (Ed M, Ed D); English-Spanish translation (MA); entrepreneurship and management (MBA); integrated management of digital animation (MA); international business (MIB); international corporate law (LL M); internet technologies (MS); manufacturing systems (MMS); occupational health (MS); philosophy (MA, PhD); power electronics (MS); quality systems (MQS); renewable energy (MS); social evaluation of projects (MBA); strategic market research (MBA); tax law (MA); teaching mathematics (MA).

Université de Montréal, Faculty of Arts and Sciences, Department of Literatures and Modern Languages, Program in Hispanic Studies, Montréal, QC H3C 3J7, Canada. Offers MA. *Degree requirements:* For master's, 2 foreign languages, thesis. Electronic applications accepted. *Faculty research:* Spanish literature and culture, Latin American literature and culture.

Université Laval, Faculty of Letters, Department of Literature, Programs in Spanish Literatures, Québec, QC G1K 7P4, Canada. Offers MA, PhD. Part-time programs available. Terminal master's awarded for partial completion of doctoral program. *Degree requirements:* For master's, thesis; for doctorate, comprehensive exam, thesis/dissertation. *Entrance requirements:* For master's and doctorate, linguistics exams, knowledge of French and Spanish. Electronic applications accepted.

University at Albany, State University of New York, College of Arts and Sciences, Department of Languages, Literatures, and Cultures, Program in Spanish, Albany, NY 12222-0001. Offers MA, PhD. *Degree requirements:* For doctorate, thesis/dissertation. *Entrance requirements:* For doctorate, GRE General Test.

University at Buffalo, the State University of New York, Graduate School, College of Arts and Sciences, Department of Romance Languages and Literatures, Buffalo, NY 14260. Offers French (MA, PhD); Spanish (MA, PhD). Part-time programs available. *Faculty:* 15 full-time (9 women), 7 part-time/adjunct (6 women). *Students:* 28 full-time (22 women), 11 part-time (9 women); includes 1 Asian, non-Hispanic/Latino; 12 Two or more races, non-Hispanic/Latino. Average age 31. 16 applicants, 75% accepted, 6 enrolled. In 2010, 3 master's, 4 doctorates awarded. Terminal master's awarded for partial completion of doctoral program. *Degree requirements:* For master's, one foreign language, comprehensive exam, thesis; for doctorate, 2 foreign languages, comprehensive exam, thesis/dissertation. *Entrance requirements:* For master's and doctorate, GRE. Additional exam requirements/recommendations for international students: Required—TOEFL (minimum score 550 paper-based; 213 computer-based; 79 iBT). *Application deadline:* For fall admission, 1/15 priority date for domestic and international students. Applications are processed on a rolling basis. Application fee: $75. Electronic applications accepted. *Financial support:* In 2010–11, 26 students received support, including fellowships with full tuition reimbursements available (averaging $6,000 per year), teaching assistantships with full tuition reimbursements available (averaging $13,415 per year); Federal Work-Study, institutionally sponsored loans, and health care benefits also available. Financial award application deadline: 2/28; financial award applicants required to submit FAFSA. *Faculty research:* Romance linguistics, cultural studies, literary studies, literature and philosophy. *Unit head:* Dr. David Castillo, Chair, 716-645-0869, Fax: 716-645-5981, E-mail: dc63@buffalo.edu. *Application contact:* Dr. Justin Read, Director of Graduate Studies, 716-645-0878, Fax: 716-645-5981, E-mail: jread2@buffalo.edu.

University at Buffalo, the State University of New York, Graduate School, Graduate School of Education, Department of Learning and Instruction, Buffalo, NY 14260. Offers biology education (Ed M, Certificate); chemistry education (Ed M, Certificate); childhood education (Ed M); childhood education with bilingual extension (Ed M); early childhood education (Ed M); earth science education (Ed M, Certificate); educational technology and new literacies (Certificate); elementary education (Ed D, PhD); English education (Ed M, PhD, Certificate); English for speakers of other languages (Ed M); foreign and second language education (PhD); French education (Ed M, Certificate); general education (Ed M); German education (Ed M, Certificate); gifted education (online) (Certificate); Latin education (Ed M, Certificate); literary specialist (Ed M); mathematics education (Ed M, PhD, Certificate); music education (Ed M, Certificate); physics education (Ed M, Certificate); reading education (PhD); science and the public (online) (Ed M); science education (PhD); social studies education (Ed M, Certificate); Spanish education (Ed M, Certificate); special education (PhD); teaching and leading for diversity (Certificate); teaching English to speakers of other languages (Ed M). Part-time and evening/weekend programs available. Postbaccalaureate distance learning degree programs offered (no on-campus study). *Faculty:* 32 full-time (22 women), 53 part-time/adjunct (43 women). *Students:* 343 full-time (237 women), 340 part-time (261 women); includes 17 Black or African American, non-Hispanic/Latino; 3 American Indian or Alaska Native, non-Hispanic/Latino; 13 Asian, non-Hispanic/Latino; 13 Hispanic/Latino, 76 international. Average age 29. 587 applicants, 75% accepted, 281 enrolled. In 2010, 212 master's, 16 doctorates, 37 other advanced degrees awarded. *Degree requirements:* For master's, comprehensive exam; for doctorate, thesis/dissertation, research analysis exam, research experience component. *Entrance requirements:* For doctorate, GRE General Test or MAT, interview, writing sample, letters of recommendation. Additional exam requirements/recommendations for international students: Required—TOEFL (minimum score 600 paper-based; 96 iBT). *Application deadline:* For fall admission, 2/1 priority date for domestic and international students; for spring admission, 11/15 priority date for domestic students, 10/1 for international students. Applications are processed on a rolling basis. Application fee: $50. Electronic applications accepted. *Financial support:* In 2010–11, 21 fellowships with full tuition reimbursements (averaging $9,000 per year), 42 research assistantships with full tuition reimbursements (averaging $10,589 per year) were awarded; teaching assistantships with full tuition reimbursements, career-related internships or fieldwork, Federal Work-Study, institutionally sponsored loans, scholarships/grants, tuition waivers (partial), and unspecified assistantships also available. Financial award application deadline: 2/28; financial award applicants required to submit FAFSA. *Faculty research:* Science assessment, foreign language teaching and learning, early learning, new literacies, gender and education. *Unit head:* Dr. Jim Collins, Chair, 716-645-2455, Fax: 716-645-3161, E-mail: jcollins@buffalo.edu. *Application contact:* Cathy Dimino, Admissions Assistant, 716-645-2110, Fax: 716-645-7937, E-mail: cadimino@buffalo.edu.

The University of Akron, Graduate School, Buchtel College of Arts and Sciences, Department of Modern Languages, Program in Spanish, Akron, OH 44325. Offers MA. Part-time and evening/weekend programs available. *Faculty:* 8 full-time (6 women), 2 part-time/adjunct (both women). *Students:* 6 full-time (all women), 3 part-time (1 woman); includes 4 minority (all Hispanic/Latino). Average age 28. 10 applicants, 80% accepted, 4 enrolled. In 2010, 4 master's awarded. *Degree requirements:* For master's, one foreign language, comprehensive exam, oral exam, essay, research paper. *Entrance requirements:* For master's, minimum GPA of 2.75, proficiency in Spanish, three letters of recommendation, interview. Additional exam requirements/recommendations for international students: Required—TOEFL (minimum score 550 paper-based; 213 computer-based; 79 iBT). *Application deadline:* Applications are processed on a rolling basis. Application fee: $30 ($40 for international students). Electronic applications accepted. *Expenses:* Tuition, state resident: full-time $6800; part-time $378 per credit hour. Tuition, nonresident: full-time $11,644; part-time $647 per credit hour. Required fees: $1265. One-time fee: $30 full-time. *Financial support:* Teaching assistantships with full tuition reimbursements, institutionally sponsored loans available. *Unit head:* Dr. Parizad Dejbord-Sawan, Director of Graduate Studies, 330-972-7824, E-mail: parizad@uakron.edu. *Application contact:* Dr. Parizad Dejbord-Sawan, Director of Graduate Studies, 330-972-7824, E-mail: parizad@uakron.edu.

The University of Alabama, Graduate School, College of Arts and Sciences, Department of Modern Languages and Classics, Tuscaloosa, AL 35487. Offers French (MA, PhD); French and Spanish (PhD); German (MA); Romance languages (MA, PhD); Spanish (MA, PhD). Part-time programs available. *Faculty:* 25 full-time (12 women). *Students:* 50 full-time (33 women), 31 part-time (19 women); includes 11 minority (2 Black or African American, non-Hispanic/Latino; 8 Hispanic/Latino; 1 Two or more races, non-Hispanic/Latino), 19 international. Average age 31. 24 applicants, 83% accepted, 11 enrolled. In 2010, 17 master's, 1 doctorate awarded. *Degree requirements:* For master's, comprehensive exam, thesis optional; for doctorate, one foreign language, thesis/dissertation, preliminary exam. *Entrance requirements:* For master's and doctorate, minimum GPA of 3.0, writing sample. Additional exam requirements/recommendations for international students: Required—TOEFL or IELTS. *Application deadline:* For fall admission, 7/6 priority date for domestic students, 1/15 priority date for international students; for spring admission, 12/5 priority date for domestic students, 6/1 priority date for international students. Applications are processed on a rolling basis. Application fee: $50 ($60 for international students). Electronic applications accepted. *Expenses:* Tuition, state resident: full-time $7900. Tuition, nonresident: full-time $20,500. *Financial support:* In 2010–11, 7 students received support, including 1 fellowship, research assistantships with full tuition reimbursements available (averaging $10,291 per year), 6 teaching assistantships with full tuition reimbursements available (averaging $10,291 per year); career-related internships or fieldwork, Federal Work-Study, institutionally sponsored loans, and scholarships/grants also available. Financial award application deadline: 7/14. *Faculty research:* Non-English literature, linguistics, culture, film. *Unit head:* Dr. Michael Picone, Chair and Professor, 205-348-5054, Fax: 205-348-2042, E-mail: mpicone@bama.ua.edu. *Application contact:* Dr. K. Barbara Fischer, Graduate Director and Associate Professor, 205-348-8465, Fax: 205-348-2042, E-mail: bfischer@bama.ua.edu.

The University of Arizona, College of Humanities, Department of Spanish and Portuguese, Tucson, AZ 85721. Offers Spanish (MA, PhD). *Faculty:* 16 full-time (10 women), 3 part-time/adjunct (0 women). *Students:* 53 full-time (33 women), 19 part-time (14 women); includes 38 minority (all Hispanic/Latino), 14 international. Average age 35. 36 applicants, 28% accepted, 7 enrolled. In 2010, 6 master's, 11 doctorates awarded. Terminal master's awarded for partial completion of doctoral program. *Degree requirements:* For master's, one foreign language, comprehensive exam, thesis optional; for doctorate, 3 foreign languages, comprehensive exam, thesis/dissertation. *Entrance requirements:* For master's, GRE General Test, minimum GPA of 3.3, writing sample, 3 letters of recommendation, audio sample; for doctorate, GRE General Test, minimum GPA of 3.4, 3 letters of recommendation, statement of purpose, writing sample, audio sample. Additional exam requirements/recommendations for international students: Required—TOEFL (minimum score 550 paper-based; 213 computer-based; 79 iBT). *Application deadline:* For fall admission, 2/15 for domestic and international students; for spring admission, 8/1 for domestic and international students. Application fee: $75. Electronic applications accepted. *Expenses:* Tuition, state resident: full-time $7692. *Financial support:* In 2010–11, 5 research assistantships with full tuition reimbursements (averaging $19,114 per year), 83 teaching assistantships with full tuition reimbursements (averaging $19,862 per year) were awarded; institutionally sponsored loans, scholarships/grants, health care benefits, tuition waivers (full), and unspecified assistantships also available. Financial award application deadline: 2/15. *Faculty research:* Spanish and Latin American literature and linguistics, literary theory. Total annual research expenditures: $5,243. *Unit head:* Dr. Malcolm A. Compitello, Head, 520-621-3123, E-mail: compitel@email.arizona.edu. *Application contact:* Isela Gonzales, Administrative Assistant, 520-621-3125, Fax: 520-621-6104, E-mail: iselag@email.arizona.edu.

University of Arkansas, Graduate School, J. William Fulbright College of Arts and Sciences, Department of World Languages, Literature and Cultures, Program in Spanish, Fayetteville, AR 72701-1201. Offers MA. *Faculty:* 6 full-time (4 women). *Students:* 11 full-time (4 women), 2 part-time (1 woman); includes 1 minority (Hispanic/Latino), 6 international. 10 applicants, 100% accepted. In 2010, 7 master's awarded. *Degree requirements:* For master's, one foreign language, comprehensive exam, thesis optional. *Entrance requirements:* Additional exam requirements/recommendations for international students: Required—TOEFL (minimum score 550 paper-based; 213 computer-based), IELTS (minimum score 6.5). *Application deadline:* For fall admission, 1/15 priority date for domestic students, 4/1 for international students; for spring admission, 9/15 priority date for domestic students, 10/1 for international students. Applications are processed on a rolling basis. Application fee: $40 ($50 for international students). Electronic applications accepted. *Financial support:* In 2010–11, fellowships with tuition reimbursements (averaging $2,178 per year), 2 research assistantships, 9 teaching assistantships (averaging $8,200 per year) were awarded; career-related internships or fieldwork and Federal Work-Study also available. Support available to part-time students. Financial award application deadline: 1/15; financial award applicants required to submit FAFSA. *Faculty research:* Medieval and Golden Age poetry, colonial Latin America, contemporary Latin America. *Unit head:* Dr. Joan Turner, Department Chair, 479-575-2951, Fax: 479-575-6795, E-mail: joant@uark.edu. *Application contact:* Dr. M. Reina Ruiz, Graduate Coordinator, 479-575-6590, E-mail: rruiz@uark.edu.

University of California, Berkeley, Graduate Division, College of Letters and Science, Group in Romance Languages and Literature, Berkeley, CA 94720-1500. Offers French (PhD); Italian (PhD); Spanish (PhD). *Degree requirements:* For doctorate, thesis/dissertation, qualifying exam. *Entrance requirements:* For doctorate, GRE General Test, minimum GPA of 3.0, 3 letters of recommendation. Additional exam requirements/recommendations for international students: Required—TOEFL (minimum score 570 paper-based; 230 computer-based).

University of California, Davis, Graduate Studies, Program in Spanish, Davis, CA 95616. Offers MA, PhD. Terminal master's awarded for partial completion of doctoral program. *Degree requirements:* For master's, comprehensive exam (for some programs), thesis (for some programs); for doctorate, 2 foreign languages, thesis/dissertation. *Entrance requirements:* For master's, GRE General Test, minimum GPA of 3.0; for doctorate, GRE General Test, master's degree, minimum GPA of 3.0. Additional exam requirements/recommendations for international students: Required—TOEFL (minimum score 550 paper-based; 213 computer-based). *Faculty research:* Medieval Spanish language and literature, Spanish linguistics, Latin American literature, nineteenth century Peninsular literature.

University of California, Irvine, School of Humanities, Department of Spanish and Portuguese, Irvine, CA 92697. Offers Spanish (MA, MAT, PhD). *Students:* 42 full-time (22 women); includes 27 minority (1 Asian, non-Hispanic/Latino; 26 Hispanic/Latino). Average age 28. 29 applicants, 28% accepted, 5 enrolled. In 2010, 6 master's, 2 doctorates awarded. *Degree requirements:* For doctorate, thesis/dissertation. *Entrance requirements:* For master's and doctorate, GRE General Test, minimum GPA of 3.0. Additional exam requirements/recommendations for international students: Required—TOEFL (minimum score 550 paper-based; 213 computer-based). *Application deadline:* For fall admission, 1/2 priority date for domestic students, 1/2 for international students. Applications are processed on a rolling basis. Application fee: $80 ($100 for international students). Electronic applications accepted. *Financial support:* Fellowships, teaching assistantships, institutionally sponsored loans, traineeships, health care benefits, and unspecified assistantships available. Financial award application deadline: 3/1; financial award applicants required to submit FAFSA. *Faculty research:* Latin American literature, Spanish literature, Spanish linguistics in Creole studies, Hispanic literature in the U. S., Luso-Brazilian literature. *Unit head:* Prof. Horacio Legras, Chair, 949-824-7265, Fax: 949-824-2803, E-mail: hlegras@uci.edu. *Application contact:* June DeTurk, Graduate Program Coordinator, 949-824-8793, Fax: 949-824-2803, E-mail: jdeturk@uci.edu.

University of California, Los Angeles, Graduate Division, College of Letters and Science, Department of Spanish and Portuguese, Program in Spanish, Los Angeles, CA 90095. Offers MA. *Students:* 8 full-time (5 women); includes 2 minority (both Hispanic/Latino), 1 international. Average age 29. 27 applicants, 7% accepted, 2 enrolled. In 2010, 2 master's awarded. Terminal master's awarded for partial completion of doctoral program. *Degree requirements:* For master's, one foreign language, comprehensive exam or thesis. *Entrance requirements:* For master's, GRE General Test, minimum GPA of 3.0, sample of written work (recommended). *Application deadline:* For fall admission, 12/31 for domestic and international students. Application fee: $70 ($90 for international students). Electronic applications accepted. *Financial support:* In 2010–11, 6 fellowships with full and partial tuition reimbursements, 1 research assistantship with full and partial tuition reimbursement, 5 teaching assistantships with full and partial tuition reimbursements were awarded; Federal Work-Study, scholarships/grants, health care benefits, tuition waivers (full and partial), and unspecified assistantships also available. Financial award application deadline: 3/1; financial award applicants required to submit FAFSA. *Unit head:* Dr.

Spanish

University of California, Los Angeles (continued)
Maarten Van Delden, Chair, 310-825-1220, E-mail: mvandelden@humnet.ucla.edu. *Application contact:* Departmental Office, 310-825-1036, E-mail: peinado@humnet.ucla.edu.

University of California, Riverside, Graduate Division, Department of Hispanic Studies, Riverside, CA 92521-0102. Offers Spanish (MA, PhD). Terminal master's awarded for partial completion of doctoral program. *Degree requirements:* For master's, one foreign language, comprehensive exam; for doctorate, one foreign language, thesis/dissertation, qualifying exams, 1 quarter of teaching experience. *Entrance requirements:* For master's and doctorate, GRE General Test, minimum GPA of 3.2. Additional exam requirements/recommendations for international students: Required—TOEFL (minimum score 550 paper-based; 213 computer-based; 80 iBT). Electronic applications accepted. *Faculty research:* Spanish literature of sixteenth, seventeenth and twentieth century; pre-Columbian and colonial Latin American literature; nineteenth and twentieth century Latin American literature.

University of California, San Diego, Office of Graduate Studies, Department of Literature, Program in Spanish Literature, La Jolla, CA 92093. Offers MA. *Degree requirements:* For master's, thesis. *Entrance requirements:* For master's, GRE General Test, GRE Subject Test. Electronic applications accepted.

University of California, Santa Barbara, Graduate Division, College of Letters and Sciences, Division of Humanities and Fine Arts, Department of Spanish and Portuguese, Santa Barbara, CA 93106-4150. Offers Hispanic languages and literature (PhD), including European medieval studies, feminist studies, Hispanic linguistics, Hispanic literature, Luso-Brazilian literature; Hispanic linguistics (MA); Luso-Brazilian literature (MA); Spanish or Spanish-American literature (MA); MA/PhD. Spanish Language Institute available during summer session. *Faculty:* 16 full-time (7 women). *Students:* 32 full-time (22 women); includes 1 Black or African American, non-Hispanic/Latino; 1 Asian, non-Hispanic/Latino; 9 Hispanic/Latino. Average age 32. 34 applicants, 26% accepted, 5 enrolled. In 2010, 3 master's, 3 doctorates awarded. Terminal master's awarded for partial completion of doctoral program. *Degree requirements:* For master's, 2 foreign languages, comprehensive exam (for some programs), thesis optional; for doctorate, 3 foreign languages, comprehensive exam, thesis/dissertation. *Entrance requirements:* For master's and doctorate, GRE. Additional exam requirements/recommendations for international students: Required—TOEFL (minimum score 550 paper-based; 80 iBT), IELTS (minimum score 7). *Application deadline:* For fall admission, 12/15 for domestic and international students. Application fee: $70 ($90 for international students). Electronic applications accepted. *Financial support:* In 2010–11, 32 students received support, including 12 fellowships with full and partial tuition reimbursements available (averaging $10,016 per year), 27 teaching assistantships with full and partial tuition reimbursements available (averaging $14,583 per year); career-related internships or fieldwork, Federal Work-Study, tuition waivers (full and partial), and unspecified assistantships also available. Financial award application deadline: 12/15; financial award applicants required to submit FAFSA. *Faculty research:* Nineteenth century Spanish and Portuguese literature, Spanish and Spanish American literature, nineteenth and twentieth century Portuguese and Brazilian literatures, Hispanic linguistics, Catalan language and culture. *Unit head:* Prof. Francisco A. Lomeli, Chair, 805-893-5715, Fax: 805-893-8341, E-mail: lomeli@spanport.ucsb.edu. *Application contact:* Ashley Bradbury, Graduate Program Assistant, 805-893-2131, Fax: 805-893-8341, E-mail: ashley@hfa.ucsb.edu.

University of Central Florida, College of Arts and Humanities, Department of Modern Languages and Literatures, Program in Spanish, Orlando, FL 32816. Offers MA. Part-time and evening/weekend programs available. *Students:* 9 full-time (7 women), 19 part-time (13 women); includes 1 Black or African American, non-Hispanic/Latino; 1 Asian, non-Hispanic/Latino; 20 Hispanic/Latino, 2 international. Average age 38. 10 applicants, 100% accepted, 8 enrolled. In 2010, 5 master's awarded. *Degree requirements:* For master's, one foreign language, comprehensive exam, thesis or alternative. *Entrance requirements:* For master's, GRE General Test, minimum GPA of 3.0 in last 60 hours. Additional exam requirements/recommendations for international students: Required—TOEFL. *Application deadline:* For fall admission, 6/1 for domestic students; for spring admission, 12/1 for domestic students. Application fee: $30. Electronic applications accepted. *Expenses:* Tuition, state resident: part-time $256.56 per credit hour. Tuition, nonresident: part-time $1011.52 per credit hour. Part-time tuition and fees vary according to program. *Financial support:* In 2010–11, 5 students received support, including 5 teaching assistantships with partial tuition reimbursements available (averaging $8,000 per year); career-related internships or fieldwork, Federal Work-Study, institutionally sponsored loans, tuition waivers (partial), and unspecified assistantships also available. Financial award application deadline: 3/1; financial award applicants required to submit FAFSA.

University of Chicago, Division of the Humanities, Department of Romance Languages and Literatures, Chicago, IL 60637-1513. Offers French (AM, PhD); Italian (AM, PhD); Spanish (AM, PhD). Terminal master's awarded for partial completion of doctoral program. *Degree requirements:* For master's, 2 foreign languages, thesis; for doctorate, 3 foreign languages, thesis/dissertation. *Entrance requirements:* For master's and doctorate, GRE General Test, GRE Subject Test. Additional exam requirements/recommendations for international students: Required—TOEFL.

University of Cincinnati, Graduate School, McMicken College of Arts and Sciences, Department of Romance Languages and Literature, Program in Spanish, Cincinnati, OH 45221. Offers MA, PhD. Terminal master's awarded for partial completion of doctoral program. *Degree requirements:* For master's, thesis optional; for doctorate, 2 foreign languages, thesis/dissertation. *Entrance requirements:* For master's, minimum GPA of 3.0. Electronic applications accepted. *Faculty research:* Applied linguistics, Spanish essay, Latin American culture, women's studies, poetry.

University of Colorado Boulder, Graduate School, College of Arts and Sciences, Department of Spanish and Portuguese, Boulder, CO 80309. Offers Hispanic linguistics (MA); medieval/early modern Hispanic literatures (PhD); Spanish and Spanish American literatures (MA, PhD). Part-time programs available. *Faculty:* 15 full-time (6 women). *Students:* 48 full-time (30 women), 1 (woman) part-time; includes 9 minority (all Hispanic/Latino), 18 international. Average age 32. 52 applicants, 15 enrolled. In 2010, 10 master's, 2 doctorates awarded. Terminal master's awarded for partial completion of doctoral program. *Degree requirements:* For master's, one foreign language, comprehensive exam, thesis or alternative; for doctorate, 2 foreign languages, thesis/dissertation. *Entrance requirements:* For master's, minimum undergraduate GPA of 2.75. *Application deadline:* For fall admission, 12/15 priority date for domestic students, 12/15 for international students. Applications are processed on a rolling basis. Application fee: $50 ($60 for international students). *Financial support:* In 2010–11, 7 fellowships with full tuition reimbursements (averaging $3,436 per year), 19 research assistantships (averaging $12,128 per year) were awarded; tuition waivers (full) also available. Financial award application deadline: 12/15. *Faculty research:* Spanish peninsular and Spanish-American literatures; Hispanic linguistics; medieval, Golden Age, eighteenth and nineteenth century literatures.

University of Colorado Denver, College of Liberal Arts and Sciences, Department of Modern Languages, Denver, CO 80217-3364. Offers Spanish (MA). Part-time programs available. *Faculty:* 10 full-time (6 women). *Students:* 6 full-time (all women), 18 part-time (15 women); includes 5 Hispanic/Latino. Average age 39. 6 applicants, 67% accepted, 4 enrolled. In 2010, 8 master's awarded. *Degree requirements:* For master's, comprehensive exam, thesis (for some programs), 33 credit hours of course work. *Entrance requirements:* For master's, BA in Spanish from accredited institution, or BA in another discipline plus language skills that meet department's standards; minimum GPA of 2.5, 3.0 in all Spanish courses; written and oral proficiency at advanced level. Additional exam requirements/recommendations for international students: Required—TOEFL. *Application deadline:* For fall admission, 3/15 for domestic students; for spring admission, 10/15 for domestic students. Application fee: $50 ($75 for international students). Electronic applications accepted. *Expenses:* Tuition, state resident: full-time $7332; part-time $355 per credit hour. Tuition, nonresident: full-time $18,990; part-time $1055 per credit hour. Required fees: $998. Tuition and fees vary according to course level, course load, degree level, campus/location, program, reciprocity agreements and student level. *Financial support:* Teaching assistantships, Federal Work-Study and scholarships/grants available. Financial award application deadline: 4/1. *Faculty research:* Spanish-American literature; sociolinguistics, bilingualism, phonology and historical linguistics; Spanish peninsular literature; applied linguistics, pragmatics and second language acquisition. *Unit head:* Dr. Michael Abeyta, Associate Professor of Spanish American Literature, 303-556-4008, E-mail: michael.abeyta@ucdenver.edu. *Application contact:* Dr. Michael Abeyta, Associate Professor of Spanish American Literature, 303-556-4008, E-mail: michael.abeyta@ucdenver.edu.

University of Connecticut, Graduate School, College of Liberal Arts and Sciences, Department of Modern and Classical Languages, Field of Spanish, Storrs, CT 06269. Offers MA, PhD. Terminal master's awarded for partial completion of doctoral program. *Degree requirements:* For master's, one foreign language, comprehensive exam; for doctorate, 2 foreign languages, thesis/dissertation. *Entrance requirements:* For master's and doctorate, GRE General Test, GRE Subject Test. Additional exam requirements/recommendations for international students: Required—TOEFL (minimum score 550 paper-based; 213 computer-based). Electronic applications accepted.

University of Delaware, College of Arts and Sciences, Department of Foreign Languages and Literatures, Newark, DE 19716. Offers foreign languages and literatures (MA), including French, German, Spanish; foreign languages pedagogy (MA), including French, German, Spanish; technical Chinese translation (MA). *Degree requirements:* For master's, one foreign language, comprehensive exam, thesis optional. *Entrance requirements:* For master's, GRE General Test, letters of recommendation, writing sample. Additional exam requirements/recommendations for international students: Required—TOEFL. Electronic applications accepted. *Faculty research:* Medieval to Modern French and Spanish literature, Twentieth Century German, French, Spanish literature by women, computer-assisted instruction.

University of Florida, Graduate School, College of Liberal Arts and Sciences, Department of Languages, Literatures, and Cultures, Program in Spanish, Gainesville, FL 32611. Offers MA, PhD. Part-time programs available. *Faculty:* 11 full-time (6 women). *Students:* 22 full-time (14 women), 11 part-time (10 women); includes 1 Black or African American, non-Hispanic/Latino; 13 Hispanic/Latino, 10 international. Average age 29. 58 applicants, 31% accepted, 15 enrolled. In 2010, 2 master's, 5 doctorates awarded. Terminal master's awarded for partial completion of doctoral program. *Degree requirements:* For master's, one foreign language, comprehensive exam, thesis or extended research paper; for doctorate, 2 foreign languages, comprehensive exam, thesis/dissertation, qualifying exam. *Entrance requirements:* For master's and doctorate, GRE General Test (minimum score of 1000), minimum GPA of 3.0. Additional exam requirements/recommendations for international students: Required—TOEFL (minimum score 550 paper-based; 213 computer-based; 80 iBT), IELTS (minimum score 6). *Application deadline:* For fall admission, 12/1 priority date for domestic and international students; for winter admission, 2/1 for domestic and international students. Applications are processed on a rolling basis. Application fee: $30. Electronic applications accepted. *Expenses:* Tuition, state resident: full-time $10,915.92. Tuition, nonresident: full-time $28,309. *Financial support:* In 2010–11, 31 students received support, including 9 fellowships with full tuition reimbursements available, 3 research assistantships with full tuition reimbursements available (averaging $14,953 per year), 22 teaching assistantships with full tuition reimbursements available (averaging $19,032 per year). Financial award application deadline: 12/15; financial award applicants required to submit FAFSA. *Faculty research:* Spanish linguistics; second language acquisition and teaching; Spanish literature, film and culture; Latin American literature, film and culture; Portuguese literature, film and culture. *Unit head:* Dr. Gillian Lord, Chair, 352-273-3749 Ext. 242, E-mail: glord@ufl.edu. *Application contact:* Dr. Luis Alvarez-Castro, Graduate Coordinator, 352-273-3755, E-mail: lacastro@ufl.edu.

University of Georgia, College of Arts and Sciences, Department of Romance Languages, Program in Spanish, Athens, GA 30602. Offers MA. *Students:* 12 full-time (7 women), 2 part-time (both women); includes 3 Hispanic/Latino, 2 international. 26 applicants, 38% accepted, 6 enrolled. In 2010, 9 master's awarded. *Degree requirements:* For master's, one foreign language, thesis (MA). *Entrance requirements:* For master's, GRE General Test. *Application deadline:* For fall admission, 7/1 priority date for domestic students; for spring admission, 11/15 for domestic students. Application fee: $50. Electronic applications accepted. *Expenses:* Tuition, state resident: full-time $7200; part-time $344 per credit hour. Tuition, nonresident: full-time $21,900; part-time $944 per credit hour. Tuition and fees vary according to course load and program. *Financial support:* Fellowships, research assistantships, teaching assistantships, unspecified assistantships available. *Unit head:* Dr. Nina Hellerstein, Interim Head, 706-542-3122, E-mail: hellerst@uga.edu. *Application contact:* Dr. Catherine M. Jones, Graduate Coordinator, 706-542-3159, Fax: 706-542-2272, E-mail: cmjones@uga.edu.

University of Hawaii at Manoa, Graduate Division, College of Languages, Linguistics and Literature, Department of Languages and Literatures of Europe and the Americas, Program in Spanish, Honolulu, HI 96822. Offers MA. Part-time programs available. *Students:* 10 full-time (6 women), 2 part-time (both women); includes 9 minority (1 Black or African American, non-Hispanic/Latino; 1 Asian, non-Hispanic/Latino; 4 Hispanic/Latino; 3 Two or more races, non-Hispanic/Latino). Average age 33. 14 applicants, 86% accepted, 9 enrolled. In 2010, 6 master's awarded. *Degree requirements:* For master's, one foreign language, thesis optional. *Entrance requirements:* For master's, GRE General Test. Additional exam requirements/recommendations for international students: Required—TOEFL (minimum score 580 paper-based; 237 computer-based; 92 iBT), IELTS (minimum score 5). *Application deadline:* For fall admission, 3/1 for domestic students, 2/1 for international students; for spring admission, 9/1 for domestic students, 8/15 for international students. Application fee: $60. *Financial support:* In 2010–11, 10 students received support, including 1 fellowship (averaging $2,250 per year), 9 teaching assistantships (averaging $14,382 per year). *Application contact:* Robert Ball, Graduate Chair, 808-956-4187, Fax: 808-956-9536, E-mail: rball@hawaii.edu.

University of Houston, College of Liberal Arts and Social Sciences, Department of Hispanic Studies, Houston, TX 77204. Offers Spanish (MA, PhD). Part-time programs available. *Students:* 29 full-time (23 women), 45 part-time (34 women); includes 46 Hispanic/Latino; 1 Two or more races, non-Hispanic/Latino, 8 international. Average age 38. 29 applicants, 59% accepted, 10 enrolled. In 2010, 4 master's, 3 doctorates awarded. *Degree requirements:* For master's, comprehensive exam, thesis optional; for doctorate, 2 foreign languages, comprehensive exam, thesis/dissertation. *Entrance requirements:* For master's and doctorate, GRE. Additional exam requirements/recommendations for international students: Required—TOEFL (minimum score 550 paper-based; 79 iBT); Recommended—IELTS (minimum score 6.5). *Application deadline:* For fall admission, 2/25 for domestic and international students; for spring admission, 9/30 for domestic and international students. Applications are processed on a rolling basis. Application fee: $75. Electronic applications accepted. *Expenses:* Tuition, state resident: full-time $8592; part-time $358 per credit hour. Tuition, nonresident: full-time $16,032; part-time $668 per credit hour. Required fees: $2889. Tuition and fees vary according to course load and program. *Financial support:* In 2010–11, 5 research assistantships with full tuition reimbursements (averaging $10,400 per year), 10 teaching assistantships with full tuition reimbursements (averaging $9,992 per year) were awarded. *Unit head:* Dr. Anadeli Bencomo, Chairperson, 713-743-3068, Fax: 713-743-0935, E-mail: abencomo@uh.edu. *Application contact:* Gabriela Ventura, Director of Graduate Studies, 713-743-3259, E-mail: gbventura@uh.edu.

University of Houston, College of Liberal Arts and Social Sciences, Department of Modern and Classical Languages, Houston, TX 77204. Offers world cultures and literatures (MA). *Faculty:* 11 full-time (6 women), 4 part-time/adjunct (all women). *Students:* 1 (woman) part-time. Average age 29. 7 applicants, 29% accepted, 1 enrolled. *Degree requirements:* For master's, one foreign language, thesis optional. *Entrance requirements:* For master's, GRE General Test, minimum GPA of 3.0 in last 60 hours of course work. Additional exam requirements/recommendations for international students: Required—TOEFL (minimum score 500 paper-based). *Application deadline:* For fall admission, 4/15 for domestic and international students; for spring admission, 11/1 for domestic and international students. Applications are processed on a rolling basis. Electronic applications accepted. *Expenses:* Tuition, state resident: full-time

$8592; part-time $358 per credit hour. Tuition, nonresident: full-time $16,032; part-time $668 per credit hour. Required fees: $2889. Tuition and fees vary according to course load and program. *Financial support:* In 2010–11, 2 teaching assistantships with full tuition reimbursements (averaging $9,060 per year) were awarded; career-related internships or fieldwork, Federal Work-Study, institutionally sponsored loans, scholarships/grants, health care benefits, and unspecified assistantships also available. Support available to part-time students. Financial award applicants required to submit FAFSA. *Unit head:* Dr. Hildegard Glass, Chairperson, 713-743-8350, Fax: 713-743-2693, E-mail: hfglass@uh.edu. *Application contact:* Alessandro Carrera, 713-743-3069, E-mail: alessandro.carrera@mail.uh.edu.

University of Illinois at Chicago, Graduate College, College of Liberal Arts and Sciences, Department of Spanish, French, Italian and Portuguese, Program in Hispanic Studies, Chicago, IL 60607-7128. Offers Hispanic linguistics (MA, PhD); Hispanic literary and cultural studies (MA, PhD). Part-time programs available. Terminal master's awarded for partial completion of doctoral program. *Degree requirements:* For master's, one foreign language, departmental qualifying exam. *Entrance requirements:* For master's, GRE General Test, minimum GPA of 2.75, undergraduate major in Spanish. Additional exam requirements/recommendations for international students: Required—TOEFL. Electronic applications accepted.

University of Illinois at Urbana–Champaign, Graduate College, College of Liberal Arts and Sciences, School of Literatures, Cultures and Linguistics, Department of Spanish, Italian and Portuguese, Champaign, IL 61820. Offers Italian (MA, PhD); Portuguese (MA, PhD); Spanish (MA, PhD). *Faculty:* 17 full-time (10 women). *Students:* 39 full-time (29 women), 2 part-time (both women); includes 14 minority (all Hispanic/Latino), 16 international. 52 applicants, 23% accepted, 3 enrolled. In 2010, 12 master's, 6 doctorates awarded. *Entrance requirements:* For master's, GRE General Test, minimum GPA of 3.0; writing sample; for doctorate, GRE, minimum GPA of 3.0; writing sample. Additional exam requirements/recommendations for international students: Required—TOEFL (minimum score 88 iBT). *Application deadline:* Applications are processed on a rolling basis. Application fee: $75 ($90 for international students). Electronic applications accepted. *Financial support:* In 2010–11, 7 fellowships, 2 research assistantships, 39 teaching assistantships were awarded; tuition waivers (full and partial) also available. *Unit head:* Diane Musumeci, Head, 217-333-3390, Fax: 217-244-8430, E-mail: musumeci@illinois.edu. *Application contact:* Lynn Stanke, Office Support Specialist, 217-333-6269, Fax: 217-244-3050, E-mail: stanke@illinois.edu.

The University of Iowa, Graduate College, College of Liberal Arts and Sciences, Department of Spanish and Portuguese, Iowa City, IA 52242-1316. Offers Spanish (MA, PhD). *Degree requirements:* For master's, thesis optional, exam; for doctorate, comprehensive exam, thesis/dissertation. *Entrance requirements:* For master's and doctorate, GRE General Test, minimum GPA of 3.0. Additional exam requirements/recommendations for international students: Required—TOEFL (minimum score 600 paper-based; 250 computer-based; 100 iBT). Electronic applications accepted.

The University of Kansas, Graduate Studies, College of Liberal Arts and Sciences, Department of Spanish and Portuguese, Lawrence, KS 66045. Offers Spanish (MA, PhD). *Faculty:* 16 full-time (8 women). *Students:* 30 full-time (15 women), 1 (woman) part-time; includes 7 minority (all Hispanic/Latino), 3 international. Average age 30. 34 applicants, 47% accepted, 7 enrolled. In 2010, 5 master's, 6 doctorates awarded. *Degree requirements:* For master's, 2 foreign languages; for doctorate, 3 foreign languages, thesis/dissertation. *Entrance requirements:* Additional exam requirements/recommendations for international students: Required—TOEFL. *Application deadline:* For fall admission, 5/15 priority date for domestic students, 12/15 priority date for international students; for spring admission, 10/15 priority date for domestic students, 5/15 priority date for international students. Applications are processed on a rolling basis. Application fee: $55 ($65 for international students). Electronic applications accepted. *Expenses:* Tuition, state resident: full-time $7092; part-time $295.50 per credit hour. Tuition, nonresident: full-time $16,590; part-time $691.25 per credit hour. Required fees: $858; $71.49 per credit hour. Tuition and fees vary according to course load, campus/location and program. *Financial support:* Fellowships with tuition reimbursements, research assistantships, teaching assistantships with full and partial tuition reimbursements, unspecified assistantships available. Financial award application deadline: 1/15. *Faculty research:* Latin American literary and cultural studies; medieval, early modern and contemporary Spanish literary and cultural studies. *Unit head:* Dr. Stuart Day, Chair, 785-864-3851, Fax: 785-864-3819, E-mail: spanport@ku.edu. *Application contact:* Shirley Wheeler, Graduate Coordinator, 785-864-0279, Fax: 785-864-3819, E-mail: wheeler@ku.edu.

University of Lethbridge, School of Graduate Studies, Lethbridge, AB T1K 3M4, Canada. Offers accounting (MScM); addictions counseling (M Sc); agricultural biotechnology (M Sc); agricultural studies (M Sc, MA); anthropology (MA); archaeology (MA); art (MA, MFA); biochemistry (M Sc); biological sciences (M Sc); biomolecular science (PhD); biosystems and biodiversity (PhD); Canadian studies (MA); chemistry (M Sc); computer science (M Sc); computer science and geographical information science (M Sc); counseling psychology (M Ed); dramatic arts (MA); earth, space, and physical science (PhD); economics (MA); educational leadership (M Ed); English (MA); environmental science (M Sc); evolution and behavior (PhD); exercise science (M Sc); finance (MScM); French (MA); French/German (MA); French/Spanish (MA); general education (M Ed); general management (MScM); geography (M Sc, MA); German (MA); health science (M Sc); history (MA); human resource management and labour relations (MScM); individualized multidisciplinary (M Sc, MA); information systems (MScM); international management (MScM); kinesiology (M Sc, MA); management (M Sc, MA); marketing (MScM); mathematics (M Sc); music (M Mus, MA); Native American studies (MA); neuroscience (M Sc, PhD); new media (MA); nursing (M Sc); philosophy (MA); physics (M Sc); policy and strategy (MScM); political science (MA); psychology (M Sc, MA); religious studies (MA); social sciences (MA); sociology (MA); theatre and dramatic arts (MFA); theoretical and computational science (PhD); urban and regional studies (MA); women's studies (MA). Part-time and evening/weekend programs available. *Degree requirements:* For doctorate, comprehensive exam, thesis/dissertation. *Entrance requirements:* For master's, GMAT (M Sc in management), bachelor's degree in related field, minimum GPA of 3.0 during previous 20 graded semester courses, 2 years teaching or related experience (M Ed); for doctorate, master's degree, minimum graduate GPA of 3.5. Additional exam requirements/recommendations for international students: Required—TOEFL. *Faculty research:* Movement and brain plasticity, gibberellin physiology, photosynthesis, carbon cycling, molecular properties of main-group ring components.

University of Louisville, Graduate School, College of Arts and Sciences, Department of Classical and Modern Languages, Louisville, KY 40292-0001. Offers French (MA); Spanish (MA). Part-time and evening/weekend programs available. *Faculty:* 22 full-time (13 women), 1 (woman) part-time/adjunct. *Students:* 11 full-time (8 women), 14 part-time (8 women); includes 2 Black or African American, non-Hispanic/Latino; 5 Hispanic/Latino, 1 international. Average age 31. 17 applicants, 76% accepted, 10 enrolled. In 2010, 18 master's awarded. *Degree requirements:* For master's, one foreign language, thesis optional. *Entrance requirements:* For master's, GRE General Test: Recommended, but not required. Additional exam requirements/recommendations for international students: Required—TOEFL (minimum score 550 paper-based; 79 computer-based). *Application deadline:* Applications are processed on a rolling basis. Application fee: $50. Electronic applications accepted. *Expenses:* Tuition, state resident: full-time $9144; part-time $508 per credit hour. Tuition, nonresident: full-time $19,026; part-time $1057 per credit hour. Tuition and fees vary according to program and reciprocity agreements. *Financial support:* In 2010–11, 9 students received support, including 8 teaching assistantships with full tuition reimbursements available (averaging $12,000 per year); fellowships, institutionally sponsored loans, scholarships/grants, health care benefits, and unspecified assistantships also available. Financial award applicants required to submit FAFSA. *Faculty research:* Hispanic cultural studies, sociolinguistics, translation, contemporary France, medieval literature. *Unit head:* Dr. Augustus A. Mastri, Chair, 502-852-0403, Fax: 502-852-8885, E-mail: mastri@louisville.edu. *Application contact:* Libby Leggett, Director, Graduate Admissions, 502-852-3101, Fax: 502-852-6536, E-mail: gradadm@louisville.edu.

The University of Manchester, School of Languages, Linguistics and Cultures, Manchester, United Kingdom. Offers Arab world studies (PhD); Chinese studies (M Phil, PhD); East Asian studies (M Phil, PhD); English language (PhD); French studies (M Phil, PhD); German studies (M Phil, PhD); interpreting studies (PhD); Italian studies (M Phil, PhD); Japanese studies (M Phil, PhD); Latin American cultural studies (M Phil, PhD); linguistics (M Phil, PhD); Middle Eastern studies (M Phil, PhD); Polish studies (M Phil, PhD); Portuguese studies (M Phil, PhD); Russian studies (M Phil, PhD); Spanish studies (M Phil, PhD); translation and intercultural studies (M Phil, PhD).

University of Maryland, College Park, Academic Affairs, College of Arts and Humanities, School of Languages, Literature, and Cultures, Department of Spanish and Portuguese, College Park, MD 20742. Offers MA, PhD. *Students:* 33 full-time (25 women), 2 part-time (1 woman); includes 6 Hispanic/Latino, 16 international. 35 applicants, 46% accepted, 5 enrolled. In 2010, 4 master's, 3 doctorates awarded. *Degree requirements:* For master's, comprehensive exam, thesis optional, scholarly paper; for doctorate, 2 foreign languages, thesis/dissertation. *Entrance requirements:* For master's, minimum GPA of 3.0, interview, sample research paper, minimum of 12 credits in upper-level literature, 3 letters of recommendation; for doctorate, minimum GPA of 3.0, interview, sample research paper, minimum of 12 credits in upper-level literature. Additional exam requirements/recommendations for international students: Required—TOEFL. *Application deadline:* For fall admission, 1/7 for domestic and international students; for spring admission, 6/1 for international students. Applications are processed on a rolling basis. Application fee: $75. Electronic applications accepted. *Expenses:* Tuition, state resident: part-time $471 per credit hour. Tuition, nonresident: part-time $1016 per credit hour. Required fees: $337 per term. *Financial support:* In 2010–11, 7 fellowships with partial tuition reimbursements (averaging $9,891 per year), 17 teaching assistantships (averaging $19,772 per year) were awarded; Federal Work-Study also available. Support available to part-time students. Financial award applicants required to submit FAFSA. *Unit head:* Carol A. Mossman, Director, School of Languages, Literatures, and Cultures, 301-405-4025, Fax: 301-314-9928, E-mail: cmossman@umd.edu. *Application contact:* Dr. Charles A. Caramello, Dean of Graduate School, 301-405-0358, Fax: 301-314-9305, E-mail: ccaramel@umd.edu.

University of Massachusetts Amherst, Graduate School, College of Humanities and Fine Arts, Department of Languages, Literatures, and Cultures, Programs in Hispanic Literatures, Cultures and Linguistics, Amherst, MA 01003. Offers Hispanic literatures, cultures and linguistics (MA, PhD); teaching Spanish (MAT). Part-time programs available. *Faculty:* 13 full-time (6 women). *Students:* 25 full-time (19 women), 29 part-time (16 women); includes 17 minority (1 Asian, non-Hispanic/Latino; 16 Hispanic/Latino), 19 international. Average age 35. 42 applicants, 60% accepted, 14 enrolled. In 2010, 9 master's, 3 doctorates awarded. Terminal master's awarded for partial completion of doctoral program. *Degree requirements:* For master's, one foreign language, thesis or alternative; for doctorate, 2 foreign languages, comprehensive exam, thesis/dissertation. *Entrance requirements:* For master's and doctorate, GRE General Test, sample academic term paper. Additional exam requirements/recommendations for international students: Required—TOEFL (minimum score 550 paper-based; 213 computer-based; 80 iBT), IELTS (minimum score 6.5). *Application deadline:* For fall admission, 2/1 for domestic and international students. Applications are processed on a rolling basis. Application fee: $50 ($65 for international students). Electronic applications accepted. *Expenses:* Tuition, state resident: full-time $2640. Required fees: $8282. One-time fee: $357 full-time. *Financial support:* In 2010–11, 32 teaching assistantships with full tuition reimbursements (averaging $15,272 per year) were awarded; fellowships, research assistantships, career-related internships or fieldwork, Federal Work-Study, scholarships/grants, traineeships, health care benefits, tuition waivers (full), and unspecified assistantships also available. Support available to part-time students. Financial award application deadline: 2/1; financial award applicants required to submit FAFSA. *Unit head:* Dr. Frank C. Fagundes, Graduate Program Director, 413-545-0544, Fax: 413-545-3178. *Application contact:* Jean M. Ames, Supervisor of Admissions, 413-545-0722, Fax: 413-577-0010, E-mail: gradadm@grad.umass.edu.

University of Memphis, Graduate School, College of Arts and Sciences, Department of Foreign Languages and Literatures, Memphis, TN 38152. Offers French (MA); Spanish (MA). Part-time programs available. *Faculty:* 12 full-time (5 women), 1 part-time/adjunct (0 women). *Students:* 14 full-time (11 women), 58 part-time (57 women); includes 5 minority (3 Black or African American, non-Hispanic/Latino; 2 Hispanic/Latino), 4 international. Average age 34. 12 applicants, 92% accepted, 5 enrolled. In 2010, 7 master's awarded. *Degree requirements:* For master's, 2 foreign languages, comprehensive exam. *Entrance requirements:* For master's, GRE, interview in language of concentration. Additional exam requirements/recommendations for international students: Required—TOEFL (minimum score 79 iBT). *Application deadline:* For fall admission, 5/15 for domestic students, 4/5 for international students; for spring admission, 11/30 for domestic students, 10/5 for international students. Applications are processed on a rolling basis. Application fee: $35 ($60 for international students). Electronic applications accepted. *Financial support:* In 2010–11, 11 students received support; research assistantships with full tuition reimbursements available, teaching assistantships with full tuition reimbursements available, Federal Work-Study, scholarships/grants, and unspecified assistantships available. Financial award application deadline: 2/15; financial award applicants required to submit FAFSA. *Faculty research:* Latin American studies, Brazilian culture and literature, modernity and postmodernity, Hispanic studies, French studies, French and Hispanic culture and literature, Hispanic linguistics, applied linguistics. *Unit head:* Dr. Ralph Albanese, Professor and Chair, 901-678-2507, E-mail: ralbanes@memphis.edu. *Application contact:* Dr. Fernando Burgos, Professor and Coordinator of Graduate Studies, 901-678-3158, E-mail: fburgos@memphis.edu.

University of Miami, Graduate School, College of Arts and Sciences, Department of Modern Languages and Literatures, Coral Gables, FL 33124. Offers romance studies (PhD), including French, Spanish. *Degree requirements:* For doctorate, 2 foreign languages, thesis/dissertation, area exam, qualifying exam. *Entrance requirements:* For doctorate, 1 writing sample in English and 1 writing sample in French or Spanish, minimum GPA of 3.0, oral interview, letters of recommendation. Additional exam requirements/recommendations for international students: Required—TOEFL (minimum score 550 paper-based; 213 computer-based; 59 iBT). Electronic applications accepted. *Faculty research:* Transatlantic studies, Caribbean studies, comparative literature, gender theory, cultural studies.

University of Miami, Graduate School, School of Communication, Coral Gables, FL 33124. Offers communication (PhD); communication studies (MA); film studies (MA, PhD); motion pictures (MFA), including production, producing, and screenwriting; print journalism (MA); public relations (MA); Spanish language journalism (MA); television broadcast journalism (MA). *Accreditation:* ACEJMC. Part-time programs available. *Degree requirements:* For master's, comprehensive exam (for some programs), thesis (for some programs); for doctorate, comprehensive exam, thesis/dissertation. *Entrance requirements:* For master's, GRE General Test; for doctorate, GRE General Test, master's thesis or scholarly research. Additional exam requirements/recommendations for international students: Required—TOEFL (minimum score 600 paper-based; 250 computer-based; 100 iBT). Electronic applications accepted. *Faculty research:* Communication studies, mass communication, international/interpersonal communication, film studies, journalism.

University of Michigan, Horace H. Rackham School of Graduate Studies, College of Literature, Science, and the Arts, Department of Romance Languages and Literatures, Program in Spanish, Ann Arbor, MI 48109. Offers PhD. *Faculty:* 17 full-time (6 women). *Students:* 30 full-time (15 women); includes 15 Hispanic/Latino. Average age 30. 45 applicants, 18% accepted, 4 enrolled. In 2010, 5 doctorates awarded. *Degree requirements:* For doctorate, 2 foreign languages, thesis/dissertation, oral defense of dissertation, preliminary exams. *Entrance requirements:* For doctorate, GRE General Test. Additional exam requirements/recommendations for international students: Required—TOEFL or Michigan English Language Assessment Battery. *Application deadline:* For fall admission, 1/1 for domestic and international students. Application fee: $65 ($75 for international students). Electronic applications accepted. *Expenses:* Tuition, state resident: full-time $17,784; part-time $1116 per credit hour. Tuition, nonresident: full-time

Spanish

University of Michigan (continued)

$35,944; part-time $2125 per credit hour. International tuition: $35,994 full-time. Required fees: $95 per semester. Tuition and fees vary according to course load, degree level and program. *Financial support:* In 2010–11, 23 students received support, including 6 fellowships with full tuition reimbursements available (averaging $20,000 per year), 31 teaching assistantships with full tuition reimbursements available (averaging $20,000 per year); institutionally sponsored loans, scholarships/grants, and unspecified assistantships also available. Financial award application deadline: 1/1. *Faculty research:* Comparative Romance studies, medieval and early modern studies, postcolonial and minority literatures, culture and materiality, reflection in the nature and function of scholarship. *Unit head:* Dr. Cristina Moreiras-Menor, Chair, 734-764-5344, Fax: 734-764-8163. *Application contact:* Annette Herbert, Graduate Assistant, 734-764-8164, Fax: 734-764-8163, E-mail: rll-admissions@umich.edu.

University of Minnesota, Twin Cities Campus, Graduate School, College of Liberal Arts, Department of Spanish and Portuguese Studies, Minneapolis, MN 55455-0213. Offers Hispanic and Lusophone literatures, cultures and linguistics (PhD); Hispanic linguistics (MA); Hispanic literature (MA); Lusophone literature (MA). *Degree requirements:* For master's, 2 foreign languages, comprehensive exam, thesis or alternative; for doctorate, 2 foreign languages, comprehensive exam, thesis/dissertation. *Entrance requirements:* For master's and doctorate, GRE General Test, samples of written work, 3 letters of recommendation, voice sample, statement of purpose. Additional exam requirements/recommendations for international students: Required—TOEFL (minimum score 550 paper-based; 213 computer-based; 79 iBT). Electronic applications accepted. *Faculty research:* Sociohistorical approaches to literature and culture, feminist studies, literary theory, ideologies and literature, pragmatics and sociolinguistics.

University of Mississippi, Graduate School, College of Liberal Arts, Department of Modern Languages, Oxford, University, MS 38677. Offers French (MA); German (MA); Spanish (MA). *Students:* 39 full-time (28 women), 19 part-time (17 women); includes 8 Black or African American, non-Hispanic/Latino; 1 American Indian or Alaska Native, non-Hispanic/Latino; 7 Asian, non-Hispanic/Latino; 10 Hispanic/Latino; 1 Two or more races, non-Hispanic/Latino. In 2010, 17 master's awarded. *Degree requirements:* For master's, thesis (for some programs). *Entrance requirements:* For master's, GRE General Test, minimum GPA of 3.0. Additional exam requirements/recommendations for international students: Required—TOEFL. *Application deadline:* For fall admission, 2/1 for domestic students; for spring admission, 10/1 for domestic students. Applications are processed on a rolling basis. Application fee: $25. Electronic applications accepted. *Financial support:* Scholarships/grants available. Financial award application deadline: 3/1; financial award applicants required to submit FAFSA. *Unit head:* Dr. Donald L. Dyer, Chair, 662-915-7298, Fax: 662-915-1086, E-mail: mlangs@olemiss.edu. *Application contact:* Dr. Christy M. Wyandt, Associate Dean, 662-915-7474, Fax: 662-915-7577, E-mail: cwyandt@olemiss.edu.

University of Missouri, Graduate School, College of Arts and Sciences, Department of Romance Languages and Literature, Program in Spanish, Columbia, MO 65211. Offers MA, PhD. *Degree requirements:* For master's, one foreign language; for doctorate, 4 foreign languages, thesis/dissertation. *Entrance requirements:* For master's and doctorate, GRE General Test, minimum GPA of 3.0. Additional exam requirements/recommendations for international students: Required—TOEFL (minimum score 500 paper-based; 173 computer-based).

The University of Montana, Graduate School, College of Arts and Sciences, Department of Modern and Classical Languages and Literatures, Missoula, MT 59812-0002. Offers French (MA); German (MA); Spanish (MA). *Degree requirements:* For master's, one foreign language. *Entrance requirements:* For master's, GRE General Test. Additional exam requirements/recommendations for international students: Required—TOEFL.

University of Nebraska–Lincoln, Graduate College, College of Arts and Sciences, Department of Modern Languages and Literatures, Lincoln, NE 68588. Offers French (MA, PhD); German (MA, PhD); Spanish (MA, PhD). *Degree requirements:* For master's, thesis optional; for doctorate, comprehensive exam, thesis/dissertation. *Entrance requirements:* For master's and doctorate, writing sample in target language. Additional exam requirements/recommendations for international students: Required—TOEFL (minimum score 550 paper-based; 213 computer-based). Electronic applications accepted. *Faculty research:* French, German, and Spanish language, literature, and culture.

University of Nevada, Reno, Graduate School, College of Liberal Arts, Department of Foreign Languages and Literatures, Reno, NV 89557. Offers French (MA); German (MA); Spanish (MA). *Degree requirements:* For master's, one foreign language, thesis optional. *Entrance requirements:* For master's, GRE General Test, minimum GPA of 2.75. Additional exam requirements/recommendations for international students: Required—TOEFL (minimum score 500 paper-based; 173 computer-based; 61 iBT), IELTS (minimum score 6). *Expenses:* Tuition, state resident: full-time $2219; part-time $246 per credit. Tuition, nonresident: part-time $510 per credit. International tuition: $9009 full-time. Required fees: $59 per term. One-time fee: $101. Tuition and fees vary according to course load. *Faculty research:* Thirteenth century mysticism, contemporary Spanish and Latin American poetry and theater, French interrelation between narration and photography, exile literature and Holocaust.

University of New Hampshire, Graduate School, College of Liberal Arts, Program in Spanish, Durham, NH 03824. Offers MA. *Faculty:* 9 full-time (6 women). *Students:* 5 full-time (3 women), 12 part-time (all women); includes 3 minority (all Hispanic/Latino), 1 international. Average age 34. 7 applicants, 86% accepted, 6 enrolled. In 2010, 5 master's awarded. *Degree requirements:* For master's, one foreign language, thesis or alternative. *Entrance requirements:* Additional exam requirements/recommendations for international students: Required—TOEFL (minimum score 550 paper-based; 213 computer-based; 80 iBT). *Application deadline:* For fall admission, 6/1 priority date for domestic students, 4/1 for international students; for spring admission, 12/1 priority date for domestic students. Applications are processed on a rolling basis. Application fee: $65. Electronic applications accepted. *Financial support:* In 2010–11, 4 students received support, including 4 teaching assistantships; fellowships, research assistantships, career-related internships or fieldwork, Federal Work-Study, scholarships/grants, and tuition waivers (full and partial) also available. Support available to part-time students. Financial award application deadline: 2/15. *Unit head:* Dr. Piero Garofalo, Chairperson, 603-862-4005. *Application contact:* Holly Harris, Administrative Assistant, 603-862-3121, E-mail: spanish.master@unh.edu.

University of New Mexico, Graduate School, College of Arts and Sciences, Department of Spanish and Portuguese, Albuquerque, NM 87131-2039. Offers Portuguese (MA); Spanish (MA); Spanish and Portuguese (PhD). Part-time programs available. *Faculty:* 24 full-time (14 women), 60 part-time/adjunct (39 women). *Students:* 51 full-time (35 women), 9 part-time (8 women); includes 1 Black or African American, non-Hispanic/Latino; 36 Hispanic/Latino, 12 international. Average age 34. 45 applicants, 53% accepted, 14 enrolled. In 2010, 9 master's, 1 doctorate awarded. *Degree requirements:* For master's, one foreign language, comprehensive exam, thesis optional; for doctorate, one foreign language, comprehensive exam, thesis/dissertation. *Entrance requirements:* For master's, Versant test for Teaching assistantship, BA in Spanish or Portuguese, 3 letters of recommendation, letter of intent; for doctorate, GRE, Versant test for Teaching assistantship, 3 letters of recommendation, letter of intent, sample research paper. Additional exam requirements/recommendations for international students: Required—TOEFL (minimum score 550 paper-based; 213 computer-based). *Application deadline:* For fall admission, 1/15 priority date for domestic students; for spring admission, 11/15 for domestic students. Applications are processed on a rolling basis. Application fee: $50. Electronic applications accepted. *Expenses:* Tuition, state resident: full-time $5991; part-time $251 per credit hour. Tuition, nonresident: full-time $14,405; part-time $800.20 per credit hour. Tuition and fees vary according to course level, course load, program and reciprocity agreements. *Financial support:* In 2010–11, 53 students received support, including 2 fellowships (averaging $9,350 per year), 3 research assistantships (averaging $5,067 per year), 45 teaching assistantships with full tuition reimbursements available (averaging $12,773 per

year); Federal Work-Study, institutionally sponsored loans, scholarships/grants, health care benefits, and unspecified assistantships also available. Support available to part-time students. Financial award application deadline: 3/1; financial award applicants required to submit FAFSA. *Faculty research:* Languages and literatures from the Iberian Peninsula, Latin America and the American Southwest. *Unit head:* Dr. Enrique Lamadrid, Chair, 505-277-5907, Fax: 505-277-3885, E-mail: lamadrid@unm.edu. *Application contact:* Martha Hurd, Graduate Administration Assistant, 505-277-2974, E-mail: marthah@unm.edu.

The University of North Carolina at Chapel Hill, Graduate School, College of Arts and Sciences, Department of Romance Languages, Chapel Hill, NC 27599. Offers French (MA, PhD); Italian (MA, PhD); Portuguese (MA, PhD); Romance languages (MA, PhD); Romance philology (MA, PhD); Spanish (MA, PhD). *Degree requirements:* For master's, one foreign language, comprehensive exam, thesis; for doctorate, 2 foreign languages, comprehensive exam, thesis/dissertation. *Entrance requirements:* For master's and doctorate, GRE General Test, minimum GPA of 3.0. Additional exam requirements/recommendations for international students: Required—TOEFL (minimum score 550 paper-based; 213 computer-based). Electronic applications accepted.

The University of North Carolina at Charlotte, Graduate School, College of Arts and Sciences, Department of Languages and Culture Studies, Charlotte, NC 28223-0001. Offers Spanish (MA). Part-time and evening/weekend programs available. *Faculty:* 19 full-time (9 women). *Students:* 5 full-time (3 women), 18 part-time (14 women); includes 7 minority (5 Black or African American, non-Hispanic/Latino; 2 Hispanic/Latino), 1 international. Average age 23. 7 applicants, 100% accepted, 4 enrolled. In 2010, 5 master's awarded. *Degree requirements:* For master's, thesis optional. *Entrance requirements:* For master's, GRE, 3 letters of reference, minimum GPA of 2.75. Additional exam requirements/recommendations for international students: Required—TOEFL (minimum score 557 paper-based; 220 computer-based; 83 iBT). *Application deadline:* For fall admission, 7/15 for domestic students, 5/1 for international students; for spring admission, 11/15 for domestic students, 10/1 for international students. Applications are processed on a rolling basis. Application fee: $55. Electronic applications accepted. *Expenses:* Tuition, state resident: full-time $3464. Tuition, nonresident: full-time $14,297. Required fees: $2094. Tuition and fees vary according to course load. *Financial support:* In 2010–11, 9 students received support, including 9 teaching assistantships (averaging $5,839 per year); career-related internships or fieldwork, institutionally sponsored loans, and scholarships/grants also available. Support available to part-time students. Financial award application deadline: 4/1; financial award applicants required to submit FAFSA. *Faculty research:* Twentieth and twenty-first century Spanish literature, Central American literature, Caribbean literature, Mexican literature, literature of the Southern Cone. Total annual research expenditures: $15,571. *Unit head:* Robert L. Reimer, Chair, 704-687-8767, Fax: 704-687-3496, E-mail: rcreimer@uncc.edu. *Application contact:* Kathy B. Giddings, Director of Graduate Admissions, 704-687-5503, Fax: 704-687-3279, E-mail: gradadm@uncc.edu.

The University of North Carolina at Greensboro, Graduate School, College of Arts and Sciences, Department of Romance Languages, Program in Spanish, Greensboro, NC 27412-5001. Offers advanced Spanish language and Hispanic cultural studies (Certificate); Spanish (MA). *Degree requirements:* For master's, one foreign language, comprehensive exam, thesis or alternative. *Entrance requirements:* For master's, GRE General Test, 3-5 minute tape demonstrating foreign language proficiency, composition in Spanish, sample paper in English. Additional exam requirements/recommendations for international students: Required—TOEFL. Electronic applications accepted.

The University of North Carolina Wilmington, College of Arts and Sciences, Department of Foreign Languages and Literature, Wilmington, NC 28403-3297. Offers Hispanic studies (Graduate Certificate); Spanish (MA). Part-time programs available. Postbaccalaureate distance learning degree programs offered. *Faculty:* 12 full-time (6 women). *Students:* 1 full-time (0 women), 2 part-time (0 women); includes 1 Black or African American, non-Hispanic/Latino; 1 Hispanic/Latino. Average age 34. 13 applicants, 62% accepted, 3 enrolled. In 2010, 3 master's awarded. *Degree requirements:* For master's, one foreign language, comprehensive exam, thesis or alternative. *Entrance requirements:* For master's, GRE. Additional exam requirements/recommendations for international students: Required—TOEFL (minimum score 550 paper-based; 217 computer-based; 79 iBT), IELTS (minimum score 6.5). Application fee: $60. *Financial support:* In 2010–11, 4 teaching assistantships with full and partial tuition reimbursements (averaging $9,500 per year) were awarded. *Unit head:* Dr. Raymond Burt, Chair, 910-962-4095, E-mail: burtr@uncw.edu. *Application contact:* Dr. R. Terry Mount, Graduate Coordinator, 910-962-3344, E-mail: mountt@uncw.edu.

University of Northern Colorado, Graduate School, College of Humanities and Social Sciences, School of Modern Languages and Cultural Studies, Program in Foreign Languages, Greeley, CO 80639. Offers Spanish/teaching (MA). Part-time programs available. *Faculty:* 14 full-time (9 women). *Students:* 1 part-time (0 women); minority (Hispanic/Latino). Average age 51. 1 applicant, 100% accepted, 0 enrolled. In 2010, 4 master's awarded. *Degree requirements:* For master's, comprehensive exam, thesis or alternative. *Entrance requirements:* For master's, minimum undergraduate GPA of 3.0, BA in Spanish, 1 year of secondary teaching. *Application deadline:* Applications are processed on a rolling basis. Application fee: $50 ($60 for international students). Electronic applications accepted. *Expenses:* Tuition, state resident: full-time $6199; part-time $344 per credit hour. Tuition, nonresident: full-time $14,834; part-time $824 per credit hour. Required fees: $1091; $60.60 per credit hour. Tuition and fees vary according to course load, degree level and program. *Financial support:* In 2010–11, 1 teaching assistantship (averaging $11,969 per year) was awarded; fellowships, research assistantships, unspecified assistantships also available. Financial award application deadline: 3/1; financial award applicants required to submit FAFSA. *Unit head:* Dr. Joy Landeira, Program Coordinator, 970-351-2221, Fax: 970-351-1571. *Application contact:* Linda Sisson, Graduate Student Admission Coordinator, 970-351-1807, Fax: 970-351-2371, E-mail: linda.sisson@unco.edu.

University of Northern Iowa, Graduate College, College of Humanities and Fine Arts, Department of Modern Languages, Program in Spanish, Cedar Falls, IA 50614. Offers Spanish (MA); teaching English to speakers of other languages/Spanish (MA). Part-time and evening/weekend programs available. *Students:* 10 full-time (9 women), 7 part-time (6 women); includes 5 minority (all Hispanic/Latino), 3 international. 11 applicants, 64% accepted, 6 enrolled. In 2010, 11 master's awarded. *Degree requirements:* For master's, one foreign language, comprehensive exam, thesis or alternative. *Entrance requirements:* For master's, minimum GPA of 3.0, valid teaching license, documentation of successful teaching experience. Additional exam requirements/recommendations for international students: Required—TOEFL (minimum score 600 paper-based; 250 computer-based; 100 iBT). *Application deadline:* For fall admission, 8/1 priority date for domestic students. Applications are processed on a rolling basis. Application fee: $50 ($70 for international students). Electronic applications accepted. *Financial support:* Career-related internships or fieldwork, Federal Work-Study, and tuition waivers (full and partial) available. Support available to part-time students. Financial award application deadline: 2/1. *Unit head:* Dr. Juan C. Castillo, Coordinator, 319-273-6200, Fax: 319-273-2848, E-mail: juan.castillo@uni.edu. *Application contact:* Laurie S. Russell, Record Analyst, 319-273-2623, Fax: 319-273-2885, E-mail: laurie.russell@uni.edu.

University of North Texas, Toulouse Graduate School, College of Arts and Sciences, Department of Foreign Languages and Literatures, Denton, TX 76203. Offers French (MA); Spanish (MA). Part-time programs available. *Degree requirements:* For master's, 2 foreign languages, comprehensive exam, thesis optional. *Entrance requirements:* For master's, GRE General Test, minimum undergraduate GPA of 3.0, curriculum vitae, 250-word essay in French or Spanish, 12 advanced credits in French or Spanish. Additional exam requirements/recommendations for international students: Recommended—TOEFL (minimum score 550 paper-based; 213 computer-based; 79 iBT). *Expenses:* Tuition, state resident: full-time $4298; part-time $239 per credit hour. Tuition, nonresident: full-time $10,782; part-time $549 per credit hour. Required fees: $1292; $270 per credit hour. *Financial support:* Fellowships, teaching assistantships, career-related internships or fieldwork, Federal Work-Study, and institutionally sponsored loans available. Financial award application deadline: 4/1; financial award applicants required to submit FAFSA. *Faculty research:* Literature of Austria, France, Germany, Latin America, Spain; culture/civilization; applied linguistics. *Unit head:* Chair. *Application contact:* Chair.

University of Notre Dame, Graduate School, College of Arts and Letters, Division of Humanities, Department of Romance Languages and Literatures, Notre Dame, IN 46556. Offers French and Francophone studies (MA); Iberian and Latin American studies (MA); Italian studies (MA); Romance literatures (MA). *Degree requirements:* For master's, 2 foreign languages, comprehensive exam, thesis optional. *Entrance requirements:* For master's, GRE General Test, BA in target language. Additional exam requirements/recommendations for international students: Required—TOEFL (minimum score 600 paper-based; 250 computer-based; 80 iBT). Electronic applications accepted. *Faculty research:* Literature of discovery and exploration, modern literature, literary criticism, medieval literature, feminist critical theory.

University of Oklahoma, College of Arts and Sciences, Department of Modern Languages, Program in Spanish, Norman, OK 73019. Offers MA, PhD, MBA/MA. Part-time programs available. *Students:* 19 full-time (12 women), 1 (woman) part-time; includes 3 minority (1 American Indian or Alaska Native, non-Hispanic/Latino; 2 Hispanic/Latino), 3 international. Average age 38. 8 applicants, 88% accepted, 3 enrolled. In 2010, 2 master's awarded. *Degree requirements:* For master's, one foreign language, comprehensive exam, thesis optional, departmental qualifying exam; for doctorate, 2 foreign languages, comprehensive exam, thesis/dissertation, departmental qualifying exam. *Entrance requirements:* For master's, BA in Spanish literature, minimum GPA of 3.0 in last 60 hours, 3 letters of recommendation; for doctorate, MA in Spanish, 3 letters of recommendation, minimum graduate GPA of 3.5. Additional exam requirements/recommendations for international students: Required—TOEFL (minimum score 550 paper-based; 213 computer-based; 79 iBT). *Application deadline:* For fall admission, 2/1 for domestic and international students; for spring admission, 10/1 for domestic students, 9/1 for international students. Application fee: $40 ($90 for international students). Electronic applications accepted. *Expenses:* Tuition, state resident: full-time $3893; part-time $162.20 per credit hour. Tuition, nonresident: full-time $14,167; part-time $590.30 per credit hour. Required fees: $2523; $94.60 per credit hour. Tuition and fees vary according to course load and degree level. *Financial support:* Scholarships/grants, health care benefits, and unspecified assistantships available. Financial award applicants required to submit FAFSA. *Faculty research:* Spanish and Latin American literatures, twentieth century literature of Latin American social issues, women writers, medieval and early modern intellectual history, Golden Age drama. *Unit head:* Dr. Pamela Genova, Chairperson, 405-325-6181, Fax: 405-325-0103, E-mail: pgenova@ou.edu. *Application contact:* Dr. Logan E. Whalen, Graduate Liaison, 405-325-5088, Fax: 405-325-0103, E-mail: mlllgradinfo@ou.edu.

University of Oregon, Graduate School, College of Arts and Sciences, Department of Romance Languages, Program in Spanish, Eugene, OR 97403. Offers MA. Part-time programs available. *Degree requirements:* For master's, one foreign language. *Entrance requirements:* For master's, GRE General Test, minimum GPA of 3.0. Additional exam requirements/recommendations for international students: Required—TOEFL.

University of Ottawa, Faculty of Graduate and Postdoctoral Studies, Faculty of Arts, Department of Modern Languages and Literatures, Ottawa, ON K1N 6N5, Canada. Offers Spanish (MA, PhD). Part-time and evening/weekend programs available. *Degree requirements:* For master's, one foreign language, thesis or alternative; for doctorate, one foreign language, comprehensive exam, thesis/dissertation. *Entrance requirements:* For master's, BA with honors in Spanish, minimum B average; for doctorate, MA in Spanish or equivalent, minimum B average. Electronic applications accepted. *Faculty research:* Spanish American literature, Mexican literature and film studies, Spanish golden age literature, twentieth century Spanish literature, Hispanic linguistics with special emphasis on linguistic theory.

University of Pennsylvania, School of Arts and Sciences, Graduate Group in Romance Languages, Philadelphia, PA 19104. Offers French (AM, PhD); Italian (AM, PhD); Spanish (AM, PhD). *Faculty:* 58 full-time (23 women), 4 part-time/adjunct (1 woman). *Students:* 61 full-time (34 women), 2 part-time (both women); includes 1 American Indian or Alaska Native, non-Hispanic/Latino; 12 Hispanic/Latino, 19 international. 114 applicants, 15% accepted, 11 enrolled. In 2010, 11 master's, 6 doctorates awarded. Terminal master's awarded for partial completion of doctoral program. *Degree requirements:* For master's, one foreign language, thesis or alternative; for doctorate, 2 foreign languages, thesis/dissertation. *Entrance requirements:* For master's and doctorate, GRE General Test. Additional exam requirements/recommendations for international students: Required—TOEFL. *Application deadline:* For fall admission, 12/1 priority date for domestic students. Application fee: $70. Electronic applications accepted. *Expenses:* Tuition: Full-time $25,660; part-time $4758 per course. Required fees: $2152; $270 per course. Tuition and fees vary according to course load, degree level and program. *Financial support:* In 2010–11, 23 fellowships, 2 research assistantships, 39 teaching assistantships were awarded; institutionally sponsored loans, scholarships/grants, traineeships, health care benefits, and unspecified assistantships also available. Financial award application deadline: 12/15. *Faculty research:* Literary theory and criticism, cultural studies, history of Romance literatures, gender studies. *Application contact:* Graduate Coordinator, 215-898-7429.

University of Pittsburgh, School of Arts and Sciences, Program in Hispanic Linguistics, Pittsburgh, PA 15260. Offers MA, PhD. Part-time programs available. *Faculty:* 1 (woman) full-time. *Students:* 7 full-time (5 women); includes 1 Hispanic/Latino, 3 international. Average age 30. 8 applicants, 50% accepted, 2 enrolled. In 2010, 1 master's awarded. Terminal master's awarded for partial completion of doctoral program. *Degree requirements:* For master's, one foreign language, thesis; for doctorate, 2 foreign languages, comprehensive exam, thesis/dissertation. *Entrance requirements:* For master's, GRE General Test; for doctorate, GRE General Test, MA in linguistics. Additional exam requirements/recommendations for international students: Required—TOEFL (minimum score 600 paper-based; 250 computer-based; 100 iBT). *Application deadline:* For fall admission, 12/15 for domestic and international students. Applications are processed on a rolling basis. Application fee: $50. Electronic applications accepted. *Expenses:* Tuition, state resident: full-time $17,304; part-time $701 per credit. Tuition, nonresident: full-time $29,554; part-time $1210 per credit. Required fees: $740; $214 per term. Tuition and fees vary according to program. *Financial support:* In 2010–11, 5 students received support, including 6 fellowships (averaging $15,675 per year); teaching assistantships, scholarships/grants, health care benefits, and unspecified assistantships also available. Financial award application deadline: 12/15. *Faculty research:* Hispanic linguistics. *Unit head:* Dr. Yasuhiro Shirai, Chair, 412-624-5933, Fax: 412-624-6130, E-mail: yshirai@pitt.edu. *Application contact:* Allison M. Thompson, Department Administrator, 412-624-5938, Fax: 412-624-6130, E-mail: lingpitt@pitt.edu.

University of Rhode Island, Graduate School, College of Arts and Sciences, Department of Modern and Classical Languages and Literatures, Kingston, RI 02881. Offers Spanish (MA). Part-time programs available. *Faculty:* 24 full-time (10 women), 1 (woman) part-time/adjunct. *Students:* 5 full-time (all women), 11 part-time (10 women); includes 7 minority (all Hispanic/Latino), 1 international. In 2010, 4 master's awarded. *Degree requirements:* For master's, one foreign language, comprehensive exam, thesis optional. *Entrance requirements:* For master's, 2 letters of recommendation. Additional exam requirements/recommendations for international students: Required—TOEFL (minimum score 550 paper-based; 213 computer-based). *Application deadline:* For fall admission, 7/15 for domestic students, 2/1 for international students; for spring admission, 11/15 for domestic students, 7/15 for international students. Application fee: $65. Electronic applications accepted. *Expenses:* Tuition, state resident: full-time $9588; part-time $533 per credit hour. Tuition, nonresident: full-time $22,968; part-time $1276 per credit hour. Required fees: $1282; $68 per semester. Tuition and fees vary according to program. *Financial support:* In 2010–11, 3 teaching assistantships with full and partial tuition reimbursements (averaging $13,894 per year) were awarded. Financial award application deadline: 7/15; financial award applicants required to submit FAFSA. Total annual research expenditures: $429,664. *Unit head:* Dr. Norbert Hedderich, Department Chair, 401-874-4710, Fax: 401-874-4694, E-mail: hedderich@uri.edu. *Application contact:* Dr. Clement White, Director of Graduate Studies, 401-874-5472, Fax: 401-874-4694, E-mail: clement@uri.edu.

University of Rochester, School of Arts and Sciences, Department of Modern Languages and Cultures, Program in Spanish, Rochester, NY 14627.

University of South Africa, College of Human Sciences, Pretoria, South Africa. Offers adult education (M Ed); African languages (MA, PhD); African politics (MA, PhD); Afrikaans (MA, PhD); ancient history (MA, PhD); ancient Near Eastern studies (MA, PhD); anthropology (MA, PhD); applied linguistics (MA); Arabic (MA, PhD); archaeology (MA); art history (MA); Biblical archaeology (MA); Biblical studies (M Th, D Th, PhD); Christian spirituality (M Th, D Th); church history (M Th, D Th); classical studies (MA, PhD); clinical psychology (MA); communication (MA, PhD); comparative education (M Ed, Ed D); consulting psychology (D Admin, D Com, PhD); curriculum studies (M Ed, Ed D); development studies (M Admin, MA, D Admin, PhD); didactics (M Ed, Ed D); education (M Tech); education management (M Ed, Ed D); educational psychology (M Ed); English (MA); environmental education (M Ed); French (MA, PhD); German (MA, PhD); Greek (MA); guidance and counseling (M Ed); health studies (MA, PhD), including health sciences education (MA), health services management (MA), medical and surgical nursing science (critical care general) (MA), midwifery and neonatal nursing science (MA), trauma and emergency care (MA); history (MA, PhD); history of education (Ed D); inclusive education (M Ed, Ed D); information and communications technology policy and regulation (MA); information science (MA, MIS, PhD); international politics (MA, PhD); Islamic studies (MA, PhD); Italian (MA, PhD); Judaica (MA, PhD); linguistics (MA, PhD); mathematical education (M Ed); mathematics education (MA); missiology (M Th, D Th); modern Hebrew (MA, PhD); musicology (MA, MMus, D Mus, PhD); natural science education (M Ed); New Testament (M Th, D Th); Old Testament (D Th); pastoral therapy (M Th, D Th); philosophy (MA); philosophy of education (M Ed, Ed D); politics (MA, PhD); Portuguese (MA, PhD); practical theology (M Th, D Th); psychology (MA, MS, PhD); psychology of education (M Ed, Ed D); public health (MA); religious studies (MA, D Th, PhD); Romance languages (MA); Russian (MA, PhD); Semitic languages (MA, PhD); social behavior studies in HIV/AIDS (MA); social science (mental health) (MA); social science in development studies (MA); social science in psychology (MA); social science in social work (MA); social science in sociology (MA); social work (MSW, DSW, PhD); socio-education (M Ed, Ed D); sociolinguistics (MA); sociology (MA, PhD); Spanish (MA, PhD); systematic theology (M Th, D Th); TESOL (teaching English to speakers of other languages) (MA); theological ethics (M Th, D Th); theory of literature (MA, PhD); urban ministries (D Th); urban ministry (M Th).

University of South Carolina, The Graduate School, College of Arts and Sciences, Department of Languages, Literatures, and Cultures, Columbia, SC 29208. Offers comparative literature (MA, PhD); foreign languages (MAT), including French, German, Spanish; French (MA); German (MA); Spanish (MA). MAT offered in cooperation with the College of Education. Part-time programs available. *Degree requirements:* For master's, one foreign language, comprehensive exam, thesis optional; for doctorate, 2 foreign languages, comprehensive exam, thesis/dissertation. *Entrance requirements:* For master's and doctorate, GRE General Test, writing sample. Additional exam requirements/recommendations for international students: Required—TOEFL (minimum score 230 computer-based; 75 iBT). Electronic applications accepted. *Faculty research:* Modern literature, linguistics, literature and culture, medieval literature, literary theory.

University of Southern California, Graduate School, Dana and David Dornsife College of Letters, Arts and Sciences, Comparative Studies in Literature and Culture Doctoral Program, Los Angeles, CA 90089. Offers comparative literature (PhD); comparative media and culture (PhD); Spanish and Latin American studies (PhD). *Faculty:* 16 full-time (7 women). *Students:* 27 full-time (17 women), 1 part-time (0 women); includes 6 minority (2 Black or African American, non-Hispanic/Latino; 2 Asian, non-Hispanic/Latino; 2 Hispanic/Latino), 6 international. In 2010, 1 doctorate awarded. *Median time to degree:* Of those who began their doctoral program in fall 2002, 50% received their degree in 8 years or less. *Degree requirements:* For doctorate, 2 foreign languages, comprehensive exam, thesis/dissertation. *Entrance requirements:* For doctorate, GRE, competence in language other than English (highly recommended). Additional exam requirements/recommendations for international students: Required—TOEFL. *Application deadline:* For fall admission, 12/1 priority date for domestic and international students. Application fee: $85. Electronic applications accepted. *Expenses:* Tuition: Full-time $31,240; part-time $1420 per unit. Required fees: $600. One-time fee: $35 full-time. Full-time tuition and fees vary according to degree level and program. *Financial support:* In 2010–11, 25 students received support, including 8 fellowships with full tuition reimbursements available (averaging $51,000 per year), 17 teaching assistantships with full tuition reimbursements available (averaging $51,000 per year). Financial award applicants required to submit FAFSA. *Faculty research:* Literary theory, Japanese film and contemporary fiction, Francophone literature and cinema, Latin American and Caribbean literature, Spanish literature and film, nineteenth and twentieth century British and American literature. *Unit head:* Prof. Peggy Kamuf, Director of Comparative Studies in Literature and Culture Doctoral Program, 213-740-0101, Fax: 213-740-8058, E-mail: kamuf@usc.edu. *Application contact:* Katherine Guevarra, Administrative Assistant, 213-740-0102, Fax: 213-740-0858, E-mail: kguevarr@usc.edu.

University of South Florida, Graduate School, College of Arts and Sciences, World Languages Department, Tampa, FL 33620-9951. Offers classics: Latin/Greek (MA); French (MA); linguistics (MA); linguistics: ESL (MA); Spanish (MA). Part-time and evening/weekend programs available. *Faculty:* 10 full-time (6 women). *Students:* 38 full-time (28 women), 25 part-time (17 women); includes 3 Black or African American, non-Hispanic/Latino; 2 American Indian or Alaska Native, non-Hispanic/Latino; 3 Asian, non-Hispanic/Latino; 18 Hispanic/Latino; 1 Two or more races, non-Hispanic/Latino, 6 international. Average age 35. 65 applicants, 48% accepted, 23 enrolled. In 2010, 23 master's awarded. *Degree requirements:* For master's, comprehensive exam, thesis. *Entrance requirements:* For master's, GRE General Test, minimum GPA of 3.0 in last 60 hours. Additional exam requirements/recommendations for international students: Required—TOEFL (minimum score 600 paper-based; 250 computer-based). *Application deadline:* For fall admission, 2/15 for domestic students, 1/2 for international students; for spring admission, 10/15 for domestic students, 6/1 for international students. Application fee: $30. Electronic applications accepted. *Financial support:* In 2010–11, 31 teaching assistantships with tuition reimbursements (averaging $9,272 per year) were awarded; tuition waivers (partial) and unspecified assistantships also available. Financial award application deadline: 6/30. *Faculty research:* Second language writing, academic literacy. Total annual research expenditures: $116,653. *Unit head:* Dr. Victor Peppard, Chairperson, 813-974-2012, Fax: 813-974-1718, E-mail: peppard@.cas.usf.edu. *Application contact:* Dr. Victor Peppard, Chairperson, 813-974-2012, Fax: 813-974-1718, E-mail: peppard@.cas.usf.edu.

The University of Tennessee, Graduate School, College of Arts and Sciences, Department of Modern Foreign Languages and Literatures, Program in Modern Foreign Languages, Knoxville, TN 37996. Offers applied linguistics (PhD); French (PhD); German (PhD); Italian (PhD); Portuguese (PhD); Russian (PhD); Spanish (PhD). *Degree requirements:* For doctorate, 2 foreign languages, thesis/dissertation. *Entrance requirements:* For doctorate, minimum GPA of 2.7. Additional exam requirements/recommendations for international students: Required—TOEFL. Electronic applications accepted. *Expenses:* Tuition, state resident: full-time $7440; part-time $414 per credit hour. Tuition, nonresident: full-time $22,478; part-time $1250 per credit hour. Required fees: $922; $43 per credit hour. Tuition and fees vary according to program.

The University of Tennessee, Graduate School, College of Arts and Sciences, Department of Modern Foreign Languages and Literatures, Program in Spanish, Knoxville, TN 37996. Offers MA. *Degree requirements:* For master's, one foreign language, thesis or alternative. *Entrance requirements:* For master's, minimum GPA of 2.7. Additional exam requirements/recommendations for international students: Required—TOEFL. Electronic applications accepted. *Expenses:* Tuition, state resident: full-time $7440; part-time $414 per credit hour. Tuition,

Spanish

The University of Tennessee (continued)
nonresident: full-time $22,478; part-time $1250 per credit hour. Required fees: $922; $43 per credit hour. Tuition and fees vary according to program.

The University of Texas at Arlington, Graduate School, College of Liberal Arts, Department of Modern Languages, Arlington, TX 76019. Offers French (MA); Spanish (MA). Part-time and evening/weekend programs available. *Faculty:* 8 full-time (5 women), 1 (woman) part-time/adjunct. *Students:* 18 full-time (9 women), 23 part-time (16 women); includes 20 minority (6 Black or African American, non-Hispanic/Latino; 1 Asian, non-Hispanic/Latino; 11 Hispanic/Latino; 1 Native Hawaiian or other Pacific Islander, non-Hispanic/Latino; 1 Two or more races, non-Hispanic/Latino), 2 international. 14 applicants, 100% accepted, 11 enrolled. In 2010, 6 master's awarded. *Degree requirements:* For master's, 2 foreign languages, comprehensive exam, thesis optional. *Entrance requirements:* For master's, GRE General Test, minimum GPA of 3.0, 3 letters of recommendation. Additional exam requirements/recommendations for international students: Required—TOEFL (minimum score 550 paper-based; 213 computer-based). *Application deadline:* For fall admission, 6/15 for domestic students. Applications are processed on a rolling basis. Application fee: $35 ($50 for international students). *Expenses:* Tuition, state resident: full-time $7500. Tuition, nonresident: full-time $13,080. International tuition: $13,250 full-time. *Financial support:* In 2010–11, 4 fellowships with full tuition reimbursements, 14 teaching assistantships (averaging $12,000 per year) were awarded; research assistantships. Financial award application deadline: 6/1; financial award applicants required to submit FAFSA. *Unit head:* Dr. Antoinette Sol, Chair, 817-272-3161, Fax: 817-272-5408, E-mail: amsol@uta.edu. *Application contact:* Dr. Ignacio Ruiz-Perez, Graduate Advisor, 817-272-3161, Fax: 817-272-5408, E-mail: iruiz@uta.edu.

The University of Texas at Austin, Graduate School, College of Liberal Arts, Department of Spanish and Portuguese, Austin, TX 78712-1111. Offers Hispanic linguistics (MA, PhD); Hispanic literature (MA, PhD); Luso-Brazilian literature (MA, PhD). *Degree requirements:* For master's, 2 foreign languages, thesis or alternative; for doctorate, 3 foreign languages, thesis/dissertation. *Entrance requirements:* For master's and doctorate, GRE General Test. Electronic applications accepted.

The University of Texas at Brownsville, Graduate Studies, College of Liberal Arts, Department of Modern Languages, Brownsville, TX 78520-4991. Offers interdisciplinary studies (MAIS); Spanish (MA). Part-time and evening/weekend programs available. *Degree requirements:* For master's, comprehensive exam, thesis optional. *Entrance requirements:* For master's, GRE General Test, letters of recommendation, interview. Additional exam requirements/recommendations for international students: Required—TOEFL. *Faculty research:* Children's literature, Hispanic folklore, translation.

The University of Texas at El Paso, Graduate School, College of Liberal Arts, Department of Creative Writing, El Paso, TX 79968-0001. Offers creative writing (on-line) (MFA); creative writing in English (MFA); creative writing in Spanish (MFA). Part-time and evening/weekend programs available. Postbaccalaureate distance learning degree programs offered (no on-campus study). *Students:* 47 (25 women); includes 1 Black or African American, non-Hispanic/Latino; 20 Hispanic/Latino, 13 international. Average age 34. In 2010, 7 master's awarded. *Degree requirements:* For master's, thesis. *Entrance requirements:* For master's, minimum GPA of 3.0, letters of recommendation, writing sample. Additional exam requirements/recommendations for international students: Required—TOEFL; Recommended—IELTS. *Application deadline:* For fall admission, 8/1 priority date for domestic students, 3/1 for international students; for spring admission, 11/1 for domestic students, 9/1 for international students. Applications are processed on a rolling basis. Application fee: $45 ($80 for international students). Electronic applications accepted. *Financial support:* In 2010–11, research assistantships (averaging $18,625 per year), teaching assistantships with partial tuition reimbursements (averaging $14,900 per year) were awarded; fellowships with partial tuition reimbursements, institutionally sponsored loans, scholarships/grants, health care benefits, tuition waivers (partial), and unspecified assistantships also available. Support available to part-time students. Financial award application deadline: 3/15; financial award applicants required to submit FAFSA. *Unit head:* Dr. Johnny Payne, Chair, 915-747-5713, Fax: 915-747-5523, E-mail: jpayne@utep.edu. *Application contact:* Dr. Patricia D. Witherspoon, Dean of the Graduate School, 915-747-5491, Fax: 915-747-5788, E-mail: withersp@utep.edu.

The University of Texas at El Paso, Graduate School, College of Liberal Arts, Department of Languages and Linguistics, El Paso, TX 79968-0001. Offers linguistics (MA); Spanish (MA); teaching English to speakers of other languages (Certificate). Part-time and evening/weekend programs available. *Students:* 28 (12 women); includes 15 Hispanic/Latino, 4 international. Average age 34. In 2010, 10 master's awarded. *Degree requirements:* For master's, thesis optional. *Entrance requirements:* For master's, GRE General Test, departmental exam, minimum GPA of 3.0, letters of recommendation. Additional exam requirements/recommendations for international students: Required—TOEFL; Recommended—IELTS. *Application deadline:* For fall admission, 8/1 for domestic students, 3/1 for international students; for spring admission, 11/1 for domestic students, 9/1 for international students. Applications are processed on a rolling basis. Application fee: $45 ($80 for international students). Electronic applications accepted. *Financial support:* In 2010–11, research assistantships with partial tuition reimbursements (averaging $18,625 per year), teaching assistantships with partial tuition reimbursements (averaging $14,900 per year) were awarded; fellowships with partial tuition reimbursements, institutionally sponsored loans, scholarships/grants, health care benefits, tuition waivers (partial), and unspecified assistantships also available. Support available to part-time students. Financial award application deadline: 3/15; financial award applicants required to submit FAFSA. *Unit head:* Dr. Kirsten F. Nigro, Chair, 915-747-5767, Fax: 915-747-5292, E-mail: kfnigro@utep.edu. *Application contact:* Dr. Patricia D. Witherspoon, Dean of the Graduate School, 915-747-5491, Fax: 915-747-5788, E-mail: withersp@utep.edu.

The University of Texas at San Antonio, College of Liberal and Fine Arts, Department of Modern Languages and Literatures, San Antonio, TX 78249-0617. Offers Spanish (MA). Part-time and evening/weekend programs available. *Faculty:* 5 full-time (1 woman), 1 (woman) part-time/adjunct. *Students:* 8 full-time (7 women), 19 part-time (14 women); includes 23 minority (1 Black or African American, non-Hispanic/Latino; 22 Hispanic/Latino). Average age 33. 8 applicants, 63% accepted, 5 enrolled. In 2010, 9 master's awarded. *Degree requirements:* For master's, one foreign language, comprehensive exam (for some programs), thesis (for some programs). *Entrance requirements:* For master's, GRE, minimum GPA of 3.0, sample of written and spoken work. Additional exam requirements/recommendations for international students: Required—TOEFL (minimum score 500 paper-based; 173 computer-based; 61 iBT), IELTS (minimum score 5). *Application deadline:* For fall admission, 7/1 for domestic students, 4/1 for international students; for spring admission, 11/1 for domestic students, 9/1 for international students. Applications are processed on a rolling basis. Application fee: $45 ($80 for international students). Electronic applications accepted. *Expenses:* Tuition, state resident: full-time $4172; part-time $231.75 per credit hour. Tuition, nonresident: full-time $15,332; part-time $851.75 per credit hour. *Financial support:* In 2010–11, 14 students received support, including 1 research assistantship (averaging $7,904 per year), 3 teaching assistantships (averaging $3,990 per year); career-related internships or fieldwork, institutionally sponsored loans, scholarships/grants, tuition waivers, and unspecified assistantships also available. Support available to part-time students. *Unit head:* Dr. Marita Nummikosi, Department Chair, 210-458-4373, Fax: 210-458-5672, E-mail: marita.nummikoski@utsa.edu. *Application contact:* Veronica Ramirez, Assistant Dean of the Graduate School, 210-458-4330, Fax: 210-458-4332, E-mail: graduatestudies@utsa.edu.

The University of Texas of the Permian Basin, Office of Graduate Studies, College of Arts and Sciences, Department of Literature and Languages, Odessa, TX 79762-0001. Offers English (MA); Spanish (MA). *Degree requirements:* For master's, comprehensive exam (for some programs), thesis (for some programs). *Entrance requirements:* For master's, GRE General Test. Additional exam requirements/recommendations for international students: Required—TOEFL (minimum score 550 paper-based; 213 computer-based).

The University of Texas–Pan American, College of Arts and Humanities, Department of Modern Languages and Literatures, Edinburg, TX 78539. Offers Spanish (MA). Part-time programs available. *Degree requirements:* For master's, comprehensive exam, thesis or alternative. *Entrance requirements:* For master's, GRE General Test, minimum GPA of 3.0. *Faculty research:* Latin American literature, women's literature, Caribbean literature, Latina/o studies, sociolinguistics, applied linguistics, creative writing.

The University of Toledo, College of Graduate Studies, College of Language, Literature and Social Sciences, Department of Foreign Languages, Toledo, OH 43606-3390. Offers French (MA); German (MA); Spanish (MA). Part-time programs available. *Faculty:* 6. *Students:* 2 full-time (both women), 3 part-time (2 women); includes 1 minority (Hispanic/Latino). Average age 35. 8 applicants, 25% accepted, 2 enrolled. In 2010, 2 master's awarded. *Degree requirements:* For master's, one foreign language, comprehensive exam, comprehensive reading exam in 1 additional foreign language. *Entrance requirements:* For master's, A minimum 2.7 cumulative point-hour ratio (on a 4.0 scale) for all previous academic work. Additional exam requirements/recommendations for international students: Required—TOEFL (minimum score 550 paper-based; 213 computer-based; 80 iBT), IELTS (minimum score 6.5). *Application deadline:* For fall admission, 1/15 priority date for domestic and international students. Applications are processed on a rolling basis. Application fee: $45 ($75 for international students). Electronic applications accepted. *Expenses:* Tuition, state resident: full-time $11,426; part-time $476 per credit hour. Tuition, nonresident: full-time $21,660; part-time $903 per credit hour. One-time fee: $62. *Financial support:* Teaching assistantships with full tuition reimbursements, Federal Work-Study, institutionally sponsored loans, scholarships/grants, tuition waivers (full), and unspecified assistantships available. Support available to part-time students. *Unit head:* Dr. Ruth Hottell, Chair, 419-530-4651, E-mail: ruth.hottell@utoledo.edu. *Application contact:* Graduate School Office, 419-530-4723, Fax: 419-530-4724, E-mail: grdsch@utnet.utoledo.edu.

University of Toronto, School of Graduate Studies, Humanities Division, Department of Spanish and Portuguese, Toronto, ON M5S 1A1, Canada. Offers MA, PhD. Part-time programs available. *Degree requirements:* For doctorate, thesis/dissertation. *Entrance requirements:* For master's, minimum B average in final year, 2 letters of reference; for doctorate, minimum A– average, 2 letters of reference, writing sample. Additional exam requirements/recommendations for international students: Required—TOEFL, Michigan English Language Assessment Battery, IELTS or COPE.

University of Utah, Graduate School, College of Humanities, Department of Languages and Literature, Salt Lake City, UT 84112. Offers comparative literary and cultural studies (MA, PhD); French (MA, MALP); German (MA, MALP, PhD); Spanish (MA, MALP, PhD); world languages with secondary teaching licensure (MA). *Faculty:* 36 full-time (21 women). *Students:* 35 full-time (24 women), 9 part-time (7 women); includes 7 minority (1 American Indian or Alaska Native, non-Hispanic/Latino; 2 Asian, non-Hispanic/Latino; 4 Hispanic/Latino), 8 international. Average age 34. 58 applicants, 57% accepted, 24 enrolled. In 2010, 17 master's, 2 doctorates awarded. Terminal master's awarded for partial completion of doctoral program. *Degree requirements:* For master's, 2 foreign languages, comprehensive exam (for some programs), thesis (for some programs), standard proficiency in 2 languages other than English; for doctorate, 3 foreign languages, comprehensive exam, thesis/dissertation, standard proficiency in 2 languages other than English and language of study, advanced proficiency in 1 language other than English and language of study. *Entrance requirements:* For master's, GRE, bachelor's degree or strong undergraduate record in target languages, minimum GPA of 3.0; for doctorate, GRE, MA, advanced proficiency in a target language. Additional exam requirements/recommendations for international students: Required—TOEFL (minimum score 500 paper-based; 173 computer-based). *Application deadline:* For fall admission, 1/15 priority date for domestic students, 12/15 priority date for international students. Application fee: $55 ($65 for international students). Electronic applications accepted. *Expenses:* Tuition, area resident: Part-time $179.19 per credit hour. Tuition, state resident: full-time $4384. Tuition, nonresident: full-time $16,684; part-time $630.67 per credit hour. Required fees: $350 per semester. Tuition and fees vary according to course load, degree level and program. *Financial support:* In 2010–11, 24 students received support, including 2 fellowships, 22 teaching assistantships with full and partial tuition reimbursements available (averaging $11,500 per year); health care benefits also available. Financial award application deadline: 1/15; financial award applicants required to submit FAFSA. *Faculty research:* Literary study, literary theory, linguistics, cultural studies, comparative studies. Total annual research expenditures: $53,399. *Unit head:* Dr. Karin Baumgartner, Director of Graduate Studies, 801-585-3001, Fax: 801-581-7581, E-mail: karin.baumgartner@hum.utah.edu. *Application contact:* Virginia Ellinwood, Academic Advisor, 801-585-9437, Fax: 801-581-7581, E-mail: v.ellinwood@utah.edu.

University of Virginia, College and Graduate School of Arts and Sciences, Department of Spanish, Italian and Portuguese, Program in Spanish, Charlottesville, VA 22903. Offers MA, PhD. *Students:* 40 full-time (29 women), 4 part-time (2 women); includes 1 Asian, non-Hispanic/Latino; 6 Hispanic/Latino; 1 Two or more races, non-Hispanic/Latino, 3 international. Average age 27. 50 applicants, 20% accepted, 8 enrolled. In 2010, 15 master's, 6 doctorates awarded. *Degree requirements:* For master's, one foreign language, comprehensive exam, thesis; for doctorate, 2 foreign languages, comprehensive exam, thesis/dissertation. *Entrance requirements:* For master's, GRE General Test, GRE Subject Test, 2 letters of recommendation; for doctorate, GRE General Test, GRE Subject Test, 2 letters of recommendation, writing sample. Additional exam requirements/recommendations for international students: Required—TOEFL (minimum score 600 paper-based; 250 computer-based; 90 iBT), IELTS (minimum score 7). *Application deadline:* For fall admission, 12/1 for domestic and international students. Applications are processed on a rolling basis. Application fee: $60. Electronic applications accepted. *Financial support:* Fellowships, teaching assistantships available. Financial award applicants required to submit FAFSA. *Unit head:* Deborah Parker, Chair, 434-924-7159, Fax: 434-924-7160, E-mail: aipinfo@virginia.edu. *Application contact:* E. Michael Gerli, Director of Graduate Studies, 434-924-7159, Fax: 434-924-7160, E-mail: sipinfo@virginia.edu.

University of Washington, Graduate School, College of Arts and Sciences, Department of Romance Languages and Literature, Division of Spanish and Portuguese Studies, Seattle, WA 98195. Offers Hispanic literary and cultural studies (MA). *Degree requirements:* For master's, 2 foreign languages, thesis optional, exam. *Entrance requirements:* For master's, GRE General Test, minimum GPA of 3.0. Additional exam requirements/recommendations for international students: Required—TOEFL. Electronic applications accepted. *Faculty research:* Medieval through modern Spanish literature and film, Latin American literature, poetry and essay, pan-Hispanic ballad, Hispanic cultural studies, second language acquisition and applied linguistics.

The University of Western Ontario, Faculty of Graduate Studies, Faculty of Arts and Humanities, Department of Comparative Literature, London, ON N6A 5B8, Canada. Offers comparative literature (MA, PhD); Spanish (MA). Part-time programs available. *Degree requirements:* For master's, 2 foreign languages, thesis (for some programs). *Entrance requirements:* For master's, honors degree in Spanish or equivalent, minimum B average. Additional exam requirements/recommendations for international students: Required—TOEFL, TOEFL (comparative literature). *Faculty research:* Spanish golden age, Latin-American, romance, medieval, film.

University of West Georgia, College of Education, Department of Curriculum and Instruction, Carrollton, GA 30118. Offers art education (M Ed); art teacher education (Ed S); biology—secondary education (M Ed); biology/secondary education (Ed S); business education (M Ed, Ed S); chemistry/secondary education (Ed S); economics/secondary teacher education (Ed S); education administration and supervision (M Ed); educational leadership (M Ed, Ed S); English teacher education (M Ed, Ed S); French language teacher education (M Ed, Ed S); history teacher education (Ed S); mathematics teacher education (M Ed, Ed S); middle grades education (M Ed, Ed S); physical education teaching and coaching (M Ed); physics/secondary education (Ed S); school improvement (Ed S); science teacher education (M Ed, Ed S); secondary education (M Ed); social science—secondary education (M Ed); social science teacher education

(M Ed); Spanish language teacher education (M Ed, Ed S); Spanish MAT (M Ed); sports management (M Ed). Part-time and evening/weekend programs available. *Faculty:* 18 full-time (15 women), 7 part-time/adjunct (6 women). *Students:* 104 full-time (68 women), 254 part-time (169 women); includes 89 Black or African American, non-Hispanic/Latino; 4 Asian, non-Hispanic/Latino; 3 Hispanic/Latino; 6 Two or more races, non-Hispanic/Latino, 1 international. Average age 37. 94 applicants, 67% accepted, 21 enrolled. In 2010, 86 master's, 55 other advanced degrees awarded. *Degree requirements:* For master's, comprehensive exam; for Ed S, research project. *Entrance requirements:* For master's, minimum GPA of 2.7; for Ed S, master's degree, minimum graduate GPA of 2.7. *Application deadline:* For fall admission, 7/17 for domestic students; for spring admission, 11/20 for domestic students. Applications are processed on a rolling basis. Application fee: $30. Electronic applications accepted. *Expenses:* Tuition, state resident: full-time $4130; part-time $173 per semester hour. Tuition, nonresident: full-time $16,524; part-time $689 per semester hour. Required fees: $1586; $44.01 per semester hour. $397 per semester. Tuition and fees vary according to program. *Financial support:* In 2010–11, 5 research assistantships with full tuition reimbursements (averaging $3,000 per year) were awarded; career-related internships or fieldwork and scholarships/grants also available. Support available to part-time students. Financial award applicants required to submit FAFSA. *Unit head:* Dr. Frank Butts, Chair, 678-839-6530, Fax: 678-839-6195, E-mail: fbutts@westga.edu. *Application contact:* Dr. Frank Butts, Chair, 678-839-6530, Fax: 678-839-6195, E-mail: fbutts@westga.edu.

University of Wisconsin–Madison, Graduate School, College of Letters and Science, Department of Spanish and Portuguese, Program in Spanish, Madison, WI 53706-1380. Offers MA, PhD. *Degree requirements:* For master's, one foreign language; for doctorate, 2 foreign languages, thesis/dissertation. *Entrance requirements:* For master's, GRE (recommended), minimum GPA of 3.25 in Spanish or Portuguese; for doctorate, GRE (recommended), minimum graduate GPA of 3.4, writing sample. Additional exam requirements/recommendations for international students: Required—TOEFL. Electronic applications accepted. *Expenses:* Tuition, state resident: full-time $9887; part-time $617.96 per credit. Tuition, nonresident: full-time $24,054; part-time $1503.40 per credit. Required fees: $67.63 per credit. Tuition and fees vary according to reciprocity agreements. *Faculty research:* Hispanic linguistics, Spanish and Spanish-American literature.

University of Wisconsin–Milwaukee, Graduate School, College of Letters and Sciences, Department of Spanish, Milwaukee, WI 53201-0413. Offers Spanish (MA); translation (Certificate). *Faculty:* 8 full-time (3 women). *Students:* 6 full-time (3 women), 10 part-time (8 women); includes 2 Black or African American, non-Hispanic/Latino; 4 Hispanic/Latino, 1 international. Average age 28. 16 applicants, 94% accepted, 8 enrolled. In 2010, 1 master's awarded. *Entrance requirements:* For master's, bachelor's degree. *Application deadline:* Applications are processed on a rolling basis. Application fee: $56 ($96 for international students). Electronic applications accepted. *Financial support:* In 2010–11, 12 teaching assistantships were awarded; fellowships, research assistantships, unspecified assistantships also available. Financial award applicants required to submit FAFSA. *Faculty research:* Sociolinguistics, Spanish-American literature, Spanish literature, Hispanic culture, Hispanic historiography. *Unit head:* Jeffrey Oxford, Chair, 414-229-4257, E-mail: oxford@uwm.edu. *Application contact:* General Information Contact, 414-229-4982, Fax: 414-229-6967, E-mail: gradschool@uwm.edu.

University of Wyoming, College of Arts and Sciences, Department of Modern and Classical Languages, Program in Spanish, Laramie, WY 82070. Offers MA. Part-time programs available. *Degree requirements:* For master's, one foreign language, thesis or alternative. *Entrance requirements:* For master's, GRE General Test, minimum GPA of 3.0. *Faculty research:* Peninsular literature, Latin American literature, theatre, science and literature, linguistics.

Vanderbilt University, Graduate School, Department of Spanish and Portuguese, Nashville, TN 37240-1001. Offers Portuguese (MA); Spanish (MA, MAT, PhD); Spanish and Portuguese (PhD). *Faculty:* 14 full-time (6 women). *Students:* 27 full-time (14 women); includes 1 Black or African American, non-Hispanic/Latino; 3 Hispanic/Latino. Average age 31. 56 applicants, 13% accepted, 5 enrolled. In 2010, 8 master's, 5 doctorates awarded. *Degree requirements:* For master's, one foreign language, thesis; for doctorate, 2 foreign languages, thesis/dissertation, final and qualifying exams. *Entrance requirements:* For master's, GRE General Test; for doctorate, GRE General Test, writing sample in Spanish. Additional exam requirements/recommendations for international students: Required—TOEFL (minimum score 570 paper-based; 230 computer-based; 88 iBT). *Application deadline:* For fall admission, 1/15 for domestic and international students. Application fee: $0. Electronic applications accepted. *Financial support:* Fellowships with full and partial tuition reimbursements, teaching assistantships with full tuition reimbursements, Federal Work-Study, institutionally sponsored loans, and health care benefits available. Financial award application deadline: 1/15; financial award applicants required to submit CSS PROFILE or FAFSA. *Faculty research:* Spanish, Portuguese, and Latin American literatures; foreign language pedagogy; Renaissance and Baroque poetry; nineteenth century Spanish novel. *Unit head:* Dr. Cathy L. Jrade, Chair, 615-322-6930, Fax: 615-343-7260, E-mail: cathy.l.jrade@vanderbilt.edu. *Application contact:* Dr. Christina Karageorgou-Bastea, Director of Graduate Studies, 615-343-4087, Fax: 615-343-7260, E-mail: christina.karageorgou@vanderbilt.edu.

Washington State University, Graduate School, College of Liberal Arts, Department of Foreign Languages and Cultures, Pullman, WA 99164. Offers foreign languages with emphasis in Spanish (MA). *Faculty:* 7. *Students:* 11 full-time (7 women); includes 4 Hispanic/Latino, 2 international. Average age 28. 21 applicants, 48% accepted, 4 enrolled. In 2010, 3 master's awarded. *Degree requirements:* For master's, comprehensive exam (for some programs), thesis (for some programs), 4 written exams, oral exam, paper. *Entrance requirements:* For master's, three current letters of recommendation; all original transcripts including an official English translation; two writing samples; letter of application stating qualifications and personal goals; brief (3-5 minute) tape recordings of two informal dialogues between applicant and native speaker. Additional exam requirements/recommendations for international students: Required—TOEFL (minimum score 550 paper-based). *Application deadline:* For fall admission, 1/1 priority date for domestic and international students; for spring admission, 7/1 priority date for domestic students, 7/1 for international students. Application fee: $50. Electronic applications accepted. *Expenses:* Tuition, state resident: full-time $8552; part-time $443 per credit. Tuition, nonresident: full-time $21,650; part-time $1083 per credit. Required fees: $846. *Financial support:* In 2010–11, fellowships (averaging $2,200 per year), teaching assistantships with full and partial tuition reimbursements (averaging $13,056 per year) were awarded; career-related internships or fieldwork, Federal Work-Study, institutionally sponsored loans, scholarships/grants, and health care benefits also available. Financial award application deadline: 2/15; financial award applicants required to submit FAFSA. *Faculty research:* Spanish and Latin American literature, film, and culture; pedagogy; computer-aided instruction. Total annual research expenditures: $98,000. *Unit head:* Dr. Eloy Gonzalez, Chair, 509-335-2756, Fax: 509-335-3708, E-mail: eloygonz@wsunix.wsu.edu. *Application contact:* Graduate School Admissions, 800-GRADWSU, Fax: 509-335-1949, E-mail: gradsch@wsu.edu.

Washington University in St. Louis, Graduate School of Arts and Sciences, Department of Romance Languages and Literatures, Program in Spanish, St. Louis, MO 63130-4899. Offers MA, PhD. Terminal master's awarded for partial completion of doctoral program. *Degree requirements:* For master's, thesis or alternative; for doctorate, thesis/dissertation. *Entrance requirements:* For master's and doctorate, GRE General Test. Electronic applications accepted.

Wayne State University, College of Liberal Arts and Sciences, Department of Classical and Modern Languages, Literatures, and Cultures, Program in Modern Languages, Detroit, MI 48202. Offers French (PhD); German (PhD); Spanish (PhD). *Faculty:* 27 full-time (13 women). *Students:* 15 full-time (14 women), 7 part-time (5 women); includes 7 minority (all Hispanic/Latino), 3 international. Average age 41. 3 applicants, 67% accepted, 2 enrolled. In 2010, 1 doctorate awarded. *Expenses:* Tuition, state resident: full-time $7662; part-time $478.85 per credit hour. Tuition, nonresident: full-time $16,920; part-time $1057.55 per credit hour. Required fees: $571.20; $35.70 per credit hour. $188.05 per semester. Tuition and fees vary according to course load and program. *Financial support:* In 2010–11, 2 fellowships (averaging $14,113 per year), 7 teaching assistantships (averaging $14,620 per year) were awarded. *Unit head:* Dr. Michael Giordano, Graduate Director, 313-577-3051, Fax: 313-577-6243, E-mail: m.j.giordano@wayne.edu. *Application contact:* Janet Hankin, Professor, 313-577-0841, E-mail: janet.hankin@wayne.edu.

Wayne State University, College of Liberal Arts and Sciences, Program in Language Learning, Detroit, MI 48202. Offers Arabic (MA); French (MA); German (MA); Italian (MA); Latin (MA); Spanish (MA). *Faculty:* 1 full-time (0 women), 1 (woman) part-time/adjunct. *Students:* 1 (woman) full-time, 12 part-time (11 women), 1 international. Average age 32. 4 applicants, 100% accepted, 3 enrolled. In 2010, 2 master's awarded. *Expenses:* Tuition, state resident: full-time $7662; part-time $478.85 per credit hour. Tuition, nonresident: full-time $16,920; part-time $1057.55 per credit hour. Required fees: $571.20; $35.70 per credit hour. $188.05 per semester. Tuition and fees vary according to course load and program. *Financial support:* In 2010–11, 1 teaching assistantship (averaging $14,620 per year) was awarded. *Unit head:* Robert Thomas, Dean, 313-577-2519, Fax: 313-577-8971, E-mail: aa0817@wayne.edu. *Application contact:* Janet Hankin, Professor, 313-577-0841, E-mail: janet.hankin@wayne.edu.

West Chester University of Pennsylvania, Office of Graduate Studies, College of Arts and Sciences, Department of Languages and Cultures, West Chester, PA 19383. Offers French (M Ed, MA, Teaching Certificate); Spanish (M Ed, MA, Teaching Certificate). Part-time and evening/weekend programs available. *Students:* 6 full-time (5 women), 13 part-time (10 women); includes 3 minority (2 Asian, non-Hispanic/Latino; 1 Hispanic/Latino). Average age 33. 16 applicants, 88% accepted, 6 enrolled. In 2010, 6 master's awarded. *Degree requirements:* For master's, one foreign language, thesis optional, exit exam, capstone project. *Entrance requirements:* For master's, placement test. Additional exam requirements/recommendations for international students: Required—TOEFL (minimum score 550 paper-based; 213 computer-based; 80 iBT). *Application deadline:* For fall admission, 4/15 priority date for domestic students, 3/15 for international students; for spring admission, 10/15 for domestic students, 9/1 for international students. Applications are processed on a rolling basis. Application fee: $35. Electronic applications accepted. *Expenses:* Tuition, state resident: full-time $6966; part-time $387 per credit. Tuition, nonresident: full-time $11,146; part-time $619 per credit. Required fees: $1614.40; $133.24 per credit. Part-time tuition and fees vary according to campus/location. *Financial support:* Unspecified assistantships available. Support available to part-time students. Financial award application deadline: 2/15; financial award applicants required to submit FAFSA. *Faculty research:* Implementation of world languages curriculum framework. *Unit head:* Dr. Jerome Williams, Chair, 610-436-2700, Fax: 610-436-3048, E-mail: jwilliams2@wcupa.edu. *Application contact:* Dr. Rebecca Pauly, Graduate Coordinator, 610-436-2382, E-mail: rpauly@wcupa.edu.

Western Kentucky University, Graduate Studies, Potter College of Arts and Letters, Department of Modern Languages, Bowling Green, KY 42101. Offers French (MA Ed); German (MA Ed); Spanish (MA Ed).

Western Michigan University, Graduate College, College of Arts and Sciences, Department of Foreign Languages and Literatures, Kalamazoo, MI 49008. Offers Spanish (MA, PhD). *Degree requirements:* For master's, oral exam.

West Virginia University, Eberly College of Arts and Sciences, Department of Foreign Languages, Morgantown, WV 26506. Offers French (MA); linguistics (MA); Spanish (MA); teaching English to speakers of other languages (MA). Part-time programs available. *Degree requirements:* For master's, one foreign language, comprehensive exam (for some programs), thesis optional. *Entrance requirements:* For master's, minimum GPA of 3.0. Electronic applications accepted. *Faculty research:* French, German, and Spanish literature; foreign language pedagogy; English as a second language; cultural studies; linguistics.

Wichita State University, Graduate School, Fairmount College of Liberal Arts and Sciences, Department of Modern and Classical Languages and Literatures, Wichita, KS 67260. Offers Spanish (MA). Part-time programs available. *Unit head:* Dr. Wilson Baldridge, Chair, 316-978-3180, Fax: 316-978-3293, E-mail: wilson.baldridge@wichita.edu. *Application contact:* Dr. Kerry Wilks, Graduate Coordinator, 316-978-3180, E-mail: kerry.wilks@wichita.edu.

Winthrop University, College of Arts and Sciences, Program in Spanish, Rock Hill, SC 29733. Offers MA. Part-time programs available. *Entrance requirements:* For master's, GRE General Test and PRAXIS, minimum GPA of 3.0, 24 hours of undergraduate Spanish, or interview. Electronic applications accepted.

Worcester State University, Graduate Studies, Program in Spanish, Worcester, MA 01602-2597. Offers MA. Part-time programs available. *Faculty:* 2 full-time (both women). *Students:* 10 part-time (8 women); includes 1 Hispanic/Latino. Average age 31. 1 applicant, 100% accepted, 1 enrolled. In 2010, 6 master's awarded. *Degree requirements:* For master's, comprehensive exam (for some programs), thesis optional. *Entrance requirements:* Additional exam requirements/recommendations for international students: Required—TOEFL (minimum score 500 paper-based; 61 iBT). *Application deadline:* Applications are processed on a rolling basis. Application fee: $40. Electronic applications accepted. *Expenses:* Tuition, state resident: full-time $2700; part-time $150 per credit. Tuition, nonresident: full-time $2700; part-time $150 per credit. Required fees: $2016; $112 per credit. *Financial support:* Career-related internships or fieldwork, scholarships/grants, and unspecified assistantships available. Financial award application deadline: 3/1; financial award applicants required to submit FAFSA. *Unit head:* Dr. Juan Orbe, Head, 508-929-8704, Fax: 508-929-8174, E-mail: jorbe@worcester.edu. *Application contact:* Sara Grady, Assistant Dean of Graduate and Continuing Education, 508-929-8787, Fax: 508-929-8100, E-mail: sara.grady@worcester.edu.

Yale University, Graduate School of Arts and Sciences, Department of Spanish and Portuguese, New Haven, CT 06520. Offers Latin American literature (PhD); Luso-Brazilian and Spanish/Spanish American literatures (PhD); Spanish peninsular literature (PhD). Terminal master's awarded for partial completion of doctoral program. *Degree requirements:* For doctorate, 3 foreign languages, thesis/dissertation. *Entrance requirements:* For doctorate, GRE General Test.

Section 10
Linguistic Studies

This section contains a directory of institutions offering graduate work in linguistic studies. Additional information about programs listed in the directory may be obtained by writing directly to the dean of a graduate school or chair of a department at the address given in the directory.

For programs offering related work, see also in this book Area and Cultural Studies, Language and Literature, and Sociology, Anthropology, and Archaeology.

CONTENTS

Program Directories

Linguistics

Arizona State University, College of Liberal Arts and Sciences, Department of English, Tempe, AZ 85287-0302. Offers applied linguistics (PhD); creative writing (MFA); English (MA, PhD), including comparative literature (MA), linguistics (MA), literature, rhetoric and composition (MA), rhetoric/composition and linguistics (PhD); linguistics (Graduate Certificate); teaching English to speakers of other languages (MTESOL). *Faculty:* 138 full-time (86 women). *Students:* 183 full-time (115 women), 98 part-time (73 women); includes 35 minority (6 Black or African American, non-Hispanic/Latino; 5 American Indian or Alaska Native, non-Hispanic/Latino; 10 Asian, non-Hispanic/Latino; 13 Hispanic/Latino; 1 Two or more races, non-Hispanic/Latino), 34 international. Average age 33. 597 applicants, 31% accepted, 88 enrolled. In 2010, 52 master's, 11 doctorates awarded. Terminal master's awarded for partial completion of doctoral program. *Degree requirements:* For master's, variable foreign language requirement, comprehensive exam (for some programs), thesis (for some programs), interactive Program of Study (iPOS) submitted before completing 50 percent of required credit hours; for doctorate, variable foreign language requirement, comprehensive exam, thesis/dissertation, interactive Program of Study (iPOS) submitted before completing 50 percent of required credit hours. *Entrance requirements:* For master's and doctorate, GRE, minimum GPA of 3.0 or equivalent in last 2 years of work leading to bachelor's degree. Additional exam requirements/recommendations for international students: Required—TOEFL, IELTS, or Pearson Test of English. *Application deadline:* For fall admission, 1/15 priority date for domestic students, 9/15 priority date for international students. Applications are processed on a rolling basis. Application fee: $70 ($90 for international students). Electronic applications accepted. *Expenses:* Tuition: state resident: full-time $8510; part-time $608 per credit. Tuition, nonresident: full-time $16,542; part-time $919 per credit. Required fees: $339; $110 per credit. Part-time tuition and fees vary according to course load. *Financial support:* In 2010–11, 12 research assistantships with tuition reimbursements (averaging $10,337 per year), 111 teaching assistantships with full and partial tuition reimbursements (averaging $13,799 per year) were awarded; fellowships with full tuition reimbursements, career-related internships or fieldwork, Federal Work-Study, institutionally sponsored loans, scholarships/grants, and tuition waivers (full and partial) also available. Financial award application deadline: 3/1; financial award applicants required to submit FAFSA. Total annual research expenditures: $734,687. *Unit head:* Dr. Maureen Goggin, Associate Chair, 480-965-1804, E-mail: maureen.goggin@asu.edu. *Application contact:* Graduate Admissions, 480-965-6113.

Ball State University, Graduate School, College of Sciences and Humanities, Department of English, Program in Linguistics, Muncie, IN 47306-1099. Offers applied linguistics (PhD); linguistics (MA). *Students:* 11 full-time (4 women), 10 part-time (6 women), 10 international. Average age 24. 39 applicants, 13% accepted, 2 enrolled. In 2010, 1 master's awarded. Application fee: $50. *Expenses:* Tuition, state resident: full-time $6160; part-time $299 per credit hour. Tuition, nonresident: full-time $16,020; part-time $783 per credit hour. Required fees: $2278; $95 per credit hour. *Financial support:* In 2010–11, 7 teaching assistantships (averaging $13,152 per year) were awarded; career-related internships or fieldwork and unspecified assistantships also available. Financial award application deadline: 3/1. *Faculty research:* Descriptive and theoretical linguistics. *Unit head:* Dr. Elizabeth Riddle, Director of Graduate Programs in English, 765-285-8415, Fax: 765-285-3765. *Application contact:* Dr. Jill Christman.

Biola University, School of Intercultural Studies, La Mirada, CA 90639-0001. Offers anthropology (MA); applied linguistics (MA); Biblical languages and linguistics (MA); intercultural education (PhD); intercultural studies (MAICS); linguistics (Certificate); missiology (D Miss); missions (MA); teaching English to speakers of other languages (MA, Certificate). Part-time and evening/weekend programs available. *Faculty:* 16 full-time (5 women), 6 part-time/adjunct (1 woman). *Students:* 66 full-time (39 women), 126 part-time (72 women); includes 48 minority (6 Black or African American, non-Hispanic/Latino; 40 Asian, non-Hispanic/Latino; 2 Two or more races, non-Hispanic/Latino), 30 international. 136 applicants, 70% accepted, 59 enrolled. In 2010, 27 master's, 10 doctorates awarded. Terminal master's awarded for partial completion of doctoral program. *Degree requirements:* For master's, one foreign language, comprehensive exam; for doctorate, one foreign language, comprehensive exam, thesis/dissertation. *Entrance requirements:* For master's, minimum undergraduate GPA of 3.0; for doctorate, MA, 3 years of ministry experience, minimum graduate GPA of 3.3. Additional exam requirements/recommendations for international students: Required—TOEFL (minimum score 550 paper-based; 213 computer-based). *Application deadline:* For fall admission, 7/1 for domestic students; for spring admission, 1/1 for domestic students. Applications are processed on a rolling basis. Application fee: $45. Electronic applications accepted. *Financial support:* Teaching assistantships, career-related internships or fieldwork, institutionally sponsored loans, and scholarships/grants available. Support available to part-time students. Financial award application deadline: 3/2; financial award applicants required to submit FAFSA. *Unit head:* Dr. Douglas Pennoyer, Dean, 562-903-4844, Fax: 562-903-4748, E-mail: douglas.pennoyer@biola.edu. *Application contact:* Roy M. Allinson, Director of Graduate Admissions, 562-903-4752, Fax: 562-903-4709, E-mail: admissions@biola.edu.

Boston College, Graduate School of Arts and Sciences, Department of Slavic and Eastern Languages, Program in Linguistics, Chestnut Hill, MA 02467-3800. Offers MA, MA/JD, MBA/MA. Part-time programs available. *Degree requirements:* For master's, 3 foreign languages, comprehensive exam, thesis or alternative. Electronic applications accepted.

Boston University, Graduate School of Arts and Sciences, Program in Applied Linguistics, Boston, MA 02215. Offers MA, PhD. Part-time programs available. *Faculty:* 17 full-time (9 women). *Students:* 14 full-time (7 women), 9 part-time (all women); includes 2 minority (both Black or African American, non-Hispanic/Latino), 5 international. Average age 34. 43 applicants, 9% accepted, 1 enrolled. Terminal master's awarded for partial completion of doctoral program. *Degree requirements:* For master's, one foreign language, project; for doctorate, 2 foreign languages, thesis/dissertation, 1 book review, 2 research papers, oral exam. *Entrance requirements:* For master's and doctorate, GRE General Test. Additional exam requirements/recommendations for international students: Required—TOEFL. *Application deadline:* For fall admission, 3/1 priority date for domestic and international students. Applications are processed on a rolling basis. Application fee: $60. Electronic applications accepted. *Expenses:* Tuition: Full-time $39,314; part-time $1228 per credit. Required fees: $40 per semester. *Financial support:* In 2010–11, 16 students received support, including 4 research assistantships with full tuition reimbursements available (averaging $18,800 per year), 2 teaching assistantships with full tuition reimbursements available (averaging $18,800 per year); Federal Work-Study, scholarships/grants, and unspecified assistantships also available. Financial award application deadline: 1/15; financial award applicants required to submit FAFSA. *Faculty research:* Psycholinguistics, sociolinguistics, neurolinguistics, language acquisition, American Sign Language. Total annual research expenditures: $900,000. *Unit head:* M. Catherine O'Connor, Director, 617-353-3318, Fax: 617-358-2353, E-mail: mco@bu.edu. *Application contact:* Hui-Wen Cheng, Program Assistant, 617-353-6197, Fax: 617-353-2353, E-mail: linguist@bu.edu.

Brandeis University, Graduate School of Arts and Sciences, Program in Computational Linguistics, Waltham, MA 02454-9110. Offers MA. Part-time programs available. *Faculty:* 13 full-time (3 women), 4 part-time/adjunct (2 women). *Students:* 13 full-time (6 women), 1 part-time (0 women); includes 1 Asian, non-Hispanic/Latino; 1 Hispanic/Latino, 3 international. 25 applicants, 68% accepted, 11 enrolled. In 2010, 4 master's awarded. *Degree requirements:* For master's, thesis. *Entrance requirements:* For master's, statement of purpose, 2 letters of recommendation, official transcripts, resume or curriculum vitae. Additional exam requirements/recommendations for international students: Required—TOEFL (minimum score 650 paper-based; 250 computer-based; 100 iBT); Recommended—IELTS (minimum score 7). *Application deadline:* Applications are processed on a rolling basis. Application fee: $75. Electronic applications accepted. *Financial support:* In 2010–11, 3 teaching assistantships with partial tuition reimbursements (averaging $3,200 per year) were awarded; institutionally sponsored loans and scholarships/grants also available. Financial award application deadline: 4/15; financial award applicants required to submit FAFSA. *Faculty research:* Computer science (artificial intelligence, theory of computation, and programming methods), language and linguistics (phonology, syntax, semantics, and pragmatics). *Unit head:* Dr. James Pustejovsky, Program Chair, 781-736-2701, Fax: 781-736-2741, E-mail: jamesp@brandeis.edu. *Application contact:* David F. Cotter, Graduate School of Arts and Sciences, 781-736-3410, Fax: 781-736-3412, E-mail: gradschool@brandeis.edu.

Brigham Young University, Graduate Studies, College of Humanities, Department of Linguistics and English Language, Provo, UT 84602. Offers general linguistics (MA); teaching English as a second language (MA, Certificate). Part-time programs available. *Faculty:* 22 full-time (6 women), 5 part-time/adjunct (all women). *Students:* 68 full-time (46 women); includes 9 Asian, non-Hispanic/Latino; 3 Hispanic/Latino. Average age 30. 73 applicants, 64% accepted, 44 enrolled. In 2010, 22 master's, 29 other advanced degrees awarded. *Degree requirements:* For master's, 2 foreign languages, thesis. *Entrance requirements:* For master's, GRE General Test, minimum GPA of 3.6 in last 60 hours of course work. Additional exam requirements/recommendations for international students: Required—TOEFL (minimum score 580 paper-based; 237 computer-based; 90 iBT), TWE. *Application deadline:* 1/15 for domestic and international students. Application fee: $50. Electronic applications accepted. *Expenses:* Tuition: Full-time $5580; part-time $310 per credit hour. Tuition and fees vary according to program and student's religious affiliation. *Financial support:* In 2010–11, 61 students received support, including 92 research assistantships with partial tuition reimbursements available (averaging $1,917 per year), 48 teaching assistantships with partial tuition reimbursements available (averaging $1,829 per year); fellowships with partial tuition reimbursements available, career-related internships or fieldwork, institutionally sponsored loans, scholarships/grants, tuition waivers (partial), unspecified assistantships, and student instructorships also available. Support available to part-time students. Financial award application deadline: 5/1. *Faculty research:* Teaching English to speakers of other languages, second language acquisition, computational linguistics, semiotics and semantics, computer-assisted language instruction. Total annual research expenditures: $197,644. *Unit head:* Dr. William G. Eggington, Chair, 801-422-2937, Fax: 801-422-0906, E-mail: bill_eggington@byu.edu. *Application contact:* LoriAnne Spear, Secretary, 801-422-9010, Fax: 801-422-0906, E-mail: lorianne_spear@byu.edu.

Brown University, Graduate School, Department of Cognitive and Linguistic Sciences, Providence, RI 02912. Offers cognitive science (Sc M, PhD); linguistics (AM, PhD). *Degree requirements:* For master's, one foreign language, thesis or alternative; for doctorate, 2 foreign languages, thesis/dissertation.

California State University, Fresno, Division of Graduate Studies, College of Arts and Humanities, Department of Linguistics, Fresno, CA 93740-8027. Offers linguistics (MA), including Teaching English as a second language. Part-time and evening/weekend programs available. *Degree requirements:* For master's, comprehensive exam. *Entrance requirements:* For master's, GRE General Test, minimum GPA of 3.0. Additional exam requirements/recommendations for international students: Required—TOEFL. Electronic applications accepted. *Faculty research:* Communication systems, bilingual education, animal communication, conflict resolution, literacy programs.

California State University, Fullerton, Graduate Studies, College of Humanities and Social Sciences, Program in Linguistics, Fullerton, CA 92834-9480. Offers analysis of specific language structures (MA); anthropological linguistics (MA); applied linguistics (MA); communication and semantics (MA); disorders of communication (MA); experimental phonetics (MA). Part-time programs available. *Students:* 12 full-time (8 women), 11 part-time (5 women); includes 4 Asian, non-Hispanic/Latino; 3 Hispanic/Latino, 6 international. Average age 34. 33 applicants, 52% accepted, 7 enrolled. In 2010, 8 master's awarded. *Degree requirements:* For master's, one foreign language, thesis or alternative, project. *Entrance requirements:* For master's, minimum GPA of 3.0, undergraduate major in linguistics or related field. Application fee: $55. *Financial support:* Career-related internships or fieldwork, Federal Work-Study, institutionally sponsored loans, and scholarships/grants available. Support available to part-time students. Financial award application deadline: 3/1; financial award applicants required to submit FAFSA. *Unit head:* Dr. Franz Muller-Gotama, Adviser, 657-278-2441. *Application contact:* Admissions/Applications, 657-278-2371.

California State University, Long Beach, Graduate Studies, College of Liberal Arts, Department of Linguistics, Long Beach, CA 90840. Offers general linguistics (MA); language and culture (MA); special concentration (MA); teaching English as a second language (MA). Part-time and evening/weekend programs available. *Faculty:* 9 full-time (6 women), 1 (woman) part-time/adjunct. *Students:* 31 full-time (21 women), 36 part-time (27 women); includes 1 American Indian or Alaska Native, non-Hispanic/Latino; 10 Asian, non-Hispanic/Latino; 9 Hispanic/Latino, 16 international. Average age 31. 62 applicants, 53% accepted, 29 enrolled. In 2010, 28 master's awarded. *Degree requirements:* For master's, one foreign language, comprehensive exam, thesis optional. *Application deadline:* For fall admission, 5/1 for domestic students. Applications are processed on a rolling basis. Application fee: $55. Electronic applications accepted. *Financial support:* Teaching assistantships, career-related internships or fieldwork, Federal Work-Study, institutionally sponsored loans, and scholarships/grants available. Financial award application deadline: 3/2. *Faculty research:* Pedagogy of language instruction, role of language in society, Khmer language instruction. *Unit head:* Dr. Malcolm Awadajin Finney, Chair, 562-985-7425, Fax: 562-985-2593, E-mail: mfinney@csulb.edu. *Application contact:* Dr. Xiaoping Liang, Graduate Advisor, 562-985-8509, Fax: 562-985-5792, E-mail: xliang@csulb.edu.

California State University, Northridge, Graduate Studies, College of Humanities, Linguistics Program, Northridge, CA 91330. Offers MA. Part-time and evening/weekend programs available. *Degree requirements:* For master's, one foreign language, comprehensive exam, thesis, or project. *Entrance requirements:* For master's, GRE General Test or minimum GPA of 3.0. Additional exam requirements/recommendations for international students: Required—TOEFL (minimum score 563 paper-based; 223 computer-based; 85 iBT). *Faculty research:* Ethnography of communication, stylistics, natural language processing, linguistics and humor, Otomanguean phonology and reconstruction.

Carleton University, Faculty of Graduate Studies, Faculty of Arts and Social Sciences, School of Linguistics and Applied Language Studies, Ottawa, ON K1S 5B6, Canada. Offers applied language studies (MA). *Degree requirements:* For master's, thesis optional. *Entrance requirements:* For master's, honors degree. Additional exam requirements/recommendations for international students: Required—TOEFL or CAEL. *Faculty research:* Language learning, acquisition and use of first and/or second languages in a variety of professional and academic contexts.

Carnegie Mellon University, College of Humanities and Social Sciences, Department of Modern Languages, Pittsburgh, PA 15213-3891. Offers second language acquisition (PhD). *Degree requirements:* For doctorate, one foreign language, comprehensive exam, thesis/dissertation. *Entrance requirements:* For doctorate, GRE General Test. Additional exam requirements/recommendations for international students: Required—TOEFL.

Case Western Reserve University, School of Graduate Studies, Department of Cognitive Science, Cleveland, OH 44106. Offers cognitive linguistics (MA). Part-time programs available. *Faculty:* 6 full-time (2 women), 2 part-time/adjunct (1 woman). *Students:* 2 full-time (0 women), 4 part-time (0 women). Average age 30. 7 applicants, 57% accepted, 2 enrolled. In 2010, 3 master's awarded. *Degree requirements:* For master's, thesis. *Entrance requirements:* For master's, GRE, recommendations, writing sample. Additional exam requirements/recommendations for international students: Required—TOEFL (minimum score 550 paper-based; 213 computer-based; 79 iBT). *Application deadline:* For fall admission, 5/1 priority date for domestic students. Application fee: $50. Electronic applications accepted. *Faculty research:*

Integrated, trans-disciplinary research into human higher-order cognition with emphases including the workings of the human mind in design, art, and technology, the interaction of brain and culture in development and evolution, the origins of human higher-order cognition. *Unit head:* Dr. Todd Oakley, Chair, 216-368-4753, E-mail: cogsci@case.edu. *Application contact:* Dr. Todd Oakley, Co-Director of Admission, 216-368-4753, E-mail: coglingadmission@case.edu.

Cleveland State University, College of Graduate Studies, College of Liberal Arts and Social Sciences, Department of Modern Languages, Cleveland, OH 44115. Offers French (M Ed); Spanish (M Ed, MA), including language and linguistics (MA), Latin American studies (MA), peninsular studies (MA), Spanish (MA). Part-time and evening/weekend programs available. *Faculty:* 12 full-time (9 women). *Students:* 7 full-time (4 women), 9 part-time (7 women); includes 1 Black or African American, non-Hispanic/Latino; 1 Asian, non-Hispanic/Latino; 3 Hispanic/Latino; 1 Two or more races, non-Hispanic/Latino, 2 international. Average age 37. 11 applicants, 100% accepted, 8 enrolled. In 2010, 9 master's awarded. *Degree requirements:* For master's, one foreign language, comprehensive exam, thesis optional, study abroad. *Entrance requirements:* For master's, undergraduate major in Spanish or equivalent, essay in Spanish, writing sample. Additional exam requirements/recommendations for international students: Required—TOEFL (minimum score 525 paper-based; 197 computer-based). *Application deadline:* For fall admission, 7/25 priority date for domestic students; for spring admission, 12/15 priority date for domestic students. Applications are processed on a rolling basis. Application fee: $30. Electronic applications accepted. *Expenses:* Tuition, state resident: full-time $8447; part-time $469 per credit hour. Tuition, nonresident: full-time $16,020; part-time $890 per credit hour. Required fees: $50. *Financial support:* In 2010–11, 6 students received support, including 6 teaching assistantships with full tuition reimbursements available (averaging $7,030 per year); Federal Work-Study also available. *Faculty research:* Second language acquisition, sociolinguistics, contemporary Spanish novel, Arabic diaspora in Latin America, border literature. *Unit head:* Dr. Tama L. Engelking, Chairperson, 216-523-7175, Fax: 216-687-4650, E-mail: t.engelking@csuohio.edu. *Application contact:* Dr. Antonio Medina-Rivera, Graduate Director, 216-523-7168, Fax: 216-687-4650, E-mail: a.medinarivera@csuohio.edu.

Concordia University, School of Graduate Studies, Faculty of Arts and Science, Department of Education, Program in Applied Linguistics, Montréal, QC H3G 1M8, Canada. Offers applied linguistics (MA); teaching English as a second language (Certificate).

Cornell University, Graduate School, Graduate Fields of Arts and Sciences, Field of Asian Studies, Ithaca, NY 14853-0001. Offers East Asian linguistics (MA); East Asian studies (MA); South Asian linguistics (MA); South Asian studies (MA); Southeast Asian linguistics (MA); Southeast Asian studies (MA). *Faculty:* 52 full-time (20 women). *Students:* 10 full-time (6 women); includes 1 Asian, non-Hispanic/Latino, 5 international. Average age 27. 75 applicants, 36% accepted, 10 enrolled. In 2010, 5 master's awarded. *Degree requirements:* For master's, one foreign language, thesis. *Entrance requirements:* For master's, GRE General Test, 3 letters of recommendation. Additional exam requirements/recommendations for international students: Required—TOEFL (minimum score 550 paper-based; 213 computer-based; 77 iBT). *Application deadline:* Applications are processed on a rolling basis. Application fee: $80. Electronic applications accepted. *Expenses:* Tuition: Full-time $29,500. Required fees: $76. Tuition and fees vary according to degree level and program. *Financial support:* In 2010–11, 2 fellowships with full tuition reimbursements, 2 teaching assistantships with full tuition reimbursements were awarded; research assistantships with full tuition reimbursements, institutionally sponsored loans, scholarships/grants, health care benefits, tuition waivers (full and partial), and unspecified assistantships also available. Financial award applicants required to submit FAFSA. *Faculty research:* East Asian studies, South Asian studies, Southeast Asian studies. *Unit head:* Director of Graduate Studies, 607-255-9099, Fax: 607-255-1345. *Application contact:* Graduate Field Assistant, 607-255-9099, Fax: 607-255-1345, E-mail: asian@cornell.edu.

Cornell University, Graduate School, Graduate Fields of Arts and Sciences, Field of Linguistics, Ithaca, NY 14853-0001. Offers applied linguistics (MA, PhD); East Asian linguistics (MA, PhD); English linguistics (MA, PhD); general linguistics (MA, PhD); Germanic linguistics (MA, PhD); Indo-European linguistics (MA, PhD); phonetics (MA, PhD); phonological theory (MA, PhD); Romance linguistics (MA, PhD); second language acquisition (MA, PhD); semantics (MA, PhD); Slavic linguistics (MA, PhD); sociolinguistics (MA, PhD); South Asian linguistics (MA, PhD); Southeast Asian linguistics (MA, PhD); syntactic theory (MA, PhD). *Faculty:* 15 full-time (7 women). *Students:* 34 full-time (18 women); includes 3 Hispanic/Latino, 15 international. Average age 28. 111 applicants, 12% accepted, 8 enrolled. In 2010, 2 master's, 6 doctorates awarded. Terminal master's awarded for partial completion of doctoral program. *Degree requirements:* For master's, one foreign language, thesis; for doctorate, one foreign language, comprehensive exam, thesis/dissertation. *Entrance requirements:* For master's and doctorate, GRE General Test, 2 letters of recommendation. Additional exam requirements/recommendations for international students: Required—TOEFL (minimum score 600 paper-based; 250 computer-based; 77 iBT). *Application deadline:* For fall admission, 1/15 for domestic students. Application fee: $80. Electronic applications accepted. *Expenses:* Tuition: Full-time $29,500. Required fees: $76. Tuition and fees vary according to degree level and program. *Financial support:* In 2010–11, 17 fellowships with full tuition reimbursements, 1 research assistantship with full tuition reimbursement, 15 teaching assistantships with full tuition reimbursements were awarded; institutionally sponsored loans, scholarships/grants, health care benefits, tuition waivers (full and partial), and unspecified assistantships also available. Financial award applicants required to submit FAFSA. *Faculty research:* Phonology and phonetics, syntax and semantics, historical linguistics, philosophy of language, language acquisition. *Unit head:* Director of Graduate Studies, 607-255-1105. *Application contact:* Graduate Field Assistant, 607-255-1105, E-mail: lingfield@cornell.edu.

Eastern Michigan University, Graduate School, College of Arts and Sciences, Department of English Language and Literature, Program in English Linguistics, Ypsilanti, MI 48197. Offers MA. Part-time and evening/weekend programs available. Postbaccalaureate distance learning degree programs offered (minimal on-campus study). *Students:* 14 full-time (7 women), 11 part-time (7 women); includes 3 minority (1 Black or African American, non-Hispanic/Latino; 2 Asian, non-Hispanic/Latino), 10 international. Average age 27. In 2010, 5 master's awarded. *Degree requirements:* For master's, thesis (for some programs). *Entrance requirements:* Additional exam requirements/recommendations for international students: Required—TOEFL. *Application deadline:* Applications are processed on a rolling basis. Application fee: $35. *Financial support:* Fellowships with tuition reimbursements, research assistantships with full tuition reimbursements, teaching assistantships with full tuition reimbursements, career-related internships or fieldwork, Federal Work-Study, institutionally sponsored loans, scholarships/grants, tuition waivers (partial), and unspecified assistantships available. Support available to part-time students. Financial award applicants required to submit FAFSA. *Application contact:* Dr. Veronica Grondona, Program Advisor, 734-487-0145, Fax: 734-483-9744, E-mail: vgrondona@emich.edu.

Florida Atlantic University, Dorothy F. Schmidt College of Arts and Letters, Department of Languages, Linguistics, and Comparative Literature, Boca Raton, FL 33431-0991. Offers comparative literature (MA); French (MA); linguistics (MA); Spanish (MA). Part-time programs available. *Faculty:* 30 full-time (24 women), 5 part-time/adjunct (all women). *Students:* 30 full-time (22 women), 19 part-time (15 women); includes 24 minority (4 Black or African American, non-Hispanic/Latino; 20 Hispanic/Latino), 6 international. Average age 34. 42 applicants, 57% accepted, 20 enrolled. In 2010, 5 master's awarded. *Degree requirements:* For master's, one foreign language, comprehensive exam, thesis optional. *Entrance requirements:* For master's, GRE General Test, minimum GPA of 3.0. *Application deadline:* For fall admission, 7/1 priority date for domestic students, 2/15 for international students; for spring admission, 11/1 for domestic students, 7/15 for international students. Applications are processed on a rolling basis. Application fee: $30. *Expenses:* Tuition, area resident: Part-time $319.96 per credit. Tuition, state resident: part-time $319.96 per credit. Tuition, nonresident: part-time $926.42 per credit. *Financial support:* Fellowships, research assistantships, teaching assistantships with partial tuition reimbursements, Federal Work-Study and tuition waivers (partial) available. Support available to part-time students. Financial award application deadline: 4/1. *Faculty research:* Modern European studies, modern Latin America, medieval Europe. *Unit head:* Dr. Michael Horswell, Chair, 561-297-3860, Fax: 561-297-2756, E-mail: horswell@fau.edu. *Application contact:* Dr. Emily Stockard, Associate Dean, 561-297-2817, Fax: 561-297-2744, E-mail: stockard@fau.edu.

Florida International University, College of Arts and Sciences, Department of English, Program in Linguistics, Miami, FL 33199. Offers MA. Part-time and evening/weekend programs available. *Students:* 18 full-time (14 women), 5 part-time (all women); includes 2 Asian, non-Hispanic/Latino; 9 Hispanic/Latino, 5 international. Average age 27. 38 applicants, 50% accepted, 18 enrolled. In 2010, 4 master's awarded. *Degree requirements:* For master's, thesis or alternative. *Entrance requirements:* For master's, minimum GPA of 3.0, letter of intent, two letters of recommendation. Additional exam requirements/recommendations for international students: Required—TOEFL (minimum score 550 paper-based; 80 iBT). *Application deadline:* For fall admission, 3/1 for domestic and international students; for spring admission, 10/1 for domestic students, 9/1 for international students. Application fee: $30. Electronic applications accepted. *Financial support:* Institutionally sponsored loans and scholarships/grants available. Financial award application deadline: 3/1; financial award applicants required to submit FAFSA. *Unit head:* Dr. James Sutton, Chair, English Department, 305-348-2874, Fax: 305-348-3878, E-mail: james.sutton@fiu.edu. *Application contact:* Dr. Feryal Yavas, Program DIrector, 305-348-3935, Fax: 305-348-3878, E-mail: yavas@fiu.edu.

Gallaudet University, The Graduate School, Washington, DC 20002-3625. Offers administration (MS); audiology (Au D, PhD); change leadership in education (Ed S); clinical psychology (PhD); deaf education (Ed D, PhD); deaf education: advanced studies (MA); deaf education: special programs in deaf education (MA); deaf history (Certificate); deaf studies (MA); education: teacher preparation (MA, MA Missions), including deaf education (MA), early childhood education and deaf education (MA), elementary education and deaf education (MA Missions), secondary education and deaf education (MA); hearing, speech and language sciences (MS); international development (MA); interpretation (MA, PhD); leadership (Certificate); leisure services administration (MS); linguistics (MA, PhD); management (Certificate); mental health counseling (MA); school counseling (MA); school counseling (summer session) (MA); school psychology (Psy S); sign language teaching (MA); social work (MSW); special education administration (PhD); speech-language pathology (PhD). Part-time programs available. *Faculty:* 116 full-time (86 women). *Students:* 291 full-time (224 women), 122 part-time (97 women); includes 142 minority (36 Black or African American, non-Hispanic/Latino; 3 American Indian or Alaska Native, non-Hispanic/Latino; 13 Asian, non-Hispanic/Latino; 29 Hispanic/Latino; 61 Two or more races, non-Hispanic/Latino), 28 international. Average age 30. 442 applicants, 52% accepted, 145 enrolled. In 2010, 116 master's, 17 doctorates, 16 other advanced degrees awarded. Terminal master's awarded for partial completion of doctoral program. *Degree requirements:* For master's, comprehensive exam (for some programs), thesis optional; for doctorate, comprehensive exam, thesis/dissertation. *Entrance requirements:* For master's and doctorate, GRE General Test or MAT, letters of recommendation, interviews, goals statement, ASL proficiency interview, written English competency. Additional exam requirements/recommendations for international students: Required—TOEFL. *Application deadline:* For fall admission, 2/15 for domestic students. Applications are processed on a rolling basis. Application fee: $50. Electronic applications accepted. *Expenses:* Tuition: Full-time $11,930; part-time $663 per credit. Required fees: $188 per semester. *Financial support:* In 2010–11, 219 students received support; fellowships, research assistantships, teaching assistantships, career-related internships or fieldwork, Federal Work-Study, scholarships/grants, tuition waivers (partial), and unspecified assistantships available. Support available to part-time students. Financial award applicants required to submit FAFSA. *Faculty research:* Bimodal bilingualism development, audiology, telecommunications access, early childhood education, linguistics, visual language and visual learning, rehabilitation and hearing enhancement. *Unit head:* Dr. Carol J. Erting, Dean, 202-651-5520, Fax: 202-651-5027, E-mail: carol.erting@gallaudet.edu. *Application contact:* Wednesday Luria, Coordinator of Prospective Graduate Student Services, 202-651-5400, Fax: 202-651-5295, E-mail: graduate.school@gallaudet.edu.

George Mason University, College of Humanities and Social Sciences, Department of English, Fairfax, VA 22030. Offers creative writing (MFA); English (MA); folklore studies (Certificate); linguistics (PhD); professional writing and rhetoric (Certificate); teaching English as a second language (Certificate). *Faculty:* 82 full-time (45 women), 35 part-time/adjunct (22 women). *Students:* 69 full-time (45 women), 208 part-time (153 women); includes 13 Black or African American, non-Hispanic/Latino; 3 American Indian or Alaska Native, non-Hispanic/Latino; 20 Asian, non-Hispanic/Latino; 6 Hispanic/Latino; 4 Two or more races, non-Hispanic/Latino, 10 international. Average age 31. 391 applicants, 56% accepted, 96 enrolled. In 2010, 116 master's, 11 other advanced degrees awarded. *Degree requirements:* For master's, thesis (for some programs), proficiency in a foreign language by course work or translation test. *Entrance requirements:* For master's, 30 credits in graduate English courses, minimum undergraduate GPA of 3.0, 2 letters of recommendation. Additional exam requirements/recommendations for international students: Required—TOEFL (minimum score 570 paper-based; 230 computer-based; 88 iBT). *Application deadline:* For fall admission, 3/15 priority date for domestic students; for spring admission, 10/15 for domestic students. Application fee: $100. Electronic applications accepted. *Expenses:* Tuition, state resident: full-time $8192; part-time $440 per credit hour. Tuition, nonresident: full-time $22,952; part-time $1055 per credit hour. Required fees: $2364; $99 per credit hour. *Financial support:* In 2010–11, 50 students received support, including 2 fellowships with full tuition reimbursements available (averaging $18,000 per year), 5 research assistantships with full and partial tuition reimbursements available (averaging $11,251 per year), 44 teaching assistantships with full and partial tuition reimbursements available (averaging $11,009 per year); Federal Work-Study, scholarships/grants, unspecified assistantships, and health care benefits (full-time research or teaching assistantship recipients) also available. Financial award application deadline: 3/1; financial award applicants required to submit FAFSA. *Faculty research:* Literature, professional writing and editing, writing of fiction or poetry. Total annual research expenditures: $1.2 million. *Unit head:* Robert Matz, Chair, 703-993-1170, E-mail: rmatz@gmu.edu. *Application contact:* Denise Albanese, Graduate Director, 703-993-1175, E-mail: dalbanes@gmu.edu.

Georgetown University, Graduate School of Arts and Sciences, Department of Linguistics, Washington, DC 20057. Offers bilingual education (Certificate); language and communication (MA); linguistics (MS, PhD), including applied linguistics, computational linguistics, sociolinguistics, theoretical linguistics; teaching English as a second language (MAT, Certificate); teaching English as a second language and bilingual education (MAT). Terminal master's awarded for partial completion of doctoral program. *Degree requirements:* For master's, one foreign language, comprehensive exam, optional research project; for doctorate, 2 foreign languages, comprehensive exam, thesis/dissertation. *Entrance requirements:* For master's and doctorate, 18 undergraduate credits in a foreign language. Additional exam requirements/recommendations for international students: Required—TOEFL.

Georgia State University, College of Arts and Sciences, Department of Applied Linguistics and English as a Second Language, Atlanta, GA 30302-3083. Offers applied linguistics (MA, PhD). Part-time programs available. *Degree requirements:* For master's, one foreign language, portfolio; for doctorate, one foreign language, comprehensive exam, thesis/dissertation, qualifying paper. *Entrance requirements:* For master's, GRE General Test; for doctorate, GRE. Additional exam requirements/recommendations for international students: Required—TOEFL (minimum score 600 paper-based; 250 computer-based; 97 iBT), TWE (minimum score 5). Electronic applications accepted. *Faculty research:* Native language and second language, second language literacy, intercultural communication, classroom-centered research, learning styles/strategies.

Graduate Institute of Applied Linguistics, Graduate Programs, Dallas, TX 75236. Offers applied linguistics (MA, Certificate); language development (MA). Part-time programs available. *Degree requirements:* For master's, one foreign language, comprehensive exam (for some programs), thesis (for some programs). *Entrance requirements:* For master's, GRE. Additional exam requirements/recommendations for international students: Required—TOEFL (minimum

Linguistics

Graduate Institute of Applied Linguistics (continued)
score 577 paper-based; 233 computer-based; 90 iBT). Electronic applications accepted. *Faculty research:* Minority languages, endangered languages, language documentation.

Graduate School and University Center of the City University of New York, Graduate Studies, Program in Anthropology, New York, NY 10016-4039. Offers anthropological linguistics (PhD); archaeology (PhD); cultural anthropology (PhD); physical anthropology (PhD). *Degree requirements:* For doctorate, one foreign language, thesis/dissertation. *Entrance requirements:* For doctorate, GRE General Test. Additional exam requirements/recommendations for international students: Required—TOEFL. Electronic applications accepted.

Graduate School and University Center of the City University of New York, Graduate Studies, Program in Linguistics, New York, NY 10016-4039. Offers MA, PhD. Terminal master's awarded for partial completion of doctoral program. *Degree requirements:* For master's, one foreign language, thesis; for doctorate, 2 foreign languages, thesis/dissertation. *Entrance requirements:* For master's and doctorate, GRE General Test. Additional exam requirements/recommendations for international students: Required—TOEFL. Electronic applications accepted.

Harvard University, Graduate School of Arts and Sciences, Department of Linguistics, Cambridge, MA 02138. Offers descriptive linguistics (PhD); historical linguistics (PhD); theoretical linguistics (PhD). *Degree requirements:* For doctorate, 4 foreign languages, thesis/dissertation, field exam, Indo-European language exam, research paper. *Entrance requirements:* For doctorate, GRE General Test. Additional exam requirements/recommendations for international students: Required—TOEFL. *Expenses:* Tuition: Full-time $34,976. Required fees: $1166. Full-time tuition and fees vary according to program.

Hofstra University, College of Liberal Arts and Sciences, Programs in Forensic and Applied Linguistics, Hempstead, NY 11549. Offers applied linguistics (TESOL) (MA); linguistics (MA), including forensic linguistics. Part-time programs available. *Faculty:* 13 full-time (6 women), 1 part-time/adjunct (0 women). *Students:* 8 full-time (5 women), 2 part-time (both women), 3 international. Average age 32. 17 applicants, 76% accepted, 6 enrolled. *Degree requirements:* For master's, thesis, 36 credits; capstone. *Entrance requirements:* For master's, Bachelor's degree in related area; Interview; 2 letters of recommendation. Additional exam requirements/recommendations for international students: Required—TOEFL (minimum score 550 paper-based; 213 computer-based; 80 iBT). *Application deadline:* Applications are processed on a rolling basis. Application fee: $70 ($75 for international students). Electronic applications accepted. *Expenses:* Tuition: Full-time $18,000; part-time $1000 per credit hour. Required fees: $970; $145 per term. Tuition and fees vary according to program. *Financial support:* In 2010–11, 7 students received support; fellowships with full and partial tuition reimbursements available, research assistantships with full and partial tuition reimbursements available, Federal Work-Study, institutionally sponsored loans, scholarships/grants, tuition waivers (full and partial), and unspecified assistantships available. Support available to part-time students. Financial award applicants required to submit FAFSA. *Faculty research:* Application of linguistics to forensic data, interrogation techniques and invalid confessions, authorship analysis, forensic linguistically-enhanced threat assessment, second language acquisition, second language writing. *Unit head:* Dr. George L. Greaney, Director, 516-463-5651, E-mail: cllglg@hofstra.edu. *Application contact:* Carol Drummer, Dean of Graduate Admissions, 516-463-4876, Fax: 516-463-4664, E-mail: gradstudent@hofstra.edu.

Hofstra University, School of Education, Health, and Human Services, Programs in Learning and Teaching, Hempstead, NY 11549. Offers learning and teaching (Ed D), including applied linguistics, art education, arts and humanities, early childhood education, English education, human development, math education, math, science, and technology, multicultural education, physical education, science education, social studies education, special education. Part-time and evening/weekend programs available. *Students:* 2 full-time (both women), 26 part-time (21 women); includes 2 Black or African American, non-Hispanic/Latino, 1 international. Average age 36. 26 applicants, 38% accepted, 9 enrolled. *Degree requirements:* For doctorate, comprehensive exam, thesis/dissertation. *Entrance requirements:* For doctorate, GRE, 3 letters of recommendation, essay, interview, 2 years full-time teaching. Additional exam requirements/recommendations for international students: Required—TOEFL (minimum score 550 paper-based; 213 computer-based; 80 iBT). *Application deadline:* Applications are processed on a rolling basis. Application fee: $70 ($75 for international students). Electronic applications accepted. *Expenses:* Tuition: Full-time $18,000; part-time $1000 per credit hour. Required fees: $970; $145 per term. Tuition and fees vary according to program. *Financial support:* In 2010–11, 27 students received support, including 22 fellowships with full and partial tuition reimbursements available (averaging $5,468 per year); research assistantships with full and partial tuition reimbursements available, Federal Work-Study, institutionally sponsored loans, scholarships/grants, tuition waivers (full and partial), and scholarships also available. Support available to part-time students. Financial award applicants required to submit FAFSA. *Faculty research:* Critical thinking, professional development, teacher quality, quantitative research. *Unit head:* Dr. Esther Fusco, Chairperson, 516-463-7704, Fax: 516-463-6196, E-mail: catajs@hofstra.edu. *Application contact:* Carol Drummer, Dean of Graduate Admissions, 516-463-4876, Fax: 516-463-4664, E-mail: gradstudent@hofstra.edu.

Indiana State University, College of Graduate and Professional Studies, College of Arts and Sciences, Department of Languages, Literatures, and Linguistics, Terre Haute, IN 47809. Offers linguistics/teaching English as a second language (MA); TESL/TEFL (CAS). *Degree requirements:* For master's, comprehensive exam. Electronic applications accepted.

Indiana University Bloomington, University Graduate School, College of Arts and Sciences, Department of French and Italian, Bloomington, IN 47405-7000. Offers French (MA, PhD), including French instruction (MA), French linguistics, French literature; Italian (MA, PhD). Part-time programs available. *Faculty:* 19 full-time (7 women). *Students:* 69 full-time (43 women), 5 part-time (2 women); includes 2 minority (1 American Indian or Alaska Native, non-Hispanic/Latino; 1 Hispanic/Latino), 23 international. Average age 30. 73 applicants, 67% accepted, 14 enrolled. In 2010, 14 master's, 6 doctorates awarded. Terminal master's awarded for partial completion of doctoral program. *Degree requirements:* For master's, one foreign language, comprehensive exam, thesis optional; for doctorate, 2 foreign languages, comprehensive exam, thesis/dissertation. *Entrance requirements:* For master's and doctorate, GRE General Test. Additional exam requirements/recommendations for international students: Required—TOEFL (minimum score 550 paper-based; 213 computer-based; 79 iBT). *Application deadline:* For fall admission, 1/15 priority date for domestic students, 12/1 priority date for international students; for spring admission, 9/1 priority date for domestic and international students. Application fee: $55 ($65 for international students). Electronic applications accepted. *Financial support:* In 2010–11, 2 fellowships with partial tuition reimbursements (averaging $14,000 per year), 4 research assistantships with partial tuition reimbursements (averaging $13,913 per year), 20 teaching assistantships with partial tuition reimbursements (averaging $12,944 per year) were awarded. Financial award application deadline: 1/15. *Faculty research:* All periods of French and Italian literature and various areas of French linguistics, including the novel and political theory, literature and fine arts, literary theory, postcolonialism, French-Creole studies, French literature of Africa and its Diaspora, humanism, medieval folklore and mythology, humor in medieval and Renaissance literature, cinema Old Occitan and Old French, emigration, second language acquisition, syntax, sociolinguistics, phonology, lexicography. *Unit head:* Prof. Emanuel Mickel, Interim Chairman, 812-855-5458, Fax: 812-855-8877, E-mail: fritchr@indiana.edu. *Application contact:* Jocelyn Karlan, Secretary, 812-855-1088, Fax: 812-855-8877, E-mail: fritgs@indiana.edu.

Indiana University Bloomington, University Graduate School, College of Arts and Sciences, Department of Germanic Studies, Bloomington, IN 47405-7000. Offers German philology and linguistics (PhD); German studies (MA, PhD), including German (MA), German literature and culture (MA), German literature and linguistics (MA); medieval German studies (PhD); teaching German (MAT). *Faculty:* 13 full-time (4 women), 6 part-time/adjunct (2 women). *Students:* 35 full-time (19 women), 2 part-time (1 woman); includes 1 Black or African American, non-Hispanic/

Latino; 1 Hispanic/Latino, 8 international. Average age 31. 34 applicants, 41% accepted, 5 enrolled. In 2010, 6 master's, 3 doctorates awarded. Terminal master's awarded for partial completion of doctoral program. *Degree requirements:* For master's, one foreign language, project; for doctorate, one foreign language, comprehensive exam, thesis/dissertation. *Entrance requirements:* For master's, GRE General Test, BA in German or equivalent; for doctorate, GRE General Test, MA in German or equivalent. Additional exam requirements/recommendations for international students: Required—TOEFL. *Application deadline:* For fall admission, 1/15 priority date for domestic students, 12/15 for international students; for spring admission, 9/1 priority date for domestic students, 9/1 for international students. Applications are processed on a rolling basis. Application fee: $55 ($65 for international students). *Financial support:* In 2010–11, 7 fellowships with full and partial tuition reimbursements (averaging $16,000 per year), 17 teaching assistantships with full tuition reimbursements (averaging $13,455 per year) were awarded; research assistantships, Federal Work-Study, institutionally sponsored loans, scholarships/grants, and unspecified assistantships also available. Support available to part-time students. Financial award application deadline: 1/15; financial award applicants required to submit FAFSA. *Faculty research:* German and other European literature: medieval to modern/postmodern, German and culture studies, Germanic philology, literary theory, literature and the other arts. *Unit head:* William Rasch, Department Chairman, 812-855-7947, Fax: 812-855-8292, E-mail: wrasch@indiana.edu. *Application contact:* Michelle Dunbar, Graduate Secretary, 812-855-7947, E-mail: midunbar@indiana.edu.

Indiana University Bloomington, University Graduate School, College of Arts and Sciences, Department of Linguistics, Bloomington, IN 47405-7000. Offers African languages and linguistics (PhD); computational linguistics (MA, PhD); linguistics (MA, PhD). *Faculty:* 10 full-time (1 woman), 18 part-time/adjunct (7 women). *Students:* 78 full-time (42 women); includes 6 minority (3 Black or African American, non-Hispanic/Latino; 2 Asian, non-Hispanic/Latino; 1 Hispanic/Latino), 28 international. Average age 32. 71 applicants, 44% accepted, 7 enrolled. In 2010, 10 master's, 12 doctorates awarded. Terminal master's awarded for partial completion of doctoral program. *Degree requirements:* For master's, one foreign language, thesis optional; for doctorate, one foreign language, comprehensive exam, thesis/dissertation, proficiency in research tool appropriate to research area. *Entrance requirements:* For master's and doctorate, GRE General Test. Additional exam requirements/recommendations for international students: Required—TOEFL (minimum score 580 paper-based; 237 computer-based; 92 iBT). *Application deadline:* For fall admission, 1/15 priority date for domestic students, 12/1 priority date for international students. Application fee: $55 ($65 for international students). Electronic applications accepted. *Financial support:* In 2010–11, 7 fellowships with full tuition reimbursements (averaging $18,150 per year), 5 research assistantships with full tuition reimbursements (averaging $12,580 per year), 22 teaching assistantships with full tuition reimbursements (averaging $12,660 per year) were awarded; unspecified assistantships also available. *Faculty research:* African linguistics and language, semantics, phonology, syntactic theory, historical linguistics, phonetics-phonology, syntax, sociolinguistics, computational linguistics. Total annual research expenditures: $100,000. *Unit head:* Dr. Stuart Davis, Chair, 812-855-6456, Fax: 812-855-5363, E-mail: davis@indiana.edu. *Application contact:* Margaret Anderson, Secretary, 812-855-6456, Fax: 812-855-5363, E-mail: maraande@indiana.edu.

Indiana University of Pennsylvania, School of Graduate Studies and Research, College of Humanities and Social Sciences, Department of English, Indiana, PA 15705-1087. Offers composition and teaching English to speakers of other languages (MA, MAT, PhD), including composition and teaching English to speakers of other languages (PhD), teaching English (MAT), teaching English to speakers of other languages (MA); literature and criticism (MA, PhD), including generalist (MA), literature (MA), literature and criticism (PhD); rhetoric and linguistics (PhD). Part-time programs available. *Faculty:* 30 full-time (12 women). *Students:* 113 full-time (71 women), 254 part-time (155 women); includes 25 minority (11 Black or African American, non-Hispanic/Latino; 1 American Indian or Alaska Native, non-Hispanic/Latino; 7 Asian, non-Hispanic/Latino; 5 Hispanic/Latino; 1 Two or more races, non-Hispanic/Latino), 99 international. Average age 35. 350 applicants, 37% accepted, 63 enrolled. In 2010, 31 master's, 36 doctorates awarded. *Degree requirements:* For master's, thesis optional; for doctorate, one foreign language, comprehensive exam, thesis/dissertation. *Entrance requirements:* For master's and doctorate, 2 letters of recommendation. Additional exam requirements/recommendations for international students: Required—TOEFL. *Application deadline:* For fall admission, 7/1 priority date for domestic students; for spring admission, 11/1 for domestic students. Applications are processed on a rolling basis. Application fee: $40. *Financial support:* In 2010–11, 8 fellowships (averaging $1,063 per year), 32 research assistantships with full and partial tuition reimbursements (averaging $6,053 per year), 21 teaching assistantships with partial tuition reimbursements (averaging $12,679 per year) were awarded. Financial award application deadline: 3/15; financial award applicants required to submit FAFSA. *Unit head:* Dr. Gail I. Berlin, Chairperson, 724-357-2261, E-mail: ivy@iup.edu. *Application contact:* Dr. Gail I. Berlin, Chairperson, 724-357-2261, E-mail: ivy@iup.edu.

Instituto Tecnologico de Santo Domingo, Graduate School, Area of Humanities and Social Sciences, Santo Domingo, Dominican Republic. Offers accounting (Certificate); adult education (Certificate); applied linguistics (MA); economics (MA); education (M Ed); educational psychology (MA, Certificate); gender and development (MA, Certificate); humanistic studies (MA); international marketing management (Certificate); international relations in the Caribbean basin (Certificate); intervention systems in family therapy (MA); linguistic and literary communication (Certificate); pedagogical support (MA); social science education (M Ed); sustainable human development (MA); terminal illness and death psychology (Certificate); youth and adult education (M Ed).

Louisiana State University and Agricultural and Mechanical College, Graduate School, College of Humanities and Social Sciences, Interdepartmental Program in Linguistics, Baton Rouge, LA 70803. Offers MA, PhD. *Students:* 9 full-time (8 women), 2 part-time (both women); includes 1 Black or African American, non-Hispanic/Latino, 6 international. Average age 34. 1 applicant, 0% accepted, 0 enrolled. In 2010, 3 master's, 2 doctorates awarded. Terminal master's awarded for partial completion of doctoral program. *Degree requirements:* For master's, one foreign language, thesis or alternative; for doctorate, one foreign language, thesis/dissertation. *Entrance requirements:* For master's, GRE General Test, minimum GPA of 3.0; for doctorate, GRE General Test. Additional exam requirements/recommendations for international students: Required—TOEFL (minimum score 550 paper-based; 213 computer-based; 79 iBT) or IELTS (minimum score 6.5). *Application deadline:* For fall admission, 1/25 priority date for domestic students, 5/15 for international students; for spring admission, 10/15 for international students. Applications are processed on a rolling basis. Application fee: $50 ($70 for international students). Electronic applications accepted. *Financial support:* In 2010–11, 6 students received support, including 1 research assistantship with partial tuition reimbursement available (averaging $12,000 per year), 4 teaching assistantships with partial tuition reimbursements available (averaging $10,725 per year); fellowships with full and partial tuition reimbursements available, health care benefits also available. Financial award application deadline: 5/1; financial award applicants required to submit FAFSA. *Faculty research:* Neurolinguistics, speech science, English as a second language, Hispanic linguistics, anthropological linguistics. *Unit head:* Dr. Lisi Oliver, Director, 225-578-4252, E-mail: lolive1@lsu.edu. *Application contact:* Dr. Lisi Oliver, Director, 225-578-4252, E-mail: lolive1@lsu.edu.

Massachusetts Institute of Technology, School of Humanities, Arts, and Social Sciences, Department of Linguistics and Philosophy, Linguistics Section, Cambridge, MA 02139. Offers PhD. *Faculty:* 13 full-time (4 women). *Students:* 41 full-time (13 women), 1 (woman) part-time; includes 4 minority (1 American Indian or Alaska Native, non-Hispanic/Latino; 2 Asian, non-Hispanic/Latino; 1 Two or more races, non-Hispanic/Latino), 28 international. Average age 28. 172 applicants, 8% accepted, 12 enrolled. In 2010, 3 doctorates awarded. *Degree requirements:* For doctorate, one foreign language, comprehensive exam, thesis/dissertation. *Entrance requirements:* Additional exam requirements/recommendations for international students: Required—TOEFL (minimum score 577 paper-based; 233 computer-based; 90 iBT), IELTS (minimum score 6.5). *Application deadline:* For fall admission, 1/2 for domestic and international students. Application fee: $75. Electronic applications accepted. *Expenses:* Tuition:

Full-time $38,940; part-time $605 per unit. Required fees: $272. *Financial support:* In 2010–11, 27 fellowships with tuition reimbursements (averaging $32,245 per year), 12 research assistantships with tuition reimbursements (averaging $33,060 per year) were awarded; teaching assistantships with tuition reimbursements, Federal Work-Study, institutionally sponsored loans, scholarships/grants, health care benefits, and unspecified assistantships also available. *Unit head:* Prof. Irene Heim, Department Head and Linguistics Chair, 617-253-4141, Fax: 617-253-5017. *Application contact:* Graduate Admissions, 617-253-4141, Fax: 617-253-5017, E-mail: lp-admissions@mit.edu.

McGill University, Faculty of Graduate and Postdoctoral Studies, Faculty of Arts, Department of Linguistics, Montréal, QC H3A 2T5, Canada. Offers language acquisition (PhD); linguistics (MA, PhD).

Memorial University of Newfoundland, School of Graduate Studies, Department of Linguistics, St. John's, NL A1C 5S7, Canada. Offers MA, PhD. *Degree requirements:* For master's, one foreign language, thesis or comprehensive exam; for doctorate, 2 foreign languages, comprehensive exam, thesis/dissertation, oral defense of thesis. *Entrance requirements:* For master's, BA in linguistics; for doctorate, master's degree in linguistics. Electronic applications accepted. *Faculty research:* Aboriginal languages of eastern North America, historical/comparative linguistics, languages and dialects of Newfoundland and Labrador.

Michigan State University, The Graduate School, College of Arts and Letters, Department of Linguistics and Germanic, Slavic, Asian, and African Languages, East Lansing, MI 48824. Offers German studies (MA, PhD); linguistics (MA, PhD); teaching English to speakers of other languages (MA). Part-time and evening/weekend programs available. *Entrance requirements:* For master's, GRE General Test, minimum GPA of 3.2 in last 2 undergraduate years, 2 years of college-level foreign language, 3 letters of recommendation, portfolio (German studies); for doctorate, GRE General Test, minimum graduate GPA of 3.5, 3 letters of recommendation, master's degree or sufficient graduate course work in linguistics or language of study, master's thesis or major research paper. Additional exam requirements/recommendations for international students: Required—TOEFL. Electronic applications accepted.

Michigan State University, The Graduate School, College of Arts and Letters, Department of Spanish and Portuguese, East Lansing, MI 48824. Offers applied Spanish linguistics (MA); Hispanic cultural studies (PhD); Hispanic literatures (MA). *Entrance requirements:* Additional exam requirements/recommendations for international students: Required—TOEFL. Electronic applications accepted.

Midwestern Baptist Theological Seminary, Graduate and Professional Programs, Kansas City, MO 64118-4697. Offers Biblical archaeology (MA); Biblical languages (MA); Christian education (M Div, MACE); Christian foundations—lay ministry (Graduate Certificate); collegiate ministries (M Div); counseling (MA); educational ministry (D Ed Min); international church planting (M Div); ministry (M Div, D Min); North American church planting (M Div); sacred music (MCM); urban ministry (M Div); worship leadership (M Div); youth ministry (M Div). *Accreditation:* ATS. Part-time programs available. Postbaccalaureate distance learning degree programs offered (minimal on-campus study). *Degree requirements:* For doctorate, thesis/dissertation; for M Div, 2 foreign languages. *Entrance requirements:* For doctorate, MAT. Electronic applications accepted. *Faculty research:* Ministerial studies, Biblical and theological studies, missions, counseling.

Montclair State University, The Graduate School, College of Humanities and Social Sciences, Department of Linguistics, Montclair, NJ 07043-1624. Offers applied linguistics (MA); teaching English as a second language (Certificate). Part-time and evening/weekend programs available. *Faculty:* 7 full-time (6 women), 22 part-time/adjunct (19 women). *Students:* 15 full-time (11 women), 19 part-time (16 women); includes 3 Black or African American, non-Hispanic/Latino; 2 Asian, non-Hispanic/Latino; 5 Hispanic/Latino, 3 international. Average age 36. 14 applicants, 64% accepted, 5 enrolled. In 2010, 11 master's, 1 other advanced degree awarded. *Degree requirements:* For master's, comprehensive exam. *Entrance requirements:* For master's, GRE General Test, 2 letters of recommendation. Additional exam requirements/recommendations for international students: Required—TOEFL (minimum iBT score of 83) or IELTS. *Application deadline:* For fall admission, 6/1 for international students; for spring admission, 10/1 for international students. Applications are processed on a rolling basis. Application fee: $60. Electronic applications accepted. *Expenses:* Tuition, state resident: part-time $501.34 per credit. Tuition, nonresident: part-time $773.88 per credit. Required fees: $71.15 per credit. *Financial support:* In 2010–11, 3 research assistantships with full tuition reimbursements (averaging $7,000 per year) were awarded; Federal Work-Study, scholarships/grants, and unspecified assistantships also available. Support available to part-time students. Financial award application deadline: 3/1; financial award applicants required to submit FAFSA. *Faculty research:* Cognitive processing of first and second languages, questions in institutional discourse, cognitive modeling of bilingualism, acquisition of sign languages, computer-mediated communication, rapid multilingual computer resource development, computer modeling of deception. Total annual research expenditures: $110,000. *Unit head:* Dr. Eileen Fitzpatrick, Chairperson, 973-655-4480. *Application contact:* Amy Aiello, Director of Graduate Admissions and Operations, 973-655-5147, E-mail: graduate.school@montclair.edu.

New York University, Graduate School of Arts and Science, Department of Linguistics, New York, NY 10012-1019. Offers MA, PhD. Part-time programs available. *Faculty:* 8 full-time (2 women). *Students:* 39 full-time (19 women), 3 part-time (2 women); includes 2 Black or African American, non-Hispanic/Latino; 1 Hispanic/Latino, 16 international. Average age 30. 126 applicants, 9% accepted, 6 enrolled. In 2010, 2 master's, 10 doctorates awarded. Terminal master's awarded for partial completion of doctoral program. *Degree requirements:* For master's, one foreign language, comprehensive exam, thesis optional; for doctorate, one foreign language, thesis/dissertation, 2 publishable papers. *Entrance requirements:* For master's and doctorate, GRE General Test. Additional exam requirements/recommendations for international students: Required—TOEFL. *Application deadline:* For fall admission, 1/4 priority date for domestic students. Application fee: $90. *Financial support:* Fellowships with tuition reimbursements, teaching assistantships with tuition reimbursements, Federal Work-Study, institutionally sponsored loans, scholarships/grants, health care benefits, and unspecified assistantships available. Financial award application deadline: 1/4; financial award applicants required to submit FAFSA. *Faculty research:* Phonology, syntax, sociolinguistics, cognitive science. *Unit head:* Alec Marantz, Chairman, 212-998-7950, Fax: 212-995-4707, E-mail: linguistics@nyu.edu. *Application contact:* Chris Barker, Director of Graduate Studies, 212-998-7950, Fax: 212-995-4707, E-mail: linguistics@nyu.edu.

New York University, Steinhardt School of Culture, Education, and Human Development, Department of Teaching and Learning, Program in English Education, New York, NY 10012-1019. Offers secondary and college (PhD), including applied linguistics, comparative education, curriculum, literature and reading, media education; teachers of English 7-12 (MA); teachers of English language and literature in college (Advanced Certificate). *Accreditation:* Teacher Education Accreditation Council. Part-time programs available. *Faculty:* 4 full-time (3 women). *Students:* 43 full-time (35 women), 22 part-time (19 women); includes 5 Black or African American, non-Hispanic/Latino; 3 Asian, non-Hispanic/Latino; 2 Hispanic/Latino, 2 international. Average age 30. 95 applicants, 71% accepted, 14 enrolled. In 2010, 25 master's, 1 doctorate, 1 other advanced degree awarded. *Degree requirements:* For master's, thesis (for some programs); for doctorate, thesis/dissertation. *Entrance requirements:* For doctorate, GRE General Test, interview; for Advanced Certificate, master's degree. Additional exam requirements/recommendations for international students: Required—TOEFL. *Application deadline:* For fall admission, 12/1 priority date for domestic and international students; for spring admission, 11/1 for domestic and international students. Applications are processed on a rolling basis. Application fee: $75. Electronic applications accepted. *Financial support:* Fellowships with full and partial tuition reimbursements, teaching assistantships with full and partial tuition reimbursements, career-related internships or fieldwork, Federal Work-Study, institutionally sponsored loans, scholarships/grants, tuition waivers (partial), and unspecified assistantships available. Support available to part-time students. Financial award application deadline: 2/1; financial award applicants required to submit FAFSA. *Faculty research:* Making meaning of literature, teaching of literature, urban adolescent literacy and equity, literacy development and globalization, digital media and literacy. *Unit head:* Director, 212-998-5460, Fax: 212-995-4049. *Application contact:* 212-998-5030, Fax: 212-995-4328, E-mail: steinhardt.gradadmissions@nyu.edu.

Northeastern Illinois University, Graduate College, College of Arts and Sciences, Department of Linguistics, Program in Linguistics, Chicago, IL 60625-4699. Offers linguistics (MA); TESL (MA). Part-time and evening/weekend programs available. *Faculty:* 7 full-time (5 women), 3 part-time/adjunct (2 women). *Students:* 35 full-time (22 women), 113 part-time (84 women); includes 30 minority (10 Black or African American, non-Hispanic/Latino; 10 Asian, non-Hispanic/Latino; 8 Hispanic/Latino; 2 Two or more races, non-Hispanic/Latino), 7 international. Average age 32. 60 applicants, 83% accepted, 47 enrolled. In 2010, 50 master's awarded. *Degree requirements:* For master's, one foreign language, comprehensive exam, thesis optional. *Entrance requirements:* For master's, 9 undergraduate hours in a foreign language or equivalent, minimum GPA of 2.75. Additional exam requirements/recommendations for international students: Required—TOEFL (minimum score 550 paper-based; 213 computer-based; 79 iBT). *Application deadline:* Applications are processed on a rolling basis. Application fee: $30. Electronic applications accepted. *Financial support:* In 2010–11, 41 students received support, including 6 research assistantships with full and partial tuition reimbursements available (averaging $6,600 per year); career-related internships or fieldwork, Federal Work-Study, institutionally sponsored loans, scholarships/grants, tuition waivers (full and partial), and unspecified assistantships also available. Support available to part-time students. Financial award applicants required to submit FAFSA. *Faculty research:* Acquisition of literacy, Mayan language, Rotuman language, English as a second language methodology, Farsi language. *Unit head:* Dr. Lawrence N. Berlin, Department Chair. *Application contact:* Dr. Lawrence N. Berlin, Department Chair.

Northern Arizona University, Graduate College, College of Arts and Letters, Department of English, Flagstaff, AZ 86011. Offers applied linguistics (PhD); English (MA), including creative writing, general English studies, literacy, technology and professional writing, literature, secondary English education; professional writing (Certificate); teaching English as a second language (MA, Certificate). Part-time programs available. *Faculty:* 42 full-time (30 women). *Students:* 107 full-time (70 women), 100 part-time (77 women); includes 39 minority (9 Black or African American, non-Hispanic/Latino; 4 American Indian or Alaska Native, non-Hispanic/Latino; 3 Asian, non-Hispanic/Latino; 15 Hispanic/Latino; 8 Two or more races, non-Hispanic/Latino), 27 international. Average age 31. 238 applicants, 68% accepted, 90 enrolled. In 2010, 84 master's, 2 doctorates, 20 other advanced degrees awarded. *Degree requirements:* For master's, comprehensive exam (for some programs), thesis (for some programs), departmental qualifying exam; for doctorate, comprehensive exam, thesis/dissertation, departmental qualifying exam. *Entrance requirements:* For master's, minimum GPA of 3.0 or GRE; for doctorate, GRE General Test. Additional exam requirements/recommendations for international students: Required—TOEFL (minimum score 550 paper-based; 213 computer-based; 80 iBT), IELTS (minimum score 7), TOEFL (600 paper, 250 computer, 100 iBT for PhD; 570 paper, 237 computer, 89 iBT for MA). *Application deadline:* For fall admission, 4/15 priority date for domestic students, 2/15 priority date for international students; for spring admission, 11/15 priority date for domestic and international students. Applications are processed on a rolling basis. Application fee: $65. Electronic applications accepted. *Financial support:* In 2010–11, 72 teaching assistantships with partial tuition reimbursements (averaging $11,623 per year) were awarded; Federal Work-Study, scholarships/grants, health care benefits, tuition waivers (full and partial), and unspecified assistantships also available. Financial award applicants required to submit FAFSA. *Unit head:* Dr. J. Allen Woodman, Chair, 928-523-5651, Fax: 928-523-7074, E-mail: allen.woodman@nau.edu. *Application contact:* Giovanina Bucci, Secretary, 928-523-4911, Fax: 928-523-7074, E-mail: giovanina.bucci@nau.edu.

Northwestern University, The Graduate School, Judd A. and Marjorie Weinberg College of Arts and Sciences, Department of Linguistics, Evanston, IL 60208. Offers MA, PhD, JD/PhD. Admissions and degrees offered through The Graduate School. Part-time programs available. Terminal master's awarded for partial completion of doctoral program. *Degree requirements:* For master's, one foreign language, thesis; for doctorate, 2 foreign languages, thesis/dissertation, 2 qualifying papers. *Entrance requirements:* For master's and doctorate, GRE General Test. Additional exam requirements/recommendations for international students: Required—TOEFL. Electronic applications accepted. *Faculty research:* Theoretical linguistics, empirical approaches to the study of language, language and cognition.

Oakland University, Graduate Study and Lifelong Learning, College of Arts and Sciences, Department of Linguistics, Rochester, MI 48309-4401. Offers linguistics (MA); teaching English as a second language (Certificate). Part-time and evening/weekend programs available. *Entrance requirements:* For master's, minimum GPA of 3.0 for unconditional admission. Additional exam requirements/recommendations for international students: Required—TOEFL (minimum score 550 paper-based; 213 computer-based).

The Ohio State University, Graduate School, College of Arts and Sciences, Division of Arts and Humanities, Department of Linguistics, Columbus, OH 43210. Offers MA, PhD. *Faculty:* 16. *Students:* 26 full-time (11 women), 25 part-time (14 women); includes 1 Black or African American, non-Hispanic/Latino; 3 Asian, non-Hispanic/Latino; 2 Hispanic/Latino; 2 Two or more races, non-Hispanic/Latino, 14 international. Average age 29. In 2010, 2 master's, 6 doctorates awarded. *Degree requirements:* For master's, one foreign language, exam or thesis; for doctorate, 2 foreign languages, thesis/dissertation, exam. *Entrance requirements:* For master's and doctorate, GRE General Test. Additional exam requirements/recommendations for international students: Required—TOEFL (minimum score 600 paper-based; 250 computer-based). *Application deadline:* For fall admission, 8/15 priority date for domestic students, 7/1 priority date for international students; for winter admission, 12/1 priority date for domestic students, 11/1 priority date for international students; for spring admission, 3/1 priority date for domestic students, 2/1 priority date for international students. Applications are processed on a rolling basis. Application fee: $40 ($50 for international students). Electronic applications accepted. *Expenses:* Tuition, state resident: full-time $10,605. Tuition, nonresident: full-time $26,535. Tuition and fees vary according to course load and program. *Financial support:* Fellowships, research assistantships, teaching assistantships, Federal Work-Study and institutionally sponsored loans available. Support available to part-time students. *Faculty research:* Experimental phonetics, nonlinear phonology, process morphology (synchronically and diachronically), syntactic theory (GB, GPSG, HPSG, Categorical Grammar, Relational Grammar), Montague semantics. *Unit head:* Elizabeth Hume, Chair, 614-292-2577, E-mail: hume-ohaire.1@osu.edu. *Application contact:* 614-292-9444, Fax: 614-292-3895, E-mail: domestic.grad@osu.edu.

The Ohio State University, Graduate School, College of Arts and Sciences, Division of Arts and Humanities, Department of Slavic and East European Languages and Literatures, Columbus, OH 43210. Offers linguistics (MA); literature (MA); Russian literature (PhD); Slavic linguistics (PhD). *Faculty:* 13. *Students:* 21 full-time (12 women), 8 part-time (4 women); includes 1 Asian, non-Hispanic/Latino, 4 international. Average age 31. In 2010, 2 master's, 3 doctorates awarded. *Degree requirements:* For master's, variable foreign language requirement, thesis optional; for doctorate, variable foreign language requirement, thesis/dissertation. *Entrance requirements:* For master's and doctorate, GRE General Test. Additional exam requirements/recommendations for international students: Required—TOEFL (minimum score 600 paper-based; 250 computer-based). *Application deadline:* For fall admission, 8/15 priority date for domestic students, 7/1 priority date for international students; for winter admission, 12/1 priority date for domestic students, 11/1 priority date for international students; for spring admission, 3/1 priority date for domestic students, 2/1 priority date for international students. Applications are processed on a rolling basis. Application fee: $40 ($50 for international students). Electronic applications accepted. *Expenses:* Tuition, state resident: full-time $10,605. Tuition, nonresident: full-time $26,535. Tuition and fees vary according to course load and program. *Financial support:* Fellowships, research assistantships, teaching assistantships,

Linguistics

The Ohio State University (continued)
Federal Work-Study and institutionally sponsored loans available. Support available to part-time students. *Faculty research:* Polish literature. *Unit head:* Helena Goscilo, Chair, 614-247-1790, E-mail: goscilo.1@osu.edu. *Application contact:* 614-292-9444, Fax: 614-292-3895, E-mail: domestic.grad@osu.edu.

Ohio University, Graduate College, College of Arts and Sciences, Department of Linguistics, Athens, OH 45701-2979. Offers applied linguistics/TESOL (MA). Part-time programs available. *Students:* 32 full-time (21 women), 1 part-time (0 women); includes 1 minority (Hispanic/Latino), 18 international. 75 applicants, 57% accepted, 22 enrolled. In 2010, 23 master's awarded. *Degree requirements:* For master's, one foreign language, thesis or alternative. *Entrance requirements:* For master's, minimum GPA of 3.0. Additional exam requirements/recommendations for international students: Required—TOEFL (minimum score 600 paper-based; 100 iBT) or IELTS (minimum score 7). *Application deadline:* For fall admission, 2/15 priority date for domestic and international students. Application fee: $50 ($55 for international students). Electronic applications accepted. *Financial support:* In 2010–11, 2 fellowships with tuition reimbursements were awarded; research assistantships with tuition reimbursements, teaching assistantships with tuition reimbursements, Federal Work-Study, institutionally sponsored loans, tuition waivers (partial), and unspecified assistantships also available. Financial award application deadline: 2/15. *Faculty research:* Syntax, language learning, language teaching, computers for teaching, sociolinguistics. *Unit head:* Dr. Chris Thompson, Chair, 740-593-0666, E-mail: thompsoc@ohio.edu. *Application contact:* Dr. Hiroyuki Oshita, Graduate Chair, 740-593-4570, Fax: 740-593-2967, E-mail: oshita@ohio.edu.

Old Dominion University, College of Arts and Letters, Program in Applied Linguistics, Norfolk, VA 23529. Offers MA. Part-time programs available. *Faculty:* 4 full-time (all women). *Students:* 17 full-time (12 women), 14 part-time (11 women); includes 5 minority (3 Black or African American, non-Hispanic/Latino; 1 Asian, non-Hispanic/Latino; 1 Two or more races, non-Hispanic/Latino), 6 international. Average age 30. 19 applicants, 63% accepted, 11 enrolled. In 2010, 7 master's awarded. *Degree requirements:* For master's, one foreign language, comprehensive exam, thesis optional. *Entrance requirements:* For master's, GRE General Test, sample of written work, 12 hours in English, 9 on the upper level, minimum B average. Additional exam requirements/recommendations for international students: Required—TOEFL (minimum score 570 paper-based; 88 iBT). *Application deadline:* For fall admission, 6/1 priority date for domestic students, 4/15 priority date for international students; for spring admission, 11/1 priority date for domestic students, 10/1 priority date for international students. Applications are processed on a rolling basis. Application fee: $50. Electronic applications accepted. *Expenses:* Tuition, state resident: full-time $8592; part-time $358 per credit. Tuition, nonresident: full-time $21,672; part-time $903 per credit. Required fees: $119 per semester. One-time fee: $50. *Financial support:* In 2010–11, 5 students received support, including 1 research assistantship (averaging $10,000 per year), 3 teaching assistantships (averaging $10,000 per year); career-related internships or fieldwork, institutionally sponsored loans, and unspecified assistantships also available. Financial award application deadline: 2/15. *Faculty research:* Discourse analysis, phonology, syntax, second language acquisition, gender, sociolinguistics. *Unit head:* Dr. Joanne Scheibman, Graduate Program Director, 757-683-3879, Fax: 757-683-3241, E-mail: linggpd@odu.edu. *Application contact:* Dr. Robert Wojtowicz, Associate Dean, 757-683-6077, Fax: 757-683-5746, E-mail: rwojtowi@odu.edu.

Penn State University Park, Graduate School, College of the Liberal Arts, Department of Linguistics and Applied Language Studies, State College, University Park, PA 16802-1503. Offers MA, PhD. *Unit head:* Dr. Joan Kelly Hall, Head, 814-865-7365, Fax: 814-865-7944, E-mail: jkh11@psu.edu. *Application contact:* Cynthia E. Nicosia, Director, Graduate Enrollment Services, 814-865-1795, Fax: 814-865-4627, E-mail: cey1@psu.edu.

Purdue University, Graduate School, College of Liberal Arts, Department of English, West Lafayette, IN 47907. Offers creative writing (MFA); literature (MA, PhD), including linguistics, literature and philosophy (PhD), rhetoric and composition, theory and cultural studies (PhD). Part-time programs available. *Degree requirements:* For master's, one foreign language; for doctorate, one foreign language, thesis/dissertation. *Entrance requirements:* For master's and doctorate, GRE General Test, sample of written work. Additional exam requirements/recommendations for international students: Required—TOEFL. Electronic applications accepted. *Faculty research:* Cultural studies, postmodern narrative, contemporary women writers, composition theory, slave narratives.

Purdue University, Graduate School, College of Liberal Arts, Department of Speech, Language, and Hearing Sciences, West Lafayette, IN 47907. Offers audiology (MS, Au D, PhD); linguistics (MS, PhD); speech and hearing science (MS, PhD); speech-language pathology (MS, PhD). *Accreditation:* ASHA. *Degree requirements:* For master's, thesis optional; for doctorate, thesis/dissertation. *Entrance requirements:* For master's and doctorate, GRE. Additional exam requirements/recommendations for international students: Required—TOEFL. Electronic applications accepted. *Faculty research:* Psychoacoustics, speech perception, speech physiology, stuttering, child language.

Purdue University, Graduate School, College of Liberal Arts, Program in Linguistics, West Lafayette, IN 47907. Offers MS, PhD. *Entrance requirements:* For master's and doctorate, GRE, minimum GPA of 3.4. Additional exam requirements/recommendations for international students: Required—TOEFL. Electronic applications accepted. *Faculty research:* Sign languages, sociolinguistics and African American English, computational linguistics, indigenous languages, theoretical linguistics.

Queens College of the City University of New York, Division of Graduate Studies, Arts and Humanities Division, Department of Linguistics and Communication Disorders, Program in Applied Linguistics, Flushing, NY 11367-1597. Offers MA. Part-time and evening/weekend programs available. *Faculty:* 8 full-time (5 women). *Students:* 9 part-time (7 women); includes 1 Black or African American, non-Hispanic/Latino; 2 Asian, non-Hispanic/Latino; 3 Hispanic/Latino. 18 applicants, 33% accepted, 4 enrolled. In 2010, 3 master's awarded. *Degree requirements:* For master's, thesis optional. *Entrance requirements:* For master's, minimum GPA of 3.0. Additional exam requirements/recommendations for international students: Required—TOEFL. *Application deadline:* For fall admission, 4/1 for domestic students; for spring admission, 11/1 for domestic students. Applications are processed on a rolling basis. Application fee: $125. *Financial support:* Career-related internships or fieldwork, Federal Work-Study, institutionally sponsored loans, and tuition waivers (partial) available. Support available to part-time students. Financial award application deadline: 4/1; financial award applicants required to submit FAFSA. *Unit head:* Dr. Robert M. Vago, Chairperson, 718-997-2875. *Application contact:* Mario Caruso, Director of Graduate Admissions, 718-997-5200, Fax: 718-997-5193, E-mail: graduate_admissions@qc.edu.

Rice University, Graduate Programs, School of Humanities, Department of Linguistics, Houston, TX 77251-1892. Offers MA, PhD. Terminal master's awarded for partial completion of doctoral program. *Degree requirements:* For master's, one foreign language, thesis; for doctorate, 2 foreign languages, thesis/dissertation, 3 research papers. *Entrance requirements:* For master's and doctorate, GRE General Test, minimum GPA of 3.0. Additional exam requirements/recommendations for international students: Required—TOEFL (minimum score 600 paper-based; 250 computer-based; 90 iBT). Electronic applications accepted. *Faculty research:* Typology, fieldwork and language description, cognitive grammar, historical linguistics, corpus linguistics.

Rutgers, The State University of New Jersey, New Brunswick, Graduate School-New Brunswick, Department of Linguistics, Piscataway, NJ 08854-8097. Offers PhD. *Degree requirements:* For doctorate, thesis/dissertation, 2 qualifying papers. *Entrance requirements:* For doctorate, GRE General Test, 3 letters of recommendation, writing sample. Electronic applications accepted. *Expenses:* Tuition, state resident: full-time $7200; part-time $600 per credit. Tuition, nonresident: full-time $11,124; part-time $927 per credit. *Faculty research:* Theoretical linguistics, syntax, semantics, phonology, computational linguistics, phoenetics.

San Diego State University, Graduate and Research Affairs, College of Arts and Letters, Department of Linguistics and Oriental Languages, San Diego, CA 92182. Offers applied linguistics and English as a second language (CAL); computational linguistics (MA); English as a second language/applied linguistics (MA); general linguistics (MA). *Degree requirements:* For master's, one foreign language, comprehensive exam, thesis optional. *Entrance requirements:* For master's, GRE General Test, 2 letters of recommendation. Additional exam requirements/recommendations for international students: Required—TOEFL (minimum score 570 paper-based). Electronic applications accepted. *Faculty research:* Cross-cultural linguistic studies of semantics.

San Francisco State University, Division of Graduate Studies, College of Humanities, Department of English Language and Literature, Program in Linguistics, San Francisco, CA 94132-1722. Offers MA. Part-time programs available. *Degree requirements:* For master's, 2 foreign languages, thesis (for some programs). *Application deadline:* Applications are processed on a rolling basis. *Faculty research:* Mental lexicon, endangered languages, language and gender, linguistics, discourse analysis. *Unit head:* Dr. Bruce Avery, Chair, 415-338-2264, E-mail: english@sfsu.edu. *Application contact:* Troi Carleton, Graduate Coordinator, 415-338-2264, E-mail: troi@sfsu.edu.

San Jose State University, Graduate Studies and Research, College of Humanities and the Arts, Department of Linguistics and Language Development, San Jose, CA 95192-0001. Offers computational linguistics (Certificate); linguistics (MA); teaching English to speakers of other languages (MA, Certificate). *Entrance requirements:* Additional exam requirements/recommendations for international students: Required—TOEFL (minimum score 570 paper-based; 230 computer-based). Electronic applications accepted.

Simon Fraser University, Graduate Studies, Faculty of Arts and Social Sciences, Department of Linguistics, Burnaby, BC V5A 1S6, Canada. Offers MA, PhD. *Degree requirements:* For master's, one foreign language, thesis; for doctorate, 2 foreign languages, thesis/dissertation. *Entrance requirements:* For master's, minimum GPA of 3.0; for doctorate, minimum GPA of 3.5. Additional exam requirements/recommendations for international students: Required—TOEFL or IELTS. *Faculty research:* History of linguistics, syntactic theory, relational grammar, experimental phonetics, pragmatics.

Southern Illinois University Carbondale, Graduate School, College of Liberal Arts, Department of Applied Linguistics, Carbondale, IL 62901-4701. Offers applied linguistics (MA); teaching English to speakers of other languages (MA). *Degree requirements:* For master's, one foreign language, thesis. *Entrance requirements:* For master's, minimum GPA of 3.0. Additional exam requirements/recommendations for international students: Required—TOEFL. *Faculty research:* Theory and methods, second language acquisition, pidgin and Creole languages, cognitive grammar.

Stanford University, School of Humanities and Sciences, Department of Linguistics, Stanford, CA 94305-9991. Offers MA, PhD. *Degree requirements:* For master's, one foreign language, thesis; for doctorate, 2 foreign languages, thesis/dissertation, oral exam, qualifying papers. *Entrance requirements:* For master's and doctorate, GRE General Test. Additional exam requirements/recommendations for international students: Required—TOEFL. Electronic applications accepted. *Expenses:* Tuition: Full-time $38,700; part-time $860 per unit. One-time fee: $200 full-time.

Stony Brook University, State University of New York, Graduate School, College of Arts and Sciences, Department of Linguistics, Program in Linguistics, Stony Brook, NY 11794. Offers MA, PhD. *Faculty:* 14 full-time (8 women), 4 part-time/adjunct (all women). *Students:* 30 full-time (20 women); includes 1 Asian, non-Hispanic/Latino, 18 international. Average age 31. 46 applicants, 28% accepted, 3 enrolled. In 2010, 2 doctorates awarded. *Application deadline:* For fall admission, 1/15 for domestic students. Application fee: $100. *Expenses:* Tuition, state resident: full-time $8370; part-time $349 per credit. Tuition, nonresident: full-time $13,780; part-time $574 per credit. Required fees: $994. *Financial support:* Fellowships, research assistantships, teaching assistantships available. *Unit head:* Dr. Robert Hoberman, Chair, 631-632-7774, Fax: 631-632-9789. *Application contact:* Michelle Carbone, 631-632-7774, Fax: 631-632-9789.

Syracuse University, College of Arts and Sciences, Program in Linguistic Studies, Syracuse, NY 13244. Offers MA. Part-time programs available. *Students:* 18 full-time (15 women), 2 part-time (1 woman); includes 1 minority (Black or African American, non-Hispanic/Latino), 13 international. Average age 28. 32 applicants, 50% accepted, 8 enrolled. In 2010, 9 master's awarded. *Degree requirements:* For master's, comprehensive exam, thesis or alternative. *Entrance requirements:* For master's, GRE General Test. Additional exam requirements/recommendations for international students: Required—TOEFL (minimum score 100 iBT). *Application deadline:* For fall admission, 1/10 priority date for domestic and international students. Application fee: $75. Electronic applications accepted. *Expenses:* Tuition: Part-time $1162 per credit. *Financial support:* Fellowships with full tuition reimbursements, teaching assistantships with full tuition reimbursements available. Financial award application deadline: 1/1; financial award applicants required to submit FAFSA. *Unit head:* Dr. Jaklin Kornfilt, Director, 315-443-2175, Fax: 315-443-5376, E-mail: kornfilt@syr.edu. *Application contact:* Barbara Moon, Recruiting Contact, 315-443-5906, E-mail: bamoon@syr.edu.

Teachers College, Columbia University, Graduate Faculty of Education, Department of Arts and Humanities, Program in Applied Linguistics, New York, NY 10027. Offers Ed M, MA, Ed D. Part-time and evening/weekend programs available. *Faculty:* 5 full-time (3 women), 7 part-time/adjunct (4 women). *Students:* 8 full-time (7 women), 71 part-time (56 women); includes 14 minority (1 Black or African American, non-Hispanic/Latino; 8 Asian, non-Hispanic/Latino; 5 Hispanic/Latino), 26 international. Average age 34. 78 applicants, 62% accepted, 18 enrolled. In 2010, 12 master's, 3 doctorates awarded. Terminal master's awarded for partial completion of doctoral program. *Degree requirements:* For master's, essay (for MA), project (for Ed M); for doctorate, comprehensive exam, thesis/dissertation. *Entrance requirements:* For master's, MA in applied linguistics, TESOL, or related field (for Ed M); for doctorate, MA in applied linguistics, TESOL, or related field. Additional exam requirements/recommendations for international students: Required—TOEFL (minimum score 600 paper-based; 250 computer-based; 102 iBT), IELTS (minimum score 7), TWE (minimum score 5), TWE: Test of Spoken English (minimum 50), CEP: Cambridge Certificate of Proficiency in English (minimum B). *Application deadline:* For fall admission, 1/15 priority date for domestic students; for spring admission, 11/1 for domestic students. Application fee: $65. Electronic applications accepted. *Expenses:* Tuition: Full-time $28,272; part-time $1178 per credit. Required fees: $756; $378 per semester. *Financial support:* Fellowships, research assistantships, teaching assistantships, career-related internships or fieldwork, Federal Work-Study, institutionally sponsored loans, and tuition waivers (full and partial) available. Support available to part-time students. Financial award application deadline: 2/1. *Faculty research:* Linguistics applied to education and other professions, sociolinguistics and second language acquisition, rude speech and social rules of speaking. *Unit head:* Prof. James E. Purpura, Program Coordinator, 212-678-3795, E-mail: appliedlinguistics@columbia.edu. *Application contact:* Prof. James E. Purpura, Program Coordinator, 212-678-3795, E-mail: appliedlinguistics@columbia.edu.

Temple University, Health Sciences Center and Graduate School, College of Health Professions, Department of Communication Sciences, Philadelphia, PA 19122-6096. Offers communication sciences (PhD); linguistics (MA); speech-language-hearing (MA). *Accreditation:* ASHA. Part-time and evening/weekend programs available. *Faculty:* 9 full-time (3 women). *Students:* 61 full-time (60 women), 4 part-time (all women); includes 2 Asian, non-Hispanic/Latino; 2 Hispanic/Latino, 1 international. 363 applicants, 20% accepted, 28 enrolled. In 2010, 20 master's, 1 doctorate awarded. *Degree requirements:* For doctorate, thesis/dissertation. *Entrance requirements:* For master's and doctorate, GRE General Test, minimum GPA of 3.0.

Additional exam requirements/recommendations for international students: Required—TOEFL (minimum score 550 paper-based; 213 computer-based; 79 iBT). Application fee: $50. Electronic applications accepted. *Financial support:* Fellowships, research assistantships, teaching assistantships with full tuition reimbursements, career-related internships or fieldwork, Federal Work-Study, institutionally sponsored loans, and tuition waivers (partial) available. Financial award application deadline: 1/15. *Faculty research:* Fluency, infants and families, multilingual/multicultural communication, geriatrics, conflict process, language, health communication. Total annual research expenditures: $1.1 million. *Unit head:* Dr. Carol Scheffner Hammer, Interim Chair, 215-204-7543, E-mail: cjhammer@temple.edu. *Application contact:* Dr. Carol Scheffner Hammer, Interim Chair, 215-204-7543, E-mail: cjhammer@temple.edu.

Texas Tech University, Graduate School, College of Arts and Sciences, Department of Classical and Modern Languages and Literatures, MA in Applied Linguistics Program, Lubbock, TX 79409. Offers MA. *Students:* 21 full-time (14 women), 3 part-time (1 woman); includes 1 Hispanic/Latino, 15 international. Average age 27. 19 applicants, 58% accepted, 7 enrolled. In 2010, 17 master's awarded. *Entrance requirements:* For master's, GRE General Test. Additional exam requirements/recommendations for international students: Required—TOEFL (minimum score 550 paper-based; 213 computer-based; 79 iBT). *Application deadline:* For fall admission, 6/1 priority date for domestic students, 1/15 priority date for international students; for spring admission, 9/1 priority date for domestic students, 6/15 priority date for international students. Applications are processed on a rolling basis. Application fee: $50 ($75 for international students). Electronic applications accepted. *Expenses:* Tuition, state resident: full-time $5495.76; part-time $228.99 per credit hour. Tuition, nonresident: full-time $12,936; part-time $538.99 per credit hour. Required fees: $2674; $36 per credit hour. $905 per semester. *Financial support:* Application deadline: 4/15. *Faculty research:* Second language acquisition, second language instruction, language processing, assessment, general linguistics. *Unit head:* Dr. Bill VanPatten, Director and Professor, 860-742-3145 Ext. 232, Fax: 860-742-3306, E-mail: bill.vanpatten@ttu.edu. *Application contact:* Liz Hildebrand, Senior Advisor, 806-742-4055, Fax: 806-742-3306, E-mail: liz.hildebrand@ttu.edu.

Trinity Western University, School of Graduate Studies, Program in Linguistics, Langley, BC V2Y 1Y1, Canada. Offers MA. *Degree requirements:* For master's, essay (for non-thesis students). *Entrance requirements:* For master's, minimum GPA of 2.7, 3.0 in last two years; 12 seminar hours; linguistic prerequisites; 1 foreign language. Additional exam requirements/recommendations for international students: Required—TOEFL (minimum score 600 paper-based; 250 computer-based). Electronic applications accepted. *Expenses:* Contact institution. *Faculty research:* Syntax, phonology, tone, historical and comparative, discourse analysis.

Universidad de las Américas–Puebla, Division of Graduate Studies, School of Humanities, Program in Applied Linguistics, Puebla, Mexico. Offers linguistics (MA). Part-time and evening/weekend programs available. *Degree requirements:* For master's, one foreign language, thesis. *Entrance requirements:* Additional exam requirements/recommendations for international students: Required—TOEFL. *Faculty research:* English linguistics, teaching English to speakers of other languages.

Université de Montréal, Faculty of Arts and Sciences, Department of Linguistics and Translation, Montréal, QC H3C 3J7, Canada. Offers linguistics (MA, PhD); translation (MA, PhD, DESS). *Degree requirements:* For master's, thesis, general exam; for doctorate, thesis/dissertation, general exam. Electronic applications accepted.

Université de Sherbrooke, Faculty of Letters and Human Sciences, Department of Letters and Communications, Sherbrooke, QC J1K 2R1, Canada. Offers comparative Canadian literature (MA, PhD); French literature (MA, PhD); linguistics (MA); theatre (MA). *Degree requirements:* For master's, thesis or alternative; for doctorate, thesis/dissertation. *Entrance requirements:* For master's, minimum GPA of 2.8; for doctorate, minimum GPA of 3.0.

Université du Québec à Chicoutimi, Graduate Programs, Program in Linguistics, Chicoutimi, QC G7H 2B1, Canada. Offers MA. Part-time programs available. *Degree requirements:* For master's, thesis. *Entrance requirements:* For master's, appropriate bachelor's degree, proficiency in French.

Université du Québec à Montréal, Graduate Programs, Program in Linguistics, Montréal, QC H3C 3P8, Canada. Offers MA, PhD. Part-time programs available. *Degree requirements:* For master's, thesis optional; for doctorate, thesis/dissertation. *Entrance requirements:* For master's, appropriate bachelor's degree or equivalent, proficiency in French; for doctorate, appropriate master's degree or equivalent, proficiency in French.

Université Laval, Faculty of Letters, Department of Languages, Linguistics and Translations, Programs in Linguistics, Québec, QC G1K 7P4, Canada. Offers MA, PhD. Terminal master's awarded for partial completion of doctoral program. *Degree requirements:* For master's, thesis (for some programs); for doctorate, comprehensive exam, thesis/dissertation. *Entrance requirements:* For master's, English test (comprehension of written English), knowledge of French; for doctorate, English exam (comprehension of written English), knowledge of French. Electronic applications accepted.

University at Buffalo, the State University of New York, Graduate School, College of Arts and Sciences, Department of Linguistics, Buffalo, NY 14260. Offers MA, PhD. *Faculty:* 15 full-time (5 women), 2 part-time/adjunct (1 woman). *Students:* 60 full-time (28 women), 4 part-time (2 women); includes 1 American Indian or Alaska Native, non-Hispanic/Latino; 1 Asian, non-Hispanic/Latino, 34 international. Average age 30. 69 applicants, 71% accepted, 19 enrolled. In 2010, 6 master's, 3 doctorates awarded. Terminal master's awarded for partial completion of doctoral program. *Degree requirements:* For master's, exam, project, or thesis; for doctorate, thesis/dissertation, qualifying paper. *Entrance requirements:* For master's and doctorate, GRE General Test. Additional exam requirements/recommendations for international students: Required—TOEFL (minimum score 600 paper-based; 250 computer-based; 100 iBT). *Application deadline:* For fall admission, 4/1 for domestic students, 3/1 for international students. Application fee: $75. Electronic applications accepted. *Financial support:* In 2010–11, 23 students received support, including 4 fellowships with full tuition reimbursements available (averaging $5,000 per year), 2 research assistantships with full tuition reimbursements available (averaging $16,500 per year), 19 teaching assistantships with full tuition reimbursements available (averaging $13,436 per year); scholarships/grants and unspecified assistantships also available. Financial award application deadline: 1/10; financial award applicants required to submit FAFSA. *Faculty research:* Cognitive linguistics, cross-linguistic studies, psycholinguistics, syntax, semantics. *Unit head:* Dr. Karin Michelson, Professor and Chair, 716-645-2177, Fax: 716-645-3825, E-mail: kmich@buffalo.edu. *Application contact:* Jodi L. Reiner, Secretary, 716-645-3794 Ext. 785, Fax: 716-645-3825, E-mail: jlreiner@buffalo.edu.

University of Alaska Fairbanks, College of Liberal Arts, Program in Linguistics, Fairbanks, AK 99775-6280. Offers applied linguistics (MA), including language documentation, second language acquisition teacher education. Part-time programs available. *Faculty:* 1 (woman) full-time. *Students:* 6 full-time (3 women), 8 part-time (5 women); includes 6 minority (5 American Indian or Alaska Native, non-Hispanic/Latino; 1 Asian, non-Hispanic/Latino). Average age 40. 10 applicants, 60% accepted, 4 enrolled. In 2010, 16 master's awarded. *Degree requirements:* For master's, comprehensive exam, thesis or alternative. *Entrance requirements:* Additional exam requirements/recommendations for international students: Required—TOEFL (minimum score 550 paper-based; 213 computer-based; 80 iBT). *Application deadline:* For fall admission, 6/1 for domestic students, 3/1 for international students; for spring admission, 10/15 for domestic students, 9/1 for international students. Application fee: $60. *Expenses:* Tuition, state resident: full-time $5688; part-time $316 per credit. Tuition, nonresident: full-time $11,628; part-time $646 per credit. Required fees: $289 per semester. Tuition and fees vary according to course load and reciprocity agreements. *Financial support:* In 2010–11, 2 research assistantships with tuition reimbursements (averaging $5,977 per year), 1 teaching assistantship with tuition reimbursement (averaging $11,955 per year) were awarded; fellowships with tuition reimbursements, career-related internships or fieldwork, Federal Work-Study, scholarships/grants, health care benefits, and unspecified assistantships also available. Support available to part-time students. Financial award application deadline: 7/1; financial award applicants required to submit FAFSA. *Faculty research:* Second language acquisition/teaching, INUPIAQ, Athabaskan languages, language maintenance and shift, phonology, morphology. Total annual research expenditures: $80,404. *Unit head:* Dr. Siri Tuttle, Program Head, 907-474-7876, Fax: 907-474-6586, E-mail: ffamb@uaf.edu. *Application contact:* Dr. Siri Tuttle, Program Head, 907-474-7876, Fax: 907-474-6586, E-mail: ffamb@uaf.edu.

University of Alberta, Faculty of Graduate Studies and Research, Department of Linguistics, Edmonton, AB T6G 2E1, Canada. Offers experimental linguistics (M Sc, PhD). *Degree requirements:* For master's, thesis (for some programs); for doctorate, thesis/dissertation. *Entrance requirements:* For master's, BA in linguistics; for doctorate, M Sc or MA in linguistics. Additional exam requirements/recommendations for international students: Required—TOEFL. *Faculty research:* Experimental phonetics, psycholinguistics, phonology, endangered languages, language acquisition.

University of Alberta, Faculty of Graduate Studies and Research, Department of Modern Languages and Cultural Studies, Edmonton, AB T6G 2E1, Canada. Offers applied linguistics (Germanic, Romance, Slavic) (MA); French language, literatures and linguistics (PhD); French language, literatures, and linguistics (MA); Germanic languages, literatures and linguistics (PhD); Germanic languages, literatures, and linguistics (MA); Italian studies (MA); Slavic languages and literatures (Russian, Ukrainian) (MA, PhD); Slavic linguistics (Russian, Ukrainian) (MA, PhD); Spanish and Latin American studies (MA, PhD); Ukrainian folklore (MA, PhD). Part-time programs available. *Degree requirements:* For master's, one foreign language, thesis; for doctorate, 2 foreign languages, comprehensive exam, thesis/dissertation. *Entrance requirements:* For master's and doctorate, 1 language other than English. Additional exam requirements/recommendations for international students: Required—Michigan English Language Assessment Battery or TOEFL (minimum score 550 paper-based; 213 computer-based). Electronic applications accepted. *Faculty research:* Russian/Ukrainian studies; German studies; contemporary Latin American, French and Francophone studies; Italian studies.

The University of Arizona, College of Social and Behavioral Sciences, Department of Linguistics, Tucson, AZ 85721. Offers human language technology (MS); linguistics and anthropology (PhD); Native American linguistics (MA); theoretical linguistics (PhD). PhD (linguistics and anthropology) offered jointly with Department of Anthropology. *Faculty:* 16 full-time (9 women). *Students:* 32 full-time (16 women), 14 part-time (8 women); includes 1 American Indian or Alaska Native, non-Hispanic/Latino; 1 Asian, non-Hispanic/Latino; 1 Hispanic/Latino; 7 Two or more races, non-Hispanic/Latino, 10 international. Average age 31. 82 applicants, 10% accepted, 2 enrolled. In 2010, 3 master's, 5 doctorates awarded. Terminal master's awarded for partial completion of doctoral program. *Degree requirements:* For master's, one foreign language, thesis; for doctorate, one foreign language, comprehensive exam, thesis/dissertation. *Entrance requirements:* For master's, GRE General Test, 3 letters of recommendation, writing sample, resume; for doctorate, GRE General Test, 3 letters of recommendation, statement of purpose, writing sample, resume. Additional exam requirements/recommendations for international students: Required—TOEFL (minimum score 550 paper-based; 213 computer-based; 79 iBT). *Application deadline:* Applications are processed on a rolling basis. Application fee: $65. Electronic applications accepted. *Expenses:* Tuition, state resident: full-time $7692. *Financial support:* In 2010–11, 7 research assistantships with full tuition reimbursements (averaging $19,279 per year), 20 teaching assistantships with full tuition reimbursements (averaging $19,652 per year) were awarded; career-related internships or fieldwork, institutionally sponsored loans, scholarships/grants, health care benefits, tuition waivers (full and partial), and unspecified assistantships also available. Support available to part-time students. Financial award application deadline: 4/15. *Faculty research:* Semantic, syntactic, morphological, and phonological theories of natural languages; native languages of the American Southwest, psycholinguistics and computational linguistics. Total annual research expenditures: $234,017. *Unit head:* Dr. Michael Hammond, Head, 520-621-5759, Fax: 520-626-9014, E-mail: hammond@u.arizona.edu. *Application contact:* Jennifer Columbus, Information Contact, 520-621-2113, Fax: 520-626-9014, E-mail: jennife2@email.arizona.edu.

The University of Arizona, College of Social and Behavioral Sciences, Program in Human Language Technology, Tucson, AZ 85721. Offers MS. *Students:* 1 (woman) full-time, all international. Average age 25. 6 applicants, 33% accepted. In 2010, 5 master's awarded. *Expenses:* Tuition, state resident: full-time $7692. *Unit head:* Dr. Sandiway Fong, Program Coordinator, 520-626-6146, E-mail: sadc@email.arizona.edu. *Application contact:* Jennifer Columbus, Information Contact, 520-621-2113, Fax: 520-626-9014, E-mail: jennife2@email.arizona.edu.

The University of British Columbia, Faculty of Arts and Faculty of Graduate Studies, Department of Linguistics, Vancouver, BC V6T 1Z1, Canada. Offers MA, PhD. Part-time programs available. *Degree requirements:* For master's, one foreign language, thesis optional; for doctorate, 2 foreign languages, thesis/dissertation, 2 qualifying papers. *Entrance requirements:* Additional exam requirements/recommendations for international students: Required—TOEFL (minimum score 550 paper-based; 213 computer-based). Electronic applications accepted. Tuition charges are reported in Canadian dollars. *Expenses:* Tuition, area resident: Full-time $4179 Canadian dollars. International tuition: $7344 Canadian dollars full-time. *Faculty research:* Linguistic theory (phonology, syntax, semantics), Native American languages, African languages, first language acquisition, experimental phonetics.

University of Calgary, Faculty of Graduate Studies, Faculty of Social Sciences, Department of Linguistics, Calgary, AB T2N 1N4, Canada. Offers MA, PhD. *Degree requirements:* For master's, one foreign language, thesis; for doctorate, one foreign language, comprehensive exam, thesis/dissertation. *Entrance requirements:* For doctorate, MA. Additional exam requirements/recommendations for international students: Required—TOEFL (minimum score 560 paper-based; 220 computer-based). Electronic applications accepted. *Faculty research:* Theoretical linguistics, historical linguistics, language acquisition, Amerindian.

University of California, Berkeley, Graduate Division, College of Letters and Science, Department of Linguistics, Berkeley, CA 94720-1500. Offers PhD. *Degree requirements:* For doctorate, thesis/dissertation, qualifying exam. *Entrance requirements:* For doctorate, GRE General Test, minimum GPA of 3.0, 3 letters of recommendation.

University of California, Davis, Graduate Studies, Graduate Group in Linguistics, Davis, CA 95616. Offers applied linguistics (MA, PhD); linguistics (MA). *Degree requirements:* For master's, one foreign language, comprehensive exam (for some programs), thesis (for some programs); for doctorate, thesis/dissertation. *Entrance requirements:* For master's and doctorate, GRE General Test, minimum GPA of 3.0. Additional exam requirements/recommendations for international students: Required—TOEFL (minimum score 550 paper-based; 213 computer-based). Electronic applications accepted. *Faculty research:* Grammatical analysis and theory, sociolinguistics, historical linguistics, Romance linguistics, neurolinguistics.

University of California, Los Angeles, Graduate Division, College of Letters and Science, Department of Applied Linguistics and Teaching English as a Second Language, Program in Applied Linguistics, Los Angeles, CA 90095. Offers PhD. *Students:* 48 full-time (36 women); includes 11 minority (6 Asian, non-Hispanic/Latino; 5 Hispanic/Latino), 21 international. Average age 33. 111 applicants, 14% accepted, 8 enrolled. In 2010, 1 doctorate awarded. *Degree requirements:* For doctorate, one foreign language, thesis/dissertation, oral and written qualifying exams. *Entrance requirements:* For doctorate, GRE General Test, MA in relevant field, thesis or related research paper. *Application deadline:* For fall admission, 12/15 for domestic students. Application fee: $70 ($90 for international students). Electronic applications accepted. *Financial support:* In 2010–11, 32 fellowships with full and partial tuition reimbursements, 21 research assistantships with full and partial tuition reimbursements, 28 teaching assistantships with full and partial tuition reimbursements were awarded; Federal Work-Study, institutionally sponsored loans, scholarships/grants, and tuition waivers (full and partial) also available. Financial award

Linguistics

University of California, Los Angeles (continued)
application deadline: 3/1; financial award applicants required to submit FAFSA. *Unit head:* Dr. Olga Yokoyama, Chair, 310-825-4631, E-mail: appling@ucla.edu. *Application contact:* Department Office, 310-825-4631, Fax: 310-206-4118, E-mail: appling@ucla.edu.

University of California, Los Angeles, Graduate Division, College of Letters and Science, Department of Linguistics, Los Angeles, CA 90095. Offers MA, PhD. *Faculty:* 20 full-time (9 women). *Students:* 35 full-time (19 women); includes 2 minority (both Asian, non-Hispanic/Latino), 10 international. Average age 26. 163 applicants, 9% accepted, 7 enrolled. In 2010, 2 master's, 4 doctorates awarded. Terminal master's awarded for partial completion of doctoral program. *Degree requirements:* For master's, one foreign language, comprehensive exam or thesis; for doctorate, thesis/dissertation, oral and written qualifying exams. *Entrance requirements:* For master's, GRE General Test, minimum GPA of 3.0, sample of written work; for doctorate, GRE General Test, minimum undergraduate GPA of 3.0, sample of written work; statement of purpose. *Application deadline:* For fall admission, 12/15 for domestic and international students. Application fee: $70 ($90 for international students). Electronic applications accepted. *Financial support:* In 2010–11, 32 fellowships with full and partial tuition reimbursements, 24 research assistantships with full and partial tuition reimbursements, 18 teaching assistantships with full and partial tuition reimbursements were awarded; Federal Work-Study, institutionally sponsored loans, scholarships/grants, health care benefits, tuition waivers (full and partial), and unspecified assistantships also available. Financial award application deadline: 3/1; financial award applicants required to submit FAFSA. *Faculty research:* Phonetics, nonlinear phonology, formal syntax, formal semantics, natural language processing. *Unit head:* Dr. Anoop Mahajan, Chair, 310-850-2662, E-mail: mahajan@ucla.edu. *Application contact:* Department Office, 310-825-0634, E-mail: linguist@humnet.ucla.edu.

University of California, San Diego, Office of Graduate Studies, Department of Linguistics, La Jolla, CA 92093. Offers PhD. *Degree requirements:* For doctorate, thesis/dissertation. *Entrance requirements:* For doctorate, GRE General Test. Electronic applications accepted.

University of California, San Diego, Office of Graduate Studies, Interdisciplinary Program in Cognitive Science, La Jolla, CA 92093. Offers cognitive science/anthropology (PhD); cognitive science/communication (PhD); cognitive science/computer science and engineering (PhD); cognitive science/linguistics (PhD); cognitive science/neuroscience (PhD); cognitive science/philosophy (PhD); cognitive science/psychology (PhD); cognitive science/sociology (PhD). Admissions offered through affiliated departments. *Degree requirements:* For doctorate, thesis/dissertation. *Entrance requirements:* For doctorate, GRE General Test, acceptance into one of the eight participating departments. *Faculty research:* Language and cognition, philosophy of mind, visual perception, biological anthropology, sociolinguistics.

University of California, Santa Barbara, Graduate Division, College of Letters and Sciences, Division of Humanities and Fine Arts, Department of Linguistics, Santa Barbara, CA 93106-9580. Offers applied linguistics (PhD); cognitive science (PhD); language, interaction, and social organizations (PhD); linguistics (PhD); translation studies (PhD); MA/PhD. *Faculty:* 9 full-time (5 women), 1 part-time/adjunct (0 women). *Students:* 28 full-time (14 women); includes 1 Asian, non-Hispanic/Latino. Average age 31. 62 applicants, 23% accepted, 8 enrolled. In 2010, 2 doctorates awarded. Terminal master's awarded for partial completion of doctoral program. *Degree requirements:* For doctorate, one foreign language, comprehensive exam, thesis/dissertation. *Entrance requirements:* For doctorate, GRE. Additional exam requirements/recommendations for international students: Required—TOEFL (minimum score 550 paper-based; 80 iBT), IELTS (minimum score 7). *Application deadline:* For fall admission, 12/1 for domestic and international students. Application fee: $70 ($90 for international students). Electronic applications accepted. *Financial support:* In 2010–11, 22 students received support, including 20 fellowships with full and partial tuition reimbursements available (averaging $16,513 per year), 2 research assistantships with full and partial tuition reimbursements available (averaging $12,185 per year), 10 teaching assistantships with full and partial tuition reimbursements available (averaging $6,586 per year). Financial award application deadline: 12/1; financial award applicants required to submit FAFSA. *Faculty research:* Sociolinguistics, linguistic theory, discourse, psycho-linguistics, anthropological linguistics. *Unit head:* Joni Schwartz, Director, 805-893-3237, Fax: 805-893-7492, E-mail: joni@hfa.ucsb.edu. *Application contact:* Cami Helmuth, Graduate Program Advisor, 805-893-7490, Fax: 805-893-7492, E-mail: helmuth@hfa.uscb.edu.

University of California, Santa Barbara, Graduate Division, College of Letters and Sciences, Division of Humanities and Fine Arts, Department of Spanish and Portuguese, Santa Barbara, CA 93106-4150. Offers Hispanic languages and literature (PhD), including European medieval studies, feminist studies, Hispanic linguistics, Hispanic literature, Luso-Brazilian literature; Hispanic linguistics (MA); Luso-Brazilian literature (MA); Spanish or Spanish-American literature (MA); MA/PhD. Spanish Language Institute available during summer session. *Faculty:* 16 full-time (7 women). *Students:* 32 full-time (22 women); includes 1 Black or African American, non-Hispanic/Latino; 1 Asian, non-Hispanic/Latino; 9 Hispanic/Latino. Average age 32. 34 applicants, 26% accepted, 5 enrolled. In 2010, 3 master's, 3 doctorates awarded. Terminal master's awarded for partial completion of doctoral program. *Degree requirements:* For master's, 2 foreign languages, comprehensive exam (for some programs), thesis optional; for doctorate, 3 foreign languages, comprehensive exam, thesis/dissertation. *Entrance requirements:* For master's and doctorate, GRE. Additional exam requirements/recommendations for international students: Required—TOEFL (minimum score 550 paper-based; 80 iBT), IELTS (minimum score 7). *Application deadline:* For fall admission, 12/15 for domestic and international students. Application fee: $70 ($90 for international students). Electronic applications accepted. *Financial support:* In 2010–11, 32 students received support, including 12 fellowships with full and partial tuition reimbursements available (averaging $10,016 per year), 27 teaching assistantships with full and partial tuition reimbursements available (averaging $14,583 per year); career-related internships or fieldwork, Federal Work-Study, tuition waivers (full and partial), and unspecified assistantships also available. Financial award application deadline: 12/15; financial award applicants required to submit FAFSA. *Faculty research:* Nineteenth century Spanish and Portuguese literature, Spanish and Spanish American literature, nineteenth and twentieth century Portuguese and Brazilian literatures, Hispanic linguistics, Catalan language and culture. *Unit head:* Prof. Francisco A. Lomeli, Chair, 805-893-5715, Fax: 805-893-8341, E-mail: lomeli@spanport.ucsb.edu. *Application contact:* Ashley Bradbury, Graduate Program Assistant, 805-893-2131, Fax: 805-893-8341, E-mail: ashley@hfa.ucsb.edu.

University of California, Santa Cruz, Division of Graduate Studies, Division of Humanities, Department of Linguistics, Santa Cruz, CA 95064. Offers MA, PhD. *Students:* 22 full-time (8 women); includes 3 minority (1 Asian, non-Hispanic/Latino; 2 Hispanic/Latino), 1 international. Average age 26. 61 applicants, 20% accepted, 6 enrolled. In 2010, 11 master's, 4 doctorates awarded. Terminal master's awarded for partial completion of doctoral program. *Degree requirements:* For master's, one foreign language, research paper; for doctorate, one foreign language, thesis/dissertation, qualifying exam. *Entrance requirements:* For master's and doctorate, GRE General Test. Additional exam requirements/recommendations for international students: Required—TOEFL (minimum score 550 paper-based; 220 computer-based; 83 iBT); Recommended—IELTS (minimum score 8). *Application deadline:* For fall admission, 12/15 for domestic and international students. Application fee: $70 ($90 for international students). Electronic applications accepted. *Financial support:* Fellowships, research assistantships, teaching assistantships, institutionally sponsored loans and tuition waivers available. Financial award application deadline: 1/15; financial award applicants required to submit FAFSA. *Faculty research:* Theoretical and descriptive linguistics: syntax, semantics and phonology. *Unit head:* Ashley Hardisty, Graduate Program Coordinator, 831-459-2905, E-mail: ashleyh@ucsc.edu. *Application contact:* Ashley Hardisty, Graduate Program Coordinator, 831-459-2905, E-mail: ashleyh@ucsc.edu.

University of Chicago, Division of the Humanities, Department of Linguistics, Chicago, IL 60637-1513. Offers anthropology and linguistics (PhD); linguistics (AM, PhD). Terminal master's awarded for partial completion of doctoral program. *Degree requirements:* For master's, one foreign language, thesis; for doctorate, 2 foreign languages, thesis/dissertation. *Entrance requirements:* For master's and doctorate, GRE General Test. Additional exam requirements/recommendations for international students: Required—TOEFL.

University of Colorado Boulder, Graduate School, College of Arts and Sciences, Department of Linguistics, Boulder, CO 80309. Offers MA, PhD. Part-time programs available. *Faculty:* 8 full-time (6 women). *Students:* 60 full-time (32 women), 16 part-time (11 women); includes 6 minority (2 American Indian or Alaska Native, non-Hispanic/Latino; 2 Asian, non-Hispanic/Latino; 2 Hispanic/Latino), 8 international. Average age 31. 114 applicants, 24 enrolled. In 2010, 19 master's, 6 doctorates awarded. Terminal master's awarded for partial completion of doctoral program. *Degree requirements:* For master's, comprehensive exam, thesis optional; for doctorate, one foreign language, thesis/dissertation. *Entrance requirements:* For master's, GRE General Test, minimum undergraduate GPA of 2.75; for doctorate, GRE General Test. *Application deadline:* For fall admission, 1/15 priority date for domestic students, 12/1 for international students. Applications are processed on a rolling basis. Application fee: $50 ($60 for international students). *Financial support:* In 2010–11, 9 fellowships (averaging $1,617 per year), 22 research assistantships (averaging $9,385 per year) were awarded; Federal Work-Study and tuition waivers (full) also available. Financial award application deadline: 1/15. *Faculty research:* Synchronic linguistics, discourse analysis, language acquisition, diachronic linguistics, lexicography, American Indian linguistics, psycholinguistics, African linguistics. Total annual research expenditures: $1.5 million.

University of Colorado Denver, College of Liberal Arts and Sciences, Department of English, Denver, CO 80217. Offers applied linguistics (MA); literature (MA); rhetoric and teaching of writing (MA). Part-time and evening/weekend programs available. *Faculty:* 23 full-time (13 women). *Students:* 45 full-time (27 women), 22 part-time (15 women); includes 3 Hispanic/Latino, 3 international. Average age 30. 39 applicants, 77% accepted, 18 enrolled. In 2010, 18 master's awarded. *Degree requirements:* For master's, variable foreign language requirement, comprehensive exam (for some programs), thesis (for some programs), minimum of 33 credit hours (for literature), 30 (for rhetoric and teaching of writing and applied linguistics). *Entrance requirements:* For master's, GRE General Test, minimum GPA of 3.0, critical writing sample, letters of recommendation, completion of 24 semester hours in English courses (at least 16 at the upper-division). *Application deadline:* For fall admission, 4/1 for domestic students; for spring admission, 10/1 for domestic students. Application fee: $50 ($75 for international students). Electronic applications accepted. *Expenses:* Tuition, state resident: full-time $7332; part-time $355 per credit hour. Tuition, nonresident: full-time $18,990; part-time $1055 per credit hour. Required fees: $998. Tuition and fees vary according to course level, course load, degree level, campus/location, program, reciprocity agreements and student level. *Financial support:* Fellowships, teaching assistantships, Federal Work-Study, scholarships/grants, and unspecified assistantships available. Financial award application deadline: 4/1; financial award applicants required to submit FAFSA. *Faculty research:* Literature, rhetoric, teaching of writing, applied linguistics. *Unit head:* Prof. Nancy Ciccone, Chair, 303-556-8395, Fax: 303-556-2959, E-mail: nancy.ciccone@ucdenver.edu. *Application contact:* English Department, 303-556-2584, Fax: 303-556-2959.

University of Connecticut, Graduate School, College of Liberal Arts and Sciences, Department of Linguistics, Storrs, CT 06269. Offers MA, PhD. *Degree requirements:* For doctorate, thesis/dissertation. *Entrance requirements:* For doctorate, GRE General Test. Additional exam requirements/recommendations for international students: Required—TOEFL (minimum score 550 paper-based; 213 computer-based). Electronic applications accepted.

University of Delaware, College of Arts and Sciences, Department of Linguistics, Newark, DE 19716. Offers MA, PhD. *Degree requirements:* For doctorate, one foreign language, comprehensive exam, thesis/dissertation, publishable research papers. *Entrance requirements:* For master's, GRE General Test; for doctorate, GRE General Test, writing sample. Additional exam requirements/recommendations for international students: Required—TOEFL (minimum score 600 paper-based; 250 computer-based). Electronic applications accepted. *Faculty research:* East Asian, Austronesian and Romance languages, phonology, phonetics, syntax, cognitive science, semantics, psycholinguistics, language acquisition, endangered languages.

University of Florida, Graduate School, College of Liberal Arts and Sciences, Program in Linguistics, Gainesville, FL 32611. Offers linguistics (MA, PhD); teaching English as a second language (Certificate). Part-time programs available. *Faculty:* 11 full-time (8 women), 1 (woman) part-time/adjunct. *Students:* 48 full-time (22 women), 7 part-time (6 women); includes 1 Black or African American, non-Hispanic/Latino; 1 Asian, non-Hispanic/Latino; 1 Hispanic/Latino, 26 international. Average age 33. 73 applicants, 30% accepted, 8 enrolled. In 2010, 10 master's, 10 doctorates awarded. Terminal master's awarded for partial completion of doctoral program. *Degree requirements:* For master's, one foreign language, comprehensive exam, thesis (for some programs); for doctorate, 2 foreign languages, comprehensive exam, thesis/dissertation. *Entrance requirements:* For master's and doctorate, GRE General Test, minimum GPA of 3.0. Additional exam requirements/recommendations for international students: Required—TOEFL (minimum score 550 paper-based; 213 computer-based; 80 iBT), IELTS (minimum score 6). *Application deadline:* For fall admission, 12/15 priority date for domestic students, 12/15 for international students. Applications are processed on a rolling basis. Application fee: $30. Electronic applications accepted. *Expenses:* Tuition, state resident: full-time $10,915.92. Tuition, nonresident: full-time $28,309. *Financial support:* In 2010–11, 30 students received support, including 7 fellowships with tuition reimbursements available, 7 research assistantships (averaging $15,919 per year), 16 teaching assistantships with tuition reimbursements available (averaging $14,100 per year); institutionally sponsored loans and unspecified assistantships also available. Financial award application deadline: 12/15; financial award applicants required to submit FAFSA. *Faculty research:* Theoretical, applied, and descriptive linguistics. *Unit head:* Dr. Caroline R. Wiltshire, Chair, 352-392-0639 Ext. 224, Fax: 352-392-8480, E-mail: wiltshir@ufl.edu. *Application contact:* Dr. Ratree Wayland, Graduate Coordinator, 352-392-0639 Ext. 225, Fax: 352-392-8480, E-mail: ratree@ufl.edu.

University of Georgia, College of Arts and Sciences, Program in Linguistics, Athens, GA 30602. Offers MA, PhD. *Students:* 33 full-time (17 women), 12 part-time (6 women); includes 4 Hispanic/Latino; 1 Two or more races, non-Hispanic/Latino, 4 international. 49 applicants, 43% accepted, 10 enrolled. In 2010, 5 master's, 6 doctorates awarded. *Degree requirements:* For master's, one foreign language, thesis; for doctorate, 2 foreign languages, comprehensive exam, thesis/dissertation. *Entrance requirements:* For master's and doctorate, GRE General Test. *Application deadline:* For fall admission, 7/1 priority date for domestic students; for spring admission, 11/15 for domestic students. Application fee: $50. Electronic applications accepted. *Expenses:* Contact institution. *Financial support:* In 2010–11, 3 fellowships, 7 research assistantships, 8 teaching assistantships were awarded; Federal Work-Study and institutionally sponsored loans also available. Financial award application deadline: 2/15. *Faculty research:* Applied linguistics, English linguistics, dialectology, lexicography, discourse analysis. *Unit head:* Dr. Jared Stephen Klein, Director, 706-542-9261, Fax: 706-542-2897, E-mail: jklein@uga.edu. *Application contact:* Dr. Jonathan Evans, Graduate Coordinator, 706-542-2229, E-mail: jdmevans@uga.edu.

University of Hawaii at Manoa, Graduate Division, College of Languages, Linguistics and Literature, Department of Linguistics, Honolulu, HI 96822. Offers MA, PhD. Part-time programs available. *Faculty:* 34 full-time (14 women), 1 part-time/adjunct (0 women). *Students:* 57 full-time (35 women), 2 part-time (both women); includes 18 minority (1 American Indian or Alaska Native, non-Hispanic/Latino; 12 Asian, non-Hispanic/Latino; 1 Hispanic/Latino; 2 Native Hawaiian or other Pacific Islander, non-Hispanic/Latino; 2 Two or more races, non-Hispanic/Latino), 24 international. Average age 32. 65 applicants, 45% accepted, 15 enrolled. In 2010, 12 master's, 3 doctorates awarded. Terminal master's awarded for partial completion of doctoral program. *Degree requirements:* For master's, 2 foreign languages, thesis optional; for doctorate, 2 foreign languages, comprehensive exam, thesis/dissertation. *Entrance requirements:* For master's and doctorate, GRE General Test. Additional exam requirements/recommendations for international students: Required—TOEFL (minimum score 600 paper-based; 250 computer-based; 100 iBT), IELTS (minimum score 7). *Application deadline:* For fall admission, 1/10 for domestic and international students; for spring admission, 9/1 for domestic and international students. Applications are processed on a rolling basis. Application fee: $60. *Financial support:* In 2010–11, 24 fellowships (averaging $3,832 per year), 2 research assistantships (averaging $17,847 per year), 29 teaching assistantships (averaging $14,785 per year) were awarded; career-related internships or fieldwork, Federal Work-Study, scholarships/grants, and tuition waivers (full and partial) also available. Support available to part-time students. Financial award application deadline: 3/1. *Faculty research:* Languages of the Pacific and Asia. Total annual research expenditures: $139,000. *Application contact:* Patricia Donegan, Graduate Chair, 808-956-8602, Fax: 808-956-9166, E-mail: donegan@hawaii.edu.

University of Houston, College of Liberal Arts and Social Sciences, Department of English, Houston, TX 77204. Offers applied English linguistics (MA); creative writing (MFA); creative writing and literature (MA, PhD); English (MA, PhD). *Faculty:* 27 full-time (11 women), 5 part-time/adjunct (2 women). *Students:* 104 full-time (60 women), 38 part-time (29 women); includes 5 Black or African American, non-Hispanic/Latino; 15 Asian, non-Hispanic/Latino; 7 Hispanic/Latino; 1 Two or more races, non-Hispanic/Latino, 5 international. Average age 31. 379 applicants, 14% accepted, 34 enrolled. In 2010, 17 master's, 8 doctorates awarded. *Degree requirements:* For master's, one foreign language, comprehensive exam (for some programs), thesis (MFA); for doctorate, 2 foreign languages, comprehensive exam, thesis/ dissertation. *Entrance requirements:* For master's, GRE General Test, minimum GPA of 3.0 in last 60 hours of course work; for doctorate, GRE General Test, GRE Subject Test (literature), writing sample. Additional exam requirements/recommendations for international students: Required—TOEFL (minimum score 550 paper-based; 79 iBT). *Application deadline:* For fall admission, 2/1 for domestic and international students; for spring admission, 11/1 for domestic and international students. Application fee: $50 ($75 for international students). Electronic applications accepted. *Expenses:* Tuition, state resident: full-time $8592; part-time $358 per credit hour. Tuition, nonresident: full-time $16,032; part-time $668 per credit hour. Required fees: $2889. Tuition and fees vary according to course load and program. *Financial support:* In 2010–11, 14 fellowships with full tuition reimbursements (averaging $6,430 per year), 38 teaching assistantships with full tuition reimbursements (averaging $10,016 per year) were awarded; career-related internships or fieldwork, Federal Work-Study, institutionally sponsored loans, scholarships/grants, health care benefits, and unspecified assistantships also available. Support available to part-time students. Financial award application deadline: 2/1. *Unit head:* Wyman Henderson, Chairperson, 713-743-3004, Fax: 713-743-3215, E-mail: whh@uh.edu. *Application contact:* Julie Kofford, Academic Advisor, 713-743-3004, E-mail: jkofford@central. uh.edu.

University of Illinois at Chicago, Graduate College, College of Liberal Arts and Sciences, Department of English, Program in Linguistics, Chicago, IL 60607-7128. Offers teaching English to speakers of other languages/applied linguistics (MA). Part-time programs available. *Degree requirements:* For master's, one foreign language, comprehensive exam, thesis (for some programs). *Entrance requirements:* For master's, minimum GPA of 3.0. Additional exam requirements/recommendations for international students: Required—TOEFL. Electronic applications accepted. *Faculty research:* Second language acquisition, methodology of second language teaching, lexicography, language, sex and gender.

University of Illinois at Urbana–Champaign, Graduate College, College of Liberal Arts and Sciences, School of Literatures, Cultures and Linguistics, Department of Linguistics, Champaign, IL 61820. Offers linguistics (MA, PhD); teaching of English as a second language (MA). *Faculty:* 16 full-time (5 women). *Students:* 76 full-time (52 women), 41 part-time (34 women); includes 18 minority (3 Black or African American, non-Hispanic/Latino; 11 Asian, non-Hispanic/ Latino; 4 Hispanic/Latino), 58 international. 202 applicants, 20% accepted, 27 enrolled. In 2010, 30 master's, 4 doctorates awarded. *Entrance requirements:* For master's, GRE, minimum GPA of 3.0; writing sample; for doctorate, GRE, minimum GPA of 3.5; writing sample. Additional exam requirements/recommendations for international students: Required—TOEFL (minimum score 88 iBT). *Application deadline:* Applications are processed on a rolling basis. Application fee: $75 ($90 for international students). Electronic applications accepted. *Financial support:* In 2010–11, 15 fellowships, 21 research assistantships, 65 teaching assistantships were awarded; tuition waivers (full and partial) also available. *Unit head:* Hye Suk James Yoon, Acting Head, 217-244-3055, E-mail: jyoon@illinois.edu. *Application contact:* Lynn Stanke, Office Support Specialist, 217-333-6269, Fax: 217-244-3050, E-mail: stanke@illinois.edu.

The University of Iowa, Graduate College, College of Liberal Arts and Sciences, Department of Linguistics, Iowa City, IA 52242-1316. Offers linguistics (MA, PhD); linguistics with TESL (MA). Linguistics with TESL option offered as part of dual degree that begins at undergraduate level. *Degree requirements:* For master's, thesis optional, exam; for doctorate, comprehensive exam, thesis/dissertation. *Entrance requirements:* For master's and doctorate, GRE General Test, minimum GPA of 3.0. Additional exam requirements/recommendations for international students: Required—TOEFL (minimum score 550 paper-based; 213 computer-based; 81 iBT). Electronic applications accepted.

The University of Kansas, Graduate Studies, College of Liberal Arts and Sciences, Department of Linguistics, Lawrence, KS 66045. Offers MA, PhD. *Faculty:* 8 full-time (3 women), 1 (woman) part-time/adjunct. *Students:* 34 full-time (17 women), 1 part-time (0 women), 21 international. Average age 31. 47 applicants, 38% accepted, 7 enrolled. In 2010, 2 master's, 2 doctorates awarded. Terminal master's awarded for partial completion of doctoral program. *Degree requirements:* For master's, one foreign language, thesis or alternative, 33 credit hours; for doctorate, one foreign language, comprehensive exam, thesis/dissertation, 24 credit hours post-MA, research skills, two papers. *Entrance requirements:* For master's and doctorate, GRE General Test, curriculum vitae, statement of purpose, 3 letters of recommendation. Additional exam requirements/recommendations for international students: Required—TOEFL (minimum score 53 paper-based; 20 computer-based; 20 iBT). *Application deadline:* For fall admission, 1/1 for domestic and international students. Application fee: $55 ($65 for international students). Electronic applications accepted. *Expenses:* Tuition, state resident: full-time $7092; part-time $295.50 per credit hour. Tuition, nonresident: full-time $16,590; part-time $691.25 per credit hour. Required fees: $858; $71.49 per credit hour. Tuition and fees vary according to course load, campus/location and program. *Financial support:* Fellowships with full and partial tuition reimbursements, research assistantships with full and partial tuition reimbursements, teaching assistantships with full and partial tuition reimbursements, scholarships/grants available. Financial award application deadline: 1/1. *Faculty research:* Phonetics and phonology, syntax and semantics, psycholinguistics, neurolinguistics, first and second language acquisition. *Unit head:* Dr. Allard Jongman, Chair, 785-864-2384, Fax: 785-864-5724, E-mail: jongman@ku.edu. *Application contact:* Dr. Jie Zhang, Director of Graduate Studies, 785-864-2879, Fax: 785-864-5724, E-mail: zhang@ku.edu.

The University of Manchester, School of Languages, Linguistics and Cultures, Manchester, United Kingdom. Offers Arab world studies (PhD); Chinese studies (M Phil, PhD); East Asian studies (M Phil, PhD); English language (PhD); French studies (M Phil, PhD); German studies (M Phil, PhD); interpreting studies (PhD); Italian studies (M Phil, PhD); Japanese studies (M Phil, PhD); Latin American cultural studies (M Phil, PhD); linguistics (M Phil, PhD); Middle Eastern studies (M Phil, PhD); Polish studies (M Phil, PhD); Portuguese studies (M Phil, PhD); Russian studies (M Phil, PhD); Spanish studies (M Phil, PhD); translation and intercultural studies (M Phil, PhD).

University of Manitoba, Faculty of Graduate Studies, Faculty of Arts, Department of Linguistics, Winnipeg, MB R3T 2N2, Canada. Offers MA, PhD.

University of Maryland, Baltimore County, Graduate School, College of Arts, Humanities and Social Sciences, Department of Modern Languages and Linguistics, Program in Intercultural Communication, Baltimore, MD 21250. Offers MA. Part-time and evening/weekend programs available. *Faculty:* 18 full-time (6 women), 3 part-time/adjunct (2 women). *Students:* 17 full-time (13 women), 12 part-time (10 women); includes 1 minority (Hispanic/Latino), 11 international. 24 applicants, 83% accepted, 15 enrolled. In 2010, 13 master's awarded. *Degree requirements:*

For master's, one foreign language, comprehensive exam (for some programs), thesis (for some programs). *Entrance requirements:* For master's, GRE General Test, minimum GPA of 3.0, 3 letters of recommendation, self-evaluation and statement of support, resume. Additional exam requirements/recommendations for international students: Required—TOEFL (minimum score 550 paper-based; 213 computer-based; 80 iBT). *Application deadline:* For fall admission, 1/31 for domestic and international students. Application fee: $50. Electronic applications accepted. *Financial support:* In 2010–11, 8 students received support, including 5 teaching assistantships with full tuition reimbursements available (averaging $11,324 per year); tuition waivers also available. Financial award applicants required to submit FAFSA. *Faculty research:* Comparative television research-cross-cultural; cultural studies; social developments in Latin America; intercultural communication; French civilization and cultural studies; language, gender and sexuality; sociolinguistics; African linguistics; immigrants in U. S. and Latin American societies. *Unit head:* Dr. Denis Provencher, Director, 410-455-2109 Ext. 2636, Fax: 410-455-2636, E-mail: provench@umbc.edu. *Application contact:* Dr. Denis Provencher, Director, 410-455-2109 Ext. 2636, Fax: 410-455-2636, E-mail: provench@umbc.edu.

University of Maryland, College Park, Academic Affairs, College of Arts and Humanities, Department of Linguistics, College Park, MD 20742. Offers MA, PhD. *Faculty:* 23 full-time (9 women), 2 part-time/adjunct (both women). *Students:* 38 full-time (19 women); includes 5 minority (1 Black or African American, non-Hispanic/Latino; 1 Asian, non-Hispanic/Latino; 2 Hispanic/Latino; 1 Two or more races, non-Hispanic/Latino), 15 international. 139 applicants, 5% accepted, 5 enrolled. In 2010, 1 master's, 6 doctorates awarded. *Degree requirements:* For master's, thesis or alternative; for doctorate, thesis/dissertation. *Entrance requirements:* For master's, GRE General Test, minimum GPA of 3.0, sample of work, 3 letters of recommendation; for doctorate, GRE General Test, minimum GPA of 3.0, sample of work. Additional exam requirements/recommendations for international students: Required—TOEFL. *Application deadline:* For fall admission, 5/15 for domestic students, 2/1 for international students. Applications are processed on a rolling basis. Application fee: $75. Electronic applications accepted. *Expenses:* Tuition, state resident: part-time $471 per credit hour. Tuition, nonresident: part-time $1016 per credit hour. Required fees: $337 per term. *Financial support:* In 2010–11, 15 fellowships with full and partial tuition reimbursements (averaging $14,208 per year), 2 research assistantships (averaging $18,408 per year), 28 teaching assistantships (averaging $17,964 per year) were awarded; Federal Work-Study and scholarships/grants also available. Support available to part-time students. Financial award applicants required to submit FAFSA. *Faculty research:* Psycholinguistics, computational linguistics. Total annual research expenditures: $767,487. *Unit head:* Dr. Norbert Hornstein, Chairman, 301-405-7002, Fax: 301-314-7104, E-mail: nhorste@umd.edu. *Application contact:* Dean of Graduate School, 301-405-0376, Fax: 301-314-9305.

University of Massachusetts Amherst, Graduate School, College of Humanities and Fine Arts, Department of Linguistics, Amherst, MA 01003. Offers MA, PhD. Part-time programs available. *Faculty:* 15 full-time (7 women). *Students:* 35 full-time (19 women), 9 part-time (7 women); includes 4 minority (1 Black or African American, non-Hispanic/Latino; 1 Hispanic/ Latino; 2 Two or more races, non-Hispanic/Latino), 17 international. Average age 28. 123 applicants, 12% accepted, 9 enrolled. In 2010, 3 master's, 2 doctorates awarded. *Degree requirements:* For master's, thesis or alternative; for doctorate, comprehensive exam, thesis/ dissertation. *Entrance requirements:* For doctorate, GRE General Test. Additional exam requirements/recommendations for international students: Required—TOEFL (minimum score 550 paper-based; 213 computer-based; 80 iBT), IELTS (minimum score 6.5). *Application deadline:* For fall admission, 1/15 for domestic and international students. Applications are processed on a rolling basis. Application fee: $50 ($65 for international students). Electronic applications accepted. *Expenses:* Tuition, state resident: full-time $2640. Required fees: $8282. One-time fee: $357 full-time. *Financial support:* In 2010–11, 3 fellowships with full tuition reimbursements (averaging $27,749 per year), 18 research assistantships with full tuition reimbursements (averaging $7,716 per year), 32 teaching assistantships with full tuition reimbursements (averaging $12,043 per year) were awarded; career-related internships or fieldwork, Federal Work-Study, scholarships/grants, traineeships, health care benefits, tuition waivers (full), and unspecified assistantships also available. Support available to part-time students. Financial award application deadline: 1/15; financial award applicants required to submit FAFSA. *Unit head:* Dr. Joseph V. Pater, Graduate Program Director, 413-545-0885, Fax: 413-545-2792. *Application contact:* Jean M. Ames, Supervisor of Admissions, 413-545-0722, Fax: 413-577-0010, E-mail: gradadm@grad.umass.edu.

University of Massachusetts Boston, Office of Graduate Studies, College of Liberal Arts, Program in Applied Linguistics, Boston, MA 02125-3393. Offers bilingual education (MA); English as a second language (MA); foreign language pedagogy (MA). Part-time and evening/ weekend programs available. *Degree requirements:* For master's, one foreign language, comprehensive exam. *Entrance requirements:* For master's, minimum GPA of 2.75. *Faculty research:* Multicultural theory and curriculum development, foreign language pedagogy, language and culture, applied psycholinguistics, bilingual education.

University of Memphis, Graduate School, College of Arts and Sciences, Department of English, Memphis, TN 38152. Offers African-American literature (Graduate Certificate); applied linguistics (PhD); composition studies (PhD); creative writing (MFA); English as a second language (MA); linguistics (MA); literary and cultural studies (PhD), including African-American literature; literature (MA); professional writing (MA, PhD); teaching English as a second language (Graduate Certificate). Part-time and evening/weekend programs available. Post-baccalaureate distance learning degree programs offered (no on-campus study). *Faculty:* 31 full-time (15 women), 2 part-time/adjunct (both women). *Students:* 108 full-time (70 women), 107 part-time (69 women); includes 15 minority (2 Black or African American, non-Hispanic/ Latino; 2 Asian, non-Hispanic/Latino; 6 Hispanic/Latino; 5 Two or more races, non-Hispanic/ Latino), 8 international. Average age 34. 128 applicants, 71% accepted, 29 enrolled. In 2010, 38 master's, 4 doctorates, 21 other advanced degrees awarded. Terminal master's awarded for partial completion of doctoral program. *Degree requirements:* For master's, one foreign language, comprehensive exam, thesis optional; for doctorate, 2 foreign languages, comprehensive exam, thesis/dissertation. *Entrance requirements:* For master's and doctorate, GRE. Additional exam requirements/recommendations for international students: Required—TOEFL. *Application deadline:* For fall admission, 7/1 for domestic students; for spring admission, 10/15 for domestic students. Applications are processed on a rolling basis. Application fee: $35 ($60 for international students). Electronic applications accepted. *Financial support:* In 2010–11, 123 students received support; research assistantships with full tuition reimbursements available, teaching assistantships with full tuition reimbursements available, Federal Work-Study, scholarships/grants, and unspecified assistantships available. Financial award application deadline: 2/15; financial award applicants required to submit FAFSA. *Faculty research:* Applied linguistics, British and American literature, professional writing, composition studies. *Unit head:* Dr. Verner D. Mitchell, Chair, 901-678-3099, Fax: 901-678-2226, E-mail: vdmtchll@memphis.edu. *Application contact:* Dr. Verner D. Mitchell, Director, Graduate Studies, 901-678-3099, Fax: 901-678-2226, E-mail: vdmtchll@memphis.edu.

University of Michigan, Horace H. Rackham School of Graduate Studies, College of Literature, Science, and the Arts, Department of Linguistics, Ann Arbor, MI 48109. Offers linguistics (PhD); linguistics and Romance languages and literatures (PhD). *Faculty:* 16 full-time (7 women), 2 part-time/adjunct (both women). *Students:* 25 full-time (11 women); includes 1 Black or African American, non-Hispanic/Latino; 3 Asian, non-Hispanic/Latino, 9 international. Average age 30. 100 applicants, 9% accepted, 4 enrolled. In 2010, 5 doctorates awarded. *Degree requirements:* For doctorate, 2 foreign languages, thesis/dissertation, oral defense of dissertation. *Entrance requirements:* For doctorate, GRE General Test. Additional exam requirements/recommendations for international students: Required—Michigan English Language Assessment Battery; Recommended—TOEFL (minimum score 620 paper-based; 260 computer-based; 95 iBT). *Application deadline:* For fall admission, 12/7 for domestic students, 12/8 for international students. Application fee: $65 ($75 for international students). Electronic applications accepted. *Expenses:* Tuition, state resident: full-time $17,784; part-time $1116 per credit hour. Tuition, nonresident: full-time $35,944; part-time $2125 per credit hour.

Linguistics

University of Michigan (continued)

International tuition: $35,994 full-time. Required fees: $95 per semester. Tuition and fees vary according to course load, degree level and program. *Financial support:* In 2010–11, 23 students received support, including 13 fellowships with full tuition reimbursements available (averaging $16,800 per year), 2 research assistantships with full tuition reimbursements available (averaging $17,270 per year), 12 teaching assistantships with full tuition reimbursements available (averaging $17,270 per year); health care benefits and tuition waivers (full) also available. Financial award application deadline: 12/8. *Faculty research:* Broad-based approach to linguistics as a cognitive and social science including theoretical, experimental and computational approaches. Total annual research expenditures: $140,405. *Unit head:* Prof. Sarah Thomason, Professor/Chair, 734-764-0353, Fax: 734-936-3406, E-mail: linguistics@umich.edu. *Application contact:* Sylvia Suttor, Senior Student Services Assistant, 734-936-3403, Fax: 734-936-3406, E-mail: linggradadmissions@umich.edu.

University of Michigan, Horace H. Rackham School of Graduate Studies, College of Literature, Science, and the Arts, Department of Romance Languages and Literatures, Ann Arbor, MI 48109. Offers French (PhD); Italian (PhD); Romance linguistics (PhD); Spanish (PhD). *Faculty:* 28 full-time (13 women), 2 part-time/adjunct (1 woman). *Students:* 47 full-time (24 women); includes 27 Hispanic/Latino. Average age 27. 89 applicants, 20% accepted, 8 enrolled. In 2010, 5 doctorates awarded. *Degree requirements:* For doctorate, 2 foreign languages, thesis/dissertation, oral defense of dissertation, preliminary exams. *Entrance requirements:* For doctorate, GRE General Test. Additional exam requirements/recommendations for international students: Required—TOEFL or Michigan English Language Assessment Battery. *Application deadline:* For fall admission, 1/1 for domestic and international students. Application fee: $65 ($75 for international students). Electronic applications accepted. *Expenses:* Tuition, state resident: full-time $17,784; part-time $1116 per credit hour. Tuition, nonresident: full-time $35,944; part-time $2125 per credit hour. International tuition: $35,994 full-time. Required fees: $95 per semester. Tuition and fees vary according to course load, degree level and program. *Financial support:* In 2010–11, 1 teaching assistantship with full tuition reimbursement was awarded; fellowships with full tuition reimbursements, institutionally sponsored loans, scholarships/grants, and unspecified assistantships also available. Financial award application deadline: 1/1. *Faculty research:* Comparative Romance studies, medieval and early modern studies, postcolonial and minority literatures, culture and materiality, reflection on the nature and function of scholarship. *Unit head:* Dr. Cristina Moreiras-Menor, Chair, 734-764-5344, Fax: 734-764-8163. *Application contact:* Annette Herbert, Graduate Assistant, 734-764-8164, Fax: 734-764-8163, E-mail: rll-admissions@umich.edu.

University of Minnesota, Twin Cities Campus, Graduate School, College of Liberal Arts, Institute of Linguistics, English as a Second Language, and Slavic Languages and Literatures (ILES), Program in Linguistics, Minneapolis, MN 55455-0213. Offers MA, PhD. Terminal master's awarded for partial completion of doctoral program. *Degree requirements:* For master's, one foreign language, comprehensive exam, thesis; for doctorate, 2 foreign languages, comprehensive exam, thesis/dissertation. *Entrance requirements:* For master's and doctorate, GRE General Test, 3 letters of recommendation, unit questionnaire. Additional exam requirements/recommendations for international students: Required—TOEFL (minimum score 550 paper-based; 213 computer-based; 79 iBT). Electronic applications accepted. *Faculty research:* Pragmatics and language processing, syntactic theory, language policy and planning, contact linguistics, language and cognition.

University of Missouri–St. Louis, College of Arts and Sciences, Department of English, St. Louis, MO 63121. Offers American literature (MA); creative writing (MFA); English literature (MA); linguistics (MA); teaching of writing (Certificate). Part-time and evening/weekend programs available. *Faculty:* 19 full-time (9 women), 2 part-time/adjunct (1 woman). *Students:* 25 full-time (12 women), 95 part-time (62 women); includes 13 minority (6 Black or African American, non-Hispanic/Latino; 2 American Indian or Alaska Native, non-Hispanic/Latino; 3 Asian, non-Hispanic/Latino; 1 Hispanic/Latino; 1 Two or more races, non-Hispanic/Latino), 1 international. Average age 30. 103 applicants, 41% accepted, 24 enrolled. In 2010, 241 master's, 5 other advanced degrees awarded. *Degree requirements:* For master's, thesis optional. *Entrance requirements:* For master's, two letters of recommendation; writing sample (MFA). Additional exam requirements/recommendations for international students: Required—TOEFL (minimum score 550 paper-based; 213 computer-based). *Application deadline:* For fall admission, 7/1 priority date for domestic and international students; for spring admission, 12/1 priority date for domestic and international students. Applications are processed on a rolling basis. Application fee: $35 ($40 for international students). Electronic applications accepted. *Expenses:* Tuition, state resident: full-time $5522; part-time $306.80 per credit hour. Tuition, nonresident: full-time $14,253; part-time $792.10 per credit hour. Required fees: $658; $49 per credit hour. One-time fee: $12. Tuition and fees vary according to program. *Financial support:* In 2010–11, 6 research assistantships with full and partial tuition reimbursements (averaging $5,666 per year), 10 teaching assistantships with full and partial tuition reimbursements (averaging $9,000 per year) were awarded. Financial award applicants required to submit FAFSA. *Faculty research:* Victorian literature, Shakespeare and Renaissance literature, eighteenth century literature, composition theory. *Unit head:* Dr. Frank Grady, Director of Graduate Studies, 314-516-5541, Fax: 314-516-5781, E-mail: fgrady@umsl.edu. *Application contact:* 314-516-5458, Fax: 314-516-5310, E-mail: gradadm@umsl.edu.

The University of Montana, Graduate School, College of Arts and Sciences, Department of Anthropology, Missoula, MT 59812-0002. Offers anthropology (MA); cultural heritage (MA); cultural heritage studies (PhD); forensic anthropology (MA); historical anthropology (PhD); linguistics (MA). *Degree requirements:* For master's, thesis (for some programs). *Entrance requirements:* For master's, GRE General Test. Additional exam requirements/recommendations for international students: Required—TOEFL. *Faculty research:* Historical preservation, plateau-plains archaeology and ethnohistory.

The University of Montana, Graduate School, College of Arts and Sciences, Program in Linguistics, Missoula, MT 59812-0002. Offers MA. *Entrance requirements:* For master's, GRE General Test. Additional exam requirements/recommendations for international students: Required—TOEFL.

University of New Hampshire, Graduate School, College of Liberal Arts, Department of English, Durham, NH 03824. Offers English (MFA, PhD); English education (MST); language and linguistics (MA); literature (MA); writing (MA). Part-time programs available. *Faculty:* 35 full-time (18 women). *Students:* 60 full-time (33 women), 68 part-time (45 women); includes 5 minority (1 Black or African American, non-Hispanic/Latino; 1 Hispanic/Latino; 3 Two or more races, non-Hispanic/Latino), 5 international. Average age 33. 291 applicants, 47% accepted, 50 enrolled. In 2010, 39 master's, 6 doctorates awarded. *Degree requirements:* For master's, one foreign language; for doctorate, 2 foreign languages, thesis/dissertation. *Entrance requirements:* For master's, GRE General Test, sample of written work; for doctorate, GRE General Test, GRE Subject Test, sample of written work. Additional exam requirements/recommendations for international students: Required—TOEFL (minimum score 550 paper-based; 213 computer-based; 80 iBT). *Application deadline:* For fall admission, 6/1 priority date for domestic students, 2/15 for international students; for spring admission, 12/1 for domestic students. Applications are processed on a rolling basis. Application fee: $65. Electronic applications accepted. *Financial support:* In 2010–11, 63 students received support, including 1 fellowship, 46 teaching assistantships; research assistantships, career-related internships or fieldwork, Federal Work-Study, scholarships/grants, and tuition waivers (full and partial) also available. Support available to part-time students. Financial award application deadline: 2/15. *Unit head:* Dr. Andrew Merton, Chairperson, 603-862-3963. *Application contact:* Jamie Auger, Administrative Assistant, 603-862-3963, E-mail: engl.grad@unh.edu.

University of New Mexico, Graduate School, College of Arts and Sciences, Department of Linguistics, Albuquerque, NM 87131-2039. Offers MA, PhD. Part-time programs available. *Faculty:* 21 full-time (16 women), 19 part-time/adjunct (12 women). *Students:* 37 full-time (20 women), 15 part-time (11 women); includes 1 Black or African American, non-Hispanic/Latino;

4 American Indian or Alaska Native, non-Hispanic/Latino; 1 Asian, non-Hispanic/Latino; 1 Hispanic/Latino; 1 Two or more races, non-Hispanic/Latino, 15 international. Average age 34. 56 applicants, 43% accepted, 17 enrolled. In 2010, 4 master's, 2 doctorates awarded. *Degree requirements:* For master's, comprehensive exam, thesis optional; for doctorate, one foreign language, comprehensive exam, thesis/dissertation. *Entrance requirements:* For master's, minimum GPA of 3.0, 3 letters of recommendation, letter of intent; for doctorate, MA in linguistics or equivalent, paper of publishable quality, 3 letters of recommendation, letter of intent. Additional exam requirements/recommendations for international students: Required—TOEFL (minimum score 520 paper-based; 190 computer-based; 68 iBT), IELTS. *Application deadline:* For fall admission, 12/15 priority date for domestic and international students. Application fee: $50. Electronic applications accepted. *Expenses:* Tuition, state resident: full-time $5991; part-time $251 per credit hour. Tuition, nonresident: full-time $14,405; part-time $800.20 per credit hour. Tuition and fees vary according to course level, course load, program and reciprocity agreements. *Financial support:* In 2010–11, 40 students received support, including 2 fellowships with full tuition reimbursements available (averaging $7,350 per year), 2 research assistantships (averaging $8,452 per year), 24 teaching assistantships with full and partial tuition reimbursements available (averaging $10,679 per year); Federal Work-Study, health care benefits, and tuition waivers (full and partial) also available. Financial award application deadline: 1/15; financial award applicants required to submit FAFSA. *Faculty research:* American Sign Language, functional/cognitive linguistics, sociolinguistics, Spanish linguistics, Native American linguistics, signed language linguistics, language processing, Navajo/Dine Language, Spanish linguistics, typology, discourse, language acquisition. Total annual research expenditures: $37,817. *Unit head:* Dr. Sherman Wilcox, Chair, 505-277-6353, Fax: 505-277-6355, E-mail: wilcox@unm.edu. *Application contact:* Jessica Slocum, Administrative Assistant III, 505-277-6353, Fax: 505-277-6355, E-mail: jslocum@unm.edu.

University of New Mexico, Graduate School, College of Education, Department of Language, Literacy and Sociocultural Studies, Program in Educational Linguistics, Albuquerque, NM 87131-2039. Offers PhD. Part-time programs available. *Students:* 4 full-time (2 women), 9 part-time (8 women); includes 2 Asian, non-Hispanic/Latino; 2 Hispanic/Latino; 1 Two or more races, non-Hispanic/Latino, 4 international. Average age 44. 10 applicants, 50% accepted, 3 enrolled. In 2010, 2 doctorates awarded. *Degree requirements:* For doctorate, comprehensive exam, thesis/dissertation. *Entrance requirements:* For doctorate, master's degree in linguistics or complementary field (recommended). Additional exam requirements/recommendations for international students: Required—TOEFL (minimum score 550 paper-based; 213 computer-based; 79 iBT). *Application deadline:* For fall admission, 12/1 for domestic and international students. Application fee: $50. Electronic applications accepted. *Expenses:* Tuition, state resident: full-time $5991; part-time $251 per credit hour. Tuition, nonresident: full-time $14,405; part-time $800.20 per credit hour. Tuition and fees vary according to course level, course load, program and reciprocity agreements. *Financial support:* In 2010–11, 6 students received support, including 3 teaching assistantships with tuition reimbursements available (averaging $9,583 per year); career-related internships or fieldwork, institutionally sponsored loans, scholarships/grants, and unspecified assistantships also available. Support available to part-time students. Financial award application deadline: 1/15; financial award applicants required to submit FAFSA. *Faculty research:* Bilingualism, language maintenance and loss, bilingual deaf education, Spanish dialectical studies, English as a second language, writing/composition, Native American language issues, language and thought, language policy studies, global English issues, assessment. *Unit head:* Dr. Holbrook Mahn, Graduate Director, 505-277-5887, Fax: 505-277-8362, E-mail: hmahn@unm.edu. *Application contact:* Mary Gurule Vernon, Program Administrator, 505-277-5282, Fax: 505-277-8362, E-mail: mgurule2@unm.edu.

The University of North Carolina at Chapel Hill, Graduate School, College of Arts and Sciences, Department of Germanic Languages, Chapel Hill, NC 27599. Offers literature and linguistics (MA, PhD). Part-time programs available. Terminal master's awarded for partial completion of doctoral program. *Degree requirements:* For master's, comprehensive exam, thesis; for doctorate, one foreign language, comprehensive exam, thesis/dissertation. *Entrance requirements:* For master's and doctorate, GRE General Test, minimum GPA of 3.0. *Faculty research:* Gender and sexuality, literature and politics, German and Jewish culture, medieval through modern literature, Germanic linguistics.

The University of North Carolina at Chapel Hill, Graduate School, College of Arts and Sciences, Department of Linguistics, Chapel Hill, NC 27599. Offers MA. *Faculty:* 4 full-time (2 women). *Students:* 17 full-time (11 women); includes 1 Black or African American, non-Hispanic/Latino, 5 international. Average age 30. 33 applicants, 33% accepted, 6 enrolled. In 2010, 2 master's awarded. *Degree requirements:* For master's, one foreign language, comprehensive exam, thesis. *Entrance requirements:* For master's, GRE General Test, minimum GPA of 3.0. Additional exam requirements/recommendations for international students: Required—TOEFL (minimum score 213 computer-based; 79 iBT). *Application deadline:* For fall admission, 12/15 priority date for domestic and international students. Application fee: $77. Electronic applications accepted. *Financial support:* In 2010–11, 9 students received support, including 13 teaching assistantships with full tuition reimbursements available (averaging $15,000 per year). Financial award application deadline: 1/1. *Faculty research:* Phonetics, phonology, morphology, syntax, semantics, historical linguistics, language acquisition, Mayan linguistics. *Unit head:* Prof. Paul T. Roberge, Interim Chair, 919-962-1192, Fax: 919-962-5859, E-mail: ptr@email.unc.edu. *Application contact:* Elliott Moreton, Director of Graduate Admissions, 919-962-1192, Fax: 919-962-5859, E-mail: moreton@email.unc.edu.

University of North Dakota, Graduate School, College of Arts and Sciences, Program in Linguistics, Grand Forks, ND 58202. Offers MA. *Faculty:* 18 full-time (5 women). *Students:* 6 part-time (3 women). Average age 33. 1 applicant, 0% accepted, 0 enrolled. In 2010, 3 master's awarded. *Degree requirements:* For master's, one foreign language, thesis, final examination. *Entrance requirements:* For master's, minimum GPA of 3.0. Additional exam requirements/recommendations for international students: Required—TOEFL (minimum score 550 paper-based; 213 computer-based; 79 iBT), IELTS (minimum score 6.5). *Application deadline:* For fall admission, 3/1 priority date for domestic and international students. Applications are processed on a rolling basis. Application fee: $35. Electronic applications accepted. *Expenses:* Tuition, state resident: full-time $5857; part-time $306.74 per credit. Tuition, nonresident: full-time $15,666; part-time $729.77 per credit. Required fees: $53.42 per credit. Tuition and fees vary according to course load, program and reciprocity agreements. *Financial support:* Fellowships with full and partial tuition reimbursements, research assistantships with full and partial tuition reimbursements, teaching assistantships with full and partial tuition reimbursements, Federal Work-Study, institutionally sponsored loans, tuition waivers (full and partial), and unspecified assistantships available. Support available to part-time students. Financial award application deadline: 3/15; financial award applicants required to submit FAFSA. *Faculty research:* Practice-based field studies. *Unit head:* Dr. John Clifton, Graduate Director, 701-777-2011. *Application contact:* Matt Anderson, Admissions Associate, 701-777-2947, Fax: 701-777-3619, E-mail: matthew.anderson@gradschool.und.edu.

University of Oregon, Graduate School, College of Arts and Sciences, Department of Linguistics, Eugene, OR 97403. Offers MA, PhD. Terminal master's awarded for partial completion of doctoral program. *Degree requirements:* For master's, 2 foreign languages; for doctorate, thesis/dissertation. *Entrance requirements:* For master's and doctorate, GRE General Test, minimum GPA of 3.0. Additional exam requirements/recommendations for international students: Required—TOEFL. *Faculty research:* Functional syntax, discourse, empirical methods.

University of Ottawa, Faculty of Graduate and Postdoctoral Studies, Faculty of Arts, Department of Linguistics, Ottawa, ON K1N 6N5, Canada. Offers MA, PhD. *Degree requirements:* For master's, one foreign language, thesis or alternative; for doctorate, 2 foreign languages, comprehensive exam, thesis/dissertation. *Entrance requirements:* For master's, honors degree or equivalent, minimum B average; for doctorate, master's degree, minimum B+ average. Electronic applications accepted. *Faculty research:* Empirical linguistics, formal linguistics.

University of Pennsylvania, Graduate School of Education, Division of Language in Education, Programs in Teaching English to Speakers of Other Languages and Intercultural Communication, Philadelphia, PA 19104. Offers educational linguistics (PhD); intercultural communication (MS Ed); teaching English to speakers of other languages (MS Ed). Part-time programs available. Postbaccalaureate distance learning degree programs offered (minimal on-campus study). *Students:* 109 full-time (95 women), 19 part-time (17 women); includes 2 Black or African American, non-Hispanic/Latino; 7 Asian, non-Hispanic/Latino; 1 Hispanic/Latino, 105 international. 182 applicants, 77% accepted, 74 enrolled. In 2010, 38 master's awarded. Terminal master's awarded for partial completion of doctoral program. *Degree requirements:* For master's, comprehensive exam, thesis (for some programs); for doctorate, one foreign language, thesis/dissertation, preliminary exam. *Entrance requirements:* For master's and doctorate, GRE General Test or MAT. Additional exam requirements/recommendations for international students: Required—TOEFL. *Application deadline:* For fall admission, 12/15 priority date for domestic students. Applications are processed on a rolling basis. Application fee: $70. Electronic applications accepted. *Expenses:* Contact institution. *Financial support:* Fellowships, research assistantships, institutionally sponsored loans, scholarships/grants, traineeships, health care benefits, and unspecified assistantships available. *Faculty research:* Second language acquisition, social linguistics, English as a second language. *Application contact:* Penny Creedon, 215-898-3245, E-mail: pennyc@gse.upenn.edu.

University of Pennsylvania, School of Arts and Sciences, Graduate Group in Linguistics, Philadelphia, PA 19104. Offers AM, PhD. *Faculty:* 21 full-time (4 women). *Students:* 31 full-time (19 women), 1 (woman) part-time; includes 1 Asian, non-Hispanic/Latino, 8 international. 124 applicants, 7% accepted, 4 enrolled. In 2010, 3 master's, 6 doctorates awarded. Terminal master's awarded for partial completion of doctoral program. *Degree requirements:* For master's, thesis; for doctorate, 2 foreign languages, thesis/dissertation. *Entrance requirements:* For master's and doctorate, GRE General Test. Additional exam requirements/recommendations for international students: Required—TOEFL. *Application deadline:* For fall admission, 12/1 priority date for domestic students. Application fee: $70. Electronic applications accepted. *Expenses:* Tuition: Full-time $25,660; part-time $4758 per course. Required fees: $2152; $270 per course. Tuition and fees vary according to course load, degree level and program. *Financial support:* Fellowships, research assistantships, teaching assistantships, institutionally sponsored loans, scholarships/grants, traineeships, health care benefits, and unspecified assistantships available. Financial award application deadline: 12/15. *Unit head:* Anthony Kroch, Department Chair, Linguistics, 215-898-3212, E-mail: kroch@change.ling.upenn.edu. *Application contact:* Anthony Kroch, Department Chair, Linguistics, 215-898-3212, E-mail: kroch@change.ling.upenn.edu.

University of Pittsburgh, School of Arts and Sciences, Department of Linguistics, Pittsburgh, PA 15260. Offers applied linguistics (PhD); linguistics (MA); sociolinguistics (PhD). Part-time programs available. *Faculty:* 7 full-time (2 women), 1 (woman) part-time/adjunct. *Students:* 28 full-time (20 women), 2 part-time (both women); includes 2 Black or African American, non-Hispanic/Latino, 8 international. Average age 30. 113 applicants, 19% accepted, 6 enrolled. In 2010, 3 master's awarded. Terminal master's awarded for partial completion of doctoral program. *Degree requirements:* For master's, one foreign language, thesis; for doctorate, 2 foreign languages, comprehensive exam, thesis/dissertation. *Entrance requirements:* For master's, GRE General Test; for doctorate, GRE General Test, MA in linguistics. Additional exam requirements/recommendations for international students: Required—TOEFL (minimum score 600 paper-based; 250 computer-based; 100 iBT). *Application deadline:* For fall admission, 12/15 priority date for domestic and international students. Applications are processed on a rolling basis. Application fee: $50. Electronic applications accepted. *Expenses:* Tuition, state resident: full-time $17,304; part-time $701 per credit. Tuition, nonresident: full-time $29,554; part-time $1210 per credit. Required fees: $740; $214 per term. Tuition and fees vary according to program. *Financial support:* In 2010–11, 19 students received support, including 4 fellowships with full and partial tuition reimbursements available (averaging $15,000 per year), 4 research assistantships with full and partial tuition reimbursements available (averaging $12,300 per year), 11 teaching assistantships with full and partial tuition reimbursements available (averaging $15,065 per year); scholarships/grants, health care benefits, and unspecified assistantships also available. Financial award application deadline: 12/15. *Faculty research:* Second language acquisition, applied linguistics, sociolinguistics, language contact. Total annual research expenditures: $279,685. *Unit head:* Dr. Yasuhiro Shirai, Chair, 412-624-5933, Fax: 412-624-6130, E-mail: yshirai@pitt.edu. *Application contact:* Allison M. Thompson, Department Administrator, 412-624-5938, Fax: 412-624-6130, E-mail: lingpitt@pitt.edu.

University of Puerto Rico, Río Piedras, College of Humanities, Department of Hispanic Studies, San Juan, PR 00931-3300. Offers Hispanic linguistics (PhD); Hispanic studies (MA); Latin American literature (PhD); Puerto Rican literature (PhD); Spanish literature (PhD). Part-time programs available. *Degree requirements:* For master's, one foreign language, comprehensive exam, thesis; for doctorate, one foreign language, comprehensive exam, thesis/dissertation. *Entrance requirements:* For master's, PAEG or GRE, interview, minimum GPA of 3.0, letter of recommendation (2); for doctorate, PAEG or GRE, interview, master's degree, minimum GPA of 3.0, letter of recommendation (2). *Faculty research:* Poetry of Luis Palés Matos, short stories in Puerto Rico, language in the social process, 'Decima Popular", Anglicism.

University of Puerto Rico, Río Piedras, College of Humanities, Department of Linguistics, San Juan, PR 00931-3300. Offers MA. Part-time programs available. *Degree requirements:* For master's, one foreign language, comprehensive exam, thesis. *Entrance requirements:* For master's, PAEG or GRE, interview, minimum GPA of 3.0, letter of recommendation (2).

University of Regina, Faculty of Graduate Studies and Research, Faculty of Arts, Program in Linguistics, Regina, SK S4S 0A2, Canada. Offers MA. Offered as special case program. Part-time programs available. *Faculty:* 3 full-time (1 woman). *Students:* 1 (woman) full-time. *Degree requirements:* For master's, thesis. *Entrance requirements:* Additional exam requirements/recommendations for international students: Required—TOEFL (minimum score 580 paper-based). *Application deadline:* Applications are processed on a rolling basis. Application fee: $100. Electronic applications accepted. Tuition and fees charges are reported in Canadian dollars. *Expenses:* Tuition, area resident: Full-time $3244.50 Canadian dollars; part-time $180.25 Canadian dollars per credit hour. International tuition: $4744.50 Canadian dollars full-time. Required fees: $494 Canadian dollars; $115.25 Canadian dollars per credit hour. $115.25 Canadian dollars per semester. Tuition and fees vary according to program. *Financial support:* Fellowships, research assistantships, teaching assistantships, scholarships/grants available. Financial award application deadline: 6/15. *Faculty research:* Advanced phonology, advanced morphology, advanced syntax, advanced semantics, diachronic linguistics. *Unit head:* Dr. Arok Wolvengrey, Program Coordinator, 306-790-5950 Ext. 3310, Fax: 306-790-5994, E-mail: awolvengrey@firstnations.university.ca. *Application contact:* Dr. Arok Wolvengrey, Graduate Program Coordinator, 306-790-5950 Ext. 3310, Fax: 306-790-5994, E-mail: awolvengrey@firstnations.university.ca.

University of Rochester, School of Arts and Sciences, Department of Linguistics, Rochester, NY 14627.

University of South Africa, College of Human Sciences, Pretoria, South Africa. Offers adult education (M Ed); African languages (MA, PhD); African politics (MA, PhD); Afrikaans (MA, PhD); ancient history (MA, PhD); ancient Near Eastern studies (MA, PhD); anthropology (MA, PhD); applied linguistics (MA); Arabic (MA, PhD); archaeology (MA); art history (MA); Biblical archaeology (MA); Biblical studies (M Th, D Th, PhD); Christian spirituality (M Th, D Th); church history (M Th, D Th); classical studies (MA, PhD); clinical psychology (MA); communication (MA, PhD); comparative education (M Ed, Ed D); consulting psychology (D Admin, D Com, PhD); curriculum studies (M Ed, Ed D); development studies (M Admin, MA, D Admin, PhD); didactics (M Ed, Ed D); education (M Tech); education management (M Ed, Ed D); educational psychology (M Ed); English (MA); environmental education (M Ed); French (MA, PhD); German (MA, PhD); Greek (MA); guidance and counseling (M Ed); health studies (MA, PhD), including health sciences education (MA), health services management (MA), medical and surgical nursing science (critical care general) (MA), midwifery and neonatal nursing science (MA), trauma and emergency care (MA); history (MA, PhD); history of education (Ed D); inclusive education (M Ed, Ed D); information and communications technology policy and regulation (MA); information science (MA, MIS, PhD); international politics (MA, PhD); Islamic studies (MA, PhD); Italian (MA, PhD); Judaica (MA, PhD); linguistics (MA, PhD); mathematical education (M Ed); mathematics education (MA); missiology (M Th, D Th); modern Hebrew (MA, PhD); musicology (MA, MMus, D Mus, PhD); natural science education (M Ed); New Testament (M Th, D Th); Old Testament (D Th); pastoral therapy (M Th, D Th); philosophy (MA); philosophy of education (M Ed, Ed D); politics (MA, PhD); Portuguese (MA, PhD); practical theology (M Th, D Th); psychology (MA, MS, PhD); psychology of education (M Ed, Ed D); public health (MA); religious studies (MA, D Th, PhD); Romance languages (MA); Russian (MA, PhD); Semitic languages (MA, PhD); social behavior studies in HIV/AIDS (MA); social science (mental health) (MA); social science in development studies (MA); social science in psychology (MA); social science in social work (MA); social science in sociology (MA); social work (MSW, DSW, PhD); socio-education (M Ed, Ed D); sociolinguistics (MA); sociology (MA, PhD); Spanish (MA, PhD); systematic theology (M Th, D Th); TESOL (teaching English to speakers of other languages) (MA); theological ethics (M Th, D Th); theory of literature (MA, PhD); urban ministries (D Th); urban ministry (M Th).

University of South Carolina, The Graduate School, College of Arts and Sciences, Linguistics Program, Columbia, SC 29208. Offers linguistics (MA, PhD); teaching English to speakers of other languages (Certificate). Part-time programs available. Terminal master's awarded for partial completion of doctoral program. *Degree requirements:* For master's, one foreign language, comprehensive exam, thesis optional; for doctorate, 3 foreign languages, comprehensive exam, thesis/dissertation. *Entrance requirements:* For master's and Certificate, GRE General Test, minimum GPA of 3.0; for doctorate, GRE General Test, minimum GPA of 3.5. Additional exam requirements/recommendations for international students: Required—TOEFL. Electronic applications accepted. *Faculty research:* Second language acquisition, sociolinguistics, syntax, historical linguistics and phonology.

University of Southern California, Graduate School, Dana and David Dornsife College of Letters, Arts and Sciences, Department of East Asian Languages and Cultures, Los Angeles, CA 90089. Offers classical Chinese literature (MA, PhD); classical Japanese literature (MA, PhD); linguistics (MA, PhD); modern Chinese literature (MA, PhD); modern Japanese literature (MA, PhD); modern Korean literature (MA, PhD). *Faculty:* 14 full-time (7 women). *Students:* 19 full-time (14 women), 1 (woman) part-time; includes 5 minority (1 Black or African American, non-Hispanic/Latino; 4 Asian, non-Hispanic/Latino), 10 international. 37 applicants, 16% accepted, 6 enrolled. In 2010, 5 master's, 1 doctorate awarded. *Degree requirements:* For master's, thesis; for doctorate, 2 foreign languages, comprehensive exam, thesis/dissertation. *Entrance requirements:* For master's and doctorate, GRE, BA in relevant field. Additional exam requirements/recommendations for international students: Required—TOEFL. *Application deadline:* For fall admission, 12/1 priority date for domestic and international students. Application fee: $85. Electronic applications accepted. *Expenses:* Tuition: Full-time $31,240; part-time $1420 per unit. Required fees: $600. One-time fee: $35 full-time. Full-time tuition and fees vary according to degree level and program. *Financial support:* In 2010–11, 25 students received support, including 4 fellowships with full tuition reimbursements available (averaging $30,000 per year), 25 teaching assistantships with partial tuition reimbursements available (averaging $19,800 per year); scholarships/grants, health care benefits, and unspecified assistantships also available. Financial award application deadline: 12/1. *Faculty research:* Gender, visual studies, multimedia, ecocriticism, second language acquisition. *Unit head:* Dominic Cheung, Chair, 213-740-3708, Fax: 213-740-9295, E-mail: dcheung@usc.edu. *Application contact:* Sherall R. Preyer, Administrative Coordinator, 213-740-3709, Fax: 213-740-9295, E-mail: preyer@college.usc.edu.

University of Southern California, Graduate School, Dana and David Dornsife College of Letters, Arts and Sciences, Department of Linguistics, Los Angeles, CA 90089. Offers East Asian linguistics (PhD); Hispanic linguistics (PhD); linguistics (PhD); Slavic linguistics (PhD). *Faculty:* 15 full-time (10 women), 5 part-time/adjunct (3 women). *Students:* 40 full-time (26 women), 2 part-time (1 woman); includes 7 minority (5 Asian, non-Hispanic/Latino; 1 Hispanic/Latino; 1 Two or more races, non-Hispanic/Latino), 23 international. 76 applicants, 24% accepted, 7 enrolled. In 2010, 1 doctorate awarded. *Degree requirements:* For doctorate, comprehensive exam, thesis/dissertation. *Entrance requirements:* For doctorate, GRE. Additional exam requirements/recommendations for international students: Required—TOEFL (minimum score 100 iBT). *Application deadline:* For fall admission, 12/1 priority date for domestic and international students. Application fee: $85. Electronic applications accepted. *Expenses:* Tuition: Full-time $31,240; part-time $1420 per unit. Required fees: $600. One-time fee: $35 full-time. Full-time tuition and fees vary according to degree level and program. *Financial support:* In 2010–11, 37 students received support, including 12 fellowships with full tuition reimbursements available (averaging $20,000 per year), 3 research assistantships with full tuition reimbursements available (averaging $19,250 per year), 22 teaching assistantships with full tuition reimbursements available (averaging $19,250 per year); scholarships/grants, health care benefits, and unspecified assistantships also available. *Faculty research:* Syntax, phonology, phonetics, semantics, sociolinguistics, psycholinguistics. *Unit head:* Dr. James Higginbotham, Chair, 213-740-2986, Fax: 213-740-9306, E-mail: higgy@usc.edu. *Application contact:* Joyce Perez, Student Services Advisor, 213-740-3891, Fax: 213-740-9306, E-mail: jpperez@usc.edu.

University of South Florida, Graduate School, College of Arts and Sciences, World Languages Department, Tampa, FL 33620-9951. Offers classics: Latin/Greek (MA); French (MA); linguistics (MA); linguistics: ESL (MA); Spanish (MA). Part-time and evening/weekend programs available. *Faculty:* 10 full-time (6 women). *Students:* 38 full-time (28 women), 25 part-time (17 women); includes 3 Black or African American, non-Hispanic/Latino; 2 American Indian or Alaska Native, non-Hispanic/Latino; 3 Asian, non-Hispanic/Latino; 18 Hispanic/Latino; 1 Two or more races, non-Hispanic/Latino, 6 international. Average age 35. 65 applicants, 48% accepted, 23 enrolled. In 2010, 23 master's awarded. *Degree requirements:* For master's, comprehensive exam, thesis. *Entrance requirements:* For master's, GRE General Test, minimum GPA of 3.0 in last 60 hours. Additional exam requirements/recommendations for international students: Required—TOEFL (minimum score 600 paper-based; 250 computer-based). *Application deadline:* For fall admission, 2/15 for domestic students, 1/2 for international students; for spring admission, 10/15 for domestic students, 6/1 for international students. Application fee: $30. Electronic applications accepted. *Financial support:* In 2010–11, 31 teaching assistantships with tuition reimbursements (averaging $9,272 per year) were awarded; tuition waivers (partial) and unspecified assistantships also available. Financial award application deadline: 6/30. *Faculty research:* Second language writing, academic literacy. Total annual research expenditures: $116,653. *Unit head:* Dr. Victor Peppard, Chairperson, 813-974-2012, Fax: 813-974-1718, E-mail: peppard@.cas.usf.edu. *Application contact:* Dr. Victor Peppard, Chairperson, 813-974-2012, Fax: 813-974-1718, E-mail: peppard@.cas.usf.edu.

The University of Tennessee, Graduate School, College of Arts and Sciences, Department of Modern Foreign Languages and Literatures, Program in Modern Foreign Languages, Knoxville, TN 37996. Offers applied linguistics (PhD); French (PhD); German (PhD); Italian (PhD); Portuguese (PhD); Russian (PhD); Spanish (PhD). *Degree requirements:* For doctorate, 2 foreign languages, thesis/dissertation. *Entrance requirements:* For doctorate, minimum GPA of 2.7. Additional exam requirements/recommendations for international students: Required—TOEFL. Electronic applications accepted. *Expenses:* Tuition, state resident: full-time $7440; part-time $414 per credit hour. Tuition, nonresident: full-time $22,478; part-time $1250 per credit hour. Required fees: $922; $43 per credit hour. Tuition and fees vary according to program.

The University of Texas at Arlington, Graduate School, College of Liberal Arts, Department of Linguistics and TESOL, Program in Linguistics, Arlington, TX 76019. Offers MA, PhD. Part-time and evening/weekend programs available. *Faculty:* 7 full-time (4 women), 2 part-time/adjunct (0 women). *Students:* 27 full-time (16 women), 22 part-time (13 women); includes 9 minority (3 Black or African American, non-Hispanic/Latino; 4 Asian, non-Hispanic/Latino; 2 Hispanic/Latino), 10 international. 28 applicants, 57% accepted, 14 enrolled. In 2010, 14

Linguistics

The University of Texas at Arlington (continued)
master's, 6 doctorates awarded. Terminal master's awarded for partial completion of doctoral program. *Degree requirements:* For master's, one foreign language, comprehensive exam (for some programs), thesis optional; for doctorate, 2 foreign languages, comprehensive exam, thesis/dissertation, qualifying exam, dissertation proposal defense, professional development. *Entrance requirements:* For master's, GRE General Test, minimum undergraduate GPA of 3.0, 9 credits of undergraduate foundation courses; for doctorate, GRE General Test, 30 hours of graduate work in linguistics or a related discipline, minimum GPA of 3.5. Additional exam requirements/recommendations for international students: Required—TOEFL (minimum score 550 paper-based; 213 computer-based). *Application deadline:* For fall admission, 6/15 for domestic students. Applications are processed on a rolling basis. Application fee: $35 ($50 for international students). Electronic applications accepted. *Expenses:* Tuition, state resident: full-time $7500. Tuition, nonresident: full-time $13,080. International tuition: $13,250 full-time. *Financial support:* In 2010–11, 3 fellowships (averaging $1,000 per year), 1 research assistantship (averaging $11,500 per year), 7 teaching assistantships with full tuition reimbursements (averaging $12,000 per year) were awarded; career-related internships or fieldwork and institutionally sponsored loans also available. Financial award application deadline: 3/1; financial award applicants required to submit FAFSA. *Faculty research:* Field linguistics, discourse analysis, text linguistics, phonology, teaching English as a second language. *Unit head:* Dr. Jerrold Edmonson, Chair, 817-272-3133, Fax: 817-272-2731, E-mail: jerry@uta.edu. *Application contact:* Dr. Laurel Stvan, Graduate Advisor, 817-272-3133, Fax: 817-272-2731.

The University of Texas at Austin, Graduate School, College of Liberal Arts, Department of French and Italian, Austin, TX 78712-1111. Offers French (MA, PhD); French linguistics (MA, PhD); Italian studies (MA, PhD); Romance linguistics (MA, PhD). Part-time programs available. *Degree requirements:* For master's, one foreign language, thesis; for doctorate, 2 foreign languages, thesis/dissertation. *Entrance requirements:* For master's, GRE General Test, minimum GPA of 3.0, bachelor's degree in French or equivalent; for doctorate, GRE General Test, minimum GPA of 3.0, master's degree in French. Additional exam requirements/recommendations for international students: Required—TOEFL. Electronic applications accepted. *Faculty research:* Nineteenth-century Italian literature, Italian Renaissance, twentieth-century French literature, Francophone literature, fifteenth-century literature and culture.

The University of Texas at Austin, Graduate School, College of Liberal Arts, Department of Linguistics, Austin, TX 78712-1111. Offers MA, PhD. *Degree requirements:* For master's, one foreign language, thesis; for doctorate, 2 foreign languages, thesis/dissertation. *Entrance requirements:* For master's and doctorate, GRE General Test. Electronic applications accepted. *Faculty research:* Theoretical linguistics, sociolinguistics, documentary and descriptive linguistics, computational linguistics.

The University of Texas at El Paso, Graduate School, College of Liberal Arts, Department of Languages and Linguistics, El Paso, TX 79968-0001. Offers linguistics (MA); Spanish (MA); teaching English to speakers of other languages (Certificate). Part-time and evening/weekend programs available. *Students:* 28 (12 women); includes 15 Hispanic/Latino, 4 international. Average age 34. In 2010, 10 master's awarded. *Degree requirements:* For master's, thesis optional. *Entrance requirements:* For master's, GRE General Test, departmental exam, minimum GPA of 3.0, letters of recommendation. Additional exam requirements/recommendations for international students: Required—TOEFL; Recommended—IELTS. *Application deadline:* For fall admission, 8/1 for domestic students, 3/1 for international students; for spring admission, 11/1 for domestic students, 9/1 for international students. Applications are processed on a rolling basis. Application fee: $45 ($80 for international students). Electronic applications accepted. *Financial support:* In 2010–11, research assistantships with partial tuition reimbursements (averaging $18,625 per year), teaching assistantships with partial tuition reimbursements (averaging $14,900 per year) were awarded; fellowships with partial tuition reimbursements, institutionally sponsored loans, scholarships/grants, health care benefits, tuition waivers (partial), and unspecified assistantships also available. Support available to part-time students. Financial award application deadline: 3/15; financial award applicants required to submit FAFSA. *Unit head:* Dr. Kirsten F. Nigro, Chair, 915-747-5767, Fax: 915-747-5292, E-mail: kfnigro@utep.edu. *Application contact:* Dr. Patricia D. Witherspoon, Dean of the Graduate School, 915-747-5491, Fax: 915-747-5788, E-mail: withersp@utep.edu.

University of Toronto, School of Graduate Studies, Humanities Division, Department of Linguistics, Toronto, ON M5S 1A1, Canada. Offers MA, PhD. Part-time programs available. *Degree requirements:* For master's, 2 foreign languages; for doctorate, thesis/dissertation, oral thesis proposal. *Entrance requirements:* For master's, BA in linguistics; for doctorate, MA in linguistics.

University of Utah, Graduate School, College of Humanities, Department of Linguistics, Salt Lake City, UT 84112-0492. Offers applied linguistics (MA, PhD); linguistics (MA, PhD). *Faculty:* 8 full-time (4 women), 1 part-time/adjunct (0 women). *Students:* 20 full-time (12 women), 14 part-time (10 women); includes 4 minority (2 Asian, non-Hispanic/Latino; 1 Hispanic/Latino; 1 Two or more races, non-Hispanic/Latino), 6 international. Average age 33. 48 applicants, 35% accepted, 11 enrolled. In 2010, 8 master's, 1 doctorate awarded. *Degree requirements:* For master's, 2 foreign languages, comprehensive exam; for doctorate, 2 foreign languages, comprehensive exam, thesis/dissertation. *Entrance requirements:* For master's and doctorate, GRE General Test, minimum undergraduate GPA of 3.0. Additional exam requirements/recommendations for international students: Required—TOEFL (minimum score 600 paper-based; 250 computer-based; 100 iBT). *Application deadline:* For fall admission, 12/15 for domestic students, 11/30 for international students. Application fee: $55 ($65 for international students). Electronic applications accepted. *Expenses:* Tuition, area resident: Part-time $179.19 per credit hour. Tuition, state resident: full-time $4384. Tuition, nonresident: full-time $16,684; part-time $630.67 per credit hour. Required fees: $350 per semester. Tuition and fees vary according to course load, degree level and program. *Financial support:* In 2010–11, 2 students received support, including 1 fellowship with full tuition reimbursement available (averaging $6,000 per year), 2 research assistantships with full tuition reimbursements available (averaging $11,500 per year), 14 teaching assistantships with full and partial tuition reimbursements available (averaging $11,500 per year); scholarships/grants, tuition waivers (partial), and unspecified assistantships also available. Financial award application deadline: 2/1; financial award applicants required to submit FAFSA. *Faculty research:* American Indian languages, applied linguistics phonology, sociolinguistics, syntax. Total annual research expenditures: $1,357. *Unit head:* Dr. Edward Rubin, Chair, 801-581-8047, Fax: 801-585-7351, E-mail: e.rubin@utah.edu. *Application contact:* Kate Lythgoe, Academic Coordinator, 801-581-6516, Fax: 801-585-7351, E-mail: kate.lythgoe@linguistics.utah.edu.

University of Utah, Graduate School, College of Humanities, Program in Middle East Studies, Salt Lake City, UT 84112. Offers anthropology (MA); Arabic (MA, PhD); Arabic and linguistics (MA, PhD); Hebrew (MA); history (MA, PhD); Persian (MA, PhD); political science (MA, PhD); Turkish (MA). *Students:* 20 full-time (10 women), 15 part-time (5 women), 8 international. Average age 33. 28 applicants, 29% accepted, 3 enrolled. In 2010, 3 master's awarded. Terminal master's awarded for partial completion of doctoral program. *Degree requirements:* For master's, 2 foreign languages, comprehensive exam, thesis optional; for doctorate, 3 foreign languages, comprehensive exam, thesis/dissertation. *Entrance requirements:* For master's, GRE General Test, minimum GPA of 3.2; for doctorate, GRE General Test, MA in Middle East studies or equivalent, minimum GPA of 3.2. Additional exam requirements/recommendations for international students: Required—TOEFL (minimum score 580 paper-based; 237 computer-based; 92 iBT). *Application deadline:* For fall admission, 1/15 priority date for domestic and international students. Application fee: $55 ($65 for international students). Electronic applications accepted. *Expenses:* Tuition, area resident: Part-time $179.19 per credit hour. Tuition, state resident: full-time $4384. Tuition, nonresident: full-time $16,684; part-time $630.67 per credit hour. Required fees: $350 per semester. Tuition and fees vary according to course load, degree level and program. *Financial support:* In 2010–11, 17 students received support, including 11 fellowships with full tuition reimbursements available (averaging $14,000 per year), 6 teaching assistantships with full tuition reimbursements available (averaging $12,000 per year); unspecified assistantships also available. Financial award application deadline: 1/15. *Faculty research:* Arabic linguistics; Islamic studies; Middle Eastern history; political science; Judaic studies; anthropology; Arabic, Persian, Hebrew, and Turkish language and literature. *Application contact:* Peter von Sivers, Director of Graduate Studies, 801-581-8073, Fax: 801-581-6183, E-mail: peter.vonsivers@utah.edu.

University of Victoria, Faculty of Graduate Studies, Faculty of Humanities, Department of Linguistics, Victoria, BC V8W 2Y2, Canada. Offers applied linguistics (MA); linguistics (MA, PhD). Part-time programs available. *Degree requirements:* For master's, one foreign language, thesis, colloquium; for doctorate, 2 foreign languages, comprehensive exam, thesis/dissertation, candidacy exam. *Entrance requirements:* For master's, GRE; for doctorate, GRE, sample of written work. Additional exam requirements/recommendations for international students: Required—TOEFL. Electronic applications accepted. *Faculty research:* Grammatical theory, syntactic analysis, morphology, Western Amerindian languages, Salishan, applied linguistics.

University of Virginia, College and Graduate School of Arts and Sciences, Program in Linguistics, Charlottesville, VA 22903. Offers MA. *Students:* 8 full-time (5 women); includes 1 Hispanic/Latino, 3 international. Average age 23. 21 applicants, 48% accepted, 4 enrolled. In 2010, 3 master's awarded. *Degree requirements:* For master's, one foreign language, comprehensive exam, thesis optional, reading knowledge of French or German. *Entrance requirements:* For master's, GRE General Test. Additional exam requirements/recommendations for international students: Required—TOEFL (minimum score 600 paper-based; 250 computer-based; 90 iBT), IELTS (minimum score 7). *Application deadline:* For fall admission, 2/15 for domestic and international students. Applications are processed on a rolling basis. Application fee: $60. Electronic applications accepted. *Financial support:* Teaching assistantships available. Financial award applicants required to submit FAFSA. *Unit head:* Lise Dobrin, 434-924-7048, E-mail: ld4n@virginia.edu. *Application contact:* Lise Dobrin, 434-924-7048, E-mail: ld4n@virginia.edu.

University of Washington, Graduate School, College of Arts and Sciences, Department of Linguistics, Seattle, WA 98195. Offers computational linguistics (MA); linguistics (MA, PhD); Romance linguistics (MA, PhD). Part-time programs available. Terminal master's awarded for partial completion of doctoral program. *Degree requirements:* For master's, one foreign language, thesis; for doctorate, 2 foreign languages, thesis/dissertation. *Entrance requirements:* For master's, GRE General Test, minimum GPA of 3.0; for doctorate, GRE, minimum GPA of 3.0. Additional exam requirements/recommendations for international students: Required—TOEFL. Electronic applications accepted. *Faculty research:* Syntax, phonology, semantics, phonetics, sociolinguistics.

University of Washington, Graduate School, College of Arts and Sciences, Department of Slavic Languages and Literatures, Seattle, WA 98195. Offers Russian literature (MA, PhD); Slavic linguistics (MA, PhD). *Degree requirements:* For master's, 2 foreign languages, thesis optional; for doctorate, 3 foreign languages, thesis/dissertation. *Entrance requirements:* For master's and doctorate, GRE General Test, minimum GPA of 3.0. Additional exam requirements/recommendations for international students: Required—TOEFL. Electronic applications accepted. *Faculty research:* Modern and medieval East European languages and literatures, comparative literature, Russian folk literature, Slavic literary theory and criticism, computerized morphology of Russian.

University of Wisconsin–Madison, Graduate School, College of Letters and Science, Department of East Asian Languages and Literature, Program in Japanese Linguistics, Madison, WI 53706-1380. Offers MA, PhD. Part-time programs available. Terminal master's awarded for partial completion of doctoral program. *Degree requirements:* For master's, one foreign language, seminars, written exam; for doctorate, 3 foreign languages, thesis/dissertation, seminars, preliminary exams, oral exam. *Entrance requirements:* For master's, GRE General Test, bachelor's degree or equivalent in Japanese; for doctorate, GRE General Test, master's degree or equivalent in Japanese. Electronic applications accepted. *Expenses:* Tuition, state resident: full-time $9887; part-time $617.96 per credit. Tuition, nonresident: full-time $24,054; part-time $1503.40 per credit. Required fees: $67.63 per credit. Tuition and fees vary according to reciprocity agreements. *Faculty research:* Modern and historical Japanese linguistics, modern Japanese fiction and poetry, classical Japanese literature, language pedagogy.

University of Wisconsin–Madison, Graduate School, College of Letters and Science, Department of English, Madison, WI 53706-1380. Offers applied English linguistics (MA); composition and rhetoric (PhD); creative writing (MFA); English language and linguistics (PhD); literary studies (MA, PhD). *Degree requirements:* For doctorate, thesis/dissertation. *Expenses:* Tuition, state resident: full-time $9887; part-time $617.96 per credit. Tuition, nonresident: full-time $24,054; part-time $1503.40 per credit. Required fees: $67.63 per credit. Tuition and fees vary according to reciprocity agreements.

University of Wisconsin–Madison, Graduate School, College of Letters and Science, Department of Linguistics, Madison, WI 53706-1380. Offers MA, PhD. Part-time programs available. Terminal master's awarded for partial completion of doctoral program. *Degree requirements:* For master's, 2 foreign languages; for doctorate, 3 foreign languages, thesis/dissertation. Electronic applications accepted. *Expenses:* Tuition, state resident: full-time $9887; part-time $617.96 per credit. Tuition, nonresident: full-time $24,054; part-time $1503.40 per credit. Required fees: $67.63 per credit. Tuition and fees vary according to reciprocity agreements. *Faculty research:* Formal linguistics, acoustic phonetics, American studies, Indo-European linguistics.

University of Wisconsin–Milwaukee, Graduate School, College of Letters and Sciences, Department of English, Milwaukee, WI 53201-0413. Offers creative writing (PhD); English (MA); international technical communication (Certificate); linguistics (PhD); professional writing (PhD); professional writing and communication (Certificate); rhetoric and composition (PhD); MLIS/MA. *Faculty:* 40 full-time (19 women). *Students:* 106 full-time (62 women), 65 part-time (45 women); includes 4 Black or African American, non-Hispanic/Latino; 5 Asian, non-Hispanic/Latino, 17 international. Average age 34. 208 applicants, 54% accepted, 29 enrolled. In 2010, 19 master's, 14 doctorates awarded. *Degree requirements:* For master's, thesis or alternative; for doctorate, one foreign language, thesis/dissertation. *Entrance requirements:* For master's, GRE General Test, GRE Subject Test; for doctorate, GRE. Additional exam requirements/recommendations for international students: Required—TOEFL (minimum score 550 paper-based; 79 iBT), IELTS (minimum score 6.5). *Application deadline:* For fall admission, 1/1 priority date for domestic students; for spring admission, 9/1 for domestic students. Applications are processed on a rolling basis. Application fee: $56 ($96 for international students). Electronic applications accepted. *Financial support:* In 2010–11, 4 fellowships, 1 research assistantship, 84 teaching assistantships were awarded; career-related internships or fieldwork, unspecified assistantships, and project assistantships also available. Support available to part-time students. Financial award application deadline: 4/15; financial award applicants required to submit FAFSA. Total annual research expenditures: $36,259. *Unit head:* Tasha Oren, Representative, 414-229-6625, Fax: 414-229-2643, E-mail: tgoren@uwm.edu. *Application contact:* General Information Contact, 414-229-4982, Fax: 414-229-6967, E-mail: gradschool@uwm.edu.

Wayne State University, College of Liberal Arts and Sciences, Interdisciplinary Program in Linguistics, Detroit, MI 48202. Offers MA. *Faculty:* 9 full-time (5 women), 1 part-time/adjunct (0 women). *Students:* 5 full-time (2 women), 10 part-time (8 women); includes 2 minority (1 Black or African American, non-Hispanic/Latino; 1 Hispanic/Latino), 2 international. Average age 31. 18 applicants, 72% accepted, 5 enrolled. In 2010, 3 master's awarded. *Degree requirements:* For master's, one foreign language, thesis. *Entrance requirements:* Additional exam requirements/recommendations for international students: Required—TOEFL (minimum score 550 paper-based; 213 computer-based); Recommended—TWE (minimum score 6). *Application deadline:* For fall admission, 7/1 for domestic students, 6/1 for international students; for winter admission, 10/1 for international students; for spring admission, 2/1 for international students.

Application fee: $30 ($50 for international students). Electronic applications accepted. *Expenses:* Tuition, state resident: full-time $7662; part-time $478.85 per credit hour. Tuition, nonresident: full-time $16,920; part-time $1057.55 per credit hour. Required fees: $571.20; $35.70 per credit hour. $188.05 per semester. Tuition and fees vary according to course load and program. *Faculty research:* Formal linguistics, psycholinguistics, sociolinguistics, historical linguistics, language acquisition. *Unit head:* Patricia Siple, Director, 313-577-8642. *Application contact:* Patricia Siple, Director, 313-577-8642.

West Virginia University, Eberly College of Arts and Sciences, Department of Foreign Languages, Morgantown, WV 26506. Offers French (MA); linguistics (MA); Spanish (MA); teaching English to speakers of other languages (MA). Part-time programs available. *Degree requirements:* For master's, one foreign language, comprehensive exam (for some programs), thesis optional. *Entrance requirements:* For master's, minimum GPA of 3.0. Electronic applications accepted. *Faculty research:* French, German, and Spanish literature; foreign language pedagogy; English as a second language; cultural studies; linguistics.

Yale University, Graduate School of Arts and Sciences, Department of Linguistics, New Haven, CT 06520. Offers PhD. *Degree requirements:* For doctorate, 2 foreign languages, thesis/dissertation. *Entrance requirements:* For doctorate, GRE General Test.

York University, Faculty of Graduate Studies, Faculty of Arts, Program in Theoretical and Applied Linguistics, Toronto, ON M3J 1P3, Canada. Offers MA, PhD. *Degree requirements:* For master's, thesis.

Translation and Interpretation

American University, College of Arts and Sciences, Department of Language and Foreign Studies, Washington, DC 20016-8045. Offers French (Certificate), including translation; Russian (Certificate), including translation; Spanish: Latin American studies (MA, Certificate), including Spanish: Latin American studies (MA), translation (Certificate); teaching English to speakers of other languages (MA, Certificate). Part-time and evening/weekend programs available. *Faculty:* 41 full-time (29 women), 43 part-time/adjunct (34 women). *Students:* 22 full-time (17 women), 39 part-time (31 women); includes 8 minority (1 Black or African American, non-Hispanic/Latino; 3 Asian, non-Hispanic/Latino; 3 Hispanic/Latino; 1 Native Hawaiian or other Pacific Islander, non-Hispanic/Latino), 6 international. Average age 34. 64 applicants, 64% accepted, 14 enrolled. In 2010, 24 master's, 28 other advanced degrees awarded. *Degree requirements:* For master's, one foreign language, comprehensive exam, thesis or alternative, portfolio, research; for Certificate, minimum 15 credit hours related coursework. *Entrance requirements:* For master's, GRE, writing sample; for Certificate, bachelor's degree. Additional exam requirements/recommendations for international students: Required—TOEFL. *Application deadline:* For fall admission, 2/1 for domestic students; for spring admission, 10/1 for domestic students. Application fee: $80. *Financial support:* Fellowships, career-related internships or fieldwork, Federal Work-Study, institutionally sponsored loans, and tuition waivers (partial) available. Financial award application deadline: 2/1. *Unit head:* Olga Rojer, Chair, 202-885-2139, Fax: 202-885-1076, E-mail: orojer@american.edu. *Application contact:* Kathleen Clowery, Director of Graduate Admissions, 202-885-3621, Fax: 202-885-1505, E-mail: clowery@american.edu.

American University of Sharjah, Graduate Programs, Sharjah, United Arab Emirates. Offers business (EMBA, GEMPA, MBA); chemical engineering (MS Ch E); civil engineering (MSCE); computer engineering (MS); electrical engineering (MSEE); mechanical engineering (MSME); mechatronics engineering (MS); public administration (MPA); teaching English to speakers of other languages (MA); translation and interpreting (MA); urban planning (MUP). Part-time and evening/weekend programs available. *Entrance requirements:* For master's, GMAT (MBA). Additional exam requirements/recommendations for international students: Required—TOEFL (minimum score 550 paper-based; 213 computer-based; 80 iBT), TWE (minimum score 5). Electronic applications accepted. *Faculty research:* Chemical engineering, civil engineering, computer engineering, electrical engineering, linguistics, translation.

Babel University School of Translation, Program in Translation, Honolulu, HI 96815-1302. Offers MS. Part-time and evening/weekend programs available. Postbaccalaureate distance learning degree programs offered (no on-campus study). *Degree requirements:* For master's, comprehensive exam, thesis. *Entrance requirements:* For master's, translation exam. Additional exam requirements/recommendations for international students: Recommended—TOEFL (minimum score 550 paper-based).

Concordia University, School of Graduate Studies, Faculty of Arts and Science, Department of Études Françaises, Montréal, QC H3G 1M8, Canada. Offers écriture (Certificate); anglais-français en langue et techniques de localisation (Certificate); littératures francophones et résonances médiatiques (MA); traductologie (MA); translation (Diploma). *Degree requirements:* For other advanced degree, one foreign language.

Drew University, Caspersen School of Graduate Studies, Program in Poetry, Madison, NJ 07940-1493. Offers poetry (MFA); poetry in translation (MFA). *Degree requirements:* For master's, thesis. *Entrance requirements:* For master's, transcripts, writing sample, recommendations. *Expenses:* Contact institution.

Gallaudet University, The Graduate School, Washington, DC 20002-3625. Offers administration (MS); audiology (Au D, PhD); change leadership in education (Ed S); clinical psychology (PhD); deaf education (Ed D, PhD); deaf education: advanced studies (MA); deaf education: special programs in deaf education (MA); deaf history (Certificate); deaf studies (MA); education: teacher preparation (MA, MA Missions), including deaf education (MA), early childhood education and deaf education (MA), elementary education and deaf education (MA Missions), secondary education and deaf education (MA); hearing, speech and language sciences (MS); international development (MA); interpretation (MA, PhD); leadership (Certificate); leisure services administration (MS); linguistics (MA, PhD); management (Certificate); mental health counseling (MA); school counseling (MA); school counseling (summer session) (MA); school psychology (Psy S); sign language teaching (MA); social work (MSW); special education administration (PhD); speech-language pathology (PhD). Part-time programs available. *Faculty:* 116 full-time (86 women). *Students:* 291 full-time (224 women), 122 part-time (97 women); includes 142 minority (36 Black or African American, non-Hispanic/Latino; 3 American Indian or Alaska Native, non-Hispanic/Latino; 13 Asian, non-Hispanic/Latino; 29 Hispanic/Latino; 61 Two or more races, non-Hispanic/Latino), 28 international. Average age 30. 442 applicants, 52% accepted, 145 enrolled. In 2010, 116 master's, 17 doctorates, 16 other advanced degrees awarded. Terminal master's awarded for partial completion of doctoral program. *Degree requirements:* For master's, comprehensive exam (for some programs), thesis optional; for doctorate, comprehensive exam, thesis/dissertation. *Entrance requirements:* For master's and doctorate, GRE General Test or MAT, letters of recommendation, interviews, goals statement, ASL proficiency interview, written English competency. Additional exam requirements/recommendations for international students: Required—TOEFL. *Application deadline:* For fall admission, 2/15 for domestic students. Applications are processed on a rolling basis. Application fee: $50. Electronic applications accepted. *Expenses:* Tuition: Full-time $11,930; part-time $663 per credit. Required fees: $188 per semester. *Financial support:* In 2010–11, 219 students received support; fellowships, research assistantships, teaching assistantships, career-related internships or fieldwork, Federal Work-Study, scholarships/grants, tuition waivers (partial), and unspecified assistantships available. Support available to part-time students. Financial award applicants required to submit FAFSA. *Faculty research:* Bimodal bilingualism development, audiology, telecommunications access, early childhood education, linguistics, visual language and visual learning, rehabilitation and hearing enhancement. *Unit head:* Dr. Carol J. Erting, Dean, 202-651-5520, Fax: 202-651-5027, E-mail: carol.erting@gallaudet.edu. *Application contact:* Wednesday Luria, Coordinator of Prospective Graduate Student Services, 202-651-5400, Fax: 202-651-5295, E-mail: graduate.school@gallaudet.edu.

Georgia State University, College of Arts and Sciences, Department of Modern and Classical Languages, Program in Translation and Interpretation, Atlanta, GA 30302-3083. Offers French (Certificate); German (Certificate); Spanish (Certificate). Electronic applications accepted.

Kent State University, College of Arts and Sciences, Department of Modern and Classical Language Studies, Kent, OH 44242-0001. Offers French literature (MA); French, Spanish, German and Latin pedagogy (MA); German literature (MA); Spanish literature (MA); translation (MA), including French, German, Japanese, Russian, Spanish; translation studies (PhD). Part-time and evening/weekend programs available. *Degree requirements:* For master's, one foreign language, comprehensive exam (for some programs), thesis (for some programs); for doctorate, comprehensive exam, thesis/dissertation (for some programs). *Entrance requirements:* For master's, minimum GPA of 3.0, writing sample, audio tape or CD; for doctorate, 3 recommendations. Additional exam requirements/recommendations for international students: Required—TOEFL (minimum score 197 computer-based). Electronic applications accepted. *Expenses:* Tuition, state resident: full-time $7866; part-time $437 per credit hour. Tuition, nonresident: full-time $14,022; part-time $779 per credit hour. *Faculty research:* Literature, pedagogy, applied linguistics, translation studies.

Marygrove College, Graduate Division, Program in Modern Language Translation, Detroit, MI 48221-2599. Offers Certificate.

Montclair State University, The Graduate School, College of Humanities and Social Sciences, Department of Spanish and Italian, Montclair, NJ 07043-1624. Offers Italian (Certificate); Spanish (MA, Certificate); translation and interpretation in Spanish (Certificate). Part-time and evening/weekend programs available. *Faculty:* 21 full-time (13 women), 25 part-time/adjunct (16 women). *Students:* 4 full-time (3 women), 20 part-time (17 women); includes 1 American Indian or Alaska Native, non-Hispanic/Latino; 11 Hispanic/Latino. Average age 33. 10 applicants, 90% accepted, 6 enrolled. In 2010, 7 master's awarded. *Degree requirements:* For master's, comprehensive exam, thesis or alternative. *Entrance requirements:* For master's, GRE General Test, 2 letters of recommendation. Additional exam requirements/recommendations for international students: Required—TOEFL (minimum iBT score of 83) or IELTS. *Application deadline:* For fall admission, 6/1 for international students; for spring admission, 11/1 for international students. Applications are processed on a rolling basis. Application fee: $60. Electronic applications accepted. *Expenses:* Tuition, state resident: part-time $501.34 per credit. Tuition, nonresident: part-time $773.88 per credit. Required fees: $71.15 per credit. *Financial support:* In 2010–11, 1 research assistantship with full tuition reimbursement (averaging $7,000 per year) was awarded; Federal Work-Study, scholarships/grants, and unspecified assistantships also available. Support available to part-time students. Financial award application deadline: 3/1; financial award applicants required to submit FAFSA. *Unit head:* Dr. Linda Gould Levine, Chairperson, 973-655-7506. *Application contact:* Amy Aiello, Director of Graduate Admissions and Operations, 973-655-5147, Fax: 973-655-7869, E-mail: graduate.school@montclair.edu.

Monterey Institute of International Studies, Graduate School of Translation, Interpretation and Language Education, Program in Translation and Interpretation, Monterey, CA 93940-2691. Offers conference interpretation (MA); translation (MA); translation and interpretation (MA); translation and localization management (MA). *Degree requirements:* For master's, one foreign language, thesis or alternative, exams. *Entrance requirements:* For master's, minimum GPA of 3.0, proficiency in a foreign language. Additional exam requirements/recommendations for international students: Required—TOEFL (minimum score 600 paper-based; 250 computer-based; 100 iBT). Electronic applications accepted. *Expenses:* Tuition: Full-time $32,000; part-time $1525 per credit hour. Required fees: $56. *Faculty research:* Assessment and testing in translation and interpretation, translation and interpretation pedagogy and curricula, integration of translation technology, language policy and planning.

New York University, NYU in Madrid, Madrid, NY 10012-1019, Spain. Offers creative writing in Spanish (MFA); Spanish (PhD); Spanish and Latin American literatures and cultures (MA); Spanish language and translation (MA).

New York University, School of Continuing and Professional Studies, Division of Liberal Studies and Allied Arts, New York, NY 10012-1019. Offers translation (MS).

Rutgers, The State University of New Jersey, New Brunswick, Graduate School-New Brunswick, Program in Spanish, Piscataway, NJ 08854-8097. Offers bilingualism and second language acquisition (MA, PhD); Spanish (MA, MAT, PhD); Spanish literature (MA, PhD); translation (MA). Part-time programs available. *Degree requirements:* For master's, comprehensive exam (for some programs), thesis (for some programs); for doctorate, 2 foreign languages, comprehensive exam, thesis/dissertation. *Entrance requirements:* For master's and doctorate, GRE General Test. Additional exam requirements/recommendations for international students: Required—TOEFL. Electronic applications accepted. *Expenses:* Tuition, state resident: full-time $7200; part-time $600 per credit. Tuition, nonresident: full-time $11,124; part-time $927 per credit. *Faculty research:* Hispanic literature, Luso-Brazilian literature, Spanish linguistics, Spanish translation.

State University of New York at Binghamton, Graduate School, School of Arts and Sciences, Department of Romance Languages and Literatures, Program in Spanish, Binghamton, NY 13902-6000. Offers Spanish (MA); translation (Certificate). *Students:* 2 full-time (0 women), 4 part-time (all women); includes 1 Hispanic/Latino, 1 international. Average age 30. 6 applicants, 83% accepted, 4 enrolled. In 2010, 2 master's awarded. *Degree requirements:* For master's, one foreign language, comprehensive exam, thesis or alternative. *Entrance requirements:* For master's, GRE General Test, GRE Subject Test. Additional exam requirements/recommendations for international students: Required—TOEFL (minimum score 550 paper-based; 213 computer-based; 80 iBT). *Application deadline:* For fall admission, 2/15 priority date for domestic and international students; for spring admission, 11/15 priority date for domestic and international students. Applications are processed on a rolling basis. Application fee: $60. Electronic applications accepted. *Financial support:* In 2010–11, 1 student received support, including 1 teaching assistantship with full tuition reimbursement available (averaging $9,500 per year); career-related internships or fieldwork, Federal Work-Study, institutionally sponsored loans, scholarships/grants, health care benefits, and unspecified assistantships also available. Financial award application deadline: 2/15; financial award applicants required to submit FAFSA. *Unit head:* Dr. Antonio Sobejano-Moran, Chairperson, 607-777-4635, E-mail: antobianco@msn.com. *Application contact:* Catherine Smith, Recruiting and Admissions Coordinator, 607-777-2151, Fax: 607-777-2501, E-mail: cmsmith@binghamton.edu.

State University of New York at Binghamton, Graduate School, School of Arts and Sciences, Translation Research and Instruction Program, Binghamton, NY 13902-6000. Offers

Translation and Interpretation

State University of New York at Binghamton (continued)
Certificate. Part-time programs available. *Faculty:* 1 (woman) part-time/adjunct. *Students:* 14 full-time (7 women), 12 part-time (10 women), 15 international. Average age 37. 15 applicants, 47% accepted, 4 enrolled. In 2010, 2 Certificates awarded. *Entrance requirements:* For degree, GRE General Test. Additional exam requirements/recommendations for international students: Required—TOEFL (minimum score 550 paper-based; 213 computer-based; 80 iBT). *Application deadline:* For fall admission, 1/15 priority date for domestic and international students; for spring admission, 10/15 priority date for domestic and international students. Applications are processed on a rolling basis. Application fee: $60. Electronic applications accepted. *Financial support:* In 2010–11, 5 students received support, including 1 research assistantship with full tuition reimbursement available (averaging $14,500 per year), 3 teaching assistantships with full tuition reimbursements available (averaging $14,500 per year); career-related internships or fieldwork, Federal Work-Study, institutionally sponsored loans, scholarships/grants, health care benefits, and unspecified assistantships also available. Financial award application deadline: 2/15; financial award applicants required to submit FAFSA. *Unit head:* Dr. Marilyn Gaddis Rose, Director, 607-777-6726, E-mail: mgrose@binghamton.edu. *Application contact:* Catherine Smith, Recruiting and Admissions Coordinator, 607-777-2151, Fax: 607-777-2501, E-mail: cmsmith@binghamton.edu.

Universidad Autonoma de Guadalajara, Graduate Programs, Guadalajara, Mexico. Offers administrative law and justice (LL M); advertising and corporate communications (MA); architecture (M Arch); business (MBA); computational science (MCC); education (Ed M, Ed D); English-Spanish translation (MA); entrepreneurship and management (MBA); integrated management of digital animation (MA); international business (MIB); international corporate law (LL M); internet technologies (MS); manufacturing systems (MMS); occupational health (MS); philosophy (MA, PhD); power electronics (MS); quality systems (MQS); renewable energy (MS); social evaluation of projects (MBA); strategic market research (MBA); tax law (MA); teaching mathematics (MA).

Université de Montréal, Faculty of Arts and Sciences, Department of Linguistics and Translation, Montréal, QC H3C 3J7, Canada. Offers linguistics (MA, PhD); translation (MA, PhD, DESS). *Degree requirements:* For master's, thesis, general exam; for doctorate, thesis/dissertation, general exam. Electronic applications accepted.

Université Laval, Faculty of Letters, Department of Languages, Linguistics and Translations, Programs in Terminology and Translation, Québec, QC G1K 7P4, Canada. Offers MA, Diploma. Part-time programs available. *Degree requirements:* For master's, thesis (for some programs). *Entrance requirements:* For master's and Diploma, knowledge of French and English. Electronic applications accepted.

University at Albany, State University of New York, College of Arts and Sciences, Department of Languages, Literatures, and Cultures, Program in Russian, Albany, NY 12222-0001. Offers Russian (MA); Russian translation (Certificate). *Faculty research:* Translation, phonology and morphology of modern Russian.

University of Arkansas, Graduate School, J. William Fulbright College of Arts and Sciences, Department of English, Program in Translation, Fayetteville, AR 72701-1201. Offers MFA. *Students:* 3 part-time (2 women). *Degree requirements:* For master's, thesis. *Application deadline:* For fall admission, 4/1 for international students; for spring admission, 10/1 for international students. Applications are processed on a rolling basis. Application fee: $40 ($50 for international students). Electronic applications accepted. *Financial support:* In 2010–11, 3 teaching assistantships were awarded; fellowships, research assistantships, career-related internships or fieldwork and Federal Work-Study also available. Support available to part-time students. Financial award application deadline: 4/1; financial award applicants required to submit FAFSA. *Unit head:* Dr. Joseph Candido, Department Head, 479-575-4301, E-mail: candido@uark.edu. *Application contact:* Dr. Joseph Candido, Department Head, 479-575-4301, E-mail: candido@uark.edu.

University of California, Santa Barbara, Graduate Division, College of Letters and Sciences, Division of Humanities and Fine Arts, Department of East Asian Languages and Cultural Studies, Santa Barbara, CA 93106-7075. Offers East Asian language and cultural studies (MA, PhD); translation studies (PhD). *Faculty:* 14 full-time, 7 part-time/adjunct. *Students:* 13 full-time (8 women). Average age 27. 76 applicants, 28% accepted, 6 enrolled. In 2010, 2 master's awarded. *Degree requirements:* For master's, one foreign language, thesis or alternative; for doctorate, 2 foreign languages, thesis/dissertation. *Entrance requirements:* For master's and doctorate, GRE, 3 letters of recommendation, statement of purpose, personal achievements/contributions statement, resume/curriculum vitae, transcripts for post-secondary institutions attended. Additional exam requirements/recommendations for international students: Required—TOEFL (minimum score 550 paper-based; 213 computer-based; 80 iBT) or IELTS (minimum score 7). *Application deadline:* For fall admission, 4/1 for domestic and international students. Application fee: $70 ($90 for international students). Electronic applications accepted. *Financial support:* In 2010–11, 13 students received support, including 5 fellowships with full and partial tuition reimbursements available (averaging $11,651 per year), 13 teaching assistantships with partial tuition reimbursements available (averaging $8,745 per year); Federal Work-Study, institutionally sponsored loans, scholarships/grants, health care benefits, and unspecified assistantships also available. Financial award application deadline: 12/15; financial award applicants required to submit FAFSA. *Faculty research:* Chinese literature, Chinese film, Japanese society, Japanese literature, East Asian cultural studies. *Unit head:* Dr. William Powell, Chair, 805-893-4455, Fax: 805-893-3011, E-mail: bpowell@religion.ucsb.edu. *Application contact:* Sally Lombrozo, Graduate Program Assistant, 805-893-2744, Fax: 805-893-7671, E-mail: lombrozo@hfa.ucsb.edu.

University of California, Santa Barbara, Graduate Division, College of Letters and Sciences, Division of Humanities and Fine Arts, Department of Linguistics, Santa Barbara, CA 93106-9580. Offers applied linguistics (PhD); cognitive science (PhD); language, interaction, and social organizations (PhD); linguistics (PhD); translation studies (PhD); MA/PhD. *Faculty:* 9 full-time (5 women), 1 part-time/adjunct (0 women). *Students:* 28 full-time (14 women); includes 1 Asian, non-Hispanic/Latino. Average age 31. 62 applicants, 23% accepted, 8 enrolled. In 2010, 2 doctorates awarded. Terminal master's awarded for partial completion of doctoral program. *Degree requirements:* For doctorate, one foreign language, comprehensive exam, thesis/dissertation. *Entrance requirements:* For doctorate, GRE. Additional exam requirements/recommendations for international students: Required—TOEFL (minimum score 550 paper-based; 80 iBT), IELTS (minimum score 7). *Application deadline:* For fall admission, 12/1 for domestic and international students. Application fee: $70 ($90 for international students). Electronic applications accepted. *Financial support:* In 2010–11, 22 students received support, including 20 fellowships with full and partial tuition reimbursements available (averaging $16,513 per year), 2 research assistantships with full and partial tuition reimbursements available (averaging $12,185 per year), 10 teaching assistantships with full and partial tuition reimbursements available (averaging $6,586 per year). Financial award application deadline: 12/1; financial award applicants required to submit FAFSA. *Faculty research:* Sociolinguistics, linguistic theory, discourse, psycho-linguistics, anthropological linguistics. *Unit head:* Joni Schwartz, Director, 805-893-3237, Fax: 805-893-7492, E-mail: joni@hfa.ucsb.edu. *Application contact:* Cami Helmuth, Graduate Program Advisor, 805-893-7490, Fax: 805-893-7492, E-mail: helmuth@hfa.uscb.edu.

University of California, Santa Barbara, Graduate Division, College of Letters and Sciences, Division of Humanities and Fine Arts, Department of Religious Studies, Santa Barbara, CA 93106-3130. Offers ancient Mediterranean studies (PhD); European medieval studies (PhD); feminist studies (PhD); global studies (PhD); religious studies (MA, PhD); translation studies (PhD); MA/PhD. *Faculty:* 19 full-time (9 women), 8 part-time/adjunct (3 women). *Students:* 79 full-time (29 women); includes 2 Black or African American, non-Hispanic/Latino; 1 American Indian or Alaska Native, non-Hispanic/Latino; 9 Asian, non-Hispanic/Latino; 5 Hispanic/Latino. Average age 31. 139 applicants, 22% accepted, 10 enrolled. In 2010, 11 master's, 10 doctorates awarded. *Degree requirements:* For master's, one foreign language, comprehensive exam (for some programs), thesis (for some programs), colloquium; for doctorate, one foreign language, thesis/dissertation, methodology, colloquium. *Entrance requirements:* For master's and doctorate, GRE General Test. Additional exam requirements/recommendations for international students: Required—TOEFL (minimum score 550 paper-based; 80 iBT), IELTS (minimum score 7). *Application deadline:* For fall admission, 12/1 for domestic and international students. Application fee: $70 ($90 for international students). Electronic applications accepted. *Financial support:* In 2010–11, 64 students received support, including 31 fellowships with full tuition reimbursements available (averaging $12,351 per year), 4 research assistantships with full and partial tuition reimbursements available (averaging $4,147 per year), 37 teaching assistantships with partial tuition reimbursements available (averaging $9,573 per year); career-related internships or fieldwork, scholarships/grants, tuition waivers (full and partial), and associateships also available. Financial award application deadline: 12/1; financial award applicants required to submit FAFSA. *Faculty research:* Area studies; religious traditions; theory and method in the study of religion; religion, culture, and politics; spirituality and religious experience. *Unit head:* Prof. Jose I. Cabezon, Professor and Chair, 805-893-3564, Fax: 805-893-7671, E-mail: jcabezon@religion.ucsb.edu. *Application contact:* Sally J. Lombrozo, Graduate Program Assistant, 805-893-2744, Fax: 805-893-7671, E-mail: lombrozo@hfa.ucsb.edu.

University of California, Santa Barbara, Graduate Division, College of Letters and Sciences, Division of Humanities and Fine Arts, Program in Comparative Literature, Santa Barbara, CA 93106-4130. Offers comparative literature (PhD); East Asian literatures (PhD); feminist studies (PhD); French (PhD); global studies (PhD); translation studies (PhD); MA/PhD. *Faculty:* 63 full-time (31 women). *Students:* 21 full-time (14 women); includes 3 Asian, non-Hispanic/Latino; 2 Hispanic/Latino. Average age 31. 41 applicants, 12% accepted, 2 enrolled. In 2010, 1 doctorate awarded. *Degree requirements:* For doctorate, 2 foreign languages, comprehensive exam, thesis/dissertation. *Entrance requirements:* For doctorate, GRE. Additional exam requirements/recommendations for international students: Required—TOEFL (minimum score 550 paper-based; 80 iBT), IELTS (minimum score 7). *Application deadline:* For fall admission, 12/15 for domestic and international students. Application fee: $70 ($90 for international students). Electronic applications accepted. *Financial support:* In 2010–11, 19 students received support, including 14 fellowships with full and partial tuition reimbursements available (averaging $16,232 per year), 12 teaching assistantships with partial tuition reimbursements available (averaging $12,826 per year); research assistantships, Federal Work-Study, institutionally sponsored loans, scholarships/grants, health care benefits, and tuition waivers (full and partial) also available. Financial award application deadline: 12/15; financial award applicants required to submit FAFSA. *Faculty research:* Comparative literary studies in global context, critical theory, translation studies, mediatechnological studies, trauma studies. *Unit head:* Prof. Susan Derwin, Chair, 805-893-4399, Fax: 805-893-8341, E-mail: derwin@gss.ucsb.edu. *Application contact:* Ashley Bradbury, Graduate Program Assistant, 805-893-2131, Fax: 805-893-8341, E-mail: ashley@hfa.ucsb.edu.

University of Delaware, College of Arts and Sciences, Department of Foreign Languages and Literatures, Newark, DE 19716. Offers foreign languages and literatures (MA), including French, German, Spanish; foreign languages pedagogy (MA), including French, German, Spanish; technical Chinese translation (MA). *Degree requirements:* For master's, one foreign language, comprehensive exam, thesis optional. *Entrance requirements:* For master's, GRE General Test, letters of recommendation, writing sample. Additional exam requirements/recommendations for international students: Required—TOEFL. Electronic applications accepted. *Faculty research:* Medieval to Modern French and Spanish literature, Twentieth Century German, French, Spanish literature by women, computer-assisted instruction.

University of Denver, University College, Denver, CO 80208. Offers arts and culture (MLS, Certificate), including art, literature, and culture, arts development and program management (Certificate), creative writing; environmental policy and management (MAS, Certificate), including energy and sustainability (Certificate), environmental assessment of nuclear power (Certificate), environmental health and safety (Certificate), environmental management, natural resource management (Certificate); geographic information systems (MAS, Certificate); global affairs (MLS, Certificate), including translation studies, world history and culture; healthcare leadership (MPH, Certificate), including healthcare policy, law, and ethics, medical and healthcare information technologies, strategic management of healthcare; information and communications technology (MCIS, Certificate), including database design and administration (Certificate), geographic information systems (MCIS), information security systems security (Certificate), information systems security (MCIS), project management (MCIS, MPS, Certificate), software design and administration (Certificate), software design and programming (MCIS), technology management, telecommunications technology (MCIS), Web design and development; leadership and organizations (MPS, Certificate), including human capital in organizations, philanthropic leadership, project management (MCIS, MPS, Certificate), strategic innovation and change; organizational and professional communication (MPS, Certificate), including alternative dispute resolution, organizational communication, organizational development and training, public relations and marketing; security management (MAS, Certificate), including emergency planning and response, information security (MAS), organizational security; strategic human resource management (MPS, Certificate), including global human resources (MPS), human resource management and development (MPS). Part-time and evening/weekend programs available. Postbaccalaureate distance learning degree programs offered (no on-campus study). *Faculty:* 7 full-time (2 women), 212 part-time/adjunct (83 women). *Students:* 52 full-time (19 women), 1,044 part-time (625 women); includes 196 minority (81 Black or African American, non-Hispanic/Latino; 7 American Indian or Alaska Native, non-Hispanic/Latino; 30 Asian, non-Hispanic/Latino; 66 Hispanic/Latino; 3 Native Hawaiian or other Pacific Islander, non-Hispanic/Latino; 9 Two or more races, non-Hispanic/Latino), 76 international. Average age 36. 488 applicants, 91% accepted, 339 enrolled. In 2010, 286 master's, 130 other advanced degrees awarded. *Entrance requirements:* Additional exam requirements/recommendations for international students: Required—TOEFL (minimum score 550 paper-based; 80 iBT). *Application deadline:* For fall admission, 6/22 priority date for domestic students, 6/10 priority date for international students; for winter admission, 9/15 priority date for domestic students, 9/6 priority date for international students; for spring admission, 2/3 priority date for domestic students, 12/15 priority date for international students. Applications are processed on a rolling basis. Application fee: $75. Electronic applications accepted. *Expenses:* Contact institution. *Financial support:* Applicants required to submit FAFSA. *Unit head:* Dr. James Davis, Dean, 303-871-2291, Fax: 303-871-4047, E-mail: jdavis@du.edu. *Application contact:* Information Contact, 303-871-3155, Fax: 303-871-4047, E-mail: ucolinfo@du.edu.

The University of Iowa, Graduate College, College of Liberal Arts and Sciences, Department of Cinema and Comparative Literature, Program in Comparative Literature Translation, Iowa City, IA 52242-1316. Offers MFA. *Degree requirements:* For master's, thesis, exam. *Entrance requirements:* For master's, GRE General Test, minimum GPA of 3.0. Additional exam requirements/recommendations for international students: Required—TOEFL (minimum score 550 paper-based; 213 computer-based; 81 iBT). Electronic applications accepted.

The University of Manchester, School of Languages, Linguistics and Cultures, Manchester, United Kingdom. Offers Arab world studies (PhD); Chinese studies (M Phil, PhD); East Asian studies (M Phil, PhD); English language (PhD); French studies (M Phil, PhD); German studies (M Phil, PhD); interpreting studies (PhD); Italian studies (M Phil, PhD); Japanese studies (M Phil, PhD); Latin American cultural studies (M Phil, PhD); linguistics (M Phil, PhD); Middle Eastern studies (M Phil, PhD); Polish studies (M Phil, PhD); Portuguese studies (M Phil, PhD); Russian studies (M Phil, PhD); Spanish studies (M Phil, PhD); translation and intercultural studies (M Phil, PhD).

University of North Florida, College of Education and Human Services, Department of Exceptional Student and Deaf Education, Jacksonville, FL 32224. Offers American sign language/English interpreting (M Ed); applied behavior analysis (M Ed); autism (M Ed); deaf education (M Ed); disability services (M Ed); exceptional student education (M Ed). *Accreditation:* NCATE. Part-time and evening/weekend programs available. *Faculty:* 11 full-time (9 women), 2 part-time/adjunct (both women). *Students:* 30 full-time (28 women), 51 part-time (49 women); includes 4 Black or African American, non-Hispanic/Latino; 3 Asian, non-Hispanic/Latino; 7 Hispanic/Latino, 1 international. Average age 30. 54 applicants, 74% accepted, 32 enrolled. In 2010, 22 master's awarded. *Entrance requirements:* For master's, GRE General Test, minimum GPA of 3.0 in last 60 hours, interview, 3 letters of recommendation. Additional exam requirements/recommendations for international students: Required—TOEFL (minimum score 500 paper-based; 173 computer-based). *Application deadline:* For fall admission, 7/1 priority date for domestic students, 5/1 for international students; for spring admission, 11/1 priority date for domestic students, 10/1 for international students. Applications are processed on a rolling basis. Application fee: $30. Electronic applications accepted. *Expenses:* Tuition, state resident: full-time $7646.40; part-time $318.60 per credit hour. Tuition, nonresident: full-time $23,502; part-time $979.24 per credit hour. Required fees: $1208.88; $50.37 per credit hour. Tuition and fees vary according to course load and program. *Financial support:* In 2010–11, 38 students received support, including 1 research assistantship (averaging $6,150 per year); teaching assistantships, career-related internships or fieldwork, Federal Work-Study, scholarships/grants, tuition waivers (partial), and unspecified assistantships also available. Support available to part-time students. Financial award application deadline: 4/1; financial award applicants required to submit FAFSA. *Faculty research:* Transition, integrating technology into teacher education, written language development, professional school development, learning strategies. Total annual research expenditures: $892,583. *Unit head:* Dr. Karen Patterson, Chair, 904-620-2930, Fax: 904-620-3895, E-mail: karen.patterson@unf.edu. *Application contact:* Lillith Richardson, Assistant Director, The Graduate School, 904-620-1360, Fax: 904-620-1362, E-mail: graduateschool@unf.edu.

University of Ottawa, Faculty of Graduate and Postdoctoral Studies, Faculty of Arts, Institute of Canadian Studies, Ottawa, ON K1N 6N5, Canada. Offers economics (PhD); English (PhD); geography (PhD); history (PhD); lettres Françaises (PhD); linguistics (PhD); philosophy (PhD); political science (PhD); psychology (PhD); religious studies (PhD); translation studies (PhD). *Degree requirements:* For doctorate, comprehensive exam, thesis/dissertation.

University of Ottawa, Faculty of Graduate and Postdoctoral Studies, Faculty of Arts, School of Translation and Interpretation, Ottawa, ON K1N 6N5, Canada. Offers interpreting (MA); Spanish translation (MA); translation (MA); translation studies (PhD). *Degree requirements:* For master's, one foreign language, thesis or alternative, research paper; for doctorate, thesis/dissertation, doctoral exam. *Entrance requirements:* For master's, school-administered exam, honors degree or equivalent, minimum B average; for doctorate, master's degree, minimum B+ average. Electronic applications accepted. *Faculty research:* Theory of translation, Spanish translation, conference interpreting, legal translation, translation-oriented lexicology and terminology.

University of Puerto Rico, Río Piedras, College of Humanities, Program in Translation, San Juan, PR 00931-3300. Offers MA, Certificate. Part-time and evening/weekend programs available. *Degree requirements:* For master's, 2 foreign languages, comprehensive exam, thesis. *Entrance requirements:* For master's, PAEG, minimum GPA of 3.0, graduate-level knowledge of 2 languages (English, French, or Spanish), letter of recommendation.

University of Rochester, School of Arts and Sciences, Interdisciplinary Program in Literary Translation Studies, Rochester, NY 14627.

University of Wisconsin–Milwaukee, Graduate School, College of Letters and Sciences, Department of Spanish, Milwaukee, WI 53201-0413. Offers Spanish (MA); translation (Certificate). *Faculty:* 8 full-time (3 women). *Students:* 6 full-time (3 women), 10 part-time (8 women); includes 2 Black or African American, non-Hispanic/Latino; 4 Hispanic/Latino, 1 international. Average age 28. 16 applicants, 94% accepted, 8 enrolled. In 2010, 1 master's awarded. *Entrance requirements:* For master's, bachelor's degree. *Application deadline:* Applications are processed on a rolling basis. Application fee: $56 ($96 for international students). Electronic applications accepted. *Financial support:* In 2010–11, 12 teaching assistantships were awarded; fellowships, research assistantships, unspecified assistantships also available. Financial award applicants required to submit FAFSA. *Faculty research:* Sociolinguistics, Spanish-American literature, Spanish literature, Hispanic culture, Hispanic historiography. *Unit head:* Jeffrey Oxford, Chair, 414-229-4257, E-mail: oxford@uwm.edu. *Application contact:* General Information Contact, 414-229-4982, Fax: 414-229-6967, E-mail: gradschool@uwm.edu.

University of Wisconsin–Milwaukee, Graduate School, College of Letters and Sciences, Interdepartmental Program in Foreign Language and Literature, Milwaukee, WI 53201-0413. Offers classics and Hebrew studies (MAFLL); comparative literature (MAFLL); French and Italian (MAFLL); German (MAFLL); Slavic studies (MAFLL); translation (Certificate). Part-time programs available. *Faculty:* 29 full-time (14 women). *Students:* 35 full-time (27 women), 29 part-time (20 women); includes 1 Hispanic/Latino. Average age 40. 30 applicants, 67% accepted, 19 enrolled. In 2010, 24 master's awarded. *Degree requirements:* For master's, 2 foreign languages, thesis or alternative. *Entrance requirements:* Additional exam requirements/recommendations for international students: Required—TOEFL (minimum score 550 paper-based; 79 iBT), IELTS (minimum score 6.5). *Application deadline:* For fall admission, 1/1 priority date for domestic students; for spring admission, 9/1 for domestic students. Applications are processed on a rolling basis. Application fee: $56 ($96 for international students). Electronic applications accepted. *Financial support:* In 2010–11, 1 fellowship, 2 research assistantships, 26 teaching assistantships were awarded; career-related internships or fieldwork, health care benefits, unspecified assistantships, and project assistantships also available. Support available to part-time students. Financial award application deadline: 4/15; financial award applicants required to submit FAFSA. Total annual research expenditures: $304,210. *Unit head:* Gabrielle Verdier, Representative, 414-229-3346, Fax: 414-229-2741, E-mail: verdier@uwm.edu. *Application contact:* General Information Contact, 414-229-4982, Fax: 414-229-6967, E-mail: gradschool@uwm.edu.

York University, Faculty of Graduate Studies, Glendon College, Program in Translation, Toronto, ON M3J 1P3, Canada. Offers MA. *Degree requirements:* For master's, thesis or alternative. *Entrance requirements:* For master's, professional translating experience. Electronic applications accepted.

Section 11
Philosophy and Ethics

This section contains a directory of institutions offering graduate work in philosophy and ethics. Additional information about programs listed in the directory may be obtained by writing directly to the dean of a graduate school or chair of a department at the address given in the directory.

For programs offering related work, see also in this book Area and Cultural Studies, History, Humanities, Religious Studies, and Social Sciences.

CONTENTS

Program Directories

Ethics

American University, College of Arts and Sciences, Department of Philosophy and Religion, Washington, DC 22016-8056. Offers ethics, peace, and global affairs (MA); philosophy (MA), including history of philosophy, philosophy and social policy. Part-time and evening/weekend programs available. *Faculty:* 10 full-time (6 women), 9 part-time/adjunct (4 women). *Students:* 10 full-time (5 women), 2 part-time (0 women); includes 1 Hispanic/Latino. Average age 23. 49 applicants, 55% accepted, 8 enrolled. In 2010, 10 master's awarded. *Degree requirements:* For master's, one foreign language, comprehensive exam, thesis (for some programs). *Entrance requirements:* For master's, GRE, writing sample. Additional exam requirements/recommendations for international students: Required—TOEFL. *Application deadline:* For fall admission, 2/1 for domestic students; for spring admission, 10/1 for domestic students. Application fee: $80. *Financial support:* Fellowships, teaching assistantships, Federal Work-Study and institutionally sponsored loans available. Support available to part-time students. Financial award application deadline: 2/1. *Faculty research:* Oriental religion, classical and medieval philosophy, philosophy of law and ethics, comparative religion, philosophy of science. *Unit head:* Dr. Amy Oliver, Chair, 202-885-2140. *Application contact:* Kathleen Clowery, Director, Graduate Admissions, 202-885-3621, Fax: 202-885-1505.

American University, School of International Service, Washington, DC 20016-8071. Offers comparative and regional studies (Certificate); cross-cultural communication (Certificate); development management (MS); ethics, peace, and global affairs (MA); European studies (Certificate); global environmental policy (MA, Certificate); international affairs (MA), including comparative and regional studies, environmental policy, international economic policy, international politics, natural resources and sustainable development, U. S. foreign policy; international communication (MA, Certificate); international development (MA, Certificate); international development management (Certificate); international economic policy (Certificate); international economic relations (Certificate); international media (MA); international peace and conflict resolution (MA, Certificate); international relations (PhD); international service (MIS); peace building (Certificate); the Americas (Certificate); United States foreign policy (Certificate); JD/MA. Part-time and evening/weekend programs available. *Faculty:* 91 full-time (35 women), 48 part-time/adjunct (16 women). *Students:* 591 full-time (383 women), 367 part-time (229 women); includes 164 minority (51 Black or African American, non-Hispanic/Latino; 4 American Indian or Alaska Native, non-Hispanic/Latino; 42 Asian, non-Hispanic/Latino; 63 Hispanic/Latino; 4 Two or more races, non-Hispanic/Latino), 94 international. Average age 27. 2,115 applicants, 59% accepted, 360 enrolled. In 2010, 370 master's, 7 doctorates awarded. Terminal master's awarded for partial completion of doctoral program. *Degree requirements:* For master's, one foreign language, comprehensive exam, thesis or alternative; for doctorate, one foreign language, comprehensive exam, thesis/dissertation, research practicum; for Certificate, minimum 15 credit hours related course work. *Entrance requirements:* For master's, GRE, 24 credits of course work in related social sciences, minimum GPA of 3.5, 2 letters of recommendation, bachelor's degree, resume; for doctorate, GRE, 2 letters of recommendation, 24 credits in related social sciences; for Certificate, bachelor's degree. Additional exam requirements/recommendations for international students: Required—TOEFL (minimum score 600 paper-based; 250 computer-based; 100 iBT). *Application deadline:* For fall admission, 1/15 priority date for domestic students; for spring admission, 10/1 priority date for domestic students. Applications are processed on a rolling basis. Application fee: $50. *Financial support:* Career-related internships or fieldwork, Federal Work-Study, and institutionally sponsored loans available. Financial award application deadline: 1/15. *Faculty research:* International intellectual property, international environmental issues, international law and legal order, international telecommunications/technology, international sustainable development. *Unit head:* Dr. Louis W. Goodman, Dean, 202-885-1600, Fax: 202-885-2494. *Application contact:* Yasmin Quianzon, Director of Graduate Admissions and Financial Aid, 202-885-2496, Fax: 202-885-1109.

Arizona State University, College of Liberal Arts and Sciences, School of Life Sciences, Tempe, AZ 85287-4601. Offers animal behavior (PhD); applied ethics (biomedical and health ethics) (MA); biological design (PhD); biology (MS, PhD); biology (biology and society) (MS, PhD); environmental life sciences (PhD); evolutionary biology (PhD); human and social dimensions of science and technology (PhD); microbiology (PhD); molecular and cellular biology (PhD); neuroscience (PhD); philosophy (history and philosophy of science) (MA); sustainability (PhD). *Faculty:* 102 full-time (26 women), 4 part-time/adjunct (1 woman). *Students:* 188 full-time (95 women), 45 part-time (29 women); includes 31 minority (3 Black or African American, non-Hispanic/Latino; 2 American Indian or Alaska Native, non-Hispanic/Latino; 12 Asian, non-Hispanic/Latino; 12 Hispanic/Latino; 2 Two or more races, non-Hispanic/Latino), 39 international. Average age 30. 203 applicants, 41% accepted, 60 enrolled. In 2010, 17 master's, 21 doctorates awarded. Terminal master's awarded for partial completion of doctoral program. *Degree requirements:* For master's, thesis (for some programs), interactive Program of Study (iPOS) submitted before completing 50 percent of required credit hours; for doctorate, variable foreign language requirement, comprehensive exam, thesis/dissertation, interactive Program of Study (iPOS) submitted before completing 50 percent of required credit hours. *Entrance requirements:* For master's and doctorate, GRE, minimum GPA of 3.0 or equivalent in last 2 years of work leading to bachelor's degree. Additional exam requirements/recommendations for international students: Required—TOEFL (minimum score 600 paper-based; 250 computer-based; 100 iBT). *Application deadline:* For fall admission, 12/15 for domestic and international students. Application fee: $70 ($90 for international students). Electronic applications accepted. *Expenses:* Tuition, state resident: full-time $8510; part-time $608 per credit. Tuition, nonresident: full-time $16,542; part-time $919 per credit. Required fees: $339; $110 per credit. Part-time tuition and fees vary according to course load. *Financial support:* In 2010–11, 80 research assistantships with full and partial tuition reimbursements (averaging $17,888 per year), 101 teaching assistantships with full and partial tuition reimbursements (averaging $17,327 per year) were awarded; fellowships with full tuition reimbursements, career-related internships or fieldwork, Federal Work-Study, institutionally sponsored loans, scholarships/grants, and tuition waivers (full and partial) also available. Financial award application deadline: 3/1; financial award applicants required to submit FAFSA. Total annual research expenditures: $29.3 million. *Unit head:* Dr. Robert E. Page, Director, 480-965-0803, E-mail: robert.page@asu.edu. *Application contact:* Graduate Admissions, 480-965-6113.

Arizona State University, New College of Interdisciplinary Arts and Sciences, Phoenix, AZ 85069-7100. Offers applied ethics and the professions (MA); communication studies (MA); interdisciplinary studies (MA); psychology (MS); social justice and human rights (MA). Part-time and evening/weekend programs available. *Faculty:* 109 full-time (53 women), 4 part-time/adjunct (3 women). *Students:* 97 full-time (65 women), 82 part-time (54 women); includes 39 minority (17 Black or African American, non-Hispanic/Latino; 5 American Indian or Alaska Native, non-Hispanic/Latino; 4 Asian, non-Hispanic/Latino; 11 Hispanic/Latino; 2 Two or more races, non-Hispanic/Latino), 8 international. Average age 31. 159 applicants, 72% accepted, 74 enrolled. In 2010, 35 master's awarded. *Degree requirements:* For master's, thesis (for some programs), interactive Program of Study (iPOS) submitted before completing 50 percent of required credit hours. *Entrance requirements:* For master's, GRE, minimum GPA of 3.0 or equivalent in last 2 years of work leading to bachelor's degree. Additional exam requirements/recommendations for international students: Required—TOEFL, IELTS, or Pearson Test of English. *Application deadline:* For fall admission, 7/1 for domestic and international students; for spring admission, 12/1 for domestic and international students. Applications are processed on a rolling basis. Application fee: $70 ($90 for international students). Electronic applications accepted. *Expenses:* Tuition, state resident: full-time $8510; part-time $608 per credit. Tuition, nonresident: full-time $16,542; part-time $919 per credit. Required fees: $339; $110 per credit. Part-time tuition and fees vary according to course load. *Financial support:* In 2010–11, 10 research assistantships with full and partial tuition reimbursements (averaging $6,102 per year) were awarded; teaching assistantships with full and partial tuition reimbursements, career-related internships or fieldwork, Federal Work-Study, institutionally sponsored loans, scholarships/grants, and tuition waivers (full and partial) also available. Support available to part-time students. Financial award application deadline: 3/1; financial award applicants required to submit FAFSA. Total annual research expenditures: $755,902. *Unit head:* Dr. Elizabeth Langland, Vice President and Dean, 602-543-6033, Fax: 602-543-6032, E-mail: elizabeth.langland@asu.edu. *Application contact:* Sheryl Gordon, Coordinator, Student Support Services, 602-543-6241, Fax: 602-543-6032, E-mail: sheryl.gordon@asu.edu.

Arizona State University, School of Letters and Sciences, Program in Applied Ethics and the Professions, Tempe, AZ 85287-4503. Offers applied ethics and the professions (biomedical and health ethics) (MA); applied ethics and the professions (ethics and emerging technologies) (MA); applied ethics and the professions (public administration, policy and ethics) (MA); applied ethics and the professions (science, technology and ethics) (MA). Part-time and evening/weekend programs available. *Students:* 14 full-time (11 women), 10 part-time (6 women); includes 6 minority (3 Black or African American, non-Hispanic/Latino; 1 American Indian or Alaska Native, non-Hispanic/Latino; 1 Asian, non-Hispanic/Latino; 1 Hispanic/Latino), 1 international. Average age 41. 19 applicants, 79% accepted, 12 enrolled. *Degree requirements:* For master's, thesis or alternative, applied project, interactive Program of Study (iPOS) submitted before completing 50 percent of required credit hours. *Entrance requirements:* For master's, GRE (for ethics and emerging technologies concentration), minimum GPA of 3.0 or equivalent in last 2 years of work leading to bachelor's degree, 2 letters of recommendation, resume, personal statement of interest and qualifications. Additional exam requirements/recommendations for international students: Required—TOEFL (minimum score 550 paper-based; 213 computer-based; 80 iBT). *Application deadline:* For fall admission, 2/15 for domestic and international students. Application fee: $70 ($90 for international students). Electronic applications accepted. *Expenses:* Tuition, state resident: full-time $8510; part-time $608 per credit. Tuition, nonresident: full-time $16,542; part-time $919 per credit. Required fees: $339; $110 per credit. Part-time tuition and fees vary according to course load. *Financial support:* In 2010–11, 1 research assistantship with full and partial tuition reimbursement (averaging $15,715 per year), 1 teaching assistantship with full and partial tuition reimbursement (averaging $15,715 per year) were awarded; institutionally sponsored loans, scholarships/grants, and tuition waivers (full and partial) also available. Financial award application deadline: 3/1; financial award applicants required to submit FAFSA. *Application contact:* Graduate Admissions, 480-965-6113.

Azusa Pacific University, Haggard Graduate School of Theology, Program in Theological Studies, Program in Religion: Theology and Ethics, Azusa, CA 91702-7000. Offers MA. *Students:* 5 full-time (1 woman), 6 part-time (3 women); includes 5 minority (2 Black or African American, non-Hispanic/Latino; 1 Asian, non-Hispanic/Latino; 2 Hispanic/Latino), 1 international. Average age 38. In 2010, 15 master's awarded. Application fee: $45 ($65 for international students). *Unit head:* Dr. Scott Daniels, Dean, 626-387-5750. *Application contact:* Dr. Scott Daniels, Dean, 626-387-5750.

Biola University, Talbot School of Theology, La Mirada, CA 90639-0001. Offers Biblical studies (MA); Christian education (MACE); Christian ministry and leadership (MA); divinity (M Div); education (PhD); ministry (MA Min); New Testament (MA); Old Testament (MA); philosophy of religion and ethics (MA); spiritual formation (MA); spiritual formation and soul care (MA); theological studies (MA); theology (MA, Th M, D Min). *Accreditation:* ATS. Part-time and evening/weekend programs available. *Faculty:* 45 full-time (5 women), 40 part-time/adjunct (10 women). *Students:* 611 full-time (123 women), 573 part-time (144 women); includes 382 minority (48 Black or African American, non-Hispanic/Latino; 1 American Indian or Alaska Native, non-Hispanic/Latino; 300 Asian, non-Hispanic/Latino; 5 Native Hawaiian or other Pacific Islander, non-Hispanic/Latino; 28 Two or more races, non-Hispanic/Latino), 153 international. Average age 31. 515 applicants, 76% accepted, 277 enrolled. In 2010, 47 first professional degrees, 152 master's, 9 doctorates awarded. *Degree requirements:* For master's, variable foreign language requirement, thesis or alternative; for doctorate, variable foreign language requirement, thesis/dissertation; for M Div, thesis/dissertation or alternative. *Entrance requirements:* For M Div, minimum GPA of 2.6; for master's, minimum undergraduate GPA of 3.0; for doctorate, minimum GPA of 3.25. Additional exam requirements/recommendations for international students: Required—TOEFL (minimum score 550 paper-based; 213 computer-based). *Application deadline:* For fall admission, 7/1 for domestic students; for spring admission, 1/1 for domestic students. Applications are processed on a rolling basis. Application fee: $45. *Financial support:* Research assistantships, teaching assistantships, career-related internships or fieldwork, institutionally sponsored loans, and scholarships/grants available. Support available to part-time students. Financial award application deadline: 3/2; financial award applicants required to submit FAFSA. *Faculty research:* Moral development; biological, medical, and social ethics; ancient Near Eastern historical philosophy. *Unit head:* Dr. Dennis Dirks, Dean, 562-903-4816, Fax: 562-903-4748, E-mail: dennis_dirks@peter.biola.edu. *Application contact:* Roy M. Allinson, Director of Graduate Admissions, 562-903-4752, Fax: 562-903-4709, E-mail: admissions@biola.edu.

Chicago Theological Seminary, Graduate and Professional Programs, Chicago, IL 60637-1507. Offers preaching (D Min); religion and health (D Min); religious studies (MA); spirituality and spiritual direction (D Min); theology (M Div); theology, ethics and the human sciences (PhD); M Div/MSW. *Accreditation:* ACIPE; ATS. Part-time programs available. *Degree requirements:* For master's, thesis; for doctorate, 2 foreign languages, comprehensive exam, thesis/dissertation; for M Div, thesis/dissertation. *Entrance requirements:* For doctorate, GRE General Test. Additional exam requirements/recommendations for international students: Required—TOEFL (minimum score 217 computer-based). *Faculty research:* Bible, culture and hermeneutics, theology, gender and sexuality, black faith and life, spirituality and psychology, practical theology.

Claremont Graduate University, Graduate Programs, School of Religion, Claremont, CA 91711-6160. Offers Hebrew Bible (MA, PhD); history of Christianity and religions of North America (MA, PhD); New Testament (MA, PhD); philosophy of religion and theology (MA, PhD); theology, ethics and culture (MA, PhD); women's studies in religion (MA, PhD); MA/PhD; MBA/PhD. Part-time programs available. *Faculty:* 6 full-time (2 women), 2 part-time/adjunct (0 women). *Students:* 218 full-time (87 women), 10 part-time (4 women); includes 13 Black or African American, non-Hispanic/Latino; 11 Asian, non-Hispanic/Latino; 12 Hispanic/Latino; 1 Two or more races, non-Hispanic/Latino, 29 international. Average age 37. In 2010, 13 master's, 12 doctorates awarded. Terminal master's awarded for partial completion of doctoral program. *Entrance requirements:* For master's and doctorate, GRE General Test. Additional exam requirements/recommendations for international students: Required—TOEFL (minimum score 550 paper-based; 213 computer-based; 80 iBT). *Application deadline:* For fall admission, 2/1 priority date for domestic students. Applications are processed on a rolling basis. Application fee: $60. Electronic applications accepted. *Expenses:* Tuition: Full-time $35,748; part-time $1554 per unit. Required fees: $215 per semester. *Financial support:* Fellowships, research assistantships, teaching assistantships, Federal Work-Study, institutionally sponsored loans, and scholarships/grants available. Support available to part-time students. Financial award application deadline: 2/15; financial award applicants required to submit FAFSA. *Unit head:* Anselm Min, Dean, 909-607-3214, Fax: 909-621-9587, E-mail: anselm.min@cgu.edu. *Application contact:* Brent Smith, Recruiter, 909-607-2653, Fax: 909-607-9587, E-mail: brent.smith@cgu.edu.

Claremont School of Theology, Graduate and Professional Programs, Program in Religion, Claremont, CA 91711-3199. Offers practical theology (PhD), including religious education, spiritual care and counseling; religion (PhD), including Hebrew Bible, New Testament and Christian origins, process studies, religion, ethics, and society; religion and theology (MA); religious education (MARE). *Accreditation:* ACIPE; ATS. Terminal master's awarded for partial completion of doctoral program. *Degree requirements:* For master's, thesis; for doctorate, 2 foreign languages, thesis/dissertation. *Entrance requirements:* For doctorate, GRE General Test. Additional exam requirements/recommendations for international students: Required—TOEFL (minimum score 250 computer-based). Electronic applications accepted.

Columbia University, Graduate School of Business, MBA Program, New York, NY 10027. Offers accounting (MBA); decision, risk, and operations (MBA); entrepreneurship (MBA); finance and economics (MBA); healthcare and pharmaceutical management (MBA); human resource management (MBA); international business (MBA); leadership and ethics (MBA); management (MBA); marketing (MBA); media (MBA); private equity (MBA); real estate (MBA); social enterprise (MBA); value investing (MBA); DDS/MBA; JD/MBA; MBA/MIA; MBA/MPH; MBA/MS; MD/MBA. *Entrance requirements:* For master's, GMAT, 2 letters of recommendation. Additional exam requirements/recommendations for international students: Required—TOEFL. Electronic applications accepted. *Expenses:* Contact institution. *Faculty research:* Human decision making and behavioral research; real estate market and mortgage defaults; financial crisis and corporate governance; international business; security analysis and accounting.

Duquesne University, School of Leadership and Professional Advancement, Pittsburgh, PA 15282-0001. Offers leadership (MS), including business ethics, community leadership, global leadership, information technology, leadership, liberal studies, professional administration, sports leadership. Part-time and evening/weekend programs available. Postbaccalaureate distance learning degree programs offered (no on-campus study). *Faculty:* 1 full-time (0 women), 70 part-time/adjunct (35 women). *Students:* 275 full-time, 171 part-time; includes 20 Black or African American, non-Hispanic/Latino; 1 American Indian or Alaska Native, non-Hispanic/Latino; 6 Asian, non-Hispanic/Latino; 3 Hispanic/Latino. Average age 31. 161 applicants, 73% accepted, 103 enrolled. In 2010, 108 master's awarded. *Degree requirements:* For master's, capstone course. *Entrance requirements:* For master's, professional work experience, 500-word essay. Additional exam requirements/recommendations for international students: Required—TOEFL. *Application deadline:* Applications are processed on a rolling basis. Application fee: $0. Electronic applications accepted. *Expenses:* Tuition: Part-time $884 per credit. Required fees: $84 per credit. Tuition and fees vary according to course load. *Financial support:* Applicants required to submit FAFSA. *Unit head:* Dr. Dorothy Bassett, Dean, 412-396-2141, Fax: 412-396-4711, E-mail: bassettd@duq.edu. *Application contact:* Marianne Leister, Director of Student Services, 412-396-4933, Fax: 412-396-5072, E-mail: leister@duq.edu.

Emory University, Candler School of Theology, Atlanta, GA 30322. Offers formation and witness (M Div); history, scripture and tradition (MTS); leadership in church and community (M Div); modern religious thought and experience (MTS); pastoral counseling (Th D); religion and race (M Div); religion, health and science (M Div); scripture and interpretation (M Div); society and personality (M Div); theology (Th M); theology and ethics (M Div); theology and the arts (M Div); traditions of the church (M Div); women and religion (M Div); JD/M Div; JD/MTS; M Div/MBA; M Div/MPH; MBA/MTS; MTS/MPH. *Accreditation:* ACIPE; ATS. Part-time programs available. *Faculty:* 45 full-time (11 women), 26 part-time/adjunct (12 women). *Students:* 411 full-time (206 women), 44 part-time (29 women); includes 113 Black or African American, non-Hispanic/Latino; 1 American Indian or Alaska Native, non-Hispanic/Latino; 8 Asian, non-Hispanic/Latino; 8 Hispanic/Latino; 1 Two or more races, non-Hispanic/Latino, 40 international. Average age 32. 603 applicants, 74% accepted, 191 enrolled. In 2010, 141 first professional degrees, 48 master's, 1 doctorate awarded. *Degree requirements:* For master's, thesis optional; for doctorate, comprehensive exam, thesis/dissertation; for M Div, thesis/dissertation optional. *Entrance requirements:* For M Div, minimum undergraduate GPA of 2.75; for master's, minimum undergraduate GPA of 3.0; for doctorate, GRE, M Div, 8 units of course work in clinical pastoral education. Additional exam requirements/recommendations for international students: Required—TOEFL (minimum score 600 paper-based; 250 computer-based; 95 iBT). *Application deadline:* For fall admission, 7/1 for domestic and international students; for spring admission, 11/1 for domestic and international students. Applications are processed on a rolling basis. Application fee: $50. Electronic applications accepted. *Expenses:* Contact institution. *Financial support:* In 2010–11, 422 students received support, including 343 fellowships (averaging $12,216 per year); career-related internships or fieldwork, institutionally sponsored loans, scholarships/grants, and student employment also available. Support available to part-time students. Financial award application deadline: 1/15; financial award applicants required to submit FAFSA. *Faculty research:* Biblical studies, church history, ethics, ministry practice, pastoral care. *Unit head:* Shelly E. Hart, Registrar, 404-727-6480, Fax: 404-727-4373, E-mail: candlerregistrar@emory.edu. *Application contact:* Mary Lou Greenwood Boice, Associate Dean of Admissions and Financial Aid, 404-727-6326, Fax: 404-727-2915, E-mail: candleradmissions@emory.edu.

Fordham University, Graduate School of Arts and Sciences, Center for Ethics Education, New York, NY 10458. Offers ethics and society (MA); health care ethics (Certificate). Part-time programs available. *Students:* 4 full-time (2 women), 10 part-time (7 women); includes 1 Hispanic/Latino, 1 international. 9 applicants, 100% accepted, 8 enrolled. *Entrance requirements:* Additional exam requirements/recommendations for international students: Required—TOEFL. *Application deadline:* For fall admission, 1/4 priority date for domestic students; for spring admission, 10/31 for domestic students. Application fee: $65. Electronic applications accepted. *Financial support:* In 2010–11, 1 student received support. Federal Work-Study, institutionally sponsored loans, scholarships/grants, tuition waivers (partial), and unspecified assistantships available. Financial award application deadline: 1/4. Total annual research expenditures: $49,033. *Unit head:* Dr. Celia Fisher, Director, 718-817-3793, Fax: 212-759-2009, E-mail: fisher@fordham.edu. *Application contact:* Charlene Dundie, Director of Graduate Admissions, 718-817-4420, Fax: 718-817-3566, E-mail: dundie@fordham.edu.

Freed-Hardeman University, Program in Business Administration, Henderson, TN 38340-2399. Offers accounting (MBA); corporate responsibility (MBA); leadership (MBA). *Accreditation:* ACBSP. Part-time and evening/weekend programs available. Postbaccalaureate distance learning degree programs offered (no on-campus study). *Entrance requirements:* For master's, GMAT. Additional exam requirements/recommendations for international students: Required—TOEFL (minimum score 500 paper-based; 173 computer-based).

George Mason University, School of Public Policy, Arlington, VA 22201. Offers culture and values in social policy (Certificate); global medical policy (Certificate); global trade management (Certificate); health and medical policy (MS); international commerce and policy (MA); national security and public policy (Certificate); organization development and knowledge management (MS); peace operations (MS); public policy (EMPP, MPP, PhD); transportation and logistics policy (Certificate); transportation policy, operations and logistics (MA). Part-time and evening/weekend programs available. *Faculty:* 66 full-time (24 women), 15 part-time/adjunct (3 women). *Students:* 344 full-time (199 women), 607 part-time (310 women); includes 55 Black or African American, non-Hispanic/Latino; 1 American Indian or Alaska Native, non-Hispanic/Latino; 33 Asian, non-Hispanic/Latino; 55 Hispanic/Latino; 5 Two or more races, non-Hispanic/Latino, 106 international. Average age 31. 842 applicants, 62% accepted, 280 enrolled. In 2010, 291 master's, 15 doctorates, 12 other advanced degrees awarded. *Degree requirements:* For master's, thesis or alternative; for doctorate, comprehensive exam, thesis/dissertation. *Entrance requirements:* For master's, GRE (for students seeking merit-based scholarships), minimum undergraduate GPA of 3.0, resume, 2 letters of recommendation; for doctorate, GMAT or GRE General Test, resume, writing sample, master's degree, goals statement, 2 letters of recommendation; for Certificate, minimum undergraduate GPA of 3.0, resume, 2 letters of recommendation, goals statement. Additional exam requirements/recommendations for international students: Required—TOEFL (minimum score 570 paper-based; 230 computer-based; 88 iBT). *Application deadline:* Applications are processed on a rolling basis. Application fee: $100. Electronic applications accepted. *Expenses:* Contact institution. *Financial support:* In 2010–11, 43 students received support, including 2 fellowships with full tuition reimbursements available (averaging $18,000 per year), 41 research assistantships with full and partial tuition reimbursements available (averaging $18,104 per year), 2 teaching assistantships (averaging $10,408 per year); career-related internships or fieldwork, Federal Work-Study, scholarships/grants, unspecified assistantships, and health care benefits (full-time research or teaching assistantship recipients) also available. Financial award application deadline: 3/1; financial award applicants required to submit FAFSA. *Faculty research:* Governance, regional and economic development, international commerce and policy, science and technology policy, entrepreneurship, culture and values. Total annual research expenditures: $8 million. *Unit head:* Dr. Edward Rhodes, Dean, 703-993-2280, Fax: 703-993-8215, E-mail: edrhodes@gmu.edu. *Application contact:* Tennille Haegele, Director of Graduate Admissions, School of Public Policy, 703-993-3183, Fax: 703-993-4876, E-mail: thaegele@gmu.edu.

Georgetown University, Graduate School of Arts and Sciences, School of Continuing Studies, Washington, DC 20057. Offers American studies (MALS); Catholic studies (MALS); classical civilizations (MALS); disability studies (MPS); ethics and the professions (MALS); human resources management (MPS); humanities (MALS); individualized study (MALS); international affairs (MALS); Islam and Muslim-Christian relations (MALS); journalism (MPS); liberal studies (DLS); literature and society (MALS); medieval and early modern European studies (MALS); public relations and corporate communications (MPS); real estate (MPS); religious studies (MALS); social and public policy (MALS); sports industry management (MPS); the theory and practice of American democracy (MALS); visual culture (MALS). *Entrance requirements:* Additional exam requirements/recommendations for international students: Required—TOEFL.

Graduate Theological Union, Graduate Programs, Berkeley, CA 94709-1212. Offers art and religion (MA, PhD, Th D); biblical languages (MA); biblical studies (MA); Biblical studies (PhD, Th D); Buddhist studies (MA); Christian spirituality (MA, PhD, Th D); cultural and historical studies of religions (MA, PhD, Th D); ethics and social theory (PhD, Th D); history (MA, PhD, Th D); homiletics (MA, PhD, Th D); interdisciplinary studies (PhD, Th D); Jewish studies (MA, PhD, Th D, Certificate); liturgical studies (MA, PhD, Th D); Near Eastern religions (PhD, Th D); Orthodox Christian studies (MA); religion and psychology (MA, PhD, Th D); religion and society/ethics and social theory (MA); systematic and philosophical theology (MA, PhD, Th D). PhD programs in Jewish studies and Near Eastern religions offered jointly with University of California, Berkeley. *Accreditation:* ATS. Terminal master's awarded for partial completion of doctoral program. *Degree requirements:* For master's, one foreign language, thesis; for doctorate, one foreign language, comprehensive exam, thesis/dissertation. *Entrance requirements:* For master's, GRE General Test; for doctorate, GRE General Test, MA or M Div. Additional exam requirements/recommendations for international students: Required—TOEFL. Electronic applications accepted.

John Brown University, Graduate Business Programs, Siloam Springs, AR 72761-2121. Offers business administration (MBA), including international business, leadership and ethics; international community development leadership (MS); leadership and ethics (MS); leadership and higher education (MS). Part-time and evening/weekend programs available. Postbaccalaureate distance learning degree programs offered (minimal on-campus study). *Entrance requirements:* For master's, MAT, GMAT or GRE if undergraduate GPA is less than 3.0, recommendation forms from three people, 200-word essay describing professional plans and reason for seeking acceptance. Additional exam requirements/recommendations for international students: Required—TOEFL (minimum score 550 paper-based; 173 computer-based; 70 iBT). Electronic applications accepted.

Lancaster Theological Seminary, Graduate and Professional Programs, Lancaster, PA 17603-2812. Offers biblical studies (MAR); Christian education (MAR); Christianity and the arts (MAR); church history (MAR); congregational life (MAR); lay leadership (Certificate); theological studies (M Div); theology (D Min); theology and ethics (MAR). *Accreditation:* ACIPE; ATS. *Degree requirements:* For doctorate, thesis/dissertation; for M Div, one foreign language.

Lutheran Theological Seminary, Graduate and Professional Programs, Saskatoon, SK S7N 0X3, Canada. Offers Biblical studies (MTS); church history (MTS); ethics/church and society (MTS); history of Christianity (STM); New Testament (STM); Old Testament (STM); pastoral studies (STM); pastoral theology (MTS); systematic theology (MTS); systematic theology and philosophy of religion (STM); theology (M Div, D Div). STM programs offered jointly with College of Emmanuel and St. Chad and St. Andrew's College. *Accreditation:* ATS. Part-time programs available. *Degree requirements:* For master's, thesis; for M Div, Greek, Hebrew.

Marquette University, Graduate School, College of Arts and Sciences, Department of Philosophy, Milwaukee, WI 53201-1881. Offers ancient philosophy (PhD); British empiricism and analytic philosophy (PhD); Christian philosophy (PhD); early modern European philosophy (PhD); ethics (PhD); German philosophy (PhD); history of philosophy (MA); medieval philosophy (PhD); phenomenology and existentialism (PhD); philosophy of religion (PhD); social and applied philosophy (MA); JD/MA. Part-time programs available. *Faculty:* 25 full-time (5 women), 18 part-time/adjunct (5 women). *Students:* 43 full-time (10 women), 20 part-time (2 women); includes 5 minority (1 Black or African American, non-Hispanic/Latino; 4 Asian, non-Hispanic/Latino), 5 international. Average age 31. 96 applicants, 41% accepted, 9 enrolled. In 2010, 2 master's, 6 doctorates awarded. *Degree requirements:* For master's, variable foreign language requirement, comprehensive exam, thesis or alternative; for doctorate, 2 foreign languages, thesis/dissertation, written and oral qualifying exams. *Entrance requirements:* For master's and doctorate, GRE General Test, official transcripts from all current and previous colleges/universities except Marquette, statement of purpose, at least three letters of recommendation, sample of philosophical writing. Additional exam requirements/recommendations for international students: Required—TOEFL (minimum score 530 paper-based; 78 computer-based). *Application deadline:* For fall admission, 2/15 for domestic and international students. Applications are processed on a rolling basis. Application fee: $50. Electronic applications accepted. *Expenses:* Tuition: Full-time $16,290; part-time $905 per credit hour. Tuition and fees vary according to program. *Financial support:* In 2010–11, 1 fellowship, 6 research assistantships, 9 teaching assistantships were awarded; Federal Work-Study, institutionally sponsored loans, scholarships/grants, and tuition waivers (full and partial) also available. Support available to part-time students. Financial award application deadline: 2/15. *Faculty research:* Aristotle, Augustine, Descartes, Hegel, Heidegger. Total annual research expenditures: $109,819. *Unit head:* Dr. James South, Chair, 414-288-6857, Fax: 414-288-1578. *Application contact:* Dr. Pol Vandevelde, Director of Graduate Studies, 414-288-5962, Fax: 414-288-1578.

Marquette University, Graduate School, College of Arts and Sciences, Department of Theology, Milwaukee, WI 53201-1881. Offers historical theology (MA, PhD); Judaism and Christianity in antiquity (MA, PhD); systematic theology (MA, PhD); theological ethics (PhD); theology (MACD); theology and society (PhD). Part-time and evening/weekend programs available. Postbaccalaureate distance learning degree programs offered (no on-campus study). *Faculty:* 30 full-time (7 women), 19 part-time/adjunct (3 women). *Students:* 65 full-time (17 women), 45 part-time (13 women); includes 6 minority (3 Black or African American, non-Hispanic/Latino; 3 Hispanic/Latino), 3 international. Average age 36. 167 applicants, 39% accepted, 16 enrolled. In 2010, 114 master's, 8 doctorates awarded. Terminal master's awarded for partial completion of doctoral program. *Degree requirements:* For master's, one foreign language, comprehensive exam, thesis or alternative; for doctorate, 2 foreign languages, comprehensive exam, thesis/dissertation. *Entrance requirements:* For master's, GRE General Test, official transcripts from all current and previous colleges/universities except Marquette, three letters of recommendation, short personal statement; for doctorate, GRE General Test, official transcripts from all current and previous colleges/universities except Marquette, three letters of recommendation, short personal statement, academic writing sample. Additional exam requirements/recommendations for international students: Required—TOEFL (minimum score 530 paper-based; 78 computer-based). *Application deadline:* For fall admission, 12/15 for domestic and international students. Application fee: $50. Electronic applications accepted. *Expenses:* Tuition: Full-time $16,290; part-time $905 per credit hour. Tuition and fees vary according to program. *Financial support:* In 2010–11, 10 fellowships, 22 teaching assistantships were awarded; research assistantships, Federal Work-Study, institutionally sponsored loans, scholarships/grants, and tuition waivers (full and partial) also available. Support available to part-time students. Financial award application deadline: 2/15. *Faculty research:* Old Testament theology, New Testament theology, church history, Christian ethics. Total annual research expenditures: $4,625. *Unit head:* Dr. Susan Wood, Chair, 414-288-7170, Fax: 414-288-5548. *Application contact:* Dr. M. Therese Lysaught, Director of Graduate Studies, 414-288-3740.

New England College of Business and Finance, Program in Business Ethics and Compliance, Boston, MA 02111-2645. Offers MS. Postbaccalaureate distance learning degree programs offered (no on-campus study).

Ethics

Northwestern University, School of Continuing Studies, Program in Liberal Studies, Evanston, IL 60208. Offers American studies (MA); history (MA); religious and ethical studies (MA).

Phillips Theological Seminary, Programs in Theology, Tulsa, OK 74116. Offers administration of church agencies (M Div); campus ministry (M Div); church-related social work (M Div); college and seminary teaching (M Div); global mission work (M Div); institutional chaplaincy (M Div); ministerial vocations in Christian education (M Div); ministry (D Min), including parish ministry, pastoral counseling, practices of ministry; ministry and culture (MAMC), including Christian education, congregational leadership, history and practice of Christian spirituality, theology, ethics, and culture; ministry of music (M Div); pastoral care and counseling (M Div); pastoral ministry (M Div); theological studies (MTS). *Accreditation:* ATS. Part-time programs available. Postbaccalaureate distance learning degree programs offered (minimal on-campus study). *Degree requirements:* For master's, thesis (for some programs); for doctorate, thesis/dissertation. *Entrance requirements:* For master's, minimum GPA of 2.5; for doctorate, M Div, minimum GPA of 3.0. *Faculty research:* Biblical studies, historical studies, theology and culture, practical theology, theology and film.

St. Edward's University, School of Management and Business, Program in Organizational Leadership and Ethics, Austin, TX 78704. Offers MS. Part-time and evening/weekend programs available. *Students:* 42 part-time (29 women); includes 21 minority (6 Black or African American, non-Hispanic/Latino; 1 American Indian or Alaska Native, non-Hispanic/Latino; 14 Hispanic/Latino). Average age 37. 11 applicants, 100% accepted, 10 enrolled. In 2010, 20 master's awarded. *Degree requirements:* For master's, minimum of 24 hours in residence. *Entrance requirements:* For master's, GMAT or GRE General Test, minimum GPA of 2.75 in last 60 hours of course work. Additional exam requirements/recommendations for international students: Required—TOEFL (minimum score 550 paper-based; 213 computer-based; 79 iBT) or IELTS (minimum score 6). *Application deadline:* For fall admission, 7/1 for domestic and international students; for spring admission, 11/1 for domestic and international students. Applications are processed on a rolling basis. Application fee: $45 ($50 for international students). Electronic applications accepted. *Expenses:* Tuition: Full-time $16,200; part-time $900 per credit hour. Required fees: $50 per trimester. Full-time tuition and fees vary according to course load and program. *Financial support:* Scholarships/grants available. *Faculty research:* Spirituality and work, Asian (Eastern) ethics, Birkman Method impact on college retention. *Unit head:* Dr. Tom Sechrest, Director, 512-637-1954, Fax: 512-448-8492, E-mail: thomasl@stedwards.edu. *Application contact:* Kay Lynn Arnold, Assistant Director of Admission, 512-233-1636, Fax: 512-428-1032, E-mail: kayla@stedwards.edu.

Southeastern Baptist Theological Seminary, Graduate and Professional Programs, Wake Forest, NC 27588-1889. Offers advanced biblical studies (M Div); Christian education (M Div, MACE); Christian ethics (PhD); Christian ministry (M Div); Christian planting (M Div); church music (MACM); counseling (MACO); evangelism (PhD); language (M Div); ministry (D Min); New Testament (PhD); Old Testament (PhD); philosophy (PhD); theology (Th M, PhD); women's studies (M Div). *Accreditation:* ACIPE; ATS (one or more programs are accredited). *Degree requirements:* For master's, thesis (for some programs), oral exam; for doctorate, thesis/dissertation, fieldwork; for M Div, supervised ministry. *Entrance requirements:* For master's, Cooperative English Test, minimum GPA of 2.0, M Div or equivalent (Th M); for doctorate, GRE General Test or MAT, Cooperative English Test, M Div or equivalent, 3 years of professional experience.

Spring Hill College, Graduate Programs, Program in Liberal Arts, Mobile, AL 36608-1791. Offers fine arts (MLA); history and social science (MLA); leadership and ethics (MLA); literature (MLA). Part-time and evening/weekend programs available. *Faculty:* 5 full-time (2 women), 2 part-time/adjunct (1 woman). *Students:* 3 full-time (2 women), 31 part-time (19 women); includes 10 minority (9 Black or African American, non-Hispanic/Latino; 1 Hispanic/Latino). Average age 37. In 2010, 12 master's awarded. *Degree requirements:* For master's, capstone course, completion of program within 6 years of initial admittance. *Entrance requirements:* For master's, bachelor's degree with minimum undergraduate GPA of 3.0 or graduate/professional degree. Additional exam requirements/recommendations for international students: Required—TOEFL (minimum score 550 paper-based; 213 computer-based; 80 iBT), IELTS (minimum score 6.5), CPE or CAE (score: C), MELAB (score: 90). *Application deadline:* For fall admission, 8/1 priority date for domestic and international students; for spring admission, 12/1 priority date for domestic and international students. Applications are processed on a rolling basis. Application fee: $25 ($35 for international students). Electronic applications accepted. *Expenses:* Contact institution. *Financial support:* Applicants required to submit FAFSA. *Unit head:* Dr. Alexander R. Landi, Director, 251-380-3056, Fax: 251-460-2115, E-mail: landi@shc.edu. *Application contact:* Donna B. Tarasavage, Director of Admissions, Graduate and Continuing Studies, 251-380-3067, Fax: 251-460-2190, E-mail: dtarasavage@shc.edu.

Suffolk University, College of Arts and Sciences, Program in Ethics and Public Policy, Boston, MA 02108-2770. Offers MS. Part-time and evening/weekend programs available. *Faculty:* 5 full-time (2 women). *Students:* 10 full-time (5 women), 5 part-time (2 women). Average age 28. 29 applicants, 72% accepted, 10 enrolled. In 2010, 8 master's awarded. *Degree requirements:* For master's, internship or thesis. *Entrance requirements:* For master's, GRE General Test, MAT, GMAT, statement of professional goals, official transcripts, 2 letters of recommendation, resume. Additional exam requirements/recommendations for international students: Required—TOEFL (minimum score 550 paper-based; 213 computer-based; 80 iBT). *Application deadline:* For fall and spring admission, 6/15 priority date for domestic and international students. Applications are processed on a rolling basis. Application fee: $50. Electronic applications accepted. *Expenses:* Contact institution. *Financial support:* In 2010–11, 13 students received support, including 11 fellowships (averaging $6,264 per year); career-related internships or fieldwork, Federal Work-Study, institutionally sponsored loans, and unspecified assistantships also available. Support available to part-time students. Financial award application deadline: 4/1; financial award applicants required to submit FAFSA. *Faculty research:* History of philosophy, ethics, political philosophy, continental philosophy and phenomenology, applied ethics. *Unit head:* Dr. Greg Fried, Chair of Philosophy Department, 617-573-8109, E-mail: gfried@suffolk.edu. *Application contact:* Judith Reynolds, Director of Graduate Admissions, 617-573-8302, Fax: 617-305-1733, E-mail: grad.admission@suffolk.edu.

Union Institute & University, PhD Program in Interdisciplinary Studies, Cincinnati, OH 45206-1925. Offers ethical and creative leadership (PhD), including Martin Luther King studies; humanities and culture (PhD), including Martin Luther King studies; public policy and social change (PhD), including Martin Luther King studies. Program requires participation in brief on-campus residencies twice each year (January and July). Postbaccalaureate distance learning degree programs offered (minimal on-campus study). *Faculty:* 4 full-time (1 woman), 14 part-time/adjunct (9 women). *Students:* 103 full-time (60 women), 3 part-time (1 woman); includes 42 minority (40 Black or African American, non-Hispanic/Latino; 1 American Indian or Alaska Native, non-Hispanic/Latino; 1 Hispanic/Latino). Average age 46. In 2010, 2 doctorates awarded. *Degree requirements:* For doctorate, comprehensive exam, thesis/dissertation. *Entrance requirements:* For doctorate, master's degree, letters of recommendation, interview. *Application deadline:* Applications are processed on a rolling basis. Application fee: $50. *Expenses:* Tuition: Full-time $16,430; part-time $685 per credit hour. Required fees: $174; $44 per term. Tuition and fees vary according to course load, degree level and program. *Financial support:* Federal Work-Study, scholarships/grants, and tuition waivers (partial) available. Financial award application deadline: 5/1; financial award applicants required to submit FAFSA. *Faculty research:* Social responsibility, ethical leadership, Martin Luther King studies. *Unit head:* Dr. Larry Preston, Dean, 513-861-6400 Ext. 1151, E-mail: larry.preston@myunion.edu. *Application contact:* Michelle Flick, Admissions Counselor, 800-486-3116 Ext. 1225.

Université de Sherbrooke, Faculty of Theology, Ethics and Philosophy, Sherbrooke, QC J1K 2R1, Canada. Offers applied ethics (Diploma); human science of religions (MA); intercultural training (Diploma); philosophy (MA, PhD); spiritual anthropology (Diploma); theology (MA, PhD, Diploma). Part-time and evening/weekend programs available. Postbaccalaureate distance learning degree programs offered. Terminal master's awarded for partial completion of doctoral program. *Entrance requirements:* For master's, bachelor's degree in related discipline; for doctorate, master's degree in related discipline. *Faculty research:* Faith and culture interrelation.

Université du Québec à Chicoutimi, Graduate Programs, Program in Ethics, Chicoutimi, QC G7H 2B1, Canada. Offers Diploma. *Entrance requirements:* For degree, appropriate bachelor's degree, proficiency in French.

Université du Québec à Rimouski, Graduate Programs, Program in Ethics, Rimouski, QC G5L 3A1, Canada. Offers MA, Diploma. Part-time programs available. *Degree requirements:* For master's, thesis. *Entrance requirements:* For master's, appropriate bachelor's degree, proficiency in French.

Université Laval, Faculty of Theology and Religious Sciences, Program in Applied Ethics, Québec, QC G1K 7P4, Canada. Offers DESS. Part-time programs available. *Entrance requirements:* For degree, knowledge of French. Electronic applications accepted.

University of Baltimore, Graduate School, The Yale Gordon College of Liberal Arts, Program in Legal and Ethical Studies, Baltimore, MD 21201-5779. Offers MA. Part-time and evening/weekend programs available. *Degree requirements:* For master's, thesis optional. *Entrance requirements:* For master's, minimum GPA of 3.0. Additional exam requirements/recommendations for international students: Required—TOEFL (minimum score 550 paper-based; 213 computer-based). Electronic applications accepted. *Faculty research:* Morality in law and economics, religion in lawmaking, comparative legal history, law and social change, critical issues in constitutional law, theories of justice.

University of Nevada, Las Vegas, Graduate College, College of Liberal Arts, Department of Political Science, Program in Ethics and Policy Studies, Las Vegas, NV 89154-5029. Offers MA. Part-time programs available. *Faculty:* 2 full-time (0 women), 2 part-time/adjunct (both women). *Students:* 7 part-time (2 women); includes 4 minority (2 Asian, non-Hispanic/Latino; 2 Hispanic/Latino). Average age 33. 1 applicant, 0% accepted, 0 enrolled. In 2010, 1 master's awarded. *Degree requirements:* For master's, thesis. *Entrance requirements:* For master's, GRE General Test. Additional exam requirements/recommendations for international students: Required—TOEFL (minimum score 550 paper-based; 213 computer-based; 80 iBT), IELTS (minimum score 7). Application fee: $60 ($95 for international students). *Expenses:* Tuition, area resident: Part-time $239.50 per credit. Tuition, state resident: part-time $239.50 per credit. Tuition, nonresident: part-time $503 per credit. Required fees: $108 per semester. Tuition and fees vary according to course load, program and reciprocity agreements. *Financial support:* Institutionally sponsored loans, scholarships/grants, health care benefits, and unspecified assistantships available. Financial award application deadline: 3/1. *Faculty research:* Ancient political philosophy, international security, globalization, Islamic law, informal education in Senegal. *Unit head:* Dr. John Tuman, Chair/ Associate Professor, 702-895-5258, Fax: 702-895-1065, E-mail: john.tuman@unlv.edu. *Application contact:* Graduate College Admissions Evaluator, 702-895-3320, Fax: 702-895-4180, E-mail: gradcollege@unlv.edu.

University of New England, College of Arts and Sciences, Program in Education, Biddeford, ME 04005-9526. Offers advanced educational leadership (CAGS); curriculum and instruction strategies (CAGS); curriculum and instruction strategy (MS Ed); educational leadership (MS Ed, CAGS); general studies (MS Ed); inclusion education (MS Ed); leadership, ethics and change (CAGS); literacy K-12 (MS Ed, CAGS); teaching methodologies (MS Ed). Part-time programs available. Postbaccalaureate distance learning degree programs offered (minimal on-campus study). *Faculty:* 10 part-time/adjunct. *Students:* 596 full-time (451 women), 195 part-time (160 women); includes 33 Black or African American, non-Hispanic/Latino; 6 American Indian or Alaska Native, non-Hispanic/Latino; 4 Asian, non-Hispanic/Latino; 16 Hispanic/Latino; 7 Two or more races, non-Hispanic/Latino. In 2010, 349 master's, 66 CAGSs awarded. *Degree requirements:* For master's, collaborative action research project, integrative seminar portfolio. *Entrance requirements:* For master's, teaching certificate, 2 years of teaching experience. Additional exam requirements/recommendations for international students: Required—TOEFL. *Application deadline:* For fall admission, 9/15 for domestic students; for spring admission, 1/15 for domestic students. Applications are processed on a rolling basis. Application fee: $40. Electronic applications accepted. *Expenses:* Contact institution. *Financial support:* Application deadline: 5/1. *Faculty research:* Distance learning, effective teaching, transition planning, adult learning. *Unit head:* Dr. Doug Lynch, Chair of Education Department, 207-283-0171 Ext. 2888, E-mail: dlynch@une.edu. *Application contact:* Stacy Gato, Assistant Director of Graduate Admissions, 207-221-4225, Fax: 207-221-4898, E-mail: gradadmissions@une.edu.

The University of North Carolina at Charlotte, Graduate School, College of Arts and Sciences, Department of Philosophy, Charlotte, NC 28223-0001. Offers applied ethics (Certificate); ethics and applied philosophy (MA). *Faculty:* 10 full-time (4 women). *Students:* 3 full-time (2 women), 11 part-time (2 women); includes 1 minority (Black or African American, non-Hispanic/Latino). Average age 30. 10 applicants, 70% accepted, 5 enrolled. In 2010, 1 master's awarded. *Degree requirements:* For master's, thesis or alternative. *Application deadline:* For fall admission, 7/15 for domestic students, 5/1 for international students; for spring admission, 11/15 for domestic students, 10/1 for international students. Applications are processed on a rolling basis. Electronic applications accepted. *Expenses:* Tuition, state resident: full-time $3464. Tuition, nonresident: full-time $14,297. Required fees: $2094. Tuition and fees vary according to course load. *Financial support:* In 2010–11, 5 students received support, including 2 teaching assistantships (averaging $2,000 per year); administrative assistantship also available. Total annual research expenditures: $23,076. *Unit head:* Dr. Marvin J. Croy, Interim Chair, 704-687-2174, E-mail: mjcroy@uncc.edu. *Application contact:* Prof. William Gay, Coordinator, 704-687-2161, E-mail: mcgay@uncc.edu.

University of North Florida, College of Arts and Sciences, Department of Philosophy, Jacksonville, FL 32224. Offers applied ethics (Graduate Certificate); practical philosophy and applied ethics (MA). Part-time and evening/weekend programs available. *Faculty:* 10 full-time (3 women). *Students:* 7 full-time (3 women), 8 part-time (5 women); includes 1 Asian, non-Hispanic/Latino. Average age 37. 9 applicants, 78% accepted, 4 enrolled. *Entrance requirements:* For master's, GRE General Test, minimum GPA of 3.0 in last 60 hours, 3 letters of recommendation, writing sample. Additional exam requirements/recommendations for international students: Required—TOEFL (minimum score 500 paper-based; 173 computer-based; 61 iBT). *Application deadline:* For fall admission, 7/1 priority date for domestic students, 5/1 for international students. Applications are processed on a rolling basis. Application fee: $30. Electronic applications accepted. *Expenses:* Tuition, state resident: full-time $7646.40; part-time $318.60 per credit hour. Tuition, nonresident: full-time $23,502; part-time $979.24 per credit hour. Required fees: $1208.88; $50.37 per credit hour. Tuition and fees vary according to course load and program. *Financial support:* In 2010–11, 3 students received support, including 1 research assistantship (averaging $6,315 per year); teaching assistantships, Federal Work-Study, scholarships/grants, tuition waivers, and unspecified assistantships also available. Financial award application deadline: 4/1; financial award applicants required to submit FAFSA. *Faculty research:* Late modern philosophy, pragmatism, religion and American culture, hermeneutics, philosophy of mind. Total annual research expenditures: $42,164. *Unit head:* Dr. Hans-Herbert Koegler, 904-620-1330, Fax: 904-620-1840, E-mail: hkoegler@unf.edu. *Application contact:* Lillith Richardson, Assistant Director, The Graduate School, 904-620-1360, Fax: 904-620-1362, E-mail: graduateschool@unf.edu.

University of Pennsylvania, Wharton School, Legal Studies and Business Ethics Department, Philadelphia, PA 19104. Offers MBA, PhD. *Expenses:* Tuition: Full-time $25,660; part-time $4758 per course. Required fees: $2152; $270 per course. Tuition and fees vary according to course load, degree level and program.

University of South Africa, College of Human Sciences, Pretoria, South Africa. Offers adult education (M Ed); African languages (MA, PhD); African politics (MA, PhD); Afrikaans (MA, PhD); ancient history (MA, PhD); ancient Near Eastern studies (MA, PhD); anthropology (MA, PhD); applied linguistics (MA); Arabic (MA, PhD); archaeology (MA); art history (MA); Biblical archaeology (MA); Biblical studies (M Th, D Th, PhD); Christian spirituality (M Th, D Th);

church history (M Th, D Th); classical studies (MA, PhD); clinical psychology (MA); communication (MA, PhD); comparative education (M Ed, Ed D); consulting psychology (D Admin, D Com, PhD); curriculum studies (M Ed, Ed D); development studies (M Admin, MA, D Admin, PhD); didactics (M Ed, Ed D); education (M Tech); education management (M Ed, Ed D); educational psychology (M Ed); English (MA); environmental education (M Ed); French (MA, PhD); German (MA, PhD); Greek (MA); guidance and counseling (M Ed); health studies (MA, PhD), including health sciences education (MA), health services management (MA), medical and surgical nursing science (critical care general) (MA), midwifery and neonatal nursing science (MA), trauma and emergency care (MA); history (MA, PhD); history of education (Ed D); inclusive education (M Ed, Ed D); information and communications technology policy and regulation (MA); information science (MA, MIS, PhD); international politics (MA, PhD); Islamic studies (MA, PhD); Italian (MA, PhD); Judaica (MA, PhD); linguistics (MA, PhD); mathematical education (M Ed); mathematics education (MA); missiology (M Th, D Th); modern Hebrew (MA, PhD); musicology (MA, MMus, D Mus, PhD); natural science education (M Ed); New Testament (M Th, D Th); Old Testament (D Th); pastoral therapy (M Th, D Th); philosophy (MA); philosophy of education (M Ed, Ed D); politics (MA, PhD); Portuguese (MA, PhD); practical theology (M Th, D Th); psychology (MA, MS, PhD); psychology of education (M Ed, Ed D); public health (MA); religious studies (MA, D Th, PhD); Romance languages (MA); Russian (MA, PhD); Semitic languages (MA, PhD); social behavior studies in HIV/AIDS (MA); social science (mental health) (MA); social science in development studies (MA); social science in psychology (MA); social science in social work (MA); social science in sociology (MA); social work (MSW, DSW, PhD); socio-education (M Ed, Ed D); sociolinguistics (MA); sociology (MA, PhD); Spanish (MA, PhD); systematic theology (M Th, D Th); TESOL (teaching English to speakers of other languages) (MA); theological ethics (M Th, D Th); theory of literature (MA, PhD); urban ministries (D Th); urban ministry (M Th).

Valparaiso University, Graduate School, Programs in Liberal Studies, Concentration in Ethics and Values, Valparaiso, IN 46383. Offers MALS, Post-Master's Certificate, JD/MALS. Part-time and evening/weekend programs available. *Students:* 2 full-time (1 woman). Average age 27. In 2010, 1 master's awarded. *Entrance requirements:* For master's, minimum GPA of 3.0. Additional exam requirements/recommendations for international students: Required—TOEFL (minimum score 550 paper-based; 213 computer-based; 80 iBT). *Application deadline:* Applications are processed on a rolling basis. Application fee: $30 ($50 for international students). Electronic applications accepted. *Expenses:* Tuition: Full-time $9540; part-time $530 per credit hour. Required fees: $292; $95 per semester. Tuition and fees vary according to program. *Financial support:* Available to part-time students. Applicants required to submit FAFSA. *Unit head:* Dr. David L. Rowland, Dean, Graduate School and Continuing Education/Associate Provost, 219-464-5313, Fax: 219-464-5381, E-mail: david.rowland@valpo.edu. *Application contact:* Laura Groth, Coordinator of Student Services and Support, 219-464-5313, Fax: 219-464-5381, E-mail: laura.groth@valpo.edu.

Warner Pacific College, Graduate Programs, Portland, OR 97215-4099. Offers biblical and theological studies (MA); biblical studies (M Rel); education (M Ed); management/organizational leadership (MS); pastoral ministries (M Rel); religion and ethics (M Rel); teaching (MA); theology (M Rel). Part-time programs available. *Degree requirements:* For master's, thesis or alternative, presentation of defense. *Entrance requirements:* For master's, interview, minimum GPA of 2.5, letters of recommendations. *Faculty research:* New Testament studies, nineteenth-century Wesleyan theology, preaching and church growth, Christian ethics.

West Chester University of Pennsylvania, Office of Graduate Studies, College of Arts and Sciences, Department of Philosophy, West Chester, PA 19383. Offers business ethics (Certificate); healthcare ethics (Certificate); philosophy: applied ethics (MA); philosophy: general (MA). Part-time and evening/weekend programs available. *Students:* 12 full-time (1 woman), 13 part-time (4 women); includes 2 minority (both Hispanic/Latino). Average age 30. 17 applicants, 94% accepted, 14 enrolled. In 2010, 5 master's awarded. *Degree requirements:* For master's, thesis or comprehensive exam. *Entrance requirements:* For master's, GRE or writing sample, three letters of reference. Additional exam requirements/recommendations for international students: Required—TOEFL (minimum score 550 paper-based; 213 computer-based; 80 iBT). *Application deadline:* For fall admission, 4/15 priority date for domestic students, 3/15 for international students; for spring admission, 10/15 for domestic students, 9/1 for international students. Applications are processed on a rolling basis. Application fee: $35. Electronic applications accepted. *Expenses:* Tuition, state resident: full-time $6966; part-time $387 per credit. Tuition, nonresident: full-time $11,146; part-time $619 per credit. Required fees: $1614.40; $133.24 per credit. Part-time tuition and fees vary according to campus/location. *Financial support:* Unspecified assistantships available. Support available to part-time students. Financial award application deadline: 2/15; financial award applicants required to submit FAFSA. *Faculty research:* International studies. *Unit head:* Dr. Joan Woolfrey, Chair, 610-436-1004, E-mail: jwoolfrey@wcupa.edu. *Application contact:* Dr. Helen Daley Schroepfer, Graduate Coordinator, 610-436-2429, E-mail: hschroepfer@wcupa.edu.

Philosophy

American University, College of Arts and Sciences, Department of Philosophy and Religion, Washington, DC 22016-8056. Offers ethics, peace, and global affairs (MA); philosophy (MA), including history of philosophy, philosophy and social policy. Part-time and evening/weekend programs available. *Faculty:* 10 full-time (6 women), 9 part-time/adjunct (4 women). *Students:* 10 full-time (5 women), 2 part-time (0 women); includes 1 Hispanic/Latino. Average age 23. 49 applicants, 55% accepted, 8 enrolled. In 2010, 10 master's awarded. *Degree requirements:* For master's, one foreign language, comprehensive exam, thesis (for some programs). *Entrance requirements:* For master's, GRE, writing sample. Additional exam requirements/recommendations for international students: Required—TOEFL. *Application deadline:* For fall admission, 2/1 for domestic students; for spring admission, 10/1 for domestic students. Application fee: $80. *Financial support:* Fellowships, teaching assistantships, Federal Work-Study and institutionally sponsored loans available. Support available to part-time students. Financial award application deadline: 2/1. *Faculty research:* Oriental religion, classical and medieval philosophy, philosophy of law and ethics, comparative religion, philosophy of science. *Unit head:* Dr. Amy Oliver, Chair, 202-885-2140. *Application contact:* Kathleen Clowery, Director, Graduate Admissions, 202-885-3621, Fax: 202-885-1505.

American University of Beirut, Graduate Programs, Faculty of Arts and Sciences, Beirut, Lebanon. Offers anthropology (MA); Arabic language and literature (MA); archaeology (MA); biology (MS); chemistry (MS); computational science (MS); computer science (MS); economics (MA); education (MA); English language (MA); English literature (MA); environmental policy planning (MSES); financial economics (MAFE); geology (MS); history (MA); mathematics (MA, MS); Middle Eastern studies (MA); philosophy (MA); physics (MS); political studies (MA); psychology (MA); public administration (MA); sociology (MA); statistics (MA, MS). Part-time programs available. *Faculty:* 229 full-time (98 women), 136 part-time/adjunct (79 women). *Students:* 158 full-time (104 women), 263 part-time (171 women). Average age 25. 356 applicants, 59% accepted, 127 enrolled. In 2010, 57 master's awarded. *Degree requirements:* For master's, one foreign language, comprehensive exam, thesis (for some programs). *Entrance requirements:* For master's, GRE, letter of recommendation. Additional exam requirements/recommendations for international students: Required—TOEFL (minimum score 600 paper-based; 250 computer-based; 97 iBT), IELTS (minimum score 7). *Application deadline:* For fall admission, 4/30 for domestic and international students; for spring admission, 11/1 for domestic and international students. Application fee: $50. *Expenses:* Tuition: Full-time $12,294; part-time $683 per credit. Required fees: $499; $499 per credit. Tuition and fees vary according to course load and program. *Financial support:* In 2010–11, 33 students received support. Career-related internships or fieldwork, institutionally sponsored loans, scholarships/grants, health care benefits, and unspecified assistantships available. Financial award application deadline: 2/4; financial award applicants required to submit FAFSA. *Faculty research:* Modern and contemporary world theatre; mineralogy, petrology, and geochemistry; cell differentiation and transformation; combinatorial technologies; philosophy of action; continental philosophy; Phoenician epigraphy; nascent complex societies and urbanism; the economies of the Arab world; environmental economics; tectonophysics; host-parasite interactions; innate immunity; insect-plant interactions; history of the Ottoman archives; decentralization; transparency and corruption. Total annual research expenditures: $622,243. *Unit head:* Dr. Patrick McGreevy, Dean, 961-137-4374 Ext. 3800, Fax: 961-174-4461, E-mail: pm07@aub.edu.lb. *Application contact:* Dr. Salim Kanaan, Director, Admissions Office, 961-135-0000 Ext. 2594, Fax: 961-175-0775, E-mail: sk00@aub.edu.lb.

Arizona State University, College of Liberal Arts and Sciences, School of Historical, Philosophical and Religious Studies, Tempe, AZ 85287-4301. Offers East/Southeast Asian history (MA, PhD); European history (MA, PhD); Latin American studies (MA, PhD); North American history (MA, PhD); philosophy (MA, PhD); public history (MA); religious studies (MA, PhD); scholarly publishing (Graduate Certificate). Part-time programs available. *Faculty:* 70 full-time (29 women), 2 part-time/adjunct (0 women). *Students:* 125 full-time (58 women), 68 part-time (37 women); includes 21 minority (5 Black or African American, non-Hispanic/Latino; 3 American Indian or Alaska Native, non-Hispanic/Latino; 1 Asian, non-Hispanic/Latino; 11 Hispanic/Latino; 1 Two or more races, non-Hispanic/Latino), 16 international. Average age 34. 221 applicants, 51% accepted, 41 enrolled. In 2010, 24 master's, 10 doctorates, 3 other advanced degrees awarded. Terminal master's awarded for partial completion of doctoral program. *Degree requirements:* For master's, thesis or alternative, interactive Program of Study (iPOS) submitted before completing 50 percent of required credit hours; for doctorate, variable foreign language requirement, comprehensive exam, thesis/dissertation, interactive Program of Study (iPOS) submitted before completing 50 percent of required credit hours. *Entrance requirements:* For master's and doctorate, GRE, minimum GPA of 3.0 or equivalent in last 2 years of work leading to bachelor's degree. Additional exam requirements/recommendations for international students: Required—TOEFL, IELTS, or Pearson Test of English. *Application deadline:* For fall admission, 1/1 for domestic and international students. Applications are processed on a rolling basis. Application fee: $70 ($90 for international students). Electronic applications accepted. *Expenses:* Tuition, state resident: full-time $8510; part-time $608 per credit. Tuition, nonresident: full-time $16,542; part-time $919 per credit. Required fees: $339; $110 per credit. Part-time tuition and fees vary according to course load. *Financial support:* In 2010–11, 26 research assistantships with full and partial tuition reimbursements (averaging $12,900 per year), 69 teaching assistantships with full and partial tuition reimbursements (averaging $11,771 per year) were awarded; fellowships with full tuition reimbursements, career-related internships or fieldwork, institutionally sponsored loans, scholarships/grants, and tuition waivers (partial) also available. Financial award application deadline: 3/1; financial award applicants required to submit FAFSA. Total annual research expenditures: $1.3 million. *Unit head:* Mark Von Hagen, Director, 480-965-4186, E-mail: mark.vonhagen@asu.edu. *Application contact:* Graduate Admissions, 480-965-6113.

Baylor University, Graduate School, College of Arts and Sciences, Department of Philosophy, Waco, TX 76798. Offers MA, PhD. *Students:* 28 full-time (6 women), 4 part-time (0 women), 2 international. In 2010, 3 master's, 2 doctorates awarded. *Degree requirements:* For master's, one foreign language, thesis or alternative. *Entrance requirements:* For master's, GRE General Test. Additional exam requirements/recommendations for international students: Required—TOEFL. *Application deadline:* Applications are processed on a rolling basis. Application fee: $25. *Financial support:* Teaching assistantships, Federal Work-Study, institutionally sponsored loans, and unspecified assistantships available. *Unit head:* Dr. Bob Roberts, Graduate Program Director, 254-710-6363, Fax: 254-710-3838, E-mail: robert_roberts@baylor.edu. *Application contact:* Marilyn McKinney, Administrative Assistant, 254-710-4237, Fax: 254-710-3870, E-mail: marilyn_mckinney@baylor.edu.

Boston College, Graduate School of Arts and Sciences, Department of Philosophy, Chestnut Hill, MA 02467-3800. Offers MA, PhD. Terminal master's awarded for partial completion of doctoral program. *Degree requirements:* For master's, one foreign language, thesis optional; for doctorate, 2 foreign languages, thesis/dissertation. *Entrance requirements:* For master's and doctorate, GRE General Test. Additional exam requirements/recommendations for international students: Required—TOEFL (minimum score 600 paper-based; 250 computer-based; 100 iBT). *Faculty research:* History of philosophy, metaphysics, ethics.

Boston University, Graduate School of Arts and Sciences, Department of Philosophy, Boston, MA 02215. Offers MA, PhD, JD/MA. *Students:* 50 full-time (19 women), 5 part-time (0 women); includes 2 minority (1 Asian, non-Hispanic/Latino; 1 Two or more races, non-Hispanic/Latino), 13 international. Average age 30. 268 applicants, 13% accepted, 17 enrolled. In 2010, 25 master's, 6 doctorates awarded. Terminal master's awarded for partial completion of doctoral program. *Degree requirements:* For master's, one foreign language, thesis; for doctorate, one foreign language, comprehensive exam, thesis/dissertation. *Entrance requirements:* For master's and doctorate, GRE General Test, sample of written work, 3 letters of recommendation. Additional exam requirements/recommendations for international students: Required—TOEFL (minimum score 600 paper-based; 250 computer-based). *Application deadline:* For fall admission, 1/15 for domestic and international students. Application fee: $70. Electronic applications accepted. *Expenses:* Tuition: Full-time $39,314; part-time $1228 per credit. Required fees: $40 per semester. *Financial support:* In 2010–11, 11 fellowships with full tuition reimbursements (averaging $18,800 per year), 2 research assistantships with full tuition reimbursements (averaging $18,800 per year), 18 teaching assistantships with full tuition reimbursements (averaging $18,800 per year) were awarded; Federal Work-Study and scholarships/grants also available. Financial award application deadline: 1/15; financial award applicants required to submit FAFSA. *Unit head:* Dr. Daniel Dahlstrom, Chairman, 617-353-4583, Fax: 617-353-6805, E-mail: dahlstro@bu.edu. *Application contact:* Lesley Moreau, Senior Program Coordinator, 617-353-2571, Fax: 617-353-6805, E-mail: casphilo@bu.edu.

Bowling Green State University, Graduate College, College of Arts and Sciences, Department of Philosophy, Bowling Green, OH 43403. Offers applied philosophy (PhD); institutional theory and history (PhD); philosophy (MA). Part-time programs available. Terminal master's awarded for partial completion of doctoral program. *Degree requirements:* For master's, thesis or alternative; for doctorate, comprehensive exam, thesis/dissertation, foreign language or research tool. *Entrance requirements:* For master's and doctorate, GRE General Test. Additional exam requirements/recommendations for international students: Required—TOEFL. Electronic applications accepted. *Faculty research:* Moral philosophy and ethics, political and social philosophy, decision theory, applied ethics, public policy.

Brandeis University, Graduate School of Arts and Sciences, Department of Philosophy, Waltham, MA 02454-9110. Offers MA. Part-time programs available. *Faculty:* 10 full-time (3 women), 2 part-time/adjunct (both women). *Students:* 25 full-time (5 women); includes 1 Black

Philosophy

Brandeis University (continued)
or African American, non-Hispanic/Latino; 1 Two or more races, non-Hispanic/Latino, 4 international. 104 applicants, 44% accepted, 13 enrolled. In 2010, 3 master's awarded. *Degree requirements:* For master's, thesis. *Entrance requirements:* For master's, GRE, official transcript(s), 3 recommendation letters, curriculum vitae or resume, statement of purpose, writing sample. Additional exam requirements/recommendations for international students: Required—TOEFL (minimum score 600 paper-based; 250 computer-based; 100 iBT); Recommended—IELTS (minimum score 7). *Application deadline:* For fall admission, 2/15 priority date for domestic students. Applications are processed on a rolling basis. Application fee: $75. Electronic applications accepted. *Financial support:* In 2010–11, 27 teaching assistantships with partial tuition reimbursements (averaging $3,200 per year) were awarded; scholarships/grants also available. Financial award application deadline: 4/15; financial award applicants required to submit FAFSA. *Faculty research:* Metaphysics and epistemology, ethics, social and political philosophy, philosophy of language, logic, philosophy of mind and cognitive science, early modern philosophy, aesthetics, the philosophy of law. *Unit head:* Prof. Kate Moran, Director of Graduate Studies, 781-736-2695, Fax: 781-736-8562, E-mail: kmoran@brandeis.edu. *Application contact:* Julie Seeger, Department Administrator, 781-736-2789, Fax: 781-736-8562, E-mail: jseeger@brandeis.edu.

Brock University, Faculty of Graduate Studies, Faculty of Humanities, Program in Philosophy, St. Catharines, ON L2S 3A1, Canada. Offers MA. Part-time programs available. *Degree requirements:* For master's, thesis optional. *Entrance requirements:* For master's, honors BA in philosophy. Additional exam requirements/recommendations for international students: Required—TOEFL (minimum score 550 paper-based; 213 computer-based; 80 iBT), IELTS (minimum score 6.5), TWE (minimum score 4). Electronic applications accepted. *Faculty research:* Contemporary continental philosophy, Chinese and comparative philosophy, Indian philosophy, ethics.

Brown University, Graduate School, Department of Philosophy, Providence, RI 02912. Offers MA, PhD. *Degree requirements:* For master's, thesis or alternative; for doctorate, variable foreign language requirement, thesis/dissertation. *Entrance requirements:* For master's and doctorate, GRE General Test.

California Institute of Integral Studies, School of Consciousness and Transformation, San Francisco, CA 94103. Offers creative inquiry/interdisciplinary arts (MFA); cultural anthropology and social transformation (MA); East-West psychology (MA, PhD); integrative health studies (MA); philosophy and religion (MA, PhD), including Asian and comparative studies, philosophy, cosmology, and consciousness, women's spirituality; social and cultural anthropology (PhD); transformative leadership (MA); transformative studies (PhD); writing and consciousness (MFA). Part-time and evening/weekend programs available. Postbaccalaureate distance learning degree programs offered (minimal on-campus study). *Students:* 455 full-time (315 women), 133 part-time (90 women); includes 47 Black or African American, non-Hispanic/Latino; 3 American Indian or Alaska Native, non-Hispanic/Latino; 21 Asian, non-Hispanic/Latino; 41 Hispanic/Latino, 40 international. Average age 37. 265 applicants, 91% accepted, 163 enrolled. In 2010, 64 master's, 22 doctorates awarded. Terminal master's awarded for partial completion of doctoral program. *Degree requirements:* For master's, thesis optional; for doctorate, comprehensive exam, thesis/dissertation, 1 foreign language (Asian comparative studies). *Entrance requirements:* For master's, minimum GPA of 3.0, letters of recommendation, writing sample; for doctorate, master's degree, minimum GPA of 3.0, letters of recommendation, writing sample. Additional exam requirements/recommendations for international students: Required—TOEFL. *Application deadline:* For fall admission, 2/1 priority date for domestic and international students; for spring admission, 10/15 priority date for domestic and international students. Applications are processed on a rolling basis. Application fee: $65. Electronic applications accepted. *Expenses:* Tuition: Full-time $15,660; part-time $870 per semester hour. Required fees: $95 per semester. *Financial support:* In 2010–11, 255 students received support; research assistantships, teaching assistantships, career-related internships or fieldwork, Federal Work-Study, scholarships/grants, and tuition waivers (partial) available. Support available to part-time students. Financial award application deadline: 4/15; financial award applicants required to submit FAFSA. *Faculty research:* Ecology and sustainability, philosophy and religion, East-West psychology, integrative health, social and cultural anthropology, transformative leadership. *Application contact:* Allyson Werner, Associate Director of Admissions, 415-575-6155, Fax: 415-575-1268.

California State University, Long Beach, Graduate Studies, College of Liberal Arts, Department of Philosophy, Long Beach, CA 90840. Offers MA. Part-time programs available. *Faculty:* 7 full-time (1 woman). *Students:* 8 full-time (2 women), 12 part-time (3 women); includes 2 Asian, non-Hispanic/Latino; 2 Hispanic/Latino. Average age 30. 38 applicants, 39% accepted, 9 enrolled. In 2010, 6 master's awarded. *Degree requirements:* For master's, comprehensive exam or thesis. *Application deadline:* For fall admission, 7/1 for domestic students. Applications are processed on a rolling basis. Application fee: $55. Electronic applications accepted. *Financial support:* Federal Work-Study, institutionally sponsored loans, and scholarships/grants available. Financial award application deadline: 3/2. *Faculty research:* Philosophy of science, ethics. *Unit head:* Dr. Martin Herman, Interim Chair, 562-985-4331, Fax: 562-985-7135, E-mail: mherman@csulb.edu. *Application contact:* Dr. Cory Wright, Graduate Advisor, 562-985-4245, Fax: 562-985-4331, E-mail: cdwright@csulb.edu.

California State University, Los Angeles, Graduate Studies, College of Arts and Letters, Department of Philosophy, Los Angeles, CA 90032-8530. Offers MA. Part-time and evening/weekend programs available. *Faculty:* 6 full-time (2 women), 1 (woman) part-time/adjunct. *Students:* 20 full-time (6 women), 30 part-time (9 women); includes 21 minority (3 Black or African American, non-Hispanic/Latino; 1 American Indian or Alaska Native, non-Hispanic/Latino; 5 Asian, non-Hispanic/Latino; 11 Hispanic/Latino; 1 Two or more races, non-Hispanic/Latino), 1 international. Average age 32. 50 applicants, 100% accepted, 24 enrolled. In 2010, 18 master's awarded. *Degree requirements:* For master's, comprehensive exam. *Entrance requirements:* Additional exam requirements/recommendations for international students: Required—TOEFL (minimum score 500 paper-based; 173 computer-based). *Application deadline:* For fall admission, 5/1 for domestic and international students. Applications are processed on a rolling basis. Application fee: $55. Electronic applications accepted. *Financial support:* Career-related internships or fieldwork and Federal Work-Study available. Support available to part-time students. Financial award application deadline: 3/1. *Faculty research:* Aesthetics, philosophy of language, ethics, philosophy of science, history of philosophy. *Unit head:* Dr. Kayley Vernallis, Chair, 323-343-4180, Fax: 323-343-4193, E-mail: kvernal@calstatela.edu. *Application contact:* Dr. Alan Muchlinski, Dean of Graduate Studies, 323-343-3820, Fax: 323-343-5653, E-mail: amuchli@exchange.calstatela.edu.

Carleton University, Faculty of Graduate Studies, Faculty of Arts and Social Sciences, Department of Philosophy, Ottawa, ON K1S 5B6, Canada. Offers MA. *Degree requirements:* For master's, thesis optional. *Entrance requirements:* For master's, honors degree. Additional exam requirements/recommendations for international students: Required—TOEFL. *Faculty research:* Application of philosophical theory to issues of current concern, history of philosophy, contemporary philosophy in North America and Europe.

Carnegie Mellon University, College of Humanities and Social Sciences, Department of Philosophy, Pittsburgh, PA 15213-3891. Offers logic, computation and methodology (MS, PhD); philosophy (MA). Part-time programs available. *Faculty:* 18 full-time (3 women), 4 part-time/adjunct (3 women). *Students:* 35 full-time (5 women), 1 part-time (0 women); includes 5 minority (1 Black or African American, non-Hispanic/Latino; 3 Asian, non-Hispanic/Latino; 1 Hispanic/Latino), 3 international. Average age 25. 67 applicants, 24% accepted, 11 enrolled. In 2010, 6 master's, 4 doctorates awarded. *Degree requirements:* For master's, thesis; for doctorate, comprehensive exam, thesis/dissertation. *Entrance requirements:* For master's and doctorate, GRE General Test. Additional exam requirements/recommendations for international students: Required—TOEFL. *Application deadline:* For fall admission, 1/2 priority date for domestic and international students. Application fee: $30. Electronic applications accepted. *Financial support:* In 2010–11, 27 students received support, including 3 research assistantships with full tuition reimbursements available (averaging $15,000 per year); fellowships, teaching assistantships, career-related internships or fieldwork, Federal Work-Study, institutionally sponsored loans, scholarships/grants, and health care benefits also available. Support available to part-time students. Financial award application deadline: 2/1; financial award applicants required to submit FAFSA. *Faculty research:* Philosophy of science, artificial intelligence. *Unit head:* Prof. David Danks, Director of Graduate Studies, 412-268-8569, Fax: 412-268-1440, E-mail: ddanks@andrew.cmu.edu. *Application contact:* Adm. Jan Mary Puhl, Academic Coordinator, 412-268-8569, Fax: 412-268-1440, E-mail: jp10@andrew.cmu.edu.

The Catholic University of America, School of Philosophy, Washington, DC 20064. Offers MA, PhD, Ph L, MA/JD. Part-time programs available. *Faculty:* 20 full-time (5 women), 2 part-time/adjunct (1 woman). *Students:* 62 full-time (8 women), 76 part-time (16 women); includes 1 Black or African American, non-Hispanic/Latino; 3 Asian, non-Hispanic/Latino; 6 Hispanic/Latino, 9 international. Average age 31. 134 applicants, 58% accepted, 41 enrolled. In 2010, 18 master's, 8 doctorates awarded. *Degree requirements:* For master's, one foreign language, thesis, oral exam; for doctorate, 2 foreign languages, comprehensive exam, thesis/dissertation, oral exam. *Entrance requirements:* For master's, GRE General Test, statement of purpose, official copies of academic transcripts, three letters of recommendation, writing sample; for doctorate, GRE General Test, statement of purpose, official copies of academic transcripts, three letters of recommendation. Additional exam requirements/recommendations for international students: Required—TOEFL (minimum score 580 paper-based; 237 computer-based). *Application deadline:* For fall admission, 8/1 priority date for domestic students, 7/15 for international students; for spring admission, 12/1 priority date for domestic students, 10/15 for international students. Applications are processed on a rolling basis. Application fee: $55. Electronic applications accepted. *Expenses:* Tuition: Full-time $33,580; part-time $1315 per credit hour. Required fees: $80; $40 per semester hour. One-time fee: $425. *Financial support:* Fellowships, research assistantships, teaching assistantships, Federal Work-Study, scholarships/grants, tuition waivers (full and partial), and unspecified assistantships available. Financial award application deadline: 2/1; financial award applicants required to submit FAFSA. *Faculty research:* Ancient philosophy, modern philosophy, metaphysics, ethics, phenomenology. Total annual research expenditures: $57,792. *Unit head:* Dr. John McCarthy, OP, Interim Dean, 202-319-6649, Fax: 202-319-4731, E-mail: mccartjc@cua.edu. *Application contact:* Andrew Woodall, Director of Graduate Admissions, 202-319-5057, Fax: 202-319-6533, E-mail: cua-admissions@cua.edu.

Central European University, Graduate Studies, School of Social Sciences and Humanities, Budapest, Hungary. Offers economics (MA, PhD); gender studies (MA, PhD); international relations and European studies (MA, PhD); mathematics and its applications (MS, PhD); medieval studies (MA, PhD); nationalism studies (MA, PhD); philosophy (MA, PhD); political science (MA, PhD); public policy (MA, PhD); sociology and social anthropology (MA, PhD). *Faculty:* 90 full-time (29 women), 13 part-time/adjunct (7 women). *Students:* 732 full-time (404 women). Average age 28. 3,639 applicants, 22% accepted, 416 enrolled. In 2010, 278 master's, 16 doctorates awarded. Terminal master's awarded for partial completion of doctoral program. *Degree requirements:* For master's, one foreign language, thesis; for doctorate, one foreign language, comprehensive exam, thesis/dissertation. *Entrance requirements:* For master's, interview; for doctorate, GRE, CEU subject test, interview. Additional exam requirements/recommendations for international students: Required—TOEFL (minimum score 570 paper-based; 230 computer-based); Recommended—IELTS (minimum score 6.5). *Application deadline:* For fall admission, 1/15 priority date for domestic and international students. Application fee: $0. Electronic applications accepted. Tuition and fees charges are reported in euros. *Expenses:* Tuition: Full-time 11,000 euros. Required fees: 250 euros. One-time fee: 200 euros full-time. Tuition and fees vary according to degree level, program, reciprocity agreements and student level. *Financial support:* In 2010–11, 402 students received support, including 416 fellowships with full and partial tuition reimbursements available (averaging $6,200 per year); career-related internships or fieldwork, institutionally sponsored loans, and scholarships/grants also available. Financial award application deadline: 1/5. *Faculty research:* Civil society, fiscal decentralization, party politics, political philosophy (especially liberalism, theory of democracy). Total annual research expenditures: $35,000. *Unit head:* Dr. Katalin Farkas, Provost/Academic Pro Rector, 361-327-3000 Ext. 2227, E-mail: farkask@ceu.hu. *Application contact:* Zsuzsanna Jaszberenyi, Admissions Officer, 361-327-3009, Fax: 361-327-3211, E-mail: admissions@ceu.hu.

Claremont Graduate University, Graduate Programs, School of Arts and Humanities, Department of Philosophy, Claremont, CA 91711-6160. Offers MA, PhD, MA/PhD, MBA/MA, MBA/PhD. Part-time programs available. *Faculty:* 3 full-time (1 woman). *Students:* 28 full-time (8 women), 3 part-time; includes 3 Black or African American, non-Hispanic/Latino; 3 Asian, non-Hispanic/Latino; 2 Hispanic/Latino; 1 Two or more races, non-Hispanic/Latino, 1 international. Average age 38. In 2010, 9 master's, 1 doctorate awarded. *Degree requirements:* For doctorate, research folio. *Entrance requirements:* For master's and doctorate, GRE General Test. Additional exam requirements/recommendations for international students: Required—TOEFL (minimum score 550 paper-based; 213 computer-based; 80 iBT). *Application deadline:* For fall admission, 2/1 priority date for domestic students. Applications are processed on a rolling basis. Application fee: $60. Electronic applications accepted. *Expenses:* Tuition: Full-time $35,748; part-time $1554 per unit. Required fees: $215 per semester. *Financial support:* Fellowships, research assistantships, Federal Work-Study, institutionally sponsored loans, and scholarships/grants available. Support available to part-time students. Financial award application deadline: 2/15; financial award applicants required to submit FAFSA. *Faculty research:* Ancient philosophy, philosophy of science, probability theory, philosophical logic, philosophy of logic. *Unit head:* Charles Young, Chair, 909-607-3926, Fax: 909-607-1221, E-mail: charles.young@cgu.edu. *Application contact:* Susan Hampson, Admissions Coordinator, 909-607-1278, Fax: 909-607-1221, E-mail: humanities@cgu.edu.

Cleveland State University, College of Graduate Studies, College of Liberal Arts and Social Sciences, Department of Philosophy, Cleveland, OH 44115. Offers bioethics (MA, Certificate), including bioethics (MA); philosophy (MA), including philosophy. Part-time and evening/weekend programs available. *Faculty:* 8 full-time (4 women), 1 part-time/adjunct (0 women). *Students:* 6 full-time (3 women), 7 part-time (2 women); includes 2 Black or African American, non-Hispanic/Latino. Average age 30. 13 applicants, 46% accepted, 2 enrolled. In 2010, 4 master's awarded. *Degree requirements:* For master's, comprehensive exam, thesis optional. *Entrance requirements:* For master's, minimum GPA of 2.75. Additional exam requirements/recommendations for international students: Required—TOEFL (minimum score 525 paper-based; 197 computer-based). *Application deadline:* For fall admission, 5/1 priority date for domestic and international students. Applications are processed on a rolling basis. Application fee: $30. *Expenses:* Tuition, state resident: full-time $8447; part-time $469 per credit hour. Tuition, nonresident: full-time $16,020; part-time $890 per credit hour. Required fees: $50. *Financial support:* In 2010–11, research assistantships with full tuition reimbursements (averaging $3,480 per year), 6 teaching assistantships with full tuition reimbursements (averaging $3,480 per year) were awarded; tuition waivers (full) and unspecified assistantships also available. *Faculty research:* Ethics, history of philosophy, bioethics, social and political philosophy. *Unit head:* Dr. Diane Steinberg, Chairperson, 216-687-3900, Fax: 216-523-7482, E-mail: d.steinberg@csuohio.edu. *Application contact:* Dr. Giannina Pianalto, Director of Graduate Admissions, 216-687-5599, Fax: 216-687-5400, E-mail: g.pianalto@csuohio.edu.

Collège Dominicain de Philosophie et de Théologie, Graduate Programs, Faculty of Philosophy, Ottawa, ON K1R 7G3, Canada. Offers MA Ph, PhD. *Degree requirements:* For master's, thesis; for doctorate, 2 foreign languages, thesis/dissertation, candidacy exam. *Entrance requirements:* For master's, honors degree in philosophy, minimum B average in undergraduate course work; for doctorate, master's degree in philosophy, minimum A average in graduate course work. *Faculty research:* Ethics, philosophy of Kant.

College of the Humanities and Sciences, Harrison Middleton University, Graduate Program, Tempe, AZ 85282. Offers education (MA, Ed D); humanities (MA); imaginative literature (MA);

interdisciplinary studies (DA); jurisprudence (MA); natural science (MA); philosophy and religion (MA); social science (MA). Part-time and evening/weekend programs available. Post-baccalaureate distance learning degree programs offered (no on-campus study). *Faculty:* 17 full-time (7 women), 14 part-time/adjunct (6 women). *Students:* 52 full-time (20 women). In 2010, 4 master's awarded. *Degree requirements:* For master's and doctorate, capstone project. *Entrance requirements:* For doctorate, 3 academic letters of reference, interview. *Application deadline:* Applications are processed on a rolling basis. Application fee: $50. Electronic applications accepted. *Expenses:* Tuition: Part-time $300 per credit hour. One-time fee: $350 part-time. *Faculty research:* Japanese animation, educational leadership, war art, John Muir's wilderness. *Application contact:* Deborah Deacon, Dean of Graduate Studies, 877-248-6724, Fax: 800-762-1622, E-mail: ddeacon@hmu.edu.

Colorado State University, Graduate School, College of Liberal Arts, Department of Philosophy, Fort Collins, CO 80523-1781. Offers MA. Part-time programs available. *Faculty:* 13 full-time (3 women), 1 part-time/adjunct (0 women). *Students:* 8 full-time (3 women), 12 part-time (1 woman); includes 2 minority (both Hispanic/Latino). Average age 27. 43 applicants, 40% accepted, 5 enrolled. In 2010, 13 master's awarded. *Degree requirements:* For master's, variable foreign language requirement, comprehensive exam (for some programs), thesis (for some programs). *Entrance requirements:* For master's, GRE General Test, minimum GPA of 3.25, 3 letters of recommendation, writing sample. Additional exam requirements/recommendations for international students: Required—TOEFL. *Application deadline:* For fall admission, 2/15 priority date for domestic and international students; for spring admission, 8/1 priority date for domestic and international students. Applications are processed on a rolling basis. Application fee: $50. Electronic applications accepted. *Expenses:* Tuition, state resident: full-time $7434; part-time $413 per credit. Tuition, nonresident: full-time $19,022; part-time $1057 per credit. Required fees: $1729; $88 per credit. *Financial support:* In 2010–11, 12 students received support, including 12 teaching assistantships with full tuition reimbursements available (averaging $12,330 per year); fellowships, research assistantships, career-related internships or fieldwork, Federal Work-Study, institutionally sponsored loans, scholarships/grants, traineeships, and unspecified assistantships also available. Support available to part-time students. Financial award application deadline: 3/1; financial award applicants required to submit FAFSA. *Faculty research:* Animal ethics, environmental ethics, history of philosophy, comparative philosophy, epistemology. *Unit head:* Dr. Jane E. Kneller, Chair, 970-491-7614, Fax: 970-491-4900, E-mail: jane.kneller@colostate.edu. *Application contact:* Dr. Michael Losonsky, Graduate Studies Coordinator, 970-491-6734, Fax: 970-491-4900, E-mail: losonsky@lamar.colostate.edu.

Columbia University, Graduate School of Arts and Sciences, Division of Humanities, Department of Philosophy, New York, NY 10027. Offers M Phil, MA, PhD, JD/MA, JD/PhD. Part-time programs available. *Degree requirements:* For master's, one foreign language; for doctorate, 2 foreign languages, thesis/dissertation. *Entrance requirements:* For master's and doctorate, GRE General Test, writing sample. Additional exam requirements/recommendations for international students: Required—TOEFL.

Columbia University, Graduate School of Arts and Sciences, Division of Natural Sciences, Department of Physics, Program in Philosophical Foundations of Physics, New York, NY 10027. Offers MA.

Concordia University, School of Graduate Studies, Faculty of Arts and Science, Department of Philosophy, Montréal, QC H3G 1M8, Canada. Offers MA. *Degree requirements:* For master's, comprehensive exam, thesis or alternative. *Entrance requirements:* For master's, honors degree in philosophy or equivalent. *Faculty research:* Anglo-American analytic thought, Continental thought, pragmatic thought.

Cornell University, Graduate School, Graduate Fields of Arts and Sciences, Field of Philosophy, Ithaca, NY 14853-0001. Offers PhD. *Faculty:* 16 full-time (4 women). *Students:* 38 full-time (8 women); includes 1 Black or African American, non-Hispanic/Latino; 1 Hispanic/Latino, 21 international. Average age 29. 308 applicants, 6% accepted, 9 enrolled. In 2010, 4 doctorates awarded. *Degree requirements:* For doctorate, comprehensive exam, thesis/dissertation, teaching experience. *Entrance requirements:* For doctorate, sample of written work in philosophy, 2 letters of recommendation. Additional exam requirements/recommendations for international students: Required—TOEFL (minimum score 550 paper-based; 213 computer-based; 77 iBT). *Application deadline:* For fall admission, 1/15 for domestic students. Application fee: $80. Electronic applications accepted. *Expenses:* Tuition: Full-time $29,500. Required fees: $76. Tuition and fees vary according to degree level and program. *Financial support:* In 2010–11, 14 fellowships with full tuition reimbursements, 20 teaching assistantships with full tuition reimbursements were awarded; research assistantships with full tuition reimbursements, institutionally sponsored loans, scholarships/grants, health care benefits, tuition waivers (full and partial), and unspecified assistantships also available. Financial award applicants required to submit FAFSA. *Unit head:* Director of Graduate Studies, 607-255-3687, Fax: 607-255-8177. *Application contact:* Graduate Field Assistant, 607-255-3687, Fax: 607-255-8177, E-mail: philosophy@cornell.edu.

Dalhousie University, Faculty of Arts and Social Science, Department of Philosophy, Halifax, NS B3H 4R2, Canada. Offers MA, PhD. *Entrance requirements:* For doctorate, MA in philosophy. Additional exam requirements/recommendations for international students: Required—TOEFL, IELTS, CANTEST, CAEL, or Michigan English Language Assessment Battery. Electronic applications accepted. *Faculty research:* Ethical and political philosophy; epistemology; philosophy of language, history, and logic; bioethics; feminist theory.

DePaul University, College of Liberal Arts and Sciences, Department of Philosophy, Chicago, IL 60604-2287. Offers MA, PhD. Part-time and evening/weekend programs available. *Faculty:* 21 full-time (8 women). *Students:* 17 full-time (6 women), 30 part-time (14 women); includes 1 Black or African American, non-Hispanic/Latino; 1 Hispanic/Latino, 7 international. Average age 29. 157 applicants, 4% accepted, 6 enrolled. In 2010, 6 master's, 2 doctorates awarded. Terminal master's awarded for partial completion of doctoral program. *Degree requirements:* For master's, one foreign language, thesis optional; for doctorate, 2 foreign languages, thesis/dissertation, oral exam, 28 courses in philosophy. *Entrance requirements:* For master's, GRE General Test, sample of written work, BA, two letters of recommendation; for doctorate, GRE General Test, MA in philosophy, sample of written work, two letters of recommendation. Additional exam requirements/recommendations for international students: Required—TOEFL. *Application deadline:* For fall admission, 12/15 for domestic students; for winter admission, 12/15 for domestic students. Applications are processed on a rolling basis. Application fee: $40. Electronic applications accepted. *Financial support:* In 2010–11, 12 fellowships with full tuition reimbursements (averaging $18,000 per year), 24 teaching assistantships with full tuition reimbursements (averaging $15,500 per year) were awarded; tuition waivers (partial) also available. Financial award application deadline: 12/15. *Faculty research:* German idealism, contemporary Continental philosophy, social and political philosophy, critical race theory, Renaissance and early modern philosophy. *Unit head:* Richard A. Lee, Chair, 773-325-4502, Fax: 773-325-7268, E-mail: rlee17@depaul.edu. *Application contact:* Avery M. Goldman, Director of Recruitment, 773-325-4811, Fax: 773-325-7268, E-mail: agoldman@depaul.edu.

Dominican School of Philosophy and Theology, Graduate Programs, Department of Philosophy, Berkeley, CA 94708. Offers MA, MA/MA. Part-time programs available. *Faculty:* 11 full-time (1 woman), 10 part-time/adjunct (2 women). *Students:* 8 full-time (0 women), 2 part-time (0 women); includes 4 minority (1 American Indian or Alaska Native, non-Hispanic/Latino; 1 Asian, non-Hispanic/Latino; 1 Hispanic/Latino; 1 Two or more races, non-Hispanic/Latino). Average age 33. 4 applicants, 75% accepted, 2 enrolled. In 2010, 6 master's awarded. *Degree requirements:* For master's, one foreign language, thesis. *Entrance requirements:* For master's, GRE General Test, minimum GPA of 3.0. Additional exam requirements/recommendations for international students: Required—TOEFL (minimum score 550 paper-based; 68 computer-based; 80 iBT). *Application deadline:* For fall admission, 3/15 priority date for domestic and international students; for spring admission, 10/15 priority date for domestic and international students. Applications are processed on a rolling basis. Application fee: $40. *Expenses:* Tuition: Full-time $14,160; part-time $590 per unit. *Financial support:* In 2010–11, 4 students received support. Institutionally sponsored loans, scholarships/grants, and tuition waivers (partial) available. Financial award application deadline: 4/1; financial award applicants required to submit FAFSA. *Faculty research:* Pre-modernism philosophy, philosophy and science, human suffering, philosophy of language, classical philosophy. *Unit head:* Fr. Anselm Ramelow, OP, Chair, 510-883-2074, Fax: 510-849-1372, E-mail: aramelow@dspt.edu. *Application contact:* John D. Knutsen, Director of Admissions, 510-883-2083, Fax: 510-849-1372, E-mail: admissions@dspt.edu.

Duke University, Graduate School, Department of Philosophy, Durham, NC 27708. Offers AM, PhD, JD/AM. *Faculty:* 14 full-time. *Students:* 28 full-time (10 women); includes 1 American Indian or Alaska Native, non-Hispanic/Latino; 2 Asian, non-Hispanic/Latino; 1 Hispanic/Latino, 4 international. 6 applicants, 100% accepted, 3 enrolled. In 2010, 1 master's, 2 doctorates awarded. *Degree requirements:* For doctorate, one foreign language, thesis/dissertation. *Entrance requirements:* For doctorate, GRE General Test. Additional exam requirements/recommendations for international students: Required—TOEFL (minimum score 550 paper-based; 213 computer-based; 83 iBT), IELTS (minimum score 7). *Application deadline:* For fall admission, 12/8 priority date for domestic and international students. Application fee: $75. Electronic applications accepted. *Financial support:* Fellowships, research assistantships, teaching assistantships, Federal Work-Study available. Financial award application deadline: 12/8. *Unit head:* Karen Neander, Director of Graduate Studies, 919-660-3048, Fax: 919-660-3060, E-mail: rjjc77@duke.edu. *Application contact:* Elizabeth Hutton, Director of Admissions, 919-684-3913, Fax: 919-684-2277, E-mail: grad-admissions@duke.edu.

Duquesne University, Graduate School of Liberal Arts, Department of Philosophy, Pittsburgh, PA 15282-0001. Offers MA, PhD. Part-time and evening/weekend programs available. *Faculty:* 10 full-time (3 women), 4 part-time/adjunct (2 women). *Students:* 95 full-time (23 women), 8 part-time (0 women); includes 1 Black or African American, non-Hispanic/Latino; 1 Hispanic/Latino, 6 international. Average age 32. 123 applicants, 26% accepted, 18 enrolled. In 2010, 20 master's, 5 doctorates awarded. Terminal master's awarded for partial completion of doctoral program. *Degree requirements:* For master's, one foreign language; for doctorate, 2 foreign languages, comprehensive exam, thesis/dissertation. *Entrance requirements:* For master's, GRE General Test, bachelor's degree in philosophy, minimum GPA of 3.5; for doctorate, GRE General Test, master's degree in philosophy, minimum GPA of 3.75. Additional exam requirements/recommendations for international students: Required—TOEFL. *Application deadline:* For fall admission, 2/15 for domestic and international students. Electronic applications accepted. *Expenses:* Tuition: Part-time $884 per credit. Required fees: $84 per credit. Tuition and fees vary according to course load. *Financial support:* In 2010–11, 17 teaching assistantships with full tuition reimbursements (averaging $15,000 per year) were awarded; research assistantships with full tuition reimbursements, Federal Work-Study, scholarships/grants, tuition waivers (partial), and unspecified assistantships also available. Financial award application deadline: 5/1. *Faculty research:* Phenomenology, twentieth century Continental philosophy, history of philosophy. *Unit head:* Dr. James Swindal, Chair, 412-396-6572, E-mail: swiindalj@duq.edu. *Application contact:* Dr. James Swindal, Chair, 412-396-6572, E-mail: swindalj@duq.edu.

Emory University, Laney Graduate School, Department of Comparative Literature, Atlanta, GA 30322-1100. Offers comparative literature (PhD); English (Certificate); French (Certificate); Middle Eastern studies (PhD); philosophy (Certificate); psychoanalytic studies (PhD); religion (PhD); Spanish (Certificate); women studies (Certificate). *Degree requirements:* For doctorate, 2 foreign languages, comprehensive exam, thesis/dissertation. *Entrance requirements:* For doctorate, GRE General Test, minimum GPA of 3.0. Additional exam requirements/recommendations for international students: Required—TOEFL. Electronic applications accepted. *Expenses:* Tuition: Full-time $33,800. Required fees: $1300. *Faculty research:* Literary theory, psychoanalysis trauma and testimony, literature and religion, literature and technology, literature and philosophy, politics and global culture, literature and aesthetics.

Emory University, Laney Graduate School, Department of Philosophy, Atlanta, GA 30322-1100. Offers PhD. *Degree requirements:* For doctorate, 2 foreign languages, comprehensive exam, thesis/dissertation. *Entrance requirements:* For doctorate, GRE General Test, minimum GPA of 3.0. Additional exam requirements/recommendations for international students: Required—TOEFL. Electronic applications accepted. *Expenses:* Tuition: Full-time $33,800. Required fees: $1300. *Faculty research:* History of philosophy, German idealism, twentieth century Continental philosophy, ethics, social theory.

Florida State University, The Graduate School, College of Arts and Sciences, Department of Philosophy, Tallahassee, FL 32306-1500. Offers history and philosophy of science (MA); philosophy (MA, PhD). *Faculty:* 14 full-time (2 women), 3 part-time/adjunct (2 women). *Students:* 40 full-time (11 women), 4 part-time (1 woman); includes 3 minority (1 Black or African American, non-Hispanic/Latino; 2 Hispanic/Latino), 1 international. Average age 29. 78 applicants, 17% accepted, 6 enrolled. In 2010, 7 master's, 4 doctorates awarded. Terminal master's awarded for partial completion of doctoral program. *Degree requirements:* For master's, one foreign language, comprehensive exam (for some programs), thesis (for some programs); for doctorate, one foreign language, thesis/dissertation. *Entrance requirements:* For master's and doctorate, GRE General Test. Additional exam requirements/recommendations for international students: Required—TOEFL (minimum score 550 paper-based; 213 computer-based; 80 iBT). *Application deadline:* For fall admission, 1/3 priority date for domestic and international students. Applications are processed on a rolling basis. Application fee: $30. Electronic applications accepted. *Expenses:* Tuition, state resident: full-time $8238.24. *Financial support:* In 2010–11, 1 student received support, including 2 fellowships with partial tuition reimbursements available (averaging $20,000 per year), 2 research assistantships with partial tuition reimbursements available (averaging $5,000 per year), 35 teaching assistantships with partial tuition reimbursements available (averaging $12,000 per year); Federal Work-Study, scholarships/grants, and health care benefits also available. Financial award application deadline: 1/3; financial award applicants required to submit FAFSA. *Faculty research:* Philosophy of biology, Greek philosophy, ethics, action theory, philosophy of mind. *Unit head:* Dr. John Piers Rawling, Chairman, 850-644-1483, Fax: 850-644-3832, E-mail: prawling@fsu.edu. *Application contact:* Douglas Lee Bowen, Academic Support Assistant, 850-644-1483, Fax: 850-644-3832, E-mail: philosophy@admin.fsu.edu.

Fordham University, Graduate School of Arts and Sciences, Department of Philosophy, New York, NY 10458. Offers philosophical resources (MA); philosophy (MA, PhD). Part-time and evening/weekend programs available. *Faculty:* 31 full-time (10 women). *Students:* 52 full-time (8 women), 25 part-time (7 women); includes 1 Asian, non-Hispanic/Latino, 4 international. Average age 30. 195 applicants, 16% accepted, 14 enrolled. In 2010, 16 master's, 7 doctorates awarded. Terminal master's awarded for partial completion of doctoral program. *Degree requirements:* For master's, one foreign language, comprehensive exam; for doctorate, 2 foreign languages, comprehensive exam, thesis/dissertation. *Entrance requirements:* For master's and doctorate, GRE General Test. Additional exam requirements/recommendations for international students: Required—TOEFL (minimum score 650 paper-based; 280 computer-based). *Application deadline:* For fall admission, 1/4 priority date for domestic students; for spring admission, 11/1 for domestic students. Application fee: $70. Electronic applications accepted. *Financial support:* In 2010–11, 45 students received support, including 2 fellowships with tuition reimbursements available (averaging $21,175 per year), 20 research assistantships with tuition reimbursements available (averaging $17,782 per year), 23 teaching assistantships with tuition reimbursements available (averaging $15,293 per year); institutionally sponsored loans, tuition waivers (full and partial), and unspecified assistantships also available. Support available to part-time students. Financial award application deadline: 1/4. *Faculty research:* Contemporary continental philosophy (including German idealism), philosophy of religion, medieval philosophy, ethics, epistemology. *Unit head:* Dr. John Drummond, SJ, Chair, 718-817-3270, Fax: 718-817-3300, E-mail: drummond@fordham.edu. *Application contact:* Charlene Dundie, Director of Graduate Admissions, 718-817-4420, Fax: 718-817-3566, E-mail: dundie@fordham.edu.

Philosophy

Franciscan University of Steubenville, Graduate Programs, Department of Philosophy, Steubenville, OH 43952-1763. Offers MA. Part-time programs available. *Degree requirements:* For master's, one foreign language, thesis. *Entrance requirements:* For master's, minimum undergraduate GPA of 3.0.

George Mason University, College of Humanities and Social Sciences, Department of Philosophy, Fairfax, VA 22030. Offers MA. *Faculty:* 10 full-time (2 women), 6 part-time/adjunct (0 women). *Students:* 7 full-time (1 woman), 16 part-time (6 women); includes 1 Two or more races, non-Hispanic/Latino, 2 international. Average age 36. 17 applicants, 53% accepted, 5 enrolled. In 2010, 6 master's awarded. *Entrance requirements:* For master's, 3 letters of recommendation, current transcript, expanded goals statement, writing sample, resume. Additional exam requirements/recommendations for international students: Required—TOEFL (minimum score 570 paper-based; 230 computer-based; 88 iBT). *Application deadline:* For fall admission, 4/15 priority date for domestic students; for spring admission, 11/1 for domestic students. Applications are processed on a rolling basis. Application fee: $100. Electronic applications accepted. *Expenses:* Tuition, state resident: full-time $8192; part-time $440 per credit hour. Tuition, nonresident: full-time $22,952; part-time $1055 per credit hour. Required fees: $2364; $99 per credit hour. *Financial support:* In 2010–11, 1 student received support, including 1 research assistantship (averaging $10,000 per year); Federal Work-Study, scholarships/grants, unspecified assistantships, and health care benefits (full-time research or teaching assistantship recipients) also available. Financial award application deadline: 3/1; financial award applicants required to submit FAFSA. *Faculty research:* Cultural studies, political theory philosophy, social and political philosophy, feminist theory, analytical and continental philosophy, philosophy of science. *Unit head:* Ted Kinnaman, Chair/Associate Professor, 703-993-4328, E-mail: tkinnama@gmu.edu. *Application contact:* Rose Cherubin, Graduate Coordinator, 703-993-1332, E-mail: rcherubi@gmu.edu.

Georgetown University, Graduate School of Arts and Sciences, Department of Philosophy, Washington, DC 20057. Offers bioethics (MA); philosophy (PhD); JD/MA; JD/PhD; MD/PhD. *Degree requirements:* For master's, thesis or alternative; for doctorate, 2 foreign languages, comprehensive exam, thesis/dissertation. *Entrance requirements:* For master's and doctorate, GRE General Test. Additional exam requirements/recommendations for international students: Required—TOEFL.

The George Washington University, Columbian College of Arts and Sciences, Department of Philosophy, Washington, DC 20052. Offers philosophy and social policy (MA). *Students:* 13 full-time (7 women), 10 part-time (5 women); includes 3 minority (all Black or African American, non-Hispanic/Latino), 2 international. Average age 26. 15 applicants, 87% accepted, 8 enrolled. In 2010, 5 master's awarded. *Degree requirements:* For master's, comprehensive exam, thesis or alternative. *Entrance requirements:* For master's, GRE General Test, interview, minimum GPA of 3.0. Additional exam requirements/recommendations for international students: Required—TOEFL (minimum score 600 paper-based; 250 computer-based; 100 iBT). *Application deadline:* For fall admission, 4/1 priority date for domestic and international students; for spring admission, 10/1 priority date for domestic students, 9/1 priority date for international students. Applications are processed on a rolling basis. Application fee: $60. Electronic applications accepted. *Financial support:* In 2010–11, 2 students received support; fellowships with tuition reimbursements available, Federal Work-Study and institutionally sponsored loans available. Financial award application deadline: 1/15. *Unit head:* Dr. William B. Griffith, Academic Director, 202-994-8684, E-mail: wbg@gwu.edu. *Application contact:* Information Contact, 202-994-6265, Fax: 202-994-8683, E-mail: philosop@gwu.edu.

Georgia State University, College of Arts and Sciences, Department of Philosophy, Atlanta, GA 30302-4089. Offers MA, MA/JD. Part-time programs available. *Degree requirements:* For master's, thesis. *Entrance requirements:* For master's, GRE General Test, sample of written work. Additional exam requirements/recommendations for international students: Required—TOEFL. Electronic applications accepted. *Faculty research:* Ethics, ancient philosophy, German philosophy, philosophy of mind/neurophilosophy.

Gonzaga University, College of Arts and Sciences, Program in Philosophy, Spokane, WA 99258. Offers MA. Part-time programs available. *Degree requirements:* For master's, comprehensive exam. *Entrance requirements:* For master's, GRE General Test or MAT, minimum GPA of 3.0. Additional exam requirements/recommendations for international students: Required—TOEFL.

Graduate School and University Center of the City University of New York, Graduate Studies, Program in Philosophy, New York, NY 10016-4039. Offers MA, PhD. Terminal master's awarded for partial completion of doctoral program. *Degree requirements:* For master's, thesis; for doctorate, one foreign language, comprehensive exam, thesis/dissertation. *Entrance requirements:* For master's, GRE General Test; for doctorate, GRE General Test, 3 letters of recommendation, writing sample. Additional exam requirements/recommendations for international students: Required—TOEFL. Electronic applications accepted.

Harvard University, Graduate School of Arts and Sciences, Department of Philosophy, Cambridge, MA 02138. Offers classical philosophy (PhD); philosophy (PhD). *Degree requirements:* For doctorate, 2 foreign languages, thesis/dissertation, final exams. *Entrance requirements:* For doctorate, GRE General Test. Additional exam requirements/recommendations for international students: Required—TOEFL. *Expenses:* Tuition: Full-time $34,976. Required fees: $1166. Full-time tuition and fees vary according to program.

Harvard University, Graduate School of Arts and Sciences, Department of Sanskrit and Indian Studies, Cambridge, MA 02138. Offers Indian philosophy (AM, PhD); Pali (AM, PhD); Sanskrit (AM, PhD); Tibetan (AM, PhD); Urdu (AM, PhD). Terminal master's awarded for partial completion of doctoral program. *Degree requirements:* For master's, 3 foreign languages; for doctorate, 3 foreign languages, thesis/dissertation. *Entrance requirements:* For master's, GRE General Test; for doctorate, GRE General Test, proficiency in French and German. Additional exam requirements/recommendations for international students: Required—TOEFL. *Expenses:* Tuition: Full-time $34,976. Required fees: $1166. Full-time tuition and fees vary according to program.

Harvard University, Graduate School of Arts and Sciences, Department of the Classics, Cambridge, MA 02138. Offers Byzantine Greek (PhD); classical archaeology (PhD); classical philology (PhD); classical philosophy (PhD); medieval Latin (PhD). *Degree requirements:* For doctorate, 4 foreign languages, thesis/dissertation, preliminary and special exams. *Entrance requirements:* For doctorate, GRE General Test. Additional exam requirements/recommendations for international students: Required—TOEFL. *Expenses:* Tuition: Full-time $34,976. Required fees: $1166. Full-time tuition and fees vary according to program.

Howard University, Graduate School, Department of Philosophy, Washington, DC 20059-0002. Offers MA. Part-time programs available. *Degree requirements:* For master's, one foreign language, comprehensive exam, thesis. *Entrance requirements:* For master's, GRE General Test. Additional exam requirements/recommendations for international students: Required—TOEFL. *Faculty research:* African and African-American philosophy, social and political philosophy, ethics, philosophy of culture, applied philosophy.

Indiana University Bloomington, University Graduate School, College of Arts and Sciences, Department of Philosophy, Bloomington, IN 47405. Offers MA, PhD. *Faculty:* 17 full-time (5 women). *Students:* 35 full-time (7 women); includes 7 minority (5 Asian, non-Hispanic/Latino; 1 Hispanic/Latino; 1 Two or more races, non-Hispanic/Latino), 6 international. Average age 31. 138 applicants, 8% accepted, 7 enrolled. In 2010, 2 master's, 4 doctorates awarded. Terminal master's awarded for partial completion of doctoral program. *Degree requirements:* For master's, variable foreign language requirement, thesis optional; for doctorate, comprehensive exam, thesis/dissertation, qualifying paper. *Entrance requirements:* For master's and doctorate, GRE General Test, writing sample. Additional exam requirements/recommendations for international students: Required—TOEFL. *Application deadline:* For fall admission, 12/15 priority date for domestic students, 12/15 for international students; for spring admission, 9/1 priority date for domestic students. Applications are processed on a rolling basis. Application fee: $55 ($65 for international students). Electronic applications accepted. *Financial support:* In 2010–11, 7 fellowships with partial tuition reimbursements (averaging $16,000 per year), 29 teaching assistantships with partial tuition reimbursements (averaging $15,119 per year) were awarded; research assistantships. Financial award application deadline: 4/15. *Faculty research:* Algebraic logic, cognitive science, history of modern philosophy, ancient and Jewish philosophy, medieval logic and semantics, epistemology, ethics, history, philosophy of mind, philosophy of language. *Unit head:* Timothy W. O'Connor, Chair and Professor, 812-855-1093, Fax: 812-855-3777, E-mail: toconnor@indiana.edu. *Application contact:* Marge Clark, Administrative Secretary, 812-855-7088, Fax: 812-855-3777, E-mail: clarkma@indiana.edu.

Indiana University–Purdue University Indianapolis, School of Liberal Arts, Department of Philosophy, Indianapolis, IN 46202-2896. Offers American philosophy (Certificate); bioethics (Certificate); philosophy (MA); JD/MA; MD/MA. Part-time programs available. *Faculty:* 13 full-time (2 women), 1 part-time/adjunct (0 women). *Students:* 4 full-time (2 women), 11 part-time (6 women); includes 1 minority (Black or African American, non-Hispanic/Latino). Average age 32. 6 applicants, 67% accepted, 3 enrolled. In 2010, 10 master's, 1 other advanced degree awarded. *Degree requirements:* For master's, thesis optional. *Entrance requirements:* For master's, GRE. Additional exam requirements/recommendations for international students: Required—TOEFL. *Application deadline:* For fall admission, 3/1 priority date for domestic and international students; for spring admission, 11/15 for domestic and international students. Applications are processed on a rolling basis. Application fee: $55 ($65 for international students). Electronic applications accepted. *Financial support:* In 2010–11, 6 students received support, including 1 fellowship (averaging $1,000 per year), 4 teaching assistantships (averaging $4,330 per year); research assistantships with full tuition reimbursements available. Financial award application deadline: 1/15; financial award applicants required to submit FAFSA. *Faculty research:* American philosophy, Peirce bioethics, metaphysics, ethical theory. *Unit head:* Dr. John Tilley, Associate Professor and Chair, 317-274-4690, Fax: 317-278-4579, E-mail: jtilley@iupui.edu. *Application contact:* Dr. Jason Thomas Eberl, Assistant Professor and Graduate Co-Director, 317-278-9239, Fax: 317-278-4579, E-mail: jeberl@iupui.edu.

Institute for Christian Studies, Graduate Programs, Toronto, ON M5T 1R4, Canada. Offers education (M Phil F, PhD); history of philosophy (M Phil F, PhD); philosophical aesthetics (M Phil F, PhD); philosophy of religion (M Phil F, PhD); political theory (M Phil F, PhD); systematic philosophy (M Phil F, PhD); theology (M Phil F, PhD); worldview studies (MWS). Part-time programs available. Postbaccalaureate distance learning degree programs offered (minimal on-campus study). *Degree requirements:* For master's, one foreign language, thesis; for doctorate, 2 foreign languages, thesis/dissertation. *Entrance requirements:* For master's and doctorate, philosophy background. Additional exam requirements/recommendations for international students: Required—TOEFL (minimum score 600 paper-based; 250 computer-based). *Faculty research:* Human rights, anthropology of self, medieval discourse, gender and body, post-modern thought; biblical hermeneutics, creational aesthetics, ecumenism, epistemology, political theory and public policy, relational psychotherapy.

Institute for Doctoral Studies in the Visual Arts, PhD Program in Visual Art: Philosophy, Aesthetics, and Art Theory, Portland, ME 04102. Offers aesthetics (PhD); art theory (PhD); philosophy (PhD). Postbaccalaureate distance learning degree programs offered (minimal on-campus study). *Faculty:* 2 full-time (1 woman), 11 part-time/adjunct (3 women). *Students:* 24 full-time (19 women); includes 3 Black or African American, non-Hispanic/Latino; 1 Asian, non-Hispanic/Latino; 1 Hispanic/Latino. Average age 38. *Degree requirements:* For doctorate, comprehensive exam, thesis/dissertation, dissertation defense. *Entrance requirements:* For doctorate, curriculum vitae, writing sample, letter of purpose, portfolio, artist's statement, interview. *Application deadline:* Applications are processed on a rolling basis. Application fee: $50. Electronic applications accepted. *Expenses:* Tuition: Full-time $24,000. *Financial support:* In 2010–11, 22 students received support, including 1 fellowship (averaging $2,000 per year); scholarships/grants also available. *Faculty research:* Visual culture, sonic art, cultural studies, feminism, contemporary art. *Unit head:* Amy Curtis, Executive Vice President, 207-879-8757, E-mail: acurtis@idsva.org. *Application contact:* Diane Einsiedler, Assistant to the Executive Vice President, 207-771-8887, E-mail: info@idsva.org.

The Johns Hopkins University, Zanvyl Krieger School of Arts and Sciences, Department of Philosophy, Baltimore, MD 21218-2699. Offers MA, PhD. *Faculty:* 10 full-time (3 women). *Students:* 24 full-time (4 women); includes 2 minority (1 Asian, non-Hispanic/Latino; 1 Two or more races, non-Hispanic/Latino), 8 international. Average age 29. 96 applicants, 7% accepted, 4 enrolled. In 2010, 10 master's, 5 doctorates awarded. *Degree requirements:* For doctorate, thesis/dissertation. *Entrance requirements:* For master's and doctorate, GRE General Test. Additional exam requirements/recommendations for international students: Required—TOEFL. *Application deadline:* For fall admission, 1/15 for domestic students. Application fee: $65. Electronic applications accepted. *Financial support:* In 2010–11, 9 fellowships with partial tuition reimbursements (averaging $17,500 per year), 1 research assistantship with partial tuition reimbursement (averaging $12,000 per year), 15 teaching assistantships with tuition reimbursements (averaging $17,500 per year) were awarded; Federal Work-Study also available. Financial award application deadline: 1/15; financial award applicants required to submit FAFSA. *Faculty research:* Historical and analytical research on range of philosophical topics. Total annual research expenditures: $198,561. *Unit head:* Dr. Richard Bett, Acting Chair/Graduate Advisor/Professor, 410-516-6863, Fax: 410-516-6848, E-mail: rbett1@jhu.edu. *Application contact:* Alicia V. Burley, Academic Program Coordinator, 410-516-7524, Fax: 410-516-6848, E-mail: aburley1@jhu.edu.

Kent State University, College of Arts and Sciences, Department of Philosophy, Kent, OH 44242-0001. Offers MA. Part-time programs available. *Degree requirements:* For master's, thesis optional. *Entrance requirements:* For master's, GRE, minimum GPA of 3.0. Electronic applications accepted. *Expenses:* Tuition, state resident: full-time $7866; part-time $437 per credit hour. Tuition, nonresident: full-time $14,022; part-time $779 per credit hour.

Louisiana State University and Agricultural and Mechanical College, Graduate School, College of Humanities and Social Sciences, Department of Philosophy and Religious Studies, Baton Rouge, LA 70803. Offers philosophy (MA). Part-time programs available. *Faculty:* 17 full-time (3 women). *Students:* 11 full-time (1 woman); includes 1 Hispanic/Latino. Average age 28. 19 applicants, 89% accepted, 3 enrolled. In 2010, 2 master's awarded. *Degree requirements:* For master's, one foreign language, thesis (for some programs). *Entrance requirements:* For master's, GRE General Test, minimum GPA of 3.0. Additional exam requirements/recommendations for international students: Required—TOEFL (minimum score 550 paper-based; 213 computer-based; 79 iBT) or IELTS (minimum score 6.5). *Application deadline:* For fall admission, 4/25 priority date for domestic students, 5/15 for international students; for spring admission, 10/15 for international students. Applications are processed on a rolling basis. Application fee: $50 ($70 for international students). Electronic applications accepted. *Financial support:* In 2010–11, 9 students received support, including 5 teaching assistantships with partial tuition reimbursements available (averaging $8,569 per year); fellowships, research assistantships with partial tuition reimbursements available, Federal Work-Study, institutionally sponsored loans, scholarships/grants, health care benefits, and unspecified assistantships also available. Support available to part-time students. Financial award applicants required to submit FAFSA. *Faculty research:* Analytic philosophy, continental philosophy, history of philosophy, philosophy and religion, existential value theory. Total annual research expenditures: $45,587. *Unit head:* Dr. Delbert Burkett, Chair, 225-578-2220, Fax: 225-578-4897, E-mail: dburket@lsu.edu. *Application contact:* Dr. Greg Schufrieder, Professor, 225-578-2276, Fax: 225-578-4897, E-mail: gschufr@lsu.edu.

Loyola Marymount University, College of Liberal Arts, Department of Philosophy, Program in Philosophy, Los Angeles, CA 90045. Offers MA. *Faculty:* 18 full-time (5 women). *Students:* 22 full-time (8 women), 3 part-time (1 woman); includes 2 Black or African American, non-Hispanic/Latino; 2 Asian, non-Hispanic/Latino; 2 Hispanic/Latino; 1 Two or more races, non-Hispanic/

Latino. Average age 27. 37 applicants, 76% accepted, 14 enrolled. In 2010, 18 master's awarded. *Degree requirements:* For master's, one foreign language, comprehensive exam. *Entrance requirements:* For master's, GRE General Test, writing sample (10-15 pages), 2 letters of recommendation, personal statement (4 pages). Additional exam requirements/recommendations for international students: Required—TOEFL (minimum score 600 paper-based; 250 computer-based; 100 iBT). *Application deadline:* For fall admission, 3/15 for domestic students; for spring admission, 11/1 for domestic students. Application fee: $50. *Financial support:* In 2010–11, 25 students received support, including 5 research assistantships (averaging $1,152 per year), 5 teaching assistantships (averaging $3,500 per year); unspecified assistantships also available. Financial award application deadline: 6/1; financial award applicants required to submit FAFSA. *Unit head:* Dr. Mark D. Morelli, Graduate Director, 310-338-7384, E-mail: mmorelli@lmu.edu. *Application contact:* Chake H. Kouyoumjian, Associate Dean of Graduate Studies, 310-338-2721, Fax: 310-338-6086, E-mail: ckouyoum@lmu.edu.

Loyola University Chicago, Graduate School, Department of Philosophy, Chicago, IL 60660. Offers MA, PhD. Part-time and evening/weekend programs available. *Faculty:* 21 full-time (7 women), 1 part-time/adjunct (0 women). *Students:* 77 full-time (18 women), 7 part-time (3 women); includes 10 minority (1 Black or African American, non-Hispanic/Latino; 5 Asian, non-Hispanic/Latino; 4 Hispanic/Latino), 9 international. Average age 32. 223 applicants, 15% accepted, 20 enrolled. In 2010, 12 master's, 9 doctorates awarded. Terminal master's awarded for partial completion of doctoral program. *Degree requirements:* For master's, comprehensive exam (for some programs), thesis (for some programs), oral exam; for doctorate, one foreign language, thesis/dissertation, oral exam. *Entrance requirements:* For master's and doctorate, GRE General Test. Additional exam requirements/recommendations for international students: Required—TOEFL. *Application deadline:* For fall admission, 1/15 priority date for domestic and international students. Application fee: $50. Electronic applications accepted. *Expenses:* Tuition: Full-time $14,940; part-time $830 per credit hour. Required fees: $87 per semester. Part-time tuition and fees vary according to course load and program. *Financial support:* In 2010–11, 22 students received support, including 4 fellowships with full tuition reimbursements available (averaging $20,000 per year), 4 research assistantships with full tuition reimbursements available (averaging $18,000 per year), 13 teaching assistantships with full tuition reimbursements available (averaging $18,000 per year); institutionally sponsored loans, health care benefits, and unspecified assistantships also available. Financial award application deadline: 1/15; financial award applicants required to submit FAFSA. *Faculty research:* Social philosophy, ethics, medical ethics, analytic philosophy, contemporary Continental philosophy. *Unit head:* Dr. Paul Moser, Chair, 773-508-8481, Fax: 773-508-3292, E-mail: acutrof@luc.edu. *Application contact:* Dr. Mark Waymack, Graduate Program Director, 773-508-2738, Fax: 773-508-2292, E-mail: mwaymac@luc.edu.

Marquette University, Graduate School, College of Arts and Sciences, Department of Philosophy, Milwaukee, WI 53201-1881. Offers ancient philosophy (PhD); British empiricism and analytic philosophy (PhD); Christian philosophy (PhD); early modern European philosophy (PhD); ethics (PhD); German philosophy (PhD); history of philosophy (MA); medieval philosophy (PhD); phenomenology and existentialism (PhD); philosophy of religion (PhD); social and applied philosophy (MA); JD/MA. Part-time programs available. *Faculty:* 25 full-time (5 women), 18 part-time/adjunct (5 women). *Students:* 43 full-time (10 women), 20 part-time (2 women); includes 5 minority (1 Black or African American, non-Hispanic/Latino; 4 Asian, non-Hispanic/Latino), 5 international. Average age 31. 96 applicants, 41% accepted, 9 enrolled. In 2010, 2 master's, 6 doctorates awarded. *Degree requirements:* For master's, variable foreign language requirement, comprehensive exam, thesis or alternative; for doctorate, 2 foreign languages, thesis/dissertation, written and oral qualifying exams. *Entrance requirements:* For master's and doctorate, GRE General Test, official transcripts from all current and previous colleges/universities except Marquette, statement of purpose, at least three letters of recommendation, sample of philosophical writing. Additional exam requirements/recommendations for international students: Required—TOEFL (minimum score 530 paper-based; 78 computer-based). *Application deadline:* For fall admission, 2/15 for domestic and international students. Applications are processed on a rolling basis. Application fee: $50. Electronic applications accepted. *Expenses:* Tuition: Full-time $16,290; part-time $905 per credit hour. Tuition and fees vary according to program. *Financial support:* In 2010–11, 1 fellowship, 6 research assistantships, 9 teaching assistantships were awarded; Federal Work-Study, institutionally sponsored loans, scholarships/grants, and tuition waivers (full and partial) also available. Support available to part-time students. Financial award application deadline: 2/15. *Faculty research:* Aristotle, Augustine, Descartes, Hegel, Heidegger. Total annual research expenditures: $109,819. *Unit head:* Dr. James South, Chair, 414-288-6857, Fax: 414-288-1578. *Application contact:* Dr. Pol Vandevelde, Director of Graduate Studies, 414-288-5962, Fax: 414-288-1578.

Massachusetts Institute of Technology, School of Humanities, Arts, and Social Sciences, Department of Linguistics and Philosophy, Philosophy Section, Cambridge, MA 02139-4307. Offers PhD. *Faculty:* 13 full-time (3 women). *Students:* 26 full-time (9 women); includes 2 minority (both Two or more races, non-Hispanic/Latino), 8 international. Average age 26. 241 applicants, 4% accepted, 5 enrolled. In 2010, 6 doctorates awarded. *Degree requirements:* For doctorate, comprehensive exam, thesis/dissertation. *Entrance requirements:* Additional exam requirements/recommendations for international students: Required—TOEFL (minimum score 577 paper-based; 233 computer-based; 90 iBT), IELTS (minimum score 6.5). *Application deadline:* For fall admission, 1/2 for domestic and international students. Application fee: $75. Electronic applications accepted. *Expenses:* Tuition: Full-time $38,940; part-time $605 per unit. Required fees: $272. *Financial support:* In 2010–11, 13 fellowships with tuition reimbursements (averaging $31,927 per year), 9 teaching assistantships with tuition reimbursements (averaging $31,766 per year) were awarded; research assistantships with tuition reimbursements, Federal Work-Study, institutionally sponsored loans, scholarships/grants, health care benefits, and unspecified assistantships also available. *Faculty research:* Metaphysics, philosophy of mind, philosophy of language, ethics, feminist philosophy. *Unit head:* Prof. Richard Holton, Chair, 617-253-4141, Fax: 617-253-5017. *Application contact:* Graduate Admissions, 617-253-4141, Fax: 617-253-5017, E-mail: lp-admissions@mit.edu.

McGill University, Faculty of Graduate and Postdoctoral Studies, Faculty of Arts, Department of Philosophy, Montréal, QC H3A 2T5, Canada. Offers bioethics (MA); philosophy (PhD).

McMaster University, School of Graduate Studies, Faculty of Humanities, Department of Philosophy, Hamilton, ON L8S 4M2, Canada. Offers MA, PhD. Part-time programs available. *Degree requirements:* For master's, thesis; for doctorate, one foreign language, thesis/dissertation. *Entrance requirements:* For master's, honors degree in philosophy; minimum average B+; for doctorate, master's degree in philosophy. Additional exam requirements/recommendations for international students: Required—TOEFL (minimum score 580 paper-based; 237 computer-based). *Faculty research:* Twentieth-century European philosophy, twentieth-century Anglo-American philosophy, political philosophy, ethics, argumentation.

Memorial University of Newfoundland, School of Graduate Studies, Department of Philosophy, St. John's, NL A1C 5S7, Canada. Offers MA. Part-time programs available. *Degree requirements:* For master's, thesis. *Entrance requirements:* For master's, first-class undergraduate degree in philosophy. Electronic applications accepted. *Faculty research:* History of philosophy, philosophy of science, phenomenology and existentialism, contemporary metaphysics.

Miami University, Graduate School, College of Arts and Science, Department of Philosophy, Oxford, OH 45056. Offers MA. *Students:* 9 full-time (4 women); includes 2 minority (1 Asian, non-Hispanic/Latino; 1 Two or more races, non-Hispanic/Latino). Average age 24. In 2010, 3 master's awarded. *Entrance requirements:* For master's, minimum undergraduate GPA of 3.0 during previous 2 years or 2.75 overall. Additional exam requirements/recommendations for international students: Required—TOEFL. *Application deadline:* For fall admission, 2/15 for domestic and international students. Application fee: $50. Electronic applications accepted. *Expenses:* Tuition, state resident: full-time $11,616; part-time $484 per credit hour. Tuition, nonresident: full-time $25,656; part-time $1069 per credit hour. Required fees: $528. *Financial support:* Fellowships with full tuition reimbursements, research assistantships, teaching assistant-

ships, Federal Work-Study, institutionally sponsored loans, health care benefits, tuition waivers (full), and unspecified assistantships available. Financial award application deadline: 3/1; financial award applicants required to submit FAFSA. *Unit head:* Dr. Emily Zakin, Chair, 513-529-2440, Fax: 513-529-4731, E-mail: zakinea@muohio.edu. *Application contact:* Dr. Elaine Miller, Director of the Graduate Program, 513-529-2440, Fax: 513-529-4731, E-mail: millerep@muohio.edu.

Michigan State University, The Graduate School, College of Arts and Letters, Department of Philosophy, East Lansing, MI 48824. Offers MA, PhD. *Entrance requirements:* Additional exam requirements/recommendations for international students: Required—TOEFL. Electronic applications accepted.

Montclair State University, The Graduate School, College of Education and Human Services, Center of Pedagogy, Montclair, NJ 07043-1624. Offers pedagogy and philosophy (Ed D). Part-time programs available. *Faculty:* 1 (woman) full-time. *Students:* 5 full-time (2 women), 22 part-time (12 women); includes 2 Black or African American, non-Hispanic/Latino; 2 Asian, non-Hispanic/Latino; 1 Hispanic/Latino, 4 international. Average age 40. 2 applicants, 0% accepted, 0 enrolled. *Degree requirements:* For doctorate, thesis/dissertation. *Entrance requirements:* For doctorate, GRE, 3 letters of recommendation. Additional exam requirements/recommendations for international students: Required—TOEFL or IELTS. *Application deadline:* For fall admission, 2/1 for domestic students, 11/15 for international students. Application fee: $60. Electronic applications accepted. *Expenses:* Tuition, state resident: part-time $501.34 per credit. Tuition, nonresident: part-time $773.88 per credit. Required fees: $71.15 per credit. *Financial support:* In 2010–11, 3 research assistantships (averaging $7,000 per year), 3 teaching assistantships (averaging $12,000 per year) were awarded; Federal Work-Study, institutionally sponsored loans, scholarships/grants, and unspecified assistantships also available. Support available to part-time students. Financial award application deadline: 3/1; financial award applicants required to submit FAFSA. *Faculty research:* Minority teacher recruitment, parental involvement. Total annual research expenditures: $1.4 million. *Unit head:* Jennifer Robinson, Director, 973-655-4262. *Application contact:* Amy Aiello, Director of Graduate Admissions and Operations, 973-655-5147, Fax: 973-655-7869, E-mail: graduate.school@montclair.edu.

Montclair State University, The Graduate School, College of Education and Human Services, Department of Educational Foundations, Montclair, NJ 07043-1624. Offers philosophy for children (Certificate). Part-time and evening/weekend programs available. *Faculty:* 9 full-time (5 women), 1 part-time/adjunct (0 women). *Entrance requirements:* Additional exam requirements/recommendations for international students: Required—TOEFL (minimum iBT score of 83) or IELTS. *Application deadline:* For fall admission, 2/1 for domestic students, 2/15 for international students; for spring admission, 10/15 for domestic and international students. Applications are processed on a rolling basis. Application fee: $60. Electronic applications accepted. *Expenses:* Tuition, state resident: part-time $501.34 per credit. Tuition, nonresident: part-time $773.88 per credit. Required fees: $71.15 per credit. *Financial support:* In 2010–11, 4 research assistantships with full tuition reimbursements (averaging $7,000 per year) were awarded; Federal Work-Study and scholarships/grants also available. Support available to part-time students. Financial award application deadline: 3/1; financial award applicants required to submit FAFSA. *Faculty research:* Pragmatism and education: theoretical and practical, history of education, children and philosophy, academic development, developing theory and practice—transforming K-12 school pedagogy. Total annual research expenditures: $39,725. *Unit head:* Dr. Jeremy Price, Chairperson, 973-655-7039. *Application contact:* Amy Aiello, Director of Graduate Admissions and Operations, 973-655-5147, Fax: 973-655-7869, E-mail: graduate.school@montclair.edu.

Mount St. Mary's University, Program in Philosophical Studies, Emmitsburg, MD 21727-7799. Offers MA. Part-time programs available. *Faculty:* 4 full-time (1 woman). *Students:* 1 full-time (0 women), 3 part-time (0 women). Average age 30. In 2010, 3 master's awarded. *Degree requirements:* For master's, one foreign language, thesis. *Entrance requirements:* For master's, undergraduate degree, minimum cumulative undergraduate GPA of 3.0. Additional exam requirements/recommendations for international students: Required—TOEFL (minimum score 550 paper-based; 213 computer-based). *Expenses:* Tuition: Full-time $8640; part-time $480 per credit hour. Tuition and fees vary according to program. *Financial support:* Unspecified assistantships available. Financial award applicants required to submit FAFSA. *Unit head:* Dr. Christopher Anadale, Director, 301-447-5368 Ext. 4307, E-mail: anadale@msmary.edu. *Application contact:* Dr. Christopher Anadale, Director, 301-447-5368 Ext. 4307, E-mail: anadale@msmary.edu.

The New School: A University, The New School for Social Research, Department of Philosophy, New York, NY 10003. Offers MA, DS Sc, PhD. Part-time and evening/weekend programs available. Terminal master's awarded for partial completion of doctoral program. *Degree requirements:* For master's, one foreign language, exam or thesis; for doctorate, 2 foreign languages, comprehensive exam, thesis/dissertation, qualifying exam. *Entrance requirements:* For master's, GRE General Test; for doctorate, GRE General Test, MA. Additional exam requirements/recommendations for international students: Required—TOEFL (minimum score 600 paper-based; 250 computer-based; 100 iBT). Electronic applications accepted. *Faculty research:* Continental philosophy, history of philosophy, political philosophy, aesthetics, pragmatism.

New York University, Graduate School of Arts and Science, Department of Philosophy, New York, NY 10012-1019. Offers MA, PhD, JD/MA, JD/PhD, MD/MA. Part-time programs available. *Faculty:* 16 full-time (1 woman). *Students:* 47 full-time (12 women); includes 2 Asian, non-Hispanic/Latino, 15 international. Average age 28. 321 applicants, 4% accepted, 7 enrolled. In 2010, 3 doctorates awarded. *Degree requirements:* For master's, thesis or alternative; for doctorate, one foreign language, thesis/dissertation. *Entrance requirements:* For master's and doctorate, GRE General Test, sample of written work. Additional exam requirements/recommendations for international students: Required—TOEFL. *Application deadline:* For fall admission, 1/4 for domestic students. Application fee: $90. *Financial support:* Fellowships with tuition reimbursements, teaching assistantships with tuition reimbursements, Federal Work-Study, institutionally sponsored loans, scholarships/grants, health care benefits, and unspecified assistantships available. Financial award application deadline: 1/4; financial award applicants required to submit FAFSA. *Faculty research:* Philosophy of mind and language, metaphysics, ethics and political philosophy. *Unit head:* Don Garrett, Chair, 212-998-8320, Fax: 212-995-4179, E-mail: philosophy.admissions@nyu.edu. *Application contact:* James Pryor, Director of Admissions, 212-998-8320, Fax: 212-995-4179, E-mail: philosophy.admissions@nyu.edu.

Northern Illinois University, Graduate School, College of Liberal Arts and Sciences, Department of Philosophy, De Kalb, IL 60115-2854. Offers MA. Part-time programs available. *Faculty:* 12 full-time (2 women), 1 part-time/adjunct (0 women). *Students:* 19 full-time (1 woman), 14 part-time (3 women); includes 1 Black or African American, non-Hispanic/Latino; 2 Asian, non-Hispanic/Latino; 3 Hispanic/Latino; 1 Two or more races, non-Hispanic/Latino, 2 international. Average age 25. 125 applicants, 30% accepted, 14 enrolled. In 2010, 9 master's awarded. *Degree requirements:* For master's, comprehensive exam, thesis optional. *Entrance requirements:* For master's, GRE General Test, minimum GPA of 2.75, writing sample, major or minor in philosophy. Additional exam requirements/recommendations for international students: Required—TOEFL (minimum score 550 paper-based; 213 computer-based). *Application deadline:* For fall admission, 3/1 priority date for domestic students, 5/1 for international students; for spring admission, 11/1 for domestic students, 10/1 for international students. Applications are processed on a rolling basis. Application fee: $30. Electronic applications accepted. *Expenses:* Tuition, state resident: full-time $7200; part-time $300 per credit hour. Tuition, nonresident: full-time $14,400; part-time $600 per credit hour. Required fees: $79 per credit hour. *Financial support:* In 2010–11, 14 teaching assistantships with full tuition reimbursements were awarded; fellowships with full tuition reimbursements, research assistantships with full tuition reimbursements, Federal Work-Study, scholarships/grants, tuition waivers (full), and unspecified assistantships also available. Support available to part-time students. Financial

Philosophy

Northern Illinois University (continued)
award applicants required to submit FAFSA. *Faculty research:* Epistemology, philosophy of biology, animal rights, philosophy of war, international ethics. *Unit head:* Dr. David J. Buller, Chair, 815-753-6299, Fax: 815-753-6302, E-mail: buller@niu.edu. *Application contact:* Dr. David Buller, Graduate Director, 815-753-6411, E-mail: askphilosophy@niu.edu.

Northwestern University, The Graduate School, Judd A. and Marjorie Weinberg College of Arts and Sciences, Department of Philosophy, Evanston, IL 60208. Offers PhD. Admissions and degrees offered through The Graduate School. *Degree requirements:* For doctorate, 2 foreign languages, thesis/dissertation. *Entrance requirements:* For doctorate, GRE General Test, sample of written work. Additional exam requirements/recommendations for international students: Required—TOEFL. Electronic applications accepted. *Faculty research:* Phenomenology, philosophy of science, history of philosophy, ethics, social and political philosophy, epistemology.

The Ohio State University, Graduate School, College of Arts and Sciences, Division of Arts and Humanities, Department of Philosophy, Columbus, OH 43210. Offers MA, PhD. *Faculty:* 26. *Students:* 19 full-time (6 women), 21 part-time (4 women); includes 1 Asian, non-Hispanic/Latino; 1 Hispanic/Latino, 4 international. Average age 28. In 2010, 3 doctorates awarded. *Degree requirements:* For master's, thesis optional; for doctorate, thesis/dissertation. *Entrance requirements:* For master's and doctorate, GRE General Test. Additional exam requirements/recommendations for international students: Required—TOEFL (minimum score 600 paper-based; 250 computer-based). *Application deadline:* For fall admission, 8/15 priority date for domestic students, 7/1 priority date for international students; for winter admission, 12/1 priority date for domestic students, 11/1 priority date for international students; for spring admission, 3/1 priority date for domestic students, 2/1 priority date for international students. Applications are processed on a rolling basis. Application fee: $40 ($50 for international students). Electronic applications accepted. *Expenses:* Tuition, state resident: full-time $10,605. Tuition, nonresident: full-time $26,535. Tuition and fees vary according to course load and program. *Financial support:* Fellowships, research assistantships, teaching assistantships, Federal Work-Study, institutionally sponsored loans, and unspecified assistantships available. Support available to part-time students. *Unit head:* Don Hubin, Chair, 614-292-2510, E-mail: hubin.1@osu.edu. *Application contact:* 614-292-9444, Fax: 614-292-3895, E-mail: domestic.grad@osu.edu.

Ohio University, Graduate College, College of Arts and Sciences, Department of Philosophy, Athens, OH 45701-2979. Offers MA. Part-time programs available. *Students:* 11 full-time (2 women). Average age 27. 20 applicants, 75% accepted, 7 enrolled. In 2010, 7 master's awarded. *Degree requirements:* For master's, thesis. *Entrance requirements:* For master's, 28 hours in philosophy including logic, ancient and modern philosophy; minimum GPA of 3.0; sample of philosophical writing. Additional exam requirements/recommendations for international students: Required—TOEFL (minimum score 550 paper-based; 80 iBT) or IELTS (minimum score 6.5). *Application deadline:* For fall admission, 3/1 priority date for domestic and international students; for winter admission, 4/1 for domestic and international students; for spring admission, 9/1 for domestic and international students. Applications are processed on a rolling basis. Application fee: $50 ($55 for international students). Electronic applications accepted. *Financial support:* Teaching assistantships with tuition reimbursements, Federal Work-Study, institutionally sponsored loans, tuition waivers (partial), and unspecified assistantships available. Financial award application deadline: 3/1. *Faculty research:* Ethics, phenomenology, applied ethics, Aristotle, Kant, epistemology. *Unit head:* Dr. Arthur Zucker, Chair, 740-593-4588, E-mail: philosophy.department@ohio.edu. *Application contact:* Dr. John W. Bender, Graduate Chair, 740-593-4599, Fax: 740-593-4597, E-mail: bender@ohio.edu.

Oklahoma City University, Petree College of Arts and Sciences, Program in Liberal Arts, Oklahoma City, OK 73106-1402. Offers art (MLA); general studies (MLA); leadership/management (MLA); literature (MLA); mass communications (MLA); philosophy (MLA); writing (MLA). Part-time and evening/weekend programs available. *Degree requirements:* For master's, comprehensive exam, thesis optional. *Entrance requirements:* Additional exam requirements/recommendations for international students: Required—TOEFL (minimum score 550 paper-based).

Oklahoma State University, College of Arts and Sciences, Department of Philosophy, Stillwater, OK 74078. Offers MA. *Faculty:* 15 full-time (6 women), 2 part-time/adjunct (1 woman). *Students:* 8 full-time (0 women), 6 part-time (1 woman); includes 2 Asian, non-Hispanic/Latino. Average age 28. 15 applicants, 53% accepted, 4 enrolled. In 2010, 1 master's awarded. *Degree requirements:* For master's, comprehensive exam, thesis. *Entrance requirements:* For master's, GRE, 2 letters of recommendation. Additional exam requirements/recommendations for international students: Required—TOEFL (minimum score 550 paper-based; 79 iBT). *Application deadline:* For fall admission, 3/1 priority date for international students; for spring admission, 8/1 priority date for international students. Applications are processed on a rolling basis. Application fee: $40 ($75 for international students). Electronic applications accepted. *Expenses:* Tuition, state resident: full-time $3716; part-time $154.85 per credit hour. Tuition, nonresident: full-time $14,892; part-time $621 per credit hour. Required fees: $2044; $85.20 per credit hour. One-time fee: $50. Tuition and fees vary according to course load and campus/location. *Financial support:* In 2010–11, 9 teaching assistantships (averaging $13,203 per year) were awarded; career-related internships or fieldwork, Federal Work-Study, scholarships/grants, health care benefits, tuition waivers (partial), and unspecified assistantships also available. Support available to part-time students. Financial award application deadline: 3/1; financial award applicants required to submit FAFSA. *Faculty research:* Theoretical and applied ethics, history and philosophy of science, east/west comparative philosophy, social/political/legal philosophy, truth and theory of knowledge. *Unit head:* Dr. Doren Recker, Head, 405-744-0487, Fax: 405-744-4635. *Application contact:* Dr. Gordon Emslie, Dean, 405-744-6368, Fax: 405-744-0355, E-mail: grad-i@okstate.edu.

Penn State University Park, Graduate School, College of the Liberal Arts, Department of Philosophy, State College, University Park, PA 16802-1503. Offers MA, PhD. *Unit head:* Dr. Shannon W. Sullivan, Head, 814-865-1618, Fax: 814-865-0119, E-mail: sws10@psu.edu. *Application contact:* Dr. Shannon W. Sullivan, Head, 814-865-1618, Fax: 814-865-0119, E-mail: sws10@psu.edu.

Princeton University, Graduate School, Department of Classics, Princeton, NJ 08544-1019. Offers classical and hellenic studies (PhD); classical philosophy (PhD); history (the ancient world) (PhD); literature and philology (PhD). *Degree requirements:* For doctorate, thesis/dissertation. *Entrance requirements:* For doctorate, GRE General Test, sample of written work. Additional exam requirements/recommendations for international students: Required—TOEFL (minimum score 600 paper-based; 250 computer-based). Electronic applications accepted.

Princeton University, Graduate School, Department of Philosophy, Princeton, NJ 08544-1019. Offers classical philosophy (PhD); philosophy (PhD); philosophy of science (PhD). *Degree requirements:* For doctorate, variable foreign language requirement, thesis/dissertation. *Entrance requirements:* For doctorate, GRE General Test, sample of written work. Additional exam requirements/recommendations for international students: Required—TOEFL (minimum score 600 paper-based; 250 computer-based). Electronic applications accepted.

Princeton University, Graduate School, Department of Politics, Princeton, NJ 08544-1019. Offers political philosophy (PhD); politics (PhD). *Degree requirements:* For doctorate, comprehensive exam, thesis/dissertation, teaching experience. *Entrance requirements:* For doctorate, GRE General Test, sample of written work, letters of recommendation. Additional exam requirements/recommendations for international students: Required—TOEFL (minimum score 600 paper-based; 250 computer-based). Electronic applications accepted. *Faculty research:* American politics, comparative politics, formal and quantitative methods, international relations, public law, political theory.

Purdue University, Graduate School, College of Liberal Arts, Department of Philosophy, West Lafayette, IN 47907. Offers MA, PhD. Part-time programs available. Terminal master's awarded for partial completion of doctoral program. *Degree requirements:* For master's, thesis optional; for doctorate, one foreign language, thesis/dissertation. *Entrance requirements:* For master's and doctorate, GRE General Test. Additional exam requirements/recommendations for international students: Required—TOEFL. Electronic applications accepted. *Faculty research:* Continental philosophy, ethics and social philosophy, analytic philosophy, history of philosophy, logic.

Queen's University at Kingston, School of Graduate Studies and Research, Faculty of Arts and Sciences, Department of Philosophy, Kingston, ON K7L 3N6, Canada. Offers MA, PhD. Part-time programs available. *Degree requirements:* For master's, thesis; for doctorate, comprehensive exam, thesis/dissertation. *Entrance requirements:* Additional exam requirements/recommendations for international students: Required—TOEFL. Electronic applications accepted. *Faculty research:* Ethics, social and political philosophy, philosophy of language, epistemology, metaphysics.

Regis College, Graduate and Professional Programs, Toronto, ON M5S 2Z5, Canada. Offers eastern Christian studies (Certificate); Ignatian studies (Diploma); Lonergan studies (Diploma); ministry (D Min); ministry and spirituality (MAMS); philosophical studies (Diploma); retreat direction (Certificate); sacred theology (STB, STM, STD, STL); spiritual direction (Diploma); spiritual theology (Diploma); theological studies (MTS, Diploma); theology (M Div, MA, Th M, PhD, Th D); M Div/MA. *Accreditation:* ATS (one or more programs are accredited). Terminal master's awarded for partial completion of doctoral program. *Degree requirements:* For master's, 2 foreign languages, thesis; for doctorate, 3 foreign languages, comprehensive exam, thesis/dissertation; for first professional degree, comprehensive exam. *Entrance requirements:* For first professional degree and other advanced degree, minimum GPA of 3.0; for master's, minimum GPA of 3.3; for doctorate, minimum GPA of 3.7. Additional exam requirements/recommendations for international students: Required—TOEFL (minimum score 580 paper-based; 237 computer-based; 93 iBT), TWE (minimum score 5).

Rice University, Graduate Programs, School of Humanities, Department of Philosophy, Houston, TX 77251-1892. Offers MA, PhD. Terminal master's awarded for partial completion of doctoral program. *Degree requirements:* For master's, one foreign language; for doctorate, one foreign language, comprehensive exam, thesis/dissertation. *Entrance requirements:* For master's and doctorate, GRE General Test, minimum GPA of 3.0. Additional exam requirements/recommendations for international students: Required—TOEFL (minimum score 600 paper-based; 250 computer-based; 90 iBT). Electronic applications accepted. *Faculty research:* Metaphysics, philosophy of law, philosophy of science, medical ethics, philosophy of language.

Rutgers, The State University of New Jersey, New Brunswick, Graduate School-New Brunswick, Program in Philosophy, Piscataway, NJ 08854-8097. Offers PhD. *Degree requirements:* For doctorate, comprehensive exam, thesis/dissertation. *Entrance requirements:* For doctorate, GRE General Test, writing sample. Electronic applications accepted. *Expenses:* Tuition, state resident: full-time $7200; part-time $600 per credit. Tuition, nonresident: full-time $11,124; part-time $927 per credit. *Faculty research:* Philosophy of mind, epistemology, philosophy of language, philosophy of science, metaphysics.

St. John's University, St. John's College of Liberal Arts and Sciences, Department of Philosophy, Queens, NY 11439. Offers MA. Part-time and evening/weekend programs available. *Entrance requirements:* Additional exam requirements/recommendations for international students: Required—TOEFL (minimum score 600 paper-based; 250 computer-based; 100 iBT), IELTS (minimum score 7). *Application deadline:* For fall admission, 5/1 priority date for domestic and international students; for spring admission, 11/1 priority date for domestic and international students. *Expenses:* Tuition: Full-time $17,100; part-time $950 per credit. Required fees: $340; $170 per semester. Tuition and fees vary according to program. *Financial support:* Career-related internships or fieldwork and scholarships/grants available. Support available to part-time students. *Unit head:* Dr. Paul Gaffney, Chair, 718-990-5256, E-mail: gaffneyp@stjohns.edu. *Application contact:* Kathleen Davis, Director of Graduate Admission, 718-990-1601, Fax: 718-990-5686, E-mail: gradhelp@stjohns.edu.

Saint Louis University, Graduate Education, College of Arts and Sciences and Graduate Education, Department of Philosophy, St. Louis, MO 63103-2097. Offers MA, MA-R, PhD. Part-time programs available. *Degree requirements:* For master's, one foreign language, thesis, comprehensive oral and written exams; for doctorate, 2 foreign languages, thesis/dissertation, preliminary exams, comprehensive oral and written exams. *Entrance requirements:* For master's, GRE General Test, letters of recommendation, resume, writing sample, interview; for doctorate, GRE General Test, letters of recommendation, resumé, writing sample, interview, goal statement, transcripts. Additional exam requirements/recommendations for international students: Required—TOEFL (minimum score 550 paper-based; 213 computer-based). Electronic applications accepted. *Faculty research:* Medieval philosophy, philosophy of religion, political philosophy, ethics, epistemology.

Saint Mary's University, Faculty of Arts, Department of Philosophy, Halifax, NS B3H 3C3, Canada. Offers MA. *Degree requirements:* For master's, thesis. *Entrance requirements:* For master's, 3 letters of recommendation, 2 samples of written work. Additional exam requirements/recommendations for international students: Required—TOEFL. *Faculty research:* History of philosophy, analytic philosophy, ethics, social philosophy, logic.

San Diego State University, Graduate and Research Affairs, College of Arts and Letters, Department of Philosophy, San Diego, CA 92182. Offers MA. Part-time programs available. *Entrance requirements:* For master's, GRE General Test. Additional exam requirements/recommendations for international students: Required—TOEFL. Electronic applications accepted. *Faculty research:* Ancient philosophy, modern philosophy, philosophy of technology, logic, philosophy of mind.

San Francisco State University, Division of Graduate Studies, College of Humanities, Department of Philosophy, San Francisco, CA 94132-1722. Offers philosophy (MA); teaching critical thinking (Certificate). Part-time programs available. *Application deadline:* Applications are processed on a rolling basis. *Unit head:* Dr. Anita Silvers, Chair, 415-338-1596. *Application contact:* Dr. Alice Sowaal, Graduate Coordinator, 415-338-1596, E-mail: asowaal@sfsu.edu.

San Jose State University, Graduate Studies and Research, College of Humanities and the Arts, Department of Philosophy, San Jose, CA 95192-0001. Offers MA. *Degree requirements:* For master's, one foreign language, thesis or alternative. Electronic applications accepted.

Simon Fraser University, Graduate Studies, Faculty of Arts and Social Sciences, Department of Philosophy, Burnaby, BC V5A 1S6, Canada. Offers MA, PhD. PhD offered jointly with The University of British Columbia. Terminal master's awarded for partial completion of doctoral program. *Degree requirements:* For master's, thesis or alternative; for doctorate, thesis/dissertation. *Entrance requirements:* For master's, minimum GPA of 3.33; for doctorate, minimum GPA of 3.67. Additional exam requirements/recommendations for international students: Required—TOEFL or IELTS. Electronic applications accepted. *Faculty research:* Epistemology, philosophy of mind, philosophy of science, value theory, logic.

Southeastern Baptist Theological Seminary, Graduate and Professional Programs, Wake Forest, NC 27588-1889. Offers advanced biblical studies (M Div); Christian education (M Div, MACE); Christian ethics (PhD); Christian ministry (M Div); Christian planting (M Div); church music (MACM); counseling (MACO); evangelism (PhD); language (M Div); ministry (D Min); New Testament (PhD); Old Testament (PhD); philosophy (PhD); theology (Th M, PhD); women's studies (M Div). *Accreditation:* ACIPE; ATS (one or more programs are accredited). *Degree requirements:* For master's, thesis (for some programs), oral exam; for doctorate, thesis/dissertation, fieldwork; for M Div, supervised ministry. *Entrance requirements:* For master's,

Cooperative English Test, minimum GPA of 2.0, M Div or equivalent (Th M); for doctorate, GRE General Test or MAT, Cooperative English Test, M Div or equivalent, 3 years of professional experience.

Southern Baptist Theological Seminary, School of Theology, Louisville, KY 40280-0004. Offers applied theology (D Min); biblical and theological studies (M Div); biblical counseling (M Div, MA, D Min); biblical spirituality (D Min); Christian ministry (M Div); expository preaching (D Min); pastoral studies (M Div); theological studies (MA); theology (Th M, PhD); worldview and apologetics (M Div). *Accreditation:* ATS. Part-time and evening/weekend programs available. Postbaccalaureate distance learning degree programs offered (minimal on-campus study). *Degree requirements:* For master's, 2 foreign languages, thesis; for doctorate, 4 foreign languages, thesis/dissertation; for M Div, 2 foreign languages. *Entrance requirements:* For master's, GRE General Test, MAT, M Div; for doctorate, GRE General Test, MAT, interview, M Div, field essay. Additional exam requirements/recommendations for international students: Required—TOEFL, TWE. *Faculty research:* Biblical studies, contemporary theology, church history, pastoral care, ministry/missions studies.

Southern Evangelical Seminary, Graduate Programs, Matthews, NC 28105. Offers apologetics (MA, Certificate); Christian education (MA); church ministry (MA, Certificate); divinity (Certificate), including apologetics (M Div, Certificate); Islamic studies (MA, Certificate); Jewish studies (MA); philosophy (MA); religion (MA); theology (M Div), including apologetics (M Div, Certificate), Biblical studies; youth ministry (MA). Part-time and evening/weekend programs available. Postbaccalaureate distance learning degree programs offered. *Degree requirements:* For master's, thesis (for some programs); for doctorate, 2 foreign languages, comprehensive exam (for some programs), thesis/dissertation; for M Div, one foreign language. *Entrance requirements:* Additional exam requirements/recommendations for international students: Required—TOEFL (minimum score 600 paper-based; 250 computer-based). *Application deadline:* For fall admission, 8/15 priority date for domestic students, 8/5 priority date for international students; for winter admission, 12/15 priority date for domestic and international students; for spring admission, 1/15 priority date for domestic and international students. Applications are processed on a rolling basis. Application fee: $25. *Expenses:* Tuition: Full-time $9405; part-time $313.50 per credit hour. Required fees: $150; $50 per semester. *Financial support:* Scholarships/grants available. *Unit head:* Dr. Barry R. Leventhal, Dean, 704-847-5600 Ext. 204, Fax: 704-845-1747, E-mail: dean@ses.edu. *Application contact:* Duke Hale, Director of Recruitment, 704-847-5600 Ext. 216, Fax: 704-845-1747, E-mail: dhale@ses.edu.

Southern Illinois University Carbondale, Graduate School, College of Liberal Arts, Department of Philosophy, Carbondale, IL 62901-4701. Offers MA, PhD. *Degree requirements:* For master's, one foreign language, thesis; for doctorate, 2 foreign languages, thesis/dissertation. *Entrance requirements:* For master's, GRE General Test, minimum GPA of 2.7; for doctorate, GRE General Test, minimum GPA of 3.25. Additional exam requirements/recommendations for international students: Required—TOEFL. *Faculty research:* Continental philosophy, American philosophy, philosophy of mind, Asian philosophy.

Stanford University, School of Humanities and Sciences, Department of Philosophy, Stanford, CA 94305-9991. Offers MA, PhD. Terminal master's awarded for partial completion of doctoral program. *Degree requirements:* For master's, oral exam; for doctorate, thesis/dissertation, oral exam. *Entrance requirements:* For master's and doctorate, GRE General Test. Additional exam requirements/recommendations for international students: Required—TOEFL. Electronic applications accepted. *Expenses:* Tuition: Full-time $38,700; part-time $860 per unit. One-time fee: $200 full-time.

State University of New York at Binghamton, Graduate School, School of Arts and Sciences, Department of Philosophy, Binghamton, NY 13902-6000. Offers MA, PhD. *Faculty:* 14 full-time (5 women). *Students:* 2 full-time (1 woman), 1 (woman) part-time; includes 1 Asian, non-Hispanic/Latino. Average age 22. 1 applicant, 100% accepted, 1 enrolled. In 2010, 1 master's awarded. *Degree requirements:* For master's, 2 foreign languages, thesis or alternative; for doctorate, thesis/dissertation. *Entrance requirements:* For master's and doctorate, GRE General Test, GRE Subject Test. Additional exam requirements/recommendations for international students: Required—TOEFL (minimum score 550 paper-based; 213 computer-based; 80 iBT). *Application deadline:* Applications are processed on a rolling basis. Application fee: $60. Electronic applications accepted. *Financial support:* Career-related internships or fieldwork, Federal Work-Study, institutionally sponsored loans, scholarships/grants, health care benefits, tuition waivers (full and partial), and unspecified assistantships available. Financial award application deadline: 2/15; financial award applicants required to submit FAFSA. *Unit head:* Dr. Max Pensky, Chairperson, 607-777-4163, E-mail: mpensky@binghamton.edu. *Application contact:* Catherine Smith, Recruiting and Admissions Coordinator, 607-777-2151, Fax: 607-777-2501, E-mail: cmsmith@binghamton.edu.

State University of New York at Binghamton, Graduate School, School of Arts and Sciences, Philosophy, Interpretation and Culture Program, Binghamton, NY 13902-6000. Offers MA, PhD. *Faculty:* 2 full-time (1 woman), 1 part-time/adjunct (0 women). *Students:* 13 full-time (7 women), 34 part-time (17 women); includes 4 Black or African American, non-Hispanic/Latino; 2 Asian, non-Hispanic/Latino; 6 Hispanic/Latino, 19 international. Average age 36. 29 applicants, 38% accepted, 5 enrolled. In 2010, 9 master's, 8 doctorates awarded. Application fee: $60. *Financial support:* In 2010–11, 9 students received support, including 5 fellowships with full tuition reimbursements available (averaging $14,500 per year), 6 teaching assistantships with full tuition reimbursements available (averaging $14,500 per year); career-related internships or fieldwork, Federal Work-Study, institutionally sponsored loans, scholarships/grants, health care benefits, and unspecified assistantships also available. Financial award application deadline: 2/15; financial award applicants required to submit FAFSA. *Unit head:* Dr. Joshua Price, Director, 607-777-2348, E-mail: jmprice@binghamton.edu. *Application contact:* Catherine Smith, Recruiting and Admissions Coordinator, 607-777-2151, Fax: 607-777-2501, E-mail: cmsmith@binghamton.edu.

State University of New York at Binghamton, Graduate School, School of Arts and Sciences, Program in Social, Political, Ethical and Legal Philosophy, Binghamton, NY 13902-6000. Offers MA, PhD. *Students:* 21 full-time (10 women), 17 part-time (4 women); includes 3 Black or African American, non-Hispanic/Latino; 1 American Indian or Alaska Native, non-Hispanic/Latino; 2 Asian, non-Hispanic/Latino; 3 Hispanic/Latino, 3 international. Average age 29. 43 applicants, 40% accepted, 8 enrolled. In 2010, 3 master's, 4 doctorates awarded. Application fee: $60. *Financial support:* In 2010–11, 23 students received support, including 3 fellowships with full tuition reimbursements available (averaging $14,500 per year), 20 teaching assistantships with full tuition reimbursements available (averaging $14,500 per year); career-related internships or fieldwork, Federal Work-Study, institutionally sponsored loans, scholarships/grants, health care benefits, tuition waivers (full and partial), and unspecified assistantships also available. Financial award application deadline: 2/15; financial award applicants required to submit FAFSA. *Unit head:* Dr. Max Pensky, Chairperson, 607-777-4163, E-mail: mpensky@binghamton.edu. *Application contact:* Catherine Smith, Recruiting and Admissions Coordinator, 607-777-2151, Fax: 607-777-2501, E-mail: cmsmith@binghamton.edu.

Stony Brook University, State University of New York, Graduate School, College of Arts and Sciences, Department of Philosophy, Stony Brook, NY 11794. Offers MA, PhD. Evening/weekend programs available. *Faculty:* 21 full-time (5 women), 1 part-time/adjunct (0 women). *Students:* 76 full-time (26 women), 8 part-time (5 women); includes 1 Black or African American, non-Hispanic/Latino; 1 Asian, non-Hispanic/Latino; 9 Hispanic/Latino, 13 international. Average age 29. 229 applicants, 16% accepted, 22 enrolled. In 2010, 26 master's, 9 doctorates awarded. *Degree requirements:* For doctorate, one foreign language, thesis/dissertation. *Entrance requirements:* For master's and doctorate, GRE General Test. Additional exam requirements/recommendations for international students: Required—TOEFL. *Application deadline:* For fall admission, 1/15 for domestic students. Application fee: $100. *Expenses:* Tuition, state resident: full-time $8370; part-time $349 per credit. Tuition, nonresident: full-time $13,780; part-time $574 per credit. Required fees: $994. *Financial support:* In 2010–11, 1 research assistantship, 39 teaching assistantships were awarded; fellowships also available. *Faculty research:* Philosophy of science, philosophy of language, analytical philosophy, phenomenology, structuralism. Total annual research expenditures: $84,693. *Unit head:* Dr. Robert Crease, Chair, 631-632-7590, Fax: 631-632-7522. *Application contact:* Dr. Harvey Cormier, Director of Graduate Studies, 631-632-7312, Fax: 631-632-7522, E-mail: harvey.cormier@notes.cc.sunysb.edu.

Syracuse University, College of Arts and Sciences, Program in Philosophy, Syracuse, NY 13244. Offers MA, PhD. Part-time programs available. *Students:* 39 full-time (10 women), 6 part-time (1 woman); includes 8 minority (1 Black or African American, non-Hispanic/Latino; 3 Asian, non-Hispanic/Latino; 3 Hispanic/Latino; 1 Native Hawaiian or other Pacific Islander, non-Hispanic/Latino), 6 international. Average age 30. 141 applicants, 17% accepted, 11 enrolled. In 2010, 1 master's, 3 doctorates awarded. *Degree requirements:* For master's, thesis or alternative; for doctorate, thesis/dissertation. *Entrance requirements:* For master's and doctorate, GRE, writing sample. Additional exam requirements/recommendations for international students: Required—TOEFL (minimum score 100 iBT). *Application deadline:* For fall admission, 1/10 priority date for domestic and international students. Application fee: $75. Electronic applications accepted. *Expenses:* Tuition: Part-time $1162 per credit. *Financial support:* Fellowships with full and partial tuition reimbursements, research assistantships, teaching assistantships with full tuition reimbursements available. Financial award application deadline: 1/1; financial award applicants required to submit FAFSA. *Faculty research:* Ethics, metaphysics, epistemology, philosophy of language. *Unit head:* Dr. Thomas McKay, Graduate Studies Director, 315-443-2536, Fax: 315-443-5675. *Application contact:* Lisa Farnsworth, Information Contact, 315-443-2245, E-mail: lfarmswo@syr.edu.

Temple University, College of Liberal Arts, Department of Philosophy, Philadelphia, PA 19122-6096. Offers MA, PhD. Part-time programs available. *Faculty:* 10 full-time (3 women). *Students:* 41 full-time (16 women), 4 part-time (3 women); includes 2 Black or African American, non-Hispanic/Latino; 1 Hispanic/Latino, 6 international. 57 applicants, 40% accepted, 9 enrolled. In 2010, 4 master's, 2 doctorates awarded. Terminal master's awarded for partial completion of doctoral program. *Degree requirements:* For master's, thesis or alternative; for doctorate, one foreign language, thesis/dissertation. *Entrance requirements:* For master's and doctorate, GRE General Test. Additional exam requirements/recommendations for international students: Required—TOEFL (minimum score 550 paper-based; 213 computer-based; 79 iBT). *Application deadline:* For fall admission, 1/15 for domestic students, 12/15 for international students; for spring admission, 10/1 for domestic students, 8/1 for international students. Applications are processed on a rolling basis. Application fee: $50. Electronic applications accepted. *Financial support:* Fellowships with full tuition reimbursements, teaching assistantships with full tuition reimbursements, institutionally sponsored loans and tuition waivers (partial) available. Financial award application deadline: 1/15; financial award applicants required to submit FAFSA. *Faculty research:* Philosophy of mind, aesthetics, philosophy of science, nineteenth century German philosophy, phenomenology. *Unit head:* Dr. David Wolfsdorf, Chair, 215-204-1742, Fax: 215-204-6266, E-mail: dwolfsdo@temple.edu. *Application contact:* Dr. David Wolfsdorf, Chair, 215-204-1742, Fax: 215-204-6266, E-mail: dwolfsdo@temple.edu.

Texas A&M University, College of Liberal Arts, Department of Philosophy, College Station, TX 77843. Offers MA, PhD. Part-time programs available. *Faculty:* 12. *Students:* 21 full-time (8 women), 4 part-time (2 women); includes 4 Hispanic/Latino, 1 international. Average age 27. In 2010, 5 master's awarded. Terminal master's awarded for partial completion of doctoral program. *Degree requirements:* For master's, thesis optional; for doctorate, comprehensive exam, thesis/dissertation. *Entrance requirements:* For master's, GRE General Test, letter of recommendation, resume, writing sample; for doctorate, GRE General Test, letters of recommendation, resume, writing sample. *Application deadline:* For fall admission, 1/15 for domestic students, 3/1 for international students; for winter admission, 8/1 for international students; for spring admission, 10/15 priority date for domestic students. Application fee: $50 ($75 for international students). Electronic applications accepted. *Financial support:* In 2010–11, fellowships with partial tuition reimbursements (averaging $16,000 per year), research assistantships with partial tuition reimbursements (averaging $15,000 per year), teaching assistantships with partial tuition reimbursements (averaging $9,000 per year) were awarded; career-related internships or fieldwork, institutionally sponsored loans, scholarships/grants, and unspecified assistantships also available. Financial award application deadline: 1/15; financial award applicants required to submit FAFSA. *Faculty research:* American philosophy, applied ethics, philosophy of mind, philosophy of religion, history and philosophy of logic. *Unit head:* Dr. Daniel Conway, Head, 979-845-5696, E-mail: conway@philosophy.tamu.edu. *Application contact:* Dr. Daniel Conway, Head, 979-845-5696, E-mail: conway@philosophy.tamu.edu.

Texas Tech University, Graduate School, College of Arts and Sciences, Department of Philosophy, Lubbock, TX 79409. Offers MA. Part-time programs available. *Faculty:* 6 full-time (2 women). *Students:* 19 full-time (2 women), 3 part-time (1 woman); includes 1 Hispanic/Latino; 1 Two or more races, non-Hispanic/Latino, 2 international. Average age 24. 40 applicants, 53% accepted, 12 enrolled. In 2010, 8 master's awarded. *Degree requirements:* For master's, thesis or alternative. *Entrance requirements:* For master's, GRE General Test. Additional exam requirements/recommendations for international students: Required—TOEFL (minimum score 550 paper-based; 213 computer-based; 79 iBT). *Application deadline:* For fall admission, 6/1 priority date for domestic students, 1/15 priority date for international students; for spring admission, 9/1 priority date for domestic students, 6/15 priority date for international students. Applications are processed on a rolling basis. Application fee: $50 ($75 for international students). Electronic applications accepted. *Expenses:* Tuition, state resident: full-time $5495.76; part-time $228.99 per credit hour. Tuition, nonresident: full-time $12,936; part-time $538.99 per credit hour. Required fees: $2674; $36 per credit hour. $905 per semester. *Financial support:* In 2010–11, 18 students received support, including 14 teaching assistantships with partial tuition reimbursements available (averaging $7,890 per year). Financial award application deadline: 4/15; financial award applicants required to submit FAFSA. *Faculty research:* Aesthetics, ethics, history of philosophy, philosophy of mind, philosophy of science. Total annual research expenditures: $31,260. *Unit head:* Dr. Mark O. Webb, Chair, 806-742-3275 Ext. 323, Fax: 806-742-0730, E-mail: mark.webb@ttu.edu. *Application contact:* Dr. Daniel O. Nathan, Director of Graduate Studies, 806-742-0373 Ext. 340, Fax: 806-742-0730, E-mail: daniel.nathan@ttu.edu.

Trinity Western University, School of Graduate Studies, Program in Interdisciplinary Humanities, Langley, BC V2Y 1Y1, Canada. Offers general humanities (MAIH); specialized (MAIH), including English, history, philosophy. Part-time programs available. *Degree requirements:* For master's, thesis or alternative, 36 semester hours. *Entrance requirements:* For master's, strong undergraduate degree in humanities or English, history or philosophy. Electronic applications accepted. *Faculty research:* Literary theory, gender, medieval and early modern literature, philosophy of religion, Thomas Merton's poetics.

Tufts University, Graduate School of Arts and Sciences, Department of Philosophy, Medford, MA 02155. Offers MA. *Degree requirements:* For master's, one foreign language, comprehensive exam, departmental qualifying exam. *Entrance requirements:* For master's, GRE General Test, writing sample. Additional exam requirements/recommendations for international students: Required—TOEFL (minimum score 550 paper-based; 213 computer-based; 80 iBT). Electronic applications accepted. *Expenses:* Tuition: Full-time $39,624; part-time $3962 per course. Required fees: $40 per year. Full-time tuition and fees vary according to degree level, program and student level. Part-time tuition and fees vary according to course load.

Tulane University, School of Liberal Arts, Department of Philosophy, New Orleans, LA 70118-5669. Offers MA, PhD. *Degree requirements:* For master's, thesis or alternative; for doctorate, one foreign language, thesis/dissertation. *Entrance requirements:* For master's, GRE General Test, minimum B average in undergraduate course work; for doctorate, GRE General Test. Additional exam requirements/recommendations for international students: Required—TOEFL. Electronic applications accepted.

Philosophy

Universidad Autonoma de Guadalajara, Graduate Programs, Guadalajara, Mexico. Offers administrative law and justice (LL M); advertising and corporate communications (MA); architecture (M Arch); business (MBA); computational science (MCC); education (Ed M, Ed D); English-Spanish translation (MA); entrepreneurship and management (MBA); integrated management of digital animation (MA); international business (MIB); international corporate law (LL M); internet technologies (MS); manufacturing systems (MMS); occupational health (MS); philosophy (MA, PhD); power electronics (MS); quality systems (MQS); renewable energy (MS); social evaluation of projects (MBA); strategic market research (MBA); tax law (MA); teaching mathematics (MA).

Université de Montréal, Faculty of Arts and Sciences, Department of Philosophy, Montréal, QC H3C 3J7, Canada. Offers MA, PhD. *Degree requirements:* For master's, 2 foreign languages, thesis; for doctorate, thesis/dissertation, general exam. Electronic applications accepted. *Faculty research:* Ancient and modern philosophy; logic and philosophy of language, ethics, and politics; contemporary Continental philosophy.

Université de Sherbrooke, Faculty of Letters and Human Sciences, Department of Human Sciences, Sherbrooke, QC J1K 2R1, Canada. Offers history (MA); philosophy (MA). *Degree requirements:* For master's, thesis. *Entrance requirements:* For master's, minimum GPA of 2.75. *Faculty research:* Political, social, and urban history; history of women.

Université de Sherbrooke, Faculty of Theology, Ethics and Philosophy, Sherbrooke, QC J1K 2R1, Canada. Offers applied ethics (Diploma); human science of religions (MA); intercultural training (Diploma); philosophy (MA, PhD); spiritual anthropology (Diploma); theology (MA, PhD, Diploma). Part-time and evening/weekend programs available. Postbaccalaureate distance learning degree programs offered. Terminal master's awarded for partial completion of doctoral program. *Entrance requirements:* For master's, bachelor's degree in related discipline; for doctorate, master's degree in related discipline. *Faculty research:* Faith and culture interrelation.

Université du Québec à Montréal, Graduate Programs, Program in Philosophy, Montréal, QC H3C 3P8, Canada. Offers MA, PhD. PhD offered jointly with Université du Québec à Trois-Rivières. Part-time programs available. *Degree requirements:* For master's, thesis; for doctorate, thesis/dissertation. *Entrance requirements:* For master's, appropriate bachelor's degree or equivalent, proficiency in French; for doctorate, appropriate master's degree or equivalent, proficiency in French.

Université du Québec à Trois-Rivières, Graduate Programs, Program in Philosophy, Trois-Rivières, QC G9A 5H7, Canada. Offers MA, PhD. PhD offered jointly with Université du Québec à Montréal. Part-time programs available. *Degree requirements:* For master's, thesis; for doctorate, thesis/dissertation. *Entrance requirements:* For master's, appropriate bachelor's degree, proficiency in French; for doctorate, appropriate master's degree, proficiency in French.

Université Laval, Faculty of Philosophy, Programs in Philosophy, Québec, QC G1K 7P4, Canada. Offers MA, PhD. Terminal master's awarded for partial completion of doctoral program. *Degree requirements:* For master's, thesis; for doctorate, comprehensive exam, thesis/dissertation. *Entrance requirements:* For master's and doctorate, French exam. Electronic applications accepted.

University at Albany, State University of New York, College of Arts and Sciences, Department of Philosophy, Albany, NY 12222-0001. Offers MA, PhD. *Degree requirements:* For master's, one foreign language, thesis; for doctorate, thesis/dissertation. *Entrance requirements:* For master's and doctorate, GRE General Test. Additional exam requirements/recommendations for international students: Required—TOEFL (minimum score 550 paper-based; 213 computer-based). Electronic applications accepted. *Faculty research:* Philosophical logic, ethics, ancient philosophy/metaphysics, aesthetics, biomedical ethics.

University at Buffalo, the State University of New York, Graduate School, College of Arts and Sciences, Department of Philosophy, Buffalo, NY 14260. Offers MA, PhD. *Faculty:* 20 full-time (2 women). *Students:* 31 full-time (8 women), 26 part-time (5 women); includes 6 Asian, non-Hispanic/Latino; 1 Hispanic/Latino, 3 international. Average age 31. 49 applicants, 78% accepted, 17 enrolled. In 2010, 4 master's, 7 doctorates awarded. Terminal master's awarded for partial completion of doctoral program. *Degree requirements:* For master's, variable foreign language requirement, thesis or alternative; for doctorate, variable foreign language requirement, comprehensive exam, thesis/dissertation. *Entrance requirements:* For master's, GRE General Test, minimum GPA of 2.67; for doctorate, GRE General Test, minimum GPA of 3.0. Additional exam requirements/recommendations for international students: Required—TOEFL (minimum score 550 paper-based; 213 computer-based; 79 iBT). *Application deadline:* For fall admission, 12/15 for domestic and international students. Applications are processed on a rolling basis. Application fee: $75. Electronic applications accepted. *Financial support:* In 2010–11, 10 fellowships with full tuition reimbursements (averaging $4,000 per year), 25 teaching assistantships with full tuition reimbursements (averaging $13,250 per year) were awarded; research assistantships, Federal Work-Study, institutionally sponsored loans, tuition waivers, and unspecified assistantships also available. Financial award application deadline: 1/20; financial award applicants required to submit FAFSA. *Faculty research:* Logic, metaphysics (historical and contemporary), aesthetics, epistemology, ethics (historical and contemporary), ontology. Total annual research expenditures: $3.7 million. *Unit head:* Dr. David B. Hershenov, Chair, 716-645-0150, Fax: 716-645-6139, E-mail: dh25@buffalo.edu. *Application contact:* Dr. William H. Baumer, Director of Graduate Studies, 716-645-0164, Fax: 716-645-6139, E-mail: whbaumer@buffalo.edu.

University of Alberta, Faculty of Graduate Studies and Research, Department of Philosophy, Edmonton, AB T6G 2E1, Canada. Offers MA, PhD. Part-time programs available. *Degree requirements:* For master's, thesis; for doctorate, thesis/dissertation. *Entrance requirements:* Additional exam requirements/recommendations for international students: Required—TOEFL (minimum score 550 paper-based; 213 computer-based). Electronic applications accepted. *Faculty research:* Philosophy of science, cognitive science, social and political philosophy, philosophy of language and logic, environmental aesthetics.

The University of Arizona, College of Social and Behavioral Sciences, Department of Philosophy, Tucson, AZ 85721. Offers MA, PhD, JD/PhD. Part-time programs available. *Faculty:* 16 full-time (4 women), 4 part-time/adjunct (2 women). *Students:* 41 full-time (9 women), 5 part-time (2 women); includes 1 Hispanic/Latino; 1 Two or more races, non-Hispanic/Latino, 7 international. Average age 31. 160 applicants, 5% accepted, 8 enrolled. In 2010, 1 master's, 1 doctorate awarded. Terminal master's awarded for partial completion of doctoral program. *Degree requirements:* For master's, exams, qualifying paper; for doctorate, thesis/dissertation, preliminary exams. *Entrance requirements:* For doctorate, GRE General Test, 3 letters of recommendation, writing sample. Additional exam requirements/recommendations for international students: Required—TOEFL (minimum score 550 paper-based; 213 computer-based; 79 iBT). *Application deadline:* For fall admission, 1/2 for domestic and international students. Applications are processed on a rolling basis. Application fee: $65. Electronic applications accepted. *Expenses:* Tuition, state resident: full-time $7692. *Financial support:* In 2010–11, 35 teaching assistantships with full tuition reimbursements (averaging $19,296 per year) were awarded; research assistantships, scholarships/grants, health care benefits, tuition waivers (full), and unspecified assistantships also available. Financial award application deadline: 1/15. *Faculty research:* Law, social, and political philosophy; epistemology; philosophy of mind; cognitive science. *Unit head:* Dr. J. Christopher Maloney, Head, 520-621-3120. *Application contact:* Debbie Jackson, Program Coordinator, 520-621-5045, Fax: 520-621-9559, E-mail: debbiej@email.arizona.edu.

University of Arkansas, Graduate School, J. William Fulbright College of Arts and Sciences, Department of Philosophy, Fayetteville, AR 72701-1201. Offers MA, PhD. Part-time programs available. *Students:* 14 full-time (5 women), 15 part-time (1 woman); includes 3 minority (2 Asian, non-Hispanic/Latino; 1 Hispanic/Latino), 1 international. 11 applicants, 73% accepted. In 2010, 4 master's awarded. *Degree requirements:* For master's, thesis; for doctorate, 2 foreign languages, thesis/dissertation. *Application deadline:* For fall admission, 4/1 for international students; for spring admission, 10/1 for international students. Applications are processed on a rolling basis. Application fee: $40 ($50 for international students). Electronic applications accepted. *Financial support:* In 2010–11, 1 fellowship with tuition reimbursement, 1 research assistantship, 10 teaching assistantships were awarded; career-related internships or fieldwork and Federal Work-Study also available. Support available to part-time students. Financial award application deadline: 4/1; financial award applicants required to submit FAFSA. *Unit head:* Dr. Thomas Senor, Departmental Chairperson, 479-575-3551, Fax: 479-575-2642, E-mail: senor@uark.edu. *Application contact:* Dr. Jack Lyons, Graduate Coordinator, 479-575-5825, E-mail: jclyons@uark.edu.

The University of British Columbia, Faculty of Arts and Faculty of Graduate Studies; Department of Philosophy, Vancouver, BC V6T 1Z1, Canada. Offers MA, PhD. *Accreditation:* NCATE. Part-time programs available. *Degree requirements:* For master's, thesis (for some programs); for doctorate, comprehensive exam, thesis/dissertation. *Entrance requirements:* For master's, bachelor's degree with minimum average of 76% or minimum GPA of 3.0 in 3rd- and 4th-year coursework; 3 credits in formal logic; 6 credits at the upper-level in the history of philosophy and in metaphysics, epistemology, or philosophy; 3 credits at the upper-level in ethics or value theory; for doctorate, MA, honors BA with first class standing, or BA with first class standing in philosophy. Additional exam requirements/recommendations for international students: Required—TOEFL (minimum score 600 paper-based; 250 computer-based), IELTS (minimum score 6.5), Michigan English Language Assessment Battery: minimum overall score of 81. Electronic applications accepted. Tuition charges are reported in Canadian dollars. *Expenses:* Tuition, area resident: Full-time $4179 Canadian dollars. International tuition: $7344 Canadian dollars full-time. *Faculty research:* Ethics and applied ethics, metaphysics and epistemology, history of philosophy, philosophy of science, philosophy of biology.

University of Calgary, Faculty of Graduate Studies, Faculty of Arts, Department of Philosophy, Calgary, AB T2N 1N4, Canada. Offers MA, PhD. Part-time programs available. *Degree requirements:* For master's, comprehensive exam (for some programs), thesis (for some programs); for doctorate, thesis/dissertation, candidacy exam. *Entrance requirements:* Additional exam requirements/recommendations for international students: Required—TOEFL (minimum score 550 paper-based; 213 computer-based). Electronic applications accepted. *Faculty research:* Ethics and political philosophy, metaphysics, philosophy of mind, philosophy of language.

University of California, Berkeley, Graduate Division, College of Letters and Science, Department of Philosophy, Berkeley, CA 94720-1500. Offers PhD. *Degree requirements:* For doctorate, thesis/dissertation, qualifying exam. *Entrance requirements:* For doctorate, GRE General Test, minimum GPA of 3.0, writing sample, 3 letters of recommendation.

University of California, Davis, Graduate Studies, Program in Philosophy, Davis, CA 95616. Offers MA, PhD. Terminal master's awarded for partial completion of doctoral program. *Degree requirements:* For doctorate, thesis/dissertation. *Entrance requirements:* For master's and doctorate, GRE General Test, minimum GPA of 3.0. Additional exam requirements/recommendations for international students: Required—TOEFL (minimum score 550 paper-based; 213 computer-based). Electronic applications accepted. *Faculty research:* Moral and political philosophy, philosophy of language, metaphysics, philosophy of science, history of philosophy.

University of California, Irvine, School of Humanities, Department of Philosophy, Irvine, CA 92697. Offers MA, PhD. *Students:* 34 full-time (8 women), 4 part-time (1 woman); includes 1 minority (Two or more races, non-Hispanic/Latino), 2 international. Average age 28. 74 applicants, 18% accepted, 9 enrolled. In 2010, 7 master's, 4 doctorates awarded. *Degree requirements:* For master's, thesis; for doctorate, thesis/dissertation. *Entrance requirements:* For master's and doctorate, GRE General Test, minimum GPA of 3.0. Additional exam requirements/recommendations for international students: Required—TOEFL (minimum score 550 paper-based; 213 computer-based). *Application deadline:* For fall admission, 1/15 priority date for domestic students, 1/15 for international students. Applications are processed on a rolling basis. Application fee: $80 ($100 for international students). Electronic applications accepted. *Financial support:* Fellowships with tuition reimbursements, teaching assistantships with partial tuition reimbursements, institutionally sponsored loans, traineeships, health care benefits, and unspecified assistantships available. Financial award application deadline: 3/1; financial award applicants required to submit FAFSA. *Faculty research:* Philosophy of action and decision theory, philosophy of language, philosophy of mathematics, virtue ethics, modern and contemporary Continental philosophy. *Unit head:* Sven Dietrich Bernecker, Chair, 949-824-3896, Fax: 949-824-6520, E-mail: ns.bernecker@uci.edu. *Application contact:* Lumen Chi-Young Hwang, Graduate Coordinator, 949-824-6525, Fax: 949-824-6520, E-mail: hwangl@uci.edu.

University of California, Irvine, School of Social Sciences, Department of Logic and Philosophy of Science, Irvine, CA 92697. Offers philosophy (PhD). *Students:* 19 full-time (3 women); includes 4 minority (1 Hispanic/Latino; 3 Two or more races, non-Hispanic/Latino). Average age 28. 53 applicants, 23% accepted, 6 enrolled. In 2010, 3 doctorates awarded. *Entrance requirements:* For doctorate, GRE, minimum GPA of 3.0. Additional exam requirements/recommendations for international students: Required—TOEFL (minimum score 550 paper-based; 213 computer-based). *Application deadline:* For fall admission, 1/15 for domestic and international students. Application fee: $80 ($100 for international students). *Financial support:* Fellowships, research assistantships with full tuition reimbursements, teaching assistantships, institutionally sponsored loans, traineeships, health care benefits, and unspecified assistantships available. Financial award application deadline: 3/1. *Unit head:* Lumen Hwang, Graduate Program Administrator, 949-824-6525, Fax: 949-824-6520, E-mail: hwangl@uci.edu. *Application contact:* Alice Decker, Manager, 949-824-8457, Fax: 949-824-6520, E-mail: adecker@uci.edu.

University of California, Los Angeles, Graduate Division, College of Letters and Science, Department of Philosophy, Los Angeles, CA 90095. Offers MA, PhD. *Faculty:* 15 full-time (3 women). *Students:* 50 full-time (18 women); includes 5 minority (3 Asian, non-Hispanic/Latino; 2 Hispanic/Latino), 2 international. Average age 30. 153 applicants, 7% accepted, 5 enrolled. In 2010, 7 master's, 4 doctorates awarded. Terminal master's awarded for partial completion of doctoral program. *Degree requirements:* For master's, one foreign language, comprehensive exam; for doctorate, one foreign language, thesis/dissertation, oral and written qualifying exams, teaching experience. *Entrance requirements:* For master's, GRE General Test, minimum GPA of 3.0, sample of written work; for doctorate, GRE General Test, minimum undergraduate GPA of 3.0, sample of written work. Additional exam requirements/recommendations for international students: Required—TOEFL. *Application deadline:* For fall admission, 1/10 for domestic and international students. Application fee: $70 ($90 for international students). Electronic applications accepted. *Financial support:* In 2010–11, 47 fellowships with full and partial tuition reimbursements, 17 research assistantships with full and partial tuition reimbursements, 42 teaching assistantships with full and partial tuition reimbursements were awarded; Federal Work-Study, institutionally sponsored loans, scholarships/grants, health care benefits, tuition waivers (full and partial), and unspecified assistantships also available. Financial award application deadline: 3/1; financial award applicants required to submit FAFSA. *Unit head:* Dr. John Carriero, Chair, 310-206-3475, E-mail: carriero@humnet.ucla.edu. *Application contact:* Department Office, 310-206-1356, E-mail: philcounselor@humnet.ucla.edu.

University of California, Riverside, Graduate Division, Department of Philosophy, Riverside, CA 92521-0102. Offers MA, PhD. Terminal master's awarded for partial completion of doctoral program. *Degree requirements:* For master's, logic exam, professional paper; for doctorate, one foreign language, thesis/dissertation, logic exam, proposition papers, qualifying exams. *Entrance requirements:* For master's, GRE General Test, minimum GPA of 3.2; for doctorate, GRE General Test, master's degree in philosophy, minimum GPA of 3.2. Additional exam requirements/recommendations for international students: Required—TOEFL (minimum score 550 paper-based; 213 computer-based; 80 iBT). Electronic applications accepted. *Faculty research:* Moral philosophy, philosophy of science, history of philosophy, philosophy of language, Continental philosophy.

University of California, San Diego, Office of Graduate Studies, Department of Philosophy, La Jolla, CA 92093. Offers philosophy (PhD); science studies (PhD). *Degree requirements:* For doctorate, thesis/dissertation. *Entrance requirements:* For doctorate, GRE General Test, GRE Subject Test. Electronic applications accepted.

University of California, San Diego, Office of Graduate Studies, Interdisciplinary Program in Cognitive Science, La Jolla, CA 92093. Offers cognitive science/anthropology (PhD); cognitive science/communication (PhD); cognitive science/computer science and engineering (PhD); cognitive science/linguistics (PhD); cognitive science/neuroscience (PhD); cognitive science/philosophy (PhD); cognitive science/psychology (PhD); cognitive science/sociology (PhD). Admissions offered through affiliated departments. *Degree requirements:* For doctorate, thesis/dissertation. *Entrance requirements:* For doctorate, GRE General Test, acceptance into one of the eight participating departments. *Faculty research:* Language and cognition, philosophy of mind, visual perception, biological anthropology, sociolinguistics.

University of California, Santa Barbara, Graduate Division, College of Letters and Sciences, Division of Humanities and Fine Arts, Department of Philosophy, Santa Barbara, CA 93106-9580. Offers PhD, MA/PhD. *Faculty:* 11 full-time (1 woman). *Students:* 37 full-time (4 women); includes 6 Asian, non-Hispanic/Latino. Average age 30. 79 applicants, 13% accepted, 5 enrolled. In 2010, 2 doctorates awarded. Terminal master's awarded for partial completion of doctoral program. *Degree requirements:* For doctorate, thesis/dissertation. *Entrance requirements:* For doctorate, GRE. Additional exam requirements/recommendations for international students: Required—TOEFL (minimum score 550 paper-based; 80 iBT), IELTS (minimum score 7). *Application deadline:* For fall admission, 1/15 priority date for domestic and international students; for winter admission, 11/1 for domestic students, 11/1 priority date for international students; for spring admission, 2/1 for domestic students, 2/1 priority date for international students. Applications are processed on a rolling basis. Application fee: $70 ($90 for international students). Electronic applications accepted. *Financial support:* In 2010–11, 29 students received support, including 12 fellowships with full and partial tuition reimbursements available (averaging $11,277 per year), 1 research assistantship with full and partial tuition reimbursement available (averaging $8,370 per year), 24 teaching assistantships with full and partial tuition reimbursements available (averaging $13,518 per year); career-related internships or fieldwork also available. Financial award application deadline: 12/1; financial award applicants required to submit FAFSA. *Faculty research:* Epistemology, philosophy of language, philosophy of mind, history of philosophy, logic. *Unit head:* Joni Schwartz, Director, 805-893-3237, Fax: 805-893-7492, E-mail: joni@hfa.ucsb.edu. *Application contact:* Cami Helmuth, Graduate Program Advisor, 805-893-7490, Fax: 805-893-7492, E-mail: helmuth@hfa.ucsb.edu.

University of California, Santa Cruz, Division of Graduate Studies, Division of Humanities, Department of Philosophy, Santa Cruz, CA 95064. Offers MA, PhD. *Students:* 14 full-time (4 women); includes 4 minority (1 Black or African American, non-Hispanic/Latino; 1 Asian, non-Hispanic/Latino; 2 Hispanic/Latino), 2 international. Average age 30. 45 applicants, 22% accepted, 6 enrolled. In 2010, 2 master's, 2 doctorates awarded. *Degree requirements:* For doctorate, thesis/dissertation, qualifying exam. *Entrance requirements:* For master's, GRE, 3 letters of recommendation; for doctorate, GRE, official transcripts, 3 letters of recommendation. Additional exam requirements/recommendations for international students: Required—TOEFL (minimum score 550 paper-based; 220 computer-based; 83 iBT); Recommended—IELTS (minimum score 8). *Application deadline:* For fall admission, 1/15 for domestic and international students. Application fee: $70 ($90 for international students). Electronic applications accepted. *Financial support:* Fellowships, research assistantships, teaching assistantships, institutionally sponsored loans and tuition waivers (full and partial) available. Financial award applicants required to submit FAFSA. *Faculty research:* Philosophy of science. *Unit head:* Holly Clausnitzer, Graduate Program Coordinator, 831-459-4578, Fax: 831-459-2650, E-mail: hclausni@ucsc.edu. *Application contact:* Holly Clausnitzer, Graduate Program Coordinator, 831-459-4578, Fax: 831-459-2650, E-mail: hclausni@ucsc.edu.

University of Chicago, Division of the Humanities, Department of Philosophy, Chicago, IL 60637-1513. Offers ancient philosophy (AM, PhD); philosophy (AM, PhD). Terminal master's awarded for partial completion of doctoral program. *Degree requirements:* For master's, thesis; for doctorate, one foreign language, thesis/dissertation. *Entrance requirements:* For master's and doctorate, GRE General Test. Additional exam requirements/recommendations for international students: Required—TOEFL.

University of Cincinnati, Graduate School, McMicken College of Arts and Sciences, Department of Philosophy, Cincinnati, OH 45221. Offers MA, PhD. Terminal master's awarded for partial completion of doctoral program. *Degree requirements:* For master's, thesis; for doctorate, one foreign language, comprehensive exam, thesis/dissertation. *Entrance requirements:* For master's and doctorate, GRE General Test, BA in philosophy or equivalent experience. Additional exam requirements/recommendations for international students: Required—TOEFL (minimum score 240 computer-based). Electronic applications accepted.

University of Colorado Boulder, Graduate School, College of Arts and Sciences, Department of Philosophy, Boulder, CO 80309. Offers MA, PhD. *Faculty:* 23 full-time (5 women). *Students:* 47 full-time (10 women), 3 part-time (1 woman); includes 7 minority (3 Asian, non-Hispanic/Latino; 4 Hispanic/Latino). Average age 29. 273 applicants, 10 enrolled. In 2010, 16 master's, 10 doctorates awarded. Terminal master's awarded for partial completion of doctoral program. *Degree requirements:* For master's, comprehensive exam, thesis; for doctorate, one foreign language, thesis/dissertation, logic and qualifying papers, oral exam. *Entrance requirements:* For master's, GRE General Test, writing sample, minimum undergraduate GPA of 2.75; for doctorate, GRE General Test. *Application deadline:* For fall admission, 1/15 priority date for domestic students, 12/1 for international students. Applications are processed on a rolling basis. Application fee: $50 ($60 for international students). *Financial support:* In 2010–11, 15 fellowships (averaging $4,522 per year), 23 research assistantships (averaging $5,071 per year) were awarded; Federal Work-Study, institutionally sponsored loans, and tuition waivers (full) also available. Financial award application deadline: 1/15. *Faculty research:* Metaphysics and epistemology, classical philosophy, philosophy of science, moral and political philosophy.

University of Connecticut, Graduate School, College of Liberal Arts and Sciences, Department of Philosophy, Storrs, CT 06269. Offers MA, PhD. Terminal master's awarded for partial completion of doctoral program. *Degree requirements:* For master's, comprehensive exam; for doctorate, 2 foreign languages, thesis/dissertation. *Entrance requirements:* For master's and doctorate, GRE General Test. Additional exam requirements/recommendations for international students: Required—TOEFL (minimum score 550 paper-based; 213 computer-based). Electronic applications accepted.

University of Dallas, Braniff Graduate School of Liberal Arts, Institute of Philosophic Studies, Doctoral Program in Philosophy, Irving, TX 75062-4736. Offers PhD. *Degree requirements:* For doctorate, 2 foreign languages, comprehensive exam, thesis/dissertation, qualifying exams. *Entrance requirements:* For doctorate, GRE General Test. *Expenses:* Tuition: Full-time $7500; part-time $720 per credit hour. Required fees: $500; $60 per credit hour. $300 per semester. One-time fee: $150. Tuition and fees vary according to program and student level. *Faculty research:* Aesthetics, postmodernism, Hegel, ethics, Aristotle.

University of Dallas, Braniff Graduate School of Liberal Arts, Master's Program in Philosophy, Irving, TX 75062-4736. Offers MA. *Degree requirements:* For master's, one foreign language, comprehensive exam, thesis. *Entrance requirements:* For master's, GRE General Test. Additional exam requirements/recommendations for international students: Required—TOEFL. *Expenses:* Tuition: Full-time $7500; part-time $720 per credit hour. Required fees: $500; $60 per credit hour. $300 per semester. One-time fee: $150. Tuition and fees vary according to program and student level. *Faculty research:* Aesthetics, postmodernism, Hegel, ethics, Aristotle.

University of Florida, Graduate School, College of Liberal Arts and Sciences, Department of Philosophy, Gainesville, FL 32611. Offers MA, PhD. Part-time programs available. *Faculty:* 8 full-time (0 women), 1 part-time/adjunct (0 women). *Students:* 13 full-time (1 woman), 2 part-time (0 women); includes 1 Black or African American, non-Hispanic/Latino; 2 Hispanic/Latino, 3 international. Average age 37. 17 applicants, 41% accepted, 5 enrolled. In 2010, 3 master's, 2 doctorates awarded. *Degree requirements:* For doctorate, one foreign language, comprehensive exam, thesis/dissertation. *Entrance requirements:* For master's and doctorate, GRE General Test, minimum GPA of 3.0. Additional exam requirements/recommendations for international students: Required—TOEFL (minimum score 550 paper-based; 213 computer-based; 80 iBT), IELTS (minimum score 6). *Application deadline:* For fall admission, 1/15 priority date for domestic students, 1/15 for international students. Applications are processed on a rolling basis. Application fee: $30. Electronic applications accepted. *Expenses:* Tuition, state resident: full-time $10,915.92. Tuition, nonresident: full-time $28,309. *Financial support:* In 2010–11, 13 students received support, including 1 fellowship with tuition reimbursement available, 12 teaching assistantships with tuition reimbursements available (averaging $17,404 per year); unspecified assistantships also available. Financial award application deadline: 1/15; financial award applicants required to submit FAFSA. *Faculty research:* Philosophy of mind, metaphysics, philosophy of science, ancient philosophy, philosophical logic. *Unit head:* Dr. Gene Witmer, Chair, 352-273-1830, Fax: 352-392-5577, E-mail: gwitmer@ufl.edu. *Application contact:* Dr. Chuang Liu, Graduate Coordinator, 352-392-2084 Ext. 333, Fax: 352-392-5577, E-mail: logics@ufl.edu.

University of Georgia, College of Arts and Sciences, Department of Philosophy, Athens, GA 30602. Offers MA, PhD. Part-time programs available. *Faculty:* 13 full-time (6 women). *Students:* 27 full-time (4 women), 12 part-time (2 women); includes 2 Hispanic/Latino; 1 Native Hawaiian or other Pacific Islander, non-Hispanic/Latino, 4 international. 40 applicants, 50% accepted, 10 enrolled. In 2010, 2 doctorates awarded. *Degree requirements:* For master's, one foreign language, thesis; for doctorate, one foreign language, thesis/dissertation. *Entrance requirements:* For master's and doctorate, GRE General Test. Additional exam requirements/recommendations for international students: Required—TOEFL. *Application deadline:* For fall admission, 1/1 priority date for domestic and international students; for spring admission, 11/15 for domestic students. Application fee: $50. Electronic applications accepted. *Expenses:* Tuition, state resident: full-time $7200; part-time $344 per credit hour. Tuition, nonresident: full-time $21,900; part-time $944 per credit hour. Tuition and fees vary according to course load and program. *Financial support:* In 2010–11, 19 students received support, including 4 teaching assistantships with partial tuition reimbursements available (averaging $13,342 per year); unspecified assistantships also available. Financial award application deadline: 1/1. *Unit head:* Dr. Victoria M. Davion, Head, 706-542-2823, Fax: 706-542-2839, E-mail: vdavion@uga.edu. *Application contact:* Dr. Richard D. Winfield, Graduate Coordinator, 706-583-2811, Fax: 706-542-2839, E-mail: winfield@uga.edu.

University of Guelph, Graduate Studies, College of Arts, Department of Philosophy, Guelph, ON N1G 2W1, Canada. Offers MA, PhD. PhD offered jointly with McMaster University, Wilfrid Laurier University. Part-time programs available. *Degree requirements:* For master's, thesis (for some programs); for doctorate, one foreign language, thesis/dissertation. *Entrance requirements:* For master's, minimum B- average during previous 2 years of course work; for doctorate, minimum B average. Additional exam requirements/recommendations for international students: Required—TOEFL (minimum score 550 paper-based; 213 computer-based). Electronic applications accepted. *Faculty research:* Philosophy of science, ethics, modern philosophy, social philosophy, Continental philosophy.

University of Hawaii at Manoa, Graduate Division, College of Arts and Humanities, Department of Philosophy, Honolulu, HI 96822. Offers MA, PhD. Part-time programs available. *Faculty:* 14 full-time (4 women). *Students:* 58 full-time (10 women), 33 part-time (4 women); includes 11 minority (6 Asian, non-Hispanic/Latino; 1 Hispanic/Latino; 1 Native Hawaiian or other Pacific Islander, non-Hispanic/Latino; 3 Two or more races, non-Hispanic/Latino), 5 international. Average age 29. 53 applicants, 42% accepted, 14 enrolled. In 2010, 8 master's, 2 doctorates awarded. *Degree requirements:* For master's, variable foreign language requirement, thesis optional, culminating exam; for doctorate, variable foreign language requirement, comprehensive exam, thesis/dissertation, final oral presentation. *Entrance requirements:* For master's and doctorate, GRE General Test. Additional exam requirements/recommendations for international students: Required—TOEFL (minimum score 600 paper-based; 100 iBT), IELTS (minimum score 7). *Application deadline:* For fall admission, 2/1 for domestic students, 1/15 for international students; for spring admission, 9/1 for domestic students, 8/1 for international students. Applications are processed on a rolling basis. Application fee: $60. *Financial support:* In 2010–11, 28 students received support, including 17 fellowships (averaging $5,390 per year), 1 research assistantship with full tuition reimbursement available (averaging $21,288 per year), 9 teaching assistantships with full tuition reimbursements available (averaging $15,562 per year); Federal Work-Study, scholarships/grants, and unspecified assistantships also available. Support available to part-time students. Financial award application deadline: 3/1; financial award applicants required to submit FAFSA. *Faculty research:* Renaissance philosophy, Indian philosophy, logic, ethics, philosophy of science, philosophy of mathematics, Chinese philosophy. Total annual research expenditures: $158,000. *Application contact:* Ron Bontekoe, Graduate Chair, 808-956-8410, Fax: 808-956-9228, E-mail: bontekoe@hawaii.edu.

University of Houston, College of Liberal Arts and Social Sciences, Department of Philosophy, Houston, TX 77204. Offers MA. *Faculty:* 7 full-time (1 woman), 1 part-time/adjunct (0 women). *Students:* 16 full-time (3 women), 8 part-time (1 woman); includes 2 Hispanic/Latino, 1 international. Average age 26. 46 applicants, 96% accepted, 13 enrolled. In 2010, 10 master's awarded. *Degree requirements:* For master's, thesis (for some programs), thesis or additional course requirements. *Entrance requirements:* For master's, GRE General Test, minimum of 18 hours of course work in philosophy; minimum GPA of 3.3 in last 60 hours. Additional exam requirements/recommendations for international students: Required—TOEFL (minimum score 550 paper-based; 79 iBT). *Application deadline:* For fall admission, 3/15 for domestic students, 4/1 for international students. Applications are processed on a rolling basis. Application fee: $40. Electronic applications accepted. *Expenses:* Tuition, state resident: full-time $8592; part-time $358 per credit hour. Tuition, nonresident: full-time $16,032; part-time $668 per credit hour. Required fees: $2889. Tuition and fees vary according to course load and program. *Financial support:* In 2010–11, 9 teaching assistantships with full tuition reimbursements (averaging $8,816 per year) were awarded; career-related internships or fieldwork, Federal Work-Study, institutionally sponsored loans, scholarships/grants, health care benefits, and unspecified assistantships also available. Support available to part-time students. Financial award application deadline: 3/10. *Faculty research:* Skepticism, nominalism, history of philosophy, cognitive science. *Unit head:* Dr. Cynthia Freeland, Chairperson, 713-743-3010, Fax: 713-743-5162, E-mail: cfreeland@uh.edu. *Application contact:* Dr. Cynthia Freeland, Chairperson, 713-743-3010, Fax: 713-743-5162, E-mail: cfreeland@uh.edu.

University of Illinois at Chicago, Graduate College, College of Liberal Arts and Sciences, Department of Philosophy, Chicago, IL 60607-7128. Offers MA, PhD. Terminal master's awarded for partial completion of doctoral program. *Degree requirements:* For doctorate, thesis/dissertation, preliminary exams. *Entrance requirements:* For master's and doctorate, minimum GPA of 2.75. Additional exam requirements/recommendations for international students: Required—TOEFL. Electronic applications accepted. *Faculty research:* Philosophy of science, philosophy of language, epistemology and metaphysics, ethics, aesthetics.

University of Illinois at Urbana–Champaign, Graduate College, College of Liberal Arts and Sciences, Department of Philosophy, Champaign, IL 61820. Offers MA, PhD, PhD/JD. *Faculty:* 10 full-time (2 women), 1 part-time/adjunct (0 women). *Students:* 31 full-time (4 women), 4 part-time (0 women), 3 international. 68 applicants, 15% accepted, 10 enrolled. In 2010, 2 doctorates awarded. *Entrance requirements:* For doctorate, GRE, minimum GPA of 3.0; writing sample. Additional exam requirements/recommendations for international students: Required—TOEFL (minimum score 600 paper-based; 100 iBT). *Application deadline:* Applications are processed on a rolling basis. Application fee: $75 ($90 for international students). Electronic applications accepted. *Financial support:* In 2010–11, 8 fellowships, 1 research assistantship, 33 teaching assistantships were awarded; tuition waivers (full and partial) also available. *Unit head:* Robert C. Cummins, Chair, 217-333-2889, Fax: 217-244-8355, E-mail: rcummins@

Philosophy

University of Illinois at Urbana–Champaign (continued)
illinois.edu. *Application contact:* Peggy Wells, Office Support Specialist, 217-244-2646, Fax: 217-244-8355, E-mail: pwells@illinois.edu.

The University of Iowa, Graduate College, College of Liberal Arts and Sciences, Department of Philosophy, Iowa City, IA 52242-1316. Offers MA, PhD, JD/MA. *Degree requirements:* For master's, thesis optional, exam; for doctorate, comprehensive exam, thesis/dissertation. *Entrance requirements:* For master's, GRE General Test or LSAT, minimum GPA of 3.0; for doctorate, GRE General Test, minimum GPA of 3.0. Additional exam requirements/recommendations for international students: Required—TOEFL (minimum score 550 paper-based; 213 computer-based; 81 iBT). Electronic applications accepted.

The University of Kansas, Graduate Studies, College of Liberal Arts and Sciences, Department of Philosophy, Lawrence, KS 66045. Offers MA, PhD, JD/MA. *Faculty:* 11 full-time (2 women), 1 (woman) part-time/adjunct. *Students:* 35 full-time (8 women), 3 part-time (1 woman); includes 3 minority (1 Black or African American, non-Hispanic/Latino; 1 Asian, non-Hispanic/Latino; 1 Two or more races, non-Hispanic/Latino), 4 international. Average age 31. 28 applicants, 54% accepted, 5 enrolled. In 2010, 5 master's, 1 doctorate awarded. Terminal master's awarded for partial completion of doctoral program. *Degree requirements:* For master's, comprehensive exam, thesis or alternative; for doctorate, one foreign language, comprehensive exam, thesis/dissertation. *Entrance requirements:* For master's and doctorate, GRE. Additional exam requirements/recommendations for international students: Required—TOEFL. *Application deadline:* For fall admission, 2/1 priority date for domestic students, 6/15 for international students. Applications are processed on a rolling basis. Application fee: $55 ($65 for international students). Electronic applications accepted. *Expenses:* Tuition, state resident: full-time $7092; part-time $295.50 per credit hour. Tuition, nonresident: full-time $16,590; part-time $691.25 per credit hour. Required fees: $858; $71.49 per credit hour. Tuition and fees vary according to course load, campus/location and program. *Financial support:* Fellowships, teaching assistantships with full tuition reimbursements available. Financial award application deadline: 1/5. *Faculty research:* Theoretical and applied ethics, social and political philosophy, history of philosophy, analytic philosophy, philosophy of mind and language. *Unit head:* Prof. Ben Eggleston, Chair, 785-864-2332, Fax: 785-864-4298, E-mail: eggleston@ku.edu. *Application contact:* Prof. Dale Dorsey, Director of Graduate Studies, 785-864-2139, Fax: 785-864-4298, E-mail: ddorsey@ku.edu.

University of Kentucky, Graduate School, College of Arts and Sciences, Program in Philosophy, Lexington, KY 40506-0032. Offers MA, PhD. *Degree requirements:* For master's, one foreign language, comprehensive exam, thesis; for doctorate, one foreign language, comprehensive exam, thesis/dissertation. *Entrance requirements:* For master's, GRE General Test, minimum undergraduate GPA of 2.75; for doctorate, GRE General Test, minimum graduate GPA of 3.0. Additional exam requirements/recommendations for international students: Required—TOEFL (minimum score 550 paper-based; 213 computer-based). Electronic applications accepted. *Faculty research:* History of philosophy, history and philosophy of science, ethics, social and political philosophy.

University of Lethbridge, School of Graduate Studies, Lethbridge, AB T1K 3M4, Canada. Offers accounting (MScM); addictions counseling (M Sc); agricultural biotechnology (M Sc); agricultural studies (M Sc, MA); anthropology (MA); archaeology (MA); art (MA, MFA); biochemistry (M Sc); biological sciences (M Sc); biomolecular science (PhD); biosystems and biodiversity (PhD); Canadian studies (MA); chemistry (M Sc); computer science (M Sc); computer science and geographical information science (M Sc); counseling psychology (M Ed); dramatic arts (MA); earth, space, and physical science (PhD); economics (MA); educational leadership (M Ed); English (MA); environmental science (M Sc); evolution and behavior (PhD); exercise science (M Sc); finance (MScM); French (MA); French/German (MA); French/Spanish (MA); general education (M Ed); general management (MScM); geography (M Sc, MA); German (MA); health science (M Sc); history (MA); human resource management and labour relations (MScM); individualized multidisciplinary (M Sc, MA); information systems (MScM); international management (MScM); kinesiology (M Sc, MA); management (M Sc, MA); marketing (MScM); mathematics (M Sc); music (M Mus, MA); Native American studies (MA); neuroscience (M Sc, PhD); new media (MA); nursing (M Sc); philosophy (MA); physics (M Sc); policy and strategy (MScM); political science (MA); psychology (M Sc, MA); religious studies (MA); social sciences (MA); sociology (MA); theatre and dramatic arts (MFA); theoretical and computational science (PhD); urban and regional studies (MA); women's studies (MA). Part-time and evening/weekend programs available. *Degree requirements:* For doctorate, comprehensive exam, thesis/dissertation. *Entrance requirements:* For master's, GMAT (M Sc in management), bachelor's degree in related field, minimum GPA of 3.0 during previous 20 graded semester courses, 2 years teaching or related experience (M Ed); for doctorate, master's degree, minimum graduate GPA of 3.5. Additional exam requirements/recommendations for international students: Required—TOEFL. *Faculty research:* Movement and brain plasticity, gibberellin physiology, photosynthesis, carbon cycling, molecular properties of main-group ring components.

University of Louisville, Graduate School, College of Arts and Sciences, Department of Philosophy, Louisville, KY 40292-0001. Offers MA. *Degree requirements:* For master's, one foreign language, thesis or alternative. *Entrance requirements:* For master's, GRE General Test. *Application deadline:* Applications are processed on a rolling basis. Application fee: $50. *Expenses:* Tuition, state resident: full-time $9144; part-time $508 per credit hour. Tuition, nonresident: full-time $19,026; part-time $1057 per credit hour. Tuition and fees vary according to program and reciprocity agreements. *Unit head:* Dr. Robert Kimball, Chair, 502-852-0488, Fax: 502-852-0459, E-mail: robert.kimball@louisville.edu. *Application contact:* Libby Leggett, Director, Graduate Admissions, 502-852-3101, Fax: 502-852-6536, E-mail: gradadm@louisville.edu.

The University of Manchester, School of Social Sciences, Manchester, United Kingdom. Offers ethnographic documentary (M Phil); interdisciplinary study of culture (PhD); philosophy (PhD); politics (PhD); social anthropology (PhD); social anthropology with visual media (PhD); social change (PhD); social statistics (PhD); sociology (PhD); visual anthropology (M Phil).

University of Manitoba, Faculty of Graduate Studies, Faculty of Arts, Department of Philosophy, Winnipeg, MB R3T 2N2, Canada. Offers MA. *Degree requirements:* For master's, variable foreign language requirement, thesis or alternative.

University of Maryland, College Park, Academic Affairs, College of Arts and Humanities, Department of Philosophy, College Park, MD 20742. Offers MA, PhD. *Faculty:* 19 full-time (5 women), 6 part-time/adjunct (1 woman). *Students:* 32 full-time (5 women), 5 part-time (0 women); includes 5 minority (1 American Indian or Alaska Native, non-Hispanic/Latino; 2 Asian, non-Hispanic/Latino; 2 Hispanic/Latino), 10 international. 151 applicants, 3% accepted, 3 enrolled. In 2010, 3 master's, 3 doctorates awarded. *Degree requirements:* For master's, thesis optional; for doctorate, thesis/dissertation, 2 semesters of undergraduate teaching, qualification in symbolic logic. *Entrance requirements:* For master's, GRE General Test, minimum GPA of 3.0, philosophy paper, writing sample, 3 letters of recommendation; for doctorate, GRE General Test, minimum GPA of 3.0, philosophy paper, writing sample. *Application deadline:* For fall admission, 1/3 for domestic and international students. Applications are processed on a rolling basis. Application fee: $75. Electronic applications accepted. *Expenses:* Tuition, state resident: part-time $471 per credit hour. Tuition, nonresident: part-time $1016 per credit hour. Required fees: $337 per term. *Financial support:* In 2010–11, 1 fellowship with partial tuition reimbursement (averaging $10,800 per year), 31 teaching assistantships (averaging $17,173 per year) were awarded; research assistantships, Federal Work-Study and scholarships/grants also available. Support available to part-time students. Financial award applicants required to submit FAFSA. *Faculty research:* Contemporary British and American philosophy, the relationship between philosophy and other disciplines, ethical and conceptual issues in public policy. Total annual research expenditures: $107,217. *Unit head:* Paul Pietroski, Chair, 301-405-5718, E-mail: pietro@umd.edu. *Application contact:* Dr. Charles A. Caramello, Dean of Graduate School, 301-405-0358, Fax: 301-314-9305, E-mail: ccaramel@umd.edu.

University of Massachusetts Amherst, Graduate School, College of Humanities and Fine Arts, Department of Philosophy, Amherst, MA 01003. Offers MA, PhD. Part-time programs available. *Faculty:* 17 full-time (5 women). *Students:* 25 full-time (8 women), 13 part-time (1 woman); includes 3 minority (1 Black or African American, non-Hispanic/Latino; 1 Hispanic/Latino; 1 Two or more races, non-Hispanic/Latino), 7 international. Average age 30. 145 applicants, 14% accepted, 7 enrolled. In 2010, 2 master's, 5 doctorates awarded. Terminal master's awarded for partial completion of doctoral program. *Degree requirements:* For master's, thesis optional; for doctorate, comprehensive exam, thesis/dissertation. *Entrance requirements:* For master's and doctorate, GRE General Test, writing sample, 3 letters of recommendation. Additional exam requirements/recommendations for international students: Required—TOEFL (minimum score 550 paper-based; 213 computer-based; 80 iBT), IELTS (minimum score 6.5). *Application deadline:* For fall admission, 1/2 for domestic and international students. Applications are processed on a rolling basis. Application fee: $50 ($65 for international students). Electronic applications accepted. *Expenses:* Tuition, state resident: full-time $2640. Required fees: $8282. One-time fee: $357 full-time. *Financial support:* In 2010–11, 6 fellowships with full tuition reimbursements (averaging $10,417 per year), 1 research assistantship with full tuition reimbursement (averaging $3,629 per year), 24 teaching assistantships with full tuition reimbursements (averaging $10,831 per year) were awarded; career-related internships or fieldwork, Federal Work-Study, scholarships/grants, traineeships, health care benefits, tuition waivers (full), and unspecified assistantships also available. Support available to part-time students. Financial award application deadline: 1/2; financial award applicants required to submit FAFSA. *Unit head:* Dr. Fred A. Feldman, Graduate Program Director, 413-545-2330, Fax: 413-577-3800. *Application contact:* Jean M. Ames, Supervisor of Admissions, 413-545-0722, Fax: 413-577-0010, E-mail: gradadm@grad.umass.edu.

University of Memphis, Graduate School, College of Arts and Sciences, Department of Philosophy, Memphis, TN 38152. Offers MA, PhD. Part-time and evening/weekend programs available. *Faculty:* 9 full-time (3 women), 1 part-time/adjunct (0 women). *Students:* 26 full-time (11 women), 9 part-time (6 women); includes 7 Black or African American, non-Hispanic/Latino; 1 Asian, non-Hispanic/Latino; 1 Hispanic/Latino, 4 international. Average age 30. 95 applicants, 26% accepted, 7 enrolled. In 2010, 14 master's, 2 doctorates awarded. Terminal master's awarded for partial completion of doctoral program. *Degree requirements:* For master's, comprehensive exam, thesis optional, 33 hours of class work; for doctorate, 2 foreign languages, comprehensive exam, thesis/dissertation, 72 hours of class work. *Entrance requirements:* For master's, GRE General Test, minimum GPA of 2.5, 18 hours of undergraduate course work in philosophy, 3 letters of recommendation, writing sample; for doctorate, GRE General Test, minimum GPA of 3.0, bachelor's degree in philosophy, 3 letters of recommendation, writing sample. Additional exam requirements/recommendations for international students: Required—TOEFL (minimum score 550 paper-based; 210 computer-based). *Application deadline:* For fall admission, 1/15 for domestic students. Application fee: $35 ($60 for international students). *Financial support:* In 2010–11, 9 students received support; fellowships with full tuition reimbursements available, research assistantships with full tuition reimbursements available, teaching assistantships with full tuition reimbursements available, Federal Work-Study, scholarships/grants, tuition waivers (full), and unspecified assistantships available. Financial award application deadline: 2/15; financial award applicants required to submit FAFSA. *Faculty research:* Continental philosophy, ethics, analytic philosophy, feminist theory, Africana philosophy. *Unit head:* Dr. Deborah Tollefsen, Chair, 901-678-2535, Fax: 901-678-4365, E-mail: dtollfsn@memphis.edu. *Application contact:* Dr. Mary Beth Mader, Coordinator of Admission, 901-678-4526.

University of Miami, Graduate School, College of Arts and Sciences, Department of Philosophy, Coral Gables, FL 33124. Offers MA, PhD. Part-time programs available. Terminal master's awarded for partial completion of doctoral program. *Degree requirements:* For master's, thesis or alternative; for doctorate, comprehensive exam, thesis/dissertation. *Entrance requirements:* For master's, GRE General Test; for doctorate, GRE General Test, minimum GPA of 3.0, 3 letters of recommendation, writing sample. Additional exam requirements/recommendations for international students: Required—TOEFL. Electronic applications accepted. *Faculty research:* Ethics, epistemology, pragmatism, philosophy of science, metaphysics.

University of Michigan, Horace H. Rackham School of Graduate Studies, College of Literature, Science, and the Arts, Department of Philosophy, Ann Arbor, MI 48109. Offers AM, PhD. *Faculty:* 21 full-time (5 women), 2 part-time/adjunct (0 women). *Students:* 34 full-time (6 women); includes 1 American Indian or Alaska Native, non-Hispanic/Latino; 2 Asian, non-Hispanic/Latino; 1 Hispanic/Latino, 8 international. Average age 28. 209 applicants, 9% accepted, 6 enrolled. In 2010, 8 master's, 8 doctorates awarded. Terminal master's awarded for partial completion of doctoral program. *Degree requirements:* For doctorate, one foreign language, thesis/dissertation, oral defense of dissertation. *Entrance requirements:* For master's and doctorate, GRE General Test, 3 letters of recommendation, writing sample. Additional exam requirements/recommendations for international students: Required—TOEFL (minimum score 560 paper-based; 84 iBT). *Application deadline:* For fall admission, 1/15 for domestic and international students. Application fee: $65 ($75 for international students). Electronic applications accepted. *Expenses:* Tuition, state resident: full-time $17,784; part-time $1116 per credit hour. Tuition, nonresident: full-time $35,944; part-time $2125 per credit hour. International tuition: $35,994 full-time. Required fees: $95 per semester. Tuition and fees vary according to course load, degree level and program. *Financial support:* In 2010–11, 32 students received support, including fellowships with full tuition reimbursements available (averaging $17,200 per year), teaching assistantships with full tuition reimbursements available (averaging $17,200 per year); health care benefits also available. Financial award application deadline: 1/15. *Faculty research:* Ethics, metaphysics, philosophy of language and mind, political and social philosophy, philosophy of science. *Unit head:* Laura Ruetsche, Chair, 734-764-6285, Fax: 734-763-8071, E-mail: ruetsche@umich.edu. *Application contact:* Linda Shultes, Graduate Program Coordinator, 734-764-3260, Fax: 734-763-8071, E-mail: phil-admissions@umich.edu.

University of Minnesota, Twin Cities Campus, Graduate School, College of Liberal Arts, Department of Philosophy, Minneapolis, MN 55455-0213. Offers MA, PhD. Part-time programs available. Terminal master's awarded for partial completion of doctoral program. *Degree requirements:* For master's, comprehensive exam, thesis or 3 papers; oral exam; for doctorate, comprehensive exam, thesis/dissertation. *Entrance requirements:* For master's and doctorate, GRE. Additional exam requirements/recommendations for international students: Required—TOEFL (minimum score 550 paper-based; 213 computer-based), IELTS (minimum score 6.5), or Michigan English Language Assessment Battery (minimum score 80). Electronic applications accepted. *Faculty research:* Philosophy of science; ethics and social/political philosophy; logic, language, and mind.

University of Mississippi, Graduate School, College of Liberal Arts, Department of Philosophy and Religions, Oxford, University, MS 38677. Offers philosophy (MA). *Students:* 7 full-time (2 women), 2 part-time (0 women). In 2010, 4 master's awarded. *Degree requirements:* For master's, thesis. *Entrance requirements:* For master's, GRE General Test, minimum GPA of 3.0. Additional exam requirements/recommendations for international students: Required—TOEFL. *Application deadline:* For fall admission, 4/1 for domestic students; for spring admission, 10/1 for domestic students. Applications are processed on a rolling basis. Application fee: $25. Electronic applications accepted. *Financial support:* Scholarships/grants available. Financial award application deadline: 3/1; financial award applicants required to submit FAFSA. *Unit head:* Dr. William Lawhead, Chair, 662-915-7020, Fax: 662-915-5654, E-mail: wlawhead@olemiss.edu. *Application contact:* Dr. Christy M. Wyandt, Associate Dean, 662-915-7474, Fax: 662-915-7577, E-mail: cwyandt@olemiss.edu.

University of Missouri, Graduate School, College of Arts and Sciences, Department of Philosophy, Columbia, MO 65211. Offers MA, PhD. *Faculty:* 14 full-time (2 women), 4 part-time/adjunct (1 woman). *Students:* 23 full-time (3 women), 5 international. Average age 29. 41 applicants, 20% accepted, 5 enrolled. In 2010, 5 master's, 3 doctorates awarded. Terminal master's awarded for partial completion of doctoral program. *Degree requirements:* For doctorate, one foreign language, comprehensive exam, thesis/dissertation. *Entrance requirements:* For master's and doctorate, GRE General Test (minimum score 650 verbal, 700 quantitative), minimum GPA of 3.0, 3.9 in major. Additional exam requirements/recommendations for international students: Required—TOEFL (minimum score 500 paper-based; 173 computer-based; 61 iBT). *Application deadline:* For fall admission, 1/15 priority date for domestic students. Applications are processed on a rolling basis. Application fee: $45 ($60 for international students). Electronic applications accepted. *Financial support:* In 2010–11, 3 fellowships with full tuition reimbursements, 1 research assistantship with full tuition reimbursement, 22 teaching assistantships with full tuition reimbursements were awarded; institutionally sponsored loans, health care benefits, and unspecified assistantships also available. Financial award application deadline: 2/1. *Faculty research:* Epistemology, political philosophy, philosophy of biology, decision/game/rational choice theory, ethics, philosophy of mind and psychology, Indian philosophy, metaphysics, action theory. *Unit head:* Dr. Andrew Melnyk, Department Chair, 573-882-1278, E-mail: melnyka@missouri.edu. *Application contact:* Jonni Paxton, Administrative Assistant, 573-882-2871, E-mail: paxtonj@missouri.edu.

University of Missouri–St. Louis, College of Arts and Sciences, Department of Philosophy, St. Louis, MO 63121. Offers MA. *Faculty:* 10 full-time (4 women), 4 part-time/adjunct (0 women). *Students:* 15 full-time (6 women), 12 part-time (1 woman); includes 2 minority (1 Asian, non-Hispanic/Latino; 1 Hispanic/Latino). Average age 27. 33 applicants, 76% accepted, 10 enrolled. In 2010, 11 master's awarded. *Entrance requirements:* For master's, writing sample, 3 letters of recommendation. Additional exam requirements/recommendations for international students: Required—TOEFL (minimum score 550 paper-based; 213 computer-based). *Application deadline:* For fall admission, 7/1 priority date for domestic and international students; for spring admission, 12/1 priority date for domestic and international students. Applications are processed on a rolling basis. Application fee: $35 ($40 for international students). Electronic applications accepted. *Expenses:* Tuition, state resident: full-time $5522; part-time $306.80 per credit hour. Tuition, nonresident: full-time $14,253; part-time $792.10 per credit hour. Required fees: $658; $49 per credit hour. One-time fee: $12. Tuition and fees vary according to program. *Financial support:* In 2010–11, 1 research assistantship with full and partial tuition reimbursement (averaging $5,400 per year), 15 teaching assistantships with full and partial tuition reimbursements (averaging $6,615 per year) were awarded. Financial award applicants required to submit FAFSA. *Faculty research:* Ethics, philosophy and history of science, philosophical social science, aesthetics. *Unit head:* Dr. Berit Brogaard, Graduate Program Director, 314-516-5631, Fax: 314-516-5816, E-mail: brogaardb@umsl.edu. *Application contact:* 314-516-5458, Fax: 314-516-6996, E-mail: gradadm@umsl.edu.

The University of Montana, Graduate School, College of Arts and Sciences, Department of Philosophy, Missoula, MT 59812-0002. Offers MA. *Degree requirements:* For master's, thesis or additional course work/professional paper. *Entrance requirements:* For master's, GRE General Test. Additional exam requirements/recommendations for international students: Required—TOEFL (minimum score 525 paper-based; 197 computer-based). *Faculty research:* Philosophy of law, natural science, feminism, and technology; environmental, business, and medical ethics.

University of Nebraska–Lincoln, Graduate College, College of Arts and Sciences, Department of Philosophy, Lincoln, NE 68588. Offers MA, PhD. *Degree requirements:* For master's, thesis optional; for doctorate, comprehensive exam, thesis/dissertation. *Entrance requirements:* For master's and doctorate, GRE General Test, writing sample. Additional exam requirements/recommendations for international students: Required—TOEFL (minimum score 600 paper-based; 250 computer-based). Electronic applications accepted. *Faculty research:* Ethics, epistemology, metaphysics, cognitive science, history of philosophy.

University of Nevada, Reno, Graduate School, College of Liberal Arts, Department of Philosophy, Reno, NV 89557. Offers MA. *Degree requirements:* For master's, thesis optional. *Entrance requirements:* For master's, GRE General Test, minimum GPA of 2.75. Additional exam requirements/recommendations for international students: Required—TOEFL (minimum score 500 paper-based; 173 computer-based; 61 iBT), IELTS (minimum score 6). Electronic applications accepted. *Expenses:* Tuition, state resident: full-time $2219; part-time $246 per credit. Tuition, nonresident: part-time $510 per credit. International tuition: $9009 full-time. Required fees: $59 per term. One-time fee: $101. Tuition and fees vary according to course load. *Faculty research:* Ancient philosophy (Aristotle), ethics, political theory, violence, Continental philosophy.

University of New Brunswick Fredericton, School of Graduate Studies, Policy Studies Program, Fredericton, NB E3B 5A3, Canada. Offers people, property and alternative dispute resolution (M Phil); philosophy politics and economics (M Phil); sustainable development (M Phil). Part-time programs available. *Faculty:* 7 full-time (4 women), 8 part-time/adjunct (4 women). *Students:* 4 full-time (2 women), 5 part-time (3 women). In 2010, 3 master's awarded. *Degree requirements:* For master's, thesis, report. *Entrance requirements:* For master's, minimum GPA of 3.5. Additional exam requirements/recommendations for international students: Required—TWE (minimum score 4), TOEFL (minimum score 600 paper-based; 250 computer-based; 100 iBT) or IELTS (minimum score 7). Application fee: $50 Canadian dollars. *Expenses:* Tuition, area resident: Full-time $3708; part-time $927 per term. International tuition: $6300 full-time. Required fees: $50 per term. *Financial support:* In 2010–11, 3 fellowships, research assistantships (averaging $5,600 per year), teaching assistantships (averaging $4,400 per year) were awarded. *Unit head:* Dr. Linda Eyre, Dean of Graduate Studies, 506-447-3044, Fax: 506-453-4817, E-mail: gradidst@unb.ca. *Application contact:* Janet Amurault, Graduate Secretary, 506-458-7558, Fax: 506-453-4817, E-mail: jamiraul@unb.ca.

University of New Mexico, Graduate School, College of Arts and Sciences, Department of Philosophy, Albuquerque, NM 87131-2039. Offers MA, PhD. Part-time programs available. *Faculty:* 25 full-time (6 women), 20 part-time/adjunct (6 women). *Students:* 32 full-time (7 women), 16 part-time (4 women); includes 1 American Indian or Alaska Native, non-Hispanic/Latino; 2 Asian, non-Hispanic/Latino; 4 Hispanic/Latino; 1 Two or more races, non-Hispanic/Latino, 3 international. Average age 32. 88 applicants, 34% accepted, 14 enrolled. In 2010, 4 master's, 2 doctorates awarded. Terminal master's awarded for partial completion of doctoral program. *Degree requirements:* For master's, thesis (for some programs); for doctorate, one foreign language, comprehensive exam, thesis/dissertation. *Entrance requirements:* For master's and doctorate, GRE. Additional exam requirements/recommendations for international students: Required—TOEFL. *Application deadline:* For fall admission, 1/31 for domestic and international students; for spring admission, 11/1 for domestic and international students. Application fee: $50. Electronic applications accepted. *Expenses:* Tuition, state resident: full-time $5991; part-time $251 per credit hour. Tuition, nonresident: full-time $14,405; part-time $800.20 per credit hour. Tuition and fees vary according to course level, course load, program and reciprocity agreements. *Financial support:* In 2010–11, 35 students received support, including fellowships with tuition reimbursements available (averaging $7,200 per year), 1 research assistantship (averaging $10,000 per year), 13 teaching assistantships with tuition reimbursements available (averaging $13,286 per year). Financial award application deadline: 1/31; financial award applicants required to submit FAFSA. *Faculty research:* Continental philosophy, Indian philosophy, history of philosophy, ethics, phenomenology, philosophy of art and literature. *Unit head:* Dr. John Bussanich, Chair, 505-277-8938, Fax: 505-277-6362, E-mail: john.bussanich@gmail.edu. *Application contact:* Shannon Kindilien, Administrative Assistant II, 505-277-2405, Fax: 505-277-6362, E-mail: thinker@unm.edu.

The University of North Carolina at Chapel Hill, Graduate School, College of Arts and Sciences, Department of Philosophy, Chapel Hill, NC 27599. Offers MA, PhD. *Degree requirements:* For master's, comprehensive exam, thesis; for doctorate, comprehensive exam, thesis/dissertation. *Entrance requirements:* For master's and doctorate, GRE General Test, minimum GPA of 3.0.

The University of North Carolina at Charlotte, Graduate School, College of Arts and Sciences, Department of Philosophy, Charlotte, NC 28223-0001. Offers applied ethics (Certificate); ethics and applied philosophy (MA). *Faculty:* 10 full-time (4 women). *Students:* 3 full-time (2 women), 11 part-time (2 women); includes 1 minority (Black or African American, non-Hispanic/Latino). Average age 30. 10 applicants, 70% accepted, 5 enrolled. In 2010, 1 master's awarded. *Degree requirements:* For master's, thesis or alternative. *Application deadline:* For fall admission, 7/15 for domestic students, 5/1 for international students; for spring admission, 11/15 for domestic students, 10/1 for international students. Applications are processed on a rolling basis. Electronic applications accepted. *Expenses:* Tuition, state resident: full-time $3464. Tuition, nonresident: full-time $14,297. Required fees: $2094. Tuition and fees vary according to course load. *Financial support:* In 2010–11, 5 students received support, including 2 teaching assistantships (averaging $2,000 per year); administrative assistantship also available. Total annual research expenditures: $23,076. *Unit head:* Dr. Marvin J. Croy, Interim Chair, 704-687-2174, E-mail: mjcroy@uncc.edu. *Application contact:* Prof. William Gay, Coordinator, 704-687-2161, E-mail: mcgay@uncc.edu.

University of North Florida, College of Arts and Sciences, Department of Philosophy, Jacksonville, FL 32224. Offers applied ethics (Graduate Certificate); practical philosophy and applied ethics (MA). Part-time and evening/weekend programs available. *Faculty:* 10 full-time (3 women). *Students:* 7 full-time (3 women), 8 part-time (5 women); includes 1 Asian, non-Hispanic/Latino. Average age 37. 9 applicants, 78% accepted, 4 enrolled. *Entrance requirements:* For master's, GRE General Test, minimum GPA of 3.0 in last 60 hours, 3 letters of recommendation, writing sample. Additional exam requirements/recommendations for international students: Required—TOEFL (minimum score 500 paper-based; 173 computer-based; 61 iBT). *Application deadline:* For fall admission, 7/1 priority date for domestic students, 5/1 for international students. Applications are processed on a rolling basis. Application fee: $30. Electronic applications accepted. *Expenses:* Tuition, state resident: full-time $7646.40; part-time $318.60 per credit hour. Tuition, nonresident: full-time $23,502; part-time $979.24 per credit hour. Required fees: $1208.88; $50.37 per credit hour. Tuition and fees vary according to course load and program. *Financial support:* In 2010–11, 3 students received support, including 1 research assistantship (averaging $6,315 per year); teaching assistantships, Federal Work-Study, scholarships/grants, tuition waivers, and unspecified assistantships also available. Financial award application deadline: 4/1; financial award applicants required to submit FAFSA. *Faculty research:* Late modern philosophy, pragmatism, religion and American culture, hermeneutics, philosophy of mind. Total annual research expenditures: $42,164. *Unit head:* Dr. Hans-Herbert Koegler, 904-620-1330, Fax: 904-620-1840, E-mail: hkoegler@unf.edu. *Application contact:* Lillith Richardson, Assistant Director, The Graduate School, 904-620-1360, Fax: 904-620-1362, E-mail: graduateschool@unf.edu.

University of North Texas, Toulouse Graduate School, College of Arts and Sciences, Department of Philosophy and Religion Studies, Denton, TX 76203. Offers philosophy (MA, PhD). *Degree requirements:* For master's, one foreign language, thesis or alternative; for doctorate, one foreign language, comprehensive exam, thesis/dissertation. *Entrance requirements:* For master's, GRE General Test. Additional exam requirements/recommendations for international students: Recommended—TOEFL (minimum score 550 paper-based; 213 computer-based; 79 iBT). *Expenses:* Tuition, state resident: full-time $4298; part-time $239 per credit hour. Tuition, nonresident: full-time $10,782; part-time $549 per credit hour. Required fees: $1292; $270 per credit hour. *Financial support:* Application deadline: 4/1. *Application contact:* Associate Dean, 940-565-2383, Fax: 940-565-2141.

University of Notre Dame, Graduate School, College of Arts and Letters, Division of Humanities, Department of Philosophy, Notre Dame, IN 46556. Offers PhD. *Degree requirements:* For doctorate, 2 foreign languages, thesis/dissertation, candidacy exam. *Entrance requirements:* For doctorate, GRE General Test. Additional exam requirements/recommendations for international students: Required—TOEFL (minimum score 600 paper-based; 250 computer-based; 80 iBT). Electronic applications accepted. *Faculty research:* History of philosophy, ethics, philosophy of science and logic, philosophy of religion, Continental philosophy, metaphysics.

University of Oklahoma, College of Arts and Sciences, Department of Philosophy, Norman, OK 73019. Offers MA, PhD. Part-time and evening/weekend programs available. *Faculty:* 14 full-time (3 women). *Students:* 26 full-time (1 woman), 10 part-time (2 women); includes 2 minority (1 Asian, non-Hispanic/Latino; 1 Hispanic/Latino). Average age 29. 40 applicants, 45% accepted, 9 enrolled. In 2010, 4 master's, 3 doctorates awarded. Terminal master's awarded for partial completion of doctoral program. *Degree requirements:* For master's, thesis optional; for doctorate, thesis/dissertation, oral and written exams. *Entrance requirements:* For master's and doctorate, GRE General Test, 3 letters of recommendation, writing sample. Additional exam requirements/recommendations for international students: Required—TOEFL (minimum score 550 paper-based; 213 computer-based; 79 iBT). *Application deadline:* For fall admission, 2/1 priority date for domestic and international students; for spring admission, 11/1 for domestic students, 9/1 for international students. Applications are processed on a rolling basis. Application fee: $40 ($90 for international students). Electronic applications accepted. *Expenses:* Tuition, state resident: full-time $3893; part-time $162.20 per credit hour. Tuition, nonresident: full-time $14,167; part-time $590.30 per credit hour. Required fees: $2523; $94.60 per credit hour. Tuition and fees vary according to course load and degree level. *Financial support:* In 2010–11, 35 students received support, including 2 fellowships (averaging $5,000 per year), 3 research assistantships with partial tuition reimbursements available (averaging $15,471 per year), 18 teaching assistantships with partial tuition reimbursements available (averaging $12,693 per year); health care benefits and unspecified assistantships also available. Financial award application deadline: 2/28; financial award applicants required to submit FAFSA. *Faculty research:* Metaphysics, epistemology, aesthetics, ethics, Chinese philosophy. Total annual research expenditures: $99,210. *Unit head:* Dr. Hugh Benson, Chair, 405-325-6324, Fax: 405-325-2660, E-mail: hbenson@ou.edu. *Application contact:* Wayne Riggs, Director of Graduate Studies, 405-325-6324, Fax: 405-325-2660, E-mail: wriggs@ou.edu.

University of Oregon, Graduate School, College of Arts and Sciences, Department of Philosophy, Eugene, OR 97403. Offers MA, PhD. Terminal master's awarded for partial completion of doctoral program. *Degree requirements:* For master's, one foreign language, thesis or alternative; for doctorate, one foreign language, thesis/dissertation. *Entrance requirements:* For master's and doctorate, GRE General Test. Additional exam requirements/recommendations for international students: Required—TOEFL. *Faculty research:* Social and political philosophy, feminist philosophy, American philosophy, aesthetics, philosophy of mind.

University of Ottawa, Faculty of Graduate and Postdoctoral Studies, Faculty of Arts, Department of Philosophy, Ottawa, ON K1N 6N5, Canada. Offers MA, PhD. *Degree requirements:* For master's, thesis or alternative; for doctorate, comprehensive exam, thesis/dissertation. *Entrance requirements:* For master's, honors degree or equivalent, minimum B average; for doctorate, master's degree, minimum B+ average. Electronic applications accepted. *Faculty research:* History of philosophy (ancient, medieval, modern and contemporary); metaphysics/epistemology; value theory: political philosophy, ethics.

University of Pennsylvania, School of Arts and Sciences, Graduate Group in Philosophy, Philadelphia, PA 19104. Offers AM, PhD, JD/PhD. *Faculty:* 16 full-time (6 women), 2 part-time/adjunct (0 women). *Students:* 30 full-time (11 women), 1 (woman) part-time; includes 1 Hispanic/Latino, 10 international. 143 applicants, 8% accepted, 5 enrolled. In 2010, 1 master's, 3 doctorates awarded. Terminal master's awarded for partial completion of doctoral program. *Degree requirements:* For master's, thesis; for doctorate, thesis/dissertation, 1 year of teaching experience. *Application deadline:* For fall admission, 12/1 priority date for domestic students. Application fee: $70. Electronic applications accepted. *Expenses:* Tuition: Full-time $25,660; part-time $4758 per course. Required fees: $2152; $270 per course. Tuition and fees vary according to course load, degree level and program. *Financial support:* Fellowships, teaching assistantships, institutionally sponsored loans, scholarships/grants, traineeships, health care benefits, and unspecified assistantships available. Financial award application deadline: 12/15. *Unit head:* Susan Meyer, Department Chair, Philosophy, 215-898-8950, E-mail: smeyer@phil.upenn.edu. *Application contact:* Susan Meyer, Department Chair, Philosophy, 215-898-8950, E-mail: smeyer@phil.upenn.edu.

University of Pittsburgh, School of Arts and Sciences, Department of History and Philosophy of Science, Pittsburgh, PA 15260. Offers MA, PhD. *Faculty:* 8 full-time (1 woman), 1 part-time/

Philosophy

University of Pittsburgh (continued)

adjunct (0 women). *Students:* 30 full-time (9 women), 1 part-time (0 women); includes 5 Asian, non-Hispanic/Latino, 5 international. Average age 29. 63 applicants, 11% accepted, 3 enrolled. In 2010, 1 doctorate awarded. Terminal master's awarded for partial completion of doctoral program. *Degree requirements:* For master's, one foreign language, comprehensive exam; for doctorate, 2 foreign languages, comprehensive exam, thesis/dissertation. *Entrance requirements:* For master's and doctorate, GRE General Test. Additional exam requirements/recommendations for international students: Required—TOEFL (minimum score 550 paper-based; 213 computer-based). *Application deadline:* For fall admission, 1/10 for domestic and international students. Application fee: $50. Electronic applications accepted. *Expenses:* Tuition, state resident: full-time $17,304; part-time $701 per credit. Tuition, nonresident: full-time $29,554; part-time $1210 per credit. Required fees: $740; $214 per term. Tuition and fees vary according to program. *Financial support:* In 2010–11, 25 students received support, including 14 fellowships with full tuition reimbursements available, 11 teaching assistantships with full tuition reimbursements available; health care benefits also available. Financial award application deadline: 1/10. *Faculty research:* History and philosophy of biology, psychology, neuroscience; history and philosophy of physics; early modern science; rhetoric of science; philosophy of social science. *Unit head:* Dr. Sandra Mitchell, Chairman, 412-624-5896, Fax: 412-624-6825, E-mail: smitchel@pitt.edu. *Application contact:* Joann McIntyre, Graduate Admissions Secretary, 412-624-5896, Fax: 412-624-6825, E-mail: vanna@pitt.edu.

University of Pittsburgh, School of Arts and Sciences, Department of Philosophy, Pittsburgh, PA 15260. Offers MA, PhD. *Faculty:* 18 full-time (2 women). *Students:* 69 full-time (18 women); includes 2 Black or African American, non-Hispanic/Latino; 1 American Indian or Alaska Native, non-Hispanic/Latino; 6 Asian, non-Hispanic/Latino; 1 Hispanic/Latino, 21 international. 212 applicants, 8% accepted, 7 enrolled. In 2010, 3 master's, 6 doctorates awarded. Terminal master's awarded for partial completion of doctoral program. *Degree requirements:* For master's, one foreign language; for doctorate, one foreign language, thesis/dissertation. *Entrance requirements:* For master's and doctorate, GRE General Test. Additional exam requirements/recommendations for international students: Required—TOEFL (minimum score 550 paper-based; 213 computer-based; 79 iBT), IELTS (minimum score 6.5). *Application deadline:* For fall admission, 1/10 for domestic and international students. Application fee: $50. Electronic applications accepted. *Expenses:* Tuition, state resident: full-time $17,304; part-time $701 per credit. Tuition, nonresident: full-time $29,554; part-time $1210 per credit. Required fees: $740; $214 per term. Tuition and fees vary according to program. *Financial support:* In 2010–11, 52 students received support, including 20 fellowships with full tuition reimbursements available (averaging $24,774 per year), 2 research assistantships with full tuition reimbursements available (averaging $16,140 per year), 30 teaching assistantships with full tuition reimbursements available (averaging $16,140 per year); Federal Work-Study, scholarships/grants, health care benefits, and tuition waivers (full and partial) also available. Financial award application deadline: 1/10. *Faculty research:* Metaphysics and epistemology, ethics, philosophy of science, history of philosophy, logic. *Unit head:* Dr. Mark Wilson, Chairman, 412-624-5768, Fax: 412-624-5377, E-mail: mawilson@pitt.edu. *Application contact:* Dr. Mark Wilson, Chairman, 412-624-5768, Fax: 412-624-5377, E-mail: mawilson@pitt.edu.

University of Puerto Rico, Río Piedras, College of Humanities, Department of Philosophy, San Juan, PR 00931-3300. Offers MA. Part-time programs available. *Degree requirements:* For master's, one foreign language, comprehensive exam, thesis. *Entrance requirements:* For master's, PAEG or GRE, interview, minimum GPA of 3.0, letter of recommendation (2).

University of Regina, Faculty of Graduate Studies and Research, Faculty of Arts, Department of Philosophy, Regina, SK S4S 0A2, Canada. Offers MA. Part-time programs available. *Faculty:* 5 full-time (0 women), 1 part-time/adjunct (0 women). *Students:* 2 full-time (1 woman), 1 (woman) part-time. *Degree requirements:* For master's, thesis. *Entrance requirements:* Additional exam requirements/recommendations for international students: Required—TOEFL (minimum score 580 paper-based; 80 iBT). *Application deadline:* Applications are processed on a rolling basis. Application fee: $100. Electronic applications accepted. Tuition and fees charges are reported in Canadian dollars. *Expenses:* Tuition, area resident: Full-time $3244.50 Canadian dollars; part-time $180.25 Canadian dollars per credit hour. International tuition: $4744.50 Canadian dollars full-time. Required fees: $494 Canadian dollars; $115.25 Canadian dollars per credit hour. $115.25 Canadian dollars per semester. Tuition and fees vary according to program. *Financial support:* In 2010–11, 2 teaching assistantships (averaging $6,759 per year) were awarded; fellowships, research assistantships, scholarships/grants also available. Financial award application deadline: 6/15. *Faculty research:* Ethics, politics, religion, history, critical thinking. *Unit head:* Dr. Phillip Hansen, Head, 306-585-4389, Fax: 306-585-4827, E-mail: phillip.hansen@uregina.ca. *Application contact:* Dr. Phillip Hansen, Graduate Program Coordinator, 306-585-4389, Fax: 306-585-7827, E-mail: phillip.hansen@uregina.ca.

University of Regina, Faculty of Graduate Studies and Research, Faculty of Arts, Program in Social and Political Thought, Regina, SK S4S 0A2, Canada. Offers MA. Part-time programs available. *Faculty:* 1 (woman) full-time. *Students:* 3 full-time (1 woman). 1 applicant, 100% accepted. In 2010, 3 master's awarded. *Degree requirements:* For master's, thesis. *Entrance requirements:* Additional exam requirements/recommendations for international students: Required—TOEFL (minimum score 580 paper-based; 80 iBT). *Application deadline:* For fall admission, 3/15 for domestic and international students. Application fee: $100. Electronic applications accepted. Tuition and fees charges are reported in Canadian dollars. *Expenses:* Tuition, area resident: Full-time $3244.50 Canadian dollars; part-time $180.25 Canadian dollars per credit hour. International tuition: $4744.50 Canadian dollars full-time. Required fees: $494 Canadian dollars; $115.25 Canadian dollars per credit hour. $115.25 Canadian dollars per semester. Tuition and fees vary according to program. *Financial support:* In 2010–11, 1 research assistantship (averaging $16,500 per year) was awarded; fellowships, teaching assistantships, scholarships/grants also available. Financial award application deadline: 5/15. *Faculty research:* Liberalism and freedom, neo-conservatism, Aristotle's ethics, Kant's ethical theory and political philosophy, Hegel's philosophy of right. *Unit head:* Dr. Shadia Drury, Program Coordinator, 306-585-4073, E-mail: shadia.drury@uregina.ca. *Application contact:* Dr. Shadia Drury, Graduate Program Coordinator, 306-585-4073, E-mail: shadia.drury@uregina.ca.

University of Rochester, School of Arts and Sciences, Department of Philosophy, Rochester, NY 14627. Offers MA, PhD. Terminal master's awarded for partial completion of doctoral program. *Degree requirements:* For doctorate, thesis/dissertation, qualifying exam. *Entrance requirements:* For master's, GRE General Test; for doctorate, GRE General Test, sample of written work. Additional exam requirements/recommendations for international students: Required—TOEFL.

University of St. Thomas, Center for Thomistic Studies, Houston, TX 77006-4696. Offers philosophy (MA, PhD). Part-time programs available. *Faculty:* 7 full-time (1 woman). *Students:* 9 full-time (2 women), 22 part-time (2 women); includes 7 minority (2 Asian, non-Hispanic/Latino; 5 Hispanic/Latino), 3 international. Average age 33. 16 applicants, 75% accepted, 8 enrolled. In 2010, 3 master's awarded. Terminal master's awarded for partial completion of doctoral program. *Degree requirements:* For master's, one foreign language, comprehensive exam, thesis (for some programs); for doctorate, 2 foreign languages, comprehensive exam, thesis/dissertation. *Entrance requirements:* For master's, GRE, bachelor's degree with minimum GPA of 3.0 and at least 18 hours of undergraduate philosophy coursework, 3 letters of recommendation from professional educators, writing sample; for doctorate, GRE, MA in philosophy, 3 letters of recommendation from professional educators, writing sample, fulfillment of Latin language requirement (if not available at time of admission, must be completed no later than the third semester of doctoral study). Additional exam requirements/recommendations for international students: Required—TOEFL (minimum score 550 paper-based; 213 computer-based; 80 iBT), ELS exam (level 112). *Application deadline:* Applications are processed on a rolling basis. Application fee: $35. Electronic applications accepted. *Expenses:* Tuition: Full-time $15,696; part-time $872 per credit hour. Required fees: $236; $83 per term. One-time fee: $100. Tuition and fees vary according to course load, campus/location and program. *Financial support:* In 2010–11, 9 students received support. Federal Work-Study, scholarships/grants, unspecified assistantships, and state work-study, institutional employment available. Support available to part-time students. Financial award application deadline: 4/15; financial award applicants required to submit FAFSA. *Faculty research:* Biomedical ethnics, Islamic philosophy, metaphysics, virtue ethics, semiotics. *Unit head:* Dr. Mary Catherine Sommers, Director, 713-525-3591, Fax: 713-942-3464, E-mail: sommers@stthom.edu. *Application contact:* Valerie Hall, Administrative Assistant II, 713-525-3591, Fax: 713-942-3464, E-mail: hallvl@stthom.edu.

University of Saskatchewan, College of Graduate Studies and Research, College of Arts and Sciences, Department of Philosophy, Saskatoon, SK S7N 5A2, Canada. Offers MA. *Degree requirements:* For master's, thesis. *Entrance requirements:* Additional exam requirements/recommendations for international students: Required—TOEFL (minimum score 80 iBT); Recommended—IELTS (minimum score 6.5). Electronic applications accepted.

University of South Africa, College of Human Sciences, Pretoria, South Africa. Offers adult education (M Ed); African languages (MA, PhD); African politics (MA, PhD); Afrikaans (MA, PhD); ancient history (MA, PhD); ancient Near Eastern studies (MA, PhD); anthropology (MA, PhD); applied linguistics (MA); Arabic (MA, PhD); archaeology (MA); art history (MA); Biblical archaeology (MA); Biblical studies (M Th, D Th, PhD); Christian spirituality (M Th, D Th); church history (M Th, D Th); classical studies (MA, PhD); clinical psychology (MA); communication (MA, PhD); comparative education (M Ed, Ed D); consulting psychology (D Admin, D Com, PhD); curriculum studies (M Ed, Ed D); development studies (M Admin, MA, D Admin, PhD); didactics (M Ed, Ed D); education (M Tech); education management (M Ed, Ed D); educational psychology (M Ed); English (MA); environmental education (M Ed); French (MA, PhD); German (MA, PhD); Greek (MA); guidance and counseling (M Ed); health studies (MA, PhD), including health sciences education (MA), health services management (MA), medical and surgical nursing science (critical care general) (MA), midwifery and neonatal nursing science (MA), trauma and emergency care (MA); history (MA, PhD); history of education (Ed D); inclusive education (M Ed, Ed D); information and communications technology policy and regulation (MA); information science (MA, MIS, PhD); international politics (MA, PhD); Islamic studies (MA, PhD); Italian (MA, PhD); Judaica (MA, PhD); linguistics (MA, PhD); mathematical education (M Ed); mathematics education (MA); missiology (M Th, D Th); modern Hebrew (MA, PhD); musicology (MA, MMus, D Mus, PhD); natural science education (M Ed); New Testament (M Th, D Th); Old Testament (D Th); pastoral therapy (M Th, D Th); philosophy (MA); philosophy of education (M Ed, Ed D); politics (MA, PhD); Portuguese (MA, PhD); practical theology (M Th, D Th); psychology (MA, MS, PhD); psychology of education (M Ed, Ed D); public health (MA); religious studies (MA, D Th, PhD); Romance languages (MA); Russian (MA, PhD); Semitic languages (MA, PhD); social behavior studies in HIV/AIDS (MA); social science (mental health) (MA); social science in development studies (MA); social science in psychology (MA); social science in social work (MA); social science in sociology (MA); social work (MSW, DSW, PhD); socio-education (M Ed, Ed D); sociolinguistics (MA); sociology (MA, PhD); Spanish (MA, PhD); systematic theology (M Th, D Th); TESOL (teaching English to speakers of other languages) (MA); theological ethics (M Th, D Th); theory of literature (MA, PhD); urban ministries (D Th); urban ministry (M Th).

University of South Carolina, The Graduate School, College of Arts and Sciences, Department of Philosophy, Columbia, SC 29208. Offers MA, PhD. Part-time programs available. *Degree requirements:* For master's, one foreign language, comprehensive exam, thesis optional; for doctorate, one foreign language, comprehensive exam, thesis/dissertation, candidacy exam. *Entrance requirements:* For master's and doctorate, GRE General Test, 18 hours in philosophy, 3 letters of recommendation, writing sample. Additional exam requirements/recommendations for international students: Required—TOEFL (minimum score 590 paper-based; 243 computer-based). Electronic applications accepted. *Faculty research:* History of philosophy, ethics, philosophy of science, social philosophy.

University of Southern California, Graduate School, Dana and David Dornsife College of Letters, Arts and Sciences, School of Philosophy, Los Angeles, CA 90089. Offers MA, PhD, MA/JD. *Faculty:* 22 full-time (5 women). *Students:* 48 full-time (10 women), 1 (woman) part-time; includes 5 minority (4 Asian, non-Hispanic/Latino; 1 Hispanic/Latino), 13 international. 122 applicants, 12% accepted, 15 enrolled. In 2010, 5 doctorates awarded. *Degree requirements:* For doctorate, one foreign language, thesis/dissertation, area exam, qualifying exam. *Entrance requirements:* For doctorate, GRE general test. Additional exam requirements/recommendations for international students: Required—TOEFL. *Application deadline:* For fall admission, 12/15 priority date for domestic students, 12/1 priority date for international students. Application fee: $85. Electronic applications accepted. *Expenses:* Tuition: Full-time $31,240; part-time $1420 per unit. Required fees: $600. One-time fee: $35 full-time. Full-time tuition and fees vary according to degree level and program. *Financial support:* In 2010–11, 43 students received support, including 20 fellowships with full tuition reimbursements available (averaging $19,000 per year), 1 research assistantship with full tuition reimbursement available (averaging $19,500 per year), 22 teaching assistantships with full tuition reimbursements available (averaging $19,000 per year). Financial award application deadline: 1/1; financial award applicants required to submit FAFSA. *Faculty research:* Logic, epistemology, ethics/metaethics, philosophy of language, philosophy of law. *Unit head:* Dr. Scott Soames, Distinguished Professor and Director, 213-740-0798, Fax: 213-740-5174, E-mail: soames@usc.edu. *Application contact:* Barrington Smith-Seetachitt, Administrative Assistant, 213-740-4084, Fax: 213-740-5174, E-mail: smithsee@usc.edu.

University of South Florida, Graduate School, College of Arts and Sciences, Department of Philosophy, Tampa, FL 33620-9951. Offers MA, PhD. Part-time and evening/weekend programs available. *Faculty:* 9 full-time (3 women). *Students:* 45 full-time (10 women), 24 part-time (4 women); includes 1 Asian, non-Hispanic/Latino; 6 Hispanic/Latino, 4 international. Average age 33. 38 applicants, 61% accepted, 11 enrolled. In 2010, 9 master's, 4 doctorates awarded. Terminal master's awarded for partial completion of doctoral program. *Degree requirements:* For master's, one foreign language, comprehensive exam, thesis or alternative; for doctorate, 2 foreign languages, comprehensive exam, thesis/dissertation. *Entrance requirements:* For master's, GRE General Test, minimum GPA of 3.0 in last 60 hours, references; for doctorate, GRE General Test, writing sample, statement of purpose, references. Additional exam requirements/recommendations for international students: Required—TOEFL (minimum score 550 paper-based; 213 computer-based). *Application deadline:* For fall admission, 2/15 for domestic and international students; for spring admission, 10/15 for domestic students, 8/1 for international students. Application fee: $30. Electronic applications accepted. *Financial support:* In 2010–11, 34 students received support, including 32 teaching assistantships with tuition reimbursements available (averaging $11,361 per year); unspecified assistantships also available. Financial award application deadline: 1/1. *Faculty research:* Ancient philosophy, social philosophy, ethics, continental philosophy, philosophy of science. Total annual research expenditures: $122,832. *Unit head:* Dr. Roger Ariew, Chairperson, 813-974-8207, Fax: 813-974-5914, E-mail: rariew@cas.usf.edu. *Application contact:* Alex Levine, Director, 813-974-5508, Fax: 813-974-5914, E-mail: alevine@cas.usf.edu.

The University of Tennessee, Graduate School, College of Arts and Sciences, Department of Philosophy, Knoxville, TN 37996. Offers medical ethics (MA, PhD); philosophy (MA, PhD); religious studies (MA). Part-time programs available. *Degree requirements:* For master's, thesis or alternative; for doctorate, one foreign language, thesis/dissertation. *Entrance requirements:* For master's and doctorate, GRE General Test, minimum GPA of 2.7. Additional exam requirements/recommendations for international students: Required—TOEFL. Electronic applications accepted. *Expenses:* Tuition, state resident: full-time $7440; part-time $414 per credit hour. Tuition, nonresident: full-time $22,478; part-time $1250 per credit hour. Required fees: $922; $43 per credit hour. Tuition and fees vary according to program.

The University of Texas at Austin, Graduate School, College of Liberal Arts, Department of Philosophy, Austin, TX 78712-1111. Offers PhD. Part-time programs available. Terminal master's awarded for partial completion of doctoral program. *Degree requirements:* For doctorate, one foreign language, thesis/dissertation. *Entrance requirements:* For doctorate, GRE General Test. Electronic applications accepted. *Faculty research:* Ancient philosophy, cognitive science, continental philosophy, history and philosophy of science.

The University of Texas at Dallas, School of Arts and Humanities, Program in Humanities, Richardson, TX 75080. Offers aesthetic studies (MA, MAT, PhD); history (MA); history of ideas (MA, MAT, PhD); humanities (MA, PhD); Latin American studies (MA); studies in literature (MA, MAT, PhD). *Faculty:* 44 full-time (14 women). *Students:* 161 full-time (95 women), 178 part-time (104 women); includes 71 minority (22 Black or African American, non-Hispanic/Latino; 4 American Indian or Alaska Native, non-Hispanic/Latino; 16 Asian, non-Hispanic/Latino; 24 Hispanic/Latino; 5 Two or more races, non-Hispanic/Latino), 22 international. Average age 38. 156 applicants, 70% accepted, 79 enrolled. In 2010, 46 master's, 20 doctorates awarded. *Degree requirements:* For master's, one foreign language, portfolio, thesis, or capstone project; for doctorate, one foreign language, thesis/dissertation. *Entrance requirements:* For master's, minimum GPA of 3.3 in upper-level coursework in field; for doctorate, doctoral field examinations, minimum GPA of 3.3 in upper-level coursework in field. Additional exam requirements/recommendations for international students: Required—TOEFL (minimum score 550 paper-based; 215 computer-based). *Application deadline:* For fall admission, 7/15 for domestic students, 5/1 priority date for international students; for spring admission, 11/15 for domestic students, 9/1 priority date for international students. Applications are processed on a rolling basis. Application fee: $50 ($100 for international students). Electronic applications accepted. *Expenses:* Tuition, state resident: full-time $10,248; part-time $569 per credit hour. Tuition, nonresident: full-time $18,544; part-time $1030 per credit hour. Tuition and fees vary according to course load. *Financial support:* In 2010–11, 151 students received support, including 5 research assistantships with partial tuition reimbursements available (averaging $10,905 per year), 82 teaching assistantships with partial tuition reimbursements available (averaging $10,156 per year); career-related internships or fieldwork, Federal Work-Study, institutionally sponsored loans, scholarships/grants, and unspecified assistantships also available. Support available to part-time students. Financial award application deadline: 4/30; financial award applicants required to submit FAFSA. *Faculty research:* Holocaust studies, U. S. /Mexico studies, translation studies, art history research, Chinese studies. *Unit head:* Dr. Michael Wilson, Associate Dean for Graduate Education, 972-883-2080, E-mail: mwilson@utdallas.edu. *Application contact:* Dr. Michael Wilson, Associate Dean of Graduate Studies, 972-883-2756, Fax: 972-883-2989, E-mail: mwilson@utdallas.edu.

The University of Texas at El Paso, Graduate School, College of Liberal Arts, Department of Philosophy, El Paso, TX 79968-0001. Offers MA. *Degree requirements:* For master's, thesis, oral examination. *Entrance requirements:* For master's, GRE, 2 letters of recommendation. *Unit head:* Jules Simon, Chair, 915-747-7912, E-mail: jsimon@utep.edu. *Application contact:* Lorena Chavez, Admissions Contact, 915-747-7912, E-mail: philos@utep.edu.

The University of Toledo, College of Graduate Studies, College of Language, Literature and Social Sciences, Department of Philosophy, Toledo, OH 43606-3390. Offers MA. Part-time programs available. *Faculty:* 10. *Students:* 10 full-time (2 women), 3 part-time (1 woman). Average age 32. 17 applicants, 65% accepted, 6 enrolled. In 2010, 4 master's awarded. *Degree requirements:* For master's, comprehensive exam, thesis, exam. *Entrance requirements:* For master's, GRE encouraged for students applying for an assistantship. A minimum 2.7 cumulative point-hour ratio (on a 4.0 scale) for all previous academic work. Three Letters of Recommendation. Additional exam requirements/recommendations for international students: Required—TOEFL (minimum score 550 paper-based; 213 computer-based; 80 iBT), IELTS (minimum score 6.5). *Application deadline:* For fall admission, 1/15 priority date for domestic and international students. Applications are processed on a rolling basis. Application fee: $45 ($75 for international students). Electronic applications accepted. *Expenses:* Tuition, state resident: full-time $11,426; part-time $476 per credit hour. Tuition, nonresident: full-time $21,660; part-time $903 per credit hour. One-time fee: $62. *Financial support:* Research assistantships with tuition reimbursements, teaching assistantships with tuition reimbursements, Federal Work-Study, institutionally sponsored loans, scholarships/grants, tuition waivers (full), and unspecified assistantships available. Support available to part-time students. *Faculty research:* History of philosophy, ethics, social/political philosophy, philosophy of science, European philosophy. *Unit head:* Dr. John Sarnecki, Chair, 419-530-4524, Fax: 419-530-6189, E-mail: john.sarnecki@utoledo.edu. *Application contact:* Graduate College Office, 419-530-4723, Fax: 419-530-4724, E-mail: grdsch@utnet.utoledo.edu.

University of Toronto, School of Graduate Studies, Humanities Division, Department of Philosophy, Toronto, ON M5S 1A1, Canada. Offers MA, PhD. Part-time programs available. *Degree requirements:* For doctorate, one foreign language, thesis/dissertation. *Entrance requirements:* For master's, GRE, 6 courses in philosophy; minimum A– average in philosophy courses, B overall; 2 letters of reference; writing sample; for doctorate, GRE, MA in philosophy, minimum A– average, 2 letters of reference, writing sample. Additional exam requirements/recommendations for international students: Required—TOEFL (minimum score 600 paper-based), TWE (minimum score 5).

University of Utah, Graduate School, College of Humanities, Department of Philosophy, Salt Lake City, UT 84112. Offers MA, MS, PhD. Part-time programs available. *Faculty:* 18 full-time (7 women). *Students:* 15 full-time (6 women), 21 part-time (4 women); includes 3 minority (1 Black or African American, non-Hispanic/Latino; 2 Asian, non-Hispanic/Latino), 1 international. Average age 32. 26 applicants, 23% accepted, 6 enrolled. In 2010, 3 master's, 3 doctorates awarded. *Degree requirements:* For master's, comprehensive exam, thesis or alternative; for doctorate, thesis/dissertation, qualifying oral exam. *Entrance requirements:* For master's, GRE General Test, minimum undergraduate GPA of 3.0; for doctorate, GRE General Test. Additional exam requirements/recommendations for international students: Required—TOEFL (minimum score 650 paper-based). *Application deadline:* For fall admission, 1/15 priority date for domestic students, 12/15 priority date for international students. Applications are processed on a rolling basis. Application fee: $55 ($65 for international students). Electronic applications accepted. *Expenses:* Tuition, area resident: Part-time $179.19 per credit hour. Tuition, state resident: full-time $4384. Tuition, nonresident: full-time $16,684; part-time $630.67 per credit hour. Required fees: $350 per semester. Tuition and fees vary according to course load, degree level and program. *Financial support:* In 2010–11, 1 student received support, including 1 fellowship with full tuition reimbursement available (averaging $11,500 per year), 1 research assistantship (averaging $18,000 per year), 15 teaching assistantships with full tuition reimbursements available (averaging $11,500 per year); Federal Work-Study, institutionally sponsored loans, scholarships/grants, health care benefits, and unspecified assistantships also available. Financial award application deadline: 2/15; financial award applicants required to submit FAFSA. *Faculty research:* Philosophy of biology, philosophy of science, applied ethics, practical reasoning, political philosophy, philosophy of cognitive science. Total annual research expenditures: $46,694. *Unit head:* Dr. Stephen Matthew Downes, Chair, 801-581-6094, Fax: 801-585-5195, E-mail: s.downes@.utah.edu. *Application contact:* Connie Celadden Corbett, Academic Coordinator, 801-581-8162, Fax: 801-585-5195, E-mail: c.corbett@utah.edu.

University of Victoria, Faculty of Graduate Studies, Faculty of Humanities, Department of Philosophy, Victoria, BC V8W 2Y2, Canada. Offers MA. Part-time and evening/weekend programs available. *Degree requirements:* For master's, thesis. *Entrance requirements:* For master's, writing sample. Additional exam requirements/recommendations for international students: Required—TOEFL (minimum score 575 paper-based; 233 computer-based), IELTS (minimum score 7). *Faculty research:* Ethics, metaphysics, philosophy of mind, history of philosophy, political philosophy.

University of Virginia, College and Graduate School of Arts and Sciences, Department of Philosophy, Charlottesville, VA 22903. Offers MA, PhD, JD/MA. *Faculty:* 14 full-time (4 women). *Students:* 31 full-time (6 women); includes 1 Asian, non-Hispanic/Latino, 3 international. Average age 29. 149 applicants, 7% accepted, 6 enrolled. In 2010, 2 master's, 3 doctorates awarded. *Degree requirements:* For master's, 2 papers; for doctorate, thesis/dissertation, 2 papers. *Entrance requirements:* For master's, GRE General Test, GRE Subject Test, 3 letters of recommendation, writing sample; for doctorate, GRE General Test, GRE Subject Test, 3 letters of recommendation; writing sample. Additional exam requirements/recommendations for international students: Required—TOEFL (minimum score 600 paper-based; 250 computer-based; 90 iBT), IELTS. *Application deadline:* For fall admission, 1/1 for domestic students, 1/5 for international students. Applications are processed on a rolling basis. Application fee: $60. Electronic applications accepted. *Financial support:* Fellowships, teaching assistantships available. Financial award applicants required to submit FAFSA. *Unit head:* Jorge Secada, Chair, 434-924-7701, Fax: 434-924-6927, E-mail: jes2f@virginia.edu. *Application contact:* Mitch Green, Director of Graduate Admissions, 434-924-7701, Fax: 434-924-6927, E-mail: msg6m@virginia.edu.

University of Washington, Graduate School, College of Arts and Sciences, Department of Philosophy, Seattle, WA 98195. Offers classics and philosophy (PhD); philosophy (MA, PhD). Terminal master's awarded for partial completion of doctoral program. *Degree requirements:* For master's, 3 papers; for doctorate, thesis/dissertation, general exam. *Entrance requirements:* For master's and doctorate, GRE, minimum GPA of 3.0. Additional exam requirements/recommendations for international students: Required—TOEFL. *Faculty research:* History and philosophy of science, epistemology, Aristotle's metaphysics, ethics and politics, causation in modern philosophy.

University of Waterloo, Graduate Studies, Faculty of Arts, Department of Philosophy, Waterloo, ON N2L 3G1, Canada. Offers MA, PhD. *Degree requirements:* For master's, thesis or alternative; for doctorate, one foreign language, thesis/dissertation. *Entrance requirements:* For master's, honors degree, minimum B+ average, writing sample, resume; for doctorate, master's degree, minimum A- average, resumé. Additional exam requirements/recommendations for international students: Required—TOEFL, TWE. Electronic applications accepted. *Faculty research:* Logic, ethics, social/political, cognitive science, philosophy of science.

The University of Western Ontario, Faculty of Graduate Studies, Faculty of Arts and Humanities, Department of Philosophy, London, ON N6A 5B8, Canada. Offers MA, PhD. *Degree requirements:* For master's, 1 competency exam; for doctorate, comprehensive exam, thesis/dissertation, 2 competency exams. *Entrance requirements:* For master's, honors degree. Additional exam requirements/recommendations for international students: Required—TOEFL (minimum score 600 paper-based; 250 computer-based). Electronic applications accepted. *Faculty research:* Philosophy of science, history of philosophy, philosophy of law, ethics, epistemology.

University of Windsor, Faculty of Graduate Studies, Faculty of Arts and Social Sciences, Department of Philosophy, Windsor, ON N9B 3P4, Canada. Offers MA. Part-time programs available. *Degree requirements:* For master's, thesis. *Entrance requirements:* For master's, minimum B average. Additional exam requirements/recommendations for international students: Required—TOEFL (minimum score 600 paper-based; 250 computer-based). Electronic applications accepted. *Faculty research:* Informal logic, contemporary Continental philosophy, epistemology.

University of Wisconsin–Madison, Graduate School, College of Letters and Science, Department of Philosophy, Madison, WI 53706-1380. Offers MA, PhD. Part-time programs available. Terminal master's awarded for partial completion of doctoral program. *Degree requirements:* For master's, thesis, preliminary exams; for doctorate, thesis/dissertation, preliminary exams. *Entrance requirements:* For doctorate, GRE, BA in philosophy or related area. Additional exam requirements/recommendations for international students: Required—TOEFL. Electronic applications accepted. *Expenses:* Tuition, state resident: full-time $9887; part-time $617.96 per credit. Tuition, nonresident: full-time $24,054; part-time $1503.40 per credit. Required fees: $67.63 per credit. Tuition and fees vary according to reciprocity agreements. *Faculty research:* History of philosophy, logic, philosophy of science, philosophy of mind, metaphysics.

University of Wisconsin–Milwaukee, Graduate School, College of Letters and Sciences, Department of Philosophy, Milwaukee, WI 53201-0413. Offers MA. Part-time programs available. *Faculty:* 14 full-time (4 women). *Students:* 21 full-time (6 women); includes 3 Asian, non-Hispanic/Latino, 1 international. Average age 25. 120 applicants, 27% accepted, 9 enrolled. In 2010, 10 master's awarded. *Degree requirements:* For master's, thesis or alternative. *Entrance requirements:* For master's, GRE General Test. Additional exam requirements/recommendations for international students: Required—TOEFL (minimum score 550 paper-based; 79 iBT), IELTS (minimum score 6.5). *Application deadline:* For fall admission, 1/1 priority date for domestic students; for spring admission, 9/1 for domestic students. Applications are processed on a rolling basis. Application fee: $56 ($96 for international students). Electronic applications accepted. *Financial support:* In 2010–11, 2 fellowships, 19 teaching assistantships were awarded; career-related internships or fieldwork, unspecified assistantships, and project assistantships also available. Support available to part-time students. Financial award application deadline: 4/15; financial award applicants required to submit FAFSA. Total annual research expenditures: $1,290. *Unit head:* Richard J. Tierney, Chair, 414-229-4736, Fax: 414-229-5022, E-mail: rtierney@uwm.edu. *Application contact:* Carla Bagnoli, General Information Contact, 414-229-5215, Fax: 414-229-6967, E-mail: cbagnoli@uwm.edu.

University of Wyoming, College of Arts and Sciences, Department of Philosophy, Laramie, WY 82070. Offers MA. Part-time programs available. *Degree requirements:* For master's, thesis, logic proficiency, first-year paper. *Entrance requirements:* For master's, GRE General Test, minimum GPA of 3.0. Additional exam requirements/recommendations for international students: Required—TOEFL (minimum score 525 paper-based; 197 computer-based). Electronic applications accepted. *Faculty research:* Philosophy of science, political and ethical theory, philosophy of language, epistemology, philosophy of mind, early modern philosophy.

Vanderbilt University, Graduate School, Department of Philosophy, Nashville, TN 37240-1001. Offers MA, PhD. *Faculty:* 16 full-time (5 women). *Students:* 41 full-time (20 women); includes 1 Black or African American, non-Hispanic/Latino; 1 American Indian or Alaska Native, non-Hispanic/Latino; 1 Asian, non-Hispanic/Latino; 2 Hispanic/Latino; 1 Two or more races, non-Hispanic/Latino. Average age 31. 173 applicants, 8% accepted, 8 enrolled. In 2010, 2 master's, 6 doctorates awarded. Terminal master's awarded for partial completion of doctoral program. *Degree requirements:* For doctorate, one foreign language, comprehensive exam, thesis/dissertation, final and qualifying exams. *Entrance requirements:* For doctorate, GRE General Test, writing sample. Additional exam requirements/recommendations for international students: Required—TOEFL (minimum score 570 paper-based; 230 computer-based; 88 iBT). *Application deadline:* For fall admission, 1/15 for domestic and international students. Application fee: $0. Electronic applications accepted. *Financial support:* Fellowships with full tuition reimbursements, teaching assistantships with full tuition reimbursements, Federal Work-Study, institutionally sponsored loans, scholarships/grants, and health care benefits available. Financial award application deadline: 1/15; financial award applicants required to submit CSS PROFILE or FAFSA. *Faculty research:* Ancient, medieval, and modern philosophy; philosophy of science; ethics; philosophy of language; philosophy of religion. *Unit head:* Jeffrey Tlumak, Chair, 615-343-5909, Fax: 615-343-7259, E-mail: jeffrey.tlumak@vanderbilt.edu. *Application contact:* Robert Talisse, Director of Graduate Studies, 615-343-8671, Fax: 615-343-7259, E-mail: robert.talisse@vanderbilt.edu.

Villanova University, Graduate School of Liberal Arts and Sciences, Department of Philosophy, Villanova, PA 19085-1699. Offers PhD. Part-time and evening/weekend programs available. *Faculty:* 6 full-time (2 women). *Students:* 54 full-time (20 women); includes 5 minority (1 Asian, non-Hispanic/Latino; 4 Hispanic/Latino), 7 international. Average age 28. 126 applicants, 10% accepted, 7 enrolled. In 2010, 1 doctorate awarded. *Degree requirements:* For doctorate, 2 foreign languages, comprehensive exam, thesis/dissertation. *Entrance requirements:* For doctorate, GRE General Test, GRE Subject Test, minimum GPA of 3.5. Additional exam requirements/recommendations for international students: Required—TOEFL. *Application deadline:* For fall admission, 2/1 priority date for domestic and international students. Applications are processed on a rolling basis. Application fee: $50. Electronic applications accepted.

Philosophy

Villanova University (continued)
Expenses: Tuition: Part-time $700 per credit. Part-time tuition and fees vary according to degree level and program. *Financial support:* Research assistantships, teaching assistantships, Federal Work-Study available. Financial award applicants required to submit FAFSA. *Unit head:* Dr. Walter Brogan, Chairman, 610-519-4690. *Application contact:* Dr. Adele Lindenmeyr, Dean, Graduate School of Liberal Arts and Sciences, 610-519-7093, Fax: 610-519-7096.

Virginia Polytechnic Institute and State University, Graduate School, College of Liberal Arts and Human Sciences, Department of Philosophy, Blacksburg, VA 24061. Offers MA. *Faculty:* 12 full-time (3 women). *Students:* 19 full-time (6 women), 1 part-time (0 women), 1 international. Average age 26. 69 applicants, 49% accepted, 8 enrolled. In 2010, 10 master's awarded. *Degree requirements:* For master's, comprehensive exam (for some programs), thesis (for some programs). *Entrance requirements:* For master's, GRE. Additional exam requirements/recommendations for international students: Required—TOEFL (minimum score 550 paper-based; 213 computer-based). *Application deadline:* For fall admission, 7/1 for domestic and international students; for spring admission, 12/1 for domestic and international students. Applications are processed on a rolling basis. Application fee: $65. Electronic applications accepted. *Expenses:* Tuition, state resident: full-time $9399; part-time $488 per credit hour. Tuition, nonresident: full-time $17,854; part-time $957.75 per credit hour. Required fees: $1534. Full-time tuition and fees vary according to program. *Financial support:* In 2010–11, 9 teaching assistantships with full tuition reimbursements (averaging $10,202 per year) were awarded; career-related internships or fieldwork, Federal Work-Study, scholarships/grants, health care benefits, and unspecified assistantships also available. Financial award application deadline: 1/15. *Faculty research:* History of philosophy, ethics, history and philosophy of science and philosophy. Total annual research expenditures: $11,487. *Unit head:* Dr. James Klagge, UNIT HEAD, 540-231-8487, Fax: 540-231-6367, E-mail: jklagge@vt.edu. *Application contact:* William Fitzpatrick, Contact, 540-231-7543, Fax: 540-231-6367, E-mail: william.fitzpatrick@vt.edu.

Washington State University, Graduate School, College of Liberal Arts, Department of Philosophy, Pullman, WA 99164. Offers MA. *Faculty:* 7. *Students:* 9 full-time (3 women); includes 1 Black or African American, non-Hispanic/Latino. 15 applicants, 73% accepted, 3 enrolled. In 2010, 5 master's awarded. *Degree requirements:* For master's, comprehensive exam (for some programs), thesis (for some programs). *Entrance requirements:* For master's, GRE, minimum GPA of 3.0, 3 letters of recommendation, writing sample. Additional exam requirements/recommendations for international students: Required—TOEFL, IELTS. *Application deadline:* For fall admission, 1/10 for domestic and international students; for spring admission, 7/1 for domestic and international students. Application fee: $50. *Expenses:* Tuition, state resident: full-time $8552; part-time $443 per credit. Tuition, nonresident: full-time $21,650; part-time $1083 per credit. Required fees: $846. *Financial support:* In 2010–11, 7 teaching assistantships with tuition reimbursements (averaging $13,056 per year) were awarded. *Faculty research:* Philosophy of language and mind, philosophy of race and ethnicity, social and political philosophy. *Unit head:* Dr. David L. Shier, Chair, 509-335-1415, E-mail: shier@wsu.edu. *Application contact:* Graduate School Admissions, 800-GRADWSU, Fax: 509-335-1949, E-mail: gradsch@wsu.edu.

Washington University in St. Louis, Graduate School of Arts and Sciences, Department of Philosophy, St. Louis, MO 63130-4899. Offers philosophy (MA, PhD); philosophy/neuroscience/psychology (PhD). Terminal master's awarded for partial completion of doctoral program. *Degree requirements:* For master's, thesis optional; for doctorate, thesis/dissertation. *Entrance requirements:* For master's and doctorate, GRE General Test, sample of written work. Electronic applications accepted.

Wayne State University, College of Liberal Arts and Sciences, Department of Philosophy, Detroit, MI 48202. Offers MA, PhD. *Faculty:* 6 full-time (1 woman). *Students:* 21 full-time (3 women), 2 part-time (0 women); includes 7 minority (3 Black or African American, non-Hispanic/Latino; 1 American Indian or Alaska Native, non-Hispanic/Latino; 2 Asian, non-Hispanic/Latino; 1 Hispanic/Latino). Average age 29. 16 applicants, 50% accepted, 6 enrolled. In 2010, 3 master's, 1 doctorate awarded. Terminal master's awarded for partial completion of doctoral program. *Degree requirements:* For master's, thesis; for doctorate, one foreign language, thesis/dissertation. *Entrance requirements:* For master's, GRE General Test or minimum GPA of 3.0; for doctorate, minimum undergraduate GPA of 3.0. Additional exam requirements/recommendations for international students: Required—TOEFL (minimum score 550 paper-based; 213 computer-based); Recommended—TWE (minimum score 6). *Application deadline:*

For fall admission, 7/1 priority date for domestic students, 6/1 for international students; for winter admission, 10/1 for international students; for spring admission, 2/1 for international students. Applications are processed on a rolling basis. Application fee: $30 ($50 for international students). Electronic applications accepted. *Expenses:* Tuition, state resident: full-time $7662; part-time $478.85 per credit hour. Tuition, nonresident: full-time $16,920; part-time $1057.55 per credit hour. Required fees: $571.20; $35.70 per credit hour. $188.05 per semester. Tuition and fees vary according to course load and program. *Financial support:* In 2010–11, 1 fellowship with tuition reimbursement (averaging $15,750 per year), 8 teaching assistantships with tuition reimbursements (averaging $14,620 per year) were awarded. Financial award application deadline: 4/1. *Faculty research:* Metaphysics, ancient philosophy, philosophy of art, ethics, philosophy of science. *Unit head:* Robert Yanal, Chair, 313-577-6099, E-mail: r.yanal@wayne.edu. *Application contact:* Robert Yanal, Chair, 313-577-6099, E-mail: r.yanal@wayne.edu.

West Chester University of Pennsylvania, Office of Graduate Studies, College of Arts and Sciences, Department of Philosophy, West Chester, PA 19383. Offers business ethics (Certificate); healthcare ethics (Certificate); philosophy: applied ethics (MA); philosophy: general (MA). Part-time and evening/weekend programs available. *Students:* 12 full-time (1 woman), 13 part-time (4 women); includes 2 minority (both Hispanic/Latino). Average age 30. 17 applicants, 94% accepted, 14 enrolled. In 2010, 5 master's awarded. *Degree requirements:* For master's, thesis or comprehensive exam. *Entrance requirements:* For master's, GRE or writing sample, three letters of reference. Additional exam requirements/recommendations for international students: Required—TOEFL (minimum score 550 paper-based; 213 computer-based; 80 iBT). *Application deadline:* For fall admission, 4/15 priority date for domestic students, 3/15 for international students; for spring admission, 10/15 for domestic students, 9/1 for international students. Applications are processed on a rolling basis. Application fee: $35. Electronic applications accepted. *Expenses:* Tuition, state resident: full-time $6966; part-time $387 per credit. Tuition, nonresident: full-time $11,146; part-time $619 per credit. Required fees: $1614.40; $133.24 per credit. Part-time tuition and fees vary according to campus/location. *Financial support:* Unspecified assistantships available. Support available to part-time students. Financial award application deadline: 2/15; financial award applicants required to submit FAFSA. *Faculty research:* International studies. *Unit head:* Dr. Joan Woolfrey, Chair, 610-436-1004, E-mail: jwoolfrey@wcupa.edu. *Application contact:* Dr. Helen Daley Schroepfer, Graduate Coordinator, 610-436-2429, E-mail: hschroepfer@wcupa.edu.

Western Michigan University, Graduate College, College of Arts and Sciences, Department of Philosophy, Kalamazoo, MI 49008. Offers MA. *Degree requirements:* For master's, thesis optional.

Wilfrid Laurier University, Faculty of Graduate and Postdoctoral Studies, Faculty of Arts, Department of Philosophy, Waterloo, ON N2L 3C5, Canada. Offers agency (MA); community (MA); self (MA). *Faculty:* 9 full-time (2 women), 1 (woman) part-time/adjunct. *Students:* 7 full-time (3 women), 1 (woman) part-time. 17 applicants, 76% accepted, 5 enrolled. In 2010, 9 master's awarded. *Entrance requirements:* For master's, honours BA in philosophy or equivalent with minimum B+ average in philosophy and in final year. Additional exam requirements/recommendations for international students: Required—TOEFL (minimum score 89 iBT). *Application deadline:* For fall admission, 2/1 priority date for domestic and international students. Application fee: $100. Electronic applications accepted. Tuition and fees charges are reported in Canadian dollars. *Expenses:* Tuition, area resident: Full-time $15,300 Canadian dollars; part-time $1200 Canadian dollars per credit. International tuition: $21,300 Canadian dollars full-time. Required fees: $650 Canadian dollars; $100 Canadian dollars per credit. Tuition and fees vary according to course load, degree level, campus/location and program. *Financial support:* In 2010–11, 10 fellowships, 10 teaching assistantships were awarded; career-related internships or fieldwork, scholarships/grants, health care benefits, and unspecified assistantships also available. *Faculty research:* Self, agency, community. *Unit head:* Dr. Jill Rusin, Graduate Coordinator, 519-884-0710 Ext. 3274, Fax: 519-883-0991, E-mail: jrusin@wlu.ca. *Application contact:* Jennifer Williams, Graduate Admission and Records Officer, 519-884-0710 Ext. 3536, Fax: 519-884-1020, E-mail: gradstudies@wlu.ca.

Yale University, Graduate School of Arts and Sciences, Department of Philosophy, New Haven, CT 06520. Offers PhD. *Degree requirements:* For doctorate, 2 foreign languages, thesis/dissertation. *Entrance requirements:* For doctorate, GRE General Test.

York University, Faculty of Graduate Studies, Faculty of Arts, Program in Philosophy, Toronto, ON M3J 1P3, Canada. Offers MA, PhD. Part-time programs available. *Degree requirements:* For master's, thesis or alternative; for doctorate, one foreign language, thesis/dissertation. Electronic applications accepted.

Section 12
Religious Studies

This section contains a directory of institutions offering graduate work in religious studies. Additional information about programs listed in the directory may be obtained by writing directly to the dean of a graduate school or chair of a department at the address given in the directory.

For programs offering related work, see also in this book *Area and Cultural Studies, History, Humanities,* and *Philosophy.* In another guide in this series:

Graduate Programs in Business, Education, Health, Information Studies, Law & Social Work
See *Subject Areas (Religious Education)*

CONTENTS

Program Directories

Close-Up

Missions and Missiology

Abilene Christian University, Graduate School, College of Biblical Studies, Graduate School of Theology, Program in Missions, Abilene, TX 79699-9100. Offers MA, MAMI. Part-time programs available. *Students:* 2 full-time (both women), 5 part-time (0 women); includes 1 Black or African American, non-Hispanic/Latino; 1 Hispanic/Latino, 2 international. 4 applicants, 100% accepted, 3 enrolled. In 2010, 3 master's awarded. *Degree requirements:* For master's, comprehensive exam, thesis. *Entrance requirements:* For master's, GRE, MAT. Additional exam requirements/recommendations for international students: Required—TOEFL (minimum score 550 paper-based; 213 computer-based). *Application deadline:* For fall admission, 4/1 priority date for domestic students; for spring admission, 11/1 for domestic students. Applications are processed on a rolling basis. Application fee: $40. Electronic applications accepted. *Expenses:* Tuition: Full-time $12,906; part-time $717 per hour. Required fees: $1250; $61.50 per unit. *Financial support:* In 2010–11, 2 students received support; teaching assistantships, career-related internships or fieldwork available. Financial award application deadline: 4/1; financial award applicants required to submit FAFSA. *Faculty research:* Animism, contextualization, missions education. *Unit head:* Dr. Chris Flanders, Graduate Adviser, 325-674-3742, Fax: 325-674-6180, E-mail: clf03c@acu.edu. *Application contact:* David Pittman, Graduate Admissions Counselor, 325-674-2656, Fax: 325-674-6717, E-mail: gradinfo@acu.edu.

Ambrose University College, Ambrose Seminary, Calgary, AB T2P 3T5, Canada. Offers biblical/theological studies (MA); Chinese ministries (Certificate); Christian studies (M Div, MA, Diploma); foundations for ministry (Certificate); intercultural ministries (M Div, MA, Certificate, Diploma); leadership and ministry (MA, Certificate, Diploma). *Accreditation:* ATS (one or more programs are accredited). Part-time programs available. *Faculty:* 7 full-time (0 women), 24 part-time/adjunct (2 women). *Students:* 55 full-time (16 women), 98 part-time (52 women); includes 49 minority (5 Black or African American, non-Hispanic/Latino; 2 American Indian or Alaska Native, non-Hispanic/Latino; 41 Asian, non-Hispanic/Latino; 1 Hispanic/Latino). Average age 41. *Degree requirements:* For master's, 2 foreign languages, internship; for M Div, one foreign language, internship. *Entrance requirements:* For master's, bachelor's degree. Additional exam requirements/recommendations for international students: Required—TOEFL or IELTS. *Application deadline:* For fall admission, 7/31 priority date for domestic students, 3/1 priority date for international students; for winter admission, 11/30 priority date for domestic students, 6/1 priority date for international students. Applications are processed on a rolling basis. Application fee: $50. Electronic applications accepted. Tuition and fees charges are reported in Canadian dollars. *Expenses:* Tuition: Full-time $9270 Canadian dollars; part-time $309 Canadian dollars per credit hour. Required fees: $510 Canadian dollars. *Financial support:* Career-related internships or fieldwork and scholarships/grants available. Support available to part-time students. Financial award application deadline: 3/30. *Faculty research:* Evangelicalism and sociology, missiological trends, chaplaincy, intertestamental studies, postmodernism. *Unit head:* Dr. Paul Spilsbury, Vice-President of Academic Affairs, 403-410-2000 Ext. 6905, Fax: 403-571-2556, E-mail: pspilsbury@ambrose.edu. *Application contact:* Dr. Paul Spilsbury, Vice-President of Academic Affairs, 403-410-2000 Ext. 6905, Fax: 403-571-2556, E-mail: pspilsbury@ambrose.edu.

Anderson University, School of Theology, Anderson, IN 46012-3495. Offers missions (MA); theology (M Div, MTS, D Min). *Accreditation:* ACIPE; ATS. Part-time programs available. *Degree requirements:* For master's, one foreign language, thesis, integrative senior seminar; for doctorate, thesis/dissertation; for M Div, thesis/dissertation (for some programs). *Faculty research:* Small-church/bivocational ministry, women in ministry.

Asbury Theological Seminary, Graduate and Professional Programs, Wilmore, KY 40390-1199. Offers MA, MACE, MACL, MAMFC, MAMHC, MAPC, MAYM, Th M, PhD, Certificate. *Accreditation:* ATS. Part-time programs available. Postbaccalaureate distance learning degree programs offered (minimal on-campus study). *Faculty:* 63 full-time (12 women), 74 part-time/adjunct (14 women). *Students:* 719 full-time (251 women), 855 part-time (276 women); includes 178 minority (87 Black or African American, non-Hispanic/Latino; 4 American Indian or Alaska Native, non-Hispanic/Latino; 35 Asian, non-Hispanic/Latino; 40 Hispanic/Latino; 3 Native Hawaiian or other Pacific Islander, non-Hispanic/Latino; 9 Two or more races, non-Hispanic/Latino), 109 international. Average age 38. 772 applicants, 71% accepted, 406 enrolled. In 2010, 101 master's, 37 doctorates, 3 other advanced degrees awarded. Terminal master's awarded for partial completion of doctoral program. *Degree requirements:* For master's, thesis (for some programs); for doctorate, thesis/dissertation, qualifying exam. *Entrance requirements:* For master's, minimum GPA of 2.75; for doctorate, minimum GPA of 3.0. Additional exam requirements/recommendations for international students: Required—TOEFL, IELTS. *Application deadline:* Applications are processed on a rolling basis. Application fee: $50. Electronic applications accepted. *Expenses:* Tuition: Full-time $12,120; part-time $505 per credit hour. One-time fee: $100. *Financial support:* In 2010–11, 1,317 students received support. Career-related internships or fieldwork, Federal Work-Study, institutionally sponsored loans, and scholarships/grants available. Support available to part-time students. Financial award applicants required to submit FAFSA. *Unit head:* Dr. Leslie A. Andrews, Provost, 859-858-2206, Fax: 859-858-2025, E-mail: leslie.andrews@asburyseminary.edu. *Application contact:* Kevin Bush, Vice President of Enrollment Management, 859-858-2211, Fax: 859-858-2287, E-mail: admissions.office@asburyseminary.edu.

Assemblies of God Theological Seminary, Graduate and Professional Programs, Springfield, MO 65802. Offers Christian ministries (MA); counseling (MA); divinity (M Div); intercultural ministry (MA); intercultural studies (PhD); ministry (D Min); missiology (D Miss); theological studies (MA). *Accreditation:* ATS. Part-time and evening/weekend programs available. Postbaccalaureate distance learning degree programs offered (minimal on-campus study). *Faculty:* 12 full-time (3 women), 20 part-time/adjunct (6 women). *Students:* 176 full-time (59 women), 211 part-time (48 women); includes 55 minority (16 Black or African American, non-Hispanic/Latino; 7 American Indian or Alaska Native, non-Hispanic/Latino; 16 Asian, non-Hispanic/Latino; 14 Hispanic/Latino; 2 Native Hawaiian or other Pacific Islander, non-Hispanic/Latino), 9 international. Average age 40. 96 applicants, 79% accepted, 53 enrolled. In 2010, 26 first professional degrees, 65 master's, 9 doctorates awarded. *Degree requirements:* For master's, analytical reflection paper, comprehensive exam or field education research project; for doctorate, thesis/dissertation; for M Div, one foreign language, analytical reflection paper or field education research project. *Entrance requirements:* For M Div, minimum GPA of 2.5; for master's, minimum GPA of 2.5; for doctorate, minimum GPA of 3.0. Additional exam requirements/recommendations for international students: Required—TOEFL (minimum score 550 paper-based; 213 computer-based; 80 iBT). *Application deadline:* For fall admission, 7/1 priority date for domestic students, 6/1 priority date for international students; for spring admission, 12/1 priority date for domestic students, 11/1 priority date for international students. Applications are processed on a rolling basis. Application fee: $75. Electronic applications accepted. *Expenses:* Tuition: Full-time $12,192; part-time $508 per credit hour. *Financial support:* Career-related internships or fieldwork, Federal Work-Study, and scholarships/grants available. Support available to part-time students. Financial award application deadline: 7/15; financial award applicants required to submit FAFSA. *Unit head:* Stephen Lim, Academic Dean, 417-268-1000, Fax: 417-268-1001, E-mail: slim@agts.edu. *Application contact:* Stephen Lim, Academic Dean, 417-268-1000, Fax: 417-268-1001, E-mail: slim@agts.edu.

Associated Mennonite Biblical Seminary, Graduate and Professional Programs, Elkhart, IN 46517-1999. Offers Christian formation (MA); divinity (M Div); mission and evangelism (MA); peace studies (MA); theological studies (MA, Certificate). *Accreditation:* ACIPE; ATS. Part-time programs available. *Degree requirements:* For master's, comprehensive exam, thesis optional; for M Div, integration paper. *Entrance requirements:* For M Div, master's, and Certificate, 3 letters of reference. Additional exam requirements/recommendations for international students: Required—TOEFL (minimum score 550 paper-based; 213 computer-based). Electronic applications accepted. *Faculty research:* Biblical studies, theology, church history, church leadership.

Baptist Bible College of Pennsylvania, Baptist Bible Seminary, Clarks Summit, PA 18411-1297. Offers biblical studies (PhD); church planting (M Div); global missions (M Div); military

chaplaincy (M Div); ministry (M Min, D Min); pastor of church education (M Div); pastor of outreach (M Div); pastoral counseling (M Div); pastoral leadership (M Div); theology (M Div, Th M); youth pastor (M Div). Part-time and evening/weekend programs available. Postbaccalaureate distance learning degree programs offered (minimal on-campus study). *Faculty:* 10 full-time (0 women). *Students:* 71 full-time (0 women), 79 part-time (0 women); includes 16 minority (10 Black or African American, non-Hispanic/Latino; 4 Asian, non-Hispanic/Latino; 2 Hispanic/Latino), 7 international. Average age 38. In 2010, 23 master's, 4 doctorates awarded. Terminal master's awarded for partial completion of doctoral program. *Degree requirements:* For master's, 2 foreign languages, thesis; for doctorate, 2 foreign languages, comprehensive exam (for some programs), thesis/dissertation, oral exam; for M Div, 2 foreign languages, thesis/dissertation, oral exam. *Entrance requirements:* For doctorate, Greek and Hebrew entrance exams (PhD). *Application deadline:* Applications are processed on a rolling basis. Application fee: $30. Electronic applications accepted. *Expenses:* Tuition: Full-time $7488; part-time $416 per credit. Required fees: $522; $29 per credit. Full-time tuition and fees vary according to degree level and campus/location. *Financial support:* Career-related internships or fieldwork and scholarships/grants available. Support available to part-time students. *Unit head:* Dr. Michael Stallard, Seminary Academic Dean, 570-585-9348, Fax: 570-585-4057, E-mail: mstallard@bbc.edu. *Application contact:* Paul Golden, Director of Seminary Admissions, 570-586-9396, Fax: 570-585-4057, E-mail: pgolden@bbc.edu.

Bethel Seminary, Graduate and Professional Programs, St. Paul, MN 55112-6998. Offers Anglican studies (Certificate); applied ministry (MA, Certificate); biblical studies (Certificate); children's and family ministry (MACFM); Christian education (MACE); Christian thought (MACT); community ministry leadership (MA, Certificate); global and contextual studies (MA); Greek and Hebrew language track (M Div); Greek language track (M Div); Hebrew language track (M Div); lay ministry (Certificate); marriage and family therapy (MAMFT, Certificate); men's ministry leadership (Certificate); ministry (D Min); ministry leadership (Certificate); spiritual formation (Certificate); theological studies (MATS, Certificate); transformational leadership (MATL, Certificate); young life youth ministry (Certificate). *Accreditation:* ACIPE; ATS (one or more programs are accredited). Part-time and evening/weekend programs available. Postbaccalaureate distance learning degree programs offered (minimal on-campus study). *Faculty:* 26 full-time (3 women), 74 part-time/adjunct (29 women). *Students:* 729 full-time (275 women), 274 part-time (118 women); includes 75 minority (34 Black or African American, non-Hispanic/Latino; 1 American Indian or Alaska Native, non-Hispanic/Latino; 12 Asian, non-Hispanic/Latino; 16 Hispanic/Latino; 1 Native Hawaiian or other Pacific Islander, non-Hispanic/Latino; 11 Two or more races, non-Hispanic/Latino), 16 international. Average age 38. 525 applicants, 76% accepted, 265 enrolled. In 2010, 149 master's, 13 doctorates awarded. *Degree requirements:* For master's, variable foreign language requirement, thesis (for some programs); for doctorate, thesis/dissertation; for M Div, one foreign language. *Entrance requirements:* For M Div and master's, letters of reference, transcripts, personal statement; for doctorate, M Div, letters of reference, organizational support. Additional exam requirements/recommendations for international students: Required—TOEFL (minimum score 550 paper-based; 213 computer-based; 87 iBT). *Application deadline:* For fall admission, 8/1 priority date for domestic students, 3/1 for international students; for winter admission, 12/1 priority date for domestic students; for spring admission, 3/1 priority date for domestic students. Applications are processed on a rolling basis. Application fee: $20. Electronic applications accepted. *Financial support:* In 2010–11, 655 students received support, including 18 teaching assistantships; career-related internships or fieldwork, Federal Work-Study, scholarships/grants, and tuition waivers (full) also available. Financial award application deadline: 7/15; financial award applicants required to submit FAFSA. *Faculty research:* Nature of theology, ethics, Biblical commentaries, nature of God, science and theology. *Unit head:* Dr. David Ridder, Vice President and Dean, 651-638-6553. *Application contact:* Joseph V. Dworak, Director of Admissions, 651-638-6288, Fax: 651-638-6002, E-mail: j-dworak@bethel.edu.

Biblical Theological Seminary, Graduate and Professional Programs, Hatfield, PA 19440-2499. Offers advanced missional leadership (D Min); advanced pastoral studies (Certificate); biblical counseling (Certificate); biblical studies (MA, Certificate); counseling (MA); ministry (M Div, MA); missional theology (MA). *Accreditation:* ATS. Part-time and evening/weekend programs available. *Faculty:* 11 full-time (0 women), 27 part-time/adjunct (9 women). *Students:* 205 applicants, 52% accepted, 84 enrolled. In 2010, 23 first professional degrees, 24 master's, 10 doctorates awarded. *Degree requirements:* For M Div, thesis/dissertation. *Entrance requirements:* Additional exam requirements/recommendations for international students: Required—TOEFL (minimum score 550 paper-based; 213 computer-based; 80 iBT). *Application deadline:* Applications are processed on a rolling basis. Application fee: $30. *Expenses:* Tuition: Full-time $10,728; part-time $447 per credit. Required fees: $25 per term. One-time fee: $30. *Financial support:* In 2010–11, 174 students received support. Career-related internships or fieldwork, institutionally sponsored loans, and scholarships/grants available. Support available to part-time students. Financial award application deadline: 8/30; financial award applicants required to submit FAFSA. *Faculty research:* Theology, culture, Biblical interpretation. *Unit head:* Pamela Jean Smith, Vice President for Student Advancement, 215-368-5000 Ext. 122, Fax: 215-368-7002, E-mail: psmith@biblical.edu. *Application contact:* Rev. Darryl John Lang, Director of Recruitment and Student Life, 215-368-5000 Ext. 147, Fax: 215-368-7002, E-mail: dlang@biblical.edu.

Biola University, School of Intercultural Studies, La Mirada, CA 90639-0001. Offers anthropology (MA); applied linguistics (MA); Biblical languages and linguistics (MA); intercultural education (PhD); intercultural studies (MAICS); linguistics (Certificate); missiology (D Miss); missions (MA); teaching English to speakers of other languages (MA, Certificate). Part-time and evening/weekend programs available. *Faculty:* 16 full-time (5 women), 6 part-time/adjunct (1 woman). *Students:* 66 full-time (39 women), 126 part-time (72 women); includes 48 minority (6 Black or African American, non-Hispanic/Latino; 40 Asian, non-Hispanic/Latino; 2 Two or more races, non-Hispanic/Latino), 30 international. 136 applicants, 70% accepted, 59 enrolled. In 2010, 27 master's, 10 doctorates awarded. Terminal master's awarded for partial completion of doctoral program. *Degree requirements:* For master's, one foreign language, comprehensive exam; for doctorate, one foreign language, comprehensive exam, thesis/dissertation. *Entrance requirements:* For master's, minimum undergraduate GPA of 3.0; for doctorate, MA, 3 years of ministry experience, minimum graduate GPA of 3.3. Additional exam requirements/recommendations for international students: Required—TOEFL (minimum score 550 paper-based; 213 computer-based). *Application deadline:* For fall admission, 7/1 for domestic students; for spring admission, 1/1 for domestic students. Applications are processed on a rolling basis. Application fee: $45. Electronic applications accepted. *Financial support:* Teaching assistantships, career-related internships or fieldwork, institutionally sponsored loans, and scholarships/grants available. Support available to part-time students. Financial award application deadline: 3/2; financial award applicants required to submit FAFSA. *Unit head:* Dr. Douglas Pennoyer, Dean, 562-903-4844, Fax: 562-903-4748, E-mail: douglas.pennoyer@biola.edu. *Application contact:* Roy M. Allinson, Director of Graduate Admissions, 562-903-4752, Fax: 562-903-4709, E-mail: admissions@biola.edu.

Briercrest Seminary, Graduate Programs, Program in Christian Ministries, Caronport, SK S0H 0S0, Canada. Offers leadership (MA); marriage and family counseling (MA); missions (MA); pastoral counseling (MA); worship (MA); youth and family ministry (MA). Part-time programs available. *Degree requirements:* For master's, comprehensive exam, thesis optional. *Entrance requirements:* Additional exam requirements/recommendations for international students: Required—TOEFL (minimum score 550 paper-based; 213 computer-based).

Calvin Theological Seminary, Graduate and Professional Programs, Grand Rapids, MI 49546-4387. Offers Bible and theology (MA); divinity (M Div), including ancient near eastern languages and literature, contextual ministry, evangelism and teaching, history of Christianity, new church development, New Testament, Old Testament, pastoral care and leadership, preaching and worship, theological studies, youth and family ministries; educational ministry

(MA); historical theology (PhD); missions and evangelism (MA); pastoral care (MA); philosophical and moral theology (PhD); systematic theology (PhD); theological studies (MTS); theology (Th M); worship (MA); youth and family ministries (MA). *Accreditation:* ACIPE; ATS. Part-time programs available. *Degree requirements:* For master's, thesis (for some programs); for doctorate, 4 foreign languages, comprehensive exam, thesis/dissertation; for M Div, 2 foreign languages. *Entrance requirements:* For doctorate, GRE General Test, Hebrew, Greek, and a modern foreign language. Additional exam requirements/recommendations for international students: Required—TOEFL (minimum score 550 paper-based; 213 computer-based), TWE (minimum score 4). Electronic applications accepted. *Faculty research:* Recent Trinity theory, Christian anthropology, Proverbs, reformed confessions, Paul's view of law.

Catholic Theological Union at Chicago, Graduate and Professional Programs, Chicago, IL 60615-5698. Offers biblical spirituality (Certificate); cross-cultural ministries (D Min); cross-cultural missions (Certificate); divinity (M Div); liturgical studies (Certificate); liturgy (D Min); pastoral studies (MAPS, Certificate); spiritual formation (Certificate); spirituality (D Min); theology (MA); M Div/MA; M Div/MSW; M Div/PhD. M Div/PhD offered jointly with University of Chicago; M Div/MSW with Loyola University Chicago and University of Chicago. *Accreditation:* ACIPE; ATS (one or more programs are accredited). Part-time and evening/weekend programs available. *Degree requirements:* For master's, one foreign language, comprehensive exam (for some programs), thesis (for some programs); for doctorate, thesis/dissertation. *Entrance requirements:* For doctorate, master's degree, 5 years of active ministry. *Faculty research:* Doctrine, sacraments, ethics, Bible.

Central Baptist Theological Seminary, Graduate and Professional Programs, Shawnee, KS 66226. Offers missional church studies (MA); theological studies (MA); theology (M Div, Diploma). *Accreditation:* ACIPE; ATS (one or more programs are accredited). Part-time programs available. *Degree requirements:* For master's, thesis optional, MMPI, Myers-Briggs, Enneagram; for M Div, thesis/dissertation optional. *Entrance requirements:* For master's, accredited bachelor's degree with minimum GPA of 2.3. Additional exam requirements/recommendations for international students: Required—TOEFL (minimum score 547 paper-based; 210 computer-based; 77 iBT). Electronic applications accepted.

Columbia International University, Columbia Biblical Seminary and School of Missions, Columbia, SC 29230-3122. Offers academic ministries (M Div); bible exposition (M Div, MABE); biblical studies (Certificate); counseling ministries (Certificate); divinity (M Div); educational ministries (M Div, MAEM, Certificate); intercultural studies (M Div, MAIS, Certificate); leadership (D Min); leadership for evangelism/mobilization (MALM); member care (D Min); ministry (Certificate); missions (D Min); pastoral counseling and spiritual formation (M Div, MAPS); preaching (D Min); theology (MA). *Accreditation:* ATS (one or more programs are accredited). Part-time and evening/weekend programs available. *Degree requirements:* For master's, integrative seminar; for doctorate, comprehensive exam, thesis/dissertation; for M Div, internship. *Entrance requirements:* For master's, minimum GPA of 2.7; for doctorate, 3 years of ministerial experience, M Div. Additional exam requirements/recommendations for international students: Required—TOEFL. Electronic applications accepted.

Dallas Baptist University, College of Adult Education, Liberal Arts Program, Dallas, TX 75211-9299. Offers arts (MLA); Christian ministry (MLA); English (MLA); English as a second language (MLA); fine arts (MLA); history (MLA); missions (MLA); political science (MLA). Part-time and evening/weekend programs available. *Entrance requirements:* For master's, minimum GPA of 3.0. Additional exam requirements/recommendations for international students: Required—TOEFL. Electronic applications accepted. *Expenses:* Tuition: Full-time $11,394; part-time $633 per credit hour. *Faculty research:* Milton and seventeenth-century Puritans, inter-Biblical years, nineteenth-century literature, Latin American and Texas history.

Dallas Baptist University, College of Adult Education, Professional Development Program, Dallas, TX 75211-9299. Offers accounting (MA); church leadership (MA); counseling (MA); criminal justice (MA); English as a second language (MA); finance (MA); higher education (MA); leadership studies (MA); management (MA); management information systems (MA); marketing (MA); missions (MA). Part-time and evening/weekend programs available. *Entrance requirements:* For master's, minimum GPA of 3.0. Additional exam requirements/recommendations for international students: Required—TOEFL, IELTS. *Expenses:* Tuition: Full-time $11,394; part-time $633 per credit hour.

Dallas Baptist University, Gary Cook School of Leadership, Program in Christian Education, Dallas, TX 75211-9299. Offers adult ministry (MA); business ministry (MA); childhood ministry (MA); collegiate ministry (MA); communication ministry (MA); counseling ministry (MA); education ministry (MA); general ministry (MA); missions ministry (MA); student ministry (MA); worship ministry (MA). Part-time and evening/weekend programs available. *Entrance requirements:* For master's, minimum GPA of 3.0. Additional exam requirements/recommendations for international students: Required—TOEFL. Electronic applications accepted. *Expenses:* Tuition: Full-time $11,394; part-time $633 per credit hour.

Dallas Baptist University, Gary Cook School of Leadership, Program in Global Leadership, Dallas, TX 75211-9299. Offers business communication (MA); Christian education/missions (MA); ESL (MA); general studies (MA); global studies (MA); international business (MA); missions (MA); worship/missions (MA). Part-time and evening/weekend programs available. *Entrance requirements:* For master's, minimum GPA of 3.0. Additional exam requirements/recommendations for international students: Required—TOEFL, IELTS. *Expenses:* Tuition: Full-time $11,394; part-time $633 per credit hour.

Dallas Theological Seminary, Graduate Programs, Dallas, TX 75204-6499. Offers academic ministries (Th M); Bible translation (Th M); biblical and theological studies (CGS); biblical counseling (MA, Th M); biblical exegesis and linguistics (MA); biblical exposition (PhD); biblical studies (MA); Christian education (MA, D Min); cross-cultural ministries (MA, Th M); educational leadership (Th M); evangelism and discipleship (Th M); interdisciplinary studies (Th M); media and communication (MA); media arts in ministry (Th M); ministry (D Min); New Testament studies (Th M, PhD); Old Testament studies (PhD); parachurch ministries (Th M); pastoral ministries (Th M); sacred theology (STM); theological studies (PhD); women's ministry (Th M). *Accreditation:* ATS (one or more programs are accredited). Part-time and evening/weekend programs available. *Degree requirements:* For master's, variable foreign language requirement, thesis (for some programs); for doctorate, 2 foreign languages, thesis/dissertation. *Entrance requirements:* Additional exam requirements/recommendations for international students: Required—TOEFL, TWE. Electronic applications accepted.

Eastern University, Palmer Theological Seminary, Program in Renewal of the Church for Mission, St. Davids, PA 19087-3696. Offers D Min. *Degree requirements:* For doctorate, thesis/dissertation.

Emmanuel Christian Seminary, Graduate and Professional Programs, Johnson City, TN 37601-9438. Offers Christian care and counseling (M Div); Christian doctrine (MAR); Christian education (M Div); Christian ministry (M Div); church history (MAR); divinity (M Div); ministry (D Min); New Testament (MAR); Old Testament (MAR); urban ministry (M Div); world missions (M Div). *Accreditation:* ACIPE; ATS. Part-time programs available. *Faculty:* 9 full-time (2 women), 9 part-time/adjunct (1 woman). *Students:* 90 full-time (27 women), 57 part-time (10 women); includes 2 Black or African American, non-Hispanic/Latino; 3 Hispanic/Latino, 17 international. Average age 27. 30 applicants, 97% accepted, 22 enrolled. In 2010, 17 first professional degrees, 1 master's, 1 doctorate awarded. *Degree requirements:* For master's, 2 foreign languages, thesis or alternative, portfolio; for doctorate, thesis/dissertation; for M Div, 2 foreign languages, thesis/dissertation or alternative, portfolio. *Entrance requirements:* For M Div and master's, bachelor's degree from accredited institution; for doctorate, Minnesota Multiphasic Personality Inventory, M Div or equivalent. Additional exam requirements/recommendations for international students: Required—TOEFL (minimum score 80 computer-based). *Application deadline:* For fall admission, 8/1 for domestic and international students; for spring admission, 1/20 for domestic and international students. Applications are processed on a rolling basis. Application fee: $25. *Expenses:* Tuition: Full-time $11,700; part-time $390 per credit hour. Required fees: $162.50 per semester. One-time fee: $240. Tuition and fees vary according to reciprocity agreements. *Financial support:* In 2010–11, 136 students received support; teaching assistantships with partial tuition reimbursements available, career-related internships or fieldwork, scholarships/grants, and tuition waivers (partial) available. Support available to part-time students. Financial award application deadline: 3/1; financial award applicants required to submit FAFSA. *Faculty research:* Theology of Old Testament prophets, spiritual formation for Christian leaders, history of African churches and religions, social world of early Christianity, lay pastoral counseling, ANE epigraphy. Total annual research expenditures: $12,000. *Unit head:* Dr. Jack Holland, Dean and Professor of Christian Care and Counseling, 423-461-1524, Fax: 423-926-6198, E-mail: jholland@ecs.edu. *Application contact:* Erin Layton, Director of Admissions, 423-461-1535, Fax: 423-926-6198, E-mail: elayton@ecs.edu.

Evangelical Theological Seminary, Graduate and Professional Programs, Myerstown, PA 17067-1212. Offers Biblical studies (MAR); congregational ministry (M Div); global and contextual studies (M Div, MAR); historical and theological studies (MAR); interdisciplinary studies (MAR); marriage and family counseling (M Div); marriage and family therapy (MA); New Testament (MAR); Old Testament (MAR); spiritual formation (MAR); teaching ministry (M Div); youth ministry (M Div). *Accreditation:* ATS (one or more programs are accredited). Part-time programs available. Postbaccalaureate distance learning degree programs offered (minimal on-campus study). *Degree requirements:* For master's, 2 foreign languages; for M Div, 2 foreign languages, ministry internship. *Entrance requirements:* For M Div and master's, minimum GPA of 2.5. Additional exam requirements/recommendations for international students: Required—TOEFL (minimum score 550 paper-based; 213 computer-based). *Faculty research:* Literary form and structure within the Hebrew and Greek scriptures, Wesley studies, esoteric biblical languages, the Mosaic law and the Christian, ethics.

Faulkner University, College of Biblical Studies, Montgomery, AL 36109-3398. Offers ministry (MABS); missions (MABS); New Testament (MABS); Old Testament (MABS); youth and family ministry (MABS).

Fresno Pacific University, Fresno Pacific Biblical Seminary, Program in Intercultural Mission, Fresno, CA 93702-4709. Offers MA.

Fuller Theological Seminary, Graduate School of Theology, Pasadena, CA 91182. Offers Christian leadership (MACL); evangelism (MA); family life education (MA); ministry (M Div, D Min); pastoral ministry (MA); recovery ministry (MA); theology (MAT, Th M, PhD); worship music ministry (MA); worship, theology, and the arts (MA); youth, family, and culture (MA). M Div offered jointly with Denver Conservative Baptist Seminary; D Min with Tyndale University College & Seminary. *Accreditation:* ACIPE; ATS (one or more programs are accredited). Part-time and evening/weekend programs available. *Degree requirements:* For doctorate, variable foreign language requirement, thesis/dissertation; for M Div, 2 foreign languages. *Entrance requirements:* For doctorate, GRE General Test. *Faculty research:* New Testament, Old Testament, systematic theology, history, practical theology.

Fuller Theological Seminary, School of Intercultural Studies, Program in Global Ministries, Pasadena, CA 91182. Offers global leadership (MA); global ministries (D Min); global ministry (Korean language) (D Min). D Min offered jointly with Tyndale University College & Seminary. *Degree requirements:* For doctorate, one foreign language, thesis/dissertation. *Entrance requirements:* For doctorate, qualifying exam.

Fuller Theological Seminary, School of Intercultural Studies, Program in Intercultural Studies, Pasadena, CA 91182. Offers cross-cultural studies (MA); intercultural studies (MA, Th M, PhD); intercultural studies (Korean language) (MA). *Degree requirements:* For master's, one foreign language, thesis optional; for doctorate, one foreign language, thesis/dissertation. *Entrance requirements:* For doctorate, qualifying exam, minimum GPA of 3.7, Th M and MA degrees from Graduate School of World Mission. Additional exam requirements/recommendations for international students: Required—TOEFL.

Fuller Theological Seminary, School of Intercultural Studies, Program in Missiology, Pasadena, CA 91182. Offers missiology (D Miss); missiology (Korean language) (Th M). *Degree requirements:* For doctorate, one foreign language, thesis/dissertation. *Entrance requirements:* For doctorate, qualifying exam, minimum GPA of 3.4 (D Miss), 3.7 (PhD); Th M and MA from Graduate School of World Mission. Additional exam requirements/recommendations for international students: Required—TOEFL.

Gardner-Webb University, School of Divinity, Boiling Springs, NC 28017. Offers biblical studies (M Div); Christian education and formation (M Div); ministry (D Min); missiology (M Div); pastoral care and counseling (M Div); pastoral studies (M Div); M Div/MA; M Div/MBA. *Accreditation:* ACIPE; ATS. Part-time programs available. *Faculty:* 11 full-time (9 women), 5 part-time/adjunct (2 women). *Students:* 138 full-time (63 women), 81 part-time (26 women); includes 74 Black or African American, non-Hispanic/Latino; 1 Asian, non-Hispanic/Latino; 3 Hispanic/Latino, 2 international. Average age 40. In 2010, 56 first professional degrees, 1 doctorate awarded. *Degree requirements:* For M Div, 2 foreign languages. *Entrance requirements:* For M Div, minimum GPA of 2.0; for doctorate, minimum GPA of 2.75. *Application deadline:* For fall admission, 8/1 priority date for domestic students; for spring admission, 12/15 priority date for domestic students. Applications are processed on a rolling basis. Application fee: $40. *Expenses:* Contact institution. *Financial support:* Fellowships, institutionally sponsored loans and unspecified assistantships available. Support available to part-time students. Financial award application deadline: 5/15. *Faculty research:* Jewish Christian dialogue, Islam. *Unit head:* Dr. Robert W. Canoy, Dean, 704-406-4400, Fax: 704-406-3935, E-mail: rcanoy@gardner-webb.edu. *Application contact:* Jeremy Fern, Director of Admissions, 704-406-3205, Fax: 704-406-3935, E-mail: jfern@gardner-webb.edu.

George Fox University, George Fox Evangelical Seminary, Newberg, OR 97132-2697. Offers Biblical studies (M Div); Christian earthkeeping (M Div); Christian history and theology (M Div); clinical pastoral education and hospital chaplaincy (M Div); leadership and spiritual formation (D Min), including global missional leadership, semiotics and future studies; military chaplaincy (M Div); ministry leadership (MA); pastoral studies (M Div); spiritual formation (MA, Certificate); spiritual formation and discipleship (M Div); theological studies (MA). *Accreditation:* ACIPE; ATS. Part-time programs available. Postbaccalaureate distance learning degree programs offered (minimal on-campus study). *Faculty:* 7 full-time (2 women), 23 part-time/adjunct (6 women). *Students:* 122 full-time (41 women), 236 part-time (76 women); includes 6 Black or African American, non-Hispanic/Latino; 2 American Indian or Alaska Native, non-Hispanic/Latino; 11 Asian, non-Hispanic/Latino; 4 Hispanic/Latino; 4 Two or more races, non-Hispanic/Latino, 14 international. Average age 40. 141 applicants, 94% accepted, 95 enrolled. In 2010, 19 first professional degrees, 33 master's, 17 doctorates, 3 other advanced degrees awarded. *Degree requirements:* For master's, variable foreign language requirement, thesis optional, internship; for doctorate, comprehensive exam (for some programs), thesis/dissertation, internship. *Entrance requirements:* For master's, resume, three references (one pastoral, one academic or professional, one personal), one official transcript from each college or university attended; for doctorate, resume, 3 references (1 professional, 1 academic, 1 personal). Additional exam requirements/recommendations for international students: Required—TOEFL (minimum score 577 paper-based; 233 computer-based; 90 iBT). *Application deadline:* For fall admission, 7/1 for domestic and international students; for winter admission, 11/1 for domestic and international students; for spring admission, 4/1 for domestic and international students. Applications are processed on a rolling basis. Application fee: $40. Electronic applications accepted. *Expenses:* Contact institution. *Financial support:* Career-related internships or fieldwork and scholarships/grants available. Financial award application deadline: 5/1; financial award applicants required to submit FAFSA. *Unit head:* Dr. Chuck Conniry, Professor of Theology/Vice President and Dean, 503-554-6152, E-mail: cconniry@georgefox.edu. *Application contact:* Sheila Bartlett, Admissions Counselor, 800-631-0921, Fax: 503-554-6122, E-mail: gfes@georgefox.edu.

Missions and Missiology

Global University, Graduate School of Theology, Springfield, MO 65804. Offers biblical studies (MA); divinity (M Div); ministerial studies (MA), including education, leadership, missions, New Testament, Old Testament. Part-time and evening/weekend programs available. Postbaccalaureate distance learning degree programs offered (no on-campus study). *Degree requirements:* For master's, thesis (for some programs). *Entrance requirements:* For M Div, minimum undergraduate GPA of 3.0; for master's, minimum undergraduate GPA of 3.0, 15 undergraduate credit hours of course work in Bible or theology. Electronic applications accepted. *Faculty research:* Higher education, cross-cultural missions.

Gordon-Conwell Theological Seminary, Graduate and Professional Programs, South Hamilton, MA 01982. Offers Biblical languages (MABL); church history (MACH); counseling (MACO); ministry (D Min); missions/evangelism (MAME); New Testament (MANT); Old Testament (MAOT); religion (MAR); theology (M Div, MATH, Th M, Th D). *Accreditation:* ACIPE; ATS (one or more programs are accredited). Part-time and evening/weekend programs available. *Degree requirements:* For master's, one foreign language, thesis optional; for doctorate, 2 foreign languages, thesis/dissertation; for M Div, 2 foreign languages. *Entrance requirements:* For M Div and master's, minimum GPA of 2.5; for doctorate, minimum GPA of 3.0.

Grace Theological Seminary, Graduate and Professional Programs, Winona Lake, IN 46590-9907. Offers biblical studies (Certificate); camp administration (MA); counseling (M Div); exegetical studies (MA); intercultural studies (M Div, MA); local church studies (MA); pastoral studies (M Div); theological studies (MA); theology (D Min, Diploma). Part-time programs available. Postbaccalaureate distance learning degree programs offered (no on-campus study). *Degree requirements:* For master's, thesis optional; for doctorate, 2 foreign languages, thesis/dissertation; for M Div, 2 foreign languages, thesis/dissertation optional. *Entrance requirements:* For M Div and master's, MAT, minimum GPA of 2.5. Electronic applications accepted. *Faculty research:* Biblical theology, language, and church ministries.

Grand Rapids Theological Seminary of Cornerstone University, Graduate Programs, Grand Rapids, MI 49525-5897. Offers biblical counseling (MA); Biblical counseling (M Div); chaplaincy (M Div); Christian education (M Div, MA); intercultural studies (M Div, MA); New Testament (MA, Th M); Old Testament (MA, Th M); pastoral studies (M Div); systematic theology (MA); theology (Th M). *Accreditation:* ATS. Part-time programs available. Postbaccalaureate distance learning degree programs offered (minimal on-campus study). *Entrance requirements:* Additional exam requirements/recommendations for international students: Required—TOEFL (minimum score 577 paper-based; 233 computer-based; 90 iBT). Electronic applications accepted.

Hope International University, School of Graduate and Professional Studies, Programs in Ministry, Fullerton, CA 92831-3138. Offers Christian leadership (MCM); church music (MA); church music (Korean track) (MCM); church planting (MCM); intercultural studies (MCM); worship (MCM). Part-time and evening/weekend programs available. Postbaccalaureate distance learning degree programs offered (minimal on-campus study). *Degree requirements:* For master's, thesis (for some programs), project. *Entrance requirements:* For master's, minimum GPA of 3.0, MCM program requires an undergraduate degree in music, 2 references. Additional exam requirements/recommendations for international students: Required—TOEFL (minimum score 550 paper-based; 213 computer-based; 86 iBT); Recommended—IELTS (minimum score 6.5). Electronic applications accepted. *Expenses:* Contact institution. *Faculty research:* Church dynamics, growth methodologies.

Knox Theological Seminary, Graduate Programs, Program in Evangelism, Fort Lauderdale, FL 33308. Offers ME. Part-time and evening/weekend programs available. *Entrance requirements:* Additional exam requirements/recommendations for international students: Required—TOEFL, TWE (minimum score 5).

Luther Rice University, Graduate Programs, Lithonia, GA 30038-2454. Offers Bible/theology (M Div); Christian education (M Div); Christian studies (MA); church ministry (D Min); counseling (M Div); discipleship counseling (MA); ministry (M Div, MA); missions/evangelism (M Div). Part-time programs available. Postbaccalaureate distance learning degree programs offered (no on-campus study). *Degree requirements:* For doctorate, thesis/dissertation. *Entrance requirements:* Additional exam requirements/recommendations for international students: Required—TOEFL (minimum score 500 paper-based; 173 computer-based).

Midwestern Baptist Theological Seminary, Graduate and Professional Programs, Kansas City, MO 64118-4697. Offers Biblical archaeology (MA); Biblical languages (MA); Christian education (M Div, MACE); Christian foundations—lay ministry (Graduate Certificate); collegiate ministries (M Div); counseling (MA); educational ministry (D Ed Min); international church planting (M Div); ministry (M Div, D Min); North American church planting (M Div); sacred music (MCM); urban ministry (M Div); worship leadership (M Div); youth ministry (M Div). *Accreditation:* ATS. Part-time programs available. Postbaccalaureate distance learning degree programs offered (minimal on-campus study). *Degree requirements:* For doctorate, thesis/dissertation; for M Div, 2 foreign languages. *Entrance requirements:* For doctorate, MAT. Electronic applications accepted. *Faculty research:* Ministerial studies, Biblical and theological studies, missions, counseling.

Nazarene Theological Seminary, Graduate and Professional Programs, Kansas City, MO 64131-1263. Offers Christian education (MA); intercultural studies (MA); theological studies (MA); theology (M Div, D Min). *Accreditation:* ACIPE; ATS. Part-time programs available. *Degree requirements:* For master's, comprehensive exam (for some programs), thesis (for some programs); for doctorate, thesis/dissertation. *Entrance requirements:* Additional exam requirements/recommendations for international students: Required—TOEFL. Electronic applications accepted.

Northwest Nazarene University, Graduate Studies, Program in Religion, Nampa, ID 83686-5897. Offers Christian education (MA); missional leadership (MA); pastoral ministry (MA); religion (M Div); spiritual formation (MA). Part-time and evening/weekend programs available. Postbaccalaureate distance learning degree programs offered (no on-campus study). *Faculty:* 7 full-time (1 woman), 10 part-time/adjunct (1 woman). *Students:* 119 full-time (33 women), 11 part-time (3 women); includes 8 minority (4 Black or African American, non-Hispanic/Latino; 1 American Indian or Alaska Native, non-Hispanic/Latino; 2 Hispanic/Latino; 1 Native Hawaiian or other Pacific Islander, non-Hispanic/Latino), 1 international. In 2010, 42 master's awarded. *Application deadline:* Applications are processed on a rolling basis. Application fee: $50. Electronic applications accepted. *Unit head:* Dr. Jay Akkerman, Director, Graduate Studies, 208-467-8437, Fax: 208-467-8252. *Application contact:* Jill Jones, Program Assistant, 208-467-8368, Fax: 208-467-8252, E-mail: jdjones@nnu.edu.

Northwest University, College of Ministry, Kirkland, WA 98033. Offers ministry (MA); missional leadership (MA); theology and culture (MA). Evening/weekend programs available. *Faculty:* 9 full-time (1 woman), 21 part-time/adjunct (2 women). *Students:* 17 full-time (3 women), 43 part-time (9 women); includes 7 minority (5 Black or African American, non-Hispanic/Latino; 1 Asian, non-Hispanic/Latino; 1 Hispanic/Latino), 2 international. 32 applicants, 97% accepted, 29 enrolled. In 2010, 6 master's awarded. *Entrance requirements:* Additional exam requirements/recommendations for international students: Required—TOEFL (minimum score 550 paper-based). Application fee: $75. Tuition and fees vary according to program. *Unit head:* Dr. Wayde Goodall, Dean, 425-889-5253, E-mail: wayde.goodall@northwestu.edu. *Application contact:* Aaron Oosterwyk, Director of Graduate and Professional Studies Enrollment, 425-889-7799, Fax: 425-803-3059, E-mail: gpse@northwestu.edu.

Oral Roberts University, School of Theology and Missions, Tulsa, OK 74171. Offers biblical literature (MA), including advanced languages, Judaic-Christian studies; Christian counseling (MA), including marriage and family therapy; divinity (M Div); missions (MA); practical theology (MA); theological/historical studies (MA); theology (D Min). Part-time programs available. Postbaccalaureate distance learning degree programs offered (minimal on-campus study). *Degree requirements:* For master's, thesis (for some programs), practicum/internship; for doctorate, thesis/dissertation, applied research project; for M Div, one foreign language, field experience. *Entrance requirements:* For M Div and master's, GRE General Test or MAT, minimum GPA of 2.5; for doctorate, M Div, minimum GPA of 3.0, 3 years of full-time ministry experience. Additional exam requirements/recommendations for international students: Required—TOEFL (minimum score 550 paper-based; 213 computer-based; 79 iBT). Electronic applications accepted.

Phillips Theological Seminary, Programs in Theology, Tulsa, OK 74116. Offers administration of church agencies (M Div); campus ministry (M Div); church-related social work (M Div); college and seminary teaching (M Div); global mission work (M Div); institutional chaplaincy (M Div); ministerial vocations in Christian education (M Div); ministry (D Min), including parish ministry, pastoral counseling, practices of ministry; ministry and culture (MAMC), including Christian education, congregational leadership, history and practice of Christian spirituality, theology, ethics, and culture; ministry of music (M Div); pastoral care and counseling (M Div); pastoral ministry (M Div); theological studies (MTS). *Accreditation:* ATS. Part-time programs available. Postbaccalaureate distance learning degree programs offered (minimal on-campus study). *Degree requirements:* For master's, thesis (for some programs); for doctorate, thesis/dissertation. *Entrance requirements:* For master's, minimum GPA of 2.5; for doctorate, M Div, minimum GPA of 3.0. *Faculty research:* Biblical studies, historical studies, theology and culture, practical theology, theology and film.

Providence College and Theological Seminary, Theological Seminary, Otterburne, MB R0A 1G0, Canada. Offers children's ministry (Certificate); Christian studies (MA, Certificate); counseling (MA); cross-cultural discipleship (Certificate); divinity (M Div); educational studies (MA), including counseling psychology, educational ministries, student development, teaching English to speakers of other languages, training teachers of English to speakers of other languages; global studies (MA); lay counseling (Diploma); ministry (D Min); teaching English to speakers of other languages (Certificate); theological studies (MA); training teacher of English to speakers of other languages (Certificate); youth ministry (Certificate). *Accreditation:* ATS. Part-time programs available. *Degree requirements:* For master's, variable foreign language requirement, thesis (for some programs); for doctorate, thesis/dissertation; for M Div, 2 foreign languages, comprehensive exam, thesis/dissertation (for some programs). *Entrance requirements:* Additional exam requirements/recommendations for international students: Recommended—TOEFL (minimum score 550 paper-based; 213 computer-based). *Faculty research:* Studies in Isaiah, theology of sin.

Reformed Theological Seminary–Jackson Campus, Graduate and Professional Programs, Jackson, MS 39209-3099. Offers Bible, theology, and missions (Certificate); biblical studies (MA); Christian education (M Div, MA); counseling (M Div); divinity (M Div, Diploma); marriage and family therapy (MA); ministry (D Min); missions (M Div, MA, D Min); New Testament (Th M); Old Testament (Th M); theological studies (MA); theology (Th M); M Div/MA. *Accreditation:* AAMFT/COAMFTE (one or more programs are accredited); ATS (one or more programs are accredited). *Degree requirements:* For master's, thesis (for some programs), fieldwork; for doctorate, 2 foreign languages, thesis/dissertation; for M Div, 2 foreign languages, thesis/dissertation (for some programs). *Entrance requirements:* For M Div and master's, minimum GPA of 2.6; for doctorate, minimum GPA of 3.0. Additional exam requirements/recommendations for international students: Required—TOEFL.

Regent University, Graduate School, School of Divinity, Virginia Beach, VA 23464-9800. Offers Biblical studies (MA); leadership and renewal (D Min); missiology (M Div, MA); practical theology (M Div, MA); renewal studies (PhD); M Div/M Ed; M Div/MA; M Div/MBA; M Ed/MA; MBA/MA. *Accreditation:* ACIPE; ATS. Part-time programs available. Postbaccalaureate distance learning degree programs offered (minimal on-campus study). *Faculty:* 20 full-time (4 women), 26 part-time/adjunct (5 women). *Students:* 128 full-time (60 women), 524 part-time (225 women); includes 278 Black or African American, non-Hispanic/Latino; 4 American Indian or Alaska Native, non-Hispanic/Latino; 16 Asian, non-Hispanic/Latino; 24 Hispanic/Latino, 20 international. Average age 41. 361 applicants, 64% accepted, 154 enrolled. In 2010, 32 first professional degrees, 61 master's, 9 doctorates awarded. *Degree requirements:* For master's, comprehensive exam, thesis or alternative, internship; for doctorate, thesis/dissertation or alternative; for M Div, internship. *Entrance requirements:* For M Div, GRE General Test or MAT, minimum undergraduate GPA of 3.0, minimum 3 years of ministry experience, transcripts, recommendations; for master's, GRE General Test or MAT, minimum undergraduate GPA of 2.75, writing sample, clergy recommendation; for doctorate, M Div or theological master's degree; minimum graduate GPA of 3.5 (PhD), 3.0 (D Min); recommendations; writing sample; transcripts. Additional exam requirements/recommendations for international students: Required—TOEFL (minimum score 577 paper-based; 233 computer-based). *Application deadline:* For fall admission, 5/1 priority date for domestic students. Applications are processed on a rolling basis. Application fee: $50. Electronic applications accepted. *Expenses:* Contact institution. *Financial support:* Fellowships with full and partial tuition reimbursements, career-related internships or fieldwork, scholarships/grants, tuition waivers (full and partial), and unspecified assistantships available. Support available to part-time students. Financial award application deadline: 9/1; financial award applicants required to submit FAFSA. *Faculty research:* Greek and Hebrew, theology, spiritual formation, global missions and world Christianity, women's studies. *Unit head:* Dr. Michael Palmer, Dean, 757-352-4406, Fax: 757-352-4597, E-mail: mpalmer@regent.edu. *Application contact:* Matthew Chadwick, Director of Enrollment Support Services, 800-373-5504, Fax: 757-352-4381, E-mail: admissions@regent.edu.

Rochester College, Center for Missional Leadership, Rochester Hills, MI 48307-2764. Offers MRE.

Saint Paul University, Faculty of Human Sciences, Program in Mission and Interreligious Studies, Ottawa, ON K1S 1C4, Canada. Offers MA. *Degree requirements:* For master's, one foreign language, thesis. *Entrance requirements:* For master's, honors BA in mission, minimum B average. *Faculty research:* Theology of mission; mission and sociology; history of mission; faith, religion, and culture; world religions; practice of mission; religious anthropology; sociocultural anthropology.

Simpson University, A.W. Tozer Theological Seminary, Redding, CA 96003-8606. Offers intellectual leadership (MA); ministry (M Div). Part-time and evening/weekend programs available. Postbaccalaureate distance learning degree programs offered (minimal on-campus study). *Degree requirements:* For master's, student portfolio. *Entrance requirements:* For master's, GRE General Test (if undergraduate GPA less than 2.5), 2 letters of reference, Christian Experience statement. Additional exam requirements/recommendations for international students: Required—TOEFL. Electronic applications accepted. *Expenses:* Contact institution.

Southeastern Baptist Theological Seminary, Graduate and Professional Programs, Wake Forest, NC 27588-1889. Offers advanced biblical studies (M Div); Christian education (M Div, MACE); Christian ethics (PhD); Christian ministry (M Div); Christian planting (M Div); church music (MACM); counseling (MACO); evangelism (PhD); language (M Div); ministry (D Min); New Testament (PhD); Old Testament (PhD); philosophy (PhD); theology (Th M, PhD); women's studies (M Div). *Accreditation:* ACIPE; ATS (one or more programs are accredited). *Degree requirements:* For master's, thesis (for some programs), oral exam; for doctorate, thesis/dissertation, fieldwork; for M Div, supervised ministry. *Entrance requirements:* For master's, Cooperative English Test, minimum GPA of 2.0, M Div or equivalent (Th M); for doctorate, GRE General Test or MAT, Cooperative English Test, M Div or equivalent, 3 years of professional experience.

Southern Adventist University, School of Religion, Collegedale, TN 37315-0370. Offers Biblical and theological studies (MA); church leadership and management (M Min); church ministry and homiletics (M Min); evangelism and world mission (M Min); religious studies (MA). Part-time programs available. *Degree requirements:* For master's, comprehensive exam, thesis (for some programs). *Entrance requirements:* For master's, GRE. Additional exam requirements/recommendations for international students: Required—TOEFL (minimum score 600 paper-based; 250 computer-based). *Faculty research:* Biblical archaeology.

Southern Baptist Theological Seminary, Billy Graham School of Missions, Evangelism and Church Growth, Louisville, KY 40280-0004. Offers Christian mission/world religion (PhD); evangelism/church growth (PhD); ministry (D Min); missiology (MA, D Miss); missions, evangelism and church growth (M Div); religion (Th M); theological studies (MA). *Accreditation:* ATS. Part-time and evening/weekend programs available. Postbaccalaureate distance learning degree programs offered (minimal on-campus study). *Degree requirements:* For master's and M Div, 2 foreign languages; for doctorate, 4 foreign languages, thesis/dissertation. *Entrance requirements:* For doctorate, GRE General Test, MAT, M Div. Additional exam requirements/ recommendations for international students: Required—TOEFL, TWE. *Faculty research:* Assimilation of church congregants, effective methodologies of evangelism, expectations of church members, spiritual warfare literature, formative church discipline.

Southern Evangelical Seminary, Graduate Programs, Matthews, NC 28105. Offers apologetics (MA, Certificate); Christian education (MA); church ministry (MA, Certificate); divinity (Certificate), including apologetics (M Div, Certificate); Islamic studies (MA, Certificate); Jewish studies (MA); philosophy (MA); religion (MA); theology (M Div), including apologetics (M Div, Certificate), Biblical studies; youth ministry (MA). Part-time and evening/weekend programs available. Postbaccalaureate distance learning degree programs offered. *Degree requirements:* For master's, thesis (for some programs); for doctorate, 2 foreign languages, comprehensive exam (for some programs), thesis/dissertation; for M Div, one foreign language. *Entrance requirements:* Additional exam requirements/recommendations for international students: Required—TOEFL (minimum score 600 paper-based; 250 computer-based). *Application deadline:* For fall admission, 8/15 priority date for domestic students, 8/5 priority date for international students; for winter admission, 12/15 priority date for domestic and international students; for spring admission, 1/15 priority date for domestic and international students. Applications are processed on a rolling basis. Application fee: $25. *Expenses:* Tuition: Full-time $9405; part-time $313.50 per credit hour. Required fees: $150; $50 per semester. *Financial support:* Scholarships/grants available. *Unit head:* Dr. Barry R. Leventhal, Dean, 704-847-5600 Ext. 204, Fax: 704-845-1747, E-mail: dean@ses.edu. *Application contact:* Duke Hale, Director of Recruitment, 704-847-5600 Ext. 216, Fax: 704-845-1747, E-mail: dhale@ses.edu.

Southwestern Assemblies of God University, Thomas F. Harrison School of Graduate Studies, Program in Theological Studies, Waxahachie, TX 75165-5735. Offers Bible and theology (MS); Biblical studies (M Div); counseling (M Div); cross cultural missions (M Div); practical theology (M Div); theological studies (M Div). Postbaccalaureate distance learning degree programs offered. *Degree requirements:* For master's, comprehensive written and oral exams. *Entrance requirements:* For master's, GRE General Test, minimum GPA of 2.5. Electronic applications accepted.

Southwestern Christian University, Program in Ministry, Bethany, OK 73008-0340. Offers church planting (M Min); church revitalization and renewal (M Min); intercultural studies (M Min); leadership (M Min); life coaching (M Min); pastoral ministries (M Min); work place ministries (M Min). Part-time programs available. *Degree requirements:* For master's, thesis. *Entrance requirements:* For master's, minimum GPA of 2.5. Additional exam requirements/ recommendations for international students: Required—TOEFL (minimum score 500 paper-based). Electronic applications accepted.

Taylor College and Seminary, Graduate and Professional Programs, Edmonton, AB T6J 4T3, Canada. Offers Christian studies (Diploma); intercultural studies (MA, Diploma), including intercultural studies (Diploma), TESOL; theology (M Div, MTS). *Accreditation:* ATS. Part-time programs available. Postbaccalaureate distance learning degree programs offered (minimal on-campus study). *Degree requirements:* For master's, thesis optional. *Entrance requirements:* Additional exam requirements/recommendations for international students: Required—TOEFL (minimum score 550 paper-based; 80 iBT), IELTS (minimum score 6.5). *Faculty research:* Biblical studies, administration and organization, world religions, ethics, missiology.

Trinity International University, Trinity Evangelical Divinity School, Deerfield, IL 60015-1284. Offers Biblical and Near Eastern archaeology and languages (MA); Christian studies (MA, Certificate); Christian thought (MA); church history (MA, Th M); congregational ministry: pastor-teacher (M Div); congregational ministry: team ministry (M Div); counseling ministries (MA); counseling psychology (MA); cross-cultural ministry (M Div); educational studies (PhD); evangelism (MA); history of Christianity in America (MA); intercultural studies (MA, PhD); leadership and ministry management (D Min); military chaplaincy (D Min); ministry (MA); mission and evangelism (Th M); missions and evangelism (D Min); New Testament (MA, Th M); Old Testament (Th M); Old Testament and Semitic languages (MA); pastoral care (M Div); pastoral care and counseling (D Min); pastoral counseling and psychology (Th M); pastoral theology (Th M); philosophy of religion (MA); preaching (D Min); religion (MA); research ministry (M Div); systematic theology (Th M); theological studies (PhD); urban ministry (MA). *Accreditation:* ATS (one or more programs are accredited). Part-time programs available. Postbaccalaureate distance learning degree programs offered (minimal on-campus study). *Degree requirements:* For master's, comprehensive exam, thesis, fieldwork; for doctorate, comprehensive exam (for some programs), thesis/dissertation; for M Div, 2 foreign languages, fieldwork; for Certificate, comprehensive exam, integrative papers. *Entrance requirements:* For M Div, GRE, MAT; for master's, GRE, MAT, minimum cumulative undergraduate GPA of 3.0; for doctorate, GRE, minimum cumulative graduate GPA of 3.2; for Certificate, GRE, MAT, minimum undergraduate GPA of 2.5. Additional exam requirements/recommendations for international students: Required—TOEFL (minimum score 580 paper-based; 237 computer-based), TWE (minimum score 4). Electronic applications accepted.

Trinity School for Ministry, Graduate Programs, Ambridge, PA 15003-2397. Offers Anglican studies (Diploma); basic Christian studies (Diploma); divinity (M Div); ministry (D Min); mission and evangelism (MAME, Diploma); religion (MAR); youth ministry (Diploma). *Accreditation:* ATS (one or more programs are accredited). Part-time programs available. *Degree requirements:* For master's, thesis optional; for doctorate, thesis/dissertation; for M Div, thesis/dissertation optional, Greek and Hebrew. *Entrance requirements:* Additional exam requirements/ recommendations for international students: Required—TOEFL. *Faculty research:* Pauline Epistles, contemporary theology, history of Anglican liturgy, book of Ruth, biblical theology.

Tyndale University College & Seminary, Graduate Programs, Toronto, ON M2M 4B3, Canada. Offers Biblical studies (M Div); Christian foundations (MTS); Christian studies (Diploma); counseling (M Div); educational ministry (M Div); missions (M Div, Diploma); pastoral and Chinese ministry (M Div); pastoral ministry (M Div); Pentecostal studies (MTS); spiritual formation (M Div, Diploma); theological studies (M Div); theology (Th M); worship and liturgy (M Div, MTS); youth and family ministry (M Div). *Accreditation:* ATS. Part-time programs available. Postbaccalaureate distance learning degree programs offered (no on-campus study). *Degree requirements:* For M Div, one foreign language, thesis/dissertation optional. *Entrance requirements:* For M Div, master's, and Diploma, minimum C+ average in undergraduate course work. Additional exam requirements/recommendations for international students: Required—TOEFL (minimum score 570 paper-based; 230 computer-based), TWE (minimum score 5). Electronic applications accepted. *Faculty research:* Canadian church history, Chinese church history, Old Testament, counseling ministries (narrative therapy), world religions.

University of South Africa, College of Human Sciences, Pretoria, South Africa. Offers adult education (M Ed); African languages (MA, PhD); African politics (MA, PhD); Afrikaans (MA, PhD); ancient history (MA, PhD); ancient Near Eastern studies (MA, PhD); anthropology (MA, PhD); applied linguistics (MA); Arabic (MA, PhD); archaeology (MA); art history (MA); Biblical archaeology (MA); Biblical studies (M Th, D Th, PhD); Christian spirituality (M Th, D Th); church history (M Th, D Th); classical studies (MA, PhD); clinical psychology (MA); communication (MA, PhD); comparative education (M Ed, Ed D); consulting psychology (D Admin, D Com, PhD); curriculum studies (M Ed, Ed D); development studies (M Admin, MA, D Admin, PhD); didactics (M Ed, Ed D); education (M Tech); education management (M Ed, Ed D); educational psychology (M Ed); English (MA); environmental education (M Ed); French (MA, PhD); German (MA, PhD); Greek (MA); guidance and counseling (M Ed); health studies (MA, PhD), including health sciences education (MA), health services management (MA), medical and surgical nursing science (critical care general) (MA), midwifery and neonatal nursing science (MA), trauma and emergency care (MA); history (MA, PhD); history of education (Ed D); inclusive education (M Ed, Ed D); information and communications technology policy and regulation (MA); information science (MA, MIS, PhD); international politics (MA, PhD); Islamic studies (MA, PhD); Italian (MA, PhD); Judaica (MA, PhD); linguistics (MA, PhD); mathematical education (M Ed); mathematics education (MA); missiology (M Th, D Th); modern Hebrew (MA, PhD); musicology (MA, MMus, D Mus, PhD); natural science education (M Ed); New Testament (M Th, D Th); Old Testament (D Th); pastoral therapy (M Th, D Th); philosophy (MA); philosophy of education (M Ed, Ed D); politics (MA, PhD); Portuguese (MA, PhD); practical theology (M Th, D Th); psychology (MA, MS, PhD); psychology of education (M Ed, Ed D); public health (MA); religious studies (MA, D Th, PhD); Romance languages (MA); Russian (MA, PhD); Semitic languages (MA, PhD); social behavior studies in HIV/AIDS (MA); social science (mental health) (MA); social science in development studies (MA); social science in psychology (MA); social science in social work (MA); social science in sociology (MA); social work (MSW, DSW, PhD); socio-education (M Ed, Ed D); sociolinguistics (MA); sociology (MA, PhD); Spanish (MA, PhD); systematic theology (M Th, D Th); TESOL (teaching English to speakers of other languages) (MA); theological ethics (M Th, D Th); theory of literature (MA, PhD); urban ministries (D Th); urban ministry (M Th).

Villanova University, Villanova School of Business, Master of Science in Church Management Program, Villanova, PA 19085-1699. Offers MSCM. *Expenses:* Tuition: Part-time $700 per credit. Part-time tuition and fees vary according to degree level and program.

Wesley Biblical Seminary, Graduate Programs, Jackson, MS 39206. Offers apologetics (MA); Biblical studies (MA); Christian studies (MA); evangelism (M Div); family life ministry (M Div); honors research (M Div); missions (M Div); pastoral ministry (M Div); teaching (M Div); theological studies (MA). *Accreditation:* ATS. Part-time programs available. *Degree requirements:* For master's, thesis. *Entrance requirements:* Additional exam requirements/recommendations for international students: Required—TOEFL. Electronic applications accepted. *Faculty research:* Patristics, missiology, culture, hermeneutics.

Westminster Theological Seminary, Graduate and Professional Programs, Philadelphia, PA 19118. Offers apologetics (Th M); Biblical and urban studies (Certificate); Biblical counseling (MA); biblical studies (MAR); Christian studies (Certificate); church history (Th M); counseling (M Div); general studies (M Div, MAR); hermeneutics and Bible interpretations (PhD); historical and theological studies (PhD); historical theology (Th M); New Testament (Th M); Old Testament (Th M); pastoral counseling (D Min); pastoral ministry (M Div, D Min); systematic theology (Th M); theological studies (MAR); urban missions (M Div, MA, MAR, D Min). *Accreditation:* ATS. Part-time programs available. Terminal master's awarded for partial completion of doctoral program. *Degree requirements:* For master's, thesis (for some programs); for doctorate, 4 foreign languages, comprehensive exam (for some programs), thesis/dissertation; for M Div, 2 foreign languages. *Entrance requirements:* For doctorate, GRE General Test. Additional exam requirements/recommendations for international students: Required—TOEFL, TWE.

Wheaton College, Graduate School, Department of Intercultural Studies, Wheaton, IL 60187-5593. Offers evangelism (MA); intercultural studies (MA); intercultural studies/teaching English as a second language (MA); missions (MA); teaching English as a second language (Certificate). Part-time programs available. *Degree requirements:* For master's, thesis or alternative. *Entrance requirements:* For master's, GRE General Test, MAT. Electronic applications accepted.

Pastoral Ministry and Counseling

Abilene Christian University, Graduate School, College of Biblical Studies, Graduate School of Theology, Program in Ministry, Abilene, TX 79699-9100. Offers D Min. Part-time programs available. *Students:* 22 part-time (0 women), 1 international. 14 applicants, 93% accepted, 11 enrolled. In 2010, 2 doctorates awarded. *Degree requirements:* For doctorate, one foreign language, comprehensive exam, thesis/dissertation. *Entrance requirements:* For doctorate, GRE, MAT. Additional exam requirements/recommendations for international students: Required—TOEFL (minimum score 550 paper-based; 213 computer-based). *Application deadline:* For fall admission, 4/1 priority date for domestic students; for spring admission, 11/1 for domestic students. Applications are processed on a rolling basis. Application fee: $40. *Expenses:* Tuition: Full-time $12,906; part-time $717 per hour. Required fees: $1250; $61.50 per unit. *Financial support:* In 2010–11, 8 students received support. Application deadline: 4/1. *Faculty research:* Church growth, ministry evaluation, leadership. *Unit head:* Dr. Charles Siburt, Graduate Adviser, 325-674-3732, Fax: 325-674-6716, E-mail: siburt@bible.acu.edu. *Application contact:* David Pittman, Graduate Admissions Counselor, 325-674-2656, Fax: 325-674-6717, E-mail: gradinfo@acu.edu.

Abilene Christian University, Graduate School, College of Biblical Studies, Graduate School of Theology, Programs in Christian Ministry, Abilene, TX 79699-9100. Offers MACM. Part-time programs available. *Students:* 5 full-time (1 woman), 35 part-time (5 women); includes 1 Black or African American, non-Hispanic/Latino; 1 Asian, non-Hispanic/Latino; 2 Hispanic/Latino; 1 Two or more races, non-Hispanic/Latino, 1 international. 24 applicants, 79% accepted, 15 enrolled. In 2010, 18 master's awarded. *Degree requirements:* For master's, comprehensive exam, thesis. *Entrance requirements:* For master's, GRE General Test or MAT. Additional exam requirements/recommendations for international students: Required—TOEFL (minimum score 550 paper-based; 213 computer-based). *Application deadline:* For fall admission, 4/1 priority date for domestic students; for spring admission, 11/1 for domestic students. Applications are processed on a rolling basis. Application fee: $40. Electronic applications accepted. *Expenses:* Tuition: Full-time $12,906; part-time $717 per hour. Required fees: $1250; $61.50 per unit. *Financial support:* In 2010–11, 4 students received support. Application deadline: 4/1. *Faculty research:* Program innovation, instruments for educational evaluation. *Unit head:* Dr. Tim Sensing, Graduate Advisor, 325-674-3792, Fax: 325-674-6180, E-mail: sensingt@acu.edu. *Application contact:* David Pittman, Graduate Admissions Counselor, 325-674-2656, Fax: 325-674-6717, E-mail: gradinfo@acu.edu.

American Baptist Seminary of the West, Graduate and Professional Programs, Berkeley, CA 94704-3029. Offers community leadership (MA); theology (M Div, MA). MA program in theology offered jointly with Graduate Theological Union. *Accreditation:* ACIPE; ATS (one or more programs are accredited). Part-time and evening/weekend programs available. *Faculty:* 6 full-time (4 women), 7 part-time/adjunct (2 women). *Students:* 42 full-time (13 women), 33 part-time (15 women); includes 38 Black or African American, non-Hispanic/Latino; 11 Asian, non-Hispanic/Latino; 1 Hispanic/Latino; 1 Native Hawaiian or other Pacific Islander, non-Hispanic/Latino, 16 international. In 2010, 22 first professional degrees awarded. *Entrance*

Pastoral Ministry and Counseling

American Baptist Seminary of the West (continued)

requirements: For M Div, minimum GPA of 2.5; for master's, minimum GPA of 3.0. Additional exam requirements/recommendations for international students: Required—TOEFL (minimum score 550 paper-based; 250 computer-based). *Application deadline:* For fall admission, 4/15 priority date for domestic students, 4/15 for international students. Applications are processed on a rolling basis. Application fee: $25. Electronic applications accepted. *Expenses:* Tuition: Full-time $14,040; part-time $540 per credit. Required fees: $240 per semester. One-time fee: $340. *Financial support:* Career-related internships or fieldwork, Federal Work-Study, institutionally sponsored loans, scholarships/grants, tuition waivers (partial), and tuition discount available. Support available to part-time students. Financial award application deadline: 4/15; financial award applicants required to submit FAFSA. *Unit head:* Dr. Paul M. Martin, President, 510-841-1905 Ext. 224, Fax: 510-841-2446, E-mail: pmartin@absw.edu. *Application contact:* Rev. Michelle M. Holmes, Vice President, 510-841-1905 Ext. 225, Fax: 510-841-2446, E-mail: mmholmes@absw.edu.

Amridge University, Graduate and Professional Programs, Montgomery, AL 36117. Offers behavioral leadership and management (MA); Biblical exposition (MA); biblical studies (MA, PhD); family therapy (D Min); historical and theological studies (MA); leadership and management (MS); marriage and family therapy (M Div, MA, PhD); ministerial leadership (M Div, MS); pastoral counseling (M Div, MS); practical ministry (MA); professional counseling (M Div, MA, PhD); theology (D Min). Part-time and evening/weekend programs available. Postbaccalaureate distance learning degree programs offered (no on-campus study). *Faculty:* 39 full-time (6 women), 39 part-time/adjunct (5 women). *Students:* 119 full-time (54 women), 260 part-time (149 women); includes 160 minority (153 Black or African American, non-Hispanic/Latino; 1 Asian, non-Hispanic/Latino; 6 Hispanic/Latino). Average age 35. *Degree requirements:* For master's, one foreign language, comprehensive exam (for some programs), thesis (for some programs); for doctorate, comprehensive exam (for some programs), thesis/dissertation; for M Div, comprehensive exam (for some programs). *Entrance requirements:* For M Div, master's, and doctorate, GRE General Test or MAT. Additional exam requirements/recommendations for international students: Required—TOEFL. *Application deadline:* For fall admission, 9/1 priority date for domestic students; for spring admission, 1/1 priority date for domestic students. Applications are processed on a rolling basis. Application fee: $75. Electronic applications accepted. *Financial support:* Federal Work-Study and scholarships/grants available. Support available to part-time students. Financial award applicants required to submit FAFSA. *Faculty research:* Homiletics, hermeneutics, ancient Near Eastern history. *Unit head:* Director of Enrollment Management, 800-351-4040 Ext. 7513, Fax: 334-387-3878. *Application contact:* Ora Davis, Admissions Officer, 334-387-3877 Ext. 7524, Fax: 334-387-3878, E-mail: admissions@amridgeuniversity.edu.

Anderson University, School of Christian Ministry, Anderson, SC 29621-4035. Offers M Min. Postbaccalaureate distance learning degree programs offered. *Degree requirements:* For master's, capstone course, ministry project. *Entrance requirements:* For master's, 3 references. *Expenses:* Tuition: Part-time $320 per semester hour. *Unit head:* Dr. Michael Duduit, Dean, 800-542-3594, E-mail: ministry@andersonuniversity.edu. *Application contact:* Dr. Michael Duduit, Dean, 800-542-3594, E-mail: ministry@andersonuniversity.edu.

Andrews University, School of Graduate Studies, Seventh-day Adventist Theological Seminary, Berrien Springs, MI 49104. Offers ministry (M Div, D Min); pastoral ministry (MA); religious education (MA, Ed D, PhD, Ed S); theology (M Th, Th D); youth ministry (MA). *Accreditation:* ATS. *Degree requirements:* For master's, thesis optional; for doctorate, variable foreign language requirement, thesis/dissertation; for M Div, one foreign language, thesis/dissertation optional. *Entrance requirements:* For master's, GRE Subject Test, minimum GPA of 2.0. Additional exam requirements/recommendations for international students: Required—TOEFL (minimum score 550 paper-based).

Anna Maria College, Graduate Division, Program in Pastoral Ministry, Paxton, MA 01612. Offers MA. Part-time and evening/weekend programs available. *Degree requirements:* For master's, pastoral project. *Entrance requirements:* For master's, interview. Additional exam requirements/recommendations for international students: Required—TOEFL (minimum score 500 paper-based). Electronic applications accepted.

Appalachian Bible College, Graduate School, Bradley, WV 25818. Offers ministry (MA). Postbaccalaureate distance learning degree programs offered (no on-campus study). *Entrance requirements:* For master's, ABHE Bible Content Exam, bachelor's degree, 3 references, minimum undergraduate cumulative GPA of 2.75. Additional exam requirements/recommendations for international students: Required—TOEFL (minimum score 550 paper-based; 213 computer-based).

Aquinas Institute of Theology, Graduate and Professional Programs, St. Louis, MO 63108. Offers biblical studies (Certificate); health care mission (MAHCM); ministry (M Div); pastoral care (Certificate); pastoral ministry (MAPM); pastoral studies (MAPS); preaching (D Min); spiritual direction (Certificate); theology (M Div, MA); Thomistic studies (Certificate); M Div/MA; MAPS/MSW. *Accreditation:* ATS (one or more programs are accredited). Part-time and evening/weekend programs available. Postbaccalaureate distance learning degree programs offered (minimal on-campus study). *Degree requirements:* For master's, one foreign language, comprehensive exam, thesis or major paper; for doctorate, thesis/dissertation. *Entrance requirements:* For M Div, master's, and Certificate, MAT; for doctorate, 3 years of ministerial experience, 6 hours of graduate course work in homiletics, M Div or the equivalent, minimum GPA of 3.0. Additional exam requirements/recommendations for international students: Required—TOEFL. *Faculty research:* Theology of preaching, hermeneutics, lay ecclesial ministry, pastoral and practical theology.

Argosy University, Sarasota, College of Psychology and Behavioral Sciences, Sarasota, FL 34235. Offers community counseling (MA); counseling psychology (Ed D); counselor education and supervision (Ed D); forensic psychology (MA); marriage and family therapy (MA); mental health counseling (MA); pastoral community counseling (Ed D).

See Close-Up on page 1147.

Asbury Theological Seminary, Graduate and Professional Programs, Wilmore, KY 40390-1199. Offers MA, MACE, MACL, MAMFC, MAMHC, MAPC, MAYM, Th M, PhD, Certificate. *Accreditation:* ATS. Part-time programs available. Postbaccalaureate distance learning degree programs offered (minimal on-campus study). *Faculty:* 63 full-time (12 women), 74 part-time/adjunct (14 women). *Students:* 719 full-time (251 women), 855 part-time (276 women); includes 178 minority (87 Black or African American, non-Hispanic/Latino; 4 American Indian or Alaska Native, non-Hispanic/Latino; 35 Asian, non-Hispanic/Latino; 40 Hispanic/Latino; 3 Native Hawaiian or other Pacific Islander, non-Hispanic/Latino; 9 Two or more races, non-Hispanic/Latino), 109 international. Average age 38. 772 applicants, 71% accepted, 406 enrolled. In 2010, 101 master's, 37 doctorates, 3 other advanced degrees awarded. Terminal master's awarded for partial completion of doctoral program. *Degree requirements:* For master's, thesis (for some programs); for doctorate, thesis/dissertation, qualifying exam. *Entrance requirements:* For master's, minimum GPA of 2.75; for doctorate, minimum GPA of 3.0. Additional exam requirements/recommendations for international students: Required—TOEFL, IELTS. *Application deadline:* Applications are processed on a rolling basis. Application fee: $50. Electronic applications accepted. *Expenses:* Tuition: Full-time $12,120; part-time $505 per credit hour. One-time fee: $100. *Financial support:* In 2010–11, 1,317 students received support. Career-related internships or fieldwork, Federal Work-Study, institutionally sponsored loans, and scholarships/grants available. Support available to part-time students. Financial award applicants required to submit FAFSA. *Unit head:* Dr. Leslie A. Andrews, Provost, 859-858-2206, Fax: 859-858-2025, E-mail: leslie.andrews@asburyseminary.edu. *Application contact:* Kevin Bush, Vice President of Enrollment Management, 859-858-2211, Fax: 859-858-2287, E-mail: admissions.office@asburyseminary.edu.

Ashland Theological Seminary, Graduate Programs, Ashland, OH 44805. Offers biblical and theological studies (MA, MAR), including New Testament (MA), Old Testament (MA); Christian ministry (MAPT); Christian studies (Diploma); clinical counseling (MAC, MACC); historical studies (MA), including church history; ministry (D Min); pastoral ministry (M Div); theological studies (MA). *Accreditation:* ATS. Part-time programs available. *Faculty:* 23 full-time (6 women), 38 part-time/adjunct (15 women). *Students:* 464 full-time (258 women), 117 part-time (70 women); includes 240 minority (221 Black or African American, non-Hispanic/Latino; 4 American Indian or Alaska Native, non-Hispanic/Latino; 8 Asian, non-Hispanic/Latino; 7 Hispanic/Latino), 11 international. Average age 43. 89 applicants, 100% accepted, 88 enrolled. In 2010, 34 first professional degrees, 100 master's, 27 doctorates, 2 other advanced degrees awarded. *Degree requirements:* For master's, 2 foreign languages, comprehensive exam (for some programs), thesis (for some programs); for doctorate, thesis/dissertation; for M Div, 2 foreign languages, comprehensive exam (for some programs). *Entrance requirements:* For M Div, minimum GPA of 2.75; for master's, minimum undergraduate GPA of 2.75; for doctorate, M Div, minimum undergraduate GPA of 3.0. Additional exam requirements/recommendations for international students: Required—TOEFL (minimum score 500 paper-based; 173 computer-based; 65 iBT). *Application deadline:* For fall admission, 8/30 for domestic students. Applications are processed on a rolling basis. Application fee: $30. Electronic applications accepted. *Financial support:* In 2010–11, 156 students received support, including 17 teaching assistantships; research assistantships, career-related internships or fieldwork, institutionally sponsored loans, scholarships/grants, and unspecified assistantships also available. Support available to part-time students. Financial award application deadline: 5/15; financial award applicants required to submit FAFSA. *Faculty research:* Semitic languages and linguistics, rhetorical and social-scientific criticism, Anabaptist studies, inner spiritual healing, African-American clergy in film and literature. *Unit head:* Dr. John C. Shultz, President, 419-289-5160, Fax: 419-289-5969, E-mail: jshultz@ashland.edu. *Application contact:* Glenn Black, Director of Enrollment Management, 419-289-5151, Fax: 419-289-5969, E-mail: gblack@ashland.edu.

Assemblies of God Theological Seminary, Graduate and Professional Programs, Springfield, MO 65802. Offers Christian ministries (MA); counseling (MA); divinity (M Div); intercultural ministry (MA); intercultural studies (PhD); ministry (D Min); missiology (D Miss); theological studies (MA). *Accreditation:* ATS. Part-time and evening/weekend programs available. Postbaccalaureate distance learning degree programs offered (minimal on-campus study). *Faculty:* 12 full-time (3 women), 20 part-time/adjunct (6 women). *Students:* 176 full-time (59 women), 211 part-time (48 women); includes 55 minority (16 Black or African American, non-Hispanic/Latino; 7 American Indian or Alaska Native, non-Hispanic/Latino; 16 Asian, non-Hispanic/Latino; 14 Hispanic/Latino; 2 Native Hawaiian or other Pacific Islander, non-Hispanic/Latino), 9 international. Average age 40. 96 applicants, 79% accepted, 53 enrolled. In 2010, 26 first professional degrees, 65 master's, 9 doctorates awarded. *Degree requirements:* For master's, analytical reflection paper, comprehensive exam or field education research project; for doctorate, thesis/dissertation; for M Div, one foreign language, analytical reflection paper or field education research project. *Entrance requirements:* For M Div, minimum GPA of 2.5; for master's, minimum GPA of 2.5; for doctorate, minimum GPA of 3.0. Additional exam requirements/recommendations for international students: Required—TOEFL (minimum score 550 paper-based; 213 computer-based; 80 iBT). *Application deadline:* For fall admission, 7/1 priority date for domestic students, 6/1 priority date for international students; for spring admission, 12/1 priority date for domestic students, 11/1 priority date for international students. Applications are processed on a rolling basis. Application fee: $75. Electronic applications accepted. *Expenses:* Tuition: Full-time $12,192; part-time $508 per credit hour. *Financial support:* Career-related internships or fieldwork, Federal Work-Study, and scholarships/grants available. Support available to part-time students. Financial award application deadline: 7/15; financial award applicants required to submit FAFSA. *Unit head:* Stephen Lim, Academic Dean, 417-268-1000, Fax: 417-268-1001, E-mail: slim@agts.edu. *Application contact:* Stephen Lim, Academic Dean, 417-268-1000, Fax: 417-268-1001, E-mail: slim@agts.edu.

The Athenaeum of Ohio, Graduate Programs, Cincinnati, OH 45230-5900. Offers biblical studies (MABS); divinity (M Div); lay ministry (Certificate); pastoral counseling (MAPC); pastoral ministry (MA); theology (MA Th); M Div/MA Th; M Div/MABS; M Div/MAPC. *Accreditation:* ATS (one or more programs are accredited). Part-time and evening/weekend programs available. *Degree requirements:* For master's, one foreign language, comprehensive exam (for some programs), thesis optional; for M Div, comprehensive exam.

Atlantic School of Theology, Graduate and Professional Programs, Halifax, NS B3H 3B5, Canada. Offers ministry (M Div); theological studies (Graduate Certificate). *Accreditation:* ATS. Part-time programs available. Postbaccalaureate distance learning degree programs offered (minimal on-campus study). *Degree requirements:* For master's, thesis. *Entrance requirements:* For M Div, master's, and Graduate Certificate, minimum B average in undergraduate course work. *Faculty research:* Ethics and biology; death, dying and pastoral care; theology and the economy; adult education; John and anti-Judaism.

Austin Presbyterian Theological Seminary, Graduate and Professional Programs, Austin, TX 78705-5797. Offers divinity (M Div); ministry (D Min); theological studies (MA); M Div/MSSW. *Accreditation:* ACIPE; ATS. Part-time programs available. *Faculty:* 18 full-time (5 women), 6 part-time/adjunct (2 women). *Students:* 96 full-time (56 women), 100 part-time (49 women); includes 27 minority (15 Black or African American, non-Hispanic/Latino; 1 American Indian or Alaska Native, non-Hispanic/Latino; 5 Asian, non-Hispanic/Latino; 6 Hispanic/Latino), 6 international. 89 applicants, 61% accepted, 41 enrolled. In 2010, 52 first professional degrees, 10 master's, 5 doctorates awarded. *Degree requirements:* For doctorate, thesis/dissertation; for M Div, Greek, Hebrew. *Entrance requirements:* References. Additional exam requirements/recommendations for international students: Required—TOEFL (minimum score 550 paper-based; 213 computer-based; 79 iBT). *Application deadline:* For fall admission, 5/1 for domestic students, 1/1 for international students; for spring admission, 9/1 for domestic students. Applications are processed on a rolling basis. Application fee: $65. *Expenses:* Tuition: Part-time $190 per credit. Required fees: $30 per semester. One-time fee: $150 part-time. Tuition and fees vary according to degree level and program. *Financial support:* In 2010–11, 130 students received support; fellowships, career-related internships or fieldwork, institutionally sponsored loans, scholarships/grants, and tutorships available. Support available to part-time students. Financial award application deadline: 6/1; financial award applicants required to submit FAFSA. *Faculty research:* Mystical theology, religious pluralism, narrative preaching, social ethics, pastoral care and healing. *Unit head:* Rev. Dr. Allan Hugh Cole, Academic Dean, 512-404-4821, Fax: 512-479-0738, E-mail: dean@austinseminary.edu. *Application contact:* Dr. Jack Barden, Director of Admissions, 512-404-4827, Fax: 512-472-7089, E-mail: admissions@austinseminary.edu.

Ave Maria University, Graduate Programs, Ave Maria, FL 34142. Offers pastoral theology (MTS); theology (MA, PhD). Terminal master's awarded for partial completion of doctoral program. *Degree requirements:* For master's, one foreign language, thesis; for doctorate, 3 foreign languages, comprehensive exam, thesis/dissertation. *Entrance requirements:* For master's, GRE; for doctorate, GRE, M Div or equivalent; MA or MTS in religion, theology, or philosophy; bachelor's degree with strong background in religion, theology, and/or philosophy.

Ave Maria University, Institute for Pastoral Theology, Ave Maria, FL 34142. Offers MTS. Part-time and evening/weekend programs available.

Azusa Pacific University, College of Liberal Arts and Sciences, Program in Transformational Urban Leadership, Azusa, CA 91702-7000. Offers MA. *Unit head:* Dr. David Weeks, Dean, 626-969-3434 Ext. 3500, E-mail: dweeks@apu.edu. *Application contact:* Director of Graduate Admissions, 626-812-3037, Fax: 626-969-7180.

Azusa Pacific University, Haggard Graduate School of Theology, Program in Divinity, Azusa, CA 91702-7000. Offers M Div. *Students:* 147 full-time (38 women), 73 part-time (18 women); includes 99 minority (19 Black or African American, non-Hispanic/Latino; 48 Asian, non-Hispanic/Latino; 32 Hispanic/Latino), 50 international. Average age 39. In 2010, 33 M Divs awarded. Application fee: $45 ($65 for international students). *Unit head:* Dr. Scott Daniels, Dean,

626-387-5750, E-mail: ezone@apu.edu. *Application contact:* Dr. Scott Daniels, Dean, 626-387-5750, E-mail: ezone@apu.edu.

Azusa Pacific University, Haggard Graduate School of Theology, Program in Pastoral Studies, Concentration in Church Leadership and Development, Azusa, CA 91702-7000. Offers MAPS. *Students:* 12 full-time (3 women), 10 part-time (2 women); includes 8 minority (6 Black or African American, non-Hispanic/Latino; 2 Hispanic/Latino), 2 international. Average age 39. In 2010, 4 master's awarded. Application fee: $45 ($65 for international students). *Unit head:* Dr. Scott Daniels, ean, 626-387-5750. *Application contact:* Dr. Scott Daniels, ean, 626-387-5750.

Azusa Pacific University, Haggard Graduate School of Theology, Program in Pastoral Studies, Program in Worship Leadership, Azusa, CA 91702-7000. Offers MAPS. *Students:* 6 full-time (2 women), 6 part-time (3 women); includes 4 minority (1 Black or African American, non-Hispanic/Latino; 1 Asian, non-Hispanic/Latino; 2 Hispanic/Latino), 4 international. Average age 38. In 2010, 3 master's awarded. Application fee: $45 ($65 for international students). *Unit head:* Dr. Scott Daniels, Dean, 626-387-5750, E-mail: ezone@apu.edu. *Application contact:* Dr. Scott Daniels, Dean, 626-387-5750, E-mail: ezone@apu.edu.

Bakke Graduate University, Programs in Pastoral Ministry and Business, Seattle, WA 98104. Offers business (MBA); global urban leadership (MA); social and civic entrepreneurship (MA); transformational leadership for the global city (D Min). Part-time programs available. Postbaccalaureate distance learning degree programs offered (minimal on-campus study). *Faculty:* 7 full-time (2 women), 30 part-time/adjunct (4 women). *Students:* 78 full-time (15 women), 301 part-time (105 women); includes 199 minority (99 Black or African American, non-Hispanic/Latino; 1 American Indian or Alaska Native, non-Hispanic/Latino; 90 Asian, non-Hispanic/Latino; 9 Hispanic/Latino). Average age 38. 41 applicants, 98% accepted, 25 enrolled. In 2010, 11 master's, 37 doctorates awarded. *Degree requirements:* For master's, thesis; for doctorate, thesis/dissertation. *Entrance requirements:* For master's, 2 years of ministry experience, BA in Biblical studies or theology; for doctorate, 3 years of ministry experience, M Div. Additional exam requirements/recommendations for international students: Required—TOEFL (minimum score 60 computer-based). *Application deadline:* For fall admission, 7/1 priority date for domestic students; for winter admission, 12/1 for domestic students; for spring admission, 3/15 for domestic students. Applications are processed on a rolling basis. Application fee: $75. Electronic applications accepted. *Expenses:* Tuition: Full-time $5000; part-time $500 per credit. Required fees: $175; $50 per course. *Financial support:* In 2010–11, 140 students received support. Scholarships/grants and tuition waivers (partial) available. Financial award applicants required to submit FAFSA. *Faculty research:* Theological systems, church management, worship. *Unit head:* Dr. Gwen Dewey, Academic Dean, 206-264-9100 Ext. 119, Fax: 206-264-8828, E-mail: gwend@bgu.edu. *Application contact:* Addie Tolle, Registrar, 206-246-9100 Ext. 110, Fax: 206-264-8828.

Baptist Bible College, Graduate School of Theology, Springfield, MO 65803-3498. Offers biblical counseling (MA); biblical studies (MA); church ministry (MA); intercultural studies (MA); theology (M Div). Part-time programs available. *Degree requirements:* For master's, 2 foreign languages, thesis (for some programs); for M Div, 2 foreign languages, thesis/dissertation (for some programs). *Entrance requirements:* For master's, outcomes test. Electronic applications accepted.

Baptist Bible College of Pennsylvania, Baptist Bible Seminary, Clarks Summit, PA 18411-1297. Offers biblical studies (PhD); church planting (M Div); global missions (M Div); military chaplaincy (M Div); ministry (M Min, D Min); pastor of church education (M Div); pastor of outreach (M Div); pastoral counseling (M Div); pastoral leadership (M Div); theology (M Div, Th M); youth pastor (M Div). Part-time and evening/weekend programs available. Postbaccalaureate distance learning degree programs offered (minimal on-campus study). *Faculty:* 10 full-time (0 women). *Students:* 71 full-time (0 women), 79 part-time (0 women); includes 16 minority (10 Black or African American, non-Hispanic/Latino; 4 Asian, non-Hispanic/Latino; 2 Hispanic/Latino), 7 international. Average age 38. In 2010, 23 master's, 4 doctorates awarded. Terminal master's awarded for partial completion of doctoral program. *Degree requirements:* For master's, 2 foreign languages, thesis; for doctorate, 2 foreign languages, comprehensive exam (for some programs), thesis/dissertation, oral exam; for M Div, 2 foreign languages, thesis/dissertation, oral exam. *Entrance requirements:* For doctorate, Greek and Hebrew entrance exams (PhD). *Application deadline:* Applications are processed on a rolling basis. Application fee: $30. Electronic applications accepted. *Expenses:* Tuition: Full-time $7488; part-time $416 per credit. Required fees: $522; $29 per credit. Full-time tuition and fees vary according to degree level and campus/location. *Financial support:* Career-related internships or fieldwork and scholarships/grants available. Support available to part-time students. *Unit head:* Dr. Michael Stallard, Seminary Academic Dean, 570-585-9348, Fax: 570-585-4057, E-mail: mstallard@bbc.edu. *Application contact:* Paul Golden, Director of Seminary Admissions, 570-586-9396, Fax: 570-585-4057, E-mail: pgolden@bbc.edu.

Baptist Theological Seminary at Richmond, Graduate and Professional Programs, Richmond, VA 23227. Offers biblical interpretation (M Div); Christian education (M Div); theological studies (MATS); theology (D Min); youth and student ministries (M Div); M Div/MS; M Div/MSW. *Accreditation:* ATS. Part-time programs available. Postbaccalaureate distance learning degree programs offered (minimal on-campus study). *Faculty:* 8 full-time (2 women), 19 part-time/adjunct (7 women). *Students:* 71 full-time (36 women), 30 part-time (13 women); includes 10 minority (9 Black or African American, non-Hispanic/Latino; 1 Hispanic/Latino), 3 international. Average age 46. 40 applicants, 88% accepted, 30 enrolled. In 2010, 24 first professional degrees, 4 doctorates awarded. *Degree requirements:* For doctorate, one foreign language, comprehensive exam, thesis/dissertation, field study, independent study; for M Div, one foreign language, comprehensive exam (for some programs), thesis/dissertation optional, mission immersion experience, internship. *Entrance requirements:* For doctorate, MAT, M Div, 3 years of full-time ministry experience. Additional exam requirements/recommendations for international students: Required—TOEFL (minimum score 550 paper-based; 213 computer-based). *Application deadline:* For fall admission, 8/1 priority date for domestic students, 5/1 priority date for international students; for winter admission, 12/1 priority date for domestic students, 9/1 priority date for international students; for spring admission, 1/1 priority date for domestic students, 10/1 priority date for international students. Applications are processed on a rolling basis. Application fee: $35. *Expenses:* Tuition: Full-time $9000; part-time $900 per credit. Required fees: $135 per year. *Financial support:* In 2010–11, 12 teaching assistantships (averaging $1,650 per year) were awarded; scholarships/grants and tuition waivers (partial) also available. Financial award application deadline: 2/1. *Faculty research:* Biblical studies, pastoral care, church history, theology, ministry. *Unit head:* Dr. Ronald W. Crawford, President, 804-204-1201, Fax: 804-355-8182, E-mail: rcrawford@btsr.edu. *Application contact:* Tiffany Kellogg Pittman, Director of Admissions, 804-204-1208, Fax: 804-355-8182, E-mail: admissions@btsr.edu.

Barry University, School of Arts and Sciences, Department of Theology and Philosophy, Miami Shores, FL 33161-6695. Offers ministry (D Min); pastoral ministry for Hispanics (MA); pastoral theology (MA); practical theology (MA). *Accreditation:* ATS. Part-time and evening/weekend programs available. *Degree requirements:* For master's, comprehensive exam, thesis optional; for doctorate, thesis/dissertation. *Entrance requirements:* For master's, GRE General Test or MAT, minimum GPA of 3.0. Electronic applications accepted. *Faculty research:* Fundamental morals, bioethics, social ethics, liturgical and sacramental theology, biblical studies.

Bethany Theological Seminary, Graduate and Professional Programs, Richmond, IN 47374-4019. Offers biblical studies (MA Th); ministry studies (M Div); peace studies (M Div, MA Th); theological studies (MA Th, CATS); youth ministry (M Div). *Accreditation:* ACIPE; ATS. Part-time programs available. Postbaccalaureate distance learning degree programs offered (minimal on-campus study). *Degree requirements:* For master's, thesis. *Entrance requirements:* For M Div, letters of reference, minimum GPA of 2.75; for master's, letters of reference, minimum GPA of 3.0. Additional exam requirements/recommendations for international students: Required—TOEFL (minimum score 550 paper-based; 218 computer-based).

Bethel College, Division of Graduate Studies, Program in Christian Ministries, Mishawaka, IN 46545-5591. Offers M Min. Part-time and evening/weekend programs available. *Faculty:* 1 full-time (0 women), 9 part-time/adjunct (0 women). *Students:* 6 full-time (3 women), 49 part-time (16 women); includes 6 minority (4 Black or African American, non-Hispanic/Latino; 1 Hispanic/Latino; 1 Two or more races, non-Hispanic/Latino), 2 international. 17 applicants, 100% accepted, 15 enrolled. In 2010, 17 master's awarded. *Degree requirements:* For master's, thesis or alternative. *Entrance requirements:* Additional exam requirements/recommendations for international students: Required—TOEFL (minimum score 540 paper-based; 207 computer-based). *Application deadline:* For fall admission, 5/1 for international students; for spring admission, 10/1 for international students. Applications are processed on a rolling basis. Application fee: $25. Electronic applications accepted. Tuition and fees vary according to program. *Financial support:* Career-related internships or fieldwork available. Financial award applicants required to submit FAFSA. *Unit head:* Dr. Gene Carpenter, Director, 574-257-3332, E-mail: carpeng@bethelcollege.edu. *Application contact:* Dr. John Dendiu, Advisor, 574-257-2675, Fax: 574-257-3385, E-mail: dendiuj@bethelcollege.edu.

Bethel Seminary, Graduate and Professional Programs, St. Paul, MN 55112-6998. Offers Anglican studies (Certificate); applied ministry (MA, Certificate); biblical studies (Certificate); children's and family ministry (MACFM); Christian education (MACE); Christian thought (MACT); community ministry leadership (MA, Certificate); global and contextual studies (MA); Greek and Hebrew language track (M Div); Greek language track (M Div); Hebrew language track (M Div); lay ministry (Certificate); marriage and family therapy (MAMFT, Certificate); men's ministry leadership (Certificate); ministry (D Min); ministry leadership (Certificate); spiritual formation (Certificate); theological studies (MATS, Certificate); transformational leadership (MATL, Certificate); young life youth ministry (Certificate). *Accreditation:* ACIPE; ATS (one or more programs are accredited). Part-time and evening/weekend programs available. Postbaccalaureate distance learning degree programs offered (minimal on-campus study). *Faculty:* 26 full-time (3 women), 74 part-time/adjunct (29 women). *Students:* 729 full-time (275 women), 274 part-time (118 women); includes 75 minority (34 Black or African American, non-Hispanic/Latino; 1 American Indian or Alaska Native, non-Hispanic/Latino; 12 Asian, non-Hispanic/Latino; 16 Hispanic/Latino; 1 Native Hawaiian or other Pacific Islander, non-Hispanic/Latino; 11 Two or more races, non-Hispanic/Latino), 16 international. Average age 38. 525 applicants, 76% accepted, 265 enrolled. In 2010, 149 master's, 13 doctorates awarded. *Degree requirements:* For master's, variable foreign language requirement, thesis (for some programs); for doctorate, thesis/dissertation; for M Div, one foreign language. *Entrance requirements:* For M Div and master's, letters of reference, transcripts, personal statement; for doctorate, M Div, letters of reference, organizational support. Additional exam requirements/recommendations for international students: Required—TOEFL (minimum score 550 paper-based; 213 computer-based; 87 iBT). *Application deadline:* For fall admission, 8/1 priority date for domestic students, 3/1 for international students; for winter admission, 12/1 priority date for domestic students; for spring admission, 3/1 priority date for domestic students. Applications are processed on a rolling basis. Application fee: $20. Electronic applications accepted. *Financial support:* In 2010–11, 655 students received support, including 18 teaching assistantships; career-related internships or fieldwork, Federal Work-Study, scholarships/grants, and tuition waivers (full) also available. Financial award application deadline: 7/15; financial award applicants required to submit FAFSA. *Faculty research:* Nature of theology, ethics, Biblical commentaries, nature of God, science and theology. *Unit head:* Dr. David Ridder, Vice President and Dean, 651-638-6553. *Application contact:* Joseph V. Dworak, Director of Admissions, 651-638-6288, Fax: 651-638-6002, E-mail: j-dworak@bethel.edu.

Biblical Theological Seminary, Graduate and Professional Programs, Hatfield, PA 19440-2499. Offers advanced missional leadership (D Min); advanced pastoral studies (Certificate); biblical counseling (Certificate); biblical studies (MA, Certificate); counseling (MA); ministry (M Div, MA); missional theology (MA). *Accreditation:* ATS. Part-time and evening/weekend programs available. *Faculty:* 11 full-time (0 women), 27 part-time/adjunct (9 women). *Students:* 205 applicants, 52% accepted, 84 enrolled. In 2010, 23 first professional degrees, 24 master's, 10 doctorates awarded. *Degree requirements:* For M Div, thesis/dissertation. *Entrance requirements:* Additional exam requirements/recommendations for international students: Required—TOEFL (minimum score 550 paper-based; 213 computer-based; 80 iBT). *Application deadline:* Applications are processed on a rolling basis. Application fee: $30. *Expenses:* Tuition: Full-time $10,728; part-time $447 per credit. Required fees: $25 per term. One-time fee: $30. *Financial support:* In 2010–11, 174 students received support. Career-related internships or fieldwork, institutionally sponsored loans, and scholarships/grants available. Support available to part-time students. Financial award application deadline: 8/30; financial award applicants required to submit FAFSA. *Faculty research:* Theology, culture, Biblical interpretation. *Unit head:* Pamela Jean Smith, Vice President for Student Advancement, 215-368-5000 Ext. 122, Fax: 215-368-7002, E-mail: psmith@biblical.edu. *Application contact:* Rev. Darryl John Lang, Director of Recruitment and Student Life, 215-368-5000 Ext. 147, Fax: 215-368-7002, E-mail: dlang@biblical.edu.

Bob Jones University, Graduate Programs, Greenville, SC 29614. Offers accountancy (MS); Bible (MA); Bible translation (MA); Biblical studies (Certificate); broadcast management (MS); business administration (MBA); church history (MA, PhD); church ministries (MA); church music (MM); cinema and video production (MA); counseling (MS); curriculum and instruction (Ed D); divinity (M Div); dramatic production (MA); educational leadership (MS, Ed D, Ed S); elementary education (M Ed, MAT); English (M Ed, MA, MAT); fine arts (MA); graphic design (MA); history (M Ed, MA); illustration (MA); interpretative speech (MA); mathematics (M Ed, MAT); medical missions (Certificate); ministry (MM, D Min); multi-categorical special education (M Ed, MAT); music (M Ed); New Testament interpretation (PhD); Old Testament interpretation (PhD); orchestral instrument performance (MM); organ performance (MM); pastoral studies (MA); personnel services (MS, Ed S); piano pedagogy (MM); piano performance (MM); platform arts (MA); radio and television broadcasting (MS); rhetoric and public address (MA); secondary education (M Ed); studio art (MA); teaching Bible (MA); theology (MA, PhD); voice performance (MM); youth ministries (MA); M Div/MM.

Boston College, School of Theology and Ministry, Chestnut Hill, MA 02467-3800. Offers church leadership (MA); divinity (M Div); pastoral ministry (MA), including Hispanic ministry, liturgy and worship, pastoral care and counseling, spirituality; religious education (MA, PhD); sacred theology (STD, STL); social justice/social ministry (MA); spiritual direction (MA); theological studies (MTS); theology (Th M, PhD); youth ministry (MA); MA/MA; MS/MA; MSW/MA. *Accreditation:* Teacher Education Accreditation Council. Part-time programs available. *Degree requirements:* For doctorate, one foreign language, thesis/dissertation. *Entrance requirements:* For doctorate, GRE. Additional exam requirements/recommendations for international students: Required—TOEFL (minimum score 550 paper-based; 213 computer-based). Electronic applications accepted. *Faculty research:* Philosophy and practice of religious education, pastoral psychology, liturgical and spiritual theology, spiritual formation for the practice of ministry.

Briercrest Seminary, Graduate Programs, Program in Christian Ministries, Caronport, SK S0H 0S0, Canada. Offers leadership (MA); marriage and family counseling (MA); missions (MA); pastoral counseling (MA); worship (MA); youth and family ministry (MA). Part-time programs available. *Degree requirements:* For master's, comprehensive exam, thesis optional. *Entrance requirements:* Additional exam requirements/recommendations for international students: Required—TOEFL (minimum score 550 paper-based; 213 computer-based).

Briercrest Seminary, Graduate Programs, Program in Theology, Caronport, SK S0H 0S0, Canada. Offers Biblical studies (M Div); leadership and management (M Div); New Testament (MATS); Old Testament (MATS); pastoral counseling (M Div); pastoral ministry (M Div); theological studies (M Div); theology (MATS); worship (M Div); youth and family ministry (M Div). *Accreditation:* ATS. Part-time programs available. *Degree requirements:* For master's, comprehensive exam, thesis optional. *Entrance requirements:* Additional exam requirements/recommendations for international students: Required—TOEFL (minimum score 550 paper-based; 213 computer-based).

Pastoral Ministry and Counseling

Caldwell College, Graduate Studies, Program in Pastoral Ministry, Caldwell, NJ 07006-6195. Offers MA. Part-time and evening/weekend programs available. *Degree requirements:* For master's, thesis. *Entrance requirements:* For master's, minimum GPA of 3.0, 2 years of ministry experience. Additional exam requirements/recommendations for international students: Required—TOEFL (minimum score 580 paper-based; 237 computer-based). Electronic applications accepted.

California Baptist University, Program in Counseling Ministry, Riverside, CA 92504-3206. Offers MA. Part-time programs available. *Faculty:* 4 full-time (0 women). *Students:* 8 full-time (all women), 3 part-time (2 women); includes 4 Black or African American, non-Hispanic/Latino; 2 Hispanic/Latino. 3 applicants, 100% accepted, 3 enrolled. In 2010, 1 master's awarded. *Degree requirements:* For master's, thesis or alternative. *Entrance requirements:* For master's, Minnesota Multiphasic Personality Inventory-2, Meyers-Briggs Type Indicator, minimum undergraduate GPA of 2.75. Additional exam requirements/recommendations for international students: Required—TOEFL (minimum score 575 paper-based; 230 computer-based; 89 iBT). *Application deadline:* For fall admission, 8/1 priority date for domestic students, 7/1 for international students; for spring admission, 12/1 priority date for domestic students, 10/15 for international students. Applications are processed on a rolling basis. Application fee: $45. Electronic applications accepted. *Expenses:* Contact institution. *Financial support:* Federal Work-Study and scholarships/grants available. Support available to part-time students. Financial award applicants required to submit FAFSA. *Unit head:* Dr. Nathan Lewis, Director, 951-343-4348, Fax: 951-343-4569, E-mail: nlewis@calbaptist.edu. *Application contact:* Gail Ronveaux, Dean of Graduate Enrollment, 951-343-5045, Fax: 951-343-5095, E-mail: graduateadmissions@calbaptist.edu.

California Baptist University, Program in Counseling Psychology, Riverside, CA 92504-3206. Offers professional counseling (MS); professional ministry (MS). Part-time programs available. *Faculty:* 13 full-time (8 women), 15 part-time/adjunct (8 women). *Students:* 151 full-time (126 women), 50 part-time (42 women); includes 107 minority (34 Black or African American, non-Hispanic/Latino; 2 American Indian or Alaska Native, non-Hispanic/Latino; 7 Asian, non-Hispanic/Latino; 61 Hispanic/Latino; 3 Two or more races, non-Hispanic/Latino), 1 international. 97 applicants, 91% accepted, 76 enrolled. In 2010, 51 master's awarded. *Degree requirements:* For master's, comprehensive exam, 24 hours (individual) or 50 hours (group) psychotherapy, 300 hours of field work. *Entrance requirements:* For master's, Minnesota Multiphasic Personality Inventory, Myers-Briggs Type Indicator, course work in developmental psychology, theories of personality, and statistics; minimum undergraduate GPA of 2.75. Additional exam requirements/recommendations for international students: Required—TOEFL (minimum score 575 paper-based; 230 computer-based; 89 iBT). *Application deadline:* For fall admission, 9/1 for domestic students, 7/1 for international students; for spring admission, 1/3 for domestic students, 10/15 for international students. Applications are processed on a rolling basis. Application fee: $45. Electronic applications accepted. *Expenses:* Contact institution. *Financial support:* Career-related internships or fieldwork, Federal Work-Study, scholarships/grants, traineeships, and unspecified assistantships available. Support available to part-time students. Financial award applicants required to submit FAFSA. *Unit head:* Dr. Mischa Routon, Director, 951-343-4206, Fax: 951-343-4569, E-mail: mrouton@calbaptist.edu. *Application contact:* Gail Ronveaux, Dean of Graduate Enrollment, 951-343-5045, Fax: 951-343-5095, E-mail: graduateadmissions@calbaptist.edu.

Calvary Bible College and Theological Seminary, Calvary Theological Seminary, Kansas City, MO 64147-1341. Offers Bible and theology (MS); Biblical counseling (MA); Biblical studies (MA); Christian ministry (MA); Christian studies (MS); Christian theology (MA); New Testament (MA); Old Testament (MA); pastoral studies (M Div). Part-time and evening/weekend programs available. *Faculty:* 5 full-time, 2 part-time/adjunct. *Students:* 14 full-time (5 women), 36 part-time (10 women); includes 4 Black or African American, non-Hispanic/Latino; 1 Asian, non-Hispanic/Latino; 1 Native Hawaiian or other Pacific Islander, non-Hispanic/Latino. Average age 40. In 2010, 14 master's awarded. *Degree requirements:* For master's, one foreign language, comprehensive exam, thesis; for M Div, 2 foreign languages, comprehensive exam, thesis/dissertation. *Entrance requirements:* For M Div and master's, minimum GPA of 2.5, 50 semester hours of course work in liberal arts, BA or BS, doctrine agreement. Additional exam requirements/recommendations for international students: Required—TOEFL (minimum score 550 paper-based; 213 computer-based). *Application deadline:* For fall admission, 7/15 priority date for domestic and international students; for spring admission, 12/1 priority date for domestic and international students. Application fee: $25. *Expenses:* Tuition: Full-time $5580; part-time $310 per hour. Required fees: $258 per semester. *Financial support:* Scholarships/grants available. Financial award application deadline: 11/5. *Unit head:* Dr. Thomas Baurain, Academic Dean, 816-322-0110 Ext. 1502, Fax: 816-331-4474, E-mail: thomas.baurain@calvary.edu. *Application contact:* Bob Crank, Director of Admissions, 800-326-3960 Ext. 1321, Fax: 816-331-4474, E-mail: admissions@calvary.edu.

Calvin Theological Seminary, Graduate and Professional Programs, Grand Rapids, MI 49546-4387. Offers Bible and theology (MA); divinity (M Div), including ancient near eastern languages and literature, contextual ministry, evangelism and teaching, history of Christianity, new church development, New Testament, Old Testament, pastoral care and leadership, preaching and worship, theological studies, youth and family ministries; educational ministry (MA); historical theology (PhD); missions and evangelism (MA); pastoral care (MA); philosophical and moral theology (PhD); systematic theology (PhD); theological studies (MTS); theology (Th M); worship (MA); youth and family ministries (MA). *Accreditation:* ACIPE; ATS. Part-time programs available. *Degree requirements:* For master's, thesis (for some programs); for doctorate, 4 foreign languages, comprehensive exam, thesis/dissertation; for M Div, 2 foreign languages. *Entrance requirements:* For doctorate, GRE General Test, Hebrew, Greek, and a modern foreign language. Additional exam requirements/recommendations for international students: Required—TOEFL (minimum score 550 paper-based; 213 computer-based), TWE (minimum score 4). Electronic applications accepted. *Faculty research:* Recent Trinity theory, Christian anthropology, Proverbs, reformed confessions, Paul's view of law.

Capital Bible Seminary, Graduate and Professional Programs, Lanham, MD 20706-3599. Offers biblical studies (MA, Certificate); Christian counseling (MA); Christian counseling and discipleship (Certificate); ministry leadership (MA); theology (M Div, Th M). *Accreditation:* ATS (one or more programs are accredited). Part-time and evening/weekend programs available. *Degree requirements:* For master's, 2 foreign languages, comprehensive exam, thesis (for some programs); for M Div, 2 foreign languages, comprehensive exam. *Entrance requirements:* For M Div and master's, GRE General Test, Greek exam for those with 2 years of Greek, proficiency exam in theology, previous course work in Biblical studies. Additional exam requirements/recommendations for international students: Required—TOEFL (minimum score 550 paper-based; 213 computer-based). *Faculty research:* Dead Sea Scrolls, spiritual gifts, hermeneutics.

Cardinal Stritch University, College of Arts and Sciences, Department of Religious Studies, Milwaukee, WI 53217-3985. Offers lay ministries (MA); ministry (MA); religious studies (MA). Part-time and evening/weekend programs available. *Degree requirements:* For master's, comprehensive exam, thesis, faculty recommendation, research project. *Entrance requirements:* For master's, interview, minimum GPA of 2.75.

Carolina Evangelical Divinity School, Ministry Program, High Point, NC 27265. Offers D Min. *Degree requirements:* For doctorate, project. *Entrance requirements:* For doctorate, MAT, M Div or equivalent, minimum GPA of 3.0 on all previous graduate study, 3 years of ministry experience.

Catholic Theological Union at Chicago, Graduate and Professional Programs, Chicago, IL 60615-5698. Offers biblical spirituality (Certificate); cross-cultural ministries (D Min); cross-cultural missions (Certificate); divinity (M Div); liturgical studies (Certificate); liturgy (D Min); pastoral studies (MAPS, Certificate); spiritual formation (Certificate); spirituality (D Min); theology (MA); M Div/MA; M Div/MSW; M Div/PhD. M Div/PhD offered jointly with University of Chicago; M Div/MSW with Loyola University Chicago and University of Chicago. *Accreditation:* ACIPE; ATS (one or more programs are accredited). Part-time and evening/weekend programs available. *Degree requirements:* For master's, one foreign language, comprehensive exam (for some programs), thesis (for some programs); for doctorate, thesis/dissertation. *Entrance requirements:* For doctorate, master's degree, 5 years of active ministry. *Faculty research:* Doctrine, sacraments, ethics, Bible.

The Catholic University of America, School of Theology and Religious Studies, Washington, DC 20064. Offers M Div, STB, MA, MRE, D Min, PhD, STD, Certificate, STL, MSLS/MA. *Accreditation:* ATS (one or more programs are accredited). Part-time programs available. *Faculty:* 40 full-time (6 women), 10 part-time/adjunct (2 women). *Students:* 161 full-time (28 women), 235 part-time (61 women); includes 7 Black or African American, non-Hispanic/Latino; 1 American Indian or Alaska Native, non-Hispanic/Latino; 10 Asian, non-Hispanic/Latino; 11 Hispanic/Latino; 1 Native Hawaiian or other Pacific Islander, non-Hispanic/Latino, 69 international. Average age 36. 259 applicants, 64% accepted, 73 enrolled. In 2010, 7 first professional degrees, 29 master's, 29 doctorates awarded. *Degree requirements:* For master's, variable foreign language requirement, comprehensive exam, thesis (for some programs); for doctorate, variable foreign language requirement, comprehensive exam, thesis/dissertation. *Entrance requirements:* For first professional degree, master's, and doctorate, GRE General Test, statement of purpose, official copies of academic transcripts, three letters of recommendation. Additional exam requirements/recommendations for international students: Required—TOEFL (minimum score 580 paper-based; 237 computer-based). *Application deadline:* For fall admission, 8/1 priority date for domestic students, 7/15 for international students; for spring admission, 12/1 priority date for domestic students, 10/15 for international students. Applications are processed on a rolling basis. Application fee: $55. Electronic applications accepted. *Expenses:* Tuition: Full-time $33,580; part-time $1315 per credit hour. Required fees: $80; $40 per semester hour. One-time fee: $425. *Financial support:* Fellowships, research assistantships, teaching assistantships, Federal Work-Study, scholarships/grants, tuition waivers (full and partial), and unspecified assistantships available. Financial award application deadline: 2/1; financial award applicants required to submit FAFSA. *Faculty research:* Historical and systematic theology, religious education and catechetics, moral theology and ethics, Biblical studies, liturgical studies and sacramental theology. Total annual research expenditures: $66,740. *Unit head:* Msgr. Kevin W. Irwin, Dean, 202-319-5684, Fax: 202-319-5704, E-mail: irwin@cua.edu. *Application contact:* Andrew Woodall, Director of Graduate Admissions, 202-319-5057, Fax: 202-319-6533, E-mail: cua-admissions@cua.edu.

Chaminade University of Honolulu, Graduate Services, Program in Pastoral Leadership, Honolulu, HI 96816-1578. Offers MAPL. Part-time and evening/weekend programs available. Postbaccalaureate distance learning degree programs offered (minimal on-campus study). *Degree requirements:* For master's, internship or thesis. *Entrance requirements:* For master's, 2 letters of recommendation. Additional exam requirements/recommendations for international students: Required—TOEFL (minimum score 550 paper-based). Electronic applications accepted.

Chaminade University of Honolulu, Graduate Services, Program in Pastoral Theology, Honolulu, HI 96816-1578. Offers MPT. Part-time and evening/weekend programs available. Postbaccalaureate distance learning degree programs offered. *Degree requirements:* For master's, capstone course. *Entrance requirements:* For master's, 2 letters of recommendation. Additional exam requirements/recommendations for international students: Required—TOEFL (minimum score 550 paper-based). Electronic applications accepted.

Chicago Theological Seminary, Graduate and Professional Programs, Chicago, IL 60637-1507. Offers preaching (D Min); religion and health (D Min); religious studies (MA); spirituality and spiritual direction (D Min); theology (M Div); theology, ethics and the human sciences (PhD); M Div/MSW. *Accreditation:* ACIPE; ATS. Part-time programs available. *Degree requirements:* For master's, thesis; for doctorate, 2 foreign languages, comprehensive exam, thesis/dissertation; for M Div, thesis/dissertation. *Entrance requirements:* For doctorate, GRE General Test. Additional exam requirements/recommendations for international students: Required—TOEFL (minimum score 217 computer-based). *Faculty research:* Bible, culture and hermeneutics, theology, gender and sexuality, black faith and life, spirituality and psychology, practical theology.

Christian Theological Seminary, Graduate and Professional Programs, Indianapolis, IN 46208-3301. Offers educational and arts ministries (MA); marriage and family therapy (MA); pastoral care and counseling (D Min); psychotherapy and faith (MA); theological studies (MTS); theology (M Div). *Accreditation:* AAMFT/COAMFTE (one or more programs are accredited); ACIPE; ATS. Part-time programs available. Terminal master's awarded for partial completion of doctoral program. *Degree requirements:* For master's, comprehensive exam (for some programs), thesis (for some programs); for doctorate, comprehensive exam, thesis/dissertation; for M Div, comprehensive exam, thesis/dissertation (for some programs), missionary and cross-cultural experience. *Entrance requirements:* For master's, GRE General Test, MAT; for doctorate, M Div. Electronic applications accepted. *Faculty research:* Faith formation, peer learning post graduation.

Christ the King Seminary, Graduate and Professional Programs, East Aurora, NY 14052. Offers divinity (M Div); pastoral ministry (MA); theology (MA). *Accreditation:* ATS. Part-time and evening/weekend programs available. *Faculty:* 9 full-time (0 women), 11 part-time/adjunct (3 women). *Students:* 22 full-time (4 women), 60 part-time (34 women); includes 12 minority (8 Black or African American, non-Hispanic/Latino; 4 Hispanic/Latino). Average age 38. 20 applicants, 90% accepted, 17 enrolled. In 2010, 5 first professional degrees, 12 master's awarded. *Degree requirements:* For master's, comprehensive exam, thesis; for M Div, comprehensive exam. *Entrance requirements:* For M Div and master's, previous course work in philosophy and religious studies. *Application deadline:* For fall admission, 8/15 priority date for domestic students; for spring admission, 1/5 priority date for domestic students. Applications are processed on a rolling basis. Application fee: $40. *Expenses:* Tuition: Full-time $7110. Required fees: $220. *Financial support:* Career-related internships or fieldwork and scholarships/grants available. Support available to part-time students. Financial award application deadline: 8/1; financial award applicants required to submit FAFSA. *Unit head:* Dr. Dennis Castillo, Academic Dean, 716-652-8900, E-mail: dcastillo@cks.edu. *Application contact:* Cindy Vogel, Assistant to the Academic Dean, 716-652-8900 Ext. 7088, Fax: 716-652-8903, E-mail: cvogel@cks.edu.

Cincinnati Christian University, Graduate School, Program in Counseling, Cincinnati, OH 45204-3200. Offers MAC. *Degree requirements:* For master's, thesis or alternative, integration paper. *Entrance requirements:* For master's, GRE General Test, interview, minimum undergraduate GPA of 3.0. Additional exam requirements/recommendations for international students: Required—TOEFL. Electronic applications accepted. *Expenses:* Contact institution.

Claremont School of Theology, Graduate and Professional Programs, Program in Ministry, Claremont, CA 91711-3199. Offers D Min. *Accreditation:* ACIPE. *Degree requirements:* For doctorate, thesis/dissertation. *Entrance requirements:* For doctorate, GRE General Test. Additional exam requirements/recommendations for international students: Required—TOEFL (minimum score 230 computer-based). Electronic applications accepted.

Claremont School of Theology, Graduate and Professional Programs, Program in Religion, Claremont, CA 91711-3199. Offers practical theology (PhD), including religious education, spiritual care and counseling; religion (PhD), including Hebrew Bible, New Testament and Christian origins, process studies, religion, ethics, and society; religion and theology (MA); religious education (MARE). *Accreditation:* ACIPE; ATS. Terminal master's awarded for partial completion of doctoral program. *Degree requirements:* For master's, thesis; for doctorate, 2 foreign languages, thesis/dissertation. *Entrance requirements:* For doctorate, GRE General Test. Additional exam requirements/recommendations for international students: Required—TOEFL (minimum score 250 computer-based). Electronic applications accepted.

College of Mount St. Joseph, Graduate Program in Religious Studies, Cincinnati, OH 45233-1670. Offers religious education (Certificate); spiritual and pastoral care (MA, Certificate); spiritual direction (Certificate). Part-time and evening/weekend programs available. *Faculty:* 4 full-time (3 women). *Students:* 24 part-time (17 women); includes 1 minority (Black or African American, non-Hispanic/Latino). Average age 47. 20 applicants, 90% accepted, 10 enrolled. In 2010, 5 master's awarded. *Degree requirements:* For master's, comprehensive exam, integrating project. *Entrance requirements:* For master's, 3 letters of recommendation, interview, minimum GPA of 3.0. Additional exam requirements/recommendations for international students: Required—TOEFL (minimum score 560 paper-based; 220 computer-based; 83 iBT). *Application deadline:* Applications are processed on a rolling basis. Application fee: $50. Electronic applications accepted. *Financial support:* In 2010–11, 20 students received support. Scholarships/grants available. Financial award applicants required to submit FAFSA. *Faculty research:* Contextual/cultural/systematic theology, historical/spiritual theology, business/economics ethics, social justice, Biblical/cultural/pastoral theology. *Unit head:* Dr. John Trokan, Chair of Religious/Pastoral Studies, 513-244-4272, Fax: 513-244-4222, E-mail: john_trokan@mail.msj.edu. *Application contact:* Marilyn Hoskins, Assistant Director of Graduate Recruitment, 513-244-4723, Fax: 513-244-4629, E-mail: marilyn_hoskins@mail.msj.edu.

Columbia International University, Columbia Biblical Seminary and School of Missions, Columbia, SC 29230-3122. Offers academic ministries (M Div); bible exposition (M Div, MABE); biblical studies (Certificate); counseling ministries (Certificate); divinity (M Div); educational ministries (M Div, MAEM, Certificate); intercultural studies (M Div, MAIS, Certificate); leadership (D Min); leadership for evangelism/mobilization (MALM); member care (D Min); ministry (Certificate); missions (D Min); pastoral counseling and spiritual formation (M Div, MAPS); preaching (D Min); theology (MA). *Accreditation:* ATS (one or more programs are accredited). Part-time and evening/weekend programs available. *Degree requirements:* For master's, integrative seminar; for doctorate, comprehensive exam, thesis/dissertation; for M Div, internship. *Entrance requirements:* For master's, minimum GPA of 2.7; for doctorate, 3 years of ministerial experience, M Div. Additional exam requirements/recommendations for international students: Required—TOEFL. Electronic applications accepted.

Concordia University, Nebraska, Graduate Programs in Education, Program in Family Life Ministry, Seward, NE 68434-1599. Offers MS. Part-time and evening/weekend programs available. *Degree requirements:* For master's, thesis or alternative. *Entrance requirements:* For master's, GRE, MAT, or NTE, minimum GPA of 3.0, BS in education or equivalent.

Concordia University, St. Paul, College of Vocation and Ministry, St. Paul, MN 55104-5494. Offers Christian education (Certificate); Christian outreach (MA, Certificate). Evening/weekend programs available. Postbaccalaureate distance learning degree programs offered (minimal on-campus study). *Faculty:* 2 full-time (0 women), 5 part-time/adjunct (2 women). *Students:* 11 full-time (3 women); includes 1 Asian, non-Hispanic/Latino. Average age 40. In 2010, 7 master's awarded. *Application deadline:* Applications are processed on a rolling basis. Application fee: $50. Electronic applications accepted. *Expenses:* Tuition: Full-time $7500; part-time $460 per credit. Required fees: $460 per credit. Tuition and fees vary according to program. *Financial support:* Applicants required to submit FAFSA. *Unit head:* Dr. David Lumpp, Dean, 651-641-8217, E-mail: lumpp@csp.edu. *Application contact:* Kimberly Craig, Director of Graduate and Cohort Admission, 651-603-6223, Fax: 651-603-6320, E-mail: craig@csp.edu.

Corban University, Graduate School, Program in Counseling, Salem, OR 97301-9392. Offers MA. *Degree requirements:* For master's, internship, practicum.

The Criswell College, Graduate School of the Bible, Dallas, TX 75246-1537. Offers biblical studies (M Div); Christian leadership (MA); counseling (MA); Jewish studies (MA); ministry (MA); theological and biblical studies (MA). Part-time programs available. *Degree requirements:* For master's, 2 foreign languages, thesis optional; for M Div, 2 foreign languages, thesis/dissertation optional. *Entrance requirements:* For M Div and master's, GRE General Test, minimum GPA of 2.5. Electronic applications accepted. *Faculty research:* Emphasis on biblical languages (Hebrew and Greek), expository preaching and evangelism in the local church.

Dallas Baptist University, College of Adult Education, Professional Development Program, Dallas, TX 75211-9299. Offers accounting (MA); church leadership (MA); counseling (MA); criminal justice (MA); English as a second language (MA); finance (MA); higher education (MA); leadership studies (MA); management (MA); management information systems (MA); marketing (MA); missions (MA). Part-time and evening/weekend programs available. *Entrance requirements:* For master's, minimum GPA of 3.0. Additional exam requirements/recommendations for international students: Required—TOEFL, IELTS. *Expenses:* Tuition: Full-time $11,394; part-time $633 per credit hour.

Dallas Baptist University, Gary Cook School of Leadership, Program in Christian Education, Dallas, TX 75211-9299. Offers adult ministry (MA); business ministry (MA); childhood ministry (MA); collegiate ministry (MA); communication ministry (MA); counseling ministry (MA); education ministry (MA); general ministry (MA); missions ministry (MA); student ministry (MA); worship ministry (MA). Part-time and evening/weekend programs available. *Entrance requirements:* For master's, minimum GPA of 3.0. Additional exam requirements/recommendations for international students: Required—TOEFL. Electronic applications accepted. *Expenses:* Tuition: Full-time $11,394; part-time $633 per credit hour.

Dallas Baptist University, Gary Cook School of Leadership, Program in Christian Education: Childhood Ministry, Dallas, TX 75211-9299. Offers MA. Part-time and evening/weekend programs available. *Entrance requirements:* For master's, minimum GPA of 3.0. Additional exam requirements/recommendations for international students: Required—TOEFL, IELTS. *Expenses:* Tuition: Full-time $11,394; part-time $633 per credit hour.

Dallas Baptist University, Gary Cook School of Leadership, Program in Christian Education: Student Ministry, Dallas, TX 75211-9299. Offers MA. Part-time and evening/weekend programs available. *Entrance requirements:* For master's, minimum GPA of 3.0. Additional exam requirements/recommendations for international students: Required—TOEFL, IELTS. *Expenses:* Tuition: Full-time $11,394; part-time $633 per credit hour.

Dallas Baptist University, Gary Cook School of Leadership, Program in Global Leadership, Dallas, TX 75211-9299. Offers business communication (MA); Christian education/missions (MA); ESL (MA); general studies (MA); global studies (MA); international business (MA); missions (MA); worship/missions (MA). Part-time and evening/weekend programs available. *Entrance requirements:* For master's, minimum GPA of 3.0. Additional exam requirements/recommendations for international students: Required—TOEFL, IELTS. *Expenses:* Tuition: Full-time $11,394; part-time $633 per credit hour.

Dallas Baptist University, Gary Cook School of Leadership, Program in Worship Leadership, Dallas, TX 75211-9299. Offers MA. Part-time and evening/weekend programs available. *Entrance requirements:* For master's, minimum GPA of 3.0. Additional exam requirements/recommendations for international students: Required—TOEFL, IELTS. *Expenses:* Tuition: Full-time $11,394; part-time $633 per credit hour.

Dallas Theological Seminary, Graduate Programs, Dallas, TX 75204-6499. Offers academic ministries (Th M); Bible translation (Th M); biblical and theological studies (CGS); biblical counseling (MA, Th M); biblical exegesis and linguistics (MA); biblical exposition (PhD); biblical studies (MA); Christian education (MA, D Min); cross-cultural ministries (MA, Th M); educational leadership (Th M); evangelism and discipleship (Th M); interdisciplinary studies (Th M); media and communication (MA); media arts in ministry (Th M); ministry (D Min); New Testament studies (Th M, PhD); Old Testament studies (PhD); parachurch ministries (Th M); pastoral ministries (Th M); sacred theology (STM); theological studies (PhD); women's ministry (Th M). *Accreditation:* ATS (one or more programs are accredited). Part-time and evening/weekend programs available. *Degree requirements:* For master's, variable foreign language requirement, thesis (for some programs); for doctorate, 2 foreign languages, thesis/dissertation. *Entrance requirements:* Additional exam requirements/recommendations for international students: Required—TOEFL, TWE. Electronic applications accepted.

Denver Seminary, Graduate and Professional Programs, Littleton, CO 80120. Offers apologetics (Certificate); biblical studies (MA); Christian formation and soul care (MA, Certificate); Christian studies (MA, Certificate); church and parachurch leadership (D Min); counseling licensure (MA); counseling ministry (MA); intercultural ministry (Certificate); leadership (MA, Certificate); marriage and family counseling (D Min); pastoral ministry (D Min); philosophy of religion (MA); spiritual guidance (Certificate); theology (M Div, Certificate); worship (Certificate); youth and family ministry (MA). *Accreditation:* ACA; ACIPE; ATS (one or more programs are accredited). Part-time and evening/weekend programs available. Postbaccalaureate distance learning degree programs offered. *Degree requirements:* For master's, 2 foreign languages, thesis (for some programs); for doctorate, 2 foreign languages, thesis/dissertation; for M Div, 2 foreign languages. *Entrance requirements:* For M Div, minimum undergraduate GPA of 2.5; for master's, minimum undergraduate GPA of 3.0; for doctorate, M Div, 3 years of ministry experience. Additional exam requirements/recommendations for international students: Required—TOEFL (minimum score 575 paper-based; 233 computer-based; 90 iBT). Electronic applications accepted.

Dominican University, School of Leadership and Continuing Studies, River Forest, IL 60305-1099. Offers family ministry (MA); organizational leadership (MSOL). Part-time and evening/weekend programs available. *Entrance requirements:* Additional exam requirements/recommendations for international students: Required—TOEFL (minimum score 550 paper-based; 213 computer-based; 79 iBT). *Expenses:* Contact institution.

Eastern Mennonite University, Eastern Mennonite Seminary, Harrisonburg, VA 22802-2462. Offers church leadership (MA); divinity (M Div); ministry studies (Certificate); online theological studies (Certificate); religion (MA); theological studies (Certificate). *Accreditation:* ATS. Part-time programs available. *Degree requirements:* For master's, thesis (for some programs); for M Div, thesis/dissertation (for some programs), supervised field education. *Entrance requirements:* For M Div and master's, minimum GPA of 2.5. Additional exam requirements/recommendations for international students: Required—TOEFL (minimum score 550 paper-based; 213 computer-based). *Expenses:* Contact institution. *Faculty research:* Spiritual direction and culture of call, leadership coaching: an approach to leadership in a culture of call, clarity of call in the probationary process for United Methodist clergy in Virginia, EMS women's experiences of culture of call efforts, practices of excellent and fruitful Mennonite pastoral ministry.

Eastern Mennonite University, Program in Counseling, Harrisonburg, VA 22802-2462. Offers MA, M Div/MA. *Accreditation:* ACA (one or more programs are accredited); ACIPE. Part-time programs available. *Degree requirements:* For master's, practicum, internship. *Entrance requirements:* For master's, minimum GPA of 3.0. Additional exam requirements/recommendations for international students: Required—TOEFL (minimum score 550 paper-based). *Expenses:* Contact institution. *Faculty research:* Career and gender, empathy and consciousness, pastoral counseling, education models.

Eastern University, Palmer Theological Seminary, Program in Ministry, St. Davids, PA 19087-3696. Offers marriage and family (D Min). Part-time programs available. *Degree requirements:* For doctorate, thesis/dissertation. *Entrance requirements:* For doctorate, 3 years of experience, involvement in ministry, church endorsement. *Expenses:* Contact institution.

Ecumenical Theological Seminary, Program in Ministry, Detroit, MI 48201. Offers D Min. *Accreditation:* ACIPE.

Emmanuel Christian Seminary, Graduate and Professional Programs, Johnson City, TN 37601-9438. Offers Christian care and counseling (M Div); Christian doctrine (MAR); Christian education (M Div); Christian ministry (M Div); church history (MAR); divinity (M Div); ministry (D Min); New Testament (MAR); Old Testament (MAR); urban ministry (M Div); world missions (M Div). *Accreditation:* ACIPE; ATS. Part-time programs available. *Faculty:* 9 full-time (2 women), 9 part-time/adjunct (1 woman). *Students:* 90 full-time (27 women), 57 part-time (10 women); includes 2 Black or African American, non-Hispanic/Latino; 3 Hispanic/Latino, 17 international. Average age 27. 30 applicants, 97% accepted, 22 enrolled. In 2010, 17 first professional degrees, 1 master's, 1 doctorate awarded. *Degree requirements:* For master's, 2 foreign languages, thesis or alternative, portfolio; for doctorate, thesis/dissertation; for M Div, 2 foreign languages, thesis/dissertation or alternative, portfolio. *Entrance requirements:* For M Div and master's, bachelor's degree from accredited institution; for doctorate, Minnesota Multiphasic Personality Inventory, M Div or equivalent. Additional exam requirements/recommendations for international students: Required—TOEFL (minimum score 80 computer-based). *Application deadline:* For fall admission, 8/1 for domestic and international students; for spring admission, 1/20 for domestic and international students. Applications are processed on a rolling basis. Application fee: $25. *Expenses:* Tuition: Full-time $11,700; part-time $390 per credit hour. Required fees: $162.50 per semester. One-time fee: $240. Tuition and fees vary according to reciprocity agreements. *Financial support:* In 2010–11, 136 students received support; teaching assistantships with partial tuition reimbursements available, career-related internships or fieldwork, scholarships/grants, and tuition waivers (partial) available. Support available to part-time students. Financial award application deadline: 3/1; financial award applicants required to submit FAFSA. *Faculty research:* Theology of Old Testament prophets, spiritual formation for Christian leaders, history of African churches and religions, social world of early Christianity, lay pastoral counseling, ANE epigraphy. Total annual research expenditures: $12,000. *Unit head:* Dr. Jack Holland, Dean and Professor of Christian Care and Counseling, 423-461-1524, Fax: 423-926-6198, E-mail: jholland@ecs.edu. *Application contact:* Erin Layton, Director of Admissions, 423-461-1535, Fax: 423-926-6198, E-mail: elayton@ecs.edu.

Emory University, Candler School of Theology, Atlanta, GA 30322. Offers formation and witness (M Div); history, scripture and tradition (MTS); leadership in church and community (M Div); modern religious thought and experience (MTS); pastoral counseling (Th D); religion and race (M Div); religion, health and science (M Div); scripture and interpretation (M Div); society and personality (M Div); theology (Th M); theology and ethics (M Div); theology and the arts (M Div); traditions of the church (M Div); women and religion (M Div); JD/M Div; JD/MTS; M Div/MBA; M Div/MPH; MBA/MTS; MTS/MPH. *Accreditation:* ACIPE; ATS. Part-time programs available. *Faculty:* 45 full-time (11 women), 26 part-time/adjunct (12 women). *Students:* 411 full-time (206 women), 44 part-time (29 women); includes 113 Black or African American, non-Hispanic/Latino; 1 American Indian or Alaska Native, non-Hispanic/Latino; 8 Asian, non-Hispanic/Latino; 8 Hispanic/Latino; 1 Two or more races, non-Hispanic/Latino, 40 international. Average age 32. 603 applicants, 74% accepted, 191 enrolled. In 2010, 141 first professional degrees, 48 master's, 1 doctorate awarded. *Degree requirements:* For master's, thesis optional; for doctorate, comprehensive exam, thesis/dissertation; for M Div, thesis/dissertation optional. *Entrance requirements:* For M Div, minimum undergraduate GPA of 2.75; for master's, minimum undergraduate GPA of 3.0; for doctorate, GRE, M Div, 8 units of course work in clinical pastoral education. Additional exam requirements/recommendations for international students: Required—TOEFL (minimum score 600 paper-based; 250 computer-based; 95 iBT). *Application deadline:* For fall admission, 7/1 for domestic and international students; for spring admission, 11/1 for domestic and international students. Applications are processed on a rolling basis. Application fee: $50. Electronic applications accepted. *Expenses:* Contact institution. *Financial support:* In 2010–11, 422 students received support, including 343 fellowships (averaging $12,216 per year); career-related internships or fieldwork, institutionally sponsored loans, scholarships/grants, and student employment also available. Support available to part-time students. Financial award application deadline: 1/15; financial award applicants required to submit FAFSA. *Faculty research:* Biblical studies, church history, ethics, ministry practice, pastoral care. *Unit head:* Shelly E. Hart, Registrar, 404-727-6480, Fax: 404-727-4373, E-mail: candlerregistrar@emory.edu. *Application contact:* Mary Lou Greenwood Boice, Associate Dean of Admissions and Financial Aid, 404-727-6326, Fax: 404-727-2915, E-mail: candleradmissions@emory.edu.

Evangelical Theological Seminary, Graduate and Professional Programs, Myerstown, PA 17067-1212. Offers Biblical studies (MAR); congregational ministry (M Div); global and contextual studies (M Div, MAR); historical and theological studies (MAR); interdisciplinary studies (MAR);

Pastoral Ministry and Counseling

Evangelical Theological Seminary (continued)
marriage and family counseling (M Div); marriage and family therapy (MA); New Testament (MAR); Old Testament (MAR); spiritual formation (MAR); teaching ministry (M Div); youth ministry (M Div). *Accreditation:* ATS (one or more programs are accredited). Part-time programs available. Postbaccalaureate distance learning degree programs offered (minimal on-campus study). *Degree requirements:* For master's, 2 foreign languages; for M Div, 2 foreign languages, ministry internship. *Entrance requirements:* For M Div and master's, minimum GPA of 2.5. Additional exam requirements/recommendations for international students: Required—TOEFL (minimum score 550 paper-based; 213 computer-based). *Faculty research:* Literary form and structure within the Hebrew and Greek scriptures, Wesley studies, esoteric biblical languages, the Mosaic law and the Christian, ethics.

Faith Baptist Bible College and Theological Seminary, Graduate Program, Ankeny, IA 50023. Offers biblical studies (MA); pastoral studies (M Div); pastoral training (MA); religion (MA); theological studies (MA). Part-time programs available. *Faculty:* 4 full-time (0 women), 4 part-time/adjunct (0 women). *Students:* 14 full-time (1 woman), 25 part-time (0 women); includes 3 Asian, non-Hispanic/Latino, 1 international. Average age 29. In 2010, 5 first professional degrees, 14 master's awarded. *Degree requirements:* For master's, thesis or alternative; for M Div, 2 foreign languages. *Entrance requirements:* Additional exam requirements/recommendations for international students: Required—TOEFL (minimum score 550 paper-based; 197 computer-based). *Application deadline:* For fall admission, 8/1 priority date for domestic students, 8/1 for international students; for spring admission, 12/15 for domestic and international students. Applications are processed on a rolling basis. Application fee: $25. *Financial support:* Career-related internships or fieldwork and scholarships/grants available. Support available to part-time students. Financial award application deadline: 3/1; financial award applicants required to submit FAFSA. *Faculty research:* Baptist theology, American church history. *Unit head:* Dr. Ernest Schmidt, Dean of Seminary, 515-964-0601, E-mail: schmidte@faith.edu. *Application contact:* Carrie Johnson, Admissions Administrative Assistant, 888-FAITH4U, Fax: 515-964-1638, E-mail: admissions@faith.edu.

Faulkner University, College of Biblical Studies, Montgomery, AL 36109-3398. Offers ministry (MABS); missions (MABS); New Testament (MABS); Old Testament (MABS); youth and family ministry (MABS).

Fordham University, Graduate School of Religion and Religious Education, New York, NY 10458. Offers pastoral counseling and spiritual care (MA); pastoral ministry/spirituality/pastoral counseling (D Min); religion and religious education (MA); religious education (MS, PhD, PD); spiritual direction (Certificate). Part-time programs available. Terminal master's awarded for partial completion of doctoral program. *Degree requirements:* For master's, research paper; for doctorate, comprehensive exam, thesis/dissertation. *Entrance requirements:* For doctorate, MAT. Electronic applications accepted. *Expenses:* Contact institution. *Faculty research:* Spirituality and spiritual direction, pastoral care and counseling, adult family and community, growth and young adult.

Freed-Hardeman University, School of Biblical Studies, Program in Ministry, Henderson, TN 38340-2399. Offers M Min. Part-time programs available. *Degree requirements:* For master's, comprehensive exam, internship. *Entrance requirements:* For master's, GRE General Test or MAT. Additional exam requirements/recommendations for international students: Required—TOEFL (minimum score 500 paper-based; 173 computer-based).

Fresno Pacific University, Fresno Pacific Biblical Seminary, Program in Christian Ministry, Fresno, CA 93702-4709. Offers MA. Part-time programs available. Postbaccalaureate distance learning degree programs offered (minimal on-campus study). *Entrance requirements:* Additional exam requirements/recommendations for international students: Required—TOEFL (minimum score 550 paper-based; 213 computer-based).

Fuller Theological Seminary, Graduate School of Theology, Pasadena, CA 91182. Offers Christian leadership (MACL); evangelism (MA); family life education (MA); ministry (M Div, D Min); pastoral ministry (MA); recovery ministry (MA); theology (MAT, Th M, PhD); worship music ministry (MA); worship, theology, and the arts (MA); youth, family, and culture (MA). M Div offered jointly with Denver Conservative Baptist Seminary; D Min with Tyndale University College & Seminary. *Accreditation:* ACIPE; ATS (one or more programs are accredited). Part-time and evening/weekend programs available. *Degree requirements:* For doctorate, variable foreign language requirement, thesis/dissertation; for M Div, 2 foreign languages. *Entrance requirements:* For doctorate, GRE General Test. *Faculty research:* New Testament, Old Testament, systematic theology, history, practical theology.

Gannon University, School of Graduate Studies, College of Humanities, Education, and Social Sciences, School of Humanities, Program in Pastoral Studies, Erie, PA 16541-0001. Offers MA, Certificate. Part-time and evening/weekend programs available. *Students:* 1 (woman) full-time, 7 part-time (4 women). Average age 48. 4 applicants, 75% accepted, 0 enrolled. In 2010, 3 master's awarded. *Degree requirements:* For master's, comprehensive exam, thesis or alternative, research project, internship, written evaluation. *Entrance requirements:* For master's, interview; minimum 10 credits of course work in philosophy, religious studies, or theology. Additional exam requirements/recommendations for international students: Required—TOEFL (minimum score 79 iBT). *Application deadline:* Applications are processed on a rolling basis. Application fee: $25. Electronic applications accepted. *Expenses:* Tuition: Full-time $14,670; part-time $815 per credit. Required fees: $430; $18 per credit. Tuition and fees vary according to class time, course load, degree level, campus/location and program. *Financial support:* Career-related internships or fieldwork, scholarships/grants, and unspecified assistantships available. Financial award application deadline: 7/1; financial award applicants required to submit FAFSA. *Unit head:* Dr. Mary Anne Rivera, Director, 814-871-5646, E-mail: rivera006@gannon.edu. *Application contact:* Kara Morgan, Assistant Director of Graduate Admissions, 814-871-5831, Fax: 814-871-5827, E-mail: graduate@gannon.edu.

Gardner-Webb University, School of Divinity, Boiling Springs, NC 28017. Offers biblical studies (M Div); Christian education and formation (M Div); ministry (D Min); missiology (M Div); pastoral care and counseling (M Div); pastoral studies (M Div); M Div/MA; M Div/MBA. *Accreditation:* ACIPE; ATS. Part-time programs available. *Faculty:* 11 full-time (9 women), 5 part-time/adjunct (2 women). *Students:* 138 full-time (63 women), 81 part-time (26 women); includes 74 Black or African American, non-Hispanic/Latino; 1 Asian, non-Hispanic/Latino; 3 Hispanic/Latino, 2 international. Average age 40. In 2010, 56 first professional degrees, 1 doctorate awarded. *Degree requirements:* For M Div, 2 foreign languages. *Entrance requirements:* For M Div, minimum GPA of 2.0; for doctorate, minimum GPA of 2.75. *Application deadline:* For fall admission, 8/1 priority date for domestic students; for spring admission, 12/15 priority date for domestic students. Applications are processed on a rolling basis. Application fee: $40. *Expenses:* Contact institution. *Financial support:* Fellowships, institutionally sponsored loans and unspecified assistantships available. Support available to part-time students. Financial award application deadline: 5/15. *Faculty research:* Jewish Christian dialogue, Islam. *Unit head:* Dr. Robert W. Canoy, Dean, 704-406-4400, Fax: 704-406-3935, E-mail: rcanoy@gardner-webb.edu. *Application contact:* Jeremy Fern, Director of Admissions, 704-406-3205, Fax: 704-406-3935, E-mail: jfern@gardner-webb.edu.

Garrett-Evangelical Theological Seminary, Graduate and Professional Programs, Evanston, IL 60201-3298. Offers Bible and culture (PhD); Christian education (MA); Christian education and congregational studies (PhD); contemporary theology and culture (PhD); divinity (M Div); ethics, church, and society (MA); liturgical studies (PhD); ministry (D Min); music ministry (MA); pastoral care and counseling (MA); pastoral theology, personality, and culture (PhD); spiritual formation and evangelism (MA); theological studies (MTS); M Div/MSW. M Div/MSW offered jointly with Loyola University Chicago. *Accreditation:* ACIPE; ATS (one or more programs are accredited). Part-time programs available. *Degree requirements:* For master's, thesis (for some programs); for doctorate, thesis/dissertation. *Entrance requirements:* For doctorate, GRE (PhD). Additional exam requirements/recommendations for international students: Required—TOEFL (minimum score 560 paper-based; 230 computer-based). Electronic applications accepted.

General Theological Seminary, Graduate and Professional Programs, New York, NY 10011-4977. Offers Anglican studies (STM, Th D, Certificate); ascetical theology (Certificate); biblical studies (Certificate); congregational development (Certificate); divinity (M Div); historical and theological studies (Certificate); spiritual direction (MASD, STM, Certificate); theology (MA). *Accreditation:* ACIPE; ATS. Part-time and evening/weekend programs available. Terminal master's awarded for partial completion of doctoral program. *Degree requirements:* For master's, thesis; for doctorate, 2 foreign languages, thesis/dissertation. *Entrance requirements:* For M Div, GRE General Test, bishop's endorsement; for master's, GRE General Test; for doctorate, GRE, M Div or MA. Additional exam requirements/recommendations for international students: Required—TOEFL. *Faculty research:* Liturgy, New Testament, ethics, history, ecumenical relations.

George Fox University, George Fox Evangelical Seminary, Newberg, OR 97132-2697. Offers Biblical studies (M Div); Christian earthkeeping (M Div); Christian history and theology (M Div); clinical pastoral education and hospital chaplaincy (M Div); leadership and spiritual formation (D Min), including global missional leadership, semiotics and future studies; military chaplaincy (M Div); ministry leadership (MA); pastoral studies (M Div); spiritual formation (MA, Certificate); spiritual formation and discipleship (M Div); theological studies (MA). *Accreditation:* ACIPE; ATS. Part-time programs available. Postbaccalaureate distance learning degree programs offered (minimal on-campus study). *Faculty:* 7 full-time (2 women), 23 part-time/adjunct (6 women). *Students:* 122 full-time (41 women), 236 part-time (76 women); includes 6 Black or African American, non-Hispanic/Latino; 2 American Indian or Alaska Native, non-Hispanic/Latino; 11 Asian, non-Hispanic/Latino; 4 Hispanic/Latino; 4 Two or more races, non-Hispanic/Latino, 14 international. Average age 40. 141 applicants, 94% accepted, 95 enrolled. In 2010, 19 first professional degrees, 33 master's, 17 doctorates, 3 other advanced degrees awarded. *Degree requirements:* For master's, variable foreign language requirement, thesis optional, internship; for doctorate, comprehensive exam (for some programs), thesis/dissertation, internship. *Entrance requirements:* For master's, resume, three references (one pastoral, one academic or professional, one personal), one official transcript from each college or university attended; for doctorate, resume, 3 references (1 professional, 1 academic, 1 personal). Additional exam requirements/recommendations for international students: Required—TOEFL (minimum score 577 paper-based; 233 computer-based; 90 iBT). *Application deadline:* For fall admission, 7/1 for domestic and international students; for winter admission, 11/1 for domestic and international students; for spring admission, 4/1 for domestic and international students. Applications are processed on a rolling basis. Application fee: $40. Electronic applications accepted. *Expenses:* Contact institution. *Financial support:* Career-related internships or fieldwork and scholarships/grants available. Financial award application deadline: 5/1; financial award applicants required to submit FAFSA. *Unit head:* Dr. Chuck Conniry, Professor of Theology/Vice President and Dean, 503-554-6152, E-mail: cconniry@georgefox.edu. *Application contact:* Sheila Bartlett, Admissions Counselor, 800-631-0921, Fax: 503-554-6122, E-mail: gfes@georgefox.edu.

Georgian Court University, School of Arts and Sciences, Lakewood, NJ 08701-2697. Offers biology (MA); Catholic school leadership (Certificate); clinical mental health counseling (MA); holistic health studies (MA); mathematics (MA); pastoral ministry (Certificate); religious education (Certificate); school psychology (Certificate); theology (MA, Certificate). Part-time and evening/weekend programs available. *Faculty:* 19 full-time (11 women), 7 part-time/adjunct (5 women). *Students:* 61 full-time (59 women), 143 part-time (113 women); includes 20 minority (5 Black or African American, non-Hispanic/Latino; 3 Asian, non-Hispanic/Latino; 11 Hispanic/Latino; 1 Two or more races, non-Hispanic/Latino), 1 international. Average age 39. 139 applicants, 59% accepted, 50 enrolled. In 2010, 5 master's awarded. *Degree requirements:* For master's, comprehensive exam (for some programs), thesis (for some programs). *Entrance requirements:* For master's, GRE, MAT, or NTE/PRAXIS, 3 letters of recommendation. Additional exam requirements/recommendations for international students: Required—TOEFL (minimum score 550 paper-based; 213 computer-based). *Application deadline:* For fall admission, 8/1 priority date for domestic students, 4/1 for international students; for spring admission, 1/1 priority date for domestic students, 7/1 for international students. Applications are processed on a rolling basis. Application fee: $40. Electronic applications accepted. *Expenses:* Tuition: Full-time $12,510; part-time $695 per credit. Required fees: $416 per year. Tuition and fees vary according to campus/location and program. *Financial support:* Scholarships/grants, health care benefits, and unspecified assistantships available. Financial award application deadline: 4/15; financial award applicants required to submit FAFSA. *Unit head:* Dr. Linda James, Dean, 732-987-2617, Fax: 732-987-2007. *Application contact:* Patrick Givens, Assistant Director of Admissions, 732-987-2736, Fax: 732-987-2084, E-mail: graduateadmissions@georgian.edu.

Golden Gate Baptist Theological Seminary, Graduate and Professional Programs, Mill Valley, CA 94941-3197. Offers divinity (M Div); early childhood education (Certificate); education leadership (MAEL, Diploma); ministry (D Min); theological studies (MTS); theology (Th M); youth ministry (Certificate). *Accreditation:* ACIPE; ATS (one or more programs are accredited). Part-time and evening/weekend programs available. *Degree requirements:* For master's, thesis (for some programs); for doctorate, 2 foreign languages, thesis/dissertation; for M Div, 2 foreign languages. *Entrance requirements:* For doctorate, MAT. Additional exam requirements/recommendations for international students: Required—TOEFL (minimum score 550 paper-based; 213 computer-based). Electronic applications accepted.

Gonzaga University, College of Arts and Sciences, Department of Religious Studies, Spokane, WA 99258. Offers pastoral ministry (MA); religious studies (MA); spirituality (MA). *Degree requirements:* For master's, comprehensive exam. *Entrance requirements:* For master's, GRE General Test or MAT, minimum GPA of 3.0. Additional exam requirements/recommendations for international students: Required—TOEFL.

Gordon-Conwell Theological Seminary, Graduate and Professional Programs, South Hamilton, MA 01982. Offers Biblical languages (MABL); church history (MACH); counseling (MACO); ministry (D Min); missions/evangelism (MAME); New Testament (MANT); Old Testament (MAOT); religion (MAR); theology (M Div, MATH, Th M, Th D). *Accreditation:* ACIPE; ATS (one or more programs are accredited). Part-time and evening/weekend programs available. *Degree requirements:* For master's, one foreign language, thesis optional; for doctorate, 2 foreign languages, thesis/dissertation; for M Div, 2 foreign languages. *Entrance requirements:* For M Div and master's, minimum GPA of 2.5; for doctorate, minimum GPA of 3.0.

Graceland University, Community of Christ Seminary, Independence, MO 64050. Offers Christian ministry (MACM); religion (MAR). Part-time programs available. Postbaccalaureate distance learning degree programs offered (minimal on-campus study). *Faculty:* 2 full-time (1 woman), 9 part-time/adjunct (3 women). *Students:* 4 full-time (all women), 13 part-time (8 women); includes 1 Black or African American, non-Hispanic/Latino, 1 international. Average age 41. 15 applicants, 80% accepted, 7 enrolled. In 2010, 6 master's awarded. *Degree requirements:* For master's, thesis optional, portfolio or thesis (MAR), practicum (MACM). *Entrance requirements:* For master's, minimum cumulative GPA of 3.0. Additional exam requirements/recommendations for international students: Required—TOEFL. *Application deadline:* For fall admission, 8/15 priority date for domestic students; for winter admission, 10/15 priority date for domestic students; for spring admission, 4/15 priority date for domestic students. Applications are processed on a rolling basis. Application fee: $50. *Expenses:* Contact institution. *Financial support:* Scholarships/grants available. Financial award application deadline: 12/15; financial award applicants required to submit FAFSA. *Faculty research:* Theology, scripture. *Unit head:* Dr. Don H. Compier, Dean, 800-833-0524 Ext. 4900, Fax: 816-833-2990, E-mail: dcompier@graceland.edu. *Application contact:* Judy K. Luffman, Executive Assistant, 816-833-0524 Ext. 4508, Fax: 816-833-2990, E-mail: luffman@graceland.edu.

Grace Theological Seminary, Graduate and Professional Programs, Winona Lake, IN 46590-9907. Offers biblical studies (Certificate); camp administration (MA); counseling (M Div); exegetical studies (MA); intercultural studies (M Div, MA); local church studies (MA); pastoral studies (M Div); theological studies (MA); theology (D Min, Diploma). Part-time programs available. Postbaccalaureate distance learning degree programs offered (no on-campus study). *Degree requirements:* For master's, thesis optional; for doctorate, 2 foreign languages, thesis/dissertation; for M Div, 2 foreign languages, thesis/dissertation optional. *Entrance requirements:* For M Div and master's, MAT, minimum GPA of 2.5. Electronic applications accepted. *Faculty research:* Biblical theology, language, and church ministries.

Grace University, College of Graduate Studies, Counseling Program, Omaha, NE 68108. Offers MA. *Entrance requirements:* For master's, minimum undergraduate GPA of 3.0.

Grand Rapids Theological Seminary of Cornerstone University, Graduate Programs, Grand Rapids, MI 49525-5897. Offers biblical counseling (MA); Biblical counseling (M Div); chaplaincy (M Div); Christian education (M Div, MA); intercultural studies (M Div, MA); New Testament (MA, Th M); Old Testament (MA, Th M); pastoral studies (M Div); systematic theology (MA); theology (Th M). *Accreditation:* ATS. Part-time programs available. Postbaccalaureate distance learning degree programs offered (minimal on-campus study). *Entrance requirements:* Additional exam requirements/recommendations for international students: Required—TOEFL (minimum score 577 paper-based; 233 computer-based; 90 iBT). Electronic applications accepted.

Greenville College, Program in Leadership and Ministry, Greenville, IL 62246-0159. Offers MA. Part-time programs available. *Degree requirements:* For master's, 6 hours of research/practicum in applied ministry. *Entrance requirements:* For master's, 1 year of work experience in Christian ministry, interview. Additional exam requirements/recommendations for international students: Required—TOEFL (minimum score 525 paper-based; 197 computer-based). Electronic applications accepted.

Hampton University, Graduate College, College of Education and Continuing Studies, Program in Counseling, Hampton, VA 23668. Offers college student development (MA); community agency counseling (MA); pastoral counseling (MA); school counseling (MA). *Accreditation:* NCATE. Part-time and evening/weekend programs available. *Entrance requirements:* For master's, GRE General Test.

Harding University, College of Bible and Religion, Master of Ministry Program, Searcy, AR 72149-0001. Offers M Min. Part-time and evening/weekend programs available. Postbaccalaureate distance learning degree programs offered. *Faculty:* 4 part-time/adjunct (0 women). *Students:* 1 full-time (0 women), 37 part-time (3 women); includes 3 Black or African American, non-Hispanic/Latino; 1 American Indian or Alaska Native, non-Hispanic/Latino; 1 Hispanic/Latino, 3 international. Average age 38. 10 applicants, 100% accepted, 10 enrolled. In 2010, 5 master's awarded. *Degree requirements:* For master's, 3 practica (1 hour each), portfolio, capstone project. *Entrance requirements:* For master's, 16 hours course work in Bible, minimum GPA of 2.75. *Application deadline:* For fall admission, 8/1 priority date for domestic and international students; for spring admission, 12/1 priority date for domestic students, 12/15 priority date for international students. Applications are processed on a rolling basis. Application fee: $25. Electronic applications accepted. *Expenses:* Tuition: Full-time $10,098; part-time $561 per credit hour. Required fees: $22.50 per credit hour. *Financial support:* In 2010–11, 36 students received support. Scholarships/grants and unspecified assistantships available. *Unit head:* Dr. Bill Richardson, Director/Associate Professor, 501-279-4252, Fax: 501-279-4081, E-mail: mmin@harding.edu. *Application contact:* Debbie Stewart, Information Contact, 501-279-4252, E-mail: dstewart@harding.edu.

Harding University Graduate School of Religion, Graduate Programs, Memphis, TN 38117-5499. Offers Christian ministry (MA); counseling (MA); ministry (M Div, D Min); religion (MA). *Accreditation:* ATS. Part-time programs available. Postbaccalaureate distance learning degree programs offered (minimal on-campus study). *Degree requirements:* For master's, variable foreign language requirement, thesis (for some programs); for doctorate, one foreign language, thesis/dissertation; for M Div, 2 foreign languages, thesis/dissertation optional. *Entrance requirements:* For M Div, GRE General Test (for graduates of non-accredited schools), minimum GPA of 2.5; for master's, minimum GPA of 2.7; for doctorate, minimum GPA of 3.0. Additional exam requirements/recommendations for international students: Required—TOEFL (minimum score 550 paper-based; 213 computer-based; 79 iBT). Electronic applications accepted.

Hardin-Simmons University, Graduate School, Logsdon School of Theology, Logsdon Seminary, Seminary Program in Family Ministry, Abilene, TX 79698-0001. Offers MA. Part-time programs available. *Faculty:* 2 full-time (0 women). *Students:* 10 full-time (5 women), 7 part-time (3 women); includes 2 Black or African American, non-Hispanic/Latino. Average age 31. 9 applicants, 67% accepted, 5 enrolled. In 2010, 5 master's awarded. *Degree requirements:* For master's, comprehensive exam, clinical experience, project. *Entrance requirements:* For master's, minimum undergraduate GPA of 3.0 in major, 2.7 overall; 6 hours each of course work in psychology and Old and New Testament; interview; writing sample; references. Additional exam requirements/recommendations for international students: Required—TOEFL (minimum score 555 paper-based; 213 computer-based; 75 iBT). *Application deadline:* For fall admission, 8/15 priority date for domestic students, 4/1 for international students; for spring admission, 1/5 priority date for domestic students, 9/1 for international students. Applications are processed on a rolling basis. Application fee: $50. *Expenses:* Tuition: Full-time $12,150; part-time $675 per credit hour. Required fees: $650; $110 per semester. Tuition and fees vary according to degree level. *Financial support:* In 2010–11, 17 students received support; fellowships, career-related internships or fieldwork and scholarships/grants available. Support available to part-time students. Financial award application deadline: 6/30; financial award applicants required to submit FAFSA. *Unit head:* Dr. Randall Maurer, Director, 325-670-1599, Fax: 325-670-1406, E-mail: rmaurer@hsutx.edu. *Application contact:* Dr. Nancy Kucinski, Dean of Graduate Studies, 325-670-1298, Fax: 325-670-1564, E-mail: gradoff@hsutx.edu.

Hardin-Simmons University, Graduate School, Logsdon School of Theology, Logsdon Seminary, Seminary Program in Ministry, Abilene, TX 79698-0001. Offers D Min. Part-time programs available. *Faculty:* 9 full-time (0 women). *Students:* 18 part-time (0 women); includes 1 Hispanic/Latino. Average age 40. 9 applicants, 100% accepted, 9 enrolled. *Degree requirements:* For doctorate, ministry project. *Entrance requirements:* For doctorate, GRE or MAT, M Div or equivalent, minimum graduate GPA of 3.0, minimum 3 years ministry experience, active current ministry involvement, interview, 4 letters of recommendation, church endorsement. *Application deadline:* For fall admission, 4/30 for domestic students. Application fee: $50. *Expenses:* Tuition: Full-time $12,150; part-time $675 per credit hour. Required fees: $650; $110 per semester. Tuition and fees vary according to degree level. *Financial support:* In 2010–11, 17 students received support. Application deadline: 6/30. *Unit head:* Dr. Larry Baker, Director, 325-671-2110, E-mail: lbaker@hsutx.edu. *Application contact:* Dr. Nancy Kucinski, Dean of Graduate Studies, 325-670-1298, Fax: 325-670-1564, E-mail: gradoff@hsutx.edu.

Hartford Seminary, Graduate Programs, Hartford, CT 06105-2279. Offers Islamic studies (MA); ministry (D Min); religious studies (MA); spirituality (Certificate). *Accreditation:* ATS (one or more programs are accredited). Part-time and evening/weekend programs available. Postbaccalaureate distance learning degree programs offered (no on-campus study). *Faculty:* 15 full-time (3 women), 19 part-time/adjunct (7 women). *Students:* 37 full-time (17 women), 121 part-time (68 women); includes 35 minority (27 Black or African American, non-Hispanic/Latino; 5 Asian, non-Hispanic/Latino; 3 Hispanic/Latino), 25 international. *Degree requirements:* For master's, thesis optional, oral exam; for doctorate, thesis/dissertation, oral exam. *Entrance requirements:* For doctorate, experience in ministry, M Div. Additional exam requirements/recommendations for international students: Required—TOEFL (minimum score 550 paper-based; 213 computer-based; 80 iBT). *Application deadline:* For fall admission, 7/15 priority date for domestic students, 5/1 priority date for international students; for winter admission, 12/1 priority date for domestic students, 4/1 priority date for international students; for spring admission, 4/5 priority date for domestic students, 3/1 priority date for international students. Applications are processed on a rolling basis. Application fee: $50. *Expenses:* Tuition: Full-time $10,680; part-time $1780 per course. *Financial support:* In 2010–11, 74 students received support. Scholarships/grants and tuition waivers (partial) available. Support available to part-time students. Financial award application deadline: 6/1. *Faculty research:* Liturgy and social justice, professional leadership in ministry, congregational studies, Christian-Muslim relations, American religion. *Unit head:* Dr. Efrain Agosto, Dean, 860-509-9554, E-mail: eagosto@hartsem.edu. *Application contact:* Dr. Vanessa Avery, Admissions and Recruitment Manager, 860-509-9552, Fax: 860-509-9509, E-mail: vavery@hartsem.edu.

Heritage Baptist College and Heritage Theological Seminary, Program in Theological Studies, Cambridge, ON N3C 3T2, Canada. Offers chaplaincy (M Div); counselling (M Div); general (M Div); ministry (D Min); pastoral (M Div); research (M Div); theological studies (MA, Certificate). *Accreditation:* ATS.

Heritage Christian University, Graduate Programs, Florence, AL 35630. Offers counseling (MM); Greek (MA); ministry (MM); New Testament (MA). *Degree requirements:* For master's, practicum (MM), major research paper (MA). *Entrance requirements:* For master's, MAT or GRE, bachelor's degree in Bible from an accredited college or university, minimum GPA of 2.75, 3 letters of recommendation.

Hillsdale Free Will Baptist College, Department of Bible Studies, Moore, OK 73160-1208. Offers ministry (MA). Part-time and evening/weekend programs available. *Degree requirements:* For master's, thesis optional. *Entrance requirements:* Additional exam requirements/recommendations for international students: Recommended—TOEFL (minimum score 500 paper-based).

Holmes Institute, Graduate Program, Burbank, CA 91505. Offers consciousness studies (MS). Postbaccalaureate distance learning degree programs offered. *Faculty:* 50. *Students:* 72 part-time (51 women). *Degree requirements:* For master's, comprehensive exam, 2 spiritual retreats per year, internship (1 per term), 2 spiritual conferences. *Entrance requirements:* For master's, 3 letters of recommendation, interview, background check, official transcripts. *Application deadline:* Applications are processed on a rolling basis. Application fee: $300. *Unit head:* Rev. Dr. Lynn Connolly, Director of Education, 720-279-8990, Fax: 303-526-0913, E-mail: lconnolly@religiousscience.org. *Application contact:* Maureen Thurston, Administrative Registrar, 720-279-8992, Fax: 303-526-0913, E-mail: mthurston@religiousscience.org.

Holy Names University, Graduate Division, Department of Counseling Psychology, Oakland, CA 94619-1699. Offers counseling psychology (MA); forensic psychology (MA, Certificate); pastoral counseling (MA, Certificate). Part-time and evening/weekend programs available. *Faculty:* 1 (woman) full-time, 9 part-time/adjunct (5 women). *Students:* 49 full-time (39 women), 25 part-time (24 women); includes 30 Black or African American, non-Hispanic/Latino; 4 Asian, non-Hispanic/Latino; 13 Hispanic/Latino, 1 international. Average age 32. 22 applicants, 68% accepted, 11 enrolled. In 2010, 13 master's awarded. *Degree requirements:* For master's, comprehensive paper, seminars. *Entrance requirements:* For master's, minimum undergraduate GPA of 2.6 overall, 3.0 in major. Additional exam requirements/recommendations for international students: Required—TOEFL (minimum score 550 paper-based; 213 computer-based; 80 iBT). *Application deadline:* For fall admission, 8/1 priority date for domestic students, 8/1 for international students; for spring admission, 12/1 priority date for domestic students, 12/1 for international students. Applications are processed on a rolling basis. Application fee: $0. *Expenses:* Tuition: Full-time $13,788; part-time $766 per credit. Required fees: $340; $170 per semester. *Financial support:* In 2010–11, 38 students received support. Available to part-time students. Application deadline: 3/2. *Faculty research:* Cognitive psychology, anger management, grief and grief counseling, post-modernism and psychotherapy, spirituality and psychology. *Unit head:* Dr. Helen Shoemaker, Program Director, 510-436-1543, E-mail: shoemaker@hnu.edu. *Application contact:* 800-430-1321, Fax: 510-436-1325, E-mail: adulted@hnu.edu.

Holy Names University, Graduate Division, Program in Pastoral Ministries, Oakland, CA 94619-1699. Offers MA, Certificate. Part-time programs available. Postbaccalaureate distance learning degree programs offered (no on-campus study). *Degree requirements:* For master's, ministry project. *Entrance requirements:* Additional exam requirements/recommendations for international students: Required—TOEFL (minimum score 550 paper-based; 213 computer-based; 80 iBT). *Expenses:* Tuition: Full-time $13,788; part-time $766 per credit. Required fees: $340; $170 per semester. *Faculty research:* Ethics, cross-cultural management, faith development through liturgy, multi-cultural community building.

Houston Baptist University, College of Education and Behavioral Sciences, Program in Christian Counseling, Houston, TX 77074-3298. Offers MACC. *Degree requirements:* For master's, comprehensive exam. *Entrance requirements:* For master's, GRE General Test, minimum GPA of 3.0. Additional exam requirements/recommendations for international students: Required—TOEFL (minimum score 550 paper-based; 213 computer-based).

Houston Graduate School of Theology, Graduate School, Houston, TX 77092. Offers counseling (MA); pastoral ministry (M Div, D Min); theology (MA). *Accreditation:* ATS (one or more programs are accredited). Part-time and evening/weekend programs available. *Degree requirements:* For master's, thesis (for some programs); for doctorate, thesis/dissertation; for M Div, thesis/dissertation optional. *Entrance requirements:* For doctorate, GRE General Test or MAT, M Div or equivalent. Additional exam requirements/recommendations for international students: Required—TOEFL (minimum score 550 paper-based; 213 computer-based). *Faculty research:* Hermeneutics, spirituality, religion of Eastern Europe.

Howard Payne University, Program in Youth Ministry, Brownwood, TX 76801-2715. Offers MA. *Degree requirements:* For master's, internship. *Entrance requirements:* For master's, baccalaureate degree, 3 references, interview.

Huntington University, Graduate School, Huntington, IN 46750-1299. Offers counseling (MA), including licensed mental health counselor; education (M Ed); youth ministry leadership (MA). Part-time programs available. Postbaccalaureate distance learning degree programs offered (minimal on-campus study). *Degree requirements:* For master's, thesis. *Entrance requirements:* For master's, GRE (for counseling and education students only). Additional exam requirements/recommendations for international students: Required—TOEFL. Electronic applications accepted. *Faculty research:* Leadership, educational technology trends, evangelism, youth ministry, mental health.

Iliff School of Theology, Graduate and Professional Programs, Denver, CO 80210-4798. Offers biblical studies (MA); church history (MA); religion (MA); religion and social change (MA); specialized ministry (MASM), including justice and peace, pastoral theology and care, religious leadership; theology (M Div, MTS, D Min, PhD), including Biblical studies (PhD), religion and psychological studies (PhD), religion and social change (PhD), theology, philosophy and culture (PhD); theology/ethics (MA). PhD offered jointly with University of Denver. *Accreditation:* ACIPE; ATS. Part-time and evening/weekend programs available. *Degree requirements:* For master's, one foreign language, thesis (for some programs); for doctorate, 2 foreign languages, comprehensive exam, thesis/dissertation; for M Div, thesis/dissertation optional. *Entrance requirements:* For M Div, minimum GPA of 2.75, references; for master's, minimum GPA of 3.0, writing sample, references; for doctorate, GRE General Test, minimum GPA of 3.0, writing sample, letters of recommendation. Additional exam requirements/recommendations for international students: Required—TOEFL (minimum score 550 paper-based). Electronic applications accepted. *Faculty research:* Pastoral care, history, church music, contemporary church, biblical studies.

Indiana Wesleyan University, Graduate School, Wesley Seminary, Program in Ministry, Marion, IN 46953-4974. Offers ministerial leadership (MA); youth ministry (MA). Part-time programs available. Postbaccalaureate distance learning degree programs offered (minimal on-campus study). *Degree requirements:* For master's, one foreign language, capstone practicum and/or project. *Entrance requirements:* Additional exam requirements/recommendations for international students: Required—TOEFL. Electronic applications accepted. *Expenses:*

Pastoral Ministry and Counseling

Indiana Wesleyan University (continued)
Contact institution. *Faculty research:* History of worship innovation, history of New Testament afterlife traditions, second century mantanism, cross-cultural ministry, church health and growth, leadership in Christian organizations, managing change in the church, effective youth ministry, women in ministry, biblical hermeneutics.

Institute of Transpersonal Psychology, Low-Residency Programs, Palo Alto, CA 94303. Offers counseling psychology (online) (MA); spiritual guidance (MA); women's spirituality (MA). Postbaccalaureate distance learning degree programs offered (minimal on-campus study).

Inter American University of Puerto Rico, Metropolitan Campus, Graduate Programs, Program in Pastoral Theology, San Juan, PR 00919-1293. Offers PhD.

International Baptist College, Program in Ministry, Chandler, AZ 85286. Offers M Min, D Min.

Iona College, School of Arts and Science, Department of Family and Pastoral Counseling, New Rochelle, NY 10801-1890. Offers marriage and family therapy (MS, Certificate). *Accreditation:* AAMFT/COAMFTE. Part-time and evening/weekend programs available. *Faculty:* 4 full-time (0 women), 1 (woman) part-time/adjunct. *Students:* 30 full-time (23 women), 10 part-time (all women); includes 15 minority (7 Black or African American, non-Hispanic/Latino; 8 Hispanic/Latino). Average age 33. 49 applicants, 57% accepted, 15 enrolled. In 2010, 20 master's, 1 other advanced degree awarded. *Degree requirements:* For master's, thesis, project. *Entrance requirements:* For master's, draw-a-person test, sentence completion test, interview, minimum GPA of 3.0. *Application deadline:* Applications are processed on a rolling basis. Application fee: $50. Electronic applications accepted. *Expenses:* Contact institution. *Financial support:* Career-related internships or fieldwork, tuition waivers (partial), and unspecified assistantships available. Support available to part-time students. Financial award application deadline: 4/15; financial award applicants required to submit FAFSA. *Faculty research:* Marriage counseling. *Unit head:* Jerry Rubino, Chair, 914-633-2418, E-mail: jrubino@iona.edu. *Application contact:* Veronica Jarek-Prinz, Director of Graduate Admissions, 914-633-2420, Fax: 914-633-2277, E-mail: vjarekprinz@iona.edu.

Jewish University of America, Graduate School, Abrams Institute of Pastoral Counseling, Skokie, IL 60077-3248. Offers counseling (MA); pastoral counseling (MPC, DPC). *Degree requirements:* For master's, thesis optional; for doctorate, one foreign language, thesis/dissertation. *Entrance requirements:* For master's and doctorate, interview.

John Brown University, Graduate Ministry Programs, Siloam Springs, AR 72761-2121. Offers MA. Part-time and evening/weekend programs available. *Entrance requirements:* For master's, GRE or MAT if undergraduate GPA is less than 3.0, graduate of Kanakuk Institute. Additional exam requirements/recommendations for international students: Required—TOEFL (minimum score 550 paper-based; 173 computer-based; 70 iBT). Electronic applications accepted.

Knox Theological Seminary, Graduate Programs, Program in Ministry, Fort Lauderdale, FL 33308. Offers D Min. Part-time programs available. *Degree requirements:* For doctorate, thesis/dissertation. *Entrance requirements:* For doctorate, M Div or equivalent. Additional exam requirements/recommendations for international students: Required—TOEFL, TWE (minimum score 5).

Lancaster Bible College, Graduate School, Lancaster, PA 17601-5036. Offers adult ministries (MA); Bible (MA); children and family ministry (MA); consulting resource teacher (M Ed); elementary school counseling (M Ed); leadership (PhD); leadership studies (MA); marriage and family counseling (MA); mental health counseling (MA); pastoral studies (MA); secondary school counseling (M Ed); student ministry (MA). Part-time and evening/weekend programs available. *Faculty:* 8 full-time (1 woman), 5 part-time/adjunct (1 woman). *Students:* 94 full-time (47 women), 89 part-time (45 women); includes 21 minority (15 Black or African American, non-Hispanic/Latino; 5 Asian, non-Hispanic/Latino; 1 Hispanic/Latino). Average age 36. *Degree requirements:* For master's, comprehensive exam (for some programs), thesis (for some programs). *Entrance requirements:* For master's, bachelor's degree with a minimum of 30 credits of course work in Bible, minimum undergraduate GPA of 3.0, interview. Additional exam requirements/recommendations for international students: Required—TOEFL. *Application deadline:* Applications are processed on a rolling basis. Application fee: $25. *Expenses:* Tuition: Part-time $1491 per course. Required fees: $35 per semester. *Financial support:* In 2010–11, 31 students received support; teaching assistantships, scholarships/grants and unspecified assistantships available. Support available to part-time students. Financial award application deadline: 6/1; financial award applicants required to submit FAFSA. *Unit head:* Dr. Gary Bredfeldt, Associate Vice President/Dean of iLead Center, 717-560-8297, Fax: 717-560-8236. *Application contact:* Mark Wilson, Admissions Counselor, 717-560-8229, E-mail: mwilson@lbc.edu.

La Salle University, School of Arts and Sciences, Program in Theological, Pastoral and Liturgical Studies, Philadelphia, PA 19141-1199. Offers pastoral studies (MA); religion (MA); theological studies (MA). Part-time and evening/weekend programs available. *Entrance requirements:* For master's, 26 credits in humanistic subjects, religion, theology, or ministry-related work.

La Sierra University, School of Religion, Riverside, CA 92515. Offers pastoral ministry (M Div); religion (MA); religious education (MA); religious studies (MA). Part-time programs available. *Degree requirements:* For master's, one foreign language, thesis or alternative. *Entrance requirements:* For master's, GRE General Test, minimum GPA of 3.0.

Lee University, Program in Religion, Cleveland, TN 37320-3450. Offers biblical studies (MA); ministry studies (MA); theological studies (MA). Part-time programs available. *Faculty:* 8 full-time (2 women), 1 part-time/adjunct (0 women). *Students:* 13 full-time (5 women), 14 part-time (5 women); includes 1 Black or African American; non-Hispanic/Latino; 1 Asian, non-Hispanic/Latino; 2 Hispanic/Latino; 1 Two or more races, non-Hispanic/Latino, 1 international. Average age 29. 11 applicants, 100% accepted, 11 enrolled. In 2010, 5 master's awarded. *Degree requirements:* For master's, comprehensive exam, thesis. *Entrance requirements:* For master's, GRE or MAT, minimum GPA of 3.0, 2 letters of recommendation, interview. Additional exam requirements/recommendations for international students: Required—TOEFL (minimum score 450 paper-based; 45 computer-based). *Application deadline:* For fall admission, 4/1 priority date for domestic students; for spring admission, 10/1 priority date for domestic students. Applications are processed on a rolling basis. Application fee: $25. *Expenses:* Tuition: Full-time $12,120; part-time $506 per credit hour. Required fees: $560; $305 per semester. Part-time tuition and fees vary according to course load and campus/location. *Financial support:* Teaching assistantships, career-related internships or fieldwork, Federal Work-Study, institutionally sponsored loans, scholarships/grants, and unspecified assistantships available. Financial award application deadline: 3/1; financial award applicants required to submit FAFSA. *Faculty research:* Book of Isaiah, Gospel of Mark, school of St. Victor of the twelfth century, spirit Christology, people groups of New Testament and work. Total annual research expenditures: $3,000. *Unit head:* Dr. Bob Bayles, Director, 423-614-8338, E-mail: bbayles@leeuniversity.edu. *Application contact:* Vicki Glasscock, Graduate Admissions Director, 423-614-8059, E-mail: vglasscock@leeuniversity.edu.

Liberty University, College of Arts and Sciences, Lynchburg, VA 24502. Offers counseling (MA); human services (MA); nursing (MSN); pastoral care and counseling (PhD); professional counseling (PhD). *Accreditation:* AACN. Part-time programs available. Postbaccalaureate distance learning degree programs offered (minimal on-campus study). *Students:* 2,021 full-time (1,587 women), 4,301 part-time (3,346 women); includes 1,698 minority (1,424 Black or African American, non-Hispanic/Latino; 20 American Indian or Alaska Native, non-Hispanic/Latino; 59 Asian, non-Hispanic/Latino; 181 Hispanic/Latino; 10 Native Hawaiian or other Pacific Islander, non-Hispanic/Latino; 4 Two or more races, non-Hispanic/Latino), 93 international. Average age 36. In 2010, 865 master's, 12 doctorates awarded. *Degree requirements:* For master's, comprehensive exam (for some programs); for doctorate, comprehensive exam, thesis/dissertation. *Entrance requirements:* For master's, GRE General Test (MSN), minimum undergraduate GPA of 3.0; for doctorate, GRE General Test, minimum master's GPA of 3.25. Additional exam requirements/recommendations for international students: Required—TOEFL (minimum score 600 paper-based; 250 computer-based; 100 iBT). *Application deadline:* For fall admission, 6/1 priority date for domestic students; for spring admission, 11/1 priority date for domestic students. Applications are processed on a rolling basis. Application fee: $50. Electronic applications accepted. *Financial support:* Teaching assistantships with tuition reimbursements, Federal Work-Study available. *Faculty research:* God concept and adult attachment, building marital strength, image of God and gender, breastfeeding behavior among adolescent mothers, osteoporosis. *Unit head:* Dr. Ronald E. Hawkins, Dean, 434-592-4030, Fax: 434-522-0416, E-mail: rehawkin@liberty.edu. *Application contact:* Jay Bridge, Director of Graduate Admissions, 800-424-9595, Fax: 800-628-7977, E-mail: gradadmissions@liberty.edu.

Lincoln Christian Seminary, Graduate and Professional Programs, Lincoln, IL 62656-2167. Offers Bible and theology (MA); Christian ministries (MA); counseling (MA); divinity (M Div); leadership ministry (D Min); religious education (MRE). *Accreditation:* ACIPE; ATS. Part-time programs available. *Degree requirements:* For master's, 2 foreign languages, thesis; for doctorate, thesis/dissertation; for M Div, 2 foreign languages. *Entrance requirements:* For M Div and master's, minimum GPA of 2.5; for doctorate, M Div or equivalent. Additional exam requirements/recommendations for international students: Required—TOEFL (minimum score 550 paper-based; 213 computer-based). Electronic applications accepted.

Loma Linda University, Faculty of Religion, Program in Clinical Ministry, Loma Linda, CA 92350. Offers MA, Certificate. *Degree requirements:* For master's, comprehensive exam, thesis optional. *Entrance requirements:* For master's, minimum GPA of 3.0. Additional exam requirements/recommendations for international students: Required—TOEFL. Electronic applications accepted.

Loras College, Graduate Division, Program in Theology and Ministry, Dubuque, IA 52004-0178. Offers ministry (MA); theology (MA). Part-time and evening/weekend programs available. *Degree requirements:* For master's, comprehensive exam (for some programs), thesis (for some programs). *Entrance requirements:* For master's, bachelor's degree or undergraduate minor in religious studies or equivalent, minimum undergraduate GPA of 2.75.

Loyola Marymount University, College of Liberal Arts, Department of Theological Studies, Program in Pastoral Theology, Los Angeles, CA 90045-8400. Offers MA. Part-time and evening/weekend programs available. *Faculty:* 23 full-time (5 women), 3 part-time/adjunct (2 women). *Students:* 15 full-time (10 women), 37 part-time (23 women); includes 10 Asian, non-Hispanic/Latino; 17 Hispanic/Latino; 1 Native Hawaiian or other Pacific Islander, non-Hispanic/Latino, 1 international. Average age 43. 13 applicants, 62% accepted, 7 enrolled. In 2010, 32 master's awarded. *Degree requirements:* For master's, comprehensive exam, thesis or alternative. *Entrance requirements:* For master's, GRE General Test or MAT (recommended), 2 letters of recommendation, personal statement. Additional exam requirements/recommendations for international students: Required—TOEFL (minimum score 600 paper-based; 250 computer-based; 100 iBT). *Application deadline:* For fall admission, 3/1 priority date for domestic students. Application fee: $50. Electronic applications accepted. *Financial support:* In 2010–11, 47 students received support. Scholarships/grants and unspecified assistantships available. Support available to part-time students. Financial award application deadline: 6/1; financial award applicants required to submit FAFSA. Total annual research expenditures: $39,474. *Unit head:* Dr. Jonathan Rothchild, Graduate Director, 310-338-1716, E-mail: jrothchild@lmu.edu.

Loyola University Chicago, Institute of Pastoral Studies, Program in Pastoral Counseling, Chicago, IL 60660. Offers MA, Certificate. *Accreditation:* ACIPE. Part-time programs available. *Faculty:* 6 full-time (2 women), 12 part-time/adjunct (7 women). *Students:* 31 full-time (14 women), 25 part-time (19 women); includes 13 minority (4 Black or African American, non-Hispanic/Latino; 3 Asian, non-Hispanic/Latino; 5 Hispanic/Latino; 1 Two or more races, non-Hispanic/Latino), 7 international. Average age 41. 33 applicants, 82% accepted, 16 enrolled. In 2010, 13 master's awarded. *Degree requirements:* For master's, thesis or alternative, integration project. *Application deadline:* For fall admission, 2/15 priority date for domestic students. Applications are processed on a rolling basis. Application fee: $50. Electronic applications accepted. *Expenses:* Tuition: Full-time $14,940; part-time $830 per credit hour. Required fees: $87 per semester. Part-time tuition and fees vary according to course load and program. *Financial support:* In 2010–11, 7 students received support. Career-related internships or fieldwork, Federal Work-Study, and institutionally sponsored loans available. Support available to part-time students. Financial award application deadline: 3/1; financial award applicants required to submit FAFSA. *Faculty research:* Pastoral psychotherapy, enrichment outcome, marriage and family therapy, marriage and family spirituality, gender and ethnicity issues, theological anthropology. *Unit head:* Dr. Paul R. Giblin, Associate Professor, 312-915-7483, Fax: 312-915-7410, E-mail: pgibli@luc.edu. *Application contact:* Dr. Paul R. Giblin, Associate Professor, 312-915-7483, Fax: 312-915-7410, E-mail: pgibli@luc.edu.

Loyola University Chicago, Institute of Pastoral Studies, Program in Pastoral Studies, Chicago, IL 60660. Offers MA. *Accreditation:* ACIPE. *Faculty:* 6 full-time (2 women). *Students:* 17 full-time (11 women), 68 part-time (50 women); includes 5 minority (3 Black or African American, non-Hispanic/Latino; 2 Hispanic/Latino), 4 international. Average age 45. 38 applicants, 68% accepted, 19 enrolled. In 2010, 19 master's awarded. *Application deadline:* For fall admission, 8/1 priority date for domestic students; for spring admission, 12/1 for domestic students. Applications are processed on a rolling basis. Application fee: $50. *Expenses:* Tuition: Full-time $14,940; part-time $830 per credit hour. Required fees: $87 per semester. Part-time tuition and fees vary according to course load and program. *Financial support:* Career-related internships or fieldwork, Federal Work-Study, institutionally sponsored loans, and scholarships/grants available. Support available to part-time students. Financial award application deadline: 3/1. *Unit head:* Dr. Peter Gilmour, Director, 312-915-7400, Fax: 312-915-7410, E-mail: pgilmou@luc.edu. *Application contact:* Randy Gibbons, Administrative Assistant, 312-915-7450, Fax: 312-915-7410, E-mail: rgibbon@luc.edu.

Loyola University Maryland, Graduate Programs, Loyola College of Arts and Sciences, Department of Pastoral Counseling, Program in Pastoral Counseling, Baltimore, MD 21210-2699. Offers MS, PhD, CAS. Part-time and evening/weekend programs available. *Entrance requirements:* For master's, doctorate, and CAS, GRE General Test, GRE Subject Test (recommended). Additional exam requirements/recommendations for international students: Required—TOEFL (minimum score 550 paper-based; 213 computer-based).

Loyola University Maryland, Graduate Programs, Loyola College of Arts and Sciences, Department of Pastoral Counseling, Program in Spiritual and Pastoral Care, Baltimore, MD 21210-2699. Offers MA. Part-time and evening/weekend programs available. *Entrance requirements:* For master's, GRE General Test, GRE Subject Test (recommended). Additional exam requirements/recommendations for international students: Required—TOEFL (minimum score 550 paper-based; 213 computer-based).

Lutheran School of Theology at Chicago, Graduate and Professional Programs, Chicago, IL 60615-5199. Offers ministry (MAM, D Min); theological studies (MATS, PhD); theology (M Div, Th M). *Accreditation:* ACIPE; ATS (one or more programs are accredited). Part-time programs available. *Faculty:* 20 full-time (6 women), 18 part-time/adjunct (5 women). *Students:* 195 full-time (96 women), 87 part-time (48 women). Terminal master's awarded for partial completion of doctoral program. *Degree requirements:* For master's, variable foreign language requirement; for doctorate, variable foreign language requirement, comprehensive exam, thesis/dissertation; for M Div, 2 foreign languages. *Entrance requirements:* For master's, GRE (Th M), M Div or equivalent (Th M); for doctorate, GRE, M Div or equivalent, 3 years of professional experience (D Min). Additional exam requirements/recommendations for international students: Required—TOEFL (for Th M). *Application deadline:* Applications are processed on a rolling basis. Application fee: $50. *Expenses:* Tuition: Full-time $12,294; part-time $1366 per course. Required fees: $35 per semester. Tuition and fees vary according to degree level and program. *Financial support:* Career-related internships or fieldwork and scholarships/grants available. Support available to part-time students. *Unit head:* Michael Shelley, Dean, 773-256-0722, Fax: 773-256-0782, E-mail: mshelley@lstc.edu. *Application contact:* Dorothy C. Dominiak, Director of Financial Aid and Admissions, 773-256-0726, Fax: 773-256-0782, E-mail: ddominia@lstc.edu.

Lutheran Theological Seminary, Graduate and Professional Programs, Saskatoon, SK S7N 0X3, Canada. Offers Biblical studies (MTS); church history (MTS); ethics/church and society (MTS); history of Christianity (STM); New Testament (STM); Old Testament (STM); pastoral studies (STM); pastoral theology (MTS); systematic theology (MTS); systematic theology and philosophy of religion (STM); theology (M Div, D Div). STM programs offered jointly with College of Emmanuel and St. Chad and St. Andrew's College. *Accreditation:* ATS. Part-time programs available. *Degree requirements:* For master's, thesis; for M Div, Greek, Hebrew.

Lutheran Theological Seminary at Gettysburg, Graduate and Professional Programs, Gettysburg, PA 17325-1795. Offers divinity (M Div); ministerial studies (MAMS); outdoor ministry (MAR); parish ministry (D Min); theology (STM). *Accreditation:* ACIPE; ATS (one or more programs are accredited). Part-time programs available. Postbaccalaureate distance learning degree programs offered (no on-campus study). *Degree requirements:* For master's, thesis (for some programs); for M Div, one foreign language. Electronic applications accepted.

The Lutheran Theological Seminary at Philadelphia, Graduate School, Philadelphia, PA 19119-1794. Offers divinity (M Div); ministry (D Min); public leadership (MA); religion (MAR); social ministry (Certificate); theology (STM, PhD). *Accreditation:* ACIPE; ATS. Part-time and evening/weekend programs available. *Faculty:* 18 full-time (5 women), 22 part-time/adjunct (8 women). *Students:* 121 full-time (56 women), 204 part-time (97 women); includes 92 minority (80 Black or African American, non-Hispanic/Latino; 2 Asian, non-Hispanic/Latino; 10 Hispanic/Latino), 14 international. 123 applicants, 86% accepted, 84 enrolled. *Degree requirements:* For master's, one foreign language, comprehensive exam (for some programs), thesis (for some programs); for doctorate, thesis/dissertation; for M Div, 2 foreign languages. *Entrance requirements:* For M Div and master's, minimum undergraduate GPA of 2.8; for doctorate, minimum first professional GPA of 3.0. Additional exam requirements/recommendations for international students: Required—TOEFL (minimum score 550 paper-based; 213 computer-based), TWE. *Application deadline:* For fall admission, 6/1 priority date for domestic students. Applications are processed on a rolling basis. Application fee: $35. Electronic applications accepted. *Expenses:* Tuition: Full-time $13,900; part-time $1470 per course. Required fees: $2484; $75 per semester. Tuition and fees vary according to degree level. *Financial support:* In 2010–11, 102 students received support; research assistantships with tuition reimbursements available, teaching assistantships with tuition reimbursements available, career-related internships or fieldwork and Federal Work-Study available. Financial award application deadline: 7/1; financial award applicants required to submit FAFSA. *Unit head:* Rev. Dr. J. Paul Rajashekar, Dean, 215-248-6379, Fax: 215-248-4577, E-mail: rajashekar@ltsp.edu. *Application contact:* Rev. Louise Johnson, Director of Admissions, 800-286-4616 Ext. 6321, Fax: 215-248-7315, E-mail: admissions@ltsp.edu.

Luther Rice University, Graduate Programs, Lithonia, GA 30038-2454. Offers Bible/theology (M Div); Christian education (M Div); Christian studies (MA); church ministry (D Min); counseling (M Div); discipleship counseling (MA); ministry (M Div, MA); missions/evangelism (M Div). Part-time programs available. Postbaccalaureate distance learning degree programs offered (no on-campus study). *Degree requirements:* For doctorate, thesis/dissertation. *Entrance requirements:* Additional exam requirements/recommendations for international students: Required—TOEFL (minimum score 500 paper-based; 173 computer-based).

Madonna University, Program in Religious Studies, Livonia, MI 48150-1173. Offers pastoral ministry (MA).

Maple Springs Baptist Bible College and Seminary, Graduate and Professional Programs, Capitol Heights, MD 20743. Offers biblical studies (MA, Certificate); Christian counseling (MA); church administration (MA); divinity (M Div); ministry (D Min); religious education (MRE).

Maranatha Baptist Bible College, Program in Biblical Counseling, Watertown, WI 53094. Offers MA. Part-time programs available. *Faculty:* 4 full-time (0 women), 5 part-time/adjunct (0 women). *Students:* 6 full-time (3 women), 12 part-time (7 women). Average age 24. 2 applicants, 100% accepted, 2 enrolled. *Application deadline:* Applications are processed on a rolling basis. Application fee: $50. *Expenses:* Tuition: Full-time $4160; part-time $260 per credit hour. Required fees: $350; $23 per credit hour. *Financial support:* In 2010–11, 2 students received support. Scholarships/grants and tuition waivers (full and partial) available. Support available to part-time students. *Unit head:* Dr. Larry Oats, Dean of Maranatha Baptist Seminary, 920-206-2324, Fax: 920-261-9109, E-mail: loats@mbbc.edu. *Application contact:* Dr. Jim Harrison, Director of Admissions, 920-206-2327, Fax: 920-261-9109, E-mail: admissions@mbbc.edu.

Martin University, Graduate School of Urban Ministry, Indianapolis, IN 46218-3867. Offers urban ministry studies (MA). Part-time and evening/weekend programs available. *Degree requirements:* For master's, Greek, oral and written comprehensive exam or thesis. *Faculty research:* How to bridge the gap between black theology and the black church.

Marymount University, School of Education and Human Services, Program in Pastoral Counseling, Arlington, VA 22207-4299. Offers pastoral and spiritual care (MA); pastoral counseling (MA, Certificate). Part-time and evening/weekend programs available. *Degree requirements:* For master's, thesis or alternative. *Entrance requirements:* For master's, GRE, 2 letters of recommendation, interview, resume; for Certificate, master's degree in counseling. Additional exam requirements/recommendations for international students: Required—TOEFL (minimum score 600 paper-based; 250 computer-based; 96 iBT), IELTS (minimum score 6.5). Electronic applications accepted.

The Master's College and Seminary, The Master's Seminary, Santa Clarita, CA 91321-1200. Offers biblical counseling (MABC); New Testament (Th D); Old Testament (Th D); preaching (D Min); theology (M Div, M Th, Th D). Part-time programs available. *Degree requirements:* For master's, 2 foreign languages, thesis; for doctorate, 4 foreign languages, thesis/dissertation; for M Div, 2 foreign languages, thesis/dissertation. *Entrance requirements:* For M Div, minimum 2 years of college; for master's, minimum GPA of 2.75; for doctorate, Th M, minimum GPA of 3.5. Additional exam requirements/recommendations for international students: Required—TOEFL (minimum score 550 paper-based).

McCormick Theological Seminary, Graduate and Professional Programs, Chicago, IL 60615. Offers ministry (D Min); theological studies (MATS, Certificate); theology (M Div); M Div/MSW. M Div/MSW offered jointly with Loyola University Chicago, University of Chicago, and University of Illinois at Chicago. *Accreditation:* ACIPE; ATS (one or more programs are accredited). Part-time and evening/weekend programs available. *Degree requirements:* For master's, thesis (for some programs); for doctorate, thesis/dissertation. *Entrance requirements:* For M Div and master's, minimum GPA of 3.0; for doctorate, M Div, minimum 3 years in pastorate. *Faculty research:* Faith formation, families, biblical literature, Dead Sea scrolls, women in antiquity.

McMaster University, McMaster Divinity College, Hamilton, ON L8S 4M2, Canada. Offers biblical studies (M Div); Biblical studies (MA, MTS, Diploma); Christian interpretation/history (M Div, MA, MTS, Diploma); Christian ministry (M Div, MA, MTS, Diploma); Christian Studies (Certificate); Christian theology (PhD). Affiliated with the Toronto School of Theology. *Accreditation:* ATS. Part-time programs available. *Degree requirements:* For master's, one foreign language, thesis optional; for doctorate, 3 foreign languages, comprehensive exam, thesis/dissertation; for other advanced degree, 2 foreign languages, thesis. *Entrance requirements:* For master's, minimum B average in undergraduate course work, 3 letters of reference; for doctorate, minimum B+ average in bachelor's and master's, appropriate modern/ancient language, interview; for other advanced degree, 6 units of related Biblical language, minimum B+ average in undergraduate course work, minimum 15 units of course work in related area of study, 3 letters of recommendation. Additional exam requirements/recommendations for international students: Required—TOEFL (minimum score 550 paper-based; 237 computer-based). *Faculty research:* Ethics, Biblical studies, language studies, church history, Christian ministry.

Meadville Lombard Theological School, Graduate and Professional Programs, Chicago, IL 60637-1602. Offers divinity (M Div); ministry (D Min); religion (MA); M Div/MSW. M Div/MSW offered jointly with University of Chicago. *Accreditation:* ACIPE; ATS. Part-time programs available. Postbaccalaureate distance learning degree programs offered (minimal on-campus study). *Entrance requirements:* For M Div and master's, bachelor's degree; for doctorate, bachelor's and masters degrees, 3 years of ministry.

Messiah College, Program in Youth and Young Adult Ministries, Grantham, PA 17027. Offers MA.

Mid-America Christian University, Program in Counseling, Oklahoma City, OK 73170-4504. Offers marital and family therapy (MS); pastoral/spiritual direction (MS); professional counselor (MS). *Entrance requirements:* For master's, MAT, bachelor's degree from a regionally accredited college or university, minimum overall cumulative GPA of 2.75 of bachelor course work. Additional exam requirements/recommendations for international students: Required—TOEFL (minimum score 550 paper-based; 213 computer-based).

Midwestern Baptist Theological Seminary, Graduate and Professional Programs, Kansas City, MO 64118-4697. Offers Biblical archaeology (MA); Biblical languages (MA); Christian education (M Div, MACE); Christian foundations—lay ministry (Graduate Certificate); collegiate ministries (M Div); counseling (MA); educational ministry (D Ed Min); international church planting (M Div); ministry (M Div, D Min); North American church planting (M Div); sacred music (MCM); urban ministry (M Div); worship leadership (M Div); youth ministry (M Div). *Accreditation:* ATS. Part-time programs available. Postbaccalaureate distance learning degree programs offered (minimal on-campus study). *Degree requirements:* For doctorate, thesis/dissertation; for M Div, 2 foreign languages. *Entrance requirements:* For doctorate, MAT. Electronic applications accepted. *Faculty research:* Ministerial studies, Biblical and theological studies, missions, counseling.

Missouri Baptist University, Graduate Programs, St. Louis, MO 63141-8660. Offers business administration (MBA); Christian ministries (MACM); counseling (MAC); education (MSE); education administration (MEA); educational leadership (MSE, Ed S); teaching (MAT).

Moody Bible Institute, Graduate School, Chicago, IL 60610-3284. Offers biblical studies (MABS, Graduate Certificate); intercultural studies (MAIS, Graduate Certificate); ministry (M Div, M Min); spiritual formation and discipleship (MASF, Graduate Certificate); urban studies (MA, Graduate Certificate). Part-time programs available. *Degree requirements:* For master's, 2 foreign languages, fieldwork (MABS); colloquium, field research project (MA Min). *Entrance requirements:* For master's, 30 hours in Bible/theology, 2 years of ministry experience (MA Min).

Moravian Theological Seminary, Graduate and Professional Programs, Bethlehem, PA 18018-6614. Offers divinity (M Div); formative spirituality (M Div, MAPC, MATS); pastoral counseling (MAPC); theological studies (MATS). *Accreditation:* ACIPE; ATS (one or more programs are accredited). Part-time programs available. *Faculty:* 7 full-time (3 women), 11 part-time/adjunct (5 women). *Students:* 27 full-time (12 women), 49 part-time (34 women); includes 14 minority (5 Black or African American, non-Hispanic/Latino; 1 Asian, non-Hispanic/Latino; 8 Hispanic/Latino), 2 international. Average age 45. 44 applicants, 86% accepted, 36 enrolled. In 2010, 6 M Divs, 16 master's awarded. *Degree requirements:* For master's, thesis. *Entrance requirements:* Additional exam requirements/recommendations for international students: Required—TOEFL. *Application deadline:* For fall admission, 4/1 priority date for international students; for spring admission, 9/1 priority date for international students. Applications are processed on a rolling basis. Application fee: $35. *Expenses:* Tuition: Full-time $13,800; part-time $3078 per semester. Required fees: $90 per semester. *Financial support:* In 2010–11, 72 students received support. Career-related internships or fieldwork, Federal Work-Study, and scholarships/grants available. Support available to part-time students. Financial award application deadline: 5/1; financial award applicants required to submit FAFSA. *Unit head:* Rev. Dr. Frank L. Crouch, Dean and Vice President, 610-861-1516. *Application contact:* Ann Gibson, Director of Enrollment, 610-861-1512, Fax: 610-861-1569, E-mail: agibson@moravian.edu.

Mount Marty College, Graduate Studies Division, Yankton, SD 57078-3724. Offers business administration (MBA); nurse anesthesia (MS); nursing (MSN); pastoral ministries (MPM). *Accreditation:* AANA/CANAEP (one or more programs are accredited). *Degree requirements:* For master's, thesis or alternative. *Entrance requirements:* For master's, GRE General Test, minimum GPA of 3.0. Electronic applications accepted. *Faculty research:* Clinical anesthesia, professional characteristics, motivations of applicants.

Mount Mary College, Graduate Programs, Program in Community Counseling, Milwaukee, WI 53222-4597. Offers community counseling (MS); pastoral counseling (MS); school counseling (MS). Part-time and evening/weekend programs available. *Degree requirements:* For master's, comprehensive exam, thesis or alternative. *Entrance requirements:* For master's, minimum GPA of 3.0. Additional exam requirements/recommendations for international students: Required—TOEFL (minimum score 500 paper-based; 173 computer-based). *Faculty research:* Cognitive behavioral interventions for depression, eating disorders and compliance.

Neumann University, Program in Pastoral Counseling, Aston, PA 19014-1298. Offers pastoral counseling (MS, CAS); spiritual direction (CSD). Part-time and evening/weekend programs available. *Degree requirements:* For master's, clinical case study. *Entrance requirements:* Additional exam requirements/recommendations for international students: Required—TOEFL. Electronic applications accepted. *Faculty research:* Development of an integrated model of religion/psychology for remediation and prevention of emotional disturbance.

New Brunswick Theological Seminary, Graduate and Professional Programs, Program in Metro-Urban Ministry, New Brunswick, NJ 08901-1196. Offers theological studies (D Min). Part-time programs available. *Degree requirements:* For doctorate, thesis/dissertation. *Entrance requirements:* For doctorate, M Div. *Faculty research:* Urban-land use planning, theology of the city.

New Orleans Baptist Theological Seminary, Graduate and Professional Programs, Division of Pastoral Ministries, New Orleans, LA 70126-4858. Offers M Div, MAMFC, D Min, PhD. *Accreditation:* ACIPE. Postbaccalaureate distance learning degree programs offered. *Faculty:* 16 full-time (4 women). *Students:* 639 full-time (102 women), 375 part-time (43 women); includes 70 Black or African American, non-Hispanic/Latino; 46 Asian, non-Hispanic/Latino; 21 Hispanic/Latino, 60 international. Average age 36. 76 applicants, 75% accepted, 57 enrolled. In 2010, 23 first professional degrees, 44 master's awarded. *Degree requirements:* For master's, 2 foreign languages, thesis (for some programs); for doctorate, 3 foreign languages, comprehensive exam, thesis/dissertation; for M Div, 2 foreign languages, comprehensive exam, project report. *Entrance requirements:* For master's and doctorate, GRE General Test. Additional exam requirements/recommendations for international students: Required—TOEFL. *Application deadline:* For fall admission, 7/20 priority date for domestic students; for spring admission, 11/20 for domestic students. Applications are processed on a rolling basis. Application fee: $25. *Expenses:* Tuition: Full-time $3040. Required fees: $160 per credit hour. $80 per semester. One-time fee: $80 full-time. Tuition and fees vary according to course load and student's religious affiliation. *Unit head:* Dr. Preston Nix, Chairman, 504-282-4455. *Application contact:* Dr. Paul E. Gregoire, Director of Admissions and Registrar, 504-282-4455 Ext. 3337, Fax: 504-286-3591, E-mail: registrar@nobts.edu.

Pastoral Ministry and Counseling

The Nigerian Baptist Theological Seminary, Graduate Studies, Ogbomoso, Nigeria. Offers church music (M Div, M Th, Diploma); divinity (M Div); ministry (D Min); religious education (M Div, M Th, PhD); theological studies (MATS); theology (M Th, PhD). Part-time programs available. *Degree requirements:* For master's, thesis, 2 Nigerian languages; for M Div, thesis/dissertation (for some programs), 2 biblical languages; for Diploma, thesis or alternative.

Northern Baptist Theological Seminary, Graduate and Professional Programs, Lombard, IL 60148-5698. Offers Biblical studies (M Div); Christian ministries (MACM); ministry (D Min); theology (M Div). *Accreditation:* ATS. Part-time programs available. *Faculty:* 7 full-time (0 women), 24 part-time/adjunct (3 women). *Students:* 78 full-time (29 women), 79 part-time (37 women); includes 69 minority (55 Black or African American, non-Hispanic/Latino; 8 Asian, non-Hispanic/Latino; 6 Hispanic/Latino), 4 international. Average age 40. 100 applicants, 70% accepted, 50 enrolled. In 2010, 18 master's, 5 doctorates awarded. *Degree requirements:* For doctorate, thesis/dissertation. *Entrance requirements:* For master's, all official transcripts, letter of reference from pastor, autobiographical statement (400 words or more); for doctorate, M Div, 3 years in the ministry post-M Div, 3 letters of reference. Additional exam requirements/recommendations for international students: Required—TOEFL (minimum score 550 paper-based; 213 computer-based). *Application deadline:* For fall admission, 8/25 for domestic students, 2/1 for international students; for winter admission, 12/10 for domestic students, 2/1 for international students; for spring admission, 3/15 for domestic students, 2/1 for international students. Applications are processed on a rolling basis. Application fee: $35. Electronic applications accepted. *Expenses:* Tuition: Full-time $15,840. Required fees: $115 per quarter. *Financial support:* In 2010–11, 69 students received support. Career-related internships or fieldwork and scholarships/grants available. Support available to part-time students. Financial award application deadline: 9/1; financial award applicants required to submit FAFSA. *Faculty research:* Theology, worship studies, church history, evangelism, Bible. *Unit head:* Dr. J. Alistair Brown, Chief Academic Officer, 630-620-2101, Fax: 630-620-2190. *Application contact:* Greg Henson, Executive Director of External Relations, 630-620-2180, Fax: 630-620-2190, E-mail: admissions@seminary.edu.

North Greenville University, T. Walter Brashier Graduate School, Greer, SC 29651. Offers Christian ministry (MCM); human resources (MBA). Part-time and evening/weekend programs available. Postbaccalaureate distance learning degree programs offered (no on-campus study). *Faculty:* 4 full-time (1 woman), 16 part-time/adjunct (1 woman). *Students:* 80 full-time (33 women), 148 part-time (53 women); includes 48 minority (37 Black or African American, non-Hispanic/Latino; 1 American Indian or Alaska Native, non-Hispanic/Latino; 3 Asian, non-Hispanic/Latino; 5 Hispanic/Latino; 2 Two or more races, non-Hispanic/Latino). Average age 32. 180 applicants, 98% accepted, 170 enrolled. In 2010, 29 master's awarded. *Degree requirements:* For master's, comprehensive exam (for some programs), thesis or alternative, capstone course. *Entrance requirements:* For master's, GMAT, GRE, minimum GPA of 2.25 overall, 2.5 in major. Additional exam requirements/recommendations for international students: Required—TOEFL (minimum score 550 paper-based; 213 computer-based). *Application deadline:* For fall admission, 8/1 for domestic students, 6/1 for international students; for winter admission, 1/1 for domestic students, 10/1 for international students; for spring admission, 3/1 for domestic students, 1/1 for international students. Applications are processed on a rolling basis. Application fee: $30. Electronic applications accepted. *Expenses:* Required fees: $280 per credit hour. One-time fee: $30. *Financial support:* In 2010–11, 112 students received support. Federal Work-Study, institutionally sponsored loans, scholarships/grants, and tuition waivers (partial) available. Support available to part-time students. Financial award applicants required to submit FAFSA. *Faculty research:* Organizational behavior, church growth, homiletics, human resources, business strategy. *Unit head:* Dr. Joseph Samuel Isgett, Vice President for Graduate Studies, 864-877-3052, Fax: 864-877-1653, E-mail: sisgett@ngu.edu. *Application contact:* Tawana P. Scott, Director of Graduate Enrollment, 864-877-1598, Fax: 864-877-1653, E-mail: tscott@ngu.edu.

North Park Theological Seminary, Graduate and Professional Programs, Program in Christian Ministry, Chicago, IL 60625-4895. Offers MACM, MA/MBA, MA/MM.

North Park Theological Seminary, Graduate and Professional Programs, Program in Christian Studies, Chicago, IL 60625-4895. Offers adult ministry (Certificate); camping and retreat ministry (Certificate); children and family ministry (Certificate); Christian formation (Certificate); faith and health (Certificate); intercultural studies (Certificate); justice ministry (Certificate); leadership and administration (Certificate); spiritual direction (Certificate); youth ministry (Certificate). *Accreditation:* ACIPE. Part-time programs available. *Entrance requirements:* For degree, minimum GPA of 2.5. Additional exam requirements/recommendations for international students: Required—TOEFL.

Northwest Nazarene University, Graduate Studies, Program in Religion, Nampa, ID 83686-5897. Offers Christian education (MA); missional leadership (MA); pastoral ministry (MA); religion (M Div); spiritual formation (MA). Part-time and evening/weekend programs available. Postbaccalaureate distance learning degree programs offered (no on-campus study). *Faculty:* 7 full-time (1 woman), 10 part-time/adjunct (1 woman). *Students:* 119 full-time (33 women), 11 part-time (3 women); includes 8 minority (4 Black or African American, non-Hispanic/Latino; 1 American Indian or Alaska Native, non-Hispanic/Latino; 2 Hispanic/Latino; 1 Native Hawaiian or other Pacific Islander, non-Hispanic/Latino), 1 international. In 2010, 42 master's awarded. *Application deadline:* Applications are processed on a rolling basis. Application fee: $50. Electronic applications accepted. *Unit head:* Dr. Jay Akkerman, Director, Graduate Studies, 208-467-8437, Fax: 208-467-8252. *Application contact:* Jill Jones, Program Assistant, 208-467-8368, Fax: 208-467-8252, E-mail: jdjones@nnu.edu.

Northwest University, College of Ministry, Kirkland, WA 98033. Offers ministry (MA); missional leadership (MA); theology and culture (MA). Evening/weekend programs available. *Faculty:* 9 full-time (1 woman), 21 part-time/adjunct (2 women). *Students:* 17 full-time (3 women), 43 part-time (9 women); includes 7 minority (5 Black or African American, non-Hispanic/Latino; 1 Asian, non-Hispanic/Latino; 1 Hispanic/Latino), 2 international. 32 applicants, 97% accepted, 29 enrolled. In 2010, 6 master's awarded. *Entrance requirements:* Additional exam requirements/recommendations for international students: Required—TOEFL (minimum score 550 paper-based). Application fee: $75. Tuition and fees vary according to program. *Unit head:* Dr. Wayde Goodall, Dean, 425-889-5253, E-mail: wayde.goodall@northwestu.edu. *Application contact:* Aaron Oosterwyk, Director of Graduate and Professional Studies Enrollment, 425-889-7799, Fax: 425-803-3059, E-mail: gpse@northwestu.edu.

Notre Dame College, Graduate Studies, South Euclid, OH 44121-4293. Offers accounting (Certificate); creative critical thinking (M Ed); financial services management (Certificate); information systems (Certificate); learning disabilities (M Ed); management (Certificate); paralegal (Certificate); pastoral ministry (Certificate); reading (M Ed); security policy studies (MA); teacher education (Certificate). Part-time and evening/weekend programs available. *Degree requirements:* For master's, thesis. *Entrance requirements:* For master's, GRE General Test, MAT, minimum GPA of 2.75, valid teaching certificate. *Faculty research:* Cognitive psychology, teaching critical thinking in the classroom.

Nyack College, Alliance Theological Seminary, Nyack, NY 10960-3698. Offers Biblical literature (MA), including New Testament, Old Testament; Christian ministry (MPS); intercultural studies (MA); ministry (D Min); theology (M Div); urban ministry (MPS). *Accreditation:* ATS. Part-time programs available. *Students:* 256 full-time (96 women), 482 part-time (251 women); includes 231 Black or African American, non-Hispanic/Latino; 2 American Indian or Alaska Native, non-Hispanic/Latino; 123 Asian, non-Hispanic/Latino; 187 Hispanic/Latino; 12 Two or more races, non-Hispanic/Latino, 80 international. Average age 40. In 2010, 47 first professional degrees, 45 master's awarded. *Degree requirements:* For master's, comprehensive exam (for some programs), thesis optional, internship; for doctorate, thesis/dissertation; for M Div, internship. *Entrance requirements:* Additional exam requirements/recommendations for international students: Required—TOEFL (minimum score 213 computer-based; 78 iBT). *Application deadline:* Applications are processed on a rolling basis. Application fee: $30. Electronic applications accepted. Tuition and fees vary according to program. *Financial support:* Teaching assistantships, career-related internships or fieldwork, Federal Work-Study, and scholarships/grants available. Financial award applicants required to submit FAFSA. *Unit head:* Dr. Ron Walborn, Dean, 845-770-5715, Fax: 845-358-1663. *Application contact:* Traci Piescki, Director of Admissions, 845-770-5701, Fax: 845-348-3912, E-mail: admissions.ats@nyack.edu.

Oakwood University, Program in Pastoral Studies, Huntsville, AL 35896. Offers MA. *Entrance requirements:* For master's, Biblical Literacy Entrance Test (BLET), minimum cumulative GPA of 2.5, 2 letters of recommendation, current resume, 3 years of pastoral or local church leadership experience. Additional exam requirements/recommendations for international students: Required—TOEFL (minimum score 500 paper-based; 173 computer-based).

Oblate School of Theology, Graduate and Professional Programs, San Antonio, TX 78216-6693. Offers divinity (M Div); Hispanic ministry (D Min); pastoral ministry (MAP Min); pastoral studies (Certificate); spirituality (MA Sp); supervision (D Min), including clinical pastoral education, general supervision; theology (MA Th); M Div/MA Th. *Accreditation:* ACIPE; ATS (one or more programs are accredited). Part-time programs available. *Faculty:* 19 full-time (6 women), 2 part-time/adjunct (0 women). *Students:* 91 full-time (7 women), 59 part-time (34 women); includes 4 Black or African American, non-Hispanic/Latino; 1 American Indian or Alaska Native, non-Hispanic/Latino; 18 Asian, non-Hispanic/Latino; 39 Hispanic/Latino, 36 international. 24 applicants, 100% accepted, 24 enrolled. In 2010, 13 first professional degrees, 17 master's, 4 doctorates awarded. *Degree requirements:* For master's, thesis (for some programs), practicum; for doctorate, paper, practicum; for M Div, one foreign language, seminar. *Entrance requirements:* For M Div, MAT, interview, course work in philosophy and theology; for master's, MAT, interview, course work in theology or religious studies, minimum GPA of 2.5; for doctorate, M Div. Additional exam requirements/recommendations for international students: Required—TOEFL (minimum score 197 computer-based; 71 iBT). *Application deadline:* For fall admission, 6/15 priority date for domestic and international students; for spring admission, 11/30 for domestic and international students. Applications are processed on a rolling basis. Application fee: $50. *Expenses:* Tuition: Full-time $12,350; part-time $475 per credit hour. Required fees: $175 per semester. One-time fee: $90. Tuition and fees vary according to course level, course load and degree level. *Financial support:* Scholarships/grants available. Support available to part-time students. Financial award application deadline: 8/1; financial award applicants required to submit FAFSA. *Unit head:* Dr. Scott Woodward, Academic Dean, 210-341-1366, Fax: 210-341-4519, E-mail: swoodward@ost.edu. *Application contact:* James Oberhausen, Director of Admission/Registrar, 210-341-1366 Ext. 212, Fax: 210-341-4519, E-mail: registrar@ost.edu.

Oklahoma Christian University, Graduate School of Theology, Oklahoma City, OK 73136-1100. Offers family life ministry (MA); ministry (M Div, MA); youth ministry (MA). Part-time programs available. Postbaccalaureate distance learning degree programs offered (minimal on-campus study). *Degree requirements:* For master's, one foreign language, comprehensive exam, field experience; for M Div, 2 foreign languages, comprehensive exam, field experience. *Entrance requirements:* For M Div and master's, minimum undergraduate GPA of 3.0. Additional exam requirements/recommendations for international students: Required—TOEFL (minimum score 550 paper-based; 213 computer-based). Electronic applications accepted. *Faculty research:* Early marriage adjustment, new religions, Ethiopic language, church health, Hebrew rhetoric.

Oral Roberts University, School of Theology and Missions, Tulsa, OK 74171. Offers biblical literature (MA), including advanced languages, Judaic-Christian studies; Christian counseling (MA), including marriage and family therapy; divinity (M Div); missions (MA); practical theology (MA); theological/historical studies (MA); theology (D Min). Part-time programs available. Postbaccalaureate distance learning degree programs offered (minimal on-campus study). *Degree requirements:* For master's, thesis (for some programs), practicum/internship; for doctorate, thesis/dissertation, applied research project; for M Div, one foreign language, field experience. *Entrance requirements:* For M Div and master's, GRE General Test or MAT, minimum GPA of 2.5; for doctorate, M Div, minimum GPA of 3.0, 3 years of full-time ministry experience. Additional exam requirements/recommendations for international students: Required—TOEFL (minimum score 550 paper-based; 213 computer-based; 79 iBT). Electronic applications accepted.

Ottawa University, Graduate Studies-Arizona, Program in Professional Counseling, Ottawa, KS 66067-3399. Offers Christian counseling (MA); expressive arts therapy (MA); marriage and family therapy (MA); treatment of trauma, abuse and deprivation (MA). Programs offered in Mesa, Phoenix, Tempe and West Valley, AZ. Part-time and evening/weekend programs available. Postbaccalaureate distance learning degree programs offered. *Degree requirements:* For master's, comprehensive exam, thesis or alternative, field experience, practicum. *Entrance requirements:* For master's, minimum undergraduate GPA of 3.0; course work in theories of personality, abnormal psychology, and human growth and development. Additional exam requirements/recommendations for international students: Required—TOEFL (minimum score 550 paper-based; 213 computer-based).

Pentecostal Theological Seminary, Graduate and Professional Programs, Cleveland, TN 37320-3330. Offers counseling (MA); discipleship and Christian formations (MA); ministry (D Min); theology (M Div). *Accreditation:* ACIPE; ATS. Part-time programs available. *Degree requirements:* For M Div, 2 foreign languages, thesis/dissertation, internship. *Faculty research:* Biblical exegesis.

Pepperdine University, Seaver College, Division of Religion, Master of Science in Ministry Program, Malibu, CA 90263. Offers MS. *Students:* 1 (woman) full-time, 1 (woman) part-time. 3 applicants, 33% accepted, 1 enrolled. In 2010, 2 master's awarded. *Entrance requirements:* For master's, GRE, letters of recommendation, writing sample. Additional exam requirements/recommendations for international students: Required—TOEFL. *Application deadline:* For fall admission, 2/1 priority date for domestic students. Applications are processed on a rolling basis. Application fee: $55. Electronic applications accepted. *Unit head:* Dr. Timothy Willis, Chair/Professor of Religion, 310-506-4352, E-mail: timothy.willis@pepperdine.edu. *Application contact:* Michael A. Truschke, Dean of Admission and Enrollment Management, 310-506-6165, Fax: 310-506-4861, E-mail: admission-seaver@pepperdine.edu.

Philadelphia Biblical University, Department of Christian Counseling, Langhorne, PA 19047-2990. Offers MSCC. Part-time and evening/weekend programs available. *Faculty:* 2 full-time (0 women), 10 part-time/adjunct (8 women). *Students:* 1 (woman) full-time, 120 part-time (86 women); includes 48 minority (37 Black or African American, non-Hispanic/Latino; 5 Asian, non-Hispanic/Latino; 5 Hispanic/Latino; 1 Two or more races, non-Hispanic/Latino), 4 international. Average age 37. 78 applicants, 54% accepted, 38 enrolled. In 2010, 37 master's awarded. *Entrance requirements:* Additional exam requirements/recommendations for international students: Required—TOEFL (minimum score 550 paper-based; 213 computer-based). *Application deadline:* Applications are processed on a rolling basis. Application fee: $25. Electronic applications accepted. *Expenses:* Tuition: Full-time $10,710; part-time $595 per credit. Tuition and fees vary according to program. *Financial support:* In 2010–11, 23 students received support. Scholarships/grants available. Support available to part-time students. Financial award applicants required to submit FAFSA. *Unit head:* Dr. Jeff Black, Chair, 215-702-4347, E-mail: jblack@pbu.edu. *Application contact:* Gwen Dorsey, Enrollment Counselor, Graduate Counseling, 800-572-2472, Fax: 215-702-4248, E-mail: gdorsey@pbu.edu.

Phillips Theological Seminary, Programs in Theology, Doctor of Ministry Program, Tulsa, OK 74116. Offers parish ministry (D Min); pastoral counseling (D Min); practices of ministry (D Min). *Accreditation:* ATS. Part-time programs available. *Degree requirements:* For doctorate, thesis/dissertation. *Entrance requirements:* For doctorate, M Div, minimum GPA of 3.0, 3 years of post-M Div pastoral experience. *Expenses:* Contact institution. *Faculty research:* Politics and theology, media and theology, ecology and theology.

Phoenix Seminary, Graduate Programs, Phoenix, AZ 85018. Offers Biblical and theological studies (Graduate Diploma); Biblical communication (M Div); Biblical leadership (MA); Christian counseling (Graduate Diploma); counseling and family (M Div); leadership development (M Div); ministry (D Min); professional counseling (MA). *Accreditation:* ATS (one or more programs are accredited). Part-time and evening/weekend programs available. *Faculty:* 6 full-time (0 women), 7 part-time/adjunct (0 women). *Students:* 30 full-time (4 women), 160 part-time (50 women); includes 40 minority (18 Black or African American, non-Hispanic/Latino; 8 Asian, non-Hispanic/Latino; 12 Hispanic/Latino; 2 Two or more races, non-Hispanic/Latino). Average age 37. 49 applicants, 96% accepted, 37 enrolled. In 2010, 21 master's, 5 doctorates, 8 other advanced degrees awarded. *Degree requirements:* For master's, 2 foreign languages, comprehensive exam; for doctorate, 2 foreign languages, thesis/dissertation. *Entrance requirements:* For master's, undergraduate degree with minimum GPA of 2.5; for doctorate, M Div (94 hours) with minimum GPA of 3.0. Additional exam requirements/recommendations for international students: Required—TOEFL (minimum score 587 paper-based; 240 computer-based; 92 iBT), TWE (minimum score 4.5). *Application deadline:* For fall admission, 6/1 for domestic students; for spring admission, 11/1 for domestic students. Applications are processed on a rolling basis. Application fee: $90. *Expenses:* Tuition: Full-time $10,105; part-time $430 per semester hour. Required fees: $430 per semester hour. $60 per semester. One-time fee: $160. *Financial support:* In 2010–11, 123 students received support. Institutionally sponsored loans and scholarships/grants available. Support available to part-time students. Financial award application deadline: 6/1; financial award applicants required to submit FAFSA. *Application contact:* Roma Royer, Director of Admissions and Academic Services, 602-850-8000 Ext. 111, Fax: 602-850-8080, E-mail: rroyer@ps.edu.

Providence College and Theological Seminary, Theological Seminary, Otterburne, MB R0A 1G0, Canada. Offers children's ministry (Certificate); Christian studies (MA, Certificate); counseling (MA); cross-cultural discipleship (Certificate); divinity (M Div); educational studies (MA), including counseling psychology, educational ministries, student development, teaching English to speakers of other languages, training teachers of English to speakers of other languages; global studies (MA); lay counseling (Diploma); ministry (D Min); teaching English to speakers of other languages (Certificate); theological studies (MA); training teacher of English to speakers of other languages (Certificate); youth ministry (Certificate). *Accreditation:* ATS. Part-time programs available. *Degree requirements:* For master's, variable foreign language requirement, thesis (for some programs); for doctorate, thesis/dissertation; for M Div, 2 foreign languages, comprehensive exam, thesis/dissertation (for some programs). *Entrance requirements:* Additional exam requirements/recommendations for international students: Recommended—TOEFL (minimum score 550 paper-based; 213 computer-based). *Faculty research:* Studies in Isaiah, theology of sin.

Reformed Theological Seminary–Charlotte Campus, Graduate and Professional Programs, Charlotte, NC 28226-6318. Offers biblical studies (MA); ministry (D Min); pastoral ministry (M Div); theological studies (MA). Part-time programs available. *Degree requirements:* For master's, comprehensive exam; for doctorate, thesis/dissertation; for M Div, 2 foreign languages, comprehensive exam. *Entrance requirements:* For master's, minimum GPA of 2.6; for doctorate, minimum GPA of 3.0. Additional exam requirements/recommendations for international students: Required—TOEFL (minimum score 550 paper-based; 213 computer-based). Electronic applications accepted.

Reformed Theological Seminary–Jackson Campus, Graduate and Professional Programs, Jackson, MS 39209-3099. Offers Bible, theology, and missions (Certificate); biblical studies (MA); Christian education (M Div, MA); counseling (M Div); divinity (M Div, Diploma); marriage and family therapy (MA); ministry (D Min); missions (M Div, MA, D Min); New Testament (Th M); Old Testament (Th M); theological studies (MA); theology (Th M); M Div/MA. *Accreditation:* AAMFT/COAMFTE (one or more programs are accredited); ATS (one or more programs are accredited). *Degree requirements:* For master's, thesis (for some programs), fieldwork; for doctorate, 2 foreign languages, thesis/dissertation; for M Div, 2 foreign languages, thesis/dissertation (for some programs). *Entrance requirements:* For M Div and master's, minimum GPA of 2.6; for doctorate, minimum GPA of 3.0. Additional exam requirements/recommendations for international students: Required—TOEFL.

Reformed Theological Seminary–Orlando Campus, Graduate Program, Oviedo, FL 32765-7197. Offers biblical studies (MA); counseling (MA); ministry (D Min); reformation studies (Th M); theological studies (MA); theology (M Div); MA/Certificate. Ma/Certificate offered jointly with University of Central Florida. Part-time programs available. Postbaccalaureate distance learning degree programs offered (minimal on-campus study). *Entrance requirements:* For M Div and master's, minimum GPA of 2.6. Electronic applications accepted.

Regent University, Graduate School, School of Divinity, Virginia Beach, VA 23464-9800. Offers Biblical studies (MA); leadership and renewal (D Min); missiology (M Div, MA); practical theology (M Div, MA); renewal studies (PhD); M Div/M Ed; M Div/MA; M Div/MBA; M Ed/MA; MBA/MA. *Accreditation:* ACIPE; ATS. Part-time programs available. Postbaccalaureate distance learning degree programs offered (minimal on-campus study). *Faculty:* 20 full-time (4 women), 26 part-time/adjunct (5 women). *Students:* 128 full-time (60 women), 524 part-time (225 women); includes 278 Black or African American, non-Hispanic/Latino; 4 American Indian or Alaska Native, non-Hispanic/Latino; 16 Asian, non-Hispanic/Latino; 24 Hispanic/Latino, 20 international. Average age 41. 361 applicants, 64% accepted, 154 enrolled. In 2010, 32 first professional degrees, 61 master's, 9 doctorates awarded. *Degree requirements:* For master's, comprehensive exam, thesis or alternative, internship; for doctorate, thesis/dissertation or alternative; for M Div, internship. *Entrance requirements:* For M Div, GRE General Test or MAT, minimum undergraduate GPA of 3.0, minimum 3 years of ministry experience, transcripts, recommendations; for master's, GRE General Test or MAT, minimum undergraduate GPA of 2.75, writing sample, clergy recommendation; for doctorate, M Div or theological master's degree; minimum graduate GPA of 3.5 (PhD), 3.0 (D Min); recommendations; writing sample; transcripts. Additional exam requirements/recommendations for international students: Required—TOEFL (minimum score 577 paper-based; 233 computer-based). *Application deadline:* For fall admission, 5/1 priority date for domestic students. Applications are processed on a rolling basis. Application fee: $50. Electronic applications accepted. *Expenses:* Contact institution. *Financial support:* Fellowships with full and partial tuition reimbursements, career-related internships or fieldwork, scholarships/grants, tuition waivers (full and partial), and unspecified assistantships available. Support available to part-time students. Financial award application deadline: 9/1; financial award applicants required to submit FAFSA. *Faculty research:* Greek and Hebrew, theology, spiritual formation, global missions and world Christianity, women's studies. *Unit head:* Dr. Michael Palmer, Dean, 757-352-4406, Fax: 757-352-4597, E-mail: mpalmer@regent.edu. *Application contact:* Matthew Chadwick, Director of Enrollment Support Services, 800-373-5504, Fax: 757-352-4381, E-mail: admissions@regent.edu.

Regis College, Graduate and Professional Programs, Toronto, ON M5S 2Z5, Canada. Offers eastern Christian studies (Certificate); Ignatian studies (Diploma); Lonergan studies (Diploma); ministry (D Min); ministry and spirituality (MAMS); philosophical studies (Diploma); retreat direction (Certificate); sacred theology (STB, STM, STD, STL); spiritual direction (Diploma); spiritual theology (Diploma); theological studies (MTS, Diploma); theology (M Div, MA, Th M, PhD, Th D); M Div/MA. *Accreditation:* ATS (one or more programs are accredited). Terminal master's awarded for partial completion of doctoral program. *Degree requirements:* For master's, 2 foreign languages, thesis; for doctorate, 3 foreign languages, comprehensive exam, thesis/dissertation; for first professional degree, comprehensive exam. *Entrance requirements:* For first professional degree and other advanced degree, minimum GPA of 3.0; for master's, minimum GPA of 3.3; for doctorate, minimum GPA of 3.7. Additional exam requirements/recommendations for international students: Required—TOEFL (minimum score 580 paper-based; 237 computer-based; 93 iBT), TWE (minimum score 5).

Roberts Wesleyan College, Division of Social Sciences, Rochester, NY 14624-1997. Offers counseling in ministry (MA); school counseling (MS); school psychology (MS).

Sacred Heart Major Seminary, School of Theology, Detroit, MI 48206-1799. Offers pastoral studies (MAPS); theology (M Div, MA). *Accreditation:* ACIPE; ATS. Part-time and evening/weekend programs available. *Degree requirements:* For master's, one foreign language, thesis optional, integrating project; for M Div, integrating seminar. *Entrance requirements:* For M Div and master's, GRE, previous course work in philosophy and theology. *Faculty research:* Local church history, patristics, spirituality, religious education.

St. Ambrose University, College of Arts and Sciences, Program in Pastoral Theology, Davenport, IA 52803-2898. Offers MP Th. Part-time programs available. *Faculty:* 2 full-time (1 woman), 1 part-time/adjunct (0 women). *Students:* 27 part-time (12 women). Average age 55. 1 applicant, 100% accepted, 0 enrolled. In 2010, 2 master's awarded. *Degree requirements:* For master's, integration project. *Entrance requirements:* For master's, minimum GPA of 2.6, prior pastoral experience, 9 credits of course work in theology. Additional exam requirements/recommendations for international students: Required—TOEFL. *Application deadline:* For fall admission, 8/15 priority date for domestic students; for winter admission, 12/15 priority date for domestic students; for spring admission, 1/1 priority date for domestic students. Applications are processed on a rolling basis. Application fee: $25. Electronic applications accepted. *Expenses:* Contact institution. *Financial support:* Career-related internships or fieldwork, scholarships/grants, and tuition waivers (partial) available. Financial award application deadline: 8/15; financial award applicants required to submit FAFSA. *Faculty research:* Theological education, ecclesiology, spirituality and liturgy, medical ethics. *Unit head:* Dr. Corinne M. Winter, Director, 563-333-6442, Fax: 563-333-6243, E-mail: wintercorinnem@sau.edu. *Application contact:* Dr. Corinne M. Winter, Director, 563-333-6442, Fax: 563-333-6243, E-mail: wintercorinnem@sau.edu.

St. Augustine's Seminary of Toronto, Graduate and Professional Programs, Scarborough, ON M1M 1M3, Canada. Offers divinity (M Div); lay ministry (Diploma); religious education (MRE); theological studies (MTS, Diploma). *Accreditation:* ATS. Part-time and evening/weekend programs available. *Degree requirements:* For M Div, comprehensive exam (for some programs), thesis/dissertation optional, field education. *Entrance requirements:* Course work in philosophy. Additional exam requirements/recommendations for international students: Required—TOEFL (minimum score 580 paper-based; 237 computer-based), TWE (minimum score 5).

Saint Bernard's School of Theology and Ministry, Graduate and Professional Programs, Rochester, NY 14618. Offers pastoral studies (MA, Certificate); theological studies (MA); theology (M Div). *Accreditation:* ATS (one or more programs are accredited). Part-time and evening/weekend programs available. *Faculty:* 3 full-time (all women), 8 part-time/adjunct (4 women). *Students:* 7 full-time (2 women), 106 part-time (50 women); includes 1 Black or African American, non-Hispanic/Latino; 1 Asian, non-Hispanic/Latino; 2 Hispanic/Latino. Average age 50. 17 applicants, 94% accepted, 16 enrolled. In 2010, 3 first professional degrees, 14 master's awarded. *Degree requirements:* For master's, variable foreign language requirement, thesis (for some programs). *Entrance requirements:* For M Div, minimum GPA of 2.0; for master's, minimum GPA of 2.5. *Application deadline:* Applications are processed on a rolling basis. Application fee: $75. *Expenses:* Tuition: Full-time $9144; part-time $1524 per course. Required fees: $30 per semester. *Financial support:* In 2010–11, 31 students received support; fellowships, research assistantships, teaching assistantships, career-related internships or fieldwork, scholarships/grants, and tuition waivers (partial) available. Support available to part-time students. Financial award application deadline: 4/15; financial award applicants required to submit FAFSA. *Unit head:* Dr. Patricia Schoelles, President, 585-271-3657 Ext. 276, Fax: 585-271-2045, E-mail: pschoelles@stbernards.edu. *Application contact:* Laura Smith, Director of Admissions and Financial Aid, 585-271-3657 Ext. 289, Fax: 585-271-2045, E-mail: admissions@stbernards.edu.

St. Catherine University, Graduate Programs, Program in Theology, St. Paul, MN 55105. Offers catechetical ministry (Certificate); pastoral ministry (Certificate); spiritual direction (Certificate); theology (MA). *Faculty:* 8 full-time (2 women). *Students:* 12 full-time (11 women), 22 part-time (20 women); includes 4 minority (2 Black or African American, non-Hispanic/Latino; 1 Asian, non-Hispanic/Latino; 1 Two or more races, non-Hispanic/Latino). Average age 47. 6 applicants, 83% accepted, 5 enrolled. In 2010, 14 master's awarded. *Degree requirements:* For master's, comprehensive exam, thesis (for some programs). *Entrance requirements:* For master's, MAT, minimum GPA of 3.0. Additional exam requirements/recommendations for international students: Required—Michigan English Language Assessment Battery or TOEFL (minimum score 600 paper-based; 250 computer-based; 100 iBT). *Application deadline:* For fall admission, 8/1 priority date for domestic students. Applications are processed on a rolling basis. Application fee: $35. *Expenses:* Contact institution. *Financial support:* In 2010–11, 9 students received support; research assistantships, career-related internships or fieldwork and institutionally sponsored loans available. Support available to part-time students. Financial award application deadline: 4/1; financial award applicants required to submit FAFSA. *Faculty research:* Feminist scholarship, historical theology, symbols, rites of purification, spirituality. *Unit head:* Dr. William McDonough, Director, 651-690-6072, Fax: 651-690-6024. *Application contact:* 651-690-6933, Fax: 651-690-6064.

Saint Francis Seminary, Graduate and Professional Programs, St. Francis, WI 53235-3795. Offers M Div, MAPS. *Accreditation:* ACIPE; ATS. Part-time programs available. *Degree requirements:* For master's, comprehensive exam; for M Div, thesis/dissertation. *Entrance requirements:* For M Div and master's, Otis IQ Test, Terman Concept Mastery Test, interview. Additional exam requirements/recommendations for international students: Required—TOEFL (minimum score 550 paper-based).

St. John's Seminary, Graduate and Professional Programs, Camarillo, CA 93012-2598. Offers divinity (M Div); pastoral ministry (MAPM); theology (MA). *Accreditation:* ATS. Part-time programs available. *Faculty:* 23 full-time (5 women), 7 part-time/adjunct (1 woman). *Students:* 77 full-time (5 women), 12 part-time (6 women); includes 14 Asian, non-Hispanic/Latino; 32 Hispanic/Latino; 1 Native Hawaiian or other Pacific Islander, non-Hispanic/Latino, 19 international. Average age 34. 19 applicants, 100% accepted, 16 enrolled. In 2010, 6 first professional degrees, 1 master's awarded. *Degree requirements:* For master's, comprehensive exam (for some programs), thesis optional, comprehensive integration paper (MAPM); for M Div, parish internship. *Entrance requirements:* For M Div, GRE General Test, bishop's approbation; for master's, GRE General Test, minimum GPA of 3.5 (MA), 2.5 (MAPM). Additional exam requirements/recommendations for international students: Required—TOEFL (minimum score 550 paper-based; 213 computer-based; 79 iBT). *Application deadline:* For fall admission, 7/15 priority date for domestic students. Applications are processed on a rolling basis. Application fee: $0. Electronic applications accepted. *Expenses:* Tuition: Full-time $14,000; part-time $467 per unit. One-time fee: $5201.96 full-time; $105 part-time. Full-time tuition and fees vary according to course load and program. *Faculty research:* Biblical studies, moral theology, historical studies, systematic theology, spiritual theology. *Unit head:* Rev. Kevin McCracken, CM, Interim Academic Dean, 805-482-2755 Ext. 1012, Fax: 805-482-3470, E-mail: kmccracken@stjohnsem.edu. *Application contact:* Esme M. Takahashi, Registrar, 805-482-2755 Ext. 1014, Fax: 805-482-3470, E-mail: esme@stjohnsem.edu.

St. John's University, St. John's College of Liberal Arts and Sciences, Department of Theology and Religious Studies, Queens, NY 11439. Offers pastoral ministry (Certificate); priestly studies (M Div); theology (MA, Certificate). *Accreditation:* ACIPE. Part-time and evening/weekend programs available. *Students:* 18 full-time (4 women), 21 part-time (15 women); includes 12 minority (5 Black or African American, non-Hispanic/Latino; 4 Asian, non-Hispanic/Latino; 3 Hispanic/Latino), 11 international. Average age 43. 32 applicants, 63% accepted, 10 enrolled. In 2010, 11 master's awarded. *Degree requirements:* For master's, comprehensive exam, thesis optional; for M Div, thesis/dissertation optional. *Entrance requirements:* For M Div and master's, minimum GPA of 3.0. Additional exam requirements/recommendations for international students: Required—TOEFL (minimum score 600 paper-based; 250 computer-based; 100 iBT), IELTS (minimum score 5.5). *Application deadline:* For fall admission, 5/1 priority date for domestic and international students; for spring admission, 11/1 priority date for domestic and international students. Applications are processed on a rolling basis. Application fee: $70. Electronic applications accepted. *Expenses:* Tuition: Full-time $17,100; part-time $950 per credit. Required fees: $340; $170 per semester. Tuition and fees vary according to program.

Pastoral Ministry and Counseling

St. John's University (continued)

Financial support: Research assistantships, scholarships/grants available. Support available to part-time students. Financial award application deadline: 3/1; financial award applicants required to submit FAFSA. *Faculty research:* Systematic theology, moral theory, Biblical studies, pastoral theology, church history. *Unit head:* Fr. Michael Whalen, Chair, 718-990-1556, E-mail: whalenm@stjohns.edu. *Application contact:* Kathleen Davis, Director of Graduate Admission, 718-990-1601, Fax: 718-990-5686, E-mail: gradhelp@stjohns.edu.

Saint John's University, Saint John's School of Theology and Seminary, Collegeville, MN 56321. Offers divinity (M Div); liturgical music (MA); liturgical studies (MA); pastoral ministry (MA); theology (MA), including church history, liturgy, monastic studies, scripture, spirituality, systematics; M Div/MA. *Accreditation:* ATS. Part-time programs available. Postbaccalaureate distance learning degree programs offered (no on-campus study). *Degree requirements:* For master's, one foreign language, comprehensive exam (for some programs), thesis (for some programs). *Entrance requirements:* For master's, GRE General Test or MAT. Electronic applications accepted. *Faculty research:* Religious education, biblical literature.

Saint Leo University, Graduate Studies in Theology, Saint Leo, FL 33574-6665. Offers theology (MA). Part-time and evening/weekend programs available. *Faculty:* 8 full-time (0 women), 1 part-time/adjunct (0 women). *Students:* 184 full-time (37 women), 1 part-time (0 women); includes 20 minority (10 Black or African American, non-Hispanic/Latino; 1 American Indian or Alaska Native, non-Hispanic/Latino; 2 Asian, non-Hispanic/Latino; 7 Hispanic/Latino). Average age 52. In 2010, 6 master's awarded. *Degree requirements:* For master's, comprehensive project. *Entrance requirements:* For master's, bachelor's degree from regionally-accredited college or university with minimum GPA of 3.0, letter of recommendation. Additional exam requirements/recommendations for international students: Required—TOEFL (minimum score 550 paper-based; 213 computer-based; 80 iBT). *Application deadline:* For fall admission, 7/1 priority date for domestic and international students; for spring admission, 11/1 priority date for domestic and international students. Applications are processed on a rolling basis. Application fee: $75. Electronic applications accepted. *Expenses:* Tuition: Part-time $609 per semester hour. Required fees: $115 per course. Tuition and fees vary according to campus/location and program. *Financial support:* In 2010–11, 4 students received support. Federal Work-Study, scholarships/grants, and health care benefits available. Financial award applicants required to submit FAFSA. *Faculty research:* Ecclesiology and the Second Vatican Council, sacramental theology and the liturgical movement, Christian and Eastern religious traditions, ecumenism, ministry and technology. *Unit head:* Fr. Anthony Kissel, Director, 352-588-7297, Fax: 352-588-8404, E-mail: anthony.kissel@saintleo.edu. *Application contact:* Jared Welling, Director, Graduate/Weekend and Evening Admission, 800-707-8846, Fax: 352-588-7873, E-mail: grad.admissions@saintleo.edu.

Saint Mary-of-the-Woods College, Program in Pastoral Theology, Saint Mary-of-the-Woods, IN 47876. Offers pastoral theology (MA); youth ministry (Graduate Certificate). Part-time and evening/weekend programs available. Postbaccalaureate distance learning degree programs offered (minimal on-campus study). *Degree requirements:* For master's, thesis, qualifying exam.

St. Mary's University, Graduate School, Department of Theology, San Antonio, TX 78228-8507. Offers pastoral ministry (MA); theology (MA); JD/MA. Part-time and evening/weekend programs available. Postbaccalaureate distance learning degree programs offered (no on-campus study). *Degree requirements:* For master's, comprehensive exam, practicum (pastoral administration). *Entrance requirements:* For master's, GRE General Test, MAT, 12 credit hours in theology/philosophy. Additional exam requirements/recommendations for international students: Required—TOEFL (minimum score 550 paper-based; 213 computer-based; 80 iBT). Electronic applications accepted. *Faculty research:* Bioethics; perceptions of ministry; Marian doctrines and the contemporary church; Jaspers, peace, and justice.

Saint Mary's University of Minnesota, Schools of Graduate and Professional Programs, Graduate School of Health and Human Services, Institute in Pastoral Ministries, Winona, MN 55987-1399. Offers Canon Law (Certificate); pastoral administration (MA); pastoral ministries (MA). *Application contact:* Jami Spitzer, Information Contact, 507-457-7500, E-mail: jspitzer@smumn.edu.

Saint Paul University, Faculty of Canon Law, Ottawa, ON K1S 1C4, Canada. Offers canon law (MCL, JCD, PhD, Graduate Certificate, JCL); canonical practice (Graduate Certificate); ecclesiastical administration (Graduate Certificate). Part-time programs available. *Faculty:* 9 full-time (1 woman), 7 part-time/adjunct (1 woman). *Students:* 58 full-time (9 women), 14 part-time (8 women); includes 17 Black or African American, non-Hispanic/Latino; 15 Asian, non-Hispanic/Latino; 1 Hispanic/Latino. Average age 40. 78 applicants, 92% accepted, 72 enrolled. In 2010, 15 master's, 3 doctorates, 33 other advanced degrees awarded. *Degree requirements:* For master's, one foreign language; for doctorate, one foreign language, comprehensive exam, thesis/dissertation; for other advanced degree, one foreign language, comprehensive exam and seminar paper (JCL). *Entrance requirements:* For master's, appropriate bachelor's degree, 18 credits in theology; for doctorate, JCL or MCL; for other advanced degree, B Th or equivalent (JCL), appropriate bachelor's degree, 18 credits in theology. *Application deadline:* For fall admission, 8/15 priority date for domestic students, 3/1 priority date for international students. Applications are processed on a rolling basis. Application fee: $75 Canadian dollars. *Financial support:* Scholarships/grants and bursaries available. *Faculty research:* Questions related to Church law. *Unit head:* Dr. Anne Asselin, Dean, 613-751-4018, Fax: 613-751-4036, E-mail: canonlaw@ustpaul.ca. *Application contact:* Beverly Ruth Kavanaugh, Administrative Assistant, 613-751-4018, Fax: 613-751-4036, E-mail: bkavanaugh@ustpaul.ca.

Saint Paul University, Faculty of Human Sciences, Program in Counseling and Spirituality, Ottawa, ON K1S 1C4, Canada. Offers individual or marital/couple counseling (MA); spiritual care (MA). Part-time programs available. *Degree requirements:* For master's, research project or thesis. *Entrance requirements:* For master's, honors BA in human sciences, minimum B average, 12 theology credits.

Saints Cyril and Methodius Seminary, Graduate and Professional Programs, Orchard Lake, MI 48324. Offers pastoral ministry (MAPM); religious education (MARE); theology (M Div, MA). *Accreditation:* ATS. Part-time programs available.

St. Stephen's College, Programs in Theology, Edmonton, AB T6G 2J6, Canada. Offers ministry (D Min); pastoral counseling (MA); social transformation ministry (MA); spirituality and liturgy (MA); theological studies (MTS); theology (M Th). Part-time and evening/weekend programs available. Postbaccalaureate distance learning degree programs offered (minimal on-campus study). Terminal master's awarded for partial completion of doctoral program. *Degree requirements:* For master's, thesis; for doctorate, thesis/dissertation. *Entrance requirements:* Additional exam requirements/recommendations for international students: Required—TOEFL. Electronic applications accepted. *Faculty research:* Methodology for theological education, practice and supervision for ministry.

St. Thomas University, School of Theology and Ministry, Institute for Pastoral Ministries, Miami Gardens, FL 33054-6459. Offers pastoral ministries (MA, Certificate); practical theology (PhD). Part-time and evening/weekend programs available. *Degree requirements:* For master's, comprehensive exam; for doctorate, comprehensive exam, thesis/dissertation. *Entrance requirements:* For master's, interview, minimum GPA of 3.0 or GRE; for doctorate, GRE, MA in theology. Additional exam requirements/recommendations for international students: Required—TOEFL (minimum score 550 paper-based; 213 computer-based; 79 iBT). Electronic applications accepted.

Santa Clara University, College of Arts and Sciences, Program in Pastoral Ministries, Santa Clara, CA 95053. Offers MA. Part-time and evening/weekend programs available. *Students:* 9 full-time (6 women), 22 part-time (16 women); includes 8 minority (4 Asian, non-Hispanic/

Latino; 3 Hispanic/Latino; 1 Native Hawaiian or other Pacific Islander, non-Hispanic/Latino), 2 international. Average age 43. 15 applicants, 73% accepted, 7 enrolled. In 2010, 13 master's awarded. *Degree requirements:* For master's, comprehensive exam, thesis optional, recital (for liturgical music students). *Entrance requirements:* For master's, 3 letters of recommendation, essay, resume, interview, statement of purpose. Additional exam requirements/recommendations for international students: Required—TOEFL. *Application deadline:* Applications are processed on a rolling basis. Application fee: $50. Electronic applications accepted. *Expenses:* Contact institution. *Financial support:* Fellowships, research assistantships, career-related internships or fieldwork, Federal Work-Study, institutionally sponsored loans, and scholarships/grants available. Support available to part-time students. Financial award applicants required to submit FAFSA. *Unit head:* Fr. Paul Crowley, Department Chair of Religious Studies, 408-554-4542. *Application contact:* Fr. Paul Crowley, Department Chair of Religious Studies, 408-554-4542.

Seattle University, School of Theology and Ministry, Program in Pastoral Counseling, Seattle, WA 98122-1090. Offers MA.

Seattle University, School of Theology and Ministry, Program in Pastoral Studies, Seattle, WA 98122-1090. Offers MAPS. Part-time and evening/weekend programs available. *Degree requirements:* For master's, project. *Entrance requirements:* For master's, interview, minimum GPA of 2.75, 2 years of experience in field.

Seminary of the Immaculate Conception, School of Theology, Huntington, NY 11743-1696. Offers pastoral studies (MA); theology (M Div, MA, D Min, Certificate). *Accreditation:* ATS (one or more programs are accredited). Part-time and evening/weekend programs available. *Faculty:* 9 full-time (2 women), 15 part-time/adjunct (2 women). *Students:* 39 full-time (1 woman), 89 part-time (40 women); includes 24 minority (8 Black or African American, non-Hispanic/Latino; 7 Asian, non-Hispanic/Latino; 9 Hispanic/Latino), 6 international. Average age 49. 19 applicants, 100% accepted, 19 enrolled. In 2010, 6 first professional degrees, 37 master's awarded. *Degree requirements:* For master's, seminar and paper/thesis; for doctorate, thesis/dissertation; for M Div, one foreign language, thesis/dissertation. *Entrance requirements:* For M Div, degree in philosophy-theology; for master's, undergraduate degree; for doctorate, MA plus 30 credits or M Div; for Certificate, MA in theology. *Application deadline:* For fall admission, 8/30 priority date for domestic students; for spring admission, 1/20 priority date for domestic students. Applications are processed on a rolling basis. Application fee: $75. *Expenses:* Tuition: Full-time $12,000; part-time $450 per credit. Required fees: $300; $50 per semester. One-time fee: $200 part-time. *Financial support:* In 2010–11, 19 students received support. Scholarships/grants available. *Unit head:* Sr. Mary Louise Brink, SC, Academic Dean, 631-423-0483 Ext. 130, Fax: 631-432-2346, E-mail: mlbrink@icseminary.edu. *Application contact:* Kathryn L. Zahner, Registrar, 631-423-0483 Ext. 147, Fax: 631-423-2346, E-mail: kzahner@icseminary.edu.

Seminary of the Southwest, Graduate and Professional Programs, Austin, TX 78768-2247. Offers Anglican studies (Advanced Diploma); chaplaincy (MCPC, JD/MAC); counseling (MAC); divinity (M Div); religion (MAR); spiritual formation (MAPM, MSF); theological studies (Advanced Diploma); JD/MAC. *Accreditation:* ACIPE; ATS (one or more programs are accredited). Part-time and evening/weekend programs available. *Faculty:* 11 full-time (3 women), 26 part-time/adjunct (7 women). *Students:* 69 full-time (40 women), 47 part-time (34 women); includes 11 minority (4 Black or African American, non-Hispanic/Latino; 4 Hispanic/Latino; 3 Two or more races, non-Hispanic/Latino), 3 international. Average age 45. 57 applicants, 93% accepted, 46 enrolled. In 2010, 13 first professional degrees, 8 master's, 6 other advanced degrees awarded. *Degree requirements:* For master's, thesis (for some programs). *Entrance requirements:* For M Div and master's, GRE, MAT, interview; for Advanced Diploma, interview. *Application deadline:* For fall admission, 7/1 for domestic students; for spring admission, 11/1 for domestic students. Applications are processed on a rolling basis. Application fee: $50. *Expenses:* Tuition: Full-time $13,152; part-time $548 per credit hour. Required fees: $75. One-time fee: $20 part-time. *Financial support:* Career-related internships or fieldwork and scholarships/grants available. Support available to part-time students. Financial award application deadline: 6/15. *Unit head:* Very Rev. Douglas Travis, Dean and President, 512-472-4133 Ext. 307, Fax: 512-472-3098, E-mail: dtravis@ssw.edu. *Application contact:* Jennielle Strother, Director of Admissions, 512-472-4133 Ext. 375, Fax: 512-472-3098, E-mail: jstrother@ssw.edu.

Seton Hall University, Immaculate Conception Seminary School of Theology, South Orange, NJ 07079-2697. Offers Christian spirituality (Certificate); great spiritual books (Certificate); pastoral ministry (M Div, MA, Certificate); scripture studies (Certificate); Seminary's Theological Education for Parish Services (STEPS) (Certificate); theology (MA); youth ministry (Certificate). *Accreditation:* ATS (one or more programs are accredited). Part-time and evening/weekend programs available. *Faculty:* 13 full-time (2 women), 12 part-time/adjunct (1 woman). *Students:* 105 full-time (7 women), 112 part-time (43 women); includes 4 Black or African American, non-Hispanic/Latino; 9 Asian, non-Hispanic/Latino; 31 Hispanic/Latino, 72 international. Average age 39. 74 applicants, 100% accepted, 69 enrolled. In 2010, 16 first professional degrees, 32 master's, 6 other advanced degrees awarded. *Degree requirements:* For master's, one foreign language, comprehensive exam, thesis (for some programs), final project; for M Div, one foreign language, thesis/dissertation, final project and seminar, field education, spiritual formation. *Entrance requirements:* For M Div, GRE, MAT; for master's, GRE General Test or MAT. Additional exam requirements/recommendations for international students: Required—TOEFL (minimum score 600 paper-based; 250 computer-based; 100 iBT). *Application deadline:* For fall admission, 8/1 priority date for domestic and international students; for spring admission, 12/15 priority date for domestic and international students. Applications are processed on a rolling basis. Application fee: $50. Electronic applications accepted. *Expenses:* Contact institution. *Financial support:* In 2010–11, 217 students received support. Career-related internships or fieldwork, Federal Work-Study, scholarships/grants, tuition waivers (partial), and unspecified assistantships available. Support available to part-time students. Financial award application deadline: 8/1; financial award applicants required to submit FAFSA. *Faculty research:* Pauline literature, history of Biblical interpretation and theological exegesis, spirituality of St. Edith Stein, Thomism, history of Catholicism in America. *Unit head:* Rev. Msgr. Robert F. Coleman, Rector and Dean, 973-761-9016, Fax: 973-761-9577, E-mail: robert.coleman@shu.edu. *Application contact:* Rev. Msgr. Joseph R. Chapel, Associate Dean, 973-761-9633, Fax: 973-761-9577, E-mail: theology@shu.edu.

Shasta Bible College, Program in Biblical Counseling, Redding, CA 96002. Offers biblical counseling and Christian family life education (MA). Part-time programs available. *Degree requirements:* For master's, comprehensive exam (for some programs), thesis or alternative. *Entrance requirements:* For master's, minimum GPA of 2.5. Additional exam requirements/recommendations for international students: Required—TOEFL (minimum score 550 paper-based; 213 computer-based).

Shasta Bible College, Program in Christian Ministry, Redding, CA 96002. Offers MA. Part-time programs available. Postbaccalaureate distance learning degree programs offered (minimal on-campus study). *Entrance requirements:* Additional exam requirements/recommendations for international students: Required—TOEFL (minimum score 550 paper-based; 213 computer-based).

Simpson University, A.W. Tozer Theological Seminary, Redding, CA 96003-8606. Offers intellectual leadership (MA); ministry (M Div). Part-time and evening/weekend programs available. Postbaccalaureate distance learning degree programs offered (minimal on-campus study). *Degree requirements:* For master's, student portfolio. *Entrance requirements:* For master's, GRE General Test (if undergraduate GPA less than 2.5), 2 letters of reference, Christian Experience statement. Additional exam requirements/recommendations for international students: Required—TOEFL. Electronic applications accepted. *Expenses:* Contact institution.

Sioux Falls Seminary, Graduate and Professional Programs, Professional Program in Pastoral Ministry, Sioux Falls, SD 57105-1599. Offers M Div. *Accreditation:* ACIPE. Part-time programs available. *Entrance requirements:* Minimum GPA of 2.5.

Sioux Falls Seminary, Graduate and Professional Programs, Program in Counseling, Sioux Falls, SD 57105-1599. Offers MA. Part-time programs available. *Entrance requirements:* For master's, minimum GPA of 2.5.

Southeastern University, College of Christian Ministries and Religion, Lakeland, FL 33801-6099. Offers ministerial leadership (MA). Evening/weekend programs available. Postbaccalaureate distance learning degree programs offered. *Degree requirements:* For master's, thesis/project.

Southern Baptist Theological Seminary, Billy Graham School of Missions, Evangelism and Church Growth, Louisville, KY 40280-0004. Offers Christian mission/world religion (PhD); evangelism/church growth (PhD); ministry (D Min); missiology (MA, D Miss); missions, evangelism and church growth (M Div); religion (Th M); theological studies (MA). *Accreditation:* ATS. Part-time and evening/weekend programs available. Postbaccalaureate distance learning degree programs offered (minimal on-campus study). *Degree requirements:* For master's and M Div, 2 foreign languages; for doctorate, 4 foreign languages, thesis/dissertation. *Entrance requirements:* For doctorate, GRE General Test, MAT, M Div. Additional exam requirements/recommendations for international students: Required—TOEFL, TWE. *Faculty research:* Assimilation of church congregants, effective methodologies of evangelism, expectations of church members, spiritual warfare literature, formative church discipline.

Southern Baptist Theological Seminary, School of Church Ministries, Louisville, KY 40280-0004. Offers children's and family ministry (M Div, MA); church music (M Div, MA, MCM); college ministry (M Div, MA); discipleship and family ministry (M Div, MA); family ministry (PhD); higher education (PhD); leadership (M Div, MA, PhD); ministry (D Ed Min, D Min); women's leadership (M Div, MA); worship leadership (M Div, MA); youth and family ministry (M Div, MA). Part-time programs available. Postbaccalaureate distance learning degree programs offered (minimal on-campus study). *Degree requirements:* For doctorate, thesis/dissertation; for M Div, 2 foreign languages. *Entrance requirements:* For doctorate, GRE General Test, interview, M Div or MACE. Additional exam requirements/recommendations for international students: Required—TWE. *Faculty research:* Gerontology, creative teaching methods, faith development in children, faith development in youth, transformational learning.

Southern Baptist Theological Seminary, School of Theology, Louisville, KY 40280-0004. Offers applied theology (D Min); biblical and theological studies (M Div); biblical counseling (M Div, MA, D Min); biblical spirituality (D Min); Christian ministry (M Div); expository preaching (D Min); pastoral studies (M Div); theological studies (MA); theology (Th M, PhD); worldview and apologetics (M Div). *Accreditation:* ATS. Part-time and evening/weekend programs available. Postbaccalaureate distance learning degree programs offered (minimal on-campus study). *Degree requirements:* For master's, 2 foreign languages, thesis; for doctorate, 4 foreign languages, thesis/dissertation; for M Div, 2 foreign languages. *Entrance requirements:* For master's, GRE General Test, MAT, M Div; for doctorate, GRE General Test, MAT, interview, M Div, field essay. Additional exam requirements/recommendations for international students: Required—TOEFL, TWE. *Faculty research:* Biblical studies, contemporary theology, church history, pastoral care, ministry/missions studies.

Southern Evangelical Seminary, Graduate Programs, Matthews, NC 28105. Offers apologetics (MA, Certificate); Christian education (MA); church ministry (MA, Certificate); divinity (Certificate), including apologetics (M Div, Certificate); Islamic studies (MA, Certificate); Jewish studies (MA); philosophy (MA); religion (MA); theology (M Div), including apologetics (M Div, Certificate), Biblical studies; youth ministry (MA). Part-time and evening/weekend programs available. Postbaccalaureate distance learning degree programs offered. *Degree requirements:* For master's, thesis (for some programs); for doctorate, 2 foreign languages, comprehensive exam (for some programs), thesis/dissertation; for M Div, one foreign language. *Entrance requirements:* Additional exam requirements/recommendations for international students: Required—TOEFL (minimum score 600 paper-based; 250 computer-based). *Application deadline:* For fall admission, 8/15 priority date for domestic students, 8/5 priority date for international students; for winter admission, 12/15 priority date for domestic and international students; for spring admission, 1/15 priority date for domestic and international students. Applications are processed on a rolling basis. Application fee: $25. *Expenses:* Tuition: Full-time $9405; part-time $313.50 per credit hour. Required fees: $150; $50 per semester. *Financial support:* Scholarships/grants available. *Unit head:* Dr. Barry R. Leventhal, Dean, 704-847-5600 Ext. 204, Fax: 704-845-1747, E-mail: dean@ses.edu. *Application contact:* Duke Hale, Director of Recruitment, 704-847-5600 Ext. 216, Fax: 704-845-1747, E-mail: dhale@ses.edu.

Southern Wesleyan University, Program in Christian Ministries, Central, SC 29630-1020. Offers M Min. Part-time and evening/weekend programs available. *Faculty:* 3 full-time (2 women). *Students:* 5 full-time (2 women); includes 2 minority (both Black or African American, non-Hispanic/Latino). Average age 45. *Entrance requirements:* For master's, GRE General Test or MAT, biographical paper; 12 semester credit hours of undergraduate work in religion, Bible, or ethics; 2 years of full-time Christian ministry experience. Additional exam requirements/recommendations for international students: Required—TOEFL (minimum score 500 paper-based; 173 computer-based). *Application deadline:* Applications are processed on a rolling basis. Application fee: $50. *Expenses:* Tuition: Full-time $8925; part-time $425 per credit hour. Required fees: $1659; $230 per course. *Unit head:* Dr. Christina Accornero, Chair, Religion Division, 864-644-5226, Fax: 864-644-5902, E-mail: caccornero@swu.edu. *Application contact:* Corrie Creasman, Enrollment Services Coordinator, 877-644-5577, Fax: 864-644-5972, E-mail: ccreasman@swu.edu.

Southwestern Assemblies of God University, Thomas F. Harrison School of Graduate Studies, Program in Theological Studies, Waxahachie, TX 75165-5735. Offers Bible and theology (MS); Biblical studies (M Div); counseling (M Div); cross cultural missions (M Div); practical theology (M Div); theological studies (M Div). Postbaccalaureate distance learning degree programs offered. *Degree requirements:* For master's, comprehensive written and oral exams. *Entrance requirements:* For master's, GRE General Test, minimum GPA of 2.5. Electronic applications accepted.

Southwestern Christian University, Program in Ministry, Bethany, OK 73008-0340. Offers church planting (M Min); church revitalization and renewal (M Min); intercultural studies (M Min); leadership (M Min); life coaching (M Min); pastoral ministries (M Min); work place ministries (M Min). Part-time programs available. *Degree requirements:* For master's, thesis. *Entrance requirements:* For master's, minimum GPA of 2.5. Additional exam requirements/recommendations for international students: Required—TOEFL (minimum score 500 paper-based). Electronic applications accepted.

Spring Arbor University, School of Arts and Sciences, Spring Arbor, MI 49283-9799. Offers communication (MA); spiritual formation and leadership (MA). Part-time programs available. Postbaccalaureate distance learning degree programs offered (no on-campus study). *Faculty:* 6 full-time (1 woman), 9 part-time/adjunct (6 women). *Students:* 92 full-time (60 women), 75 part-time (57 women); includes 6 Black or African American, non-Hispanic/Latino; 1 Asian, non-Hispanic/Latino; 1 Hispanic/Latino. Average age 39. In 2010, 37 master's awarded. *Degree requirements:* For master's, thesis (for some programs). *Entrance requirements:* For master's, GRE (minimum score of 40th percentile and taken within last 5 years), bachelor's degree from regionally-accredited college or university, minimum GPA of 3.0 for at least the last two years of the bachelor's degree, at least two recommendations from professional/academic individuals. Additional exam requirements/recommendations for international students: Required—TOEFL (minimum score 600 paper-based; 220 computer-based). Application fee: $40. *Expenses:* Contact institution. *Financial support:* Applicants required to submit FAFSA. *Unit head:* Dr. Wally Metts, Chair of the Department of Communication, 517-750-1200 Ext. 1491, E-mail: wmetts@arbor.edu. *Application contact:* Dale Glinz, Lead Recruitment Specialist/Trainer, Graduate and Professional Studies, 517-750-6703, E-mail: dglinz@arbor.edu.

Spring Hill College, Graduate Programs, Programs in Theology and Ministry, Mobile, AL 36608-1791. Offers pastoral studies (MPS); theological studies (MTS); theology (MA). Part-time and evening/weekend programs available. *Faculty:* 5 full-time (0 women), 4 part-time/adjunct (1 woman). *Students:* 1 full-time (0 women), 51 part-time (23 women); includes 6 minority (4 Black or African American, non-Hispanic/Latino; 2 Hispanic/Latino). Average age 47. In 2010, 13 master's awarded. *Degree requirements:* For master's, variable foreign language requirement, comprehensive exam, thesis (for some programs), completion of program within 6 calendar years of initial enrollment (MTS, MPS), 4½ calendar years (MA). *Entrance requirements:* For master's, bachelor's degree with minimum undergraduate GPA of 3.0; six hours of undergraduate theology, religious studies, or unquestioned equivalency. Additional exam requirements/recommendations for international students: Required—TOEFL (minimum score 550 paper-based; 213 computer-based; 80 iBT), IELTS (minimum score 6.5), CPE or CAE (score: C), MELAB (score: 90). *Application deadline:* For fall admission, 8/1 priority date for domestic and international students; for spring admission, 12/1 priority date for domestic and international students. Applications are processed on a rolling basis. Application fee: $25 ($35 for international students). Electronic applications accepted. *Expenses:* Tuition: Full-time $5364; part-time $298 per credit hour. Tuition and fees vary according to program. *Financial support:* Applicants required to submit FAFSA. *Unit head:* Dr. John B. Switzer, Director, 251-380-4669, Fax: 251-460-2194, E-mail: jswitzer@shc.edu. *Application contact:* Donna B. Tarasavage, Director of Admissions, Graduate and Continuing Studies, 251-380-3067, Fax: 251-460-2190, E-mail: dtarasavage@shc.edu.

Trinity Baptist College, Graduate Programs, Jacksonville, FL 32221. Offers educational leadership (M Ed); ministry (MA); special education (M Ed). Postbaccalaureate distance learning degree programs offered. *Faculty:* 4 full-time (1 woman), 3 part-time/adjunct (0 women). *Students:* 7 part-time (1 woman). *Entrance requirements:* For master's, GRE (M Ed), 2 letters of recommendation; minimum GPA of 2.5 (M Min) or 3.0 (M Ed); computer proficiency. *Unit head:* Dr. Matthew Beemer, Senior Vice President, 904-596-2400, Fax: 904-596-2531, E-mail: mbeemer@tbc.edu. *Application contact:* Michael Nichols, Director of Graduate Studies, 904-596-2449, E-mail: graduatestudies@tbc.edu.

Trinity International University, Trinity Evangelical Divinity School, Deerfield, IL 60015-1284. Offers Biblical and Near Eastern archaeology and languages (MA); Christian studies (MA, Certificate); Christian thought (MA); church history (MA, Th M); congregational ministry: pastor-teacher (M Div); congregational ministry: team ministry (M Div); counseling ministries (MA); counseling psychology (MA); cross-cultural ministry (M Div); educational studies (PhD); evangelism (MA); history of Christianity in America (MA); intercultural studies (MA, PhD); leadership and ministry management (D Min); military chaplaincy (D Min); ministry (MA); mission and evangelism (Th M); missions and evangelism (D Min); New Testament (MA, Th M); Old Testament (Th M); Old Testament and Semitic languages (MA); pastoral care (M Div); pastoral care and counseling (D Min); pastoral counseling and psychology (Th M); pastoral theology (Th M); philosophy of religion (MA); preaching (D Min); religion (MA); research ministry (M Div); systematic theology (Th M); theological studies (PhD); urban ministry (MA). *Accreditation:* ATS (one or more programs are accredited). Part-time programs available. Postbaccalaureate distance learning degree programs offered (minimal on-campus study). *Degree requirements:* For master's, comprehensive exam, thesis, fieldwork; for doctorate, comprehensive exam (for some programs), thesis/dissertation; for M Div, 2 foreign languages, fieldwork; for Certificate, comprehensive exam, integrative papers. *Entrance requirements:* For M Div, GRE, MAT; for master's, GRE, MAT, minimum cumulative undergraduate GPA of 3.0; for doctorate, GRE, minimum cumulative graduate GPA of 3.2; for Certificate, GRE, MAT, minimum undergraduate GPA of 2.5. Additional exam requirements/recommendations for international students: Required—TOEFL (minimum score 580 paper-based; 237 computer-based), TWE (minimum score 4). Electronic applications accepted.

Trinity Lutheran Seminary, Graduate and Professional Programs, Columbus, OH 43209-2334. Offers Christian education (MA); church music (MA); divinity (M Div); sacred theology (STM); theological studies (MTS); youth and family ministry (MA); MSN/MTS; MTS/JD. *Accreditation:* ACIPE; ATS. Part-time programs available. *Faculty:* 15 full-time (7 women), 7 part-time/adjunct (2 women). *Students:* 110 full-time (42 women), 35 part-time (19 women); includes 21 minority (15 Black or African American, non-Hispanic/Latino; 4 Asian, non-Hispanic/Latino; 2 Hispanic/Latino), 4 international. Average age 35. 71 applicants, 77% accepted, 49 enrolled. In 2010, 29 first professional degrees, 9 master's awarded. *Degree requirements:* For master's, comprehensive exam (for some programs), thesis (for some programs); for M Div, 2 foreign languages, internship. *Entrance requirements:* For master's, M Div or equivalent (STM). Additional exam requirements/recommendations for international students: Required—TOEFL (minimum score 500 paper-based; 173 computer-based; 61 iBT). *Application deadline:* For fall admission, 7/15 priority date for domestic and international students. Applications are processed on a rolling basis. Application fee: $25. *Expenses:* Tuition: Full-time $13,020; part-time $434 per semester hour. Required fees: $165 per semester. One-time fee: $150. *Financial support:* In 2010–11, 102 students received support. Career-related internships or fieldwork, Federal Work-Study, institutionally sponsored loans, and scholarships/grants available. Support available to part-time students. Financial award application deadline: 5/1; financial award applicants required to submit FAFSA. *Unit head:* Dr. James Childs, Interim Academic Dean, 614-235-4136 Ext. 4670, Fax: 614-384-4635. *Application contact:* Rev. Sheri L. Ayers, Director of Admissions, 614-235-4136 Ext. 4614, Fax: 866-610-8572, E-mail: sayers@tls.edu.

Trinity School for Ministry, Graduate Programs, Ambridge, PA 15003-2397. Offers Anglican studies (Diploma); basic Christian studies (Diploma); divinity (M Div); ministry (D Min); mission and evangelism (MAME, Diploma); religion (MAR); youth ministry (Diploma). *Accreditation:* ATS (one or more programs are accredited). Part-time programs available. *Degree requirements:* For master's, thesis optional; for doctorate, thesis/dissertation; for M Div, thesis/dissertation optional, Greek and Hebrew. *Entrance requirements:* Additional exam requirements/recommendations for international students: Required—TOEFL. *Faculty research:* Pauline Epistles, contemporary theology, history of Anglican liturgy, book of Ruth, biblical theology.

Trinity Western University, ACTS Seminaries, Langley, BC V2Y 1Y1, Canada. Offers Christian studies (MA); cross cultural ministry (MA); theology (M Div, M Th, MAMFT, MLE, MTS, D Min). *Accreditation:* ATS. Part-time programs available. *Degree requirements:* For master's, thesis (for some programs), internship. *Entrance requirements:* For doctorate, MDiv or equivalent. Additional exam requirements/recommendations for international students: Required—TOEFL. *Expenses:* Contact institution. *Faculty research:* Theology of leadership.

Tyndale University College & Seminary, Graduate Programs, Toronto, ON M2M 4B3, Canada. Offers Biblical studies (M Div); Christian foundations (MTS); Christian studies (Diploma); counseling (M Div); educational ministry (M Div); missions (M Div, Diploma); pastoral and Chinese ministry (M Div); pastoral ministry (M Div); Pentecostal studies (MTS); spiritual formation (M Div, Diploma); theological studies (M Div); theology (Th M); worship and liturgy (M Div, MTS); youth and family ministry (M Div). *Accreditation:* ATS. Part-time programs available. Postbaccalaureate distance learning degree programs offered (no on-campus study). *Degree requirements:* For M Div, one foreign language, thesis/dissertation optional. *Entrance requirements:* For M Div, master's, and Diploma, minimum C+ average in undergraduate course work. Additional exam requirements/recommendations for international students: Required—TOEFL (minimum score 570 paper-based; 230 computer-based), TWE (minimum score 5). Electronic applications accepted. *Faculty research:* Canadian church history, Chinese church history, Old Testament, counseling ministries (narrative therapy), world religions.

Unification Theological Seminary, Graduate Program, Main Campus, Barrytown, NY 12507. Offers divinity (M Div); ministry (D Min); religious education (MRE); religious studies (MA). Part-time and evening/weekend programs available. *Faculty:* 4 full-time (1 woman), 3 part-time/adjunct (0 women). *Students:* 37 full-time (9 women), 1 part-time (0 women); includes 10 Black or African American, non-Hispanic/Latino; 1 American Indian or Alaska Native, non-Hispanic/Latino; 4 Asian, non-Hispanic/Latino; 1 Hispanic/Latino, 9 international. Average age 45. In 2010, 2 first professional degrees, 14 master's, 3 doctorates awarded. *Degree*

Pastoral Ministry and Counseling

Unification Theological Seminary (continued)
requirements: For master's, one foreign language, thesis (for some programs), project; for doctorate, thesis/dissertation; for M Div, one foreign language, thesis/dissertation. *Entrance requirements:* For M Div and master's, bachelor's degree; for doctorate, M Div or equivalency. Additional exam requirements/recommendations for international students: Required—TOEFL (minimum score 450 paper-based; 133 computer-based; 45 iBT). *Application deadline:* For fall admission, 8/15 priority date for domestic students; for spring admission, 1/15 priority date for domestic students. Applications are processed on a rolling basis. Application fee: $30. *Expenses:* Tuition: Full-time $10,440; part-time $435 per credit. Required fees: $125 per semester. *Financial support:* Career-related internships or fieldwork, institutionally sponsored loans, scholarships/grants, and tuition waivers (partial) available. Support available to part-time students. Financial award applicants required to submit FAFSA. *Faculty research:* Church leadership, church history, world religions, ecumenism, interfaith peace building, service-learning. *Unit head:* Dr. Kathy Winings, Academic Dean, 845-752-3000 Ext. 228, Fax: 845-752-3014, E-mail: academics@uts.edu. *Application contact:* Davetta Ogunlola, Director of Admissions, 212-563-6647 Ext. 105, Fax: 212-563-6431, E-mail: d.ogunlola@uts.edu.

Union University, School of Christian Studies, Jackson, TN 38305-3697. Offers Christian studies (MCS); expository preaching (D Min).

United Theological Seminary of the Twin Cities, Graduate Programs, New Brighton, MN 55112-2598. Offers advanced theological studies (Diploma); justice and peace studies (M Div, MA); leadership toward racial justice (M Div, MA, Certificate); Methodist studies (M Div, MA, Certificate); ministry (D Min); ministry renewal and professional development (Certificate); pastoral care and counseling (M Div, MA, MARL); religion and theology (MA); theological and religious studies (Certificate); theology and the arts (M Div, MA); urban ministry (M Div, MA, MARL); women's studies: religion, theology and ministry (M Div, MA). *Accreditation:* ACIPE; ATS. Part-time and evening/weekend programs available. *Faculty:* 8 full-time (5 women), 28 part-time/adjunct (16 women). *Students:* 57 full-time (41 women), 94 part-time (61 women); includes 6 minority (5 Black or African American, non-Hispanic/Latino; 1 Hispanic/Latino), 1 international. Average age 47. 49 applicants, 98% accepted, 41 enrolled. In 2010, 10 first professional degrees, 6 master's, 4 doctorates, 2 other advanced degrees awarded. *Degree requirements:* For master's, thesis; for doctorate, comprehensive exam, thesis/dissertation; for M Div, integrative notebook, spiritual chronicle. *Entrance requirements:* For M Div and master's, minimum GPA of 2.75; strong analytical, reflective thinking and writing skills; vocational and academic goals compatible with those of Seminary; for doctorate, M Div or equivalent, minimum GPA of 3.0, 3 years experience in professional ministry; for other advanced degree, BA or equivalent life experience; strong analytical, reflective thinking and writing skills (Certificate); proficiency in English language, previous study of theology at a theological school, recommendation of student's denomination (Diploma). Additional exam requirements/recommendations for international students: Required—TOEFL (minimum score 550 paper-based). *Application deadline:* For fall admission, 7/1 priority date for domestic students, 11/1 priority date for international students; for winter admission, 11/1 priority date for domestic students; for spring admission, 11/15 priority date for domestic students. Applications are processed on a rolling basis. Application fee: $50. *Expenses:* Tuition: Full-time $13,014; part-time $482 per credit hour. One-time fee: $170. Tuition and fees vary according to course load, degree level and program. *Financial support:* In 2010–11, 120 students received support. Career-related internships or fieldwork, institutionally sponsored loans, and scholarships/grants available. Support available to part-time students. Financial award application deadline: 5/1; financial award applicants required to submit FAFSA. *Unit head:* Prof. Susan K. Ebbers, Dean of the Seminary, 651-255-6143 Ext. 108, Fax: 651-633-4315, E-mail: sebbers@unitedseminary.edu. *Application contact:* Rev. Glen Herrington-Hall, Director of Admissions, 651-255-6107 Ext. 107, Fax: 651-633-4315, E-mail: gherrington-hall@unitedseminary.edu.

Universidad Adventista de las Antillas, EGECED Department, Mayagüez, PR 00681-0118. Offers curriculum and instruction (M Ed); health education (M Ed); medical surgical nursing (MN); pastoral theology (M Div); school administration and supervision (M Ed). *Faculty:* 4 part-time/adjunct (3 women). *Students:* 25 full-time (21 women), 17 part-time (all women). *Degree requirements:* For master's, comprehensive exam (for some programs), thesis (for some programs). *Entrance requirements:* For master's, EXADEP or GRE General Test, recommendations. Application fee: $175. Electronic applications accepted. *Expenses:* Tuition: Full-time $1152; part-time $836 per year. Required fees: $260 per semester. *Financial support:* Fellowships, Federal Work-Study available. *Unit head:* Director, 787-834-9595 Ext. 2282, Fax: 787-834-9595. *Application contact:* Prof. Yolanda Ferrer, Director of Admission, 787-834-9595 Ext. 2261, Fax: 787-834-9597, E-mail: admissions@uaa.edu.

University of Dallas, Institute for Religious and Pastoral Studies, Irving, TX 75062-4736. Offers MCSL, MPM, MRE, MTS. *Accreditation:* ACIPE. Part-time and evening/weekend programs available. Postbaccalaureate distance learning degree programs offered (no on-campus study). *Expenses:* Tuition: Full-time $7500; part-time $720 per credit hour. Required fees: $500; $60 per credit hour. $300 per semester. One-time fee: $150. Tuition and fees vary according to program and student level. *Faculty research:* Scripture, pastoral theology, ecclesiology, systematic theology, theological anthropology.

University of Dayton, Graduate School, College of Arts and Sciences, Department of Religious Studies, Dayton, OH 45469-1300. Offers pastoral ministry (MA); theological studies (MA); theology (PhD). Part-time and evening/weekend programs available. *Faculty:* 19 full-time (5 women), 5 part-time/adjunct (3 women). *Students:* 61 full-time (25 women), 21 part-time (11 women); includes 8 minority (1 Black or African American, non-Hispanic/Latino; 1 American Indian or Alaska Native, non-Hispanic/Latino; 2 Asian, non-Hispanic/Latino; 4 Hispanic/Latino), 1 international. Average age 34. 63 applicants, 56% accepted, 22 enrolled. In 2010, 12 master's awarded. Terminal master's awarded for partial completion of doctoral program. *Degree requirements:* For master's, thesis or alternative; for doctorate, 2 foreign languages, comprehensive exam, thesis/dissertation. *Entrance requirements:* For master's, minimum undergraduate GPA of 3.0, 3 letters of recommendation, personal statement, official transcript(s); for doctorate, GRE General Test (minimum score 600 verbal), minimum GPA of 3.5, academic writing sample, 3 letters of recommendation. Additional exam requirements/recommendations for international students: Required—TOEFL (minimum score 550 paper-based; 213 computer-based; 80 iBT). *Application deadline:* For fall admission, 3/1 priority date for domestic and international students; for winter admission, 7/1 priority date for international students; for spring admission, 1/1 priority date for international students. Applications are processed on a rolling basis. Application fee: $0 ($50 for international students). Electronic applications accepted. *Expenses:* Contact institution. *Financial support:* In 2010–11, 4 fellowships with full tuition reimbursements (averaging $15,814 per year), 8 research assistantships with full tuition reimbursements (averaging $9,457 per year), 16 teaching assistantships with full tuition reimbursements (averaging $15,814 per year) were awarded; career-related internships or fieldwork, institutionally sponsored loans, scholarships/grants, health care benefits, tuition waivers (full), and unspecified assistantships also available. Support available to part-time students. Financial award application deadline: 3/1; financial award applicants required to submit FAFSA. *Faculty research:* Practical/constructive theology, theological ethics, U. S. Catholic/Christian life and thought, methodologies in Biblical studies, religion and science. *Unit head:* Dr. Sandra Yocum, Chair, 937-229-4321, Fax: 937-229-4330, E-mail: sandra.yocum@notes.udayton.edu. *Application contact:* Alexander Popovski, Associate Director of Graduate and International Admissions, 937-229-2357, Fax: 937-229-4729, E-mail: alex.popovski@notes.udayton.edu.

University of Portland, College of Arts and Sciences, Department of Theology, Portland, OR 97203-5798. Offers pastoral ministry (MA). *Students:* 6 full-time (5 women), 25 part-time (14 women); includes 1 Asian, non-Hispanic/Latino; 1 Hispanic/Latino; 3 Two or more races, non-Hispanic/Latino. Average age 50. In 2010, 3 master's awarded. *Entrance requirements:* For master's, GRE or MAT, 3 letters of recommendation, minimum GPA of 3.0. Additional exam requirements/recommendations for international students: Required—TOEFL (minimum score 550 paper-based; 80 iBT), IELTS (minimum score 7). *Application deadline:* For fall admission, 7/15 priority date for domestic and international students. Application fee: $45. *Expenses:* Tuition: Part-time $940 per credit hour. Tuition and fees vary according to program. *Financial support:* Federal Work-Study and scholarships/grants available. Financial award application deadline: 3/1; financial award applicants required to submit FAFSA. *Unit head:* Dr. Matt Baasten, Head, 503-943-7160. *Application contact:* Dr. Mary Labarre, Director, 503-943-7365, E-mail: labarre@up.edu.

University of Puget Sound, Graduate Studies, School of Education, Program in Counseling, Tacoma, WA 98416. Offers mental health counseling (M Ed); pastoral counseling (M Ed); school counseling (M Ed). *Accreditation:* NCATE. Part-time programs available. *Entrance requirements:* For master's, GRE General Test, minimum GPA of 3.0. Additional exam requirements/recommendations for international students: Required—TOEFL (minimum score 550 paper-based; 213 computer-based; 80 iBT). Electronic applications accepted. *Expenses:* Contact institution. *Faculty research:* Cross-role professional preparation, suicide prevention.

University of Saint Francis, Graduate School, Department of Psychology and Counseling, Fort Wayne, IN 46808-3994. Offers general psychology (MS); mental health counseling (MS); pastoral counseling (MS); school counseling (MS Ed). Part-time and evening/weekend programs available. *Entrance requirements:* For master's, interview, minimum undergraduate GPA of 3.0. *Expenses:* Tuition: Part-time $770 per semester hour. Part-time tuition and fees vary according to program.

University of St. Michael's College, Faculty of Theology, Toronto, ON M5S 1J4, Canada. Offers Catholic leadership (MA); eastern Christian studies (Diploma); religious education (Diploma); theological studies (Diploma); theology (M Div, MA, MRE, MTS, D Min, PhD, Th D); theology and Jewish studies (MA). Th D offered jointly with University of Toronto. *Accreditation:* ATS (one or more programs are accredited). Part-time programs available. *Degree requirements:* For master's, thesis (for some programs), 1 foreign language (MA), 2 foreign languages (Th M); for doctorate, 3 foreign languages, comprehensive exam, thesis/dissertation; for M Div, thesis/dissertation optional; for other advanced degree, thesis optional. *Entrance requirements:* For M Div and other advanced degree, minimum GPA of 2.7; for master's, M Div or BA, course work in an ancient or modern language, minimum GPA of 3.3; for doctorate, MA in theology, Th M, or M Div with thesis, minimum GPA of 3.7. Additional exam requirements/recommendations for international students: Required—TOEFL (minimum score 600 paper-based; 250 computer-based). Electronic applications accepted. *Expenses:* Contact institution. *Faculty research:* Patristics, eastern Christianity, ecology and theology, ecumenism, Jewish Christian studies.

University of St. Thomas, Graduate Studies, The Saint Paul Seminary School of Divinity, Saint Paul, MN 55105. Offers M Div, MA, MARE. *Accreditation:* ACIPE; ATS. Part-time and evening/weekend programs available. *Faculty:* 13 full-time (5 women), 5 part-time/adjunct (2 women). *Students:* 97 full-time (5 women), 20 part-time (10 women); includes 2 minority (both Hispanic/Latino), 10 international. Average age 30. 32 applicants, 100% accepted, 30 enrolled. In 2010, 9 first professional degrees, 23 master's awarded. *Degree requirements:* For master's, one foreign language, comprehensive exam (for some programs), thesis (for some programs). *Entrance requirements:* For M Div, GRE General Test or MAT, BA with minimum undergraduate GPA of 3.0, interview; for master's, GRE, 3 letters of recommendation, interview. Additional exam requirements/recommendations for international students: Required—TOEFL (minimum score 550 paper-based; 213 computer-based). *Application deadline:* For fall admission, 6/1 priority date for domestic students. Applications are processed on a rolling basis. Application fee: $40. Electronic applications accepted. *Expenses:* Contact institution. *Financial support:* In 2010–11, 52 students received support; fellowships, research assistantships, institutionally sponsored loans and scholarships/grants available. Support available to part-time students. Financial award application deadline: 4/1; financial award applicants required to submit FAFSA. *Faculty research:* Theological education. *Unit head:* Rev. Msgr. Aloysius R. Callaghan, Rector, 651-962-5052, Fax: 651-962-5790, E-mail: arcallaghan@stthomas.edu. *Application contact:* Rev. Peter A. Laird, Vice Rector and Admissions Chair, 651-962-5070, Fax: 651-962-5790, E-mail: palaird@stthomas.edu.

University of South Africa, College of Human Sciences, Pretoria, South Africa. Offers adult education (M Ed); African languages (MA, PhD); African politics (MA, PhD); Afrikaans (MA, PhD); ancient history (MA, PhD); ancient Near Eastern studies (MA, PhD); anthropology (MA, PhD); applied linguistics (MA); Arabic (MA, PhD); archaeology (MA); art history (MA); Biblical archaeology (MA); Biblical studies (M Th, D Th, PhD); Christian spirituality (M Th, D Th); church history (M Th, D Th); classical studies (MA, PhD); clinical psychology (MA); communication (MA, PhD); comparative education (M Ed, Ed D); consulting psychology (D Admin, D Com, PhD); curriculum studies (M Ed, Ed D); development studies (M Admin, MA, D Admin, PhD); didactics (M Ed, Ed D); education (M Tech); education management (M Ed, Ed D); educational psychology (M Ed); English (MA); environmental education (M Ed); French (MA, PhD); German (MA, PhD); Greek (MA); guidance and counseling (M Ed); health studies (MA, PhD), including health sciences education (MA), health services management (MA), medical and surgical nursing science (critical care general) (MA), midwifery and neonatal nursing science (MA), trauma and emergency care (MA); history (MA, PhD); history of education (Ed D); inclusive education (M Ed, Ed D); information and communications technology policy and regulation (MA); information science (MA, MIS, PhD); international politics (MA, PhD); Islamic studies (MA, PhD); Italian (MA, PhD); Judaica (MA, PhD); linguistics (MA, PhD); mathematical education (M Ed); mathematics education (MA); missiology (M Th, D Th); modern Hebrew (MA, PhD); musicology (MA, MMus, D Mus, PhD); natural science education (M Ed); New Testament (M Th, D Th); Old Testament (D Th); pastoral therapy (M Th, D Th); philosophy (MA); philosophy of education (M Ed, Ed D); politics (MA, PhD); Portuguese (MA, PhD); practical theology (M Th, D Th); psychology (MA, MS, PhD); psychology of education (M Ed, Ed D); public health (MA); religious studies (MA, D Th, PhD); Romance languages (MA); Russian (MA, PhD); Semitic languages (MA, PhD); social behavior studies in HIV/AIDS (MA); social science (mental health) (MA); social science in development studies (MA); social science in psychology (MA); social science in social work (MA); social science in sociology (MA); social work (MSW, DSW, PhD); socio-education (M Ed, Ed D); sociolinguistics (MA); sociology (MA, PhD); Spanish (MA, PhD); systematic theology (M Th, D Th); TESOL (teaching English to speakers of other languages) (MA); theological ethics (M Th, D Th); theory of literature (MA, PhD); urban ministries (D Th); urban ministry (M Th).

University of Trinity College, Faculty of Divinity, Toronto, ON M5S 1H8, Canada. Offers ministry (Diploma); ministry for church musicians (Diploma); theology (M Div, MA, MTS, Th M, D Min, PhD, Th D, Diploma, L Th); M Div/MA. *Accreditation:* ATS. Part-time programs available. *Faculty:* 3 full-time (1 woman), 31 part-time/adjunct (4 women). *Students:* 50 full-time (15 women), 84 part-time (39 women). Average age 45. *Degree requirements:* For master's, 2 foreign languages, thesis (for some programs); for doctorate, 3 foreign languages, comprehensive exam, thesis/dissertation; for M Div, thesis/dissertation optional; for other advanced degree, thesis (for some programs). *Entrance requirements:* For M Div, interview; for master's, 1 language (modern or ancient), interview; for doctorate, 2 languages (modern and ancient). Additional exam requirements/recommendations for international students: Required—TOEFL, TWE. *Application deadline:* For fall admission, 3/31 priority date for domestic and international students; for winter admission, 12/31 for domestic and international students; for spring admission, 4/30 priority date for domestic and international students. Applications are processed on a rolling basis. Application fee: $0. *Financial support:* Fellowships, teaching assistantships, career-related internships or fieldwork, institutionally sponsored loans, and bursaries available. Support available to part-time students. Financial award application deadline: 5/15. *Faculty research:* Interreligious dialogue, feminist theology, systematic theology, philosophy of religion, pastoral theology. *Unit head:* Dr. David Neelands, Dean, 416-978-7750, Fax: 416-978-4949, E-mail: divdean@trinity.utoronto.ca. *Application contact:* Rachel Richards, Administrative Assistant to the Dean, 416-978-2133, Fax: 416-978-4949, E-mail: divinity@trinity.utoronto.ca.

Warner Pacific College, Graduate Programs, Portland, OR 97215-4099. Offers biblical and theological studies (MA); biblical studies (M Rel); education (M Ed); management/organizational leadership (MS); pastoral ministries (M Rel); religion and ethics (M Rel); teaching (MA); theology (M Rel). Part-time programs available. *Degree requirements:* For master's, thesis or alternative, presentation of defense. *Entrance requirements:* For master's, interview, minimum GPA of 2.5, letters of recommendations. *Faculty research:* New Testament studies, nineteenth-century Wesleyan theology, preaching and church growth, Christian ethics.

Wayland Baptist University, Graduate Programs, Programs in Religion, Plainview, TX 79072-6998. Offers Christian ministry (MCM); religion (MA). Part-time and evening/weekend programs available. Postbaccalaureate distance learning degree programs offered (no on-campus study). *Degree requirements:* For master's, comprehensive exam. *Entrance requirements:* For master's, GRE or MAT. Additional exam requirements/recommendations for international students: Required—TOEFL (minimum score 500 paper-based; 173 computer-based; 61 iBT). Electronic applications accepted.

Wesley Biblical Seminary, Graduate Programs, Jackson, MS 39206. Offers apologetics (MA); Biblical studies (MA); Christian studies (MA); evangelism (M Div); family life ministry (M Div); honors research (M Div); missions (M Div); pastoral ministry (M Div); teaching (M Div); theological studies (MA). *Accreditation:* ATS. Part-time programs available. *Degree requirements:* For master's, thesis. *Entrance requirements:* Additional exam requirements/recommendations for international students: Required—TOEFL. Electronic applications accepted. *Faculty research:* Patristics, missiology, culture, hermeneutics.

Western Seminary, Graduate Programs, Program in Counseling, Portland, OR 97215-3367. Offers counseling (MA, Certificate); pastoral counseling (M Div); M Div/MA. Part-time and evening/weekend programs available. *Faculty:* 93 full-time (38 women), 586 part-time/adjunct (198 women). *Students:* 265 applicants, 77% accepted, 155 enrolled. In 2010, 93 master's, 6 other advanced degrees awarded. *Degree requirements:* For master's, practicum; for M Div, 2 foreign languages, practicum. *Entrance requirements:* Additional exam requirements/recommendations for international students: Required—TOEFL. *Application deadline:* For fall admission, 7/18 priority date for domestic students; for winter admission, 11/7 priority date for domestic students; for spring admission, 3/13 priority date for domestic students. Applications are processed on a rolling basis. Application fee: $50. *Expenses:* Contact institution. *Financial support:* Career-related internships or fieldwork and institutionally sponsored loans available. Financial award application deadline: 7/15; financial award applicants required to submit FAFSA. *Unit head:* Dr. Kay Bruce, Director, 503-517-1875, E-mail: kbruce@westernseminary.edu. *Application contact:* Dr. Robert W. Wiggins, Registrar/Dean of Student Development, 503-517-1820, Fax: 503-517-1801, E-mail: rwiggins@westernseminary.edu.

Western Seminary, Graduate Programs, Program in Intercultural Studies, Portland, OR 97215-3367. Offers MA, D Miss, Certificate, G Dip. Part-time and evening/weekend programs available. *Faculty:* 2 full-time (1 woman), 5 part-time/adjunct (1 woman). *Students:* 265 applicants, 77% accepted, 155 enrolled. In 2010, 93 master's, 19 doctorates, 6 other advanced degrees awarded. *Degree requirements:* For master's, practicum; for doctorate, 2 foreign languages, thesis/dissertation. *Entrance requirements:* Additional exam requirements/recommendations for international students: Required—TOEFL. *Application deadline:* For fall admission, 7/18 priority date for domestic students; for winter admission, 11/7 priority date for domestic students; for spring admission, 3/13 priority date for domestic students. Applications are processed on a rolling basis. Application fee: $50. *Expenses:* Tuition: Part-time $425 per credit. *Financial support:* Career-related internships or fieldwork available. Financial award applicants required to submit FAFSA. *Unit head:* Dr. Enoch Wan, Director, 503-233-1804, Fax: 503-517-1889, E-mail: ewan@westernseminary.edu. *Application contact:* Dr. Robert W. Wiggins, Registrar/Dean of Student Development, 503-517-1820, Fax: 503-517-1801, E-mail: rwiggins@westernseminary.edu.

Western Seminary, Graduate Programs, Program in Ministry and Leadership, Portland, OR 97215-3367. Offers chaplaincy (MA); coaching (MA); Jewish ministry (MA); pastoral care to women (MA); youth ministry (MA). *Students:* 265 applicants, 77% accepted, 155 enrolled. In 2010, 93 master's awarded. *Degree requirements:* For master's, practicum. *Entrance requirements:* Additional exam requirements/recommendations for international students: Required—TOEFL. *Application deadline:* For fall admission, 7/18 priority date for domestic students; for winter admission, 11/7 priority date for domestic students; for spring admission, 3/13 priority date for domestic students. Applications are processed on a rolling basis. Application fee: $50. *Expenses:* Tuition: Part-time $425 per credit. *Financial support:* Applicants required to submit FAFSA. *Unit head:* Beverly Hislop, Director, 503-517-1881, E-mail: bhislop@westernseminary.edu. *Application contact:* Dr. Robert W. Wiggins, Registrar/Dean of Student Development, 503-517-1820, Fax: 503-517-1801, E-mail: rwiggins@westernseminary.edu.

Western Seminary–Sacramento Campus, Graduate Certificate Programs, Sacramento, CA 95821. Offers Bible (Graduate Certificate); coaching (Graduate Certificate); pastoral care to women (Graduate Certificate); theology (Graduate Certificate); youth and family (Graduate Certificate). Postbaccalaureate distance learning degree programs offered. *Entrance requirements:* For degree, essays, undergraduate transcripts, 4 recommendations. Additional exam requirements/recommendations for international students: Required—TOEFL.

Western Seminary–Sacramento Campus, Graduate Diploma Programs, Sacramento, CA 95821. Offers Bible and theology (Graduate Diploma); ministry (Graduate Diploma); pastoral care to women (Graduate Diploma). *Entrance requirements:* For degree, essays, undergraduate transcripts, 4 recommendations. Additional exam requirements/recommendations for international students: Required—TOEFL.

Western Seminary–Sacramento Campus, Program in Ministry and Leadership, Sacramento, CA 95821. Offers MA. *Entrance requirements:* For master's, essays, undergraduate transcripts, 4 recommendations. Additional exam requirements/recommendations for international students: Required—TOEFL.

Western Seminary–San Jose Campus, Graduate Programs, Los Gatos, CA 95032-4520. Offers Biblical and theological studies (MA); exposition ministry (M Div); marital and family therapy (MA); ministry and leadership (MA); open track (M Div); pastoral ministry (M Div); theology (Graduate Diploma). Postbaccalaureate distance learning degree programs offered. *Degree requirements:* For master's, 2 foreign languages; for M Div, 3 foreign languages. *Entrance requirements:* For M Div, minimum GPA of 2.5; for master's, minimum GPA of 3.0. *Expenses:* Tuition: Part-time $445 per unit.

Westminster Theological Seminary, Graduate and Professional Programs, Philadelphia, PA 19118. Offers apologetics (Th M); Biblical and urban studies (Certificate); Biblical counseling (MA); biblical studies (MAR); Christian studies (Certificate); church history (Th M); counseling (M Div); general studies (M Div, MAR); hermeneutics and Bible interpretations (PhD); historical and theological studies (PhD); historical theology (Th M); New Testament (Th M); Old Testament (Th M); pastoral counseling (D Min); pastoral ministry (M Div, D Min); systematic theology (Th M); theological studies (MAR); urban missions (M Div, MA, MAR, D Min). *Accreditation:* ATS. Part-time programs available. Terminal master's awarded for partial completion of doctoral program. *Degree requirements:* For master's, thesis (for some programs); for doctorate, 4 foreign languages, comprehensive exam (for some programs), thesis/dissertation; for M Div, 2 foreign languages. *Entrance requirements:* For doctorate, GRE General Test. Additional exam requirements/recommendations for international students: Required—TOEFL, TWE.

Wheaton College, Graduate School, Department of Psychology, Wheaton, IL 60187-5593. Offers clinical psychology (MA, Psy D); counseling ministries (MA). *Accreditation:* APA (one or more programs are accredited). Terminal master's awarded for partial completion of doctoral program. *Degree requirements:* For master's, thesis or alternative; for doctorate, thesis/dissertation, internship. *Entrance requirements:* For master's, GRE General Test, 18 hours of course work in psychology; for doctorate, GRE General Test.

Wilfrid Laurier University, Waterloo Lutheran Seminary, Waterloo, ON N2L 3C5, Canada. Offers divinity (M Div); multifaith spiritual care and counseling (Diploma); pastoral leadership (D Min); spiritual care and counseling (D Min); theology (M Th, MTS); M Div/MTS/MSW. *Accreditation:* ATS. Part-time programs available. *Degree requirements:* For master's, one foreign language, thesis (for some programs); for doctorate, thesis/dissertation; for M Div, one foreign language, thesis/dissertation. *Entrance requirements:* For M Div, denominational endorsement, two letters of reference; for master's, two letters of reference; for doctorate, M Div, two letters of reference. Additional exam requirements/recommendations for international students: Required—TOEFL (minimum score 573 paper-based; 230 computer-based; 89 iBT), IELTS (minimum score 7). *Application deadline:* For fall admission, 5/1 for domestic and international students; for winter admission, 9/1 for domestic and international students; for spring admission, 1/1 for domestic and international students. Applications are processed on a rolling basis. Application fee: $50. Electronic applications accepted. *Expenses:* Contact institution. *Financial support:* Career-related internships or fieldwork, institutionally sponsored loans, and scholarships/grants available. Financial award application deadline: 10/1. *Faculty research:* Biblical study, church history, systematic theology. *Unit head:* Dr. David Pfrimmer, Principal-Dean/Registrar, 519-884-0710 Ext. 3229, E-mail: dpfrimmer@wlu.ca. *Application contact:* Sarina Wheeler, Student Advisor and Admissions Coordinator, 519-884-0710 Ext. 3498, Fax: 519-725-2434, E-mail: swheeler@wlu.ca.

Xavier University, College of Arts and Sciences, Department of Theology, Cincinnati, OH 45207. Offers health care mission integration (MA); theology (MA), including religious education, social and pastoral ministry, theology. Part-time and evening/weekend programs available. *Faculty:* 5 full-time (4 women). *Students:* 4 full-time (3 women), 19 part-time (5 women); includes 1 minority (Hispanic/Latino). Average age 35. 6 applicants, 83% accepted, 4 enrolled. In 2010, 9 master's awarded. *Degree requirements:* For master's, thesis optional, final paper (or thesis) and defense. *Entrance requirements:* For master's, MAT or GRE, letters of recommendation. Additional exam requirements/recommendations for international students: Required—TOEFL (minimum score 550 paper-based; 213 computer-based). *Application deadline:* Applications are processed on a rolling basis. Application fee: $35. Electronic applications accepted. *Expenses:* Tuition: Part-time $718 per credit hour. Tuition and fees vary according to degree level, campus/location and program. *Financial support:* In 2010–11, 20 students received support. Scholarships/grants and unspecified assistantships available. Financial award applicants required to submit FAFSA. *Faculty research:* Scripture, ethics, constructive theology, historical theology. *Unit head:* Dr. Sarah Melcher, Chair, 513-745-2043, Fax: 513-745-3215, E-mail: melcher@xavier.edu. *Application contact:* Dr. Sarah Melcher, Chair, 513-745-2043, Fax: 513-745-3215, E-mail: melcher@xavier.edu.

Xavier University of Louisiana, Graduate School, Institute for Black Catholic Studies, New Orleans, LA 70125-1098. Offers pastoral theology (Th M). Part-time programs available. *Degree requirements:* For master's, comprehensive exam, practicum. *Entrance requirements:* For master's, GRE General Test, MAT, minimum GPA of 2.5. Additional exam requirements/recommendations for international students: Required—TOEFL.

Religion

Ambrose University College, Ambrose Seminary, Calgary, AB T2P 3T5, Canada. Offers biblical/theological studies (MA); Chinese ministries (Certificate); Christian studies (M Div, MA, Diploma); foundations for ministry (Certificate); intercultural ministries (M Div, MA, Certificate, Diploma); leadership and ministry (MA, Certificate, Diploma). *Accreditation:* ATS (one or more programs are accredited). Part-time programs available. *Faculty:* 7 full-time (0 women), 24 part-time/adjunct (2 women). *Students:* 55 full-time (16 women), 98 part-time (52 women); includes 49 minority (5 Black or African American, non-Hispanic/Latino; 2 American Indian or Alaska Native, non-Hispanic/Latino; 41 Asian, non-Hispanic/Latino; 1 Hispanic/Latino). Average age 41. *Degree requirements:* For master's, 2 foreign languages, internship; for M Div, one foreign language, internship. *Entrance requirements:* For master's, bachelor's degree. Additional exam requirements/recommendations for international students: Required—TOEFL or IELTS. *Application deadline:* For fall admission, 7/31 priority date for domestic students, 3/1 priority date for international students; for winter admission, 11/30 priority date for domestic students, 6/1 priority date for international students. Applications are processed on a rolling basis. Application fee: $50. Electronic applications accepted. Tuition and fees charges are reported in Canadian dollars. *Expenses:* Tuition: Full-time $9270 Canadian dollars; part-time $309 Canadian dollars per credit hour. Required fees: $510 Canadian dollars. *Financial support:* Career-related internships or fieldwork and scholarships/grants available. Support available to part-time students. Financial award application deadline: 3/30. *Faculty research:* Evangelicalism and sociology, missiological trends, chaplaincy, intertestamental studies, postmodernism. *Unit head:* Dr. Paul Spilsbury, Vice-President of Academic Affairs, 403-410-2000 Ext. 6905, Fax: 403-571-2556, E-mail: pspilsbury@ambrose.edu. *Application contact:* Dr. Paul Spilsbury, Vice-President of Academic Affairs, 403-410-2000 Ext. 6905, Fax: 403-571-2556, E-mail: pspilsbury@ambrose.edu.

Amridge University, Graduate and Professional Programs, Montgomery, AL 36117. Offers behavioral leadership and management (MA); Biblical exposition (MA); biblical studies (MA, PhD); family therapy (D Min); historical and theological studies (MA); leadership and management (MS); marriage and family therapy (M Div, MA, PhD); ministerial leadership (M Div, MS); pastoral counseling (M Div, MS); practical ministry (MA); professional counseling (M Div, MA, PhD); theology (D Min). Part-time and evening/weekend programs available. Postbaccalaureate distance learning degree programs offered (no on-campus study). *Faculty:* 39 full-time (6 women), 39 part-time/adjunct (5 women). *Students:* 119 full-time (54 women), 260 part-time (149 women); includes 160 minority (153 Black or African American, non-Hispanic/Latino; 1 Asian, non-Hispanic/Latino; 6 Hispanic/Latino). Average age 35. *Degree requirements:* For master's, one foreign language, comprehensive exam (for some programs), thesis (for some programs); for doctorate, comprehensive exam (for some programs), thesis/dissertation; for M Div, comprehensive exam (for some programs). *Entrance requirements:* For M Div, master's, and doctorate, GRE General Test or MAT. Additional exam requirements/recommendations for international students: Required—TOEFL. *Application deadline:* For fall admission, 9/1 priority date for domestic students; for spring admission, 1/1 priority date for domestic students. Applications are processed on a rolling basis. Application fee: $75. Electronic applications accepted. *Financial support:* Federal Work-Study and scholarships/grants available. Support available to part-time students. Financial award applicants required to submit FAFSA. *Faculty research:* Homiletics, hermeneutics, ancient Near Eastern history. *Unit head:* Director of Enrollment Management, 800-351-4040 Ext. 7513, Fax: 334-387-3878. *Application contact:* Ora Davis, Admissions Officer, 334-387-3877 Ext. 7524, Fax: 334-387-3878, E-mail: admissions@amridgeuniversity.edu.

Religion

Arizona State University, College of Liberal Arts and Sciences, School of Historical, Philosophical and Religious Studies, Tempe, AZ 85287-4301. Offers East/Southeast Asian history (MA, PhD); European history (MA, PhD); Latin American studies (MA, PhD); North American history (MA, PhD); philosophy (MA, PhD); public history (MA); religious studies (MA, PhD); scholarly publishing (Graduate Certificate). Part-time programs available. *Faculty:* 70 full-time (29 women), 2 part-time/adjunct (0 women). *Students:* 125 full-time (58 women), 68 part-time (37 women); includes 21 minority (5 Black or African American, non-Hispanic/Latino; 3 American Indian or Alaska Native, non-Hispanic/Latino; 1 Asian, non-Hispanic/Latino; 11 Hispanic/Latino; 1 Two or more races, non-Hispanic/Latino), 16 international. Average age 34. 221 applicants, 51% accepted, 41 enrolled. In 2010, 24 master's, 10 doctorates, 3 other advanced degrees awarded. Terminal master's awarded for partial completion of doctoral program. *Degree requirements:* For master's, thesis or alternative, interactive Program of Study (iPOS) submitted before completing 50 percent of required credit hours; for doctorate, variable foreign language requirement, comprehensive exam, thesis/dissertation, interactive Program of Study (iPOS) submitted before completing 50 percent of required credit hours. *Entrance requirements:* For master's and doctorate, GRE, minimum GPA of 3.0 or equivalent in last 2 years of work leading to bachelor's degree. Additional exam requirements/recommendations for international students: Required—TOEFL, IELTS, or Pearson Test of English. *Application deadline:* For fall admission, 1/1 for domestic and international students. Applications are processed on a rolling basis. Application fee: $70 ($90 for international students). Electronic applications accepted. *Expenses:* Tuition, state resident: full-time $8510; part-time $608 per credit. Tuition, nonresident: full-time $16,542; part-time $919 per credit. Required fees: $339; $110 per credit. Part-time tuition and fees vary according to course load. *Financial support:* In 2010–11, 26 research assistantships with full and partial tuition reimbursements (averaging $12,900 per year), 69 teaching assistantships with full and partial tuition reimbursements (averaging $11,771 per year) were awarded; fellowships with full tuition reimbursements, career-related internships or fieldwork, institutionally sponsored loans, scholarships/grants, and tuition waivers (partial) also available. Financial award application deadline: 3/1; financial award applicants required to submit FAFSA. Total annual research expenditures: $1.3 million. *Unit head:* Mark Von Hagen, Director, 480-965-4186, E-mail: mark.vonhagen@asu.edu. *Application contact:* Graduate Admissions, 480-965-6113.

Baptist Bible College of Pennsylvania, Baptist Bible Seminary, Clarks Summit, PA 18411-1297. Offers biblical studies (PhD); church planting (M Div); global missions (M Div); military chaplaincy (M Div); ministry (M Min, D Min); pastor of church education (M Div); pastor of outreach (M Div); pastoral counseling (M Div); pastoral leadership (M Div); theology (M Div, Th M); youth pastor (M Div). Part-time and evening/weekend programs available. Postbaccalaureate distance learning degree programs offered (minimal on-campus study). *Faculty:* 10 full-time (0 women). *Students:* 71 full-time (0 women), 79 part-time (0 women); includes 16 minority (10 Black or African American, non-Hispanic/Latino; 4 Asian, non-Hispanic/Latino; 2 Hispanic/Latino), 7 international. Average age 38. In 2010, 23 master's, 4 doctorates awarded. Terminal master's awarded for partial completion of doctoral program. *Degree requirements:* For master's, 2 foreign languages, thesis; for doctorate, 2 foreign languages, comprehensive exam (for some programs), thesis/dissertation, oral exam; for M Div, 2 foreign languages, thesis/dissertation, oral exam. *Entrance requirements:* For doctorate, Greek and Hebrew entrance exams (PhD). *Application deadline:* Applications are processed on a rolling basis. Application fee: $30. Electronic applications accepted. *Expenses:* Tuition: Full-time $7488; part-time $416 per credit. Required fees: $522; $29 per credit. Full-time tuition and fees vary according to degree level and campus/location. *Financial support:* Career-related internships or fieldwork and scholarships/grants available. Support available to part-time students. *Unit head:* Dr. Michael Stallard, Seminary Academic Dean, 570-585-9348, Fax: 570-585-4057, E-mail: mstallard@bbc.edu. *Application contact:* Paul Golden, Director of Seminary Admissions, 570-586-9396, Fax: 570-585-4057, E-mail: pgolden@bbc.edu.

Baptist Theological Seminary at Richmond, Graduate and Professional Programs, Richmond, VA 23227. Offers biblical interpretation (M Div); Christian education (M Div); theological studies (MATS); theology (D Min); youth and student ministries (M Div); M Div/MS; M Div/MSW. *Accreditation:* ATS. Part-time programs available. Postbaccalaureate distance learning degree programs offered (minimal on-campus study). *Faculty:* 8 full-time (2 women), 19 part-time/adjunct (7 women). *Students:* 71 full-time (36 women), 30 part-time (13 women); includes 10 minority (9 Black or African American, non-Hispanic/Latino; 1 Hispanic/Latino), 3 international. Average age 46. 40 applicants, 88% accepted, 30 enrolled. In 2010, 24 first professional degrees, 4 doctorates awarded. *Degree requirements:* For doctorate, one foreign language, comprehensive exam, thesis/dissertation, field study, independent study; for M Div, one foreign language, comprehensive exam (for some programs), thesis/dissertation optional, mission immersion experience, internship. *Entrance requirements:* For doctorate, MAT, M Div, 3 years of full-time ministry experience. Additional exam requirements/recommendations for international students: Required—TOEFL (minimum score 550 paper-based; 213 computer-based). *Application deadline:* For fall admission, 8/1 priority date for domestic students, 5/1 priority date for international students; for winter admission, 12/1 priority date for domestic students, 9/1 priority date for international students; for spring admission, 1/1 priority date for domestic students, 10/1 priority date for international students. Applications are processed on a rolling basis. Application fee: $35. *Expenses:* Tuition: Full-time $9000; part-time $900 per credit. Required fees: $135 per year. *Financial support:* In 2010–11, 12 teaching assistantships (averaging $1,650 per year) were awarded; scholarships/grants and tuition waivers (partial) also available. Financial award application deadline: 2/1. *Faculty research:* Biblical studies, pastoral care, church history, theology, ministry. *Unit head:* Dr. Ronald W. Crawford, President, 804-204-1201, Fax: 804-355-8182, E-mail: rcrawford@btsr.edu. *Application contact:* Tiffany Kellogg Pittman, Director of Admissions, 804-204-1208, Fax: 804-355-8182, E-mail: admissions@btsr.edu.

Baylor University, Graduate School, College of Arts and Sciences, Department of Religion, Waco, TX 76798. Offers MA, PhD. *Students:* 62 full-time (9 women), 8 part-time (4 women); includes 8 minority (1 American Indian or Alaska Native, non-Hispanic/Latino; 3 Asian, non-Hispanic/Latino; 2 Hispanic/Latino; 2 Two or more races, non-Hispanic/Latino), 7 international. In 2010, 1 master's, 10 doctorates awarded. Terminal master's awarded for partial completion of doctoral program. *Degree requirements:* For master's, one foreign language, thesis; for doctorate, 2 foreign languages, thesis/dissertation. *Entrance requirements:* For master's and doctorate, GRE General Test. *Application deadline:* Applications are processed on a rolling basis. Application fee: $25. *Financial support:* Fellowships, research assistantships, teaching assistantships, Federal Work-Study, institutionally sponsored loans, and scholarships/grants available. *Unit head:* Dr. Bill Pitts, Graduate Program Director, 254-710-6321, Fax: 254-710-3740, E-mail: william_pitts@baylor.edu. *Application contact:* Lisa M. Long, Administrative Assistant, 254-710-3742, Fax: 254-710-3870, E-mail: lisa_m_long@baylor.edu.

Baylor University, Graduate School, College of Arts and Sciences, J. M. Dawson Institute of Church-State Studies, Waco, TX 76798. Offers MA, PhD. *Students:* 40 full-time (15 women), 3 part-time (2 women); includes 9 minority (2 Black or African American, non-Hispanic/Latino; 1 Asian, non-Hispanic/Latino; 4 Hispanic/Latino; 2 Two or more races, non-Hispanic/Latino), 7 international. In 2010, 3 master's, 2 doctorates awarded. *Degree requirements:* For master's, thesis, oral exam; for doctorate, one foreign language, thesis/dissertation, preliminary exams. *Entrance requirements:* For master's, GRE General Test; for doctorate, GRE General Test, MA or equivalent. *Application deadline:* For fall admission, 3/1 for domestic students. Applications are processed on a rolling basis. Application fee: $25. *Financial support:* Fellowships, research assistantships, teaching assistantships, Federal Work-Study and institutionally sponsored loans available. Financial award application deadline: 3/1. *Faculty research:* Religion and politics, religion and public education, religious freedom and international politics, First Amendment jurisprudence. *Unit head:* Dr. Christopher Marsh, Graduate Program Director, 254-710-4412, Fax: 254-710-1571, E-mail: chris_marsh@baylor.edu. *Application contact:* Suzanne Seller, Administrative Assistant, 254-710-1510, Fax: 254-710-1571, E-mail: suzanne_sellers@baylor.edu.

Bellarmine University, Bellarmine College of Arts and Sciences, Louisville, KY 40205-0671. Offers spirituality (MA). *Faculty:* 3 full-time (1 woman), 3 part-time/adjunct (1 woman). *Students:* 13 part-time (11 women); includes 1 Black or African American, non-Hispanic/Latino. Average age 43. In 2010, 1 master's awarded. *Entrance requirements:* For master's, minimum GPA of 2.8, letter of recommendation, spirituality autobiography. Additional exam requirements/recommendations for international students: Required—TOEFL (minimum score 550 paper-based; 213 computer-based; 80 iBT). *Application deadline:* For spring admission, 3/15 for domestic students. Application fee: $25. *Expenses:* Contact institution. *Faculty research:* Early Christianity, Catholic social teaching, Christian spirituality, social justice. *Unit head:* Dr. Gregory Hillis, Program Director, 502-272-3800, E-mail: ghillis@bellarmine.edu. *Application contact:* Sara Pettingill, Dean of Graduate Admission, 502-272-8401, E-mail: spettingill@bellarmine.edu.

Bethany Theological Seminary, Graduate and Professional Programs, Richmond, IN 47374-4019. Offers biblical studies (MA Th); ministry studies (M Div); peace studies (M Div, MA Th); theological studies (MA Th, CATS); youth ministry (M Div). *Accreditation:* ACIPE; ATS. Part-time programs available. Postbaccalaureate distance learning degree programs offered (minimal on-campus study). *Degree requirements:* For master's, thesis. *Entrance requirements:* For M Div, letters of reference, minimum GPA of 2.75; for master's, letters of reference, minimum GPA of 3.0. Additional exam requirements/recommendations for international students: Required—TOEFL (minimum score 550 paper-based; 218 computer-based).

Bethel Seminary, Graduate and Professional Programs, St. Paul, MN 55112-6998. Offers Anglican studies (Certificate); applied ministry (MA, Certificate); biblical studies (Certificate); children's and family ministry (MACFM); Christian education (MACE); Christian thought (MACT); community ministry leadership (MA, Certificate); global and contextual studies (MA); Greek and Hebrew language track (M Div); Greek language track (M Div); Hebrew language track (M Div); lay ministry (Certificate); marriage and family therapy (MAMFT, Certificate); men's ministry leadership (Certificate); ministry (D Min); ministry leadership (Certificate); spiritual formation (Certificate); theological studies (MATS, Certificate); transformational leadership (MATL, Certificate); young life youth ministry (Certificate). *Accreditation:* ACIPE; ATS (one or more programs are accredited). Part-time and evening/weekend programs available. Postbaccalaureate distance learning degree programs offered (minimal on-campus study). *Faculty:* 26 full-time (3 women), 74 part-time/adjunct (29 women). *Students:* 729 full-time (275 women), 274 part-time (118 women); includes 75 minority (34 Black or African American, non-Hispanic/Latino; 1 American Indian or Alaska Native, non-Hispanic/Latino; 12 Asian, non-Hispanic/Latino; 16 Hispanic/Latino; 1 Native Hawaiian or other Pacific Islander, non-Hispanic/Latino; 11 Two or more races, non-Hispanic/Latino), 16 international. Average age 38. 525 applicants, 76% accepted, 265 enrolled. In 2010, 149 master's, 13 doctorates awarded. *Degree requirements:* For master's, variable foreign language requirement, thesis (for some programs); for doctorate, thesis/dissertation; for M Div, one foreign language. *Entrance requirements:* For M Div and master's, letters of reference, transcripts, personal statement; for doctorate, M Div, letters of reference, organizational support. Additional exam requirements/recommendations for international students: Required—TOEFL (minimum score 550 paper-based; 213 computer-based; 87 iBT). *Application deadline:* For fall admission, 8/1 priority date for domestic students, 3/1 for international students; for winter admission, 12/1 priority date for domestic students; for spring admission, 3/1 priority date for domestic students. Applications are processed on a rolling basis. Application fee: $20. Electronic applications accepted. *Financial support:* In 2010–11, 655 students received support, including 18 teaching assistantships; career-related internships or fieldwork, Federal Work-Study, scholarships/grants, and tuition waivers (full) also available. Financial award application deadline: 7/15; financial award applicants required to submit FAFSA. *Faculty research:* Nature of theology, ethics, Biblical commentaries, nature of God, science and theology. *Unit head:* Dr. David Ridder, Vice President and Dean, 651-638-6553. *Application contact:* Joseph V. Dworak, Director of Admissions, 651-638-6288, Fax: 651-638-6002, E-mail: j-dworak@bethel.edu.

Bethesda Christian University, Graduate and Professional Programs, Anaheim, CA 92801. Offers biblical studies (MA); music (MA); theology (M Div). *Entrance requirements:* For M Div and master's, interview.

Beulah Heights University, Graduate School, Atlanta, GA 30316. Offers biblical studies (MA); leadership studies (MA). *Entrance requirements:* Additional exam requirements/recommendations for international students: Required—TOEFL (minimum score 500 paper-based). Electronic applications accepted.

Biola University, School of Arts and Sciences, La Mirada, CA 90639-0001. Offers science and religion (MS). Part-time and evening/weekend programs available. *Faculty:* 8 full-time (5 women), 10 part-time/adjunct (7 women). *Students:* 26 full-time (5 women), 173 part-time (38 women); includes 35 minority (7 Black or African American, non-Hispanic/Latino; 14 Asian, non-Hispanic/Latino; 9 Hispanic/Latino; 5 Two or more races, non-Hispanic/Latino), 6 international. 118 applicants, 85% accepted, 83 enrolled. In 2010, 49 master's awarded. *Degree requirements:* For master's, thesis or alternative, minimum GPA of 2.5, completion of program within 5 years. *Entrance requirements:* For master's, minimum GPA of 3.0, bachelor's degree in related field. Additional exam requirements/recommendations for international students: Required—TOEFL (minimum score 550 paper-based; 213 computer-based). *Application deadline:* For fall admission, 7/1 for domestic students; for spring admission, 12/1 for domestic students. Applications are processed on a rolling basis. Application fee: $45. Electronic applications accepted. *Expenses:* Contact institution. *Financial support:* Career-related internships or fieldwork, institutionally sponsored loans, and scholarships/grants available. Support available to part-time students. Financial award application deadline: 3/2; financial award applicants required to submit FAFSA. *Application contact:* Roy M. Allinson, Director of Graduate Admissions, 562-903-4752, Fax: 562-903-4709, E-mail: admissions@biola.edu.

Biola University, Talbot School of Theology, La Mirada, CA 90639-0001. Offers Biblical studies (MA); Christian education (MACE); Christian ministry and leadership (MA); divinity (M Div); education (PhD); ministry (MA Min); New Testament (MA); Old Testament (MA); philosophy of religion and ethics (MA); spiritual formation (MA); spiritual formation and soul care (MA); theological studies (MA); theology (MA, Th M, D Min). *Accreditation:* ATS. Part-time and evening/weekend programs available. *Faculty:* 45 full-time (5 women), 40 part-time/adjunct (10 women). *Students:* 611 full-time (123 women), 573 part-time (144 women); includes 382 minority (48 Black or African American, non-Hispanic/Latino; 1 American Indian or Alaska Native, non-Hispanic/Latino; 300 Asian, non-Hispanic/Latino; 5 Native Hawaiian or other Pacific Islander, non-Hispanic/Latino; 28 Two or more races, non-Hispanic/Latino), 153 international. Average age 31. 515 applicants, 76% accepted, 277 enrolled. In 2010, 47 first professional degrees, 152 master's, 9 doctorates awarded. *Degree requirements:* For master's, variable foreign language requirement, thesis or alternative; for doctorate, variable foreign language requirement, thesis/dissertation; for M Div, thesis/dissertation or alternative. *Entrance requirements:* For M Div, minimum GPA of 2.6; for master's, minimum undergraduate GPA of 3.0; for doctorate, minimum GPA of 3.25. Additional exam requirements/recommendations for international students: Required—TOEFL (minimum score 550 paper-based; 213 computer-based). *Application deadline:* For fall admission, 7/1 for domestic students; for spring admission, 1/1 for domestic students. Applications are processed on a rolling basis. Application fee: $45. *Financial support:* Research assistantships, teaching assistantships, career-related internships or fieldwork, institutionally sponsored loans, and scholarships/grants available. Support available to part-time students. Financial award application deadline: 3/2; financial award applicants required to submit FAFSA. *Faculty research:* Moral development; biological, medical, and social ethics; ancient Near Eastern historical philosophy. *Unit head:* Dr. Dennis Dirks, Dean, 562-903-4816, Fax: 562-903-4748, E-mail: dennis_dirks@peter.biola.edu. *Application contact:* Roy M. Allinson, Director of Graduate Admissions, 562-903-4752, Fax: 562-903-4709, E-mail: admissions@biola.edu.

Bob Jones University, Graduate Programs, Greenville, SC 29614. Offers accountancy (MS); Bible (MA); Bible translation (MA); Biblical studies (Certificate); broadcast management (MS); business administration (MBA); church history (MA, PhD); church ministries (MA); church music (MM); cinema and video production (MA); counseling (MS); curriculum and instruction (Ed D); divinity (M Div); dramatic production (MA); educational leadership (MS, Ed D, Ed S);

elementary education (M Ed, MAT); English (M Ed, MA, MAT); fine arts (MA); graphic design (MA); history (M Ed, MA); illustration (MA); interpretative speech (MA); mathematics (M Ed, MAT); medical missions (Certificate); ministry (MM, D Min); multi-categorical special education (M Ed, MAT); music (M Ed); New Testament interpretation (PhD); Old Testament interpretation (PhD); orchestral instrument performance (MM); organ performance (MM); pastoral studies (MA); personnel services (MS, Ed S); piano pedagogy (MM); piano performance (MM); platform arts (MA); radio and television broadcasting (MS); rhetoric and public address (MA); secondary education (M Ed); studio art (MA); teaching Bible (MA); theology (MA, PhD); voice performance (MM); youth ministries (MA); M Div/MM.

Boston University, Graduate School of Arts and Sciences, Division of Religious and Theological Studies, Boston, MA 02215. Offers MA, PhD. *Students:* 52 full-time (21 women), 11 part-time (7 women); includes 10 minority (2 Black or African American, non-Hispanic/Latino; 4 Asian, non-Hispanic/Latino; 2 Hispanic/Latino; 2 Two or more races, non-Hispanic/Latino), 9 international. Average age 34. 149 applicants, 15% accepted, 5 enrolled. In 2010, 5 master's, 9 doctorates awarded. Terminal master's awarded for partial completion of doctoral program. *Degree requirements:* For master's, one foreign language, comprehensive exam, thesis; for doctorate, 2 foreign languages, comprehensive exam, thesis/dissertation. *Entrance requirements:* For master's and doctorate, GRE General Test, 3 letters of recommendation, academic writing sample. Additional exam requirements/recommendations for international students: Required—TOEFL (minimum score 550 paper-based; 213 computer-based). *Application deadline:* For fall admission, 1/1 for domestic and international students. Application fee: $70. Electronic applications accepted. *Expenses:* Tuition: Full-time $39,314; part-time $1228 per credit. Required fees: $40 per semester. *Financial support:* In 2010–11, 36 students received support, including 2 fellowships with full tuition reimbursements available (averaging $19,300 per year), 1 research assistantship with full tuition reimbursement available (averaging $18,800 per year), 6 teaching assistantships with full tuition reimbursements available (averaging $18,800 per year); career-related internships or fieldwork, Federal Work-Study, tuition waivers (partial), and unspecified assistantships also available. Support available to part-time students. Financial award application deadline: 1/1; financial award applicants required to submit FAFSA. *Unit head:* John Berthrong, Acting Director, 617-353-3050, Fax: 617-353-5441, E-mail: jhb@bu.edu. *Application contact:* Karen Nardella, Department Administrator, 617-353-2636, Fax: 617-353-5441, E-mail: kcn@bu.edu.

Briercrest Seminary, Graduate Programs, Program in Christian Ministries, Caronport, SK S0H 0S0, Canada. Offers leadership (MA); marriage and family counseling (MA); missions (MA); pastoral counseling (MA); worship (MA); youth and family ministry (MA). Part-time programs available. *Degree requirements:* For master's, comprehensive exam, thesis optional. *Entrance requirements:* Additional exam requirements/recommendations for international students: Required—TOEFL (minimum score 550 paper-based; 213 computer-based).

Briercrest Seminary, Graduate Programs, Program in Theology, Caronport, SK S0H 0S0, Canada. Offers Biblical studies (M Div); leadership and management (M Div); New Testament (MATS); Old Testament (MATS); pastoral counseling (M Div); pastoral ministry (M Div); theological studies (M Div); theology (MATS); worship (M Div); youth and family ministry (M Div). *Accreditation:* ATS. Part-time programs available. *Degree requirements:* For master's, comprehensive exam, thesis optional. *Entrance requirements:* Additional exam requirements/recommendations for international students: Required—TOEFL (minimum score 550 paper-based; 213 computer-based).

Brown University, Graduate School, Department of Religious Studies, Providence, RI 02912. Offers ancient Judaism (PhD); early Christianity (PhD); religion and critical thought (PhD); religion in the ancient Mediterranean (PhD); religion, culture, and comparison (PhD). *Degree requirements:* For doctorate, 2 foreign languages, thesis/dissertation. *Entrance requirements:* For doctorate, GRE General Test.

Bryn Athyn College of the New Church, Academy of the New Church Theological School, Bryn Athyn, PA 19009-0717. Offers divinity (M Div); religious studies (MA). Part-time programs available. Postbaccalaureate distance learning degree programs offered (minimal on-campus study). *Degree requirements:* For master's, thesis; for M Div, 3 foreign languages, thesis/dissertation. *Entrance requirements:* Additional exam requirements/recommendations for international students: Required—TOEFL.

California Institute of Integral Studies, School of Consciousness and Transformation, San Francisco, CA 94103. Offers creative inquiry/interdisciplinary arts (MFA); cultural anthropology and social transformation (MA); East-West psychology (MA, PhD); integrative health studies (MA); philosophy and religion (MA, PhD), including Asian and comparative studies, philosophy, cosmology, and consciousness, women's spirituality; social and cultural anthropology (PhD); transformative leadership (MA); transformative studies (PhD); writing and consciousness (MFA). Part-time and evening/weekend programs available. Postbaccalaureate distance learning degree programs offered (minimal on-campus study). *Students:* 455 full-time (315 women), 133 part-time (90 women); includes 47 Black or African American, non-Hispanic/Latino; 3 American Indian or Alaska Native, non-Hispanic/Latino; 21 Asian, non-Hispanic/Latino; 41 Hispanic/Latino, 40 international. Average age 37. 265 applicants, 91% accepted, 163 enrolled. In 2010, 64 master's, 22 doctorates awarded. Terminal master's awarded for partial completion of doctoral program. *Degree requirements:* For master's, thesis optional; for doctorate, comprehensive exam, thesis/dissertation, 1 foreign language (Asian comparative studies). *Entrance requirements:* For master's, minimum GPA of 3.0, letters of recommendation, writing sample; for doctorate, master's degree, minimum GPA of 3.0, letters of recommendation, writing sample. Additional exam requirements/recommendations for international students: Required—TOEFL. *Application deadline:* For fall admission, 2/1 priority date for domestic and international students; for spring admission, 10/15 priority date for domestic and international students. Applications are processed on a rolling basis. Application fee: $65. Electronic applications accepted. *Expenses:* Tuition: Full-time $15,660; part-time $870 per semester hour. Required fees: $95 per semester. *Financial support:* In 2010–11, 255 students received support; research assistantships, teaching assistantships, career-related internships or fieldwork, Federal Work-Study, scholarships/grants, and tuition waivers (partial) available. Support available to part-time students. Financial award application deadline: 4/15; financial award applicants required to submit FAFSA. *Faculty research:* Ecology and sustainablility, philosophy and religion, East-West psychology, integrative health, social and cultural anthropology, transformative leadership. *Application contact:* Allyson Werner, Associate Director of Admissions, 415-575-6155, Fax: 415-575-1268.

California State University, Long Beach, Graduate Studies, College of Liberal Arts, Department of Religious Studies, Long Beach, CA 90840. Offers MA. Part-time and evening/weekend programs available. *Faculty:* 5 full-time (1 woman). *Students:* 11 full-time (6 women), 13 part-time (8 women); includes 2 Asian, non-Hispanic/Latino; 7 Hispanic/Latino. Average age 34. 22 applicants, 59% accepted, 10 enrolled. In 2010, 8 master's awarded. *Entrance requirements:* Additional exam requirements/recommendations for international students: Required—TOEFL. *Application deadline:* For fall admission, 3/15 for domestic students, 7/1 for international students; for spring admission, 12/1 for international students. Applications are processed on a rolling basis. Application fee: $55. Electronic applications accepted. *Financial support:* Application deadline: 3/2. *Unit head:* Dr. Peter Lowentrout, Chair, 562-985-4906, Fax: 562-985-5540. *Application contact:* Dr. Carlos R. Piar, Graduate Advisor, 562-985-8727, Fax: 562-985-5540, E-mail: crpiar@csulb.edu.

Calvin Theological Seminary, Graduate and Professional Programs, Grand Rapids, MI 49546-4387. Offers Bible and theology (MA); divinity (M Div), including ancient near eastern languages and literature, contextual ministry, evangelism and teaching, history of Christianity, new church development, New Testament, Old Testament, pastoral care and leadership, preaching and worship, theological studies, youth and family ministries; educational ministry (MA); historical theology (PhD); missions and evangelism (MA); pastoral care (MA); philosophical and moral theology (PhD); systematic theology (PhD); theological studies (MTS); theology (Th M); worship (MA); youth and family ministries (MA). *Accreditation:* ACIPE; ATS. Part-time programs available. *Degree requirements:* For master's, thesis (for some programs); for doctorate, 4 foreign languages, comprehensive exam, thesis/dissertation; for M Div, 2 foreign languages. *Entrance requirements:* For doctorate, GRE General Test, Hebrew, Greek, and a modern foreign language. Additional exam requirements/recommendations for international students: Required—TOEFL (minimum score 550 paper-based; 213 computer-based), TWE (minimum score 4). Electronic applications accepted. *Faculty research:* Recent Trinity theory, Christian anthropology, Proverbs, reformed confessions, Paul's view of law.

Cardinal Stritch University, College of Arts and Sciences, Department of Religious Studies, Milwaukee, WI 53217-3985. Offers lay ministries (MA); ministry (MA); religious studies (MA). Part-time and evening/weekend programs available. *Degree requirements:* For master's, comprehensive exam, thesis, faculty recommendation, research project. *Entrance requirements:* For master's, interview, minimum GPA of 2.75.

The Catholic University of America, School of Arts and Sciences, Program in Early Christian Studies, Washington, DC 20064. Offers MA, PhD. Part-time programs available. *Faculty:* 1 full-time (0 women). *Students:* 3 full-time (1 woman), 6 part-time (2 women), 2 international. Average age 33. 14 applicants, 36% accepted, 3 enrolled. *Degree requirements:* For master's, one foreign language, comprehensive exam; for doctorate, 2 foreign languages, comprehensive exam, thesis/dissertation. *Entrance requirements:* For master's and doctorate, GRE General Test, statement of purpose, official copies of academic transcripts, three letters of recommendation. Additional exam requirements/recommendations for international students: Required—TOEFL (minimum score 580 paper-based; 237 computer-based). *Application deadline:* For fall admission, 8/1 priority date for domestic students, 7/15 for international students; for spring admission, 12/1 priority date for domestic students, 10/15 for international students. Applications are processed on a rolling basis. Application fee: $55. Electronic applications accepted. *Expenses:* Tuition: Full-time $33,580; part-time $1315 per credit hour. Required fees: $80; $40 per semester hour. One-time fee: $425. *Financial support:* Fellowships, research assistantships, teaching assistantships, Federal Work-Study, scholarships/grants, tuition waivers (full and partial), and unspecified assistantships available. Financial award application deadline: 2/1; financial award applicants required to submit FAFSA. *Faculty research:* Languages and literatures of the Christian Near East, systematic and fundamental theology, Greek and Latin patristics, early Christian poetry and hagiography, ancient and late antique philosophy. *Unit head:* Dr. Philip Rousseau, Director, 202-319-6217, Fax: 202-319-6609, E-mail: rousseau@cua.edu. *Application contact:* Andrew Woodall, Director of Graduate Admissions, 202-319-5057, Fax: 202-319-6533, E-mail: cua-admissions@cua.edu.

The Catholic University of America, School of Theology and Religious Studies, Washington, DC 20064. Offers M Div, STB, MA, MRE, D Min, PhD, STD, Certificate, STL, MSLS/MA. *Accreditation:* ATS (one or more programs are accredited). Part-time programs available. *Faculty:* 40 full-time (6 women), 10 part-time/adjunct (2 women). *Students:* 161 full-time (28 women), 235 part-time (61 women); includes 7 Black or African American, non-Hispanic/Latino; 1 American Indian or Alaska Native, non-Hispanic/Latino; 10 Asian, non-Hispanic/Latino; 11 Hispanic/Latino; 1 Native Hawaiian or other Pacific Islander, non-Hispanic/Latino, 69 international. Average age 36. 259 applicants, 64% accepted, 73 enrolled. In 2010, 7 first professional degrees, 29 master's, 29 doctorates awarded. *Degree requirements:* For master's, variable foreign language requirement, comprehensive exam, thesis (for some programs); for doctorate, variable foreign language requirement, comprehensive exam, thesis/dissertation. *Entrance requirements:* For first professional degree, master's, and doctorate, GRE General Test, statement of purpose, official copies of academic transcripts, three letters of recommendation. Additional exam requirements/recommendations for international students: Required—TOEFL (minimum score 580 paper-based; 237 computer-based). *Application deadline:* For fall admission, 8/1 priority date for domestic students, 7/15 for international students; for spring admission, 12/1 priority date for domestic students, 10/15 for international students. Applications are processed on a rolling basis. Application fee: $55. Electronic applications accepted. *Expenses:* Tuition: Full-time $33,580; part-time $1315 per credit hour. Required fees: $80; $40 per semester hour. One-time fee: $425. *Financial support:* Fellowships, research assistantships, teaching assistantships, Federal Work-Study, scholarships/grants, tuition waivers (full and partial), and unspecified assistantships available. Financial award application deadline: 2/1; financial award applicants required to submit FAFSA. *Faculty research:* Historical and systematic theology, religious education and catechetics, moral theology and ethics, Biblical studies, liturgical studies and sacramental theology. Total annual research expenditures: $66,740. *Unit head:* Msgr. Kevin W. Irwin, Dean, 202-319-5684, Fax: 202-319-5704, E-mail: irwin@cua.edu. *Application contact:* Andrew Woodall, Director of Graduate Admissions, 202-319-5057, Fax: 202-319-6533, E-mail: cua-admissions@cua.edu.

Chestnut Hill College, School of Graduate Studies, Department of Religious Studies and Philosophy, Philadelphia, PA 19118-2693. Offers holistic spirituality (MA); holistic spirituality and healthcare (MA); holistic spirituality and spiritual direction (MA); holistic spirituality/health care (CAS); spiritual direction (CAS); spirituality (CAS); supervision of spiritual directors (CAS). Part-time and evening/weekend programs available. *Faculty:* 6 full-time (5 women), 1 (woman) part-time/adjunct. *Students:* 1 (woman) full-time, 29 part-time (25 women); includes 1 minority (Black or African American, non-Hispanic/Latino). Average age 51. 4 applicants, 75% accepted, 3 enrolled. In 2010, 4 master's awarded. *Degree requirements:* For master's, thesis optional, practicum (spiritual direction and healthcare tracks). *Entrance requirements:* For master's, MAT or GRE, writing sample. Additional exam requirements/recommendations for international students: Required—TOEFL (minimum score 500 paper-based; 213 computer-based). *Application deadline:* For fall admission, 7/17 priority date for domestic students, 7/15 priority date for international students; for spring admission, 12/15 priority date for domestic and international students. Applications are processed on a rolling basis. Application fee: $55. *Expenses:* Tuition: Part-time $560 per credit hour. One-time fee: $55. Tuition and fees vary according to degree level and program. *Faculty research:* Interfaith spiritual direction, supervisory issues for spiritual directors, ecclesial responsibility of reconciliation, globalization of the Magdalene laundry system, ethical issues at the end of life. *Unit head:* Dr. Marie Conn, Department Chair, 215-248-7044, Fax: 215-248-7155, E-mail: mconn@chc.edu. *Application contact:* Amy Boorse, Administrative Assistant, School of Graduate Studies Office, 215-248-7170, Fax: 215-248-7161, E-mail: gradadmissions@chc.edu.

Chicago Theological Seminary, Graduate and Professional Programs, Chicago, IL 60637-1507. Offers preaching (D Min); religion and health (D Min); religious studies (MA); spirituality and spiritual direction (D Min); theology (M Div); theology, ethics and the human sciences (PhD); M Div/MSW. *Accreditation:* ACIPE; ATS. Part-time programs available. *Degree requirements:* For master's, thesis; for doctorate, 2 foreign languages, comprehensive exam, thesis/dissertation; for M Div, thesis/dissertation. *Entrance requirements:* For doctorate, GRE General Test. Additional exam requirements/recommendations for international students: Required—TOEFL (minimum score 217 computer-based). *Faculty research:* Bible, culture and hermeneutics, theology, gender and sexuality, black faith and life, spirituality and psychology, practical theology.

Christian Brothers University, School of Arts, Memphis, TN 38104-5581. Offers Catholic studies (MACS); educational leadership (MSEL); teacher-leadership (M Ed); teaching (MAT). Part-time and evening/weekend programs available. *Faculty:* 6 full-time (3 women), 13 part-time/adjunct (11 women). *Students:* 51 full-time (42 women), 154 part-time (119 women); includes 77 minority (67 Black or African American, non-Hispanic/Latino; 3 Asian, non-Hispanic/Latino; 4 Hispanic/Latino; 1 Native Hawaiian or other Pacific Islander, non-Hispanic/Latino; 2 Two or more races, non-Hispanic/Latino), 3 international. Average age 33. In 2010, 89 master's awarded. *Entrance requirements:* For master's, GRE, GMAT, PRAXIS II. *Application deadline:* Applications are processed on a rolling basis. Application fee: $35. *Expenses:* Contact institution. *Financial support:* Institutionally sponsored loans available. Support available to part-time students. *Unit head:* Dr. Paul A. Haught, Dean, 901-321-3579, Fax: 901-321-4340, E-mail: phaught@cbu.edu. *Application contact:* Dr. Talana L. Vogel, Director, 901-321-4101, Fax: 901-321-3408, E-mail: tvogel@cbu.edu.

Religion

Christian Theological Seminary, Graduate and Professional Programs, Indianapolis, IN 46208-3301. Offers educational and arts ministries (MA); marriage and family therapy (MA); pastoral care and counseling (D Min); psychotherapy and faith (MA); theological studies (MTS); theology (M Div). *Accreditation:* AAMFT/COAMFTE (one or more programs are accredited); ACIPE; ATS. Part-time programs available. Terminal master's awarded for partial completion of doctoral program. *Degree requirements:* For master's, comprehensive exam (for some programs), thesis (for some programs); for doctorate, comprehensive exam, thesis/dissertation; for M Div, comprehensive exam, thesis/dissertation (for some programs), missionary and cross-cultural experience. *Entrance requirements:* For master's, GRE General Test, MAT; for doctorate, M Div. Electronic applications accepted. *Faculty research:* Faith formation, peer learning post graduation.

Cincinnati Christian University, Graduate School, Cincinnati, OH 45204-3200. Offers biblical studies (MA); church history (MA); counseling (MAC); divinity (M Div); ministry (M Min); practical ministries (MA); theological studies (MA). *Accreditation:* ATS. Part-time programs available. *Degree requirements:* For master's, thesis (for some programs); for M Div, 2 foreign languages, oral exam. *Entrance requirements:* For master's, GRE General Test. Additional exam requirements/recommendations for international students: Required—TOEFL. Electronic applications accepted.

Claremont Graduate University, Graduate Programs, School of Religion, Claremont, CA 91711-6160. Offers Hebrew Bible (MA, PhD); history of Christianity and religions of North America (MA, PhD); New Testament (MA, PhD); philosophy of religion and theology (MA, PhD); theology, ethics and culture (MA, PhD); women's studies in religion (MA, PhD); MA/PhD; MBA/PhD. Part-time programs available. *Faculty:* 6 full-time (2 women), 2 part-time/adjunct (0 women). *Students:* 218 full-time (87 women), 10 part-time (4 women); includes 13 Black or African American, non-Hispanic/Latino; 11 Asian, non-Hispanic/Latino; 12 Hispanic/Latino; 1 Two or more races, non-Hispanic/Latino, 29 international. Average age 37. In 2010, 13 master's, 12 doctorates awarded. Terminal master's awarded for partial completion of doctoral program. *Entrance requirements:* For master's and doctorate, GRE General Test. Additional exam requirements/recommendations for international students: Required—TOEFL (minimum score 550 paper-based; 213 computer-based; 80 iBT). *Application deadline:* For fall admission, 2/1 priority date for domestic students. Applications are processed on a rolling basis. Application fee: $60. Electronic applications accepted. *Expenses:* Tuition: Full-time $35,748; part-time $1554 per unit. Required fees: $215 per semester. *Financial support:* Fellowships, research assistantships, teaching assistantships, Federal Work-Study, institutionally sponsored loans, and scholarships/grants available. Support available to part-time students. Financial award application deadline: 2/15; financial award applicants required to submit FAFSA. *Unit head:* Anselm Min, Dean, 909-607-3214, Fax: 909-621-9587, E-mail: anselm.min@cgu.edu. *Application contact:* Brent Smith, Recruiter, 909-607-2653, Fax: 909-607-9587, E-mail: brent.smith@cgu.edu.

Claremont School of Theology, Graduate and Professional Programs, Program in Religion, Claremont, CA 91711-3199. Offers practical theology (PhD), including religious education, spiritual care and counseling; religion (PhD), including Hebrew Bible, New Testament and Christian origins, process studies, religion, ethics, and society; religion and theology (MA); religious education (MARE). *Accreditation:* ACIPE; ATS. Terminal master's awarded for partial completion of doctoral program. *Degree requirements:* For master's, thesis; for doctorate, 2 foreign languages, thesis/dissertation. *Entrance requirements:* For doctorate, GRE General Test. Additional exam requirements/recommendations for international students: Required—TOEFL (minimum score 250 computer-based). Electronic applications accepted.

College of the Humanities and Sciences, Harrison Middleton University, Graduate Program, Tempe, AZ 85282. Offers education (MA, Ed D); humanities (MA); imaginative literature (MA); interdisciplinary studies (DA); jurisprudence (MA); natural science (MA); philosophy and religion (MA); social science (MA). Part-time and evening/weekend programs available. Postbaccalaureate distance learning degree programs offered (no on-campus study). *Faculty:* 17 full-time (7 women), 14 part-time/adjunct (6 women). *Students:* 52 full-time (20 women). In 2010, 4 master's awarded. *Degree requirements:* For master's and doctorate, capstone project. *Entrance requirements:* For doctorate, 3 academic letters of reference, interview. *Application deadline:* Applications are processed on a rolling basis. Application fee: $50. Electronic applications accepted. *Expenses:* Tuition: Part-time $300 per credit hour. One-time fee: $350 part-time. *Faculty research:* Japanese animation, educational leadership, war art, John Muir's wilderness. *Application contact:* Deborah Deacon, Dean of Graduate Studies, 877-248-6724, Fax: 800-762-1622, E-mail: ddeacon@hmu.edu.

Columbia University, Graduate School of Arts and Sciences, Division of Humanities, Department of Religion, New York, NY 10027. Offers M Phil, MA, PhD. *Degree requirements:* For master's, 2 foreign languages, thesis, oral and written exams; for doctorate, variable foreign language requirement, thesis/dissertation. *Entrance requirements:* For master's and doctorate, GRE General Test. Additional exam requirements/recommendations for international students: Required—TOEFL.

Concordia University, School of Graduate Studies, Faculty of Arts and Science, Department of Religion, Program in History and Philosophy of Religion, Montréal, QC H3G 1M8, Canada. Offers MA. *Degree requirements:* For master's, comprehensive exam, thesis optional. *Entrance requirements:* For master's, honors degree in religion or equivalent. *Faculty research:* Comparative ethics, social theory and political society, Judaic studies.

Concordia University, School of Graduate Studies, Faculty of Arts and Science, Department of Religion, Program in Religion, Montréal, QC H3G 1M8, Canada. Offers PhD. Program offered jointly with Université du Québec à Montréal. *Degree requirements:* For doctorate, one foreign language, comprehensive exam, thesis/dissertation.

Concordia University, School of Theology, Irvine, CA 92612-3299. Offers Christian leadership (MA); research in theology (MA); theology and culture (MA). Part-time and evening/weekend programs available. *Faculty:* 8 full-time (1 woman), 2 part-time/adjunct (0 women). *Students:* 30 full-time (3 women), 7 part-time (3 women); includes 5 minority (1 Black or African American, non-Hispanic/Latino; 1 Asian, non-Hispanic/Latino; 3 Hispanic/Latino), 4 international. Average age 34. 11 applicants, 55% accepted, 5 enrolled. In 2010, 2 master's awarded. *Degree requirements:* For master's, project/thesis or vicarage. *Entrance requirements:* For master's, official college transcript(s), statement of intent, 2 references, graduate health form, interview. Additional exam requirements/recommendations for international students: Required—TOEFL. *Application deadline:* For fall admission, 7/1 priority date for domestic students, 6/1 for international students; for spring admission, 11/30 priority date for domestic students, 10/1 for international students. Applications are processed on a rolling basis. Application fee: $50 ($125 for international students). Electronic applications accepted. *Expenses:* Contact institution. *Financial support:* Scholarships/grants and unspecified assistantships available. Financial award applicants required to submit FAFSA. *Unit head:* Rev. Dr. James Bachman, Dean of Graduate Studies, 949-214-3387, E-mail: james.bachman@cui.edu. *Application contact:* Carrie Donohoe, Christ College Program Coordinator, 949-214-3389, E-mail: carrie.donohoe@cui.edu.

Concordia University Chicago, College of Graduate and Innovative Programs, Program in Religion, River Forest, IL 60305-1499. Offers MA. Part-time and evening/weekend programs available. *Degree requirements:* For master's, comprehensive exam, thesis. *Entrance requirements:* For master's, minimum GPA of 2.9. Additional exam requirements/recommendations for international students: Required—TOEFL (minimum score 550 paper-based; 195 computer-based). Electronic applications accepted. *Faculty research:* Dead Sea Scrolls, cultural construction of gender in early modern Europe, Luther, Luther's theology of the cross, gospels of Mark and John.

Concordia University College of Alberta, Program in Biblical and Christian Studies, Edmonton, AB T5B 4E4, Canada. Offers MA.

Cornell University, Graduate School, Graduate Fields of Arts and Sciences, Field of Asian Religions, Ithaca, NY 14853-0001. Offers PhD. *Faculty:* 8 full-time (4 women). *Students:* 7 full-time (3 women), 1 international. Average age 30. 18 applicants, 11% accepted, 2 enrolled. In 2010, 1 doctorate awarded. *Degree requirements:* For doctorate, comprehensive exam, thesis/dissertation. *Entrance requirements:* For doctorate, GRE General Test, academic writing sample, 3 letters of recommendation. Additional exam requirements/recommendations for international students: Required—TOEFL (minimum score 600 paper-based; 250 computer-based; 77 iBT). *Application deadline:* For fall admission, 1/15 for domestic students. Application fee: $80. Electronic applications accepted. *Expenses:* Tuition: Full-time $29,500. Required fees: $76. Tuition and fees vary according to degree level and program. *Financial support:* In 2010–11, 2 fellowships with full tuition reimbursements, 4 teaching assistantships with full tuition reimbursements were awarded; research assistantships with full tuition reimbursements, institutionally sponsored loans, scholarships/grants, health care benefits, and unspecified assistantships also available. *Unit head:* Director of Graduate Studies, 607-255-9099, Fax: 607-255-1345. *Application contact:* Graduate Field Assistant, 607-255-9099, Fax: 607-255-1345, E-mail: asian-religions@cornell.edu.

Denver Seminary, Graduate and Professional Programs, Littleton, CO 80120. Offers apologetics (Certificate); biblical studies (MA); Christian formation and soul care (MA, Certificate); Christian studies (MA, Certificate); church and parachurch leadership (D Min); counseling licensure (MA); counseling ministry (MA); intercultural ministry (Certificate); leadership (MA, Certificate); marriage and family counseling (D Min); pastoral ministry (D Min); philosophy of religion (MA); spiritual guidance (Certificate); theology (M Div, Certificate); worship (Certificate); youth and family ministry (MA). *Accreditation:* ACA; ACIPE; ATS (one or more programs are accredited). Part-time and evening/weekend programs available. Postbaccalaureate distance learning degree programs offered. *Degree requirements:* For master's, 2 foreign languages, thesis (for some programs); for doctorate, 2 foreign languages, thesis/dissertation; for M Div, 2 foreign languages. *Entrance requirements:* For M Div, minimum undergraduate GPA of 2.5; for master's, minimum undergraduate GPA of 3.0; for doctorate, M Div, 3 years of ministry experience. Additional exam requirements/recommendations for international students: Required—TOEFL (minimum score 575 paper-based; 233 computer-based; 90 iBT). Electronic applications accepted.

Duke University, Graduate School, Department of Religion, Durham, NC 27708. Offers MA, PhD, JD/MA. Part-time programs available. *Faculty:* 45 full-time. *Students:* 81 full-time (33 women); includes 4 Black or African American, non-Hispanic/Latino; 8 Asian, non-Hispanic/Latino; 1 Hispanic/Latino, 12 international. 215 applicants, 20% accepted, 23 enrolled. In 2010, 15 master's, 13 doctorates awarded. Terminal master's awarded for partial completion of doctoral program. *Degree requirements:* For master's, one foreign language, thesis or alternative; for doctorate, 2 foreign languages, thesis/dissertation. *Entrance requirements:* For master's and doctorate, GRE General Test. Additional exam requirements/recommendations for international students: Required—TOEFL (minimum score 550 paper-based; 213 computer-based; 83 iBT), IELTS (minimum score 7). *Application deadline:* For fall admission, 12/8 priority date for domestic and international students. Application fee: $75. Electronic applications accepted. *Financial support:* Fellowships, research assistantships, teaching assistantships, Federal Work-Study available. Financial award application deadline: 12/8; financial award applicants required to submit FAFSA. *Unit head:* Grant Wacker, Director of Graduate Studies, 919-660-3512, Fax: 919-660-3530, E-mail: lisa.bradick@duke.edu. *Application contact:* Elizabeth Hutton, Director of Admissions, 919-684-3913, Fax: 919-684-2277, E-mail: elizabeth.hutton@duke.edu.

Earlham School of Religion, Graduate Programs, Richmond, IN 47374. Offers religion (MA); theology (M Div, M Min). *Accreditation:* ACIPE; ATS. Part-time programs available. Postbaccalaureate distance learning degree programs offered (minimal on-campus study). *Faculty:* 9 full-time (4 women), 8 part-time/adjunct (5 women). *Students:* 111 full-time (71 women), 38 part-time (21 women); includes 2 Black or African American, non-Hispanic/Latino; 1 American Indian or Alaska Native, non-Hispanic/Latino; 1 Asian, non-Hispanic/Latino; 3 Hispanic/Latino, 6 international. Average age 45. 37 applicants, 97% accepted, 34 enrolled. In 2010, 15 first professional degrees, 2 master's awarded. *Degree requirements:* For master's, one foreign language, comprehensive exam, thesis; for M Div, internship. *Entrance requirements:* For M Div and master's, 3 references. Additional exam requirements/recommendations for international students: Required—TOEFL (minimum score 550 paper-based; 218 computer-based; 82 iBT). *Application deadline:* For fall admission, 7/15 priority date for domestic students; for winter admission, 12/15 priority date for domestic students. Applications are processed on a rolling basis. Application fee: $35. Electronic applications accepted. *Financial support:* Scholarships/grants and tuition waivers (full and partial) available. Financial award application deadline: 4/15; financial award applicants required to submit FAFSA. *Faculty research:* Digitizing Quaker texts, vital Quaker ministry, research in Quaker Studies and other seminary areas. *Unit head:* Jay W. Marshall, Dean, 800-432-1377, Fax: 765-983-1688, E-mail: marshja@earlham.edu. *Application contact:* Valerie K. Hurwitz, Director of Recruitment and Admissions, 800-432-1377, Fax: 765-983-1688, E-mail: hurwiva@earlham.edu.

Eastern Mennonite University, Eastern Mennonite Seminary, Harrisonburg, VA 22802-2462. Offers church leadership (MA); divinity (M Div); ministry studies (Certificate); online theological studies (Certificate); religion (MA); theological studies (Certificate). *Accreditation:* ATS. Part-time programs available. *Degree requirements:* For master's, thesis (for some programs); for M Div, thesis/dissertation (for some programs), supervised field education. *Entrance requirements:* For M Div and master's, minimum GPA of 2.5. Additional exam requirements/recommendations for international students: Required—TOEFL (minimum score 550 paper-based; 213 computer-based). *Expenses:* Contact institution. *Faculty research:* Spiritual direction and culture of call, leadership coaching: an approach to leadership in a culture of call, clarity of call in the probationary process for United Methodist clergy in Virginia, EMS women's experiences of culture of call efforts, practices of excellent and fruitful Mennonite pastoral ministry.

Edgewood College, Program in Religious Studies, Madison, WI 53711-1997. Offers MA. Part-time and evening/weekend programs available. In 2010, 1 master's awarded. *Entrance requirements:* For master's, minimum GPA of 2.75, 2 letters of reference. Additional exam requirements/recommendations for international students: Required—TOEFL (minimum score 213 computer-based). *Application deadline:* For fall admission, 8/24 for domestic students, 8/1 for international students; for spring admission, 1/10 for domestic students, 10/1 for international students. Applications are processed on a rolling basis. Application fee: $25. Electronic applications accepted. *Expenses:* Tuition: Part-time $719 per credit hour. *Financial support:* Career-related internships or fieldwork, institutionally sponsored loans, scholarships/grants, and tuition waivers (partial) available. *Faculty research:* Interpretation theory and New Testament, women and religion, theology and literature, Hebrew poetry. *Unit head:* Dr. John Leonard, Chair, 608-663-2823, Fax: 608-663-3291, E-mail: jleonard@edgewood.edu. *Application contact:* Joann Eastman, Admissions Counselor, 608-663-3250, Fax: 608-663-2214, E-mail: gps@edgewood.edu.

Elms College, Religious Studies Department, Chicopee, MA 01013-2839. Offers MAAT. Part-time and evening/weekend programs available. *Degree requirements:* For master's, thesis. *Entrance requirements:* For master's, minimum GPA of 3.0. Additional exam requirements/recommendations for international students: Required—TOEFL.

Emmanuel Christian Seminary, Graduate and Professional Programs, Johnson City, TN 37601-9438. Offers Christian care and counseling (M Div); Christian doctrine (MAR); Christian education (M Div); Christian ministry (M Div); church history (MAR); divinity (M Div); ministry (D Min); New Testament (MAR); Old Testament (MAR); urban ministry (M Div); world missions (M Div). *Accreditation:* ACIPE; ATS. Part-time programs available. *Faculty:* 9 full-time (2 women), 9 part-time/adjunct (1 woman). *Students:* 90 full-time (27 women), 57 part-time (10 women); includes 2 Black or African American, non-Hispanic/Latino; 3 Hispanic/Latino, 17 international. Average age 27. 30 applicants, 97% accepted, 22 enrolled. In 2010, 17 first professional degrees, 1 master's, 1 doctorate awarded. *Degree requirements:* For master's, 2 foreign languages, thesis or alternative, portfolio; for doctorate, thesis/dissertation; for M Div, 2 foreign languages, thesis/dissertation or alternative, portfolio. *Entrance requirements:* For M Div and master's, bachelor's degree from accredited institution; for doctorate, Minnesota Multiphasic Personality Inventory, M Div or equivalent. Additional exam requirements/recommendations for international students: Required—TOEFL (minimum score 80 computer-based). *Application deadline:* For fall admission, 8/1 for domestic and international students; for spring admission, 1/20 for domestic and international students. Applications are processed on a rolling basis. Application fee: $25. *Expenses:* Tuition: Full-time $11,700; part-time $390 per credit hour. Required fees: $162.50 per semester. One-time fee: $240. Tuition and fees vary according to reciprocity agreements. *Financial support:* In 2010–11, 136 students received support; teaching assistantships with partial tuition reimbursements available, career-related internships or fieldwork, scholarships/grants, and tuition waivers (partial) available. Support available to part-time students. Financial award application deadline: 3/1; financial award applicants required to submit FAFSA. *Faculty research:* Theology of Old Testament prophets, spiritual formation for Christian leaders, history of African churches and religions, social world of early Christianity, lay pastoral counseling, ANE epigraphy. Total annual research expenditures: $12,000. *Unit head:* Dr. Jack Holland, Dean and Professor of Christian Care and Counseling, 423-461-1524, Fax: 423-926-6198, E-mail: jholland@ecs.edu. *Application contact:* Erin Layton, Director of Admissions, 423-461-1535, Fax: 423-926-6198, E-mail: elayton@ecs.edu.

Emory University, Laney Graduate School, Department of Comparative Literature, Atlanta, GA 30322-1100. Offers comparative literature (PhD); English (Certificate); French (Certificate); Middle Eastern studies (PhD); philosophy (Certificate); psychoanalytic studies (PhD); religion (PhD); Spanish (Certificate); women studies (Certificate). *Degree requirements:* For doctorate, 2 foreign languages, comprehensive exam, thesis/dissertation. *Entrance requirements:* For doctorate, GRE General Test, minimum GPA of 3.0. Additional exam requirements/recommendations for international students: Required—TOEFL. Electronic applications accepted. *Expenses:* Tuition: Full-time $33,800. Required fees: $1300. *Faculty research:* Literary theory, psychoanalysis trauma and testimony, literature and religion, literature and technology, literature and philosophy, politics and global culture, literature and aesthetics.

Emory University, Laney Graduate School, Division of Religion, Atlanta, GA 30322-1100. Offers PhD. *Degree requirements:* For doctorate, 2 foreign languages, comprehensive exam, thesis/dissertation. *Entrance requirements:* For doctorate, GRE General Test, minimum GPA of 3.0. Additional exam requirements/recommendations for international students: Required—TOEFL. Electronic applications accepted. *Expenses:* Tuition: Full-time $33,800. Required fees: $1300. *Faculty research:* Systematic and historical theology, biblical studies.

Faith Baptist Bible College and Theological Seminary, Graduate Program, Ankeny, IA 50023. Offers biblical studies (MA); pastoral studies (M Div); pastoral training (MA); religion (MA); theological studies (MA). Part-time programs available. *Faculty:* 4 full-time (0 women), 4 part-time/adjunct (0 women). *Students:* 14 full-time (1 woman), 25 part-time (0 women); includes 3 Asian, non-Hispanic/Latino, 1 international. Average age 29. In 2010, 5 first professional degrees, 14 master's awarded. *Degree requirements:* For master's, thesis or alternative; for M Div, 2 foreign languages. *Entrance requirements:* Additional exam requirements/recommendations for international students: Required—TOEFL (minimum score 550 paper-based; 197 computer-based). *Application deadline:* For fall admission, 8/1 priority date for domestic students, 8/1 for international students; for spring admission, 12/15 for domestic and international students. Applications are processed on a rolling basis. Application fee: $25. *Financial support:* Career-related internships or fieldwork and scholarships/grants available. Support available to part-time students. Financial award application deadline: 3/1; financial award applicants required to submit FAFSA. *Faculty research:* Baptist theology, American church history. *Unit head:* Dr. Ernest Schmidt, Dean of Seminary, 515-964-0601, E-mail: schmidte@faith.edu. *Application contact:* Carrie Johnson, Admissions Administrative Assistant, 888-FAITH4U, Fax: 515-964-1638, E-mail: admissions@faith.edu.

Florida International University, College of Arts and Sciences, Department of Religious Studies, Miami, FL 33199. Offers MA. Part-time and evening/weekend programs available. *Faculty:* 12 full-time (8 women), 10 part-time/adjunct (2 women). *Students:* 16 full-time (9 women), 9 part-time (4 women); includes 1 Black or African American, non-Hispanic/Latino; 8 Hispanic/Latino, 3 international. Average age 28. 23 applicants, 43% accepted, 10 enrolled. In 2010, 10 master's awarded. *Degree requirements:* For master's, thesis or alternative. *Entrance requirements:* For master's, minimum GPA of 3.0, 2 letters of recommendation. Additional exam requirements/recommendations for international students: Required—TOEFL (minimum score 550 paper-based; 80 iBT). *Application deadline:* For fall admission, 2/15 for domestic and international students; for spring admission, 10/1 for domestic students, 9/1 for international students. Application fee: $30. Electronic applications accepted. *Financial support:* Institutionally sponsored loans and scholarships/grants available. Financial award application deadline: 3/1; financial award applicants required to submit FAFSA. *Unit head:* Dr. Christine Gudorf, Chair, 305-348-2186, Fax: 305-348-1879, E-mail: religion@fiu.edu. *Application contact:* Dr. Oren Stier, Graduate Program Director, 305-348-2186, Fax: 305-348-1879, E-mail: religion@fiu.edu.

Florida State University, The Graduate School, College of Arts and Sciences, Department of Religion, Tallahassee, FL 32306-1520. Offers humanities (PhD), including religion; religion (MA, PhD). *Faculty:* 18 full-time (6 women), 4 part-time/adjunct (2 women). *Students:* 57 full-time (26 women), 5 part-time (2 women); includes 2 Black or African American, non-Hispanic/Latino; 1 American Indian or Alaska Native, non-Hispanic/Latino; 1 Asian, non-Hispanic/Latino; 2 Hispanic/Latino. Average age 26. 78 applicants, 27% accepted, 15 enrolled. In 2010, 7 master's, 2 doctorates awarded. Terminal master's awarded for partial completion of doctoral program. *Degree requirements:* For master's, one foreign language, comprehensive exam (for some programs), thesis (for some programs); for doctorate, 2 foreign languages, thesis/dissertation. *Entrance requirements:* For master's, GRE General Test, minimum GPA of 3.0; for doctorate, GRE General Test, MA in religion. Additional exam requirements/recommendations for international students: Required—TOEFL. *Application deadline:* For fall admission, 1/15 for domestic students, 1/5 for international students. Application fee: $30. Electronic applications accepted. *Expenses:* Tuition, state resident: full-time $8238.24. *Financial support:* In 2010–11, 55 students received support, including 4 fellowships with partial tuition reimbursements available (averaging $8,650 per year), 20 research assistantships with partial tuition reimbursements available (averaging $8,100 per year), 35 teaching assistantships with partial tuition reimbursements available (averaging $10,165 per year); institutionally sponsored loans and unspecified assistantships also available. Financial award application deadline: 3/15; financial award applicants required to submit FAFSA. *Faculty research:* American religious history, comparative religious ethics, religions of western antiquity, Asian religions and culture, method and theory. *Unit head:* Dr. John Corrigan, Chair, 850-644-1020, Fax: 850-644-7225, E-mail: john.corrigan@fsu.edu. *Application contact:* Dr. Bryan Cuevas, Director of Graduate Studies, 850-644-1020, Fax: 850-644-7225, E-mail: bcuevas@fsu.edu.

Fordham University, Graduate School of Religion and Religious Education, New York, NY 10458. Offers pastoral counseling and spiritual care (MA); pastoral ministry/spirituality/pastoral counseling (D Min); religion and religious education (MA); religious education (MS, PhD, PD); spiritual direction (Certificate). Part-time programs available. Terminal master's awarded for partial completion of doctoral program. *Degree requirements:* For master's, research paper; for doctorate, comprehensive exam, thesis/dissertation. *Entrance requirements:* For doctorate, MAT. Electronic applications accepted. *Expenses:* Contact institution. *Faculty research:* Spirituality and spiritual direction, pastoral care and counseling, adult family and community, growth and young adult.

Gardner-Webb University, Graduate School, Department of Religious Studies and Philosophy, Boiling Springs, NC 28017. Offers religion (MA). *Expenses:* Tuition: Part-time $325 per credit hour.

General Theological Seminary, Graduate and Professional Programs, New York, NY 10011-4977. Offers Anglican studies (STM, Th D, Certificate); ascetical theology (Certificate); biblical studies (Certificate); congregational development (Certificate); divinity (M Div); historical and theological studies (Certificate); spiritual direction (MASD, STM, Certificate); theology (MA). *Accreditation:* ACIPE; ATS. Part-time and evening/weekend programs available. Terminal master's awarded for partial completion of doctoral program. *Degree requirements:* For master's, thesis; for doctorate, 2 foreign languages, thesis/dissertation. *Entrance requirements:* For M Div, GRE General Test, bishop's endorsement; for master's, GRE General Test; for doctorate, GRE, M Div or MA. Additional exam requirements/recommendations for international students: Required—TOEFL. *Faculty research:* Liturgy, New Testament, ethics, history, ecumenical relations.

Georgetown University, Graduate School of Arts and Sciences, School of Continuing Studies, Washington, DC 20057. Offers American studies (MALS); Catholic studies (MALS); classical civilizations (MALS); disability studies (MPS); ethics and the professions (MALS); human resources management (MPS); humanities (MALS); individualized study (MALS); international affairs (MALS); Islam and Muslim-Christian relations (MALS); journalism (MPS); liberal studies (DLS); literature and society (MALS); medieval and early modern European studies (MALS); public relations and corporate communications (MPS); real estate (MPS); religious studies (MALS); social and public policy (MALS); sports industry management (MPS); the theory and practice of American democracy (MALS); visual culture (MALS). *Entrance requirements:* Additional exam requirements/recommendations for international students: Required—TOEFL.

The George Washington University, Columbian College of Arts and Sciences, Department of Religion, Washington, DC 20052. Offers Hinduism and Islam (MA). Part-time and evening/weekend programs available. *Faculty:* 7 full-time (3 women), 7 part-time/adjunct (3 women). *Students:* 1 (woman) full-time, 1 part-time (0 women); includes 1 Asian, non-Hispanic/Latino, 1 international. Average age 28. 7 applicants, 57% accepted, 0 enrolled. In 2010, 2 master's awarded. *Degree requirements:* For master's, one foreign language, comprehensive exam, thesis. *Entrance requirements:* For master's, GRE General Test, interview, minimum GPA of 3.0. Additional exam requirements/recommendations for international students: Required—TOEFL (minimum score 550 paper-based; 213 computer-based; 80 iBT). *Application deadline:* For fall admission, 4/1 priority date for domestic students, 1/15 priority date for international students; for spring admission, 10/1 priority date for domestic students, 9/1 priority date for international students. Applications are processed on a rolling basis. Application fee: $75. Electronic applications accepted. *Financial support:* In 2010–11, 1 student received support. Federal Work-Study and tuition waivers available. *Unit head:* Dr. Alfred Hiltebeitel, Chair, 202-994-1674, Fax: 202-994-9379, E-mail: religion@gwu.edu. *Application contact:* Information Contact, 202-994-6325, Fax: 202-994-9379, E-mail: religion@gwu.edu.

Georgia State University, College of Arts and Sciences, Department of Religious Studies, Atlanta, GA 30302-4089. Offers MA. Part-time programs available. *Degree requirements:* For master's, thesis optional. *Entrance requirements:* For master's, GRE, 3 letters of recommendation, writing sample. Electronic applications accepted. *Faculty research:* Comparative religions; history of religions; religious ethics; comparative religious ritual; Islam, Judaism, and the Middle East.

Gonzaga University, College of Arts and Sciences, Department of Religious Studies, Spokane, WA 99258. Offers pastoral ministry (MA); religious studies (MA); spirituality (MA). *Degree requirements:* For master's, comprehensive exam. *Entrance requirements:* For master's, GRE General Test or MAT, minimum GPA of 3.0. Additional exam requirements/recommendations for international students: Required—TOEFL.

Gordon-Conwell Theological Seminary, Graduate and Professional Programs, South Hamilton, MA 01982. Offers Biblical languages (MABL); church history (MACH); counseling (MACO); ministry (D Min); missions/evangelism (MAME); New Testament (MANT); Old Testament (MAOT); religion (MAR); theology (M Div, MATH, Th M, Th D). *Accreditation:* ACIPE; ATS (one or more programs are accredited). Part-time and evening/weekend programs available. *Degree requirements:* For master's, one foreign language, thesis optional; for doctorate, 2 foreign languages, thesis/dissertation; for M Div, 2 foreign languages. *Entrance requirements:* For M Div and master's, minimum GPA of 2.5; for doctorate, minimum GPA of 3.0.

Graceland University, Community of Christ Seminary, Independence, MO 64050. Offers Christian ministry (MACM); religion (MAR). Part-time programs available. Postbaccalaureate distance learning degree programs offered (minimal on-campus study). *Faculty:* 2 full-time (1 woman), 9 part-time/adjunct (3 women). *Students:* 4 full-time (all women), 13 part-time (8 women); includes 1 Black or African American, non-Hispanic/Latino, 1 international. Average age 41. 15 applicants, 80% accepted, 7 enrolled. In 2010, 6 master's awarded. *Degree requirements:* For master's, thesis optional, portfolio or thesis (MAR), practicum (MACM). *Entrance requirements:* For master's, minimum cumulative GPA of 3.0. Additional exam requirements/recommendations for international students: Required—TOEFL. *Application deadline:* For fall admission, 8/15 priority date for domestic students; for winter admission, 10/15 priority date for domestic students; for spring admission, 4/15 priority date for domestic students. Applications are processed on a rolling basis. Application fee: $50. *Expenses:* Contact institution. *Financial support:* Scholarships/grants available. Financial award application deadline: 12/15; financial award applicants required to submit FAFSA. *Faculty research:* Theology, scripture. *Unit head:* Dr. Don H. Compier, Dean, 800-833-0524 Ext. 4900, Fax: 816-833-2990, E-mail: dcompier@graceland.edu. *Application contact:* Judy K. Luffman, Executive Assistant, 816-833-0524 Ext. 4508, Fax: 816-833-2990, E-mail: luffman@graceland.edu.

Graduate Theological Union, Graduate Programs, Berkeley, CA 94709-1212. Offers art and religion (MA, PhD, Th D); biblical languages (MA); biblical studies (MA); Biblical studies (PhD, Th D); Buddhist studies (MA); Christian spirituality (MA, PhD, Th D); cultural and historical studies of religions (MA, PhD, Th D); ethics and social theory (PhD, Th D); history (MA, PhD, Th D); homiletics (MA, PhD, Th D); interdisciplinary studies (PhD, Th D); Jewish studies (MA, PhD, Th D, Certificate); liturgical studies (MA, PhD, Th D); Near Eastern religions (PhD, Th D); Orthodox Christian studies (MA); religion and psychology (MA, PhD, Th D); religion and society/ethics and social theory (MA); systematic and philosophical theology (MA, PhD, Th D). PhD programs in Jewish studies and Near Eastern religions offered jointly with University of California, Berkeley. *Accreditation:* ATS. Terminal master's awarded for partial completion of doctoral program. *Degree requirements:* For master's, one foreign language, thesis; for doctorate, one foreign language, comprehensive exam, thesis/dissertation. *Entrance requirements:* For master's, GRE General Test; for doctorate, GRE General Test, MA or M Div. Additional exam requirements/recommendations for international students: Required—TOEFL. Electronic applications accepted.

Grand Rapids Theological Seminary of Cornerstone University, Graduate Programs, Grand Rapids, MI 49525-5897. Offers biblical counseling (MA); Biblical counseling (M Div); chaplaincy (M Div); Christian education (M Div, MA); intercultural studies (M Div, MA); New Testament (MA, Th M); Old Testament (MA, Th M); pastoral studies (M Div); systematic theology (MA); theology (Th M). *Accreditation:* ATS. Part-time programs available. Postbaccalaureate distance learning degree programs offered (minimal on-campus study). *Entrance requirements:* Additional exam requirements/recommendations for international students: Required—TOEFL (minimum score 577 paper-based; 233 computer-based; 90 iBT). Electronic applications accepted.

Harding University Graduate School of Religion, Graduate Programs, Memphis, TN 38117-5499. Offers Christian ministry (MA); counseling (MA); ministry (M Div, D Min); religion (MA). *Accreditation:* ATS. Part-time programs available. Postbaccalaureate distance learning degree programs offered (minimal on-campus study). *Degree requirements:* For master's, variable foreign language requirement, thesis (for some programs); for doctorate, one foreign language, thesis/dissertation; for M Div, 2 foreign languages, thesis/dissertation optional. *Entrance requirements:* For M Div, GRE General Test (for graduates of non-accredited schools), minimum GPA of 2.5; for master's, minimum GPA of 2.7; for doctorate, minimum GPA of 3.0. Additional exam requirements/recommendations for international students: Required—TOEFL (minimum score 550 paper-based; 213 computer-based; 79 iBT). Electronic applications accepted.

Religion

Hardin-Simmons University, Graduate School, Logsdon School of Theology, Program in Religion, Abilene, TX 79698-0001. Offers MA. Part-time programs available. *Faculty:* 16 full-time (1 woman), 7 part-time/adjunct (2 women). *Students:* 5 full-time (2 women), 8 part-time (3 women). Average age 27. 6 applicants, 83% accepted, 5 enrolled. *Degree requirements:* For master's, one foreign language, comprehensive exam, thesis or alternative. *Entrance requirements:* For master's, minimum undergraduate GPA of 3.0 in major, 2.7 overall, 18 hours of course work in religious studies, interview. Additional exam requirements/recommendations for international students: Required—TOEFL (minimum score 550 paper-based; 213 computer-based; 75 iBT). *Application deadline:* For fall admission, 8/15 priority date for domestic students, 4/1 for international students; for spring admission, 1/5 priority date for domestic students, 9/1 for international students. Applications are processed on a rolling basis. Application fee: $50. *Expenses:* Tuition: Full-time $12,150; part-time $675 per credit hour. Required fees: $650; $110 per semester. Tuition and fees vary according to degree level. *Financial support:* In 2010–11, 13 students received support; fellowships, scholarships/grants available. Support available to part-time students. Financial award application deadline: 6/30; financial award applicants required to submit FAFSA. *Faculty research:* Archaeology research in Christian origins, Hebrew grammar, history of Christian education, training of ministers into the twenty-first century, role of women in the Old Testament, contemporary ethical issues. *Unit head:* Dr. Travis Frampton, Director, 325-670-1270, Fax: 325-670-1406, E-mail: frampton@hsutx.edu. *Application contact:* Dr. Nancy Kucinski, Dean of Graduate Studies, 325-670-1298, Fax: 325-670-1564, E-mail: gradoff@hsutx.edu.

Hartford Seminary, Graduate Programs, Hartford, CT 06105-2279. Offers Islamic studies (MA); ministry (D Min); religious studies (MA); spirituality (Certificate). *Accreditation:* ATS (one or more programs are accredited). Part-time and evening/weekend programs available. Postbaccalaureate distance learning degree programs offered (no on-campus study). *Faculty:* 15 full-time (3 women), 19 part-time/adjunct (7 women). *Students:* 37 full-time (17 women), 121 part-time (68 women); includes 35 minority (27 Black or African American, non-Hispanic/Latino; 5 Asian, non-Hispanic/Latino; 3 Hispanic/Latino), 25 international. *Degree requirements:* For master's, thesis optional, oral exam; for doctorate, thesis/dissertation, oral exam. *Entrance requirements:* For doctorate, experience in ministry, M Div. Additional exam requirements/recommendations for international students: Required—TOEFL (minimum score 550 paper-based; 213 computer-based; 80 iBT). *Application deadline:* For fall admission, 7/15 priority date for domestic students, 5/1 priority date for international students; for winter admission, 12/1 priority date for domestic students, 4/1 priority date for international students; for spring admission, 4/5 priority date for domestic students, 3/1 priority date for international students. Applications are processed on a rolling basis. Application fee: $50. *Expenses:* Tuition: Full-time $10,680; part-time $1780 per course. *Financial support:* In 2010–11, 74 students received support. Scholarships/grants and tuition waivers (partial) available. Support available to part-time students. Financial award application deadline: 6/1. *Faculty research:* Liturgy and social justice, professional leadership in ministry, congregational studies, Christian-Muslim relations, American religion. *Unit head:* Dr. Efrain Agosto, Dean, 860-509-9554, E-mail: eagosto@hartsem.edu. *Application contact:* Dr. Vanessa Avery, Admissions and Recruitment Manager, 860-509-9552, Fax: 860-509-9509, E-mail: vavery@hartsem.edu.

Harvard University, Graduate School of Arts and Sciences, Committee on the Study of Religion, Cambridge, MA 02138. Offers PhD. *Degree requirements:* For doctorate, 2 foreign languages, thesis/dissertation. *Entrance requirements:* For doctorate, GRE General Test. Additional exam requirements/recommendations for international students: Required—TOEFL. *Expenses:* Tuition: Full-time $34,976. Required fees: $1166. Full-time tuition and fees vary according to program.

Heritage Christian University, Graduate Programs, Florence, AL 35630. Offers counseling (MM); Greek (MA); ministry (MM); New Testament (MA). *Degree requirements:* For master's, practicum (MM), major research paper (MA). *Entrance requirements:* For master's, MAT or GRE, bachelor's degree in Bible from an accredited college or university, minimum GPA of 2.75, 3 letters of recommendation.

Holy Names University, Graduate Division, Sophia Center in Culture and Spirituality, Oakland, CA 94619-1699. Offers MA, Certificate. *Degree requirements:* For master's, thesis or alternative. *Entrance requirements:* For master's, minimum undergraduate GPA of 2.6 overall, 3.0 in major. Additional exam requirements/recommendations for international students: Required—TOEFL. *Expenses:* Tuition: Full-time $13,788; part-time $766 per credit. Required fees: $340; $170 per semester. *Faculty research:* Medieval mystics, environmental justice, work and spirituality.

Hope International University, School of Graduate and Professional Studies, Programs in Ministry, Fullerton, CA 92831-3138. Offers Christian leadership (MCM); church music (MA); church music (Korean track) (MCM); church planting (MCM); intercultural studies (MCM); worship (MCM). Part-time and evening/weekend programs available. Postbaccalaureate distance learning degree programs offered (minimal on-campus study). *Degree requirements:* For master's, thesis (for some programs), project. *Entrance requirements:* For master's, minimum GPA of 3.0, MCM program requires an undergraduate degree in music, 2 references. Additional exam requirements/recommendations for international students: Required—TOEFL (minimum score 550 paper-based; 213 computer-based; 86 iBT); Recommended—IELTS (minimum score 6.5). Electronic applications accepted. *Expenses:* Contact institution. *Faculty research:* Church dynamics, growth methodologies.

Iliff School of Theology, Graduate and Professional Programs, Denver, CO 80210-4798. Offers biblical studies (MA); church history (MA); religion (MA); religion and social change (MA); specialized ministry (MASM), including justice and peace, pastoral theology and care, religions leadership; theology (M Div, MTS, D Min, PhD), including Biblical studies (PhD), religion and psychological studies (PhD), religion and social change (PhD), theology, philosophy and culture (PhD); theology/ethics (MA). PhD offered jointly with University of Denver. *Accreditation:* ACIPE; ATS. Part-time and evening/weekend programs available. *Degree requirements:* For master's, one foreign language, thesis (for some programs); for doctorate, 2 foreign languages, comprehensive exam, thesis/dissertation; for M Div, thesis/dissertation optional. *Entrance requirements:* For M Div, minimum GPA of 2.75, references; for master's, minimum GPA of 3.0, writing sample, references; for doctorate, GRE General Test, minimum GPA of 3.0, writing sample, letters of recommendation. Additional exam requirements/recommendations for international students: Required—TOEFL (minimum score 550 paper-based). Electronic applications accepted. *Faculty research:* Pastoral care, history, church music, contemporary church, biblical studies.

Indiana University Bloomington, University Graduate School, College of Arts and Sciences, Department of Religious Studies, Bloomington, IN 47405-7005. Offers MA, PhD. Part-time programs available. *Faculty:* 15 full-time (6 women). *Students:* 30 full-time (18 women); includes 2 Asian, non-Hispanic/Latino; 1 Hispanic/Latino, 4 international. Average age 32. 120 applicants, 1% accepted, 1 enrolled. In 2010, 1 master's, 6 doctorates awarded. Terminal master's awarded for partial completion of doctoral program. *Degree requirements:* For master's, variable foreign language requirement, thesis or alternative; for doctorate, 2 foreign languages, thesis/dissertation. *Entrance requirements:* For master's, GRE General Test; for doctorate, GRE, MA, writing sample. Additional exam requirements/recommendations for international students: Required—TOEFL. *Application deadline:* For fall admission, 12/15 priority date for domestic students, 12/1 priority date for international students. Application fee: $55 ($65 for international students). Electronic applications accepted. *Financial support:* In 2010–11, 2 fellowships with full tuition reimbursements (averaging $15,000 per year), 15 teaching assistantships with full tuition reimbursements (averaging $11,380 per year) were awarded; research assistantships with full tuition reimbursements, Federal Work-Study and institutionally sponsored loans also available. Financial award application deadline: 2/1. *Unit head:* Prof. David Brakke, Chair, 812-855-3531, Fax: 812-855-4687, E-mail: dbrakke@indiana.edu. *Application contact:* Debra Melsheimer, Graduate Secretary, 812-855-3531, Fax: 812-855-4687, E-mail: dmelshei@indiana.edu.

The Jewish Theological Seminary, The Graduate School, New York, NY 10027-4649. Offers ancient Judaism (MA, DHL, PhD); Bible and ancient Semitic languages (MA, DHL, PhD); interdepartmental studies (MA); Jewish art and visual culture (MA); Jewish gender and women's studies (MA); Jewish history (MA, DHL, PhD); Jewish literature (MA, DHL, PhD); Jewish philosophy (DHL); Jewish thought (MA, PhD); liturgy (MA, DHL, PhD); medieval Jewish studies (MA, DHL, PhD); Midrash (DHL); Midrash and scriptural interpretation (MA, PhD); modern Jewish studies (MA, DHL, PhD); Talmud and rabbinics (MA, DHL, PhD); MA/MSW. MA/MSW offered jointly with Columbia University. *Accreditation:* ACIPE. Part-time programs available. Terminal master's awarded for partial completion of doctoral program. *Degree requirements:* For master's, one foreign language, comprehensive exam (for some programs), thesis (for some programs); for doctorate, 3 foreign languages, comprehensive exam (for some programs), thesis/dissertation. *Entrance requirements:* For master's, GRE or MAT, 3 letters of recommendation, writing sample; for doctorate, GRE or MAT, 3 letters of recommendation, writing research sample. Additional exam requirements/recommendations for international students: Required—TOEFL (minimum score 100 computer-based).

John Carroll University, Graduate School, Department of Religious Studies, University Heights, OH 44118-4581. Offers MA. Part-time and evening/weekend programs available. *Degree requirements:* For master's, comprehensive exam, research essay or thesis, foreign language proficiency. *Entrance requirements:* For master's, GRE General Test or MAT, minimum GPA of 2.5. Additional exam requirements/recommendations for international students: Required—TOEFL. Electronic applications accepted. *Faculty research:* Ethics, women's studies, contemporary theology, Bible studies, Latin American theology.

Kentucky Christian University, Graduate School, Grayson, KY 41143-2205. Offers Biblical studies (MA); Christian leadership (MA). Part-time programs available. *Faculty:* 8 part-time/adjunct (0 women). *Students:* 6 full-time (3 women), 36 part-time (9 women), 3 international. Average age 33. 14 applicants, 86% accepted, 11 enrolled. *Degree requirements:* For master's, comprehensive exam (for some programs), thesis optional. *Entrance requirements:* For master's, minimum cumulative GPA of 2.75 in major or 2.5 overall; 6 additional hours in Bible (for non-Biblical undergraduate majors). Additional exam requirements/recommendations for international students: Required—TOEFL (minimum score 550 paper-based; 213 computer-based). *Application deadline:* Applications are processed on a rolling basis. Application fee: $35. Electronic applications accepted. *Expenses:* Tuition: Part-time $258.33 per credit. *Financial support:* Teaching assistantships with full tuition reimbursements, scholarships/grants and unspecified assistantships available. Support available to part-time students. *Unit head:* Dr. David Fiensy, Dean, 606-474-3263, Fax: 606-474-3189, E-mail: dfiensy@kcu.edu. *Application contact:* Jane Shick, Academic Office Manager, 877-811-6391, Fax: 606-474-3189, E-mail: gradstudies@kcu.edu.

Knox Theological Seminary, Graduate Programs, Program in Christianity and Culture, Fort Lauderdale, FL 33308. Offers MA. Part-time and evening/weekend programs available. *Entrance requirements:* Additional exam requirements/recommendations for international students: Required—TOEFL (minimum score 520 paper-based; 213 computer-based; 83 iBT), TWE (minimum score 5).

Lancaster Theological Seminary, Graduate and Professional Programs, Lancaster, PA 17603-2812. Offers biblical studies (MAR); Christian education (MAR); Christianity and the arts (MAR); church history (MAR); congregational life (MAR); lay leadership (Certificate); theological studies (M Div); theology (D Min); theology and ethics (MAR). *Accreditation:* ACIPE; ATS. *Degree requirements:* For doctorate, thesis/dissertation; for M Div, one foreign language.

La Salle University, School of Arts and Sciences, Program in Theological, Pastoral and Liturgical Studies, Philadelphia, PA 19141-1199. Offers pastoral studies (MA); religion (MA); theological studies (MA). Part-time and evening/weekend programs available. *Entrance requirements:* For master's, 26 credits in humanistic subjects, religion, theology, or ministry-related work.

La Sierra University, School of Religion, Riverside, CA 92515. Offers pastoral ministry (M Div); religion (MA); religious education (MA); religious studies (MA). Part-time programs available. *Degree requirements:* For master's, one foreign language, thesis or alternative. *Entrance requirements:* For master's, GRE General Test, minimum GPA of 3.0.

Lee University, Program in Religion, Cleveland, TN 37320-3450. Offers biblical studies (MA); ministry studies (MA); theological studies (MA). Part-time programs available. *Faculty:* 8 full-time (2 women), 1 part-time/adjunct (0 women). *Students:* 13 full-time (5 women), 14 part-time (5 women); includes 1 Black or African American, non-Hispanic/Latino; 1 Asian, non-Hispanic/Latino; 2 Hispanic/Latino; 1 Two or more races, non-Hispanic/Latino, 1 international. Average age 29. 11 applicants, 100% accepted, 11 enrolled. In 2010, 5 master's awarded. *Degree requirements:* For master's, comprehensive exam, thesis. *Entrance requirements:* For master's, GRE or MAT, minimum GPA of 3.0, 2 letters of recommendation, interview. Additional exam requirements/recommendations for international students: Required—TOEFL (minimum score 450 paper-based; 45 computer-based). *Application deadline:* For fall admission, 4/1 priority date for domestic students; for spring admission, 10/1 priority date for domestic students. Applications are processed on a rolling basis. Application fee: $25. *Expenses:* Tuition: Full-time $12,120; part-time $506 per credit hour. Required fees: $560; $305 per semester. Part-time tuition and fees vary according to course load and campus/location. *Financial support:* Teaching assistantships, career-related internships or fieldwork, Federal Work-Study, institutionally sponsored loans, scholarships/grants, and unspecified assistantships available. Financial award application deadline: 3/1; financial award applicants required to submit FAFSA. *Faculty research:* Book of Isaiah, Gospel of Mark, school of St. Victor of the twelfth century, spirit Christology, people groups of New Testament and work. Total annual research expenditures: $3,000. *Unit head:* Dr. Bob Bayles, Director, 423-614-8338, E-mail: bbayles@leeuniversity.edu. *Application contact:* Vicki Glasscock, Graduate Admissions Director, 423-614-8059, E-mail: vglasscock@leeuniversity.edu.

Liberty University, Liberty Theological Seminary and Graduate School, Lynchburg, VA 24502. Offers religious studies (M Div, MA, MAR, MRE, D Min); theology (Th M). Part-time programs available. Postbaccalaureate distance learning degree programs offered (minimal on-campus study). *Students:* 2,825 full-time (645 women), 3,515 part-time (828 women); includes 1,336 minority (996 Black or African American, non-Hispanic/Latino; 32 American Indian or Alaska Native, non-Hispanic/Latino; 108 Asian, non-Hispanic/Latino; 185 Hispanic/Latino; 11 Native Hawaiian or other Pacific Islander, non-Hispanic/Latino; 4 Two or more races, non-Hispanic/Latino), 258 international. Average age 38. In 2010, 236 first professional degrees, 1,088 master's, 76 doctorates awarded. *Degree requirements:* For master's, 2 foreign languages, thesis (for some programs); for doctorate, 2 foreign languages, thesis/dissertation. *Entrance requirements:* For M Div, minimum undergraduate GPA of 2.0; for master's, minimum undergraduate GPA of 2.0, 9 credit hours of course work in Greek, 9 credit hours of course work in Hebrew (Th M); for doctorate, GRE General Test or MAT. Additional exam requirements/recommendations for international students: Required—TOEFL (minimum score 550 paper-based; 250 computer-based; 100 iBT). *Application deadline:* For fall admission, 6/1 priority date for domestic students; for spring admission, 11/1 for domestic students. Applications are processed on a rolling basis. Application fee: $50. Electronic applications accepted. *Expenses:* Contact institution. *Financial support:* Teaching assistantships with tuition reimbursements, career-related internships or fieldwork and Federal Work-Study available. *Unit head:* Dr. Elmer Towns, Dean, 434-582-2169, Fax: 434-582-2766, E-mail: eltowns@liberty.edu. *Application contact:* Jay Bridge, Director of Graduate Admissions, 800-424-9595, Fax: 800-628-7977, E-mail: gradadmissions@liberty.edu.

Lipscomb University, Hazelip School of Theology, Nashville, TN 37204-3951. Offers biblical studies (MA); Christian studies (MA); divinity (M Div); ministry (MA); New Testament (MA); Old Testament (MA); theological studies (MTS); theology (MA). *Accreditation:* ATS. Part-time and evening/weekend programs available. *Faculty:* 10 full-time (0 women), 2 part-time/adjunct (0 women). *Students:* 18 full-time (7 women), 82 part-time (13 women); includes 15 Black or

African American, non-Hispanic/Latino; 1 Hispanic/Latino, 1 international. Average age 35. 38 applicants, 97% accepted, 20 enrolled. In 2010, 7 first professional degrees, 6 master's awarded. *Degree requirements:* For master's, 2 foreign languages, comprehensive exam (for some programs); for M Div, 2 foreign languages. *Entrance requirements:* For M Div and master's, 2 references. Additional exam requirements/recommendations for international students: Required—TOEFL (minimum score 570 paper-based; 230 computer-based). *Application deadline:* For fall admission, 8/14 priority date for domestic students; for spring admission, 12/31 for domestic students. Applications are processed on a rolling basis. Application fee: $0 ($75 for international students). Electronic applications accepted. *Expenses:* Tuition: Full-time $18,149; part-time $943 per hour. Tuition and fees vary according to program. *Financial support:* Scholarships/grants available. Support available to part-time students. Financial award application deadline: 3/1; financial award applicants required to submit FAFSA. *Faculty research:* Status of Churches of Christ in foreign nations, Hebrew grammar, marriage and family. *Unit head:* Dr. Mark Black, Director, 615-966-1000 Ext. 5799, Fax: 615-966-1808, E-mail: mark.black@lipscomb.edu. *Application contact:* Kellye McCool, Information Contact, 615-966-6051, Fax: 615-966-6052, E-mail: kellye.mccool@lipscomb.edu.

Loma Linda University, Faculty of Religion, Program in Religion and Science, Loma Linda, CA 92350. Offers MA. *Degree requirements:* For master's, comprehensive exam, thesis optional. *Entrance requirements:* Additional exam requirements/recommendations for international students: Required—TOEFL. Electronic applications accepted.

Louisville Presbyterian Theological Seminary, Graduate and Professional Programs, Louisville, KY 40205-1798. Offers Bible (MAR); divinity (M Div); ministry (D Min); religious thought (MAR); theology (Th M); JD/M Div; M Div/MBA; M Div/MS; M Div/MSW. JD/M Div, M Div/MBA; and M Div/MSW offered jointly with University of Louisville. *Accreditation:* AAMFT/COAMFTE (one or more programs are accredited); ACIPE; ATS (one or more programs are accredited). Part-time and evening/weekend programs available. *Degree requirements:* For master's, one foreign language; for doctorate, thesis/dissertation; for M Div, 2 foreign languages. *Entrance requirements:* For master's, interview; for doctorate, M Div. Additional exam requirements/recommendations for international students: Required—TOEFL (minimum score 550 paper-based; 213 computer-based). Electronic applications accepted. *Expenses:* Tuition: Full-time $9660; part-time $322 per credit hour. Required fees: $143 per semester.

Lutheran Theological Seminary, Graduate and Professional Programs, Saskatoon, SK S7N 0X3, Canada. Offers Biblical studies (MTS); church history (MTS); ethics/church and society (MTS); history of Christianity (STM); New Testament (STM); Old Testament (STM); pastoral studies (STM); pastoral theology (MTS); systematic theology (MTS); systematic theology and philosophy of religion (STM); theology (M Div, D Div). STM programs offered jointly with College of Emmanuel and St. Chad and St. Andrew's College. *Accreditation:* ATS. Part-time programs available. *Degree requirements:* For master's, thesis; for M Div, Greek, Hebrew.

Lutheran Theological Seminary at Gettysburg, Graduate and Professional Programs, Gettysburg, PA 17325-1795. Offers divinity (M Div); ministerial studies (MAMS); outdoor ministry (MAR); parish ministry (D Min); theology (STM). *Accreditation:* ACIPE; ATS (one or more programs are accredited). Part-time programs available. Postbaccalaureate distance learning degree programs offered (no on-campus study). *Degree requirements:* For master's, thesis (for some programs); for M Div, one foreign language. Electronic applications accepted.

The Lutheran Theological Seminary at Philadelphia, Graduate School, Philadelphia, PA 19119-1794. Offers divinity (M Div); ministry (D Min); public leadership (MA); religion (MAR); social ministry (Certificate); theology (STM, PhD). *Accreditation:* ACIPE; ATS. Part-time and evening/weekend programs available. *Faculty:* 18 full-time (5 women), 22 part-time/adjunct (8 women). *Students:* 121 full-time (56 women), 204 part-time (97 women); includes 92 minority (80 Black or African American, non-Hispanic/Latino; 2 Asian, non-Hispanic/Latino; 10 Hispanic/Latino), 14 international. 123 applicants, 86% accepted, 84 enrolled. *Degree requirements:* For master's, one foreign language, comprehensive exam (for some programs), thesis (for some programs); for doctorate, thesis/dissertation; for M Div, 2 foreign languages. *Entrance requirements:* For M Div and master's, minimum undergraduate GPA of 2.8; for doctorate, minimum first professional GPA of 3.0. Additional exam requirements/recommendations for international students: Required—TOEFL (minimum score 550 paper-based; 213 computer-based), TWE. *Application deadline:* For fall admission, 6/1 priority date for domestic students. Applications are processed on a rolling basis. Application fee: $35. Electronic applications accepted. *Expenses:* Tuition: Full-time $13,900; part-time $1470 per course. Required fees: $2484; $75 per semester. Tuition and fees vary according to degree level. *Financial support:* In 2010–11, 102 students received support; research assistantships with tuition reimbursements available, teaching assistantships with tuition reimbursements available, career-related internships or fieldwork and Federal Work-Study available. Financial award application deadline: 7/1; financial award applicants required to submit FAFSA. *Unit head:* Rev. Dr. J. Paul Rajashekar, Dean, 215-248-6379, Fax: 215-248-4577, E-mail: rajashekar@ltsp.edu. *Application contact:* Rev. Louise Johnson, Director of Admissions, 800-286-4616 Ext. 6321, Fax: 215-248-7315, E-mail: admissions@ltsp.edu.

Maranatha Baptist Bible College, Program in English Bible, Watertown, WI 53094. Offers MA. Part-time programs available. Postbaccalaureate distance learning degree programs offered (no on-campus study). *Faculty:* 4 full-time (0 women), 5 part-time/adjunct (0 women). *Students:* 20 part-time (0 women). Average age 28. 10 applicants, 100% accepted, 10 enrolled. Application fee: $50. *Expenses:* Tuition: Full-time $4160; part-time $260 per credit hour. Required fees: $350; $23 per credit hour. *Unit head:* Dr. Larry Oats, Dean of Maranatha Baptist Seminary, 920-206-2324, Fax: 920-261-9109, E-mail: loats@mbbc.edu. *Application contact:* Dr. Jim Harrison, Director of Admissions, 920-206-2327, Fax: 920-261-9109, E-mail: admissions@mbbc.edu.

Marquette University, Graduate School, College of Arts and Sciences, Department of Theology, Milwaukee, WI 53201-1881. Offers historical theology (MA, PhD); Judaism and Christianity in antiquity (MA, PhD); systematic theology (MA, PhD); theological ethics (PhD); theology (MACD); theology and society (PhD). Part-time and evening/weekend programs available. Postbaccalaureate distance learning degree programs offered (no on-campus study). *Faculty:* 30 full-time (7 women), 19 part-time/adjunct (3 women). *Students:* 65 full-time (17 women), 45 part-time (13 women); includes 6 minority (3 Black or African American, non-Hispanic/Latino; 3 Hispanic/Latino), 3 international. Average age 36. 167 applicants, 39% accepted, 16 enrolled. In 2010, 114 master's, 8 doctorates awarded. Terminal master's awarded for partial completion of doctoral program. *Degree requirements:* For master's, one foreign language, comprehensive exam, thesis or alternative; for doctorate, 2 foreign languages, comprehensive exam, thesis/dissertation. *Entrance requirements:* For master's, GRE General Test, official transcripts from all current and previous colleges/universities except Marquette, three letters of recommendation, short personal statement; for doctorate, GRE General Test, official transcripts from all current and previous colleges/universities except Marquette, three letters of recommendation, short personal statement, academic writing sample. Additional exam requirements/recommendations for international students: Required—TOEFL (minimum score 530 paper-based; 78 computer-based). *Application deadline:* For fall admission, 12/15 for domestic and international students. Application fee: $50. Electronic applications accepted. *Expenses:* Tuition: Full-time $16,290; part-time $905 per credit hour. Tuition and fees vary according to program. *Financial support:* In 2010–11, 10 fellowships, 22 teaching assistantships were awarded; research assistantships, Federal Work-Study, institutionally sponsored loans, scholarships/grants, and tuition waivers (full and partial) also available. Support available to part-time students. Financial award application deadline: 2/15. *Faculty research:* Old Testament theology, New Testament theology, church history, Christian ethics. Total annual research expenditures: $4,625. *Unit head:* Dr. Susan Wood, Chair, 414-288-7170, Fax: 414-288-5548. *Application contact:* Dr. M. Therese Lysaught, Director of Graduate Studies, 414-288-3740.

Mars Hill Graduate School, Graduate Programs, Seattle, WA 98121. Offers Christian studies (MA); counseling psychology (MA); divinity (MS). Part-time programs available. *Entrance requirements:* For master's, MAT.

McGill University, Faculty of Graduate and Postdoctoral Studies, Faculty of Religious Studies, Montréal, QC H3A 2T5, Canada. Offers MA, STM, PhD. *Accreditation:* ATS.

McMaster University, School of Graduate Studies, Faculty of Social Sciences, Department of Religious Studies, Hamilton, ON L8S 4M2, Canada. Offers MA, PhD. Part-time programs available. *Degree requirements:* For master's, one foreign language, thesis; for doctorate, 2 foreign languages, comprehensive exam, thesis/dissertation. *Entrance requirements:* For master's, minimum B+ average. Additional exam requirements/recommendations for international students: Required—TOEFL (minimum score 580 paper-based; 237 computer-based). *Faculty research:* Hellenistic Judaism, religious biographies in Asia, medieval India, synoptic gospels, ritual and belief systems.

Memorial University of Newfoundland, School of Graduate Studies, Department of Religious Studies, St. John's, NL A1C 5S7, Canada. Offers MA. Part-time programs available. *Degree requirements:* For master's, one foreign language, thesis. *Entrance requirements:* For master's, honors degree in religious studies or equivalent. Electronic applications accepted. *Faculty research:* Biblical studies, Christian thought and history, world religions, ethics, contemporary spirituality.

Miami University, Graduate School, College of Arts and Science, Department of Comparative Religion, Oxford, OH 45056. Offers MA. Part-time programs available. *Students:* 5 full-time (4 women). Average age 25. In 2010, 2 master's awarded. *Entrance requirements:* For master's, minimum undergraduate GPA of 3.0 during previous 2 years or 2.75 overall. Additional exam requirements/recommendations for international students: Required—TOEFL. Application fee: $50. *Expenses:* Tuition, state resident: full-time $11,616; part-time $484 per credit hour. Tuition, nonresident: full-time $25,656; part-time $1069 per credit hour. Required fees: $528. *Financial support:* Fellowships with full tuition reimbursements, research assistantships, teaching assistantships, Federal Work-Study, health care benefits, tuition waivers (full), and unspecified assistantships available. Financial award application deadline: 3/1; financial award applicants required to submit FAFSA. *Unit head:* Dr. Elizabeth Wilson, Chair, 513-529-4300, E-mail: wilsone@muohio.edu. *Application contact:* Dr. Lisa Poirier, Director of Graduate Studies, 513-529-4300, Fax: 513-529-1774, E-mail: poirelj@muohio.edu.

Michigan Theological Seminary, Graduate Programs, Plymouth, MI 48170. Offers Bible (Graduate Certificate); Christian education (MA); counseling psychology (MA); divinity (M Div); theological studies (MA). Part-time and evening/weekend programs available. *Degree requirements:* For master's, one foreign language, thesis; for M Div, 2 foreign languages. *Faculty research:* Judaism, cults, world religions.

Midwestern Baptist Theological Seminary, Graduate and Professional Programs, Kansas City, MO 64118-4697. Offers Biblical archaeology (MA); Biblical languages (MA); Christian education (M Div, MACE); Christian foundations—lay ministry (Graduate Certificate); collegiate ministries (M Div); counseling (MA); educational ministry (D Ed Min); international church planting (M Div); ministry (M Div, D Min); North American church planting (M Div); sacred music (MCM); urban ministry (M Div); worship leadership (M Div); youth ministry (M Div). *Accreditation:* ATS. Part-time programs available. Postbaccalaureate distance learning degree programs offered (minimal on-campus study). *Degree requirements:* For doctorate, thesis/dissertation; for M Div, 2 foreign languages. *Entrance requirements:* For doctorate, MAT. Electronic applications accepted. *Faculty research:* Ministerial studies, Biblical and theological studies, missions, counseling.

Missouri State University, Graduate College, College of Humanities and Public Affairs, Department of Religious Studies, Springfield, MO 65897. Offers MA. Part-time programs available. *Degree requirements:* For master's, one foreign language, comprehensive exam, thesis or alternative. *Entrance requirements:* For master's, GRE, minimum GPA of 3.2. Additional exam requirements/recommendations for international students: Required—TOEFL (minimum score 550 paper-based; 213 computer-based; 79 iBT). Electronic applications accepted. *Expenses:* Tuition, state resident: full-time $3348; part-time $186 per credit hour. Tuition, nonresident: full-time $6696; part-time $372 per credit hour. Required fees: $238 per semester. Tuition and fees vary according to course level, course load and program. *Faculty research:* Apocalyptic literature, Protestantism in American society, contemporary Hinduism, Christian history.

Mount St. Mary's College, Graduate Division, Program in Religious Studies, Los Angeles, CA 90049-1599. Offers MA. Part-time and evening/weekend programs available. *Degree requirements:* For master's, thesis. *Entrance requirements:* For master's, minimum GPA of 3.0. Additional exam requirements/recommendations for international students: Required—TOEFL (minimum score 550 paper-based). *Faculty research:* Scripture, systematics, ethics, religious education for Mexican-Americans.

Naropa University, Graduate Programs, Program in Indo-Tibetan Buddhism, Boulder, CO 80302-6697. Offers MA. *Faculty:* 6 full-time (2 women), 10 part-time/adjunct (5 women). *Students:* 2 full-time, 2 part-time. Average age 36. 3 applicants, 67% accepted, 1 enrolled. In 2010, 5 master's awarded. *Degree requirements:* For master's, comprehensive exam, thesis. *Entrance requirements:* For master's, writing sample, interview (by phone or in-person), 3 letters of recommendation, letter of interest, resume. Additional exam requirements/recommendations for international students: Required—TOEFL (minimum score 600 paper-based; 250 computer-based). *Application deadline:* For fall admission, 1/15 priority date for domestic and international students. Applications are processed on a rolling basis. Application fee: $60. Electronic applications accepted. *Expenses:* Tuition: Full-time $17,820; part-time $810 per credit. Required fees: $305 per semester. Tuition and fees vary according to course load, program and reciprocity agreements. *Financial support:* In 2010–11, 5 research assistantships with partial tuition reimbursements (averaging $3,000 per year), 2 teaching assistantships with partial tuition reimbursements (averaging $3,000 per year) were awarded; career-related internships or fieldwork, Federal Work-Study, scholarships/grants, health care benefits, tuition waivers (partial), and unspecified assistantships also available. Support available to part-time students. Financial award application deadline: 3/1; financial award applicants required to submit FAFSA. *Unit head:* Phillip Stanley, Co-Chair, 303-245-4728. *Application contact:* Donna McIntyre, Assistant Director of Graduate Admissions, 303-546-3555, Fax: 303-546-3583, E-mail: donna@naropa.edu.

Naropa University, Graduate Programs, Program in Indo-Tibetan Buddhism with Language, Boulder, CO 80302-6697. Offers MA. *Faculty:* 6 full-time (2 women), 10 part-time/adjunct (5 women). *Students:* 15 full-time (1 woman), 4 part-time (0 women); includes 1 American Indian or Alaska Native, non-Hispanic/Latino; 1 Asian, non-Hispanic/Latino; 1 Hispanic/Latino, 1 international. Average age 32. 19 applicants, 84% accepted, 8 enrolled. In 2010, 5 master's awarded. *Degree requirements:* For master's, comprehensive exam, thesis. *Entrance requirements:* For master's, writing sample, interview (by phone or in-person), resume, letter of interest, 3 letters of recommendation. Additional exam requirements/recommendations for international students: Required—TOEFL (minimum score 600 paper-based; 250 computer-based). *Application deadline:* For fall admission, 1/15 priority date for domestic and international students. Applications are processed on a rolling basis. Application fee: $60. Electronic applications accepted. *Expenses:* Tuition: Full-time $17,820; part-time $810 per credit. Required fees: $305 per semester. Tuition and fees vary according to course load, program and reciprocity agreements. *Financial support:* In 2010–11, 11 students received support, including 5 research assistantships with partial tuition reimbursements available (averaging $3,000 per year), 2 teaching assistantships with partial tuition reimbursements available (averaging $3,000 per year); career-related internships or fieldwork, Federal Work-Study, scholarships/grants, health care benefits, tuition waivers (partial), and unspecified assistantships also available. Support available to part-time students. Financial award application deadline: 3/1; financial award applicants required to submit FAFSA. *Unit head:* Roger Dorris, Co-Chair, 303-546-0937. *Application contact:* Donna McIntyre, Assistant Director of Admissions, 303-546-3555, Fax: 303-546-3583, E-mail: donna@naropa.edu.

Religion

Naropa University, Graduate Programs, Program in Religious Studies, Boulder, CO 80302-6697. Offers MA. *Faculty:* 5 full-time (1 woman), 7 part-time/adjunct (5 women). *Students:* 15 full-time (6 women), 2 part-time (1 woman); includes 2 minority (1 American Indian or Alaska Native, non-Hispanic/Latino; 1 Two or more races, non-Hispanic/Latino). Average age 27. 25 applicants, 80% accepted, 8 enrolled. In 2010, 4 master's awarded. *Degree requirements:* For master's, comprehensive exam, thesis. *Entrance requirements:* For master's, interview (by phone or in-person), writing sample, letter of interest, resume, 3 letters of recommendation. Additional exam requirements/recommendations for international students: Required—TOEFL (minimum score 600 paper-based; 250 computer-based). *Application deadline:* For fall admission, 1/15 priority date for domestic and international students. Applications are processed on a rolling basis. Application fee: $60. Electronic applications accepted. *Expenses:* Tuition: Full-time $17,820; part-time $810 per credit. Required fees: $305 per semester. Tuition and fees vary according to course load, program and reciprocity agreements. *Financial support:* In 2010–11, 12 students received support, including 2 research assistantships with partial tuition reimbursements available (averaging $1,314 per year); teaching assistantships with partial tuition reimbursements available, career-related internships or fieldwork, Federal Work-Study, scholarships/grants, health care benefits, tuition waivers (partial), and unspecified assistantships also available. Support available to part-time students. Financial award application deadline: 3/1; financial award applicants required to submit FAFSA. *Unit head:* Jane Carpenter, Director, School of Humanities and Interdisciplinary Studies, 303-245-4602, E-mail: jane@naropa.edu. *Application contact:* Krista Stuchlik, Senior Graduate Admissions Counselor, 303-546-3528, Fax: 303-546-3583, E-mail: kstuchlik@naropa.edu.

Naropa University, Graduate Programs, Program in Religious Studies with Language, Boulder, CO 80302-6697. Offers MA. *Faculty:* 5 full-time (1 woman), 7 part-time/adjunct (5 women). *Students:* 20 full-time (9 women), 2 part-time (1 woman); includes 6 minority (1 Black or African American, non-Hispanic/Latino; 1 American Indian or Alaska Native, non-Hispanic/Latino; 4 Two or more races, non-Hispanic/Latino). Average age 27. 36 applicants, 67% accepted, 13 enrolled. In 2010, 1 master's awarded. *Degree requirements:* For master's, thesis. *Entrance requirements:* For master's, interview, writing sample, resume, 3 letters of recommendation, letter of interest. Additional exam requirements/recommendations for international students: Required—TOEFL (minimum score 600 paper-based; 250 computer-based). *Application deadline:* For fall admission, 1/15 priority date for domestic and international students. Applications are processed on a rolling basis. Application fee: $60. Electronic applications accepted. *Expenses:* Tuition: Full-time $17,820; part-time $810 per credit. Required fees: $305 per semester. Tuition and fees vary according to course load, program and reciprocity agreements. *Financial support:* In 2010–11, 14 students received support, including 3 research assistantships with partial tuition reimbursements available (averaging $1,875 per year), 3 teaching assistantships with partial tuition reimbursements available (averaging $1,875 per year); career-related internships or fieldwork, Federal Work-Study, scholarships/grants, health care benefits, tuition waivers (partial), and unspecified assistantships also available. Support available to part-time students. Financial award application deadline: 3/1; financial award applicants required to submit FAFSA. *Unit head:* Jane Carpenter, Director, School of Humanities and Interdisciplinary Studies, 303-245-4602, E-mail: jane@naropa.edu. *Application contact:* Krista Stuchlik, Senior Graduate Admissions Counselor, 303-546-3528, E-mail: kstuchlik@naropa.edu.

New Life Theological Seminary, Graduate Program, Charlotte, NC 28206-7901. Offers urban Christian ministry (MA), including Biblical studies, church planting, divinity, youth/music. Part-time and evening/weekend programs available. *Degree requirements:* For master's, thesis. Electronic applications accepted.

New Saint Andrews College, Graduate Studies, Moscow, ID 83843. Offers classical Christian studies (Graduate Certificate); Trinitarian theology and culture (MA). Part-time programs available. *Degree requirements:* For master's, final oral exam. *Entrance requirements:* For master's, GRE, 2 letters of recommendation; for Graduate Certificate, GRE, bachelor's degree, essays, 2 letters of recommendation. Electronic applications accepted.

New York University, Graduate School of Arts and Science, Draper Interdisciplinary Program in Humanities and Social Thought, New York, NY 10012-1019. Offers humanities and social thought (MA); religion (Advanced Certificate); social theory (Advanced Certificate). Part-time programs available. *Faculty:* 6 full-time (3 women). *Students:* 115 full-time (69 women), 118 part-time (76 women); includes 12 Black or African American, non-Hispanic/Latino; 9 Asian, non-Hispanic/Latino; 18 Hispanic/Latino, 19 international. Average age 28. 415 applicants, 51% accepted, 97 enrolled. In 2010, 69 master's awarded. *Degree requirements:* For master's, thesis, comprehensive exam or essay. *Entrance requirements:* For degree, master's degree. Additional exam requirements/recommendations for international students: Required—TOEFL. *Application deadline:* For fall admission, 7/1 for domestic students; for spring admission, 12/1 for domestic students. Applications are processed on a rolling basis. Application fee: $90. *Financial support:* Teaching assistantships with tuition reimbursements, Federal Work-Study, institutionally sponsored loans, and tuition waivers (partial) available. Financial award application deadline: 7/1; financial award applicants required to submit FAFSA. *Faculty research:* Art world, gender politics, global histories, literary cultures, the city. *Unit head:* Robin Nagle, Director, 212-998-8070, Fax: 212-995-4691, E-mail: draper.program@nyu.edu. *Application contact:* Robert Dimit, Associate Director, 212-998-8070, Fax: 212-995-4691, E-mail: draper.program@nyu.edu.

New York University, Graduate School of Arts and Science, Program in Religious Studies, New York, NY 10012-1019. Offers MA. Part-time programs available. *Students:* 12 full-time (7 women), 6 part-time (4 women), 6 international. Average age 29. 35 applicants, 54% accepted, 5 enrolled. In 2010, 5 master's awarded. *Degree requirements:* For master's, one foreign language, thesis. *Entrance requirements:* For master's, GRE General Test. Additional exam requirements/recommendations for international students: Required—TOEFL. *Application deadline:* For fall admission, 1/4 priority date for domestic students. Application fee: $90. *Financial support:* Teaching assistantships with tuition reimbursements, Federal Work-Study and institutionally sponsored loans available. Financial award application deadline: 1/4; financial award applicants required to submit FAFSA. *Faculty research:* Biblical and rabbinic Judaism, New Testament and early Christianity, comparative mysticism, gender and embodiment, East Asian religions. *Unit head:* Adam Becker, Director, 212-998-3756, Fax: 212-995-4827, E-mail: religious.studies@nyu.edu. *Application contact:* J. Mercer Crenshaw, Department Administrator, 212-998-3756, Fax: 212-995-4827, E-mail: religious.studies@nyu.edu.

Northwestern University, School of Continuing Studies, Program in Liberal Studies, Evanston, IL 60208. Offers American studies (MA); history (MA); religious and ethical studies (MA).

Northwest Nazarene University, Graduate Studies, Program in Religion, Nampa, ID 83686-5897. Offers Christian education (MA); missional leadership (MA); pastoral ministry (MA); religion (M Div); spiritual formation (MA). Part-time and evening/weekend programs available. Postbaccalaureate distance learning degree programs offered (no on-campus study). *Faculty:* 7 full-time (1 woman), 10 part-time/adjunct (1 woman). *Students:* 119 full-time (33 women), 11 part-time (3 women); includes 8 minority (4 Black or African American, non-Hispanic/Latino; 1 American Indian or Alaska Native, non-Hispanic/Latino; 2 Hispanic/Latino; 1 Native Hawaiian or other Pacific Islander, non-Hispanic/Latino), 1 international. In 2010, 42 master's awarded. *Application deadline:* Applications are processed on a rolling basis. Application fee: $50. Electronic applications accepted. *Unit head:* Dr. Jay Akkerman, Director, Graduate Studies, 208-467-8437, Fax: 208-467-8252. *Application contact:* Jill Jones, Program Assistant, 208-467-8368, Fax: 208-467-8252, E-mail: jdjones@nnu.edu.

Oblate School of Theology, Graduate and Professional Programs, San Antonio, TX 78216-6693. Offers divinity (M Div); Hispanic ministry (D Min); pastoral ministry (MAP Min); pastoral studies (Certificate); spirituality (MA Sp); supervision (D Min), including clinical pastoral education, general supervision; theology (MA Th); M Div/MA Th. *Accreditation:* ACIPE; ATS (one or more programs are accredited). Part-time programs available. *Faculty:* 19 full-time (6 women), 2 part-time/adjunct (0 women). *Students:* 91 full-time (7 women), 59 part-time (34 women); includes 4 Black or African American, non-Hispanic/Latino; 1 American Indian or Alaska Native, non-Hispanic/Latino; 18 Asian, non-Hispanic/Latino; 39 Hispanic/Latino, 36 international. 24 applicants, 100% accepted, 24 enrolled. In 2010, 13 first professional degrees, 17 master's, 4 doctorates awarded. *Degree requirements:* For master's, thesis (for some programs), practicum; for doctorate, paper, practicum; for M Div, one foreign language, seminar. *Entrance requirements:* For M Div, MAT, interview, course work in philosophy and theology; for master's, MAT, interview, course work in theology or religious studies, minimum GPA of 2.5; for doctorate, M Div. Additional exam requirements/recommendations for international students: Required—TOEFL (minimum score 197 computer-based; 71 iBT). *Application deadline:* For fall admission, 6/15 priority date for domestic and international students; for spring admission, 11/30 for domestic and international students. Applications are processed on a rolling basis. Application fee: $50. *Expenses:* Tuition: Full-time $12,350; part-time $475 per credit hour. Required fees: $175 per semester. One-time fee: $90. Tuition and fees vary according to course level, course load and degree level. *Financial support:* Scholarships/grants available. Support available to part-time students. Financial award application deadline: 8/1; financial award applicants required to submit FAFSA. *Unit head:* Dr. Scott Woodward, Academic Dean, 210-341-1366, Fax: 210-341-4519, E-mail: swoodward@ost.edu. *Application contact:* James Oberhausen, Director of Admission/Registrar, 210-341-1366 Ext. 212, Fax: 210-341-4519, E-mail: registrar@ost.edu.

Oklahoma City University, Petree College of Arts and Sciences, Wimberly School of Religion and Graduate Theological Center, Oklahoma City, OK 73106-1402. Offers M Rel. Part-time and evening/weekend programs available. *Degree requirements:* For master's, thesis optional. *Entrance requirements:* For master's, minimum GPA of 3.0. Additional exam requirements/recommendations for international students: Required—TOEFL (minimum score 550 paper-based). *Faculty research:* Biblical studies, church history, social ethics, world religions.

Olivet Nazarene University, Graduate School, Division of Religion, Bourbonnais, IL 60914. Offers biblical literature (MA); religion (MA); theology (MA). Part-time programs available. *Degree requirements:* For master's, thesis or alternative.

Oxford Graduate School, Graduate Programs, Dayton, TN 37321-6736. Offers family life education (M Litt); organizational leadership (M Litt); sociological integration of religion and society (D Phil). *Faculty:* 10 full-time (2 women), 22 part-time/adjunct (7 women). *Students:* 105 full-time (40 women). *Application contact:* Joanne Phillips, Information Contact, 423-775-6596, Fax: 423-775-6599, E-mail: oxfordgraduateschool@ogs.edu.

Pacific School of Religion, Graduate and Professional Programs, Berkeley, CA 94709-1323. Offers M Div, MA, MTS, D Min, PhD, Th D, CAPS, CMS, CSS, CTS. MA, PhD, Th D offered jointly with Graduate Theological Union; D Min with Church Divinity School of the Pacific. *Accreditation:* ACIPE; ATS (one or more programs are accredited). Part-time programs available. *Degree requirements:* For master's, one foreign language, thesis (for some programs); for doctorate, thesis/dissertation. *Entrance requirements:* For M Div and master's, minimum GPA of 3.0; for doctorate, M Div, minimum GPA of 3.0 (D Min); for other advanced degree, M Div, minimum GPA of 3.0 (CAPS). Additional exam requirements/recommendations for international students: Required—TOEFL (minimum score 550 paper-based; 213 computer-based). Electronic applications accepted. *Faculty research:* Medical ethics, gay/lesbian studies in religion, Asian-American religion, race, culture and theology, theology in context.

Pepperdine University, Seaver College, Division of Religion, Malibu, CA 90263. Offers divinity (M Div); ministry (MS); religion (MA). Part-time and evening/weekend programs available. *Students:* 2 full-time (0 women), 8 part-time (4 women). 6 applicants, 83% accepted, 2 enrolled. *Entrance requirements:* For master's, GRE General Test, letters of recommendation, writing sample. Additional exam requirements/recommendations for international students: Required—TOEFL. *Application deadline:* For fall admission, 2/1 priority date for domestic students. Applications are processed on a rolling basis. Application fee: $55. Electronic applications accepted. *Financial support:* Applicants required to submit FAFSA. *Unit head:* Dr. Timothy Willis, Chair/Professor, 310-506-4352, Fax: 310-506-7271, E-mail: timothy.willis@pepperdine.edu. *Application contact:* Michael Truschke, Dean of Admission and Enrollment Management, 310-506-6165, Fax: 310-506-4861, E-mail: admission-seaver@pepperdine.edu.

Point Loma Nazarene University, Program in Religion, San Diego, CA 92106-2899. Offers M Min, MA. Part-time programs available. *Degree requirements:* For master's, thesis optional. *Entrance requirements:* For master's, GRE General Test, letters of recommendation, writing sample. *Faculty research:* Theology, Christian education, church administration.

Princeton Theological Seminary, Graduate and Professional Programs, Princeton, NJ 08542-0803. Offers M Div, MA, Th M, D Min, PhD. *Accreditation:* ACIPE; ATS. Part-time programs available. Terminal master's awarded for partial completion of doctoral program. *Degree requirements:* For doctorate, 2 foreign languages, thesis/dissertation, comprehensive exam (PhD), French and German. *Entrance requirements:* For doctorate, GRE General Test. Additional exam requirements/recommendations for international students: Required—TOEFL. Electronic applications accepted.

Princeton University, Graduate School, Department of Religion, Princeton, NJ 08544-1019. Offers PhD. *Degree requirements:* For doctorate, variable foreign language requirement, comprehensive exam, thesis/dissertation. *Entrance requirements:* For doctorate, GRE General Test. Additional exam requirements/recommendations for international students: Required—TOEFL (minimum score 600 paper-based; 250 computer-based). Electronic applications accepted.

Providence College, Graduate Studies, Department of Religious Studies, Providence, RI 02918. Offers Biblical studies (MA); theology (MA, MTS). Part-time and evening/weekend programs available. *Faculty:* 12 full-time (4 women), 1 (woman) part-time/adjunct. *Students:* 4 full-time (2 women), 25 part-time (6 women); includes 1 minority (Two or more races, non-Hispanic/Latino). Average age 40. 4 applicants, 100% accepted. In 2010, 14 master's awarded. *Degree requirements:* For master's, comprehensive exam, Greek and Hebrew (biblical studies). *Entrance requirements:* Additional exam requirements/recommendations for international students: Required—TOEFL (minimum score 550 paper-based; 213 computer-based; 80 iBT). *Application deadline:* For fall admission, 8/1 priority date for domestic and international students; for spring admission, 12/1 priority date for domestic and international students. Applications are processed on a rolling basis. Application fee: $55. *Expenses:* Tuition: Part-time $367 per credit. Required fees: $367. *Financial support:* In 2010–11, 4 research assistantships with full tuition reimbursements (averaging $8,400 per year) were awarded; career-related internships or fieldwork and unspecified assistantships also available. Support available to part-time students. Financial award application deadline: 8/1; financial award applicants required to submit FAFSA. *Unit head:* Rev. Thomas McCreesh, Director, 401-865-1150, Fax: 401-865-1830, E-mail: tmccrees@providence.edu. *Application contact:* Rev. Thomas McCreesh, Director, 401-865-1150, Fax: 401-865-1830, E-mail: tmccrees@providence.edu.

Queen's University at Kingston, School of Graduate Studies and Research, Faculty of Arts and Sciences, Department of Religious Studies, Kingston, ON K7L 3N6, Canada. Offers MA. *Degree requirements:* For master's, one foreign language, essay. *Entrance requirements:* For master's, honors BA in religious studies or equivalent. Additional exam requirements/recommendations for international students: Required—TOEFL (minimum score 600 paper-based; 250 computer-based). *Faculty research:* Modernity, culture, feminism, world religions, traditions.

Reformed Theological Seminary–Charlotte Campus, Graduate and Professional Programs, Charlotte, NC 28226-6318. Offers biblical studies (MA); ministry (D Min); pastoral ministry (M Div); theological studies (MA). Part-time programs available. *Degree requirements:* For master's, comprehensive exam; for doctorate, thesis/dissertation; for M Div, 2 foreign languages, comprehensive exam. *Entrance requirements:* For master's, minimum GPA of 2.6; for doctorate, minimum GPA of 3.0. Additional exam requirements/recommendations for international students: Required—TOEFL (minimum score 550 paper-based; 213 computer-based). Electronic applications accepted.

Reformed Theological Seminary–Washington D.C., Graduate and Professional Programs, McLean, VA 22101. Offers Bible (M Div); practical theology (M Div); religion (MA); theology (M Div). Part-time and evening/weekend programs available. *Faculty:* 2 full-time (0 women), 5 part-time/adjunct (0 women). *Students:* 13 full-time (1 woman), 69 part-time (7 women); includes 4 Black or African American, non-Hispanic/Latino; 20 Asian, non-Hispanic/Latino; 2 Hispanic/Latino, 1 international. Average age 35. 30 applicants, 77% accepted, 15 enrolled. In 2010, 11 master's awarded. *Degree requirements:* For master's, integrative paper. *Entrance requirements:* For master's, minimum undergraduate GPA of 2.6. Additional exam requirements/recommendations for international students: Required—TOEFL (minimum score 550 paper-based; 213 computer-based), TWE. *Application deadline:* Applications are processed on a rolling basis. Application fee: $75. Electronic applications accepted. *Expenses:* Tuition: Full-time $7020; part-time $1755 per semester. Tuition and fees vary according to course load. *Financial support:* In 2010–11, 76 students received support, including 7 fellowships (averaging $1,000 per year); institutionally sponsored loans, scholarships/grants, tuition waivers (partial), and unspecified assistantships also available. Support available to part-time students. Financial award application deadline: 6/1. *Faculty research:* Theology, Biblical studies, cultural studies. *Unit head:* Hugh C. Whelchel, Executive Director, 703-448-3393, Fax: 703-738-7389, E-mail: hwhelchel@rts.edu. *Application contact:* Geoff M. Sackett, Director of Admissions, 703-448-3393, Fax: 703-738-7389, E-mail: gsackett@rts.edu.

Rice University, Graduate Programs, School of Humanities, Department of Religious Studies, Houston, TX 77251-1892. Offers African religions (PhD); African-American religions (PhD); contemplative studies (PhD); ghosticism, esotericism, mysticism (PhD); Islam (PhD); Jewish thought and philosophy (PhD); modern Christianity in thought and popular culture (PhD); psychology of religion (PhD); the Bible and beyond (PhD). *Degree requirements:* For doctorate, 2 foreign languages, comprehensive exam, thesis/dissertation. *Entrance requirements:* For doctorate, GRE, letters of recommendation, writing sample. Additional exam requirements/recommendations for international students: Required—TOEFL (minimum score 600 paper-based; 90 iBT). Electronic applications accepted. *Faculty research:* Origins and historical development of Islam, history of Christianity, the study of comparative religion, African-American religion, religion and culture.

The Robert E. Webber Institute for Worship Studies, Doctor of Worship Studies Program, Orange Park, FL 32073. Offers DWS. *Degree requirements:* For doctorate, thesis/dissertation, practicum.

The Robert E. Webber Institute for Worship Studies, Master of Worship Studies Program, Orange Park, FL 32073. Offers MWS. *Degree requirements:* For master's, internship.

Sacred Heart University, Graduate Programs, College of Arts and Sciences, Department of Philosophy and Religious Studies, Fairfield, CT 06825-1000. Offers religious studies (MA). Part-time programs available. *Degree requirements:* For master's, comprehensive exam. *Entrance requirements:* Additional exam requirements/recommendations for international students: Required—TOEFL (minimum score 550 paper-based; 213 computer-based). Electronic applications accepted. *Expenses:* Contact institution.

St. Bonaventure University, School of Graduate Studies, School of Franciscan Studies, St. Bonaventure, NY 14778-2284. Offers MA. Part-time programs available. *Faculty:* 2 full-time (0 women). *Students:* 5 part-time (3 women), 2 international. Average age 48. 12 applicants, 83% accepted. In 2010, 8 master's awarded. *Degree requirements:* For master's, comprehensive exam, thesis optional. *Entrance requirements:* For master's, letter of intent, bachelor's degree, transcripts, letters of recommendation. Additional exam requirements/recommendations for international students: Required—TOEFL (minimum score 550 paper-based; 213 computer-based). *Application deadline:* For fall admission, 3/15 priority date for domestic students, 2/1 priority date for international students. Applications are processed on a rolling basis. Application fee: $30. Electronic applications accepted. *Expenses:* Tuition: Part-time $670 per credit hour. *Financial support:* In 2010–11, 1 research assistantship with full and partial tuition reimbursement was awarded; Federal Work-Study, scholarships/grants, health care benefits, tuition waivers (full and partial), and unspecified assistantships also available. Support available to part-time students. Financial award application deadline: 4/15; financial award applicants required to submit FAFSA. *Unit head:* Fr. Edward Coughlin, Interim Dean, 716-375-2032, E-mail: coughlin@sbu.edu. *Application contact:* Bruce E. Campbell, Director, Graduate Admissions, 716-375-2429, Fax: 716-375-7834, E-mail: gradsch@sbu.edu.

St. Charles Borromeo Seminary, Overbrook, Graduate and Professional Programs, Division of Religious Studies, Wynnewood, PA 19096. Offers MA. Part-time programs available. *Faculty:* 3 full-time (2 women), 3 part-time/adjunct (1 woman). *Students:* 46 part-time (26 women); includes 8 minority (4 Black or African American, non-Hispanic/Latino; 2 Asian, non-Hispanic/Latino; 2 Hispanic/Latino), 1 international. Average age 42. 19 applicants, 100% accepted, 18 enrolled. In 2010, 14 master's awarded. *Degree requirements:* For master's, comprehensive exam. *Entrance requirements:* For master's, 18 undergraduate credits in theology and/or philosophy or the equivalent. Additional exam requirements/recommendations for international students: Required—TOEFL. *Application deadline:* For fall admission, 7/15 for domestic students, 3/15 for international students; for spring admission, 11/15 for domestic students. Applications are processed on a rolling basis. Application fee: $0. *Expenses:* Tuition: Full-time $18,888; part-time $1548 per course. Required fees: $1140. *Unit head:* Rev. Joseph W. Bongard, Acting Academic Dean, 610-785-6287, Fax: 610-667-4122, E-mail: frjbongard@adphila.org. *Application contact:* Jared Haselbarth, Assistant Academic Dean, 610-785-6287, Fax: 610-667-1422, E-mail: jhaselba@adphila.org.

Saint John's Seminary, Graduate Programs, Brighton, MA 02135. Offers M Div, MA Th, MAM. *Accreditation:* ATS.

Saint Mary's University, Faculty of Arts, Department of Religious Studies, Halifax, NS B3H 3C3, Canada. Offers theology and religious studies (MA).

Seminary of the Southwest, Graduate and Professional Programs, Austin, TX 78768-2247. Offers Anglican studies (Advanced Diploma); chaplaincy (MCPC, JD/MAC); counseling (MAC); divinity (M Div); religion (MAR); spiritual formation (MAPM, MSF); theological studies (Advanced Diploma); JD/MAC. *Accreditation:* ACIPE; ATS (one or more programs are accredited). Part-time and evening/weekend programs available. *Faculty:* 11 full-time (3 women), 26 part-time/adjunct (7 women). *Students:* 69 full-time (40 women), 47 part-time (34 women); includes 11 minority (4 Black or African American, non-Hispanic/Latino; 4 Hispanic/Latino; 3 Two or more races, non-Hispanic/Latino), 3 international. Average age 45. 57 applicants, 93% accepted, 46 enrolled. In 2010, 13 first professional degrees, 8 master's, 6 other advanced degrees awarded. *Degree requirements:* For master's, thesis (for some programs). *Entrance requirements:* For M Div and master's, GRE, MAT, interview; for Advanced Diploma, interview. *Application deadline:* For fall admission, 7/1 for domestic students; for spring admission, 11/1 for domestic students. Applications are processed on a rolling basis. Application fee: $50. *Expenses:* Tuition: Full-time $13,152; part-time $548 per credit hour. Required fees: $75. One-time fee: $20 part-time. *Financial support:* Career-related internships or fieldwork and scholarships/grants available. Support available to part-time students. Financial award application deadline: 6/15. *Unit head:* Very Rev. Douglas Travis, Dean and President, 512-472-4133 Ext. 307, Fax: 512-472-3098, E-mail: dtravis@ssw.edu. *Application contact:* Jennielle Strother, Director of Admissions, 512-472-4133 Ext. 375, Fax: 512-472-3098, E-mail: jstrother@ssw.edu.

Seton Hall University, College of Arts and Sciences, Department of Jewish-Christian Studies, South Orange, NJ 07079-2697. Offers Holocaust studies (MA); Jewish-Christian Studies (MA). Part-time and evening/weekend programs available. *Degree requirements:* For master's, thesis optional. *Entrance requirements:* For master's, interview or suitable correspondence with department chair. Additional exam requirements/recommendations for international students:

Required—TOEFL. Electronic applications accepted. *Faculty research:* Jewish-Christian issues, Biblical studies, Holocaust studies.

Seton Hall University, Immaculate Conception Seminary School of Theology, South Orange, NJ 07079-2697. Offers Christian spirituality (Certificate); great spiritual books (Certificate); pastoral ministry (M Div, MA, Certificate); scripture studies (Certificate); Seminary's Theological Education for Parish Services (STEPS) (Certificate); theology (MA); youth ministry (Certificate). *Accreditation:* ATS (one or more programs are accredited). Part-time and evening/weekend programs available. *Faculty:* 13 full-time (2 women), 12 part-time/adjunct (1 woman). *Students:* 105 full-time (7 women), 112 part-time (43 women); includes 4 Black or African American, non-Hispanic/Latino; 9 Asian, non-Hispanic/Latino; 31 Hispanic/Latino, 72 international. Average age 39. 74 applicants, 100% accepted, 69 enrolled. In 2010, 16 first professional degrees, 32 master's, 6 other advanced degrees awarded. *Degree requirements:* For master's, one foreign language, comprehensive exam, thesis (for some programs), final project; for M Div, one foreign language, thesis/dissertation, final project and seminar, field education, spiritual formation. *Entrance requirements:* For M Div, GRE, MAT; for master's, GRE General Test or MAT. Additional exam requirements/recommendations for international students: Required—TOEFL (minimum score 600 paper-based; 250 computer-based; 100 iBT). *Application deadline:* For fall admission, 8/1 priority date for domestic and international students; for spring admission, 12/15 priority date for domestic and international students. Applications are processed on a rolling basis. Application fee: $50. Electronic applications accepted. *Expenses:* Contact institution. *Financial support:* In 2010–11, 217 students received support. Career-related internships or fieldwork, Federal Work-Study, scholarships/grants, tuition waivers (partial), and unspecified assistantships available. Support available to part-time students. Financial award application deadline: 8/1; financial award applicants required to submit FAFSA. *Faculty research:* Pauline literature, history of Biblical interpretation and theological exegesis, spirituality of St. Edith Stein, Thomism, history of Catholicism in America. *Unit head:* Rev. Msgr. Robert F. Coleman, Rector and Dean, 973-761-9016, Fax: 973-761-9577, E-mail: robert.coleman@shu.edu. *Application contact:* Rev. Msgr. Joseph R. Chapel, Associate Dean, 973-761-9633, Fax: 973-761-9577, E-mail: theology@shu.edu.

Sioux Falls Seminary, Graduate and Professional Programs, Program in Christian Leadership, Sioux Falls, SD 57105-1599. Offers MA.

Southern Adventist University, School of Religion, Collegedale, TN 37315-0370. Offers Biblical and theological studies (MA); church leadership and management (M Min); church ministry and homiletics (M Min); evangelism and world mission (M Min); religious studies (MA). Part-time programs available. *Degree requirements:* For master's, comprehensive exam, thesis (for some programs). *Entrance requirements:* For master's, GRE. Additional exam requirements/recommendations for international students: Required—TOEFL (minimum score 600 paper-based; 250 computer-based). *Faculty research:* Biblical archaeology.

Southern Baptist Theological Seminary, Billy Graham School of Missions, Evangelism and Church Growth, Louisville, KY 40280-0004. Offers Christian mission/world religion (PhD); evangelism/church growth (PhD); ministry (D Min); missiology (MA, D Miss); missions, evangelism and church growth (M Div); religion (Th M); theological studies (MA). *Accreditation:* ATS. Part-time and evening/weekend programs available. Postbaccalaureate distance learning degree programs offered (minimal on-campus study). *Degree requirements:* For master's and M Div, 2 foreign languages; for doctorate, 4 foreign languages, thesis/dissertation. *Entrance requirements:* For doctorate, GRE General Test, MAT, M Div. Additional exam requirements/recommendations for international students: Required—TOEFL, TWE. *Faculty research:* Assimilation of church congregants, effective methodologies of evangelism, expectations of church members, spiritual warfare literature, formative church discipline.

Southern Baptist Theological Seminary, School of Theology, Louisville, KY 40280-0004. Offers applied theology (D Min); biblical and theological studies (M Div); biblical counseling (M Div, MA, D Min); biblical spirituality (D Min); Christian ministry (M Div); expository preaching (D Min); pastoral studies (M Div); theological studies (MA); theology (Th M, PhD); worldview and apologetics (M Div). *Accreditation:* ATS. Part-time and evening/weekend programs available. Postbaccalaureate distance learning degree programs offered (minimal on-campus study). *Degree requirements:* For master's, 2 foreign languages, thesis; for doctorate, 4 foreign languages, thesis/dissertation; for M Div, 2 foreign languages. *Entrance requirements:* For master's, GRE General Test, MAT, M Div; for doctorate, GRE General Test, MAT, interview, M Div, field essay. Additional exam requirements/recommendations for international students: Required—TOEFL, TWE. *Faculty research:* Biblical studies, contemporary theology, church history, pastoral care, ministry/missions studies.

Southern California Seminary, Graduate and Professional Programs, El Cajon, CA 92019. Offers Biblical studies (MABS); counseling psychology (MACP); marriage and family therapy (MAMFT); psychology (Psy D); religious studies (MRS); theology (M Div). Part-time and evening/weekend programs available. Postbaccalaureate distance learning degree programs offered (minimal on-campus study). *Students:* 37 full-time (8 women), 80 part-time (37 women); includes 55 minority (20 Black or African American, non-Hispanic/Latino; 14 Asian, non-Hispanic/Latino; 16 Hispanic/Latino; 1 Native Hawaiian or other Pacific Islander, non-Hispanic/Latino; 4 Two or more races, non-Hispanic/Latino), 5 international. Average age 41. In 2010, 7 first professional degrees, 50 master's, 4 doctorates awarded. *Degree requirements:* For master's, thesis (for some programs); for doctorate, thesis/dissertation; for M Div, 2 foreign languages. *Entrance requirements:* For doctorate, master's degree in psychology. Additional exam requirements/recommendations for international students: Required—TOEFL (minimum score 550 paper-based). *Application deadline:* For fall admission, 8/13 for domestic and international students; for spring admission, 12/11 for domestic students, 12/15 for international students. Applications are processed on a rolling basis. Application fee: $31 ($126 for international students). Electronic applications accepted. *Expenses:* Tuition: Part-time $339 per unit. Part-time tuition and fees vary according to degree level, campus/location and program. *Financial support:* In 2010–11, 14 students received support. Federal Work-Study, scholarships/grants, and tuition waivers (partial) available. Financial award application deadline: 3/1; financial award applicants required to submit FAFSA. *Unit head:* Dr. Chuck Emert, Vice-President of Academics, 619-201-8995, Fax: 619-201-8975. *Application contact:* Thomas Pittman, Admissions Officer and Director of Student Services, 888-389-7244, Fax: 619-201-8975, E-mail: thpittman@socalsem.edu.

Southern Evangelical Seminary, Graduate Programs, Matthews, NC 28105. Offers apologetics (MA, Certificate); Christian education (MA); church ministry (MA, Certificate); divinity (Certificate), including apologetics (M Div, Certificate); Islamic studies (MA, Certificate); Jewish studies (MA); philosophy (MA); religion (MA); theology (M Div, including apologetics (M Div, Certificate), Biblical studies; youth ministry (MA). Part-time and evening/weekend programs available. Postbaccalaureate distance learning degree programs offered. *Degree requirements:* For master's, thesis (for some programs); for doctorate, 2 foreign languages, comprehensive exam (for some programs), thesis/dissertation; for M Div, one foreign language. *Entrance requirements:* Additional exam requirements/recommendations for international students: Required—TOEFL (minimum score 600 paper-based; 250 computer-based). *Application deadline:* For fall admission, 8/15 priority date for domestic students, 8/5 priority date for international students; for winter admission, 12/15 priority date for domestic and international students; for spring admission, 1/15 priority date for domestic and international students. Applications are processed on a rolling basis. Application fee: $25. *Expenses:* Tuition: Full-time $9405; part-time $313.50 per credit hour. Required fees: $150; $50 per semester. *Financial support:* Scholarships/grants available. *Unit head:* Dr. Barry R. Leventhal, Dean, 704-847-5600 Ext. 204, Fax: 704-845-1747, E-mail: dean@ses.edu. *Application contact:* Duke Hale, Director of Recruitment, 704-847-5600 Ext. 216, Fax: 704-845-1747, E-mail: dhale@ses.edu.

Southern Methodist University, Dedman College, Graduate Program in Religious Studies, Dallas, TX 75275-0133. Offers MA, PhD. *Faculty:* 16 full-time (5 women). *Students:* 30 full-time (10 women); includes 1 Black or African American, non-Hispanic/Latino; 1 American

Religion

Southern Methodist University *(continued)*
Indian or Alaska Native, non-Hispanic/Latino, 3 international. Average age 35. 60 applicants, 12% accepted, 5 enrolled. In 2010, 8 doctorates awarded. Terminal master's awarded for partial completion of doctoral program. *Degree requirements:* For master's, one foreign language, thesis, oral and written exams; for doctorate, variable foreign language requirement, thesis/dissertation, oral and written exams. *Entrance requirements:* For master's and doctorate, GRE General Test, minimum GPA of 3.0, course work in religion. Additional exam requirements/recommendations for international students: Required—TOEFL (minimum score 550 paper-based; 210 computer-based; 79 iBT). *Application deadline:* For fall admission, 1/15 for domestic and international students. Application fee: $75. Electronic applications accepted. *Financial support:* In 2010–11, 30 students received support, including 27 fellowships with full and partial tuition reimbursements available (averaging $13,555 per year), 5 research assistantships with full and partial tuition reimbursements available (averaging $650 per year), 3 teaching assistantships with full and partial tuition reimbursements available (averaging $2,000 per year); institutionally sponsored loans, scholarships/grants, and tuition waivers (full and partial) also available. Financial award application deadline: 2/1; financial award applicants required to submit FAFSA. *Faculty research:* Theology, religious ethics, Biblical studies, history of Christianity, religion and culture. *Unit head:* Prof. Bruce D. Marshall, Director, 214-768-2432, Fax: 214-768-2117. *Application contact:* Lucy Cobbe, Assistant to Director, 214-768-2432, Fax: 214-768-2117, E-mail: gradreli@mail.smu.edu.

Southern Nazarene University, Graduate College, Department of Philosophy and Religion, Bethany, OK 73008. Offers theology (MA). Part-time programs available. *Degree requirements:* For master's, one foreign language, thesis optional. *Entrance requirements:* For master's, GMAT, English proficiency exam, minimum GPA of 3.0 in last 60 hours/major, 2.7 overall. *Expenses:* Tuition: Part-time $575 per credit hour.

Southwestern Assemblies of God University, Thomas F. Harrison School of Graduate Studies, Program in Theological Studies, Waxahachie, TX 75165-5735. Offers Bible and theology (MS); Biblical studies (M Div); counseling (M Div); cross cultural missions (M Div); practical theology (M Div); theological studies (M Div). Postbaccalaureate distance learning degree programs offered. *Degree requirements:* For master's, comprehensive written and oral exams. *Entrance requirements:* For master's, GRE General Test, minimum GPA of 2.5. Electronic applications accepted.

Stanford University, School of Humanities and Sciences, Department of Religious Studies, Stanford, CA 94305-9991. Offers MA, PhD. Terminal master's awarded for partial completion of doctoral program. *Degree requirements:* For master's, one foreign language, thesis optional; for doctorate, 2 foreign languages, thesis/dissertation, qualifying exam. *Entrance requirements:* For master's and doctorate, GRE General Test. Additional exam requirements/recommendations for international students: Required—TOEFL. Electronic applications accepted. *Expenses:* Tuition: Full-time $38,700; part-time $860 per unit. One-time fee: $200 full-time.

Syracuse University, College of Arts and Sciences, Program in Religion, Syracuse, NY 13244. Offers MA, PhD. Part-time programs available. *Students:* 38 full-time (22 women), 10 part-time (3 women); includes 3 minority (1 Asian, non-Hispanic/Latino; 1 Hispanic/Latino; 1 Two or more races, non-Hispanic/Latino), 5 international. Average age 35. 55 applicants, 16% accepted, 2 enrolled. In 2010, 3 master's, 6 doctorates awarded. Terminal master's awarded for partial completion of doctoral program. *Degree requirements:* For master's, one foreign language, comprehensive exam, thesis optional; for doctorate, 2 foreign languages, comprehensive exam, thesis/dissertation. *Entrance requirements:* For master's and doctorate, GRE General Test. Additional exam requirements/recommendations for international students: Required—TOEFL (minimum score 100 iBT). *Application deadline:* For fall admission, 1/10 priority date for domestic and international students. Application fee: $75. Electronic applications accepted. *Expenses:* Tuition: Part-time $1162 per credit. *Financial support:* Fellowships with full tuition reimbursements, teaching assistantships with full tuition reimbursements, tuition waivers (partial) available. Financial award application deadline: 1/1; financial award applicants required to submit FAFSA. *Unit head:* Dr. Joanne P. Waghorne, Director of Graduate Studies, 315-443-3861, Fax: 315-443-3958, E-mail: jpwaghor@syr.edu. *Application contact:* Jackie Borowre, Recruiting Contact, 315-443-3861, E-mail: jborowre@syr.edu.

Taylor University, Master of Arts in Religious Studies Program, Upland, IN 46989-1001. Offers biblical studies (MA); world religions (MA). Part-time programs available. *Faculty:* 1 (woman) full-time, 2 part-time/adjunct (0 women). *Students:* 2 full-time (1 woman), 4 part-time (1 woman); includes 1 Black or African American, non-Hispanic/Latino. Average age 31. In 2010, 1 master's awarded. *Degree requirements:* For master's, thesis. *Application deadline:* Applications are processed on a rolling basis. Application fee: $100. *Expenses:* Contact institution. *Financial support:* In 2010–11, 1 student received support, including 2 fellowships (averaging $1,500 per year). Financial award applicants required to submit FAFSA. *Unit head:* Dr. Sheri Klouda, Chair, 765-998-4786, Fax: 765-998-4930, E-mail: shklouda@taylor.edu. *Application contact:* Kari Manganello, Program Assistant, 765-998-5148, Fax: 765-998-4930, E-mail: krmangane@taylor.edu.

Temple Baptist Seminary, Program in Theology, Chattanooga, TN 37404-3530. Offers biblical languages (M Div); Biblical studies (MABS); Christian education (MACE); English Bible û language tools (M Div); theology (MM, D Min). Part-time and evening/weekend programs available. Postbaccalaureate distance learning degree programs offered (minimal on-campus study). *Degree requirements:* For doctorate, thesis/dissertation; for M Div, proficiency in Greek and Hebrew. *Entrance requirements:* For doctorate, minimum GPA of 3.0, M Div.

Temple University, College of Liberal Arts, Department of Religion, Philadelphia, PA 19122-6096. Offers MA, PhD. Part-time programs available. *Faculty:* 12 full-time (4 women). *Students:* 54 full-time (19 women), 12 part-time (5 women); includes 6 Black or African American, non-Hispanic/Latino; 1 American Indian or Alaska Native, non-Hispanic/Latino; 2 Asian, non-Hispanic/Latino; 1 Hispanic/Latino; 1 Two or more races, non-Hispanic/Latino, 7 international. 61 applicants, 64% accepted, 17 enrolled. In 2010, 10 master's, 1 doctorate awarded. *Degree requirements:* For doctorate, variable foreign language requirement, thesis/dissertation. *Entrance requirements:* For doctorate, GRE General Test, minimum GPA of 3.0. Additional exam requirements/recommendations for international students: Required—TOEFL (minimum score 550 paper-based; 213 computer-based; 79 iBT). *Application deadline:* For fall admission, 1/15 for domestic students, 12/15 for international students. Application fee: $50. Electronic applications accepted. *Financial support:* Fellowships, teaching assistantships, Federal Work-Study, institutionally sponsored loans, and tuition waivers (full and partial) available. Financial award application deadline: 1/15; financial award applicants required to submit FAFSA. *Faculty research:* Textural and historical origins; philosophy of religion and religious thought; religion, culture, and society. *Unit head:* Dr. Terry Rey, Chair, 215-204-7973, Fax: 215-204-2535, E-mail: religion@temple.edu. *Application contact:* Dr. Terry Rey, Chair, 215-204-7973, Fax: 215-204-2535, E-mail: religion@temple.edu.

Trevecca Nazarene University, Graduate Division, Graduate Religion Programs, Nashville, TN 37210-2877. Offers biblical studies (MA); preaching and practical theology (MA); systematic theology/historical theology (MA). Part-time programs available. *Faculty:* 4 full-time (0 women). *Students:* 17 full-time (0 women), 22 part-time (9 women); includes 9 Black or African American, non-Hispanic/Latino. Average age 34. In 2010, 6 master's awarded. *Degree requirements:* For master's, comprehensive exam, thesis optional. *Entrance requirements:* For master's, GRE General Test or MAT, minimum GPA of 2.7, 2 letters of recommendation. Additional exam requirements/recommendations for international students: Required—TOEFL (minimum score 550 paper-based; 213 computer-based). *Application deadline:* Applications are processed on a rolling basis. Application fee: $25. Electronic applications accepted. *Expenses:* Contact institution. *Financial support:* Applicants required to submit FAFSA. *Unit head:* Dr. Tim Green, Dean/Director, 615-248-1378, Fax: 615-248-7417, E-mail: admissions_rel@trevecca.edu. *Application contact:* Center of Lifelong Learning, 615-248-1200, E-mail: cll@trevecca.edu.

Trinity International University, South Florida Campus, Divinity School, Miami, FL 33132-1996. Offers MA, Certificate.

Trinity School for Ministry, Graduate Programs, Ambridge, PA 15003-2397. Offers Anglican studies (Diploma); basic Christian studies (Diploma); divinity (M Div); ministry (D Min); mission and evangelism (MAME, Diploma); religion (MAR); youth ministry (Diploma). *Accreditation:* ATS (one or more programs are accredited). Part-time programs available. *Degree requirements:* For master's, thesis optional; for doctorate, thesis/dissertation; for M Div, thesis/dissertation optional, Greek and Hebrew. *Entrance requirements:* Additional exam requirements/recommendations for international students: Required—TOEFL. *Faculty research:* Pauline Epistles, contemporary theology, history of Anglican liturgy, book of Ruth, biblical theology.

Unification Theological Seminary, Graduate Program, Main Campus, Barrytown, NY 12507. Offers divinity (M Div); ministry (D Min); religious education (MRE); religious studies (MA). Part-time and evening/weekend programs available. *Faculty:* 4 full-time (1 woman), 3 part-time/adjunct (0 women). *Students:* 37 full-time (9 women), 1 part-time (0 women); includes 10 Black or African American, non-Hispanic/Latino; 1 American Indian or Alaska Native, non-Hispanic/Latino; 4 Asian, non-Hispanic/Latino; 1 Hispanic/Latino, 9 international. Average age 45. In 2010, 2 first professional degrees, 14 master's, 3 doctorates awarded. *Degree requirements:* For master's, one foreign language, thesis (for some programs), project; for doctorate, thesis/dissertation; for M Div, one foreign language, thesis/dissertation. *Entrance requirements:* For M Div and master's, bachelor's degree; for doctorate, M Div or equivalency. Additional exam requirements/recommendations for international students: Required—TOEFL (minimum score 450 paper-based; 133 computer-based; 45 iBT). *Application deadline:* For fall admission, 8/15 priority date for domestic students; for spring admission, 1/15 priority date for domestic students. Applications are processed on a rolling basis. Application fee: $30. *Expenses:* Tuition: Full-time $10,440; part-time $435 per credit. Required fees: $125 per semester. *Financial support:* Career-related internships or fieldwork, institutionally sponsored loans, scholarships/grants, and tuition waivers (partial) available. Support available to part-time students. Financial award applicants required to submit FAFSA. *Faculty research:* Church leadership, church history, world religions, ecumenism, interfaith peace building, service-learning. *Unit head:* Dr. Kathy Winings, Academic Dean, 845-752-3000 Ext. 228, Fax: 845-752-3014, E-mail: academics@uts.edu. *Application contact:* Davetta Ogunlola, Director of Admissions, 212-563-6647 Ext. 105, Fax: 212-563-6431, E-mail: d.ogunlola@uts.edu.

Unification Theological Seminary, Graduate Program, New York Extension, New York, NY 10036. Offers divinity (M Div); religious education (MRE); religious studies (MA). Part-time and evening/weekend programs available. *Faculty:* 3 full-time (0 women), 9 part-time/adjunct (2 women). *Students:* 42 full-time (17 women), 21 part-time (12 women); includes 25 Black or African American, non-Hispanic/Latino; 2 Asian, non-Hispanic/Latino; 1 Hispanic/Latino, 30 international. Average age 40. *Degree requirements:* For master's, thesis (for some programs), project; for M Div, thesis/dissertation. *Entrance requirements:* For M Div and master's, bachelor's degree. Additional exam requirements/recommendations for international students: Required—TOEFL (minimum score 450 paper-based; 133 computer-based). *Application deadline:* For fall admission, 8/15 priority date for domestic students; for spring admission, 1/15 priority date for domestic students. Applications are processed on a rolling basis. Application fee: $30. *Expenses:* Tuition: Full-time $10,440; part-time $435 per credit. Required fees: $125 per semester. *Financial support:* Career-related internships or fieldwork, institutionally sponsored loans, scholarships/grants, and tuition waivers (partial) available. Support available to part-time students. Financial award applicants required to submit FAFSA. *Faculty research:* Church history, world religions, ecumenism, interfaith peace building, service-learning. *Unit head:* Dr. Kathy Winings, Academic Dean, 212-563-6647 Ext. 101, Fax: 212-563-6431, E-mail: academics@uts.edu. *Application contact:* Davetta Ogunlola, Admissions Officer, 212-563-6647 Ext. 105, Fax: 212-563-6431, E-mail: d.ogunlola@uts.edu.

Union University, School of Christian Studies, Jackson, TN 38305-3697. Offers Christian studies (MCS); expository preaching (D Min).

United Theological Seminary of the Twin Cities, Graduate Programs, New Brighton, MN 55112-2598. Offers advanced theological studies (Diploma); justice and peace studies (M Div, MA); leadership toward racial justice (M Div, MA, Certificate); Methodist studies (M Div, MA, Certificate); ministry (D Min); ministry renewal and professional development (Certificate); pastoral care and counseling (M Div, MA, MARL); religion and theology (MA); theological and religious studies (Certificate); theology and the arts (M Div, MA); urban ministry (M Div, MA, MARL); women's studies: religion, theology and ministry (M Div, MA). *Accreditation:* ACIPE; ATS. Part-time and evening/weekend programs available. *Faculty:* 8 full-time (5 women), 28 part-time/adjunct (16 women). *Students:* 57 full-time (41 women), 94 part-time (61 women); includes 6 minority (5 Black or African American, non-Hispanic/Latino; 1 Hispanic/Latino), 1 international. Average age 47. 49 applicants, 98% accepted, 41 enrolled. In 2010, 10 first professional degrees, 6 master's, 4 doctorates, 2 other advanced degrees awarded. *Degree requirements:* For master's, thesis; for doctorate, comprehensive exam, thesis/dissertation; for M Div, integrative notebook, spiritual chronicle. *Entrance requirements:* For M Div and master's, minimum GPA of 2.75; strong analytical, reflective thinking and writing skills; vocational and academic goals compatible with those of Seminary; for doctorate, M Div or equivalent, minimum GPA of 3.0, 3 years experience in professional ministry; for other advanced degree, BA or equivalent life experience; strong analytical, reflective thinking and writing skills (Certificate); proficiency in English language, previous study of theology at a theological school, recommendation of student's denomination (Diploma). Additional exam requirements/recommendations for international students: Required—TOEFL (minimum score 550 paper-based). *Application deadline:* For fall admission, 7/1 priority date for domestic students, 11/1 priority date for international students; for winter admission, 11/1 priority date for domestic students; for spring admission, 11/15 priority date for domestic students. Applications are processed on a rolling basis. Application fee: $50. *Expenses:* Tuition: Full-time $13,014; part-time $482 per credit hour. One-time fee: $170. Tuition and fees vary according to course load, degree level and program. *Financial support:* In 2010–11, 120 students received support. Career-related internships or fieldwork, institutionally sponsored loans, and scholarships/grants available. Support available to part-time students. Financial award application deadline: 5/1; financial award applicants required to submit FAFSA. *Unit head:* Prof. Susan K. Ebbers, Dean of the Seminary, 651-255-6143 Ext. 108, Fax: 651-633-4315, E-mail: sebbers@unitedseminary.edu. *Application contact:* Rev. Glen Herrington-Hall, Director of Admissions, 651-255-6107 Ext. 107, Fax: 651-633-4315, E-mail: gherrington-hall@unitedseminary.edu.

Université de Montréal, Faculty of Theology and Sciences of Religions, Montréal, QC H3C 3J7, Canada. Offers health, spirituality and bioethics (DESS); practical theology (MA, PhD); religious sciences (MA, PhD); theology (MA, D Th, PhD, L Th); theology-Biblical studies (PhD). *Degree requirements:* For master's, one foreign language; for doctorate, 2 foreign languages, thesis/dissertation, general exam. Electronic applications accepted.

Université de Sherbrooke, Faculty of Theology, Ethics and Philosophy, Sherbrooke, QC J1K 2R1, Canada. Offers applied ethics (Diploma); human science of religions (MA); intercultural training (Diploma); philosophy (MA, PhD); spiritual anthropology (Diploma); theology (MA, PhD, Diploma). Part-time and evening/weekend programs available. Postbaccalaureate distance learning degree programs offered. Terminal master's awarded for partial completion of doctoral program. *Entrance requirements:* For master's, bachelor's degree in related discipline; for doctorate, master's degree in related discipline. *Faculty research:* Faith and culture interrelation.

Université du Québec à Montréal, Graduate Programs, Program in Religious Sciences, Montréal, QC H3C 3P8, Canada. Offers MA, PhD. MA offered jointly with Concordia University. Part-time programs available. *Degree requirements:* For master's, thesis; for doctorate, thesis/dissertation. *Entrance requirements:* For master's, appropriate bachelor's degree or equivalent, proficiency in French; for doctorate, appropriate master's degree or equivalent, proficiency in French.

Université Laval, Faculty of Theology and Religious Sciences, Programs in Human Sciences of Religion, Québec, QC G1K 7P4, Canada. Offers MA, PhD. Terminal master's awarded for partial completion of doctoral program. *Degree requirements:* For master's, thesis (for some programs); for doctorate, comprehensive exam, thesis/dissertation. *Entrance requirements:* For master's, knowledge of French, comprehension of a second language; for doctorate, knowledge of French and English. Electronic applications accepted.

The University of British Columbia, Faculty of Arts and Faculty of Graduate Studies, Department of Classical, Near Eastern and Religious Studies, Program in Religious Studies, Vancouver, BC V6T 1Z1, Canada. Offers MA, PhD. Part-time programs available. *Degree requirements:* For master's, 2 foreign languages, comprehensive exam, thesis optional; for doctorate, 2 foreign languages, comprehensive exam, thesis/dissertation. *Entrance requirements:* For doctorate, MA. Additional exam requirements/recommendations for international students: Required—TOEFL (minimum score 600 paper-based; 250 computer-based), IELTS. Electronic applications accepted. Tuition charges are reported in Canadian dollars. *Expenses:* Tuition, area resident: Full-time $4179 Canadian dollars. International tuition: $7344 Canadian dollars full-time. *Faculty research:* Hebrew Bible in ancient Near Eastern context, Christian scriptures in Greco-Roman context, mystical aspects of religion, the feminine in western traditions, modern Jewish experience.

The University of British Columbia, Faculty of Arts and Faculty of Graduate Studies, Department of Classical, Near Eastern and Religious Studies, Programmes in Classics, Vancouver, BC V6T 1Z1, Canada. Offers ancient culture, religion, and ethnicity (MA); classical and near eastern archaeology (MA); classics (MA, PhD). Part-time programs available. *Degree requirements:* For master's, 2 foreign languages, thesis or comprehensive exam; for doctorate, 2 foreign languages, comprehensive exam, thesis/dissertation. *Entrance requirements:* For doctorate, MA. Additional exam requirements/recommendations for international students: Required—TOEFL (minimum score 600 paper-based; 250 computer-based), IELTS (minimum score 7.5). Electronic applications accepted. Tuition charges are reported in Canadian dollars. *Expenses:* Tuition, area resident: Full-time $4179 Canadian dollars. International tuition: $7344 Canadian dollars full-time. *Faculty research:* Classical archaeology, ancient historians, late antiquity, ancient prose fiction, epigraphy.

University of Calgary, Faculty of Graduate Studies, Faculty of Arts, Department of Religious Studies, Calgary, AB T2N 1N4, Canada. Offers MA, PhD. Part-time programs available. *Degree requirements:* For master's, one foreign language, thesis; for doctorate, 2 foreign languages, thesis/dissertation, candidacy exam. *Entrance requirements:* For master's, minimum GPA of 3.3; for doctorate, minimum GPA of 3.5. Additional exam requirements/recommendations for international students: Required—TOEFL (minimum score 550 paper-based; 213 computer-based). *Faculty research:* Eastern religions, Western religions, nature of religion.

University of California, Berkeley, Graduate Division, College of Letters and Science, Department of Near Eastern Studies, Group in Near Eastern Religions, Berkeley, CA 94720-1500. Offers PhD. Program offered jointly with Graduate Theological Union. *Degree requirements:* For doctorate, 2 foreign languages, thesis/dissertation, qualifying exam. *Entrance requirements:* For doctorate, GRE General Test, MA or equivalent in Near Eastern studies or related field; minimum GPA of 3.0, 3 letters of recommendation.

University of California, Berkeley, Graduate Division, College of Letters and Science, Group in Buddhist Studies, Berkeley, CA 94720-1500. Offers PhD. *Degree requirements:* For doctorate, 4 foreign languages, thesis/dissertation, dissertation defense, qualifying exam. *Entrance requirements:* For doctorate, GRE General Test, MA in Japanese, Chinese, or Sanskrit; minimum GPA of 3.0, 3 letters of recommendation. Electronic applications accepted.

University of California, Santa Barbara, Graduate Division, College of Letters and Sciences, Division of Humanities and Fine Arts, Department of Religious Studies, Santa Barbara, CA 93106-3130. Offers ancient Mediterranean studies (PhD); European medieval studies (PhD); feminist studies (PhD); global studies (PhD); religious studies (MA, PhD); translation studies (PhD); MA/PhD. *Faculty:* 19 full-time (9 women), 8 part-time/adjunct (3 women). *Students:* 79 full-time (29 women); includes 2 Black or African American, non-Hispanic/Latino; 1 American Indian or Alaska Native, non-Hispanic/Latino; 9 Asian, non-Hispanic/Latino; 5 Hispanic/Latino. Average age 31. 139 applicants, 22% accepted, 10 enrolled. In 2010, 11 master's, 10 doctorates awarded. *Degree requirements:* For master's, one foreign language, comprehensive exam (for some programs), thesis (for some programs), colloquium; for doctorate, one foreign language, thesis/dissertation, methodology, colloquium. *Entrance requirements:* For master's and doctorate, GRE General Test. Additional exam requirements/recommendations for international students: Required—TOEFL (minimum score 550 paper-based; 80 iBT), IELTS (minimum score 7). *Application deadline:* For fall admission, 12/1 for domestic and international students. Application fee: $70 ($90 for international students). Electronic applications accepted. *Financial support:* In 2010–11, 64 students received support, including 31 fellowships with full tuition reimbursements available (averaging $12,351 per year), 4 research assistantships with full and partial tuition reimbursements available (averaging $4,147 per year), 37 teaching assistantships with partial tuition reimbursements available (averaging $9,573 per year); career-related internships or fieldwork, scholarships/grants, tuition waivers (full and partial), and associateships also available. Financial award application deadline: 12/1; financial award applicants required to submit FAFSA. *Faculty research:* Area studies; religious traditions; theory and method in the study of religion; religion, culture, and politics; spirituality and religious experience. *Unit head:* Prof. Jose I. Cabezon, Professor and Chair, 805-893-3564, Fax: 805-893-7671, E-mail: jcabezon@religion.ucsb.edu. *Application contact:* Sally J. Lombrozo, Graduate Program Assistant, 805-893-2744, Fax: 805-893-7671, E-mail: lombrozo@hfa.ucsb.edu.

University of California, Santa Barbara, Graduate Division, College of Letters and Sciences, Division of Social Sciences, Department of Global and International Studies, Santa Barbara, CA 93106-7065. Offers global culture and religion (MA); global government and human rights (MA); political economy, sustainable development, and the environment (MA). *Faculty:* 14 full-time (5 women), 4 part-time/adjunct (1 woman). *Students:* 37 full-time (25 women); includes 6 Asian, non-Hispanic/Latino; 2 Hispanic/Latino; 1 Native Hawaiian or other Pacific Islander, non-Hispanic/Latino. Average age 28. 55 applicants, 42% accepted, 12 enrolled. In 2010, 14 master's awarded. *Degree requirements:* For master's, one foreign language, thesis or alternative, 2 years of a second language. *Entrance requirements:* For master's, GRE, 2 years of a second language with minimum B grade, 3 letters of recommendation, resume/curriculum vitae. Additional exam requirements/recommendations for international students: Required—TOEFL (minimum score 600 paper-based; 80 iBT), IELTS (minimum score 7). *Application deadline:* For fall admission, 12/15 for domestic and international students. Application fee: $70 ($90 for international students). Electronic applications accepted. *Financial support:* In 2010–11, 36 students received support, including 29 fellowships with partial tuition reimbursements available (averaging $6,805 per year), 31 teaching assistantships with partial tuition reimbursements available (averaging $8,175 per year); career-related internships or fieldwork also available. Financial award application deadline: 12/15; financial award applicants required to submit FAFSA. *Faculty research:* Global culture religion, global governance human rights, political economy, environment, sustainable development. Total annual research expenditures: $240,000. *Unit head:* Prof. Giles Gunn, Chair, 805-893-4299, Fax: 805-893-8003, E-mail: ggunn@global.ucsb.edu. *Application contact:* Jessea Gay Marie, Graduate Program Advisor/Internship Assistance Officer, 805-893-4668, Fax: 805-893-8003, E-mail: gd-global@global.ucsb.edu.

University of Chicago, Divinity School, Chicago, IL 60637-1513. Offers M Div, AM, AMRS, PhD, JD/M Div, JD/MA, JD/PhD, MPP/M Div, MSW/M Div. *Accreditation:* ATS (one or more programs are accredited). Part-time programs available. *Degree requirements:* For master's and M Div, one foreign language; for doctorate, 2 foreign languages, comprehensive exam, thesis/dissertation. *Entrance requirements:* For M Div, master's, and doctorate, GRE General Test. Additional exam requirements/recommendations for international students: Required—TOEFL (minimum score 600 paper-based; 250 computer-based). Electronic applications accepted. *Expenses:* Contact institution. *Faculty research:* Theology, history of religion, ethics, biblical studies, philosophy of religion.

University of Colorado Boulder, Graduate School, College of Arts and Sciences, Department of Religious Studies, Boulder, CO 80309. Offers MA. *Faculty:* 8 full-time (4 women). *Students:* 29 full-time (15 women), 8 part-time (4 women); includes 4 minority (1 American Indian or Alaska Native, non-Hispanic/Latino; 1 Asian, non-Hispanic/Latino; 2 Hispanic/Latino), 3 international. Average age 29. 38 applicants, 13 enrolled. In 2010, 7 master's awarded. *Degree requirements:* For master's, one foreign language, comprehensive exam, thesis. *Entrance requirements:* For master's, minimum undergraduate GPA of 2.75. *Application deadline:* For fall admission, 1/15 priority date for domestic students, 1/31 for international students; for spring admission, 10/15 for domestic students, 9/15 for international students. Applications are processed on a rolling basis. Application fee: $50 ($60 for international students). *Financial support:* In 2010–11, 6 fellowships (averaging $6,063 per year), 5 research assistantships (averaging $6,388 per year) were awarded; tuition waivers (full) also available. Financial award application deadline: 1/15. *Faculty research:* Comparative studies in religion, methodologies in the study of religion, religion and dance, history of religions (including Hinduism, Buddhism, religions of China and Japan, Islam, and Christianity). Total annual research expenditures: $45,000.

University of Denver, Division of Arts, Humanities and Social Sciences, Department of Religious Studies, Denver, CO 80208. Offers MA. *Faculty:* 11 full-time (7 women), 1 part-time/adjunct (0 women). *Students:* 2 full-time (both women), 10 part-time (5 women); includes 3 minority (all Hispanic/Latino). Average age 36. 11 applicants, 82% accepted, 5 enrolled. In 2010, 2 master's awarded. *Degree requirements:* For master's, comprehensive exam, thesis. *Entrance requirements:* For master's, GRE General Test. Additional exam requirements/recommendations for international students: Required—TOEFL (minimum score 550 paper-based; 80 iBT). *Application deadline:* Applications are processed on a rolling basis. Application fee: $60. Electronic applications accepted. *Expenses:* Tuition: Full-time $35,604; part-time $29,670 per year. Required fees: $687 per year. Tuition and fees vary according to program. *Financial support:* Applicants required to submit FAFSA. *Unit head:* Dr. Ginette Ishimatsu, Chair, 303-871-2755, Fax: 303-871-2750, E-mail: gishimat@du.edu. *Application contact:* Dr. Carl Raschke, Professor, 303-371-3206, Fax: 303-871-2750, E-mail: rlgs@du.edu.

University of Denver, DU-Iliff Joint PhD Program in Religious and Theological Studies, Denver, CO 80208. Offers PhD. Program jointly offered with Iliff School of Theology. Part-time programs available. *Faculty:* 20 full-time (10 women), 3 part-time/adjunct (0 women). *Students:* 42 full-time (20 women), 50 part-time (20 women); includes 13 minority (3 Black or African American, non-Hispanic/Latino; 2 American Indian or Alaska Native, non-Hispanic/Latino; 2 Asian, non-Hispanic/Latino; 5 Hispanic/Latino; 1 Two or more races, non-Hispanic/Latino), 3 international. Average age 39. 53 applicants, 49% accepted, 15 enrolled. In 2010, 8 doctorates awarded. *Degree requirements:* For doctorate, one foreign language, comprehensive exam, thesis/dissertation. *Entrance requirements:* For doctorate, GRE General Test. Additional exam requirements/recommendations for international students: Required—TOEFL (minimum score 550 paper-based; 80 iBT). *Application deadline:* For fall admission, 1/15 for domestic students. Application fee: $60. *Expenses:* Tuition: Full-time $35,604; part-time $29,670 per year. Required fees: $687 per year. Tuition and fees vary according to program. *Unit head:* Dr. Ted Vial, Director, 303-765-3166, E-mail: tvial@iliff.edu. *Application contact:* Meghan Laurvick, Coordinator, 303-765-3166, E-mail: jointphd@iliff.edu.

University of Detroit Mercy, College of Liberal Arts and Education, Department of Religious Studies, Detroit, MI 48221. Offers MA. *Degree requirements:* For master's, thesis or alternative. *Entrance requirements:* For master's, minimum GPA of 3.0. *Faculty research:* History of religions, textual studies (Old and New Testaments), ethical and cultural studies.

University of Florida, Graduate School, College of Liberal Arts and Sciences, Department of Religion, Gainesville, FL 32611. Offers religion and nature (MA); religion in the Americas (MA); religions of Asia (MA, PhD). Part-time programs available. *Faculty:* 10 full-time (3 women), 3 part-time/adjunct (1 woman). *Students:* 24 full-time (12 women), 7 part-time (6 women); includes 1 American Indian or Alaska Native, non-Hispanic/Latino; 4 Asian, non-Hispanic/Latino; 3 Hispanic/Latino, 1 international. Average age 34. 36 applicants, 58% accepted, 12 enrolled. In 2010, 1 master's, 1 doctorate awarded. *Degree requirements:* For master's, one foreign language, thesis optional; for doctorate, one foreign language, comprehensive exam, thesis/dissertation. *Entrance requirements:* For master's, GRE General Test, minimum GPA of 3.0. Additional exam requirements/recommendations for international students: Required—TOEFL (minimum score 550 paper-based; 213 computer-based; 80 iBT), IELTS (minimum score 6). *Application deadline:* For fall admission, 6/1 priority date for domestic students. Applications are processed on a rolling basis. Application fee: $30. Electronic applications accepted. *Expenses:* Tuition, state resident: full-time $10,915.92. Tuition, nonresident: full-time $28,309. *Financial support:* In 2010–11, 18 students received support, including 5 fellowships, 1 research assistantship (averaging $16,965 per year), 12 teaching assistantships (averaging $13,539 per year); Federal Work-Study and unspecified assistantships also available. Financial award applicants required to submit FAFSA. *Faculty research:* Religion in America, Christian thought, Islam, religions of India, comparative religion. *Unit head:* Dr. Vasudha Narayanan, Chair, 352-392-1625, E-mail: vasu@ufl.edu. *Application contact:* Dr. Manuel Vasquez, Graduate Coordinator, 352-392-1625 Ext. 229, Fax: 352-392-7395, E-mail: manuelv@ufl.edu.

University of Georgia, College of Arts and Sciences, Department of Religion, Athens, GA 30602. Offers MA. *Faculty:* 11 full-time (1 woman). *Students:* 24 full-time (12 women), 8 part-time (3 women); includes 3 Black or African American, non-Hispanic/Latino; 1 Two or more races, non-Hispanic/Latino, 3 international. 38 applicants, 74% accepted, 16 enrolled. In 2010, 11 master's awarded. *Degree requirements:* For master's, one foreign language, thesis. *Entrance requirements:* For master's, GRE General Test. *Application deadline:* For fall admission, 7/1 priority date for domestic students; for spring admission, 11/15 for domestic students. Application fee: $50. Electronic applications accepted. *Expenses:* Tuition, state resident: full-time $7200; part-time $344 per credit hour. Tuition, nonresident: full-time $21,900; part-time $944 per credit hour. Tuition and fees vary according to course load and program. *Financial support:* Fellowships, research assistantships, teaching assistantships, unspecified assistantships available. *Unit head:* Dr. Sandy D. Martin, Head, 706-542-1485, Fax: 706-542-6724, E-mail: martin@uga.edu. *Application contact:* Dr. Carolyn Medine, Graduate Coordinator, 706-543-0308, Fax: 706-542-6724, E-mail: medine@uga.edu.

University of Hawaii at Manoa, Graduate Division, College of Arts and Humanities, Department of Religion, Honolulu, HI 96822. Offers MA. Part-time programs available. *Faculty:* 10 full-time (1 woman). *Students:* 11 full-time (9 women), 3 part-time (2 women); includes 7 minority (2 Asian, non-Hispanic/Latino; 1 Native Hawaiian or other Pacific Islander, non-Hispanic/Latino; 4 Two or more races, non-Hispanic/Latino). Average age 31. 20 applicants, 35% accepted, 5 enrolled. In 2010, 5 master's awarded. *Degree requirements:* For master's, one foreign language, thesis optional. *Entrance requirements:* For master's, GRE General Test. Additional exam requirements/recommendations for international students: Required—TOEFL (minimum score 600 paper-based; 250 computer-based; 100 iBT), IELTS (minimum score 7). *Application deadline:* For fall admission, 3/1 for domestic students, 1/15 for international students; for spring admission, 9/1 for international students. Applications are processed on a rolling basis. Application fee: $60. *Financial support:* In 2010–11, 4 fellowships (averaging $4,125 per year), 8 teaching assistantships (averaging $14,382 per year) were awarded; career-related internships or fieldwork, scholarships/grants, and tuition waivers (full and partial) also available. Financial award application deadline: 3/1. *Faculty research:* Buddhism, East Asian religion, South Asian religion, Polynesian religion, Western religions. *Application contact:* Michael Mohr, Graduate Field Chairperson, 808-956-8299, Fax: 808-956-9894, E-mail: mmohr@hawaii.edu.

The University of Iowa, Graduate College, College of Liberal Arts and Sciences, Department of Religious Studies, Iowa City, IA 52242-1316. Offers MA, PhD, JD/MA. Terminal master's awarded for partial completion of doctoral program. *Degree requirements:* For master's, thesis optional, exam; for doctorate, comprehensive exam, thesis/dissertation. *Entrance requirements:*

Religion

The University of Iowa (continued)

For master's and doctorate, GRE General Test, minimum GPA of 3.0. Additional exam requirements/recommendations for international students: Required—TOEFL (minimum score 550 paper-based; 213 computer-based; 81 iBT). Electronic applications accepted. *Faculty research:* Eastern and Western religion.

The University of Kansas, Graduate Studies, College of Liberal Arts and Sciences, Department of Religious Studies, Lawrence, KS 66045. Offers MA. Part-time programs available. *Faculty:* 8 full-time (0 women), 4 part-time/adjunct (2 women). *Students:* 13 full-time (6 women), 4 part-time (2 women); includes 1 minority (Black or African American, non-Hispanic/Latino). Average age 28. 16 applicants, 69% accepted, 9 enrolled. In 2010, 8 master's awarded. *Degree requirements:* For master's, comprehensive exam, thesis optional. *Entrance requirements:* For master's, minimum GPA of 3.0. Additional exam requirements/recommendations for international students: Required—TOEFL. *Application deadline:* For fall admission, 2/1 for domestic and international students. Application fee: $55 ($65 for international students). Electronic applications accepted. *Expenses:* Tuition, state resident: full-time $7092; part-time $295.50 per credit hour. Tuition, nonresident: full-time $16,590; part-time $691.25 per credit hour. Required fees: $858; $71.49 per credit hour. Tuition and fees vary according to course load, campus/location and program. *Financial support:* Fellowships, teaching assistantships with full tuition reimbursements, scholarships/grants and unspecified assistantships available. Financial award application deadline: 1/1. *Faculty research:* Judaism and Christianity, Islam, religions in Asia, methods and theories, American and Native American religion. *Unit head:* Daniel B. Stevenson, Chair, 785-864-7258, Fax: 785-864-5205, E-mail: rstudies@ku.edu. *Application contact:* William Lindsey, Graduate Director, 785-864-5582, Fax: 785-864-5205, E-mail: brl@ku.edu.

University of Lethbridge, School of Graduate Studies, Lethbridge, AB T1K 3M4, Canada. Offers accounting (MScM); addictions counseling (M Sc); agricultural biotechnology (M Sc); agricultural studies (M Sc, MA); anthropology (MA); archaeology (MA); art (MA, MFA); biochemistry (M Sc); biological sciences (M Sc); biomolecular science (PhD); biosystems and biodiversity (PhD); Canadian studies (MA); chemistry (M Sc); computer science (M Sc); computer science and geographical information science (M Sc); counseling psychology (M Ed); dramatic arts (MA); earth, space, and physical science (PhD); economics (MA); educational leadership (M Ed); English (MA); environmental science (M Sc); evolution and behavior (PhD); exercise science (M Sc); finance (MScM); French (MA); French/German (MA); French/Spanish (MA); general education (M Ed); general management (MScM); geography (M Sc, MA); German (MA); health science (M Sc); history (MA); human resource management and labour relations (MScM); individualized multidisciplinary (M Sc, MA); information systems (MScM); international management (MScM); kinesiology (M Sc, MA); management (M Sc, MA); marketing (MScM); mathematics (M Sc); music (M Mus, MA); Native American studies (MA); neuroscience (M Sc, PhD); new media (MA); nursing (M Sc); philosophy (MA); physics (M Sc); policy and strategy (MScM); political science (MA); psychology (M Sc, MA); religious studies (MA); social sciences (MA); sociology (MA); theatre and dramatic arts (MFA); theoretical and computational science (PhD); urban and regional studies (MA); women's studies (MA). Part-time and evening/weekend programs available. *Degree requirements:* For doctorate, comprehensive exam, thesis/dissertation. *Entrance requirements:* For master's, GMAT (M Sc in management), bachelor's degree in related field, minimum GPA of 3.0 during previous 20 graded semester courses, 2 years teaching or related experience (M Ed); for doctorate, master's degree, minimum graduate GPA of 3.5. Additional exam requirements/recommendations for international students: Required—TOEFL. *Faculty research:* Movement and brain plasticity, gibberellin physiology, photosynthesis, carbon cycling, molecular properties of main-group ring components.

The University of Manchester, School of Arts, Histories and Cultures, Manchester, United Kingdom. Offers anthropology, media and performance (PhD); applied theatre professional (PhD); archaeology (PhD); art history and visual studies (PhD); arts management and cultural policy (PhD); classics and ancient history (PhD); composition (PhD); creative writing (PhD); drama (PhD); economic and social history (PhD); electroacoustic composition (PhD); English and American studies (PhD); history (PhD); humanitarianism and conflict response (PhD); museology (PhD); music (PhD); musicology (PhD); religions and theology (PhD).

University of Manitoba, Faculty of Graduate Studies, Faculty of Arts, Department of Religion, Winnipeg, MB R3T 2N2, Canada. Offers MA, PhD. MA offered jointly with The University of Winnipeg. *Degree requirements:* For master's, one foreign language, thesis or alternative.

University of Michigan, Horace H. Rackham School of Graduate Studies, College of Literature, Science, and the Arts, Department of Near Eastern Studies, Ann Arbor, MI 48109. Offers ancient Near Eastern studies (AM, PhD); Arabic for professional purposes (AM); Arabic language and literature (AM, PhD); Armenian studies (AM, PhD); Christianity in late antiquity (AM, PhD); Egyptology (AM, PhD); Hebrew Bible and ancient Israel (AM, PhD); Hebrew literature (AM, PhD); Islamic studies (AM, PhD); Jewish cultural studies (AM, PhD); Jewish mysticism (AM, PhD); Persian and Iranian studies (AM, PhD); Rabbinic literature (AM, PhD); Second Temple Judaism (AM, PhD); teaching of Arabic as a foreign language (AM); Turkish studies (AM, PhD). Part-time programs available. Terminal master's awarded for partial completion of doctoral program. *Degree requirements:* For master's, 2 foreign languages; for doctorate, 4 foreign languages, comprehensive exam, thesis/dissertation. *Entrance requirements:* For master's, GRE General Test; for doctorate, GRE General Test, master's degree. Additional exam requirements/recommendations for international students: Required—TOEFL (minimum score 560 paper-based; 220 computer-based; 84 iBT). Electronic applications accepted. *Expenses:* Tuition, state resident: full-time $17,784; part-time $1116 per credit hour. Tuition, nonresident: full-time $35,944; part-time $2125 per credit hour. International tuition: $35,994 full-time. Required fees: $95 per semester. Tuition and fees vary according to course load, degree level and program. *Faculty research:* Middle and Near Eastern literatures, languages, cultures from ancient times to the present.

University of Minnesota, Twin Cities Campus, Graduate School, College of Liberal Arts, Department of Classical and Near Eastern Studies, Minneapolis, MN 55455-0213. Offers ancient and medieval art and archaeology (MA, PhD); classics (MA, PhD); Greek (MA, PhD); Latin (MA, PhD); religions in antiquity (MA). Part-time programs available. Terminal master's awarded for partial completion of doctoral program. *Degree requirements:* For master's, 2 foreign languages, comprehensive exam, thesis or alternative; for doctorate, variable foreign language requirement, comprehensive exam, thesis/dissertation. *Entrance requirements:* For master's and doctorate, GRE, 3 letters of recommendation, writing sample, copies of transcripts, personal statement. Additional exam requirements/recommendations for international students: Required—TOEFL. Electronic applications accepted. *Faculty research:* Greek and Latin literature, religions in antiquity, ancient Near East.

University of Missouri, Graduate School, College of Arts and Sciences, Department of Religious Studies, Columbia, MO 65211. Offers MA. *Entrance requirements:* For master's, GRE General Test, minimum GPA of 3.0. Additional exam requirements/recommendations for international students: Required—TOEFL (minimum score 550 paper-based; 213 computer-based; 79 iBT). Electronic applications accepted. *Faculty research:* American religious history; biblical studies; history of Christianity; religion and society; religions of East Asia; religions of Indigenous peoples; religions of South Asia; women and religion.

University of Mobile, Graduate Programs, Program in Religious Studies, Mobile, AL 36613. Offers biblical/theological studies (MA); marriage and family counseling (MA). Part-time and evening/weekend programs available. *Faculty:* 6 full-time (0 women). *Students:* 12 full-time (7 women), 53 part-time (41 women); includes 34 Black or African American, non-Hispanic/Latino; 3 American Indian or Alaska Native, non-Hispanic/Latino, 2 international. Average age 34. 18 applicants, 94% accepted, 16 enrolled. In 2010, 10 master's awarded. *Degree requirements:* For master's, 2 foreign languages, comprehensive exam, thesis optional. *Entrance requirements:* For master's, GRE General Test. Additional exam requirements/recommendations for international students: Required—TOEFL (minimum score 550 paper-based; 213 computer-based; 80 iBT). *Application deadline:* For fall admission, 8/3 priority date for domestic students; for spring admission, 12/23 for domestic students. Applications are processed on a rolling basis. Application fee: $40 ($50 for international students). *Expenses:* Tuition: Full-time $3915; part-time $435 per credit hour. Required fees: $63 per semester. *Financial support:* Federal Work-Study available. Support available to part-time students. Financial award application deadline: 8/1. *Unit head:* Dr. Cecil Taylor, Dean, School of Christian Studies, 251-442-2255, Fax: 251-442-2523, E-mail: ctaylor@mail.umobile.edu. *Application contact:* Tammy C. Eubanks, Administrative Assistant to Dean of Graduate Programs, 251-442-2270, Fax: 251-442-2523, E-mail: teubanks@umobile.edu.

The University of North Carolina at Chapel Hill, Graduate School, College of Arts and Sciences, Department of Religious Studies, Chapel Hill, NC 27599. Offers MA, PhD. *Faculty:* 16 full-time (4 women), 12 part-time/adjunct (1 woman). *Students:* 39 full-time (19 women); includes 3 Asian, non-Hispanic/Latino; 2 Hispanic/Latino. Average age 31. 99 applicants, 10% accepted, 5 enrolled. In 2010, 3 master's, 2 doctorates awarded. Terminal master's awarded for partial completion of doctoral program. *Degree requirements:* For master's, one foreign language, comprehensive exam, thesis; for doctorate, 2 foreign languages, comprehensive exam, thesis/dissertation. *Entrance requirements:* For master's and doctorate, GRE General Test, minimum GPA of 3.0. Additional exam requirements/recommendations for international students: Required—TOEFL. *Application deadline:* For fall admission, 12/15 for domestic and international students. Application fee: $60 ($77 for international students). Electronic applications accepted. *Financial support:* In 2010–11, 29 students received support, including 3 fellowships with full tuition reimbursements available (averaging $22,333 per year), 1 research assistantship with full tuition reimbursement available (averaging $18,000 per year), 24 teaching assistantships with full tuition reimbursements available (averaging $15,140 per year). Financial award application deadline: 3/1; financial award applicants required to submit FAFSA. *Faculty research:* Religion. *Unit head:* Prof. Laurie Maffly-Kipp, Chair, 919-962-3927, Fax: 919-962-1567, E-mail: maffly@email.unc.edu. *Application contact:* Myra Covington Quick, Registrar/Program Coordinator, 919-962-5667, Fax: 919-962-1567, E-mail: quick@unc.edu.

The University of North Carolina at Charlotte, Graduate School, College of Arts and Sciences, Department of Religious Studies, Charlotte, NC 28223-0001. Offers MA. *Faculty:* 10 full-time (2 women). *Students:* 7 full-time (5 women), 21 part-time (7 women); includes 1 minority (Black or African American, non-Hispanic/Latino). Average age 31. 18 applicants, 78% accepted, 7 enrolled. In 2010, 2 master's awarded. *Degree requirements:* For master's, comprehensive exam, thesis. *Entrance requirements:* For master's, GRE or MAT, 3 letters of reference. Additional exam requirements/recommendations for international students: Required—TOEFL (minimum score 557 paper-based; 220 computer-based; 83 iBT). *Application deadline:* For fall admission, 7/15 for domestic students, 5/1 for international students; for spring admission, 11/15 for domestic students, 10/1 for international students. Applications are processed on a rolling basis. Application fee: $55. Electronic applications accepted. *Expenses:* Tuition, state resident: full-time $3464. Tuition, nonresident: full-time $14,297. Required fees: $2094. Tuition and fees vary according to course load. *Financial support:* In 2010–11, 3 students received support, including 3 teaching assistantships (averaging $9,000 per year); career-related internships or fieldwork, institutionally sponsored loans, scholarships/grants, and unspecified assistantships also available. Support available to part-time students. Financial award application deadline: 4/1; financial award applicants required to submit FAFSA. Total annual research expenditures: $5,036. *Unit head:* Dr. James D. Tabor, Chair, 704-687-2783, Fax: 704-687-3002, E-mail: jdtabor@uncc.edu. *Application contact:* Kathy B. Giddings, Director of Graduate Admissions, 704-687-5503, Fax: 704-687-3279, E-mail: gradadm@uncc.edu.

University of North Texas, Toulouse Graduate School, College of Arts and Sciences, Department of Philosophy and Religion Studies, Denton, TX 76203. Offers philosophy (MA, PhD). *Degree requirements:* For master's, one foreign language, thesis or alternative; for doctorate, one foreign language, comprehensive exam, thesis/dissertation. *Entrance requirements:* For master's, GRE General Test. Additional exam requirements/recommendations for international students: Recommended—TOEFL (minimum score 550 paper-based; 213 computer-based; 79 iBT). *Expenses:* Tuition, state resident: full-time $4298; part-time $239 per credit hour. Tuition, nonresident: full-time $10,782; part-time $549 per credit hour. Required fees: $1292; $270 per credit hour. *Financial support:* Application deadline: 4/1. *Application contact:* Associate Dean, 940-565-2383, Fax: 940-565-2141.

University of Notre Dame, Graduate School, College of Arts and Letters, Division of Humanities, Program in Early Christian Studies, Notre Dame, IN 46556. Offers MA. *Degree requirements:* For master's, 3 foreign languages, comprehensive exam. *Entrance requirements:* For master's, GRE General Test. Additional exam requirements/recommendations for international students: Required—TOEFL (minimum score 600 paper-based; 250 computer-based; 80 iBT). Electronic applications accepted. *Faculty research:* Early Christian theology, worship and scriptural interpretation; late antique and Byzantine history; art and culture; Greek and Latin literature.

University of Ottawa, Faculty of Graduate and Postdoctoral Studies, Faculty of Arts, Department of Classics and Religious Studies, Ottawa, ON K1N 6N5, Canada. Offers classical studies (MA); religious studies (PhD). *Degree requirements:* For master's, comprehensive exam, thesis or alternative; for doctorate, comprehensive exam, thesis/dissertation. *Entrance requirements:* For master's, honors degree or equivalent, minimum B average; for doctorate, master's degree, minimum B+ average. Electronic applications accepted. *Faculty research:* Religions in Canada, including Amerindian and Inuit religions; religion and culture; late antiquity.

University of Pennsylvania, School of Arts and Sciences, Graduate Group in Religious Studies, Philadelphia, PA 19104. Offers PhD. *Faculty:* 21 full-time (10 women), 7 part-time/adjunct (0 women). *Students:* 18 full-time (8 women), 4 part-time (2 women); includes 1 Asian, non-Hispanic/Latino, 4 international. 43 applicants, 2% accepted, 0 enrolled. In 2010, 3 doctorates awarded. *Degree requirements:* For doctorate, thesis/dissertation, approved specialty languages, preliminary and final exams. *Entrance requirements:* For doctorate, GRE. Additional exam requirements/recommendations for international students: Required—TOEFL. *Application deadline:* For fall admission, 12/1 priority date for domestic students. Application fee: $70. Electronic applications accepted. *Expenses:* Tuition: Full-time $25,660; part-time $4758 per course. Required fees: $2152; $270 per course. Tuition and fees vary according to course load, degree level and program. *Financial support:* In 2010–11, 10 students received support, including 2 fellowships, 1 research assistantship, 3 teaching assistantships; institutionally sponsored loans, scholarships/grants, traineeships, health care benefits, and unspecified assistantships also available. Financial award application deadline: 12/15. *Faculty research:* Judaism and Christianity (ancient, medieval, modern), Islam, Hinduism, Buddhism, modern religious thought. *Unit head:* Anthea Butler, Graduate Studies Chair, 215-898-5441, E-mail: antheab@sas.upenn.edu. *Application contact:* Ernestine Williams, Graduate Coordinator, 215-573-0250, E-mail: ernestin@sas.upenn.edu.

University of Pittsburgh, School of Arts and Sciences, Cooperative Doctoral Program in Religion, Pittsburgh, PA 15260. Offers PhD. *Faculty:* 10 full-time (3 women), 7 part-time/adjunct (2 women). *Students:* 14 full-time (8 women), 1 part-time (0 women); includes 1 Hispanic/Latino, 1 international. 23 applicants, 43% accepted, 5 enrolled. In 2010, 1 doctorate awarded. *Degree requirements:* For doctorate, 2 foreign languages, comprehensive exam, thesis/dissertation, preliminary exam. *Entrance requirements:* For doctorate, GRE General Test, sample of research or written work, 3 letters of recommendation. Additional exam requirements/recommendations for international students: Required—TOEFL (minimum score 600 paper-based; 250 computer-based; 100 iBT). *Application deadline:* For fall admission, 1/15 for domestic and international students. Application fee: $50. Electronic applications accepted. *Expenses:* Tuition, state resident: full-time $17,304; part-time $701 per credit. Tuition, nonresident: full-time $29,554; part-time $1210 per credit. Required fees: $740; $214 per term. Tuition and fees vary according to program. *Financial support:* In 2010–11, 12 students received support, including 1 fellowship with full tuition reimbursement available (averaging $16,000 per year), 2 teaching assistantships with full tuition reimbursements available (averaging $15,000 per year); research assistantships, health care benefits, tuition waivers (partial), and unspecified assistantships also available. Financial award application deadline: 1/15. *Faculty research:* Contemporary Catholicism and religion in America, Buddhism and East Asian religions, philosophy and religion and religious thought and language, medieval to modern Jewish history, theories and methods in the study of religion. *Unit head:* Dr. Adam Shear, Director of Graduate Studies, 412-624-2280, Fax: 412-624-5994, E-mail: ashear@pitt.edu. *Application contact:* Donna L. Walker, Department Administrator, 412-624-5990, Fax: 412-624-5994, E-mail: dlw5@pitt.edu.

University of Pittsburgh, School of Arts and Sciences, Department of Religious Studies, Pittsburgh, PA 15260. Offers MA. *Faculty:* 8 full-time (3 women), 3 part-time/adjunct (1 woman). *Students:* 2 full-time (1 woman). 21 applicants, 5% accepted, 0 enrolled. In 2010, 3 master's awarded. *Degree requirements:* For master's, comprehensive exam, thesis. *Entrance requirements:* For master's, GRE General Test, sample of written work, 3 letters of recommendation. Additional exam requirements/recommendations for international students: Required—TOEFL (minimum score 600 paper-based; 250 computer-based; 100 iBT). *Application deadline:* For fall admission, 1/15 for domestic and international students. Application fee: $50. Electronic applications accepted. *Expenses:* Tuition, state resident: full-time $17,304; part-time $701 per credit. Tuition, nonresident: full-time $29,554; part-time $1210 per credit. Required fees: $740; $214 per term. Tuition and fees vary according to program. *Financial support:* In 2010–11, 2 students received support, including fellowships (averaging $16,000 per year), research assistantships with full tuition reimbursements available (averaging $16,000 per year), 2 teaching assistantships with full tuition reimbursements available (averaging $16,000 per year); health care benefits and unspecified assistantships also available. Financial award application deadline: 1/15. *Faculty research:* Contemporary Catholicism and religion in America, Buddhism and East Asian religions, philosophy and religion and religious thought and language, medieval to modern Jewish history, theories and methods in the study of religion. *Unit head:* Dr. Adam Shear, Director of Graduate Studies, 412-624-2280, Fax: 412-624-5994, E-mail: ashear@pitt.edu. *Application contact:* Donna L. Walker, Department Administrator, 412-624-5990, Fax: 412-624-5994, E-mail: dlw5@pitt.edu.

University of Regina, Faculty of Graduate Studies and Research, Faculty of Arts, Department of Religious Studies, Regina, SK S4S 0A2, Canada. Offers MA. Part-time programs available. *Faculty:* 9 full-time (3 women). *Students:* 7 full-time (3 women), 2 part-time (1 woman). 3 applicants, 100% accepted. In 2010, 2 master's awarded. *Degree requirements:* For master's, thesis. *Entrance requirements:* Additional exam requirements/recommendations for international students: Required—TOEFL (minimum score 580 paper-based; 80 iBT). *Application deadline:* Applications are processed on a rolling basis. Application fee: $100. Electronic applications accepted. Tuition and fees charges are reported in Canadian dollars. *Expenses:* Tuition, area resident: Full-time $3244.50 Canadian dollars; part-time $180.25 Canadian dollars per credit hour. International tuition: $4744.50 Canadian dollars full-time. Required fees: $494 Canadian dollars; $115.25 Canadian dollars per credit hour. $115.25 Canadian dollars per semester. Tuition and fees vary according to program. *Financial support:* In 2010–11, 1 fellowship (averaging $18,000 per year), 1 research assistantship (averaging $16,500 per year), 2 teaching assistantships (averaging $6,759 per year) were awarded; scholarships/grants also available. Financial award application deadline: 6/15. *Faculty research:* Comparative religion; religious traditions; thematic and methodological studies; advanced studies in Christianity, Islam, and ancient religions. *Unit head:* Dr. Leona Anderson, Head, 306-585-4580, Fax: 306-585-4815, E-mail: leona.anderson@uregina.ca. *Application contact:* Dr. Leona Anderson, Graduate Program Coordinator, 306-585-4580, Fax: 306-585-4815, E-mail: leona.anderson@uregina.ca.

University of St. Thomas, Center for Faith and Culture, Houston, TX 77006-4696. Offers MA. Part-time programs available. *Faculty:* 1 full-time (0 women), 2 part-time/adjunct (0 women). *Students:* 6 full-time (3 women), 6 part-time (2 women); includes 5 minority (1 Black or African American, non-Hispanic/Latino; 1 Asian, non-Hispanic/Latino; 2 Hispanic/Latino; 1 Two or more races, non-Hispanic/Latino), 1 international. Average age 38. 13 applicants, 100% accepted, 12 enrolled. *Degree requirements:* For master's, capstone, integrating presentation. *Entrance requirements:* For master's, bachelor's degree with minimum GPA of 2.75 or advanced degree; 3 letters of recommendation: 1 personal and 2 professional/academic; essay on student goals and expectations; interviews with 2 faculty members and admissions committee; writing sample. Additional exam requirements/recommendations for international students: Required—TOEFL (minimum score 550 paper-based; 213 computer-based; 79 iBT), ELS exam (level 112); Recommended—IELTS (minimum score 6.5). *Application deadline:* Applications are processed on a rolling basis. Application fee: $35. Electronic applications accepted. *Expenses:* Tuition: Full-time $15,696; part-time $872 per credit hour. Required fees: $236; $83 per term. One-time fee: $100. Tuition and fees vary according to course load, campus/location and program. *Financial support:* In 2010–11, 12 students received support. Federal Work-Study, scholarships/grants, and state work-study, institutional employment available. Support available to part-time students. Financial award application deadline: 4/15; financial award applicants required to submit FAFSA. *Unit head:* Fr. Donald S. Nesti, Director, 713-942-5066, E-mail: cfc@stthom.edu. *Application contact:* Dr. Adam Martinez, Program Director, 713-942-5066, E-mail: cfc@stthom.edu.

University of St. Thomas, Graduate Studies, College of Arts and Sciences, Program in Catholic Studies, St. Paul, MN 55105-1096. Offers MA. Part-time and evening/weekend programs available. *Faculty:* 8 full-time (1 woman), 4 part-time/adjunct (1 woman). *Students:* 15 full-time (8 women), 40 part-time (20 women); includes 1 Hispanic/Latino. Average age 33. 24 applicants, 96% accepted, 14 enrolled. In 2010, 16 master's awarded. *Degree requirements:* For master's, thesis. *Entrance requirements:* For master's, bachelor's degree with minimum GPA of 3.0, writing sample, personal statement, 3 letters of recommendation. Additional exam requirements/recommendations for international students: Required—TOEFL (minimum score 550 paper-based). *Application deadline:* For fall admission, 3/1 for domestic and international students; for spring admission, 11/1 for domestic and international students. Application fee: $0. Electronic applications accepted. *Financial support:* In 2010–11, 16 students received support, including 4 fellowships with full tuition reimbursements available (averaging $8,000 per year), 1 research assistantship (averaging $1,500 per year); tuition waivers (partial) also available. *Unit head:* Dr. John F. Boyle, Director, 651-962-5714, Fax: 651-962-5710, E-mail: jfboyle@stthomas.edu. *Application contact:* Theresa R. Klein, Program Manager, 651-962-5704, Fax: 651-962-5710, E-mail: gradcath@stthomas.edu.

University of Saskatchewan, College of Graduate Studies and Research, College of Arts and Sciences, Department of Religious Studies and Anthropology, Saskatoon, SK S7N 5A2, Canada. Offers MA. *Degree requirements:* For master's, thesis. *Entrance requirements:* Additional exam requirements/recommendations for international students: Required—TOEFL (minimum score 80 iBT); Recommended—IELTS (minimum score 6.5). Electronic applications accepted.

University of South Africa, College of Human Sciences, Pretoria, South Africa. Offers adult education (M Ed); African languages (MA, PhD); African politics (MA, PhD); Afrikaans (MA, PhD); ancient history (MA, PhD); ancient Near Eastern studies (MA, PhD); anthropology (MA, PhD); applied linguistics (MA); Arabic (MA, PhD); archaeology (MA); art history (MA); Biblical archaeology (MA); Biblical studies (M Th, D Th, PhD); Christian spirituality (M Th, D Th); church history (M Th, D Th); classical studies (MA, PhD); clinical psychology (MA); communication (MA, PhD); comparative education (M Ed, Ed D); consulting psychology (D Admin, D Com, PhD); curriculum studies (M Ed, Ed D); development studies (M Admin, MA, D Admin, PhD); didactics (M Ed, Ed D); education (M Tech); education management (M Ed, Ed D); educational psychology (M Ed); English (MA); environmental education (M Ed); French (MA, PhD); German (MA, PhD); Greek (MA); guidance and counseling (M Ed); health studies (MA, PhD), including health sciences education (MA), health services management (MA), medical and surgical nursing science (critical care general) (MA), midwifery and neonatal nursing science (MA), trauma and emergency care (MA); history (MA, PhD); history of education (Ed D); inclusive education (M Ed, Ed D); information and communications technology policy and regulation (MA); information science (MA, MIS, PhD); international politics (MA, PhD); Islamic studies (MA, PhD); Italian (MA, PhD); Judaica (MA, PhD); linguistics (MA, PhD); mathematical education (M Ed); mathematics education (MA); missiology (M Th, D Th); modern Hebrew (MA, PhD); musicology (MA, MMus, D Mus, PhD); natural science education (M Ed); New Testament (M Th, D Th); Old Testament (D Th); pastoral therapy (M Th, D Th); philosophy (MA); philosophy of education (M Ed, Ed D); politics (MA, PhD); Portuguese (MA, PhD); practical theology (M Th, D Th); psychology (MA, MS, PhD); psychology of education (M Ed, Ed D); public health (MA); religious studies (MA, D Th, PhD); Romance languages (MA); Russian (MA, PhD); Semitic languages (MA, PhD); social behavior studies in HIV/AIDS (MA); social science (mental health) (MA); social science in development studies (MA); social science in psychology (MA); social science in social work (MA); social science in sociology (MA); social work (MSW, DSW, PhD); socio-education (M Ed, Ed D); sociolinguistics (MA); sociology (MA, PhD); Spanish (MA, PhD); systematic theology (M Th, D Th); TESOL (teaching English to speakers of other languages) (MA); theological ethics (M Th, D Th); theory of literature (MA, PhD); urban ministries (D Th); urban ministry (M Th).

University of South Carolina, The Graduate School, College of Arts and Sciences, Department of Religious Studies, Columbia, SC 29208. Offers MA. Part-time programs available. *Degree requirements:* For master's, one foreign language, comprehensive exam, thesis. *Entrance requirements:* For master's, GRE General Test or MAT. Additional exam requirements/recommendations for international students: Required—TOEFL. Electronic applications accepted. *Faculty research:* Biblical and Near Eastern studies, theology and religious thought, religion and culture, South Asian religions, Islamic studies.

University of South Florida, Graduate School, College of Arts and Sciences, Department of Religious Studies, Tampa, FL 33620-9951. Offers MA. Part-time and evening/weekend programs available. *Faculty:* 5 full-time (0 women). *Students:* 13 full-time (6 women), 6 part-time (all women); includes 1 Black or African American, non-Hispanic/Latino; 1 American Indian or Alaska Native, non-Hispanic/Latino; 1 Asian, non-Hispanic/Latino; 3 Hispanic/Latino. Average age 30. 16 applicants, 50% accepted, 6 enrolled. In 2010, 12 master's awarded. *Degree requirements:* For master's, comprehensive exam, thesis. *Entrance requirements:* For master's, GRE General Test, minimum GPA of 3.0 in last 60 hours. Additional exam requirements/recommendations for international students: Required—TOEFL (minimum score 550 paper-based; 213 computer-based). *Application deadline:* For fall admission, 2/15 priority date for domestic students, 1/2 priority date for international students; for spring admission, 10/15 priority date for domestic students, 6/1 priority date for international students. Applications are processed on a rolling basis. Application fee: $30. Electronic applications accepted. *Financial support:* In 2010–11, 10 teaching assistantships with tuition reimbursements (averaging $9,001 per year) were awarded; unspecified assistantships also available. Financial award applicants required to submit FAFSA. *Faculty research:* Scripture and history of Judaism, Christianity, and Islam; religion and society; new religions; comparative religious ethics; narrative and religion. Total annual research expenditures: $27,955. *Unit head:* Dr. Mozella G. Mitchell, Chairperson, 813-974-1852, Fax: 813-974-1853, E-mail: mitchellm@usf.edu. *Application contact:* Dr. Paul Schneider, Director, 813-974-2730, Fax: 813-974-1853, E-mail: pgschnei@cas.usf.edu.

The University of Tennessee, Graduate School, College of Arts and Sciences, Department of Philosophy, Knoxville, TN 37996. Offers medical ethics (MA, PhD); philosophy (MA, PhD); religious studies (MA). Part-time programs available. *Degree requirements:* For master's, thesis or alternative; for doctorate, one foreign language, thesis/dissertation. *Entrance requirements:* For master's and doctorate, GRE General Test, minimum GPA of 2.7. Additional exam requirements/recommendations for international students: Required—TOEFL. Electronic applications accepted. *Expenses:* Tuition, state resident: full-time $7440; part-time $414 per credit hour. Tuition, nonresident: full-time $22,478; part-time $1250 per credit hour. Required fees: $922; $43 per credit hour. Tuition and fees vary according to program.

University of the Cumberlands, Program in Christian Studies, Williamsburg, KY 40769-1372. Offers MA. Part-time and evening/weekend programs available. Postbaccalaureate distance learning degree programs offered (no on-campus study). *Faculty:* 4 full-time (0 women), 4 part-time/adjunct (0 women). *Students:* 9 full-time (2 women), 2 part-time (1 woman); includes 1 Black or African American, non-Hispanic/Latino. Average age 28. *Entrance requirements:* For master's, GRE of Miller Analogies Test. Additional exam requirements/recommendations for international students: Required—TOEFL. *Application deadline:* Applications are processed on a rolling basis. Application fee: $30. Electronic applications accepted. *Expenses:* Tuition: Full-time $6984; part-time $291 per credit hour. Required fees: $50 per term. Tuition and fees vary according to course level, course load and program. *Unit head:* Dr. Keith Goforth, Director, 606-539-4222, E-mail: macs@ucumberlands.edu. *Application contact:* Donna Stanfill, Director, Graduate Admissions, 606-549-2200 Ext. 4496, Fax: 606-539-4534, E-mail: donna.stanfill@cumberlandcollege.edu.

University of the Incarnate Word, School of Graduate Studies and Research, College of Humanities, Arts, and Social Sciences, Program in Religious Studies, San Antonio, TX 78209-6397. Offers MA. Part-time programs available. *Faculty:* 1 (woman) full-time, 1 part-time/adjunct (0 women). *Students:* 16 part-time (10 women); includes 7 minority (1 Black or African American, non-Hispanic/Latino; 6 Hispanic/Latino). Average age 42. In 2010, 6 master's awarded. *Degree requirements:* For master's, pastoral project. *Entrance requirements:* For master's, recommendation letters, 12 credit hours of related undergraduate coursework. Additional exam requirements/recommendations for international students: Required—TOEFL (minimum score 560 paper-based; 220 computer-based; 83 iBT). *Application deadline:* Applications are processed on a rolling basis. Application fee: $20. Electronic applications accepted. *Expenses:* Tuition: Part-time $725 per contact hour. Required fees: $890 per semester. *Financial support:* Federal Work-Study, scholarships/grants, and tuition waivers (partial) available. Financial award applicants required to submit FAFSA. *Unit head:* Sr. Eilish Ryan, Chair, 210-829-3871, Fax: 210-829-3880, E-mail: eryan@uiwtx.edu. *Application contact:* Andrea Cyterski-Acosta, Dean of Enrollment, 210-829-6005, Fax: 210-829-3921, E-mail: admis@uiwtx.edu.

University of the West, Department of Religious Studies, Rosemead, CA 91770. Offers Buddhist studies (MA, DBS); comparative religions (MA); religious studies (PhD). Part-time and evening/weekend programs available. *Degree requirements:* For master's, thesis or comprehensive exam, competency in language associated with Buddhist Canon literature; for doctorate, one foreign language, comprehensive exam, thesis/dissertation.

University of Toronto, School of Graduate Studies, Humanities Division, Centre for the Study of Religion, Toronto, ON M5S 1A1, Canada. Offers MA, PhD. Part-time programs available. *Degree requirements:* For master's, one foreign language, research paper, language requirement examination; for doctorate, 2 foreign languages, thesis/dissertation, language examinations, general examinations, oral examination. *Entrance requirements:* For master's, BA in religion or a related field; minimum A- average in final year, 3 letters of recommendation, resume; for doctorate, MA in religion, minimum average of A- in MA courses with no individual grade below a B, 3 letters of recommendation, resumé, brief writing sample. Additional exam requirements/recommendations for international students: Required—TOEFL (minimum score 600 paper-based; 250 computer-based), TWE (minimum score 5).

University of Virginia, College and Graduate School of Arts and Sciences, Department of Religious Studies, Charlottesville, VA 22903. Offers MA, PhD. *Faculty:* 28 full-time (7 women), 1 part-time/adjunct (0 women). *Students:* 93 full-time (30 women), 2 part-time (1 woman); includes 1 Black or African American, non-Hispanic/Latino; 1 Asian, non-Hispanic/Latino; 2 Two or more races, non-Hispanic/Latino, 8 international. Average age 31. 164 applicants, 23% accepted, 26 enrolled. In 2010, 10 master's, 5 doctorates awarded. *Degree requirements:* For master's, one foreign language, thesis optional; for doctorate, 2 foreign languages, comprehensive exam, thesis/dissertation. *Entrance requirements:* For master's and doctorate, GRE General Test, 3 letters of recommendation. Additional exam requirements/recommendations for international students: Required—TOEFL (minimum score 600 paper-based; 250 computer-based; 90 iBT), IELTS (minimum score 7). *Application deadline:* For fall admission, 12/1 for

Religion

University of Virginia (continued)

domestic students, 12/3 for international students. Applications are processed on a rolling basis. Application fee: $60. Electronic applications accepted. *Financial support:* Fellowships, teaching assistantships available. Financial award applicants required to submit FAFSA. *Unit head:* Kevin Hart, Chair, 434-924-6705, Fax: 434-924-1467. *Application contact:* Elizabeth Smith, Graduate and Fiscal Coordinator, 434-924-6706, Fax: 434-924-1467, E-mail: eas5x@virginia.edu.

University of Washington, Graduate School, College of Arts and Sciences, Department of Asian Languages and Literature, Seattle, WA 98195. Offers Buddhist studies (MA, PhD); Chinese language and literature (MA, PhD); Japanese language and literature (MA, PhD); Korean language and literature (MA, PhD); South Asian language and literature (MA, PhD). *Degree requirements:* For master's, 2 foreign languages, general exam, thesis or 2 research papers; for doctorate, 3 foreign languages, thesis/dissertation, general exam. *Entrance requirements:* For master's, GRE, minimum GPA of 3.0; for doctorate, GRE, master's degree in related field, minimum GPA of 3.0. Additional exam requirements/recommendations for international students: Required—TOEFL. Electronic applications accepted. *Faculty research:* Textual, linguistic, philological, and literary study of languages and literatures of Asia.

University of Washington, Graduate School, College of Arts and Sciences, Henry M. Jackson School of International Studies, Comparative Religion Program, Seattle, WA 98195. Offers MAIS. *Faculty:* 21 full-time (9 women). *Students:* 11 full-time (4 women); includes 1 Asian, non-Hispanic/Latino; 1 Hispanic/Latino. 29 applicants, 66% accepted, 6 enrolled. In 2010, 2 master's awarded. *Degree requirements:* For master's, 2 foreign languages. *Entrance requirements:* For master's, GRE General Test, minimum GPA of 3.00 (last two years). Additional exam requirements/recommendations for international students: Required—TOEFL (minimum score 500 paper-based; 213 computer-based; 92 iBT) or IELTS (minimum score 7). *Application deadline:* For fall admission, 1/5 for domestic and international students. Application fee: $75. Electronic applications accepted. *Financial support:* In 2010–11, 1 fellowship, 2 teaching assistantships with full tuition reimbursements were awarded; research assistantships, career-related internships or fieldwork, Federal Work-Study, institutionally sponsored loans, scholarships/grants, and tuition waivers (partial) also available. Financial award application deadline: 1/5; financial award applicants required to submit FAFSA. *Unit head:* Prof. James K. Wellman, Chair, 206-543-0339, E-mail: jwellman@u.washington.edu. *Application contact:* 206-543-6001, Fax: 206-616-3170, E-mail: jsisinfo@u.washington.edu.

University of Waterloo, Graduate Studies, Faculty of Arts, Department of Religious Studies, Waterloo, ON N2L 3G1, Canada. Offers religious diversity in North America (PhD). *Degree requirements:* For doctorate, thesis/dissertation. *Entrance requirements:* Additional exam requirements/recommendations for international students: Required—TOEFL. Electronic applications accepted. *Faculty research:* Religious diversity in North America.

The University of Winnipeg, Graduate Studies, Department of Religious Studies, Winnipeg, MB R3B 2E9, Canada. Offers MA. Program offered jointly with University of Manitoba. Part-time programs available. *Faculty research:* Religion and culture, social ethics, religious liberalism, history of Canaanite and Israelite religion, literary criticism of the Hebrew Bible.

Valley Forge Christian College, Program in Christian Leadership, Phoenixville, PA 19460. Offers MA. *Degree requirements:* For master's, project.

Valley Forge Christian College, Program in Worship Studies, Phoenixville, PA 19460. Offers MA.

Vanderbilt University, Graduate School, Department of Religion, Nashville, TN 37240-1001. Offers MA, PhD. *Faculty:* 25 full-time (8 women). *Students:* 104 full-time (52 women), 1 part-time (0 women); includes 14 Black or African American, non-Hispanic/Latino; 4 Asian, non-Hispanic/Latino; 3 Hispanic/Latino; 2 Two or more races, non-Hispanic/Latino. Average age 35. 224 applicants, 13% accepted, 20 enrolled. In 2010, 14 master's, 9 doctorates awarded. *Degree requirements:* For master's, one foreign language, thesis; for doctorate, 2 foreign languages, thesis/dissertation, final and qualifying exams. *Entrance requirements:* For master's and doctorate, GRE General Test. Additional exam requirements/recommendations for international students: Required—TOEFL (minimum score 570 paper-based; 230 computer-based; 88 iBT). *Application deadline:* For fall admission, 1/15 for domestic and international students. Application fee: $0. Electronic applications accepted. *Financial support:* Fellowships with full and partial tuition reimbursements, teaching assistantships with full and partial tuition reimbursements, Federal Work-Study, institutionally sponsored loans, health care benefits, and tuition waivers (full and partial) available. Support available to part-time students. Financial award application deadline: 1/15; financial award applicants required to submit CSS PROFILE or FAFSA. *Faculty research:* Hebrew Bible, New Testament, church history, theology, ethics. *Unit head:* John S. McClure, Chair, 615-343-3989, Fax: 615-343-5449, E-mail: john.s.mcclure@vanderbilt.edu. *Application contact:* James P. Byrd, Director of Graduate Studies, 615-343-3976, Fax: 615-343-5449, E-mail: james.p.byrd@vanderbilt.edu.

Vanguard University of Southern California, Graduate Programs in Religion, Costa Mesa, CA 92626-9601. Offers leadership studies (MA); theological studies (MTS). Part-time and evening/weekend programs available. *Degree requirements:* For master's, comprehensive exam (for some programs), thesis (for some programs). *Entrance requirements:* For master's, minimum GPA of 3.0 (MA), 2.5 (MTS). Additional exam requirements/recommendations for international students: Required—TOEFL (minimum score 550 paper-based; 213 computer-based; 79 iBT). Electronic applications accepted. *Expenses:* Contact institution. *Faculty research:* Narrative theology, ecumenism and Pentecost, leadership studies.

Virginia Polytechnic Institute and State University, Graduate School, College of Liberal Arts and Human Sciences, Department of Religion and Culture, Blacksburg, VA 24061. Offers liberal arts (Certificate); religious studies (Certificate). *Expenses:* Tuition, state resident: full-time $9399; part-time $488 per credit hour. Tuition, nonresident: full-time $17,854; part-time $957.75 per credit hour. Required fees: $1534. Full-time tuition and fees vary according to program.

Virginia University of Lynchburg, Graduate Programs, Lynchburg, VA 24501-6417. Offers Christian ministry (M Div).

Wake Forest University, Graduate School of Arts and Sciences, Department of Religion, Winston-Salem, NC 27109. Offers MA. *Accreditation:* ACIPE. Part-time programs available. *Degree requirements:* For master's, one foreign language, thesis. *Entrance requirements:* For master's, GRE General Test. Additional exam requirements/recommendations for international students: Required—TOEFL (minimum score 213 computer-based; 79 iBT). Electronic applications accepted. *Faculty research:* Christian origins, biblical archaeology, psychology and religion, religion and literature.

Warner Pacific College, Graduate Programs, Portland, OR 97215-4099. Offers biblical and theological studies (MA); biblical studies (M Rel); education (M Ed); management/organizational leadership (MS); pastoral ministries (M Rel); religion and ethics (M Rel); teaching (MA); theology (M Rel). Part-time programs available. *Degree requirements:* For master's, thesis or alternative, presentation of defense. *Entrance requirements:* For master's, interview, minimum GPA of 2.5, letters of recommendations. *Faculty research:* New Testament studies, nineteenth-century Wesleyan theology, preaching and church growth, Christian ethics.

Washington Adventist University, Program in Religion, Takoma Park, MD 20912. Offers MAR. Part-time programs available.

Wayland Baptist University, Graduate Programs, Programs in Religion, Plainview, TX 79072-6998. Offers Christian ministry (MCM); religion (MA). Part-time and evening/weekend programs available. Postbaccalaureate distance learning degree programs offered (no on-campus study). *Degree requirements:* For master's, comprehensive exam. *Entrance requirements:* For master's, GRE or MAT. Additional exam requirements/recommendations for international students: Required—TOEFL (minimum score 500 paper-based; 173 computer-based; 61 iBT). Electronic applications accepted.

Wesley Biblical Seminary, Graduate Programs, Jackson, MS 39206. Offers apologetics (MA); Biblical studies (MA); Christian studies (MA); evangelism (M Div); family life ministry (M Div); honors research (M Div); missions (M Div); pastoral ministry (M Div); teaching (M Div); theological studies (MA). *Accreditation:* ATS. Part-time programs available. *Degree requirements:* For master's, thesis. *Entrance requirements:* Additional exam requirements/recommendations for international students: Required—TOEFL. Electronic applications accepted. *Faculty research:* Patristics, missiology, culture, hermeneutics.

Western Michigan University, Graduate College, College of Arts and Sciences, Department of Comparative Religion, Kalamazoo, MI 49008. Offers MA. *Degree requirements:* For master's, one foreign language, thesis optional, oral exam.

Western Seminary, Graduate Programs, Program in Biblical and Theological Studies, Portland, OR 97215-3367. Offers biblical and theological studies (MA, G Dip); biblical studies (Certificate); theology (Th M). *Accreditation:* ATS. Part-time and evening/weekend programs available. *Faculty:* 93 full-time (38 women), 586 part-time/adjunct (198 women). *Students:* 265 applicants, 77% accepted, 155 enrolled. In 2010, 93 master's, 6 other advanced degrees awarded. *Degree requirements:* For master's, thesis or alternative, practicum. *Entrance requirements:* Additional exam requirements/recommendations for international students: Required—TOEFL. *Application deadline:* For fall admission, 7/18 priority date for domestic students; for winter admission, 11/7 priority date for domestic students; for spring admission, 3/13 priority date for domestic students. Applications are processed on a rolling basis. Application fee: $50. *Expenses:* Tuition: Part-time $425 per credit. *Financial support:* Fellowships, career-related internships or fieldwork available. Financial award applicants required to submit FAFSA. *Unit head:* Dr. Gerry Breshears, Director, 503-517-1870, E-mail: gbreshears@westernseminary.edu. *Application contact:* Dr. Robert W. Wiggins, Registrar/Dean of Student Development, 503-517-1820, Fax: 503-517-1820, E-mail: rwiggins@westernseminary.edu.

Westminster Seminary California, Programs in Theology, Escondido, CA 92027-4128. Offers Biblical studies (MA); historical theology (MA); theological studies (M Div, MA). *Accreditation:* ATS. Part-time and evening/weekend programs available. *Degree requirements:* For master's, 2 foreign languages, thesis (for some programs); for M Div, 2 foreign languages, internship. *Entrance requirements:* For M Div and master's, 2 letters of reference. Additional exam requirements/recommendations for international students: Required—TOEFL (minimum score 570 paper-based; 230 computer-based; 89 iBT), TWE (minimum score 4.5). *Faculty research:* Neo-paganism, New Testament background, eschatology, Protestant scholasticism, Ezekiel.

Westminster Theological Seminary, Graduate and Professional Programs, Philadelphia, PA 19118. Offers apologetics (Th M); Biblical and urban studies (Certificate); Biblical counseling (MA); biblical studies (MAR); Christian studies (Certificate); church history (Th M); counseling (M Div); general studies (M Div, MAR); hermeneutics and Bible interpretations (PhD); historical and theological studies (PhD); historical theology (Th M); New Testament (Th M); Old Testament (Th M); pastoral counseling (D Min); pastoral ministry (M Div, D Min); systematic theology (Th M); theological studies (MAR); urban missions (M Div, MA, MAR, D Min). *Accreditation:* ATS. Part-time programs available. Terminal master's awarded for partial completion of doctoral program. *Degree requirements:* For master's, thesis (for some programs); for doctorate, 4 foreign languages, comprehensive exam (for some programs), thesis/dissertation; for M Div, 2 foreign languages. *Entrance requirements:* For doctorate, GRE General Test. Additional exam requirements/recommendations for international students: Required—TOEFL, TWE.

Wheaton College, Graduate School, Department of Biblical and Theological Studies, Program in Religion in American Life, Wheaton, IL 60187-5593. Offers MA. Part-time programs available. *Degree requirements:* For master's, thesis optional. *Entrance requirements:* For master's, GRE General Test, MAT. Electronic applications accepted.

Wilfrid Laurier University, Faculty of Graduate and Postdoctoral Studies, Faculty of Arts, Department of Religion and Culture, Waterloo, ON N2L 3C5, Canada. Offers religion and culture (MA); religious diversity of North America (PhD). Part-time programs available. *Faculty:* 10 full-time (5 women). *Students:* 24 full-time (13 women), 1 part-time. 43 applicants, 35% accepted, 9 enrolled. In 2010, 11 master's, 1 doctorate awarded. *Degree requirements:* For master's, thesis optional; for doctorate, thesis/dissertation. *Entrance requirements:* For master's, honors BA or the equivalent in religious studies or other interdisciplinary social science or humanities program, minimum B average in overall undergraduate course work, B+ average in the undergraduate major; for doctorate, MA in religious studies, minimum A- average. Additional exam requirements/recommendations for international students: Required—TOEFL (minimum score 89 iBT). *Application deadline:* For fall admission, 2/1 priority date for domestic and international students. Application fee: $100. Electronic applications accepted. Tuition and fees charges are reported in Canadian dollars. *Expenses:* Tuition, area resident: Full-time $15,300 Canadian dollars; part-time $1200 Canadian dollars per credit. International tuition: $21,300 Canadian dollars full-time. Required fees: $650 Canadian dollars; $100 Canadian dollars per credit. Tuition and fees vary according to course load, degree level, campus/location and program. *Financial support:* In 2010–11, 31 fellowships, 31 teaching assistantships were awarded; career-related internships or fieldwork, scholarships/grants, health care benefits, and unspecified assistantships also available. *Faculty research:* Religious diversity in North America. *Unit head:* Dr. Janet McLellan, Graduate Coordinator, 519-884-0710 Ext. 2895, Fax: 519-884-9387, E-mail: jmclellan@wlu.ca. *Application contact:* Jennifer Williams, Graduate Admission and Records Officer, 519-884-0710 Ext. 3536, Fax: 519-884-1020, E-mail: gradstudies@wlu.ca.

WON Institute of Graduate Studies, Applied Meditation Studies Program, Glenside, PA 19038. Offers MA. Part-time and evening/weekend programs available. *Faculty:* 2 full-time (1 woman). *Students:* 5 part-time (4 women), 1 international. 3 applicants, 100% accepted, 3 enrolled. In 2010, 1 master's awarded. *Entrance requirements:* For master's, 2 letters recommendation, essay. *Application deadline:* For fall admission, 7/15 for domestic students. Applications are processed on a rolling basis. Application fee: $75. *Expenses:* Tuition: Full-time $16,900; part-time $400 per credit. Required fees: $150 per trimester. *Unit head:* Dr. Glenn Wallis, Chair, 215-884-8942, Fax: 215-884-9002, E-mail: glenn.wallis@woninstitute.edu. *Application contact:* Dr. Glenn Wallis, Chair, 215-884-8942, Fax: 215-884-9002, E-mail: glenn.wallis@woninstitute.edu.

WON Institute of Graduate Studies, Won Buddhist Studies Program, Glenside, PA 19038. Offers MA. Part-time programs available. *Faculty:* 2 full-time (both women). *Students:* 5 full-time (4 women), 2 part-time (1 woman); includes 1 Black or African American, non-Hispanic/Latino, 5 international. Average age 27. 5 applicants, 100% accepted, 5 enrolled. In 2010, 2 master's awarded. *Degree requirements:* For master's, comprehensive exam. *Entrance requirements:* For master's, bachelor's degree or one-year preparatory course in Won Buddhist studies; recommendation from Won Buddhist Diocese. Additional exam requirements/recommendations for international students: Required—TOEFL (minimum score 550 paper-based; 213 computer-based; 79 iBT). *Application deadline:* For fall admission, 7/15 for domestic students, 2/15 for international students. Applications are processed on a rolling basis. Application fee: $75. *Expenses:* Tuition: Full-time $16,900; part-time $400 per credit. Required fees: $150 per trimester. *Financial support:* In 2010–11, 7 students received support. Application deadline: 8/1. *Unit head:* Dr. Chungnam HA, Chair, 215-884-8942, E-mail: wbschair@woninstitute.edu. *Application contact:* Dr. Chungnam HA, Chair, 215-884-8942, E-mail: wbschair@woninstitute.edu.

Wycliffe College, Division of Advanced Degree Studies, Toronto, ON M5S 1H7, Canada. Offers MA, Th M, D Min, PhD, Th D. PhD, D Min, MA offered jointly with Toronto School of Theology; Th D, Th M with University of Toronto. *Accreditation:* ATS (one or more programs are accredited). Part-time programs available. Terminal master's awarded for partial completion of doctoral program. *Degree requirements:* For master's, 2 foreign languages, thesis (for some programs); for doctorate, 3 foreign languages, thesis/dissertation. *Entrance requirements:*

Additional exam requirements/recommendations for international students: Required—TOEFL (minimum score 600 paper-based; 250 computer-based). *Expenses:* Contact institution. *Faculty research:* Old and New Testament, doctrine, ethics, philosophy, history.

Wycliffe College, Division of Basic Degree Studies, Toronto, ON M5S 1H7, Canada. Offers Christian Studies (Diploma); theology (M Div, M Rel, MTS). M Div, M Rel, MTS offered jointly with University of Toronto. *Accreditation:* ATS. Part-time programs available. *Degree requirements:* For master's, one foreign language, thesis; for M Div, thesis/dissertation optional. *Entrance requirements:* Additional exam requirements/recommendations for international students: Required—TOEFL (minimum score 580 paper-based).

Yale University, Graduate School of Arts and Sciences, Department of Religious Studies, New Haven, CT 06520. Offers PhD. *Degree requirements:* For doctorate, 2 foreign languages, thesis/dissertation. *Entrance requirements:* For doctorate, GRE General Test.

Yeshiva Derech Chaim, Graduate Program, Brooklyn, NY 11218. Offers PhD. *Accreditation:* AARTS.

Theology

Abilene Christian University, Graduate School, College of Biblical Studies, Graduate School of Theology, Program in Divinity, Abilene, TX 79699-9100. Offers M Div. *Accreditation:* ATS. Part-time and evening/weekend programs available. *Students:* 39 full-time (4 women), 28 part-time (3 women); includes 2 Black or African American, non-Hispanic/Latino; 1 American Indian or Alaska Native, non-Hispanic/Latino; 1 Asian, non-Hispanic/Latino; 5 Hispanic/Latino. 22 applicants, 77% accepted, 16 enrolled. *Degree requirements:* For M Div, one foreign language, comprehensive exam. *Entrance requirements:* GMAT, GRE, or MAT. Additional exam requirements/recommendations for international students: Required—TOEFL (minimum score 550 paper-based; 213 computer-based). *Application deadline:* For fall admission, 4/1 priority date for domestic students; for spring admission, 11/1 for domestic students. Applications are processed on a rolling basis. Application fee: $40. Electronic applications accepted. *Expenses:* Tuition: Full-time $12,906; part-time $717 per hour. Required fees: $1250; $61.50 per unit. *Financial support:* In 2010–11, 7 students received support. Applicants required to submit FAFSA. *Unit head:* Dr. Tim Sensing, Graduate Advisor, 325-674-3792, Fax: 325-674-6716, E-mail: sensingt@acu.edu. *Application contact:* David Pittman, Graduate Admissions Counselor, 325-674-2656, Fax: 325-674-6717, E-mail: gradinfo@acu.edu.

Abilene Christian University, Graduate School, College of Biblical Studies, Graduate School of Theology, Program in History and Theology, Abilene, TX 79699-9100. Offers MA. Part-time programs available. *Students:* 7 full-time (0 women), 8 part-time (0 women); includes 2 Black or African American, non-Hispanic/Latino, 1 international. 7 applicants, 43% accepted, 3 enrolled. In 2010, 2 master's awarded. *Degree requirements:* For master's, comprehensive exam, thesis. *Entrance requirements:* For master's, GRE. Additional exam requirements/recommendations for international students: Required—TOEFL (minimum score 550 paper-based; 213 computer-based). *Application deadline:* For fall admission, 4/1 priority date for domestic students; for spring admission, 11/1 for domestic students. Applications are processed on a rolling basis. Application fee: $40. Electronic applications accepted. *Expenses:* Tuition: Full-time $12,906; part-time $717 per hour. Required fees: $1250; $61.50 per unit. *Financial support:* In 2010–11, 3 students received support. Application deadline: 4/1. *Unit head:* Dr. Douglas Foster, Graduate Advisor, 325-674-3730, Fax: 325-674-6180, E-mail: foster@bible.acu.edu. *Application contact:* David Pittman, Graduate Admissions Counselor, 325-674-2656, Fax: 325-674-6717, E-mail: gradinfo@acu.edu.

Abilene Christian University, Graduate School, College of Biblical Studies, Graduate School of Theology, Program in New Testament, Abilene, TX 79699-9100. Offers MA. *Accreditation:* ATS. Part-time programs available. *Students:* 2 full-time (0 women), 1 part-time (0 women). 2 applicants, 100% accepted, 2 enrolled. In 2010, 1 master's awarded. *Degree requirements:* For master's, comprehensive exam, thesis. *Entrance requirements:* For master's, GRE General Test or MAT. Additional exam requirements/recommendations for international students: Required—TOEFL (minimum score 550 paper-based; 213 computer-based). *Application deadline:* For fall admission, 4/1 priority date for domestic students; for spring admission, 11/1 for domestic students. Applications are processed on a rolling basis. Application fee: $40. Electronic applications accepted. *Expenses:* Tuition: Full-time $12,906; part-time $717 per hour. Required fees: $1250; $61.50 per unit. *Financial support:* In 2010–11, 1 student received support. Application deadline: 4/1. *Unit head:* Dr. James Thompson, Graduate Advisor, 325-674-3781, Fax: 325-674-6180, E-mail: thompsonja@acu.edu. *Application contact:* David Pittman, Graduate Admissions Counselor, 325-674-2656, Fax: 325-674-6717, E-mail: gradinfo@acu.edu.

Abilene Christian University, Graduate School, College of Biblical Studies, Graduate School of Theology, Program in Old Testament, Abilene, TX 79699-9100. Offers MA. Part-time programs available. *Students:* 6 full-time (1 woman), 2 part-time (0 women), 1 international. 3 applicants, 100% accepted, 3 enrolled. *Degree requirements:* For master's, comprehensive exam, thesis. *Entrance requirements:* For master's, GRE. Additional exam requirements/recommendations for international students: Required—TOEFL (minimum score 550 paper-based; 213 computer-based). *Application deadline:* For fall admission, 4/1 priority date for domestic students; for spring admission, 11/1 for domestic students. Applications are processed on a rolling basis. Application fee: $40. Electronic applications accepted. *Expenses:* Tuition: Full-time $12,906; part-time $717 per hour. Required fees: $1250; $61.50 per unit. *Financial support:* In 2010–11, 1 student received support. Application deadline: 4/1. *Unit head:* Dr. Mark Hamilton, Graduate Advisor, 325-674-3765, Fax: 325-674-6180, E-mail: wmh00c@acu.edu. *Application contact:* David Pittman, Graduate Admissions Counselor, 325-674-2656, Fax: 325-674-6717, E-mail: gradinfo@acu.edu.

Acadia University, Divinity College, Wolfville, NS B4P 2R6, Canada. Offers divinity (M Div); theology (MA, D Min), including Biblical studies (MA), church history (MA), theology (MA). *Accreditation:* ATS. Part-time programs available. *Faculty:* 12 full-time (2 women), 12 part-time/adjunct (1 woman). *Students:* 34 full-time (9 women), 29 part-time (11 women). Average age 43. In 2010, 53 master's, 7 doctorates awarded. *Degree requirements:* For master's, one foreign language, thesis (for some programs); for doctorate, one foreign language, comprehensive exam, thesis/dissertation. *Entrance requirements:* For M Div, minimum GPA of 2.0; for master's, minimum GPA of 3.0; for doctorate, minimum GPA of 3.0, 3 years ministry experience. Additional exam requirements/recommendations for international students: Required—TOEFL. *Application deadline:* For fall admission, 6/30 priority date for domestic students, 4/1 priority date for international students; for spring admission, 4/30 priority date for domestic students. Applications are processed on a rolling basis. Application fee: $50. *Expenses:* Contact institution. *Financial support:* In 2010–11, 8 teaching assistantships (averaging $1,000 per year) were awarded; career-related internships or fieldwork, institutionally sponsored loans, and scholarships/grants also available. Support available to part-time students. Financial award application deadline: 8/12. *Faculty research:* Biblical canon, Jesus, Dead Sea Scrolls, Baptist studies, Old Testament-Septuagint. *Unit head:* Dr. Harry Gardner, President, 902-585-2212, Fax: 902-585-2233, E-mail: harry.gardner@acadiau.ca. *Application contact:* Shawna Peverill, Registrar, 902-585-2215, Fax: 902-585-2233, E-mail: shawna.peverill@acadiau.ca.

Ambrose University College, Ambrose Seminary, Calgary, AB T2P 3T5, Canada. Offers biblical/theological studies (MA); Chinese ministries (Certificate); Christian studies (M Div, MA, Diploma); foundations for ministry (Certificate); intercultural ministries (M Div, MA, Certificate, Diploma); leadership and ministry (MA, Certificate, Diploma). *Accreditation:* ATS (one or more programs are accredited). Part-time programs available. *Faculty:* 7 full-time (0 women), 24 part-time/adjunct (2 women). *Students:* 55 full-time (16 women), 98 part-time (52 women); includes 49 minority (5 Black or African American, non-Hispanic/Latino; 2 American Indian or Alaska Native, non-Hispanic/Latino; 41 Asian, non-Hispanic/Latino; 1 Hispanic/Latino). Average age 41. *Degree requirements:* For master's, 2 foreign languages, internship; for M Div, one foreign language, internship. *Entrance requirements:* For master's, bachelor's degree. Additional exam requirements/recommendations for international students: Required—TOEFL or IELTS. *Application deadline:* For fall admission, 7/31 priority date for domestic students, 3/1 priority date for international students; for winter admission, 11/30 priority date for domestic students, 6/1 priority date for international students. Applications are processed on a rolling basis. Application fee: $50. Electronic applications accepted. Tuition and fees charges are reported in Canadian dollars. *Expenses:* Tuition: Full-time $9270 Canadian dollars; part-time $309 Canadian dollars per credit hour. Required fees: $510 Canadian dollars. *Financial support:* Career-related internships or fieldwork and scholarships/grants available. Support available to part-time students. Financial award application deadline: 3/30. *Faculty research:* Evangelicalism and sociology, missiological trends, chaplaincy, intertestamental studies, postmodernism. *Unit head:* Dr. Paul Spilsbury, Vice-President of Academic Affairs, 403-410-2000 Ext. 6905, Fax: 403-571-2556, E-mail: pspilsbury@ambrose.edu. *Application contact:* Dr. Paul Spilsbury, Vice-President of Academic Affairs, 403-410-2000 Ext. 6905, Fax: 403-571-2556, E-mail: pspilsbury@ambrose.edu.

American Baptist Seminary of the West, Graduate and Professional Programs, Berkeley, CA 94704-3029. Offers community leadership (MA); theology (M Div, MA). MA program in theology offered jointly with Graduate Theological Union. *Accreditation:* ACIPE; ATS (one or more programs are accredited). Part-time and evening/weekend programs available. *Faculty:* 6 full-time (4 women), 7 part-time/adjunct (2 women). *Students:* 42 full-time (13 women), 33 part-time (15 women); includes 38 Black or African American, non-Hispanic/Latino; 11 Asian, non-Hispanic/Latino; 1 Hispanic/Latino; 1 Native Hawaiian or other Pacific Islander, non-Hispanic/Latino, 16 international. In 2010, 22 first professional degrees awarded. *Entrance requirements:* For M Div, minimum GPA of 2.5; for master's, minimum GPA of 3.0. Additional exam requirements/recommendations for international students: Required—TOEFL (minimum score 550 paper-based; 250 computer-based). *Application deadline:* For fall admission, 4/15 priority date for domestic students, 4/15 for international students. Applications are processed on a rolling basis. Application fee: $25. Electronic applications accepted. *Expenses:* Tuition: Full-time $14,040; part-time $540 per credit. Required fees: $240 per semester. One-time fee: $340. *Financial support:* Career-related internships or fieldwork, Federal Work-Study, institutionally sponsored loans, scholarships/grants, tuition waivers (partial), and tuition discount available. Support available to part-time students. Financial award application deadline: 4/15; financial award applicants required to submit FAFSA. *Unit head:* Dr. Paul M. Martin, President, 510-841-1905 Ext. 224, Fax: 510-841-2446, E-mail: pmartin@absw.edu. *Application contact:* Rev. Michelle M. Holmes, Vice President, 510-841-1905 Ext. 225, Fax: 510-841-2446, E-mail: mmholmes@absw.edu.

American Jewish University, Ziegler School of Rabbinic Studies, Bel Air, CA 90077-1599. Offers MARS. *Degree requirements:* For master's, one foreign language. *Entrance requirements:* For master's, GRE General Test, interview. Additional exam requirements/recommendations for international students: Required—TOEFL.

Amridge University, Graduate and Professional Programs, Montgomery, AL 36117. Offers behavioral leadership and management (MA); Biblical exposition (MA); biblical studies (MA, PhD); family therapy (D Min); historical and theological studies (MA); leadership and management (MS); marriage and family therapy (M Div, MA, PhD); ministerial leadership (M Div, MS); pastoral counseling (M Div, MS); practical ministry (MA); professional counseling (M Div, MA, PhD); theology (D Min). Part-time and evening/weekend programs available. Postbaccalaureate distance learning degree programs offered (no on-campus study). *Faculty:* 39 full-time (6 women), 39 part-time/adjunct (5 women). *Students:* 119 full-time (54 women), 260 part-time (149 women); includes 160 minority (153 Black or African American, non-Hispanic/Latino; 1 Asian, non-Hispanic/Latino; 6 Hispanic/Latino). Average age 35. *Degree requirements:* For master's, one foreign language, comprehensive exam (for some programs), thesis (for some programs); for doctorate, comprehensive exam (for some programs), thesis/dissertation; for M Div, comprehensive exam (for some programs). *Entrance requirements:* For M Div, master's, and doctorate, GRE General Test or MAT. Additional exam requirements/recommendations for international students: Required—TOEFL. *Application deadline:* For fall admission, 9/1 priority date for domestic students; for spring admission, 1/1 priority date for domestic students. Applications are processed on a rolling basis. Application fee: $75. Electronic applications accepted. *Financial support:* Federal Work-Study and scholarships/grants available. Support available to part-time students. Financial award applicants required to submit FAFSA. *Faculty research:* Homiletics, hermeneutics, ancient Near Eastern history. *Unit head:* Director of Enrollment Management, 800-351-4040 Ext. 7513, Fax: 334-387-3878. *Application contact:* Ora Davis, Admissions Officer, 334-387-3877 Ext. 7524, Fax: 334-387-3878, E-mail: admissions@amridgeuniversity.edu.

Anderson University, School of Theology, Anderson, IN 46012-3495. Offers missions (MA); theology (M Div, MTS, D Min). *Accreditation:* ACIPE; ATS. Part-time programs available. *Degree requirements:* For master's, one foreign language, thesis, integrative senior seminar; for doctorate, thesis/dissertation; for M Div, thesis/dissertation (for some programs). *Faculty research:* Small-church/bivocational ministry, women in ministry.

Andover Newton Theological School, Graduate and Professional Programs, Newton Centre, MA 02459-2243. Offers divinity (M Div); religious education (MA); theological research (MA); theological studies (MA); theology (D Min). *Accreditation:* ACIPE; ATS. Part-time programs available. *Faculty:* 15 full-time (7 women), 49 part-time/adjunct (21 women). *Students:* 58 full-time (28 women), 234 part-time (160 women). *Degree requirements:* For master's, comprehensive exam (for some programs), thesis (for some programs); for doctorate, comprehensive exam, thesis/dissertation. *Entrance requirements:* For doctorate, M Div or equivalent. Additional exam requirements/recommendations for international students: Required—TOEFL (minimum score 550 paper-based; 213 computer-based). *Application deadline:* For fall admission, 7/1 priority date for domestic students, 4/1 for international students; for winter admission, 11/1 for domestic students; for spring admission, 12/1 priority date for domestic students. Applications are processed on a rolling basis. Application fee: $20 ($50 for international students). Electronic applications accepted. *Financial support:* Teaching assistantships with partial tuition reimbursements, career-related internships or fieldwork, Federal Work-Study, scholarships/grants, and tuition waivers (full) available. Support available to part-time students. Financial award application deadline: 4/15; financial award applicants required to submit FAFSA. *Unit head:* Nick Carter, President, 617-964-1100 Ext. 2410, Fax: 617-965-9756, E-mail: ncarter@ants.edu. *Application contact:* Margaret L. Carroll, Director of Enrollment, 800-964-2687 Ext. 2428, Fax: 617-558-9785, E-mail: admissions@ants.edu.

Andrews University, School of Graduate Studies, Seventh-day Adventist Theological Seminary, Berrien Springs, MI 49104. Offers ministry (M Div, D Min); pastoral ministry (MA); religious

Theology

Andrews University (continued)
education (MA, Ed D, PhD, Ed S); theology (M Th, Th D); youth ministry (MA). *Accreditation:* ATS. *Degree requirements:* For master's, thesis optional; for doctorate, variable foreign language requirement, thesis/dissertation; for M Div, one foreign language, thesis/dissertation optional. *Entrance requirements:* For master's, GRE Subject Test, minimum GPA of 2.0. Additional exam requirements/recommendations for international students: Required—TOEFL (minimum score 550 paper-based).

Apex School of Theology, Graduate Programs, Durham, NC 27703. Offers M Div, MACC, MCE, D Min. *Faculty:* 4 full-time (1 woman), 11 part-time/adjunct (6 women). *Students:* 111 full-time (76 women), 27 part-time (10 women). Average age 45.Application fee: $50. *Expenses:* Tuition: Part-time $675 per course. *Faculty research:* Sociology, educational sciences, economics. *Unit head:* Dr. LaFayette Maxwell, Academic Dean, 919-572-1625, Fax: 919-572-1762, E-mail: lmaxwell@apexsot.edu. *Application contact:* Dr. Henry O. Wells, Registrar, 919-572-1625, Fax: 919-572-1762, E-mail: registrar@apexsot.edu.

Aquinas Institute of Theology, Graduate and Professional Programs, St. Louis, MO 63108. Offers biblical studies (Certificate); health care mission (MAHCM); ministry (M Div); pastoral care (Certificate); pastoral ministry (MAPM); pastoral studies (MAPS); preaching (D Min); spiritual direction (Certificate); theology (M Div, MA); Thomistic studies (Certificate); M Div/MA; MAPS/MSW. *Accreditation:* ATS (one or more programs are accredited). Part-time and evening/weekend programs available. Postbaccalaureate distance learning degree programs offered (minimal on-campus study). *Degree requirements:* For master's, one foreign language, comprehensive exam, thesis or major paper; for doctorate, thesis/dissertation. *Entrance requirements:* For M Div, master's, and Certificate, MAT; for doctorate, 3 years of ministerial experience, 6 hours of graduate course work in homiletics, M Div or the equivalent, minimum GPA of 3.0. Additional exam requirements/recommendations for international students: Required—TOEFL. *Faculty research:* Theology of preaching, hermeneutics, lay ecclesial ministry, pastoral and practical theology.

Asbury Theological Seminary, Graduate and Professional Programs, Wilmore, KY 40390-1199. Offers MA, MACE, MACL, MAMFC, MAMHC, MAPC, MAYM, Th M, PhD, Certificate. *Accreditation:* ATS. Part-time programs available. Postbaccalaureate distance learning degree programs offered (minimal on-campus study). *Faculty:* 63 full-time (12 women), 74 part-time/adjunct (14 women). *Students:* 719 full-time (251 women), 855 part-time (276 women); includes 178 minority (87 Black or African American, non-Hispanic/Latino; 4 American Indian or Alaska Native, non-Hispanic/Latino; 35 Asian, non-Hispanic/Latino; 40 Hispanic/Latino; 3 Native Hawaiian or other Pacific Islander, non-Hispanic/Latino; 9 Two or more races, non-Hispanic/Latino), 109 international. Average age 38. 772 applicants, 71% accepted, 406 enrolled. In 2010, 101 master's, 37 doctorates, 3 other advanced degrees awarded. Terminal master's awarded for partial completion of doctoral program. *Degree requirements:* For master's, thesis (for some programs); for doctorate, thesis/dissertation, qualifying exam. *Entrance requirements:* For master's, minimum GPA of 2.75; for doctorate, minimum GPA of 3.0. Additional exam requirements/recommendations for international students: Required—TOEFL, IELTS. *Application deadline:* Applications are processed on a rolling basis. Application fee: $50. Electronic applications accepted. *Expenses:* Tuition: Full-time $12,120; part-time $505 per credit hour. One-time fee: $100. *Financial support:* In 2010–11, 1,317 students received support. Career-related internships or fieldwork, Federal Work-Study, institutionally sponsored loans, and scholarships/grants available. Support available to part-time students. Financial award applicants required to submit FAFSA. *Unit head:* Dr. Leslie A. Andrews, Provost, 859-858-2206, Fax: 859-858-2025, E-mail: leslie.andrews@asburyseminary.edu. *Application contact:* Kevin Bush, Vice President of Enrollment Management, 859-858-2211, Fax: 859-858-2287, E-mail: admissions.office@asburyseminary.edu.

Ashland Theological Seminary, Graduate Programs, Ashland, OH 44805. Offers biblical and theological studies (MA, MAR), including New Testament (MA), Old Testament (MA); Christian ministry (MAPT); Christian studies (Diploma); clinical counseling (MAC, MACC); historical studies (MA), including church history; ministry (D Min); pastoral ministry (M Div); theological studies (MA). *Accreditation:* ATS. Part-time programs available. *Faculty:* 23 full-time (6 women), 38 part-time/adjunct (15 women). *Students:* 464 full-time (258 women), 117 part-time (70 women); includes 240 minority (221 Black or African American, non-Hispanic/Latino; 4 American Indian or Alaska Native, non-Hispanic/Latino; 8 Asian, non-Hispanic/Latino; 7 Hispanic/Latino), 11 international. Average age 43. 89 applicants, 100% accepted, 88 enrolled. In 2010, 34 first professional degrees, 100 master's, 27 doctorates, 2 other advanced degrees awarded. *Degree requirements:* For master's, 2 foreign languages, comprehensive exam (for some programs), thesis (for some programs); for doctorate, thesis/dissertation; for M Div, 2 foreign languages, comprehensive exam (for some programs). *Entrance requirements:* For M Div, minimum GPA of 2.75; for master's, minimum undergraduate GPA of 2.75; for doctorate, M Div, minimum undergraduate GPA of 3.0. Additional exam requirements/recommendations for international students: Required—TOEFL (minimum score 500 paper-based; 173 computer-based; 65 iBT). *Application deadline:* For fall admission, 8/30 for domestic students. Applications are processed on a rolling basis. Application fee: $30. Electronic applications accepted. *Financial support:* In 2010–11, 156 students received support, including 17 teaching assistantships; research assistantships, career-related internships or fieldwork, institutionally sponsored loans, scholarships/grants, and unspecified assistantships also available. Support available to part-time students. Financial award application deadline: 5/15; financial award applicants required to submit FAFSA. *Faculty research:* Semitic languages and linguistics, rhetorical and social-scientific criticism, Anabaptist studies, inner spiritual healing, African-American clergy in film and literature. *Unit head:* Dr. John C. Shultz, President, 419-289-5160, Fax: 419-289-5969, E-mail: jshultz@ashland.edu. *Application contact:* Glenn Black, Director of Enrollment Management, 419-289-5151, Fax: 419-289-5969, E-mail: gblack@ashland.edu.

Assemblies of God Theological Seminary, Graduate and Professional Programs, Springfield, MO 65802. Offers Christian ministries (MA); counseling (MA); divinity (M Div); intercultural ministry (MA); intercultural studies (PhD); ministry (D Min); missiology (D Miss); theological studies (MA). *Accreditation:* ATS. Part-time and evening/weekend programs available. Postbaccalaureate distance learning degree programs offered (minimal on-campus study). *Faculty:* 12 full-time (3 women), 20 part-time/adjunct (6 women). *Students:* 176 full-time (59 women), 211 part-time (48 women); includes 55 minority (16 Black or African American, non-Hispanic/Latino; 7 American Indian or Alaska Native, non-Hispanic/Latino; 16 Asian, non-Hispanic/Latino; 14 Hispanic/Latino; 2 Native Hawaiian or other Pacific Islander, non-Hispanic/Latino), 9 international. Average age 40. 96 applicants, 79% accepted, 53 enrolled. In 2010, 26 first professional degrees, 65 master's, 9 doctorates awarded. *Degree requirements:* For master's, analytical reflection paper, comprehensive exam or field education research project; for doctorate, thesis/dissertation; for M Div, one foreign language, analytical reflection paper or field education research project. *Entrance requirements:* For M Div, minimum GPA of 2.5; for master's, minimum GPA of 2.5; for doctorate, minimum GPA of 3.0. Additional exam requirements/recommendations for international students: Required—TOEFL (minimum score 550 paper-based; 213 computer-based; 80 iBT). *Application deadline:* For fall admission, 7/1 priority date for domestic students, 6/1 priority date for international students; for spring admission, 12/1 priority date for domestic students, 11/1 priority date for international students. Applications are processed on a rolling basis. Application fee: $75. Electronic applications accepted. *Expenses:* Tuition: Full-time $12,192; part-time $508 per credit hour. *Financial support:* Career-related internships or fieldwork, Federal Work-Study, and scholarships/grants available. Support available to part-time students. Financial award application deadline: 7/15; financial award applicants required to submit FAFSA. *Unit head:* Stephen Lim, Academic Dean, 417-268-1000, Fax: 417-268-1001, E-mail: slim@agts.edu. *Application contact:* Stephen Lim, Academic Dean, 417-268-1000, Fax: 417-268-1001, E-mail: slim@agts.edu.

Associated Mennonite Biblical Seminary, Graduate and Professional Programs, Elkhart, IN 46517-1999. Offers Christian formation (MA); divinity (M Div); mission and evangelism (MA); peace studies (MA); theological studies (MA, Certificate). *Accreditation:* ACIPE; ATS. Part-time programs available. *Degree requirements:* For master's, comprehensive exam, thesis optional; for M Div, integration paper. *Entrance requirements:* For M Div, master's, and Certificate, 3 letters of reference. Additional exam requirements/recommendations for international students: Required—TOEFL (minimum score 550 paper-based; 213 computer-based). Electronic applications accepted. *Faculty research:* Biblical studies, theology, church history, church leadership.

The Athenaeum of Ohio, Graduate Programs, Cincinnati, OH 45230-5900. Offers biblical studies (MABS); divinity (M Div); lay ministry (Certificate); pastoral counseling (MAPC); pastoral ministry (MA); theology (MA Th); M Div/MA Th; M Div/MABS; M Div/MAPC. *Accreditation:* ATS (one or more programs are accredited). Part-time and evening/weekend programs available. *Degree requirements:* For master's, one foreign language, comprehensive exam (for some programs), thesis optional; for M Div, comprehensive exam.

Atlantic School of Theology, Graduate and Professional Programs, Halifax, NS B3H 3B5, Canada. Offers ministry (M Div); theological studies (Graduate Certificate). *Accreditation:* ATS. Part-time programs available. Postbaccalaureate distance learning degree programs offered (minimal on-campus study). *Degree requirements:* For master's, thesis. *Entrance requirements:* For M Div, master's, and Graduate Certificate, minimum B average in undergraduate course work. *Faculty research:* Ethics and biology; death, dying and pastoral care; theology and the economy; adult education; John and anti-Judaism.

Austin Graduate School of Theology, Program in Theological Studies, Austin, TX 78752. Offers MATS. Part-time programs available. *Degree requirements:* For master's, 2 foreign languages, comprehensive exam, faculty forums. *Entrance requirements:* For master's, 3 letters of reference. Additional exam requirements/recommendations for international students: Required—TOEFL (minimum score 530 paper-based). *Faculty research:* Revelation, synoptic problem, Acadian, Biblical archaeology, worship.

Austin Presbyterian Theological Seminary, Graduate and Professional Programs, Austin, TX 78705-5797. Offers divinity (M Div); ministry (D Min); theological studies (MA); M Div/MSSW. *Accreditation:* ACIPE; ATS. Part-time programs available. *Faculty:* 18 full-time (5 women), 6 part-time/adjunct (2 women). *Students:* 96 full-time (56 women), 100 part-time (49 women); includes 27 minority (15 Black or African American, non-Hispanic/Latino; 1 American Indian or Alaska Native, non-Hispanic/Latino; 5 Asian, non-Hispanic/Latino; 6 Hispanic/Latino), 6 international. 89 applicants, 61% accepted, 41 enrolled. In 2010, 52 first professional degrees, 10 master's, 5 doctorates awarded. *Degree requirements:* For doctorate, thesis/dissertation; for M Div, Greek, Hebrew. *Entrance requirements:* References. Additional exam requirements/recommendations for international students: Required—TOEFL (minimum score 550 paper-based; 213 computer-based; 79 iBT). *Application deadline:* For fall admission, 5/1 for domestic students, 1/1 for international students; for spring admission, 9/1 for domestic students. Applications are processed on a rolling basis. Application fee: $65. *Expenses:* Tuition: Part-time $190 per credit. Required fees: $30 per semester. One-time fee: $150 part-time. Tuition and fees vary according to degree level and program. *Financial support:* In 2010–11, 130 students received support; fellowships, career-related internships or fieldwork, institutionally sponsored loans, scholarships/grants, and tutorships available. Support available to part-time students. Financial award application deadline: 6/1; financial award applicants required to submit FAFSA. *Faculty research:* Mystical theology, religious pluralism, narrative preaching, social ethics, pastoral care and healing. *Unit head:* Rev. Dr. Allan Hugh Cole, Academic Dean, 512-404-4821, Fax: 512-479-0738, E-mail: dean@austinseminary.edu. *Application contact:* Dr. Jack Barden, Director of Admissions, 512-404-4827, Fax: 512-472-7089, E-mail: admissions@austinseminary.edu.

Ave Maria University, Graduate Programs, Ave Maria, FL 34142. Offers pastoral theology (MTS); theology (MA, PhD). Terminal master's awarded for partial completion of doctoral program. *Degree requirements:* For master's, one foreign language, thesis; for doctorate, 3 foreign languages, comprehensive exam, thesis/dissertation. *Entrance requirements:* For master's, GRE; for doctorate, GRE, M Div or equivalent; MA or MTS in religion, theology, or philosophy; bachelor's degree with strong background in religion, theology, and/or philosophy.

Ave Maria University, Institute for Pastoral Theology, Ave Maria, FL 34142. Offers MTS. Part-time and evening/weekend programs available.

Azusa Pacific University, Haggard Graduate School of Theology, Program in Ministry, Azusa, CA 91702-7000. Offers D Min. *Students:* 13 part-time (2 women); includes 7 minority (all Asian, non-Hispanic/Latino), 6 international. Average age 44.Application fee: $45 ($65 for international students). *Unit head:* Dr. Scott Daniels, Associate Dean, 626-387-5750. *Application contact:* Dr. Scott Daniels, Associate Dean, 626-387-5750.

Azusa Pacific University, Haggard Graduate School of Theology, Program in Religion: Biblical Studies, Azusa, CA 91702-7000. Offers MAR. *Students:* 7 full-time (2 women), 10 part-time (4 women); includes 6 minority (3 Black or African American, non-Hispanic/Latino; 1 Asian, non-Hispanic/Latino; 2 Hispanic/Latino), 3 international. Average age 38. In 2010, 2 master's awarded. Application fee: $45 ($65 for international students). *Unit head:* Dr. Scott Daniels, ean, 626-387-5750. *Application contact:* Dr. Scott Daniels, ean, 626-387-5750.

Azusa Pacific University, Haggard Graduate School of Theology, Program in Theological Studies, Program in Religion: Theology and Ethics, Azusa, CA 91702-7000. Offers MA. *Students:* 5 full-time (1 woman), 6 part-time (3 women); includes 5 minority (2 Black or African American, non-Hispanic/Latino; 1 Asian, non-Hispanic/Latino; 2 Hispanic/Latino), 1 international. Average age 38. In 2010, 15 master's awarded. Application fee: $45 ($65 for international students). *Unit head:* Dr. Scott Daniels, Dean, 626-387-5750. *Application contact:* Dr. Scott Daniels, Dean, 626-387-5750.

Bangor Theological Seminary, Professional Program, Bangor, ME 04401-4699. Offers M Div, MA, MTS, D Min. M Div not offered at Portland, ME campus. *Accreditation:* ACIPE; ATS. Part-time programs available. *Degree requirements:* For master's, thesis optional; for doctorate, project, report; for M Div, thesis/dissertation optional. *Entrance requirements:* For M Div and master's, Bachelor degree; for doctorate, M Div, 3 years in ministry. Additional exam requirements/recommendations for international students: Required—TOEFL (minimum score 550 paper-based; 213 computer-based; 80 iBT). *Faculty research:* Formation of the New Testament canon, critical pedagogy, history of theological education, human sexuality, the Isaiah Scroll.

Baptist Bible College, Graduate School of Theology, Springfield, MO 65803-3498. Offers biblical counseling (MA); biblical studies (MA); church ministry (MA); intercultural studies (MA); theology (M Div). Part-time programs available. *Degree requirements:* For master's, 2 foreign languages, thesis (for some programs); for M Div, 2 foreign languages, thesis/dissertation (for some programs). *Entrance requirements:* For master's, outcomes test. Electronic applications accepted.

Baptist Bible College of Pennsylvania, Baptist Bible Seminary, Clarks Summit, PA 18411-1297. Offers biblical studies (PhD); church planting (M Div); global missions (M Div); military chaplaincy (M Div); ministry (M Min, D Min); pastor of church education (M Div); pastor of outreach (M Div); pastoral counseling (M Div); pastoral leadership (M Div); theology (M Div, Th M); youth pastor (M Div). Part-time and evening/weekend programs available. Postbaccalaureate distance learning degree programs offered (minimal on-campus study). *Faculty:* 10 full-time (0 women). *Students:* 71 full-time (0 women), 79 part-time (0 women); includes 16 minority (10 Black or African American, non-Hispanic/Latino; 4 Asian, non-Hispanic/Latino; 2 Hispanic/Latino), 7 international. Average age 38. In 2010, 23 master's, 4 doctorates awarded. Terminal master's awarded for partial completion of doctoral program. *Degree requirements:* For master's, 2 foreign languages, thesis; for doctorate, 2 foreign languages, comprehensive exam (for some programs), thesis/dissertation, oral exam; for M Div, 2 foreign languages, thesis/dissertation, oral exam. *Entrance requirements:* For doctorate, Greek and Hebrew entrance exams (PhD). *Application deadline:* Applications are processed on a rolling basis. Application fee: $30. Electronic applications accepted. *Expenses:* Tuition: Full-time $7488;

part-time $416 per credit. Required fees: $522; $29 per credit. Full-time tuition and fees vary according to degree level and campus/location. *Financial support:* Career-related internships or fieldwork and scholarships/grants available. Support available to part-time students. *Unit head:* Dr. Michael Stallard, Seminary Academic Dean, 570-585-9348, Fax: 570-585-4057, E-mail: mstallard@bbc.edu. *Application contact:* Paul Golden, Director of Seminary Admissions, 570-586-9396, Fax: 570-585-4057, E-mail: pgolden@bbc.edu.

Baptist Bible College of Pennsylvania, Graduate School, Clarks Summit, PA 18411-1297. Offers Bible (MA); counseling (MS); education (MS). Part-time and evening/weekend programs available. Postbaccalaureate distance learning degree programs offered (no on-campus study). *Faculty:* 2 full-time (0 women), 1 part-time/adjunct (0 women). *Students:* 45 full-time (21 women), 68 part-time (41 women); includes 10 minority (9 Black or African American, non-Hispanic/Latino; 1 Hispanic/Latino), 1 international. Average age 31. In 2010, 14 master's awarded. *Entrance requirements:* Additional exam requirements/recommendations for international students: Required—TOEFL (minimum score 500 paper-based; 173 computer-based). *Application deadline:* Applications are processed on a rolling basis. Application fee: $30. *Expenses:* Tuition: Full-time $7488; part-time $416 per credit. Required fees: $522; $29 per credit. Full-time tuition and fees vary according to degree level and campus/location. *Financial support:* In 2010–11, 75 students received support. Institutionally sponsored loans and scholarships/grants available. Financial award application deadline: 8/20; financial award applicants required to submit FAFSA. *Unit head:* Dr. James Lytle, Provost, 570-586-2400 Ext. 9222, Fax: 570-586-1753. *Application contact:* Drew Whipple, Assistant Director of Enrollment, 570-585-9370, Fax: 570-585-9299, E-mail: gradadmissions@bbc.edu.

Baptist Missionary Association Theological Seminary, Graduate and Professional Programs, Jacksonville, TX 75766-5407. Offers M Div, MAR. Part-time programs available. *Degree requirements:* For master's, thesis optional; for M Div, 2 foreign languages, thesis/dissertation optional. *Entrance requirements:* Additional exam requirements/recommendations for international students: Required—TOEFL (minimum score 550 paper-based; 213 computer-based). Electronic applications accepted. *Faculty research:* Education, Biblical studies.

Baptist Theological Seminary at Richmond, Graduate and Professional Programs, Richmond, VA 23227. Offers biblical interpretation (M Div); Christian education (M Div); theological studies (MATS); theology (D Min); youth and student ministries (M Div); M Div/MS; M Div/MSW. *Accreditation:* ATS. Part-time programs available. Postbaccalaureate distance learning degree programs offered (minimal on-campus study). *Faculty:* 8 full-time (2 women), 19 part-time/adjunct (7 women). *Students:* 71 full-time (36 women), 30 part-time (13 women); includes 10 minority (9 Black or African American, non-Hispanic/Latino; 1 Hispanic/Latino), 3 international. Average age 46. 40 applicants, 88% accepted, 30 enrolled. In 2010, 24 first professional degrees, 4 doctorates awarded. *Degree requirements:* For doctorate, one foreign language, comprehensive exam, thesis/dissertation, field study, independent study; for M Div, one foreign language, comprehensive exam (for some programs), thesis/dissertation optional, mission immersion experience, internship. *Entrance requirements:* For doctorate, MAT, M Div, 3 years of full-time ministry experience. Additional exam requirements/recommendations for international students: Required—TOEFL (minimum score 550 paper-based; 213 computer-based). *Application deadline:* For fall admission, 8/1 priority date for domestic students, 5/1 priority date for international students; for winter admission, 12/1 priority date for domestic students, 9/1 priority date for international students; for spring admission, 1/1 priority date for domestic students, 10/1 priority date for international students. Applications are processed on a rolling basis. Application fee: $35. *Expenses:* Tuition: Full-time $9000; part-time $900 per credit. Required fees: $135 per year. *Financial support:* In 2010–11, 12 teaching assistantships (averaging $1,650 per year) were awarded; scholarships/grants and tuition waivers (partial) also available. Financial award application deadline: 2/1. *Faculty research:* Biblical studies, pastoral care, church history, theology, ministry. *Unit head:* Dr. Ronald W. Crawford, President, 804-204-1201, Fax: 804-355-8182, E-mail: rcrawford@btsr.edu. *Application contact:* Tiffany Kellogg Pittman, Director of Admissions, 804-204-1208, Fax: 804-355-8182, E-mail: admissions@btsr.edu.

Barry University, School of Arts and Sciences, Department of Theology and Philosophy, Miami Shores, FL 33161-6695. Offers ministry (D Min); pastoral ministry for Hispanics (MA); pastoral theology (MA); practical theology (MA). *Accreditation:* ATS. Part-time and evening/weekend programs available. *Degree requirements:* For master's, comprehensive exam, thesis optional; for doctorate, thesis/dissertation. *Entrance requirements:* For master's, GRE General Test or MAT, minimum GPA of 3.0. Electronic applications accepted. *Faculty research:* Fundamental morals, bioethics, social ethics, liturgical and sacramental theology, biblical studies.

Baylor University, George W. Truett Theological Seminary, Waco, TX 76798. Offers M Div, MTS, D Min, M Div/MM, M Div/MSW, MTS/MSW. *Accreditation:* ATS. *Faculty:* 17 full-time (3 women), 7 part-time/adjunct (1 woman). *Students:* 289 full-time (107 women), 80 part-time (28 women); includes 76 minority (41 Black or African American, non-Hispanic/Latino; 1 American Indian or Alaska Native, non-Hispanic/Latino; 3 Asian, non-Hispanic/Latino; 20 Hispanic/Latino; 1 Native Hawaiian or other Pacific Islander, non-Hispanic/Latino; 10 Two or more races, non-Hispanic/Latino), 23 international. Average age 29. 144 applicants, 94% accepted, 102 enrolled. In 2010, 68 first professional degrees, 112 master's, 6 doctorates awarded. *Entrance requirements:* Additional exam requirements/recommendations for international students: Required—TOEFL (minimum score 82 computer-based). *Application deadline:* For fall admission, 5/1 for domestic and international students; for spring admission, 11/1 for domestic and international students. Applications are processed on a rolling basis. Application fee: $35. Electronic applications accepted. *Financial support:* In 2010–11, 207 students received support, including 1 research assistantship, 12 teaching assistantships; career-related internships or fieldwork, institutionally sponsored loans, scholarships/grants, tuition waivers (partial), and unspecified assistantships also available. Support available to part-time students. Financial award application deadline: 8/1; financial award applicants required to submit FAFSA. *Unit head:* Dr. David E. Garland, Dean, 254-710-3755, Fax: 254-710-3753, E-mail: david_e_garland@baylor.edu. *Application contact:* Dr. Edward Grear Howard, Director of Student Services, 254-710-6087, Fax: 254-710-7233, E-mail: grear_howard@baylor.edu.

Bethany Theological Seminary, Graduate and Professional Programs, Richmond, IN 47374-4019. Offers biblical studies (MA Th); ministry studies (M Div); peace studies (M Div, MA Th); theological studies (MA Th, CATS); youth ministry (M Div). *Accreditation:* ACIPE; ATS. Part-time programs available. Postbaccalaureate distance learning degree programs offered (minimal on-campus study). *Degree requirements:* For master's, thesis. *Entrance requirements:* For M Div, letters of reference, minimum GPA of 2.75; for master's, letters of reference, minimum GPA of 3.0. Additional exam requirements/recommendations for international students: Required—TOEFL (minimum score 550 paper-based; 218 computer-based).

Bethel College, Division of Graduate Studies, Program in Theological Studies, Mishawaka, IN 46545-5591. Offers MATS. Part-time and evening/weekend programs available. *Faculty:* 1 full-time (0 women), 9 part-time/adjunct (0 women). *Students:* 3 full-time (1 woman), 16 part-time (7 women); includes 5 minority (all Black or African American, non-Hispanic/Latino), 1 international. 9 applicants, 100% accepted, 7 enrolled. In 2010, 9 master's awarded. *Entrance requirements:* Additional exam requirements/recommendations for international students: Required—TOEFL (minimum score 540 paper-based; 207 computer-based). *Application deadline:* For fall admission, 5/1 for international students; for spring admission, 10/1 for international students. Applications are processed on a rolling basis. Application fee: $25. Electronic applications accepted. Tuition and fees vary according to program. *Financial support:* Career-related internships or fieldwork available. Financial award applicants required to submit FAFSA. Total annual research expenditures: $9. *Unit head:* Dr. Eugene Carpenter, Director, 574-257-3332, E-mail: carpeng@bethelcollege.edu. *Application contact:* Dr. John Dendiu, Advisor, 574-257-2675, Fax: 574-257-3385, E-mail: dendiuj@bethelcollege.edu.

Bethel Seminary, Graduate and Professional Programs, St. Paul, MN 55112-6998. Offers Anglican studies (Certificate); applied ministry (MA, Certificate); biblical studies (Certificate);

children's and family ministry (MACFM); Christian education (MACE); Christian thought (MACT); community ministry leadership (MA, Certificate); global and contextual studies (MA); Greek and Hebrew language track (M Div); Greek language track (M Div); Hebrew language track (M Div); lay ministry (Certificate); marriage and family therapy (MAMFT, Certificate); men's ministry leadership (Certificate); ministry (D Min); ministry leadership (Certificate); spiritual formation (Certificate); theological studies (MATS, Certificate); transformational leadership (MATL, Certificate); young life youth ministry (Certificate). *Accreditation:* ACIPE; ATS (one or more programs are accredited). Part-time and evening/weekend programs available. Postbaccalaureate distance learning degree programs offered (minimal on-campus study). *Faculty:* 26 full-time (3 women), 74 part-time/adjunct (29 women). *Students:* 729 full-time (275 women), 274 part-time (118 women); includes 75 minority (34 Black or African American, non-Hispanic/Latino; 1 American Indian or Alaska Native, non-Hispanic/Latino; 12 Asian, non-Hispanic/Latino; 16 Hispanic/Latino; 1 Native Hawaiian or other Pacific Islander, non-Hispanic/Latino; 11 Two or more races, non-Hispanic/Latino), 16 international. Average age 38. 525 applicants, 76% accepted, 265 enrolled. In 2010, 149 master's, 13 doctorates awarded. *Degree requirements:* For master's, variable foreign language requirement, thesis (for some programs); for doctorate, thesis/dissertation; for M Div, one foreign language. *Entrance requirements:* For M Div and master's, letters of reference, transcripts, personal statement; for doctorate, M Div, letters of reference, organizational support. Additional exam requirements/recommendations for international students: Required—TOEFL (minimum score 550 paper-based; 213 computer-based; 87 iBT). *Application deadline:* For fall admission, 8/1 priority date for domestic students, 3/1 for international students; for winter admission, 12/1 priority date for domestic students; for spring admission, 3/1 priority date for domestic students. Applications are processed on a rolling basis. Application fee: $20. Electronic applications accepted. *Financial support:* In 2010–11, 655 students received support, including 18 teaching assistantships; career-related internships or fieldwork, Federal Work-Study, scholarships/grants, and tuition waivers (full) also available. Financial award application deadline: 7/15; financial award applicants required to submit FAFSA. *Faculty research:* Nature of theology, ethics; Biblical commentaries, nature of God, science and theology. *Unit head:* Dr. David Ridder, Vice President and Dean, 651-638-6553. *Application contact:* Joseph V. Dworak, Director of Admissions, 651-638-6288, Fax: 651-638-6002, E-mail: j-dworak@bethel.edu.

Bethesda Christian University, Graduate and Professional Programs, Anaheim, CA 92801. Offers biblical studies (MA); music (MA); theology (M Div). *Entrance requirements:* For M Div and master's, interview.

Beth HaMedrash Shaarei Yosher Institute, Graduate Programs, Brooklyn, NY 11204. *Accreditation:* AARTS.

Beth Hatalmud Rabbinical College, Graduate Programs, Brooklyn, NY 11214. *Accreditation:* AARTS.

Beth Medrash Govoha, Graduate Programs, Lakewood, NJ 08701-2797. *Accreditation:* AARTS.

Bethune-Cookman University, School of Graduate and Professional Studies, Daytona Beach, FL 32114-3099. Offers transformative leadership (MS). Postbaccalaureate distance learning degree programs offered (minimal on-campus study). *Degree requirements:* For master's, thesis. *Entrance requirements:* For master's, GRE or MAT, minimum GPA of 2.75 in the last 60 semester hours; 3 letters of recommendation. Additional exam requirements/recommendations for international students: Required—TOEFL (minimum score 550 paper-based; 213 computer-based). Electronic applications accepted. *Faculty research:* Civic engagement, communication ethics, service learning in higher education women in leadership.

Bexley Hall Episcopal Seminary, Graduate Programs, Columbus, OH 43209-2325. Offers M Div, MA. *Accreditation:* ATS.

Biblical Theological Seminary, Graduate and Professional Programs, Hatfield, PA 19440-2499. Offers advanced missional leadership (D Min); advanced pastoral studies (Certificate); biblical counseling (Certificate); biblical studies (MA, Certificate); counseling (MA); ministry (M Div, MA); missional theology (MA). *Accreditation:* ATS. Part-time and evening/weekend programs available. *Faculty:* 11 full-time (0 women), 27 part-time/adjunct (9 women). *Students:* 205 applicants, 52% accepted, 84 enrolled. In 2010, 23 first professional degrees, 24 master's, 10 doctorates awarded. *Degree requirements:* For M Div, thesis/dissertation. *Entrance requirements:* Additional exam requirements/recommendations for international students: Required—TOEFL (minimum score 550 paper-based; 213 computer-based; 80 iBT). *Application deadline:* Applications are processed on a rolling basis. Application fee: $30. *Expenses:* Tuition: Full-time $10,728; part-time $447 per credit. Required fees: $25 per term. One-time fee: $30. *Financial support:* In 2010–11, 174 students received support. Career-related internships or fieldwork, institutionally sponsored loans, and scholarships/grants available. Support available to part-time students. Financial award application deadline: 8/30; financial award applicants required to submit FAFSA. *Faculty research:* Theology, culture, Biblical interpretation. *Unit head:* Pamela Jean Smith, Vice President for Student Advancement, 215-368-5000 Ext. 122, Fax: 215-368-7002, E-mail: psmith@biblical.edu. *Application contact:* Rev. Darryl John Lang, Director of Recruitment and Student Life, 215-368-5000 Ext. 147, Fax: 215-368-7002, E-mail: dlang@biblical.edu.

Biola University, School of Professional Studies, La Mirada, CA 90639-0001. Offers Christian apologetics (MA); organizational leadership (MA). Part-time and evening/weekend programs available. *Faculty:* 4 full-time (0 women), 40 part-time/adjunct (12 women). *Students:* 5 full-time (2 women), 44 part-time (22 women); includes 6 Black or African American, non-Hispanic/Latino; 6 Asian, non-Hispanic/Latino; 6 Hispanic/Latino. 184 applicants, 65% accepted. In 2010, 72 master's awarded. *Entrance requirements:* For master's, minimum undergraduate GPA of 3.0. Additional exam requirements/recommendations for international students: Required—TOEFL (minimum score 550 paper-based; 213 computer-based). *Application deadline:* For fall admission, 7/1 for domestic students; for spring admission, 12/1 for domestic students. Applications are processed on a rolling basis. Application fee: $45. Electronic applications accepted. *Financial support:* Institutionally sponsored loans and scholarships/grants available. Support available to part-time students. Financial award application deadline: 3/2; financial award applicants required to submit FAFSA. *Unit head:* Dr. Ed Norman, Dean, 562-903-4715, E-mail: ed.norman@biola.edu. *Application contact:* Roy M. Allinson, Director of Graduate Admissions, 562-903-4752, Fax: 562-903-4709, E-mail: admissions@biola.edu.

Biola University, Talbot School of Theology, La Mirada, CA 90639-0001. Offers Biblical studies (MA); Christian education (MACE); Christian ministry and leadership (MA); divinity (M Div); education (PhD); ministry (MA Min); New Testament (MA); Old Testament (MA); philosophy of religion and ethics (MA); spiritual formation (MA); spiritual formation and soul care (MA); theological studies (MA); theology (MA, Th M, D Min). *Accreditation:* ATS. Part-time and evening/weekend programs available. *Faculty:* 45 full-time (5 women), 40 part-time/adjunct (10 women). *Students:* 611 full-time (123 women), 573 part-time (144 women); includes 382 minority (48 Black or African American, non-Hispanic/Latino; 1 American Indian or Alaska Native, non-Hispanic/Latino; 300 Asian, non-Hispanic/Latino; 5 Native Hawaiian or other Pacific Islander, non-Hispanic/Latino; 28 Two or more races, non-Hispanic/Latino), 153 international. Average age 31. 515 applicants, 76% accepted, 277 enrolled. In 2010, 47 first professional degrees, 152 master's, 9 doctorates awarded. *Degree requirements:* For master's, variable foreign language requirement, thesis or alternative; for doctorate, variable foreign language requirement, thesis/dissertation; for M Div, thesis/dissertation or alternative. *Entrance requirements:* For M Div, minimum GPA of 2.6; for master's, minimum undergraduate GPA of 3.0; for doctorate, minimum GPA of 3.25. Additional exam requirements/recommendations for international students: Required—TOEFL (minimum score 550 paper-based; 213 computer-based). *Application deadline:* For fall admission, 7/1 for domestic students; for spring admission, 1/1 for domestic students. Applications are processed on a rolling basis. Application fee: $45. *Financial support:* Research assistantships, teaching assistantships, career-related internships or fieldwork, institutionally sponsored loans, and scholarships/grants available. Support available to part-time students. Financial award application deadline: 3/2; financial award

Theology

Biola University *(continued)*
applicants required to submit FAFSA. *Faculty research:* Moral development; biological, medical, and social ethics; ancient Near Eastern historical philosophy. *Unit head:* Dr. Dennis Dirks, Dean, 562-903-4816, Fax: 562-903-4748, E-mail: dennis_dirks@peter.biola.edu. *Application contact:* Roy M. Allinson, Director of Graduate Admissions, 562-903-4752, Fax: 562-903-4709, E-mail: admissions@biola.edu.

Blessed John XXIII National Seminary, School of Theology, Weston, MA 02493-2618. Offers M Div. *Accreditation:* ATS. *Entrance requirements:* Bachelor's degree or equivalent in life experience.

Bob Jones University, Graduate Programs, Greenville, SC 29614. Offers accountancy (MS); Bible (MA); Bible translation (MA); Biblical studies (Certificate); broadcast management (MS); business administration (MBA); church history (MA, PhD); church ministries (MA); church music (MM); cinema and video production (MA); counseling (MS); curriculum and instruction (Ed D); divinity (M Div); dramatic production (MA); educational leadership (MS, Ed D, Ed S); elementary education (M Ed, MAT); English (M Ed, MA, MAT); fine arts (MA); graphic design (MA); history (M Ed, MA); illustration (MA); interpretative speech (MA); mathematics (M Ed, MAT); medical missions (Certificate); ministry (MM, D Min); multi-categorical special education (M Ed, MAT); music (M Ed); New Testament interpretation (PhD); Old Testament interpretation (PhD); orchestral instrument performance (MM); organ performance (MM); pastoral studies (MA); personnel services (MS, Ed S); piano pedagogy (MM); piano performance (MM); platform arts (MA); radio and television broadcasting (MS); rhetoric and public address (MA); secondary education (M Ed); studio art (MA); teaching Bible (MA); theology (MA, PhD); voice performance (MM); youth ministries (MA); M Div/MM.

Boston College, Graduate School of Arts and Sciences, Department of Theology, Chestnut Hill, MA 02467-3800. Offers PhD. *Accreditation:* ATS. Part-time programs available. Terminal master's awarded for partial completion of doctoral program. *Degree requirements:* For doctorate, thesis/dissertation. *Entrance requirements:* For doctorate, GRE General Test. Additional exam requirements/recommendations for international students: Required—TOEFL (minimum score 590 paper-based; 250 computer-based; 91 iBT). Electronic applications accepted. *Faculty research:* Roman Catholic theology, Christian social ethics, Bible, history of Christian life and thought.

Boston College, School of Theology and Ministry, Chestnut Hill, MA 02467-3800. Offers church leadership (MA); divinity (M Div); pastoral ministry (MA), including Hispanic ministry, liturgy and worship, pastoral care and counseling, spirituality; religious education (MA, PhD); sacred theology (STD, STL); social justice/social ministry (MA); spiritual direction (MA); theological studies (MTS); theology (Th M, PhD); youth ministry (MA); MA/MA; MS/MA; MSW/MA. *Accreditation:* Teacher Education Accreditation Council. Part-time programs available. *Degree requirements:* For doctorate, one foreign language, thesis/dissertation. *Entrance requirements:* For doctorate, GRE. Additional exam requirements/recommendations for international students: Required—TOEFL (minimum score 550 paper-based; 213 computer-based). Electronic applications accepted. *Faculty research:* Philosophy and practice of religious education, pastoral psychology, liturgical and spiritual theology, spiritual formation for the practice of ministry.

Boston University, School of Theology, Boston, MA 02215. Offers M Div, MSM, MTS, STM, D Min, Th D, D Min/MSW, M Div/MSM, M Div/MSW, MTS/MSW. *Accreditation:* ACIPE; ATS. Part-time programs available. *Faculty:* 24 full-time (10 women), 18 part-time/adjunct (5 women). *Students:* 252 full-time (110 women), 19 part-time (7 women); includes 38 minority (13 Black or African American, non-Hispanic/Latino; 2 American Indian or Alaska Native, non-Hispanic/Latino; 10 Asian, non-Hispanic/Latino; 10 Hispanic/Latino; 3 Two or more races, non-Hispanic/Latino), 77 international. Average age 34. In 2010, 25 first professional degrees, 38 master's, 8 doctorates awarded. *Degree requirements:* For master's, comprehensive exam; for doctorate, 2 foreign languages, comprehensive exam, thesis/dissertation. *Entrance requirements:* For M Div and master's, GRE General Test or MAT, minimum GPA of 3.0; for doctorate, GRE General Test or MAT, minimum GPA of 3.3. *Application deadline:* For fall admission, 1/15 priority date for domestic students; for spring admission, 10/1 priority date for domestic students. Applications are processed on a rolling basis. Application fee: $70. Electronic applications accepted. *Expenses:* Contact institution. *Financial support:* Fellowships, research assistantships, teaching assistantships, Federal Work-Study, institutionally sponsored loans, and scholarships/grants available. Support available to part-time students. Financial award application deadline: 7/15; financial award applicants required to submit FAFSA. *Faculty research:* Israelite literature in its social and cultural context, New Testament literature in its social and cultural context, Reformation history, women in the church, social ethics. *Unit head:* Mary Elizabeth Moore, Interim Dean, 617-353-3050, Fax: 617-353-3061. *Application contact:* Anastasia Kidd, Director of Admissions, 617-353-3036, Fax: 617-358-0140, E-mail: sthadmis@bu.edu.

Briercrest Seminary, Graduate Programs, Program in Theology, Caronport, SK S0H 0S0, Canada. Offers Biblical studies (M Div); leadership and management (M Div); New Testament (MATS); Old Testament (MATS); pastoral counseling (M Div); pastoral ministry (M Div); theological studies (M Div); theology (MATS); worship (M Div); youth and family ministry (M Div). *Accreditation:* ATS. Part-time programs available. *Degree requirements:* For master's, comprehensive exam, thesis optional. *Entrance requirements:* Additional exam requirements/recommendations for international students: Required—TOEFL (minimum score 550 paper-based; 213 computer-based).

Bryn Athyn College of the New Church, Academy of the New Church Theological School, Bryn Athyn, PA 19009-0717. Offers divinity (M Div); religious studies (MA). Part-time programs available. Postbaccalaureate distance learning degree programs offered (minimal on-campus study). *Degree requirements:* For master's, thesis; for M Div, 3 foreign languages, thesis/dissertation. *Entrance requirements:* Additional exam requirements/recommendations for international students: Required—TOEFL.

California Institute of Integral Studies, School of Consciousness and Transformation, San Francisco, CA 94103. Offers creative inquiry/interdisciplinary arts (MFA); cultural anthropology and social transformation (MA); East-West psychology (MA, PhD); integrative health studies (MA); philosophy and religion (MA, PhD), including Asian and comparative studies, philosophy, cosmology, and consciousness, women's spirituality; social and cultural anthropology (PhD); transformative leadership (MA); transformative studies (PhD); writing and consciousness (MFA). Part-time and evening/weekend programs available. Postbaccalaureate distance learning degree programs offered (minimal on-campus study). *Students:* 455 full-time (315 women), 133 part-time (90 women); includes 47 Black or African American, non-Hispanic/Latino; 3 American Indian or Alaska Native, non-Hispanic/Latino; 21 Asian, non-Hispanic/Latino; 41 Hispanic/Latino, 40 international. Average age 37. 265 applicants, 91% accepted, 163 enrolled. In 2010, 64 master's, 22 doctorates awarded. Terminal master's awarded for partial completion of doctoral program. *Degree requirements:* For master's, thesis optional; for doctorate, comprehensive exam, thesis/dissertation, 1 foreign language (Asian comparative studies). *Entrance requirements:* For master's, minimum GPA of 3.0, letters of recommendation, writing sample; for doctorate, master's degree, minimum GPA of 3.0, letters of recommendation, writing sample. Additional exam requirements/recommendations for international students: Required—TOEFL. *Application deadline:* For fall admission, 2/1 priority date for domestic and international students; for spring admission, 10/15 priority date for domestic and international students. Applications are processed on a rolling basis. Application fee: $65. Electronic applications accepted. *Expenses:* Tuition: Full-time $15,660; part-time $870 per semester hour. Required fees: $95 per semester. *Financial support:* In 2010–11, 255 students received support; research assistantships, teaching assistantships, career-related internships or fieldwork, Federal Work-Study, scholarships/grants, and tuition waivers (partial) available. Support available to part-time students. Financial award application deadline: 4/15; financial award applicants required to submit FAFSA. *Faculty research:* Ecology and sustainability, philosophy and religion, East-West psychology, integrative health, social and cultural anthropology, transformative

leadership. *Application contact:* Allyson Werner, Associate Director of Admissions, 415-575-6155, Fax: 415-575-1268.

Calvary Baptist Theological Seminary, Graduate Programs, Landsdale, PA 19446. Offers M Div, MACM, MATS, Th M, D Min.

Calvary Bible College and Theological Seminary, Calvary Theological Seminary, Kansas City, MO 64147-1341. Offers Bible and theology (MS); Biblical counseling (MA); Biblical studies (MA); Christian ministry (MA); Christian studies (MS); Christian theology (MA); New Testament (MA); Old Testament (MA); pastoral studies (M Div). Part-time and evening/weekend programs available. *Faculty:* 5 full-time, 2 part-time/adjunct. *Students:* 14 full-time (5 women), 36 part-time (10 women); includes 4 Black or African American, non-Hispanic/Latino; 1 Asian, non-Hispanic/Latino; 1 Native Hawaiian or other Pacific Islander, non-Hispanic/Latino. Average age 40. In 2010, 14 master's awarded. *Degree requirements:* For master's, one foreign language, comprehensive exam, thesis; for M Div, 2 foreign languages, comprehensive exam, thesis/dissertation. *Entrance requirements:* For M Div and master's, minimum GPA of 2.5, 50 semester hours of course work in liberal arts, BA or BS, doctrine agreement. Additional exam requirements/recommendations for international students: Required—TOEFL (minimum score 550 paper-based; 213 computer-based). *Application deadline:* For fall admission, 7/15 priority date for domestic and international students; for spring admission, 12/1 priority date for domestic and international students. Application fee: $25. *Expenses:* Tuition: Full-time $5580; part-time $310 per hour. Required fees: $258 per semester. *Financial support:* Scholarships/grants available. Financial award application deadline: 11/5. *Unit head:* Dr. Thomas Baurain, Academic Dean, 816-322-0110 Ext. 1502, Fax: 816-331-4474, E-mail: thomas.baurain@calvary.edu. *Application contact:* Bob Crank, Director of Admissions, 800-326-3960 Ext. 1321, Fax: 816-331-4474, E-mail: admissions@calvary.edu.

Calvin Theological Seminary, Graduate and Professional Programs, Grand Rapids, MI 49546-4387. Offers Bible and theology (MA); divinity (M Div), including ancient near eastern languages and literature, contextual ministry, evangelism and teaching, history of Christianity, new church development, New Testament, Old Testament, pastoral care and leadership, preaching and worship, theological studies, youth and family ministries; educational ministry (MA); historical theology (PhD); missions and evangelism (MA); pastoral care (MA); philosophical and moral theology (PhD); systematic theology (PhD); theological studies (MTS); theology (Th M); worship (MA); youth and family ministries (MA). *Accreditation:* ACIPE; ATS. Part-time programs available. *Degree requirements:* For master's, thesis (for some programs); for doctorate, 4 foreign languages, comprehensive exam, thesis/dissertation; for M Div, 2 foreign languages. *Entrance requirements:* For doctorate, GRE General Test, Hebrew, Greek, and a modern foreign language. Additional exam requirements/recommendations for international students: Required—TOEFL (minimum score 550 paper-based; 213 computer-based), TWE (minimum score 4). Electronic applications accepted. *Faculty research:* Recent Trinity theory, Christian anthropology, Proverbs, reformed confessions, Paul's view of law.

Campbellsville University, School of Theology, Campbellsville, KY 42718-2799. Offers theology (M Th). Part-time programs available. *Degree requirements:* For master's, comprehensive exam, thesis optional. *Entrance requirements:* For master's, GRE General Test, minimum GPA of 3.0 in major, minimum GPA of 2.75 overall, 18 hours of undergraduate coursework in Christian studies. Electronic applications accepted. *Expenses:* Tuition: Full-time $7110; part-time $395 per contact hour. Required fees: $250; $75 per course. *Faculty research:* Clergy needing graduate theology education, trinity and Christian faith, Old Testament David narratives, leadership Principles on Christian University integration of Christian principles in counseling process.

Campbell University, Graduate and Professional Programs, Divinity School, Buies Creek, NC 27506. Offers Christian education (MA); divinity (M Div); ministry (D Min); M Div/MA; M Div/MBA. *Accreditation:* ATS. *Degree requirements:* For doctorate, final project. *Entrance requirements:* For master's, minimum GPA of 2.5; for doctorate, MAT, M Div, minimum graduate GPA of 3.0. Additional exam requirements/recommendations for international students: Required—TOEFL (minimum score 580 paper-based; 237 computer-based). *Expenses:* Contact institution. *Faculty research:* New Testament, theology, spiritual formation, Old Testament, Christian leadership.

Canadian Southern Baptist Seminary, Graduate Programs, Cochrane, AB T4C 2G1, Canada. Offers Christian education (MACE); ministry (M Div). *Accreditation:* ATS. Part-time programs available. *Faculty:* 8 full-time (0 women), 2 part-time/adjunct (0 women). *Students:* 7 full-time (2 women), 28 part-time (6 women); includes 2 Black or African American, non-Hispanic/Latino; 12 Asian, non-Hispanic/Latino; 3 Hispanic/Latino, 1 international. 11 applicants, 91% accepted, 8 enrolled. In 2010, 9 master's awarded. *Entrance requirements:* Additional exam requirements/recommendations for international students: Required—TOEFL (minimum score 560 paper-based; 220 computer-based), IELTS (minimum score 6.5). *Application deadline:* For fall admission, 7/1 priority date for domestic and international students; for winter admission, 11/15 priority date for domestic and international students. Applications are processed on a rolling basis. Application fee: $50. *Expenses:* Tuition: Full-time $5800; part-time $240 per credit hour. Required fees: $20 per credit hour. *Unit head:* Steve Booth, Academic Dean, 403-932-6622. *Application contact:* Kathleen McNaughton, Registrar, 403-932-6622 Ext. 221, E-mail: kathleen.mcnaughton@csbs.ca.

Capital Bible Seminary, Graduate and Professional Programs, Lanham, MD 20706-3599. Offers biblical studies (MA, Certificate); Christian counseling (MA); Christian counseling and discipleship (Certificate); ministry leadership (MA); theology (M Div, Th M). *Accreditation:* ATS (one or more programs are accredited). Part-time and evening/weekend programs available. *Degree requirements:* For master's, 2 foreign languages, comprehensive exam, thesis (for some programs); for M Div, 2 foreign languages, comprehensive exam. *Entrance requirements:* For M Div and master's, GRE General Test, Greek exam for those with 2 years of Greek, proficiency exam in theology, previous course work in Biblical studies. Additional exam requirements/recommendations for international students: Required—TOEFL (minimum score 550 paper-based; 213 computer-based). *Faculty research:* Dead Sea Scrolls, spiritual gifts, hermeneutics.

Carey Theological College, Graduate Programs, Vancouver, BC V6T 1J6, Canada. Offers M Div, MASF, D Min. *Accreditation:* ATS. Part-time programs available. *Degree requirements:* For doctorate, thesis/dissertation. *Entrance requirements:* For master's, undergraduate degree with minimum GPA of 2.7; for doctorate, M Div with minimum GPA of 3.5. Additional exam requirements/recommendations for international students: Required—TOEFL (minimum score 577 paper-based; 233 computer-based; 90 iBT). Electronic applications accepted. *Faculty research:* Missional church, new monasticism, women in leadership, spiritual formation, applied theology.

Carolina Evangelical Divinity School, Divinity Program, High Point, NC 27265. Offers M Div.

Carolina Evangelical Divinity School, Program in Theological Studies, High Point, NC 27265. Offers MA.

Carson-Newman College, Program in Applied Theology, Jefferson City, TN 37760. Offers MA. *Faculty:* 2 full-time (0 women). *Students:* 12 part-time (4 women). *Application deadline:* For fall admission, 7/15 priority date for domestic students. Applications are processed on a rolling basis. *Expenses:* Tuition: Full-time $6750; part-time $375 per credit hour. Required fees: $200. *Application contact:* Graduate Admissions and Services Adviser, 865-473-3468, Fax: 865-472-3475.

The Catholic Distance University, Graduate Programs, Hamilton, VA 20158. Offers religious studies (MRS); theology (MA). Part-time and evening/weekend programs available. Postbaccalaureate distance learning degree programs offered (no on-campus study). *Degree requirements:* For master's, comprehensive exam, capstone paper or project.

Catholic Theological Union at Chicago, Graduate and Professional Programs, Chicago, IL 60615-5698. Offers biblical spirituality (Certificate); cross-cultural ministries (D Min); cross-cultural missions (Certificate); divinity (M Div); liturgical studies (Certificate); liturgy (D Min); pastoral studies (MAPS, Certificate); spiritual formation (Certificate); spirituality (D Min); theology (MA); M Div/MA; M Div/MSW; M Div/PhD. M Div/PhD offered jointly with University of Chicago; M Div/MSW with Loyola University Chicago and University of Chicago. *Accreditation:* ACIPE; ATS (one or more programs are accredited). Part-time and evening/weekend programs available. *Degree requirements:* For master's, one foreign language, comprehensive exam (for some programs), thesis (for some programs); for doctorate, thesis/dissertation. *Entrance requirements:* For doctorate, master's degree, 5 years of active ministry. *Faculty research:* Doctrine, sacraments, ethics, Bible.

The Catholic University of America, School of Canon Law, Washington, DC 20064. Offers JCD, JCL, JD/JCL. Part-time programs available. *Faculty:* 6 full-time (1 woman), 1 part-time/adjunct (0 women). *Students:* 37 full-time (8 women), 49 part-time (3 women); includes 2 Black or African American, non-Hispanic/Latino; 4 Asian, non-Hispanic/Latino; 6 Hispanic/Latino, 13 international. Average age 40. 40 applicants, 65% accepted, 22 enrolled. In 2010, 5 doctorates awarded. *Degree requirements:* For doctorate, 2 foreign languages, thesis/dissertation, fluency in canonical Latin. *Entrance requirements:* For doctorate, GRE General Test, minimum GPA of A-, JCL. Additional exam requirements/recommendations for international students: Required—TOEFL (minimum score 580 paper-based; 237 computer-based). *Application deadline:* For fall admission, 8/1 priority date for domestic students, 7/15 for international students; for spring admission, 12/1 priority date for domestic students, 10/15 for international students. Applications are processed on a rolling basis. Application fee: $55. Electronic applications accepted. *Expenses:* Tuition: Full-time $33,580; part-time $1315 per credit hour. Required fees: $80; $40 per semester hour. One-time fee: $425. *Financial support:* Fellowships, research assistantships, teaching assistantships, Federal Work-Study, scholarships/grants, tuition waivers (full and partial), and unspecified assistantships available. Financial award application deadline: 2/1; financial award applicants required to submit FAFSA. *Faculty research:* Ecclesiology and the Sacrament of Orders, procedural law, temporal goods, matrimonial jurisprudence, sacramental and liturgical law. *Unit head:* Rev. Robert Kaslyn, SJ, Dean, 202-319-5492, Fax: 202-319-4187, E-mail: cua-canonlaw@cua.edu. *Application contact:* Andrew Woodall, Director of Graduate Admissions, 202-319-5057, Fax: 202-319-6533, E-mail: cua-admissions@cua.edu.

The Catholic University of America, School of Theology and Religious Studies, Washington, DC 20064. Offers M Div, STB, MA, MRE, D Min, PhD, STD, Certificate, STL, MSLS/MA. *Accreditation:* ATS (one or more programs are accredited). Part-time programs available. *Faculty:* 40 full-time (6 women), 10 part-time/adjunct (2 women). *Students:* 161 full-time (28 women), 235 part-time (61 women); includes 7 Black or African American, non-Hispanic/Latino; 1 American Indian or Alaska Native, non-Hispanic/Latino; 10 Asian, non-Hispanic/Latino; 11 Hispanic/Latino; 1 Native Hawaiian or other Pacific Islander, non-Hispanic/Latino, 69 international. Average age 36. 259 applicants, 64% accepted, 73 enrolled. In 2010, 7 first professional degrees, 29 master's, 29 doctorates awarded. *Degree requirements:* For master's, variable foreign language requirement, comprehensive exam, thesis (for some programs); for doctorate, variable foreign language requirement, comprehensive exam, thesis/dissertation. *Entrance requirements:* For first professional degree, master's, and doctorate, GRE General Test, statement of purpose, official copies of academic transcripts, three letters of recommendation. Additional exam requirements/recommendations for international students: Required—TOEFL (minimum score 580 paper-based; 237 computer-based). *Application deadline:* For fall admission, 8/1 priority date for domestic students, 7/15 for international students; for spring admission, 12/1 priority date for domestic students, 10/15 for international students. Applications are processed on a rolling basis. Application fee: $55. Electronic applications accepted. *Expenses:* Tuition: Full-time $33,580; part-time $1315 per credit hour. Required fees: $80; $40 per semester hour. One-time fee: $425. *Financial support:* Fellowships, research assistantships, teaching assistantships, Federal Work-Study, scholarships/grants, tuition waivers (full and partial), and unspecified assistantships available. Financial award application deadline: 2/1; financial award applicants required to submit FAFSA. *Faculty research:* Historical and systematic theology, religious education and catechetics, moral theology and ethics, Biblical studies, liturgical studies and sacramental theology. Total annual research expenditures: $66,740. *Unit head:* Msgr. Kevin W. Irwin, Dean, 202-319-5684, Fax: 202-319-5704, E-mail: irwin@cua.edu. *Application contact:* Andrew Woodall, Director of Graduate Admissions, 202-319-5057, Fax: 202-319-6533, E-mail: cua-admissions@cua.edu.

Central Baptist Theological Seminary, Graduate and Professional Programs, Shawnee, KS 66226. Offers missional church studies (MA); theological studies (MA); theology (M Div, Diploma). *Accreditation:* ACIPE; ATS (one or more programs are accredited). Part-time programs available. *Degree requirements:* For master's, thesis optional, MMPI, Myers-Briggs, Enneagram; for M Div, thesis/dissertation optional. *Entrance requirements:* For master's, accredited bachelor's degree with minimum GPA of 2.3. Additional exam requirements/recommendations for international students: Required—TOEFL (minimum score 547 paper-based; 210 computer-based; 77 iBT). Electronic applications accepted.

Central Baptist Theological Seminary of Virginia Beach, Graduate Programs, Virginia Beach, VA 23464. Offers M Div, MBS, Th M. *Entrance requirements:* For M Div, GRE, interview, M Div or equivalent from an accredited seminary, minimum cumulative GPA of 2.7, church endorsement, 4 recommendations; for master's, GRE, interview, minimum cumulative GPA of 2.4, church endorsement, 4 recommendations. Electronic applications accepted.

Central Yeshiva Tomchei Tmimim-Lubavitch, Graduate Programs, Brooklyn, NY 11230. *Accreditation:* AARTS.

Chaminade University of Honolulu, Graduate Services, Program in Pastoral Theology, Honolulu, HI 96816-1578. Offers MPT. Part-time and evening/weekend programs available. Postbaccalaureate distance learning degree programs offered. *Degree requirements:* For master's, capstone course. *Entrance requirements:* For master's, 2 letters of recommendation. Additional exam requirements/recommendations for international students: Required—TOEFL (minimum score 550 paper-based). Electronic applications accepted.

Chicago Theological Seminary, Graduate and Professional Programs, Chicago, IL 60637-1507. Offers preaching (D Min); religion and health (D Min); religious studies (MA); spirituality and spiritual direction (D Min); theology (M Div); theology, ethics and the human sciences (PhD); M Div/MSW. *Accreditation:* ACIPE; ATS. Part-time programs available. *Degree requirements:* For master's, thesis; for doctorate, 2 foreign languages, comprehensive exam, thesis/dissertation; for M Div, thesis/dissertation. *Entrance requirements:* For doctorate, GRE General Test. Additional exam requirements/recommendations for international students: Required—TOEFL (minimum score 217 computer-based). *Faculty research:* Bible, culture and hermeneutics, theology, gender and sexuality, black faith and life, spirituality and psychology, practical theology.

Christendom College, Notre Dame Graduate School, Front Royal, VA 22630-5103. Offers theological studies (MA). Part-time and evening/weekend programs available. *Degree requirements:* For master's, one foreign language, thesis or alternative. Electronic applications accepted.

Christian Theological Seminary, Graduate and Professional Programs, Indianapolis, IN 46208-3301. Offers educational and arts ministries (MA); marriage and family therapy (MA); pastoral care and counseling (D Min); psychotherapy and faith (MA); theological studies (MTS); theology (M Div). *Accreditation:* AAMFT/COAMFTE (one or more programs are accredited); ACIPE; ATS. Part-time programs available. Terminal master's awarded for partial completion of doctoral program. *Degree requirements:* For master's, comprehensive exam (for some programs), thesis (for some programs); for doctorate, comprehensive exam, thesis/dissertation; for M Div, comprehensive exam, thesis/dissertation (for some programs), missionary and cross-cultural experience. *Entrance requirements:* For master's, GRE General Test, MAT; for doctorate, M Div. Electronic applications accepted. *Faculty research:* Faith formation, peer learning post graduation.

Christ the King Seminary, Graduate and Professional Programs, East Aurora, NY 14052. Offers divinity (M Div); pastoral ministry (MA); theology (MA). *Accreditation:* ATS. Part-time and evening/weekend programs available. *Faculty:* 9 full-time (0 women), 11 part-time/adjunct (3 women). *Students:* 22 full-time (4 women), 60 part-time (34 women); includes 12 minority (8 Black or African American, non-Hispanic/Latino; 4 Hispanic/Latino). Average age 38. 20 applicants, 90% accepted, 17 enrolled. In 2010, 5 first professional degrees, 12 master's awarded. *Degree requirements:* For master's, comprehensive exam, thesis; for M Div, comprehensive exam. *Entrance requirements:* For M Div and master's, previous course work in philosophy and religious studies. *Application deadline:* For fall admission, 8/15 priority date for domestic students; for spring admission, 1/5 priority date for domestic students. Applications are processed on a rolling basis. Application fee: $40. *Expenses:* Tuition: Full-time $7110. Required fees: $220. *Financial support:* Career-related internships or fieldwork and scholarships/grants available. Support available to part-time students. Financial award application deadline: 8/1; financial award applicants required to submit FAFSA. *Unit head:* Dr. Dennis Castillo, Academic Dean, 716-652-8900, E-mail: dcastillo@cks.edu. *Application contact:* Cindy Vogel, Assistant to the Academic Dean, 716-652-8900 Ext. 7088, Fax: 716-652-8903, E-mail: cvogel@cks.edu.

Church Divinity School of the Pacific, Graduate and Professional Programs, Berkeley, CA 94709-1217. Offers M Div, MA, MTS, D Min, Certificate. MA program offered jointly with Graduate Theological Union. *Accreditation:* ACIPE; ATS (one or more programs are accredited). Part-time programs available. *Degree requirements:* For master's, one foreign language, thesis; for doctorate, thesis/dissertation; for M Div, one foreign language. *Entrance requirements:* For M Div, master's, and Certificate, GRE General Test, letters of reference; for doctorate, letters of reference. Additional exam requirements/recommendations for international students: Required—TOEFL. Electronic applications accepted.

Cincinnati Christian University, Graduate School, Cincinnati, OH 45204-3200. Offers biblical studies (MA); church history (MA); counseling (MAC); divinity (M Div); ministry (M Min); practical ministries (MA); theological studies (MA). *Accreditation:* ATS. Part-time programs available. *Degree requirements:* For master's, thesis (for some programs); for M Div, 2 foreign languages, oral exam. *Entrance requirements:* For master's, GRE General Test. Additional exam requirements/recommendations for international students: Required—TOEFL. Electronic applications accepted.

Claremont Graduate University, Graduate Programs, School of Religion, Claremont, CA 91711-6160. Offers Hebrew Bible (MA, PhD); history of Christianity and religions of North America (MA, PhD); New Testament (MA, PhD); philosophy of religion and theology (MA, PhD); theology, ethics and culture (MA, PhD); women's studies in religion (MA, PhD); MA/PhD; MBA/PhD. Part-time programs available. *Faculty:* 6 full-time (2 women), 2 part-time/adjunct (0 women). *Students:* 218 full-time (87 women), 10 part-time (4 women); includes 13 Black or African American, non-Hispanic/Latino; 11 Asian, non-Hispanic/Latino; 12 Hispanic/Latino; 1 Two or more races, non-Hispanic/Latino, 29 international. Average age 37. In 2010, 13 master's, 12 doctorates awarded. Terminal master's awarded for partial completion of doctoral program. *Entrance requirements:* For master's and doctorate, GRE General Test. Additional exam requirements/recommendations for international students: Required—TOEFL (minimum score 550 paper-based; 213 computer-based; 80 iBT). *Application deadline:* For fall admission, 2/1 priority date for domestic students. Applications are processed on a rolling basis. Application fee: $60. Electronic applications accepted. *Expenses:* Tuition: Full-time $35,748; part-time $1554 per unit. Required fees: $215 per semester. *Financial support:* Fellowships, research assistantships, teaching assistantships, Federal Work-Study, institutionally sponsored loans, and scholarships/grants available. Support available to part-time students. Financial award application deadline: 2/15; financial award applicants required to submit FAFSA. *Unit head:* Anselm Min, Dean, 909-607-3214, Fax: 909-621-9587, E-mail: anselm.min@cgu.edu. *Application contact:* Brent Smith, Recruiter, 909-607-2653, Fax: 909-607-9587, E-mail: brent.smith@cgu.edu.

Claremont School of Theology, Graduate and Professional Programs, Master of Divinity Program, Claremont, CA 91711-3199. Offers M Div. *Accreditation:* ACIPE; ATS. Part-time programs available. *Entrance requirements:* Additional exam requirements/recommendations for international students: Required—TOEFL (minimum score 230 computer-based). Electronic applications accepted.

Claremont School of Theology, Graduate and Professional Programs, Program in Religion, Claremont, CA 91711-3199. Offers practical theology (PhD), including religious education, spiritual care and counseling; religion (PhD), including Hebrew Bible, New Testament and Christian origins, process studies, religion, ethics, and society; religion and theology (MA); religious education (MARE). *Accreditation:* ACIPE; ATS. Terminal master's awarded for partial completion of doctoral program. *Degree requirements:* For master's, thesis; for doctorate, 2 foreign languages, thesis/dissertation. *Entrance requirements:* For doctorate, GRE General Test. Additional exam requirements/recommendations for international students: Required—TOEFL (minimum score 250 computer-based). Electronic applications accepted.

Colgate Rochester Crozer Divinity School, Graduate and Professional Programs, Rochester, NY 14620-2530. Offers M Div, MA, D Min, Certificate. *Accreditation:* ACIPE; ATS (one or more programs are accredited). Part-time programs available. Postbaccalaureate distance learning degree programs offered (minimal on-campus study). *Faculty:* 8 full-time (4 women), 14 part-time/adjunct (6 women). *Students:* 79 full-time, 35 part-time; includes 28 Black or African American, non-Hispanic/Latino; 2 Asian, non-Hispanic/Latino; 2 Hispanic/Latino, 4 international. Average age 42. 35 applicants, 86% accepted, 26 enrolled. In 2010, 15 first professional degrees, 6 master's, 6 doctorates awarded. *Degree requirements:* For master's, thesis; for doctorate, thesis/dissertation; for M Div, supervised ministry year. *Entrance requirements:* For M Div and master's, BA/BS, personal statement, 4 recommendations; for doctorate, M Div, 3 years professional experience, writing sample, personal statement, curriculum vitae, 4 recommendations. Additional exam requirements/recommendations for international students: Required—TOEFL (minimum score 600 paper-based; 237 computer-based; 93 iBT). *Application deadline:* For fall admission, 7/1 priority date for domestic students, 3/1 for international students; for spring admission, 12/1 priority date for domestic students, 9/1 for international students. Applications are processed on a rolling basis. Application fee: $35. *Expenses:* Tuition: Full-time $12,640; part-time $1580 per course. Required fees: $215; $35 per course. Tuition and fees vary according to degree level and program. *Financial support:* In 2010–11, 63 students received support. Scholarships/grants available. Financial award application deadline: 9/1; financial award applicants required to submit FAFSA. *Faculty research:* Old Testament, New Testament, Christian ethics, black church studies, woman and gender studies. *Unit head:* Rev. Jack M. McKelvey, President, 585-271-1320 Ext. 680, Fax: 585-271-8013. *Application contact:* Melissa M. Morral, Vice President for Enrollment Services, 585-340-9500, Fax: 585-340-9644, E-mail: mmorral@crcds.edu.

Collège Dominicain de Philosophie et de Théologie, Graduate Programs, Faculty of Theology, Ottawa, ON K1R 7G3, Canada. Offers M Th, MA Th, PhD, Th D, L Th. Part-time and evening/weekend programs available. *Degree requirements:* For master's, 2 foreign languages, research paper; for doctorate, 2 foreign languages, thesis/dissertation, candidacy exam. *Entrance requirements:* For master's, B Th or equivalent, minimum A- average in undergraduate course work; for doctorate, MA Th or equivalent, minimum A- average in graduate course work. *Faculty research:* Exegese, bioethics, history of church, New Testament.

College of Emmanuel and St. Chad, Bachelor of Theology Program, Saskatoon, SK S7N 0W6, Canada. Offers B Th. Part-time programs available. Postbaccalaureate distance learning degree programs offered (minimal on-campus study). *Degree requirements:* For B Th, internship. *Entrance requirements:* 1 year of university-level work or equivalent. Additional exam

Theology

College of Emmanuel and St. Chad (continued)

requirements/recommendations for international students: Required—TOEFL. *Faculty research:* Pauline studies, New Testament, ethics, congregational development, trauma and spirituality.

College of Emmanuel and St. Chad, Graduate Programs, Saskatoon, SK S7N 0W6, Canada. Offers M Div, MTS, STM. STM program offered jointly with Lutheran Theological Seminary and St. Andrew's College. Part-time programs available. *Degree requirements:* For master's, thesis optional. *Entrance requirements:* For master's, M Div or MTS (STM). Additional exam requirements/recommendations for international students: Required—TOEFL. *Faculty research:* New Testament, systematics, Christian education, theology, ethics.

College of Mount St. Joseph, Graduate Program in Religious Studies, Cincinnati, OH 45233-1670. Offers religious education (Certificate); spiritual and pastoral care (MA, Certificate); spiritual direction (Certificate). Part-time and evening/weekend programs available. *Faculty:* 4 full-time (3 women). *Students:* 24 part-time (17 women); includes 1 minority (Black or African American, non-Hispanic/Latino). Average age 47. 20 applicants, 90% accepted, 10 enrolled. In 2010, 5 master's awarded. *Degree requirements:* For master's, comprehensive exam, integrating project. *Entrance requirements:* For master's, 3 letters of recommendation, interview, minimum GPA of 3.0. Additional exam requirements/recommendations for international students: Required—TOEFL (minimum score 560 paper-based; 220 computer-based; 83 iBT). *Application deadline:* Applications are processed on a rolling basis. Application fee: $50. Electronic applications accepted. *Financial support:* In 2010–11, 20 students received support. Scholarships/grants available. Financial award applicants required to submit FAFSA. *Faculty research:* Contextual/cultural/systematic theology, historical/spiritual theology, business/economics ethics, social justice, Biblical/cultural/pastoral theology. *Unit head:* Dr. John Trokan, Chair of Religious/Pastoral Studies, 513-244-4272, Fax: 513-244-4222, E-mail: john_trokan@mail.msj.edu. *Application contact:* Marilyn Hoskins, Assistant Director of Graduate Recruitment, 513-244-4723, Fax: 513-244-4629, E-mail: marilyn_hoskins@mail.msj.edu.

College of Saint Elizabeth, Department of Theology, Morristown, NJ 07960-6989. Offers MA. Part-time and evening/weekend programs available. *Faculty:* 3 full-time (2 women), 4 part-time/adjunct (0 women). *Students:* 12 part-time (8 women); includes 1 Black or African American, non-Hispanic/Latino; 1 Asian, non-Hispanic/Latino. Average age 53. 7 applicants, 71% accepted, 4 enrolled. In 2010, 8 master's awarded. *Degree requirements:* For master's, thesis or alternative, 3 essays, oral exam. *Entrance requirements:* For master's, interview, minimum GPA of 3.0. Additional exam requirements/recommendations for international students: Required—TOEFL (minimum score 550 paper-based). *Application deadline:* For fall admission, 3/1 priority date for domestic students; for spring admission, 9/1 for domestic students. Applications are processed on a rolling basis. Application fee: $35. Electronic applications accepted. *Expenses:* Tuition: Part-time $857 per credit. Required fees: $70 per credit. *Financial support:* Tuition waivers (partial) and unspecified assistantships available. Support available to part-time students. Financial award applicants required to submit FAFSA. *Unit head:* Sr. Kathleen Flanagan, Director of the Graduate Program, 973-290-4336, Fax: 973-290-4312, E-mail: kflanagan@cse.edu. *Application contact:* Dean Donna Tatarka, Dean of Admission, 973-290-4705, Fax: 973-290-4710, E-mail: dtatarka@cse.edu.

Columbia International University, Columbia Biblical Seminary and School of Missions, Columbia, SC 29230-3122. Offers academic ministries (M Div); bible exposition (M Div, MABE); biblical studies (Certificate); counseling ministries (Certificate); divinity (M Div); educational ministries (M Div, MAEM, Certificate); intercultural studies (M Div, MAIS, Certificate); leadership (D Min); leadership for evangelism/mobilization (MALM); member care (D Min); ministry (Certificate); missions (D Min); pastoral counseling and spiritual formation (M Div, MAPS); preaching (D Min); theology (MA). *Accreditation:* ATS (one or more programs are accredited). Part-time and evening/weekend programs available. *Degree requirements:* For master's, integrative seminar; for doctorate, comprehensive exam, thesis/dissertation; for M Div, internship. *Entrance requirements:* For master's, minimum GPA of 2.7; for doctorate, 3 years of ministerial experience, M Div. Additional exam requirements/recommendations for international students: Required—TOEFL. Electronic applications accepted.

Columbia Theological Seminary, Graduate and Professional Programs, Decatur, GA 30031-0520. Offers M Div, MATS, Th M, D Min, Th D. Th D program offered jointly with Emory University; D Min with Interdenominational Theological Center. *Accreditation:* ACIPE; ATS (one or more programs are accredited). Terminal master's awarded for partial completion of doctoral program. *Degree requirements:* For master's, thesis (for some programs); for doctorate, one foreign language, thesis/dissertation; for M Div, 2 foreign languages. *Entrance requirements:* For doctorate, M Div or equivalent, 3 years practice of ministry. Additional exam requirements/recommendations for international students: Required—TOEFL.

Concordia Lutheran Seminary, Graduate and Professional Programs, Edmonton, AB T5B 4E3, Canada. Offers M Div, Graduate Certificate. *Accreditation:* ATS (one or more programs are accredited). Part-time programs available. *Degree requirements:* For M Div, 2 foreign languages, thesis/dissertation. *Entrance requirements:* GRE General Test, 1 year of Greek, 1 year of Hebrew, minimum GPA of 2.0. Additional exam requirements/recommendations for international students: Required—TOEFL. *Faculty research:* Lutheran Pietism, Christianity and culture, missiology, Christian worship, homiletics.

Concordia Seminary, Graduate Programs, St. Louis, MO 63105-3199. Offers M Div, MA, STM, D Min, PhD, Certificate. *Accreditation:* ACIPE; ATS (one or more programs are accredited). Terminal master's awarded for partial completion of doctoral program. *Degree requirements:* For master's, 3 foreign languages, thesis optional; for doctorate, 4 foreign languages, thesis/dissertation; for M Div, 2 foreign languages, comprehensive exam (for some programs), thesis/dissertation (for some programs). *Entrance requirements:* For M Div, GRE General Test, previous course work in public speaking, Greek, Hebrew, Old Testament, New Testament, and Christian Doctrine; for master's, GRE General Test; for doctorate, GRE General Test, theological essay in English (foreign students only). Additional exam requirements/recommendations for international students: Required—TOEFL. *Faculty research:* Family counseling, educational administration, contemporary theology, pastoral office, humanism and education.

Concordia Theological Seminary, Graduate and Professional Programs, Fort Wayne, IN 46825-4996. Offers M Div, MA, STM, D Min, PhD. *Accreditation:* ATS. Part-time programs available. *Degree requirements:* For master's, 2 foreign languages, thesis, oral exam, language exam, comprehensive exam (STM); for doctorate, comprehensive exam, thesis/dissertation, oral exam; for M Div, one foreign language, 1 year of vicarage. *Entrance requirements:* GRE General Test, minimum GPA of 2.25.

Concordia University, School of Graduate Studies, Faculty of Arts and Science, Department of Theological Studies, Montréal, QC H3G 1M8, Canada. Offers MA. *Degree requirements:* For master's, one foreign language, research papers or thesis. *Entrance requirements:* For master's, minimum B average in theology. *Faculty research:* Interpretation theory, theological methodology.

Concordia University, School of Theology, Irvine, CA 92612-3299. Offers Christian leadership (MA); research in theology (MA); theology and culture (MA). Part-time and evening/weekend programs available. *Faculty:* 8 full-time (1 woman), 2 part-time/adjunct (0 women). *Students:* 30 full-time (3 women), 7 part-time (3 women); includes 5 minority (1 Black or African American, non-Hispanic/Latino; 1 Asian, non-Hispanic/Latino; 3 Hispanic/Latino), 4 international. Average age 34. 11 applicants, 55% accepted, 5 enrolled. In 2010, 2 master's awarded. *Degree requirements:* For master's, project/thesis or vicarage. *Entrance requirements:* For master's, official college transcript(s), statement of intent, 2 references, graduate health form, interview. Additional exam requirements/recommendations for international students: Required—TOEFL. *Application deadline:* For fall admission, 7/1 priority date for domestic students, 6/1 for international students; for spring admission, 11/30 priority date for domestic students, 10/1 for international students. Applications are processed on a rolling basis. Application fee: $50 ($125 for international students). Electronic applications accepted. *Expenses:* Contact institution. *Financial support:* Scholarships/grants and unspecified assistantships available. Financial award applicants required to submit FAFSA. *Unit head:* Rev. Dr. James Bachman, Dean of Graduate Studies, 949-214-3387, E-mail: james.bachman@cui.edu. *Application contact:* Carrie Donohoe, Christ College Program Coordinator, 949-214-3389, E-mail: carrie.donohoe@cui.edu.

Concordia University College of Alberta, Program in Biblical and Christian Studies, Edmonton, AB T5B 4E4, Canada. Offers MA.

Concordia University, St. Paul, College of Vocation and Ministry, St. Paul, MN 55104-5494. Offers Christian education (Certificate); Christian outreach (MA, Certificate). Evening/weekend programs available. Postbaccalaureate distance learning degree programs offered (minimal on-campus study). *Faculty:* 2 full-time (0 women), 5 part-time/adjunct (2 women). *Students:* 11 full-time (3 women); includes 1 Asian, non-Hispanic/Latino. Average age 40. In 2010, 7 master's awarded. *Application deadline:* Applications are processed on a rolling basis. Application fee: $50. Electronic applications accepted. *Expenses:* Tuition: Full-time $7500; part-time $460 per credit. Required fees: $460 per credit. Tuition and fees vary according to program. *Financial support:* Applicants required to submit FAFSA. *Unit head:* Dr. David Lumpp, Dean, 651-641-8217, E-mail: lumpp@csp.edu. *Application contact:* Kimberly Craig, Director of Graduate and Cohort Admission, 651-603-6223, Fax: 651-603-6320, E-mail: craig@csp.edu.

Covenant Theological Seminary, Graduate and Professional Programs, St. Louis, MO 63141-8697. Offers M Div, MA, MAC, MAEM, Th M, D Min, Certificate. *Accreditation:* ATS (one or more programs are accredited). Part-time and evening/weekend programs available. Postbaccalaureate distance learning degree programs offered (minimal on-campus study). *Degree requirements:* For master's, 2 foreign languages, thesis (for some programs); for doctorate, 2 foreign languages, thesis/dissertation; for M Div and Certificate, 2 foreign languages. *Entrance requirements:* For doctorate and Certificate, M Div. Additional exam requirements/recommendations for international students: Required—TOEFL (minimum score 550 paper-based; 213 computer-based). Electronic applications accepted.

Creighton University, Graduate School, College of Arts and Sciences, Department of Theology, Omaha, NE 68178-0001. Offers Christian spirituality (MA); ministry (MA); theology (MA). Part-time and evening/weekend programs available. Postbaccalaureate distance learning degree programs offered (minimal on-campus study). *Faculty:* 20 full-time (6 women), 3 part-time/adjunct (0 women). *Students:* 2 full-time (1 woman), 28 part-time (17 women); includes 3 minority (2 Black or African American, non-Hispanic/Latino; 1 American Indian or Alaska Native, non-Hispanic/Latino). Average age 44. 8 applicants, 75% accepted, 6 enrolled. In 2010, 10 master's awarded. *Degree requirements:* For master's, thesis (for some programs). *Entrance requirements:* For master's, GRE General Test, 9 hours of theology course work, 3 letters of recommendation. Additional exam requirements/recommendations for international students: Required—TOEFL (minimum score 550 paper-based; 213 computer-based; 80 iBT). *Application deadline:* For fall admission, 3/1 for domestic and international students; for winter admission, 10/1 for domestic students, 5/1 for international students; for spring admission, 4/1 for domestic students, 10/1 for international students. Applications are processed on a rolling basis. Application fee: $50. *Expenses:* Tuition: Full-time $12,168; part-time $676 per credit hour. Required fees: $131 per semester. Tuition and fees vary according to program. *Financial support:* Scholarships/grants and tuition waivers (partial) available. Support available to part-time students. Financial award applicants required to submit FAFSA. *Unit head:* Dr. Richard Miller, Director, 402-280-3618, E-mail: richardmiller@creighton.edu. *Application contact:* Taunya Plater, Senior Program Coordinator, 402-280-2870, Fax: 402-280-2899, E-mail: taunyaplater@creighton.edu.

The Criswell College, Graduate School of the Bible, Dallas, TX 75246-1537. Offers biblical studies (M Div); Christian leadership (MA); counseling (MA); Jewish studies (MA); ministry (MA); theological and biblical studies (MA). Part-time programs available. *Degree requirements:* For master's, 2 foreign languages, thesis optional; for M Div, 2 foreign languages, thesis/dissertation optional. *Entrance requirements:* For M Div and master's, GRE General Test, minimum GPA of 2.5. Electronic applications accepted. *Faculty research:* Emphasis on biblical languages (Hebrew and Greek), expository preaching and evangelism in the local church.

Crown College, Adult and Graduate Studies, St. Bonifacius, MN 55375-9001. Offers Christian studies (MA); instructional leadership (MA); international leadership (MA); ministry leadership (MA); organizational leadership (MA). Part-time and evening/weekend programs available. Postbaccalaureate distance learning degree programs offered (no on-campus study). *Faculty:* 10 full-time (2 women), 19 part-time/adjunct (6 women). *Students:* 138 full-time (53 women), 27 part-time (11 women); includes 16 minority (4 Black or African American, non-Hispanic/Latino; 1 American Indian or Alaska Native, non-Hispanic/Latino; 8 Asian, non-Hispanic/Latino; 3 Hispanic/Latino). Average age 37. 53 applicants, 91% accepted, 44 enrolled. In 2010, 40 master's awarded. *Degree requirements:* For master's, thesis optional. *Entrance requirements:* For master's, 12 credits in foundational studies, minimum GPA of 2.5 and bachelor's degree from regionally-accredited college. Additional exam requirements/recommendations for international students: Required—TOEFL (minimum score 550 paper-based; 213 computer-based; 80 iBT). *Application deadline:* For fall admission, 8/1 priority date for domestic students; for winter admission, 1/1 priority date for domestic students; for spring admission, 6/1 priority date for domestic students. Applications are processed on a rolling basis. Application fee: $20. Electronic applications accepted. *Financial support:* In 2010–11, 71 students received support, including 3 teaching assistantships with full tuition reimbursements available (averaging $7,200 per year); scholarships/grants also available. Financial award application deadline: 8/1; financial award applicants required to submit FAFSA. *Unit head:* Matt Newby, Director, 952-446-4224, Fax: 952-416-4349, E-mail: grad@crown.edu. *Application contact:* Nate Erickson, Enrollment Coordinator, 952-446-4370, Fax: 952-446-4349, E-mail: grad@crown.edu.

Dallas Theological Seminary, Graduate Programs, Dallas, TX 75204-6499. Offers academic ministries (Th M); Bible translation (Th M); biblical and theological studies (CGS); biblical counseling (MA, Th M); biblical exegesis and linguistics (MA); biblical exposition (PhD); biblical studies (MA); Christian education (MA, D Min); cross-cultural ministries (MA, Th M); educational leadership (Th M); evangelism and discipleship (Th M); interdisciplinary studies (Th M); media and communication (MA); media arts in ministry (Th M); ministry (D Min); New Testament studies (Th M, PhD); Old Testament studies (PhD); parachurch ministries (Th M); pastoral ministries (Th M); sacred theology (STM); theological studies (PhD); women's ministry (Th M). *Accreditation:* ATS (one or more programs are accredited). Part-time and evening/weekend programs available. *Degree requirements:* For master's, variable foreign language requirement, thesis (for some programs); for doctorate, 2 foreign languages, thesis/dissertation. *Entrance requirements:* Additional exam requirements/recommendations for international students: Required—TOEFL, TWE. Electronic applications accepted.

Darkei Noam Rabbinical College, Graduate Programs, Brooklyn, NY 11210.

Denver Seminary, Graduate and Professional Programs, Littleton, CO 80120. Offers apologetics (Certificate); biblical studies (MA); Christian formation and soul care (MA, Certificate); Christian studies (MA, Certificate); church and parachurch leadership (D Min); counseling licensure (MA); counseling ministry (MA); intercultural ministry (Certificate); leadership (MA, Certificate); marriage and family counseling (D Min); pastoral ministry (D Min); philosophy of religion (MA); spiritual guidance (Certificate); theology (M Div, Certificate); worship (Certificate); youth and family ministry (MA). *Accreditation:* ACA; ACIPE; ATS (one or more programs are accredited). Part-time and evening/weekend programs available. Postbaccalaureate distance learning degree programs offered. *Degree requirements:* For master's, 2 foreign languages, thesis (for some programs); for doctorate, 2 foreign languages, thesis/dissertation; for M Div, 2 foreign languages. *Entrance requirements:* For M Div, minimum undergraduate GPA of 2.5; for master's, minimum undergraduate GPA of 3.0; for doctorate, M Div, 3 years of ministry experience. Additional exam requirements/recommendations for international students: Required—TOEFL (minimum score 575 paper-based; 233 computer-based; 90 iBT). Electronic applications accepted.

Dominican House of Studies, Pontifical Faculty of the Immaculate Conception, Graduate and Professional Programs in Theology, Washington, DC 20017-1585. Offers moral theology (STL); sacred scripture (STL); systematic theology (STL); theology (M Div, STB, MA); Thomistic studies (MA, STL). *Accreditation:* ATS (one or more programs are accredited). Part-time programs available. *Faculty:* 17 full-time (1 woman), 6 part-time/adjunct (2 women). *Students:* 56 full-time (4 women), 15 part-time (5 women); includes 2 Asian, non-Hispanic/Latino; 3 Hispanic/Latino, 13 international. Average age 33. 33 applicants, 94% accepted, 22 enrolled. In 2010, 10 first professional degrees, 6 master's, 10 other advanced degrees awarded. *Degree requirements:* For master's, one foreign language, thesis, thesis defense; for first professional degree, 2 foreign languages, comprehensive exam; for STL, 3 foreign languages, comprehensive exam (for some programs), thesis (for some programs), lecture. *Entrance requirements:* For first professional degree, 18 credits of philosophy (36 for STB); reading knowledge of Latin; BA with minimum GPA of 3.0 (3.25 for STB); for master's, 18 credits of philosophy, reading knowledge of Latin, BA with a minimum GPA of 3.0. Additional exam requirements/recommendations for international students: Required—TOEFL (minimum score 550 paper-based; 215 computer-based; 79 iBT). *Application deadline:* For fall admission, 7/1 priority date for domestic and international students; for spring admission, 12/1 priority date for domestic and international students. Applications are processed on a rolling basis. Application fee: $50. *Expenses:* Tuition: Full-time $15,120; part-time $630 per credit. Required fees: $50 per semester. One-time fee: $50. *Financial support:* In 2010–11, 8 students received support. Career-related internships or fieldwork and Federal Work-Study available. Support available to part-time students. Financial award application deadline: 6/30; financial award applicants required to submit FAFSA. *Faculty research:* Sacred scripture, moral theology, systematic theology, philosophy, languages. Total annual research expenditures: $13,118. *Unit head:* Rev. Gabriel O'Donnell, Vice-President/Academic Dean, 202-495-3832, Fax: 202-495-3873, E-mail: dean@dhs.edu. *Application contact:* Tobias John Nathe, Registrar, 202-495-3836, Fax: 202-495-3873, E-mail: registrar@dhs.edu.

Dominican School of Philosophy and Theology, Graduate Programs, Department of Theology, Berkeley, CA 94708. Offers M Div, MTS, Certificate, M Div/MA, MA/MA. *Accreditation:* ATS (one or more programs are accredited). Part-time programs available. *Faculty:* 11 full-time (1 woman), 10 part-time/adjunct (2 women). *Students:* 52 full-time (10 women), 20 part-time (11 women); includes 28 minority (15 Asian, non-Hispanic/Latino; 5 Hispanic/Latino; 8 Two or more races, non-Hispanic/Latino). Average age 36. 53 applicants, 96% accepted, 36 enrolled. In 2010, 1 first professional degree, 14 master's awarded. *Degree requirements:* For master's, one foreign language, thesis. *Entrance requirements:* For M Div, minimum GPA of 2.3; for master's, GRE, minimum GPA of 3.0. Additional exam requirements/recommendations for international students: Required—TOEFL (minimum score 550 paper-based; 68 computer-based; 80 iBT). *Application deadline:* For fall admission, 3/15 priority date for domestic and international students; for spring admission, 10/15 priority date for domestic and international students. Applications are processed on a rolling basis. Application fee: $40. Electronic applications accepted. *Expenses:* Tuition: Full-time $14,160; part-time $590 per unit. *Financial support:* In 2010–11, 15 students received support. Institutionally sponsored loans, scholarships/grants, and tuition waivers (partial) available. Financial award application deadline: 4/1; financial award applicants required to submit FAFSA. *Unit head:* Sr. Marianne Farina, CSC, Chair, 510-883-2081, Fax: 510-849-1372, E-mail: mfarina@dspt.edu. *Application contact:* John D. Knutsen, Director of Admissions, 510-883-2073, Fax: 510-849-1372, E-mail: admissions@dspt.edu.

Drew University, Theological School, Madison, NJ 07940-1493. Offers M Div, MA, MA Min, STM, D Min, Certificate. *Accreditation:* ACIPE; ATS. Part-time programs available. Post-baccalaureate distance learning degree programs offered (minimal on-campus study). *Faculty:* 25 full-time (11 women), 24 part-time/adjunct (12 women). *Students:* 200 full-time (114 women), 165 part-time (81 women); includes 111 minority (85 Black or African American, non-Hispanic/Latino; 1 American Indian or Alaska Native, non-Hispanic/Latino; 15 Asian, non-Hispanic/Latino; 10 Hispanic/Latino), 73 international. Average age 35. 237 applicants, 57% accepted, 76 enrolled. In 2010, 68 master's, 22 doctorates awarded. *Degree requirements:* For doctorate, thesis/dissertation. *Entrance requirements:* For M Div, 3 years professional ministry experience; for master's, minimum GPA of 3.0. Additional exam requirements/recommendations for international students: Required—TOEFL (minimum score 580 paper-based; 230 computer-based; 88 iBT), TWE. *Application deadline:* For fall admission, 3/1 priority date for domestic and international students; for spring admission, 12/1 priority date for domestic students, 10/1 priority date for international students. Applications are processed on a rolling basis. Application fee: $35. Electronic applications accepted. *Expenses:* Contact institution. *Financial support:* Fellowships, career-related internships or fieldwork, Federal Work-Study, institutionally sponsored loans, and scholarships/grants available. Support available to part-time students. Financial award application deadline: 4/15; financial award applicants required to submit FAFSA. *Faculty research:* Biblical studies, constructive theology, ecology and religion, gender and religion, race/ethnicity and religion. *Unit head:* Dr. Kah-Jin Jeffrey Kuan, Dean, 973-408-3258, Fax: 973-408-3534, E-mail: jkuan@drew.edu. *Application contact:* Rev. Dr. Kevin D. Miller, Director of Theological Admissions, 973-408-3111, Fax: 973-408-3242, E-mail: kmiller@drew.edu.

Duke University, Divinity School, Durham, NC 27708-0586. Offers M Div, MTS, Th M, Th D, JD/MTS, M Div/MSW. *Accreditation:* ACIPE; ATS. Part-time programs available. *Degree requirements:* For master's, thesis optional; for doctorate, 2 foreign languages, thesis/dissertation; for M Div, field experience, spiritual formation, faculty evaluation. *Entrance requirements:* For M Div, 5 letters of reference, 2 essays; for master's, 5 letters of reference; for doctorate, GRE, 4 letters of reference, 2-page statement of purpose, one sample of academic writing. Additional exam requirements/recommendations for international students: Required—TOEFL (minimum score 580 paper-based; 93 iBT). Electronic applications accepted. *Expenses:* Contact institution. *Faculty research:* Biblical studies, historical church studies, theological studies, church ministry studies.

Duquesne University, Graduate School of Liberal Arts, Department of Theology, Pittsburgh, PA 15282-0001. Offers pastoral ministry (MA); religious education (MA); systematic theology (PhD); theology (MA). Part-time and evening/weekend programs available. *Faculty:* 13 full-time (4 women). *Students:* 93 full-time (39 women), 19 part-time (all women); includes 2 Black or African American, non-Hispanic/Latino, 14 international. Average age 35. 47 applicants, 51% accepted, 15 enrolled. In 2010, 6 master's, 6 doctorates awarded. *Degree requirements:* For master's, comprehensive exam; for doctorate, 2 foreign languages, comprehensive exam, thesis/dissertation. *Entrance requirements:* For master's and doctorate, GRE General Test. Additional exam requirements/recommendations for international students: Required—TOEFL. *Application deadline:* For fall admission, 2/1 for domestic and international students. Electronic applications accepted. *Expenses:* Tuition: Part-time $884 per credit. Required fees: $84 per credit. Tuition and fees vary according to course load. *Financial support:* In 2010–11, 10 teaching assistantships with full tuition reimbursements (averaging $15,000 per year) were awarded; career-related internships or fieldwork, scholarships/grants, tuition waivers (partial), and unspecified assistantships also available. Support available to part-time students. Financial award application deadline: 5/1. *Unit head:* Dr. George Worgul, Chair, 412-396-6530. *Application contact:* Dr. Marie Baird, Director, 412-396-6530.

Earlham School of Religion, Graduate Programs, Richmond, IN 47374. Offers religion (MA); theology (M Div, M Min). *Accreditation:* ACIPE; ATS. Part-time programs available. Post-baccalaureate distance learning degree programs offered (minimal on-campus study). *Faculty:* 9 full-time (4 women), 8 part-time/adjunct (5 women). *Students:* 111 full-time (71 women), 38 part-time (21 women); includes 2 Black or African American, non-Hispanic/Latino; 1 American Indian or Alaska Native, non-Hispanic/Latino; 1 Asian, non-Hispanic/Latino; 3 Hispanic/Latino, 6 international. Average age 45. 37 applicants, 97% accepted, 34 enrolled. In 2010, 15 first professional degrees, 2 master's awarded. *Degree requirements:* For master's, one foreign language, comprehensive exam, thesis; for M Div, internship. *Entrance requirements:* For M Div and master's, 3 references. Additional exam requirements/recommendations for international students: Required—TOEFL (minimum score 550 paper-based; 218 computer-based; 82 iBT). *Application deadline:* For fall admission, 7/15 priority date for domestic students; for winter admission, 12/15 priority date for domestic students. Applications are processed on a rolling basis. Application fee: $35. Electronic applications accepted. *Financial support:* Scholarships/grants and tuition waivers (full and partial) available. Financial award application deadline: 4/15; financial award applicants required to submit FAFSA. *Faculty research:* Digitizing Quaker texts, vital Quaker ministry, research in Quaker Studies and other seminary areas. *Unit head:* Jay W. Marshall, Dean, 800-432-1377, Fax: 765-983-1688, E-mail: marshja@earlham.edu. *Application contact:* Valerie K. Hurwitz, Director of Recruitment and Admissions, 800-432-1377, Fax: 765-983-1688, E-mail: hurwiva@earlham.edu.

Eastern Mennonite University, Eastern Mennonite Seminary, Harrisonburg, VA 22802-2462. Offers church leadership (MA); divinity (M Div); ministry studies (Certificate); online theological studies (Certificate); religion (MA); theological studies (Certificate). *Accreditation:* ATS. Part-time programs available. *Degree requirements:* For master's, thesis (for some programs); for M Div, thesis/dissertation (for some programs), supervised field education. *Entrance requirements:* For M Div and master's, minimum GPA of 2.5. Additional exam requirements/recommendations for international students: Required—TOEFL (minimum score 550 paper-based; 213 computer-based). *Expenses:* Contact institution. *Faculty research:* Spiritual direction and culture of call, leadership coaching: an approach to leadership in a culture of call, clarity of call in the probationary process for United Methodist clergy in Virginia, EMS women's experiences of culture of call efforts, practices of excellent and fruitful Mennonite pastoral ministry.

Eastern University, Palmer Theological Seminary, Wynnewood, PA 19096-3430. Offers M Div, MTS, D Min, M Div/MBA, M Div/MSW. *Accreditation:* ACIPE; ATS; MSA/CIHE. Part-time and evening/weekend programs available. *Entrance requirements:* Additional exam requirements/recommendations for international students: Required—TOEFL.

Ecumenical Theological Seminary, Professional Program, Detroit, MI 48201. Offers M Div. *Accreditation:* ACIPE; ATS.

Eden Theological Seminary, Graduate and Professional Programs, St. Louis, MO 63119-3192. Offers M Div, MAPS, MTS, D Min. *Accreditation:* ACIPE; ATS. *Degree requirements:* For master's, comprehensive exam (for some programs), thesis (for some programs), 2 oral exams; for doctorate, professional essay, supervised in-service projects; for M Div, thesis/dissertation optional, 2 oral exams. *Entrance requirements:* For M Div and master's, interview, minimum GPA of 2.7; for doctorate, interview, minimum GPA of 3.0. Additional exam requirements/recommendations for international students: Required—TOEFL (minimum score 550 paper-based). Electronic applications accepted. *Faculty research:* Psalms, pastoral ethics, historical Jesus, leadership roles, congregational life.

Emmanuel Christian Seminary, Graduate and Professional Programs, Johnson City, TN 37601-9438. Offers Christian care and counseling (M Div); Christian doctrine (MAR); Christian education (M Div); Christian ministry (M Div); church history (MAR); divinity (M Div); ministry (D Min); New Testament (MAR); Old Testament (MAR); urban ministry (M Div); world missions (M Div). *Accreditation:* ACIPE; ATS. Part-time programs available. *Faculty:* 9 full-time (2 women), 9 part-time/adjunct (1 woman). *Students:* 90 full-time (27 women), 57 part-time (10 women); includes 2 Black or African American, non-Hispanic/Latino; 3 Hispanic/Latino, 17 international. Average age 27. 30 applicants, 97% accepted, 22 enrolled. In 2010, 17 first professional degrees, 1 master's, 1 doctorate awarded. *Degree requirements:* For master's, 2 foreign languages, thesis or alternative, portfolio; for doctorate, thesis/dissertation; for M Div, 2 foreign languages, thesis/dissertation or alternative, portfolio. *Entrance requirements:* For M Div and master's, bachelor's degree from accredited institution; for doctorate, Minnesota Multiphasic Personality Inventory, M Div or equivalent. Additional exam requirements/recommendations for international students: Required—TOEFL (minimum score 80 computer-based). *Application deadline:* For fall admission, 8/1 for domestic and international students; for spring admission, 1/20 for domestic and international students. Applications are processed on a rolling basis. Application fee: $25. *Expenses:* Tuition: Full-time $11,700; part-time $390 per credit hour. Required fees: $162.50 per semester. One-time fee: $240. Tuition and fees vary according to reciprocity agreements. *Financial support:* In 2010–11, 136 students received support; teaching assistantships with partial tuition reimbursements available, career-related internships or fieldwork, scholarships/grants, and tuition waivers (partial) available. Support available to part-time students. Financial award application deadline: 3/1; financial award applicants required to submit FAFSA. *Faculty research:* Theology of Old Testament prophets, spiritual formation for Christian leaders, history of African churches and religions, social world of early Christianity, lay pastoral counseling, ANE epigraphy. Total annual research expenditures: $12,000. *Unit head:* Dr. Jack Holland, Dean and Professor of Christian Care and Counseling, 423-461-1524, Fax: 423-926-6198, E-mail: jholland@ecs.edu. *Application contact:* Erin Layton, Director of Admissions, 423-461-1535, Fax: 423-926-6198, E-mail: elayton@ecs.edu.

Emory University, Candler School of Theology, Atlanta, GA 30322. Offers formation and witness (M Div); history, scripture and tradition (MTS); leadership in church and community (M Div); modern religious thought and experience (MTS); pastoral counseling (Th D); religion and race (M Div); religion, health and science (M Div); scripture and interpretation (M Div); society and personality (M Div); theology (Th M); theology and ethics (M Div); theology and the arts (M Div); traditions of the church (M Div); women and religion (M Div); JD/M Div; JD/MTS; M Div/MBA; M Div/MPH; MBA/MTS; MTS/MPH. *Accreditation:* ACIPE; ATS. Part-time programs available. *Faculty:* 45 full-time (11 women), 26 part-time/adjunct (12 women). *Students:* 411 full-time (206 women), 44 part-time (29 women); includes 113 Black or African American, non-Hispanic/Latino; 1 American Indian or Alaska Native, non-Hispanic/Latino; 8 Asian, non-Hispanic/Latino; 8 Hispanic/Latino; 1 Two or more races, non-Hispanic/Latino, 40 international. Average age 32. 603 applicants, 74% accepted, 191 enrolled. In 2010, 141 first professional degrees, 48 master's, 1 doctorate awarded. *Degree requirements:* For master's, thesis optional; for doctorate, comprehensive exam, thesis/dissertation; for M Div, thesis/dissertation optional. *Entrance requirements:* For M Div, minimum undergraduate GPA of 2.75; for master's, minimum undergraduate GPA of 3.0; for doctorate, GRE, M Div, 8 units of course work in clinical pastoral education. Additional exam requirements/recommendations for international students: Required—TOEFL (minimum score 600 paper-based; 250 computer-based; 95 iBT). *Application deadline:* For fall admission, 7/1 for domestic and international students; for spring admission, 11/1 for domestic and international students. Applications are processed on a rolling basis. Application fee: $50. Electronic applications accepted. *Expenses:* Contact institution. *Financial support:* In 2010–11, 422 students received support, including 343 fellowships (averaging $12,216 per year); career-related internships or fieldwork, institutionally sponsored loans, scholarships/grants, and student employment also available. Support available to part-time students. Financial award application deadline: 1/15; financial award applicants required to submit FAFSA. *Faculty research:* Biblical studies, church history, ethics, ministry practice, pastoral care. *Unit head:* Shelly E. Hart, Registrar, 404-727-6480, Fax: 404-727-4373, E-mail: candlerregistrar@emory.edu. *Application contact:* Mary Lou Greenwood Boice, Associate Dean of Admissions and Financial Aid, 404-727-6326, Fax: 404-727-2915, E-mail: candleradmissions@emory.edu.

Episcopal Divinity School, Graduate and Professional Programs, Cambridge, MA 02138-3494. Offers M Div, MATS, D Min, CTS. *Accreditation:* ACIPE; ATS (one or more programs are accredited). Part-time programs available. *Degree requirements:* For master's, thesis optional; for doctorate, thesis/dissertation, project; for M Div, thesis/dissertation optional, fieldwork. *Entrance requirements:* For M Div and master's, GRE General Test or MAT, 2 interviews, 4 letters of recommendation, 1500-word autobiographical statement; for doctorate, interview, M Div or equivalent, 3 letters of recommendation, 1500-word autobiographical statement; for CTS, GRE General Test, MAT, or advanced degree; interview; 2 letters of recommendation, 1000-word autobiographical statement. Additional exam requirements/recommendations for international students: Required—TOEFL. *Faculty research:* Anglican, global, and ecumenical studies; congregational studies; feminist liberation theologies.

Erskine Theological Seminary, Graduate and Professional Programs, Due West, SC 29639-0668. Offers M Div, MACE, MACM, MAPM, MATS, MCM, D Min. M Div program offered jointly with Columbia International University, Interdenominational Theological Center, Lutheran Theological Southern Seminary, and Reformed Theological Seminary–Charlotte Campus;

Theology

Erskine Theological Seminary (continued)
D Min with Columbia Theological Seminary, Interdenominational Theologial Center, and Emory University's Candler School of Theology. *Accreditation:* ATS. Part-time and evening/weekend programs available. *Degree requirements:* For doctorate, thesis/dissertation; for M Div, 2 foreign languages. *Entrance requirements:* For master's, Myers-Briggs Type Indicator, Taylor Johnson Temperament Analysis, Ministry Specialties Test (MACM), minimum GPA of 3.0, interview with committee (MACM); for doctorate, minimum GPA of 3.0 during M Div. Additional exam requirements/recommendations for international students: Required—TOEFL (minimum score 550 paper-based). Electronic applications accepted. *Faculty research:* Church administration, biblical studies.

Evangelical Seminary of Puerto Rico, Graduate and Professional Programs, San Juan, PR 00925-2207. Offers M Div, MAR, D Min. *Accreditation:* ATS. Part-time programs available. *Faculty:* 8 full-time (1 woman), 11 part-time/adjunct (0 women). *Students:* 59 full-time (27 women), 181 part-time (82 women); includes all Hispanic/Latino. Average age 45. In 2010, 15 first professional degrees, 6 master's awarded. *Degree requirements:* For master's, comprehensive exam; for M Div, integration essay. *Entrance requirements:* For M Div, Admission Test for Graduate Studies, denominational endorsement; for doctorate, 3 years experience in ministry service. Additional exam requirements/recommendations for international students: Required—TOEFL. *Application deadline:* For fall admission, 5/31 priority date for domestic students; for spring admission, 10/30 priority date for domestic students. Application fee: $50. *Financial support:* Scholarships/grants available. Support available to part-time students. Financial award application deadline: 8/30; financial award applicants required to submit FAFSA. *Faculty research:* Protestantism in Puerto Rico. *Unit head:* Dr. Sergio Ojeda, President, 787-763-6700 Ext. 243, Fax: 787-751-0847. *Application contact:* Marie L. Rivera, Registrar, 787-763-6700 Ext. 224, Fax: 787-766-0938, E-mail: registro@seminarioevangelicopr.org.

Evangelical Theological Seminary, Graduate and Professional Programs, Myerstown, PA 17067-1212. Offers Biblical studies (MAR); congregational ministry (M Div); global and contextual studies (M Div, MAR); historical and theological studies (MAR); interdisciplinary studies (MAR); marriage and family counseling (M Div); marriage and family therapy (MA); New Testament (MAR); Old Testament (MAR); spiritual formation (MAR); teaching ministry (M Div); youth ministry (M Div). *Accreditation:* ATS (one or more programs are accredited). Part-time programs available. Postbaccalaureate distance learning degree programs offered (minimal on-campus study). *Degree requirements:* For master's, 2 foreign languages; for M Div, 2 foreign languages, ministry internship. *Entrance requirements:* For M Div and master's, minimum GPA of 2.5. Additional exam requirements/recommendations for international students: Required—TOEFL (minimum score 550 paper-based; 213 computer-based). *Faculty research:* Literary form and structure within the Hebrew and Greek scriptures, Wesley studies, esoteric biblical languages, the Mosaic law and the Christian, ethics.

Faith Baptist Bible College and Theological Seminary, Graduate Program, Ankeny, IA 50023. Offers biblical studies (MA); pastoral studies (M Div); pastoral training (MA); religion (MA); theological studies (MA). Part-time programs available. *Faculty:* 4 full-time (0 women), 4 part-time/adjunct (0 women). *Students:* 14 full-time (1 woman), 25 part-time (0 women); includes 3 Asian, non-Hispanic/Latino, 1 international. Average age 29. In 2010, 5 first professional degrees, 14 master's awarded. *Degree requirements:* For master's, thesis or alternative; for M Div, 2 foreign languages. *Entrance requirements:* Additional exam requirements/recommendations for international students: Required—TOEFL (minimum score 550 paper-based; 197 computer-based). *Application deadline:* For fall admission, 8/1 priority date for domestic students, 8/1 for international students; for spring admission, 12/15 for domestic and international students. Applications are processed on a rolling basis. Application fee: $25. *Financial support:* Career-related internships or fieldwork and scholarships/grants available. Support available to part-time students. Financial award application deadline: 3/1; financial award applicants required to submit FAFSA. *Faculty research:* Baptist theology, American church history. *Unit head:* Dr. Ernest Schmidt, Dean of Seminary, 515-964-0601, E-mail: schmidte@faith.edu. *Application contact:* Carrie Johnson, Admissions Administrative Assistant, 888-FAITH4U, Fax: 515-964-1638, E-mail: admissions@faith.edu.

Faith Evangelical Lutheran Seminary, Graduate and Professional Programs, Tacoma, WA 98407. Offers B Th, M Div, MCM, MTS, D Min. Part-time and evening/weekend programs available. Postbaccalaureate distance learning degree programs offered (minimal on-campus study). *Degree requirements:* For master's, thesis optional; for doctorate, thesis/dissertation; for first professional degree, thesis/dissertation (for some programs). *Entrance requirements:* For first professional degree and master's, minimum undergraduate GPA of 2.7; for doctorate, minimum graduate GPA of 3.0. Additional exam requirements/recommendations for international students: Required—TOEFL (minimum score 550 paper-based; 213 computer-based).

Faith Theological Seminary, Graduate Programs, Baltimore, MD 21212. Offers M Div, D Min, Th D.

Faulkner University, College of Biblical Studies, Montgomery, AL 36109-3398. Offers ministry (MABS); missions (MABS); New Testament (MABS); Old Testament (MABS); youth and family ministry (MABS).

Fordham University, Graduate School of Arts and Sciences, Department of Theology, New York, NY 10458. Offers MA, PhD. Part-time and evening/weekend programs available. *Faculty:* 22 full-time (7 women). *Students:* 30 full-time (15 women), 47 part-time (15 women); includes 4 minority (1 Black or African American, non-Hispanic/Latino; 1 American Indian or Alaska Native, non-Hispanic/Latino; 1 Asian, non-Hispanic/Latino; 1 Hispanic/Latino), 1 international. Average age 36. 89 applicants, 42% accepted, 13 enrolled. In 2010, 3 master's, 5 doctorates awarded. Terminal master's awarded for partial completion of doctoral program. *Degree requirements:* For master's, one foreign language, comprehensive exam; for doctorate, 2 foreign languages, comprehensive exam, thesis/dissertation. *Entrance requirements:* For master's and doctorate, GRE General Test. Additional exam requirements/recommendations for international students: Required—TOEFL (minimum score 650 paper-based; 280 computer-based). *Application deadline:* For fall admission, 1/4 priority date for domestic students; for spring admission, 11/1 for domestic students. Application fee: $70. Electronic applications accepted. *Financial support:* In 2010–11, 28 students received support, including 2 fellowships with tuition reimbursements available (averaging $19,800 per year), 17 research assistantships with tuition reimbursements available (averaging $18,541 per year), 9 teaching assistantships with tuition reimbursements available (averaging $20,711 per year); institutionally sponsored loans, tuition waivers (full and partial), and unspecified assistantships also available. Support available to part-time students. Financial award application deadline: 1/4. *Faculty research:* History of Christian tradition, contemporary systematic theology, theological/feminist ethics, American Catholicism, Biblical exegesis and theology. Total annual research expenditures: $10,000. *Unit head:* Dr. Terrence Tilley, Chair, 718-817-3245, E-mail: ttilley@fordham.edu. *Application contact:* Charlene Dundie, Director of Graduate Admissions, 718-817-4420, Fax: 718-817-3566, E-mail: dundie@fordham.edu.

Franciscan School of Theology, Graduate and Professional Programs, Berkeley, CA 94709-1294. Offers M Div, MA, MAMC, MTS. *Accreditation:* ATS (one or more programs are accredited). Part-time programs available. *Degree requirements:* For master's, one foreign language, thesis. *Entrance requirements:* For master's, GRE General Test (MA). Additional exam requirements/recommendations for international students: Required—TOEFL (minimum score 550 paper-based; 213 computer-based). *Faculty research:* Church history, multicultural ministries, ethics and morality, catechesis, biblical studies.

Franciscan University of Steubenville, Graduate Programs, Department of Theology, Steubenville, OH 43952-1763. Offers theology and Christian ministry (MA). Part-time programs available. Postbaccalaureate distance learning degree programs offered (minimal on-campus study). *Degree requirements:* For master's, comprehensive exam. *Entrance requirements:* For master's, minimum undergraduate GPA of 3.0.

Freed-Hardeman University, School of Biblical Studies, Program in Divinity, Henderson, TN 38340-2399. Offers M Div. Part-time programs available. *Entrance requirements:* Additional exam requirements/recommendations for international students: Required—TOEFL (minimum score 500 paper-based; 173 computer-based).

Freed-Hardeman University, School of Biblical Studies, Program in New Testament, Henderson, TN 38340-2399. Offers MA. Part-time programs available. *Degree requirements:* For master's, one foreign language, comprehensive exam, thesis. *Entrance requirements:* For master's, GRE General Test or MAT. Additional exam requirements/recommendations for international students: Required—TOEFL (minimum score 500 paper-based; 173 computer-based).

Fresno Pacific University, Fresno Pacific Biblical Seminary, Program in Divinity, Fresno, CA 93702-4709. Offers M Div. *Accreditation:* ATS. *Degree requirements:* For M Div, one foreign language.

Fresno Pacific University, Fresno Pacific Biblical Seminary, Programs in New Testament, Old Testament, and Theology, Fresno, CA 93702-4709. Offers New Testament (MA); Old Testament (MA); theology (MA). Part-time programs available. *Entrance requirements:* Additional exam requirements/recommendations for international students: Required—TOEFL (minimum score 550 paper-based; 213 computer-based).

Friends University, Graduate School, Wichita, KS 67213. Offers accounting (MBA); business administration (MBA); business law (MBL); Christian ministry (MACM); family therapy (MSFT); global leadership and management (MA); health care leadership (MHCL); management information systems (MMIS); operations management (MSOM); organization development (MSOD); teaching (MAT). Part-time and evening/weekend programs available. Postbaccalaureate distance learning degree programs offered (minimal on-campus study). *Faculty:* 14 full-time (5 women), 2 part-time/adjunct (1 woman). *Students:* 166 full-time (122 women), 507 part-time (290 women); includes 134 minority (64 Black or African American, non-Hispanic/Latino; 6 American Indian or Alaska Native, non-Hispanic/Latino; 24 Asian, non-Hispanic/Latino; 30 Hispanic/Latino; 1 Native Hawaiian or other Pacific Islander, non-Hispanic/Latino; 9 Two or more races, non-Hispanic/Latino). Average age 38. 445 applicants, 69% accepted, 236 enrolled. In 2010, 345 master's awarded. *Degree requirements:* For master's, research project. *Entrance requirements:* Additional exam requirements/recommendations for international students: Required—TOEFL (minimum score 560 paper-based; 220 computer-based). *Application deadline:* Applications are processed on a rolling basis. Application fee: $45 ($65 for international students). Electronic applications accepted. Tuition and fees vary according to course load, campus/location and program. *Financial support:* Applicants required to submit FAFSA. *Unit head:* Dr. Evelyn Hume, Dean, 800-794-6945 Ext. 5859, Fax: 316-295-5040, E-mail: evelyn_hume@friends.edu. *Application contact:* Jeanette Hanson, Executive Director of Adult Recruitment, 800-794-6945, Fax: 316-295-5050, E-mail: jeanette@friends.edu.

Fuller Theological Seminary, Graduate School of Theology, Pasadena, CA 91182. Offers Christian leadership (MACL); evangelism (MA); family life education (MA); ministry (M Div, D Min); pastoral ministry (MA); recovery ministry (MA); theology (MAT, Th M, PhD); worship music ministry (MA); worship, theology, and the arts (MA); youth, family, and culture (MA). M Div offered jointly with Denver Conservative Baptist Seminary; D Min with Tyndale University College & Seminary. *Accreditation:* ACIPE; ATS (one or more programs are accredited). Part-time and evening/weekend programs available. *Degree requirements:* For doctorate, variable foreign language requirement, thesis/dissertation; for M Div, 2 foreign languages. *Entrance requirements:* For doctorate, GRE General Test. *Faculty research:* New Testament, Old Testament, systematic theology, history, practical theology.

Gardner-Webb University, School of Divinity, Boiling Springs, NC 28017. Offers biblical studies (M Div); Christian education and formation (M Div); ministry (D Min); missiology (M Div); pastoral care and counseling (M Div); pastoral studies (M Div); M Div/MA; M Div/MBA. *Accreditation:* ACIPE; ATS. Part-time programs available. *Faculty:* 11 full-time (9 women), 5 part-time/adjunct (2 women). *Students:* 138 full-time (63 women), 81 part-time (26 women); includes 74 Black or African American, non-Hispanic/Latino; 1 Asian, non-Hispanic/Latino; 3 Hispanic/Latino, 2 international. Average age 40. In 2010, 56 first professional degrees, 1 doctorate awarded. *Degree requirements:* For M Div, 2 foreign languages. *Entrance requirements:* For M Div, minimum GPA of 2.0; for doctorate, minimum GPA of 2.75. *Application deadline:* For fall admission, 8/1 priority date for domestic students; for spring admission, 12/15 priority date for domestic students. Applications are processed on a rolling basis. Application fee: $40. *Expenses:* Contact institution. *Financial support:* Fellowships, institutionally sponsored loans and unspecified assistantships available. Support available to part-time students. Financial award application deadline: 5/15. *Faculty research:* Jewish Christian dialogue, Islam. *Unit head:* Dr. Robert W. Canoy, Dean, 704-406-4400, Fax: 704-406-3935, E-mail: rcanoy@gardner-webb.edu. *Application contact:* Jeremy Fern, Director of Admissions, 704-406-3205, Fax: 704-406-3935, E-mail: jfern@gardner-webb.edu.

Garrett-Evangelical Theological Seminary, Graduate and Professional Programs, Evanston, IL 60201-3298. Offers Bible and culture (PhD); Christian education (MA); Christian education and congregational studies (PhD); contemporary theology and culture (PhD); divinity (M Div); ethics, church, and society (MA); liturgical studies (PhD); ministry (D Min); music ministry (MA); pastoral care and counseling (MA); pastoral theology, personality, and culture (PhD); spiritual formation and evangelism (MA); theological studies (MTS); M Div/MSW. M Div/MSW offered jointly with Loyola University Chicago. *Accreditation:* ACIPE; ATS (one or more programs are accredited). Part-time programs available. *Degree requirements:* For master's, thesis (for some programs); for doctorate, thesis/dissertation. *Entrance requirements:* For doctorate, GRE (PhD). Additional exam requirements/recommendations for international students: Required—TOEFL (minimum score 560 paper-based; 230 computer-based). Electronic applications accepted.

General Theological Seminary, Graduate and Professional Programs, New York, NY 10011-4977. Offers Anglican studies (STM, Th D, Certificate); ascetical theology (Certificate); biblical studies (Certificate); congregational development (Certificate); divinity (M Div); historical and theological studies (Certificate); spiritual direction (MASD, STM, Certificate); theology (MA). *Accreditation:* ACIPE; ATS. Part-time and evening/weekend programs available. Terminal master's awarded for partial completion of doctoral program. *Degree requirements:* For master's, thesis; for doctorate, 2 foreign languages, thesis/dissertation. *Entrance requirements:* For M Div, GRE General Test, bishop's endorsement; for master's, GRE General Test; for doctorate, GRE, M Div or MA. Additional exam requirements/recommendations for international students: Required—TOEFL. *Faculty research:* Liturgy, New Testament, ethics, history, ecumenical relations.

George Fox University, George Fox Evangelical Seminary, Newberg, OR 97132-2697. Offers Biblical studies (M Div); Christian earthkeeping (M Div); Christian history and theology (M Div); clinical pastoral education and hospital chaplaincy (M Div); leadership and spiritual formation (D Min), including global missional leadership, semiotics and future studies; military chaplaincy (M Div); ministry leadership (MA); pastoral studies (M Div); spiritual formation (MA, Certificate); spiritual formation and discipleship (M Div); theological studies (MA). *Accreditation:* ACIPE; ATS. Part-time programs available. Postbaccalaureate distance learning degree programs offered (minimal on-campus study). *Faculty:* 7 full-time (2 women), 23 part-time/adjunct (6 women). *Students:* 122 full-time (41 women), 236 part-time (76 women); includes 6 Black or African American, non-Hispanic/Latino; 2 American Indian or Alaska Native, non-Hispanic/Latino; 11 Asian, non-Hispanic/Latino; 4 Hispanic/Latino; 4 Two or more races, non-Hispanic/Latino, 14 international. Average age 40. 141 applicants, 94% accepted, 95 enrolled. In 2010, 19 first professional degrees, 33 master's, 17 doctorates, 3 other advanced degrees awarded. *Degree requirements:* For master's, variable foreign language requirement, thesis optional, internship; for doctorate, comprehensive exam (for some programs), thesis/dissertation, internship. *Entrance requirements:* For master's, resume, three references (one pastoral, one academic or professional, one personal), one official transcript from each college or university attended; for doctorate, resume, 3 references (1 professional, 1 academic, 1 personal). Additional exam requirements/recommendations for international students: Required—TOEFL (minimum score 577 paper-based; 233 computer-based; 90 iBT). *Application deadline:* For fall admission, 7/1 for domestic and international students; for winter admission, 11/1 for domestic and international students; for spring admission, 4/1 for domestic and international students. Applications are processed on a rolling basis. Application fee: $40. Electronic applications accepted. *Expenses:* Contact institution. *Financial support:* Career-related internships or fieldwork and scholarships/grants available. Financial award application deadline: 5/1; financial award applicants required to submit FAFSA. *Unit head:* Dr. Chuck Conniry, Professor of Theology/Vice President and Dean, 503-554-6152, E-mail: cconniry@georgefox.edu. *Application contact:* Sheila Bartlett, Admissions Counselor, 800-631-0921, Fax: 503-554-6122, E-mail: gfes@georgefox.edu.

Georgetown University, Graduate School of Arts and Sciences, Department of Theology, Washington, DC 20057. Offers PhD.

Georgian Court University, School of Arts and Sciences, Lakewood, NJ 08701-2697. Offers biology (MA); Catholic school leadership (Certificate); clinical mental health counseling (MA); holistic health studies (MA); mathematics (MA); pastoral ministry (Certificate); religious education (Certificate); school psychology (Certificate); theology (MA, Certificate). Part-time and evening/weekend programs available. *Faculty:* 19 full-time (11 women), 7 part-time/adjunct (5 women). *Students:* 61 full-time (59 women), 143 part-time (113 women); includes 20 minority (5 Black or African American, non-Hispanic/Latino; 3 Asian, non-Hispanic/Latino; 11 Hispanic/Latino; 1 Two or more races, non-Hispanic/Latino), 1 international. Average age 39. 139 applicants, 59% accepted, 50 enrolled. In 2010, 5 master's awarded. *Degree requirements:* For master's, comprehensive exam (for some programs), thesis (for some programs). *Entrance requirements:* For master's, GRE, MAT, or NTE/PRAXIS, 3 letters of recommendation. Additional exam requirements/recommendations for international students: Required—TOEFL (minimum score 550 paper-based; 213 computer-based). *Application deadline:* For fall admission, 8/1 priority date for domestic students, 4/1 for international students; for spring admission, 1/1 priority date for domestic students, 7/1 for international students. Applications are processed on a rolling basis. Application fee: $40. Electronic applications accepted. *Expenses:* Tuition: Full-time $12,510; part-time $695 per credit. Required fees: $416 per year. Tuition and fees vary according to campus/location and program. *Financial support:* Scholarships/grants, health care benefits, and unspecified assistantships available. Financial award application deadline: 4/15; financial award applicants required to submit FAFSA. *Unit head:* Dr. Linda James, Dean, 732-987-2617, Fax: 732-987-2007. *Application contact:* Patrick Givens, Assistant Director of Admissions, 732-987-2736, Fax: 732-987-2084, E-mail: graduateadmissions@georgian.edu.

Global University, Graduate School of Theology, Springfield, MO 65804. Offers biblical studies (MA); divinity (M Div); ministerial studies (MA), including education, leadership, missions, New Testament, Old Testament. Part-time and evening/weekend programs available. Postbaccalaureate distance learning degree programs offered (no on-campus study). *Degree requirements:* For master's, thesis (for some programs). *Entrance requirements:* For M Div, minimum undergraduate GPA of 3.0; for master's, minimum undergraduate GPA of 3.0, 15 undergraduate credit hours of course work in Bible or theology. Electronic applications accepted. *Faculty research:* Higher education, cross-cultural missions.

Golden Gate Baptist Theological Seminary, Graduate and Professional Programs, Mill Valley, CA 94941-3197. Offers divinity (M Div); early childhood education (Certificate); education leadership (MAEL, Diploma); ministry (D Min); theological studies (MTS); theology (Th M); youth ministry (Certificate). *Accreditation:* ACIPE; ATS (one or more programs are accredited). Part-time and evening/weekend programs available. *Degree requirements:* For master's, thesis (for some programs); for doctorate, 2 foreign languages, thesis/dissertation; for M Div, 2 foreign languages. *Entrance requirements:* For doctorate, MAT. Additional exam requirements/recommendations for international students: Required—TOEFL (minimum score 550 paper-based; 213 computer-based). Electronic applications accepted.

Gordon-Conwell Theological Seminary, Graduate and Professional Programs, South Hamilton, MA 01982. Offers Biblical languages (MABL); church history (MACH); counseling (MACO); ministry (D Min); missions/evangelism (MAME); New Testament (MANT); Old Testament (MAOT); religion (MAR); theology (M Div, MATH, Th M, Th D). *Accreditation:* ACIPE; ATS (one or more programs are accredited). Part-time and evening/weekend programs available. *Degree requirements:* For master's, one foreign language, thesis optional; for doctorate, 2 foreign languages, thesis/dissertation; for M Div, 2 foreign languages. *Entrance requirements:* For M Div and master's, minimum GPA of 2.5; for doctorate, minimum GPA of 3.0.

Graceland University, Community of Christ Seminary, Independence, MO 64050. Offers Christian ministry (MACM); religion (MAR). Part-time programs available. Postbaccalaureate distance learning degree programs offered (minimal on-campus study). *Faculty:* 2 full-time (1 woman), 9 part-time/adjunct (3 women). *Students:* 4 full-time (all women), 13 part-time (8 women); includes 1 Black or African American, non-Hispanic/Latino, 1 international. Average age 41. 15 applicants, 80% accepted, 7 enrolled. In 2010, 6 master's awarded. *Degree requirements:* For master's, thesis optional, portfolio or thesis (MAR), practicum (MACM). *Entrance requirements:* For master's, minimum cumulative GPA of 3.0. Additional exam requirements/recommendations for international students: Required—TOEFL. *Application deadline:* For fall admission, 8/15 priority date for domestic students; for winter admission, 10/15 priority date for domestic students; for spring admission, 4/15 priority date for domestic students. Applications are processed on a rolling basis. Application fee: $50. *Expenses:* Contact institution. *Financial support:* Scholarships/grants available. Financial award application deadline: 12/15; financial award applicants required to submit FAFSA. *Faculty research:* Theology, scripture. *Unit head:* Dr. Don H. Compier, Dean, 800-833-0524 Ext. 4900, Fax: 816-833-2990, E-mail: dcompier@graceland.edu. *Application contact:* Judy K. Luffman, Executive Assistant, 816-833-0524 Ext. 4508, Fax: 816-833-2990, E-mail: luffman@graceland.edu.

Grace Theological Seminary, Graduate and Professional Programs, Winona Lake, IN 46590-9907. Offers biblical studies (Certificate); camp administration (MA); counseling (M Div); exegetical studies (MA); intercultural studies (M Div, MA); local church studies (MA); pastoral studies (M Div); theological studies (MA); theology (D Min, Diploma). Part-time programs available. Postbaccalaureate distance learning degree programs offered (no on-campus study). *Degree requirements:* For master's, thesis optional; for doctorate, 2 foreign languages, thesis/dissertation; for M Div, 2 foreign languages, thesis/dissertation optional. *Entrance requirements:* For M Div and master's, MAT, minimum GPA of 2.5. Electronic applications accepted. *Faculty research:* Biblical theology, language, and church ministries.

Grace University, College of Graduate Studies, Bible Department, Omaha, NE 68108. Offers MA. *Degree requirements:* For master's, thesis optional. *Entrance requirements:* For master's, minimum undergraduate GPA of 3.0. Electronic applications accepted.

Graduate Theological Union, Graduate Programs, Berkeley, CA 94709-1212. Offers art and religion (MA, PhD, Th D); biblical languages (MA); biblical studies (MA); Biblical studies (PhD, Th D); Buddhist studies (MA); Christian spirituality (MA, PhD, Th D); cultural and historical studies of religions (MA, PhD, Th D); ethics and social theory (PhD, Th D); history (MA, PhD, Th D); homiletics (MA, PhD, Th D); interdisciplinary studies (PhD, Th D); Jewish studies (MA, PhD, Th D, Certificate); liturgical studies (MA, PhD, Th D); Near Eastern religions (PhD, Th D); Orthodox Christian studies (MA); religion and psychology (MA, PhD, Th D); religion and society/ethics and social theory (MA); systematic and philosophical theology (MA, PhD, Th D). PhD programs in Jewish studies and Near Eastern religions offered jointly with University of California, Berkeley. *Accreditation:* ATS. Terminal master's awarded for partial completion of doctoral program. *Degree requirements:* For master's, one foreign language, thesis; for doctorate, one foreign language, comprehensive exam, thesis/dissertation. *Entrance requirements:* For master's, GRE General Test; for doctorate, GRE General Test, MA or M Div. Additional exam requirements/recommendations for international students: Required—TOEFL. Electronic applications accepted.

Grand Rapids Theological Seminary of Cornerstone University, Graduate Programs, Grand Rapids, MI 49525-5897. Offers biblical counseling (MA); Biblical counseling (M Div); chaplaincy (M Div); Christian education (M Div, MA); intercultural studies (M Div, MA); New Testament (MA, Th M); Old Testament (MA, Th M); pastoral studies (M Div); systematic theology (MA); theology (Th M). *Accreditation:* ATS. Part-time programs available. Postbaccalaureate distance learning degree programs offered (minimal on-campus study). *Entrance requirements:* Additional exam requirements/recommendations for international students: Required—TOEFL (minimum score 577 paper-based; 233 computer-based; 90 iBT). Electronic applications accepted.

Harding University Graduate School of Religion, Graduate Programs, Memphis, TN 38117-5499. Offers Christian ministry (MA); counseling (MA); ministry (M Div, D Min); religion (MA). *Accreditation:* ATS. Part-time programs available. Postbaccalaureate distance learning degree programs offered (minimal on-campus study). *Degree requirements:* For master's, variable foreign language requirement, thesis (for some programs); for doctorate, one foreign language, thesis/dissertation; for M Div, 2 foreign languages, thesis/dissertation optional. *Entrance requirements:* For M Div, GRE General Test (for graduates of non-accredited schools), minimum GPA of 2.5; for master's, minimum GPA of 2.7; for doctorate, minimum GPA of 3.0. Additional exam requirements/recommendations for international students: Required—TOEFL (minimum score 550 paper-based; 213 computer-based; 79 iBT). Electronic applications accepted.

Hardin-Simmons University, Graduate School, Logsdon School of Theology, Abilene, TX 79698-0001. Offers M Div, MA, D Min. Part-time and evening/weekend programs available. *Faculty:* 18 full-time (1 woman), 7 part-time/adjunct (2 women). *Students:* 57 full-time (15 women), 75 part-time (14 women); includes 8 Black or African American, non-Hispanic/Latino; 2 American Indian or Alaska Native, non-Hispanic/Latino; 1 Asian, non-Hispanic/Latino; 9 Hispanic/Latino. Average age 33. 49 applicants, 80% accepted, 35 enrolled. In 2010, 17 first professional degrees, 5 master's awarded. *Entrance requirements:* Additional exam requirements/recommendations for international students: Required—TOEFL (minimum score 550 paper-based; 213 computer-based; 75 iBT). *Application deadline:* For fall admission, 8/15 priority date for domestic students, 4/1 for international students; for spring admission, 1/5 priority date for domestic students, 9/1 for international students. Applications are processed on a rolling basis. Application fee: $50. *Expenses:* Tuition: Full-time $12,150; part-time $675 per credit hour. Required fees: $650; $110 per semester. Tuition and fees vary according to degree level. *Financial support:* In 2010–11, 102 students received support; fellowships, scholarships/grants available. Support available to part-time students. Financial award application deadline: 6/30; financial award applicants required to submit FAFSA. *Unit head:* Dr. Don Williford, Interim Dean, 325-670-1266, Fax: 325-670-1406, E-mail: willifrd@hsutx.edu. *Application contact:* Dr. Nancy Kucinski, Dean of Graduate Studies, 325-670-1298, Fax: 325-670-1564, E-mail: gradoff@hsutx.edu.

Hardin-Simmons University, Graduate School, Logsdon School of Theology, Logsdon Seminary, Seminary Program in Theology, Abilene, TX 79698-0001. Offers M Div. *Accreditation:* ATS. Part-time programs available. *Faculty:* 16 full-time (1 woman), 7 part-time/adjunct (2 women). *Students:* 42 full-time (8 women), 42 part-time (8 women); includes 6 Black or African American, non-Hispanic/Latino; 2 American Indian or Alaska Native, non-Hispanic/Latino; 1 Asian, non-Hispanic/Latino; 8 Hispanic/Latino. Average age 32. 25 applicants, 76% accepted, 16 enrolled. In 2010, 17 M Divs awarded. *Degree requirements:* For M Div, 2 foreign languages, chapel/spiritual formations, colloquium, ministry retreat and formation conferences. *Entrance requirements:* Minimum GPA of 2.0, interview, 3 letters of recommendation. Additional exam requirements/recommendations for international students: Required—TOEFL (minimum score 550 paper-based; 213 computer-based; 75 iBT). *Application deadline:* For fall admission, 8/15 priority date for domestic students, 4/1 for international students; for spring admission, 1/5 priority date for domestic students, 9/1 for international students. Applications are processed on a rolling basis. Application fee: $50. *Expenses:* Tuition: Full-time $12,150; part-time $675 per credit hour. Required fees: $650; $110 per semester. Tuition and fees vary according to degree level. *Financial support:* In 2010–11, 54 students received support; fellowships, career-related internships or fieldwork and scholarships/grants available. Support available to part-time students. Financial award application deadline: 6/30; financial award applicants required to submit FAFSA. *Faculty research:* Hebrew grammar, history of Christian education, training of ministers into the twenty-first century, role of women in the Old Testament, contemporary ethical issues, Ricouer in contemporary theology. *Unit head:* Dr. Robert Ellis, Director, 325-670-5841, E-mail: rellis@hsutx.edu. *Application contact:* Dr. Nancy Kucinski, Dean of Graduate Studies, 325-670-1298, Fax: 325-670-1564, E-mail: gradoff@hsutx.edu.

Hartford Seminary, Graduate Programs, Hartford, CT 06105-2279. Offers Islamic studies (MA); ministry (D Min); religious studies (MA); spirituality (Certificate). *Accreditation:* ATS (one or more programs are accredited). Part-time and evening/weekend programs available. Postbaccalaureate distance learning degree programs offered (no on-campus study). *Faculty:* 15 full-time (3 women), 19 part-time/adjunct (7 women). *Students:* 37 full-time (17 women), 121 part-time (68 women); includes 35 minority (27 Black or African American, non-Hispanic/Latino; 5 Asian, non-Hispanic/Latino; 3 Hispanic/Latino), 25 international. *Degree requirements:* For master's, thesis optional, oral exam; for doctorate, thesis/dissertation, oral exam. *Entrance requirements:* For doctorate, experience in ministry, M Div. Additional exam requirements/recommendations for international students: Required—TOEFL (minimum score 550 paper-based; 213 computer-based; 80 iBT). *Application deadline:* For fall admission, 7/15 priority date for domestic students, 5/1 priority date for international students; for winter admission, 12/1 priority date for domestic students, 4/1 priority date for international students; for spring admission, 4/5 priority date for domestic students, 3/1 priority date for international students. Applications are processed on a rolling basis. Application fee: $50. *Expenses:* Tuition: Full-time $10,680; part-time $1780 per course. *Financial support:* In 2010–11, 74 students received support. Scholarships/grants and tuition waivers (partial) available. Support available to part-time students. Financial award application deadline: 6/1. *Faculty research:* Liturgy and social justice, professional leadership in ministry, congregational studies, Christian-Muslim relations, American religion. *Unit head:* Dr. Efrain Agosto, Dean, 860-509-9554, E-mail: eagosto@hartsem.edu. *Application contact:* Dr. Vanessa Avery, Admissions and Recruitment Manager, 860-509-9552, Fax: 860-509-9509, E-mail: vavery@hartsem.edu.

Harvard University, Harvard Divinity School, Cambridge, MA 02138. Offers M Div, MTS, Th M, Th D. *Accreditation:* ACIPE; ATS. *Faculty:* 45 full-time (19 women), 58 part-time/adjunct (23 women). *Students:* 362 full-time (191 women); includes 24 Black or African American, non-Hispanic/Latino; 2 American Indian or Alaska Native, non-Hispanic/Latino; 19 Asian, non-Hispanic/Latino; 28 Hispanic/Latino; 13 Two or more races, non-Hispanic/Latino, 37 international. Average age 26. 481 applicants, 42% accepted, 130 enrolled. In 2010, 56 M Divs, 94 master's, 5 doctorates awarded. *Degree requirements:* For master's, one foreign language, thesis (for some programs); for doctorate, 3 foreign languages, comprehensive exam, thesis/dissertation; for M Div, one foreign language, thesis/dissertation, field education. *Entrance requirements:* For M Div, master's, and doctorate, GRE General Test. Additional exam requirements/recommendations for international students: Required—TOEFL (minimum score 600 paper-based; 250 computer-based; 100 iBT). *Application deadline:* For fall admission, 1/11 for domestic and international students. Application fee: $75. Electronic applications accepted. *Expenses:* Contact institution. *Financial support:* In 2010–11, 317 students received support, including 317 fellowships with tuition reimbursements available (averaging $26,986 per year); teaching assistantships, career-related internships or fieldwork, Federal Work-Study, and scholarships/grants also available. Support available to part-time students. Financial award application deadline: 2/1; financial award applicants required to submit FAFSA. *Faculty research:* Theology, women's studies, history, comparative religion. *Unit head:* William A.

Theology

Harvard University (continued)

Graham, Dean of the Faculty of Divinity, 917-495-4513, Fax: 617-496-8026. *Application contact:* Loida Feliz, Director of Admissions, 617-495-5796, Fax: 617-495-0345, E-mail: admissions@hds.harvard.edu.

Hebrew College, Rabbinical School, Newton Centre, MA 02459. Offers MA. *Entrance requirements:* For master's, interview. Additional exam requirements/recommendations for international students: Required—TOEFL.

Hebrew Union College–Jewish Institute of Religion, Rabbinical School, New York, NY 10012-1186. Offers MAHL. *Degree requirements:* For MAHL, one foreign language, thesis/dissertation, fieldwork, sermons. *Entrance requirements:* GRE, language exam, minimum GPA of 3.0, minimum 2 years of college-level Hebrew. Additional exam requirements/recommendations for international students: Required—TOEFL. *Faculty research:* Philosophy and theology, Bible, Hebrew, pastoral care, history and Rabbinics.

Hebrew Union College–Jewish Institute of Religion, School of Graduate Studies, Program in Pastoral Counseling, New York, NY 10012-1186. Offers D Min. *Accreditation:* ACIPE. *Degree requirements:* For doctorate, thesis/dissertation. *Entrance requirements:* For doctorate, M Div (or higher), ordination/certification for ministry. Additional exam requirements/recommendations for international students: Required—TOEFL. *Expenses:* Contact institution. *Faculty research:* Philosophy and theology, Bible, Hebrew, pastoral care, history and Rabbinics.

Heritage Baptist College and Heritage Theological Seminary, Program in Theological Studies, Cambridge, ON N3C 3T2, Canada. Offers chaplaincy (M Div); counselling (M Div); general (M Div); ministry (D Min); pastoral (M Div); research (M Div); theological studies (MA, Certificate). *Accreditation:* ATS.

Holy Apostles College and Seminary, Department of Theology, Cromwell, CT 06416-2005. Offers bioethics (MA, Certificate, Post Master's Certificate); church history (MA, Certificate, Post Master's Certificate); dogmatic theology (MA, Certificate, Post Master's Certificate); liturgical music (MA, Certificate, Post Master's Certificate); liturgy (MA, Certificate, Post Master's Certificate); moral theology (MA, Certificate, Post Master's Certificate); philosophical theology (MA, Certificate, Post Master's Certificate); religious education (MA, Certificate, Post Master's Certificate); sacred scripture (MA, Post Master's Certificate); sacred scriptures (Certificate); theology (M Div). Part-time and evening/weekend programs available. Postbaccalaureate distance learning degree programs offered (no on-campus study). *Degree requirements:* For master's, one foreign language, comprehensive exam, thesis optional; for other advanced degree, culminating paper. *Entrance requirements:* For M Div, interview; for master's, minimum undergraduate GPA of 3.0; for other advanced degree, minimum graduate GPA of 3.0. Electronic applications accepted. *Faculty research:* Roman Catholic theology, philosophy.

Holy Cross Greek Orthodox School of Theology, Theological Programs, Brookline, MA 02445-7496. Offers M Div, MTS, Th M. *Accreditation:* ATS. Part-time programs available. *Faculty:* 10 full-time (1 woman), 10 part-time/adjunct (2 women). *Students:* 136 full-time (15 women), 11 part-time (2 women); includes 1 Black or African American, non-Hispanic/Latino; 1 Hispanic/Latino, 14 international. Average age 25. 62 applicants, 87% accepted, 46 enrolled. In 2010, 22 M Divs, 14 master's awarded. *Degree requirements:* For master's, 2 foreign languages, thesis (for some programs); for M Div, 2 foreign languages, thesis/dissertation (for some programs). *Entrance requirements:* For M Div and master's, GRE General Test, interview, written submission, official transcripts, letters of recommendation, health form. Additional exam requirements/recommendations for international students: Required—TOEFL (minimum score 550 paper-based; 213 computer-based; 80 iBT). *Application deadline:* For fall admission, 8/15 for domestic students, 8/1 for international students; for spring admission, 1/3 for domestic students. Application fee: $50. *Expenses:* Tuition: Full-time $19,136; part-time $797.34 per credit. Required fees: $500. *Financial support:* In 2010–11, 26 students received support, including 20 teaching assistantships (averaging $525 per year); research assistantships, Federal Work-Study, scholarships/grants, and tuition waivers (partial) also available. Financial award application deadline: 4/1; financial award applicants required to submit FAFSA. *Faculty research:* Spirituality, liturgies, ecumenism, church history. *Unit head:* Rev. Dr. Thomas FitzGerald, Dean, 617-731-3500 Ext. 1213, Fax: 617-850-1460, E-mail: tfitzgerald@hchc.edu. *Application contact:* Gregory Floor, Director of Admissions, 617-731-3500 Ext. 1285, Fax: 617-850-1460, E-mail: gfloor@hchc.edu.

Hood Theological Seminary, Graduate and Professional Programs, Salisbury, NC 28144. Offers M Div, MTS, D Min. *Accreditation:* ATS. Evening/weekend programs available. *Degree requirements:* For master's, thesis optional; for doctorate, thesis/dissertation; for M Div, thesis/dissertation optional. *Faculty research:* Old Testament human sexuality, preaching and the vulnerable, socio-historical issues, Pauline studies, multiculturalism/African-American studies.

Houston Baptist University, College of Arts and Humanities, Program in Theological Studies, Houston, TX 77074-3298. Offers MATS. Part-time and evening/weekend programs available. *Degree requirements:* For master's, comprehensive exam. *Entrance requirements:* For master's, GRE General Test, 6 hours of course work in Greek or Hebrew (optional), interview, minimum GPA of 2.5. Additional exam requirements/recommendations for international students: Required—TOEFL (minimum score 550 paper-based; 213 computer-based). *Expenses:* Contact institution.

Houston Graduate School of Theology, Graduate School, Houston, TX 77092. Offers counseling (MA); pastoral ministry (M Div, D Min); theology (MA). *Accreditation:* ATS (one or more programs are accredited). Part-time and evening/weekend programs available. *Degree requirements:* For master's, thesis (for some programs); for doctorate, thesis/dissertation; for M Div, thesis/dissertation optional. *Entrance requirements:* For doctorate, GRE General Test or MAT, M Div or equivalent. Additional exam requirements/recommendations for international students: Required—TOEFL (minimum score 550 paper-based; 213 computer-based). *Faculty research:* Hermeneutics, spirituality, religion of Eastern Europe.

Howard University, School of Divinity, Washington, DC 20017. Offers M Div, MARS, D Min. *Accreditation:* ACIPE; ATS. Part-time and evening/weekend programs available. *Degree requirements:* For master's, thesis; for doctorate, thesis/dissertation; for M Div, thesis/dissertation optional. *Entrance requirements:* For M Div, minimum GPA of 2.0; for master's and doctorate, minimum GPA of 3.0. Electronic applications accepted. *Faculty research:* African-American religious experience, women in ministry, ecumenics, biblical studies.

Iliff School of Theology, Graduate and Professional Programs, Denver, CO 80210-4798. Offers biblical studies (MA); church history (MA); religion (MA); religion and social change (MA); specialized ministry (MASM), including justice and peace, pastoral theology and care, religions leadership; theology (M Div, MTS, D Min, PhD), including Biblical studies (PhD), religion and psychological studies (PhD), religion and social change (PhD), theology, philosophy and culture (PhD); theology/ethics (MA). PhD offered jointly with University of Denver. *Accreditation:* ACIPE; ATS. Part-time and evening/weekend programs available. *Degree requirements:* For master's, one foreign language, thesis (for some programs); for doctorate, 2 foreign languages, comprehensive exam, thesis/dissertation; for M Div, thesis/dissertation optional. *Entrance requirements:* For M Div, minimum GPA of 2.75, references; for master's, minimum GPA of 3.0, writing sample, references; for doctorate, GRE General Test, minimum GPA of 3.0, writing sample, letters of recommendation. Additional exam requirements/recommendations for international students: Required—TOEFL (minimum score 550 paper-based). Electronic applications accepted. *Faculty research:* Pastoral care, history, church music, contemporary church, biblical studies.

Indiana Wesleyan University, Graduate School, Wesley Seminary, Master of Divinity Program, Marion, IN 46953-4974. Offers M Div. Postbaccalaureate distance learning degree programs offered (minimal on-campus study). *Degree requirements:* For M Div, capstone. *Expenses:*

Tuition: Full-time $7902; part-time $439 per credit hour. One-time fee: $290. Tuition and fees vary according to degree level, campus/location and program.

Institute for Christian Studies, Graduate Programs, Toronto, ON M5T 1R4, Canada. Offers education (M Phil F, PhD); history of philosophy (M Phil F, PhD); philosophical aesthetics (M Phil F, PhD); philosophy of religion (M Phil F, PhD); political theory (M Phil F, PhD); systematic philosophy (M Phil F, PhD); theology (M Phil F, PhD); worldview studies (MWS). Part-time programs available. Postbaccalaureate distance learning degree programs offered (minimal on-campus study). *Degree requirements:* For master's, one foreign language, thesis; for doctorate, 2 foreign languages, thesis/dissertation. *Entrance requirements:* For master's and doctorate, philosophy background. Additional exam requirements/recommendations for international students: Required—TOEFL (minimum score 600 paper-based; 250 computer-based). *Faculty research:* Human rights, anthropology of self, medieval discourse, gender and body, post-modern thought; biblical hermeneutics, creational aesthetics, ecumenism, epistemology, political theory and public policy, relational psychotherapy.

Inter American University of Puerto Rico, Metropolitan Campus, Graduate Programs, Program in Theological Studies, San Juan, PR 00919-1293. Offers PhD.

Interdenominational Theological Center, Graduate and Professional Programs, Atlanta, GA 30314-4112. Offers M Div, MACE, MACM, D Min, Th D, M Div/MACE, M Div/MACM, MACM/MACE. D Min and Th D programs offered jointly with Columbia Theological Seminary and Emory University's Candler School of Theology. *Accreditation:* ACIPE; ATS (one or more programs are accredited). Part-time and evening/weekend programs available. Postbaccalaureate distance learning degree programs offered (minimal on-campus study). *Faculty:* 20 full-time (6 women), 26 part-time/adjunct (12 women). *Students:* 236 full-time (96 women), 167 part-time (73 women); includes 388 Black or African American, non-Hispanic/Latino; 1 Asian, non-Hispanic/Latino; 1 Hispanic/Latino; 1 Two or more races, non-Hispanic/Latino, 6 international. 160 applicants, 81% accepted, 104 enrolled. In 2010, 93 first professional degrees, 4 master's awarded. *Degree requirements:* For doctorate, thesis/dissertation. *Entrance requirements:* For M Div, bachelor's degree; for doctorate, master's degree. *Application deadline:* For fall admission, 7/1 for domestic and international students; for spring admission, 11/1 for domestic and international students. Applications are processed on a rolling basis. Application fee: $50. *Expenses:* Tuition: Full-time $11,212; part-time $657 per credit. Required fees: $425 per semester. *Financial support:* Research assistantships, career-related internships or fieldwork and Federal Work-Study available. Support available to part-time students. Financial award application deadline: 6/15; financial award applicants required to submit FAFSA. *Unit head:* Dr. Ronald E. Peters, President, 404-527-7702, Fax: 404-527-7770, E-mail: rpeters@itc.edu. *Application contact:* Walter Cabassa, Office of Admission and Recruitment, 404-527-7792, E-mail: wcabassa@itc.edu.

International Baptist College, Program in Biblical Studies, Chandler, AZ 85286. Offers MA.

The Jewish Theological Seminary, The Graduate School, New York, NY 10027-4649. Offers ancient Judaism (MA, DHL, PhD); Bible and ancient Semitic languages (MA, DHL, PhD); interdepartmental studies (MA); Jewish art and visual culture (MA); Jewish gender and women's studies (MA); Jewish history (MA, DHL, PhD); Jewish literature (MA, DHL, PhD); Jewish philosophy (DHL); Jewish thought (MA, PhD); liturgy (MA, DHL, PhD); medieval Jewish studies (MA, DHL, PhD); Midrash (DHL); Midrash and scriptural interpretation (MA, PhD); modern Jewish studies (MA, DHL, PhD); Talmud and rabbinics (MA, DHL, PhD); MA/MSW. MA/MSW offered jointly with Columbia University. *Accreditation:* ACIPE. Part-time programs available. Terminal master's awarded for partial completion of doctoral program. *Degree requirements:* For master's, one foreign language, comprehensive exam (for some programs), thesis (for some programs); for doctorate, 3 foreign languages, comprehensive exam (for some programs), thesis/dissertation. *Entrance requirements:* For master's, GRE or MAT, 3 letters of recommendation, writing sample; for doctorate, GRE or MAT, 3 letters of recommendation, writing research sample. Additional exam requirements/recommendations for international students: Required—TOEFL (minimum score 100 computer-based).

The Jewish Theological Seminary, The Rabbinical School, New York, NY 10027-4649. Offers MA, Rabbi. *Accreditation:* ACIPE. *Degree requirements:* For master's and Rabbi, one foreign language, competency exams. *Entrance requirements:* For master's and Rabbi, GRE, interview, writing sample. Additional exam requirements/recommendations for international students: Required—TOEFL. *Expenses:* Contact institution.

Johnson University, Program in New Testament, Knoxville, TN 37998-1001. Offers preaching (MA); research (MA). Part-time and evening/weekend programs available. Postbaccalaureate distance learning degree programs offered (no on-campus study). *Degree requirements:* For master's, one foreign language, comprehensive exam, thesis (for some programs). *Entrance requirements:* For master's, minimum GPA of 2.5. Additional exam requirements/recommendations for international students: Required—TOEFL. *Expenses:* Tuition: Full-time $8300; part-time $320 per credit hour. Required fees: $800; $32 per hour. Part-time tuition and fees vary according to course load and program.

Kehilath Yakov Rabbinical Seminary, Graduate Programs, Ossining, NY 10562. *Accreditation:* AARTS.

Kenrick-Glennon Seminary, Graduate and Professional Programs, St. Louis, MO 63119-4330. Offers M Div, MA. *Accreditation:* ATS. *Degree requirements:* For master's, thesis optional. *Entrance requirements:* MAT.

Kentucky Christian University, Graduate School, Grayson, KY 41143-2205. Offers Biblical studies (MA); Christian leadership (MA). Part-time programs available. *Faculty:* 8 part-time/adjunct (0 women). *Students:* 6 full-time (3 women), 36 part-time (9 women), 3 international. Average age 33. 14 applicants, 86% accepted, 11 enrolled. *Degree requirements:* For master's, comprehensive exam (for some programs), thesis optional. *Entrance requirements:* For master's, minimum cumulative GPA of 2.75 in major or 2.5 overall; 6 additional hours in Bible (for non-Biblical undergraduate majors). Additional exam requirements/recommendations for international students: Required—TOEFL (minimum score 550 paper-based; 213 computer-based). *Application deadline:* Applications are processed on a rolling basis. Application fee: $35. Electronic applications accepted. *Expenses:* Tuition: Part-time $258.33 per credit. *Financial support:* Teaching assistantships with full tuition reimbursements, scholarships/grants and unspecified assistantships available. Support available to part-time students. *Unit head:* Dr. David Fiensy, Dean, 606-474-3263, Fax: 606-474-3189, E-mail: dfiensy@kcu.edu. *Application contact:* Jane Shick, Academic Office Manager, 877-811-6391, Fax: 606-474-3189, E-mail: gradstudies@kcu.edu.

Knox College, College of Theology, Toronto, ON M5S 2E6, Canada. Offers M Div, MRE, MTS, Th M, D Min, Th D. Applicants for D Min, Th M, and Th D must apply to Toronto School of Theology; MRE, M Div, MTS, Th D, and Th M programs offered jointly with University of Toronto. *Accreditation:* ATS. Part-time programs available. *Degree requirements:* For master's, one foreign language, thesis (for some programs); for doctorate, 2 foreign languages, thesis/dissertation. *Entrance requirements:* For doctorate, M Div. Additional exam requirements/recommendations for international students: Required—TOEFL (minimum score 580 paper-based; 237 computer-based), TWE (minimum score 5). *Faculty research:* Nineteenth century theologians.

Knox Theological Seminary, Graduate Programs, Program in Biblical Studies, Fort Lauderdale, FL 33308. Offers CBS. *Accreditation:* ATS. Part-time and evening/weekend programs available. *Entrance requirements:* Additional exam requirements/recommendations for international students: Required—TOEFL (minimum score 520 paper-based; 213 computer-based; 83 iBT), TWE (minimum score 5).

Knox Theological Seminary, Graduate Programs, Program in Divinity, Fort Lauderdale, FL 33308. Offers M Div. *Accreditation:* ATS. Part-time and evening/weekend programs available.

Entrance requirements: Additional exam requirements/recommendations for international students: Required—TOEFL (minimum score 520 paper-based; 213 computer-based; 83 iBT), TWE (minimum score 5).

Knox Theological Seminary, Graduate Programs, Program in New and Old Testament, Fort Lauderdale, FL 33308. Offers MBT. *Accreditation:* ATS. Part-time and evening/weekend programs available. *Degree requirements:* For master's, one foreign language, thesis. *Entrance requirements:* Additional exam requirements/recommendations for international students: Required—TOEFL, TWE (minimum score 5).

Kol Yaakov Torah Center, Graduate Program, Monsey, NY 10952-2954. Offers Advanced Rabbinic Degree. *Accreditation:* AARTS. Part-time and evening/weekend programs available. *Faculty research:* Talmud, Jewish law.

Lakeland College, Graduate Studies Division, Program in Theology, Sheboygan, WI 53082-0359. Offers MAT.

Lancaster Bible College, Graduate School, Lancaster, PA 17601-5036. Offers adult ministries (MA); Bible (MA); children and family ministry (MA); consulting resource teacher (M Ed); elementary school counseling (M Ed); leadership (PhD); leadership studies (MA); marriage and family counseling (MA); mental health counseling (MA); pastoral studies (MA); secondary school counseling (M Ed); student ministry (MA). Part-time and evening/weekend programs available. *Faculty:* 8 full-time (1 woman), 5 part-time/adjunct (1 woman). *Students:* 94 full-time (47 women), 89 part-time (45 women); includes 21 minority (15 Black or African American, non-Hispanic/Latino; 5 Asian, non-Hispanic/Latino; 1 Hispanic/Latino). Average age 36. *Degree requirements:* For master's, comprehensive exam (for some programs), thesis (for some programs). *Entrance requirements:* For master's, bachelor's degree with a minimum of 30 credits of course work in Bible, minimum undergraduate GPA of 3.0, interview. Additional exam requirements/recommendations for international students: Required—TOEFL. *Application deadline:* Applications are processed on a rolling basis. Application fee: $25. *Expenses:* Tuition: Part-time $1491 per course. Required fees: $35 per semester. *Financial support:* In 2010–11, 31 students received support; teaching assistantships, scholarships/grants and unspecified assistantships available. Support available to part-time students. Financial award application deadline: 6/1; financial award applicants required to submit FAFSA. *Unit head:* Dr. Gary Bredfeldt, Associate Vice President/Dean of iLead Center, 717-560-8297, Fax: 717-560-8236. *Application contact:* Mark Wilson, Admissions Counselor, 717-560-8229, E-mail: mwilson@lbc.edu.

Lancaster Theological Seminary, Graduate and Professional Programs, Lancaster, PA 17603-2812. Offers biblical studies (MAR); Christian education (MAR); Christianity and the arts (MAR); church history (MAR); congregational life (MAR); lay leadership (Certificate); theological studies (M Div); theology (D Min); theology and ethics (MAR). *Accreditation:* ACIPE; ATS. *Degree requirements:* For doctorate, thesis/dissertation; for M Div, one foreign language.

La Salle University, School of Arts and Sciences, Program in Theological, Pastoral and Liturgical Studies, Philadelphia, PA 19141-1199. Offers pastoral studies (MA); religion (MA); theological studies (MA). Part-time and evening/weekend programs available. *Entrance requirements:* For master's, 26 credits in humanistic subjects, religion, theology, or ministry-related work.

Lee University, Program in Religion, Cleveland, TN 37320-3450. Offers biblical studies (MA); ministry studies (MA); theological studies (MA). Part-time programs available. *Faculty:* 8 full-time (2 women), 1 part-time/adjunct (0 women). *Students:* 13 full-time (5 women), 14 part-time (5 women); includes 1 Black or African American, non-Hispanic/Latino; 1 Asian, non-Hispanic/Latino; 2 Hispanic/Latino; 1 Two or more races, non-Hispanic/Latino, 1 international. Average age 29. 11 applicants, 100% accepted, 11 enrolled. In 2010, 5 master's awarded. *Degree requirements:* For master's, comprehensive exam, thesis. *Entrance requirements:* For master's, GRE or MAT, minimum GPA of 3.0, 2 letters of recommendation, interview. Additional exam requirements/recommendations for international students: Required—TOEFL (minimum score 450 paper-based; 45 computer-based). *Application deadline:* For fall admission, 4/1 priority date for domestic students; for spring admission, 10/1 priority date for domestic students. Applications are processed on a rolling basis. Application fee: $25. *Expenses:* Tuition: Full-time $12,120; part-time $506 per credit hour. Required fees: $560; $305 per semester. Part-time tuition and fees vary according to course load and campus/location. *Financial support:* Teaching assistantships, career-related internships or fieldwork, Federal Work-Study, institutionally sponsored loans, scholarships/grants, and unspecified assistantships available. Financial award application deadline: 3/1; financial award applicants required to submit FAFSA. *Faculty research:* Book of Isaiah, Gospel of Mark, school of St. Victor of the twelfth century, spirit Christology, people groups of New Testament and work. Total annual research expenditures: $3,000. *Unit head:* Dr. Bob Bayles, Director, 423-614-8338, E-mail: bbayles@leeuniversity.edu. *Application contact:* Vicki Glasscock, Graduate Admissions Director, 423-614-8059, E-mail: vglasscock@leeuniversity.edu.

Lexington Theological Seminary, Graduate and Professional Programs, Lexington, KY 40508-3218. Offers M Div, MA, MAPS, D Min, M Div/MSW. M Div/MSW offered jointly with University of Kentucky. *Accreditation:* ACIPE; ATS. Part-time and evening/weekend programs available. *Degree requirements:* For master's, thesis; for doctorate, thesis/dissertation. *Entrance requirements:* Additional exam requirements/recommendations for international students: Required—TOEFL (minimum score 600 paper-based; 250 computer-based). *Faculty research:* History of biblical interpretation, biblical apocalyptic, psalms, history of Stone-Campbell traditions.

Liberty University, Liberty Theological Seminary and Graduate School, Lynchburg, VA 24502. Offers religious studies (M Div, MA, MAR, MRE, D Min); theology (Th M). Part-time programs available. Postbaccalaureate distance learning degree programs offered (minimal on-campus study). *Students:* 2,825 full-time (645 women), 3,515 part-time (828 women); includes 1,336 minority (996 Black or African American, non-Hispanic/Latino; 32 American Indian or Alaska Native, non-Hispanic/Latino; 108 Asian, non-Hispanic/Latino; 185 Hispanic/Latino; 11 Native Hawaiian or other Pacific Islander, non-Hispanic/Latino; 4 Two or more races, non-Hispanic/Latino), 258 international. Average age 38. In 2010, 236 first professional degrees, 1,088 master's, 76 doctorates awarded. *Degree requirements:* For master's, 2 foreign languages, thesis (for some programs); for doctorate, 2 foreign languages, thesis/dissertation. *Entrance requirements:* For M Div, minimum undergraduate GPA of 2.0; for master's, minimum undergraduate GPA of 2.0, 9 credit hours of course work in Greek, 9 credit hours of course work in Hebrew (Th M); for doctorate, GRE General Test or MAT. Additional exam requirements/recommendations for international students: Required—TOEFL (minimum score 550 paper-based; 250 computer-based; 100 iBT). *Application deadline:* For fall admission, 6/1 priority date for domestic students; for spring admission, 11/1 for domestic students. Applications are processed on a rolling basis. Application fee: $50. Electronic applications accepted. *Expenses:* Contact institution. *Financial support:* Teaching assistantships with tuition reimbursements, career-related internships or fieldwork and Federal Work-Study available. *Unit head:* Dr. Elmer Towns, Dean, 434-582-2169, Fax: 434-582-2766, E-mail: eltowns@liberty.edu. *Application contact:* Jay Bridge, Director of Graduate Admissions, 800-424-9595, Fax: 800-628-7977, E-mail: gradadmissions@liberty.edu.

Lincoln Christian Seminary, Graduate and Professional Programs, Lincoln, IL 62656-2167. Offers Bible and theology (MA); Christian ministries (MA); counseling (MA); divinity (M Div); leadership ministry (D Min); religious education (MRE). *Accreditation:* ACIPE; ATS. Part-time programs available. *Degree requirements:* For master's, 2 foreign languages, thesis; for doctorate, thesis/dissertation; for M Div, 2 foreign languages. *Entrance requirements:* For M Div and master's, minimum GPA of 2.5; for doctorate, M Div or equivalent. Additional exam requirements/recommendations for international students: Required—TOEFL (minimum score 550 paper-based; 213 computer-based). Electronic applications accepted.

Lipscomb University, Hazelip School of Theology, Nashville, TN 37204-3951. Offers biblical studies (MA); Christian studies (MA); divinity (M Div); ministry (MA); New Testament (MA); Old Testament (MA); theological studies (MTS); theology (MA). *Accreditation:* ATS. Part-time and evening/weekend programs available. *Faculty:* 10 full-time (0 women), 2 part-time/adjunct (0 women). *Students:* 18 full-time (7 women), 82 part-time (13 women); includes 15 Black or African American, non-Hispanic/Latino; 1 Hispanic/Latino, 1 international. Average age 35. 38 applicants, 97% accepted, 20 enrolled. In 2010, 7 first professional degrees, 6 master's awarded. *Degree requirements:* For master's, 2 foreign languages, comprehensive exam (for some programs); for M Div, 2 foreign languages. *Entrance requirements:* For M Div and master's, 2 references. Additional exam requirements/recommendations for international students: Required—TOEFL (minimum score 570 paper-based; 230 computer-based). *Application deadline:* For fall admission, 8/14 priority date for domestic students; for spring admission, 12/31 for domestic students. Applications are processed on a rolling basis. Application fee: $0 ($75 for international students). Electronic applications accepted. *Expenses:* Tuition: Full-time $18,149; part-time $943 per hour. Tuition and fees vary according to program. *Financial support:* Scholarships/grants available. Support available to part-time students. Financial award application deadline: 3/1; financial award applicants required to submit FAFSA. *Faculty research:* Status of Churches of Christ in foreign nations, Hebrew grammar, marriage and family. *Unit head:* Dr. Mark Black, Director, 615-966-1000 Ext. 5799, Fax: 615-966-1808, E-mail: mark.black@lipscomb.edu. *Application contact:* Kellye McCool, Information Contact, 615-966-6051, Fax: 615-966-6052, E-mail: kellye.mccool@lipscomb.edu.

Logos Evangelical Seminary, Graduate Programs, El Monte, CA 91731. Offers M Div, MA, Th M, D Min. *Accreditation:* ATS (one or more programs are accredited). Part-time programs available. *Faculty:* 10 full-time (2 women), 7 part-time/adjunct (1 woman). *Students:* 89 full-time (36 women), 61 part-time (41 women); includes 106 Asian, non-Hispanic/Latino, 44 international. Average age 48. 45 applicants, 98% accepted, 37 enrolled. In 2010, 10 first professional degrees, 4 master's, 3 doctorates awarded. *Degree requirements:* For master's, 2 foreign languages, comprehensive exam, thesis; for doctorate, thesis/dissertation; for M Div, one foreign language, field education. *Entrance requirements:* For M Div, BA with a minimum GPA of 2.66, 2 recommendations, 3 years post-baptism; for master's, MA in Biblical studies with a minimum GPA of 3.33, 1.5 years of a Biblical language, 2 recommendations, 1 research paper; for doctorate, M Div with a minimum GPA of 3.0, 3 years ministry experience, 2 recommendations. Additional exam requirements/recommendations for international students: Required—TOEFL (minimum score 450 paper-based; 133 computer-based; 45 iBT). *Application deadline:* For fall admission, 7/15 for domestic students, 5/15 for international students; for spring admission, 12/15 for domestic students, 10/15 for international students. Applications are processed on a rolling basis. Application fee: $25 ($50 for international students). Electronic applications accepted. *Expenses:* Tuition: Full-time $8320; part-time $260 per credit. *Financial support:* Application deadline: 3/1. *Faculty research:* Asian-American hermaneutics, narrative theology, Biblical studies, pastors' mental health. *Unit head:* Dr. Jeffrey Lu, Academic Dean, 626-571-5110 Ext. 126, Fax: 626-571-5119, E-mail: jefl@les.edu. *Application contact:* Becky Perng, Admission Officer, 626-571-5110 Ext. 112, Fax: 626-571-5119, E-mail: admission@les.edu.

Loras College, Graduate Division, Program in Theology and Ministry, Dubuque, IA 52004-0178. Offers ministry (MA); theology (MA). Part-time and evening/weekend programs available. *Degree requirements:* For master's, comprehensive exam (for some programs), thesis (for some programs). *Entrance requirements:* For master's, bachelor's degree or undergraduate minor in religious studies or equivalent, minimum undergraduate GPA of 2.75.

Louisville Presbyterian Theological Seminary, Graduate and Professional Programs, Louisville, KY 40205-1798. Offers Bible (MAR); divinity (M Div); ministry (D Min); religious thought (MAR); theology (Th M); JD/M Div; M Div/MBA; M Div/MS; M Div/MSW. JD/M Div, M Div/MBA, and M Div/MSW offered jointly with University of Louisville. *Accreditation:* AAMFT/COAMFTE (one or more programs are accredited); ACIPE; ATS (one or more programs are accredited). Part-time and evening/weekend programs available. *Degree requirements:* For master's, one foreign language; for doctorate, thesis/dissertation; for M Div, 2 foreign languages. *Entrance requirements:* For master's, interview; for doctorate, M Div. Additional exam requirements/recommendations for international students: Required—TOEFL (minimum score 550 paper-based; 213 computer-based). Electronic applications accepted. *Expenses:* Tuition: Full-time $9660; part-time $322 per credit hour. Required fees: $143 per semester.

Loyola Marymount University, College of Liberal Arts, Department of Theological Studies, Program in Theology, Los Angeles, CA 90045-8400. Offers MA. *Accreditation:* ATS. *Faculty:* 23 full-time (5 women), 3 part-time/adjunct (2 women). *Students:* 25 full-time (11 women), 23 part-time (10 women); includes 1 Black or African American, non-Hispanic/Latino; 5 Asian, non-Hispanic/Latino; 11 Hispanic/Latino; 2 Two or more races, non-Hispanic/Latino, 1 international. Average age 39. 26 applicants, 77% accepted, 12 enrolled. In 2010, 12 master's awarded. *Degree requirements:* For master's, comprehensive exam, thesis or alternative. *Entrance requirements:* For master's, GRE or MAT (recommended), 2 letters of recommendation, personal statement. Additional exam requirements/recommendations for international students: Required—TOEFL (minimum score 600 paper-based; 250 computer-based; 100 iBT). *Application deadline:* For fall admission, 3/1 priority date for domestic students. Application fee: $50. Electronic applications accepted. *Financial support:* In 2010–11, 33 students received support, including 7 research assistantships (averaging $1,537 per year); Federal Work-Study, scholarships/grants, and unspecified assistantships also available. Support available to part-time students. Financial award application deadline: 6/1; financial award applicants required to submit FAFSA. Total annual research expenditures: $39,474. *Application contact:* Dr. Jonathan Rothchild, Graduate Director, 310-338-1716, E-mail: jrothchild@lmu.edu.

Loyola University Chicago, Graduate School, Department of Theology, Chicago, IL 60660. Offers MA, PhD. Part-time and evening/weekend programs available. *Faculty:* 25 full-time (11 women). *Students:* 84 full-time (24 women), 7 part-time (1 woman); includes 4 minority (1 Black or African American, non-Hispanic/Latino; 1 Asian, non-Hispanic/Latino; 2 Hispanic/Latino), 6 international. Average age 33. 77 applicants, 52% accepted, 16 enrolled. In 2010, 8 master's, 5 doctorates awarded. Terminal master's awarded for partial completion of doctoral program. *Degree requirements:* For master's, comprehensive exam; for doctorate, 2 foreign languages, comprehensive exam, thesis/dissertation. *Entrance requirements:* For master's, GRE General Test, minimum GPA of 3.0, 9 hours of course work in theology; for doctorate, GRE General Test, minimum GPA of 3.0, master's degree or equivalent. Additional exam requirements/recommendations for international students: Required—TOEFL. *Application deadline:* For fall admission, 1/15 for domestic and international students; for spring admission, 12/1 for domestic and international students. Application fee: $50. Electronic applications accepted. *Expenses:* Tuition: Full-time $14,940; part-time $830 per credit hour. Required fees: $87 per semester. Part-time tuition and fees vary according to course load and program. *Financial support:* In 2010–11, 12 students received support, including 12 research assistantships (averaging $16,500 per year); fellowships, teaching assistantships, institutionally sponsored loans also available. Financial award application deadline: 1/15; financial award applicants required to submit FAFSA. *Faculty research:* Systematics, historical theology, constructive theology, scripture, theological ethics. *Unit head:* Dr. Wendy J. Cotter, CSJ, Department Chair, 773-508-8457, Fax: 773-508-2386, E-mail: wcotter@luc.edu. *Application contact:* Dr. Wendy J. Cotter, CSJ, Department Chair, 773-508-8457, Fax: 773-508-2386, E-mail: wcotter@luc.edu.

Loyola University Chicago, Institute of Pastoral Studies, Professional Program in Divinity, Chicago, IL 60660. Offers M Div, M Div/MA, M Div/MSW. *Accreditation:* ACIPE. *Faculty:* 8 full-time (2 women), 26 part-time/adjunct (12 women). *Students:* 12 full-time (6 women), 19 part-time (10 women); includes 3 minority (2 Black or African American, non-Hispanic/Latino; 1 Hispanic/Latino). Average age 41. 18 applicants, 78% accepted, 6 enrolled. In 2010, 6 first professional degrees awarded. *Degree requirements:* For M Div, project. *Entrance requirements:* Minimum GPA of 3.0, 1 year of ministry experience. Additional exam requirements/recommendations for international students: Required—TOEFL. *Application deadline:* For fall admission, 8/1 priority date for domestic students; for spring admission, 12/1 priority date for

Theology

Loyola University Chicago (continued)
domestic students. Applications are processed on a rolling basis. Application fee: $50. Electronic applications accepted. *Expenses:* Contact institution. *Financial support:* In 2010–11, 9 students received support. Career-related internships or fieldwork, Federal Work-Study, institutionally sponsored loans, and scholarships/grants available. Support available to part-time students. Financial award application deadline: 2/1; financial award applicants required to submit FAFSA. *Faculty research:* Women leadership development for professionals in ministry, religious memoirs, passing on the values of Jesus, justice. *Unit head:* Dr. Robert T. O'Gorman, Professor, 312-915-7485, Fax: 312-915-7410, E-mail: rogorma@luc.edu. *Application contact:* Randy Gibbons, Administrative Assistant, 312-915-7450, Fax: 312-915-7410, E-mail: rgibbon@luc.edu.

Loyola University Chicago, Institute of Pastoral Studies, Program in Pastoral Counseling, Chicago, IL 60660. Offers MA, Certificate. *Accreditation:* ACIPE. Part-time programs available. *Faculty:* 6 full-time (2 women), 12 part-time/adjunct (7 women). *Students:* 31 full-time (14 women), 25 part-time (19 women); includes 13 minority (4 Black or African American, non-Hispanic/Latino; 3 Asian, non-Hispanic/Latino; 5 Hispanic/Latino; 1 Two or more races, non-Hispanic/Latino), 7 international. Average age 41. 33 applicants, 82% accepted, 16 enrolled. In 2010, 13 master's awarded. *Degree requirements:* For master's, thesis or alternative, integration project. *Application deadline:* For fall admission, 2/15 priority date for domestic students. Applications are processed on a rolling basis. Application fee: $50. Electronic applications accepted. *Expenses:* Tuition: Full-time $14,940; part-time $830 per credit hour. Required fees: $87 per semester. Part-time tuition and fees vary according to course load and program. *Financial support:* In 2010–11, 7 students received support. Career-related internships or fieldwork, Federal Work-Study, and institutionally sponsored loans available. Support available to part-time students. Financial award application deadline: 3/1; financial award applicants required to submit FAFSA. *Faculty research:* Pastoral psychotherapy, enrichment outcome, marriage and family therapy, marriage and family spirituality, gender and ethnicity issues, theological anthropology. *Unit head:* Dr. Paul R. Giblin, Associate Professor, 312-915-7483, Fax: 312-915-7410, E-mail: pgibli@luc.edu. *Application contact:* Dr. Paul R. Giblin, Associate Professor, 312-915-7483, Fax: 312-915-7410, E-mail: pgibli@luc.edu.

Loyola University Chicago, Institute of Pastoral Studies, Program in Spirituality/Spiritual Direction, Chicago, IL 60660. Offers contemporary spirituality (MA); spirituality (MA, Certificate). *Students:* 5 full-time (0 women), 25 part-time (20 women); includes 4 minority (1 Black or African American, non-Hispanic/Latino; 2 Asian, non-Hispanic/Latino; 1 Hispanic/Latino), 2 international. Average age 51. 12 applicants, 67% accepted, 7 enrolled. In 2010, 7 master's awarded. *Expenses:* Tuition: Full-time $14,940; part-time $830 per credit hour. Required fees: $87 per semester. Part-time tuition and fees vary according to course load and program. *Unit head:* Dr. Robert A. Ludwig. *Application contact:* Randy Gibbons, Administrative Assistant, 312-915-7450, Fax: 312-915-7410, E-mail: rgibbon@luc.edu.

Loyola University New Orleans, College of Social Sciences, Loyola Institute for Ministry, New Orleans, LA 70118-6195. Offers pastoral studies (MPS); religious education (MRE); theology and ministry (Certificate). Part-time and evening/weekend programs available. Postbaccalaureate distance learning degree programs offered (no on-campus study). *Students:* 5 full-time (3 women), 305 part-time (206 women); includes 19 Black or African American, non-Hispanic/Latino; 4 American Indian or Alaska Native, non-Hispanic/Latino; 2 Asian, non-Hispanic/Latino; 30 Hispanic/Latino, 2 international. Average age 51. 84 applicants, 99% accepted, 56 enrolled. In 2010, 62 master's, 40 other advanced degrees awarded. *Entrance requirements:* For master's, minimum GPA of 2.5, resume, 2 letters of recommendation, work experience. Additional exam requirements/recommendations for international students: Required—TOEFL (minimum score 550 paper-based; 213 computer-based). *Application deadline:* Applications are processed on a rolling basis. Application fee: $20. Electronic applications accepted. *Financial support:* Career-related internships or fieldwork, scholarships/grants, health care benefits, tuition waivers (partial), and room and board assistance available. Support available to part-time students. Financial award application deadline: 5/1; financial award applicants required to submit FAFSA. *Faculty research:* Practical theology, ministry education, small Christian communities, religion and ecology, Christian spirituality. *Unit head:* Dr. Tom Ryan, Director, 504-865-2069, Fax: 504-865-2066, E-mail: tfryan@loyno.edu. *Application contact:* Cecelia M. Bennett, Associate Director, 504-865-3398, Fax: 504-865-2066, E-mail: abennett@loyno.edu.

Lubbock Christian University, Graduate Biblical Studies, Lubbock, TX 79407-2099. Offers Bible and ministry (MS); biblical interpretation (MA). Part-time programs available. *Degree requirements:* For master's, one foreign language, thesis (for some programs). *Entrance requirements:* For master's, GRE General Test or MAT. *Faculty research:* Commentary on John, commentary on First and Second Thessalonians, mission teams, church leadership, family systems.

Lutheran School of Theology at Chicago, Graduate and Professional Programs, Chicago, IL 60615-5199. Offers ministry (MAM, D Min); theological studies (MATS, PhD); theology (M Div, Th M). *Accreditation:* ACIPE; ATS (one or more programs are accredited). Part-time programs available. *Faculty:* 20 full-time (6 women), 18 part-time/adjunct (5 women). *Students:* 195 full-time (96 women), 87 part-time (48 women). Terminal master's awarded for partial completion of doctoral program. *Degree requirements:* For master's, variable foreign language requirement; for doctorate, variable foreign language requirement, comprehensive exam, thesis/dissertation; for M Div, 2 foreign languages. *Entrance requirements:* For master's, GRE (Th M), M Div or equivalent (Th M); for doctorate, GRE, M Div or equivalent, 3 years of professional experience (D Min). Additional exam requirements/recommendations for international students: Required—TOEFL (for Th M). *Application deadline:* Applications are processed on a rolling basis. Application fee: $50. *Expenses:* Tuition: Full-time $12,294; part-time $1366 per course. Required fees: $35 per semester. Tuition and fees vary according to degree level and program. *Financial support:* Career-related internships or fieldwork and scholarships/grants available. Support available to part-time students. *Unit head:* Michael Shelley, Dean, 773-256-0722, Fax: 773-256-0782, E-mail: mshelley@lstc.edu. *Application contact:* Dorothy C. Dominiak, Director of Financial Aid and Admissions, 773-256-0726, Fax: 773-256-0782, E-mail: ddominia@lstc.edu.

Lutheran Theological Seminary, Graduate and Professional Programs, Saskatoon, SK S7N 0X3, Canada. Offers Biblical studies (MTS); church history (MTS); ethics/church and society (MTS); history of Christianity (STM); New Testament (STM); Old Testament (STM); pastoral studies (STM); pastoral theology (MTS); systematic theology (MTS); systematic theology and philosophy of religion (STM); theology (M Div, D Div). STM programs offered jointly with College of Emmanuel and St. Chad and St. Andrew's College. *Accreditation:* ATS. Part-time programs available. *Degree requirements:* For master's, thesis; for M Div, Greek, Hebrew.

Lutheran Theological Seminary at Gettysburg, Graduate and Professional Programs, Gettysburg, PA 17325-1795. Offers divinity (M Div); ministerial studies (MAMS); outdoor ministry (MAR); parish ministry (D Min); theology (STM). *Accreditation:* ACIPE; ATS (one or more programs are accredited). Part-time programs available. Postbaccalaureate distance learning degree programs offered (no on-campus study). *Degree requirements:* For master's, thesis (for some programs); for M Div, one foreign language. Electronic applications accepted.

The Lutheran Theological Seminary at Philadelphia, Graduate School, Philadelphia, PA 19119-1794. Offers divinity (M Div); ministry (D Min); public leadership (MA); religion (MAR); social ministry (Certificate); theology (STM, PhD). *Accreditation:* ACIPE; ATS. Part-time and evening/weekend programs available. *Faculty:* 18 full-time (5 women), 22 part-time/adjunct (8 women). *Students:* 121 full-time (56 women), 204 part-time (97 women); includes 92 minority (80 Black or African American, non-Hispanic/Latino; 2 Asian, non-Hispanic/Latino; 10 Hispanic/Latino), 14 international. 123 applicants, 86% accepted, 84 enrolled. *Degree requirements:* For master's, one foreign language, comprehensive exam (for some programs), thesis (for some programs); for doctorate, thesis/dissertation; for M Div, 2 foreign languages. *Entrance requirements:* For M Div and master's, minimum undergraduate GPA of 2.8; for doctorate, minimum first professional GPA of 3.0. Additional exam requirements/recommendations for international students: Required—TOEFL (minimum score 550 paper-based; 213 computer-based), TWE. *Application deadline:* For fall admission, 6/1 priority date for domestic students. Applications are processed on a rolling basis. Application fee: $35. Electronic applications accepted. *Expenses:* Tuition: Full-time $13,900; part-time $1470 per course. Required fees: $2484; $75 per semester. Tuition and fees vary according to degree level. *Financial support:* In 2010–11, 102 students received support; research assistantships with tuition reimbursements available, teaching assistantships with tuition reimbursements available, career-related internships or fieldwork and Federal Work-Study available. Financial award application deadline: 7/1; financial award applicants required to submit FAFSA. *Unit head:* Rev. Dr. J. Paul Rajashekar, Dean, 215-248-6379, Fax: 215-248-4577, E-mail: rajashekar@ltsp.edu. *Application contact:* Rev. Louise Johnson, Director of Admissions, 800-286-4616 Ext. 6321, Fax: 215-248-7315, E-mail: admissions@ltsp.edu.

Lutheran Theological Southern Seminary, Graduate and Professional Programs, Columbia, SC 29203. Offers M Div, MAR, STM, D Min. *Accreditation:* ACIPE; ATS. Part-time programs available. *Faculty:* 15 full-time (4 women), 4 part-time/adjunct (3 women). *Students:* 135 full-time (65 women), 49 part-time (22 women); includes 15 minority (all Black or African American, non-Hispanic/Latino), 1 international. Average age 37. 73 applicants, 96% accepted, 45 enrolled. In 2010, 28 first professional degrees, 12 master's awarded. *Degree requirements:* For master's, comprehensive exam (for some programs), thesis (for some programs); for M Div, 2 foreign languages. *Application deadline:* For fall admission, 5/15 priority date for domestic students, 10/1 for international students; for spring admission, 12/1 priority date for domestic students. Applications are processed on a rolling basis. Application fee: $35. *Financial support:* In 2010–11, 94 students received support; teaching assistantships, career-related internships or fieldwork, institutionally sponsored loans, scholarships/grants, health care benefits, tuition waivers (partial), unspecified assistantships, and on-campus employment available. Support available to part-time students. Financial award application deadline: 3/15; financial award applicants required to submit FAFSA. *Faculty research:* Theology in the twenty-first century, Biblical interpretation. *Unit head:* Rev. Dr. Marcus J. Miller, President, 803-786-5150, Fax: 803-786-6499, E-mail: mmiller@ltss.edu. *Application contact:* Jenny Tomalka, Director of Admissions, 800-804-5233, E-mail: jtomalka@ltss.edu.

Luther Rice University, Graduate Programs, Lithonia, GA 30038-2454. Offers Bible/theology (M Div); Christian education (M Div); Christian studies (MA); church ministry (D Min); counseling (M Div); discipleship counseling (MA); ministry (M Div, MA); missions/evangelism (M Div). Part-time programs available. Postbaccalaureate distance learning degree programs offered (no on-campus study). *Degree requirements:* For doctorate, thesis/dissertation. *Entrance requirements:* Additional exam requirements/recommendations for international students: Required—TOEFL (minimum score 500 paper-based; 173 computer-based).

Luther Seminary, Graduate and Professional Programs, St. Paul, MN 55108-1445. Offers M Div, M Th, MA, MSM, D Min, PhD. *Accreditation:* ACIPE; ATS. *Degree requirements:* For master's, thesis or alternative; for doctorate, 2 foreign languages, thesis/dissertation; for M Div, 2 foreign languages, 1 year internship. *Entrance requirements:* For M Div, minimum GPA of 3.0; for master's, minimum GPA of 2.8; for doctorate, GRE General Test. Electronic applications accepted. *Faculty research:* Theology, psychology (pastoral care), church history, Bible, Islamic studies.

Machzikei Hadath Rabbinical College, Graduate Programs, Brooklyn, NY 11204-1805. Offers First Talmudic Degree. *Accreditation:* AARTS.

Madonna University, Program in Religious Studies, Livonia, MI 48150-1173. Offers pastoral ministry (MA).

Malone University, Graduate Program in Theological Studies, Canton, OH 44709. Offers theological studies: general track (MA). Part-time and evening/weekend programs available. *Faculty:* 5 full-time (0 women), 4 part-time/adjunct (0 women). *Students:* 3 full-time (1 woman), 34 part-time (14 women); includes 10 Black or African American, non-Hispanic/Latino; 1 Asian, non-Hispanic/Latino. Average age 37. 29 applicants, 69% accepted, 12 enrolled. In 2010, 8 master's awarded. *Entrance requirements:* For master's, minimum GPA of 3.0. Additional exam requirements/recommendations for international students: Required—TOEFL (minimum score 550 paper-based; 213 computer-based; 79 iBT). *Application deadline:* Applications are processed on a rolling basis. Application fee: $25. *Expenses:* Contact institution. *Financial support:* Tuition waivers (partial) and unspecified assistantships available. Support available to part-time students. Financial award application deadline: 6/30. *Faculty research:* Pauline theology, history of Biblical interpretation, Johannine epistles, miracles in the New Testament, God's judgment and love. *Unit head:* Dr. Larry D. Reinhart, Director, 330-471-8198, Fax: 330-471-8477, E-mail: lreinhart@malone.edu. *Application contact:* Heather Pritchard, Recruiter/Adviser, 330-471-8134, Fax: 330-471-8343, E-mail: hpritchard@malone.edu.

Maple Springs Baptist Bible College and Seminary, Graduate and Professional Programs, Capitol Heights, MD 20743. Offers biblical studies (MA, Certificate); Christian counseling (MA); church administration (MA); divinity (M Div); ministry (D Min); religious education (MRE).

Maranatha Baptist Bible College, Program in Biblical Studies, Watertown, WI 53094. Offers MA. Part-time programs available. *Faculty:* 4 full-time (0 women), 5 part-time/adjunct (0 women). *Students:* 10 full-time (0 women), 12 part-time (0 women); includes 1 Asian, non-Hispanic/Latino; 1 Hispanic/Latino. Average age 27. 3 applicants, 100% accepted, 3 enrolled. In 2010, 8 master's awarded. *Degree requirements:* For master's, one foreign language, fieldwork. *Application deadline:* Applications are processed on a rolling basis. Application fee: $50. *Expenses:* Tuition: Full-time $4160; part-time $260 per credit hour. Required fees: $350; $23 per credit hour. *Financial support:* In 2010–11, 8 students received support. Scholarships/grants and tuition waivers (full and partial) available. Support available to part-time students. *Faculty research:* Bible structure, counseling techniques, church history. *Unit head:* Dr. Larry Oats, Dean of Maranatha Baptist Seminary, 920-206-2324, Fax: 920-261-9109, E-mail: loats@mbbc.edu. *Application contact:* Dr. Jim Harrison, Director of Admissions, 920-206-2327, Fax: 920-261-9109, E-mail: admissions@mbbc.edu.

Maranatha Baptist Bible College, Program in Divinity, Watertown, WI 53094. Offers M Div. Part-time programs available. *Faculty:* 4 full-time (0 women), 5 part-time/adjunct (0 women). *Students:* 12 full-time (0 women), 10 part-time (0 women); includes 1 Asian, non-Hispanic/Latino; 1 Hispanic/Latino. Average age 25. 4 applicants, 100% accepted, 4 enrolled. *Application deadline:* Applications are processed on a rolling basis. Application fee: $50. *Expenses:* Tuition: Full-time $4160; part-time $260 per credit hour. Required fees: $350; $23 per credit hour. *Financial support:* In 2010–11, 4 students received support. Scholarships/grants and tuition waivers (full and partial) available. Support available to part-time students. *Faculty research:* Church history, Counseling techniques, Bible structure, ancient language. *Unit head:* Dr. Larry Oats, Dean of Maranatha Baptist Seminary, 920-206-2324, Fax: 920-261-9109, E-mail: loats@mbbc.edu. *Application contact:* Dr. Jim Harrison, Director of Admissions, 920-206-2327, Fax: 920-261-9109, E-mail: admissions@mbbc.edu.

Marquette University, Graduate School, College of Arts and Sciences, Department of Theology, Milwaukee, WI 53201-1881. Offers historical theology (MA, PhD); Judaism and Christianity in antiquity (MA, PhD); systematic theology (MA, PhD); theological ethics (PhD); theology (MACD); theology and society (PhD). Part-time and evening/weekend programs available. Postbaccalaureate distance learning degree programs offered (no on-campus study). *Faculty:* 30 full-time (7 women), 19 part-time/adjunct (3 women). *Students:* 65 full-time (17 women), 45 part-time (13 women); includes 6 minority (3 Black or African American, non-Hispanic/Latino; 3 Hispanic/Latino), 3 international. Average age 36. 167 applicants, 39% accepted, 16 enrolled. In 2010, 114 master's, 8 doctorates awarded. Terminal master's awarded for partial completion of doctoral program. *Degree requirements:* For master's, one foreign language, comprehensive exam, thesis or alternative; for doctorate, 2 foreign languages, comprehensive exam, thesis/

dissertation. *Entrance requirements:* For master's, GRE General Test, official transcripts from all current and previous colleges/universities except Marquette, three letters of recommendation, short personal statement; for doctorate, GRE General Test, official transcripts from all current and previous colleges/universities except Marquette, three letters of recommendation, short personal statement, academic writing sample. Additional exam requirements/recommendations for international students: Required—TOEFL (minimum score 530 paper-based; 78 computer-based). *Application deadline:* For fall admission, 12/15 for domestic and international students. Application fee: $50. Electronic applications accepted. *Expenses:* Tuition: Full-time $16,290; part-time $905 per credit hour. Tuition and fees vary according to program. *Financial support:* In 2010–11, 10 fellowships, 22 teaching assistantships were awarded; research assistantships, Federal Work-Study, institutionally sponsored loans, scholarships/ grants, and tuition waivers (full and partial) also available. Support available to part-time students. Financial award application deadline: 2/15. *Faculty research:* Old Testament theology, New Testament theology, church history, Christian ethics. Total annual research expenditures: $4,625. *Unit head:* Dr. Susan Wood, Chair, 414-288-7170, Fax: 414-288-5548. *Application contact:* Dr. M. Therese Lysaught, Director of Graduate Studies, 414-288-3740.

Mars Hill Graduate School, Graduate Programs, Seattle, WA 98121. Offers Christian studies (MA); counseling psychology (MA); divinity (MS). Part-time programs available. *Entrance requirements:* For master's, MAT.

Marylhurst University, Department of Religious Studies–Applied Theology Program, Marylhurst, OR 97036-0261. Offers applied theology (MA). Part-time and evening/weekend programs available. *Faculty:* 2 full-time (1 woman), 8 part-time/adjunct (3 women). *Students:* 15 part-time (12 women). Average age 48. 4 applicants, 50% accepted, 2 enrolled. In 2010, 2 master's awarded. *Degree requirements:* For master's, thesis. *Entrance requirements:* For master's, MAT, resume, 3 letters of recommendation, interview, autobiography. Additional exam requirements/recommendations for international students: Recommended—TOEFL (minimum score 550 paper-based; 213 computer-based; 80 iBT). *Application deadline:* For fall admission, 6/30 priority date for domestic students, 6/30 for international students; for winter admission, 11/30 priority date for domestic students, 11/30 for international students; for spring admission, 3/30 priority date for domestic students, 3/30 for international students. Applications are processed on a rolling basis. Application fee: $50. Electronic applications accepted. *Expenses:* Tuition: Full-time $13,932; part-time $516 per credit. Tuition and fees vary according to course load and program. *Financial support:* Fellowships, research assistantships, teaching assistantships, scholarships/grants available. Support available to part-time students. Financial award applicants required to submit FAFSA. *Faculty research:* Pastoral care, scripture, world religions. *Unit head:* Dr. Jerry Roussell, Chair, 503-636-8141, Fax: 503-697-5597, E-mail: jroussell@ marylhurst.edu. *Application contact:* Maruksa Lynch, Graduate Admissions Specialist, 800-634-9982 Ext. 6322, Fax: 503-699-6320, E-mail: admissions@marylhurst.edu.

Marylhurst University, Department of Religious Studies–Divinity Program, Marylhurst, OR 97036-0261. Offers M Div. Part-time and evening/weekend programs available. *Faculty:* 2 full-time (1 woman), 8 part-time/adjunct (3 women). *Students:* 12 full-time (9 women), 23 part-time (15 women); includes 1 Hispanic/Latino; 1 Two or more races, non-Hispanic/Latino. Average age 47. 8 applicants, 88% accepted, 7 enrolled. *Degree requirements:* For M Div, thesis/dissertation. *Entrance requirements:* MAT, resume, 3 letters of recommendation, interview. Additional exam requirements/recommendations for international students: Required—TOEFL (minimum score 550 paper-based; 213 computer-based; 80 iBT). *Application deadline:* For fall admission, 6/30 for domestic students; for winter admission, 11/30 for domestic students; for spring admission, 3/30 for domestic students. Applications are processed on a rolling basis. Application fee: $50. Electronic applications accepted. *Expenses:* Tuition: Full-time $13,932; part-time $516 per credit. Tuition and fees vary according to course load and program. *Financial support:* Fellowships, research assistantships, teaching assistantships, scholarships/ grants available. Support available to part-time students. Financial award applicants required to submit FAFSA. *Faculty research:* Scripture-Biblical studies, theology, history, ministry, spirituality. *Unit head:* Dr. Jerry Roussell, Chair, 503-636-8141, Fax: 503-697-5597, E-mail: jroussell@marylhurst.edu. *Application contact:* Maruska Lynch, Graduate Admissions Specialist, 800-634-9982 Ext. 6322, Fax: 503-699-6320, E-mail: admissions@marylhurst.edu.

The Master's College and Seminary, The Master's Seminary, Santa Clarita, CA 91321-1200. Offers biblical counseling (MABC); New Testament (Th D); Old Testament (Th D); preaching (D Min); theology (M Div, M Th, Th D). Part-time programs available. *Degree requirements:* For master's, 2 foreign languages, thesis; for doctorate, 4 foreign languages, thesis/dissertation; for M Div, 2 foreign languages, thesis/dissertation. *Entrance requirements:* For M Div, minimum 2 years of college; for master's, minimum GPA of 2.75; for doctorate, Th M, minimum GPA of 3.5. Additional exam requirements/recommendations for international students: Required— TOEFL (minimum score 550 paper-based).

McCormick Theological Seminary, Graduate and Professional Programs, Chicago, IL 60615. Offers ministry (D Min); theological studies (MATS, Certificate); theology (M Div); M Div/MSW. M Div/MSW offered jointly with Loyola University Chicago, University of Chicago, and University of Illinois at Chicago. *Accreditation:* ACIPE; ATS (one or more programs are accredited). Part-time and evening/weekend programs available. *Degree requirements:* For master's, thesis (for some programs); for doctorate, thesis/dissertation. *Entrance requirements:* For M Div and master's, minimum GPA of 3.0; for doctorate, M Div, minimum 3 years in pastorate. *Faculty research:* Faith formation, families, biblical literature, Dead Sea scrolls, women in antiquity.

McGill University, Faculty of Graduate and Postdoctoral Studies, Faculty of Religious Studies, Montréal, QC H3A 2T5, Canada. Offers MA, STM, PhD. *Accreditation:* ATS.

McMaster University, McMaster Divinity College, Hamilton, ON L8S 4M2, Canada. Offers biblical studies (M Div); Biblical studies (MA, MTS, Diploma); Christian interpretation/history (M Div, MA, MTS, Diploma); Christian ministry (M Div, MA, MTS, Diploma); Christian Studies (Certificate); Christian theology (PhD). Affiliated with the Toronto School of Theology. *Accreditation:* ATS. Part-time programs available. *Degree requirements:* For master's, one foreign language, thesis optional; for doctorate, 3 foreign languages, comprehensive exam, thesis/dissertation; for other advanced degree, 2 foreign languages, thesis. *Entrance requirements:* For master's, minimum B average in undergraduate course work, 3 letters of reference; for doctorate, minimum B+ average in bachelor's and master's, appropriate modern/ ancient language, interview; for other advanced degree, 6 units of related Biblical language, minimum B+ average in undergraduate course work, minimum 15 units of course work in related area of study, 3 letters of recommendation. Additional exam requirements/ recommendations for international students: Required—TOEFL (minimum score 550 paper-based; 237 computer-based). *Faculty research:* Ethics, Biblical studies, language studies, church history, Christian ministry.

Meadville Lombard Theological School, Graduate and Professional Programs, Chicago, IL 60637-1602. Offers divinity (M Div); ministry (D Min); religion (MA); M Div/MSW. M Div/MSW offered jointly with University of Chicago. *Accreditation:* ACIPE; ATS. Part-time programs available. Postbaccalaureate distance learning degree programs offered (minimal on-campus study). *Entrance requirements:* For M Div and master's, bachelor's degree; for doctorate, bachelor's and masters degrees, 3 years of ministry.

Memphis Theological Seminary, Graduate and Professional Programs, Memphis, TN 38104-4395. Offers M Div, MAR, D Min. *Accreditation:* ATS. Part-time programs available. *Faculty:* 11 full-time (4 women), 7 part-time/adjunct (0 women). *Students:* 163 full-time (76 women), 119 part-time (60 women); includes 96 minority (94 Black or African American, non-Hispanic/ Latino; 1 American Indian or Alaska Native, non-Hispanic/Latino; 1 Asian, non-Hispanic/ Latino), 1 international. Average age 43. *Degree requirements:* For doctorate, thesis/dissertation. *Entrance requirements:* For doctorate, M Div, 3 years in ministry. *Application deadline:* For fall admission, 8/10 for domestic students; for spring admission, 1/10 for domestic students. Applications are processed on a rolling basis. Application fee: $35. *Expenses:* Tuition: Part-time $400 per semester hour. *Financial support:* Career-related internships or fieldwork and

scholarships/grants available. Support available to part-time students. Financial award application deadline: 4/15. *Unit head:* Dr. Daniel J. Earheart-Brown, President, 901-458-8232, Fax: 901-452-4501, E-mail: jebrown@memphisseminary.edu. *Application contact:* Barry L. Anderson, Director of Admissions, 901-458-8232 Ext. 109, Fax: 901-452-4501, E-mail: banderson@ memphisseminary.edu.

Mercer University, Graduate Studies, Cecil B. Day Campus, James and Carolyn McAfee School of Theology, Macon, GA 31207-0003. Offers M Div, MACM, D Min, M Div/MBA, M Div/MM, M Div/MS. *Accreditation:* ATS. Part-time programs available. *Faculty:* 13 full-time (3 women), 7 part-time/adjunct (2 women). *Students:* 173 full-time (94 women), 92 part-time (45 women); includes 127 minority (121 Black or African American, non-Hispanic/Latino; 1 American Indian or Alaska Native, non-Hispanic/Latino; 1 Asian, non-Hispanic/Latino; 3 Hispanic/ Latino; 1 Two or more races, non-Hispanic/Latino), 3 international. Average age 35. 140 applicants, 70% accepted, 60 enrolled. In 2010, 40 first professional degrees, 5 master's, 5 doctorates awarded. *Degree requirements:* For doctorate, thesis/dissertation, fieldwork, seminars; for M Div, 2 foreign languages. *Entrance requirements:* For M Div, letters of recommendation, minimum B+ average in undergraduate course work; for master's, bachelor's degree with liberal arts core from regionally accredited college/university; for doctorate, MAT or GRE, minimum B+ average in undergraduate course work, letters of recommendation. Additional exam requirements/recommendations for international students: Required—TOEFL (minimum score 550 paper-based; 215 computer-based; 79 iBT). *Application deadline:* For fall admission, 7/1 for domestic students, 2/1 for international students; for spring admission, 1/4 for domestic students. Applications are processed on a rolling basis. Application fee: $35. *Expenses:* Contact institution. *Financial support:* In 2010–11, 30 students received support. Career-related internships or fieldwork, Federal Work-Study, institutionally sponsored loans, and merit-based scholarships available. Support available to part-time students. Financial award applicants required to submit FAFSA. *Faculty research:* Biblical studies, Baptist heritage, Christian heritage, theology, pastoral care, ethics, global missions, academic research. *Unit head:* Dr. R. Alan Culpepper, Dean, 678-547-6470, Fax: 678-547-6478, E-mail: culpepper_ra@ mercer.edu. *Application contact:* Dr. Ryan A. Clark, Director of Admissions, 678-547-6451, Fax: 678-547-6478, E-mail: clark_ra@mercer.edu.

Mesivta of Eastern Parkway–Yeshiva Zichron Meilech, Graduate Programs, Brooklyn, NY 11218-5559. *Accreditation:* AARTS.

Mesivta Tifereth Jerusalem of America, Graduate Programs, New York, NY 10002-6301. *Accreditation:* AARTS.

Mesivta Torah Vodaath Rabbinical Seminary, Graduate Programs, Brooklyn, NY 11218-5299. *Accreditation:* AARTS.

Methodist Theological School in Ohio, Graduate and Professional Programs, Delaware, OH 43015-8004. Offers M Div, MACE, MACM, MTS, D Min. *Accreditation:* ACIPE; ATS. Part-time programs available. *Entrance requirements:* For master's, 3 letters of recommendation. Additional exam requirements/recommendations for international students: Required—TOEFL (minimum score 577 paper-based; 233 computer-based; 90 iBT).

Michigan Theological Seminary, Graduate Programs, Plymouth, MI 48170. Offers Bible (Graduate Certificate); Christian education (MA); counseling psychology (MA); divinity (M Div); theological studies (MA). Part-time and evening/weekend programs available. *Degree requirements:* For master's, one foreign language, thesis; for M Div, 2 foreign languages. *Faculty research:* Judaism, cults, world religions.

Mid-America Baptist Theological Seminary, Graduate and Professional Programs, Cordova, TN 38016. Offers M Div, MACE, MCE, MM, D Min, PhD. *Degree requirements:* For doctorate, 4 foreign languages, thesis/dissertation; for M Div, 2 foreign languages. *Entrance requirements:* For doctorate, MAT. Additional exam requirements/recommendations for international students: Required—TOEFL (minimum score 600 paper-based; 250 computer-based). Electronic applications accepted.

Mid-America Baptist Theological Seminary Northeast Branch, Program in Theology, Schenectady, NY 12303-3463. Offers M Div. Part-time and evening/weekend programs available. *Degree requirements:* For M Div, 2 foreign languages. *Entrance requirements:* Additional exam requirements/recommendations for international students: Required—TOEFL. Electronic applications accepted.

Mid-America Reformed Seminary, Graduate Programs, Dyer, IN 46311. Offers M Div, MTS. *Degree requirements:* For M Div, comprehensive exam. *Entrance requirements:* Additional exam requirements/recommendations for international students: Required—TOEFL (minimum score 550 paper-based).

Midwestern Baptist Theological Seminary, Graduate and Professional Programs, Kansas City, MO 64118-4697. Offers Biblical archaeology (MA); Biblical languages (MA); Christian education (M Div, MACE); Christian foundations—lay ministry (Graduate Certificate); collegiate ministries (M Div); counseling (MA); educational ministry (D Ed Min); international church planting (M Div); ministry (M Div, D Min); North American church planting (M Div); sacred music (MCM); urban ministry (M Div); worship leadership (M Div); youth ministry (M Div). *Accreditation:* ATS. Part-time programs available. Postbaccalaureate distance learning degree programs offered (minimal on-campus study). *Degree requirements:* For doctorate, thesis/ dissertation; for M Div, 2 foreign languages. *Entrance requirements:* For doctorate, MAT. Electronic applications accepted. *Faculty research:* Ministerial studies, Biblical and theological studies, missions, counseling.

Midwest University, Graduate Programs, Wentzville, MO 63385. Offers social work (DSW); teaching English to speakers of other languages (MA); theology (M Div, MA, D Min). Part-time programs available. Postbaccalaureate distance learning degree programs offered (minimal on-campus study). *Degree requirements:* For master's, thesis (for some programs); for doctorate, thesis/dissertation; for M Div, thesis/dissertation (for some programs). *Entrance requirements:* Additional exam requirements/recommendations for international students: Recommended— TOEFL (minimum score 550 paper-based).

Mirrer Yeshiva, Graduate Programs, Brooklyn, NY 11223-2010. *Accreditation:* AARTS.

Moody Bible Institute, Graduate School, Chicago, IL 60610-3284. Offers biblical studies (MABS, Graduate Certificate); intercultural studies (MAIS, Graduate Certificate); ministry (M Div, M Min); spiritual formation and discipleship (MASF, Graduate Certificate); urban studies (MA, Graduate Certificate). Part-time programs available. *Degree requirements:* For master's, 2 foreign languages, fieldwork (MABS); colloquium, field research project (MA Min). *Entrance requirements:* For master's, 30 hours in Bible/theology, 2 years of ministry experience (MA Min).

Moravian Theological Seminary, Graduate and Professional Programs, Bethlehem, PA 18018-6614. Offers divinity (M Div); formative spirituality (M Div, MAPC, MATS); pastoral counseling (MAPC); theological studies (MATS). *Accreditation:* ACIPE; ATS (one or more programs are accredited). Part-time programs available. *Faculty:* 7 full-time (3 women), 11 part-time/adjunct (5 women). *Students:* 27 full-time (12 women), 49 part-time (34 women); includes 14 minority (5 Black or African American, non-Hispanic/Latino; 1 Asian, non-Hispanic/ Latino; 8 Hispanic/Latino), 2 international. Average age 45. 44 applicants, 86% accepted, 36 enrolled. In 2010, 6 M Divs, 16 master's awarded. *Degree requirements:* For master's, thesis. *Entrance requirements:* Additional exam requirements/recommendations for international students: Required—TOEFL. *Application deadline:* For fall admission, 4/1 priority date for international students; for spring admission, 9/1 priority date for international students. Applications are processed on a rolling basis. Application fee: $35. *Expenses:* Tuition: Full-time $13,800; part-time $3078 per semester. Required fees: $90 per semester. *Financial support:* In 2010–11, 72 students received support. Career-related internships or fieldwork, Federal Work-Study, and scholarships/grants available. Support available to part-time students. Financial award application deadline: 5/1; financial award applicants required to submit FAFSA. *Unit*

Theology

Moravian Theological Seminary *(continued)*
head: Rev. Dr. Frank L. Crouch, Dean and Vice President, 610-861-1516. *Application contact:* Ann Gibson, Director of Enrollment, 610-861-1512, Fax: 610-861-1569, E-mail: agibson@moravian.edu.

Mount Angel Seminary, Program in Theology, Saint Benedict, OR 97373. Offers M Div, MA. *Accreditation:* ACIPE; ATS. Part-time programs available. *Degree requirements:* For master's, thesis optional.

Mount St. Mary's University, Graduate Seminary, Emmitsburg, MD 21727-7799. Offers M Div, MA. *Accreditation:* ATS. *Faculty:* 12 full-time (0 women), 5 part-time/adjunct (3 women). *Students:* 148 full-time (0 women), 3 part-time (1 woman); includes 9 minority (1 Black or African American, non-Hispanic/Latino; 3 Asian, non-Hispanic/Latino; 5 Hispanic/Latino), 18 international. Average age 29. 67 applicants, 97% accepted, 54 enrolled. In 2010, 26 first professional degrees, 12 master's awarded. *Degree requirements:* For master's, one foreign language, comprehensive exam, thesis, language proficiency exams. *Entrance requirements:* For M Div, 24 credits of course work in philosophy; for master's, 18 credits of course work in philosophy. Additional exam requirements/recommendations for international students: Required—TOEFL (minimum score 550 paper-based; 213 computer-based). *Application deadline:* For fall admission, 8/1 for domestic and international students. Application fee: $0. *Expenses:* Contact institution. *Financial support:* Career-related internships or fieldwork and scholarships/grants available. Financial award applicants required to submit FAFSA. *Faculty research:* Permanence of marriage, priestly spirituality, medieval catechesis, medical ethics, eschatology. *Unit head:* Rev. Steven P. Rohlfs, Vice President/Rector, 301-447-5295, Fax: 301-447-5636, E-mail: rohlfs@msmary.edu. *Application contact:* Susan Nield, Seminary Admissions, 301-447-7423, Fax: 301-447-7402, E-mail: nield@msmary.edu.

Mount Vernon Nazarene University, Program in Ministry, Mount Vernon, OH 43050-9500. Offers M Min. Part-time and evening/weekend programs available. *Degree requirements:* For master's, project. *Faculty research:* Pastoral effectiveness and professional development.

Naropa University, Graduate Programs, Program in Divinity, Boulder, CO 80302-6697. Offers M Div. *Faculty:* 5 full-time (1 woman), 7 part-time/adjunct (5 women). *Students:* 22 full-time (10 women), 6 part-time (5 women); includes 1 Black or African American, non-Hispanic/Latino; 1 Asian, non-Hispanic/Latino; 1 Hispanic/Latino; 2 Two or more races, non-Hispanic/Latino. Average age 40. 21 applicants, 71% accepted, 9 enrolled. *Entrance requirements:* In-person interview, writing sample. Additional exam requirements/recommendations for international students: Required—TOEFL (minimum score 600 paper-based; 250 computer-based). *Application deadline:* For fall admission, 1/15 priority date for domestic and international students. Applications are processed on a rolling basis. Application fee: $60. Electronic applications accepted. *Expenses:* Tuition: Full-time $17,820; part-time $810 per credit. Required fees: $305 per semester. Tuition and fees vary according to course load, program and reciprocity agreements. *Financial support:* In 2010–11, 15 students received support, including 2 research assistantships with partial tuition reimbursements available (averaging $2,250 per year), 2 teaching assistantships with partial tuition reimbursements available (averaging $2,250 per year); career-related internships or fieldwork, Federal Work-Study, scholarships/grants, health care benefits, tuition waivers (partial), and unspecified assistantships also available. Support available to part-time students. Financial award application deadline: 3/1; financial award applicants required to submit FAFSA. *Unit head:* Jane Carpenter, Director, School of Humanities and Interdisciplinary Studies, 303-245-4602, E-mail: jane@naropa.edu. *Application contact:* Krista Shuchlik, Senior Graduate Admissions Counselor, 303-546-3528, Fax: 303-546-3583, E-mail: kstuchlik@naropa.edu.

Nashotah House, School of Theology, Nashotah, WI 53058-9793. Offers M Div, MTS, STM, Certificate. *Accreditation:* ACIPE; ATS (one or more programs are accredited). Part-time programs available. *Degree requirements:* For master's, thesis optional; for M Div, 2 foreign languages, thesis/dissertation optional, clinical experience. *Entrance requirements:* For M Div, master's, and Certificate, GRE General Test or MAT, interview. Additional exam requirements/recommendations for international students: Required—TOEFL. *Faculty research:* Formation for parochial ministry, ancient Semitic epigraphy.

Nazarene Theological Seminary, Graduate and Professional Programs, Kansas City, MO 64131-1263. Offers Christian education (MA); intercultural studies (MA); theological studies (MA); theology (M Div, D Min). *Accreditation:* ACIPE; ATS. Part-time programs available. *Degree requirements:* For master's, comprehensive exam (for some programs), thesis (for some programs); for doctorate, thesis/dissertation. *Entrance requirements:* Additional exam requirements/recommendations for international students: Required—TOEFL. Electronic applications accepted.

Ner Israel Rabbinical College, Graduate Programs, Baltimore, MD 21208. Offers MTL, DTL, Professional Certificate. *Accreditation:* AARTS.

Ner Israel Yeshiva College of Toronto, Graduate Programs, Thornhill, ON L4J 8A7, Canada. *Accreditation:* AARTS.

New Brunswick Theological Seminary, Graduate and Professional Programs, New Brunswick, NJ 08901-1196. Offers metro-urban ministry (D Min), including theological studies; theological studies (M Div, MA); M Div/MA. *Accreditation:* ACIPE; ATS. Part-time and evening/weekend programs available. *Degree requirements:* For master's, thesis optional. *Entrance requirements:* For M Div, minimum GPA of 2.0; for master's, minimum GPA of 3.0; for doctorate, M Div. Additional exam requirements/recommendations for international students: Required—TOEFL. Electronic applications accepted.

Newman Theological College, Theology Programs, Edmonton, AB T6V 1H3, Canada. Offers M Div, M Th, MTS. *Accreditation:* ATS. Part-time programs available. *Faculty:* 13 full-time (3 women), 23 part-time/adjunct (8 women). *Students:* 27 full-time (4 women), 31 part-time (13 women). Average age 39. 8 applicants, 100% accepted, 7 enrolled. In 2010, 10 first professional degrees, 1 master's awarded. *Degree requirements:* For master's, comprehensive exam, thesis; for M Div, comprehensive exam, thesis/dissertation. *Entrance requirements:* For M Div, bachelor's degree including 12 credits in philosophy; for master's, M Div. Additional exam requirements/recommendations for international students: Required—TOEFL (minimum score 560 paper-based; 220 computer-based; 86 iBT). *Application deadline:* For fall admission, 8/7 priority date for domestic students; for winter admission, 1/3 priority date for domestic students; for spring admission, 5/1 priority date for domestic students. Applications are processed on a rolling basis. Application fee: $45 ($250 for international students). Tuition and fees charges are reported in Canadian dollars. *Expenses:* Tuition: Full-time $5700 Canadian dollars; part-time $570 Canadian dollars per course. Required fees: $55 Canadian dollars per semester. Tuition and fees vary according to course load and campus/location. *Financial support:* In 2010–11, 14 students received support. Tuition bursaries available. Support available to part-time students. Financial award application deadline: 5/31. *Unit head:* Fr. Stefano Penna, Dean, 780-392-2450 Ext. 5223, Fax: 780-462-4013, E-mail: stefano.penna@newman.edu. *Application contact:* Maria Saulnier, Registrar, 780-392-2450 Ext. 5227, Fax: 780-462-4013, E-mail: registrar@newman.edu.

Newman University, School of Arts and Humanities, Wichita, KS 67213-2097. Offers theological studies (MTS); theology (MA). Part-time programs available. Postbaccalaureate distance learning degree programs offered (minimal on-campus study). *Faculty:* 3 full-time (0 women). *Students:* 56 part-time (31 women); includes 1 Black or African American, non-Hispanic/Latino; 1 Asian, non-Hispanic/Latino; 5 Hispanic/Latino, 1 international. Average age 45. 25 applicants, 92% accepted, 19 enrolled. *Degree requirements:* For master's, 2 foreign languages, comprehensive exam (for some programs). *Entrance requirements:* For master's, letter of recommendation from pastor; bachelor's degree in theology or related field (MA), in any field (MTS). Additional exam requirements/recommendations for international students: Required—TOEFL (minimum score 600 paper-based; 250 computer-based; 100 iBT). *Application deadline:* For fall admission,

8/1 priority date for domestic students. Application fee: $25 ($40 for international students). *Expenses:* Contact institution. *Financial support:* In 2010–11, 55 students received support. Federal Work-Study available. Financial award application deadline: 8/15; financial award applicants required to submit FAFSA. *Unit head:* Fr. Gile Joseph, Assistant Professor of Theology and Graduate Theology Director, 316-942-4291 Ext. 2861, Fax: 316-942-4483, E-mail: gilej@newmanu.edu. *Application contact:* Linda Kay Sabala, Director of Graduate Admissions, 316-942-4291 Ext. 2230, E-mail: sabalal@newmanu.edu.

New Orleans Baptist Theological Seminary, Graduate and Professional Programs, Division of Biblical Studies, New Orleans, LA 70126-4858. Offers M Div, MA, PhD. *Accreditation:* ACIPE; ATS (one or more programs are accredited). *Faculty:* 11 full-time (0 women). *Students:* 72 full-time (11 women), 41 part-time (10 women); includes 6 Black or African American, non-Hispanic/Latino; 2 Asian, non-Hispanic/Latino; 2 Hispanic/Latino, 10 international. Average age 35. 26 applicants, 69% accepted, 17 enrolled. In 2010, 6 master's, 2 doctorates awarded. *Degree requirements:* For master's, 2 foreign languages, comprehensive exam (for some programs), thesis (for some programs); for doctorate, 4 foreign languages, comprehensive exam, thesis/dissertation. *Entrance requirements:* For doctorate, GRE General Test. *Application deadline:* For fall admission, 7/20 priority date for domestic students; for spring admission, 11/20 for domestic students. Applications are processed on a rolling basis. Application fee: $25. *Expenses:* Tuition: Full-time $3040. Required fees: $160 per credit hour. $80 per semester. One-time fee: $80 full-time. Tuition and fees vary according to course load and student's religious affiliation. *Unit head:* Dr. Dennis Cole, Chairman, 504-282-4455. *Application contact:* Dr. Paul E. Gregoire, Director of Admissions and Registrar, 504-282-4455 Ext. 3337, Fax: 504-286-3591, E-mail: registrar@nobts.edu.

New Orleans Baptist Theological Seminary, Graduate and Professional Programs, Division of Theological and Historical Studies, New Orleans, LA 70126-4858. Offers M Div, MA, D Min, PhD. *Accreditation:* ACIPE; ATS (one or more programs are accredited). Postbaccalaureate distance learning degree programs offered (minimal on-campus study). *Faculty:* 9 full-time (0 women). *Students:* 59 full-time (3 women), 21 part-time (4 women); includes 5 Black or African American, non-Hispanic/Latino; 1 Asian, non-Hispanic/Latino; 1 Hispanic/Latino, 2 international. Average age 33. 22 applicants, 82% accepted, 18 enrolled. In 2010, 1 doctorate awarded. *Degree requirements:* For master's, 2 foreign languages, comprehensive exam (for some programs), thesis (for some programs); for doctorate, 3 foreign languages, comprehensive exam, thesis/dissertation; for M Div, 2 foreign languages. *Entrance requirements:* For doctorate, GRE General Test. Additional exam requirements/recommendations for international students: Required—TOEFL. *Application deadline:* For fall admission, 7/15 priority date for domestic students; for spring admission, 12/20 for domestic students. Applications are processed on a rolling basis. Application fee: $25. *Expenses:* Tuition: Full-time $3040. Required fees: $160 per credit hour. $80 per semester. One-time fee: $80 full-time. Tuition and fees vary according to course load and student's religious affiliation. *Unit head:* Dr. Daniel Holcomb, Chairman, 504-282-4455. *Application contact:* Dr. Paul E. Gregoire, Director of Admissions and Registrar, 504-282-4455 Ext. 3337, Fax: 504-286-3591, E-mail: registrar@nobts.edu.

New Saint Andrews College, Graduate Studies, Moscow, ID 83843. Offers classical Christian studies (Graduate Certificate); Trinitarian theology and culture (MA). Part-time programs available. *Degree requirements:* For master's, final oral exam. *Entrance requirements:* For master's, GRE, 2 letters of recommendation; for Graduate Certificate, GRE, bachelor's degree, essays, 2 letters of recommendation. Electronic applications accepted.

New York Theological Seminary, Graduate and Professional Programs, New York, NY 10115. Offers M Div, MPS, MSW, D Min. MSW offered jointly with Fordham University. *Accreditation:* ACIPE; ATS (one or more programs are accredited). Part-time programs available. *Degree requirements:* For doctorate, thesis/dissertation; for M Div, thesis/dissertation, supervised ministry. *Entrance requirements:* For M Div, interview; for doctorate, M Div, 3 years of ministry experience, interview. Additional exam requirements/recommendations for international students: Required—TOEFL. *Faculty research:* Women in leadership; crime and punishment; church history; culture, politics and theology.

The Nigerian Baptist Theological Seminary, Graduate Studies, Ogbomoso, Nigeria. Offers church music (M Div, M Th, Diploma); divinity (M Div); ministry (D Min); religious education (M Div, M Th, PhD); theological studies (MATS); theology (M Th, PhD). Part-time programs available. *Degree requirements:* For master's, thesis, 2 Nigerian languages; for M Div, thesis/dissertation (for some programs), 2 biblical languages; for Diploma, thesis or alternative.

Northeastern Seminary at Roberts Wesleyan College, Graduate and Professional Programs, Rochester, NY 14624. Offers ministry (D Min); theological studies (MA); theology (M Div); M Div/MSW. M Div/MSW offered jointly with Roberts Wesleyan College. *Accreditation:* ATS. Evening/weekend programs available. *Degree requirements:* For master's, thesis (for some programs); for doctorate, one foreign language, thesis/dissertation. *Entrance requirements:* For doctorate, M Div, 3 years of full-time ministry experience. Additional exam requirements/recommendations for international students: Required—TOEFL (minimum score 550 paper-based). Electronic applications accepted. *Faculty research:* Historical theology, spiritual formation, biblical theology, counseling education.

Northern Baptist Theological Seminary, Graduate and Professional Programs, Lombard, IL 60148-5698. Offers Biblical studies (M Div); Christian ministries (MACM); ministry (D Min); theology (M Div). *Accreditation:* ATS. Part-time programs available. *Faculty:* 7 full-time (0 women), 24 part-time/adjunct (3 women). *Students:* 78 full-time (29 women), 79 part-time (37 women); includes 69 minority (55 Black or African American, non-Hispanic/Latino; 8 Asian, non-Hispanic/Latino; 6 Hispanic/Latino), 4 international. Average age 40. 100 applicants, 70% accepted, 50 enrolled. In 2010, 18 master's, 5 doctorates awarded. *Degree requirements:* For doctorate, thesis/dissertation. *Entrance requirements:* For master's, all official transcripts, letter of reference from pastor, autobiographical statement (400 words or more); for doctorate, M Div, 3 years in the ministry post-M Div, 3 letters of reference. Additional exam requirements/recommendations for international students: Required—TOEFL (minimum score 550 paper-based; 213 computer-based). *Application deadline:* For fall admission, 8/25 for domestic students, 2/1 for international students; for winter admission, 12/10 for domestic students, 2/1 for international students; for spring admission, 3/15 for domestic students, 2/1 for international students. Applications are processed on a rolling basis. Application fee: $35. Electronic applications accepted. *Expenses:* Tuition: Full-time $15,840. Required fees: $115 per quarter. *Financial support:* In 2010–11, 69 students received support. Career-related internships or fieldwork and scholarships/grants available. Support available to part-time students. Financial award application deadline: 9/1; financial award applicants required to submit FAFSA. *Faculty research:* Theology, worship studies, church history, evangelism, Bible. *Unit head:* Dr. J. Alistair Brown, Chief Academic Officer, 630-620-2101, Fax: 630-620-2190. *Application contact:* Greg Henson, Executive Director of External Relations, 630-620-2180, Fax: 630-620-2190, E-mail: admissions@seminary.edu.

North Park Theological Seminary, Graduate and Professional Programs, Professional Program, Chicago, IL 60625-4895. Offers M Div, M Div/MBA, M Div/MM. M Div/MBA offered jointly with North Park University. *Accreditation:* ACIPE; ATS. Part-time programs available. *Degree requirements:* For M Div, 2 foreign languages. *Entrance requirements:* Minimum GPA of 2.5. Additional exam requirements/recommendations for international students: Required—TOEFL.

North Park Theological Seminary, Graduate and Professional Programs, Program in Christian Formation, Chicago, IL 60625-4895. Offers MA, MA/MM.

North Park Theological Seminary, Graduate and Professional Programs, Program in Preaching, Chicago, IL 60625-4895. Offers D Min. Program offered jointly with Chicago Theological Seminary, Lutheran School of Theology at Chicago, McCormick Theological Seminary, Seabury-Western Theological Seminary. *Accreditation:* ACIPE; ATS. *Degree* *requirements:* For doctorate, thesis/dissertation. *Entrance requirements:* For doctorate, 3 years of preaching experience.

North Park Theological Seminary, Graduate and Professional Programs, Program in Theological Studies, Chicago, IL 60625-4895. Offers MATS, MATS/MBA, MATS/MM, MATS/MBA offered jointly with North Park University. *Accreditation:* ACIPE; ATS. Part-time programs available. *Degree requirements:* For master's, comprehensive exam or thesis. *Entrance requirements:* For master's, minimum GPA of 2.5. Additional exam requirements/recommendations for international students: Required—TOEFL.

Northwest Baptist Seminary, Programs in Theology, Tacoma, WA 98407. Offers M Div, M Min, MTS, STM, Th M, D Min, Certificate. Part-time and evening/weekend programs available. *Degree requirements:* For master's, thesis; for M Div, thesis/dissertation (for some programs). *Entrance requirements:* Greek placement exam. Additional exam requirements/recommendations for international students: Required—TOEFL (minimum score 550 paper-based; 213 computer-based), IELTS (minimum score 6).

Northwestern College, Program in Theological Studies, St. Paul, MN 55113-1598. Offers MATS. Evening/weekend programs available.

Northwest University, College of Ministry, Kirkland, WA 98033. Offers ministry (MA); missional leadership (MA); theology and culture (MA). Evening/weekend programs available. *Faculty:* 9 full-time (1 woman), 21 part-time/adjunct (2 women). *Students:* 17 full-time (3 women), 43 part-time (9 women); includes 7 minority (5 Black or African American, non-Hispanic/Latino; 1 Asian, non-Hispanic/Latino; 1 Hispanic/Latino), 2 international. 32 applicants, 97% accepted, 29 enrolled. In 2010, 6 master's awarded. *Entrance requirements:* Additional exam requirements/recommendations for international students: Required—TOEFL (minimum score 550 paper-based). Application fee: $75. Tuition and fees vary according to program. *Unit head:* Dr. Wayde Goodall, Dean, 425-889-5253, E-mail: wayde.goodall@northwestu.edu. *Application contact:* Aaron Oosterwyk, Director of Graduate and Professional Studies Enrollment, 425-889-7799, Fax: 425-803-3059, E-mail: gpse@northwestu.edu.

Notre Dame Seminary, Graduate School of Theology, New Orleans, LA 70118-4391. Offers M Div, MA. *Accreditation:* ACIPE; ATS. Part-time programs available. *Degree requirements:* For master's, one foreign language, comprehensive exam, thesis. *Entrance requirements:* For M Div, GRE, previous course work in philosophy; for master's, GRE. Additional exam requirements/recommendations for international students: Required—TOEFL.

Nyack College, Alliance Theological Seminary, Nyack, NY 10960-3698. Offers Biblical literature (MA), including New Testament, Old Testament; Christian ministry (MPS); intercultural studies (MA); ministry (D Min); theology (M Div); urban ministry (MPS). *Accreditation:* ATS. Part-time programs available. *Students:* 256 full-time (96 women), 482 part-time (251 women); includes 231 Black or African American, non-Hispanic/Latino; 2 American Indian or Alaska Native, non-Hispanic/Latino; 123 Asian, non-Hispanic/Latino; 187 Hispanic/Latino; 12 Two or more races, non-Hispanic/Latino, 80 international. Average age 40. In 2010, 47 first professional degrees, 45 master's awarded. *Degree requirements:* For master's, comprehensive exam (for some programs), thesis optional, internship; for doctorate, thesis/dissertation; for M Div, internship. *Entrance requirements:* Additional exam requirements/recommendations for international students: Required—TOEFL (minimum score 213 computer-based; 78 iBT). *Application deadline:* Applications are processed on a rolling basis. Application fee: $30. Electronic applications accepted. Tuition and fees vary according to program. *Financial support:* Teaching assistantships, career-related internships or fieldwork, Federal Work-Study, and scholarships/grants available. Financial award applicants required to submit FAFSA. *Unit head:* Dr. Ron Walborn, Dean, 845-770-5715, Fax: 845-358-1663. *Application contact:* Traci Piescki, Director of Admissions, 845-770-5701, Fax: 845-348-3912, E-mail: admissions.ats@nyack.edu.

Oakland City University, Chapman Seminary, Oakland City, IN 47660-1099. Offers M Div, D Min. *Accreditation:* ATS. Part-time programs available. *Faculty:* 5 full-time (0 women), 5 part-time/adjunct (1 woman). *Students:* 7 full-time (1 woman), 5 part-time (1 woman); includes 1 minority (Black or African American, non-Hispanic/Latino). Average age 33. 11 applicants, 100% accepted, 8 enrolled. In 2010, 2 M Divs awarded. *Degree requirements:* For doctorate, thesis/dissertation. *Entrance requirements:* For M Div, GRE General Test, minimum GPA of 2.75 in undergraduate major or 2.5 overall; for doctorate, GRE, MAT, letters of recommendation. Additional exam requirements/recommendations for international students: Required—TOEFL. *Application deadline:* Applications are processed on a rolling basis. Application fee: $35. *Expenses:* Contact institution. *Financial support:* In 2010–11, 10 students received support. Career-related internships or fieldwork and Federal Work-Study available. Support available to part-time students. Financial award applicants required to submit FAFSA. *Faculty research:* Pastoral ministry, Christian education, missions. *Unit head:* Dr. Douglas Low, Dean, 812-749-1280, Fax: 812-749-1308, E-mail: dlow@oak.edu. *Application contact:* Dr. Douglas Low, Dean, 812-749-1280, Fax: 812-749-1308, E-mail: dlow@oak.edu.

Oblate School of Theology, Graduate and Professional Programs, San Antonio, TX 78216-6693. Offers divinity (M Div); Hispanic ministry (D Min); pastoral ministry (MAP Min); pastoral studies (Certificate); spirituality (MA Sp); supervision (D Min), including clinical pastoral education, general supervision; theology (MA Th); M Div/MA Th. *Accreditation:* ACIPE; ATS (one or more programs are accredited). Part-time programs available. *Faculty:* 19 full-time (6 women), 2 part-time/adjunct (0 women). *Students:* 91 full-time (7 women), 59 part-time (34 women); includes 4 Black or African American, non-Hispanic/Latino; 1 American Indian or Alaska Native, non-Hispanic/Latino; 18 Asian, non-Hispanic/Latino; 39 Hispanic/Latino, 36 international. 24 applicants, 100% accepted, 24 enrolled. In 2010, 13 first professional degrees, 17 master's, 4 doctorates awarded. *Degree requirements:* For master's, thesis (for some programs), practicum; for doctorate, paper, practicum; for M Div, one foreign language, seminar. *Entrance requirements:* For M Div, MAT, interview, course work in philosophy and theology; for master's, MAT, interview, course work in theology or religious studies, minimum GPA of 2.5; for doctorate, M Div. Additional exam requirements/recommendations for international students: Required—TOEFL (minimum score 197 computer-based; 71 iBT). *Application deadline:* For fall admission, 6/15 priority date for domestic and international students; for spring admission, 11/30 for domestic and international students. Applications are processed on a rolling basis. Application fee: $50. *Expenses:* Tuition: Full-time $12,350; part-time $475 per credit hour. Required fees: $175 per semester. One-time fee: $90. Tuition and fees vary according to course level, course load and degree level. *Financial support:* Scholarships/grants available. Support available to part-time students. Financial award application deadline: 8/1; financial award applicants required to submit FAFSA. *Unit head:* Dr. Scott Woodward, Academic Dean, 210-341-1366, Fax: 210-341-4519, E-mail: swoodward@ost.edu. *Application contact:* James Oberhausen, Director of Admission/Registrar, 210-341-1366 Ext. 212, Fax: 210-341-4519, E-mail: registrar@ost.edu.

Ohio Dominican University, Graduate Programs, Division of Theology, Arts and Ideas, Columbus, OH 43219-2099. Offers theology (MA). Part-time and evening/weekend programs available. *Students:* 10 full-time (4 women), 8 part-time (6 women); includes 1 minority (Hispanic/Latino), 1 international. Average age 38. In 2010, 9 master's awarded. *Degree requirements:* For master's, thesis or alternative. *Entrance requirements:* For master's, 20 undergraduate semester hours of theology or the equivalent, 3 letters of recommendation, interview. Additional exam requirements/recommendations for international students: Required—TOEFL (minimum score 550 paper-based; 213 computer-based), IELTS (minimum score 6.5). *Application deadline:* For fall admission, 7/15 priority date for domestic students, 7/18 priority date for international students; for spring admission, 12/18 priority date for domestic and international students. Applications are processed on a rolling basis. Application fee: $25. *Expenses:* Tuition: Part-time $485 per credit hour. *Financial support:* Applicants required to submit FAFSA. *Unit head:* Dr. Leo Madden, Program Director, 614-251-4720, E-mail: maddenl@ohiodominican.edu. *Application contact:* Jill M. Westerfeld, Assistant Director Graduate Admissions, 614-251-4725, Fax: 614-251-6654, E-mail: westerfj@ohiodominican.edu.

Ohr Hameir Theological Seminary, Graduate Programs, Cortlandt Manor, NY 10567. *Accreditation:* AARTS.

Oklahoma Christian University, Graduate School of Theology, Oklahoma City, OK 73136-1100. Offers family life ministry (MA); ministry (M Div, MA); youth ministry (MA). Part-time programs available. Postbaccalaureate distance learning degree programs offered (minimal on-campus study). *Degree requirements:* For master's, one foreign language, comprehensive exam, field experience; for M Div, 2 foreign languages, comprehensive exam, field experience. *Entrance requirements:* For M Div and master's, minimum undergraduate GPA of 3.0. Additional exam requirements/recommendations for international students: Required—TOEFL (minimum score 550 paper-based; 213 computer-based). Electronic applications accepted. *Faculty research:* Early marriage adjustment, new religions, Ethiopic language, church health, Hebrew rhetoric.

Olivet Nazarene University, Graduate School, Department of Practical Ministries, Bourbonnais, IL 60914. Offers MPM. Part-time programs available. *Degree requirements:* For master's, thesis or alternative.

Olivet Nazarene University, Graduate School, Division of Religion, Bourbonnais, IL 60914. Offers biblical literature (MA); religion (MA); theology (MA). Part-time programs available. *Degree requirements:* For master's, thesis or alternative.

Oral Roberts University, School of Theology and Missions, Tulsa, OK 74171. Offers biblical literature (MA), including advanced languages, Judaic-Christian studies; Christian counseling (MA), including marriage and family therapy; divinity (M Div); missions (MA); practical theology (MA); theological/historical studies (MA); theology (D Min). Part-time programs available. Post-baccalaureate distance learning degree programs offered (minimal on-campus study). *Degree requirements:* For master's, thesis (for some programs), practicum/internship; for doctorate, thesis/dissertation, applied research project; for M Div, one foreign language, field experience. *Entrance requirements:* For M Div and master's, GRE General Test or MAT, minimum GPA of 2.5; for doctorate, M Div, minimum GPA of 3.0, 3 years of full-time ministry experience. Additional exam requirements/recommendations for international students: Required—TOEFL (minimum score 550 paper-based; 213 computer-based; 79 iBT). Electronic applications accepted.

Pacific Lutheran Theological Seminary, Graduate and Professional Programs, Berkeley, CA 94708-1597. Offers M Div, MA, MCM, MTS, PhD, Th D, Certificate, M Div/MA. MA, Th D, PhD offered jointly with Graduate Theological Union; PhD with University of California, Berkeley. *Accreditation:* ACIPE; ATS (one or more programs are accredited). Part-time programs available. *Degree requirements:* For master's, variable foreign language requirement, thesis or alternative; for M Div, one foreign language. *Entrance requirements:* Minimum cumulative GPA of 2.5, two semesters of Greek. *Faculty research:* Theology and genetics, power and prayer, liturgy and ethics, Christianity and Confucianism, religion and abuse.

Pacific School of Religion, Graduate and Professional Programs, Berkeley, CA 94709-1323. Offers M Div, MA, MTS, D Min, PhD, Th D, CAPS, CMS, CSS, CTS. MA, PhD, Th D offered jointly with Graduate Theological Union; D Min with Church Divinity School of the Pacific. *Accreditation:* ACIPE; ATS (one or more programs are accredited). Part-time programs available. *Degree requirements:* For master's, one foreign language, thesis (for some programs); for doctorate, thesis/dissertation. *Entrance requirements:* For M Div and master's, minimum GPA of 3.0; for doctorate, M Div, minimum GPA of 3.0 (D Min); for other advanced degree, M Div, minimum GPA of 3.0 (CAPS). Additional exam requirements/recommendations for international students: Required—TOEFL (minimum score 550 paper-based; 213 computer-based). Electronic applications accepted. *Faculty research:* Medical ethics, gay/lesbian studies in religion, Asian-American religion, race, culture and theology, theology in context.

Payne Theological Seminary, Program in Theology, Wilberforce, OH 45384-3474. Offers M Div. *Accreditation:* ACIPE; ATS. Part-time and evening/weekend programs available. Postbaccalaureate distance learning degree programs offered (minimal on-campus study). *Degree requirements:* For M Div, 2 foreign languages, thesis/dissertation.

Pentecostal Theological Seminary, Graduate and Professional Programs, Cleveland, TN 37320-3330. Offers counseling (MA); discipleship and Christian formations (MA); ministry (D Min); theology (M Div). *Accreditation:* ACIPE; ATS. Part-time programs available. *Degree requirements:* For M Div, 2 foreign languages, thesis/dissertation, internship. *Faculty research:* Biblical exegesis.

Pepperdine University, Seaver College, Division of Religion, Master of Divinity Program, Malibu, CA 90263. Offers M Div. *Students:* 2 full-time (0 women), 5 part-time (2 women); includes 2 minority (both Asian, non-Hispanic/Latino). 3 applicants, 100% accepted, 3 enrolled. *Entrance requirements:* Additional exam requirements/recommendations for international students: Required—TOEFL. *Application deadline:* For fall admission, 2/1 priority date for domestic students. Applications are processed on a rolling basis. Application fee: $55. Electronic applications accepted. *Financial support:* Applicants required to submit FAFSA. *Unit head:* Dr. Timothy Willis, Chair/Professor of Religion, 310-506-4352, E-mail: timothy.willis@pepperdine.edu. *Application contact:* Michael Truschke, Dean of Admission and Enrollment Management, 310-506-6165, Fax: 310-506-4861, E-mail: admission-seaver@pepperdine.edu.

Pfeiffer University, Program in Practical Theology, Misenheimer, NC 28109-0960. Offers MA. Part-time and evening/weekend programs available. *Entrance requirements:* For master's, minimum GPA of 2.75.

Philadelphia Biblical University, School of Biblical Studies, Langhorne, PA 19047-2990. Offers M Div, MSB. Part-time and evening/weekend programs available. *Faculty:* 8 full-time (0 women), 1 part-time/adjunct (0 women). *Students:* 17 full-time (7 women), 66 part-time (17 women); includes 40 minority (35 Black or African American, non-Hispanic/Latino; 4 Asian, non-Hispanic/Latino; 1 Hispanic/Latino), 2 international. Average age 39. 38 applicants, 47% accepted, 9 enrolled. In 2010, 6 M Divs, 3 master's awarded. *Entrance requirements:* Additional exam requirements/recommendations for international students: Required—TOEFL (minimum score 550 paper-based; 213 computer-based). *Application deadline:* Applications are processed on a rolling basis. Application fee: $25. Electronic applications accepted. *Expenses:* Tuition: Full-time $10,710; part-time $595 per credit. Tuition and fees vary according to program. *Financial support:* In 2010–11, 15 students received support. Scholarships/grants available. Support available to part-time students. Financial award applicants required to submit FAFSA. *Unit head:* Dr. O. Herbert Hirt, Dean, 215-702-4354, Fax: 215-702-4359, E-mail: bible@pbu.edu. *Application contact:* Timothy Nessler, Assistant Director, Graduate Admissions, 800-572-2472, Fax: 215-702-4248, E-mail: tnessler@pbu.edu.

Phillips Theological Seminary, Programs in Theology, Tulsa, OK 74116. Offers administration of church agencies (M Div); campus ministry (M Div); church-related social work (M Div); college and seminary teaching (M Div); global mission work (M Div); institutional chaplaincy (M Div); ministerial vocations in Christian education (M Div); ministry (D Min), including parish ministry, pastoral counseling, practices of ministry; ministry and culture (MAMC), including Christian education, congregational leadership, history and practice of Christian spirituality, theology, ethics, and culture; ministry of music (M Div); pastoral care and counseling (M Div); pastoral ministry (M Div); theological studies (MTS). *Accreditation:* ATS. Part-time programs available. Postbaccalaureate distance learning degree programs offered (minimal on-campus study). *Degree requirements:* For master's, thesis (for some programs); for doctorate, thesis/dissertation. *Entrance requirements:* For master's, minimum GPA of 2.5; for doctorate, M Div, minimum GPA of 3.0. *Faculty research:* Biblical studies, historical studies, theology and culture, practical theology, theology and film.

Phoenix Seminary, Graduate Programs, Phoenix, AZ 85018. Offers Biblical and theological studies (Graduate Diploma); Biblical communication (M Div); Biblical leadership (MA); Christian counseling (Graduate Diploma); counseling and family (M Div); leadership development (M Div);

Theology

Phoenix Seminary (continued)
ministry (D Min); professional counseling (MA). *Accreditation:* ATS (one or more programs are accredited). Part-time and evening/weekend programs available. *Faculty:* 6 full-time (0 women), 7 part-time/adjunct (0 women). *Students:* 30 full-time (4 women), 160 part-time (50 women); includes 40 minority (18 Black or African American, non-Hispanic/Latino; 8 Asian, non-Hispanic/Latino; 12 Hispanic/Latino; 2 Two or more races, non-Hispanic/Latino). Average age 37. 49 applicants, 96% accepted, 37 enrolled. In 2010, 21 master's, 5 doctorates, 8 other advanced degrees awarded. *Degree requirements:* For master's, 2 foreign languages, comprehensive exam; for doctorate, 2 foreign languages, thesis/dissertation. *Entrance requirements:* For master's, undergraduate degree with minimum GPA of 2.5; for doctorate, M Div (94 hours) with minimum GPA of 3.0. Additional exam requirements/recommendations for international students: Required—TOEFL (minimum score 587 paper-based; 240 computer-based; 92 iBT), TWE (minimum score 4.5). *Application deadline:* For fall admission, 6/1 for domestic students; for spring admission, 11/1 for domestic students. Applications are processed on a rolling basis. Application fee: $90. *Expenses:* Tuition: Full-time $10,105; part-time $430 per semester hour. Required fees: $430 per semester hour. $60 per semester. One-time fee: $160. *Financial support:* In 2010–11, 123 students received support. Institutionally sponsored loans and scholarships/grants available. Support available to part-time students. Financial award application deadline: 6/1; financial award applicants required to submit FAFSA. *Application contact:* Roma Royer, Director of Admissions and Academic Services, 602-850-8000 Ext. 111, Fax: 602-850-8080, E-mail: rroyer@ps.edu.

Piedmont Baptist College and Graduate School, Piedmont Baptist Graduate School, Winston-Salem, NC 27101-5197. Offers chaplaincy track (MABS); non-language track (MABS); PhD preparation track (MABS); theology (M Min, PhD). Part-time programs available. Post-baccalaureate distance learning degree programs offered (no on-campus study). *Degree requirements:* For master's, 2 foreign languages, comprehensive exam, thesis or alternative; for doctorate, 2 foreign languages, comprehensive exam. *Entrance requirements:* For master's, GRE General Test; for doctorate, Hebrew and Greek proficiency, MA. Electronic applications accepted. *Faculty research:* Theological and biblical studies.

Pittsburgh Theological Seminary, Graduate and Professional Programs, Pittsburgh, PA 15206-2596. Offers divinity (M Div); ministry (D Min); theology (MA, STM); JD/M Div; M Div/MS; M Div/MSW. M Div/MSW offered jointly with University of Pittsburgh; JD/M Div with Duquesne University; M Div/MS with Carnegie Mellon University. *Accreditation:* ATS (one or more programs are accredited). Part-time and evening/weekend programs available. *Faculty:* 17 full-time (3 women), 9 part-time/adjunct (3 women). *Students:* 248 full-time (87 women), 57 part-time (29 women); includes 38 Black or African American, non-Hispanic/Latino; 4 Asian, non-Hispanic/Latino; 2 Hispanic/Latino, 9 international. Average age 36. 123 applicants, 80% accepted, 68 enrolled. In 2010, 37 first professional degrees, 17 master's, 23 doctorates awarded. *Degree requirements:* For master's, comprehensive exam (for some programs), thesis (for some programs); for doctorate, thesis/dissertation; for M Div, one foreign language. *Entrance requirements:* For M Div and master's, bachelor's degree with minimum GPA of 2.7, interview, references; for doctorate, interview, references. Additional exam requirements/recommendations for international students: Required—TOEFL (minimum score 570 paper-based; 230 computer-based; 89 iBT). *Application deadline:* For fall admission, 6/30 priority date for domestic students, 12/1 for international students; for winter admission, 10/15 priority date for domestic students; for spring admission, 1/15 priority date for domestic students. Applications are processed on a rolling basis. Application fee: $40. *Expenses:* Tuition: Full-time $2574; part-time $303 per credit hour. Required fees: $51 per term. Tuition and fees vary according to course load. *Financial support:* In 2010–11, 104 students received support. Career-related internships or fieldwork, scholarships/grants, and institutional work-study available. Financial award application deadline: 3/30; financial award applicants required to submit FAFSA. *Unit head:* Dr. Byron H. Jackson, Dean of Faculty and Vice President for Academic Affairs, 412-924-1374, Fax: 412-924-1774, E-mail: bjackson@pts.edu. *Application contact:* Sherry Sparks, Associate Dean of Admissions, 412-924-1382, Fax: 412-924-1782, E-mail: ssparks@pts.edu.

Pontifical Catholic University of Puerto Rico, College of Arts and Humanities, Department of Theology and Philosophy, Ponce, PR 00717-0777. Offers M Div.

Pontifical College Josephinum, School of Theology, Columbus, OH 43235. Offers M Div, MA. *Accreditation:* ATS. Part-time programs available. *Degree requirements:* For master's, 3 foreign languages, comprehensive exam, thesis; for M Div, 2 foreign languages, thesis/dissertation. *Entrance requirements:* For M Div, GRE General Test, 24 credit hours of course work in philosophy, 12 credit hours of course work in theology; for master's, GRE General Test, 15 credit hours of course work in philosophy, 6 credit hours of course work in scripture. Additional exam requirements/recommendations for international students: Required—TOEFL (minimum score 600 paper-based; 250 computer-based).

Princeton Theological Seminary, Graduate and Professional Programs, Princeton, NJ 08542-0803. Offers M Div, MA, Th M, D Min, PhD. *Accreditation:* ACIPE; ATS. Part-time programs available. Terminal master's awarded for partial completion of doctoral program. *Degree requirements:* For doctorate, 2 foreign languages, thesis/dissertation, comprehensive exam (PhD), French and German. *Entrance requirements:* For doctorate, GRE General Test. Additional exam requirements/recommendations for international students: Required—TOEFL. Electronic applications accepted.

Providence College, Graduate Studies, Department of Religious Studies, Providence, RI 02918. Offers Biblical studies (MA); theology (MA, MTS). Part-time and evening/weekend programs available. *Faculty:* 12 full-time (4 women), 1 (woman) part-time/adjunct. *Students:* 4 full-time (2 women), 25 part-time (6 women); includes 1 minority (Two or more races, non-Hispanic/Latino). Average age 40. 4 applicants, 100% accepted. In 2010, 14 master's awarded. *Degree requirements:* For master's, comprehensive exam, Greek and Hebrew (biblical studies). *Entrance requirements:* Additional exam requirements/recommendations for international students: Required—TOEFL (minimum score 550 paper-based; 213 computer-based; 80 iBT). *Application deadline:* For fall admission, 8/1 priority date for domestic and international students; for spring admission, 12/1 priority date for domestic and international students. Applications are processed on a rolling basis. Application fee: $55. *Expenses:* Tuition: Part-time $367 per credit. Required fees: $367. *Financial support:* In 2010–11, 4 research assistantships with full tuition reimbursements (averaging $8,400 per year) were awarded; career-related internships or fieldwork and unspecified assistantships also available. Support available to part-time students. Financial award application deadline: 8/1; financial award applicants required to submit FAFSA. *Unit head:* Rev. Thomas McCreesh, Director, 401-865-1150, Fax: 401-865-1830, E-mail: tmccrees@providence.edu. *Application contact:* Rev. Thomas McCreesh, Director, 401-865-1150, Fax: 401-865-1830, E-mail: tmccrees@providence.edu.

Providence College and Theological Seminary, Theological Seminary, Otterburne, MB R0A 1G0, Canada. Offers children's ministry (Certificate); Christian studies (MA, Certificate); counseling (MA); cross-cultural discipleship (Certificate); divinity (M Div); educational studies (MA), including counseling psychology, educational ministries, student development, teaching English to speakers of other languages, training teachers of English to speakers of other languages; global studies (MA); lay counseling (Diploma); ministry (D Min); teaching English to speakers of other languages (Certificate); theological studies (MA); training teacher of English to speakers of other languages (Certificate); youth ministry (Certificate). *Accreditation:* ATS. Part-time programs available. *Degree requirements:* For master's, variable foreign language requirement, thesis (for some programs); for doctorate, thesis/dissertation; for M Div, 2 foreign languages, comprehensive exam, thesis/dissertation (for some programs). *Entrance requirements:* Additional exam requirements/recommendations for international students: Recommended—TOEFL (minimum score 550 paper-based; 213 computer-based). *Faculty research:* Studies in Isaiah, theology of sin.

Queen's University at Kingston, Queen's Theological College, Kingston, ON K7L 3N6, Canada. Offers M Div, MTS, Certificate. *Accreditation:* ATS. Part-time programs available. *Degree requirements:* For master's, thesis (for some programs); for M Div, 2 foreign languages. *Entrance requirements:* For master's, minimum undergraduate B average. Additional exam requirements/recommendations for international students: Required—TOEFL (minimum score 580 paper-based). *Faculty research:* Early Christian group formations, pastoral care and spiritual direction, feminist theology, public religion, interpretation of Biblical texts using psychologies of shame and trauma.

Quincy University, Program in Theological Studies, Quincy, IL 62301-2699. Offers MTS. Part-time and evening/weekend programs available. *Faculty:* 2 full-time (0 women). *Students:* 4 part-time (1 woman); includes 1 Black or African American, non-Hispanic/Latino. *Entrance requirements:* For master's, MAT or GRE. Additional exam requirements/recommendations for international students: Required—TOEFL (minimum score 550 paper-based). *Application deadline:* Applications are processed on a rolling basis. Application fee: $25. Electronic applications accepted. *Expenses:* Tuition: Full-time $8880; part-time $370 per semester hour. Required fees: $360; $15 per semester hour. Tuition and fees vary according to course load, campus/location and program. *Financial support:* Applicants required to submit FAFSA. *Unit head:* Dr. Daniel Strudwick, Director, 217-228-5432 Ext. 3202, E-mail: strudda@quincy.edu. *Application contact:* Jennifer Bang, Coordinator of Adult Studies, 217-228-5404, Fax: 217-228-5479, E-mail: admissions@quincy.edu.

Rabbi Isaac Elchanan Theological Seminary, Graduate Program, New York, NY 10033-1807. Offers Certificate of Advanced Ordination, Certificate of Ordination. *Degree requirements:* For other advanced degree, one foreign language, comprehensive exam. *Entrance requirements:* For degree, oral exam, 2 interview, undergraduate major in Jewish studies or equivalent. *Faculty research:* Talmud, rabbinics.

Rabbinical Academy Mesivta Rabbi Chaim Berlin, Graduate Program, Brooklyn, NY 11230-4715. Offers Advanced Talmudic Degree, Second Talmudic Degree. *Accreditation:* AARTS. *Degree requirements:* For other advanced degree, 2 foreign languages. *Entrance requirements:* For degree, must be a graduate of a rabbinical school.

Rabbinical College Beth Shraga, Graduate Programs, Monsey, NY 10952-3035. *Accreditation:* AARTS.

Rabbinical College Bobover Yeshiva B'nei Zion, Graduate Programs, Brooklyn, NY 11219. *Accreditation:* AARTS.

Rabbinical College Ch'san Sofer, Graduate Programs, Brooklyn, NY 11204. *Accreditation:* AARTS.

Rabbinical College of Long Island, Graduate Programs, Long Beach, NY 11561-3305. *Accreditation:* AARTS.

Rabbinical Seminary M'kor Chaim, Graduate Programs, Brooklyn, NY 11219. *Accreditation:* AARTS.

Rabbinical Seminary of America, Graduate Programs, Flushing, NY 11367. School offers a master's and first professional degree. *Accreditation:* AARTS.

Reconstructionist Rabbinical College, Graduate Programs, Wyncote, PA 19095-1898. Offers Jewish studies (MAJS); rabbinics (MAHL, DHL); women's studies (Certificate). Certificate offered jointly with Temple University. Part-time programs available. *Faculty:* 8 full-time (4 women), 25 part-time/adjunct (14 women). *Students:* 52 full-time (37 women), 7 part-time (4 women). 25 applicants, 52% accepted, 11 enrolled. *Degree requirements:* For master's, one foreign language, thesis (MAJS), completion of rabbinical program (MAHL); for doctorate and MAHL, one foreign language. *Entrance requirements:* For MAHL and doctorate, GRE General Test, placement examinations in Hebrew and Judaism; for master's, GRE General Test. *Application deadline:* Applications are processed on a rolling basis. Application fee: $50. *Financial support:* In 2010–11, 46 students received support, including 4 fellowships with full tuition reimbursements available (averaging $11,000 per year), 1 research assistantship with partial tuition reimbursement available (averaging $5,500 per year), 5 teaching assistantships (averaging $5,500 per year); career-related internships or fieldwork, institutionally sponsored loans, and scholarships/grants also available. Financial award application deadline: 4/15. *Faculty research:* Bible, Hebrew Semitic texts, contemporary Judaism. *Unit head:* Rabbi Dan Ehrenkrantz, President, 215-576-0800 Ext. 129, Fax: 215-576-6143, E-mail: dehrenkrantz@rrc.edu. *Application contact:* Rabbi Amber Powers, Dean of Recruitment and Admissions, 215-576-0800 Ext. 145, Fax: 215-576-6143, E-mail: apowers@rrc.edu.

Reformed Presbyterian Theological Seminary, Graduate and Professional Programs, Pittsburgh, PA 15208-2594. Offers M Div, MTS, D Min. *Accreditation:* ATS. Part-time and evening/weekend programs available. Electronic applications accepted. *Faculty research:* Prayer.

Reformed Theological Seminary–Atlanta Campus, Graduate Programs, Atlanta, GA 30327. Offers M Div, MABS, MAR, D Min, Certificate.

Reformed Theological Seminary–Charlotte Campus, Graduate and Professional Programs, Charlotte, NC 28226-6318. Offers biblical studies (MA); ministry (D Min); pastoral ministry (M Div); theological studies (MA). Part-time programs available. *Degree requirements:* For master's, comprehensive exam; for doctorate, thesis/dissertation; for M Div, 2 foreign languages, comprehensive exam. *Entrance requirements:* For master's, minimum GPA of 2.6; for doctorate, minimum GPA of 3.0. Additional exam requirements/recommendations for international students: Required—TOEFL (minimum score 550 paper-based; 213 computer-based). Electronic applications accepted.

Reformed Theological Seminary–Jackson Campus, Graduate and Professional Programs, Jackson, MS 39209-3099. Offers Bible, theology, and missions (Certificate); biblical studies (MA); Christian education (M Div, MA); counseling (M Div); divinity (M Div, Diploma); marriage and family therapy (MA); ministry (D Min); missions (M Div, MA, D Min); New Testament (Th M); Old Testament (Th M); theological studies (MA); theology (Th M); M Div/MA. *Accreditation:* AAMFT/COAMFTE (one or more programs are accredited); ATS (one or more programs are accredited). *Degree requirements:* For master's, thesis (for some programs), fieldwork; for doctorate, 2 foreign languages, thesis/dissertation; for M Div, 2 foreign languages, thesis/dissertation (for some programs). *Entrance requirements:* For M Div and master's, minimum GPA of 2.6; for doctorate, minimum GPA of 3.0. Additional exam requirements/recommendations for international students: Required—TOEFL.

Reformed Theological Seminary–Orlando Campus, Graduate Program, Oviedo, FL 32765-7197. Offers biblical studies (MA); counseling (MA); ministry (D Min); reformation studies (Th M); theological studies (MA); theology (M Div); MA/Certificate. Ma/Certificate offered jointly with University of Central Florida. Part-time programs available. Postbaccalaureate distance learning degree programs offered (minimal on-campus study). *Entrance requirements:* For M Div and master's, minimum GPA of 2.6. Electronic applications accepted.

Reformed Theological Seminary–Washington D.C., Graduate and Professional Programs, McLean, VA 22101. Offers Bible (M Div); practical theology (M Div); religion (MA); theology (M Div). Part-time and evening/weekend programs available. *Faculty:* 2 full-time (0 women), 5 part-time/adjunct (0 women). *Students:* 13 full-time (1 woman), 69 part-time (7 women); includes 4 Black or African American, non-Hispanic/Latino; 20 Asian, non-Hispanic/Latino; 2 Hispanic/Latino, 1 international. Average age 35. 30 applicants, 77% accepted, 15 enrolled. In 2010, 11 master's awarded. *Degree requirements:* For master's, integrative paper. *Entrance requirements:* For master's, minimum undergraduate GPA of 2.6. Additional exam requirements/recommendations for international students: Required—TOEFL (minimum score 550 paper-based; 213 computer-based), TWE. *Application deadline:* Applications are processed on a rolling basis. Application fee: $75. Electronic applications accepted. *Expenses:* Tuition: Full-time $7020; part-time $1755 per semester. Tuition and fees vary according to course load. *Financial* *support:* In 2010–11, 76 students received support, including 7 fellowships (averaging $1,000 per year); institutionally sponsored loans, scholarships/grants, tuition waivers (partial), and unspecified assistantships also available. Support available to part-time students. Financial award application deadline: 6/1. *Faculty research:* Theology, Biblical studies, cultural studies. *Unit head:* Hugh C. Whelchel, Executive Director, 703-448-3393, Fax: 703-738-7389, E-mail: hwhelchel@rts.edu. *Application contact:* Geoff M. Sackett, Director of Admissions, 703-448-3393, Fax: 703-738-7389, E-mail: gsackett@rts.edu.

Regent College, Program in Theology, Vancouver, BC V6T 2E4, Canada. Offers M Div, MCS, Th M, Dip CS. *Accreditation:* ATS (one or more programs are accredited). Part-time programs available. *Faculty:* 16 full-time (3 women), 16 part-time/adjunct (6 women). *Students:* 220 full-time (76 women), 233 part-time (94 women); includes 2 Black or African American, non-Hispanic/Latino; 1 American Indian or Alaska Native, non-Hispanic/Latino; 113 Asian, non-Hispanic/Latino; 7 Hispanic/Latino. Average age 33. 220 applicants, 88% accepted, 133 enrolled. In 2010, 51 M Divs, 81 master's, 64 other advanced degrees awarded. *Degree requirements:* For master's, thesis (for some programs). *Entrance requirements:* For M Div and Dip CS, minimum GPA of 2.8; for master's, minimum GPA of 2.8 (MCS), 3.5 (Th M). Additional exam requirements/recommendations for international students: Required—TOEFL (minimum score 575 paper-based; 230 computer-based; 90 iBT). *Application deadline:* For fall admission, 2/1 priority date for domestic students, 1/1 priority date for international students; for winter admission, 7/1 priority date for domestic and international students; for spring admission, 2/1 priority date for domestic students, 1/1 priority date for international students. Applications are processed on a rolling basis. Application fee: $60 Canadian dollars. Electronic applications accepted. *Financial support:* In 2010–11, 130 students received support, including 112 teaching assistantships (averaging $2,365 per year); career-related internships or fieldwork, scholarships/grants, and health care benefits also available. Financial award application deadline: 3/1. *Faculty research:* Integration of theology with secular life, Biblical studies. *Unit head:* Dr. Rod Wilson, President, 604-221-3318, Fax: 604-224-3097, E-mail: presidentsoffice@regent-college.edu. *Application contact:* Amy Petroelje, Housing and Inquiries Coordinator, 604-224-3245 Ext. 355, Fax: 604-224-3097, E-mail: admissions@regent-college.edu.

Regent University, Graduate School, School of Divinity, Virginia Beach, VA 23464-9800. Offers Biblical studies (MA); leadership and renewal (D Min); missiology (M Div, MA); practical theology (M Div, MA); renewal studies (PhD); M Div/M Ed; M Div/MA; M Div/MBA; M Ed/MA; MBA/MA. *Accreditation:* ACIPE; ATS. Part-time programs available. Postbaccalaureate distance learning degree programs offered (minimal on-campus study). *Faculty:* 20 full-time (4 women), 26 part-time/adjunct (5 women). *Students:* 128 full-time (60 women), 524 part-time (225 women); includes 278 Black or African American, non-Hispanic/Latino; 4 American Indian or Alaska Native, non-Hispanic/Latino; 16 Asian, non-Hispanic/Latino; 24 Hispanic/Latino, 20 international. Average age 41. 361 applicants, 64% accepted, 154 enrolled. In 2010, 32 first professional degrees, 61 master's, 9 doctorates awarded. *Degree requirements:* For master's, comprehensive exam, thesis or alternative, internship; for doctorate, thesis/dissertation or alternative; for M Div, internship. *Entrance requirements:* For M Div, GRE General Test or MAT, minimum undergraduate GPA of 3.0, minimum 3 years of ministry experience, transcripts, recommendations; for master's, GRE General Test or MAT, minimum undergraduate GPA of 2.75, writing sample, clergy recommendation; for doctorate, M Div or theological master's degree; minimum graduate GPA of 3.5 (PhD), 3.0 (D Min); recommendations; writing sample; transcripts. Additional exam requirements/recommendations for international students: Required—TOEFL (minimum score 577 paper-based; 233 computer-based). *Application deadline:* For fall admission, 5/1 priority date for domestic students. Applications are processed on a rolling basis. Application fee: $50. Electronic applications accepted. *Expenses:* Contact institution. *Financial support:* Fellowships with full and partial tuition reimbursements, career-related internships or fieldwork, scholarships/grants, tuition waivers (full and partial), and unspecified assistantships available. Support available to part-time students. Financial award application deadline: 9/1; financial award applicants required to submit FAFSA. *Faculty research:* Greek and Hebrew, theology, spiritual formation, global missions and world Christianity, women's studies. *Unit head:* Dr. Michael Palmer, Dean, 757-352-4406, Fax: 757-352-4597, E-mail: mpalmer@regent.edu. *Application contact:* Matthew Chadwick, Director of Enrollment Support Services, 800-373-5504, Fax: 757-352-4381, E-mail: admissions@regent.edu.

Regis College, Graduate and Professional Programs, Toronto, ON M5S 2Z5, Canada. Offers eastern Christian studies (Certificate); Ignatian studies (Diploma); Lonergan studies (Diploma); ministry (D Min); ministry and spirituality (MAMS); philosophical studies (Diploma); retreat direction (Certificate); sacred theology (STB, STM, STD, STL); spiritual direction (Diploma); spiritual theology (Diploma); theological studies (MTS, Diploma); theology (M Div, MA, Th M, PhD, Th D); M Div/MA. *Accreditation:* ATS (one or more programs are accredited). Terminal master's awarded for partial completion of doctoral program. *Degree requirements:* For master's, 2 foreign languages, thesis; for doctorate, 3 foreign languages, comprehensive exam, thesis/dissertation; for first professional degree, comprehensive exam. *Entrance requirements:* For first professional degree and other advanced degree, minimum GPA of 3.0; for master's, minimum GPA of 3.3; for doctorate, minimum GPA of 3.7. Additional exam requirements/recommendations for international students: Required—TOEFL (minimum score 580 paper-based; 237 computer-based; 93 iBT), TWE (minimum score 5).

Sacred Heart Major Seminary, School of Theology, Detroit, MI 48206-1799. Offers pastoral studies (MAPS); theology (M Div, MA). *Accreditation:* ACIPE; ATS. Part-time and evening/weekend programs available. *Degree requirements:* For master's, one foreign language, thesis optional, integrating project; for M Div, integrating seminar. *Entrance requirements:* For M Div and master's, GRE, previous course work in philosophy and theology. *Faculty research:* Local church history, patristics, spirituality, religious education.

Sacred Heart School of Theology, Graduate and Professional Programs, Hales Corners, WI 53130-0429. Offers theology (M Div, MA). *Accreditation:* ACIPE; ATS. Part-time programs available. *Faculty:* 29 full-time (6 women), 14 part-time/adjunct (6 women). *Students:* 89 full-time (0 women), 18 part-time (8 women); includes 11 minority (4 Black or African American, non-Hispanic/Latino; 2 American Indian or Alaska Native, non-Hispanic/Latino; 2 Asian, non-Hispanic/Latino; 1 Hispanic/Latino; 2 Native Hawaiian or other Pacific Islander, non-Hispanic/Latino), 18 international. Average age 47. 39 applicants, 100% accepted, 39 enrolled. In 2010, 11 first professional degrees, 5 master's awarded. *Degree requirements:* For master's, essay or comprehensive exam; for M Div, integrating seminar. *Entrance requirements:* For master's, MAT, 6 hours of course work each in philosophy and theology, letter of recommendation. Additional exam requirements/recommendations for international students: Required—TOEFL. *Application deadline:* For fall admission, 8/1 for domestic students; for spring admission, 12/1 for domestic students. Applications are processed on a rolling basis. Application fee: $50. *Expenses:* Tuition: Full-time $14,100; part-time $480 per credit. Required fees: $25 per term. *Financial support:* In 2010–11, 5 students received support. Career-related internships or fieldwork and scholarships/grants available. Financial award application deadline: 9/30; financial award applicants required to submit FAFSA. *Unit head:* Very Rev. Jan de Jong, President-Rector, 414-425-8300 Ext. 6972, Fax: 414-529-6999, E-mail: jdejong@shst.edu. *Application contact:* Rev. Thomas L. Knoebel, Director of Admissions, 414-425-8300 Ext. 6984, Fax: 414-529-6999, E-mail: tknoebel@shst.edu.

St. Andrew's College, Graduate Programs in Theology, Saskatoon, SK S7N 0W3, Canada. Offers M Div, MTS, STM. *Accreditation:* ATS. *Faculty:* 4 full-time (3 women), 2 part-time/adjunct (both women). *Students:* 10 full-time (4 women), 16 part-time (12 women). Tuition and fees charges are reported in Canadian dollars. *Expenses:* Tuition: Full-time $6500 Canadian dollars; part-time $650 Canadian dollars per course. Required fees: $150 Canadian dollars. One-time fee: $150 Canadian dollars part-time. Tuition and fees vary according to course level and degree level.

St. Andrew's College in Winnipeg, Graduate Programs, Winnipeg, MB R3T 2M7, Canada. Offers M Div. *Degree requirements:* For M Div, one foreign language, thesis/dissertation. *Faculty research:* Church history, doctrine, liturgical theology.

St. Augustine's Seminary of Toronto, Graduate and Professional Programs, Scarborough, ON M1M 1M3, Canada. Offers divinity (M Div); lay ministry (Diploma); religious education (MRE); theological studies (MTS, Diploma). *Accreditation:* ATS. Part-time and evening/weekend programs available. *Degree requirements:* For M Div, comprehensive exam (for some programs), thesis/dissertation optional, field education. *Entrance requirements:* Course work in philosophy. Additional exam requirements/recommendations for international students: Required—TOEFL (minimum score 580 paper-based; 237 computer-based), TWE (minimum score 5).

Saint Bernard's School of Theology and Ministry, Graduate and Professional Programs, Rochester, NY 14618. Offers pastoral studies (MA, Certificate); theological studies (MA); theology (M Div). *Accreditation:* ATS (one or more programs are accredited). Part-time and evening/weekend programs available. *Faculty:* 3 full-time (all women), 8 part-time/adjunct (4 women). *Students:* 7 full-time (2 women), 106 part-time (50 women); includes 1 Black or African American, non-Hispanic/Latino; 1 Asian, non-Hispanic/Latino; 2 Hispanic/Latino. Average age 50. 17 applicants, 94% accepted, 16 enrolled. In 2010, 3 first professional degrees, 14 master's awarded. *Degree requirements:* For master's, variable foreign language requirement, thesis (for some programs). *Entrance requirements:* For M Div, minimum GPA of 2.0; for master's, minimum GPA of 2.5. *Application deadline:* Applications are processed on a rolling basis. Application fee: $75. *Expenses:* Tuition: Full-time $9144; part-time $1524 per course. Required fees: $30 per semester. *Financial support:* In 2010–11, 31 students received support; fellowships, research assistantships, teaching assistantships, career-related internships or fieldwork, scholarships/grants, and tuition waivers (partial) available. Support available to part-time students. Financial award application deadline: 4/15; financial award applicants required to submit FAFSA. *Unit head:* Dr. Patricia Schoelles, President, 585-271-3657 Ext. 276, Fax: 585-271-2045, E-mail: pschoelles@stbernards.edu. *Application contact:* Laura Smith, Director of Admissions and Financial Aid, 585-271-3657 Ext. 289, Fax: 585-271-2045, E-mail: admissions@stbernards.edu.

St. Catherine University, Graduate Programs, Program in Theology, St. Paul, MN 55105. Offers catechetical ministry (Certificate); pastoral ministry (Certificate); spiritual direction (Certificate); theology (MA). *Faculty:* 8 full-time (2 women). *Students:* 12 full-time (11 women), 22 part-time (20 women); includes 4 minority (2 Black or African American, non-Hispanic/Latino; 1 Asian, non-Hispanic/Latino; 1 Two or more races, non-Hispanic/Latino). Average age 47. 6 applicants, 83% accepted, 5 enrolled. In 2010, 14 master's awarded. *Degree requirements:* For master's, comprehensive exam, thesis (for some programs). *Entrance requirements:* For master's, MAT, minimum GPA of 3.0. Additional exam requirements/recommendations for international students: Required—Michigan English Language Assessment Battery or TOEFL (minimum score 600 paper-based; 250 computer-based; 100 iBT). *Application deadline:* For fall admission, 8/1 priority date for domestic students. Applications are processed on a rolling basis. Application fee: $35. *Expenses:* Contact institution. *Financial support:* In 2010–11, 9 students received support; research assistantships, career-related internships or fieldwork and institutionally sponsored loans available. Support available to part-time students. Financial award application deadline: 4/1; financial award applicants required to submit FAFSA. *Faculty research:* Feminist scholarship, historical theology, symbols, rites of purification, spirituality. *Unit head:* Dr. William McDonough, Director, 651-690-6072, Fax: 651-690-6024. *Application contact:* 651-690-6933, Fax: 651-690-6064.

St. Charles Borromeo Seminary, Overbrook, Graduate and Professional Programs, Division of Theology, Wynnewood, PA 19096. Offers M Div, MA. *Accreditation:* ATS. Part-time programs available. *Faculty:* 12 full-time (3 women), 9 part-time/adjunct (2 women). *Students:* 59 full-time (0 women); includes 3 minority (2 Asian, non-Hispanic/Latino; 1 Two or more races, non-Hispanic/Latino). Average age 27. 34 applicants, 100% accepted, 33 enrolled. In 2010, 13 first professional degrees, 12 master's awarded. *Degree requirements:* For master's, comprehensive exam, research papers; for M Div, comprehensive exam. *Entrance requirements:* For M Div, previous course work in philosophy and theology; for master's, M Div. Additional exam requirements/recommendations for international students: Required—TOEFL. *Application deadline:* For fall admission, 7/15 for domestic students, 3/15 for international students; for spring admission, 11/15 for domestic students. Applications are processed on a rolling basis. Application fee: $0. *Expenses:* Tuition: Full-time $18,888; part-time $1548 per course. Required fees: $1140. *Financial support:* Federal Work-Study and scholarships/grants available. *Unit head:* Rev. Robert A. Pesarchick, Academic Dean, 610-785-6204, Fax: 610-667-1422, E-mail: academicdcdscs@adphila.org. *Application contact:* Rev. Joseph W. Bongard, Vice Rector, 610-785-6271, Fax: 610-617-9267, E-mail: frjbongard@adphila.org.

Saint Francis Seminary, Graduate and Professional Programs, St. Francis, WI 53235-3795. Offers M Div, MAPS. *Accreditation:* ACIPE; ATS. Part-time programs available. *Degree requirements:* For master's, comprehensive exam; for M Div, thesis/dissertation. *Entrance requirements:* For M Div and master's, Otis IQ Test, Terman Concept Mastery Test, interview. Additional exam requirements/recommendations for international students: Required—TOEFL (minimum score 550 paper-based).

St. John's Seminary, Graduate and Professional Programs, Camarillo, CA 93012-2598. Offers divinity (M Div); pastoral ministry (MAPM); theology (MA). *Accreditation:* ATS. Part-time programs available. *Faculty:* 23 full-time (5 women), 7 part-time/adjunct (1 woman). *Students:* 77 full-time (5 women), 12 part-time (6 women); includes 14 Asian, non-Hispanic/Latino; 32 Hispanic/Latino; 1 Native Hawaiian or other Pacific Islander, non-Hispanic/Latino, 19 international. Average age 34. 19 applicants, 100% accepted, 16 enrolled. In 2010, 6 first professional degrees, 1 master's awarded. *Degree requirements:* For master's, comprehensive exam (for some programs), thesis optional, comprehensive integration paper (MAPM); for M Div, parish internship. *Entrance requirements:* For M Div, GRE General Test, bishop's approbation; for master's, GRE General Test, minimum GPA of 3.5 (MA), 2.5 (MAPM). Additional exam requirements/recommendations for international students: Required—TOEFL (minimum score 550 paper-based; 213 computer-based; 79 iBT). *Application deadline:* For fall admission, 7/15 priority date for domestic students. Applications are processed on a rolling basis. Application fee: $0. Electronic applications accepted. *Expenses:* Tuition: Full-time $14,000; part-time $467 per unit. One-time fee: $5201.96 full-time; $105 part-time. Full-time tuition and fees vary according to course load and program. *Faculty research:* Biblical studies, moral theology, historical studies, systematic theology, spiritual theology. *Unit head:* Rev. Kevin McCracken, CM, Interim Academic Dean, 805-482-2755 Ext. 1012, Fax: 805-482-3470, E-mail: kmccracken@stjohnsem.edu. *Application contact:* Esme M. Takahashi, Registrar, 805-482-2755 Ext. 1014, Fax: 805-482-3470, E-mail: esme@stjohnsem.edu.

Saint John's Seminary, Graduate Programs, Brighton, MA 02135. Offers M Div, MA Th, MAM. *Accreditation:* ATS.

St. John's University, St. John's College of Liberal Arts and Sciences, Department of Theology and Religious Studies, Queens, NY 11439. Offers pastoral ministry (Certificate); priestly studies (M Div); theology (MA, Certificate). *Accreditation:* ACIPE. Part-time and evening/weekend programs available. *Students:* 18 full-time (4 women), 21 part-time (15 women); includes 12 minority (5 Black or African American, non-Hispanic/Latino; 4 Asian, non-Hispanic/Latino; 3 Hispanic/Latino), 11 international. Average age 43. 32 applicants, 63% accepted, 10 enrolled. In 2010, 11 master's awarded. *Degree requirements:* For master's, comprehensive exam, thesis optional; for M Div, thesis/dissertation optional. *Entrance requirements:* For M Div and master's, minimum GPA of 3.0. Additional exam requirements/recommendations for international students: Required—TOEFL (minimum score 600 paper-based; 250 computer-based; 100 iBT), IELTS (minimum score 5.5). *Application deadline:* For fall admission, 5/1 priority date for domestic and international students; for spring admission, 11/1 priority date for domestic and international students. Applications are processed on a rolling basis. Application fee: $70. Electronic applications accepted. *Expenses:* Tuition: Full-time $17,100; part-time $950 per credit. Required fees: $340; $170 per semester. Tuition and fees vary according to program. *Financial support:* Research assistantships, scholarships/grants available. Support available to part-time students. Financial award application deadline: 3/1; financial award applicants

Theology

St. John's University (continued)

required to submit FAFSA. *Faculty research:* Systematic theology, moral theory, Biblical studies, pastoral theology, church history. *Unit head:* Fr. Michael Whalen, Chair, 718-990-1556, E-mail: whalenm@stjohns.edu. *Application contact:* Kathleen Davis, Director of Graduate Admission, 718-990-1601, Fax: 718-990-5686, E-mail: gradhelp@stjohns.edu.

Saint John's University, Saint John's School of Theology and Seminary, Collegeville, MN 56321. Offers divinity (M Div); liturgical music (MA); liturgical studies (MA); pastoral ministry (MA); theology (MA), including church history, liturgy, monastic studies, scripture, spirituality, systematics; M Div/MA. *Accreditation:* ATS. Part-time programs available. Postbaccalaureate distance learning degree programs offered (no on-campus study). *Degree requirements:* For master's, one foreign language, comprehensive exam (for some programs), thesis (for some programs). *Entrance requirements:* For master's, GRE General Test or MAT. Electronic applications accepted. *Faculty research:* Religious education, biblical literature.

St. Joseph's Seminary, Institute of Religious Studies, Yonkers, NY 10704. Offers MA. *Accreditation:* ATS. Part-time and evening/weekend programs available. *Degree requirements:* For master's, comprehensive exam. *Entrance requirements:* For master's, 18 hours in theology and/or philosophy. Electronic applications accepted. *Expenses:* Contact institution. *Faculty research:* Medical ethics, mystical theology of Karl Rahner, medieval church history.

St. Joseph's Seminary, Professional Program, Yonkers, NY 10704. Offers divinity (M Div); theology (MA). *Accreditation:* ATS. *Degree requirements:* For master's, one foreign language, thesis; for M Div, comprehensive exam. *Entrance requirements:* For M Div and master's, 27 credits in philosophy and 9 in theology.

Saint Leo University, Graduate Studies in Theology, Saint Leo, FL 33574-6665. Offers theology (MA). Part-time and evening/weekend programs available. *Faculty:* 8 full-time (0 women), 1 part-time/adjunct (0 women). *Students:* 184 full-time (37 women), 1 part-time (0 women); includes 20 minority (10 Black or African American, non-Hispanic/Latino; 1 American Indian or Alaska Native, non-Hispanic/Latino; 2 Asian, non-Hispanic/Latino; 7 Hispanic/Latino). Average age 52. In 2010, 6 master's awarded. *Degree requirements:* For master's, comprehensive project. *Entrance requirements:* For master's, bachelor's degree from regionally-accredited college or university with minimum GPA of 3.0, letter of recommendation. Additional exam requirements/recommendations for international students: Required—TOEFL (minimum score 550 paper-based; 213 computer-based; 80 iBT). *Application deadline:* For fall admission, 7/1 priority date for domestic and international students; for spring admission, 11/1 priority date for domestic and international students. Applications are processed on a rolling basis. Application fee: $75. Electronic applications accepted. *Expenses:* Tuition: Part-time $609 per semester hour. Required fees: $115 per course. Tuition and fees vary according to campus/location and program. *Financial support:* In 2010–11, 4 students received support. Federal Work-Study, scholarships/grants, and health care benefits available. Financial award applicants required to submit FAFSA. *Faculty research:* Ecclesiology and the Second Vatican Council, sacramental theology and the liturgical movement, Christian and Eastern religious traditions, ecumenism, ministry and technology. *Unit head:* Fr. Anthony Kissel, Director, 352-588-7297, Fax: 352-588-8404, E-mail: anthony.kissel@saintleo.edu. *Application contact:* Jared Welling, Director, Graduate/Weekend and Evening Admission, 800-707-8846, Fax: 352-588-7873, E-mail: grad.admissions@saintleo.edu.

Saint Louis University, Graduate Education, College of Arts and Sciences and Graduate Education, Department of Theological Studies, St. Louis, MO 63103-2097. Offers historical theology (MA, PhD); theology (MA). Part-time programs available. *Degree requirements:* For master's, comprehensive exam; for doctorate, 4 foreign languages, comprehensive exam, thesis/dissertation, preliminary exams. *Entrance requirements:* For master's, GRE General Test, letters of recommendation, resume; for doctorate, GRE General Test, letters of recommendation, resumé, interview, transcripts, goal statement. Additional exam requirements/recommendations for international students: Required—TOEFL (minimum score 550 paper-based; 213 computer-based). Electronic applications accepted. *Faculty research:* Biblical and early church studies, medieval and renaissance studies, modern and American Christianity, comparative and interreligious studies, moral and ethical theology.

Saint Mary-of-the-Woods College, Program in Pastoral Theology, Saint Mary-of-the-Woods, IN 47876. Offers pastoral theology (MA); youth ministry (Graduate Certificate). Part-time and evening/weekend programs available. Postbaccalaureate distance learning degree programs offered (minimal on-campus study). *Degree requirements:* For master's, thesis, qualifying exam.

Saint Mary Seminary and Graduate School of Theology, School of Theology, Wickliffe, OH 44092-2527. Offers M Div, MA, D Min. *Accreditation:* ATS. Part-time programs available. *Degree requirements:* For master's, comprehensive exam, symposium; for doctorate, thesis/dissertation, final project, symposium; for M Div, one foreign language, evaluation by faculty for ordination. *Entrance requirements:* For M Div, GRE General Test, previous course work in religion and philosophy; for master's, GRE General Test, previous course work in religion; for doctorate, M Div or equivalent, 3 years in full-time ministry, interviews, ministry profile report. *Faculty research:* Pastoral ministry, theology of ministry, ecclesiology, American Catholics.

St. Mary's Seminary and University, Ecumenical Institute of Theology, Baltimore, MD 21210-1994. Offers church ministries (MA); theology (MA Th, Certificate). *Accreditation:* ATS. Part-time and evening/weekend programs available. *Degree requirements:* For master's, thesis or alternative, comprehensive exam or colloquium. *Expenses:* Contact institution. *Faculty research:* Scripture and ethics, theology and literature, early Christianity and Judaism, medical and social ethics.

St. Mary's Seminary and University, School of Theology, Baltimore, MD 21210-1994. Offers M Div, STB, MA Th, STD, STL. *Accreditation:* ATS (one or more programs are accredited). Part-time programs available. Terminal master's awarded for partial completion of doctoral program. *Degree requirements:* For master's and first professional degree, comprehensive exam. *Entrance requirements:* For master's, Computerized Adaptive Placement Assessment and Support System.

Saint Mary's University, Faculty of Arts, Department of Religious Studies, Halifax, NS B3H 3C3, Canada. Offers theology and religious studies (MA).

St. Mary's University, Graduate School, Department of Theology, San Antonio, TX 78228-8507. Offers pastoral ministry (MA); theology (MA); JD/MA. Part-time and evening/weekend programs available. Postbaccalaureate distance learning degree programs offered (no on-campus study). *Degree requirements:* For master's, comprehensive exam, practicum (pastoral administration). *Entrance requirements:* For master's, GRE General Test, MAT, 12 credit hours in theology/philosophy. Additional exam requirements/recommendations for international students: Required—TOEFL (minimum score 550 paper-based; 213 computer-based; 80 iBT). Electronic applications accepted. *Faculty research:* Bioethics; perceptions of ministry; Marian doctrines and the contemporary church; Jaspers, peace, and justice.

Saint Meinrad School of Theology, Professional Program, Saint Meinrad, IN 47577. Offers M Div. *Accreditation:* ATS. *Entrance requirements:* 30 credits in philosophy, 12 credits in theology. Additional exam requirements/recommendations for international students: Required—TOEFL (minimum score 550 paper-based).

Saint Meinrad School of Theology, Program in Catholic Thought and Life, Saint Meinrad, IN 47577. Offers MA. *Accreditation:* ATS. Part-time and evening/weekend programs available. *Degree requirements:* For master's, comprehensive exam.

Saint Meinrad School of Theology, Program in Theological Studies, Saint Meinrad, IN 47577. Offers MTS. *Accreditation:* ATS. Part-time and evening/weekend programs available. *Degree requirements:* For master's, thesis.

Saint Michael's College, Graduate Programs, Program in Theology and Pastoral Ministry, Colchester, VT 05439. Offers theology (MA, CAS, Certificate). Part-time and evening/weekend programs available. *Degree requirements:* For master's, thesis optional, 1 foreign language if thesis option selected. *Entrance requirements:* For master's, bachelor's degree in arts, science, philosophy, theology, or education; minimum GPA of 3.0; 24 hours of course work in theology and other humanistic disciplines. Additional exam requirements/recommendations for international students: Required—TOEFL (minimum score 550 paper-based; 213 computer-based; 80 iBT), IELTS (minimum score 6). Electronic applications accepted. *Expenses:* Contact institution.

St. Norbert College, Program in Theological Studies, De Pere, WI 54115-2099. Offers MTS. Part-time programs available. *Faculty:* 9 part-time/adjunct (3 women). *Students:* 57 part-time (43 women); includes 1 Asian, non-Hispanic/Latino; 6 Hispanic/Latino. 2 applicants, 100% accepted, 2 enrolled. In 2010, 5 master's awarded. *Degree requirements:* For master's, comprehensive exam, thesis. *Entrance requirements:* For master's, minimum of 8 credits of course work in theology/religious studies, BA from accredited institution. *Application deadline:* Applications are processed on a rolling basis. Application fee: $50. Electronic applications accepted. *Expenses:* Tuition: Part-time $390 per credit hour. *Financial support:* In 2010–11, 13 students received support. Scholarships/grants available. Support available to part-time students. *Faculty research:* Practical theology, Holocaust, Rahner, women in the Bible and Christian ethics. *Unit head:* Dr. Howard Ebert, Director, 920-403-3956, Fax: 920-403-4086, E-mail: howard.ebert@snc.edu. *Application contact:* Dinah Grassel, Program Coordinator, 920-403-3957, Fax: 920-403-4086, E-mail: dinah.grassel@snc.edu.

St. Patrick's Seminary & University, School of Theology, Menlo Park, CA 94025-3596. Offers M Div, STB, MA. STB offered jointly with St. Mary's Seminary and University. *Accreditation:* ATS (one or more programs are accredited). Part-time programs available. *Degree requirements:* For master's, comprehensive exam, thesis or alternative. *Entrance requirements:* For first professional degree, GRE General Test or MAT, minimum GPA of 2.0, interview; for master's, GRE General Test, minimum GPA of 3.0, interview. Additional exam requirements/recommendations for international students: Required—TOEFL (minimum score 550 paper-based; 215 computer-based; 80 iBT), TWE. *Faculty research:* Systematic theology, sacred scripture, moral theology, liturgy.

Saint Paul School of Theology, Graduate and Professional Programs, Kansas City, MO 64127-2440. Offers M Div, MA, MTS, D Min. *Accreditation:* ACIPE; ATS. Part-time programs available. *Degree requirements:* For doctorate, thesis/dissertation. *Entrance requirements:* For M Div and master's, minimum GPA of 2.75; for doctorate, minimum GPA of 3.0. Additional exam requirements/recommendations for international students: Required—TOEFL. *Faculty research:* Religion and aging; leadership development; feminist, African-American, and liberation theology; rural ministry; worship and the arts.

Saint Paul University, Faculty of Canon Law, Ottawa, ON K1S 1C4, Canada. Offers canon law (MCL, JCD, PhD, Graduate Certificate, JCL); canonical practice (Graduate Certificate); ecclesiastical administration (Graduate Certificate). Part-time programs available. *Faculty:* 9 full-time (1 woman), 7 part-time/adjunct (1 woman). *Students:* 58 full-time (9 women), 14 part-time (8 women); includes 17 Black or African American, non-Hispanic/Latino; 15 Asian, non-Hispanic/Latino; 1 Hispanic/Latino. Average age 40. 78 applicants, 92% accepted, 72 enrolled. In 2010, 15 master's, 3 doctorates, 33 other advanced degrees awarded. *Degree requirements:* For master's, one foreign language; for doctorate, one foreign language, comprehensive exam, thesis/dissertation; for other advanced degree, one foreign language, comprehensive exam and seminar paper (JCL). *Entrance requirements:* For master's, appropriate bachelor's degree, 18 credits in theology; for doctorate, JCL or MCL; for other advanced degree, B Th or equivalent (JCL), appropriate bachelor's degree, 18 credits in theology. *Application deadline:* For fall admission, 8/15 priority date for domestic students, 3/1 priority date for international students. Applications are processed on a rolling basis. Application fee: $75 Canadian dollars. *Financial support:* Scholarships/grants and bursaries available. *Faculty research:* Questions related to Church law. *Unit head:* Dr. Anne Asselin, Dean, 613-751-4018, Fax: 613-751-4036, E-mail: canonlaw@ustpaul.ca. *Application contact:* Beverly Ruth Kavanaugh, Administrative Assistant, 613-751-4018, Fax: 613-751-4036, E-mail: bkavanaugh@ustpaul.ca.

Saint Paul University, Faculty of Human Sciences, Program in Counseling and Spirituality, Ottawa, ON K1S 1C4, Canada. Offers individual or marital/couple counseling (MA); spiritual care (MA). Part-time programs available. *Degree requirements:* For master's, research project or thesis. *Entrance requirements:* For master's, honors BA in human sciences, minimum B average, 12 theology credits.

Saint Paul University, Faculty of Theology, Ottawa, ON K1S 1C4, Canada. Offers MA Th, MP Th, MRE, D Min, D Th, PhD, L Th. *Degree requirements:* For master's and L Th, one foreign language; for doctorate, one foreign language, comprehensive exam, thesis/dissertation. *Entrance requirements:* For master's, B Th; for doctorate, MA Th, L Th, MP Th, M Div. *Faculty research:* Biblical studies, systematic and historical theology, ethics, spirituality, Eastern Christian studies, applied theology.

St. Peter's Seminary, Department of Theology, London, ON N6A 3Y1, Canada. Offers M Div, MTS. *Accreditation:* ATS.

Saints Cyril and Methodius Seminary, Graduate and Professional Programs, Orchard Lake, MI 48324. Offers pastoral ministry (MAPM); religious education (MARE); theology (M Div, MA). *Accreditation:* ATS. Part-time programs available.

St. Stephen's College, Programs in Theology, Edmonton, AB T6G 2J6, Canada. Offers ministry (D Min); pastoral counseling (MA); social transformation ministry (MA); spirituality and liturgy (MA); theological studies (MTS); theology (M Th). Part-time and evening/weekend programs available. Postbaccalaureate distance learning degree programs offered (minimal on-campus study). Terminal master's awarded for partial completion of doctoral program. *Degree requirements:* For master's, thesis; for doctorate, thesis/dissertation. *Entrance requirements:* Additional exam requirements/recommendations for international students: Required—TOEFL. Electronic applications accepted. *Faculty research:* Methodology for theological education, practice and supervision for ministry.

St. Thomas University, School of Theology and Ministry, Institute for Pastoral Ministries, Miami Gardens, FL 33054-6459. Offers pastoral ministries (MA, Certificate); practical theology (PhD). Part-time and evening/weekend programs available. *Degree requirements:* For master's, comprehensive exam; for doctorate, comprehensive exam, thesis/dissertation. *Entrance requirements:* For master's, interview, minimum GPA of 3.0 or GRE; for doctorate, GRE, MA in theology. Additional exam requirements/recommendations for international students: Required—TOEFL (minimum score 550 paper-based; 213 computer-based; 79 iBT). Electronic applications accepted.

St. Tikhon's Orthodox Theological Seminary, Divinity Program, South Canaan, PA 18459. Offers M Div. *Accreditation:* ATS. *Faculty:* 8 full-time (1 woman), 6 part-time/adjunct (0 women). *Students:* 51 full-time (1 woman), 6 part-time (0 women); includes 1 Black or African American, non-Hispanic/Latino, 4 international. 35 applicants, 80% accepted, 28 enrolled. *Degree requirements:* For M Div, one foreign language, thesis/dissertation optional. *Entrance requirements:* Letters of recommendation, baccalaureate degree. *Application deadline:* For fall admission, 7/30 for domestic students, 6/30 for international students. Applications are processed on a rolling basis. Application fee: $28. *Expenses:* Tuition: Full-time $2100. Required fees: $400. One-time fee: $30 full-time. *Financial support:* Fellowships with partial tuition reimbursements, career-related internships or fieldwork, institutionally sponsored loans, scholarships/grants, and tuition waivers (partial) available. *Faculty research:* Church history, patristics, scripture, spirituality. *Unit head:* Bp. Tikhon Mollard, Rector, 570-937-9331, Fax: 570-937-4139, E-mail: bp.tikhon@stots.edu. *Application contact:* Fr. Alexander Atty, Dean and Director of Admissions, 570-561-1818 Ext. 191, E-mail: father.alexander@stots.edu.

Saint Vincent de Paul Regional Seminary, Graduate and Professional Programs, Boynton Beach, FL 33436-4899. Offers theology (M Div, MA Th). *Accreditation:* ATS. Part-time programs available. *Degree requirements:* For master's, comprehensive exam (for some programs), thesis optional; for M Div, one foreign language. *Entrance requirements:* For M Div and master's, GRE General Test, MAT. Additional exam requirements/recommendations for international students: Required—TOEFL.

Saint Vincent Seminary, School of Theology, Latrobe, PA 15650-2690. Offers M Div, MA. *Accreditation:* ATS. Part-time programs available. *Degree requirements:* For master's, one foreign language, comprehensive exam; for M Div, one foreign language. *Entrance requirements:* For M Div, minimum GPA of 2.5; for master's, minimum GPA of 3.0. Additional exam requirements/recommendations for international students: Required—TOEFL (minimum score 550 paper-based; 220 computer-based). Electronic applications accepted. *Faculty research:* Church history, preaching, psychology of religion, Biblical studies, moral theology.

St. Vladimir's Orthodox Theological Seminary, Graduate School of Theology, Crestwood, NY 10707-1699. Offers general theological studies (MA); liturgical music (MA); religious education (MA); theology (M Div, M Th, D Min); M Div/MA. MA in general theological studies, M Div offered jointly with St. Nersess Seminary. *Accreditation:* ATS. Part-time programs available. *Degree requirements:* For master's, one foreign language, thesis, fieldwork; for doctorate, thesis/dissertation, fieldwork; for M Div, one foreign language, thesis/dissertation, fieldwork. *Entrance requirements:* For doctorate, M Div, minimum GPA of 3.0. Additional exam requirements/recommendations for international students: Required—TOEFL (minimum score 250 computer-based).

Samford University, Beeson School of Divinity, Birmingham, AL 35229. Offers M Div, MATS, D Min, JD/M Div, JD/MATS, M Div/MBA, M Div/MM, M Div/MSE. *Accreditation:* ATS. *Faculty:* 14 full-time (3 women), 2 part-time/adjunct (1 woman). *Students:* 176 full-time (26 women), 8 part-time (4 women); includes 24 minority (21 Black or African American, non-Hispanic/Latino; 3 Hispanic/Latino), 2 international. Average age 30. 55 applicants, 76% accepted, 31 enrolled. In 2010, 13 first professional degrees, 34 master's awarded. *Degree requirements:* For master's, one foreign language, thesis optional; for doctorate, thesis/dissertation; for M Div, 2 foreign languages, thesis/dissertation optional, 4 internships (including 1 cross-cultural experience). *Entrance requirements:* For M Div and master's, minimum GPA of 2.5; for doctorate, minimum GPA of 3.0. Additional exam requirements/recommendations for international students: Required—TOEFL (minimum score 550 paper-based; 213 computer-based). *Application deadline:* For fall admission, 3/1 for domestic and international students; for spring admission, 10/1 for domestic and international students. Application fee: $25. Electronic applications accepted. *Expenses:* Contact institution. *Financial support:* In 2010–11, 135 students received support. Scholarships/grants and tuition waivers (full and partial) available. Financial award applicants required to submit FAFSA. *Faculty research:* New Testament theology, exegesis of Psalms, doctrinal preaching, history of Anglicanism, racial reconciliation. *Unit head:* Dr. Timothy George, Dean, 205-726-2632, E-mail: tfgeorge@samford.edu. *Application contact:* Sherri Spurling Brown, Director of Admission, 205-726-2066, Fax: 205-726-4120, E-mail: sbrown5@samford.edu.

San Francisco Theological Seminary, Graduate and Professional Programs, San Anselmo, CA 94960-2997. Offers M Div, MA, MATS, D Min, PhD, Th D, M Div/MA. MA, Th D, PhD, M Div/MA offered jointly with Graduate Theological Union. *Accreditation:* ACIPE; ATS (one or more programs are accredited). Part-time programs available. *Degree requirements:* For master's, one foreign language, thesis (for some programs); for doctorate, thesis/dissertation; for M Div, one foreign language, internship. *Entrance requirements:* For master's, minimum GPA of 3.0; for doctorate, M Div. Additional exam requirements/recommendations for international students: Required—TOEFL.

Santa Clara University, Jesuit School of Theology, Santa Clara, CA 95053. Offers M Div, STB, MA, MTS, Th M, STD, STL, MA/M Div. *Accreditation:* ATS. Part-time and evening/weekend programs available. *Faculty:* 15 full-time (3 women), 5 part-time/adjunct (3 women). *Students:* 98 full-time (29 women), 46 part-time (19 women); includes 21 minority (1 Black or African American, non-Hispanic/Latino; 13 Asian, non-Hispanic/Latino; 6 Hispanic/Latino; 1 Native Hawaiian or other Pacific Islander, non-Hispanic/Latino), 65 international. Average age 37. 102 applicants, 82% accepted, 64 enrolled. In 2010, 26 master's, 4 doctorates, 10 other advanced degrees awarded. *Degree requirements:* For doctorate, thesis/dissertation (for some programs). *Entrance requirements:* For first professional degree, resume, statement of purpose; for master's, GRE; for doctorate, GRE, master's degree or equivalent. Additional exam requirements/recommendations for international students: Required—TOEFL (minimum score 550 paper-based; 213 computer-based; 79 iBT). *Application deadline:* For fall admission, 8/15 priority date for domestic and international students; for spring admission, 1/10 priority date for domestic and international students. Applications are processed on a rolling basis. Application fee: $50. Electronic applications accepted. Tuition and fees vary according to course load and program. *Financial support:* Application deadline: 3/2. *Unit head:* Kevin F. Burke, SJ, Dean, 510-549-5040, E-mail: kburke@jstb.edu. *Application contact:* Grace Hogan, Associate Director of Enrollment Management, 510-549-5013, Fax: 510-841-8536, E-mail: ghogan@jstb.edu.

Seabury-Western Theological Seminary, School of Theology, Evanston, IL 60201-2976. Offers advanced theological studies (Certificate); church music and liturgy (MTS); congregational development (D Min); preaching (D Min); theological studies (MA); theology (M Div, L Th). D Min in congregational development offered in summer only; D Min in preaching offered jointly with Chicago Theological Seminary, Lutheran School of Theology at Chicago, McCormick Theological Seminary, and Northern Baptist Theological Seminary. *Accreditation:* ACIPE; ATS (one or more programs are accredited). Part-time programs available. *Degree requirements:* For master's, thesis; for doctorate, thesis/dissertation; for other advanced degree, thesis (for some programs). *Entrance requirements:* For M Div and master's, interview, sample of written work. *Faculty research:* Liturgical interpretations of baptism, trinitarian theology, congregational development, post modern biblical criticism-Matthew.

Seattle Pacific University, Master of Arts in Theology Program, Seattle, WA 98119-1997. Offers MA. *Faculty:* 6 full-time (1 woman), 1 (woman) part-time/adjunct. *Students:* 7 full-time (3 women), 7 part-time (3 women); includes 3 minority (1 Black or African American, non-Hispanic/Latino; 2 Asian, non-Hispanic/Latino). Average age 37. 15 applicants, 33% accepted, 5 enrolled. *Degree requirements:* For master's, internship or thesis. *Entrance requirements:* For master's, minimum GPA of 3.0. Additional exam requirements/recommendations for international students: Required—TOEFL (minimum score 550 paper-based; 213 computer-based). *Application deadline:* For fall admission, 6/15 for domestic and international students. Applications are processed on a rolling basis. Application fee: $50. Electronic applications accepted. *Financial support:* In 2010–11, 8 students received support. Application deadline: 4/1. *Unit head:* Dr. Douglas Strong, Dean, 206-281-2473, E-mail: dstrong@spu.edu. *Application contact:* John Glancy, Director, Graduate Admissions and Marketing, 206-281-2325, Fax: 206-281-2877, E-mail: jglancy@spu.edu.

Seattle Pacific University, The Master of Divinity Program, Seattle, WA 98119-1997. Offers M Div. *Faculty:* 5 full-time (1 woman), 2 part-time/adjunct (1 woman). *Students:* 21 full-time (9 women), 8 part-time (0 women); includes 7 minority (1 American Indian or Alaska Native, non-Hispanic/Latino; 4 Asian, non-Hispanic/Latino; 1 Hispanic/Latino; 1 Two or more races, non-Hispanic/Latino). Average age 30. 22 applicants, 64% accepted, 14 enrolled. *Entrance requirements:* Additional exam requirements/recommendations for international students: Required—TOEFL (minimum score 550 paper-based; 213 computer-based). *Application deadline:* For fall admission, 6/15 for domestic students. Application fee: $50. *Financial support:* In 2010–11, 11 students received support. Scholarships/grants available. Financial award applicants required to submit FAFSA. *Unit head:* Douglas Strong, Dean, 206-281-2473, E-mail: dstrong@spu.edu. *Application contact:* John Glancy, Director, Graduate Admissions and Marketing, 206-281-2325, Fax: 206-281-2877, E-mail: jglancy@spu.edu.

Seattle University, School of Theology and Ministry, Program in Divinity, Seattle, WA 98122-1090. Offers M Div. *Accreditation:* ATS. Part-time and evening/weekend programs available. *Degree requirements:* For M Div, project. *Entrance requirements:* Interview, minimum GPA of 2.75.

Seattle University, School of Theology and Ministry, Program in Transforming Spirituality, Seattle, WA 98122-1090. Offers MATS, Certificate. *Accreditation:* ATS. Part-time and evening/weekend programs available. *Degree requirements:* For master's, project. *Entrance requirements:* For master's, interview, minimum GPA of 2.75.

Seminary of the Immaculate Conception, School of Theology, Huntington, NY 11743-1696. Offers pastoral studies (MA); theology (M Div, MA, D Min, Certificate). *Accreditation:* ATS (one or more programs are accredited). Part-time and evening/weekend programs available. *Faculty:* 9 full-time (2 women), 15 part-time/adjunct (2 women). *Students:* 39 full-time (1 woman), 89 part-time (40 women); includes 24 minority (8 Black or African American, non-Hispanic/Latino; 7 Asian, non-Hispanic/Latino; 9 Hispanic/Latino), 6 international. Average age 49. 19 applicants, 100% accepted, 19 enrolled. In 2010, 6 first professional degrees, 37 master's awarded. *Degree requirements:* For master's, seminar and paper/thesis; for doctorate, thesis/dissertation; for M Div, one foreign language, thesis/dissertation. *Entrance requirements:* For M Div, degree in philosophy-theology; for master's, undergraduate degree; for doctorate, MA plus 30 credits or M Div; for Certificate, MA in theology. *Application deadline:* For fall admission, 8/30 priority date for domestic students; for spring admission, 1/20 priority date for domestic students. Applications are processed on a rolling basis. Application fee: $75. *Expenses:* Tuition: Full-time $12,000; part-time $450 per credit. Required fees: $300; $50 per semester. One-time fee: $200 part-time. *Financial support:* In 2010–11, 19 students received support. Scholarships/grants available. *Unit head:* Sr. Mary Louise Brink, SC, Academic Dean, 631-423-0483 Ext. 130, Fax: 631-432-2346, E-mail: mlbrink@icseminary.edu. *Application contact:* Kathryn L. Zahner, Registrar, 631-423-0483 Ext. 147, Fax: 631-423-2346, E-mail: kzahner@icseminary.edu.

Seminary of the Southwest, Graduate and Professional Programs, Austin, TX 78768-2247. Offers Anglican studies (Advanced Diploma); chaplaincy (MCPC, JD/MAC); counseling (MAC); divinity (M Div); religion (MAR); spiritual formation (MAPM, MSF); theological studies (Advanced Diploma); JD/MAC. *Accreditation:* ACIPE; ATS (one or more programs are accredited). Part-time and evening/weekend programs available. *Faculty:* 11 full-time (3 women), 26 part-time/adjunct (7 women). *Students:* 69 full-time (40 women), 47 part-time (34 women); includes 11 minority (4 Black or African American, non-Hispanic/Latino; 4 Hispanic/Latino; 3 Two or more races, non-Hispanic/Latino), 3 international. Average age 45. 57 applicants, 93% accepted, 46 enrolled. In 2010, 13 first professional degrees, 8 master's, 6 other advanced degrees awarded. *Degree requirements:* For master's, thesis (for some programs). *Entrance requirements:* For M Div and master's, GRE, MAT, interview; for Advanced Diploma, interview. *Application deadline:* For fall admission, 7/1 for domestic students; for spring admission, 11/1 for domestic students. Applications are processed on a rolling basis. Application fee: $50. *Expenses:* Tuition: Full-time $13,152; part-time $548 per credit hour. Required fees: $75. One-time fee: $20 part-time. *Financial support:* Career-related internships or fieldwork and scholarships/grants available. Support available to part-time students. Financial award application deadline: 6/15. *Unit head:* Very Rev. Douglas Travis, Dean and President, 512-472-4133 Ext. 307, Fax: 512-472-3098, E-mail: dtravis@ssw.edu. *Application contact:* Jennielle Strother, Director of Admissions, 512-472-4133 Ext. 375, Fax: 512-472-3098, E-mail: jstrother@ssw.edu.

Seton Hall University, Immaculate Conception Seminary School of Theology, South Orange, NJ 07079-2697. Offers Christian spirituality (Certificate); great spiritual books (Certificate); pastoral ministry (M Div, MA, Certificate); scripture studies (Certificate); Seminary's Theological Education for Parish Services (STEPS) (Certificate); theology (MA); youth ministry (Certificate). *Accreditation:* ATS (one or more programs are accredited). Part-time and evening/weekend programs available. *Faculty:* 13 full-time (2 women), 12 part-time/adjunct (1 woman). *Students:* 105 full-time (7 women), 112 part-time (43 women); includes 4 Black or African American, non-Hispanic/Latino; 9 Asian, non-Hispanic/Latino; 31 Hispanic/Latino, 72 international. Average age 39. 74 applicants, 100% accepted, 69 enrolled. In 2010, 16 first professional degrees, 32 master's, 6 other advanced degrees awarded. *Degree requirements:* For master's, one foreign language, comprehensive exam, thesis (for some programs), final project; for M Div, one foreign language, thesis/dissertation, final project and seminar, field education, spiritual formation. *Entrance requirements:* For M Div, GRE, MAT; for master's, GRE General Test or MAT. Additional exam requirements/recommendations for international students: Required—TOEFL (minimum score 600 paper-based; 250 computer-based; 100 iBT). *Application deadline:* For fall admission, 8/1 priority date for domestic and international students; for spring admission, 12/15 priority date for domestic and international students. Applications are processed on a rolling basis. Application fee: $50. Electronic applications accepted. *Expenses:* Contact institution. *Financial support:* In 2010–11, 217 students received support. Career-related internships or fieldwork, Federal Work-Study, scholarships/grants, tuition waivers (partial), and unspecified assistantships available. Support available to part-time students. Financial award application deadline: 8/1; financial award applicants required to submit FAFSA. *Faculty research:* Pauline literature, history of Biblical interpretation and theological exegesis, spirituality of St. Edith Stein, Thomism, history of Catholicism in America. *Unit head:* Rev. Msgr. Robert F. Coleman, Rector and Dean, 973-761-9016, Fax: 973-761-9577, E-mail: robert.coleman@shu.edu. *Application contact:* Rev. Msgr. Joseph R. Chapel, Associate Dean, 973-761-9633, Fax: 973-761-9577, E-mail: theology@shu.edu.

Sewanee: The University of the South, School of Theology, Sewanee, TN 37383. Offers M Div, MA, STM, D Min. *Accreditation:* ACIPE; ATS. Part-time programs available. *Degree requirements:* For master's, thesis; for doctorate, thesis/dissertation. *Entrance requirements:* For M Div, GRE General Test, interview; for master's, GRE General Test, M Div (STM); for doctorate, M Div. Additional exam requirements/recommendations for international students: Required—TOEFL (minimum score 550 paper-based).

Shaw University, Divinity School, Raleigh, NC 27601-2399. Offers M Div, MRE. *Accreditation:* ATS. Part-time and evening/weekend programs available. *Degree requirements:* For master's, thesis; for M Div, thesis/dissertation. *Entrance requirements:* For M Div and master's, letters of reference. Electronic applications accepted. *Faculty research:* HIV/AIDS awareness through faith-based curriculum, domestic abuse and violence prevention, pedagogy for non-traditional theology education, health disparities in the African-American community, technology and theological education.

Sh'or Yoshuv Rabbinical College, Graduate Programs, Far Rockaway, NY 11691-4002. *Accreditation:* AARTS.

Sioux Falls Seminary, Graduate and Professional Programs, Program in Bible and Theology, Sioux Falls, SD 57105-1599. Offers MA. *Accreditation:* ACIPE; ATS. Part-time programs available. *Degree requirements:* For master's, 2 foreign languages, thesis or alternative. *Entrance requirements:* For master's, minimum GPA of 2.5.

Sioux Falls Seminary, Graduate and Professional Programs, Program in Ministry, Sioux Falls, SD 57105-1599. Offers D Min. *Accreditation:* ACIPE. Part-time programs available. *Degree requirements:* For doctorate, thesis/dissertation. *Entrance requirements:* For doctorate, M Div, 3 years of ministry.

Sioux Falls Seminary, Graduate and Professional Programs, Program in Theological Studies, Sioux Falls, SD 57105-1599. Offers Certificate.

Southeastern Baptist Theological Seminary, Graduate and Professional Programs, Wake Forest, NC 27588-1889. Offers advanced biblical studies (M Div); Christian education (M Div, MACE); Christian ethics (PhD); Christian ministry (M Div); Christian planting (M Div); church music (MACM); counseling (MACO); evangelism (PhD); language (M Div); ministry (D Min); New Testament (PhD); Old Testament (PhD); philosophy (PhD); theology (Th M, PhD); women's studies (M Div). *Accreditation:* ACIPE; ATS (one or more programs are accredited). *Degree requirements:* For master's, thesis (for some programs), oral exam; for doctorate, thesis/

Theology

Southeastern Baptist Theological Seminary (continued)
dissertation, fieldwork; for M Div, supervised ministry. *Entrance requirements:* For master's, Cooperative English Test, minimum GPA of 2.0, M Div or equivalent (Th M); for doctorate, GRE General Test or MAT, Cooperative English Test, M Div or equivalent, 3 years of professional experience.

Southern Adventist University, School of Religion, Collegedale, TN 37315-0370. Offers Biblical and theological studies (MA); church leadership and management (M Min); church ministry and homiletics (M Min); evangelism and world mission (M Min); religious studies (MA). Part-time programs available. *Degree requirements:* For master's, comprehensive exam, thesis (for some programs). *Entrance requirements:* For master's, GRE. Additional exam requirements/recommendations for international students: Required—TOEFL (minimum score 600 paper-based; 250 computer-based). *Faculty research:* Biblical archaeology.

Southern Baptist Theological Seminary, Billy Graham School of Missions, Evangelism and Church Growth, Louisville, KY 40280-0004. Offers Christian mission/world religion (PhD); evangelism/church growth (PhD); ministry (D Min); missiology (MA, D Miss); missions, evangelism and church growth (M Div); religion (Th M); theological studies (MA). *Accreditation:* ATS. Part-time and evening/weekend programs available. Postbaccalaureate distance learning degree programs offered (minimal on-campus study). *Degree requirements:* For master's and M Div, 2 foreign languages; for doctorate, 4 foreign languages, thesis/dissertation. *Entrance requirements:* For doctorate, GRE General Test, MAT, M Div. Additional exam requirements/recommendations for international students: Required—TOEFL, TWE. *Faculty research:* Assimilation of church congregants, effective methodologies of evangelism, expectations of church members, spiritual warfare literature, formative church discipline.

Southern Baptist Theological Seminary, School of Theology, Louisville, KY 40280-0004. Offers applied theology (D Min); biblical and theological studies (M Div); biblical counseling (M Div, MA, D Min); biblical spirituality (D Min); Christian ministry (M Div); expository preaching (D Min); pastoral studies (M Div); theological studies (MA); theology (Th M, PhD); worldview and apologetics (M Div). *Accreditation:* ATS. Part-time and evening/weekend programs available. Postbaccalaureate distance learning degree programs offered (minimal on-campus study). *Degree requirements:* For master's, 2 foreign languages, thesis; for doctorate, 4 foreign languages, thesis/dissertation; for M Div, 2 foreign languages. *Entrance requirements:* For master's, GRE General Test, MAT, M Div; for doctorate, GRE General Test, MAT, interview, M Div, field essay. Additional exam requirements/recommendations for international students: Required—TOEFL, TWE. *Faculty research:* Biblical studies, contemporary theology, church history, pastoral care, ministry/missions studies.

Southern California Seminary, Graduate and Professional Programs, El Cajon, CA 92019. Offers Biblical studies (MABS); counseling psychology (MACP); marriage and family therapy (MAMFT); psychology (Psy D); religious studies (MRS); theology (M Div). Part-time and evening/weekend programs available. Postbaccalaureate distance learning degree programs offered (minimal on-campus study). *Students:* 37 full-time (8 women), 80 part-time (37 women); includes 55 minority (20 Black or African American, non-Hispanic/Latino; 14 Asian, non-Hispanic/Latino; 16 Hispanic/Latino; 1 Native Hawaiian or other Pacific Islander, non-Hispanic/Latino; 4 Two or more races, non-Hispanic/Latino), 5 international. Average age 41. In 2010, 7 first professional degrees, 50 master's, 4 doctorates awarded. *Degree requirements:* For master's, thesis (for some programs); for doctorate, thesis/dissertation; for M Div, 2 foreign languages. *Entrance requirements:* For doctorate, master's degree in psychology. Additional exam requirements/recommendations for international students: Required—TOEFL (minimum score 550 paper-based). *Application deadline:* For fall admission, 8/13 for domestic and international students; for spring admission, 12/11 for domestic students, 12/15 for international students. Applications are processed on a rolling basis. Application fee: $31 ($126 for international students). Electronic applications accepted. *Expenses:* Tuition: Part-time $339 per unit. Part-time tuition and fees vary according to degree level, campus/location and program. *Financial support:* In 2010–11, 14 students received support. Federal Work-Study, scholarships/grants, and tuition waivers (partial) available. Financial award application deadline: 3/1; financial award applicants required to submit FAFSA. *Unit head:* Dr. Chuck Emert, Vice-President of Academics, 619-201-8995, Fax: 619-201-8975. *Application contact:* Thomas Pittman, Admissions Officer and Director of Student Services, 888-389-7244, Fax: 619-201-8975, E-mail: thpittman@socalsem.edu.

Southern Evangelical Seminary, Graduate Programs, Matthews, NC 28105. Offers apologetics (MA, Certificate); Christian education (MA); church ministry (MA, Certificate); divinity (Certificate), including apologetics (M Div, Certificate); Islamic studies (MA, Certificate); Jewish studies (MA); philosophy (MA); religion (MA); theology (M Div), including apologetics (M Div, Certificate), Biblical studies; youth ministry (MA). Part-time and evening/weekend programs available. Postbaccalaureate distance learning degree programs offered. *Degree requirements:* For master's, thesis (for some programs); for doctorate, 2 foreign languages, comprehensive exam (for some programs), thesis/dissertation; for M Div, one foreign language. *Entrance requirements:* Additional exam requirements/recommendations for international students: Required—TOEFL (minimum score 600 paper-based; 250 computer-based). *Application deadline:* For fall admission, 8/15 priority date for domestic students, 8/5 priority date for international students; for winter admission, 12/15 priority date for domestic and international students; for spring admission, 1/15 priority date for domestic and international students. Applications are processed on a rolling basis. Application fee: $25. *Expenses:* Tuition: Full-time $9405; part-time $313.50 per credit hour. Required fees: $150; $50 per semester. *Financial support:* Scholarships/grants available. *Unit head:* Dr. Barry R. Leventhal, Dean, 704-847-5600 Ext. 204, Fax: 704-845-1747, E-mail: dean@ses.edu. *Application contact:* Duke Hale, Director of Recruitment, 704-847-5600 Ext. 216, Fax: 704-845-1747, E-mail: dhale@ses.edu.

Southern Methodist University, Perkins School of Theology, Dallas, TX 75275. Offers M Div, CMM, MSM, MTS, D Min. *Accreditation:* ACIPE; ATS. Part-time programs available. *Faculty:* 27 full-time (11 women), 8 part-time/adjunct (4 women). *Students:* 180 full-time (91 women), 173 part-time (89 women); includes 92 minority (64 Black or African American, non-Hispanic/Latino; 1 American Indian or Alaska Native, non-Hispanic/Latino; 6 Asian, non-Hispanic/Latino; 18 Hispanic/Latino; 1 Native Hawaiian or other Pacific Islander, non-Hispanic/Latino; 2 Two or more races, non-Hispanic/Latino), 17 international. Average age 39. 162 applicants, 80% accepted, 92 enrolled. In 2010, 56 M Divs, 25 master's, 4 doctorates awarded. *Degree requirements:* For master's, thesis (for some programs), internship; for doctorate, internship, oral exam, professional project; for M Div, internship. *Entrance requirements:* For M Div and master's, minimum GPA of 2.75; for doctorate, minimum graduate GPA of 3.0, M Div or equivalent, 3 years of ministry experience. Additional exam requirements/recommendations for international students: Required—TOEFL (minimum score 600 paper-based; 250 computer-based; 100 iBT), TWE. *Application deadline:* For fall admission, 5/1 for domestic students, 12/15 for international students; for spring admission, 11/1 for domestic students. Applications are processed on a rolling basis. Application fee: $50. *Expenses:* Contact institution. *Financial support:* In 2010–11, 188 students received support, including 3 fellowships with full tuition reimbursements available (averaging $5,000 per year); career-related internships or fieldwork, Federal Work-Study, scholarships/grants, and minister's family tuition awards also available. Support available to part-time students. Financial award application deadline: 3/1; financial award applicants required to submit FAFSA. Total annual research expenditures: $271,008. *Unit head:* Dr. William B. Lawrence, Dean, 214-768-2534, Fax: 214-768-2966. *Application contact:* Rev. Herbert S. Coleman, Director, Recruitment and Admissions, 214-768-2139, Fax: 214-768-4245, E-mail: theology@smu.edu.

Southern Nazarene University, Graduate College, Department of Philosophy and Religion, Bethany, OK 73008. Offers theology (MA). Part-time programs available. *Degree requirements:* For master's, one foreign language, thesis optional. *Entrance requirements:* For master's, GMAT, English proficiency exam, minimum GPA of 3.0 in last 60 hours/major, 2.7 overall. *Expenses:* Tuition: Part-time $575 per credit hour.

Southwestern Assemblies of God University, Thomas F. Harrison School of Graduate Studies, Program in Theological Studies, Waxahachie, TX 75165-5735. Offers Bible and theology (MS); Biblical studies (M Div); counseling (M Div); cross cultural missions (M Div); practical theology (M Div); theological studies (M Div). Postbaccalaureate distance learning degree programs offered. *Degree requirements:* For master's, comprehensive written and oral exams. *Entrance requirements:* For master's, GRE General Test, minimum GPA of 2.5. Electronic applications accepted.

Southwestern Baptist Theological Seminary, School of Theology, Fort Worth, TX 76122-0000. Offers M Div, MA Islamic, MA Miss, MA Th, Th M, D Min, PhD, SPTH. *Accreditation:* ACIPE; ATS (one or more programs are accredited). Part-time and evening/weekend programs available. Terminal master's awarded for partial completion of doctoral program. *Degree requirements:* For master's, 2 foreign languages, thesis (for some programs); for doctorate, 2 foreign languages, comprehensive exam, thesis/dissertation, oral exams; for M Div, 2 foreign languages, thesis/dissertation (for some programs). *Entrance requirements:* For doctorate, GRE, M Div or equivalent. Additional exam requirements/recommendations for international students: Required—TOEFL. Electronic applications accepted.

Southwestern College, Professional Studies Programs, Wichita, KS 67207. Offers business administration (MBA); leadership (MS); management (MS); security administration (MS); specialized ministries (MA); theological studies (MA). Part-time and evening/weekend programs available. Postbaccalaureate distance learning degree programs offered (minimal on-campus study). *Faculty:* 12 part-time/adjunct (5 women). *Students:* 154 part-time (62 women); includes 29 minority (20 Black or African American, non-Hispanic/Latino; 1 American Indian or Alaska Native, non-Hispanic/Latino; 4 Hispanic/Latino; 4 Two or more races, non-Hispanic/Latino). Average age 35. 91 applicants, 66% accepted, 52 enrolled. In 2010, 112 master's awarded. *Degree requirements:* For master's, practicum/capstone project. *Entrance requirements:* For master's, baccalaureate degree; minimum GPA of 2.5, 3.0 for MBA. Additional exam requirements/recommendations for international students: Required—TOEFL (minimum score 550 paper-based; 213 computer-based). *Application deadline:* For fall admission, 8/1 for domestic students; for spring admission, 12/1 for domestic students. Applications are processed on a rolling basis. Application fee: $0. Electronic applications accepted. *Expenses:* Tuition: Full-time $7470; part-time $415 per credit hour. Tuition and fees vary according to program. *Financial support:* In 2010–11, 6 students received support. Federal Work-Study, tuition waivers (partial), and unspecified assistantships available. Financial award application deadline: 4/1; financial award applicants required to submit FAFSA. *Unit head:* Gail Cullen, Director of Academic Affairs, 888-684-5335 Ext. 203, Fax: 316-688-5218, E-mail: gail.cullen@sckans.edu. *Application contact:* Gail Cullen, Director of Academic Affairs, 888-684-5335 Ext. 203, Fax: 316-688-5218, E-mail: gail.cullen@sckans.edu.

Spring Arbor University, School of Arts and Sciences, Spring Arbor, MI 49283-9799. Offers communication (MA); spiritual formation and leadership (MA). Part-time programs available. Postbaccalaureate distance learning degree programs offered (no on-campus study). *Faculty:* 6 full-time (1 woman), 9 part-time/adjunct (6 women). *Students:* 92 full-time (60 women), 75 part-time (57 women); includes 6 Black or African American, non-Hispanic/Latino; 1 Asian, non-Hispanic/Latino; 1 Hispanic/Latino. Average age 39. In 2010, 37 master's awarded. *Degree requirements:* For master's, thesis (for some programs). *Entrance requirements:* For master's, GRE (minimum score of 40th percentile and taken within last 5 years), bachelor's degree from regionally-accredited college or university, minimum GPA of 3.0 for at least the last two years of the bachelor's degree, at least two recommendations from professional/academic individuals. Additional exam requirements/recommendations for international students: Required—TOEFL (minimum score 600 paper-based; 220 computer-based). Application fee: $40. *Expenses:* Contact institution. *Financial support:* Applicants required to submit FAFSA. *Unit head:* Dr. Wally Metts, Chair of the Department of Communication, 517-750-1200 Ext. 1491, E-mail: wmetts@arbor.edu. *Application contact:* Dale Glinz, Lead Recruitment Specialist/Trainer, Graduate and Professional Studies, 517-750-6703, E-mail: dglinz@arbor.edu.

Spring Hill College, Graduate Programs, Programs in Theology and Ministry, Mobile, AL 36608-1791. Offers pastoral studies (MPS); theological studies (MTS); theology (MA). Part-time and evening/weekend programs available. *Faculty:* 5 full-time (0 women), 4 part-time/adjunct (1 woman). *Students:* 1 full-time (0 women), 51 part-time (23 women); includes 6 minority (4 Black or African American, non-Hispanic/Latino; 2 Hispanic/Latino). Average age 47. In 2010, 13 master's awarded. *Degree requirements:* For master's, variable foreign language requirement, comprehensive exam, thesis (for some programs), completion of program within 6 calendar years of initial enrollment (MTS, MPS), 4½ calendar years (MA). *Entrance requirements:* For master's, bachelor's degree with minimum undergraduate GPA of 3.0; six hours of undergraduate theology, religious studies, or unquestioned equivalency. Additional exam requirements/recommendations for international students: Required—TOEFL (minimum score 550 paper-based; 213 computer-based; 80 iBT), IELTS (minimum score 6.5), CPE or CAE (score: C), MELAB (score: 90). *Application deadline:* For fall admission, 8/1 priority date for domestic and international students; for spring admission, 12/1 priority date for domestic and international students. Applications are processed on a rolling basis. Application fee: $25 ($35 for international students). Electronic applications accepted. *Expenses:* Tuition: Full-time $5364; part-time $298 per credit hour. Tuition and fees vary according to program. *Financial support:* Applicants required to submit FAFSA. *Unit head:* Dr. John B. Switzer, Director, 251-380-4669, Fax: 251-460-2194, E-mail: jswitzer@shc.edu. *Application contact:* Donna B. Tarasavage, Director of Admissions, Graduate and Continuing Studies, 251-380-3067, Fax: 251-460-2190, E-mail: dtarasavage@shc.edu.

Starr King School for the Ministry, Professional Program, Berkeley, CA 94709-1209. Offers M Div. *Accreditation:* ACIPE; ATS.

Talmudic College of Florida, Program in Talmudic Law, Miami Beach, FL 33139. Offers MRE. *Accreditation:* AARTS. *Degree requirements:* For master's, 2 foreign languages. *Entrance requirements:* For master's, oral exam, undergraduate Judaic studies degree.

Taylor College and Seminary, Graduate and Professional Programs, Edmonton, AB T6J 4T3, Canada. Offers Christian studies (Diploma); intercultural studies (MA, Diploma), including intercultural studies (Diploma), TESOL; theology (M Div, MTS). *Accreditation:* ATS. Part-time programs available. Postbaccalaureate distance learning degree programs offered (minimal on-campus study). *Degree requirements:* For master's, thesis optional. *Entrance requirements:* Additional exam requirements/recommendations for international students: Required—TOEFL (minimum score 550 paper-based; 80 iBT), IELTS (minimum score 6.5). *Faculty research:* Biblical studies, administration and organization, world religions, ethics, missiology.

Temple Baptist Seminary, Program in Theology, Chattanooga, TN 37404-3530. Offers biblical languages (M Div); Biblical studies (MABS); Christian education (MACE); English Bible û language tools (M Div); theology (MM, D Min). Part-time and evening/weekend programs available. Postbaccalaureate distance learning degree programs offered (minimal on-campus study). *Degree requirements:* For doctorate, thesis/dissertation; for M Div, proficiency in Greek and Hebrew. *Entrance requirements:* For doctorate, minimum GPA of 3.0, M Div.

Toronto School of Theology, Graduate Programs, Toronto, ON M5S 2C3, Canada. Offers M Div, M Mus, M Rel, MA, MAMS, MPS, MRE, MTS, Th M, D Min, PhD, Th D. Federation of seven Toronto-area theological colleges; basic degrees offered through the member colleges jointly with the University of Toronto. *Accreditation:* ATS. Postbaccalaureate distance learning degree programs offered (minimal on-campus study). Terminal master's awarded for partial completion of doctoral program. *Degree requirements:* For master's, 2 foreign languages, thesis; for doctorate, 3 foreign languages, comprehensive exam, thesis/dissertation. *Entrance requirements:* For master's, language exams, minimum B+ average in undergraduate course work; for doctorate, language exams, first-class standing in master's program. Additional exam requirements/recommendations for international students: Required—TOEFL. Electronic applications accepted.

Trevecca Nazarene University, Graduate Division, Graduate Religion Programs, Nashville, TN 37210-2877. Offers biblical studies (MA); preaching and practical theology (MA); systematic theology/historical theology (MA). Part-time programs available. *Faculty:* 4 full-time (0 women). *Students:* 17 full-time (0 women), 22 part-time (9 women); includes 9 Black or African American, non-Hispanic/Latino. Average age 34. In 2010, 6 master's awarded. *Degree requirements:* For master's, comprehensive exam, thesis optional. *Entrance requirements:* For master's, GRE General Test or MAT, minimum GPA of 2.7, 2 letters of recommendation. Additional exam requirements/recommendations for international students: Required—TOEFL (minimum score 550 paper-based; 213 computer-based). *Application deadline:* Applications are processed on a rolling basis. Application fee: $25. Electronic applications accepted. *Expenses:* Contact institution. *Financial support:* Applicants required to submit FAFSA. *Unit head:* Dr. Tim Green, Dean/Director, 615-248-1378, Fax: 615-248-7417, E-mail: admissions_rel@trevecca.edu. *Application contact:* Center of Lifelong Learning, 615-248-1200, E-mail: cll@trevecca.edu.

Trinity International University, Trinity Evangelical Divinity School, Deerfield, IL 60015-1284. Offers Biblical and Near Eastern archaeology and languages (MA); Christian studies (MA, Certificate); Christian thought (MA); church history (MA, Th M); congregational ministry: pastor-teacher (M Div); congregational ministry: team ministry (M Div); counseling ministries (MA); counseling psychology (MA); cross-cultural ministry (M Div); educational studies (PhD); evangelism (MA); history of Christianity in America (MA); intercultural studies (MA, PhD); leadership and ministry management (D Min); military chaplaincy (D Min); ministry (MA); mission and evangelism (Th M); missions and evangelism (D Min); New Testament (MA, Th M); Old Testament (Th M); Old Testament and Semitic languages (MA); pastoral care (M Div); pastoral care and counseling (D Min); pastoral counseling and psychology (Th M); pastoral theology (Th M); philosophy of religion (MA); preaching (D Min); religion (MA); research ministry (M Div); systematic theology (Th M); theological studies (PhD); urban ministry (MA). *Accreditation:* ATS (one or more programs are accredited). Part-time programs available. Postbaccalaureate distance learning degree programs offered (minimal on-campus study). *Degree requirements:* For master's, comprehensive exam, thesis, fieldwork; for doctorate, comprehensive exam (for some programs), thesis/dissertation; for M Div, 2 foreign languages, fieldwork; for Certificate, comprehensive exam, integrative papers. *Entrance requirements:* For M Div, GRE, MAT; for master's, GRE, MAT, minimum cumulative undergraduate GPA of 3.0; for doctorate, GRE, minimum cumulative graduate GPA of 3.2; for Certificate, GRE, MAT, minimum undergraduate GPA of 2.5. Additional exam requirements/recommendations for international students: Required—TOEFL (minimum score 580 paper-based; 237 computer-based), TWE (minimum score 4). Electronic applications accepted.

Trinity Lutheran Seminary, Graduate and Professional Programs, Columbus, OH 43209-2334. Offers Christian education (MA); church music (MA); divinity (M Div); sacred theology (STM); theological studies (MTS); youth and family ministry (MA); MSN/MTS; MTS/JD. *Accreditation:* ACIPE; ATS. Part-time programs available. *Faculty:* 15 full-time (7 women), 7 part-time/adjunct (2 women). *Students:* 110 full-time (42 women), 35 part-time (19 women); includes 21 minority (15 Black or African American, non-Hispanic/Latino; 4 Asian, non-Hispanic/Latino; 2 Hispanic/Latino), 4 international. Average age 35. 71 applicants, 77% accepted, 49 enrolled. In 2010, 29 first professional degrees, 9 master's awarded. *Degree requirements:* For master's, comprehensive exam (for some programs), thesis (for some programs); for M Div, 2 foreign languages, internship. *Entrance requirements:* For master's, M Div or equivalent (STM). Additional exam requirements/recommendations for international students: Required—TOEFL (minimum score 500 paper-based; 173 computer-based; 61 iBT). *Application deadline:* For fall admission, 7/15 priority date for domestic and international students. Applications are processed on a rolling basis. Application fee: $25. *Expenses:* Tuition: Full-time $13,020; part-time $434 per semester hour. Required fees: $165 per semester. One-time fee: $150. *Financial support:* In 2010–11, 102 students received support. Career-related internships or fieldwork, Federal Work-Study, institutionally sponsored loans, and scholarships/grants available. Support available to part-time students. Financial award application deadline: 5/1; financial award applicants required to submit FAFSA. *Unit head:* Dr. James Childs, Interim Academic Dean, 614-235-4136 Ext. 4670, Fax: 614-384-4635. *Application contact:* Rev. Sheri L. Ayers, Director of Admissions, 614-235-4136 Ext. 4614, Fax: 866-610-8572, E-mail: sayers@tls.edu.

Trinity School for Ministry, Graduate Programs, Ambridge, PA 15003-2397. Offers Anglican studies (Diploma); basic Christian studies (Diploma); divinity (M Div); ministry (D Min); mission and evangelism (MAME, Diploma); religion (MAR); youth ministry (Diploma). *Accreditation:* ATS (one or more programs are accredited). Part-time programs available. *Degree requirements:* For master's, thesis optional; for doctorate, thesis/dissertation; for M Div, thesis/dissertation optional, Greek and Hebrew. *Entrance requirements:* Additional exam requirements/recommendations for international students: Required—TOEFL. *Faculty research:* Pauline Epistles, contemporary theology, history of Anglican liturgy, book of Ruth, biblical theology.

Trinity Western University, ACTS Seminaries, Langley, BC V2Y 1Y1, Canada. Offers Christian studies (MA); cross cultural ministry (MA); theology (M Div, M Th, MAMFT, MLE, MTS, D Min). *Accreditation:* ATS. Part-time programs available. *Degree requirements:* For master's, thesis (for some programs), internship. *Entrance requirements:* For doctorate, MDiv or equivalent. Additional exam requirements/recommendations for international students: Required—TOEFL. *Expenses:* Contact institution. *Faculty research:* Theology of leadership.

Trinity Western University, School of Graduate Studies, Program in Biblical Studies, Langley, BC V2Y 1Y1, Canada. Offers MA. *Accreditation:* ATS. Part-time programs available. *Degree requirements:* For master's, 2 foreign languages, thesis, 2 years Greek, 2 years Hebrew. *Entrance requirements:* For master's, minimum GPA of 3.0, degree in biblical studies, master of divinity or 42 hours Biblical Study credit. Additional exam requirements/recommendations for international students: Required—TOEFL (minimum score 600 paper-based; 250 computer-based). Electronic applications accepted. *Faculty research:* Intertestamental literature, Dead Sea Scrolls, Biblical literature, history of Jesus, ancient languages.

Tyndale University College & Seminary, Graduate Programs, Toronto, ON M2M 4B3, Canada. Offers Biblical studies (M Div); Christian foundations (MTS); Christian studies (Diploma); counseling (M Div); educational ministry (M Div); missions (M Div, Diploma); pastoral and Chinese ministry (M Div); pastoral ministry (M Div); Pentecostal studies (MTS); spiritual formation (M Div, Diploma); theological studies (M Div); theology (Th M); worship and liturgy (M Div, MTS); youth and family ministry (M Div). *Accreditation:* ATS. Part-time programs available. Postbaccalaureate distance learning degree programs offered (no on-campus study). *Degree requirements:* For M Div, one foreign language, thesis/dissertation optional. *Entrance requirements:* For M Div, master's, and Diploma, minimum C+ average in undergraduate course work. Additional exam requirements/recommendations for international students: Required—TOEFL (minimum score 570 paper-based; 230 computer-based), TWE (minimum score 5). Electronic applications accepted. *Faculty research:* Canadian church history, Chinese church history, Old Testament, counseling ministries (narrative therapy), world religions.

Unification Theological Seminary, Graduate Program, Main Campus, Barrytown, NY 12507. Offers divinity (M Div); ministry (D Min); religious education (MRE); religious studies (MA). Part-time and evening/weekend programs available. *Faculty:* 4 full-time (1 woman), 3 part-time/adjunct (0 women). *Students:* 37 full-time (9 women), 1 part-time (0 women); includes 10 Black or African American, non-Hispanic/Latino; 1 American Indian or Alaska Native, non-Hispanic/Latino; 4 Asian, non-Hispanic/Latino; 1 Hispanic/Latino, 9 international. Average age 45. In 2010, 2 first professional degrees, 14 master's, 3 doctorates awarded. *Degree requirements:* For master's, one foreign language, thesis (for some programs), project; for doctorate, thesis/dissertation; for M Div, one foreign language, thesis/dissertation. *Entrance requirements:* For M Div and master's, bachelor's degree; for doctorate, M Div or equivalency. Additional exam requirements/recommendations for international students: Required—TOEFL (minimum score 450 paper-based; 133 computer-based; 45 iBT). *Application deadline:* For fall admission, 8/15 priority date for domestic students; for spring admission, 1/15 priority date for domestic students. Applications are processed on a rolling basis. Application fee: $30. *Expenses:* Tuition: Full-time $10,440; part-time $435 per credit. Required fees: $125 per semester. *Financial support:* Career-related internships or fieldwork, institutionally sponsored loans, scholarships/grants, and tuition waivers (partial) available. Support available to part-time students. Financial award applicants required to submit FAFSA. *Faculty research:* Church leadership, church history, world religions, ecumenism, interfaith peace building, service-learning. *Unit head:* Dr. Kathy Winings, Academic Dean, 845-752-3000 Ext. 228, Fax: 845-752-3014, E-mail: academics@uts.edu. *Application contact:* Davetta Ogunlola, Director of Admissions, 212-563-6647 Ext. 105, Fax: 212-563-6431, E-mail: d.ogunlola@uts.edu.

Unification Theological Seminary, Graduate Program, New York Extension, New York, NY 10036. Offers divinity (M Div); religious education (MRE); religious studies (MA). Part-time and evening/weekend programs available. *Faculty:* 3 full-time (0 women), 9 part-time/adjunct (2 women). *Students:* 42 full-time (17 women), 21 part-time (12 women); includes 25 Black or African American, non-Hispanic/Latino; 2 Asian, non-Hispanic/Latino; 1 Hispanic/Latino, 30 international. Average age 40. *Degree requirements:* For master's, thesis (for some programs), project; for M Div, thesis/dissertation. *Entrance requirements:* For M Div and master's, bachelor's degree. Additional exam requirements/recommendations for international students: Required—TOEFL (minimum score 450 paper-based; 133 computer-based). *Application deadline:* For fall admission, 8/15 priority date for domestic students; for spring admission, 1/15 priority date for domestic students. Applications are processed on a rolling basis. Application fee: $30. *Expenses:* Tuition: Full-time $10,440; part-time $435 per credit. Required fees: $125 per semester. *Financial support:* Career-related internships or fieldwork, institutionally sponsored loans, scholarships/grants, and tuition waivers (partial) available. Support available to part-time students. Financial award applicants required to submit FAFSA. *Faculty research:* Church history, world religions, ecumenism, interfaith peace building, service-learning. *Unit head:* Dr. Kathy Winings, Academic Dean, 212-563-6647 Ext. 101, Fax: 212-563-6431, E-mail: academics@uts.edu. *Application contact:* Davetta Ogunlola, Admissions Officer, 212-563-6647 Ext. 105, Fax: 212-563-6431, E-mail: d.ogunlola@uts.edu.

Union Theological Seminary in the City of New York, Graduate and Professional Programs, New York, NY 10027-5710. Offers M Div, MA, STM, Ed D, PhD, M Div/MSSW. Ed D offered jointly with Teachers College, Columbia University; M Div/MSSW with Columbia University. *Accreditation:* ACIPE; ATS (one or more programs are accredited). Part-time programs available. *Degree requirements:* For master's, one foreign language, thesis; for doctorate, 2 foreign languages, thesis/dissertation; for M Div, one foreign language, thesis/dissertation. *Entrance requirements:* For doctorate, GRE General Test, sample of written work. *Faculty research:* American religious history, psychiatry and religion, Christian ethics, New Testament.

United Talmudical Seminary, Graduate Programs, Brooklyn, NY 11211. *Accreditation:* AARTS.

United Theological Seminary, Graduate and Professional Programs, Trotwood, OH 45426. Offers M Div, MA, MATS, D Min, M Div/MA. *Accreditation:* ATS. Part-time and evening/weekend programs available. Postbaccalaureate distance learning degree programs offered (minimal on-campus study). *Faculty:* 14 full-time (5 women), 30 part-time/adjunct (9 women). *Students:* 311 full-time (123 women), 49 part-time (22 women); includes 183 minority (171 Black or African American, non-Hispanic/Latino; 9 Asian, non-Hispanic/Latino; 3 Hispanic/Latino), 3 international. *Degree requirements:* For master's, thesis (for some programs), comprehensive evaluation; for doctorate, thesis/dissertation, final exam; for M Div, comprehensive evaluation. *Entrance requirements:* For M Div, minimum GPA of 2.5, 5 letters of recommendation, interview; for master's, minimum GPA of 2.5, interview, 5 letters of recommendation; for doctorate, minimum GPA of 3.0, 2 letters of recommendation, interview. Additional exam requirements/recommendations for international students: Required—TOEFL (minimum score 550 paper-based; 213 computer-based). *Application deadline:* For fall admission, 8/1 for domestic students, 1/15 for international students; for spring admission, 1/1 for domestic students. Applications are processed on a rolling basis. Application fee: $40. Electronic applications accepted. *Expenses:* Tuition: Full-time $10,836; part-time $477 per credit hour. Required fees: $105 per semester. Tuition and fees vary according to course load and program. *Financial support:* Career-related internships or fieldwork, Federal Work-Study, and scholarships/grants available. Financial award application deadline: 4/1; financial award applicants required to submit CSS PROFILE or FAFSA. *Unit head:* Dr. Richard Eslinger, Academic Dean, 937-529-2201, E-mail: reslinger@united.edu. *Application contact:* Evan Abla, Admissions Officer, 937-529-2201, E-mail: utsadmis@united.edu.

United Theological Seminary of the Twin Cities, Graduate Programs, New Brighton, MN 55112-2598. Offers advanced theological studies (Diploma); justice and peace studies (M Div, MA); leadership toward racial justice (M Div, MA, Certificate); Methodist studies (M Div, MA, Certificate); ministry (D Min); ministry renewal and professional development (Certificate); pastoral care and counseling (M Div, MA, MARL); religion and theology (MA); theological and religious studies (Certificate); theology and the arts (M Div, MA); urban ministry (M Div, MA, MARL); women's studies: religion, theology and ministry (M Div, MA). *Accreditation:* ACIPE; ATS. Part-time and evening/weekend programs available. *Faculty:* 8 full-time (5 women), 28 part-time/adjunct (16 women). *Students:* 57 full-time (41 women), 94 part-time (61 women); includes 6 minority (5 Black or African American, non-Hispanic/Latino; 1 Hispanic/Latino), 1 international. Average age 47. 49 applicants, 98% accepted, 41 enrolled. In 2010, 10 first professional degrees, 6 master's, 4 doctorates, 2 other advanced degrees awarded. *Degree requirements:* For master's, thesis; for doctorate, comprehensive exam, thesis/dissertation; for M Div, integrative notebook, spiritual chronicle. *Entrance requirements:* For M Div and master's, minimum GPA of 2.75; strong analytical, reflective thinking and writing skills; vocational and academic goals compatible with those of Seminary; for doctorate, M Div or equivalent, minimum GPA of 3.0, 3 years experience in professional ministry; for other advanced degree, BA or equivalent life experience; strong analytical, reflective thinking and writing skills (Certificate); proficiency in English language, previous study of theology at a theological school, recommendation of student's denomination (Diploma). Additional exam requirements/recommendations for international students: Required—TOEFL (minimum score 550 paper-based). *Application deadline:* For fall admission, 7/1 priority date for domestic students, 11/1 priority date for international students; for winter admission, 11/1 priority date for domestic students; for spring admission, 11/15 priority date for domestic students. Applications are processed on a rolling basis. Application fee: $50. *Expenses:* Tuition: Full-time $13,014; part-time $482 per credit hour. One-time fee: $170. Tuition and fees vary according to course load, degree level and program. *Financial support:* In 2010–11, 120 students received support. Career-related internships or fieldwork, institutionally sponsored loans, and scholarships/grants available. Support available to part-time students. Financial award application deadline: 5/1; financial award applicants required to submit FAFSA. *Unit head:* Prof. Susan K. Ebbers, Dean of the Seminary, 651-255-6143 Ext. 108, Fax: 651-633-4315, E-mail: sebbers@unitedseminary.edu. *Application contact:* Rev. Glen Herrington-Hall, Director of Admissions, 651-255-6107 Ext. 107, Fax: 651-633-4315, E-mail: gherrington-hall@unitedseminary.edu.

Universidad FLET, Department of Graduate Studies, Miami, FL 33186. Offers education (M Ed); theological studies (MTS). *Degree requirements:* For master's, thesis or project. *Entrance requirements:* For master's, letter of recommendation.

Université de Montréal, Faculty of Theology and Sciences of Religions, Montréal, QC H3C 3J7, Canada. Offers health, spirituality and bioethics (DESS); practical theology (MA, PhD); religious sciences (MA, PhD); theology (MA, D Th, PhD, L Th); theology-Biblical studies (PhD). *Degree requirements:* For master's, one foreign language; for doctorate, 2 foreign languages, thesis/dissertation, general exam. Electronic applications accepted.

Université de Sherbrooke, Faculty of Theology, Ethics and Philosophy, Sherbrooke, QC J1K 2R1, Canada. Offers applied ethics (Diploma); human science of religions (MA); intercultural training (Diploma); philosophy (MA, PhD); spiritual anthropology (Diploma); theology (MA, PhD, Diploma). Part-time and evening/weekend programs available. Postbaccalaureate distance learning degree programs offered. Terminal master's awarded for partial completion of doctoral program. *Entrance requirements:* For master's, bachelor's degree in related discipline; for doctorate, master's degree in related discipline. *Faculty research:* Faith and culture interrelation.

Theology

Université du Québec à Chicoutimi, Graduate Programs, Program in Theology (Pastoral Studies), Chicoutimi, QC G7H 2B1, Canada. Offers MA, PhD. Programs offered jointly with Université de Montréal. Part-time programs available. *Degree requirements:* For doctorate, thesis/dissertation. *Entrance requirements:* For master's, appropriate bachelor's degree, proficiency in French; for doctorate, appropriate master's degree, proficiency in French.

Université Laval, Faculty of Theology and Religious Sciences, Program in Practical Theology, Québec, QC G1K 7P4, Canada. Offers D Th P. Part-time programs available. *Degree requirements:* For doctorate, comprehensive exam, thesis/dissertation. *Entrance requirements:* For doctorate, knowledge of French and English. Electronic applications accepted.

Université Laval, Faculty of Theology and Religious Sciences, Programs in Theology, Québec, QC G1K 7P4, Canada. Offers MA, PhD. Terminal master's awarded for partial completion of doctoral program. *Degree requirements:* For master's, thesis (for some programs); for doctorate, comprehensive exam, thesis/dissertation. *Entrance requirements:* For master's and doctorate, knowledge of French, comprehension of written English. Electronic applications accepted.

University of Chicago, Divinity School, Chicago, IL 60637-1513. Offers M Div, AM, AMRS, PhD, JD/M Div, JD/MA, JD/PhD, MPP/M Div, MSW/M Div. *Accreditation:* ATS (one or more programs are accredited). Part-time programs available. *Degree requirements:* For master's and M Div, one foreign language; for doctorate, 2 foreign languages, comprehensive exam, thesis/dissertation. *Entrance requirements:* For M Div, master's, and doctorate, GRE General Test. Additional exam requirements/recommendations for international students: Required—TOEFL (minimum score 600 paper-based; 250 computer-based). Electronic applications accepted. *Expenses:* Contact institution. *Faculty research:* Theology, history of religion, ethics, biblical studies, philosophy of religion.

University of Dallas, Braniff Graduate School of Liberal Arts, Department of Theology, Irving, TX 75062-4736. Offers M Th, MA. Part-time programs available. *Degree requirements:* For master's, one foreign language, comprehensive exam, thesis (for some programs). *Entrance requirements:* For master's, GRE General Test. *Expenses:* Tuition: Full-time $7500; part-time $720 per credit hour. Required fees: $500; $60 per credit hour. $300 per semester. One-time fee: $150. Tuition and fees vary according to program and student level. *Faculty research:* Patristics, justice in the Old and New Testament, Pauline literature, Christology, theology of the Trinity.

University of Dayton, Graduate School, College of Arts and Sciences, Department of Religious Studies, Dayton, OH 45469-1300. Offers pastoral ministry (MA); theological studies (MA); theology (PhD). Part-time and evening/weekend programs available. *Faculty:* 19 full-time (5 women), 5 part-time/adjunct (3 women). *Students:* 61 full-time (25 women), 21 part-time (11 women); includes 8 minority (1 Black or African American, non-Hispanic/Latino; 1 American Indian or Alaska Native, non-Hispanic/Latino; 2 Asian, non-Hispanic/Latino; 4 Hispanic/Latino), 1 international. Average age 34. 63 applicants, 56% accepted, 22 enrolled. In 2010, 12 master's awarded. Terminal master's awarded for partial completion of doctoral program. *Degree requirements:* For master's, thesis or alternative; for doctorate, 2 foreign languages, comprehensive exam, thesis/dissertation. *Entrance requirements:* For master's, minimum undergraduate GPA of 3.0, 3 letters of recommendation, personal statement, official transcript(s); for doctorate, GRE General Test (minimum score 600 verbal), minimum GPA of 3.5, academic writing sample, 3 letters of recommendation. Additional exam requirements/recommendations for international students: Required—TOEFL (minimum score 550 paper-based; 213 computer-based; 80 iBT). *Application deadline:* For fall admission, 3/1 priority date for domestic and international students; for winter admission, 7/1 priority date for international students; for spring admission, 1/1 priority date for international students. Applications are processed on a rolling basis. Application fee: $0 ($50 for international students). Electronic applications accepted. *Expenses:* Contact institution. *Financial support:* In 2010–11, 4 fellowships with full tuition reimbursements (averaging $15,814 per year), 8 research assistantships with full tuition reimbursements (averaging $9,457 per year), 16 teaching assistantships with full tuition reimbursements (averaging $15,814 per year) were awarded; career-related internships or fieldwork, institutionally sponsored loans, scholarships/grants, health care benefits, tuition waivers (full), and unspecified assistantships also available. Support available to part-time students. Financial award application deadline: 3/1; financial award applicants required to submit FAFSA. *Faculty research:* Practical/constructive theology, theological ethics, U. S. Catholic/Christian life and thought, methodologies in Biblical studies, religion and science. *Unit head:* Dr. Sandra Yocum, Chair, 937-229-4321, Fax: 937-229-4330, E-mail: sandra.yocum@notes.udayton.edu. *Application contact:* Alexander Popovski, Associate Director of Graduate and International Admissions, 937-229-2357, Fax: 937-229-4729, E-mail: alex.popovski@notes.udayton.edu.

University of Denver, DU-Iliff Joint PhD Program in Religious and Theological Studies, Denver, CO 80208. Offers PhD. Program jointly offered with Iliff School of Theology. Part-time programs available. *Faculty:* 20 full-time (10 women), 3 part-time/adjunct (0 women). *Students:* 42 full-time (20 women), 50 part-time (20 women); includes 13 minority (3 Black or African American, non-Hispanic/Latino; 2 American Indian or Alaska Native, non-Hispanic/Latino; 2 Asian, non-Hispanic/Latino; 5 Hispanic/Latino; 1 Two or more races, non-Hispanic/Latino), 3 international. Average age 39. 53 applicants, 49% accepted, 15 enrolled. In 2010, 8 doctorates awarded. *Degree requirements:* For doctorate, one foreign language, comprehensive exam, thesis/dissertation. *Entrance requirements:* For doctorate, GRE General Test. Additional exam requirements/recommendations for international students: Required—TOEFL (minimum score 550 paper-based; 80 iBT). *Application deadline:* For fall admission, 1/15 for domestic students. Application fee: $60. *Expenses:* Tuition: Full-time $35,604; part-time $29,670 per year. Required fees: $687 per year. Tuition and fees vary according to program. *Unit head:* Dr. Ted Vial, Director, 303-765-3166, E-mail: tvial@iliff.edu. *Application contact:* Meghan Laurvick, Coordinator, 303-765-3166, E-mail: jointphd@iliff.edu.

University of Dubuque, Theological Seminary, Dubuque, IA 52001-5099. Offers M Div, MAMC, D Min. *Accreditation:* ACIPE; ATS. Postbaccalaureate distance learning degree programs offered (minimal on-campus study). *Faculty:* 12 full-time (3 women), 8 part-time/adjunct (4 women). *Students:* 142 full-time (56 women), 16 part-time (9 women); includes 4 Black or African American, non-Hispanic/Latino; 1 American Indian or Alaska Native, non-Hispanic/Latino; 1 Asian, non-Hispanic/Latino; 3 Hispanic/Latino, 5 international. Average age 41. 72 applicants, 92% accepted, 56 enrolled. In 2010, 28 master's, 3 doctorates awarded. *Degree requirements:* For doctorate, thesis/dissertation. *Entrance requirements:* Additional exam requirements/recommendations for international students: Recommended—TOEFL (minimum score 550 paper-based; 220 computer-based; 80 iBT). *Application deadline:* For fall admission, 4/15 priority date for domestic students, 12/1 priority date for international students; for spring admission, 11/1 priority date for domestic students. Applications are processed on a rolling basis. Application fee: $30. *Financial support:* In 2010–11, 69 students received support. Career-related internships or fieldwork, Federal Work-Study, institutionally sponsored loans, scholarships/grants, and tuition waivers (full and partial) available. Support available to part-time students. Financial award application deadline: 6/1; financial award applicants required to submit FAFSA. *Faculty research:* biblical theology, reformed history and theology, pastoral theology, homiletics. Total annual research expenditures: $8,458. *Unit head:* Dr. Bradley Longfield, Dean, 319-589-3122, Fax: 319-589-3110, E-mail: blongfie@dbq.edu. *Application contact:* Peggy Sell, Director, Seminary Admissions, 563-589-3267, E-mail: psell@dbq.edu.

The University of Manchester, School of Arts, Histories and Cultures, Manchester, United Kingdom. Offers anthropology, media and performance (PhD); applied theatre professional (PhD); archaeology (PhD); art history and visual studies (PhD); arts management and cultural policy (PhD); classics and ancient history (PhD); composition (PhD); creative writing (PhD); drama (PhD); economic and social history (PhD); electroacoustic composition (PhD); English and American studies (PhD); history (PhD); humanitarianism and conflict response (PhD); museology (PhD); music (PhD); musicology (PhD); religions and theology (PhD).

University of Mobile, Graduate Programs, Program in Religious Studies, Mobile, AL 36613. Offers biblical/theological studies (MA); marriage and family counseling (MA). Part-time and evening/weekend programs available. *Faculty:* 6 full-time (0 women). *Students:* 12 full-time (7 women), 53 part-time (41 women); includes 34 Black or African American, non-Hispanic/Latino; 3 American Indian or Alaska Native, non-Hispanic/Latino, 2 international. Average age 34. 18 applicants, 94% accepted, 16 enrolled. In 2010, 10 master's awarded. *Degree requirements:* For master's, 2 foreign languages, comprehensive exam, thesis optional. *Entrance requirements:* For master's, GRE General Test. Additional exam requirements/recommendations for international students: Required—TOEFL (minimum score 550 paper-based; 213 computer-based; 80 iBT). *Application deadline:* For fall admission, 8/3 priority date for domestic students; for spring admission, 12/23 for domestic students. Applications are processed on a rolling basis. Application fee: $40 ($50 for international students). *Expenses:* Tuition: Full-time $3915; part-time $435 per credit hour. Required fees: $63 per semester. *Financial support:* Federal Work-Study available. Support available to part-time students. Financial award application deadline: 8/1. *Unit head:* Dr. Cecil Taylor, Dean, School of Christian Studies, 251-442-2255, Fax: 251-442-2523, E-mail: ctaylor@mail.umobile.edu. *Application contact:* Tammy C. Eubanks, Administrative Assistant to Dean of Graduate Programs, 251-442-2270, Fax: 251-442-2523, E-mail: teubanks@umobile.edu.

University of Notre Dame, Graduate School, College of Arts and Letters, Division of Humanities, Department of Theology, Notre Dame, IN 46556. Offers M Div, MA, MSM, MTS, PhD. *Accreditation:* ACIPE; ATS. Terminal master's awarded for partial completion of doctoral program. *Degree requirements:* For master's, one foreign language, comprehensive exam, thesis or alternative; for doctorate, 3 foreign languages, comprehensive exam, thesis/dissertation, candidacy exam. *Entrance requirements:* For M Div, master's, and doctorate, GRE General Test. Additional exam requirements/recommendations for international students: Required—TOEFL (minimum score 600 paper-based; 250 computer-based; 80 iBT). Electronic applications accepted. *Faculty research:* Liturgy, ethics, historical studies, Biblical studies, systematic theology.

University of Notre Dame, Graduate School, College of Arts and Letters, Division of Humanities, Program in History and Philosophy of Science, Notre Dame, IN 46556. Offers history and philosophy of science (MA, PhD); theology and science (PhD). *Degree requirements:* For doctorate, 2 foreign languages, comprehensive exam, thesis/dissertation, candidacy exam. *Entrance requirements:* For doctorate, GRE General Test. Additional exam requirements/recommendations for international students: Required—TOEFL (minimum score 600 paper-based; 250 computer-based; 80 iBT). Electronic applications accepted. *Faculty research:* Philosophy of physics, science and ethics, history and philosophy of biology, history of medicine and technology, history and philosophy of economics.

University of Philosophical Research, Program in Consciousness Studies, Los Angeles, CA 90027. Offers MA. *Degree requirements:* For master's, thesis.

University of Philosophical Research, Program in Transformational Psychology, Los Angeles, CA 90027. Offers MA. *Degree requirements:* For master's, thesis.

University of Saint Mary of the Lake–Mundelein Seminary, Graduate School of Theology, Mundelein, IL 60060. Offers M Div, MA, D Min. *Accreditation:* ATS (one or more programs are accredited). *Faculty:* 42 full-time (6 women), 15 part-time/adjunct (3 women). *Students:* 212 full-time (13 women); includes 10 minority (2 Black or African American, non-Hispanic/Latino; 3 Asian, non-Hispanic/Latino; 5 Hispanic/Latino), 78 international. 95 applicants, 75% accepted, 71 enrolled. *Degree requirements:* For doctorate, thesis/dissertation; for M Div, thesis/dissertation (for some programs). *Entrance requirements:* For M Div, master's, and doctorate, bachelor's degree. Additional exam requirements/recommendations for international students: Required—TOEFL. *Application deadline:* Applications are processed on a rolling basis. Application fee: $0. Electronic applications accepted. *Expenses:* Tuition: Full-time $20,622. Required fees: $250. *Financial support:* Career-related internships or fieldwork available. *Unit head:* Rev. Raymond J. Webb, Academic Dean, 847-566-6401. *Application contact:* Rev. Raymond J. Webb, Academic Dean, 847-566-6401.

University of St. Michael's College, Faculty of Theology, Toronto, ON M5S 1J4, Canada. Offers Catholic leadership (MA); eastern Christian studies (Diploma); religious education (Diploma); theological studies (Diploma); theology (M Div, MA, MRE, MTS, D Min, PhD, Th D); theology and Jewish studies (MA). Th D offered jointly with University of Toronto. *Accreditation:* ATS (one or more programs are accredited). Part-time programs available. *Degree requirements:* For master's, thesis (for some programs), 1 foreign language (MA), 2 foreign languages (Th M); for doctorate, 3 foreign languages, comprehensive exam, thesis/dissertation; for M Div, thesis/dissertation optional; for other advanced degree, thesis optional. *Entrance requirements:* For M Div and other advanced degree, minimum GPA of 2.7; for master's, M Div or BA, course work in an ancient or modern language, minimum GPA of 3.3; for doctorate, MA in theology, Th M, or M Div with thesis, minimum GPA of 3.7. Additional exam requirements/recommendations for international students: Required—TOEFL (minimum score 600 paper-based; 250 computer-based). Electronic applications accepted. *Expenses:* Contact institution. *Faculty research:* Patristics, eastern Christianity, ecology and theology, ecumenism, Jewish Christian studies.

University of St. Thomas, Graduate Studies, The Saint Paul Seminary School of Divinity, Saint Paul, MN 55105. Offers M Div, MA, MARE. *Accreditation:* ACIPE; ATS. Part-time and evening/weekend programs available. *Faculty:* 13 full-time (5 women), 5 part-time/adjunct (2 women). *Students:* 97 full-time (5 women), 20 part-time (10 women); includes 2 minority (both Hispanic/Latino), 10 international. Average age 30. 32 applicants, 100% accepted, 30 enrolled. In 2010, 9 first professional degrees, 23 master's awarded. *Degree requirements:* For master's, one foreign language, comprehensive exam (for some programs), thesis (for some programs). *Entrance requirements:* For M Div, GRE General Test or MAT, BA with minimum undergraduate GPA of 3.0, interview; for master's, GRE, 3 letters of recommendation, interview. Additional exam requirements/recommendations for international students: Required—TOEFL (minimum score 550 paper-based; 213 computer-based). *Application deadline:* For fall admission, 6/1 priority date for domestic students. Applications are processed on a rolling basis. Application fee: $40. Electronic applications accepted. *Expenses:* Contact institution. *Financial support:* In 2010–11, 52 students received support; fellowships, research assistantships, institutionally sponsored loans and scholarships/grants available. Support available to part-time students. Financial award application deadline: 4/1; financial award applicants required to submit FAFSA. *Faculty research:* Theological education. *Unit head:* Rev. Msgr. Aloysius R. Callaghan, Rector, 651-962-5052, Fax: 651-962-5790, E-mail: arcallaghan@stthomas.edu. *Application contact:* Rev. Peter A. Laird, Vice Rector and Admissions Chair, 651-962-5070, Fax: 651-962-5790, E-mail: palaird@stthomas.edu.

University of St. Thomas, School of Theology, Houston, TX 77006-4696. Offers M Div, MAPS, MAT. *Accreditation:* ATS. Part-time programs available. *Faculty:* 8 full-time (2 women), 5 part-time/adjunct (0 women). *Students:* 91 full-time (5 women), 113 part-time (39 women); includes 71 minority (9 Black or African American, non-Hispanic/Latino; 21 Asian, non-Hispanic/Latino; 38 Hispanic/Latino; 3 Two or more races, non-Hispanic/Latino), 21 international. Average age 41. 43 applicants, 100% accepted, 35 enrolled. In 2010, 13 first professional degrees, 23 master's awarded. *Degree requirements:* For master's, variable foreign language requirement, comprehensive exam. *Entrance requirements:* For M Div, BA, BS or equivalent with minimum GPA of 2.0; personal essay; undergraduate philosophy or theology courses; 2 letters of recommendation; evidence of certification through diocesan programs; for master's, BA, BS or equivalent; personal essay (for some programs); undergraduate philosophy or theology courses; 2 letters of recommendation; evidence of certification through diocesan programs. Additional exam requirements/recommendations for international students: Required—TOEFL (minimum score 550 paper-based; 213 computer-based; 79 iBT). *Application deadline:* Applications are processed on a rolling basis. Application fee: $35. Electronic applications accepted. *Expenses:* Contact institution. *Financial support:* In 2010–11, 10 students received support. Federal Work-Study, scholarships/grants, and state work-study, institutional employment available. Support available to part-time students. Financial award application deadline: 4/15; financial award applicants required to submit FAFSA. *Unit head:* Dr. Sandra C. Magie, Dean, 713-686-4345, Fax: 713-683-8673, E-mail: sms@stthom.edu. *Application contact:* Connie Henry, Office Manager, 713-686-4345, Fax: 713-683-8673, E-mail: sms@stthom.edu.

The University of Scranton, College of Graduate and Continuing Education, Program in Theology, Scranton, PA 18510. Offers MA. Part-time and evening/weekend programs available. *Faculty:* 14 full-time (5 women). *Students:* 4 full-time (1 woman), 8 part-time (3 women). Average age 35. 9 applicants, 33% accepted. In 2010, 1 master's awarded. *Degree requirements:* For master's, thesis (for some programs), capstone experience. *Entrance requirements:* For master's, minimum GPA of 2.75. Additional exam requirements/recommendations for international students: Required—TOEFL (minimum score 500 paper-based; 173 computer-based), IELTS (minimum score 5.5). *Application deadline:* Applications are processed on a rolling basis. Application fee: $0. *Expenses:* Contact institution. *Financial support:* In 2010–11, 2 students received support, including 2 teaching assistantships with full tuition reimbursements available (averaging $4,400 per year); career-related internships or fieldwork, Federal Work-Study, and unspecified assistantships also available. Support available to part-time students. Financial award application deadline: 3/1. *Unit head:* Dr. Charles R. Pinches, Chair, 570-941-4302, Fax: 570-941-6369, E-mail: pinchesc1@scranton.edu. *Application contact:* Joseph M. Roback, Director of Admissions, 570-941-4385, Fax: 570-941-5928, E-mail: robackj2@scranton.edu.

University of South Africa, College of Human Sciences, Pretoria, South Africa. Offers adult education (M Ed); African languages (MA, PhD); African politics (MA, PhD); Afrikaans (MA, PhD); ancient history (MA, PhD); ancient Near Eastern studies (MA, PhD); anthropology (MA, PhD); applied linguistics (MA); Arabic (MA, PhD); archaeology (MA); art history (MA); Biblical archaeology (MA); Biblical studies (M Th, D Th, PhD); Christian spirituality (M Th, D Th); church history (M Th, D Th); classical studies (MA, PhD); clinical psychology (MA); communication (MA, PhD); comparative education (M Ed, Ed D); consulting psychology (D Admin, D Com, PhD); curriculum studies (M Ed, Ed D); development studies (M Admin, MA, D Admin, PhD); didactics (M Ed, Ed D); education (M Tech); education management (M Ed, Ed D); educational psychology (M Ed); English (MA); environmental education (M Ed); French (MA, PhD); German (MA, PhD); Greek (MA); guidance and counseling (M Ed); health studies (MA, PhD), including health sciences education (MA), health services management (MA), medical and surgical nursing science (critical care general) (MA), midwifery and neonatal nursing science (MA), trauma and emergency care (MA); history (MA, PhD); history of education (Ed D); inclusive education (M Ed, Ed D); information and communications technology policy and regulation (MA); information science (MA, MIS, PhD); international politics (MA, PhD); Islamic studies (MA, PhD); Italian (MA, PhD); Judaica (MA, PhD); linguistics (MA, PhD); mathematical education (M Ed); mathematics education (MA); missiology (M Th, D Th); modern Hebrew (MA, PhD); musicology (MA, MMus, D Mus, PhD); natural science education (M Ed); New Testament (M Th, D Th); Old Testament (D Th); pastoral therapy (M Th, D Th); philosophy (MA); philosophy of education (M Ed, Ed D); politics (MA, PhD); Portuguese (MA, PhD); practical theology (M Th, D Th); psychology (MA, MS, PhD); psychology of education (M Ed, Ed D); public health (MA); religious studies (MA, D Th, PhD); Romance languages (MA); Russian (MA, PhD); Semitic languages (MA, PhD); social behavior studies in HIV/AIDS (MA); social science (mental health) (MA); social science in development studies (MA); social science in psychology (MA); social science in social work (MA); social science in sociology (MA); social work (MSW, DSW, PhD); socio-education (M Ed, Ed D); sociolinguistics (MA); sociology (MA, PhD); Spanish (MA, PhD); systematic theology (M Th, D Th); TESOL (teaching English to speakers of other languages) (MA); theological ethics (M Th, D Th); theory of literature (MA, PhD); urban ministries (D Th); urban ministry (M Th).

University of Trinity College, Faculty of Divinity, Toronto, ON M5S 1H8, Canada. Offers ministry (Diploma); ministry for church musicians (Diploma); theology (M Div, MA, MTS, Th M, D Min, PhD, Th D, Diploma, L Th); M Div/MA. *Accreditation:* ATS. Part-time programs available. *Faculty:* 3 full-time (1 woman), 31 part-time/adjunct (4 women). *Students:* 50 full-time (15 women), 84 part-time (39 women). Average age 45. *Degree requirements:* For master's, 2 foreign languages, thesis (for some programs); for doctorate, 3 foreign languages, comprehensive exam, thesis/dissertation; for M Div, thesis/dissertation optional; for other advanced degree, thesis (for some programs). *Entrance requirements:* For M Div, interview; for master's, 1 language (modern or ancient), interview; for doctorate, 2 languages (modern and ancient). Additional exam requirements/recommendations for international students: Required—TOEFL, TWE. *Application deadline:* For fall admission, 3/31 priority date for domestic and international students; for winter admission, 12/31 for domestic and international students; for spring admission, 4/30 priority date for domestic and international students. Applications are processed on a rolling basis. Application fee: $0. *Financial support:* Fellowships, teaching assistantships, career-related internships or fieldwork, institutionally sponsored loans, and bursaries available. Support available to part-time students. Financial award application deadline: 5/15. *Faculty research:* Interreligious dialogue, feminist theology, systematic theology, philosophy of religion, pastoral theology. *Unit head:* Dr. David Neelands, Dean, 416-978-7750, Fax: 416-978-4949, E-mail: divdean@trinity.utoronto.ca. *Application contact:* Rachel Richards, Administrative Assistant to the Dean, 416-978-2133, Fax: 416-978-4949, E-mail: divinity@trinity.utoronto.ca.

The University of Winnipeg, Faculty of Theology, Winnipeg, MB R3B 2E9, Canada. Offers marriage and family therapy (MMFT, Certificate); sacred theology (STM); theology (M Div). *Accreditation:* AAMFT/COAMFTE; ATS. Part-time programs available. *Degree requirements:* For M Div, thesis/dissertation optional.

Ursuline College, School of Graduate Studies, Graduate Program in Ministry, Pepper Pike, OH 44124-4398. Offers MA. Part-time programs available. *Faculty:* 1 (woman) full-time, 1 (woman) part-time/adjunct. *Students:* 18 part-time (16 women); includes 2 Black or African American, non-Hispanic/Latino. Average age 47. 3 applicants, 100% accepted, 3 enrolled. In 2010, 4 master's awarded. *Degree requirements:* For master's, thesis. *Entrance requirements:* For master's, minimum undergraduate GPA of 3.0, interview. Additional exam requirements/recommendations for international students: Required—TOEFL (minimum score 500 paper-based; 173 computer-based). *Application deadline:* For fall admission, 8/1 priority date for domestic students. Applications are processed on a rolling basis. Application fee: $25. *Expenses:* Contact institution. *Financial support:* In 2010–11, 11 students received support. Federal Work-Study available. Financial award application deadline: 3/1; financial award applicants required to submit FAFSA. *Unit head:* Dr. Linda Martin, Co-Director, 440-646-8191, Fax: 440-684-6088, E-mail: lmartin@ursuline.edu. *Application contact:* Melanie Steele, Graduate Admission Assistant, 440-646-8199, Fax: 440-684-6138, E-mail: graduateadmissions@ursuline.edu.

Valley Forge Christian College, Program in Theology, Phoenixville, PA 19460. Offers MA. *Degree requirements:* For master's, project.

Valparaiso University, Graduate School, Programs in Liberal Studies, Concentration in Theology, Valparaiso, IN 46383. Offers MALS, Post-Master's Certificate, JD/MALS. Part-time and evening/weekend programs available. *Entrance requirements:* For master's, minimum GPA of 3.0. Additional exam requirements/recommendations for international students: Required—TOEFL (minimum score 550 paper-based; 213 computer-based; 80 iBT). *Application deadline:* Applications are processed on a rolling basis. Application fee: $30 ($50 for international students). Electronic applications accepted. *Expenses:* Tuition: Full-time $9540; part-time $530 per credit hour. Required fees: $292; $95 per semester. Tuition and fees vary according to program. *Financial support:* Available to part-time students. Applicants required to submit FAFSA. *Unit head:* Dr. David L. Rowland, Dean, Graduate School and Continuing Education/Associate Provost, 219-464-5313, Fax: 219-464-5381, E-mail: david.rowland@valpo.edu. *Application contact:* Laura Groth, Coordinator of Student Services and Support, 219-464-5313, Fax: 219-464-5381, E-mail: laura.groth@valpo.edu.

Valparaiso University, Graduate School, Programs in Liberal Studies, Concentration in Theology and Ministry, Valparaiso, IN 46383. Offers MALS, Post-Master's Certificate. Part-time and evening/weekend programs available. *Entrance requirements:* For master's, minimum GPA of 3.0. Additional exam requirements/recommendations for international students: Required—TOEFL (minimum score 550 paper-based; 213 computer-based; 80 iBT). *Application deadline:* Applications are processed on a rolling basis. Application fee: $30 ($50 for international students). Electronic applications accepted. *Expenses:* Tuition: Full-time $9540; part-time $530 per credit hour. Required fees: $292; $95 per semester. Tuition and fees vary according to program. *Financial support:* Available to part-time students. Applicants required to submit FAFSA. *Unit head:* Dr. David L. Rowland, Dean, Graduate School and Continuing Education/Associate Provost, 219-464-5313, Fax: 219-464-5381, E-mail: david.rowland@valpo.edu. *Application contact:* Laura Groth, Coordinator of Student Services and Support, 219-464-5313, Fax: 219-464-5381, E-mail: laura.groth@valpo.edu.

Vancouver School of Theology, Graduate and Professional Programs, Vancouver, BC V6T 1L4, Canada. Offers spiritual direction (Graduate Diploma); theological studies (MATS); theology (M Div, Th M, Dip CS). *Accreditation:* ATS. Part-time programs available. *Degree requirements:* For master's, comprehensive exam (for some programs), thesis (for some programs); for M Div, thesis/dissertation (for some programs); for other advanced degree, one foreign language, thesis. *Entrance requirements:* Additional exam requirements/recommendations for international students: Required—TOEFL. Electronic applications accepted. *Faculty research:* Old Testament studies, pastoral theology, New Testament studies, field education, church history, systematic theology, spirituality.

Vanderbilt University, Divinity School, Nashville, TN 37240. Offers M Div, MTS, JD/M Div, JD/MTS, MBA/M Div, MBA/MTS, MD/M Div, MD/MTS, MSN/M Div, MSN/MTS. *Accreditation:* ACIPE; ATS. Part-time programs available. *Faculty:* 38 full-time (13 women), 3 part-time/adjunct (1 woman). *Students:* 246 full-time (131 women), 4 part-time (all women); includes 62 minority (48 Black or African American, non-Hispanic/Latino; 1 American Indian or Alaska Native, non-Hispanic/Latino; 9 Asian, non-Hispanic/Latino; 4 Hispanic/Latino). Average age 29. 201 applicants, 83% accepted, 86 enrolled. In 2010, 40 first professional degrees, 42 master's awarded. *Entrance requirements:* Additional exam requirements/recommendations for international students: Required—TOEFL (minimum score 630 paper-based; 250 computer-based; 100 iBT). *Application deadline:* For winter admission, 1/15 priority date for domestic and international students; for spring admission, 4/1 for domestic and international students. Applications are processed on a rolling basis. Application fee: $50. Electronic applications accepted. *Expenses:* Contact institution. *Financial support:* In 2010–11, 246 students received support. Career-related internships or fieldwork, Federal Work-Study, institutionally sponsored loans, scholarships/grants, and tuition waivers (full and partial) available. Financial award application deadline: 5/1; financial award applicants required to submit CSS PROFILE or FAFSA. *Unit head:* Dr. James Hudnut-Beumler, Dean, 615-322-2776, Fax: 615-343-9957, E-mail: james.d.hudnut-beumler@vanderbilt.edu. *Application contact:* Rev. Katherine H. Smith, Director of Admissions and Student Services, 615-343-3963, Fax: 615-322-0691, E-mail: katherine.smith@vanderbilt.edu.

Vanguard University of Southern California, Graduate Programs in Religion, Costa Mesa, CA 92626-9601. Offers leadership studies (MA); theological studies (MTS). Part-time and evening/weekend programs available. *Degree requirements:* For master's, comprehensive exam (for some programs), thesis (for some programs). *Entrance requirements:* For master's, minimum GPA of 3.0 (MA), 2.5 (MTS). Additional exam requirements/recommendations for international students: Required—TOEFL (minimum score 550 paper-based; 213 computer-based; 79 iBT). Electronic applications accepted. *Expenses:* Contact institution. *Faculty research:* Narrative theology, ecumenism and Pentecost, leadership studies.

Victoria University, Emmanuel College, Toronto, ON M5S 1K7, Canada. Offers M Div, MA, MPS, MRE, MSMus, MTS, Th M, D Min, PhD, Th D, Certificate, Diploma, L Th, M Div/MA, M Div/MPS, M Div/MRE. M Div, MRE, Th M, Th D, M Div/MA, M Div/MRE, M Div/MPS offered jointly with University of Toronto; MA, PhD with University of St. Michael's College. *Accreditation:* ATS. Terminal master's awarded for partial completion of doctoral program. *Degree requirements:* For master's, 2 foreign languages, thesis (for some programs); for doctorate, 2 foreign languages, thesis/dissertation; for M Div, thesis/dissertation optional. *Entrance requirements:* For M Div, BA, BSc, BMus; for master's and other advanced degree, BA, BSc; for doctorate, MDiv, MA, MTS, ThM. Additional exam requirements/recommendations for international students: Required—TOEFL (minimum score 600 paper-based; 250 computer-based; 100 iBT), IELTS (minimum score 7), TWE (minimum score 5). Electronic applications accepted. *Faculty research:* New Testament and Old Testament hermeneutics, religious symbolism, Reformation, liberation theology, Canadian church history.

Villanova University, Graduate School of Liberal Arts and Sciences, Department of Theology, Villanova, PA 19085-1699. Offers MA. Part-time and evening/weekend programs available. *Faculty:* 9 full-time (3 women). *Students:* 35 full-time (18 women), 7 part-time (4 women); includes 7 minority (3 Black or African American, non-Hispanic/Latino; 3 Asian, non-Hispanic/Latino; 1 Two or more races, non-Hispanic/Latino), 1 international. Average age 34. 18 applicants, 100% accepted, 16 enrolled. In 2010, 16 master's awarded. *Degree requirements:* For master's, one foreign language, comprehensive exam, thesis optional. *Entrance requirements:* For master's, GRE, minimum GPA of 3.0. Additional exam requirements/recommendations for international students: Required—TOEFL. *Application deadline:* For fall admission, 3/1 priority date for domestic and international students; for spring admission, 11/15 priority date for domestic students, 11/15 for international students. Applications are processed on a rolling basis. Application fee: $50. Electronic applications accepted. *Expenses:* Tuition: Part-time $700 per credit. Part-time tuition and fees vary according to degree level and program. *Financial support:* Research assistantships, Federal Work-Study, scholarships/grants, and unspecified assistantships available. Financial award applicants required to submit FAFSA. *Unit head:* Dr. Bernard Prusak, Chair, 610-519-7423. *Application contact:* Dr. Adele Lindenmeyr, Dean, Graduate School of Liberal Arts and Sciences, 610-519-7093, Fax: 610-519-7096.

Virginia Theological Seminary, Graduate and Professional Programs, Alexandria, VA 22304. Offers M Div, MACE, MTS, D Min. *Accreditation:* ATS. Part-time programs available. *Degree requirements:* For master's, 2 foreign languages, thesis; for doctorate, thesis/dissertation. *Entrance requirements:* For M Div, master's, and doctorate, GRE General Test.

Virginia Union University, School of Theology, Richmond, VA 23220-1170. Offers M Div, D Min. *Accreditation:* ACIPE; ATS. Part-time and evening/weekend programs available. *Entrance requirements:* Additional exam requirements/recommendations for international students: Required—TOEFL.

Walsh University, Graduate Studies, Program in Theology, North Canton, OH 44720-3396. Offers MA. Part-time and evening/weekend programs available. *Faculty:* 2 full-time (1 woman), 3 part-time/adjunct (2 women). *Students:* 17 part-time (11 women). Average age 48. 5 applicants, 80% accepted, 4 enrolled. In 2010, 1 master's awarded. *Degree requirements:* For master's, thesis. *Entrance requirements:* For master's, MAT or GRE, minimum GPA of 3.0. *Application deadline:* For fall admission, 7/15 priority date for domestic students. Applications are processed on a rolling basis. Application fee: $25. Electronic applications accepted. *Expenses:* Tuition: Full-time $13,080; part-time $545 per credit hour. *Financial support:* In 2010–11, 9 students received support; research assistantships available. Financial award application deadline: 12/31. *Faculty research:* Historical theology, patristics, twentieth century Catholic theologians, theological anthropology, peace studies. *Unit head:* Dr. Patrick Manning, Chair, 330-244-4922, Fax: 330-244-4955, E-mail: pmanning@walsh.edu. *Application contact:* Christine Haver, Assistant Director for Graduate and Transfer Admissions, 330-490-7177, Fax: 330-244-4925, E-mail: chaver@walsh.edu.

Warner Pacific College, Graduate Programs, Portland, OR 97215-4099. Offers biblical and theological studies (MA); biblical studies (M Rel); education (M Ed); management/organizational leadership (MS); pastoral ministries (M Rel); religion and ethics (M Rel); teaching (MA); theology (M Rel). Part-time programs available. *Degree requirements:* For master's, thesis or alternative, presentation of defense. *Entrance requirements:* For master's, interview, minimum GPA of 2.5,

Theology

Warner Pacific College (continued)
letters of recommendations. *Faculty research:* New Testament studies, nineteenth-century Wesleyan theology, preaching and church growth, Christian ethics.

Wartburg Theological Seminary, Graduate and Professional Programs, Dubuque, IA 52004-5004. Offers diaconal ministry (MA); ministry (M Div); theology (MA, MATDE, STM). *Accreditation:* ACIPE; ATS. *Faculty:* 19 full-time (6 women), 9 part-time/adjunct (3 women). *Students:* 141 full-time (72 women), 12 part-time (8 women); includes 4 Black or African American, non-Hispanic/Latino; 2 American Indian or Alaska Native, non-Hispanic/Latino; 2 Asian, non-Hispanic/Latino; 2 Hispanic/Latino, 1 international. Average age 34. 58 applicants, 88% accepted, 50 enrolled. In 2010, 39 first professional degrees, 14 master's awarded. *Degree requirements:* For master's, thesis (for some programs); for M Div, thesis/dissertation optional. *Entrance requirements:* For M Div, minimum GPA of 2.5; for master's, minimum GPA of 3.0 (STM). Additional exam requirements/recommendations for international students: Required—TOEFL (minimum score 500 paper-based; 173 computer-based; 80 iBT). *Application deadline:* For fall admission, 5/15 priority date for domestic students, 10/1 priority date for international students; for winter admission, 10/1 for international students; for spring admission, 12/15 priority date for domestic students, 10/1 for international students. Applications are processed on a rolling basis. Application fee: $0. Electronic applications accepted. *Expenses:* Tuition: Full-time $13,000; part-time $625 per semester hour. Required fees: $505; $50 per term. *Financial support:* In 2010–11, 100 students received support, including 13 research assistantships with partial tuition reimbursements available (averaging $1,125 per year); career-related internships or fieldwork, Federal Work-Study, institutionally sponsored loans, and scholarships/grants also available. Support available to part-time students. Financial award application deadline: 6/15; financial award applicants required to submit FAFSA. *Unit head:* Rev. Dr. Craig L. Nessan, Academic Dean, 563-589-0207, Fax: 563-589-0333. *Application contact:* Rev. Karla Wildberger, Director of Admissions, 563-589-0203, Fax: 563-589-0333, E-mail: admissions@wartburgseminary.edu.

Washington Theological Union, Graduate and Professional Programs, Washington, DC 20012. Offers M Div, MA, MAPS, MTS, D Min, M Div/MA. *Accreditation:* ACIPE; ATS. Part-time programs available. Postbaccalaureate distance learning degree programs offered. *Faculty:* 18 full-time (3 women), 9 part-time/adjunct (2 women). *Students:* 43 full-time (6 women), 197 part-time (75 women). Average age 32. 149 applicants, 95% accepted. In 2010, 19 first professional degrees, 22 master's awarded. *Degree requirements:* For master's, one foreign language, comprehensive exam, thesis. *Entrance requirements:* For M Div, 18 hours of course work in philosophy; for master's, 18 hours of course work in philosophy and religious studies. *Application deadline:* For fall admission, 4/1 priority date for domestic students; for spring admission, 11/15 priority date for domestic students. Applications are processed on a rolling basis. Application fee: $50. *Expenses:* Tuition: Part-time $660 per credit hour. Required fees: $90 per semester. *Financial support:* In 2010–11, 40 students received support. Career-related internships or fieldwork and scholarships/grants available. Support available to part-time students. Financial award application deadline: 3/15; financial award applicants required to submit FAFSA. *Unit head:* Very Rev. Frederick J. Tillotson, OCARM, President, 202-541-5228, Fax: 202-726-1716. *Application contact:* Cynthia Cameron, Director of Recruitment and Enrollment Services, 202-541-5210, Fax: 202-726-1716, E-mail: admissions@wtu.edu.

Wesley Biblical Seminary, Graduate Programs, Jackson, MS 39206. Offers apologetics (MA); Biblical studies (MA); Christian studies (MA); evangelism (M Div); family life ministry (M Div); honors research (M Div); missions (M Div); pastoral ministry (M Div); teaching (M Div); theological studies (MA). *Accreditation:* ATS. Part-time programs available. *Degree requirements:* For master's, thesis. *Entrance requirements:* Additional exam requirements/recommendations for international students: Required—TOEFL. Electronic applications accepted. *Faculty research:* Patristics, missiology, culture, hermeneutics.

Wesley Theological Seminary, Graduate and Professional Programs, Washington, DC 20016-5690. Offers M Div, MA, MTS, D Min, M Div/MA, M Div/MTS. *Accreditation:* ACIPE; ATS. Part-time programs available. *Degree requirements:* For master's, thesis; for doctorate, thesis/dissertation; for M Div, thesis/dissertation or alternative. *Entrance requirements:* For M Div and master's, minimum GPA of 2.7; for doctorate, minimum GPA of 3.0.

Western Seminary, Graduate Programs, Master of Divinity Program, Portland, OR 97215-3367. Offers M Div. *Faculty:* 3 full-time (1 woman), 3 part-time/adjunct (0 women). *Students:* 265 applicants, 77% accepted, 155 enrolled. *Degree requirements:* For M Div, thesis/dissertation or alternative, practicum. *Entrance requirements:* Additional exam requirements/recommendations for international students: Required—TOEFL. *Application deadline:* For fall admission, 7/18 priority date for domestic students; for winter admission, 11/7 priority date for domestic students; for spring admission, 3/13 priority date for domestic students. Applications are processed on a rolling basis. Application fee: $50. *Expenses:* Tuition: Part-time $425 per credit. *Financial support:* Fellowships, career-related internships or fieldwork available. Support available to part-time students. Financial award applicants required to submit FAFSA. *Unit head:* Dr. Art Azurdia, Director, 503-517-1873, E-mail: aazurdia@westernseminary.edu. *Application contact:* Dr. Robert W. Wiggins, Registrar/Dean of Student Development, 503-517-1820, Fax: 503-517-1801, E-mail: rwiggins@westernseminary.edu.

Western Seminary, Graduate Programs, Program in Biblical and Theological Studies, Portland, OR 97215-3367. Offers biblical and theological studies (MA, G Dip); biblical studies (Certificate); theology (Th M). *Accreditation:* ATS. Part-time and evening/weekend programs available. *Faculty:* 93 full-time (38 women), 586 part-time/adjunct (198 women). *Students:* 265 applicants, 77% accepted, 155 enrolled. In 2010, 93 master's, 6 other advanced degrees awarded. *Degree requirements:* For master's, thesis or alternative, practicum. *Entrance requirements:* Additional exam requirements/recommendations for international students: Required—TOEFL. *Application deadline:* For fall admission, 7/18 priority date for domestic students; for winter admission, 11/7 priority date for domestic students; for spring admission, 3/13 priority date for domestic students. Applications are processed on a rolling basis. Application fee: $50. *Expenses:* Tuition: Part-time $425 per credit. *Financial support:* Fellowships, career-related internships or fieldwork available. Financial award applicants required to submit FAFSA. *Unit head:* Dr. Gerry Breshears, Director, 503-517-1870, E-mail: gbreshears@westernseminary.edu. *Application contact:* Dr. Robert W. Wiggins, Registrar/Dean of Student Development, 503-517-1820, Fax: 503-517-1820, E-mail: rwiggins@westernseminary.edu.

Western Seminary–Sacramento Campus, Graduate Certificate Programs, Sacramento, CA 95821. Offers Bible (Graduate Certificate); coaching (Graduate Certificate); pastoral care to women (Graduate Certificate); theology (Graduate Certificate); youth and family (Graduate Certificate). Postbaccalaureate distance learning degree programs offered. *Entrance requirements:* For degree, essays, undergraduate transcripts, 4 recommendations. Additional exam requirements/recommendations for international students: Required—TOEFL.

Western Seminary–Sacramento Campus, Graduate Diploma Programs, Sacramento, CA 95821. Offers Bible and theology (Graduate Diploma); ministry (Graduate Diploma); pastoral care to women (Graduate Diploma). *Entrance requirements:* For degree, essays, undergraduate transcripts, 4 recommendations. Additional exam requirements/recommendations for international students: Required—TOEFL.

Western Seminary–Sacramento Campus, Master of Divinity Program, Sacramento, CA 95821. Offers M Div. *Entrance requirements:* Essays, undergraduate transcripts, 4 recommendations. Additional exam requirements/recommendations for international students: Required—TOEFL.

Western Seminary–Sacramento Campus, Program in Biblical and Theological Studies, Sacramento, CA 95821. Offers MA. *Entrance requirements:* For master's, essays, undergraduate transcripts, 4 recommendations. Additional exam requirements/recommendations for international students: Required—TOEFL.

Western Seminary–San Jose Campus, Graduate Programs, Los Gatos, CA 95032-4520. Offers Biblical and theological studies (MA); exposition ministry (M Div); marital and family therapy (MA); ministry and leadership (MA); open track (M Div); pastoral ministry (M Div); theology (Graduate Diploma). Postbaccalaureate distance learning degree programs offered. *Degree requirements:* For master's, 2 foreign languages; for M Div, 3 foreign languages. *Entrance requirements:* For M Div, minimum GPA of 2.5; for master's, minimum GPA of 3.0. *Expenses:* Tuition: Part-time $445 per unit.

Western Theological Seminary, Graduate and Professional Programs, Holland, MI 49423-3622. Offers M Div, M Th, D Min. *Accreditation:* ACIPE; ATS. Part-time programs available. Postbaccalaureate distance learning degree programs offered (minimal on-campus study). *Faculty:* 18 full-time (4 women), 9 part-time/adjunct (5 women). *Students:* 170 full-time (67 women), 69 part-time (23 women); includes 24 minority (19 Black or African American, non-Hispanic/Latino; 1 Asian, non-Hispanic/Latino; 4 Hispanic/Latino), 1 international. 82 applicants, 98% accepted, 64 enrolled. In 2010, 35 first professional degrees, 5 master's, 1 doctorate awarded. *Degree requirements:* For doctorate, 2 foreign languages, thesis/dissertation; for M Div, 2 foreign languages. *Entrance requirements:* For doctorate, 5 years of experience in the ministry (must be ordained). Additional exam requirements/recommendations for international students: Required—TOEFL. *Application deadline:* For fall admission, 5/1 priority date for domestic students. Applications are processed on a rolling basis. Application fee: $50. *Expenses:* Tuition: Full-time $11,680; part-time $365 per credit hour. Required fees: $90. *Financial support:* Career-related internships or fieldwork, institutionally sponsored loans, and scholarships/grants available. Support available to part-time students. Financial award applicants required to submit FAFSA. *Unit head:* Dr. Timothy Brown, President, 616-392-8555, Fax: 616-392-7717, E-mail: tim.brown@westernsem.edu. *Application contact:* Rev. Mark Poppen, Director of Admissions, 616-392-8555, Fax: 616-392-7717, E-mail: mark@westernsem.edu.

Westminster Seminary California, Programs in Theology, Escondido, CA 92027-4128. Offers Biblical studies (MA); historical theology (MA); theological studies (M Div, MA). *Accreditation:* ATS. Part-time and evening/weekend programs available. *Degree requirements:* For master's, 2 foreign languages, thesis (for some programs); for M Div, 2 foreign languages, internship. *Entrance requirements:* For M Div and master's, 2 letters of reference. Additional exam requirements/recommendations for international students: Required—TOEFL (minimum score 570 paper-based; 230 computer-based; 89 iBT), TWE (minimum score 4.5). *Faculty research:* Neo-paganism, New Testament background, eschatology, Protestant scholasticism, Ezekiel.

Westminster Theological Seminary, Graduate and Professional Programs, Philadelphia, PA 19118. Offers apologetics (Th M); Biblical and urban studies (Certificate); Biblical counseling (MA); biblical studies (MAR); Christian studies (Certificate); church history (Th M); counseling (M Div); general studies (M Div, MAR); hermeneutics and Bible interpretations (PhD); historical and theological studies (PhD); historical theology (Th M); New Testament (Th M); Old Testament (Th M); pastoral counseling (D Min); pastoral ministry (M Div, D Min); systematic theology (Th M); theological studies (MAR); urban missions (M Div, MA, MAR, D Min). *Accreditation:* ATS. Part-time programs available. Terminal master's awarded for partial completion of doctoral program. *Degree requirements:* For master's, thesis (for some programs); for doctorate, 4 foreign languages, comprehensive exam (for some programs), thesis/dissertation; for M Div, 2 foreign languages. *Entrance requirements:* For doctorate, GRE General Test. Additional exam requirements/recommendations for international students: Required—TOEFL, TWE.

Wheaton College, Graduate School, Department of Biblical and Theological Studies, Program in Biblical and Theological Studies, Wheaton, IL 60187-5593. Offers PhD. *Degree requirements:* For doctorate, thesis/dissertation. *Entrance requirements:* For doctorate, GRE. Electronic applications accepted.

Wheaton College, Graduate School, Department of Biblical and Theological Studies, Program in Biblical Archaeology, Wheaton, IL 60187-5593. Offers MA. *Degree requirements:* For master's, thesis or alternative, semester of study in Israel. *Entrance requirements:* For master's, GRE General Test or MAT. Electronic applications accepted.

Wheaton College, Graduate School, Department of Biblical and Theological Studies, Program in Biblical Exegesis, Wheaton, IL 60187-5593. Offers MA. *Degree requirements:* For master's, 2 foreign languages, thesis or alternative. *Entrance requirements:* For master's, GRE General Test or MAT. Electronic applications accepted.

Wheaton College, Graduate School, Department of Biblical and Theological Studies, Program in Biblical Studies, Wheaton, IL 60187-5593. Offers MA. Part-time programs available. *Degree requirements:* For master's, one foreign language, thesis optional. *Entrance requirements:* For master's, GRE General Test, MAT. Electronic applications accepted.

Wheaton College, Graduate School, Department of Biblical and Theological Studies, Program in General History of Christianity, Wheaton, IL 60187-5593. Offers biblical and theological studies (MA). Part-time and evening/weekend programs available. *Degree requirements:* For master's, thesis optional. *Entrance requirements:* For master's, GRE General Test, MAT.

Wheaton College, Graduate School, Department of Biblical and Theological Studies, Program in Historical and Systematic Theology, Wheaton, IL 60187-5593. Offers biblical and theological studies (MA). Electronic applications accepted.

Whitworth University, Master of Arts in Theology Program, Spokane, WA 99251-0001. Offers MA. Part-time and evening/weekend programs available. Tuition and fees vary according to course load and program.

Wilfrid Laurier University, Waterloo Lutheran Seminary, Waterloo, ON N2L 3C5, Canada. Offers divinity (M Div); multifaith spiritual care and counseling (Diploma); pastoral leadership (D Min); spiritual care and counseling (D Min); theology (M Th, MTS); M Div/MTS/MSW. *Accreditation:* ATS. Part-time programs available. *Degree requirements:* For master's, one foreign language, thesis (for some programs); for doctorate, thesis/dissertation; for M Div, one foreign language, thesis/dissertation. *Entrance requirements:* For M Div, denominational endorsement, two letters of reference; for master's, two letters of reference; for doctorate, M Div, two letters of reference. Additional exam requirements/recommendations for international students: Required—TOEFL (minimum score 573 paper-based; 230 computer-based; 89 iBT), IELTS (minimum score 7). *Application deadline:* For fall admission, 5/1 for domestic and international students; for winter admission, 9/1 for domestic and international students; for spring admission, 1/1 for domestic and international students. Applications are processed on a rolling basis. Application fee: $50. Electronic applications accepted. *Expenses:* Contact institution. *Financial support:* Career-related internships or fieldwork, institutionally sponsored loans, and scholarships/grants available. Financial award application deadline: 10/1. *Faculty research:* Biblical study, church history, systematic theology. *Unit head:* Dr. David Pfrimmer, Principal-Dean/Registrar, 519-884-0710 Ext. 3229, E-mail: dpfrimmer@wlu.ca. *Application contact:* Sarina Wheeler, Student Advisor and Admissions Coordinator, 519-884-0710 Ext. 3498, Fax: 519-725-2434, E-mail: swheeler@wlu.ca.

Winebrenner Theological Seminary, Graduate Programs, Findlay, OH 45840. Offers church development (MA); family ministry (MA); theological study (MA); theological/ministerial studies (D Min); theology/ministerial studies (M Div). *Accreditation:* ATS (one or more programs are accredited). Part-time and evening/weekend programs available. *Faculty:* 7 full-time (1 woman), 2 part-time/adjunct (1 woman). *Students:* 38 full-time (7 women), 44 part-time (17 women); includes 11 Black or African American, non-Hispanic/Latino; 1 Two or more races, non-Hispanic/Latino, 2 international. Average age 40. 23 applicants, 100% accepted, 19 enrolled. In 2010, 12 first professional degrees, 17 master's, 3 doctorates awarded. *Degree requirements:* For master's, variable foreign language requirement, thesis (for some programs), supervised ministry, theological summit; for doctorate, thesis/dissertation, research project; for M Div, 2 foreign languages, supervised ministry, theological summit, thesis (for some programs). *Entrance requirements:* For doctorate, 3 years of post-M Div full-time ministry. Additional exam requirements/recommendations for international students: Required—TOEFL (minimum score

550 paper-based; 213 computer-based; 80 iBT). *Application deadline:* For fall admission, 8/15 priority date for domestic students, 7/15 priority date for international students; for winter admission, 12/15 priority date for domestic students, 11/15 priority date for international students; for spring admission, 4/15 priority date for domestic students, 3/15 priority date for international students. Applications are processed on a rolling basis. Application fee: $30. Electronic applications accepted. *Expenses:* Tuition: Full-time $10,920; part-time $426 per credit hour. Required fees: $115 per term. Tuition and fees vary according to degree level and program. *Financial support:* In 2010–11, 26 students received support, including 1 research assistantship with partial tuition reimbursement available, 2 teaching assistantships with partial tuition reimbursements available; institutionally sponsored loans, scholarships/grants, and tuition waivers (partial) also available. Support available to part-time students. Financial award applicants required to submit FAFSA. *Faculty research:* Online theological education, building more resilient pastors, missiology, Celtic spirituality, reasons clergy leave ministry. *Unit head:* Prof. Joel W. Cocklin, Interim Academic Dean, 419-434-4250, Fax: 419-434-4267, E-mail: jcocklin@winebrenner.edu. *Application contact:* Jim Wilder, Regional Coordinator, 419-434-4220, Fax: 419-434-4267, E-mail: admissions@winebrenner.edu.

Wycliffe College, Division of Advanced Degree Studies, Toronto, ON M5S 1H7, Canada. Offers MA, Th M, D Min, PhD, Th D. PhD, D Min, MA offered jointly with Toronto School of Theology; Th D, Th M with University of Toronto. *Accreditation:* ATS (one or more programs are accredited). Part-time programs available. Terminal master's awarded for partial completion of doctoral program. *Degree requirements:* For master's, 2 foreign languages, thesis (for some programs); for doctorate, 3 foreign languages, thesis/dissertation. *Entrance requirements:* Additional exam requirements/recommendations for international students: Required—TOEFL (minimum score 600 paper-based; 250 computer-based). *Expenses:* Contact institution. *Faculty research:* Old and New Testament, doctrine, ethics, philosophy, history.

Wycliffe College, Division of Basic Degree Studies, Toronto, ON M5S 1H7, Canada. Offers Christian Studies (Diploma); theology (M Div, M Rel, MTS). M Div, M Rel, MTS offered jointly with University of Toronto. *Accreditation:* ATS. Part-time programs available. *Degree requirements:* For master's, one foreign language, thesis; for M Div, thesis/dissertation optional. *Entrance requirements:* Additional exam requirements/recommendations for international students: Required—TOEFL (minimum score 580 paper-based).

Xavier University, College of Arts and Sciences, Department of Theology, Cincinnati, OH 45207. Offers health care mission integration (MA); theology (MA), including religious education, social and pastoral ministry, theology. Part-time and evening/weekend programs available. *Faculty:* 5 full-time (4 women). *Students:* 4 full-time (3 women), 19 part-time (5 women); includes 1 minority (Hispanic/Latino). Average age 35. 6 applicants, 83% accepted, 4 enrolled.

In 2010, 9 master's awarded. *Degree requirements:* For master's, thesis optional, final paper (or thesis) and defense. *Entrance requirements:* For master's, MAT or GRE, letters of recommendation. Additional exam requirements/recommendations for international students: Required—TOEFL (minimum score 550 paper-based; 213 computer-based). *Application deadline:* Applications are processed on a rolling basis. Application fee: $35. Electronic applications accepted. *Expenses:* Tuition: Part-time $718 per credit hour. Tuition and fees vary according to degree level, campus/location and program. *Financial support:* In 2010–11, 20 students received support. Scholarships/grants and unspecified assistantships available. Financial award applicants required to submit FAFSA. *Faculty research:* Scripture, ethics, constructive theology, historical theology. *Unit head:* Dr. Sarah Melcher, Chair, 513-745-2043, Fax: 513-745-3215, E-mail: melcher@xavier.edu. *Application contact:* Dr. Sarah Melcher, Chair, 513-745-2043, Fax: 513-745-3215, E-mail: melcher@xavier.edu.

Xavier University of Louisiana, Graduate School, Institute for Black Catholic Studies, New Orleans, LA 70125-1098. Offers pastoral theology (Th M). Part-time programs available. *Degree requirements:* For master's, comprehensive exam, practicum. *Entrance requirements:* For master's, GRE General Test, MAT, minimum GPA of 2.5. Additional exam requirements/recommendations for international students: Required—TOEFL.

Yale University, Divinity School, New Haven, CT 06511. Offers M Div, MAR, STM, JD/M Div, JD/MAR, M Div/MBA, M Div/MF, M Div/MSN, M Div/MSW, MAR/MSN, MAR/MSW, MD/M Div, MD/MAR. *Accreditation:* ACIPE; ATS. Part-time programs available. *Entrance requirements:* Additional exam requirements/recommendations for international students: Required—IELTS (minimum score 7). Electronic applications accepted. *Expenses:* Contact institution.

Yeshiva Beth Moshe, Graduate Programs, Scranton, PA 18505-2124. Offers Second Talmudical Degree, Talmudic Fellow Degree. *Accreditation:* AARTS.

Yeshiva Karlin Stolin Rabbinical Institute, Graduate Programs, Brooklyn, NY 11204. Offers Advanced Rabbinical Degree. *Accreditation:* AARTS.

Yeshiva of Nitra Rabbinical College, Graduate Programs, Mount Kisco, NY 10549. *Accreditation:* AARTS.

Yeshiva Shaar Hatorah Talmudic Research Institute, Graduate Programs, Kew Gardens, NY 11418-1469. *Accreditation:* AARTS.

Yeshivath Zichron Moshe, Graduate Programs, South Fallsburg, NY 12779. Offers Advanced Talmudic Degree, Talmudic Scholar Degree. *Accreditation:* AARTS. Part-time programs available.

Yeshiva Toras Chaim Talmudical Seminary, Graduate Programs, Denver, CO 80204-1415.

Section 13
Writing

This section contains a directory of institutions offering graduate work in writing, followed by in-depth entries submitted by institutions that chose to prepare detailed program descriptions. Additional information about programs listed in the directory but not augmented by an in-depth entry may be obtained by writing directly to the dean of a graduate school or chair of a department at the address given in the directory.

For programs offering related work, see also in this book *Communication* and *Media* and *Language and Literature.*

CONTENTS

Technical Writing

Carnegie Mellon University, College of Humanities and Social Sciences, Department of English, Program in Professional Writing, Pittsburgh, PA 15213-3891. Offers editing and publishing (MAPW); policy and non-profit communication (MAPW); public and media relations / corporate communications (MAPW); science or healthcare communication (MAPW); technical writing (MAPW); writing for new media (MAPW); writing for print media (MAPW). Part-time programs available. *Entrance requirements:* For master's, GRE General Test. Additional exam requirements/recommendations for international students: Required—TOEFL, TWE.

Colorado State University, Graduate School, College of Liberal Arts, Department of Journalism and Technical Communication, Fort Collins, CO 80523-1785. Offers public communication and technology (MS, PhD); technical communication (MS). Part-time programs available. *Faculty:* 17 full-time (7 women), 1 (woman) part-time/adjunct. *Students:* 31 full-time (23 women), 34 part-time (23 women); includes 6 minority (4 Hispanic/Latino; 2 Two or more races, non-Hispanic/Latino), 2 international. Average age 33. 56 applicants, 50% accepted, 21 enrolled. In 2010, 14 master's awarded. *Degree requirements:* For master's, variable foreign language requirement, comprehensive exam (for some programs), thesis (for some programs); for doctorate, variable foreign language requirement, comprehensive exam (for some programs), thesis/dissertation (for some programs). *Entrance requirements:* For master's, GRE General Test, samples of written work, letters of recommendation, resume or curriculum vitae, 3 writing/communication projects; for doctorate, GRE General Test, master's degree, minimum GPA of 3.0, scholarly/professional work, letters of recommendation, statement of career plans, resume. Additional exam requirements/recommendations for international students: Required—TOEFL (minimum score 550 paper-based; 213 computer-based; 80 iBT). *Application deadline:* For fall admission, 2/15 priority date for domestic students, 12/15 priority date for international students; for spring admission, 6/15 priority date for domestic students. Applications are processed on a rolling basis. Application fee: $50. Electronic applications accepted. *Expenses:* Tuition, state resident: full-time $7434; part-time $413 per credit. Tuition, nonresident: full-time $19,022; part-time $1057 per credit. Required fees: $1729; $88 per credit. *Financial support:* In 2010–11, 35 students received support, including 2 research assistantships with full and partial tuition reimbursements available (averaging $9,269 per year), 33 teaching assistantships with partial tuition reimbursements available (averaging $10,636 per year); fellowships with partial tuition reimbursements available, career-related internships or fieldwork, Federal Work-Study, institutionally sponsored loans, scholarships/grants, traineeships, and unspecified assistantships also available. Support available to part-time students. Financial award application deadline: 3/1; financial award applicants required to submit FAFSA. *Faculty research:* Technical/ science communication, public relations, health/risk communication, Web/new media technologies, environmental communication. Total annual research expenditures: $250,177. *Unit head:* Dr. Greg Luft, Chair, 970-491-1979, Fax: 970-491-2908, E-mail: greg.luft@colostate.edu. *Application contact:* Dr. Craig Trumbo, Graduate Program Coordinator, 970-491-2077, Fax: 970-491-2908, E-mail: craig.trumbo@colostate.edu.

Drexel University, College of Arts and Sciences, Department of Culture and Communication, Philadelphia, PA 19104-2875. Offers communication (MS), including public communication, science communication, technical communication; publication management (MS). Part-time and evening/weekend programs available. *Degree requirements:* For master's, internship, professional portfolio. *Entrance requirements:* Additional exam requirements/recommendations for international students: Required—TOEFL. Electronic applications accepted. *Faculty research:* Science information and attitudes, science influence on literature, process of technical writing, document design, software documentation.

Fitchburg State University, Division of Graduate and Continuing Education, Program in Applied Communications, Fitchburg, MA 01420-2697. Offers applied communications (MS, Certificate); health communication (MS); library media (MS); technical and professional writing (MS). Part-time and evening/weekend programs available. *Students:* 2 full-time (1 woman), 18 part-time (11 women), 3 international. Average age 34. 4 applicants, 100% accepted, 1 enrolled. In 2010, 8 master's awarded. *Entrance requirements:* For master's, GRE General Test or MAT, minimum 2 years of related experience, letters of recommendation, resume. Additional exam requirements/recommendations for international students: Required—TOEFL (minimum score 550 paper-based; 213 computer-based; 79 iBT). *Application deadline:* Applications are processed on a rolling basis. Application fee: $25 ($50 for international students). *Expenses:* Tuition, area resident: Part-time $150 per credit. Tuition, state resident: part-time $150 per credit. Tuition, nonresident: part-time $150 per credit. Required fees: $127 per credit. *Financial support:* In 2010–11, research assistantships with partial tuition reimbursements (averaging $5,500 per year); Federal Work-Study, scholarships/grants, and unspecified assistantships also available. Support available to part-time students. Financial award application deadline: 3/1; financial award applicants required to submit FAFSA. *Unit head:* Dr. John Chetro-Szivos, Chair, 978-665-3261, Fax: 978-665-3658, E-mail: gce@fitchburgstate.edu. *Application contact:* Director of Admissions, 978-665-3144, Fax: 978-665-4540, E-mail: admissions@fsc.edu.

Illinois Institute of Technology, Graduate College, College of Science and Letters, Lewis Department of Humanities, Chicago, IL 60616-3793. Offers information architecture (MS); technical communication (PhD); technical communication and information design (MS). Part-time programs available. *Faculty:* 18 full-time (8 women), 16 part-time/adjunct (12 women). *Students:* 29 full-time (15 women), 16 part-time (12 women); includes 13 minority (10 Black or African American, non-Hispanic/Latino; 2 Asian, non-Hispanic/Latino; 1 Hispanic/Latino), 6 international. Average age 34. 34 applicants, 56% accepted, 11 enrolled. In 2010, 9 master's, 1 doctorate awarded. *Degree requirements:* For master's, comprehensive exam, thesis or alternative; for doctorate, comprehensive exam, thesis/dissertation. *Entrance requirements:* For master's and doctorate, GRE General Test (minimum score 500 Quantitative, 500 Verbal, and 3.0 Analytical Writing), minimum undergraduate GPA of 3.0. Additional exam requirements/recommendations for international students: Required—TOEFL (minimum score 523 paper-based; 70 iBT). *Application deadline:* For fall admission, 5/1 for domestic and international students; for spring admission, 10/15 for domestic and international students. Applications are processed on a rolling basis. Application fee: $50. Electronic applications accepted. *Expenses:* Tuition: Full-time $18,576; part-time $1032 per credit hour. Required fees: $583 per semester. One-time fee: $150. Tuition and fees vary according to program and student level. *Financial support:* In 2010–11, 4 research assistantships with partial tuition reimbursements (averaging $8,300 per year), 13 teaching assistantships with partial tuition reimbursements (averaging $7,553 per year) were awarded; fellowships with partial tuition reimbursements, career-related internships or fieldwork, Federal Work-Study, institutionally sponsored loans, scholarships/grants, health care benefits, tuition waivers (partial), and unspecified assistantships also available. Support available to part-time students. Financial award applicants required to submit FAFSA. *Faculty research:* Aesthetics, document and online design, ethics in the professions, history of art and architecture, humanizing technology. Total annual research expenditures: $180,587. *Unit head:* Dr. Maureen Flanagan, Professor and Chair, 312-567-3563, Fax: 312-567-5187, E-mail: maureen.flanagan@iit.edu. *Application contact:* Deborah Gibson, Director, Graduate Admission, 866-472-3448, Fax: 312-567-3138, E-mail: inquiry.grad@iit.edu.

James Madison University, The Graduate School, College of Arts and Letters, School of Writing, Rhetoric, and Technical Communication, Harrisonburg, VA 22807. Offers MA, MS. Part-time programs available. *Faculty:* 6 full-time (3 women), 2 part-time/adjunct (1 woman). *Students:* 16 full-time (10 women), 5 part-time (all women); includes 1 minority (Asian, non-Hispanic/Latino), 1 international. Average age 27. In 2010, 7 master's awarded. *Degree requirements:* For master's, one foreign language, thesis, internship, practicum. *Entrance requirements:* For master's, GRE General Test, GRE Subject Test, TSC application dossier, 3 letters of recommendation, 20-30 page writing samples. Additional exam requirements/recommendations for international students: Required—TOEFL (minimum score 550 paper-based). *Application deadline:* For fall admission, 5/31 priority date for domestic students; for spring admission, 8/31 priority date for domestic students. Applications are processed on a

rolling basis. Application fee: $55. Electronic applications accepted. *Financial support:* In 2010–11, 9 students received support, including 3 teaching assistantships with full tuition reimbursements available (averaging $8,664 per year); Federal Work-Study, unspecified assistantships, and 6 graduate assistantships ($7382) also available. Financial award application deadline: 3/1; financial award applicants required to submit FAFSA. *Unit head:* Dr. Larry W. Burton, Interim Director, 540-568-2334, E-mail: burtonlw@jmu.edu. *Application contact:* Lynette M. Bible, Director of Graduate Admissions, 540-568-6395, Fax: 540-568-7860, E-mail: biblelm@jmu.edu.

The Johns Hopkins University, Zanvyl Krieger School of Arts and Sciences, The Writing Seminars, Baltimore, MD 21218-2699. Offers fiction writing (MFA); poetry (MFA); science writing (MA). *Faculty:* 7 full-time (3 women), 1 (woman) part-time/adjunct. *Students:* 28 full-time (19 women); includes 2 Asian, non-Hispanic/Latino, 1 international. Average age 29. 273 applicants, 9% accepted, 17 enrolled. In 2010, 13 master's awarded. *Degree requirements:* For master's, one foreign language, thesis, foreign language exam (MFA). *Entrance requirements:* For master's, GRE General Test, GRE Subject Test (recommended), foreign language exam, sample of written work, 3 letters of recommendation, transcripts of all college/ university course work. Additional exam requirements/recommendations for international students: Required—TOEFL (minimum score 600 paper-based; 250 computer-based; 100 iBT). *Application deadline:* For fall admission, 1/15 for domestic and international students. Application fee: $75. Electronic applications accepted. *Financial support:* In 2010–11, 24 students received support, including 1 fellowship (averaging $5,000 per year), 1 research assistantship with full tuition reimbursement available (averaging $18,900 per year), 22 teaching assistantships with full tuition reimbursements available (averaging $18,900 per year); Federal Work-Study, institutionally sponsored loans, scholarships/grants, health care benefits, tuition waivers (partial), and two teaching assistantships with $5000 stipend and full tuition also available. Financial award application deadline: 3/1; financial award applicants required to submit FAFSA. *Faculty research:* Contemporary fiction and poetry, film history, literary criticism, psychoanalysis. *Unit head:* Jean McGarry, Professor and Co-Chair, 410-516-5276, Fax: 410-516-6828, E-mail: mcgarry@jhu.edu. *Application contact:* Gina Woloszyn, Application Contact, 410-516-6286, Fax: 410-516-6828, E-mail: regina@jhu.edu.

Laurentian University, School of Graduate Studies and Research, Programme in Science Communication, Sudbury, ON P3E 2C6, Canada. Offers G Dip.

Massachusetts Institute of Technology, School of Humanities, Arts, and Social Sciences, Program in Science Writing, Cambridge, MA 02139-4307. Offers SM. *Faculty:* 10 full-time (2 women). *Students:* 7 full-time (6 women); includes 1 minority (Two or more races, non-Hispanic/ Latino), 1 international. Average age 23. 59 applicants, 19% accepted, 7 enrolled. In 2010, 7 master's awarded. *Degree requirements:* For master's, thesis, internship. *Entrance requirements:* For master's, GRE General Test. Additional exam requirements/recommendations for international students: Required—TOEFL (minimum score 600 paper-based; 250 computer-based), IELTS (minimum score 7.5). *Application deadline:* For fall admission, 1/15 for domestic and international students. Application fee: $75. Electronic applications accepted. *Expenses:* Tuition: Full-time $38,940; part-time $605 per unit. Required fees: $272. *Financial support:* In 2010–11, 7 students received support, including 7 fellowships with tuition reimbursements available (averaging $13,270 per year); teaching assistantships with tuition reimbursements available, career-related internships or fieldwork, Federal Work-Study, institutionally sponsored loans, scholarships/grants, health care benefits, and unspecified assistantships also available. Total annual research expenditures: $11,000. *Unit head:* Prof. Thomas Levenson, Program Head, 617-253-6668. *Application contact:* Science Writing Graduate Admissions, 617-253-6668, Fax: 617-452-5100, E-mail: sciwrite-www@mit.edu.

Metropolitan State University, College of Arts and Sciences, St. Paul, MN 55106-5000. Offers computer science (MS); liberal studies (MA); technical communication (MS). Part-time and evening/weekend programs available. *Students:* 38 full-time (16 women), 72 part-time (49 women); includes 4 Black or African American, non-Hispanic/Latino; 8 Asian, non-Hispanic/ Latino; 3 Hispanic/Latino, 13 international. Average age 38. In 2010, 22 master's awarded. *Entrance requirements:* For master's, minimum GPA of 2.75, resume. Additional exam requirements/recommendations for international students: Required—TOEFL (minimum score 550 paper-based; 213 computer-based). *Application deadline:* For fall admission, 8/1 priority date for domestic students, 3/15 for international students; for winter admission, 10/15 for international students; for spring admission, 12/1 priority date for domestic students, 3/15 for international students. Applications are processed on a rolling basis. Application fee: $20. Electronic applications accepted. *Expenses:* Tuition, state resident: full-time $5827; part-time $291 per credit hour. Tuition, nonresident: full-time $11,654; part-time $583 per credit hour. Required fees: $10 per credit hour. Tuition and fees vary according to degree level. *Financial support:* Research assistantships available. Financial award applicants required to submit FAFSA. *Unit head:* Dr. Becky Omdahl, Dean, 651-793-1443, Fax: 651-793-1446, E-mail: becky.omdahli@metrostate.edu. *Application contact:* Lucille Maghrak, Graduate Studies Coordinator, 651-793-1932, E-mail: lucille.maghrak@metrostate.edu.

Northern Arizona University, Graduate College, College of Arts and Letters, Department of English, Flagstaff, AZ 86011. Offers applied linguistics (PhD); English (MA), including creative writing, general English studies, literacy, technology and professional writing, literature, secondary English education; professional writing (Certificate); teaching English as a second language (MA, Certificate). Part-time programs available. *Faculty:* 42 full-time (30 women). *Students:* 107 full-time (70 women), 100 part-time (77 women); includes 39 minority (9 Black or African American, non-Hispanic/Latino; 4 American Indian or Alaska Native, non-Hispanic/Latino; 3 Asian, non-Hispanic/Latino; 15 Hispanic/Latino; 8 Two or more races, non-Hispanic/Latino), 27 international. Average age 31. 238 applicants, 68% accepted, 90 enrolled. In 2010, 84 master's, 2 doctorates, 20 other advanced degrees awarded. *Degree requirements:* For master's, comprehensive exam (for some programs), thesis (for some programs), departmental qualifying exam; for doctorate, comprehensive exam, thesis/dissertation, departmental qualifying exam. *Entrance requirements:* For master's, minimum GPA of 3.0 or GRE; for doctorate, GRE General Test. Additional exam requirements/recommendations for international students: Required—TOEFL (minimum score 550 paper-based; 213 computer-based; 80 iBT), IELTS (minimum score 7), TOEFL (600 paper, 250 computer, 100 iBT for PhD; 570 paper, 237 computer, 89 iBT for MA). *Application deadline:* For fall admission, 4/15 priority date for domestic students, 2/15 priority date for international students; for spring admission, 11/15 priority date for domestic and international students. Applications are processed on a rolling basis. Application fee: $65. Electronic applications accepted. *Financial support:* In 2010–11, 72 teaching assistantships with partial tuition reimbursements (averaging $11,623 per year) were awarded; Federal Work-Study, scholarships/grants, health care benefits, tuition waivers (full and partial), and unspecified assistantships also available. Financial award applicants required to submit FAFSA. *Unit head:* Dr. J. Allen Woodman, Chair, 928-523-5651, Fax: 928-523-7074, E-mail: allen.woodman@nau.edu. *Application contact:* Giovanina Bucci, Secretary, 928-523-4911, Fax: 928-523-7074, E-mail: giovanina.bucci@nau.edu.

Polytechnic Institute of NYU, Department of Humanities and Social Sciences, Major in Technical Writing and Specialized Journalism, Brooklyn, NY 11201-2990. Offers MS. *Students:* 1 (woman) full-time; minority (Black or African American, non-Hispanic/Latino). Average age 33. 2 applicants, 100% accepted, 0 enrolled. Application fee: $75. *Expenses:* Tuition: Full-time $21,492; part-time $1194 per credit. Required fees: $385 per semester. Tuition and fees vary according to course load. *Unit head:* Kristen Day, Head, 718-260-3899, E-mail: kday@poly.edu. *Application contact:* Kristen Day, Head, 718-260-3899, E-mail: kday@poly.edu.

Regis University, College for Professional Studies, School of Humanities and Social Sciences, MA Program, Denver, CO 80221-1099. Offers communication (MA); fine arts (Certificate); interdisciplinary studies (MA); mediation and conflict resolution (Certificate); psychology (MA);

social justice, peace, and reconciliation (Certificate); technical communication (Certificate). Program also offered in Henderson and Las Vegas (Summerlin), NV. Part-time and evening/weekend programs available. Postbaccalaureate distance learning degree programs offered (minimal on-campus study). *Degree requirements:* For master's, thesis, research project. *Entrance requirements:* For master's, resume, recommendations. Additional exam requirements/recommendations for international students: Required—TOEFL (minimum score 213 computer-based), TWE (minimum score 5). Electronic applications accepted. *Expenses:* Contact institution. *Faculty research:* Independent/nonresidential graduate study: new methods and models, adult learning and the capstone experience, Goal Setting, behavior of Adult students, Innovative Studies for Community Colleges.

Texas Tech University, Graduate School, College of Arts and Sciences, Department of English, Lubbock, TX 79409. Offers English (MA, PhD); technical communication (MA); technical communication and rhetoric (PhD). Part-time programs available. *Faculty:* 38 full-time (16 women), 1 (woman) part-time/adjunct. *Students:* 106 full-time (62 women), 89 part-time (55 women); includes 4 Black or African American, non-Hispanic/Latino; 2 American Indian or Alaska Native, non-Hispanic/Latino; 7 Asian, non-Hispanic/Latino; 4 Hispanic/Latino, 18 international. Average age 34. 242 applicants, 21% accepted, 34 enrolled. In 2010, 25 master's, 11 doctorates awarded. *Degree requirements:* For master's, one foreign language, thesis (for some programs); for doctorate, one foreign language, thesis/dissertation (for some programs). *Entrance requirements:* For master's and doctorate, GRE General Test. Additional exam requirements/recommendations for international students: Required—TOEFL (minimum score 550 paper-based; 213 computer-based; 79 iBT). *Application deadline:* For fall admission, 6/1 priority date for domestic students, 1/15 priority date for international students; for spring admission, 9/1 priority date for domestic students, 6/15 priority date for international students. Applications are processed on a rolling basis. Application fee: $50 ($75 for international students). Electronic applications accepted. *Expenses:* Tuition, state resident: full-time $5495.76; part-time $228.99 per credit hour. Tuition, nonresident: full-time $12,936; part-time $538.99 per credit hour. Required fees: $2674; $36 per credit hour. $905 per semester. *Financial support:* In 2010–11, 110 students received support, including 10 research assistantships with partial tuition reimbursements available (averaging $8,815 per year), 48 teaching assistantships with partial tuition reimbursements available (averaging $6,362 per year). Financial award application deadline: 4/15; financial award applicants required to submit FAFSA. *Faculty research:* Computers and writing, technical communication and rhetoric, creative writing, nineteenth century studies, literature of social justice and the environment. *Unit head:* Dr. Sam Dragga, Chair, 806-742-2501, Fax: 806-742-0989, E-mail: sam.dragga@ttu.edu. *Application contact:* Dr. Brian McFadden, Director of Graduate Studies, 806-742-2501, Fax: 806-742-0989, E-mail: english.gradadvisor@ttu.edu.

The University of Alabama in Huntsville, School of Graduate Studies, College of Liberal Arts, Department of English, Huntsville, AL 35899. Offers English (MA); teaching of English to speakers of other languages (Certificate); technical communications (Certificate). Part-time and evening/weekend programs available. *Faculty:* 13 full-time (9 women). *Students:* 16 full-time (12 women), 39 part-time (30 women); includes 15 minority (12 Black or African American, non-Hispanic/Latino; 1 American Indian or Alaska Native, non-Hispanic/Latino; 2 Hispanic/Latino). Average age 32. 34 applicants, 85% accepted, 18 enrolled. In 2010, 17 master's, 2 other advanced degrees awarded. *Degree requirements:* For master's, one foreign language, comprehensive exam, thesis or alternative, oral and written exams. *Entrance requirements:* For master's and Certificate, GRE General Test, minimum GPA of 3.0. Additional exam requirements/recommendations for international students: Required—TOEFL (minimum score 500 paper-based; 173 computer-based; 62 iBT). *Application deadline:* For fall admission, 7/15 for domestic students, 4/1 for international students; for spring admission, 11/30 for

domestic students, 9/1 for international students. Applications are processed on a rolling basis. Application fee: $40 ($50 for international students). Electronic applications accepted. *Expenses:* Tuition, state resident: full-time $7250; part-time $407.75 per credit hour. Tuition, nonresident: full-time $17,358; part-time $970.05 per credit hour. Required fees: $246.80 per semester. Tuition and fees vary according to course load and program. *Financial support:* In 2010–11, 9 students received support, including 5 teaching assistantships with full and partial tuition reimbursements available (averaging $8,460 per year); career-related internships or fieldwork, Federal Work-Study, institutionally sponsored loans, scholarships/grants, health care benefits, tuition waivers, and unspecified assistantships also available. Support available to part-time students. Financial award application deadline: 4/1; financial award applicants required to submit FAFSA. *Faculty research:* American and British literature, linguistics, technical writing, women's studies, rhetoric. Total annual research expenditures: $26,119. *Unit head:* Dr. Dan Schenker, Chair, 256-824-6320, Fax: 256-824-6949, E-mail: schenkd@uah.edu. *Application contact:* Kathy Biggs, Graduate Studies Admissions Manager, 256-824-6199, Fax: 256-824-6405, E-mail: deangrad@uah.edu.

University of Arkansas at Little Rock, Graduate School, College of Arts, Humanities, and Social Science, Department of Rhetoric and Writing, Little Rock, AR 72204-1099. Offers professional and technical writing (MA). Part-time and evening/weekend programs available. *Degree requirements:* For master's, thesis or alternative, oral defense of final project. *Entrance requirements:* For master's, GRE, minimum GPA of 3.0, writing portfolio. *Faculty research:* Writing for industry, science, business, and government; composition and rhetorical theory; writing nonfiction; teaching of writing.

The University of North Carolina at Greensboro, Graduate School, College of Arts and Sciences, Department of English, Greensboro, NC 27412-5001. Offers creative writing (MFA); English (M Ed, MA, PhD, Certificate), including American literature (PhD), English (M Ed, MA), English literature (PhD), rhetoric and composition (PhD), technical writing (Certificate), women's studies (Certificate). *Degree requirements:* For master's, comprehensive exam; for doctorate, variable foreign language requirement, thesis/dissertation, preliminary exam. *Entrance requirements:* For master's, GRE General Test, minimum GPA of 3.0; for doctorate, GRE General Test, GRE Subject Test, critical writing sample, minimum GPA of 3.0. Additional exam requirements/recommendations for international students: Required—TOEFL. Electronic applications accepted.

University of the Sciences in Philadelphia, College of Graduate Studies, Program in Biomedical Writing, Philadelphia, PA 19104-4495. Offers biomedical writing (MS); medical marketing writing (Certificate); regulatory affairs writing (Certificate). Part-time and evening/weekend programs available. Postbaccalaureate distance learning degree programs offered (minimal on-campus study). *Entrance requirements:* For master's, GRE General Test. Additional exam requirements/recommendations for international students: Required—TOEFL, TWE. *Expenses:* Contact institution. *Faculty research:* History of medical writing and publishing, compliance, regulatory.

University of Waterloo, Graduate Studies, Faculty of Arts, Department of English, Language and Literature, Waterloo, ON N2L 3G1, Canada. Offers English language and literature (PhD); literary studies (MA); rhetoric and communication design (MA). Part-time programs available. *Degree requirements:* For master's, one foreign language, thesis optional; for doctorate, 2 foreign languages, thesis/dissertation. *Entrance requirements:* For master's, honors degree, minimum B+ average; for doctorate, master's degree, minimum A- average. Additional exam requirements/recommendations for international students: Required—TOEFL, TWE. Electronic applications accepted. *Faculty research:* Shakespeare, American literature, rhetoric, Romantics, moderns.

Writing

Abilene Christian University, Graduate School, College of Arts and Sciences, Department of English, Abilene, TX 79699-9100. Offers composition/rhetoric (MA); literature (MA); writing (MA). Part-time programs available. *Faculty:* 16 part-time/adjunct (7 women). *Students:* 15 full-time (8 women); includes 1 Two or more races, non-Hispanic/Latino, 1 international. 18 applicants, 72% accepted, 6 enrolled. In 2010, 5 master's awarded. *Degree requirements:* For master's, one foreign language, comprehensive exam (for some programs), thesis (for some programs). *Entrance requirements:* For master's, GRE General Test. Additional exam requirements/recommendations for international students: Required—TOEFL (minimum score 550 paper-based; 213 computer-based). *Application deadline:* For fall admission, 4/1 priority date for domestic students; for spring admission, 11/1 for domestic students. Applications are processed on a rolling basis. Application fee: $40. Electronic applications accepted. *Expenses:* Tuition: Full-time $12,906; part-time $717 per hour. Required fees: $1250; $61.50 per unit. *Financial support:* In 2010–11, 14 students received support; teaching assistantships, Federal Work-Study available. Support available to part-time students. Financial award application deadline: 4/1; financial award applicants required to submit FAFSA. *Faculty research:* Feminism, Shakespearean dimensions of new literature, poetic consciousness, deconstruction myths. *Unit head:* Dr. Dana McMichael, Graduate Adviser, 325-674-2083, Fax: 325-674-2408, E-mail: dana.mcmichael@acu.edu. *Application contact:* David Pittman, Graduate Admissions Counselor, 325-674-2656, Fax: 325-674-6717, E-mail: gradinfo@acu.edu.

Adelphi University, Graduate School of Arts and Sciences, Program in Creative Writing, Garden City, NY 11530-0701. Offers MFA. Part-time and evening/weekend programs available. *Students:* 12 full-time (6 women), 22 part-time (15 women); includes 2 Black or African American, non-Hispanic/Latino; 2 Asian, non-Hispanic/Latino; 4 Hispanic/Latino. Average age 30. In 2010, 9 master's awarded. *Degree requirements:* For master's, thesis. *Entrance requirements:* For master's, 3 letters of reference, manuscript in chosen genre (poetry, fiction, playwriting). Additional exam requirements/recommendations for international students: Required—TOEFL (minimum score 550 paper-based; 213 computer-based; 80 iBT). *Application deadline:* For fall admission, 5/1 priority date for international students; for spring admission, 11/1 priority date for international students. Applications are processed on a rolling basis. Application fee: $50. Electronic applications accepted. *Financial support:* Fellowships, Federal Work-Study available. *Unit head:* Judith Baumel, Director, 516-877-4031, E-mail: baumel@adelphi.edu. *Application contact:* Christine Murphy, Director of Admissions, 516-877-3050, Fax: 516-877-3039, E-mail: graduateadmissions@adelphi.edu.

See Close-Up on page 573.

Albertus Magnus College, Master of Fine Arts in Writing Program, New Haven, CT 06511-1189. Offers MFA. *Faculty:* 5 full-time (3 women), 2 part-time/adjunct (1 woman). *Students:* 4 full-time (all women), 5 part-time (all women); includes 2 Black or African American, non-Hispanic/Latino; 1 Hispanic/Latino. Average age 35. 12 applicants, 83% accepted, 9 enrolled. *Degree requirements:* For master's, thesis. *Application deadline:* For fall admission, 8/15 for domestic students; for spring admission, 1/15 for domestic students. Application fee: $35. *Expenses:* Tuition: Full-time $12,582; part-time $2097 per course. Required fees: $90; $25 per course. *Unit head:* Dr. John Donohue, Provost and Vice President for Academic Affairs, 203-777-8539, Fax: 203-777-3701, E-mail: jdonohue@albertus.edu. *Application contact:* Sarah Wallman, Director of Master of Fine Arts Program, 203-777-4473, Fax: 203-777-3701, E-mail: swallman@albertus.edu.

American University, College of Arts and Sciences, Department of Literature, Washington, DC 20016-8047. Offers creative writing (MFA); literature (MA). Part-time and evening/weekend

programs available. *Faculty:* 43 full-time (25 women), 22 part-time/adjunct (14 women). *Students:* 51 full-time (33 women), 36 part-time (21 women); includes 12 minority (10 Black or African American, non-Hispanic/Latino; 2 Hispanic/Latino, 5 international. Average age 29. 212 applicants, 59% accepted, 27 enrolled. In 2010, 21 master's awarded. *Degree requirements:* For master's, comprehensive exam. *Entrance requirements:* For master's, GRE, writing sample, minimum GPA of 3.0, 2 letters of recommendation. Additional exam requirements/recommendations for international students: Required—TOEFL. *Application deadline:* For fall admission, 2/1 for domestic students. Application fee: $80. *Financial support:* Fellowships, research assistantships, teaching assistantships, career-related internships or fieldwork, Federal Work-Study, institutionally sponsored loans, and tuition waivers (full and partial) available. Support available to part-time students. Financial award application deadline: 2/1. *Faculty research:* British, American, Irish, Russian, and Third World literature; cinema studies; literary theory; feminist criticism. *Unit head:* Dr. Keith Leonard, Chair, 202-885-2998, Fax: 202-885-2938, E-mail: jloesbe@american.edu. *Application contact:* Kathleen Clowery, Director of Graduate Admissions, 202-885-3621, Fax: 202-885-1505.

Antioch University Los Angeles, Graduate Programs, Program in Creative Writing, Culver City, CA 90230. Offers creative writing (MFA); pedagogy of creative writing (Certificate). Postbaccalaureate distance learning degree programs offered (minimal on-campus study). *Degree requirements:* For master's, thesis. *Entrance requirements:* For master's, sample of written work. Additional exam requirements/recommendations for international students: Required—TOEFL. *Faculty research:* Creative nonfiction, fiction, poetry.

Antioch University Midwest, Graduate Programs, Individualized Liberal and Professional Studies Program, Yellow Springs, OH 45387-1609. Offers liberal and professional studies (MA), including counseling, creative writing, education, film studies, liberal studies, management, modern literature, psychology, theatre, visual arts. Part-time and evening/weekend programs available. Postbaccalaureate distance learning degree programs offered (minimal on-campus study). *Faculty:* 2 full-time (1 woman), 2 part-time/adjunct (both women). *Students:* 15 full-time (11 women), 34 part-time (22 women); includes 11 minority (8 Black or African American, non-Hispanic/Latino; 3 Hispanic/Latino). Average age 40. 13 applicants, 69% accepted, 5 enrolled. In 2010, 18 master's awarded. *Degree requirements:* For master's, thesis or alternative. *Entrance requirements:* For master's, resume, goal statement, interview. *Application deadline:* For fall admission, 8/1 for domestic students; for winter admission, 12/1 for domestic students; for spring admission, 3/10 for domestic students. Applications are processed on a rolling basis. Application fee: $50. Electronic applications accepted. *Expenses:* Contact institution. *Financial support:* Federal Work-Study available. Financial award applicants required to submit FAFSA. *Unit head:* Dr. Joseph Cronin, Chair, 937-769-1894, Fax: 937-769-1807, E-mail: jcronin@antioch.edu. *Application contact:* Seth Gordon, Assistant Director of Admissions, 937-769-1800 Ext. 1825, Fax: 937-769-1804, E-mail: sgordon@antioch.edu.

Arizona State University, College of Liberal Arts and Sciences, Department of English, Interdisciplinary Program in Creative Writing, Tempe, AZ 85287-0302. Offers MFA. *Faculty:* 13 full-time (7 women). *Students:* 35 full-time (18 women), 3 part-time (1 woman); includes 5 minority (1 Black or African American, non-Hispanic/Latino; 2 Asian, non-Hispanic/Latino; 2 Hispanic/Latino). Average age 28. 269 applicants, 5% accepted, 11 enrolled. In 2010, 17 master's awarded. *Degree requirements:* For master's, thesis, practicum (9 hours). *Entrance requirements:* For master's, undergraduate major in English or creative writing (preferred), minimum GPA of 3.0, 3 letters of recommendation, resume or curriculum vitae, personal

Writing

Arizona State University (continued)
statement, official transcripts, 3 copies of manuscript sample (20 pages of poetry, 30 pages of prose, or both). Additional exam requirements/recommendations for international students: Required—TOEFL, IELTS, or Pearson Test of English. *Application deadline:* For fall admission, 1/15 for domestic and international students. Application fee: $70 ($90 for international students). Electronic applications accepted. *Expenses:* Tuition, state resident: full-time $8510; part-time $608 per credit. Tuition, nonresident: full-time $16,542; part-time $919 per credit. Required fees: $339; $110 per credit. Part-time tuition and fees vary according to course load. *Financial support:* In 2010–11, 35 teaching assistantships with full and partial tuition reimbursements (averaging $12,971 per year) were awarded; fellowships with full and partial tuition reimbursements, career-related internships or fieldwork, institutionally sponsored loans, scholarships/grants, and tuition waivers (partial) also available. Financial award application deadline: 3/1; financial award applicants required to submit FAFSA. *Unit head:* Dr. Peter Turchi, Director, 480-965-6856, E-mail: peter.turchi@asu.edu. *Application contact:* Graduate Admissions, 480-965-6113.

Asbury University, School of Graduate and Professional Studies, Wilmore, KY 40390-1198. Offers biology: alternative certificate (MA Ed); chemistry: alternative certificate (MA Ed); English (MA Ed); English as a second language (MA Ed); ESL (MA Ed); French (MA Ed); Latin: alternative certificate (MA Ed); mathematics: alternative certificate (MA Ed); reading/writing endorsement (MA Ed); social studies (MA Ed); social work (MSW), including child and family services; Spanish (MA Ed); special education (MA Ed); special education: alternative certificate (MA Ed); teacher as leader endorsement (MA Ed). *Accreditation:* NCATE. Part-time programs available. *Degree requirements:* For master's, action research project, portfolio. *Entrance requirements:* For master's, PRAXIS/NTE, minimum GPA of 2.75, letters of recommendation. Additional exam requirements/recommendations for international students: Required—TOEFL (minimum score 550 paper-based). Electronic applications accepted.

Ashland University, College of Arts and Sciences, Program in Creative Writing, Ashland, OH 44805-3702. Offers MFA. Postbaccalaureate distance learning degree programs offered (minimal on-campus study). *Faculty:* 10 part-time/adjunct (5 women). *Students:* 41 full-time (31 women); includes 4 minority (1 Black or African American, non-Hispanic/Latino; 2 American Indian or Alaska Native, non-Hispanic/Latino; 1 Hispanic/Latino). Average age 42. 33 applicants, 100% accepted, 18 enrolled. In 2010, 13 master's awarded. *Degree requirements:* For master's, thesis. *Entrance requirements:* For master's, writing sample, minimum GPA of 2.75. *Application deadline:* For fall admission, 2/1 priority date for domestic students; for winter admission, 10/1 priority date for domestic students. Application fee: $30. Electronic applications accepted. *Expenses:* Contact institution. *Financial support:* Career-related internships or fieldwork, Federal Work-Study, and institutionally sponsored loans available. Financial award application deadline: 4/15; financial award applicants required to submit FAFSA. *Unit head:* Dr. Stephen Haven, Director, MFA Program, 419-289-5979, Fax: 419-289-5255, E-mail: shaven@ashland.edu. *Application contact:* Sarah Marie Wells, Administrative Director, MFA Program, 419-289-5957, Fax: 419-289-5255, E-mail: swells@ashland.edu.

Ball State University, Graduate School, College of Sciences and Humanities, Department of English, Muncie, IN 47306-1099. Offers English (MA, PhD), including composition, creative writing (MA), general (MA), literature; linguistics (MA, PhD), including applied linguistics (PhD), linguistics (MA); linguistics and teaching English to speakers of other languages (MA); teaching English to speakers of other languages (MA). *Faculty:* 38. *Students:* 44 full-time (23 women), 67 part-time (42 women); includes 5 minority (1 American Indian or Alaska Native, non-Hispanic/Latino; 2 Hispanic/Latino; 2 Two or more races, non-Hispanic/Latino), 23 international. Average age 27. 160 applicants, 32% accepted, 24 enrolled. In 2010, 18 master's, 5 doctorates awarded. *Degree requirements:* For doctorate, variable foreign language requirement, thesis/dissertation. *Entrance requirements:* For master's, GRE General Test, writing sample; for doctorate, GRE General Test, GRE Subject Test, minimum graduate GPA of 3.2, writing sample. Application fee: $25 ($35 for international students). *Expenses:* Tuition, state resident: full-time $6160; part-time $299 per credit hour. Tuition, nonresident: full-time $16,020; part-time $783 per credit hour. Required fees: $2278; $95 per credit hour. *Financial support:* In 2010–11, 48 teaching assistantships with full tuition reimbursements (averaging $15,324 per year) were awarded; fellowships, career-related internships or fieldwork and unspecified assistantships also available. Financial award application deadline: 3/1. *Faculty research:* American literature; literary editing; medieval, Renaissance, and eighteenth century British literature; rhetoric. *Unit head:* Dr. Elizabeth Riddle, Chairperson, 765-285-8535, Fax: 765-285-3765. *Application contact:* Dr. Jill Christman.

Belmont University, College of Arts and Sciences, Department of English, Nashville, TN 37212-3757. Offers literature (MA); writing (MA). Part-time and evening/weekend programs available. *Faculty:* 16 full-time (12 women). *Students:* 4 full-time (2 women), 38 part-time (29 women); includes 4 minority (all Black or African American, non-Hispanic/Latino). Average age 30. 15 applicants, 80% accepted, 12 enrolled. In 2010, 10 master's awarded. *Degree requirements:* For master's, one foreign language, comprehensive exam (for some programs), thesis optional. *Entrance requirements:* For master's, GRE, letters of recommendation, writing sample, transcripts, statement of purpose. Additional exam requirements/recommendations for international students: Required—TOEFL. *Application deadline:* For fall admission, 8/1 for domestic and international students; for spring admission, 12/1 for domestic and international students. Applications are processed on a rolling basis. Application fee: $50. Electronic applications accepted. *Expenses:* Contact institution. *Financial support:* In 2010–11, 20 students received support. Federal Work-Study and scholarships/grants available. Financial award application deadline: 8/1; financial award applicants required to submit FAFSA. *Faculty research:* Gender, creative writing, Shakespeare, popular culture, world literature. *Unit head:* Dr. Annette M. Sisson, Director of Graduate Program, 615-460-6803, Fax: 615-460-5720, E-mail: annette.sisson@belmont.edu. *Application contact:* Dr. Annette M. Sisson, Director of Graduate Program, 615-460-6803, Fax: 615-460-5720, E-mail: annette.sisson@belmont.edu.

Bennington College, Graduate Programs, The Bennington Writing Seminars, Bennington, VT 05201. Offers creative writing (MFA). Postbaccalaureate distance learning degree programs offered (minimal on-campus study). *Faculty:* 17 full-time (7 women), 3 part-time/adjunct (2 women). *Students:* 105 full-time (77 women); includes 2 Black or African American, non-Hispanic/Latino; 1 American Indian or Alaska Native, non-Hispanic/Latino; 6 Asian, non-Hispanic/Latino; 4 Hispanic/Latino. Average age 41. 155 applicants, 41% accepted, 29 enrolled. In 2010, 53 master's awarded. *Degree requirements:* For master's, thesis, collection of essays or poems, or collection of short stories and/or a novel. *Entrance requirements:* For master's, manuscript. *Application deadline:* For fall admission, 3/1 for domestic students; for spring admission, 9/1 for domestic students. Application fee: $60. *Expenses:* Contact institution. *Financial support:* In 2010–11, 10 students received support. Scholarships/grants available. Financial award application deadline: 4/1; financial award applicants required to submit FAFSA. *Unit head:* Sven Birkerts, Director, 802-440-4452, Fax: 802-440-4453, E-mail: writing@bennington.edu. *Application contact:* Victoria Clausi, Associate Director, 802-440-4454, Fax: 802-440-4453, E-mail: writing@bennington.edu.

Boise State University, Graduate College, College of Arts and Sciences, Department of English, Program in Creative Writing, Boise, ID 83725-0399. Offers MFA. *Degree requirements:* For master's, thesis. *Entrance requirements:* For master's, GRE General Test, minimum GPA of 3.0.

Boston University, Graduate School of Arts and Sciences, Creative Writing Program, Boston, MA 02215. Offers MFA. *Students:* 25 full-time (14 women), 11 part-time (7 women); includes 7 minority (1 Black or African American, non-Hispanic/Latino; 3 Asian, non-Hispanic/Latino; 1 Hispanic/Latino; 1 Native Hawaiian or other Pacific Islander, non-Hispanic/Latino; 1 Two or more races, non-Hispanic/Latino). Average age 30. 318 applicants, 8% accepted, 26 enrolled. In 2010, 26 master's awarded. *Entrance requirements:* Additional exam requirements/recommendations for international students: Required—TOEFL. *Application deadline:* For fall admission, 3/1 for domestic and international students. Application fee: $70. Electronic applications accepted. *Expenses:* Tuition: Full-time $39,314; part-time $1228 per credit. Required fees: $40 per semester. *Financial support:* In 2010–11, 22 students received support, including teaching assistantships with partial tuition reimbursements available (averaging $18,800 per year); Federal Work-Study and unspecified assistantships also available. Support available to part-time students. Financial award application deadline: 3/1; financial award applicants required to submit FAFSA. *Unit head:* Leslie Epstein, Director, 617-353-2510, Fax: 617-353-3653, E-mail: leslieep@bu.edu. *Application contact:* Caroline Woods, Administrative Coordinator, 617-353-2510, Fax: 617-353-3653, E-mail: crwr@bu.edu.

Boston University, Graduate School of Arts and Sciences, Department of English, Boston, MA 02215. Offers creative writing (MA); English (MA, PhD). *Students:* 54 full-time (33 women), 7 part-time (4 women); includes 1 minority (Asian, non-Hispanic/Latino), 1 international. Average age 28. 278 applicants, 7% accepted, 15 enrolled. In 2010, 15 master's, 7 doctorates awarded. Terminal master's awarded for partial completion of doctoral program. *Degree requirements:* For master's, one foreign language, thesis; for doctorate, 2 foreign languages, comprehensive exam, thesis/dissertation, qualifying/oral exam. *Entrance requirements:* For master's and doctorate, GRE General Test, GRE Subject Test, sample of written work, 2 letters of recommendation. Additional exam requirements/recommendations for international students: Required—TOEFL (minimum score 550 paper-based; 213 computer-based). *Application deadline:* For fall admission, 1/1 for domestic and international students. Application fee: $70. Electronic applications accepted. *Expenses:* Tuition: Full-time $39,314; part-time $1228 per credit. Required fees: $40 per semester. *Financial support:* In 2010–11, 36 students received support, including 2 fellowships with full tuition reimbursements available (averaging $19,300 per year), 25 teaching assistantships with partial tuition reimbursements available (averaging $18,800 per year); Federal Work-Study, scholarships/grants, and unspecified assistantships also available. Financial award application deadline: 1/15; financial award applicants required to submit FAFSA. *Unit head:* William C. Carroll, Interim Chairman, 617-353-2509, Fax: 617-353-3653, E-mail: wcarroll@bu.edu. *Application contact:* Amanda Trainor, Administrative Assistant, 617-353-2509, Fax: 617-353-3653, E-mail: hlane@bu.edu.

Boston University, Graduate School of Arts and Sciences, Editorial Institute, Boston, MA 02215. Offers MA, PhD. *Students:* 14 full-time (9 women), 2 part-time (0 women), 1 international. Average age 39. 13 applicants, 38% accepted, 5 enrolled. *Degree requirements:* For master's, one foreign language, thesis; for doctorate, one foreign language, comprehensive exam, thesis/dissertation. *Entrance requirements:* For master's and doctorate, GRE General Test, thesis proposal, 3 letters of recommendation. Additional exam requirements/recommendations for international students: Required—TOEFL (minimum score 550 paper-based; 213 computer-based). *Application deadline:* For fall admission, 3/30 for domestic and international students. Application fee: $70. Electronic applications accepted. *Expenses:* Tuition: Full-time $39,314; part-time $1228 per credit. Required fees: $40 per semester. *Financial support:* In 2010–11, 14 students received support, including 3 teaching assistantships with full tuition reimbursements available (averaging $18,800 per year); Federal Work-Study, scholarships/grants, and unspecified assistantships also available. Support available to part-time students. Financial award application deadline: 1/15; financial award applicants required to submit FAFSA. *Unit head:* Archie Burnett, Co-Director, 617-353-6631, E-mail: burnetta@bu.edu. *Application contact:* Katy Evans, Administrative Assistant, 617-358-1937, Fax: 617-353-6917, E-mail: editinst@bu.edu.

Bowling Green State University, Graduate College, College of Arts and Sciences, Department of English, Program in Creative Writing, Bowling Green, OH 43403. Offers fiction (MFA); poetry (MFA). Part-time programs available. *Degree requirements:* For master's, thesis or alternative. *Entrance requirements:* For master's, GRE General Test. Additional exam requirements/recommendations for international students: Required—TOEFL. Electronic applications accepted. *Faculty research:* Poetry, criticism, novels, translation, travel writing.

Bowling Green State University, Graduate College, College of Arts and Sciences, Department of English, Program in English, Bowling Green, OH 43403. Offers English (MA, PhD); literature (MA); rhetoric and writing (PhD); scientific and technical communication (MA). Part-time programs available. *Degree requirements:* For master's, thesis or alternative; for doctorate, comprehensive exam, thesis/dissertation, foreign language or proficiency in Old English. *Entrance requirements:* For master's and doctorate, GRE General Test. Additional exam requirements/recommendations for international students: Required—TOEFL. Electronic applications accepted. *Faculty research:* Postmodern literary theory, rhetorical theory, ethnic American literature, literature and culture, composition pedagogy.

Brigham Young University, Graduate Studies, College of Humanities, Department of English, Provo, UT 84602-1001. Offers creative writing (MFA); literature (MA); rhetoric/composition (MA). *Faculty:* 50 full-time (16 women). *Students:* 63 full-time (44 women), 5 part-time (2 women); includes 1 Hispanic/Latino. Average age 24. 103 applicants, 34% accepted, 31 enrolled. In 2010, 30 master's awarded. *Degree requirements:* For master's, thesis. *Entrance requirements:* For master's, GRE General Test, creative portfolio (for MFA). Additional exam requirements/recommendations for international students: Required—TOEFL. *Application deadline:* For fall admission, 1/15 for domestic and international students. Application fee: $50. Electronic applications accepted. *Expenses:* Tuition: Full-time $5580; part-time $310 per credit hour. Tuition and fees vary according to program and student's religious affiliation. *Financial support:* In 2010–11, 79 students received support, including 10 research assistantships (averaging $3,000 per year), 62 teaching assistantships (averaging $6,000 per year); career-related internships or fieldwork, institutionally sponsored loans, scholarships/grants, and tuition waivers (partial) also available. Support available to part-time students. Financial award application deadline: 3/15. *Faculty research:* English literature, American literature, rhetoric, creative writing. *Unit head:* Prof. Ed Cutler, Head, 801-422-3581, Fax: 801-422-0221, E-mail: ed_cutler@byu.edu. *Application contact:* Lou Ann C. Crisler, Graduate Secretary, 801-422-8673, Fax: 801-422-0221, E-mail: louann_crisler@byu.edu.

Brooklyn College of the City University of New York, Division of Graduate Studies, Department of English, Program in Creative Writing, Brooklyn, NY 11210-2889. Offers fiction (MFA); playwriting (MFA); poetry (MFA). Part-time and evening/weekend programs available. *Students:* 5 full-time (4 women), 61 part-time (32 women); includes 15 minority (5 Black or African American, non-Hispanic/Latino; 6 Asian, non-Hispanic/Latino; 4 Hispanic/Latino), 6 international. Average age 29. 579 applicants, 9% accepted, 33 enrolled. In 2010, 31 master's awarded. *Degree requirements:* For master's, comprehensive exam, thesis or alternative, 36 credits. *Entrance requirements:* For master's, 12 undergraduate advanced credits in English, writing sample, 2 letters of recommendation, manuscript. Additional exam requirements/recommendations for international students: Required—TOEFL (minimum score 650 paper-based; 280 computer-based; 114 iBT). *Application deadline:* For fall admission, 1/15 priority date for domestic students, 1/15 for international students. Applications are processed on a rolling basis. Application fee: $125. Electronic applications accepted. *Expenses:* Tuition, state resident: full-time $7360; part-time $310 per credit hour. Tuition, nonresident: full-time $13,800; part-time $575 per credit hour. Required fees: $190 per semester. *Financial support:* Federal Work-Study, institutionally sponsored loans, and scholarships/grants available. Support available to part-time students. Financial award application deadline: 5/1; financial award applicants required to submit FAFSA. *Faculty research:* Postmodern fiction. *Unit head:* Dr. James Davis, Graduate Deputy Chairperson, 718-951-5195, E-mail: jcdavis@brooklyn.cuny.edu. *Application contact:* Hernan Sierra, Graduate Admissions Coordinator, 718-951-4536, Fax: 718-951-4506, E-mail: grads@brooklyn.cuny.edu.

Brown University, Graduate School, Department of English, Program in Nonfiction Writing, Providence, RI 02912. Offers MFA. *Degree requirements:* For master's, thesis. *Entrance requirements:* For master's, GRE General Test, GRE Subject Test.

California College of the Arts, Graduate Programs, Program in Writing, San Francisco, CA 94107. Offers MFA. *Faculty:* 3 full-time (1 woman), 29 part-time/adjunct (17 women). *Students:* 66 full-time (40 women), 6 part-time (1 woman); includes 4 Black or African American, non-Hispanic/Latino; 5 Asian, non-Hispanic/Latino; 11 Hispanic/Latino, 2 international. Average age 30. 136 applicants, 89% accepted, 31 enrolled. In 2010, 25 master's awarded. *Degree* *requirements:* For master's, thesis. *Entrance requirements:* For master's, appropriate bachelor's degree, portfolio, transcripts, letters of recommendation. Additional exam requirements/recommendations for international students: Required—TOEFL (minimum score 600 paper-based; 250 computer-based; 100 iBT). *Application deadline:* For fall admission, 1/5 for domestic and international students. Application fee: $70. Electronic applications accepted. *Expenses:* Tuition: Full-time $38,550; part-time $1285 per unit. One-time fee: $185 full-time. *Financial support:* In 2010–11, 7 fellowships (averaging $18,000 per year), teaching assistantships (averaging $2,000 per year) were awarded; career-related internships or fieldwork, Federal Work-Study, scholarships/grants, and health care benefits also available. Financial award application deadline: 3/2; financial award applicants required to submit FAFSA. *Unit head:* Joseph Lease, Chair, 415-551-9285, E-mail: jlease@cca.edu. *Application contact:* Heidi Geis, Assistant Director of Graduate Admissions, 415-703-9523 Ext. 9533, Fax: 415-703-9539, E-mail: hgeis@cca.edu.

California Institute of Integral Studies, School of Consciousness and Transformation, San Francisco, CA 94103. Offers creative inquiry/interdisciplinary arts (MFA); cultural anthropology and social transformation (MA); East-West psychology (MA, PhD); integrative health studies (MA); philosophy and religion (MA, PhD), including Asian and comparative studies, philosophy, cosmology, and consciousness, women's spirituality; social and cultural anthropology (PhD); transformative leadership (MA); transformative studies (PhD); writing and consciousness (MFA). Part-time and evening/weekend programs available. Postbaccalaureate distance learning degree programs offered (minimal on-campus study). *Students:* 455 full-time (315 women), 133 part-time (90 women); includes 47 Black or African American, non-Hispanic/Latino; 3 American Indian or Alaska Native, non-Hispanic/Latino; 21 Asian, non-Hispanic/Latino; 41 Hispanic/Latino, 40 international. Average age 37. 265 applicants, 91% accepted, 163 enrolled. In 2010, 64 master's, 22 doctorates awarded. Terminal master's awarded for partial completion of doctoral program. *Degree requirements:* For master's, thesis optional; for doctorate, comprehensive exam, thesis/dissertation, 1 foreign language (Asian comparative studies). *Entrance requirements:* For master's, minimum GPA of 3.0, letters of recommendation, writing sample; for doctorate, master's degree, minimum GPA of 3.0, letters of recommendation, writing sample. Additional exam requirements/recommendations for international students: Required—TOEFL. *Application deadline:* For fall admission, 2/1 priority date for domestic and international students; for spring admission, 10/15 priority date for domestic and international students. Applications are processed on a rolling basis. Application fee: $65. Electronic applications accepted. *Expenses:* Tuition: Full-time $15,660; part-time $870 per semester hour. Required fees: $95 per semester. *Financial support:* In 2010–11, 255 students received support; research assistantships, teaching assistantships, career-related internships or fieldwork, Federal Work-Study, scholarships/grants, and tuition waivers (partial) available. Support available to part-time students. Financial award application deadline: 4/15; financial award applicants required to submit FAFSA. *Faculty research:* Ecology and sustainablility, philosophy and religion, East-West psychology, integrative health, social and cultural anthropology, transformative leadership. *Application contact:* Allyson Werner, Associate Director of Admissions, 415-575-6155, Fax: 415-575-1268.

California Institute of the Arts, School of Critical Studies, Valencia, CA 91355-2340. Offers writing (MFA, Adv C). *Entrance requirements:* For master's, portfolio. Additional exam requirements/recommendations for international students: Required—TOEFL.

California Institute of the Arts, School of Theatre, Valencia, CA 91355-2340. Offers acting (MFA, Adv C); design and technology (Adv C); directing (MFA); performing arts design and technology (MFA); theater management (MFA, Adv C); writing for performance (MFA). *Accreditation:* NAST. *Degree requirements:* For master's, thesis (for some programs), faculty review, performance or portfolio. *Entrance requirements:* For master's, audition or portfolio, interview. Additional exam requirements/recommendations for international students: Required—TOEFL. Electronic applications accepted.

California State University, Fresno, Division of Graduate Studies, College of Arts and Humanities, Department of English, Fresno, CA 93740-8027. Offers composition theory (MA); creative writing (MFA); literature (MA). Part-time and evening/weekend programs available. *Degree requirements:* For master's, one foreign language, thesis. *Entrance requirements:* For master's, GRE General Test, minimum GPA of 3.0, writing sample. Additional exam requirements/recommendations for international students: Required—TOEFL. Electronic applications accepted. *Faculty research:* American literature, Renaissance literature, foreign literature.

California State University, Long Beach, Graduate Studies, College of Liberal Arts, Department of English, Long Beach, CA 90840. Offers creative writing (MFA); English (MA). Part-time programs available. *Faculty:* 24 full-time (10 women), 4 part-time/adjunct (2 women). *Students:* 67 full-time (49 women), 97 part-time (68 women); includes 3 Black or African American, non-Hispanic/Latino; 4 American Indian or Alaska Native, non-Hispanic/Latino; 13 Asian, non-Hispanic/Latino; 23 Hispanic/Latino, 2 international. Average age 30. 222 applicants, 41% accepted, 57 enrolled. In 2010, 45 master's awarded. *Degree requirements:* For master's, one foreign language, comprehensive exam or thesis. *Entrance requirements:* For master's, GRE Subject Test, minimum GPA of 3.0 in English. *Application deadline:* For fall admission, 5/1 for domestic students. Applications are processed on a rolling basis. Application fee: $55. Electronic applications accepted. *Financial support:* Federal Work-Study, institutionally sponsored loans, and scholarships/grants available. Financial award application deadline: 3/2. *Faculty research:* English and American literature, literary theory, linguistics, rhetoric and composition. *Unit head:* Dr. Eileen S. Klink, Chair, 562-985-4223, Fax: 562-985-2369, E-mail: eklink@csulb.edu. *Application contact:* Dr. Beth Lau, Graduate Adviser, 562-985-4252, Fax: 562-985-4223, E-mail: blau@csulb.edu.

California State University, Northridge, Graduate Studies, College of Humanities, Department of English, Northridge, CA 91330. Offers creative writing (MA); literature (MA); rhetoric and composition theory (MA). Part-time and evening/weekend programs available. *Degree requirements:* For master's, thesis or alternative. *Entrance requirements:* For master's, writing proficiency test, GRE General Test or minimum GPA of 3.0. Additional exam requirements/recommendations for international students: Required—TOEFL. *Faculty research:* Reading improvement, professional writing, Dickens, Shaw, English as a second language.

California State University, Sacramento, Graduate Studies, College of Arts and Letters, Department of English, Sacramento, CA 95819. Offers creative writing (MA); teaching English to speakers of other languages (MA). Part-time programs available. *Degree requirements:* For master's, thesis, project, or comprehensive exam; writing proficiency exam. *Entrance requirements:* For master's, portfolio (creative writing); minimum GPA of 3.0 in English, 2.75 overall during previous 2 years. Additional exam requirements/recommendations for international students: Required—TOEFL. Electronic applications accepted. *Faculty research:* Teaching composition, remedial writing.

California State University, San Bernardino, Graduate Studies, College of Arts and Letters, Department of English, San Bernardino, CA 92407-2397. Offers creative writing (MFA); English composition (MA). Part-time and evening/weekend programs available. *Degree requirements:* For master's, one foreign language, thesis. *Entrance requirements:* For master's, BA in English or linguistics, minimum GPA of 3.0. Additional exam requirements/recommendations for international students: Required—TOEFL. *Faculty research:* Composition and literary theory, theatrical theory, creative writing, relationship between evaluating writing and teaching composition.

California State University, San Marcos, College of Arts and Sciences, Program in Literature and Writing Studies, San Marcos, CA 92096-0001. Offers MA. Part-time and evening/weekend programs available. *Degree requirements:* For master's, one foreign language, thesis. *Entrance requirements:* For master's, GRE General Test, minimum GPA of 3.0, writing sample. *Faculty research:* Postcolonialism, feminism rhetoric, cultural studies, creative writing, critical theory.

California State University, Stanislaus, College of Humanities and Social Sciences, Program in English (MA), Turlock, CA 95382. Offers literature (Certificate); rhetoric and teaching writing (MA); teaching English to speakers of other languages (MA). Part-time programs available. *Faculty:* 21. *Students:* 10 full-time (7 women), 42 part-time (30 women); includes 19 minority (3 Black or African American, non-Hispanic/Latino; 1 Asian, non-Hispanic/Latino; 10 Hispanic/Latino; 1 Native Hawaiian or other Pacific Islander, non-Hispanic/Latino; 4 Two or more races, non-Hispanic/Latino), 1 international. Average age 35. 28 applicants, 68% accepted, 15 enrolled. In 2010, 19 master's awarded. *Degree requirements:* For master's, comprehensive exam, thesis or alternative. *Entrance requirements:* For master's, GRE, minimum GPA of 3.0, 2 letters of reference, personal statement. Additional exam requirements/recommendations for international students: Required—TOEFL (minimum score 575 paper-based; 233 computer-based), TWE (minimum score 4). *Application deadline:* For fall admission, 5/1 for domestic students; for spring admission, 9/15 for domestic students. Application fee: $55. Electronic applications accepted. Tuition and fees vary according to program. *Financial support:* Fellowships, research assistantships, teaching assistantships, career-related internships or fieldwork and Federal Work-Study available. Financial award application deadline: 3/1; financial award applicants required to submit FAFSA. *Faculty research:* Transnational literacies, Renaissance and medieval literature, abolition writings and slave narratives, qualitative writing. *Unit head:* Dr. Scott Davis, English Department Chair, 209-667-3361, Fax: 209-667-3720, E-mail: english@csustan.edu. *Application contact:* Graduate School, 209-667-3129, Fax: 209-664-7025, E-mail: graduate_school@csustan.edu.

Carlow University, Humanities Division, Pittsburgh, PA 15213-3165. Offers creative writing (MFA), including fiction, nonfiction, poetry. Part-time and evening/weekend programs available. Postbaccalaureate distance learning degree programs offered (minimal on-campus study). *Students:* 34 part-time (31 women); includes 3 Black or African American, non-Hispanic/Latino. Average age 41. 1 applicant, 100% accepted, 1 enrolled. In 2010, 11 master's awarded. *Degree requirements:* For master's, thesis or alternative. *Entrance requirements:* For master's, minimum GPA of 3.0, resume, writing samples, 2 letters of recommendation. Additional exam requirements/recommendations for international students: Required—TOEFL (minimum score 550 paper-based; 213 computer-based). *Application deadline:* For fall admission, 6/15 priority date for domestic and international students; for spring admission, 11/15 priority date for domestic and international students. Applications are processed on a rolling basis. Application fee: $20. *Expenses:* Tuition: Full-time $9900; part-time $660 per credit. Tuition and fees vary according to course load, degree level and program. *Financial support:* Career-related internships or fieldwork, Federal Work-Study, and scholarships/grants available. Support available to part-time students. Financial award application deadline: 4/1; financial award applicants required to submit FAFSA. *Unit head:* Dr. Ellie Wymard, Director of MFA Program, 412-578-6597, Fax: 412-578-8706, E-mail: wymardex@carlow.edu. *Application contact:* Jo Danhires, Administrative Assistant of Admissions, 412-578-6059, Fax: 412-578-6321, E-mail: gradstudies@carlow.edu.

Carnegie Mellon University, College of Humanities and Social Sciences, Department of English, Program in Professional Writing, Pittsburgh, PA 15213-3891. Offers editing and publishing (MAPW); policy and non-profit communication (MAPW); public and media relations / corporate communications (MAPW); science or healthcare communication (MAPW); technical writing (MAPW); writing for new media (MAPW); writing for print media (MAPW). Part-time programs available. *Entrance requirements:* For master's, GRE General Test. Additional exam requirements/recommendations for international students: Required—TOEFL, TWE.

Central Michigan University, College of Graduate Studies, College of Humanities and Social and Behavioral Sciences, Department of English Language and Literature, Mount Pleasant, MI 48859. Offers English composition and communication (MA); English language and literature (MA), including children's and young adult literature, creative writing, general concentration; teaching English to speakers of other languages (MA). Part-time and evening/weekend programs available. *Faculty:* 16 full-time (10 women). *Students:* 23 full-time (15 women), 61 part-time (38 women); includes 1 American Indian or Alaska Native, non-Hispanic/Latino; 1 Hispanic/Latino, 16 international. Average age 32. *Degree requirements:* For master's, thesis or alternative. *Application deadline:* For fall admission, 6/1 for international students; for spring admission, 10/1 for international students. Applications are processed on a rolling basis. Application fee: $35 ($45 for international students). Electronic applications accepted. *Expenses:* Tuition, state resident: full-time $8208; part-time $456 per credit hour. Tuition, nonresident: full-time $13,788; part-time $766 per credit hour. One-time fee: $25. *Financial support:* Fellowships with tuition reimbursements, research assistantships with tuition reimbursements, teaching assistantships with tuition reimbursements, career-related internships or fieldwork, Federal Work-Study, unspecified assistantships, and out-of-state merit awards, non-resident graduate awards available. *Faculty research:* Composition theory, science fiction history and bibliography, children's and young adult literature, nineteenth-century American literature, applied linguistics. *Unit head:* Dr. William H. Wandless, Chairperson, 989-774-3171, Fax: 989-774-1271, E-mail: wandl1wh@cmich.edu. *Application contact:* Dr. Jeffrey A. Weinstock, Coordinator, Graduate Studies in English, 989-774-3101, Fax: 989-774-1271, E-mail: weins1ja@cmich.edu.

Chapman University, Graduate Studies, Wilkinson College of Humanities and Social Sciences, Department of English, Orange, CA 92866. Offers creative writing (MFA); English (MA). Part-time and evening/weekend programs available. *Faculty:* 22 full-time (11 women), 20 part-time/adjunct (6 women). *Students:* 32 full-time (18 women), 29 part-time (21 women); includes 12 minority (4 Black or African American, non-Hispanic/Latino; 1 Asian, non-Hispanic/Latino; 5 Hispanic/Latino; 2 Two or more races, non-Hispanic/Latino). Average age 33. 53 applicants, 70% accepted, 19 enrolled. In 2010, 26 master's awarded. *Degree requirements:* For master's, comprehensive exam (for some programs), thesis (for some programs). *Entrance requirements:* For master's, GRE or MAT, minimum undergraduate GPA of 2.5. Additional exam requirements/recommendations for international students: Required—TOEFL (minimum score 550 paper-based; 213 computer-based; 80 iBT). *Application deadline:* For fall admission, 5/1 priority date for domestic students; for winter admission, 11/1 priority date for domestic students. Applications are processed on a rolling basis. Application fee: $60. Electronic applications accepted. *Expenses:* Contact institution. *Financial support:* Fellowships, Federal Work-Study and scholarships/grants available. Financial award applicants required to submit FAFSA. *Unit head:* Dr. Mark Axelrod, Director of Graduate Programs, 714-997-6586, E-mail: axelrod@chapman.edu. *Application contact:* Priscilla Garcia Powers, Graduate Admission Counselor, 714-997-6711, E-mail: pgarcia@chapman.edu.

Chapman University, Graduate Studies, Wilkinson College of Humanities and Social Sciences, Program in Creative Writing, Orange, CA 92866. Offers MFA. Part-time and evening/weekend programs available. *Faculty:* 19 full-time (8 women), 19 part-time/adjunct (11 women). *Students:* 33 full-time (21 women), 25 part-time (13 women); includes 1 Black or African American, non-Hispanic/Latino; 2 Asian, non-Hispanic/Latino; 4 Hispanic/Latino. Average age 29. 40 applicants, 80% accepted, 22 enrolled. In 2010, 19 master's awarded. *Degree requirements:* For master's, thesis, project. *Entrance requirements:* For master's, GRE General Test or MAT, minimum undergraduate GPA of 3.0, sample of creative writing. Additional exam requirements/recommendations for international students: Required—TOEFL (minimum score 550 paper-based). *Application deadline:* Applications are processed on a rolling basis. Application fee: $55. Electronic applications accepted. *Expenses:* Contact institution. *Financial support:* Fellowships, Federal Work-Study and scholarships/grants available. Financial award application deadline: 6/30; financial award applicants required to submit FAFSA. *Unit head:* Dr. Richard Ruppel, Chair, 714-997-6754, E-mail: ruppel@chapman.edu. *Application contact:* Jim Blaylock, Coordinator, 714-997-6750, E-mail: blaylock@chapman.edu.

Chatham University, Program in Writing, Pittsburgh, PA 15232-2826. Offers children's writing (MFA); fiction (MFA); non-fiction (MFA); poetry (MFA); professional writing (MPW); screenwriting (MFA). Part-time and evening/weekend programs available. Postbaccalaureate distance learning degree programs offered (minimal on-campus study). *Entrance requirements:* For master's, minimum GPA of 3.0, writing sample, recommendation letters. Additional exam requirements/recommendations for international students: Required—TOEFL (minimum score 600 paper-

Writing

Chatham University (continued)
based; 250 computer-based; 100 iBT), IELTS (minimum score 6.5), TWE. Electronic applications accepted. *Faculty research:* Ecopoetics; environment and culture; wilderness and literature; literature of exploration, exile, and home.

Chicago State University, School of Graduate and Professional Studies, College of Arts and Sciences, Department of English, Chicago, IL 60628. Offers creative writing (MFA); English (MA). *Degree requirements:* For master's, comprehensive exam. *Entrance requirements:* For master's, minimum GPA of 2.75.

City College of the City University of New York, Graduate School, College of Liberal Arts and Science, Division of the Humanities and Arts, Department of English, Program in Creative Writing, New York, NY 10031-9198. Offers MA, MFA. *Degree requirements:* For master's, one foreign language, comprehensive exam, thesis. *Entrance requirements:* For master's, minimum GPA of 3.0, 10-15 poems or 30-50 pages of fiction (short stories or novel excerpt). Additional exam requirements/recommendations for international students: Required—TOEFL (minimum score 600 paper-based; 100 iBT). Electronic applications accepted.

Claremont Graduate University, Graduate Programs, School of Arts and Humanities, Department of English, Claremont, CA 91711-6160. Offers American studies (MA, PhD); critical theory (MA, PhD); early modern studies (MA, PhD); English (M Phil, MA, PhD); literary theory (PhD); literature (MA, PhD); literature and creative writing (MA); literature and film (MA); MBA/MA; MBA/PhD. Part-time programs available. *Faculty:* 2 full-time (both women), 4 part-time/adjunct (1 woman). *Students:* 88 full-time (56 women), 14 part-time (12 women); includes 1 Black or African American, non-Hispanic/Latino; 9 Asian, non-Hispanic/Latino; 7 Hispanic/Latino; 5 Two or more races, non-Hispanic/Latino, 7 international. Average age 34. In 2010, 9 master's, 10 doctorates awarded. *Entrance requirements:* For master's and doctorate, GRE General Test. Additional exam requirements/recommendations for international students: Required—TOEFL (minimum score 550 paper-based; 213 computer-based; 80 iBT). *Application deadline:* For fall admission, 2/1 priority date for domestic students. Applications are processed on a rolling basis. Application fee: $60. Electronic applications accepted. *Expenses:* Tuition: Full-time $35,748; part-time $1554 per unit. Required fees: $215 per semester. *Financial support:* Fellowships, Federal Work-Study, institutionally sponsored loans, and scholarships/grants available. Support available to part-time students. Financial award application deadline: 2/15; financial award applicants required to submit FAFSA. *Faculty research:* American, comparative, and English Renaissance literature; modernism; feminist literature and theory. *Unit head:* Elysabeth Flores Griffith, Administrative Director, 909-607-3877, E-mail: elysabeth.flores@cgu.edu. *Application contact:* Susan Hampson, Admissions Coordinator, 909-607-1278, Fax: 909-607-1221, E-mail: humanities@cgu.edu.

Clemson University, Graduate School, College of Architecture, Arts, and Humanities, Department of English, Program in Professional Communication, Clemson, SC 29634. Offers MA. Part-time programs available. *Students:* 25 full-time (20 women), 3 part-time (2 women); includes 1 Black or African American, non-Hispanic/Latino; 2 Two or more races, non-Hispanic/Latino, 3 international. Average age 28. 42 applicants, 33% accepted, 11 enrolled. In 2010, 16 master's awarded. *Degree requirements:* For master's, one foreign language, thesis optional, oral exam. *Entrance requirements:* For master's, GRE General Test, minimum GPA of 3.0. Additional exam requirements/recommendations for international students: Required—TOEFL, IELTS. *Application deadline:* For fall admission, 2/1 priority date for domestic students, 4/15 for international students; for spring admission, 11/1 priority date for domestic students, 9/15 for international students. Applications are processed on a rolling basis. Application fee: $70 ($80 for international students). Electronic applications accepted. *Expenses:* Tuition, state resident: full-time $6492; part-time $400 per credit hour. Tuition, nonresident: full-time $13,634; part-time $800 per credit hour. Required fees: $262 per semester. Part-time tuition and fees vary according to course load and program. *Financial support:* In 2010–11, 27 students received support, including 1 research assistantship with partial tuition reimbursement available (averaging $15,000 per year), 19 teaching assistantships with partial tuition reimbursements available (averaging $12,171 per year); fellowships with full and partial tuition reimbursements available, career-related internships or fieldwork, institutionally sponsored loans, scholarships/grants, health care benefits, and unspecified assistantships also available. Support available to part-time students. Financial award application deadline: 4/1; financial award applicants required to submit FAFSA. *Faculty research:* Usability testing, rhetoric, communication across the curriculum, intercultural communication. *Unit head:* Dr. Lee Morrissey, Coordinator, 864-656-3151, Fax: 864-656-1345, E-mail: lmorris@clemson.edu. *Application contact:* Dr. Summer Taylor, Graduate Coordinator, 864-656-6689, Fax: 864-656-1345, E-mail: slsmith@clemson.edu.

Cleveland State University, College of Graduate Studies, College of Liberal Arts and Social Sciences, Department of English, Cleveland, OH 44115. Offers creative writing (MFA); English (MA). Part-time and evening/weekend programs available. *Faculty:* 8 full-time (2 women), 5 part-time/adjunct (1 woman). *Students:* 14 full-time (9 women), 64 part-time (43 women); includes 15 Black or African American, non-Hispanic/Latino; 1 Asian, non-Hispanic/Latino; 1 Hispanic/Latino, 2 international. Average age 34. 59 applicants, 61% accepted, 16 enrolled. In 2010, 17 master's awarded. *Degree requirements:* For master's, comprehensive exam, thesis. *Entrance requirements:* For master's, minimum GPA of 2.75, undergraduate concentration in English, writing sample, portfolio. Additional exam requirements/recommendations for international students: Required—TOEFL (525 paper-based; 197 computer-based) or IELTS (6 paper-based). *Application deadline:* For fall admission, 7/15 priority date for domestic students, 5/15 for international students; for spring admission, 12/15 for domestic students, 11/1 for international students. Applications are processed on a rolling basis. Application fee: $30. Electronic applications accepted. *Expenses:* Tuition, state resident: full-time $8447; part-time $469 per credit hour. Tuition, nonresident: full-time $16,020; part-time $890 per credit hour. Required fees: $50. *Financial support:* In 2010–11, 20 students received support, including 1 fellowship (averaging $1,000 per year), 5 research assistantships with full and partial tuition reimbursements available (averaging $3,480 per year), 7 teaching assistantships with full and partial tuition reimbursements available (averaging $3,480 per year); Federal Work-Study, institutionally sponsored loans, tuition waivers (full and partial), and unspecified assistantships also available. Support available to part-time students. Financial award application deadline: 2/15. *Faculty research:* Literary history and criticism, linguistics, literature. Total annual research expenditures: $5,000. *Unit head:* Dr. David M. Larson, Chairperson, 216-687-3951, Fax: 216-687-6943, E-mail: d.larson@csuohio.edu. *Application contact:* Dr. Jennifer M. Jeffers, Graduate Director, 216-687-3975, Fax: 216-687-6943, E-mail: j.m.jeffers53@csuohio.edu.

Coastal Carolina University, Thomas W. and Robin W. Edwards College of Humanities and Fine Arts, Conway, SC 29528-6054. Offers writing (MA). Part-time and evening/weekend programs available. *Faculty:* 6 full-time (5 women), 2 part-time/adjunct (1 woman). *Students:* 1 full-time (0 women), 9 part-time (6 women). Average age 39. 18 applicants, 67% accepted, 10 enrolled. *Degree requirements:* For master's, thesis. *Entrance requirements:* For master's, GRE, official transcripts, 2 letters of recommendation. Additional exam requirements/recommendations for international students: Required—TOEFL (minimum score 550 paper-based; 213 computer-based; 79 iBT). *Application deadline:* For fall admission, 5/1 priority date for domestic and international students; for spring admission, 11/15 priority date for domestic and international students. Applications are processed on a rolling basis. Application fee: $45. Electronic applications accepted. *Expenses:* Tuition, state resident: full-time $10,080; part-time $420 per credit hour. Tuition, nonresident: full-time $12,840; part-time $535 per credit hour. Required fees: $80; $40 per semester. Tuition and fees vary according to program. *Financial support:* Fellowships, research assistantships, unspecified assistantships available. Support available to part-time students. Financial award application deadline: 3/1; financial award applicants required to submit FAFSA. *Unit head:* Jason E. Ockert, Associate Dean, 843-349-2531, E-mail: jockert@coastal.edu. *Application contact:* Dr. Deborah A. Vrooman, Interim Director of Graduate Studies, 843-349-2783, Fax: 843-349-6444, E-mail: vroomand@coastal.edu.

The College at Brockport, State University of New York, School of the Arts, Humanities and Social Sciences, Department of English, Brockport, NY 14420-2997. Offers English (MA), including creative writing, literature. Part-time programs available. *Students:* 20 full-time (14 women), 31 part-time (18 women). 25 applicants, 44% accepted, 10 enrolled. In 2010, 15 master's awarded. *Degree requirements:* For master's, thesis. *Entrance requirements:* For master's, minimum GPA of 3.0, letters of recommendation, writing sample. Additional exam requirements/recommendations for international students: Required—TOEFL (minimum score 550 paper-based; 213 computer-based; 79 iBT). *Application deadline:* For fall admission, 4/15 priority date for domestic and international students; for spring admission, 11/15 priority date for domestic and international students. Application fee: $50. Electronic applications accepted. *Financial support:* In 2010–11, 3 teaching assistantships with full tuition reimbursements (averaging $6,000 per year) were awarded; Federal Work-Study, scholarships/grants, and unspecified assistantships also available. Support available to part-time students. Financial award application deadline: 3/15; financial award applicants required to submit FAFSA. *Faculty research:* British and American literature, creative writing, film studies, children's literature, ancient and modern world literature. *Unit head:* Dr. J. Roger Kurtz, Chairperson, 585-395-2503, Fax: 585-395-2391, E-mail: rkurtz@brockport.edu. *Application contact:* Dr. Miriam Burstein, Graduate Program Director, 585-395-5827, Fax: 585-395-2391, E-mail: mburstei@brockport.edu.

Colorado State University, Graduate School, College of Liberal Arts, Department of English, Fort Collins, CO 80523-1773. Offers creative writing (MFA); English (MA). Part-time programs available. *Faculty:* 30 full-time (19 women), 1 part-time/adjunct (0 women). *Students:* 101 full-time (60 women), 46 part-time (32 women); includes 11 minority (1 American Indian or Alaska Native, non-Hispanic/Latino; 4 Asian, non-Hispanic/Latino; 5 Hispanic/Latino; 1 Two or more races, non-Hispanic/Latino), 15 international. Average age 30. 362 applicants, 26% accepted, 53 enrolled. In 2010, 48 master's awarded. *Degree requirements:* For master's, variable foreign language requirement, thesis (for some programs), exams. *Entrance requirements:* For master's, GRE, writing sample, BA/BS with minimum GPA of 3.0, letters of recommendation. Additional exam requirements/recommendations for international students: Required—TOEFL (minimum score 550 paper-based; 213 computer-based; 80 iBT). *Application deadline:* For fall admission, 4/1 priority date for domestic students; for spring admission, 9/1 priority date for domestic students. Applications are processed on a rolling basis. Application fee: $50. Electronic applications accepted. *Expenses:* Tuition, state resident: full-time $7434; part-time $413 per credit. Tuition, nonresident: full-time $19,022; part-time $1057 per credit. Required fees: $1729; $88 per credit. *Financial support:* In 2010–11, 40 students received support, including 40 teaching assistantships with full tuition reimbursements available (averaging $12,377 per year); fellowships, research assistantships, career-related internships or fieldwork, Federal Work-Study, institutionally sponsored loans, scholarships/grants, traineeships, and unspecified assistantships also available. Support available to part-time students. Financial award application deadline: 5/1; financial award applicants required to submit FAFSA. *Faculty research:* Computers and writing, environmental writing, cultural studies, new historicism, performance and identity. Total annual research expenditures: $58,341. *Unit head:* Dr. Bruce Ronda, Chair, 970-491-6428, Fax: 970-491-5601, E-mail: bruce.ronda@colostate.edu. *Application contact:* Marnie Leonard, Administrative Assistant, 970-491-2403, Fax: 970-491-7541, E-mail: marnie.leonard@colostate.edu.

Columbia College Chicago, Graduate School, Department of Fiction Writing, Chicago, IL 60605-1996. Offers creative writing (MFA); teaching of writing (MA); MFA/MA. Part-time programs available. *Students:* 32 full-time (15 women), 19 part-time (8 women); includes 4 Black or African American, non-Hispanic/Latino; 2 Hispanic/Latino. Average age 31. 131 applicants, 21% accepted, 12 enrolled. In 2010, 19 master's awarded. *Degree requirements:* For master's, thesis. *Entrance requirements:* For master's, minimum GPA of 3.0, work sample, thirty pages of manuscript in roughly equal amounts of fiction and expository prose. Additional exam requirements/recommendations for international students: Required—TOEFL (minimum score 550 paper-based; 213 computer-based). *Application deadline:* For fall admission, 1/14 for domestic and international students. Applications are processed on a rolling basis. Application fee: $55. Electronic applications accepted. *Expenses:* Tuition: Full-time $16,966; part-time $684 per credit. Required fees: $520; $113 per semester. One-time fee: $150 full-time. Tuition and fees vary according to course load and program. *Financial support:* Fellowships, career-related internships or fieldwork, Federal Work-Study, and scholarships/grants available. Support available to part-time students. Financial award application deadline: 8/13; financial award applicants required to submit FAFSA. *Unit head:* Alexis Pride, Chairperson, 312-369-7829, E-mail: apride@colum.edu. *Application contact:* Cate Lagueux, Director of Graduate Admissions, 312-369-7260, Fax: 312-369-8047, E-mail: clagueux@colum.edu.

Columbia College Chicago, Graduate School, Program in Nonfiction Writing, Chicago, IL 60605-1996. Offers MFA. *Students:* 8 full-time (5 women), 1 (woman) part-time; includes 1 Black or African American, non-Hispanic/Latino; 1 Two or more races, non-Hispanic/Latino. Average age 29. 27 applicants, 93% accepted. *Application deadline:* For fall admission, 1/14 for domestic and international students. *Expenses:* Tuition: Full-time $16,966; part-time $684 per credit. Required fees: $520; $113 per semester. One-time fee: $150 full-time. Tuition and fees vary according to course load and program. *Financial support:* Teaching assistantships available. *Unit head:* Nicole Wilson, Associate Director, Creative Writing Programs, 312-369-8819, E-mail: nwilson@colum.edu. *Application contact:* Cate Lagueux, Director of Graduate Admissions, 312-369-7260, Fax: 312-369-8047, E-mail: gradstudy@colum.edu.

Columbia College Chicago, Graduate School, Program in Poetry, Chicago, IL 60605-1996. Offers MFA. Part-time programs available. *Students:* 23 full-time (10 women), 1 (woman) part-time; includes 1 Black or African American, non-Hispanic/Latino; 2 Hispanic/Latino. Average age 25. 85 applicants, 59% accepted, 14 enrolled. In 2010, 10 master's awarded. *Degree requirements:* For master's, thesis. *Entrance requirements:* For master's, interview, writing sample, minimum GPA of 3.0. Additional exam requirements/recommendations for international students: Required—TOEFL (minimum score 550 paper-based; 213 computer-based). *Application deadline:* For fall admission, 1/14 for domestic and international students. Application fee: $55. Electronic applications accepted. *Expenses:* Tuition: Full-time $16,966; part-time $684 per credit. Required fees: $520; $113 per semester. One-time fee: $150 full-time. Tuition and fees vary according to course load and program. *Financial support:* Fellowships, Federal Work-Study and scholarships/grants available. Support available to part-time students. Financial award application deadline: 8/13; financial award applicants required to submit FAFSA. *Unit head:* Lisa Fishman, Director, 312-369-8825, E-mail: lfishman@colum.edu. *Application contact:* Cate Lagueux, Director of Graduate Admissions, 312-369-7260, Fax: 312-369-8047, E-mail: gradstudy@colum.edu.

Columbia University, School of the Arts, Writing Division, New York, NY 10027. Offers fiction (MFA); nonfiction (MFA); poetry (MFA). *Degree requirements:* For master's, thesis. *Entrance requirements:* For master's, 3 letters of recommendation, writing sample. Additional exam requirements/recommendations for international students: Required—TOEFL (minimum score 600 paper-based; 250 computer-based). Electronic applications accepted.

See Close-Up on page 295.

Concordia University, School of Graduate Studies, Faculty of Arts and Science, Department of English, Program in Creative Writing, Montréal, QC H3G 1M8, Canada. Offers MA. *Degree requirements:* For master's, one foreign language, thesis. *Entrance requirements:* For master's, honors degree in English, minimum GPA of 3.3 in English literature, portfolio. *Faculty research:* Fiction, poetry, prose, drama.

Cornell University, Graduate School, Graduate Fields of Arts and Sciences, Field of English Language and Literature, Ithaca, NY 14853-0001. Offers African-American literature (PhD); American literature after 1865 (PhD); American literature to 1865 (PhD); American studies (PhD); colonial and postcolonial literature (PhD); creative writing (MFA); cultural studies (PhD); dramatic literature (PhD); English poetry (PhD); English Renaissance to 1660 (PhD); lesbian, bisexual, and gay literature studies (PhD); literary criticism and theory (PhD); nineteenth century (PhD); Old and Middle English (PhD); prose fiction (PhD); Restoration and eighteenth century (PhD); twentieth century (PhD); women's literature (PhD); MFA/PhD. *Faculty:* 56 full-time (29 women). *Students:* 100 full-time (56 women); includes 5 Black or African American, non-Hispanic/Latino; 3 American Indian or Alaska Native, non-Hispanic/Latino; 10 Asian, non-Hispanic/Latino; 8 Hispanic/Latino, 12 international. Average age 27. 1,091 applicants, 4% accepted, 21 enrolled. In 2010, 25 master's, 12 doctorates awarded. Terminal master's awarded for partial completion of doctoral program. *Degree requirements:* For master's, one foreign language, thesis; for doctorate, one foreign language, comprehensive exam, thesis/dissertation, teaching experience. *Entrance requirements:* For master's, GRE General Test, 3 letters of recommendation, creative writing sample; for doctorate, GRE General Test, GRE Subject Test (English), 3 letters of recommendation, writing sample. Additional exam requirements/recommendations for international students: Required—TOEFL (minimum score 600 paper-based; 250 computer-based; 77 iBT). *Application deadline:* For fall admission, 1/10 for domestic students. Application fee: $80. Electronic applications accepted. *Expenses:* Tuition: Full-time $29,500. Required fees: $76. Tuition and fees vary according to degree level and program. *Financial support:* In 2010–11, 32 fellowships with full tuition reimbursements, 60 teaching assistantships with full tuition reimbursements were awarded; research assistantships with full tuition reimbursements, institutionally sponsored loans, scholarships/grants, health care benefits, tuition waivers (full and partial), and unspecified assistantships also available. Financial award applicants required to submit FAFSA. *Faculty research:* English and American literature, women's writing, ethnic and post-colonial literature, critical theory, medievalism. *Unit head:* Director of Graduate Studies, 607-255-7989, Fax: 607-255-6661. *Application contact:* Graduate Field Assistant, 607-255-7989, Fax: 607-255-6661, E-mail: english_grad@cornell.edu.

Creighton University, Graduate School, College of Arts and Sciences, Department of English, Omaha, NE 68178-0001. Offers creative writing (MA). Part-time programs available. *Faculty:* 16 full-time (8 women). *Students:* 11 full-time (6 women), 3 part-time (1 woman); includes 1 minority (Hispanic/Latino), 3 international. Average age 26. 13 applicants, 85% accepted, 2 enrolled. In 2010, 2 master's awarded. *Degree requirements:* For master's, thesis optional. *Entrance requirements:* For master's, GRE, 10-15 page writing sample, 3 letters of recommendation. Additional exam requirements/recommendations for international students: Required—TOEFL (minimum score 550 paper-based; 213 computer-based; 80 iBT). *Application deadline:* For fall admission, 3/15 priority date for domestic and international students. Application fee: $50. Electronic applications accepted. *Expenses:* Tuition: Full-time $12,168; part-time $676 per credit hour. Required fees: $131 per semester. Tuition and fees vary according to program. *Financial support:* In 2010–11, 5 fellowships with full and partial tuition reimbursements (averaging $10,698 per year) were awarded; tuition waivers (partial) and unspecified assistantships also available. Financial award applicants required to submit FAFSA. *Unit head:* Dr. Brent Spencer, Director, 402-280-2292, E-mail: brentspencer@creighton.edu. *Application contact:* Taunya Plater, Senior Program Coordinator, 402-280-2870, Fax: 402-280-2899, E-mail: taunyaplater@creighton.edu.

DePaul University, College of Liberal Arts and Sciences, Department of English, Master of Arts in Writing and Publishing Program, Chicago, IL 60604-2287. Offers MA. *Students:* 103 full-time (70 women), 40 part-time (28 women); includes 8 Black or African American, non-Hispanic/Latino; 3 Asian, non-Hispanic/Latino; 6 Hispanic/Latino; 1 Native Hawaiian or other Pacific Islander, non-Hispanic/Latino. *Unit head:* Christine Tardy, Director, 773-325-4145. *Application contact:* Dr. Lesley Kordecki, Director, 773-325-1786, Fax: 773-325-8607, E-mail: lkordeck@depaul.edu.

Drew University, Caspersen School of Graduate Studies, Program in Poetry, Madison, NJ 07940-1493. Offers poetry (MFA); poetry in translation (MFA). *Degree requirements:* For master's, thesis. *Entrance requirements:* For master's, transcripts, writing sample, recommendations. *Expenses:* Contact institution.

Eastern Kentucky University, The Graduate School, College of Arts and Sciences, Department of English and Theatre, Richmond, KY 40475-3102. Offers creative writing (MFA); English (MA). Part-time and evening/weekend programs available. *Degree requirements:* For master's, thesis optional. *Entrance requirements:* For master's, GRE General Test, minimum GPA of 2.5, minor in English with 3.0 GPA. *Faculty research:* Old English, Victorian studies, women's studies, rhetoric, popular culture, novel studies.

Eastern Michigan University, Graduate School, College of Arts and Sciences, Department of English Language and Literature, Program in Creative Writing, Ypsilanti, MI 48197. Offers MA. Part-time and evening/weekend programs available. Postbaccalaureate distance learning degree programs offered (minimal on-campus study). *Students:* 11 part-time (1 woman); includes 1 minority (American Indian or Alaska Native, non-Hispanic/Latino). Average age 30. In 2010, 4 master's awarded. *Entrance requirements:* Additional exam requirements/recommendations for international students: Required—TOEFL. *Application deadline:* Applications are processed on a rolling basis. Application fee: $35. *Financial support:* Fellowships, research assistantships with full tuition reimbursements, teaching assistantships with full tuition reimbursements, career-related internships or fieldwork, Federal Work-Study, institutionally sponsored loans, scholarships/grants, tuition waivers (partial), and unspecified assistantships available. Support available to part-time students. Financial award applicants required to submit FAFSA. *Application contact:* Christine Hume, Program Advisor, 734-487-1310, Fax: 734-483-9744, E-mail: chume@emich.edu.

Eastern Michigan University, Graduate School, College of Arts and Sciences, Department of English Language and Literature, Program in Teaching of Writing, Ypsilanti, MI 48197. Offers MA, Graduate Certificate. *Students:* 3 part-time (all women); includes 1 minority (Hispanic/Latino). Average age 35. In 2010, 1 other advanced degree awarded. Application fee: $35. *Application contact:* Prof. Steve Krause, Program Advisor, 734-487-3172, Fax: 734-483-9744, E-mail: skrause@emich.edu.

Eastern Michigan University, Graduate School, College of Arts and Sciences, Department of English Language and Literature, Program in Written Communication, Ypsilanti, MI 48197. Offers technical communications (MA, Graduate Certificate); written communications (MA). Part-time and evening/weekend programs available. Postbaccalaureate distance learning degree programs offered (minimal on-campus study). *Students:* 8 full-time (6 women), 38 part-time (30 women); includes 5 minority (4 Black or African American, non-Hispanic/Latino; 1 Hispanic/Latino), 1 international. Average age 34. In 2010, 11 master's awarded. *Entrance requirements:* Additional exam requirements/recommendations for international students: Required—TOEFL. *Application deadline:* Applications are processed on a rolling basis. Application fee: $35. *Financial support:* Fellowships, research assistantships with full tuition reimbursements, teaching assistantships with full tuition reimbursements, career-related internships or fieldwork, Federal Work-Study, institutionally sponsored loans, scholarships/grants, tuition waivers (partial), and unspecified assistantships available. Support available to part-time students. Financial award applicants required to submit FAFSA. *Application contact:* Prof. Steve Krause, Program Advisor, 734-487-3172, Fax: 734-483-9744, E-mail: skrause@emich.edu.

Eastern Washington University, Graduate Studies, College of Arts and Letters, Inland Northwest Center for Writers, Cheney, WA 99004-2431. Offers MFA. *Degree requirements:* For master's, comprehensive exam, thesis. *Entrance requirements:* For master's, GRE General Test, minimum GPA of 3.0, sample of written work.

Emerson College, Graduate Studies, School of the Arts, Department of Writing, Literature and Publishing, Program in Creative Writing, Boston, MA 02116-4624. Offers MFA. Part-time and evening/weekend programs available. *Entrance requirements:* For master's, GRE General Test, 15 page writing sample. Additional exam requirements/recommendations for international students: Required—TOEFL (minimum score 550 paper-based; 213 computer-based; 80 iBT), IELTS (minimum score 6.5). Electronic applications accepted.

Emerson College, Graduate Studies, School of the Arts, Department of Writing, Literature and Publishing, Program in Publishing and Writing, Boston, MA 02116-4624. Offers MA. Part-time and evening/weekend programs available. *Degree requirements:* For master's, thesis or alternative. *Entrance requirements:* For master's, GRE General Test, 15 page writing sample. Additional exam requirements/recommendations for international students: Required—TOEFL (minimum score 550 paper-based; 213 computer-based; 80 iBT), IELTS (minimum score 6.5). Electronic applications accepted. *Faculty research:* Publishing.

Fairfield University, College of Arts and Sciences, Fairfield, CT 06824-5195. Offers American studies (MA); communication (MA); creative writing (MFA); mathematics (MS). Part-time and evening/weekend programs available. Postbaccalaureate distance learning degree programs offered (minimal on-campus study). *Faculty:* 46 full-time (20 women), 15 part-time/adjunct (7 women). *Students:* 96 full-time (65 women), 97 part-time (63 women); includes 7 Black or African American, non-Hispanic/Latino; 5 Hispanic/Latino; 2 Two or more races, non-Hispanic/Latino, 7 international. Average age 41. 114 applicants, 62% accepted, 38 enrolled. In 2010, 36 master's awarded. *Degree requirements:* For master's, capstone research course. *Entrance requirements:* For master's, minimum GPA of 3.0, 2 letters of recommendation, resume. Additional exam requirements/recommendations for international students: Required—TOEFL (minimum score 550 paper-based; 213 computer-based; 80 iBT). *Application deadline:* For fall admission, 5/15 for international students; for spring admission, 10/15 for international students. Applications are processed on a rolling basis. Application fee: $60. Electronic applications accepted. *Expenses:* Tuition: Part-time $600 per hour. Part-time tuition and fees vary according to degree level and program. *Financial support:* In 2010–11, 19 students received support. Unspecified assistantships available. Financial award applicants required to submit FAFSA. *Faculty research:* Non-commutative algebra, partial differential equations, writing (fiction, non-fiction and poetry), communication for social change, comparative media systems, negotiation and management. *Unit head:* Dr. Robbin Crabtree, Dean, 203-254-4000 Ext. 3263, Fax: 203-254-4119, E-mail: rcrabtree@fairfield.edu. *Application contact:* Marianne Gumpper, Director of Graduate and Continuing Studies Admissions, 203-254-4184, Fax: 203-254-4073, E-mail: gradadmis@fairfield.edu.

Fairleigh Dickinson University, College at Florham, Maxwell Becton College of Arts and Sciences, Department of English, Communication and Philosophy, Program in Creative Writing, Madison, NJ 07940-1099. Offers MFA. *Students:* 45 full-time (30 women), 9 part-time (3 women). Average age 34. 62 applicants, 29% accepted, 14 enrolled. In 2010, 12 master's awarded. *Application deadline:* Applications are processed on a rolling basis. Application fee: $40. *Application contact:* Susan Brooman, University Director, Graduate Admissions, 973-443-8905, Fax: 973-443-8088, E-mail: grad@fdu.edu.

Fairleigh Dickinson University, College at Florham, Maxwell Becton College of Arts and Sciences, Department of English, Communication and Philosophy, Program in Creative Writing and Literature for Educators, Madison, NJ 07940-1099. Offers MA. *Students:* 11 full-time (10 women). Average age 37. 11 applicants, 100% accepted, 0 enrolled.Application fee: $40. *Application contact:* Susan Brooman, University Director, Graduate Admissions, 973-443-8905, Fax: 973-443-8088, E-mail: grad@fdu.edu.

Florida Atlantic University, Dorothy F. Schmidt College of Arts and Letters, Department of English, Boca Raton, FL 33431-0991. Offers British and American literature (MA); creative nonfiction (MFA); creative writing (MA); fiction (MFA); multicultural literatures and literacies (MA); poetry (MFA); science fiction and fantasy (MA); teaching English (MAT). Part-time programs available. *Faculty:* 59 full-time (32 women), 3 part-time/adjunct (2 women). *Students:* 33 full-time (17 women), 25 part-time (18 women); includes 14 minority (2 Black or African American, non-Hispanic/Latino; 1 Asian, non-Hispanic/Latino; 11 Hispanic/Latino). Average age 30. 60 applicants, 47% accepted, 20 enrolled. In 2010, 20 master's awarded. *Degree requirements:* For master's, one foreign language, thesis. *Entrance requirements:* For master's, GRE General Test, minimum GPA of 3.0, writing samples, 2 letters of recommendation. *Application deadline:* For fall admission, 3/1 for domestic students, 2/15 for international students; for spring admission, 11/1 for domestic students, 7/15 for international students. Applications are processed on a rolling basis. Application fee: $30. Electronic applications accepted. *Expenses:* Tuition, area resident: Part-time $319.96 per credit. Tuition, state resident: part-time $319.96 per credit. Tuition, nonresident: part-time $926.42 per credit. *Financial support:* Fellowships, teaching assistantships with partial tuition reimbursements, Federal Work-Study and tuition waivers available. Support available to part-time students. Financial award application deadline: 3/1. *Faculty research:* African-American writers, critical theory, British-American, Asian-American. *Unit head:* Dr. Wenying Xu, Chair, 561-297-2065, Fax: 561-297-3807, E-mail: wxu@fau.edu. *Application contact:* Dr. Andrew Furman, Director of Graduate Studies, 561-297-3835, Fax: 561-297-3807, E-mail: afurman@fau.edu.

Florida International University, College of Arts and Sciences, Department of English, Program in Creative Writing, Miami, FL 33199. Offers MFA. Part-time and evening/weekend programs available. *Students:* 25 full-time (14 women), 27 part-time (17 women); includes 3 Black or African American, non-Hispanic/Latino; 1 American Indian or Alaska Native, non-Hispanic/Latino; 10 Hispanic/Latino. Average age 37. 70 applicants, 23% accepted, 16 enrolled. In 2010, 8 master's awarded. *Degree requirements:* For master's, comprehensive exam. *Entrance requirements:* For master's, GRE General Test, minimum undergraduate GPA of 3.0, writing sample, 2 letters of recommendation. Additional exam requirements/recommendations for international students: Required—TOEFL (minimum score 550 paper-based; 80 iBT). *Application deadline:* For fall admission, 1/15 for domestic and international students. Application fee: $30. Electronic applications accepted. *Financial support:* Institutionally sponsored loans and scholarships/grants available. Financial award application deadline: 3/1; financial award applicants required to submit FAFSA. *Unit head:* Dr. James Sutton, Chair, English Department, 305-348-2874, Fax: 305-348-3778, E-mail: james.sutton@fiu.edu. *Application contact:* Dr. Kimberly Harrision, Director, 305-348-2874, Fax: 305-348-3778, E-mail: kimberly.harrison@fiu.edu.

Florida State University, The Graduate School, College of Arts and Sciences, Department of English, Tallahassee, FL 32312. Offers creative writing (MFA); English (PhD), including creative writing, literature, rhetoric and composition; literature (MA); rhetoric and composition (MA). Part-time programs available. *Faculty:* 48 full-time (23 women), 6 part-time/adjunct (1 woman). *Students:* 150 full-time (90 women), 20 part-time (10 women); includes 15 Black or African American, non-Hispanic/Latino; 1 American Indian or Alaska Native, non-Hispanic/Latino; 5 Asian, non-Hispanic/Latino; 10 Hispanic/Latino. Average age 30. 480 applicants, 21% accepted, 58 enrolled. In 2010, 22 master's, 14 doctorates awarded. *Degree requirements:* For master's, one foreign language, thesis or alternative; for doctorate, comprehensive exam, thesis/dissertation, 27 hours of coursework, 24 hours of dissertation work. *Entrance requirements:* For master's and doctorate, GRE General Test, GRE Subject Test (literature only), sample of written work, 3 letters of recommendation, resume. Additional exam requirements/recommendations for international students: Required—TOEFL. *Application deadline:* For fall admission, 1/1 priority date for domestic and international students. Application fee: $30. Electronic applications accepted. *Expenses:* Tuition, state resident: full-time $8238.24. *Financial support:* In 2010–11, 126 students received support, including 5 fellowships, teaching assistantships (averaging $11,375 per year); career-related internships or fieldwork, Federal Work-Study, and institutionally sponsored loans also available. Financial award application deadline: 1/1; financial award applicants required to submit FAFSA. *Faculty research:* British and Irish literature, American literature, creative writing, rhetoric and composition, multiethnic transnational literature. *Unit head:* Dr. Ralph Berry, Chairman, 850-644-4230, Fax: 850-644-0811, E-mail: rberry@fsu.edu. *Application contact:* Dr. Ralph Berry, Chairman, 850-644-4230, Fax: 850-644-0811, E-mail: rberry@fsu.edu.

Full Sail University, Creative Writing Master of Fine Arts Program—Online, Winter Park, FL 32792-7437. Offers MFA. Postbaccalaureate distance learning degree programs offered (no on-campus study).

George Mason University, College of Humanities and Social Sciences, Department of English, Program in Creative Writing, Fairfax, VA 22030. Offers MFA. *Faculty:* 8 full-time (5 women), 1 (woman) part-time/adjunct. *Students:* 33 full-time (21 women), 73 part-time (48 women);

Writing

George Mason University (continued)
includes 4 Black or African American, non-Hispanic/Latino; 1 American Indian or Alaska Native, non-Hispanic/Latino; 7 Asian, non-Hispanic/Latino; 3 Hispanic/Latino; 3 Two or more races, non-Hispanic/Latino, 2 international. Average age 30. 242 applicants, 51% accepted, 39 enrolled. In 2010, 41 master's awarded. *Degree requirements:* For master's, one foreign language, thesis, exam or project. *Entrance requirements:* For master's, minimum GPA of 3.0 in last 60 hours, portfolio, 2 letters of recommendation. Additional exam requirements/recommendations for international students: Required—TOEFL (minimum score 570 paper-based; 230 computer-based; 88 iBT). *Application deadline:* For fall admission, 1/2 priority date for domestic students. Application fee: $100. Electronic applications accepted. *Expenses:* Tuition, state resident: full-time $8192; part-time $440 per credit hour. Tuition, nonresident: full-time $22,952; part-time $1055 per credit hour. Required fees: $2364; $99 per credit hour. *Financial support:* In 2010–11, 42 students received support, including 4 research assistantships with full and partial tuition reimbursements available (averaging $11,739 per year), 39 teaching assistantships with full and partial tuition reimbursements available (averaging $11,128 per year); career-related internships or fieldwork, Federal Work-Study, scholarships/grants, unspecified assistantships, and health care benefits (full-time research or teaching assistantship recipients) also available. Support available to part-time students. Financial award application deadline: 3/1; financial award applicants required to submit FAFSA. *Faculty research:* British Romantic poetry and literary celebrity, Arab feminist novelists in the West, masculinity and African-American culture, public rhetoric and the South African Truth Commission, the origins of children's literature in eighteenth and nineteenth century Britain. *Unit head:* Denise Albanese, Graduate Director, Associate Professor, 703-993-1175, E-mail: dalbanes@gmu.edu. *Application contact:* Jennifer Stone, Graduate Programs Manager, 703-993-1180, E-mail: jstone22@gmu.edu.

Georgia College & State University, Graduate School, College of Arts and Sciences, Department of English and Rhetoric, Program in Creative Writing, Milledgeville, GA 31061. Offers MFA. Part-time and evening/weekend programs available. *Students:* 8 full-time (3 women), 19 part-time (13 women); includes 2 minority (1 Hispanic/Latino; 1 Two or more races, non-Hispanic/Latino). Average age 29. 54 applicants, 26% accepted, 9 enrolled. In 2010, 12 master's awarded. *Degree requirements:* For master's, one foreign language, thesis. *Entrance requirements:* For master's, GRE or MAT, writing portfolio, letters of recommendation. Additional exam requirements/recommendations for international students: Recommended—TOEFL (minimum score 550 paper-based; 213 computer-based; 79 iBT). *Application deadline:* For fall admission, 2/1 for domestic students. Application fee: $40. Electronic applications accepted. *Expenses:* Tuition, state resident: full-time $4806; part-time $267 per hour. Tuition, nonresident: full-time $17,802; part-time $989 per hour. Tuition and fees vary according to course load. *Financial support:* In 2010–11, 22 teaching assistantships with full tuition reimbursements were awarded; unspecified assistantships also available. Financial award applicants required to submit FAFSA. *Unit head:* Dr. Martin Lammon, Coordinator, 478-445-3508, E-mail: mfa@gcsu.edu. *Application contact:* Dr. Martin Lammon, Coordinator, 478-445-3508, E-mail: mfa@gcsu.edu.

Georgia State University, College of Arts and Sciences, Department of English, Program in Creative Writing, Atlanta, GA 30302-3083. Offers fiction/poetry (MA, MFA). Part-time programs available. *Degree requirements:* For master's, variable foreign language requirement, comprehensive exam, thesis; for doctorate, one foreign language, comprehensive exam, thesis/dissertation. *Entrance requirements:* For master's and doctorate, GRE General Test, portfolio. Additional exam requirements/recommendations for international students: Required—TOEFL (minimum score 0 paper-based; 0 computer-based). Electronic applications accepted. *Faculty research:* Poetry and fiction.

Goddard College, Graduate Division, Master of Fine Arts in Creative Writing Program, Plainfield, VT 05667-9432. Offers MFA. Program residency available in Plainfield, VT or Port Townsend, WA. Postbaccalaureate distance learning degree programs offered (minimal on-campus study). *Degree requirements:* For master's, thesis, completed manuscript, teaching practicum, 3 critical papers, reading of 45 to 60 literary works. *Entrance requirements:* For master's, 3 letters of recommendation, preliminary study plan and bibliography, creative writing sample or samples, current resume. Electronic applications accepted. *Expenses:* Contact institution.

Goucher College, Program in Creative Nonfiction, Baltimore, MD 21204-2794. Offers MFA. Part-time and evening/weekend programs available. Postbaccalaureate distance learning degree programs offered (minimal on-campus study). *Faculty:* 9 part-time/adjunct (4 women). *Students:* 41 full-time (28 women), 3 part-time (2 women); includes 2 Black or African American, non-Hispanic/Latino. Average age 40. In 2010, 16 master's awarded. *Degree requirements:* For master's, manuscript, portfolio. *Entrance requirements:* For master's, writing sample. *Application deadline:* For fall admission, 2/26 for domestic students. Applications are processed on a rolling basis. Application fee: $50. *Expenses:* Contact institution. *Financial support:* Career-related internships or fieldwork and institutionally sponsored loans available. Financial award application deadline: 3/15; financial award applicants required to submit FAFSA. *Unit head:* Patsy Sims, Director, 410-337-6200, Fax: 410-337-6085, E-mail: psims@goucher.edu. *Application contact:* Megan Cornett, Director of Marketing and Communications, 410-337-6200, Fax: 410-337-6085, E-mail: mcornett@goucher.edu.

Hamline University, Graduate School of Liberal Studies, St. Paul, MN 55104-1284. Offers liberal studies (MALS, CALS); writing (MFA); writing for children and young adults (MFA). Part-time and evening/weekend programs available. Postbaccalaureate distance learning degree programs offered (minimal on-campus study). *Faculty:* 6 full-time (4 women), 7 part-time/adjunct (5 women). *Students:* 94 full-time (76 women), 119 part-time (85 women); includes 8 minority (6 Black or African American, non-Hispanic/Latino; 1 American Indian or Alaska Native, non-Hispanic/Latino; 1 Hispanic/Latino), 1 international. Average age 37. 73 applicants, 70% accepted, 30 enrolled. In 2010, 60 master's awarded. *Degree requirements:* For master's, thesis. *Entrance requirements:* For master's, official transcripts, 20-page writing sample (MFA), letters of recommendation. *Application deadline:* For fall admission, 1/5 for domestic and international students; for spring admission, 9/1 for domestic and international students. Applications are processed on a rolling basis. Application fee: $0. Electronic applications accepted. *Expenses:* Contact institution. *Financial support:* Federal Work-Study and scholarships/grants available. Support available to part-time students. Financial award applicants required to submit FAFSA. *Unit head:* Mary Rockcastle, Dean, 651-523-2047, Fax: 651-523-2490, E-mail: mrockcastle@gw.hamline.edu. *Application contact:* Rae A. Lenway, Director, Graduate Recruitment and Admission, 651-523-2900, Fax: 651-523-3058, E-mail: rlenway01@gw.hamline.edu.

Hofstra University, College of Liberal Arts and Sciences, Department of English, Hempstead, NY 11549. Offers creative writing (MFA); English literature (MA). Part-time programs available. *Faculty:* 13 full-time (6 women), 1 part-time/adjunct (0 women). *Students:* 16 full-time (13 women), 15 part-time (12 women); includes 4 minority (2 Black or African American, non-Hispanic/Latino; 2 Hispanic/Latino). Average age 29. 33 applicants, 85% accepted, 8 enrolled. In 2010, 10 master's awarded. *Degree requirements:* For master's, thesis optional. *Entrance requirements:* For master's, Writing sample; Minimum GPA of 3.0 in literature courses. Additional exam requirements/recommendations for international students: Required—TOEFL (minimum score 550 paper-based; 213 computer-based; 80 iBT). *Application deadline:* Applications are processed on a rolling basis. Application fee: $70 ($75 for international students). Electronic applications accepted. *Expenses:* Tuition: Full-time $18,000; part-time $1000 per credit hour. Required fees: $970; $145 per term. Tuition and fees vary according to program. *Financial support:* In 2010–11, 10 students received support, including 2 fellowships with full and partial tuition reimbursements available (averaging $3,375 per year); research assistantships with full and partial tuition reimbursements available, Federal Work-Study, institutionally sponsored loans, scholarships/grants, and tuition waivers (full and partial) also available. Support available to part-time students. Financial award applicants required to submit FAFSA. *Faculty research:* Herman Melville, disability studies, early American literature, queer theory, trauma theory, critical theory, twentieth century popular culture, Jane Austen, Toni Morrison, John Milton, William Shakespeare, British Modernism, Renaissance studies, the long eighteenth century, Victorian literature. *Unit head:* Dr. Joseph A. Fichtelberg, Chairperson, 516-463-5455, Fax: 516-463-6395, E-mail: engjaf@hofstra.edu. *Application contact:* Carol Drummer, Dean of Graduate Admissions, 516-463-4876, Fax: 516-463-4664, E-mail: gradstudent@hofstra.edu.

Hofstra University, School of Education, Health, and Human Services, Department of Literacy Studies, Hempstead, NY 11549. Offers advanced literacy studies (PD), including birth-grade 6 (MA, MS Ed, PD); advanced literary studies (PD), including grades 5-12 (MA, MS Ed, PD); birth-grade 6 (MS Ed, CAS); grades 5-12 (CAS); literacy studies (MS Ed, Ed D, PhD), including birth-grade 6 (MA, MS Ed, PD), grades 5-12 (MA, MS Ed, PD); literacy studies and special education (MS Ed); special education (MS Ed), including birth-grade 2; teaching of writing (MA), including birth-grade 6 (MA, MS Ed, PD), grades 5-12 (MA, MS Ed, PD). Part-time and evening/weekend programs available. *Students:* 35 full-time (all women), 110 part-time (103 women); includes 11 Black or African American, non-Hispanic/Latino; 2 Asian, non-Hispanic/Latino; 9 Hispanic/Latino, 1 international. Average age 32. 71 applicants, 59% accepted, 32 enrolled. In 2010, 49 master's, 2 doctorates, 12 other advanced degrees awarded. *Degree requirements:* For master's, comprehensive exam, portfolio; for doctorate, one foreign language, comprehensive exam, thesis/dissertation, qualifying hearing. *Entrance requirements:* For master's, interview, teaching certificate, 2 letters of recommendation; for doctorate, GRE or MAT, interview, resume, essay, master's degree, 3 letters of recommendation, writing sample; for other advanced degree, 2 letters of recommendation, interview, teaching certificate, essay, master's degree. Additional exam requirements/recommendations for international students: Required—TOEFL (minimum score 550 paper-based; 213 computer-based; 80 iBT). *Application deadline:* Applications are processed on a rolling basis. Application fee: $70 ($75 for international students). Electronic applications accepted. *Expenses:* Tuition: Full-time $18,000; part-time $1000 per credit hour. Required fees: $970; $145 per term. Tuition and fees vary according to program. *Financial support:* In 2010–11, 78 students received support, including 26 fellowships with full and partial tuition reimbursements available (averaging $3,579 per year); research assistantships with full and partial tuition reimbursements available, career-related internships or fieldwork, Federal Work-Study, institutionally sponsored loans, scholarships/grants, tuition waivers (full and partial), unspecified assistantships, and scholarships also available. Support available to part-time students. Financial award applicants required to submit FAFSA. *Faculty research:* Research literacy practices of immigrant and urban youth, literature for children and adolescents, eye movement/miscue analysis, digital literacy, transnational literacies. *Unit head:* Dr. Esther Fusco, Chairperson, 516-463-7704, Fax: 516-463-6196, E-mail: catezf@hofstra.edu. *Application contact:* Carol Drummer, Dean of Graduate Admissions, 516-463-4876, Fax: 516-463-4664, E-mail: gradstudent@hofstra.edu.

Hollins University, Graduate Programs, Program in Creative Writing, Roanoke, VA 24020-1603. Offers MFA. *Degree requirements:* For master's, comprehensive exam, thesis. *Entrance requirements:* For master's, manuscripts, 3 letters of recommendation. Additional exam requirements/recommendations for international students: Required—TOEFL (minimum score 550 paper-based; 213 computer-based; 79 iBT). Electronic applications accepted. *Expenses:* Contact institution. *Faculty research:* Poetry, fiction, creative nonfiction, literary criticism, literary theory.

Holy Names University, Graduate Division, Masters of Creative Writing Program, Oakland, CA 94619-1699. Offers MA. *Expenses:* Tuition: Full-time $13,788; part-time $766 per credit. Required fees: $340; $170 per semester.

Hunter College of the City University of New York, Graduate School, School of Arts and Sciences, Department of English, Program in Creative Writing, New York, NY 10021-5085. Offers creative writing (MFA); fiction (MFA); nonfiction (MFA); poetry (MFA). Part-time and evening/weekend programs available. *Faculty:* 24 full-time (14 women), 1 part-time/adjunct (0 women). *Students:* 34 part-time (24 women); includes 4 Black or African American, non-Hispanic/Latino; 2 Hispanic/Latino, 4 international. Average age 29. 719 applicants, 2% accepted, 16 enrolled. In 2010, 17 master's awarded. *Degree requirements:* For master's, thesis. *Entrance requirements:* For master's, creative writing manuscript (up to 10 pages of poetry or 25-30 pages of fiction or nonfiction), nonfiction proposal (for nonfiction applicants only). *Application deadline:* For fall admission, 2/1 for domestic and international students. Application fee: $125. *Financial support:* In 2010–11, 18 students received support, including 12 fellowships (averaging $5,000 per year); Federal Work-Study and tuition waivers (partial) also available. Support available to part-time students. Financial award application deadline: 4/15. *Unit head:* Sue Nacey, Coordinator, 212-772-5164, Fax: 212-772-5076, E-mail: mfa@hunter.cuny.edu. *Application contact:* Elena Georgiou, Coordinator, 212-772-5164, Fax: 212-772-5076, E-mail: egeorgio@hunter.cuny.edu.

Hunter College of the City University of New York, Graduate School, School of Arts and Sciences, Department of Theatre, New York, NY 10021-5085. Offers playwriting (MFA); theatre (MA). Part-time and evening/weekend programs available. *Faculty:* 5 full-time (4 women), 1 part-time/adjunct (0 women). *Students:* 1 full-time (0 women), 41 part-time (27 women); includes 4 Black or African American, non-Hispanic/Latino; 3 Hispanic/Latino, 5 international. Average age 34. 18 applicants, 56% accepted, 7 enrolled. In 2010, 5 master's awarded. *Degree requirements:* For master's, comprehensive exam, thesis. *Entrance requirements:* For master's, GRE General Test. Additional exam requirements/recommendations for international students: Required—TOEFL. *Application deadline:* For fall admission, 4/1 for domestic students, 2/1 for international students; for spring admission, 11/1 for domestic students, 9/1 for international students. Application fee: $125. *Financial support:* In 2010–11, 1 fellowship (averaging $3,000 per year), 4 teaching assistantships were awarded; research assistantships, career-related internships or fieldwork, Federal Work-Study, and tuition waivers (partial) also available. Support available to part-time students. Financial award application deadline: 4/15. *Faculty research:* Modern French mimes, acting techniques, directing, New York avant-garde theater and popular entertainment, playwriting. *Unit head:* Dr. Barbara Bosch, Chairperson, 212-772-5148, Fax: 212-650-3584, E-mail: bbosch@hunter.cuny.edu. *Application contact:* Mira Felner, Graduate Advisor, 212-772-4642, E-mail: theatre@hunter.cuny.edu.

Illinois State University, Graduate School, College of Arts and Sciences, Department of English, Program in Writing, Normal, IL 61790-2200. Offers MA, MS. *Degree requirements:* For master's, comprehensive exam, internship or practicum. *Entrance requirements:* For master's, GRE General Test, minimum GPA of 3.0 in last 60 hours.

Indiana State University, College of Graduate and Professional Studies, College of Arts and Sciences, Department of English, Terre Haute, IN 47809. Offers English teaching (MA); history (MA); literature (MA). Part-time and evening/weekend programs available. *Degree requirements:* For master's, one foreign language, thesis optional. *Entrance requirements:* For master's, minimum GPA of 2.75 in all English courses above freshman level. Additional exam requirements/recommendations for international students: Required—TOEFL (minimum score 550 paper-based). Electronic applications accepted.

Indiana University Bloomington, University Graduate School, College of Arts and Sciences, Department of English, Bloomington, IN 47405. Offers composition, literacy, and culture (PhD); creative writing (MA, MFA), including fiction, poetry; language (MA); literature (MA, PhD); writing (MA). Part-time programs available. *Faculty:* 51 full-time (23 women). *Students:* 219 full-time (144 women), 6 part-time (4 women); includes 29 minority (6 Black or African American, non-Hispanic/Latino; 11 Asian, non-Hispanic/Latino; 8 Hispanic/Latino; 4 Two or more races, non-Hispanic/Latino), 8 international. Average age 30. 677 applicants, 8% accepted, 26 enrolled. In 2010, 31 master's, 16 doctorates awarded. Terminal master's awarded for partial completion of doctoral program. *Degree requirements:* For master's, 30-36 credit hours plus one language proficiency (for MA); 60 credit hours plus thesis (for MFA); for doctorate, one foreign language, thesis/dissertation, qualifying exam, 90 credit hours. *Entrance requirements:* For master's, GRE General Test, GRE Subject Test (for all but MFA and MA in creative writing), minimum GPA of 3.5; for doctorate, GRE General Test, GRE Subject Test, minimum GPA of 3.7. Additional exam requirements/recommendations for international students: Required—TOEFL.

Application deadline: For fall admission, 1/2 priority date for domestic students, 12/15 for international students. Application fee: $55 ($65 for international students). Electronic applications accepted. *Financial support:* In 2010–11, 8 fellowships with full and partial tuition reimbursements (averaging $15,000 per year), 96 teaching assistantships with full tuition reimbursements (averaging $15,142 per year) were awarded; research assistantships with partial tuition reimbursements, career-related internships or fieldwork and health care benefits also available. Financial award application deadline: 2/1. *Unit head:* Jonathan Elmer, Chair, 812-855-8225, Fax: 812-855-9535, E-mail: elmerj@indiana.edu. *Application contact:* Patricia Ingham, Director of Graduate Studies, 812-855-1543, Fax: 812-855-9535, E-mail: pingham@indiana.edu.

Indiana University of Pennsylvania, School of Graduate Studies and Research, College of Humanities and Social Sciences, Department of English, Program in Composition and Teaching English to Speakers of Other Languages, Indiana, PA 15705-1087. Offers composition and teaching English to speakers of other languages (PhD); teaching English (MAT); teaching English to speakers of other languages (MA). *Faculty:* 30 full-time (12 women). *Students:* 27 full-time (17 women), 135 part-time (86 women); includes 10 minority (3 Black or African American, non-Hispanic/Latino; 5 Asian, non-Hispanic/Latino; 2 Hispanic/Latino), 40 international. Average age 39. 152 applicants, 26% accepted, 17 enrolled. In 2010, 19 doctorates awarded. *Degree requirements:* For master's, thesis optional; for doctorate, one foreign language, comprehensive exam, thesis/dissertation. *Entrance requirements:* For master's and doctorate, 2 letters of recommendation. Additional exam requirements/recommendations for international students: Required—TOEFL. *Application deadline:* For fall admission, 7/1 priority date for domestic students; for spring admission, 11/1 for domestic students. Applications are processed on a rolling basis. Application fee: $40. *Financial support:* In 2010–11, 1 fellowship (averaging $1,000 per year), 21 research assistantships with full and partial tuition reimbursements (averaging $5,716 per year), 10 teaching assistantships with partial tuition reimbursements (averaging $12,936 per year) were awarded. Financial award application deadline: 3/15; financial award applicants required to submit FAFSA. *Unit head:* Dr. Ben Rafoth, Graduate Coordinator, 724-357-2272. *Application contact:* Dr. Ben Rafoth, Graduate Coordinator, 724-357-2272.

Iowa State University of Science and Technology, Graduate College, College of Liberal Arts and Sciences, Department of English, Ames, IA 50011. Offers creative writing (MFA); English (MA); rhetoric and professional communication (PhD). *Faculty:* 46 full-time (21 women), 9 part-time/adjunct (8 women). *Students:* 118 full-time (77 women), 45 part-time (32 women); includes 2 Black or African American, non-Hispanic/Latino; 1 Asian, non-Hispanic/Latino; 6 Hispanic/Latino, 36 international. 135 applicants, 56% accepted, 48 enrolled. In 2010, 27 master's, 5 doctorates awarded. *Degree requirements:* For master's, thesis or alternative; for doctorate, thesis/dissertation. *Entrance requirements:* For master's, GRE General Test, sample of written work, resume, portfolio in creative writing; for doctorate, GRE General Test, sample of written work, resume. Additional exam requirements/recommendations for international students: Required—TOEFL (minimum score 600 paper-based; 100 iBT), IELTS (minimum score 7). *Application deadline:* For fall admission, 1/5 priority date for domestic and international students. Application fee: $40 ($90 for international students). Electronic applications accepted. *Financial support:* In 2010–11, 7 research assistantships with full and partial tuition reimbursements (averaging $10,211 per year), 86 teaching assistantships with full and partial tuition reimbursements (averaging $13,238 per year) were awarded; fellowships, scholarships/grants, health care benefits, and unspecified assistantships also available. *Faculty research:* Creative writing, literature, rhetoric, composition and professional communication, teaching English as a second language, applied linguistics. *Unit head:* Dr. Charles Kostelnick, Chair, 515-294-2477, Fax: 515-294-2125, E-mail: englgrad@iastate.edu. *Application contact:* Dr. Constance Post, Director of Graduate Education, 515-294-3175, E-mail: englgrad@iastate.edu.

The Johns Hopkins University, Zanvyl Krieger School of Arts and Sciences, Advanced Academic Programs, Program in Writing, Baltimore, MD 21218-2699. Offers MA. Part-time and evening/weekend programs available. *Faculty:* 1 full-time (0 women), 19 part-time/adjunct (9 women). *Students:* 3 full-time (2 women), 167 part-time (119 women); includes 27 minority (11 Black or African American, non-Hispanic/Latino; 7 Asian, non-Hispanic/Latino; 3 Hispanic/Latino; 6 Two or more races, non-Hispanic/Latino), 3 international. Average age 36. 95 applicants, 54% accepted, 47 enrolled. In 2010, 37 master's awarded. *Degree requirements:* For master's, thesis. *Entrance requirements:* Additional exam requirements/recommendations for international students: Required—TOEFL (minimum score 600 paper-based; 250 computer-based; 100 iBT). *Application deadline:* For fall admission, 5/31 priority date for domestic students, 4/30 for international students; for spring admission, 10/31 priority date for domestic students, 10/31 for international students. Application fee: $75. *Financial support:* Applicants required to submit FAFSA. *Unit head:* Prof. David Everett, Associate Program Chair, 202-452-0758, Fax: 202-452-8713, E-mail: deverett@jhu.edu. *Application contact:* Valana M. McMickens, Admissions Manager, 202-452-1941, Fax: 202-452-1970, E-mail: aapadmissions@jhu.edu.

The Johns Hopkins University, Zanvyl Krieger School of Arts and Sciences, The Writing Seminars, Baltimore, MD 21218-2699. Offers fiction writing (MFA); poetry (MFA); science writing (MA). *Faculty:* 7 full-time (3 women), 1 (woman) part-time/adjunct. *Students:* 28 full-time (19 women); includes 2 Asian, non-Hispanic/Latino, 1 international. Average age 29. 273 applicants, 9% accepted, 17 enrolled. In 2010, 13 master's awarded. *Degree requirements:* For master's, one foreign language, thesis, foreign language exam (MFA). *Entrance requirements:* For master's, GRE General Test, GRE Subject Test (recommended), foreign language exam, sample of written work, 3 letters of recommendation, transcripts of all college/university course work. Additional exam requirements/recommendations for international students: Required—TOEFL (minimum score 600 paper-based; 250 computer-based; 100 iBT). *Application deadline:* For fall admission, 1/15 for domestic and international students. Application fee: $75. Electronic applications accepted. *Financial support:* In 2010–11, 24 students received support, including 1 fellowship (averaging $5,000 per year), 1 research assistantship with full tuition reimbursement available (averaging $18,900 per year), 22 teaching assistantships with full tuition reimbursements available (averaging $18,900 per year); Federal Work-Study, institutionally sponsored loans, scholarships/grants, health care benefits, tuition waivers (partial), and two teaching assistantships with $5000 stipend and full tuition also available. Financial award application deadline: 3/1; financial award applicants required to submit FAFSA. *Faculty research:* Contemporary fiction and poetry, film history, literary criticism, psychoanalysis. *Unit head:* Jean McGarry, Professor and Co-Chair, 410-516-5276, Fax: 410-516-6828, E-mail: mcgarry@jhu.edu. *Application contact:* Gina Woloszyn, Application Contact, 410-516-6286, Fax: 410-516-6828, E-mail: regina@jhu.edu.

Kean University, College of Humanities and Social Sciences, Program in English Writing, Union, NJ 07083. Offers MA. Part-time and evening/weekend programs available. *Faculty:* 21 full-time (11 women). *Students:* 3 full-time (1 woman), 8 part-time (6 women); includes 2 Black or African American, non-Hispanic/Latino; 2 Asian, non-Hispanic/Latino; 1 Hispanic/Latino. Average age 28. 9 applicants, 100% accepted, 7 enrolled. *Degree requirements:* For master's, thesis. *Entrance requirements:* For master's, GRE General Test, minimum GPA of 3.0, 12 credits in English or related area, 2 letters of recommendation, transcripts, interview. *Application deadline:* For fall admission, 6/1 for domestic students; for spring admission, 11/1 for domestic students. Application fee: $75 ($150 for international students). Electronic applications accepted. *Expenses:* Tuition, state resident: full-time $10,872; part-time $500 per credit. Tuition, nonresident: full-time $14,736; part-time $614 per credit. Required fees: $2740.80; $125 per credit. Part-time tuition and fees vary according to course load and degree level. *Financial support:* In 2010–11, 3 research assistantships with full tuition reimbursements (averaging $3,263 per year) were awarded; unspecified assistantships also available. Financial award applicants required to submit FAFSA. *Unit head:* Dr. Sarah Chandler, Program Coordinator, 908-737-0377, E-mail: schandler@kean.edu. *Application contact:* Ann-Marie Kay, Assistant Director of Graduate Admissions, 908-737-5922, Fax: 908-737-5925, E-mail: akay@kean.edu.

Kennesaw State University, College of Humanities and Social Sciences, Program in Professional Writing, Kennesaw, GA 30144-5591. Offers MAPW. Part-time and evening/weekend programs available. *Students:* 29 full-time (20 women), 66 part-time (50 women); includes 22 minority (16 Black or African American, non-Hispanic/Latino; 1 American Indian or Alaska Native, non-Hispanic/Latino; 1 Asian, non-Hispanic/Latino; 1 Hispanic/Latino; 1 Native Hawaiian or other Pacific Islander, non-Hispanic/Latino; 2 Two or more races, non-Hispanic/Latino). Average age 37. 57 applicants, 63% accepted, 30 enrolled. In 2010, 30 master's awarded. *Entrance requirements:* For master's, GRE General Test, minimum GPA of 2.5, writing sample. Additional exam requirements/recommendations for international students: Required—TOEFL (minimum score 550 paper-based; 213 computer-based; 80 iBT), IELTS (minimum score 6). *Application deadline:* For fall admission, 2/1 for domestic and international students. Application fee: $60. Electronic applications accepted. *Expenses:* Tuition, state resident: full-time $5500; part-time $225 per credit hour. Tuition, nonresident: full-time $16,100; part-time $813 per credit hour. Required fees: $673 per semester. *Financial support:* In 2010–11, 2 research assistantships with full tuition reimbursements (averaging $4,000 per year) were awarded; Federal Work-Study also available. Support available to part-time students. Financial award application deadline: 6/15; financial award applicants required to submit FAFSA. *Unit head:* Dr. Jim Elledge, Director, 678-797-2039, E-mail: jellege1@kennesaw.edu. *Application contact:* Tamara Hutto, Admissions Counselor, 770-420-4377, Fax: 770-423-6885, E-mail: ksugrad@kennesaw.edu.

Kent State University, College of Arts and Sciences, Department of English, Kent, OH 44242-0001. Offers comparative literature (MA); creative writing (MFA); English (PhD); English for teachers (MA); literature and writing (MA); rhetoric and composition (PhD); teaching English as a second language (MA). MFA program offered jointly with Cleveland State University, The University of Akron, and Youngstown State University. Part-time programs available. Terminal master's awarded for partial completion of doctoral program. *Degree requirements:* For master's, one foreign language, thesis optional; for doctorate, one foreign language, thesis/dissertation, qualifying exams. *Entrance requirements:* For master's and doctorate, GRE General Test, writing sample, letters of recommendation. Additional exam requirements/recommendations for international students: Required—TOEFL (minimum score 600 paper-based). Electronic applications accepted. *Expenses:* Tuition, state resident: full-time $7866; part-time $437 per credit hour. Tuition, nonresident: full-time $14,022; part-time $779 per credit hour. *Faculty research:* British and American literature, textual editing, rhetoric and composition, cultural studies, linguistic and critical theories.

La Sierra University, College of Arts and Sciences, Department of English and Communication, Riverside, CA 92515. Offers communication (MA), including public relations/advertising, theory emphasis; English (MA), including literary emphasis, writing emphasis. Part-time programs available. *Degree requirements:* For master's, one foreign language. *Entrance requirements:* For master's, GRE General Test.

Lesley University, Graduate School of Arts and Social Sciences, Program in Creative Writing, Cambridge, MA 02138-2790. Offers MFA. Part-time programs available. Postbaccalaureate distance learning degree programs offered (minimal on-campus study). *Degree requirements:* For master's, intensive residency. *Entrance requirements:* For master's, writing sample. Additional exam requirements/recommendations for international students: Required—TOEFL (minimum score 550 paper-based; 213 computer-based; 80 iBT). *Expenses:* Contact institution.

Lindenwood University, Graduate Programs, College of Individualized Education, St. Charles, MO 63301-1695. Offers administration (MSA); business administration (MBA); communications (MA); criminal justice and administration (MS); gerontology (MA); health management (MS); human resource management (MS); information technology (MBA, Certificate); managing information technology (MS); writing (MFA). Part-time and evening/weekend programs available. *Faculty:* 15 full-time (8 women), 128 part-time/adjunct (53 women). *Students:* 828 full-time (527 women), 80 part-time (50 women); includes 284 minority (265 Black or African American, non-Hispanic/Latino; 3 American Indian or Alaska Native, non-Hispanic/Latino; 6 Asian, non-Hispanic/Latino; 10 Hispanic/Latino), 23 international. Average age 35. 223 applicants, 44% accepted, 87 enrolled. In 2010, 478 master's awarded. *Degree requirements:* For master's, thesis (for some programs), 1 colloquium per term. *Entrance requirements:* For master's, interview, minimum GPA of 3.0. Additional exam requirements/recommendations for international students: Required—TOEFL (minimum score 550 paper-based; 213 computer-based; 80 iBT). *Application deadline:* For fall admission, 10/2 priority date for domestic and international students; for winter admission, 1/8 priority date for domestic and international students; for spring admission, 4/8 priority date for domestic and international students. Applications are processed on a rolling basis. Application fee: $30 ($100 for international students). Electronic applications accepted. *Expenses:* Tuition: Full-time $13,260; part-time $380 per credit hour. Required fees: $340. One-time fee: $30. Tuition and fees vary according to course level and course load. *Financial support:* In 2010–11, 631 students received support. Career-related internships or fieldwork, institutionally sponsored loans, tuition waivers (partial), and unspecified assistantships available. Financial award application deadline: 6/30; financial award applicants required to submit FAFSA. *Unit head:* Dan Kemper, Dean, 636-949-4501, Fax: 636-949-4505, E-mail: dkemper@lindenwood.edu. *Application contact:* Brett Barger, Dean of Evening Admissions and Extension Campuses, 636-949-4934, Fax: 636-949-4109, E-mail: adultadmissions@lindenwood.edu.

Long Island University, Brooklyn Campus, Richard L. Conolly College of Liberal Arts and Sciences, Department of English, Brooklyn, NY 11201-8423. Offers creative writing (MFA); literature (MA); professional writing (MA); writing and rhetoric (MA). Part-time and evening/weekend programs available. *Degree requirements:* For master's, thesis or alternative. *Entrance requirements:* For master's, 2 letters of recommendation (at least 1 from a former professor or teacher). Additional exam requirements/recommendations for international students: Required—TOEFL (minimum score 550 paper-based; 173 computer-based). Electronic applications accepted.

Longwood University, Office of Graduate Studies, Department of English and Modern Languages, Farmville, VA 23909. Offers 6-12 initial teaching/licensure (MA); creative writing (MA); English education and writing (MA); literature (MA). Part-time programs available. *Degree requirements:* For master's, comprehensive exam (for some programs), thesis (for some programs). *Entrance requirements:* For master's, minimum GPA of 2.75. Additional exam requirements/recommendations for international students: Required—TOEFL (minimum score 550 paper-based; 213 computer-based).

Louisiana State University and Agricultural and Mechanical College, Graduate School, College of Humanities and Social Sciences, Department of English, Baton Rouge, LA 70803. Offers creative writing (MFA); English (MA, PhD). Part-time programs available. *Faculty:* 49 full-time (21 women), 1 (woman) part-time/adjunct. *Students:* 77 full-time (44 women), 9 part-time (4 women); includes 2 Black or African American, non-Hispanic/Latino; 1 Asian, non-Hispanic/Latino; 3 Hispanic/Latino; 2 Two or more races, non-Hispanic/Latino, 5 international. Average age 31. 302 applicants, 10% accepted, 19 enrolled. In 2010, 10 master's, 7 doctorates awarded. Terminal master's awarded for partial completion of doctoral program. *Degree requirements:* For master's, comprehensive exam; for doctorate, one foreign language, comprehensive exam, thesis/dissertation. *Entrance requirements:* For master's, GRE General Test, minimum GPA of 3.0; for doctorate, GRE General Test, GRE Subject Test, minimum GPA of 3.0. Additional exam requirements/recommendations for international students: Required—TOEFL (minimum score 550 paper-based; 213 computer-based; 79 iBT) or IELTS (minimum score 6.5). *Application deadline:* For fall admission, 5/15 priority date for domestic students, 5/15 for international students; for spring admission, 10/15 priority date for domestic students, 10/15 for international students. Applications are processed on a rolling basis. Application fee: $50 ($70 for international students). Electronic applications accepted. *Financial support:* In 2010–11, 80 students received support, including 1 fellowship with full tuition reimbursement available (averaging $13,435 per year), 5 research assistantships with partial tuition reimbursements available (averaging $17,000 per year), 70 teaching assistantships with partial tuition reimbursements available (averaging $16,764 per year); career-related internships or fieldwork, Federal Work-Study, traineeships, and health care benefits also available. Financial award application deadline: 2/1; financial award applicants required to submit FAFSA. *Faculty research:*

Writing

Louisiana State University and Agricultural and Mechanical College (continued)

American literature, British literature, cultural studies, rhetoric and composition, folklore. Total annual research expenditures: $214,726. *Unit head:* Dr. Richard Morland, Chair, 225-578-0812, Fax: 225-578-2214, E-mail: english@lsu.edu. *Application contact:* Dr. Sharon Weltman, Director of Graduate Studies, 225-578-0812, Fax: 225-578-4129, E-mail: egs@lsu.edu.

Loyola Marymount University, School of Film and Television, Department of Screenwriting, Program in Screen Writing, Los Angeles, CA 90045-8347. Offers MFA. *Faculty:* 6 full-time (3 women), 2 part-time/adjunct (1 woman). *Students:* 32 full-time (13 women), 1 part-time (0 women); includes 3 Black or African American, non-Hispanic/Latino; 1 American Indian or Alaska Native, non-Hispanic/Latino; 6 Hispanic/Latino; 1 Two or more races, non-Hispanic/Latino, 7 international. Average age 26. 56 applicants, 57% accepted, 10 enrolled. In 2010, 7 master's awarded. *Degree requirements:* For master's, thesis, project or script. *Entrance requirements:* For master's, GRE General Test, writing sample, 2 letters of recommendation, personal statement. Additional exam requirements/recommendations for international students: Required—TOEFL (minimum score 600 paper-based; 250 computer-based; 100 iBT). *Application deadline:* For fall admission, 2/15 for domestic students. Application fee: $50. Electronic applications accepted. *Financial support:* In 2010–11, 29 students received support, including 3 research assistantships (averaging $1,200 per year); career-related internships or fieldwork and scholarships/grants also available. Support available to part-time students. Financial award application deadline: 6/1; financial award applicants required to submit FAFSA. *Unit head:* Kennedy Wheatley, Chair, 310-338-7834. *Application contact:* Chake H. Kouyoumjian, Associate Dean of Graduate Admissions, 310-338-2721, Fax: 310-338-6086, E-mail: ckouyoum@lmu.edu.

Manhattanville College, Graduate Programs, Humanities and Social Sciences Programs, Program in Writing, Purchase, NY 10577-2132. Offers MA. Part-time and evening/weekend programs available. *Students:* 1 full-time (0 women), 41 part-time (26 women); includes 1 Asian, non-Hispanic/Latino; 2 Hispanic/Latino. In 2010, 17 master's awarded. *Degree requirements:* For master's, thesis. *Entrance requirements:* For master's, interview, 2 letters of recommendation. Additional exam requirements/recommendations for international students: Required—TOEFL. *Application deadline:* Applications are processed on a rolling basis. Application fee: $75. *Expenses:* Tuition: Full-time $16,110; part-time $895 per credit. Required fees: $50 per semester. *Financial support:* Career-related internships or fieldwork, Federal Work-Study, institutionally sponsored loans, and unspecified assistantships available. Financial award application deadline: 3/1; financial award applicants required to submit FAFSA. *Faculty research:* Published writers: fiction, poetry, essay. *Unit head:* Karen Sirabian, Dean Emeritus, 914-694-5239, Fax: 914-694-2200, E-mail: sirabiank@mville.edu. *Application contact:* Office of Admissions for Graduate and Professional Studies, 914-323-5418, E-mail: gps@mville.edu.

Massachusetts Institute of Technology, School of Humanities, Arts, and Social Sciences, Program in Science Writing, Cambridge, MA 02139-4307. Offers SM. *Faculty:* 10 full-time (2 women). *Students:* 7 full-time (6 women); includes 1 minority (Two or more races, non-Hispanic/Latino), 1 international. Average age 23. 59 applicants, 19% accepted, 7 enrolled. In 2010, 7 master's awarded. *Degree requirements:* For master's, thesis, internship. *Entrance requirements:* For master's, GRE General Test. Additional exam requirements/recommendations for international students: Required—TOEFL (minimum score 600 paper-based; 250 computer-based), IELTS (minimum score 7.5). *Application deadline:* For fall admission, 1/15 for domestic and international students. Application fee: $75. Electronic applications accepted. *Expenses:* Tuition: Full-time $38,940; part-time $605 per unit. Required fees: $272. *Financial support:* In 2010–11, 7 students received support, including 7 fellowships with tuition reimbursements available (averaging $13,270 per year); teaching assistantships with tuition reimbursements available, career-related internships or fieldwork, Federal Work-Study, institutionally sponsored loans, scholarships/grants, health care benefits, and unspecified assistantships also available. Total annual research expenditures: $11,000. *Unit head:* Prof. Thomas Levenson, Program Head, 617-253-6668. *Application contact:* Science Writing Graduate Admissions, 617-253-6668, Fax: 617-452-5100, E-mail: sciwrite-www@mit.edu.

McNeese State University, Doré School of Graduate Studies, College of Liberal Arts, Department of English and Foreign Languages, Program in Creative Writing, Lake Charles, LA 70609. Offers MFA. Evening/weekend programs available. *Faculty:* 14 full-time (9 women). *Students:* 19 full-time (9 women); includes 3 minority (1 Black or African American, non-Hispanic/Latino; 2 Asian, non-Hispanic/Latino). In 2010, 11 master's awarded. *Degree requirements:* For master's, thesis, public reading. *Entrance requirements:* For master's, GRE, writing sample. *Application deadline:* For fall admission, 5/15 priority date for domestic and international students; for spring admission, 10/15 priority date for domestic and international students. Applications are processed on a rolling basis. Application fee: $20 ($30 for international students). Tuition and fees vary according to course load. *Financial support:* Teaching assistantships available. Financial award application deadline: 5/1. *Unit head:* Dr. Jacob D. Blevins, Head, 337-475-5325, Fax: 337-475-5327, E-mail: jblevins@mcneese.edu. *Application contact:* Dr. George F. Mead, Interim Dean of Dore' School of Graduate Studies, 337-475-5396, Fax: 337-475-5397, E-mail: admissions@mcneese.edu.

Michigan State University, The Graduate School, College of Arts and Letters, Program in Rhetoric and Writing, East Lansing, MI 48824. Offers critical studies in literacy and pedagogy (MA); digital rhetoric and professional writing (MA); rhetoric and writing (PhD). *Entrance requirements:* Additional exam requirements/recommendations for international students: Required—TOEFL. Electronic applications accepted. *Faculty research:* Rhetoric, writing and communication studies; media studies; technical communication, writing for digital environments.

Mills College, Graduate Studies, Department of English, Oakland, CA 94613-1000. Offers book art and creative writing (MFA); creative writing, poetry (MFA); creative writing, prose (MFA); English and American literature (MA). Part-time programs available. *Faculty:* 14 full-time (11 women), 15 part-time/adjunct (12 women). *Students:* 94 full-time (81 women), 2 part-time (both women); includes 8 Black or African American, non-Hispanic/Latino; 4 Asian, non-Hispanic/Latino; 7 Hispanic/Latino; 1 Native Hawaiian or other Pacific Islander, non-Hispanic/Latino; 1 Two or more races, non-Hispanic/Latino. Average age 31. 155 applicants, 88% accepted, 48 enrolled. In 2010, 63 master's awarded. *Degree requirements:* For master's, comprehensive exam, thesis. *Entrance requirements:* For master's, manuscript, writing sample. Additional exam requirements/recommendations for international students: Required—TOEFL (minimum score 600 paper-based; 250 computer-based; 100 iBT), IELTS (minimum score 7). *Application deadline:* For fall admission, 12/15 priority date for domestic students, 12/15 for international students. Applications are processed on a rolling basis. Application fee: $50. Electronic applications accepted. *Expenses:* Tuition: Full-time $28,280; part-time $7070 per course. Required fees: $1058; $1058 per year. Tuition and fees vary according to program. *Financial support:* In 2010–11, 120 fellowships (averaging $5,723 per year), 37 teaching assistantships with partial tuition reimbursements (averaging $3,081 per year) were awarded; scholarships/grants also available. Support available to part-time students. Financial award application deadline: 2/1; financial award applicants required to submit FAFSA. *Faculty research:* Creative writing, African-American literature, Victorian women writers, theories of sexuality, Shakespeare. *Unit head:* Dr. Cynthia Scheinberg, Chair, 510-430-2213, E-mail: cyns@mills.edu. *Application contact:* Jessica King, Graduate Admission Specialist, 510-430-3305, Fax: 510-430-2159, E-mail: grad-studies@mills.edu.

Mills College, Graduate Studies, Program in Book Art and Creative Writing, Oakland, CA 94613-1000. Offers MFA. *Faculty:* 1 (woman) full-time, 1 (woman) part-time/adjunct. *Students:* 6 full-time (5 women). 22 applicants, 59% accepted, 5 enrolled. *Degree requirements:* For master's, thesis project. *Application deadline:* For fall admission, 12/15 priority date for domestic students, 12/15 for international students. *Expenses:* Tuition: Full-time $28,280; part-time $7070 per course. Required fees: $1058; $1058 per year. Tuition and fees vary according to program. *Financial support:* In 2010–11, 9 fellowships (averaging $6,167 per year), 3 teaching assistantships (averaging $3,000 per year) were awarded. *Unit head:* Carol Langlois, Administrative Dean for Graduate Recruitment and Enrollment, 510-430-3118, Fax: 510-430-2159, E-mail: clangloi@mills.edu. *Application contact:* Jessica King, Graduate Admission Specialist, 510-430-3305, Fax: 510-430-2159, E-mail: grad-studies@mills.edu.

Minnesota State University Mankato, College of Graduate Studies, College of Arts and Humanities, Department of English, Mankato, MN 56001. Offers creative writing (MFA); English (MAT); English studies (MA); teaching English as a second language (MA, Certificate); technical communication (MA, Certificate). Part-time programs available. *Students:* 46 full-time (28 women), 147 part-time (97 women). *Degree requirements:* For master's, one foreign language, comprehensive exam, thesis or alternative. *Entrance requirements:* For master's, minimum GPA of 3.0 during previous 2 years, writing sample (MFA). Additional exam requirements/recommendations for international students: Required—TOEFL (minimum score 500 paper-based; 61 iBT). *Application deadline:* For fall admission, 7/1 for domestic students, 5/1 for international students. Applications are processed on a rolling basis. Application fee: $40. Electronic applications accepted. *Financial support:* Research assistantships with full tuition reimbursements, teaching assistantships with full tuition reimbursements, career-related internships or fieldwork, Federal Work-Study, and unspecified assistantships available. Financial award application deadline: 3/15; financial award applicants required to submit FAFSA. *Faculty research:* Keats and Christianity. *Unit head:* Dr. John Banschbach, Chairperson, 507-389-2117. *Application contact:* 507-389-2321, E-mail: grad@mnsu.edu.

Minnesota State University Moorhead, Graduate Studies, College of Arts and Humanities, Program in Creative Writing, Moorhead, MN 56563-0002. Offers MFA. Part-time programs available. *Degree requirements:* For master's, thesis, final manuscript, final oral exam. *Entrance requirements:* For master's, manuscript, minimum GPA of 2.75, 3 letters of recommendation. Additional exam requirements/recommendations for international students: Required—TOEFL (minimum score 550 paper-based; 213 computer-based). Electronic applications accepted.

Missouri Western State University, Program in Written Communication, St. Joseph, MO 64507-2294. Offers technical communication (MAS); writing studies (MAS). *Expenses:* Tuition, state resident: full-time $5544; part-time $308 per credit hour. Tuition, nonresident: full-time $10,206; part-time $567 per credit hour. Required fees: $30 per semester. One-time fee: $45 full-time.

Monmouth University, The Graduate School, Department of English, West Long Branch, NJ 07764-1898. Offers creative writing (MA); New Jersey studies (MA); rhetoric and writing (MA). Part-time and evening/weekend programs available. *Faculty:* 12 full-time (8 women). *Students:* 9 full-time (7 women), 30 part-time (21 women); includes 1 Black or African American, non-Hispanic/Latino; 1 Asian, non-Hispanic/Latino; 1 Hispanic/Latino. Average age 32. 30 applicants, 93% accepted, 14 enrolled. In 2010, 9 master's awarded. *Degree requirements:* For master's, comprehensive exam (for some programs), thesis (for some programs). *Entrance requirements:* For master's, minimum overall GPA of 2.75, at least 15 credits in literary studies. Additional exam requirements/recommendations for international students: Required—TOEFL (minimum score 550 paper-based; 213 computer-based; 79 iBT), IELTS (minimum score 5), Michigan English Language Assessment Battery (minimum score 77), Cambridge A, B, C. *Application deadline:* For fall admission, 7/15 for domestic students, 6/1 for international students; for spring admission, 11/15 for domestic students, 11/1 for international students. Application fee: $50. *Expenses:* Tuition: Full-time $19,572; part-time $816 per credit. Required fees: $628; $157 per semester. *Financial support:* In 2010–11, 28 students received support, including 28 fellowships (averaging $1,689 per year), 5 research assistantships (averaging $4,502 per year); career-related internships or fieldwork, scholarships/grants, and unspecified assistantships also available. Support available to part-time students. Financial award applicants required to submit FAFSA. *Faculty research:* Renaissance and medieval literature, nineteenth century American literature, eighteenth century British literature and women's studies, Old English and Middle English, African diaspora and African post-colonial literature. *Unit head:* Dr. Hiede Estes, Program Director, 732-571-7547, E-mail: hestes@monmouth.edu. *Application contact:* Kevin Roane, Director, Office of Graduate Admission, 732-571-3452, Fax: 732-263-5123, E-mail: gradadm@monmouth.edu.

Montclair State University, The Graduate School, College of Humanities and Social Sciences, Department of English, Montclair, NJ 07043-1624. Offers elementary school specialization: language arts/literature 5-9 (Certificate); English (MA); teaching writing (Certificate). Part-time and evening/weekend programs available. *Faculty:* 45 full-time (29 women), 55 part-time/adjunct (39 women). *Students:* 16 full-time (11 women), 60 part-time (48 women); includes 1 Asian, non-Hispanic/Latino; 3 Hispanic/Latino, 1 international. Average age 34. 34 applicants, 68% accepted, 18 enrolled. In 2010, 11 master's, 2 other advanced degrees awarded. *Degree requirements:* For master's, thesis. *Entrance requirements:* For master's, GRE General Test, 2 letters of recommendation. Additional exam requirements/recommendations for international students: Required—TOEFL (minimum score: 83 iBT) or IELTS. *Application deadline:* For fall admission, 6/1 for international students; for spring admission, 10/1 for international students. Applications are processed on a rolling basis. Application fee: $60. Electronic applications accepted. *Expenses:* Tuition, state resident: part-time $501.34 per credit. Tuition, nonresident: part-time $773.88 per credit. Required fees: $71.15 per credit. *Financial support:* In 2010–11, 8 research assistantships with full tuition reimbursements (averaging $7,000 per year) were awarded; Federal Work-Study, scholarships/grants, and unspecified assistantships also available. Support available to part-time students. Financial award application deadline: 3/1; financial award applicants required to submit FAFSA. *Faculty research:* Modernism, Shakespeare, Victorian poetry, contemporary European film, nineteenth century American literature. *Unit head:* Dr. Dan Bronson, Chairperson, 973-655-4274. *Application contact:* Amy Aiello, Director of Graduate Admissions and Operations, 973-655-5147, Fax: 973-655-7869, E-mail: graduate.school@montclair.edu.

Murray State University, College of Humanities and Fine Arts, Department of English and Philosophy, Program in Creative Writing, Murray, KY 42071. Offers MFA.

Naropa University, Graduate Programs, Program in Creative Writing, Boulder, CO 80302-6697. Offers MFA. Program is offered online only. Part-time and evening/weekend programs available. Postbaccalaureate distance learning degree programs offered (minimal on-campus study). *Faculty:* 6 full-time (2 women), 9 part-time/adjunct (6 women). *Students:* 9 full-time (6 women), 19 part-time (11 women); includes 4 minority (2 Black or African American, non-Hispanic/Latino; 1 American Indian or Alaska Native, non-Hispanic/Latino; 1 Hispanic/Latino), 1 international. Average age 39. 32 applicants, 59% accepted, 5 enrolled. In 2010, 12 master's awarded. *Degree requirements:* For master's, manuscript. *Entrance requirements:* For master's, manuscript/writing sample; resume, 3 letters of recommendation, letter of interest, technology check list. Additional exam requirements/recommendations for international students: Required—TOEFL (minimum score 600 paper-based; 250 computer-based). *Application deadline:* For fall admission, 1/15 priority date for domestic and international students; for spring admission, 10/15 for domestic students, 10/15 priority date for international students. Applications are processed on a rolling basis. Application fee: $60. Electronic applications accepted. *Expenses:* Tuition: Full-time $17,820; part-time $810 per credit. Required fees: $305 per semester. Tuition and fees vary according to course load, program and reciprocity agreements. *Financial support:* In 2010–11, 3 students received support, including research assistantships with partial tuition reimbursements available (averaging $3,000 per year), 1 teaching assistantship with partial tuition reimbursement available (averaging $3,000 per year); career-related internships or fieldwork, Federal Work-Study, scholarships/grants, health care benefits, tuition waivers (partial), and unspecified assistantships also available. Support available to part-time students. Financial award application deadline: 3/1; financial award applicants required to submit FAFSA. *Unit head:* Michelle Naka Pierce, Director, Jack Kerouac School of Disembodied Poetics, 303-245-4808, E-mail: michelle@naropa.edu. *Application contact:* Donna McIntyre, Associate Director of Graduate Admissions, 303-546-3555, Fax: 303-546-3583, E-mail: donna@naropa.edu.

Naropa University, Graduate Programs, Program in Writing and Poetics, Boulder, CO 80302-6697. Offers MFA. *Faculty:* 6 full-time (2 women), 9 part-time/adjunct (6 women). *Students:* 35

full-time (20 women), 10 part-time (8 women); includes 7 minority (1 Black or African American, non-Hispanic/Latino; 1 American Indian or Alaska Native, non-Hispanic/Latino; 3 Hispanic/Latino; 2 Two or more races, non-Hispanic/Latino), 1 international. Average age 28. 76 applicants, 86% accepted, 23 enrolled. In 2010, 20 master's awarded. *Degree requirements:* For master's, thesis. *Entrance requirements:* For master's, manuscript; resume, 3 letters of recommendation, statement of interest. Additional exam requirements/recommendations for international students: Required—TOEFL (minimum score 600 paper-based; 250 computer-based). *Application deadline:* For fall admission, 1/15 priority date for domestic and international students; for spring admission, 10/15 priority date for domestic and international students. Applications are processed on a rolling basis. Application fee: $60. Electronic applications accepted. *Expenses:* Tuition: Full-time $17,820; part-time $810 per credit. Required fees: $305 per semester. Tuition and fees vary according to course load, program and reciprocity agreements. *Financial support:* In 2010–11, 14 students received support, including 6 research assistantships with partial tuition reimbursements available (averaging $2,060 per year), 2 teaching assistantships with partial tuition reimbursements available (averaging $1,920 per year); career-related internships or fieldwork, Federal Work-Study, scholarships/grants, health care benefits, tuition waivers (partial), and unspecified assistantships also available. Support available to part-time students. Financial award application deadline: 3/1; financial award applicants required to submit FAFSA. *Unit head:* Michelle Naka Pierce, Director, Jack Kerouac School of Disembodied Poetics, 303-245-4808, E-mail: michelle@naropa.edu. *Application contact:* Donna McIntyre, Associate Director of Graduate Admissions, 303-546-3555, Fax: 303-546-3583, E-mail: donna@naropa.edu.

National-Louis University, College of Arts and Sciences, Chicago, IL 60603. Offers counseling and human services (MS); language and academic development (M Ed, Certificate); psychology (MA, PhD, Certificate); public policy (MA); written communication (MS, Certificate). Part-time and evening/weekend programs available. Postbaccalaureate distance learning degree programs offered (minimal on-campus study). *Students:* 29 full-time (22 women), 489 part-time (405 women); includes 186 minority (137 Black or African American, non-Hispanic/Latino; 8 Asian, non-Hispanic/Latino; 32 Hispanic/Latino; 9 Two or more races, non-Hispanic/Latino), 2 international. Average age 38. In 2010, 245 master's, 9 doctorates, 24 other advanced degrees awarded. *Degree requirements:* For master's and Certificate, comprehensive exam (for some programs), thesis (for some programs); for doctorate, thesis/dissertation. *Entrance requirements:* For master's, MAT or GRE, 3 professional or academic references, interview, minimum GPA of 3.0; for doctorate, GRE General Test, MAT, or Watson-Glaser Critical Thinking Appraisal, three professional or academic references, statement of academic and professional goals, 3 years of experience in field, interview, master's degree, resume, writing sample; for Certificate, GRE, MAT, or Watson-Glaser Critical Thinking Appraisal, three professional or academic references, statement of academic and professional goals, interview, minimum GPA of 3.0. Additional exam requirements/recommendations for international students: Required—Department of Language Studies Assessment or TOEFL (minimum score 550 paper-based; 213 computer-based; 79 iBT). *Application deadline:* Applications are processed on a rolling basis. Application fee: $40. Electronic applications accepted. *Financial support:* Career-related internships or fieldwork, Federal Work-Study, institutionally sponsored loans, scholarships/grants, and tuition waivers available. Support available to part-time students. Financial award applicants required to submit FAFSA. *Unit head:* Dr. Stephen Thompson, Interim Dean, 224-233-2539, Fax: 224-233-2539, E-mail: sthompson@nl.edu. *Application contact:* Dr. George Valcourt, Vice President of Enrollment and Student Services, 888-658-8632, Fax: 312-261-3550, E-mail: george.valcourt@nl.edu.

National University, Academic Affairs, College of Letters and Sciences, Department of Art and Humanities, La Jolla, CA 92037-1011. Offers creative writing (MFA); English (MA); history (MA). Part-time and evening/weekend programs available. Postbaccalaureate distance learning degree programs offered (no on-campus study). *Faculty:* 17 full-time (6 women), 198 part-time/adjunct (110 women). *Students:* 198 full-time (144 women), 534 part-time (364 women); includes 99 Black or African American, non-Hispanic/Latino; 6 American Indian or Alaska Native, non-Hispanic/Latino; 10 Asian, non-Hispanic/Latino; 54 Hispanic/Latino; 14 Two or more races, non-Hispanic/Latino. Average age 38. 424 applicants, 100% accepted, 289 enrolled. In 2010, 222 master's awarded. *Degree requirements:* For master's, thesis (for some programs). *Entrance requirements:* For master's, interview, minimum GPA of 2.5. Additional exam requirements/recommendations for international students: Required—TOEFL (minimum score 550 paper-based; 213 computer-based; 79 iBT), IELTS (minimum score 6). *Application deadline:* Applications are processed on a rolling basis. Application fee: $60 ($65 for international students). Electronic applications accepted. *Expenses:* Tuition: Full-time $9450; part-time $350 per unit. Required fees: $350 per unit. One-time fee: $60. *Financial support:* Career-related internships or fieldwork, institutionally sponsored loans, scholarships/grants, and tuition waivers (partial) available. Support available to part-time students. Financial award application deadline: 6/30; financial award applicants required to submit FAFSA. *Unit head:* Dr. Janet Baker, Chair, 858-642-8472, Fax: 858-642-8715, E-mail: jbaker@nu.edu. *Application contact:* Dominick Giovanniello, Associate Regional Dean—San Diego, 800-NAT-UNIV, Fax: 858-541-7792, E-mail: dgiovann@nu.edu.

New England College, Programs in Writing, Henniker, NH 03242-3293. Offers poetry (MFA); professional writing (MA). Part-time and evening/weekend programs available. Electronic applications accepted. *Faculty research:* Poetry collections.

New Mexico Highlands University, Graduate Studies, College of Arts and Sciences, Department of Humanities, Las Vegas, NM 87701. Offers English (MA), including creative writing, language, rhetoric and composition, literature. *Faculty:* 8 full-time (5 women). *Students:* 13 full-time (5 women), 2 part-time (both women); includes 1 Hispanic/Latino; 2 Two or more races, non-Hispanic/Latino. Average age 36. 10 applicants, 100% accepted, 7 enrolled. In 2010, 4 master's awarded. *Degree requirements:* For master's, comprehensive exam, thesis. *Entrance requirements:* For master's, minimum undergraduate GPA of 3.0. Additional exam requirements/recommendations for international students: Required—TOEFL (minimum score 540 paper-based; 207 computer-based). *Application deadline:* For fall admission, 8/1 priority date for domestic students. Applications are processed on a rolling basis. Application fee: $15. *Expenses:* Tuition, state resident: full-time $2544. Required fees: $624; $132 per credit hour. *Financial support:* In 2010–11, 11 students received support. Career-related internships or fieldwork, Federal Work-Study, institutionally sponsored loans, scholarships/grants, tuition waivers (full and partial), and unspecified assistantships available. Support available to part-time students. Financial award application deadline: 3/1; financial award applicants required to submit FAFSA. *Faculty research:* Twentieth century literature, life path writing in homeless shelters, native American philosophy, medieval intellectual and cultural history, creating pedagogical tools for teaching law. *Unit head:* Dr. Barbara Risch, Department Head, 505-454-3451, E-mail: barbararisch@nmhu.edu. *Application contact:* Diane Trujillo, Administrative Assistant, Graduate Studies, 505-454-3266, Fax: 505-426-2117, E-mail: dtrujillo@nmhu.edu.

New Mexico State University, Graduate School, College of Arts and Sciences, Department of English, Las Cruces, NM 88003-8001. Offers creative writing (MFA); English (MA); rhetoric and professional communication (PhD). Part-time programs available. *Faculty:* 22 full-time (13 women), 1 (woman) part-time/adjunct. *Students:* 71 full-time (39 women), 31 part-time (17 women); includes 22 minority (5 Black or African American, non-Hispanic/Latino; 2 Asian, non-Hispanic/Latino; 14 Hispanic/Latino; 1 Two or more races, non-Hispanic/Latino), 4 international. Average age 32. 109 applicants, 58% accepted, 27 enrolled. In 2010, 30 master's, 2 doctorates awarded. *Degree requirements:* For master's, one foreign language, thesis (for some programs); for doctorate, comprehensive exam, thesis/dissertation, internship. *Entrance requirements:* For master's and doctorate, sample of written work. Additional exam requirements/recommendations for international students: Required—TOEFL (minimum score 550 paper-based; 79 iBT), IELTS (minimum score 6.5). *Application deadline:* For fall admission, 2/1 for domestic and international students. Application fee: $30 ($50 for international students). Electronic applications accepted. *Expenses:* Tuition, state resident: full-time $4536; part-time $242 per credit. Tuition, nonresident: full-time $15,816; part-time $712 per credit. Required fees: $636 per term. *Financial support:* In 2010–11, 3 research assistantships (averaging $6,817 per year), 49 teaching assistantships (averaging $15,105 per year) were awarded; fellowships, career-related internships or fieldwork, Federal Work-Study, institutionally sponsored loans, scholarships/grants, health care benefits, and unspecified assistantships also available. Financial award application deadline: 2/1; financial award applicants required to submit FAFSA. *Faculty research:* Composition research, history and theory of rhetoric, technical/professional communication, creative writing, English and American literature. *Unit head:* Dr. Monica F. Torres, Head, 575-646-2319, Fax: 575-646-7725, E-mail: mftorres@nmsu.edu. *Application contact:* Dr. Elizabeth Schirmer, Director of Graduate Studies, 575-646-1733, E-mail: eschirme@nmsu.edu.

The New School: A University, The New School for General Studies, Program in Creative Writing, New York, NY 10011. Offers MFA. Evening/weekend programs available. *Degree requirements:* For master's, thesis, literature project. *Entrance requirements:* For master's, portfolio. Additional exam requirements/recommendations for international students: Required—TOEFL (minimum score 600 paper-based; 250 computer-based; 100 iBT). Electronic applications accepted. *Expenses:* Contact institution.

New York University, Graduate School of Arts and Science, Department of English, Program in Creative Writing, New York, NY 10012-1019. Offers MA, MFA. Part-time and evening/weekend programs available. *Students:* 84 full-time (53 women), 24 part-time (8 women); includes 2 Black or African American, non-Hispanic/Latino; 7 Asian, non-Hispanic/Latino; 4 Hispanic/Latino, 8 international. Average age 28. 798 applicants, 8% accepted, 43 enrolled. In 2010, 36 master's awarded. *Degree requirements:* For master's, one foreign language, thesis or alternative. *Entrance requirements:* For master's, GRE General Test, sample of written work. Additional exam requirements/recommendations for international students: Required—TOEFL. *Application deadline:* For fall admission, 12/15 for domestic students. Application fee: $90. *Financial support:* Fellowships with tuition reimbursements, teaching assistantships with tuition reimbursements, Federal Work-Study, institutionally sponsored loans, scholarships/grants, health care benefits, tuition waivers (full and partial), and unspecified assistantships available. Financial award application deadline: 12/15; financial award applicants required to submit FAFSA. *Faculty research:* Fiction, poetry. *Unit head:* Deborah Landau, Director, 212-998-8816, Fax: 212-995-4864, E-mail: creative.writing@nyu.edu. *Application contact:* Jessica Flynn, Program Coordinator, 212-998-8816, Fax: 212-995-4864, E-mail: creative.writing@nyu.edu.

New York University, NYU in Madrid, Madrid, NY 10012-1019, Spain. Offers creative writing in Spanish (MFA); Spanish (PhD); Spanish and Latin American literatures and cultures (MA); Spanish language and translation (MA).

New York University, Tisch School of the Arts Asia, Singapore, NY 248923, Singapore. Offers animation and digital arts (MFA); dramatic writing (MFA); film production (MFA). *Entrance requirements:* Additional exam requirements/recommendations for international students: Required—TOEFL (minimum score 610 paper-based; 250 computer-based; 105 iBT). Electronic applications accepted.

New York University, Tisch School of the Arts, Rita and Burton Goldberg Department of Dramatic Writing, New York, NY 10012-1019. Offers MFA. *Faculty:* 15 full-time, 16 part-time/adjunct. *Students:* 41 full-time (17 women); includes 6 Black or African American, non-Hispanic/Latino; 4 Asian, non-Hispanic/Latino; 2 Hispanic/Latino. Average age 30. 238 applicants, 15% accepted, 22 enrolled. In 2010, 20 master's awarded. *Degree requirements:* For master's, thesis, play or screenplay, internship. *Entrance requirements:* For master's, writing sample. Additional exam requirements/recommendations for international students: Required—TOEFL or IELTS. *Application deadline:* For fall admission, 12/1 for domestic and international students. Application fee: $60. Electronic applications accepted. *Financial support:* In 2010–11, 19 students received support, including 5 fellowships with full and partial tuition reimbursements available; career-related internships or fieldwork, Federal Work-Study, institutionally sponsored loans, and scholarships/grants also available. Financial award application deadline: 2/15; financial award applicants required to submit FAFSA. *Faculty research:* Craft of screenwriting film story analysis, production elements in film and theatre. *Unit head:* Dr. Richard Wesley, Chair, 212-998-1940, Fax: 212-995-4069. *Application contact:* Dan Sandford, Director of Graduate Admissions, 212-998-1918, Fax: 212-995-4060, E-mail: tisch.gradadmissions@nyu.edu.

North Carolina State University, Graduate School, College of Humanities and Social Sciences, Department of English, Program in Creative Writing, Raleigh, NC 27695. Offers MFA. *Degree requirements:* For master's, thesis optional. *Entrance requirements:* For master's, GRE. Electronic applications accepted. *Faculty research:* Science fiction, Asian poetry, translation, Southern writers, satiric fiction.

Northeastern Illinois University, Graduate College, College of Arts and Sciences, Department of English, Programs in English, Chicago, IL 60625-4699. Offers composition/writing (MA); literature (MA). Part-time and evening/weekend programs available. *Faculty:* 14 full-time (4 women). *Students:* 9 full-time (8 women), 32 part-time (21 women); includes 6 minority (1 Asian, non-Hispanic/Latino; 5 Hispanic/Latino). Average age 40. 25 applicants, 44% accepted. In 2010, 7 master's awarded. *Degree requirements:* For master's, comprehensive exam, thesis optional. *Entrance requirements:* For master's, 30 hours of undergraduate course work in literature and composition (literature), BA in English or approval (composition/writing), minimum GPA of 2.75. Additional exam requirements/recommendations for international students: Required—TOEFL (minimum score 550 paper-based; 213 computer-based; 79 iBT). *Application deadline:* Applications are processed on a rolling basis. Application fee: $30. Electronic applications accepted. *Financial support:* In 2010–11, 13 students received support, including 3 research assistantships with full tuition reimbursements available (averaging $6,600 per year); career-related internships or fieldwork, Federal Work-Study, institutionally sponsored loans, scholarships/grants, tuition waivers (full and partial), and unspecified assistantships also available. Support available to part-time students. Financial award applicants required to submit FAFSA. *Faculty research:* Arthurian literature, Southern American literature, rhetoric and theories of authorship. *Unit head:* Dr. Timothy R. Libretti, Graduate Adviser, 773-442-5820, Fax: 773-442-5490, E-mail: t-libretti@neiu.edu. *Application contact:* Dr. Timothy R. Libretti, Graduate Adviser, 773-442-5820, Fax: 773-442-5490, E-mail: t-libretti@neiu.edu.

Northern Arizona University, Graduate College, College of Arts and Letters, Department of English, Flagstaff, AZ 86011. Offers applied linguistics (PhD); English (MA), including creative writing, general English studies, literacy, technology and professional writing, literature, secondary English education; professional writing (Certificate); teaching English as a second language (MA, Certificate). Part-time programs available. *Faculty:* 42 full-time (30 women). *Students:* 107 full-time (70 women), 100 part-time (77 women); includes 39 minority (9 Black or African American, non-Hispanic/Latino; 4 American Indian or Alaska Native, non-Hispanic/Latino; 3 Asian, non-Hispanic/Latino; 15 Hispanic/Latino; 8 Two or more races, non-Hispanic/Latino), 27 international. Average age 31. 238 applicants, 68% accepted, 90 enrolled. In 2010, 84 master's, 2 doctorates, 20 other advanced degrees awarded. *Degree requirements:* For master's, comprehensive exam (for some programs), thesis (for some programs), departmental qualifying exam; for doctorate, comprehensive exam, thesis/dissertation, departmental qualifying exam. *Entrance requirements:* For master's, minimum GPA of 3.0 or GRE; for doctorate, GRE General Test. Additional exam requirements/recommendations for international students: Required—TOEFL (minimum score 550 paper-based; 213 computer-based; 80 iBT), IELTS (minimum score 7), TOEFL (600 paper, 250 computer, 100 iBT for PhD; 570 paper, 237 computer, 89 iBT for MA). *Application deadline:* For fall admission, 4/15 priority date for domestic students, 2/15 priority date for international students; for spring admission, 11/15 priority date for domestic and international students. Applications are processed on a rolling basis. Application fee: $65. Electronic applications accepted. *Financial support:* In 2010–11, 72 teaching assistantships with partial tuition reimbursements (averaging $11,623 per year) were awarded; Federal Work-Study, scholarships/grants, health care benefits, tuition waivers (full and partial), and unspecified assistantships also available. Financial award applicants required to submit FAFSA. *Unit head:* Dr. J. Allen Woodman, Chair, 928-523-5651, Fax: 928-523-7074,

Writing

Northern Arizona University (continued)

E-mail: allen.woodman@nau.edu. *Application contact:* Giovanina Bucci, Secretary, 928-523-4911, Fax: 928-523-7074, E-mail: giovanina.bucci@nau.edu.

Northern Kentucky University, Office of Graduate Programs, College of Arts and Sciences, Program in English, Highland Heights, KY 41099. Offers composition and rhetoric (Certificate); creative writing (Certificate); cultural studies (Certificate); English (MA); professional writing (Certificate). Part-time and evening/weekend programs available. *Faculty:* 11 full-time (6 women). *Students:* 8 full-time (5 women), 66 part-time (53 women); includes 6 minority (4 Black or African American, non-Hispanic/Latino; 1 Hispanic/Latino; 1 Two or more races, non-Hispanic/Latino). Average age 34. 36 applicants, 94% accepted, 32 enrolled. In 2010, 3 master's awarded. *Degree requirements:* For master's, comprehensive exam (for some programs), comprehensive exam, thesis, project, or portfolio. *Entrance requirements:* For master's, minimum GPA of 3.0, two letters of reference. Additional exam requirements/recommendations for international students: Required—TOEFL (minimum score 550 paper-based; 213 computer-based; 79 iBT); Recommended—IELTS (minimum score 6.5). *Application deadline:* For fall admission, 7/1 priority date for domestic students, 6/1 priority date for international students; for spring admission, 11/1 for domestic students, 10/1 for international students. Applications are processed on a rolling basis. Application fee: $40. Electronic applications accepted. *Expenses:* Tuition, state resident: full-time $7254; part-time $403 per credit hour. Tuition, nonresident: full-time $12,492; part-time $694 per credit hour. Tuition and fees vary according to degree level and program. *Financial support:* Unspecified assistantships available. Financial award applicants required to submit FAFSA. *Faculty research:* Composition and rhetoric, creative writing, English and American literature, professional writing, cultural studies. *Unit head:* Dr. Roxanne Kent-Drury, Coordinator, 859-572-6636, Fax: 859-572-6093, E-mail: rkdrury@nku.edu. *Application contact:* Dr. Peg Griffin, Director of Graduate Programs, 859-572-6934, Fax: 859-572-6670, E-mail: griffinp@nku.edu.

Northern Michigan University, College of Graduate Studies, College of Arts and Sciences, Department of English, Marquette, MI 49855-5301. Offers creative writing (MFA); literature (MA); pedagogy (MA); writing (MA). Part-time programs available. *Degree requirements:* For master's, thesis or alternative. *Entrance requirements:* For master's, minimum GPA of 2.75.

Northwestern University, Medill School of Journalism, Evanston, IL 60208. Offers broadcast journalism (MSJ); integrated marketing communications (MSIMC), including advertising/sales promotion, direct database and e-commerce marketing, general studies, public relations; magazine publishing (MSJ); new media (MSJ); reporting and writing (MSJ). *Accreditation:* ACEJMC (one or more programs are accredited). *Entrance requirements:* For master's, GRE General Test, GMAT or LSAT (MSJ). Additional exam requirements/recommendations for international students: Required—TOEFL. Electronic applications accepted. *Expenses:* Contact institution. *Faculty research:* Web business journalism, cultural stereotypes, voter apathy, digital television.

Northwestern University, School of Continuing Studies, Program in Creative Writing, Evanston, IL 60208. Offers MA, MFA.

Oklahoma City University, Petree College of Arts and Sciences, Program in Liberal Arts, Oklahoma City, OK 73106-1402. Offers art (MLA); general studies (MLA); leadership/management (MLA); literature (MLA); mass communications (MLA); philosophy (MLA); writing (MLA). Part-time and evening/weekend programs available. *Degree requirements:* For master's, comprehensive exam, thesis optional. *Entrance requirements:* Additional exam requirements/recommendations for international students: Required—TOEFL (minimum score 550 paper-based).

Oklahoma State University, College of Arts and Sciences, Department of English, Stillwater, OK 74078. Offers creative writing (MFA); English (MA, PhD). *Faculty:* 52 full-time (31 women), 3 part-time/adjunct (all women). *Students:* 10 full-time (7 women), 145 part-time (71 women); includes 1 Black or African American, non-Hispanic/Latino; 8 American Indian or Alaska Native, non-Hispanic/Latino; 2 Asian, non-Hispanic/Latino; 5 Hispanic/Latino, 20 international. Average age 32. 148 applicants, 34% accepted, 32 enrolled. In 2010, 21 master's, 4 doctorates awarded. *Degree requirements:* For master's, comprehensive exam, thesis; for doctorate, comprehensive exam, thesis/dissertation. *Entrance requirements:* For master's, GRE General Test, minimum GPA of 3.0, writing sample; for doctorate, GRE General Test, minimum GPA of 3.5, writing sample. Additional exam requirements/recommendations for international students: Required—TOEFL (minimum score 550 paper-based; 79 iBT). *Application deadline:* For fall admission, 3/1 priority date for international students; for spring admission, 8/1 priority date for international students. Applications are processed on a rolling basis. Application fee: $40 ($75 for international students). Electronic applications accepted. *Expenses:* Tuition, state resident: full-time $3716; part-time $154.85 per credit hour. Tuition, nonresident: full-time $14,892; part-time $621 per credit hour. Required fees: $2044; $85.20 per credit hour. One-time fee: $50. Tuition and fees vary according to course load and campus/location. *Financial support:* In 2010–11, 2 research assistantships (averaging $12,960 per year), 107 teaching assistantships (averaging $14,625 per year) were awarded; career-related internships or fieldwork, Federal Work-Study, scholarships/grants, health care benefits, tuition waivers (partial), and unspecified assistantships also available. Support available to part-time students. Financial award application deadline: 3/1; financial award applicants required to submit FAFSA. *Faculty research:* American and British novels, poetry, and autobiography; Native American languages and literature; institutional history of American film, history, and adaptations; rhetoric and theories of human communication; learning strategies of second language learners. *Unit head:* Dr. Carol Moder, Head, 405-744-9474, Fax: 405-744-6326. *Application contact:* Dr. Gordon Emslie, Dean, 405-744-6368, Fax: 405-744-0355, E-mail: grad-i@okstate.edu.

Old Dominion University, College of Arts and Letters, MFA Program in Creative Writing, Norfolk, VA 23529. Offers MFA. Part-time programs available. *Faculty:* 6 full-time (3 women), 1 part-time/adjunct (0 women). *Students:* 24 full-time (12 women), 5 part-time (3 women); includes 1 minority (Hispanic/Latino). Average age 35. 56 applicants, 55% accepted, 12 enrolled. In 2010, 9 master's awarded. *Degree requirements:* For master's, comprehensive exam, thesis. *Entrance requirements:* For master's, GRE General Test, 24 hours previous course work in English, sample of written work. Additional exam requirements/recommendations for international students: Required—TOEFL. *Application deadline:* For fall admission, 2/15 for domestic students. Application fee: $40. Electronic applications accepted. *Expenses:* Tuition, state resident: full-time $8592; part-time $358 per credit. Tuition, nonresident: full-time $21,672; part-time $903 per credit. Required fees: $119 per semester. One-time fee: $50. *Financial support:* In 2010–11, 13 students received support, including 2 fellowships with tuition reimbursements available (averaging $13,000 per year), 3 research assistantships with tuition reimbursements available (averaging $10,000 per year), 8 teaching assistantships with tuition reimbursements available (averaging $10,000 per year); scholarships/grants and unspecified assistantships also available. Financial award application deadline: 2/15. *Faculty research:* Literary fiction, nonfiction, poetry. Total annual research expenditures: $35,000. *Unit head:* Dr. Luisa Igloria, Graduate Program Director, 757-683-3929, Fax: 757-683-3241, E-mail: cwgpd@odu.edu. *Application contact:* Dr. Robert Wojtowicz, Associate Dean, 757-683-6077, Fax: 757-683-5746, E-mail: rwojtowi@odu.edu.

Otis College of Art and Design, Program in Writing, Los Angeles, CA 90045-9785. Offers MFA. *Faculty:* 1 full-time (0 women), 7 part-time/adjunct (1 woman). *Students:* 15 full-time (12 women), 14 part-time (11 women); includes 11 minority (3 Black or African American, non-Hispanic/Latino; 2 Asian, non-Hispanic/Latino; 5 Hispanic/Latino; 1 Two or more races, non-Hispanic/Latino), 3 international. Average age 34. 40 applicants, 55% accepted, 6 enrolled. In 2010, 8 master's awarded. *Degree requirements:* For master's, thesis. *Entrance requirements:* For master's, writing sample. *Application deadline:* For fall admission, 1/15 for domestic and international students; for spring admission, 11/1 for domestic and international students. Application fee: $60. Electronic applications accepted. *Expenses:* Tuition: Full-time $33,900; part-time $1107 per unit. Required fees: $700. *Financial support:* Federal Work-Study, scholarships/grants, and tuition waivers (partial) available. Financial award applicants required to submit FAFSA. *Unit head:* Paul Vangelisti, Chair, 310-665-6891, Fax: 310-665-6890, E-mail: pvangel@otis.edu. *Application contact:* Information Contact, 310-665-6820, Fax: 310-665-6821, E-mail: admissions@otis.edu.

Our Lady of the Lake University of San Antonio, College of Arts and Sciences, Program in English, San Antonio, TX 78207-4689. Offers communication arts (MA); English and literature (MA); English education (MA); writing (MA). Program offered jointly with University of the Incarnate Word, St. Mary's University. Part-time and evening/weekend programs available. *Students:* 6 full-time (5 women), 18 part-time (14 women); includes 17 minority (1 Black or African American, non-Hispanic/Latino; 1 American Indian or Alaska Native, non-Hispanic/Latino; 15 Hispanic/Latino). Average age 35. In 2010, 8 master's awarded. *Degree requirements:* For master's, comprehensive exam, thesis optional. *Entrance requirements:* For master's, GRE General Test or MAT, minimum GPA of 3.0 in last 60 hours, 2.5 overall. Additional exam requirements/recommendations for international students: Required—TOEFL. *Application deadline:* Applications are processed on a rolling basis. Application fee: $25 ($50 for international students). Electronic applications accepted. *Expenses:* Tuition: Full-time $13,500; part-time $750 per contact hour. Required fees: $330. Tuition and fees vary according to course level, degree level and campus/location. *Financial support:* Research assistantships, teaching assistantships, career-related internships or fieldwork, Federal Work-Study, institutionally sponsored loans, and tuition waivers (partial) available. Financial award application deadline: 4/15. *Faculty research:* Writing theory and research, contemporary Southern literature, popular culture, poetry, literature of the Southwest. *Unit head:* Dr. Michael Lueker, Chair, 210-434-6711 Ext. 2242, E-mail: luekm@lake.ollusa.edu. *Application contact:* 210-434-6711, Fax: 210-431-4036, E-mail: gradadm@lake.ollusa.edu.

Pacific Lutheran University, Division of Graduate Studies, Division of Humanities, Tacoma, WA 98447. Offers creative writing (MFA). Offered during summer only. Part-time programs available. *Degree requirements:* For master's, thesis, final residency including teaching class. *Entrance requirements:* For master's, portfolio, book review. Additional exam requirements/recommendations for international students: Required—TOEFL. Electronic applications accepted. *Expenses:* Contact institution.

Pacific University, Program in Writing, Forest Grove, OR 97116-1797. Offers MFA. Part-time programs available.

Penn State University Park, Graduate School, College of the Liberal Arts, Department of English, State College, University Park, PA 16802-1503. Offers MA, MFA, PhD.

Pepperdine University, Seaver College, Humanities and Teacher Education Division, Master of Fine Arts Program in Writing for Screen and Television, Malibu, CA 90263. Offers MFA. *Students:* 6 full-time (1 woman), 14 part-time (3 women); includes 1 minority (Asian, non-Hispanic/Latino). 23 applicants, 65% accepted, 8 enrolled. *Entrance requirements:* For master's, GRE General Test, statement of purpose and intent for writing as a vocation, script writing sample, letters of recommendation. Additional exam requirements/recommendations for international students: Required—TOEFL. *Application deadline:* For fall admission, 2/1 priority date for domestic students. Application fee: $55. Electronic applications accepted. *Unit head:* Dr. Maire Mullins, Chair/Professor of English, Humanities and Teacher Education Division, 310-506-4894, E-mail: maire.mullins@pepperdine.edu. *Application contact:* Michael Truschke, Dean of Admission and Enrollment Management, 310-506-6165, Fax: 310-506-4861, E-mail: admission-seaver@pepperdine.edu.

Perelandra College, Program in Creative Writing, La Mesa, CA 91941. Offers MA. *Degree requirements:* For master's, thesis.

Purdue University, Graduate School, College of Liberal Arts, Department of English, West Lafayette, IN 47907. Offers creative writing (MFA); literature (MA, PhD), including linguistics, literature and philosophy (PhD), rhetoric and composition, theory and cultural studies (PhD). Part-time programs available. *Degree requirements:* For master's, one foreign language; for doctorate, one foreign language, thesis/dissertation. *Entrance requirements:* For master's and doctorate, GRE General Test, sample of written work. Additional exam requirements/recommendations for international students: Required—TOEFL. Electronic applications accepted. *Faculty research:* Cultural studies, postmodern narrative, contemporary women writers, composition theory, slave narratives.

Queens College of the City University of New York, Division of Graduate Studies, Arts and Humanities Division, Department of English, Flushing, NY 11367-1597. Offers creative writing (MA); English language and literature (MA). Part-time and evening/weekend programs available. *Faculty:* 53 full-time (25 women). *Students:* 5 full-time (all women), 125 part-time (88 women); includes 16 Black or African American, non-Hispanic/Latino; 9 Asian, non-Hispanic/Latino; 14 Hispanic/Latino, 2 international. 158 applicants, 38% accepted, 38 enrolled. In 2010, 32 master's awarded. *Degree requirements:* For master's, one foreign language, thesis (for some programs), oral exam (English language and literature). *Entrance requirements:* For master's, manuscript (creative writing), minimum GPA of 3.0. Additional exam requirements/recommendations for international students: Required—TOEFL. *Application deadline:* For fall admission, 4/1 for domestic students; for spring admission, 11/1 for domestic students. Applications are processed on a rolling basis. Application fee: $125. *Financial support:* Career-related internships or fieldwork, Federal Work-Study, institutionally sponsored loans, and tuition waivers (partial) available. Support available to part-time students. Financial award application deadline: 4/1; financial award applicants required to submit FAFSA. *Unit head:* Dr. Nancy Comley, Chairperson, 718-997-4600, E-mail: nancy_comley@qc.edu. *Application contact:* Dr. Talia Schaffer, Graduate Adviser, 718-997-4600, E-mail: talia_schaffer@qc.edu.

Queens University of Charlotte, College of Arts and Sciences, Charlotte, NC 28274-0002. Offers creative writing (MFA). Part-time programs available. Postbaccalaureate distance learning degree programs offered (minimal on-campus study). Electronic applications accepted.

Rhode Island College, School of Graduate Studies, Faculty of Arts and Sciences, Department of English, Providence, RI 02908-1991. Offers creative writing (MA, CGS); English (MA); literature (CGS). Part-time and evening/weekend programs available. *Faculty:* 11 full-time (4 women). *Students:* 1 (woman) full-time, 14 part-time (7 women). Average age 34. In 2010, 12 master's awarded. *Degree requirements:* For master's, thesis (for some programs). *Entrance requirements:* For master's, GRE General Test, 3 letters of recommendation, interview. Additional exam requirements/recommendations for international students: Recommended—TOEFL (minimum score 550 paper-based; 213 computer-based; 79 iBT). *Application deadline:* For fall admission, 3/1 for domestic students; for spring admission, 11/1 for domestic students. Applications are processed on a rolling basis. Application fee: $50. *Expenses:* Tuition, state resident: full-time $8208; part-time $342 per credit hour. Tuition, nonresident: full-time $16,080; part-time $670 per credit hour. Required fees: $554; $20 per credit. $72 per term. *Financial support:* In 2010–11, 1 teaching assistantship with full tuition reimbursement (averaging $4,550 per year) was awarded; career-related internships or fieldwork, Federal Work-Study, scholarships/grants, health care benefits, and unspecified assistantships also available. Support available to part-time students. Financial award application deadline: 5/15; financial award applicants required to submit FAFSA. *Unit head:* Dr. Maureen Reddy, Chair, 401-456-8028. *Application contact:* Graduate Studies, 401-456-8700.

Rivier College, School of Graduate Studies, Department of English, Nashua, NH 03060. Offers English (MAT); writing and literature (MA). Part-time and evening/weekend programs available. *Faculty:* 3 full-time (1 woman). *Students:* 6 full-time (all women), 17 part-time (13 women). Average age 31. 14 applicants, 14% accepted, 1 enrolled. In 2010, 13 master's awarded. *Degree requirements:* For master's, comprehensive exam (for some programs). *Entrance requirements:* For master's, GRE Subject Test. *Application deadline:* Applications are processed on a rolling basis. Application fee: $25. *Expenses:* Tuition: Part-time $456 per credit. *Financial support:* Available to part-time students. Application deadline: 2/1. *Unit head:* Dr. Brad Stull, Chairman, 603-897-8238, E-mail: bstull@rivier.edu. *Application contact:* Mathew

Kittredge, Director of Graduate Admissions, 603-897-8229, Fax: 603-897-8810, E-mail: mkittredge@rivier.edu.

Roosevelt University, Graduate Division, College of Arts and Sciences, Department of Literature and Languages, Program in Creative Writing, Chicago, IL 60605. Offers MFA. Part-time and evening/weekend programs available. *Faculty research:* Poetry, fiction, nonfiction, script writing.

Rosemont College, Schools of Graduate and Professional Studies, Program in Creative Writing, Rosemont, PA 19010-1699. Offers MFA. *Expenses:* Tuition: Full-time $11,700; part-time $650 per credit.

Rowan University, Graduate School, College of Communication, Program in Writing, Glassboro, NJ 08028-1701. Offers MA. Part-time and evening/weekend programs available. *Faculty:* 3 full-time (2 women), 1 (woman) part-time/adjunct. *Students:* 8 full-time (7 women), 16 part-time (9 women); includes 2 Asian, non-Hispanic/Latino. Average age 30. 11 applicants, 100% accepted, 8 enrolled. In 2010, 11 master's awarded. *Degree requirements:* For master's, thesis. *Entrance requirements:* For master's, GRE General Test. Additional exam requirements/recommendations for international students: Required—TOEFL. *Application deadline:* Applications are processed on a rolling basis. Application fee: $65 ($200 for international students). Electronic applications accepted. *Expenses:* Tuition, area resident: Part-time $602 per semester hour. Tuition, nonresident: part-time $602 per semester hour. Required fees: $100 per semester hour. One-time fee: $10 part-time. *Financial support:* Career-related internships or fieldwork, scholarships/grants, and health care benefits available. Support available to part-time students. *Unit head:* Dr. Horacio Sosa, Dean, College of Graduate and Continuing Education, 856-256-4747, Fax: 856-256-5638, E-mail: sosa@rowan.edu. *Application contact:* Karen Haynes, Graduate Coordinator, 856-256-4052, E-mail: haynes@rowan.edu.

Rutgers, The State University of New Jersey, Camden, Graduate School of Arts and Sciences, Program in Creative Writing, Camden, NJ 08102. Offers MFA. Part-time and evening/weekend programs available. *Faculty:* 4 full-time (2 women), 3 part-time/adjunct (2 women). *Students:* 10 full-time (2 women), 20 part-time (14 women); includes 2 Black or African American, non-Hispanic/Latino; 2 Hispanic/Latino. Average age 34. 104 applicants, 27% accepted, 12 enrolled. *Degree requirements:* For master's, thesis, 42 credits. *Entrance requirements:* For master's, GRE (for assistantships), 2 letters of recommendation, writing sample, statement of personal, professional, and academic goals. Additional exam requirements/recommendations for international students: Required—TOEFL, IELTS. *Application deadline:* For fall admission, 1/15 for domestic students. Application fee: $65. Electronic applications accepted. *Expenses:* Tuition, state resident: full-time $4963; part-time $319 per credit. Tuition, nonresident: full-time $10,493; part-time $680 per credit. *Financial support:* In 2010–11, 25 students received support, including 8 fellowships with partial tuition reimbursements available (averaging $3,325 per year), 5 teaching assistantships with full tuition reimbursements available (averaging $26,000 per year); Federal Work-Study, scholarships/grants, and tuition waivers (partial) also available. Financial award application deadline: 3/15; financial award applicants required to submit FAFSA. *Faculty research:* Poetry, fiction, nonfiction. *Unit head:* Prof. Lisa Zeidner, Director, 856-225-6121, E-mail: mfa@camden.rutgers.edu. *Application contact:* Prof. Lisa Zeidner, Director, 856-225-6121, E-mail: mfa@camden.rutgers.edu.

Rutgers, The State University of New Jersey, Newark, Graduate School, Program in Creative Writing, Newark, NJ 07102. Offers MFA. *Faculty:* 1 (woman) full-time. *Students:* 32 full-time (19 women), 19 part-time (9 women); includes 7 Black or African American, non-Hispanic/Latino; 6 Asian, non-Hispanic/Latino; 6 Hispanic/Latino. 170 applicants, 35% accepted, 29 enrolled. In 2010, 17 master's awarded. *Entrance requirements:* For master's, GRE, minimum undergraduate B average. Application fee: $60. *Expenses:* Tuition, state resident: part-time $600 per credit. Tuition, nonresident: full-time $10,694. *Financial support:* In 2010–11, 9 teaching assistantships with full and partial tuition reimbursements (averaging $23,112 per year) were awarded. *Unit head:* Dr. Jayne Ann Phillips, Program Director, 973-353-5279, E-mail: japhillips@andromeda.rutgers.edu. *Application contact:* Jason Hand, Director of Admissions, 973-353-5205, Fax: 973-353-1440.

Rutgers, The State University of New Jersey, New Brunswick, Mason Gross School of the Arts, Theater Arts Department, New Brunswick, NJ 08901. Offers acting (MFA); design (MFA); directing (MFA); playwriting (MFA); stage management (MFA). *Faculty:* 13 full-time (8 women), 21 part-time/adjunct (6 women). *Students:* 67 full-time (41 women); includes 10 Black or African American, non-Hispanic/Latino; 1 Hispanic/Latino. Average age 27. 183 applicants, 17% accepted, 27 enrolled. In 2010, 22 master's awarded. *Degree requirements:* For master's, thesis (for some programs), performance project. *Entrance requirements:* For master's, audition, interview, portfolio. Additional exam requirements/recommendations for international students: Required—TOEFL (minimum score 550 paper-based; 213 computer-based), IELTS (minimum score 7). *Application deadline:* For fall admission, 3/1 for domestic and international students. Application fee: $65. Electronic applications accepted. *Expenses:* Tuition, state resident: full-time $7200; part-time $600 per credit. Tuition, nonresident: full-time $11,124; part-time $927 per credit. *Financial support:* In 2010–11, 16 fellowships (averaging $1,000 per year), 62 teaching assistantships with partial tuition reimbursements (averaging $3,700 per year) were awarded; career-related internships or fieldwork, Federal Work-Study, scholarships/grants, and health care benefits also available. Financial award application deadline: 3/1; financial award applicants required to submit FAFSA. *Faculty research:* Faculty of working professional. *Unit head:* Michael Miller, Interim Chair, 732-932-9891 Ext. 10, Fax: 732-932-1409. *Application contact:* Barbara Harwanko, Administrative Assistant, 732-932-9891 Ext. 10, Fax: 732-932-1409, E-mail: harwanko@masongross.rutgers.edu.

Saint Joseph's University, College of Arts and Sciences, Program in Writing Studies, Philadelphia, PA 19131-1395. Offers MA. Part-time and evening/weekend programs available. *Faculty:* 10 full-time (5 women), 1 (woman) part-time/adjunct. *Students:* 11 full-time (10 women), 39 part-time (27 women); includes 9 Black or African American, non-Hispanic/Latino; 1 Asian, non-Hispanic/Latino; 1 Hispanic/Latino. Average age 30. 25 applicants, 100% accepted, 15 enrolled. In 2010, 13 master's awarded. *Entrance requirements:* For master's, 2 letters of recommendation, resume, 2 writing samples. Additional exam requirements/recommendations for international students: Required—TOEFL (minimum score 550 paper-based; 213 computer-based; 79 iBT). *Application deadline:* For fall admission, 7/15 priority date for domestic students, 4/15 priority date for international students; for winter admission, 1/15 priority date for international students; for spring admission, 11/15 priority date for domestic students, 10/15 priority date for international students. Applications are processed on a rolling basis. Application fee: $35. Electronic applications accepted. *Expenses:* Tuition: Part-time $729 per credit. Tuition and fees vary according to course load, degree level and program. *Financial support:* Unspecified assistantships available. Financial award applicants required to submit FAFSA. *Unit head:* Dr. Ann Green, Director, 610-660-1889, E-mail: agreen@sju.edu. *Application contact:* Kate McConnell, Director, Graduate College of Arts and Sciences Admissions and Retention, 610-660-3184, Fax: 610-660-3230, E-mail: kate.mcconnell@sju.edu.

Saint Mary's College of California, School of Liberal Arts, MFA Program in Creative Writing, Moraga, CA 94556. Offers MFA. *Faculty:* 6 full-time (3 women), 4 part-time/adjunct (3 women). *Students:* 47 full-time (26 women), 1 (woman) part-time; includes 3 Asian, non-Hispanic/Latino; 1 Hispanic/Latino. Average age 29. In 2010, 19 master's awarded. *Degree requirements:* For master's, thesis. *Entrance requirements:* For master's, sample of written work. *Application deadline:* For fall admission, 1/31 for domestic students, 10/31 for international students. Application fee: $50. Electronic applications accepted. *Financial support:* In 2010–11, 22 students received support, including 3 fellowships (averaging $6,000 per year), 20 teaching assistantships (averaging $2,000 per year); career-related internships or fieldwork and Federal Work-Study also available. Support available to part-time students. Financial award application deadline: 1/31; financial award applicants required to submit FAFSA. *Faculty research:* Poetry, fiction, nonfiction. *Unit head:* Marilyn Abildskov, Director, 925-631-4457, Fax: 925-631-4471, E-mail: mabildsk@stmarys-ca.edu. *Application contact:* Thomas Cooney, MFA Program Coordinator, 925-631-4762, Fax: 925-631-4471, E-mail: writers@stmarys-ca.edu.

Saint Xavier University, Graduate Studies, School of Arts and Sciences, Department of English, Chicago, IL 60655-3105. Offers English (CAS); literary studies (MA); teaching of writing (MA); writing pedagogy (CAS). Part-time and evening/weekend programs available. *Entrance requirements:* For master's, MAT or GRE, minimum GPA of 3.0.

Salisbury University, Graduate Division, Program in English, Salisbury, MD 21801-6837. Offers composition, language and rhetoric (MA); literature (MA); teaching English to speakers of other languages (MA). Part-time and evening/weekend programs available. *Faculty:* 11 full-time (6 women). *Students:* 14 full-time (12 women), 17 part-time (10 women); includes 2 minority (both Two or more races, non-Hispanic/Latino). Average age 27. 31 applicants, 52% accepted, 2 enrolled. In 2010, 19 master's awarded. *Degree requirements:* For master's, comprehensive exam (for some programs), thesis optional. *Entrance requirements:* For master's, GRE General Test, MAT or PRAXIS, minimum GPA of 3.0, 2 letters of recommendation. Additional exam requirements/recommendations for international students: Required—TOEFL (minimum score 550 paper-based; 213 computer-based; 79 iBT). *Application deadline:* For fall admission, 8/1 for domestic students; for spring admission, 1/1 for domestic students. Applications are processed on a rolling basis. Application fee: $45. Electronic applications accepted. *Financial support:* In 2010–11, 9 students received support, including 14 teaching assistantships with full tuition reimbursements available; career-related internships or fieldwork and scholarships/grants also available. Support available to part-time students. Financial award applicants required to submit FAFSA. *Faculty research:* Shakespeare, Keats, J. D. Salinger, Samuel Johnson, post-colonial theory. *Unit head:* Dr. John D. Kalb, Director, 410-543-6049, Fax: 410-548-2142, E-mail: jdkalb@salisbury.edu. *Application contact:* Dr. John D. Kalb, Director, 410-543-6049, Fax: 410-548-2142, E-mail: jdkalb@salisbury.edu.

San Diego State University, Graduate and Research Affairs, College of Arts and Letters, Department of English and Comparative Literature, San Diego, CA 92182. Offers creative writing (MFA); English (MA). *Degree requirements:* For master's, one foreign language, comprehensive exam (for some programs), thesis (for some programs). *Entrance requirements:* For master's, GRE General Test, minimum GPA of 2.85, writing sample, 3 letters of recommendation. Additional exam requirements/recommendations for international students: Required—TOEFL. Electronic applications accepted.

San Diego State University, Graduate and Research Affairs, College of Arts and Letters, Department of Rhetoric and Writing, San Diego, CA 92182. Offers MA. Part-time programs available. *Degree requirements:* For master's, thesis. *Entrance requirements:* For master's, GRE General Test, writing sample, 3 letters of reference. Additional exam requirements/recommendations for international students: Required—TOEFL. Electronic applications accepted.

San Francisco State University, Division of Graduate Studies, College of Humanities, Department of Creative Writing, San Francisco, CA 94132-1722. Offers MA, MFA. Part-time programs available. *Degree requirements:* For master's, thesis. *Financial support:* Career-related internships or fieldwork and Federal Work-Study available. *Unit head:* Maxine Chernoff, Chair, 415-338-1891, Fax: 415-405-2142, E-mail: cwriting@sfsu.edu. *Application contact:* Barbara Eaton, Academic Office Coordinator, 415-338-1891, E-mail: cwriting@sfsu.edu.

Sarah Lawrence College, Graduate Studies, Program in Writing, Bronxville, NY 10708-5999. Offers creative non-fiction (MFA); fiction (MFA); poetry (MFA). Part-time programs available. *Degree requirements:* For master's, thesis. *Entrance requirements:* For master's, sample of creative writing, minimum B average in undergraduate course work. Additional exam requirements/recommendations for international students: Required—TOEFL (minimum score 600 paper-based).

Savannah College of Art and Design, Graduate School, Program in Professional Writing, Savannah, GA 31402-3146. Offers MFA. Part-time programs available. *Faculty:* 5 full-time (2 women). *Students:* 36 full-time (28 women), 9 part-time (8 women); includes 6 Black or African American, non-Hispanic/Latino; 1 American Indian or Alaska Native, non-Hispanic/Latino; 1 Hispanic/Latino; 1 Two or more races, non-Hispanic/Latino, 1 international. Average age 29. In 2010, 2 master's awarded. *Degree requirements:* For master's, thesis. *Entrance requirements:* Additional exam requirements/recommendations for international students: Required—TOEFL (minimum score 450 paper-based; 133 computer-based). *Application deadline:* For fall admission, 4/1 priority date for domestic and international students. Applications are processed on a rolling basis. Application fee: $50. Electronic applications accepted. *Expenses:* Tuition: Full-time $29,520; part-time $3280 per quarter. Tuition and fees vary according to campus/location. *Financial support:* Fellowships, career-related internships or fieldwork, Federal Work-Study, and scholarships/grants available. Financial award application deadline: 4/1; financial award applicants required to submit FAFSA. *Unit head:* James Lough, Acting Chair, 912-525-5117, Fax: 912-525-5886, E-mail: jlough@scad.edu. *Application contact:* Elizabeth Mathis, Director of Graduate Recruitment, 912-525-5965, Fax: 912-525-5985, E-mail: admission@scad.edu.

School of the Art Institute of Chicago, Graduate Division, Program in Writing, Chicago, IL 60603-3103. Offers MFA, Certificate. *Entrance requirements:* Additional exam requirements/recommendations for international students: Required—TOEFL.

Seattle Pacific University, Masters of Fine Arts in Creative Writing Program, Seattle, WA 98119-1997. Offers MFA. Part-time programs available. *Faculty:* 1 full-time (0 women), 6 part-time/adjunct (4 women). *Students:* 25 part-time (14 women); includes 1 minority (Two or more races, non-Hispanic/Latino), 1 international. Average age 37. 1 applicant, 0% accepted, 0 enrolled. In 2010, 5 master's awarded. *Degree requirements:* For master's, thesis. *Entrance requirements:* For master's, 10 pages of poetry or 25 to 30 double-spaced pages of prose (fiction or creative nonfiction) in chosen genre. *Application deadline:* For winter admission, 10/1 for domestic students. Application fee: $50. Electronic applications accepted. *Financial support:* In 2010–11, 14 students received support. Applicants required to submit FAFSA. *Unit head:* Dr. Gregory Wolfe, Director, 206-281-2109, E-mail: gwolfe@spu.edu. *Application contact:* The Graduate Center, 206-281-2091.

Seton Hall University, College of Arts and Sciences, Department of English, South Orange, NJ 07079-2697. Offers English (MA), including literature, writing. Part-time and evening/weekend programs available. *Degree requirements:* For master's, one foreign language, comprehensive exam, thesis. *Entrance requirements:* For master's, GRE, minimum of 21 undergraduate credits in English. Additional exam requirements/recommendations for international students: Required—TOEFL. Electronic applications accepted. *Faculty research:* The essay, modern poetry, the novel, medieval poetry, Renaissance drama.

Seton Hill University, Program in Writing Popular Fiction, Greensburg, PA 15601. Offers MFA, Certificate. Part-time programs available. Postbaccalaureate distance learning degree programs offered (minimal on-campus study). *Faculty:* 4 full-time (2 women), 22 part-time/adjunct (11 women). *Students:* 81 full-time (59 women), 20 part-time (16 women); includes 4 Black or African American, non-Hispanic/Latino; 1 American Indian or Alaska Native, non-Hispanic/Latino; 8 Hispanic/Latino, 3 international. Average age 40. 95 applicants, 36% accepted, 19 enrolled. In 2010, 3 master's awarded. *Degree requirements:* For master's, thesis or alternative. *Entrance requirements:* For master's, writing sample, minimum GPA of 3.0, 3 letters of recommendation. Additional exam requirements/recommendations for international students: Required—TOEFL (minimum score 650 paper-based; 280 computer-based), IELTS (minimum score 7). *Application deadline:* For fall admission, 6/1 for domestic students; for spring admission, 12/15 for domestic students. Applications are processed on a rolling basis. Application fee: $35. Electronic applications accepted. *Expenses:* Tuition: Full-time $13,050; part-time $725 per credit. Required fees: $700; $34 per credit. $50 per semester. Tuition and fees vary according to course load and program. *Financial support:* Scholarships/grants, tuition waivers (partial), and unspecified assistantships available. Support available to part-time students. Financial award application deadline: 8/15; financial award applicants required to submit FAFSA. *Faculty research:* Writing novels, writing books on writing, editing books on writing. *Unit head:* Dr. Albert Wendland, Director, 724-830-1019, Fax: 724-830-1294, E-mail:

Writing

Seton Hill University (continued)
wendland@setonhill.edu. Application contact: Laurel Komarny, Program Counselor, 724-838-4209, Fax: 724-830-1891, E-mail: 1komarny@setonhill.edu.

Sewanee: The University of the South, Sewanee School of Letters, Sewanee, TN 37383-1000. Offers American and English literature (MA); creative writing (MFA). Programs offered only during the summer. Part-time programs available. Degree requirements: For master's, thesis (for some programs). Entrance requirements: For master's, writing sample, 2 letters of recommendation. Electronic applications accepted. Expenses: Contact institution.

Sonoma State University, Department of English, Rohnert Park, CA 94928. Offers American literature (MA); creative writing (MA); English literature (MA); world literature (MA). Part-time and evening/weekend programs available. Faculty: 6 full-time (4 women), 1 part-time/adjunct (0 women). Students: 24 full-time (16 women), 17 part-time (11 women); includes 4 minority (all Two or more races, non-Hispanic/Latino), 1 international. Average age 31. 27 applicants, 78% accepted, 9 enrolled. In 2010, 7 master's awarded. Degree requirements: For master's, one foreign language, thesis or alternative. Entrance requirements: For master's, minimum GPA of 2.5. Additional exam requirements/recommendations for international students: Required—TOEFL (minimum score 500 paper-based; 173 computer-based). Application deadline: For fall admission, 11/30 priority date for domestic students. Application fee: $55. Financial support: Teaching assistantships, career-related internships or fieldwork and Federal Work-Study available. Financial award application deadline: 3/2; financial award applicants required to submit FAFSA. Unit head: Dr. Thaine Stearns, Chair of Graduate Studies, 707-661-2882, E-mail: thaine.stearns@sonoma.edu. Application contact: Dr. Sherril Jaffe, 707-664-2508, E-mail: sherril.jaffe@sonoma.edu.

Southeastern Louisiana University, College of Arts, Humanities and Social Sciences, Department of English, Hammond, LA 70402. Offers creative writing (MA); language and theory (MA); professional writing (MA). Part-time and evening/weekend programs available. Faculty: 14 full-time (7 women), 1 (woman) part-time/adjunct. Students: 23 full-time (13 women), 36 part-time (25 women); includes 3 minority (2 Black or African American, non-Hispanic/Latino; 1 Native Hawaiian or other Pacific Islander, non-Hispanic/Latino). Average age 29. 25 applicants, 72% accepted, 13 enrolled. In 2010, 5 master's awarded. Degree requirements: For master's, one foreign language, comprehensive exam, thesis (for some programs). Entrance requirements: For master's, GRE General Test (850 or better), 24 undergraduate credit hours in English, minimum GPA of 2.5. Additional exam requirements/recommendations for international students: Required—TOEFL (minimum score 500 paper-based; 173 computer-based; 61 iBT). Application deadline: For fall admission, 7/15 priority date for domestic students, 6/1 priority date for international students; for spring admission, 12/1 priority date for domestic students, 10/1 priority date for international students. Applications are processed on a rolling basis. Application fee: $20 ($30 for international students). Electronic applications accepted. Expenses: Tuition, state resident: full-time $3533. Tuition, nonresident: full-time $12,002. Required fees: $907. Tuition and fees vary according to degree level. Financial support: In 2010–11, 15 students received support, including 2 fellowships (averaging $11,700 per year), 7 research assistantships (averaging $9,300 per year); career-related internships or fieldwork, Federal Work-Study, institutionally sponsored loans, scholarships/grants, and administrative assistantship, professional assistantships also available. Support available to part-time students. Financial award application deadline: 5/1; financial award applicants required to submit FAFSA. Faculty research: Composition/rhetoric, professional and technical writing, film and performance studies, literary criticism, creative writing. Unit head: Dr. David Hanson, Department Head, 985-549-2100, Fax: 985-549-5021, E-mail: dhanson@selu.edu. Application contact: Sandra Meyers, Graduate Admissions Analyst, 985-549-5620, Fax: 985-549-5632, E-mail: admissions@selu.edu.

Southern Illinois University Carbondale, Graduate School, College of Liberal Arts, Department of English, Program in Creative Writing, Carbondale, IL 62901-4701. Offers MFA. Degree requirements: For master's, one foreign language, thesis. Entrance requirements: For master's, GRE General Test, GRE Subject Test, minimum GPA of 2.7. Additional exam requirements/recommendations for international students: Required—TOEFL.

Southern Illinois University Edwardsville, Graduate School, College of Arts and Sciences, Department of English Language and Literature, Program in Creative Writing, Edwardsville, IL 62026-0001. Offers MA. Part-time programs available. Students: 7 full-time (4 women), 16 part-time (13 women); includes 3 minority (1 Black or African American, non-Hispanic/Latino; 1 Asian, non-Hispanic/Latino; 1 Hispanic/Latino). Average age 26. In 2010, 6 master's awarded. Degree requirements: For master's, one foreign language, thesis. Entrance requirements: Additional exam requirements/recommendations for international students: Required—TOEFL (minimum score 550 paper-based; 213 computer-based; 79 iBT), IELTS (minimum score 6.5). Application deadline: For fall admission, 7/22 for domestic students, 6/1 for international students; for spring admission, 12/9 for domestic students, 10/1 for international students. Applications are processed on a rolling basis. Application fee: $30. Electronic applications accepted. Expenses: Tuition, state resident: full-time $6012; part-time $1503 per semester. Tuition, nonresident: full-time $15,030; part-time $3758 per semester. Required fees: $1711; $675 per semester. Financial support: Fellowships with full tuition reimbursements, research assistantships with full tuition reimbursements, teaching assistantships with full tuition reimbursements available. Financial award application deadline: 3/1; financial award applicants required to submit FAFSA. Unit head: Dr. Joel Hardman, Director, 618-650-5978, E-mail: jhardma@siue.edu. Application contact: Dr. Joel Hardman, Director, 618-650-5978, E-mail: jhardma@siue.edu.

Southern New Hampshire University, School of Liberal Arts, Manchester, NH 03106-1045. Offers clinical services for adults psychiatric disabilities (Certificate); clinical services for children and adolescents with psychiatric disabilities (Certificate); clinical services for persons with co-occurring substance abuse and psychiatric disabilities (Certificate); community mental health (MS); fiction writing (MFA); non-fiction writing (MFA); teaching English as a foreign language (MS). Part-time and evening/weekend programs available. Degree requirements: For master's, one foreign language, thesis. Entrance requirements: For master's, minimum GPA of 2.75: MS-TEFL, 3.0: MFA. Additional exam requirements/recommendations for international students: Required—TOEFL (minimum score 550 paper-based; 213 computer-based; 79 iBT), IELTS (minimum score 6.5), TWE (minimum score 5). Electronic applications accepted. Expenses: Contact institution. Faculty research: Action research, state of the art practice in behavioral health services, wraparound approaches to working with youth, learning styles.

Spalding University, Graduate Studies, College of Social Sciences and Humanities, Program in Writing, Louisville, KY 40203-2188. Offers MFA. Postbaccalaureate distance learning degree programs offered (minimal on-campus study). Faculty: 1 (woman) full-time, 1 (woman) part-time/adjunct. Students: 151 full-time (113 women), 1 (woman) part-time; includes 21 minority (11 Black or African American, non-Hispanic/Latino; 1 Asian, non-Hispanic/Latino; 3 Hispanic/Latino; 6 Two or more races, non-Hispanic/Latino). Average age 43. 58 applicants, 57% accepted, 32 enrolled. In 2010, 45 master's awarded. Degree requirements: For master's, thesis. Entrance requirements: For master's, writing sample, letters of recommendation. Additional exam requirements/recommendations for international students: Required—TOEFL (minimum score 535 paper-based; 203 computer-based). Application deadline: For fall admission, 7/1 priority date for domestic and international students; for spring admission, 1/15 priority date for domestic and international students. Applications are processed on a rolling basis. Application fee: $29. Electronic applications accepted. Financial support: In 2010–11, 55 students received support. Scholarships/grants and unspecified assistantships available. Financial award application deadline: 3/15; financial award applicants required to submit FAFSA. Faculty research: Fiction, creative nonfiction, poetry, writing for children, playwriting/screenwriting. Unit head: Dr. Sena Jeter Naslund, Director, 502-585-9911 Ext. 2876, Fax: 502-585-7158, E-mail: mfa@spalding.edu. Application contact: Karen J. Mann, Administrative Director, 502-585-9911 Ext. 2786, Fax: 502-585-7158, E-mail: mfa@spalding.edu.

Stony Brook University, State University of New York, Graduate School, College of Arts and Sciences, Department of English, Program in Composition Studies, Stony Brook, NY 11794. Offers Certificate. Expenses: Tuition, state resident: full-time $8370; part-time $349 per credit. Tuition, nonresident: full-time $13,780; part-time $574 per credit. Required fees: $994. Unit head: Dr. Stephen Spector, Chair, 631-632-7420, Fax: 631-632-7568. Application contact: Dr. Helen M. Cooper, Director, 631-632-7784, Fax: 631-632-7568, E-mail: hcooper@notes.cc.sunysb.edu.

Stony Brook University, State University of New York, Stony Brook Southampton, Program in Writing and Literature, Stony Brook, NY 11794. Offers fiction (MFA); poetry (MFA); scientific writing (MFA), including environmental, medical, technological; scriptwriting (MFA). Faculty: 14 full-time (12 women), 9 part-time/adjunct (0 women). Students: 22 full-time (14 women), 56 part-time (42 women); includes 5 Black or African American, non-Hispanic/Latino; 1 American Indian or Alaska Native, non-Hispanic/Latino; 2 Asian, non-Hispanic/Latino; 5 Hispanic/Latino. 52 applicants, 71% accepted, 10 enrolled. In 2010, 4 master's awarded. Application deadline: For fall admission, 1/15 for domestic students. Application fee: $100. Expenses: Tuition, state resident: full-time $8370; part-time $349 per credit. Tuition, nonresident: full-time $13,780; part-time $574 per credit. Required fees: $994. Financial support: Teaching assistantships available. Unit head: Dr. Robert Reeves, Director, 631-632-5030, Fax: 631-632-2576, E-mail: southamptonwriters@notes.cc.sunysb.edu. Application contact: Director of Graduate Admissions and Program Administration.

Syracuse University, College of Arts and Sciences, Program in Composition and Cultural Rhetoric, Syracuse, NY 13244. Offers PhD. Students: 29 full-time (19 women), 8 part-time (3 women); includes 6 minority (3 Black or African American, non-Hispanic/Latino; 2 Hispanic/Latino; 1 Two or more races, non-Hispanic/Latino), 1 international. Average age 36. 30 applicants, 17% accepted, 4 enrolled. In 2010, 4 doctorates awarded. Degree requirements: For doctorate, comprehensive exam, thesis/dissertation. Entrance requirements: For doctorate, GRE. Additional exam requirements/recommendations for international students: Required—TOEFL (minimum score 100 iBT). Application deadline: For fall admission, 2/1 priority date for domestic and international students. Application fee: $75. Electronic applications accepted. Expenses: Tuition: Part-time $1162 per credit. Financial support: Fellowships with full tuition reimbursements, teaching assistantships with full tuition reimbursements available. Financial award application deadline: 1/1; financial award applicants required to submit FAFSA. Unit head: Prof. Gwendolyn Pough, Graduate Director, 315-443-5146, E-mail: gdpough@syr.edu. Application contact: Velita Degraft, 315-443-5146, E-mail: vsdegraf@syr.edu.

Syracuse University, College of Arts and Sciences, Program in Creative Writing, Syracuse, NY 13244. Offers MFA. Students: 34 full-time (19 women), 1 (woman) part-time; includes 6 minority (1 Black or African American, non-Hispanic/Latino; 2 Asian, non-Hispanic/Latino; 3 Hispanic/Latino), 1 international. Average age 30. 560 applicants, 3% accepted, 12 enrolled. In 2010, 10 master's awarded. Degree requirements: For master's, thesis. Entrance requirements: For master's, GRE General Test, sample of written work. Additional exam requirements/recommendations for international students: Required—TOEFL (minimum score 100 iBT). Application deadline: For fall admission, 1/10 priority date for domestic and international students. Application fee: $75. Electronic applications accepted. Expenses: Tuition: Part-time $1162 per credit. Financial support: Fellowships with full tuition reimbursements, teaching assistantships with full tuition reimbursements available. Financial award application deadline: 1/1. Unit head: Christopher Kennedy, Director, 315-443-3755, Fax: 315-443-3660, E-mail: ckennedy@syr.edu. Application contact: Terri Zollo, Information Contact, 315-443-2174, E-mail: tazollo@syr.edu.

Temple University, College of Liberal Arts, Department of English, Program in Creative Writing, Philadelphia, PA 19122-6096. Offers MA, MFA. Part-time programs available. Students: 26 full-time (12 women), 4 part-time (1 woman); includes 1 Black or African American, non-Hispanic/Latino. In 2010, 8 master's awarded. Degree requirements: For master's, comprehensive exam, manuscript. Entrance requirements: For master's, GRE General Test, minimum GPA of 3.0. Additional exam requirements/recommendations for international students: Required—TOEFL (minimum score 550 paper-based; 213 computer-based; 79 iBT). Application deadline: For fall admission, 1/15 for domestic students, 12/15 for international students. Application fee: $50. Electronic applications accepted. Financial support: Fellowships, teaching assistantships available. Financial award application deadline: 1/15; financial award applicants required to submit FAFSA. Faculty research: Poetry, fiction, cultural studies. Unit head: Dr. Samuel Delany, Director, 215-204-3014, Fax: 215-204-2662, E-mail: creatwrt@temple.edu. Application contact: Dr. Samuel Delany, Director, 215-204-3014, Fax: 215-204-2662, E-mail: creatwrt@temple.edu.

Texas State University–San Marcos, Graduate School, College of Liberal Arts, Department of English, Program in Creative Writing, San Marcos, TX 78666. Offers MFA. Part-time and evening/weekend programs available. Faculty: 8 full-time (3 women). Students: 58 full-time (29 women), 15 part-time (8 women); includes 15 minority (2 Black or African American, non-Hispanic/Latino; 2 Asian, non-Hispanic/Latino; 9 Hispanic/Latino; 1 Native Hawaiian or other Pacific Islander, non-Hispanic/Latino; 1 Two or more races, non-Hispanic/Latino), 1 international. Average age 29. 161 applicants, 35% accepted, 25 enrolled. In 2010, 19 master's awarded. Degree requirements: For master's, comprehensive exam, thesis. Entrance requirements: For master's, 24 hours of undergraduate course work in English (12 advanced) with minimum GPA of 3.25, 6 hours of course work in foreign language, minimum GPA of 2.75 in last 60 hours, writing portfolios (3 copies), 3 letters of recommendation. Additional exam requirements/recommendations for international students: Required—TOEFL (minimum score 550 paper-based; 213 computer-based; 78 iBT). Application deadline: For fall admission, 1/15 priority date for domestic students, 1/15 for international students; for spring admission, 11/1 priority date for domestic students, 10/1 for international students. Applications are processed on a rolling basis. Application fee: $40 ($90 for international students). Electronic applications accepted. Expenses: Tuition, state resident: full-time $6024; part-time $251 per credit hour. Tuition, nonresident: full-time $13,536; part-time $564 per credit hour. Required fees: $1776; $50 per credit hour. $306 per semester. Financial support: In 2010–11, 39 students received support, including 1 research assistantship (averaging $6,290 per year), 44 teaching assistantships (averaging $5,789 per year); Federal Work-Study and institutionally sponsored loans also available. Support available to part-time students. Financial award application deadline: 4/1; financial award applicants required to submit FAFSA. Unit head: Tom Grimes, Graduate Adviser, 512-245-2163, Fax: 512-245-8546, E-mail: tg02@txstate.edu. Application contact: Dr. J. Michael Willoughby, Dean of Graduate School, 512-245-2581, Fax: 512-245-8365, E-mail: gradcollege@txstate.edu.

Towson University, Program in Professional Writing, Towson, MD 21252-0001. Offers MS. Part-time and evening/weekend programs available. Students: 21 full-time (9 women), 51 part-time (41 women); includes 13 minority (10 Black or African American, non-Hispanic/Latino; 1 American Indian or Alaska Native, non-Hispanic/Latino; 1 Asian, non-Hispanic/Latino; 1 Hispanic/Latino). Average age 32. In 2010, 13 master's awarded. Degree requirements: For master's, thesis optional, exam. Entrance requirements: For master's, sample of written work, minimum GPA of 3.0, 2 letters of recommendation. Application deadline: For fall admission, 3/1 for domestic students; for spring admission, 10/1 for domestic students. Application fee: $50. Electronic applications accepted. Expenses: Tuition, state resident: part-time $324 per credit. Tuition, nonresident: part-time $681 per credit. Required fees: $95 per term. Financial support: Federal Work-Study and unspecified assistantships available. Financial award application deadline: 4/1; financial award applicants required to submit FAFSA. Faculty research: Creative writing, essay writing, sociopsychological linguistics, interdisciplinary rhetoric, global communication. Unit head: Prof. Geoffrey Becker, Graduate Program Director, 410-704-5196, Fax: 410-704-3434, E-mail: gbecker@towson.edu. Application contact: 410-704-2501, Fax: 410-704-4675, E-mail: grads@towson.edu.

Union Institute & University, Master of Arts Program–Online, Montpelier, VT 05602. Offers creativity studies (MA); education (MA); health and wellness (MA); history and culture (MA);

leadership, public policy, and social issues (MA); literature and writing (MA); psychology (MA). Part-time programs available. Postbaccalaureate distance learning degree programs offered (no on-campus study). *Faculty:* 2 full-time (1 woman), 18 part-time/adjunct (11 women). *Students:* 27 full-time (26 women), 119 part-time (98 women); includes 34 minority (25 Black or African American, non-Hispanic/Latino; 3 American Indian or Alaska Native, non-Hispanic/Latino; 6 Hispanic/Latino). Average age 40. In 2010, 26 master's awarded. *Degree requirements:* For master's, thesis. *Application deadline:* Applications are processed on a rolling basis. Application fee: $50. Electronic applications accepted. *Expenses:* Tuition: Full-time $16,430; part-time $685 per credit hour. Required fees: $174; $44 per term. Tuition and fees vary according to course load, degree level and program. *Financial support:* Career-related internships or fieldwork and tuition waivers available. Financial award applicants required to submit FAFSA. *Unit head:* Dr. Brian Webb, Program Director, 802-828-8777, E-mail: brian.webb@tui.edu. *Application contact:* Diane Robinson, Director of Admissions, 888-828-8575, E-mail: diane.robinson@myunion.edu.

The University of Akron, Graduate School, Buchtel College of Arts and Sciences, Department of English, Akron, OH 44325. Offers composition (MA); creative writing (MFA); literature (MA). Part-time programs available. *Faculty:* 28 full-time (14 women), 71 part-time/adjunct (47 women). *Students:* 42 full-time (18 women), 39 part-time (24 women); includes 6 Black or African American, non-Hispanic/Latino. Average age 32. 51 applicants, 90% accepted, 22 enrolled. In 2010, 27 master's awarded. *Degree requirements:* For master's, thesis optional. *Entrance requirements:* For master's, BA in English, minimum GPA of 2.75, writing portfolio, statement of purpose. Additional exam requirements/recommendations for international students: Required—TOEFL (minimum score 580 paper-based; 237 computer-based; 92 iBT). *Application deadline:* Applications are processed on a rolling basis. Application fee: $30 ($40 for international students). Electronic applications accepted. *Expenses:* Tuition, state resident: full-time $6800; part-time $378 per credit hour. Tuition, nonresident: full-time $11,644; part-time $647 per credit hour. Required fees: $1265. One-time fee: $30 full-time. *Financial support:* In 2010–11, 1 research assistantship with full tuition reimbursement, 25 teaching assistantships with full tuition reimbursements were awarded. *Faculty research:* British and American literary studies, literary theory, creative writing, applied linguistics. Total annual research expenditures: $51,119. *Unit head:* Dr. Michael Schuldiner, Chair, 330-972-8556, E-mail: schuldi@uakron.edu. *Application contact:* Dr. Hillary Nunn, Director of Graduate Studies, 330-972-7601, E-mail: nunn@uakron.edu.

The University of Alabama, Graduate School, College of Arts and Sciences, Department of English, Tuscaloosa, AL 35487. Offers composition and rhetoric (PhD); creative writing (MFA), including fiction, poetry; literature (MA, PhD); rhetoric and composition (MA); teaching English as a second language (MATESOL). *Faculty:* 31 full-time (14 women). *Students:* 64 full-time (46 women), 75 part-time (44 women); includes 15 minority (11 Black or African American, non-Hispanic/Latino; 1 Asian, non-Hispanic/Latino; 1 Hispanic/Latino; 1 Native Hawaiian or other Pacific Islander, non-Hispanic/Latino; 1 Two or more races, non-Hispanic/Latino), 7 international. Average age 28. 364 applicants, 20% accepted, 46 enrolled. In 2010, 40 master's, 7 doctorates awarded. *Degree requirements:* For master's, one foreign language, comprehensive exam, thesis (for some programs); for doctorate, 2 foreign languages, comprehensive exam, thesis/dissertation. *Entrance requirements:* For master's and doctorate, GRE, minimum GPA of 3.0, critical writing sample. Additional exam requirements/recommendations for international students: Required—TOEFL. *Application deadline:* For fall admission, 1/15 priority date for domestic students, 1/15 for international students. Application fee: $50 ($60 for international students). Electronic applications accepted. *Expenses:* Tuition, state resident: full-time $7900. Tuition, nonresident: full-time $20,500. *Financial support:* In 2010–11, 7 fellowships with full tuition reimbursements (averaging $15,000 per year), 1 research assistantship (averaging $11,708 per year), 106 teaching assistantships with full tuition reimbursements (averaging $11,708 per year) were awarded; career-related internships or fieldwork, scholarships/grants, health care benefits, and unspecified assistantships also available. Financial award application deadline: 1/15. *Faculty research:* Critical theory; modern, Renaissance, and African-American literature. *Unit head:* Dr. Catherine E. Davies, Director of Graduate Studies, 205-348-8499, E-mail: cdavies@bama.ua.edu. *Application contact:* Vernita W. James, Office Assistant II, 205-348-0766, Fax: 205-348-1388, E-mail: vwjames@bama.ua.edu.

University of Alaska Anchorage, College of Arts and Sciences, Program in Creative Writing and Literary Arts, Anchorage, AK 99508. Offers MFA. Part-time programs available. *Degree requirements:* For master's, comprehensive exam, thesis or alternative. *Entrance requirements:* For master's, portfolio, minimum GPA of 3.0. Additional exam requirements/recommendations for international students: Required—TOEFL (minimum score 550 paper-based; 213 computer-based). *Faculty research:* Alaska Quarterly Review publications, feminist studies, ecocriticism and native writing, poetry.

University of Alaska Fairbanks, College of Liberal Arts, Department of English, Fairbanks, AK 99775-5720. Offers creative writing (MFA); literature (MA); MA/MFA. Part-time programs available. *Faculty:* 16 full-time (7 women). *Students:* 28 full-time (13 women), 13 part-time (9 women); includes 8 minority (1 American Indian or Alaska Native, non-Hispanic/Latino; 3 Asian, non-Hispanic/Latino; 1 Hispanic/Latino; 3 Two or more races, non-Hispanic/Latino). Average age 31. 50 applicants, 44% accepted, 14 enrolled. In 2010, 19 master's awarded. *Degree requirements:* For master's, comprehensive exam, thesis or alternative, oral exams, oral defense. *Entrance requirements:* For master's, GRE General Test, academic writing sample. Additional exam requirements/recommendations for international students: Required—TOEFL (minimum score 550 paper-based; 213 computer-based; 80 iBT). *Application deadline:* For fall admission, 6/1 for domestic students, 3/1 for international students; for spring admission, 10/15 for domestic students, 9/1 for international students. Applications are processed on a rolling basis. Application fee: $60. Electronic applications accepted. *Expenses:* Tuition, state resident: full-time $5688; part-time $316 per credit. Tuition, nonresident: full-time $11,628; part-time $646 per credit. Required fees: $289 per semester. Tuition and fees vary according to course load and reciprocity agreements. *Financial support:* In 2010–11, 23 teaching assistantships with tuition reimbursements (averaging $11,643 per year) were awarded; fellowships with tuition reimbursements, research assistantships with tuition reimbursements, Federal Work-Study, scholarships/grants, health care benefits, and unspecified assistantships also available. Support available to part-time students. Financial award application deadline: 7/1; financial award applicants required to submit FAFSA. *Faculty research:* Traditional Alaskan native literature, British literature, pedagogy, American literature, rhetoric/composition history. *Unit head:* Richard Carr, Department Chair, 907-474-7193, Fax: 907-474-5247, E-mail: faengl@uaf.edu. *Application contact:* Richard Carr, Department Chair, 907-474-7193, Fax: 907-474-5247, E-mail: faengl@uaf.edu.

The University of Arizona, College of Humanities, Department of English, Program in Creative Writing, Tucson, AZ 85721. Offers MFA. *Students:* 38 full-time (23 women), 5 part-time (1 woman); includes 6 Hispanic/Latino; 1 Two or more races, non-Hispanic/Latino, 1 international. Average age 29. 306 applicants, 16% accepted, 24 enrolled. In 2010, 25 master's awarded. *Entrance requirements:* Additional exam requirements/recommendations for international students: Required—TOEFL (minimum score 550 paper-based; 213 computer-based; 79 iBT). *Application deadline:* For fall admission, 1/1 for domestic students, 12/1 for international students. Applications are processed on a rolling basis. Application fee: $75. Electronic applications accepted. *Expenses:* Tuition, state resident: full-time $7692. *Financial support:* Career-related internships or fieldwork, institutionally sponsored loans, and tuition waivers (partial) available. *Unit head:* Aurelie Sheehan, Director, 520-621-3880, E-mail: sheehan@email.arizona.edu. *Application contact:* Marlene Cooksey, Graduate Secretary, 520-621-3880, Fax: 520-621-7397, E-mail: mcooksey@email.arizona.edu.

University of Arkansas, Graduate School, J. William Fulbright College of Arts and Sciences, Department of English, Program in Creative Writing, Fayetteville, AR 72701-1201. Offers MFA. *Students:* 9 full-time (4 women), 28 part-time (12 women); includes 2 minority (1 Asian, non-Hispanic/Latino; 1 Hispanic/Latino). 14 applicants, 14% accepted. In 2010, 10 master's awarded. *Degree requirements:* For master's, thesis. *Application deadline:* For fall admission, 4/1 for international students; for spring admission, 10/1 for international students. Applications are processed on a rolling basis. Application fee: $40 ($50 for international students). Electronic applications accepted. *Financial support:* In 2010–11, 1 research assistantship, 29 teaching assistantships were awarded; fellowships with tuition reimbursements, career-related internships or fieldwork and Federal Work-Study also available. Support available to part-time students. Financial award application deadline: 4/1; financial award applicants required to submit FAFSA. *Unit head:* Dr. Joseph Candido, Interim Director, 479-575-4301, Fax: 479-575-5919, E-mail: candido@uark.edu. *Application contact:* Dr. Joseph Candido, Interim Director, 479-575-4301, Fax: 479-575-5919, E-mail: candido@uark.edu.

University of Arkansas at Little Rock, Graduate School, College of Arts, Humanities, and Social Science, Department of Rhetoric and Writing, Little Rock, AR 72204-1099. Offers professional and technical writing (MA). Part-time and evening/weekend programs available. *Degree requirements:* For master's, thesis or alternative, oral defense of final project. *Entrance requirements:* For master's, GRE, minimum GPA of 3.0, writing portfolio. *Faculty research:* Writing for industry, science, business, and government; composition and rhetorical theory; writing nonfiction; teaching of writing.

University of Baltimore, Graduate School, The Yale Gordon College of Liberal Arts, Program in Creative Writing and Publishing Arts, Baltimore, MD 21201-5779. Offers MFA. Part-time and evening/weekend programs available. *Entrance requirements:* Additional exam requirements/recommendations for international students: Required—TOEFL.

University of Baltimore, Graduate School, The Yale Gordon College of Liberal Arts, Program in Publications Design, Baltimore, MD 21201-5779. Offers MA. Part-time and evening/weekend programs available. *Degree requirements:* For master's, seminar project. *Entrance requirements:* For master's, minimum GPA of 3.0, portfolio, interview. Additional exam requirements/recommendations for international students: Required—TOEFL (minimum score 550 paper-based; 213 computer-based). Electronic applications accepted. *Faculty research:* Communication theory, graphic design, media technology.

The University of British Columbia, Faculty of Arts, Creative Writing Program, Vancouver, BC V6T 1Z1, Canada. Offers creative writing (MFA); creative writing and film (MFA); creative writing and theatre (MFA). Part-time programs available. Postbaccalaureate distance learning degree programs offered (minimal on-campus study). *Degree requirements:* For master's, thesis. *Entrance requirements:* For master's, sample of written work. Additional exam requirements/recommendations for international students: Required—TOEFL (minimum score 550 paper-based; 213 computer-based). Electronic applications accepted. *Expenses:* Contact institution. *Faculty research:* Writing of fiction; poetry, creative nonfiction, plays for stage, screen, television, radio, writing for children and translation, song lyrics and libretto, new media and graphic novel.

The University of British Columbia, Faculty of Arts and Faculty of Graduate Studies, Department of Theatre and Film, Film Program, Vancouver, BC V6T 1Z2, Canada. Offers creative writing and film production (MFA); film production (MFA, Diploma); film studies (MA). *Degree requirements:* For master's, variable foreign language requirement, comprehensive exam, thesis (MA), thesis or project (MFA). *Entrance requirements:* For master's, portfolio (MFA). Additional exam requirements/recommendations for international students: Required—TOEFL (minimum score 600 paper-based; 250 computer-based). Electronic applications accepted. Tuition charges are reported in Canadian dollars. *Expenses:* Tuition, area resident: Full-time $4179 Canadian dollars. International tuition: $7344 Canadian dollars full-time. *Faculty research:* Film theory and violence; American and European cinema; cult cinema; Irish cinema.

University of California, Berkeley, UC Berkeley Extension, Certificate Programs in Writing, Editing and Technical Communication, Berkeley, CA 94720-1500. Offers writing (Postbaccalaureate Certificate). Postbaccalaureate distance learning degree programs offered.

University of California, Davis, Graduate Studies, Program in English, Davis, CA 95616. Offers creative writing (MA); English (MA, PhD). Terminal master's awarded for partial completion of doctoral program. *Degree requirements:* For master's, one foreign language, thesis optional; for doctorate, 2 foreign languages, thesis/dissertation. *Entrance requirements:* For master's and doctorate, GRE General Test, GRE Subject Test, minimum GPA of 3.0, writing sample. Additional exam requirements/recommendations for international students: Required—TOEFL (minimum score 550 paper-based; 213 computer-based). Electronic applications accepted. *Faculty research:* Feminist theory, ethnic literature, literary theory, history of literature, literature of nature.

University of California, Irvine, School of Humanities, Department of English and Comparative Literature, Program in Writing, Irvine, CA 92697. Offers creative writing (MFA), including fiction, poetry. *Students:* 29 full-time (14 women); includes 6 minority (1 Black or African American, non-Hispanic/Latino; 4 Asian, non-Hispanic/Latino; 1 Hispanic/Latino). Average age 28. 584 applicants, 2% accepted, 12 enrolled. In 2010, 14 master's awarded. *Degree requirements:* For master's, thesis. *Entrance requirements:* For master's, minimum GPA of 3.0, sample of written work. *Application deadline:* For fall admission, 1/15 for domestic and international students. Application fee: $80 ($100 for international students). Electronic applications accepted. *Financial support:* Fellowships with full and partial tuition reimbursements, research assistantships, teaching assistantships with partial tuition reimbursements, institutionally sponsored loans and tuition waivers (full and partial) available. Financial award application deadline: 3/1; financial award applicants required to submit FAFSA. *Unit head:* Lynh My Tran, Graduate Program Administrator: M.F.A., 949-824-6718, Fax: 949-824-2916, E-mail: lynh.tran@uci.edu. *Application contact:* Lynh My Tran, Graduate Program Administrator: M.F.A., 949-824-6718, Fax: 949-824-2916, E-mail: lynh.tran@uci.edu.

University of California, Riverside, Graduate Division, Department of Creative Writing, Palm Desert, CA 92211. Offers creative writing and writing for the performing arts (MFA). Program also offered at Palm Desert Graduate Center. Part-time programs available. *Faculty:* 15 part-time/adjunct (5 women). *Students:* 66 part-time (39 women); includes 8 Black or African American, non-Hispanic/Latino; 4 Hispanic/Latino; 1 Native Hawaiian or other Pacific Islander, non-Hispanic/Latino. Average age 39. 57 applicants, 53% accepted, 27 enrolled. *Degree requirements:* For master's, thesis, final project. *Entrance requirements:* For master's, writing sample. Additional exam requirements/recommendations for international students: Required—TOEFL (minimum score 550 paper-based; 213 computer-based; 80 iBT). *Application deadline:* For fall admission, 8/1 for domestic students, 6/1 for international students; for winter admission, 11/1 for domestic students, 8/1 for international students; for spring admission, 2/1 for domestic students, 12/1 for international students. Applications are processed on a rolling basis. Application fee: $70 ($75 for international students). Electronic applications accepted. *Financial support:* In 2010–11, 1 fellowship with partial tuition reimbursement (averaging $12,000 per year) was awarded; research assistantships, teaching assistantships with partial tuition reimbursements. *Faculty research:* Non-fiction, playwriting, screenwriting, poetry, fiction. *Unit head:* Tod Goldberg, Administrative Director, 760-834-0928, Fax: 760-834-0800, E-mail: tod.goldberg@ucr.edu. *Application contact:* Michelle Harding, Program Manager, 760-834-0926, Fax: 760-834-0796, E-mail: michelle.harding@ucr.edu.

University of California, Santa Cruz, Division of Graduate Studies, Division of Social Sciences, Program in Social Documentation, Santa Cruz, CA 95064. Offers MA. *Students:* 14 full-time (11 women); includes 5 minority (3 Hispanic/Latino; 1 Native Hawaiian or other Pacific Islander, non-Hispanic/Latino; 1 Two or more races, non-Hispanic/Latino). Average age 27. 30 applicants, 50% accepted, 8 enrolled. In 2010, 4 master's awarded. *Entrance requirements:* For master's, resume or curriculum vitae, sample of documentary production work. Additional exam requirements/recommendations for international students: Required—TOEFL (minimum score 550 paper-based; 220 computer-based; 83 iBT); Recommended—IELTS (minimum score 8). *Application deadline:* For fall admission, 1/14 for domestic and international students. Application fee: $70 ($90 for international students). Electronic applications accepted. *Financial support:* Fellowships, research assistantships, teaching assistantships, institutionally sponsored

Writing

University of California, Santa Cruz (continued)
loans and tuition waivers available. Financial award applicants required to submit FAFSA. *Faculty research:* Documentation of underrepresented areas of community life. *Unit head:* Robert Valiente-Neighbours, Graduate Program Coordinator, 831-459-4706, E-mail: rneighbo@ucsc.edu. *Application contact:* Robert Valiente-Neighbours, Graduate Program Coordinator, 831-459-4706, E-mail: rneighbo@ucsc.edu.

University of Central Florida, College of Arts and Humanities, Department of English, Program in English, Orlando, FL 32816. Offers creative writing (MFA); English (MA); professional writing (Certificate). *Students:* 49 full-time (25 women), 51 part-time (33 women); includes 7 Black or African American, non-Hispanic/Latino; 1 Asian, non-Hispanic/Latino; 4 Hispanic/Latino; 2 Two or more races, non-Hispanic/Latino. Average age 30. 103 applicants, 55% accepted, 42 enrolled. In 2010, 16 master's, 14 other advanced degrees awarded. Application fee: $30. Electronic applications accepted. *Expenses:* Tuition, state resident: part-time $256.56 per credit hour. Tuition, nonresident: part-time $1011.52 per credit hour. Part-time tuition and fees vary according to program. *Financial support:* In 2010–11, 30 students received support, including 6 fellowships with partial tuition reimbursements available (averaging $9,200 per year), 8 research assistantships with partial tuition reimbursements available (averaging $6,200 per year), 24 teaching assistantships with partial tuition reimbursements available (averaging $6,700 per year).

University of Central Oklahoma, College of Graduate Studies and Research, College of Liberal Arts, Department of English, Edmond, OK 73034-5209. Offers composition skills (MA); contemporary literature (MA); creative writing (MA); teaching English as a second language (MA); traditional studies (MA). Part-time programs available. *Degree requirements:* For master's, one foreign language. *Entrance requirements:* For master's, 24 hours of course work in English language and literature. Additional exam requirements/recommendations for international students: Required—TOEFL (minimum score 550 paper-based; 213 computer-based). Electronic applications accepted. *Faculty research:* John Milton, Harriet Beecher Stowe.

University of Colorado Boulder, Graduate School, College of Arts and Sciences, Department of English, Boulder, CO 80309. Offers literature (MA, PhD), including creative writing (MA). Part-time programs available. *Faculty:* 45 full-time (25 women). *Students:* 113 full-time (64 women), 10 part-time (8 women); includes 12 minority (4 Black or African American, non-Hispanic/Latino; 1 American Indian or Alaska Native, non-Hispanic/Latino; 3 Asian, non-Hispanic/Latino; 4 Hispanic/Latino), 1 international. Average age 31. 405 applicants, 39 enrolled. In 2010, 27 master's, 8 doctorates awarded. *Degree requirements:* For master's, one foreign language, comprehensive exam, thesis or alternative; for doctorate, 2 foreign languages, comprehensive exam, thesis/dissertation. *Entrance requirements:* For master's, GRE General Test, GRE Subject Test, minimum undergraduate GPA of 3.0; for doctorate, GRE General Test, GRE Subject Test. *Application deadline:* For fall admission, 1/1 for domestic students, 12/1 for international students. Application fee: $50 ($60 for international students). *Financial support:* In 2010–11, 22 fellowships (averaging $3,976 per year), 42 research assistantships (averaging $11,068 per year) were awarded; Federal Work-Study and tuition waivers (full) also available. Financial award application deadline: 1/1; financial award applicants required to submit FAFSA. *Faculty research:* Creative writing, literature, language, critical theory. Total annual research expenditures: $1.7 million.

University of Colorado Denver, School of Education and Human Development, Teacher Education Programs, Denver, CO 80217. Offers elementary linguistically diverse education (MA); elementary math and science education (MA); elementary math education (MA); elementary reading and writing (MA); elementary science education (MA); secondary English education (MA); secondary linguistically diverse education (MA); secondary math education (MA); secondary reading and writing (MA); secondary science education (MA); special education (MA). *Accreditation:* NCATE. Part-time and evening/weekend programs available. *Students:* 504 full-time (387 women), 273 part-time (235 women); includes 12 Black or African American, non-Hispanic/Latino; 4 American Indian or Alaska Native, non-Hispanic/Latino; 23 Asian, non-Hispanic/Latino; 52 Hispanic/Latino; 1 Two or more races, non-Hispanic/Latino, 11 international. Average age 31. 310 applicants, 80% accepted, 198 enrolled. In 2010, 222 master's awarded. *Degree requirements:* For master's, comprehensive exam. *Entrance requirements:* For master's, GRE or MAT (required for those with GPA below 2.75), transcripts, resume, letters of recommendation, written statement. Additional exam requirements/recommendations for international students: Required—TOEFL (minimum score 525 paper-based; 197 computer-based). *Application deadline:* For fall admission, 2/15 priority date for domestic students; for spring admission, 9/15 priority date for domestic students. Applications are processed on a rolling basis. Application fee: $50 ($75 for international students). Electronic applications accepted. *Expenses:* Contact institution. *Financial support:* Research assistantships, teaching assistantships, Federal Work-Study available. Financial award application deadline: 4/1; financial award applicants required to submit FAFSA. *Faculty research:* Linguistically diverse education/ESL, elementary reading and writing, elementary teacher education, secondary teacher education, special education. *Unit head:* Cindy Gutierrez, Director, 303-315-4982, E-mail: cindy.gutierrez@ucdenver.edu. *Application contact:* Student Services Center, 303-315-6300, E-mail: education@ucdenver.edu.

University of Denver, Division of Arts, Humanities and Social Sciences, Department of English, Denver, CO 80208. Offers creative writing (PhD); literary studies (MA, PhD); rhetoric and theory (PhD). Part-time programs available. *Faculty:* 18 full-time (7 women), 1 (woman) part-time/adjunct. *Students:* 32 full-time (17 women), 10 part-time (9 women), 1 international. Average age 32. 195 applicants, 11% accepted, 18 enrolled. In 2010, 3 master's, 6 doctorates awarded. *Degree requirements:* For master's, one foreign language, comprehensive exam, thesis; for doctorate, 2 foreign languages, comprehensive exam, thesis/dissertation. *Entrance requirements:* For master's and doctorate, GRE General Test, GRE Subject Test. Additional exam requirements/recommendations for international students: Required—TOEFL (minimum score 570 paper-based; 88 iBT). *Application deadline:* Applications are processed on a rolling basis. Application fee: $60. Electronic applications accepted. *Expenses:* Tuition: Full-time $35,604; part-time $29,670 per year. Required fees: $687 per year. Tuition and fees vary according to program. *Financial support:* In 2010–11, 31 teaching assistantships with full and partial tuition reimbursements (averaging $16,910 per year) were awarded; Federal Work-Study, institutionally sponsored loans, scholarships/grants, and unspecified assistantships also available. Support available to part-time students. Financial award application deadline: 3/1; financial award applicants required to submit FAFSA. *Faculty research:* Cultural studies, creative nonfiction, eighteenth century colonial literature, multicultural literature, Cervantes. *Unit head:* Dr. Clark Davis, Chair, 303-871-2900, Fax: 303-871-2853, E-mail: cldavis@du.edu. *Application contact:* Niki Herrera, Graduate Student Services Assistant, 303-871-4313, Fax: 303-871-2853, E-mail: niki.herrera@du.edu.

University of Denver, University College, Denver, CO 80208. Offers arts and culture (MLS, Certificate), including art, literature, and culture, arts development and program management (Certificate), creative writing; environmental policy and management (MAS, Certificate), including energy and sustainability (Certificate), environmental assessment of nuclear power (Certificate), environmental health and safety (Certificate), environmental management, natural resource management (Certificate); geographic information systems (MAS, Certificate); global affairs (MLS, Certificate), including translation studies, world history and culture; healthcare leadership (MPH, Certificate), including healthcare policy, law, and ethics, medical and healthcare information technologies, strategic management of healthcare; information and communications technology (MCIS, Certificate), including database design and administration (Certificate), geographic information systems (MCIS), information security systems security (Certificate), information systems security (MCIS), project management (MCIS, MPS, Certificate), software design and administration (Certificate), software design and programming (MCIS), technology management, telecommunications technology (MCIS), Web design and development; leadership and organizations (MPS, Certificate), including human capital in organizations, philanthropic leadership, project management (MCIS, MPS, Certificate), strategic innovation and change; organizational and professional communication (MPS, Certificate), including alternative dispute resolution, organizational communication, organizational development and training, public relations and marketing; security management (MAS, Certificate), including emergency planning and response, information security (MAS), organizational security; strategic human resource management (MPS, Certificate), including global human resources (MPS), human resource management and development (MPS). Part-time and evening/weekend programs available. Postbaccalaureate distance learning degree programs offered (no on-campus study). *Faculty:* 7 full-time (2 women), 212 part-time/adjunct (83 women). *Students:* 52 full-time (19 women), 1,044 part-time (625 women); includes 196 minority (81 Black or African American, non-Hispanic/Latino; 7 American Indian or Alaska Native, non-Hispanic/Latino; 30 Asian, non-Hispanic/Latino; 66 Hispanic/Latino; 3 Native Hawaiian or other Pacific Islander, non-Hispanic/Latino; 9 Two or more races, non-Hispanic/Latino), 76 international. Average age 36. 488 applicants, 91% accepted, 339 enrolled. In 2010, 286 master's, 130 other advanced degrees awarded. *Entrance requirements:* Additional exam requirements/recommendations for international students: Required—TOEFL (minimum score 550 paper-based; 80 iBT). *Application deadline:* For fall admission, 6/22 priority date for domestic students, 6/10 priority date for international students; for winter admission, 9/15 priority date for domestic students, 9/6 priority date for international students; for spring admission, 2/3 priority date for domestic students, 12/15 priority date for international students. Applications are processed on a rolling basis. Application fee: $75. Electronic applications accepted. *Expenses:* Contact institution. *Financial support:* Applicants required to submit FAFSA. *Unit head:* Dr. James Davis, Dean, 303-871-2291, Fax: 303-871-4047, E-mail: jdavis@du.edu. *Application contact:* Information Contact, 303-871-3155, Fax: 303-871-4047, E-mail: ucolinfo@du.edu.

University of Florida, Graduate School, College of Liberal Arts and Sciences, Department of English, Gainesville, FL 32611. Offers creative writing (MFA); English (MA, PhD). *Faculty:* 42 full-time (15 women), 4 part-time/adjunct (3 women). *Students:* 148 full-time (75 women), 10 part-time (5 women); includes 8 Black or African American, non-Hispanic/Latino; 5 Asian, non-Hispanic/Latino; 20 Hispanic/Latino, 12 international. Average age 28. 366 applicants, 11% accepted, 23 enrolled. In 2010, 18 master's, 23 doctorates awarded. *Degree requirements:* For master's, one foreign language, comprehensive exam, thesis or alternative; for doctorate, one foreign language, comprehensive exam, thesis/dissertation. *Entrance requirements:* For master's and doctorate, GRE General Test, minimum GPA of 3.0. Additional exam requirements/recommendations for international students: Required—TOEFL (minimum score 550 paper-based; 213 computer-based; 80 iBT), IELTS (minimum score 6). *Application deadline:* For spring admission, 1/1 for domestic and international students. Application fee: $30. Electronic applications accepted. *Expenses:* Tuition, state resident: full-time $10,915.92. Tuition, nonresident: full-time $28,309. *Financial support:* In 2010–11, 179 students received support, including 52 fellowships with tuition reimbursements available, 30 research assistantships with tuition reimbursements available (averaging $8,003 per year), 97 teaching assistantships with tuition reimbursements available (averaging $14,593 per year); unspecified assistantships also available. Financial award application deadline: 1/15; financial award applicants required to submit FAFSA. *Faculty research:* Modern global literatures in English, film and media studies, cultural studies and critical theory, American literature, English literature. *Unit head:* Dr. Kenneth Kidd, Chair, 352-392-6650 Ext. 302, Fax: 352-392-0860, E-mail: kbkidd@ufl.edu. *Application contact:* Dr. Phillip Wegner, Graduate Coordinator, 352-392-6650 Ext. 261, Fax: 352-392-0860, E-mail: pwegner@english.ufl.edu.

University of Georgia, College of Arts and Sciences, Department of English, Athens, GA 30602. Offers creative writing (MFA, PhD); English (MA, MAT, PhD). *Faculty:* 37 full-time (16 women), 1 part-time/adjunct (0 women). *Students:* 70 full-time (38 women), 18 part-time (10 women); includes 7 Black or African American, non-Hispanic/Latino; 1 Asian, non-Hispanic/Latino, 1 international. 280 applicants, 12% accepted, 14 enrolled. In 2010, 11 master's, 14 doctorates awarded. *Degree requirements:* For master's, one foreign language, thesis (MA); for doctorate, 2 foreign languages, thesis/dissertation. *Entrance requirements:* For master's and doctorate, GRE General Test. Additional exam requirements/recommendations for international students: Required—TWE. *Application deadline:* For fall admission, 7/1 priority date for domestic students; for spring admission, 11/15 for domestic students. Application fee: $50. Electronic applications accepted. *Expenses:* Tuition, state resident: full-time $7200; part-time $344 per credit hour. Tuition, nonresident: full-time $21,900; part-time $944 per credit hour. Tuition and fees vary according to course load and program. *Financial support:* Fellowships, research assistantships, teaching assistantships, unspecified assistantships available. *Unit head:* Dr. Doug Anderson, Head, 706-543-2248, Fax: 706-542-2181, E-mail: anderson@uga.edu. *Application contact:* Dr. Adam Parkes, Graduate Coordinator, 706-542-3100, E-mail: aparkes@uga.edu.

University of Houston, College of Liberal Arts and Social Sciences, Department of English, Houston, TX 77204. Offers applied English linguistics (MA); creative writing (MFA); creative writing and literature (MA, PhD); English (MA, PhD). *Faculty:* 27 full-time (11 women), 5 part-time/adjunct (2 women). *Students:* 104 full-time (60 women), 38 part-time (29 women); includes 5 Black or African American, non-Hispanic/Latino; 15 Asian, non-Hispanic/Latino; 7 Hispanic/Latino; 1 Two or more races, non-Hispanic/Latino, 5 international. Average age 31. 379 applicants, 14% accepted, 34 enrolled. In 2010, 17 master's, 8 doctorates awarded. *Degree requirements:* For master's, one foreign language, comprehensive exam (for some programs), thesis (MFA); for doctorate, 2 foreign languages, comprehensive exam, thesis/dissertation. *Entrance requirements:* For master's, GRE General Test, minimum GPA of 3.0 in last 60 hours of course work; for doctorate, GRE General Test, GRE Subject Test (literature), writing sample. Additional exam requirements/recommendations for international students: Required—TOEFL (minimum score 550 paper-based; 79 iBT). *Application deadline:* For fall admission, 2/1 for domestic and international students; for spring admission, 11/1 for domestic and international students. Application fee: $50 ($75 for international students). Electronic applications accepted. *Expenses:* Tuition, state resident: full-time $8592; part-time $358 per credit hour. Tuition, nonresident: full-time $16,032; part-time $668 per credit hour. Required fees: $2889. Tuition and fees vary according to course load and program. *Financial support:* In 2010–11, 14 fellowships with full tuition reimbursements (averaging $6,430 per year), 38 teaching assistantships with full tuition reimbursements (averaging $10,016 per year) were awarded; career-related internships or fieldwork, Federal Work-Study, institutionally sponsored loans, scholarships/grants, health care benefits, and unspecified assistantships also available. Support available to part-time students. Financial award application deadline: 2/1. *Unit head:* Wyman Henderson, Chairperson, 713-743-3004, Fax: 713-743-3215, E-mail: whh@uh.edu. *Application contact:* Julie Kofford, Academic Advisor, 713-743-3004, E-mail: jkofford@central.uh.edu.

University of Houston–Downtown, College of Humanities and Social Sciences, Department of English, Houston, TX 77002. Offers professional writing and technical communication (MS). Part-time and evening/weekend programs available. *Faculty:* 9 full-time (4 women). *Students:* 4 full-time (all women), 17 part-time (12 women); includes 4 Black or African American, non-Hispanic/Latino; 1 Asian, non-Hispanic/Latino; 2 Hispanic/Latino, 1 international. Average age 35. 6 applicants, 83% accepted, 4 enrolled. In 2010, 7 master's awarded. *Degree requirements:* For master's, thesis optional, graduation portfolio with oral defense. *Entrance requirements:* For master's, GRE (including Analytical Writing section), personal application statement, resume, writing sample, 3 letters of recommendation. Additional exam requirements/recommendations for international students: Required—TOEFL (minimum score 600 paper-based; 250 computer-based; 86 iBT). *Application deadline:* For fall admission, 3/15 for domestic and international students; for spring admission, 11/15 for domestic and international students. Application fee: $35 ($60 for international students). Electronic applications accepted. *Expenses:* Tuition, state resident: full-time $4280; part-time $183 per credit hour. Tuition, nonresident: full-time $9230; part-time $458 per credit hour. Required fees: $390 per term. *Financial support:* Applicants required to submit FAFSA. *Faculty research:* Environmental rhetoric, instructional design, usability, assessment, presentation slides. *Unit head:* Dr. Robert Jarrett, Chair, 713-221-8013, Fax: 713-226-5205, E-mail: jarrettr@uhd.edu. *Application contact:* Dr.

Michelle Moosally, Coordinator of MS in Professional Writing and Technical Communication and Professor, Department of English, 713-221-8013, Fax: 713-226-5205, E-mail: mspwtc@uhd.edu.

University of Idaho, College of Graduate Studies, College of Letters, Arts and Social Sciences, Department of English, Program in Creative Writing, Moscow, ID 83844-2282. Offers MFA. *Students:* 33 full-time, 3 part-time. Average age 30. In 2010, 6 master's awarded. *Entrance requirements:* For master's, minimum GPA of 2.8. *Application deadline:* For fall admission, 8/1 for domestic students; for spring admission, 12/15 for domestic students. Applications are processed on a rolling basis. Application fee: $60. Electronic applications accepted. *Expenses:* Tuition, nonresident: part-time $580 per credit. Required fees: $306 per credit. *Financial support:* Applicants required to submit FAFSA. *Unit head:* Dr. Gary Williams, Chair, 208-883-6156. *Application contact:* Dr. Gary Williams, Chair, 208-883-6156.

University of Illinois at Chicago, Graduate College, College of Liberal Arts and Sciences, Department of English, Chicago, IL 60607-7128. Offers English (MA, PhD), including creative writing (PhD), English education (MA), English studies, writing (MA); linguistics (MA), including teaching English to speakers of other languages/applied linguistics. Part-time and evening/weekend programs available. *Degree requirements:* For doctorate, variable foreign language requirement, thesis/dissertation, written and oral exams. *Entrance requirements:* For master's, GRE General Test, GRE Subject Test; for doctorate, GRE General Test, GRE Subject Test, minimum GPA of 2.0. Additional exam requirements/recommendations for international students: Required—TOEFL. Electronic applications accepted. *Faculty research:* Literary history and theory.

University of Illinois at Urbana–Champaign, Graduate College, College of Liberal Arts and Sciences, Department of English, Champaign, IL 61820. Offers creative writing (MFA); English (MA, PhD). *Faculty:* 49 full-time (22 women), 1 (woman) part-time/adjunct. *Students:* 72 full-time (49 women), 71 part-time (49 women); includes 3 Black or African American, non-Hispanic/Latino; 9 Asian, non-Hispanic/Latino; 12 Hispanic/Latino, 12 international. 412 applicants, 8% accepted, 12 enrolled. In 2010, 20 master's, 14 doctorates awarded. *Entrance requirements:* For master's, GRE General Test, GRE Subject Test, minimum GPA of 3.0; writing sample. Additional exam requirements/recommendations for international students: Required—TOEFL (minimum score 550 paper-based; 213 computer-based). *Application deadline:* Applications are processed on a rolling basis. Application fee: $75 ($90 for international students). Electronic applications accepted. *Financial support:* In 2010–11, 42 fellowships, 31 research assistantships, 113 teaching assistantships were awarded; tuition waivers (full and partial) also available. *Faculty research:* English and American literature, cultural studies and critical theory. *Unit head:* Curtis Perry, Head, 217-333-2391, Fax: 217-333-4321, E-mail: cperry@illinois.edu. *Application contact:* Stephanie J. Shockey, Office Support Specialist, 217-333-3646, Fax: 217-333-4321, E-mail: shockey@illinois.edu.

The University of Iowa, Graduate College, College of Liberal Arts and Sciences, Department of English, Iowa City, IA 52242-1316. Offers English (PhD); literary criticism (PhD); literary history (PhD); literary studies (MA); nonfiction writing (MFA); rhetorical theory and stylistics (PhD); writer's workshop (MFA); JD/PhD. *Degree requirements:* For master's, thesis (for some programs), exam; for doctorate, comprehensive exam, thesis/dissertation. *Entrance requirements:* For master's and doctorate, GRE General Test, minimum GPA of 3.0. Additional exam requirements/recommendations for international students: Required—TOEFL (minimum score 640 paper-based; 273 computer-based; 111 iBT). Electronic applications accepted.

The University of Kansas, Graduate Studies, College of Liberal Arts and Sciences, Department of English, Lawrence, KS 66045. Offers creative writing (MFA); English (MA, PhD). Part-time programs available. *Faculty:* 39 full-time (18 women). *Students:* 93 full-time (63 women), 12 part-time (6 women); includes 16 minority (7 Black or African American, non-Hispanic/Latino; 1 American Indian or Alaska Native, non-Hispanic/Latino; 6 Hispanic/Latino; 2 Two or more races, non-Hispanic/Latino), 4 international. Average age 32. 173 applicants, 21% accepted, 21 enrolled. In 2010, 12 master's, 6 doctorates awarded. *Degree requirements:* For master's, one foreign language, comprehensive exam (for some programs), thesis or alternative; for doctorate, 2 foreign languages, comprehensive exam, thesis/dissertation. *Entrance requirements:* For master's and doctorate, GRE General Test, minimum GPA of 3.3. Additional exam requirements/recommendations for international students: Required—TOEFL. *Application deadline:* For fall admission, 12/31 for domestic and international students. Application fee: $55 ($65 for international students). Electronic applications accepted. *Expenses:* Tuition, state resident: full-time $7092; part-time $295.50 per credit hour. Tuition, nonresident: full-time $16,590; part-time $691.25 per credit hour. Required fees: $858; $71.49 per credit hour. Tuition and fees vary according to course load, campus/location and program. *Financial support:* Fellowships with full tuition reimbursements, research assistantships with full and partial tuition reimbursements, teaching assistantships with full and partial tuition reimbursements, unspecified assistantships available. Financial award application deadline: 12/31. *Faculty research:* African-American literature, twentieth century American literature, Renaissance literature, creative writing. *Unit head:* Marta Caminero-Santangelo, Chair, 785-864-4520, E-mail: camsan@ku.edu. *Application contact:* Joseph Harrington, Director of Graduate Studies, 785-864-4520, E-mail: jharring@ku.edu.

University of Louisiana at Lafayette, College of Liberal Arts, Department of English, Lafayette, LA 70504. Offers British and American literature (MA), including creative writing, folklore, rhetoric; creative writing (PhD); literature (PhD); rhetoric (PhD). Part-time programs available. Terminal master's awarded for partial completion of doctoral program. *Degree requirements:* For master's, one foreign language, thesis or alternative; for doctorate, 2 foreign languages, comprehensive exam, thesis/dissertation. *Entrance requirements:* For master's, GRE General Test, minimum GPA of 2.75; for doctorate, GRE General Test, minimum GPA of 3.0. Additional exam requirements/recommendations for international students: Required—TOEFL (minimum score 550 paper-based; 213 computer-based). Electronic applications accepted. *Faculty research:* Composition theory, Southern literature, medieval literature.

University of Louisville, Graduate School, College of Arts and Sciences, Department of English, Louisville, KY 40292. Offers English (MA), including creative writing, literature, rhetoric and composition (MA, PhD); English rhetoric and composition (PhD), including rhetoric and composition (MA, PhD). Part-time programs available. *Faculty:* 40 full-time (22 women). *Students:* 78 full-time (41 women), 25 part-time (12 women); includes 3 Black or African American, non-Hispanic/Latino; 1 American Indian or Alaska Native, non-Hispanic/Latino; 2 Asian, non-Hispanic/Latino; 2 Hispanic/Latino, 7 international. Average age 30. 97 applicants, 64% accepted, 38 enrolled. In 2010, 21 master's, 8 doctorates awarded. *Degree requirements:* For master's, one foreign language, thesis or culminating project; for doctorate, 2 foreign languages, comprehensive exam, thesis/dissertation. *Entrance requirements:* For master's, GRE General Test, 2 academic letters of recommendation; for doctorate, GRE General Test, 15-20 page critical writing sample, 1000-word statement of professional goals, 3 academic letters of recommendation, transcripts of all college work. Additional exam requirements/recommendations for international students: Required—TOEFL (minimum score 600 paper-based; 210 computer-based; 100 iBT). *Application deadline:* For fall admission, 8/1 for domestic students, 1/5 for international students; for spring admission, 12/1 for domestic students. Applications are processed on a rolling basis. Application fee: $50. Electronic applications accepted. *Expenses:* Tuition, state resident: full-time $9144; part-time $508 per credit hour. Tuition, nonresident: full-time $19,026; part-time $1057 per credit hour. Tuition and fees vary according to program and reciprocity agreements. *Financial support:* In 2010–11, 49 students received support, including 9 fellowships with full tuition reimbursements available, 40 teaching assistantships with full tuition reimbursements available; health care benefits and unspecified assistantships also available. Financial award application deadline: 1/5. *Faculty research:* American and English literatures and cultures, rhetoric and composition, critical theory and cultural studies, creative writing. Total annual research expenditures: $278,898. *Unit head:* Dr. Susan Griffin, Chair, 502-852-6801, Fax: 502-852-4182, E-mail: smgriff01@louisville.edu. *Application contact:* Libby Leggett, Director, Graduate Admissions, 502-852-3101, Fax: 502-852-6536, E-mail: gradadm@louisville.edu.

University of Maine, Graduate School, College of Liberal Arts and Sciences, Department of English, Orono, ME 04469. Offers composition and pedagogy (MA); creative (MA); gender and literature (MA); poetry and poetics (MA). Part-time and evening/weekend programs available. *Faculty:* 18 full-time (7 women), 20 part-time/adjunct (10 women). *Students:* 25 full-time (8 women), 6 part-time (5 women). Average age 28. 36 applicants, 47% accepted, 14 enrolled. In 2010, 13 degrees awarded. *Degree requirements:* For master's, one foreign language, thesis optional. *Entrance requirements:* For master's, GRE General Test, minimum GPA of 3.0. Additional exam requirements/recommendations for international students: Required—TOEFL. *Application deadline:* For fall admission, 2/1 priority date for domestic students. Applications are processed on a rolling basis. Application fee: $65. Electronic applications accepted. *Expenses:* Tuition, state resident: full-time $400. Tuition, nonresident: full-time $1050. *Financial support:* In 2010–11, 21 teaching assistantships with tuition reimbursements (averaging $12,790 per year) were awarded; Federal Work-Study and tuition waivers (full and partial) also available. Financial award application deadline: 3/1. *Faculty research:* Contemporary poetics, contemporary criticism, composition theory and pedagogy, feminist approaches to literature. *Unit head:* Dr. Naomi Jacobs, Chair, 207-581-3822, Fax: 207-581-1604. *Application contact:* Scott G. Delcourt, Associate Dean of the Graduate School, 207-581-3291, Fax: 207-581-3232, E-mail: graduate@maine.edu.

The University of Manchester, School of Arts, Histories and Cultures, Manchester, United Kingdom. Offers anthropology, media and performance (PhD); applied theatre professional (PhD); archaeology (PhD); art history and visual studies (PhD); arts management and cultural policy (PhD); classics and ancient history (PhD); composition (PhD); creative writing (PhD); drama (PhD); economic and social history (PhD); electroacoustic composition (PhD); English and American studies (PhD); history (PhD); humanitarianism and conflict response (PhD); museology (PhD); music (PhD); musicology (PhD); religions and theology (PhD).

University of Maryland, College Park, Academic Affairs, College of Arts and Humanities, Department of English, Creative Writing Program, College Park, MD 20742. Offers MA, MFA, PhD. *Students:* 31 full-time (19 women), 19 part-time (8 women); includes 2 Black or African American, non-Hispanic/Latino; 5 Asian, non-Hispanic/Latino; 1 Hispanic/Latino, 1 international. 190 applicants, 25% accepted, 19 enrolled. In 2010, 7 master's awarded. *Degree requirements:* For master's, thesis optional, written exam; for doctorate, one foreign language, oral and written exams. *Entrance requirements:* For master's, GRE General Test, minimum GPA of 3.5, writing sample, 3 letters of recommendation. Additional exam requirements/recommendations for international students: Required—TOEFL. *Application deadline:* For fall admission, 1/15 for domestic and international students. Applications are processed on a rolling basis. Application fee: $75. Electronic applications accepted. *Expenses:* Tuition, state resident: part-time $471 per credit hour. Tuition, nonresident: part-time $1016 per credit hour. Required fees: $337 per term. *Financial support:* In 2010–11, 19 teaching assistantships (averaging $15,771 per year) were awarded; fellowships, research assistantships also available. Financial award applicants required to submit FAFSA. *Faculty research:* Early British literature, American literature. *Unit head:* Kent Cartwright, Chair, 301-405-3807, E-mail: kcartwri@umd.edu. *Application contact:* Dean of Graduate School, 301-405-0376, Fax: 301-314-9305.

University of Massachusetts Amherst, Graduate School, College of Humanities and Fine Arts, Department of English, Amherst, MA 01003. Offers creative writing (MFA); English and American literature (MA, PhD). Part-time programs available. *Faculty:* 46 full-time (22 women). *Students:* 98 full-time (55 women), 95 part-time (63 women); includes 27 minority (6 Black or African American, non-Hispanic/Latino; 1 American Indian or Alaska Native, non-Hispanic/Latino; 8 Asian, non-Hispanic/Latino; 10 Hispanic/Latino; 2 Two or more races, non-Hispanic/Latino), 7 international. Average age 31. 623 applicants, 13% accepted, 38 enrolled. In 2010, 33 master's, 7 doctorates awarded. Terminal master's awarded for partial completion of doctoral program. *Degree requirements:* For master's, one foreign language, thesis optional; for doctorate, one foreign language, comprehensive exam, thesis/dissertation. *Entrance requirements:* For master's, GRE General Test, GRE Subject Test (MA), writing sample (MFA); for doctorate, GRE General Test, GRE Subject Test. Additional exam requirements/recommendations for international students: Required—TOEFL (minimum score 550 paper-based; 213 computer-based; 80 iBT), IELTS (minimum score 6.5). *Application deadline:* For fall admission, 12/1 for domestic and international students. Applications are processed on a rolling basis. Application fee: $50 ($65 for international students). Electronic applications accepted. *Expenses:* Tuition, state resident: full-time $2640. Required fees: $8282. One-time fee: $357 full-time. *Financial support:* In 2010–11, 3 fellowships with full tuition reimbursements (averaging $5,839 per year), 8 research assistantships with full tuition reimbursements (averaging $8,705 per year), 51 teaching assistantships with full tuition reimbursements (averaging $9,896 per year) were awarded; career-related internships or fieldwork, Federal Work-Study, scholarships/grants, traineeships, health care benefits, tuition waivers (full), and unspecified assistantships also available. Support available to part-time students. Financial award application deadline: 12/1; financial award applicants required to submit FAFSA. *Unit head:* Dr. Joseph F. Bartolomeo, Department Head, 413-545-2575, Fax: 413-545-3880. *Application contact:* Jean M. Ames, Supervisor of Admissions, 413-545-0722, Fax: 413-577-0010, E-mail: gradadm@grad.umass.edu.

University of Massachusetts Dartmouth, Graduate School, College of Arts and Sciences, Program in Professional Writing, North Dartmouth, MA 02747-2300. Offers MA, Post-baccalaureate Certificate. Part-time programs available. *Faculty:* 24 full-time (12 women), 37 part-time/adjunct (24 women). *Students:* 6 full-time (5 women), 19 part-time (12 women); includes 1 Hispanic/Latino. Average age 35. 12 applicants, 42% accepted, 4 enrolled. In 2010, 8 master's awarded. *Degree requirements:* For master's, thesis. *Entrance requirements:* For master's, MAT or GRE, portfolio or writing sample (10-30 pages), 3 letters of recommendation. Additional exam requirements/recommendations for international students: Required—TOEFL (minimum score 500 paper-based). *Application deadline:* For fall admission, 4/1 for domestic students, 2/1 for international students; for spring admission, 11/1 for domestic students, 9/1 for international students. Application fee: $40 ($60 for international students). Electronic applications accepted. *Expenses:* Tuition, state resident: full-time $2071; part-time $86 per credit. Tuition, nonresident: full-time $8099; part-time $337 per credit. Required fees: $9446; $394 per credit. One-time fee: $75. Part-time tuition and fees vary according to class time, course load, degree level and reciprocity agreements. *Financial support:* In 2010–11, 9 teaching assistantships with full tuition reimbursements (averaging $10,450 per year) were awarded; career-related internships or fieldwork, Federal Work-Study, and unspecified assistantships also available. Support available to part-time students. Financial award application deadline: 3/1; financial award applicants required to submit FAFSA. *Faculty research:* Rhetoric/communication studies, ethnic literatures, technology transfer, women writers, pedagogy. Total annual research expenditures: $2,589. *Unit head:* Dr. Christopher Eisenhart, Director, 508-910-6468, Fax: 508-999-9235, E-mail: ceisenhart@umassd.edu. *Application contact:* Elan Turcotte-Shamski, Graduate Admissions Officer, 508-999-8604, Fax: 508-999-8183, E-mail: graduate@umassd.edu.

University of Memphis, Graduate School, College of Arts and Sciences, Department of English, Memphis, TN 38152. Offers African-American literature (Graduate Certificate); applied linguistics (PhD); composition studies (PhD); creative writing (MFA); English as a second language (MA); linguistics (MA); literary and cultural studies (PhD), including African-American literature; literature (MA); professional writing (MA, PhD); teaching English as a second language (Graduate Certificate). Part-time and evening/weekend programs available. Post-baccalaureate distance learning degree programs offered (no on-campus study). *Faculty:* 31 full-time (15 women), 2 part-time/adjunct (both women). *Students:* 108 full-time (70 women), 107 part-time (69 women); includes 15 minority (2 Black or African American, non-Hispanic/Latino; 2 Asian, non-Hispanic/Latino; 6 Hispanic/Latino; 5 Two or more races, non-Hispanic/Latino), 8 international. Average age 34. 128 applicants, 71% accepted, 29 enrolled. In 2010, 38 master's, 4 doctorates, 21 other advanced degrees awarded. Terminal master's awarded

Writing

University of Memphis (continued)

for partial completion of doctoral program. *Degree requirements:* For master's, one foreign language, comprehensive exam, thesis optional; for doctorate, 2 foreign languages, comprehensive exam, thesis/dissertation. *Entrance requirements:* For master's and doctorate, GRE. Additional exam requirements/recommendations for international students: Required—TOEFL. *Application deadline:* For fall admission, 7/1 for domestic students; for spring admission, 10/15 for domestic students. Applications are processed on a rolling basis. Application fee: $35 ($60 for international students). Electronic applications accepted. *Financial support:* In 2010–11, 123 students received support; research assistantships with full tuition reimbursements available, teaching assistantships with full tuition reimbursements available, Federal Work-Study, scholarships/grants, and unspecified assistantships available. Financial award application deadline: 2/15; financial award applicants required to submit FAFSA. *Faculty research:* Applied linguistics, British and American literature, professional writing, composition studies. *Unit head:* Dr. Verner D. Mitchell, Chair, 901-678-3099, Fax: 901-678-2226, E-mail: vdmtchll@memphis.edu. *Application contact:* Dr. Verner D. Mitchell, Director, Graduate Studies, 901-678-3099, Fax: 901-678-2226, E-mail: vdmtchll@memphis.edu.

University of Miami, Graduate School, College of Arts and Sciences, Department of English, Coral Gables, FL 33124. Offers creative writing (MFA); English (MA, PhD). Part-time programs available. Terminal master's awarded for partial completion of doctoral program. *Degree requirements:* For master's, one foreign language, thesis optional; for doctorate, one foreign language, thesis/dissertation. *Entrance requirements:* For master's and doctorate, GRE General Test. Electronic applications accepted. *Faculty research:* Anglo-Irish literature, feminist criticism and theory, Caribbean literature, early modern literature and culture, postcolonial and ethnic studies.

University of Michigan, Horace H. Rackham School of Graduate Studies, College of Literature, Science, and the Arts, Department of English Language and Literature, Creative Writing Program, Ann Arbor, MI 48109. Offers MFA. *Faculty:* 10 full-time (5 women). *Students:* 46 full-time (28 women); includes 12 minority (7 Black or African American, non-Hispanic/Latino; 4 Asian, non-Hispanic/Latino; 1 Hispanic/Latino), 2 international. 1,072 applicants, 3% accepted, 22 enrolled. In 2010, 22 master's awarded. *Degree requirements:* For master's, comprehensive exam, thesis. *Entrance requirements:* For master's, writing sample. Additional exam requirements/recommendations for international students: Required—TOEFL (minimum score 620 paper-based; 260 computer-based; 106 iBT). *Application deadline:* For fall admission, 1/1 for domestic and international students. Application fee: $65 ($75 for international students). Electronic applications accepted. *Expenses:* Tuition, state resident: full-time $17,784; part-time $1116 per credit hour. Tuition, nonresident: full-time $35,944; part-time $2125 per credit hour. International tuition: $35,994 full-time. Required fees: $95 per semester. Tuition and fees vary according to course load, degree level and program. *Financial support:* In 2010–11, 46 students received support; fellowships with tuition reimbursements available, teaching assistantships with tuition reimbursements available, health care benefits and summer funding available. *Faculty research:* Prose, poetry. *Unit head:* Prof. Michael Byers, Director, 734-763-2267. *Application contact:* Graduate Admissions Office, 734-936-2274, Fax: 734-763-3128, E-mail: grad.eng.admis@um.cc.umich.edu.

University of Missouri–Kansas City, College of Arts and Sciences, Department of English Language and Literature, Kansas City, MO 64110-2499. Offers creative writing and media arts (MFA); English (MA, PhD). PhD (interdisciplinary) offered through the School of Graduate Studies. Part-time and evening/weekend programs available. *Faculty:* 22 full-time (15 women), 21 part-time/adjunct (10 women). *Students:* 11 full-time (7 women), 47 part-time (23 women); includes 6 minority (5 Black or African American, non-Hispanic/Latino; 1 Asian, non-Hispanic/Latino). Average age 30. 75 applicants, 40% accepted, 22 enrolled. In 2010, 11 master's awarded. *Degree requirements:* For master's, one foreign language; for doctorate, 2 foreign languages, comprehensive exam, thesis/dissertation. *Entrance requirements:* For master's, GRE General Test, 3 letters of recommendation. Additional exam requirements/recommendations for international students: Required—TOEFL (minimum score 550 paper-based; 213 computer-based; 80 iBT). *Application deadline:* For fall admission, 1/15 for domestic students, 1/15 priority date for international students. Applications are processed on a rolling basis. Application fee: $45 ($50 for international students). Electronic applications accepted. *Expenses:* Tuition, state resident: full-time $5522.40; part-time $306.80 per credit hour. Tuition, nonresident: full-time $7128; part-time $792 per credit hour. Required fees: $261.15 per term. *Financial support:* In 2010–11, 12 teaching assistantships (averaging $13,358 per year) were awarded; career-related internships or fieldwork, Federal Work-Study, and institutionally sponsored loans also available. Support available to part-time students. Financial award application deadline: 3/1; financial award applicants required to submit FAFSA. *Faculty research:* Creative writing: poetry and prose, computational linguistics, rhetoric and composition, African-American and British literature, print culture. Total annual research expenditures: $13,729. *Unit head:* Dr. Jeff Rydberg-Cox, Co-Chair, 816-235-2560, Fax: 816-235-1308, E-mail: rydbergcoxj@umkc.edu. *Application contact:* Dr. Laurie Ellinghausen, Director of Graduate Studies, 816-235-6032, E-mail: ellinghausenl@umkc.edu.

University of Missouri–St. Louis, College of Arts and Sciences, Department of English, St. Louis, MO 63121. Offers American literature (MA); creative writing (MFA); English literature (MA); linguistics (MA); teaching of writing (Certificate). Part-time and evening/weekend programs available. *Faculty:* 19 full-time (9 women), 2 part-time/adjunct (1 woman). *Students:* 25 full-time (12 women), 95 part-time (62 women); includes 13 minority (6 Black or African American, non-Hispanic/Latino; 2 American Indian or Alaska Native, non-Hispanic/Latino; 3 Asian, non-Hispanic/Latino; 1 Hispanic/Latino; 1 Two or more races, non-Hispanic/Latino), 1 international. Average age 30. 103 applicants, 41% accepted, 24 enrolled. In 2010, 241 master's, 5 other advanced degrees awarded. *Degree requirements:* For master's, thesis optional. *Entrance requirements:* For master's, two letters of recommendation; writing sample (MFA). Additional exam requirements/recommendations for international students: Required—TOEFL (minimum score 550 paper-based; 213 computer-based). *Application deadline:* For fall admission, 7/1 priority date for domestic and international students; for spring admission, 12/1 priority date for domestic and international students. Applications are processed on a rolling basis. Application fee: $35 ($40 for international students). Electronic applications accepted. *Expenses:* Tuition, state resident: full-time $5522; part-time $306.80 per credit hour. Tuition, nonresident: full-time $14,253; part-time $792.10 per credit hour. Required fees: $658; $49 per credit hour. One-time fee: $12. Tuition and fees vary according to program. *Financial support:* In 2010–11, 6 research assistantships with full and partial tuition reimbursements (averaging $5,666 per year), 10 teaching assistantships with full and partial tuition reimbursements (averaging $9,000 per year) were awarded. Financial award applicants required to submit FAFSA. *Faculty research:* Victorian literature, Shakespeare and Renaissance literature, eighteenth century literature, composition theory. *Unit head:* Dr. Frank Grady, Director of Graduate Studies, 314-516-5541, Fax: 314-516-5781, E-mail: fgrady@umsl.edu. *Application contact:* 314-516-5458, Fax: 314-516-5310, E-mail: gradadm@umsl.edu.

The University of Montana, Graduate School, College of Arts and Sciences, Department of English, Program in Creative Writing, Missoula, MT 59812-0002. Offers fiction (MFA); non-fiction (MFA); poetry (MFA). *Degree requirements:* For master's, final creative paper. *Entrance requirements:* For master's, GRE General Test, sample of written work. Additional exam requirements/recommendations for international students: Required—TOEFL. *Faculty research:* Fiction, poetry, nonfiction.

University of Nebraska at Kearney, College of Graduate Study, College of Fine Arts and Humanities, Department of English, Kearney, NE 68849-0001. Offers creative writing (MA); literature (MA). Part-time and evening/weekend programs available. *Degree requirements:* For master's, thesis optional. *Entrance requirements:* For master's, GRE General Test. Additional exam requirements/recommendations for international students: Required—TOEFL (minimum score 550 paper-based; 213 computer-based). Electronic applications accepted. *Faculty research:* Narrative theory, popular culture, western and plains literature, women's studies, media studies.

University of Nebraska at Omaha, Graduate Studies, College of Arts and Sciences, Department of English, Omaha, NE 68182. Offers advanced writing (Certificate); English (MA); teaching English to speakers of other languages (Certificate); technical communication (Certificate). Part-time and evening/weekend programs available. *Faculty:* 16 full-time (8 women). *Students:* 22 full-time (9 women), 58 part-time (44 women); includes 3 minority (1 Asian, non-Hispanic/Latino; 2 Two or more races, non-Hispanic/Latino), 2 international. Average age 32. 48 applicants, 79% accepted, 27 enrolled. In 2010, 17 master's, 15 other advanced degrees awarded. *Degree requirements:* For master's, comprehensive exam, thesis (for some programs). *Entrance requirements:* For master's, minimum GPA of 3.0, 3 letters of recommendation, writing sample. Additional exam requirements/recommendations for international students: Required—TOEFL (minimum score 600 paper-based; 250 computer-based; 100 iBT). *Application deadline:* For fall admission, 8/1 priority date for domestic students; for spring admission, 12/1 priority date for domestic students. Applications are processed on a rolling basis. Application fee: $45. Electronic applications accepted. *Financial support:* In 2010–11, 46 students received support; fellowships, teaching assistantships with tuition reimbursements available, Federal Work-Study, institutionally sponsored loans, scholarships/grants, tuition waivers (partial), and unspecified assistantships available. Support available to part-time students. Financial award application deadline: 3/1; financial award applicants required to submit FAFSA. *Unit head:* Dr. Robert Darcy, Chairperson, 402-554-3636. *Application contact:* Dr. Tracy Bridgeford, Student Contact, 402-554-3636.

University of Nebraska at Omaha, Graduate Studies, Program in Writing, Omaha, NE 68182. Offers MFA. Postbaccalaureate distance learning degree programs offered (no on-campus study). *Faculty:* 4 full-time (2 women). *Students:* 15 full-time (10 women); includes 3 minority (1 Black or African American, non-Hispanic/Latino; 2 Hispanic/Latino). Average age 38. 22 applicants, 64% accepted, 9 enrolled. In 2010, 9 master's awarded. *Degree requirements:* For master's, comprehensive exam. *Entrance requirements:* For master's, portfolio, letters of recommendation. Additional exam requirements/recommendations for international students: Required—TOEFL (minimum score 550 paper-based; 213 computer-based; 80 iBT). *Application deadline:* For fall admission, 2/15 priority date for domestic students; for spring admission, 7/15 priority date for domestic students. Applications are processed on a rolling basis. Application fee: $45. Electronic applications accepted. *Financial support:* Scholarships/grants and tuition waivers (partial) available. Financial award application deadline: 3/1; financial award applicants required to submit FAFSA. *Unit head:* Dr. Arthur Homer, Director, 402-554-4801. *Application contact:* Dr. Arthur Homer, Director, Graduate Studies, 402-554-2341, Fax: 402-554-3143, E-mail: graduate@unomaha.edu.

University of Nebraska–Lincoln, Graduate College, College of Arts and Sciences, Department of English, Lincoln, NE 68588-0333. Offers composition and rhetoric (MA, PhD); creative writing (MA, PhD); literature studies (MA, PhD). *Degree requirements:* For master's, thesis optional; for doctorate, one foreign language, comprehensive exam, thesis/dissertation. *Entrance requirements:* For master's, writing sample; for doctorate, GRE General Test, writing sample. Additional exam requirements/recommendations for international students: Required—TOEFL (minimum score 600 paper-based; 250 computer-based). Electronic applications accepted. *Faculty research:* Creative writing, composition and rhetoric, women's studies, North American literature, medieval/Renaissance studies.

University of Nevada, Las Vegas, Graduate College, College of Liberal Arts, Department of English, Las Vegas, NV 89154-5011. Offers creative writing (MFA); English (MA, PhD). Part-time programs available. *Faculty:* 32 full-time (12 women), 5 part-time/adjunct (0 women). *Students:* 67 full-time (34 women), 26 part-time (14 women); includes 35 minority (1 Black or African American, non-Hispanic/Latino; 7 Hispanic/Latino; 1 Native Hawaiian or other Pacific Islander, non-Hispanic/Latino; 26 Two or more races, non-Hispanic/Latino), 4 international. Average age 33. 202 applicants, 13% accepted, 25 enrolled. In 2010, 16 master's, 4 doctorates awarded. *Degree requirements:* For master's, one foreign language, comprehensive exam, thesis (for some programs); for doctorate, 2 foreign languages, comprehensive exam, thesis/dissertation. *Entrance requirements:* For master's, GRE General Test (verbal); for doctorate, GRE General Test (verbal), GRE Subject Test. Additional exam requirements/recommendations for international students: Required—TOEFL (minimum score 550 paper-based; 213 computer-based; 80 iBT), IELTS (minimum score 7). *Application deadline:* For fall admission, 2/15 priority date for domestic and international students; for spring admission, 11/1 priority date for domestic and international students. Applications are processed on a rolling basis. Application fee: $60 ($95 for international students). Electronic applications accepted. *Expenses:* Tuition, area resident: Part-time $239.50 per credit. Tuition, state resident: part-time $239.50 per credit. Tuition, nonresident: part-time $503 per credit. Required fees: $108 per semester. Tuition and fees vary according to course load, program and reciprocity agreements. *Financial support:* In 2010–11, 68 students received support, including 1 fellowship with full tuition reimbursement available (averaging $14,000 per year), 12 research assistantships with partial tuition reimbursements available (averaging $13,782 per year), 55 teaching assistantships with partial tuition reimbursements available (averaging $11,127 per year); institutionally sponsored loans, scholarships/grants, health care benefits, and unspecified assistantships also available. Financial award application deadline: 3/1. *Faculty research:* Professional and technical writing, Renaissance literature, modern American and British literature, writing of novels and poetry, eighteenth- and nineteenth-century British literature. *Unit head:* Dr. Richard Harp, Chair/ Professor, 702-895-0919, Fax: 702-895-4801, E-mail: richard.harp@unlv.edu. *Application contact:* Graduate College Admissions Evaluator, 702-895-3320, Fax: 702-895-4180, E-mail: gradcollege@unlv.edu.

University of New Hampshire, Graduate School, College of Liberal Arts, Department of English, Durham, NH 03824. Offers English (MFA, PhD); English education (MST); language and linguistics (MA); literature (MA); writing (MA). Part-time programs available. *Faculty:* 35 full-time (18 women). *Students:* 60 full-time (33 women), 68 part-time (45 women); includes 5 minority (1 Black or African American, non-Hispanic/Latino; 1 Hispanic/Latino; 3 Two or more races, non-Hispanic/Latino), 5 international. Average age 33. 291 applicants, 47% accepted, 50 enrolled. In 2010, 39 master's, 6 doctorates awarded. *Degree requirements:* For master's, one foreign language; for doctorate, 2 foreign languages, thesis/dissertation. *Entrance requirements:* For master's, GRE General Test, sample of written work; for doctorate, GRE General Test, GRE Subject Test, sample of written work. Additional exam requirements/recommendations for international students: Required—TOEFL (minimum score 550 paper-based; 213 computer-based; 80 iBT). *Application deadline:* For fall admission, 6/1 priority date for domestic students, 2/15 for international students; for spring admission, 12/1 for domestic students. Applications are processed on a rolling basis. Application fee: $65. Electronic applications accepted. *Financial support:* In 2010–11, 63 students received support, including 1 fellowship, 46 teaching assistantships; research assistantships, career-related internships or fieldwork, Federal Work-Study, scholarships/grants, and tuition waivers (full and partial) also available. Support available to part-time students. Financial award application deadline: 2/15. *Unit head:* Dr. Andrew Merton, Chairperson, 603-862-3963. *Application contact:* Jamie Auger, Administrative Assistant, 603-862-3963, E-mail: engl.grad@unh.edu.

University of New Mexico, Graduate School, College of Arts and Sciences, Department of English, Albuquerque, NM 87131-2039. Offers creative writing (MFA); English (MA, PhD). Part-time programs available. *Faculty:* 81 full-time (54 women), 121 part-time/adjunct (80 women). *Students:* 89 full-time (61 women), 26 part-time (16 women); includes 23 minority (2 Black or African American, non-Hispanic/Latino; 2 American Indian or Alaska Native, non-Hispanic/Latino; 2 Asian, non-Hispanic/Latino; 16 Hispanic/Latino; 1 Two or more races, non-Hispanic/Latino), 2 international. Average age 35. 201 applicants, 27% accepted, 34 enrolled. In 2010, 6 master's, 10 doctorates awarded. *Degree requirements:* For master's, one foreign language, comprehensive exam (for some programs), portfolio; thesis (MFA); for doctorate, 2 foreign languages, comprehensive exam, thesis/dissertation. *Entrance requirements:* For master's, GRE General Test, writing sample; for doctorate, GRE General Test, GRE Subject Test (literature), writing sample. *Application deadline:* For fall admission, 1/15 for domestic students. Application fee: $50. Electronic applications accepted. *Expenses:* Tuition, state resident: full-time $5991; part-time $251 per credit hour. Tuition, nonresident: full-time

$14,405; part-time $800.20 per credit hour. Tuition and fees vary according to course level, course load, program and reciprocity agreements. *Financial support:* In 2010–11, 95 students received support, including 2 research assistantships (averaging $2,600 per year), 70 teaching assistantships with full tuition reimbursements available (averaging $13,924 per year); fellowships, career-related internships or fieldwork, scholarships/grants, health care benefits, and unspecified assistantships also available. Financial award application deadline: 1/15; financial award applicants required to submit FAFSA. *Faculty research:* American literature, Native American literature, Chicana/o literature, British and Irish literature, creative writing, rhetoric and writing. Total annual research expenditures: $3,000. *Unit head:* Dr. Gail Turley Houston, Chair, 505-277-6347, Fax: 505-277-0021, E-mail: ghouston@unm.edu. *Application contact:* N. Ezra Meier, Graduate Advisor, 505-277-4437, Fax: 505-277-0021, E-mail: nezra@unm.edu.

University of New Mexico, Graduate School, College of Arts and Sciences, Program in Creative Writing, Albuquerque, NM 87131-2039. Offers MFA. Part-time programs available. *Students:* 25 full-time (17 women), 10 part-time (7 women); includes 1 Black or African American, non-Hispanic/Latino; 1 American Indian or Alaska Native, non-Hispanic/Latino; 2 Asian, non-Hispanic/Latino; 8 Hispanic/Latino. Average age 37. 129 applicants, 14% accepted, 12 enrolled. In 2010, 7 master's awarded. *Degree requirements:* For master's, comprehensive exam, thesis. *Entrance requirements:* For master's, writing sample. *Application deadline:* For fall admission, 1/15 for domestic and international students. Application fee: $50. Electronic applications accepted. *Expenses:* Tuition, state resident: full-time $5991; part-time $251 per credit hour. Tuition, nonresident: full-time $14,405; part-time $800.20 per credit hour. Tuition and fees vary according to course level, course load, program and reciprocity agreements. *Financial support:* In 2010–11, 30 students received support, including 18 teaching assistantships with full and partial tuition reimbursements available (averaging $13,084 per year); health care benefits and unspecified assistantships also available. Financial award application deadline: 1/15. *Faculty research:* Creative writing, fiction, creative non-fiction, poetry. *Unit head:* Dr. Gail Turley Houston, Chair, 505-277-6347, Fax: 505-277-0021, E-mail: ghouston@unm.edu. *Application contact:* Ezra Meir, Graduate Advisor, 505-277-4437, Fax: 505-277-0021, E-mail: nezra@unm.edu.

University of New Mexico, Graduate School, College of Fine Arts, Department of Theatre and Dance, Albuquerque, NM 87131-2039. Offers dance (MFA); dance history (MA); dramatic writing (MFA); theatre education and outreach (MA). *Accreditation:* NASD; NAST. *Faculty:* 23 full-time (11 women), 15 part-time/adjunct (10 women). *Students:* 19 full-time (16 women), 4 part-time (all women); includes 9 minority (1 American Indian or Alaska Native, non-Hispanic/Latino; 2 Asian, non-Hispanic/Latino; 6 Hispanic/Latino). Average age 31. 33 applicants, 21% accepted, 7 enrolled. In 2010, 3 master's awarded. *Degree requirements:* For master's, comprehensive exam (for some programs), thesis (for some programs). *Entrance requirements:* For master's, minimum GPA of 3.0; undergraduate major in theatre, dance or closely related field; 3 letters of recommendation; letter of intent; BA, BFA, BS, or MA in dance movement science or related field, or equivalent experience (for MFA in dance). *Application deadline:* For fall admission, 4/15 for domestic students; for spring admission, 11/10 for domestic students. Application fee: $50. Electronic applications accepted. *Expenses:* Tuition, state resident: full-time $5991; part-time $251 per credit hour. Tuition, nonresident: full-time $14,405; part-time $800.20 per credit hour. Tuition and fees vary according to course level, course load, program and reciprocity agreements. *Financial support:* In 2010–11, 20 students received support, including 1 fellowship (averaging $7,200 per year), 1 research assistantship with partial tuition reimbursement available (averaging $3,750 per year), 3 teaching assistantships with partial tuition reimbursements available (averaging $4,482 per year); Federal Work-Study, health care benefits, tuition waivers (partial), and unspecified assistantships also available. Financial award application deadline: 3/1; financial award applicants required to submit FAFSA. *Faculty research:* Theater education and outreach, choreography, dramatic writing, dance history/criticism. *Unit head:* Bill Liotta, Chair, 505-277-4332, Fax: 505-277-8921, E-mail: wliotta@unm.edu. *Application contact:* Christina Squire, Administrator II, 505-277-7362, Fax: 505-277-8921, E-mail: csquire@unm.edu.

The University of North Carolina at Charlotte, Graduate School, College of Arts and Sciences, Department of English, Charlotte, NC 28223-0001. Offers English (MA); English education (MA); technical/professional writing (Certificate). Part-time and evening/weekend programs available. *Faculty:* 34 full-time (19 women), 1 part-time/adjunct (0 women). *Students:* 45 full-time (30 women), 76 part-time (55 women); includes 20 minority (13 Black or African American, non-Hispanic/Latino; 6 Asian, non-Hispanic/Latino; 1 Two or more races, non-Hispanic/Latino), 2 international. Average age 29. 46 applicants, 89% accepted, 31 enrolled. In 2010, 28 master's awarded. *Degree requirements:* For master's, comprehensive exam, thesis optional. *Entrance requirements:* For master's, GRE General Test, minimum undergraduate GPA of 3.0 in major, 2.75 overall. Additional exam requirements/recommendations for international students: Required—TOEFL (minimum score 557 paper-based; 220 computer-based; 83 iBT). *Application deadline:* For fall admission, 7/15 for domestic students, 5/1 for international students; for spring admission, 11/15 for domestic students, 10/1 for international students. Applications are processed on a rolling basis. Application fee: $55. Electronic applications accepted. *Expenses:* Tuition, state resident: full-time $3464. Tuition, nonresident: full-time $14,297. Required fees: $2094. Tuition and fees vary according to course load. *Financial support:* In 2010–11, 16 students received support, including 16 teaching assistantships (averaging $7,625 per year); career-related internships or fieldwork, institutionally sponsored loans, scholarships/grants, and unspecified assistantships also available. Support available to part-time students. Financial award application deadline: 4/1; financial award applicants required to submit FAFSA. *Faculty research:* English as a second language (ESL), composition theory and pedagogy, children's literature, technical and professional writing, English for specific purposes (ESP). Total annual research expenditures: $190,607. *Unit head:* Dr. Malin Pereira, Chair, 704-687-2299, Fax: 704-687-3961, E-mail: mpereira@uncc.edu. *Application contact:* Kathy B. Giddings, Director of Graduate Admissions, 704-687-5503, Fax: 704-687-3279, E-mail: gradadm@uncc.edu.

The University of North Carolina at Greensboro, Graduate School, College of Arts and Sciences, Department of English, Program in Creative Writing, Greensboro, NC 27412-5001. Offers MFA. *Degree requirements:* For master's, comprehensive exam, thesis. *Entrance requirements:* For master's, GRE General Test, minimum GPA of 3.0, writing sample. Additional exam requirements/recommendations for international students: Required—TOEFL. Electronic applications accepted. *Faculty research:* Fiction, poetry, science fiction, film studies.

The University of North Carolina Wilmington, College of Arts and Sciences, Department of Creative Writing, Wilmington, NC 28403-3297. Offers MFA. Part-time programs available. *Faculty:* 14 full-time (6 women). *Students:* 50 full-time (37 women), 25 part-time (16 women); includes 1 Black or African American, non-Hispanic/Latino; 3 Asian, non-Hispanic/Latino; 2 Hispanic/Latino; 2 Two or more races, non-Hispanic/Latino, 1 international. Average age 29. 299 applicants, 24% accepted, 25 enrolled. In 2010, 18 master's awarded. *Degree requirements:* For master's, comprehensive exam, thesis. *Entrance requirements:* For master's, writing sample. Additional exam requirements/recommendations for international students: Required—TOEFL (minimum score 550 paper-based; 217 computer-based; 79 iBT), IELTS (minimum score 6.5). *Application deadline:* For fall admission, 3/1 for domestic students. Application fee: $60. *Financial support:* In 2010–11, 16 teaching assistantships with full and partial tuition reimbursements (averaging $14,000 per year) were awarded; career-related internships or fieldwork and Federal Work-Study also available. Support available to part-time students. Financial award application deadline: 3/15. *Unit head:* Dr. Philip Gerard, Chair, 910-962-3329, Fax: 910-962-7461, E-mail: gerardp@uncw.edu. *Application contact:* Lisa Bertini, Program Assistant, 910-962-3070, E-mail: bertinil@uncw.edu.

University of Northern Iowa, Graduate College, College of Humanities and Fine Arts, Department of English Language and Literature, Cedar Falls, IA 50614. Offers creative writing (MA); English (MA); literature (MA); teaching English in secondary schools (TESS) (MA), including middle/junior high and senior high; teaching English to speakers of other languages (MA). Part-time and evening/weekend programs available. *Students:* 32 full-time (22 women), 43 part-time (39 women); includes 7 minority (3 Black or African American, non-Hispanic/Latino; 2 Asian, non-Hispanic/Latino; 1 Hispanic/Latino; 1 Two or more races, non-Hispanic/Latino), 7 international. 53 applicants, 57% accepted, 21 enrolled. In 2010, 21 master's awarded. *Degree requirements:* For master's, one foreign language, comprehensive exam, thesis or alternative, portfolio. *Entrance requirements:* For master's, minimum GPA of 3.0. Additional exam requirements/recommendations for international students: Required—TOEFL (minimum score 600 paper-based; 250 computer-based; 100 iBT). *Application deadline:* For fall admission, 8/1 priority date for domestic students. Applications are processed on a rolling basis. Application fee: $50 ($70 for international students). Electronic applications accepted. *Financial support:* Career-related internships or fieldwork, Federal Work-Study, scholarships/grants, and tuition waivers (full and partial) available. Support available to part-time students. Financial award application deadline: 2/1. *Unit head:* Dr. Jeffrey S. Copeland, Head, 319-273-3855, Fax: 319-273-5807, E-mail: jeffrey.copeland@uni.edu. *Application contact:* Laurie S. Russell, Record Analyst, 319-273-2623, Fax: 319-273-2885, E-mail: laurie.russell@uni.edu.

University of North Florida, College of Arts and Sciences, Department of English, Jacksonville, FL 32224. Offers MA. Part-time and evening/weekend programs available. *Faculty:* 18 full-time (8 women). *Students:* 11 full-time (6 women), 31 part-time (20 women); includes 1 American Indian or Alaska Native, non-Hispanic/Latino; 1 Asian, non-Hispanic/Latino; 1 Two or more races, non-Hispanic/Latino. Average age 30. 22 applicants, 36% accepted, 4 enrolled. In 2010, 12 master's awarded. *Degree requirements:* For master's, comprehensive exam, thesis optional. *Entrance requirements:* For master's, GRE General Test, minimum GPA of 3.0 in last 60 hours, writing sample. Additional exam requirements/recommendations for international students: Required—TOEFL (minimum score 500 paper-based; 173 computer-based; 61 iBT). *Application deadline:* For fall admission, 7/1 priority date for domestic students, 5/1 for international students; for spring admission, 11/1 priority date for domestic students, 10/1 for international students. Applications are processed on a rolling basis. Application fee: $30. Electronic applications accepted. *Expenses:* Tuition, state resident: full-time $7646.40; part-time $318.60 per credit hour. Tuition, nonresident: full-time $23,502; part-time $979.24 per credit hour. Required fees: $1208.88; $50.37 per credit hour. Tuition and fees vary according to course load and program. *Financial support:* In 2010–11, 7 students received support; research assistantships, teaching assistantships, Federal Work-Study and scholarships/grants available. Financial award application deadline: 4/1; financial award applicants required to submit FAFSA. *Faculty research:* Genre, period, and individual author studies in British, American, and world literature; literary criticism and theory—psychological, new historical and cultural, deconstructive, feminist, narrative, mythic; film and popular culture; online poetry publishing. *Unit head:* Dr. Samuel A. Kimball, Chair, 904-620-2273, Fax: 904-620-3940, E-mail: skimball@unf.edu. *Application contact:* Lillith Richardson, Assistant Director, The Graduate School, 904-620-1360, Fax: 904-620-1362, E-mail: graduateschool@unf.edu.

University of North Texas, Toulouse Graduate School, College of Arts and Sciences, Department of English, Denton, TX 76203. Offers creative writing (MA); English (MA, PhD). Terminal master's awarded for partial completion of doctoral program. *Degree requirements:* For master's, one foreign language, comprehensive exam, thesis optional; for doctorate, one foreign language, comprehensive exam, thesis/dissertation. *Entrance requirements:* For master's, GRE General Test, minimum GPA of 3.0, personal statement, current curriculum vitae/resume, writing sample (for creative writing program); for doctorate, GRE General Test, minimum GPA of 3.5, 3 letters of recommendation, personal statement, writing sample. Additional exam requirements/recommendations for international students: Recommended—TOEFL (minimum score 550 paper-based; 213 computer-based; 79 iBT). *Expenses:* Tuition, state resident: full-time $4298; part-time $239 per credit hour. Tuition, nonresident: full-time $10,782; part-time $549 per credit hour. Required fees: $1292; $270 per credit hour. *Financial support:* Fellowships with full tuition reimbursements, teaching assistantships with partial tuition reimbursements, career-related internships or fieldwork, Federal Work-Study, institutionally sponsored loans, scholarships/grants, health care benefits, and unspecified assistantships available. Financial award application deadline: 4/1; financial award applicants required to submit FAFSA. *Faculty research:* Creative writing, British and American literature, composition and rhetoric. *Application contact:* Chair of Graduate Studies, 940-565-2114, Fax: 940-565-4355.

University of Notre Dame, Graduate School, College of Arts and Letters, Division of Humanities, Department of English, Creative Writing Program, Notre Dame, IN 46556. Offers MFA. *Degree requirements:* For master's, thesis. *Entrance requirements:* For master's, GRE General Test, minimum GPA of 3.0. Additional exam requirements/recommendations for international students: Required—TOEFL (minimum score 600 paper-based; 250 computer-based; 80 iBT). Electronic applications accepted. *Faculty research:* Novels, stories, poetry.

University of Oklahoma, College of Arts and Sciences, Department of English, Norman, OK 73019. Offers English (MA, PhD), including composition/rhetoric/literacy studies, creative writing (MA), literary studies. Part-time programs available. *Faculty:* 34 full-time (15 women). *Students:* 61 full-time (36 women), 6 part-time (5 women); includes 11 minority (1 Black or African American, non-Hispanic/Latino; 8 American Indian or Alaska Native, non-Hispanic/Latino; 2 Hispanic/Latino), 4 international. Average age 31. 56 applicants, 55% accepted, 21 enrolled. In 2010, 4 master's, 3 doctorates awarded. *Degree requirements:* For master's, one foreign language, thesis or alternative, qualifying exam; for doctorate, 2 foreign languages, comprehensive exam, thesis/dissertation, qualifying exam. *Entrance requirements:* For master's, GRE General Test, minimum GPA of 3.0, BA with 27 hours of course work in English or 15 hours of upper-level courses; for doctorate, GRE General Test, GRE Subject Test (English literature), minimum graduate GPA of 3.5. Additional exam requirements/recommendations for international students: Required—TOEFL (minimum score 550 paper-based; 213 computer-based; 79 iBT). *Application deadline:* For fall admission, 4/1 priority date for domestic students, 4/1 for international students; for spring admission, 11/1 for domestic students, 9/1 for international students. Applications are processed on a rolling basis. Application fee: $40 ($90 for international students). Electronic applications accepted. *Expenses:* Tuition, state resident: full-time $3893; part-time $162.20 per credit hour. Tuition, nonresident: full-time $14,167; part-time $590.30 per credit hour. Required fees: $2523; $94.60 per credit hour. Tuition and fees vary according to course load and degree level. *Financial support:* In 2010–11, 1 fellowship with full tuition reimbursement (averaging $2,500 per year), 3 research assistantships with partial tuition reimbursements (averaging $12,765 per year), 58 teaching assistantships with partial tuition reimbursements (averaging $12,462 per year) were awarded; scholarships/grants, health care benefits, and unspecified assistantships also available. Financial award applicants required to submit FAFSA. *Faculty research:* Literary theory, cultural studies, Native American studies, composition and rhetoric, British and American literature. *Unit head:* David Mair, Chair, 405-325-4661, Fax: 405-325-0831, E-mail: dmair@ou.edu. *Application contact:* Zara Cougher, Graduate Secretary, 405-325-0489, Fax: 405-325-0831, E-mail: scougher@ou.edu.

University of Oklahoma, Gaylord College of Journalism and Mass Communication, Program in Journalism and Mass Communication, Norman, OK 73019-0390. Offers advertising and public relations (MA); information gathering and distribution (MA); mass communication management and policy (MA); professional writing (MA); telecommunications and new technologies (MA). Part-time programs available. *Students:* 21 full-time (16 women), 26 part-time (13 women); includes 7 minority (4 Black or African American, non-Hispanic/Latino; 2 American Indian or Alaska Native, non-Hispanic/Latino; 1 Hispanic/Latino), 6 international. Average age 27. 29 applicants, 76% accepted, 10 enrolled. In 2010, 20 master's awarded. *Degree requirements:* For master's, thesis optional. *Entrance requirements:* For master's, GRE General Test, minimum GPA of 3.2, 9 hours of course work in journalism, course work in statistics. Additional exam requirements/recommendations for international students: Required—TOEFL (minimum score 600 paper-based; 250 computer-based; 100 iBT), TWE (minimum score 5). *Application deadline:* For fall admission, 2/1 for domestic students, 4/1 for international students; for spring admission, 11/1 for domestic students, 9/1 for international students. Application fee: $40 ($90 for international students). Electronic applications accepted. *Expenses:* Tuition, state resident: full-time $3893; part-time $162.20 per credit hour. Tuition, nonresident: full-time $14,167; part-time $590.30 per credit hour. Required fees: $2523; $94.60 per credit hour.

Writing

University of Oklahoma (continued)

Tuition and fees vary according to course load and degree level. *Financial support:* In 2010–11, 30 students received support. Career-related internships or fieldwork, scholarships/grants, health care benefits, and unspecified assistantships available. *Faculty research:* Organizational management, strategic communications, rhetorical theories and mass communication, interactive messaging and audience response; mass media history and law. *Unit head:* Dr. Joe Foote, Dean, 405-325-2721, Fax: 405-325-7565, E-mail: jfoote@ou.edu. *Application contact:* Kelly Storm, Graduate Advisor, 405-325-2722, Fax: 405-325-7565, E-mail: kstorm@ou.edu.

University of Oklahoma, Gaylord College of Journalism and Mass Communication, Program in Professional Writing, Norman, OK 73019-0390. Offers MPW. Part-time programs available. *Students:* 9 full-time (6 women), 11 part-time (6 women); includes 4 minority (3 American Indian or Alaska Native, non-Hispanic/Latino; 1 Asian, non-Hispanic/Latino). Average age 30. 5 applicants, 100% accepted, 3 enrolled. In 2010, 5 master's awarded. *Degree requirements:* For master's, project. *Entrance requirements:* For master's, GRE General Test, 2 letters of recommendation, resume, writing sample. Additional exam requirements/recommendations for international students: Required—TOEFL (minimum score 600 paper-based; 250 computer-based; 100 iBT), TWE (minimum score 5). *Application deadline:* For fall admission, 7/1 for domestic students, 4/1 for international students; for spring admission, 11/1 for domestic students, 9/1 for international students. Application fee: $40 ($90 for international students). Electronic applications accepted. *Expenses:* Tuition, state resident: full-time $3893; part-time $162.20 per credit hour. Tuition, nonresident: full-time $14,167; part-time $590.30 per credit hour. Required fees: $2523; $94.60 per credit hour. Tuition and fees vary according to course load and degree level. *Financial support:* In 2010–11, 13 students received support. Career-related internships or fieldwork, scholarships/grants, health care benefits, and unspecified assistantships available. Financial award applicants required to submit FAFSA. *Faculty research:* Creative writing, script writing, nonfiction. *Unit head:* Dr. Joe Foote, Dean, 405-325-2721, Fax: 405-325-7565, E-mail: jfoote@ou.edu. *Application contact:* Kelly Storm, Graduate Advisor, 405-325-2722, Fax: 405-325-7565, E-mail: kstorm@ou.edu.

University of Oregon, Graduate School, College of Arts and Sciences, Department of Creative Writing, Eugene, OR 97403. Offers MFA. *Degree requirements:* For master's, thesis, exam. *Entrance requirements:* For master's, minimum GPA of 3.0. Additional exam requirements/recommendations for international students: Required—TOEFL. *Faculty research:* Poetry, fiction, literary nonfiction.

University of Pennsylvania, Graduate School of Education, Division of Language in Education, Program in Reading, Writing, and Literacy, Philadelphia, PA 19104. Offers MS Ed, Ed D, PhD. Part-time programs available. *Students:* 97 full-time (86 women), 43 part-time (40 women); includes 23 Black or African American, non-Hispanic/Latino; 13 Asian, non-Hispanic/Latino; 3 Hispanic/Latino, 2 international. 127 applicants, 67% accepted, 48 enrolled. In 2010, 19 master's, 2 doctorates awarded. *Degree requirements:* For master's, comprehensive exam; for doctorate, one foreign language, thesis/dissertation, preliminary exam. *Entrance requirements:* For master's and doctorate, GRE General Test or MAT. Additional exam requirements/recommendations for international students: Required—TOEFL. *Application deadline:* For fall admission, 12/15 priority date for domestic students. Applications are processed on a rolling basis. Application fee: $70. Electronic applications accepted. *Expenses:* Contact institution. *Financial support:* Fellowships, institutionally sponsored loans, scholarships/grants, traineeships, health care benefits, and unspecified assistantships available. *Faculty research:* Reading and writing relationships, classroom teachers as researchers, comprehension processes. *Application contact:* Penny Creedon, 215-898-3245, E-mail: pennyc@gse.upenn.edu.

University of Pittsburgh, School of Arts and Sciences, Department of English, Pittsburgh, PA 15260. Offers cultural and critical studies (PhD); English (MA); writing (MFA). Part-time programs available. *Faculty:* 51 full-time (26 women), 1 (woman) part-time/adjunct. *Students:* 117 full-time (79 women), 28 part-time (21 women); includes 15 minority (1 Black or African American, non-Hispanic/Latino; 5 Asian, non-Hispanic/Latino; 4 Hispanic/Latino; 5 Two or more races, non-Hispanic/Latino), 10 international. Average age 29. 344 applicants, 16% accepted, 17 enrolled. In 2010, 22 master's, 10 doctorates awarded. *Degree requirements:* For master's, one foreign language; for doctorate, 2 foreign languages, comprehensive exam, thesis/dissertation. *Entrance requirements:* For master's and doctorate, GRE General Test, writing sample. Additional exam requirements/recommendations for international students: Required—TOEFL (minimum score 550 paper-based; 213 computer-based; 80 iBT). *Application deadline:* For fall admission, 12/10 for domestic and international students. Application fee: $50. Electronic applications accepted. *Expenses:* Tuition, state resident: full-time $17,304; part-time $701 per credit. Tuition, nonresident: full-time $29,554; part-time $1210 per credit. Required fees: $740; $214 per term. Tuition and fees vary according to program. *Financial support:* In 2010–11, 100 students received support, including 22 fellowships with full tuition reimbursements available (averaging $17,822 per year), 5 research assistantships with full and partial tuition reimbursements available (averaging $12,300 per year), 70 teaching assistantships with full tuition reimbursements available (averaging $15,065 per year); Federal Work-Study, tuition waivers (full and partial), and unspecified assistantships also available. Financial award application deadline: 12/12. *Faculty research:* Cultural studies, literary history and theory, film, composition. *Unit head:* Dr. H. David Brumble, Chair, 412-624-6509, Fax: 412-624-6639, E-mail: brumble@pitt.edu. *Application contact:* Duane Walsh, Graduate Administrator, 412-624-6549, Fax: 412-624-6639, E-mail: engrad@pitt.edu.

University of San Francisco, College of Arts and Sciences, Program in Writing, San Francisco, CA 94117-1080. Offers MFA. Part-time and evening/weekend programs available. *Faculty:* 2 full-time (1 woman), 13 part-time/adjunct (5 women). *Students:* 78 full-time (55 women), 8 part-time (6 women); includes 27 minority (1 Black or African American, non-Hispanic/Latino; 14 Asian, non-Hispanic/Latino; 9 Hispanic/Latino; 3 Two or more races, non-Hispanic/Latino), 1 international. Average age 36. 234 applicants, 45% accepted, 43 enrolled. In 2010, 28 master's awarded. *Degree requirements:* For master's, thesis. *Entrance requirements:* For master's, minimum overall GPA of 2.7, writing sample, 2 letters of recommendation, resume, interview. Additional exam requirements/recommendations for international students: Required—TOEFL (minimum score 550 paper-based; 79 iBT). *Application deadline:* For fall admission, 2/1 for domestic students. Applications are processed on a rolling basis. Application fee: $55 ($65 for international students). *Expenses:* Tuition: Full-time $20,070; part-time $1115 per credit hour. Tuition and fees vary according to course load, degree level and program. *Financial support:* In 2010–11, 59 students received support; fellowships, institutionally sponsored loans available. Support available to part-time students. Financial award application deadline: 3/2; financial award applicants required to submit FAFSA. *Faculty research:* Techniques of teaching the novel to writers, oral history. *Unit head:* Dr. Aaron Shurin, Director, 415-422-5357, Fax: 415-422-6996, E-mail: mfaw@usfca.edu. *Application contact:* Dr. Aaron Shurin, Director, 415-422-5357, Fax: 415-422-6996, E-mail: mfaw@usfca.edu.

University of South Carolina, The Graduate School, College of Arts and Sciences, Department of English Language and Literature, Columbia, SC 29208. Offers creative writing (MFA); English (MA, PhD); English education (MAT); MLIS/MA. MAT offered in cooperation with the College of Education. Part-time programs available. *Degree requirements:* For master's, one foreign language, comprehensive exam, thesis; for doctorate, 2 foreign languages, comprehensive exam, thesis/dissertation. *Entrance requirements:* For master's, GRE General Test (MFA), GRE Subject Test (MA, MAT), sample of written work; for doctorate, GRE General Test, GRE Subject Test, sample of written work. Additional exam requirements/recommendations for international students: Required—TOEFL. Electronic applications accepted. *Faculty research:* American literature, British literature, composition and rhetoric, linguistics, speech communication.

University of Southern California, Graduate School, Dana and David Dornsife College of Letters, Arts and Sciences, Department of English, Los Angeles, CA 90089. Offers English (MA, PhD); literature and creative writing (PhD). *Faculty:* 37 full-time (18 women), 12 part-time/adjunct (5 women). *Students:* 98 full-time (57 women), 1 part-time (0 women); includes 22 minority (1 Black or African American, non-Hispanic/Latino; 1 American Indian or Alaska Native, non-Hispanic/Latino; 3 Asian, non-Hispanic/Latino; 14 Hispanic/Latino; 3 Two or more races, non-Hispanic/Latino), 8 international. In 2010, 5 master's, 21 doctorates awarded. Terminal master's awarded for partial completion of doctoral program. *Degree requirements:* For doctorate, one foreign language, comprehensive exam, thesis/dissertation. *Entrance requirements:* For doctorate, GRE General Test, GRE Subject Test (English literature). Additional exam requirements/recommendations for international students: Required—TOEFL. *Application deadline:* For fall admission, 12/1 for domestic and international students. Application fee: $85. Electronic applications accepted. *Expenses:* Tuition: Full-time $31,240; part-time $1420 per unit. Required fees: $600. One-time fee: $35 full-time. Full-time tuition and fees vary according to degree level and program. *Financial support:* In 2010–11, 54 students received support, including 12 fellowships with full tuition reimbursements available (averaging $25,500 per year), 2 research assistantships with full tuition reimbursements available (averaging $19,250 per year), 32 teaching assistantships with full tuition reimbursements available (averaging $19,800 per year); scholarships/grants, health care benefits, tuition waivers, and unspecified assistantships also available. *Faculty research:* Creative writing and literature; early modern studies; gender and sexuality; narrative studies; poetry and poetics; media, film, and popular culture; studies in race and minority literature. *Unit head:* Prof. Margaret Russett, Chair, 213-740-3727, Fax: 213-741-0377, E-mail: russett@usc.edu. *Application contact:* Flora Ruiz, Graduate Coordinator of Student Affairs, 213-740-3728, Fax: 213-741-0377, E-mail: fruiz@usc.edu.

University of Southern California, Graduate School, Dana and David Dornsife College of Letters, Arts and Sciences, Master of Professional Writing Program, Los Angeles, CA 90089. Offers MPW. Part-time and evening/weekend programs available. *Faculty:* 5 full-time (4 women), 16 part-time/adjunct (8 women). *Students:* 49 full-time (25 women), 48 part-time (30 women); includes 29 minority (9 Black or African American, non-Hispanic/Latino; 7 Asian, non-Hispanic/Latino; 13 Hispanic/Latino), 6 international. 45 applicants, 89% accepted, 31 enrolled. In 2010, 54 master's awarded. *Degree requirements:* For master's, thesis. *Entrance requirements:* For master's, GRE. Additional exam requirements/recommendations for international students: Required—TOEFL. *Application deadline:* For fall admission, 6/1 priority date for domestic and international students; for spring admission, 11/1 priority date for domestic and international students. Applications are processed on a rolling basis. Application fee: $50. Electronic applications accepted. *Expenses:* Tuition: Full-time $31,240; part-time $1420 per unit. Required fees: $600. One-time fee: $35 full-time. Full-time tuition and fees vary according to degree level and program. *Financial support:* In 2010–11, 10 students received support, including 10 teaching assistantships with full tuition reimbursements available (averaging $19,800 per year). Financial award application deadline: 12/1. *Faculty research:* Creative writing including fiction, creative nonfiction, screenwriting, television writing, playwriting, poetry, Internet writing; publishing in electronic media; book and film reviewing; teaching. *Unit head:* Brighde Mullins, Director, 213-740-4718, Fax: 213-740-5002, E-mail: bmullins@college.usc.edu. *Application contact:* Natalie Inouye, Student Service Advisor, 213-740-1384, Fax: 213-740-5002, E-mail: natalie.inouye@college.usc.edu.

University of Southern Maine, College of Arts and Sciences, Program in Creative Writing, Portland, ME 04104. Offers MFA.

University of Southern Mississippi, Graduate School, College of Arts and Letters, Department of English, Hattiesburg, MS 39406-0001. Offers creative writing (MA, PhD); English literature (MA, PhD). *Faculty:* 26 full-time (13 women), 1 part-time/adjunct (0 women). *Students:* 56 full-time (27 women), 20 part-time (15 women); includes 2 Black or African American, non-Hispanic/Latino; 3 Hispanic/Latino; 3 Two or more races, non-Hispanic/Latino, 4 international. Average age 33. 81 applicants, 59% accepted, 20 enrolled. In 2010, 11 master's, 8 doctorates awarded. *Degree requirements:* For master's, one foreign language, comprehensive exam, thesis; for doctorate, 2 foreign languages, comprehensive exam, thesis/dissertation. *Entrance requirements:* For master's, GRE General Test, minimum GPA of 3.0 in field of study, 2.75 in last 2 years; for doctorate, GRE General Test, minimum GPA of 3,5. Additional exam requirements/recommendations for international students: Required—TOEFL, IELTS. *Application deadline:* For fall admission, 3/15 priority date for domestic students, 3/15 for international students. Application fee: $50. Electronic applications accepted. *Financial support:* In 2010–11, 1 fellowship (averaging $14,000 per year), 2 research assistantships with full tuition reimbursements (averaging $10,000 per year), 44 teaching assistantships with full tuition reimbursements (averaging $10,000 per year) were awarded; Federal Work-Study, institutionally sponsored loans, scholarships/grants, and unspecified assistantships also available. Financial award application deadline: 3/15; financial award applicants required to submit FAFSA. *Faculty research:* English and American literature, critical theory and cultural studies, creative writing. *Unit head:* Dr. Eric Tribunella, Chair, 601-266-4319, Fax: 601-266-5757. *Application contact:* Dr. Monika Gehlawalk Lares, Graduate Coordinator, 601-266-4320, Fax: 601-266-5757.

The University of Tennessee at Chattanooga, Graduate School, College of Arts and Sciences, Department of English, Chattanooga, TN 37403. Offers creative writing (MA); literary study (MA); rhetoric and writing (MA, Graduate Certificate). Part-time and evening/weekend programs available. *Faculty:* 12 full-time (7 women). *Students:* 19 full-time (13 women), 26 part-time (15 women); includes 1 minority (Two or more races, non-Hispanic/Latino), 1 international. Average age 29. 33 applicants, 88% accepted, 23 enrolled. In 2010, 20 master's awarded. *Degree requirements:* For master's, one foreign language, comprehensive exam, thesis. *Entrance requirements:* For master's, GRE General Test or GRE Subject Test (literature), minimum GPA of 3.0 in English. Additional exam requirements/recommendations for international students: Required—TOEFL (minimum score 550 paper-based; 213 computer-based; 79 iBT), IELTS (minimum score 6). *Application deadline:* For fall admission, 8/1 priority date for domestic students, 6/1 for international students; for spring admission, 12/1 priority date for domestic students, 10/1 for international students. Applications are processed on a rolling basis. Application fee: $35. Electronic applications accepted. *Financial support:* In 2010–11, 6 research assistantships with full and partial tuition reimbursements (averaging $5,500 per year) were awarded; career-related internships or fieldwork, scholarships/grants, and unspecified assistantships also available. Support available to part-time students. *Faculty research:* Technical writing, African-American literature, Milton, creative writing and poetry, American modernism and gender theory. Total annual research expenditures: $74,953. *Unit head:* Dr. Verbie Prevost, Head, 423-425-4238, Fax: 423-785-2282, E-mail: verbie-prevost@utc.edu. *Application contact:* Dr. Jerald Ainsworth, Dean of Graduate Studies, 423-425-4478, Fax: 423-425-5223, E-mail: jerald-ainsworth@utc.edu.

The University of Texas at Austin, Graduate School, College of Liberal Arts, Department of English, Austin, TX 78712-1111. Offers creative writing (MA); English (MA, PhD). Part-time programs available. Terminal master's awarded for partial completion of doctoral program. *Degree requirements:* For master's, 2 foreign languages; for doctorate, variable foreign language requirement. *Entrance requirements:* For master's and doctorate, GRE General Test. Electronic applications accepted.

The University of Texas at Austin, Graduate School, Program in Writing, Austin, TX 78712-1111. Offers MFA. Electronic applications accepted.

The University of Texas at El Paso, Graduate School, College of Liberal Arts, Department of Creative Writing, El Paso, TX 79968-0001. Offers creative writing (on-line) (MFA); creative writing in English (MFA); creative writing in Spanish (MFA). Part-time and evening/weekend programs available. Postbaccalaureate distance learning degree programs offered (no on-campus study). *Students:* 47 (25 women); includes 1 Black or African American, non-Hispanic/Latino; 20 Hispanic/Latino, 13 international. Average age 34. In 2010, 7 master's awarded. *Degree requirements:* For master's, thesis. *Entrance requirements:* For master's, minimum GPA of 3.0, letters of recommendation, writing sample. Additional exam requirements/recommendations for international students: Required—TOEFL; Recommended—IELTS. *Application deadline:* For fall admission, 8/1 priority date for domestic students, 3/1 for international students; for spring admission, 11/1 for domestic students, 9/1 for international students. Applications are processed on a rolling basis. Application fee: $45 ($80 for international students). Electronic applications accepted. *Financial support:* In 2010–11, research assistantships (averaging $18,625 per year), teaching assistantships with partial tuition reimbursements (averaging $14,900 per year) were awarded; fellowships with partial tuition reimbursements, institutionally sponsored loans, scholarships/grants, health care benefits, tuition waivers (partial), and unspecified assistantships also available. Support available to part-time students. Financial award application deadline: 3/15; financial award applicants required to submit FAFSA. *Unit head:* Dr. Johnny Payne, Chair, 915-747-5713, Fax: 915-747-5523, E-mail: jpayne@utep.edu. *Application contact:* Dr. Patricia D. Witherspoon, Dean of the Graduate School, 915-747-5491, Fax: 915-747-5788, E-mail: withersp@utep.edu.

The University of Texas at El Paso, Graduate School, College of Liberal Arts, Department of English, El Paso, TX 79968-0001. Offers bilingual professional writing (Certificate); English and American literature (MA); rhetoric and composition (PhD); rhetoric and writing studies (MA); teaching English (MAT). Part-time and evening/weekend programs available. *Students:* 68 (47 women); includes 1 Black or African American, non-Hispanic/Latino; 1 Asian, non-Hispanic/Latino; 36 Hispanic/Latino, 2 international. Average age 34. In 2010, 18 master's awarded. *Degree requirements:* For master's, thesis optional. *Entrance requirements:* For master's, GRE General Test, minimum GPA of 3.0. Additional exam requirements/recommendations for international students: Required—TOEFL. *Application deadline:* For fall admission, 7/1 priority date for domestic students, 3/1 for international students; for spring admission, 11/1 priority date for domestic students, 9/1 for international students. Applications are processed on a rolling basis. Application fee: $15 ($65 for international students). Electronic applications accepted. *Financial support:* In 2010–11, research assistantships with partial tuition reimbursements (averaging $20,555 per year), teaching assistantships with partial tuition reimbursements (averaging $16,444 per year) were awarded; Federal Work-Study, institutionally sponsored loans, scholarships/grants, and tuition waivers (partial) also available. Financial award application deadline: 3/15; financial award applicants required to submit FAFSA. *Faculty research:* Literature, creative writing, literary theory. *Unit head:* Evelyn Posey, Chair, 915-747-5731. *Application contact:* Dr. Charles H. Ambler, Dean of the Graduate School, 915-747-5491 Ext. 7886, Fax: 915-747-5788, E-mail: cambler@utep.edu.

University of the Sacred Heart, Graduate Programs, Department of Communication, San Juan, PR 00914-0383. Offers contemporary culture and media (MA); digital journalism (MA, Certificate); editing for media (MA, Certificate); public relations (MA, Certificate); publicity (MA, Certificate); scriptwriting (MA, Certificate). Part-time and evening/weekend programs available. *Degree requirements:* For master's, thesis.

University of the Sacred Heart, Graduate Programs, Program in Creative Writing, San Juan, PR 00914-0383. Offers MFA, Certificate.

The University of Toledo, College of Graduate Studies, College of Language, Literature and Social Sciences, Department of English, Toledo, OH 43606-3390. Offers English as a second language (MA); literature (MA); teaching of writing (Certificate). Part-time programs available. *Faculty:* 15. *Students:* 37 full-time (23 women), 12 part-time (10 women); includes 3 minority (all Black or African American, non-Hispanic/Latino), 6 international. Average age 29. 45 applicants, 73% accepted, 26 enrolled. In 2010, 19 master's, 1 other advanced degree awarded. *Degree requirements:* For master's, thesis. *Entrance requirements:* For master's, GRE if GPA is less than 3.0 for domestic students and GRE and TOEFL required for foreign students. A minimum 2.7 cumulative point-hour ratio (on a 4.0 scale) for all previous academic work. Three Letters of Recommendation, transcripts from all prior institutions attended. A critical essay for review by admissions committee. Additional exam requirements/recommendations for international students: Required—TOEFL (minimum score 550 paper-based; 213 computer-based; 80 iBT), IELTS (minimum score 6.5). *Application deadline:* For fall admission, 1/15 priority date for domestic students, 1/5 priority date for international students. Applications are processed on a rolling basis. Application fee: $45 ($75 for international students). Electronic applications accepted. *Expenses:* Tuition: state resident: full-time $11,426; part-time $476 per credit hour. Tuition, nonresident: full-time $21,660; part-time $903 per credit hour. One-time fee: $62. *Financial support:* Teaching assistantships with full tuition reimbursements, Federal Work-Study, institutionally sponsored loans, scholarships/grants, tuition waivers (full), and unspecified assistantships available. Support available to part-time students. *Faculty research:* Literary criticism, linguistics, creative writing, folklore and cultural studies. *Unit head:* Dr. Sara Lundquist, Chair, 419-530-2506, Fax: 419-530-2590, E-mail: sara.lundquist@utoledo.edu. *Application contact:* Graduate School Office, 419-530-4723, Fax: 419-530-4724, E-mail: grdsch@utoledo.edu.

University of Utah, Graduate School, College of Humanities, Department of English, Program in Creative Writing, Salt Lake City, UT 84112. Offers rhetoric/composition (MA, PhD). *Students:* 5 full-time (2 women), 5 part-time (3 women); includes 2 minority (1 Black or African American, non-Hispanic/Latino; 1 American Indian or Alaska Native, non-Hispanic/Latino). Average age 31. 58 applicants, 2% accepted, 1 enrolled. In 2010, 5 master's awarded. *Degree requirements:* For master's, variable foreign language requirement, comprehensive exam, thesis optional; for doctorate, variable foreign language requirement, comprehensive exam, thesis/dissertation. *Entrance requirements:* For master's and doctorate, GRE. *Application deadline:* For fall admission, 1/15 for domestic students. Application fee: $55 ($65 for international students). *Expenses:* Tuition, area resident: Part-time $179.19 per credit hour. Tuition, state resident: full-time $4384. Tuition, nonresident: full-time $16,684; part-time $630.67 per credit hour. Required fees: $350 per semester. Tuition and fees vary according to course load, degree level and program. *Financial support:* In 2010–11, 9 teaching assistantships with full tuition reimbursements (averaging $12,430 per year) were awarded; institutionally sponsored loans, scholarships/grants, health care benefits, and unspecified assistantships also available. *Unit head:* Dr. Maureen Ann Mathison, Director, 801-581-7090, E-mail: maureen.mathison@hum.utah.edu. *Application contact:* Pauline Frances Light, Office Support Coordinator, 801-581-7098, E-mail: plight@utah.edu.

University of Victoria, Faculty of Graduate Studies, Faculty of Fine Arts, Department of Writing, Victoria, BC V8W 2Y2, Canada. Offers MFA. *Entrance requirements:* For master's, portfolio, 2 letters of reference.

University of Virginia, College and Graduate School of Arts and Sciences, Department of English Language and Literature, Program in Creative Writing, Charlottesville, VA 22903. Offers MFA. *Faculty:* 8 full-time (5 women). *Students:* 27 full-time (18 women); includes 1 Black or African American, non-Hispanic/Latino; 1 Asian, non-Hispanic/Latino; 2 Hispanic/Latino; 1 Native Hawaiian or other Pacific Islander, non-Hispanic/Latino, 1 international. Average age 27. 801 applicants, 1% accepted, 10 enrolled. In 2010, 13 master's awarded. *Degree requirements:* For master's, comprehensive exam, thesis. *Entrance requirements:* For master's, GRE General Test, writing sample. Additional exam requirements/recommendations for international students: Required—TOEFL (minimum score 600 paper-based; 250 computer-based; 90 iBT), IELTS (minimum score 7). *Application deadline:* For fall admission, 1/1 for domestic students, 1/4 for international students. Application fee: $60. Electronic applications accepted. *Financial support:* Fellowships, teaching assistantships available. Financial award application deadline: 1/4; financial award applicants required to submit FAFSA. *Unit head:* Christopher Tilghman, Director, 434-924-6675, Fax: 434-924-1478, E-mail: ct2a@virginia.edu. *Application contact:* Barbara Moriarty, Administrative Assistant, 434-924-6074, Fax: 434-924-1478, E-mail: bam9s@virginia.edu.

University of Washington, Graduate School, College of Arts and Sciences, Department of English, Program in Creative Writing, Seattle, WA 98195. Offers MFA. *Entrance requirements:* For master's, GRE, GMAT. Additional exam requirements/recommendations for international students: Required—TOEFL (minimum score 550 paper-based; 213 computer-based). Electronic applications accepted.

University of West Florida, College of Arts and Sciences: Arts, Department of English and Foreign Languages, Pensacola, FL 32514-5750. Offers creative writing (MA); literature (MA). Part-time and evening/weekend programs available. *Faculty:* 7 full-time (3 women). *Students:*

13 full-time (9 women), 33 part-time (19 women); includes 2 Black or African American, non-Hispanic/Latino; 2 American Indian or Alaska Native, non-Hispanic/Latino; 2 Hispanic/Latino. Average age 33. 20 applicants, 55% accepted, 7 enrolled. In 2010, 7 master's awarded. *Degree requirements:* For master's, thesis. *Entrance requirements:* For master's, GRE General Test, minimum GPA of 3.0. Additional exam requirements/recommendations for international students: Required—TOEFL (minimum score 550 paper-based; 213 computer-based). *Application deadline:* For fall admission, 6/1 for domestic students, 5/15 for international students; for spring admission, 10/1 for domestic and international students. Applications are processed on a rolling basis. Application fee: $30. *Expenses:* Tuition, state resident: full-time $4982; part-time $208 per credit hour. Tuition, nonresident: full-time $20,059; part-time $836 per credit hour. Required fees: $1365; $57 per credit hour. *Financial support:* In 2010–11, 6 fellowships with partial tuition reimbursements (averaging $924 per year), 24 research assistantships with partial tuition reimbursements (averaging $3,280 per year), 18 teaching assistantships with partial tuition reimbursements (averaging $5,571 per year) were awarded; unspecified assistantships also available. Financial award application deadline: 4/15; financial award applicants required to submit FAFSA. *Faculty research:* Faulkner, Shakespeare, American humor, women's studies, poetry. *Unit head:* Dr. Bob Yeager, Chairperson, 850-474-2923. *Application contact:* Terry McCray, Assistant Director of Graduate Admissions, 850-473-7718, Fax: 850-473-7714, E-mail: gradadmissions@uwf.edu.

University of Windsor, Faculty of Graduate Studies, Faculty of Arts and Social Sciences, Department of English Language, Literature and Creative Writing, Windsor, ON N9B 3P4, Canada. Offers English: creative writing and language and literature (MA); English: language and literature (MA). Part-time programs available. *Degree requirements:* For master's, thesis. *Entrance requirements:* For master's, minimum B average, portfolio. Additional exam requirements/recommendations for international students: Required—TOEFL (minimum score 600 paper-based; 250 computer-based). Electronic applications accepted. *Faculty research:* Use of gender-related terms in popular culture; international and Aboriginal literatures: expression of cultural identity; critical analysis of authors: Pope, Munroe, Lady Morgan, Orwell, Thomas; the 'feminine' voice in literature and contemporary culture.

University of Wisconsin–Eau Claire, College of Arts and Sciences, Program in English, Eau Claire, WI 54702-4004. Offers literature and textual interpretation (MA); writing (MA). Part-time programs available. *Faculty:* 24 full-time (16 women). *Students:* 8 full-time (3 women), 11 part-time (10 women); includes 2 minority (1 Hispanic/Latino; 1 Two or more races, non-Hispanic/Latino). Average age 31. 15 applicants, 80% accepted, 8 enrolled. In 2010, 6 master's awarded. *Degree requirements:* For master's, thesis, oral defense with thesis. *Entrance requirements:* For master's, minimum GPA of 3.25 in English, 3.0 overall; bachelor's degree with minimum of 24 credits in English. Additional exam requirements/recommendations for international students: Required—TOEFL (minimum score 550 paper-based; 213 computer-based; 79 iBT); Recommended—IELTS (minimum score 7). *Application deadline:* For fall admission, 7/1 priority date for domestic students, 6/1 priority date for international students; for spring admission, 12/1 priority date for domestic students, 11/1 priority date for international students. Applications are processed on a rolling basis. Application fee: $56. *Expenses:* Tuition, state resident: full-time $7001; part-time $389 per credit. Tuition, nonresident: full-time $16,771; part-time $932 per credit. Required fees: $1057; $58.49 per credit. *Financial support:* In 2010–11, 13 students received support, including 3 fellowships (averaging $2,013 per year); Federal Work-Study and unspecified assistantships also available. Financial award application deadline: 3/1; financial award applicants required to submit FAFSA. *Unit head:* Dr. Jack Bushnell, Chair, 715-836-2639, Fax: 715-836-5996, E-mail: bushnejp@uwec.edu. *Application contact:* Dr. Jennifer Shaddock, Director, 715-836-5476, E-mail: shaddoj@uwec.edu.

University of Wisconsin–Madison, Graduate School, College of Letters and Science, Department of English, Madison, WI 53706-1380. Offers applied English linguistics (MA); composition and rhetoric (PhD); creative writing (MFA); English language and linguistics (PhD); literary studies (MA, PhD). *Degree requirements:* For doctorate, thesis/dissertation. *Expenses:* Tuition, state resident: full-time $9887; part-time $617.96 per credit. Tuition, nonresident: full-time $24,054; part-time $1503.40 per credit. Required fees: $67.63 per credit. Tuition and fees vary according to reciprocity agreements.

University of Wisconsin–Milwaukee, Graduate School, College of Letters and Sciences, Department of English, Milwaukee, WI 53201-0413. Offers creative writing (PhD); English (MA); international technical communication (Certificate); linguistics (PhD); professional writing (PhD); professional writing and communication (Certificate); rhetoric and composition (PhD); MLIS/MA. *Faculty:* 40 full-time (19 women). *Students:* 106 full-time (62 women), 65 part-time (45 women); includes 4 Black or African American, non-Hispanic/Latino; 5 Asian, non-Hispanic/Latino, 17 international. Average age 34. 208 applicants, 54% accepted, 29 enrolled. In 2010, 19 master's, 14 doctorates awarded. *Degree requirements:* For master's, thesis or alternative; for doctorate, one foreign language, thesis/dissertation. *Entrance requirements:* For master's, GRE General Test, GRE Subject Test; for doctorate, GRE. Additional exam requirements/recommendations for international students: Required—TOEFL (minimum score 550 paper-based; 79 iBT), IELTS (minimum score 6.5). *Application deadline:* For fall admission, 1/1 priority date for domestic students; for spring admission, 9/1 for domestic students. Applications are processed on a rolling basis. Application fee: $56 ($96 for international students). Electronic applications accepted. *Financial support:* In 2010–11, 4 fellowships, 1 research assistantship, 84 teaching assistantships were awarded; career-related internships or fieldwork, unspecified assistantships, and project assistantships also available. Support available to part-time students. Financial award application deadline: 4/15; financial award applicants required to submit FAFSA. Total annual research expenditures: $36,259. *Unit head:* Tasha Oren, Representative, 414-229-6625, Fax: 414-229-2643, E-mail: tgoren@uwm.edu. *Application contact:* General Information Contact, 414-229-4982, Fax: 414-229-6967, E-mail: gradschool@uwm.edu.

University of Wyoming, College of Arts and Sciences, Department of English, Laramie, WY 82070. Offers creative writing (MFA); English (MA). Part-time programs available. *Degree requirements:* For master's, thesis or alternative, internship. *Entrance requirements:* For master's, GRE General Test, minimum GPA of 3.0. Electronic applications accepted. *Faculty research:* Literature and theory, creative writing, English as a second language, ethnic and women's studies, composition.

Utah State University, School of Graduate Studies, College of Humanities, Arts and Social Sciences, Department of English, Logan, UT 84322. Offers American studies (MA, MS), including folklore, western American literature and culture; English (MA, MS), including literature and writing, technical writing. Part-time and evening/weekend programs available. *Degree requirements:* For master's, thesis or alternative. *Entrance requirements:* For master's, GRE General Test or MAT, minimum GPA of 3.0, recommendation letters, writing samples. Additional exam requirements/recommendations for international students: Required—TOEFL. *Faculty research:* Scottish enlightenment, material culture, composition theory, creative nonfiction, literary criticism.

Vanderbilt University, Graduate School, Program in Creative Writing, Nashville, TN 37240-1001. Offers MFA. *Faculty:* 33 full-time (17 women). *Students:* 7 full-time (6 women), 5 part-time (3 women); includes 1 Asian, non-Hispanic/Latino. Average age 29. 526 applicants, 2% accepted, 6 enrolled. In 2010, 5 master's awarded. *Degree requirements:* For master's, comprehensive exam, thesis. *Entrance requirements:* For master's, GRE General Test, sample of written work. Additional exam requirements/recommendations for international students: Required—TOEFL (minimum score 570 paper-based; 230 computer-based; 88 iBT). *Application deadline:* For fall admission, 1/15 for domestic and international students. Application fee: $0. Electronic applications accepted. *Financial support:* Fellowships with full and partial tuition reimbursements, teaching assistantships with full and partial tuition reimbursements, Federal Work-Study, institutionally sponsored loans, and health care benefits available. Financial award application deadline: 1/15; financial award applicants required to submit CSS PROFILE or FAFSA. *Unit head:* Dr. Mark Jarman, Director, 615-322-2618, E-mail: mark.jarman@

Writing

Vanderbilt University (continued)

vanderbilt.edu. *Application contact:* Margaret Quigley, MFA Graduate Assistant, 615-322-6527, E-mail: creativewriting@vanderbilt.edu.

Vermont College of Fine Arts, Program in Writing, Montpelier, VT 05602. Offers MFA. Postbaccalaureate distance learning degree programs offered (minimal on-campus study). *Faculty:* 31 full-time, 15 part-time/adjunct. *Students:* 137 full-time (98 women); includes 1 Black or African American, non-Hispanic/Latino; 2 Asian, non-Hispanic/Latino; 2 Hispanic/Latino. Average age 38. 161 applicants, 61% accepted, 47 enrolled. *Application deadline:* For fall admission, 2/1 for domestic and international students; for spring admission, 8/1 for domestic and international students. Application fee: $75. *Expenses:* Tuition: Full-time $17,820. Required fees: $270. *Financial support:* Scholarships/grants available. *Unit head:* Louise Crowley, Program Director, 802-828-8840, E-mail: louise.crowley@vermontcollege.edu. *Application contact:* Jason Lamb, Assistant Director of Admissions, 802-828-8829, E-mail: jason.lamb@vermontcollege.edu.

Vermont College of Fine Arts, Program in Writing for Children and Young Adults, Montpelier, VT 05602. Offers MFA. Postbaccalaureate distance learning degree programs offered (minimal on-campus study). *Faculty:* 20 full-time, 10 part-time/adjunct. *Students:* 88 full-time (78 women); includes 2 Black or African American, non-Hispanic/Latino; 1 Asian, non-Hispanic/Latino. Average age 38. 61 applicants, 74% accepted, 33 enrolled. *Application deadline:* For fall admission, 3/1 for domestic and international students; for spring admission, 10/1 for domestic and international students. Application fee: $75. *Expenses:* Tuition: Full-time $17,820. Required fees: $270. *Financial support:* Traineeships available. Financial award applicants required to submit FAFSA. *Unit head:* Melissa Fisher, Program Director, 802-828-8696, E-mail: melissa.fisher@vermontcollege.edu. *Application contact:* Jason Lamb, Assistant Director of Admissions, 802-828-8829, E-mail: jason.lamb@vermontcollege.edu.

Virginia Commonwealth University, Graduate School, College of Humanities and Sciences, Department of English, Program in Creative Writing, Richmond, VA 23284-9005. Offers fiction (MFA); fictional poetry (MFA); poetry (MFA). Part-time programs available. *Students:* 24 full-time (16 women), 4 part-time (3 women); includes 4 minority (2 Black or African American, non-Hispanic/Latino; 1 Asian, non-Hispanic/Latino; 1 Two or more races, non-Hispanic/Latino). 108 applicants, 18% accepted, 9 enrolled. In 2010, 9 master's awarded. *Entrance requirements:* For master's, GRE General Test, portfolio. Additional exam requirements/recommendations for international students: Required—Either TOEFL (minimum score: paper-based 600, computer-based 250) or IELTS (6.5). *Application deadline:* For fall admission, 2/1 priority date for domestic students. Applications are processed on a rolling basis. Application fee: $50. Electronic applications accepted. *Expenses:* Tuition, state resident: full-time $4308; part-time $479 per credit hour. Tuition, nonresident: full-time $8942; part-time $994 per credit hour. Required fees: $2000; $85 per credit hour. Tuition and fees vary according to course level, course load, degree level, campus/location and program. *Financial support:* Federal Work-Study, institutionally sponsored loans, and tuition waivers (full and partial) available. Support available to part-time students. Financial award applicants required to submit FAFSA. *Faculty research:* Poetry, fiction. *Unit head:* Clint McCown, Director of Creative Writing, 804-828-1329, E-mail: jcmccown@vcu.edu. *Application contact:* Thom Didato, Graduate Programs Advisor, 804-828-1329, E-mail: tndidato@vcu.edu.

Virginia Commonwealth University, Graduate School, College of Humanities and Sciences, Department of English, Program in English, Richmond, VA 23284-9005. Offers literature (MA); writing and rhetoric (MA). Part-time programs available. *Students:* 30 full-time (16 women), 28 part-time (18 women); includes 10 minority (5 Black or African American, non-Hispanic/Latino; 1 American Indian or Alaska Native, non-Hispanic/Latino; 1 Asian, non-Hispanic/Latino; 2 Hispanic/Latino; 1 Two or more races, non-Hispanic/Latino), 1 international. 39 applicants, 69% accepted, 15 enrolled. In 2010, 16 master's awarded. *Entrance requirements:* For master's, GRE General Test. Additional exam requirements/recommendations for international students: Required—TWE, Either TOEFL (minimum score: paper-based 600, computer-based 250) or IELTS (6.5). *Application deadline:* For fall admission, 3/1 for domestic students; for spring admission, 11/15 for domestic students. Applications are processed on a rolling basis. Application fee: $50. Electronic applications accepted. *Expenses:* Tuition, state resident: full-time $4308; part-time $479 per credit hour. Tuition, nonresident: full-time $8942; part-time $994 per credit hour. Required fees: $2000; $85 per credit hour. Tuition and fees vary according to course level, course load, degree level, campus/location and program. *Financial support:* Federal Work-Study, institutionally sponsored loans, and tuition waivers (full and partial) available. Support available to part-time students. Financial award applicants required to submit FAFSA. *Faculty research:* Literature, writing, rhetoric. *Unit head:* Dr. Katherine C. Bassard, Program Director, 804-828-1329, E-mail: kcbassar@vcu.edu. *Application contact:* Thom N. Didato, Director, 804-828-1329, E-mail: tndidato@vcu.edu.

Warren Wilson College, MFA Program for Writers, Swannanoa, Asheville, NC 28815-9000. Offers MFA. Postbaccalaureate distance learning degree programs offered (minimal on-campus study). *Degree requirements:* For master's, thesis, public reading, teaching experience. *Entrance requirements:* For master's, manuscript of creative work. *Faculty research:* Analytic writing, creative and analytic study of literature.

Washington University in St. Louis, Graduate School of Arts and Sciences, Department of English and American Literature, Writing Program, St. Louis, MO 63130-4899. Offers MFAW. *Degree requirements:* For master's, thesis or written exam. *Entrance requirements:* For master's, GRE General Test, sample of written work. Electronic applications accepted.

Wayne State University, College of Liberal Arts and Sciences, Department of English, Detroit, MI 48202. Offers comparative literature (MA); English (MA, PhD). *Faculty:* 26 full-time (14 women), 1 part-time/adjunct (0 women). *Students:* 94 full-time (54 women), 35 part-time (23 women); includes 13 minority (8 Black or African American, non-Hispanic/Latino; 3 Asian, non-Hispanic/Latino; 2 Hispanic/Latino), 9 international. Average age 34. 81 applicants, 43% accepted, 20 enrolled. In 2010, 8 master's, 9 doctorates awarded. *Degree requirements:* For master's, one foreign language, essay or thesis; for doctorate, one foreign language, thesis/dissertation. *Entrance requirements:* For master's, GRE General Test, minimum GPA of 3.25 in English, 3.0 overall; references; for doctorate, GRE General Test, GRE Subject Test, statement of purpose, references, sample essay. Additional exam requirements/recommendations for international students: Required—TOEFL (minimum score 550 paper-based; 213 computer-based); Recommended—TWE (minimum score 6). *Application deadline:* For fall admission, 6/1 for international students; for winter admission, 10/1 for international students; for spring admission, 2/1 for international students. Applications are processed on a rolling basis. Application fee: $30 ($50 for international students). Electronic applications accepted. *Expenses:* Tuition, state resident: full-time $7662; part-time $478.85 per credit hour. Tuition, nonresident: full-time $16,920; part-time $1057.55 per credit hour. Required fees: $571.20; $35.70 per credit hour. $188.05 per semester. Tuition and fees vary according to course load and program. *Financial support:* In 2010–11, 8 fellowships (averaging $15,320 per year), 30 teaching assistantships (averaging $14,658 per year) were awarded; research assistantships, career-related internships or fieldwork, institutionally sponsored loans, and tuition waivers (full and partial) also available. Support available to part-time students. Financial award application deadline: 3/1. *Faculty research:* English and American literature, cultural studies, composition, linguistics, film. *Unit head:* Dr. Richard Grusin, Chair, 313-577-7692, Fax: 313-577-8618, E-mail: aj4671@wayne.edu. *Application contact:* Ross Pudaloff, Graduate Director, 313-577-7699, E-mail: r.pudaloff@wayne.edu.

Western Connecticut State University, Division of Graduate Studies and External Programs, School of Arts and Sciences, Department of English, Danbury, CT 06810-6885. Offers English (MA); literature option (MA); TESOL option (MA); writing option (MA). Part-time programs available. *Students:* 4 full-time (2 women), 23 part-time (18 women); includes 3 minority (2 Hispanic/Latino; 1 Two or more races, non-Hispanic/Latino). Average age 41. In 2010, 9 master's awarded. *Degree requirements:* For master's, thesis (writing option), completion of program in 6 years. *Entrance requirements:* For master's, minimum GPA of 2.5, writing sample. Additional exam requirements/recommendations for international students: Recommended—TOEFL (minimum score 550 paper-based; 213 computer-based; 79 iBT), IELTS (minimum score 6). *Application deadline:* For fall admission, 8/5 priority date for domestic students; for spring admission, 1/5 priority date for domestic students. Applications are processed on a rolling basis. Application fee: $50. *Expenses:* Tuition, state resident: full-time $5012; part-time $417 per credit hour. Tuition, nonresident: full-time $13,962; part-time $423 per credit hour. Required fees: $3886. Full-time tuition and fees vary according to course load, degree level and program. *Financial support:* Application deadline: 5/1. *Unit head:* Dr. Shouhua Qi, Co-Coordinator, 203-837-9048, Fax: 203-837-8525, E-mail: qis@wcsu.edu. *Application contact:* Chris Shankle, Associate Director of Graduate Studies, 203-837-9005, Fax: 203-837-8326, E-mail: shanklec@wcsu.edu.

Western Connecticut State University, Division of Graduate Studies and External Programs, School of Arts and Sciences, Department of Writing, Linguistics, and Creative Process, Danbury, CT 06810-6885. Offers professional writing (MFA). Part-time programs available. *Students:* 25 full-time (16 women), 11 part-time (8 women); includes 4 minority (3 Black or African American, non-Hispanic/Latino; 1 Hispanic/Latino). Average age 38. In 2010, 7 master's awarded. *Degree requirements:* For master's, thesis, completion of program within 4 years, enrichment project that compliments course of study. *Entrance requirements:* For master's, 2 writing samples: a 20-50 page portfolio of previous writing and a brief essay. Additional exam requirements/recommendations for international students: Recommended—TOEFL (minimum score 550 paper-based; 213 computer-based; 79 iBT), IELTS (minimum score 6). *Application deadline:* For fall admission, 8/5 priority date for domestic students; for spring admission, 1/5 priority date for domestic students. Application fee: $50. *Expenses:* Contact institution. *Financial support:* In 2010–11, 1 student received support. Scholarships/grants available. *Unit head:* Dr. Brian Clements, MFA Coordinator, 203-837-8876, Fax: 636-246-7589, E-mail: clementsb@wcsu.edu. *Application contact:* Chris Shankle, Associate Director of Graduate Admissions, 203-837-9005, Fax: 203-837-8326, E-mail: shanklec@wcsu.edu.

Western Illinois University, School of Graduate Studies, College of Arts and Sciences, Department of English and Journalism, Macomb, IL 61455-1390. Offers English (MA); literary studies (Certificate); professional writing (Certificate); teaching writing (Certificate). Part-time programs available. *Students:* 13 full-time (11 women), 27 part-time (20 women); includes 4 minority (1 Black or African American, non-Hispanic/Latino; 2 Hispanic/Latino; 1 Two or more races, non-Hispanic/Latino), 3 international. Average age 28. 21 applicants, 86% accepted. In 2010, 15 master's, 3 other advanced degrees awarded. *Degree requirements:* For master's, thesis or alternative. *Entrance requirements:* Additional exam requirements/recommendations for international students: Required—TOEFL (minimum score 575 paper-based; 230 computer-based; 88 iBT). *Application deadline:* Applications are processed on a rolling basis. Application fee: $30. Electronic applications accepted. *Expenses:* Tuition, state resident: full-time $6370; part-time $265.40 per credit hour. Tuition, nonresident: full-time $12,740; part-time $530.80 per credit hour. Required fees: $75.67 per credit hour. *Financial support:* In 2010–11, 16 students received support, including 8 research assistantships with full tuition reimbursements available (averaging $7,280 per year), 8 teaching assistantships with full tuition reimbursements available (averaging $8,400 per year). Financial award applicants required to submit FAFSA. *Unit head:* Dr. Mark Mossman, Chairperson, 309-298-1103. *Application contact:* Evelyn Hoing, Assistant Director of Graduate Studies, 309-298-1806, Fax: 309-298-2345, E-mail: grad-office@wiu.edu.

Western Kentucky University, Graduate Studies, Potter College of Arts and Letters, Department of English, Bowling Green, KY 42101. Offers education (MA); English (MA Ed); literature (MA), including American literature, British literature, literary theory, women writers, world literature; teaching English as a second language (MA); writing (MA). Part-time and evening/weekend programs available. *Degree requirements:* For master's, comprehensive exam, thesis optional, final exam. *Entrance requirements:* For master's, GRE General Test, minimum GPA of 2.75. Additional exam requirements/recommendations for international students: Required—TOEFL (minimum score 555 paper-based; 213 computer-based; 79 iBT). *Faculty research:* Improving writing, linking teacher knowledge and performance, Victorian women writers, Kentucky women writers, Kentucky poets.

Western Michigan University, Graduate College, College of Arts and Sciences, Department of English, Kalamazoo, MI 49008. Offers creative writing (MFA, PhD); English (MA, PhD); English education (MA, PhD). *Degree requirements:* For master's, oral exams; for doctorate, one foreign language, thesis/dissertation, oral exam, written exams. *Entrance requirements:* For master's and doctorate, GRE General Test, GRE Subject Test.

Western State College of Colorado, Program in Creative Writing, Gunnison, CO 81231. Offers mainstream genre fiction (MFA); poetry (MFA); screenwriting (MFA). Postbaccalaureate distance learning degree programs offered (minimal on-campus study). *Degree requirements:* For master's, thesis.

See Display on next page and Close-Up on page 575.

Westminster College, Program in Professional Communication, Salt Lake City, UT 84105-3697. Offers MPC. Part-time and evening/weekend programs available. *Faculty:* 7 full-time (3 women), 5 part-time/adjunct (3 women). *Students:* 14 full-time (8 women), 50 part-time (37 women); includes 1 Native Hawaiian or other Pacific Islander, non-Hispanic/Latino; 1 Two or more races, non-Hispanic/Latino, 2 international. Average age 32. 35 applicants, 66% accepted, 17 enrolled. In 2010, 15 master's awarded. *Degree requirements:* For master's, field project. *Entrance requirements:* For master's, resume, professional writing sample, 2 letters of recommendation, official transcripts. Additional exam requirements/recommendations for international students: Required—TOEFL (minimum score 600 paper-based; 250 computer-based; 100 iBT), IELTS (minimum score 7). *Application deadline:* For fall admission, 7/9 for domestic and international students. Applications are processed on a rolling basis. Application fee: $50. Electronic applications accepted. *Expenses:* Contact institution. *Financial support:* In 2010–11, 38 students received support. Career-related internships or fieldwork and tuition reimbursement, tuition remission available. Support available to part-time students. Financial award applicants required to submit FAFSA. *Faculty research:* Critical communication pedagogy, sexuality and gender, autoethnography, regulation of broadcast indecency, hypertext theory. *Unit head:* Dr. Helen Hodgson, Director, 801-832-2821, Fax: 801-832-3102, E-mail: hhodgson@westminstercollege.edu. *Application contact:* Joel Bauman, Vice President of Enrollment Services, 801-832-2200, Fax: 801-832-3101, E-mail: admission@westminstercollege.edu.

West Virginia University, Eberly College of Arts and Sciences, Department of English, Program in Creative Writing, Morgantown, WV 26506. Offers MFA. Part-time and evening/weekend programs available.

Wichita State University, Graduate School, Fairmount College of Liberal Arts and Sciences, Department of English, Wichita, KS 67260. Offers creative writing (MFA); English (MA). Part-time and evening/weekend programs available. *Entrance requirements:* For master's, writing sample (MFA). *Unit head:* Dr. Donald Wineke, Chair, 316-978-3130, Fax: 316-978-3548, E-mail: donald.wineke@wichita.edu. *Application contact:* Dr. Donald Wineke, Chair, 316-978-3130, Fax: 316-978-3548, E-mail: donald.wineke@wichita.edu.

Wilkes University, College of Graduate and Professional Studies, College of Arts, Humanities and Social Sciences, Program in Creative Writing, Wilkes-Barre, PA 18766-0002. Offers MA, MFA. Part-time programs available. Postbaccalaureate distance learning degree programs offered (minimal on-campus study). *Students:* 81 full-time (48 women), 18 part-time (10 women); includes 17 minority (7 Black or African American, non-Hispanic/Latino; 1 Asian, non-Hispanic/Latino; 7 Hispanic/Latino; 1 Native Hawaiian or other Pacific Islander, non-Hispanic/Latino; 1 Two or more races, non-Hispanic/Latino). Average age 37. In 2010, 45 master's awarded. *Entrance requirements:* Additional exam requirements/recommendations for international students: Required—TOEFL (minimum score 550 paper-based; 213 computer-based; 79 iBT). *Application deadline:* Applications are processed on a rolling basis. Application fee: $35. Electronic applications accepted. *Expenses:* Contact institution. *Financial support:* Application deadline: 3/1. *Unit head:* Dr. Bonnie Culver, Director, 570-408-4527, Fax: 570-408-7846, E-mail: bonnie.culver@wilkes.edu. *Application contact:* Kathleen Houlihan, Director of Graduate Studies, 570-408-3235, Fax: 570-408-7846, E-mail: kathleen.houlihan@wilkes.edu.

Wright State University, School of Graduate Studies, College of Liberal Arts, Department of English Language and Literatures, Dayton, OH 45435. Offers composition and rhetoric (MA); English (MA); literature (MA); teaching English to speakers of other languages (MA). *Degree requirements:* For master's, thesis optional, portfolio. *Entrance requirements:* For master's, 20 hours in upper-level English. Additional exam requirements/recommendations for international students: Required—TOEFL. *Faculty research:* American literature, world literature in English, applied linguistics, writing theory and pedagogy.

ADELPHI UNIVERSITY

College of the Arts and Sciences
Program in Creative Writing

Program of Study

The Master of Fine Arts (M.F.A.) in creative writing offers students the opportunity to specialize in three major genres—fiction, poetry, and playwriting. This cross-genre program is distinctive from the traditional two-genre M.F.A. programs in which students study either fiction or poetry. Its unique Professional Development Practicum introduces students to the professional and practical life of writers across many disciplines.

Taught by distinguished faculty members who have published extensively, the program prepares students for careers in writing, teaching, and/or more advanced graduate studies through training in creative writing, language and literary studies, research, and teaching. Most classes are seminars that are held in the evenings once a week, either from 4 to 6:30 p.m. or from 7 to 9:30 p.m. Students must complete 37 credits in a plan of study that includes writing workshops (16 credits) and literature classes (12 credits). Students must also complete a 4-credit thesis colloquium. The 1-credit Professional Development Practicum meets once a week in the spring semester of the first year. Through meetings with writers and agents, students learn firsthand about the professional life of a writer. They also learn the practical procedures of submitting a manuscript or applying for a grant. Students and their advisers determine the appropriate plan of study. A student thesis is required in all programs.

Research Facilities

The University's primary research holdings are at Swirbul Library and include 600,000 volumes (including bound periodicals and government publications), 806,000 items in microformats, 33,000 audiovisual items, and access to over 61,000 electronic journal titles. Online access is provided to more than 221 research databases.

Financial Aid

All applicants are eligible for financial aid and are automatically considered for one of six partial (one-half) tuition remissions. Second-year students and students entering with a previous M.A. degree are eligible for graduate teaching fellowships in the Department of English. There are also opportunities for work-study positions, for community service teaching grants, or for positions at the Writing Center and the Learning Center.

Cost of Study

For the 2011–12 academic year, the tuition rate is $930 per credit. University fees range from $315 to $550 per semester.

Living and Housing Costs

The University assists single and married students in finding suitable accommodations whenever possible. The cost of living is dependent upon location and the number of rooms rented.

Location

Located in historic Garden City, New York, 45 minutes from Manhattan and 20 minutes from Queens, Adelphi's 75-acre suburban campus is known for the beauty of its landscape and architecture. The campus is a short walk from the Long Island Rail Road and is convenient to New York's major airports and several major highways. Off-campus centers are located in Manhattan, Hauppauge, and Poughkeepsie.

The University and The College

Founded in 1896, Adelphi is a fully accredited, private university with nearly 8,000 undergraduate, graduate, and returning-adult students in the arts and sciences, business, clinical psychology, education, nursing, and social work. Students come from forty-one states and from forty-eight countries. *The Princeton Review* named Adelphi University a Best College in the Northeastern Region, and *Fiske Guide to Colleges* recognized Adelphi as a "Best Buy" in higher education for a fifth year in a row. The University is one of only twenty-four private institutions in the nation to earn this recognition.

Mindful of the cultural inheritance of the past, the College of Arts and Sciences encompasses those realms of inquiry that have characterized the modern pursuit of knowledge. The faculty members of the College place a high priority on their students' intellectual development in and out of the classroom and structure programs and opportunities to foster that growth. Students analyze original research or other creative work, develop firsthand facility with creative or research methodologies, undertake collaborative work with peers and mentors, engage in serious internships, and hone communicative skills.

Applying

A baccalaureate degree is required for admission (the degree does not have to be in English or literature). A student must submit the completed application form, the $50 application fee, official college transcripts, two letters of reference from people familiar with the student's writing, a personal statement (of no more than 1,000 words and about the student's writing life and goals), and a manuscript in one genre only (poetry, fiction, or playwriting). The application deadlines are January 15 for fall enrollment and September 15 for spring enrollment. After those dates, rolling admissions are made on a space-available basis.

Correspondence and Information

Jaqueline Jones LaMon, Director of the M.F.A. Program
Harvey Hall, Room 215
College of Arts and Sciences
Adelphi University
Garden City, New York 11530-0701
Phone: 516-877-4164
Fax: 516-877-4038
E-mail: lamon@adelphi.edu
Web site: http://academics.adelphi.edu/artsci/creativewriting/

Adelphi University

THE FACULTY AND THEIR RESEARCH

CREATIVE WRITING

Judith Baumel, Associate Professor; M.A., Johns Hopkins, 1978. Contemporary poetry.

Martha Cooley, Associate Professor; B.A., Trinity, 1977. Creative writing, modern and contemporary American literature, world literatures in translation (particularly Italian).

Anton Dudley, Assistant Professor; M.F.A., NYU, 2001. Dramatic writing.

Kermit Frazier, Chair of the English Department and Associate Professor; M.F.A., NYU, 1977; M.A., Syracuse, 1970. Playwriting, television writing, contemporary drama, African American drama, the literature of AIDS.

Jacqueline Jones LaMon, Director of the M.F.A. Program in Creative Writing and Associate Professor; J.D., UCLA, 1987; M.F.A., Indiana, 2006.

Vincent Passaro, Assistant Professor, M.F.A., Columbia, 1988. Modern and contemporary fiction, the history of the novel.

Igor Webb, Professor; Ph.D., Stanford, 1971. The nineteenth-century novel.

LITERATURE

Craig Carson, Assistant Professor, Ph.D., California, Irvine, 2007. Politics and theater, Restoration/eighteenth-century literature.

Jennifer Fleischner, Professor; Ph.D., Columbia, 1988. Twentieth-century American literature, race and slavery, women's literature.

Michael Matto, Associate Professor; Ph.D., NYU, 1998. History of the English language, history of rhetoric, Old English literature and culture, theories of metaphor, history of subjectivity.

Christopher Mayo, Assistant Professor; Ph.D., Brandeis, 2004. Restoration and eighteenth-century British literature and culture.

Lahney Preston-Matto, Associate Professor; Ph.D., NYU, 2000. Twentieth-century medievalism, translation theory, gender, twentieth-century Irish poetry, cultural studies.

Steven J. Rubin, Professor, Ph.D., Michigan, 1970. American Jewish literature, ethnic studies.

Susan Weisser, Professor; Ph.D., Columbia, 1987. The nineteenth-century novel, autobiography, romantic love and gender.

Peter West, Assistant Professor, Ph.D., Emory, 2001. Urban literature, the literature of slavery, nineteenth-century American literature and culture.

Adelphi's campus in historic Garden City, Long Island, New York.

A registered arboretum, Adelphi is truly a green campus.

WESTERN STATE COLLEGE OF COLORADO

Master of Fine Arts in Creative Writing Program

Programs of Study

The Western State College low-residency M.F.A. program offers disciplined writers the opportunity to pursue their passion, network with noted writers, and realize a deeper understanding of their broader audiences. Mentored by a dedicated and accomplished faculty, students establish the skills, networks, and industry knowledge needed to turn their passion into their career.

Students engage in four semesters of rigorous online course work that includes a combination of online writing submissions and critiques as well as regular discussion with individual faculty mentors. Students must earn and successfully complete 60 credits. The program includes a two-week, on-campus residency during each of three consecutive summers for 9 credits and a capstone thesis for 3 credits. The master's candidate earns a degree in one of three concentrations: mainstream/genre fiction, poetry with an emphasis in verse craft, and screenwriting.

The program enables students to realize their role as active participants in the creation of fiction, verse, and film. Through online course work, student and faculty readings, workshops, and master classes, students discover a noncompetitive, cohesive community devoted to their development. Western's low student-faculty ratio ensures that each student receives individualized feedback and support. The low-residency model allows students to engage their passions and pursue a degree in creative writing while maintaining the responsibilities and meeting the demands of adult life.

Concentration in Mainstream/Genre Fiction: This concentration explores the themes, ideas, and questions of each writer's imagination that inspire and demand retelling. Students master the art of writing for such forms as science fiction, the mystery, narrative nonfiction, and mainstream commercial fiction. Through the study of long and short written forms as well as explorations of forms for alternative media such as public performance, audio, and Internet media, students explore the world of writing that targets audiences beyond traditional academic circles. Through a rigorous curriculum of workshops, independent study projects, and residencies, students realize the skills and industry knowledge needed to reinvigorate their writing and reach a larger audience.

Concentration in Poetry with an Emphasis in Verse Craft: Verse is not only a way of saying something; it also is a way of doing something that prose cannot. That is why, in this program, students study the greatest possible range of how to do these things, from meters to stanzas, sonnet to ghazal, aubade to serenade, verse drama to verse satire. Students come to Western with something to say—the curriculum helps poets master how to say it.

This concentration requires that students achieve demonstrable mastery of a wide range of poetic forms and techniques along with acquiring historical and analytical knowledge about them. Students who complete the program are required to demonstrate their readiness to participate fully in the literary world through public speaking and relevant prose (book reviews, metrical analysis, historical investigation, etc.). Poetry applicants must have sufficient preparation in a foreign language (ancient or modern) to work on translation with the aid of a dictionary and other supporting texts during their second year of studies.

Concentration in Screenwriting: The screenwriting concentration examines the history and analysis as well as the future of classical and contemporary screenwriting texts and the resulting films. Students explore the visual narrative, three-act structure, four-act structure, character development, thematic development, conflict, genre, story arc, dialogue, and voice-over. The program emphasizes the Hollywood or independent feature-length screenplay, teaching students how to communicate their vision through written screenplays and see their vision realized on the big screen. The program introduces students to the process by which an idea becomes a film, from writing their initial screenplay to pitching and marketing their work. The curriculum also includes television drama and situation comedy writing as well as screenwriting contests, festivals, and opportunities for marketing the students' work. A master's thesis project in the form of a 100-page feature-length screenplay must be completed as a part of the degree requirements.

Publishing Certificate: This program presents a unique opportunity for writers to learn about the publishing industry through hands-on work. Students work with experts in the publishing industry, have opportunities for internships after completing the certificate, and become better prepared to enter the publishing field as agents or editors. The course of studies includes summer face-to-face classes, a series of integrated self-paced modules, and synchronous discussions in an online environment.

Students come to Western's campus for two weeks during two consecutive summers in late July to study the publishing industry, workshop their writing, and learn how to present their work to editors and agents. In addition to the summer residency, students participate during the fall and spring terms in an online editorial board to plan and prepare a book for publication through Western's press. Students also learn about publishing house operations including acquisitions, editorials, design, marketing, and sales, as well as record keeping and fulfillment.

Residencies

Surrounded by the unspoiled mountain landscapes and rugged beauty of western Colorado, the residency immerses students in the writer's life. For two weeks each summer, M.F.A. and publishing certificate students gather from across the country to inspire, direct, and connect with one another through intensive and illuminating workshops, critiques, panels, and student and faculty readings. Students realize a vibrant literary community while enjoying the natural playgrounds all around them. Students may stay in College residence halls or explore various housing options in the towns of Gunnison and Crested Butte. Students have access to the Leslie J. Savage Library along with multiple computer labs.

During the summer residency, the M.F.A. program hosts the Writing the Rockies conference. Led by celebrated authors, editors, and industry professionals, the conference offers students additional opportunities to explore their craft while learning the ins and outs of the publishing industry. In addition to workshops, panels, and readings, celebrated poets and critics gather at the Critical Path Poets Symposium to discuss, debate, and explore modern criticism. Students may attend those tracks and sessions that interest them most. These events include opportunities for pitch sessions with agents, producers, and acquisition editors.

Financial Aid

For graduate students in good standing, FAFSA loans are available for up to $20,500 for each year of full-time study. Half-time study is also eligible for loan awards. Colorado Opportunity Fund (COF) stipends are not available to graduate students.

Cost of Study

The total tuition cost for the two-year M.F.A. program (60 credits) for 2010–11 was $42,600 for both in-state and out-of-state students. Textbook costs and fees range from $100 to $350 for each year of the program. The total cost for the Publishing certificate for 2010–11 was $6300 for both in-state and out-of-state students.

Living and Housing Costs

Because of the low-residency structure of the program, students are able to participate in this M.F.A. program while maintaining their existing responsibilities and residencies. Summer residency requires on-site attendance for two weeks. Rooms in one-bedroom campus apartments with kitchenettes are also available for $25 to $40 per night. Other short-term housing is available in the community.

Location

At an altitude of 7,700 feet, Western's campus among the Colorado Rocky Mountains in Gunnison is beautiful and inspiring. Students have an unmatched opportunity to extend the academic experience beyond the classroom in this rugged alpine playground. Whether skiing, biking, climbing, hiking, or reveling within breathtaking horizons, students can immerse themselves in the pure and simple Colorado environment. The quaint mountain towns are safe and relaxing and offer something for everyone. Crested Butte, just 30 miles from Western's campus, is known as Colorado's last great ski town and is the official Wildflower Capitol of Colorado. Only minutes from campus is some of the world's best powder for skiing, granite faces for bouldering and climbing, a whitewater park perfect for kayaking, and miles of trails to hike and mountain bike.

The College

Founded in 1901, Western State College of Colorado is committed to a different kind of higher education experience. Academics at Western are characterized by quality education in the classroom enriched by hands-on learning experiences. Students experience a dedicated faculty, a supportive community, and endless opportunities to expand their curiosity, test their limits, and pursue academic excellence.

Applying

Prospective students should submit an online application for admission, official college transcripts demonstrating evidence of literary and/or film studies of at least four undergraduate or graduate courses, an 800- to 1,000-word personal statement describing writing experience and commitment to writing, a 20- to 30-page writing sample in the appropriate genre, three letters of recommendation, and a $50 application fee. Applications are accepted year-round on a rolling basis.

Correspondence and Information

Extended Studies Graduate Program
Western State College of Colorado
600 North Adams Street
Gunnison, Colorado 81231

Phone: 970-943-2885
  800-876-5309 Ext. 7 (toll-free)
Fax: 970-943-2212
E-mail: extendedstudies@western.edu
Web site: http://western.edu/graduate

Western State College of Colorado

THE FACULTY

Western State College's faculty members are established industry professionals dedicated to the growth and success of its students, both within and beyond the program. Each has been nationally recognized for their excellence, not only as writers but as teachers of writing. Together, they have published more than 100 books, produced dozens of films, documentaries, and television pilots, and have been awarded nearly every major literary and film award in the United States. Please visit the Web site at http://western.edu/directory/creative-writing-faculty/ for detailed information on Western's faculty members.

Barbara Chepaitis, Concentration Director, Mainstream and Genre Fiction; Ph.D., SUNY at Albany. Barbara Chepaitis has six published novels, including *A Lunatic Fear* (Wildside Press, 2004), *Something Unpredictable* (Simon & Schuster, 2003), *These Dreams* (Simon & Schuster, 2002), and three other novels with Bantam and Ace. She was a finalist in the 2003 Sundance screenwriters contest and has written four other screenplays. She has numerous shorter works collected in a variety of anthologies, and she also has experience in radio drama, voice-over work, and editing.

Russell Davis, Visiting Professor of Mainstream and Genre Fiction; M.F.A. Russell Davis has written and sold more than fifty-six novels and dozens of short stories in virtually every genre of fiction under numerous names to major publishers in both the United States and Canada. As an editor, he has worked with authors of both short fiction and novels, and he has acquired and edited novels and anthologies in romance, science fiction, fantasy, women's fiction, mystery, and Westerns. He is a regular speaker at conferences and schools where he teaches on writing, editing, and the fundamentals of the publishing industry. He has served as the president of Science Fiction & Fantasy Writers of America, Inc. (SFWA).

Mayank Gupta, Visiting Professor of Screenwriting, M.F.A., Loyola Marymount. Studio insider Mayank Gupta lives the life of a Hollywood screenwriter, pitching his own scripts, reworking others' works, collaborating and networking with Studio City heavyweights like producers Bruce Cohen (*American Beauty, Big Fish, Milk*), Derek Dauchy (*xXx, Across the Universe*), and Steve McEveety (*Passion of the Christ, Braveheart, What Women Want*). His musical film *Supernumerary* recently won the top prize at the Action on Film Festival, and has played at the Newport Beach Film Festival. His previous films have been shown at the London International film festival, Reynolda Film Festival and several others. He was invited by Robert DeNiro to the prestigious 2010 Tribeca All Access program. He is represented by Hollywood's foremost literary management company—Circle of Confusion. He has several screenplays and TV projects in development all over Hollywood.

Karla Kuban, Visiting Professor of Mainstream and Genre Fiction; M.F.A. Karla Kuban is author of the critically acclaimed and *New York Times* bestselling novel, *Marchlands*, published by Simon & Schuster, Inc. She was a student at the Johns Hopkins University Writing Program, a James A. Michener Fellow, and winner of two Pushcart Prizes for short stories. She currently divides her time between California and Aspen, Colorado. Her writing specialties bridge literary with mainstream fiction as well as autobiographical and narrative nonfiction.

John "Jack" Lucido, Professor of Screenwriting. M.F.A., North Carolina at Greensboro. Jack Lucido teaches film production, theory, aesthetics, and screenwriting. His film *Chill Out* won the National Wildlife Federation's Climate Action on Campus Award in 2010. *Jackson Sandwich*, his personal documentary about autism, was awarded the prestigious Cine Golden Eagle Award and has been broadcast on public television in several states. Lucido received an Emmy nomination as a producer at KEET-TV, a PBS-member station, for directing the one-hour documentary film on engineering wonders on California's Redwood Coast.

Teresa Milbrodt, Visiting Professor of Mainstream/Genre Fiction; M.F.A., Bowling Green State. Teresa Milbrodt served as Assistant Fiction Editor at *Mid-American Review* for several years. Her short story collection, *Bearded Women: Stories*, from Chizine Publications is slated for publication in fall 2011. Her work has appeared or is forthcoming in *Nimrod, North American Review, Crazyhorse, The Cream City Review, Hayden's Ferry Review, New Orleans Review, PANK, Natural Bridge, Indiana Review, Sycamore Review, Passages North, Main Street Rag, Eureka Literary Magazine,* and guernicamag.com, among other literary journals. Three of her stories have been nominated for the Pushcart Prize.

David J. Rothman, Concentration Director, Poetry with a Focus in Verse Craft; Ph.D., NYU. Award-winning poet David J. Rothman has been an editor, reviewer, publisher, and judge in poetry circles for over two decades. His own work has a distinguished record in such literary journals as *The Atlantic Monthly, The Kenyon Review, The Lyric, Prism, The Gettysburg Review,* and many others. He has three collections of published poetry (*Beauty at Night,* 2002; *The Elephant's Chiropractor,* 1999; *Dominion of Shadow,* 1996), and a fourth collection, *Go Big,* forthcoming from Red Hen Press. He is also owner/publisher of award-winning Conundrum Press.

Michaela Roessner-Herman, Visiting Professor of Mainstream and Genre Fiction; M.F.A., Southern Maine. Michaela Roessner has had four novels published, as well as assorted short fiction and nonfiction in publications that include *Asimov's Magazine, The Magazine of Fantasy and Science Fiction, OMNI Magazine,* Canada's *Room Magazine,* and anthologies that include *Full Spectrum 2* and *Intersections.* Her first novel, *Walkabout Woman,* won the Crawford and John W. Campbell awards. She has had work shortlisted for the Calvino Prize, the Tiptree Award, and the Millennium Publishing short fiction contest. Her current projects include a number of short fiction pieces, finishing up her fifth novel, *The Waters of Babylon,* and an experimental fiction chapbook, *The Book of Clever Women—A Hagiology.*

Bob Shayne, Visiting Professor of Screenwriting; M.F.A. Bob Shayne has been an active and successful screenwriter for years, both in New York and Los Angeles. He's sold eighteen prime-time pilots and written sixteen of them for the major TV networks in all genres, six of which were shot, two of which went to series, and most of which he produced. He's worked on staff of both sitcoms and one-hour dramas; been a show-runner on sitcom, drama, MOW and pilots; written well over 100 episodes; written and produced TV movies; written two 4-hour miniseries, written both live-action and animated features, and adapted four novels into screenplays (not counting his own). He's won or been nominated for awards including Best TV Movie of the Year from the Writers Guild of America, Edgar for Best TV Movie of the Year from the Mystery Writers of America, Edgar for Best TV Episode of the Year from the Mystery Writers of America, two Emmys from the TV Academy (for Best Talk Show and Best Documentary), and a Grammy for Best Comedy Album.

Mark Todd, Director of the M.F.A. Program; Ph.D., Texas Tech. Mark Todd has served on the faculty at Western for over twenty years. He also teaches in Western's undergraduate creative writing emphasis. His own works include two collections of poetry (*Wire Song,* 2001; *Tamped, But Loose Enough to Breathe,* 2008), and three novels—two adventure comedies cowritten with wife Kym O'Connell-Todd (*The Silverville Swindle,* 2006; *The Silverville Curse,* pending publication) and one science fiction novel, *Strange Attractors,* currently agented. He and his wife have also written a screenplay adaptation to the first Silverville novel called *Little Greed Men,* currently under development, as well as an original screenplay, *Dough Baby,* currently under consideration.

David Yezzi, Professor of Poetry with a Focus in Versecraft; M.F.A., Columbia. David Yezzi, acclaimed poet and executive editor of *The New Criterion,* is a former director of the Unterberg Poetry Center of the 92nd Street Y in New York, where he also currently teaches poetry in the center's writing program. David Yezzi's books of poetry are *The Hidden Model,* and *Azores,* a *Slate*-magazine best book of the year. He is the editor of *The Swallow Anthology of New American Poets,* with a foreword by J. D. McClatchy. His poems and reviews have appeared in *The Atlantic, The New Yorker, The Paris Review, The New Republic, the New York Times, The Best American Poetry,* and elsewhere.

ACADEMIC AND
PROFESSIONAL PROGRAMS IN
INTERDISCIPLINARY STUDIES

Section 14
Interdisciplinary Studies

This section contains a directory of institutions offering graduate work in interdisciplinary studies. Additional information about programs listed in the directory may be obtained by writing directly to the dean of a graduate school or chair of a department at the address given in the directory.

For programs offering related work, see also in this book *Comparative and Interdisciplinary Arts, Humanities,* and *Social Sciences.*

CONTENTS

Interdisciplinary Studies

Alaska Pacific University, Graduate Programs, Liberal Studies Department, Self-Designed Programs, Anchorage, AK 99508-4672. Offers MA. Part-time and evening/weekend programs available. *Degree requirements:* For master's, thesis or project. *Entrance requirements:* For master's, MAT (preferred), GRE General Test or GMAT. *Expenses:* Contact institution.

Amberton University, Graduate School, Program in Professional Development, Garland, TX 75041-5595. Offers MA. *Entrance requirements:* For master's, minimum GPA of 3.0.

American University, College of Arts and Sciences, Interdisciplinary Programs, Washington, DC 20016-8001. Offers MA.

Angelo State University, College of Graduate Studies, Program in Interdisciplinary Studies, San Angelo, TX 76909. Offers MA, MS. Part-time and evening/weekend programs available. Postbaccalaureate distance learning degree programs offered (minimal on-campus study). *Students:* 1 (woman) part-time; includes Black or African American, non-Hispanic/Latino. Average age 23. 1 applicant, 0% accepted, 0 enrolled. *Degree requirements:* For master's, comprehensive exam. *Entrance requirements:* For master's, essay. Additional exam requirements/recommendations for international students: Required—TOEFL or IELTS. *Application deadline:* For fall admission, 7/15 priority date for domestic students, 6/10 for international students; for spring admission, 12/1 priority date for domestic students, 11/1 for international students. Applications are processed on a rolling basis. Application fee: $40 ($50 for international students). Electronic applications accepted. *Expenses:* Tuition, state resident: full-time $4560; part-time $152 per credit hour. Tuition, nonresident: full-time $13,860; part-time $462 per credit hour. Required fees: $2132. Tuition and fees vary according to course load. *Financial support:* Federal Work-Study and scholarships/grants available. Support available to part-time students. Financial award application deadline: 3/1; financial award applicants required to submit FAFSA. *Unit head:* Dr. Brian J. May, Dean of Graduate Studies, 325-942-2169, Fax: 325-942-2194, E-mail: brian.may@angelo.edu. *Application contact:* Aly Hunter, Graduate Admissions Assistant, 325-942-2169, Fax: 325-942-2194, E-mail: aly.hunter@angelo.edu.

Antioch University New England, Graduate School, Department of Environmental Studies, Individualized Program, Keene, NH 03431-3552. Offers MS. *Degree requirements:* For master's, practicum, seminar, thesis or project. *Entrance requirements:* For master's, detailed proposal.

Arizona State University, New College of Interdisciplinary Arts and Sciences, Program in Interdisciplinary Studies, Phoenix, AZ 85069-7100. Offers MA. Part-time and evening/weekend programs available. *Faculty:* 34 full-time (18 women), 1 (woman) part-time/adjunct. *Students:* 19 full-time (11 women), 34 part-time (20 women); includes 11 minority (6 Black or African American, non-Hispanic/Latino; 1 American Indian or Alaska Native, non-Hispanic/Latino; 1 Asian, non-Hispanic/Latino; 2 Hispanic/Latino; 1 Two or more races, non-Hispanic/Latino). Average age 35. 28 applicants, 86% accepted, 22 enrolled. In 2010, 21 master's awarded. *Degree requirements:* For master's, thesis or alternative, research paper or applied project; interactive Program of Study (iPOS) submitted before completing 50 percent of required credit hours. *Entrance requirements:* For master's, GRE (if GPA less than 3.0 in last 60 hours of undergraduate study), minimum GPA of 3.0 or equivalent in last 2 years of work leading to bachelor's degree, 3 letters of recommendation, official transcripts, personal statement, writing sample of scholarly work or example of professional activities. Additional exam requirements/recommendations for international students: Required—TOEFL, IELTS, or Pearson Test of English. *Application deadline:* For fall admission, 7/1 priority date for domestic and international students; for spring admission, 12/15 priority date for domestic and international students. Applications are processed on a rolling basis. Application fee: $70 ($90 for international students). Electronic applications accepted. *Expenses:* Tuition, state resident: full-time $8510; part-time $608 per credit. Tuition, nonresident: full-time $16,542; part-time $919 per credit. Required fees: $339; $110 per credit. Part-time tuition and fees vary according to course load. *Financial support:* Research assistantships with full and partial tuition reimbursements, institutionally sponsored loans, scholarships/grants, and tuition waivers (full and partial) available. Financial award application deadline: 3/1; financial award applicants required to submit FAFSA. *Faculty research:* Comparative politics, foreign policy, world religions, African and African American folklore, British modernism, English renaissance drama, physiological psychology, sociology of health and illness, gender/race/class/sexuality, applied ethics, borderland theories. *Unit head:* Dr. Patrick Bixby, Director, 602-543-3010, E-mail: patrick.bixby@asu.edu. *Application contact:* Graduate Admissions, 480-965-6113.

Athabasca University, Centre for Integrated Studies, Athabasca, AB T9S 3A3, Canada. Offers adult education (MA); community studies (MA); cultural studies (MA); educational studies (MA); global change (MA); work, organization, and leadership (MA). Part-time and evening/weekend programs available. Postbaccalaureate distance learning degree programs offered (no on-campus study). *Degree requirements:* For master's, project. *Entrance requirements:* Additional exam requirements/recommendations for international students: Required—TOEFL (minimum score 560 paper-based; 220 computer-based). Electronic applications accepted. *Faculty research:* Women's history, literature and culture studies, sustainable development, labor and education.

Baylor University, Graduate School, College of Arts and Sciences, J. M. Dawson Institute of Church-State Studies, Waco, TX 76798. Offers MA, PhD. *Students:* 40 full-time (15 women), 3 part-time (2 women); includes 9 minority (2 Black or African American, non-Hispanic/Latino; 1 Asian, non-Hispanic/Latino; 4 Hispanic/Latino; 2 Two or more races, non-Hispanic/Latino), 7 international. In 2010, 3 master's, 2 doctorates awarded. *Degree requirements:* For master's, thesis, oral exam; for doctorate, one foreign language, thesis/dissertation, preliminary exams. *Entrance requirements:* For master's, GRE General Test; for doctorate, GRE General Test, MA or equivalent. *Application deadline:* For fall admission, 3/1 for domestic students. Applications are processed on a rolling basis. Application fee: $25. *Financial support:* Fellowships, research assistantships, teaching assistantships, Federal Work-Study and institutionally sponsored loans available. Financial award application deadline: 3/1. *Faculty research:* Religion and politics, religion and public education, religious freedom and international politics, First Amendment jurisprudence. *Unit head:* Dr. Christopher Marsh, Graduate Program Director, 254-710-4412, Fax: 254-710-1571, E-mail: chris_marsh@baylor.edu. *Application contact:* Suzanne Seller, Administrative Assistant, 254-710-1510, Fax: 254-710-1571, E-mail: suzanne_sellers@baylor.edu.

Boise State University, Graduate College, College of Arts and Sciences, Program in Interdisciplinary Studies, Boise, ID 83725-0399. Offers MA, MS. Part-time programs available. *Degree requirements:* For master's, thesis. *Entrance requirements:* For master's, minimum GPA of 3.0. Electronic applications accepted.

Bowling Green State University, Graduate College, Interdisciplinary Studies, Bowling Green, OH 43403. Offers M Ed, MA, MS, PhD. Part-time programs available. *Degree requirements:* For master's, thesis or alternative; for doctorate, comprehensive exam, thesis/dissertation. *Entrance requirements:* For master's and doctorate, GRE General Test. Additional exam requirements/recommendations for international students: Required—TOEFL. Electronic applications accepted.

Buffalo State College, State University of New York, The Graduate School, Program in Multidisciplinary Studies, Buffalo, NY 14222-1095. Offers MA, MS. Part-time and evening/weekend programs available. *Degree requirements:* For master's, thesis or project. *Entrance requirements:* For master's, minimum GPA of 2.5. Additional exam requirements/recommendations for international students: Required—TOEFL (minimum score 550 paper-based; 213 computer-based).

California Institute of Integral Studies, School of Consciousness and Transformation, San Francisco, CA 94103. Offers creative inquiry/interdisciplinary arts (MFA); cultural anthropology and social transformation (MA); East-West psychology (MA, PhD); integrative health studies (MA); philosophy and religion (MA, PhD), including Asian and comparative studies, philosophy, cosmology, and consciousness, women's spirituality; social and cultural anthropology (PhD); transformative leadership (MA); transformative studies (PhD); writing and consciousness (MFA). Part-time and evening/weekend programs available. Postbaccalaureate distance learning degree programs offered (minimal on-campus study). *Students:* 455 full-time (315 women), 133 part-time (90 women); includes 47 Black or African American, non-Hispanic/Latino; 3 American Indian or Alaska Native, non-Hispanic/Latino; 21 Asian, non-Hispanic/Latino; 41 Hispanic/Latino, 40 international. Average age 37. 265 applicants, 91% accepted, 163 enrolled. In 2010, 64 master's, 22 doctorates awarded. Terminal master's awarded for partial completion of doctoral program. *Degree requirements:* For master's, thesis optional; for doctorate, comprehensive exam, thesis/dissertation, 1 foreign language (Asian comparative studies). *Entrance requirements:* For master's, minimum GPA of 3.0, letters of recommendation, writing sample; for doctorate, master's degree, minimum GPA of 3.0, letters of recommendation, writing sample. Additional exam requirements/recommendations for international students: Required—TOEFL. *Application deadline:* For fall admission, 2/1 priority date for domestic and international students; for spring admission, 10/15 priority date for domestic and international students. Applications are processed on a rolling basis. Application fee: $65. Electronic applications accepted. *Expenses:* Tuition: Full-time $15,660; part-time $870 per semester hour. Required fees: $95 per semester. *Financial support:* In 2010–11, 255 students received support; research assistantships, teaching assistantships, career-related internships or fieldwork, Federal Work-Study, scholarships/grants, and tuition waivers (partial) available. Support available to part-time students. Financial award application deadline: 4/15; financial award applicants required to submit FAFSA. *Faculty research:* Ecology and sustainablility, philosophy and religion, East-West psychology, integrative health, social and cultural anthropology, transformative leadership. *Application contact:* Allyson Werner, Associate Director of Admissions, 415-575-6155, Fax: 415-575-1268.

California State University, Bakersfield, Division of Graduate Studies, Program in Interdisciplinary Studies, Bakersfield, CA 93311. Offers MA. *Degree requirements:* For master's, thesis or project. *Entrance requirements:* For master's, minimum GPA of 3.0 in last 90 quarter units. Additional exam requirements/recommendations for international students: Required—TOEFL (minimum score 550 paper-based; 213 computer-based). *Faculty research:* Ethics, physical education and health.

California State University, Chico, Graduate School, Interdisciplinary Programs, Chico, CA 95929-0722. Offers interdisciplinary studies (MA, MS); science teaching (MS); simulation science (MS). Part-time programs available. *Students:* 22 full-time (18 women), 8 part-time (7 women); includes 1 Black or African American, non-Hispanic/Latino; 1 Asian, non-Hispanic/Latino; 5 Hispanic/Latino, 8 international. Average age 35. 22 applicants, 77% accepted, 8 enrolled. In 2010, 6 master's awarded. *Degree requirements:* For master's, thesis or alternative, oral exam. *Entrance requirements:* For master's, GRE General Test or MAT, 3 letters of recommendation. Additional exam requirements/recommendations for international students: Required—TOEFL (minimum score 550 paper-based; 213 computer-based; 80 iBT), IELTS (minimum score 6.5). *Application deadline:* For fall admission, 3/1 priority date for domestic students, 3/1 for international students; for spring admission, 9/15 priority date for domestic students, 9/15 for international students. Applications are processed on a rolling basis. Application fee: $55. *Financial support:* Fellowships, Federal Work-Study available. Support available to part-time students. *Unit head:* Dr. Sara Trechter, Graduate Coordinator, 530-898-5447. *Application contact:* School of Graduate, International, and Interdisciplinary Studies, 530-898-6880, Fax: 530-898-6889, E-mail: grin@csuchico.edu.

California State University, East Bay, Office of Academic Programs and Graduate Studies, Interdisciplinary Programs, Hayward, CA 94542-3000. Offers MA, MS. Part-time programs available. *Students:* 3 full-time (2 women), 3 part-time (all women); includes 1 Black or African American, non-Hispanic/Latino, 1 international. Average age 40. 5 applicants, 40% accepted, 0 enrolled. In 2010, 1 master's awarded. *Degree requirements:* For master's, comprehensive exam, project or thesis. *Entrance requirements:* Additional exam requirements/recommendations for international students: Required—TOEFL (minimum score 550 paper-based; 213 computer-based). *Application deadline:* For fall admission, 6/30 for domestic and international students; for winter admission, 10/31 for domestic students; for spring admission, 11/30 for domestic students. Applications are processed on a rolling basis. Application fee: $55. Electronic applications accepted. *Financial support:* Fellowships, teaching assistantships, Federal Work-Study, institutionally sponsored loans, and scholarships/grants available. Support available to part-time students. Financial award application deadline: 3/2; financial award applicants required to submit FAFSA. *Unit head:* Dr. Susan Opp, Associate Vice President, 510-885-3716, Fax: 510-885-4777, E-mail: susan.opp@csueastbay.edu. *Application contact:* Dr. Donna Wiley, Interim Associate Director, 510-885-2928, Fax: 510-885-4777, E-mail: donna.wiley@csueastbay.edu.

California State University, Long Beach, Graduate Studies, Interdisciplinary Studies Program, Long Beach, CA 90840. Offers MA, MS. Part-time programs available. *Students:* 6 part-time (5 women); includes 1 American Indian or Alaska Native, non-Hispanic/Latino; 1 Hispanic/Latino. Average age 41. In 2010, 3 master's awarded. *Degree requirements:* For master's, thesis. *Entrance requirements:* For master's, minimum undergraduate GPA of 3.0. *Application deadline:* For fall admission, 3/30 for domestic students. Applications are processed on a rolling basis. Application fee: $55. Electronic applications accepted. *Financial support:* Federal Work-Study, institutionally sponsored loans, and scholarships/grants available. Financial award application deadline: 3/2. *Unit head:* Dr. Cecile Lindsay, Director, 562-985-8225, Fax: 562-985-1680, E-mail: clindsay@csulb.edu. *Application contact:* Dr. Cecile Lindsay, Director, 562-985-8225, Fax: 562-985-1680, E-mail: clindsay@csulb.edu.

California State University, Monterey Bay, College of Science, Media Arts and Technology, School of Information Technology and Communication Design, Seaside, CA 93955-8001. Offers interdisciplinary studies (MA), including instructional science and technology; management and information technology (MA). *Degree requirements:* For master's, capstone or thesis. *Entrance requirements:* For master's, GRE, 2 letters of recommendation, minimum GPA of 3.0, technology screening assessment. Additional exam requirements/recommendations for international students: Required—TOEFL (minimum score 550 paper-based; 213 computer-based; 71 iBT). Electronic applications accepted. *Faculty research:* Electronic commerce, e-learning, knowledge management, international business, business and public policy.

California State University, Northridge, Graduate Studies, Interdisciplinary Studies, Northridge, CA 91330. Offers MA, MS. *Entrance requirements:* For master's, GRE (if cumulative undergraduate GPA less than 3.0). Additional exam requirements/recommendations for international students: Required—TOEFL.

California State University, San Bernardino, Graduate Studies, Interdisciplinary Programs, San Bernardino, CA 92407-2397. Offers MA. Part-time and evening/weekend programs available. *Degree requirements:* For master's, thesis or alternative, advancement to candidacy. *Entrance requirements:* For master's, writing exam, minimum overall undergraduate GPA of 2.5; 3.0 in major.

California State University, Stanislaus, College of Humanities and Social Sciences, Programs in Interdisciplinary Studies (MA/MS), Turlock, CA 95382. Offers MA, MS. Part-time and evening/weekend programs available. *Students:* 5 full-time (4 women), 17 part-time (11 women); includes 5 minority (1 Black or African American, non-Hispanic/Latino; 3 Hispanic/Latino; 1 Two or more races, non-Hispanic/Latino), 1 international. Average age 38. 8 applicants, 100% accepted, 4 enrolled. In 2010, 4 master's awarded. *Degree requirements:* For master's, thesis. *Entrance requirements:* For master's, GRE, minimum GPA of 3.0, personal statement. Additional exam requirements/recommendations for international students: Required—TOEFL (minimum score 550 paper-based; 213 computer-based). *Application deadline:* For fall admission, 5/1 for domestic students; for spring admission, 1/7 for domestic students. Application fee: $55. Electronic applications accepted. Tuition and fees vary according to program. *Financial support:* Research assistantships, teaching assistantships, Federal Work-Study available. Financial award application deadline: 3/1; financial award applicants required to submit FAFSA. *Unit head:* Dr. Dennis Sayers, Program Director, 209-667-3129, E-mail: dsayers@csustan.edu. *Application contact:* Graduate School, 209-667-3129, Fax: 209-664-7025, E-mail: graduate_school@csustan.edu.

Cambridge College, School of Education, Cambridge, MA 02138-5304. Offers autism specialist (M Ed); autism/behavior analyst (M Ed); behavior analyst (Post-Master's Certificate); behavioral management (M Ed); early childhood teacher (M Ed); education specialist in curriculum and instruction (CAGS); educational leadership (Ed D); elementary teacher (M Ed); English as a second language (M Ed, Certificate); general science (M Ed); health education (Post-Master's Certificate); health/family and consumer sciences (M Ed); history (M Ed); individualized (M Ed); information technology literacy (M Ed); instructional technology (M Ed); interdisciplinary studies (M Ed); library teacher (M Ed); literacy education (M Ed); mathematics (M Ed); mathematics specialist (Certificate); middle school mathematics and science (M Ed); school administration (M Ed, CAGS); school guidance counselor (M Ed); school nurse education (M Ed); school social worker/school adjustment counselor (M Ed); special education administrator (CAGS); special education/moderate disabilities (M Ed); teaching skills and methodologies (M Ed). Part-time and evening/weekend programs available. Postbaccalaureate distance learning degree programs offered (minimal on-campus study). *Faculty:* 8 full-time (2 women), 245 part-time/adjunct (166 women). *Students:* 846 full-time (664 women), 930 part-time (714 women); includes 972 minority (802 Black or African American, non-Hispanic/Latino; 3 American Indian or Alaska Native, non-Hispanic/Latino; 18 Asian, non-Hispanic/Latino; 148 Hispanic/Latino; 1 Two or more races, non-Hispanic/Latino), 23 international. Average age 38. In 2010, 724 master's, 162 other advanced degrees awarded. *Degree requirements:* For master's, thesis, internship/practicum (licensure program only); for doctorate, thesis/dissertation; for other advanced degree, thesis. *Entrance requirements:* For master's, interview, resume, documentation of licensure, 2 professional references; for doctorate, official transcripts, interview, resume, documentation of licensure (if any), written personal statement/essay, portfolio of scholarly and professional work, qualifying assessment, 2 professional references, health insurance, immunizations form; for other advanced degree, official transcripts, interview, resume, documentation of licensure (if any), written personal statement/essay, 2 professional references, health insurance, immunizations form. Additional exam requirements/recommendations for international students: Required—TOEFL (minimum score 550 paper-based; 213 computer-based; 79 iBT); Recommended—IELTS (minimum score 6). *Application deadline:* Applications are processed on a rolling basis. Application fee: $30. Electronic applications accepted. *Expenses:* Contact institution. *Financial support:* Career-related internships or fieldwork, Federal Work-Study, and scholarships/grants available. Financial award applicants required to submit FAFSA. *Faculty research:* Adult education, accelerated learning, mathematics education, brain compatible learning, special education and law. *Unit head:* Dr. N. Alan Sheppard, Interim Associate Dean, 617-873-0619, E-mail: alan.sheppard@cambridgecollege.edu. *Application contact:* Elaine M. Lapomardo, Dean of Enrollment Management, 617-873-0274, Fax: 617-349-3561, E-mail: elaine.lapomardo@cambridgecollege.edu.

Campbell University, Graduate and Professional Programs, School of Education, Buies Creek, NC 27506. Offers administration (MSA); community counseling (MA); elementary education (M Ed); English education (M Ed); interdisciplinary studies (M Ed); mathematics education (M Ed); middle grades education (M Ed); physical education (M Ed); school counseling (M Ed); secondary education (M Ed); social science education (M Ed). *Accreditation:* NCATE. Part-time and evening/weekend programs available. *Degree requirements:* For master's, comprehensive exam. *Entrance requirements:* For master's, GRE General Test, minimum GPA of 2.7. *Faculty research:* Spiritual values and wellness issues in counseling, stress and professional burnout among counselors, thinking strategies, leadership, adaptive technology.

Central Washington University, Graduate Studies and Research, Individual Studies Program, Ellensburg, WA 98926. Offers M Ed, MA, MS. Part-time programs available. *Degree requirements:* For master's, thesis. *Entrance requirements:* For master's, GRE General Test, minimum GPA of 3.0. Additional exam requirements/recommendations for international students: Required—TOEFL (minimum score 550 paper-based; 213 computer-based; 79 iBT).

College of the Humanities and Sciences, Harrison Middleton University, Graduate Program, Tempe, AZ 85282. Offers education (MA, Ed D); humanities (MA); imaginative literature (MA); interdisciplinary studies (DA); jurisprudence (MA); natural science (MA); philosophy and religion (MA); social science (MA). Part-time and evening/weekend programs available. Postbaccalaureate distance learning degree programs offered (no on-campus study). *Faculty:* 17 full-time (7 women), 14 part-time/adjunct (6 women). *Students:* 52 full-time (20 women). In 2010, 4 master's awarded. *Degree requirements:* For master's and doctorate, capstone project. *Entrance requirements:* For doctorate, 3 academic letters of reference, interview. *Application deadline:* Applications are processed on a rolling basis. Application fee: $50. Electronic applications accepted. *Expenses:* Tuition: Part-time $300 per credit hour. One-time fee: $350 part-time. *Faculty research:* Japanese animation, educational leadership, war art, John Muir's wilderness. *Application contact:* Deborah Deacon, Dean of Graduate Studies, 877-248-6724, Fax: 800-762-1622, E-mail: ddeacon@hmu.edu.

Columbia University, Graduate School of Arts and Sciences, Program in Liberal Studies, New York, NY 10027. Offers American studies (MA); East Asian studies (MA); human rights studies (MA); Islamic culture studies (MA); Jewish studies (MA); medieval studies (MA); modern European studies (MA); South Asian studies (MA). Part-time and evening/weekend programs available. *Degree requirements:* For master's, thesis.

Concordia University, School of Graduate Studies, Special Individualized Programs, Montréal, QC H3G 1M8, Canada. Offers M Sc, MA, PhD. *Degree requirements:* For master's, comprehensive exam, thesis; for doctorate, one foreign language, comprehensive exam, thesis/dissertation.

Dalhousie University, Faculty of Graduate Studies, Interdisciplinary PhD Program, Halifax, NS B3H 4H6, Canada. Offers PhD. *Degree requirements:* For doctorate, thesis/dissertation. *Entrance requirements:* Additional exam requirements/recommendations for international students: Required—TOEFL, IELTS, CANTEST, CAEL, or Michigan English Language Assessment Battery. Electronic applications accepted. *Expenses:* Contact institution.

Dallas Baptist University, College of Adult Education, Professional Development Program, Dallas, TX 75211-9299. Offers accounting (MA); church leadership (MA); counseling (MA); criminal justice (MA); English as a second language (MA); finance (MA); higher education (MA); leadership studies (MA); management (MA); management information systems (MA); marketing (MA); missions (MA). Part-time and evening/weekend programs available. *Entrance requirements:* For master's, minimum GPA of 3.0. Additional exam requirements/recommendations for international students: Required—TOEFL, IELTS. *Expenses:* Tuition: Full-time $11,394; part-time $633 per credit hour.

DePaul University, College of Liberal Arts and Sciences, Department of Interdisciplinary Studies, Chicago, IL 60614. Offers MA, MS. Part-time and evening/weekend programs available. *Degree requirements:* For master's, thesis optional.

Drew University, Caspersen School of Graduate Studies, Program in Arts and Letters, Madison, NJ 07940-1493. Offers holocaust and genocide studies (Certificate); interdisciplinary studies (M Litt, D Litt). Part-time and evening/weekend programs available. Terminal master's awarded for partial completion of doctoral program. *Degree requirements:* For master's, thesis optional; for doctorate, thesis/dissertation. *Entrance requirements:* For master's and doctorate, transcripts, writing sample, personal statement, recommendations. Additional exam requirements/recommendations for international students: Required—TOEFL (minimum score 585 paper-

based; 240 computer-based; 95 iBT), TWE. *Expenses:* Contact institution. *Faculty research:* Interdisciplinary studies across art, literature, music, philosophy, religion, and history.

Eastern Washington University, Graduate Studies, Interdisciplinary Studies, Cheney, WA 99004-2431. Offers MA, MS. *Degree requirements:* For master's, comprehensive exam, thesis or alternative. *Entrance requirements:* For master's, minimum GPA of 3.0.

Embry-Riddle Aeronautical University–Daytona, Daytona Beach Campus Graduate Program, Department of Aerospace Engineering, Daytona Beach, FL 32114-3900. Offers aerospace engineering (MSAE); multidisciplinary engineering (MSE). Part-time programs available. *Faculty:* 8 full-time (0 women). *Students:* 110 full-time (17 women), 25 part-time (3 women); includes 19 minority (3 Black or African American, non-Hispanic/Latino; 7 Asian, non-Hispanic/Latino; 6 Hispanic/Latino; 3 Two or more races, non-Hispanic/Latino), 48 international. Average age 23. 110 applicants, 63% accepted, 37 enrolled. In 2010, 31 master's awarded. *Degree requirements:* For master's, thesis. *Entrance requirements:* For master's, BS in aeronautical engineering or equivalent; minimum GPA of 3.0 in last 2 undergraduate years, 2.5 overall. Additional exam requirements/recommendations for international students: Required—TOEFL (minimum score 550 paper-based; 213 computer-based; 79 iBT). *Application deadline:* For fall admission, 8/1 priority date for domestic students; for spring admission, 12/1 priority date for domestic students. Applications are processed on a rolling basis. Application fee: $50. Electronic applications accepted. *Expenses:* Tuition: Full-time $14,040; part-time $1170 per credit hour. *Financial support:* In 2010–11, 59 students received support, including 6 research assistantships with full and partial tuition reimbursements available (averaging $6,092 per year), 15 teaching assistantships with full and partial tuition reimbursements available (averaging $6,092 per year); career-related internships or fieldwork, Federal Work-Study, and unspecified assistantships also available. Support available to part-time students. Financial award application deadline: 4/15; financial award applicants required to submit FAFSA. *Faculty research:* Propulsion research: CFD research, composite torque research, establishing software engineering domain expertise, assessment of software tools for safety critical real-time systems, student NASA eagle eye satellite, structural blade testing support, remote airport lighting system (RALS). Total annual research expenditures: $377,487. *Unit head:* Dr. Y. Zhao, Graduate Program Coordinator, 386-226-6746, Fax: 386-226-6747, E-mail: yi.zhao@erau.edu. *Application contact:* Keith Deaton, Director, International and Graduate Admissions, 800-388-3728, Fax: 386-226-7070, E-mail: graduate.admissions@erau.edu.

Emory University, Laney Graduate School, Graduate Institute of Liberal Arts, Atlanta, GA 30322-1100. Offers PhD. *Degree requirements:* For doctorate, one foreign language, comprehensive exam, thesis/dissertation. *Entrance requirements:* For doctorate, GRE General Test. Electronic applications accepted. *Expenses:* Tuition: Full-time $33,800. Required fees: $1300. *Faculty research:* American cultural criticism, intellectual history, psychoanalysis, history of science, popular culture.

Fitchburg State University, Division of Graduate and Continuing Education, Program in Interdisciplinary Studies, Fitchburg, MA 01420-2697. Offers CAGS. Part-time and evening/weekend programs available. *Students:* 5 full-time (4 women), 37 part-time (32 women), 1 international. Average age 41. 19 applicants, 100% accepted, 9 enrolled. In 2010, 24 CAGSs awarded. *Entrance requirements:* For degree, master's degree, letters of recommendation, resume. Additional exam requirements/recommendations for international students: Required—TOEFL (minimum score 550 paper-based; 213 computer-based; 79 iBT). *Application deadline:* Applications are processed on a rolling basis. Application fee: $25 ($50 for international students). *Expenses:* Tuition, area resident: Part-time $150 per credit. Tuition, state resident: part-time $150 per credit. Tuition, nonresident: part-time $150 per credit. Required fees: $127 per credit. *Financial support:* In 2010–11, research assistantships with partial tuition reimbursements (averaging $5,500 per year); Federal Work-Study, scholarships/grants, and unspecified assistantships also available. Support available to part-time students. Financial award application deadline: 3/1; financial award applicants required to submit FAFSA. *Unit head:* Dr. Harry Semerjian, Chair, 978-665-3279, Fax: 978-665-3658, E-mail: gce@fitchburgstate.edu. *Application contact:* Director of Admissions, 978-665-3144, Fax: 978-665-4540, E-mail: admissions@fitchburgstate.edu.

Florida Gulf Coast University, College of Health Professions, Department of Health Sciences, Fort Myers, FL 33965-6565. Offers MS. Part-time and evening/weekend programs available. Postbaccalaureate distance learning degree programs offered (no on-campus study). *Faculty:* 45 full-time (35 women), 28 part-time/adjunct (18 women). *Students:* 36 full-time (26 women), 7 part-time (6 women); includes 6 Black or African American, non-Hispanic/Latino; 1 American Indian or Alaska Native, non-Hispanic/Latino; 1 Asian, non-Hispanic/Latino; 4 Hispanic/Latino. Average age 33. 20 applicants, 55% accepted, 10 enrolled. In 2010, 9 master's awarded. *Degree requirements:* For master's, final project or thesis. *Entrance requirements:* For master's, GRE General Test or MAT, minimum GPA of 3.0. Additional exam requirements/recommendations for international students: Required—TOEFL (minimum score 550 paper-based; 213 computer-based). *Application deadline:* For fall admission, 7/1 priority date for domestic students; for spring admission, 11/15 for domestic students. Applications are processed on a rolling basis. Application fee: $30. Electronic applications accepted. *Expenses:* Tuition, state resident: part-time $322.08 per credit hour. Tuition, nonresident: part-time $1117.08 per credit hour. *Financial support:* Career-related internships or fieldwork available. *Faculty research:* Health services administration, gerontology, therapeutic recreation, health professions education, exercise physiology. *Unit head:* Dr. Joan Glacken, Chair, 239-590-7498, Fax: 239-590-7474, E-mail: jglacken@fgcu.edu. *Application contact:* Dr. Joan Glacken, Chair, 239-590-7498, Fax: 239-590-7474, E-mail: jglacken@fgcu.edu.

Florida Institute of Technology, Graduate Programs, College of Science, Department of Physics and Space Sciences, Melbourne, FL 32901-6975. Offers interdisciplinary science (MS); physics (MS, PhD); space sciences (MS, PhD). Part-time programs available. *Faculty:* 12 full-time (1 woman). *Students:* 33 full-time (12 women), 10 part-time (2 women); includes 4 minority (2 Asian, non-Hispanic/Latino; 2 Hispanic/Latino), 12 international. Average age 29. 75 applicants, 44% accepted, 7 enrolled. In 2010, 7 master's, 4 doctorates awarded. Terminal master's awarded for partial completion of doctoral program. *Degree requirements:* For master's, comprehensive exam, thesis optional, oral exam, 6 credits of math methodology; for doctorate, one foreign language, comprehensive exam, thesis/dissertation, publication in referred journal, seminar on dissertation research, dissertation published in a major journal. *Entrance requirements:* For master's, minimum GPA of 3.0, resume, 3 letters of recommendation, vector analysis, statement of objectives; for doctorate, GRE General and Subject Tests (recommended), minimum GPA of 3.2, resume, 3 letters of recommendation, statement of objectives. Additional exam requirements/recommendations for international students: Required—TOEFL (minimum score 550 paper-based; 213 computer-based; 79 iBT). *Application deadline:* For fall admission, 4/1 for international students; for spring admission, 9/30 for international students. Applications are processed on a rolling basis. Application fee: $50. Electronic applications accepted. *Expenses:* Tuition: Part-time $1040 per credit hour. Tuition and fees vary according to campus/location. *Financial support:* In 2010–11, 13 research assistantships with full and partial tuition reimbursements (averaging $13,018 per year), 16 teaching assistantships with full and partial tuition reimbursements (averaging $12,769 per year) were awarded; career-related internships or fieldwork, institutionally sponsored loans, tuition waivers (partial), unspecified assistantships, and tuition remissions also available. Support available to part-time students. Financial award application deadline: 3/1; financial award applicants required to submit FAFSA. *Faculty research:* Lasers, semiconductors, magnetism, quantum devices, high energy physics. Total annual research expenditures: $2.9 million. *Unit head:* Dr. Terry D. Oswalt, Department Head, 321-674-7325, Fax: 321-674-7482, E-mail: toswalt@fit.edu. *Application contact:* Cheryl A. Brown, Associate Director of Graduate Admissions, 321-674-7581, Fax: 321-723-9468, E-mail: cbrown@fit.edu.

Franklin Pierce University, Graduate Studies, Rindge, NH 03461-0060. Offers curriculum and instruction (M Ed); emerging network technology (Graduate Certificate); health administration (MBA, Graduate Certificate); human resource management (MBA, Graduate Certificate);

Interdisciplinary Studies

Franklin Pierce University (continued)
information technology management (MS); leadership (MBA, DA); nursing (MS); physical therapy (DPT); physician assistant studies (MPAS); special education (M Ed); sports management (MS). *Accreditation:* APTA. Part-time programs available. Postbaccalaureate distance learning degree programs offered (no on-campus study). *Faculty:* 28 full-time (18 women), 72 part-time/adjunct (44 women). *Students:* 100 full-time (63 women), 487 part-time (306 women); includes 42 minority (25 Black or African American, non-Hispanic/Latino; 10 Asian, non-Hispanic/Latino; 6 Hispanic/Latino; 1 Two or more races, non-Hispanic/Latino), 67 international. Average age 38. 227 applicants, 97% accepted, 185 enrolled. In 2010, 76 master's, 46 doctorates awarded. *Degree requirements:* For master's, concentrated original research projects; student teaching; fieldwork and/or internship; leadership project; PRAXIS I and II (for M Ed); for doctorate, concentrated original research projects, clinical fieldwork and/or internship, leadership project. *Entrance requirements:* For master's, minimum GPA of 2.5, 3 letters of recommendation; competencies in accounting, economics, statistics, and computer skills through life experience or undergraduate coursework (for MBA); certification/e-portfolio, minimum C grade in all education courses (for M Ed); license to practice as RN (for MS in nursing); for doctorate, GRE, BA/BS, 3 letters of recommendation, personal mission statement, interview; writing sample (for DA program)For DPT: 80 hours of observation/work in PT settings, completion of anatomy, chemistry, physics, an statistics, all > 3.0 GPAFor DA: 2.8 cum. GPA, Master's degree completion. Additional exam requirements/recommendations for international students: Required—TOEFL (minimum score 550 paper-based; 195 computer-based; 61 iBT). *Application deadline:* Applications are processed on a rolling basis. Application fee: $0. Electronic applications accepted. *Expenses:* Tuition: Part-time $573 per credit hour. Part-time tuition and fees vary according to degree level and program. *Financial support:* In 2010–11, 121 students received support, including 32 teaching assistantships with full and partial tuition reimbursements available (averaging $8,000 per year); career-related internships or fieldwork and unspecified assistantships also available. Support available to part-time students. Financial award applicants required to submit FAFSA. *Faculty research:* Evidence-based practice in sports physical therapy, human resource management in economic crisis, leadership in nursing, innovation in sports facility management, differentiated learning and understanding by design. *Unit head:* Dr. Patricia Brown, Interim Dean of Graduate and Professional Studies, 603-899-4316, Fax: 603-229-4580, E-mail: brownp@franklinpierce.edu.

Fresno Pacific University, Graduate Programs, Individualized Study Program, Fresno, CA 93702-4709. Offers MA. Part-time and evening/weekend programs available. *Degree requirements:* For master's, thesis. *Entrance requirements:* For master's, GMAT, GRE General Test, or MAT, 2 writing samples, interview. Additional exam requirements/recommendations for international students: Required—TOEFL (minimum score 550 paper-based; 213 computer-based). Electronic applications accepted.

Frostburg State University, Graduate School, College of Education, Department of Educational Professions, Program in Interdisciplinary Education, Frostburg, MD 21532-1099. Offers M Ed. Part-time and evening/weekend programs available. *Degree requirements:* For master's, thesis or alternative. *Entrance requirements:* Additional exam requirements/recommendations for international students: Required—TOEFL. Electronic applications accepted.

George Mason University, College of Humanities and Social Sciences, Interdisciplinary Studies Program, Fairfax, VA 22030. Offers interdisciplinary studies (MAIS). Part-time and evening/weekend programs available. *Faculty:* 6 full-time (3 women), 5 part-time/adjunct (2 women). *Students:* 15 full-time (12 women), 97 part-time (64 women); includes 6 Black or African American, non-Hispanic/Latino; 1 American Indian or Alaska Native, non-Hispanic/Latino; 5 Asian, non-Hispanic/Latino; 11 Hispanic/Latino, 3 international. Average age 33. 104 applicants, 47% accepted, 29 enrolled. In 2010, 42 master's awarded. *Degree requirements:* For master's, project or thesis. *Entrance requirements:* For master's, minimum GPA of 3.0 in last 60 hours of course work, resume, 3 letters of recommendation, writing sample. Additional exam requirements/recommendations for international students: Required—TOEFL (minimum score 570 paper-based; 230 computer-based; 88 iBT). *Application deadline:* For fall admission, 3/1 priority date for domestic students; for spring admission, 10/15 for domestic students. Application fee: $100. Electronic applications accepted. *Expenses:* Tuition, state resident: full-time $8192; part-time $440 per credit hour. Tuition, nonresident: full-time $22,952; part-time $1055 per credit hour. Required fees: $2364; $99 per credit hour. *Financial support:* In 2010–11, 2 students received support, including 2 research assistantships (averaging $8,103 per year), 1 teaching assistantship (averaging $1,590 per year); career-related internships or fieldwork, Federal Work-Study, scholarships/grants, unspecified assistantships, and health care benefits (full-time research or teaching assistantship recipients) also available. Financial award application deadline: 3/1; financial award applicants required to submit FAFSA. *Faculty research:* Combined English and folklore, religious and cultural studies (Christianity and Muslim society). *Unit head:* Clare Snyder-Hall, Chair, 703-993-2308, E-mail: rcsnyder@gmu.edu. *Application contact:* Charles Milling, Administrative Coordinator, 703-993-8762, E-mail: cmilling@gmu.edu.

Georgetown University, Graduate School of Arts and Sciences, School of Continuing Studies, Washington, DC 20057. Offers American studies (MALS); Catholic studies (MALS); classical civilizations (MALS); disability studies (MPS); ethics and the professions (MALS); human resources management (MPS); humanities (MALS); individualized study (MALS); international affairs (MALS); Islam and Muslim-Christian relations (MALS); journalism (MPS); liberal studies (DLS); literature and society (MALS); medieval and early modern European studies (MALS); public relations and corporate communications (MPS); real estate (MPS); religious studies (MALS); social and public policy (MALS); sports industry management (MPS); the theory and practice of American democracy (MALS); visual culture (MALS). *Entrance requirements:* Additional exam requirements/recommendations for international students: Required—TOEFL.

Goddard College, Graduate Division, Master of Arts in Individualized Studies Program, Plainfield, VT 05667-9432. Offers consciousness studies (MA); environmental studies (MA); transformative language arts (MA). Postbaccalaureate distance learning degree programs offered (minimal on-campus study). *Degree requirements:* For master's, thesis. *Entrance requirements:* For master's, 3 letters of recommendation, study plan, bibliography/resource list, interview. Electronic applications accepted. *Expenses:* Contact institution.

Graduate School and University Center of the City University of New York, Graduate Studies, Interdisciplinary Studies, New York, NY 10016-4039. Offers language in social context (PhD); medieval studies (PhD); public policy (MA, PhD); urban studies (MA, PhD); women's studies (MA, PhD). Terminal master's awarded for partial completion of doctoral program. *Degree requirements:* For master's, thesis; for doctorate, comprehensive exam, thesis/dissertation. *Entrance requirements:* For master's and doctorate, GRE General Test.

Hiram College, Graduate Studies, Hiram, OH 44234-0067. Offers MAIS. Part-time and evening/weekend programs available. *Faculty:* 12 full-time (6 women), 2 part-time/adjunct (1 woman). *Students:* 30 part-time (23 women). Average age 40. *Degree requirements:* For master's, two seminars, capstone research project. *Entrance requirements:* For master's, bachelor's degree from an accredited institution, 2 letters of recommendation, writing sample, interview. *Application deadline:* For fall admission, 7/1 for domestic students; for spring admission, 12/1 for domestic students. *Expenses:* Tuition: Part-time $450 per semester hour. Required fees: $100 per semester. *Unit head:* Cathy Mansor, Dean, 330-569-6111, Fax: 330-569-5003, E-mail: mansorcn@hiram.edu. *Application contact:* Terrie Nielsen, Admissions Counselor, 330-569-5180, Fax: 330-569-5003, E-mail: nielsenta@hiram.edu.

Hodges University, Graduate Programs, Naples, FL 34119. Offers business administration (MBA); computer information technology (MS); criminal justice (MCJ); education (MPS); information systems management (MIS); interdisciplinary (MPS); legal studies (MS); management (MSM); mental health counseling (MS); psychology (MPS); public administration (MPA). Part-time and evening/weekend programs available. Postbaccalaureate distance learning degree programs offered (no on-campus study). *Faculty:* 25 full-time (9 women), 5 part-time/adjunct (4 women). *Students:* 27 full-time (15 women), 228 part-time (146 women); includes 76 minority (35 Black or African American, non-Hispanic/Latino; 5 Asian, non-Hispanic/Latino; 36 Hispanic/Latino). Average age 36. 92 applicants, 91% accepted, 81 enrolled. In 2010, 92 master's awarded. *Degree requirements:* For master's, comprehensive exam (for some programs), thesis (for some programs). *Entrance requirements:* For master's, in-house entrance exam. *Application deadline:* Applications are processed on a rolling basis. Application fee: $50. Electronic applications accepted. *Expenses:* Tuition: Full-time $16,605; part-time $615 per credit hour. Required fees: $190 per trimester. *Financial support:* In 2010–11, 200 students received support. Federal Work-Study and scholarships/grants available. Financial award application deadline: 7/9; financial award applicants required to submit FAFSA. *Unit head:* Terry McMahan, President, 239-513-1122, Fax: 239-598-6253, E-mail: tmcmahan@hodges.edu. *Application contact:* Rita Lampus, Vice President of Student Enrollment Management, 239-513-1122, Fax: 239-598-6253, E-mail: rlampus@hodges.edu.

Hollins University, Graduate Programs, Program in Liberal Studies, Roanoke, VA 24020-1603. Offers humanities (MALS); interdisciplinary studies (MALS); justice and legal studies (MALS); liberal studies (CAS); social science (MALS); visual and performing arts (MALS). Part-time and evening/weekend programs available. *Degree requirements:* For master's, thesis. *Entrance requirements:* For master's, letters of recommendation, interview. Additional exam requirements/recommendations for international students: Required—TOEFL (minimum score 550 paper-based; 213 computer-based; 79 iBT). Electronic applications accepted. *Faculty research:* Elderly blacks, film, feminist economics, US voting patterns, Wagner, diversity.

Idaho State University, Office of Graduate Studies, Department of Interdisciplinary Studies, Pocatello, ID 83209. Offers general interdisciplinary (M Ed, MA, MNS); waste management and environmental science (MS). Part-time programs available. *Degree requirements:* For master's, comprehensive exam, thesis optional. *Entrance requirements:* For master's, GRE General Test or MAT, minimum GPA of 3.0. Additional exam requirements/recommendations for international students: Required—TOEFL (minimum score 550 paper-based; 213 computer-based; 80 iBT).

Iowa State University of Science and Technology, Graduate College, Interdisciplinary Programs, Program in Interdisciplinary Graduate Studies, Ames, IA 50011. Offers MA, MS. *Students:* 22 full-time (7 women), 58 part-time (42 women); includes 8 Black or African American, non-Hispanic/Latino; 2 American Indian or Alaska Native, non-Hispanic/Latino; 2 Asian, non-Hispanic/Latino; 2 Hispanic/Latino, 8 international. 27 applicants, 56% accepted, 6 enrolled. In 2010, 15 master's awarded. *Degree requirements:* For master's, thesis or alternative. *Entrance requirements:* Additional exam requirements/recommendations for international students: Recommended—TOEFL (minimum score 550 paper-based; 79 iBT), IELTS (minimum score 6.5). *Application deadline:* Applications are processed on a rolling basis. Application fee: $40 ($90 for international students). Electronic applications accepted. *Financial support:* In 2010–11, 5 research assistantships with full and partial tuition reimbursements (averaging $8,534 per year), 3 teaching assistantships with full and partial tuition reimbursements (averaging $9,504 per year) were awarded; fellowships, scholarships/grants, health care benefits, and unspecified assistantships also available. *Unit head:* Chair, Supervisory Committee, 515-294-1170. *Application contact:* Linda Thorson, Information Contact, 515-294-1170, Fax: 515-294-3003, E-mail: grad_admissions@iastate.edu.

John F. Kennedy University, Graduate School of Holistic Studies, Department of Integral Studies, Program in Consciousness Studies, Pleasant Hill, CA 94523-4817. Offers MA. Part-time and evening/weekend programs available. *Degree requirements:* For master's, thesis or alternative. *Entrance requirements:* For master's, interview. Additional exam requirements/recommendations for international students: Required—TOEFL.

Lehigh University, P. C. Rossin College of Engineering and Applied Science and College of Arts and Sciences, Center for Polymer Science and Engineering, Bethlehem, PA 18015. Offers M Eng, MS, PhD. Part-time and evening/weekend programs available. Postbaccalaureate distance learning degree programs offered (no on-campus study). *Students:* 5 full-time (1 woman), 8 part-time (2 women); includes 1 minority (Hispanic/Latino), 2 international. Average age 33. In 2010, 3 master's, 1 doctorate awarded. Terminal master's awarded for partial completion of doctoral program. *Degree requirements:* For master's, thesis (for some programs); for doctorate, thesis/dissertation. *Entrance requirements:* For master's and doctorate, GRE General Test. Additional exam requirements/recommendations for international students: Required—TOEFL (minimum score 487 paper-based; 216 computer-based; 85 iBT). *Application deadline:* For fall admission, 7/15 for domestic students, 1/15 for international students; for spring admission, 12/1 for domestic and international students. Applications are processed on a rolling basis. Application fee: $75. Electronic applications accepted. *Financial support:* In 2010–11, 3 students received support, including 5 research assistantships (averaging $24,200 per year), teaching assistantships (averaging $24,200 per year). Financial award application deadline: 1/15. *Faculty research:* Polymer colloids, polymer coatings, blends and composites, polymer interfaces, emulsion polymer. *Unit head:* Dr. Raymond A. Pearson, Director, 610-758-3857, Fax: 610-758-3526, E-mail: rp02@lehigh.edu. *Application contact:* James E. Roberts, Chair, Polymer Education Committee, 610-758-4841, Fax: 610-758-6536, E-mail: jer1@lehigh.edu.

Lesley University, Graduate School of Arts and Social Sciences, Self-Designed Master's Program in Interdisciplinary Studies, Cambridge, MA 02138-2790. Offers individualized studies (MA); integrative holistic health (MA); women's studies (MA). Part-time and evening/weekend programs available. Postbaccalaureate distance learning degree programs offered (no on-campus study). *Entrance requirements:* For master's, 3 letters of recommendation. Additional exam requirements/recommendations for international students: Required—TOEFL (minimum score 550 paper-based; 213 computer-based; 80 iBT).

Long Island University, C.W. Post Campus, College of Liberal Arts and Sciences, Program in Interdisciplinary Studies, Brookville, NY 11548-1300. Offers MA, MS. Part-time and evening/weekend programs available. *Degree requirements:* For master's, thesis. *Entrance requirements:* For master's, minimum GPA of 3.0. Electronic applications accepted.

Marquette University, Graduate School, Interdisciplinary PhD and Transfusion Medicine Programs, Milwaukee, WI 53201-1881. Offers interdisciplinary studies (PhD); transfusion medicine (MS), including business administration, education, science. Part-time programs available. *Students:* 4 full-time (1 woman), 9 part-time (6 women); includes 1 Black or African American, non-Hispanic/Latino; 1 Hispanic/Latino, 4 international. Average age 40. 5 applicants, 60% accepted, 2 enrolled. In 2010, 3 doctorates awarded. *Degree requirements:* For master's, thesis (for some programs); for doctorate, thesis/dissertation. *Entrance requirements:* For master's, GRE General Test, official transcripts from all current and previous colleges/universities except Marquette, three letters of recommendation; for doctorate, GRE General Test. Additional exam requirements/recommendations for international students: Required—TOEFL (minimum score 630 paper-based; 78 computer-based). *Application deadline:* Applications are processed on a rolling basis. Application fee: $50. Electronic applications accepted. *Expenses:* Tuition: Full-time $16,290; part-time $905 per credit hour. Tuition and fees vary according to program. *Financial support:* In 2010–11, 1 fellowship, 1 research assistantship were awarded; teaching assistantships, career-related internships or fieldwork, Federal Work-Study, institutionally sponsored loans, scholarships/grants, and tuition waivers (full and partial) also available. Support available to part-time students. Financial award application deadline: 2/15. *Unit head:* Dr. Jeanne Hossenlopp, Vice Provost for Research/Dean, 414-288-1532, Fax: 414-288-1578. *Application contact:* Erin Fox, Director of Graduate Admissions, 414-288-7182, Fax: 414-288-1902, E-mail: erin.fox@marquette.edu.

Marylhurst University, Department of Interdisciplinary Studies, Marylhurst, OR 97036-0261. Offers MA. Part-time and evening/weekend programs available. *Faculty:* 2 full-time (both women), 1 part-time/adjunct (0 women). *Students:* 3 full-time (2 women), 33 part-time (27 women); includes 2 Hispanic/Latino; 1 Two or more races, non-Hispanic/Latino. Average age 50. 12 applicants, 83% accepted, 7 enrolled. In 2010, 4 master's awarded. *Degree requirements:*

For master's, thesis. *Entrance requirements:* For master's, 2 letters of recommendation, writing sample, interview. Additional exam requirements/recommendations for international students: Recommended—TOEFL (minimum score 550 paper-based; 213 computer-based; 80 iBT). *Application deadline:* Applications are processed on a rolling basis. Application fee: $50. Electronic applications accepted. *Expenses:* Tuition: Full-time $13,932; part-time $516 per credit. Tuition and fees vary according to course load and program. *Financial support:* Federal Work-Study and scholarships/grants available. Support available to part-time students. Financial award applicants required to submit FAFSA. *Faculty research:* World religions, spirituality and literature, philosophy, humanities. *Unit head:* Dr. Debrah B. Bokowski, Chair, 503-636-8141, Fax: 503-697-5597, E-mail: dbokowski@marylhurst.edu. *Application contact:* Maruska Lynch, Graduate Admissions Specialist, 800-634-9982 Ext. 6322, Fax: 503-699-6320, E-mail: admissions@marylhurst.edu.

Marywood University, Academic Affairs, Insalaco College of Creative and Performing Arts, Department of Communication Arts, Program in Communication Arts, Scranton, PA 18509-1598. Offers interdisciplinary (MA); media management (MA); production (MA). *Entrance requirements:* Additional exam requirements/recommendations for international students: Required—TOEFL (minimum score 550 paper-based; 213 computer-based; 79 iBT). Electronic applications accepted. *Expenses:* Tuition: Part-time $735 per credit. Required fees: $470 per semester. Tuition and fees vary according to degree level and campus/location.

Mills College, Graduate Studies, Program in Computer Science, Oakland, CA 94613-1000. Offers computer science (Certificate); interdisciplinary computer science (MA). Part-time programs available. *Faculty:* 7 full-time (6 women), 1 (woman) part-time/adjunct. *Students:* 9 full-time (5 women), 3 part-time (2 women); includes 1 Black or African American, non-Hispanic/Latino; 1 Hispanic/Latino. Average age 31. 13 applicants, 85% accepted, 7 enrolled. In 2010, 2 master's awarded. *Degree requirements:* For master's, thesis. *Entrance requirements:* Additional exam requirements/recommendations for international students: Required—TOEFL. *Application deadline:* For fall admission, 2/1 priority date for domestic students, 12/15 for international students; for spring admission, 11/1 priority date for domestic students, 10/1 for international students. Applications are processed on a rolling basis. Application fee: $50. Electronic applications accepted. *Expenses:* Tuition: Full-time $28,280; part-time $7070 per course. Required fees: $1058; $1058 per year. Tuition and fees vary according to program. *Financial support:* In 2010–11, 11 students received support, including 11 fellowships (averaging $2,614 per year), 11 teaching assistantships (averaging $2,614 per year); career-related internships or fieldwork and residence awards also available. Financial award application deadline: 2/1; financial award applicants required to submit FAFSA. *Faculty research:* Dynamical systems, linear programming, theory of computer viruses, interface design, intelligent tutoring systems. *Unit head:* Susan S. Wang, Department Head, 510-430-2138, E-mail: wang@mills.edu. *Application contact:* Jessica King, Graduate Admission Specialist, 510-430-3305, Fax: 510-430-2159, E-mail: rmcglaut@mills.edu.

Minnesota State University Mankato, College of Graduate Studies, Program in Cross-disciplinary Studies, Mankato, MN 56001. Offers MS. Part-time and evening/weekend programs available. *Students:* 4 part-time (3 women). *Degree requirements:* For master's, comprehensive exam, thesis or alternative. *Entrance requirements:* For master's, GRE General Test, minimum GPA of 3.0 during previous 2 years. Additional exam requirements/recommendations for international students: Required—TOEFL. *Application deadline:* For fall admission, 7/1 priority date for domestic students; for spring admission, 11/1 for domestic students. Applications are processed on a rolling basis. Application fee: $40. Electronic applications accepted. *Financial support:* Research assistantships with full tuition reimbursements, teaching assistantships with full tuition reimbursements, career-related internships or fieldwork, Federal Work-Study, and unspecified assistantships available. Support available to part-time students. Financial award application deadline: 3/15; financial award applicants required to submit FAFSA. *Unit head:* Chris Mickle, Graduate Coordinator, 507-389-2321. *Application contact:* 507-389-2321, E-mail: grad@mnsu.edu.

Mississippi State University, College of Arts and Sciences, Department of Biological Sciences, Mississippi State, MS 39762. Offers biological sciences (MS, PhD); general biology (MS); interdisciplinary sciences (MA), including biological sciences. MS (general biology), MA only offered online. Postbaccalaureate distance learning degree programs offered (minimal on-campus study). *Faculty:* 14 full-time (8 women), 1 part-time/adjunct (0 women). *Students:* 34 full-time (20 women), 135 part-time (100 women); includes 21 minority (14 Black or African American, non-Hispanic/Latino; 2 Asian, non-Hispanic/Latino; 2 Hispanic/Latino; 3 Two or more races, non-Hispanic/Latino), 12 international. Average age 33. 134 applicants, 69% accepted, 76 enrolled. In 2010, 25 master's, 3 doctorates awarded. Terminal master's awarded for partial completion of doctoral program. *Degree requirements:* For master's, one foreign language, thesis, comprehensive oral or written exam; for doctorate, one foreign language, thesis/dissertation, comprehensive oral or written exam. *Entrance requirements:* For master's, GRE General Test, minimum GPA of 2.75 on last two years of undergraduate courses; for doctorate, GRE General Test. Additional exam requirements/recommendations for international students: Required—TOEFL (minimum score 550 paper-based; 213 computer-based; 79 iBT). *Application deadline:* For fall admission, 7/1 for domestic students, 5/1 for international students; for spring admission, 11/1 for domestic students, 9/1 for international students. Applications are processed on a rolling basis. Application fee: $40. Electronic applications accepted. *Expenses:* Tuition, state resident: full-time $2730.50; part-time $304 per credit hour. Tuition, nonresident: full-time $6901; part-time $767 per credit hour. *Financial support:* In 2010–11, 3 research assistantships with full and partial tuition reimbursements (averaging $13,873 per year), 25 teaching assistantships with full and partial tuition reimbursements (averaging $14,491 per year) were awarded; Federal Work-Study, institutionally sponsored loans, scholarships/grants, and unspecified assistantships also available. Financial award applicants required to submit FAFSA. *Faculty research:* Botany, zoology, microbiology, ecology. Total annual research expenditures: $5 million. *Unit head:* Dr. Nancy Reichert, Professor/Head, 662-325-3483, Fax: 662-325-7939, E-mail: nreichert@biology.msstate.edu. *Application contact:* Dr. Gary Ervin, Associate Dean/Graduate Coordinator, 662-325-1203, Fax: 662-325-7939, E-mail: gervin@biology.msstate.edu.

Mississippi State University, College of Arts and Sciences, Department of Chemistry, Mississippi State, MS 39762. Offers chemistry (MS, PhD); interdisciplinary sciences (MA), including chemistry. MA program is only available online. *Faculty:* 12 full-time (0 women), 1 part-time/adjunct (0 women). *Students:* 50 full-time (16 women), 7 part-time (1 woman); includes 2 minority (1 Black or African American, non-Hispanic/Latino; 1 Asian, non-Hispanic/Latino), 41 international. Average age 30. 116 applicants, 10% accepted, 10 enrolled. In 2010, 3 doctorates awarded. Terminal master's awarded for partial completion of doctoral program. *Degree requirements:* For master's, thesis, comprehensive oral or written exam; for doctorate, thesis/dissertation, comprehensive oral or written exam. *Entrance requirements:* For master's, minimum GPA of 2.75 on last two years of undergraduate courses; for doctorate, minimum GPA of 2.75. Additional exam requirements/recommendations for international students: Required—TOEFL (minimum score 475 paper-based; 153 computer-based). *Application deadline:* For fall admission, 7/1 for domestic students, 5/1 for international students; for spring admission, 11/1 for domestic students, 9/1 for international students. Applications are processed on a rolling basis. Application fee: $40. Electronic applications accepted. *Expenses:* Tuition, state resident: full-time $2730.50; part-time $304 per credit hour. Tuition, nonresident: full-time $6901; part-time $767 per credit hour. *Financial support:* In 2010–11, 9 research assistantships with full tuition reimbursements (averaging $16,835 per year), 41 teaching assistantships with full tuition reimbursements (averaging $17,092 per year) were awarded; Federal Work-Study, institutionally sponsored loans, scholarships/grants, and unspecified assistantships also available. Financial award application deadline: 4/1; financial award applicants required to submit FAFSA. *Faculty research:* Spectroscopy, fluorometry, organic and inorganic synthesis, electrochemistry. Total annual research expenditures: $4.8 million. *Unit head:* Dr. Edwin A. Lewis, Department Head, 662-325-3584, Fax: 662-325-1618, E-mail: elewis@chemistry.msstate.edu. *Application contact:* Dr. Stephen Foster, Graduate Coordinator, 662-325-8854, E-mail: grad@chemistry.msstate.edu.

Montana State University Billings, College of Education, Department of Educational Theory and Practice, Option in Interdisciplinary Studies, Billings, MT 59101-0298. Offers M Ed. *Degree requirements:* For master's, thesis or alternative. *Entrance requirements:* For master's, GRE General Test or MAT, minimum GPA of 3.0 (undergraduate), 3.25 (graduate).

Montana Tech of The University of Montana, Graduate School, Interdisciplinary Program, Butte, MT 59701-8997. Offers MS. Part-time programs available. *Students:* 4 full-time (2 women), 1 international. 2 applicants, 0% accepted, 0 enrolled. In 2010, 1 master's awarded. *Degree requirements:* For master's, comprehensive exam (for some programs), thesis optional. *Entrance requirements:* For master's, GRE General Test, minimum GPA of 3.0. Additional exam requirements/recommendations for international students: Required—TOEFL (minimum score 525 paper-based; 195 computer-based; 71 iBT). *Application deadline:* For fall admission, 4/1 for domestic students, 3/1 priority date for international students; for spring admission, 10/1 for domestic students, 7/1 priority date for international students. Application fee: $30. *Expenses:* Tuition, state resident: full-time $5084. Tuition, nonresident: full-time $15,104. *Financial support:* In 2010–11, 3 students received support, including 2 teaching assistantships (averaging $8,000 per year); research assistantships, career-related internships or fieldwork, tuition waivers (full and partial), and unspecified assistantships also available. *Unit head:* Dr. Joseph Figueira, Associate Vice Chancellor of Academic Affairs and Research/Dean of the Graduate School, 406-496-4456. *Application contact:* Fred Sullivan, Administrator, Graduate School, 406-496-4304, Fax: 406-496-4710, E-mail: fsullivan@mtech.edu.

Mountain State University, School of Graduate Studies, Program in Interdisciplinary Studies, Beckley, WV 25802-9003. Offers MA, MS. Part-time and evening/weekend programs available. Postbaccalaureate distance learning degree programs offered (no on-campus study). *Faculty:* 7 full-time (3 women), 3 part-time/adjunct (0 women). *Students:* 26 full-time (20 women), 17 part-time (13 women); includes 15 minority (12 Black or African American, non-Hispanic/Latino; 1 American Indian or Alaska Native, non-Hispanic/Latino; 1 Asian, non-Hispanic/Latino; 1 Hispanic/Latino), 1 international. Average age 39. 49 applicants, 59% accepted, 16 enrolled. In 2010, 6 master's awarded. *Degree requirements:* For master's, thesis or alternative. *Entrance requirements:* Additional exam requirements/recommendations for international students: Required—TOEFL (minimum score 550 paper-based; 213 computer-based); Recommended—IELTS (minimum score 6.5). *Application deadline:* For fall admission, 5/31 priority date for domestic and international students. Applications are processed on a rolling basis. Application fee: $25 ($50 for international students). Electronic applications accepted. *Expenses:* Tuition: Full-time $4800; part-time $400 per credit hour. Required fees: $2250; $2250 per credit hour. Tuition and fees vary according to degree level and program. *Financial support:* Federal Work-Study, scholarships/grants, and unspecified assistantships available. Support available to part-time students. Financial award applicants required to submit FAFSA. *Unit head:* Dr. William White, Interim Dean, School of Graduate Studies/Dean, School of Leadership and Professional Development, 304-929-1658, Fax: 304-929-1637, E-mail: wwhite@mountainstate.edu. *Application contact:* Anita Diaz, Enrollment Coordinator for Graduate Studies, 304-929-1731, Fax: 304-929-1710, E-mail: adiaz@mountainstate.edu.

New Mexico State University, Graduate School, Interdisciplinary Program, Las Cruces, NM 88003-8001. Offers MA, MS, PhD. Part-time programs available. Postbaccalaureate distance learning degree programs offered (minimal on-campus study). *Faculty:* 1 (woman) full-time. *Students:* 102 full-time (52 women), 265 part-time (179 women); includes 199 minority (17 Black or African American, non-Hispanic/Latino; 7 American Indian or Alaska Native, non-Hispanic/Latino; 6 Asian, non-Hispanic/Latino; 168 Hispanic/Latino; 1 Two or more races, non-Hispanic/Latino), 8 international. Average age 35. 397 applicants, 97% accepted, 284 enrolled. In 2010, 16 master's, 1 doctorate awarded. *Degree requirements:* For master's, comprehensive exam, thesis; for doctorate, comprehensive exam, thesis/dissertation. *Entrance requirements:* For master's, GRE General Test, minimum GPA of 2.5; for doctorate, GRE General Test, minimum GPA of 3.0. Additional exam requirements/recommendations for international students: Required—TOEFL (minimum score 550 paper-based; 213 computer-based; 79 iBT), IELTS. *Application deadline:* Applications are processed on a rolling basis. Application fee: $30 ($50 for international students). *Expenses:* Tuition, state resident: full-time $4536; part-time $242 per credit. Tuition, nonresident: full-time $15,816; part-time $712 per credit. Required fees: $636 per term. *Financial support:* In 2010–11, 2 research assistantships with full tuition reimbursements (averaging $7,177 per year), 3 teaching assistantships with full tuition reimbursements (averaging $9,250 per year) were awarded; fellowships, career-related internships or fieldwork, Federal Work-Study, and health care benefits also available. Financial award application deadline: 3/1. *Faculty research:* Bioinformatics, molecular genetics, plant pathology. *Unit head:* Dr. Linda Lacey, Dean, 575-646-5745, Fax: 575-646-7758, E-mail: lacey@nmsu.edu. *Application contact:* Dr. Linda Lacey, Dean, 575-646-5745, Fax: 575-646-7758, E-mail: lacey@nmsu.edu.

New York University, Gallatin School of Individualized Study, New York, NY 10003. Offers MA. Part-time and evening/weekend programs available. *Faculty:* 52 full-time (28 women), 102 part-time/adjunct (44 women). *Students:* 64 full-time (52 women), 135 part-time (94 women); includes 15 Black or African American, non-Hispanic/Latino; 1 American Indian or Alaska Native, non-Hispanic/Latino; 13 Asian, non-Hispanic/Latino; 10 Hispanic/Latino. Average age 34. 330 applicants, 41% accepted, 56 enrolled. In 2010, 58 master's awarded. *Degree requirements:* For master's, thesis. *Entrance requirements:* Additional exam requirements/recommendations for international students: Required—TOEFL. *Application deadline:* For fall admission, 1/15 priority date for domestic and international students; for spring admission, 10/15 for domestic and international students. Applications are processed on a rolling basis. Application fee: $50. Electronic applications accepted. *Expenses:* Contact institution. *Financial support:* In 2010–11, 88 students received support, including 3 fellowships with tuition reimbursements available (averaging $25,000 per year), 4 research assistantships with full tuition reimbursements available (averaging $17,284 per year); Federal Work-Study, scholarships/grants, and unspecified assistantships also available. Support available to part-time students. Financial award application deadline: 2/1; financial award applicants required to submit FAFSA. *Faculty research:* Arts and culture, gender studies, political and social thought, literature, environmental and global studies. *Unit head:* Dr. Susanne L. Wofford, Dean, 212-998-7370. *Application contact:* Frances R. Levin, Director of Enrollment, 212-998-7370, Fax: 212-995-4150, E-mail: gallatin.gradadmissions@nyu.edu.

Niagara University, Graduate Division of Arts and Sciences, Program in Interdisciplinary Studies, Niagara Falls, Niagara University, NY 14109. Offers MA. Part-time programs available. *Faculty:* 1 full-time (0 women). *Students:* 6 full-time (5 women), 15 part-time (10 women); includes 2 Black or African American, non-Hispanic/Latino. Average age 35. In 2010, 4 master's awarded. *Entrance requirements:* Additional exam requirements/recommendations for international students: Required—TOEFL. *Application deadline:* For fall admission, 8/1 for domestic students. Applications are processed on a rolling basis. *Expenses:* Tuition: Full-time $13,230; part-time $735 per credit hour. Required fees: $50. One-time fee: $120 full-time. *Financial support:* Fellowships available. Financial award applicants required to submit FAFSA. *Unit head:* Dr. Thomas A. Chambers, Director, 716-286-8091, E-mail: chambers@niagara.edu. *Application contact:* Dr. Talia Harmon, Director, 716-286-8093, Fax: 716-286-8061, E-mail: tharmon@niagara.edu.

Northeastern University, College of Engineering, Program in Interdisciplinary Engineering, Boston, MA 02115-5096. Offers PhD. *Students:* 8 full-time (3 women). Average age 25. 2 applicants, 50% accepted, 1 enrolled. *Entrance requirements:* Additional exam requirements/recommendations for international students: Required—TOEFL (minimum score 550 paper-based; 213 computer-based). *Application deadline:* For fall admission, 1/15 priority date for domestic and international students. Applications are processed on a rolling basis. Application fee: $50. Electronic applications accepted. *Financial support:* In 2010–11, 3 students received support, including 3 research assistantships with full tuition reimbursements available (averaging $18,325 per year), 2 teaching assistantships with full tuition reimbursements available (averaging $18,325 per year); fellowships, career-related internships or fieldwork, Federal Work-Study, scholarships/grants, tuition waivers, and unspecified assistantships also available. Support

Interdisciplinary Studies

Northeastern University (continued)
available to part-time students. Financial award application deadline: 1/15. *Unit head:* Dr. Yaman Yener, Associate Dean of Engineering for Research and Graduate Studies, 617-373-2711, Fax: 617-373-2501. *Application contact:* Jeffery Hengel, Admissions Specialist, 617-373-2711, Fax: 617-373-2501, E-mail: grad-eng@coe.neu.edu.

Nova Southeastern University, Graduate School of Humanities and Social Sciences, Department of Multi-Disciplinary Studies, Program in Cross-Disciplinary Studies, Fort Lauderdale, FL 33314-7796. Offers MA. Part-time programs available. Postbaccalaureate distance learning degree programs offered (minimal on-campus study). *Faculty:* 1 (woman) full-time, 52 part-time/adjunct (30 women). *Students:* 6 full-time (5 women), 41 part-time (33 women); includes 16 Black or African American, non-Hispanic/Latino; 11 Hispanic/Latino, 1 international. Average age 31. 25 applicants, 52% accepted, 10 enrolled. In 2010, 9 master's awarded. *Degree requirements:* For master's, comprehensive exam, thesis optional, portfolio. *Entrance requirements:* For master's, interview, minimum GPA of 3.0. Additional exam requirements/recommendations for international students: Required—TOEFL. *Application deadline:* For fall admission, 7/1 priority date for domestic and international students; for winter admission, 11/1 priority date for domestic and international students; for spring admission, 3/1 priority date for domestic and international students. Applications are processed on a rolling basis. Application fee: $50. Electronic applications accepted. *Financial support:* In 2010–11, 1 research assistantship (averaging $15,000 per year) was awarded; Federal Work-Study also available. *Unit head:* Dr. Judith McKay, Chair, 954-262-3060. *Application contact:* Marcia Arango, Student Recruitment Coordinator, 954-262-3006, Fax: 954-262-3968, E-mail: marango@nsu.nova.edu.

The Ohio State University, Graduate School, College of Arts and Sciences, Division of Arts and Humanities, Department of Comparative Studies, Columbus, OH 43210. Offers MA, PhD. *Faculty:* 71. *Students:* 15 full-time (4 women), 8 part-time (7 women); includes 3 Black or African American, non-Hispanic/Latino; 1 Asian, non-Hispanic/Latino, 5 international. Average age 33. In 2010, 4 master's, 3 doctorates awarded. *Entrance requirements:* For master's and doctorate, GRE General Test. Additional exam requirements/recommendations for international students: Required—TOEFL (minimum score 600 paper-based; 250 computer-based). *Application deadline:* For fall admission, 8/15 priority date for domestic students, 7/1 priority date for international students; for winter admission, 12/1 priority date for domestic students, 11/1 priority date for international students; for spring admission, 3/1 priority date for domestic students, 2/1 priority date for international students. Applications are processed on a rolling basis. Application fee: $40 ($50 for international students). Electronic applications accepted. *Expenses:* Tuition, state resident: full-time $10,605. Tuition, nonresident: full-time $26,535. Tuition and fees vary according to course load and program. *Financial support:* Fellowships, research assistantships, teaching assistantships, Federal Work-Study, institutionally sponsored loans, and unspecified assistantships available. Support available to part-time students. *Unit head:* Eugene Holland, Chair, 614-688-5437, E-mail: holland.1@osu.edu. *Application contact:* 614-292-9444, Fax: 614-292-3895, E-mail: domestic.grad@osu.edu.

Oregon State University, Graduate School, Program in Interdisciplinary Studies, Corvallis, OR 97331. Offers MAIS. Program focuses on three areas of study and must include at least one area of study in liberal arts. Part-time programs available. *Degree requirements:* For master's, thesis optional. *Entrance requirements:* For master's, minimum GPA of 3.0 in last 90 hours of course work. Additional exam requirements/recommendations for international students: Required—TOEFL.

Polytechnic Institute of NYU, Department of Interdisciplinary Studies, Brooklyn, NY 11201-2990. Offers bioinformatics (MS); industrial engineering (MS); manufacturing engineering (MS). Part-time programs available. *Faculty:* 3 full-time (0 women), 14 part-time/adjunct (2 women). *Students:* 62 full-time (24 women), 42 part-time (20 women); includes 4 Black or African American, non-Hispanic/Latino; 5 Asian, non-Hispanic/Latino; 3 Hispanic/Latino, 50 international. Average age 29. 127 applicants, 47% accepted, 28 enrolled. In 2010, 41 master's awarded. *Degree requirements:* For master's, comprehensive exam (for some programs), thesis (for some programs). *Entrance requirements:* Additional exam requirements/recommendations for international students: Required—TOEFL (minimum score 550 paper-based; 213 computer-based; 80 iBT); Recommended—IELTS (minimum score 6.5). *Application deadline:* For fall admission, 7/31 priority date for domestic students, 4/30 priority date for international students; for spring admission, 12/31 priority date for domestic students, 11/30 priority date for international students. Applications are processed on a rolling basis. Application fee: $75. Electronic applications accepted. *Expenses:* Tuition: Full-time $21,492; part-time $1194 per credit. Required fees: $385 per semester. Tuition and fees vary according to course load. *Financial support:* Institutionally sponsored loans, scholarships/grants, and unspecified assistantships available. Support available to part-time students. *Unit head:* Prof. Michael Greenstein, Department Head, 718-260-3835, E-mail: mgreenst@poly.edu. *Application contact:* JeanCarlo Bonilla, Dir. Graduate Enrollment Management, 718-260-3182, Fax: 718-260-3624, E-mail: gradinfo@poly.edu.

Polytechnic Institute of NYU, Long Island Graduate Center, Graduate Programs, Department of Interdisciplinary Studies, Melville, NY 11747. Offers bioinformatics (MS); industrial engineering (MS); manufacturing engineering (MS). Part-time and evening/weekend programs available. *Students:* 4 part-time (2 women); includes 1 minority (Black or African American, non-Hispanic/Latino). Average age 37. 1 applicant, 100% accepted, 1 enrolled. In 2010, 3 master's awarded. *Entrance requirements:* Additional exam requirements/recommendations for international students: Required—TOEFL (minimum score 550 paper-based; 213 computer-based; 80 iBT); Recommended—IELTS (minimum score 6.5). *Application deadline:* For fall admission, 7/31 priority date for domestic students, 4/30 priority date for international students; for spring admission, 12/31 priority date for domestic students, 11/30 priority date for international students. Applications are processed on a rolling basis. Application fee: $75. Electronic applications accepted. *Expenses:* Tuition: Full-time $21,492; part-time $1194 per credit. Required fees: $385 per semester. Tuition and fees vary according to course load. *Financial support:* Institutionally sponsored loans, scholarships/grants, and unspecified assistantships available. Support available to part-time students. *Application contact:* JeanCarlo Bonilla, Director of Graduate Enrollment Management, 718-260-3182, Fax: 718-260-3624, E-mail: gradinfo@poly.edu.

Polytechnic Institute of NYU, Westchester Graduate Center, Graduate Programs, Department of Interdisciplinary Studies, Hawthorne, NY 10532-1507. Offers bioinformatics (MS); industrial engineering (MS); manufacturing engineering (MS); wireless innovation (ME). *Students:* 1 part-time (0 women). Average age 35. 2 applicants, 0% accepted, 0 enrolled. *Entrance requirements:* Additional exam requirements/recommendations for international students: Required—TOEFL (minimum score 550 paper-based; 213 computer-based; 80 iBT); Recommended—IELTS (minimum score 6.5). *Application deadline:* For fall admission, 7/31 priority date for domestic students, 4/30 priority date for international students; for spring admission, 12/31 priority date for domestic students, 11/30 priority date for international students. Applications are processed on a rolling basis. Application fee: $75. Electronic applications accepted. *Expenses:* Tuition: Full-time $21,492; part-time $1194 per credit. Required fees: $385 per semester. Tuition and fees vary according to course load. *Financial support:* Institutionally sponsored loans, scholarships/grants, and unspecified assistantships available. Support available to part-time students. *Application contact:* JeanCarlo Bonilla, Director of Graduate Enrollment Management, 718-260-3182, Fax: 718-260-3624, E-mail: gradinfo@poly.edu.

Quinnipiac University, School of Nursing, Care of the Individual Track, Hamden, CT 06518-1940. Offers DNP. *Expenses:* Tuition: Part-time $810 per credit. Required fees: $35 per credit.

Regis University, College for Professional Studies, School of Humanities and Social Sciences, MA Program, Denver, CO 80221-1099. Offers communication (MA); fine arts (Certificate); interdisciplinary studies (MA); mediation and conflict resolution (Certificate); psychology (MA); social justice, peace, and reconciliation (Certificate); technical communication (Certificate);

Program also offered in Henderson and Las Vegas (Summerlin), NV. Part-time and evening/weekend programs available. Postbaccalaureate distance learning degree programs offered (minimal on-campus study). *Degree requirements:* For master's, thesis, research project. *Entrance requirements:* For master's, resume, recommendations. Additional exam requirements/recommendations for international students: Required—TOEFL (minimum score 213 computer-based), TWE (minimum score 5). Electronic applications accepted. *Expenses:* Contact institution. *Faculty research:* Independent/nonresidential graduate study: new methods and models, adult learning and the capstone experience, Goal Setting, behavior of Adult students, Innovative Studies for Community Colleges.

Rensselaer Polytechnic Institute, Graduate School, School of Science, Program in Multi-Disciplinary Science, Troy, NY 12180-3590. Offers MS, PhD. Part-time programs available. *Students:* 5 full-time (1 woman), 1 international. Average age 26. 8 applicants, 13% accepted, 1 enrolled.Terminal master's awarded for partial completion of doctoral program. *Degree requirements:* For master's, comprehensive exam (for some programs), thesis optional; for doctorate, comprehensive exam, thesis/dissertation. *Entrance requirements:* For doctorate, GRE General Test. Additional exam requirements/recommendations for international students: Required—TOEFL. *Application deadline:* For fall admission, 1/15 priority date for domestic and international students. Applications are processed on a rolling basis. Application fee: $75. Electronic applications accepted. *Expenses:* Tuition: Full-time $39,600; part-time $1650 per credit. Required fees: $1896. *Financial support:* In 2010–11, 5 students received support, including 1 fellowship with full tuition reimbursement available (averaging $18,000 per year), 3 research assistantships with full tuition reimbursements available (averaging $16,500 per year), 1 teaching assistantship with full tuition reimbursement available (averaging $16,500 per year); career-related internships or fieldwork and institutionally sponsored loans also available. Financial award application deadline: 2/1. *Faculty research:* Bioinformatics, astrobiology, nanotechnology, biotechnology, scientific computation. *Unit head:* Dr. William L. Siegmann, Associate Dean for Graduate Education and Research, 518-276-6905, Fax: 518-276-2825, E-mail: siegmw@rpi.edu. *Application contact:* Dr. William L. Siegmann, Associate Dean for Graduate Education and Research, 518-276-6905, Fax: 518-276-2825, E-mail: siegmw@rpi.edu.

Rochester Institute of Technology, Graduate Enrollment Services, Center for Multidisciplinary Studies, Program in Professional Studies, Rochester, NY 14623-5603. Offers MS. Part-time and evening/weekend programs available. Postbaccalaureate distance learning degree programs offered (no on-campus study). *Students:* 43 full-time (18 women), 131 part-time (73 women); includes 11 Black or African American, non-Hispanic/Latino; 2 Asian, non-Hispanic/Latino; 5 Hispanic/Latino, 19 international. Average age 35. 107 applicants, 41% accepted, 40 enrolled. In 2010, 28 master's awarded. *Degree requirements:* For master's, thesis or alternative. *Entrance requirements:* For master's, minimum GPA of 3.0. Additional exam requirements/recommendations for international students: Required—TOEFL (minimum score 550 paper-based; 213 computer-based; 79 iBT) or IELTS (minimum score 6.5). *Application deadline:* For fall admission, 2/15 priority date for domestic and international students; for winter admission, 11/1 for domestic and international students; for spring admission, 2/1 for domestic and international students. Applications are processed on a rolling basis. *Expenses:* Tuition: Full-time $33,234; part-time $924 per credit hour. Required fees: $219. *Financial support:* In 2010–11, 42 students received support. Career-related internships or fieldwork available. Support available to part-time students. Financial award application deadline: 2/15; financial award applicants required to submit FAFSA. *Unit head:* Dr. Samuel McQuade, Graduate Program Director, 585-475-5230, Fax: 585-475-6292, E-mail: scmcms@rit.edu. *Application contact:* Diane Ellison, Assistant Vice President, Graduate Enrollment Services, 585-475-2229, Fax: 585-475-7164, E-mail: gradinfo@rit.edu.

Rosalind Franklin University of Medicine and Science, College of Health Professions, Department of Interprofessional Healthcare Studies, Interprofessional Healthcare Studies Program, North Chicago, IL 60064-3095. Offers interprofessional studies (D Sc). Part-time programs available. Postbaccalaureate distance learning degree programs offered (minimal on-campus study). *Degree requirements:* For doctorate, comprehensive exam, thesis/dissertation. *Entrance requirements:* For doctorate, GRE. Additional exam requirements/recommendations for international students: Required—TOEFL. *Faculty research:* Interprofessional education.

Rutgers, The State University of New Jersey, New Brunswick, Graduate School-New Brunswick, BioMaPS Institute for Quantitative Biology, Piscataway, NJ 08854-8097. Offers computational biology and molecular biophysics (PhD). *Degree requirements:* For doctorate, comprehensive exam, thesis/dissertation. *Entrance requirements:* For doctorate, GRE. Additional exam requirements/recommendations for international students: Required—TOEFL. Electronic applications accepted. *Expenses:* Tuition, state resident: full-time $7200; part-time $600 per credit. Tuition, nonresident: full-time $11,124; part-time $927 per credit. *Faculty research:* Structural biology, systems biology, bioinformatics, translational medicine, genomics.

San Diego State University, Graduate and Research Affairs, Interdisciplinary Studies, San Diego, CA 92182. Offers MA, MS. Part-time programs available. *Degree requirements:* For master's, thesis. *Entrance requirements:* For master's, GRE General Test. Additional exam requirements/recommendations for international students: Required—TOEFL. Electronic applications accepted.

San Jose State University, Graduate Studies and Research, Program in Interdisciplinary Studies, San Jose, CA 95192-0001. Offers MA, MS. Electronic applications accepted.

Sarah Lawrence College, Graduate Studies, Individualized Study Program, Bronxville, NY 10708-5999. Offers MA. Part-time programs available. *Degree requirements:* For master's, thesis.

Sonoma State University, Institute of Interdisciplinary Studies/Special Major, Rohnert Park, CA 94928. Offers special major (MA, MS). Part-time programs available. *Faculty:* 2 full-time (1 woman). *Students:* 4 full-time (2 women), 29 part-time (18 women); includes 1 Hispanic/Latino; 3 Two or more races, non-Hispanic/Latino. Average age 38. 17 applicants, 76% accepted, 8 enrolled. In 2010, 12 master's awarded. *Degree requirements:* For master's, thesis or alternative. *Entrance requirements:* For master's, written English proficiency test, minimum GPA of 3.0 in last 60 hours. Additional exam requirements/recommendations for international students: Required—TOEFL (minimum score 500 paper-based; 173 computer-based). *Application deadline:* For fall admission, 1/31 for domestic students; for spring admission, 10/31 for domestic students. Application fee: $55. *Financial support:* Career-related internships or fieldwork, Federal Work-Study, and institutionally sponsored loans available. Support available to part-time students. Financial award applicants required to submit FAFSA. *Unit head:* Dr. Ellen Carlton, Coordinator, 707-664-3918, E-mail: ellen.carlton@sonoma.edu. *Application contact:* Elaine Sundberg, Associate Vice Provost, Academic Programs/Graduate Studies, 707-664-2215, Fax: 707-664-4060, E-mail: elaine.sundberg@sonoma.edu.

Southern Oregon University, Graduate Studies, College of Arts and Sciences, Program in Interdisciplinary Studies, Ashland, OR 97520. Offers MIS. Part-time programs available. Postbaccalaureate distance learning degree programs offered (no on-campus study). *Faculty:* 144 full-time (55 women), 27 part-time/adjunct (11 women). *Students:* 10 full-time (7 women), 8 part-time (4 women); includes 2 minority (1 American Indian or Alaska Native, non-Hispanic/Latino; 1 Two or more races, non-Hispanic/Latino). Average age 50. 14 applicants, 79% accepted, 8 enrolled. In 2010, 6 master's awarded. *Degree requirements:* For master's, thesis optional. *Entrance requirements:* For master's, GRE General Test, minimum GPA of 3.0. *Application deadline:* Applications are processed on a rolling basis. Application fee: $50. *Expenses:* Tuition, state resident: full-time $9450; part-time $350 per credit. Tuition, nonresident: full-time $15,000; part-time $350 per credit. Required fees: $400 per quarter. *Unit head:* Dr. Bill Gholson, Director, 541-552-6630, E-mail: gholson@sou.edu. *Application contact:* Mark Bottorff, Director of Admissions, 541-552-6411, Fax: 541-552-8403, E-mail: admissions@sou.edu.

Stanford University, School of Education, Program in Social Sciences, Policy, and Educational Practice, Stanford, CA 94305-9991. Offers administration and policy analysis (Ed D, PhD); anthropology of education (PhD); economics of education (PhD); educational linguistics (PhD); evaluation (MA), including interdisciplinary studies; higher education (PhD); history of education (PhD); interdisciplinary studies (PhD); international comparative education (MA, PhD); international education administration and policy analysis (MA); philosophy of education (PhD); policy analysis (MA); prospective principal's program (MA); sociology of education (PhD). *Degree requirements:* For master's, thesis (for some programs); for doctorate, thesis/dissertation. *Entrance requirements:* For master's and doctorate, GRE General Test. Electronic applications accepted. *Expenses:* Tuition: Full-time $38,700; part-time $860 per unit. One-time fee: $200 full-time.

State University of New York at Fredonia, Graduate Studies, Graduate Programs in Interdisciplinary Studies, Fredonia, NY 14063-1136. Offers MA, MS. Part-time and evening/weekend programs available. *Degree requirements:* For master's, thesis optional. *Expenses:* Tuition, state resident: full-time $8370; part-time $349 per credit hour. Tuition, nonresident: full-time $13,250; part-time $552 per credit hour. Required fees: $1328; $55.15 per credit hour.

Stephen F. Austin State University, Graduate School, College of Applied Arts and Science, Program in Interdisciplinary Studies, Nacogdoches, TX 75962. Offers MIS. Part-time programs available. *Degree requirements:* For master's, comprehensive exam, thesis optional. *Entrance requirements:* For master's, GRE General Test. Additional exam requirements/recommendations for international students: Required—TOEFL (minimum score 550 paper-based; 213 computer-based).

Teachers College, Columbia University, Graduate Faculty of Education, Interdisciplinary Programs, New York, NY 10027-6696. Offers Ed M, MA, Ed D. Part-time programs available. *Students:* 9 full-time (6 women), 22 part-time (12 women); includes 8 minority (2 Black or African American, non-Hispanic/Latino; 1 American Indian or Alaska Native, non-Hispanic/Latino; 2 Asian, non-Hispanic/Latino; 2 Hispanic/Latino; 1 Two or more races, non-Hispanic/Latino), 3 international. Average age 41. 1 applicant, 0% accepted, 0 enrolled. In 2010, 2 doctorates awarded. Terminal master's awarded for partial completion of doctoral program. *Degree requirements:* For doctorate, thesis/dissertation. Application fee: $65. *Expenses:* Tuition: Full-time $28,272; part-time $1178 per credit. Required fees: $756; $378 per semester. *Financial support:* Fellowships, career-related internships or fieldwork, Federal Work-Study, institutionally sponsored loans, and tuition waivers (full and partial) available. Support available to part-time students. Financial award application deadline: 2/1. *Unit head:* William J. Baldwin, Vice Provost. *Application contact:* Thomas P. Rock, Executive Director of Enrollment Services, 212-678-3710, Fax: 212-678-4171.

Texas A&M University–Texarkana, Graduate Studies and Research, College of Education and Liberal Arts, Texarkana, TX 75505-5518. Offers adult education (MS); curriculum and instruction (M Ed); education (MS); educational administration (M Ed); English (MA); instructional technology (MS); interdisciplinary studies (MA, MS); special education (MS). Part-time and evening/weekend programs available. *Degree requirements:* For master's, comprehensive exam (for some programs), thesis optional. *Entrance requirements:* For master's, minimum GPA of 2.5 on last 60 hours of bachelor's degree. Additional exam requirements/recommendations for international students: Required—TOEFL. Electronic applications accepted.

Texas State University–San Marcos, Graduate School, College of Liberal Arts, Department of Sociology, Interdisciplinary Studies Program in Applied Sociology, San Marcos, TX 78666. Offers MS. Part-time and evening/weekend programs available. *Faculty:* 13 full-time (8 women), 1 part-time/adjunct (0 women). *Students:* 5 full-time (3 women), 8 part-time (5 women); includes 3 minority (1 Black or African American, non-Hispanic/Latino; 2 Hispanic/Latino). Average age 31. 6 applicants, 83% accepted, 4 enrolled. In 2010, 2 master's awarded. *Degree requirements:* For master's, comprehensive exam. *Entrance requirements:* For master's, minimum GPA of 3.0 on last 60 hours of undergraduate work, 3 letters of reference, letter of intent. Additional exam requirements/recommendations for international students: Required—TOEFL (minimum score 550 paper-based; 213 computer-based; 78 iBT). *Application deadline:* For fall admission, 6/15 priority date for domestic students, 6/1 for international students; for spring admission, 10/15 priority date for domestic students, 10/1 for international students. Applications are processed on a rolling basis. Application fee: $40 ($90 for international students). Electronic applications accepted. *Expenses:* Tuition, state resident: full-time $6024; part-time $251 per credit hour. Tuition, nonresident: full-time $13,536; part-time $564 per credit hour. Required fees: $1776; $50 per credit hour. $306 per semester. *Financial support:* In 2010–11, 2 students received support, including 3 teaching assistantships (averaging $5,558 per year); Federal Work-Study, institutionally sponsored loans, scholarships/grants, health care benefits, and unspecified assistantships also available. Support available to part-time students. Financial award application deadline: 4/1; financial award applicants required to submit FAFSA. *Unit head:* Dr. Audwin Anderson, Head, 512-245-2113, E-mail: aa04@txstate.edu. *Application contact:* Dr. J. Michael Willoughby, Dean of Graduate School, 512-245-2581, Fax: 512-245-8365, E-mail: gradcollege@txstate.edu.

Texas State University–San Marcos, Graduate School, College of Liberal Arts, Department of Sociology, Interdisciplinary Studies Program in Criminal Justice, San Marcos, TX 78666. Offers MSIS. Part-time and evening/weekend programs available. *Faculty:* 13 full-time (8 women), 1 part-time/adjunct (0 women). *Students:* 22 full-time (14 women), 29 part-time (20 women); includes 22 minority (9 Black or African American, non-Hispanic/Latino; 1 Asian, non-Hispanic/Latino; 10 Hispanic/Latino; 2 Two or more races, non-Hispanic/Latino). Average age 29. 30 applicants, 93% accepted, 19 enrolled. In 2010, 4 master's awarded. *Degree requirements:* For master's, comprehensive exam, thesis optional. *Entrance requirements:* For master's, minimum GPA of 2.75 in last 60 hours of undergraduate work. Additional exam requirements/recommendations for international students: Required—TOEFL (minimum score 550 paper-based; 213 computer-based; 78 iBT). *Application deadline:* For fall admission, 6/15 priority date for domestic students, 6/1 for international students; for spring admission, 10/15 priority date for domestic students, 10/1 for international students. Applications are processed on a rolling basis. Application fee: $40 ($90 for international students). Electronic applications accepted. *Expenses:* Tuition, state resident: full-time $6024; part-time $251 per credit hour. Tuition, nonresident: full-time $13,536; part-time $564 per credit hour. Required fees: $1776; $50 per credit hour. $306 per semester. *Financial support:* In 2010–11, 17 students received support, including 13 teaching assistantships (averaging $5,297 per year); research assistantships, Federal Work-Study, institutionally sponsored loans, scholarships/grants, health care benefits, and unspecified assistantships also available. Support available to part-time students. Financial award application deadline: 4/1; financial award applicants required to submit FAFSA. *Unit head:* Dr. Audwin Anderson, Graduate Advisor, 512-245-2174, Fax: 512-245-2174, E-mail: aa04@txstate.edu. *Application contact:* Dr. J. Michael Willoughby, Dean of Graduate School, 512-245-2581, Fax: 512-245-8365, E-mail: gradcollege@txstate.edu.

Texas State University–San Marcos, Graduate School, Interdisciplinary Studies in Political Science, San Marcos, TX 78666. Offers MAIS. *Degree requirements:* For master's, comprehensive exam, thesis optional. *Entrance requirements:* For master's, minimum GPA of 2.9 or GRE (minimum combined score of 900 Verbal and Quantitative preferred). Additional exam requirements/recommendations for international students: Required—TOEFL (minimum score 550 paper-based; 213 computer-based; 78 iBT). *Application deadline:* For fall admission, 6/15 priority date for domestic students, 6/1 for international students; for spring admission, 10/15 priority date for domestic students, 10/1 for international students. Applications are processed on a rolling basis. Application fee: $40 ($90 for international students). *Expenses:* Tuition, state resident: full-time $6024; part-time $251 per credit hour. Tuition, nonresident: full-time $13,536; part-time $564 per credit hour. Required fees: $1776; $50 per credit hour. $306 per semester. *Financial support:* Application deadline: 4/1. *Unit head:* Dr. Cecilia Castillio, Graduate Advisor, 512-245-3255, Fax: 512-345-7815, E-mail: cr09@txstate.edu. *Application contact:* Dr. J. Michael Willoughby, Dean of Graduate School, 512-245-2581, Fax: 512-245-8365, E-mail: gradcollege@txstate.edu.

Texas State University–San Marcos, Graduate School, Interdisciplinary Studies Program in Biology, San Marcos, TX 78666. Offers MSIS. *Degree requirements:* For master's, comprehensive exam, thesis optional. *Entrance requirements:* For master's, GRE (minimum score 1000 verbal and quantitative preferred), bachelor's degree in biology or related field, minimum GPA of 3.0 in last 60 hours of undergraduate work. Additional exam requirements/recommendations for international students: Required—TOEFL (minimum score 550 paper-based; 213 computer-based; 78 iBT). *Application deadline:* For fall admission, 6/15 priority date for domestic students, 6/1 for international students; for spring admission, 10/15 priority date for domestic students, 10/1 for international students. Applications are processed on a rolling basis. Application fee: $40 ($90 for international students). *Expenses:* Tuition, state resident: full-time $6024; part-time $251 per credit hour. Tuition, nonresident: full-time $13,536; part-time $564 per credit hour. Required fees: $1776; $50 per credit hour. $306 per semester. *Financial support:* Research assistantships, teaching assistantships, Federal Work-Study, institutionally sponsored loans, scholarships/grants, health care benefits, and unspecified assistantships available. Support available to part-time students. Financial award application deadline: 4/1; financial award applicants required to submit FAFSA. *Unit head:* Dr. David Lemker, Graduate Advisor, 512-245-2178, E-mail: dl10@txstate.edu. *Application contact:* Dr. J. Michael Willoughby, Dean of Graduate School, 512-245-2581, Fax: 512-245-8365, E-mail: gradcollege@txstate.edu.

Texas State University–San Marcos, Graduate School, Interdisciplinary Studies Program in Educational Administration and Psychological Services, San Marcos, TX 78666. Offers MAIS. *Degree requirements:* For master's, comprehensive exam. *Entrance requirements:* Additional exam requirements/recommendations for international students: Required—TOEFL (minimum score 550 paper-based; 213 computer-based; 78 iBT). *Application deadline:* For fall admission, 6/15 priority date for domestic students; for spring admission, 10/15 priority date for domestic students. Applications are processed on a rolling basis. Application fee: $40 ($90 for international students). *Expenses:* Tuition, state resident: full-time $6024; part-time $251 per credit hour. Tuition, nonresident: full-time $13,536; part-time $564 per credit hour. Required fees: $1776; $50 per credit hour. $306 per semester. *Financial support:* Application deadline: 4/1. *Unit head:* Dr. Stan Carpenter, Dean, 512-245-2575, Fax: 512-245-8345, E-mail: sc33@txstate.edu. *Application contact:* Dr. J. Michael Willoughby, Dean of Graduate School, 512-245-2581, Fax: 512-245-8365, E-mail: gradcollege@txstate.edu.

Texas State University–San Marcos, Graduate School, Interdisciplinary Studies Program in Elementary Mathematics, Science, and Technology, San Marcos, TX 78666. Offers MSIS. *Students:* 2 part-time (both women). Average age 33. In 2010, 1 master's awarded. *Degree requirements:* For master's, comprehensive exam, thesis optional. *Entrance requirements:* For master's, minimum GPA of 2.75 in the last 60 hours of undergraduate work. Additional exam requirements/recommendations for international students: Required—TOEFL (minimum score 550 paper-based; 213 computer-based; 78 iBT). *Application deadline:* For fall admission, 6/15 priority date for domestic students, 6/1 priority date for international students; for spring admission, 10/15 priority date for domestic students, 10/1 priority date for international students. Applications are processed on a rolling basis. Application fee: $40 ($90 for international students). Electronic applications accepted. *Expenses:* Tuition, state resident: full-time $6024; part-time $251 per credit hour. Tuition, nonresident: full-time $13,536; part-time $564 per credit hour. Required fees: $1776; $50 per credit hour. $306 per semester. *Financial support:* In 2010–11, 1 research assistantship (averaging $308 per year) was awarded; teaching assistantships, Federal Work-Study, institutionally sponsored loans, scholarships/grants, health care benefits, and unspecified assistantships also available. Support available to part-time students. Financial award application deadline: 4/1; financial award applicants required to submit FAFSA. *Unit head:* Dr. Sandra Mody, Acting Dean, 512-245-3360, Fax: 512-245-8095, E-mail: sw04@txstate.edu. *Application contact:* Dr. J. Michael Willoughby, Dean of Graduate School, 512-245-2581, Fax: 512-245-8365, E-mail: gradcollege@txstate.edu.

Texas State University–San Marcos, Graduate School, Interdisciplinary Studies Program in Health, Physical Education, and Recreation, San Marcos, TX 78666. Offers MAIS. Part-time and evening/weekend programs available. *Students:* 2 full-time (both women). Average age 32. 4 applicants, 75% accepted, 1 enrolled. In 2010, 2 master's awarded. *Degree requirements:* For master's, comprehensive exam, thesis optional. *Entrance requirements:* For master's, GRE General Test, minimum GPA of 2.75 in last 60 hours of course work. Additional exam requirements/recommendations for international students: Required—TOEFL (minimum score 550 paper-based; 213 computer-based; 78 iBT). *Application deadline:* For fall admission, 6/15 priority date for domestic students, 6/1 for international students; for spring admission, 10/15 priority date for domestic students, 10/1 for international students. Applications are processed on a rolling basis. Application fee: $40 ($90 for international students). *Expenses:* Tuition, state resident: full-time $6024; part-time $251 per credit hour. Tuition, nonresident: full-time $13,536; part-time $564 per credit hour. Required fees: $1776; $50 per credit hour. $306 per semester. *Financial support:* Teaching assistantships, career-related internships or fieldwork, Federal Work-Study, institutionally sponsored loans, scholarships/grants, health care benefits, and unspecified assistantships available. Support available to part-time students. Financial award application deadline: 4/1; financial award applicants required to submit FAFSA. *Unit head:* Dr. Lisa Lloyd, Graduate Advisor, 512-245-2561, Fax: 512-245-8678, E-mail: ll12@txstate.edu. *Application contact:* Dr. J. Michael Willoughby, Dean of Graduate School, 512-245-2581, Fax: 512-245-8365, E-mail: gradcollege@txstate.edu.

Texas State University–San Marcos, Graduate School, Interdisciplinary Studies Program in Modern Languages, San Marcos, TX 78666. Offers MAIS. *Degree requirements:* For master's, comprehensive exam, thesis optional. *Entrance requirements:* For master's, minimum GPA of 2.75 in last 60 hours of course work. Additional exam requirements/recommendations for international students: Required—TOEFL (minimum score 550 paper-based; 213 computer-based; 78 iBT). *Application deadline:* For fall admission, 6/15 priority date for domestic students, 6/1 for international students; for spring admission, 10/15 priority date for domestic students, 10/1 for international students. Applications are processed on a rolling basis. Application fee: $40 ($90 for international students). *Expenses:* Tuition, state resident: full-time $6024; part-time $251 per credit hour. Tuition, nonresident: full-time $13,536; part-time $564 per credit hour. Required fees: $1776; $50 per credit hour. $306 per semester. *Financial support:* Application deadline: 4/1. *Unit head:* Dr. Catherine Jaffe, Advisor, 512-245-2360, Fax: 512-245-8298, E-mail: cj10@txstate.edu. *Application contact:* Dr. Catherine Jaffe, Advisor, 512-245-2360, Fax: 512-245-8298, E-mail: cj10@txstate.edu.

Texas State University–San Marcos, Graduate School, Interdisciplinary Studies Program in Occupational Education, San Marcos, TX 78666. Offers MAIS, MSIS. *Faculty:* 3 full-time (1 woman), 1 part-time/adjunct (0 women). *Students:* 11 full-time (5 women), 46 part-time (24 women); includes 24 minority (7 Black or African American, non-Hispanic/Latino; 1 Asian, non-Hispanic/Latino; 16 Hispanic/Latino). Average age 40. 18 applicants, 100% accepted, 14 enrolled. In 2010, 17 master's awarded. *Degree requirements:* For master's, comprehensive exam, thesis optional. *Entrance requirements:* For master's, minimum GPA of 2.75 for undergraduate work, statement of personal goals. Additional exam requirements/recommendations for international students: Required—TOEFL (minimum score 550 paper-based; 213 computer-based; 78 iBT). *Application deadline:* For fall admission, 6/15 priority date for domestic students, 6/1 priority date for international students; for spring admission, 10/15 priority date for domestic students, 10/1 priority date for international students. Applications are processed on a rolling basis. Application fee: $40 ($90 for international students). Electronic applications accepted. *Expenses:* Tuition, state resident: full-time $6024; part-time $251 per credit hour. Tuition, nonresident: full-time $13,536; part-time $564 per credit hour. Required fees: $1776; $50 per credit hour. $306 per semester. *Financial support:* In 2010–11, 18 students received support, including 3 research assistantships (averaging $5,837 per year), 1 teaching assistantship (averaging $5,076 per year); Federal Work-Study, institutionally sponsored loans, scholarships/grants, health care benefits, and unspecified assistantships also available. Support available to part-time students. Financial award application deadline: 4/1; financial award applicants required to submit FAFSA. *Unit head:* Dr. Stephen Springer, Director, 512-245-2115, E-mail: ss01@txstate.edu. *Application contact:* Dr. J. Michael Willoughby, Dean of Graduate School, 512-245-2581, Fax: 512-245-8365, E-mail: gradcollege@txstate.edu.

Interdisciplinary Studies

Texas State University–San Marcos, Graduate School, Interdisciplinary Studies Program in Psychology, San Marcos, TX 78666. Offers MAIS, MSIS. *Degree requirements:* For master's, comprehensive exam. *Entrance requirements:* Additional exam requirements/recommendations for international students: Required—TOEFL (minimum score 550 paper-based; 213 computer-based; 78 iBT). *Application deadline:* For fall admission, 6/15 priority date for domestic students, 6/1 for international students; for spring admission, 10/15 priority date for domestic students, 10/1 for international students. Applications are processed on a rolling basis. Application fee: $40 ($90 for international students). *Expenses:* Tuition, state resident: full-time $6024; part-time $251 per credit hour. Tuition, nonresident: full-time $13,536; part-time $564 per credit hour. Required fees: $1776; $50 per credit hour. $306 per semester. *Financial support:* Application deadline: 4/1. *Unit head:* Dr. Paula Williams, Advisor, 512-245-3159, E-mail: pw04@txstate.edu. *Application contact:* Dr. J. Michael Willoughby, Dean of Graduate School, 512-245-2581, Fax: 512-245-8365, E-mail: gradcollege@txstate.edu.

Texas Tech University, Graduate School, Program in Interdisciplinary Studies, Lubbock, TX 79409. Offers MA, MS. Part-time and evening/weekend programs available. *Faculty:* 2 full-time (0 women). *Students:* 90 full-time (46 women), 92 part-time (53 women); includes 11 Black or African American, non-Hispanic/Latino; 1 American Indian or Alaska Native, non-Hispanic/Latino; 5 Asian, non-Hispanic/Latino; 34 Hispanic/Latino; 4 Two or more races, non-Hispanic/Latino, 15 international. Average age 29. 109 applicants, 80% accepted, 72 enrolled. In 2010, 32 master's awarded. *Degree requirements:* For master's, comprehensive exam, thesis or alternative. *Entrance requirements:* For master's, GRE General Test. Additional exam requirements/recommendations for international students: Required—TOEFL (minimum score 550 paper-based; 213 computer-based; 79 iBT). *Application deadline:* For fall admission, 6/1 priority date for domestic students, 1/15 priority date for international students; for spring admission, 9/1 priority date for domestic students, 6/15 priority date for international students. Applications are processed on a rolling basis. Application fee: $50 ($75 for international students). Electronic applications accepted. *Expenses:* Tuition, state resident: full-time $5495.76; part-time $228.99 per credit hour. Tuition, nonresident: full-time $12,936; part-time $538.99 per credit hour. Required fees: $2674; $36 per credit hour. $905 per semester. *Financial support:* Teaching assistantships with partial tuition reimbursements available. Financial award application deadline: 4/15; financial award applicants required to submit FAFSA. *Faculty research:* Literature-short story, comparative literature. *Unit head:* Dr. Wendell Aycock, Associate Dean, 806-742-2781 Ext. 228, E-mail: wendell.aycock@ttu.edu. *Application contact:* Graduate Adviser, 806-742-2781 Ext. 228.

Trinity Western University, School of Graduate Studies, Program in Interdisciplinary Humanities, Langley, BC V2Y 1Y1, Canada. Offers general humanities (MAIH); specialized (MAIH), including English, history, philosophy. Part-time programs available. *Degree requirements:* For master's, thesis or alternative, 36 semester hours. *Entrance requirements:* For master's, strong undergraduate degree in humanities or English, history or philosophy. Electronic applications accepted. *Faculty research:* Literary theory, gender, medieval and early modern literature, philosophy of religion, Thomas Merton's poetics.

Tulane University, School of Science and Engineering, Interdisciplinary PhD Program, New Orleans, LA 70118-5669. Offers PhD.

Union Institute & University, Master of Arts Program–Online, Montpelier, VT 05602. Offers creativity studies (MA); education (MA); health and wellness (MA); history and culture (MA); leadership, public policy, and social issues (MA); literature and writing (MA); psychology (MA). Part-time programs available. Postbaccalaureate distance learning degree programs offered (no on-campus study). *Faculty:* 2 full-time (1 woman), 18 part-time/adjunct (11 women). *Students:* 27 full-time (26 women), 119 part-time (98 women); includes 34 minority (25 Black or African American, non-Hispanic/Latino; 3 American Indian or Alaska Native, non-Hispanic/Latino; 6 Hispanic/Latino). Average age 40. In 2010, 26 master's awarded. *Degree requirements:* For master's, thesis. *Application deadline:* Applications are processed on a rolling basis. Application fee: $50. Electronic applications accepted. *Expenses:* Tuition: Full-time $16,430; part-time $685 per credit hour. Required fees: $174; $44 per term. Tuition and fees vary according to course load, degree level and program. *Financial support:* Career-related internships or fieldwork and tuition waivers available. Financial award applicants required to submit FAFSA. *Unit head:* Dr. Brian Webb, Program Director, 802-828-8777, E-mail: brian.webb@tui.edu. *Application contact:* Diane Robinson, Director of Admissions, 888-828-8575, E-mail: diane.robinson@myunion.edu.

Union Institute & University, PhD Program in Interdisciplinary Studies, Cincinnati, OH 45206-1925. Offers ethical and creative leadership (PhD), including Martin Luther King studies; humanities and culture (PhD), including Martin Luther King studies; public policy and social change (PhD), including Martin Luther King studies. Program requires participation in brief on-campus residencies twice each year (January and July). Postbaccalaureate distance learning degree programs offered (minimal on-campus study). *Faculty:* 4 full-time (1 woman), 14 part-time/adjunct (9 women). *Students:* 103 full-time (60 women), 3 part-time (1 woman); includes 42 minority (40 Black or African American, non-Hispanic/Latino; 1 American Indian or Alaska Native, non-Hispanic/Latino; 1 Hispanic/Latino). Average age 46. In 2010, 2 doctorates awarded. *Degree requirements:* For doctorate, comprehensive exam, thesis/dissertation. *Entrance requirements:* For doctorate, master's degree, letters of recommendation, interview. *Application deadline:* Applications are processed on a rolling basis. Application fee: $50. *Expenses:* Tuition: Full-time $16,430; part-time $685 per credit hour. Required fees: $174; $44 per term. Tuition and fees vary according to course load, degree level and program. *Financial support:* Federal Work-Study, scholarships/grants, and tuition waivers (partial) available. Financial award application deadline: 5/1; financial award applicants required to submit FAFSA. *Faculty research:* Social responsibility, ethical leadership, Martin Luther King studies. *Unit head:* Dr. Larry Preston, Dean, 513-861-6400 Ext. 1151, E-mail: larry.preston@myunion.edu. *Application contact:* Michelle Flick, Admissions Counselor, 800-486-3116 Ext. 1225.

The University of Alabama, Interdisciplinary Programs, Tuscaloosa, AL 35487. Offers PhD. *Faculty:* 2 full-time (0 women). *Students:* 6 full-time (2 women), 6 part-time (4 women); includes 3 minority (all Black or African American, non-Hispanic/Latino). Average age 39. 4 applicants, 25% accepted, 0 enrolled. *Expenses:* Tuition, state resident: full-time $7900. Tuition, nonresident: full-time $20,500. *Application contact:* Patrick D. Fuller, Senior Graduate Admissions Counselor, 205-348-5923, Fax: 205-348-0400, E-mail: patrick.d.fuller@ua.edu.

The University of Alabama at Birmingham, School of Engineering, Program in Interdisciplinary Engineering, Birmingham, AL 35294. Offers PhD. *Students:* 11 full-time (2 women), 7 part-time (0 women); includes 5 minority (4 Black or African American, non-Hispanic/Latino; 1 Hispanic/Latino), 6 international. Average age 33. 8 applicants, 100% accepted, 3 enrolled. *Degree requirements:* For doctorate, comprehensive exam, thesis/dissertation. *Entrance requirements:* For doctorate, GRE, undergraduate degree in a supporting field, official transcripts. Additional exam requirements/recommendations for international students: Required—TOEFL (minimum score 550 paper-based; 100 iBT). *Expenses:* Tuition, state resident: full-time $5482. Tuition, nonresident: full-time $12,430. Tuition and fees vary according to program. *Unit head:* Melinda Lalor, 205-934-8410. *Application contact:* Julie Bryant, Director of Graduate Admissions, 205-934-8227, Fax: 205-934-8413, E-mail: jbryant@uab.edu.

The University of Alabama in Huntsville, School of Graduate Studies, Interdisciplinary Studies, Huntsville, AL 35899. Offers MS, PhD, Certificate. Part-time and evening/weekend programs available. *Faculty:* 66 full-time (8 women), 7 part-time/adjunct (0 women). *Students:* 36 full-time (16 women), 31 part-time (7 women); includes 10 minority (7 Black or African American, non-Hispanic/Latino; 2 American Indian or Alaska Native, non-Hispanic/Latino; 1 Asian, non-Hispanic/Latino), 19 international. Average age 34. 78 applicants, 54% accepted, 32 enrolled. In 2010, 3 master's, 5 doctorates, 8 other advanced degrees awarded. *Degree requirements:* For master's, comprehensive exam, thesis or alternative, oral and written exams; for doctorate, comprehensive exam, thesis/dissertation, oral and written exams. *Entrance requirements:* For master's and doctorate, GRE General Test, minimum GPA of 3.0; for Certificate, GMAT (minimum score 500), minimum AACSB index of 1080. Additional exam requirements/recommendations for international students: Required—TOEFL (minimum score 500 paper-based; 173 computer-based; 62 iBT). *Application deadline:* For fall admission, 7/15 for domestic students, 4/1 for international students; for spring admission, 11/30 for domestic students, 9/1 for international students. Applications are processed on a rolling basis. Application fee: $40 ($50 for international students). Electronic applications accepted. *Expenses:* Tuition, state resident: full-time $7250; part-time $407.75 per credit hour. Tuition, nonresident: full-time $17,358; part-time $970.05 per credit hour. Required fees: $246.80 per semester. Tuition and fees vary according to course load and program. *Financial support:* In 2010–11, 32 students received support, including 14 research assistantships with full and partial tuition reimbursements available (averaging $13,049 per year), 18 teaching assistantships with full and partial tuition reimbursements available (averaging $11,208 per year); career-related internships or fieldwork, Federal Work-Study, institutionally sponsored loans, scholarships/grants, health care benefits, and unspecified assistantships also available. Support available to part-time students. Financial award application deadline: 4/1; financial award applicants required to submit FAFSA. *Faculty research:* Service discovery, laser technology, macromolecular materials, simulation interoperability, protein structure and function. Total annual research expenditures: $3.4 million. *Unit head:* Dr. Rhonda Kay Gaede, Dean of Graduate Studies, 256-824-6002, Fax: 256-824-6405, E-mail: rhonda.gaede@uah.edu. *Application contact:* Kathy Biggs, Graduate Studies Admissions Manager, 256-824-6199, Fax: 256-824-6405, E-mail: deangrad@uah.edu.

University of Alaska Anchorage, College of Arts and Sciences, Program in Interdisciplinary Studies, Anchorage, AK 99508. Offers MA, MS. Part-time programs available. *Entrance requirements:* For master's, GRE General Test, GRE Subject Test, minimum GPA of 3.0. Additional exam requirements/recommendations for international students: Required—TOEFL (minimum score 550 paper-based; 213 computer-based).

University of Alaska Fairbanks, Graduate School for Interdisciplinary Studies, Fairbanks, AK 99775-7560. Offers indigenous studies (PhD); interdisciplinary studies (MA, MS, PhD). Part-time programs available. *Students:* 2 full-time (both women), 18 part-time (14 women); includes 9 minority (7 American Indian or Alaska Native, non-Hispanic/Latino; 2 Two or more races, non-Hispanic/Latino). Average age 48. 25 applicants, 52% accepted, 13 enrolled. In 2010, 2 master's, 4 doctorates awarded. Terminal master's awarded for partial completion of doctoral program. *Degree requirements:* For master's, comprehensive exam (for some programs), thesis (for some programs); for doctorate, one foreign language, comprehensive exam, thesis/dissertation, oral defense, oral exam. *Entrance requirements:* For master's and doctorate, GRE General Test. Additional exam requirements/recommendations for international students: Required—TOEFL (minimum score 550 paper-based; 213 computer-based; 80 iBT). *Application deadline:* For fall admission, 6/1 for domestic students, 3/1 for international students; for spring admission, 10/15 for domestic students, 9/1 for international students. Applications are processed on a rolling basis. Application fee: $60. Electronic applications accepted. *Expenses:* Tuition, state resident: full-time $5688; part-time $316 per credit. Tuition, nonresident: full-time $11,628; part-time $646 per credit. Required fees: $289 per semester. Tuition and fees vary according to course load and reciprocity agreements. *Financial support:* In 2010–11, 1 teaching assistantship with tuition reimbursement (averaging $7,300 per year) was awarded; fellowships with tuition reimbursements, research assistantships with tuition reimbursements, career-related internships or fieldwork, Federal Work-Study, scholarships/grants, health care benefits, and unspecified assistantships also available. Support available to part-time students. Financial award application deadline: 2/15; financial award applicants required to submit FAFSA. *Unit head:* Lawrence Duffy, Interim Dean, 907-474-7716, Fax: 907-474-1984, E-mail: fyinds@uaf.edu. *Application contact:* Lawrence Duffy, Interim Dean, 907-474-7716, Fax: 907-474-1984, E-mail: fyinds@uaf.edu.

The University of Arizona, Graduate Interdisciplinary Programs, Tucson, AZ 85721. Offers American Indian studies (MA, PhD); applied mathematics (MS, PMS, PhD), including applied mathematics (MS, PhD), mathematical sciences (PMS); biomedical engineering (MS, PhD); cancer biology (PhD); entomology (MA); entomology and insect science (MS, PhD); genetics (MS, PhD); neuroscience (PhD); physiological sciences (MS, PhD); second language acquisition and teaching (PhD); statistics (MS, PhD); JD/MA. Part-time programs available. *Faculty:* 8 full-time (6 women). *Students:* 275 full-time (156 women), 61 part-time (27 women); includes 8 Black or African American, non-Hispanic/Latino; 9 American Indian or Alaska Native, non-Hispanic/Latino; 8 Asian, non-Hispanic/Latino; 27 Hispanic/Latino; 50 Two or more races, non-Hispanic/Latino, 59 international. Average age 36. 529 applicants, 31% accepted, 80 enrolled. In 2010, 42 master's, 42 doctorates awarded. *Entrance requirements:* Additional exam requirements/recommendations for international students: Required—TOEFL (minimum score 550 paper-based; 213 computer-based; 79 iBT). *Application deadline:* For fall admission, 2/1 for domestic students, 1/15 for international students. Application fee: $65. *Expenses:* Tuition, state resident: full-time $7692. *Financial support:* In 2010–11, 115 research assistantships with full tuition reimbursements (averaging $22,536 per year), 38 teaching assistantships with full tuition reimbursements (averaging $21,205 per year) were awarded; career-related internships or fieldwork, Federal Work-Study, institutionally sponsored loans, scholarships/grants, health care benefits, tuition waivers (full and partial), and unspecified assistantships also available. Support available to part-time students. Total annual research expenditures: $9.9 million. *Unit head:* Dr. Andrew Comrie, Dean, 520-621-3512, Fax: 520-621-4101, E-mail: gradadm@grad.arizona.edu. *Application contact:* Jolene M. Gruener, Associate Director, 520-621-8368, E-mail: gidp@email.arizona.edu.

University of Arkansas, Graduate School, Interdisciplinary Program in Comparative Literature and Cultural Studies, Fayetteville, AR 72701-1201. Offers MA, PhD. *Degree requirements:* For doctorate, 2 foreign languages, comprehensive exam, thesis/dissertation optional. *Entrance requirements:* For doctorate, GRE General Test, official transcripts of all undergraduate and graduate work, three letters of recommendation, writing sample, statement of purpose. Additional exam requirements/recommendations for international students: Required—TOEFL (minimum paper-based score 550, computer-based 213, iBT 80) or IELTS (6.5). Application fee: $40 ($50 for international students). *Financial support:* Fellowships, research assistantships, teaching assistantships, Federal Work-Study and institutionally sponsored loans available. *Faculty research:* Literary and cultural theory, cultural studies, postcolonial theory, gender studies, world literature. *Unit head:* Prof. M. Keith Booker, Director, 479-575-2951, Fax: 479-575-6795, E-mail: kbooker@uark.edu. *Application contact:* Graduate Admissions, 479-575-6246, Fax: 479-575-5908, E-mail: gradinfo@uark.edu.

University of Arkansas, Graduate School, Interdisciplinary Program in Environmental Dynamics, Fayetteville, AR 72701-1201. Offers PhD. *Students:* 2 full-time (both women), 21 part-time (11 women); includes 3 minority (all Black or African American, non-Hispanic/Latino), 4 international. 7 applicants, 71% accepted. In 2010, 5 doctorates awarded. *Degree requirements:* For doctorate, thesis/dissertation. *Application deadline:* For fall admission, 4/1 for international students; for spring admission, 10/1 for international students. Applications are processed on a rolling basis. Application fee: $40 ($50 for international students). Electronic applications accepted. *Financial support:* In 2010–11, 12 fellowships with tuition reimbursements, 4 research assistantships, 9 teaching assistantships were awarded. Financial award application deadline: 4/1. *Unit head:* Dr. Stephen Boss, Head, 479-575-6603, Fax: 479-575-3469, E-mail: sboss@uark.edu. *Application contact:* Graduate Admissions, 479-575-6246, Fax: 479-575-5908, E-mail: gradinfo@uark.edu.

The University of British Columbia, College for Interdisciplinary Studies, Vancouver, BC V6T 1Z1, Canada. Offers MA. Tuition charges are reported in Canadian dollars. *Expenses:* Tuition, area resident: Full-time $4179 Canadian dollars. International tuition: $7344 Canadian dollars full-time.

University of California, Santa Cruz, Division of Graduate Studies, Division of the Arts, Department of Music, Santa Cruz, CA 95064. Offers ethnomusicology (MA); music (PhD), including cross-cultural and interdisciplinary studies; music composition (MA, DMA), including world music composition (DMA); music composition (DMA), including computer-assisted (algorithmic) composition; performance practice (MA). *Students:* 21 full-time (6 women), 4 part-time (1 woman); includes 7 minority (1 Black or African American, non-Hispanic/Latino; 4 Asian, non-Hispanic/Latino; 1 Native Hawaiian or other Pacific Islander, non-Hispanic/Latino; 1 Two or more races, non-Hispanic/Latino), 4 international. Average age 36. 33 applicants, 36% accepted, 6 enrolled. In 2010, 6 master's, 1 doctorate awarded. *Degree requirements:* For master's, one foreign language, thesis, recital; for doctorate, one foreign language, thesis/dissertation, qualifying and final examinations. *Entrance requirements:* For master's, GRE General Test, 3 letters of recommendation, writing or composition sample, 10-20 minute unedited recording; for doctorate, GRE General Test, 3 letters of recommendation, writing sample. Additional exam requirements/recommendations for international students: Required—TOEFL (minimum score 550 paper-based; 220 computer-based; 83 iBT); Recommended—IELTS (minimum score 8). *Application deadline:* For fall admission, 1/5 for domestic and international students. Application fee: $70 ($90 for international students). Electronic applications accepted. *Financial support:* Fellowships, research assistantships, teaching assistantships, institutionally sponsored loans and tuition waivers available. Financial award applicants required to submit FAFSA. *Faculty research:* Western music history, new music, composition, ethnomusicology, musicology. *Unit head:* Laura McShane, Graduate Program Coordinator, 831-459-3199, E-mail: lmcshane@ucsc.edu. *Application contact:* Laura McShane, Graduate Program Coordinator, 831-459-3199, E-mail: lmcshane@ucsc.edu.

University of Central Florida, College of Graduate Studies, Program in Interdisciplinary Studies, Orlando, FL 32816. Offers MA, MS. *Students:* 10 full-time (5 women), 17 part-time (9 women); includes 1 Asian, non-Hispanic/Latino; 3 Hispanic/Latino. Average age 32. 28 applicants, 75% accepted, 16 enrolled. In 2010, 9 master's awarded. *Degree requirements:* For master's, thesis or alternative. *Entrance requirements:* For master's, GRE General Test, minimum GPA of 3.0 in last 60 hours. Additional exam requirements/recommendations for international students: Required—TOEFL. Application fee: $30. Electronic applications accepted. *Expenses:* Tuition, state resident: part-time $256.56 per credit hour. Tuition, nonresident: part-time $1011.52 per credit hour. Part-time tuition and fees vary according to program. *Financial support:* In 2010–11, 4 students received support, including 2 fellowships (averaging $10,000 per year), 2 teaching assistantships (averaging $8,000 per year). *Unit head:* Dr. Michael Hampton, Director, 407-823-2136, E-mail: mhampton@mail.ucf.edu. *Application contact:* Dr. Michael Hampton, Director, 407-823-2136, E-mail: mhampton@mail.ucf.edu.

University of Chicago, Division of Biological Sciences, The Interdisciplinary Scientist Training Program, Chicago, IL 60637-1513. Offers PhD. *Degree requirements:* For doctorate, thesis/dissertation, ethics class, 2 teaching assistantships. *Entrance requirements:* Additional exam requirements/recommendations for international students: Required—TOEFL (minimum score 600 paper-based; 250 computer-based; 104 iBT), IELTS (minimum score 7). Electronic applications accepted.

University of Cincinnati, Graduate School, McMicken College of Arts and Sciences, Interdisciplinary Studies Program, Cincinnati, OH 45221. Offers PhD. *Entrance requirements:* For doctorate, GRE General Test. Electronic applications accepted.

University of Denver, School of Engineering and Computer Science, Department of Mechanical and Materials Engineering, Denver, CO 80208. Offers bioengineering (MS); engineering (MS, PhD); interdisciplinary engineering (PhD); materials science (MS, PhD); mechanical engineering (MS, PhD); nanoscale science and engineering (PhD). Part-time programs available. *Faculty:* 8 full-time (1 woman), 5 part-time/adjunct (1 woman). *Students:* 3 full-time (1 woman), 21 part-time (5 women), 7 international. Average age 33. 63 applicants, 65% accepted, 5 enrolled. In 2010, 5 master's, 1 doctorate awarded. Terminal master's awarded for partial completion of doctoral program. *Degree requirements:* For master's, thesis or alternative; for doctorate, comprehensive exam, thesis/dissertation. *Entrance requirements:* For master's and doctorate, GRE General Test. Additional exam requirements/recommendations for international students: Required—TOEFL (minimum score 550 paper-based; 80 iBT). *Application deadline:* Applications are processed on a rolling basis. Application fee: $60. Electronic applications accepted. *Expenses:* Tuition: Full-time $35,604; part-time $29,670 per year. Required fees: $687 per year. Tuition and fees vary according to program. *Financial support:* In 2010–11, 7 research assistantships with full and partial tuition reimbursements (averaging $10,795 per year), 5 teaching assistantships with full and partial tuition reimbursements (averaging $13,230 per year) were awarded; Federal Work-Study, scholarships/grants, and unspecified assistantships also available. Financial award applicants required to submit FAFSA. *Faculty research:* Aerosols, biomechanics, composite materials, photo optics, drug delivery. *Unit head:* Dr. Daniel Armentrout, Chair, 303-871-3580, Fax: 303-871-4450, E-mail: darmentr@du.edu. *Application contact:* Renee Carvalho, Assistant to the Chair, 303-871-2107, Fax: 303-871-4450, E-mail: renee.carvalho@du.edu.

University of Houston–Victoria, School of Arts and Sciences, Program in Interdisciplinary Studies, Victoria, TX 77901-4450. Offers MAIS. Part-time and evening/weekend programs available. Postbaccalaureate distance learning degree programs offered (minimal on-campus study). *Students:* 36 full-time (21 women), 62 part-time (44 women); includes 16 Black or African American, non-Hispanic/Latino; 10 Asian, non-Hispanic/Latino; 17 Hispanic/Latino, 1 international. Average age 33. 54 applicants, 80% accepted, 29 enrolled. In 2010, 16 master's awarded. *Degree requirements:* For master's, comprehensive exam or thesis. *Entrance requirements:* For master's, GRE General Test. Additional exam requirements/recommendations for international students: Required—TOEFL (minimum score 550 paper-based; 213 computer-based). *Application deadline:* For fall admission, 6/1 for international students; for spring admission, 10/1 for international students. Applications are processed on a rolling basis. Application fee: $0. Electronic applications accepted. *Expenses:* Tuition, state resident: full-time $4050; part-time $225 per credit hour. Tuition, nonresident: full-time $8730; part-time $485 per credit hour. Required fees: $810; $54 per credit hour. Tuition and fees vary according to course load. *Financial support:* In 2010–11, research assistantships with partial tuition reimbursements (averaging $2,000 per year), teaching assistantships with partial tuition reimbursements (averaging $2,000 per year) were awarded; Federal Work-Study, scholarships/grants, and unspecified assistantships also available. Support available to part-time students. Financial award application deadline: 4/15. *Unit head:* Dr. Horace Fairlamb, 361-570-4204, Fax: 361-570-4229, E-mail: fairlambh@uhv.edu. *Application contact:* Tracey Fox, Director of Services, 361-570-4233, Fax: 361-580-5507, E-mail: foxt@uhv.edu.

University of Idaho, College of Graduate Studies, Department of Bioregional Planning and Community Design, Moscow, ID 83844-2282. Offers MS. *Faculty:* 5 full-time, 1 part-time/adjunct. *Students:* 23 full-time, 2 part-time. Average age 30. In 2010, 3 master's awarded. *Application deadline:* Applications are processed on a rolling basis. Application fee: $60. Electronic applications accepted. *Expenses:* Tuition, nonresident: part-time $580 per credit. Required fees: $306 per credit. *Financial support:* Applicants required to submit FAFSA. *Faculty research:* Environment and behavior interaction, geographic trade, design development, economic development, natural resource policy. *Unit head:* Mark Hoversten, Dean, 208-885-7448, E-mail: bioregionalplanning@uidaho.edu. *Application contact:* Mark Hoversten, Dean, 208-885-7448, E-mail: bioregionalplanning@uidaho.edu.

University of Idaho, College of Graduate Studies, Program in Interdisciplinary Studies, Moscow, ID 83844-2282. Offers MA, MS. *Students:* 3 full-time, 2 part-time. Average age 37. In 2010, 1 master's awarded. *Entrance requirements:* For master's, minimum GPA of 2.8. *Application deadline:* For fall admission, 8/1 for domestic students; for spring admission, 12/15 for domestic students. Applications are processed on a rolling basis. Application fee: $60. Electronic applications accepted. *Expenses:* Tuition, nonresident: part-time $580 per credit. Required fees: $306 per credit. *Financial support:* Applicants required to submit FAFSA. *Unit head:* Dr. Nilsa Bosque-Perez, Interim Dean of Graduate Studies, 208-885-6243, E-mail: uigrad@uidaho.edu. *Application contact:* Dr. Nilsa Bosque-Perez, Interim Dean of Graduate Studies, 208-885-6243, E-mail: uigrad@uidaho.edu.

University of Illinois at Springfield, Graduate Programs, College of Liberal Arts and Sciences, Individual Option Program, Springfield, IL 62703-5407. Offers MA. Part-time and evening/weekend programs available. *Degree requirements:* For master's, project or thesis. *Entrance requirements:* For master's, 2 letters of reference, interview. Additional exam requirements/recommendations for international students: Required—TOEFL (minimum score 500 paper-based; 176 computer-based; 61 iBT). *Expenses:* Tuition, state resident: full-time $6774; part-time $282.25 per credit hour. Tuition, nonresident: full-time $15,078; part-time $628.25 per credit hour. Required fees: $15.25 per credit hour. $492 per term.

The University of Kansas, University of Kansas Medical Center, School of Medicine, Interdisciplinary Graduate Program in Biomedical Sciences (IGPBS), Kansas City, KS 66160. Offers MA, MPH, MS, PhD, MD/MPH, MD/MS, MD/PhD. *Students:* 21 full-time (13 women), 9 international. Average age 25. 222 applicants, 18% accepted, 21 enrolled.Terminal master's awarded for partial completion of doctoral program. *Degree requirements:* For master's, thesis; for doctorate, comprehensive exam, thesis/dissertation. *Entrance requirements:* For master's and doctorate, GRE. Additional exam requirements/recommendations for international students: Required—TOEFL. *Application deadline:* For fall admission, 1/15 priority date for domestic and international students. Applications are processed on a rolling basis. Application fee: $0. Electronic applications accepted. *Expenses:* Tuition, state resident: full-time $7092; part-time $295.50 per credit hour. Tuition, nonresident: full-time $16,590; part-time $691.25 per credit hour. Required fees: $858; $71.49 per credit hour. Tuition and fees vary according to course load, campus/location and program. *Financial support:* Research assistantships with full tuition reimbursements, teaching assistantships with full tuition reimbursements, scholarships/grants and unspecified assistantships available. Financial award application deadline: 2/14; financial award applicants required to submit FAFSA. *Faculty research:* Cardiovascular biology, neurosciences, signal transduction and cancer biology, molecular biology and genetics, developmental biology. *Unit head:* Dr. Michael J. Werle, Director, 913-588-7491, Fax: 913-588-2710, E-mail: mwerle@kumc.edu. *Application contact:* Miranda Olenhouse, Coordinator, 913-588-2719, Fax: 913-588-2711, E-mail: molenhouse@kumc.edu.

University of Louisville, School of Interdisciplinary and Graduate Studies, Louisville, KY 40292. Offers MA, MS, PhD. Part-time and evening/weekend programs available. *Students:* 9 full-time (5 women), 8 part-time (4 women); includes 2 Black or African American, non-Hispanic/Latino; 1 Asian, non-Hispanic/Latino. Average age 33. 27 applicants, 70% accepted, 10 enrolled. In 2010, 3 master's awarded. Terminal master's awarded for partial completion of doctoral program. *Degree requirements:* For master's, thesis (for some programs); for doctorate, thesis/dissertation. *Entrance requirements:* For master's, GRE General Test, baccalaureate degree, minimum GPA of 3.0; for doctorate, GRE General Test, minimum GPA of 3.0. Additional exam requirements/recommendations for international students: Required—TOEFL (minimum score 550 paper-based; 213 computer-based; 79 iBT), IELTS (minimum score 6.5). *Application deadline:* For fall admission, 5/1 for international students; for spring admission, 11/1 for international students. Applications are processed on a rolling basis. Application fee: $50. Electronic applications accepted. *Expenses:* Tuition, state resident: full-time $9144; part-time $508 per credit hour. Tuition, nonresident: full-time $19,026; part-time $1057 per credit hour. Tuition and fees vary according to program and reciprocity agreements. *Financial support:* In 2010–11, 61 fellowships with full tuition reimbursements (averaging $18,068 per year) were awarded; career-related internships or fieldwork, Federal Work-Study, institutionally sponsored loans, scholarships/grants, health care benefits, and tuition waivers (full and partial) also available. Financial award application deadline: 2/1; financial award applicants required to submit FAFSA. *Unit head:* Dr. Beth A. Boehm, Interim Dean/Associate Provost for Faculty Personnel/Professor of English, 502-852-6590, Fax: 502-852-6616, E-mail: beth.boehm@louisville.edu. *Application contact:* Libby Leggett, Executive Director of Graduate Admissions and Recruitment, 502-852-3108, Fax: 502-852-3111, E-mail: melegg02@louisville.edu.

University of Maine, Graduate School, Interdisciplinary Doctoral Program, Orono, ME 04469. Offers communication (PhD); functional genomics (PhD); mass communication (PhD); ocean engineering (PhD). Part-time and evening/weekend programs available. *Students:* 22 full-time (13 women), 25 part-time (14 women); includes 2 minority (1 Black or African American, non-Hispanic/Latino; 1 Asian, non-Hispanic/Latino), 4 international. Average age 37. 17 applicants, 41% accepted, 7 enrolled. In 2010, 10 doctorates awarded. *Degree requirements:* For doctorate, comprehensive exam, thesis/dissertation. *Entrance requirements:* For doctorate, GRE General Test. Additional exam requirements/recommendations for international students: Required—TOEFL. *Application deadline:* For fall admission, 4/1 for domestic students; for spring admission, 11/1 for domestic students. Applications are processed on a rolling basis. Application fee: $65. Electronic applications accepted. *Expenses:* Tuition, state resident: full-time $400. Tuition, nonresident: full-time $1050. *Unit head:* Scott G. Delcourt, Associate Dean of the Graduate School, 207-581-3291, Fax: 207-581-3232, E-mail: graduate@maine.edu. *Application contact:* Scott G. Delcourt, Associate Dean of the Graduate School, 207-581-3291, Fax: 207-581-3232, E-mail: graduate@maine.edu.

University of Maine, Graduate School, Interdisciplinary Program in Information Systems, Orono, ME 04469. Offers MS. Part-time programs available. *Faculty:* 4 full-time (1 woman), 3 part-time/adjunct (1 woman). *Students:* 2 full-time (0 women), 1 part-time (0 women); includes 1 minority (Hispanic/Latino). Average age 30. 8 applicants, 50% accepted, 3 enrolled. In 2010, 1 master's awarded. *Entrance requirements:* For master's, GRE General Test or GMAT. Additional exam requirements/recommendations for international students: Required—TOEFL. *Application deadline:* For fall admission, 2/1 priority date for domestic students. Applications are processed on a rolling basis. Application fee: $65. Electronic applications accepted. *Expenses:* Tuition, state resident: full-time $400. Tuition, nonresident: full-time $1050. *Financial support:* In 2010–11, 4 teaching assistantships with tuition reimbursements (averaging $12,790 per year) were awarded; Federal Work-Study also available. *Unit head:* Dr. Owen Smith, Associate Dean of the Graduate School, 207-581-4358, Fax: 207-581-4357, E-mail: graduate@maine.edu. *Application contact:* Dr. Owen Smith, Associate Dean of the Graduate School, 207-581-4358, Fax: 207-581-4357, E-mail: graduate@maine.edu.

University of Manitoba, Faculty of Graduate Studies, Interdisciplinary Programs, Individual Interdisciplinary Programs, Winnipeg, MB R3T 2N2, Canada. Offers M Sc, MA, PhD.

University of Massachusetts Worcester, Graduate School of Biomedical Sciences, Worcester, MA 01655-0115. Offers biochemistry and molecular pharmacology (PhD); bioinformatics and computational biology (PhD); cancer biology (PhD); cell biology (PhD); clinical and population health research (PhD); clinical investigation (MS); immunology and virology (PhD); interdisciplinary graduate program (PhD); molecular genetics and microbiology (PhD); neuroscience (PhD); DVM/PhD; MD/PhD. *Faculty:* 1,059 full-time (357 women), 145 part-time/adjunct (100 women). *Students:* 438 full-time (239 women), 1 (woman) part-time; includes 44 minority (9 Black or African American, non-Hispanic/Latino; 31 Asian, non-Hispanic/Latino; 4 Hispanic/Latino), 148 international. Average age 29. 687 applicants, 28% accepted, 116 enrolled. In 2010, 6 master's, 45 doctorates awarded. Terminal master's awarded for partial completion of doctoral program. *Degree requirements:* For master's, thesis; for doctorate, thesis/dissertation. *Entrance requirements:* For master's, bachelor's degree; for doctorate, GRE General Test, MS, MA, or MPH (for some programs). Additional exam requirements/recommendations for international students: Required—TOEFL (minimum score 600 paper-based; 250 computer-based). *Application deadline:* For fall admission, 12/15 for domestic and international students; for winter admission, 1/15 for domestic students; for spring admission, 5/15 for domestic students. Application fee: $35. Electronic applications accepted. *Expenses:* Contact institution. *Financial support:* In 2010–11, 439 students received support, including 439 research assistantships with full tuition reimbursements available (averaging $28,350 per year); scholarships/grants, health care benefits, tuition waivers (full), and unspecified assistantships also available. Financial award application deadline: 4/20. *Faculty research:* RNA interference, gene therapy, cell biology, bioinformatics, clinical research. Total annual research expenditures: $232 million. *Unit head:* Dr. Anthony Carruthers, Dean, 508-856-4135, E-mail: anthony.carruthers@umassmed.edu. *Application contact:* Dr. Kendall Knight, Associate Dean and Interim Director of Admissions and Recruitment, 508-856-5628, Fax: 508-856-3659, E-mail: kendall.knight@umassmed.edu.

University of Medicine and Dentistry of New Jersey, School of Health Related Professions, Department of Interdisciplinary Studies, Program in Health Sciences, Newark, NJ 07107-1709.

Interdisciplinary Studies

University of Medicine and Dentistry of New Jersey (continued)
Offers cardiopulmonary sciences (PhD); clinical laboratory sciences (PhD); health sciences (MS); interdisciplinary studies (PhD); nutrition (PhD); physical therapy/movement science (PhD). Part-time and evening/weekend programs available. Postbaccalaureate distance learning degree programs offered (no on-campus study). *Students:* 6 full-time (4 women), 125 part-time (94 women); includes 12 Black or African American, non-Hispanic/Latino; 5 Asian, non-Hispanic/ Latino; 8 Hispanic/Latino, 5 international. Average age 40. 78 applicants, 46% accepted, 29 enrolled. In 2010, 14 master's, 2 doctorates awarded. *Degree requirements:* For doctorate, thesis/dissertation. *Entrance requirements:* For doctorate, interview, writing sample. Additional exam requirements/recommendations for international students: Required—TOEFL. *Application deadline:* For fall admission, 3/1 for domestic students. Applications are processed on a rolling basis. Application fee: $50. Electronic applications accepted. *Unit head:* Dr. Margaret Kildoff, Director, 973-972-4989, Fax: 973-972-7854, E-mail: ms-phd-hs@umdnj.edu. *Application contact:* Douglas Lomonaco, Assistant Dean, 973-972-5454, Fax: 973-972-7463, E-mail: shrpadm@umdnj.edu.

University of Memphis, Graduate School, College of Arts and Sciences, Department of Earth Sciences, Memphis, TN 38152. Offers archaeology (MS); earth sciences (PhD); geographic information systems (Graduate Certificate); geography (MA, MS); geology (MS); geophysics (MS); interdisciplinary (MS). Part-time and evening/weekend programs available. *Faculty:* 15 full-time (3 women), 6 part-time/adjunct (2 women). *Students:* 35 full-time (7 women), 28 part-time (13 women); includes 5 Black or African American, non-Hispanic/Latino; 1 Asian, non-Hispanic/Latino, 15 international. Average age 33. 48 applicants, 69% accepted, 18 enrolled. In 2010, 2 master's, 2 doctorates, 1 other advanced degree awarded. Terminal master's awarded for partial completion of doctoral program. *Degree requirements:* For master's, comprehensive exam, thesis, seminar presentation; for doctorate, thesis/dissertation. *Entrance requirements:* For master's, GRE General Test, 3 letters of recommendation, statement of research interests; for doctorate, GRE General Test, 2 letters of recommendation, resume, personal statement. Additional exam requirements/recommendations for international students: Required—TOEFL (minimum score 550 paper-based; 210 computer-based). *Application deadline:* For fall admission, 1/31 for domestic students; for spring admission, 11/1 for domestic students. Applications are processed on a rolling basis. Application fee: $35 ($60 for international students). Electronic applications accepted. *Financial support:* In 2010–11, 18 students received support; fellowships with full tuition reimbursements available, research assistantships with full tuition reimbursements available, teaching assistantships with full tuition reimbursements available, Federal Work-Study, scholarships/grants, and unspecified assistantships available. Financial award application deadline: 2/15; financial award applicants required to submit FAFSA. *Faculty research:* Hazards, active tectonics, geophysics, hydrology and water resources, spatial analysis. *Unit head:* Dr. M. Jerry Bartholomew, Chair, 901-678-4536, Fax: 901-678-4467, E-mail: jbrthlm1@memphis.edu. *Application contact:* Dr. Arlene Hill, Associate Professor and Graduate Program Coordinator, 901-678-4358, Fax: 901-678-2178, E-mail: dlarsen@memphis.edu.

University of Minnesota, Twin Cities Campus, Graduate School, College of Liberal Arts, Department of Cultural Studies and Comparative Literature, Program in Comparative Studies in Discourse and Society, Minneapolis, MN 55455-0213. Offers PhD. *Degree requirements:* For doctorate, 2 foreign languages, thesis/dissertation. *Entrance requirements:* For doctorate, GRE General Test, sample of written work. Additional exam requirements/recommendations for international students: Required—TOEFL. *Faculty research:* Cultural theory; music; architecture, space, and urbanism; body and gender; film and popular culture.

University of Missouri–Kansas City, School of Graduate Studies, Kansas City, MO 64110-2499. Offers interdisciplinary studies (PhD), including art history, cell biology and biophysics, chemistry, computer and electrical engineering, computer science and informatics, economics, education, engineering, English, entrepreneurship and innovation, geosciences, history, mathematics and statistics, molecular biology and biochemistry, music education, oral biology, pharmaceutical sciences, pharmacology, physics, political science, psychology, public affairs and administration, religious studies, social science consortium, sociology, telecommunications and computer networking, urban leadership and policy studies in education. *Students:* 73 full-time (32 women), 316 part-time (127 women); includes 32 minority (16 Black or African American, non-Hispanic/Latino; 9 Asian, non-Hispanic/Latino; 6 Hispanic/Latino; 1 Two or more races, non-Hispanic/Latino), 169 international. Average age 35. 335 applicants, 26% accepted, 69 enrolled. In 2010, 32 doctorates awarded. *Degree requirements:* For doctorate, comprehensive exam, thesis/dissertation, residency. *Entrance requirements:* For doctorate, GRE General Test, minimum GPA of 2.75 (undergraduate), 3.0 (graduate). Additional exam requirements/recommendations for international students: Required—TOEFL (minimum score 550 paper-based; 213 computer-based; 80 iBT), TWE (minimum score 4). *Application deadline:* For fall admission, 1/15 priority date for domestic and international students. Applications are processed on a rolling basis. Application fee: $45 ($50 for international students). Electronic applications accepted. *Expenses:* Tuition, state resident: full-time $5522.40; part-time $306.80 per credit hour. Tuition, nonresident: full-time $7128; part-time $792 per credit hour. Required fees: $261.15 per term. *Financial support:* Career-related internships or fieldwork, Federal Work-Study, tuition waivers (partial), and unspecified assistantships available. Support available to part-time students. Financial award application deadline: 3/1; financial award applicants required to submit FAFSA. *Unit head:* Dr. Ronald MacQuarrie, Dean, 816-235-1301, Fax: 816-235-1310, E-mail: macquarrier@umkc.edu. *Application contact:* Qunicy Bennett Johnson, Administrative Assistant, 816-235-1559, Fax: 816-235-1310, E-mail: bennettq@umkc.edu.

University of Missouri–St. Louis, College of Arts and Sciences, Interdisciplinary Programs, St. Louis, MO 63121. Offers gender studies (Certificate); international studies (Certificate). *Expenses:* Tuition, state resident: full-time $5522; part-time $306.80 per credit hour. Tuition, nonresident: full-time $14,253; part-time $792.10 per credit hour. Required fees: $658; $49 per credit hour. One-time fee: $12. Tuition and fees vary according to program. *Unit head:* Dr. Ronald Yasbin, Dean, 314-516-5501. *Application contact:* Graduate Admissions, 314-516-5458, Fax: 314-516-6996, E-mail: gradadm@umsl.edu.

The University of Montana, Graduate School, Program in Interdisciplinary Studies, Missoula, MT 59812-0002. Offers individual interdisciplinary programs (IIP) (PhD); interdisciplinary studies (MIS). *Degree requirements:* For doctorate, thesis/dissertation. *Entrance requirements:* For master's, GRE General Test. Additional exam requirements/recommendations for international students: Required—TOEFL.

University of New Brunswick Fredericton, School of Graduate Studies, Interdisciplinary Studies Program, Fredericton, NB E3B 5A3, Canada. Offers M IDST, PhD. *Faculty:* 44 full-time (32 women), 13 part-time/adjunct (8 women). *Students:* 39 full-time (32 women), 10 part-time (6 women). In 2010, 3 master's, 2 doctorates awarded. *Degree requirements:* For master's, thesis; for doctorate, comprehensive exam, thesis/dissertation. *Entrance requirements:* For master's, BA honours degree with minimum A- average, minimum GPA of 3.3; for doctorate, master's degree with thesis; minimum A- average. Additional exam requirements/recommendations for international students: Required—TWE (minimum score 4), TOEFL (minimum score 600 paper-based; 250 computer-based; 100 iBT) or IELTS (minimum score 7). Application fee: $50 Canadian dollars. *Expenses:* Tuition, area resident: Full-time $3708; part-time $927 per term. International tuition: $6300 full-time. Required fees: $50 per term. *Financial support:* In 2010–11, 8 fellowships, 10 research assistantships, 5 teaching assistantships were awarded. *Unit head:* Dr. Linda Eyre, Assistant Dean of Graduate Studies, 506-447-3044, Fax: 506-453-4817, E-mail: gradidst@unb.ca. *Application contact:* Janet Amirault, Graduate Secretary, 506-458-7558, Fax: 506-453-4817, E-mail: jamiraul@unb.ca.

The University of North Carolina at Charlotte, Graduate School, College of Arts and Sciences, Program in Interdisciplinary Studies, Charlotte, NC 28223-0001. Offers gerontology (MA, Certificate); Latin American studies (MA); liberal studies (MA); women's studies (Certificate). *Faculty:* 2 full-time (1 woman), 2 part-time/adjunct (both women). *Students:* 15 full-time (14 women), 53 part-time (39 women); includes 20 minority (11 Black or African American, non-Hispanic/Latino; 8 Hispanic/Latino; 1 Two or more races, non-Hispanic/Latino), 5 international. Average age 30. 24 applicants, 96% accepted, 15 enrolled. In 2010, 16 master's awarded. *Degree requirements:* For master's, thesis optional, comprehensive exam or project. *Entrance requirements:* For master's, GRE General Test or MAT, minimum GPA of 3.0 during previous 2 years, 2.75 overall. Additional exam requirements/recommendations for international students: Required—TOEFL (minimum score 557 paper-based; 220 computer-based; 83 iBT). *Application deadline:* For fall admission, 7/1 for domestic students, 5/1 for international students; for spring admission, 11/1 for domestic students, 10/1 for international students. Applications are processed on a rolling basis. Application fee: $55. Electronic applications accepted. *Expenses:* Tuition, state resident: full-time $3464. Tuition, nonresident: full-time $14,297. Required fees: $2094. Tuition and fees vary according to course load. *Financial support:* In 2010–11, 7 students received support, including 2 research assistantships (averaging $3,025 per year), 5 teaching assistantships (averaging $7,950 per year); career-related internships or fieldwork, institutionally sponsored loans, scholarships/grants, and unspecified assistantships also available. Support available to part-time students. Financial award application deadline: 4/1; financial award applicants required to submit FAFSA. *Unit head:* Dr. Paula Eckard, Interim Director, 704-687-4309, Fax: 704-687-4347, E-mail: pgeckard@uncc.edu. *Application contact:* Kathy B. Giddings, Director of Graduate Admissions, 704-687-5503, Fax: 704-687-3279, E-mail: gradadm@uncc.edu.

University of Northern British Columbia, Office of Graduate Studies, Prince George, BC V2N 4Z9, Canada. Offers business administration (Diploma); community health science (M Sc); disability management (MA); education (M Ed); first nations studies (MA); gender studies (MA); history (MA); interdisciplinary studies (MA); international studies (MA); mathematical, computer and physical sciences (M Sc); natural resources and environmental studies (M Sc, MA, MNRES, PhD); political science (MA); psychology (M Sc, PhD); social work (MSW). Part-time and evening/weekend programs available. Postbaccalaureate distance learning degree programs offered (no on-campus study). *Degree requirements:* For master's, thesis; for doctorate, thesis/dissertation. *Entrance requirements:* For master's, GRE, minimum B average in undergraduate course work; for doctorate, candidacy exam, minimum A average in graduate course work.

University of North Texas, Toulouse Graduate School, Interdisciplinary Studies, Denton, TX 76203. Offers MA, MS. Part-time programs available. *Degree requirements:* For master's, comprehensive exam, thesis optional. *Entrance requirements:* For master's, GRE General Test, minimum GPA of 2.8, 3 letters of reference. Additional exam requirements/recommendations for international students: Recommended—TOEFL (minimum score 550 paper-based; 213 computer-based; 79 iBT). *Application deadline:* Applications are processed on a rolling basis. Electronic applications accepted. *Expenses:* Tuition, state resident: full-time $4298; part-time $239 per credit hour. Tuition, nonresident: full-time $10,782; part-time $549 per credit hour. Required fees: $1292; $270 per credit hour. *Financial support:* Fellowships, career-related internships or fieldwork, Federal Work-Study, and institutionally sponsored loans available. Financial award application deadline: 4/1; financial award applicants required to submit FAFSA.

University of Oklahoma, Graduate College, Program in Interdisciplinary Studies, Norman, OK 73019-0390. Offers MA, MS, PhD. Part-time and evening/weekend programs available. *Students:* 117 full-time (46 women), 463 part-time (172 women); includes 99 minority (42 Black or African American, non-Hispanic/Latino; 6 American Indian or Alaska Native, non-Hispanic/ Latino; 15 Asian, non-Hispanic/Latino; 28 Hispanic/Latino; 3 Native Hawaiian or other Pacific Islander, non-Hispanic/Latino; 5 Two or more races, non-Hispanic/Latino), 5 international. Average age 34. 135 applicants, 93% accepted, 70 enrolled. In 2010, 132 master's, 6 doctorates awarded. *Entrance requirements:* Additional exam requirements/recommendations for international students: Recommended—TOEFL (minimum score 550 paper-based; 213 computer-based; 79 iBT). *Application deadline:* For fall admission, 6/1 for domestic students, 4/1 for international students; for spring admission, 11/1 for domestic students, 9/1 for international students. Applications are processed on a rolling basis. Application fee: $40 ($90 for international students). Electronic applications accepted. *Expenses:* Tuition, state resident: full-time $3893; part-time $162.20 per credit hour. Tuition, nonresident: full-time $14,167; part-time $590.30 per credit hour. Required fees: $2523; $94.60 per credit hour. Tuition and fees vary according to course load and degree level. *Financial support:* In 2010–11, 53 students received support, including 11 research assistantships (averaging $10,070 per year); tuition waivers (full and partial) and unspecified assistantships also available. Financial award applicants required to submit FAFSA. Total annual research expenditures: $164,726. *Unit head:* Lee Williams, Dean, 405-325-3811, Fax: 405-325-5346, E-mail: lwilliams@ou.edu. *Application contact:* Angela Castillo, Academic Counselor II, 405-325-3841, Fax: 405-325-5346, E-mail: acastillo@ou.edu.

University of Oregon, Graduate School, Interdisciplinary Program in Applied Information Management, Eugene, OR 97403. Offers MS. Part-time and evening/weekend programs available. *Degree requirements:* For master's, project. *Entrance requirements:* For master's, GMAT, GRE, or MAT. Additional exam requirements/recommendations for international students: Required—TOEFL. Electronic applications accepted. *Expenses:* Contact institution. *Faculty research:* Business management, information design.

University of Ottawa, Faculty of Graduate and Postdoctoral Studies, Interdisciplinary Programs, Ottawa, ON K1N 6N5, Canada. Offers e-business (Certificate); e-commerce (Certificate); finance (Certificate); health services and policies research (Diploma); population health (PhD); population health risk assessment and management (Certificate); public management and governance (Certificate); systems science (Certificate).

University of Pittsburgh, School of Medicine, Graduate Programs in Medicine, Interdisciplinary Biomedical Sciences Program, Pittsburgh, PA 15260. Offers PhD. *Faculty:* 301 full-time (78 women). *Students:* 28 full-time (20 women); includes 1 Asian, non-Hispanic/Latino; 1 Hispanic/ Latino; 1 Two or more races, non-Hispanic/Latino, 8 international. Average age 27. 486 applicants, 14% accepted, 28 enrolled. In 2010, 43 doctorates awarded. *Degree requirements:* For doctorate, comprehensive exam, thesis/dissertation. *Entrance requirements:* For doctorate, GRE General Test, GRE Subject Test, minimum QPA of 3.0. Additional exam requirements/ recommendations for international students: Required—TOEFL (minimum score 600 paper-based; 100 iBT), IELTS (minimum score 7). *Application deadline:* For fall admission, 12/15 priority date for domestic and international students. Application fee: $50. Electronic applications accepted. *Expenses:* Tuition, state resident: full-time $17,304; part-time $701 per credit. Tuition, nonresident: full-time $29,554; part-time $1210 per credit. Required fees: $740; $214 per term. Tuition and fees vary according to program. *Financial support:* In 2010–11, 28 research assistantships with full tuition reimbursements (averaging $25,500 per year) were awarded; teaching assistantships, institutionally sponsored loans, scholarships/grants, traineeships, and unspecified assistantships also available. *Faculty research:* Cell biology and molecular physiology, cellular and molecular pathology, immunology, molecular genetics and developmental biology, molecular pharmacology and molecular virology and microbiology. *Unit head:* Dr. John P. Horn, Associate Dean for Graduate Studies, 412-648-8957, Fax: 412-648-1077, E-mail: gradstudies@medschool.pitt.edu. *Application contact:* Graduate Studies Administrator, 412-648-8957, Fax: 412-648-1077, E-mail: gradstudies@medschool.pitt.edu.

The University of South Dakota, Graduate School, Interdisciplinary Studies Program, Vermillion, SD 57069-2390. Offers interdisciplinary studies (MA). Part-time programs available. Postbaccalaureate distance learning degree programs offered. *Degree requirements:* For master's, thesis or alternative. *Entrance requirements:* For master's, minimum GPA of 2.7; supplemental packet. Additional exam requirements/recommendations for international students: Required—TOEFL (minimum score 550 paper-based; 213 computer-based; 79 iBT). Electronic applications accepted.

University of South Florida, Graduate School, College of Marine Science, Saint Petersburg, FL 33701. Offers biological oceanography (MS, PhD); chemical oceanography (MS, PhD); geological oceanography (MS, PhD); interdisciplinary (MS, PhD); marine resource assessment (MS, PhD); physical oceanography (MS, PhD). Part-time programs available. *Faculty:* 24

full-time (6 women). *Students:* 69 full-time (41 women), 35 part-time (20 women); includes 6 Black or African American, non-Hispanic/Latino; 11 Hispanic/Latino; 1 Two or more races, non-Hispanic/Latino, 11 international. Average age 31. 98 applicants, 29% accepted, 15 enrolled. In 2010, 7 master's, 7 doctorates awarded. Terminal master's awarded for partial completion of doctoral program. *Degree requirements:* For master's, thesis, successful oral defense; for doctorate, comprehensive exam, thesis/dissertation, successful oral defense. *Entrance requirements:* For master's, GRE General Test; for doctorate, GRE General Test, bachelor's degree or equivalent from regionally-accredited university, minimum B average or GPA of 3.0 in all upper-division work attempted. Additional exam requirements/recommendations for international students: Required—TOEFL (minimum score 550 paper-based; 213 computer-based; 79 iBT). *Application deadline:* For fall admission, 1/15 for domestic students, 1/2 for international students; for spring admission, 10/1 for domestic students, 7/1 for international students. Applications are processed on a rolling basis. Application fee: $30. *Financial support:* In 2010–11, 73 students received support. Health care benefits and unspecified assistantships available. Financial award application deadline: 1/15. *Faculty research:* Trace metal chemistry, water quality, organic and isotopic geochemistry, physical chemistry, nutrient chemistry. Total annual research expenditures: $9.2 million. *Unit head:* Dr. Edward S. Van Vleet, Professor and Director of Academic Programs and Student Affairs, 727-553-1165, Fax: 727-553-1189, E-mail: vanvleet@marine.usf.edu. *Application contact:* Dawna L. Ishler, Academic Services Administrator, 727-553-3944, Fax: 727-553-1189, E-mail: dishler@usf.edu.

The University of Texas at Arlington, Graduate School, School of Urban and Public Affairs, Department of Interdisciplinary Science, Arlington, TX 76019. Offers MA. Part-time and evening/weekend programs available. *Faculty:* 3 full-time (0 women). *Students:* 23 full-time (8 women); includes 10 minority (8 Black or African American, non-Hispanic/Latino; 2 Hispanic/Latino). 22 applicants, 100% accepted, 21 enrolled. In 2010, 1 master's awarded. *Entrance requirements:* For master's, GRE. Additional exam requirements/recommendations for international students: Required—TOEFL (minimum score 550 paper-based; 213 computer-based). *Application deadline:* For fall admission, 6/1 for domestic students, 4/1 for international students; for spring admission, 10/15 for domestic students, 9/15 for international students. Application fee: $35 ($50 for international students). Electronic applications accepted. *Expenses:* Tuition, state resident: full-time $7500. Tuition, nonresident: full-time $13,080. International tuition: $13,250 full-time. *Unit head:* Dr. James Welch, Interim Director, 817-272-1023, E-mail: welchj4@uta.edu. *Application contact:* Megan Topham, Academic Advisor, 817-272-5988.

The University of Texas at Brownsville, Graduate Studies, College of Liberal Arts, Department of English, Brownsville, TX 78520-4991. Offers English (MA); interdisciplinary studies (MAIS). Part-time and evening/weekend programs available. *Degree requirements:* For master's, comprehensive exam or thesis. *Entrance requirements:* For master's, GRE General Test. Additional exam requirements/recommendations for international students: Required—TOEFL. *Faculty research:* Sandra Cisneros, Nathaniel Hawthorne, Rodolfo Araya, Isabel Allende, linguistics.

The University of Texas at Brownsville, Graduate Studies, College of Liberal Arts, Department of Modern Languages, Brownsville, TX 78520-4991. Offers interdisciplinary studies (MAIS); Spanish (MA). Part-time and evening/weekend programs available. *Degree requirements:* For master's, comprehensive exam, thesis optional. *Entrance requirements:* For master's, GRE General Test, letters of recommendation, interview. Additional exam requirements/recommendations for international students: Required—TOEFL. *Faculty research:* Children's literature, Hispanic folklore, translation.

The University of Texas at Dallas, School of Interdisciplinary Studies, Richardson, TX 75080. Offers MA. Part-time and evening/weekend programs available. *Faculty:* 3 full-time (2 women). *Students:* 13 full-time (10 women), 26 part-time (15 women); includes 16 minority (7 Black or African American, non-Hispanic/Latino; 4 Asian, non-Hispanic/Latino; 5 Hispanic/Latino), 1 international. Average age 39. 17 applicants, 82% accepted, 11 enrolled. In 2010, 13 master's awarded. *Degree requirements:* For master's, research project, seminar. *Entrance requirements:* For master's, GRE General Test, minimum GPA of 3.0. Additional exam requirements/recommendations for international students: Required—TOEFL (minimum score 550 paper-based; 215 computer-based). *Application deadline:* For fall admission, 7/15 for domestic students, 5/1 priority date for international students; for spring admission, 11/15 for domestic students, 9/1 priority date for international students. Applications are processed on a rolling basis. Application fee: $50 ($100 for international students). Electronic applications accepted. *Expenses:* Tuition, state resident: full-time $10,248; part-time $569 per credit hour. Tuition, nonresident: full-time $18,544; part-time $1030 per credit hour. Tuition and fees vary according to course load. *Financial support:* In 2010–11, 14 students received support; research assistantships with partial tuition reimbursements available, teaching assistantships with partial tuition reimbursements available, career-related internships or fieldwork, Federal Work-Study, institutionally sponsored loans, and scholarships/grants available. Support available to part-time students. Financial award application deadline: 4/30; financial award applicants required to submit FAFSA. *Faculty research:* Psychology of gender, education of homeless children and youths. Total annual research expenditures: $69,239. *Unit head:* Dr. George Fair, Dean, 972-883-2350, Fax: 972-883-2440, E-mail: gwfair@utdallas.edu. *Application contact:* Dr. Elizabeth Salter, Associate Dean, 972-883-2323, Fax: 972-883-2440, E-mail: emsalter@utdallas.edu.

The University of Texas at El Paso, Graduate School, College of Liberal Arts, Interdisciplinary Program in Liberal Arts, El Paso, TX 79968-0001. Offers MAIS. Part-time and evening/weekend programs available. *Students:* 12 (5 women); includes 5 Hispanic/Latino, 4 international. Average age 34. In 2010, 5 master's awarded. *Entrance requirements:* For master's, GRE, minimum GPA of 3.0, letters of recommendation. Additional exam requirements/recommendations for international students: Required—TOEFL; Recommended—IELTS. *Application deadline:* For fall admission, 8/1 priority date for domestic students, 3/1 for international students; for spring admission, 11/1 priority date for domestic students, 9/1 for international students. Applications are processed on a rolling basis. Application fee: $45 ($80 for international students). Electronic applications accepted. *Financial support:* In 2010–11, research assistantships with tuition reimbursements (averaging $18,625 per year), teaching assistantships with partial tuition reimbursements (averaging $14,900 per year) were awarded; fellowships with partial tuition reimbursements, institutionally sponsored loans, scholarships/grants, health care benefits, tuition waivers (partial), and unspecified assistantships also available. Support available to part-time students. Financial award application deadline: 3/15; financial award applicants required to submit FAFSA. *Unit head:* Dr. Ronald Weber, Director, 915-747-7073, E-mail: rweber@utep.edu. *Application contact:* Dr. Patricia D. Witherspoon, Dean of the Graduate School, 915-747-5491, Fax: 915-747-5788, E-mail: withersp@utep.edu.

The University of Texas at El Paso, Graduate School, College of Science, Interdisciplinary Studies Program, El Paso, TX 79968-0001. Offers MSIS. Part-time and evening/weekend programs available. *Students:* 6 (3 women); includes 4 Hispanic/Latino, 2 international. Average age 34. In 2010, 4 master's awarded. *Degree requirements:* For master's, thesis optional. *Entrance requirements:* For master's, GRE. Additional exam requirements/recommendations for international students: Required—TOEFL; Recommended—IELTS. *Application deadline:* For fall admission, 8/1 priority date for domestic students, 3/1 for international students; for spring admission, 11/1 priority date for domestic students, 9/1 for international students. Applications are processed on a rolling basis. Application fee: $45 ($80 for international students). Electronic applications accepted. *Financial support:* In 2010–11, research assistantships (averaging $21,812 per year), teaching assistantships (averaging $17,450 per year) were awarded; fellowships with partial tuition reimbursements, institutionally sponsored loans, scholarships/grants, health care benefits, tuition waivers (partial), and unspecified assistantships also available. Support available to part-time students. Financial award application deadline: 3/15; financial award applicants required to submit FAFSA. *Unit head:* Joel Gilbert, Program Coordinator, 915-747-5554, E-mail: esci@utep.edu. *Application contact:* Dr. Patricia D. Witherspoon, Dean of the Graduate School, 915-747-5491, Fax: 915-747-5788, E-mail: withersp@utep.edu.

The University of Texas at San Antonio, College of Education and Human Development, Department of Interdisciplinary Learning and Teaching, San Antonio, TX 78249-0617. Offers adult learning and teaching (MA); education (MA), including curriculum and instruction, early childhood and elementary education, instructional technology, literacy education, special education; interdisciplinary learning and teaching (PhD). Part-time and evening/weekend programs available. *Faculty:* 25 full-time (21 women), 1 (woman) part-time/adjunct. *Students:* 114 full-time (88 women), 379 part-time (312 women); includes 275 minority (34 Black or African American, non-Hispanic/Latino; 1 American Indian or Alaska Native, non-Hispanic/Latino; 10 Asian, non-Hispanic/Latino; 221 Hispanic/Latino; 9 Two or more races, non-Hispanic/Latino), 19 international. Average age 34. 235 applicants, 84% accepted, 133 enrolled. In 2010, 104 master's awarded. *Degree requirements:* For master's, comprehensive exam (for some programs), thesis (for some programs). *Entrance requirements:* For master's, GRE General Test, minimum GPA of 3.0. Additional exam requirements/recommendations for international students: Required—TOEFL (minimum score 500 paper-based; 173 computer-based; 61 iBT), IELTS (minimum score 5). *Application deadline:* For fall admission, 7/1 for domestic students, 4/1 for international students; for spring admission, 11/1 for domestic students, 9/1 for international students. Applications are processed on a rolling basis. Application fee: $45 ($80 for international students). Electronic applications accepted. *Expenses:* Tuition, state resident: full-time $4172; part-time $231.75 per credit hour. Tuition, nonresident: full-time $15,332; part-time $851.75 per credit hour. *Financial support:* In 2010–11, 76 students received support, including 24 research assistantships (averaging $11,539 per year), 6 teaching assistantships (averaging $8,800 per year); scholarships/grants, tuition waivers, and unspecified assistantships also available. Support available to part-time students. *Faculty research:* Adult education; early childhood education; literacy; special education; science, technology, engineering and math fields. Total annual research expenditures: $57,097. *Unit head:* Dr. Christine Moesley, Department Chair, 210-458-5969, Fax: 210-458-7281, E-mail: christine.moseley@utsa.edu. *Application contact:* Veronica Ramirez, Assistant Dean, 210-458-4330, Fax: 210-458-4332, E-mail: graduatestudies@utsa.edu.

The University of Texas at Tyler, College of Arts and Sciences, Department of Art and Art History, Tyler, TX 75799-0001. Offers art history (MA); interdisciplinary (MAIS); studio art (MFA). *Degree requirements:* For master's, thesis, graduate committee review. *Entrance requirements:* For master's, minimum GPA of 3.0. Additional exam requirements/recommendations for international students: Required—TOEFL (minimum score 79 computer-based). *Faculty research:* Classical myths in contemporary art, social issues in contemporary art, casting methods, Renaissance art.

The University of Texas at Tyler, College of Arts and Sciences, Department of Biology, Tyler, TX 75799-0001. Offers biology (MS); interdisciplinary studies (MSIS). *Degree requirements:* For master's, comprehensive exam, thesis, oral qualifying exam, thesis defense. *Entrance requirements:* For master's, GRE General Test, GRE Subject Test, bachelor's degree in biology or equivalent. Additional exam requirements/recommendations for international students: Required—TOEFL (minimum score 79 computer-based). Electronic applications accepted. *Faculty research:* Phenotypic plasticity and heritability of life history traits, invertebrate ecology and genetics, systematics and phylogenetics of reptiles, hibernation physiology in turtles, landscape ecology, host-microbe interaction, outer membrane proteins in bacteria.

The University of Texas at Tyler, College of Arts and Sciences, Department of Literature and Languages, Tyler, TX 75799-0001. Offers English (MA); interdisciplinary studies (MAIS). Part-time and evening/weekend programs available. *Degree requirements:* For master's, one foreign language, comprehensive exam, thesis optional. *Entrance requirements:* For master's, GRE General Test, minimum GPA of 3.0; four semesters or the equivalent of one foreign language. Additional exam requirements/recommendations for international students: Required—TOEFL (minimum score 79 computer-based). Electronic applications accepted. *Faculty research:* Medieval and Tudor drama, Shakespeare, British Romanticism, British and Irish modernism, American realism, Greek drama, nineteenth century American literature.

The University of Texas at Tyler, College of Education and Psychology, Department of Psychology and Counseling, Tyler, TX 75799-0001. Offers clinical psychology (MS), including neuropsychology, school psychology; counseling psychology (MA), including general, marriage and family; interdisciplinary studies (MSIS); school counseling (MA). Part-time and evening/weekend programs available. *Degree requirements:* For master's, comprehensive exam, thesis optional. *Entrance requirements:* For master's, GRE General Test, minimum GPA of 3.0. Additional exam requirements/recommendations for international students: Required—TOEFL (minimum score 79 computer-based). Electronic applications accepted. *Faculty research:* Neuropsychology, child abuse, psychometric properties of psychological instruments, maternal behavior, clinical practice issues, victimization of women, post-traumatic stress disorder.

The University of Texas at Tyler, College of Engineering and Computer Science, Department of Computer Science, Tyler, TX 75799-0001. Offers computer science (MS); interdisciplinary studies (MSIS). *Degree requirements:* For master's, comprehensive exam, thesis optional. *Entrance requirements:* For master's, GRE General Test, previous course work in data structures and computer organization, 6 hours of course work in calculus and statistics. Additional exam requirements/recommendations for international students: Required—TOEFL (minimum score 79 computer-based). Electronic applications accepted. *Faculty research:* Database design, software engineering, client-server architecture, visual programming, data mining, computer security, digital image processing, simulation and modeling, computer science education.

The University of Texas–Pan American, College of Arts and Humanities, Program in Interdisciplinary Studies, Edinburg, TX 78539. Offers MAIS, MSIS. Part-time and evening/weekend programs available. *Degree requirements:* For master's, comprehensive exam, thesis or alternative. *Entrance requirements:* For master's, GRE General Test, minimum GPA of 3.0.

University of the Incarnate Word, School of Graduate Studies and Research, College of Humanities, Arts, and Social Sciences, Program in Multidisciplinary Studies, San Antonio, TX 78209-6397. Offers MA. Part-time and evening/weekend programs available. *Students:* 1 (woman) full-time, 7 part-time (5 women); includes 7 Hispanic/Latino. Average age 36. *Degree requirements:* For master's, thesis or capstone experience in one area of focus which incorporates the integration of all disciplines from which work is taken. *Entrance requirements:* For master's, GRE (minimum score 800 verbal and quantitative, 3.5 analytical), MAT (minimum score 40), GMAT (minimum score 450). Additional exam requirements/recommendations for international students: Required—TOEFL (minimum score 560 paper-based; 220 computer-based; 83 iBT). *Application deadline:* Applications are processed on a rolling basis. Application fee: $20. Electronic applications accepted. *Expenses:* Tuition: Part-time $725 per contact hour. Required fees: $890 per semester. *Financial support:* Federal Work-Study and scholarships/grants available. Financial award applicants required to submit FAFSA. *Unit head:* Dr. Kevin Vichcales, Dean, School of Graduate Studies and Research, 210-829-3157. *Application contact:* Andrea Cyterski-Acosta, Dean of Enrollment, 210-829-6005, Fax: 210-829-3921, E-mail: admis@uiwtx.edu.

University of the Incarnate Word, School of Graduate Studies and Research, School of Mathematics, Science, and Engineering, Program in Multidisciplinary Sciences, San Antonio, TX 78209-6397. Offers MA. Part-time and evening/weekend programs available. *Faculty:* 4 full-time (2 women). *Students:* 17 part-time (12 women); includes 1 Asian, non-Hispanic/Latino; 11 Hispanic/Latino. Average age 36. In 2010, 3 master's awarded. *Degree requirements:* For master's, capstone. *Entrance requirements:* For master's, GRE (minimum score 800 verbal and quantitative, 3.5 analytical), elementary certification with science endorsement (18 hours of science) or secondary certification, or equivalent professional experience teaching service. Additional exam requirements/recommendations for international students: Required—TOEFL (minimum score 560 paper-based; 220 computer-based; 83 iBT). *Application deadline:* Applications are processed on a rolling basis. Application fee: $20. Electronic applications accepted. *Expenses:* Tuition: Part-time $725 per contact hour. Required fees: $890 per semester. *Financial support:* Federal Work-Study and scholarships/grants available. Financial award applicants required to submit FAFSA. *Faculty research:* Professional development of

Interdisciplinary Studies

University of the Incarnate Word (continued)
in-service high school science teachers. Total annual research expenditures: $20,000. *Unit head:* Dr. Alakananda Chaudhuri, 210-829-3145, Fax: 210-829-3153, E-mail: alakanan@uiwtx.edu. *Application contact:* Andrea Cyterski-Acosta, Dean of Enrollment, 210-829-6005, Fax: 210-829-3921, E-mail: admis@uiwtx.edu.

University of Vermont, Graduate College, College of Education and Social Services, Department of Integrated Professional Studies, Interdisciplinary Major, Burlington, VT 05405. Offers M Ed. *Students:* 27 (22 women); includes 2 Black or African American, non-Hispanic/Latino; 1 Asian, non-Hispanic/Latino; 3 Hispanic/Latino, 1 international. 15 applicants, 80% accepted, 3 enrolled. In 2010, 11 master's awarded. *Degree requirements:* For master's, thesis or alternative. *Entrance requirements:* Additional exam requirements/recommendations for international students: Required—TOEFL (minimum score 550 paper-based; 213 computer-based; 80 iBT). *Application deadline:* For fall admission, 8/1 priority date for domestic students. Applications are processed on a rolling basis. Application fee: $40. Electronic applications accepted. *Expenses:* Tuition, state resident: part-time $537 per credit hour. Tuition, nonresident: part-time $1355 per credit hour. *Financial support:* Research assistantships, teaching assistantships available. Financial award application deadline: 3/1. *Unit head:* Dr. R. Nash, Coordinator, 802-656-2030. *Application contact:* Dr. R. Nash, Coordinator, 802-656-2030.

University of Virginia, College and Graduate School of Arts and Sciences, Program in Art and Architectural History, Charlottesville, VA 22903. Offers MA, PhD. *Faculty:* 19 full-time (7 women), 3 part-time/adjunct (all women). *Students:* 54 full-time (41 women); includes 1 Hispanic/Latino; 1 Two or more races, non-Hispanic/Latino, 1 international. Average age 31. 120 applicants, 23% accepted, 10 enrolled. In 2010, 7 master's, 3 doctorates awarded. *Degree requirements:* For master's, one foreign language, comprehensive exam, thesis; for doctorate, 2 foreign languages, thesis/dissertation, oral exam. *Entrance requirements:* For master's and doctorate, GRE, 2 letters of recommendation. *Application deadline:* For fall admission, 12/7 for domestic and international students. Applications are processed on a rolling basis. Electronic applications accepted. *Financial support:* Application deadline: 12/7. *Unit head:* Howard Singerman, Chair, 434-924-6123, Fax: 434-924-3647, E-mail: artdept@virginia.edu. *Application contact:* Douglas Fordham, Director of Graduate Studies, 434-924-6130, Fax: 434-924-3647, E-mail: df2p@virginia.edu.

University of Washington, Tacoma, Graduate Programs, Interdisciplinary Studies Program, Tacoma, WA 98402-3100. Offers MA. Part-time and evening/weekend programs available. *Faculty:* 60 full-time (34 women), 24 part-time/adjunct (13 women). *Students:* 23 full-time (14 women), 27 part-time (18 women); includes 2 Black or African American, non-Hispanic/Latino; 2 American Indian or Alaska Native, non-Hispanic/Latino; 2 Asian, non-Hispanic/Latino; 4 Hispanic/Latino. Average age 37. 22 applicants, 73% accepted, 12 enrolled. In 2010, 15 master's awarded. *Degree requirements:* For master's, thesis or project. *Entrance requirements:* For master's, GRE, statement of intended area of focus, two official transcripts from every college attended, copy of current resume, three recommendations. Additional exam requirements/recommendations for international students: Required—TOEFL. *Application deadline:* For fall admission, 5/1 priority date for domestic students; for winter admission, 11/1 for domestic students. Applications are processed on a rolling basis. Application fee: $65. Electronic applications accepted. *Financial support:* Applicants required to submit FAFSA. *Faculty research:* American history, political and social theory, political economy of labor, human rights; African-American, labor, and ethnic studies; South Asian art, aesthetics, semiotics, and modes of creative practice; social movements. *Unit head:* Dr. Lawrence M. Knopp, Director, 253-692-4450, Fax: 253-692-5718, E-mail: ias@u.washington.edu. *Application contact:* Dr. Linda Kachinsky, Adviser, 253-692-4450, Fax: 253-692-5718, E-mail: ias@u.washington.edu.

The University of Western Ontario, Faculty of Graduate Studies, Center for the Study of Theory and Criticism, London, ON N6A 5B8, Canada. Offers MA, PhD. *Degree requirements:* For master's, one foreign language, thesis; for doctorate, one foreign language, comprehensive exam, thesis/dissertation. *Entrance requirements:* For master's, honors degree or equivalent, minimum B+ average, 2 samples of written work; for doctorate, MA in humanitites or social sciences.

University of Wisconsin–Milwaukee, Graduate School, Program in Multidisciplinary Studies, Milwaukee, WI 53201-0413. Offers PhD. *Students:* 1 (woman) full-time, 1 (woman) part-time. Average age 53. *Degree requirements:* For doctorate, thesis/dissertation. *Application deadline:* For fall admission, 1/1 priority date for domestic students; for spring admission, 9/1 for domestic students. Applications are processed on a rolling basis. Application fee: $56 ($96 for international students). Electronic applications accepted. *Financial support:* Career-related internships or fieldwork and unspecified assistantships available. Support available to part-time students. Financial award application deadline: 4/15; financial award applicants required to submit FAFSA. *Application contact:* Patricia J. Hayes, Senior Student Services Specialist, 414-229-6263, Fax: 414-229-6967, E-mail: hayes@uwm.edu.

Virginia Commonwealth University, Graduate School, Program in Interdisciplinary Studies, Richmond, VA 23284-9005. Offers MIS. Part-time programs available. *Students:* 4 full-time (3 women), 14 part-time (10 women); includes 3 minority (all Black or African American, non-Hispanic/Latino). 10 applicants, 90% accepted, 6 enrolled. *Degree requirements:* For master's, thesis optional. *Entrance requirements:* For master's, GRE General Test, minimum GPA of 3.0. Additional exam requirements/recommendations for international students: Required—TOEFL (minimum score 600 paper-based; 250 computer-based; 100 iBT); Recommended—IELTS (minimum score 6.5). *Application deadline:* For fall admission, 5/1 for domestic students; for spring admission, 10/1 for domestic students. Applications are processed on a rolling basis. Application fee: $50. Electronic applications accepted. *Expenses:* Tuition, state resident: full-time $4308; part-time $479 per credit hour. Tuition, nonresident: full-time $8942; part-time $994 per credit hour. Required fees: $2000; $85 per credit hour. Tuition and fees vary according to course level, course load, degree level, campus/location and program. *Financial support:* Federal Work-Study and institutionally sponsored loans available. Support available to part-time students. *Unit head:* Dr. Sherry Sandkam, Associate Dean, 804-827-4546, Fax: 804-828-6949, E-mail: ssandkam@vcu.edu. *Application contact:* K. Stone, Education support specialist, 804-827-4546, Fax: 804-827-6949, E-mail: stoneke@vcu.edu.

Virginia Polytechnic Institute and State University, Graduate School, College of Liberal Arts and Human Sciences, Alliance for Social, Political, Ethical, and Cultural Thought, Blacksburg, VA 24061. Offers PhD, Certificate. *Expenses:* Tuition, state resident: full-time $9399; part-time $488 per credit hour. Tuition, nonresident: full-time $17,854; part-time $957.75 per credit hour. Required fees: $1534. Full-time tuition and fees vary according to program.

Virginia Polytechnic Institute and State University, Graduate School, College of Natural Resources and Environment, Department of Geography, Program in Geospatial and Environmental Analysis, Blacksburg, VA 24061. Offers PhD. *Expenses:* Tuition, state resident: full-time $9399; part-time $488 per credit hour. Tuition, nonresident: full-time $17,854; part-time $957.75 per credit hour. Required fees: $1534. Full-time tuition and fees vary according to program.

Virginia Polytechnic Institute and State University, Graduate School, College of Natural Resources and Environment, Program in Natural Resources, Blacksburg, VA 24061. Offers MNR, Certificate. *Students:* 11 full-time (6 women), 5 part-time (2 women); includes 1 Asian, non-Hispanic/Latino, 7 international. Average age 33. 13 applicants, 15% accepted, 2 enrolled. *Degree requirements:* For master's, comprehensive exam (for some programs), thesis (for some programs). *Entrance requirements:* For master's, GRE. Additional exam requirements/recommendations for international students: Required—TOEFL (minimum score 550 paper-based; 213 computer-based). *Application deadline:* For fall admission, 7/1 for domestic and international students; for spring admission, 12/1 for domestic and international students. Applications are processed on a rolling basis. Application fee: $65. Electronic applications accepted. *Expenses:* Tuition, state resident: full-time $9399; part-time $488 per credit hour. Tuition, nonresident: full-time $17,854; part-time $957.75 per credit hour. Required fees: $1534. Full-time tuition and fees vary according to program. *Financial support:* In 2010–11, 1 research assistantship with full tuition reimbursement (averaging $13,483 per year) was awarded; career-related internships or fieldwork, Federal Work-Study, scholarships/grants, health care benefits, and unspecified assistantships also available. Financial award application deadline: 1/15. Total annual research expenditures: $255,144. *Unit head:* Dr. Paul M. Winistorfer, UNIT HEAD, 540-231-8834, Fax: 540-231-5481, E-mail: pwinisto@vt.edu. *Application contact:* Peggy Quarterman, Contact, 540-231-5481, Fax: 540-231-5481, E-mail: pquarter@vt.edu.

Virginia Polytechnic Institute and State University, Graduate School, Intercollege, Blacksburg, VA 24061. Offers MIT, MS, PhD, Certificate. *Students:* 743 full-time (250 women), 148 part-time (64 women); includes 80 Black or African American, non-Hispanic/Latino; 2 American Indian or Alaska Native, non-Hispanic/Latino; 74 Asian, non-Hispanic/Latino; 29 Hispanic/Latino, 124 international. Average age 33. 756 applicants, 77% accepted, 390 enrolled. In 2010, 79 master's, 11 doctorates, 135 other advanced degrees awarded. *Degree requirements:* For master's, comprehensive exam (for some programs), thesis (for some programs); for doctorate, comprehensive exam (for some programs), thesis/dissertation (for some programs). *Entrance requirements:* For master's and doctorate, GRE. Additional exam requirements/recommendations for international students: Required—TOEFL (minimum score 550 paper-based; 213 computer-based). *Application deadline:* For fall admission, 7/1 for domestic and international students; for spring admission, 12/1 for domestic and international students. Applications are processed on a rolling basis. Application fee: $65. Electronic applications accepted. *Expenses:* Tuition, state resident: full-time $9399; part-time $488 per credit hour. Tuition, nonresident: full-time $17,854; part-time $957.75 per credit hour. Required fees: $1534. Full-time tuition and fees vary according to program. *Financial support:* In 2010–11, 19 fellowships with full tuition reimbursements (averaging $23,872 per year), 134 research assistantships with full tuition reimbursements (averaging $20,375 per year), 59 teaching assistantships with full tuition reimbursements (averaging $15,212 per year) were awarded; career-related internships or fieldwork, Federal Work-Study, scholarships/grants, health care benefits, and unspecified assistantships also available. Financial award application deadline: 1/15.

Virginia State University, School of Graduate Studies, Research, and Outreach, Program in Interdisciplinary Studies, Petersburg, VA 23806-0001. Offers MIS. Program offered jointly with Virginia Commonwealth University. *Degree requirements:* For master's, thesis optional. *Expenses:* Tuition, state resident: full-time $5576; part-time $335 per credit hour. Tuition, nonresident: full-time $13,402; part-time $670 per credit hour.

Washington State University, Graduate School, Individual Interdisciplinary Doctoral Program, Pullman, WA 99164. Offers PhD. *Students:* 4 full-time (1 woman), 5 part-time (2 women); includes 2 Black or African American, non-Hispanic/Latino, 2 international. 9 applicants, 44% accepted, 4 enrolled. In 2010, 8 doctorates awarded. *Degree requirements:* For doctorate, comprehensive exam, thesis/dissertation. *Entrance requirements:* For doctorate, minimum GPA of 3.5, master's degree from an accredited institution. Additional exam requirements/recommendations for international students: Required—TOEFL. *Application deadline:* For fall admission, 2/15 for domestic students, 3/1 for international students; for spring admission, 9/15 for domestic students, 7/1 for international students. Application fee: $50. *Expenses:* Tuition, state resident: full-time $8552; part-time $443 per credit. Tuition, nonresident: full-time $21,650; part-time $1083 per credit. Required fees: $846. *Financial support:* In 2010–11, 8 students received support, including 1 fellowship (averaging $4,000 per year), 2 research assistantships with tuition reimbursements available (averaging $13,917 per year), 2 teaching assistantships with tuition reimbursements available (averaging $13,056 per year). *Unit head:* Dr. Lori Wiest, Coordinator, 509-335-1337, Fax: 509-335-1949, E-mail: lwiest@wsu.edu. *Application contact:* Graduate School Admissions, 800-GRADWSU, Fax: 509-335-1949, E-mail: gradsch@wsu.edu.

Wayland Baptist University, Graduate Programs, Program in Multidisciplinary Science, Plainview, TX 79072-6998. Offers MS. Part-time and evening/weekend programs available. *Degree requirements:* For master's, comprehensive exam. *Entrance requirements:* For master's, GRE or MAT. Additional exam requirements/recommendations for international students: Required—TOEFL (minimum score 500 paper-based; 173 computer-based; 61 iBT). Electronic applications accepted.

Western Kentucky University, Graduate Studies, College of Education and Behavioral Sciences, School of Teacher Education, Bowling Green, KY 42101. Offers elementary education (MAE, Ed S); exceptional education: learning and behavioral disorders (MAE); exceptional education: moderate and severe disabilities (MAE); instructional design (MS); interdisciplinary early childhood education (MAE); library media education (MS); literacy education (MAE); middle grades education (MAE); secondary education (MAE, Ed S). Part-time and evening/weekend programs available. Postbaccalaureate distance learning degree programs offered (minimal on-campus study). *Degree requirements:* For master's, comprehensive exam. *Entrance requirements:* For master's, GRE General Test. Additional exam requirements/recommendations for international students: Required—TOEFL (minimum score 555 paper-based; 213 computer-based; 79 iBT). *Faculty research:* Teacher preparation in moderate/severe disabilities.

Western New Mexico University, Graduate Division, Interdisciplinary Studies, Silver City, NM 88062-0680. Offers MA. Part-time programs available. *Degree requirements:* For master's, comprehensive exam (for some programs), thesis optional. *Entrance requirements:* For master's, GRE General Test, GRE Subject Test, minimum GPA of 3.2 in last 64 hours of undergraduate study. Additional exam requirements/recommendations for international students: Required—TOEFL (minimum score 550 paper-based; 213 computer-based).

West Texas A&M University, Program in Interdisciplinary Studies, Canyon, TX 79016-0001. Offers MA, MS. Part-time and evening/weekend programs available. Postbaccalaureate distance learning degree programs offered (minimal on-campus study). *Degree requirements:* For master's, comprehensive exam, thesis or alternative. *Entrance requirements:* For master's, GRE General Test, interview with graduate Dean. Additional exam requirements/recommendations for international students: Required—TOEFL (minimum score 550 paper-based). Electronic applications accepted.

Worcester Polytechnic Institute, Graduate Studies, Department of Social Science and Policy Studies, Worcester, MA 01609-2280. Offers interdisciplinary social science (PhD); system dynamics (MS, Graduate Certificate). Part-time and evening/weekend programs available. Postbaccalaureate distance learning degree programs offered (no on-campus study). *Faculty:* 4 full-time (1 woman), 3 part-time/adjunct (0 women). *Students:* 8 part-time (1 woman); includes 1 Hispanic/Latino; 1 Native Hawaiian or other Pacific Islander, non-Hispanic/Latino, 1 international. 23 applicants, 61% accepted, 2 enrolled. In 2010, 2 master's awarded. *Entrance requirements:* For master's, GRE General Test, 3 letters of recommendation. Additional exam requirements/recommendations for international students: Required—TOEFL (minimum score 550 paper-based; 213 computer-based; 79 iBT), IELTS (minimum score 6.5). *Application deadline:* For fall admission, 1/1 priority date for domestic students, 1/15 for international students; for spring admission, 10/1 priority date for domestic students, 10/1 for international students. Applications are processed on a rolling basis. Application fee: $70. Electronic applications accepted. *Expenses:* Tuition: Full-time $20,862; part-time $1159 per term. One-time fee: $15. *Financial support:* Career-related internships or fieldwork, institutionally sponsored loans, scholarships/grants, and unspecified assistantships available. Financial award application deadline: 1/1; financial award applicants required to submit FAFSA. *Faculty research:* Microeconomics, political economy, system dynamics, systems thinking, social simulation. *Unit head:* Dr. James K. Doyle, Head, 508-831-5296, Fax: 508-831-5896, E-mail: doyle@wpi.edu. *Application contact:* Dr. Oleg Pavlov, Graduate Coordinator, 508-831-5296, Fax: 508-831-5896, E-mail: opavlov@wpi.edu.

Worcester Polytechnic Institute, Graduate Studies, Programs in Interdisciplinary Studies, Worcester, MA 01609-2280. Offers bioscience administration (MS); impact engineering (MS); manufacturing engineering management (MS); power systems management (MS); social science (PhD); systems modeling (MS). Part-time and evening/weekend programs available.

Faculty: 1 part-time/adjunct (0 women). *Students:* 6 full-time (1 woman), 146 part-time (25 women); includes 1 Black or African American, non-Hispanic/Latino; 6 Hispanic/Latino; 11 Native Hawaiian or other Pacific Islander, non-Hispanic/Latino, 1 international. 151 applicants, 76% accepted, 79 enrolled. In 2010, 47 master's awarded. *Degree requirements:* For master's, thesis; for doctorate, comprehensive exam, thesis/dissertation. *Entrance requirements:* For master's and doctorate, 3 letters of recommendation. Additional exam requirements/recommendations for international students: Required—TOEFL (minimum score 550 paper-based; 213 computer-based; 79 iBT), IELTS (minimum score 6.5). *Application deadline:* For fall admission, 1/1 priority date for domestic students, 1/1 for international students; for spring admission, 10/1 priority date for domestic students, 10/1 for international students. Application fee: $70. *Expenses:* Tuition: Full-time $20,862; part-time $1159 per term. One-time fee: $15. *Financial support:* Institutionally sponsored loans, scholarships/grants, and unspecified assistant-

ships available. Financial award application deadline: 1/1; financial award applicants required to submit FAFSA. *Unit head:* Dr. Fred J. Looft, Head, 508-831-5231, Fax: 508-831-5491, E-mail: fjlooft@wpi.edu. *Application contact:* Lynne Dougherty, Administrative Assistant, 508-831-5301, Fax: 508-831-5717, E-mail: grad@wpi.edu.

Wright State University, School of Graduate Studies, Interdisciplinary Programs, Program in Interdisciplinary Studies, Dayton, OH 45435. Offers MA, MS. *Degree requirements:* For master's, thesis optional. *Entrance requirements:* Additional exam requirements/recommendations for international students: Required—TOEFL.

York University, Faculty of Graduate Studies, Program in Interdisciplinary Studies, Toronto, ON M3J 1P3, Canada. Offers MA. Part-time programs available. *Degree requirements:* For master's, thesis or alternative. Electronic applications accepted.

ACADEMIC AND PROFESSIONAL PROGRAMS IN THE SOCIAL SCIENCES

Section 15
Area and Cultural Studies

This section contains a directory of institutions offering graduate work in area and cultural studies, followed by in-depth entries submitted by institutions that chose to prepare detailed program descriptions. Additional information about programs listed in the directory but not augmented by an in-depth entry may be obtained by writing directly to the dean of a graduate school or chair of a department at the address given in the directory.

For programs offering related work, see also in this book *Geography, History, Language and Literature, Political Science and International Affairs,* and *Sociology, Anthropology, and Archaeology.*

CONTENTS

African-American Studies

Arizona State University, College of Liberal Arts and Sciences, School of Justice and Social Inquiry, Tempe, AZ 85287-4902. Offers African American diaspora studies (Graduate Certificate); gender studies (PhD, Graduate Certificate); justice studies (MS, PhD); socio-economic justice (Graduate Certificate); PhD/JD. Part-time programs available. *Faculty:* 55 full-time (37 women). *Students:* 52 full-time (37 women), 28 part-time (23 women); includes 23 minority (4 Black or African American, non-Hispanic/Latino; 1 American Indian or Alaska Native, non-Hispanic/Latino; 5 Asian, non-Hispanic/Latino; 12 Hispanic/Latino; 1 Two or more races, non-Hispanic/Latino), 12 international. Average age 32. 83 applicants, 41% accepted, 22 enrolled. In 2010, 8 master's, 12 doctorates, 3 other advanced degrees awarded. Terminal master's awarded for partial completion of doctoral program. *Degree requirements:* For master's, thesis or alternative, interactive Program of Study (iPOS) submitted before completing 50 percent of required credit hours; for doctorate, comprehensive exam, thesis/dissertation, interactive Program of Study (iPOS) submitted before completing 50 percent of required credit hours. *Entrance requirements:* For master's, GRE or LSAT, minimum GPA of 3.0 or equivalent in last 2 years of work leading to bachelor's degree; for doctorate, GRE or LSAT (for justice studies program), minimum GPA of 3.0 or equivalent in last 2 years of work leading to bachelor's degree. Additional exam requirements/recommendations for international students: Required—TOEFL, IELTS, or Pearson Test of English. *Application deadline:* For fall admission, 12/14 for domestic and international students. Applications are processed on a rolling basis. Application fee: $70 ($90 for international students). Electronic applications accepted. *Expenses:* Tuition, state resident: full-time $8510; part-time $608 per credit. Tuition, nonresident: full-time $16,542; part-time $919 per credit. Required fees: $339; $110 per credit. Part-time tuition and fees vary according to course load. *Financial support:* In 2010–11, 4 research assistantships with full and partial tuition reimbursements (averaging $12,586 per year), 27 teaching assistantships with full and partial tuition reimbursements (averaging $14,093 per year) were awarded; fellowships with full tuition reimbursements, career-related internships or fieldwork, Federal Work-Study, institutionally sponsored loans, scholarships/grants, and tuition waivers (full) also available. Financial award application deadline: 3/1; financial award applicants required to submit FAFSA. Total annual research expenditures: $1.7 million. *Unit head:* Dr. Mary Margaret Fonow, Director, 480-965-2358, E-mail: marymargaret.fonow@asu.edu. *Application contact:* Graduate Admissions, 480-965-6113.

Boston University, Graduate School of Arts and Sciences, Program in African American Studies, Boston, MA 02215. Offers MA. *Students:* 2 full-time (0 women); includes 1 minority (Black or African American, non-Hispanic/Latino), 1 international. Average age 25. 7 applicants, 57% accepted. In 2010, 3 master's awarded. *Degree requirements:* For master's, one foreign language, comprehensive exam. *Entrance requirements:* For master's, GRE General Test, 2 letters of recommendation. Additional exam requirements/recommendations for international students: Required—TOEFL (minimum score 550 paper-based; 213 computer-based). *Application deadline:* For fall admission, 7/1 for domestic and international students. Application fee: $70. Electronic applications accepted. *Expenses:* Tuition: Full-time $39,314; part-time $1228 per credit. Required fees: $40 per semester. *Financial support:* In 2010–11, 2 students received support. Career-related internships or fieldwork, Federal Work-Study, scholarships/grants, and unspecified assistantships available. Support available to part-time students. Financial award application deadline: 1/15; financial award applicants required to submit FAFSA. *Unit head:* Linda Heywood, Director, 617-358-3389, Fax: 617-353-0455, E-mail: heywood@bu.edu. *Application contact:* Deirdre James, Program Administrator, 617-358-1421, Fax: 617-353-0455, E-mail: dejames@bu.edu.

Carnegie Mellon University, College of Humanities and Social Sciences, Department of History, Pittsburgh, PA 15213-3891. Offers African and African-American diaspora (PhD); culture and power (PhD); gender and the family (PhD); history (MA, MS); history and policy (MA); labor and politics (PhD); science, technology, medicine and environment (PhD). Part-time programs available. *Degree requirements:* For doctorate, oral and written comprehensive exams, dissertation defense. *Entrance requirements:* For doctorate, GRE General Test. Additional exam requirements/recommendations for international students: Required—TOEFL. Electronic applications accepted. *Faculty research:* Anthropology and history, African American history, technology/environment, cultural history analysis.

Clark Atlanta University, School of Arts and Sciences, Department of African-American Studies, Atlanta, GA 30314. Offers MA, DAH. Part-time programs available. *Faculty:* 1 full-time (0 women), 1 (woman) part-time/adjunct. *Students:* 12 full-time (5 women), 28 part-time (14 women); includes 36 Black or African American, non-Hispanic/Latino, 3 international. Average age 38. 12 applicants, 92% accepted, 11 enrolled. In 2010, 4 master's awarded. *Degree requirements:* For master's, one foreign language, comprehensive exam, thesis optional; for doctorate, one foreign language, comprehensive exam, thesis/dissertation. *Entrance requirements:* For master's, GRE General Test, minimum GPA of 2.5. Additional exam requirements/recommendations for international students: Required—TOEFL (minimum score 500 paper-based; 173 computer-based; 61 iBT). *Application deadline:* For fall admission, 4/1 for domestic and international students; for spring admission, 11/1 for domestic and international students. Applications are processed on a rolling basis. Application fee: $40 ($55 for international students). Electronic applications accepted. *Expenses:* Tuition: Full-time $12,942; part-time $719 per credit hour. Required fees: $710; $355 per semester. *Financial support:* Scholarships/grants available. Financial award application deadline: 4/30; financial award applicants required to submit FAFSA. *Unit head:* Dr. Josephine Bradley, Chairperson, 404-880-6810, E-mail: jbradley@cau.edu. *Application contact:* Michelle Clark-Davis, Graduate Program Admissions, 404-880-6605, E-mail: cauadmissions@cau.edu.

Clark Atlanta University, School of Arts and Sciences, Department of Africana Women's Studies, Atlanta, GA 30314. Offers MA, DAH. Part-time programs available. *Faculty:* 1 (woman) full-time, 1 (woman) part-time/adjunct. *Students:* 5 full-time (all women), 10 part-time (9 women); includes 12 Black or African American, non-Hispanic/Latino, 1 international. Average age 35. 6 applicants, 100% accepted, 4 enrolled. In 2010, 2 master's awarded. *Degree requirements:* For master's, one foreign language, comprehensive exam, thesis optional; for doctorate, one foreign language, comprehensive exam, thesis/dissertation. *Entrance requirements:* For master's, GRE General Test, minimum GPA of 2.5; for doctorate, GRE General Test, minimum graduate GPA of 3.0. Additional exam requirements/recommendations for international students: Required—TOEFL (minimum score 500 paper-based; 173 computer-based; 61 iBT). *Application deadline:* For fall admission, 4/1 for domestic and international students; for spring admission, 11/1 for domestic and international students. Applications are processed on a rolling basis. Application fee: $40 ($55 for international students). Electronic applications accepted. *Expenses:* Tuition: Full-time $12,942; part-time $719 per credit hour. Required fees: $710; $355 per semester. *Financial support:* Scholarships/grants available. Financial award application deadline: 4/30; financial award applicants required to submit FAFSA. *Faculty research:* Concerns of women of African descent globally. *Unit head:* Dr. Josephine Bradley, Chairperson, 404-880-6810, E-mail: jbradley@cau.edu. *Application contact:* Michelle Clark-Davis, Graduate Program Admissions, 404-880-6605, E-mail: cauadmissions@cau.edu.

Columbia University, Graduate School of Arts and Sciences, Program in African-American Studies, New York, NY 10027. Offers MA. Part-time programs available.

Cornell University, Graduate School, Graduate Fields of Arts and Sciences, Field of African and African-American Studies, Ithaca, NY 14853-0001. Offers African studies (MPS); African-American studies (MPS). *Faculty:* 22 full-time (9 women). *Students:* 10 full-time (6 women); includes 5 Black or African American, non-Hispanic/Latino; 1 Hispanic/Latino, 2 international. Average age 26. 33 applicants, 21% accepted, 5 enrolled. In 2010, 6 master's awarded. *Degree requirements:* For master's, thesis. *Entrance requirements:* For master's, GRE General Test (recommended), 3 letters of recommendation. Additional exam requirements/recommendations for international students: Required—TOEFL (minimum score 550 paper-based; 213 computer-based; 77 iBT). *Application deadline:* For fall admission, 1/30 for domestic students. Application fee: $80. Electronic applications accepted. *Expenses:* Tuition: Full-time $29,500. Required fees: $76. Tuition and fees vary according to degree level and program. *Financial support:* In 2010–11, 10 fellowships with full tuition reimbursements were awarded; research assistantships, teaching assistantships with full tuition reimbursements, institutionally sponsored loans, scholarships/grants, health care benefits, tuition waivers (full and partial), and unspecified assistantships also available. Financial award applicants required to submit FAFSA. *Faculty research:* African-American literature, art, cinema and theater; African-American politics and public policy; African history, politics and art; Caribbean politics and Africana Diaspora. *Unit head:* Director of Graduate Studies, 607-255-4625, Fax: 607-255-0784. *Application contact:* Graduate Field Assistant, 607-255-4625, Fax: 607-255-0784, E-mail: spt1@cornell.edu.

Cornell University, Graduate School, Graduate Fields of Arts and Sciences, Field of English Language and Literature, Ithaca, NY 14853-0001. Offers African-American literature (PhD); American literature after 1865 (PhD); American literature to 1865 (PhD); American studies (PhD); colonial and postcolonial literature (PhD); creative writing (MFA); cultural studies (PhD); dramatic literature (PhD); English poetry (PhD); English Renaissance to 1660 (PhD); lesbian, bisexual, and gay literature studies (PhD); literary criticism and theory (PhD); nineteenth century (PhD); Old and Middle English (PhD); prose fiction (PhD); Restoration and eighteenth century (PhD); twentieth century (PhD); women's literature (PhD); MFA/PhD. *Faculty:* 56 full-time (29 women). *Students:* 100 full-time (56 women); includes 5 Black or African American, non-Hispanic/Latino; 3 American Indian or Alaska Native, non-Hispanic/Latino; 10 Asian, non-Hispanic/Latino; 8 Hispanic/Latino, 12 international. Average age 27. 1,091 applicants, 4% accepted, 21 enrolled. In 2010, 25 master's, 12 doctorates awarded. Terminal master's awarded for partial completion of doctoral program. *Degree requirements:* For master's, one foreign language, thesis; for doctorate, one foreign language, comprehensive exam, thesis/dissertation, teaching experience. *Entrance requirements:* For master's, GRE General Test, 3 letters of recommendation, creative writing sample; for doctorate, GRE General Test, GRE Subject Test (English), 3 letters of recommendation, writing sample. Additional exam requirements/recommendations for international students: Required—TOEFL (minimum score 600 paper-based; 250 computer-based; 77 iBT). *Application deadline:* For fall admission, 1/10 for domestic students. Application fee: $80. Electronic applications accepted. *Expenses:* Tuition: Full-time $29,500. Required fees: $76. Tuition and fees vary according to degree level and program. *Financial support:* In 2010–11, 32 fellowships with full tuition reimbursements, 60 teaching assistantships with full tuition reimbursements were awarded; research assistantships with full tuition reimbursements, institutionally sponsored loans, scholarships/grants, health care benefits, tuition waivers (full and partial), and unspecified assistantships also available. Financial award applicants required to submit FAFSA. *Faculty research:* English and American literature, women's writing, ethnic and post-colonial literature, critical theory, medievalism. *Unit head:* Director of Graduate Studies, 607-255-7989, Fax: 607-255-6661. *Application contact:* Graduate Field Assistant, 607-255-7989, Fax: 607-255-6661, E-mail: english_grad@cornell.edu.

Eastern Michigan University, Graduate School, College of Arts and Sciences, Department of African-American Studies, Ypsilanti, MI 48197. Offers Graduate Certificate. *Faculty:* 3 full-time (0 women). *Students:* 1 (woman) full-time, 4 part-time (3 women); includes 4 minority (all Black or African American, non-Hispanic/Latino). Average age 36. 7 applicants, 71% accepted, 3 enrolled. In 2010, 5 Graduate Certificates awarded. *Entrance requirements:* For degree, bachelor's degree with minimum GPA of 2.7, two letters of reference. *Application deadline:* Applications are processed on a rolling basis. Application fee: $35. *Unit head:* Dr. Victor Okafor, Head, 734-487-3460, Fax: 734-487-6891, E-mail: victor.okafor@emich.edu. *Application contact:* Dr. Robert Perry, Graduate Advisor, 734-487-3460, Fax: 734-487-6891, E-mail: robert.perry@emich.edu.

Florida Agricultural and Mechanical University, Division of Graduate Studies, Research, and Continuing Education, College of Arts and Sciences, Division of History and Political Sciences, Program in Applied Social Science, Tallahassee, FL 32307-3200. Offers African American history (MASS); criminal justice (MASS); economics (MASS); history (MASS); political science (MASS); public administration (MASS); public management (MASS); social work (MASS); sociology (MASS). Part-time programs available. *Degree requirements:* For master's, thesis optional. *Entrance requirements:* For master's, GRE General Test, minimum GPA of 3.0. *Faculty research:* Southern history, black history, election trends, presidential history.

Harvard University, Graduate School of Arts and Sciences, Department of African and African American Studies, Cambridge, MA 02138. Offers PhD. *Expenses:* Tuition: Full-time $34,976. Required fees: $1166. Full-time tuition and fees vary according to program.

Indiana University Bloomington, University Graduate School, College of Arts and Sciences, Department of African American and African Diaspora Studies, Bloomington, IN 47405-7000. Offers MA. Part-time programs available. *Faculty:* 3 full-time (1 woman). *Students:* 17 full-time (13 women), 3 part-time (2 women); includes 17 minority (15 Black or African American, non-Hispanic/Latino; 2 Two or more races, non-Hispanic/Latino), 2 international. Average age 30. 52 applicants, 52% accepted, 10 enrolled. In 2010, 7 master's awarded. *Entrance requirements:* For master's, GRE, minimum GPA of 3.0. Additional exam requirements/recommendations for international students: Required—TOEFL. *Application deadline:* For fall admission, 1/15 priority date for domestic students, 12/15 for international students; for spring admission, 9/1 for domestic and international students. Applications are processed on a rolling basis. Application fee: $55 ($65 for international students). Electronic applications accepted. *Financial support:* In 2010–11, 1 fellowship with tuition reimbursement (averaging $10,000 per year), 1 research assistantship with tuition reimbursement (averaging $12,485 per year), 7 teaching assistantships with tuition reimbursements (averaging $11,214 per year) were awarded. *Unit head:* Dr. Valerie Grim, Chair, 812-855-3875. *Application contact:* Yunika Jackson, Department Secretary, 812-855-3875, E-mail: ytjackso@indiana.edu.

Michigan State University, The Graduate School, College of Arts and Letters, Program in African American and African Studies, East Lansing, MI 48824. Offers MA, PhD. *Entrance requirements:* Additional exam requirements/recommendations for international students: Required—TOEFL. Electronic applications accepted. *Faculty research:* Black American and diasporic studies, comparative communities of color.

Morgan State University, School of Graduate Studies, College of Liberal Arts, Department of History and Geography, Baltimore, MD 21251. Offers African-American studies (MA); history (MA, PhD). Part-time and evening/weekend programs available. *Degree requirements:* For master's, comprehensive exam, thesis; for doctorate, comprehensive exam, thesis/dissertation. *Entrance requirements:* For master's, minimum GPA of 2.5; for doctorate, GRE or MAT. Additional exam requirements/recommendations for international students: Required—TOEFL (minimum score 550 paper-based; 213 computer-based). *Faculty research:* Women's history, African diaspora history, urban history.

North Carolina Agricultural and Technical State University, Graduate School, College of Arts and Sciences, Department of English, Program in English and Afro-American Literature, Greensboro, NC 27411. Offers MA. Part-time and evening/weekend programs available. *Degree requirements:* For master's, comprehensive exam, qualifying exam. *Entrance requirements:* For master's, GRE General Test, minimum GPA of 3.0.

Northwestern University, The Graduate School, Judd A. and Marjorie Weinberg College of Arts and Sciences, Department of African American Studies, Evanston, IL 60208. Offers PhD.

The Ohio State University, Graduate School, College of Arts and Sciences, Division of Arts and Humanities, Department of African-American and African Studies, Columbus, OH 43210. Offers MA. *Faculty:* 18. *Students:* 11 full-time (5 women); includes 6 Black or African American, non-Hispanic/Latino, 1 international. Average age 25. *Degree requirements:* For master's, comprehensive exam, internship or thesis. *Entrance requirements:* For master's, GRE General Test. Additional exam requirements/recommendations for international students: Required—TOEFL (minimum score 600 paper-based; 250 computer-based). *Application deadline:* For fall admission, 8/15 priority date for domestic students, 7/1 priority date for international students; for winter admission, 12/1 priority date for domestic students, 11/1 priority date for international students; for spring admission, 3/1 priority date for domestic students, 2/1 priority date for international students. Applications are processed on a rolling basis. Application fee: $40 ($50 for international students). Electronic applications accepted. *Expenses:* Tuition, state resident: full-time $10,605. Tuition, nonresident: full-time $26,535. Tuition and fees vary according to course load and program. *Financial support:* In 2010–11, 9 teaching assistantships were awarded; fellowships, research assistantships, Federal Work-Study, institutionally sponsored loans, and unspecified assistantships also available. Support available to part-time students. *Unit head:* H. Ike Okafor-Newsum, Chair, 614-292-2114, E-mail: newsum.2@osu.edu. *Application contact:* 614-292-9444, Fax: 614-292-3895, E-mail: domestic.grad@osu.edu.

Rutgers, The State University of New Jersey, New Brunswick, Graduate School-New Brunswick, Program in History, Piscataway, NJ 08854-8097. Offers African-American history (PhD); early American history (PhD); early modern European history (PhD); east Asian history (PhD); global and comparative history (PhD); history (PhD); history of diplomacy and foreign relations (PhD); history of technology, environment and health (PhD); history of the Atlantic cultures and African diaspora (PhD); Latin American history (PhD); medieval history (PhD); modern European history (PhD); nineteenth and twentieth century American history (PhD); women's and gender history (PhD). *Degree requirements:* For doctorate, thesis/dissertation. *Entrance requirements:* For doctorate, GRE General Test, sample of written work. Electronic applications accepted. *Expenses:* Tuition, state resident: full-time $7200; part-time $600 per credit. Tuition, nonresident: full-time $11,124; part-time $927 per credit. *Faculty research:* American history, European history, Afro-American history, women's history, Latin American history.

Syracuse University, College of Arts and Sciences, Program in Pan-African Studies, Syracuse, NY 13244. Offers MA. *Students:* 13 full-time (10 women); includes 8 minority (all Black or African American, non-Hispanic/Latino), 4 international. Average age 26. 27 applicants, 30% accepted, 3 enrolled. In 2010, 3 master's awarded. *Degree requirements:* For master's, thesis. *Entrance requirements:* For master's, GRE General Test. Additional exam requirements/recommendations for international students: Required—TOEFL (minimum score 100 iBT). *Application deadline:* For fall admission, 1/10 priority date for domestic and international students. Application fee: $75. Electronic applications accepted. *Expenses:* Tuition: Part-time $1162 per credit. *Financial support:* Fellowships with tuition reimbursements available. Financial award application deadline: 1/1; financial award applicants required to submit FAFSA. *Unit head:* Dr. Linda Carter, Graduate Studies Director, 315-443-5599, E-mail: lcarty@syr.edu. *Application contact:* Aja Brown, Information Contact, 315-443-5599, E-mail: aabrow02@syr.edu.

Temple University, College of Liberal Arts, Department of African American Studies, Philadelphia, PA 19122-6096. Offers MA, PhD. *Faculty:* 7 full-time (4 women). *Students:* 31 full-time (15 women), 9 part-time (5 women); includes 35 Black or African American, non-Hispanic/Latino; 1 American Indian or Alaska Native, non-Hispanic/Latino; 1 Hispanic/Latino, 2 international. 49 applicants, 31% accepted, 10 enrolled. In 2010, 8 master's, 2 doctorates awarded. Terminal master's awarded for partial completion of doctoral program. *Degree requirements:* For master's, comprehensive exam; for doctorate, one foreign language, thesis/dissertation, oral and written qualifying exams. *Entrance requirements:* For doctorate, MA in African American studies. Additional exam requirements/recommendations for international students: Required—TOEFL (minimum score 550 paper-based; 213 computer-based; 79 iBT). *Application deadline:* For fall admission, 1/15 for domestic students, 12/15 for international students. Applications are processed on a rolling basis. Application fee: $50. Electronic applications accepted. *Financial support:* Teaching assistantships, Federal Work-Study available. Financial award application deadline: 1/15; financial award applicants required to submit FAFSA. *Faculty research:* Afrocentric theory; African-American youth; centered drama, literature, and history; comparative analysis; South and West Africa; Nile Valley. Total annual research expenditures: $10,000. *Unit head:* Dr. Nathaniel Norment, Chair, 215-204-8491, Fax: 215-204-5953, E-mail: afam@temple.edu. *Application contact:* Dr. Nathaniel Norment, Chair, 215-204-8491, Fax: 215-204-5953, E-mail: afam@temple.edu.

University at Albany, State University of New York, College of Arts and Sciences, Department of Africana Studies, Albany, NY 12222-0001. Offers African studies (MA); Afro-American studies (MA). Part-time and evening/weekend programs available. *Entrance requirements:* Additional exam requirements/recommendations for international students: Required—TOEFL (minimum score 550 paper-based; 213 computer-based). Electronic applications accepted. *Faculty research:* The black family, Afro-centricity in poetry, black women in U.S. literature, African economic development, African American history.

University of California, Berkeley, Graduate Division, College of Letters and Science, Department of African American Studies, Berkeley, CA 94720-1500. Offers PhD. *Degree requirements:* For doctorate, one foreign language, thesis/dissertation. *Entrance requirements:* For doctorate, minimum GPA of 3.0, 3 letters of recommendation. Additional exam requirements/recommendations for international students: Required—TOEFL (minimum score 570 paper-based; 230 computer-based) or IELTS (minimum score 7). *Faculty research:* Black influence on U. S. foreign policy, black intellectuals, ethnic space in urban society, representation in museums of African-Americans and British Americans during slavery.

University of California, Los Angeles, Graduate Division, College of Letters and Science, Interdepartmental Program in Afro-American Studies, Los Angeles, CA 90095. Offers MA, MA/JD. *Students:* 20 full-time (14 women); includes 17 minority (16 Black or African American, non-Hispanic/Latino; 1 Asian, non-Hispanic/Latino). Average age 29. 26 applicants, 42% accepted, 6 enrolled. In 2010, 11 master's awarded. *Degree requirements:* For master's, one foreign language, comprehensive exam or thesis. *Entrance requirements:* For master's, GRE General Test, minimum GPA of 3.0, sample of written work. *Application deadline:* For fall admission, 12/15 for domestic and international students. Application fee: $70 ($90 for international students). Electronic applications accepted. *Financial support:* In 2010–11, 18 fellowships with full and partial tuition reimbursements, 2 research assistantships with full and partial tuition reimbursements, 2 teaching assistantships with full and partial tuition reimbursements were awarded; Federal Work-Study, institutionally sponsored loans, scholarships/grants, health care benefits, tuition waivers (full and partial), and unspecified assistantships also available. Financial award application deadline: 3/1; financial award applicants required to submit FAFSA. *Unit head:* Brenda Stevenson, Chair, 310-825-9420. *Application contact:* Department Office, 310-825-9821, E-mail: idpstaff@bunche.ucla.edu.

The University of Iowa, Graduate College, College of Liberal Arts and Sciences, Program in African American World Studies, Iowa City, IA 52242-1316. Offers MA. *Degree requirements:* For master's, thesis optional, exam. *Entrance requirements:* For master's, GRE General Test, minimum GPA of 3.0. Additional exam requirements/recommendations for international students: Required—TOEFL (minimum score 550 paper-based; 213 computer-based; 81 iBT). Electronic applications accepted.

The University of Kansas, Graduate Studies, College of Liberal Arts and Sciences, Department of African and African-American Studies, Lawrence, KS 66045. Offers African and African-American studies (MA); African Studies (Graduate Certificate). Part-time programs available. *Faculty:* 11 full-time (5 women), 35 part-time/adjunct (18 women). *Students:* 7 full-time (5 women), 1 (woman) part-time; includes 4 minority (all Black or African American, non-Hispanic/Latino). Average age 30. 11 applicants, 73% accepted, 5 enrolled. *Degree requirements:* For master's, variable foreign language requirement, thesis or alternative. *Entrance requirements:* For master's, GRE, all academic transcripts, 3 letters of recommendation, personal statement of purpose, writing sample. Additional exam requirements/recommendations for international students: Required—TOEFL. *Application deadline:* For fall admission, 5/1 for domestic students. Applications are processed on a rolling basis. Application fee: $55 ($65 for international students). Electronic applications accepted. *Expenses:* Tuition, state resident: full-time $7092; part-time $295.50 per credit hour. Tuition, nonresident: full-time $16,590; part-time $691.25 per credit hour. Required fees: $858; $71.49 per credit hour. Tuition and fees vary according to course load, campus/location and program. *Faculty research:* African theatre, YaKuur culture, interracial communication, African development and urban planning, African literature, Muslim women in West Africa, identity formation in African and Disaporan settings, African-American history, North African and Arab societies, civil rights. *Unit head:* Dr. Peter Ukpokodu, Chair, 785-864-3054, Fax: 785-864-5330, E-mail: afs@ku.edu. *Application contact:* Lisa Brown, Administrative Associate Sr, 785-864-3054, Fax: 785-864-5330, E-mail: lisabrown@ku.edu.

University of Louisville, Graduate School, College of Arts and Sciences, Department of Pan-African Studies, Louisville, KY 40292. Offers African and Diaspora studies (MA); African-American studies (MA); MA/MSW; MSSW/MA. Part-time programs available. *Faculty:* 12 full-time (8 women), 2 part-time/adjunct (1 woman). *Students:* 16 full-time (12 women), 6 part-time (4 women); includes 18 Black or African American, non-Hispanic/Latino, 3 international. Average age 28. 22 applicants, 59% accepted, 9 enrolled. In 2010, 6 master's awarded. *Degree requirements:* For master's, comprehensive exam, thesis optional. *Entrance requirements:* For master's, GRE General Test. Additional exam requirements/recommendations for international students: Recommended—TOEFL (minimum score 550 paper-based; 213 computer-based; 79 iBT). *Application deadline:* For fall admission, 3/15 for domestic and international students; for spring admission, 10/15 for domestic and international students. Application fee: $50. Electronic applications accepted. *Expenses:* Tuition, state resident: full-time $9144; part-time $508 per credit hour. Tuition, nonresident: full-time $19,026; part-time $1057 per credit hour. Tuition and fees vary according to program and reciprocity agreements. *Financial support:* In 2010–11, 10 students received support; teaching assistantships available. Financial award application deadline: 3/3; financial award applicants required to submit FAFSA. *Faculty research:* African popular culture, black male identity development, education and retention, contemporary politics in Nigeria, poverty in the Caribbean. *Unit head:* Dr. Theresa Rajack-Talley, Chair, 502-852-4192, Fax: 502-852-5954, E-mail: tatall01@louisville.edu. *Application contact:* Dr. Kaila A. Story, Acting Director, PAS Graduate Program, 502-852-5985, Fax: 502-852-5954, E-mail: kastor03@louisville.edu.

University of Massachusetts Amherst, Graduate School, College of Humanities and Fine Arts, Department of Afro-American Studies, Amherst, MA 01003. Offers MA, PhD. Part-time programs available. *Faculty:* 13 full-time (5 women). *Students:* 29 full-time (16 women); includes 22 minority (19 Black or African American, non-Hispanic/Latino; 2 Hispanic/Latino; 1 Two or more races, non-Hispanic/Latino), 3 international. Average age 32. 45 applicants, 16% accepted, 5 enrolled. In 2010, 2 master's, 4 doctorates awarded. *Degree requirements:* For master's, thesis or alternative; for doctorate, comprehensive exam, thesis/dissertation. *Entrance requirements:* For master's, 3 letters of recommendation; for doctorate, writing sample, 3 letters of recommendation. Additional exam requirements/recommendations for international students: Required—TOEFL (minimum score 550 paper-based; 213 computer-based; 80 iBT), IELTS (minimum score 6.5). *Application deadline:* For fall admission, 1/15 for domestic and international students. Applications are processed on a rolling basis. Application fee: $50 ($65 for international students). Electronic applications accepted. *Expenses:* Tuition, state resident: full-time $2640. Required fees: $8282. One-time fee: $357 full-time. *Financial support:* In 2010–11, 4 fellowships with full tuition reimbursements (averaging $7,902 per year), 4 teaching assistantships with full tuition reimbursements (averaging $12,218 per year) were awarded; research assistantships with full tuition reimbursements, career-related internships or fieldwork, Federal Work-Study, scholarships/grants, traineeships, health care benefits, tuition waivers (full), and unspecified assistantships also available. Support available to part-time students. Financial award application deadline: 1/15; financial award applicants required to submit FAFSA. *Unit head:* Dr. Manish Sinha, Graduate Program Director, 413-545-2751, Fax: 413-545-0628. *Application contact:* Jean M. Ames, Supervisor of Admissions, 413-545-0722, Fax: 413-577-0100, E-mail: gradadm@grad.umass.edu.

University of Memphis, Graduate School, College of Arts and Sciences, Department of English, Memphis, TN 38152. Offers African-American literature (Graduate Certificate); applied linguistics (PhD); composition studies (PhD); creative writing (MFA); English as a second language (MA); linguistics (MA); literary and cultural studies (PhD), including African-American literature; literature (MA); professional writing (MA, PhD); teaching English as a second language (Graduate Certificate). Part-time and evening/weekend programs available. Postbaccalaureate distance learning degree programs offered (no on-campus study). *Faculty:* 31 full-time (15 women), 2 part-time/adjunct (both women). *Students:* 108 full-time (70 women), 107 part-time (69 women); includes 15 minority (2 Black or African American, non-Hispanic/Latino; 2 Asian, non-Hispanic/Latino; 6 Hispanic/Latino; 5 Two or more races, non-Hispanic/Latino), 8 international. Average age 34. 128 applicants, 71% accepted, 29 enrolled. In 2010, 38 master's, 4 doctorates, 21 other advanced degrees awarded. Terminal master's awarded for partial completion of doctoral program. *Degree requirements:* For master's, one foreign language, comprehensive exam, thesis optional; for doctorate, 2 foreign languages, comprehensive exam, thesis/dissertation. *Entrance requirements:* For master's and doctorate, GRE. Additional exam requirements/recommendations for international students: Required—TOEFL. *Application deadline:* For fall admission, 7/1 for domestic students; for spring admission, 10/15 for domestic students. Applications are processed on a rolling basis. Application fee: $35 ($60 for international students). Electronic applications accepted. *Financial support:* In 2010–11, 123 students received support; research assistantships with full tuition reimbursements available, teaching assistantships with full tuition reimbursements available, Federal Work-Study, scholarships/grants, and unspecified assistantships available. Financial award application deadline: 2/15; financial award applicants required to submit FAFSA. *Faculty research:* Applied linguistics, British and American literature, professional writing, composition studies. *Unit head:* Dr. Verner D. Mitchell, Chair, 901-678-3099, Fax: 901-678-2226, E-mail: vdmtchll@memphis.edu. *Application contact:* Dr. Verner D. Mitchell, Director, Graduate Studies, 901-678-3099, Fax: 901-678-2226, E-mail: vdmtchll@memphis.edu.

University of Wisconsin–Madison, Graduate School, College of Letters and Science, Department of Afro-American Studies, Madison, WI 53706-1380. Offers MA. *Degree requirements:* For master's, thesis or alternative. *Entrance requirements:* For master's, bachelor's degree in related field, minimum GPA of 3.0. Additional exam requirements/recommendations for international students: Required—TOEFL. Electronic applications accepted. *Expenses:* Tuition, state resident: full-time $9887; part-time $617.96 per credit. Tuition, nonresident: full-time $24,054; part-time $1503.40 per credit. Required fees: $67.63 per credit. Tuition and fees vary according to reciprocity agreements. *Faculty research:* Afro American art, history, music, literature, and culture.

West Virginia University, Eberly College of Arts and Sciences, Department of History, Morgantown, WV 26506. Offers African history (MA, PhD); African-American history (MA, PhD); American history (MA, PhD); Appalachian/regional history (MA, PhD); East Asian history (MA, PhD); European history (MA, PhD); history of science and technology (MA, PhD); Latin American history (MA). Part-time programs available. *Degree requirements:* For master's, one foreign language, thesis (for some programs), oral exam, thesis defense; for doctorate, one foreign language, comprehensive exam, thesis/dissertation, dissertation defense. *Entrance requirements:* For master's, GRE General Test, minimum GPA of 3.0; for doctorate, GRE General Test. Additional exam requirements/recommendations for international students: Required—TOEFL (minimum score 550 paper-based), IELTS (minimum score 6.5). Electronic applications accepted. *Faculty research:* U.S., Appalachia, modern Europe, Africa, colonial and post-colonial societies.

Yale University, Graduate School of Arts and Sciences, Interdisciplinary Program in African-American Studies, New Haven, CT 06520. Offers PhD. *Entrance requirements:* For doctorate, GRE General Test.

African Studies

Boston University, Graduate School of Arts and Sciences, Department of International Relations, Boston, MA 02215. Offers African studies (Certificate); international relations (MA); international relations and environmental policy management (MA); international relations and international communication (MA); JD/MA; MBA/MA. *Students:* 49 full-time (36 women), 12 part-time (7 women); includes 10 minority (2 Black or African American, non-Hispanic/Latino; 5 Asian, non-Hispanic/Latino; 1 Hispanic/Latino; 2 Two or more races, non-Hispanic/Latino), 10 international. Average age 26. 417 applicants, 59% accepted, 50 enrolled. In 2010, 41 master's awarded. *Degree requirements:* For master's, one foreign language, comprehensive exam, thesis. *Entrance requirements:* For master's, GRE General Test, 3 letters of recommendation; for Certificate, GRE General Test. Additional exam requirements/recommendations for international students: Required—TOEFL (minimum score 600 paper-based; 250 computer-based). *Application deadline:* For fall admission, 4/15 for domestic and international students; for spring admission, 10/15 for domestic and international students. Application fee: $70. Electronic applications accepted. *Expenses:* Tuition: Full-time $39,314; part-time $1228 per credit. Required fees: $40 per semester. *Financial support:* In 2010–11, 19 students received support. Federal Work-Study, scholarships/grants, and unspecified assistantships available. Support available to part-time students. Financial award application deadline: 1/15; financial award applicants required to submit FAFSA. *Unit head:* William Grimes, Chairman, 617-353-9420, Fax: 617-353-9290, E-mail: wgrimes@bu.edu. *Application contact:* Michael Williams, Graduate Program Administrator, 617-353-9349, Fax: 617-353-9290, E-mail: mawillia@bu.edu.

California State University, Long Beach, Graduate Studies, College of Liberal Arts, Department of History, Long Beach, CA 90840. Offers Africa and the Middle East (MA); ancient/medieval Europe (MA); Asia (MA); Latin America (MA); modern Europe (MA); United States (MA); world (MA). Part-time and evening/weekend programs available. *Faculty:* 12 full-time (7 women). *Students:* 18 full-time (6 women), 51 part-time (18 women); includes 3 Black or African American, non-Hispanic/Latino; 1 American Indian or Alaska Native, non-Hispanic/Latino; 3 Asian, non-Hispanic/Latino; 16 Hispanic/Latino, 1 international. Average age 30. 80 applicants, 53% accepted, 30 enrolled. In 2010, 11 master's awarded. *Degree requirements:* For master's, one foreign language, comprehensive exam or thesis. *Application deadline:* For fall admission, 3/1 for domestic students. Applications are processed on a rolling basis. Application fee: $55. Electronic applications accepted. *Financial support:* Research assistantships, Federal Work-Study, institutionally sponsored loans, and scholarships/grants available. Financial award application deadline: 3/2. *Faculty research:* All periods of European and American history, recent Asian and African history. *Unit head:* Dr. Nancy Quam-Wickham, Department Chair, 562-985-4431, Fax: 562-985-5431, E-mail: quamwick@csulb.edu. *Application contact:* Dr. Houri Berberian, Graduate Advisor, 562-985-4524, Fax: 562-985-4431, E-mail: hberber@csulb.edu.

Carnegie Mellon University, College of Humanities and Social Sciences, Department of History, Pittsburgh, PA 15213-3891. Offers African and African-American diaspora (PhD); culture and power (PhD); gender and the family (PhD); history (MA, MS); history and policy (MA); labor and politics (PhD); science, technology, medicine and environment (PhD). Part-time programs available. *Degree requirements:* For doctorate, oral and written comprehensive exams, dissertation defense. *Entrance requirements:* For doctorate, GRE General Test. Additional exam requirements/recommendations for international students: Required—TOEFL. Electronic applications accepted. *Faculty research:* Anthropology and history, African American history, technology/environment, cultural history analysis.

Claremont Graduate University, Graduate Programs, School of Arts and Humanities, Department of History, Claremont, CA 91711-6160. Offers Africana history (Certificate); American studies and U. S. history (MA, PhD); archival studies (MA); early modern studies (MA, PhD); European studies (MA, PhD); oral history (MA, PhD); MBA/MA; MBA/PhD. *Faculty:* 4 full-time (2 women), 1 part-time/adjunct (0 women). *Students:* 75 full-time (36 women), 2 part-time (1 woman); includes 25 minority (3 Black or African American, non-Hispanic/Latino; 1 American Indian or Alaska Native, non-Hispanic/Latino; 6 Asian, non-Hispanic/Latino; 9 Hispanic/Latino; 1 Native Hawaiian or other Pacific Islander, non-Hispanic/Latino; 5 Two or more races, non-Hispanic/Latino), 2 international. Average age 36. In 2010, 12 master's, 2 doctorates awarded. Terminal master's awarded for partial completion of doctoral program. *Entrance requirements:* For master's and doctorate, GRE General Test. Additional exam requirements/recommendations for international students: Required—TOEFL (minimum score 550 paper-based; 213 computer-based; 80 iBT). *Application deadline:* For fall admission, 2/1 priority date for domestic students. Applications are processed on a rolling basis. Application fee: $60. Electronic applications accepted. *Expenses:* Tuition: Full-time $35,748; part-time $1554 per unit. Required fees: $215 per semester. *Financial support:* Fellowships, research assistantships, Federal Work-Study, institutionally sponsored loans, and scholarships/grants available. Support available to part-time students. Financial award application deadline: 2/15; financial award applicants required to submit FAFSA. *Faculty research:* Intellectual and social history, cultural studies, gender studies, Western history, Chicano history. *Unit head:* Janet Farrell Brodie, Chair, 909-621-8880, Fax: 909-621-8609, E-mail: janet.brodie@cgu.edu. *Application contact:* Susan Hampson, Admissions Coordinator, 909-607-1278, E-mail: humanities@cgu.edu.

Claremont Graduate University, Graduate Programs, School of Educational Studies, Claremont, CA 91711-6160. Offers Africana education (Certificate); education and policy (MA, PhD); higher education/student affairs (MA, PhD); human development (MA, PhD); public school administration (MA, PhD); quantitative evaluation (MA, PhD); special education (MA, PhD); teacher education (MA); teaching and learning (MA, PhD); urban leadership (PhD); MBA/PhD. PhD program offered jointly with San Diego State University. Part-time programs available. *Faculty:* 16 full-time (8 women), 2 part-time/adjunct (1 woman). *Students:* 296 full-time (200 women), 154 part-time (112 women); includes 228 minority (55 Black or African American, non-Hispanic/Latino; 4 American Indian or Alaska Native, non-Hispanic/Latino; 48 Asian, non-Hispanic/Latino; 99 Hispanic/Latino; 3 Native Hawaiian or other Pacific Islander, non-Hispanic/Latino; 19 Two or more races, non-Hispanic/Latino), 11 international. Average age 38. In 2010, 83 master's, 26 doctorates, 9 other advanced degrees awarded. Terminal master's awarded for partial completion of doctoral program. *Entrance requirements:* For master's and doctorate, GRE General Test. Additional exam requirements/recommendations for international students: Required—TOEFL (minimum score 550 paper-based; 213 computer-based; 80 iBT). *Application deadline:* For fall admission, 2/1 priority date for domestic students. Applications are processed on a rolling basis. Application fee: $60. Electronic applications accepted. *Expenses:* Tuition: Full-time $35,748; part-time $1554 per unit. Required fees: $215 per semester. *Financial support:* Fellowships, research assistantships, Federal Work-Study, institutionally sponsored loans, and scholarships/grants available. Support available to part-time students. Financial award application deadline: 2/15; financial award applicants required to submit FAFSA. *Faculty research:* Education administration, K-12 and higher education, multicultural education, education policy, diversity in higher education, faculty issues. *Unit head:* Margaret Grogan, Dean, 909-621-8075, Fax: 909-621-8734, E-mail: margaret.grogan@cgu.edu. *Application contact:* Margaret Grogan, Dean, 909-621-8075, Fax: 909-621-8734, E-mail: margaret.grogan@cgu.edu.

Columbia University, School of International and Public Affairs, Institute of African Studies, New York, NY 10027. Offers Certificate. Students must be enrolled in a separate graduate degree program at Columbia University. Electronic applications accepted.

Cornell University, Graduate School, Graduate Fields of Arts and Sciences, Field of African and African-American Studies, Ithaca, NY 14853-0001. Offers African studies (MPS); African-American studies (MPS). *Faculty:* 22 full-time (9 women). *Students:* 10 full-time (6 women); includes 5 Black or African American, non-Hispanic/Latino; 1 Hispanic/Latino, 2 international. Average age 26. 33 applicants, 21% accepted, 5 enrolled. In 2010, 6 master's awarded. *Degree requirements:* For master's, thesis. *Entrance requirements:* For master's, GRE General Test (recommended), 3 letters of recommendation. Additional exam requirements/recommendations for international students: Required—TOEFL (minimum score 550 paper-based; 213 computer-based; 77 iBT). *Application deadline:* For fall admission, 1/30 for domestic students. Application fee: $80. Electronic applications accepted. *Expenses:* Tuition: Full-time $29,500. Required fees: $76. Tuition and fees vary according to degree level and program. *Financial support:* In 2010–11, 10 fellowships with full tuition reimbursements were awarded; research assistantships, teaching assistantships with full tuition reimbursements, institutionally sponsored loans, scholarships/grants, health care benefits, tuition waivers (full and partial), and unspecified assistantships also available. Financial award applicants required to submit FAFSA. *Faculty research:* African-American literature, art, cinema and theater; African-American politics and public policy; African history, politics and art; Caribbean politics and Africana Diaspora. *Unit head:* Director of Graduate Studies, 607-255-4625, Fax: 607-255-0784. *Application contact:* Graduate Field Assistant, 607-255-4625, Fax: 607-255-0784, E-mail: spt1@cornell.edu.

Cornell University, Graduate School, Graduate Fields of Arts and Sciences, Field of History, Ithaca, NY 14853-0001. Offers African history (MA, PhD); American history (MA, PhD); ancient history (MA, PhD); early modern European history (MA, PhD); English history (MA, PhD); French history (MA, PhD); German history (MA, PhD); history of science (MA, PhD); Latin American history (MA, PhD); medieval Chinese history (MA, PhD); medieval history (MA, PhD); modern Chinese history (MA, PhD); modern European history (MA, PhD); modern Japanese history (MA, PhD); premodern Islamic history (MA, PhD); premodern Japanese history (MA, PhD); Renaissance history (MA, PhD); Russian history (MA, PhD); Southeast Asian history (MA, PhD). *Faculty:* 53 full-time (15 women). *Students:* 59 full-time (30 women); includes 3 Black or African American, non-Hispanic/Latino; 2 Asian, non-Hispanic/Latino; 4 Hispanic/Latino, 22 international. Average age 30. 217 applicants, 6% accepted, 8 enrolled. In 2010, 9 master's, 5 doctorates awarded. Terminal master's awarded for partial completion of doctoral program. *Degree requirements:* For master's, thesis; for doctorate, 2 foreign languages, comprehensive exam, thesis/dissertation, 1 year of teaching experience. *Entrance requirements:* For master's and doctorate, GRE General Test, writing sample, 3 letters of recommendation. Additional exam requirements/recommendations for international students: Required—TOEFL (minimum score 550 paper-based; 213 computer-based; 77 iBT). *Application deadline:* For fall admission, 1/15 for domestic students. Application fee: $80. Electronic applications accepted. *Expenses:* Tuition: Full-time $29,500. Required fees: $76. Tuition and fees vary according to degree level and program. *Financial support:* In 2010–11, 26 fellowships with full tuition reimbursements, 27 teaching assistantships with full tuition reimbursements were awarded; research assistantships with full tuition reimbursements, institutionally sponsored loans, scholarships/grants, health care benefits, tuition waivers (full and partial), and unspecified assistantships also available. Financial award applicants required to submit FAFSA. *Unit head:* Director of Graduate Studies, 607-255-6738, Fax: 607-255-0469. *Application contact:* Graduate Field Assistant, 607-255-6738, Fax: 607-255-0469, E-mail: history_grad_info@cornell.edu.

Florida International University, College of Arts and Sciences, Program in African-New World Studies, Miami, FL 33199. Offers MA. Part-time and evening/weekend programs available. *Faculty:* 1 full-time (0 women), 1 (woman) part-time/adjunct. *Students:* 3 full-time (1 woman), 5 part-time (2 women); includes 3 Black or African American, non-Hispanic/Latino; 2 Hispanic/Latino, 1 international. Average age 31. 11 applicants, 36% accepted, 4 enrolled. In 2010, 3 master's awarded. Terminal master's awarded for partial completion of doctoral program. *Degree requirements:* For master's, one foreign language, thesis optional, minimum GPA of 3.0. *Entrance requirements:* For master's, GRE General Test, BA with minimum GPA of 3.0, 2 letters of recommendation, examples of written work. Additional exam requirements/recommendations for international students: Required—TOEFL (minimum score 80 iBT). *Application deadline:* For fall admission, 2/1 for domestic and international students; for spring admission, 10/1 for domestic students, 9/1 for international students. Application fee: $30. Electronic applications accepted. *Financial support:* Institutionally sponsored loans, scholarships/grants, and unspecified assistantships available. Financial award application deadline: 3/1; financial award applicants required to submit FAFSA. *Faculty research:* African Diaspora in Latin America, Haitian Creole phonology and culture, racial/ethnic minority sexual health, African-American labor and southern history, gendered perspective of the development of racial science. *Unit head:* Dr. Jean Muteba Rahier, Director, African—African Diaspora Studies, 305-348-6860, Fax: 305-348-3270, E-mail: africana@fiu.edu. *Application contact:* Dr. Alex Lichtenstein, Director of Graduate Studies, 305-348-1535, Fax: 305-348-3270, E-mail: africana@fiu.edu.

Harvard University, Graduate School of Arts and Sciences, Department of African and African American Studies, Cambridge, MA 02138. Offers PhD. *Expenses:* Tuition: Full-time $34,976. Required fees: $1166. Full-time tuition and fees vary according to program.

Howard University, Graduate School, Department of African Studies, Washington, DC 20059-0002. Offers MA, PhD. Part-time programs available. *Degree requirements:* For master's, one foreign language, comprehensive exam, thesis, internship; for doctorate, 2 foreign languages, comprehensive exam, thesis/dissertation, field research for some. *Entrance requirements:* For master's, GRE General Test, minimum GPA of 3.0; for doctorate, GRE General Test, minimum GPA of 3.5. Electronic applications accepted. *Faculty research:* African literature and film, economics of Africa, international relations, public policy analysis, gender.

Indiana University Bloomington, University Graduate School, College of Arts and Sciences, African Studies Program, Bloomington, IN 47405-7000. Offers MA. *Students:* 8 full-time (3 women), 1 (woman) part-time; includes 1 minority (Black or African American, non-Hispanic/Latino), 3 international. Average age 31. 20 applicants, 85% accepted, 6 enrolled. In 2010, 2 master's awarded. Application fee: $55 ($65 for international students). *Financial support:* In 2010–11, 5 students received support, including 3 fellowships with tuition reimbursements available (averaging $15,000 per year). *Unit head:* Dr. Samuel Obeng, Director, 812-855-8284, E-mail: sobeng@indiana.edu. *Application contact:* Sue Hanson, Graduate Secretary, 812-855-8284, E-mail: shanson@indiana.edu.

Michigan State University, The Graduate School, College of Arts and Letters, Program in African American and African Studies, East Lansing, MI 48824. Offers MA, PhD. *Entrance requirements:* Additional exam requirements/recommendations for international students: Required—TOEFL. Electronic applications accepted. *Faculty research:* Black American and diasporic studies, comparative communities of color.

New York University, Graduate School of Arts and Science, Department of History, New York, NY 10012-1019. Offers African diaspora (PhD); African history (PhD); archival management and historical editing (Advanced Certificate); Atlantic history (PhD); French studies/history (PhD); Hebrew and Judaic studies/history (PhD); history (MA, PhD), including Europe (PhD), Latin American and the Caribbean (PhD), United States (PhD), women's history (MA); Middle Eastern history (MA); Middle Eastern studies/history (PhD); public history (Advanced Certificate); world history (MA); JD/MA; MA/Advanced Certificate. Part-time programs available. *Faculty:* 43 full-time (19 women). *Students:* 135 full-time (84 women), 42 part-time (30 women); includes 15 Black or African American, non-Hispanic/Latino; 2 Asian, non-Hispanic/Latino; 11 Hispanic/Latino, 41 international. Average age 30. 541 applicants, 21% accepted, 43 enrolled. In 2010, 28 master's, 14 doctorates, 3 other advanced degrees awarded. Terminal master's awarded for partial completion of doctoral program. *Degree requirements:* For master's, seminar paper; for doctorate, one foreign language, thesis/dissertation, oral and written exams; for Advanced Certificate, internship. *Entrance requirements:* For master's, GRE General Test, minimum GPA of 3.0, writing sample; for doctorate, GRE. Additional exam requirements/recommendations for international students: Required—TOEFL. *Application deadline:* For fall admission, 12/15 for domestic students. Application fee: $90. *Financial support:* Fellowships with tuition reimbursements, research assistantships, teaching assistantships with tuition reimbursements, career-related internships or fieldwork, Federal Work-Study, institutionally sponsored loans, scholarships/grants, health care benefits, and unspecified assistantships available. Financial award application deadline: 12/15; financial award applicants required to submit FAFSA. *Faculty research:* African, East Asian, medieval, early modern, and modern European history; U. S. history; African and African Diaspora; Latin American history; Atlantic World. *Unit head:* Joanna Waley-Cohen, Chair, 212-998-8600, Fax: 212-995-4017, E-mail: history.dept@nyu.edu. *Application contact:* Fiona Griffiths, Director of Graduate Studies, 212-998-8600, Fax: 212-995-4017, E-mail: history.dept@nyu.edu.

New York University, Graduate School of Arts and Science, Program in Africana Studies, New York, NY 10012-1019. Offers MA. *Students:* 11 full-time (7 women), 6 part-time (5 women); includes 10 Black or African American, non-Hispanic/Latino, 5 international. Average age 26. 40 applicants, 55% accepted, 8 enrolled. In 2010, 6 master's awarded. *Degree requirements:* For master's, thesis or alternative. *Entrance requirements:* For master's, GRE, sample of written work. Additional exam requirements/recommendations for international students: Required—TOEFL. *Application deadline:* For fall admission, 4/15 for domestic students. Application fee: $90. *Financial support:* Fellowships with tuition reimbursements, Federal Work-Study and institutionally sponsored loans available. Financial award application deadline: 4/15; financial award applicants required to submit FAFSA. *Faculty research:* Pan-Africanism, black urban studies, film and literature of black Diaspora, cultural politics and theory, politics of identity. *Unit head:* Awam Amkpa, Director, 212-992-9650, Fax: 212-995-4665, E-mail: africana@nyu.edu. *Application contact:* Jennifer Morgan, Director of Graduate Studies, 212-998-9650, Fax: 212-995-4665, E-mail: africana@nyu.edu.

New York University, Graduate School of Arts and Science, Program in Museum Studies, New York, NY 10012-1019. Offers museum studies (MA, Advanced Certificate), including Africana studies (MA), Hebrew and Judaic studies (MA), Latin American and Caribbean studies (MA), Near Eastern studies (MA). Part-time and evening/weekend programs available. *Students:* 61 full-time (56 women), 16 part-time (13 women); includes 1 Black or African American, non-Hispanic/Latino; 1 American Indian or Alaska Native, non-Hispanic/Latino; 6 Asian, non-Hispanic/Latino; 5 Hispanic/Latino, 14 international. Average age 26. 200 applicants, 50% accepted, 38 enrolled. In 2010, 40 master's, 3 other advanced degrees awarded. *Entrance requirements:* For degree, master's degree or PhD. Additional exam requirements/recommendations for international students: Required—TOEFL. *Application deadline:* For fall admission, 2/15 for domestic students; for spring admission, 11/1 for domestic students. Application fee: $90. *Financial support:* Application deadline: 2/15. *Faculty research:* Modern and contemporary art, history of museums and exhibitions, conservation of cultural materials, museum anthropology, ethnography. *Unit head:* Bruce Altshuler, Director, 212-998-8080, Fax: 212-995-4185, E-mail: museum.studies@nyu.edu. *Application contact:* Tatiana Kamorina, Department Administrator, 212-998-8080, Fax: 212-995-4185, E-mail: museum.studies@nyu.edu.

Northwestern University, The Graduate School, Program of African Studies, Evanston, IL 60208. Offers Certificate. *Degree requirements:* For Certificate, one foreign language. *Faculty research:* Collapsing states in Africa, HIV/AIDS in Africa, Islam in Africa, African philosophy.

The Ohio State University, Graduate School, College of Arts and Sciences, Division of Arts and Humanities, Department of African-American and African Studies, Columbus, OH 43210. Offers MA. *Faculty:* 18. *Students:* 11 full-time (5 women); includes 6 Black or African American, non-Hispanic/Latino, 1 international. Average age 25. *Degree requirements:* For master's, comprehensive exam, internship or thesis. *Entrance requirements:* For master's, GRE General Test. Additional exam requirements/recommendations for international students: Required—TOEFL (minimum score 600 paper-based; 250 computer-based). *Application deadline:* For fall admission, 8/15 priority date for domestic students, 7/1 priority date for international students; for winter admission, 12/1 priority date for domestic students, 11/1 priority date for international students; for spring admission, 3/1 priority date for domestic students, 2/1 priority date for international students. Applications are processed on a rolling basis. Application fee: $40 ($50 for international students). Electronic applications accepted. *Expenses:* Tuition, state resident: full-time $10,605. Tuition, nonresident: full-time $26,535. Tuition and fees vary according to course load and program. *Financial support:* In 2010–11, 9 teaching assistantships were awarded; fellowships, research assistantships, Federal Work-Study, institutionally sponsored loans, and unspecified assistantships also available. Support available to part-time students. *Unit head:* H. Ike Okafor-Newsum, Chair, 614-292-2114, E-mail: newsum.2@osu.edu. *Application contact:* 614-292-9444, Fax: 614-292-3895, E-mail: domestic.grad@osu.edu.

Ohio University, Graduate College, Center for International Studies, Program in African Studies, Athens, OH 45701. Offers MA. Part-time programs available. *Students:* 21 full-time (14 women), 4 part-time (2 women); includes 5 minority (all Black or African American, non-Hispanic/Latino), 10 international. Average age 30. 67 applicants, 60% accepted, 10 enrolled. In 2010, 24 master's awarded. *Degree requirements:* For master's, one foreign language, thesis optional. *Entrance requirements:* For master's, minimum GPA of 3.0. Additional exam requirements/recommendations for international students: Required—TOEFL (minimum score 550 paper-based; 213 computer-based; 80 iBT), IELTS (minimum score 6.5). *Application deadline:* For fall admission, 1/1 for domestic and international students. Application fee: $50 ($55 for international students). *Financial support:* In 2010–11, fellowships with full tuition reimbursements (averaging $15,000 per year), research assistantships with full tuition reimbursements (averaging $11,499 per year), teaching assistantships with full tuition reimbursements (averaging $11,499 per year) were awarded; Federal Work-Study, institutionally sponsored loans, scholarships/grants, tuition waivers (partial), and unspecified assistantships also available. Financial award application deadline: 1/1. *Faculty research:* African social sciences and the humanities. Total annual research expenditures: $110,000. *Unit head:* Dr. William Stephen Howard, Director, 740-593-1840, E-mail: showard1@ohio.edu. *Application contact:* Joan Kraynanski, Administrative Assistant, 740-593-1840, Fax: 740-593-1837, E-mail: kraynans@ohio.edu.

Rice University, Graduate Programs, School of Humanities, Department of Religious Studies, Houston, TX 77251-1892. Offers African religions (PhD); African-American religions (PhD); contemplative studies (PhD); ghosticism, esotericism, mysticism (PhD); Islam (PhD); Jewish thought and philosophy (PhD); modern Christianity in thought and popular culture (PhD); psychology of religion (PhD); the Bible and beyond (PhD). *Degree requirements:* For doctorate, 2 foreign languages, comprehensive exam, thesis/dissertation. *Entrance requirements:* For doctorate, GRE, letters of recommendation, writing sample. Additional exam requirements/recommendations for international students: Required—TOEFL (minimum score 600 paper-based; 90 iBT). Electronic applications accepted. *Faculty research:* Origins and historical development of Islam, history of Christianity, the study of comparative religion, African-American religion, religion and culture.

Rutgers, The State University of New Jersey, New Brunswick, Graduate School-New Brunswick, Program in History, Piscataway, NJ 08854-8097. Offers African-American history (PhD); early American history (PhD); early modern European history (PhD); east Asian history (PhD); global and comparative history (PhD); history (PhD); history of diplomacy and foreign relations (PhD); history of technology, environment and health (PhD); history of the Atlantic cultures and African diaspora (PhD); Latin American history (PhD); medieval history (PhD); modern European history (PhD); nineteenth and twentieth century American history (PhD); women's and gender history (PhD). *Degree requirements:* For doctorate, thesis/dissertation. *Entrance requirements:* For doctorate, GRE General Test, sample of written work. Electronic applications accepted. *Expenses:* Tuition, state resident: full-time $7200; part-time $600 per credit. Tuition, nonresident: full-time $11,124; part-time $927 per credit. *Faculty research:* American history, European history, Afro-American history, women's history, Latin American history.

St. John's University, St. John's College of Liberal Arts and Sciences, Institute of Asian Studies, Queens, NY 11439. Offers Asian and African cultural studies (Adv C); Asian studies

(Adv C); Chinese studies (MA, Adv C); East Asian culture studies (Adv C); East Asian studies (MA). Part-time and evening/weekend programs available. *Students:* 8 full-time (6 women), 6 part-time (4 women); includes 7 minority (1 Black or African American, non-Hispanic/Latino; 4 Asian, non-Hispanic/Latino; 2 Hispanic/Latino), 7 international. Average age 32. 15 applicants, 73% accepted, 1 enrolled. In 2010, 3 master's awarded. *Degree requirements:* For master's, one foreign language, comprehensive exam, thesis optional. *Entrance requirements:* For master's, 6 semester hours of course work in the field, minimum GPA of 3.0. Additional exam requirements/recommendations for international students: Required—TOEFL (minimum score 600 paper-based; 250 computer-based; 100 iBT), IELTS (minimum score 5.5). *Application deadline:* For fall admission, 5/1 priority date for domestic and international students; for spring admission, 11/1 priority date for domestic and international students. Applications are processed on a rolling basis. Application fee: $70. Electronic applications accepted. *Expenses:* Tuition: Full-time $17,100; part-time $950 per credit. Required fees: $340; $170 per semester. Tuition and fees vary according to program. *Financial support:* Research assistantships, scholarships/grants available. Support available to part-time students. Financial award application deadline: 3/1; financial award applicants required to submit FAFSA. *Faculty research:* East Asian philosophy and religions, government and politics of East Asia, business and economy of East Asia, legal systems and trade relations of East Asian countries, Chinese language and civilization, Japanese language and civilization, Korean language and civilization, modern China, modern Japan, modern Korea, Chinese art and history, Japanese art and history, Korean art and history. *Unit head:* Dr. Bernadette Li, Chair, 718-990-1657, Fax: 718-990-1881, E-mail: lib@stjohns.edu. *Application contact:* Kathleen Davis, Director of Graduate Admission, 718-990-1601, Fax: 718-990-5686, E-mail: gradhelp@stjohns.edu.

Stony Brook University, State University of New York, Graduate School, College of Arts and Sciences, Department of Africana Studies, Stony Brook, NY 11794. Offers MA. *Faculty:* 8 full-time (4 women), 1 part-time/adjunct (0 women). *Students:* 1 (woman) full-time, 2 part-time (1 woman); includes 2 Black or African American, non-Hispanic/Latino. 9 applicants, 89% accepted, 3 enrolled. *Degree requirements:* For master's, research thesis project, research seminar. *Entrance requirements:* For master's, GRE General Test, minimum GPA of 3.0, 3 letters of recommendation. *Expenses:* Tuition, state resident: full-time $8370; part-time $349 per credit. Tuition, nonresident: full-time $13,780; part-time $574 per credit. Required fees: $994. *Unit head:* Dr. E. Anthony Hurley, Chairperson, 631-632-1366, E-mail: anthony.hurley@sunysb.edu. *Application contact:* Graduate Program Director, 631-632-7470, Fax: 631-632-5703, E-mail: ahurley@notes.cc.sunysb.edu.

Syracuse University, College of Arts and Sciences, Program in Pan-African Studies, Syracuse, NY 13244. Offers MA. *Students:* 13 full-time (10 women); includes 8 minority (all Black or African American, non-Hispanic/Latino), 4 international. Average age 26. 27 applicants, 30% accepted, 3 enrolled. In 2010, 3 master's awarded. *Degree requirements:* For master's, thesis. *Entrance requirements:* For master's, GRE General Test. Additional exam requirements/recommendations for international students: Required—TOEFL (minimum score 100 iBT). *Application deadline:* For fall admission, 1/10 priority date for domestic and international students. Application fee: $75. Electronic applications accepted. *Expenses:* Tuition: Part-time $1162 per credit. *Financial support:* Fellowships with tuition reimbursements available. Financial award application deadline: 1/1; financial award applicants required to submit FAFSA. *Unit head:* Dr. Linda Carter, Graduate Studies Director, 315-443-5599, E-mail: lcarty@syr.edu. *Application contact:* Aja Brown, Information Contact, 315-443-5599, E-mail: aabrow02@syr.edu.

University at Albany, State University of New York, College of Arts and Sciences, Department of Africana Studies, Albany, NY 12222-0001. Offers African studies (MA); Afro-American studies (MA). Part-time and evening/weekend programs available. *Entrance requirements:* Additional exam requirements/recommendations for international students: Required—TOEFL (minimum score 550 paper-based; 213 computer-based). Electronic applications accepted. *Faculty research:* The black family, Afro-centricity in poetry, black women in U.S. literature, African economic development, African American history.

University of California, Los Angeles, Graduate Division, International Institute, Interdepartmental Program in African Studies, Los Angeles, CA 90095. Offers MA, MPH/MA. *Students:* 8 full-time (3 women); includes 3 Black or African American, non-Hispanic/Latino, 1 international. Average age 25. 19 applicants, 58% accepted, 5 enrolled. In 2010, 8 master's awarded. *Degree requirements:* For master's, one foreign language, comprehensive exam or thesis. *Entrance requirements:* For master's, GRE General Test, minimum GPA of 3.0, sample of research writing. *Application deadline:* For fall admission, 12/15 for domestic and international students. Application fee: $70 ($90 for international students). Electronic applications accepted. *Financial support:* In 2010–11, 12 fellowships with full and partial tuition reimbursements, 2 teaching assistantships with full and partial tuition reimbursements were awarded; research assistantships with full and partial tuition reimbursements, Federal Work-Study, institutionally sponsored loans, scholarships/grants, health care benefits, tuition waivers (full and partial), and unspecified assistantships also available. Financial award application deadline: 3/1; financial award applicants required to submit FAFSA. *Unit head:* Dr. Ghislaine Lydon, Chair, 310-825-4214. *Application contact:* Department Office, 310-825-4214, E-mail: idpgrads@international.ucla.edu.

University of Connecticut, Graduate School, College of Liberal Arts and Sciences, Field of International Studies, Program in African Studies, Storrs, CT 06269. Offers MA. *Degree requirements:* For master's, comprehensive exam. *Entrance requirements:* For master's, GRE General Test. Additional exam requirements/recommendations for international students: Required—TOEFL (minimum score 550 paper-based; 213 computer-based). Electronic applications accepted.

University of Florida, Graduate School, College of Liberal Arts and Sciences, Center for African Studies, Gainesville, FL 32611. Offers Certificate. Part-time programs available. *Application deadline:* For fall admission, 6/1 priority date for domestic students; for spring admission, 11/1 for domestic students. Application fee: $30. *Expenses:* Tuition, state resident: full-time $10,915.92. Tuition, nonresident: full-time $28,309. *Financial support:* Federal Work-Study and institutionally sponsored loans available. Financial award application deadline: 2/15. *Faculty research:* Governance, human rights, African archaeology, southern African history, wildlife conservation and natural resources. *Unit head:* Dr. Leonardo A. Villalon, Director and Graduate Coordinator, 352-392-2183, Fax: 352-392-2435, E-mail: villalon@ufl.edu. *Application contact:* Dr. Leonardo A. Villalon, Director and Graduate Coordinator, 352-392-2183, Fax: 352-392-2435, E-mail: villalon@ufl.edu.

University of Florida, Graduate School, College of Liberal Arts and Sciences, Department of History, Gainesville, FL 32611. Offers African history (MA, PhD); American history (MA, PhD); European history (MA, PhD); Latin American history (MA, PhD); JD/MA; JD/PhD. Part-time programs available. *Faculty:* 31 full-time (10 women), 5 part-time/adjunct (4 women). *Students:* 81 full-time (33 women), 17 part-time (8 women); includes 3 Black or African American, non-Hispanic/Latino; 2 American Indian or Alaska Native, non-Hispanic/Latino; 2 Asian, non-Hispanic/Latino; 1 Hispanic/Latino, 12 international. Average age 30. 150 applicants, 29% accepted, 21 enrolled. In 2010, 19 master's, 8 doctorates awarded. Terminal master's awarded for partial completion of doctoral program. *Degree requirements:* For master's, variable foreign language requirement, thesis optional, 30 credit hours; for doctorate, variable foreign language requirement, comprehensive exam, thesis/dissertation, 90 credit hours. *Entrance requirements:* For master's and doctorate, GRE General Test, minimum GPA of 3.0. Additional exam requirements/recommendations for international students: Required—TOEFL (minimum score 550 paper-based; 213 computer-based; 80 iBT), IELTS (minimum score 6). *Application deadline:* For fall admission, 1/1 priority date for domestic students, 1/1 for international students. Applications are processed on a rolling basis. Application fee: $30. Electronic applications accepted. *Expenses:* Tuition, state resident: full-time $10,915.92. Tuition, nonresident: full-time $28,309. *Financial support:* In 2010–11, 70 students received support, including 30 fellowships, 13 research assistantships (averaging $16,665 per year), 27 teaching assistantships (averaging $16,733 per year); career-related internships or fieldwork and unspecified assistant-

African Studies

University of Florida (continued)

ships also available. Financial award application deadline: 1/15; financial award applicants required to submit FAFSA. *Faculty research:* Latin America and Caribbean history, nineteenth-century U. S. history, medieval Europe history, African history and Atlantic world history. *Unit head:* Dr. Ida L. Altman, Chair, 352-392-9634, E-mail: ialtman@ufl.edu. *Application contact:* Nina Caputo, Graduate Coordinator, 352-273-3379, Fax: 352-392-6927, E-mail: ncaputo@ufl.edu.

University of Illinois at Urbana–Champaign, Graduate College, College of Liberal Arts and Sciences, Center for African Studies, Champaign, IL 61820. Offers MA. *Students:* 11 full-time (4 women), 1 part-time (0 women); includes 3 Black or African American, non-Hispanic/Latino, 3 international. 19 applicants, 53% accepted, 6 enrolled. In 2010, 3 master's awarded. *Entrance requirements:* For master's, minimum GPA of 3.0. Additional exam requirements/recommendations for international students: Required—TOEFL (minimum score 550 paper-based; 213 computer-based; 79 iBT). *Application deadline:* Applications are processed on a rolling basis. Application fee: $75 ($90 for international students). Electronic applications accepted. *Financial support:* In 2010–11, 1 fellowship, 2 research assistantships, 3 teaching assistantships were awarded; tuition waivers (full and partial) also available. *Unit head:* Merle L. Bowen, Director, 217-333-6335, Fax: 217-244-2429, E-mail: bowen@illinois.edu. *Application contact:* Maimouna Barro, Associate Director, 217-333-6335, Fax: 217-244-2429, E-mail: barro@illinois.edu.

The University of Kansas, Graduate Studies, College of Liberal Arts and Sciences, Department of African and African-American Studies, Lawrence, KS 66045. Offers African and African-American studies (MA); African Studies (Graduate Certificate). Part-time programs available. *Faculty:* 11 full-time (5 women), 35 part-time/adjunct (18 women). *Students:* 7 full-time (5 women), 1 (woman) part-time; includes 4 minority (all Black or African American, non-Hispanic/Latino). Average age 30. 11 applicants, 73% accepted, 5 enrolled. *Degree requirements:* For master's, variable foreign language requirement, thesis or alternative. *Entrance requirements:* For master's, GRE, all academic transcripts, 3 letters of recommendation, personal statement of purpose, writing sample. Additional exam requirements/recommendations for international students: Required—TOEFL. *Application deadline:* For fall admission, 5/1 for domestic students. Applications are processed on a rolling basis. Application fee: $55 ($65 for international students). Electronic applications accepted. *Expenses:* Tuition, state resident: full-time $7092; part-time $295.50 per credit hour. Tuition, nonresident: full-time $16,590; part-time $691.25 per credit hour. Required fees: $858; $71.49 per credit hour. Tuition and fees vary according to course load, campus/location and program. *Faculty research:* African theatre, YaKuur culture, interracial communication, African development and urban planning, African literature, Muslim women in West Africa, identity formation in African and Disaporan settings, African-American history, North African and Arab societies, civil rights. *Unit head:* Dr. Peter Ukpokodu, Chair, 785-864-3054, Fax: 785-864-5330, E-mail: afs@ku.edu. *Application contact:* Lisa Brown, Administrative Associate Sr, 785-864-3054, Fax: 785-864-5330, E-mail: lisabrown@ku.edu.

University of Louisville, Graduate School, College of Arts and Sciences, Department of Pan-African Studies, Louisville, KY 40292. Offers African and Diaspora studies (MA); African-American studies (MA); MA/MSW; MSSW/MA. Part-time programs available. *Faculty:* 12 full-time (8 women), 2 part-time/adjunct (1 woman). *Students:* 16 full-time (12 women), 6 part-time (4 women); includes 18 Black or African American, non-Hispanic/Latino, 3 international. Average age 28. 22 applicants, 59% accepted, 9 enrolled. In 2010, 6 master's awarded. *Degree requirements:* For master's, comprehensive exam, thesis optional. *Entrance requirements:* For master's, GRE General Test. Additional exam requirements/recommendations for international students: Recommended—TOEFL (minimum score 550 paper-based; 213 computer-based; 79 iBT). *Application deadline:* For fall admission, 3/15 for domestic and international students; for spring admission, 10/15 for domestic and international students. Application fee: $50. Electronic applications accepted. *Expenses:* Tuition, state resident: full-time $9144; part-time $508 per credit hour. Tuition, nonresident: full-time $19,026; part-time $1057 per credit hour. Tuition and fees vary according to program and reciprocity agreements. *Financial support:* In 2010–11, 10 students received support; teaching assistantships available. Financial award application deadline: 3/3; financial award applicants required to submit FAFSA. *Faculty research:* African popular culture, black male identity development, education and retention, contemporary politics in Nigeria, poverty in the Caribbean. *Unit head:* Dr. Theresa Rajack-Talley, Chair, 502-852-4192, Fax: 502-852-5954, E-mail: tatall01@louisville.edu. *Application contact:* Dr. Kaila A. Story, Acting Director, PAS Graduate Program, 502-852-5985, Fax: 502-852-5954, E-mail: kastor03@louisville.edu.

University of Pennsylvania, School of Arts and Sciences, Program in Africana Studies, Philadelphia, PA 19104. Offers MA, PhD. *Faculty:* 25 full-time (13 women), 1 part-time/adjunct (0 women). *Students:* 6 full-time (3 women); includes 3 Black or African American, non-Hispanic/Latino; 1 Hispanic/Latino, 1 international. 57 applicants, 4% accepted, 2 enrolled. In 2010, 1 master's awarded. Application fee: $70. *Expenses:* Tuition: Full-time $25,660; part-time $4758 per course. Required fees: $2152; $270 per course. Tuition and fees vary according to course load, degree level and program. *Unit head:* Dr. Barbara Savage, Program Chair, 215-898-4965, Fax: 215-573-2052, E-mail: africana-grad@sas.upenn.edu. *Application contact:* Patricia Rea, Associate Director for Admissions, 215-573-5816, Fax: 215-573-8068, E-mail: gdasadmis@sas.upenn.edu.

University of Pittsburgh, University Center for International Studies, Pittsburgh, PA 15260. Offers African studies (Certificate); Asian studies (Certificate); European Union studies (Certificate); global studies (Certificate); Latin American studies (Certificate); Russian and East European studies (Certificate); West European studies (Certificate). *Students:* 322 full-time (192 women), 19 part-time (14 women); includes 22 minority (8 Black or African American, non-Hispanic/Latino; 3 Asian, non-Hispanic/Latino; 6 Hispanic/Latino; 5 Two or more races,

non-Hispanic/Latino), 134 international. In 2010, 61 Certificates awarded. *Degree requirements:* For Certificate, one foreign language, study abroad. *Application deadline:* Applications are processed on a rolling basis. *Expenses:* Tuition, state resident: full-time $17,304; part-time $701 per credit. Tuition, nonresident: full-time $29,554; part-time $1210 per credit. Required fees: $740; $214 per term. Tuition and fees vary according to program. *Unit head:* Dr. Lawrence F. Feick, Director, University Center for International Studies, 412-648-7374, Fax: 412-624-4672, E-mail: feick@pitt.edu. *Application contact:* Information Contact, 412-624-4141, E-mail: graduate@pitt.edu.

University of South Florida, Graduate School, College of Arts and Sciences, Department of Africana Studies, Tampa, FL 33620-9951. Offers MLA. *Faculty:* 2 full-time (1 woman). *Degree requirements:* For master's, comprehensive exam, thesis. *Entrance requirements:* For master's, GRE, 3 letters of recommendation. Additional exam requirements/recommendations for international students: Required—TOEFL (minimum score 550 paper-based; 213 computer-based). *Application deadline:* For fall admission, 2/15 for domestic students, 1/2 for international students; for spring admission, 10/15 for domestic students, 6/1 for international students. Application fee: $30. *Financial support:* In 2010–11, 4 teaching assistantships with tuition reimbursements (averaging $9,061 per year) were awarded; tuition waivers (full) also available. Financial award applicants required to submit FAFSA. *Unit head:* Eric D. Duke, Director, 813-974-4442, Fax: 813-974-2668, E-mail: eduke@cas.usf.edu. *Application contact:* Eric D. Duke, Director, 813-974-4442, Fax: 813-974-2668, E-mail: eduke@cas.usf.edu.

The University of Texas at Austin, Graduate School, College of Liberal Arts, John L. Warfield Center for African and African American Studies, Austin, TX 78712-1111. Offers African Diaspora studies (MA, PhD). Part-time programs available. *Degree requirements:* For master's, one foreign language, thesis. *Entrance requirements:* For master's, GRE General Test. Electronic applications accepted.

University of Wisconsin–Madison, Graduate School, College of Letters and Science, Department of African Languages and Literature, Madison, WI 53706-1380. Offers MA, PhD. Part-time programs available. *Degree requirements:* For master's, one foreign language, thesis; for doctorate, 2 foreign languages, comprehensive exam, thesis/dissertation. *Entrance requirements:* For master's, BA in African language and literature; for doctorate, MA in African language and literature. Electronic applications accepted. *Expenses:* Tuition, state resident: full-time $9887; part-time $617.96 per credit. Tuition, nonresident: full-time $24,054; part-time $1503.40 per credit. Required fees: $67.63 per credit. Tuition and fees vary according to reciprocity agreements. *Faculty research:* Oral traditions, language pedagogy, stylistics, sociolinguistics, literary criticism.

University of Wisconsin–Madison, Graduate School, College of Letters and Science, Department of History, Madison, WI 53706-1380. Offers African history (MA, PhD); Central Asian history (MA, PhD); comparative world history (MA, PhD); East Asian history (MA, PhD); European history (MA, PhD); gender and women's history (MA, PhD); Latin American and Caribbean history (MA, PhD); Middle Eastern history (MA, PhD); South Asian history (MA, PhD); Southeast Asian history (MA, PhD); United States history (MA, PhD). Terminal master's awarded for partial completion of doctoral program. *Degree requirements:* For master's, thesis (for some programs); for doctorate, variable foreign language requirement, thesis/dissertation. *Entrance requirements:* For master's and doctorate, GRE General Test. Additional exam requirements/recommendations for international students: Required—Michigan English Language Assessment Battery or TOEFL. Electronic applications accepted. *Expenses:* Tuition, state resident: full-time $9887; part-time $617.96 per credit. Tuition, nonresident: full-time $24,054; part-time $1503.40 per credit. Required fees: $67.63 per credit. Tuition and fees vary according to reciprocity agreements. *Faculty research:* American, African, European, Asian, Latin American, and Middle Eastern history.

University of Wisconsin–Milwaukee, Graduate School, College of Letters and Sciences, Department of Africology, Milwaukee, WI 53201-0413. Offers PhD. *Faculty:* 10 full-time (6 women). *Students:* 12 applicants, 75% accepted, 4 enrolled. *Degree requirements:* For doctorate, comprehensive exam. *Entrance requirements:* For doctorate, GRE General Test. Additional exam requirements/recommendations for international students: Required—TOEFL (minimum score 550 paper-based; 79 iBT), IELTS (minimum score 6.5). *Application deadline:* Applications are processed on a rolling basis. Application fee: $56 ($96 for international students). Electronic applications accepted. *Financial support:* In 2010–11, 1 fellowship, 5 teaching assistantships were awarded; research assistantships, unspecified assistantships also available. Total annual research expenditures: $20,652. *Unit head:* Abera Gelan, Representative, 414-229-4155, E-mail: agelan@uwm.edu. *Application contact:* General Information Contact, 414-229-4982, Fax: 414-229-6967, E-mail: gradschool@uwm.edu.

West Virginia University, Eberly College of Arts and Sciences, Department of History, Morgantown, WV 26506. Offers African history (MA, PhD); African-American history (MA, PhD); American history (MA, PhD); Appalachian/regional history (MA, PhD); East Asian history (MA, PhD); European history (MA, PhD); history of science and technology (MA, PhD); Latin American history (MA). Part-time programs available. *Degree requirements:* For master's, one foreign language, thesis (for some programs), oral exam, thesis defense; for doctorate, one foreign language, comprehensive exam, thesis/dissertation, dissertation defense. *Entrance requirements:* For master's, GRE General Test, minimum GPA of 3.0; for doctorate, GRE General Test. Additional exam requirements/recommendations for international students: Required—TOEFL (minimum score 550 paper-based), IELTS (minimum score 6.5). Electronic applications accepted. *Faculty research:* U.S., Appalachia, modern Europe, Africa, colonial and post-colonial societies.

Yale University, Graduate School of Arts and Sciences, Interdisciplinary Program in African Studies, New Haven, CT 06520. Offers MA. *Degree requirements:* For master's, one foreign language, thesis. *Entrance requirements:* For master's, GRE General Test.

American Indian/Native American Studies

Central Michigan University, College of Graduate Studies, College of Humanities and Social and Behavioral Sciences, Program in Humanities, Mount Pleasant, MI 48859. Offers humanities (MA), including contemporary issues in the humanities: race, class, and gender, images and ideas of self, Native American issues in modern culture, popular culture studies, the rise of industrial society. Part-time and evening/weekend programs available. *Students:* 2 full-time (both women), 10 part-time (6 women); includes 1 American Indian or Alaska Native, non-Hispanic/Latino; 2 Hispanic/Latino. Average age 37. *Degree requirements:* For master's, thesis or alternative. *Application deadline:* For fall admission, 6/1 for international students; for spring admission, 10/1 for international students. Applications are processed on a rolling basis. Application fee: $35 ($45 for international students). Electronic applications accepted. *Expenses:* Tuition, state resident: full-time $8208; part-time $456 per credit hour. Tuition, nonresident: full-time $13,788; part-time $766 per credit hour. One-time fee: $25. *Financial support:* Fellowships with tuition reimbursements, Federal Work-Study, unspecified assistantships, and out-of-state merit awards, non-resident graduate awards available. *Faculty research:* Rise of industrial society; images and ideas of self; contemporary issues of race, class, and gender; popular culture; Native American issues in modern culture. *Unit head:* Dr. Susan A. Schiller, Director, 989-774-3681, Fax: 989-774-7106, E-mail: schil1sa@cmich.edu. *Application contact:* Judith L. Prince, Director of Graduate Student Services, 989-774-1059, Fax: 989-774-1857, E-mail: judith.l.prince@cmich.edu.

Montana State University, College of Graduate Studies, College of Letters and Science, Department of Native American Studies, Bozeman, MT 59717. Offers MA. Part-time programs available. Postbaccalaureate distance learning degree programs offered (no on-campus study). *Faculty:* 5 full-time (1 woman). *Students:* 8 full-time (5 women), 14 part-time (9 women); includes 13 minority (8 American Indian or Alaska Native, non-Hispanic/Latino; 3 Hispanic/Latino; 2 Two or more races, non-Hispanic/Latino). Average age 42. 14 applicants, 79% accepted, 9 enrolled. *Degree requirements:* For master's, comprehensive exam. *Entrance requirements:* For master's, minimum GPA of 3.0; 3 letters of recommendation; 2 academic writing samples; statement of purpose. Additional exam requirements/recommendations for international students: Required—TOEFL (minimum score 550 paper-based; 213 computer-based). *Application deadline:* For fall admission, 7/15 priority date for domestic students, 5/15 priority date for international students; for spring admission, 12/1 priority date for domestic students, 10/1 priority date for international students. Applications are processed on a rolling basis. Application fee: $30. Electronic applications accepted. *Expenses:* Tuition, state resident: full-time $5553.90. Tuition, nonresident: full-time $14,646. Required fees: $1233. *Financial support:* In 2010–11, 4 teaching assistantships with partial tuition reimbursements (averaging $10,000 per year) were awarded; unspecified assistantships also available. Financial award application deadline: 3/1; financial award applicants required to submit FAFSA. *Faculty research:* Federal Indian law and policy, contemporary Native film and literature, tribal colleges and

Native Americans in higher education, Native veterans, native land rights. Total annual research expenditures: $1,614. *Unit head:* Dr. Walter Fleming, Head, 406-994-3881, Fax: 406-994-6879, E-mail: wfleming@montana.edu. *Application contact:* Dr. Carl A. Fox, Vice Provost for Graduate Education, 406-994-4145, Fax: 406-994-7433, E-mail: gradstudy@montana.edu.

Trent University, Graduate Studies, The Frost Centre for Canadian Studies and Indigenous Studies, Peterborough, ON K9J 7B8, Canada. Offers Canadian studies (PhD); Canadian studies and indigenous studies (MA). Part-time programs available. *Degree requirements:* For master's, thesis. *Entrance requirements:* For master's, honors degree. *Faculty research:* Native community-based socioeconomic development, environmental and social impact inventory, regional studies.

Trent University, Graduate Studies, Program in Indigenous Studies, Peterborough, ON K9J 7B8, Canada. Offers PhD. Part-time programs available. *Degree requirements:* For doctorate, thesis/dissertation. *Entrance requirements:* For doctorate, master's degree.

The University of Arizona, Graduate Interdisciplinary Programs, Graduate Interdisciplinary Program in American Indian Studies, Tucson, AZ 85721. Offers MA, PhD, JD/MA. Part-time programs available. *Faculty:* 7 full-time (6 women). *Students:* 32 full-time (24 women), 24 part-time (13 women); includes 1 Black or African American, non-Hispanic/Latino; 9 American Indian or Alaska Native, non-Hispanic/Latino; 3 Hispanic/Latino; 26 Two or more races, non-Hispanic/Latino, 5 international. Average age 39. 24 applicants, 58% accepted, 9 enrolled. In 2010, 7 master's, 2 doctorates awarded. *Degree requirements:* For master's, thesis; for doctorate, one foreign language, comprehensive exam, thesis/dissertation. *Entrance requirements:* For master's, 3 letters of recommendation, 2 writing samples, resume; for doctorate, statement of purpose, 3 letters of recommendation, 2 writing samples, resume. Additional exam requirements/recommendations for international students: Required—TOEFL (minimum score 550 paper-based; 213 computer-based; 79 iBT). *Application deadline:* For fall admission, 1/15 for domestic and international students; for spring admission, 8/1 for domestic and international students. Application fee: $65. Electronic applications accepted. *Expenses:* Tuition, state resident: full-time $7692. *Financial support:* In 2010–11, 13 teaching assistantships with full tuition reimbursements (averaging $16,835 per year) were awarded; institutionally sponsored loans, scholarships/grants, health care benefits, tuition waivers (partial), and unspecified assistantships also available. Support available to part-time students. Financial award application deadline: 1/15. *Faculty research:* Indian law and policy, Indian societies, Indian language and literature, Indian education. *Unit head:* Dr. Jospeh Hiller, Head, 520-626-9772, Fax: 520-621-7952, E-mail: jghiller@cals.arizona.edu. *Application contact:* Beverly Larson, Administrative Secretary, 520-621-7108, Fax: 520-621-7952, E-mail: aisp@email.arizona.edu.

University of California, Davis, Graduate Studies, Program in Native American Studies, Davis, CA 95616. Offers MA, PhD. Terminal master's awarded for partial completion of doctoral program. *Degree requirements:* For master's, comprehensive exam (for some programs), thesis (for some programs); for doctorate, thesis/dissertation. *Entrance requirements:* For doctorate, GRE. Additional exam requirements/recommendations for international students: Required—TOEFL (minimum score 550 paper-based; 213 computer-based).

University of California, Los Angeles, Graduate Division, College of Letters and Science, Interdepartmental Program in American Indian Studies, Los Angeles, CA 90095. Offers MA, JD/MA. *Students:* 16 full-time (11 women); includes 12 minority (7 American Indian or Alaska Native, non-Hispanic/Latino; 4 Hispanic/Latino; 1 Two or more races, non-Hispanic/Latino). Average age 29. 18 applicants, 61% accepted, 6 enrolled. In 2010, 6 master's awarded. *Degree requirements:* For master's, comprehensive exam or thesis. *Entrance requirements:* For master's, GRE General Test (recommended), minimum GPA of 3.0, sample of written work. *Application deadline:* For fall admission, 12/15 for domestic and international students. Application fee: $70 ($90 for international students). Electronic applications accepted. *Financial support:* In 2010–11, 15 fellowships with full and partial tuition reimbursements, 4 research assistantships with full and partial tuition reimbursements, 2 teaching assistantships with full and partial tuition reimbursements were awarded; Federal Work-Study, institutionally sponsored loans, scholarships/grants, health care benefits, tuition waivers (full and partial), and unspecified assistantships also available. Financial award application deadline: 3/1; financial award applicants required to submit FAFSA. *Unit head:* Dr. Felicia Hodge, Chair, 310-794-9997. *Application contact:* Department Office, 310-794-9997, E-mail: aisc@ucla.edu.

University of Idaho, College of Law, Moscow, ID 83844-2321. Offers law (JD); Native American law (JD); natural resources and environmental law (JD). *Accreditation:* ABA. *Faculty:* 12 full-time, 1 part-time/adjunct. *Students:* 342 full-time, 7 part-time. Average age 27. In 2010, 96 JDs awarded. *Entrance requirements:* LSAT, Law School Admission Council Credential Assembly Service (CAS) Report. *Application deadline:* For fall admission, 2/15 for domestic students. Applications are processed on a rolling basis. Application fee: $50 ($60 for international students). Electronic applications accepted. *Expenses:* Tuition, nonresident: part-time $580 per credit. Required fees: $306 per credit. *Financial support:* Career-related internships or fieldwork, Federal Work-Study, and institutionally sponsored loans available. Financial award applicants required to submit FAFSA. *Faculty research:* Transboundary river governance, tribal protection and stewardship, regional water issues, environmental law. *Unit head:* Donald L. Burnett, Dean, 208-885-4977, E-mail: uilaw@uidaho.edu. *Application contact:* Donald L. Burnett, Dean, 208-885-4977, E-mail: uilaw@uidaho.edu.

The University of Kansas, Graduate Studies, College of Liberal Arts and Sciences, Global Indigenous Nations Studies Program, Lawrence, KS 66045-7515. Offers MA, JD/MA. Part-time programs available. *Faculty:* 16. *Students:* 12 full-time (8 women), 8 part-time (4 women); includes 15 minority (12 American Indian or Alaska Native, non-Hispanic/Latino; 3 Two or more races, non-Hispanic/Latino). Average age 33. 8 applicants, 88% accepted, 6 enrolled. In 2010, 3 master's awarded. *Degree requirements:* For master's, thesis or alternative. *Entrance requirements:* For master's, GRE, resume, writing sample, minimum GPA of 3.0 (preferred), 3 recommendations, one original transcript. Additional exam requirements/recommendations for international students: Required—TOEFL. *Application deadline:* For fall admission, 3/15 priority date for domestic and international students. Applications are processed on a rolling basis. Application fee: $55 ($65 for international students). Electronic applications accepted. *Expenses:* Tuition, state resident: full-time $7092; part-time $295.50 per credit hour. Tuition, nonresident: full-time $16,590; part-time $691.25 per credit hour. Required fees: $858; $71.49 per credit hour. Tuition and fees vary according to course load, campus/location and program. *Financial support:* Fellowships, research assistantships, teaching assistantships, Federal Work-Study, institutionally sponsored loans, and scholarships/grants available. Support available to part-time students. Financial award application deadline: 3/15; financial award applicants required to submit FAFSA. *Faculty research:* American Indian history, religion, literature, law, languages, decolonization, sovereignty, cultures of Latin America, Siberia, ethnobotany, nutrition, anthropology, geography. *Unit head:* Dr. John Hoopes, Director, 785-864-2660, Fax: 785-864-0370, E-mail: indigenous@ku.edu. *Application contact:* Prof. Sharon O'Brien, Graduate Coordinator, 785-864-2660, Fax: 785-864-0370, E-mail: indigenous@ku.edu.

University of Lethbridge, School of Graduate Studies, Lethbridge, AB T1K 3M4, Canada. Offers accounting (MScM); addictions counseling (M Sc); agricultural biotechnology (M Sc); agricultural studies (M Sc, MA); anthropology (MA); archaeology (MA); art (MA, MFA); biochemistry (M Sc); biological sciences (M Sc); biomolecular science (PhD); biosystems and biodiversity (PhD); Canadian studies (MA); chemistry (M Sc); computer science (M Sc); computer science and geographical information science (M Sc); counseling psychology (M Ed); dramatic arts (MA); earth, space, and physical science (PhD); economics (MA); educational leadership (M Ed); English (MA); environmental science (M Sc); evolution and behavior (PhD); exercise science (M Sc); finance (MScM); French (MA); French/German (MA); French/Spanish (MA); general education (M Ed); general management (MScM); geography (M Sc, MA); German (MA); health science (M Sc); history (MA); human resource management and labour relations (MScM); individualized multidisciplinary (M Sc, MA); information systems (MScM); international management (MScM); kinesiology (M Sc, MA); management (M Sc, MA); marketing (MScM); mathematics (M Sc); music (M Mus, MA); Native American studies (MA); neuroscience (M Sc, PhD); new media (MA); nursing (M Sc); philosophy (MA); physics (M Sc); policy and strategy (MScM); political science (MA); psychology (M Sc, MA); religious studies (MA); social sciences (MA); sociology (MA); theatre and dramatic arts (MFA); theoretical and computational science (PhD); urban and regional studies (MA); women's studies (MA). Part-time and evening/weekend programs available. *Degree requirements:* For doctorate, comprehensive exam, thesis/dissertation. *Entrance requirements:* For master's, GMAT (M Sc in management), bachelor's degree in related field, minimum GPA of 3.0 during previous 20 graded semester courses, 2 years teaching or related experience (M Ed); for doctorate, master's degree, minimum graduate GPA of 3.5. Additional exam requirements/recommendations for international students: Required—TOEFL. *Faculty research:* Movement and brain plasticity, gibberellin physiology, photosynthesis, carbon cycling, molecular properties of main-group ring components.

University of Manitoba, Faculty of Graduate Studies, Faculty of Arts, Department of Native Studies, Winnipeg, MB R3T 2N2, Canada. Offers MA.

University of Oklahoma, College of Arts and Sciences, Department of Native American Studies, Norman, OK 73019. Offers MA, JD/MA. Part-time programs available. *Faculty:* 23 full-time (10 women). *Students:* 18 full-time (12 women), 13 part-time (12 women); includes 22 minority (all American Indian or Alaska Native, non-Hispanic/Latino), 1 international. Average age 32. 9 applicants, 89% accepted, 7 enrolled. In 2010, 3 master's awarded. *Degree requirements:* For master's, thesis. *Entrance requirements:* For master's, minimum undergraduate GPA of 3.0, 3 letters of recommendation. Additional exam requirements/recommendations for international students: Required—TOEFL (minimum score 550 paper-based; 213 computer-based; 79 iBT). *Application deadline:* For fall admission, 2/1 for domestic students, 4/1 for international students; for spring admission, 11/1 for domestic students, 9/1 for international students. Applications are processed on a rolling basis. Application fee: $40 ($90 for international students). Electronic applications accepted. *Expenses:* Tuition, state resident: full-time $3893; part-time $162.20 per credit hour. Tuition, nonresident: full-time $14,167; part-time $590.30 per credit hour. Required fees: $2523; $94.60 per credit hour. Tuition and fees vary according to course load and degree level. *Financial support:* In 2010–11, 26 students received support, including 7 teaching assistantships with partial tuition reimbursements available (averaging $10,286 per year); Federal Work-Study, institutionally sponsored loans, scholarships/grants, and unspecified assistantships also available. Support available to part-time students. Financial award application deadline: 2/1; financial award applicants required to submit FAFSA. *Faculty research:* Indigenous archaeology, tribal economic development, Oklahoma tribal history, American Indian student retention, contemporary native artists. Total annual research expenditures: $60,000. *Unit head:* Joe Watkins, Director, 405-325-2312, Fax: 405-325-0842, E-mail: jwatkins@ou.edu. *Application contact:* Barbara T. Hobson, Assistant Director, 405-325-2324, Fax: 405-325-0842, E-mail: bhobson@ou.edu.

University of Tulsa, Graduate School, Program in Museum Science and Management, Tulsa, OK 74104-3189. Offers anthropology (MA); general (MA); history (MA); Native American (MA). Part-time programs available. *Faculty:* 9 full-time (1 woman). *Students:* 6 full-time (all women); includes 1 minority (Black or African American, non-Hispanic/Latino). Average age 29. 14 applicants, 86% accepted, 6 enrolled. *Degree requirements:* For master's, final semester internship or independent research project. *Entrance requirements:* For master's, GRE General Test. Additional exam requirements/recommendations for international students: Required—TOEFL (minimum score 575 paper-based; 231 computer-based; 91 iBT), IELTS (minimum score 6.5). *Application deadline:* Applications are processed on a rolling basis. Application fee: $40. Electronic applications accepted. *Expenses:* Tuition: Full-time $16,902; part-time $939 per credit hour. Required fees: $1020; $4 per credit hour. Tuition and fees vary according to course load. *Financial support:* In 2010–11, 4 students received support, including 1 research assistantship with full and partial tuition reimbursement available (averaging $5,504 per year), 3 teaching assistantships with full and partial tuition reimbursements available (averaging $13,040 per year); fellowships with full and partial tuition reimbursements available, career-related internships or fieldwork, Federal Work-Study, scholarships/grants, health care benefits, tuition waivers (full and partial), and unspecified assistantships also available. Support available to part-time students. Total annual research expenditures: $12,000. *Unit head:* Dr. Bob Pickering, Senior Curator, 918-596-2706, Fax: 918-596-2770, E-mail: bob-pickering@utulsa.edu. *Application contact:* Graduate School, 918-631-2336, Fax: 918-631-2156, E-mail: grad@utulsa.edu.

American Studies

American University, School of International Service, Washington, DC 20016-8071. Offers comparative and regional studies (Certificate); cross-cultural communication (Certificate); development management (MS); ethics, peace, and global affairs (MA); European studies (Certificate); global environmental policy (MA, Certificate); international affairs (MA), including comparative and regional studies, environmental policy, international economic policy, international politics, natural resources and sustainable development, U. S. foreign policy; international communication (MA, Certificate); international development (MA, Certificate); international development management (Certificate); international economic policy (Certificate); international economic relations (Certificate); international media (MA); international peace and conflict resolution (MA, Certificate); international relations (PhD); international service (MIS); peace building (Certificate); the Americas (Certificate); United States foreign policy (Certificate); JD/MA. Part-time and evening/weekend programs available. *Faculty:* 91 full-time (35 women), 48 part-time/adjunct (16 women). *Students:* 591 full-time (383 women), 367 part-time (229 women); includes 164 minority (51 Black or African American, non-Hispanic/Latino; 4 American Indian or Alaska Native, non-Hispanic/Latino; 42 Asian, non-Hispanic/Latino; 63 Hispanic/Latino; 4 Two or more races, non-Hispanic/Latino), 94 international. Average age 27. 2,115 applicants, 59% accepted, 360 enrolled. In 2010, 370 master's, 7 doctorates awarded. Terminal master's awarded for partial completion of doctoral program. *Degree requirements:* For master's, one foreign language, comprehensive exam, thesis or alternative; for doctorate, one foreign language, comprehensive exam, thesis/dissertation, research practicum; for Certificate, minimum 15 credit hours related course work. *Entrance requirements:* For master's, GRE, 24 credits of course work in related social sciences, minimum GPA of 3.5, 2 letters of recommendation, bachelor's degree, resume; for doctorate, GRE, 2 letters of recommendation, 24 credits in related social sciences; for Certificate, bachelor's degree. Additional exam requirements/recommendations for international students: Required—TOEFL (minimum score 600 paper-based; 250 computer-based; 100 iBT). *Application deadline:* For fall admission, 1/15 priority date for domestic students; for spring admission, 10/1 priority date for domestic students. Applications are processed on a rolling basis. Application fee: $50.

American Studies

American University (continued)
Financial support: Career-related internships or fieldwork, Federal Work-Study, and institutionally sponsored loans available. Financial award application deadline: 1/15. *Faculty research:* International intellectual property, international environmental issues, international law and legal order, international telecommunications/technology, international sustainable development. *Unit head:* Dr. Louis W. Goodman, Dean, 202-885-1600, Fax: 202-885-2494. *Application contact:* Yasmin Quianzon, Director of Graduate Admissions and Financial Aid, 202-885-2496, Fax: 202-885-1109.

Appalachian State University, Cratis D. Williams Graduate School, Center for Appalachian Studies, Boone, NC 28608. Offers culture (MA); music (MA); sustainable development (MA). Part-time programs available. *Faculty:* 14 full-time (5 women). *Students:* 25 full-time (15 women), 5 part-time (4 women); includes 1 Hispanic/Latino. 20 applicants, 85% accepted, 12 enrolled. In 2010, 11 master's awarded. *Degree requirements:* For master's, one foreign language, comprehensive exam, thesis optional. *Entrance requirements:* For master's, GRE General Test, 3 letters of recommendation. Additional exam requirements/recommendations for international students: Required—TOEFL (minimum score 570 paper-based; 230 computer-based; 79 iBT), IELTS (minimum score 6.5). *Application deadline:* For fall admission, 7/1 for domestic students, 2/1 for international students; for spring admission, 11/1 for domestic students, 7/1 for international students. Applications are processed on a rolling basis. Application fee: $55. Electronic applications accepted. *Expenses:* Tuition, state resident: full-time $3428; part-time $428 per unit. Tuition, nonresident: full-time $14,518; part-time $1814 per unit. Required fees: $2320; $344 per unit. Tuition and fees vary according to campus/location. *Financial support:* In 2010–11, 8 research assistantships (averaging $8,000 per year) were awarded; fellowships, teaching assistantships, career-related internships or fieldwork, Federal Work-Study, scholarships/grants, and unspecified assistantships also available. Financial award application deadline: 4/1; financial award applicants required to submit FAFSA. *Faculty research:* Appalachian culture, sustainable development, Appalachian music. Total annual research expenditures: $35,275. *Unit head:* Dr. Pat Beaver, Director, 828-262-2550, E-mail: beaverpd@appstate.edu. *Application contact:* Dr. Katherine Ledford, Graduate Program Director, 828-262-4089, E-mail: ledfordke@appstate.edu.

Baylor University, Graduate School, College of Arts and Sciences, Program in American Studies, Waco, TX 76798. Offers MA. *Students:* 2 full-time (both women), 2 part-time (0 women), 1 international. In 2010, 3 master's awarded. *Degree requirements:* For master's, thesis, final oral exam. *Entrance requirements:* For master's, GRE General Test, 24 semester hours of course work in subjects with American content. *Application deadline:* For fall admission, 8/1 for domestic students. Applications are processed on a rolling basis. Application fee: $25. *Financial support:* Fellowships, Federal Work-Study and institutionally sponsored loans available. Financial award application deadline: 4/15. *Unit head:* Dr. Doug Ferdon, Graduate Program Director, 254-710-6350, Fax: 254-710-3600, E-mail: doug_ferdon@baylor.edu. *Application contact:* Margaret Kramer, Administrative Assistant, 254-710-4350, Fax: 254-710-3870, E-mail: margaret_kramer@baylor.edu.

Boston University, Graduate School of Arts and Sciences, Program in American and New England Studies, Boston, MA 02215. Offers PhD. *Students:* 37 full-time (23 women), 11 part-time (2 women); includes 4 minority (2 Black or African American, non-Hispanic/Latino; 2 Two or more races, non-Hispanic/Latino), 2 international. Average age 34. 80 applicants, 18% accepted, 8 enrolled. In 2010, 3 doctorates awarded. *Degree requirements:* For doctorate, one foreign language, comprehensive exam, thesis/dissertation. *Entrance requirements:* For doctorate, GRE General Test, scholarly writing sample, 3 letters of recommendation. Additional exam requirements/recommendations for international students: Required—TOEFL (minimum score 550 paper-based; 213 computer-based). *Application deadline:* For fall admission, 1/15 for domestic and international students. Application fee: $70. Electronic applications accepted. *Expenses:* Tuition: Full-time $39,314; part-time $1228 per credit. Required fees: $40 per semester. *Financial support:* In 2010–11, 15 students received support, including 1 fellowship with full tuition reimbursement available (averaging $19,300 per year), 1 research assistantship with full tuition reimbursement available (averaging $18,800 per year), 4 teaching assistantships with full tuition reimbursements available (averaging $18,800 per year); career-related internships or fieldwork, Federal Work-Study, scholarships/grants, and unspecified assistantships also available. Support available to part-time students. Financial award application deadline: 1/15; financial award applicants required to submit FAFSA. *Unit head:* Kim Sichel, Director, 617-353-9912, Fax: 617-353-2556, E-mail: ksichel@bu.edu. *Application contact:* Benjamin Tocchi, Senior Program Coordinator, 617-353-2948, Fax: 617-353-2556, E-mail: btocchi@bu.edu.

Bowling Green State University, Graduate College, College of Arts and Sciences, American Culture Studies Program, Bowling Green, OH 43403. Offers MA, PhD. Part-time programs available. *Degree requirements:* For master's, thesis or alternative; for doctorate, comprehensive exam, thesis/dissertation. *Entrance requirements:* For master's and doctorate, GRE General Test. Additional exam requirements/recommendations for international students: Required—TOEFL. Electronic applications accepted. *Faculty research:* Race and ethnicity, gender, popular culture.

Bowling Green State University, Graduate College, College of Arts and Sciences, Department of Popular Culture, Bowling Green, OH 43403. Offers MA. Part-time programs available. *Degree requirements:* For master's, thesis or alternative. *Entrance requirements:* For master's, GRE General Test. Additional exam requirements/recommendations for international students: Required—TOEFL. Electronic applications accepted. *Faculty research:* Mass media (popular film, TV, and music); folklore/folklife; ritual, festival, celebration, and holidays; global, international, and popular culture; nineteenth century everyday life.

Brown University, Graduate School, Department of American Civilization, Providence, RI 02912. Offers American civilization (MA, PhD); public humanities (MA). *Degree requirements:* For doctorate, thesis/dissertation, preliminary exam.

California State University, Fullerton, Graduate Studies, College of Humanities and Social Sciences, Department of American Studies, Fullerton, CA 92834-9480. Offers MA. Part-time programs available. *Students:* 16 full-time (8 women), 36 part-time (26 women); includes 16 minority (1 American Indian or Alaska Native, non-Hispanic/Latino; 3 Asian, non-Hispanic/Latino; 9 Hispanic/Latino; 3 Two or more races, non-Hispanic/Latino), 3 international. Average age 28. 33 applicants, 61% accepted, 17 enrolled. In 2010, 16 master's awarded. *Degree requirements:* For master's, comprehensive exam or thesis. *Entrance requirements:* For master's, minimum GPA of 3.0 in major, 2.5 in last 60 hours. Application fee: $55. *Financial support:* Federal Work-Study, institutionally sponsored loans, and scholarships/grants available. Support available to part-time students. Financial award application deadline: 3/1; financial award applicants required to submit FAFSA. *Unit head:* Dr. Jesse Battan, Chair, 657-278-2441. *Application contact:* Admissions/Applications, 657-278-2371.

California State University, Long Beach, Graduate Studies, College of Liberal Arts, Department of History, Long Beach, CA 90840. Offers Africa and the Middle East (MA); ancient/medieval Europe (MA); Asia (MA); Latin America (MA); modern Europe (MA); United States (MA); world (MA). Part-time and evening/weekend programs available. *Faculty:* 12 full-time (7 women). *Students:* 18 full-time (6 women), 51 part-time (18 women); includes 3 Black or African American, non-Hispanic/Latino; 1 American Indian or Alaska Native, non-Hispanic/Latino; 3 Asian, non-Hispanic/Latino; 16 Hispanic/Latino, 1 international. Average age 30. 80 applicants, 53% accepted, 30 enrolled. In 2010, 11 master's awarded. *Degree requirements:* For master's, one foreign language, comprehensive exam or thesis. *Application deadline:* For fall admission, 3/1 for domestic students. Applications are processed on a rolling basis. Application fee: $55. Electronic applications accepted. *Financial support:* Research assistantships, Federal Work-Study, institutionally sponsored loans, and scholarships/grants available. Financial award application deadline: 3/2. *Faculty research:* All periods of European and American history, recent Asian and African history. *Unit head:* Dr. Nancy Quam-Wickham, Department Chair, 562-985-4431, Fax: 562-985-5431, E-mail: quamwick@csulb.edu. *Application contact:* Dr. Houri Berberian, Graduate Advisor, 562-985-4524, Fax: 562-985-4431, E-mail: hberber@csulb.edu.

Central Michigan University, College of Graduate Studies, College of Humanities and Social and Behavioral Sciences, Department of History, Mount Pleasant, MI 48859. Offers European history (Graduate Certificate); history (MA, PhD); modern history (Graduate Certificate); United States history (Graduate Certificate). Part-time programs available. *Faculty:* 15 full-time (4 women). *Students:* 38 full-time (11 women), 23 part-time (8 women); includes 2 Black or African American, non-Hispanic/Latino; 1 Asian, non-Hispanic/Latino, 5 international. Average age 30. *Degree requirements:* For master's, thesis or alternative; for doctorate, comprehensive exam, thesis/dissertation. Application fee: $35 ($45 for international students). Electronic applications accepted. *Expenses:* Tuition, state resident: full-time $8208; part-time $456 per credit hour. Tuition, nonresident: full-time $13,788; part-time $766 per credit hour. One-time fee: $25. *Financial support:* Fellowships with tuition reimbursements, research assistantships with tuition reimbursements, teaching assistantships with tuition reimbursements, Federal Work-Study, unspecified assistantships, and out-of-state merit awards, non-resident graduate awards available. *Faculty research:* Colonial and revolutionary United States history, modern European history, Latin American and transatlantic history, transnational and comparative history, United States social history. *Unit head:* Dr. Mitchell K. Hall, Chairperson, 989-773-3374, Fax: 989-774-1156, E-mail: hall1mk@cmich.edu. *Application contact:* Dr. Mitchell K. Hall, Chairperson, 989-773-3374, Fax: 989-774-1156, E-mail: hall1mk@cmich.edu.

Claremont Graduate University, Graduate Programs, School of Arts and Humanities, Department of English, Claremont, CA 91711-6160. Offers American studies (MA, PhD); critical theory (MA, PhD); early modern studies (MA, PhD); English (M Phil, MA, PhD); literary theory (PhD); literature (MA, PhD); literature and creative writing (MA); literature and film (MA); MBA/MA; MBA/PhD. Part-time programs available. *Faculty:* 2 full-time (both women), 4 part-time/adjunct (1 woman). *Students:* 88 full-time (56 women), 14 part-time (12 women); includes 1 Black or African American, non-Hispanic/Latino; 9 Asian, non-Hispanic/Latino; 7 Hispanic/Latino; 5 Two or more races, non-Hispanic/Latino, 7 international. Average age 34. In 2010, 9 master's, 10 doctorates awarded. *Entrance requirements:* For master's and doctorate, GRE General Test. Additional exam requirements/recommendations for international students: Required—TOEFL (minimum score 550 paper-based; 213 computer-based; 80 iBT). *Application deadline:* For fall admission, 2/1 priority date for domestic students. Applications are processed on a rolling basis. Application fee: $60. Electronic applications accepted. *Expenses:* Tuition: Full-time $35,748; part-time $1554 per unit. Required fees: $215 per semester. *Financial support:* Fellowships, Federal Work-Study, institutionally sponsored loans, and scholarships/grants available. Support available to part-time students. Financial award application deadline: 2/15; financial award applicants required to submit FAFSA. *Faculty research:* American, comparative, and English Renaissance literature; modernism; feminist literature and theory. *Unit head:* Elysabeth Flores Griffith, Administrative Director, 909-607-3877, E-mail: elysabeth.flores@cgu.edu. *Application contact:* Susan Hampson, Admissions Coordinator, 909-607-1278, Fax: 909-607-1221, E-mail: humanities@cgu.edu.

Claremont Graduate University, Graduate Programs, School of Arts and Humanities, Department of History, Claremont, CA 91711-6160. Offers Africana history (Certificate); American studies and U. S. history (MA, PhD); archival studies (MA); early modern studies (MA, PhD); European studies (MA, PhD); oral history (MA, PhD); MBA/MA; MBA/PhD. *Faculty:* 4 full-time (2 women), 1 part-time/adjunct (0 women). *Students:* 75 full-time (36 women), 2 part-time (1 woman); includes 25 minority (3 Black or African American, non-Hispanic/Latino; 1 American Indian or Alaska Native, non-Hispanic/Latino; 6 Asian, non-Hispanic/Latino; 9 Hispanic/Latino; 1 Native Hawaiian or other Pacific Islander, non-Hispanic/Latino; 5 Two or more races, non-Hispanic/Latino), 2 international. Average age 36. In 2010, 12 master's, 2 doctorates awarded. Terminal master's awarded for partial completion of doctoral program. *Entrance requirements:* For master's and doctorate, GRE General Test. Additional exam requirements/recommendations for international students: Required—TOEFL (minimum score 550 paper-based; 213 computer-based; 80 iBT). *Application deadline:* For fall admission, 2/1 priority date for domestic students. Applications are processed on a rolling basis. Application fee: $60. Electronic applications accepted. *Expenses:* Tuition: Full-time $35,748; part-time $1554 per unit. Required fees: $215 per semester. *Financial support:* Fellowships, research assistantships, Federal Work-Study, institutionally sponsored loans, and scholarships/grants available. Support available to part-time students. Financial award application deadline: 2/15; financial award applicants required to submit FAFSA. *Faculty research:* Intellectual and social history, cultural studies, gender studies, Western history, Chicano history. *Unit head:* Janet Farrell Brodie, Chair, 909-621-8880, Fax: 909-621-8609, E-mail: janet.brodie@cgu.edu. *Application contact:* Susan Hampson, Admissions Coordinator, 909-607-1278, E-mail: humanities@cgu.edu.

Clark University, Graduate School, Department of History, Program in American History, Worcester, MA 01610-1477. Offers MA, PhD. *Students:* 11 full-time (5 women), 1 part-time (0 women). Average age 29. 13 applicants, 23% accepted, 2 enrolled. In 2010, 1 master's awarded. *Application deadline:* For fall admission, 1/15 for domestic students. Application fee: $50. *Expenses:* Tuition: Full-time $37,000; part-time $1156 per credit hour. Required fees: $30; $1156 per credit hour. *Financial support:* In 2010–11, fellowships with full and partial tuition reimbursements (averaging $11,850 per year), research assistantships with full and partial tuition reimbursements (averaging $11,850 per year), teaching assistantships with full and partial tuition reimbursements (averaging $11,850 per year) were awarded. *Faculty research:* American political history, comparative history, American family history. Total annual research expenditures: $15,000. *Unit head:* Dr. Amy Richter, Chair, 508-793-7288. *Application contact:* Diane Fenner, Academic Secretary, 508-793-7288, Fax: 508-793-8816, E-mail: history@clarku.edu.

The College at Brockport, State University of New York, School of the Arts, Humanities and Social Sciences, Department of History, Brockport, NY 14420-2997. Offers history (MA), including American history, American/world history, world history. Part-time and evening/weekend programs available. *Students:* 27 full-time (12 women), 28 part-time (12 women); includes 4 minority (2 American Indian or Alaska Native, non-Hispanic/Latino; 2 Hispanic/Latino). 26 applicants, 65% accepted, 17 enrolled. In 2010, 7 master's awarded. *Degree requirements:* For master's, thesis or alternative. *Entrance requirements:* For master's, minimum GPA of 3.0, writing sample, letters of recommendation, statement of objectives. Additional exam requirements/recommendations for international students: Required—TOEFL (minimum score 550 paper-based; 213 computer-based; 79 iBT). *Application deadline:* For fall admission, 6/1 priority date for domestic and international students; for spring admission, 11/15 priority date for domestic and international students. Application fee: $50. Electronic applications accepted. *Financial support:* In 2010–11, 1 fellowship with tuition reimbursement (averaging $1,600 per year), 2 teaching assistantships with full tuition reimbursements (averaging $6,000 per year) were awarded; Federal Work-Study, scholarships/grants, and unspecified assistantships also available. Support available to part-time students. Financial award application deadline: 3/15; financial award applicants required to submit FAFSA. *Faculty research:* American history, women's history, European history, world history, cultural history. *Unit head:* Dr. Alison Parker, Chairperson, 585-395-5694, Fax: 585-395-2620, E-mail: aparker@brockport.edu. *Application contact:* Dr. Morag Martin, Graduate Director, 585-395-5690, Fax: 585-395-2620, E-mail: mmartin@brockport.edu.

The College of William and Mary, Faculty of Arts and Sciences, Program in American Studies, Williamsburg, VA 23187-8795. Offers MA, PhD, JD/MA. Part-time programs available. *Faculty:* 5 full-time (2 women). *Students:* 42 full-time (28 women), 3 part-time (all women); includes 8 minority (5 Black or African American, non-Hispanic/Latino; 1 Asian, non-Hispanic/Latino; 2 Two or more races, non-Hispanic/Latino), 1 international. Average age 31. 96 applicants, 22% accepted, 9 enrolled. In 2010, 7 master's, 4 doctorates awarded. Terminal master's awarded for partial completion of doctoral program. *Degree requirements:* For master's, thesis; for doctorate, one foreign language, comprehensive exam, thesis/dissertation. *Entrance* *requirements:* For master's, GRE; for doctorate, GRE, MA. Additional exam requirements/recommendations for international students: Required—TOEFL. *Application deadline:* For fall admission, 1/1 for domestic and international students. Application fee: $45. Electronic applications accepted. *Expenses:* Tuition, state resident: full-time $6400; part-time $345 per credit hour. Tuition, nonresident: full-time $19,720; part-time $920 per credit hour. Required fees: $4368. *Financial support:* In 2010–11, 24 students received support, including 20 fellowships with full tuition reimbursements available (averaging $17,000 per year), 4 research assistantships with full tuition reimbursements available (averaging $4,000 per year); career-related internships or fieldwork, tuition waivers (full), and unspecified assistantships also available. Financial award application deadline: 3/15; financial award applicants required to submit FAFSA. *Faculty research:* Native American literature and environment, Guadalcanal and memory, twentieth century African-American celebrity, African-Americans' relation to war, American religious nationalism. *Unit head:* Dr. Chandos M. Brown, Director, 757-221-1271, Fax: 757-221-1287, E-mail: cmbrow@wm.edu. *Application contact:* Jean Brown, Program Administrator, 757-221-1275, Fax: 757-221-1287, E-mail: jxbrow@wm.edu.

The Colorado College, Department of Education, Experienced Teacher Program, Colorado Springs, CO 80903-3294. Offers arts and humanities (MAT); liberal arts (MAT); Southwest studies (MAT). Programs offered during summer only. Part-time programs available. *Degree requirements:* For master's, thesis, oral exam, 50-page paper. *Expenses:* Contact institution.

Columbia University, Graduate School of Arts and Sciences, Program in Liberal Studies, New York, NY 10027. Offers American studies (MA); East Asian studies (MA); human rights studies (MA); Islamic culture studies (MA); Jewish studies (MA); medieval studies (MA); modern European studies (MA); South Asian studies (MA). Part-time and evening/weekend programs available. *Degree requirements:* For master's, thesis.

Cornell University, Graduate School, Graduate Fields of Arts and Sciences, Field of English Language and Literature, Ithaca, NY 14853-0001. Offers African-American literature (PhD); American literature after 1865 (PhD); American literature to 1865 (PhD); American studies (PhD); colonial and postcolonial literature (PhD); creative writing (MFA); cultural studies (PhD); dramatic literature (PhD); English poetry (PhD); English Renaissance to 1660 (PhD); lesbian, bisexual, and gay literature studies (PhD); literary criticism and theory (PhD); nineteenth century (PhD); Old and Middle English (PhD); prose fiction (PhD); Restoration and eighteenth century (PhD); twentieth century (PhD); women's literature (PhD); MFA/PhD. *Faculty:* 56 full-time (29 women). *Students:* 100 full-time (56 women); includes 5 Black or African American, non-Hispanic/Latino; 3 American Indian or Alaska Native, non-Hispanic/Latino; 10 Asian, non-Hispanic/Latino; 8 Hispanic/Latino, 12 international. Average age 27. 1,091 applicants, 4% accepted, 21 enrolled. In 2010, 25 master's, 12 doctorates awarded. Terminal master's awarded for partial completion of doctoral program. *Degree requirements:* For master's, one foreign language, thesis; for doctorate, one foreign language, comprehensive exam, thesis/dissertation, teaching experience. *Entrance requirements:* For master's, GRE General Test, 3 letters of recommendation, creative writing sample; for doctorate, GRE General Test, GRE Subject Test (English), 3 letters of recommendation, writing sample. Additional exam requirements/recommendations for international students: Required—TOEFL (minimum score 600 paper-based; 250 computer-based; 77 iBT). *Application deadline:* For fall admission, 1/10 for domestic students. Application fee: $80. Electronic applications accepted. *Expenses:* Tuition: Full-time $29,500. Required fees: $76. Tuition and fees vary according to degree level and program. *Financial support:* In 2010–11, 32 fellowships with full tuition reimbursements, 60 teaching assistantships with full tuition reimbursements were awarded; research assistantships with tuition reimbursements, institutionally sponsored loans, scholarships/grants, health care benefits, tuition waivers (full and partial), and unspecified assistantships also available. Financial award applicants required to submit FAFSA. *Faculty research:* English and American literature, women's writing, ethnic and post-colonial literature, critical theory, medievalism. *Unit head:* Director of Graduate Studies, 607-255-7989, Fax: 607-255-6661. *Application contact:* Graduate Field Assistant, 607-255-7989, Fax: 607-255-6661, E-mail: english_grad@cornell.edu.

Cornell University, Graduate School, Graduate Fields of Arts and Sciences, Field of History, Ithaca, NY 14853-0001. Offers African history (MA, PhD); American history (MA, PhD); ancient history (MA, PhD); early modern European history (MA, PhD); English history (MA, PhD); French history (MA, PhD); German history (MA, PhD); history of science (MA, PhD); Latin American history (MA, PhD); medieval Chinese history (MA, PhD); medieval history (MA, PhD); modern Chinese history (MA, PhD); modern European history (MA, PhD); modern Japanese history (MA, PhD); premodern Islamic history (MA, PhD); premodern Japanese history (MA, PhD); Renaissance history (MA, PhD); Russian history (MA, PhD); Southeast Asian history (MA, PhD). *Faculty:* 53 full-time (15 women). *Students:* 59 full-time (30 women); includes 3 Black or African American, non-Hispanic/Latino; 2 Asian, non-Hispanic/Latino; 4 Hispanic/Latino, 22 international. Average age 30. 217 applicants, 6% accepted, 8 enrolled. In 2010, 9 master's, 5 doctorates awarded. Terminal master's awarded for partial completion of doctoral program. *Degree requirements:* For master's, thesis; for doctorate, 2 foreign languages, comprehensive exam, thesis/dissertation, 1 year of teaching experience. *Entrance requirements:* For master's and doctorate, GRE General Test, writing sample, 3 letters of recommendation. Additional exam requirements/recommendations for international students: Required—TOEFL (minimum score 550 paper-based; 213 computer-based; 77 iBT). *Application deadline:* For fall admission, 1/15 for domestic students. Application fee: $80. Electronic applications accepted. *Expenses:* Tuition: Full-time $29,500. Required fees: $76. Tuition and fees vary according to degree level and program. *Financial support:* In 2010–11, 26 fellowships with full tuition reimbursements, 27 teaching assistantships with full tuition reimbursements were awarded; research assistantships with full tuition reimbursements, institutionally sponsored loans, scholarships/grants, health care benefits, tuition waivers (full and partial), and unspecified assistantships also available. Financial award applicants required to submit FAFSA. *Unit head:* Director of Graduate Studies, 607-255-6738, Fax: 607-255-0469. *Application contact:* Graduate Field Assistant, 607-255-6738, Fax: 607-255-0469, E-mail: history_grad_info@cornell.edu.

Cornell University, Graduate School, Graduate Fields of Arts and Sciences, Field of History of Art, Archaeology and Visual Studies, Ithaca, NY 14853. Offers American art (PhD); ancient art and archaeology (PhD); Asian art (PhD); Baroque art (PhD); medieval art (PhD); modern art (PhD); Renaissance art (PhD); Southeast Asian art (PhD); theory and criticism (PhD). *Faculty:* 24 full-time (15 women). *Students:* 21 full-time (19 women); includes 1 Black or African American, non-Hispanic/Latino; 2 American Indian or Alaska Native, non-Hispanic/Latino; 1 Hispanic/Latino, 7 international. Average age 31. 71 applicants, 7% accepted, 5 enrolled. In 2010, 2 doctorates awarded. *Degree requirements:* For doctorate, one foreign language, comprehensive exam, thesis/dissertation, general exams in 3 areas. *Entrance requirements:* For doctorate, GRE General Test, sample of written work, 3 letters of recommendation. Additional exam requirements/recommendations for international students: Required—TOEFL (minimum score 550 paper-based; 213 computer-based; 77 iBT). *Application deadline:* For fall admission, 1/15 for domestic students. Application fee: $80. Electronic applications accepted. *Expenses:* Tuition: Full-time $29,500. Required fees: $76. Tuition and fees vary according to degree level and program. *Financial support:* In 2010–11, 8 fellowships with full tuition reimbursements, 11 teaching assistantships with full tuition reimbursements were awarded; research assistantships with full tuition reimbursements, institutionally sponsored loans, scholarships/grants, health care benefits, tuition waivers (full and partial), and unspecified assistantships also available. Financial award applicants required to submit FAFSA. *Unit head:* Director of Graduate Studies, 607-255-4905, Fax: 607-255-0566, E-mail: art_history@cornell.edu. *Application contact:* Graduate Field Assistant, 607-255-4905, Fax: 607-255-0566, E-mail: art_history@cornell.edu.

East Carolina University, Graduate School, Thomas Harriot College of Arts and Sciences, Department of History, Greenville, NC 27858-4353. Offers American history (MA); European history (MA); maritime history (MA). Part-time and evening/weekend programs available. *Degree requirements:* For master's, one foreign language, comprehensive exam, thesis. *Entrance requirements:* For master's, GRE General Test, GRE Subject Test. Additional exam requirements/recommendations for international students: Required—TOEFL. *Expenses:* Tuition, state resident: full-time $3130; part-time $391.25 per credit hour. Tuition, nonresident: full-time $13,817; part-time $1727.13 per credit hour. Required fees: $1916; $239.50 per credit hour. Tuition and fees vary according to campus/location and program.

Eastern Michigan University, Graduate School, College of Arts and Sciences, Department of History and Philosophy, Programs in Social Sciences, Ypsilanti, MI 48197. Offers social science (MA, Graduate Certificate); social science and American culture (MLS). Part-time and evening/weekend programs available. Postbaccalaureate distance learning degree programs offered (minimal on-campus study). *Students:* 4 full-time (3 women), 18 part-time (8 women); includes 3 minority (all Black or African American, non-Hispanic/Latino). Average age 34. In 2010, 6 master's awarded. *Degree requirements:* For master's, thesis optional. *Entrance requirements:* Additional exam requirements/recommendations for international students: Required—TOEFL. *Application deadline:* Applications are processed on a rolling basis. Application fee: $35. *Financial support:* Fellowships, research assistantships with full tuition reimbursements, teaching assistantships with full tuition reimbursements, career-related internships or fieldwork, Federal Work-Study, institutionally sponsored loans, scholarships/grants, tuition waivers (partial), and unspecified assistantships available. Support available to part-time students. Financial award applicants required to submit FAFSA. *Application contact:* Dr. Ronald Delph, Coordinator, 734-487-0053, Fax: 734-487-6835, E-mail: rdelph@emich.edu.

Emory & Henry College, Graduate Programs, Emory, VA 24327-0947. Offers American history (MA Ed); organizational leadership (MOL); professional studies (M Ed); reading specialist (MA Ed). Part-time and evening/weekend programs available. *Entrance requirements:* For master's, GRE or PRAXIS I, recommendations, writing sample.

Fairfield University, College of Arts and Sciences, Fairfield, CT 06824-5195. Offers American studies (MA); communication (MA); creative writing (MFA); mathematics (MS). Part-time and evening/weekend programs available. Postbaccalaureate distance learning degree programs offered (minimal on-campus study). *Faculty:* 46 full-time (20 women), 15 part-time/adjunct (7 women). *Students:* 96 full-time (65 women), 97 part-time (63 women); includes 7 Black or African American, non-Hispanic/Latino; 5 Hispanic/Latino; 2 Two or more races, non-Hispanic/Latino, 7 international. Average age 41. 114 applicants, 62% accepted, 38 enrolled. In 2010, 36 master's awarded. *Degree requirements:* For master's, capstone research course. *Entrance requirements:* For master's, minimum GPA of 3.0, 2 letters of recommendation, resume. Additional exam requirements/recommendations for international students: Required—TOEFL (minimum score 550 paper-based; 213 computer-based; 80 iBT). *Application deadline:* For fall admission, 5/15 for international students; for spring admission, 10/15 for international students. Applications are processed on a rolling basis. Application fee: $60. Electronic applications accepted. *Expenses:* Tuition: Part-time $600 per hour. Part-time tuition and fees vary according to degree level and program. *Financial support:* In 2010–11, 19 students received support. Unspecified assistantships available. Financial award applicants required to submit FAFSA. *Faculty research:* Non-commutative algebra, partial differential equations, writing (fiction, non-fiction and poetry), communication for social change, comparative media systems, negotiation and management. *Unit head:* Dr. Robbin Crabtree, Dean, 203-254-4000 Ext. 3263, Fax: 203-254-4119, E-mail: rcrabtree@fairfield.edu. *Application contact:* Marianne Gumpper, Director of Graduate and Continuing Studies Admissions, 203-254-4184, Fax: 203-254-4073, E-mail: gradadmis@fairfield.edu.

Georgetown University, Graduate School of Arts and Sciences, School of Continuing Studies, Washington, DC 20057. Offers American studies (MALS); Catholic studies (MALS); classical civilizations (MALS); disability studies (MPS); ethics and the professions (MALS); human resources management (MPS); humanities (MALS); individualized study (MALS); international affairs (MALS); Islam and Muslim-Christian relations (MALS); journalism (MPS); liberal studies (DLS); literature and society (MALS); medieval and early modern European studies (MALS); public relations and corporate communications (MPS); real estate (MPS); religious studies (MALS); social and public policy (MALS); sports industry management (MPS); the theory and practice of American democracy (MALS); visual culture (MALS). *Entrance requirements:* Additional exam requirements/recommendations for international students: Required—TOEFL.

The George Washington University, Columbian College of Arts and Sciences, Department of American Studies, Washington, DC 20052. Offers American studies (PhD); folklife (MA); historic preservation (MA); material culture (MA). Part-time and evening/weekend programs available. *Faculty:* 11 full-time (5 women), 4 part-time/adjunct (2 women). *Students:* 24 full-time (17 women), 29 part-time (13 women); includes 4 Black or African American, non-Hispanic/Latino; 2 Asian, non-Hispanic/Latino; 1 Hispanic/Latino, 1 international. Average age 29. 134 applicants, 49% accepted, 19 enrolled. In 2010, 8 master's, 7 doctorates awarded. Terminal master's awarded for partial completion of doctoral program. *Degree requirements:* For master's, comprehensive exam; for doctorate, one foreign language, thesis/dissertation, general exam. *Entrance requirements:* For master's and doctorate, GRE General Test, minimum GPA of 3.0. Additional exam requirements/recommendations for international students: Required—TOEFL (minimum score 550 paper-based; 213 computer-based; 80 iBT). *Application deadline:* For fall admission, 1/15 priority date for domestic and international students; for spring admission, 10/1 for domestic students. Application fee: $75. *Financial support:* In 2010–11, 22 students received support; fellowships, research assistantships, teaching assistantships, career-related internships or fieldwork, Federal Work-Study, institutionally sponsored loans, and tuition waivers available. Financial award application deadline: 1/15. *Unit head:* James A. Miller, Chair, 202-994-6743, E-mail: jam@gwu.edu. *Application contact:* Information Contact, 202-994-6070, Fax: 202-994-8651, E-mail: amst@gwu.edu.

Harvard University, Graduate School of Arts and Sciences, Committee on History of American Civilization, Cambridge, MA 02138. Offers PhD. *Degree requirements:* For doctorate, 2 foreign languages, thesis/dissertation. *Entrance requirements:* For doctorate, GRE General Test, GRE Subject Test (recommended). Additional exam requirements/recommendations for international students: Required—TOEFL. *Expenses:* Tuition: Full-time $34,976. Required fees: $1166. Full-time tuition and fees vary according to program. *Faculty research:* American history, literature, and religion in the Colonial era; twentieth century American history, literature, and law; Southern literature, history, and sociology.

Inter American University of Puerto Rico, Metropolitan Campus, Graduate Programs, Program in History, San Juan, PR 00919-1293. Offers American history (PhD); history (MA, PhD).

Kennesaw State University, College of Humanities and Social Sciences, Master of Arts in American Studies Program, Kennesaw, GA 30144-5591. Offers MA. Part-time programs available. *Students:* 9 full-time (7 women), 20 part-time (13 women); includes 7 minority (2 Black or African American, non-Hispanic/Latino; 4 Hispanic/Latino; 1 Two or more races, non-Hispanic/Latino). Average age 34. 12 applicants, 83% accepted, 9 enrolled. In 2010, 1 master's awarded. *Degree requirements:* For master's, one foreign language. *Entrance requirements:* For master's, GRE. Additional exam requirements/recommendations for international students: Required—TOEFL (minimum score 550 paper-based; 213 computer-based; 80 iBT), IELTS (minimum score 6). *Application deadline:* For fall admission, 5/1 for domestic and international students; for winter admission, 11/1 for domestic and international students. Applications are processed on a rolling basis. Application fee: $60. Electronic applications accepted. *Expenses:* Tuition, state resident: full-time $5500; part-time $225 per credit hour. Tuition, nonresident: full-time $16,100; part-time $813 per credit hour. Required fees: $673 per semester. *Unit head:* Rebecca Hill, 770-794-7543. *Application contact:* Tamara Hutto, Admissions Counselor, 770-420-4377, Fax: 770-423-6885, E-mail: ksugrad@kennesaw.edu.

Lehigh University, College of Arts and Sciences, Department of History, Bethlehem, PA 18015. Offers American history (PhD); British history (PhD); history (MA). Part-time programs available. *Faculty:* 16 full-time (5 women). *Students:* 20 full-time (10 women), 16 part-time (2 women). Average age 32. 33 applicants, 73% accepted, 11 enrolled. In 2010, 3 master's, 2 doctorates awarded. Terminal master's awarded for partial completion of doctoral program.

American Studies

Lehigh University (continued)
Degree requirements: For master's, thesis optional, comprehensive exam or thesis; for doctorate, comprehensive exam, thesis/dissertation. *Entrance requirements:* For master's, GRE General Test, recommendations; for doctorate, GRE General Test, recommendations, writing samples. Additional exam requirements/recommendations for international students: Required—TOEFL. *Application deadline:* For fall admission, 7/15 for domestic students; for winter admission, 1/15 priority date for domestic and international students. Applications are processed on a rolling basis. Application fee: $65. Electronic applications accepted. *Financial support:* In 2010–11, 34 students received support, including fellowships with full tuition reimbursements available (averaging $25,000 per year), research assistantships with full tuition reimbursements available (averaging $15,600 per year), 10 teaching assistantships with full tuition reimbursements available (averaging $18,400 per year); institutionally sponsored loans, scholarships/grants, tuition waivers (full and partial), and unspecified assistantships also available. Support available to part-time students. Financial award application deadline: 1/15. *Faculty research:* Colonial America, modern America, history of technology. *Unit head:* Dr. Stephen H. Cutcliffe, Chairman, 610-758-3360, Fax: 610-758-6554, E-mail: shc0@lehigh.edu. *Application contact:* Dr. Roger D. Simon, Graduate Coordinator, 610-758-3368, Fax: 610-758-6554, E-mail: rds2@lehigh.edu.

Lehigh University, College of Arts and Sciences, Program in American Studies, Bethlehem, PA 18015. Offers MA. Part-time programs available. *Students:* 9 full-time (all women), 4 part-time (all women); includes 1 minority (Native Hawaiian or other Pacific Islander, non-Hispanic/Latino), 3 international. Average age 26. 9 applicants, 67% accepted, 4 enrolled. In 2010, 4 master's awarded. *Degree requirements:* For master's, thesis. *Entrance requirements:* For master's, GRE, writing sample, essay, minimum GPA of 2.75. Additional exam requirements/recommendations for international students: Required—TOEFL. *Application deadline:* For fall admission, 1/15 for domestic students, 7/15 for international students; for spring admission, 12/1 for domestic and international students. Applications are processed on a rolling basis. Application fee: $65. Electronic applications accepted. *Financial support:* In 2010–11, 4 students received support, including 1 fellowship with full tuition reimbursement available; institutionally sponsored loans, scholarships/grants, tuition waivers (full), and unspecified assistantships also available. Support available to part-time students. Financial award application deadline: 1/15; financial award applicants required to submit FAFSA. *Faculty research:* War, media and video games, social movements, community identity and narrative, traditional eighteenth/nineteenth/twentieth century literature and history, gender and popular culture. *Unit head:* Prof. Edward Whitley, Director, 610-758-4745, Fax: 610-758-6554, E-mail: amstdgrad@lehigh.edu. *Application contact:* Mary T. Harnett, Coordinator, 610-758-4745, Fax: 610-758-6554, E-mail: amstdgrad@lehigh.edu.

Lindenwood University, Graduate Programs, School of American Studies, St. Charles, MO 63301-1695. Offers MA. Part-time and evening/weekend programs available. *Faculty:* 2 full-time (0 women), 9 part-time/adjunct (5 women). *Students:* 5 full-time (2 women), 1 international. Average age 33. *Degree requirements:* For master's, project. *Entrance requirements:* For master's, baccalaureate degree from accredited institution. Additional exam requirements/recommendations for international students: Required—TOEFL (minimum score 550 paper-based; 213 computer-based; 80 iBT). *Application deadline:* For fall admission, 8/27 for domestic and international students; for spring admission, 1/28 for domestic and international students. Application fee: $30 ($100 for international students). *Expenses:* Tuition: Full-time $13,260; part-time $380 per credit hour. Required fees: $340. One-time fee: $30. Tuition and fees vary according to course level and course load. *Financial support:* In 2010–11, 3 students received support. Career-related internships or fieldwork, Federal Work-Study, institutionally sponsored loans, and tuition waivers (partial) available. Financial award application deadline: 6/30; financial award applicants required to submit FAFSA. *Unit head:* Dr. David Knotts, Dean, 636-798-2166, E-mail: dknotts@lindenwood.edu. *Application contact:* Brett Barger, Dean of Evening Admissions and Extension Campuses, 636-949-4934, Fax: 636-949-4109, E-mail: adultadmissions@lindenwood.edu.

Lindenwood University, Graduate Programs, School of Humanities, St. Charles, MO 63301-1695. Offers American studies (MA); international studies (MA). Part-time programs available. *Faculty:* 4 full-time (2 women), 5 part-time/adjunct (1 woman). *Students:* 18 full-time (13 women), 2 part-time (1 woman); includes 1 minority (Black or African American, non-Hispanic/Latino), 10 international. Average age 26. 8 applicants, 6 enrolled. In 2010, 2 master's awarded. *Degree requirements:* For master's, minimum cumulative GPA of 3.0. *Entrance requirements:* For master's, minimum GPA of 2.5, 2 letters of recommendation. Additional exam requirements/recommendations for international students: Required—TOEFL (minimum score 550 paper-based; 213 computer-based; 80 iBT). *Application deadline:* For fall admission, 8/27 priority date for domestic and international students; for spring admission, 1/28 for domestic students, 1/28 priority date for international students. Applications are processed on a rolling basis. Application fee: $30 ($100 for international students). Electronic applications accepted. *Expenses:* Tuition: Full-time $13,260; part-time $380 per credit hour. Required fees: $340. One-time fee: $30. Tuition and fees vary according to course level and course load. *Financial support:* In 2010–11, 19 students received support. Career-related internships or fieldwork, institutionally sponsored loans, tuition waivers (partial), and unspecified assistantships available. Financial award application deadline: 6/30; financial award applicants required to submit FAFSA. *Unit head:* Dr. Ana Schnellmann, Dean, 636-949-4873, E-mail: aschnellmann@lindenwood.edu. *Application contact:* Brett Barger, Dean of Evening Admissions and Extension Campuses, 636-949-4934, Fax: 636-949-4109, E-mail: adultadmissions@lindenwood.edu.

Michigan State University, The Graduate School, College of Arts and Letters, Program in American Studies, East Lansing, MI 48824. Offers MA, PhD. *Entrance requirements:* Additional exam requirements/recommendations for international students: Required—TOEFL. Electronic applications accepted.

Mississippi State University, College of Arts and Sciences, Department of History, Mississippi State, MS 39762. Offers history (PhD); U. S. and European history (MA). Part-time programs available. *Faculty:* 17 full-time (6 women). *Students:* 36 full-time (15 women), 9 part-time (3 women); includes 2 minority (1 Black or African American, non-Hispanic/Latino; 1 Asian, non-Hispanic/Latino). Average age 30. 35 applicants, 74% accepted, 18 enrolled. In 2010, 10 master's, 4 doctorates awarded. *Degree requirements:* For master's, one foreign language, comprehensive exam, thesis optional; for doctorate, 2 foreign languages, thesis/dissertation, comprehensive oral and written exam. *Entrance requirements:* For master's, minimum GPA of 3.0 on last two years of undergraduate courses; for doctorate, GRE, writing sample, minimum graduate GPA of 3.0. Additional exam requirements/recommendations for international students: Required—TOEFL (minimum score 475 paper-based; 153 computer-based; 53 iBT); Recommended—IELTS (minimum score 4.5). *Application deadline:* For fall admission, 4/1 for domestic students, 5/1 for international students; for spring admission, 11/1 for domestic students, 9/1 for international students. Applications are processed on a rolling basis. Application fee: $40. Electronic applications accepted. *Expenses:* Tuition, state resident: full-time $2730.50; part-time $304 per credit hour. Tuition, nonresident: full-time $6901; part-time $767 per credit hour. *Financial support:* In 2010–11, 31 teaching assistantships with full tuition reimbursements (averaging $10,977 per year) were awarded; Federal Work-Study, institutionally sponsored loans, scholarships/grants, and unspecified assistantships also available. Financial award application deadline: 4/1; financial award applicants required to submit FAFSA. *Faculty research:* U. S. political, diplomatic, military, social, and cultural history; modern Europe; Latin America; Asian history; African history. *Unit head:* Dr. Alan I. Marcus, Head, 662-325-3604, Fax: 662-325-1139, E-mail: aim10@msstate.edu. *Application contact:* Dr. Peter Messer, Associate Professor and Graduate Coordinator, 662-325-3604, Fax: 662-325-1139, E-mail: pmesser@history.msstate.edu.

Monmouth University, The Graduate School, Department of History, West Long Branch, NJ 07764-1898. Offers European specialization (MA); U. S. specialization (MA); world specialization (MA). Part-time and evening/weekend programs available. *Faculty:* 12 full-time (3 women). *Students:* 5 full-time (4 women), 56 part-time (28 women); includes 1 Black or African American, non-Hispanic/Latino; 1 Asian, non-Hispanic/Latino; 3 Hispanic/Latino; 1 Two or more races, non-Hispanic/Latino. Average age 36. 22 applicants, 100% accepted, 17 enrolled. In 2010, 16 master's awarded. *Degree requirements:* For master's, comprehensive exam, thesis or alternative. *Entrance requirements:* For master's, minimum GPA of 3.0 in major, 2.5 overall. Additional exam requirements/recommendations for international students: Required—TOEFL (minimum score 550 paper-based; 213 computer-based; 79 iBT), IELTS (minimum score 5) or Michigan English Language Assessment Battery (minimum score 77), Cambridge A, B, C. *Application deadline:* For fall admission, 7/15 priority date for domestic students, 6/1 for international students; for spring admission, 11/15 priority date for domestic students, 11/1 for international students. Applications are processed on a rolling basis. Application fee: $50. Electronic applications accepted. *Expenses:* Tuition: Full-time $19,572; part-time $816 per credit. Required fees: $628; $157 per semester. *Financial support:* In 2010–11, 46 students received support, including 39 fellowships (averaging $1,073 per year), 5 research assistantships (averaging $4,934 per year); career-related internships or fieldwork, scholarships/grants, and unspecified assistantships also available. Support available to part-time students. Financial award applicants required to submit FAFSA. *Faculty research:* U. S. business; labor; British, German, and French Revolutions; Soviet Union; Africa. *Unit head:* Dr. Maryann Rhett, Program Director, 732-263-5768, Fax: 732-263-5112, E-mail: mrhett@monmouth.edu. *Application contact:* Kevin Roane, Director, Office of Graduate Admission, 732-571-3452, Fax: 732-263-5123, E-mail: gradadm@monmouth.edu.

New Mexico Highlands University, Graduate Studies, College of Arts and Sciences, Program in Southwest Studies, Las Vegas, NM 87701. Offers MA, MS. Program is interdisciplinary. Part-time programs available. *Faculty:* 6 full-time (0 women). *Students:* 13 full-time (2 women), 3 part-time (2 women); includes 6 Hispanic/Latino, 9 international. Average age 26. 17 applicants, 100% accepted, 5 enrolled. In 2010, 6 master's awarded. *Degree requirements:* For master's, comprehensive exam, thesis or alternative. *Entrance requirements:* Additional exam requirements/recommendations for international students: Required—TOEFL (minimum score 540 paper-based; 207 computer-based). *Application deadline:* For fall admission, 8/1 priority date for domestic students. Applications are processed on a rolling basis. Application fee: $15. *Expenses:* Tuition, state resident: full-time $2544. Required fees: $624; $132 per credit hour. *Financial support:* In 2010–11, 14 students received support. Career-related internships or fieldwork, Federal Work-Study, institutionally sponsored loans, scholarships/grants, tuition waivers (full and partial), and unspecified assistantships available. Support available to part-time students. Financial award application deadline: 3/1; financial award applicants required to submit FAFSA. *Unit head:* Dr. John Jeffries, Department Head of Computer and Mathematical Sciences, 505-454-3480, E-mail: jjeffries@nmhu.edu. *Application contact:* Diane Trujillo, Administrative Assistant, Graduate Studies, 505-454-3266, Fax: 505-426-2117, E-mail: dtrujillo@nmhu.edu.

New York University, Graduate School of Arts and Science, Program in American Studies, New York, NY 10012-1019. Offers MA, PhD. Part-time programs available. *Faculty:* 4 full-time (1 woman), 2 part-time/adjunct (0 women). *Students:* 38 full-time (25 women), 7 part-time (4 women); includes 11 Black or African American, non-Hispanic/Latino; 1 American Indian or Alaska Native, non-Hispanic/Latino; 5 Asian, non-Hispanic/Latino; 7 Hispanic/Latino, 3 international. Average age 33. 222 applicants, 7% accepted, 7 enrolled. In 2010, 5 master's, 7 doctorates awarded. *Degree requirements:* For master's, one foreign language, thesis; for doctorate, 2 foreign languages, thesis/dissertation. *Entrance requirements:* For master's and doctorate, GRE General Test, writing sample. Additional exam requirements/recommendations for international students: Required—TOEFL. *Application deadline:* For fall admission, 12/15 for domestic students. Application fee: $90. *Financial support:* Fellowships with tuition reimbursements, teaching assistantships with tuition reimbursements, Federal Work-Study, institutionally sponsored loans, and unspecified assistantships available. Financial award application deadline: 12/15; financial award applicants required to submit FAFSA. *Faculty research:* Cultural politics; race, gender, and sexuality studies; nationalism and transnationalism; science and technology; urban and suburban studies. *Unit head:* Nikhil Singh, Director, 212-998-9650, Fax: 212-995-4665, E-mail: amstudies@nyu.edu. *Application contact:* Jennifer Morgan, Director of Graduate Studies, 212-998-9650, Fax: 212-995-4665, E-mail: amstudies@nyu.edu.

New York University, Graduate School of Arts and Science, Program in Irish and Irish American Studies, New York, NY 10012-1019. Offers MA. Part-time programs available. *Students:* 2 full-time (both women), 15 part-time (9 women), 1 international. Average age 38. 38 applicants, 37% accepted, 12 enrolled. In 2010, 8 master's awarded. *Degree requirements:* For master's, one foreign language. *Entrance requirements:* For master's, GRE General Test. Additional exam requirements/recommendations for international students: Required—TOEFL. *Application deadline:* For fall admission, 3/1 priority date for domestic students. Application fee: $90. *Financial support:* Federal Work-Study, scholarships/grants, health care benefits, and unspecified assistantships available. Financial award application deadline: 3/1. *Unit head:* John Waters, Director of Graduate Studies, 212-998-3950, Fax: 212-995-4373, E-mail: gsas.irishstudies.ma@nyu.edu. *Application contact:* Anne Solari, Program Coordinator, 212-998-3950, Fax: 212-995-4373, E-mail: gsas.irishstudies.ma@nyu.edu.

Northeastern State University, Graduate College, College of Liberal Arts, Program in American Studies, Tahlequah, OK 74464-2399. Offers MA. Part-time and evening/weekend programs available. *Students:* 7 full-time (3 women), 13 part-time (8 women); includes 7 minority (1 Black or African American, non-Hispanic/Latino; 6 American Indian or Alaska Native, non-Hispanic/Latino). In 2010, 7 master's awarded. *Degree requirements:* For master's, thesis, written and oral examinations. *Entrance requirements:* For master's, GRE, minimum GPA of 2.5. Additional exam requirements/recommendations for international students: Required—TOEFL (minimum score 213 computer-based). *Application deadline:* For fall admission, 6/1 priority date for domestic students. Applications are processed on a rolling basis. Application fee: $0 ($25 for international students). Electronic applications accepted. *Expenses:* Tuition, state resident: part-time $144 per credit hour. Tuition, nonresident: part-time $384.05 per credit hour. Required fees: $34.90 per credit hour. Tuition and fees vary according to program. *Financial support:* Teaching assistantships, Federal Work-Study available. Financial award application deadline: 3/1. *Unit head:* Dr. Chris Owen, Coordinator, 918-456-5511, Fax: 918-458-2390, E-mail: owen@nsuok.edu. *Application contact:* Margie Railey, Administrative Assistant, 918-456-5511 Ext. 2093, Fax: 918-458-2061, E-mail: railey@nsouk.edu.

Northwestern University, School of Continuing Studies, Program in Liberal Studies, Evanston, IL 60208. Offers American studies (MA); history (MA); religious and ethical studies (MA).

Norwich University, School of Graduate and Continuing Studies, Program in Military History, Northfield, VT 05663. Offers race and gender in military history (MA); total war (MA); U. S. military history (MA). Evening/weekend programs available. *Faculty:* 33 part-time/adjunct (2 women). *Students:* 127 full-time (23 women); includes 2 Black or African American, non-Hispanic/Latino; 7 Hispanic/Latino. Average age 42. 157 applicants, 96% accepted, 127 enrolled. In 2010, 127 master's awarded. *Entrance requirements:* For master's, minimum undergraduate GPA of 2.75. Additional exam requirements/recommendations for international students: Required—TOEFL (minimum score 550 paper-based; 212 computer-based; 83 iBT). *Application deadline:* For fall admission, 8/10 for domestic and international students; for winter admission, 11/7 for domestic and international students; for spring admission, 2/6 for domestic and international students. Application fee: $50. Electronic applications accepted. *Expenses:* Tuition: Full-time $17,380; part-time $645 per credit. Tuition and fees vary according to program. *Financial support:* Scholarships/grants available. Financial award applicants required to submit FAFSA. *Unit head:* Dr. James Ehrman, Program Director, 802-485-2567, Fax: 802-485-2533. *Application contact:* Lars Nielsen, Administrative Director, 802-485-2853, Fax: 802-485-2533, E-mail: lnielsen@norwich.edu.

Penn State Harrisburg, Graduate School, School of Humanities, Middletown, PA 17057-4898. Offers American studies (MA). Evening/weekend programs available. *Unit head:* Dr. Kathryn Robinson, Director, 717-948-6470, E-mail: kdr12@psu.edu. *Application contact:* Robert Coffman, Director of Admissions, 717-948-6250, Fax: 717-948-6325, E-mail: ric1@psu.edu.

Pepperdine University, Seaver College, Humanities and Teacher Education Division, Malibu, CA 90263. Offers American studies (MA); history (MA); writing for screen and television (MFA). Part-time programs available. *Students:* 23 part-time (16 women); includes 1 minority (Asian, non-Hispanic/Latino). 8 applicants, 88% accepted, 7 enrolled. In 2010, 3 master's awarded. *Degree requirements:* For master's, oral and written exams. *Entrance requirements:* For master's, GRE General Test, writing sample, letters of recommendation. Additional exam requirements/recommendations for international students: Required—TOEFL. *Application deadline:* For fall admission, 2/1 priority date for domestic students. Applications are processed on a rolling basis. Application fee: $55. *Financial support:* Applicants required to submit FAFSA. *Unit head:* Dr. Maire Mullins, Chair/Professor of English, 310-506-4235, Fax: 310-506-7307, E-mail: maire.mullins@pepperdine.edu. *Application contact:* Michael Truschke, Dean of Admission and Enrollment Management, 310-506-6165, Fax: 310-506-4861, E-mail: admission-seaver@pepperdine.edu.

Providence College, Graduate Studies, Department of History, Providence, RI 02918. Offers American history (MA); European history (MA). Part-time and evening/weekend programs available. *Faculty:* 14 part-time/adjunct (3 women). *Students:* 23 full-time (7 women), 37 part-time (15 women); includes 1 minority (Black or African American, non-Hispanic/Latino). Average age 30. 14 applicants, 100% accepted. In 2010, 28 master's awarded. *Degree requirements:* For master's, comprehensive exam, thesis optional. *Entrance requirements:* Additional exam requirements/recommendations for international students: Required—TOEFL (minimum score 550 paper-based; 213 computer-based; 80 iBT). *Application deadline:* For fall admission, 8/1 priority date for domestic and international students; for spring admission, 12/31 priority date for domestic students, 12/1 priority date for international students. Applications are processed on a rolling basis. Application fee: $55. *Expenses:* Tuition: Part-time $367 per credit. Required fees: $367. *Financial support:* In 2010–11, 8 research assistantships with full tuition reimbursements (averaging $8,400 per year) were awarded; career-related internships or fieldwork, institutionally sponsored loans, and unspecified assistantships also available. Support available to part-time students. Financial award application deadline: 8/1; financial award applicants required to submit FAFSA. *Faculty research:* Modern Europe, American social and political history, modern Ireland, Rhode Island, eastern European history. *Unit head:* Dr. Paul O'Malley, Director of Graduate Programs, 401-865-2193, Fax: 401-865-1193, E-mail: pomalley@providence.edu. *Application contact:* Phyllis S. Cardullo, Senior Administrative Coordinator, 401-865-2193, Fax: 401-865-1193, E-mail: pcardull@providence.edu.

Purdue University, Graduate School, College of Liberal Arts, Program in American Studies, West Lafayette, IN 47907. Offers MA, PhD. *Degree requirements:* For master's, essay; for doctorate, one foreign language, thesis/dissertation. *Entrance requirements:* For master's and doctorate, GRE General Test, sample of written work. Additional exam requirements/recommendations for international students: Required—TOEFL, TWE. Electronic applications accepted. *Faculty research:* American history, literature, politics, sociology, women's studies, African-American studies, mass culture.

Regent University, Graduate School, Robertson School of Government, Virginia Beach, VA 23464. Offers American government (MA); international politics (MA); political theory (MA); public administration (MA); JD/MA; M Div/MA; M Ed/MA; MBA/MA. Part-time and evening/weekend programs available. Postbaccalaureate distance learning degree programs offered (minimal on-campus study). *Faculty:* 6 full-time (1 woman), 11 part-time/adjunct (2 women). *Students:* 91 full-time (57 women), 62 part-time (37 women); includes 41 Black or African American, non-Hispanic/Latino; 3 Asian, non-Hispanic/Latino; 7 Hispanic/Latino, 1 international. Average age 30. 149 applicants, 61% accepted, 40 enrolled. In 2010, 59 master's awarded. *Degree requirements:* For master's, thesis optional, internship. *Entrance requirements:* For master's, GRE General Test or LSAT, minimum undergraduate GPA of 3.0, writing sample, resume, interview, references. Additional exam requirements/recommendations for international students: Required—TOEFL (minimum score 577 paper-based; 233 computer-based). *Application deadline:* For fall admission, 5/1 priority date for domestic students; for spring admission, 11/1 priority date for domestic students. Applications are processed on a rolling basis. Application fee: $50. Electronic applications accepted. *Expenses:* Contact institution. *Financial support:* Career-related internships or fieldwork, scholarships/grants, tuition waivers (full and partial), and unspecified assistantships available. Support available to part-time students. Financial award application deadline: 9/1; financial award applicants required to submit FAFSA. *Faculty research:* Education reform, political character issues, social capital concerns, administrative ethics, Biblical law and public policy. *Unit head:* Dr. Gary Roberts, Interim Dean, 757-352-4962, Fax: 757-352-4735, E-mail: garyrob@regent.edu. *Application contact:* Matthew Chadwick, Director of Enrollment Support Services, 800-373-5504, Fax: 757-352-4381, E-mail: admissions@regent.edu.

Rice University, Graduate Programs, School of Humanities, Department of Religious Studies, Houston, TX 77251-1892. Offers African religions (PhD); African-American religions (PhD); contemplative studies (PhD); ghosticism, esotericism, mysticism (PhD); Islam (PhD); Jewish thought and philosophy (PhD); modern Christianity in thought and popular culture (PhD); psychology of religion (PhD); the Bible and beyond (PhD). *Degree requirements:* For doctorate, 2 foreign languages, comprehensive exam, thesis/dissertation. *Entrance requirements:* For doctorate, GRE, letters of recommendation, writing sample. Additional exam requirements/recommendations for international students: Required—TOEFL (minimum score 600 paper-based; 90 iBT). Electronic applications accepted. *Faculty research:* Origins and historical development of Islam, history of Christianity, the study of comparative religion, African-American religion, religion and culture.

Rutgers, The State University of New Jersey, Newark, Graduate School, Program in American Studies, Newark, NJ 07102. Offers MA, PhD. *Faculty:* 1 full-time (0 women). *Students:* 13 full-time (6 women), 9 part-time (3 women); includes 5 Black or African American, non-Hispanic/Latino; 1 Asian, non-Hispanic/Latino; 5 Hispanic/Latino. 67 applicants, 27% accepted, 9 enrolled. *Entrance requirements:* For master's and doctorate, GRE, minimum undergraduate B average. Application fee: $60. *Expenses:* Tuition, state resident: part-time $600 per credit. Tuition, nonresident: full-time $10,694. *Financial support:* In 2010–11, 9 teaching assistantships with full and partial tuition reimbursements (averaging $23,112 per year) were awarded. *Unit head:* Dr. Charles Russell, Program Director, 973-353-5279, E-mail: crr@andromeda.rutgers.edu. *Application contact:* Jason Hand, Director of Admissions, 973-353-5205, Fax: 973-353-1440.

Saint Louis University, Graduate Education, College of Arts and Sciences and Graduate Education, Department of American Studies, St. Louis, MO 63103-2097. Offers MA, MA-R, PhD. Part-time programs available. *Degree requirements:* For master's, thesis optional, comprehensive written and oral exams; for doctorate, one foreign language, comprehensive exam, thesis/dissertation, preliminary exams. *Entrance requirements:* For master's, GRE General Test, letters of recommendation, resume; for doctorate, GRE General Test, letters of recommendation, resumé, goal statement, transcripts. Additional exam requirements/recommendations for international students: Required—TOEFL (minimum score 525 paper-based; 194 computer-based). Electronic applications accepted. *Faculty research:* Urban studies, American religion, intellectual history, southern culture, African-American literature.

State University of New York College at Cortland, Graduate Studies, School of Arts and Sciences, Program in American Civilization and Culture, Cortland, NY 13045. Offers CAS. Part-time and evening/weekend programs available. *Entrance requirements:* Additional exam requirements/recommendations for international students: Required—TOEFL.

Trinity College, Graduate Programs, Program in American Studies, Hartford, CT 06106-3100. Offers MA. Part-time and evening/weekend programs available. *Degree requirements:* For master's, thesis or alternative. *Entrance requirements:* For master's, minimum GPA of 3.0.

Universidad de las Américas–Puebla, Division of Graduate Studies, School of Social Sciences, Program in American Studies, Puebla, Mexico. Offers MA. Part-time and evening/weekend programs available. *Degree requirements:* For master's, one foreign language, thesis. *Faculty research:* NAFTA, technology, culture, politics and economics in NAFTA region.

University at Buffalo, the State University of New York, Graduate School, College of Arts and Sciences, Department of American Studies, Buffalo, NY 14260. Offers MA, PhD. Postbaccalaureate distance learning degree programs offered (minimal on-campus study). *Faculty:* 6 full-time (2 women), 2 part-time/adjunct (1 woman). *Students:* 77 full-time (47 women), 1 (woman) part-time; includes 10 Black or African American, non-Hispanic/Latino; 7 American Indian or Alaska Native, non-Hispanic/Latino; 1 Asian, non-Hispanic/Latino; 4 Hispanic/Latino; 1 Native Hawaiian or other Pacific Islander, non-Hispanic/Latino, 13 international. Average age 38. 123 applicants, 50% accepted. In 2010, 1 master's, 2 doctorates awarded. Terminal master's awarded for partial completion of doctoral program. *Degree requirements:* For master's, comprehensive exam, thesis (for some programs); for doctorate, comprehensive exam, thesis/dissertation. *Entrance requirements:* For master's, minimum GPA of 3.0; for doctorate, GRE, minimum GPA of 3.0. Additional exam requirements/recommendations for international students: Required—TOEFL (minimum score 550 paper-based; 213 computer-based; 79 iBT). *Application deadline:* For fall admission, 12/15 for domestic and international students; for winter admission, 2/1 priority date for domestic and international students; for spring admission, 4/8 priority date for domestic and international students. Applications are processed on a rolling basis. Application fee: $75. Electronic applications accepted. *Financial support:* In 2010–11, 11 students received support, including 3 fellowships with tuition reimbursements available (averaging $11,000 per year), 6 teaching assistantships with tuition reimbursements available (averaging $10,000 per year); career-related internships or fieldwork, institutionally sponsored loans, scholarships/grants, traineeships, health care benefits, tuition waivers (partial), and unspecified assistantships also available. *Faculty research:* Native American studies, intercultural studies, indigenous people's studies, multiculturalism, border theory, cultural studies, American popular culture. Total annual research expenditures: $1,500. *Unit head:* Dr. Donald A. Grinde, Chair, 716-645-0828, Fax: 716-645-5977, E-mail: dgrinde@buffalo.edu. *Application contact:* Alison Blaszak, Graduate Secretary, 716-645-2546, Fax: 716-645-5976, E-mail: ablaszak@buffalo.edu.

The University of Alabama, Graduate School, College of Arts and Sciences, Department of American Studies, Tuscaloosa, AL 35487. Offers MA. Part-time programs available. *Faculty:* 8 full-time (2 women). *Students:* 17 full-time (12 women), 5 part-time (4 women); includes 1 minority (Asian, non-Hispanic/Latino). Average age 28. 13 applicants, 77% accepted, 9 enrolled. In 2010, 8 master's awarded. *Degree requirements:* For master's, comprehensive exam, thesis optional. *Entrance requirements:* For master's, GRE or MAT. Additional exam requirements/recommendations for international students: Required—TOEFL. *Application deadline:* For fall admission, 1/15 priority date for domestic and international students; for spring admission, 11/30 priority date for domestic and international students. Applications are processed on a rolling basis. Application fee: $50 ($60 for international students). Electronic applications accepted. *Expenses:* Tuition, state resident: full-time $7900. Tuition, nonresident: full-time $20,500. *Financial support:* In 2010–11, 12 students received support; teaching assistantships, career-related internships or fieldwork, tuition waivers (full), and unspecified assistantships available. *Faculty research:* Social and cultural history, popular music, African-American arts, the South, women's history, Asian-American studies, sports, Latino Studies. *Unit head:* Dr. Lynne M. Adrian, Associate Professor, 205-348-5940, Fax: 205-348-9766, E-mail: ladrian@tenhoor.as.ua.edu. *Application contact:* Dr. Lynne M. Adrian, Associate Professor, 205-348-5940, Fax: 205-348-9766, E-mail: ladrian@tenhoor.as.ua.edu.

University of Central Oklahoma, College of Graduate Studies and Research, College of Liberal Arts, Department of History, Edmond, OK 73034-5209. Offers history (MA); museum studies (MA); social studies teaching (MA); Southwestern studies (MA). Part-time programs available. *Degree requirements:* For master's, thesis optional. *Entrance requirements:* Additional exam requirements/recommendations for international students: Required—TOEFL (minimum score 550 paper-based; 213 computer-based). Electronic applications accepted. *Faculty research:* China, Russia, civil war, American naval logistics.

University of Colorado Denver, College of Liberal Arts and Sciences, Department of History, Denver, CO 80217. Offers European history (MA); global history (MA); public history (MA); U. S. history (MA). Part-time and evening/weekend programs available. *Faculty:* 12 full-time (6 women), 2 part-time/adjunct (1 woman). *Students:* 29 full-time (17 women), 30 part-time (12 women); includes 1 Black or African American, non-Hispanic/Latino; 1 American Indian or Alaska Native, non-Hispanic/Latino; 3 Hispanic/Latino. Average age 36. 25 applicants, 60% accepted, 10 enrolled. In 2010, 17 master's awarded. *Degree requirements:* For master's, comprehensive exam, thesis optional, 36 semester hours (12 courses). *Entrance requirements:* For master's, GRE General Test, writing sample, minimum GPA of 3.25, letters of recommendation. Additional exam requirements/recommendations for international students: Required—TOEFL (minimum score 525 paper-based; 197 computer-based). *Application deadline:* For fall admission, 4/1 for domestic students; for spring admission, 10/1 for domestic students. Applications are processed on a rolling basis. Application fee: $50 ($75 for international students). Electronic applications accepted. *Expenses:* Tuition, state resident: full-time $7332; part-time $355 per credit hour. Tuition, nonresident: full-time $18,990; part-time $1055 per credit hour. Required fees: $998. Tuition and fees vary according to course level, course load, degree level, campus/location, program, reciprocity agreements and student level. *Financial support:* Research assistantships, teaching assistantships, Federal Work-Study available. Financial award application deadline: 4/1; financial award applicants required to submit FAFSA. *Faculty research:* Uses of pre-modern Islamic heritage in modern India; relationship between liberal understandings of democracy, crime, and police discretion; relationships between gender, class, health, and welfare in nineteenth and early twentieth century England; U. S. business cultures and their influences on marketing and personnel practices; intersection of business and political ideologies; social and environmental history of the Rocky Mountain West. *Unit head:* Dr. Marjorie Levine-Clark, Associate Professor and Chair, 303-556-2896. *Application contact:* Tabitha Fitzpatrick, Program Assistant, 303-556-4830, E-mail: tabitha.fitzpatrick@ucdenver.edu.

University of Dallas, Braniff Graduate School of Liberal Arts, Program in American Studies, Irving, TX 75062-4736. Offers MAS. Part-time programs available. *Degree requirements:* For master's, comprehensive exam. *Entrance requirements:* For master's, GRE General Test. *Expenses:* Tuition: Full-time $7500; part-time $720 per credit hour. Required fees: $500; $60 per credit hour. $300 per semester. One-time fee: $150. Tuition and fees vary according to program and student level. *Faculty research:* Shakespeare, Milton, Melville, Hawthorne, liberty and American literature.

University of Delaware, College of Arts and Sciences, Winterthur Program in Early American Culture, Newark, DE 19716. Offers MA. *Degree requirements:* For master's, thesis. *Entrance requirements:* For master's, GRE General Test, minimum GPA of 3.0. Electronic applications accepted. *Faculty research:* American material culture, American studies, decorative arts.

University of Florida, Graduate School, College of Liberal Arts and Sciences, Department of History, Gainesville, FL 32611. Offers African history (MA, PhD); American history (MA, PhD); European history (MA, PhD); Latin American history (MA, PhD); JD/MA; JD/PhD. Part-time programs available. *Faculty:* 31 full-time (10 women), 5 part-time/adjunct (4 women). *Students:* 81 full-time (33 women), 17 part-time (8 women); includes 3 Black or African American, non-Hispanic/Latino; 2 American Indian or Alaska Native, non-Hispanic/Latino; 2 Asian, non-Hispanic/Latino; 1 Hispanic/Latino, 12 international. Average age 30. 150 applicants, 29% accepted, 21 enrolled. In 2010, 19 master's, 8 doctorates awarded. Terminal master's awarded for partial completion of doctoral program. *Degree requirements:* For master's, variable foreign language requirement, thesis optional, 30 credit hours; for doctorate, variable foreign language requirement, comprehensive exam, thesis/dissertation, 90 credit hours. *Entrance requirements:* For master's and doctorate, GRE General Test, minimum GPA of 3.0. Additional exam requirements/recommendations for international students: Required—TOEFL (minimum score 550 paper-based; 213 computer-based; 80 iBT), IELTS (minimum score 6). *Application deadline:* For fall admission, 1/1 priority date for domestic students, 1/1 for international students.

American Studies

University of Florida (continued)

Applications are processed on a rolling basis. Application fee: $30. Electronic applications accepted. *Expenses:* Tuition, state resident: full-time $10,915.92. Tuition, nonresident: full-time $28,309. *Financial support:* In 2010–11, 70 students received support, including 30 fellowships, 13 research assistantships (averaging $16,665 per year), 27 teaching assistantships (averaging $16,733 per year); career-related internships or fieldwork and unspecified assistantships also available. Financial award application deadline: 1/15; financial award applicants required to submit FAFSA. *Faculty research:* Latin America and Caribbean history, nineteenth-century U. S. history, medieval Europe history, African history and Atlantic world history. *Unit head:* Dr. Ida L. Altman, Chair, 352-392-9634, E-mail: ialtman@ufl.edu. *Application contact:* Nina Caputo, Graduate Coordinator, 352-273-3379, Fax: 352-392-6927, E-mail: ncaputo@ufl.edu.

University of Florida, Graduate School, College of Liberal Arts and Sciences, Department of Religion, Gainesville, FL 32611. Offers religion and nature (MA); religion in the Americas (MA); religions of Asia (MA, PhD). Part-time programs available. *Faculty:* 10 full-time (3 women), 3 part-time/adjunct (1 woman). *Students:* 24 full-time (12 women), 7 part-time (6 women); includes 1 American Indian or Alaska Native, non-Hispanic/Latino; 4 Asian, non-Hispanic/Latino; 3 Hispanic/Latino, 1 international. Average age 34. 36 applicants, 58% accepted, 12 enrolled. In 2010, 1 master's, 1 doctorate awarded. *Degree requirements:* For master's, one foreign language, thesis optional; for doctorate, one foreign language, comprehensive exam, thesis/dissertation. *Entrance requirements:* For master's, GRE General Test, minimum GPA of 3.0. Additional exam requirements/recommendations for international students: Required—TOEFL (minimum score 550 paper-based; 213 computer-based; 80 iBT), IELTS (minimum score 6). *Application deadline:* For fall admission, 6/1 priority date for domestic students. Applications are processed on a rolling basis. Application fee: $30. Electronic applications accepted. *Expenses:* Tuition, state resident: full-time $10,915.92. Tuition, nonresident: full-time $28,309. *Financial support:* In 2010–11, 18 students received support, including 5 fellowships, 1 research assistantship (averaging $16,965 per year), 12 teaching assistantships (averaging $13,539 per year); Federal Work-Study and unspecified assistantships also available. Financial award applicants required to submit FAFSA. *Faculty research:* Religion in America, Christian thought, Islam, religions of India, comparative religion. *Unit head:* Dr. Vasudha Narayanan, Chair, 352-392-1625, E-mail: vasu@ufl.edu. *Application contact:* Dr. Manuel Vasquez, Graduate Coordinator, 352-392-1625 Ext. 229, Fax: 352-392-7395, E-mail: manuelv@ufl.edu.

University of Hawaii at Manoa, Graduate Division, College of Arts and Humanities, Department of American Studies, Honolulu, HI 96822. Offers American studies (MA, PhD); historic preservation (Graduate Certificate); museum studies (Graduate Certificate). Part-time programs available. *Faculty:* 17 full-time (7 women), 2 part-time/adjunct (1 woman). *Students:* 47 full-time (32 women), 25 part-time (16 women); includes 33 minority (2 American Indian or Alaska Native, non-Hispanic/Latino; 13 Asian, non-Hispanic/Latino; 1 Hispanic/Latino; 5 Native Hawaiian or other Pacific Islander, non-Hispanic/Latino; 12 Two or more races, non-Hispanic/Latino), 12 international. Average age 32. 52 applicants, 62% accepted, 27 enrolled. In 2010, 6 master's awarded. *Degree requirements:* For master's, comprehensive exam (for some programs), thesis (for some programs); for doctorate, comprehensive exam, thesis/dissertation. *Entrance requirements:* For master's and doctorate, GRE General Test. Additional exam requirements/recommendations for international students: Required—TOEFL (minimum score 600 paper-based; 100 iBT), IELTS (minimum score 7). *Application deadline:* For fall admission, 2/1 for domestic students, 1/15 for international students; for spring admission, 9/1 for domestic students, 8/1 for international students. Application fee: $60. *Financial support:* In 2010–11, 5 students received support, including 14 fellowships (averaging $1,127 per year), 2 research assistantships (averaging $17,496 per year), 6 teaching assistantships (averaging $15,362 per year); institutionally sponsored loans and tuition waivers (full and partial) also available. Support available to part-time students. Financial award application deadline: 3/31. *Faculty research:* Ethnicity and race, popular culture, historic preservation, arts and culture, international relations. Total annual research expenditures: $23,000. *Application contact:* Robert Perkinson, Graduate Chairperson, 808-956-8570, Fax: 808-956-4733, E-mail: perk@hawaii.edu.

The University of Iowa, Graduate College, College of Liberal Arts and Sciences, Department of American Studies, Iowa City, IA 52242-1316. Offers MA, PhD. *Degree requirements:* For master's, thesis optional, exam; for doctorate, comprehensive exam, thesis/dissertation. *Entrance requirements:* For master's and doctorate, GRE General Test, minimum GPA of 3.0. Additional exam requirements/recommendations for international students: Required—TOEFL (minimum score 550 paper-based; 213 computer-based; 81 iBT). Electronic applications accepted.

The University of Kansas, Graduate Studies, College of Liberal Arts and Sciences, Program in American Studies, Lawrence, KS 66045. Offers MA, PhD, MUP/MA. Part-time programs available. *Faculty:* 10 full-time (5 women). *Students:* 32 full-time (19 women), 6 part-time (3 women); includes 6 minority (3 Black or African American, non-Hispanic/Latino; 1 Hispanic/Latino; 2 Two or more races, non-Hispanic/Latino), 6 international. Average age 33. 34 applicants, 76% accepted, 12 enrolled. In 2010, 2 master's, 6 doctorates awarded. Terminal master's awarded for partial completion of doctoral program. *Degree requirements:* For master's, thesis or alternative; for doctorate, comprehensive exam, thesis/dissertation. *Entrance requirements:* For master's and doctorate, GRE General Test. Additional exam requirements/recommendations for international students: Required—TOEFL. *Application deadline:* For fall admission, 12/1 for domestic and international students; for spring admission, 5/1 for domestic and international students. Applications are processed on a rolling basis. Application fee: $55 ($65 for international students). Electronic applications accepted. *Expenses:* Tuition, state resident: full-time $7092; part-time $295.50 per credit hour. Tuition, nonresident: full-time $16,590; part-time $691.25 per credit hour. Required fees: $858; $71.49 per credit hour. Tuition and fees vary according to course load, campus/location and program. *Financial support:* Fellowships with full tuition reimbursements, research assistantships with partial tuition reimbursements, teaching assistantships with full and partial tuition reimbursements, Federal Work-Study, scholarships/grants, health care benefits, and unspecified assistantships available. Financial award application deadline: 12/21. *Faculty research:* Transnational and global American studies of race, gender, class, religion, ethnicity, sexuality, jazz studies, public health and medicine; migration and immigration; Latino/a studies; African-American studies; Jewish studies; women's studies; oral history; ethnography; environmental studies. *Unit head:* Dr. Henry Bial, Chair, 785-864-2309, Fax: 785-864-5772, E-mail: hbial@ku.edu. *Application contact:* Kay Isbell, Administrative Associate, 785-864-2306, Fax: 785-864-5772, E-mail: kisbell@ku.edu.

University of Louisiana at Lafayette, College of Liberal Arts, Department of Modern Languages, Program in Francophone Studies, Lafayette, LA 70504. Offers PhD. *Degree requirements:* For doctorate, 2 foreign languages, comprehensive exam, thesis/dissertation. *Entrance requirements:* For doctorate, GRE General Test, minimum GPA of 2.75. Additional exam requirements/recommendations for international students: Required—TOEFL (minimum score 550 paper-based; 213 computer-based). Electronic applications accepted. *Faculty research:* Louisiana folklore, eighteenth century French literature, contemporary criticism.

University of Maine, Graduate School, College of Liberal Arts and Sciences, Department of History, Orono, ME 04469. Offers American studies (MA, PhD); Canadian studies (MA, PhD); East Asian (MA); environmental (MA); European (MA); technology (MA). *Faculty:* 11 full-time (1 woman), 2 part-time/adjunct (1 woman). *Students:* 24 full-time (8 women), 35 part-time (13 women); includes 4 minority (2 American Indian or Alaska Native, non-Hispanic/Latino; 2 Hispanic/Latino). Average age 38. 43 applicants, 40% accepted, 15 enrolled. In 2010, 5 master's, 3 doctorates awarded. Terminal master's awarded for partial completion of doctoral program. *Degree requirements:* For master's, variable foreign language requirement, thesis optional; for doctorate, one foreign language, thesis/dissertation. *Entrance requirements:* For master's and doctorate, GRE General Test. Additional exam requirements/recommendations for international students: Required—TOEFL. *Application deadline:* For fall admission, 2/1 priority date for domestic students. Applications are processed on a rolling basis. Application fee: $65. Electronic applications accepted. *Expenses:* Tuition, state resident: full-time $400. Tuition, nonresident: full-time $1050. *Financial support:* In 2010–11, 9 teaching assistantships with tuition reimbursements (averaging $12,790 per year) were awarded; career-related internships or fieldwork, Federal Work-Study, and tuition waivers (full and partial) also available. Support available to part-time students. Financial award application deadline: 3/1. *Faculty research:* Canadian labor and working classes; American social, cultural, and urban history. *Unit head:* Dr. Nathan Godfried, Chair, 207-581-1923, Fax: 207-581-1817. *Application contact:* Scott G. Delcourt, Associate Dean of the Graduate School, 207-581-3291, Fax: 207-581-3232, E-mail: graduate@maine.edu.

University of Maine, Graduate School, Program in Liberal Studies, Orono, ME 04469. Offers Maine studies (MA); new media (MA); peace studies (MA). Part-time and evening/weekend programs available. *Students:* 2 full-time (both women), 19 part-time (13 women); includes 2 American Indian or Alaska Native, non-Hispanic/Latino, 1 international. Average age 47. 5 applicants, 40% accepted, 2 enrolled. In 2010, 6 master's awarded. *Degree requirements:* For master's, project. *Entrance requirements:* Additional exam requirements/recommendations for international students: Required—TOEFL. *Application deadline:* For fall admission, 4/1 for domestic students; for spring admission, 11/1 for domestic students. Applications are processed on a rolling basis. Application fee: $65. Electronic applications accepted. *Expenses:* Tuition, state resident: full-time $400. Tuition, nonresident: full-time $1050. *Financial support:* Federal Work-Study and institutionally sponsored loans available. Financial award application deadline: 3/1. *Unit head:* Amaranta Ruiz-Nelson, Coordinator, 207-581-3222, Fax: 207-581-3232, E-mail: graduate@maine.edu. *Application contact:* Amaranta Ruiz-Nelson, Coordinator, 207-581-3222, Fax: 207-581-3232, E-mail: graduate@maine.edu.

University of Maryland, College Park, Academic Affairs, College of Arts and Humanities, Department of American Studies, College Park, MD 20742. Offers MA, PhD. *Faculty:* 41 full-time (18 women), 6 part-time/adjunct (3 women). *Students:* 41 full-time (27 women), 6 part-time (2 women); includes 26 minority (19 Black or African American, non-Hispanic/Latino; 2 Asian, non-Hispanic/Latino; 5 Hispanic/Latino), 3 international. 120 applicants, 6% accepted, 7 enrolled. In 2010, 1 master's, 16 doctorates awarded. *Degree requirements:* For master's, thesis or scholarly paper and exam; for doctorate, thesis/dissertation, 3 comprehensive exams. *Entrance requirements:* For master's, GRE General Test, minimum GPA of 3.0, writing sample, 3 letters of recommendation; for doctorate, GRE General Test. Additional exam requirements/recommendations for international students: Required—TOEFL. *Application deadline:* For fall admission, 12/15 for domestic students, 2/1 for international students; for spring admission, 6/1 for international students. Applications are processed on a rolling basis. Application fee: $75. Electronic applications accepted. *Expenses:* Tuition, state resident: part-time $471 per credit hour. Tuition, nonresident: part-time $1016 per credit hour. Required fees: $337 per term. *Financial support:* In 2010–11, 6 fellowships with full and partial tuition reimbursements (averaging $13,240 per year), 25 teaching assistantships with tuition reimbursements (averaging $17,488 per year) were awarded; research assistantships, career-related internships or fieldwork, Federal Work-Study, and scholarships/grants also available. Support available to part-time students. Financial award applicants required to submit FAFSA. *Faculty research:* Material culture, modes of culture, cultural movements, popular culture, ethnography. *Unit head:* Nancy L. Struna, Chair, 301-405-1354, Fax: 301-314-9453, E-mail: nlstruna@umd.edu. *Application contact:* Dean of Graduate School, 301-405-0376, Fax: 301-314-9305.

University of Massachusetts Boston, Office of Graduate Studies, College of Liberal Arts, Program in American Studies, Boston, MA 02125-3393. Offers MA. Part-time and evening/weekend programs available. *Degree requirements:* For master's, thesis or capstone project. *Entrance requirements:* For master's, minimum GPA of 2.75. *Faculty research:* War in American culture, immigration history, Latin Americans, history of race and popular music, education and Asian Americans.

University of Michigan, Horace H. Rackham School of Graduate Studies, College of Literature, Science, and the Arts, Interdepartmental Program in American Culture, Ann Arbor, MI 48109-1045. Offers AM, PhD. *Faculty:* 36 full-time (19 women). *Students:* 48 full-time (30 women); includes 6 Black or African American, non-Hispanic/Latino; 4 American Indian or Alaska Native, non-Hispanic/Latino; 12 Asian, non-Hispanic/Latino; 8 Hispanic/Latino, 2 international. 111 applicants, 7% accepted, 6 enrolled. In 2010, 2 master's, 6 doctorates awarded. Terminal master's awarded for partial completion of doctoral program. *Degree requirements:* For doctorate, preliminary exams, field exams, oral defense of dissertation. *Entrance requirements:* For master's, GRE General Test; for doctorate, GRE General Test, sample of written work. Additional exam requirements/recommendations for international students: Required—TOEFL. *Application deadline:* For fall admission, 12/1 for domestic and international students. Application fee: $65 ($75 for international students). Electronic applications accepted. *Expenses:* Tuition, state resident: full-time $17,784; part-time $1116 per credit hour. Tuition, nonresident: full-time $35,944; part-time $2125 per credit hour. International tuition: $35,994 full-time. Required fees: $95 per semester. Tuition and fees vary according to course load, degree level and program. *Financial support:* In 2010–11, 19 students received support, including 11 fellowships with full tuition reimbursements available (averaging $25,800 per year), 13 teaching assistantships with full tuition reimbursements available (averaging $17,200 per year); research assistantships, health care benefits also available. *Faculty research:* Cultural studies; ethnic studies, American culture methodology, literature, history. *Unit head:* Gregory Dowd, Director, 734-763-1460, Fax: 734-936-1967, E-mail: ac.inq@umich.edu. *Application contact:* Marlene Moore, Graduate Student Coordinator, 734-647-9533, Fax: 734-936-1967, E-mail: ac.inq@umich.edu.

University of Michigan–Flint, Graduate Programs, Program in American Culture, Flint, MI 48502-1950. Offers MLS. Part-time programs available. *Degree requirements:* For master's, thesis or alternative. *Entrance requirements:* For master's, minimum GPA of 3.0, 24 undergraduate credits in humanities and social sciences. Additional exam requirements/recommendations for international students: Required—TOEFL (minimum score 560 paper-based; 220 computer-based; 84 iBT), IELTS (minimum score 6.5). Electronic applications accepted.

University of Minnesota, Twin Cities Campus, Graduate School, College of Liberal Arts, Department of American Studies, Minneapolis, MN 55455-0213. Offers PhD. *Degree requirements:* For doctorate, one foreign language, comprehensive exam, thesis/dissertation. *Entrance requirements:* For doctorate, GRE General Test, sample of written work, 3 letters of recommendation. Additional exam requirements/recommendations for international students: Required—TOEFL (minimum score 550 paper-based; 213 computer-based). *Faculty research:* American Indian history, nationalism/transnationalism, gender and sexuality, race and ethnicity.

University of Mississippi, Graduate School, College of Liberal Arts, Interdisciplinary Program in Southern Studies, Oxford, University, MS 38677. Offers MA. *Students:* 26 full-time (18 women), 2 part-time (both women); includes 4 minority (2 Black or African American, non-Hispanic/Latino; 2 Hispanic/Latino), 1 international. In 2010, 8 master's awarded. *Entrance requirements:* For master's, GRE General Test, minimum GPA of 3.0. Additional exam requirements/recommendations for international students: Required—TOEFL. *Application deadline:* For fall admission, 2/1 for domestic students; for spring admission, 10/1 for domestic students. Applications are processed on a rolling basis. Application fee: $25. Electronic applications accepted. *Financial support:* Scholarships/grants available. Financial award application deadline: 3/1; financial award applicants required to submit FAFSA. *Unit head:* Dr. Ted Ownby, Director, 662-915-5993, Fax: 662-915-5814, E-mail: cssc@olemiss.edu. *Application contact:* Dr. Christy M. Wyandt, Associate Dean, 662-915-7474, Fax: 662-915-7577, E-mail: cwyandt@olemiss.edu.

University of Missouri–St. Louis, College of Arts and Sciences, Department of Political Science, St. Louis, MO 63121. Offers American politics (MA); comparative politics (MA); international politics (MA); political process and behavior (MA); political science (PhD); public administration and public policy (MA); urban and regional politics (MA). Part-time and evening/weekend programs available. *Faculty:* 18 full-time (7 women), 1 (woman) part-time/adjunct. *Students:* 15 full-time (7 women), 39 part-time (21 women); includes 13 minority (8 Black or

African American, non-Hispanic/Latino; 2 American Indian or Alaska Native, non-Hispanic/Latino; 3 Asian, non-Hispanic/Latino), 3 international. Average age 35. 43 applicants, 47% accepted, 10 enrolled. In 2010, 4 master's, 5 doctorates awarded. Terminal master's awarded for partial completion of doctoral program. *Degree requirements:* For master's, thesis optional; for doctorate, thesis/dissertation. *Entrance requirements:* For master's, GRE General Test, 2 letters of recommendation; for doctorate, GRE General Test, 3 letters of recommendation. Additional exam requirements/recommendations for international students: Required—TOEFL (minimum score 550 paper-based; 213 computer-based). *Application deadline:* For fall admission, 2/15 priority date for domestic and international students; for spring admission, 10/15 priority date for domestic and international students. Applications are processed on a rolling basis. Application fee: $35 ($40 for international students). Electronic applications accepted. *Expenses:* Tuition, state resident: full-time $5522; part-time $306.80 per credit hour. Tuition, nonresident: full-time $14,253; part-time $792.10 per credit hour. Required fees: $658; $49 per credit hour. One-time fee: $12. Tuition and fees vary according to program. *Financial support:* In 2010–11, 8 research assistantships with full and partial tuition reimbursements (averaging $1,110 per year), 6 teaching assistantships with full and partial tuition reimbursements (averaging $10,800 per year) were awarded; fellowships, career-related internships or fieldwork also available. Support available to part-time students. Financial award application deadline: 3/15; financial award applicants required to submit FAFSA. *Faculty research:* Public policy, urban politics and administration, American government. *Unit head:* Dr. Kenneth Thomas, Director of Graduate Studies, 314-516-5521, Fax: 314-516-5268, E-mail: umslpolisci@umsl.edu. *Application contact:* 314-516-5458, Fax: 314-516-6996, E-mail: gradadm@umsl.edu.

University of New Mexico, Graduate School, College of Arts and Sciences, Department of American Studies, Albuquerque, NM 87131-2039. Offers MA, PhD. Part-time programs available. *Faculty:* 11 full-time (4 women), 15 part-time/adjunct (11 women). *Students:* 49 full-time (36 women), 11 part-time (6 women); includes 2 Black or African American, non-Hispanic/Latino; 4 American Indian or Alaska Native, non-Hispanic/Latino; 1 Asian, non-Hispanic/Latino; 15 Hispanic/Latino; 3 Two or more races, non-Hispanic/Latino, 3 international. Average age 36. 70 applicants, 29% accepted, 12 enrolled. In 2010, 2 master's, 4 doctorates awarded. Terminal master's awarded for partial completion of doctoral program. *Degree requirements:* For master's, comprehensive exam (for some programs), thesis (for some programs); for doctorate, one foreign language, comprehensive exam, thesis/dissertation. *Entrance requirements:* For master's, BA in related field; for doctorate, MA in related field, complete dossier. Additional exam requirements/recommendations for international students: Required—TOEFL. *Application deadline:* For fall admission, 1/15 for domestic and international students. Application fee: $50. Electronic applications accepted. *Expenses:* Tuition, state resident: full-time $5991; part-time $251 per credit hour. Tuition, nonresident: full-time $14,405; part-time $800.20 per credit hour. Tuition and fees vary according to course level, course load, program and reciprocity agreements. *Financial support:* In 2010–11, 48 students received support, including 13 fellowships (averaging $8,469 per year), 5 research assistantships (averaging $9,300 per year), 30 teaching assistantships with tuition reimbursements available (averaging $10,065 per year); career-related internships or fieldwork, Federal Work-Study, health care benefits, tuition waivers (full), and unspecified assistantships also available. Support available to part-time students. Financial award application deadline: 2/20; financial award applicants required to submit FAFSA. *Faculty research:* Cultural studies, environment/science/technology, gender, race/class/ethnicity, popular culture, Southwest studies. *Unit head:* Dr. Gabriel Melendez, Chair, 505-277-3929, Fax: 505-277-1208, E-mail: gabriel@unm.edu. *Application contact:* Sandy Rodrigue, Department Administrator, 505-277-3929, Fax: 505-277-1208, E-mail: amstudy@unm.edu.

University of Southern California, Graduate School, Dana and David Dornsife College of Letters, Arts and Sciences, Department of American Studies and Ethnicity, Los Angeles, CA 90089. Offers PhD. *Faculty:* 28 full-time (15 women). *Students:* 47 full-time (27 women), 2 part-time (both women); includes 40 minority (9 Black or African American, non-Hispanic/Latino; 16 Asian, non-Hispanic/Latino; 13 Hispanic/Latino; 2 Two or more races, non-Hispanic/Latino), 2 international. 165 applicants, 6% accepted, 5 enrolled. In 2010, 6 doctorates awarded. *Degree requirements:* For doctorate, one foreign language, thesis/dissertation, qualifying exam. *Entrance requirements:* For doctorate, GRE. *Application deadline:* For fall admission, 12/1 priority date for domestic students, 12/1 for international students. Application fee: $85. Electronic applications accepted. *Expenses:* Tuition: Full-time $31,240; part-time $1420 per unit. Required fees: $600. One-time fee: $35 full-time. Full-time tuition and fees vary according to degree level and program. *Financial support:* In 2010–11, 41 students received support, including 16 fellowships with full tuition reimbursements available (averaging $25,698 per year), 3 research assistantships with full tuition reimbursements available (averaging $19,250 per year), 21 teaching assistantships with full tuition reimbursements available (averaging $19,250 per year); tuition waivers (full) also available. Financial award application deadline: 2/1. *Faculty research:* Interdisciplinary study of race and ethnicity, regional focus on Los Angeles and the American West, multidisciplinary exploration of culture, interdisciplinary study of gender and sexuality. *Unit head:* Prof. Macarena Gomez-Barris, Interim Chair / Associate Professor, 213-740-2426, Fax: 213-821-0409, E-mail: gomezbar@usc.edu. *Application contact:* Kitty Lai, Graduate Staff Advisor, 213-740-2426, Fax: 213-821-0409, E-mail: kittylai@usc.edu.

University of Southern Maine, College of Arts and Sciences, Program in American and New England Studies, Portland, ME 04104-9300. Offers MA. Part-time and evening/weekend programs available. *Degree requirements:* For master's, thesis optional. *Entrance requirements:* For master's, GRE General Test or MAT. Additional exam requirements/recommendations for international students: Required—TOEFL. *Faculty research:* Social history, regional culture, landscape of literature, material culture, art and architecture.

University of South Florida, Graduate School, College of Arts and Sciences, Department of Humanities and Cultural Studies, Tampa, FL 33620-9951. Offers American studies (MA); film studies (MLA); humanities (MLA). Part-time and evening/weekend programs available. *Faculty:* 5 full-time (3 women). *Students:* 23 full-time (13 women), 18 part-time (12 women); includes 9 Black or African American, non-Hispanic/Latino; 4 Hispanic/Latino; 2 Two or more races, non-Hispanic/Latino, 1 international. Average age 34. 34 applicants, 47% accepted, 12 enrolled. In 2010, 9 master's awarded. *Degree requirements:* For master's, comprehensive exam, thesis. *Entrance requirements:* For master's, GRE General Test, minimum GPA of 3.0 in last 60 hours, academic writing sample. Additional exam requirements/recommendations for international students: Required—TOEFL (minimum score 550 paper-based; 213 computer-based). *Application deadline:* For fall admission, 2/15 priority date for domestic students, 1/2 for international students; for spring admission, 10/15 priority date for domestic students, 6/1 for international students. Application fee: $30. *Financial support:* Scholarships/grants available. Financial award application deadline: 4/1. *Faculty research:* American South, American autobiography, material culture, critical theory, cultural studies. *Unit head:* Daniel Belgrad, Chairperson, 813-974-9388, Fax: 813-974-9409, E-mail: dbelgrad@cas.usf.edu. *Application contact:* Maria Cizmic, Program Director, 813-974-9383, Fax: 813-974-9409, E-mail: mcizmic@cas.usf.edu.

The University of Texas at Austin, Graduate School, College of Liberal Arts, Department of American Studies, Austin, TX 78712-1111. Offers MA, PhD. Part-time programs available. *Degree requirements:* For master's, thesis; for doctorate, one foreign language, thesis/dissertation, qualifying oral exam. *Entrance requirements:* For master's and doctorate, GRE General Test, minimum GPA of 3.5. Electronic applications accepted. *Faculty research:* Race, gender, and ethnicity; history of the American West; American design and archaeology; literary cultural history; religion and psychology in American culture.

University of Utah, Graduate School, College of Humanities, Department of English, Salt Lake City, UT 84112. Offers American studies (PhD); British American literature (MA, PhD); creative writing (MA, MFA, PhD), including rhetoric/composition (MA, PhD); literature (PhD); rhetoric and composition (PhD). *Faculty:* 35 full-time (16 women), 1 part-time/adjunct (0 women). *Students:* 57 full-time (32 women), 19 part-time (12 women); includes 5 minority (1 Black or African American, non-Hispanic/Latino; 1 American Indian or Alaska Native, non-Hispanic/Latino; 1 Asian, non-Hispanic/Latino; 2 Two or more races, non-Hispanic/Latino), 4 international. Average age 33. 281 applicants, 11% accepted, 27 enrolled. In 2010, 13 master's, 3 doctorates awarded. Terminal master's awarded for partial completion of doctoral program. *Degree requirements:* For master's, one foreign language, comprehensive exam, thesis (for some programs), written exam; for doctorate, 2 foreign languages, comprehensive exam, thesis/dissertation, 2 standard level languages/1 advanced level language. *Entrance requirements:* For master's and doctorate, GRE General Test, minimum GPA of 3.2. Additional exam requirements/recommendations for international students: Required—TOEFL (minimum score 650 paper-based; 280 computer-based; 115 iBT); Recommended—IELTS (minimum score 9). *Application deadline:* For fall admission, 12/15 for domestic and international students. Application fee: $55 ($65 for international students). Electronic applications accepted. *Expenses:* Tuition, area resident: Part-time $179.19 per credit hour. Tuition, state resident: full-time $4384. Tuition, nonresident: full-time $16,684; part-time $630.67 per credit hour. Required fees: $350 per semester. Tuition and fees vary according to course load, degree level and program. *Financial support:* In 2010–11, 60 students received support, including 11 fellowships with full tuition reimbursements available (averaging $12,400 per year), 49 teaching assistantships with full tuition reimbursements available (averaging $12,400 per year); research assistantships, health care benefits also available. Financial award application deadline: 12/15; financial award applicants required to submit FAFSA. *Faculty research:* Poetics and modern poetry, nineteenth and twentieth century British and American literature, the American west, environmental studies, critical theory and race and gender studies, fiction. Total annual research expenditures: $32,329. *Unit head:* Prof. Vincent P. Pecora, Chair, 801-581-6168, E-mail: v.pecora@utah.edu. *Application contact:* Prof. Scott Black, Director of Graduate Studies, 801-581-5137, E-mail: scott.black@utah.edu.

University of Wisconsin–Madison, Graduate School, College of Letters and Science, Department of History, Madison, WI 53706-1380. Offers African history (MA, PhD); Central Asian history (MA, PhD); comparative world history (MA, PhD); East Asian history (MA, PhD); European history (MA, PhD); gender and women's history (MA, PhD); Latin American and Caribbean history (MA, PhD); Middle Eastern history (MA, PhD); South Asian history (MA, PhD); Southeast Asian history (MA, PhD); United States history (MA, PhD). Terminal master's awarded for partial completion of doctoral program. *Degree requirements:* For master's, thesis (for some programs); for doctorate, variable foreign language requirement, thesis/dissertation. *Entrance requirements:* For master's and doctorate, GRE General Test. Additional exam requirements/recommendations for international students: Required—Michigan English Language Assessment Battery or TOEFL. Electronic applications accepted. *Expenses:* Tuition, state resident: full-time $9887; part-time $617.96 per credit. Tuition, nonresident: full-time $24,054; part-time $1503.40 per credit. Required fees: $67.63 per credit. Tuition and fees vary according to reciprocity agreements. *Faculty research:* American, African, European, Asian, Latin American, and Middle Eastern history.

University of Wyoming, College of Arts and Sciences, American Studies Program, Laramie, WY 82070. Offers MA. Part-time programs available. *Degree requirements:* For master's, thesis optional. *Entrance requirements:* For master's, GRE General Test, minimum GPA of 3.0. *Faculty research:* Material culture, American culture, ethnicity, cultural environments, public culture.

Utah State University, School of Graduate Studies, College of Humanities, Arts and Social Sciences, Department of English and Department of History, Program in American Studies, Logan, UT 84322. Offers folklore (MA, MS); western American literature and culture (MA, MS). Part-time and evening/weekend programs available. *Degree requirements:* For master's, thesis or alternative. *Entrance requirements:* For master's, GRE General Test or MAT, minimum GPA of 3.0, 3 letters of recommendation, writing sample. Additional exam requirements/recommendations for international students: Required—TOEFL. *Faculty research:* Folklore and folklife, American culture, regional studies, material culture, Jewish folklore, Native American folklore.

Villanova University, Graduate School of Liberal Arts and Sciences, Program in Liberal Studies, Villanova, PA 19085. Offers American studies (Certificate); ancient worlds (Certificate); great books (Certificate); interdisciplinary studies (Post-Master's Certificate); liberal studies (MA); peace and justice studies (Certificate). Part-time and evening/weekend programs available. *Faculty:* 24 full-time. In 2010, 2 master's awarded. *Degree requirements:* For master's, comprehensive exam. *Entrance requirements:* For master's, bachelor's degree from institution accredited by one of the regional accrediting agencies with minimum undergraduate GPA of 3.0; transcripts; two letters of recommendation; two essays. Additional exam requirements/recommendations for international students: Required—TOEFL. *Application deadline:* For fall admission, 3/1 priority date for domestic and international students; for spring admission, 11/15 priority date for domestic and international students. Applications are processed on a rolling basis. Application fee: $50. Electronic applications accepted. *Expenses:* Tuition: Part-time $700 per credit. Part-time tuition and fees vary according to degree level and program. *Financial support:* Research assistantships, Federal Work-Study available. Financial award applicants required to submit FAFSA. *Unit head:* Dr. Marylu Hill, Director, Villanova Center for Liberal Education, 610-519-6936, E-mail: marylu.hill@villanova.edu. *Application contact:* Dr. Adele Lindenmeyr, Dean, Graduate School of Liberal Arts and Sciences, 610-519-7093, Fax: 610-519-7096.

Washington State University, Graduate School, College of Liberal Arts, Department of History, Pullman, WA 99164. Offers early and modern European history (MA, PhD); environmental history (MA, PhD); Latin American history (MA, PhD); modern East Asia history (MA, PhD); public history (MA, PhD); U. S. history (MA, PhD); women's history (MA, PhD); world history (MA, PhD). Part-time programs available. *Faculty:* 25. *Students:* 38 full-time (22 women), 10 part-time (4 women); includes 1 American Indian or Alaska Native, non-Hispanic/Latino; 2 Hispanic/Latino, 2 international. Average age 33. 57 applicants, 47% accepted, 10 enrolled. In 2010, 10 master's, 2 doctorates awarded. *Degree requirements:* For master's, comprehensive exam (for some programs), thesis, oral exam; for doctorate, one foreign language, comprehensive exam, thesis/dissertation, oral and written exam. *Entrance requirements:* For master's and doctorate, GRE General Test, official transcripts from all universities attended; three letters of recommendation; statement of purpose; writing sample; Preferred Fields of Study form; Language Background form. Additional exam requirements/recommendations for international students: Required—TOEFL (minimum score 550 paper-based), IELTS. *Application deadline:* For fall admission, 1/10 for domestic and international students; for spring admission, 7/1 for domestic and international students. Applications are processed on a rolling basis. Application fee: $50. Electronic applications accepted. *Expenses:* Tuition, state resident: full-time $8552; part-time $443 per credit. Tuition, nonresident: full-time $21,650; part-time $1083 per credit. Required fees: $846. *Financial support:* In 2010–11, 1 fellowship with partial tuition reimbursement (averaging $3,000 per year), research assistantships with full and partial tuition reimbursements (averaging $13,917 per year), 28 teaching assistantships with full and partial tuition reimbursements (averaging $13,056 per year) were awarded; career-related internships or fieldwork, Federal Work-Study, institutionally sponsored loans, scholarships/grants, and health care benefits also available. Financial award application deadline: 2/15; financial award applicants required to submit FAFSA. *Faculty research:* Public, world, environmental, women's and U. S. history. *Unit head:* Dr. Raymond Sun, Chair, 509-335-5139, Fax: 509-335-4171, E-mail: pietz@wsu.edu. *Application contact:* Graduate Studies Director, 509-335-4030, Fax: 509-335-4171, E-mail: kale@wsu.edu.

Washington State University, Graduate School, College of Liberal Arts, Program in American Studies, Pullman, WA 99164. Offers ethnic studies (MA, PhD); feminist studies (MA, PhD); history (MA, PhD); literature (MA, PhD). Part-time programs available. *Faculty:* 35. *Students:* 23 full-time (14 women), 4 part-time (2 women); includes 5 Black or African American, non-Hispanic/Latino; 4 American Indian or Alaska Native, non-Hispanic/Latino; 4 Asian, non-Hispanic/Latino; 4 Hispanic/Latino, 2 international. Average age 35. 55 applicants, 7% accepted, 3 enrolled. In 2010, 1 master's, 3 doctorates awarded. *Degree requirements:* For master's, one foreign language, comprehensive exam (for some programs), thesis optional, oral exam;

American Studies

Washington State University *(continued)*
for doctorate, one foreign language, comprehensive exam (for some programs), thesis/dissertation, oral exam. *Entrance requirements:* For master's and doctorate, GRE General Test, official college transcripts sent directly from each institution attended, 3-5 page statement of purpose describing areas of interest, minimum GPA of 3.0, writing sample, 3 letters of recommendation. Additional exam requirements/recommendations for international students: Required—TOEFL, IELTS. *Application deadline:* For fall admission, 1/10 priority date for domestic and international students; for spring admission, 7/1 priority date for domestic and international students. Applications are processed on a rolling basis. Application fee: $50. *Expenses:* Tuition, state resident: full-time $8552; part-time $443 per credit. Tuition, nonresident: full-time $21,650; part-time $1083 per credit. Required fees: $846. *Financial support:* In 2010–11, 1 fellowship (averaging $6,950 per year), 3 research assistantships with full and partial tuition reimbursements (averaging $14,634 per year), 17 teaching assistantships with full and partial tuition reimbursements (averaging $13,383 per year) were awarded; career-related internships or fieldwork, Federal Work-Study, institutionally sponsored loans, health care benefits, tuition waivers (partial), and teaching associateships also available. Financial award application deadline: 2/15; financial award applicants required to submit FAFSA. *Faculty research:* The American West in multicultural perspective; nineteenth century historical, literary, and cultural studies; comparative American ethnic literatures and cultures; American cultures and the environment; American rhetoric. *Unit head:* Dr. Rory J. Ong, Director, 509-335-1560, E-mail: rjong@mail.wsu.edu. *Application contact:* Graduate School Admissions, 800-GRADWSU, Fax: 509-335-1949, E-mail: gradsch@wsu.edu.

West Virginia University, Eberly College of Arts and Sciences, Department of History, Morgantown, WV 26506. Offers African history (MA, PhD); African-American history (MA, PhD); American history (MA, PhD); Appalachian/regional history (MA, PhD); East Asian history (MA, PhD); European history (MA, PhD); history of science and technology (MA, PhD); Latin American history (MA). Part-time programs available. *Degree requirements:* For master's, one foreign language, thesis (for some programs), oral exam, thesis defense; for doctorate, one foreign language, comprehensive exam, thesis/dissertation, dissertation defense. *Entrance requirements:* For master's, GRE General Test, minimum GPA of 3.0; for doctorate, GRE General Test. Additional exam requirements/recommendations for international students: Required—TOEFL (minimum score 550 paper-based), IELTS (minimum score 6.5). Electronic applications accepted. *Faculty research:* U.S., Appalachia, modern Europe, Africa, colonial and post-colonial societies.

Wheaton College, Graduate School, Department of Biblical and Theological Studies, Program in Religion in American Life, Wheaton, IL 60187-5593. Offers MA. Part-time programs available. *Degree requirements:* For master's, thesis optional. *Entrance requirements:* For master's, GRE General Test, MAT. Electronic applications accepted.

Wilfrid Laurier University, Faculty of Graduate and Postdoctoral Studies, Faculty of Arts, Department of Religion and Culture, Waterloo, ON N2L 3C5, Canada. Offers religion and culture (MA); religious diversity of North America (PhD). Part-time programs available. *Faculty:* 10 full-time (5 women). *Students:* 24 full-time (13 women), 1 part-time. 43 applicants, 35% accepted, 9 enrolled. In 2010, 11 master's, 1 doctorate awarded. *Degree requirements:* For master's, thesis optional; for doctorate, thesis/dissertation. *Entrance requirements:* For master's, honors BA or the equivalent in religious studies or other interdisciplinary social science or humanities program, minimum B average in overall undergraduate course work, B+ average in the undergraduate major; for doctorate, MA in religious studies, minimum A- average. Additional exam requirements/recommendations for international students: Required—TOEFL (minimum score 89 iBT). *Application deadline:* For fall admission, 2/1 priority date for domestic and international students. Application fee: $100. Electronic applications accepted. Tuition and fees charges are reported in Canadian dollars. *Expenses:* Tuition, area resident: Full-time $15,300 Canadian dollars; part-time $1200 Canadian dollars per credit. International tuition: $21,300 Canadian dollars full-time. Required fees: $650 Canadian dollars; $100 Canadian dollars per credit. Tuition and fees vary according to course load, degree level, campus/location and program. *Financial support:* In 2010–11, 31 fellowships, 31 teaching assistantships were awarded; career-related internships or fieldwork, scholarships/grants, health care benefits, and unspecified assistantships also available. *Faculty research:* Religious diversity in North America. *Unit head:* Dr. Janet McLellan, Graduate Coordinator, 519-884-0710 Ext. 2895, Fax: 519-884-9387, E-mail: jmclellan@wlu.ca. *Application contact:* Jennifer Williams, Graduate Admission and Records Officer, 519-884-0710 Ext. 3536, Fax: 519-884-1020, E-mail: gradstudies@wlu.ca.

Yale University, Graduate School of Arts and Sciences, Interdisciplinary Program in American Studies, New Haven, CT 06520. Offers PhD. *Degree requirements:* For doctorate, one foreign language, thesis/dissertation. *Entrance requirements:* For doctorate, GRE General Test.

Yorktown University, School of Government, Denver, CO 80246. Offers American culture and the life of the citizen (MA); foundations of democracy in America and Western Europe (MA); political economy (MA); political theory (MA).

Asian-American Studies

California State University, Long Beach, Graduate Studies, College of Liberal Arts, Department of Asian and Asian American Studies, Long Beach, CA 90840. Offers Asian studies (MA). Part-time programs available. *Faculty:* 8 full-time (5 women). *Students:* 9 full-time (7 women), 9 part-time (6 women); includes 10 Asian, non-Hispanic/Latino, 2 international. Average age 34. 16 applicants, 38% accepted, 4 enrolled. In 2010, 3 master's awarded. *Degree requirements:* For master's, one foreign language, comprehensive exam or thesis. *Application deadline:* For fall admission, 5/1 for domestic students. Applications are processed on a rolling basis. Application fee: $55. Electronic applications accepted. *Financial support:* Federal Work-Study, institutionally sponsored loans, and scholarships/grants available. Financial award application deadline: 3/2. *Faculty research:* South Asia, China, Japan, Southeast Asia, Asian-Americans in the U. S. *Unit head:* Dr. John N. Tsuchida, Chair, 562-985-8085, Fax: 562-985-1535, E-mail: jtsuchid@csulb.edu. *Application contact:* Dr. Linda Espana-Maram, Graduate Advisor, 562-985-4822, Fax: 562-985-1535, E-mail: lnemaram@csulb.edu.

San Francisco State University, Division of Graduate Studies, College of Ethnic Studies, Program in Asian American Studies, San Francisco, CA 94132-1722. Offers MA. *Unit head:* Dr. Lorraine Dong, Unit Head, 415-338-2968. *Application contact:* Allyson Tintiango-Cubales, Coordinator, 415-338-2698, E-mail: aas@sfsu.edu.

University of California, Los Angeles, Graduate Division, College of Letters and Science, Program in Asian-American Studies, Los Angeles, CA 90095. Offers MA, MA/MPH, MA/MSW. *Faculty:* 11 full-time (5 women). *Students:* 17 full-time (11 women); includes 15 minority (12 Asian, non-Hispanic/Latino; 2 Native Hawaiian or other Pacific Islander, non-Hispanic/Latino; 1 Two or more races, non-Hispanic/Latino), 1 international. Average age 28. 31 applicants, 26% accepted, 7 enrolled. In 2010, 6 master's awarded. *Degree requirements:* For master's, one foreign language, comprehensive exam or thesis, research tool. *Entrance requirements:* For master's, minimum GPA of 3.0, sample of written work. *Application deadline:* For fall admission, 12/15 for domestic and international students. Application fee: $70 ($90 for international students). Electronic applications accepted. *Financial support:* In 2010–11, 14 fellowships with full and partial tuition reimbursements, 4 research assistantships with full and partial tuition reimbursements, 6 teaching assistantships with full and partial tuition reimbursements were awarded; Federal Work-Study, institutionally sponsored loans, scholarships/grants, health care benefits, tuition waivers (full and partial), and unspecified assistantships also available. Financial award application deadline: 3/1; financial award applicants required to submit FAFSA. *Unit head:* Dr. Lane Hirabayashi, Chair, 310-206-8020. *Application contact:* Departmental Office, 310-267-5592, E-mail: maprogram@asianam.ucla.edu.

Asian Studies

California Institute of Integral Studies, School of Consciousness and Transformation, San Francisco, CA 94103. Offers creative inquiry/interdisciplinary arts (MFA); cultural anthropology and social transformation (MA); East-West psychology (MA, PhD); integrative health studies (MA); philosophy and religion (MA, PhD), including Asian and comparative studies, philosophy, cosmology, and consciousness, women's spirituality; social and cultural anthropology (PhD); transformative leadership (MA); transformative studies (PhD); writing and consciousness (MFA). Part-time and evening/weekend programs available. Postbaccalaureate distance learning degree programs offered (minimal on-campus study). *Students:* 455 full-time (315 women), 133 part-time (90 women); includes 47 Black or African American, non-Hispanic/Latino; 3 American Indian or Alaska Native, non-Hispanic/Latino; 21 Asian, non-Hispanic/Latino; 41 Hispanic/Latino, 40 international. Average age 37. 265 applicants, 91% accepted, 163 enrolled. In 2010, 64 master's, 22 doctorates awarded. Terminal master's awarded for partial completion of doctoral program. *Degree requirements:* For master's, thesis optional; for doctorate, comprehensive exam, thesis/dissertation, 1 foreign language (Asian comparative studies). *Entrance requirements:* For master's, minimum GPA of 3.0, letters of recommendation, writing sample; for doctorate, master's degree, minimum GPA of 3.0, letters of recommendation, writing sample. Additional exam requirements/recommendations for international students: Required—TOEFL. *Application deadline:* For fall admission, 2/1 priority date for domestic and international students; for spring admission, 10/15 priority date for domestic and international students. Applications are processed on a rolling basis. Application fee: $65. Electronic applications accepted. *Expenses:* Tuition: Full-time $15,660; part-time $870 per semester hour. Required fees: $95 per semester. *Financial support:* In 2010–11, 255 students received support; research assistantships, teaching assistantships, career-related internships or fieldwork, Federal Work-Study, scholarships/grants, and tuition waivers (partial) available. Support available to part-time students. Financial award application deadline: 4/15; financial award applicants required to submit FAFSA. *Faculty research:* Ecology and sustainability, philosophy and religion, East-West psychology, integrative health, social and cultural anthropology, transformative leadership. *Application contact:* Allyson Werner, Associate Director of Admissions, 415-575-6155, Fax: 415-575-1268.

California State University, Long Beach, Graduate Studies, College of Liberal Arts, Department of Asian and Asian American Studies, Long Beach, CA 90840. Offers Asian studies (MA). Part-time programs available. *Faculty:* 8 full-time (5 women). *Students:* 9 full-time (7 women), 9 part-time (6 women); includes 10 Asian, non-Hispanic/Latino, 2 international. Average age 34. 16 applicants, 38% accepted, 4 enrolled. In 2010, 3 master's awarded. *Degree requirements:* For master's, one foreign language, comprehensive exam or thesis. *Application deadline:* For fall admission, 5/1 for domestic students. Applications are processed on a rolling basis. Application fee: $55. Electronic applications accepted. *Financial support:* Federal Work-Study, institutionally sponsored loans, and scholarships/grants available. Financial award application deadline: 3/2. *Faculty research:* South Asia, China, Japan, Southeast Asia, Asian-Americans in the U. S. *Unit head:* Dr. John N. Tsuchida, Chair, 562-985-8085, Fax: 562-985-1535, E-mail: jtsuchid@csulb.edu. *Application contact:* Dr. Linda Espana-Maram, Graduate Advisor, 562-985-4822, Fax: 562-985-1535, E-mail: lnemaram@csulb.edu.

California State University, Long Beach, Graduate Studies, College of Liberal Arts, Department of History, Long Beach, CA 90840. Offers Africa and the Middle East (MA); ancient/medieval Europe (MA); Asia (MA); Latin America (MA); modern Europe (MA); United States (MA); world (MA). Part-time and evening/weekend programs available. *Faculty:* 12 full-time (7 women). *Students:* 18 full-time (6 women), 51 part-time (18 women); includes 3 Black or African American, non-Hispanic/Latino; 1 American Indian or Alaska Native, non-Hispanic/Latino; 3 Asian, non-Hispanic/Latino; 16 Hispanic/Latino, 1 international. Average age 30. 80 applicants, 53% accepted, 30 enrolled. In 2010, 11 master's awarded. *Degree requirements:* For master's, one foreign language, comprehensive exam or thesis. *Application deadline:* For fall admission, 3/1 for domestic students. Applications are processed on a rolling basis. Application fee: $55. Electronic applications accepted. *Financial support:* Research assistantships, Federal Work-Study, institutionally sponsored loans, and scholarships/grants available. Financial award application deadline: 3/2. *Faculty research:* All periods of European and American history, recent Asian and African history. *Unit head:* Dr. Nancy Quam-Wickham, Department Chair, 562-985-4431, Fax: 562-985-5431, E-mail: quamwick@csulb.edu. *Application contact:* Dr. Houri Berberian, Graduate Advisor, 562-985-4524, Fax: 562-985-4431, E-mail: hberber@csulb.edu.

Columbia University, Graduate School of Arts and Sciences, Division of Humanities, Department of East Asian Languages and Cultures, New York, NY 10027. Offers East Asian languages and cultures (M Phil, MA, PhD); Oriental studies (M Phil, MA, PhD). *Degree requirements:* For master's, one foreign language, comprehensive exam, thesis; for doctorate, 2 foreign languages, thesis/dissertation. *Entrance requirements:* For master's and doctorate, GRE General Test. Additional exam requirements/recommendations for international students: Required—TOEFL.

Columbia University, Graduate School of Arts and Sciences, Division of Humanities, Department of Middle East Languages and Cultures, New York, NY 10027. Offers Hebrew language and literature (M Phil, MA, PhD); Middle Eastern languages and cultures (M Phil, MA, PhD); South Asian languages and cultures (M Phil, MA, PhD). Part-time programs available.

Degree requirements: For master's, thesis, oral and written exams; for doctorate, 3 foreign languages, thesis/dissertation. *Entrance requirements:* For master's and doctorate, GRE General Test. Additional exam requirements/recommendations for international students: Required—TOEFL. *Faculty research:* Indo-Iranian, Turkish, central Asian, and Armenian studies; Arabic and ancient Semitics.

Columbia University, Graduate School of Arts and Sciences, Program in East Asian Regional Studies, New York, NY 10027. Offers MA. *Degree requirements:* For master's, 2 foreign languages. *Entrance requirements:* For master's, GRE General Test.

Columbia University, Graduate School of Arts and Sciences, Program in Liberal Studies, New York, NY 10027. Offers American studies (MA); East Asian studies (MA); human rights studies (MA); Islamic culture studies (MA); Jewish studies (MA); medieval studies (MA); modern European studies (MA); South Asian studies (MA). Part-time and evening/weekend programs available. *Degree requirements:* For master's, thesis.

Columbia University, School of International and Public Affairs, Weatherhead East Asian Institute, New York, NY 10027. Offers Asian studies (Certificate). Students must be enrolled in a separate graduate degree program at Columbia University. *Entrance requirements:* For degree, proficiency in East Asian language. Electronic applications accepted.

Columbia University, South Asia Institute, New York, NY 10027. Offers Certificate. Students must be enrolled in a separate graduate degree program at Columbia University. Electronic applications accepted.

Cornell University, Graduate School, Graduate Fields of Arts and Sciences, Field of Asian Religions, Ithaca, NY 14853-0001. Offers PhD. *Faculty:* 8 full-time (4 women). *Students:* 7 full-time (3 women), 1 international. Average age 30. 18 applicants, 11% accepted, 2 enrolled. In 2010, 1 doctorate awarded. *Degree requirements:* For doctorate, comprehensive exam, thesis/dissertation. *Entrance requirements:* For doctorate, GRE General Test, academic writing sample, 3 letters of recommendation. Additional exam requirements/recommendations for international students: Required—TOEFL (minimum score 600 paper-based; 250 computer-based; 77 iBT). *Application deadline:* For fall admission, 1/15 for domestic students. Application fee: $80. Electronic applications accepted. *Expenses:* Tuition: Full-time $29,500. Required fees: $76. Tuition and fees vary according to degree level and program. *Financial support:* In 2010–11, 2 fellowships with full tuition reimbursements, 4 teaching assistantships with full tuition reimbursements were awarded; research assistantships with full tuition reimbursements, institutionally sponsored loans, scholarships/grants, health care benefits, and unspecified assistantships also available. *Unit head:* Director of Graduate Studies, 607-255-9099, Fax: 607-255-1345. *Application contact:* Graduate Field Assistant, 607-255-9099, Fax: 607-255-1345, E-mail: asian-religions@cornell.edu.

Cornell University, Graduate School, Graduate Fields of Arts and Sciences, Field of Asian Studies, Ithaca, NY 14853-0001. Offers East Asian linguistics (MA); East Asian studies (MA); South Asian linguistics (MA); South Asian studies (MA); Southeast Asian linguistics (MA); Southeast Asian studies (MA). *Faculty:* 52 full-time (20 women). *Students:* 10 full-time (6 women); includes 1 Asian, non-Hispanic/Latino, 5 international. Average age 27. 75 applicants, 36% accepted, 10 enrolled. In 2010, 5 master's awarded. *Degree requirements:* For master's, one foreign language, thesis. *Entrance requirements:* For master's, GRE General Test, 3 letters of recommendation. Additional exam requirements/recommendations for international students: Required—TOEFL (minimum score 550 paper-based; 213 computer-based; 77 iBT). *Application deadline:* Applications are processed on a rolling basis. Application fee: $80. Electronic applications accepted. *Expenses:* Tuition: Full-time $29,500. Required fees: $76. Tuition and fees vary according to degree level and program. *Financial support:* In 2010–11, 2 fellowships with full tuition reimbursements, 2 teaching assistantships with full tuition reimbursements were awarded; research assistantships with full tuition reimbursements, institutionally sponsored loans, scholarships/grants, health care benefits, tuition waivers (full and partial), and unspecified assistantships also available. Financial award applicants required to submit FAFSA. *Faculty research:* East Asian studies, South Asian studies, Southeast Asian studies. *Unit head:* Director of Graduate Studies, 607-255-9099, Fax: 607-255-1345. *Application contact:* Graduate Field Assistant, 607-255-9099, Fax: 607-255-1345, E-mail: asian@cornell.edu.

Cornell University, Graduate School, Graduate Fields of Arts and Sciences, Field of East Asian Literature, Ithaca, NY 14853-0001. Offers Asian religions (MA, PhD); Chinese linguistics (MA, PhD); Chinese philology (MA, PhD); classical Chinese literature (MA, PhD); classical Japanese literature (MA, PhD); Japanese linguistics (MA, PhD); Korean literature (MA, PhD); modern Chinese literature (MA, PhD); modern Japanese literature (MA, PhD). *Faculty:* 15 full-time (7 women). *Students:* 19 full-time (9 women); includes 1 Black or African American, non-Hispanic/Latino; 3 Asian, non-Hispanic/Latino, 10 international. Average age 30. 37 applicants, 19% accepted, 6 enrolled. In 2010, 2 master's, 4 doctorates awarded. *Degree requirements:* For master's, 2 foreign languages, thesis, teaching experience; for doctorate, 2 foreign languages, comprehensive exam, thesis/dissertation, teaching experience. *Entrance requirements:* For master's, GRE General Test, 3 years of study in Chinese, Japanese, Korean, or Vietnamese; 3 letters of recommendation; academic writing sample; for doctorate, GRE General Test, 3 years of study in Chinese, Japanese, Korean, or Vietnamese, 3 letters of recommendation, academic writing sample. Additional exam requirements/recommendations for international students: Required—TOEFL (minimum score 600 paper-based; 250 computer-based; 77 iBT). *Application deadline:* For fall admission, 1/10 priority date for domestic students. Application fee: $80. Electronic applications accepted. *Expenses:* Tuition: Full-time $29,500. Required fees: $76. Tuition and fees vary according to degree level and program. *Financial support:* In 2010–11, 13 fellowships with full tuition reimbursements, 6 teaching assistantships with full tuition reimbursements were awarded; research assistantships with full tuition reimbursements, institutionally sponsored loans, scholarships/grants, health care benefits, tuition waivers (full and partial), and unspecified assistantships also available. Financial award applicants required to submit FAFSA. *Faculty research:* Vietnamese literature; Chinese literature, drama, and film; Japanese theater and literature; popular culture in East Asia; Korean literature; Asian linguistics. *Unit head:* Director of Graduate Studies, 607-255-9099. *Application contact:* Graduate Field Assistant, 607-255-9099, E-mail: east_asian_lit@cornell.edu.

Cornell University, Graduate School, Graduate Fields of Arts and Sciences, Field of History, Ithaca, NY 14853-0001. Offers African history (MA, PhD); American history (MA, PhD); ancient history (MA, PhD); early modern European history (MA, PhD); English history (MA, PhD); French history (MA, PhD); German history (MA, PhD); history of science (MA, PhD); Latin American history (MA, PhD); medieval Chinese history (MA, PhD); medieval history (MA, PhD); modern Chinese history (MA, PhD); modern European history (MA, PhD); modern Japanese history (MA, PhD); premodern Islamic history (MA, PhD); premodern Japanese history (MA, PhD); Renaissance history (MA, PhD); Russian history (MA, PhD); Southeast Asian history (MA, PhD). *Faculty:* 53 full-time (15 women). *Students:* 59 full-time (30 women); includes 3 Black or African American, non-Hispanic/Latino; 2 Asian, non-Hispanic/Latino; 4 Hispanic/Latino, 22 international. Average age 30. 217 applicants, 6% accepted, 8 enrolled. In 2010, 9 master's, 5 doctorates awarded. Terminal master's awarded for partial completion of doctoral program. *Degree requirements:* For master's, thesis; for doctorate, 2 foreign languages, comprehensive exam, thesis/dissertation, 1 year of teaching experience. *Entrance requirements:* For master's and doctorate, GRE General Test, writing sample, 3 letters of recommendation. Additional exam requirements/recommendations for international students: Required—TOEFL (minimum score 550 paper-based; 213 computer-based; 77 iBT). *Application deadline:* For fall admission, 1/15 for domestic students. Application fee: $80. Electronic applications accepted. *Expenses:* Tuition: Full-time $29,500. Required fees: $76. Tuition and fees vary according to degree level and program. *Financial support:* In 2010–11, 26 fellowships with full tuition reimbursements, 27 teaching assistantships with full tuition reimbursements were awarded; research assistantships with full tuition reimbursements, institutionally sponsored loans, scholarships/grants, health care benefits, tuition waivers (full and partial), and unspecified assistantships also available. Financial award applicants required to submit FAFSA. *Unit head:* Director of Graduate Studies, 607-255-6738, Fax: 607-255-0469. *Application contact:* Graduate Field Assistant, 607-255-6738, Fax: 607-255-0469, E-mail: history_grad_info@cornell.edu.

Cornell University, Graduate School, Graduate Fields of Arts and Sciences, Field of History of Art, Archaeology and Visual Studies, Ithaca, NY 14853. Offers American art (PhD); ancient art and archaeology (PhD); Asian art (PhD); Baroque art (PhD); medieval art (PhD); modern art (PhD); Renaissance art (PhD); Southeast Asian art (PhD); theory and criticism (PhD). *Faculty:* 24 full-time (15 women). *Students:* 21 full-time (19 women); includes 1 Black or African American, non-Hispanic/Latino; 2 American Indian or Alaska Native, non-Hispanic/Latino; 1 Hispanic/Latino, 7 international. Average age 31. 71 applicants, 7% accepted, 5 enrolled. In 2010, 2 doctorates awarded. *Degree requirements:* For doctorate, one foreign language, comprehensive exam, thesis/dissertation, general exams in 3 areas. *Entrance requirements:* For doctorate, GRE General Test, sample of written work, 3 letters of recommendation. Additional exam requirements/recommendations for international students: Required—TOEFL (minimum score 550 paper-based; 213 computer-based; 77 iBT). *Application deadline:* For fall admission, 1/15 for domestic students. Application fee: $80. Electronic applications accepted. *Expenses:* Tuition: Full-time $29,500. Required fees: $76. Tuition and fees vary according to degree level and program. *Financial support:* In 2010–11, 8 fellowships with full tuition reimbursements, 11 teaching assistantships with full tuition reimbursements were awarded; research assistantships with full tuition reimbursements, institutionally sponsored loans, scholarships/grants, health care benefits, tuition waivers (full and partial), and unspecified assistantships also available. Financial award applicants required to submit FAFSA. *Unit head:* Director of Graduate Studies, 607-255-4905, Fax: 607-255-0566, E-mail: art_history@cornell.edu. *Application contact:* Graduate Field Assistant, 607-255-4905, Fax: 607-255-0566, E-mail: art_history@cornell.edu.

Cornell University, Graduate School, Graduate Fields of Arts and Sciences, Field of Linguistics, Ithaca, NY 14853-0001. Offers applied linguistics (MA, PhD); East Asian linguistics (MA, PhD); English linguistics (MA, PhD); general linguistics (MA, PhD); Germanic linguistics (MA, PhD); Indo-European linguistics (MA, PhD); phonetics (MA, PhD); phonological theory (MA, PhD); Romance linguistics (MA, PhD); second language acquisition (MA, PhD); semantics (MA, PhD); Slavic linguistics (MA, PhD); sociolinguistics (MA, PhD); South Asian linguistics (MA, PhD); Southeast Asian linguistics (MA, PhD); syntactic theory (MA, PhD). *Faculty:* 15 full-time (7 women). *Students:* 34 full-time (18 women); includes 3 Hispanic/Latino, 15 international. Average age 28. 111 applicants, 12% accepted, 8 enrolled. In 2010, 2 master's, 6 doctorates awarded. Terminal master's awarded for partial completion of doctoral program. *Degree requirements:* For master's, one foreign language, thesis; for doctorate, one foreign language, comprehensive exam, thesis/dissertation. *Entrance requirements:* For master's and doctorate, GRE General Test, 2 letters of recommendation. Additional exam requirements/recommendations for international students: Required—TOEFL (minimum score 600 paper-based; 250 computer-based; 77 iBT). *Application deadline:* For fall admission, 1/15 for domestic students. Application fee: $80. Electronic applications accepted. *Expenses:* Tuition: Full-time $29,500. Required fees: $76. Tuition and fees vary according to degree level and program. *Financial support:* In 2010–11, 17 fellowships with full tuition reimbursements, 1 research assistantship with full tuition reimbursement, 15 teaching assistantships with full tuition reimbursements were awarded; institutionally sponsored loans, scholarships/grants, health care benefits, tuition waivers (full and partial), and unspecified assistantships also available. Financial award applicants required to submit FAFSA. *Faculty research:* Phonology and phonetics, syntax and semantics, historical linguistics, philosophy of language, language acquisition. *Unit head:* Director of Graduate Studies, 607-255-1105. *Application contact:* Graduate Field Assistant, 607-255-1105, E-mail: lingfield@cornell.edu.

Duke University, Graduate School, Department of East Asian Studies, Durham, NC 27708. Offers AM, Certificate. Part-time programs available. *Faculty:* 41 full-time. *Students:* 11 full-time (7 women); includes 1 Black or African American, non-Hispanic/Latino; 2 Asian, non-Hispanic/Latino, 3 international. 45 applicants, 71% accepted, 7 enrolled. In 2010, 6 master's awarded. *Entrance requirements:* For master's, GRE General Test. Additional exam requirements/recommendations for international students: Required—TOEFL (minimum score 550 paper-based; 213 computer-based; 83 iBT), IELTS (minimum score 7). *Application deadline:* For fall admission, 1/30 priority date for domestic and international students. Application fee: $75. Electronic applications accepted. *Financial support:* Application deadline: 1/30. *Unit head:* Kristina Troost, Director, 919-684-2604, Fax: 919-681-6247, E-mail: dana.watson@duke.edu. *Application contact:* Elizabeth Hutton, Director, Graduate Admissions, 919-684-3913, Fax: 919-684-2277, E-mail: grad-admissions@duke.edu.

Florida International University, College of Arts and Sciences, Program in Asian Studies, Miami, FL 33199. Offers MA. Part-time and evening/weekend programs available. *Students:* 11 full-time (7 women), 8 part-time (5 women); includes 2 Asian, non-Hispanic/Latino; 6 Hispanic/Latino, 2 international. Average age 26. 23 applicants, 35% accepted, 8 enrolled. In 2010, 8 master's awarded. *Degree requirements:* For master's, thesis. *Entrance requirements:* For master's, minimum GPA of 3.0, letter of intent, letter of recommendation. Additional exam requirements/recommendations for international students: Required—TOEFL (minimum score 550 paper-based; 80 iBT). *Application deadline:* For fall admission, 6/1 for domestic students, 4/1 for international students; for spring admission, 10/1 for domestic students, 9/1 for international students. Applications are processed on a rolling basis. Application fee: $30. Electronic applications accepted. *Financial support:* Institutionally sponsored loans, scholarships/grants, and tuition waivers available. Financial award application deadline: 3/1; financial award applicants required to submit FAFSA. *Unit head:* Dr. Steven Heine, Director, 305-348-1914, Fax: 305-348-6586, E-mail: asian@fiu.edu. *Application contact:* Nanett Rojas, Assistant Director of Graduate Admissions, 305-348-7442, Fax: 305-348-7441, E-mail: gradadm@fiu.edu.

Florida State University, The Graduate School, College of Social Sciences and Public Policy, Program in Asian Studies, Tallahassee, FL 32306. Offers MA. Part-time programs available. *Students:* 3 full-time (2 women), 9 part-time (4 women); includes 2 Asian, non-Hispanic/Latino, 2 international. Average age 24. 16 applicants, 100% accepted, 4 enrolled. In 2010, 1 master's awarded. *Degree requirements:* For master's, one foreign language, comprehensive exam, thesis optional. *Entrance requirements:* For master's, GRE General Test, minimum GPA of 3.0. Additional exam requirements/recommendations for international students: Required—TOEFL (minimum score 550 paper-based; 213 computer-based; 80 iBT). *Application deadline:* For fall admission, 7/1 for domestic and international students; for spring admission, 11/1 for domestic and international students. Applications are processed on a rolling basis. Application fee: $30. Electronic applications accepted. *Expenses:* Tuition, state resident: full-time $8238.24. *Financial support:* In 2010–11, 1 student received support, including 1 research assistantship with full tuition reimbursement available (averaging $5,000 per year); Federal Work-Study, institutionally sponsored loans, and unspecified assistantships also available. Financial award application deadline: 2/15; financial award applicants required to submit FAFSA. *Faculty research:* Art history of the Orient, Asian history and politics. *Unit head:* Dr. Lee K. Metcalf, Director, 850-644-7327, Fax: 850-645-4981, E-mail: lmetcalf@fsu.edu. *Application contact:* Kaley Boggs, Program Specialist, 850-644-4418, Fax: 850-644-4981, E-mail: plollis@.fsu.edu.

The George Washington University, Elliott School of International Affairs, Program in Asian Studies, Washington, DC 20052. Offers MA, JD/MA, MBA/MA, MPH/MA. Part-time and evening/weekend programs available. *Students:* 16 full-time (6 women), 13 part-time (3 women); includes 1 Asian, non-Hispanic/Latino; 3 Hispanic/Latino; 1 Two or more races, non-Hispanic/Latino, 4 international. Average age 26. 81 applicants, 49% accepted, 11 enrolled. In 2010, 17 master's awarded. *Degree requirements:* For master's, one foreign language, capstone project. *Entrance requirements:* For master's, GRE General Test, 2 years (or the equivalent) of an approved Asian language. Additional exam requirements/recommendations for international students: Required—TOEFL. *Application deadline:* For fall admission, 2/1 for domestic students; for spring admission, 10/1 for domestic students. Application fee: $75. Electronic applications accepted. *Financial support:* In 2010–11, 7 students received support; fellowships with tuition reimbursements available, research assistantships with tuition reimbursements available, career-related internships or fieldwork, Federal Work-Study, institutionally sponsored loans, and

Asian Studies

The George Washington University (continued)
tuition waivers (full) available. Financial award application deadline: 1/15; financial award applicants required to submit FAFSA. *Faculty research:* Sino-Soviet studies, Japanese-U. S. relations, Chinese foreign policy, economic development in China. *Unit head:* Elizabeth Chacko, Director, 202-994-5328, Fax: 202-994-2484, E-mail: echacko@gwu.edu. *Application contact:* Jeff V. Miles, Director of Graduate Admissions, 202-994-7050, Fax: 202-994-9537, E-mail: esiagrad@gwu.edu.

Harvard University, Graduate School of Arts and Sciences, Committee on Inner Asian and Altaic Studies, Cambridge, MA 02138. Offers PhD. *Degree requirements:* For doctorate, 2 foreign languages, thesis/dissertation, oral general exam. *Entrance requirements:* For doctorate, GRE General Test, proficiency in a related foreign language. Additional exam requirements/recommendations for international students: Required—TOEFL. *Expenses:* Tuition: Full-time $34,976. Required fees: $1166. Full-time tuition and fees vary according to program.

Harvard University, Graduate School of Arts and Sciences, Committee on Regional Studies–East Asia, Cambridge, MA 02138. Offers Chinese studies (AM); Japanese studies (AM); Korean studies (AM); Mongolian studies (AM); Vietnamese studies (AM). *Degree requirements:* For master's, one foreign language, seminar paper. *Entrance requirements:* For master's, GRE General Test. Additional exam requirements/recommendations for international students: Required—TOEFL. *Expenses:* Tuition: Full-time $34,976. Required fees: $1166. Full-time tuition and fees vary according to program.

Harvard University, Graduate School of Arts and Sciences, Department of Sanskrit and Indian Studies, Cambridge, MA 02138. Offers Indian philosophy (AM, PhD); Pali (AM, PhD); Sanskrit (AM, PhD); Tibetan (AM, PhD); Urdu (AM, PhD). Terminal master's awarded for partial completion of doctoral program. *Degree requirements:* For master's, 3 foreign languages; for doctorate, 3 foreign languages, thesis/dissertation. *Entrance requirements:* For master's, GRE General Test; for doctorate, GRE General Test, proficiency in French and German. Additional exam requirements/recommendations for international students: Required—TOEFL. *Expenses:* Tuition: Full-time $34,976. Required fees: $1166. Full-time tuition and fees vary according to program.

Indiana University Bloomington, University Graduate School, College of Arts and Sciences, Department of Central Eurasian Studies, Bloomington, IN 47405-7000. Offers MA, PhD. *Faculty:* 11 full-time (0 women). *Students:* 44 full-time (15 women), 1 (woman) part-time, 12 international. Average age 32. 49 applicants, 69% accepted, 8 enrolled. In 2010, 10 master's, 3 doctorates awarded. Terminal master's awarded for partial completion of doctoral program. *Degree requirements:* For master's, one foreign language, thesis; for doctorate, 2 foreign languages, thesis/dissertation, qualifying exams. *Entrance requirements:* For master's, minimum GPA of 3.0, 2 years of a foreign language; for doctorate, minimum GPA of 3.5, 1 research language. Additional exam requirements/recommendations for international students: Required—TOEFL. *Application deadline:* For fall admission, 1/15 priority date for domestic students, 12/15 for international students; for spring admission, 9/1 priority date for domestic students, 9/1 for international students. Applications are processed on a rolling basis. Application fee: $55 ($65 for international students). Electronic applications accepted. *Financial support:* In 2010–11, 19 students received support, including 12 fellowships with full tuition reimbursements available (averaging $15,000 per year), 3 research assistantships with full tuition reimbursements available (averaging $14,051 per year), 4 teaching assistantships with full tuition reimbursements available (averaging $12,360 per year); Federal Work-Study also available. Financial award application deadline: 2/15. *Faculty research:* Central Asia, Hungarian civilization, Tibetan civilization, Turkish studies, Mongolian philology. *Unit head:* Christopher Atwood, Chair, 812-855-2233, E-mail: catwood@indiana.edu. *Application contact:* April Younger, Graduate Secretary, 812-855-2233, E-mail: ayounger@indiana.edu.

Indiana University Bloomington, University Graduate School, College of Arts and Sciences, Department of East Asian Languages and Cultures, Bloomington, IN 47408. Offers Chinese (MA, PhD); Chinese language pedagogy (MA); East Asian studies (MA); Japanese (MA, PhD); Japanese language pedagogy (MA). Part-time programs available. *Faculty:* 15 full-time (7 women), 15 part-time/adjunct (7 women). *Students:* 28 full-time (18 women), 11 part-time (6 women); includes 2 Black or African American, non-Hispanic/Latino, 11 international. Average age 29. 100 applicants, 38% accepted, 18 enrolled. In 2010, 9 master's, 1 doctorate awarded. *Degree requirements:* For master's, one foreign language, thesis; for doctorate, 2 foreign languages, comprehensive exam, thesis/dissertation. *Entrance requirements:* Additional exam requirements/recommendations for international students: Required—TOEFL (minimum score 93 iBT). *Application deadline:* For fall admission, 1/15 for domestic students, 12/1 for international students. Application fee: $55 ($65 for international students). Electronic applications accepted. *Financial support:* In 2010–11, 21 students received support, including 5 fellowships with full tuition reimbursements available (averaging $15,500 per year), 18 teaching assistantships with full tuition reimbursements available (averaging $11,633 per year). Financial award application deadline: 3/1. *Faculty research:* Postwar/postmodern Japanese fiction, modern Chinese film and literature, classical Chinese literature and philosophy, Chinese and Japanese linguistics and pedagogy, East Asian politics and economics, Chinese and Japanese history, Korean language. *Unit head:* Michael Robinson, Chair, 812-855-0856, Fax: 812-855-6402, E-mail: robime@indiana.edu. *Application contact:* Natsuko Tsujimura, Director of Graduate Studies, 812-855-5884, Fax: 812-855-6402, E-mail: tsujimur@indiana.edu.

The Johns Hopkins University, Paul H. Nitze School of Advanced International Studies, Washington, DC 20036. Offers international development (MA, Certificate), including international economics (MA); international public policy (MIPP); international relations (PhD); international studies (Certificate); Japan studies (MA), including international economics; Korea Studies (MA), including international economics; South Asia studies (MA), including international economics; Southeast Asia studies (MA), including international economics; JD/MA; MBA/MA; MHS/MA. *Faculty:* 57 full-time (18 women), 125 part-time/adjunct (40 women). *Students:* 627 full-time (305 women), 39 part-time (24 women); includes 127 minority (18 Black or African American, non-Hispanic/Latino; 60 Asian, non-Hispanic/Latino; 32 Hispanic/Latino; 1 Native Hawaiian or other Pacific Islander, non-Hispanic/Latino; 16 Two or more races, non-Hispanic/Latino), 176 international. Average age 27. 1,753 applicants, 42% accepted, 307 enrolled. In 2010, 441 master's, 10 doctorates awarded. Terminal master's awarded for partial completion of doctoral program. *Degree requirements:* For master's, one foreign language, 4-6 International Economics courses, 5-6 functional or regional concentration courses, 2 core examinations, proficiency in a language other than native language, and capstone project; for doctorate, 2 foreign languages, thesis/dissertation, 3 comprehensive exams, economics, quantitative and qualitative course, dissertation prospectus and defense. *Entrance requirements:* For master's, GMAT or GRE General Test, previous course work in economics, foreign language, undergraduate degree; for doctorate, GRE General Test, master's degree. Additional exam requirements/recommendations for international students: Required—TOEFL (minimum score 600 paper-based; 250 computer-based; 100 iBT) or IELTS (minimum score 7). *Application deadline:* For fall admission, 1/7 for domestic and international students. Application fee: $85. Electronic applications accepted. *Expenses:* Contact institution. *Financial support:* In 2010–11, 450 students received support, including 450 fellowships (averaging $12,000 per year), 32 teaching assistantships (averaging $3,906 per year); career-related internships or fieldwork, Federal Work-Study, and scholarships/grants also available. Financial award application deadline: 2/15; financial award applicants required to submit FAFSA. *Faculty research:* Regional studies, international relations, international economics, energy and environment, international development. Total annual research expenditures: $8.1 million. *Unit head:* Sidney Jackson, Director of Admissions, 202-663-5700, Fax: 202-663-7788. *Application contact:* Admissions, 202-663-5700, Fax: 202-663-7788, E-mail: admissions.sais@jhu.edu.

Maharishi University of Management, Graduate Studies, Program in Maharishi Vedic Science, Fairfield, IA 52557. Offers MA, PhD. Evening/weekend programs available. *Degree requirements:* For master's, thesis; for doctorate, thesis/dissertation. *Entrance requirements:* For master's, minimum GPA of 3.0; for doctorate, GRE, minimum GPA of 3.0. Additional exam requirements/recommendations for international students: Required—TOEFL. *Faculty research:* Modern science and Vedic science, unification of knowledge, philosophy of science, Sanskrit.

McGill University, Faculty of Graduate and Postdoctoral Studies, Faculty of Arts, Department of East Asian Studies, Montréal, QC H3A 2T5, Canada. Offers MA, PhD.

New York University, Graduate School of Arts and Science, Department of East Asian Studies, New York, NY 10012-1019. Offers MA, PhD. Part-time programs available. *Students:* 17 full-time (10 women); includes 1 Asian, non-Hispanic/Latino, 11 international. Average age 31. 102 applicants, 5% accepted, 2 enrolled. In 2010, 2 master's awarded. *Degree requirements:* For master's and doctorate, one foreign language. *Entrance requirements:* For master's and doctorate, GRE General Test. Additional exam requirements/recommendations for international students: Required—TOEFL. *Application deadline:* For fall admission, 1/4 for domestic students. Application fee: $90. Electronic applications accepted. *Financial support:* Fellowships with tuition reimbursements, teaching assistantships with tuition reimbursements, Federal Work-Study, institutionally sponsored loans, scholarships/grants, health care benefits, and unspecified assistantships available. Financial award application deadline: 1/4. *Unit head:* Xudong Zhang, Chair, 212-998-7620, Fax: 212-995-4682, E-mail: gsas.eas.graduate@nyu.edu. *Application contact:* Tom Looser, Director of Graduate Studies, 212-998-7620, Fax: 212-995-4682, E-mail: gsas.eas.graduate@nyu.edu.

Ohio University, Graduate College, Center for International Studies, Program in Southeast Asian Studies, Athens, OH 45701-2979. Offers MA. Part-time programs available. *Students:* 11 full-time (6 women), 1 part-time (0 women); includes 1 minority (Hispanic/Latino), 6 international. Average age 31. 16 applicants, 81% accepted, 7 enrolled. In 2010, 12 master's awarded. *Degree requirements:* For master's, one foreign language, thesis optional. *Entrance requirements:* For master's, minimum GPA of 3.0. Additional exam requirements/recommendations for international students: Required—TOEFL (minimum score 550 paper-based; 213 computer-based). *Application deadline:* For fall admission, 1/1 for domestic and international students. Application fee: $50 ($55 for international students). Electronic applications accepted. *Financial support:* In 2010–11, research assistantships with full tuition reimbursements (averaging $11,499 per year), teaching assistantships with full tuition reimbursements (averaging $11,499 per year) were awarded; career-related internships or fieldwork, Federal Work-Study, institutionally sponsored loans, scholarships/grants, tuition waivers (partial), and unspecified assistantships also available. Financial award application deadline: 1/1. *Faculty research:* Indonesian and Malaysian political, history, literature, media, Islam, and environmental problems. Total annual research expenditures: $36,000. *Unit head:* Dr. Drewrey McDaniel, Director, 740-593-1684, E-mail: mcdanied@ohio.edu. *Application contact:* Joan Kraynanski, Administrative Assistant, 740-593-1840, Fax: 740-593-1837, E-mail: kraynans@ohio.edu.

Princeton University, Graduate School, Department of East Asian Studies, Princeton, NJ 08544-1019. Offers PhD. *Degree requirements:* For doctorate, 2 foreign languages, thesis/dissertation. *Entrance requirements:* For doctorate, GRE General Test, fluency in Japanese and/or Chinese. Additional exam requirements/recommendations for international students: Required—TOEFL (minimum score 600 paper-based; 250 computer-based). Electronic applications accepted. *Faculty research:* Modern and classical Japanese literature, premodern Chinese and Japanese history, Chinese narrative and poetry.

Rutgers, The State University of New Jersey, New Brunswick, Graduate School-New Brunswick, Program in History, Piscataway, NJ 08854-8097. Offers African-American history (PhD); early American history (PhD); early modern European history (PhD); east Asian history (PhD); global and comparative history (PhD); history (PhD); history of diplomacy and foreign relations (PhD); history of technology, environment and health (PhD); history of the Atlantic cultures and African diaspora (PhD); Latin American history (PhD); medieval history (PhD); modern European history (PhD); nineteenth and twentieth century American history (PhD); women's and gender history (PhD). *Degree requirements:* For doctorate, thesis/dissertation. *Entrance requirements:* For doctorate, GRE General Test, sample of written work. Electronic applications accepted. *Expenses:* Tuition, state resident: full-time $7200; part-time $600 per credit. Tuition, nonresident: full-time $11,124; part-time $927 per credit. *Faculty research:* American history, European history, Afro-American history, women's history, Latin American history.

St. John's College, Graduate Institute in Liberal Education, Program in Eastern Classics, Santa Fe, NM 87505. Offers MA. Part-time and evening/weekend programs available. *Entrance requirements:* For master's, 2 letters of recommendation. Additional exam requirements/recommendations for international students: Required—TOEFL, TWE. *Expenses:* Contact institution.

St. John's University, St. John's College of Liberal Arts and Sciences, Institute of Asian Studies, Queens, NY 11439. Offers Asian and African cultural studies (Adv C); Asian studies (Adv C); Chinese studies (MA, Adv C); East Asian culture studies (Adv C); East Asian studies (MA). Part-time and evening/weekend programs available. *Students:* 8 full-time (6 women), 6 part-time (4 women); includes 7 minority (1 Black or African American, non-Hispanic/Latino; 4 Asian, non-Hispanic/Latino; 2 Hispanic/Latino), 7 international. Average age 32. 15 applicants, 73% accepted, 1 enrolled. In 2010, 3 master's awarded. *Degree requirements:* For master's, one foreign language, comprehensive exam, thesis optional. *Entrance requirements:* For master's, 6 semester hours of course work in the field, minimum GPA of 3.0. Additional exam requirements/recommendations for international students: Required—TOEFL (minimum score 600 paper-based; 250 computer-based; 100 iBT), IELTS (minimum score 5.5). *Application deadline:* For fall admission, 5/1 priority date for domestic and international students; for spring admission, 11/1 priority date for domestic and international students. Applications are processed on a rolling basis. Application fee: $70. Electronic applications accepted. *Expenses:* Tuition: Full-time $17,100; part-time $950 per credit. Required fees: $340; $170 per semester. Tuition and fees vary according to program. *Financial support:* Research assistantships, scholarships/grants available. Support available to part-time students. Financial award application deadline: 3/1; financial award applicants required to submit FAFSA. *Faculty research:* East Asian philosophy and religions, government and politics of East Asia, business and economy of East Asia, legal systems and trade relations of East Asian countries, Chinese language and civilization, Japanese language and civilization, Korean language and civilization, modern China, modern Japan, modern Korea, Chinese art and history, Japanese art and history, Korean art and history. *Unit head:* Dr. Bernadette Li, Chair, 718-990-1657, Fax: 718-990-1881, E-mail: lib@stjohns.edu. *Application contact:* Kathleen Davis, Director of Graduate Admission, 718-990-1601, Fax: 718-990-5686, E-mail: gradhelp@stjohns.edu.

San Diego State University, Graduate and Research Affairs, College of Arts and Letters, Center for Asian Studies, San Diego, CA 92182. Offers MA. *Degree requirements:* For master's, one foreign language, thesis. *Entrance requirements:* For master's, GRE General Test, 3 letters of reference, writing sample. Additional exam requirements/recommendations for international students: Required—TOEFL. Electronic applications accepted. *Faculty research:* Language acquisition process, social organization of Asia, economic development.

Seton Hall University, College of Arts and Sciences, Department of Asian Studies, South Orange, NJ 07079-2697. Offers Asian languages (MA); Asian studies (MA); teaching Chinese language and culture (MA). Part-time and evening/weekend programs available. *Degree requirements:* For master's, thesis optional. *Entrance requirements:* For master's, strong background in Asian studies or related discipline. Additional exam requirements/recommendations for international students: Required—TOEFL. Electronic applications accepted. *Faculty research:* Modern Chinese history, contemporary Chinese politics, ancient Chinese history, Hinduism, Asian business, Japanese history.

Stanford University, School of Humanities and Sciences, Center for East Asian Studies, Stanford, CA 94305-9991. Offers MA. *Degree requirements:* For master's, one foreign language, thesis. *Entrance requirements:* For master's, GRE General Test. Additional exam requirements/

recommendations for international students: Required—TOEFL. Electronic applications accepted. *Expenses:* Tuition: Full-time $38,700; part-time $860 per unit. One-time fee: $200 full-time.

Texas A&M University, Bush School of Government and Public Service, College Station, TX 77843. Offers advanced international affairs (Certificate); China studies (Certificate); homeland security (Certificate); international affairs (MPIA); national security affairs (Certificate); nonprofit management (Certificate); public service and administration (MPSA). *Accreditation:* NASPAA. *Faculty:* 45. *Students:* 215 full-time (98 women), 93 part-time (32 women); includes 20 Black or African American, non-Hispanic/Latino; 2 American Indian or Alaska Native, non-Hispanic/Latino; 14 Asian, non-Hispanic/Latino; 30 Hispanic/Latino, 15 international. Average age 24. In 2010, 93 master's awarded. *Degree requirements:* For master's, summer internship. *Entrance requirements:* For master's, GRE (preferred) or GMAT. *Application deadline:* For fall admission, 1/24 for domestic and international students. Application fee: $50 ($75 for international students). Electronic applications accepted. *Financial support:* In 2010–11, fellowships (averaging $11,000 per year), research assistantships (averaging $11,250 per year) were awarded; career-related internships or fieldwork, Federal Work-Study, and institutionally sponsored loans also available. Financial award application deadline: 2/1; financial award applicants required to submit FAFSA. *Faculty research:* Public policy, presidential studies, public leadership, economic policy, social policy. *Unit head:* Ryan C. Crocker, Dean, 979-862-8007, E-mail: rcrocker@bushschool.tamu.edu. *Application contact:* Kathryn Meyer, Director of Recruiting, 979-458-4767, Fax: 979-845-4155, E-mail: kmeyer@bushschool.tamu.edu.

United Theological Seminary of the Twin Cities, Graduate Programs, New Brighton, MN 55112-2598. Offers advanced theological studies (Diploma); justice and peace studies (M Div, MA); leadership toward racial justice (M Div, MA, Certificate); Methodist studies (M Div, MA, Certificate); ministry (D Min); ministry renewal and professional development (Certificate); pastoral care and counseling (M Div, MA, MARL); religion and theology (MA); theological and religious studies (Certificate); theology and the arts (M Div, MA); urban ministry (M Div, MA, MARL); women's studies: religion, theology and ministry (M Div, MA). *Accreditation:* ACIPE; ATS. Part-time and evening/weekend programs available. *Faculty:* 8 full-time (5 women), 28 part-time/adjunct (16 women). *Students:* 57 full-time (41 women), 94 part-time (61 women); includes 6 minority (5 Black or African American, non-Hispanic/Latino; 1 Hispanic/Latino), 1 international. Average age 47. 49 applicants, 98% accepted, 41 enrolled. In 2010, 10 first professional degrees, 6 master's, 4 doctorates, 2 other advanced degrees awarded. *Degree requirements:* For master's, thesis; for doctorate, comprehensive exam, thesis/dissertation; for M Div, integrative notebook, spiritual chronicle. *Entrance requirements:* For M Div and master's, minimum GPA of 2.75; strong analytical, reflective thinking and writing skills; vocational and academic goals compatible with those of Seminary; for doctorate, M Div or equivalent, minimum GPA of 3.0, 3 years experience in professional ministry; for other advanced degree, BA or equivalent life experience; strong analytical, reflective thinking and writing skills (Certificate); proficiency in English language, previous study of theology at a theological school, recommendation of student's denomination (Diploma). Additional exam requirements/recommendations for international students: Required—TOEFL (minimum score 550 paper-based). *Application deadline:* For fall admission, 7/1 priority date for domestic students, 11/1 priority date for international students; for winter admission, 11/1 priority date for domestic students; for spring admission, 11/15 priority date for domestic students. Applications are processed on a rolling basis. Application fee: $50. *Expenses:* Tuition: Full-time $13,014; part-time $482 per credit hour. One-time fee: $170. Tuition and fees vary according to course load, degree level and program. *Financial support:* In 2010–11, 120 students received support. Career-related internships or fieldwork, institutionally sponsored loans, and scholarships/grants available. Support available to part-time students. Financial award application deadline: 5/1; financial award applicants required to submit FAFSA. *Unit head:* Prof. Susan K. Ebbers, Dean of the Seminary, 651-255-6143 Ext. 108, Fax: 651-633-4315, E-mail: sebbers@unitedseminary.edu. *Application contact:* Rev. Glen Herrington-Hall, Director of Admissions, 651-255-6107 Ext. 107, Fax: 651-633-4315, E-mail: gherrington-hall@unitedseminary.edu.

University of Alberta, Faculty of Graduate Studies and Research, Department of East Asian Studies, Edmonton, AB T6G 2E1, Canada. Offers Chinese literature (MA); East Asian interdisciplinary studies (MA); Japanese literature (MA). Part-time programs available. *Degree requirements:* For master's, one foreign language, thesis. *Entrance requirements:* Additional exam requirements/recommendations for international students: Required—TOEFL. Electronic applications accepted. *Faculty research:* Classical Chinese poetry and poetics, Chinese philosophy, modern/contemporary Chinese literature, modern Japanese literature and culture, Japanese women's writing.

The University of Arizona, College of Humanities, Department of East Asian Studies, Tucson, AZ 85721. Offers MA, PhD. Part-time programs available. *Faculty:* 8 full-time (3 women), 1 (woman) part-time/adjunct. *Students:* 21 full-time (16 women), 7 part-time (3 women); includes 3 Asian, non-Hispanic/Latino; 1 Two or more races, non-Hispanic/Latino, 17 international. Average age 32. 64 applicants, 19% accepted, 8 enrolled. In 2010, 6 master's, 4 doctorates awarded. Terminal master's awarded for partial completion of doctoral program. *Degree requirements:* For master's, one foreign language; for doctorate, 2 foreign languages. *Entrance requirements:* For master's, GRE General Test, 2 letters of recommendation; for doctorate, GRE General Test, 2 letters of recommendation, statement of purpose, writing sample. Additional exam requirements/recommendations for international students: Required—TOEFL (minimum score 550 paper-based; 213 computer-based; 79 iBT). *Application deadline:* For fall admission, 2/1 for domestic and international students. Applications are processed on a rolling basis. Application fee: $75. Electronic applications accepted. *Expenses:* Tuition, state resident: full-time $7692. *Financial support:* In 2010–11, 20 teaching assistantships with full tuition reimbursements (averaging $20,122 per year) were awarded; health care benefits, tuition waivers (partial), and unspecified assistantships also available. Financial award application deadline: 2/1. *Faculty research:* Chinese history, Chinese/Japanese linguistics, Chinese/Japanese literature, Chinese/Japanese religion. Total annual research expenditures: $30,001. *Unit head:* Dr. J. Philip Gabriel, Head, 520-621-7505, Fax: 520-621-1149, E-mail: jgabriel@u.arizona.edu. *Application contact:* Janet Kania, Administrative Associate, 520-621-5452, Fax: 520-621-1149, E-mail: kaniaj@u.arizona.edu.

The University of British Columbia, Faculty of Arts, Department of Asian Studies, Vancouver, CA V6T 1Z2, Canada. Offers MA, PhD. *Degree requirements:* For master's, one foreign language, thesis; for doctorate, 2 foreign languages, thesis/dissertation. *Entrance requirements:* For master's, BA; for doctorate, master's degree in Asian studies or equivalent. Additional exam requirements/recommendations for international students: Required—TOEFL (minimum score 570 paper-based; 230 computer-based; 85 iBT). Electronic applications accepted. Tuition charges are reported in Canadian dollars. *Expenses:* Tuition, area resident: Full-time $4179 Canadian dollars. International tuition: $7344 Canadian dollars full-time. *Faculty research:* Language; linguistics; literature; religion and philosophy; premodern history of China, Japan, Korea, South and South East Asia.

The University of British Columbia, Institute of Asian Research, Vancouver, BC V6T 1Z2, Canada. Offers MAPPS. *Degree requirements:* For master's, thesis optional. *Entrance requirements:* Additional exam requirements/recommendations for international students: Required—TOEFL (minimum score 600 paper-based; 250 computer-based; 100 iBT), GRE (recommended). Electronic applications accepted. Tuition charges are reported in Canadian dollars. *Expenses:* Tuition, area resident: Full-time $4179 Canadian dollars. International tuition: $7344 Canadian dollars full-time. *Faculty research:* Social cohesion, globalization, social safety nets, policy research, research and development alliances, knowledge-based workshops on Asia-Pacific studies.

University of California, Berkeley, Graduate Division, College of Letters and Science, Department of South and Southeast Asian Studies, Berkeley, CA 94720-1500. Offers Hindi (MA, PhD); Indonesian (MA, PhD); Sanskrit (MA, PhD); Tamil (MA, PhD). Terminal master's awarded for partial completion of doctoral program. *Degree requirements:* For master's, 2 foreign languages, thesis; for doctorate, 2 foreign languages, thesis/dissertation, oral qualifying exam. *Entrance requirements:* For master's and doctorate, GRE General Test, minimum GPA of 3.0, 3 letters of recommendation. Electronic applications accepted.

University of California, Berkeley, Graduate Division, College of Letters and Science, Group in Buddhist Studies, Berkeley, CA 94720-1500. Offers PhD. *Degree requirements:* For doctorate, 4 foreign languages, thesis/dissertation, dissertation defense, qualifying exam. *Entrance requirements:* For doctorate, GRE General Test, MA in Japanese, Chinese, or Sanskrit; minimum GPA of 3.0, 3 letters of recommendation. Electronic applications accepted.

University of California, Berkeley, Graduate Division, Group in International and Area Studies, Group in Asian Studies, Berkeley, CA 94720-1500. Offers Asian studies (PhD); East Asian studies (MA); Northeast Asian studies (MA); South Asian studies (MA); Southeast Asian studies (MA); JD/MA; MBA/MA; MJ/MA. *Degree requirements:* For master's, one foreign language, comprehensive exam or thesis; for doctorate, 2 foreign languages, thesis/dissertation, qualifying exam. *Entrance requirements:* For master's and doctorate, GRE General Test, minimum GPA of 3.0, 3 letters of recommendation.

University of California, Los Angeles, Graduate Division, College of Letters and Science, Department of Asian Languages and Cultures, Los Angeles, CA 90095. Offers MA, PhD. *Faculty:* 24 full-time (5 women). *Students:* 52 full-time (29 women); includes 13 minority (all Asian, non-Hispanic/Latino), 20 international. Average age 33. 62 applicants, 24% accepted, 8 enrolled. In 2010, 2 master's, 6 doctorates awarded. Terminal master's awarded for partial completion of doctoral program. *Degree requirements:* For master's, one foreign language, comprehensive exam or thesis; for doctorate, 2 foreign languages, thesis/dissertation, oral and written qualifying exams. *Entrance requirements:* For master's, GRE General Test, minimum GPA of 3.0, sample of written work; for doctorate, GRE General Test, minimum undergraduate GPA of 3.0, sample of research writing or thesis in English. Additional exam requirements/recommendations for international students: Required—TOEFL. *Application deadline:* For fall admission, 12/1 for domestic and international students. Application fee: $70 ($90 for international students). Electronic applications accepted. *Financial support:* In 2010–11, 36 fellowships with full and partial tuition reimbursements, 25 research assistantships with full and partial tuition reimbursements, 27 teaching assistantships with full and partial tuition reimbursements were awarded; Federal Work-Study, institutionally sponsored loans, scholarships/grants, health care benefits, tuition waivers (full and partial), and unspecified assistantships also available. Financial award application deadline: 3/1; financial award applicants required to submit FAFSA. *Unit head:* Dr. David Schaberg, Chair, 310-206-8235, E-mail: schaberg@humnet.ucla.edu. *Application contact:* Department Office, 310-267-4008, E-mail: shanshan@humnet.ucla.edu.

University of California, Los Angeles, Graduate Division, International Institute, Interdepartmental Program in East Asian Studies, Los Angeles, CA 90095. Offers MA. *Students:* 17 full-time (8 women); includes 9 minority (1 Black or African American, non-Hispanic/Latino; 7 Asian, non-Hispanic/Latino; 1 Hispanic/Latino), 2 international. Average age 29. 66 applicants, 45% accepted, 8 enrolled. In 2010, 6 master's awarded. *Degree requirements:* For master's, one foreign language, comprehensive exam. *Entrance requirements:* For master's, GRE General Test, minimum undergraduate GPA of 3.0. *Application deadline:* For fall admission, 12/15 for domestic and international students. Application fee: $70 ($90 for international students). Electronic applications accepted. *Financial support:* In 2010–11, 5 fellowships with full and partial tuition reimbursements, 2 research assistantships with full and partial tuition reimbursements, 2 teaching assistantships with full and partial tuition reimbursements were awarded; Federal Work-Study, institutionally sponsored loans, scholarships/grants, health care benefits, tuition waivers (full and partial), and unspecified assistantships also available. Financial award application deadline: 3/1; financial award applicants required to submit FAFSA. *Unit head:* Dr. Cindy Fan, Director, 310-825-3821, E-mail: fan@geog.ucla.edu. *Application contact:* Program Office, 310-206-6571, E-mail: idpgrads@international.ucla.edu.

University of California, Riverside, Graduate Division, Program in Southeast Asian Studies, Riverside, CA 92521-0102. Offers MA. *Degree requirements:* For master's, one foreign language, thesis. *Entrance requirements:* For master's, GRE, statement of purpose to indicate serious interest in Southeast Asian Studies (or specific country or area in this region), writing sample. Additional exam requirements/recommendations for international students: Required—TOEFL. Electronic applications accepted. *Faculty research:* Southeast Asian texts, rituals and performance, music and technoculture, dance ethnography, ethnomusicology.

University of California, Santa Barbara, Graduate Division, College of Letters and Sciences, Division of Humanities and Fine Arts, Department of East Asian Languages and Cultural Studies, Santa Barbara, CA 93106-7075. Offers East Asian language and cultural studies (MA, PhD); translation studies (PhD). *Faculty:* 14 full-time, 7 part-time/adjunct. *Students:* 13 full-time (8 women). Average age 27. 76 applicants, 28% accepted, 6 enrolled. In 2010, 2 master's awarded. *Degree requirements:* For master's, one foreign language, thesis or alternative; for doctorate, 2 foreign languages, thesis/dissertation. *Entrance requirements:* For master's and doctorate, GRE, 3 letters of recommendation, statement of purpose, personal achievements/contributions statement, resume/curriculum vitae, transcripts for post-secondary institutions attended. Additional exam requirements/recommendations for international students: Required—TOEFL (minimum score 550 paper-based; 213 computer-based; 80 iBT) or IELTS (minimum score 7). *Application deadline:* For fall admission, 4/1 for domestic and international students. Application fee: $70 ($90 for international students). Electronic applications accepted. *Financial support:* In 2010–11, 13 students received support, including 5 fellowships with full and partial tuition reimbursements available (averaging $11,651 per year), 13 teaching assistantships with partial tuition reimbursements available (averaging $8,745 per year); Federal Work-Study, institutionally sponsored loans, scholarships/grants, health care benefits, and unspecified assistantships also available. Financial award application deadline: 12/15; financial award applicants required to submit FAFSA. *Faculty research:* Chinese literature, Chinese film, Japanese society, Japanese literature, East Asian cultural studies. *Unit head:* Dr. William Powell, Chair, 805-893-4455, Fax: 805-893-3011, E-mail: bpowell@religion.ucsb.edu. *Application contact:* Sally Lombrozo, Graduate Program Assistant, 805-893-2744, Fax: 805-893-7671, E-mail: lombrozo@hfa.ucsb.edu.

University of Chicago, Division of the Humanities, Department of East Asian Languages and Civilizations, Chicago, IL 60637-1513. Offers AM, PhD. Terminal master's awarded for partial completion of doctoral program. *Degree requirements:* For master's, one foreign language, thesis; for doctorate, 2 foreign languages, thesis/dissertation. *Entrance requirements:* For master's and doctorate, GRE General Test. Additional exam requirements/recommendations for international students: Required—TOEFL.

University of Chicago, Division of the Humanities, Department of South Asian Languages and Civilizations, Chicago, IL 60637-1513. Offers South Asian languages and civilizations (AM, PhD), including Bengali (PhD), Hindi (PhD), Sanskrit (PhD), Tamil (PhD), Urdu (PhD). Terminal master's awarded for partial completion of doctoral program. *Degree requirements:* For master's, one foreign language, thesis; for doctorate, 2 foreign languages, thesis/dissertation. *Entrance requirements:* For master's and doctorate, GRE General Test. Additional exam requirements/recommendations for international students: Required—TOEFL.

University of Colorado Boulder, Graduate School, College of Arts and Sciences, Department of Asian Languages and Civilizations, Boulder, CO 80309. Offers Chinese (MA, PhD); Japanese (MA, PhD). Part-time programs available. *Faculty:* 12 full-time (6 women). *Students:* 26 full-time (12 women), 4 part-time (3 women); includes 6 minority (1 Black or African American, non-Hispanic/Latino; 4 Asian, non-Hispanic/Latino; 1 Hispanic/Latino), 7 international. Average age 26. 37 applicants, 13 enrolled. In 2010, 18 master's awarded. *Degree requirements:* For master's, comprehensive exam. *Entrance requirements:* For master's, BA in Chinese or Japanese, minimum undergraduate GPA of 3.0. Additional exam requirements/recommendations for international students: Required—TOEFL. *Application deadline:* For fall admission, 1/1 priority date for domestic students, 12/1 for international students; for spring admission, 10/1 for domestic students, 9/1 for international students. Applications are processed on a rolling

Asian Studies

University of Colorado Boulder (continued)
basis. Application fee: $50 ($60 for international students). *Financial support:* In 2010–11, 7 fellowships (averaging $13,865 per year), 10 research assistantships (averaging $6,596 per year) were awarded; career-related internships or fieldwork and Federal Work-Study also available. Financial award application deadline: 2/1. *Faculty research:* Chinese and Japanese modern and classical literature, religions, linguistics, language pedagogy, pre-modern and contemporary fiction, sociolinguistics. Total annual research expenditures: $757,691.

University of Florida, Graduate School, College of Liberal Arts and Sciences, Department of Religion, Gainesville, FL 32611. Offers religion and nature (MA); religion in the Americas (MA); religions of Asia (MA, PhD). Part-time programs available. *Faculty:* 10 full-time (3 women), 3 part-time/adjunct (1 woman). *Students:* 24 full-time (12 women), 7 part-time (6 women); includes 1 American Indian or Alaska Native, non-Hispanic/Latino; 4 Asian, non-Hispanic/Latino; 3 Hispanic/Latino, 1 international. Average age 34. 36 applicants, 58% accepted, 12 enrolled. In 2010, 1 master's, 1 doctorate awarded. *Degree requirements:* For master's, one foreign language, thesis optional; for doctorate, one foreign language, comprehensive exam, thesis/dissertation. *Entrance requirements:* For master's, GRE General Test, minimum GPA of 3.0. Additional exam requirements/recommendations for international students: Required—TOEFL (minimum score 550 paper-based; 213 computer-based; 80 iBT), IELTS (minimum score 6). *Application deadline:* For fall admission, 6/1 priority date for domestic students. Applications are processed on a rolling basis. Application fee: $30. Electronic applications accepted. *Expenses:* Tuition, state resident: full-time $10,915.92. Tuition, nonresident: full-time $28,309. *Financial support:* In 2010–11, 18 students received support, including 5 fellowships, 1 research assistantship (averaging $16,965 per year), 12 teaching assistantships (averaging $13,539 per year); Federal Work-Study and unspecified assistantships also available. Financial award applicants required to submit FAFSA. *Faculty research:* Religion in America, Christian thought, Islam, religions of India, comparative religion. *Unit head:* Dr. Vasudha Narayanan, Chair, 352-392-1625, E-mail: vasu@ufl.edu. *Application contact:* Dr. Manuel Vasquez, Graduate Coordinator, 352-392-1625 Ext. 229, Fax: 352-392-7395, E-mail: manuelv@ufl.edu.

University of Hawaii at Hilo, Program in China-US Relations, Hilo, HI 96720-4091. Offers MA.

University of Hawaii at Manoa, Graduate Division, School of Pacific and Asian Studies, Program in Asian Studies, Concentration in Korean Studies, Honolulu, HI 96822. Offers Graduate Certificate. Part-time programs available. *Students:* Average age 32. In 2010, 2 Graduate Certificates awarded. *Degree requirements:* For Graduate Certificate, one foreign language. *Entrance requirements:* For degree, GRE. Additional exam requirements/recommendations for international students: Required—TOEFL (minimum score 560 paper-based; 220 computer-based; 83 iBT), IELTS (minimum score 5). Application fee: $60. Total annual research expenditures: $40,000. *Application contact:* Yung-Hee Kim, Director, 808-956-2072, Fax: 808-956-9515.

University of Hawaii at Manoa, Graduate Division, School of Pacific and Asian Studies, Program in Asian Studies, Concentration in Southeast Asian Studies, Honolulu, HI 96822. Offers Graduate Certificate. Part-time programs available. *Students:* 1 full-time (0 women). Average age 31. In 2010, 7 Graduate Certificates awarded. *Degree requirements:* For Graduate Certificate, one foreign language. *Entrance requirements:* For degree, GRE. Additional exam requirements/recommendations for international students: Required—TOEFL (minimum score 560 paper-based; 220 computer-based; 83 iBT), IELTS (minimum score 5). Application fee: $60. *Financial support:* In 2010–11, 1 fellowship (averaging $2,000 per year) was awarded. *Application contact:* Stephen O'Harrow, Director, 808-956-2688, Fax: 808-956-6345, E-mail: dirseas@hawaii.edu.

University of Illinois at Urbana–Champaign, Graduate College, College of Liberal Arts and Sciences, School of Literatures, Cultures and Linguistics, Department of East Asian Languages and Cultures, Champaign, IL 61820. Offers Asian studies (MA); East Asian languages and cultures (PhD). *Faculty:* 16 full-time (6 women). *Students:* 31 full-time (19 women), 11 part-time (10 women); includes 1 American Indian or Alaska Native, non-Hispanic/Latino; 5 Asian, non-Hispanic/Latino, 25 international. 87 applicants, 16% accepted, 8 enrolled. In 2010, 7 master's, 5 doctorates awarded. *Entrance requirements:* For master's, GRE General Test, minimum GPA of 3.0; writing sample; for doctorate, GRE, minimum GPA of 3.0; writing sample. Additional exam requirements/recommendations for international students: Required—TOEFL (minimum score 103 iBT). *Application deadline:* Applications are processed on a rolling basis. Application fee: $75 ($90 for international students). Electronic applications accepted. *Financial support:* In 2010–11, 9 fellowships, 5 research assistantships, 26 teaching assistantships were awarded; tuition waivers (full and partial) also available. *Unit head:* Brian D. Ruppert, Head, 217-244-4012, Fax: 217-244-2223, E-mail: ruppert@illinois.edu. *Application contact:* Lynn Stanke, Office Support Specialist, 217-333-6269, Fax: 217-244-3050, E-mail: stanke@illinois.edu.

The University of Iowa, Graduate College, College of Liberal Arts and Sciences, Program in Asian Languages and Literature, Iowa City, IA 52242-1316. Offers MA. *Degree requirements:* For master's, thesis optional, exam. *Entrance requirements:* For master's, GRE General Test, minimum GPA of 3.0. Additional exam requirements/recommendations for international students: Required—TOEFL (minimum score 590 paper-based; 243 computer-based; 96 iBT). Electronic applications accepted.

The University of Kansas, Graduate Studies, College of Liberal Arts and Sciences, Department of East Asian Languages and Cultures, Lawrence, KS 66045. Offers MA, MBA/MA. Part-time programs available. *Faculty:* 7. *Students:* 13 full-time (6 women), 5 part-time (all women); includes 6 minority (1 Black or African American, non-Hispanic/Latino; 1 American Indian or Alaska Native, non-Hispanic/Latino; 3 Asian, non-Hispanic/Latino; 1 Two or more races, non-Hispanic/Latino), 3 international. Average age 30. 13 applicants, 46% accepted, 3 enrolled. In 2010, 1 master's awarded. *Degree requirements:* For master's, one foreign language, thesis. *Entrance requirements:* For master's, GRE, 3 letters of recommendation, writing sample. Additional exam requirements/recommendations for international students: Required—TOEFL. *Application deadline:* For fall admission, 5/1 priority date for domestic students, 5/1 for international students; for spring admission, 12/1 priority date for domestic students, 12/1 for international students. Applications are processed on a rolling basis. Application fee: $55 ($65 for international students). Electronic applications accepted. *Expenses:* Tuition, state resident: full-time $7092; part-time $295.50 per credit hour. Tuition, nonresident: full-time $16,590; part-time $691.25 per credit hour. Required fees: $858; $71.49 per credit hour. Tuition and fees vary according to course load, campus/location and program. *Financial support:* Fellowships, teaching assistantships with full and partial tuition reimbursements, unspecified assistantships available. Financial award application deadline: 2/1. *Faculty research:* Gender relations in literature, ancient Chinese law, visual culture of modern Japan, Japanese language pedagogy, Chinese paleography, Korean shamanism, folklore, traditional Chinese and Japanese literature, Chinese linguistics and language pedagogy. *Unit head:* Margaret Childs, Chair, 785-864-3100, E-mail: mgchilds@ku.edu. *Application contact:* Jennifer Newlin, Administrative Specialist, 785-864-3100, Fax: 785-864-4298, E-mail: ealc@ku.edu.

University of Maine, Graduate School, College of Liberal Arts and Sciences, Department of History, Orono, ME 04469. Offers American studies (MA, PhD); Canadian studies (MA, PhD); East Asian (MA); environmental (MA); European (MA); technology (MA). *Faculty:* 11 full-time (1 woman), 2 part-time/adjunct (1 woman). *Students:* 24 full-time (8 women), 35 part-time (13 women); includes 4 minority (2 American Indian or Alaska Native, non-Hispanic/Latino; 2 Hispanic/Latino). Average age 38. 43 applicants, 40% accepted, 15 enrolled. In 2010, 5 master's, 3 doctorates awarded. Terminal master's awarded for partial completion of doctoral program. *Degree requirements:* For master's, variable foreign language requirement, thesis optional; for doctorate, one foreign language, thesis/dissertation. *Entrance requirements:* For master's and doctorate, GRE General Test. Additional exam requirements/recommendations for international students: Required—TOEFL. *Application deadline:* For fall admission, 2/1

priority date for domestic students. Applications are processed on a rolling basis. Application fee: $65. Electronic applications accepted. *Expenses:* Tuition, state resident: full-time $400. Tuition, nonresident: full-time $1050. *Financial support:* In 2010–11, 9 teaching assistantships with tuition reimbursements (averaging $12,790 per year) were awarded; career-related internships or fieldwork, Federal Work-Study, and tuition waivers (full and partial) also available. Support available to part-time students. Financial award application deadline: 3/1. *Faculty research:* Canadian labor and working classes; American social, cultural, and urban history. *Unit head:* Dr. Nathan Godfried, Chair, 207-581-1923, Fax: 207-581-1817. *Application contact:* Scott G. Delcourt, Associate Dean of the Graduate School, 207-581-3291, Fax: 207-581-3232, E-mail: graduate@maine.edu.

The University of Manchester, School of Languages, Linguistics and Cultures, Manchester, United Kingdom. Offers Arab world studies (PhD); Chinese studies (M Phil, PhD); East Asian studies (M Phil, PhD); English language (PhD); French studies (M Phil, PhD); German studies (M Phil, PhD); interpreting studies (PhD); Italian studies (M Phil, PhD); Japanese studies (M Phil, PhD); Latin American cultural studies (M Phil, PhD); linguistics (M Phil, PhD); Middle Eastern studies (M Phil, PhD); Polish studies (M Phil, PhD); Portuguese studies (M Phil, PhD); Russian studies (M Phil, PhD); Spanish studies (M Phil, PhD); translation and intercultural studies (M Phil, PhD).

University of Michigan, Horace H. Rackham School of Graduate Studies, College of Literature, Science, and the Arts, Center for Chinese Studies, Ann Arbor, MI 48109. Offers Asian studies: China (AM, Graduate Certificate); JD/AM; MBA/AM; MPP/AM. Part-time programs available. *Faculty:* 30 full-time. *Students:* 15 full-time; includes 4 Asian, non-Hispanic/Latino. Average age 21. 44 applicants, 34% accepted, 7 enrolled. In 2010, 1 master's awarded. *Degree requirements:* For master's, one foreign language, thesis. *Entrance requirements:* For master's, GRE General Test. Additional exam requirements/recommendations for international students: Required—TOEFL. *Application deadline:* For winter admission, 1/15 for domestic and international students. Application fee: $60 ($75 for international students). Electronic applications accepted. *Expenses:* Tuition, state resident: full-time $17,784; part-time $1116 per credit hour. Tuition, nonresident: full-time $35,944; part-time $2125 per credit hour. International tuition: $35,994 full-time. Required fees: $95 per semester. Tuition and fees vary according to course load, degree level and program. *Financial support:* Fellowships, Federal Work-Study available. *Faculty research:* Economic reform in China, Chinese religion, history of late Imperial China, Chinese foreign policy, Chinese music and music history. *Unit head:* Mary Gallagher, Director, 734-764-6308, Fax: 734-764-5540. *Application contact:* Carol Stepanchuk, Student Services Coordinator, 734-936-3961, Fax: 734-764-5540, E-mail: cstep@umich.edu.

University of Michigan, Horace H. Rackham School of Graduate Studies, College of Literature, Science, and the Arts, Center for Japanese Studies, Ann Arbor, MI 48109-1106. Offers AM, JD/AM, MBA/AM. Part-time programs available. *Faculty:* 46 full-time (21 women), 12 part-time/adjunct (3 women). *Students:* 20 full-time (14 women), 1 part-time (0 women); includes 2 minority (1 Black or African American, non-Hispanic/Latino; 1 Asian, non-Hispanic/Latino), 1 international. Average age 26. 37 applicants, 54% accepted, 10 enrolled. In 2010, 3 master's awarded. *Degree requirements:* For master's, one foreign language, thesis optional, 3rd-year proficiency in Japanese language, distribution (3 disciplines), research/writing. *Entrance requirements:* For master's, GRE General Test, previous study of Japanese language (highly recommended). Additional exam requirements/recommendations for international students: Required—TOEFL (minimum score 560 paper-based; 84 iBT); Recommended—IELTS (minimum score 6.5). *Application deadline:* For fall admission, 1/10 for domestic and international students. Application fee: $65 ($75 for international students). Electronic applications accepted. *Expenses:* Tuition, state resident: full-time $17,784; part-time $1116 per credit hour. Tuition, nonresident: full-time $35,944; part-time $2125 per credit hour. International tuition: $35,994 full-time. Required fees: $95 per semester. Tuition and fees vary according to course load, degree level and program. *Financial support:* In 2010–11, 8 students received support, including 5 fellowships with full tuition reimbursements available (averaging $15,000 per year); research assistantships with full and partial tuition reimbursements available, teaching assistantships with full and partial tuition reimbursements available, career-related internships or fieldwork, Federal Work-Study, scholarships/grants, health care benefits, unspecified assistantships, and partial tuition fellowships; summer fellowships also available. Support available to part-time students. Financial award application deadline: 1/10; financial award applicants required to submit FAFSA. *Faculty research:* Japanese literature; Japanese history (premodern and modern); Japanese linguistics and language pedagogy; modern Japanese society and culture; Japanese elections and politics; gender and sexuality in Japan; Japanese art, art history and visual culture; Japanese film; Buddhism and religion in Japan; Japanese law. *Unit head:* Prof. Ken K. Ito, Director, 734-764-6307, Fax: 734-936-2948, E-mail: umcjs@umich.edu. *Application contact:* Dr. Azumi Ann Takata, Academic Services Coordinator, 734-764-6307, Fax: 734-936-2948, E-mail: cjsadmissions@umich.edu.

University of Michigan, Horace H. Rackham School of Graduate Studies, College of Literature, Science, and the Arts, Center for South Asian Studies, Ann Arbor, MI 48109. Offers MA, Certificate, MBA/MA. Part-time programs available. *Degree requirements:* For master's, one foreign language, thesis, 24 credits; for Certificate, one foreign language. *Entrance requirements:* For master's, GRE General Test, 3 letters of recommendation; for Certificate, GRE General Test, 2 letters of recommendation, transcripts. Additional exam requirements/recommendations for international students: Required—TOEFL (minimum score 560 paper-based; 220 computer-based; 84 iBT). Electronic applications accepted. *Expenses:* Tuition, state resident: full-time $17,784; part-time $1116 per credit hour. Tuition, nonresident: full-time $35,944; part-time $2125 per credit hour. International tuition: $35,994 full-time. Required fees: $95 per semester. Tuition and fees vary according to course load, degree level and program. *Faculty research:* History of Islam and South Asia; ethnicity and nationalism; global and transnational feminism; South Asian architecture and urbanism; mysticism and politics in Indian religions.

University of Michigan, Horace H. Rackham School of Graduate Studies, College of Literature, Science, and the Arts, Center for Southeast Asian Studies, Ann Arbor, MI 48109-1106. Offers MA, Graduate Certificate, MBA/MA, MPP/MA. Part-time programs available. *Degree requirements:* For master's, one foreign language, thesis, 25 credits; for Graduate Certificate, one foreign language. *Entrance requirements:* For master's, GRE General Test, 3 recommendations, curriculum vitae; for Graduate Certificate, GRE General Test, 2 recommendations, transcripts, statement of purpose. Additional exam requirements/recommendations for international students: Required—TOEFL (minimum score 560 paper-based; 220 computer-based; 84 iBT) or IELTS. Electronic applications accepted. *Expenses:* Tuition, state resident: full-time $17,784; part-time $1116 per credit hour. Tuition, nonresident: full-time $35,944; part-time $2125 per credit hour. International tuition: $35,994 full-time. Required fees: $95 per semester. Tuition and fees vary according to course load, degree level and program. *Faculty research:* Politics, political parties, civil society, the law and human rights in Southeast Asia; Nationalism and modernity in late colonial Southeast Asia; Islam, religion, language and media; urbanization, globalization and business; pre-modern Southeast Asia in a global/Eurasian context.

University of Michigan, Horace H. Rackham School of Graduate Studies, College of Literature, Science, and the Arts, Department of Asian Languages and Cultures, Ann Arbor, MI 48104. Offers MA, PhD. Students cannot apply directly to a terminal masters degree in this program. Masters are only awarded to PhD program students for partial completion of the degree. Terminal master's awarded for partial completion of doctoral program. *Degree requirements:* For master's, variable foreign language requirement, thesis; for doctorate, 2 foreign languages, thesis/dissertation, oral defense of dissertation, preliminary exam. *Entrance requirements:* For master's and doctorate, GRE General Test. Additional exam requirements/recommendations for international students: Required—TOEFL (minimum score 600 paper-based; 250 computer-based; 106 iBT). Electronic applications accepted. *Expenses:* Tuition, state resident: full-time $17,784; part-time $1116 per credit hour. Tuition, nonresident: full-time $35,944; part-time $2125 per credit hour. International tuition: $35,994 full-time. Required fees: $95 per semester. Tuition and fees vary according to course load, degree level and program. *Faculty research:* Literature, linguistics, religion, music, cinema.

University of Minnesota, Twin Cities Campus, Graduate School, College of Liberal Arts, Department of Asian Languages and Literatures, Minneapolis, MN 55455-0213. Offers Asian literatures, cultures, and media (PhD). *Degree requirements:* For doctorate, comprehensive exam, thesis/dissertation. *Entrance requirements:* For doctorate, GRE, 3 letters of recommendation. Additional exam requirements/recommendations for international students: Required—TOEFL (minimum score 550 paper-based; 213 computer-based), IELTS (minimum score 6.5). Electronic applications accepted. *Faculty research:* Gender studies, post-colonial theory, poetics and poetic theory, film studies, post modernist thought.

University of Oregon, Graduate School, College of Arts and Sciences, Program in Asian Studies, Eugene, OR 97403. Offers MA. Part-time programs available. *Degree requirements:* For master's, one foreign language, thesis or alternative. *Entrance requirements:* For master's, GRE General Test. Additional exam requirements/recommendations for international students: Required—TOEFL. *Faculty research:* East and Southeast Asia, Pacific Islands.

University of Pennsylvania, School of Arts and Sciences, Graduate Group in East Asian Languages and Civilization, Philadelphia, PA 19104. Offers AM, PhD. *Faculty:* 13 full-time (5 women), 2 part-time/adjunct (0 women). *Students:* 46 full-time (25 women), 3 part-time (all women); includes 1 Black or African American, non-Hispanic/Latino; 4 Asian, non-Hispanic/Latino; 2 Hispanic/Latino, 19 international. 85 applicants, 34% accepted, 14 enrolled. In 2010, 9 master's, 8 doctorates awarded. Application fee: $70. *Expenses:* Tuition: Full-time $25,660; part-time $4758 per course. Required fees: $2152; $270 per course. Tuition and fees vary according to course load, degree level and program. *Financial support:* Institutionally sponsored loans, scholarships/grants, traineeships, health care benefits, and unspecified assistantships available.

University of Pennsylvania, School of Arts and Sciences, Graduate Group in South Asian Regional Studies, Philadelphia, PA 19104. Offers AM, PhD. *Faculty:* 12 full-time (5 women), 9 part-time/adjunct (1 woman). *Students:* 25 full-time (15 women), 1 (woman) part-time; includes 1 American Indian or Alaska Native, non-Hispanic/Latino; 6 Asian, non-Hispanic/Latino, 5 international. 37 applicants, 41% accepted, 6 enrolled. In 2010, 3 master's, 3 doctorates awarded. Terminal master's awarded for partial completion of doctoral program. *Degree requirements:* For master's, one foreign language, thesis, written exam; for doctorate, 3 foreign languages, thesis/dissertation, written exam. *Entrance requirements:* For master's, GRE General Test. Additional exam requirements/recommendations for international students: Required—TOEFL. *Application deadline:* For fall admission, 12/1 priority date for domestic students. Application fee: $70. Electronic applications accepted. *Expenses:* Tuition: Full-time $25,660; part-time $4758 per course. Required fees: $2152; $270 per course. Tuition and fees vary according to course load, degree level and program. *Financial support:* Fellowships, research assistantships, teaching assistantships, institutionally sponsored loans, scholarships/grants, traineeships, health care benefits, and unspecified assistantships available. Financial award application deadline: 12/15. *Faculty research:* South Asian linguistics, literature, and history; economic history. *Application contact:* Sanjukta Banerjee, 215-898-7475, E-mail: sanjukta@sas.upenn.edu.

University of Pittsburgh, School of Arts and Sciences, Department of East Asian Languages and Literatures, Pittsburgh, PA 15260. Offers East Asian studies (MA). Part-time programs available. *Faculty:* 12 full-time (8 women), 5 part-time/adjunct (2 women). *Students:* 5 full-time (3 women), 2 part-time (both women), 3 international. Average age 26. 35 applicants, 54% accepted, 4 enrolled. In 2010, 3 master's awarded. *Degree requirements:* For master's, one foreign language, thesis, oral comprehensive exam. *Entrance requirements:* For master's, GRE General Test, 2 years of Chinese or Japanese, minimum QPA of 3.0. Additional exam requirements/recommendations for international students: Required—TOEFL (minimum score 600 paper-based). *Application deadline:* For fall admission, 1/15 for domestic and international students. Application fee: $50. Electronic applications accepted. *Expenses:* Tuition, state resident: full-time $17,304; part-time $701 per credit. Tuition, nonresident: full-time $29,554; part-time $1210 per credit. Required fees: $740; $214 per term. Tuition and fees vary according to program. *Financial support:* In 2010–11, 5 students received support, including 3 fellowships with full and partial tuition reimbursements available (averaging $17,304 per year); scholarships/grants, health care benefits, tuition waivers (full and partial), and unspecified assistantships also available. Financial award application deadline: 1/30. *Faculty research:* Chinese literature, film, and poetry; Japanese literature, film, and theater; Chinese society and culture; east Asian foreign policy, security studies, and economic history; Japanese performing arts and fine arts. *Unit head:* Dr. Hiroshi Nara, Chairman, 412-624-5568, Fax: 412-624-3458, E-mail: hnara@pitt.edu. *Application contact:* Paula Locante, Administrator, 412-624-5568, Fax: 412-624-3458, E-mail: plocante@pitt.edu.

University of Pittsburgh, University Center for International Studies, Pittsburgh, PA 15260. Offers African studies (Certificate); Asian studies (Certificate); European Union studies (Certificate); global studies (Certificate); Latin American studies (Certificate); Russian and East European studies (Certificate); West European studies (Certificate). *Students:* 322 full-time (192 women), 19 part-time (14 women); includes 22 minority (8 Black or African American, non-Hispanic/Latino; 3 Asian, non-Hispanic/Latino; 6 Hispanic/Latino; 5 Two or more races, non-Hispanic/Latino), 134 international. In 2010, 61 Certificates awarded. *Degree requirements:* For Certificate, one foreign language, study abroad. *Application deadline:* Applications are processed on a rolling basis. *Expenses:* Tuition, state resident: full-time $17,304; part-time $701 per credit. Tuition, nonresident: full-time $29,554; part-time $1210 per credit. Required fees: $740; $214 per term. Tuition and fees vary according to program. *Unit head:* Dr. Lawrence F. Feick, Director, University Center for International Studies, 412-648-7374, Fax: 412-624-4672, E-mail: feick@pitt.edu. *Application contact:* Information Contact, 412-624-4141, E-mail: graduate@pitt.edu.

University of San Francisco, College of Arts and Sciences, Program in Asia Pacific Studies, San Francisco, CA 94117-1080. Offers MA, MA/MBA. Part-time and evening/weekend programs available. *Faculty:* 1 full-time (0 women), 5 part-time/adjunct (4 women). *Students:* 35 full-time (22 women), 8 part-time (5 women); includes 17 minority (1 Black or African American, non-Hispanic/Latino; 10 Asian, non-Hispanic/Latino; 4 Hispanic/Latino; 2 Two or more races, non-Hispanic/Latino), 13 international. Average age 29. 47 applicants, 87% accepted, 15 enrolled. In 2010, 15 master's awarded. *Degree requirements:* For master's, one foreign language, thesis. *Entrance requirements:* For master's, minimum GPA of 3.0. *Application deadline:* Applications are processed on a rolling basis. Application fee: $55 ($65 for international students). *Expenses:* Tuition: Full-time $20,070; part-time $1115 per credit hour. Tuition and fees vary according to course load, degree level and program. *Financial support:* In 2010–11, 27 students received support. Career-related internships or fieldwork, Federal Work-Study, and institutionally sponsored loans available. Financial award application deadline: 3/2; financial award applicants required to submit FAFSA. *Faculty research:* History of Christianity in China, U. S.-China policy, East Asian economies and political systems, sociolinguistic aspects of Japanese. *Unit head:* Dr. Ken Kopp, Director, 415-422-6357, Fax: 415-422-5933. *Application contact:* Information Contact, 415-422-5135, Fax: 415-422-2217, E-mail: asgraduate@usfca.edu.

University of Southern California, Graduate School, Dana and David Dornsife College of Letters, Arts and Sciences, Department of East Asian Languages and Cultures, Los Angeles, CA 90089. Offers classical Chinese literature (MA, PhD); classical Japanese literature (MA, PhD); linguistics (MA, PhD); modern Chinese literature (MA, PhD); modern Japanese literature (MA, PhD); modern Korean literature (MA, PhD). *Faculty:* 14 full-time (7 women). *Students:* 19 full-time (14 women), 1 (woman) part-time; includes 5 minority (1 Black or African American, non-Hispanic/Latino; 4 Asian, non-Hispanic/Latino), 10 international. 37 applicants, 16% accepted, 6 enrolled. In 2010, 5 master's, 1 doctorate awarded. *Degree requirements:* For master's, thesis; for doctorate, 2 foreign languages, comprehensive exam, thesis/dissertation. *Entrance requirements:* For master's and doctorate, GRE, BA in relevant field. Additional exam requirements/recommendations for international students: Required—TOEFL. *Application deadline:* For fall admission, 12/1 priority date for domestic and international students. Application fee: $85. Electronic applications accepted. *Expenses:* Tuition: Full-time $31,240; part-time $1420 per unit. Required fees: $600. One-time fee: $35 full-time. Full-time tuition and fees vary according to degree level and program. *Financial support:* In 2010–11, 25 students received support, including 4 fellowships with full tuition reimbursements available (averaging $30,000 per year), 25 teaching assistantships with partial tuition reimbursements available (averaging $19,800 per year); scholarships/grants, health care benefits, and unspecified assistantships also available. Financial award application deadline: 12/1. *Faculty research:* Gender, visual studies, multimedia, ecocriticism, second language acquisition. *Unit head:* Dominic Cheung, Chair, 213-740-3708, Fax: 213-740-9295, E-mail: dcheung@usc.edu. *Application contact:* Sherall R. Preyer, Administrative Coordinator, 213-740-3709, Fax: 213-740-9295, E-mail: preyer@college.usc.edu.

University of Southern California, Graduate School, Dana and David Dornsife College of Letters, Arts and Sciences, East Asian Studies Center, Los Angeles, CA 90089. Offers MA, MA/MBA. Part-time programs available. *Faculty:* 11 full-time (3 women), 1 (woman) part-time/adjunct. *Students:* 10 full-time (7 women), 1 part-time (0 women); includes 4 minority (3 Asian, non-Hispanic/Latino; 1 Two or more races, non-Hispanic/Latino), 4 international. 54 applicants, 33% accepted, 7 enrolled. In 2010, 3 master's awarded. *Degree requirements:* For master's, one foreign language, thesis, language proficiency in an East Asian language (equivalent to 3 years of study). *Entrance requirements:* For master's, GRE (minimum score 1000). Additional exam requirements/recommendations for international students: Required—TOEFL (minimum score 600 paper-based; 250 computer-based; 100 iBT). *Application deadline:* For fall admission, 1/3 for domestic and international students. Application fee: $85. Electronic applications accepted. *Expenses:* Tuition: Full-time $31,240; part-time $1420 per unit. Required fees: $600. One-time fee: $35 full-time. Full-time tuition and fees vary according to degree level and program. *Financial support:* In 2010–11, 8 students received support, including 4 fellowships with full tuition reimbursements available (averaging $21,000 per year), 5 teaching assistantships with full tuition reimbursements available (averaging $19,250 per year); scholarships/grants and unspecified assistantships also available. Financial award application deadline: 5/2; financial award applicants required to submit FAFSA. *Faculty research:* East Asian visual cultures (Chinese, Japanese, and Korean film, culture and art); East Asian politics, society and history; East Asian literature and culture. Total annual research expenditures: $550,414. *Unit head:* Prof. David Kang, Interim Director, 213-821-4319, E-mail: kangdc@usc.edu. *Application contact:* Eva Luc, Program Specialist, 213-740-2992, Fax: 213-740-8409, E-mail: eluc@usc.edu.

The University of Texas at Austin, Graduate School, College of Liberal Arts, Department of Asian Studies, Austin, TX 78712-1111. Offers Asian cultures and languages (MA, PhD); Asian studies (MA). Part-time programs available. *Degree requirements:* For master's, thesis; for doctorate, 3 foreign languages, thesis/dissertation. *Entrance requirements:* For master's and doctorate, GRE General Test. Electronic applications accepted. *Faculty research:* Modern Taiwanese fiction, modern Japanese literature, religious studies in South Asia during classical period.

University of Toronto, School of Graduate Studies, Humanities Division, Centre for South Asian Studies, Toronto, ON M5S 1A1, Canada. Offers MA, PhD. Students who wish to be admitted into the Collaborative Program in South Asian Studies must apply to one of the following units: anthropology, English, history, geography, political science (PhD only), religious studies, social work. Part-time programs available. *Degree requirements:* For master's, thesis optional; for doctorate, one foreign language, thesis/dissertation.

University of Toronto, School of Graduate Studies, Humanities Division, Department of East Asian Studies, Toronto, ON M5S 1A1, Canada. Offers MA, PhD. Part-time programs available. *Degree requirements:* For master's, thesis optional; for doctorate, 2 foreign languages, comprehensive exam, thesis/dissertation. *Entrance requirements:* For master's, writing sample, 2 letters of recommendation, BA in a specialist or East Asian studies program, minimum B+ average in final year; for doctorate, writing sample, 3 letters of recommendation, MA in East Asian studies. Additional exam requirements/recommendations for international students: Required—TOEFL (minimum score 600 paper-based), TWE (minimum score 5). Electronic applications accepted.

University of Utah, Graduate School, College of Humanities, Asian Studies Program, Salt Lake City, UT 84112. Offers MA. Part-time and evening/weekend programs available. *Faculty:* 72 full-time (25 women), 5 part-time/adjunct (1 woman). *Students:* 3 full-time (2 women), 4 part-time (2 women); includes 1 minority (Asian, non-Hispanic/Latino), 1 international. Average age 31. 8 applicants, 50% accepted, 3 enrolled. *Degree requirements:* For master's, one foreign language, thesis, 3rd-year proficiency in one Asian language. *Entrance requirements:* For master's, GRE. Additional exam requirements/recommendations for international students: Required—TOEFL (minimum score 580 paper-based; 237 computer-based). *Application deadline:* For fall admission, 1/15 for domestic and international students; for spring admission, 9/15 for domestic students. Application fee: $55 ($65 for international students). Electronic applications accepted. *Expenses:* Tuition, area resident: Part-time $179.19 per credit hour. Tuition, state resident: full-time $4384. Tuition, nonresident: full-time $16,684; part-time $630.67 per credit hour. Required fees: $350 per semester. Tuition and fees vary according to course load, degree level and program. *Financial support:* In 2010–11, 1 student received support, including 1 fellowship with full tuition reimbursement available (averaging $15,000 per year); Federal Work-Study also available. Financial award application deadline: 1/15; financial award applicants required to submit FAFSA. *Faculty research:* Asian health studies, history, literature, culture, politics, economics. *Unit head:* Dr. Janet Theiss, Director, 801-585-6477, Fax: 801-581-6105, E-mail: janet.theiss@utah.edu. *Application contact:* Bryce W. Garner, Academic Advisor, 801-581-6101, Fax: 801-581-6105, E-mail: bryce.garner@utah.edu.

University of Victoria, Faculty of Graduate Studies, Faculty of Humanities, Department of Pacific and Asian Studies, Victoria, BC V8W 2Y2, Canada. Offers MA. *Degree requirements:* For master's, thesis. *Entrance requirements:* For master's, minimum B+ average, writing sample. Additional exam requirements/recommendations for international students: Required—TOEFL (minimum score 575 paper-based; 233 computer-based), IELTS (minimum score 7). Electronic applications accepted. *Faculty research:* Culture, ethnicity and identity; economy and society; gender studies; languages and linguistics; literature.

University of Virginia, College and Graduate School of Arts and Sciences, Department of East Asian Languages, Literatures, and Cultures, Charlottesville, VA 22903. Offers East Asian studies (MA); MBA/MA. *Faculty:* 16 full-time (13 women), 1 (woman) part-time/adjunct. *Students:* 9 full-time (4 women); includes 1 Hispanic/Latino. Average age 29. 34 applicants, 41% accepted, 7 enrolled. *Degree requirements:* For master's, one foreign language, comprehensive exam, thesis. *Entrance requirements:* For master's, GRE General Test, 2 letters of recommendation. Additional exam requirements/recommendations for international students: Required—TOEFL, IELTS. *Application deadline:* For fall admission, 1/15 for domestic and international students; for winter admission, 9/15 for domestic and international students. Applications are processed on a rolling basis. Application fee: $60. Electronic applications accepted. *Financial support:* Applicants required to submit FAFSA. *Unit head:* Anne Kinney, Chair, 434-982-2304, Fax: 434-924-6977, E-mail: deal-lc@virginia.edu. *Application contact:* Anne Kinney, Chair, 434-982-2304, Fax: 434-924-6977, E-mail: deal-lc@virginia.edu.

University of Virginia, College and Graduate School of Arts and Sciences, Department of Middle Eastern and South Asian Languages and Cultures, Charlottesville, VA 22903. Offers Middle Eastern and South Asian studies (MA). *Faculty:* 16 full-time (8 women). *Students:* 15 full-time (10 women); includes 1 Asian, non-Hispanic/Latino; 1 Hispanic/Latino; 1 Two or more races, non-Hispanic/Latino. Average age 26. 17 applicants, 76% accepted, 13 enrolled. *Unit head:* Daniel Lefkowitz, Chair, 434-924-3452, Fax: 434-924-6977, E-mail: dl2h@virginia.edu. *Application contact:* Daniel Lefkowitz, Chair, 434-924-3452, Fax: 434-924-6977, E-mail: dl2h@virginia.edu.

University of Washington, Graduate School, College of Arts and Sciences, Department of Asian Languages and Literature, Seattle, WA 98195. Offers Buddhist studies (MA, PhD);

Asian Studies

University of Washington (continued)
Chinese language and literature (MA, PhD); Japanese language and literature (MA, PhD); Korean language and literature (MA, PhD); South Asian language and literature (MA, PhD). *Degree requirements:* For master's, 2 foreign languages, general exam, thesis or 2 research papers; for doctorate, 3 foreign languages, thesis/dissertation, general exam. *Entrance requirements:* For master's, GRE, minimum GPA of 3.0; for doctorate, GRE, master's degree in related field, minimum GPA of 3.0. Additional exam requirements/recommendations for international students: Required—TOEFL. Electronic applications accepted. *Faculty research:* Textual, linguistic, philological, and literary study of languages and literatures of Asia.

University of Washington, Graduate School, College of Arts and Sciences, Henry M. Jackson School of International Studies, China Studies Program, Seattle, WA 98195. Offers MAIS. *Faculty:* 28 full-time (8 women). *Students:* 24 full-time (13 women); includes 1 Black or African American, non-Hispanic/Latino; 6 Asian, non-Hispanic/Latino, 5 international. 55 applicants, 60% accepted, 14 enrolled. In 2010, 4 master's awarded. *Degree requirements:* For master's, one foreign language, thesis optional. *Entrance requirements:* For master's, GRE General Test, minimum GPA of 3.00 (last two years). Additional exam requirements/recommendations for international students: Required—TOEFL (minimum score 500 paper-based; 213 computer-based; 92 iBT) or IELTS (minimum score 7). *Application deadline:* For fall admission, 1/5 for domestic and international students. Application fee: $75. Electronic applications accepted. *Financial support:* In 2010–11, 3 fellowships were awarded; research assistantships with tuition reimbursements, teaching assistantships with tuition reimbursements, career-related internships or fieldwork, Federal Work-Study, institutionally sponsored loans, and scholarships/grants also available. Financial award application deadline: 1/5; financial award applicants required to submit FAFSA. *Unit head:* Prof. Yue Dong, Chair, 206-543-4999. *Application contact:* 206-543-6001, Fax: 206-616-3170, E-mail: jsisinfo@u.washington.edu.

University of Washington, Graduate School, College of Arts and Sciences, Henry M. Jackson School of International Studies, Japan Studies Program, Seattle, WA 98195. Offers MAIS. *Faculty:* 13 full-time (5 women). *Students:* 18 full-time (6 women); includes 5 Asian, non-Hispanic/Latino, 2 international. 18 applicants, 78% accepted, 12 enrolled. In 2010, 9 master's awarded. *Degree requirements:* For master's, one foreign language. *Entrance requirements:* For master's, GRE General Test, minimum GPA of 3.00 (last two years). Additional exam requirements/recommendations for international students: Required—TOEFL (minimum score 500 paper-based; 213 computer-based; 92 iBT) or IELTS (minimum score 7). *Application deadline:* For fall admission, 1/5 for domestic and international students. Application fee: $75. Electronic applications accepted. *Financial support:* In 2010–11, 4 fellowships with full tuition reimbursements, 3 research assistantships with full and partial tuition reimbursements, 2 teaching assistantships with full and partial tuition reimbursements were awarded; career-related internships or fieldwork, Federal Work-Study, institutionally sponsored loans, scholarships/grants, and tuition waivers (partial) also available. Financial award application deadline: 1/5; financial award applicants required to submit FAFSA. *Unit head:* Prof. Gary Hamilton, Chair, 206-543-5883. *Application contact:* 206-543-6001, Fax: 206-616-3170, E-mail: jsisinfo@u.washington.edu.

University of Washington, Graduate School, College of Arts and Sciences, Henry M. Jackson School of International Studies, Korea Studies Program, Seattle, WA 98195. Offers MAIS. *Faculty:* 4 full-time (1 woman). *Students:* 11 full-time (1 woman); includes 4 Asian, non-Hispanic/Latino, 1 international. 18 applicants, 100% accepted, 4 enrolled. In 2010, 4 master's awarded. *Degree requirements:* For master's, one foreign language. *Entrance requirements:* For master's, GRE General Test, minimum GPA of 3.00 (last two years). Additional exam requirements/recommendations for international students: Required—TOEFL (minimum score 500 paper-based; 213 computer-based; 92 iBT) or IELTS (minimum score 7). *Application deadline:* For fall admission, 1/5 for domestic and international students. Application fee: $75. Electronic applications accepted. *Financial support:* In 2010–11, 1 fellowship with full tuition reimbursement was awarded; research assistantships, career-related internships or fieldwork, Federal Work-Study, institutionally sponsored loans, scholarships/grants, and summer language study awards also available. Financial award application deadline: 1/5; financial award applicants required to submit FAFSA. *Unit head:* Prof. Clark Sorensen. *Application contact:* 206-543-6001, Fax: 206-616-3170, E-mail: jsisinfo@u.washington.edu.

University of Washington, Graduate School, College of Arts and Sciences, Henry M. Jackson School of International Studies, Program in Southeast Asian Studies, Seattle, WA 98195. Offers MAIS. *Faculty:* 15 full-time (5 women). *Students:* 3 full-time (1 woman); includes 1 Asian, non-Hispanic/Latino. 12 applicants, 25% accepted, 3 enrolled. *Degree requirements:* For master's, one foreign language, thesis optional. *Entrance requirements:* For master's, GRE General Test, minimum GPA of 3.00 (last two years). Additional exam requirements/recommendations for international students: Required—TOEFL (minimum score 500 paper-based; 213 computer-based; 92 iBT) or IELTS (minimum score 7). *Application deadline:* For fall admission, 1/5 for domestic and international students. Application fee: $75. Electronic applications accepted. *Financial support:* In 2010–11, 1 fellowship with full tuition reimbursement was awarded; career-related internships or fieldwork, Federal Work-Study, institutionally sponsored loans, and summer language study awards also available. Financial award application deadline: 1/5; financial award applicants required to submit FAFSA. *Unit head:* Prof. Laurie J. Sears, Chair, 206-543-4370. *Application contact:* Prof. Laurie J. Sears, Chair, 206-543-4370.

University of Washington, Graduate School, College of Arts and Sciences, Henry M. Jackson School of International Studies, Russian, East European and Central Asian Studies Program, Seattle, WA 98195. Offers Central Asian studies (MAIS); East European studies (MAIS); Russian studies (MAIS). *Faculty:* 59 full-time (23 women). *Students:* 24 full-time (14 women); includes 2 Asian, non-Hispanic/Latino; 1 Hispanic/Latino. 30 applicants, 93% accepted, 12 enrolled. In 2010, 7 master's awarded. *Degree requirements:* For master's, one foreign language, thesis. *Entrance requirements:* For master's, GRE General Test, 2 years of relevant language, minimum GPA of 3.00 (last two years). Additional exam requirements/recommendations for international students: Required—TOEFL (minimum score 500 paper-based; 213 computer-based; 92 iBT) or IELTS. *Application deadline:* For fall admission, 1/5 for domestic and international students. Application fee: $75. Electronic applications accepted. *Financial support:* In 2010–11, 8 fellowships with full tuition reimbursements were awarded; research assistantships, teaching assistantships, career-related internships or fieldwork, Federal Work-Study, institutionally sponsored loans, and summer language study awards also available. Financial award application deadline: 1/5. *Unit head:* Prof. James Augerot, Chair, 206-543-6848, E-mail: bigjim@u.washington.edu. *Application contact:* 206-543-6001, Fax: 206-616-3170, E-mail: jsisinfo@u.washington.edu.

University of Washington, Graduate School, College of Arts and Sciences, Henry M. Jackson School of International Studies, South Asian Studies Program, Seattle, WA 98195. Offers MAIS. *Faculty:* 25 full-time (12 women). *Students:* 9 full-time (5 women); includes 1 Asian, non-Hispanic/Latino, 2 international. 14 applicants, 93% accepted, 5 enrolled. In 2010, 2 master's awarded. *Degree requirements:* For master's, one foreign language, thesis optional. *Entrance requirements:* For master's, GRE General Test, minimum GPA of 3.00 (last two years). Additional exam requirements/recommendations for international students: Required—TOEFL (minimum score 500 paper-based; 213 computer-based; 92 iBT) or IELTS (minimum score 7). *Application deadline:* For fall admission, 1/5 for domestic and international students. Application fee: $75. Electronic applications accepted. *Financial support:* In 2010–11, 4 fellowships with full tuition reimbursements were awarded; research assistantships, career-related internships or fieldwork, Federal Work-Study, institutionally sponsored loans, scholarships/grants, tuition waivers (partial), and summer language study awards also available. Financial award application deadline: 1/5; financial award applicants required to submit FAFSA. *Unit head:* Prof. Priti Ramamurthy, Chair, 206-543-6984, E-mail: priti@u.washington.edu. *Application contact:* 206-543-6001, Fax: 206-616-3170, E-mail: jsisinfo@u.washington.edu.

University of Wisconsin–Madison, Graduate School, College of Letters and Science, Center for Southeast Asian Studies, Madison, WI 53706. Offers MA. Part-time programs available. *Degree requirements:* For master's, one foreign language, oral defense of seminar paper. Electronic applications accepted. *Expenses:* Tuition, state resident: full-time $9887; part-time $617.96 per credit. Tuition, nonresident: full-time $24,054; part-time $1503.40 per credit. Required fees: $67.63 per credit. Tuition and fees vary according to reciprocity agreements. *Faculty research:* Economic development, censorship, political change, pedagogical developments in Indonesia, Philippine historical demography, environment photography.

University of Wisconsin–Madison, Graduate School, College of Letters and Science, Department of East Asian Languages and Literature, Madison, WI 53706-1380. Offers Chinese literature (MA, PhD); Chinese thought (MA, PhD); Japanese linguistics (MA, PhD); Japanese literature (MA, PhD). Part-time programs available. Terminal master's awarded for partial completion of doctoral program. *Degree requirements:* For master's, one foreign language, seminars, written exam; for doctorate, 3 foreign languages, thesis/dissertation, seminars, preliminary exams, oral exams. *Entrance requirements:* For master's, GRE General Test, BA or equivalent in major field; for doctorate, GRE General Test, MA or equivalent in major field. Electronic applications accepted. *Expenses:* Tuition, state resident: full-time $9887; part-time $617.96 per credit. Tuition, nonresident: full-time $24,054; part-time $1503.40 per credit. Required fees: $67.63 per credit. Tuition and fees vary according to reciprocity agreements. *Faculty research:* Modern and historical linguistics, literature, literary and cultural history.

University of Wisconsin–Madison, Graduate School, College of Letters and Science, Department of History, Madison, WI 53706-1380. Offers African history (MA, PhD); Central Asian history (MA, PhD); comparative world history (MA, PhD); East Asian history (MA, PhD); European history (MA, PhD); gender and women's history (MA, PhD); Latin American and Caribbean history (MA, PhD); Middle Eastern history (MA, PhD); South Asian history (MA, PhD); Southeast Asian history (MA, PhD); United States history (MA, PhD). Terminal master's awarded for partial completion of doctoral program. *Degree requirements:* For master's, thesis (for some programs); for doctorate, variable foreign language requirement, thesis/dissertation. *Entrance requirements:* For master's and doctorate, GRE General Test. Additional exam requirements/recommendations for international students: Required—Michigan English Language Assessment Battery or TOEFL. Electronic applications accepted. *Expenses:* Tuition, state resident: full-time $9887; part-time $617.96 per credit. Tuition, nonresident: full-time $24,054; part-time $1503.40 per credit. Required fees: $67.63 per credit. Tuition and fees vary according to reciprocity agreements. *Faculty research:* American, African, European, Asian, Latin American, and Middle Eastern history.

University of Wisconsin–Madison, Graduate School, College of Letters and Science, Department of Languages and Cultures of Asia, Madison, WI 53706-1380. Offers civilizations and cultures (PhD); languages and cultures of Asia (MA); languages and literatures (PhD); religions of Asia (PhD). Part-time programs available. Terminal master's awarded for partial completion of doctoral program. *Degree requirements:* For master's, one foreign language, thesis or alternative; for doctorate, 2 foreign languages, thesis/dissertation. *Entrance requirements:* For master's, minimum GPA of 3.0; for doctorate, minimum GPA of 3.25, master's degree. Electronic applications accepted. *Expenses:* Tuition, state resident: full-time $9887; part-time $617.96 per credit. Tuition, nonresident: full-time $24,054; part-time $1503.40 per credit. Required fees: $67.63 per credit. Tuition and fees vary according to reciprocity agreements. *Faculty research:* Literature, folklore, religion.

Valparaiso University, Graduate School, Program in Chinese Studies, Valparaiso, IN 46383. Offers MA, JD/MA. Part-time and evening/weekend programs available. *Faculty:* 2 part-time/adjunct (0 women). *Students:* 10 full-time (4 women), 3 part-time (1 woman); includes 7 minority (2 Black or African American, non-Hispanic/Latino; 1 American Indian or Alaska Native, non-Hispanic/Latino; 3 Asian, non-Hispanic/Latino; 1 Hispanic/Latino). Average age 28. In 2010, 7 master's awarded. *Entrance requirements:* For master's, minimum GPA of 3.0, Chinese language proficiency. Additional exam requirements/recommendations for international students: Required—TOEFL (minimum score 550 paper-based; 213 computer-based; 80 iBT). *Application deadline:* For fall admission, 4/1 priority date for domestic students. Applications are processed on a rolling basis. Application fee: $30 ($50 for international students). Electronic applications accepted. *Expenses:* Tuition: Full-time $9540; part-time $530 per credit hour. Required fees: $292; $95 per semester. Tuition and fees vary according to program. *Financial support:* Scholarships/grants and unspecified assistantships available. Support available to part-time students. Financial award applicants required to submit FAFSA. *Unit head:* Dr. David L. Rowland, Dean, Graduate School and Continuing Education/Associate Provost, 219-464-5313, Fax: 219-464-5381, E-mail: david.rowland@valpo.edu. *Application contact:* Laura Groth, Coordinator of Student Services and Support, 219-464-5313, Fax: 219-464-5381, E-mail: laura.groth@valpo.edu.

Washington State University, Graduate School, College of Liberal Arts, Department of History, Pullman, WA 99164. Offers early and modern European history (MA, PhD); environmental history (MA, PhD); Latin American history (MA, PhD); modern East Asia history (MA, PhD); public history (MA, PhD); U. S. history (MA, PhD); women's history (MA, PhD); world history (MA, PhD). Part-time programs available. *Faculty:* 25. *Students:* 38 full-time (22 women), 10 part-time (4 women); includes 1 American Indian or Alaska Native, non-Hispanic/Latino; 2 Hispanic/Latino, 2 international. Average age 33. 57 applicants, 47% accepted, 10 enrolled. In 2010, 10 master's, 2 doctorates awarded. *Degree requirements:* For master's, comprehensive exam (for some programs), thesis, oral exam; for doctorate, one foreign language, comprehensive exam, thesis/dissertation, oral and written exam. *Entrance requirements:* For master's and doctorate, GRE General Test, official transcripts from all universities attended; three letters of recommendation; statement of purpose; writing sample; Preferred Fields of Study form; Language Background form. Additional exam requirements/recommendations for international students: Required—TOEFL (minimum score 550 paper-based), IELTS. *Application deadline:* For fall admission, 1/10 for domestic and international students; for spring admission, 7/1 for domestic and international students. Applications are processed on a rolling basis. Application fee: $50. Electronic applications accepted. *Expenses:* Tuition, state resident: full-time $8552; part-time $443 per credit. Tuition, nonresident: full-time $21,650; part-time $1083 per credit. Required fees: $846. *Financial support:* In 2010–11, 1 fellowship with partial tuition reimbursement (averaging $3,000 per year), research assistantships with full and partial tuition reimbursements (averaging $13,917 per year), 28 teaching assistantships with full and partial tuition reimbursements (averaging $13,056 per year) were awarded; career-related internships or fieldwork, Federal Work-Study, institutionally sponsored loans, scholarships/grants, and health care benefits also available. Financial award application deadline: 2/15; financial award applicants required to submit FAFSA. *Faculty research:* Public, world, environmental, women's and U. S. history. *Unit head:* Dr. Raymond Sun, Chair, 509-335-5139, Fax: 509-335-4171, E-mail: pietz@wsu.edu. *Application contact:* Graduate Studies Director, 509-335-4030, Fax: 509-335-4171, E-mail: kale@wsu.edu.

Washington University in St. Louis, Graduate School of Arts and Sciences, Program in East Asian Studies, St. Louis, MO 63130-4899. Offers East Asian studies (MA); JD/MA. PhD offered through specific departments. *Entrance requirements:* For master's, GRE General Test. Electronic applications accepted.

West Virginia University, Eberly College of Arts and Sciences, Department of History, Morgantown, WV 26506. Offers African history (MA, PhD); African-American history (MA, PhD); American history (MA, PhD); Appalachian/regional history (MA, PhD); East Asian history (MA, PhD); European history (MA, PhD); history of science and technology (MA, PhD); Latin American history (MA). Part-time programs available. *Degree requirements:* For master's, one foreign language, thesis (for some programs), oral exam, thesis defense; for doctorate, one foreign language, comprehensive exam, thesis/dissertation, dissertation defense. *Entrance requirements:* For master's, GRE General Test, minimum GPA of 3.0; for doctorate, GRE

General Test. Additional exam requirements/recommendations for international students: Required—TOEFL (minimum score 550 paper-based), IELTS (minimum score 6.5). Electronic applications accepted. *Faculty research:* U.S., Appalachia, modern Europe, Africa, colonial and post-colonial societies.

Yale University, Graduate School of Arts and Sciences, Program in East Asian Studies, New Haven, CT 06520. Offers MA. *Degree requirements:* For master's, one foreign language. *Entrance requirements:* For master's, GRE General Test.

Canadian Studies

Carleton University, Faculty of Graduate Studies, Faculty of Arts and Social Sciences, School of Canadian Studies, Ottawa, ON K1S 5B6, Canada. Offers MA, PhD. PhD program offered jointly with Trent University. *Degree requirements:* For master's, one foreign language, thesis optional; for doctorate, one foreign language, thesis/dissertation. *Entrance requirements:* For master's, honors degree. Additional exam requirements/recommendations for international students: Required—TOEFL. Electronic applications accepted. *Faculty research:* Modern Canada, cultural studies, women's studies, aboriginal studies and the north, heritage conservation.

Collège universitaire de Saint-Boniface, Program in Canadian Studies, Saint-Boniface, MB R2H 0H7, Canada. Offers MA.

Queen's University at Kingston, School of Graduate Studies and Research, Faculty of Arts and Sciences, Department of Political Studies, Kingston, ON K7L 3N6, Canada. Offers Canadian politics (PhD); comparative politics (PhD); gender and politics (PhD); international relations (PhD); political theory (PhD). *Degree requirements:* For master's, thesis or alternative; for doctorate, one foreign language, thesis/dissertation, qualifying exams. *Entrance requirements:* Additional exam requirements/recommendations for international students: Required—TOEFL (minimum score 600 paper-based; 250 computer-based). *Faculty research:* Canadian politics, comparative politics, political thought, international politics, women and politics.

Saint Mary's University, Faculty of Arts, Program in Atlantic Canada Studies, Halifax, NS B3H 3C3, Canada. Offers MA, Certificate. Part-time and evening/weekend programs available. *Degree requirements:* For master's, thesis. *Entrance requirements:* For master's, honors degree. Electronic applications accepted. *Expenses:* Contact institution.

Trent University, Graduate Studies, The Frost Centre for Canadian Studies and Indigenous Studies, Peterborough, ON K9J 7B8, Canada. Offers Canadian studies (PhD); Canadian studies and indigenous studies (MA). Part-time programs available. *Degree requirements:* For master's, thesis. *Entrance requirements:* For master's, honors degree. *Faculty research:* Native community-based socioeconomic development, environmental and social impact inventory, regional studies.

Université de Sherbrooke, Faculty of Letters and Human Sciences, Department of Letters and Communications, Sherbrooke, QC J1K 2R1, Canada. Offers comparative Canadian literature (MA, PhD); French literature (MA, PhD); linguistics (MA); theatre (MA). *Degree requirements:* For master's, thesis or alternative; for doctorate, thesis/dissertation. *Entrance requirements:* For master's, minimum GPA of 2.8; for doctorate, minimum GPA of 3.0.

Université du Québec à Chicoutimi, Graduate Programs, Program in Regional Studies, Chicoutimi, QC G7H 2B1, Canada. Offers MA. Part-time programs available. *Degree requirements:* For master's, thesis. *Entrance requirements:* For master's, appropriate bachelor's degree, proficiency in French.

University of Lethbridge, School of Graduate Studies, Lethbridge, AB T1K 3M4, Canada. Offers accounting (MScM); addictions counseling (M Sc); agricultural biotechnology (M Sc); agricultural studies (M Sc, MA); anthropology (MA); archaeology (MA); art (MA, MFA); biochemistry (M Sc); biological sciences (M Sc); biomolecular science (PhD); biosystems and biodiversity (PhD); Canadian studies (MA); chemistry (M Sc); computer science (M Sc); computer science and geographical information science (M Sc); counseling psychology (M Ed); dramatic arts (MA); earth, space, and physical science (PhD); economics (MA); educational leadership (M Ed); English (MA); environmental science (M Sc); evolution and behavior (PhD); exercise science (M Sc); finance (MScM); French (MA); French/German (MA); French/Spanish (MA); general education (M Ed); general management (MScM); geography (M Sc, MA); German (MA); health science (M Sc); history (MA); human resource management and labour relations (MScM); individualized multidisciplinary (M Sc, MA); information systems (MScM); international management (MScM); kinesiology (M Sc, MA); management (M Sc, MA); marketing (MScM); mathematics (M Sc); music (M Mus, MA); Native American studies (MA); neuroscience (M Sc, PhD); new media (MA); nursing (M Sc); philosophy (MA); physics (M Sc); policy and strategy (MScM); political science (MA); psychology (M Sc, MA); religious studies (MA); social sciences (MA); sociology (MA); theatre and dramatic arts (MFA); theoretical and computational science (PhD); urban and regional studies (MA); women's studies (MA). Part-time and evening/weekend programs available. *Degree requirements:* For doctorate, comprehensive exam, thesis/dissertation. *Entrance requirements:* For master's, GMAT (M Sc in management), bachelor's degree in related field, minimum GPA of 3.0 during previous 20 graded semester courses, 2 years teaching or related experience (M Ed); for doctorate, master's degree, minimum graduate GPA of 3.5. Additional exam requirements/recommendations for international students: Required—TOEFL. *Faculty research:* Movement and brain plasticity, gibberellin physiology, photosynthesis, carbon cycling, molecular properties of main-group ring components.

University of Maine, Graduate School, College of Liberal Arts and Sciences, Department of History, Orono, ME 04469. Offers American studies (MA, PhD); Canadian studies (MA, PhD); East Asian (MA); environmental (MA); European (MA); technology (MA). *Faculty:* 11 full-time (1 woman), 2 part-time/adjunct (1 woman). *Students:* 24 full-time (8 women), 35 part-time (13 women); includes 4 minority (2 American Indian or Alaska Native, non-Hispanic/Latino; 2 Hispanic/Latino). Average age 38. 43 applicants, 40% accepted, 15 enrolled. In 2010, 5 master's, 3 doctorates awarded. Terminal master's awarded for partial completion of doctoral program. *Degree requirements:* For master's, variable foreign language requirement, thesis optional; for doctorate, one foreign language, thesis/dissertation. *Entrance requirements:* For master's and doctorate, GRE General Test. Additional exam requirements/recommendations for international students: Required—TOEFL. *Application deadline:* For fall admission, 2/1 priority date for domestic students. Applications are processed on a rolling basis. Application fee: $65. Electronic applications accepted. *Expenses:* Tuition, state resident: full-time $400. Tuition, nonresident: full-time $1050. *Financial support:* In 2010–11, 9 teaching assistantships with tuition reimbursements (averaging $12,790 per year) were awarded; career-related internships or fieldwork, Federal Work-Study, and tuition waivers (full and partial) also available. Support available to part-time students. Financial award application deadline: 3/1. *Faculty research:* Canadian labor and working classes; American social, cultural, and urban history. *Unit head:* Dr. Nathan Godfried, Chair, 207-581-1923, Fax: 207-581-1817. *Application contact:* Scott G. Delcourt, Associate Dean of the Graduate School, 207-581-3291, Fax: 207-581-3232, E-mail: graduate@maine.edu.

University of Manitoba, Faculty of Graduate Studies, College Universitaire de Saint Boniface, Program in Canadian Studies, Winnipeg, MB R3T 2N2, Canada. Offers MA.

University of Ottawa, Faculty of Graduate and Postdoctoral Studies, Faculty of Arts, Institute of Canadian Studies, Ottawa, ON K1N 6N5, Canada. Offers economics (PhD); English (PhD); geography (PhD); history (PhD); lettres Françaises (PhD); linguistics (PhD); philosophy (PhD); political science (PhD); psychology (PhD); religious studies (PhD); translation studies (PhD). *Degree requirements:* For doctorate, comprehensive exam, thesis/dissertation.

University of Regina, Faculty of Graduate Studies and Research, Faculty of Arts, Canadian Plains Studies Program, Regina, SK S4S 0A2, Canada. Offers MA, PhD. Offered as special case program. Part-time programs available. *Faculty:* 1 full-time (0 women). *Students:* 7 full-time (4 women). 1 applicant, 0% accepted. In 2010, 1 master's awarded. *Degree requirements:* For master's, thesis; for doctorate, thesis/dissertation. *Entrance requirements:* Additional exam requirements/recommendations for international students: Required—TOEFL (minimum score 580 paper-based; 80 iBT). *Application deadline:* Applications are processed on a rolling basis. Application fee: $100. Electronic applications accepted. Tuition and fees charges are reported in Canadian dollars. *Expenses:* Tuition, area resident: Full-time $3244.50 Canadian dollars; part-time $180.25 Canadian dollars per credit hour. International tuition: $4744.50 Canadian dollars full-time. Required fees: $494 Canadian dollars; $115.25 Canadian dollars per credit hour. $115.25 Canadian dollars per semester. Tuition and fees vary according to program. *Financial support:* In 2010–11, 1 fellowship (averaging $21,000 per year), 1 research assistantship (averaging $18,000 per year), 1 teaching assistantship (averaging $6,759 per year) were awarded; scholarships/grants also available. Financial award application deadline: 6/15. *Unit head:* Dr. Harry Diaz, Head, Executive Director, 306-585-4758, Fax: 306-585-4699, E-mail: harry.diaz@uregina.ca. *Application contact:* Dr. Harry Diaz, Head, Executive Director, 306-585-4758, Fax: 306-585-4699, E-mail: harry.diaz@uregina.ca.

University of Saskatchewan, College of Graduate Studies and Research, College of Arts and Sciences, Department of Native Studies, Saskatoon, SK S7N 5A2, Canada. Offers MA, PhD. *Degree requirements:* For master's, thesis; for doctorate, comprehensive exam (for some programs), thesis/dissertation. *Entrance requirements:* Additional exam requirements/recommendations for international students: Required—TOEFL (minimum score 80 iBT); Recommended—IELTS (minimum score 6.5). Electronic applications accepted.

Wilfrid Laurier University, Faculty of Graduate and Postdoctoral Studies, Faculty of Arts, Department of Political Science, Waterloo, ON N2L 3C5, Canada. Offers Canadian political studies (MA); comparative politics/international relations (MA). Part-time programs available. *Faculty:* 20 full-time (6 women). *Students:* 18 full-time (7 women), 3 part-time (1 woman), 1 international. 68 applicants, 49% accepted, 13 enrolled. In 2010, 13 master's awarded. *Degree requirements:* For master's, thesis optional. *Entrance requirements:* For master's, honors bachelor's degree or the equivalent in political science, minimum B average in undergraduate course work. Additional exam requirements/recommendations for international students: Required—TOEFL (minimum score 89 iBT). *Application deadline:* For fall admission, 2/1 priority date for domestic and international students. Application fee: $100. Electronic applications accepted. Tuition and fees charges are reported in Canadian dollars. *Expenses:* Tuition, area resident: Full-time $15,300 Canadian dollars; part-time $1200 Canadian dollars per credit. International tuition: $21,300 Canadian dollars full-time. Required fees: $650 Canadian dollars; $100 Canadian dollars per credit. Tuition and fees vary according to course load, degree level, campus/location and program. *Financial support:* In 2010–11, 26 fellowships, 5 research assistantships, 26 teaching assistantships were awarded; career-related internships or fieldwork, scholarships/grants, health care benefits, and unspecified assistantships also available. *Faculty research:* Political behavior/political psychology, Canadian political studies, comparative, politics/relations, public opinion and electoral studies, international. *Unit head:* Dr. Andrea Perella, Graduate Coordinator, 519-884-0710 Ext. 2719, Fax: 519-746-3655, E-mail: aperrella@wlu.ca. *Application contact:* Jennifer Williams, Graduate Admission and Records Officer, 519-884-0710 Ext. 3536, Fax: 519-884-1020, E-mail: gradstudies@wlu.ca.

Wilfrid Laurier University, Faculty of Graduate and Postdoctoral Studies, Faculty of Social Work, Waterloo, ON N2L 3C5, Canada. Offers Aboriginal studies (MSW); community, policy, planning and organizations (MSW); critical social policy and organizational studies (PhD); individuals, families and groups (MSW); social work practice (individuals, families, groups and communities) (PhD); social work practice: individuals, families, groups and communities (PhD). Part-time programs available. *Faculty:* 20 full-time (13 women), 50 part-time/adjunct (36 women). *Students:* 271 full-time (227 women), 111 part-time (100 women), 1 international. 621 applicants, 40% accepted, 132 enrolled. In 2010, 164 master's, 5 doctorates awarded. *Degree requirements:* For master's, thesis optional; for doctorate, thesis/dissertation. *Entrance requirements:* For master's, course work in social science, research methodology, and statistics; honors BA with a minimum B average; for doctorate, master's degree in social work, minimum A- average. Additional exam requirements/recommendations for international students: Required—TOEFL (minimum score 89 iBT). *Application deadline:* For fall admission, 1/15 priority date for domestic and international students. Application fee: $125. Electronic applications accepted. *Expenses:* Contact institution. *Financial support:* Career-related internships or fieldwork, scholarships/grants, health care benefits, and unspecified assistantships available. *Unit head:* Dr. Cheryl-Anne Cait, Associate Dean, 519-884-1970 Ext. 5224, E-mail: ccait@wlu.ca. *Application contact:* Rosemary Springett, Graduate Admission and Records Officer, 519-884-0710 Ext. 3078, E-mail: gradstudies@wlu.ca.

Cultural Studies

Ambrose University College, Ambrose Seminary, Calgary, AB T2P 3T5, Canada. Offers biblical/theological studies (MA); Chinese ministries (Certificate); Christian studies (M Div, MA, Diploma); foundations for ministry (Certificate); intercultural ministries (M Div, MA, Certificate, Diploma); leadership and ministry (MA, Certificate, Diploma). *Accreditation:* ATS (one or more programs are accredited). Part-time programs available. *Faculty:* 7 full-time (0 women), 24 part-time/adjunct (2 women). *Students:* 55 full-time (16 women), 98 part-time (52 women); includes 49 minority (5 Black or African American, non-Hispanic/Latino; 2 American Indian or Alaska Native, non-Hispanic/Latino; 41 Asian, non-Hispanic/Latino; 1 Hispanic/Latino). Average age 41. *Degree requirements:* For master's, 2 foreign languages, internship; for M Div, one foreign language, internship. *Entrance requirements:* For master's, bachelor's degree. Additional exam requirements/recommendations for international students: Required—TOEFL or IELTS. *Application deadline:* For fall admission, 7/31 priority date for domestic students, 3/1 priority date for international students; for winter admission, 11/30 priority date for domestic students, 6/1 priority date for international students. Applications are processed on a rolling basis. Application fee: $50. Electronic applications accepted. Tuition and fees charges are reported in Canadian dollars. *Expenses:* Tuition: Full-time $9270 Canadian dollars; part-time $309 Canadian dollars per credit hour. Required fees: $510 Canadian dollars. *Financial support:* Career-related internships or fieldwork and scholarships/grants available. Support available to part-time students. Financial award application deadline: 3/30. *Faculty research:* Evangelicalism and sociology, missiological trends, chaplaincy, intertestamental studies, postmodernism. *Unit head:* Dr. Paul Spilsbury, Vice-President of Academic Affairs, 403-410-2000 Ext. 6905, Fax: 403-571-2556, E-mail: pspilsbury@ambrose.edu. *Application contact:* Dr. Paul Spilsbury, Vice-President of Academic Affairs, 403-410-2000 Ext. 6905, Fax: 403-571-2556, E-mail: pspilsbury@ambrose.edu.

American University, School of International Service, Washington, DC 20016-8071. Offers comparative and regional studies (Certificate); cross-cultural communication (Certificate); development management (MS); ethics, peace, and global affairs (MA); European studies (Certificate); global environmental policy (MA, Certificate); international affairs (MA), including comparative and regional studies, environmental policy, international economic policy, international politics, natural resources and sustainable development, U. S. foreign policy; international communication (MA, Certificate); international development (MA, Certificate); international development management (Certificate); international economic policy (Certificate); international economic relations (Certificate); international media (MA); international peace and conflict resolution (MA, Certificate); international relations (PhD); international service (MIS); peace building (Certificate); the Americas (Certificate); United States foreign policy (Certificate); JD/MA. Part-time and evening/weekend programs available. *Faculty:* 91 full-time (35 women), 48 part-time/adjunct (16 women). *Students:* 591 full-time (383 women), 367 part-time (229 women); includes 164 minority (51 Black or African American, non-Hispanic/Latino; 4 American Indian or Alaska Native, non-Hispanic/Latino; 42 Asian, non-Hispanic/Latino; 63 Hispanic/Latino; 4 Two or more races, non-Hispanic/Latino), 94 international. Average age 27. 2,115 applicants, 59% accepted, 360 enrolled. In 2010, 370 master's, 7 doctorates awarded. Terminal master's awarded for partial completion of doctoral program. *Degree requirements:* For master's, one foreign language, comprehensive exam, thesis or alternative; for doctorate, one foreign language, comprehensive exam, thesis/dissertation, research practicum; for Certificate, minimum 15 credit hours related course work. *Entrance requirements:* For master's, GRE, 24 credits of course work in related social sciences, minimum GPA of 3.5, 2 letters of recommendation, bachelor's degree, resume; for doctorate, GRE, 2 letters of recommendation, 24 credits in related social sciences; for Certificate, bachelor's degree. Additional exam requirements/recommendations for international students: Required—TOEFL (minimum score 600 paper-based; 250 computer-based; 100 iBT). *Application deadline:* For fall admission, 1/15 priority date for domestic students; for spring admission, 10/1 priority date for domestic students. Applications are processed on a rolling basis. Application fee: $50. *Financial support:* Career-related internships or fieldwork, Federal Work-Study, and institutionally sponsored loans available. Financial award application deadline: 1/15. *Faculty research:* International intellectual property, international environmental issues, international law and legal order, international telecommunications/technology, international sustainable development. *Unit head:* Dr. Louis W. Goodman, Dean, 202-885-1600, Fax: 202-885-2494. *Application contact:* Yasmin Quianzon, Director of Graduate Admissions and Financial Aid, 202-885-2496, Fax: 202-885-1109.

The American University of Paris, Graduate Programs, Paris, France. Offers cross-cultural and sustainable business management (MA); cultural translation (MA); global communications (MA); global communications and civil society (MA); international affairs, conflict resolution and civil society development (MA); Middle East and Islamic studies (MA); Middle East and Islamic studies and international affairs (MA); public policy and international affairs (MA); public policy and international law (MA). *Faculty:* 14 full-time (3 women). *Students:* 151 full-time (110 women), 56 part-time (43 women). 271 applicants, 83% accepted, 104 enrolled. In 2010, 67 master's awarded. *Degree requirements:* For master's, thesis. *Entrance requirements:* For master's, minimum undergraduate GPA of 3.0. Additional exam requirements/recommendations for international students: Recommended—IELTS. *Application deadline:* For fall admission, 4/15 priority date for international students; for spring admission, 11/15 priority date for international students. Applications are processed on a rolling basis. Application fee: $75. Electronic applications accepted. *Financial support:* Scholarships/grants available. Financial award applicants required to submit FAFSA. *Unit head:* Dr. Celeste Schenck, President, 33-1 40 62 06 59, E-mail: president@aup.fr. *Application contact:* International Admissions Counselor, 33-1 40 62 07 20, Fax: 33-1 47 05 34 32, E-mail: admissions@aup.edu.

Appalachian State University, Cratis D. Williams Graduate School, Center for Appalachian Studies, Boone, NC 28608. Offers culture (MA); music (MA); sustainable development (MA). Part-time programs available. *Faculty:* 14 full-time (5 women). *Students:* 25 full-time (15 women), 5 part-time (4 women); includes 1 Hispanic/Latino. 20 applicants, 85% accepted, 12 enrolled. In 2010, 11 master's awarded. *Degree requirements:* For master's, one foreign language, comprehensive exam, thesis optional. *Entrance requirements:* For master's, GRE General Test, 3 letters of recommendation. Additional exam requirements/recommendations for international students: Required—TOEFL (minimum score 570 paper-based; 230 computer-based; 79 iBT), IELTS (minimum score 6.5). *Application deadline:* For fall admission, 7/1 for domestic students, 2/1 for international students; for spring admission, 11/1 for domestic students, 7/1 for international students. Applications are processed on a rolling basis. Application fee: $55. Electronic applications accepted. *Expenses:* Tuition, state resident: full-time $3428; part-time $428 per unit. Tuition, nonresident: full-time $14,518; part-time $1814 per unit. Required fees: $2320; $344 per unit. Tuition and fees vary according to campus/location. *Financial support:* In 2010–11, 8 research assistantships (averaging $8,000 per year) were awarded; fellowships, teaching assistantships, career-related internships or fieldwork, Federal Work-Study, scholarships/grants, and unspecified assistantships also available. Financial award application deadline: 4/1; financial award applicants required to submit FAFSA. *Faculty research:* Appalachian culture, sustainable development, Appalachian music. Total annual research expenditures: $35,275. *Unit head:* Dr. Pat Beaver, Director, 828-262-2550, E-mail: beaverpd@appstate.edu. *Application contact:* Dr. Katherine Ledford, Graduate Program Director, 828-262-4089, E-mail: ledfordke@appstate.edu.

Arizona State University, College of Liberal Arts and Sciences, Program in Film and Media Studies, Tempe, AZ 85287-0402. Offers American media and popular culture (MAS). Part-time and evening/weekend programs available. Postbaccalaureate distance learning degree programs offered (no on-campus study). *Faculty:* 10 full-time (3 women). *Students:* 5 full-time (all women), 12 part-time (4 women); includes 4 minority (all Hispanic/Latino). Average age 32. 20 applicants, 20% accepted, 3 enrolled. *Degree requirements:* For master's, integrated project. *Entrance requirements:* For master's, minimum GPA of 3.0 or equivalent in last 2 years of work leading to bachelor's degree. Additional exam requirements/recommendations for international students: Required—TOEFL, IELTS, or Pearson Test of English. *Application deadline:* For fall admission, 3/15 for domestic and international students; for spring admission, 10/15 for domestic and international students. Applications are processed on a rolling basis. Application fee: $70 ($90 for international students). Electronic applications accepted. *Expenses:* Contact institution. *Financial support:* In 2010–11, 1 teaching assistantship with full and partial tuition reimbursement (averaging $15,000 per year) was awarded; career-related internships or fieldwork, Federal Work-Study, institutionally sponsored loans, scholarships/grants, and tuition waivers (partial) also available. Financial award application deadline: 3/1; financial award applicants required to submit FAFSA. Total annual research expenditures: $198,441. *Unit head:* Dr. Bambi Haggins, Director, 480-965-6747, Fax: 480-965-9110, E-mail: bambi.haggins@asu.edu. *Application contact:* Graduate Admissions, 480-965-6113.

Arizona State University, College of Liberal Arts and Sciences, School of International Letters and Cultures, Program in Spanish, Tempe, AZ 85287-0202. Offers Spanish (cultural studies) (PhD); Spanish (linguistics) (MA), including second language acquisition/applied linguistics, sociolinguistics; Spanish (literature and culture) (MA); Spanish (literature) (PhD). Part-time programs available. *Faculty:* 11 full-time (4 women). *Students:* 53 full-time (34 women), 17 part-time (11 women); includes 35 minority (1 Black or African American, non-Hispanic/Latino; 2 Asian, non-Hispanic/Latino; 31 Hispanic/Latino; 1 Two or more races, non-Hispanic/Latino), 12 international. Average age 34. 49 applicants, 61% accepted, 19 enrolled. In 2010, 7 master's, 3 doctorates awarded. Terminal master's awarded for partial completion of doctoral program. *Degree requirements:* For master's, thesis, oral defense; written comprehensive exam (literature and culture); portfolio review (linguistics); interactive Program of Study (iPOS) submitted before completing 50 percent of required credit hours; for doctorate, comprehensive exam, thesis/dissertation, interactive Program of Study (iPOS) submitted before completing 50 percent of required credit hours. *Entrance requirements:* For master's, GRE (recommended), BA in Spanish or close equivalent from accredited institution with minimum GPA of 3.5, 3 letters of recommendation, personal statement, academic writing sample; for doctorate, GRE (recommended), MA in Spanish or equivalent from accredited institution with minimum GPA of 3.75, 3 letters of recommendation, personal statement, academic writing sample. Additional exam requirements/recommendations for international students: Required—TOEFL (minimum score 550 paper-based; 213 computer-based; 83 iBT), IELTS (minimum score 6.5). *Application deadline:* For fall admission, 1/1 for domestic and international students. Application fee: $70 ($90 for international students). Electronic applications accepted. *Expenses:* Tuition, state resident: full-time $8510; part-time $608 per credit. Tuition, nonresident: full-time $16,542; part-time $919 per credit. Required fees: $339; $110 per credit. Part-time tuition and fees vary according to course load. *Financial support:* In 2010–11, 1 research assistantship with full and partial tuition reimbursement (averaging $20,000 per year), 54 teaching assistantships with full and partial tuition reimbursements (averaging $14,235 per year) were awarded; fellowships with full and partial tuition reimbursements, institutionally sponsored loans, scholarships/grants, and tuition waivers (partial) also available. Financial award application deadline: 3/1; financial award applicants required to submit FAFSA. *Unit head:* Dr. Emil Volek, Director, 480-965-7211, E-mail: emil.volek@asu.edu. *Application contact:* Graduate Admissions, 480-965-6113.

Assemblies of God Theological Seminary, Graduate and Professional Programs, Springfield, MO 65802. Offers Christian ministries (MA); counseling (MA); divinity (M Div); intercultural ministry (MA); intercultural studies (PhD); ministry (D Min); missiology (D Miss); theological studies (MA). *Accreditation:* ATS. Part-time and evening/weekend programs available. Postbaccalaureate distance learning degree programs offered (minimal on-campus study). *Faculty:* 12 full-time (3 women), 20 part-time/adjunct (6 women). *Students:* 176 full-time (59 women), 211 part-time (48 women); includes 55 minority (16 Black or African American, non-Hispanic/Latino; 7 American Indian or Alaska Native, non-Hispanic/Latino; 16 Asian, non-Hispanic/Latino; 14 Hispanic/Latino; 2 Native Hawaiian or other Pacific Islander, non-Hispanic/Latino), 9 international. Average age 40. 96 applicants, 79% accepted, 53 enrolled. In 2010, 26 first professional degrees, 65 master's, 9 doctorates awarded. *Degree requirements:* For master's, analytical reflection paper, comprehensive exam or field education research project; for doctorate, thesis/dissertation; for M Div, one foreign language, analytical reflection paper or field education research project. *Entrance requirements:* For M Div, minimum GPA of 2.5; for master's, minimum GPA of 2.5; for doctorate, minimum GPA of 3.0. Additional exam requirements/recommendations for international students: Required—TOEFL (minimum score 550 paper-based; 213 computer-based; 80 iBT). *Application deadline:* For fall admission, 7/1 priority date for domestic students, 6/1 priority date for international students; for spring admission, 12/1 priority date for domestic students, 11/1 priority date for international students. Applications are processed on a rolling basis. Application fee: $75. Electronic applications accepted. *Expenses:* Tuition: Full-time $12,192; part-time $508 per credit hour. *Financial support:* Career-related internships or fieldwork, Federal Work-Study, and scholarships/grants available. Support available to part-time students. Financial award application deadline: 7/15; financial award applicants required to submit FAFSA. *Unit head:* Stephen Lim, Academic Dean, 417-268-1000, Fax: 417-268-1001, E-mail: slim@agts.edu. *Application contact:* Stephen Lim, Academic Dean, 417-268-1000, Fax: 417-268-1001, E-mail: slim@agts.edu.

Athabasca University, Centre for Integrated Studies, Athabasca, AB T9S 3A3, Canada. Offers adult education (MA); community studies (MA); cultural studies (MA); educational studies (MA); global change (MA); work, organization, and leadership (MA). Part-time and evening/weekend programs available. Postbaccalaureate distance learning degree programs offered (no on-campus study). *Degree requirements:* For master's, project. *Entrance requirements:* Additional exam requirements/recommendations for international students: Required—TOEFL (minimum score 560 paper-based; 220 computer-based). Electronic applications accepted. *Faculty research:* Women's history, literature and culture studies, sustainable development, labor and education.

Baptist Bible College, Graduate School of Theology, Springfield, MO 65803-3498. Offers biblical counseling (MA); biblical studies (MA); church ministry (MA); intercultural studies (MA); theology (M Div). Part-time programs available. *Degree requirements:* For master's, 2 foreign languages, thesis (for some programs); for M Div, 2 foreign languages, thesis/dissertation (for some programs). *Entrance requirements:* For master's, outcomes test. Electronic applications accepted.

Biola University, School of Intercultural Studies, La Mirada, CA 90639-0001. Offers anthropology (MA); applied linguistics (MA); Biblical languages and linguistics (MA); intercultural education (PhD); intercultural studies (MAICS); linguistics (Certificate); missiology (D Miss); missions (MA); teaching English to speakers of other languages (MA, Certificate). Part-time and evening/weekend programs available. *Faculty:* 16 full-time (5 women), 6 part-time/adjunct (1 woman). *Students:* 66 full-time (39 women), 126 part-time (72 women); includes 48 minority (6 Black or African American, non-Hispanic/Latino; 40 Asian, non-Hispanic/Latino; 2 Two or more races, non-Hispanic/Latino), 30 international. 136 applicants, 70% accepted, 59 enrolled. In 2010, 27 master's, 10 doctorates awarded. Terminal master's awarded for partial completion of doctoral program. *Degree requirements:* For master's, one foreign language, comprehensive exam; for doctorate, one foreign language, comprehensive exam, thesis/dissertation. *Entrance requirements:* For master's, minimum undergraduate GPA of 3.0; for doctorate, MA, 3 years of ministry experience, minimum graduate GPA of 3.3. Additional exam requirements/recommendations for international students: Required—TOEFL (minimum score 550 paper-based; 213 computer-based). *Application deadline:* For fall admission, 7/1 for domestic students; for spring admission, 1/1 for domestic students. Applications are processed on a rolling basis. Application fee: $45. Electronic applications accepted. *Financial support:* Teaching assistantships, career-related internships or fieldwork, institutionally sponsored loans, and scholarships/grants available. Support available to part-time students. Financial award application deadline: 3/2; financial award applicants required to submit FAFSA. *Unit head:* Dr. Douglas Pennoyer, Dean, 562-903-4844, Fax: 562-903-4748, E-mail: douglas.pennoyer@biola.edu. *Application contact:* Roy

M. Allinson, Director of Graduate Admissions, 562-903-4752, Fax: 562-903-4709, E-mail: admissions@biola.edu.

Boston University, Metropolitan College, Program in Gastronomy, Boston, MA 02215. Offers business (MLA); communications (MLA); food policy (MLA); history and culture (MLA). Part-time and evening/weekend programs available. *Faculty:* 1 (woman) full-time, 11 part-time/adjunct (5 women). *Students:* 7 full-time (all women), 64 part-time (52 women); includes 13 minority (3 Black or African American, non-Hispanic/Latino; 1 American Indian or Alaska Native, non-Hispanic/Latino; 6 Asian, non-Hispanic/Latino; 1 Hispanic/Latino; 2 Two or more races, non-Hispanic/Latino), 2 international. Average age 29. 30 applicants, 93% accepted, 26 enrolled. In 2010, 9 master's awarded. *Degree requirements:* For master's, thesis optional. *Entrance requirements:* Additional exam requirements/recommendations for international students: Required—TOEFL. *Application deadline:* Applications are processed on a rolling basis. Application fee: $70. Electronic applications accepted. *Expenses:* Tuition: Full-time $39,314; part-time $1228 per credit. Required fees: $40 per semester. *Financial support:* In 2010–11, 4 research assistantships with partial tuition reimbursements (averaging $2,500 per year), 1 teaching assistantship (averaging $2,500 per year) were awarded; career-related internships or fieldwork, scholarships/grants, and unspecified assistantships also available. Support available to part-time students. Financial award applicants required to submit FAFSA. *Faculty research:* Food studies. *Unit head:* Dr. Rachel Black, Assistant Professor, 617-353-6291, Fax: 617-353-4130, E-mail: rblack@bu.edu. *Application contact:* Dr. Rachel Black, Assistant Professor, 617-353-6291, Fax: 617-353-4130, E-mail: rblack@bu.edu.

Brock University, Faculty of Graduate Studies, Faculty of Social Sciences, Program in Popular Culture, St. Catharines, ON L2S 3A1, Canada. Offers MA. Part-time programs available. *Degree requirements:* For master's, thesis optional. *Entrance requirements:* For master's, honors BA. Additional exam requirements/recommendations for international students: Required—TOEFL (minimum score 550 paper-based; 213 computer-based; 80 iBT), IELTS (minimum score 6.5), TWE (minimum score 4). Electronic applications accepted. *Faculty research:* Film and television studies, popular music, historical aspects of popular culture, popular literature.

Carnegie Mellon University, College of Humanities and Social Sciences, Department of History, Pittsburgh, PA 15213-3891. Offers African and African-American diaspora (PhD); culture and power (PhD); gender and the family (PhD); history (MA, MS); history and policy (MA); labor and politics (PhD); science, technology, medicine and environment (PhD). Part-time programs available. *Degree requirements:* For doctorate, oral and written comprehensive exams, dissertation defense. *Entrance requirements:* For doctorate, GRE General Test. Additional exam requirements/recommendations for international students: Required—TOEFL. Electronic applications accepted. *Faculty research:* Anthropology and history, African American history, technology/environment, cultural history analysis.

The Catholic University of America, School of Architecture and Planning, Washington, DC 20064. Offers architecture studies (MS Arch St); sustainable design (MSSD). Part-time programs available. *Faculty:* 25 full-time (6 women), 38 part-time/adjunct (9 women). *Students:* 116 full-time (55 women), 31 part-time (13 women); includes 11 Black or African American, non-Hispanic/Latino; 6 Asian, non-Hispanic/Latino; 11 Hispanic/Latino, 11 international. Average age 27. 167 applicants, 70% accepted, 56 enrolled. In 2010, 55 master's awarded. *Degree requirements:* For master's, thesis. *Entrance requirements:* For master's, GRE (minimum score: 1000), minimum GPA of 2.8, portfolio, statement of purpose, official copies of academic transcripts, three letters of recommendation. Additional exam requirements/recommendations for international students: Required—TOEFL (minimum score 580 paper-based; 237 computer-based). *Application deadline:* For fall admission, 1/15 priority date for domestic students, 1/15 for international students; for spring admission, 10/15 priority date for domestic students, 10/15 for international students. Applications are processed on a rolling basis. Application fee: $55. Electronic applications accepted. *Expenses:* Contact institution. *Financial support:* Fellowships, research assistantships, teaching assistantships, Federal Work-Study, scholarships/grants, tuition waivers (full and partial), and unspecified assistantships available. Financial award application deadline: 2/1; financial award applicants required to submit FAFSA. *Faculty research:* Architectural history, cultural studies/sacred space, design technologies, digital media, real estate development, urban design. *Unit head:* Randall Ott, Dean, 202-319-5784, Fax: 202-319-2023, E-mail: ott@cua.edu. *Application contact:* Andrew Woodall, Director of Graduate Admissions, 202-319-5057, Fax: 202-319-6533, E-mail: cua-admissions@cua.edu.

Central Michigan University, College of Graduate Studies, College of Humanities and Social and Behavioral Sciences, Program in Humanities, Mount Pleasant, MI 48859. Offers humanities (MA), including contemporary issues in the humanities: race, class, and gender, images and ideas of self, Native American issues in modern culture, popular culture studies, the rise of industrial society. Part-time and evening/weekend programs available. *Students:* 2 full-time (both women), 10 part-time (6 women); includes 1 American Indian or Alaska Native, non-Hispanic/Latino; 2 Hispanic/Latino. Average age 37. *Degree requirements:* For master's, thesis or alternative. *Application deadline:* For fall admission, 6/1 for international students; for spring admission, 10/1 for international students. Applications are processed on a rolling basis. Application fee: $35 ($45 for international students). Electronic applications accepted. *Expenses:* Tuition, state resident: full-time $8208; part-time $456 per credit hour. Tuition, nonresident: full-time $13,788; part-time $766 per credit hour. One-time fee: $25. *Financial support:* Fellowships with tuition reimbursements, Federal Work-Study, unspecified assistantships, and out-of-state merit awards, non-resident graduate awards available. *Faculty research:* Rise of industrial society; images and ideas of self; contemporary issues of race, class, and gender; popular culture; Native American issues in modern culture. *Unit head:* Dr. Susan A. Schiller, Director, 989-774-3681, Fax: 989-774-7106, E-mail: schil1sa@cmich.edu. *Application contact:* Judith L. Prince, Director of Graduate Student Services, 989-774-1059, Fax: 989-774-1857, E-mail: judith.l.prince@cmich.edu.

Chapman University, Graduate Studies, College of Educational Studies, Program in Education: Cultural and Curricular Studies, Orange, CA 92866. Offers cultural and curricular studies (PhD); disability studies (PhD); school psychology (PhD). Part-time and evening/weekend programs available. *Faculty:* 23 full-time (15 women), 31 part-time/adjunct (22 women). *Students:* 2 full-time (both women), 58 part-time (46 women); includes 26 minority (3 Black or African American, non-Hispanic/Latino; 2 American Indian or Alaska Native, non-Hispanic/Latino; 11 Asian, non-Hispanic/Latino; 9 Hispanic/Latino; 1 Two or more races, non-Hispanic/Latino), 1 international. Average age 37. 45 applicants, 58% accepted, 18 enrolled. In 2010, 4 doctorates awarded. *Degree requirements:* For doctorate, thesis/dissertation. *Entrance requirements:* For doctorate, GRE. Additional exam requirements/recommendations for international students: Required—TOEFL (minimum score 550 paper-based; 213 computer-based; 80 iBT). *Application deadline:* For fall admission, 2/28 priority date for domestic students. Application fee: $60. Electronic applications accepted. *Financial support:* Fellowships, Federal Work-Study and scholarships/grants available. *Unit head:* Dr. Joel Colbert, Director, 714-744-7076. *Application contact:* Becky Campbell, School Psychology/Counseling and PhD Admission Coordinator, 714-628-7263, E-mail: rcampbel@chapman.edu.

Claremont Graduate University, Graduate Programs, School of Arts and Humanities, Department of Cultural Studies, Claremont, CA 91711-6160. Offers Africana studies (Certificate); cultural studies (MA, PhD); media studies (MA, PhD); museum studies (MA). Part-time programs available. *Faculty:* 2 full-time (1 woman), 1 (woman) part-time/adjunct. *Students:* 57 full-time (36 women), 9 part-time (8 women); includes 12 Black or African American, non-Hispanic/Latino; 1 American Indian or Alaska Native, non-Hispanic/Latino; 3 Asian, non-Hispanic/Latino; 9 Hispanic/Latino; 5 Two or more races, non-Hispanic/Latino, 6 international. Average age 36. In 2010, 9 master's, 5 doctorates awarded. *Entrance requirements:* For master's and doctorate, GRE General Test. Additional exam requirements/recommendations for international students: Required—TOEFL (minimum score 550 paper-based; 213 computer-based; 80 iBT). *Application deadline:* For fall admission, 2/1 priority date for domestic students. Applications are processed on a rolling basis. Application fee: $60. Electronic applications accepted. *Expenses:* Tuition:

Full-time $35,748; part-time $1554 per unit. Required fees: $215 per semester. *Financial support:* Fellowships, research assistantships, Federal Work-Study, institutionally sponsored loans, and scholarships/grants available. Support available to part-time students. Financial award application deadline: 2/15; financial award applicants required to submit FAFSA. *Unit head:* Eve Oishi, Chair, 909-607-7587, E-mail: eve.oishi@cgu.edu. *Application contact:* Susan Hampson, Admissions Coordinator, 909-607-1278, Fax: 909-607-1221, E-mail: humanities@cgu.edu.

Columbia International University, Columbia Biblical Seminary and School of Missions, Columbia, SC 29230-3122. Offers academic ministries (M Div); bible exposition (M Div, MABE); biblical studies (Certificate); counseling ministries (Certificate); divinity (M Div); educational ministries (M Div, MAEM, Certificate); intercultural studies (M Div, MAIS, Certificate); leadership (D Min); leadership for evangelism/mobilization (MALM); member care (D Min); ministry (Certificate); missions (D Min); pastoral counseling and spiritual formation (M Div, MAPS); preaching (D Min); theology (MA). *Accreditation:* ATS (one or more programs are accredited). Part-time and evening/weekend programs available. *Degree requirements:* For master's, integrative seminar; for doctorate, comprehensive exam, thesis/dissertation; for M Div, internship. *Entrance requirements:* For master's, minimum GPA of 2.7; for doctorate, 3 years of ministerial experience, M Div. Additional exam requirements/recommendations for international students: Required—TOEFL. Electronic applications accepted.

Concordia University, School of Theology, Irvine, CA 92612-3299. Offers Christian leadership (MA); research in theology (MA); theology and culture (MA). Part-time and evening/weekend programs available. *Faculty:* 8 full-time (1 woman), 2 part-time/adjunct (0 women). *Students:* 30 full-time (3 women), 7 part-time (3 women); includes 5 minority (1 Black or African American, non-Hispanic/Latino; 1 Asian, non-Hispanic/Latino; 3 Hispanic/Latino), 4 international. Average age 34. 11 applicants, 55% accepted, 5 enrolled. In 2010, 2 master's awarded. *Degree requirements:* For master's, project/thesis or vicarage. *Entrance requirements:* For master's, official college transcript(s), statement of intent, 2 references, graduate health form, interview. Additional exam requirements/recommendations for international students: Required—TOEFL. *Application deadline:* For fall admission, 7/1 priority date for domestic students, 6/1 for international students; for spring admission, 11/30 priority date for domestic students, 10/1 for international students. Applications are processed on a rolling basis. Application fee: $50 ($125 for international students). Electronic applications accepted. *Expenses:* Contact institution. *Financial support:* Scholarships/grants and unspecified assistantships available. Financial award applicants required to submit FAFSA. *Unit head:* Rev. Dr. James Bachman, Dean of Graduate Studies, 949-214-3387, E-mail: james.bachman@cui.edu. *Application contact:* Carrie Donohoe, Christ College Program Coordinator, 949-214-3389, E-mail: carrie.donohoe@cui.edu.

Cornell University, Graduate School, Graduate Fields of Arts and Sciences, Field of English Language and Literature, Ithaca, NY 14853-0001. Offers African-American literature (PhD); American literature after 1865 (PhD); American literature to 1865 (PhD); American studies (PhD); colonial and postcolonial literature (PhD); creative writing (MFA); cultural studies (PhD); dramatic literature (PhD); English poetry (PhD); English Renaissance to 1660 (PhD); lesbian, bisexual, and gay literature studies (PhD); literary criticism and theory (PhD); nineteenth century (PhD); Old and Middle English (PhD); prose fiction (PhD); Restoration and eighteenth century (PhD); twentieth century (PhD); women's literature (PhD); MFA/PhD. *Faculty:* 56 full-time (29 women). *Students:* 100 full-time (56 women); includes 5 Black or African American, non-Hispanic/Latino; 3 American Indian or Alaska Native, non-Hispanic/Latino; 10 Asian, non-Hispanic/Latino; 8 Hispanic/Latino, 12 international. Average age 27. 1,091 applicants, 4% accepted, 21 enrolled. In 2010, 25 master's, 12 doctorates awarded. Terminal master's awarded for partial completion of doctoral program. *Degree requirements:* For master's, one foreign language, thesis; for doctorate, one foreign language, comprehensive exam, thesis/dissertation, teaching experience. *Entrance requirements:* For master's, GRE General Test, 3 letters of recommendation, creative writing sample; for doctorate, GRE General Test, GRE Subject Test (English), 3 letters of recommendation, writing sample. Additional exam requirements/recommendations for international students: Required—TOEFL (minimum score 600 paper-based; 250 computer-based; 77 iBT). *Application deadline:* For fall admission, 1/10 for domestic students. Application fee: $80. Electronic applications accepted. *Expenses:* Tuition: Full-time $29,500. Required fees: $76. Tuition and fees vary according to degree level and program. *Financial support:* In 2010–11, 32 fellowships with full tuition reimbursements, 60 teaching assistantships with full tuition reimbursements were awarded; research assistantships with full tuition reimbursements, institutionally sponsored loans, scholarships/grants, health care benefits, tuition waivers (full and partial), and unspecified assistantships also available. Financial award applicants required to submit FAFSA. *Faculty research:* English and American literature, women's writing, ethnic and post-colonial literature, critical theory, medievalism. *Unit head:* Director of Graduate Studies, 607-255-7989, Fax: 607-255-6661. *Application contact:* Graduate Field Assistant, 607-255-7989, Fax: 607-255-6661, E-mail: english_grad@cornell.edu.

Eastern Michigan University, Graduate School, College of Education, Department of Teacher Education, Program in Culture and Diversity, Ypsilanti, MI 48197. Offers MA. *Students:* 7 part-time (all women); all minorities (all Black or African American, non-Hispanic/Latino). Average age 37. In 2010, 2 master's awarded. *Unit head:* Dr. Wendy Burke, Coordinator, 734-487-3260, Fax: 734-487-2101, E-mail: wendy.burke@emich.edu. *Application contact:* Dr. Wendy Burke, Coordinator, 734-487-3260, Fax: 734-487-2101, E-mail: wendy.burke@emich.edu.

George Mason University, College of Humanities and Social Sciences, Program in Cultural Studies, Fairfax, VA 22030. Offers PhD. Part-time and evening/weekend programs available. *Faculty:* 21 full-time (10 women), 1 (woman) part-time/adjunct. *Students:* 7 full-time (5 women), 56 part-time (35 women); includes 2 Black or African American, non-Hispanic/Latino; 3 Asian, non-Hispanic/Latino, 13 international. Average age 36. 77 applicants, 31% accepted, 5 enrolled. In 2010, 8 doctorates awarded. *Degree requirements:* For doctorate, one foreign language, comprehensive exam, thesis/dissertation, foreign language exams. *Entrance requirements:* For doctorate, GRE General Test, sample of written work, MA or simultaneous application to related MA program at George Mason University. Additional exam requirements/recommendations for international students: Required—TOEFL. *Application deadline:* For fall admission, 1/15 for domestic students. Application fee: $100. Electronic applications accepted. *Expenses:* Tuition, state resident: full-time $8192; part-time $440 per credit hour. Tuition, nonresident: full-time $22,952; part-time $1055 per credit hour. Required fees: $2364; $99 per credit hour. *Financial support:* In 2010–11, 27 students received support, including 3 fellowships with full tuition reimbursements available (averaging $18,000 per year), 1 research assistantship with full and partial tuition reimbursement available (averaging $12,875 per year), 23 teaching assistantships with full and partial tuition reimbursements available (averaging $11,981 per year); Federal Work-Study, unspecified assistantships, and health care benefits (full-time research or teaching assistantship recipients) also available. Support available to part-time students. Financial award application deadline: 1/15; financial award applicants required to submit FAFSA. *Faculty research:* Early Modern cultural studies, Shakespeare and film, feminism, Foucault, science and technology studies. *Unit head:* Roger N. Lancaster, Director, 703-993-2851, Fax: 703-993-2852, E-mail: rlancast@gmu.edu. *Application contact:* Dr. Matt Zingraff, Associate Dean, Research and Graduate Programs, 703-993-4769, E-mail: zingraff@gmu.edu.

George Mason University, School of Public Policy, Arlington, VA 22201. Offers culture and values in social policy (Certificate); global medical policy (Certificate); global trade management (Certificate); health and medical policy (MS); international commerce and policy (MA); national security and public policy (Certificate); organization development and knowledge management (MS); peace operations (MS); public policy (EMPP, MPP, PhD); transportation and logistics policy (Certificate); transportation policy, operations and logistics (MA). Part-time and evening/weekend programs available. *Faculty:* 66 full-time (24 women), 15 part-time/adjunct (3 women). *Students:* 344 full-time (199 women), 607 part-time (310 women); includes 55 Black or African American, non-Hispanic/Latino; 1 American Indian or Alaska Native, non-Hispanic/Latino; 33

Cultural Studies

George Mason University (continued)
Asian, non-Hispanic/Latino; 55 Hispanic/Latino; 5 Two or more races, non-Hispanic/Latino, 106 international. Average age 31. 842 applicants, 62% accepted, 280 enrolled. In 2010, 291 master's, 15 doctorates, 12 other advanced degrees awarded. *Degree requirements:* For master's, thesis or alternative; for doctorate, comprehensive exam, thesis/dissertation. *Entrance requirements:* For master's, GRE (for students seeking merit-based scholarships), minimum undergraduate GPA of 3.0, resume, 2 letters of recommendation; for doctorate, GMAT or GRE General Test, resume, writing sample, master's degree, goals statement, 2 letters of recommendation; for Certificate, minimum undergraduate GPA of 3.0, resume, 2 letters of recommendation, goals statement. Additional exam requirements/recommendations for international students: Required—TOEFL (minimum score 570 paper-based; 230 computer-based; 88 iBT). *Application deadline:* Applications are processed on a rolling basis. Application fee: $100. Electronic applications accepted. *Expenses:* Contact institution. *Financial support:* In 2010–11, 43 students received support, including 2 fellowships with full tuition reimbursements available (averaging $18,000 per year), 41 research assistantships with full and partial tuition reimbursements available (averaging $18,104 per year), 2 teaching assistantships (averaging $10,408 per year); career-related internships or fieldwork, Federal Work-Study, scholarships/grants, unspecified assistantships, and health care benefits (full-time research or teaching assistantship recipients) also available. Financial award application deadline: 3/1; financial award applicants required to submit FAFSA. *Faculty research:* Governance, regional and economic development, international commerce and policy, science and technology policy, entrepreneurship, culture and values. Total annual research expenditures: $8 million. *Unit head:* Dr. Edward Rhodes, Dean, 703-993-2280, Fax: 703-993-8215, E-mail: edrhodes@gmu.edu. *Application contact:* Tennille Haegele, Director of Graduate Admissions, School of Public Policy, 703-993-3183, Fax: 703-993-4876, E-mail: thaegele@gmu.edu.

Goucher College, Program in Cultural Sustainability, Baltimore, MD 21204-2794. Offers MA. Part-time programs available. Postbaccalaureate distance learning degree programs offered (minimal on-campus study). *Faculty:* 13 part-time/adjunct (5 women). *Students:* 22 full-time (20 women), 1 (woman) part-time; includes 2 Black or African American, non-Hispanic/Latino. *Degree requirements:* For master's, capstone project. *Application deadline:* For fall admission, 4/20 for domestic students; for spring admission, 10/15 for domestic students. Application fee: $50. *Financial support:* Application deadline: 3/15. *Unit head:* Rory Turner, Program Director, 410-337-6296. *Application contact:* Megan Cornett, Director of Marketing and Communications, 410-337-6200, Fax: 410-337-6085, E-mail: mcornett@goucher.edu.

Grace Theological Seminary, Graduate and Professional Programs, Winona Lake, IN 46590-9907. Offers biblical studies (Certificate); camp administration (MA); counseling (M Div); exegetical studies (MA); intercultural studies (M Div, MA); local church studies (MA); pastoral studies (M Div); theological studies (MA); theology (D Min, Diploma). Part-time programs available. Postbaccalaureate distance learning degree programs offered (no on-campus study). *Degree requirements:* For master's, thesis optional; for doctorate, 2 foreign languages, thesis/dissertation; for M Div, 2 foreign languages, thesis/dissertation optional. *Entrance requirements:* For M Div and master's, MAT, minimum GPA of 2.5. Electronic applications accepted. *Faculty research:* Biblical theology, language, and church ministries.

Graduate Theological Union, Graduate Programs, Berkeley, CA 94709-1212. Offers art and religion (MA, PhD, Th D); biblical languages (MA); biblical studies (MA); Biblical studies (PhD, Th D); Buddhist studies (MA); Christian spirituality (MA, PhD, Th D); cultural and historical studies of religions (MA, PhD, Th D); ethics and social theory (PhD, Th D); history (MA, PhD, Th D); homiletics (MA, PhD, Th D); interdisciplinary studies (PhD, Th D); Jewish studies (MA, PhD, Th D, Certificate); liturgical studies (MA, PhD, Th D); Near Eastern religions (PhD, Th D); Orthodox Christian studies (MA); religion and psychology (MA, PhD, Th D); religion and society/ethics and social theory (MA); systematic and philosophical theology (MA, PhD, Th D). PhD programs in Jewish studies and Near Eastern religions offered jointly with University of California, Berkeley. *Accreditation:* ATS. Terminal master's awarded for partial completion of doctoral program. *Degree requirements:* For master's, one foreign language, thesis; for doctorate, one foreign language, comprehensive exam, thesis/dissertation. *Entrance requirements:* For master's, GRE General Test; for doctorate, GRE General Test, MA or M Div. Additional exam requirements/recommendations for international students: Required—TOEFL. Electronic applications accepted.

Lewis & Clark College, Graduate School of Education and Counseling, Department of Counseling Psychology, Portland, OR 97219-7899. Offers addictions treatment (MA, MS); community counseling (MA, MS), including professional mental health counseling; marriage, couple and family therapy (MA, MS); psychological and cultural studies (MA, MS); school psychology (Ed S). *Accreditation:* AAMFT/COAMFTE; ACA. Part-time and evening/weekend programs available. *Faculty:* 10 full-time (6 women), 29 part-time/adjunct (19 women). *Students:* 182 full-time (148 women), 65 part-time (55 women); includes 2 Black or African American, non-Hispanic/Latino; 6 Asian, non-Hispanic/Latino; 10 Hispanic/Latino; 13 Two or more races, non-Hispanic/Latino, 4 international. Average age 31. 231 applicants, 62% accepted, 69 enrolled. In 2010, 60 master's awarded. *Degree requirements:* For master's, thesis proposal (MS). *Entrance requirements:* For master's, GRE General Test, minimum undergraduate GPA of 2.75. Additional exam requirements/recommendations for international students: Required—TOEFL (minimum score 575 paper-based; 233 computer-based). *Application deadline:* For fall admission, 2/1 priority date for domestic and international students; for spring admission, 10/1 priority date for domestic and international students. Application fee: $50. Electronic applications accepted. *Expenses:* Tuition: Part-time $713 per semester hour. Tuition and fees vary according to course level and campus/location. *Financial support:* In 2010–11, 33 students received support. Career-related internships or fieldwork, Federal Work-Study, institutionally sponsored loans, scholarships/grants, health care benefits, and tuition waivers (partial) available. Support available to part-time students. Financial award application deadline: 3/1; financial award applicants required to submit FAFSA. *Unit head:* Dr. Teresa McDowell, Chair, 503-768-6060, Fax: 503-768-6065, E-mail: cpsy@lclark.edu. *Application contact:* Becky Haas, Director of Admissions, 503-768-6200, Fax: 503-768-6205, E-mail: gseadmit@lclark.edu.

Maranatha Baptist Bible College, Program in Cross-Cultural Studies, Watertown, WI 53094. Offers MA. Part-time programs available. *Faculty:* 4 full-time (0 women), 5 part-time/adjunct (0 women). *Students:* 1 full-time (0 women), 1 part-time (0 women). Average age 24. 1 applicant, 100% accepted, 1 enrolled. *Application deadline:* Applications are processed on a rolling basis. Application fee: $50. *Expenses:* Tuition: Full-time $4160; part-time $260 per credit hour. Required fees: $350; $23 per credit hour. *Financial support:* Scholarships/grants and tuition waivers (full and partial) available. Support available to part-time students. *Unit head:* Dr. Larry Oats, Dean of Maranatha Baptist Seminary, 920-206-2324, Fax: 920-261-9109, E-mail: loats@mbbc.edu. *Application contact:* Dr. Jim Harrison, Director of Admissions, 920-206-2327, Fax: 920-261-9109, E-mail: admissions@mbbc.edu.

McMaster University, School of Graduate Studies, Faculty of Humanities, Department of English and Cultural Studies, Hamilton, ON L8S 4M2, Canada. Offers cultural studies and critical theory (MA); English (MA, PhD). Part-time programs available. *Degree requirements:* For master's, one foreign language, thesis; for doctorate, one foreign language, comprehensive exam, thesis/dissertation. *Entrance requirements:* For master's, honors degree, minimum B+ average in at least 6 full courses of English beyond year 1; for doctorate, MA; minimum A- average in two of three courses. Additional exam requirements/recommendations for international students: Required—TOEFL (minimum score 580 paper-based; 237 computer-based). *Faculty research:* Literary theory, feminist theory, literature of migration, Bakhting globalization.

New York University, NYU in Madrid, Madrid, NY 10012-1019, Spain. Offers creative writing in Spanish (MFA); Spanish (PhD); Spanish and Latin American literatures and cultures (MA); Spanish language and translation (MA).

New York University, Steinhardt School of Culture, Education, and Human Development, New York, NY 10003. Offers MA, MFA, MM, MS, DPS, DPT, Ed D, PhD, Advanced Certificate, MA/MA, MM/Advanced Certificate. *Accreditation:* Teacher Education Accreditation Council. Part-time programs available. *Faculty:* 262 full-time (154 women), 644 part-time/adjunct (524 women). *Students:* 2,305 full-time (1,758 women), 1,385 part-time (1,059 women); includes 253 Black or African American, non-Hispanic/Latino; 4 American Indian or Alaska Native, non-Hispanic/Latino; 312 Asian, non-Hispanic/Latino; 187 Hispanic/Latino, 536 international. Average age 30. 5,812 applicants, 49% accepted, 1293 enrolled. In 2010, 1,225 master's, 101 doctorates, 21 other advanced degrees awarded. *Degree requirements:* For master's, thesis (for some programs); for doctorate, comprehensive exam (for some programs), thesis/dissertation. *Entrance requirements:* For doctorate, GRE General Test, interview. Additional exam requirements/recommendations for international students: Required—TOEFL. *Application deadline:* For fall admission, 12/1 priority date for domestic students, 12/1 for international students; for spring admission, 1/1 for domestic and international students. Applications are processed on a rolling basis. Application fee: $75. Electronic applications accepted. *Expenses:* Contact institution. *Financial support:* Fellowships with full and partial tuition reimbursements, research assistantships with full and partial tuition reimbursements, teaching assistantships with full and partial tuition reimbursements, career-related internships or fieldwork, Federal Work-Study, institutionally sponsored loans, scholarships/grants, traineeships, tuition waivers (partial), and unspecified assistantships available. Support available to part-time students. Financial award application deadline: 2/1; financial award applicants required to submit FAFSA. *Faculty research:* Equity, urban adolescents, arts in education, globalization, community and public health. Total annual research expenditures: $22.8 million. *Unit head:* Dr. Mary Brabeck, Dean, 212-998-5000. *Application contact:* John Myers, Director of Enrollment Management, 212-998-5030, Fax: 212-995-4328, E-mail: steinhardt.gradadmissions@nyu.edu.

Northeastern University, College of Arts, Media and Design, Department of Communication Studies, Boston, MA 02115-5096. Offers communication, media, and cultural studies (MA). *Faculty:* 25 full-time (10 women), 6 part-time/adjunct (3 women). *Students:* 8 full-time (7 women), 1 part-time (0 women). 92 applicants, 36% accepted, 5 enrolled. In 2010, 1 master's awarded. *Degree requirements:* For master's, thesis (for some programs). *Entrance requirements:* For master's, GRE. Additional exam requirements/recommendations for international students: Required—TOEFL or IELTS. *Application deadline:* For fall admission, 2/1 priority date for domestic and international students. Applications are processed on a rolling basis. Application fee: $50. Electronic applications accepted. *Financial support:* Federal Work-Study and scholarships/grants available. *Unit head:* Dr. Joanne Morreale, Graduate Coordinator, 617-373-2506, E-mail: j.morreale@neu.edu. *Application contact:* Jo-Anne Dickinson, Admissions Contact, 617-373-5990, Fax: 617-373-7281, E-mail: gsas@neu.edu.

Northern Kentucky University, Office of Graduate Programs, College of Arts and Sciences, Program in English, Highland Heights, KY 41099. Offers composition and rhetoric (Certificate); creative writing (Certificate); cultural studies (Certificate); English (MA); professional writing (Certificate). Part-time and evening/weekend programs available. *Faculty:* 11 full-time (6 women). *Students:* 8 full-time (5 women), 66 part-time (53 women); includes 6 minority (4 Black or African American, non-Hispanic/Latino; 1 Hispanic/Latino; 1 Two or more races, non-Hispanic/Latino). Average age 34. 36 applicants, 94% accepted, 32 enrolled. In 2010, 3 master's awarded. *Degree requirements:* For master's, comprehensive exam (for some programs), comprehensive exam, thesis, project, or portfolio. *Entrance requirements:* For master's, minimum GPA of 3.0, two letters of reference. Additional exam requirements/recommendations for international students: Required—TOEFL (minimum score 550 paper-based; 213 computer-based; 79 iBT); Recommended—IELTS (minimum score 6.5). *Application deadline:* For fall admission, 7/1 priority date for domestic students, 6/1 priority date for international students; for spring admission, 11/1 for domestic students, 10/1 for international students. Applications are processed on a rolling basis. Application fee: $40. Electronic applications accepted. *Expenses:* Tuition, state resident: full-time $7254; part-time $403 per credit hour. Tuition, nonresident: full-time $12,492; part-time $694 per credit hour. Tuition and fees vary according to degree level and program. *Financial support:* Unspecified assistantships available. Financial award applicants required to submit FAFSA. *Faculty research:* Composition and rhetoric, creative writing, English and American literature, professional writing, cultural studies. *Unit head:* Dr. Roxanne Kent-Drury, Coordinator, 859-572-6636, Fax: 859-572-6093, E-mail: rkdrury@nku.edu. *Application contact:* Dr. Peg Griffin, Director of Graduate Programs, 859-572-6934, Fax: 859-572-6670, E-mail: griffinp@nku.edu.

Northwest University, College of Ministry, Kirkland, WA 98033. Offers ministry (MA); missional leadership (MA); theology and culture (MA). Evening/weekend programs available. *Faculty:* 9 full-time (1 woman), 21 part-time/adjunct (2 women). *Students:* 17 full-time (3 women), 43 part-time (9 women); includes 7 minority (5 Black or African American, non-Hispanic/Latino; 1 Asian, non-Hispanic/Latino; 1 Hispanic/Latino), 2 international. 32 applicants, 97% accepted, 29 enrolled. In 2010, 6 master's awarded. *Entrance requirements:* Additional exam requirements/recommendations for international students: Required—TOEFL (minimum score 550 paper-based). Application fee: $75. Tuition and fees vary according to program. *Unit head:* Dr. Wayde Goodall, Dean, 425-889-5253, E-mail: wayde.goodall@northwestu.edu. *Application contact:* Aaron Oosterwyk, Director of Graduate and Professional Studies Enrollment, 425-889-7799, Fax: 425-803-3059, E-mail: gpse@northwestu.edu.

St. Francis Xavier University, Graduate Studies, Department of Celtic Studies, Antigonish, NS B2G 2W5, Canada. Offers MA. *Degree requirements:* For master's, thesis. *Entrance requirements:* Additional exam requirements/recommendations for international students: Required—TOEFL (minimum score 580 paper-based; 236 computer-based). *Faculty research:* Scottish Gaelic in Nova Scotia.

San Francisco State University, Division of Graduate Studies, College of Behavioral and Social Sciences, Human Sexuality Studies Program, San Francisco, CA 94132-1722. Offers MA. *Unit head:* Dr. Rita Melendez, Chair, 415-405-3572, E-mail: rmelende@sfsu.edu. *Application contact:* Prof. David Frost, Graduate Advisor, 415-405-3570, E-mail: frost@sfsu.edu.

Savannah College of Art and Design, Graduate School, Savannah, GA 31402-3146. Offers accessory design (MA, MFA); advertising design (MA, MFA); animation (MA, MFA); architectural history (MA, MFA); architecture (M Arch); art history (MA); arts administration (MA); broadcast design (MA, MFA); cinema studies (MA); commercial photography (MA); digital photography (MA); documentary photography (MA); fashion (MA, MFA); fibers (MA, MFA); film and television (MA, MFA); furniture design (MA, MFA); graphic design (MA, MFA); historic preservation (MA, MFA, Graduate Certificate); illustration (MA, MFA); illustration design (MA); industrial design (MA, MFA); interactive design and game development (MA, MFA, Graduate Certificate); interior design (MA, MFA); international preservation (MA); luxury and fashion management (MA, MFA); metals and jewelry (MA, MFA); painting (MA, MFA); performing arts (MFA); photography (MA, MFA); printmaking (MA, MFA); production design (MA, MFA); professional education (MAT), including art, drama; professional writing (MFA); sculpture (MA, MFA); sequential art (MA, MFA); service design (MFA); sound design (MA, MFA); urban design and development (MUD); visual effects (MA, MFA). Part-time programs available. Postbaccalaureate distance learning degree programs offered (no on-campus study). *Students:* 1,576 full-time (898 women), 407 part-time (240 women); includes 208 minority (115 Black or African American, non-Hispanic/Latino; 8 American Indian or Alaska Native, non-Hispanic/Latino; 29 Asian, non-Hispanic/Latino; 45 Hispanic/Latino; 2 Native Hawaiian or other Pacific Islander, non-Hispanic/Latino; 9 Two or more races, non-Hispanic/Latino), 435 international. Average age 28. 2,826 applicants, 36% accepted, 642 enrolled. In 2010, 534 master's, 8 other advanced degrees awarded. *Degree requirements:* For master's, thesis, internship. *Entrance requirements:* For master's, interview, 3 letters of recommendation. Additional exam requirements/recommendations for international students: Required—TOEFL (minimum score 550 paper-based; 133 computer-based). *Application deadline:* For fall admission, 4/1 priority date for domestic and international students. Applications are processed on a rolling basis. Application fee: $35. Electronic applications accepted. *Expenses:* Tuition: Full-time $29,520; part-time $3280 per quarter. Tuition and fees vary according to campus/location. *Financial support:*

Fellowships, career-related internships or fieldwork, Federal Work-Study, and scholarships/grants available. Financial award application deadline: 4/1; financial award applicants required to submit FAFSA. *Unit head:* Edward Dupuy, Dean of Graduate Studies, 912-525-5838, E-mail: edupuy@scad.edu. *Application contact:* Elizabeth Mathis, Director of Graduate Recruitment, 912-525-5965, Fax: 912-525-5985, E-mail: emathis@scad.edu.

Simmons College, College of Arts and Sciences Graduate Studies, Program in Gender/Cultural Studies, Boston, MA 02115. Offers MA, MA/MAT, MA/MS. Part-time programs available. *Degree requirements:* For master's, thesis. *Entrance requirements:* For master's, academic writing sample. Additional exam requirements/recommendations for international students: Required—TOEFL (minimum score 600 paper-based; 250 computer-based; 100 iBT). Electronic applications accepted. *Faculty research:* Gender and sexuality, queer theory, gender and the media, race, feminist film theory.

Southern Illinois University Carbondale, Graduate School, College of Liberal Arts, Department of Foreign Languages and Literatures, Carbondale, IL 62901-4701. Offers MA. Part-time programs available. *Degree requirements:* For master's, one foreign language, thesis. *Entrance requirements:* For master's, minimum GPA of 2.7. Additional exam requirements/recommendations for international students: Required—TOEFL. *Faculty research:* Bibliography, historical linguistics, language pedagogy, philology, commercial facets.

State University of New York at Binghamton, Graduate School, School of Arts and Sciences, Philosophy, Interpretation and Culture Program, Binghamton, NY 13902-6000. Offers MA, PhD. *Faculty:* 2 full-time (1 woman), 1 part-time/adjunct (0 women). *Students:* 13 full-time (7 women), 34 part-time (17 women); includes 4 Black or African American, non-Hispanic/Latino; 2 Asian, non-Hispanic/Latino; 6 Hispanic/Latino, 19 international. Average age 36. 29 applicants, 38% accepted, 5 enrolled. In 2010, 9 master's, 8 doctorates awarded. Application fee: $60. *Financial support:* In 2010–11, 9 students received support, including 5 fellowships with full tuition reimbursements available (averaging $14,500 per year), 6 teaching assistantships with full tuition reimbursements available (averaging $14,500 per year); career-related internships or fieldwork, Federal Work-Study, institutionally sponsored loans, scholarships/grants, health care benefits, and unspecified assistantships also available. Financial award application deadline: 2/15; financial award applicants required to submit FAFSA. *Unit head:* Dr. Joshua Price, Director, 607-777-2348, E-mail: jmprice@binghamton.edu. *Application contact:* Catherine Smith, Recruiting and Admissions Coordinator, 607-777-2151, Fax: 607-777-2501, E-mail: cmsmith@binghamton.edu.

Stony Brook University, State University of New York, Graduate School, College of Arts and Sciences, Department of Comparative Literary and Cultural Studies, Stony Brook, NY 11794. Offers comparative literature (MA, PhD); cultural studies (PhD). Evening/weekend programs available. *Faculty:* 7 full-time (1 woman), 1 part-time/adjunct (0 women). *Students:* 29 full-time (18 women), 3 part-time (all women); includes 2 Asian, non-Hispanic/Latino, 13 international. Average age 30. 98 applicants, 31% accepted, 7 enrolled. In 2010, 5 master's, 3 doctorates awarded. Terminal master's awarded for partial completion of doctoral program. *Degree requirements:* For master's, 2 foreign languages, exam; for doctorate, 3 foreign languages, comprehensive exam, thesis/dissertation. *Entrance requirements:* For master's and doctorate, GRE General Test, minimum GPA of 3.5 in major, 3.0 overall. Additional exam requirements/recommendations for international students: Required—TOEFL. *Application deadline:* For fall admission, 1/15 for domestic students. Application fee: $100. *Expenses:* Tuition, state resident: full-time $8370; part-time $349 per credit. Tuition, nonresident: full-time $13,780; part-time $574 per credit. Required fees: $994. *Financial support:* In 2010–11, 12 teaching assistantships were awarded; fellowships, research assistantships also available. *Faculty research:* Literary theory, interdisciplinary studies, literary history. *Unit head:* Prof. Krin Gabbard, Chairman, 631-632-7456. *Application contact:* Dr. Kent Marks, Assistant Dean, Admissions and Records, 631-632-4723, Fax: 631-632-7243, E-mail: kmarks@notes.cc.sunysb.edu.

Taylor College and Seminary, Graduate and Professional Programs, Edmonton, AB T6J 4T3, Canada. Offers Christian studies (Diploma); intercultural studies (MA, Diploma), including intercultural studies (Diploma); TESOL; theology (M Div, MTS). *Accreditation:* ATS. Part-time programs available. Postbaccalaureate distance learning degree programs offered (minimal on-campus study). *Degree requirements:* For master's, thesis optional. *Entrance requirements:* Additional exam requirements/recommendations for international students: Required—TOEFL (minimum score 550 paper-based; 80 iBT), IELTS (minimum score 6.5). *Faculty research:* Biblical studies, administration and organization, world religions, ethics, missiology.

Texas A&M University, College of Education and Human Development, Department of Teaching, Learning, and Culture, College Station, TX 77843. Offers culture and curriculum (M Ed, MS); curriculum and instruction (PhD); English as a second language (M Ed, MS, PhD); mathematics education (M Ed, MS, PhD); reading and language arts education (M Ed, MS, PhD); science education (M Ed, MS, PhD); urban education (M Ed, MS, PhD). Part-time programs available. *Faculty:* 32. *Students:* 165 full-time (126 women), 259 part-time (203 women); includes 121 minority (69 Black or African American, non-Hispanic/Latino; 5 American Indian or Alaska Native, non-Hispanic/Latino; 8 Asian, non-Hispanic/Latino; 39 Hispanic/Latino), 52 international. Average age 36. In 2010, 106 master's, 26 doctorates awarded. *Degree requirements:* For master's, comprehensive exam, thesis (for some programs); for doctorate, comprehensive exam, thesis/dissertation. *Entrance requirements:* For master's, GRE General Test, minimum GPA of 3.0; for doctorate, GRE General Test, 3 years of teaching experience. Additional exam requirements/recommendations for international students: Required—TOEFL (minimum score 550 paper-based; 213 computer-based). *Application deadline:* For fall admission, 1/15 priority date for domestic and international students; for spring admission, 9/15 priority date for domestic and international students. Applications are processed on a rolling basis. Application fee: $50 ($75 for international students). Electronic applications accepted. *Financial support:* In 2010–11, fellowships with partial tuition reimbursements (averaging $3,000 per year), teaching assistantships with partial tuition reimbursements (averaging $7,200 per year) were awarded; research assistantships with partial tuition reimbursements, career-related internships or fieldwork, Federal Work-Study, institutionally sponsored loans, scholarships/grants, tuition waivers (partial), and unspecified assistantships also available. Support available to part-time students. Financial award application deadline: 4/1; financial award applicants required to submit FAFSA. *Unit head:* Dr. Dennie Smith, Head, 979-845-8384, Fax: 979-845-9663, E-mail: denniesmith@tamu.edu. *Application contact:* Kerri Smith, Senior Academic Advisor II, 979-845-8382, Fax: 979-845-9663, E-mail: krsmith@tamu.edu.

Trent University, Graduate Studies, Program in Cultural Studies, Peterborough, ON K9J 7B8, Canada. Offers PhD.

Union Institute & University, Master of Arts Program—Online, Montpelier, VT 05602. Offers creativity studies (MA); education (MA); health and wellness (MA); history and culture (MA); leadership, public policy, and social issues (MA); literature and writing (MA); psychology (MA). Part-time programs available. Postbaccalaureate distance learning degree programs offered (no on-campus study). *Faculty:* 2 full-time (1 woman), 18 part-time/adjunct (11 women). *Students:* 27 full-time (26 women), 119 part-time (98 women); includes 34 minority (25 Black or African American, non-Hispanic/Latino; 3 American Indian or Alaska Native, non-Hispanic/Latino; 6 Hispanic/Latino). Average age 40. In 2010, 26 master's awarded. *Degree requirements:* For master's, thesis. *Application deadline:* Applications are processed on a rolling basis. Application fee: $50. Electronic applications accepted. *Expenses:* Tuition: Full-time $16,430; part-time $685 per credit hour. Required fees: $174; $44 per term. Tuition and fees vary according to course load, degree level and program. *Financial support:* Career-related internships or fieldwork and tuition waivers available. Financial award applicants required to submit FAFSA. *Unit head:* Dr. Brian Webb, Program Director, 802-828-8777, E-mail: brian.webb@tui.edu. *Application contact:* Diane Robinson, Director of Admissions, 888-828-8575, E-mail: diane.robinson@myunion.edu.

Union University, Institute for International and Intercultural Studies, Jackson, TN 38305-3697. Offers MAIS. Part-time and evening/weekend programs available. *Degree requirements:* For master's, capstone course. *Entrance requirements:* For master's, GRE, minimum undergraduate GPA of 3.0, 3 letters of reference. Additional exam requirements/recommendations for international students: Required—TOEFL (minimum score 560 paper-based; 220 computer-based). Electronic applications accepted. *Faculty research:* International education, ethnographic field research, intercultural training for professionals and students, language and culture.

University at Buffalo, the State University of New York, Graduate School, College of Arts and Sciences, Program in Caribbean Cultural Studies, Buffalo, NY 14260. Offers MAH. *Unit head:* Dr. Bruce D. McCombe, Dean, 716-645-2711, Fax: 716-645-3888, E-mail: cas-dean@buffalo.edu. *Application contact:* Joseph C. Syracuse, Graduate Enrollment Manager, 716-645-2711, Fax: 716-645-3888, E-mail: jcs32@buffalo.edu.

University of Alaska Fairbanks, College of Liberal Arts, Department of Alaska Native Studies, Fairbanks, AK 99775-6300. Offers cross cultural studies (MA). *Faculty:* 4 full-time (1 woman), 1 part-time/adjunct (0 women). *Students:* 2 full-time (0 women), 4 part-time (3 women); includes 2 minority (both American Indian or Alaska Native, non-Hispanic/Latino). Average age 39. 5 applicants, 80% accepted, 4 enrolled. In 2010, 2 master's awarded. *Degree requirements:* For master's, comprehensive exam. *Entrance requirements:* Additional exam requirements/recommendations for international students: Required—TOEFL (minimum score 550 paper-based; 213 computer-based; 80 iBT). *Application deadline:* For fall admission, 6/1 for domestic students, 3/1 for international students; for spring admission, 10/15 for domestic students, 9/1 for international students. Applications are processed on a rolling basis. Application fee: $60. Electronic applications accepted. *Expenses:* Tuition, state resident: full-time $5688; part-time $316 per credit. Tuition, nonresident: full-time $11,628; part-time $646 per credit. Required fees: $289 per semester. Tuition and fees vary according to course load and reciprocity agreements. *Financial support:* Fellowships with tuition reimbursements, research assistantships with tuition reimbursements, teaching assistantships with tuition reimbursements, Federal Work-Study, scholarships/grants, health care benefits, and unspecified assistantships available. Support available to part-time students. Financial award application deadline: 7/1; financial award applicants required to submit FAFSA. *Faculty research:* Alaska native literature, oral traditions, history, law and policy; Alaska native cultures, art, native American religion and philosophy. Total annual research expenditures: $80,856. *Unit head:* Miranda Wright, Director, 907-474-6528, Fax: 907-474-6325, E-mail: fydanrd@uaf.edu. *Application contact:* Miranda Wright, Director, 907-474-6528, Fax: 907-474-6325, E-mail: fydanrd@uaf.edu.

University of California, Davis, Graduate Studies, Graduate Group in Cultural Studies, Davis, CA 95616. Offers MA, PhD. *Degree requirements:* For master's, thesis; for doctorate, thesis/dissertation. *Entrance requirements:* For doctorate, GRE. Additional exam requirements/recommendations for international students: Required—TOEFL (minimum score 550 paper-based; 213 computer-based). Electronic applications accepted.

University of California, Irvine, School of Humanities, Program in Culture and Theory, Irvine, CA 92697. Offers PhD. *Students:* 9 full-time (7 women); includes 5 minority (1 Black or African American, non-Hispanic/Latino; 4 Asian, non-Hispanic/Latino), 1 international. Average age 28. Application fee: $80 ($100 for international students). *Unit head:* Arlene Keizer, Director, 949-824-0718, Fax: 949-824-2916, E-mail: akeizer@uci.edu. *Application contact:* Janette Jovel, Program Administrator, 949-824-0578, E-mail: jjovel@uci.edu.

University of California, Santa Barbara, Graduate Division, College of Letters and Sciences, Division of Social Sciences, Department of Global and International Studies, Santa Barbara, CA 93106-7065. Offers global culture and religion (MA); global government and human rights (MA); political economy, sustainable development, and the environment (MA). *Faculty:* 14 full-time (5 women), 4 part-time/adjunct (1 woman). *Students:* 37 full-time (25 women); includes 6 Asian, non-Hispanic/Latino; 2 Hispanic/Latino; 1 Native Hawaiian or other Pacific Islander, non-Hispanic/Latino. Average age 28. 55 applicants, 42% accepted, 12 enrolled. In 2010, 14 master's awarded. *Degree requirements:* For master's, one foreign language, thesis or alternative, 2 years of a second language. *Entrance requirements:* For master's, GRE, 2 years of a second language with minimum B grade, 3 letters of recommendation, resume/curriculum vitae. Additional exam requirements/recommendations for international students: Required—TOEFL (minimum score 600 paper-based; 80 iBT), IELTS (minimum score 7). *Application deadline:* For fall admission, 12/15 for domestic and international students. Application fee: $70 ($90 for international students). Electronic applications accepted. *Financial support:* In 2010–11, 36 students received support, including 29 fellowships with partial tuition reimbursements available (averaging $6,805 per year), 31 teaching assistantships with partial tuition reimbursements available (averaging $8,175 per year); career-related internships or fieldwork also available. Financial award application deadline: 12/15; financial award applicants required to submit FAFSA. *Faculty research:* Global culture religion, global governance human rights, political economy, environment, sustainable development. Total annual research expenditures: $240,000. *Unit head:* Prof. Giles Gunn, Chair, 805-893-4299, Fax: 805-893-8003, E-mail: ggunn@global.ucsb.edu. *Application contact:* Jessea Gay Marie, Graduate Program Advisor/Internship Assistance Officer, 805-893-4668, Fax: 805-893-8003, E-mail: gd-global@global.ucsb.edu.

University of Denver, Division of Arts, Humanities and Social Sciences, Department of Media, Film and Journalism Studies, Denver, CO 80208. Offers advertising management (MS); digital media studies (MA); international and intercultural communication (MA); media, film, and journalism studies (MA); strategic communication (MS). Part-time programs available. *Faculty:* 14 full-time (7 women), 5 part-time/adjunct (3 women). *Students:* 28 full-time (24 women), 36 part-time (26 women); includes 12 minority (1 Black or African American, non-Hispanic/Latino; 3 Asian, non-Hispanic/Latino; 6 Hispanic/Latino; 2 Two or more races, non-Hispanic/Latino), 2 international. Average age 26. 155 applicants, 58% accepted, 32 enrolled. In 2010, 36 master's awarded. *Degree requirements:* For master's, thesis (for some programs). *Entrance requirements:* For master's, GRE General Test. Additional exam requirements/recommendations for international students: Required—TOEFL (minimum score 550 paper-based; 80 iBT). *Application deadline:* Applications are processed on a rolling basis. Application fee: $60. Electronic applications accepted. *Expenses:* Tuition: Full-time $35,604; part-time $29,670 per year. Required fees: $687 per year. Tuition and fees vary according to program. *Financial support:* In 2010–11, 4 teaching assistantships with full and partial tuition reimbursements (averaging $14,000 per year) were awarded; career-related internships or fieldwork, Federal Work-Study, institutionally sponsored loans, scholarships/grants, and unspecified assistantships also available. Support available to part-time students. Financial award application deadline: 3/1; financial award applicants required to submit FAFSA. *Faculty research:* Youth and civic engagement. *Unit head:* Dr. Renee Botta, Chair, 303-871-7918, Fax: 303-871-4949, E-mail: rbotta@du.edu. *Application contact:* Information Contact, 303-871-2166, E-mail: mfjs@du.edu.

University of Denver, University College, Denver, CO 80208. Offers arts and culture (MLS, Certificate), including art, literature, and culture, arts development and program management (Certificate), creative writing; environmental policy and management (MAS, Certificate), including energy and sustainability (Certificate), environmental assessment of nuclear power (Certificate), environmental health and safety (Certificate), environmental management, natural resource management (Certificate); geographic information systems (MAS, Certificate); global affairs (MLS, Certificate), including translation studies, world history and culture; healthcare leadership (MPH, Certificate), including healthcare policy, law, and ethics, medical and healthcare information technologies, strategic management of healthcare; information and communications technology (MCIS, Certificate), including database design and administration (Certificate), geographic information systems (MCIS), information security systems security (Certificate), information systems security (MCIS), project management (MCIS, MPS, Certificate), software design and administration (Certificate), software design and programming (MCIS), technology management, telecommunications technology (MCIS), Web design and development; leadership

Cultural Studies

University of Denver (continued)

and organizations (MPS, Certificate), including human capital in organizations, philanthropic leadership, project management (MCIS, MPS, Certificate), strategic innovation and change; organizational and professional communication (MPS, Certificate), including alternative dispute resolution, organizational communication, organizational development and training, public relations and marketing; security management (MAS, Certificate), including emergency planning and response, information security (MAS), organizational security; strategic human resource management (MPS, Certificate), including global human resources (MPS), human resource management and development (MPS). Part-time and evening/weekend programs available. Postbaccalaureate distance learning degree programs offered (no on-campus study). *Faculty:* 7 full-time (2 women), 212 part-time/adjunct (83 women). *Students:* 52 full-time (19 women), 1,044 part-time (625 women); includes 196 minority (81 Black or African American, non-Hispanic/Latino; 7 American Indian or Alaska Native, non-Hispanic/Latino; 30 Asian, non-Hispanic/Latino; 66 Hispanic/Latino; 3 Native Hawaiian or other Pacific Islander, non-Hispanic/Latino; 9 Two or more races, non-Hispanic/Latino), 76 international. Average age 36. 488 applicants, 91% accepted, 339 enrolled. In 2010, 286 master's, 130 other advanced degrees awarded. *Entrance requirements:* Additional exam requirements/recommendations for international students: Required—TOEFL (minimum score 550 paper-based; 80 iBT). *Application deadline:* For fall admission, 6/22 priority date for domestic students, 6/10 priority date for international students; for winter admission, 9/15 priority date for domestic students, 9/6 priority date for international students; for spring admission, 2/3 priority date for domestic students, 12/15 priority date for international students. Applications are processed on a rolling basis. Application fee: $75. Electronic applications accepted. *Expenses:* Contact institution. *Financial support:* Applicants required to submit FAFSA. *Unit head:* Dr. James Davis, Dean, 303-871-2291, Fax: 303-871-4047, E-mail: jdavis@du.edu. *Application contact:* Information Contact, 303-871-3155, Fax: 303-871-4047, E-mail: ucolinfo@du.edu.

University of Hawaii at Hilo, Program in Hawaiian and Indigenous Language and Cultural Revitalization, Hilo, HI 96720-4091. Offers PhD.

University of Hawaii at Hilo, Program in Indigenous Language and Culture Education, Hilo, HI 96720-4091. Offers MA.

University of Hawaii at Manoa, Graduate Division, International Cultural Studies Graduate Certificate Program, Honolulu, HI 96822. Offers Graduate Certificate. Part-time programs available. *Students:* 15 full-time (10 women), 3 part-time (0 women); includes 7 minority (1 American Indian or Alaska Native, non-Hispanic/Latino; 1 Asian, non-Hispanic/Latino; 1 Hispanic/Latino; 2 Native Hawaiian or other Pacific Islander, non-Hispanic/Latino; 2 Two or more races, non-Hispanic/Latino), 5 international. Average age 34. 20 applicants, 70% accepted, 8 enrolled. In 2010, 10 Graduate Certificates awarded. *Entrance requirements:* For degree, GRE General Test. Additional exam requirements/recommendations for international students: Required—TOEFL (minimum score 540 paper-based; 207 computer-based; 76 iBT), IELTS (minimum score 5). *Application deadline:* For fall admission, 3/1 for domestic and international students; for spring admission, 9/1 for domestic and international students. Application fee: $50. *Financial support:* In 2010–11, 3 fellowships (averaging $1,325 per year), 3 research assistantships (averaging $17,496 per year), 5 teaching assistantships (averaging $15,438 per year) were awarded. *Application contact:* Wimal Dissanayake, Graduate Chairperson, 808-944-7593, Fax: 808-956-4733, E-mail: ddissa@yahoo.edu.

University of Houston, College of Liberal Arts and Social Sciences, Department of Modern and Classical Languages, Houston, TX 77204. Offers world cultures and literatures (MA). *Faculty:* 11 full-time (6 women), 4 part-time/adjunct (all women). *Students:* 1 (woman) part-time. Average age 29. 7 applicants, 29% accepted, 1 enrolled. *Degree requirements:* For master's, one foreign language, thesis optional. *Entrance requirements:* For master's, GRE General Test, minimum GPA of 3.0 in last 60 hours of course work. Additional exam requirements/recommendations for international students: Required—TOEFL (minimum score 500 paper-based). *Application deadline:* For fall admission, 4/15 for domestic and international students; for spring admission, 11/1 for domestic and international students. Applications are processed on a rolling basis. Electronic applications accepted. *Expenses:* Tuition, state resident: full-time $8592; part-time $358 per credit hour. Tuition, nonresident: full-time $16,032; part-time $668 per credit hour. Required fees: $2889. Tuition and fees vary according to course load and program. *Financial support:* In 2010–11, 2 teaching assistantships with full tuition reimbursements (averaging $9,060 per year) were awarded; career-related internships or fieldwork, Federal Work-Study, institutionally sponsored loans, scholarships/grants, health care benefits, and unspecified assistantships also available. Support available to part-time students. Financial award applicants required to submit FAFSA. *Unit head:* Dr. Hildegard Glass, Chairperson, 713-743-8350, Fax: 713-743-2693, E-mail: hfglass@uh.edu. *Application contact:* Alessandro Carrera, 713-743-3069, E-mail: alessandro.carrera@mail.uh.edu.

University of Houston–Clear Lake, School of Human Sciences and Humanities, Programs in Human Sciences, Houston, TX 77058-1098. Offers behavioral sciences (MA), including criminology, cross cultural studies, general psychology, sociology; clinical psychology (MA); criminology (MA); cross cultural studies (MA); family therapy (MA); fitness and human performance (MA); school psychology (MA). *Accreditation:* AAMFT/COAMFTE. Part-time and evening/weekend programs available. Postbaccalaureate distance learning degree programs offered (minimal on-campus study). *Degree requirements:* For master's, thesis or alternative. *Entrance requirements:* For master's, GRE General Test. Additional exam requirements/recommendations for international students: Required—TOEFL (minimum score 550 paper-based; 213 computer-based). Electronic applications accepted. *Faculty research:* Smoking cessation, adolescent sexuality, white collar crime, serial murder, human factors/human computer interaction.

The University of Manchester, School of Arts, Histories and Cultures, Manchester, United Kingdom. Offers anthropology, media and performance (PhD); applied theatre professional (PhD); archaeology (PhD); art history and visual studies (PhD); arts management and cultural policy (PhD); classics and ancient history (PhD); composition (PhD); creative writing (PhD); drama (PhD); economic and social history (PhD); electroacoustic composition (PhD); English and American studies (PhD); history (PhD); humanitarianism and conflict response (PhD); museology (PhD); music (PhD); musicology (PhD); religions and theology (PhD).

The University of Manchester, School of Languages, Linguistics and Cultures, Manchester, United Kingdom. Offers Arab world studies (PhD); Chinese studies (M Phil, PhD); East Asian studies (M Phil, PhD); English language (PhD); French studies (M Phil, PhD); German studies (M Phil, PhD); interpreting studies (PhD); Italian studies (M Phil, PhD); Japanese studies (M Phil, PhD); Latin American cultural studies (M Phil, PhD); linguistics (M Phil, PhD); Middle Eastern studies (M Phil, PhD); Polish studies (M Phil, PhD); Portuguese studies (M Phil, PhD); Russian studies (M Phil, PhD); Spanish studies (M Phil, PhD); translation and intercultural studies (M Phil, PhD).

The University of Manchester, School of Social Sciences, Manchester, United Kingdom. Offers ethnographic documentary (M Phil); interdisciplinary study of culture (PhD); philosophy (PhD); politics (PhD); social anthropology (PhD); social anthropology with visual media (PhD); social change (PhD); social statistics (PhD); sociology (PhD); visual anthropology (M Phil).

University of Minnesota, Twin Cities Campus, Graduate School, College of Liberal Arts, Department of Cultural Studies and Comparative Literature, Program in Comparative Studies in Discourse and Society, Minneapolis, MN 55455-0213. Offers PhD. *Degree requirements:* For doctorate, 2 foreign languages, thesis/dissertation. *Entrance requirements:* For doctorate, GRE General Test, sample of written work. Additional exam requirements/recommendations for international students: Required—TOEFL. *Faculty research:* Cultural theory; music; architecture, space, and urbanism; body and gender; film and popular culture.

University of Missouri–St. Louis, College of Arts and Sciences, Interdisciplinary Programs, St. Louis, MO 63121. Offers gender studies (Certificate); international studies (Certificate).

Expenses: Tuition, state resident: full-time $5522; part-time $306.80 per credit hour. Tuition, nonresident: full-time $14,253; part-time $792.10 per credit hour. Required fees: $658; $49 per credit hour. One-time fee: $12. Tuition and fees vary according to program. *Unit head:* Dr. Ronald Yasbin, Dean, 314-516-5501. *Application contact:* Graduate Admissions, 314-516-5458, Fax: 314-516-6996, E-mail: gradadm@umsl.edu.

University of Pittsburgh, Program in Cultural Studies, Pittsburgh, PA 15260. Offers Certificate. *Expenses:* Tuition, state resident: full-time $17,304; part-time $701 per credit. Tuition, nonresident: full-time $29,554; part-time $1210 per credit. Required fees: $740; $214 per term. Tuition and fees vary according to program. *Financial support:* In 2010–11, 2 fellowships were awarded. *Application contact:* Information Contact, 412-624-4141, E-mail: graduate@pitt.edu.

University of Pittsburgh, School of Arts and Sciences, Department of English, Pittsburgh, PA 15260. Offers cultural and critical studies (PhD); English (MA); writing (MFA). Part-time programs available. *Faculty:* 51 full-time (26 women), 1 (woman) part-time/adjunct. *Students:* 117 full-time (79 women), 28 part-time (21 women); includes 15 minority (1 Black or African American, non-Hispanic/Latino; 5 Asian, non-Hispanic/Latino; 4 Hispanic/Latino; 5 Two or more races, non-Hispanic/Latino), 10 international. Average age 29. 344 applicants, 16% accepted, 17 enrolled. In 2010, 22 master's, 10 doctorates awarded. *Degree requirements:* For master's, one foreign language; for doctorate, 2 foreign languages, comprehensive exam, thesis/dissertation. *Entrance requirements:* For master's and doctorate, GRE General Test, writing sample. Additional exam requirements/recommendations for international students: Required—TOEFL (minimum score 550 paper-based; 213 computer-based; 80 iBT). *Application deadline:* For fall admission, 12/10 for domestic and international students. Application fee: $50. Electronic applications accepted. *Expenses:* Tuition, state resident: full-time $17,304; part-time $701 per credit. Tuition, nonresident: full-time $29,554; part-time $1210 per credit. Required fees: $740; $214 per term. Tuition and fees vary according to program. *Financial support:* In 2010–11, 100 students received support, including 22 fellowships with full tuition reimbursements available (averaging $17,822 per year), 5 research assistantships with full and partial tuition reimbursements available (averaging $12,300 per year), 70 teaching assistantships with full tuition reimbursements available (averaging $15,065 per year); Federal Work-Study, tuition waivers (full and partial), and unspecified assistantships also available. Financial award application deadline: 12/12. *Faculty research:* Cultural studies, literary history and theory, film, composition. *Unit head:* Dr. H. David Brumble, Chair, 412-624-6509, Fax: 412-624-6639, E-mail: brumble@pitt.edu. *Application contact:* Duane Walsh, Graduate Administrator, 412-624-6549, Fax: 412-624-6639, E-mail: engrad@pitt.edu.

University of Rochester, School of Arts and Sciences, Department of Modern Languages and Cultures, Rochester, NY 14627.

University of Southern California, Graduate School, Dana and David Dornsife College of Letters, Arts and Sciences, Comparative Studies in Literature and Culture Doctoral Program, Los Angeles, CA 90089. Offers comparative literature (PhD); comparative media and culture (PhD); Spanish and Latin American studies (PhD). *Faculty:* 16 full-time (7 women). *Students:* 27 full-time (17 women), 1 part-time (0 women); includes 6 minority (2 Black or African American, non-Hispanic/Latino; 2 Asian, non-Hispanic/Latino; 2 Hispanic/Latino), 6 international. In 2010, 1 doctorate awarded. *Median time to degree:* Of those who began their doctoral program in fall 2002, 50% received their degree in 8 years or less. *Degree requirements:* For doctorate, 2 foreign languages, comprehensive exam, thesis/dissertation. *Entrance requirements:* For doctorate, GRE, competence in language other than English (highly recommended). Additional exam requirements/recommendations for international students: Required—TOEFL. *Application deadline:* For fall admission, 12/1 priority date for domestic and international students. Application fee: $85. Electronic applications accepted. *Expenses:* Tuition: Full-time $31,240; part-time $1420 per unit. Required fees: $600. One-time fee: $35 full-time. Full-time tuition and fees vary according to degree level and program. *Financial support:* In 2010–11, 25 students received support, including 8 fellowships with full tuition reimbursements available (averaging $51,000 per year), 17 teaching assistantships with full tuition reimbursements available (averaging $51,000 per year). Financial award applicants required to submit FAFSA. *Faculty research:* Literary theory, Japanese film and contemporary fiction, Francophone literature and cinema, Latin American and Caribbean literature, Spanish literature and film, nineteenth and twentieth century British and American literature. *Unit head:* Prof. Peggy Kamuf, Director of Comparative Studies in Literature and Culture Doctoral Program, 213-740-0101, Fax: 213-740-8058, E-mail: kamuf@usc.edu. *Application contact:* Katherine Guevarra, Administrative Assistant, 213-740-0102, Fax: 213-740-0858, E-mail: kguevarr@usc.edu.

The University of Texas at San Antonio, College of Education and Human Development, Department of Bicultural and Bilingual Studies, San Antonio, TX 78249-0617. Offers bicultural-bilingual studies (MA); culture, literacy, and language (PhD); teaching English as a second language (MA). Part-time and evening/weekend programs available. *Faculty:* 13 full-time (8 women). *Students:* 61 full-time (46 women), 101 part-time (79 women); includes 95 minority (2 Black or African American, non-Hispanic/Latino; 7 Asian, non-Hispanic/Latino; 84 Hispanic/Latino; 1 Native Hawaiian or other Pacific Islander, non-Hispanic/Latino; 1 Two or more races, non-Hispanic/Latino), 21 international. Average age 37. 100 applicants, 81% accepted, 48 enrolled. In 2010, 37 master's, 6 doctorates awarded. *Degree requirements:* For master's, comprehensive exam (for some programs), thesis (for some programs); for doctorate, comprehensive exam, thesis/dissertation. *Entrance requirements:* For master's and doctorate, GRE General Test. Additional exam requirements/recommendations for international students: Required—TOEFL (minimum score 500 paper-based; 173 computer-based; 61 iBT), IELTS (minimum score 5). *Application deadline:* For fall admission, 7/1 for domestic students, 4/1 for international students; for spring admission, 11/1 for domestic students, 9/1 for international students. Applications are processed on a rolling basis. Application fee: $45 ($80 for international students). Electronic applications accepted. *Expenses:* Tuition, state resident: full-time $4172; part-time $231.75 per credit hour. Tuition, nonresident: full-time $15,332; part-time $851.75 per credit hour. *Financial support:* In 2010–11, 24 students received support, including 9 research assistantships (averaging $11,844 per year), 17 teaching assistantships (averaging $7,250 per year); career-related internships or fieldwork and tuition waivers also available. Support available to part-time students. *Faculty research:* Globalization, migration and immigrant education, integrating language and content in PK-12 instruction, language and cultural policies in multilingual societies, multiple literacies. *Unit head:* Dr. Robert Milk, Chair, 210-458-4426, Fax: 210-458-5962, E-mail: robert.milk@utsa.edu. *Application contact:* Veronica Ramirez, Assistant Dean of the Graduate School, 210-458-4330, Fax: 210-458-4332, E-mail: graduatestudies@utsa.edu.

University of the Sacred Heart, Graduate Programs, Department of Communication, Program in Contemporary Culture and Media, San Juan, PR 00914-0383. Offers MA. *Degree requirements:* For master's, thesis.

University of Washington, Bothell, Program in Cultural Studies, Bothell, WA 98011-8246. Offers MA. Evening/weekend programs available. *Faculty:* 9 full-time (5 women), 5 part-time/adjunct (1 woman). *Students:* 30 full-time (22 women), 1 (woman) part-time; includes 2 Black or African American, non-Hispanic/Latino; 1 American Indian or Alaska Native, non-Hispanic/Latino; 4 Asian, non-Hispanic/Latino; 2 Hispanic/Latino, 2 international. Average age 33. 39 applicants, 62% accepted, 18 enrolled. In 2010, 14 master's awarded. *Degree requirements:* For master's, thesis. *Entrance requirements:* Additional exam requirements/recommendations for international students: Required—TOEFL. *Application deadline:* For fall admission, 2/1 for domestic and international students. Application fee: $65. Electronic applications accepted. *Expenses:* Tuition, state resident: full-time $10,870; part-time $518 per quarter hour. Tuition, nonresident: full-time $24,210; part-time $1153 per quarter hour. Required fees: $495; $24 per quarter hour. Part-time tuition and fees vary according to course load, program and student level. *Financial support:* In 2010–11, 9 students received support, including 5 fellowships (averaging $1,000 per year), 1 research assistantship (averaging $1,000 per year); Federal Work-Study and unspecified assistantships also available. *Unit head:* Prof. Bruce Burgett,

Director, 425-352-5452, Fax: 425-352-3462, E-mail: bburgett@uwb.edu. *Application contact:* Andrew Brusletten, Program Manager, 425-352-5427, Fax: 425-352-3462, E-mail: abrusletten@uwb.edu.

Washington State University, Graduate School, The Edward R. Murrow College of Communication, Pullman, WA 99164-2520. Offers health communications (MA, PhD); intercultural and international communications (MA, PhD); media and society (MA, PhD); media process and effects (MA, PhD); organizational communications (MA, PhD). *Faculty:* 30. *Students:* 43 full-time (26 women), 6 part-time (4 women); includes 1 Asian, non-Hispanic/Latino; 1 Hispanic/Latino, 19 international. Average age 30. 120 applicants, 22% accepted, 19 enrolled. In 2010, 22 master's, 1 doctorate awarded. *Degree requirements:* For master's, comprehensive exam (for some programs), thesis optional, oral exam; for doctorate, comprehensive exam, thesis/dissertation. *Entrance requirements:* For master's, GRE General Test, minimum GPA of 3.25, 3 letters of recommendation; for doctorate, GRE General Test, minimum undergraduate GPA of 3.25, graduate 3.5; MA in communication; 3 letters of recommendation. Additional exam requirements/recommendations for international students: Required—TOEFL (minimum score 580 paper-based; 237 computer-based). *Application deadline:* For fall admission, 1/15 priority date for domestic students, 3/1 for international students. Applications are processed on a rolling basis. Application fee: $50. Electronic applications accepted. *Expenses:* Tuition, state resident: full-time $8552; part-time $443 per credit. Tuition, nonresident: full-time $21,650; part-time $1083 per credit. Required fees: $846. *Financial support:* In 2010–11, 46 students received support, including 2 fellowships (averaging $4,477 per year), 7 research assistantships with full and partial tuition reimbursements available (averaging $13,917 per year), 34 teaching assistantships with full and partial tuition reimbursements available (averaging $13,056 per year); career-related internships or fieldwork, Federal Work-Study, institutionally sponsored loans, tuition waivers (partial), and teaching associateships also available. Financial award application deadline: 4/1; financial award applicants required to submit FAFSA. *Faculty research:* Advocacy communication, mediated communication in decision making, communication technology policy and effects, multicultural and international psychology and physiology of communication. Total annual research expenditures: $550,455. *Unit head:* Dr. Erica Austin, Interim Director, 509-335-1556, E-mail: eaustin@wsu.edu. *Application contact:* Graduate School Admissions, 800-GRADWSU, Fax: 509-335-1949, E-mail: gradsch@wsu.edu.

Wheaton College, Graduate School, Department of Intercultural Studies, Wheaton, IL 60187-5593. Offers evangelism (MA); intercultural studies (MA); intercultural studies/teaching English as a second language (MA); missions (MA); teaching English as a second language (Certificate). Part-time programs available. *Degree requirements:* For master's, thesis or alternative. *Entrance requirements:* For master's, GRE General Test, MAT. Electronic applications accepted.

Wilfrid Laurier University, Faculty of Graduate and Postdoctoral Studies, Faculty of Arts, Cultural Analysis and Social Theory Program, Waterloo, ON N2L 3C5, Canada. Offers body politics (MA); cultural representation and social theory (MA); gender, sexuality and embodiment (MA); globalization, identity and social movements (MA). Part-time programs available. *Faculty:* 16 full-time (10 women). *Students:* 9 full-time (6 women), 2 part-time (both women). 23 applicants, 61% accepted, 7 enrolled. In 2010, 4 master's awarded. *Entrance requirements:* For master's, honours BA in humanities, social science or interdisciplinary program with social theory, minimum B+ in final year of full-time study. Additional exam requirements/recommendations for international students: Required—TOEFL (minimum score 89 iBT). *Application deadline:* For fall admission, 2/1 priority date for domestic and international students. Application fee: $100. Electronic applications accepted. Tuition and fees charges are reported in Canadian dollars. *Expenses:* Tuition, area resident: Full-time $15,300 Canadian dollars; part-time $1200 Canadian dollars per credit. International tuition: $21,300 Canadian dollars full-time. Required fees: $650 Canadian dollars; $100 Canadian dollars per credit. Tuition and fees vary according to course load, degree level, campus/location and program. *Financial support:* Career-related internships or fieldwork, scholarships/grants, and unspecified assistantships available. *Faculty research:* Globalization; identity and social movements; body politics: gender, sexuality and embodiment; cultural representation and social theory. *Unit head:* Dr. Jasmin Zine, Director, 519-884-0710 Ext. 3267, Fax: 519-884-8854, E-mail: jzine@wlu.ca. *Application contact:* Jennifer Williams, Graduate Admission and Records Officer, 519-884-0710 Ext. 3536, Fax: 519-884-1020, E-mail: gradstudies@wlu.ca.

Wilfrid Laurier University, Faculty of Graduate and Postdoctoral Studies, Faculty of Arts, Department of Communication Studies, Waterloo, ON N2L 3C5, Canada. Offers media, technology and culture (MA); visual communication and culture (MA). *Faculty:* 16 full-time (7 women). *Students:* 15 full-time (all women), 1 (woman) part-time, 1 international. 32 applicants, 56% accepted, 10 enrolled. In 2010, 7 master's awarded. *Degree requirements:* For master's, thesis optional. *Entrance requirements:* For master's, honours BA in communication studies or a cognate discipline from an approved university with a minimum B+ overall in last two years of study and in undergraduate major. Additional exam requirements/recommendations for international students: Required—TOEFL (minimum score 89 iBT). *Application deadline:* For fall admission, 2/1 priority date for domestic students, 2/1 for international students. Application fee: $100. Electronic applications accepted. Tuition and fees charges are reported in Canadian dollars. *Expenses:* Tuition, area resident: Full-time $15,300 Canadian dollars; part-time $1200 Canadian dollars per credit. International tuition: $21,300 Canadian dollars full-time. Required fees: $650 Canadian dollars; $100 Canadian dollars per credit. Tuition and fees vary according to course load, degree level, campus/location and program. *Financial support:* In 2010–11, 21 fellowships, 21 teaching assistantships were awarded; career-related internships or fieldwork, scholarships/grants, health care benefits, and unspecified assistantships also available. *Faculty research:* Visual communication and culture, media, technology and culture. *Unit head:* Dr. Martin Morris, Graduate Coordinator, 519-884-0710 Ext. 3015, E-mail: mmorris@wlu.ca. *Application contact:* Jennifer Williams, Graduate Admissions and Records Officer, 519-884-0710 Ext. 3536, Fax: 519-884-1020, E-mail: gradstudies@wlu.ca.

Wilfrid Laurier University, Faculty of Graduate and Postdoctoral Studies, Faculty of Arts, Department of English and Film Studies, Waterloo, ON N2L 3C5, Canada. Offers gender and genre (MA, PhD); nation, diaspora, culture (PhD); textuality, media and print studies (PhD). *Faculty:* 22 full-time (14 women). *Students:* 29 full-time (16 women), 1 (woman) part-time. 71 applicants, 48% accepted, 18 enrolled. In 2010, 15 master's, 2 doctorates awarded. *Degree requirements:* For master's, thesis optional; for doctorate, thesis/dissertation. *Entrance requirements:* For master's, honours BA or the equivalent in English, minimum B+ in English courses above first year level; for doctorate, MA in English, minimum A- average in graduate work. Additional exam requirements/recommendations for international students: Recommended—TOEFL (minimum score 89 iBT). *Application deadline:* For fall admission, 2/1 priority date for domestic and international students. Application fee: $100. Electronic applications accepted. Tuition and fees charges are reported in Canadian dollars. *Expenses:* Tuition, area resident: Full-time $15,300 Canadian dollars; part-time $1200 Canadian dollars per credit. International tuition: $21,300 Canadian dollars full-time. Required fees: $650 Canadian dollars; $100 Canadian dollars per credit. Tuition and fees vary according to course load, degree level, campus/location and program. *Financial support:* In 2010–11, 44 fellowships, 44 teaching assistantships were awarded; career-related internships or fieldwork, scholarships/grants, health care benefits, and unspecified assistantships also available. *Faculty research:* Gender and genre, Canadian studies, early modern studies, postcolonial studies, nineteenth century studies. *Unit head:* Dr. Tanis MacDonald, Graduate Coordinator, 519-884-0710 Ext. 2931, Fax: 519-884-8307, E-mail: tmacdonald@wlu.ca. *Application contact:* Jennifer Williams, Graduate Admissions and Records Officer, 519-884-0710 Ext. 3536, Fax: 519-884-1020, E-mail: gradstudies@wlu.ca.

East European and Russian Studies

Boston College, Graduate School of Arts and Sciences, Department of Slavic and Eastern Languages, Program in Slavic Studies, Chestnut Hill, MA 02467-3800. Offers MA, MA/JD, MBA/MA. Part-time programs available. *Degree requirements:* For master's, 3 foreign languages, comprehensive exam, thesis or alternative. *Entrance requirements:* Additional exam requirements/recommendations for international students: Required—TOEFL (minimum score 600 paper-based; 250 computer-based; 100 iBT). Electronic applications accepted.

Brown University, Graduate School, Department of Slavic Languages, Providence, RI 02912. Offers Russian language and literature (AM); Slavic languages (AM); Slavic studies (PhD). *Degree requirements:* For master's, one foreign language; for doctorate, 2 foreign languages, thesis/dissertation, preliminary exam.

Carleton University, Faculty of Graduate Studies, Faculty of Public Affairs and Management, Institute of European and Russian Studies, Ottawa, ON K1S 5B6, Canada. Offers European and European Union studies (MA); European integration studies (Diploma); Russian, Eurasian and transition studies (MA). *Degree requirements:* For master's, one foreign language, thesis optional. *Entrance requirements:* For master's, honors degree or equivalent; 2 years of Russian, German or other central east European language. Additional exam requirements/recommendations for international students: Required—TOEFL. *Faculty research:* East-West relations, minority rights in Russia and Eastern Europe.

Columbia University, Graduate School of Arts and Sciences, Program in Russian, Eurasian and East European Regional Studies, New York, NY 10027. Offers MA. Part-time programs available.

Columbia University, School of International and Public Affairs, The East Central Europe Center, New York, NY 10027. Offers Certificate. Students must be enrolled in a separate graduate degree program at Columbia University. Electronic applications accepted. *Faculty research:* Ethnic politics, modern East Central European history, post-Communist economic and political transitions, East Central European language and literature.

Columbia University, School of International and Public Affairs, The Harriman Institute, New York, NY 10027. Offers Certificate. Students must be enrolled in a separate graduate degree program at Columbia University. Part-time programs available. *Degree requirements:* For Certificate, one foreign language, thesis. *Entrance requirements:* For degree, minimum 2 years of Russian. Electronic applications accepted.

Cornell University, Graduate School, Graduate Fields of Arts and Sciences, Field of History, Ithaca, NY 14853-0001. Offers African history (MA, PhD); American history (MA, PhD); ancient history (MA, PhD); early modern European history (MA, PhD); English history (MA, PhD); French history (MA, PhD); German history (MA, PhD); history of science (MA, PhD); Latin American history (MA, PhD); medieval Chinese history (MA, PhD); medieval history (MA, PhD); modern Chinese history (MA, PhD); modern European history (MA, PhD); modern Japanese history (MA, PhD); premodern Islamic history (MA, PhD); premodern Japanese history (MA, PhD); Renaissance history (MA, PhD); Russian history (MA, PhD); Southeast Asian history (MA, PhD). *Faculty:* 53 full-time (15 women). *Students:* 59 full-time (30 women); includes 3 Black or African American, non-Hispanic/Latino; 2 Asian, non-Hispanic/Latino; 4 Hispanic/Latino, 22 international. Average age 30. 217 applicants, 6% accepted, 8 enrolled. In 2010, 9 master's, 5 doctorates awarded. Terminal master's awarded for partial completion of doctoral program. *Degree requirements:* For master's, thesis; for doctorate, 2 foreign languages, comprehensive exam, thesis/dissertation, 1 year of teaching experience. *Entrance requirements:* For master's and doctorate, GRE General Test, writing sample, 3 letters of recommendation. Additional exam requirements/recommendations for international students: Required—TOEFL (minimum score 550 paper-based; 213 computer-based; 77 iBT). *Application deadline:* For fall admission, 1/15 for domestic students. Application fee: $80. Electronic applications accepted. *Expenses:* Tuition: Full-time $29,500. Required fees: $76. Tuition and fees vary according to degree level and program. *Financial support:* In 2010–11, 26 fellowships with full tuition reimbursements, 27 teaching assistantships with full tuition reimbursements were awarded; research assistantships with full tuition reimbursements, institutionally sponsored loans, scholarships/grants, health care benefits, tuition waivers (full and partial), and unspecified assistantships also available. Financial award applicants required to submit FAFSA. *Unit head:* Director of Graduate Studies, 607-255-6738, Fax: 607-255-0469. *Application contact:* Graduate Field Assistant, 607-255-6738, Fax: 607-255-0469, E-mail: history_grad_info@cornell.edu.

Florida State University, The Graduate School, College of Social Sciences and Public Policy, Program in Russian and East European Studies, Tallahassee, FL 32306. Offers MA. Part-time programs available. *Students:* 4 full-time (2 women), 5 part-time (2 women); includes 1 Asian, non-Hispanic/Latino; 1 Hispanic/Latino. Average age 26. 9 applicants, 100% accepted, 1 enrolled. In 2010, 2 master's awarded. *Degree requirements:* For master's, one foreign language, comprehensive exam, thesis optional. *Entrance requirements:* For master's, GRE General Test, minimum GPA of 3.0. Additional exam requirements/recommendations for international students: Required—TOEFL (minimum score 550 paper-based; 213 computer-based; 80 iBT). *Application deadline:* For fall admission, 7/1 for domestic and international students; for spring admission, 11/1 for domestic and international students. Applications are processed on a rolling basis. Application fee: $30. Electronic applications accepted. *Expenses:* Tuition, state resident: full-time $8238.24. *Financial support:* In 2010–11, research assistantships with full tuition reimbursements (averaging $5,000 per year); fellowships, career-related internships or fieldwork, Federal Work-Study, institutionally sponsored loans, and unspecified assistantships also available. Financial award application deadline: 2/15; financial award applicants required to submit FAFSA. *Unit head:* Dr. Lee K. Metcalf, Director, 850-644-7327, Fax: 850-645-4981, E-mail: lmetcalf@fsu.edu. *Application contact:* Kaley Boggs, Academic Program Specialist, 850-644-4418, Fax: 850-645-4981, E-mail: kboggs@fsu.edu.

Georgetown University, Graduate School of Arts and Sciences, Program in Russian and East European Studies, Washington, DC 20057. Offers MA, MA/JD, MA/PhD. *Degree requirements:* For master's, one foreign language, comprehensive exam, thesis optional. *Entrance requirements:* For master's, GRE General Test. Additional exam requirements/recommendations for international students: Required—TOEFL. *Faculty research:* East-West trade.

The George Washington University, Elliott School of International Affairs, Program in European and Eurasian Studies, Washington, DC 20052. Offers MA, JD/MA, MBA/MA. Part-time and evening/weekend programs available. *Students:* 13 full-time (8 women), 9 part-time (4 women); includes 1 American Indian or Alaska Native, non-Hispanic/Latino, 3 international. Average age 26. 48 applicants, 75% accepted, 8 enrolled. In 2010, 9 master's awarded. *Degree requirements:* For master's, one foreign language, capstone project. *Entrance requirements:* For master's, GRE General Test, 2 years (or the equivalent) of a modern European language or Russian, 2 semesters of introductory economics (macro or micro). Additional exam requirements/recommendations for international students: Required—TOEFL. *Application*

East European and Russian Studies

The George Washington University (continued)
deadline: For fall admission, 2/1 for domestic students; for spring admission, 10/1 for domestic students. Application fee: $60. Electronic applications accepted. *Financial support:* In 2010–11, 3 students received support; fellowships with tuition reimbursements available, research assistantships with tuition reimbursements available, career-related internships or fieldwork, Federal Work-Study, institutionally sponsored loans, and tuition waivers available. Financial award application deadline: 1/15; financial award applicants required to submit FAFSA. *Faculty research:* NATO, European economics, European history, European Union. *Unit head:* Hope Harrison, Director, 202-994-5439, Fax: 202-994-5436, E-mail: hopeharr@gwu.edu. *Application contact:* Jeff V. Miles, Director of Graduate Admissions, 202-994-7050, Fax: 202-994-9537, E-mail: esiagrad@gwu.edu.

Harvard University, Graduate School of Arts and Sciences, Committee on Regional Studies-Russia, Eastern Europe, and Central Asia, Cambridge, MA 02138. Offers AM. *Degree requirements:* For master's, one foreign language. *Entrance requirements:* For master's, GRE General Test. Additional exam requirements/recommendations for international students: Required—TOEFL. *Expenses:* Tuition: Full-time $34,976. Required fees: $1166. Full-time tuition and fees vary according to program. *Faculty research:* Strategic policy, ethnography and demography of U.S.S.R., non-Russian nationality language training.

Indiana University Bloomington, University Graduate School, College of Arts and Sciences, Russian and East European Institute, Bloomington, IN 47405-7000. Offers MA, Certificate, MBA/MA, MIS/MA, MLS/MA, MPA/MA. Part-time programs available. *Students:* 25 full-time (14 women); includes 2 minority (1 Asian, non-Hispanic/Latino; 1 Hispanic/Latino). Average age 28. 40 applicants, 25% accepted, 8 enrolled. In 2010, 6 master's awarded. *Degree requirements:* For master's, one foreign language, essay, proficiency and written exams; for Certificate, one foreign language, oral and proficiency exams. *Entrance requirements:* For master's, GRE General Test, minimum 2 years of college Russian (Russian area studies); for Certificate, GRE General Test. Additional exam requirements/recommendations for international students: Required—TOEFL. *Application deadline:* For fall admission, 1/15 priority date for domestic students, 12/15 for international students; for spring admission, 9/1 priority date for domestic students, 9/1 for international students. Applications are processed on a rolling basis. Application fee: $55 ($65 for international students). *Financial support:* In 2010–11, 9 fellowships with tuition reimbursements (averaging $15,000 per year) were awarded; research assistantships, teaching assistantships, career-related internships or fieldwork, Federal Work-Study, and institutionally sponsored loans also available. Financial award application deadline: 2/15; financial award applicants required to submit FAFSA. *Faculty research:* Political and economic transition of former Soviet Union and eastern Europe, Russian and Soviet history, Slavic literature and linguistics, education and mass media of former Soviet Union and Eastern Europe. *Unit head:* David Ransel, Director, 812-855-7309, Fax: 812-855-6411, E-mail: ransel@indiana.edu. *Application contact:* Marianne Davis, Administrative Secretary, 812-855-3869, Fax: 812-855-6411, E-mail: marwdavi@indiana.edu.

La Salle University, School of Arts and Sciences, Central and Eastern European Studies Program, Philadelphia, PA 19141-1199. Offers MA. Part-time and evening/weekend programs available. *Degree requirements:* For master's, one foreign language, thesis or alternative. *Entrance requirements:* For master's, MAT. Additional exam requirements/recommendations for international students: Required—TOEFL. *Expenses:* Contact institution. *Faculty research:* Ukrainian culture, Russian studies, business in Central and Eastern European countries.

The Ohio State University, Graduate School, College of Arts and Sciences, Division of Arts and Humanities, Department of Slavic and East European Languages and Literatures, Columbus, OH 43210. Offers linguistics (MA); literature (MA); Russian literature (PhD); Slavic linguistics (PhD). *Faculty:* 13. *Students:* 21 full-time (12 women), 8 part-time (4 women); includes 1 Asian, non-Hispanic/Latino, 4 international. Average age 31. In 2010, 2 master's, 3 doctorates awarded. *Degree requirements:* For master's, variable foreign language requirement, thesis optional; for doctorate, variable foreign language requirement, thesis/dissertation. *Entrance requirements:* For master's and doctorate, GRE General Test. Additional exam requirements/recommendations for international students: Required—TOEFL (minimum score 600 paper-based; 250 computer-based). *Application deadline:* For fall admission, 8/15 priority date for domestic students, 7/1 priority date for international students; for winter admission, 12/1 priority date for domestic students, 11/1 priority date for international students; for spring admission, 3/1 priority date for domestic students, 2/1 priority date for international students. Applications are processed on a rolling basis. Application fee: $40 ($50 for international students). Electronic applications accepted. *Expenses:* Tuition, state resident: full-time $10,605. Tuition, nonresident: full-time $26,535. Tuition and fees vary according to course load and program. *Financial support:* Fellowships, research assistantships, teaching assistantships, Federal Work-Study and institutionally sponsored loans available. Support available to part-time students. *Faculty research:* Polish literature. *Unit head:* Helena Goscilo, Chair, 614-247-1790, E-mail: goscilo.1@osu.edu. *Application contact:* 614-292-9444, Fax: 614-292-3895, E-mail: domestic.grad@osu.edu.

Stanford University, School of Humanities and Sciences, Center for Russian and East European Studies, Stanford, CA 94305-9991. Offers MA. *Degree requirements:* For master's, one foreign language. *Entrance requirements:* For master's, GRE General Test. Additional exam requirements/recommendations for international students: Required—TOEFL. Electronic applications accepted. *Expenses:* Tuition: Full-time $38,700; part-time $860 per unit. One-time fee: $200 full-time.

University of Alberta, Faculty of Graduate Studies and Research, Department of Modern Languages and Cultural Studies, Edmonton, AB T6G 2E1, Canada. Offers applied linguistics (Germanic, Romance, Slavic) (MA); French language, literatures and linguistics (PhD); French language, literatures, and linguistics (MA); Germanic languages, literatures and linguistics (PhD); Germanic languages, literatures, and linguistics (MA); Italian studies (MA); Slavic languages and literatures (Russian, Ukrainian) (MA, PhD); Slavic linguistics (Russian, Ukrainian) (MA, PhD); Spanish and Latin American studies (MA, PhD); Ukrainian folklore (MA, PhD). Part-time programs available. *Degree requirements:* For master's, one foreign language, thesis; for doctorate, 2 foreign languages, comprehensive exam, thesis/dissertation. *Entrance requirements:* For master's and doctorate, 1 language other than English. Additional exam requirements/recommendations for international students: Required—Michigan English Language Assessment Battery or TOEFL (minimum score 550 paper-based; 213 computer-based). Electronic applications accepted. *Faculty research:* Russian/Ukrainian studies; German studies; contemporary Latin American, French and Francophone studies; Italian studies.

The University of British Columbia, Faculty of Arts and Faculty of Graduate Studies, Department of Central, Eastern and Northern European Studies, Vancouver, BC V6T2Z1, Canada. Offers Germanic studies (MA, PhD). Part-time programs available. *Degree requirements:* For master's, one foreign language, thesis optional, exam; for doctorate, comprehensive exam, thesis/dissertation. *Entrance requirements:* For master's, BA in German; for doctorate, MA in German. Additional exam requirements/recommendations for international students: Required—TOEFL (minimum score 550 paper-based; 213 computer-based). Electronic applications accepted. Tuition charges are reported in Canadian dollars. *Expenses:* Tuition, area resident: Full-time $4179 Canadian dollars. International tuition: $7344 Canadian dollars full-time. *Faculty research:* Second language acquisition, media theory, performance theory, gender studies, cultural studies.

University of Illinois at Urbana–Champaign, Graduate College, College of Liberal Arts and Sciences, Russian, East European and Eurasian Center, Champaign, IL 61820. Offers MA. *Students:* 6 full-time (4 women), 1 (woman) part-time. 19 applicants, 47% accepted, 2 enrolled. In 2010, 5 master's awarded. *Entrance requirements:* For master's, GRE, writing sample. Additional exam requirements/recommendations for international students: Required—TOEFL (minimum score 550 paper-based; 213 computer-based). *Application deadline:* Applications are processed on a rolling basis. Application fee: $75 ($90 for international students). Electronic applications accepted. *Financial support:* In 2010–11, 5 fellowships, 1 teaching assistantship were awarded; research assistantships, tuition waivers (full and partial) also available. *Unit head:* Richard Tempest, Director, 217-244-4720, Fax: 217-333-7310, E-mail: rtempest@illinois.edu. *Application contact:* Theresa Jo Schafroth, Office Manager, 217-333-3278, Fax: 217-333-1582, E-mail: schafrot@illinois.edu.

The University of Kansas, Graduate Studies, College of Liberal Arts and Sciences, Center for Russian, East European and Eurasian Studies, Lawrence, KS 66045. Offers MA. Part-time programs available. *Faculty:* 38 full-time (17 women), 4 part-time/adjunct (1 woman). *Students:* 14 full-time (4 women); includes 1 minority (Asian, non-Hispanic/Latino), 2 international. Average age 28. 20 applicants, 90% accepted, 6 enrolled. In 2010, 4 master's awarded. *Degree requirements:* For master's, one foreign language, comprehensive exam, interdisciplinary capstone research seminar. *Entrance requirements:* For master's, GRE General Test, 3 letters of recommendation. Additional exam requirements/recommendations for international students: Required—TOEFL. *Application deadline:* For fall admission, 1/1 priority date for domestic and international students. Application fee: $55 ($65 for international students). Electronic applications accepted. *Expenses:* Tuition, state resident: full-time $7092; part-time $295.50 per credit hour. Tuition, nonresident: full-time $16,590; part-time $691.25 per credit hour. Required fees: $858; $71.49 per credit hour. Tuition and fees vary according to course load, campus/location and program. *Financial support:* Fellowships with full tuition reimbursements, research assistantships with partial tuition reimbursements, scholarships/grants available. Financial award application deadline: 1/31; financial award applicants required to submit FAFSA. *Faculty research:* Russian and East Central European history and culture; Ukrainian, Russian, and Central Asian domestic politics and international security; Slavic languages, linguistics, and literatures. *Unit head:* Dr. Edith Clowes, Director, 785-864-4236, Fax: 785-864-3800, E-mail: crees@ku.edu. *Application contact:* Dr. Mariya Y. Omelicheva, Associate Director, 785-864-9002, Fax: 785-864-3800, E-mail: omeliche@ku.edu.

University of Michigan, Horace H. Rackham School of Graduate Studies, College of Literature, Science, and the Arts, Center for Russian and East European Studies, Ann Arbor, MI 48109-1106. Offers AM, Certificate, JD/AM, MBA/AM, MPP/AM. Part-time programs available. *Faculty:* 65 full-time (21 women), 11 part-time/adjunct (7 women). *Students:* 19 full-time (11 women), 1 international. Average age 28. 35 applicants, 57% accepted, 6 enrolled. In 2010, 4 master's awarded. *Degree requirements:* For master's and Certificate, one foreign language, thesis. *Entrance requirements:* For master's, GRE General Test. Additional exam requirements/recommendations for international students: Required—TOEFL. *Application deadline:* For fall admission, 1/15 for domestic and international students. Application fee: $65 ($75 for international students). Electronic applications accepted. *Expenses:* Tuition, state resident: full-time $17,784; part-time $1116 per credit hour. Tuition, nonresident: full-time $35,944; part-time $2125 per credit hour. International tuition: $35,994 full-time. Required fees: $95 per semester. Tuition and fees vary according to course load, degree level and program. *Financial support:* In 2010–11, 11 students received support, including 3 fellowships with full and partial tuition reimbursements available (averaging $15,000 per year), 3 teaching assistantships with full tuition reimbursements available (averaging $8,000 per year); scholarships/grants also available. Financial award application deadline: 2/1. *Faculty research:* Russia, East Europe, Eurasia, Central Asia, Caucasus. *Unit head:* Dr. Olga Maiorova, Director, 734-764-0351, Fax: 734-763-4765, E-mail: crees@umich.edu. *Application contact:* Julie E. Claus, Student Services Associate, 734-764-0351, Fax: 734-763-4765, E-mail: crees.admissions@umich.edu.

The University of North Carolina at Chapel Hill, Graduate School, College of Arts and Sciences, Department of Slavic Languages and Literatures, Curriculum in Russian and East European Studies, Chapel Hill, NC 27599. Offers MA. Part-time programs available. *Degree requirements:* For master's, one foreign language, thesis. *Entrance requirements:* For master's, GRE General Test. Additional exam requirements/recommendations for international students: Required—TOEFL. Electronic applications accepted. *Faculty research:* Language, area studies, social sciences, sciences, professional schools.

University of Pittsburgh, University Center for International Studies, Pittsburgh, PA 15260. Offers African studies (Certificate); Asian studies (Certificate); European Union studies (Certificate); global studies (Certificate); Latin American studies (Certificate); Russian and East European studies (Certificate); West European studies (Certificate). *Students:* 322 full-time (192 women), 19 part-time (14 women); includes 22 minority (8 Black or African American, non-Hispanic/Latino; 3 Asian, non-Hispanic/Latino; 6 Hispanic/Latino; 5 Two or more races, non-Hispanic/Latino), 134 international. In 2010, 61 Certificates awarded. *Degree requirements:* For Certificate, one foreign language, study abroad. *Application deadline:* Applications are processed on a rolling basis. *Expenses:* Tuition, state resident: full-time $17,304; part-time $701 per credit. Tuition, nonresident: full-time $29,554; part-time $1210 per credit. Required fees: $740; $214 per term. Tuition and fees vary according to program. *Unit head:* Dr. Lawrence F. Feick, Director, University Center for International Studies, 412-648-7374, Fax: 412-624-4672, E-mail: feick@pitt.edu. *Application contact:* Information Contact, 412-624-4141, E-mail: graduate@pitt.edu.

University of Saskatchewan, College of Graduate Studies and Research, College of Arts and Sciences, Department of Languages and Linguistics, Saskatoon, SK S7N 5A2, Canada. Offers MA. *Degree requirements:* For master's, 2 foreign languages, thesis. *Entrance requirements:* Additional exam requirements/recommendations for international students: Required—TOEFL (minimum score 80 iBT); Recommended—IELTS (minimum score 6.5). Electronic applications accepted.

The University of Texas at Austin, Graduate School, College of Liberal Arts, Center for Russian, East European, and Eurasian Studies, Austin, TX 78712-1111. Offers MA, JD/MA, MBA/MA, MP Aff/MA. Part-time programs available. *Degree requirements:* For master's, one foreign language, report or thesis. *Entrance requirements:* For master's, GRE General Test, 3 years of formal language training or equivalent, minimum GPA of 3.0. Electronic applications accepted. *Faculty research:* East European gypsies, elite transformation and democracy in Eastern Europe, elite partisanship as an intervening variable in Russian politics, post-Soviet youth in Russia.

University of Toronto, School of Graduate Studies, Social Sciences Division, Centre for European, Russian and Eurasian Studies, Toronto, ON M5S 1A1, Canada. Offers MA. *Degree requirements:* For master's, one foreign language, language proficiency test. *Entrance requirements:* For master's, minimum B+ average in final year, coursework in Russian/East European subjects, 2 years of study in a relevant language.

University of Washington, Graduate School, College of Arts and Sciences, Henry M. Jackson School of International Studies, Russian, East European and Central Asian Studies Program, Seattle, WA 98195. Offers Central Asian studies (MAIS); East European studies (MAIS); Russian studies (MAIS). *Faculty:* 59 full-time (23 women). *Students:* 24 full-time (14 women); includes 2 Asian, non-Hispanic/Latino; 1 Hispanic/Latino. 30 applicants, 93% accepted, 12 enrolled. In 2010, 7 master's awarded. *Degree requirements:* For master's, one foreign language, thesis. *Entrance requirements:* For master's, GRE General Test, 2 years of relevant language, minimum GPA of 3.00 (last two years). Additional exam requirements/recommendations for international students: Required—TOEFL (minimum score 500 paper-based; 213 computer-based; 92 iBT) or IELTS. *Application deadline:* For fall admission, 1/5 for domestic and international students. Application fee: $75. Electronic applications accepted. *Financial support:* In 2010–11, 8 fellowships with full tuition reimbursements were awarded; research assistantships, teaching assistantships, career-related internships or fieldwork, Federal Work-Study, institutionally sponsored loans, and summer language study awards also available. Financial award application deadline: 1/5. *Unit head:* Prof. James Augerot, Chair, 206-543-6848, E-mail: bigjim@u.washington.edu. *Application contact:* 206-543-6001, Fax: 206-616-3170, E-mail: jsisinfo@u.washington.edu.

Yale University, Graduate School of Arts and Sciences, Department of Slavic Languages and Literatures, New Haven, CT 06520. Offers medieval Slavic literature and philology (PhD);

Polish literature (PhD); Russian literature (PhD); Slavic languages and literatures and film studies (PhD). *Degree requirements:* For doctorate, 3 foreign languages, thesis/dissertation. *Entrance requirements:* For doctorate, GRE General Test.

Yale University, Graduate School of Arts and Sciences, Program in Russian and East European Studies, New Haven, CT 06520. Offers MA. *Degree requirements:* For master's, 2 foreign languages. *Entrance requirements:* For master's, GRE General Test.

Ethnic Studies

Cornell University, Graduate School, Graduate Fields of Arts and Sciences, Field of Sociology, Ithaca, NY 14853-0001. Offers economy and society (MA, PhD); gender and life course (MA, PhD); methodology (MA, PhD); organizations (MA, PhD); policy analysis (MA, PhD); political sociology/social movements (MA, PhD); racial and ethnic relations (MA, PhD); social networks (MA, PhD); social psychology (MA, PhD); social stratification (MA, PhD). *Faculty:* 33 full-time (12 women). *Students:* 36 full-time (18 women); includes 4 Asian, non-Hispanic/Latino, 9 international. Average age 29. 187 applicants, 7% accepted, 9 enrolled. In 2010, 3 master's, 2 doctorates awarded. Terminal master's awarded for partial completion of doctoral program. *Degree requirements:* For master's, thesis; for doctorate, thesis/dissertation, 1 year of teaching experience. *Entrance requirements:* For master's and doctorate, GRE General Test, 2 letters of recommendation, writing sample. Additional exam requirements/recommendations for international students: Required—TOEFL (minimum score 550 paper-based; 213 computer-based; 77 iBT). *Application deadline:* For fall admission, 1/15 for domestic students. Application fee: $80. Electronic applications accepted. *Expenses:* Tuition: Full-time $29,500. Required fees: $76. Tuition and fees vary according to degree level and program. *Financial support:* In 2010–11, 13 fellowships with full tuition reimbursements, 7 research assistantships with full tuition reimbursements, 14 teaching assistantships with full tuition reimbursements were awarded; institutionally sponsored loans, scholarships/grants, health care benefits, tuition waivers (full and partial), and unspecified assistantships also available. Financial award applicants required to submit FAFSA. *Faculty research:* Comparative societal analysis, work and family, simulations, social class and mobility, racial segregation and inequality. *Unit head:* Director of Graduate Studies, 607-255-4266. *Application contact:* Graduate Field Assistant, 607-255-4266, E-mail: sociology@cornell.edu.

Minnesota State University Mankato, College of Graduate Studies, College of Social and Behavioral Sciences, Department of Ethnic Studies, Mankato, MN 56001. Offers MS, Certificate. *Students:* 5 full-time (3 women), 5 part-time (2 women). *Application deadline:* For fall admission, 7/1 for domestic students, 5/1 for international students; for winter admission, 11/1 for domestic students; for spring admission, 10/1 for international students. Applications are processed on a rolling basis. Electronic applications accepted. *Unit head:* Dr. Hanh Huy Phan, Graduate Coordinator, 507-389-1185. *Application contact:* Dr. Hanh Huy Phan, Graduate Coordinator, 507-389-1185.

Northern Arizona University, Graduate College, College of Social and Behavioral Sciences, Ethnic Studies Program, Flagstaff, AZ 86011. Offers Graduate Certificate. Part-time programs available. *Faculty:* 4 full-time (2 women). *Students:* 1 (woman) part-time; includes American Indian or Alaska Native, non-Hispanic/Latino. Average age 25. In 2010, 1 Graduate Certificate awarded. *Entrance requirements:* For degree, bachelor's degree with minimum GPA of 2.5. Additional exam requirements/recommendations for international students: Required—TOEFL (minimum score 550 paper-based; 213 computer-based; 80 iBT), IELTS (minimum score 7). *Application deadline:* For fall admission, 3/1 priority date for international students; for spring admission, 9/15 priority date for international students. Applications are processed on a rolling basis. Application fee: $65. Electronic applications accepted. *Financial support:* Applicants required to submit FAFSA. *Unit head:* Dr. Sara Aleman, Director, 928-523-3886, Fax: 928-522-6777, E-mail: sara.aleman@nau.edu. *Application contact:* Dr. Sara Aleman, Director, 928-523-3886, Fax: 928-522-6777, E-mail: sara.aleman@nau.edu.

Norwich University, School of Graduate and Continuing Studies, Program in Military History, Northfield, VT 05663. Offers race and gender in military history (MA); total war (MA); U. S. military history (MA). Evening/weekend programs available. *Faculty:* 33 part-time/adjunct (2 women). *Students:* 127 full-time (23 women); includes 2 Black or African American, non-Hispanic/Latino; 7 Hispanic/Latino. Average age 42. 157 applicants, 96% accepted, 127 enrolled. In 2010, 127 master's awarded. *Entrance requirements:* For master's, minimum undergraduate GPA of 2.75. Additional exam requirements/recommendations for international students: Required—TOEFL (minimum score 550 paper-based; 212 computer-based; 83 iBT). *Application deadline:* For fall admission, 8/10 for domestic and international students; for winter admission, 11/7 for domestic and international students; for spring admission, 2/6 for domestic and international students. Application fee: $50. Electronic applications accepted. *Expenses:* Tuition: Full-time $17,380; part-time $645 per credit. Tuition and fees vary according to program. *Financial support:* Scholarships/grants available. Financial award applicants required to submit FAFSA. *Unit head:* Dr. James Erhman, Program Director, 802-485-2567, Fax: 802-485-2533. *Application contact:* Lars Nielsen, Administrative Director, 802-485-2853, Fax: 802-485-2533, E-mail: lnielsen@norwich.edu.

San Francisco State University, Division of Graduate Studies, College of Ethnic Studies, Program in Ethnic Studies, San Francisco, CA 94132-1722. Offers MA. *Unit head:* Dr. Laureen Chew, Associate Dean, 415-338-1693, E-mail: ethnicst@sfsu.edu. *Application contact:* Dr. Nancy Mirabel, Graduate Coordinator, 415-338-1693, E-mail: ethnicst@sfsu.edu.

United Theological Seminary of the Twin Cities, Graduate Programs, New Brighton, MN 55112-2598. Offers advanced theological studies (Diploma); justice and peace studies (M Div, MA); leadership toward racial justice (M Div, MA, Certificate); Methodist studies (M Div, MA, Certificate); ministry (D Min); ministry renewal and professional development (Certificate); pastoral care and counseling (M Div, MA, MARL); religion and theology (MA); theological and religious studies (Certificate); theology and the arts (M Div, MA); urban ministry (M Div, MA, MARL); women's studies: religion, theology and ministry (M Div, MA). *Accreditation:* ACIPE; ATS. Part-time and evening/weekend programs available. *Faculty:* 8 full-time (5 women), 28 part-time/adjunct (16 women). *Students:* 57 full-time (41 women), 94 part-time (61 women); includes 6 minority (5 Black or African American, non-Hispanic/Latino; 1 Hispanic/Latino), 1 international. Average age 47. 49 applicants, 98% accepted, 41 enrolled. In 2010, 10 first professional degrees, 6 master's, 4 doctorates, 2 other advanced degrees awarded. *Degree requirements:* For master's, thesis; for doctorate, comprehensive exam, thesis/dissertation; for M Div, integrative notebook, spiritual chronicle. *Entrance requirements:* For M Div and master's, minimum GPA of 2.75; strong analytical, reflective thinking and writing skills; vocational and academic goals compatible with those of Seminary; for doctorate, M Div or equivalent, minimum GPA of 3.0, 3 years experience in professional ministry; for other advanced degree, BA or equivalent life experience; strong analytical, reflective thinking and writing skills (Certificate); proficiency in English language, previous study of theology at a theological school, recommendation of student's denomination (Diploma). Additional exam requirements/recommendations for international students: Required—TOEFL (minimum score 550 paper-based). *Application deadline:* For fall admission, 7/1 priority date for domestic students, 11/1 priority date for international students; for winter admission, 11/1 priority date for domestic students; for spring admission, 11/15 priority date for domestic students. Applications are processed on a rolling basis. Application fee: $50. *Expenses:* Tuition: Full-time $13,014; part-time $482 per credit hour. One-time fee: $170. Tuition and fees vary according to course load, degree level and program. *Financial support:* In 2010–11, 120 students received support. Career-related internships or fieldwork, institutionally sponsored loans, and scholarships/grants available. Support available to part-time students. Financial award application deadline: 5/1; financial award applicants required to submit FAFSA. *Unit head:* Prof. Susan K. Ebbers, Dean of the Seminary, 651-255-6143 Ext. 108, Fax: 651-633-4315, E-mail: sebbers@unitedseminary.edu. *Application contact:* Rev. Glen Herrington-Hall, Director of Admissions, 651-255-6107 Ext. 107, Fax: 651-633-4315, E-mail: gherrington-hall@unitedseminary.edu.

Université Laval, Faculty of Letters, Department of History, Programs in Ethnology of French-Speaking People in North America, Québec, QC G1K 7P4, Canada. Offers MA, PhD. Terminal master's awarded for partial completion of doctoral program. *Degree requirements:* For master's, thesis; for doctorate, comprehensive exam, thesis/dissertation. *Entrance requirements:* For master's and doctorate, English exam (comprehension of written English), knowledge of French. Electronic applications accepted.

University of California, Berkeley, Graduate Division, College of Letters and Science, Group in Ethnic Studies, Berkeley, CA 94720-1500. Offers PhD. *Degree requirements:* For doctorate, one foreign language, thesis/dissertation, qualifying exam. *Entrance requirements:* For doctorate, minimum GPA of 3.0, 3 letters of recommendation. *Faculty research:* Gender and race, Asian American visual art, racial theory and politics, Chicana/o literature and visual arts, history of Native North Americans.

University of California, Riverside, Graduate Division, Department of Ethnic Studies, Riverside, CA 92521. Offers PhD. *Degree requirements:* For doctorate, variable foreign language requirement, comprehensive exam, thesis/dissertation. *Entrance requirements:* For doctorate, GRE, writing sample. Additional exam requirements/recommendations for international students: Required—TOEFL (minimum score 550 paper-based; 213 computer-based; 80 iBT). Electronic applications accepted. *Expenses:* Contact institution. *Faculty research:* The political economy of race, class, gender, sexuality, cultural production, the state, law, criminal justice and grass roots responses.

University of California, San Diego, Office of Graduate Studies, Department of Ethnic Studies, La Jolla, CA 92093. Offers MA, PhD. Electronic applications accepted.

University of Nevada, Las Vegas, Graduate College, College of Liberal Arts, Department of Anthropology and Ethnic Studies, Las Vegas, NV 89154-5003. Offers MA, PhD. Part-time programs available. *Faculty:* 14 full-time (7 women). *Students:* 25 full-time (18 women), 16 part-time (12 women); includes 15 minority (1 Black or African American, non-Hispanic/Latino; 1 Asian, non-Hispanic/Latino; 4 Hispanic/Latino; 9 Two or more races, non-Hispanic/Latino), 2 international. Average age 30. 38 applicants, 50% accepted, 15 enrolled. In 2010, 8 master's, 1 doctorate awarded. *Degree requirements:* For master's, thesis, oral defense of thesis; for doctorate, comprehensive exam, thesis/dissertation, oral defense of dissertation. *Entrance requirements:* For master's and doctorate, GRE General Test. Additional exam requirements/recommendations for international students: Required—TOEFL (minimum score 550 paper-based; 213 computer-based; 80 iBT), IELTS (minimum score 7). *Application deadline:* For fall admission, 2/1 priority date for domestic and international students. Applications are processed on a rolling basis. Application fee: $60 ($95 for international students). Electronic applications accepted. *Expenses:* Tuition, area resident: Part-time $239.50 per credit. Tuition, state resident: part-time $239.50 per credit. Tuition, nonresident: part-time $503 per credit. Required fees: $108 per semester. Tuition and fees vary according to course load, program and reciprocity agreements. *Financial support:* In 2010–11, 15 students received support, including 15 teaching assistantships with partial tuition reimbursements available (averaging $10,800 per year); institutionally sponsored loans, scholarships/grants, health care benefits, and unspecified assistantships also available. Financial award application deadline: 3/1. *Faculty research:* Bio-cultural evolution; foraging to farming transition (old and new world); human nutrition, health, and disease; human growth and development; human love, sexuality and family systems. Total annual research expenditures: $37,385. *Unit head:* Dr. Debra Martin, Chair/Professor, 702-895-1881, Fax: 702-8985-4823, E-mail: debra.martin@unlv.edu. *Application contact:* Graduate College Admissions Evaluator, 702-895-3320, Fax: 702-895-4180, E-mail: gradcollege@unlv.edu.

The University of North Carolina at Charlotte, Graduate School, College of Arts and Sciences, Department of Sociology, Charlotte, NC 28223-0001. Offers health research (MA); mathematical sociology and quantitative methods (MA); organizations, occupations, and work (MA); political sociology (MA); race and gender (MA); social psychology (MA); social theory (MA); sociology of education (MA); stratification (MA). Part-time and evening/weekend programs available. *Faculty:* 18 full-time (10 women). *Students:* 11 full-time (7 women), 14 part-time (8 women); includes 6 minority (4 Black or African American, non-Hispanic/Latino; 2 Asian, non-Hispanic/Latino). Average age 29. 20 applicants, 60% accepted, 8 enrolled. In 2010, 2 master's awarded. *Degree requirements:* For master's, thesis or alternative, thesis or comprehensive exam. *Entrance requirements:* For master's, GRE or MAT, minimum GPA of 3.0 in last 2 years, 2.75 overall. Additional exam requirements/recommendations for international students: Required—TOEFL (minimum score 557 paper-based; 220 computer-based; 83 iBT). *Application deadline:* For fall admission, 7/1 for domestic students, 5/1 for international students; for spring admission, 11/1 for domestic students, 10/1 for international students. Applications are processed on a rolling basis. Application fee: $55. Electronic applications accepted. *Expenses:* Tuition, state resident: full-time $3464. Tuition, nonresident: full-time $14,297. Required fees: $2094. Tuition and fees vary according to course load. *Financial support:* In 2010–11, 6 students received support, including 1 fellowship (averaging $60,000 per year), 1 research assistantship (averaging $9,000 per year), 1 teaching assistantship (averaging $9,000 per year); career-related internships or fieldwork, institutionally sponsored loans, scholarships/grants, and unspecified assistantships also available. Support available to part-time students. Financial award application deadline: 4/1; financial award applicants required to submit FAFSA. *Faculty research:* Social psychology, sociology of education, social gerontology, quantitative methodology, medical sociology. Total annual research expenditures: $61,382. *Unit head:* Dr. Lisa Rachotte, Chair, 704-687-2288, Fax: 704-687-3091, E-mail: lrashott@uncc.edu. *Application contact:* Kathy B. Giddings, Director of Graduate Admissions, 704-687-5503, Fax: 704-687-3279, E-mail: gradadm@uncc.edu.

Washington State University, Graduate School, College of Liberal Arts, Program in American Studies, Pullman, WA 99164. Offers ethnic studies (MA, PhD); feminist studies (MA, PhD); history (MA, PhD); literature (MA, PhD). Part-time programs available. *Faculty:* 35. *Students:* 23 full-time (14 women), 4 part-time (2 women); includes 5 Black or African American, non-Hispanic/Latino; 4 American Indian or Alaska Native, non-Hispanic/Latino; 4 Asian, non-Hispanic/Latino; 4 Hispanic/Latino, 2 international. Average age 35. 55 applicants, 7% accepted, 3 enrolled. In 2010, 1 master's, 3 doctorates awarded. *Degree requirements:* For master's, one foreign language, comprehensive exam (for some programs), thesis optional, oral exam; for doctorate, one foreign language, comprehensive exam (for some programs), thesis/dissertation, oral exam. *Entrance requirements:* For master's and doctorate, GRE General Test, official college transcripts sent directly from each institution attended, 3-5 page statement of purpose describing areas of interest, minimum GPA of 3.0, writing sample, 3 letters of recommendation. Additional exam requirements/recommendations for international students: Required—TOEFL, IELTS. *Application deadline:* For fall admission, 1/10 priority date for

Ethnic Studies

Washington State University (continued)
domestic and international students; for spring admission, 7/1 priority date for domestic and international students. Applications are processed on a rolling basis. Application fee: $50. *Expenses:* Tuition, state resident: full-time $8552; part-time $443 per credit. Tuition, nonresident: full-time $21,650; part-time $1083 per credit. Required fees: $846. *Financial support:* In 2010–11, 1 fellowship (averaging $6,950 per year), 3 research assistantships with full and partial tuition reimbursements (averaging $14,634 per year), 17 teaching assistantships with full and partial tuition reimbursements (averaging $13,383 per year) were awarded; career-related internships or fieldwork, Federal Work-Study, institutionally sponsored loans, health care benefits, tuition waivers (partial), and teaching associateships also available. Financial award application deadline: 2/15; financial award applicants required to submit FAFSA. *Faculty research:* The American West in multicultural perspective; nineteenth century historical, literary, and cultural studies; comparative American ethnic literatures and cultures; American cultures and the environment; American rhetoric. *Unit head:* Dr. Rory J. Ong, Director, 509-335-1560, E-mail: rjong@mail.wsu.edu. *Application contact:* Graduate School Admissions, 800-GRADWSU, Fax: 509-335-1949, E-mail: gradsch@wsu.edu.

Folklore

George Mason University, College of Humanities and Social Sciences, Department of English, Fairfax, VA 22030. Offers creative writing (MFA); English (MA); folklore studies (Certificate); linguistics (PhD); professional writing and rhetoric (Certificate); teaching English as a second language (Certificate). *Faculty:* 82 full-time (45 women), 35 part-time/adjunct (22 women). *Students:* 69 full-time (45 women), 208 part-time (153 women); includes 13 Black or African American, non-Hispanic/Latino; 3 American Indian or Alaska Native, non-Hispanic/Latino; 20 Asian, non-Hispanic/Latino; 6 Hispanic/Latino; 4 Two or more races, non-Hispanic/Latino, 10 international. Average age 31. 391 applicants, 56% accepted, 96 enrolled. In 2010, 116 master's, 11 other advanced degrees awarded. *Degree requirements:* For master's, thesis (for some programs), proficiency in a foreign language by course work or translation test. *Entrance requirements:* For master's, 30 credits in graduate English courses, minimum undergraduate GPA of 3.0, 2 letters of recommendation. Additional exam requirements/recommendations for international students: Required—TOEFL (minimum score 570 paper-based; 230 computer-based; 88 iBT). *Application deadline:* For fall admission, 3/15 priority date for domestic students; for spring admission, 10/15 for domestic students. Application fee: $100. Electronic applications accepted. *Expenses:* Tuition, state resident: full-time $8192; part-time $440 per credit hour. Tuition, nonresident: full-time $22,952; part-time $1055 per credit hour. Required fees: $2364; $99 per credit hour. *Financial support:* In 2010–11, 50 students received support, including 2 fellowships with full tuition reimbursements available (averaging $18,000 per year), 5 research assistantships with full and partial tuition reimbursements available (averaging $11,251 per year), 44 teaching assistantships with full and partial tuition reimbursements available (averaging $11,009 per year); Federal Work-Study, scholarships/grants, unspecified assistantships, and health care benefits (full-time research or teaching assistantship recipients) also available. Financial award application deadline: 3/1; financial award applicants required to submit FAFSA. *Faculty research:* Literature, professional writing and editing, writing of fiction or poetry. Total annual research expenditures: $1.2 million. *Unit head:* Robert Matz, Chair, 703-993-1170, E-mail: rmatz@gmu.edu. *Application contact:* Denise Albanese, Graduate Director, 703-993-1175, E-mail: dalbanes@gmu.edu.

The George Washington University, Columbian College of Arts and Sciences, Department of American Studies, Washington, DC 20052. Offers American studies (PhD); folklife (MA); historic preservation (MA); material culture (MA). Part-time and evening/weekend programs available. *Faculty:* 11 full-time (5 women), 4 part-time/adjunct (2 women). *Students:* 24 full-time (17 women), 29 part-time (13 women); includes 4 Black or African American, non-Hispanic/Latino; 2 Asian, non-Hispanic/Latino; 1 Hispanic/Latino, 1 international. Average age 29. 134 applicants, 49% accepted, 19 enrolled. In 2010, 8 master's, 7 doctorates awarded. Terminal master's awarded for partial completion of doctoral program. *Degree requirements:* For master's, comprehensive exam; for doctorate, one foreign language, thesis/dissertation, general exam. *Entrance requirements:* For master's and doctorate, GRE General Test, minimum GPA of 3.0. Additional exam requirements/recommendations for international students: Required—TOEFL (minimum score 550 paper-based; 213 computer-based; 80 iBT). *Application deadline:* For fall admission, 1/15 priority date for domestic and international students; for spring admission, 10/1 for domestic students. Application fee: $75. *Financial support:* In 2010–11, 22 students received support; fellowships, research assistantships, teaching assistantships, career-related internships or fieldwork, Federal Work-Study, institutionally sponsored loans, and tuition waivers available. Financial award application deadline: 1/15. *Unit head:* James A. Miller, Chair, 202-994-6743, E-mail: jam@gwu.edu. *Application contact:* Information Contact, 202-994-6070, Fax: 202-994-8651, E-mail: amst@gwu.edu.

The George Washington University, Columbian College of Arts and Sciences, Department of Anthropology, Concentration in Folklife, Washington, DC 20052. Offers MA. In 2010, 1 master's awarded. *Degree requirements:* For master's, comprehensive exam, thesis or alternative. *Entrance requirements:* For master's, GRE General Test, minimum GPA of 3.0. *Application deadline:* For fall admission, 4/1 priority date for domestic and international students; for spring admission, 10/1 priority date for domestic and international students. Application fee: $60. *Financial support:* Fellowships, teaching assistantships available. Financial award application deadline: 2/1. *Unit head:* Dr. John Vlach, Director, 202-994-7318, E-mail: jmv@gwu.edu. *Application contact:* Information Contact, 202-994-6075, E-mail: anth@gwu.edu.

Indiana University Bloomington, University Graduate School, College of Arts and Sciences, Department of Folklore and Ethnomusicology, Bloomington, IN 47408-3890. Offers folklore (MA, PhD), including ethnomusicology. Part-time programs available. *Faculty:* 17 full-time (7 women), 12 part-time/adjunct (7 women). *Students:* 115 full-time (72 women), 1 part-time (0 women); includes 14 minority (9 Black or African American, non-Hispanic/Latino; 5 Hispanic/Latino), 27 international. Average age 33. 72 applicants, 44% accepted, 18 enrolled. In 2010, 12 master's, 14 doctorates awarded. *Degree requirements:* For master's, one foreign language, comprehensive exam, project or thesis; for doctorate, 2 foreign languages, comprehensive exam, thesis/dissertation. *Entrance requirements:* For master's and doctorate, GRE General Test, minimum GPA of 3.0. Additional exam requirements/recommendations for international students: Required—TOEFL (minimum score 550 paper-based; 213 computer-based; 79 iBT). *Application deadline:* For fall admission, 1/15 for domestic students, 12/1 for international students. Application fee: $55 ($65 for international students). Electronic applications accepted. *Financial support:* In 2010–11, 80 students received support, including 1 fellowship with full tuition reimbursement available (averaging $15,000 per year), 16 research assistantships with full tuition reimbursements available (averaging $11,000 per year), 12 teaching assistantships with full tuition reimbursements available (averaging $11,300 per year); Federal Work-Study, scholarships/grants, health care benefits, and unspecified assistantships also available. Financial award application deadline: 3/1; financial award applicants required to submit FAFSA. *Faculty research:* Narrative, performance studies, material culture, popular culture, music. *Unit head:* Dr. John McDowell, Chair, 812-855-0390, Fax: 812-855-4008, E-mail: mcdowell@indiana.edu. *Application contact:* Michelle Melhouse, Graduate Recorder, 812-855-0389, Fax: 812-855-4008, E-mail: mmelhous@indiana.edu.

Memorial University of Newfoundland, School of Graduate Studies, Department of Folklore, St. John's, NL A1C 5S7, Canada. Offers MA, PhD. Part-time programs available. *Degree requirements:* For master's, thesis optional; for doctorate, one foreign language, comprehensive exam, thesis/dissertation, oral thesis defense. *Entrance requirements:* For master's, 36 credit hours of course work in folklore, humanities, or social studies; honors degree; for doctorate, MA in folklore or related field. Electronic applications accepted. *Faculty research:* Narrative, folklife, belief theory, methodology, popular culture.

University of Alberta, Faculty of Graduate Studies and Research, Department of Modern Languages and Cultural Studies, Edmonton, AB T6G 2E1, Canada. Offers applied linguistics (Germanic, Romance, Slavic) (MA); French language, literatures and linguistics (PhD); French language, literatures, and linguistics (MA); Germanic languages, literatures and linguistics (PhD); Germanic languages, literatures, and linguistics (MA); Italian studies (MA); Slavic languages and literatures (Russian, Ukrainian) (MA, PhD); Slavic linguistics (Russian, Ukrainian) (MA, PhD); Spanish and Latin American studies (MA, PhD); Ukrainian folklore (MA, PhD). Part-time programs available. *Degree requirements:* For master's, one foreign language, thesis; for doctorate, 2 foreign languages, comprehensive exam, thesis/dissertation. *Entrance requirements:* For master's and doctorate, 1 language other than English. Additional exam requirements/recommendations for international students: Required—Michigan English Language Assessment Battery or TOEFL (minimum score 550 paper-based; 213 computer-based). Electronic applications accepted. *Faculty research:* Russian/Ukrainian studies; German studies; contemporary Latin American, French and Francophone studies; Italian studies.

University of California, Berkeley, Graduate Division, College of Letters and Science, Department of Anthropology, Group in Folklore, Berkeley, CA 94720-1500. Offers MA. *Entrance requirements:* For master's, GRE General Test, minimum GPA of 3.0, 3 letters of recommendation.

University of Louisiana at Lafayette, College of Liberal Arts, Department of English, Lafayette, LA 70504. Offers British and American literature (MA), including creative writing, folklore, rhetoric; creative writing (PhD); literature (PhD); rhetoric (PhD). Part-time programs available. Terminal master's awarded for partial completion of doctoral program. *Degree requirements:* For master's, one foreign language, thesis or alternative; for doctorate, 2 foreign languages, comprehensive exam, thesis/dissertation. *Entrance requirements:* For master's, GRE General Test, minimum GPA of 2.75; for doctorate, GRE General Test, minimum GPA of 3.0. Additional exam requirements/recommendations for international students: Required—TOEFL (minimum score 550 paper-based; 213 computer-based). Electronic applications accepted. *Faculty research:* Composition theory, Southern literature, medieval literature.

The University of North Carolina at Chapel Hill, Graduate School, College of Arts and Sciences, Curriculum in Folklore, Chapel Hill, NC 27599. Offers MA. *Degree requirements:* For master's, one foreign language, comprehensive exam, thesis. *Entrance requirements:* For master's, GRE General Test, minimum GPA of 3.0, writing sample. Electronic applications accepted. *Faculty research:* Public folklore, politics of culture, folklore and feminist theory, belief and health systems, Southern culture.

University of Oregon, Graduate School, College of Arts and Sciences, Folklore Program, Eugene, OR 97403. Offers independent study: folklore (MA, MS). Part-time programs available. *Degree requirements:* For master's, one foreign language, project or thesis. *Entrance requirements:* For master's, GRE General Test, minimum GPA of 3.0. Additional exam requirements/recommendations for international students: Required—TOEFL. *Faculty research:* American folklore, East European folklore, film and folklore, folk religion and belief, ballad.

The University of Texas at Austin, Graduate School, College of Liberal Arts, Department of Anthropology, Program in Folklore and Public Culture, Austin, TX 78712-1111. Offers MA, PhD. Part-time programs available. Terminal master's awarded for partial completion of doctoral program. *Degree requirements:* For master's, one foreign language, thesis, report; for doctorate, one foreign language, thesis/dissertation. *Entrance requirements:* For master's and doctorate, GRE General Test. Electronic applications accepted. *Faculty research:* Expressive culture, gender, genre, folklore and culture of British Isles, ethnography of speaking.

University of Wisconsin–Madison, Graduate School, College of Letters and Science, Department of Scandinavian Studies, Madison, WI 53706-1380. Offers area studies (MA); folklore (PhD); literature (MA, PhD); philology (PhD). Part-time programs available. *Degree requirements:* For master's, 2 foreign languages, exam; for doctorate, thesis/dissertation, exam. *Entrance requirements:* For master's, minimum GPA of 3.25; for doctorate, minimum GPA of 3.5. Electronic applications accepted. *Expenses:* Tuition, state resident: full-time $9887; part-time $617.96 per credit. Tuition, nonresident: full-time $24,054; part-time $1503.40 per credit. Required fees: $67.63 per credit. Tuition and fees vary according to reciprocity agreements. *Faculty research:* Historical fiction, Icelandic poetry, nineteenth-century literature, theater, gender studies, folklore.

Utah State University, School of Graduate Studies, College of Humanities, Arts and Social Sciences, Department of English and Department of History, Program in American Studies, Logan, UT 84322. Offers folklore (MA, MS); western American literature and culture (MA, MS). Part-time and evening/weekend programs available. *Degree requirements:* For master's, thesis or alternative. *Entrance requirements:* For master's, GRE General Test or MAT, minimum GPA of 3.0, 3 letters of recommendation, writing sample. Additional exam requirements/recommendations for international students: Required—TOEFL. *Faculty research:* Folklore and folklife, American culture, regional studies, material culture, Jewish folklore, Native American folklore.

Gender Studies

The American University in Cairo, School of Global Affairs and Public Policy, Program in Gender and Women's Studies, Cairo, Egypt. Offers gender and development (MA, Diploma); gender and justice (MA, Diploma); gender and women's studies in the Middle East and North Africa (MA, Diploma).

Arizona State University, College of Liberal Arts and Sciences, School of Justice and Social Inquiry, Tempe, AZ 85287-4902. Offers African American diaspora studies (Graduate Certificate); gender studies (PhD, Graduate Certificate); justice studies (MS, PhD); socio-economic justice (Graduate Certificate); PhD/JD. Part-time programs available. *Faculty:* 55 full-time (37 women). *Students:* 52 full-time (37 women), 28 part-time (23 women); includes 23 minority (4 Black or African American, non-Hispanic/Latino; 1 American Indian or Alaska Native, non-Hispanic/Latino; 5 Asian, non-Hispanic/Latino; 12 Hispanic/Latino; 1 Two or more races, non-Hispanic/Latino), 12 international. Average age 32. 83 applicants, 41% accepted, 22 enrolled. In 2010, 8 master's, 12 doctorates, 3 other advanced degrees awarded. Terminal master's awarded for partial completion of doctoral program. *Degree requirements:* For master's, thesis or alternative, interactive Program of Study (iPOS) submitted before completing 50 percent of required credit hours; for doctorate, comprehensive exam, thesis/dissertation, interactive Program of Study (iPOS) submitted before completing 50 percent of required credit hours. *Entrance requirements:* For master's, GRE or LSAT, minimum GPA of 3.0 or equivalent in last 2 years of work leading to bachelor's degree; for doctorate, GRE or LSAT (for justice studies program), minimum GPA of 3.0 or equivalent in last 2 years of work leading to bachelor's degree. Additional exam requirements/recommendations for international students: Required—TOEFL, IELTS, or Pearson Test of English. *Application deadline:* For fall admission, 12/14 for domestic and international students. Applications are processed on a rolling basis. Application fee: $70 ($90 for international students). Electronic applications accepted. *Expenses:* Tuition, state resident: full-time $8510; part-time $608 per credit. Tuition, nonresident: full-time $16,542; part-time $919 per credit. Required fees: $339; $110 per credit. Part-time tuition and fees vary according to course load. *Financial support:* In 2010–11, 4 research assistantships with full and partial tuition reimbursements (averaging $12,586 per year), 27 teaching assistantships with full and partial tuition reimbursements (averaging $14,093 per year) were awarded; fellowships with full tuition reimbursements, career-related internships or fieldwork, Federal Work-Study, institutionally sponsored loans, scholarships/grants, and tuition waivers (full) also available. Financial award application deadline: 3/1; financial award applicants required to submit FAFSA. Total annual research expenditures: $1.7 million. *Unit head:* Dr. Mary Margaret Fonow, Director, 480-965-2358, E-mail: marymargaret.fonow@asu.edu. *Application contact:* Graduate Admissions, 480-965-6113.

Brandeis University, Graduate School of Arts and Sciences, Department of Anthropology, Waltham, MA 02454. Offers anthropology (MA, PhD); anthropology and women's and gender studies (MA). Part-time programs available. *Faculty:* 8 full-time (4 women), 3 part-time/adjunct (1 woman). *Students:* 43 full-time (30 women), 1 (woman) part-time; includes 4 Hispanic/Latino, 13 international. Average age 34. 40 applicants, 53% accepted, 13 enrolled. In 2010, 6 master's, 2 doctorates awarded. Terminal master's awarded for partial completion of doctoral program. *Degree requirements:* For master's, thesis; for doctorate, one foreign language, comprehensive exam, thesis/dissertation. *Entrance requirements:* For master's, GRE General Test (recommended), sample of written work, resume, letters of recommendation; for doctorate, GRE General Test, sample of written work, resume, letters of recommendation. Additional exam requirements/recommendations for international students: Required—TOEFL (minimum score 600 paper-based; 250 computer-based; 100 iBT); Recommended—IELTS (minimum score 7). *Application deadline:* For fall admission, 1/15 for domestic students. Application fee: $75. Electronic applications accepted. *Financial support:* In 2010–11, 23 students received support, including 12 fellowships with full tuition reimbursements available (averaging $20,000 per year), 11 teaching assistantships with partial tuition reimbursements available (averaging $3,200 per year); research assistantships with partial tuition reimbursements available, career-related internships or fieldwork, scholarships/grants, health care benefits, tuition waivers (full and partial), and unspecified assistantships also available. Support available to part-time students. Financial award application deadline: 4/15; financial award applicants required to submit FAFSA. *Faculty research:* Evolutionary processes, comparative social institutions, systems of meaning, gender studies, sociocultural anthropology, linguistic anthropology, archaeology, and physical anthropology. *Unit head:* Dr. Janet McIntosh, Associate Professor/Director of Graduate Studies, 781-736-2210, Fax: 781-736-2232, E-mail: janetmc@brandeis.edu. *Application contact:* Laurel Carpenter, Academic Administrator, 781-736-2210, Fax: 781-736-2232, E-mail: lcarpenter@brandeis.edu.

Brandeis University, Graduate School of Arts and Sciences, Department of English, Waltham, MA 02454-9110. Offers English (MA, PhD); English and women's and gender studies (MA). Part-time programs available. *Faculty:* 16 full-time (9 women), 8 part-time/adjunct (5 women). *Students:* 54 full-time (29 women), 1 (woman) part-time; includes 1 Asian, non-Hispanic/Latino; 2 Hispanic/Latino, 5 international. 177 applicants, 16% accepted, 10 enrolled. In 2010, 8 master's, 5 doctorates awarded. *Degree requirements:* For master's, one foreign language, thesis, symposium; for doctorate, 2 foreign languages, thesis/dissertation, field exam, symposium presentation, prospectus defense. *Entrance requirements:* For master's, GRE General Test, resume, sample of work, letters of recommendation; for doctorate, GRE General Test, GRE Subject Test, resume, sample of work, letters of recommendation. Additional exam requirements/recommendations for international students: Required—TOEFL (minimum score 600 paper-based; 250 computer-based; 100 iBT); Recommended—IELTS (minimum score 7). *Application deadline:* For fall admission, 1/5 for domestic and international students. Application fee: $75. Electronic applications accepted. *Financial support:* In 2010–11, 27 fellowships with full tuition reimbursements (averaging $20,000 per year), 4 teaching assistantships with partial tuition reimbursements (averaging $3,200 per year) were awarded; research assistantships with full tuition reimbursements, scholarships/grants, health care benefits, and tuition waivers (full and partial) also available. Financial award application deadline: 4/15; financial award applicants required to submit FAFSA. *Faculty research:* Feminist and gender theory, American literature, Anglophone literature, early modern literature, modernism. *Unit head:* Dr. Michael Gilmore, Director of Graduate Studies, 781-736-2130, Fax: 781-736-2179, E-mail: chaucer@brandeis.edu. *Application contact:* Lisa Pannella, Department Administrator, 781-736-2130, Fax: 781-736-2179, E-mail: pannella@brandeis.edu.

Brandeis University, Graduate School of Arts and Sciences, Department of Music, Waltham, MA 02454-9110. Offers composition and theory (MA, MFA, PhD); music and women's and gender studies (MA); musicology (MA, MFA, PhD). Part-time programs available. *Faculty:* 7 full-time (1 woman), 9 part-time/adjunct (4 women). *Students:* 43 full-time (18 women), 3 part-time (all women); includes 7 Black or African American, non-Hispanic/Latino; 3 Asian, non-Hispanic/Latino; 1 Hispanic/Latino, 7 international. 88 applicants, 30% accepted, 11 enrolled. In 2010, 11 master's, 2 doctorates awarded. Terminal master's awarded for partial completion of doctoral program. *Degree requirements:* For master's, one foreign language, thesis or alternative; for doctorate, 2 foreign languages, comprehensive exam, thesis/dissertation. *Entrance requirements:* For master's, GRE General Test (musicology), resume, sample of work (music composition), letters of recommendation; for doctorate, GRE General Test (musicology), resume, writing sample (musicology), letters of recommendation, sample of recording work (composition). Additional exam requirements/recommendations for international students: Required—TOEFL (minimum score 600 paper-based; 250 computer-based; 100 iBT); Recommended—IELTS (minimum score 7). *Application deadline:* For fall admission, 1/15 priority date for domestic and international students. Application fee: $75. Electronic applications accepted. *Financial support:* In 2010–11, 28 students received support, including 24 fellowships with full tuition reimbursements available (averaging $20,000 per year), 4 teaching assistantships with partial tuition reimbursements available (averaging $3,200 per year); research assistantships, scholarships/grants, health care benefits, and tuition waivers (full and partial) also available. Support available to part-time students. Financial award

application deadline: 4/15; financial award applicants required to submit FAFSA. *Faculty research:* Composition, performance, theory and analysis, music history, electronic music. *Unit head:* Prof. Mary Ruth Ray, Chair, 781-736-3310, E-mail: ray@brandeis.edu. *Application contact:* Mark Kagan, Senior Academic Administrator, 781-736-3311, E-mail: kagan@brandeis.edu.

Brandeis University, Graduate School of Arts and Sciences, Department of Near Eastern and Judaic Studies, Waltham, MA 02454-9110. Offers Near Eastern and Judaic studies (MA, PhD); Near Eastern and Judaic studies and sociology (PhD); Near Eastern and Judaic studies and women's and gender studies (MA); teaching of Hebrew (MAT). Part-time programs available. *Faculty:* 23 full-time (11 women), 7 part-time/adjunct (3 women). *Students:* 64 full-time (29 women); includes 2 Hispanic/Latino, 6 international. 123 applicants, 50% accepted, 18 enrolled. In 2010, 10 master's, 2 doctorates awarded. Terminal master's awarded for partial completion of doctoral program. *Degree requirements:* For master's, one foreign language, comprehensive exam, thesis or alternative; for doctorate, 3 foreign languages, comprehensive exam, thesis/dissertation. *Entrance requirements:* For master's and doctorate, GRE General Test (recommended), letters of recommendation, transcripts, statement of purpose. Additional exam requirements/recommendations for international students: Required—TOEFL (minimum score 600 paper-based; 250 computer-based; 100 iBT); Recommended—IELTS (minimum score 7). *Application deadline:* For fall admission, 1/15 priority date for domestic and international students. Applications are processed on a rolling basis. Application fee: $75. Electronic applications accepted. *Financial support:* In 2010–11, 17 students received support, including 14 fellowships with full tuition reimbursements available (averaging $20,000 per year); research assistantships with full and partial tuition reimbursements available, teaching assistantships, scholarships/grants, health care benefits, and tuition waivers (full and partial) also available. Support available to part-time students. Financial award application deadline: 4/15; financial award applicants required to submit FAFSA. *Faculty research:* Ancient Near East and Bible, philosophy, history, modern Middle East, Islamic studies. *Unit head:* Dr. Sylvia Fishman, Chair, 781-736-2950, Fax: 781-736-2070, E-mail: fishman@brandeis.edu. *Application contact:* Joanne Arnish, Department Administrator, 781-736-2950, Fax: 781-736-2070, E-mail: arnish@brandeis.edu.

Brandeis University, Graduate School of Arts and Sciences, Joint Master's Programs in Women's and Gender Studies, Waltham, MA 02454-9110. Offers anthropology and women's and gender studies (MA); English and women's and gender studies (MA); music and women's and gender studies (MA); Near Eastern and Judaic studies and women's and gender studies (MA); public policy and women's and gender studies (MA); sociology and women's and gender studies (MA); sustainable international development and women's/gender studies (MA). Part-time programs available. *Degree requirements:* For master's, thesis. *Entrance requirements:* For master's, GRE, sample of written work, resume. Additional exam requirements/recommendations for international students: Required—TOEFL (minimum score 600 paper-based; 250 computer-based; 100 iBT); Recommended—IELTS (minimum score 7). Electronic applications accepted.

Brandeis University, Graduate School of Arts and Sciences, MA Program in Women's and Gender Studies, Waltham, MA 02454-9110. Offers MA. *Degree requirements:* For master's, thesis. *Entrance requirements:* For master's, GRE, three letters of recommendation, curriculum vitae or resume, statement of purpose, critical writing sample. Additional exam requirements/recommendations for international students: Required—TOEFL (minimum score 600 paper-based; 250 computer-based; 100 iBT); Recommended—IELTS (minimum score 7). Electronic applications accepted. *Faculty research:* Gender and legal studies, sexuality studies, social and public policy, comparative literature and culture, anthropology, English, music, Near Eastern and Judaic Studies, public policy, sociology, sustainable international development.

Carnegie Mellon University, College of Humanities and Social Sciences, Department of History, Pittsburgh, PA 15213-3891. Offers African and African-American diaspora (PhD); culture and power (PhD); gender and the family (PhD); history (MA, MS); history and policy (MA); labor and politics (PhD); science, technology, medicine and environment (PhD). Part-time programs available. *Degree requirements:* For doctorate, oral and written comprehensive exams, dissertation defense. *Entrance requirements:* For doctorate, GRE General Test. Additional exam requirements/recommendations for international students: Required—TOEFL. Electronic applications accepted. *Faculty research:* Anthropology and history, African American history, technology/environment, cultural history analysis.

Central European University, Graduate Studies, School of Social Sciences and Humanities, Budapest, Hungary. Offers economics (MA, PhD); gender studies (MA, PhD); international relations and European studies (MA, PhD); mathematics and its applications (MS, PhD); medieval studies (MA, PhD); nationalism studies (MA, PhD); philosophy (MA, PhD); political science (MA, PhD); public policy (MA, PhD); sociology and social anthropology (MA, PhD). *Faculty:* 90 full-time (29 women), 13 part-time/adjunct (7 women). *Students:* 732 full-time (404 women). Average age 28. 3,639 applicants, 22% accepted, 416 enrolled. In 2010, 278 master's, 16 doctorates awarded. Terminal master's awarded for partial completion of doctoral program. *Degree requirements:* For master's, one foreign language, thesis; for doctorate, one foreign language, comprehensive exam, thesis/dissertation. *Entrance requirements:* For master's, interview; for doctorate, GRE, CEU subject test, interview. Additional exam requirements/recommendations for international students: Required—TOEFL (minimum score 570 paper-based; 230 computer-based); Recommended—IELTS (minimum score 6.5). *Application deadline:* For fall admission, 1/15 priority date for domestic and international students. Application fee: $0. Electronic applications accepted. Tuition and fees charges are reported in euros. *Expenses:* Tuition: Full-time 11,000 euros. Required fees: 250 euros. One-time fee: 200 euros full-time. Tuition and fees vary according to degree level, program, reciprocity agreements and student level. *Financial support:* In 2010–11, 402 students received support, including 416 fellowships with full and partial tuition reimbursements available (averaging $6,200 per year); career-related internships or fieldwork, institutionally sponsored loans, and scholarships/grants also available. Financial award application deadline: 1/5. *Faculty research:* Civil society, fiscal decentralization, party politics, political philosophy (especially liberalism, theory of democracy). Total annual research expenditures: $35,000. *Unit head:* Dr. Katalin Farkas, Provost/Academic Pro Rector, 361-327-3000 Ext. 2227, E-mail: farkask@ceu.hu. *Application contact:* Zsuzsanna Jaszberenyi, Admissions Officer, 361-327-3009, Fax: 361-327-3211, E-mail: admissions@ceu.hu.

Central Michigan University, College of Graduate Studies, College of Humanities and Social and Behavioral Sciences, Program in Humanities, Mount Pleasant, MI 48859. Offers humanities (MA), including contemporary issues in the humanities: race, class, and gender, images and ideas of self, Native American issues in modern culture, popular culture studies, the rise of industrial society. Part-time and evening/weekend programs available. *Students:* 2 full-time (both women), 10 part-time (6 women); includes 1 American Indian or Alaska Native, non-Hispanic/Latino; 2 Hispanic/Latino. Average age 37. *Degree requirements:* For master's, thesis or alternative. *Application deadline:* For fall admission, 6/1 for international students; for spring admission, 10/1 for international students. Applications are processed on a rolling basis. Application fee: $35 ($45 for international students). Electronic applications accepted. *Expenses:* Tuition, state resident: full-time $8208; part-time $456 per credit hour. Tuition, nonresident: full-time $13,788; part-time $766 per credit hour. One-time fee: $25. *Financial support:* Fellowships with tuition reimbursements, Federal Work-Study, unspecified assistantships, and out-of-state merit awards, non-resident graduate awards available. *Faculty research:* Rise of industrial society; images and ideas of self; contemporary issues of race, class, and gender; popular culture; Native American issues in modern culture. *Unit head:* Dr. Susan A. Schiller, Director, 989-774-3681, Fax: 989-774-7106, E-mail: schil1sa@cmich.edu. *Application contact:* Judith L. Prince, Director of Graduate Student Services, 989-774-1059, Fax: 989-774-1857, E-mail: judith.l.prince@cmich.edu.

Gender Studies

Cornell University, Graduate School, Graduate Fields of Arts and Sciences, Field of Sociology, Ithaca, NY 14853-0001. Offers economy and society (MA, PhD); gender and life course (MA, PhD); methodology (MA, PhD); organizations (MA, PhD); policy analysis (MA, PhD); political sociology/social movements (MA, PhD); racial and ethnic relations (MA, PhD); social networks (MA, PhD); social psychology (MA, PhD); social stratification (MA, PhD). *Faculty:* 33 full-time (12 women). *Students:* 36 full-time (18 women); includes 4 Asian, non-Hispanic/Latino, 9 international. Average age 29. 187 applicants, 7% accepted, 9 enrolled. In 2010, 3 master's, 2 doctorates awarded. Terminal master's awarded for partial completion of doctoral program. *Degree requirements:* For master's, thesis; for doctorate, thesis/dissertation, 1 year of teaching experience. *Entrance requirements:* For master's and doctorate, GRE General Test, 2 letters of recommendation, writing sample. Additional exam requirements/recommendations for international students: Required—TOEFL (minimum score 550 paper-based; 213 computer-based; 77 iBT). *Application deadline:* For fall admission, 1/15 for domestic students. Application fee: $80. Electronic applications accepted. *Expenses:* Tuition: Full-time $29,500. Required fees: $76. Tuition and fees vary according to degree level and program. *Financial support:* In 2010–11, 13 fellowships with full tuition reimbursements, 7 research assistantships with full tuition reimbursements, 14 teaching assistantships with full tuition reimbursements were awarded; institutionally sponsored loans, scholarships/grants, health care benefits, tuition waivers (full and partial), and unspecified assistantships also available. Financial award applicants required to submit FAFSA. *Faculty research:* Comparative societal analysis, work and family, simulations, social class and mobility, racial segregation and inequality. *Unit head:* Director of Graduate Studies, 607-255-4266. *Application contact:* Graduate Field Assistant, 607-255-4266, E-mail: sociology@cornell.edu.

Eastern Michigan University, Graduate School, College of Arts and Sciences, Department of Women's and Gender Studies, Ypsilanti, MI 48197. Offers MA, Graduate Certificate. Part-time and evening/weekend programs available. *Faculty:* 1 (woman) full-time. *Students:* 4 full-time (all women), 8 part-time (all women); includes 1 minority (Black or African American, non-Hispanic/Latino), 1 international. Average age 32. 18 applicants, 33% accepted, 3 enrolled. In 2010, 4 master's awarded. *Degree requirements:* For master's, thesis, research project, or practicum. *Entrance requirements:* Additional exam requirements/recommendations for international students: Required—TOEFL. *Application deadline:* For fall admission, 6/15 for domestic and international students; for winter admission, 9/15 for domestic and international students; for spring admission, 3/1 for domestic and international students. Applications are processed on a rolling basis. Application fee: $35. *Financial support:* Fellowships, research assistantships with full tuition reimbursements, teaching assistantships with full tuition reimbursements, career-related internships or fieldwork, Federal Work-Study, institutionally sponsored loans, scholarships/grants, tuition waivers (partial), and unspecified assistantships available. Support available to part-time students. Financial award applicants required to submit FAFSA. *Unit head:* Dr. Linda Pritchard, Department Head, 734-487-1177, Fax: 734-487-5029, E-mail: linda.pritchard@emich.edu. *Application contact:* Dr. Deanna Mihaly, Program Advisor, 734-487-1177, Fax: 734-487-5029, E-mail: dmihaly@emich.edu.

Indiana University Bloomington, University Graduate School, College of Arts and Sciences, Gender Studies Program, Bloomington, IN 47405-7000. Offers PhD. *Faculty:* 4 full-time (all women). *Students:* 26 full-time (21 women); includes 9 minority (2 Black or African American, non-Hispanic/Latino; 1 American Indian or Alaska Native, non-Hispanic/Latino; 4 Hispanic/Latino; 2 Two or more races, non-Hispanic/Latino), 3 international. Average age 29. 73 applicants, 15% accepted, 6 enrolled. *Application deadline:* For fall admission, 1/12 priority date for domestic students, 12/1 priority date for international students. Application fee: $55 ($65 for international students). *Financial support:* In 2010–11, 4 fellowships with tuition reimbursements (averaging $17,500 per year), 2 research assistantships with tuition reimbursements (averaging $12,485 per year), 11 teaching assistantships with tuition reimbursements (averaging $13,168 per year) were awarded. *Unit head:* Helen Gremillion, Director of Graduate Studies, 812-855-0101, E-mail: hgremill@indiana.edu. *Application contact:* Nina Taylor, Graduate Secretary, 812-855-4848, E-mail: nitaylor@indiana.edu.

Indiana University–Purdue University Indianapolis, School of Liberal Arts, Department of Sociology, Indianapolis, IN 46202-2896. Offers family/gender studies (MA); medical sociology (MA); work/occupations (MA). *Faculty:* 17 full-time (8 women). *Students:* 13 full-time (8 women), 9 part-time (5 women); includes 1 minority (Black or African American, non-Hispanic/Latino), 2 international. Average age 30. 16 applicants, 75% accepted, 10 enrolled. In 2010, 9 master's awarded. Application fee: $55 ($65 for international students). *Financial support:* In 2010–11, 2 fellowships (averaging $9,500 per year), 2 teaching assistantships (averaging $6,309 per year) were awarded. *Unit head:* Carrie Foote, Director of Graduate Studies, 317-274-8981, E-mail: sociology@iupui.edu. *Application contact:* Director of Research and Graduate Programs, 317-274-8305.

Instituto Tecnologico de Santo Domingo, Graduate School, Area of Humanities and Social Sciences, Santo Domingo, Dominican Republic. Offers accounting (Certificate); adult education (Certificate); applied linguistics (MA); economics (MA); education (M Ed); educational psychology (MA, Certificate); gender and development (MA, Certificate); humanistic studies (MA); international marketing management (Certificate); international relations in the Caribbean basin (Certificate); intervention systems in family therapy (MA); linguistic and literary communication (Certificate); pedagogical support (MA); social science education (M Ed); sustainable human development (MA); terminal illness and death psychology (Certificate); youth and adult education (M Ed).

Memorial University of Newfoundland, School of Graduate Studies, Department of Sociology, St. John's, NL A1C 5S7, Canada. Offers gender (PhD); maritime sociology (PhD); sociology (M Phil, MA); work and development (PhD). Part-time programs available. *Degree requirements:* For master's, comprehensive exam, thesis optional, program journal (M Phil); for doctorate, one foreign language, comprehensive exam, thesis/dissertation, oral defense of thesis. *Entrance requirements:* For master's, 2nd class degree from university of recognized standing in area of study; for doctorate, MA, M Phil, or equivalent. Electronic applications accepted. *Faculty research:* Work and development, gender, maritime sociology.

Minnesota State University Mankato, College of Graduate Studies, College of Social and Behavioral Sciences, Department of Gender and Women's Studies, Mankato, MN 56001. Offers MS, Certificate. Part-time programs available. *Students:* 12 full-time (11 women), 4 part-time (all women). *Degree requirements:* For master's, comprehensive exam, thesis or alternative. *Entrance requirements:* For master's, minimum GPA of 3.0 during previous 2 years of course work. Additional exam requirements/recommendations for international students: Required—TOEFL. *Application deadline:* For fall admission, 7/1 priority date for domestic students; for spring admission, 11/1 for domestic students. Applications are processed on a rolling basis. Application fee: $40. *Financial support:* Research assistantships, teaching assistantships with full tuition reimbursements, career-related internships or fieldwork, Federal Work-Study, institutionally sponsored loans, and unspecified assistantships available. Support available to part-time students. Financial award application deadline: 3/15; financial award applicants required to submit FAFSA. *Unit head:* Dr. Maria Bevacqua, Chairperson, 507-389-2077. *Application contact:* 507-389-2321, E-mail: grad@mnsu.edu.

Northern Arizona University, Graduate College, College of Social and Behavioral Sciences, Women's and Gender Studies Program, Flagstaff, AZ 86011. Offers Graduate Certificate. Part-time programs available. *Faculty:* 2 full-time (both women). *Students:* 1 (woman) full-time, 2 part-time (both women). Average age 25. 3 applicants, 67% accepted, 1 enrolled. In 2010, 5 Graduate Certificates awarded. *Entrance requirements:* Additional exam requirements/recommendations for international students: Required—TOEFL (minimum score 550 paper-based; 213 computer-based; 80 iBT). *Application deadline:* For fall admission, 3/1 priority date for international students; for spring admission, 9/15 priority date for international students. Applications are processed on a rolling basis. Application fee: $65. Electronic applications accepted. *Unit head:* Dr. Sanjam Ahluwalia, Chair, 928-523-8709, E-mail: sanjam.ahluwalia@nau.edu. *Application contact:* Dr. Sanjam Ahluwalia, Chair, 928-523-8709, E-mail: sanjam.ahluwalia@nau.edu.

Northwestern University, The Graduate School, Program in Gender Studies, Evanston, IL 60208. Offers PhD/Certificate. *Faculty research:* Anthropology, gender in Victorian period, autobiography, performance ethnographies, Slavic literature, women in the law.

Norwich University, School of Graduate and Continuing Studies, Program in Military History, Northfield, VT 05663. Offers race and gender in military history (MA); total war (MA); U. S. military history (MA). Evening/weekend programs available. *Faculty:* 33 part-time/adjunct (2 women). *Students:* 127 full-time (23 women); includes 2 Black or African American, non-Hispanic/Latino; 7 Hispanic/Latino. Average age 42. 157 applicants, 96% accepted, 127 enrolled. In 2010, 127 master's awarded. *Entrance requirements:* For master's, minimum undergraduate GPA of 2.75. Additional exam requirements/recommendations for international students: Required—TOEFL (minimum score 550 paper-based; 212 computer-based; 83 iBT). *Application deadline:* For fall admission, 8/10 for domestic and international students; for winter admission, 11/7 for domestic and international students; for spring admission, 2/6 for domestic and international students. Application fee: $50. Electronic applications accepted. *Expenses:* Tuition: Full-time $17,380; part-time $645 per credit. Tuition and fees vary according to program. *Financial support:* Scholarships/grants available. Financial award applicants required to submit FAFSA. *Unit head:* Dr. James Ehrman, Program Director, 802-485-2567, Fax: 802-485-2533. *Application contact:* Lars Nielsen, Administrative Director, 802-485-2853, Fax: 802-485-2533, E-mail: lnielsen@norwich.edu.

Queen's University at Kingston, School of Graduate Studies and Research, Faculty of Arts and Sciences, Department of Political Studies, Kingston, ON K7L 3N6, Canada. Offers Canadian politics (PhD); comparative politics (PhD); gender and politics (PhD); international relations (PhD); political theory (PhD). *Degree requirements:* For master's, thesis or alternative; for doctorate, one foreign language, thesis/dissertation, qualifying exams. *Entrance requirements:* Additional exam requirements/recommendations for international students: Required—TOEFL (minimum score 600 paper-based; 250 computer-based). *Faculty research:* Canadian politics, comparative politics, political thought, international politics, women and politics.

Roosevelt University, Graduate Division, College of Arts and Sciences, Department of Literature and Languages, Program in Women's and Gender Studies, Chicago, IL 60605. Offers MA, Certificate. Part-time and evening/weekend programs available. *Degree requirements:* For master's, thesis. *Entrance requirements:* For master's, minimum GPA of 2.7. *Faculty research:* Feminist economics; philosophy of feminism; race, class, and gender; women and art; women's history.

Rutgers, The State University of New Jersey, New Brunswick, Graduate School-New Brunswick, Program in Women's and Gender Studies, Piscataway, NJ 08854-8097. Offers MA, PhD. Part-time programs available. *Degree requirements:* For master's, thesis or alternative; for doctorate, comprehensive exam, thesis/dissertation. *Entrance requirements:* For master's and doctorate, GRE General Test, writing sample, 3 letters of recommendation. Additional exam requirements/recommendations for international students: Required—TOEFL. *Expenses:* Tuition, state resident: full-time $7200; part-time $600 per credit. Tuition, nonresident: full-time $11,124; part-time $927 per credit. *Faculty research:* Feminist theory, gender and sexuality, global and cultural studies, women in history, literature, and politics, feminist politics.

Saint Mary's University, Faculty of Arts, Program in Women and Gender Studies, Halifax, NS B3H 3C3, Canada. Offers MA. Program offered jointly with Mount Saint Vincent University. Part-time programs available. *Degree requirements:* For master's, thesis. *Entrance requirements:* For master's, honors degree.

Simmons College, College of Arts and Sciences Graduate Studies, Program in Gender/Cultural Studies, Boston, MA 02115. Offers MA, MA/MAT, MA/MS. Part-time programs available. *Degree requirements:* For master's, thesis. *Entrance requirements:* For master's, academic writing sample. Additional exam requirements/recommendations for international students: Required—TOEFL (minimum score 600 paper-based; 250 computer-based; 100 iBT). Electronic applications accepted. *Faculty research:* Gender and sexuality, queer theory, gender and the media, race, feminist film theory.

Syracuse University, College of Arts and Sciences, Program in Women's and Gender Studies, Syracuse, NY 13244. Offers CAS. *Students:* 1 applicant, 100% accepted, 0 enrolled. In 2010, 12 CASs awarded. *Entrance requirements:* For degree, Syracuse graduate program matriculation. Additional exam requirements/recommendations for international students: Required—TOEFL (minimum score 100 iBT). *Application deadline:* For fall admission, 2/1 priority date for domestic and international students. Application fee: $75. Electronic applications accepted. *Expenses:* Tuition: Part-time $1162 per credit. *Unit head:* Dr. Chandra Talpade Mohanty, Chair, 315-443-3707, E-mail: ctmohant@syr.edu. *Application contact:* Susann Democker-Shedd, Program contact, 315-443-3560, E-mail: sademock@syr.edu.

The University of Arizona, College of Social and Behavioral Sciences, Department of Gender and Women's Studies, Tucson, AZ 85721. Offers MA, PhD. Part-time programs available. *Faculty:* 5 full-time (4 women), 4 part-time/adjunct (all women). *Students:* 7 full-time (5 women), 4 part-time (all women); includes 2 Hispanic/Latino; 1 Two or more races, non-Hispanic/Latino, 2 international. Average age 29. 18 applicants, 44% accepted, 1 enrolled. In 2010, 4 master's awarded. *Degree requirements:* For master's, thesis/project. *Entrance requirements:* For master's and doctorate, GRE (minimum score: 500 verbal, 500 quantitative, 4.5 analytical), 3 letters of recommendation. Additional exam requirements/recommendations for international students: Required—TOEFL (minimum score 600 paper-based; 250 computer-based; 100 iBT). *Application deadline:* For fall admission, 12/1 for domestic and international students. Applications are processed on a rolling basis. Application fee: $65. Electronic applications accepted. *Expenses:* Tuition, state resident: full-time $7692. *Financial support:* In 2010–11, 3 research assistantships with full tuition reimbursements (averaging $18,282 per year), 12 teaching assistantships with full tuition reimbursements (averaging $18,282 per year) were awarded; career-related internships or fieldwork, scholarships/grants, health care benefits, tuition waivers (full and partial), and unspecified assistantships also available. Financial award application deadline: 1/15. *Faculty research:* Gender race and border studies, sexuality and the body, gender health and science, cultural representation and theory, public policy and social movements. Total annual research expenditures: $106,592. *Unit head:* Dr. Laura Briggs, Department Head, 520-626-9149, Fax: 520-621-1533, E-mail: lbriggs@email.arizona.edu. *Application contact:* Susan D. Whitworth, Information Contact, 520-626-5657, Fax: 520-621-1533, E-mail: whitwort@email.arizona.edu.

University of Colorado Denver, College of Liberal Arts and Sciences, Program in Humanities, Denver, CO 80217-3364. Offers community health science (MSS); humanities (MH); international studies (MSS); social science (MSS); society and the environment (MSS); women's and gender studies (MSS). Part-time and evening/weekend programs available. *Students:* 53 full-time (39 women), 35 part-time (22 women); includes 4 Black or African American, non-Hispanic/Latino; 1 American Indian or Alaska Native, non-Hispanic/Latino; 3 Asian, non-Hispanic/Latino; 7 Hispanic/Latino, 1 international. Average age 33. 41 applicants, 54% accepted, 19 enrolled. In 2010, 29 master's awarded. *Degree requirements:* For master's, thesis or alternative, 36 credit hours, project or thesis. *Entrance requirements:* For master's, writing sample, statement of purpose/letter of intent. Additional exam requirements/recommendations for international students: Required—TOEFL (minimum score 525 paper-based). *Application deadline:* For fall admission, 5/15 priority date for domestic students; for spring admission, 10/15 priority date for domestic students. Application fee: $50 ($75 for international students). Electronic applications accepted. *Expenses:* Tuition, state resident: full-time $7332; part-time $355 per credit hour. Tuition, nonresident: full-time $18,990; part-time $1055 per credit hour. Required fees: $998. Tuition and fees vary according to course level, course load, degree level, campus/location, program, reciprocity agreements and student level. *Financial support:* Federal Work-Study and scholarships/grants available. Financial award application deadline: 4/1; financial award applicants required to submit FAFSA. *Faculty research:* Women and gender in the classical Mediterranean, communication theory and democracy, relationship between psychology and philosophy. *Unit head:* Myra Bookman, Associate Director of Humanities and Social Science, 303-556-2496, Fax: 303-556-8100, E-mail: myra.bookman@ucdenver.edu. *Application contact:* Catherine Osmundson, Program Assistant, 303-556-2305, E-mail: catherine.osmundson@ucdenver.edu.

University of Florida, Graduate School, College of Liberal Arts and Sciences, Center for Women's Studies and Gender Research, Gainesville, FL 32611. Offers gender and development (Graduate Certificate); women's studies (MA, Graduate Certificate); MA/JD; MA/MA. *Faculty:* 3 full-time (all women), 3 part-time/adjunct (all women). *Students:* 7 full-time (all women), 1 (woman) part-time. Average age 27. 17 applicants, 65% accepted, 3 enrolled. In 2010, 3 master's awarded. Terminal master's awarded for partial completion of doctoral program. *Degree requirements:* For master's, thesis or project. *Entrance requirements:* For master's, GRE General Test (minimum score 1000), minimum GPA of 3.0. Additional exam requirements/recommendations for international students: Required—TOEFL (minimum score 550 paper-based; 213 computer-based; 80 iBT), IELTS (minimum score 6). *Application deadline:* For fall admission, 1/15 for domestic and international students; for spring admission, 10/1 for domestic and international students. Application fee: $30. Electronic applications accepted. *Expenses:* Tuition, state resident: full-time $10,915.92. Tuition, nonresident: full-time $28,309. *Financial support:* In 2010–11, 7 students received support, including 2 fellowships, 1 research assistantship (averaging $13,786 per year), 4 teaching assistantships (averaging $7,048 per year). Financial award application deadline: 1/15; financial award applicants required to submit FAFSA. *Faculty research:* Transnational feminism and postcolonial theory; gender, sexuality, and social movements; U. S. women of color, especially African American and Latina women; U. S. and British literature and cultural history; gender and indigenous identity in Latin America. *Unit head:* Dr. Judith Page, Director, 352-273-0387, Fax: 352-392-4873, E-mail: page7@ufl.edu. *Application contact:* Dr. Florence Babb, Graduate Coordinator, 352-273-0384, Fax: 352-392-4873, E-mail: fbabb@ufl.edu.

University of Maine, Graduate School, College of Liberal Arts and Sciences, Department of English, Orono, ME 04469. Offers composition and pedagogy (MA); creative (MA); gender and literature (MA); poetry and poetics (MA). Part-time and evening/weekend programs available. *Faculty:* 18 full-time (7 women), 20 part-time/adjunct (10 women). *Students:* 25 full-time (8 women), 6 part-time (5 women). Average age 28. 36 applicants, 47% accepted, 14 enrolled. In 2010, 13 degrees awarded. *Degree requirements:* For master's, one foreign language, thesis optional. *Entrance requirements:* For master's, GRE General Test, minimum GPA of 3.0. Additional exam requirements/recommendations for international students: Required—TOEFL. *Application deadline:* For fall admission, 2/1 priority date for domestic students. Applications are processed on a rolling basis. Application fee: $65. Electronic applications accepted. *Expenses:* Tuition, state resident: full-time $400. Tuition, nonresident: full-time $1050. *Financial support:* In 2010–11, 21 teaching assistantships with tuition reimbursements (averaging $12,790 per year) were awarded; Federal Work-Study and tuition waivers (full and partial) also available. Financial award application deadline: 3/1. *Faculty research:* Contemporary poetics, contemporary criticism, composition theory and pedagogy, feminist approaches to literature. *Unit head:* Dr. Naomi Jacobs, Chair, 207-581-3822, Fax: 207-581-1604. *Application contact:* Scott G. Delcourt, Associate Dean of the Graduate School, 207-581-3291, Fax: 207-581-3232, E-mail: graduate@maine.edu.

University of Missouri–St. Louis, College of Arts and Sciences, Interdisciplinary Programs, St. Louis, MO 63121. Offers gender studies (Certificate); international studies (Certificate). *Expenses:* Tuition, state resident: full-time $5522; part-time $306.80 per credit hour. Tuition, nonresident: full-time $14,253; part-time $792.10 per credit hour. Required fees: $658; $49 per credit hour. One-time fee: $12. Tuition and fees vary according to program. *Unit head:* Dr. Ronald Yasbin, Dean, 314-516-5501. *Application contact:* Graduate Admissions, 314-516-5458, Fax: 314-516-6996, E-mail: gradadm@umsl.edu.

The University of North Carolina at Charlotte, Graduate School, College of Arts and Sciences, Department of Sociology, Charlotte, NC 28223-0001. Offers health research (MA); mathematical sociology and quantitative methods (MA); organizations, occupations, and work (MA); political sociology (MA); race and gender (MA); social psychology (MA); social theory (MA); sociology of education (MA); stratification (MA). Part-time and evening/weekend programs available. *Faculty:* 18 full-time (10 women). *Students:* 11 full-time (7 women), 14 part-time (8 women); includes 6 minority (4 Black or African American, non-Hispanic/Latino; 2 Asian, non-Hispanic/Latino). Average age 29. 20 applicants, 60% accepted, 8 enrolled. In 2010, 2 master's awarded. *Degree requirements:* For master's, thesis or alternative, thesis or comprehensive exam. *Entrance requirements:* For master's, GRE or MAT, minimum GPA of 3.0 in last 2 years, 2.75 overall. Additional exam requirements/recommendations for international students: Required—TOEFL (minimum score 557 paper-based; 220 computer-based; 83 iBT). *Application deadline:* For fall admission, 7/1 for domestic students, 5/1 for international students; for spring admission, 11/1 for domestic students, 10/1 for international students. Applications are processed on a rolling basis. Application fee: $55. Electronic applications accepted. *Expenses:* Tuition, state resident: full-time $3464. Tuition, nonresident: full-time $14,297. Required fees: $2094. Tuition and fees vary according to course load. *Financial support:* In 2010–11, 6 students received support, including 1 fellowship (averaging $60,000 per year), 1 research assistantship (averaging $9,000 per year), 1 teaching assistantship (averaging $9,000 per year); career-related internships or fieldwork, institutionally sponsored loans, scholarships/grants, and unspecified assistantships also available. Support available to part-time students. Financial award application deadline: 4/1; financial award applicants required to submit FAFSA. *Faculty research:* Social psychology, sociology of education, social gerontology, quantitative methodology, medical sociology. Total annual research expenditures: $61,382. *Unit head:* Dr. Lisa Rachotte, Chair, 704-687-2288, Fax: 704-687-3091, E-mail: lrashott@uncc.edu. *Application contact:* Kathy B. Giddings, Director of Graduate Admissions, 704-687-5503, Fax: 704-687-3279, E-mail: gradadm@uncc.edu.

The University of North Carolina at Greensboro, Graduate School, College of Arts and Sciences, Program in Women's and Gender Studies, Greensboro, NC 27412-5001. Offers MA, Certificate. Electronic applications accepted.

University of Northern British Columbia, Office of Graduate Studies, Prince George, BC V2N 4Z9, Canada. Offers business administration (Diploma); community health science (M Sc); disability management (MA); education (M Ed); first nations studies (MA); gender studies (MA); history (MA); interdisciplinary studies (MA); international studies (MA); mathematical, computer and physical sciences (M Sc); natural resources and environmental studies (M Sc, MA, MNRES, PhD); political science (MA); psychology (M Sc, PhD); social work (MSW). Part-time and evening/weekend programs available. Postbaccalaureate distance learning degree programs offered (no on-campus study). *Degree requirements:* For master's, thesis; for doctorate, thesis/dissertation. *Entrance requirements:* For master's, GRE, minimum B average in undergraduate course work; for doctorate, candidacy exam, minimum A average in graduate course work.

University of Northern Iowa, Graduate College, Program in Women's and Gender Studies, Cedar Falls, IA 50614. Offers MA. *Students:* 8 full-time (7 women), 2 part-time (both women); includes 1 minority (Black or African American, non-Hispanic/Latino). 14 applicants, 79% accepted, 4 enrolled. In 2010, 1 master's awarded. *Degree requirements:* For master's, comprehensive exam (for some programs), thesis or alternative. *Entrance requirements:* For master's, minimum GPA of 3.0. Additional exam requirements/recommendations for international students: Required—TOEFL (minimum score 500 paper-based; 180 computer-based;

61 iBT). *Application deadline:* Applications are processed on a rolling basis. Application fee: $50 ($70 for international students). Electronic applications accepted. *Financial support:* Application deadline: 2/1. *Unit head:* Dr. Phyllis L. Baker, Director/Professor, 319-273-7102, Fax: 319-273-3053, E-mail: phyllis.baker@uni.edu. *Application contact:* Laurie S. Russell, Record Analyst, 319-273-2623, Fax: 319-273-2885, E-mail: laurie.russell@uni.edu.

University of Oklahoma, College of Arts and Sciences, Women's and Gender Studies Program, Norman, OK 73019. Offers Graduate Certificate. *Students:* 6 full-time (all women), 5 part-time (4 women); includes 1 minority (American Indian or Alaska Native, non-Hispanic/Latino), 1 international. Average age 38. 4 applicants, 100% accepted, 2 enrolled. *Entrance requirements:* Additional exam requirements/recommendations for international students: Required—TOEFL (minimum score 550 paper-based; 213 computer-based; 79 iBT). *Application deadline:* Applications are processed on a rolling basis. Application fee: $40 ($90 for international students). Electronic applications accepted. *Expenses:* Tuition, state resident: full-time $3893; part-time $162.20 per credit hour. Tuition, nonresident: full-time $14,167; part-time $590.30 per credit hour. Required fees: $2523; $94.60 per credit hour. Tuition and fees vary according to course load and degree level. *Financial support:* In 2010–11, 4 research assistantships (averaging $9,890 per year), 3 teaching assistantships (averaging $9,621 per year) were awarded. *Unit head:* Jill Irvine, Director, 405-325-3481, Fax: 405-325-3573, E-mail: jill.irvine@ou.edu. *Application contact:* Jill Irvine, Director, 405-325-3481, Fax: 405-325-3573, E-mail: jill.irvine@ou.edu.

University of Saskatchewan, College of Graduate Studies and Research, College of Arts and Sciences, Department of Women's and Gender Studies, Saskatoon, SK S7N 5A2, Canada. Offers MA, PhD. *Degree requirements:* For master's, thesis; for doctorate, comprehensive exam (for some programs), thesis/dissertation. *Entrance requirements:* Additional exam requirements/recommendations for international students: Required—TOEFL (minimum score 80 iBT); Recommended—IELTS (minimum score 6.5). Electronic applications accepted.

The University of Texas at El Paso, Graduate School, College of Liberal Arts, Women's Studies Program, El Paso, TX 79968-0001. Offers women's and gender studies (Certificate). *Unit head:* Dr. Howard C. Daudistel, Dean, 915-747-5666, Fax: 915-747-5905, E-mail: hdaudistel@utep.edu. *Application contact:* Dr. Patricia D. Witherspoon, Dean of the Graduate School, 915-747-5491, Fax: 915-747-5788, E-mail: withersp@utep.edu.

University of Toronto, School of Graduate Studies, Humanities Division, Women and Gender Studies Institute, Toronto, ON M5S 1A1, Canada. Offers MA.

Virginia Polytechnic Institute and State University, Graduate School, College of Liberal Arts and Human Sciences, Department of Sociology, Blacksburg, VA 24061. Offers race and social policy (Certificate); sociology (MS, PhD); women's and gender studies (Certificate). *Faculty:* 26 full-time (12 women), 1 (woman) part-time/adjunct. *Students:* 39 full-time (25 women), 7 part-time (3 women); includes 10 Black or African American, non-Hispanic/Latino; 2 Hispanic/Latino, 2 international. Average age 33. 27 applicants, 22% accepted, 5 enrolled. In 2010, 7 master's, 3 doctorates awarded. *Degree requirements:* For master's, comprehensive exam (for some programs), thesis (for some programs); for doctorate, comprehensive exam (for some programs), thesis/dissertation (for some programs). *Entrance requirements:* For master's and doctorate, GRE. Additional exam requirements/recommendations for international students: Required—TOEFL (minimum score 550 paper-based; 213 computer-based). *Application deadline:* For fall admission, 7/1 for domestic and international students; for spring admission, 12/1 for domestic and international students. Applications are processed on a rolling basis. Application fee: $65. Electronic applications accepted. *Expenses:* Tuition, state resident: full-time $9399; part-time $488 per credit hour. Tuition, nonresident: full-time $17,854; part-time $957.75 per credit hour. Required fees: $1534. Full-time tuition and fees vary according to program. *Financial support:* In 2010–11, 2 research assistantships with full tuition reimbursements (averaging $13,864 per year), 19 teaching assistantships with full tuition reimbursements (averaging $13,074 per year) were awarded; career-related internships or fieldwork, Federal Work-Study, scholarships/grants, health care benefits, and unspecified assistantships also available. Financial award application deadline: 1/15. *Faculty research:* Science and technology, deviance and criminology, social psychology, social organization, demography. Total annual research expenditures: $42,630. *Unit head:* Dr. John W. Ryan, UNIT HEAD, 540-231-6878, Fax: 540-231-3860, E-mail: johnryan@vt.edu. *Application contact:* Jim Hawdon, Contact, 540-231-7476, Fax: 540-231-3860, E-mail: hawdonj@vt.edu.

Wilfrid Laurier University, Faculty of Graduate and Postdoctoral Studies, Faculty of Arts, Cultural Analysis and Social Theory Program, Waterloo, ON N2L 3C5, Canada. Offers body politics (MA); cultural representation and social theory (MA); gender, sexuality and embodiment (MA); globalization, identity and social movements (MA). Part-time programs available. *Faculty:* 16 full-time (10 women). *Students:* 9 full-time (6 women), 2 part-time (both women). 23 applicants, 61% accepted, 7 enrolled. In 2010, 4 master's awarded. *Entrance requirements:* For master's, honours BA in humanities, social science or interdisciplinary program with social theory, minimum B+ in final year of full-time study. Additional exam requirements/recommendations for international students: Required—TOEFL (minimum score 89 iBT). *Application deadline:* For fall admission, 2/1 priority date for domestic and international students. Application fee: $100. Electronic applications accepted. Tuition and fees charges are reported in Canadian dollars. *Expenses:* Tuition, area resident: Full-time $15,300 Canadian dollars; part-time $1200 Canadian dollars per credit. International tuition: $21,300 Canadian dollars full-time. Required fees: $650 Canadian dollars; $100 Canadian dollars per credit. Tuition and fees vary according to course load, degree level, campus/location and program. *Financial support:* Career-related internships or fieldwork, scholarships/grants, and unspecified assistantships available. *Faculty research:* Globalization; identity and social movements; body politics: gender, sexuality and embodiment; cultural representation and social theory. *Unit head:* Dr. Jasmin Zine, Director, 519-884-0710 Ext. 3267, Fax: 519-884-8854, E-mail: jzine@wlu.ca. *Application contact:* Jennifer Williams, Graduate Admission and Records Officer, 519-884-0710 Ext. 3536, Fax: 519-884-1020, E-mail: gradstudies@wlu.ca.

Wilfrid Laurier University, Faculty of Graduate and Postdoctoral Studies, Faculty of Arts, Department of English and Film Studies, Waterloo, ON N2L 3C5, Canada. Offers gender and genre (MA, PhD); nation, diaspora, culture (PhD); textuality, media and print studies (PhD). *Faculty:* 22 full-time (14 women). *Students:* 29 full-time (16 women), 1 (woman) part-time. 71 applicants, 48% accepted, 18 enrolled. In 2010, 15 master's, 2 doctorates awarded. *Degree requirements:* For master's, thesis optional; for doctorate, thesis/dissertation. *Entrance requirements:* For master's, honours BA or the equivalent in English, minimum B+ in English courses above first year level; for doctorate, MA in English, minimum A- average in graduate work. Additional exam requirements/recommendations for international students: Recommended—TOEFL (minimum score 89 iBT). *Application deadline:* For fall admission, 2/1 priority date for domestic and international students. Application fee: $100. Electronic applications accepted. Tuition and fees charges are reported in Canadian dollars. *Expenses:* Tuition, area resident: Full-time $15,300 Canadian dollars; part-time $1200 Canadian dollars per credit. International tuition: $21,300 Canadian dollars full-time. Required fees: $650 Canadian dollars; $100 Canadian dollars per credit. Tuition and fees vary according to course load, degree level, campus/location and program. *Financial support:* In 2010–11, 44 fellowships, 44 teaching assistantships were awarded; career-related internships or fieldwork, scholarships/grants, health care benefits, and unspecified assistantships also available. *Faculty research:* Gender and genre, Canadian studies, early modern studies, postcolonial studies, nineteenth century studies. *Unit head:* Dr. Tanis MacDonald, Graduate Coordinator, 519-884-0710 Ext. 2931, Fax: 519-884-8307, E-mail: tmacdonald@wlu.ca. *Application contact:* Jennifer Williams, Graduate Admissions and Records Officer, 519-884-0710 Ext. 3536, Fax: 519-884-1020, E-mail: gradstudies@wlu.ca.

Hispanic Studies

Brown University, Graduate School, Department of Hispanic Studies, Providence, RI 02912. Offers MA, PhD. *Degree requirements:* For master's, one foreign language, thesis; for doctorate, 2 foreign languages, thesis/dissertation, preliminary exam.

California State University, Los Angeles, Graduate Studies, College of Natural and Social Sciences, Department of Chicano Studies, Los Angeles, CA 90032-8530. Offers Mexican-American studies (MA). Part-time and evening/weekend programs available. *Faculty:* 2 full-time (both women), 3 part-time/adjunct (1 woman). *Students:* 5 full-time (3 women), 10 part-time (7 women); includes 14 minority (all Hispanic/Latino). Average age 29. 13 applicants, 100% accepted, 6 enrolled. In 2010, 6 master's awarded. *Degree requirements:* For master's, one foreign language, comprehensive exam or thesis. *Entrance requirements:* For master's, undergraduate major in Mexican-American studies or related area, 12 units in Chicano studies. Additional exam requirements/recommendations for international students: Required—TOEFL (minimum score 500 paper-based; 173 computer-based). *Application deadline:* For fall admission, 5/1 for domestic and international students. Applications are processed on a rolling basis. Application fee: $55. Electronic applications accepted. *Financial support:* Career-related internships or fieldwork and Federal Work-Study available. Support available to part-time students. Financial award application deadline: 3/1. *Faculty research:* U. S.-Mexican relations, Chicano literature, community organization among Chicanos and Hispanics, Spanish language in the American Southwest. *Unit head:* Dr. Michael Soldatenko, Chair, 323-343-2400, Fax: 323-343-5609, E-mail: msoldat@calstatela.edu. *Application contact:* Dr. Alan Muchlinski, Dean of Graduate Studies, 323-343-3820, Fax: 323-343-5653, E-mail: amuchli@exchange.calstatela.edu.

California State University, Northridge, Graduate Studies, College of Humanities, Department of Chicana and Chicano Studies, Northridge, CA 91330. Offers MA. *Degree requirements:* For master's, thesis, project. *Entrance requirements:* Additional exam requirements/recommendations for international students: Required—TOEFL.

Eastern Michigan University, Graduate School, College of Arts and Sciences, Department of World Languages, Ypsilanti, MI 48197. Offers foreign languages (MA, Graduate Certificate), including French (MA), German (MA), German for business (Graduate Certificate), Hispanic language and cultures (Graduate Certificate), Japanese business practices (Graduate Certificate), Spanish (MA); language and international trade (MA); teaching English to speakers of other languages (MA, Graduate Certificate). Part-time and evening/weekend programs available. Postbaccalaureate distance learning degree programs offered (minimal on-campus study). *Faculty:* 23 full-time (13 women). *Students:* 12 full-time (9 women), 54 part-time (47 women); includes 12 minority (3 Black or African American, non-Hispanic/Latino; 2 Asian, non-Hispanic/Latino; 7 Hispanic/Latino), 13 international. Average age 35. 68 applicants, 40% accepted, 20 enrolled. In 2010, 24 master's, 3 other advanced degrees awarded. *Degree requirements:* For master's, one foreign language. *Entrance requirements:* Additional exam requirements/recommendations for international students: Required—TOEFL. *Application deadline:* Applications are processed on a rolling basis. Application fee: $35. *Financial support:* Fellowships, research assistantships with full tuition reimbursements, teaching assistantships with full tuition reimbursements, career-related internships or fieldwork, Federal Work-Study, institutionally sponsored loans, scholarships/grants, tuition waivers (partial), and unspecified assistantships available. Support available to part-time students. Financial award applicants required to submit FAFSA. *Unit head:* Dr. Rosemary Weston-Gil, Department Head, 734-487-0130, Fax: 734-487-3411, E-mail: rweston3@emich.edu. *Application contact:* Dr. Rosemary Weston-Gil, Department Head, 734-487-0130, Fax: 734-487-3411, E-mail: rweston3@emich.edu.

La Salle University, School of Arts and Sciences, Program in Bilingual/Bicultural Studies (Spanish), Philadelphia, PA 19141-1199. Offers MA. Part-time and evening/weekend programs available. *Degree requirements:* For master's, one foreign language, thesis or alternative, project. *Entrance requirements:* For master's, GRE or MAT. *Expenses:* Contact institution. *Faculty research:* Puerto Rican literature, cross-cultural communication, English as a second language methodology, Spanish language.

Louisiana State University and Agricultural and Mechanical College, Graduate School, College of Humanities and Social Sciences, Department of Foreign Languages and Literatures, Baton Rouge, LA 70803. Offers Hispanic studies (MA). Part-time programs available. *Faculty:* 22 full-time (8 women). *Students:* 10 full-time (8 women), 3 part-time (all women); includes 2 Hispanic/Latino, 2 international. Average age 27. 8 applicants, 63% accepted, 1 enrolled. In 2010, 5 master's awarded. *Degree requirements:* For master's, 2 foreign languages, thesis optional. *Entrance requirements:* For master's, GRE General Test, minimum GPA of 3.0. Additional exam requirements/recommendations for international students: Required—TOEFL (minimum score 550 paper-based; 213 computer-based; 79 iBT) or IELTS (minimum score 6.5). *Application deadline:* For fall admission, 1/25 priority date for domestic students, 5/15 for international students; for spring admission, 10/15 for international students. Applications are processed on a rolling basis. Application fee: $50 ($70 for international students). Electronic applications accepted. *Financial support:* In 2010–11, 12 students received support, including 9 teaching assistantships with partial tuition reimbursements available (averaging $10,500 per year); fellowships with full tuition reimbursements available, research assistantships with partial tuition reimbursements available, Federal Work-Study, scholarships/grants, health care benefits, and tuition waivers (full and partial) also available. Financial award application deadline: 4/1; financial award applicants required to submit FAFSA. *Faculty research:* Hispanic cultural studies, linguistics, literary and cultural theory, peninsular and Latin American literature. Total annual research expenditures: $3,905. *Unit head:* Dr. John Pizer, Chair, 225-578-6627, Fax: 225-578-5074, E-mail: pizerj@lsu.edu. *Application contact:* Dr. Eleno Castro, Graduate Adviser, 225-578-6616, Fax: 225-578-5074, E-mail: ecastro@lsu.edu.

McGill University, Faculty of Graduate and Postdoctoral Studies, Faculty of Arts, Department of Hispanic Studies, Montréal, QC H3A 2T5, Canada. Offers MA, PhD.

Michigan State University, The Graduate School, College of Arts and Letters, Department of Spanish and Portuguese, East Lansing, MI 48824. Offers applied Spanish linguistics (MA); Hispanic cultural studies (PhD); Hispanic literatures (MA). *Entrance requirements:* Additional exam requirements/recommendations for international students: Required—TOEFL. Electronic applications accepted.

New York University, NYU in Madrid, Madrid, NY 10012-1019, Spain. Offers creative writing in Spanish (MFA); Spanish (PhD); Spanish and Latin American literatures and cultures (MA); Spanish language and translation (MA).

Pontifical Catholic University of Puerto Rico, College of Arts and Humanities, Department of Hispanic Studies, Ponce, PR 00717-0777. Offers grammar and writing (Professional Certificate); Hispanic studies (MA). Part-time and evening/weekend programs available. *Degree requirements:* For master's, variable foreign language requirement, comprehensive exam, thesis or alternative. *Entrance requirements:* For master's, GRE General Test, 2 letters of recommendation, interview, minimum GPA of 2.75. Electronic applications accepted.

Queen's University at Kingston, School of Graduate Studies and Research, Faculty of Arts and Sciences, Department of Spanish and Italian, Kingston, ON K7L 3N6, Canada. Offers Spanish language and literature (MA). Part-time programs available. *Degree requirements:* For master's, one foreign language, thesis. *Entrance requirements:* Additional exam requirements/recommendations for international students: Required—TOEFL. Electronic applications accepted. *Faculty research:* Golden Age, nineteenth- and twentieth-century Peninsular novel, literary theory, colonial Latin America, nineteenth-and-twentieth century Latin America.

St. Thomas University, School of Leadership Studies, Program in Hispanic Media, Miami Gardens, FL 33054-6459. Offers MA, Certificate. Part-time and evening/weekend programs available. *Degree requirements:* For master's, comprehensive exam. *Entrance requirements:*

Additional exam requirements/recommendations for international students: Required—TOEFL (minimum score 550 paper-based; 213 computer-based; 79 iBT). Electronic applications accepted.

San Jose State University, Graduate Studies and Research, College of Social Sciences, Department of Mexican American Studies, San Jose, CA 95192-0001. Offers MA. Electronic applications accepted.

Texas A&M International University, Office of Graduate Studies and Research, College of Arts and Sciences, Department of Language and Literature, Laredo, TX 78041-1900. Offers English (MA); Hispanic studies (PhD); Spanish (MA). *Faculty:* 6 full-time (3 women). *Students:* 4 full-time (3 women), 34 part-time (22 women); includes 34 Hispanic/Latino, 1 international. Average age 33. 13 applicants, 77% accepted, 8 enrolled. In 2010, 15 master's awarded. *Entrance requirements:* For master's, GRE General Test. Additional exam requirements/recommendations for international students: Required—TOEFL (minimum score 550 paper-based; 213 computer-based). *Application deadline:* For fall admission, 4/30 priority date for domestic students; for spring admission, 11/30 for domestic students. Applications are processed on a rolling basis. Application fee: $25. *Financial support:* In 2010–11, 12 students received support, including 3 fellowships, 4 research assistantships, 2 teaching assistantships. Financial award application deadline: 11/1. *Unit head:* Dr. Manuel Broncano, Chair, 956-326-2470, E-mail: manuel.broncano@tamiu.edu. *Application contact:* Suzanne Hansen-Alford, Director of Graduate Recruiting, 956-326-3023, Fax: 956-326-3021, E-mail: enroll@tamiu.edu.

University of Alberta, Faculty of Graduate Studies and Research, Department of Modern Languages and Cultural Studies, Edmonton, AB T6G 2E1, Canada. Offers applied linguistics (Germanic, Romance, Slavic) (MA); French language, literatures and linguistics (PhD); French language, literatures, and linguistics (MA); Germanic languages, literatures and linguistics (PhD); Germanic languages, literatures, and linguistics (MA); Italian studies (MA); Slavic languages and literatures (Russian, Ukrainian) (MA, PhD); Slavic linguistics (Russian, Ukrainian) (MA, PhD); Spanish and Latin American studies (MA, PhD); Ukrainian folklore (MA, PhD). Part-time programs available. *Degree requirements:* For master's, one foreign language, thesis; for doctorate, 2 foreign languages, comprehensive exam, thesis/dissertation. *Entrance requirements:* For master's and doctorate, 1 language other than English. Additional exam requirements/recommendations for international students: Required—Michigan English Language Assessment Battery or TOEFL (minimum score 550 paper-based; 213 computer-based). Electronic applications accepted. *Faculty research:* Russian/Ukrainian studies; German studies; contemporary Latin American, French and Francophone studies; Italian studies.

The University of British Columbia, Faculty of Arts and Faculty of Graduate Studies, Department of French, Hispanic and Italian Studies, Vancouver, BC V6T 1Z1, Canada. Offers French (MA, PhD); Hispanic studies (MA, PhD). Part-time programs available. *Degree requirements:* For master's, thesis optional; for doctorate, 2 foreign languages, comprehensive exam, thesis/dissertation. *Entrance requirements:* For doctorate, MA. Additional exam requirements/recommendations for international students: Required—TOEFL (minimum score 550 paper-based; 213 computer-based; 80 iBT). Electronic applications accepted. Tuition charges are reported in Canadian dollars. *Expenses:* Tuition, area resident: Full-time $4179 Canadian dollars. International tuition: $7344 Canadian dollars full-time. *Faculty research:* Medieval and Renaissance literature, modern literature, romance philology and linguistics, cultural studies, women's literature.

University of California, Riverside, Graduate Division, Department of Hispanic Studies, Riverside, CA 92521-0102. Offers Spanish (MA, PhD). Terminal master's awarded for partial completion of doctoral program. *Degree requirements:* For master's, one foreign language, comprehensive exam; for doctorate, one foreign language, thesis/dissertation, qualifying exams, 1 quarter of teaching experience. *Entrance requirements:* For master's and doctorate, GRE General Test, minimum GPA of 3.2. Additional exam requirements/recommendations for international students: Required—TOEFL (minimum score 550 paper-based; 213 computer-based; 80 iBT). Electronic applications accepted. *Faculty research:* Spanish literature of sixteenth, seventeenth and twentieth century; pre-Columbian and colonial Latin American literature; nineteenth and twentieth century Latin American literature.

University of California, Santa Barbara, Graduate Division, College of Letters and Sciences, Division of Humanities and Fine Arts, Department of Spanish and Portuguese, Santa Barbara, CA 93106-4150. Offers Hispanic languages and literature (PhD); including European medieval studies, feminist studies, Hispanic linguistics, Hispanic literature, Luso-Brazilian literature; Hispanic linguistics (MA); Luso-Brazilian literature (MA); Spanish or Spanish-American literature (MA); MA/PhD. Spanish Language Institute available during summer session. *Faculty:* 16 full-time (7 women). *Students:* 32 full-time (22 women); includes 1 Black or African American, non-Hispanic/Latino; 1 Asian, non-Hispanic/Latino; 9 Hispanic/Latino. Average age 32. 34 applicants, 26% accepted, 5 enrolled. In 2010, 3 master's, 3 doctorates awarded. Terminal master's awarded for partial completion of doctoral program. *Degree requirements:* For master's, 2 foreign languages, comprehensive exam (for some programs), thesis optional; for doctorate, 3 foreign languages, comprehensive exam, thesis/dissertation. *Entrance requirements:* For master's and doctorate, GRE. Additional exam requirements/recommendations for international students: Required—TOEFL (minimum score 550 paper-based; 80 iBT), IELTS (minimum score 7). *Application deadline:* For fall admission, 12/15 for domestic and international students. Application fee: $70 ($90 for international students). Electronic applications accepted. *Financial support:* In 2010–11, 32 students received support, including 12 fellowships with full and partial tuition reimbursements available (averaging $10,016 per year), 27 teaching assistantships with full and partial tuition reimbursements available (averaging $14,583 per year); career-related internships or fieldwork, Federal Work-Study, tuition waivers (full and partial), and unspecified assistantships also available. Financial award application deadline: 12/15; financial award applicants required to submit FAFSA. *Faculty research:* Nineteenth century Spanish and Portuguese literature, Spanish and Spanish American literature, nineteenth and twentieth century Portuguese and Brazilian literatures, Hispanic linguistics, Catalan language and culture. *Unit head:* Prof. Francisco A. Lomeli, Chair, 805-893-5715, Fax: 805-893-8341, E-mail: lomeli@spanport.ucsb.edu. *Application contact:* Ashley Bradbury, Graduate Program Assistant, 805-893-2131, Fax: 805-893-8341, E-mail: ashley@hfa.ucsb.edu.

University of California, Santa Barbara, Graduate Division, College of Letters and Sciences, Division of Social Sciences, Department of Chicana and Chicano Studies, Santa Barbara, CA 93106-4120. Offers MA/PhD. *Faculty:* 11 full-time (6 women). *Students:* 24 full-time (14 women); includes 2 American Indian or Alaska Native, non-Hispanic/Latino; 21 Hispanic/Latino. Average age 31. 20 applicants, 25% accepted, 4 enrolled. *Entrance requirements:* Additional exam requirements/recommendations for international students: Required—TOEFL (minimum score 550 paper-based; 80 iBT), IELTS (minimum score 7). *Application deadline:* For fall admission, 12/15 for domestic and international students. Application fee: $70 ($90 for international students). Electronic applications accepted. *Financial support:* In 2010–11, 22 students received support, including 14 fellowships with full and partial tuition reimbursements available (averaging $7,254 per year), 21 teaching assistantships with full and partial tuition reimbursements available (averaging $12,742 per year); Federal Work-Study, institutionally sponsored loans, scholarships/grants, health care benefits, tuition waivers (full and partial), and unspecified assistantships also available. Financial award application deadline: 12/15; financial award applicants required to submit FAFSA. *Unit head:* Dr. Aida Hurtado, Professor/Department Chair, 805-893-3601, Fax: 805-893-4076, E-mail: aida@chicst.ucsb.edu. *Application contact:* Katherine G. Morales, Staff Graduate Advisor, 805-893-5269, Fax: 805-893-4076, E-mail: kmorales@chicst.ucsb.edu.

University of Houston, College of Liberal Arts and Social Sciences, Department of Hispanic Studies, Houston, TX 77204. Offers Spanish (MA, PhD). Part-time programs available. *Students:* 29 full-time (23 women), 45 part-time (34 women); includes 46 Hispanic/Latino; 1 Two or more races, non-Hispanic/Latino, 8 international. Average age 38. 29 applicants, 59% accepted, 10 enrolled. In 2010, 4 master's, 3 doctorates awarded. *Degree requirements:* For master's, comprehensive exam, thesis optional; for doctorate, 2 foreign languages, comprehensive exam, thesis/dissertation. *Entrance requirements:* For master's and doctorate, GRE. Additional exam requirements/recommendations for international students: Required—TOEFL (minimum score 550 paper-based; 79 iBT); Recommended—IELTS (minimum score 6.5). *Application deadline:* For fall admission, 2/25 for domestic and international students; for spring admission, 9/30 for domestic and international students. Applications are processed on a rolling basis. Application fee: $75. Electronic applications accepted. *Expenses:* Tuition, state resident: full-time $8592; part-time $358 per credit hour. Tuition, nonresident: full-time $16,032; part-time $668 per credit hour. Required fees: $2889. Tuition and fees vary according to course load and program. *Financial support:* In 2010–11, 5 research assistantships with full tuition reimbursements (averaging $10,400 per year), 10 teaching assistantships with full tuition reimbursements (averaging $9,992 per year) were awarded. *Unit head:* Dr. Anadeli Bencomo, Chairperson, 713-743-3068, Fax: 713-743-0935, E-mail: abencomo@uh.edu. *Application contact:* Gabriela Ventura, Director of Graduate Studies, 713-743-3259, E-mail: gbventura@uh.edu.

University of Illinois at Chicago, Graduate College, College of Liberal Arts and Sciences, Department of Spanish, French, Italian and Portuguese, Program in Hispanic Studies, Chicago, IL 60607-7128. Offers Hispanic linguistics (MA, PhD); Hispanic literary and cultural studies (MA, PhD). Part-time programs available. Terminal master's awarded for partial completion of doctoral program. *Degree requirements:* For master's, one foreign language, departmental qualifying exam. *Entrance requirements:* For master's, GRE General Test, minimum GPA of 2.75, undergraduate major in Spanish. Additional exam requirements/recommendations for international students: Required—TOEFL. Electronic applications accepted.

University of Kentucky, Graduate School, College of Arts and Sciences, Program in Hispanic Studies, Lexington, KY 40506-0032. Offers MA, PhD. *Degree requirements:* For master's, one foreign language, comprehensive exam, thesis optional; for doctorate, 2 foreign languages, comprehensive exam, thesis/dissertation. *Entrance requirements:* For master's, GRE General Test, minimum undergraduate GPA of 2.75; for doctorate, GRE General Test, minimum graduate GPA of 3.0. Additional exam requirements/recommendations for international students: Required—TOEFL (minimum score 550 paper-based; 213 computer-based). Electronic applications accepted. *Faculty research:* Hispanic linguistics, medieval Spanish literature and civilization, Renaissance and Golden Age literature and civilization, Spanish American literature and civilization.

The University of Manchester, School of Languages, Linguistics and Cultures, Manchester, United Kingdom. Offers Arab world studies (PhD); Chinese studies (M Phil, PhD); East Asian studies (M Phil, PhD); English language (PhD); French studies (M Phil, PhD); German studies (M Phil, PhD); interpreting studies (PhD); Italian studies (M Phil, PhD); Japanese studies (M Phil, PhD); Latin American cultural studies (M Phil, PhD); linguistics (M Phil, PhD); Middle Eastern studies (M Phil, PhD); Polish studies (M Phil, PhD); Portuguese studies (M Phil, PhD); Russian studies (M Phil, PhD); Spanish studies (M Phil, PhD); translation and intercultural studies (M Phil, PhD).

University of Nevada, Las Vegas, Graduate College, College of Liberal Arts, Department of Foreign Languages, Las Vegas, NV 89154-5047. Offers Hispanic studies (MA). Part-time programs available. *Faculty:* 5 full-time (4 women). *Students:* 1 (woman) full-time, 7 part-time (4 women); includes 6 minority (1 Asian, non-Hispanic/Latino; 5 Hispanic/Latino), 2 international. Average age 36. 5 applicants, 60% accepted, 1 enrolled. In 2010, 2 master's awarded. *Degree requirements:* For master's, one foreign language, comprehensive exam. *Entrance requirements:* Additional exam requirements/recommendations for international students: Required—TOEFL (minimum score 550 paper-based; 213 computer-based; 80 iBT), IELTS (minimum score 7). *Application deadline:* For fall admission, 8/1 priority date for domestic and international students; for spring admission, 12/1 priority date for domestic and international students. Applications are processed on a rolling basis. Application fee: $60 ($95 for international students). Electronic applications accepted. *Expenses:* Tuition, area resident: Part-time $239.50 per credit. Tuition, state resident: part-time $239.50 per credit. Tuition, nonresident: part-time $503 per credit. Required fees: $108 per semester. Tuition and fees vary according to course load, program and reciprocity agreements. *Financial support:* In 2010–11, 2 students received support, including 2 teaching assistantships with partial tuition reimbursements available (averaging $10,000 per year); institutionally sponsored loans, scholarships/grants, health care benefits, and unspecified assistantships also available. Financial award application deadline: 3/1. *Faculty research:* Spanish poetry of the twenties and thirties, Spanish literature of the post-Civil War era, modern Mexican literature, Mexican culture and film, second language acquisition of Spanish. *Unit head:* Dr. Ralph Buechler, Chair/Associate Professor, 702-895-3546, Fax: 702-895-3431, E-mail: ralph.buechler@unlv.edu. *Application contact:* Graduate College Admissions Evaluator, 702-895-3320, Fax: 702-895-4180, E-mail: gradcollege@unlv.edu.

The University of North Carolina at Greensboro, Graduate School, College of Arts and Sciences, Department of Romance Languages, Program in Spanish, Greensboro, NC 27412-5001. Offers advanced Spanish language and Hispanic cultural studies (Certificate); Spanish (MA). *Degree requirements:* For master's, one foreign language, comprehensive exam, thesis or alternative. *Entrance requirements:* For master's, GRE General Test, 3-5 minute tape demonstrating foreign language proficiency, composition in Spanish, sample paper in English. Additional exam requirements/recommendations for international students: Required—TOEFL. Electronic applications accepted.

The University of North Carolina Wilmington, College of Arts and Sciences, Department of Foreign Languages and Literature, Wilmington, NC 28403-3297. Offers Hispanic studies

(Graduate Certificate); Spanish (MA). Part-time programs available. Postbaccalaureate distance learning degree programs offered. *Faculty:* 12 full-time (6 women). *Students:* 1 full-time (0 women), 2 part-time (0 women); includes 1 Black or African American, non-Hispanic/Latino; 1 Hispanic/Latino. Average age 34. 13 applicants, 62% accepted, 3 enrolled. In 2010, 3 master's awarded. *Degree requirements:* For master's, one foreign language, comprehensive exam, thesis or alternative. *Entrance requirements:* For master's, GRE. Additional exam requirements/recommendations for international students: Required—TOEFL (minimum score 550 paper-based; 217 computer-based; 79 iBT), IELTS (minimum score 6.5). Application fee: $60. *Financial support:* In 2010–11, 4 teaching assistantships with full and partial tuition reimbursements (averaging $9,500 per year) were awarded. *Unit head:* Dr. Raymond Burt, Chair, 910-962-4095, E-mail: burtr@uncw.edu. *Application contact:* Dr. R. Terry Mount, Graduate Coordinator, 910-962-3344, E-mail: mountt@uncw.edu.

University of Puerto Rico, Mayagüez Campus, Graduate Studies, College of Arts and Sciences, Department of Hispanic Studies, Mayagüez, PR 00681-9000. Offers MA. Part-time programs available. *Students:* 22 full-time (16 women), 5 part-time (all women); includes 25 Hispanic/Latino, 2 international. 6 applicants, 50% accepted, 3 enrolled. In 2010, 2 master's awarded. *Degree requirements:* For master's, comprehensive exam, thesis. *Entrance requirements:* For master's, minimum GPA of 2.75, BA in Hispanic studies or its equivalent. *Application deadline:* For fall admission, 2/15 for domestic and international students; for spring admission, 9/15 for domestic and international students. Applications are processed on a rolling basis. Application fee: $25. *Expenses:* Tuition, state resident: full-time $1188. Tuition, nonresident: full-time $1188. International tuition: $6126 full-time. Tuition and fees vary according to course level and course load. *Financial support:* In 2010–11, 10 students received support, including 10 teaching assistantships (averaging $8,500 per year); Federal Work-Study and institutionally sponsored loans also available. *Faculty research:* Spanish literature, Hispanic-American literature, Puerto Rican literature, stylistics, linguistics. *Unit head:* Dr. Jaime Martell, Director, 787-265-3843, Fax: 787-265-3843, E-mail: jmartell@uprm.edu. *Application contact:* Dr. Maribel Acosta, Graduate Program Coordinator, 787-832-4040 Ext. 3334, Fax: 787-265-3843, E-mail: macostalugo@gmail.com.

University of Puerto Rico, Río Piedras, College of Humanities, Department of Hispanic Studies, San Juan, PR 00931-3300. Offers Hispanic linguistics (PhD); Hispanic studies (MA); Latin American literature (PhD); Puerto Rican literature (PhD); Spanish literature (PhD). Part-time programs available. *Degree requirements:* For master's, one foreign language, comprehensive exam, thesis; for doctorate, one foreign language, comprehensive exam, thesis/dissertation. *Entrance requirements:* For master's, PAEG or GRE, interview, minimum GPA of 3.0, letter of recommendation (2); for doctorate, PAEG or GRE, interview, master's degree, minimum GPA of 3.0, letter of recommendation (2). *Faculty research:* Poetry of Luis Palés Matos, short stories in Puerto Rico, language in the social process, 'Decima Popular', Anglicism.

The University of Texas at Austin, Graduate School, College of Liberal Arts, Center for Mexican American Studies, Austin, TX 78712-1111. Offers MA.

University of Victoria, Faculty of Graduate Studies, Faculty of Humanities, Department of Hispanic and Italian Studies, Victoria, BC V8W 2Y2, Canada. Offers Hispanic and Italian studies (MA); Hispanic studies (MA). *Degree requirements:* For master's, one foreign language, comprehensive exam, thesis (for some programs). *Entrance requirements:* For master's, undergraduate major in Hispanic studies, minimum B+ average. Additional exam requirements/recommendations for international students: Required—TOEFL (minimum score 575 paper-based; 233 computer-based), IELTS (minimum score 7). Electronic applications accepted. *Faculty research:* Medieval/Renaissance Spanish and Italian literature, Golden Age literature, Latin American literature.

University of Washington, Graduate School, College of Arts and Sciences, Department of Romance Languages and Literature, Seattle, WA 98195. Offers French and Italian studies (MA, PhD), including French, Italian (MA); Spanish and Portuguese (MA), including Hispanic literary and cultural studies. Terminal master's awarded for partial completion of doctoral program. *Degree requirements:* For master's, 2 foreign languages, thesis optional, exam; for doctorate, 3 foreign languages, thesis/dissertation, exams. *Entrance requirements:* For master's and doctorate, GRE General Test, minimum GPA of 3.0. Additional exam requirements/recommendations for international students: Required—TOEFL. Electronic applications accepted.

Villanova University, Graduate School of Liberal Arts and Sciences, Department of Romance Languages and Literatures, Villanova, PA 19085-1699. Offers Hispanic studies (MA). Part-time and evening/weekend programs available. *Faculty:* 4 full-time (all women). *Students:* 2 full-time (0 women), 12 part-time (4 women); includes 4 minority (all Hispanic/Latino), 4 international. Average age 30. 10 applicants, 100% accepted, 5 enrolled. In 2010, 14 master's awarded. *Degree requirements:* For master's, one foreign language, comprehensive exam. *Entrance requirements:* For master's, minimum GPA of 3.0, writing sample in Spanish. Additional exam requirements/recommendations for international students: Required—TOEFL. *Application deadline:* For fall admission, 2/1 priority date for domestic and international students; for spring admission, 11/15 priority date for domestic and international students. Applications are processed on a rolling basis. Application fee: $50. Electronic applications accepted. *Expenses:* Tuition: Part-time $700 per credit. Part-time tuition and fees vary according to degree level and program. *Financial support:* Teaching assistantships with tuition reimbursements, Federal Work-Study, scholarships/grants, and unspecified assistantships available. Financial award applicants required to submit FAFSA. *Unit head:* Mercedes Julia, Chair, 610-519-4680. *Application contact:* Dr. Adele Lindenmeyr, Dean, Graduate School of Liberal Arts and Sciences, 610-519-7093, Fax: 610-519-7096.

Holocaust and Genocide Studies

Clark University, Graduate School, Department of History, Program in Holocaust History, Worcester, MA 01610-1477. Offers PhD. *Students:* 8 full-time (4 women), 1 part-time (0 women), 4 international. Average age 29. 38 applicants, 11% accepted, 3 enrolled. In 2010, 2 doctorates awarded. *Degree requirements:* For doctorate, thesis/dissertation. *Entrance requirements:* Additional exam requirements/recommendations for international students: Required—TOEFL. *Application deadline:* For fall admission, 1/15 for domestic students. Application fee: $50. *Expenses:* Tuition: Full-time $37,000; part-time $1156 per credit hour. Required fees: $30; $1156 per credit hour. *Financial support:* In 2010–11, fellowships with full and partial tuition reimbursements (averaging $11,850 per year), research assistantships with full and partial tuition reimbursements (averaging $11,850 per year), teaching assistantships with full and partial tuition reimbursements (averaging $11,850 per year) were awarded; tuition waivers (partial) also available. *Faculty research:* Jewish persecution, children and survivors, Germany's role in the Holocaust. *Unit head:* Deborah Dwork, Professor, 508-421-3745. *Application contact:* Margaret Hillard, Program Officer, 508-793-7764, Fax: 508-793-8827, E-mail: chgs@clarku.edu.

Drew University, Caspersen School of Graduate Studies, Program in Arts and Letters, Madison, NJ 07940-1493. Offers holocaust and genocide studies (Certificate); interdisciplinary studies (M Litt, D Litt). Part-time and evening/weekend programs available. Terminal master's awarded for partial completion of doctoral program. *Degree requirements:* For master's, thesis optional; for doctorate, thesis/dissertation. *Entrance requirements:* For master's and doctorate, transcripts, writing sample, personal statement, recommendations. Additional exam requirements/

recommendations for international students: Required—TOEFL (minimum score 585 paper-based; 240 computer-based; 95 iBT), TWE. *Expenses:* Contact institution. *Faculty research:* Interdisciplinary studies across art, literature, music, philosophy, religion, and history.

Gratz College, Graduate Programs, Program in Jewish Studies, Melrose Park, PA 19027. Offers classical studies (MA); Holocaust studies (Certificate); Jewish studies (MA, Certificate); modern studies (MA). Part-time programs available. Postbaccalaureate distance learning degree programs offered. *Degree requirements:* For master's, one foreign language, comprehensive exam, thesis optional.

Kean University, Nathan Weiss Graduate College, Program in Holocaust and Genocide Studies, Union, NJ 07083. Offers MA. Part-time and evening/weekend programs available. *Students:* 1 full-time (0 women), 13 part-time (7 women); includes 1 Hispanic/Latino. Average age 33. 4 applicants, 75% accepted, 1 enrolled. In 2010, 5 master's awarded. *Degree requirements:* For master's, comprehensive exam, thesis. *Entrance requirements:* For master's, GRE General Test or MAT, minimum GPA of 3.0 or experience, 2 letters of recommendation, interview, official transcripts from all institutions attended. *Application deadline:* For fall admission, 6/1 for domestic students; for spring admission, 11/1 for domestic students. Application fee: $75 ($150 for international students). Electronic applications accepted. *Expenses:* Tuition, state resident: full-time $10,872; part-time $500 per credit. Tuition, nonresident: full-time $14,736; part-time $614 per credit. Required fees: $2740.80; $125 per credit. Part-time tuition and fees vary according to course load and degree level. *Financial support:* In 2010–11, 1

Holocaust and Genocide Studies

Kean University (continued)

research assistantship with full tuition reimbursement (averaging $3,263 per year) was awarded; unspecified assistantships also available. Financial award applicants required to submit FAFSA. *Unit head:* Dr. Keith Nunes, Program Coordinator, 908-737-5987, E-mail: knunes@kean.edu. *Application contact:* Ann-Marie Kay, Assistant Director of Graduate Admissions, 908-737-5922, Fax: 908-737-5925, E-mail: akay@kean.edu.

Laura and Alvin Siegal College of Judaic Studies, Graduate Programs, Beachwood, OH 44122-7116. Offers humanities (MA), including Holocaust studies; religious education (MAJS), including Jewish education, Judaic studies. Part-time and evening/weekend programs available. Postbaccalaureate distance learning degree programs offered (no on-campus study). *Degree requirements:* For master's, one foreign language, thesis. *Entrance requirements:* For master's, interview.

The Richard Stockton College of New Jersey, School of Graduate and Continuing Studies, Program in Holocaust and Genocide Studies, Pomona, NJ 08240-0195. Offers MA. Part-time and evening/weekend programs available. *Faculty:* 1 (woman) full-time, 3 part-time/adjunct (2 women). *Students:* 3 full-time (1 woman), 15 part-time (13 women); includes 1 minority (Black or African American, non-Hispanic/Latino). Average age 32. 15 applicants, 73% accepted, 8 enrolled. In 2010, 6 master's awarded. *Degree requirements:* For master's, thesis optional. *Entrance requirements:* Additional exam requirements/recommendations for international students: Required—TOEFL. *Application deadline:* For fall admission, 7/1 for domestic and international students; for spring admission, 12/1 for domestic and international students. Applications are processed on a rolling basis. Application fee: $50. Electronic applications accepted. *Expenses:* Tuition, state resident: full-time $9310; part-time $517.25 per credit. Tuition, nonresident: full-time $14,332; part-time $796.23 per credit. Required fees: $2600; $144 per credit. $70 per semester. Tuition and fees vary according to degree level. *Financial support:* In 2010–11, 12 students received support, including 6 fellowships with partial tuition reimbursements available, 6 research assistantships with full tuition reimbursements available; career-related internships or fieldwork, Federal Work-Study, scholarships/grants, and unspecified assistantships also available. Financial award application deadline: 3/1; financial award applicants required to submit FAFSA. *Faculty research:* Women and the Holocaust, survivor perspectives, liberty and persecution. *Unit head:* Dr. Michael Hayse, Interim Director, 609-652-4659, Fax: 609-748-5541, E-mail: mahg@stockton.edu. *Application contact:* Tara Williams, Assistant Director of Graduate Enrollment Management, 609-626-3640, Fax: 609-626-6050, E-mail: gradschools@stockton.edu.

Seton Hall University, College of Arts and Sciences, Department of Jewish-Christian Studies, South Orange, NJ 07079-2697. Offers Holocaust studies (MA); Jewish-Christian Studies (MA). Part-time and evening/weekend programs available. *Degree requirements:* For master's, thesis optional. *Entrance requirements:* For master's, interview or suitable correspondence with department chair. Additional exam requirements/recommendations for international students: Required—TOEFL. Electronic applications accepted. *Faculty research:* Jewish-Christian issues, Biblical studies, Holocaust studies.

Seton Hill University, Program in Genocide and Holocaust Studies, Greensburg, PA 15601. Offers Certificate. Part-time programs available. Postbaccalaureate distance learning degree programs offered (no on-campus study). *Faculty:* 2 full-time (1 woman), 3 part-time/adjunct (1 woman). *Students:* 4 part-time (3 women). Average age 42. 14 applicants, 57% accepted, 4 enrolled. *Entrance requirements:* For degree, 1 letter of recommendation, bachelor's degree, minimum GPA of 3.0. Additional exam requirements/recommendations for international students: Required—TOEFL (minimum score 600 paper-based; 250 computer-based), IELTS (minimum score 6.5). Application fee: $35. *Expenses:* Tuition: Full-time $13,050; part-time $725 per credit. Required fees: $700; $34 per credit. $50 per semester. Tuition and fees vary according to course load and program. *Financial support:* Scholarships/grants available. Financial award application deadline: 8/15; financial award applicants required to submit FAFSA. *Faculty research:* Interethnic conflict, human rights and international justice, Catholic social teaching, comparative genocide, the Catholic church and the Holocaust. *Unit head:* Dr. James Paharik, Program Advisor, 724-838-1073, E-mail: jpaharik@setonhill.edu. *Application contact:* Laurel Komarny, Program Counselor, 724-838-4209, Fax: 724-830-1891, E-mail: 1komarny@setonhill.edu.

West Chester University of Pennsylvania, Office of Graduate Studies, College of Arts and Sciences, Department of History, West Chester, PA 19383. Offers history (M Ed, MA); holocaust and genocide studies (MA, Certificate). Part-time and evening/weekend programs available. *Students:* 9 full-time (7 women), 34 part-time (19 women); includes 3 minority (2 Asian, non-Hispanic/Latino; 1 Hispanic/Latino). Average age 30. 30 applicants, 57% accepted, 9 enrolled. In 2010, 18 master's awarded. *Degree requirements:* For master's, comprehensive exam (for some programs), thesis optional. *Entrance requirements:* For master's, statement of professional goals, writing sample, minimum GPA of 3.0 in history, three letters of recommendation. Additional exam requirements/recommendations for international students: Required—TOEFL (minimum score 550 paper-based; 213 computer-based; 80 iBT). *Application deadline:* For fall admission, 4/15 priority date for domestic students, 3/15 for international students; for spring admission, 10/15 for domestic students, 9/1 for international students. Applications are processed on a rolling basis. Application fee: $35. Electronic applications accepted. *Expenses:* Tuition, state resident: full-time $6966; part-time $387 per credit. Tuition, nonresident: full-time $11,146; part-time $619 per credit. Required fees: $1614.40; $133.24 per credit. Part-time tuition and fees vary according to campus/location. *Financial support:* Unspecified assistantships available. Support available to part-time students. Financial award application deadline: 2/15; financial award applicants required to submit FAFSA. *Faculty research:* Oral histories, siege of Leningrad. *Unit head:* Dr. Wayne Hanley, Chair, 610-436-2201, E-mail: whanley@wcupa.edu. *Application contact:* Dr. Jonathan Friedman, Graduate Coordinator of Holocaust and Genocide Studies, 610-436-2972, E-mail: jfriedman@wcupa.edu.

Jewish Studies

American Jewish University, Graduate School of Nonprofit Management, Program in Jewish Communal Studies, Bel Air, CA 90077-1599. Offers MAJCS. *Degree requirements:* For master's, thesis. *Entrance requirements:* For master's, GMAT or GRE General Test, interview.

Brandeis University, Graduate School of Arts and Sciences, Department of Near Eastern and Judaic Studies, Waltham, MA 02454-9110. Offers Near Eastern and Judaic studies (MA, PhD); Near Eastern and Judaic studies and sociology (PhD); Near Eastern and Judaic studies and women's and gender studies (MA); teaching of Hebrew (MAT). Part-time programs available. *Faculty:* 23 full-time (11 women), 7 part-time/adjunct (3 women). *Students:* 64 full-time (29 women); includes 2 Hispanic/Latino, 6 international. 123 applicants, 50% accepted, 18 enrolled. In 2010, 10 master's, 2 doctorates awarded. Terminal master's awarded for partial completion of doctoral program. *Degree requirements:* For master's, one foreign language, comprehensive exam, thesis or alternative; for doctorate, 3 foreign languages, comprehensive exam, thesis/dissertation. *Entrance requirements:* For master's and doctorate, GRE General Test (recommended), letters of recommendation, transcripts, statement of purpose. Additional exam requirements/recommendations for international students: Required—TOEFL (minimum score 600 paper-based; 250 computer-based; 100 iBT); Recommended—IELTS (minimum score 7). *Application deadline:* For fall admission, 1/15 priority date for domestic and international students. Applications are processed on a rolling basis. Application fee: $75. Electronic applications accepted. *Financial support:* In 2010–11, 17 students received support, including 14 fellowships with full tuition reimbursements available (averaging $20,000 per year); research assistantships with full and partial tuition reimbursements available, teaching assistantships, scholarships/grants, health care benefits, and tuition waivers (full and partial) also available. Support available to part-time students. Financial award application deadline: 4/15; financial award applicants required to submit FAFSA. *Faculty research:* Ancient Near East and Bible, philosophy, history, modern Middle East, Islamic studies. *Unit head:* Dr. Sylvia Fishman, Chair, 781-736-2950, Fax: 781-736-2070, E-mail: fishman@brandeis.edu. *Application contact:* Joanne Arnish, Department Administrator, 781-736-2950, Fax: 781-736-2070, E-mail: arnish@brandeis.edu.

Brandeis University, Graduate School of Arts and Sciences, Hornstein Jewish Professional Leadership Program, Waltham, MA 02454-9110. Offers MA/MA, MBA/MA, MPP/MA. Part-time programs available. *Faculty:* 3 full-time (1 woman), 3 part-time/adjunct (1 woman). *Students:* 26 full-time (18 women), 1 (woman) part-time, 6 international. 33 applicants, 58% accepted, 12 enrolled. *Entrance requirements:* Additional exam requirements/recommendations for international students: Required—TOEFL (minimum score 600 paper-based; 250 computer-based; 100 iBT); Recommended—IELTS (minimum score 7). *Application deadline:* For fall admission, 2/15 priority date for domestic and international students. Applications are processed on a rolling basis. Application fee: $75. Electronic applications accepted. *Financial support:* In 2010–11, 2 fellowships with full tuition reimbursements were awarded; research assistantships, career-related internships or fieldwork, institutionally sponsored loans, scholarships/grants, tuition waivers (full), and living expense stipends also available. Support available to part-time students. Financial award application deadline: 3/30; financial award applicants required to submit FAFSA. *Faculty research:* Leadership, informal education, demography, Jewish identity, Israel-Diaspora relations. *Unit head:* Prof. Len Saxe, Director, 781-736-2990, Fax: 781-736-2070, E-mail: hornstein@brandeis.edu. *Application contact:* Carol Hengerle, Program Administrator, 781-736-2990, Fax: 781-736-2070, E-mail: hornstein@brandeis.edu.

Brooklyn College of the City University of New York, Division of Graduate Studies, Department of Judaic Studies, Brooklyn, NY 11210-2889. Offers MA. Part-time and evening/weekend programs available. *Students:* 1 applicant, 0% accepted, 0 enrolled. *Degree requirements:* For master's, 2 foreign languages, comprehensive exam or thesis. *Entrance requirements:* For master's, 18 upper-level credits in Judaic studies, interview, 2 letters of recommendation. Additional exam requirements/recommendations for international students: Required—TOEFL (minimum score 525 paper-based; 195 computer-based; 70 iBT). *Application deadline:* For fall admission, 3/1 priority date for domestic students, 2/1 priority date for international students; for spring admission, 11/1 priority date for domestic students, 10/1 priority date for international students. Applications are processed on a rolling basis. Application fee: $125. Electronic applications accepted. *Expenses:* Tuition, state resident: full-time $7360; part-time $310 per credit hour. Tuition, nonresident: full-time $13,800; part-time $575 per credit hour. Required fees: $190 per semester. *Financial support:* Federal Work-Study, institutionally sponsored loans, and scholarships/grants available. Support available to part-time students. Financial award application deadline: 5/1; financial award applicants required to submit FAFSA. *Faculty research:* Biblical studies, Talmud and Midrash, modern Jewish history and thought. *Unit head:* Dr. Sara Reguer, Chairperson, 718-951-5229, Fax: 718-951-4703, E-mail: sreguer@brooklyn.cuny.edu. *Application contact:* Hernan Sierra, Graduate Admissions Coordinator, 718-951-4536, Fax: 718-951-4506, E-mail: grads@brooklyn.cuny.edu.

Brown University, Graduate School, Department of Religious Studies, Providence, RI 02912. Offers ancient Judaism (PhD); early Christianity (PhD); religion and critical thought (PhD); religion in the ancient Mediterranean (PhD); religion, culture, and comparison (PhD). *Degree requirements:* For doctorate, 2 foreign languages, thesis/dissertation. *Entrance requirements:* For doctorate, GRE General Test.

Columbia University, Graduate School of Arts and Sciences, Division of Humanities, Program in Jewish Studies, New York, NY 10027. Offers M Phil, MA, PhD. *Degree requirements:* For master's, variable foreign language requirement; for doctorate, variable foreign language requirement, thesis/dissertation. *Entrance requirements:* For master's and doctorate, GRE General Test. Additional exam requirements/recommendations for international students: Required—TOEFL. *Faculty research:* Jewish history, culture, and institutions; Hebrew, Yiddish, and Jewish languages and literatures; history of Jewish philosophy and religion.

Columbia University, Graduate School of Arts and Sciences, Interdepartmental Committee on Yiddish Studies, New York, NY 10027. Offers MA. Applicants must apply for admission to one of the participating departments: Germanic Languages, History, Middle East Languages and Cultures, Religion. *Entrance requirements:* For master's, high degree of proficiency in Yiddish.

Columbia University, Graduate School of Arts and Sciences, Program in Liberal Studies, New York, NY 10027. Offers American studies (MA); East Asian studies (MA); human rights studies (MA); Islamic culture studies (MA); Jewish studies (MA); medieval studies (MA); modern European studies (MA); South Asian studies (MA). Part-time and evening/weekend programs available. *Degree requirements:* For master's, thesis.

Concordia University, School of Graduate Studies, Faculty of Arts and Science, Department of Religion, Program in Judaic Studies, Montréal, QC H3G 1M8, Canada. Offers MA. *Degree requirements:* For master's, one foreign language, comprehensive exam, thesis optional. *Entrance requirements:* For master's, Hebrew exam, honors degree in Judaic studies or equivalent. Additional exam requirements/recommendations for international students: Required—TOEFL. *Faculty research:* Jewish religious reflections and modern philosophy of religion, Judaism and modernity, Judaism in late antiquity.

Cornell University, Graduate School, Graduate Fields of Arts and Sciences, Field of Near Eastern Studies, Ithaca, NY 14853-0001. Offers ancient Near Eastern studies (MA, PhD); Arabic and Islamic studies (MA, PhD); biblical studies (MA, PhD); Hebrew and Judaic studies (MA, PhD). *Faculty:* 15 full-time (4 women). *Students:* 5 full-time (1 woman), 2 international. Average age 27. 46 applicants, 11% accepted, 1 enrolled. In 2010, 1 doctorate awarded. Terminal master's awarded for partial completion of doctoral program. *Degree requirements:* For master's, one foreign language, thesis; for doctorate, 2 foreign languages, comprehensive exam, thesis/dissertation. *Entrance requirements:* For master's and doctorate, GRE General Test, 2 years of 1 Near Eastern language, 3 letters of recommendation, writing sample. Additional exam requirements/recommendations for international students: Required—TOEFL (minimum score 550 paper-based; 213 computer-based; 77 iBT). *Application deadline:* For fall admission, 2/1 for domestic students. Application fee: $70. Electronic applications accepted. *Expenses:* Tuition: Full-time $29,500. Required fees: $76. Tuition and fees vary according to degree level and program. *Financial support:* In 2010–11, 5 students received support, including 1 fellowship with full tuition reimbursement available, 4 teaching assistantships with full tuition reimbursements available; research assistantships with full tuition reimbursements available, institutionally sponsored loans, scholarships/grants, health care benefits, tuition waivers (full and partial), and unspecified assistantships also available. Financial award applicants required to submit FAFSA. *Faculty research:* Ancient Near East (including archeology), Hebrew and

Judaic studies (including Bible), early Christianity, Arabic and Islamic studies, modern Middle East. *Unit head:* Director of Graduate Studies, 607-255-1329, Fax: 607-255-6450. *Application contact:* Graduate Field Assistant, 607-255-1329, Fax: 607-255-6450, E-mail: neareastern@cornell.edu.

The Criswell College, Graduate School of the Bible, Dallas, TX 75246-1537. Offers biblical studies (M Div); Christian leadership (MA); counseling (MA); Jewish studies (MA); ministry (MA); theological and biblical studies (MA). Part-time programs available. *Degree requirements:* For master's, 2 foreign languages, thesis optional; for M Div, 2 foreign languages, thesis/dissertation optional. *Entrance requirements:* For M Div and master's, GRE General Test, minimum GPA of 2.5. Electronic applications accepted. *Faculty research:* Emphasis on biblical languages (Hebrew and Greek), expository preaching and evangelism in the local church.

Emory University, Laney Graduate School, Program in Jewish Studies, Atlanta, GA 30322-1100. Offers MA. *Degree requirements:* For master's, one foreign language, thesis optional. *Entrance requirements:* For master's, GRE General Test, 2 years of course work in Hebrew or equivalent, writing sample. Additional exam requirements/recommendations for international students: Required—TOEFL. Electronic applications accepted. *Expenses:* Tuition: Full-time $33,800. Required fees: $1300. *Faculty research:* Medieval Jewish history and culture, Hebrew language and linguistics, Jewish law, Jewish ethics, Holocaust studies.

Graduate Theological Union, Graduate Programs, Berkeley, CA 94709-1212. Offers art and religion (MA, PhD, Th D); biblical languages (MA); biblical studies (MA); Biblical studies (PhD, Th D); Buddhist studies (MA); Christian spirituality (MA, PhD, Th D); cultural and historical studies of religions (MA, PhD, Th D); ethics and social theory (PhD, Th D); history (MA, PhD, Th D); homiletics (MA, PhD, Th D); interdisciplinary studies (PhD, Th D); Jewish studies (MA, PhD, Th D, Certificate); liturgical studies (MA, PhD, Th D); Near Eastern religions (PhD, Th D); Orthodox Christian studies (MA); religion and psychology (MA, PhD, Th D); religion and society/ethics and social theory (MA); systematic and philosophical theology (MA, PhD, Th D). PhD programs in Jewish studies and Near Eastern religions offered jointly with University of California, Berkeley. *Accreditation:* ATS. Terminal master's awarded for partial completion of doctoral program. *Degree requirements:* For master's, one foreign language, thesis; for doctorate, one foreign language, comprehensive exam, thesis/dissertation. *Entrance requirements:* For master's, GRE General Test; for doctorate, GRE General Test, MA or M Div. Additional exam requirements/recommendations for international students: Required—TOEFL. Electronic applications accepted.

Gratz College, Graduate Programs, Program in Jewish Studies, Melrose Park, PA 19027. Offers classical studies (MA); Holocaust studies (Certificate); Jewish studies (MA, Certificate); modern studies (MA). Part-time programs available. Postbaccalaureate distance learning degree programs offered. *Degree requirements:* For master's, one foreign language, comprehensive exam, thesis optional.

Harvard University, Graduate School of Arts and Sciences, Department of Near Eastern Languages and Civilizations, Cambridge, MA 02138. Offers Akkadian and Sumerian (AM, PhD); Arabic (AM, PhD); Armenian (AM, PhD); biblical history (AM, PhD); Hebrew (AM, PhD); Indo-Muslim culture (AM, PhD); Iranian (AM, PhD); Jewish history and literature (AM, PhD); Persian (AM, PhD); Semitic philology (AM, PhD); Syro-Palestinian archaeology (AM, PhD); Turkish (AM, PhD). *Degree requirements:* For doctorate, variable foreign language requirement, thesis/dissertation, general exams. *Entrance requirements:* For master's, GRE General Test; for doctorate, GRE General Test, proficiency in a Near Eastern language. Additional exam requirements/recommendations for international students: Required—TOEFL. *Expenses:* Tuition: Full-time $34,976. Required fees: $1166. Full-time tuition and fees vary according to program.

Hebrew College, Cantor Educator Program, Newton Centre, MA 02459. Offers MJ Ed. *Entrance requirements:* For master's, GRE, interview. Additional exam requirements/recommendations for international students: Required—TOEFL.

Hebrew College, Program in Jewish Studies, Newton Centre, MA 02459. Offers Jewish liturgical music (Certificate); Jewish music education (Certificate); Jewish studies (MA). Part-time and evening/weekend programs available. Postbaccalaureate distance learning degree programs offered (minimal on-campus study). *Degree requirements:* For master's, one foreign language. *Entrance requirements:* For master's, GRE, interview. Additional exam requirements/recommendations for international students: Required—TOEFL.

Hebrew Union College–Jewish Institute of Religion, School of Graduate Studies, Program in Judaic Studies, New York, NY 10012-1186. Offers MAJS. Part-time programs available. *Degree requirements:* For master's, one foreign language, thesis. *Entrance requirements:* For master's, GRE, minimum 2 years of college-level Hebrew. *Faculty research:* Philosophy and theology, Bible, Hebrew, history and Rabbinics.

The Jewish Theological Seminary, The Graduate School, New York, NY 10027-4649. Offers ancient Judaism (MA, DHL, PhD); Bible and ancient Semitic languages (MA, DHL, PhD); interdepartmental studies (MA); Jewish art and visual culture (MA); Jewish gender and women's studies (MA); Jewish history (MA, DHL, PhD); Jewish literature (MA, DHL, PhD); Jewish philosophy (DHL); Jewish thought (MA, PhD); liturgy (MA, DHL, PhD); medieval Jewish studies (MA, DHL, PhD); Midrash (DHL); Midrash and scriptural interpretation (MA, PhD); modern Jewish studies (MA, DHL, PhD); Talmud and rabbinics (MA, DHL, PhD); MA/MSW. MA/MSW offered jointly with Columbia University. *Accreditation:* ACIPE. Part-time programs available. Terminal master's awarded for partial completion of doctoral program. *Degree requirements:* For master's, one foreign language, comprehensive exam (for some programs), thesis (for some programs); for doctorate, 3 foreign languages, comprehensive exam (for some programs), thesis/dissertation. *Entrance requirements:* For master's, GRE or MAT, 3 letters of recommendation, writing sample; for doctorate, GRE or MAT, 3 letters of recommendation, writing research sample. Additional exam requirements/recommendations for international students: Required—TOEFL (minimum score 100 computer-based).

The Jewish Theological Seminary, William Davidson Graduate School of Jewish Education, New York, NY 10027-4649. Offers MA, Ed D. Offered in conjunction with Rabbinical School; H. L. Miller Cantorial School and College of Jewish Music; Teacher's College, Columbia University; and Union Theological Seminary. Part-time programs available. Postbaccalaureate distance learning degree programs offered (minimal on-campus study). *Degree requirements:* For master's, one foreign language, thesis optional; for doctorate, one foreign language, comprehensive exam, thesis/dissertation. *Entrance requirements:* For master's, GRE or MAT, 3 letters of recommendation; for doctorate, GRE or MAT, writing sample, 3 letters of recommendation.

Jewish University of America, Graduate School, Graduate Research Division, Skokie, IL 60077-3248. Offers Bible (MHL, DHL); Hebrew (MHL, DHL); history (MHL, DHL); Jewish studies (MHL, DHL); philosophy (MHL, DHL); rabbinics (MHL, DHL). Part-time programs available. *Degree requirements:* For doctorate, one foreign language, thesis/dissertation; for MHL, thesis/dissertation optional. *Entrance requirements:* For MHL and doctorate, interview.

Laura and Alvin Siegal College of Judaic Studies, Graduate Programs, Program in Religious Education, Beachwood, OH 44122-7116. Offers Jewish education (MAJS); Judaic studies (MAJS). Part-time and evening/weekend programs available. Postbaccalaureate distance learning degree programs offered (minimal on-campus study). *Degree requirements:* For master's, one foreign language, thesis. *Entrance requirements:* For master's, interview.

Marquette University, Graduate School, College of Arts and Sciences, Department of Theology, Milwaukee, WI 53201-1881. Offers historical theology (MA, PhD); Judaism and Christianity in antiquity (MA, PhD); systematic theology (MA, PhD); theological ethics (PhD); theology (MACD); theology and society (PhD). Part-time and evening/weekend programs available. Postbaccalaureate distance learning degree programs offered (no on-campus study). *Faculty:* 30 full-time (7 women), 19 part-time/adjunct (3 women). *Students:* 65 full-time (17 women), 45 part-time (13 women); includes 6 minority (3 Black or African American, non-Hispanic/Latino; 3 Hispanic/Latino), 3 international. Average age 36. 167 applicants, 39% accepted, 16 enrolled. In 2010, 114 master's, 8 doctorates awarded. Terminal master's awarded for partial completion of doctoral program. *Degree requirements:* For master's, one foreign language, comprehensive exam, thesis or alternative; for doctorate, 2 foreign languages, comprehensive exam, thesis/dissertation. *Entrance requirements:* For master's, GRE General Test, official transcripts from all current and previous colleges/universities except Marquette, three letters of recommendation, short personal statement; for doctorate, GRE General Test, official transcripts from all current and previous colleges/universities except Marquette, three letters of recommendation, short personal statement, academic writing sample. Additional exam requirements/recommendations for international students: Required—TOEFL (minimum score 530 paper-based; 78 computer-based). *Application deadline:* For fall admission, 12/15 for domestic and international students. Application fee: $50. Electronic applications accepted. *Expenses:* Tuition: Full-time $16,290; part-time $905 per credit hour. Tuition and fees vary according to program. *Financial support:* In 2010–11, 10 fellowships, 22 teaching assistantships were awarded; research assistantships, Federal Work-Study, institutionally sponsored loans, scholarships/grants, and tuition waivers (full and partial) also available. Support available to part-time students. Financial award application deadline: 2/15. *Faculty research:* Old Testament theology, New Testament theology, church history, Christian ethics. Total annual research expenditures: $4,625. *Unit head:* Dr. Susan Wood, Chair, 414-288-7170, Fax: 414-288-5548. *Application contact:* Dr. M. Therese Lysaught, Director of Graduate Studies, 414-288-3740.

McGill University, Faculty of Graduate and Postdoctoral Studies, Faculty of Arts, Department of Jewish Studies, Montréal, QC H3A 2T5, Canada. Offers MA.

New York University, Graduate School of Arts and Science, Program in Museum Studies, New York, NY 10012-1019. Offers museum studies (MA, Advanced Certificate), including Africana studies (MA), Hebrew and Judaic studies (MA), Latin American and Caribbean studies (MA), Near Eastern studies (MA). Part-time and evening/weekend programs available. *Students:* 61 full-time (56 women), 16 part-time (13 women); includes 1 Black or African American, non-Hispanic/Latino; 1 American Indian or Alaska Native, non-Hispanic/Latino; 6 Asian, non-Hispanic/Latino; 5 Hispanic/Latino, 14 international. Average age 26. 200 applicants, 50% accepted, 38 enrolled. In 2010, 40 master's, 3 other advanced degrees awarded. *Entrance requirements:* For degree, master's degree or PhD. Additional exam requirements/recommendations for international students: Required—TOEFL. *Application deadline:* For fall admission, 2/15 for domestic students; for spring admission, 11/1 for domestic students. Application fee: $90. *Financial support:* Application deadline: 2/15. *Faculty research:* Modern and contemporary art, history of museums and exhibitions, conservation of cultural materials, museum anthropology, ethnography. *Unit head:* Bruce Altshuler, Director, 212-998-8080, Fax: 212-995-4185, E-mail: museum.studies@nyu.edu. *Application contact:* Tatiana Kamorina, Department Administrator, 212-998-8080, Fax: 212-995-4185, E-mail: museum.studies@nyu.edu.

New York University, Graduate School of Arts and Science, Skirball Department of Hebrew and Judaic Studies, New York, NY 10012-1019. Offers Hebrew and Judaic studies (MA, PhD); Hebrew and Judaic studies/museum studies (MA). Part-time programs available. *Students:* 57 full-time (34 women), 34 part-time (23 women); includes 1 Black or African American, non-Hispanic/Latino; 1 Asian, non-Hispanic/Latino; 2 Hispanic/Latino, 25 international. Average age 31. 109 applicants, 39% accepted, 17 enrolled. In 2010, 7 master's, 3 doctorates awarded. Terminal master's awarded for partial completion of doctoral program. *Degree requirements:* For master's, 2 foreign languages, comprehensive exam, thesis optional; for doctorate, 4 foreign languages, comprehensive exam, thesis/dissertation. *Entrance requirements:* For master's, GRE General Test, minimum 2 years of undergraduate course work in Hebrew; for doctorate, GRE General Test. Additional exam requirements/recommendations for international students: Required—TOEFL. *Application deadline:* For fall admission, 12/15 priority date for domestic students. Application fee: $90. *Financial support:* Fellowships with tuition reimbursements, teaching assistantships with tuition reimbursements, Federal Work-Study and institutionally sponsored loans available. Financial award application deadline: 1/4; financial award applicants required to submit FAFSA. *Faculty research:* Post-Biblical and Talmudic literature and history, mysticism, Bible and ancient Near East, medieval and modern Jewish history, medieval and modern Jewish philosophy. *Unit head:* Lawrence Schiffman, Chair, 212-998-8980, Fax: 212-995-4178, E-mail: gsas.hebrewjudaic@nyu.edu. *Application contact:* David Engel, Director of Graduate Studies, 212-998-8980, Fax: 212-995-4178, E-mail: gsas.hebrewjudaic@nyu.edu.

New York University, Steinhardt School of Culture, Education, and Human Development, Department of Humanities and Social Sciences in the Professions, Program in Education and Jewish Studies, New York, NY 10012-1019. Offers MA, PhD, MA/MA. Part-time programs available. *Faculty:* 1 full-time (0 women). *Students:* 19 full-time (12 women), 10 part-time (6 women); includes 1 Hispanic/Latino, 3 international. Average age 28. 26 applicants, 58% accepted, 9 enrolled. In 2010, 1 doctorate awarded. *Degree requirements:* For doctorate, thesis/dissertation. *Entrance requirements:* For doctorate, GRE General Test, interview. Additional exam requirements/recommendations for international students: Required—TOEFL. *Application deadline:* For fall admission, 12/1 priority date for domestic and international students; for spring admission, 11/1 for domestic and international students. Applications are processed on a rolling basis. Application fee: $75. Electronic applications accepted. *Financial support:* Fellowships with full and partial tuition reimbursements, teaching assistantships with partial tuition reimbursements, career-related internships or fieldwork, Federal Work-Study, institutionally sponsored loans, scholarships/grants, tuition waivers (partial), and unspecified assistantships available. Support available to part-time students. Financial award application deadline: 2/1; financial award applicants required to submit FAFSA. *Faculty research:* Jewish education, educational history, Judaic studies. *Unit head:* Dr. Harold Wechsler, Director, 212-992-9475, Fax: 212-995-4178. *Application contact:* 212-998-5030, Fax: 212-995-4328, E-mail: steinhardt.gradadmissions@nyu.edu.

Reconstructionist Rabbinical College, Graduate Programs, Wyncote, PA 19095-1898. Offers Jewish studies (MAJS); rabbinics (MAHL, DHL); women's studies (Certificate). Certificate offered jointly with Temple University. Part-time programs available. *Faculty:* 8 full-time (4 women), 25 part-time/adjunct (14 women). *Students:* 52 full-time (37 women), 7 part-time (4 women). 25 applicants, 52% accepted, 11 enrolled. *Degree requirements:* For master's, one foreign language, thesis (MAJS), completion of rabbinical program (MAHL); for doctorate and MAHL, one foreign language. *Entrance requirements:* For MAHL and doctorate, GRE General Test, placement examinations in Hebrew and Judaism; for master's, GRE General Test. *Application deadline:* Applications are processed on a rolling basis. Application fee: $50. *Financial support:* In 2010–11, 46 students received support, including 4 fellowships with full tuition reimbursements available (averaging $11,000 per year), 1 research assistantship with partial tuition reimbursement available (averaging $5,500 per year), 5 teaching assistantships (averaging $5,500 per year); career-related internships or fieldwork, institutionally sponsored loans, and scholarships/grants also available. Financial award application deadline: 4/15. *Faculty research:* Bible, Hebrew Semitic texts, contemporary Judaism. *Unit head:* Rabbi Dan Ehrenkrantz, President, 215-576-0800 Ext. 129, Fax: 215-576-6143, E-mail: dehrenkrantz@rrc.edu. *Application contact:* Rabbi Amber Powers, Dean of Recruitment and Admissions, 215-576-0800 Ext. 145, Fax: 215-576-6143, E-mail: apowers@rrc.edu.

Rice University, Graduate Programs, School of Humanities, Department of Religious Studies, Houston, TX 77251-1892. Offers African religions (PhD); African-American religions (PhD); contemplative studies (PhD); ghosticism, esotericism, mysticism (PhD); Islam (PhD); Jewish thought and philosophy (PhD); modern Christianity in thought and popular culture (PhD); psychology of religion (PhD); the Bible and beyond (PhD). *Degree requirements:* For doctorate, 2 foreign languages, comprehensive exam, thesis/dissertation. *Entrance requirements:* For doctorate, GRE, letters of recommendation, writing sample. Additional exam requirements/recommendations for international students: Required—TOEFL (minimum score 600 paper-based; 90 iBT). Electronic applications accepted. *Faculty research:* Origins and historical

Jewish Studies

Rice University (continued)
development of Islam, history of Christianity, the study of comparative religion, African-American religion, religion and culture.

Seton Hall University, College of Arts and Sciences, Department of Jewish-Christian Studies, South Orange, NJ 07079-2697. Offers Holocaust studies (MA); Jewish-Christian Studies (MA). Part-time and evening/weekend programs available. *Degree requirements:* For master's, thesis optional. *Entrance requirements:* For master's, interview or suitable correspondence with department chair. Additional exam requirements/recommendations for international students: Required—TOEFL. Electronic applications accepted. *Faculty research:* Jewish-Christian issues, Biblical studies, Holocaust studies.

Southern Evangelical Seminary, Graduate Programs, Matthews, NC 28105. Offers apologetics (MA, Certificate); Christian education (MA); church ministry (MA, Certificate); divinity (Certificate), including apologetics (M Div, Certificate); Islamic studies (MA, Certificate); Jewish studies (MA); philosophy (MA); religion (MA); theology (M Div), including apologetics (M Div, Certificate), Biblical studies; youth ministry (MA). Part-time and evening/weekend programs available. Postbaccalaureate distance learning degree programs offered. *Degree requirements:* For master's, thesis (for some programs); for doctorate, 2 foreign languages, comprehensive exam (for some programs), thesis/dissertation; for M Div, one foreign language. *Entrance requirements:* Additional exam requirements/recommendations for international students: Required—TOEFL (minimum score 600 paper-based; 250 computer-based). *Application deadline:* For fall admission, 8/15 priority date for domestic students, 8/5 priority date for international students; for winter admission, 12/15 priority date for domestic and international students; for spring admission, 1/15 priority date for domestic and international students. Applications are processed on a rolling basis. Application fee: $25. *Expenses:* Tuition: Full-time $9405; part-time $313.50 per credit hour. Required fees: $150; $50 per semester. *Financial support:* Scholarships/grants available. *Unit head:* Dr. Barry R. Leventhal, Dean, 704-847-5600 Ext. 204, Fax: 704-845-1747, E-mail: dean@ses.edu. *Application contact:* Duke Hale, Director of Recruitment, 704-847-5600 Ext. 216, Fax: 704-845-1747, E-mail: dhale@ses.edu.

Spertus Institute of Jewish Studies, Graduate Programs, Program in Jewish Studies, Chicago, IL 60605-1901. Offers MAJS, MSJE, MSJS, DJS, DSJS. Part-time and evening/weekend programs available. Postbaccalaureate distance learning degree programs offered (minimal on-campus study). *Degree requirements:* For master's, one foreign language, thesis (for some programs); for doctorate, one foreign language, thesis/dissertation. *Entrance requirements:* For master's, interview, BAJS (MAJS); for doctorate, MAJS. Part-time tuition and fees vary according to degree level and program.

Telshe Yeshiva–Chicago, Graduate Program, Chicago, IL 60625-5598. Offers Second Talmudic Degree. *Accreditation:* AARTS.

Touro College, Graduate School of Jewish Studies, New York, NY 10010. Offers MA. Part-time programs available. *Degree requirements:* For master's, one foreign language, thesis. *Entrance requirements:* For master's, previous course work in Jewish studies, proficiency in Hebrew. *Faculty research:* Medieval and modern Jewish history, Jewish philosophy, holocaust studies, Jewish education.

Towson University, Baltimore Hebrew Institute, Towson, MD 21252. Offers Jewish communal service (MAJCS); Jewish education (MAJE, Certificate); Jewish studies (MAJS). *Students:* 19 full-time (10 women), 28 part-time (17 women); includes 4 minority (all Black or African American, non-Hispanic/Latino), 2 international. In 2010, 9 master's, 1 doctorate, 1 other advanced degree awarded. *Expenses:* Tuition, state resident: part-time $324 per credit. Tuition, nonresident: part-time $681 per credit. Required fees: $95 per term. *Unit head:* Erika Schon, Director, 410-704-7117, E-mail: eschon@towson.edu. *Application contact:* Erika Schon, Director, 410-704-7117, E-mail: eschon@towson.edu.

University of California, Berkeley, Graduate Division, College of Letters and Science, Program in Jewish Studies, Berkeley, CA 94720-1500. Offers PhD. Program held jointly with Graduate Theological Union. *Entrance requirements:* For doctorate, GRE General Test, 3 letters of recommendation.

University of California, San Diego, Office of Graduate Studies, Department of History, La Jolla, CA 92093. Offers history (MA, PhD); Judaic studies (MA); science studies (PhD). *Degree requirements:* For doctorate, thesis/dissertation. *Entrance requirements:* For master's and doctorate, GRE General Test. Electronic applications accepted.

University of Connecticut, Graduate School, College of Liberal Arts and Sciences, Field of International Studies, Program in Judaic Studies, Storrs, CT 06269. Offers MA. *Entrance requirements:* Additional exam requirements/recommendations for international students: Required—TOEFL (minimum score 550 paper-based; 213 computer-based). Electronic applications accepted.

University of Maryland, College Park, Academic Affairs, College of Arts and Humanities, Program in Jewish Studies, College Park, MD 20742. Offers MA. *Faculty:* 8 full-time (4 women), 2 part-time/adjunct (both women). *Students:* 3 full-time (1 woman). 11 applicants, 45% accepted, 2 enrolled. In 2010, 4 master's awarded. *Degree requirements:* For master's, thesis or 2 major research papers. *Entrance requirements:* For master's, GRE General Test, 3 letters of recommendation, writing sample. Additional exam requirements/recommendations for international students: Required—TOEFL. *Application deadline:* For fall admission, 12/15 for domestic and international students. Application fee: $75. *Expenses:* Tuition, state resident: part-time $471 per credit hour. Tuition, nonresident: part-time $1016 per credit hour. Required fees: $337 per term. *Financial support:* In 2010–11, 2 teaching assistantships (averaging $17,234 per year) were awarded; fellowships also available. *Unit head:* Hayim Lapin, Director, Meyerhoff Program and Center for Jewish Studies, 301-405-4734, E-mail: hlapin@umd.edu. *Application contact:* Dean of Graduate Studies, 301-405-0376, Fax: 301-314-9305.

University of Michigan, Horace H. Rackham School of Graduate Studies, College of Literature, Science, and the Arts, Department of Near Eastern Studies, Ann Arbor, MI 48109. Offers ancient Near Eastern studies (AM, PhD); Arabic for professional purposes (AM); Arabic language and literature (AM, PhD); Armenian studies (AM, PhD); Christianity in late antiquity (AM, PhD); Egyptology (AM, PhD); Hebrew Bible and ancient Israel (AM, PhD); Hebrew literature (AM, PhD); Islamic studies (AM, PhD); Jewish cultural studies (AM, PhD); Jewish mysticism (AM, PhD); Persian and Iranian studies (AM, PhD); Rabbinic literature (AM, PhD); Second Temple Judaism (AM, PhD); teaching of Arabic as a foreign language (AM); Turkish studies (AM, PhD). Part-time programs available. Terminal master's awarded for partial completion of doctoral program. *Degree requirements:* For master's, 2 foreign languages; for doctorate, 4 foreign languages, comprehensive exam, thesis/dissertation. *Entrance requirements:* For master's, GRE General Test; for doctorate, GRE General Test, master's degree. Additional exam requirements/recommendations for international students: Required—TOEFL (minimum score 560 paper-based; 220 computer-based; 84 iBT). Electronic applications accepted. *Expenses:* Tuition, state resident: full-time $17,784; part-time $1116 per credit hour. Tuition, nonresident: full-time $35,944; part-time $2125 per credit hour. International tuition: $35,994 full-time. Required fees: $95 per semester. Tuition and fees vary according to course load, degree level and program. *Faculty research:* Middle and Near Eastern literatures, languages, cultures from ancient times to the present.

University of Michigan, Horace H. Rackham School of Graduate Studies, College of Literature, Science, and the Arts, Jean and Samuel Frankel Center for Judaic Studies, Ann Arbor, MI 48178. Offers MA, Graduate Certificate. Part-time programs available. *Faculty:* 32 full-time (13 women). *Students:* 11 full-time (5 women), 1 (woman) part-time. Average age 25. 8 applicants, 88% accepted, 4 enrolled. In 2010, 1 master's, 1 other advanced degree awarded. *Degree requirements:* For master's, thesis, fourth-term proficiency in either Hebrew or Yiddish; for Graduate Certificate, capstone course (including public lecture), reading knowledge of 1 Jewish language. *Entrance requirements:* For master's, GRE General Test; for Graduate Certificate, admission to a U-M doctoral program. Additional exam requirements/recommendations for international students: Required—TOEFL (minimum score 560 paper-based; 84 computer-based). *Application deadline:* For fall admission, 1/10 for domestic and international students; for winter admission, 9/1 for domestic and international students. Application fee: $65 ($75 for international students). Electronic applications accepted. *Expenses:* Tuition, state resident: full-time $17,784; part-time $1116 per credit hour. Tuition, nonresident: full-time $35,944; part-time $2125 per credit hour. International tuition: $35,994 full-time. Required fees: $95 per semester. Tuition and fees vary according to course load, degree level and program. *Financial support:* In 2010–11, 10 fellowships (averaging $1,920 per year) were awarded; summer research fellowships also available. *Faculty research:* American Jewish experience; classical Judaism/religious studies; global and transnational studies; Jewish literature, language and translation; social science; visual studies. *Unit head:* Prof. Deborah Dash Moore, Director, 734-763-9047, Fax: 734-936-2186, E-mail: ddmoore@umich.edu. *Application contact:* Brittin Alissa Pollack, Student/Fellow Coordinator, 734-615-6097, Fax: 734-936-2186, E-mail: brittinp@umich.edu.

The University of Montana, Graduate School, School of Fine Arts, Department of Art, Missoula, MT 59812-0002. Offers fine arts (MA, MFA), including art (MA), art history (MA), ceramics (MFA), integrated arts and education (MA), media arts (MFA), painting and drawing (MFA), photography (MFA), printmaking (MFA), sculpture (MFA). *Accreditation:* NASAD (one or more programs are accredited). *Degree requirements:* For master's, thesis exhibit. *Entrance requirements:* For master's, GRE General Test, portfolio.

University of St. Michael's College, Faculty of Theology, Toronto, ON M5S 1J4, Canada. Offers Catholic leadership (MA); eastern Christian studies (Diploma); religious education (Diploma); theological studies (Diploma); theology (M Div, MA, MRE, MTS, D Min, PhD, Th D); theology and Jewish studies (MA). Th D offered jointly with University of Toronto. *Accreditation:* ATS (one or more programs are accredited). Part-time programs available. *Degree requirements:* For master's, thesis (for some programs), 1 foreign language (MA), 2 foreign languages (Th M); for doctorate, 3 foreign languages, comprehensive exam, thesis/dissertation; for M Div, thesis/dissertation optional; for other advanced degree, thesis optional. *Entrance requirements:* For M Div and other advanced degree, minimum GPA of 2.7; for master's, M Div or BA, course work in an ancient or modern language, minimum GPA of 3.3; for doctorate, MA in theology, Th M, or M Div with thesis, minimum GPA of 3.7. Additional exam requirements/recommendations for international students: Required—TOEFL (minimum score 600 paper-based; 250 computer-based). Electronic applications accepted. *Expenses:* Contact institution. *Faculty research:* Patristics, eastern Christianity, ecology and theology, ecumenism, Jewish Christian studies.

University of Wisconsin–Madison, Graduate School, College of Letters and Science, Department of Hebrew and Semitic Studies, Madison, WI 53706-1380. Offers MA, PhD. Terminal master's awarded for partial completion of doctoral program. *Degree requirements:* For master's, 2 foreign languages; for doctorate, thesis/dissertation. *Entrance requirements:* For master's and doctorate, GRE. Electronic applications accepted. *Expenses:* Tuition, state resident: full-time $9887; part-time $617.96 per credit. Tuition, nonresident: full-time $24,054; part-time $1503.40 per credit. Required fees: $67.63 per credit. Tuition and fees vary according to reciprocity agreements. *Faculty research:* Biblical language and literature, Northwest Semitic languages.

University of Wisconsin–Milwaukee, Graduate School, College of Letters and Sciences, Interdepartmental Program in Foreign Language and Literature, Milwaukee, WI 53201-0413. Offers classics and Hebrew studies (MAFLL); comparative literature (MAFLL); French and Italian (MAFLL); German (MAFLL); Slavic studies (MAFLL); translation (Certificate). Part-time programs available. *Faculty:* 29 full-time (14 women). *Students:* 35 full-time (27 women), 29 part-time (20 women); includes 1 Hispanic/Latino. Average age 40. 30 applicants, 67% accepted, 19 enrolled. In 2010, 24 master's awarded. *Degree requirements:* For master's, 2 foreign languages, thesis or alternative. *Entrance requirements:* Additional exam requirements/recommendations for international students: Required—TOEFL (minimum score 550 paper-based; 79 iBT), IELTS (minimum score 6.5). *Application deadline:* For fall admission, 1/1 priority date for domestic students; for spring admission, 9/1 for domestic students. Applications are processed on a rolling basis. Application fee: $56 ($96 for international students). Electronic applications accepted. *Financial support:* In 2010–11, 1 fellowship, 2 research assistantships, 26 teaching assistantships were awarded; career-related internships or fieldwork, health care benefits, unspecified assistantships, and project assistantships also available. Support available to part-time students. Financial award application deadline: 4/15; financial award applicants required to submit FAFSA. Total annual research expenditures: $304,210. *Unit head:* Gabrielle Verdier, Representative, 414-229-3346, Fax: 414-229-2741, E-mail: verdier@uwm.edu. *Application contact:* General Information Contact, 414-229-4982, Fax: 414-229-6967, E-mail: gradschool@uwm.edu.

Yeshiva University, Bernard Revel Graduate School of Jewish Studies, New York, NY 10033-3201. Offers MA, PhD. Part-time programs available. Terminal master's awarded for partial completion of doctoral program. *Degree requirements:* For master's, comprehensive exam; for doctorate, 2 foreign languages, comprehensive exam, thesis/dissertation. *Entrance requirements:* For master's and doctorate, GRE General Test (recommended), reading knowledge of Hebrew, minimum GPA of 3.0. *Faculty research:* Bible, Jewish history, Jewish philosophy and mysticism, Talmud, Semitic languages.

Latin American Studies

American University, College of Arts and Sciences, Department of Language and Foreign Studies, Washington, DC 20016-8045. Offers French (Certificate), including translation; Russian (Certificate), including translation; Spanish: Latin American studies (MA, Certificate), including Spanish: Latin American studies (MA), translation (Certificate); teaching English to speakers of other languages (MA, Certificate). Part-time and evening/weekend programs available. *Faculty:* 41 full-time (29 women), 43 part-time/adjunct (34 women). *Students:* 22 full-time (17 women), 39 part-time (31 women); includes 8 minority (1 Black or African American, non-Hispanic/Latino; 3 Asian, non-Hispanic/Latino; 3 Hispanic/Latino; 1 Native Hawaiian or other Pacific Islander, non-Hispanic/Latino), 6 international. Average age 34. 64 applicants, 64% accepted, 14 enrolled. In 2010, 24 master's, 28 other advanced degrees awarded. *Degree requirements:* For master's, one foreign language, comprehensive exam, thesis or alternative, portfolio, research; for Certificate, minimum 15 credit hours related coursework. *Entrance requirements:* For master's, GRE, writing sample; for Certificate, bachelor's degree. Additional exam requirements/recommendations for international students: Required—TOEFL. *Application deadline:* For fall admission, 2/1 for domestic students; for spring admission, 10/1 for domestic students. Application fee: $80. *Financial support:* Fellowships, career-related internships or fieldwork, Federal Work-Study, institutionally sponsored loans, and tuition waivers (partial) available. Financial award application deadline: 2/1. *Unit head:* Olga Rojer, Chair, 202-885-2139, Fax: 202-885-1076, E-mail: orojer@american.edu. *Application contact:* Kathleen Clowery, Director of Graduate Admissions, 202-885-3621, Fax: 202-885-1505, E-mail: clowery@american.edu.

Arizona State University, College of Liberal Arts and Sciences, School of Historical, Philosophical and Religious Studies, Tempe, AZ 85287-4301. Offers East/Southeast Asian history (MA, PhD); European history (MA, PhD); Latin American studies (MA, PhD); North American history (MA, PhD); philosophy (MA, PhD); public history (MA); religious studies (MA, PhD); scholarly publishing (Graduate Certificate). Part-time programs available. *Faculty:* 70 full-time (29 women), 2 part-time/adjunct (0 women). *Students:* 125 full-time (58 women), 68 part-time (37 women); includes 21 minority (5 Black or African American, non-Hispanic/Latino; 3 American Indian or Alaska Native, non-Hispanic/Latino; 1 Asian, non-Hispanic/Latino; 11 Hispanic/Latino; 1 Two or more races, non-Hispanic/Latino), 16 international. Average age 34. 221 applicants, 51% accepted, 41 enrolled. In 2010, 24 master's, 10 doctorates, 3 other advanced degrees awarded. Terminal master's awarded for partial completion of doctoral program. *Degree requirements:* For master's, thesis or alternative, interactive Program of Study (iPOS) submitted before completing 50 percent of required credit hours; for doctorate, variable foreign language requirement, comprehensive exam, thesis/dissertation, interactive Program of Study (iPOS) submitted before completing 50 percent of required credit hours. *Entrance requirements:* For master's and doctorate, GRE, minimum GPA of 3.0 or equivalent in last 2 years of work leading to bachelor's degree. Additional exam requirements/recommendations for international students: Required—TOEFL, IELTS, or Pearson Test of English. *Application deadline:* For fall admission, 1/1 for domestic and international students. Applications are processed on a rolling basis. Application fee: $70 ($90 for international students). Electronic applications accepted. *Expenses:* Tuition, state resident: full-time $8510; part-time $608 per credit. Tuition, nonresident: full-time $16,542; part-time $919 per credit. Required fees: $339; $110 per credit. Part-time tuition and fees vary according to course load. *Financial support:* In 2010–11, 26 research assistantships with full and partial tuition reimbursements (averaging $12,900 per year), 69 teaching assistantships with full and partial tuition reimbursements (averaging $11,771 per year) were awarded; fellowships with full tuition reimbursements, career-related internships or fieldwork, institutionally sponsored loans, scholarships/grants, and tuition waivers (partial) also available. Financial award application deadline: 3/1; financial award applicants required to submit FAFSA. Total annual research expenditures: $1.3 million. *Unit head:* Mark Von Hagen, Director, 480-965-4186, E-mail: mark.vonhagen@asu.edu. *Application contact:* Graduate Admissions, 480-965-6113.

Boricua College, Program in Latin American and Caribbean Studies (Brooklyn Campus), New York, NY 10032-1560. Offers MA. Evening/weekend programs available. *Degree requirements:* For master's, thesis. *Entrance requirements:* For master's, interview by the faculty. Additional exam requirements/recommendations for international students: Required—Boricua College's exam.

Boricua College, Program in Latin American and Caribbean Studies (Manhattan Campus), New York, NY 10032-1560. Offers MA. Evening/weekend programs available. *Degree requirements:* For master's, thesis. *Entrance requirements:* For master's, interview by the faculty. Additional exam requirements/recommendations for international students: Required—Boricua College's exam.

Brown University, Graduate School, Center for Portuguese and Brazilian Studies, Providence, RI 02912. Offers Brazilian studies (AM); Portuguese and Brazilian studies (AM, PhD); Portuguese Bilingual Education and Cross-Cultural Studies (AM); MA/PhD. *Degree requirements:* For doctorate, thesis/dissertation.

California State University, Long Beach, Graduate Studies, College of Liberal Arts, Department of History, Long Beach, CA 90840. Offers Africa and the Middle East (MA); ancient/medieval Europe (MA); Asia (MA); Latin America (MA); modern Europe (MA); United States (MA); world (MA). Part-time and evening/weekend programs available. *Faculty:* 12 full-time (7 women). *Students:* 18 full-time (6 women), 51 part-time (18 women); includes 3 Black or African American, non-Hispanic/Latino; 1 American Indian or Alaska Native, non-Hispanic/Latino; 3 Asian, non-Hispanic/Latino; 16 Hispanic/Latino, 1 international. Average age 30. 80 applicants, 53% accepted, 30 enrolled. In 2010, 11 master's awarded. *Degree requirements:* For master's, one foreign language, comprehensive exam or thesis. *Application deadline:* For fall admission, 3/1 for domestic students. Applications are processed on a rolling basis. Application fee: $55. Electronic applications accepted. *Financial support:* Research assistantships, Federal Work-Study, institutionally sponsored loans, and scholarships/grants available. Financial award application deadline: 3/2. *Faculty research:* All periods of European and American history, recent Asian and African history. *Unit head:* Dr. Nancy Quam-Wickham, Department Chair, 562-985-4431, Fax: 562-985-5431, E-mail: quamwick@csulb.edu. *Application contact:* Dr. Houri Berberian, Graduate Advisor, 562-985-4524, Fax: 562-985-4431, E-mail: hberber@csulb.edu.

California State University, Los Angeles, Graduate Studies, College of Natural and Social Sciences, Department of Latin American Studies, Los Angeles, CA 90032-8530. Offers MA. Part-time and evening/weekend programs available. *Students:* 15 full-time (9 women), 23 part-time (13 women); includes 29 minority (all Hispanic/Latino), 1 international. Average age 33. 16 applicants, 100% accepted, 11 enrolled. In 2010, 11 master's awarded. *Degree requirements:* For master's, one foreign language, comprehensive exam, thesis. *Entrance requirements:* For master's, minimum GPA of 2.5. Additional exam requirements/recommendations for international students: Required—TOEFL (minimum score 500 paper-based; 173 computer-based). *Application deadline:* For fall admission, 5/1 for domestic and international students. Applications are processed on a rolling basis. Application fee: $55. Electronic applications accepted. *Financial support:* Federal Work-Study available. Support available to part-time students. Financial award application deadline: 3/1. *Faculty research:* Central America, Cuba, Third World development, labor history, redemocratization. *Unit head:* Dr. Beth Baker-Cristales, Director, 323-343-2290, Fax: 323-343-5485, E-mail: bbakerc@calstatela.edu. *Application contact:* Dr. Alan Muchlinski, Dean of Graduate Studies, 323-343-3820, Fax: 323-343-5653, E-mail: amuchli@exchange.calstatela.edu.

Centro de Estudios Avanzados de Puerto Rico y el Caribe, Graduate Program in Puerto Rican and Caribbean Studies, Old San Juan, PR 00902-3970. Offers Puerto Rican and Caribbean history (MA, PhD); Puerto Rican and Caribbean literature (MA, PhD); Puerto Rican studies (MA). Part-time and evening/weekend programs available. *Degree requirements:* For master's, comprehensive exam, thesis; for doctorate, 2 foreign languages, comprehensive exam, thesis/dissertation. *Entrance requirements:* For master's and doctorate, interview. *Faculty research:* Literature, history, art, folklore, and culture of Puerto Rico and Caribbean countries.

Cleveland State University, College of Graduate Studies, College of Liberal Arts and Social Sciences, Department of Modern Languages, Cleveland, OH 44115. Offers French (M Ed); Spanish (M Ed, MA), including language and linguistics (MA), Latin American studies (MA), peninsular studies (MA), Spanish (MA). Part-time and evening/weekend programs available. *Faculty:* 12 full-time (9 women). *Students:* 7 full-time (4 women), 9 part-time (7 women); includes 1 Black or African American, non-Hispanic/Latino; 1 Asian, non-Hispanic/Latino; 3 Hispanic/Latino; 1 Two or more races, non-Hispanic/Latino, 2 international. Average age 37. 11 applicants, 100% accepted, 8 enrolled. In 2010, 9 master's awarded. *Degree requirements:* For master's, one foreign language, comprehensive exam, thesis optional, study abroad. *Entrance requirements:* For master's, undergraduate major in Spanish or equivalent, essay in Spanish, writing sample. Additional exam requirements/recommendations for international students: Required—TOEFL (minimum score 525 paper-based; 197 computer-based). *Application deadline:* For fall admission, 7/25 priority date for domestic students; for spring admission, 12/15 priority date for domestic students. Applications are processed on a rolling basis. Application fee: $30. Electronic applications accepted. *Expenses:* Tuition, state resident: full-time $8447; part-time $469 per credit hour. Tuition, nonresident: full-time $16,020; part-time $890 per credit hour. Required fees: $50. *Financial support:* In 2010–11, 6 students received support, including 6 teaching assistantships with full tuition reimbursements available (averaging $7,030 per year); Federal Work-Study also available. *Faculty research:* Second language acquisition, sociolinguistics, contemporary Spanish novel, Arabic diaspora in Latin America, border literature. *Unit head:* Dr. Tama L. Engelking, Chairperson, 216-523-7175, Fax: 216-687-4650, E-mail: t.engelking@csuohio.edu. *Application contact:* Dr. Antonio Medina-Rivera, Graduate Director, 216-523-7168, Fax: 216-687-4650, E-mail: a.medinarivera@csuohio.edu.

Columbia University, School of International and Public Affairs, Institute of Latin American Studies, New York, NY 10027. Offers Latin American and Caribbean studies (MA); Latin American studies (Certificate). Students must also be enrolled in a separate graduate degree program at Columbia University. *Degree requirements:* For master's, 2 foreign languages, thesis. Electronic applications accepted. *Faculty research:* Rights vs. efficiency in a globalized era, citizenship and governance in Latin America and Western Europe.

Cornell University, Graduate School, Graduate Fields of Arts and Sciences, Field of Archaeology, Ithaca, NY 14853-0001. Offers environmental archaeology (MA); historical archaeology (MA); Latin American archaeology (MA); medieval archaeology (MA); Mediterranean and Near Eastern archaeology (MA); Stone Age archaeology (MA). *Faculty:* 18 full-time (5 women). *Students:* 8 full-time (7 women); includes 1 Hispanic/Latino. Average age 24. 23 applicants, 30% accepted, 3 enrolled. *Degree requirements:* For master's, one foreign language, thesis. *Entrance requirements:* For master's, GRE General Test, 3 letters of recommendation, sample of written work. Additional exam requirements/recommendations for international students: Required—TOEFL (minimum score 550 paper-based; 213 computer-based; 77 iBT). *Application deadline:* For fall admission, 1/15 for domestic students. Application fee: $80. Electronic applications accepted. *Expenses:* Tuition: Full-time $29,500. Required fees: $76. Tuition and fees vary according to degree level and program. *Financial support:* In 2010–11, 1 fellowship with full tuition reimbursement, 3 teaching assistantships with full tuition reimbursements were awarded; research assistantships with full tuition reimbursements, institutionally sponsored loans, scholarships/grants, health care benefits, tuition waivers (full and partial), and unspecified assistantships also available. Financial award applicants required to submit FAFSA. *Faculty research:* Anatolia, Lydia, Sardis, classical and Hellenistic Greece; science in archaeology; North American Indians; Stone Age Africa; Mayan trade. *Unit head:* Director of Graduate Studies, 607-255-6768, E-mail: blj7@cornell.edu. *Application contact:* Graduate Field Assistant, 607-255-6768, E-mail: dsd6@cornell.edu.

Cornell University, Graduate School, Graduate Fields of Arts and Sciences, Field of History, Ithaca, NY 14853-0001. Offers African history (MA, PhD); American history (MA, PhD); ancient history (MA, PhD); early modern European history (MA, PhD); English history (MA, PhD); French history (MA, PhD); German history (MA, PhD); history of science (MA, PhD); Latin American history (MA, PhD); medieval Chinese history (MA, PhD); medieval history (MA, PhD); modern Chinese history (MA, PhD); modern European history (MA, PhD); modern Japanese history (MA, PhD); premodern Islamic history (MA, PhD); premodern Japanese history (MA, PhD); Renaissance history (MA, PhD); Russian history (MA, PhD); Southeast Asian history (MA, PhD). *Faculty:* 53 full-time (15 women). *Students:* 59 full-time (30 women); includes 3 Black or African American, non-Hispanic/Latino; 2 Asian, non-Hispanic/Latino; 4 Hispanic/Latino, 22 international. Average age 30. 217 applicants, 6% accepted, 8 enrolled. In 2010, 9 master's, 5 doctorates awarded. Terminal master's awarded for partial completion of doctoral program. *Degree requirements:* For master's, thesis; for doctorate, 2 foreign languages, comprehensive exam, thesis/dissertation, 1 year of teaching experience. *Entrance requirements:* For master's and doctorate, GRE General Test, writing sample, 3 letters of recommendation. Additional exam requirements/recommendations for international students: Required—TOEFL (minimum score 550 paper-based; 213 computer-based; 77 iBT). *Application deadline:* For fall admission, 1/15 for domestic students. Application fee: $80. Electronic applications accepted. *Expenses:* Tuition: Full-time $29,500. Required fees: $76. Tuition and fees vary according to degree level and program. *Financial support:* In 2010–11, 26 fellowships with full tuition reimbursements, 27 teaching assistantships with full tuition reimbursements were awarded; research assistantships with full tuition reimbursements, institutionally sponsored loans, scholarships/grants, health care benefits, tuition waivers (full and partial), and unspecified assistantships also available. Financial award applicants required to submit FAFSA. *Unit head:* Director of Graduate Studies, 607-255-6738, Fax: 607-255-0469. *Application contact:* Graduate Field Assistant, 607-255-6738, Fax: 607-255-0469, E-mail: history_grad_info@cornell.edu.

Duke University, Graduate School, Department of History, Durham, NC 27708. Offers history (AM, PhD); Latin American studies (PhD); JD/AM; MD/PhD. *Faculty:* 37 full-time. *Students:* 62 full-time (37 women); includes 8 Black or African American, non-Hispanic/Latino; 1 Hispanic/Latino, 7 international. 207 applicants, 14% accepted, 17 enrolled. In 2010, 4 master's, 4 doctorates awarded. *Degree requirements:* For doctorate, 2 foreign languages, thesis/dissertation. *Entrance requirements:* For doctorate, GRE General Test. Additional exam requirements/recommendations for international students: Required—TOEFL (minimum score 550 paper-based; 213 computer-based; 83 iBT), IELTS (minimum score 7). *Application deadline:* For fall admission, 12/8 priority date for domestic and international students. Application fee: $75. Electronic applications accepted. *Financial support:* Fellowships, research assistantships, teaching assistantships, Federal Work-Study available. Financial award application deadline: 12/8. *Unit head:* Peter Sigal, Director of Graduate Studies, 919-681-5746, Fax: 919-681-7670, E-mail: rmennis@duke.edu. *Application contact:* Elizabeth Hutton, Director, Graduate Admission, 919-684-3913, Fax: 919-684-2277, E-mail: grad-admissions@duke.edu.

Florida International University, College of Arts and Sciences, Program in Latin American and Caribbean Studies, Miami, FL 33199. Offers MA. Part-time and evening/weekend programs available. *Faculty:* 1 (woman) full-time. *Students:* 21 full-time (11 women), 2 part-time (0 women); includes 11 Hispanic/Latino, 4 international. Average age 29. 47 applicants, 36% accepted, 15 enrolled. In 2010, 7 master's awarded. *Degree requirements:* For master's, one foreign language, thesis or alternative. *Entrance requirements:* For master's, GRE General Test (minimum score 1000); GMAT, LSAT, or EXADEP (minimum 62nd percentile), minimum GPA of 3.0, 3 letters of recommendation, letter of intent. Additional exam requirements/recommendations for international students: Required—TOEFL (minimum score 550 paper-based; 80 iBT). *Application deadline:* For fall admission, 2/1 for domestic and international students; for spring admission, 10/1 for domestic students, 9/1 for international students. Applications are processed on a rolling basis. Application fee: $30. Electronic applications

Latin American Studies

Florida International University (continued)
accepted. *Financial support:* Institutionally sponsored loans and scholarships/grants available. Financial award application deadline: 3/1; financial award applicants required to submit FAFSA. *Unit head:* Dr. Cristina Eguizabal, Director, 305-348-2894, Fax: 305-348-3593, E-mail: lacc@fiu.edu.

Fordham University, Graduate School of Arts and Sciences, Program in Latin American and Latino Studies, New York, NY 10458. Offers MA, Certificate. *Students:* 4 full-time (3 women), 8 part-time (4 women); includes 3 Hispanic/Latino, 2 international. 12 applicants, 58% accepted, 3 enrolled. In 2010, 2 other advanced degrees awarded. *Entrance requirements:* Additional exam requirements/recommendations for international students: Required—TOEFL (minimum score 650 paper-based; 280 computer-based). *Application deadline:* For fall admission, 1/4 priority date for domestic students; for spring admission, 11/1 for domestic students. Application fee: $65. Electronic applications accepted. *Financial support:* Application deadline: 1/4. *Faculty research:* Latinos and Hollywood, Puerto Rican women and labor history, education and the state in El Salvador, avant-garde literature in twentieth-century Latin America. *Unit head:* Dr. Arnaldo Cruz-Malave, Director, 718-817-6571, E-mail: lalsi@fordham.edu. *Application contact:* Charlene Dundie, Director of Graduate Admissions, 718-817-4420, Fax: 718-817-3566, E-mail: dundie@fordham.edu.

Georgetown University, Graduate School of Arts and Sciences, Center for Latin American Studies, Washington, DC 20057-1026. Offers MA, MA/JD, MA/PhD. *Degree requirements:* For master's, one foreign language, comprehensive exam, thesis optional. *Entrance requirements:* For master's, GRE General Test, minimum B average. Additional exam requirements/recommendations for international students: Required—TOEFL.

The George Washington University, Elliott School of International Affairs, Program in Latin American and Hemispheric Studies, Washington, DC 20052. Offers MA, JD/MA, MBA/MA. Part-time and evening/weekend programs available. *Students:* 20 full-time (15 women), 6 part-time (5 women); includes 1 Black or African American, non-Hispanic/Latino; 9 Hispanic/Latino. Average age 25. 64 applicants, 77% accepted, 14 enrolled. In 2010, 7 master's awarded. *Degree requirements:* For master's, one foreign language, capstone project. *Entrance requirements:* For master's, GRE General Test, 2 years (or the equivalent) of Spanish or Portuguese. Additional exam requirements/recommendations for international students: Required—TOEFL. *Application deadline:* For fall admission, 2/1 for domestic students; for spring admission, 10/1 for domestic students. Application fee: $75. Electronic applications accepted. *Financial support:* In 2010–11, 4 students received support; fellowships with tuition reimbursements available, research assistantships with tuition reimbursements available, career-related internships or fieldwork, Federal Work-Study, institutionally sponsored loans, and tuition waivers (full) available. Financial award application deadline: 1/15; financial award applicants required to submit FAFSA. *Faculty research:* Democracy and change in Andean nations, rural economic development, peasant cooperatives and political change. *Unit head:* Cynthia McClintock, Director, 202-994-6589, Fax: 202-994-7743, E-mail: mcclin@gwu.edu. *Application contact:* Jeff V. Miles, Director of Graduate Admissions, 202-994-7050, Fax: 202-994-9537, E-mail: esiagrad@gwu.edu.

Georgia State University, College of Arts and Sciences, Department of History, Atlanta, GA 30302-3083. Offers heritage preservation (MHP, Certificate); history (MA, PhD); Latin American studies (Certificate). Part-time and evening/weekend programs available. *Degree requirements:* For master's, one foreign language, comprehensive exam, thesis; for doctorate, 2 foreign languages, comprehensive exam, thesis/dissertation, exam. *Entrance requirements:* For master's, GRE General Test; for doctorate, GRE General Test, sample of written work. Additional exam requirements/recommendations for international students: Required—TOEFL. Electronic applications accepted. *Faculty research:* Historic preservation, labor history, twentieth-century U.S. history, American South, world history.

Indiana University Bloomington, University Graduate School, College of Arts and Sciences, Center for Latin American and Caribbean Studies, Bloomington, IN 47405-7000. Offers MA, MBA/MA, MLS/MA, MPA/MA. Part-time programs available. *Students:* 5 full-time (3 women), 2 part-time (both women); includes 3 minority (all Hispanic/Latino). Average age 27. 28 applicants, 89% accepted, 5 enrolled. In 2010, 2 master's awarded. *Degree requirements:* For master's, one foreign language, oral and written exam. *Entrance requirements:* For master's, GRE General Test. Additional exam requirements/recommendations for international students: Required—TOEFL. *Application deadline:* For fall admission, 1/15 priority date for domestic students, 12/15 for international students; for spring admission, 9/1 priority date for domestic students, 9/1 for international students. Applications are processed on a rolling basis. Application fee: $55 ($65 for international students). *Financial support:* Fellowships with tuition reimbursements, research assistantships with tuition reimbursements, teaching assistantships with tuition reimbursements, career-related internships or fieldwork, Federal Work-Study, institutionally sponsored loans, scholarships/grants, and unspecified assistantships available. Financial award application deadline: 7/15; financial award applicants required to submit FAFSA. *Unit head:* Dr. Jeffrey Gould, Director, 812-855-9098, Fax: 812-855-5345, E-mail: gouldj@indiana.edu. *Application contact:* Amy Belcher, Information Contact, 812-855-9097, Fax: 812-855-5345, E-mail: clacs@indiana.edu.

La Salle University, School of Arts and Sciences, Program in Bilingual/Bicultural Studies (Spanish), Philadelphia, PA 19141-1199. Offers MA. Part-time and evening/weekend programs available. *Degree requirements:* For master's, one foreign language, thesis or alternative, project. *Entrance requirements:* For master's, GRE or MAT. *Expenses:* Contact institution. *Faculty research:* Puerto Rican literature, cross-cultural communication, English as a second language methodology, Spanish language.

Michigan State University, The Graduate School, College of Social Science, Program in Chicano/Latino Studies, East Lansing, MI 48824. Offers PhD. *Entrance requirements:* Additional exam requirements/recommendations for international students: Required—TOEFL. Electronic applications accepted.

New York University, Graduate School of Arts and Science, Center for Latin American and Caribbean Studies, New York, NY 10012-1019. Offers MA, JD/MA. Part-time programs available. *Students:* 23 full-time (15 women), 13 part-time (9 women); includes 12 Hispanic/Latino, 4 international. Average age 27. 57 applicants, 82% accepted, 20 enrolled. In 2010, 20 master's awarded. *Degree requirements:* For master's, one foreign language, thesis or alternative, major project. *Entrance requirements:* For master's, GRE General Test, knowledge of Portuguese or Spanish. Additional exam requirements/recommendations for international students: Required—TOEFL. *Application deadline:* For fall admission, 1/4 priority date for domestic students. Application fee: $90. *Financial support:* Fellowships with tuition reimbursements, teaching assistantships with tuition reimbursements, Federal Work-Study, institutionally sponsored loans, scholarships/grants, health care benefits, and unspecified assistantships available. Financial award application deadline: 1/4; financial award applicants required to submit FAFSA. *Faculty research:* Latin American politics, Caribbean societies, Andean history, political economy of cultural policies. *Unit head:* Ada Ferrer, Director, 212-998-8686, Fax: 212-995-4163, E-mail: clacs.info@nyu.edu. *Application contact:* Jennifer Lewis, Assistant Director, 212-998-8686, Fax: 212-995-4163, E-mail: clacs.info@nyu.edu.

New York University, Graduate School of Arts and Science, Program in Museum Studies, New York, NY 10012-1019. Offers museum studies (MA, Advanced Certificate), including Africana studies (MA), Hebrew and Judaic studies (MA), Latin American and Caribbean studies (MA), Near Eastern studies (MA). Part-time and evening/weekend programs available. *Students:* 61 full-time (56 women), 16 part-time (13 women); includes 1 Black or African American, non-Hispanic/Latino; 1 American Indian or Alaska Native, non-Hispanic/Latino; 6 Asian, non-Hispanic/Latino; 5 Hispanic/Latino, 14 international. Average age 26. 200 applicants, 50% accepted, 38 enrolled. In 2010, 40 master's, 3 other advanced degrees awarded. *Entrance requirements:* For degree, master's degree or PhD. Additional exam requirements/

recommendations for international students: Required—TOEFL. *Application deadline:* For fall admission, 2/15 for domestic students; for spring admission, 11/1 for domestic students. Application fee: $90. *Financial support:* Application deadline: 2/15. *Faculty research:* Modern and contemporary art, history of museums and exhibitions, conservation of cultural materials, museum anthropology, ethnography. *Unit head:* Bruce Altshuler, Director, 212-998-8080, Fax: 212-995-4185, E-mail: museum.studies@nyu.edu. *Application contact:* Tatiana Kamorina, Department Administrator, 212-998-8080, Fax: 212-995-4185, E-mail: museum.studies@nyu.edu.

New York University, NYU in Madrid, Madrid, NY 10012-1019, Spain. Offers creative writing in Spanish (MFA); Spanish (PhD); Spanish and Latin American literatures and cultures (MA); Spanish language and translation (MA).

Ohio University, Graduate College, Center for International Studies, Program in Latin American Studies, Athens, OH 45701-2979. Offers MA. Part-time programs available. *Students:* 15 full-time (11 women), 1 (woman) part-time; includes 5 minority (2 Black or African American, non-Hispanic/Latino; 3 Hispanic/Latino), 4 international. Average age 25. 15 applicants, 93% accepted, 7 enrolled. In 2010, 9 master's awarded. *Degree requirements:* For master's, one foreign language, thesis optional. *Entrance requirements:* For master's, minimum GPA of 3.0. Additional exam requirements/recommendations for international students: Required—TOEFL (minimum score 550 paper-based; 213 computer-based; 80 iBT), IELTS (minimum score 6.5). *Application deadline:* For fall admission, 1/1 priority date for domestic and international students. Applications are processed on a rolling basis. Application fee: $50 ($55 for international students). Electronic applications accepted. *Financial support:* In 2010–11, 4 research assistantships with full tuition reimbursements (averaging $11,499 per year) were awarded; career-related internships or fieldwork, Federal Work-Study, institutionally sponsored loans, scholarships/grants, tuition waivers (partial), and unspecified assistantships also available. Financial award application deadline: 1/1. *Faculty research:* Central America, Ecuador, Brazil, transnational migration, microfinance. *Unit head:* Dr. Jose Delgado, Director, 740-593-2765, E-mail: delgadoj@ohio.edu. *Application contact:* Joan Kraynanski, Administrative Assistant, 740-593-1840, Fax: 740-593-1837, E-mail: kraynans@ohio.edu.

San Diego State University, Graduate and Research Affairs, College of Arts and Letters, Center for Latin American Studies, San Diego, CA 92182. Offers MA, MBA/MA. *Degree requirements:* For master's, 2 foreign languages, thesis or alternative. *Entrance requirements:* For master's, GRE General Test, 3 letters of reference. Additional exam requirements/recommendations for international students: Required—TOEFL. Electronic applications accepted. *Faculty research:* Latin American politics and economics.

Simon Fraser University, Graduate Studies, Faculty of Arts and Social Sciences, Latin American Studies Program, Burnaby, BC V5A 1S6, Canada. Offers MA. *Degree requirements:* For master's, thesis. *Entrance requirements:* For master's, minimum GPA of 3.0. Additional exam requirements/recommendations for international students: Required—TOEFL or IELTS. *Faculty research:* Sociology theory, social and cultural anthropology, political sociology, religion and society, Canadian native people.

Syracuse University, Maxwell School of Citizenship and Public Affairs, Program in Latin American Studies, Syracuse, NY 13244. Offers CAS. In 2010, 6 CASs awarded. *Entrance requirements:* For degree, degree program matriculation. Additional exam requirements/recommendations for international students: Required—TOEFL (minimum score 100 iBT). *Application deadline:* For fall admission, 2/1 priority date for domestic and international students. Application fee: $75. Electronic applications accepted. *Expenses:* Tuition: Part-time $1162 per credit. *Financial support:* Application deadline: 1/1. *Unit head:* Tom Perreault, Associate Professor, 315-443-9467, Fax: 315-443-3385, E-mail: taperrea@maxwell.syr.edu. *Application contact:* Tom Perreault, Associate Professor, 315-443-9467, Fax: 315-443-3385, E-mail: taperrea@maxwell.syr.edu.

Tulane University, School of Liberal Arts, Roger Thayer Stone Center for Latin American Studies, New Orleans, LA 70118-5669. Offers MA, PhD, MBA/MA, MCL/MA. Terminal master's awarded for partial completion of doctoral program. *Degree requirements:* For master's, one foreign language, thesis optional; for doctorate, 2 foreign languages, thesis/dissertation. *Entrance requirements:* For master's, GRE General Test, minimum B average in undergraduate course work; for doctorate, GRE General Test. Additional exam requirements/recommendations for international students: Required—TOEFL. Electronic applications accepted.

See Display on next page and Close-Up on page 653.

University at Albany, State University of New York, College of Arts and Sciences, Latin American, Caribbean, and US Latino Studies, Albany, NY 12222-0001. Offers MA, Certificate. Part-time programs available. *Degree requirements:* For master's, thesis. *Entrance requirements:* For master's, ability to read and write Spanish. Additional exam requirements/recommendations for international students: Required—TOEFL (minimum score 550 paper-based; 213 computer-based). Electronic applications accepted. *Faculty research:* Meso-American anthropology, Latin American women's studies, Latinos in the U.S.

University at Buffalo, the State University of New York, Graduate School, College of Arts and Sciences, Program in Caribbean Cultural Studies, Buffalo, NY 14260. Offers MAH. *Unit head:* Dr. Bruce D. McCombe, Dean, 716-645-2711, Fax: 716-645-3888, E-mail: cas-dean@buffalo.edu. *Application contact:* Joseph C. Syracuse, Graduate Enrollment Manager, 716-645-2711, Fax: 716-645-3888, E-mail: jcs32@buffalo.edu.

The University of Arizona, College of Social and Behavioral Sciences, Center for Latin American Studies, Tucson, AZ 85721. Offers MA. Part-time programs available. *Faculty:* 2 full-time (1 woman). *Students:* 17 full-time (7 women), 9 part-time (2 women); includes 7 Hispanic/Latino; 1 Two or more races, non-Hispanic/Latino. Average age 27. 69 applicants, 52% accepted, 15 enrolled. In 2010, 10 master's awarded. *Degree requirements:* For master's, 2 foreign languages, comprehensive exam, thesis optional. *Entrance requirements:* For master's, GRE, 2 letters of recommendation, resume. Additional exam requirements/recommendations for international students: Required—TOEFL (minimum score 550 paper-based; 213 computer-based; 79 iBT). *Application deadline:* For fall admission, 2/1 for domestic students, 12/1 for international students. Application fee: $65. Electronic applications accepted. *Expenses:* Tuition, state resident: full-time $7692. *Financial support:* In 2010–11, 4 research assistantships with full tuition reimbursements (averaging $18,237 per year), 5 teaching assistantships with full tuition reimbursements (averaging $17,542 per year) were awarded; career-related internships or fieldwork, Federal Work-Study, institutionally sponsored loans, scholarships/grants, health care benefits, tuition waivers (full and partial), and unspecified assistantships also available. *Faculty research:* Comparative analyses of national identities and of democratization across Latin America, environmental problems and management along the U. S.-Mexican border, integration efforts along the Peru/Ecuador border, social justice issues in Guatemala. Total annual research expenditures: $78,887. *Unit head:* Dr. Scott Whiteford, Director, 520-626-7207, Fax: 520-626-7248, E-mail: eljete@email.arizona.edu. *Application contact:* Brittany Kaza, Information Contact, 520-626-3317, Fax: 520-626-7248, E-mail: bkaza@email.arizona.edu.

University of California, Berkeley, Graduate Division, Group in International and Area Studies, Group in Latin American Studies, Berkeley, CA 94720-1500. Offers MA, MJ/MA. *Degree requirements:* For master's, 2 foreign languages. *Entrance requirements:* For master's, GRE General Test, minimum GPA of 3.0, reading knowledge of Spanish or Portuguese, 3 letters of recommendation. Additional exam requirements/recommendations for international students: Required—TOEFL. Electronic applications accepted. *Faculty research:* Rural development, border communities, political economy, geography, history.

University of California, Los Angeles, Graduate Division, International Institute, Interdepartmental Program in Latin American Studies, Los Angeles, CA 90095. Offers MA, M Ed/MA, MA/MA, MBA/MA, MLIS/MA, MPH/MA. *Students:* 20 full-time (16 women); includes 15 minority (1 Asian, non-Hispanic/Latino; 14 Hispanic/Latino). Average age 27. 27 applicants, 78% accepted,

7 enrolled. In 2010, 11 master's awarded. *Degree requirements:* For master's, 2 foreign languages, comprehensive exam or thesis. *Entrance requirements:* For master's, GRE General Test, minimum GPA of 3.0. *Application deadline:* For fall admission, 12/15 for domestic and international students. Application fee: $70 ($90 for international students). Electronic applications accepted. *Financial support:* In 2010–11, 12 fellowships with full and partial tuition reimbursements, 3 research assistantships with full and partial tuition reimbursements, 4 teaching assistantships with full and partial tuition reimbursements were awarded; Federal Work-Study, institutionally sponsored loans, scholarships/grants, health care benefits, tuition waivers (full and partial), and unspecified assistantships also available. Financial award application deadline: 3/1; financial award applicants required to submit FAFSA. *Unit head:* Dr. Kevin Terraciano, Chair, 310-825-8410. *Application contact:* Department Office, 310-825-8410, E-mail: idpgrads@international.ucla.edu.

University of California, San Diego, Office of Graduate Studies, Department of Political Science, Latin American Studies Program, La Jolla, CA 92093. Offers MA. *Entrance requirements:* For master's, GRE General Test, GRE Subject Test. Electronic applications accepted.

University of California, Santa Barbara, Graduate Division, College of Letters and Sciences, Division of Humanities and Fine Arts, Program in Latin American and Iberian Studies, Santa Barbara, CA 93106-4150. Offers MA. *Faculty:* 70 part-time/adjunct (33 women). *Students:* 8 full-time (4 women); includes 6 Hispanic/Latino. Average age 35. 15 applicants, 87% accepted, 4 enrolled. In 2010, 7 master's awarded. *Degree requirements:* For master's, one foreign language, comprehensive exam (for some programs), thesis. *Entrance requirements:* For master's, GRE. Additional exam requirements/recommendations for international students: Required—TOEFL (minimum score 550 paper-based; 80 iBT), IELTS (minimum score 7). *Application deadline:* For fall admission, 12/15 for domestic and international students. Application fee: $70 ($90 for international students). *Financial support:* In 2010–11, 7 students received support, including 5 fellowships with full and partial tuition reimbursements available (averaging $2,010 per year), 6 teaching assistantships with partial tuition reimbursements available (averaging $10,626 per year); Federal Work-Study, institutionally sponsored loans, scholarships/grants, health care benefits, and tuition waivers (full and partial) also available. Financial award application deadline: 12/15; financial award applicants required to submit FAFSA. *Faculty research:* Political science, anthropology, history, sociology, Portuguese. *Unit head:* Prof. Gabriela Soto Laveaga, Director, 805-893-4304, Fax: 805-893-8341, E-mail: gsotolaveaga@history.ucsb.edu. *Application contact:* Ashley Bradbury, Graduate Program Assistant, 805-893-2131, Fax: 805-893-8341, E-mail: ashley@hfa.ucsb.edu.

University of Central Florida, College of Sciences, Department of Sociology, Orlando, FL 32816. Offers applied sociology (MA); Maya studies (Certificate); sociology (PhD). Part-time and evening/weekend programs available. *Faculty:* 19 full-time (10 women), 7 part-time/adjunct (6 women). *Students:* 46 full-time (35 women), 19 part-time (13 women); includes 6 Black or African American, non-Hispanic/Latino; 1 Asian, non-Hispanic/Latino; 8 Hispanic/Latino; 1 Two or more races, non-Hispanic/Latino, 2 international. Average age 30. 46 applicants, 65% accepted, 20 enrolled. In 2010, 17 master's, 4 doctorates, 2 other advanced degrees awarded. *Degree requirements:* For master's, comprehensive written exam or thesis. *Entrance requirements:* For master's, GRE General Test, minimum GPA of 3.0 in last 60 hours of course work. Additional exam requirements/recommendations for international students: Required—TOEFL. *Application deadline:* For fall admission, 7/15 for domestic students; for spring admission, 12/1 for domestic students. Application fee: $30. Electronic applications accepted. *Expenses:* Tuition, state resident: part-time $256.56 per credit hour. Tuition, nonresident: part-time $1011.52 per credit hour. Part-time tuition and fees vary according to program. *Financial support:* In

2010–11, 36 students received support, including 13 fellowships with partial tuition reimbursements available (averaging $3,700 per year), 6 research assistantships with partial tuition reimbursements available (averaging $5,900 per year), 28 teaching assistantships with partial tuition reimbursements available (averaging $8,100 per year); career-related internships or fieldwork, Federal Work-Study, institutionally sponsored loans, tuition waivers (partial), and unspecified assistantships also available. Financial award application deadline: 3/1; financial award applicants required to submit FAFSA. *Faculty research:* Religious subcultures, attitudes toward abortion, population, sport research, stratification. *Unit head:* Dr. Jay Corzine, Chair, 407-823-2227, Fax: 407-823-5156, E-mail: hcorzine@mail.ucf.edu. *Application contact:* Dr. Jay Corzine, Chair, 407-823-2227, Fax: 407-823-5156, E-mail: hcorzine@mail.ucf.edu.

University of Chicago, Division of Social Sciences and Division of the Humanities, Latin American and Caribbean Studies Program, Chicago, IL 60637-1513. Offers AM, MBA/AM. *Degree requirements:* For master's, one foreign language, thesis. *Entrance requirements:* For master's, GRE General Test. Additional exam requirements/recommendations for international students: Required—TOEFL. Electronic applications accepted.

University of Connecticut, Graduate School, College of Liberal Arts and Sciences, Field of International Studies, Program in Latin American Studies, Storrs, CT 06269. Offers MA. *Degree requirements:* For master's, comprehensive exam. *Entrance requirements:* For master's, GRE General Test. Additional exam requirements/recommendations for international students: Required—TOEFL (minimum score 550 paper-based; 213 computer-based). Electronic applications accepted.

University of Florida, Graduate School, College of Liberal Arts and Sciences, Center for Latin American Studies, Gainesville, FL 32611. Offers MA, Certificate, JD/MA. Part-time programs available. *Faculty:* 4 full-time (2 women), 9 part-time/adjunct (5 women). *Students:* 35 full-time (20 women), 6 part-time (3 women); includes 1 Black or African American, non-Hispanic/Latino; 1 Asian, non-Hispanic/Latino; 7 Hispanic/Latino, 7 international. Average age 27. 71 applicants, 48% accepted, 18 enrolled. In 2010, 12 master's awarded. *Degree requirements:* For master's, thesis. *Entrance requirements:* For master's, GRE General Test, minimum GPA of 3.0. Additional exam requirements/recommendations for international students: Required—TOEFL (minimum score 550 paper-based; 213 computer-based; 80 iBT), IELTS (minimum score 6). *Application deadline:* For fall admission, 6/1 priority date for domestic students. Applications are processed on a rolling basis. Application fee: $30. Electronic applications accepted. *Expenses:* Tuition, state resident: full-time $10,915.92. Tuition, nonresident: full-time $28,309. *Financial support:* In 2010–11, 19 students received support, including 6 fellowships, 12 research assistantships (averaging $19,385 per year), 1 teaching assistantship (averaging $20,571 per year); career-related internships or fieldwork, Federal Work-Study, institutionally sponsored loans, and unspecified assistantships also available. Financial award application deadline: 3/1; financial award applicants required to submit FAFSA. *Faculty research:* Tropical conservation and development; ethnicity in the Americas, Brazil, and Cuba; North American Free Trade Agreement. *Unit head:* Dr. Philip Williams, Director, 352-273-4702, Fax: 352-392-7682, E-mail: pjw@latam.ufl.edu. *Application contact:* Dr. Richmond F. Brown, Associate Director, 352-273-4708, Fax: 352-392-7682, E-mail: rfbrown@ufl.edu.

University of Florida, Graduate School, College of Liberal Arts and Sciences, Department of History, Gainesville, FL 32611. Offers African history (MA, PhD); American history (MA, PhD); European history (MA, PhD); Latin American history (MA, PhD); JD/MA; JD/PhD. Part-time programs available. *Faculty:* 31 full-time (10 women), 5 part-time/adjunct (4 women). *Students:* 81 full-time (33 women), 17 part-time (8 women); includes 3 Black or African American, non-Hispanic/Latino; 2 American Indian or Alaska Native, non-Hispanic/Latino; 2 Asian, non-

Latin American Studies

University of Florida (continued)
Hispanic/Latino; 1 Hispanic/Latino, 12 international. Average age 30. 150 applicants, 29% accepted, 21 enrolled. In 2010, 19 master's, 8 doctorates awarded. Terminal master's awarded for partial completion of doctoral program. *Degree requirements:* For master's, variable foreign language requirement, thesis optional, 30 credit hours; for doctorate, variable foreign language requirement, comprehensive exam, thesis/dissertation, 90 credit hours. *Entrance requirements:* For master's and doctorate, GRE General Test, minimum GPA of 3.0. Additional exam requirements/recommendations for international students: Required—TOEFL (minimum score 550 paper-based; 213 computer-based; 80 iBT), IELTS (minimum score 6). *Application deadline:* For fall admission, 1/1 priority date for domestic students, 1/1 for international students. Applications are processed on a rolling basis. Application fee: $30. Electronic applications accepted. *Expenses:* Tuition, state resident: full-time $10,915.92. Tuition, nonresident: full-time $28,309. *Financial support:* In 2010–11, 70 students received support, including 30 fellowships, 13 research assistantships (averaging $16,665 per year), 27 teaching assistantships (averaging $16,733 per year); career-related internships or fieldwork and unspecified assistantships also available. Financial award application deadline: 1/15; financial award applicants required to submit FAFSA. *Faculty research:* Latin America and Caribbean history, nineteenth-century U. S. history, medieval Europe history, African history and Atlantic world history. *Unit head:* Dr. Ida L. Altman, Chair, 352-392-9634, E-mail: ialtman@ufl.edu. *Application contact:* Nina Caputo, Graduate Coordinator, 352-273-3379, Fax: 352-392-6927, E-mail: ncaputo@ufl.edu.

University of Illinois at Urbana–Champaign, Graduate College, College of Liberal Arts and Sciences, Center for Latin American and Caribbean Studies, Champaign, IL 61820. Offers Latin American studies (MA). *Students:* 4 full-time (2 women), 1 part-time (0 women); includes 2 minority (both Hispanic/Latino), 1 international. 13 applicants, 23% accepted, 2 enrolled. In 2010, 2 master's awarded. *Entrance requirements:* For master's, GRE, minimum GPA of 3.0; writing sample. Additional exam requirements/recommendations for international students: Required—TOEFL (minimum score 550 paper-based; 213 computer-based). *Application deadline:* Applications are processed on a rolling basis. Application fee: $75 ($90 for international students). Electronic applications accepted. *Financial support:* In 2010–11, 4 fellowships were awarded; research assistantships, teaching assistantships, tuition waivers (full and partial) also available. *Unit head:* Andrew Orta, Director, 217-244-7108, Fax: 217-244-7333, E-mail: njacobse@illinois.edu. *Application contact:* Angelina Cotler, Associate Director, 217-333-8419, Fax: 217-244-7333, E-mail: cotler@illinois.edu.

The University of Kansas, Graduate Studies, College of Liberal Arts and Sciences, Center of Latin American Studies, Lawrence, KS 66045. Offers Brazilian studies (Graduate Certificate); Central American and Mexican studies (Graduate Certificate); Latin American studies (MA). Part-time programs available. *Faculty:* 73 full-time (29 women), 22 part-time/adjunct (2 women). *Students:* 11 full-time (5 women), 3 part-time (2 women); includes 4 minority (3 Hispanic/Latino; 1 Two or more races, non-Hispanic/Latino), 2 international. Average age 28. 8 applicants, 88% accepted, 4 enrolled. In 2010, 4 master's awarded. *Degree requirements:* For master's, 2 foreign languages, comprehensive exam, thesis optional. *Entrance requirements:* For master's, GRE, minimum GPA of 3.0, references, writing sample. Additional exam requirements/recommendations for international students: Required—TOEFL. *Application deadline:* For fall admission, 2/1 priority date for domestic and international students; for spring admission, 11/15 priority date for domestic and international students. Applications are processed on a rolling basis. Application fee: $55 ($65 for international students). Electronic applications accepted. *Expenses:* Tuition, state resident: full-time $7092; part-time $295.50 per credit hour. Tuition, nonresident: full-time $16,590; part-time $691.25 per credit hour. Required fees: $858; $71.49 per credit hour. Tuition and fees vary according to course load, campus/location and program. *Financial support:* Fellowships with full tuition reimbursements, research assistantships with full and partial tuition reimbursements, teaching assistantships with full and partial tuition reimbursements, scholarships/grants and unspecified assistantships available. Financial award application deadline: 2/1. *Faculty research:* Indigenous peoples, ethnicity, literature, environment, gender. *Unit head:* Jill Kuhnheim, Director, 785-864-4213, Fax: 785-864-3800, E-mail: jskuhn@ku.edu. *Application contact:* Judy Farmer, Office Manager, 785-864-4213, Fax: 785-864-3800, E-mail: jfarmer@ku.edu.

The University of Manchester, School of Languages, Linguistics and Cultures, Manchester, United Kingdom. Offers Arab world studies (PhD); Chinese studies (M Phil, PhD); East Asian studies (M Phil, PhD); English language (PhD); French studies (M Phil, PhD); German studies (M Phil, PhD); interpreting studies (PhD); Italian studies (M Phil, PhD); Japanese studies (M Phil, PhD); Latin American cultural studies (M Phil, PhD); linguistics (M Phil, PhD); Middle Eastern studies (M Phil, PhD); Polish studies (M Phil, PhD); Portuguese studies (M Phil, PhD); Russian studies (M Phil, PhD); Spanish studies (M Phil, PhD); translation and intercultural studies (M Phil, PhD).

University of Massachusetts Dartmouth, Graduate School, College of Arts and Sciences, Department of Portuguese, North Dartmouth, MA 02747-2300. Offers Luso-Afro-Brazilian studies (PhD); Portuguese (MA). Part-time programs available. *Faculty:* 6 full-time (2 women), 1 part-time/adjunct (0 women). *Students:* 12 full-time (9 women), 13 part-time (7 women); includes 5 minority (1 Black or African American, non-Hispanic/Latino; 4 Hispanic/Latino), 5 international. Average age 35. 18 applicants, 83% accepted, 9 enrolled. In 2010, 5 master's awarded. *Degree requirements:* For master's, comprehensive exam (for some programs). *Entrance requirements:* For master's, GRE (recommended), 10 page writing sample; for doctorate, GRE. Additional exam requirements/recommendations for international students: Required—TOEFL (minimum score 500 paper-based). *Application deadline:* For fall admission, 4/20 priority date for domestic students, 2/20 priority date for international students; for spring admission, 11/15 priority date for domestic students, 9/15 priority date for international students. Applications are processed on a rolling basis. Application fee: $40 ($60 for international students). Electronic applications accepted. *Expenses:* Tuition, state resident: full-time $2071; part-time $86 per credit. Tuition, nonresident: full-time $8099; part-time $337 per credit. Required fees: $9446; $394 per credit. One-time fee: $75. Part-time tuition and fees vary according to class time, course load, degree level and reciprocity agreements. *Financial support:* In 2010–11, 2 research assistantships with full tuition reimbursements (averaging $18,558 per year), 8 teaching assistantships with full tuition reimbursements (averaging $15,000 per year) were awarded. Financial award application deadline: 3/1; financial award applicants required to submit FAFSA. *Faculty research:* Translation studies, ethnicity and migration, literature in Luso-Afro-Brazilian studies, anaphoric direct objects in Portuguese. *Unit head:* Victor J. Mendes, Director, Graduate Studies, 508-999-8338, Fax: 508-999-9272, E-mail: vmendes@umassd.edu. *Application contact:* Elan Turcotte-Shamski, Graduate Admissions Officer, 508-999-8604, Fax: 508-999-8183, E-mail: graduate@umassd.edu.

University of Miami, Graduate School, College of Arts and Sciences, Department of Latin American and Caribbean Studies, Coral Gables, FL 33124. Offers Latin American studies (MA). Part-time programs available. *Degree requirements:* For master's, comprehensive exam (for some programs), thesis, linguistic competency in Spanish or Portuguese, reading competency in a second Latin American language. *Entrance requirements:* For master's, GRE, 3 letters of recommendation. Additional exam requirements/recommendations for international students: Required—TOEFL. Electronic applications accepted. *Faculty research:* Literary, media, religious, visual and cultural studies; environment and tourism studies; US-Latin American Relations and drug trafficking; migration, globalization, and social movements; democratization, regime transitions, and citizenship.

University of New Mexico, Graduate School, College of Arts and Sciences, Latin American Studies Program, Albuquerque, NM 87131. Offers MA, PhD, JD/MA, MA/MA, MBA/MA, MCRP/MA, MSN/MA. Part-time programs available. *Students:* 26 full-time (14 women), 7 part-time (5 women); includes 1 American Indian or Alaska Native, non-Hispanic/Latino; 1 Asian, non-Hispanic/Latino; 10 Hispanic/Latino, 1 international. Average age 28. 54 applicants, 57% accepted, 13 enrolled. In 2010, 9 master's, 1 doctorate awarded. *Degree requirements:* For master's, one foreign language, comprehensive exam (for some programs), thesis (for some programs); for doctorate, 2 foreign languages, comprehensive exam, thesis/dissertation. *Entrance requirements:* For master's, GRE General Test, intermediate competence in Spanish, Portuguese or indigenous Latin American language; for doctorate, GRE General Test, master's degree in related field, one Latin American language. Additional exam requirements/recommendations for international students: Required—TOEFL. *Application deadline:* For fall admission, 2/1 priority date for domestic and international students; for spring admission, 11/1 for domestic and international students. Application fee: $50. Electronic applications accepted. *Expenses:* Tuition, state resident: full-time $5991; part-time $251 per credit hour. Tuition, nonresident: full-time $14,405; part-time $800.20 per credit hour. Tuition and fees vary according to course level, course load, program and reciprocity agreements. *Financial support:* In 2010–11, 30 students received support, including 6 fellowships with full tuition reimbursements available (averaging $4,423 per year), 2 research assistantships with full tuition reimbursements available (averaging $4,500 per year), 2 teaching assistantships with full tuition reimbursements available (averaging $14,410 per year); Federal Work-Study, scholarships/grants, health care benefits, tuition waivers (full), and unspecified assistantships also available. Financial award application deadline: 2/1; financial award applicants required to submit FAFSA. *Unit head:* Dr. Susan Tiano, Director, 505-277-2961, Fax: 505-277-5989, E-mail: stiano@unm.edu. *Application contact:* Kathryn McKnight, Associate Director for Academic Programs, 505-277-7042, Fax: 505-277-5989, E-mail: mcknight@unm.edu.

The University of North Carolina at Chapel Hill, Graduate School, College of Arts and Sciences, Department of Political Science, Chapel Hill, NC 27599. Offers Latin American studies (Certificate); political science (MA, PhD); trans-Atlantic studies (MA). *Degree requirements:* For master's, comprehensive exam; for doctorate, one foreign language, comprehensive exam, thesis/dissertation. *Entrance requirements:* For master's and doctorate, GRE General Test, minimum GPA of 3.0 recommended. Electronic applications accepted.

The University of North Carolina at Charlotte, Graduate School, College of Arts and Sciences, Program in Interdisciplinary Studies, Charlotte, NC 28223-0001. Offers gerontology (MA, Certificate); Latin American studies (MA); liberal studies (MA); women's studies (Certificate). *Faculty:* 2 full-time (1 woman), 2 part-time/adjunct (both women). *Students:* 15 full-time (14 women), 53 part-time (39 women); includes 20 minority (11 Black or African American, non-Hispanic/Latino; 8 Hispanic/Latino; 1 Two or more races, non-Hispanic/Latino), 5 international. Average age 30. 24 applicants, 96% accepted, 15 enrolled. In 2010, 16 master's awarded. *Degree requirements:* For master's, thesis optional, comprehensive exam or project. *Entrance requirements:* For master's, GRE General Test or MAT, minimum GPA of 3.0 during previous 2 years, 2.75 overall. Additional exam requirements/recommendations for international students: Required—TOEFL (minimum score 557 paper-based; 220 computer-based; 83 iBT). *Application deadline:* For fall admission, 7/1 for domestic students, 5/1 for international students; for spring admission, 11/1 for domestic students, 10/1 for international students. Applications are processed on a rolling basis. Application fee: $55. Electronic applications accepted. *Expenses:* Tuition, state resident: full-time $3464. Tuition, nonresident: full-time $14,297. Required fees: $2094. Tuition and fees vary according to course load. *Financial support:* In 2010–11, 7 students received support, including 2 research assistantships (averaging $3,025 per year), 5 teaching assistantships (averaging $7,950 per year); career-related internships or fieldwork, institutionally sponsored loans, scholarships/grants, and unspecified assistantships also available. Support available to part-time students. Financial award application deadline: 4/1; financial award applicants required to submit FAFSA. *Unit head:* Dr. Paula Eckard, Interim Director, 704-687-4309, Fax: 704-687-4347, E-mail: pgeckard@uncc.edu. *Application contact:* Kathy B. Giddings, Director of Graduate Admissions, 704-687-5503, Fax: 704-687-3279, E-mail: gradadm@uncc.edu.

University of Notre Dame, Graduate School, College of Arts and Letters, Division of Humanities, Department of Romance Languages and Literatures, Notre Dame, IN 46556. Offers French and Francophone studies (MA); Iberian and Latin American studies (MA); Italian studies (MA); Romance literatures (MA). *Degree requirements:* For master's, 2 foreign languages, comprehensive exam, thesis optional. *Entrance requirements:* For master's, GRE General Test, BA in target language. Additional exam requirements/recommendations for international students: Required—TOEFL (minimum score 600 paper-based; 250 computer-based; 80 iBT). Electronic applications accepted. *Faculty research:* Literature of discovery and exploration, modern literature, literary criticism, medieval literature, feminist critical theory.

University of Pittsburgh, University Center for International Studies, Pittsburgh, PA 15260. Offers African studies (Certificate); Asian studies (Certificate); European Union studies (Certificate); global studies (Certificate); Latin American studies (Certificate); Russian and East European studies (Certificate); West European studies (Certificate). *Students:* 322 full-time (192 women), 19 part-time (14 women); includes 22 minority (8 Black or African American, non-Hispanic/Latino; 3 Asian, non-Hispanic/Latino; 6 Hispanic/Latino; 5 Two or more races, non-Hispanic/Latino), 134 international. In 2010, 61 Certificates awarded. *Degree requirements:* For Certificate, one foreign language, study abroad. *Application deadline:* Applications are processed on a rolling basis. *Expenses:* Tuition, state resident: full-time $17,304; part-time $701 per credit. Tuition, nonresident: full-time $29,554; part-time $1210 per credit. Required fees: $740; $214 per term. Tuition and fees vary according to program. *Unit head:* Dr. Lawrence F. Feick, Director, University Center for International Studies, 412-648-7374, Fax: 412-624-4672, E-mail: feick@pitt.edu. *Application contact:* Information Contact, 412-624-4141, E-mail: graduate@pitt.edu.

University of Southern California, Graduate School, Dana and David Dornsife College of Letters, Arts and Sciences, Comparative Studies in Literature and Culture Doctoral Program, Los Angeles, CA 90089. Offers comparative literature (PhD); comparative media and culture (PhD); Spanish and Latin American studies (PhD). *Faculty:* 16 full-time (7 women). *Students:* 27 full-time (17 women), 1 part-time (0 women); includes 6 minority (2 Black or African American, non-Hispanic/Latino; 2 Asian, non-Hispanic/Latino; 2 Hispanic/Latino), 6 international. In 2010, 1 doctorate awarded. *Median time to degree:* Of those who began their doctoral program in fall 2002, 50% received their degree in 8 years or less. *Degree requirements:* For doctorate, 2 foreign languages, comprehensive exam, thesis/dissertation. *Entrance requirements:* For doctorate, GRE, competence in language other than English (highly recommended). Additional exam requirements/recommendations for international students: Required—TOEFL. *Application deadline:* For fall admission, 12/1 priority date for domestic and international students. Application fee: $85. Electronic applications accepted. *Expenses:* Tuition: Full-time $31,240; part-time $1420 per unit. Required fees: $600. One-time fee: $35 full-time. Full-time tuition and fees vary according to degree level and program. *Financial support:* In 2010–11, 25 students received support, including 8 fellowships with full tuition reimbursements available (averaging $51,000 per year), 17 teaching assistantships with full tuition reimbursements available (averaging $51,000 per year). Financial award applicants required to submit FAFSA. *Faculty research:* Literary theory, Japanese film and contemporary fiction, Francophone literature and cinema, Latin American and Caribbean literature, Spanish literature and film, nineteenth and twentieth century British and American literature. *Unit head:* Prof. Peggy Kamuf, Director of Comparative Studies in Literature and Culture Doctoral Program, 213-740-0101, Fax: 213-740-8058, E-mail: kamuf@usc.edu. *Application contact:* Katherine Guevarra, Administrative Assistant, 213-740-0102, Fax: 213-740-0858, E-mail: kguevarr@usc.edu.

University of South Florida, Graduate School, College of Arts and Sciences, Department of Government and International Affairs, Tampa, FL 33620-9951. Offers government (PhD); Latin American Caribbean and Latino Studies (MA); political science (MA); public administration (MPA). Part-time and evening/weekend programs available. *Faculty:* 5 full-time (1 woman), 1 part-time/adjunct (0 women). *Students:* 57 full-time (35 women), 84 part-time (42 women); includes 23 Black or African American, non-Hispanic/Latino; 1 American Indian or Alaska Native, non-Hispanic/Latino; 4 Asian, non-Hispanic/Latino; 18 Hispanic/Latino, 2 international. Average age 32. 151 applicants, 38% accepted, 41 enrolled. In 2010, 31 master's awarded. *Degree requirements:* For master's, comprehensive exam, thesis; for doctorate, comprehensive exam, thesis/dissertation. *Entrance requirements:* For master's, GRE (minimum score 470 verbal, 470 quantitative), minimum GPA of 3.0 in last 60 hours of course work. Additional exam requirements/recommendations for international students: Required—TOEFL (minimum score 550 paper-based; 213 computer-based). *Application deadline:* For fall admission, 2/15 for domestic students, 1/2 for international students; for spring admission, 10/15 for domestic students, 6/1 for international students. Applications are processed on a rolling basis. Application fee: $30. Electronic applications accepted. *Financial support:* In 2010–11, 12 teaching assistantships with tuition reimbursements (averaging $15,000 per year) were awarded; unspecified assistantships also available. Financial award application deadline: 4/1. *Unit head:* Dr. Mohsen Milani, Chairperson, 813-974-2384, Fax: 813-974-0832, E-mail: milani@chuma1.cas.usf.edu. *Application contact:* Dr. Stephen Tauber, Graduate Coordinator, 813-974-0781, Fax: 813-974-0832, E-mail: stauber@chuma1.cas.usf.edu.

The University of Texas at Austin, Graduate School, College of Liberal Arts, Teresa Lozano Long Institute of Latin American Studies, Austin, TX 78712-1111. Offers MA, PhD, JD/MA, MBA/MA, MP Aff/MA, MSCRP/MA. *Entrance requirements:* For master's and doctorate, GRE General Test.

The University of Texas at Dallas, School of Arts and Humanities, Program in Humanities, Richardson, TX 75080. Offers aesthetic studies (MA, MAT, PhD); history (MA); history of ideas (MA, MAT, PhD); humanities (MA, PhD); Latin American studies (MA); studies in literature (MA, MAT, PhD). *Faculty:* 44 full-time (14 women). *Students:* 161 full-time (95 women), 178 part-time (104 women); includes 71 minority (22 Black or African American, non-Hispanic/Latino; 4 American Indian or Alaska Native, non-Hispanic/Latino; 16 Asian, non-Hispanic/Latino; 24 Hispanic/Latino; 5 Two or more races, non-Hispanic/Latino), 22 international. Average age 38. 156 applicants, 70% accepted, 79 enrolled. In 2010, 46 master's, 20 doctorates awarded. *Degree requirements:* For master's, one foreign language, portfolio, thesis, or capstone project; for doctorate, one foreign language, thesis/dissertation. *Entrance requirements:* For master's, minimum GPA of 3.3 in upper-level coursework in field; for doctorate, doctoral field examinations, minimum GPA of 3.3 in upper-level coursework in field. Additional exam requirements/recommendations for international students: Required—TOEFL (minimum score 550 paper-based; 215 computer-based). *Application deadline:* For fall admission, 7/15 for domestic students, 5/1 priority date for international students; for spring admission, 11/15 for domestic students, 9/1 priority date for international students. Applications are processed on a rolling basis. Application fee: $50 ($100 for international students). Electronic applications accepted. *Expenses:* Tuition, state resident: full-time $10,248; part-time $569 per credit hour. Tuition, nonresident: full-time $18,544; part-time $1030 per credit hour. Tuition and fees vary according to course load. *Financial support:* In 2010–11, 151 students received support, including 5 research assistantships with partial tuition reimbursements available (averaging $10,905 per year), 82 teaching assistantships with partial tuition reimbursements available (averaging $10,156 per year); career-related internships or fieldwork, Federal Work-Study, institutionally sponsored loans, scholarships/grants, and unspecified assistantships also available. Support available to part-time students. Financial award application deadline: 4/30; financial award applicants required to submit FAFSA. *Faculty research:* Holocaust studies, U. S. /Mexico studies, translation studies, art history research, Chinese studies. *Unit head:* Dr. Michael Wilson, Associate Dean for Graduate Education, 972-883-2080, E-mail: mwilson@utdallas.edu. *Application contact:* Dr. Michael Wilson, Associate Dean of Graduate Studies, 972-883-2756, Fax: 972-883-2989, E-mail: mwilson@utdallas.edu.

The University of Texas at El Paso, Graduate School, College of Liberal Arts, Department of Sociology and Anthropology, El Paso, TX 79968-0001. Offers Latin American and border studies (MA, Certificate); sociology (MA). Part-time and evening/weekend programs available. *Students:* 17 (11 women); includes 3 Black or African American, non-Hispanic/Latino; 10 Hispanic/Latino, 1 international. Average age 34. In 2010, 2 master's awarded. *Degree requirements:* For master's, thesis optional. *Entrance requirements:* For master's, GRE General Test, minimum GPA of 3.0. Additional exam requirements/recommendations for international students: Required—TOEFL. *Application deadline:* For fall admission, 8/15 priority date for domestic students, 3/1 for international students; for spring admission, 12/15 priority date for domestic students, 9/1 for international students. Applications are processed on a rolling basis. Application fee: $15 ($65 for international students). Electronic applications accepted. *Financial support:* In 2010–11, research assistantships with partial tuition reimbursements (averaging $18,625 per year), teaching assistantships with partial tuition reimbursements (averaging $14,900 per year) were awarded; career-related internships or fieldwork, Federal Work-Study, institutionally sponsored loans, and scholarships/grants also available. Financial award application deadline: 3/15; financial award applicants required to submit FAFSA. *Unit head:*

Josiah Heyman, Chair, 915-747-5740, E-mail: jmheyman@utep.edu. *Application contact:* Dr. Charles H. Ambler, Dean of the Graduate School, 915-747-5491 Ext. 7886, Fax: 915-747-5788, E-mail: cambler@utep.edu.

University of Wisconsin–Madison, Graduate School, College of Letters and Science, Department of History, Madison, WI 53706-1380. Offers African history (MA, PhD); Central Asian history (MA, PhD); comparative world history (MA, PhD); East Asian history (MA, PhD); European history (MA, PhD); gender and women's history (MA, PhD); Latin American and Caribbean history (MA, PhD); Middle Eastern history (MA, PhD); South Asian history (MA, PhD); Southeast Asian history (MA, PhD); United States history (MA, PhD). Terminal master's awarded for partial completion of doctoral program. *Degree requirements:* For master's, thesis (for some programs); for doctorate, variable foreign language requirement, thesis/dissertation. *Entrance requirements:* For master's and doctorate, GRE General Test. Additional exam requirements/recommendations for international students: Required—Michigan English Language Assessment Battery or TOEFL. Electronic applications accepted. *Expenses:* Tuition, state resident: full-time $9887; part-time $617.96 per credit. Tuition, nonresident: full-time $24,054; part-time $1503.40 per credit. Required fees: $67.63 per credit. Tuition and fees vary according to reciprocity agreements. *Faculty research:* American, African, European, Asian, Latin American, and Middle Eastern history.

University of Wisconsin–Madison, Graduate School, College of Letters and Science, Latin American, Caribbean and Iberian Studies Program, Madison, WI 53706-1380. Offers MA, MA/JD. *Degree requirements:* For master's, 2 foreign languages, thesis. *Entrance requirements:* For master's, minimum GPA of 3.0. Electronic applications accepted. *Expenses:* Tuition, state resident: full-time $9887; part-time $617.96 per credit. Tuition, nonresident: full-time $24,054; part-time $1503.40 per credit. Required fees: $67.63 per credit. Tuition and fees vary according to reciprocity agreements. *Faculty research:* Development, gender, social movements, cultural studies, history.

Vanderbilt University, Graduate School, Program in Latin American Studies, Nashville, TN 37240-1001. Offers MA, LL M/MA, MBA/MA. *Students:* 11 full-time (4 women); includes 2 Hispanic/Latino. Average age 27. 20 applicants, 35% accepted, 6 enrolled. In 2010, 6 master's awarded. *Degree requirements:* For master's, 2 foreign languages, thesis or alternative. *Entrance requirements:* For master's, GRE General Test. Additional exam requirements/recommendations for international students: Required—TOEFL (minimum score 570 paper-based; 230 computer-based; 88 iBT). *Application deadline:* For fall admission, 1/15 for domestic and international students. Application fee: $0. Electronic applications accepted. *Financial support:* Teaching assistantships with full tuition reimbursements, Federal Work-Study, institutionally sponsored loans, and health care benefits available. Financial award application deadline: 1/15; financial award applicants required to submit CSS PROFILE or FAFSA. *Faculty research:* Latin American and Iberian studies, anthropology, history, Spanish and Portuguese, social and political science. *Unit head:* Edward Fischer, Director, 615-322-2527, Fax: 615-322-2305, E-mail: edward.f.fischer@vanderbilt.edu. *Application contact:* Frank Robinson, Director of Graduate and Undergraduate Studies, 615-322-2527, Fax: 615-322-2305, E-mail: william.f.robinson@vanderbilt.edu.

West Virginia University, Eberly College of Arts and Sciences, Department of History, Morgantown, WV 26506. Offers African history (MA, PhD); African-American history (MA, PhD); American history (MA, PhD); Appalachian/regional history (MA, PhD); East Asian history (MA, PhD); European history (MA, PhD); history of science and technology (MA, PhD); Latin American history (MA). Part-time programs available. *Degree requirements:* For master's, one foreign language, thesis (for some programs), oral exam, thesis defense; for doctorate, one foreign language, comprehensive exam, thesis/dissertation, dissertation defense. *Entrance requirements:* For master's, GRE General Test, minimum GPA of 3.0; for doctorate, GRE General Test. Additional exam requirements/recommendations for international students: Required—TOEFL (minimum score 550 paper-based), IELTS (minimum score 6.5). Electronic applications accepted. *Faculty research:* U.S., Appalachia, modern Europe, Africa, colonial and post-colonial societies.

Yale University, Graduate School of Arts and Sciences, Department of Spanish and Portuguese, New Haven, CT 06520. Offers Latin American literature (PhD); Luso-Brazilian and Spanish/Spanish American literatures (PhD); Spanish peninsular literature (PhD). Terminal master's awarded for partial completion of doctoral program. *Degree requirements:* For doctorate, 3 foreign languages, thesis/dissertation. *Entrance requirements:* For doctorate, GRE General Test.

Near and Middle Eastern Studies

The American University in Cairo, School of Global Affairs and Public Policy, Program in Middle East Studies, Cairo, Egypt. Offers MA, Diploma. MA offered jointly with University of South Carolina. *Degree requirements:* For master's, proficiency in French or German, proficiency in Arabic for international students. *Entrance requirements:* Additional exam requirements/recommendations for international students: Required—English entrance exam and/or TOEFL.

The American University in Cairo, School of Humanities and Social Sciences, Department of Arabic and Islamic Civilizations, Cairo, Egypt. Offers Arab language and literature (MA); Islamic art and architecture (MA); Islamic studies (Diploma); Middle East studies (MA, Diploma); Middle Eastern history (MA). Part-time programs available. *Degree requirements:* For master's, thesis optional, proficiency in French or German. *Entrance requirements:* Additional exam requirements/recommendations for international students: Required—English entrance exam and/or TOEFL. Electronic applications accepted. *Faculty research:* History of early Islam, Ayubbid, and Mamluk periods; nineteenth- and twentieth-century Middle East Islamic jurisprudence; contemporary Arabic literary criticism.

The American University in Cairo, School of Humanities and Social Sciences, Department of Sociology, Anthropology, Psychology, and Egyptology, Cairo, Egypt. Offers sociology and anthropology (MA). *Degree requirements:* For master's, one foreign language, thesis. *Entrance requirements:* Additional exam requirements/recommendations for international students: Required—English entrance exam and/or TOEFL. Electronic applications accepted. *Faculty research:* Development, gender, sociopolitical economic formulations, social science indigenization, Arab world.

American University of Beirut, Graduate Programs, Faculty of Arts and Sciences, Beirut, Lebanon. Offers anthropology (MA); Arabic language and literature (MA); archaeology (MA); biology (MS); chemistry (MS); computational science (MS); computer science (MS); economics (MA); education (MA); English language (MA); English literature (MA); environmental policy planning (MSES); financial economics (MAFE); geology (MS); history (MA); mathematics (MA, MS); Middle Eastern studies (MA); philosophy (MA); physics (MS); political studies (MA); psychology (MA); public administration (MA); sociology (MA); statistics (MA, MS). Part-time programs available. *Faculty:* 229 full-time (98 women), 136 part-time/adjunct (79 women). *Students:* 158 full-time (104 women), 263 part-time (171 women). Average age 25. 356 applicants, 59% accepted, 127 enrolled. In 2010, 57 master's awarded. *Degree requirements:* For master's, one foreign language, comprehensive exam, thesis (for some programs). *Entrance requirements:* For master's, GRE, letter of recommendation. Additional exam requirements/recommendations for international students: Required—TOEFL (minimum score 600 paper-based; 250 computer-based; 97 iBT), IELTS (minimum score 7). *Application deadline:* For fall

admission, 4/30 for domestic and international students; for spring admission, 11/1 for domestic and international students. Application fee: $50. *Expenses:* Tuition: Full-time $12,294; part-time $683 per credit. Required fees: $499; $499 per credit. Tuition and fees vary according to course load and program. *Financial support:* In 2010–11, 33 students received support. Career-related internships or fieldwork, institutionally sponsored loans, scholarships/grants, health care benefits, and unspecified assistantships available. Financial award application deadline: 2/4; financial award applicants required to submit FAFSA. *Faculty research:* Modern and contemporary world theatre; mineralogy, petrology, and geochemistry; cell differentiation and transformation; combinatorial technologies; philosophy of action; continental philosophy; Phoenician epigraphy; nascent complex societies and urbanism; the economies of the Arab world; environmental economics; tectonophysics; host-parasite interactions; innate immunity; insect-plant interactions; history of the Ottoman archives; decentralization; transparency and corruption. Total annual research expenditures: $622,243. *Unit head:* Dr. Patrick McGreevy, Dean, 961-137-4374 Ext. 3800, Fax: 961-174-4461, E-mail: pm07@aub.edu.lb. *Application contact:* Dr. Salim Kanaan, Director, Admissions Office, 961-135-0000 Ext. 2594, Fax: 961-175-0775, E-mail: sk00@aub.edu.lb.

The American University of Paris, Graduate Programs, Paris, France. Offers cross-cultural and sustainable business management (MA); cultural translation (MA); global communications (MA); global communications and civil society (MA); international affairs, conflict resolution and civil society development (MA); Middle East and Islamic studies (MA); Middle East and Islamic studies and international affairs (MA); public policy and international affairs (MA); public policy and international law (MA). *Faculty:* 14 full-time (3 women). *Students:* 151 full-time (110 women), 56 part-time (43 women). 271 applicants, 83% accepted, 104 enrolled. In 2010, 67 master's awarded. *Degree requirements:* For master's, thesis. *Entrance requirements:* For master's, minimum undergraduate GPA of 3.0. Additional exam requirements/recommendations for international students: Recommended—IELTS. *Application deadline:* For fall admission, 4/15 priority date for international students; for spring admission, 11/15 priority date for international students. Applications are processed on a rolling basis. Application fee: $75. Electronic applications accepted. *Financial support:* Scholarships/grants available. Financial award applicants required to submit FAFSA. *Unit head:* Dr. Celeste Schenck, President, 33-1 40 62 06 59, E-mail: president@aup.fr. *Application contact:* International Admissions Counselor, 33-1 40 62 07 20, Fax: 33-1 47 05 34 32, E-mail: admissions@aup.edu.

Brandeis University, Graduate School of Arts and Sciences, Department of Near Eastern and Judaic Studies, Waltham, MA 02454-9110. Offers Near Eastern and Judaic studies (MA, PhD); Near Eastern and Judaic studies and sociology (PhD); Near Eastern and Judaic studies and women's and gender studies (MA); teaching of Hebrew (MAT). Part-time programs available.

Near and Middle Eastern Studies

Brandeis University *(continued)*
Faculty: 23 full-time (11 women), 7 part-time/adjunct (3 women). *Students:* 64 full-time (29 women); includes 2 Hispanic/Latino, 6 international. 123 applicants, 50% accepted, 18 enrolled. In 2010, 10 master's, 2 doctorates awarded. Terminal master's awarded for partial completion of doctoral program. *Degree requirements:* For master's, one foreign language, comprehensive exam, thesis or alternative; for doctorate, 3 foreign languages, comprehensive exam, thesis/dissertation. *Entrance requirements:* For master's and doctorate, GRE General Test (recommended), letters of recommendation, transcripts, statement of purpose. Additional exam requirements/recommendations for international students: Required—TOEFL (minimum score 600 paper-based; 250 computer-based; 100 iBT); Recommended—IELTS (minimum score 7). *Application deadline:* For fall admission, 1/15 priority date for domestic and international students. Applications are processed on a rolling basis. Application fee: $75. Electronic applications accepted. *Financial support:* In 2010–11, 17 students received support, including 14 fellowships with full tuition reimbursements available (averaging $20,000 per year); research assistantships with full and partial tuition reimbursements available, teaching assistantships, scholarships/grants, health care benefits, and tuition waivers (full and partial) also available. Support available to part-time students. Financial award application deadline: 4/15; financial award applicants required to submit FAFSA. *Faculty research:* Ancient Near East and Bible, philosophy, history, modern Middle East, Islamic studies. *Unit head:* Dr. Sylvia Fishman, Chair, 781-736-2950, Fax: 781-736-2070, E-mail: fishman@brandeis.edu. *Application contact:* Joanne Arnish, Department Administrator, 781-736-2950, Fax: 781-736-2070, E-mail: arnish@brandeis.edu.

California State University, Long Beach, Graduate Studies, College of Liberal Arts, Department of History, Long Beach, CA 90840. Offers Africa and the Middle East (MA); ancient/medieval Europe (MA); Asia (MA); Latin America (MA); modern Europe (MA); United States (MA); world (MA). Part-time and evening/weekend programs available. *Faculty:* 12 full-time (7 women). *Students:* 18 full-time (6 women), 51 part-time (18 women); includes 3 Black or African American, non-Hispanic/Latino; 1 American Indian or Alaska Native, non-Hispanic/Latino; 3 Asian, non-Hispanic/Latino; 16 Hispanic/Latino, 1 international. Average age 30. 80 applicants, 53% accepted, 30 enrolled. In 2010, 11 master's awarded. *Degree requirements:* For master's, one foreign language, comprehensive exam or thesis. *Application deadline:* For fall admission, 3/1 for domestic students. Applications are processed on a rolling basis. Application fee: $55. Electronic applications accepted. *Financial support:* Research assistantships, Federal Work-Study, institutionally sponsored loans, and scholarships/grants available. Financial award application deadline: 3/2. *Faculty research:* All periods of European and American history, recent Asian and African history. *Unit head:* Dr. Nancy Quam-Wickham, Department Chair, 562-985-4431, Fax: 562-985-5431, E-mail: quamwick@csulb.edu. *Application contact:* Dr. Houri Berberian, Graduate Advisor, 562-985-4524, Fax: 562-985-4431, E-mail: hberber@csulb.edu.

The Catholic University of America, School of Arts and Sciences, Department of Semitic and Egyptian Languages and Literatures, Washington, DC 20064. Offers Ancient Near East (Biblical Hebrew/Aramaic) (MA, PhD); Arabic (PhD); Christian Near East (Biblical Hebrew/Aramaic) (MA); Coptic (MA, PhD); Syriac (MA). Part-time programs available. *Faculty:* 3 full-time (0 women), 3 part-time/adjunct (1 woman). *Students:* 13 full-time (3 women), 15 part-time (6 women); includes 2 Black or African American, non-Hispanic/Latino; 1 Asian, non-Hispanic/Latino, 3 international. Average age 36. 18 applicants, 78% accepted, 5 enrolled. In 2010, 4 master's, 2 doctorates awarded. *Degree requirements:* For master's, one foreign language, comprehensive exam; for doctorate, 2 foreign languages, comprehensive exam, thesis/dissertation. *Entrance requirements:* For master's and doctorate, GRE General Test, statement of purpose, official copies of academic transcripts, three letters of recommendation. Additional exam requirements/recommendations for international students: Required—TOEFL (minimum score 580 paper-based; 237 computer-based). *Application deadline:* For fall admission, 8/1 priority date for domestic students, 7/15 for international students; for spring admission, 12/1 priority date for domestic students, 10/15 for international students. Applications are processed on a rolling basis. Application fee: $55. Electronic applications accepted. *Expenses:* Tuition: Full-time $33,580; part-time $1315 per credit hour. Required fees: $80; $40 per semester hour. One-time fee: $425. *Financial support:* Fellowships, research assistantships, teaching assistantships, Federal Work-Study, scholarships/grants, tuition waivers (full and partial), and unspecified assistantships available. Financial award application deadline: 2/1; financial award applicants required to submit FAFSA. *Faculty research:* Christian history and literature of the Near East, Biblical Hebrew, Arabic Christianity, Coptic, Syriac. *Unit head:* Dr. Edward M. Cook, Chair, 202-319-5083, Fax: 202-319-4735, E-mail: cooke@cua.edu. *Application contact:* Andrew Woodall, Director of Graduate Admissions, 202-319-5057, Fax: 202-319-6533, E-mail: cua-admissions@cua.edu.

Columbia University, Graduate School of Arts and Sciences, Division of Humanities, Department of Middle East Languages and Cultures, New York, NY 10027. Offers Hebrew language and literature (M Phil, MA, PhD); Middle Eastern languages and cultures (M Phil, MA, PhD); South Asian languages and cultures (M Phil, MA, PhD). Part-time programs available. *Degree requirements:* For master's, thesis, oral and written exams; for doctorate, 3 foreign languages, thesis/dissertation. *Entrance requirements:* For master's and doctorate, GRE General Test. Additional exam requirements/recommendations for international students: Required—TOEFL. *Faculty research:* Indo-Iranian, Turkish, central Asian, and Armenian studies; Arabic and ancient Semitics.

Columbia University, Graduate School of Arts and Sciences, Program in Liberal Studies, New York, NY 10027. Offers American studies (MA); East Asian studies (MA); human rights studies (MA); Islamic culture studies (MA); Jewish studies (MA); medieval studies (MA); modern European studies (MA); South Asian studies (MA). Part-time and evening/weekend programs available. *Degree requirements:* For master's, thesis.

Columbia University, School of International and Public Affairs, Middle East Institute, New York, NY 10027. Offers Certificate. Students must also be enrolled in a separate graduate degree program at Columbia University. Electronic applications accepted.

Cornell University, Graduate School, Graduate Fields of Arts and Sciences, Field of Archaeology, Ithaca, NY 14853-0001. Offers environmental archaeology (MA); historical archaeology (MA); Latin American archaeology (MA); medieval archaeology (MA); Mediterranean and Near Eastern archaeology (MA); Stone Age archaeology (MA). *Faculty:* 18 full-time (5 women). *Students:* 8 full-time (7 women); includes 1 Hispanic/Latino. Average age 24. 23 applicants, 30% accepted, 3 enrolled. *Degree requirements:* For master's, one foreign language, thesis. *Entrance requirements:* For master's, GRE General Test, 3 letters of recommendation, sample of written work. Additional exam requirements/recommendations for international students: Required—TOEFL (minimum score 550 paper-based; 213 computer-based; 77 iBT). *Application deadline:* For fall admission, 1/15 for domestic students. Application fee: $80. Electronic applications accepted. *Expenses:* Tuition: Full-time $29,500. Required fees: $76. Tuition and fees vary according to degree level and program. *Financial support:* In 2010–11, 1 fellowship with full tuition reimbursement, 3 teaching assistantships with full tuition reimbursements were awarded; research assistantships with full tuition reimbursements, institutionally sponsored loans, scholarships/grants, health care benefits, tuition waivers (full and partial), and unspecified assistantships also available. Financial award applicants required to submit FAFSA. *Faculty research:* Anatolia, Lydia, Sardis, classical and Hellenistic Greece; science in archaeology; North American Indians; Stone Age Africa; Mayan trade. *Unit head:* Director of Graduate Studies, 607-255-6768, E-mail: blj7@cornell.edu. *Application contact:* Graduate Field Assistant, 607-255-6768, E-mail: dsd6@cornell.edu.

Cornell University, Graduate School, Graduate Fields of Arts and Sciences, Field of History, Ithaca, NY 14853-0001. Offers African history (MA, PhD); American history (MA, PhD); ancient history (MA, PhD); early modern European history (MA, PhD); English history (MA, PhD); French history (MA, PhD); German history (MA, PhD); history of science (MA, PhD); Latin American history (MA, PhD); medieval Chinese history (MA, PhD); medieval history (MA, PhD); modern Chinese history (MA, PhD); modern European history (MA, PhD); modern Japanese history (MA, PhD); premodern Islamic history (MA, PhD); premodern Japanese history (MA, PhD); Renaissance history (MA, PhD); Russian history (MA, PhD); Southeast Asian history (MA, PhD). *Faculty:* 53 full-time (15 women). *Students:* 59 full-time (30 women); includes 3 Black or African American, non-Hispanic/Latino; 2 Asian, non-Hispanic/Latino; 4 Hispanic/Latino, 22 international. Average age 30. 217 applicants, 6% accepted, 8 enrolled. In 2010, 9 master's, 5 doctorates awarded. Terminal master's awarded for partial completion of doctoral program. *Degree requirements:* For master's, thesis; for doctorate, 2 foreign languages, comprehensive exam, thesis/dissertation, 1 year of teaching experience. *Entrance requirements:* For master's and doctorate, GRE General Test, writing sample, 3 letters of recommendation. Additional exam requirements/recommendations for international students: Required—TOEFL (minimum score 550 paper-based; 213 computer-based; 77 iBT). *Application deadline:* For fall admission, 1/15 for domestic students. Application fee: $80. Electronic applications accepted. *Expenses:* Tuition: Full-time $29,500. Required fees: $76. Tuition and fees vary according to degree level and program. *Financial support:* In 2010–11, 26 fellowships with full tuition reimbursements, 27 teaching assistantships with full tuition reimbursements were awarded; research assistantships with full tuition reimbursements, institutionally sponsored loans, scholarships/grants, health care benefits, tuition waivers (full and partial), and unspecified assistantships also available. Financial award applicants required to submit FAFSA. *Unit head:* Director of Graduate Studies, 607-255-6738, Fax: 607-255-0469. *Application contact:* Graduate Field Assistant, 607-255-6738, Fax: 607-255-0469, E-mail: history_grad_info@cornell.edu.

Cornell University, Graduate School, Graduate Fields of Arts and Sciences, Field of Near Eastern Studies, Ithaca, NY 14853-0001. Offers ancient Near Eastern studies (MA, PhD); Arabic and Islamic studies (MA, PhD); biblical studies (MA, PhD); Hebrew and Judaic studies (MA, PhD). *Faculty:* 15 full-time (4 women). *Students:* 5 full-time (1 woman), 2 international. Average age 27. 46 applicants, 11% accepted, 1 enrolled. In 2010, 1 doctorate awarded. Terminal master's awarded for partial completion of doctoral program. *Degree requirements:* For master's, one foreign language, thesis; for doctorate, 2 foreign languages, comprehensive exam, thesis/dissertation. *Entrance requirements:* For master's and doctorate, GRE General Test, 2 years of 1 Near Eastern language, 3 letters of recommendation, writing sample. Additional exam requirements/recommendations for international students: Required—TOEFL (minimum score 550 paper-based; 213 computer-based; 77 iBT). *Application deadline:* For fall admission, 2/1 for domestic students. Application fee: $70. Electronic applications accepted. *Expenses:* Tuition: Full-time $29,500. Required fees: $76. Tuition and fees vary according to degree level and program. *Financial support:* In 2010–11, 5 students received support, including 1 fellowship with full tuition reimbursement available, 4 teaching assistantships with full tuition reimbursements available; research assistantships with full tuition reimbursements available, institutionally sponsored loans, scholarships/grants, health care benefits, tuition waivers (full and partial), and unspecified assistantships also available. Financial award applicants required to submit FAFSA. *Faculty research:* Ancient Near East (including archeology), Hebrew and Judaic studies (including Bible), early Christianity, Arabic and Islamic studies, modern Middle East. *Unit head:* Director of Graduate Studies, 607-255-1329, Fax: 607-255-6450. *Application contact:* Graduate Field Assistant, 607-255-1329, Fax: 607-255-6450, E-mail: neareastern@cornell.edu.

Emory University, Laney Graduate School, Department of Comparative Literature, Atlanta, GA 30322-1100. Offers comparative literature (PhD); English (Certificate); French (Certificate); Middle Eastern studies (PhD); philosophy (Certificate); psychoanalytic studies (PhD); religion (PhD); Spanish (Certificate); women studies (Certificate). *Degree requirements:* For doctorate, 2 foreign languages, comprehensive exam, thesis/dissertation. *Entrance requirements:* For doctorate, GRE General Test, minimum GPA of 3.0. Additional exam requirements/recommendations for international students: Required—TOEFL. Electronic applications accepted. *Expenses:* Tuition: Full-time $33,800. Required fees: $1300. *Faculty research:* Literary theory, psychoanalysis trauma and testimony, literature and religion, literature and technology, literature and philosophy, politics and global culture, literature and aesthetics.

Georgetown University, Graduate School of Arts and Sciences, The Center for Contemporary Arab Studies, Washington, DC 20057. Offers MA, Certificate, MA/JD, MA/PhD. *Degree requirements:* For master's, comprehensive exam, proficiency in Arabic. *Entrance requirements:* For master's, GRE, minimum GPA of 3.0. Additional exam requirements/recommendations for international students: Required—TOEFL. *Faculty research:* Contemporary Arab world.

Georgetown University, Graduate School of Arts and Sciences, Department of Arabic and Islamic Studies, Washington, DC 20057. Offers Arabic area studies (PhD); Islamic studies (MA, PhD); linguistics (MA, PhD). *Degree requirements:* For master's, comprehensive exam, research project; for doctorate, one foreign language, comprehensive exam, thesis/dissertation. *Entrance requirements:* Additional exam requirements/recommendations for international students: Required—TOEFL.

The George Washington University, Elliott School of International Affairs, Program in Middle East Studies, Washington, DC 20052. Offers MA. *Students:* 52 full-time (23 women), 14 part-time (7 women); includes 2 Black or African American, non-Hispanic/Latino; 4 Asian, non-Hispanic/Latino; 1 Two or more races, non-Hispanic/Latino, 2 international. Average age 25. 145 applicants, 44% accepted, 31 enrolled. In 2010, 19 master's awarded. *Application deadline:* For fall admission, 2/1 for domestic students; for spring admission, 10/1 for domestic students. Application fee: $75. *Financial support:* In 2010–11, 7 students received support. Tuition waivers available. Financial award application deadline: 1/15. *Unit head:* Nathan J. Brown, Director, 202-994-2123, Fax: 202-994-5477, E-mail: nbrown@gwu.edu. *Application contact:* Jeff V. Miles, Director of Graduate Admissions, 202-994-7050, Fax: 202-994-9537, E-mail: esiagrad@gwu.edu.

Harvard University, Graduate School of Arts and Sciences, Committee on Middle Eastern Studies, Cambridge, MA 02138. Offers anthropology and Middle Eastern studies (PhD); economics and Middle Eastern studies (PhD); fine arts and Middle Eastern studies (PhD); history and Middle Eastern studies (PhD); regional studies–Middle East (AM). Terminal master's awarded for partial completion of doctoral program. *Degree requirements:* For master's, one foreign language; for doctorate, 2 foreign languages, thesis/dissertation. *Entrance requirements:* For master's, GRE General Test; for doctorate, GRE General Test, 1 year of course work in Middle Eastern regional studies, proficiency in a related language. Additional exam requirements/recommendations for international students: Required—TOEFL. *Expenses:* Tuition: Full-time $34,976. Required fees: $1166. Full-time tuition and fees vary according to program.

Harvard University, Graduate School of Arts and Sciences, Department of Near Eastern Languages and Civilizations, Cambridge, MA 02138. Offers Akkadian and Sumerian (AM, PhD); Arabic (AM, PhD); Armenian (AM, PhD); biblical history (AM, PhD); Hebrew (AM, PhD); Indo-Muslim culture (AM, PhD); Iranian (AM, PhD); Jewish history and literature (AM, PhD); Persian (AM, PhD); Semitic philology (AM, PhD); Syro-Palestinian archaeology (AM, PhD); Turkish (AM, PhD). *Degree requirements:* For doctorate, variable foreign language requirement, thesis/dissertation, general exams. *Entrance requirements:* For master's, GRE General Test; for doctorate, GRE General Test, proficiency in a Near Eastern language. Additional exam requirements/recommendations for international students: Required—TOEFL. *Expenses:* Tuition: Full-time $34,976. Required fees: $1166. Full-time tuition and fees vary according to program.

The Johns Hopkins University, Zanvyl Krieger School of Arts and Sciences, Department of Near Eastern Studies, Baltimore, MD 21218-2699. Offers PhD. Part-time programs available. *Faculty:* 6 full-time (1 woman), 11 part-time/adjunct (7 women). *Students:* 23 full-time (13 women); includes 1 Black or African American, non-Hispanic/Latino; 1 Hispanic/Latino, 2 international. Average age 30. 64 applicants, 16% accepted, 7 enrolled. In 2010, 4 doctorates awarded. *Degree requirements:* For doctorate, 2 foreign languages, comprehensive exam, thesis/dissertation. *Entrance requirements:* Additional exam requirements/recommendations for international students: Required—TOEFL (minimum score 600 paper-based; 250 computer-based; 100 iBT); Recommended—IELTS. *Application deadline:* For fall admission, 1/15 for domestic and international students. Application fee: $75. Electronic applications accepted.

Financial support: In 2010–11, 18 students received support, including 16 fellowships with full tuition reimbursements available (averaging $17,900 per year), 2 teaching assistantships with full tuition reimbursements available (averaging $17,900 per year); career-related internships or fieldwork, Federal Work-Study, scholarships/grants, and health care benefits also available. Financial award application deadline: 4/15; financial award applicants required to submit FAFSA. *Faculty research:* Egyptology, Assyriology, religions of ancient Israel and Syria, ancient and Biblical law, demotic Egyptian. Total annual research expenditures: $64,479. *Unit head:* Dr. Theodore Lewis, Chair, 410-516-6791, Fax: 410-516-5218, E-mail: tjl@jhu.edu. *Application contact:* Glenda Hogan, Academic Program Coordinator, 410-516-7394, Fax: 410-516-5218, E-mail: ghogan@jhu.edu.

McGill University, Faculty of Graduate and Postdoctoral Studies, Faculty of Arts, Institute of Islamic Studies, Montréal, QC H3A 2T5, Canada. Offers MA, PhD, Diploma.

New York University, Graduate School of Arts and Science, Hagop Kevorkian Center for Near Eastern Studies, Department of Middle Eastern and Islamic Studies, New York, NY 10012-1019. Offers Middle Eastern and Islamic studies (MA, PhD); Middle Eastern and Islamic studies/history (PhD). Part-time programs available. *Faculty:* 17 full-time (6 women). *Students:* 35 full-time (17 women), 3 part-time (all women); includes 5 Asian, non-Hispanic/Latino, 11 international. Average age 31. 122 applicants, 7% accepted, 5 enrolled. In 2010, 1 master's, 3 doctorates awarded. Terminal master's awarded for partial completion of doctoral program. *Degree requirements:* For master's, 2 foreign languages, thesis; for doctorate, 4 foreign languages, comprehensive exam, thesis/dissertation. *Entrance requirements:* For master's and doctorate, GRE General Test. Additional exam requirements/recommendations for international students: Required—TOEFL. *Application deadline:* For fall admission, 12/15 for domestic students. Application fee: $90. *Financial support:* Fellowships with tuition reimbursements, teaching assistantships with tuition reimbursements, Federal Work-Study and institutionally sponsored loans available. Financial award application deadline: 12/15; financial award applicants required to submit FAFSA. *Faculty research:* Middle Eastern history, Arabic/Persian/Turkish language and literature, cultures and societies of Middle East, Islamic studies. *Unit head:* Marion Katz, Acting Chair, 212-998-8880, Fax: 212-995-4689, E-mail: mideast.studies@nyu.edu. *Application contact:* Marion Katz, Director of Graduate Studies, 212-998-8880, Fax: 212-995-4689, E-mail: mideast.studies@nyu.edu.

New York University, Graduate School of Arts and Science, Hagop Kevorkian Center for Near Eastern Studies, Program in Near Eastern Studies, New York, NY 10012-1019. Offers Near Eastern studies (MA); Near Eastern studies (museum studies) (MA); Near Eastern studies/journalism (MA). Part-time programs available. *Faculty:* 2 full-time (0 women). *Students:* 37 full-time (25 women), 5 part-time (1 woman); includes 2 Asian, non-Hispanic/Latino; 1 Hispanic/Latino, 10 international. Average age 26. 120 applicants, 52% accepted, 24 enrolled. In 2010, 14 master's awarded. *Degree requirements:* For master's, one foreign language, thesis. *Entrance requirements:* For master's, GRE General Test. Additional exam requirements/recommendations for international students: Required—TOEFL. *Application deadline:* For fall admission, 1/4 for domestic students. Application fee: $90. *Financial support:* Fellowships with tuition reimbursements, teaching assistantships with tuition reimbursements, Federal Work-Study and institutionally sponsored loans available. Financial award application deadline: 1/4; financial award applicants required to submit FAFSA. *Faculty research:* Politics, political economy, anthropology, history and culture of the Middle East. *Unit head:* Michael Gilsenan, Director, 212-998-8877, Fax: 212-995-4144, E-mail: kevorkian.center@nyu.edu. *Application contact:* Greta Scharnweber, Associate Director, 212-998-8877, Fax: 212-995-4144, E-mail: kevorkian.center@nyu.edu.

New York University, Graduate School of Arts and Science, Program in Museum Studies, New York, NY 10012-1019. Offers museum studies (MA, Advanced Certificate), including Africana studies (MA), Hebrew and Judaic studies (MA), Latin American and Caribbean studies (MA), Near Eastern studies (MA). Part-time and evening/weekend programs available. *Students:* 61 full-time (56 women), 16 part-time (13 women); includes 1 Black or African American, non-Hispanic/Latino; 1 American Indian or Alaska Native, non-Hispanic/Latino; 6 Asian, non-Hispanic/Latino; 5 Hispanic/Latino, 14 international. Average age 26. 200 applicants, 50% accepted, 38 enrolled. In 2010, 40 master's, 3 other advanced degrees awarded. *Entrance requirements:* For degree, master's degree or PhD. Additional exam requirements/recommendations for international students: Required—TOEFL. *Application deadline:* For fall admission, 2/15 for domestic students; for spring admission, 11/1 for domestic students. Application fee: $90. *Financial support:* Application deadline: 2/15. *Faculty research:* Modern and contemporary art, history of museums and exhibitions, conservation of cultural materials, museum anthropology, ethnography. *Unit head:* Bruce Altshuler, Director, 212-998-8080, Fax: 212-995-4185, E-mail: museum.studies@nyu.edu. *Application contact:* Tatiana Kamorina, Department Administrator, 212-998-8080, Fax: 212-995-4185, E-mail: museum.studies@nyu.edu.

Princeton University, Graduate School, Department of Near Eastern Studies, Princeton, NJ 08544-1019. Offers MA, PhD. *Degree requirements:* For master's, one foreign language, thesis; for doctorate, 2 foreign languages, thesis/dissertation. *Entrance requirements:* For master's and doctorate, GRE General Test. Additional exam requirements/recommendations for international students: Required—TOEFL. Electronic applications accepted.

Rice University, Graduate Programs, School of Humanities, Department of Religious Studies, Houston, TX 77251-1892. Offers African religions (PhD); African-American religions (PhD); contemplative studies (PhD); gnosticism, esotericism, mysticism (PhD); Islam (PhD); Jewish thought and philosophy (PhD); modern Christianity in thought and popular culture (PhD); psychology of religion (PhD); the Bible and beyond (PhD). *Degree requirements:* For doctorate, 2 foreign languages, comprehensive exam, thesis/dissertation. *Entrance requirements:* For doctorate, GRE, letters of recommendation, writing sample. Additional exam requirements/recommendations for international students: Required—TOEFL (minimum score 600 paper-based; 90 iBT). Electronic applications accepted. *Faculty research:* Origins and historical development of Islam, history of Christianity, the study of comparative religion, African-American religion, religion and culture.

Southern Evangelical Seminary, Graduate Programs, Matthews, NC 28105. Offers apologetics (MA, Certificate); Christian education (MA); church ministry (MA, Certificate); divinity (Certificate), including apologetics (M Div, Certificate); Islamic studies (MA, Certificate); Jewish studies (MA); philosophy (MA); religion (MA); theology (M Div), including apologetics (M Div, Certificate), Biblical studies; youth ministry (MA). Part-time and evening/weekend programs available. Postbaccalaureate distance learning degree programs offered. *Degree requirements:* For master's, thesis (for some programs); for doctorate, 2 foreign languages, comprehensive exam (for some programs), thesis/dissertation; for M Div, one foreign language. *Entrance requirements:* Additional exam requirements/recommendations for international students: Required—TOEFL (minimum score 600 paper-based; 250 computer-based). *Application deadline:* For fall admission, 8/15 priority date for domestic students, 8/5 priority date for international students; for winter admission, 12/15 priority date for domestic and international students; for spring admission, 1/15 priority date for domestic and international students. Applications are processed on a rolling basis. Application fee: $25. *Expenses:* Tuition: Full-time $9405; part-time $313.50 per credit hour. Required fees: $150; $50 per semester. *Financial support:* Scholarships/grants available. *Unit head:* Dr. Barry R. Leventhal, Dean, 704-847-5600 Ext. 204, Fax: 704-845-1747, E-mail: dean@ses.edu. *Application contact:* Duke Hale, Director of Recruitment, 704-847-5600 Ext. 216, Fax: 704-845-1747, E-mail: dhale@ses.edu.

Syracuse University, College of Arts and Sciences, Program in Middle Eastern Studies, Syracuse, NY 13244. Offers CAS. Part-time programs available. *Students:* 2 applicants, 100% accepted, 0 enrolled. In 2010, 2 CASs awarded. *Entrance requirements:* For degree, Syracuse graduate program matriculation. *Application deadline:* For fall admission, 2/1 priority date for domestic students, 1/1 priority date for international students. Application fee: $75. Electronic applications accepted. *Expenses:* Tuition: Part-time $1162 per credit. *Unit head:* Mehrzad Boroujerdi, Program Contact, 315-443-9082, E-mail: mborouje@maxwell.syr.edu. *Application contact:* Mehrzad Boroujerdi, Program Contact, 315-443-9082, E-mail: mborouje@maxwell.syr.edu.

The University of Arizona, College of Social and Behavioral Sciences, Department of Near Eastern Studies, Tucson, AZ 85721. Offers MA, PhD. Part-time and evening/weekend programs available. *Faculty:* 10 full-time (3 women). *Students:* 29 full-time (17 women), 19 part-time (8 women); includes 1 Asian, non-Hispanic/Latino; 1 Hispanic/Latino; 3 Two or more races, non-Hispanic/Latino, 13 international. Average age 32. 91 applicants, 49% accepted, 24 enrolled. In 2010, 14 master's awarded. Terminal master's awarded for partial completion of doctoral program. *Degree requirements:* For master's, one foreign language; for doctorate, 3 foreign languages, thesis/dissertation. *Entrance requirements:* For master's, GRE General Test, 3 letters of recommendation, statement of purpose, curriculum vitae, writing sample; for doctorate, GRE General Test, 3 letters of recommendation, curriculum vitae, writing sample. Additional exam requirements/recommendations for international students: Required—TOEFL (minimum score 550 paper-based; 213 computer-based; 79 iBT). *Application deadline:* For fall admission, 1/15 for domestic students, 12/1 for international students; for spring admission, 10/1 for domestic students, 6/1 for international students. Applications are processed on a rolling basis. Application fee: $65. Electronic applications accepted. *Expenses:* Tuition, state resident: full-time $7692. *Financial support:* In 2010–11, 3 research assistantships with full tuition reimbursements (averaging $16,964 per year), 29 teaching assistantships with full tuition reimbursements (averaging $19,282 per year) were awarded; Federal Work-Study, institutionally sponsored loans, health care benefits, tuition waivers (full), and unspecified assistantships also available. Support available to part-time students. Total annual research expenditures: $8,946. *Unit head:* Dr. Michael E. Bonine, Head, 520-626-9140, Fax: 520-621-2333, E-mail: bonine@u.arizona.edu. *Application contact:* Kathleen A. Landeen, Graduate Coordinator, 520-626-8731, Fax: 520-621-2333, E-mail: klandeen@email.arizona.edu.

University of California, Berkeley, Graduate Division, College of Letters and Science, Department of Near Eastern Studies, Group in Near Eastern Religions, Berkeley, CA 94720-1500. Offers PhD. Program offered jointly with Graduate Theological Union. *Degree requirements:* For doctorate, 2 foreign languages, thesis/dissertation, qualifying exam. *Entrance requirements:* For doctorate, GRE General Test, MA or equivalent in Near Eastern studies or related field; minimum GPA of 3.0, 3 letters of recommendation.

University of California, Berkeley, Graduate Division, College of Letters and Science, Department of Near Eastern Studies, Program in Near Eastern Studies, Berkeley, CA 94720-1500. Offers MA, PhD. *Degree requirements:* For doctorate, 2 foreign languages, thesis/dissertation, qualifying exam. *Entrance requirements:* For master's and doctorate, GRE General Test, minimum GPA of 3.0, 3 letters of recommendation.

University of California, Los Angeles, Graduate Division, College of Letters and Science, Department of Near Eastern Languages and Cultures, Los Angeles, CA 90034. Offers MA, PhD. *Faculty:* 18 full-time (5 women). *Students:* 41 full-time (21 women); includes 3 minority (1 Black or African American, non-Hispanic/Latino; 1 Hispanic/Latino; 1 Two or more races, non-Hispanic/Latino), 2 international. Average age 29. 58 applicants, 24% accepted, 4 enrolled. In 2010, 5 master's, 2 doctorates awarded. *Degree requirements:* For master's, one foreign language, comprehensive exam; for doctorate, 2 foreign languages, thesis/dissertation, oral and written qualifying exams. *Entrance requirements:* For master's and doctorate, GRE General Test, minimum GPA of 3.25, sample of written work (recommended). Additional exam requirements/recommendations for international students: Required—TOEFL. *Application deadline:* For fall admission, 12/1 for domestic and international students. Application fee: $70 ($90 for international students). Electronic applications accepted. *Financial support:* In 2010–11, 25 fellowships with full and partial tuition reimbursements, 18 research assistantships with full and partial tuition reimbursements, 27 teaching assistantships with full and partial tuition reimbursements were awarded; Federal Work-Study, institutionally sponsored loans, scholarships/grants, health care benefits, tuition waivers (full and partial), and unspecified assistantships also available. Financial award application deadline: 3/1; financial award applicants required to submit FAFSA. *Unit head:* Dr. William M. Schniedewind, Chair, 310-206-2405, E-mail: williams@humnet.ucla.edu. *Application contact:* Departmental Office, 310-825-4165, E-mail: nreast@humnet.ucla.edu.

University of California, Los Angeles, Graduate Division, College of Letters and Science, Interdepartmental Program in Indo-European Studies, Los Angeles, CA 90095. Offers PhD. *Students:* 15 full-time (6 women), 5 international. Average age 28. 9 applicants, 44% accepted, 3 enrolled. In 2010, 2 doctorates awarded. *Degree requirements:* For doctorate, 2 foreign languages, thesis/dissertation, oral and written qualifying exams. *Entrance requirements:* For doctorate, minimum undergraduate GPA of 3.0, writing sample, competency in Classical Latin. *Application deadline:* For fall admission, 1/15 for domestic and international students. Application fee: $70 ($90 for international students). Electronic applications accepted. *Financial support:* In 2010–11, 14 fellowships with full and partial tuition reimbursements, 8 research assistantships with full and partial tuition reimbursements, 4 teaching assistantships with full and partial tuition reimbursements were awarded; Federal Work-Study, institutionally sponsored loans, scholarships/grants, health care benefits, tuition waivers (full and partial), and unspecified assistantships also available. Financial award application deadline: 3/1; financial award applicants required to submit FAFSA. *Unit head:* Dr. Stephanie Jamison, Chair, 310-206-7736. *Application contact:* Department Office, 310-206-1590, E-mail: dabugheida@humnet.ucla.edu.

University of California, Los Angeles, Graduate Division, International Institute, Interdepartmental Program in Islamic Studies, Los Angeles, CA 90095. Offers MA, PhD, MPH/MA. *Students:* 12 full-time (3 women); includes 2 minority (1 Black or African American, non-Hispanic/Latino; 1 Hispanic/Latino), 3 international. Average age 38. In 2010, 10 master's awarded. *Degree requirements:* For master's, one foreign language, comprehensive exam; for doctorate, 2 foreign languages, thesis/dissertation, oral and written qualifying exams. *Entrance requirements:* For master's, GRE General Test, minimum GPA of 3.0; for doctorate, GRE General Test, minimum undergraduate GPA of 3.0, master's degree, advanced level proficiency in Arabic. *Application deadline:* For fall admission, 12/15 for domestic students. Application fee: $70 ($90 for international students). Electronic applications accepted. *Financial support:* In 2010–11, 11 fellowships with full and partial tuition reimbursements, 3 research assistantships with full and partial tuition reimbursements, 5 teaching assistantships with full and partial tuition reimbursements were awarded; Federal Work-Study, institutionally sponsored loans, scholarships/grants, health care benefits, tuition waivers (full and partial), and unspecified assistantships also available. Financial award application deadline: 3/1; financial award applicants required to submit FAFSA. *Unit head:* Dr. Khaled Abou El Fadl, Chair, 310-206-5401. *Application contact:* Department Office, 310-206-5401, E-mail: idpgrads@international.ucla.edu.

University of Chicago, Division of Social Sciences and Division of the Humanities, Middle Eastern Studies Program, Chicago, IL 60637-1513. Offers AM, MBA/AM, MPP/AM. *Degree requirements:* For master's, one foreign language, thesis. *Entrance requirements:* For master's, GRE General Test. Additional exam requirements/recommendations for international students: Required—TOEFL. Electronic applications accepted.

University of Chicago, Division of the Humanities, Department of Near Eastern Languages and Civilizations, Chicago, IL 60637-1513. Offers AM, PhD. Terminal master's awarded for partial completion of doctoral program. *Degree requirements:* For master's, one foreign language, comprehensive exam, thesis; for doctorate, 2 foreign languages, comprehensive exam, thesis/dissertation. *Entrance requirements:* For master's and doctorate, GRE General Test. Additional exam requirements/recommendations for international students: Required—TOEFL.

The University of Kansas, Graduate Studies, College of Liberal Arts and Sciences, Center for Russian, East European and Eurasian Studies, Lawrence, KS 66045. Offers MA. Part-time programs available. *Faculty:* 38 full-time (17 women), 4 part-time/adjunct (1 woman). *Students:* 14 full-time (4 women); includes 1 minority (Asian, non-Hispanic/Latino), 2 international. Average age 28. 20 applicants, 90% accepted, 6 enrolled. In 2010, 4 master's awarded.

Near and Middle Eastern Studies

The University of Kansas (continued)

Degree requirements: For master's, one foreign language, comprehensive exam, interdisciplinary capstone research seminar. *Entrance requirements:* For master's, GRE General Test, 3 letters of recommendation. Additional exam requirements/recommendations for international students: Required—TOEFL. *Application deadline:* For fall admission, 1/1 priority date for domestic and international students. Application fee: $55 ($65 for international students). Electronic applications accepted. *Expenses:* Tuition, state resident: full-time $7092; part-time $295.50 per credit hour. Tuition, nonresident: full-time $16,590; part-time $691.25 per credit hour. Required fees: $858; $71.49 per credit hour. Tuition and fees vary according to course load, campus/location and program. *Financial support:* Fellowships with full tuition reimbursements, research assistantships with partial tuition reimbursements, scholarships/grants available. Financial award application deadline: 1/31; financial award applicants required to submit FAFSA. *Faculty research:* Russian and East Central European history and culture; Ukrainian, Russian, and Central Asian domestic politics and international security; Slavic languages, linguistics, and literatures. *Unit head:* Dr. Edith Clowes, Director, 785-864-4236, Fax: 785-864-3800, E-mail: crees@ku.edu. *Application contact:* Dr. Mariya Y. Omelicheva, Associate Director, 785-864-9002, Fax: 785-864-3800, E-mail: omeliche@ku.edu.

The University of Manchester, Faculty of Life Sciences, Manchester, United Kingdom. Offers adaptive organismal biology (M Phil, PhD); animal biology (M Phil, PhD); biochemistry (M Phil, PhD); bioinformatics (M Phil, PhD); biomolecular sciences (M Phil, PhD); biotechnology (M Phil, PhD); cell biology (M Phil, PhD); cell matrix research (M Phil, PhD); channels and transporters (M Phil, PhD); developmental biology (M Phil, PhD); Egyptology (M Phil, PhD); environmental biology (M Phil, PhD); evolutionary biology (M Phil, PhD); gene expression (M Phil, PhD); genetics (M Phil, PhD); history of science, technology and medicine (M Phil, PhD); immunology (M Phil, PhD); integrative neurobiology and behavior (M Phil, PhD); membrane trafficking (M Phil, PhD); microbiology (M Phil, PhD); molecular and cellular neuroscience (M Phil, PhD); molecular biology (M Phil, PhD); molecular cancer studies (M Phil, PhD); neuroscience (M Phil, PhD); ophthalmology (M Phil, PhD); optometry (M Phil, PhD); organelle function (M Phil, PhD); pharmacology (M Phil, PhD); physiology (M Phil, PhD); plant sciences (M Phil, PhD); stem cell research (M Phil, PhD); structural biology (M Phil, PhD); systems neuroscience (M Phil, PhD); toxicology (M Phil, PhD).

The University of Manchester, School of Languages, Linguistics and Cultures, Manchester, United Kingdom. Offers Arab world studies (PhD); Chinese studies (M Phil, PhD); East Asian studies (M Phil, PhD); English language (PhD); French studies (M Phil, PhD); German studies (M Phil, PhD); interpreting studies (PhD); Italian studies (M Phil, PhD); Japanese studies (M Phil, PhD); Latin American cultural studies (M Phil, PhD); linguistics (M Phil, PhD); Middle Eastern studies (M Phil, PhD); Polish studies (M Phil, PhD); Portuguese studies (M Phil, PhD); Russian studies (M Phil, PhD); Spanish studies (M Phil, PhD); translation and intercultural studies (M Phil, PhD).

University of Memphis, Graduate School, College of Arts and Sciences, Department of History, Memphis, TN 38152. Offers ancient Egyptian history (MA, PhD). Postbaccalaureate distance learning degree programs offered (no on-campus study). *Faculty:* 22 full-time (6 women), 3 part-time/adjunct (0 women). *Students:* 53 full-time (31 women), 59 part-time (30 women); includes 17 Black or African American, non-Hispanic/Latino; 4 Two or more races, non-Hispanic/Latino, 2 international. Average age 36. 50 applicants, 90% accepted, 15 enrolled. In 2010, 10 master's, 7 doctorates awarded. *Degree requirements:* For master's, comprehensive exam, thesis optional; for doctorate, one foreign language, comprehensive exam, thesis/dissertation, 60 credits plus 12 dissertation credits, 2 research seminars. *Entrance requirements:* For master's, GRE General Test or MAT, 18 undergraduate hours of course work in history with minimum GPA of 3.0, 2 letters of recommendation, writing sample; for doctorate, GRE General Test, GRE Subject Test, MA in history or related field, three letters of recommendation, writing sample, statement of purpose. Additional exam requirements/recommendations for international students: Required—TOEFL. *Application deadline:* For fall admission, 1/15 for domestic students; for spring admission, 9/15 for domestic students. Applications are processed on a rolling basis. Application fee: $35 ($60 for international students). Electronic applications accepted. *Financial support:* In 2010–11, 54 students received support; research assistantships with full tuition reimbursements available, teaching assistantships with full tuition reimbursements available, career-related internships or fieldwork, Federal Work-Study, scholarships/grants, and unspecified assistantships available. Financial award application deadline: 2/15; financial award applicants required to submit FAFSA. *Faculty research:* African/African-American history; U. S. history; ancient Egyptian history; modern European history; women, gender, and family studies. *Unit head:* Dr. Janann Sherman, Chairman, 901-678-2515, Fax: 901-678-2720, E-mail: sherman@memphis.edu. *Application contact:* Dr. James M. Blythe, Coordinator of Graduate Studies, 901-678-3381, Fax: 901-678-2720, E-mail: jmblythe@memphis.edu.

University of Michigan, Horace H. Rackham School of Graduate Studies, College of Literature, Science, and the Arts, Department of Near Eastern Studies, Ann Arbor, MI 48109. Offers ancient Near Eastern studies (AM, PhD); Arabic for professional purposes (AM); Arabic language and literature (AM, PhD); Armenian studies (AM, PhD); Christianity in late antiquity (AM, PhD); Egyptology (AM, PhD); Hebrew Bible and ancient Israel (AM, PhD); Hebrew literature (AM, PhD); Islamic studies (AM, PhD); Jewish cultural studies (AM, PhD); Jewish mysticism (AM, PhD); Persian and Iranian studies (AM, PhD); Rabbinic literature (AM, PhD); Second Temple Judaism (AM, PhD); teaching of Arabic as a foreign language (AM); Turkish studies (AM, PhD). Part-time programs available. Terminal master's awarded for partial completion of doctoral program. *Degree requirements:* For master's, 2 foreign languages; for doctorate, 4 foreign languages, comprehensive exam, thesis/dissertation. *Entrance requirements:* For master's, GRE General Test; for doctorate, GRE General Test, master's degree. Additional exam requirements/recommendations for international students: Required—TOEFL (minimum score 560 paper-based; 220 computer-based; 84 iBT). Electronic applications accepted. *Expenses:* Tuition, state resident: full-time $17,784; part-time $1116 per credit hour. Tuition, nonresident: full-time $35,944; part-time $2125 per credit hour. International tuition: $35,994 full-time. Required fees: $95 per semester. Tuition and fees vary according to course load, degree level and program. *Faculty research:* Middle and Near Eastern literatures, languages, cultures from ancient times to the present.

University of Michigan, Horace H. Rackham School of Graduate Studies, Interdepartmental Program in Modern Middle Eastern and North African Studies, Ann Arbor, MI 48109. Offers AM, JD/AM, MBA/AM. *Degree requirements:* For master's, one foreign language, thesis or alternative. *Entrance requirements:* For master's, GRE General Test. Additional exam requirements/recommendations for international students: Required—TOEFL (minimum score 560 paper-based; 84 iBT). Electronic applications accepted. *Expenses:* Tuition, state resident: full-time $17,784; part-time $1116 per credit hour. Tuition, nonresident: full-time $35,944; part-time $2125 per credit hour. International tuition: $35,994 full-time. Required fees: $95 per semester. Tuition and fees vary according to course load, degree level and program. *Faculty research:* Middle east and north Africa.

University of Pennsylvania, School of Arts and Sciences, Graduate Group in Near Eastern Languages and Civilization, Philadelphia, PA 19104. Offers AM, PhD. *Faculty:* 19 full-time (6 women), 2 part-time/adjunct (0 women). *Students:* 30 full-time (13 women), 12 part-time (8 women); includes 1 Asian, non-Hispanic/Latino, 7 international. 85 applicants, 11% accepted, 6 enrolled. In 2010, 4 master's, 3 doctorates awarded. Application fee: $70. *Expenses:* Tuition: Full-time $25,660; part-time $4758 per course. Required fees: $2152; $270 per course. Tuition and fees vary according to course load, degree level and program. *Financial support:* Institutionally sponsored loans, scholarships/grants, traineeships, health care benefits, and unspecified assistantships available. *Unit head:* Roger Allen, Department Chair, Near Eastern Languages and Civilizations, 215-898-6337, E-mail: rallen@sas.upenn.edu. *Application contact:* Roger Allen, Department Chair, Near Eastern Languages and Civilizations, 215-898-6337, E-mail: rallen@sas.upenn.edu.

University of South Africa, College of Human Sciences, Pretoria, South Africa. Offers adult education (M Ed); African languages (MA, PhD); African politics (MA, PhD); Afrikaans (MA, PhD); ancient history (MA, PhD); ancient Near Eastern studies (MA, PhD); anthropology (MA, PhD); applied linguistics (MA); Arabic (MA, PhD); archaeology (MA); art history (MA); Biblical archaeology (MA); Biblical studies (M Th, D Th, PhD); Christian spirituality (M Th, D Th); church history (M Th, D Th); classical studies (MA, PhD); clinical psychology (MA); communication (MA, PhD); comparative education (M Ed, Ed D); consulting psychology (D Admin, D Com, PhD); curriculum studies (M Ed, Ed D); development studies (M Admin, MA, D Admin, PhD); didactics (M Ed, Ed D); education (M Tech); education management (M Ed, Ed D); educational psychology (M Ed); English (MA); environmental education (M Ed); French (MA, PhD); German (MA, PhD); Greek (MA); guidance and counseling (M Ed); health studies (MA, PhD), including health sciences education (MA), health services management (MA), medical and surgical nursing science (critical care general) (MA), midwifery and neonatal nursing science (MA), trauma and emergency care (MA); history (MA, PhD); history of education (Ed D); inclusive education (M Ed, Ed D); information and communications technology policy and regulation (MA); information science (MA, MIS, PhD); international politics (MA, PhD); Islamic studies (MA, PhD); Italian (MA, PhD); Judaica (MA, PhD); linguistics (MA, PhD); mathematical education (M Ed); mathematics education (MA); missiology (M Th, D Th); modern Hebrew (MA, PhD); musicology (MA, MMus, D Mus, PhD); natural science education (M Ed); New Testament (M Th, D Th); Old Testament (D Th); pastoral therapy (M Th, D Th); philosophy (MA); philosophy of education (M Ed, Ed D); politics (MA, PhD); Portuguese (MA, PhD); practical theology (M Th, D Th); psychology (MA, MS, PhD); psychology of education (M Ed, Ed D); public health (MA); religious studies (MA, D Th, PhD); Romance languages (MA); Russian (MA, PhD); Semitic languages (MA, PhD); social behavior studies in HIV/AIDS (MA); social science (mental health) (MA); social science in development studies (MA); social science in psychology (MA); social science in social work (MA); social science in sociology (MA); social work (MSW, DSW, PhD); socio-education (M Ed, Ed D); sociolinguistics (MA); sociology (MA, PhD); Spanish (MA, PhD); systematic theology (M Th, D Th); TESOL (teaching English to speakers of other languages) (MA); theological ethics (M Th, D Th); theory of literature (MA, PhD); urban ministries (D Th); urban ministry (M Th).

The University of Texas at Austin, Graduate School, College of Liberal Arts, Center for Middle Eastern Studies, Austin, TX 78712-1111. Offers MA, JD/MA, MBA/MA, MLIS/MA, MP Aff/MA. *Degree requirements:* For master's, one foreign language, thesis optional. *Entrance requirements:* For master's, GRE General Test. Electronic applications accepted.

The University of Texas at Austin, Graduate School, College of Liberal Arts, Department of Middle Eastern Studies, Austin, TX 78712-1111. Offers Arabic (MA, PhD); Hebrew (MA). *Degree requirements:* For master's, one foreign language, comprehensive exam, thesis; for doctorate, 2 foreign languages, comprehensive exam, thesis/dissertation. *Entrance requirements:* For master's and doctorate, GRE General Test. Additional exam requirements/recommendations for international students: Required—TOEFL. Electronic applications accepted. *Faculty research:* Islamic studies, Persian language and literature, Hebrew language, Jewish studies, Arabic literature and language.

University of Toronto, School of Graduate Studies, Humanities Division, Department of Near and Middle Eastern Civilizations, Toronto, ON M5S 1A1, Canada. Offers MA, PhD. Part-time programs available. *Degree requirements:* For master's, thesis optional; for doctorate, 2 foreign languages, thesis/dissertation, language proficiency exams. *Entrance requirements:* For master's, BA in relevant area, minimum B+ average in final year, prior coursework in ancient Near Eastern or Islamic civilizations, 2 letters of reference; for doctorate, MA in relevant area with a minimum A– average, 2 letters of reference. Additional exam requirements/recommendations for international students: Required—TOEFL (minimum score 580 paper-based; 237 computer-based), TWE (minimum score 5).

University of Utah, Graduate School, College of Humanities, Program in Middle East Studies, Salt Lake City, UT 84112. Offers anthropology (MA); Arabic (MA, PhD); Arabic and linguistics (MA, PhD); Hebrew (MA); history (MA, PhD); Persian (MA, PhD); political science (MA, PhD); Turkish (MA). *Students:* 20 full-time (10 women), 15 part-time (5 women), 8 international. Average age 33. 28 applicants, 29% accepted, 3 enrolled. In 2010, 3 master's awarded. Terminal master's awarded for partial completion of doctoral program. *Degree requirements:* For master's, 2 foreign languages, comprehensive exam, thesis optional; for doctorate, 3 foreign languages, comprehensive exam, thesis/dissertation. *Entrance requirements:* For master's, GRE General Test, minimum GPA of 3.2; for doctorate, GRE General Test, MA in Middle East studies or equivalent, minimum GPA of 3.2. Additional exam requirements/recommendations for international students: Required—TOEFL (minimum score 580 paper-based; 237 computer-based; 92 iBT). *Application deadline:* For fall admission, 1/15 priority date for domestic and international students. Application fee: $55 ($65 for international students). Electronic applications accepted. *Expenses:* Tuition, area resident: Part-time $179.19 per credit hour. Tuition, state resident: full-time $4384. Tuition, nonresident: full-time $16,684; part-time $630.67 per credit hour. Required fees: $350 per semester. Tuition and fees vary according to course load, degree level and program. *Financial support:* In 2010–11, 17 students received support, including 11 fellowships with full tuition reimbursements available (averaging $14,000 per year), 6 teaching assistantships with full tuition reimbursements available (averaging $12,000 per year); unspecified assistantships also available. Financial award application deadline: 1/15. *Faculty research:* Arabic linguistics; Islamic studies; Middle Eastern history; political science; Judaic studies; anthropology; Arabic, Persian, Hebrew, and Turkish language and literature. *Application contact:* Peter von Sivers, Director of Graduate Studies, 801-581-8073, Fax: 801-581-6183, E-mail: peter.vonsivers@utah.edu.

University of Virginia, College and Graduate School of Arts and Sciences, Department of Middle Eastern and South Asian Languages and Cultures, Charlottesville, VA 22903. Offers Middle Eastern and South Asian studies (MA). *Faculty:* 16 full-time (8 women). *Students:* 15 full-time (10 women); includes 1 Asian, non-Hispanic/Latino; 1 Hispanic/Latino; 1 Two or more races, non-Hispanic/Latino. Average age 26. 17 applicants, 76% accepted, 13 enrolled. *Unit head:* Daniel Lefkowitz, Chair, 434-924-3452, Fax: 434-924-6977, E-mail: dl2h@virginia.edu. *Application contact:* Daniel Lefkowitz, Chair, 434-924-3452, Fax: 434-924-6977, E-mail: dl2h@virginia.edu.

University of Washington, Graduate School, College of Arts and Sciences, Department of Near Eastern Languages and Civilization, Seattle, WA 98195. Offers MA. *Degree requirements:* For master's, 2 foreign languages, exams. *Entrance requirements:* For master's, GRE, minimum GPA of 3.0. Additional exam requirements/recommendations for international students: Required—TOEFL. Electronic applications accepted. *Faculty research:* Arabic, Hebrew, Persian, and Turkish literature; Islamic civilization and religion; Central Asian Turkic language and literature; Hebrew Bible and ancient Near East; ancient Christianity.

University of Washington, Graduate School, College of Arts and Sciences, Henry M. Jackson School of International Studies, Middle East Studies Program, Seattle, WA 98195. Offers MAIS. *Faculty:* 36 full-time (12 women). *Students:* 21 full-time (9 women); includes 1 Asian, non-Hispanic/Latino, 4 international. 49 applicants, 43% accepted, 10 enrolled. In 2010, 3 master's awarded. *Degree requirements:* For master's, one foreign language, thesis optional. *Entrance requirements:* For master's, GRE General Test, minimum GPA of 3.00 (last two years). Additional exam requirements/recommendations for international students: Required—TOEFL (minimum score 500 paper-based; 213 computer-based; 92 iBT) or IELTS (minimum score 7). *Application deadline:* For fall admission, 1/5 for domestic and international students. Application fee: $75. Electronic applications accepted. *Financial support:* In 2010–11, 3 fellowships with full tuition reimbursements were awarded; research assistantships, teaching assistantships, career-related internships or fieldwork, Federal Work-Study, institutionally sponsored loans, scholarships/grants, and summer language study awards also available. Financial award application deadline: 1/5; financial award applicants required to submit FAFSA. *Unit head:* Prof. Philip D. Schuyler, Chair, 206-543-9878. *Application contact:* 206-543-6001, Fax: 206-616-3170, E-mail: jsisinfo@u.washington.edu.

University of Washington, Graduate School, Interdisciplinary Program in Near and Middle Eastern Studies, Seattle, WA 98195. Offers PhD. *Degree requirements:* For doctorate, 3 foreign languages, thesis/dissertation. *Entrance requirements:* For doctorate, GRE General Test, minimum GPA of 3.0. Additional exam requirements/recommendations for international students: Required—TOEFL. Electronic applications accepted.

University of Waterloo, Graduate Studies, Faculty of Arts, Department of Classical Studies, Waterloo, ON N2L 3G1, Canada. Offers ancient Mediterranean cultures (MA). *Degree requirements:* For master's, one foreign language. *Faculty research:* Ancient history, philosophy, anthropology, religion, culture.

University of Wisconsin–Madison, Graduate School, College of Letters and Science, Department of History, Madison, WI 53706-1380. Offers African history (MA, PhD); Central Asian history (MA, PhD); comparative world history (MA, PhD); East Asian history (MA, PhD); European history (MA, PhD); gender and women's history (MA, PhD); Latin American and Caribbean history (MA, PhD); Middle Eastern history (MA, PhD); South Asian history (MA, PhD); Southeast Asian history (MA, PhD); United States history (MA, PhD). Terminal master's awarded for partial completion of doctoral program. *Degree requirements:* For master's, thesis (for some programs); for doctorate, variable foreign language requirement, thesis/dissertation. *Entrance requirements:* For master's and doctorate, GRE General Test. Additional exam requirements/recommendations for international students: Required—Michigan English Language Assessment Battery or TOEFL. Electronic applications accepted. *Expenses:* Tuition, state resident: full-time $9887; part-time $617.96 per credit. Tuition, nonresident: full-time $24,054; part-time $1503.40 per credit. Required fees: $67.63 per credit. Tuition and fees vary according to reciprocity agreements. *Faculty research:* American, African, European, Asian, Latin American, and Middle Eastern history.

Wayne State University, College of Liberal Arts and Sciences, Department of Classical and Modern Languages, Literatures, and Cultures, Program in Near Eastern and Asian Studies, Detroit, MI 48202. Offers language learning (MA); Near Eastern studies (MA). *Faculty:* 27 full-time (13 women). *Students:* 3 full-time (2 women), 4 part-time (2 women). Average age 25. 8 applicants, 38% accepted, 2 enrolled. In 2010, 2 master's awarded. *Degree requirements:* For master's, one foreign language. *Entrance requirements:* For master's, GRE General Test. Additional exam requirements/recommendations for international students: Required—TOEFL (minimum score 550 paper-based; 213 computer-based); Recommended—TWE (minimum score 6). *Application deadline:* For fall admission, 7/1 for domestic students, 6/1 for international students; for winter admission, 10/1 for international students; for spring admission, 2/1 for international students. Applications are processed on a rolling basis. Application fee:

$30 ($50 for international students). Electronic applications accepted. *Expenses:* Tuition, state resident: full-time $7662; part-time $478.85 per credit hour. Tuition, nonresident: full-time $16,920; part-time $1057.55 per credit hour. Required fees: $571.20; $35.70 per credit hour. $188.05 per semester. Tuition and fees vary according to course load and program. *Financial support:* In 2010–11, 1 teaching assistantship with tuition reimbursement (averaging $14,620 per year) was awarded. *Faculty research:* Modern Middle East history, Arabic language and culture studies, Chinese linguistics, Islamic studies, Judaic studies. *Unit head:* Dr. May Seikaly, Chair, 313-577-6266, Fax: 313-577-3266, E-mail: ad6006@wayne.edu. *Application contact:* Janet Hankin, Professor, 313-577-0841, E-mail: janet.hankin@wayne.edu.

Wilfrid Laurier University, Faculty of Graduate and Postdoctoral Studies, Faculty of Arts, Department of Archaeology and Classical Studies, Waterloo, ON N2L 3C5, Canada. Offers MA. *Faculty:* 15 full-time (6 women), 3 part-time/adjunct (1 woman). *Students:* 6 full-time (3 women). 14 applicants, 36% accepted, 2 enrolled. *Degree requirements:* For master's, thesis optional. *Entrance requirements:* For master's, minimum B+ average in last two undergraduate years (exclusive of first year level courses in those years). Additional exam requirements/recommendations for international students: Required—TOEFL (minimum score 89 iBT). *Application deadline:* For fall admission, 2/1 priority date for domestic students, 1/1 priority date for international students. Application fee: $100. Electronic applications accepted. Tuition and fees charges are reported in Canadian dollars. *Expenses:* Tuition, area resident: Full-time $15,300 Canadian dollars; part-time $1200 Canadian dollars per credit. International tuition: $21,300 Canadian dollars full-time. Required fees: $650 Canadian dollars; $100 Canadian dollars per credit. Tuition and fees vary according to course load, degree level, campus/location and program. *Financial support:* In 2010–11, 5 fellowships, 5 teaching assistantships were awarded; career-related internships or fieldwork, scholarships/grants, health care benefits, and unspecified assistantships also available. *Faculty research:* History, languages, civilizations, archaeology. *Unit head:* Dr. Gerald Schaus, Graduate Officer, 519-884-0710 Ext. 3302, Fax: 519-883-0991, E-mail: gschaus@wlu.ca. *Application contact:* Jennifer Williams, Graduate Admissions and Records Officer, 519-884-0710 Ext. 3536, Fax: 519-884-1020, E-mail: gradstudies@wlu.ca.

Yale University, Graduate School of Arts and Sciences, Department of Near Eastern Languages and Civilizations, New Haven, CT 06520. Offers Arabic and Islamic studies (MA, PhD); archaeology of the ancient Near East (MA, PhD); Assyriology (MA, PhD); Egyptology (MA, PhD); Graeco-Arabic studies (MA, PhD); Northwest Semitic, Bible, comparative Semitics (MA, PhD). *Degree requirements:* For doctorate, 2 foreign languages, thesis/dissertation. *Entrance requirements:* For doctorate, GRE General Test.

Northern Studies

University of Alaska Fairbanks, College of Liberal Arts, Department of Northern Studies, Fairbanks, AK 99775-6460. Offers environmental politics and policy (MA); Northern history (MA). Part-time programs available. *Students:* 15 full-time (9 women), 21 part-time (13 women); includes 6 minority (1 Black or African American, non-Hispanic/Latino; 2 American Indian or Alaska Native, non-Hispanic/Latino; 1 Hispanic/Latino; 2 Two or more races, non-Hispanic/Latino), 2 international. Average age 39. 14 applicants, 57% accepted, 8 enrolled. In 2010, 9 master's awarded. *Degree requirements:* For master's, comprehensive exam, thesis or alternative. *Entrance requirements:* Additional exam requirements/recommendations for international students: Required—TOEFL (minimum score 550 paper-based; 213 computer-based; 80 iBT). *Application deadline:* For fall admission, 6/1 for domestic students, 3/1 for international students; for spring admission, 10/15 for domestic students, 9/1 for international students. Applications are processed on a rolling basis. Application fee: $60. Electronic applications accepted. *Expenses:* Tuition, state resident: full-time $5688; part-time $316 per credit. Tuition, nonresident: full-time $11,628; part-time $646 per credit. Required fees: $289 per

semester. Tuition and fees vary according to course load and reciprocity agreements. *Financial support:* In 2010–11, 9 teaching assistantships with tuition reimbursements (averaging $7,462 per year) were awarded; fellowships with tuition reimbursements, research assistantships with tuition reimbursements, career-related internships or fieldwork, Federal Work-Study, scholarships/grants, health care benefits, and unspecified assistantships also available. Support available to part-time students. Financial award application deadline: 1/1; financial award applicants required to submit FAFSA. *Faculty research:* Canadian history, environmental history, Native Alaskan history and art, fetal alcohol syndrome. *Unit head:* Mary Ehrlander, Director, 907-474-7126, Fax: 907-474-5817, E-mail: fynors@uaf.edu. *Application contact:* Mary Ehrlander, Director, 907-474-7126, Fax: 907-474-5817, E-mail: fynors@uaf.edu.

University of Manitoba, Faculty of Graduate Studies, Faculty of Arts, Department of Icelandic Language and Literature, Winnipeg, MB R3T 2N2, Canada. Offers MA.

Pacific Area/Pacific Rim Studies

University of California, San Diego, Office of Graduate Studies, Graduate School of International Relations and Pacific Studies, La Jolla, CA 92093. Offers economics and international affairs (PhD); Pacific international affairs (MPIA); political science and international affairs (PhD). *Degree requirements:* For master's, one foreign language; for doctorate, thesis/dissertation. *Entrance requirements:* For master's, GMAT or GRE General Test; for doctorate, GRE General Test. Additional exam requirements/recommendations for international students: Required—TOEFL (minimum score 550 paper-based; 213 computer-based). Electronic applications accepted. *Faculty research:* Pacific Rim as system and placement in global relations; studies in international economics, management and finance; analysis of patterns of policymaking in countries of the Pacific.

University of Guam, Office of Graduate Studies, College of Liberal Arts and Social Sciences, Micronesian Studies Program, Mangilao, GU 96923. Offers MA. *Degree requirements:* For master's, thesis. *Entrance requirements:* For master's, GRE General Test. Additional exam requirements/recommendations for international students: Required—TOEFL. *Faculty research:* Adolescent suicide in Micronesia, history of Micronesia, traditional agriculture in the Pacific, Micronesian languages, health and cultural practices.

University of Hawaii at Manoa, Graduate Division, School of Pacific and Asian Studies, Program in Pacific Island Studies, Honolulu, HI 96822. Offers MA, Graduate Certificate. Part-time programs available. *Faculty:* 27 full-time (9 women), 1 part-time/adjunct (0 women). *Students:* 14 full-time (9 women), 8 part-time (4 women); includes 2 Asian, non-Hispanic/Latino; 3 Two or more races, non-Hispanic/Latino, 5 international. Average age 35. 32 applicants, 53% accepted, 17 enrolled. In 2010, 10 master's awarded. *Degree requirements:* For master's, thesis optional. *Entrance requirements:* Additional exam requirements/recommendations for international students: Required—TOEFL (minimum score 580 paper-based; 237 computer-based; 92 iBT), IELTS (minimum score 5). *Application deadline:* For fall admission, 3/1 for domestic and international students; for spring admission, 9/1 for domestic and international students. Application fee: $60. *Financial support:* In 2010–11, 9 fellowships (averaging $6,070 per year) were awarded; research assistantships, teaching assistantships. Total annual research

expenditures: $271,000. *Application contact:* Terence Wesley-Smith, Associate Professor/Graduate Chair, 808-956-7700, Fax: 808-956-7053, E-mail: twsmith@hawaii.edu.

University of San Francisco, College of Arts and Sciences, Program in Asia Pacific Studies, San Francisco, CA 94117-1080. Offers MA, MA/MBA. Part-time and evening/weekend programs available. *Faculty:* 1 full-time (0 women), 5 part-time/adjunct (4 women). *Students:* 35 full-time (22 women), 8 part-time (5 women); includes 17 minority (1 Black or African American, non-Hispanic/Latino; 10 Asian, non-Hispanic/Latino; 4 Hispanic/Latino; 2 Two or more races, non-Hispanic/Latino), 13 international. Average age 29. 47 applicants, 87% accepted, 15 enrolled. In 2010, 15 master's awarded. *Degree requirements:* For master's, one foreign language, thesis. *Entrance requirements:* For master's, minimum GPA of 3.0. *Application deadline:* Applications are processed on a rolling basis. Application fee: $55 ($65 for international students). *Expenses:* Tuition: Full-time $20,070; part-time $1115 per credit hour. Tuition and fees vary according to course load, degree level and program. *Financial support:* In 2010–11, 27 students received support. Career-related internships or fieldwork, Federal Work-Study, and institutionally sponsored loans available. Financial award application deadline: 3/2; financial award applicants required to submit FAFSA. *Faculty research:* History of Christianity in China, U. S.-China policy, East Asian economies and political systems, sociolinguistic aspects of Japanese. *Unit head:* Dr. Ken Kopp, Director, 415-422-6357, Fax: 415-422-5933. *Application contact:* Information Contact, 415-422-5135, Fax: 415-422-2217, E-mail: asgraduate@usfca.edu.

University of Victoria, Faculty of Graduate Studies, Faculty of Humanities, Department of Pacific and Asian Studies, Victoria, BC V8W 2Y2, Canada. Offers MA. *Degree requirements:* For master's, thesis. *Entrance requirements:* For master's, minimum B+ average, writing sample. Additional exam requirements/recommendations for international students: Required—TOEFL (minimum score 575 paper-based; 233 computer-based), IELTS (minimum score 7). Electronic applications accepted. *Faculty research:* Culture, ethnicity and identity; economy and society; gender studies; languages and linguistics; literature.

Western European Studies

American University, School of International Service, Washington, DC 20016-8071. Offers comparative and regional studies (Certificate); cross-cultural communication (Certificate); development management (MS); ethics, peace, and global affairs (MA); European studies (Certificate); global environmental policy (MA, Certificate); international affairs (MA), including comparative and regional studies, environmental policy, international economic policy, international politics, natural resources and sustainable development, U. S. foreign policy; international communication (MA, Certificate); international development (MA, Certificate); international development management (Certificate); international economic policy (Certificate); international economic relations (Certificate); international media (MA); international peace and conflict resolution (MA, Certificate); international relations (PhD); international service (MIS); peace building (Certificate); the Americas (Certificate); United States foreign policy (Certificate); JD/MA. Part-time and evening/weekend programs available. *Faculty:* 91 full-time (35 women), 48 part-time/adjunct (16 women). *Students:* 591 full-time (383 women), 367 part-time (229 women); includes 164 minority (51 Black or African American, non-Hispanic/Latino; 4 American Indian or Alaska Native, non-Hispanic/Latino; 42 Asian, non-Hispanic/Latino; 63 Hispanic/Latino; 4 Two or more races, non-Hispanic/Latino), 94 international. Average age 27. 2,115 applicants, 59% accepted, 360 enrolled. In 2010, 370 master's, 7 doctorates awarded. Terminal master's awarded for partial completion of doctoral program. *Degree requirements:* For master's, one foreign language, comprehensive exam, thesis or alternative; for doctorate, one foreign language, comprehensive exam, thesis/dissertation, research practicum; for Certificate, minimum 15 credit hours related course work. *Entrance requirements:* For master's, GRE, 24 credits of course work in related social sciences, minimum GPA of 3.5, 2 letters of recommendation, bachelor's degree, resume; for doctorate, GRE, 2 letters of recommendation, 24 credits in related social sciences; for Certificate, bachelor's degree. Additional exam requirements/recommendations for international students: Required—TOEFL (minimum score 600 paper-based; 250 computer-based; 100 iBT). *Application deadline:* For fall admission, 1/15 priority date for domestic students; for spring admission, 10/1 priority date for domestic students. Applications are processed on a rolling basis. Application fee: $50. *Financial support:* Career-related internships or fieldwork, Federal Work-Study, and institutionally sponsored loans available. Financial award application deadline: 1/15. *Faculty research:* International intellectual property, international environmental issues, international law and legal order, international telecommunications/technology, international sustainable development. *Unit head:* Dr. Louis W. Goodman, Dean, 202-885-1600, Fax: 202-885-2494. *Application contact:* Yasmin Quianzon, Director of Graduate Admissions and Financial Aid, 202-885-2496, Fax: 202-885-1109.

Boston College, Graduate School of Arts and Sciences, Department of History, Chestnut Hill, MA 02467-3800. Offers European national studies (MA); history (MA, PhD); medieval studies (MA). Terminal master's awarded for partial completion of doctoral program. *Degree requirements:* For master's, one foreign language, comprehensive exam, thesis optional; for doctorate, 2 foreign languages, comprehensive exam, thesis/dissertation. *Entrance requirements:* For master's and doctorate, GRE General Test, writing sample. Additional exam requirements/recommendations for international students: Required—TOEFL (minimum score 600 paper-based; 250 computer-based; 100 iBT). Electronic applications accepted. *Faculty research:* Modern and early modern European, U. S., Russian, and Soviet history; European and U. S. intellectual history.

Brown University, Graduate School, Center for Portuguese and Brazilian Studies, Providence, RI 02912. Offers Brazilian studies (AM); Portuguese and Brazilian studies (AM, PhD); Portuguese Bilingual Education and Cross-Cultural Studies (AM); MA/PhD. *Degree requirements:* For doctorate, thesis/dissertation.

California State University, Long Beach, Graduate Studies, College of Liberal Arts, Department of History, Long Beach, CA 90840. Offers Africa and the Middle East (MA); ancient/medieval Europe (MA); Asia (MA); Latin America (MA); modern Europe (MA); United States (MA); world (MA). Part-time and evening/weekend programs available. *Faculty:* 12 full-time (7 women). *Students:* 18 full-time (6 women), 51 part-time (18 women); includes 3 Black or African American, non-Hispanic/Latino; 1 American Indian or Alaska Native, non-Hispanic/Latino; 3 Asian, non-Hispanic/Latino; 16 Hispanic/Latino, 1 international. Average age 30. 80 applicants, 53% accepted, 30 enrolled. In 2010, 11 master's awarded. *Degree requirements:* For master's, one foreign language, comprehensive exam or thesis. *Application deadline:* For fall admission, 3/1 for domestic students. Applications are processed on a rolling basis. Application fee: $55. Electronic applications accepted. *Financial support:* Research assistantships, Federal Work-Study, institutionally sponsored loans, and scholarships/grants available. Financial award application deadline: 3/2. *Faculty research:* All periods of European and American history, recent Asian and African history. *Unit head:* Dr. Nancy Quam-Wickham, Department Chair, 562-985-4431, Fax: 562-985-5431, E-mail: quamwick@csulb.edu. *Application contact:* Dr. Houri Berberian, Graduate Advisor, 562-985-4524, Fax: 562-985-4431, E-mail: hberber@csulb.edu.

Carleton University, Faculty of Graduate Studies, Faculty of Public Affairs and Management, Institute of European and Russian Studies, Ottawa, ON K1S 5B6, Canada. Offers European and European Union studies (MA); European integration studies (Diploma); Russian, Eurasian and transition studies (MA). *Degree requirements:* For master's, one foreign language, thesis optional. *Entrance requirements:* For master's, honors degree or equivalent; 2 years of Russian, German or other central east European language. Additional exam requirements/recommendations for international students: Required—TOEFL. *Faculty research:* East-West relations, minority rights in Russia and Eastern Europe.

The Catholic University of America, School of Arts and Sciences, Department of History, Washington, DC 20064. Offers history (MA, PhD); religion and society in the late medieval and early modern world (MA); MA/JD; MSLS/MA. Part-time programs available. *Faculty:* 13 full-time (7 women), 2 part-time/adjunct (0 women). *Students:* 16 full-time (12 women), 27 part-time (12 women); includes 1 American Indian or Alaska Native, non-Hispanic/Latino; 1 Hispanic/Latino, 3 international. Average age 32. 51 applicants, 41% accepted, 11 enrolled. In 2010, 5 master's, 3 doctorates awarded. *Degree requirements:* For master's, one foreign language, comprehensive exam, thesis optional; for doctorate, 2 foreign languages, comprehensive exam, thesis/dissertation. *Entrance requirements:* For master's and doctorate, GRE General Test, statement of purpose, official copies of academic transcripts, three letters of recommendation, writing sample. Additional exam requirements/recommendations for international students: Required—TOEFL (minimum score 580 paper-based; 237 computer-based). *Application deadline:* For fall admission, 8/1 priority date for domestic students, 7/15 for international students; for spring admission, 12/1 priority date for domestic students, 10/15 for international students. Applications are processed on a rolling basis. Application fee: $55. Electronic applications accepted. *Expenses:* Tuition: Full-time $33,580; part-time $1315 per credit hour. Required fees: $80; $40 per semester hour. One-time fee: $425. *Financial support:* Fellowships, research assistantships, teaching assistantships, Federal Work-Study, scholarships/grants, tuition waivers (full and partial), and unspecified assistantships available. Financial award application deadline: 2/1; financial award applicants required to submit FAFSA. *Faculty research:* Modern European intellectual history, history of mathematics and sciences, Renaissance, Catholic reformation, medieval women and gender. *Unit head:* Dr. Jerry Muller, Chair, 202-319-5484, Fax: 202-319-5569, E-mail: mullerj@cua.edu. *Application contact:* Andrew Woodall, Director of Graduate Admissions, 202-319-5057, Fax: 202-319-6533, E-mail: cua-admissions@cua.edu.

Central Michigan University, College of Graduate Studies, College of Humanities and Social and Behavioral Sciences, Department of History, Mount Pleasant, MI 48859. Offers European history (Graduate Certificate); history (MA, PhD); modern history (Graduate Certificate); United States history (Graduate Certificate). Part-time programs available. *Faculty:* 15 full-time (4 women). *Students:* 38 full-time (11 women), 23 part-time (8 women); includes 2 Black or African American, non-Hispanic/Latino; 1 Asian, non-Hispanic/Latino, 5 international. Average age 30. *Degree requirements:* For master's, thesis or alternative; for doctorate, comprehensive exam, thesis/dissertation. Application fee: $35 ($45 for international students). Electronic applications accepted. *Expenses:* Tuition, state resident: full-time $8208; part-time $456 per credit hour. Tuition, nonresident: full-time $13,788; part-time $766 per credit hour. One-time fee: $25. *Financial support:* Fellowships with tuition reimbursements, research assistantships with tuition reimbursements, teaching assistantships with tuition reimbursements, Federal Work-Study, unspecified assistantships, and out-of-state merit awards, non-resident graduate awards available. *Faculty research:* Colonial and revolutionary United States history, modern European history, Latin American and transatlantic history, transnational and comparative history, United States social history. *Unit head:* Dr. Mitchell K. Hall, Chairperson, 989-773-3374, Fax: 989-774-1156, E-mail: hall1mk@cmich.edu. *Application contact:* Dr. Mitchell K. Hall, Chairperson, 989-773-3374, Fax: 989-774-1156, E-mail: hall1mk@cmich.edu.

Claremont Graduate University, Graduate Programs, School of Arts and Humanities, Department of History, Claremont, CA 91711-6160. Offers Africana history (Certificate); American studies and U. S. history (MA, PhD); archival studies (MA); early modern studies (MA, PhD); European studies (MA, PhD); oral history (MA, PhD); MBA/MA; MBA/PhD. *Faculty:* 4 full-time (2 women), 1 part-time/adjunct (0 women). *Students:* 75 full-time (36 women), 2 part-time (1 woman); includes 25 minority (3 Black or African American, non-Hispanic/Latino; 1 American Indian or Alaska Native, non-Hispanic/Latino; 6 Asian, non-Hispanic/Latino; 9 Hispanic/Latino; 1 Native Hawaiian or other Pacific Islander, non-Hispanic/Latino; 5 Two or more races, non-Hispanic/Latino), 2 international. Average age 36. In 2010, 12 master's, 2 doctorates awarded. Terminal master's awarded for partial completion of doctoral program. *Entrance requirements:* For master's and doctorate, GRE General Test. Additional exam requirements/recommendations for international students: Required—TOEFL (minimum score 550 paper-based; 213 computer-based; 80 iBT). *Application deadline:* For fall admission, 2/1 priority date for domestic students. Applications are processed on a rolling basis. Application fee: $60. Electronic applications accepted. *Expenses:* Tuition: Full-time $35,748; part-time $1554 per unit. Required fees: $215 per semester. *Financial support:* Fellowships, research assistantships, Federal Work-Study, institutionally sponsored loans, and scholarships/grants available. Support available to part-time students. Financial award application deadline: 2/15; financial award applicants required to submit FAFSA. *Faculty research:* Intellectual and social history, cultural studies, gender studies, Western history, Chicano history. *Unit head:* Janet Farrell Brodie, Chair, 909-621-8880, Fax: 909-621-8609, E-mail: janet.brodie@cgu.edu. *Application contact:* Susan Hampson, Admissions Coordinator, 909-607-1278, E-mail: humanities@cgu.edu.

Columbia University, Graduate School of Arts and Sciences, Program in Liberal Studies, New York, NY 10027. Offers American studies (MA); East Asian studies (MA); human rights studies (MA); Islamic culture studies (MA); Jewish studies (MA); medieval studies (MA); modern European studies (MA); South Asian studies (MA). Part-time and evening/weekend programs available. *Degree requirements:* For master's, thesis.

Columbia University, School of International and Public Affairs, Institute for the Study of Europe, New York, NY 10027. Offers Certificate. Students must be enrolled in a separate graduate degree program at Columbia University. Electronic applications accepted.

Cornell University, Graduate School, Graduate Fields of Arts and Sciences, Field of History, Ithaca, NY 14853-0001. Offers African history (MA, PhD); American history (MA, PhD); ancient history (MA, PhD); early modern European history (MA, PhD); English history (MA, PhD); French history (MA, PhD); German history (MA, PhD); history of science (MA, PhD); Latin American history (MA, PhD); medieval Chinese history (MA, PhD); medieval history (MA, PhD); modern Chinese history (MA, PhD); modern European history (MA, PhD); modern Japanese history (MA, PhD); premodern Islamic history (MA, PhD); premodern Japanese history (MA, PhD); Renaissance history (MA, PhD); Russian history (MA, PhD); Southeast Asian history (MA, PhD). *Faculty:* 53 full-time (15 women). *Students:* 59 full-time (30 women); includes 3 Black or African American, non-Hispanic/Latino; 2 Asian, non-Hispanic/Latino; 4 Hispanic/Latino, 22 international. Average age 30. 217 applicants, 6% accepted, 8 enrolled. In 2010, 9 master's, 5 doctorates awarded. Terminal master's awarded for partial completion of doctoral program. *Degree requirements:* For master's, thesis; for doctorate, 2 foreign languages, comprehensive exam, thesis/dissertation, 1 year of teaching experience. *Entrance requirements:* For master's and doctorate, GRE General Test, writing sample, 3 letters of recommendation. Additional exam requirements/recommendations for international students: Required—TOEFL (minimum score 550 paper-based; 213 computer-based; 77 iBT). *Application deadline:* For fall admission, 1/15 for domestic students. Application fee: $80. Electronic applications accepted. *Expenses:* Tuition: Full-time $29,500. Required fees: $76. Tuition and fees vary according to degree level and program. *Financial support:* In 2010–11, 26 fellowships with full tuition reimbursements, 27 teaching assistantships with full tuition reimbursements were awarded; research assistantships with full tuition reimbursements, institutionally sponsored loans, scholarships/grants, health care benefits, tuition waivers (full and partial), and unspecified assistantships also available. Financial award applicants required to submit FAFSA. *Unit head:* Director of Graduate Studies, 607-255-6738, Fax: 607-255-0469. *Application contact:* Graduate Field Assistant, 607-255-6738, Fax: 607-255-0469, E-mail: history_grad_info@cornell.edu.

East Carolina University, Graduate School, Thomas Harriot College of Arts and Sciences, Department of History, Greenville, NC 27858-4353. Offers American history (MA); European history (MA); maritime history (MA). Part-time and evening/weekend programs available. *Degree requirements:* For master's, one foreign language, comprehensive exam, thesis. *Entrance requirements:* For master's, GRE General Test, GRE Subject Test. Additional exam requirements/recommendations for international students: Required—TOEFL. *Expenses:* Tuition, state resident: full-time $3130; part-time $391.25 per credit hour. Tuition, nonresident: full-time $13,817; part-time $1727.13 per credit hour. Required fees: $1916; $239.50 per credit hour. Tuition and fees vary according to campus/location and program.

Georgetown University, Graduate School of Arts and Sciences, BMW Center for German and European Studies, Washington, DC 20057. Offers MA, MA/JD, MA/PhD. *Degree requirements:* For master's, 2 foreign languages, comprehensive exam. *Entrance requirements:* For master's, GRE General Test. Additional exam requirements/recommendations for international students: Required—TOEFL. *Faculty research:* Trans-Atlantic relations, European Union, German and European Studies.

The George Washington University, Elliott School of International Affairs, Program in European and Eurasian Studies, Washington, DC 20052. Offers MA, JD/MA, MBA/MA. Part-time and evening/weekend programs available. *Students:* 13 full-time (8 women), 9 part-time (4 women); includes 1 American Indian or Alaska Native, non-Hispanic/Latino, 3 international. Average age 26. 48 applicants, 75% accepted, 8 enrolled. In 2010, 9 master's awarded. *Degree requirements:* For master's, one foreign language, capstone project. *Entrance requirements:* For master's, GRE General Test, 2 years (or the equivalent) of a modern European language or Russian, 2 semesters of introductory economics (macro or micro). Additional exam requirements/recommendations for international students: Required—TOEFL. *Application deadline:* For fall admission, 2/1 for domestic students; for spring admission, 10/1 for domestic students. Application fee: $60. Electronic applications accepted. *Financial support:* In 2010–11, 3 students received support; fellowships with tuition reimbursements available, research assistantships with tuition reimbursements available, career-related internships or fieldwork, Federal Work-Study, institutionally sponsored loans, and tuition waivers available. Financial award application deadline: 1/15; financial award applicants required to submit FAFSA. *Faculty research:* NATO, European economics, European history, European Union. *Unit head:* Hope Harrison, Director, 202-994-5439, Fax: 202-994-5436, E-mail: hopeharr@gwu.edu. *Application contact:* Jeff V. Miles, Director of Graduate Admissions, 202-994-7050, Fax: 202-994-9537, E-mail: esiagrad@gwu.edu.

Indiana University Bloomington, University Graduate School, College of Arts and Sciences, Department of West European Studies, Bloomington, IN 47405-7000. Offers MA. *Faculty:* 1 full-time (0 women). *Students:* 8 full-time (3 women), 2 part-time (1 woman); includes 1 minority (Hispanic/Latino), 1 international. Average age 30. 8 applicants, 75% accepted, 4 enrolled. In 2010, 1 master's awarded. *Degree requirements:* For master's, 2 foreign languages, thesis. *Entrance requirements:* For master's, GRE General Test. Additional exam requirements/recommendations for international students: Required—TOEFL. *Application deadline:* For fall admission, 1/15 priority date for domestic students, 12/15 for international students; for spring admission, 9/1 priority date for domestic students, 9/1 for international students. Applications are processed on a rolling basis. Application fee: $55 ($65 for international students). *Financial support:* In 2010–11, 1 fellowship with full tuition reimbursement (averaging $15,000 per year) was awarded; research assistantships with full tuition reimbursements, teaching assistantships with partial tuition reimbursements. *Faculty research:* European integration, economics of Europe, European union, European culture and identity, expansion of European union. *Unit head:* Dr. Patricia McManus, Director, 812-855-3280, E-mail: pmcmanus@indiana.edu. *Application contact:* Deborah Piston-Hatlen, Associate Director, 812-855-3280, Fax: 812-855-7695, E-mail: weur@indiana.edu.

Mississippi State University, College of Arts and Sciences, Department of History, Mississippi State, MS 39762. Offers history (PhD); U. S. and European history (MA). Part-time programs available. *Faculty:* 17 full-time (6 women). *Students:* 36 full-time (15 women), 9 part-time (3 women); includes 2 minority (1 Black or African American, non-Hispanic/Latino; 1 Asian, non-Hispanic/Latino). Average age 30. 35 applicants, 74% accepted, 18 enrolled. In 2010, 10 master's, 4 doctorates awarded. *Degree requirements:* For master's, one foreign language, comprehensive exam, thesis optional; for doctorate, 2 foreign languages, thesis/dissertation, comprehensive oral and written exam. *Entrance requirements:* For master's, minimum GPA of 3.0 on last two years of undergraduate courses; for doctorate, GRE, writing sample, minimum graduate GPA of 3.0. Additional exam requirements/recommendations for international students: Required—TOEFL (minimum score 475 paper-based; 153 computer-based; 53 iBT); Recommended—IELTS (minimum score 4.5). *Application deadline:* For fall admission, 4/1 for domestic students, 5/1 for international students; for spring admission, 11/1 for domestic students, 9/1 for international students. Applications are processed on a rolling basis. Application fee: $40. Electronic applications accepted. *Expenses:* Tuition, state resident: full-time $2730.50; part-time $304 per credit hour. Tuition, nonresident: full-time $6901; part-time $767 per credit hour. *Financial support:* In 2010–11, 31 teaching assistantships with full tuition reimbursements (averaging $10,977 per year) were awarded; Federal Work-Study, institutionally sponsored loans, scholarships/grants, and unspecified assistantships also available. Financial award application deadline: 4/1; financial award applicants required to submit FAFSA. *Faculty research:* U. S. political, diplomatic, military, social, and cultural history; modern Europe; Latin America; Asian history; African history. *Unit head:* Dr. Alan I. Marcus, Head, 662-325-3604, Fax: 662-325-1139, E-mail: aim10@msstate.edu. *Application contact:* Dr. Peter Messer, Associate Professor and Graduate Coordinator, 662-325-3604, Fax: 662-325-1139, E-mail: pmesser@history.msstate.edu.

Monmouth University, The Graduate School, Department of History, West Long Branch, NJ 07764-1898. Offers European specialization (MA); U. S. specialization (MA); world specialization (MA). Part-time and evening/weekend programs available. *Faculty:* 12 full-time (3 women). *Students:* 5 full-time (4 women), 56 part-time (28 women); includes 1 Black or African American, non-Hispanic/Latino; 1 Asian, non-Hispanic/Latino; 3 Hispanic/Latino; 1 Two or more races, non-Hispanic/Latino. Average age 36. 22 applicants, 100% accepted, 17 enrolled. In 2010, 16 master's awarded. *Degree requirements:* For master's, comprehensive exam, thesis or alternative. *Entrance requirements:* For master's, minimum GPA of 3.0 in major, 2.5 overall. Additional exam requirements/recommendations for international students: Required—TOEFL (minimum score 550 paper-based; 213 computer-based; 79 iBT), IELTS (minimum score 5) or Michigan English Language Assessment Battery (minimum score 77), Cambridge A, B, C. *Application deadline:* For fall admission, 7/15 priority date for domestic students, 6/1 for international students; for spring admission, 11/15 priority date for domestic students, 11/1 for international students. Applications are processed on a rolling basis. Application fee: $50. Electronic applications accepted. *Expenses:* Tuition: Full-time $19,572; part-time $816 per credit. Required fees: $628; $157 per semester. *Financial support:* In 2010–11, 46 students received support, including 39 fellowships (averaging $1,073 per year), 5 research assistantships (averaging $4,934 per year); career-related internships or fieldwork, scholarships/grants, and unspecified assistantships also available. Support available to part-time students. Financial award applicants required to submit FAFSA. *Faculty research:* U. S. business; labor; British, German, and French Revolutions; Soviet Union; Africa. *Unit head:* Dr. Maryann Rhett, Program Director, 732-263-5768, Fax: 732-263-5112, E-mail: mrhett@monmouth.edu. *Application contact:* Kevin Roane, Director, Office of Graduate Admission, 732-571-3452, Fax: 732-263-5123, E-mail: gradadm@monmouth.edu.

New York University, Graduate School of Arts and Science, Center for European Studies, New York, NY 10012-1019. Offers MA. *Faculty:* 4 full-time (0 women). *Students:* 16 full-time (10 women), 7 part-time (5 women), 5 international. Average age 25. 28 applicants, 86% accepted, 13 enrolled. In 2010, 9 master's awarded. *Entrance requirements:* For master's, GRE General Test. Additional exam requirements/recommendations for international students: Required—TOEFL. *Application deadline:* For fall admission, 1/1 priority date for domestic students. Application fee: $90. Electronic applications accepted. *Financial support:* Fellowships with tuition reimbursements, teaching assistantships with tuition reimbursements, career-related internships or fieldwork, Federal Work-Study, institutionally sponsored loans, and scholarships/grants available. Financial award application deadline: 1/4; financial award applicants required to submit FAFSA. *Faculty research:* Xenophobia, migration, and identity politics in Europe; European Union and political economy; Central Eastern Europe. *Unit head:* Larry Wolff, Director, 212-998-3838, Fax: 212-995-4188, E-mail: european.studies@nyu.edu. *Application contact:* Jennifer Denbo, Department Graduate Administrator, 212-998-3838, Fax: 212-995-4188, E-mail: european.studies@nyu.edu.

San Diego State University, Graduate and Research Affairs, College of Arts and Letters, Department of European Studies, San Diego, CA 92182. Offers MA. *Degree requirements:* For master's, one foreign language. *Entrance requirements:* For master's, GRE General Test. Additional exam requirements/recommendations for international students: Required—TOEFL. Electronic applications accepted.

Syracuse University, Maxwell School of Citizenship and Public Affairs, Program in European Union and Contemporary Europe, Syracuse, NY 13244. Offers CAS. Part-time programs available. *Students:* 5 applicants, 100% accepted, 0 enrolled. *Entrance requirements:* Additional exam requirements/recommendations for international students: Required—TOEFL (minimum score 100 iBT). Electronic applications accepted. *Expenses:* Tuition: Part-time $1162 per credit. *Financial support:* Application deadline: 1/1.

University of Colorado Denver, College of Liberal Arts and Sciences, Department of History, Denver, CO 80217. Offers European history (MA); global history (MA); public history (MA); U. S. history (MA). Part-time and evening/weekend programs available. *Faculty:* 12 full-time (6 women), 2 part-time/adjunct (1 woman). *Students:* 29 full-time (17 women), 30 part-time (12 women); includes 1 Black or African American, non-Hispanic/Latino; 1 American Indian or Alaska Native, non-Hispanic/Latino; 3 Hispanic/Latino. Average age 36. 25 applicants, 60% accepted, 10 enrolled. In 2010, 17 master's awarded. *Degree requirements:* For master's, comprehensive exam, thesis optional, 36 semester hours (12 courses). *Entrance requirements:* For master's, GRE General Test, writing sample, minimum GPA of 3.25, letters of recommendation. Additional exam requirements/recommendations for international students: Required—TOEFL (minimum score 525 paper-based; 197 computer-based). *Application deadline:* For fall admission, 4/1 for domestic students; for spring admission, 10/1 for domestic students. Applications are processed on a rolling basis. Application fee: $50 ($75 for international students). Electronic applications accepted. *Expenses:* Tuition, state resident: full-time $7332; part-time $355 per credit hour. Tuition, nonresident: full-time $18,990; part-time $1055

per credit hour. Required fees: $998. Tuition and fees vary according to course level, course load, degree level, campus/location, program, reciprocity agreements and student level. *Financial support:* Research assistantships, teaching assistantships, Federal Work-Study available. Financial award application deadline: 4/1; financial award applicants required to submit FAFSA. *Faculty research:* Uses of pre-modern Islamic heritage in modern India; relationship between liberal understandings of democracy, crime, and police discretion; relationships between gender, class, health, and welfare in nineteenth and early twentieth century England; U. S. business cultures and their influences on marketing and personnel practices; intersection of business and political ideologies; social and environmental history of the Rocky Mountain West. *Unit head:* Dr. Marjorie Levine-Clark, Associate Professor and Chair, 303-556-2896. *Application contact:* Tabitha Fitzpatrick, Program Assistant, 303-556-4830, E-mail: tabitha.fitzpatrick@ucdenver.edu.

University of Connecticut, Graduate School, College of Liberal Arts and Sciences, Field of International Studies, Program in European Studies, Storrs, CT 06269. Offers MA. *Degree requirements:* For master's, comprehensive exam. *Entrance requirements:* For master's, GRE General Test. Additional exam requirements/recommendations for international students: Required—TOEFL (minimum score 550 paper-based; 213 computer-based). Electronic applications accepted.

University of Connecticut, Graduate School, College of Liberal Arts and Sciences, Field of International Studies, Program in Italian History and Culture, Storrs, CT 06269. Offers MA. *Entrance requirements:* Additional exam requirements/recommendations for international students: Required—TOEFL (minimum score 550 paper-based; 213 computer-based). Electronic applications accepted.

University of Florida, Graduate School, College of Liberal Arts and Sciences, Department of History, Gainesville, FL 32611. Offers African history (MA, PhD); American history (MA, PhD); European history (MA, PhD); Latin American history (MA, PhD); JD/MA; JD/PhD. Part-time programs available. *Faculty:* 31 full-time (10 women), 5 part-time/adjunct (4 women). *Students:* 81 full-time (33 women), 17 part-time (8 women); includes 3 Black or African American, non-Hispanic/Latino; 2 American Indian or Alaska Native, non-Hispanic/Latino; 2 Asian, non-Hispanic/Latino; 1 Hispanic/Latino, 12 international. Average age 30. 150 applicants, 29% accepted, 21 enrolled. In 2010, 19 master's, 8 doctorates awarded. Terminal master's awarded for partial completion of doctoral program. *Degree requirements:* For master's, variable foreign language requirement, thesis optional, 30 credit hours; for doctorate, variable foreign language requirement, comprehensive exam, thesis/dissertation, 90 credit hours. *Entrance requirements:* For master's and doctorate, GRE General Test, minimum GPA of 3.0. Additional exam requirements/recommendations for international students: Required—TOEFL (minimum score 550 paper-based; 213 computer-based; 80 iBT), IELTS (minimum score 6). *Application deadline:* For fall admission, 1/1 priority date for domestic students, 1/1 for international students. Applications are processed on a rolling basis. Application fee: $30. Electronic applications accepted. *Expenses:* Tuition, state resident: full-time $10,915.92. Tuition, nonresident: full-time $28,309. *Financial support:* In 2010–11, 70 students received support, including 30 fellowships, 13 research assistantships (averaging $16,665 per year), 27 teaching assistantships (averaging $16,733 per year); career-related internships or fieldwork and unspecified assistantships also available. Financial award application deadline: 1/15; financial award applicants required to submit FAFSA. *Faculty research:* Latin America and Caribbean history, nineteenth-century U. S. history, medieval Europe history, African history and Atlantic world history. *Unit head:* Dr. Ida L. Altman, Chair, 352-392-9634, E-mail: ialtman@ufl.edu. *Application contact:* Nina Caputo, Graduate Coordinator, 352-273-3379, Fax: 352-392-6927, E-mail: ncaputo@ufl.edu.

University of Guelph, Graduate Studies, College of Arts, School of Languages and Literatures, Program in European Studies, Guelph, ON N1G 2W1, Canada. Offers MA. *Degree requirements:* For master's, research paper. *Entrance requirements:* For master's, curriculum vitae, writing sample, 2 letters of recommendation.

University of Illinois at Urbana–Champaign, Graduate College, College of Liberal Arts and Sciences, European Union Center, Champaign, IL 61820. Offers MA. Part-time programs available. *Students:* 5 full-time (3 women). 13 applicants, 69% accepted, 5 enrolled. *Degree requirements:* For master's, one foreign language. *Entrance requirements:* For master's, GRE, 2 years in a language of the EU. Additional exam requirements/recommendations for international students: Required—TOEFL (minimum score 550 paper-based; 213 computer-based; 79 iBT). Application fee: $75 ($90 for international students). Electronic applications accepted. *Financial support:* In 2010–11, 4 fellowships were awarded; research assistantships, teaching assistantships, tuition waivers (full and partial) also available. *Unit head:* Bryan Endres, Director, 217-333-1828, Fax: 217-333-6270, E-mail: bendres@illinois.edu. *Application contact:* Kim Rice, Office Support Specialist, 217-265-7515, Fax: 217-333-6270, E-mail: kimrice@illinois.edu.

University of Maine, Graduate School, College of Liberal Arts and Sciences, Department of History, Orono, ME 04469. Offers American studies (MA, PhD); Canadian studies (MA, PhD); East Asian (MA); environmental (MA); European (MA); technology (MA). *Faculty:* 11 full-time (1 woman), 2 part-time/adjunct (1 woman). *Students:* 24 full-time (8 women), 35 part-time (13 women); includes 4 minority (2 American Indian or Alaska Native, non-Hispanic/Latino; 2 Hispanic/Latino). Average age 38. 43 applicants, 40% accepted, 15 enrolled. In 2010, 5 master's, 3 doctorates awarded. Terminal master's awarded for partial completion of doctoral program. *Degree requirements:* For master's, variable foreign language requirement, thesis optional; for doctorate, one foreign language, thesis/dissertation. *Entrance requirements:* For master's and doctorate, GRE General Test. Additional exam requirements/recommendations for international students: Required—TOEFL. *Application deadline:* For fall admission, 2/1 priority date for domestic students. Applications are processed on a rolling basis. Application fee: $65. Electronic applications accepted. *Expenses:* Tuition, state resident: full-time $400. Tuition, nonresident: full-time $1050. *Financial support:* In 2010–11, 9 teaching assistantships with tuition reimbursements (averaging $12,790 per year) were awarded; career-related internships or fieldwork, Federal Work-Study, and tuition waivers (full and partial) also available. Support available to part-time students. Financial award application deadline: 3/1. *Faculty research:* Canadian labor and working classes; American social, cultural, and urban history. *Unit head:* Dr. Nathan Godfried, Chair, 207-581-1923, Fax: 207-581-1817. *Application contact:* Scott G. Delcourt, Associate Dean of the Graduate School, 207-581-3291, Fax: 207-581-3232, E-mail: graduate@maine.edu.

University of Nevada, Reno, Graduate School, Interdisciplinary Program in Basque Studies, Reno, NV 89557. Offers PhD. *Degree requirements:* For doctorate, thesis/dissertation. *Entrance requirements:* For doctorate, GRE General Test, master's degree in related field, minimum GPA of 3.0. Additional exam requirements/recommendations for international students: Required—TOEFL (minimum score 500 paper-based; 173 computer-based; 61 iBT), IELTS (minimum score 6). Electronic applications accepted. *Expenses:* Tuition, state resident: full-time $2219; part-time $246 per credit. Tuition, nonresident: part-time $510 per credit. International tuition: $9009 full-time. Required fees: $59 per term. One-time fee: $101. Tuition and fees vary according to course load. *Faculty research:* Ethnic groups, Basque society, migration studies, symbolic anthropology, terrorism.

University of Pittsburgh, University Center for International Studies, Pittsburgh, PA 15260. Offers African studies (Certificate); Asian studies (Certificate); European Union studies (Certificate); global studies (Certificate); Latin American studies (Certificate); Russian and East European studies (Certificate); West European studies (Certificate). *Students:* 322 full-time (192 women), 19 part-time (14 women); includes 22 minority (8 Black or African American, non-Hispanic/Latino; 3 Asian, non-Hispanic/Latino; 6 Hispanic/Latino; 5 Two or more races, non-Hispanic/Latino), 134 international. In 2010, 61 Certificates awarded. *Degree requirements:* For Certificate, one foreign language, study abroad. *Application deadline:* Applications are processed on a rolling basis. *Expenses:* Tuition, state resident: full-time $17,304; part-time $701 per credit. Tuition, nonresident: full-time $29,554; part-time $1210 per credit. Required

Western European Studies

University of Pittsburgh *(continued)*
fees: $740; $214 per term. Tuition and fees vary according to program. *Unit head:* Dr. Lawrence F. Feick, Director, University Center for International Studies, 412-648-7374, Fax: 412-624-4672, E-mail: feick@pitt.edu. *Application contact:* Information Contact, 412-624-4141, E-mail: graduate@pitt.edu.

Washington State University, Graduate School, College of Liberal Arts, Department of History, Pullman, WA 99164. Offers early and modern European history (MA, PhD); environmental history (MA, PhD); Latin American history (MA, PhD); modern East Asia history (MA, PhD); public history (MA, PhD); U. S. history (MA, PhD); women's history (MA, PhD); world history (MA, PhD). Part-time programs available. *Faculty:* 25. *Students:* 38 full-time (22 women), 10 part-time (4 women); includes 1 American Indian or Alaska Native, non-Hispanic/Latino; 2 Hispanic/Latino, 2 international. Average age 33. 57 applicants, 47% accepted, 10 enrolled. In 2010, 10 master's, 2 doctorates awarded. *Degree requirements:* For master's, comprehensive exam (for some programs), thesis, oral exam; for doctorate, one foreign language, comprehensive exam, thesis/dissertation, oral and written exam. *Entrance requirements:* For master's and doctorate, GRE General Test, official transcripts from all universities attended; three letters of recommendation; statement of purpose; writing sample; Preferred Fields of Study form; Language Background form. Additional exam requirements/recommendations for international students: Required—TOEFL (minimum score 550 paper-based), IELTS. *Application deadline:* For fall admission, 1/10 for domestic and international students; for spring admission, 7/1 for domestic and international students. Applications are processed on a rolling basis. Application fee: $50. Electronic applications accepted. *Expenses:* Tuition, state resident: full-time $8552; part-time $443 per credit. Tuition, nonresident: full-time $21,650; part-time $1083 per credit. Required fees: $846. *Financial support:* In 2010–11, 1 fellowship with partial tuition reimbursement (averaging $3,000 per year), research assistantships with full and partial tuition reimbursements (averaging $13,917 per year), 28 teaching assistantships with full and partial tuition reimbursements (averaging $13,056 per year) were awarded; career-related internships or fieldwork, Federal Work-Study, institutionally sponsored loans, scholarships/grants, and health care benefits also available. Financial award application deadline: 2/15; financial award applicants required to submit FAFSA. *Faculty research:* Public, world, environmental, women's and U. S. history. *Unit head:* Dr. Raymond Sun, Chair, 509-335-5139, Fax: 509-335-4171, E-mail: pietz@wsu.edu. *Application contact:* Graduate Studies Director, 509-335-4030, Fax: 509-335-4171, E-mail: kale@wsu.edu.

Women's Studies

The American University in Cairo, School of Global Affairs and Public Policy, Program in Gender and Women's Studies, Cairo, Egypt. Offers gender and development (MA, Diploma); gender and justice (MA, Diploma); gender and women's studies in the Middle East and North Africa (MA, Diploma).

Brandeis University, Graduate School of Arts and Sciences, Department of Anthropology, Waltham, MA 02454. Offers anthropology (MA, PhD); anthropology and women's and gender studies (MA). Part-time programs available. *Faculty:* 8 full-time (4 women), 3 part-time/adjunct (1 woman). *Students:* 43 full-time (30 women), 1 (woman) part-time; includes 4 Hispanic/Latino, 13 international. Average age 34. 40 applicants, 53% accepted, 13 enrolled. In 2010, 6 master's, 2 doctorates awarded. Terminal master's awarded for partial completion of doctoral program. *Degree requirements:* For master's, thesis; for doctorate, one foreign language, comprehensive exam, thesis/dissertation. *Entrance requirements:* For master's, GRE General Test (recommended), sample of written work, resume, letters of recommendation; for doctorate, GRE General Test, sample of written work, resume, letters of recommendation. Additional exam requirements/recommendations for international students: Required—TOEFL (minimum score 600 paper-based; 250 computer-based; 100 iBT); Recommended—IELTS (minimum score 7). *Application deadline:* For fall admission, 1/15 for domestic students. Application fee: $75. Electronic applications accepted. *Financial support:* In 2010–11, 23 students received support, including 12 fellowships with full tuition reimbursements available (averaging $20,000 per year), 11 teaching assistantships with partial tuition reimbursements available (averaging $3,200 per year); research assistantships with partial tuition reimbursements available, career-related internships or fieldwork, scholarships/grants, health care benefits, tuition waivers (full and partial), and unspecified assistantships also available. Support available to part-time students. Financial award application deadline: 4/15; financial award applicants required to submit FAFSA. *Faculty research:* Evolutionary processes, comparative social institutions, systems of meaning, gender studies, sociocultural anthropology, linguistic anthropology, archaeology, and physical anthropology. *Unit head:* Dr. Janet McIntosh, Associate Professor/Director of Graduate Studies, 781-736-2210, Fax: 781-736-2232, E-mail: janetmc@brandeis.edu. *Application contact:* Laurel Carpenter, Academic Administrator, 781-736-2210, Fax: 781-736-2232, E-mail: lcarpenter@brandeis.edu.

Brandeis University, Graduate School of Arts and Sciences, Department of English, Waltham, MA 02454-9110. Offers English (MA, PhD); English and women's and gender studies (MA). Part-time programs available. *Faculty:* 16 full-time (9 women), 8 part-time/adjunct (5 women). *Students:* 54 full-time (29 women), 1 (woman) part-time; includes 1 Asian, non-Hispanic/Latino; 2 Hispanic/Latino, 5 international. 177 applicants, 16% accepted, 10 enrolled. In 2010, 8 master's, 5 doctorates awarded. *Degree requirements:* For master's, one foreign language, thesis, symposium; for doctorate, 2 foreign languages, thesis/dissertation, field exam, symposium presentation, prospectus defense. *Entrance requirements:* For master's, GRE General Test, resume, sample of work, letters of recommendation; for doctorate, GRE General Test, GRE Subject Test, resume, sample of work, letters of recommendation. Additional exam requirements/recommendations for international students: Required—TOEFL (minimum score 600 paper-based; 250 computer-based; 100 iBT); Recommended—IELTS (minimum score 7). *Application deadline:* For fall admission, 1/5 for domestic and international students. Application fee: $75. Electronic applications accepted. *Financial support:* In 2010–11, 27 fellowships with full tuition reimbursements (averaging $20,000 per year), 4 teaching assistantships with partial tuition reimbursements (averaging $3,200 per year) were awarded; research assistantships with full tuition reimbursements, scholarships/grants, health care benefits, and tuition waivers (full and partial) also available. Financial award application deadline: 4/15; financial award applicants required to submit FAFSA. *Faculty research:* Feminist and gender theory, American literature, Anglophone literature, early modern literature, modernism. *Unit head:* Dr. Michael Gilmore, Director of Graduate Studies, 781-736-2130, Fax: 781-736-2179, E-mail: chaucer@brandeis.edu. *Application contact:* Lisa Pannella, Department Administrator, 781-736-2130, Fax: 781-736-2179, E-mail: pannella@brandeis.edu.

Brandeis University, Graduate School of Arts and Sciences, Department of Music, Waltham, MA 02454-9110. Offers composition and theory (MA, MFA, PhD); music and women's and gender studies (MA); musicology (MA, MFA, PhD). Part-time programs available. *Faculty:* 7 full-time (1 woman), 9 part-time/adjunct (4 women). *Students:* 43 full-time (18 women), 3 part-time (all women); includes 7 Black or African American, non-Hispanic/Latino; 3 Asian, non-Hispanic/Latino; 1 Hispanic/Latino, 7 international. 88 applicants, 30% accepted, 11 enrolled. In 2010, 11 master's, 2 doctorates awarded. Terminal master's awarded for partial completion of doctoral program. *Degree requirements:* For master's, one foreign language, thesis or alternative; for doctorate, 2 foreign languages, comprehensive exam, thesis/dissertation. *Entrance requirements:* For master's, GRE General Test (musicology), resume, sample of work (music composition), letters of recommendation; for doctorate, GRE General Test (musicology), resume, writing sample (musicology), letters of recommendation, sample of recording work (composition). Additional exam requirements/recommendations for international students: Required—TOEFL (minimum score 600 paper-based; 250 computer-based; 100 iBT); Recommended—IELTS (minimum score 7). *Application deadline:* For fall admission, 1/15 priority date for domestic and international students. Application fee: $75. Electronic applications accepted. *Financial support:* In 2010–11, 28 students received support, including 24 fellowships with full tuition reimbursements available (averaging $20,000 per year), 4 teaching assistantships with partial tuition reimbursements available (averaging $3,200 per year); research assistantships, scholarships/grants, health care benefits, and tuition waivers (full and partial) also available. Support available to part-time students. Financial award application deadline: 4/15; financial award applicants required to submit FAFSA. *Faculty research:* Composition, performance, theory and analysis, music history, electronic music. *Unit head:* Prof. Mary Ruth Ray, Chair, 781-736-3310, E-mail: ray@brandeis.edu. *Application contact:* Mark Kagan, Senior Academic Administrator, 781-736-3311, E-mail: kagan@brandeis.edu.

Brandeis University, Graduate School of Arts and Sciences, Department of Near Eastern and Judaic Studies, Waltham, MA 02454-9110. Offers Near Eastern and Judaic studies (MA, PhD); Near Eastern and Judaic studies and sociology (PhD); Near Eastern and Judaic studies and women's and gender studies (MA); teaching of Hebrew (MAT). Part-time programs available. *Faculty:* 23 full-time (11 women), 7 part-time/adjunct (3 women). *Students:* 64 full-time (29 women); includes 2 Hispanic/Latino, 6 international. 123 applicants, 50% accepted, 18 enrolled. In 2010, 10 master's, 2 doctorates awarded. Terminal master's awarded for partial completion of doctoral program. *Degree requirements:* For master's, one foreign language, comprehensive exam, thesis or alternative; for doctorate, 3 foreign languages, comprehensive exam, thesis/dissertation. *Entrance requirements:* For master's and doctorate, GRE General Test (recommended), letters of recommendation, transcripts, statement of purpose. Additional exam requirements/recommendations for international students: Required—TOEFL (minimum score 600 paper-based; 250 computer-based; 100 iBT); Recommended—IELTS (minimum score 7). *Application deadline:* For fall admission, 1/15 priority date for domestic and international students. Applications are processed on a rolling basis. Application fee: $75. Electronic applications accepted. *Financial support:* In 2010–11, 17 students received support, including 14 fellowships with full tuition reimbursements available (averaging $20,000 per year); research assistantships with full and partial tuition reimbursements available, teaching assistantships, scholarships/grants, health care benefits, and tuition waivers (full and partial) also available. Support available to part-time students. Financial award application deadline: 4/15; financial award applicants required to submit FAFSA. *Faculty research:* Ancient Near East and Bible, philosophy, history, modern Middle East, Islamic studies. *Unit head:* Dr. Sylvia Fishman, Chair, 781-736-2950, Fax: 781-736-2070, E-mail: fishman@brandeis.edu. *Application contact:* Joanne Arnish, Department Administrator, 781-736-2950, Fax: 781-736-2070, E-mail: arnish@brandeis.edu.

Brandeis University, Graduate School of Arts and Sciences, Joint Master's Programs in Women's and Gender Studies, Waltham, MA 02454-9110. Offers anthropology and women's and gender studies (MA); English and women's and gender studies (MA); music and women's and gender studies (MA); Near Eastern and Judaic studies and women's and gender studies (MA); public policy and women's and gender studies (MA); sociology and women's and gender studies (MA); sustainable international development and women's/gender studies (MA). Part-time programs available. *Degree requirements:* For master's, thesis. *Entrance requirements:* For master's, GRE, sample of written work, resume. Additional exam requirements/recommendations for international students: Required—TOEFL (minimum score 600 paper-based; 250 computer-based; 100 iBT); Recommended—IELTS (minimum score 7). Electronic applications accepted.

Brandeis University, Graduate School of Arts and Sciences, MA Program in Women's and Gender Studies, Waltham, MA 02454-9110. Offers MA. *Degree requirements:* For master's, thesis. *Entrance requirements:* For master's, GRE, three letters of recommendation, curriculum vitae or resume, statement of purpose, critical writing sample. Additional exam requirements/recommendations for international students: Required—TOEFL (minimum score 600 paper-based; 250 computer-based; 100 iBT); Recommended—IELTS (minimum score 7). Electronic applications accepted. *Faculty research:* Gender and legal studies, sexuality studies, social and public policy, comparative literature and culture, anthropology, English, music, Near Eastern and Judaic Studies, public policy, sociology, sustainable international development.

California Institute of Integral Studies, School of Consciousness and Transformation, San Francisco, CA 94103. Offers creative inquiry/interdisciplinary arts (MFA); cultural anthropology and social transformation (MA); East-West psychology (MA, PhD); integrative health studies (MA); philosophy and religion (MA, PhD), including Asian and comparative studies, philosophy, cosmology, and consciousness, women's spirituality; social and cultural anthropology (PhD); transformative leadership (MA); transformative studies (PhD); writing and consciousness (MFA). Part-time and evening/weekend programs available. Postbaccalaureate distance learning degree programs offered (minimal on-campus study). *Students:* 455 full-time (315 women), 133 part-time (90 women); includes 47 Black or African American, non-Hispanic/Latino; 3 American Indian or Alaska Native, non-Hispanic/Latino; 21 Asian, non-Hispanic/Latino; 41 Hispanic/Latino, 40 international. Average age 37. 265 applicants, 91% accepted, 163 enrolled. In 2010, 64 master's, 22 doctorates awarded. Terminal master's awarded for partial completion of doctoral program. *Degree requirements:* For master's, thesis optional; for doctorate, comprehensive exam, thesis/dissertation, 1 foreign language (Asian comparative studies). *Entrance requirements:* For master's, minimum GPA of 3.0, letters of recommendation, writing sample; for doctorate, master's degree, minimum GPA of 3.0, letters of recommendation, writing sample. Additional exam requirements/recommendations for international students: Required—TOEFL. *Application deadline:* For fall admission, 2/1 priority date for domestic and international students; for spring admission, 10/15 priority date for domestic and international students. Applications are processed on a rolling basis. Application fee: $65. Electronic applications accepted. *Expenses:* Tuition: Full-time $15,660; part-time $870 per semester hour. Required fees: $95 per semester. *Financial support:* In 2010–11, 255 students received support; research assistantships, teaching assistantships, career-related internships or fieldwork, Federal Work-Study, scholarships/grants, and tuition waivers (partial) available. Support available to part-time students. Financial award application deadline: 4/15; financial award applicants required to submit FAFSA. *Faculty research:* Ecology and sustainability, philosophy and religion, East-West psychology, integrative health, social and cultural anthropology, transformative leadership. *Application contact:* Allyson Werner, Associate Director of Admissions, 415-575-6155, Fax: 415-575-1268.

Claremont Graduate University, Graduate Programs, School of Arts and Humanities, Program in Applied Women's Studies, Claremont, CA 91711-6160. Offers MA. *Faculty:* 1 (woman) full-time. *Students:* 9 full-time (8 women), 1 (woman) part-time; includes 1 Black or African American, non-Hispanic/Latino; 1 Asian, non-Hispanic/Latino; 1 Hispanic/Latino; 1 Two or more races, non-Hispanic/Latino. Average age 26. In 2010, 7 master's awarded. *Entrance requirements:* For master's, GRE General Test. Additional exam requirements/recommendations for international students: Required—TOEFL (minimum score 550 paper-based; 213 computer-based; 80 iBT). *Application deadline:* For fall admission, 2/1 priority date for domestic students. Applications are processed on a rolling basis. Application fee: $60. Electronic applications accepted. *Expenses:* Tuition: Full-time $35,748; part-time $1554 per unit. Required fees: $215 per semester. *Financial support:* Fellowships, research assistantships, teaching assistantships, Federal Work-Study, institutionally sponsored loans, and scholarships/grants available. Support available to part-time students. Financial award application deadline: 2/15; financial award applicants required to submit FAFSA. *Unit head:* Linda Perkins, Director, 909-621-8696, E-mail: linda.perkins@cgu.edu. *Application contact:* Susan Hampson, Admissions Coordinator, 909-607-1278, Fax: 909-607-1221, E-mail: susan.hampson@cgu.edu.

Claremont Graduate University, Graduate Programs, School of Religion, Claremont, CA 91711-6160. Offers Hebrew Bible (MA, PhD); history of Christianity and religions of North America (MA, PhD); New Testament (MA, PhD); philosophy of religion and theology (MA, PhD); theology, ethics and culture (MA, PhD); women's studies in religion (MA, PhD); MA/PhD; MBA/PhD. Part-time programs available. *Faculty:* 6 full-time (2 women), 2 part-time/adjunct (0 women). *Students:* 218 full-time (87 women), 10 part-time (4 women); includes 13 Black or African American, non-Hispanic/Latino; 11 Asian, non-Hispanic/Latino; 12 Hispanic/Latino; 1 Two or more races, non-Hispanic/Latino, 29 international. Average age 37. In 2010, 13 master's, 12 doctorates awarded. Terminal master's awarded for partial completion of doctoral program. *Entrance requirements:* For master's and doctorate, GRE General Test. Additional exam requirements/recommendations for international students: Required—TOEFL (minimum score 550 paper-based; 213 computer-based; 80 iBT). *Application deadline:* For fall admission, 2/1 priority date for domestic students. Applications are processed on a rolling basis. Application fee: $60. Electronic applications accepted. *Expenses:* Tuition: Full-time $35,748; part-time $1554 per unit. Required fees: $215 per semester. *Financial support:* Fellowships, research assistantships, teaching assistantships, Federal Work-Study, institutionally sponsored loans, and scholarships/grants available. Support available to part-time students. Financial award application deadline: 2/15; financial award applicants required to submit FAFSA. *Unit head:* Anselm Min, Dean, 909-607-3214, Fax: 909-621-9587, E-mail: anselm.min@cgu.edu. *Application contact:* Brent Smith, Recruiter, 909-607-2653, Fax: 909-607-9587, E-mail: brent.smith@cgu.edu.

Clark Atlanta University, School of Arts and Sciences, Department of Africana Women's Studies, Atlanta, GA 30314. Offers MA, DAH. Part-time programs available. *Faculty:* 1 (woman) full-time, 1 (woman) part-time/adjunct. *Students:* 5 full-time (all women), 10 part-time (9 women); includes 12 Black or African American, non-Hispanic/Latino, 1 international. Average age 35. 6 applicants, 100% accepted, 4 enrolled. In 2010, 2 master's awarded. *Degree requirements:* For master's, one foreign language, comprehensive exam, thesis optional; for doctorate, one foreign language, comprehensive exam, thesis/dissertation. *Entrance requirements:* For master's, GRE General Test, minimum GPA of 2.5; for doctorate, GRE General Test, minimum graduate GPA of 3.0. Additional exam requirements/recommendations for international students: Required—TOEFL (minimum score 500 paper-based; 173 computer-based; 61 iBT). *Application deadline:* For fall admission, 4/1 for domestic and international students; for spring admission, 11/1 for domestic and international students. Applications are processed on a rolling basis. Application fee: $40 ($55 for international students). Electronic applications accepted. *Expenses:* Tuition: Full-time $12,942; part-time $719 per credit hour. Required fees: $710; $355 per semester. *Financial support:* Scholarships/grants available. Financial award application deadline: 4/30; financial award applicants required to submit FAFSA. *Faculty research:* Concerns of women of African descent globally. *Unit head:* Dr. Josephine Bradley, Chairperson, 404-880-6810, E-mail: jbradley@cau.edu. *Application contact:* Michelle Clark-Davis, Graduate Program Admissions, 404-880-6605, E-mail: cauadmissions@cau.edu.

Cornell University, Graduate School, Graduate Fields of Arts and Sciences, Field of English Language and Literature, Ithaca, NY 14853-0001. Offers African-American literature (PhD); American literature after 1865 (PhD); American literature to 1865 (PhD); American studies (PhD); colonial and postcolonial literature (PhD); creative writing (MFA); cultural studies (PhD); dramatic literature (PhD); English poetry (PhD); English Renaissance to 1660 (PhD); lesbian, bisexual, and gay literature studies (PhD); literary criticism and theory (PhD); nineteenth century (PhD); Old and Middle English (PhD); prose fiction (PhD); Restoration and eighteenth century (PhD); twentieth century (PhD); women's literature (PhD); MFA/PhD. *Faculty:* 56 full-time (29 women). *Students:* 100 full-time (56 women); includes 5 Black or African American, non-Hispanic/Latino; 3 American Indian or Alaska Native, non-Hispanic/Latino; 10 Asian, non-Hispanic/Latino; 8 Hispanic/Latino, 12 international. Average age 27. 1,091 applicants, 4% accepted, 21 enrolled. In 2010, 25 master's, 12 doctorates awarded. Terminal master's awarded for partial completion of doctoral program. *Degree requirements:* For master's, one foreign language, thesis; for doctorate, one foreign language, comprehensive exam, thesis/dissertation, teaching experience. *Entrance requirements:* For master's, GRE General Test, 3 letters of recommendation, creative writing sample; for doctorate, GRE General Test, GRE Subject Test (English), 3 letters of recommendation, writing sample. Additional exam requirements/recommendations for international students: Required—TOEFL (minimum score 600 paper-based; 250 computer-based; 77 iBT). *Application deadline:* For fall admission, 1/10 for domestic students. Application fee: $80. Electronic applications accepted. *Expenses:* Tuition: Full-time $29,500. Required fees: $76. Tuition and fees vary according to degree level and program. *Financial support:* In 2010–11, 32 fellowships with full tuition reimbursements, 60 teaching assistantships with full tuition reimbursements were awarded; research assistantships with full tuition reimbursements, institutionally sponsored loans, scholarships/grants, health care benefits, tuition waivers (full and partial), and unspecified assistantships also available. Financial award applicants required to submit FAFSA. *Faculty research:* English and American literature, women's writing, ethnic and post-colonial literature, critical theory, medievalism. *Unit head:* Director of Graduate Studies, 607-255-7989, Fax: 607-255-6661. *Application contact:* Graduate Field Assistant, 607-255-7989, Fax: 607-255-6661, E-mail: english_grad@cornell.edu.

Eastern Michigan University, Graduate School, College of Arts and Sciences, Department of Women's and Gender Studies, Ypsilanti, MI 48197. Offers MA, Graduate Certificate. Part-time and evening/weekend programs available. *Faculty:* 1 (woman) full-time. *Students:* 4 full-time (all women), 8 part-time (all women); includes 1 minority (Black or African American, non-Hispanic/Latino), 1 international. Average age 32. 18 applicants, 33% accepted, 3 enrolled. In 2010, 4 master's awarded. *Degree requirements:* For master's, thesis, research project, or practicum. *Entrance requirements:* Additional exam requirements/recommendations for international students: Required—TOEFL. *Application deadline:* For fall admission, 6/15 for domestic and international students; for winter admission, 9/15 for domestic and international students; for spring admission, 3/1 for domestic and international students. Applications are processed on a rolling basis. Application fee: $35. *Financial support:* Fellowships, research assistantships with full tuition reimbursements, teaching assistantships with full tuition reimbursements, career-related internships or fieldwork, Federal Work-Study, institutionally sponsored loans, scholarships/grants, tuition waivers (partial), and unspecified assistantships available. Support available to part-time students. Financial award applicants required to submit FAFSA. *Unit head:* Dr. Linda Pritchard, Department Head, 734-487-1177, Fax: 734-487-5029, E-mail: linda.pritchard@emich.edu. *Application contact:* Dr. Deanna Mihaly, Program Advisor, 734-487-1177, Fax: 734-487-5029, E-mail: dmihaly@emich.edu.

Emory University, Laney Graduate School, Department of Comparative Literature, Atlanta, GA 30322-1100. Offers comparative literature (PhD); English (Certificate); French (Certificate); Middle Eastern studies (PhD); philosophy (Certificate); psychoanalytic studies (PhD); religion (PhD); Spanish (Certificate); women studies (Certificate). *Degree requirements:* For doctorate, 2 foreign languages, comprehensive exam, thesis/dissertation. *Entrance requirements:* For doctorate, GRE General Test, minimum GPA of 3.0. Additional exam requirements/recommendations for international students: Required—TOEFL. Electronic applications accepted. *Expenses:* Tuition: Full-time $33,800. Required fees: $1300. *Faculty research:* Literary theory, psychoanalysis trauma and testimony, literature and religion, literature and technology, literature and philosophy, politics and global culture, literature and aesthetics.

Emory University, Laney Graduate School, Department of Spanish and Portuguese, Atlanta, GA 30322-1100. Offers comparative literature (Certificate); film studies (Certificate); Spanish (PhD); women's studies (Certificate). *Degree requirements:* For doctorate, 2 foreign languages, comprehensive exam, thesis/dissertation. *Entrance requirements:* For doctorate, GRE General Test. Additional exam requirements/recommendations for international students: Required—TOEFL. Electronic applications accepted. *Expenses:* Tuition: Full-time $33,800. Required fees: $1300. *Faculty research:* Spanish literature, Spanish-American literature, literary theory, criticism, cultural studies.

Emory University, Laney Graduate School, Department of Women's Studies, Atlanta, GA 30322-1100. Offers PhD. *Degree requirements:* For doctorate, comprehensive exam, thesis/dissertation. *Entrance requirements:* For doctorate, GRE General Test, writing sample. Additional exam requirements/recommendations for international students: Required—TOEFL. Electronic applications accepted. *Expenses:* Tuition: Full-time $33,800. Required fees: $1300. *Faculty research:* Feminist theory, women's literature, African-American literature, gender in cross-cultural perspective, public policy and globalization.

Florida Atlantic University, Dorothy F. Schmidt College of Arts and Letters, Women's Studies Center, Boca Raton, FL 33431-0991. Offers MA, Certificate. *Faculty:* 2 full-time (both women), 3 part-time/adjunct (all women). *Students:* 6 full-time (5 women), 3 part-time (all women); includes 1 minority (Hispanic/Latino), 2 international. Average age 32. 9 applicants, 67% accepted, 4 enrolled. In 2010, 2 master's awarded. *Degree requirements:* For master's, comprehensive exam, thesis or alternative. *Entrance requirements:* For master's, GRE General Test, minimum GPA of 3.0. *Application deadline:* For fall admission, 7/1 for domestic students, 2/15 for international students; for spring admission, 11/1 for domestic students, 7/15 for international students. Applications are processed on a rolling basis. Application fee: $30. *Expenses:* Tuition, area resident: Part-time $319.96 per credit. Tuition, state resident: part-time $319.96 per credit. Tuition, nonresident: part-time $926.42 per credit. *Financial support:* Fellowships with full and partial tuition reimbursements, teaching assistantships with full and partial tuition reimbursements, career-related internships or fieldwork, Federal Work-Study, institutionally sponsored loans, scholarships/grants, and unspecified assistantships available. Support available to part-time students. *Faculty research:* Women and science/technology, feminist theory, violence against women, women and international development, feminist medical anthropology. *Unit head:* Dr. Josephine Beoku-Betts, Director, 561-297-3865, Fax: 561-297-2127. *Application contact:* Dr. Jane Caputi, Professor, 561-297-2056, Fax: 561-297-2127, E-mail: jcaputi@fau.edu.

The George Washington University, Columbian College of Arts and Sciences, Department of Women's Studies, Washington, DC 20052. Offers MA, Certificate. Part-time and evening/weekend programs available. *Faculty:* 1 (woman) full-time, 6 part-time/adjunct (all women). *Students:* 27 full-time (26 women), 14 part-time (all women); includes 1 Black or African American, non-Hispanic/Latino; 4 Hispanic/Latino; 1 Two or more races, non-Hispanic/Latino, 3 international. Average age 27. 42 applicants, 90% accepted, 11 enrolled. In 2010, 12 master's, 3 other advanced degrees awarded. *Degree requirements:* For master's, comprehensive exam, thesis or alternative. *Entrance requirements:* For master's, GRE General Test, minimum GPA of 3.0. Additional exam requirements/recommendations for international students: Required—TOEFL (minimum score 550 paper-based; 213 computer-based; 80 iBT). *Application deadline:* For fall admission, 4/1 priority date for domestic students, 1/15 priority date for international students; for spring admission, 10/1 priority date for domestic students, 9/1 priority date for international students. Applications are processed on a rolling basis. Application fee: $75. Electronic applications accepted. *Financial support:* In 2010–11, 2 students received support; fellowships with tuition reimbursements available, teaching assistantships with tuition reimbursements available, Federal Work-Study, institutionally sponsored loans, and tuition waivers available. Financial award application deadline: 1/15. *Unit head:* Dr. Daniel Moshenberg, Director, 202-994-9086, Fax: 202-994-7249. *Application contact:* Information Contact, 202-994-6942, Fax: 202-994-2249, E-mail: wstu@gwu.edu.

Georgia State University, College of Arts and Sciences, Women's Studies Institute, Atlanta, GA 30302-3083. Offers MA, Graduate Certificate. Part-time programs available. *Degree requirements:* For master's, comprehensive exam, thesis. *Entrance requirements:* For master's, GRE General Test. Additional exam requirements/recommendations for international students: Required—TOEFL. *Faculty research:* Globalization and gender, womanism, sexuality studies, activism, feminist theories.

Graduate School and University Center of the City University of New York, Graduate Studies, Interdisciplinary Studies, New York, NY 10016-4039. Offers language in social context (PhD); medieval studies (PhD); public policy (MA, PhD); urban studies (MA, PhD); women's studies (MA, PhD). Terminal master's awarded for partial completion of doctoral program. *Degree requirements:* For master's, thesis; for doctorate, comprehensive exam, thesis/dissertation. *Entrance requirements:* For master's and doctorate, GRE General Test.

Institute of Transpersonal Psychology, Low-Residency Programs, Palo Alto, CA 94303. Offers counseling psychology (online) (MA); spiritual guidance (MA); women's spirituality (MA). Postbaccalaureate distance learning degree programs offered (minimal on-campus study).

Inter American University of Puerto Rico, Metropolitan Campus, Graduate Programs, Program in Women's and Gender Studies, San Juan, PR 00919-1293. Offers MA.

The Jewish Theological Seminary, The Graduate School, New York, NY 10027-4649. Offers ancient Judaism (MA, DHL, PhD); Bible and ancient Semitic languages (MA, DHL, PhD); interdepartmental studies (MA); Jewish art and visual culture (MA); Jewish gender and women's studies (MA); Jewish history (MA, DHL, PhD); Jewish literature (MA, DHL, PhD); Jewish philosophy (DHL); Jewish thought (MA, PhD); liturgy (MA, DHL, PhD); medieval Jewish studies (MA, DHL, PhD); Midrash (DHL); Midrash and scriptural interpretation (MA, PhD); modern Jewish studies (MA, DHL, PhD); Talmud and rabbinics (MA, DHL, PhD); MA/MSW. MA/MSW offered jointly with Columbia University. *Accreditation:* ACIPE. Part-time programs available. Terminal master's awarded for partial completion of doctoral program. *Degree requirements:* For master's, one foreign language, comprehensive exam (for some programs), thesis (for some programs); for doctorate, 3 foreign languages, comprehensive exam (for some programs), thesis/dissertation. *Entrance requirements:* For master's, GRE or MAT, 3 letters of recommendation, writing sample; for doctorate, GRE or MAT, 3 letters of recommendation, writing research sample. Additional exam requirements/recommendations for international students: Required—TOEFL (minimum score 100 computer-based).

Lakehead University, Graduate Studies, Department of History, Thunder Bay, ON P7B 5E1, Canada. Offers gerontology (MA); history (MA); women's studies (MA). Part-time programs available. *Degree requirements:* For master's, one foreign language, thesis. *Entrance requirements:* For master's, minimum B average. Additional exam requirements/recommendations for international students: Required—TOEFL. *Faculty research:* Canadian history, British history, Russian/German history, women's studies.

Lakehead University, Graduate Studies, Faculty of Education, Thunder Bay, ON P7B 5E1, Canada. Offers educational studies (PhD); gerontology (M Ed); women's studies (M Ed). Part-time and evening/weekend programs available. *Degree requirements:* For master's, project or thesis. *Entrance requirements:* For master's, minimum B average. Additional exam requirements/recommendations for international students: Required—TOEFL. *Faculty research:* Art education, AIDS education, language arts education, gerontology, women's studies.

Lakehead University, Graduate Studies, Faculty of Social Sciences and Humanities, Department of English, Thunder Bay, ON P7B 5E1, Canada. Offers English (MA); women's studies (MA). Part-time and evening/weekend programs available. *Degree requirements:* For master's, one foreign language, thesis optional. *Entrance requirements:* For master's, minimum B average. Additional exam requirements/recommendations for international students: Required—TOEFL. *Faculty research:* Rhetoric and literary studies, children's literature, nineteenth- and twentieth-century American literature, modern literature, women's studies.

Women's Studies

Lakehead University, Graduate Studies, Faculty of Social Sciences and Humanities, Department of Sociology, Thunder Bay, ON P7B 5E1, Canada. Offers gerontology (MA); health services and policy research (MA); sociology (MA); women's studies (MA). Part-time and evening/weekend programs available. *Degree requirements:* For master's, research project or thesis. *Entrance requirements:* For master's, minimum B average. Additional exam requirements/recommendations for international students: Required—TOEFL. *Faculty research:* Sociology of medicine, cultural and social change, health human resources, gerontology, women's studies.

Lakehead University, Graduate Studies, School of Social Work, Thunder Bay, ON P7B 5E1, Canada. Offers gerontology (MSW); social work (MSW); women's studies (MSW). Part-time programs available. *Degree requirements:* For master's, thesis or project. *Entrance requirements:* For master's, minimum B average. Additional exam requirements/recommendations for international students: Required—TOEFL. *Faculty research:* Clinical psychology, social work and practice theory, long-term care, health care for frail elderly, women's studies.

Lakehead University, Graduate Studies, Women's Studies Collaborative Program, Thunder Bay, ON P7B 5E1, Canada. Offers M Ed, MA, MSW. Part-time programs available. *Degree requirements:* For master's, thesis (for some programs). *Entrance requirements:* Additional exam requirements/recommendations for international students: Required—TOEFL. *Faculty research:* Feminist thought, feminist pedagogy, women of literature, Canadian women's history, well-being of women.

Lesley University, Graduate School of Arts and Social Sciences, Self-Designed Master's Program in Interdisciplinary Studies, Cambridge, MA 02138-2790. Offers individualized studies (MA); integrative holistic health (MA); women's studies (MA). Part-time and evening/weekend programs available. Postbaccalaureate distance learning degree programs offered (no on-campus study). *Entrance requirements:* For master's, 3 letters of recommendation. Additional exam requirements/recommendations for international students: Required—TOEFL (minimum score 550 paper-based; 213 computer-based; 80 iBT).

Memorial University of Newfoundland, School of Graduate Studies, Interdisciplinary Program in Women's Studies, St. John's, NL A1C 5S7, Canada. Offers MWS.

Minnesota State University Mankato, College of Graduate Studies, College of Social and Behavioral Sciences, Department of Gender and Women's Studies, Mankato, MN 56001. Offers MS, Certificate. Part-time programs available. *Students:* 12 full-time (11 women), 4 part-time (all women). *Degree requirements:* For master's, comprehensive exam, thesis or alternative. *Entrance requirements:* For master's, minimum GPA of 3.0 during previous 2 years of course work. Additional exam requirements/recommendations for international students: Required—TOEFL. *Application deadline:* For fall admission, 7/1 priority date for domestic students; for spring admission, 11/1 for domestic students. Applications are processed on a rolling basis. Application fee: $40. *Financial support:* Research assistantships, teaching assistantships with full tuition reimbursements, career-related internships or fieldwork, Federal Work-Study, institutionally sponsored loans, and unspecified assistantships available. Support available to part-time students. Financial award application deadline: 3/15; financial award applicants required to submit FAFSA. *Unit head:* Dr. Maria Bevacqua, Chairperson, 507-389-2077. *Application contact:* 507-389-2321, E-mail: grad@mnsu.edu.

Mount Saint Vincent University, Graduate Programs, Department of Women's Studies, Halifax, NS B3M 2J6, Canada. Offers MA. Program offered jointly with Dalhousie University, Saint Mary's University. Part-time programs available. *Degree requirements:* For master's, thesis. Electronic applications accepted.

Northern Arizona University, Graduate College, College of Social and Behavioral Sciences, Women's and Gender Studies Program, Flagstaff, AZ 86011. Offers Graduate Certificate. Part-time programs available. *Faculty:* 2 full-time (both women). *Students:* 1 (woman) full-time, 2 part-time (both women). Average age 25. 3 applicants, 67% accepted, 1 enrolled. In 2010, 5 Graduate Certificates awarded. *Entrance requirements:* Additional exam requirements/recommendations for international students: Required—TOEFL (minimum score 550 paper-based; 213 computer-based; 80 iBT). *Application deadline:* For fall admission, 3/1 priority date for international students; for spring admission, 9/15 priority date for international students. Applications are processed on a rolling basis. Application fee: $65. Electronic applications accepted. *Unit head:* Dr. Sanjam Ahluwalia, Chair, 928-523-8709, E-mail: sanjam.ahluwalia@nau.edu. *Application contact:* Dr. Sanjam Ahluwalia, Chair, 928-523-8709, E-mail: sanjam.ahluwalia@nau.edu.

The Ohio State University, Graduate School, College of Arts and Sciences, Division of Arts and Humanities, Department of Women's Studies, Columbus, OH 43210. Offers MA, PhD. *Faculty:* 63. *Students:* 25 full-time (24 women), 8 part-time (all women); includes 2 Black or African American, non-Hispanic/Latino; 2 Asian, non-Hispanic/Latino; 3 Hispanic/Latino, 6 international. Average age 28. In 2010, 8 master's, 3 doctorates awarded. *Degree requirements:* For master's, thesis optional. *Entrance requirements:* Additional exam requirements/recommendations for international students: Required—TOEFL (minimum score 600 paper-based; 250 computer-based). *Application deadline:* For fall admission, 8/15 priority date for domestic students, 7/1 priority date for international students; for winter admission, 12/1 priority date for domestic students, 11/1 priority date for international students; for spring admission, 3/1 priority date for domestic students, 2/1 priority date for international students. Applications are processed on a rolling basis. Application fee: $40 ($50 for international students). Electronic applications accepted. *Expenses:* Tuition, state resident: full-time $10,605. Tuition, nonresident: full-time $26,535. Tuition and fees vary according to course load and program. *Financial support:* Fellowships, research assistantships, teaching assistantships, career-related internships or fieldwork, Federal Work-Study, institutionally sponsored loans, and unspecified assistantships available. Support available to part-time students. *Unit head:* Jill Bystydzieński, Chair, 614-292-1021, E-mail: bystydzienski.1@osu.edu. *Application contact:* 614-292-9444, Fax: 614-292-3895, E-mail: domestic.grad@osu.edu.

Old Dominion University, College of Arts and Letters, Graduate Program in International Studies, Norfolk, VA 23529. Offers modeling and simulation (MA); women's studies (PhD). Part-time programs available. *Faculty:* 14 full-time (3 women). *Students:* 54 full-time (23 women), 40 part-time (16 women); includes 11 minority (5 Black or African American, non-Hispanic/Latino; 3 Asian, non-Hispanic/Latino; 3 Hispanic/Latino), 28 international. Average age 31. 99 applicants, 54% accepted, 30 enrolled. In 2010, 14 master's, 7 doctorates awarded. Terminal master's awarded for partial completion of doctoral program. *Degree requirements:* For master's, one foreign language, comprehensive exam, thesis optional; for doctorate, one foreign language, comprehensive exam, thesis/dissertation. *Entrance requirements:* For master's, GRE General Test, sample of written work, 2 letters of recommendation; for doctorate, GRE General Test, sample of written work, 3 letters of recommendation. Additional exam requirements/recommendations for international students: Required—TOEFL (minimum score 570 paper-based; 230 computer-based). *Application deadline:* For fall admission, 1/15 for domestic and international students; for spring admission, 10/15 for domestic and international students. Application fee: $40. Electronic applications accepted. *Expenses:* Tuition, state resident: full-time $8592; part-time $358 per credit. Tuition, nonresident: full-time $21,672; part-time $903 per credit. Required fees: $119 per semester. One-time fee: $50. *Financial support:* In 2010–11, 20 students received support, including 2 fellowships (averaging $13,000 per year), 5 research assistantships with tuition reimbursements available (averaging $15,000 per year), 7 teaching assistantships with tuition reimbursements available (averaging $15,000 per year); career-related internships or fieldwork, institutionally sponsored loans, scholarships/grants, and unspecified assistantships also available. Support available to part-time students. Financial award application deadline: 2/15; financial award applicants required to submit FAFSA. *Faculty research:* U. S. foreign policy, international security, transatlantic and transpacific relations, transnational issues, IPE and development. Total annual research expenditures: $330,391. *Unit head:* Dr. Regina Karp, Graduate Program Director, 757-683-5700, Fax: 757-683-5701, E-mail: rkarp@odu.edu. *Application contact:* Dr. Regina Karp, Graduate Program Director, 757-683-5700, Fax: 757-683-5701, E-mail: rkarp@odu.edu.

Queen's University at Kingston, School of Graduate Studies and Research, Faculty of Arts and Sciences, Department of Sociology, Kingston, ON K7L 3N6, Canada. Offers communication and Information technology (MA, PhD); feminist sociology (MA, PhD); socio-legal studies (MA, PhD); sociological theory (MA, PhD). Part-time programs available. *Degree requirements:* For master's, thesis; for doctorate, comprehensive exam, thesis/dissertation. *Entrance requirements:* For master's, honors bachelors degree in sociology; for doctorate, honors bachelors degree, masters degree in sociology. Additional exam requirements/recommendations for international students: Required—TOEFL. *Faculty research:* Social change and modernization, social control, deviance and criminology, surveillance.

Reconstructionist Rabbinical College, Graduate Programs, Wyncote, PA 19095-1898. Offers Jewish studies (MAJS); rabbinics (MAHL, DHL); women's studies (Certificate). Certificate offered jointly with Temple University. Part-time programs available. *Faculty:* 8 full-time (4 women), 25 part-time/adjunct (14 women). *Students:* 52 full-time (37 women), 7 part-time (4 women). 25 applicants, 52% accepted, 11 enrolled. *Degree requirements:* For master's, one foreign language, thesis (MAJS), completion of rabbinical program (MAHL); for doctorate and MAHL, one foreign language. *Entrance requirements:* For MAHL and doctorate, GRE General Test, placement examinations in Hebrew and Judaism; for master's, GRE General Test. *Application deadline:* Applications are processed on a rolling basis. Application fee: $50. *Financial support:* In 2010–11, 46 students received support, including 4 fellowships with full tuition reimbursements available (averaging $11,000 per year), 1 research assistantship with partial tuition reimbursement available (averaging $5,500 per year), 5 teaching assistantships (averaging $5,500 per year); career-related internships or fieldwork, institutionally sponsored loans, and scholarships/grants also available. Financial award application deadline: 4/15. *Faculty research:* Bible, Hebrew Semitic texts, contemporary Judaism. *Unit head:* Rabbi Dan Ehrenkrantz, President, 215-576-0800 Ext. 129, Fax: 215-576-6143, E-mail: dehrenkrantz@rrc.edu. *Application contact:* Rabbi Amber Powers, Dean of Recruitment and Admissions, 215-576-0800 Ext. 145, Fax: 215-576-6143, E-mail: apowers@rrc.edu.

Roosevelt University, Graduate Division, College of Arts and Sciences, Department of Literature and Languages, Program in Women's and Gender Studies, Chicago, IL 60605. Offers MA, Certificate. Part-time and evening/weekend programs available. *Degree requirements:* For master's, thesis. *Entrance requirements:* For master's, minimum GPA of 2.7. *Faculty research:* Feminist economics; philosophy of feminism; race, class, and gender; women and art; women's history.

Rutgers, The State University of New Jersey, New Brunswick, Graduate School-New Brunswick, Department of Political Science, Piscataway, NJ 08854-8097. Offers American politics (PhD); comparative politics (PhD); international relations (PhD); political theory (PhD); public law (PhD); women and politics (PhD). *Degree requirements:* For doctorate, one foreign language, comprehensive exam, thesis/dissertation. *Entrance requirements:* For doctorate, GRE General Test. Additional exam requirements/recommendations for international students: Required—TOEFL. *Expenses:* Tuition, state resident: full-time $7200; part-time $600 per credit. Tuition, nonresident: full-time $11,124; part-time $927 per credit.

Rutgers, The State University of New Jersey, New Brunswick, Graduate School-New Brunswick, Program in Women's and Gender Studies, Piscataway, NJ 08854-8097. Offers MA, PhD. Part-time programs available. *Degree requirements:* For master's, thesis or alternative; for doctorate, comprehensive exam, thesis/dissertation. *Entrance requirements:* For master's and doctorate, GRE General Test, writing sample, 3 letters of recommendation. Additional exam requirements/recommendations for international students: Required—TOEFL. *Expenses:* Tuition, state resident: full-time $7200; part-time $600 per credit. Tuition, nonresident: full-time $11,124; part-time $927 per credit. *Faculty research:* Feminist theory, gender and sexuality, global and cultural studies, women in history, literature, and politics, feminist politics.

Saint Mary's University, Faculty of Arts, Program in Women and Gender Studies, Halifax, NS B3H 3C3, Canada. Offers MA. Program offered jointly with Mount Saint Vincent University. Part-time programs available. *Degree requirements:* For master's, thesis. *Entrance requirements:* For master's, honors degree.

San Diego State University, Graduate and Research Affairs, College of Arts and Letters, Department of Women's Studies, San Diego, CA 92182. Offers MA. *Entrance requirements:* For master's, GRE General Test, 2 letters of reference. Additional exam requirements/recommendations for international students: Required—TOEFL. Electronic applications accepted.

San Francisco State University, Division of Graduate Studies, College of Humanities, Department of Women and Gender Studies, San Francisco, CA 94132-1722. Offers MA. Part-time and evening/weekend programs available. *Unit head:* Dr. Jillian Sandell, Interim Chair, 415-338-1388, E-mail: wgsdept@sfsu.edu. *Application contact:* Dr. Julietta Hua, Graduate Advisor, 415-338-1388.

Sarah Lawrence College, Graduate Studies, Program in Women's History, Bronxville, NY 10708-5999. Offers MA. Part-time programs available. *Degree requirements:* For master's, thesis. *Entrance requirements:* For master's, previous course work in history, minimum B average in undergraduate course work. Additional exam requirements/recommendations for international students: Required—TOEFL (minimum score 600 paper-based).

Simon Fraser University, Graduate Studies, Faculty of Arts and Social Sciences, Department of Women's Studies, Burnaby, BC V5A 1S6, Canada. Offers MA, PhD. *Degree requirements:* For master's, thesis or alternative. *Entrance requirements:* For master's, minimum GPA of 3.8. Additional exam requirements/recommendations for international students: Required—TOEFL or IELTS. *Faculty research:* Theory development, disability, economics, globalization.

Smith College, Graduate and Special Programs, Center for Women in Mathematics Post-Baccalaureate Program, Northampton, MA 01063. Offers Postbaccalaureate Certificate. Part-time programs available. *Faculty:* 12 full-time (5 women). *Students:* 10 full-time (all women); includes 1 Black or African American, non-Hispanic/Latino; 1 Asian, non-Hispanic/Latino; 1 Hispanic/Latino. Average age 26. 17 applicants, 59% accepted, 8 enrolled. In 2010, 7 Postbaccalaureate Certificates awarded. *Entrance requirements:* Additional exam requirements/recommendations for international students: Required—TOEFL. *Application deadline:* For fall admission, 7/1 for domestic students; for spring admission, 12/15 for domestic students. Applications are processed on a rolling basis. Application fee: $60. *Expenses:* Tuition: Full-time $14,520; part-time $1210 per credit. *Financial support:* In 2010–11, 10 students received support. Scholarships/grants and tuition waivers (full) available. Support available to part-time students. *Unit head:* Ruth Haas, Director, 413-585-3872, E-mail: rhaas@smith.edu. *Application contact:* Jim Henle, Director, 413-585-3867, E-mail: jhenle@smith.edu.

Southeastern Baptist Theological Seminary, Graduate and Professional Programs, Wake Forest, NC 27588-1889. Offers advanced biblical studies (M Div); Christian education (M Div, MACE); Christian ethics (PhD); Christian ministry (M Div); Christian planting (M Div); church music (MACM); counseling (MACO); evangelism (PhD); language (M Div); ministry (D Min); New Testament (PhD); Old Testament (PhD); philosophy (PhD); theology (Th M, PhD); women's studies (M Div). *Accreditation:* ACIPE; ATS (one or more programs are accredited). *Degree requirements:* For master's, thesis (for some programs), oral exam; for doctorate, thesis/dissertation, fieldwork; for M Div, supervised ministry. *Entrance requirements:* For master's, Cooperative English Test, minimum GPA of 2.0, M Div or equivalent (Th M); for doctorate, GRE General Test or MAT, Cooperative English Test, M Div or equivalent, 3 years of professional experience.

Southern Connecticut State University, School of Graduate Studies, School of Arts and Sciences, Program in Women's Studies, New Haven, CT 06515-1355. Offers MA. Part-time and evening/weekend programs available. *Faculty:* 1 (woman) full-time. *Students:* 15 full-time

(14 women), 9 part-time (all women); includes 4 Black or African American, non-Hispanic/Latino; 2 Hispanic/Latino. 24 applicants, 42% accepted, 9 enrolled. In 2010, 6 master's awarded. *Degree requirements:* For master's, thesis or alternative. *Entrance requirements:* For master's, interview. *Application deadline:* Applications are processed on a rolling basis. Application fee: $50. Electronic applications accepted. *Expenses:* Tuition, state resident: full-time $5137; part-time $518 per credit. Tuition, nonresident: part-time $542 per credit. Required fees: $4008; $55 per semester. Tuition and fees vary according to program. *Financial support:* Application deadline: 4/15. *Unit head:* Dr. Tricia Lin, Director, 203-392-6832, Fax: 203-392-5670, E-mail: liny4@southernct.edu. *Application contact:* Dr. Tricia Lin, Director, 203-392-6832, Fax: 203-392-5670, E-mail: liny4@southernct.edu.

Stony Brook University, State University of New York, Graduate School, College of Arts and Sciences, Program in Women's Studies, Stony Brook, NY 11794. Offers Certificate. *Students:* 1 (woman) part-time; includes Two or more races, non-Hispanic/Latino. 1 applicant, 0% accepted. *Degree requirements:* For Certificate, interdisciplinary research colloquium. *Entrance requirements:* For degree, GRE, minimum GPA of 2.75, 3 letters of recommendation. *Expenses:* Tuition, state resident: full-time $8370; part-time $349 per credit. Tuition, nonresident: full-time $13,780; part-time $574 per credit. Required fees: $994. *Unit head:* Dr. Nancy Squires, Dean, 631-632-6999, Fax: 631-632-6900. *Application contact:* Barbara Byrne, Assistant Dean for Finance and Budget; Admissions and Records, 631-632-4723, Fax: 631-632-7243, E-mail: barbara.byrne@stonybrook.edu.

Suffolk University, College of Arts and Sciences, Program in Women's Health, Boston, MA 02108-2770. Offers MA. *Faculty:* 9 full-time (7 women), 4 part-time/adjunct (all women). *Students:* 19 full-time (all women), 13 part-time (all women); includes 12 Black or African American, non-Hispanic/Latino; 1 Hispanic/Latino; 1 Two or more races, non-Hispanic/Latino. Average age 28. 57 applicants, 47% accepted, 17 enrolled. In 2010, 16 master's awarded. *Entrance requirements:* For master's, statement of professional goals, official transcripts, 2 letters of recommendation, resume. Additional exam requirements/recommendations for international students: Required—TOEFL (minimum score 550 paper-based; 213 computer-based; 80 iBT). *Application deadline:* For fall admission, 6/15 priority date for domestic students, 6/15 for international students; for spring admission, 11/1 priority date for domestic students, 11/1 for international students. Applications are processed on a rolling basis. Application fee: $50. Electronic applications accepted. *Expenses:* Contact institution. *Financial support:* In 2010–11, 31 students received support, including 25 fellowships (averaging $5,683 per year). Financial award applicants required to submit FAFSA. *Unit head:* Dr. Amy Agigian, Co-Director, 617-573-8487, Fax: 617-994-4278, E-mail: aagigian@suffolk.edu. *Application contact:* Judith Reynolds, Director of Graduate Admissions, 617-573-8302, Fax: 617-305-1733, E-mail: grad.admission@suffolk.edu.

Syracuse University, College of Arts and Sciences, Program in Women's and Gender Studies, Syracuse, NY 13244. Offers CAS. *Students:* 1 applicant, 100% accepted, 0 enrolled. In 2010, 12 CASs awarded. *Entrance requirements:* For degree, Syracuse graduate program matriculation. Additional exam requirements/recommendations for international students: Required—TOEFL (minimum score 100 iBT). *Application deadline:* For fall admission, 2/1 priority date for domestic and international students. Application fee: $75. Electronic applications accepted. *Expenses:* Tuition: Part-time $1162 per credit. *Unit head:* Dr. Chandra Talpade Mohanty, Chair, 315-443-3707, E-mail: ctmohant@syr.edu. *Application contact:* Susann Democker-Shedd, Program contact, 315-443-3560, E-mail: sademock@syr.edu.

Texas Woman's University, Graduate School, College of Arts and Sciences, Program in Women's Studies, Denton, TX 76201. Offers MA, PhD. Part-time and evening/weekend programs available. *Faculty:* 4 full-time (all women). *Students:* 14 full-time (12 women), 47 part-time (45 women); includes 12 Black or African American, non-Hispanic/Latino; 1 American Indian or Alaska Native, non-Hispanic/Latino; 2 Asian, non-Hispanic/Latino; 10 Hispanic/Latino, 1 international. Average age 36. 39 applicants, 72% accepted, 19 enrolled. In 2010, 8 master's awarded. *Degree requirements:* For master's, thesis. *Entrance requirements:* For master's, 2 letters of reference, personal essay; for doctorate, personal essay, writing sample, curriculum vitae, 2 reference letters. Additional exam requirements/recommendations for international students: Required—TOEFL (minimum score 550 paper-based; 213 computer-based; 79 iBT). *Application deadline:* For fall admission, 7/1 priority date for domestic students, 3/1 for international students; for spring admission, 12/1 priority date for domestic students, 7/1 for international students. Applications are processed on a rolling basis. Application fee: $50 ($75 for international students). Electronic applications accepted. *Expenses:* Tuition, state resident: full-time $3834; part-time $213 per credit hour. Tuition, nonresident: full-time $9468; part-time $526 per credit hour. Required fees: $1247; $220 per credit hour. *Financial support:* In 2010–11, 26 students received support, including 14 research assistantships (averaging $12,942 per year), 7 teaching assistantships (averaging $12,942 per year); career-related internships or fieldwork, Federal Work-Study, institutionally sponsored loans, scholarships/grants, traineeships, health care benefits, and unspecified assistantships also available. Support available to part-time students. Financial award application deadline: 3/1; financial award applicants required to submit FAFSA. *Faculty research:* Feminist/womanist theories and epistemologies, history of U. S. feminism, U. S. women of color, feminism and religion/spirituality, critical race theories. *Unit head:* Dr. Claire L. Sahlin, Director, 940-898-2119, Fax: 940-898-2101, E-mail: womenstudies@twu.edu. *Application contact:* Dr. Samuel Wheeler, Assistant Director of Admissions, 940-898-3188, Fax: 940-898-3081, E-mail: wheelersr@twu.edu.

Towson University, Program in Women's Studies, Towson, MD 21252-0001. Offers MS, Certificate. *Students:* 24 full-time (23 women), 15 part-time (14 women); includes 11 minority (8 Black or African American, non-Hispanic/Latino; 1 Asian, non-Hispanic/Latino; 2 Two or more races, non-Hispanic/Latino), 3 international. Average age 33. In 2010, 5 master's, 2 other advanced degrees awarded. *Degree requirements:* For master's, thesis optional. *Entrance requirements:* For master's, minimum GPA of 3.0, 9 credits of course work in women's studies and/or the social sciences. *Application deadline:* Applications are processed on a rolling basis. Application fee: $50. Electronic applications accepted. *Expenses:* Tuition, state resident: part-time $324 per credit. Tuition, nonresident: part-time $681 per credit. Required fees: $95 per term. *Financial support:* Application deadline: 4/1. *Faculty research:* Gender and international relations, health, economics, violence against women, public policy. *Unit head:* Celia Bardwell-Jones, Graduate Program Director, 410-704-2860, Fax: 410-704-3469, E-mail: cbardwelljones@towson.edu. *Application contact:* 410-704-2501, Fax: 410-704-4675, E-mail: grads@towson.edu.

United Theological Seminary of the Twin Cities, Graduate Programs, New Brighton, MN 55112-2598. Offers advanced theological studies (Diploma); justice and peace studies (M Div, MA); leadership toward racial justice (M Div, MA, Certificate); Methodist studies (M Div, MA, Certificate); ministry (D Min); ministry renewal and professional development (Certificate); pastoral care and counseling (M Div, MA, MARL); religion and theology (MA); theological and religious studies (Certificate); theology and the arts (M Div, MA); urban ministry (M Div, MA, MARL); women's studies: religion, theology and ministry (M Div, MA). *Accreditation:* ACIPE; ATS. Part-time and evening/weekend programs available. *Faculty:* 8 full-time (5 women), 28 part-time/adjunct (16 women). *Students:* 57 full-time (41 women), 94 part-time (61 women); includes 6 minority (5 Black or African American, non-Hispanic/Latino; 1 Hispanic/Latino), 1 international. Average age 47. 49 applicants, 98% accepted, 41 enrolled. In 2010, 10 first professional degrees, 6 master's, 4 doctorates, 2 other advanced degrees awarded. *Degree requirements:* For master's, thesis; for doctorate, comprehensive exam, thesis/dissertation; for M Div, integrative notebook, spiritual chronicle. *Entrance requirements:* For M Div and master's, minimum GPA of 2.75; strong analytical, reflective thinking and writing skills; vocational and academic goals compatible with those of Seminary; for doctorate, M Div or equivalent, minimum GPA of 3.0, 3 years experience in professional ministry; for other advanced degree, BA or equivalent life experience; strong analytical, reflective thinking and writing skills (Certificate); proficiency in English language, previous study of theology at a theological school, recommendation of student's denomination (Diploma). Additional exam requirements/recommendations for international students: Required—TOEFL (minimum score 550 paper-based). *Application deadline:* For fall admission, 7/1 priority date for domestic students, 11/1 priority date for international students; for winter admission, 11/1 priority date for domestic students; for spring admission, 11/15 priority date for domestic students. Applications are processed on a rolling basis. Application fee: $50. *Expenses:* Tuition: Full-time $13,014; part-time $482 per credit hour. One-time fee: $170. Tuition and fees vary according to course load, degree level and program. *Financial support:* In 2010–11, 120 students received support. Career-related internships or fieldwork, institutionally sponsored loans, and scholarships/grants available. Support available to part-time students. Financial award application deadline: 5/1; financial award applicants required to submit FAFSA. *Unit head:* Prof. Susan K. Ebbers, Dean of the Seminary, 651-255-6143 Ext. 108, Fax: 651-633-4315, E-mail: sebbers@unitedseminary.edu. *Application contact:* Rev. Glen Herrington-Hall, Director of Admissions, 651-255-6107 Ext. 107, Fax: 651-633-4315, E-mail: gherrington-hall@unitedseminary.edu.

Université Laval, Faculty of Social Sciences, Program in Feminist Studies, Québec, QC G1K 7P4, Canada. Offers Diploma. Part-time programs available. *Entrance requirements:* For degree, knowledge of French, comprehension of written English. Electronic applications accepted.

University at Albany, State University of New York, College of Arts and Sciences, Department of Women's Studies, Albany, NY 12222-0001. Offers MA, DA. *Entrance requirements:* Additional exam requirements/recommendations for international students: Required—TOEFL (minimum score 550 paper-based; 213 computer-based). Electronic applications accepted. *Faculty research:* Feminist pedagogy, lesbian and gay studies, women in the African diaspora, women's health policy, literature of feminism.

The University of Alabama, Graduate School, College of Arts and Sciences, Department of Gender and Race Studies, Tuscaloosa, AL 35487. Offers women's studies (MA). Part-time programs available. *Faculty:* 6 full-time (5 women). *Students:* 11 full-time (10 women), 3 part-time (all women); includes 5 minority (3 Black or African American, non-Hispanic/Latino; 1 Hispanic/Latino; 1 Two or more races, non-Hispanic/Latino). Average age 26. 9 applicants, 67% accepted, 4 enrolled. In 2010, 7 master's awarded. *Degree requirements:* For master's, comprehensive exam, thesis optional. *Entrance requirements:* For master's, MAT or GRE. Additional exam requirements/recommendations for international students: Required—TOEFL. *Application deadline:* For fall admission, 3/7 priority date for domestic students, 3/7 for international students. Applications are processed on a rolling basis. Application fee: $50 ($60 for international students). Electronic applications accepted. *Expenses:* Tuition, state resident: full-time $7900. Tuition, nonresident: full-time $20,500. *Financial support:* In 2010–11, 6 students received support, including 3 research assistantships with tuition reimbursements available (averaging $10,908 per year), 3 teaching assistantships with tuition reimbursements available (averaging $10,908 per year); health care benefits and unspecified assistantships also available. Financial award application deadline: 4/1. *Faculty research:* Black feminist theory, African-American women's discursive practices, black women's leadership, feminist theory, queer theory. *Unit head:* Dr. DoVeanna S. Minor, Chair, 205-348-8462, Fax: 205-348-3584, E-mail: dfulton@as.ua.edu. *Application contact:* Dr. DoVeanna S. Minor, Director of Graduate Studies, 205-348-8462, Fax: 205-348-3584, E-mail: dfulton@as.ua.edu.

The University of Arizona, College of Social and Behavioral Sciences, Department of Gender and Women's Studies, Tucson, AZ 85721. Offers MA, PhD. Part-time programs available. *Faculty:* 5 full-time (4 women), 4 part-time/adjunct (all women). *Students:* 7 full-time (5 women), 4 part-time (all women); includes 2 Hispanic/Latino; 1 Two or more races, non-Hispanic/Latino, 2 international. Average age 29. 18 applicants, 44% accepted, 1 enrolled. In 2010, 4 master's awarded. *Degree requirements:* For master's, thesis/project. *Entrance requirements:* For master's and doctorate, GRE (minimum score: 500 verbal, 500 quantitative, 4.5 analytical), 3 letters of recommendation. Additional exam requirements/recommendations for international students: Required—TOEFL (minimum score 600 paper-based; 250 computer-based; 100 iBT). *Application deadline:* For fall admission, 12/1 for domestic and international students. Applications are processed on a rolling basis. Application fee: $65. Electronic applications accepted. *Expenses:* Tuition, state resident: full-time $7692. *Financial support:* In 2010–11, 3 research assistantships with full tuition reimbursements (averaging $18,282 per year), 12 teaching assistantships with full tuition reimbursements (averaging $18,282 per year) were awarded; career-related internships or fieldwork, scholarships/grants, health care benefits, tuition waivers (full and partial), and unspecified assistantships also available. Financial award application deadline: 1/15. *Faculty research:* Gender race and border studies, sexuality and the body, gender health and science, cultural representation and theory, public policy and social movements. Total annual research expenditures: $106,592. *Unit head:* Dr. Laura Briggs, Department Head, 520-626-9149, Fax: 520-621-1533, E-mail: lbirggs@email.arizona.edu. *Application contact:* Susan D. Whitworth, Information Contact, 520-626-5657, Fax: 520-621-1533, E-mail: whitwort@email.arizona.edu.

University of California, Los Angeles, Graduate Division, College of Letters and Science, Program in Women's Studies, Los Angeles, CA 90095. Offers MA, PhD. *Faculty:* 7 full-time (all women). *Students:* 25 full-time (24 women); includes 13 minority (3 Black or African American, non-Hispanic/Latino; 1 American Indian or Alaska Native, non-Hispanic/Latino; 5 Asian, non-Hispanic/Latino; 4 Hispanic/Latino), 2 international. Average age 31. 37 applicants, 8% accepted, 1 enrolled. In 2010, 2 doctorates awarded. Terminal master's awarded for partial completion of doctoral program. *Degree requirements:* For master's, comprehensive exam or thesis; for doctorate, one foreign language, thesis/dissertation, written and oral exams. *Entrance requirements:* For master's, GRE General Test; for doctorate, GRE General Test, minimum undergraduate GPA of 3.0. *Application deadline:* For fall admission, 12/15 for domestic and international students. Application fee: $70 ($90 for international students). Electronic applications accepted. *Financial support:* In 2010–11, 23 fellowships with full and partial tuition reimbursements, 16 research assistantships with full and partial tuition reimbursements, 15 teaching assistantships with full and partial tuition reimbursements were awarded; Federal Work-Study, institutionally sponsored loans, scholarships/grants, health care benefits, tuition waivers (full and partial), and unspecified assistantships also available. Financial award applicants required to submit FAFSA. *Unit head:* Dr. Christine Littleton, Chair, 310-206-8101. *Application contact:* Department Office, 310-206-8101, E-mail: women@women.ucla.edu.

University of California, Santa Barbara, Graduate Division, College of Letters and Science, Division of Humanities and Fine Arts, Department of English, Santa Barbara, CA 93106-3170. Offers English (PhD); European medieval studies (PhD); feminist studies (PhD); global studies (PhD); technology and society (PhD); MA/PhD. *Faculty:* 26 full-time (13 women), 17 part-time/adjunct (12 women). *Students:* 68 full-time (37 women); includes 2 Black or African American, non-Hispanic/Latino; 5 Asian, non-Hispanic/Latino; 2 Hispanic/Latino. Average age 30. 173 applicants, 12% accepted, 8 enrolled. In 2010, 4 doctorates awarded. Terminal master's awarded for partial completion of doctoral program. *Degree requirements:* For doctorate, one foreign language, comprehensive exam, thesis/dissertation. *Entrance requirements:* For doctorate, GRE General Test, GRE Subject Test (English). Additional exam requirements/recommendations for international students: Required—TOEFL (minimum score 550 paper-based; 80 iBT), IELTS (minimum score 7). *Application deadline:* For fall admission, 12/15 priority date for domestic and international students. Application fee: $70 ($90 for international students). Electronic applications accepted. *Financial support:* In 2010–11, 68 students received support, including 38 fellowships with full and partial tuition reimbursements available (averaging $9,204 per year), 3 research assistantships with full and partial tuition reimbursements available (averaging $10,512 per year), 50 teaching assistantships with full and partial tuition reimbursements available (averaging $13,031 per year); career-related internships or fieldwork and tuition waivers (full and partial) also available. Financial award application deadline: 12/15; financial award applicants required to submit FAFSA. *Faculty research:* Medieval, Romantic, and Victorian studies; gender studies and feminist theory; literature and the mind; American literature; literature and new media/information culture. Total annual research expenditures: $25,000. *Unit head:* Prof. Ken Hiltner, Graduate Program Chair, 805-564-2304, Fax: 805-893-7492, E-mail: hiltner@english.ucsb.edu. *Application contact:* Mary Rae Staton, Graduate Program Staff Advisor, 805-893-2639, Fax: 805-893-7492, E-mail: staton@hfa.ucsb.edu.

Women's Studies

University of California, Santa Barbara, Graduate Division, College of Letters and Sciences, Division of Humanities and Fine Arts, Department of History, Santa Barbara, CA 93106-9410. Offers ancient Mediterranean studies (PhD); European medieval studies (PhD); feminist studies (PhD); global studies (PhD); history (PhD); public history (PhD); technology and society (PhD); MA/PhD. *Faculty:* 42 full-time (18 women), 10 part-time/adjunct (6 women). *Students:* 92 full-time (50 women); includes 1 Black or African American, non-Hispanic/Latino; 6 Asian, non-Hispanic/Latino; 11 Hispanic/Latino. Average age 34. 124 applicants, 19% accepted, 8 enrolled. In 2010, 20 doctorates awarded. *Degree requirements:* For doctorate, variable foreign language requirement, comprehensive exam, thesis/dissertation. *Entrance requirements:* For doctorate, GRE. Additional exam requirements/recommendations for international students: Required—TOEFL (minimum score 550 paper-based; 80 iBT), IELTS (minimum score 7). *Application deadline:* For fall admission, 12/5 priority date for domestic and international students. Application fee: $70 ($90 for international students). Electronic applications accepted. *Financial support:* In 2010–11, 92 students received support, including 68 fellowships with full and partial tuition reimbursements available (averaging $6,583 per year), 4 research assistantships with full and partial tuition reimbursements available (averaging $5,862 per year), 57 teaching assistantships with full and partial tuition reimbursements available (averaging $12,123 per year); tuition waivers (partial) also available. Financial award application deadline: 12/5; financial award applicants required to submit FAFSA. *Faculty research:* Europe, U. S., Latin America, Africa, Middle East, East Asia. *Unit head:* John Majewski, Chair, 805-893-2837, E-mail: majewski@history.ucrb.edu. *Application contact:* Sharon Farmer, Director of Graduate Studies, 805-893-3398, E-mail: farmer@history.ucsb.edu.

University of California, Santa Barbara, Graduate Division, College of Letters and Sciences, Division of Humanities and Fine Arts, Department of History of Art and Architecture, Santa Barbara, CA 93106-2014. Offers art history (PhD), including art history, European medieval studies, feminist studies; MA/PhD. *Faculty:* 18 full-time (8 women), 6 part-time/adjunct (2 women). *Students:* 45 full-time (40 women); includes 7 Asian, non-Hispanic/Latino; 4 Hispanic/Latino. Average age 32. 93 applicants, 11% accepted, 8 enrolled. In 2010, 3 doctorates awarded. Terminal master's awarded for partial completion of doctoral program. *Degree requirements:* For doctorate, 2 foreign languages, comprehensive exam, thesis/dissertation. *Entrance requirements:* For doctorate, GRE. Additional exam requirements/recommendations for international students: Required—TOEFL (minimum score 550 paper-based; 80 iBT), IELTS (minimum score 7). *Application deadline:* For fall admission, 12/15 priority date for domestic and international students. Application fee: $70 ($90 for international students). Electronic applications accepted. *Financial support:* In 2010–11, 31 students received support, including 24 fellowships with full tuition reimbursements available (averaging $9,585 per year), 1 research assistantship with full and partial tuition reimbursement available (averaging $15,896 per year), 21 teaching assistantships with partial tuition reimbursements available (averaging $11,884 per year); career-related internships or fieldwork, institutionally sponsored loans, and tuition waivers (full and partial) also available. Financial award application deadline: 12/15; financial award applicants required to submit FAFSA. *Faculty research:* History of architecture, Renaissance-Italian, Baroque, American. Total annual research expenditures: $72,000. *Unit head:* Prof. Ulrich Keller, Chair, 805-893-8710, Fax: 805-893-7117, E-mail: ukeller@arthisory.ucsb.edu. *Application contact:* Graduate Program Administrator, 805-893-2454, Fax: 805-893-7117, E-mail: lfredrickson@hfa.ucsb.edu.

University of California, Santa Barbara, Graduate Division, College of Letters and Sciences, Division of Humanities and Fine Arts, Department of Music, Santa Barbara, CA 93106-6070. Offers brass (MM); composition (MA, PhD); conducting (MM, DMA); ethnomusicology (MA, PhD); feminist studies (PhD); keyboard (MM, DMA); musicology (MA, PhD); piano accompanying (MM); strings (MM, DMA, PhD); theory (MA, PhD); voice (MM, DMA); woodwinds (MM); MA/PhD; MM/DMA. *Faculty:* 28 full-time (6 women), 17 part-time/adjunct (6 women). *Students:* 73 full-time (31 women); includes 5 Asian, non-Hispanic/Latino; 3 Hispanic/Latino; 1 Native Hawaiian or other Pacific Islander, non-Hispanic/Latino. Average age 28. 94 applicants, 28% accepted, 15 enrolled. In 2010, 8 master's, 2 doctorates awarded. *Degree requirements:* For master's, variable foreign language requirement, comprehensive exam (for some programs), thesis (for some programs); for doctorate, variable foreign language requirement, comprehensive exam, thesis/dissertation. *Entrance requirements:* For master's and doctorate, GRE. Additional exam requirements/recommendations for international students: Required—TOEFL (minimum score 550 paper-based; 80 iBT), IELTS (minimum score 7). *Application deadline:* For fall admission, 1/15 for domestic and international students. Application fee: $70 ($90 for international students). Electronic applications accepted. *Financial support:* In 2010–11, 66 students received support, including 50 fellowships with full and partial tuition reimbursements available (averaging $5,728 per year), 1 research assistantship with full and partial tuition reimbursement available (averaging $1,778 per year), 37 teaching assistantships with partial tuition reimbursements available (averaging $9,866 per year); career-related internships or fieldwork, Federal Work-Study, institutionally sponsored loans, health care benefits, tuition waivers (full and partial), and unspecified assistantships also available. Financial award application deadline: 1/15; financial award applicants required to submit FAFSA. *Faculty research:* Music theory, ethnomusicology, musicology, music performance, music composition. *Unit head:* Dr. Paul Berkowitz, Chair, Fax: 805-893-7194. *Application contact:* Carly Yartz, Student Affairs Officer, 805-893-4603, Fax: 805-893-7194, E-mail: cyartz@music.ucsb.edu.

University of California, Santa Barbara, Graduate Division, College of Letters and Sciences, Division of Humanities and Fine Arts, Department of Religious Studies, Santa Barbara, CA 93106-3130. Offers ancient Mediterranean studies (PhD); European medieval studies (PhD); feminist studies (PhD); global studies (PhD); religious studies (MA, PhD); translation studies (PhD); MA/PhD. *Faculty:* 19 full-time (9 women), 8 part-time/adjunct (3 women). *Students:* 79 full-time (29 women); includes 2 Black or African American, non-Hispanic/Latino; 1 American Indian or Alaska Native, non-Hispanic/Latino; 9 Asian, non-Hispanic/Latino; 5 Hispanic/Latino. Average age 31. 139 applicants, 22% accepted, 10 enrolled. In 2010, 11 master's, 10 doctorates awarded. *Degree requirements:* For master's, one foreign language, comprehensive exam (for some programs), thesis (for some programs), colloquium; for doctorate, one foreign language, thesis/dissertation, methodology, colloquium. *Entrance requirements:* For master's and doctorate, GRE General Test. Additional exam requirements/recommendations for international students: Required—TOEFL (minimum score 550 paper-based; 80 iBT), IELTS (minimum score 7). *Application deadline:* For fall admission, 12/1 for domestic and international students. Application fee: $70 ($90 for international students). Electronic applications accepted. *Financial support:* In 2010–11, 64 students received support, including 31 fellowships with full tuition reimbursements available (averaging $12,351 per year), 4 research assistantships with full and partial tuition reimbursements available (averaging $4,147 per year), 37 teaching assistantships with partial tuition reimbursements available (averaging $9,573 per year); career-related internships or fieldwork, scholarships/grants, tuition waivers (full and partial), and associateships also available. Financial award application deadline: 12/1; financial award applicants required to submit FAFSA. *Faculty research:* Area studies; religious traditions; theory and method in the study of religion; religion, culture, and politics; spirituality and religious experience. *Unit head:* Prof. Jose I. Cabezon, Professor and Chair, 805-893-3564, Fax: 805-893-7671, E-mail: jcabezon@religion.ucsb.edu. *Application contact:* Sally J. Lombrozo, Graduate Program Assistant, 805-893-2744, Fax: 805-893-7671, E-mail: lombrozo@hfa.ucsb.edu.

University of California, Santa Barbara, Graduate Division, College of Letters and Sciences, Division of Humanities and Fine Arts, Department of Spanish and Portuguese, Santa Barbara, CA 93106-4150. Offers Hispanic languages and literature (PhD), including European medieval studies, feminist studies, Hispanic linguistics, Hispanic literature, Luso-Brazilian literature; Hispanic linguistics (MA); Luso-Brazilian literature (MA); Spanish or Spanish-American literature (MA); MA/PhD. Spanish Language Institute available during summer session. *Faculty:* 16 full-time (7 women). *Students:* 32 full-time (22 women); includes 1 Black or African American, non-Hispanic/Latino; 1 Asian, non-Hispanic/Latino; 9 Hispanic/Latino. Average age 32. 34 applicants, 26% accepted, 5 enrolled. In 2010, 3 master's, 3 doctorates awarded. Terminal master's awarded for partial completion of doctoral program. *Degree requirements:* For master's, 2 foreign languages, comprehensive exam (for some programs), thesis optional; for doctorate, 3 foreign languages, comprehensive exam, thesis/dissertation. *Entrance requirements:* For master's and doctorate, GRE. Additional exam requirements/recommendations for international students: Required—TOEFL (minimum score 550 paper-based; 80 iBT), IELTS (minimum score 7). *Application deadline:* For fall admission, 12/15 for domestic and international students. Application fee: $70 ($90 for international students). Electronic applications accepted. *Financial support:* In 2010–11, 32 students received support, including 12 fellowships with full and partial tuition reimbursements available (averaging $10,016 per year), 27 teaching assistantships with full and partial tuition reimbursements available (averaging $14,583 per year); career-related internships or fieldwork, Federal Work-Study, tuition waivers (full and partial), and unspecified assistantships also available. Financial award application deadline: 12/15; financial award applicants required to submit FAFSA. *Faculty research:* Nineteenth century Spanish and Portuguese literature, Spanish and Spanish American literature, nineteenth and twentieth century Portuguese and Brazilian literatures, Hispanic linguistics, Catalan language and culture. *Unit head:* Prof. Francisco A. Lomeli, Chair, 805-893-5715, Fax: 805-893-8341, E-mail: lomeli@spanport.ucsb.edu. *Application contact:* Ashley Bradbury, Graduate Program Assistant, 805-893-2131, Fax: 805-893-8341, E-mail: ashley@hfa.ucsb.edu.

University of California, Santa Barbara, Graduate Division, College of Letters and Sciences, Division of Humanities and Fine Arts, Department of Theatre and Dance, Santa Barbara, CA 93106-7060. Offers theater studies (MA, PhD), including european medieval studies (PhD), feminist studies (PhD), theatre studies (PhD); MA/PhD. *Faculty:* 8 full-time (4 women). *Students:* 14 full-time (9 women); includes 2 Black or African American, non-Hispanic/Latino; 1 Hispanic/Latino. Average age 31. 22 applicants, 41% accepted, 3 enrolled. In 2010, 3 master's, 5 doctorates awarded. Terminal master's awarded for partial completion of doctoral program. *Degree requirements:* For master's, comprehensive exam, thesis; for doctorate, one foreign language, comprehensive exam, thesis/dissertation. *Entrance requirements:* For master's and doctorate, GRE. Additional exam requirements/recommendations for international students: Required—TOEFL (minimum score 550 paper-based; 80 iBT), IELTS (minimum score 7). *Application deadline:* For fall admission, 1/5 priority date for domestic and international students. Application fee: $70 ($90 for international students). Electronic applications accepted. *Financial support:* In 2010–11, 14 students received support, including 11 fellowships with full tuition reimbursements available (averaging $7,764 per year), 14 teaching assistantships with full and partial tuition reimbursements available (averaging $13,666 per year). Financial award applicants required to submit FAFSA. *Faculty research:* English and American theater and Ancient Greek; Spanish, Latin-American and Caribbean performance; Renaissance and Baroque drama, and intercultural theory; East Asian performance, gender and nationalism; Korean cultural studies, Russian literature, and Slavic folklore; history of German theater, Shakespeare, and European opera; postcolonialism, performance-based ethnography, globalism and national identity formation in Africa. *Unit head:* Prof. Simon Williams, Chairperson, 805-893-5515, Fax: 805-893-7029, E-mail: williams@theaterdance.ucsb.edu. *Application contact:* Mary Tench, Graduate Program Assistant, 805-893-3147, Fax: 805-893-7029, E-mail: mtench@theaterdance.ucsb.edu.

University of California, Santa Barbara, Graduate Division, College of Letters and Sciences, Division of Humanities and Fine Arts, Program in Comparative Literature, Santa Barbara, CA 93106-4130. Offers comparative literature (PhD); East Asian literatures (PhD); feminist studies (PhD); French (PhD); global studies (PhD); translation studies (PhD); MA/PhD. *Faculty:* 63 full-time (31 women). *Students:* 21 full-time (14 women); includes 3 Asian, non-Hispanic/Latino; 2 Hispanic/Latino. Average age 31. 41 applicants, 12% accepted, 2 enrolled. In 2010, 1 doctorate awarded. *Degree requirements:* For doctorate, 2 foreign languages, comprehensive exam, thesis/dissertation. *Entrance requirements:* For doctorate, GRE. Additional exam requirements/recommendations for international students: Required—TOEFL (minimum score 550 paper-based; 80 iBT), IELTS (minimum score 7). *Application deadline:* For fall admission, 12/15 for domestic and international students. Application fee: $70 ($90 for international students). Electronic applications accepted. *Financial support:* In 2010–11, 19 students received support, including 14 fellowships with full and partial tuition reimbursements available (averaging $16,232 per year), 12 teaching assistantships with partial tuition reimbursements available (averaging $12,826 per year); research assistantships, Federal Work-Study, institutionally sponsored loans, scholarships/grants, health care benefits, and tuition waivers (full and partial) also available. Financial award application deadline: 12/15; financial award applicants required to submit FAFSA. *Faculty research:* Comparative literary studies in global context, critical theory, translation studies, mediatechnological studies, trauma studies. *Unit head:* Prof. Susan Derwin, Chair, 805-893-4399, Fax: 805-893-8341, E-mail: derwin@gss.ucsb.edu. *Application contact:* Ashley Bradbury, Graduate Program Assistant, 805-893-2131, Fax: 805-893-8341, E-mail: ashley@hfa.ucsb.edu.

University of California, Santa Barbara, Graduate Division, College of Letters and Sciences, Division of Social Sciences, Department of Communication, Santa Barbara, CA 93106-4020. Offers cognitive science (PhD); feminist studies (PhD); quantitative methods in the social science (PhD); society and technology (PhD); MA/PhD. *Faculty:* 20 full-time (9 women). *Students:* 39 full-time (26 women); includes 3 Black or African American, non-Hispanic/Latino; 5 Asian, non-Hispanic/Latino; 6 Hispanic/Latino. Average age 30. 169 applicants, 6% accepted, 5 enrolled. In 2010, 3 doctorates awarded. Terminal master's awarded for partial completion of doctoral program. *Degree requirements:* For doctorate, comprehensive exam, thesis/dissertation. *Entrance requirements:* For doctorate, GRE. Additional exam requirements/recommendations for international students: Required—TOEFL (minimum score 550 paper-based; 80 iBT), IELTS (minimum score 7). *Application deadline:* For fall admission, 12/1 for domestic and international students. Application fee: $70 ($90 for international students). Electronic applications accepted. *Financial support:* In 2010–11, 39 students received support, including 39 fellowships with full and partial tuition reimbursements available (averaging $6,045 per year), 5 research assistantships with full and partial tuition reimbursements available (averaging $9,646 per year), 29 teaching assistantships with partial tuition reimbursements available (averaging $14,294 per year); career-related internships or fieldwork, health care benefits, and tuition waivers (full and partial) also available. Support available to part-time students. Financial award application deadline: 12/1. *Faculty research:* Interpersonal, intercultural, organizational, health, media. *Unit head:* Prof. Linda L. Putnam, Professor, 805-893-7935, Fax: 805-893-7102, E-mail: lputnam@comm.ucsb.edu. *Application contact:* Nancy Siris-Rawls, Graduate Program Assistant, 805-893-3046, Fax: 805-893-7102, E-mail: nsiris@comm.ucsb.edu.

University of California, Santa Barbara, Graduate Division, College of Letters and Sciences, Division of Social Sciences, Department of Feminist Studies, Santa Barbara, CA 93106-7110. Offers MA, PhD, MA/PhD. *Faculty:* 9 full-time (all women), 1 (woman) part-time/adjunct. *Students:* 7 full-time (all women); includes 1 Hispanic/Latino. Average age 26. 48 applicants, 10% accepted, 4 enrolled. In 2010, 1 master's awarded. Terminal master's awarded for partial completion of doctoral program. *Degree requirements:* For master's, thesis (for some programs); for doctorate, one foreign language, comprehensive exam, thesis/dissertation. *Entrance requirements:* For master's and doctorate, GRE. Additional exam requirements/recommendations for international students: Required—TOEFL (minimum score 550 paper-based; 80 iBT), IELTS (minimum score 7). *Application deadline:* For fall admission, 12/15 for domestic and international students. Application fee: $70 ($90 for international students). Electronic applications accepted. *Financial support:* In 2010–11, 4 students received support, including 3 fellowships with full and partial tuition reimbursements available (averaging $21,667 per year); tuition waivers (full and partial) also available. Financial award application deadline: 12/15; financial award applicants required to submit FAFSA. *Faculty research:* Genders and sexualities, productive and reproductive labors, race and nation, discourse and theory, media and new technologies. *Unit head:* Prof. Leila J. Rupp, Graduate Director, 805-893-6130, Fax: 805-893-8676, E-mail: lrupp@femst.ucsb.edu. *Application contact:* Christina Toy, Graduate Program Assistant, 805-893-4330, Fax: 805-893-8676, E-mail: christina@femst.ucsb.edu.

University of California, Santa Barbara, Graduate Division, College of Letters and Sciences, Division of Social Sciences, Department of Sociology, Santa Barbara, CA 93106-9430. Offers feminist studies (PhD); global studies (PhD); language, interaction and social organization (PhD); quantitative methods in the social sciences (PhD); technology and society (PhD);

MA/PhD. *Faculty:* 35 full-time (14 women). *Students:* 71 full-time (44 women); includes 5 Black or African American, non-Hispanic/Latino; 4 Asian, non-Hispanic/Latino; 21 Hispanic/Latino. Average age 30. 162 applicants, 8% accepted, 6 enrolled. In 2010, 13 doctorates awarded. Terminal master's awarded for partial completion of doctoral program. *Degree requirements:* For doctorate, comprehensive exam, thesis/dissertation. *Entrance requirements:* For doctorate, GRE General Test. Additional exam requirements/recommendations for international students: Required—TOEFL (minimum score 550 paper-based; 80 iBT), IELTS (minimum score 7). *Application deadline:* For fall admission, 12/1 for domestic and international students. Application fee: $70 ($90 for international students). Electronic applications accepted. *Financial support:* In 2010–11, 60 students received support, including 40 fellowships with full and partial tuition reimbursements available (averaging $10,059 per year), 4 research assistantships with full and partial tuition reimbursements available (averaging $10,166 per year), 43 teaching assistantships with full and partial tuition reimbursements available (averaging $11,913 per year); career-related internships or fieldwork, Federal Work-Study, institutionally sponsored loans, scholarships/grants, health care benefits, tuition waivers (full and partial), and unspecified assistantships also available. Financial award application deadline: 12/1. *Faculty research:* Feminist studies/sexualities, race ethnicity, global, culture, conversation analysis. *Unit head:* Prof. Verta Taylor, Chair, 805-893-3118, Fax: 805-893-3324. *Application contact:* Sharon Applegate, Graduate Program Assistant, 805-893-3328, Fax: 805-893-3324, E-mail: grad-soc@soc.ucsb.edu.

University of Cincinnati, Graduate School, McMicken College of Arts and Sciences, Department of Women's, Gender, and Sexuality Studies, Cincinnati, OH 45221-0164. Offers MA, Certificate, MA/JD. Part-time programs available. *Faculty:* 10 full-time (all women). *Students:* 29 full-time (28 women), 6 part-time (all women); includes 2 Black or African American, non-Hispanic/Latino; 6 Asian, non-Hispanic/Latino; 2 Hispanic/Latino, 5 international. Average age 25. 29 applicants, 83% accepted, 12 enrolled. In 2010, 8 master's awarded. *Degree requirements:* For master's, comprehensive exam, final paper/project. *Entrance requirements:* For master's, GRE General Test, 3 letters of recommendation. Additional exam requirements/recommendations for international students: Required—TOEFL (minimum score 600 paper-based), IELTS (minimum score 6.5). *Application deadline:* For fall admission, 1/15 for domestic and international students. Application fee: $45. Electronic applications accepted. *Financial support:* In 2010–11, 16 students received support, including 2 fellowships with full tuition reimbursements available (averaging $12,000 per year), 8 research assistantships with full and partial tuition reimbursements available (averaging $10,800 per year), 6 teaching assistantships with full tuition reimbursements available (averaging $10,800 per year); career-related internships or fieldwork, Federal Work-Study, institutionally sponsored loans, scholarships/grants, tuition waivers (partial), unspecified assistantships, and partial health premium waiver also available. Financial award application deadline: 1/15; financial award applicants required to submit FAFSA. *Faculty research:* Feminist legal issues, sexuality, international political economy, Latin America, cultural/literary and environmental studies. Total annual research expenditures: $80,000. *Unit head:* Dr. Deborah T. Meem, Department Head, 513-556-1793, Fax: 513-556-6771, E-mail: deborah.meem@uc.edu. *Application contact:* Dr. Amy Lind, Director of Graduate Studies, 513-656-6364, Fax: 513-556-6771, E-mail: amy.lind@uc.edu.

University of Colorado Denver, College of Liberal Arts and Sciences, Program in Humanities, Denver, CO 80217-3364. Offers community health science (MSS); humanities (MH); international studies (MSS); social science (MSS); society and the environment (MSS); women's and gender studies (MSS). Part-time and evening/weekend programs available. *Students:* 53 full-time (39 women), 35 part-time (22 women); includes 4 Black or African American, non-Hispanic/Latino; 1 American Indian or Alaska Native, non-Hispanic/Latino; 3 Asian, non-Hispanic/Latino; 7 Hispanic/Latino, 1 international. Average age 33. 41 applicants, 54% accepted, 19 enrolled. In 2010, 29 master's awarded. *Degree requirements:* For master's, thesis or alternative, 36 credit hours, project or thesis. *Entrance requirements:* For master's, writing sample, statement of purpose/letter of intent. Additional exam requirements/recommendations for international students: Required—TOEFL (minimum score 525 paper-based). *Application deadline:* For fall admission, 5/15 priority date for domestic students; for spring admission, 10/15 priority date for domestic students. Application fee: $50 ($75 for international students). Electronic applications accepted. *Expenses:* Tuition, state resident: full-time $7332; part-time $355 per credit hour. Tuition, nonresident: full-time $18,990; part-time $1055 per credit hour. Required fees: $998. Tuition and fees vary according to course level, course load, degree level, campus/location, program, reciprocity agreements and student level. *Financial support:* Federal Work-Study and scholarships/grants available. Financial award application deadline: 4/1; financial award applicants required to submit FAFSA. *Faculty research:* Women and gender in the classical Mediterranean, communication theory and democracy, relationship between psychology and philosophy. *Unit head:* Myra Bookman, Associate Director of Humanities and Social Science, 303-556-2496, Fax: 303-556-8100, E-mail: myra.bookman@ucdenver.edu. *Application contact:* Catherine Osmundson, Program Assistant, 303-556-2305, E-mail: catherine.osmundson@ucdenver.edu.

University of Florida, Graduate School, College of Liberal Arts and Sciences, Center for Women's Studies and Gender Research, Gainesville, FL 32611. Offers gender and development (Graduate Certificate); women's studies (MA, Graduate Certificate); MA/JD; MA/MA. *Faculty:* 3 full-time (all women), 3 part-time/adjunct (all women). *Students:* 7 full-time (all women), 1 (woman) part-time. Average age 27. 17 applicants, 65% accepted, 3 enrolled. In 2010, 3 master's awarded. Terminal master's awarded for partial completion of doctoral program. *Degree requirements:* For master's, thesis or project. *Entrance requirements:* For master's, GRE General Test (minimum score 1000), minimum GPA of 3.0. Additional exam requirements/recommendations for international students: Required—TOEFL (minimum score 550 paper-based; 213 computer-based; 80 iBT), IELTS (minimum score 6). *Application deadline:* For fall admission, 1/15 for domestic and international students; for spring admission, 10/1 for domestic and international students. Application fee: $30. Electronic applications accepted. *Expenses:* Tuition, state resident: full-time $10,915.92. Tuition, nonresident: full-time $28,309. *Financial support:* In 2010–11, 7 students received support, including 2 fellowships, 1 research assistantship (averaging $13,786 per year), 4 teaching assistantships (averaging $7,048 per year). Financial award application deadline: 1/15; financial award applicants required to submit FAFSA. *Faculty research:* Transnational feminism and postcolonial theory; gender, sexuality, and social movements; U. S. women of color, especially African American and Latina women; U. S. and British literature and cultural history; gender and indigenous identity in Latin America. *Unit head:* Dr. Judith Page, Director, 352-273-0387, Fax: 352-392-4873, E-mail: page7@ufl.edu. *Application contact:* Dr. Florence Babb, Graduate Coordinator, 352-273-0384, Fax: 352-392-4873, E-mail: fbabb@ufl.edu.

University of Georgia, College of Arts and Sciences, Institute for Women's Studies, Athens, GA 30602. Offers Certificate. *Students:* 1 (woman) part-time; includes Black or African American, non-Hispanic/Latino. 1 applicant, 100% accepted, 1 enrolled. *Expenses:* Tuition, state resident: full-time $7200; part-time $344 per credit hour. Tuition, nonresident: full-time $21,900; part-time $944 per credit hour. Tuition and fees vary according to course load and program. *Unit head:* Dr. Juanita Johnson-Bailey, Director, 706-542-2846, E-mail: jjb@uga.edu. *Application contact:* Dr. Susan R. Thomas, Assistant Director, 706-542-2763, Fax: 706-542-0049, E-mail: suthomas@uga.edu.

University of Hawaii at Manoa, Graduate Division, College of Social Sciences, Advanced Women's Studies Program, Honolulu, HI 96822. Offers Graduate Certificate. Part-time programs available. *Faculty:* 7 full-time (all women). *Students:* 12 full-time (10 women), 2 part-time (both women); includes 7 minority (4 Asian, non-Hispanic/Latino; 1 Native Hawaiian or other Pacific Islander, non-Hispanic/Latino; 2 Two or more races, non-Hispanic/Latino), 2 international. Average age 32. 6 applicants, 100% accepted, 5 enrolled. In 2010, 2 Graduate Certificates awarded. *Entrance requirements:* Additional exam requirements/recommendations for international students: Required—TOEFL (minimum score 500 paper-based; 173 computer-based; 61 iBT), IELTS (minimum score 5). *Application deadline:* For fall admission, 3/1 for domestic and international students. Application fee: $60. *Financial support:* In 2010–11, 2 fellowships (averaging $1,010 per year), 1 research assistantship (averaging $15,558 per year), 5 teaching assistantships (averaging $15,558 per year) were awarded. *Application contact:* Meda Chesney-Lind, Director, 808-956-6313, Fax: 808-956-9616, E-mail: meda@hawaii.edu.

The University of Iowa, Graduate College, College of Liberal Arts and Sciences, Department of Women's Studies, Iowa City, IA 52242-1316. Offers PhD. *Degree requirements:* For doctorate, comprehensive exam, thesis/dissertation. *Entrance requirements:* For doctorate, GRE General Test, minimum GPA of 3.0. Additional exam requirements/recommendations for international students: Required—TOEFL (minimum score 550 paper-based; 213 computer-based; 81 iBT).

University of Lethbridge, School of Graduate Studies, Lethbridge, AB T1K 3M4, Canada. Offers accounting (MScM); addictions counseling (M Sc); agricultural biotechnology (M Sc); agricultural studies (M Sc, MA); anthropology (MA); archaeology (MA); art (MA, MFA); biochemistry (M Sc); biological sciences (M Sc); biomolecular science (PhD); biosystems and biodiversity (PhD); Canadian studies (MA); chemistry (M Sc); computer science (M Sc); computer science and geographical information science (M Sc); counseling psychology (M Ed); dramatic arts (MA); earth, space, and physical science (PhD); economics (MA); educational leadership (M Ed); English (MA); environmental science (M Sc); evolution and behavior (PhD); exercise science (M Sc); finance (MScM); French (MA); French/German (MA); French/Spanish (MA); general education (M Ed); general management (MScM); geography (M Sc, MA); German (MA); health science (M Sc); history (MA); human resource management and labour relations (MScM); individualized multidisciplinary (M Sc, MA); information systems (MScM); international management (MScM); kinesiology (M Sc, MA); management (M Sc, MA); marketing (MScM); mathematics (M Sc); music (M Mus, MA); Native American studies (MA); neuroscience (M Sc, PhD); new media (MA); nursing (M Sc); philosophy (MA); physics (M Sc); policy and strategy (MScM); political science (MA); psychology (M Sc, MA); religious studies (MA); social sciences (MA); sociology (MA); theatre and dramatic arts (MFA); theoretical and computational science (PhD); urban and regional studies (MA); women's studies (MA). Part-time and evening/weekend programs available. *Degree requirements:* For doctorate, comprehensive exam, thesis/dissertation. *Entrance requirements:* For master's, GMAT (M Sc in management), bachelor's degree in related field, minimum GPA of 3.0 during previous 20 graded semester courses, 2 years teaching or related experience (M Ed); for doctorate, master's degree, minimum graduate GPA of 3.5. Additional exam requirements/recommendations for international students: Required—TOEFL. *Faculty research:* Movement and brain plasticity, gibberellin physiology, photosynthesis, carbon cycling, molecular properties of main-group ring components.

University of Louisville, Graduate School, College of Arts and Sciences, Department of Women's and Gender Studies, Louisville, KY 40292. Offers MA, Certificate, MSSW/MA. Part-time programs available. *Faculty:* 6 full-time (all women), 7 part-time/adjunct (6 women). *Students:* 16 full-time (14 women), 3 part-time (all women); includes 1 Black or African American, non-Hispanic/Latino. Average age 28. 14 applicants, 79% accepted, 6 enrolled. In 2010, 6 master's awarded. *Degree requirements:* For master's, thesis or alternative. *Entrance requirements:* For master's, GRE. *Application deadline:* For fall admission, 8/1 for domestic students, 7/15 for international students; for spring admission, 12/20 for domestic students, 12/1 for international students. Application fee: $50. Electronic applications accepted. *Expenses:* Tuition, state resident: full-time $9144; part-time $508 per credit hour. Tuition, nonresident: full-time $19,026; part-time $1057 per credit hour. Tuition and fees vary according to program and reciprocity agreements. *Financial support:* In 2010–11, 9 students received support, including 1 teaching assistantship with full tuition reimbursement available (averaging $12,000 per year); scholarships/grants also available. Financial award application deadline: 5/1; financial award applicants required to submit FAFSA. *Faculty research:* Gender representation in popular media; intersections of race, class, gender and sexuality in U. S. popular culture and popular music; interconnectedness between the performance of identity and racialized body politics for African diasporan women and men; nineteenth century women/gender in the U. S.; medicine as a gendered practice; gender, race, and class dynamics in parenting and the workplace. *Unit head:* Nancy M. Theriot, Chairperson, 502-852-8160, Fax: 502-852-4421, E-mail: nancyt@louisville.edu. *Application contact:* Libby Leggett, Director, Graduate Admissions, 502-852-3101, Fax: 502-852-6536, E-mail: gradadm@louisville.edu.

University of Maryland, Baltimore County, Graduate School, College of Arts, Humanities and Social Sciences, Program in Gender and Women's Studies, Baltimore, MD 21250. Offers Postbaccalaureate Certificate. Part-time and evening/weekend programs available. *Application deadline:* Applications are processed on a rolling basis. Application fee: $0. Electronic applications accepted. *Financial support:* In 2010–11, 1 teaching assistantship with partial tuition reimbursement (averaging $7,500 per year) was awarded; health care benefits and unspecified assistantships also available. *Faculty research:* Feminist theory, reproductive and sexual politics, U. S. women's history. *Unit head:* Dr. Carole McCann, Director and Associate Professor of Gender and Women's Studies, 410-455-2161, E-mail: mccann@umbc.edu. *Application contact:* Dr. Carole McCann, Director and Associate Professor of Gender and Women's Studies, 410-455-2161, E-mail: mccann@umbc.edu.

University of Maryland, College Park, Academic Affairs, College of Arts and Humanities, Department of Women's Studies, College Park, MD 20742. Offers MA, PhD. *Faculty:* 73 full-time (70 women), 4 part-time/adjunct (all women). *Students:* 25 full-time (all women), 1 (woman) part-time; includes 10 minority (6 Black or African American, non-Hispanic/Latino; 1 Asian, non-Hispanic/Latino; 1 Hispanic/Latino; 2 Two or more races, non-Hispanic/Latino), 4 international. 80 applicants, 6% accepted, 3 enrolled. In 2010, 1 master's, 1 doctorate awarded. *Degree requirements:* For master's, thesis or alternative; for doctorate, one foreign language, thesis/dissertation or alternative. *Entrance requirements:* For master's, GRE General Test, writing sample, 3 letters of recommendation. Additional exam requirements/recommendations for international students: Required—TOEFL. *Application deadline:* For fall admission, 12/1 for domestic students, 12/15 for international students; for spring admission, 6/1 for international students. Application fee: $75. *Expenses:* Tuition, state resident: part-time $471 per credit hour. Tuition, nonresident: part-time $1016 per credit hour. Required fees: $337 per term. *Financial support:* In 2010–11, 3 fellowships with partial tuition reimbursements (averaging $11,889 per year), 18 teaching assistantships (averaging $17,662 per year) were awarded; research assistantships, career-related internships or fieldwork, Federal Work-Study, and scholarships/grants also available. Support available to part-time students. *Faculty research:* Gender roles, national and global diversity, sexuality. *Unit head:* Seung-kyung Kim, Acting Chair, 301-450-7293, E-mail: skim2@umd.edu. *Application contact:* Dr. Charles A. Caramello, Dean of Graduate School, 301-405-0358, Fax: 301-314-9305, E-mail: ccaramel@umd.edu.

University of Massachusetts Boston, Office of Graduate Studies, Division of Continuing Education and John W. McCormack Graduate School of Policy Studies, Program in Women in Politics and Government, Boston, MA 02125-3393. Offers Certificate. Part-time and evening/weekend programs available. *Degree requirements:* For Certificate, practicum, final project. *Entrance requirements:* For degree, interview, minimum GPA of 2.75.

University of Massachusetts Boston, Office of Graduate Studies, John W. McCormack Graduate School of Policy Studies, Boston, MA 02125-3393. Offers gerontology (MA, MS, PhD, Certificate), including gerontology (MS, PhD, Certificate), gerontology research (MA), management in aging services (MA); public affairs (MS); public policy (PhD); women in politics and government (Certificate). Certificate program in women in politics and government offered jointly with Division of Continuing Education. Part-time and evening/weekend programs available. *Degree requirements:* For doctorate, thesis/dissertation; for Certificate, practicum, final project. *Entrance requirements:* For doctorate, GRE General Test; for Certificate, interview, minimum GPA of 2.5.

University of Michigan, Horace H. Rackham School of Graduate Studies, College of Literature, Science, and the Arts, Department of Women's Studies, Ann Arbor, MI 48109. Offers English and women's studies (PhD); history and women's studies (PhD); lesbian, gay, bisexual, transgender, queer (LGBTQ) studies (Certificate); psychology and women's studies (PhD); sociology and women's studies (PhD); women's studies (Certificate). *Faculty:* 77 full-time (71 women). *Students:* 71 full-time (63 women); includes 6 Black or African American, non-Hispanic/Latino; 11 Asian, non-Hispanic/Latino; 7 Hispanic/Latino; 4 Two or more races, non-Hispanic/

Women's Studies

University of Michigan (continued)

Latino. Average age 30. 101 applicants, 10% accepted, 9 enrolled. In 2010, 5 doctorates, 8 other advanced degrees awarded. *Degree requirements:* For doctorate, variable foreign language requirement, comprehensive exam (for some programs), thesis/dissertation. *Entrance requirements:* For doctorate, GRE General Test, previous undergraduate course work in women's studies; for Certificate, GRE General Test, previous course work in women's studies. Additional exam requirements/recommendations for international students: Required—TOEFL. *Application deadline:* For fall admission, 12/1 for domestic and international students. Application fee: $65 ($75 for international students). Electronic applications accepted. *Expenses:* Tuition, state resident: full-time $17,784; part-time $1116 per credit hour. Tuition, nonresident: full-time $35,944; part-time $2125 per credit hour. International tuition: $35,994 full-time. Required fees: $95 per semester. Tuition and fees vary according to course load, degree level and program. *Financial support:* In 2010–11, 39 students received support, including 21 fellowships with full tuition reimbursements available (averaging $16,800 per year), 18 teaching assistantships with full tuition reimbursements available (averaging $17,270 per year); career-related internships or fieldwork, institutionally sponsored loans, scholarships/grants, traineeships, health care benefits, and unspecified assistantships also available. *Faculty research:* Gender issues, LGBTQ studies, sexuality, women and science, global feminism. *Unit head:* Elizabeth R. Cole, Chair, Department of Women's Studies, Professor of Women's Studies, Professor of Afroamerican and African Studies, Professor of Psychology, 734-763-2047, Fax: 734-647-4943, E-mail: wsdgradinquiry@umich.edu. *Application contact:* Aimee Germain, Graduate Program Coordinator, 734-763-2047, Fax: 734-647-4943, E-mail: wsdgradinquiry@umich.edu.

University of Minnesota, Twin Cities Campus, Graduate School, College of Liberal Arts, Department of Gender, Women, and Sexuality Studies, Minneapolis, MN 55455-0213. Offers feminist studies (PhD). *Degree requirements:* For doctorate, comprehensive exam, thesis/dissertation. *Entrance requirements:* For doctorate, GRE. Additional exam requirements/recommendations for international students: Required—TOEFL (minimum score 550 paper-based). Electronic applications accepted. *Faculty research:* Transnational feminist theories, critical development theory, feminist postcolonialisms, feminist science studies and studying of health, literature, Asian diasporas, sexuality and queer theory.

University of Nevada, Las Vegas, Graduate College, College of Liberal Arts, Women's Studies Department, Las Vegas, NV 89154-5055. Offers Certificate. *Faculty:* 4 full-time (all women). *Students:* 2 part-time (both women); includes 1 minority (Hispanic/Latino). Average age 26. 1 applicant, 100% accepted, 0 enrolled. In 2010, 1 Certificate awarded. *Entrance requirements:* Additional exam requirements/recommendations for international students: Required—TOEFL (minimum score 550 paper-based; 213 computer-based; 80 iBT), IELTS (minimum score 7). *Application deadline:* For fall admission, 6/15 priority date for domestic students, 6/15 for international students; for spring admission, 11/15 priority date for domestic students, 11/15 for international students. Applications are processed on a rolling basis. Application fee: $60 ($95 for international students). Electronic applications accepted. *Expenses:* Tuition, area resident: Part-time $239.50 per credit. Tuition, state resident: part-time $239.50 per credit. Tuition, nonresident: part-time $503 per credit. Required fees: $108 per semester. Tuition and fees vary according to course load, program and reciprocity agreements. *Financial support:* In 2010–11, 2 students received support, including 2 research assistantships with partial tuition reimbursements available (averaging $11,000 per year); institutionally sponsored loans, scholarships/grants, health care benefits, and unspecified assistantships also available. Financial award application deadline: 3/1. *Faculty research:* Women and work; feminist activism; Chicana experience; intersectionality of gender, race, class; sexual cultures. Total annual research expenditures: $1,000. *Unit head:* Dr. Lois Helmbold, Chair/Professor, 702-895-0838, Fax: 702-895-0850, E-mail: lois.helmbold@unlv.edu. *Application contact:* Graduate College Admissions Evaluator, 702-895-3320, Fax: 702-895-4180, E-mail: gradcollege@unlv.edu.

University of New Mexico, Graduate School, College of Arts and Sciences, Program in Women Studies, Albuquerque, NM 87131-2039. Offers Graduate Certificate. *Faculty:* 4 full-time (3 women), 9 part-time/adjunct (7 women). *Students:* 2 applicants, 50% accepted, 0 enrolled. In 2010, 1 Graduate Certificate awarded. *Entrance requirements:* For degree, enrollment in degree-granting program. *Application deadline:* Applications are processed on a rolling basis. Application fee: $50. *Expenses:* Tuition, state resident: full-time $5991; part-time $251 per credit hour. Tuition, nonresident: full-time $14,405; part-time $800.20 per credit hour. Tuition and fees vary according to course level, course load, program and reciprocity agreements. *Unit head:* Dr. Rajeshwar Vallury, Director, 505-277-3854, Fax: 505-277-0267, E-mail: rvallury@unm.edu. *Application contact:* Dr. Rajeshwar Vallury, Director, 505-277-3854, Fax: 505-277-0267, E-mail: rvallury@unm.edu.

The University of North Carolina at Charlotte, Graduate School, College of Arts and Sciences, Program in Interdisciplinary Studies, Charlotte, NC 28223-0001. Offers gerontology (MA, Certificate); Latin American studies (MA); liberal studies (MA); women's studies (Certificate). *Faculty:* 2 full-time (1 woman), 2 part-time/adjunct (both women). *Students:* 15 full-time (14 women), 53 part-time (39 women); includes 20 minority (11 Black or African American, non-Hispanic/Latino; 8 Hispanic/Latino; 1 Two or more races, non-Hispanic/Latino), 5 international. Average age 30. 24 applicants, 96% accepted, 15 enrolled. In 2010, 16 master's awarded. *Degree requirements:* For master's, thesis optional, comprehensive exam or project. *Entrance requirements:* For master's, GRE General Test or MAT, minimum GPA of 3.0 during previous 2 years, 2.75 overall. Additional exam requirements/recommendations for international students: Required—TOEFL (minimum score 557 paper-based; 220 computer-based; 83 iBT). *Application deadline:* For fall admission, 7/1 for domestic students, 5/1 for international students; for spring admission, 11/1 for domestic students, 10/1 for international students. Applications are processed on a rolling basis. Application fee: $55. Electronic applications accepted. *Expenses:* Tuition, state resident: full-time $3464. Tuition, nonresident: full-time $14,297. Required fees: $2094. Tuition and fees vary according to course load. *Financial support:* In 2010–11, 7 students received support, including 2 research assistantships (averaging $3,025 per year), 5 teaching assistantships (averaging $7,950 per year); career-related internships or fieldwork, institutionally sponsored loans, scholarships/grants, and unspecified assistantships also available. Support available to part-time students. Financial award application deadline: 4/1; financial award applicants required to submit FAFSA. *Unit head:* Dr. Paula Eckard, Interim Director, 704-687-4309, Fax: 704-687-4347, E-mail: pgeckard@uncc.edu. *Application contact:* Kathy B. Giddings, Director of Graduate Admissions, 704-687-5503, Fax: 704-687-3279, E-mail: gradadm@uncc.edu.

The University of North Carolina at Greensboro, Graduate School, College of Arts and Sciences, Department of English, Greensboro, NC 27412-5001. Offers creative writing (MFA); English (M Ed, MA, PhD, Certificate), including American literature (PhD), English (M Ed, MA), English literature (PhD), rhetoric and composition (PhD), technical writing (Certificate), women's studies (Certificate). *Degree requirements:* For master's, comprehensive exam; for doctorate, variable foreign language requirement, thesis/dissertation, preliminary exam. *Entrance requirements:* For master's, GRE General Test, minimum GPA of 3.0; for doctorate, GRE General Test, GRE Subject Test, critical writing sample, minimum GPA of 3.0. Additional exam requirements/recommendations for international students: Required—TOEFL. Electronic applications accepted.

The University of North Carolina at Greensboro, Graduate School, College of Arts and Sciences, Program in Women's and Gender Studies, Greensboro, NC 27412-5001. Offers MA, Certificate. Electronic applications accepted.

University of Northern Iowa, Graduate College, Program in Women's and Gender Studies, Cedar Falls, IA 50614. Offers MA. *Students:* 8 full-time (7 women), 2 part-time (both women); includes 1 minority (Black or African American, non-Hispanic/Latino). 14 applicants, 79% accepted, 4 enrolled. In 2010, 1 master's awarded. *Degree requirements:* For master's, comprehensive exam (for some programs), thesis or alternative. *Entrance requirements:* For master's, minimum GPA of 3.0. Additional exam requirements/recommendations for inter-

national students: Required—TOEFL (minimum score 500 paper-based; 180 computer-based; 61 iBT). *Application deadline:* Applications are processed on a rolling basis. Application fee: $50 ($70 for international students). Electronic applications accepted. *Financial support:* Application deadline: 2/1. *Unit head:* Dr. Phyllis L. Baker, Director/Professor, 319-273-7102, Fax: 319-273-3053, E-mail: phyllis.baker@uni.edu. *Application contact:* Laurie S. Russell, Record Analyst, 319-273-2623, Fax: 319-273-2885, E-mail: laurie.russell@uni.edu.

University of Oklahoma, College of Arts and Sciences, Women's and Gender Studies Program, Norman, OK 73019. Offers Graduate Certificate. *Students:* 6 full-time (all women), 5 part-time (4 women); includes 1 minority (American Indian or Alaska Native, non-Hispanic/Latino), 1 international. Average age 38. 4 applicants, 100% accepted, 2 enrolled. *Entrance requirements:* Additional exam requirements/recommendations for international students: Required—TOEFL (minimum score 550 paper-based; 213 computer-based; 79 iBT). *Application deadline:* Applications are processed on a rolling basis. Application fee: $40 ($90 for international students). Electronic applications accepted. *Expenses:* Tuition, state resident: full-time $3893; part-time $162.20 per credit hour. Tuition, nonresident: full-time $14,167; part-time $590.30 per credit hour. Required fees: $2523; $94.60 per credit hour. Tuition and fees vary according to course load and degree level. *Financial support:* In 2010–11, 4 research assistantships (averaging $9,890 per year), 3 teaching assistantships (averaging $9,621 per year) were awarded. *Unit head:* Jill Irvine, Director, 405-325-3481, Fax: 405-325-3573, E-mail: jill.irvine@ou.edu. *Application contact:* Jill Irvine, Director, 405-325-3481, Fax: 405-325-3573, E-mail: jill.irvine@ou.edu.

University of Ottawa, Faculty of Graduate and Postdoctoral Studies, Faculty of Social Sciences, Institute of Women's Studies, Ottawa, ON K1N 6N5, Canada. Offers criminology (MA, MCA); education (MA); English (MA); history (MA); human kinetics (MA); law (LL M); lettres Françaises (MA); nursing (M Sc); pastoral studies (MA); political science (MA); religious studies (MA); sociology (MA). *Degree requirements:* For master's, thesis or alternative.

University of Pittsburgh, School of Arts and Sciences, Program in Women's Studies, Pittsburgh, PA 15260. Offers Doctoral Certificate, Master's Certificate. Part-time programs available. *Faculty:* 69 full-time (58 women). *Students:* 30 full-time (25 women); includes 2 Asian, non-Hispanic/Latino; 3 Hispanic/Latino. Average age 31. 3 applicants, 100% accepted, 3 enrolled. In 2010, 3 Master's Certificates awarded. *Degree requirements:* For other advanced degree, scholarly essay. *Entrance requirements:* Additional exam requirements/recommendations for international students: Required—TOEFL. *Application deadline:* Applications are processed on a rolling basis. Application fee: $50. Electronic applications accepted. *Expenses:* Tuition, state resident: full-time $17,304; part-time $701 per credit. Tuition, nonresident: full-time $29,554; part-time $1210 per credit. Required fees: $740; $214 per term. Tuition and fees vary according to program. *Financial support:* In 2010–11, 2 students received support, including 2 fellowships with full tuition reimbursements available (averaging $15,675 per year); unspecified assistantships also available. Financial award application deadline: 2/15. *Faculty research:* Global feminisms; gender and interpersonal violence; race and gender studies; representation and gender in media, arts, and literature; concepts of the body. *Unit head:* Jean Ferguson Carr, Director, 412-624-6486, Fax: 412-624-6492, E-mail: wstudies@pitt.edu. *Application contact:* Jean Ferguson Carr, Director, 412-624-6486, Fax: 412-624-6492, E-mail: wstudies@pitt.edu.

University of Regina, Faculty of Graduate Studies and Research, Faculty of Arts, Department of Women's Studies, Regina, SK S4S 0A2, Canada. Offers MA. Offered as a special case program. Part-time programs available. *Faculty:* 3 full-time (all women), 1 (woman) part-time/adjunct. *Students:* 1 (woman) full-time, 2 part-time (both women). *Degree requirements:* For master's, thesis. *Entrance requirements:* Additional exam requirements/recommendations for international students: Required—TOEFL (minimum score 580 paper-based; 80 iBT). *Application deadline:* Applications are processed on a rolling basis. Application fee: $100. Electronic applications accepted. Tuition and fees charges are reported in Canadian dollars. *Expenses:* Tuition, area resident: Full-time $3244.50 Canadian dollars; part-time $180.25 Canadian dollars per credit hour. International tuition: $4744.50 Canadian dollars full-time. Required fees: $494 Canadian dollars; $115.25 Canadian dollars per credit hour. $115.25 Canadian dollars per semester. Tuition and fees vary according to program. *Financial support:* Fellowships, research assistantships, teaching assistantships, scholarships/grants available. Financial award application deadline: 6/15. *Faculty research:* Feminist theory; mapping sexualities; mapping gender; women, feminism, and globalization. *Unit head:* Dr. Wendee Kubik, Coordinator, 306-585-4668, Fax: 306-585-4815, E-mail: wendee.kubik@uregina.ca. *Application contact:* Dr. Darlene Juschka, Graduate Program Coordinator, 306-585-5280, Fax: 306-585-4815, E-mail: darlene.juschka@uregina.ca.

University of Saskatchewan, College of Graduate Studies and Research, College of Arts and Sciences, Department of Women's and Gender Studies, Saskatoon, SK S7N 5A2, Canada. Offers MA, PhD. *Degree requirements:* For master's, thesis; for doctorate, comprehensive exam (for some programs), thesis/dissertation. *Entrance requirements:* Additional exam requirements/recommendations for international students: Required—TOEFL (minimum score 80 iBT); Recommended—IELTS (minimum score 6.5). Electronic applications accepted.

University of South Carolina, The Graduate School, College of Arts and Sciences, Program in Women's Studies, Columbia, SC 29208. Offers Certificate. Part-time programs available. *Entrance requirements:* For degree, GRE General Test or MAT. Additional exam requirements/recommendations for international students: Required—TOEFL. Electronic applications accepted. *Faculty research:* Health; pedagogy; intersection of race, class, gender; public policy; politics of culture and representations, feminist political economics.

University of South Florida, Graduate School, College of Arts and Sciences, Department of Women's Studies, Tampa, FL 33620-9951. Offers MA. Part-time programs available. *Faculty:* 10 full-time (6 women), 1 (woman) part-time/adjunct. *Students:* 12 full-time (all women), 1 (woman) part-time; includes 1 American Indian or Alaska Native, non-Hispanic/Latino, 1 international. Average age 30. 12 applicants, 25% accepted, 3 enrolled. *Degree requirements:* For master's, comprehensive exam, thesis or internship. *Entrance requirements:* For master's, GRE General Test, 3 letters of reference, writing sample, minimum GPA of 3.0 in last 60 hours. Additional exam requirements/recommendations for international students: Required—TOEFL (minimum score 550 paper-based; 213 computer-based). *Application deadline:* For fall admission, 2/15 for domestic students, 1/2 for international students; for spring admission, 10/15 for domestic students, 6/1 for international students. Applications are processed on a rolling basis. Application fee: $30. *Financial support:* In 2010–11, 7 students received support, including 11 teaching assistantships with tuition reimbursements available (averaging $9,093 per year). Financial award application deadline: 3/1. *Unit head:* Dr. Kim Vaz, Chairperson, 813-974-0985, Fax: 813-974-0336, E-mail: vaz@cas.usf.edu. *Application contact:* Marilyn Myerson, Director, 813-974-0979, Fax: 813-974-0336, E-mail: myerson@cas.l.usf.edu.

The University of Texas at El Paso, Graduate School, College of Liberal Arts, Women's Studies Program, El Paso, TX 79968-0001. Offers women's and gender studies (Certificate). *Unit head:* Dr. Howard C. Daudistel, Dean, 915-747-5666, Fax: 915-747-5905, E-mail: hdaudistel@utep.edu. *Application contact:* Dr. Patricia D. Witherspoon, Dean of the Graduate School, 915-747-5491, Fax: 915-747-5788, E-mail: withersp@utep.edu.

University of Toronto, School of Graduate Studies, Humanities Division, Women and Gender Studies Institute, Toronto, ON M5S 1A1, Canada. Offers MA.

University of Washington, Graduate School, College of Arts and Sciences, Department of Women Studies, Seattle, WA 98195. Offers PhD. Terminal master's awarded for partial completion of doctoral program. *Degree requirements:* For doctorate, one foreign language, thesis/dissertation, exam. *Entrance requirements:* For doctorate, GRE General Test. Additional exam requirements/recommendations for international students: Required—TOEFL. Electronic applications accepted. *Faculty research:* Women's history in U.S. and China; Native American ethnography and identity; women, science, and technology; political economy of development, feminism and nationalism.

University of Wisconsin–Madison, Graduate School, College of Letters and Science, Department of History, Madison, WI 53706-1380. Offers African history (MA, PhD); Central Asian history (MA, PhD); comparative world history (MA, PhD); East Asian history (MA, PhD); European history (MA, PhD); gender and women's history (MA, PhD); Latin American and Caribbean history (MA, PhD); Middle Eastern history (MA, PhD); South Asian history (MA, PhD); Southeast Asian history (MA, PhD); United States history (MA, PhD). Terminal master's awarded for partial completion of doctoral program. *Degree requirements:* For master's, thesis (for some programs); for doctorate, variable foreign language requirement, thesis/dissertation. *Entrance requirements:* For master's and doctorate, GRE General Test. Additional exam requirements/recommendations for international students: Required—Michigan English Language Assessment Battery or TOEFL. Electronic applications accepted. *Expenses:* Tuition, state resident: full-time $9887; part-time $617.96 per credit. Tuition, nonresident: full-time $24,054; part-time $1503.40 per credit. Required fees: $67.63 per credit. Tuition and fees vary according to reciprocity agreements. *Faculty research:* American, African, European, Asian, Latin American, and Middle Eastern history.

University of Wisconsin–Milwaukee, Graduate School, College of Letters and Sciences, Program in Women's Studies, Milwaukee, WI 53201-0413. Offers MA. Part-time programs available. *Students:* 4 full-time (all women), 1 international. Average age 28. 7 applicants, 86% accepted, 2 enrolled. *Entrance requirements:* For master's, three letters of recommendation, sample of written work, letter of intent. *Application deadline:* Applications are processed on a rolling basis. Application fee: $56 ($96 for international students). Electronic applications accepted. *Financial support:* In 2010–11, 2 teaching assistantships with full tuition reimbursements were awarded; fellowships, research assistantships, health care benefits and unspecified assistantships also available. Financial award applicants required to submit FAFSA. *Unit head:* Dr. Gwynne Kennedy, Director, 414-229-5918, E-mail: gkennedy@uwm.edu. *Application contact:* General Information Contact, 414-229-4982, Fax: 414-229-6967, E-mail: gradschool@uwm.edu.

Virginia Polytechnic Institute and State University, Graduate School, College of Liberal Arts and Human Sciences, Department of Sociology, Blacksburg, VA 24061. Offers race and social policy (Certificate); sociology (MS, PhD); women's and gender studies (Certificate). *Faculty:* 26 full-time (12 women), 1 (woman) part-time/adjunct. *Students:* 39 full-time (25 women), 7 part-time (3 women); includes 10 Black or African American, non-Hispanic/Latino; 2 Hispanic/Latino, 2 international. Average age 33. 27 applicants, 22% accepted, 5 enrolled. In 2010, 7 master's, 3 doctorates awarded. *Degree requirements:* For master's, comprehensive exam (for some programs), thesis (for some programs); for doctorate, comprehensive exam (for some programs), thesis/dissertation (for some programs). *Entrance requirements:* For master's and doctorate, GRE. Additional exam requirements/recommendations for international students: Required—TOEFL (minimum score 550 paper-based; 213 computer-based). *Application deadline:* For fall admission, 7/1 for domestic and international students; for spring admission, 12/1 for domestic and international students. Applications are processed on a rolling basis. Application fee: $65. Electronic applications accepted. *Expenses:* Tuition, state resident: full-time $9399; part-time $488 per credit hour. Tuition, nonresident: full-time $17,854; part-time $957.75 per credit hour. Required fees: $1534. Full-time tuition and fees vary according to program. *Financial support:* In 2010–11, 2 research assistantships with full tuition reimbursements (averaging $13,864 per year), 19 teaching assistantships with full tuition reimbursements (averaging $13,074 per year) were awarded; career-related internships or fieldwork, Federal Work-Study, scholarships/grants, health care benefits, and unspecified assistantships also available. Financial award application deadline: 1/15. *Faculty research:* Science and technology, deviance and criminology, social psychology, social organization, demography. Total annual research expenditures: $42,630. *Unit head:* Dr. John W. Ryan, UNIT HEAD, 540-231-6878, Fax: 540-231-3860, E-mail: johnryan@vt.edu. *Application contact:* Jim Hawdon, Contact, 540-231-7476, Fax: 540-231-3860, E-mail: hawdonj@vt.edu.

Washington State University, Graduate School, College of Liberal Arts, Program in American Studies, Pullman, WA 99164. Offers ethnic studies (MA, PhD); feminist studies (MA, PhD); history (MA, PhD); literature (MA, PhD). Part-time programs available. *Faculty:* 35. *Students:* 23 full-time (14 women), 4 part-time (2 women); includes 5 Black or African American, non-Hispanic/Latino; 4 American Indian or Alaska Native, non-Hispanic/Latino; 4 Asian, non-Hispanic/Latino; 4 Hispanic/Latino, 2 international. Average age 35. 55 applicants, 7% accepted, 3 enrolled. In 2010, 1 master's, 3 doctorates awarded. *Degree requirements:* For master's, one foreign language, comprehensive exam (for some programs), thesis optional, oral exam; for doctorate, one foreign language, comprehensive exam (for some programs), thesis/dissertation, oral exam. *Entrance requirements:* For master's and doctorate, GRE General Test, official college transcripts sent directly from each institution attended, 3-5 page statement of purpose describing areas of interest, minimum GPA of 3.0, writing sample, 3 letters of recommendation. Additional exam requirements/recommendations for international students: Required—TOEFL, IELTS. *Application deadline:* For fall admission, 1/10 priority date for domestic and international students; for spring admission, 7/1 priority date for domestic and international students. Applications are processed on a rolling basis. Application fee: $50. *Expenses:* Tuition, state resident: full-time $8552; part-time $443 per credit. Tuition, nonresident: full-time $21,650; part-time $1083 per credit. Required fees: $846. *Financial support:* In 2010–11, 1 fellowship (averaging $6,950 per year), 3 research assistantships with full and partial tuition reimbursements (averaging $14,634 per year), 17 teaching assistantships with full and partial tuition reimbursements (averaging $13,383 per year) were awarded; career-related internships or fieldwork, Federal Work-Study, institutionally sponsored loans, health care benefits, tuition waivers (partial), and teaching associateships also available. Financial award application deadline: 2/15; financial award applicants required to submit FAFSA. *Faculty research:* The American West in multicultural perspective; nineteenth century historical, literary, and cultural studies; comparative American ethnic literatures and cultures; American cultures and the environment; American rhetoric. *Unit head:* Dr. Rory J. Ong, Director, 509-335-1560, E-mail: rjong@mail.wsu.edu. *Application contact:* Graduate School Admissions, 800-GRADWSU, Fax: 509-335-1949, E-mail: gradsch@wsu.edu.

Western Seminary, Graduate Programs, Program in Ministry and Leadership, Portland, OR 97215-3367. Offers chaplaincy (MA); coaching (MA); Jewish ministry (MA); pastoral care to women (MA); youth ministry (MA). *Students:* 265 applicants, 77% accepted, 155 enrolled. In 2010, 93 master's awarded. *Degree requirements:* For master's, practicum. *Entrance requirements:* Additional exam requirements/recommendations for international students: Required—TOEFL. *Application deadline:* For fall admission, 7/18 priority date for domestic students; for winter admission, 11/7 priority date for domestic students; for spring admission, 3/13 priority date for domestic students. Applications are processed on a rolling basis. Application fee: $50. *Expenses:* Tuition: Part-time $425 per credit. *Financial support:* Applicants required to submit FAFSA. *Unit head:* Beverly Hislop, Director, 503-517-1881, E-mail: bhislop@westernseminary.edu. *Application contact:* Dr. Robert W. Wiggins, Registrar/Dean of Student Development, 503-517-1820, Fax: 503-517-1801, E-mail: rwiggins@westernseminary.edu.

Western Seminary–Sacramento Campus, Graduate Certificate Programs, Sacramento, CA 95821. Offers Bible (Graduate Certificate); coaching (Graduate Certificate); pastoral care to women (Graduate Certificate); theology (Graduate Certificate); youth and family (Graduate Certificate). Postbaccalaureate distance learning degree programs offered. *Entrance requirements:* For degree, essays, undergraduate transcripts, 4 recommendations. Additional exam requirements/recommendations for international students: Required—TOEFL.

Western Seminary–Sacramento Campus, Graduate Diploma Programs, Sacramento, CA 95821. Offers Bible and theology (Graduate Diploma); ministry (Graduate Diploma); pastoral care to women (Graduate Diploma). *Entrance requirements:* For degree, essays, undergraduate transcripts, 4 recommendations. Additional exam requirements/recommendations for international students: Required—TOEFL.

York University, Faculty of Graduate Studies, Faculty of Arts, Program in Women's Studies, Toronto, ON M3J 1P3, Canada. Offers MA, PhD. *Degree requirements:* For master's, thesis or alternative; for doctorate, comprehensive exam, thesis/dissertation. Electronic applications accepted.

TULANE UNIVERSITY

Stone Center for Latin American Studies

Programs of Study

Tulane's Stone Center for Latin American Studies offers one of the world's premier programs for the study of Latin America and the Caribbean. The multidisciplinary M.A. and Ph.D. programs provide basic education and training for both academic and professional careers. In addition, the Center for Latin American Studies offers joint M.A./M.B.A. and M.A./J.D. degrees and a joint Ph.D. degree program with art history. The M.A. degree requires completion of a total of 30 hours of course work distributed over a primary concentration and two supporting concentrations and demonstrated competency in at least one language of the region. Normally, students write an M.A. thesis, although a nonthesis option exists. The M.A. program can be completed in three semesters by students who elect to pursue the nonthesis option, but the Center strongly encourages students to pursue the thesis option and seeks to recruit students who are eager to accept the challenge. These students complete the program in four semesters. The M.A./M.B.A and M.A./J.D. joint-degree programs require 24 semester hours of course work in Latin American studies in addition to the requirements of the respective professional school. The Ph.D. requires 54 hours of course work in a primary concentration and two supporting concentrations, demonstrated proficiency in two foreign languages, general preliminary examinations, and a doctoral dissertation. In addition, the joint Ph.D. program with Art History requires completion of disciplinary degree requirements.

Research Facilities

The Latin American Library (LAL) at Tulane is one of three free-standing collections of its kind in U.S. universities. It has more than 425,000 volumes, with world-renowned collections of Latin American social sciences and humanities, with particular emphasis on history, anthropology, archaeology, art history, architecture, and cultural studies. It also has a Latin American photographic archive of 35,000 images. Its rare book and manuscript collections are extensive. The LAL is one of the world's leading repositories of colonial and pre-Columbian pictorials (Native American writing). Its collections also include the earliest extant original letter sent by Cortés from Mexico; the Codex Tulane, a large sixteenth-century Mixtec pictorial scroll; and Maya monument rubbings by Merle Greene Robinson. Annually, the Latin American Library hosts the Richard E. Greenleaf fellowship program, which brings scholars from Latin America and the Caribbean to conduct research for up to three months.

Tulane offers foreign study and internship programs in Costa Rica, Chile, Mexico, Guatemala, Cuba, Brazil, and Argentina. Its Schools of Law and Business offer executive master's and doctoral programs in Mexico, Ecuador, Venezuela, and Chile for residents of those countries. Every summer, an average of 25 to 30 graduate students conduct funded field research in Latin America. The Middle American Research Institute (MARI) is dedicated to research and publication in the social sciences about Mexico and Central America. The School of Public Health and Tropical Medicine operates research and teaching programs on campus and throughout the tropical world, including the Health Office for Latin America in Lima, Peru. The Payson Center for International Development operates a center for disaster mitigation in developing areas and offers an M.S. and a joint J.D./M.S. in international development.

Financial Aid

Superior students are slated to receive full tuition waivers plus stipends of $18,125 in 2011–12. The Center has a limited number of teaching assistantships reserved for advanced students. There are also several federal FLAS fellowships that require the study of Portuguese or Haitian Creole. The Center funds annual summer research projects in Latin America for a select group of graduate students. There is also funding for a limited number of students to enroll in summer intensive institutes for less commonly taught languages such as Kaqchikel Maya, Portuguese, Haitian Creole, and indigenous Latin American languages.

Cost of Study

In 2011–12, full-time tuition and fees are projected to be $41,650. Students with tuition waivers pay fees of $1824 per year (amount covers academic fee, health services fee, Reilly recreation fee, and a student activities fee). The fee for graduate student health insurance, provided through Tulane University, is $2000. Students admitted with a fellowship who elect the University's student health insurance plan will receive a $1000 credit applied against the $2000 insurance premium cost. Students must pay the difference.

Living and Housing Costs

There are many apartments close to the main campus. On average, prices range from $700 to $1000 a month. For Tulane-sponsored housing, graduate students have the option of renting at the Papillon Apartments, located uptown, or the Deming Pavilion, located downtown. More information can be found on Tulane's Housing Services Web site at http://housing.tulane.edu.

Student Group

The current interdisciplinary graduate student body numbers around 35. In addition, more than 60 graduate students specialize in the study of Latin America while pursuing degrees in such fields as anthropology, history, literature, and public health. Students come from all over the United States, Europe, and Latin America.

Location

Tulane is located in the uptown section of New Orleans, bounded by Audubon Park (which houses the Audubon Zoo), residential areas, and shopping areas where neighborhood restaurants and small shops abound. The French Quarter and Canal Street (downtown) are a short ride away via the St. Charles Avenue streetcar. New Orleans has approximately 400,000 residents; the metropolitan area has more than 1.3 million. Louisiana was a French and Spanish colony and has a legal system and many customs that have a great deal in common with Latin America and the Caribbean. The metropolitan area has a population of more than 50,000 Latin Americans, and the city has many commercial ties with Latin America.

The University and The Program

Tulane University is a private, nonsectarian institution of approximately 12,000 students. From its foundation in 1834, Tulane University has furthered a mission of leading study and research in Latin America. The Middle American Research Institute was founded in 1924 and the Center for Latin American Studies, in 1966. Today, the core faculty of more than 90 Latin Americanists represents the largest contingent of faculty members associated with any department or program at the University. Students and faculty members benefit from the holdings of the Latin American Library and a network of contacts with public officials, nongovernmental organizations, and academic leaders in Latin America.

The program has received numerous accolades. It is currently one of eighteen programs designated on a competitive basis by the U.S. Department of Education as a National Resource Center on Latin America. In addition to the academic program, which includes more than 450 courses plus independent studies, there are frequent lectures, conferences, symposia, and other events of scholarly interest on campus.

Applying

Applicants must provide complete transcripts, three letters of recommendation, and scores from the GRE General Test (taken within the last five years). The complete application packet is due by February 1. Ordinarily, to receive financial aid, students should have at least a 3.5 GPA and a combined verbal/quantitative score of at least 1200 on the GRE. All applicants, including those applying to joint-degree programs, must submit GRE scores. All potential applicants are encouraged to visit the Stone Center Web site (http://stonecenter.tulane.edu/) for more information on applying to the program.

Correspondence and Information

Stone Center for Latin American Studies
Tulane University
100 Jones Hall
New Orleans, Louisiana 70118-5698

Phone: 504-865-5164
Fax: 504-865-6719
E-mail: rtsclas@tulane.edu
Web site: http://stonecenter.tulane.edu/

Tulane University

THE FACULTY AND THEIR RESEARCH

Anthropology: William Balée, Ph.D., Columbia. Brazil, ethnoecology, ethnobotany. Marcello Canuto, Director, Middle American Research Institute; Ph.D., Pennsylvania. Mesoamerican archaeology, Maya epigraphy and iconography, archaeological theory. Dan Healan, Ph.D., Missouri. Mexico, archaeological ceramics, household and settlement patterns. Robert Hill, Ph.D., Pennsylvania. Cultural anthropology, ethnohistory, late postclassic and colonial Maya society. Katharine Jack, Ph.D., Alberta. Physical anthropology (primatology), primate behavior in Ecuador and Costa Rica. Judith Maxwell, Ph.D., Chicago. Language and linguistics, Kaqchikel Maya linguistics and culture, bilingual education, discourse analysis. Mariana Mora, Ph.D., Texas. Cultural anthropology, contemporary Mexico, indigenous rights, indigenous autonomy. Marc Perry, Ph.D., Texas. Cuba, Caribbean, African diaspora, race and identity. Christopher Rodning, Ph.D., North Carolina. Archaeology, Southeastern U.S., Native Americans. Ana Servigna, Ph.D., Syracuse. Urban and political anthropology, Venezuela. Marc Zender, Ph.D., Calgary. Archaeology, epigraphy, Mesoamerica. John Verano, Ph.D., UCLA. Peru, South American archaeology, forensic anthropology.

Architecture: Carol McMichael Reese, Ph.D., Texas. Argentina, Mexico, urban studies, architecture and urbanism in the Americas, nineteenth and twentieth centuries. Mark Thomas, Ph.D. candidate, Tulane. Building and environmental preservation, Cuba, Brazil.

Art History: Mia Bagneris, Ph.D., Harvard. African and African American studies, history of art and visual culture. Florencia Bazzano-Nelson, Ph.D., New Mexico. Modern Latin American art. Elizabeth Boone, Ph.D., Texas. Mexico, pre-Colombian art, colonial art of Mexico, Aztecs. Orlando Amado Hernández Ying, Ph.D., CUNY. Pre-Columbian and colonial art of Latin America. Thomas F. Reese, Director, Center for Latin American Studies; Ph.D., Yale. Argentina, Mexico, art/art history, area studies, Latin American and Iberian art, architecture and urbanism.

Business: Michael Burke, Ph.D., IIT. Worker safety and health training. Adrienne Colella, Ph.D., Ohio State. Organizational behavior. Mauricio González, Director, Center for Latin American Business Studies and Director, Goldring Institute for International Business; Ph.D., Tulane. Mexico, marketing strategy, marketing and international management. Ana Iglesias, Ph.D., Georgia State. Competitive dynamics and multimarket competition, strategic decision-making, top management teams, Brazil, strategic management. Pamela Shaw, Ph.D., Florida. Financial and managerial accounting. John M. Trapani III, Executive Director, Goldring Institute of International Business; Ph.D., Tulane.

Communication: Jennifer Ashley, Ph.D., Brown. Media and political movement, Chile. Ana López, Associate Provost for Faculty Affairs and Director, Cuban and Caribbean Studies Institute; Ph.D., Iowa. Mass communication, film, cultural studies, popular culture. Vicki Mayer, Ph.D., California, San Diego. Mexican Americans, mass media and cultural citizenship. Mauro Pereira Porto, Ph.D., California, San Diego. Brazil, media and politics.

Earth and Environmental Sciences: George C. Flowers, Ph.D., Berkeley. Mexico, geology of the Yucatan peninsula. Stephen A. Nelson, Ph.D., Berkeley. Volcanology, Mexican volcanoes.

Ecology and Evolutionary Biology: Steven Darwin, Ph.D., Massachusetts. Mexico, morphology and evolution of vascular plants, vascular flora of the Yucatan peninsula. Jordan Karubian, Ph.D., Chicago. Tropical research, conservation ecology and evolution. Thomas Sherry, Ph.D., UCLA. Neotropical ornithology, population, ecology of migratory birds, site suitability, preemption and the spatial scale of population regulation.

Economics: John Edwards, Ph.D., Maryland. Labor, education. Nora Lustig, Ph.D., Berkeley. Development economics, poverty and income distribution, social policies and protection, globalization, Mexico. Claudiney Pereira, Ph.D., North Carolina State. Economic growth, development economics, international trade and applied economics.

English: Guarav Desai, Ph.D., Duke. Postcolonial studies; literary, legal, and cultural theory. Supriya M. Nair, Ph.D., Texas at Austin. Cultural studies, feminist theory. Felipe Smith, Ph.D., LSU. Caribbean, African American literature, American literature, diasporan literature.

French: Wedsly Turenne Guerrier, Ph.D., Florida. Haitian Creole; Haitian literature, poetry, and culture. Thomas A. Klingler, Ph.D., Indiana. Caribbean, Haiti, language and linguistics, Creole language and culture.

History: Rosanne Adderley, Ph.D., Pennsylvania. Caribbean, formation of African diaspora culture, Atlantic slave trade. James Boyden, Ph.D., Texas at Austin. Spain, Habsburg Spain, Renaissance and Reformation, early modern Atlantic world. Guadalupe Garcia, Ph.D., North Carolina at Chapel Hill. Nineteenth and twentieth century Latin America, urban studies, race and ethnicity, Caribbean, Cuba. Kris Lane, Frances V. Scholes, Chair in Latin American Colonial History; Ph.D., Minnesota. Andes, South America. Jana Lipman, Ph.D., Yale. U.S. foreign relations, history of empire, Cuba, Caribbean. Colin M. MacLachlan, Ph.D., UCLA. Brazil, Mexico, environment and ecology. Justin Wolfe, Ph.D., UCLA. Central America, race and ethnicity. Gertrude M. Yeager, Ph.D., Texas Christian. South American historiography, Andes, women, nation-making.

Institutional Research: Dave Davis, Director, Institutional Research; Ph.D., Yale. Caribbean, archaeology and ethnohistory.

International Development: William E. Bertrand, Ph.D., Tulane. Public health and medicine, information technology, information and evaluation systems, instructional technology and design, human resource planning. Colin Crawford, Executive Director, Payson Center for International Development; J.D., Harvard. Environmental law, urban planning, Caribbean, Central America. Eamon M. Kelly, President Emeritus, Tulane and Director of Academic Programs, Payson Center for International Development; Ph.D., Columbia. Development, planning. S.W.R. de Samarasinghe. Ph.D., Cambridge. Economics, ethnic conflict.

Latin American Studies: Ana Margarida Fernandes Esteves, postdoctoral teaching fellow; Ph.D., Brown. Annie Gibson, postdoctoral teaching fellow; Ph.D., Tulane. Brazil, immigrant, cultural production, performance. James D. Huck, Assistant Director, Graduate Programs; Ph.D., Tulane. Contemporary Mexican politics and foreign relations, U.S.-Latin American relations, general Latin American foreign policy. Edith A. G. Wolfe, Assistant Director of Undergraduate Affairs; Ph.D., Texas. Latin American art, modernism in Latin America.

Law: Günther Handl, J.S.D., Yale. International environmental law. Oliver Houck, J.D., Georgetown. Environmental and natural resources law, Cuba.

Library: Hortensia Calvo, Doris Stone Librarian and Director, Latin American Library; Ph.D., Yale. Spanish and Spanish-American literature. Lance Query, Dean of Libraries and Academic Information Resources; Ph.D., Indiana. Latin American history.

Music: Daniel Sharp, Ph.D., Texas at Austin. Ethnomusicology, Brazil.

Physics: Wayne Reed, Ph.D., Clarkson. Macromolecular science, development of new instrumentation and software with strong collaborators and guidance of research programs in Mexico and Brazil.

Political Science: Mary Clark, Interim Associate Dean for Finance and Planning, School of Liberal Arts; Ph.D., Wisconsin. Costa Rica, comparative politics. Casey Kane-Love, Ph.D., Tulane. Mexico, U.S.-Latin American relations, Mexican politics. Martin Mendoza-Botelho, Ph.D., Cambridge. Comparative politics, Andes, Bolivia. Scott Pentzer, Associate Director, Honors Program; Ph.D., Tulane. Mexico, Costa Rica, social and intellectual history. Aaron Schneider, Ph.D., Berkeley. Brazil, Central America, political economy, public finance, statecraft. G. Eduardo Silva, Ph.D., California, San Diego. Latin American politics, environmental politics, sustainable development. Raymond Taras, Ph.D., Warsaw. Comparative communism, Eastern European relations with Latin America.

Psychology: Enrique Varela, Ph.D., Kansas. Mexico, clinical psychology, post-traumatic stress and anxiety expression in Mexican, Mexican-American, and Caucasian children.

Public Health and Tropical Medicine: Katherine Andrinopoulos, Ph.D., Johns Hopkins. Jamaica/Caribbean, HIV/AIDS. Antonio Barrios, Director of International Medical Affairs, Tulane Hospital and Clinic; M.D., San Carlos (Guatemala); M.P.H., Tulane. Health administration, international health. Jane Bertrand, Chair, Department of Health Systems Management, School of Public Health and Tropical Medicine; Ph.D., Chicago. Family planning and population studies, Central America, Andes. Pierre Buekens, Dean, School of Public Health and Tropical Medicine; M.D., M.P.H., Ph.D., Free University of Brussels. Obstetrics and gynecology, epidemiology, general Latin America. Carl Kendall, Ph.D., Rochester. International health and development, anthropology, social and cultural factors of community health. Kate Macintyre, Ph.D., North Carolina at Chapel Hill. Health systems analysis, international health policy analysis. Nancy Mock, Dr.P.H., Tulane. International health and development. evaluation research, information systems methodologies. Laura Murphy, Ph.D., North Carolina at Chapel Hill. International health and development, Ecuador, planning, development, household livelihoods and well-being, frontier settlement, tropical deforestation. Valerie Paz-Soldán, Director, Health Office for Latin America; Ph.D., North Carolina at Chapel Hill. Public health and tropical medicine, maternal and child health, Peru. Diego Rose, Ph.D., Berkeley. Community health science, Central America, Africa, consumer economics, international food and nutrition policy.

Sociology: Katie Acosta, Ph.D., Connecticut. Gender, sexuality, race/ethnicity, immigration, Latina studies, feminist methods. Stephanie Arnett, Ph.D., Notre Dame. Sociology of education, Mexico. Martha Huggins, Ph.D., New Hampshire. Brazil, political policing, torture and violence, urban sociology. David Ortiz, Ph.D., Notre Dame. Political sociology, social movements.

Spanish and Portuguese: Rebecca Atencio, Ph.D., Wisconsin–Madison. Luso-Brazilian literatures and cultures, postdictatorial Latin America, political violence and memory, testimonial and exile literatures. Idelber Avelar, Ph.D., Duke. Postdictatorial culture, Southern Cone and Brazilian literature and culture, identity and Latin Americanism. Laura Bass, Ph.D., Princeton. Seventeenth-century Spanish stage. Carolina Caballero, Country Director, Semester in Cuba; Ph.D., North Carolina at Chapel Hill. Contemporary Latin American literature, cultural studies, Cuba. John Charles, Ph.D., Yale. Latin American literature. Christopher Dunn, Ph.D., Brown. Cuba, cultural studies, Brazilian culture, African diaspora studies, popular music. Amy George-Hirons, Director, Basic Language Program; Ph.D., Tulane. Linguistics, Latin American literature, Mesoamerican art history. Antonio Daniel Gómez, Ph.D., Pittsburgh. Argentina, Cuba, literature of exile. Harry Howard, Ph.D., Cornell. Language, neuromimetic modeling of linguistics and allied phenomena. Marilyn Miller, Ph.D., Oregon. Colonial literatures of Latin America, postcolonial theory, Caribbean and trans-American studies. Tatjana Pavlovic, Ph.D., Washington. Film studies, feminism, critical theory. Fernando César Rivera-Díaz, Ph.D., Princeton, Contemporary Latin American narratives. Maureen Shea, Ph.D., Arizona. Literature and culture, Central American and Andean literature, testimonial literature, gender and sexuality. Ari Zighelboim, Ph.D., Tulane. Colonial Latin American literature and culture, Andean studies, Jewish–Latin American cultural expressions.

Theater and Dance: Diogo de Lima, Pavillion Arts Center, São Paulo (Brazil). Brazil, jazz, dance, modern dance. Beverly Trask, M.F.A., Southern Mississippi. Afro-Caribbean dance and performance, jazz and tap, modern dancing.

AFFILIATED INSTITUTES AND CENTERS

Center for Inter-American Policy and Research: Sergio Béjar, CIPR Postdoctoral Research Fellow; Ph.D., Notre Dame. Comparative politics in Latin America. Ludovico Feoli, Permanent Researcher and CEO, Executive Director; Ph.D., Tulane. Latin American political economy, state building. Moira B. MacKinnon, Postdoctoral Research Fellow; Ph.D., California, San Diego. Political sociology, worker's movements, Argentina. Constantino Urcuyo, Academic Director; Ph.D., Sorbonne. Central America, political science, democratic culture.

Professors Emeriti: E. Wyllys Andrews V, Ph.D., Tulane. Central America, archaeology of Central America, eastern Mesoamerica, Yucatan peninsula, Guatemala, El Salvador, Honduras. Harvey Bricker, Ph.D., Harvard. France, Mesoamerica, paleolithic archaeology in France, archaeoastronomy of the Maya. Victoria R. Bricker, Ph.D., Harvard. Mexico, Mesoamerican ethnohistory and linguistics, epigraphy, ethnography. Eugene D. Cizek, Ph.D. Tulane. Historic preservation, Guatemala. Rodolfo Cerdas Cruz, researcher and professor CIAPA; Ph.D., Sorbonne. Central America, political science and law, human rights, labor organizations, communist party. Richard Greenleaf, Ph.D., New Mexico. History, Mexico, colonial inquisition. Paul Lewis, Ph.D., North Carolina. Southern Cone, Argentine, and Paraguayan political systems. Susan Schroeder, Ph.D., UCLA. Mexico, Mesoamerican social history, early Nahuatl philology. Ralph Lee Woodward, Ph.D., Tulane. History, Central America, nation building.

Section 16
Communication and Media

This section contains a directory of institutions offering graduate work in communication and media, followed by in-depth entries submitted by institutions that chose to prepare detailed program descriptions. Additional information about programs listed in the directory but not augmented by an in-depth entry may be obtained by writing directly to the dean of a graduate school or chair of a department at the address given in the directory.

For programs offering related work, see also in this book *Film, Television, and Video; Language and Literature;* and *Psychology and Counseling.* In the other guides in this series:

Graduate Programs in Engineering & Applied Sciences
See *Computer Science and Information Technology* and *Telecommunications*

Graduate Programs in Business, Education, Health, Information Studies, Law & Social Work
See *Advertising and Public Relations*

CONTENTS

Communication—General

Abilene Christian University, Graduate School, College of Arts and Sciences, Department of Communication, Program in Communication, Abilene, TX 79699-9100. Offers MA. Part-time programs available. *Faculty:* 7 part-time/adjunct (3 women). *Students:* 13 full-time (3 women), 8 part-time (5 women); includes 2 Black or African American, non-Hispanic/Latino; 1 Hispanic/Latino, 7 international. 14 applicants, 71% accepted, 7 enrolled. In 2010, 6 master's awarded. *Degree requirements:* For master's, comprehensive exam, thesis optional. *Entrance requirements:* For master's, GRE General Test. Additional exam requirements/recommendations for international students: Required—TOEFL (minimum score 550 paper-based; 213 computer-based). *Application deadline:* For fall admission, 4/1 priority date for domestic students; for spring admission, 11/1 for domestic students. Applications are processed on a rolling basis. Application fee: $40. Electronic applications accepted. *Expenses:* Tuition: Full-time $12,906; part-time $717 per hour. Required fees: $1250; $61.50 per unit. *Financial support:* In 2010–11, 16 students received support; teaching assistantships, Federal Work-Study available. Support available to part-time students. Financial award application deadline: 4/1; financial award applicants required to submit FAFSA. *Faculty research:* Intercultural communication, family communication, forensics, organizational communication. *Unit head:* Dr. Paul Lakey, Graduate Adviser, 325-674-2292, Fax: 325-674-6966, E-mail: lakeyp@acu.edu. *Application contact:* David Pittman, Graduate Admissions Counselor, 325-674-2656, Fax: 325-674-6717, E-mail: gradinfo@acu.edu.

American University, School of Communication, Washington, DC 20016-8001. Offers MA, MFA, PhD. *Accreditation:* ACEJMC (one or more programs are accredited). Part-time and evening/weekend programs available. *Faculty:* 44 full-time (23 women). *Students:* 177 full-time (120 women), 199 part-time (119 women); includes 61 Black or African American, non-Hispanic/Latino; 1 American Indian or Alaska Native, non-Hispanic/Latino; 14 Asian, non-Hispanic/Latino; 14 Hispanic/Latino; 1 Two or more races, non-Hispanic/Latino, 22 international. Average age 27. 685 applicants, 64% accepted, 200 enrolled. In 2010, 185 master's awarded. *Degree requirements:* For master's, comprehensive exam, thesis or alternative; for doctorate, comprehensive exam, thesis/dissertation. *Entrance requirements:* For master's and doctorate, GRE General Test. Additional exam requirements/recommendations for international students: Required—TOEFL (minimum score 600 paper-based; 260 computer-based; 100 iBT), IELTS (minimum score 7). *Application deadline:* For fall admission, 2/1 priority date for domestic students, 4/1 priority date for international students; for spring admission, 11/15 for domestic and international students. Applications are processed on a rolling basis. Application fee: $50. Electronic applications accepted. *Financial support:* In 2010–11, 64 students received support, including 6 fellowships with partial tuition reimbursements available (averaging $23,000 per year), 15 research assistantships with partial tuition reimbursements available (averaging $18,000 per year), 15 teaching assistantships with partial tuition reimbursements available (averaging $18,000 per year); career-related internships or fieldwork, Federal Work-Study, institutionally sponsored loans, scholarships/grants, and tuition waivers (partial) also available. Support available to part-time students. Financial award application deadline: 2/1; financial award applicants required to submit FAFSA. *Faculty research:* New communication technology, documentaries and public broadcasting, litigation and public relations, dissident media, race and gender and the media, international journalism and human rights, social media. *Unit head:* Dean Larry Kirkman, Dean, 202-885-2058, Fax: 202-885-2099, E-mail: larry@american.edu. *Application contact:* Sharmeen Ahsan-Bracciale, Director of Graduate Services, 202-885-2040, Fax: 202-885-2019, E-mail: sharmeen@american.edu.

The American University in Cairo, School of Global Affairs and Public Policy, Department of Journalism and Mass Communication, Cairo, Egypt. Offers journalism and mass communication (MA); television and digital journalism (MA). Part-time programs available. *Degree requirements:* For master's, thesis (for some programs). *Entrance requirements:* For master's, English entrance exam, GMAT. Electronic applications accepted. *Faculty research:* Mass media and national development/censorship, intercultural photo communication, comparative journalism/television.

The American University of Paris, Graduate Programs, Paris, France. Offers cross-cultural and sustainable business management (MA); cultural translation (MA); global communications (MA); global communications and civil society (MA); international affairs, conflict resolution and civil society development (MA); Middle East and Islamic studies (MA); Middle East and Islamic studies and international affairs (MA); public policy and international affairs (MA); public policy and international law (MA). *Faculty:* 14 full-time (3 women). *Students:* 151 full-time (110 women), 56 part-time (43 women). 271 applicants, 83% accepted, 104 enrolled. In 2010, 67 master's awarded. *Degree requirements:* For master's, thesis. *Entrance requirements:* For master's, minimum undergraduate GPA of 3.0. Additional exam requirements/recommendations for international students: Recommended—IELTS. *Application deadline:* For fall admission, 4/15 priority date for international students; for spring admission, 11/15 priority date for international students. Applications are processed on a rolling basis. Application fee: $75. Electronic applications accepted. *Financial support:* Scholarships/grants available. Financial award applicants required to submit FAFSA. *Unit head:* Dr. Celeste Schenck, President, 33-1 40 62 06 59, E-mail: president@aup.fr. *Application contact:* International Admissions Counselor, 33-1 40 62 07 20, Fax: 33-1 47 05 34 32, E-mail: admissions@aup.edu.

Andrews University, School of Graduate Studies, College of Arts and Sciences, Interdisciplinary Studies in Communication Program, Berrien Springs, MI 49104. Offers MA.

Angelo State University, College of Graduate Studies, College of Liberal and Fine Arts, Department of Communication, Mass Media and Theatre, San Angelo, TX 76909. Offers communication systems management (MA). Part-time and evening/weekend programs available. *Faculty:* 2 full-time (0 women). *Students:* 15 full-time (9 women), 8 part-time (3 women); includes 2 Black or African American, non-Hispanic/Latino; 4 Hispanic/Latino, 1 international. Average age 30. 10 applicants, 70% accepted, 6 enrolled. In 2010, 5 master's awarded. *Degree requirements:* For master's, comprehensive exam, thesis optional. *Entrance requirements:* Additional exam requirements/recommendations for international students: Required—TOEFL or IELTS. *Application deadline:* For fall admission, 7/15 priority date for domestic students, 6/10 for international students; for spring admission, 12/1 priority date for domestic students, 11/1 for international students. Applications are processed on a rolling basis. Application fee: $40 ($50 for international students). Electronic applications accepted. *Expenses:* Tuition, state resident: full-time $4560; part-time $152 per credit hour. Tuition, nonresident: full-time $13,860; part-time $462 per credit hour. Required fees: $2132. Tuition and fees vary according to course load. *Financial support:* In 2010–11, 5 students received support, including 3 teaching assistantships (averaging $10,251 per year); career-related internships or fieldwork, Federal Work-Study, scholarships/grants, and unspecified assistantships also available. Support available to part-time students. Financial award application deadline: 3/1; financial award applicants required to submit FAFSA. *Unit head:* Dr. Shawn T. Wahl, Department Head, 325-942-2031 Ext. 228, Fax: 325-942-2551, E-mail: swahl1@angelo.edu. *Application contact:* Dr. Lana Marlow, Graduate Advisor, 325-942-2032 Ext. 356, Fax: 325-942-2551, E-mail: lana.marlow@angelo.edu.

Arizona State University, College of Liberal Arts and Sciences, Hugh Downs School of Human Communication, Tempe, AZ 85287. Offers communication (PhD). Evening/weekend programs available. *Faculty:* 31 full-time (14 women), 11 part-time/adjunct (8 women). *Students:* 43 full-time (29 women), 15 part-time (10 women); includes 8 minority (1 Black or African American, non-Hispanic/Latino; 1 Asian, non-Hispanic/Latino; 6 Hispanic/Latino), 5 international. Average age 31. 120 applicants, 31% accepted, 12 enrolled. In 2010, 12 doctorates awarded. *Degree requirements:* For doctorate, comprehensive exam, thesis/dissertation, interactive Program of Study (iPOS) submitted before completing 50 percent of required credit hours. *Entrance requirements:* For doctorate, GRE, minimum GPA of 3.0 or equivalent in last 2 years of work leading to bachelor's degree. Additional exam requirements/recommendations for international students: Required—TOEFL, IELTS, or Pearson Test of English. *Application*

deadline: For fall admission, 1/5 for domestic and international students. Applications are processed on a rolling basis. Application fee: $70 ($90 for international students). Electronic applications accepted. *Expenses:* Tuition, state resident: full-time $8510; part-time $608 per credit. Tuition, nonresident: full-time $16,542; part-time $919 per credit. Required fees: $339; $110 per credit. Part-time tuition and fees vary according to course load. *Financial support:* In 2010–11, 6 research assistantships with full and partial tuition reimbursements (averaging $11,771 per year), 33 teaching assistantships with full and partial tuition reimbursements (averaging $13,911 per year) were awarded; fellowships with full tuition reimbursements, career-related internships or fieldwork, Federal Work-Study, institutionally sponsored loans, scholarships/grants, and tuition waivers (full and partial) also available. Financial award application deadline: 3/1; financial award applicants required to submit FAFSA. Total annual research expenditures: $1.1 million. *Unit head:* Dr. Angela Trethewey, Director, 480-965-5095, E-mail: atreth@asu.edu. *Application contact:* Graduate Admissions, 480-965-6113.

Arizona State University, New College of Interdisciplinary Arts and Sciences, Program in Communication Studies, Phoenix, AZ 85069-7100. Offers MA. Part-time and evening/weekend programs available. *Faculty:* 11 full-time (5 women). *Students:* 23 full-time (15 women), 27 part-time (19 women); includes 9 minority (4 Black or African American, non-Hispanic/Latino; 1 American Indian or Alaska Native, non-Hispanic/Latino; 1 Asian, non-Hispanic/Latino; 3 Hispanic/Latino), 4 international. Average age 30. 38 applicants, 61% accepted, 9 enrolled. In 2010, 8 master's awarded. *Degree requirements:* For master's, thesis, applied project or written comprehensive exam; interactive Program of Study (iPOS) submitted before completing 50 percent of required credit hours. *Entrance requirements:* For master's, GRE (if GPA less than 3.0 in last 60 hours of undergraduate study), minimum GPA of 3.0 or equivalent in last 2 years of work leading to bachelor's degree, 3 letters of recommendation, official transcripts, writing sample of scholarly work or example of professional activities. Additional exam requirements/recommendations for international students: Required—TOEFL, IELTS, or Pearson Test of English. *Application deadline:* For fall admission, 4/15 for domestic and international students; for spring admission, 10/15 for domestic and international students. Application fee: $70 ($90 for international students). Electronic applications accepted. *Expenses:* Tuition, state resident: full-time $8510; part-time $608 per credit. Tuition, nonresident: full-time $16,542; part-time $919 per credit. Required fees: $339; $110 per credit. Part-time tuition and fees vary according to course load. *Financial support:* In 2010–11, 1 research assistantship with full and partial tuition reimbursement (averaging $6,343 per year) was awarded; teaching assistantships with full and partial tuition reimbursements, institutionally sponsored loans, scholarships/grants, and tuition waivers (full and partial) also available. Support available to part-time students. Financial award application deadline: 3/1; financial award applicants required to submit FAFSA. *Faculty research:* Organizational, applied, and environmental communication; intergenerational family communication and its connectedness to wellness; communication in personal and work relationships; popular culture; technology and culture; cultural dimensions of new mobile communication and computing technologies. *Unit head:* Dr. Jeffrey Kassing, Director, 602-543-6631, Fax: 602-543-6612, E-mail: jkassing@asu.edu. *Application contact:* Graduate Admissions, 480-965-6113.

Arkansas State University, Graduate School, College of Communications, Jonesboro, State University, AR 72467. Offers MA, MSMC, SCCT. Part-time programs available. *Faculty:* 13 full-time (5 women), 1 part-time/adjunct (0 women). *Students:* 33 full-time (20 women), 31 part-time (19 women); includes 27 minority (all Black or African American, non-Hispanic/Latino), 24 international. Average age 27. 63 applicants, 73% accepted, 29 enrolled. In 2010, 14 master's awarded. *Degree requirements:* For master's, one foreign language, comprehensive exam, thesis or alternative. *Entrance requirements:* For master's, GRE General Test, appropriate bachelor's degree, letters of reference; official transcripts, immunization records; for SCCT, GRE, interview, master's degree, official transcript, immunization records. Additional exam requirements/recommendations for international students: Required—TOEFL (minimum score 550 paper-based; 213 computer-based; 79 iBT), IELTS (minimum score 6), PTE: Pearson Test of English Academic (56). *Application deadline:* For fall admission, 7/1 for domestic and international students; for spring admission, 11/15 for domestic students, 11/14 for international students. Applications are processed on a rolling basis. Application fee: $30 ($40 for international students). Electronic applications accepted. *Expenses:* Tuition, state resident: full-time $3888; part-time $216 per credit hour. Tuition, nonresident: full-time $9918; part-time $551 per credit hour. International tuition: $8376 full-time. Required fees: $932; $49 per credit hour. $25 per term. One-time fee: $30. Tuition and fees vary according to course load and program. *Financial support:* In 2010–11, 23 students received support. Career-related internships or fieldwork, scholarships/grants, and unspecified assistantships available. Financial award application deadline: 7/1; financial award applicants required to submit FAFSA. *Unit head:* Dr. Osabuohien Amienyi, Interim Dean, 870-972-2468, Fax: 870-972-3856, E-mail: osami@astate.edu. *Application contact:* Dr. Andrew Sustich, Dean of the Graduate School, 870-972-3029, Fax: 870-972-3857, E-mail: sustich@astate.edu.

Arkansas Tech University, Graduate College, College of Arts and Humanities, Russellville, AR 72801. Offers communication (MLA); English (M Ed, MA); fine arts (MLA); history (MA); multi-media journalism (MA); psychology (MS); social science (MLA); Spanish (MA, MLA); teaching English as a second language (MA, MLA). Part-time programs available. *Students:* 39 full-time (23 women), 87 part-time (69 women); includes 13 minority (3 Black or African American, non-Hispanic/Latino; 1 American Indian or Alaska Native, non-Hispanic/Latino; 1 Asian, non-Hispanic/Latino; 8 Hispanic/Latino), 14 international. Average age 32. In 2010, 54 master's awarded. *Degree requirements:* For master's, comprehensive exam (for some programs), thesis (for some programs), project. *Entrance requirements:* For master's, GRE General Test or MAT. Additional exam requirements/recommendations for international students: Required—TOEFL (minimum score 550 paper-based; 213 computer-based; 79 iBT), IELTS (minimum score 6). *Application deadline:* For fall admission, 3/1 priority date for domestic students, 5/1 priority date for international students; for spring admission, 10/1 priority date for domestic and international students. Applications are processed on a rolling basis. Application fee: $0 ($50 for international students). Electronic applications accepted. *Expenses:* Tuition, state resident: full-time $4680; part-time $195 per credit hour. Tuition, nonresident: full-time $9360; part-time $390 per credit hour. Required fees: $714; $14 per credit hour. One-time fee: $326 part-time. Tuition and fees vary according to course load. *Financial support:* In 2010–11, teaching assistantships with full tuition reimbursements (averaging $4,000 per year); research assistantships, career-related internships or fieldwork, Federal Work-Study, scholarships/grants, health care benefits, and unspecified assistantships also available. Support available to part-time students. Financial award application deadline: 4/15; financial award applicants required to submit FAFSA. *Unit head:* Dr. Micheal Tarver, Dean, 479-968-0274, Fax: 479-964-0812, E-mail: mtarver@atu.edu. *Application contact:* Dr. Mary B. Gunter, Dean of Graduate College, 479-968-0398, Fax: 479-964-0542, E-mail: graduate.school@atu.edu.

Auburn University, Graduate School, College of Liberal Arts, Department of Communication and Journalism, Auburn University, AL 36849. Offers communication (MA); mass communications (MA). Part-time programs available. *Faculty:* 24 full-time (13 women), 10 part-time/adjunct (5 women). *Students:* 21 full-time (15 women), 6 part-time (4 women); includes 3 Black or African American, non-Hispanic/Latino; 1 Hispanic/Latino, 1 international. Average age 26. 26 applicants, 65% accepted, 13 enrolled. In 2010, 14 master's awarded. *Degree requirements:* For master's, thesis (for some programs). *Entrance requirements:* For master's, GRE General Test. *Application deadline:* For fall admission, 7/7 for domestic students; for spring admission, 11/24 for domestic students. Applications are processed on a rolling basis. Application fee: $50 ($60 for international students). Electronic applications accepted. *Expenses:* Tuition, state resident: full-time $7002. Tuition, nonresident: full-time $21,898. International tuition: $22,116 full-time. Required fees: $892. Tuition and fees vary according to course load and program. *Financial support:* Teaching assistantships, Federal Work-Study available. Support available to part-time students. Financial award application deadline: 3/15; financial award applicants required to submit FAFSA. *Unit head:* Dr. Mary Helen Brown, Acting Chair, 334-844-2727. *Application contact:* Dr. George Flowers, Dean of the Graduate School, 334-844-2125.

Austin Peay State University, College of Graduate Studies, College of Arts and Letters, Department of Communication, Clarksville, TN 37044. Offers communication arts (MA). Part-time and evening/weekend programs available. Postbaccalaureate distance learning degree programs offered (no on-campus study). *Faculty:* 8 full-time (5 women), 4 part-time/adjunct (3 women). *Students:* 2 full-time (both women), 63 part-time (44 women); includes 12 minority (11 Black or African American, non-Hispanic/Latino; 1 Two or more races, non-Hispanic/Latino). Average age 32. 32 applicants, 94% accepted, 23 enrolled. In 2010, 23 master's awarded. *Degree requirements:* For master's, comprehensive exam, thesis (for some programs). *Entrance requirements:* For master's, GRE General Test, 3 letters of recommendation. Additional exam requirements/recommendations for international students: Required—TOEFL (minimum score 500 paper-based; 173 computer-based). *Application deadline:* For fall admission, 7/27 priority date for domestic students; for spring admission, 12/17 priority date for domestic students. Applications are processed on a rolling basis. Application fee: $25. Electronic applications accepted. *Expenses:* Tuition, state resident: full-time $6480; part-time $324 per credit hour. Tuition, nonresident: full-time $17,960; part-time $898 per credit hour. Required fees: $1244; $61.20 per credit hour. *Financial support:* In 2010–11, research assistantships with full tuition reimbursements (averaging $5,174 per year); career-related internships or fieldwork, Federal Work-Study, institutionally sponsored loans, scholarships/grants, and unspecified assistantships also available. Support available to part-time students. Financial award application deadline: 3/1; financial award applicants required to submit FAFSA. *Unit head:* Dr. Mike Gotcher, Chair, 931-221-7378, Fax: 931-221-7265, E-mail: comm@apsu.edu. *Application contact:* Dr. Dixie Dennis, Dean, College of Graduate Studies, 931-221-7662, Fax: 931-221-7641, E-mail: dennisdi@apsu.edu.

Ball State University, Graduate School, College of Communication, Information, and Media, Muncie, IN 47306-1099. Offers MA, MS. Part-time programs available. Postbaccalaureate distance learning degree programs offered (no on-campus study). *Faculty:* 31. *Students:* 141 full-time (58 women), 74 part-time (35 women); includes 9 Black or African American, non-Hispanic/Latino; 1 American Indian or Alaska Native, non-Hispanic/Latino; 1 Asian, non-Hispanic/Latino; 3 Hispanic/Latino; 2 Two or more races, non-Hispanic/Latino, 32 international. Average age 25. 223 applicants, 61% accepted, 91 enrolled. In 2010, 92 master's awarded. *Degree requirements:* For master's, comprehensive exam (for some programs), thesis (for some programs). *Entrance requirements:* For master's, GRE (for some programs). Additional exam requirements/recommendations for international students: Required—TOEFL (minimum score 550 paper-based; 213 computer-based), IELTS (minimum score 6.5). *Application deadline:* For fall admission, 1/1 priority date for international students; for spring admission, 7/1 priority date for international students. Applications are processed on a rolling basis. Application fee: $50. Electronic applications accepted. *Expenses:* Tuition, state resident: full-time $6160; part-time $299 per credit hour. Tuition, nonresident: full-time $16,020; part-time $783 per credit hour. Required fees: $2278; $95 per credit hour. *Financial support:* In 2010–11, 8 research assistantships with full tuition reimbursements (averaging $6,668 per year), 66 teaching assistantships with full tuition reimbursements (averaging $7,976 per year) were awarded; career-related internships or fieldwork also available. Financial award application deadline: 3/1. *Unit head:* Roger Lavery, Dean, 765-285-6000, Fax: 765-285-6002. *Application contact:* Dr. Robert Morris, Associate Provost for Research and Dean of the Graduate School, 765-285-4723, Fax: 765-285-1328, E-mail: rmorris@bsu.edu.

Barry University, School of Arts and Sciences, Department of Communication, Miami Shores, FL 33161-6695. Offers broadcasting (Certificate); communication (MA), including broadcast communication, public relations and corporate communications; organizational communication (MS). Part-time and evening/weekend programs available. *Degree requirements:* For master's, thesis (for some programs). *Entrance requirements:* For master's, GRE General Test, MAT, minimum GPA of 3.0. Electronic applications accepted. *Faculty research:* Organizational communication, broadcast communication, intercultural communication, advertising, leadership.

Baylor University, Graduate School, College of Arts and Sciences, Department of Communication Studies, Waco, TX 76798. Offers MA. Part-time programs available. *Students:* 16 full-time (9 women), 6 part-time (2 women); includes 2 Asian, non-Hispanic/Latino, 1 international. Average age 22. In 2010, 3 master's awarded. *Degree requirements:* For master's, thesis or alternative. *Entrance requirements:* For master's, GRE General Test. *Application deadline:* For fall admission, 8/1 for domestic students. Applications are processed on a rolling basis. Application fee: $25. *Financial support:* In 2010–11, 12 teaching assistantships were awarded; career-related internships or fieldwork, Federal Work-Study, institutionally sponsored loans, and scholarships/grants also available. Financial award application deadline: 4/1. *Faculty research:* Rhetoric and debate, organizational communication, media studies, new technology. *Unit head:* Dr. Mark Morman, Graduate Program Director, 254-710-1621, E-mail: mark_morman@baylor.edu. *Application contact:* Marilyn Spivey, Administrative Assistant, 254-710-1621, Fax: 254-710-3870, E-mail: marilyn_spivey@baylor.edu.

Bellarmine University, School of Communication, Louisville, KY 40205-0671. Offers MA. Part-time and evening/weekend programs available. *Faculty:* 4 full-time (all women). *Students:* 40 part-time (30 women); includes 1 Black or African American, non-Hispanic/Latino; 2 Hispanic/Latino. Average age 33. In 2010, 14 master's awarded. *Entrance requirements:* For master's, GRE, GMAT or LSAT. Additional exam requirements/recommendations for international students: Required—TOEFL (minimum score 550 paper-based; 213 computer-based; 80 iBT). *Application deadline:* Applications are processed on a rolling basis. Application fee: $30. *Unit head:* Edward Manasssah, Executive Director, 502-272-8324, E-mail: emahassah@bellarmine.edu. *Application contact:* Dr. Sara Pettingill, Dean of Graduate Admission, 502-272-8401, Fax: 502-272-8002, E-mail: spettingill@bellarmine.edu.

Bethel University, Graduate School, Program in Communication, St. Paul, MN 55112-6999. Offers communication (MA); post-secondary teaching (Certificate). Part-time and evening/weekend programs available. *Faculty:* 5 full-time (3 women), 5 part-time/adjunct (1 woman). *Students:* 43 full-time (28 women), 19 part-time (9 women); includes 2 Black or African American, non-Hispanic/Latino; 1 Asian, non-Hispanic/Latino; 1 Two or more races, non-Hispanic/Latino, 2 international. Average age 38. 25 applicants, 100% accepted, 23 enrolled. In 2010, 19 master's awarded. *Degree requirements:* For master's, comprehensive exam, thesis. *Entrance requirements:* For master's, MAT, baccalaureate degree, minimum GPA of 3.0, course work in communication and statistics, references, sample of written work, interview. Additional exam requirements/recommendations for international students: Required—TOEFL (minimum score 550 paper-based; 213 computer-based; 80 iBT). *Application deadline:* For fall admission, 5/15 priority date for domestic students. Applications are processed on a rolling basis. Electronic applications accepted. *Expenses:* Tuition: Full-time $5400; part-time $450 per credit. Tuition and fees vary according to course level, course load, degree level and program. *Financial support:* Applicants required to submit FAFSA. *Unit head:* Dr. Lori J. Jass, Assistant Dean, 651-635-8000, Fax: 651-635-8039, E-mail: l-jass@bethel.edu. *Application contact:* Paul Ives, Director of Admissions, 651-635-8000, Fax: 651-635-8004, E-mail: gs@bethel.edu.

Boise State University, Graduate College, College of Social Sciences and Public Affairs, Department of Communication, Boise, ID 83725-0399. Offers MA. Part-time programs available. *Degree requirements:* For master's, thesis. *Entrance requirements:* For master's, minimum GPA of 3.0, writing sample. Electronic applications accepted.

Boston University, College of Communication, Boston, MA 02215. Offers MFA, MS, JD/MS, MBA/MS. Part-time programs available. *Faculty:* 57 full-time, 81 part-time/adjunct. *Students:* 252 full-time (178 women), 30 part-time (15 women); includes 29 minority (9 Black or African American, non-Hispanic/Latino; 8 Asian, non-Hispanic/Latino; 11 Hispanic/Latino; 1 Two or more races, non-Hispanic/Latino), 56 international. Average age 25. 875 applicants, 48% accepted. In 2010, 148 master's awarded. *Degree requirements:* For master's, comprehensive exam (for some programs), thesis (for some programs). *Entrance requirements:* For master's, GRE General Test. Additional exam requirements/recommendations for international students: Required—TOEFL (minimum score 600 paper-based; 250 computer-based; 100 iBT). *Application deadline:* For fall admission, 2/1 for domestic and international students. Application fee: $70. Electronic applications accepted. *Expenses:* Tuition: Full-time $39,314; part-time $1228 per credit. Required fees: $40 per semester. *Financial support:* In 2010–11, 18 teaching assistantships with partial tuition reimbursements were awarded; career-related internships or fieldwork, Federal Work-Study, institutionally sponsored loans, scholarships/grants, and unspecified assistantships also available. Support available to part-time students. Financial award application deadline: 2/1; financial award applicants required to submit FAFSA. *Unit head:* Thomas Fiedler, Dean, 617-353-3450, Fax: 617-358-0399, E-mail: com@bu.edu. *Application contact:* Jennifer Healey, Administrator of Graduate Services, 617-353-3481, Fax: 617-358-0399, E-mail: comgrad@bu.edu.

Bowling Green State University, Graduate College, College of Arts and Sciences, School of Communication Studies, Bowling Green, OH 43403. Offers MA, PhD. Part-time programs available. Terminal master's awarded for partial completion of doctoral program. *Degree requirements:* For master's, thesis or alternative; for doctorate, comprehensive exam, thesis/dissertation. *Entrance requirements:* For master's and doctorate, GRE General Test. Additional exam requirements/recommendations for international students: Required—TOEFL. Electronic applications accepted.

Brandeis University, Rabb School of Continuing Studies, Division of Graduate Professional Studies, Virtual Team Management and Communication Program, Waltham, MA 02454-9110. Offers MS, Graduate Certificate. Part-time programs available. Postbaccalaureate distance learning degree programs offered (no on-campus study). *Faculty:* 2 full-time (both women), 33 part-time/adjunct (5 women). *Students:* 6 part-time (2 women); includes 1 Black or African American, non-Hispanic/Latino. Average age 35. 3 applicants, 100% accepted, 3 enrolled. *Entrance requirements:* For master's, resume, official transcripts, recommendations, goal statements; for Graduate Certificate, resume, recommendations. Additional exam requirements/recommendations for international students: Recommended—TOEFL (minimum score 600 paper-based; 250 computer-based; 100 iBT). *Application deadline:* For fall admission, 6/15 priority date for domestic students; for winter admission, 10/15 priority date for domestic students; for spring admission, 2/15 priority date for domestic students. Applications are processed on a rolling basis. Application fee: $50. Electronic applications accepted. *Unit head:* Dr. Aline Yurik, Program Chair, 781-736-8787, Fax: 781-736-3420, E-mail: ayurik@brandeis.edu. *Application contact:* Frances Stearns, Associate Director of Admissions and Student Services, 781-736-8785, Fax: 781-736-3420, E-mail: fstearns@brandeis.edu.

Brigham Young University, Graduate Studies, College of Fine Arts and Communications, Department of Communications, Provo, UT 84602. Offers mass communications (MA). *Faculty:* 19 full-time (3 women). *Students:* 17 full-time (13 women), 22 part-time (10 women); includes 2 minority (1 Black or African American, non-Hispanic/Latino; 1 Hispanic/Latino). Average age 30. 25 applicants, 36% accepted, 8 enrolled. In 2010, 8 master's awarded. *Degree requirements:* For master's, comprehensive exam, thesis. *Entrance requirements:* For master's, GRE, minimum GPA of 3.0 in last 60 hours of course work. Additional exam requirements/recommendations for international students: Required—TOEFL (minimum score 580 paper-based; 237 computer-based; 85 iBT). *Application deadline:* For fall admission, 2/28 for domestic and international students. Application fee: $50. Electronic applications accepted. *Expenses:* Tuition: Full-time $5580; part-time $310 per credit hour. Tuition and fees vary according to program and student's religious affiliation. *Financial support:* In 2010–11, 24 students received support, including 15 research assistantships with full and partial tuition reimbursements available (averaging $4,877 per year), 7 teaching assistantships with full and partial tuition reimbursements available (averaging $6,103 per year); career-related internships or fieldwork, institutionally sponsored loans, scholarships/grants, unspecified assistantships, and supplementary awards also available. Financial award application deadline: 4/15; financial award applicants required to submit FAFSA. *Faculty research:* Ethics, international, magazine, newspaper, media effects. *Unit head:* Dr. Bradley L. Rawlins, Chair, 801-422-2997, Fax: 801-422-0160, E-mail: comms_secretary@byu.edu. *Application contact:* Dr. Steven R. Thomsen, Graduate Coordinator, 801-422-2078, Fax: 801-422-0160, E-mail: steven_thomsen@byu.edu.

California State University, Chico, Graduate School, College of Communication and Education, Department of Communication Arts and Sciences, Program in Communication Studies, Chico, CA 95929-0722. Offers MA. *Students:* 10 full-time (5 women), 7 part-time (6 women); includes 1 American Indian or Alaska Native, non-Hispanic/Latino; 2 Hispanic/Latino, 5 international. Average age 25. 21 applicants, 43% accepted, 5 enrolled. In 2010, 7 master's awarded. *Degree requirements:* For master's, thesis. *Entrance requirements:* Additional exam requirements/recommendations for international students: Required—TOEFL (minimum score 550 paper-based; 213 computer-based; 80 iBT), IELTS (minimum score 6.5). *Application deadline:* For fall admission, 3/1 priority date for domestic students, 3/1 for international students; for spring admission, 9/15 priority date for domestic students, 9/15 for international students. Applications are processed on a rolling basis. Application fee: $55. Electronic applications accepted. *Application contact:* Dr. Ruth Guzley, Graduate Coordinator, 530-898-5751.

California State University, East Bay, Office of Academic Programs and Graduate Studies, College of Letters, Arts, and Social Sciences, Department of Communication, Hayward, CA 94542-3000. Offers MA. Part-time programs available. *Faculty:* 7 full-time (3 women). *Students:* 8 full-time (3 women), 21 part-time (16 women); includes 7 Black or African American, non-Hispanic/Latino; 2 Asian, non-Hispanic/Latino; 4 Hispanic/Latino; 1 Two or more races, non-Hispanic/Latino, 3 international. Average age 32. 29 applicants, 62% accepted, 14 enrolled. In 2010, 3 master's awarded. *Degree requirements:* For master's, comprehensive exam, project or thesis. *Entrance requirements:* For master's, GRE, minimum GPA of 3.0 in field. Additional exam requirements/recommendations for international students: Required—TOEFL (minimum score 550 paper-based; 213 computer-based). *Application deadline:* For fall admission, 6/30 for domestic and international students. Applications are processed on a rolling basis. Application fee: $55. Electronic applications accepted. *Financial support:* Fellowships, teaching assistantships, career-related internships or fieldwork, Federal Work-Study, institutionally sponsored loans, scholarships/grants, and unspecified assistantships available. Support available to part-time students. Financial award application deadline: 3/2; financial award applicants required to submit FAFSA. *Unit head:* Dr. Gale Young, Interim Chair, 510-885-3292, Fax: 510-885-4099, E-mail: gale.young@csueastbay.edu. *Application contact:* Dr. Donna Wiley, Interim Associate Director, 510-885-2928, Fax: 510-885-4777, E-mail: donna.wiley@csueastbay.edu.

California State University, Fresno, Division of Graduate Studies, College of Arts and Humanities, Department of Communication, Fresno, CA 93740-8027. Offers MA. Part-time and evening/weekend programs available. *Degree requirements:* For master's, thesis or alternative. *Entrance requirements:* For master's, GRE General Test, minimum GPA of 3.1. Additional exam requirements/recommendations for international students: Required—TOEFL. Electronic applications accepted. *Faculty research:* Learning styles, education, critical thinking.

California State University, Fullerton, Graduate Studies, College of Communications, Department of Communications, Fullerton, CA 92834-9480. Offers advertising (MA); communications (MFA); entertainment and tourism (MA); journalism (MA); public relations (MA). Part-time programs available. *Students:* 24 full-time (15 women), 39 part-time (27 women); includes 2 Two or more races, non-Hispanic/Latino. Average age 29. 119 applicants, 40% accepted, 29 enrolled. In 2010, 30 master's awarded. *Degree requirements:* For master's, project or thesis. *Entrance requirements:* For master's, GRE General Test. Application fee: $55. *Financial support:* Teaching assistantships, career-related internships or fieldwork, Federal Work-Study, institutionally sponsored loans, and scholarships/grants available. Support available to part-time students. Financial award application deadline: 3/1; financial award applicants required to submit FAFSA. *Unit head:* Dr. Tony Fellow, Chair, 657-278-3517. *Application contact:* Coordinator, 657-278-3832.

Communication—General

California State University, Long Beach, Graduate Studies, College of Liberal Arts, Department of Communication Studies, Long Beach, CA 90840. Offers MA. Part-time programs available. *Faculty:* 6 full-time (4 women), 1 part-time/adjunct (0 women). *Students:* 9 full-time (7 women), 20 part-time (11 women); includes 1 Black or African American, non-Hispanic/Latino; 2 Asian, non-Hispanic/Latino; 7 Hispanic/Latino, 2 international. Average age 26. 71 applicants, 34% accepted, 14 enrolled. In 2010, 11 master's awarded. *Degree requirements:* For master's, comprehensive exam or thesis. *Entrance requirements:* For master's, GRE. *Application deadline:* For fall admission, 2/25 for domestic students. Applications are processed on a rolling basis. Application fee: $55. Electronic applications accepted. *Financial support:* Federal Work-Study, institutionally sponsored loans, and scholarships/grants available. Financial award application deadline: 3/2. *Faculty research:* Rhetoric, public address, communication theory, interpersonal communication, intercultural communication. *Unit head:* Dr. Sharon Downey, Chair, 562-985-4301, Fax: 562-985-4259. *Application contact:* Dr. Ann Johnson, Graduate Adviser, 562-985-9190, Fax: 562-985-4259, E-mail: ajohnso7@csulb.edu.

California State University, Los Angeles, Graduate Studies, College of Arts and Letters, Department of Communication Studies, Los Angeles, CA 90032-8530. Offers speech communication (MA); television, film and theatre (MFA). Part-time and evening/weekend programs available. *Faculty:* 11 full-time (5 women), 3 part-time/adjunct (2 women). *Students:* 85 full-time (52 women), 57 part-time (41 women); includes 58 minority (20 Black or African American, non-Hispanic/Latino; 7 Asian, non-Hispanic/Latino; 26 Hispanic/Latino; 5 Two or more races, non-Hispanic/Latino), 29 international. Average age 32. 93 applicants, 100% accepted, 54 enrolled. In 2010, 19 master's awarded. *Degree requirements:* For master's, comprehensive exam or thesis. *Entrance requirements:* For master's, minimum GPA of 2.75 in last 90 units of course work. Additional exam requirements/recommendations for international students: Required—TOEFL (minimum score 500 paper-based; 173 computer-based). *Application deadline:* For fall admission, 5/1 for domestic and international students. Applications are processed on a rolling basis. Application fee: $55. Electronic applications accepted. *Financial support:* Career-related internships or fieldwork and Federal Work-Study available. Support available to part-time students. Financial award application deadline: 3/1. *Faculty research:* Organizational, interpersonal, intercultural, and instructional communication; rhetorical theories. *Unit head:* Dr. Bryant Keith Alexander, Chair, 323-343-4200, Fax: 323-343-6467, E-mail: abryant@calstatela.edu. *Application contact:* Dr. Alan Muchlinski, Dean of Graduate Studies, 323-343-3820, Fax: 323-343-5653, E-mail: amuchli@exchange.calstatela.edu.

California State University, Northridge, Graduate Studies, College of Arts, Media, and Communication, Northridge, CA 91330. Offers MA, MFA, MM. Part-time and evening/weekend programs available. *Entrance requirements:* Additional exam requirements/recommendations for international students: Required—TOEFL.

California State University, Sacramento, Graduate Studies, College of Arts and Letters, Department of Communication Studies, Sacramento, CA 95819. Offers MA. Part-time programs available. *Degree requirements:* For master's, thesis or alternative, writing proficiency exam. *Entrance requirements:* For master's, minimum GPA of 3.25 during previous 2 years. Additional exam requirements/recommendations for international students: Required—TOEFL. Electronic applications accepted.

California State University, San Bernardino, Graduate Studies, College of Arts and Letters, Department of Communication Studies, San Bernardino, CA 92407-2397. Offers communication studies (MA); integrated marketing communication (MA). *Degree requirements:* For master's, comprehensive exam, advancement to candidacy. *Entrance requirements:* Additional exam requirements/recommendations for international students: Required—TOEFL.

Carleton University, Faculty of Graduate Studies, Faculty of Public Affairs and Management, School of Journalism and Communication, Program in Communication, Ottawa, ON K1S 5B6, Canada. Offers MA, PhD. *Degree requirements:* For master's, thesis optional; for doctorate, comprehensive exam, thesis/dissertation. *Entrance requirements:* For master's, honors degree. Additional exam requirements/recommendations for international students: Required—TOEFL. *Faculty research:* History of communication and media systems, communication/information technologies and society, communication and social relations, communication policy and political economy.

Carnegie Mellon University, College of Fine Arts, School of Design, Program in Communication Planning and Information Design, Pittsburgh, PA 15213-3891. Offers M Des. Part-time programs available. *Degree requirements:* For master's, thesis. *Entrance requirements:* For master's, GRE, portfolio of relevant work. Additional exam requirements/recommendations for international students: Required—TOEFL (minimum score 600 paper-based). *Faculty research:* Dynamic information design, communication design, systems design, strategic planning, kinetic typography and emotion.

Carnegie Mellon University, College of Humanities and Social Sciences, Department of English, Pittsburgh, PA 15213-3891. Offers communication planning and design (M Des); literary and cultural studies (MA, PhD); professional writing (MAPW), including editing and publishing, policy and non-profit communication, public and media relations / corporate communications, science or healthcare communication, technical writing, writing for new media, writing for print media; rhetoric (MA, PhD). Part-time programs available. Terminal master's awarded for partial completion of doctoral program. *Degree requirements:* For doctorate, 2 foreign languages, comprehensive exam, thesis/dissertation. *Entrance requirements:* For master's and doctorate, GRE General Test. Additional exam requirements/recommendations for international students: Required—TOEFL, TWE. *Faculty research:* Cognitive processes in discourse with emphasis on writing, testing, and evaluation.

Central Connecticut State University, School of Graduate Studies, School of Arts and Sciences, Department of Communication, New Britain, CT 06050-4010. Offers organizational communication (MS); public relations/promotions (Certificate). Part-time and evening/weekend programs available. *Faculty:* 12 full-time (4 women), 8 part-time/adjunct (2 women). *Students:* 12 full-time (6 women), 17 part-time (12 women); includes 5 minority (2 Black or African American, non-Hispanic/Latino; 1 Asian, non-Hispanic/Latino; 2 Hispanic/Latino). Average age 28. 19 applicants, 42% accepted, 5 enrolled. In 2010, 16 master's awarded. *Degree requirements:* For master's, comprehensive exam, thesis or alternative; for Certificate, qualifying exam. *Entrance requirements:* For master's, minimum undergraduate GPA of 3.0. Additional exam requirements/recommendations for international students: Required—TOEFL. *Application deadline:* For fall admission, 7/1 for domestic students; for spring admission, 12/1 for domestic students. Applications are processed on a rolling basis. Application fee: $50. Electronic applications accepted. *Expenses:* Tuition, area resident: Full-time $5012; part-time $470 per credit. Tuition, state resident: full-time $7518; part-time $482 per credit. Tuition, nonresident: full-time $13,962; part-time $482 per credit. Required fees: $3772. One-time fee: $62 part-time. *Financial support:* In 2010–11, 4 students received support, including 2 research assistantships; career-related internships or fieldwork, Federal Work-Study, scholarships/grants, and unspecified assistantships also available. Support available to part-time students. Financial award application deadline: 2/15; financial award applicants required to submit FAFSA. *Faculty research:* Organizational communication, mass communication, intercultural communication, political communication, information management. *Unit head:* Dr. Serafin Mendez-Mendez, Chair, 860-832-2690. *Application contact:* Dr. Serafin Mendez-Mendez, Chair, 860-832-2690.

Central Michigan University, College of Graduate Studies, College of Communication and Fine Arts, Department of Communication and Dramatic Arts, Mount Pleasant, MI 48859. Offers interpersonal and public communication (MA), including communication and dramatic arts. Part-time programs available. *Faculty:* 12 full-time (6 women). *Students:* 23 full-time (13 women), 5 part-time (2 women); includes 1 American Indian or Alaska Native, non-Hispanic/Latino; 2 Hispanic/Latino, 1 international. Average age 28. *Degree requirements:* For master's, thesis. *Application deadline:* For fall admission, 3/15 for domestic and international students; for winter admission, 10/15 for domestic and international students; for spring admission, 10/15 for domestic and international students. Applications are processed on a rolling basis. Application fee: $35 ($45 for international students). Electronic applications accepted. *Expenses:* Tuition, state resident: full-time $8208; part-time $456 per credit hour. Tuition, nonresident: full-time $13,788; part-time $766 per credit hour. One-time fee: $25. *Financial support:* Fellowships with tuition reimbursements, teaching assistantships with tuition reimbursements, career-related internships or fieldwork, Federal Work-Study, unspecified assistantships, and out-of-state merit awards, non-resident graduate awards available. *Faculty research:* Communication theory, interpersonal/nonverbal communication, organizational communication, family and interpersonal communication, political communication. *Unit head:* Dr. William O. Dailey, Chairperson, 989-774-3177, Fax: 989-774-2498, E-mail: daile1wo@cmich.edu. *Application contact:* Dr. Lesley Withers, Graduate Program Coordinator, 989-774-6673, Fax: 989-774-2498, E-mail: withe1la@cmich.edu.

Clarion University of Pennsylvania, Office of Research and Graduate Studies, College of Arts and Sciences, Department of Mass Media Arts, Journalism, and Communication Studies, Clarion, PA 16214. Offers MS. Part-time programs available. *Degree requirements:* For master's, comprehensive exam, thesis or alternative. *Entrance requirements:* For master's, minimum QPA of 3.0. Additional exam requirements/recommendations for international students: Required—TOEFL (minimum score 600 paper-based; 250 computer-based; 100 iBT). Electronic applications accepted.

Clark University, Graduate School, College of Professional and Continuing Education, Program in Professional Communication, Worcester, MA 01610-1477. Offers MSPC. *Students:* 33 full-time (28 women), 19 part-time (12 women); includes 1 Black or African American, non-Hispanic/Latino; 1 American Indian or Alaska Native, non-Hispanic/Latino; 1 Asian, non-Hispanic/Latino; 1 Hispanic/Latino, 16 international. Average age 27. 31 applicants, 100% accepted, 26 enrolled. In 2010, 34 master's awarded. *Degree requirements:* For master's, thesis optional. *Application deadline:* Applications are processed on a rolling basis. Application fee: $50. Electronic applications accepted. *Expenses:* Tuition: Full-time $37,000; part-time $1156 per credit hour. Required fees: $30; $1156 per credit hour. *Unit head:* Max E. Hess, Director of Graduate Studies, 508-793-7217, Fax: 508-793-7232. *Application contact:* Julia Parent, Director of Marketing, Communications, and Admissions, 508-793-7217, Fax: 508-793-7232, E-mail: jparent@clarku.edu.

Clemson University, Graduate School, College of Architecture, Arts, and Humanities, Department of English, Program in Professional Communication, Clemson, SC 29634. Offers MA. Part-time programs available. *Students:* 25 full-time (20 women), 3 part-time (2 women); includes 1 Black or African American, non-Hispanic/Latino; 2 Two or more races, non-Hispanic/Latino, 3 international. Average age 28. 42 applicants, 33% accepted, 11 enrolled. In 2010, 16 master's awarded. *Degree requirements:* For master's, one foreign language, thesis optional, oral exam. *Entrance requirements:* For master's, GRE General Test, minimum GPA of 3.0. Additional exam requirements/recommendations for international students: Required—TOEFL, IELTS. *Application deadline:* For fall admission, 2/1 priority date for domestic students, 4/15 for international students; for spring admission, 11/1 priority date for domestic students, 9/15 for international students. Applications are processed on a rolling basis. Application fee: $70 ($80 for international students). Electronic applications accepted. *Expenses:* Tuition, state resident: full-time $6492; part-time $400 per credit hour. Tuition, nonresident: full-time $13,634; part-time $800 per credit hour. Required fees: $262 per semester. Part-time tuition and fees vary according to course load and program. *Financial support:* In 2010–11, 27 students received support, including 1 research assistantship with partial tuition reimbursement available (averaging $15,000 per year), 19 teaching assistantships with partial tuition reimbursements available (averaging $12,171 per year); fellowships with full and partial tuition reimbursements available, career-related internships or fieldwork, institutionally sponsored loans, scholarships/grants, health care benefits, and unspecified assistantships also available. Support available to part-time students. Financial award application deadline: 4/1; financial award applicants required to submit FAFSA. *Faculty research:* Usability testing, rhetoric, communication across the curriculum, intercultural communication. *Unit head:* Dr. Lee Morrissey, Coordinator, 864-656-3151, Fax: 864-656-1345, E-mail: lmorris@clemson.edu. *Application contact:* Dr. Summer Taylor, Graduate Coordinator, 864-656-6689, Fax: 864-656-1345, E-mail: slsmith@clemson.edu.

Clemson University, Graduate School, College of Architecture, Arts, and Humanities, Program in Rhetorics, Communication and Information Design, Clemson, SC 29634. Offers PhD. *Students:* 20 full-time (8 women), 5 part-time (1 woman); includes 2 Black or African American, non-Hispanic/Latino; 1 Asian, non-Hispanic/Latino; 1 Hispanic/Latino; 1 Two or more races, non-Hispanic/Latino, 2 international. Average age 37. 13 applicants, 69% accepted, 4 enrolled. In 2010, 6 doctorates awarded. *Degree requirements:* For doctorate, thesis/dissertation (for some programs). *Entrance requirements:* For doctorate, GRE, master's degree in English, communications studies, art, professional communication or related field; portfolio; 3 letters of reference; minimum graduate GPA of 3.5. Additional exam requirements/recommendations for international students: Required—TOEFL (minimum score 550 paper-based; 213 computer-based). *Application deadline:* For fall admission, 2/1 priority date for domestic students, 4/15 for international students. Applications are processed on a rolling basis. Application fee: $70 ($80 for international students). Electronic applications accepted. *Expenses:* Tuition, state resident: full-time $6492; part-time $400 per credit hour. Tuition, nonresident: full-time $13,634; part-time $800 per credit hour. Required fees: $262 per semester. Part-time tuition and fees vary according to course load and program. *Financial support:* In 2010–11, 19 students received support, including 20 teaching assistantships with partial tuition reimbursements available (averaging $18,860 per year); career-related internships or fieldwork, institutionally sponsored loans, scholarships/grants, health care benefits, and unspecified assistantships also available. Support available to part-time students. *Faculty research:* Historiography and philology, multimodal writing, health communication, future of the book, readability studies, politics and rhetors. *Unit head:* Dr. Victor Vitanza, Director, 864-656-6411, Fax: 864-656-0599, E-mail: sophist@clemson.edu. *Application contact:* Dr. Victor Vitanza, Director, 864-656-6411, Fax: 864-656-0599, E-mail: sophist@clemson.edu.

Clemson University, Graduate School, College of Business and Behavioral Science, Department of Graphic Communications, Clemson, SC 29634. Offers MS. *Faculty:* 7 full-time (2 women), 2 part-time/adjunct (1 woman). *Students:* 9 full-time (6 women), 2 part-time (1 woman); includes 1 Asian, non-Hispanic/Latino, 2 international. Average age 26. 10 applicants, 70% accepted, 5 enrolled. In 2010, 7 master's awarded. *Entrance requirements:* For master's, GRE General Test. Additional exam requirements/recommendations for international students: Required—TOEFL. *Application deadline:* For fall admission, 4/15 for international students; for spring admission, 9/15 for international students. Application fee: $70 ($80 for international students). Electronic applications accepted. *Expenses:* Tuition, state resident: full-time $6492; part-time $400 per credit hour. Tuition, nonresident: full-time $13,634; part-time $800 per credit hour. Required fees: $262 per semester. Part-time tuition and fees vary according to course load and program. *Financial support:* In 2010–11, 6 students received support, including 6 teaching assistantships with partial tuition reimbursements available (averaging $6,900 per year); research assistantships with partial tuition reimbursements available, career-related internships or fieldwork, institutionally sponsored loans, scholarships/grants, health care benefits, and unspecified assistantships also available. Support available to part-time students. Financial award applicants required to submit FAFSA. *Unit head:* Dr. Samuel T. Ingram, Chair, 864-656-3447, E-mail: sting@clemson.edu. *Application contact:* Nancy Leininger, 864-656-3447, Fax: 864-656-5344, E-mail: lnancy@clemson.edu.

Cleveland State University, College of Graduate Studies, College of Liberal Arts and Social Sciences, School of Communication, Cleveland, OH 44115. Offers applied communication theory and methodology (MA); culture, communication and health care (Certificate). Part-time and evening/weekend programs available. *Faculty:* 10 full-time (5 women). *Students:* 14 full-time (8 women), 22 part-time (13 women); includes 1 Black or African American, non-Hispanic/Latino, 3 international. Average age 30. 39 applicants, 41% accepted, 12 enrolled. In 2010, 14 master's awarded. *Degree requirements:* For master's, variable foreign language requirement, comprehensive exam (for some programs), thesis optional, thesis, project, comprehensive exam, or collaborative project. *Entrance requirements:* For master's, GRE or

MAT, minimum undergraduate GPA of 2.75, 2 letters of recommendation. Additional exam requirements/recommendations for international students: Required—TOEFL (minimum score 525 paper-based; 197 computer-based; 65 iBT). *Application deadline:* For fall admission, 8/25 priority date for domestic students, 5/15 priority date for international students; for spring admission, 1/15 priority date for domestic students, 11/1 priority date for international students. Applications are processed on a rolling basis. Application fee: $30. Electronic applications accepted. *Expenses:* Tuition, state resident: full-time $8447; part-time $469 per credit hour. Tuition, nonresident: full-time $16,020; part-time $890 per credit hour. Required fees: $50. *Financial support:* In 2010–11, 14 students received support, including 5 research assistantships with full and partial tuition reimbursements available (averaging $11,000 per year), 9 teaching assistantships with full and partial tuition reimbursements available (averaging $11,000 per year); tuition waivers (full) and unspecified assistantships also available. Financial award application deadline: 8/1. *Faculty research:* Interpersonal, organizational, and mass communication; health communication. *Unit head:* Dr. Richard M. Perloff, Director, 216-687-4631, Fax: 216-687-5435, E-mail: r.perloff@csuohio.edu. *Application contact:* Dr. George Ray, 216-687-5103, Fax: 216-687-5435, E-mail: g.ray@csuohio.edu.

The College at Brockport, State University of New York, School of the Arts, Humanities and Social Sciences, Department of Communication, Brockport, NY 14420-2997. Offers MA. Part-time and evening/weekend programs available. *Students:* 11 full-time (4 women), 25 part-time (13 women); includes 2 Black or African American, non-Hispanic/Latino; 2 Asian, non-Hispanic/Latino; 2 Hispanic/Latino. 27 applicants, 85% accepted, 18 enrolled. In 2010, 10 master's awarded. *Degree requirements:* For master's, thesis or alternative, research project. *Entrance requirements:* For master's, minimum GPA of 3.0, letters of recommendation. Additional exam requirements/recommendations for international students: Required—TOEFL (minimum score 550 paper-based; 213 computer-based; 79 iBT). *Application deadline:* For fall admission, 7/15 priority date for domestic and international students; for spring admission, 11/15 priority date for domestic and international students. Application fee: $50. Electronic applications accepted. *Financial support:* In 2010–11, 3 teaching assistantships with full tuition reimbursements (averaging $6,000 per year) were awarded; Federal Work-Study, scholarships/grants, and unspecified assistantships also available. Support available to part-time students. Financial award application deadline: 3/15; financial award applicants required to submit FAFSA. *Faculty research:* Organizational communication, rhetorical theory and criticism, media theory and criticism, interpersonal communication, communication theory. *Unit head:* Dr. Monica Brasted, Chairperson, 585-395-2511, Fax: 585-395-5771, E-mail: mbrasted@brockport.edu. *Application contact:* Dr. Alex Lyon, Graduate Director, 585-395-5772, Fax: 585-395-5771, E-mail: alyon@brockport.edu.

College of Charleston, Graduate School, School of Humanities and Social Sciences, Program in Communication, Charleston, SC 29424-0001. Offers MA. Part-time and evening/weekend programs available. *Faculty:* 24 full-time (12 women). *Students:* 17 full-time (14 women), 14 part-time (13 women); includes 2 minority (1 Black or African American, non-Hispanic/Latino; 1 Two or more races, non-Hispanic/Latino). Average age 26. 18 applicants, 61% accepted, 11 enrolled. In 2010, 12 master's awarded. *Degree requirements:* For master's, comprehensive exam or thesis. *Entrance requirements:* For master's, GRE, writing sample; 2 letters of recommendation; minimum GPA of 2.75 overall, 3.0 in major. Additional exam requirements/recommendations for international students: Required—TOEFL (minimum score 81 iBT). *Application deadline:* For fall admission, 3/1 for domestic students; for spring admission, 10/1 for domestic students. Applications are processed on a rolling basis. Application fee: $45. Electronic applications accepted. *Financial support:* In 2010–11, research assistantships (averaging $13,000 per year), teaching assistantships (averaging $13,000 per year) were awarded; career-related internships or fieldwork, scholarships/grants, and unspecified assistantships also available. Financial award application deadline: 4/1; financial award applicants required to submit FAFSA. *Unit head:* Dr. Vincent Benigni, Director, 844-983-7854, E-mail: fergusond@cofc.edu. *Application contact:* Susan Hallatt, Director of Graduate Admissions, 843-953-5614, Fax: 843-953-1434, E-mail: hallatts@cofc.edu.

The College of New Rochelle, Graduate School, Division of Art and Communication Studies, Program in Communication Studies, New Rochelle, NY 10805-2308. Offers MS, Certificate. Part-time and evening/weekend programs available. *Degree requirements:* For master's, thesis or alternative. *Entrance requirements:* For master's, GRE General Test, interview, minimum GPA of 3.0. Additional exam requirements/recommendations for international students: Required—TOEFL.

College of Notre Dame of Maryland, Graduate Studies, Program in Contemporary Communication, Baltimore, MD 21210-2476. Offers MA. Part-time and evening/weekend programs available. *Degree requirements:* For master's, thesis optional. *Entrance requirements:* For master's, minimum GPA of 3.0. Additional exam requirements/recommendations for international students: Required—TOEFL (minimum score 500 paper-based; 173 computer-based; 61 iBT). Electronic applications accepted.

Columbia University, Graduate School of Business, Doctoral Program in Business, New York, NY 10027. Offers business (PhD), including accounting, decision, risk, and operations, finance and economics, management, marketing. *Accreditation:* AACSB. *Degree requirements:* For doctorate, comprehensive exam, thesis/dissertation, major field exam, research paper, thesis proposal. *Entrance requirements:* For doctorate, GMAT or GRE (finance), 2 letters of reference, resume. Additional exam requirements/recommendations for international students: Required—TOEFL. Electronic applications accepted. *Expenses:* Contact institution. *Faculty research:* Human decision making and behavioral research; real estate market and mortgage defaults; financial crisis and corporate governance; international business; security analysis and accounting.

Columbia University, Graduate School of Business, MBA Program, New York, NY 10027. Offers accounting (MBA); decision, risk, and operations (MBA); entrepreneurship (MBA); finance and economics (MBA); healthcare and pharmaceutical management (MBA); human resource management (MBA); international business (MBA); leadership and ethics (MBA); management (MBA); marketing (MBA); media (MBA); private equity (MBA); real estate (MBA); social enterprise (MBA); value investing (MBA); DDS/MBA; JD/MBA; MBA/MIA; MBA/MPH; MBA/MS; MD/MBA. *Entrance requirements:* For master's, GMAT, 2 letters of recommendation. Additional exam requirements/recommendations for international students: Required—TOEFL. Electronic applications accepted. *Expenses:* Contact institution. *Faculty research:* Human decision making and behavioral research; real estate market and mortgage defaults; financial crisis and corporate governance; international business; security analysis and accounting.

Columbia University, School of Continuing Education, Program in Communications Practice, New York, NY 10027. Offers MS. Electronic applications accepted.

Concordia University, School of Graduate Studies, Faculty of Arts and Science, Department of Communication Studies, Montréal, QC H3G 1M8, Canada. Offers communication (PhD); communication studies (Diploma); media studies (MA). PhD program offered jointly with Université de Montréal and Université du Québec à Montréal. *Degree requirements:* For master's, thesis optional; for doctorate, one foreign language, comprehensive exam, thesis/dissertation, research practicum, seminar. *Entrance requirements:* For master's, bachelor's degree in communications, 2 years of media-related experience; for doctorate, MA in communications. *Faculty research:* Communication and development, organizational communication, cultural studies, rhetoric, future studies.

Cornell University, Graduate School, Graduate Fields of Agriculture and Life Sciences, Field of Communication, Ithaca, NY 14853-0001. Offers communication (MPS, MS, PhD); communication research methods (MS, PhD); international communication (MS, PhD); science and environmental communication (MS, PhD); social psychology of communication (MS, PhD); uses and effects of communication (MS, PhD). *Faculty:* 21 full-time (9 women). *Students:* 33 full-time (23 women); includes 2 Asian, non-Hispanic/Latino; 2 Hispanic/Latino, 12 international. Average age 28. 135 applicants, 13% accepted, 13 enrolled. In 2010, 4 master's, 4 doctorates awarded. *Degree requirements:* For master's, thesis (MS); for doctorate, comprehensive exam, thesis/dissertation. *Entrance requirements:* For master's and doctorate, GRE General Test, 3 letters of recommendation. Additional exam requirements/recommendations for international students: Required—TOEFL (minimum score 600 paper-based; 250 computer-based; 100 iBT). *Application deadline:* For fall admission, 1/15 for domestic students. Application fee: $70. Electronic applications accepted. *Expenses:* Tuition: Full-time $29,500. Required fees: $76. Tuition and fees vary according to degree level and program. *Financial support:* In 2010–11, 5 fellowships with full tuition reimbursements, 11 research assistantships with full tuition reimbursements, 15 teaching assistantships with full tuition reimbursements were awarded; institutionally sponsored loans, scholarships/grants, health care benefits, tuition waivers (full and partial), and unspecified assistantships also available. Financial award applicants required to submit FAFSA. *Faculty research:* Mass communication, communication technologies, science and environmental communication. *Unit head:* Director of Graduate Studies, 607-255-2112. *Application contact:* Graduate Field Assistant, 607-255-2112, E-mail: commgrad@cornell.edu.

DePaul University, College of Communication, Chicago, IL 60614. Offers journalism (MA); media, culture and society (MA); organizational and multicultural communication (MA); public relations and advertising (MA). Part-time and evening/weekend programs available. *Faculty:* 31 full-time (17 women), 15 part-time/adjunct (7 women). *Students:* 170 full-time (129 women), 70 part-time (52 women); includes 29 Black or African American, non-Hispanic/Latino; 9 Asian, non-Hispanic/Latino; 20 Hispanic/Latino; 7 Two or more races, non-Hispanic/Latino, 17 international. Average age 29. 354 applicants, 44% accepted, 79 enrolled. In 2010, 64 master's awarded. *Degree requirements:* For master's, comprehensive exam (for some programs), final exam or thesis/project. *Entrance requirements:* For master's, GRE General Test (public relations and advertising), minimum GPA of 3.0, writing sample, letters of recommendation, resume. Additional exam requirements/recommendations for international students: Required—TOEFL (minimum score 590 paper-based; 243 computer-based; 96 iBT). Application fee: $40. Electronic applications accepted. *Financial support:* In 2010–11, 8 students received support, including 4 research assistantships with partial tuition reimbursements available, 2 teaching assistantships with full tuition reimbursements available (averaging $12,000 per year); fellowships with full tuition reimbursements available, career-related internships or fieldwork, scholarships/grants, and tuition waivers (partial) also available. Support available to part-time students. Financial award applicants required to submit FAFSA. *Faculty research:* Intercultural communication, corporate culture, diversity in the working place, organizational socialization, critical cultural studies. *Unit head:* Dr. Jacqueline Taylor, Dean, 773-325-7216, Fax: 773-325-7584, E-mail: jtaylor@depaul.edu. *Application contact:* Ann Spittle, Director of Graduate Admission, 773-325-7315, Fax: 773-325-2395, E-mail: gradcom@depaul.edu.

DeVry University, Keller Graduate School of Management, Downers Grove, IL 60515. Offers accounting and financial management (MAFM); business administration (MBA); human resources management (MHRM); information systems management (MISM); network and communications management (MNCM); project management (MPM); public administration (MPA).

Drake University, School of Journalism and Mass Communication, Des Moines, IA 50311-4516. Offers MCL. *Expenses:* Tuition: Part-time $538 per credit hour.

Drexel University, College of Arts and Sciences, Department of Culture and Communication, Philadelphia, PA 19104-2875. Offers communication (MS), including public communication, science communication, technical communication; publication management (MS). Part-time and evening/weekend programs available. *Degree requirements:* For master's, internship, professional portfolio. *Entrance requirements:* Additional exam requirements/recommendations for international students: Required—TOEFL. Electronic applications accepted. *Faculty research:* Science information and attitudes, science influence on literature, process of technical writing, document design, software documentation.

Drury University, Program in Communication, Springfield, MO 65802. Offers MA. Part-time and evening/weekend programs available. *Entrance requirements:* For master's, GMAT or MAT. Additional exam requirements/recommendations for international students: Required—TOEFL. Electronic applications accepted. *Expenses:* Contact institution.

Duquesne University, Graduate School of Liberal Arts, Department of Communication and Rhetorical Studies, Pittsburgh, PA 15282-0001. Offers communication (MA); rhetoric (PhD). Part-time and evening/weekend programs available. *Faculty:* 6 full-time (3 women), 5 part-time/adjunct (3 women). *Students:* 117 full-time (77 women), 20 part-time (16 women); includes 7 Black or African American, non-Hispanic/Latino; 1 Hispanic/Latino, 7 international. Average age 27. 66 applicants, 91% accepted, 34 enrolled. In 2010, 25 master's, 9 doctorates awarded. *Degree requirements:* For master's, thesis optional, practicum; for doctorate, 2 foreign languages, comprehensive exam, thesis/dissertation. *Entrance requirements:* For master's, GRE General Test, MAT or GMAT; for doctorate, GRE General Test. Additional exam requirements/recommendations for international students: Required—TOEFL. *Application deadline:* For fall admission, 2/1 priority date for domestic and international students; for spring admission, 11/1 priority date for domestic and international students. Applications are processed on a rolling basis. Electronic applications accepted. *Expenses:* Tuition: Part-time $884 per credit. Required fees: $84 per credit. Tuition and fees vary according to course load. *Financial support:* In 2010–11, 9 research assistantships with full tuition reimbursements (averaging $9,000 per year), 10 teaching assistantships with full tuition reimbursements (averaging $15,000 per year) were awarded; career-related internships or fieldwork, Federal Work-Study, institutionally sponsored loans, scholarships/grants, tuition waivers (full and partial), and unspecified assistantships also available. Financial award application deadline: 5/1. *Unit head:* Dr. Ronald Arnett, Chair, 412-396-5076. *Application contact:* Dr. Janie Fritz, Director, 412-396-6460.

Eastern Michigan University, Graduate School, College of Arts and Sciences, Department of Communication, Media and Theatre Arts, Program in Communication, Ypsilanti, MI 48197. Offers MA. Part-time and evening/weekend programs available. Postbaccalaureate distance learning degree programs offered (minimal on-campus study). *Students:* 15 full-time (12 women), 25 part-time (16 women); includes 7 minority (6 Black or African American, non-Hispanic/Latino; 1 Hispanic/Latino), 2 international. Average age 28. In 2010, 8 master's awarded. *Degree requirements:* For master's, thesis or alternative. *Entrance requirements:* Additional exam requirements/recommendations for international students: Required—TOEFL. *Application deadline:* Applications are processed on a rolling basis. Application fee: $35. *Financial support:* Fellowships, research assistantships with full tuition reimbursements, teaching assistantships with full tuition reimbursements, career-related internships or fieldwork, Federal Work-Study, institutionally sponsored loans, scholarships/grants, tuition waivers (partial), and unspecified assistantships available. Support available to part-time students. Financial award applicants required to submit FAFSA. *Unit head:* Dr. Doris Fields, Coordinator, 734-487-4199, Fax: 734-487-3443, E-mail: dfields1@emich.edu. *Application contact:* Graduate Coordinator.

Eastern New Mexico University, Graduate School, College of Fine Arts, Portales, NM 88130. Offers communicative arts and sciences (MA). Part-time programs available. Postbaccalaureate distance learning degree programs offered (minimal on-campus study). *Faculty:* 3 full-time (2 women), 1 part-time/adjunct (0 women). *Students:* 17 full-time (8 women), 11 part-time (6 women); includes 12 minority (1 Black or African American, non-Hispanic/Latino; 1 Asian, non-Hispanic/Latino; 10 Hispanic/Latino), 3 international. Average age 30. 26 applicants, 23% accepted, 6 enrolled. In 2010, 20 master's awarded. *Degree requirements:* For master's, comprehensive exam, thesis optional. *Entrance requirements:* For master's, minimum GPA of 3.0. Additional exam requirements/recommendations for international students: Required—TOEFL (minimum score 550 paper-based; 213 computer-based; 79 iBT), IELTS (minimum score 6). *Application deadline:* For fall admission, 7/20 priority date for domestic students, 6/20 priority date for international students; for spring admission, 12/15 priority date for domestic students, 11/15 priority date for international students. Applications are processed on a rolling basis. Application fee: $10. Electronic applications accepted. *Expenses:* Tuition, state resident: full-time $3210; part-time $130 per credit hour. Tuition, nonresident: full-time $8652; part-time $360.50 per credit hour. Required fees: $1212; $50.50 per credit hour. Tuition and fees vary

Communication—General

Eastern New Mexico University (continued)
according to course load. *Financial support:* In 2010–11, 1 fellowship (averaging $5,312 per year), 1 research assistantship with partial tuition reimbursement (averaging $8,500 per year), 9 teaching assistantships with partial tuition reimbursements (averaging $8,500 per year) were awarded; unspecified assistantships also available. Support available to part-time students. Financial award applicants required to submit FAFSA. *Unit head:* Dr. Patty Dobson, Communicative Arts and Sciences Department Chair/Interim Graduate Coordinator, 575-562-2130, Fax: 575-562-2847, E-mail: patricia.dobson@enmu.edu. *Application contact:* Simon Chavez, Department Secretary, Communicative Arts and Sciences, 575-562-2130, Fax: 575-562-2847, E-mail: simon.chavez@enmu.edu.

Eastern Washington University, Graduate Studies, College of Social and Behavioral Sciences, Department of Communication Studies, Cheney, WA 99004-2431. Offers MSC. Part-time and evening/weekend programs available. *Degree requirements:* For master's, comprehensive exam, thesis or alternative. *Entrance requirements:* For master's, GRE General Test, minimum GPA of 3.0.

East Tennessee State University, School of Graduate Studies, College of Arts and Sciences, Department of Communication, Johnson City, TN 37614. Offers MA. Part-time programs available. *Faculty:* 16 full-time (7 women). *Students:* 22 full-time (16 women), 2 part-time (1 woman); includes 2 minority (1 American Indian or Alaska Native, non-Hispanic/Latino; 1 Two or more races, non-Hispanic/Latino), 9 international. Average age 28. 25 applicants, 60% accepted, 7 enrolled. In 2010, 9 master's awarded. *Degree requirements:* For master's, comprehensive exam, thesis optional. *Entrance requirements:* For master's, GRE, minimum GPA of 3.0. Additional exam requirements/recommendations for international students: Required—TOEFL (minimum score 550 paper-based; 213 computer-based; 79 iBT). *Application deadline:* For fall admission, 6/1 for domestic students, 4/30 for international students; for spring admission, 11/1 for domestic students, 9/30 for international students. Application fee: $25 ($35 for international students). *Financial support:* In 2010–11, 3 research assistantships with full tuition reimbursements (averaging $5,500 per year) were awarded; teaching assistantships with full tuition reimbursements, career-related internships or fieldwork, institutionally sponsored loans, scholarships/grants, and unspecified assistantships also available. Financial award application deadline: 7/1; financial award applicants required to submit FAFSA. *Faculty research:* Political communications, visual communication, depictions of gender and ethnicity in print and online media and online corporate media, presidential rhetoric and newspaper coverage of presidential speeches. *Unit head:* Dr. Charles V. Roberts, Chair, 423-439-7577, Fax: 423-439-7540, E-mail: robertsc@etsu.edu. *Application contact:* Admissions and Records Clerk, 423-439-4221, Fax: 423-439-5624, E-mail: gradsch@etsu.edu.

Edinboro University of Pennsylvania, College of Arts and Sciences, Department of Communications and Media Studies, Edinboro, PA 16444. Offers communications studies (Certificate); conflict management (MA). Part-time and evening/weekend programs available. *Faculty:* 6 full-time (2 women). *Students:* 27 full-time (15 women), 16 part-time (9 women); includes 5 minority (3 Black or African American, non-Hispanic/Latino; 2 Asian, non-Hispanic/Latino). Average age 28. In 2010, 28 master's, 10 other advanced degrees awarded. *Degree requirements:* For master's, thesis or alternative, competency exam. *Entrance requirements:* For master's, GRE or MAT, minimum QPA of 2.5. *Application deadline:* Applications are processed on a rolling basis. Application fee: $30. Electronic applications accepted. *Expenses:* Tuition, state resident: full-time $6966; part-time $387 per credit. Tuition, nonresident: full-time $11,146; part-time $619 per credit. Required fees: $2401.70; $96.25 per credit. *Financial support:* In 2010–11, 13 research assistantships with full and partial tuition reimbursements (averaging $4,050 per year) were awarded; career-related internships or fieldwork, Federal Work-Study, scholarships/grants, and unspecified assistantships also available. Support available to part-time students. Financial award application deadline: 2/15; financial award applicants required to submit FAFSA. *Unit head:* Dr. Andrew Smith, Program Head, 814-732-2165, E-mail: arsmith@edinboro.edu. *Application contact:* Dr. Andrew Smith, Program Head, 814-732-2165, E-mail: arsmith@edinboro.edu.

Emerson College, Graduate Studies, School of Communication, Department of Communication Studies, Boston, MA 02116-4624. Offers communication management (MA). Part-time and evening/weekend programs available. *Entrance requirements:* For master's, GMAT or GRE General Test. Additional exam requirements/recommendations for international students: Required—TOEFL (minimum score 550 paper-based; 213 computer-based; 80 iBT), IELTS (minimum score 6.5). Electronic applications accepted.

Fairfield University, College of Arts and Sciences, Fairfield, CT 06824-5195. Offers American studies (MA); communication (MA); creative writing (MFA); mathematics (MS). Part-time and evening/weekend programs available. Postbaccalaureate distance learning degree programs offered (minimal on-campus study). *Faculty:* 46 full-time (20 women), 15 part-time/adjunct (7 women). *Students:* 96 full-time (65 women), 97 part-time (63 women); includes 7 Black or African American, non-Hispanic/Latino; 5 Hispanic/Latino; 2 Two or more races, non-Hispanic/Latino, 7 international. Average age 41. 114 applicants, 62% accepted, 38 enrolled. In 2010, 36 master's awarded. *Degree requirements:* For master's, capstone research course. *Entrance requirements:* For master's, minimum GPA of 3.0, 2 letters of recommendation, resume. Additional exam requirements/recommendations for international students: Required—TOEFL (minimum score 550 paper-based; 213 computer-based; 80 iBT). *Application deadline:* For fall admission, 5/15 for international students; for spring admission, 10/15 for international students. Applications are processed on a rolling basis. Application fee: $60. Electronic applications accepted. *Expenses:* Tuition: Part-time $600 per hour. Part-time tuition and fees vary according to degree level and program. *Financial support:* In 2010–11, 19 students received support. Unspecified assistantships available. Financial award applicants required to submit FAFSA. *Faculty research:* Non-commutative algebra, partial differential equations, writing (fiction, non-fiction and poetry), communication for social change, comparative media systems, negotiation and management. *Unit head:* Dr. Robbin Crabtree, Dean, 203-254-4000 Ext. 3263, Fax: 203-254-4119, E-mail: rcrabtree@fairfield.edu. *Application contact:* Marianne Gumpper, Director of Graduate and Continuing Studies Admissions, 203-254-4184, Fax: 203-254-4073, E-mail: gradadmis@fairfield.edu.

Fairleigh Dickinson University, Metropolitan Campus, University College: Arts, Sciences, and Professional Studies, School of Art and Media Studies, Program in Media and Communications, Teaneck, NJ 07666-1914. Offers MA. *Students:* 14 full-time (9 women), 10 part-time (8 women), 5 international. Average age 29. 16 applicants, 81% accepted, 7 enrolled. In 2010, 16 master's awarded. Application fee: $40. *Application contact:* Susan Brooman, University Director of Graduate Admissions, 201-692-2554, Fax: 201-692-2560, E-mail: globaleducation@fdu.edu.

Fitchburg State University, Division of Graduate and Continuing Education, Program in Applied Communications, Fitchburg, MA 01420-2697. Offers applied communications (MS, Certificate); health communication (MS); library media (MS); technical and professional writing (MS). Part-time and evening/weekend programs available. *Students:* 2 full-time (1 woman), 18 part-time (11 women), 3 international. Average age 34. 4 applicants, 100% accepted, 1 enrolled. In 2010, 8 master's awarded. *Entrance requirements:* For master's, GRE General Test or MAT, minimum 2 years of related experience, letters of recommendation, resume. Additional exam requirements/recommendations for international students: Required—TOEFL (minimum score 550 paper-based; 213 computer-based; 79 iBT). *Application deadline:* Applications are processed on a rolling basis. Application fee: $25 ($50 for international students). *Expenses:* Tuition, area resident: Part-time $150 per credit. Tuition, state resident: part-time $150 per credit. Tuition, nonresident: part-time $150 per credit. Required fees: $127 per credit. *Financial support:* In 2010–11, research assistantships with partial tuition reimbursements (averaging $5,500 per year); Federal Work-Study, scholarships/grants, and unspecified assistantships also available. Support available to part-time students. Financial award application deadline: 3/1; financial award applicants required to submit FAFSA. *Unit head:* Dr. John Chetro-Szivos, Chair, 978-665-3261, Fax: 978-665-3658, E-mail: gce@fitchburgstate.edu.

Application contact: Director of Admissions, 978-665-3144, Fax: 978-665-4540, E-mail: admissions@fsc.edu.

Florida Atlantic University, Dorothy F. Schmidt College of Arts and Letters, School of Communication and Multimedia Studies, Boca Raton, FL 33431-0991. Offers communication studies (MA); film and video (Certificate); film studies (MA); multimedia journalism studies (MA). Part-time programs available. *Faculty:* 28 full-time (10 women), 14 part-time/adjunct (3 women). *Students:* 19 full-time (15 women), 15 part-time (11 women); includes 8 minority (3 Black or African American, non-Hispanic/Latino; 1 American Indian or Alaska Native, non-Hispanic/Latino; 1 Asian, non-Hispanic/Latino; 1 Hispanic/Latino; 2 Two or more races, non-Hispanic/Latino), 6 international. Average age 28. 42 applicants, 26% accepted, 8 enrolled. In 2010, 3 master's awarded. *Degree requirements:* For master's, one foreign language, comprehensive exam (for some programs), thesis (for some programs). *Entrance requirements:* For master's, GRE General Test, minimum GPA of 3.0. *Application deadline:* For fall admission, 7/1 priority date for domestic students, 4/1 for international students; for spring admission, 11/1 for domestic students, 10/1 for international students. Applications are processed on a rolling basis. Application fee: $30. Electronic applications accepted. *Expenses:* Tuition, area resident: Part-time $319.96 per credit. Tuition, state resident: part-time $319.96 per credit. Tuition, nonresident: part-time $926.42 per credit. *Financial support:* Teaching assistantships with partial tuition reimbursements, Federal Work-Study and institutionally sponsored loans available. Support available to part-time students. Financial award application deadline: 3/1. *Faculty research:* Cultural studies, gender studies, film, communication theory, journalism, new media. *Unit head:* Dr. Susan S. Reilly, Director, 561-297-1095, Fax: 561-297-2615, E-mail: sreilly@fau.edu. *Application contact:* Dr. Eric M. Freedman, Graduate Coordinator, 561-297-2534, Fax: 561-297-2615, E-mail: efreedma@fau.edu.

Florida Institute of Technology, Graduate Programs, College of Psychology and Liberal Arts, Department of Humanities and Communication, Melbourne, FL 32901-6975. Offers technical and professional communication (MS). Part-time and evening/weekend programs available. *Faculty:* 3 full-time (all women), 1 (woman) part-time/adjunct. *Students:* 11 full-time (7 women), 6 part-time (5 women); includes 5 minority (2 Black or African American, non-Hispanic/Latino; 1 American Indian or Alaska Native, non-Hispanic/Latino; 1 Asian, non-Hispanic/Latino; 1 Hispanic/Latino), 1 international. Average age 38. 5 applicants, 80% accepted, 3 enrolled. In 2010, 2 master's awarded. *Degree requirements:* For master's, comprehensive exam (for some programs), thesis optional. *Entrance requirements:* For master's, GRE (minimum score 1000 verbal and analytical), minimum GPA of 3.0, 2 letters of recommendation, discursive writing sample. Additional exam requirements/recommendations for international students: Required—TOEFL (minimum score 550 paper-based; 213 computer-based; 79 iBT). *Application deadline:* For fall admission, 4/1 for international students; for spring admission, 9/30 for international students. Applications are processed on a rolling basis. Application fee: $50. Electronic applications accepted. *Expenses:* Tuition: Part-time $1040 per credit hour. Tuition and fees vary according to campus/location. *Financial support:* Career-related internships or fieldwork and tuition remissions available. Support available to part-time students. Financial award application deadline: 3/1; financial award applicants required to submit FAFSA. *Faculty research:* Communication of astronomy in the seventeenth century, persuasion and patronage in seventeenth century work, technical and cross-cultural communication. Total annual research expenditures: $4,782. *Unit head:* Dr. Robert A. Taylor, Department Head, 321-674-7384, Fax: 321-674-8109, E-mail: rotaylor@fit.edu. *Application contact:* Cheryl A. Brown, Associate Director of Graduate Admissions, 321-674-7581, Fax: 321-723-9468, E-mail: cbrown@fit.edu.

Florida State University, The Graduate School, College of Communication and Information, School of Communication, Tallahassee, FL 32306. Offers corporate and public communication (MS); integrated marketing communication (MA, MS); mass communication (PhD); media and communication studies (MA, MS); speech communication (PhD). Part-time programs available. *Faculty:* 24 full-time (9 women), 6 part-time/adjunct (1 woman). *Students:* 147 full-time (94 women), 63 part-time (38 women); includes 92 minority (26 Black or African American, non-Hispanic/Latino; 2 American Indian or Alaska Native, non-Hispanic/Latino; 45 Asian, non-Hispanic/Latino; 16 Hispanic/Latino; 1 Native Hawaiian or other Pacific Islander, non-Hispanic/Latino; 2 Two or more races, non-Hispanic/Latino). Average age 24. 268 applicants, 57% accepted, 79 enrolled. In 2010, 103 master's, 4 doctorates awarded. *Degree requirements:* For master's, thesis (for some programs); for doctorate, comprehensive exam, thesis/dissertation. *Entrance requirements:* For master's, GRE General Test, minimum GPA of 3.0; for doctorate, GRE General Test, minimum GPA of 3.3 in graduate course work. Additional exam requirements/recommendations for international students: Required—TOEFL (minimum score 600 paper-based; 250 computer-based; 100 iBT). *Application deadline:* For fall admission, 7/1 priority date for domestic students, 5/1 priority date for international students; for spring admission, 11/1 priority date for domestic and international students. Applications are processed on a rolling basis. Application fee: $30. Electronic applications accepted. *Expenses:* Tuition, state resident: full-time $8238.24. *Financial support:* In 2010–11, 52 students received support, including 1 fellowship with full tuition reimbursement available, 8 research assistantships with full tuition reimbursements available (averaging $14,000 per year), 40 teaching assistantships with full tuition reimbursements available (averaging $5,000 per year); career-related internships or fieldwork, Federal Work-Study, institutionally sponsored loans, scholarships/grants, tuition waivers (partial), and unspecified assistantships also available. Support available to part-time students. Financial award application deadline: 2/1; financial award applicants required to submit FAFSA. *Faculty research:* Communication technology and policy, marketing communication, communication content and effect, new communication/information technologies. Total annual research expenditures: $400,000. *Unit head:* Dr. Stephen D. McDowell, Director, 850-644-2276, Fax: 850-644-8642, E-mail: steve.mcdowell@cci.fsu.edu. *Application contact:* Natashia Hinson-Turner, Graduate Coordinator, 850-644-8746, Fax: 850-644-8642, E-mail: natashia.turner@cci.fsu.edu.

Fordham University, Graduate School of Arts and Sciences, Department of Communication and Media Studies, New York, NY 10458. Offers public communications (MA). Part-time and evening/weekend programs available. *Faculty:* 11 full-time (3 women). *Students:* 16 full-time (15 women), 22 part-time (13 women); includes 6 minority (3 Black or African American, non-Hispanic/Latino; 1 Asian, non-Hispanic/Latino; 2 Hispanic/Latino), 9 international. Average age 26. 77 applicants, 44% accepted, 14 enrolled. In 2010, 24 master's awarded. *Degree requirements:* For master's, thesis, internship. *Entrance requirements:* For master's, GRE General Test. Additional exam requirements/recommendations for international students: Required—TOEFL (minimum score 600 paper-based; 250 computer-based). *Application deadline:* For fall admission, 1/4 priority date for domestic students; for spring admission, 11/1 for domestic students. Application fee: $70. Electronic applications accepted. *Financial support:* In 2010–11, 3 students received support, including 3 research assistantships with tuition reimbursements available (averaging $19,000 per year); fellowships, career-related internships or fieldwork, Federal Work-Study, institutionally sponsored loans, scholarships/grants, tuition waivers (full and partial), and unspecified assistantships also available. Financial award application deadline: 1/4. Total annual research expenditures: $80,000. *Unit head:* Dr. Paul Levinson, Chair, 718-817-4860, Fax: 718-817-4868, E-mail: levinson@fordham.edu. *Application contact:* Charlene Dundie, Director of Graduate Admissions, 718-817-4420, Fax: 718-817-3566, E-mail: dundie@fordham.edu.

Fort Hays State University, Graduate School, College of Arts and Sciences, Department of Communication, Hays, KS 67601-4099. Offers MS. Part-time programs available. *Degree requirements:* For master's, comprehensive exam, thesis optional. *Entrance requirements:* Additional exam requirements/recommendations for international students: Required—TOEFL (minimum score 550 paper-based; 213 computer-based). Electronic applications accepted. *Faculty research:* Listening skills development, oral sensory motor skills, speech, reading, articulation in preschool children.

George Mason University, College of Humanities and Social Sciences, Program in Communications, Fairfax, VA 22030. Offers MA, PhD. *Faculty:* 33 full-time (12 women), 40 part-time/adjunct (18 women). *Students:* 32 full-time (21 women), 33 part-time (24 women); includes

2 Black or African American, non-Hispanic/Latino; 3 Asian, non-Hispanic/Latino; 2 Hispanic/ Latino; 2 Two or more races, non-Hispanic/Latino, 5 international. Average age 33. 140 applicants, 35% accepted, 30 enrolled. In 2010, 16 master's awarded. *Degree requirements:* For master's, comprehensive exam, thesis or project; for doctorate, comprehensive exam, thesis/dissertation. *Entrance requirements:* For master's, GRE, 3 letters of recommendation, resume; for doctorate, GRE, 3 letters of recommendation, essay addressing communication area, resume, expanded goals statement. Additional exam requirements/recommendations for international students: Required—TOEFL (minimum score 570 paper-based; 230 computer-based; 88 iBT). *Application deadline:* For fall admission, 3/1 for domestic students. Applications are processed on a rolling basis. Application fee: $100. Electronic applications accepted. *Expenses:* Tuition, state resident: full-time $8192; part-time $440 per credit hour. Tuition, nonresident: full-time $22,952; part-time $1055 per credit hour. Required fees: $2364; $99 per credit hour. *Financial support:* In 2010–11, 22 students received support, including 3 fellowships with full tuition reimbursements available (averaging $18,000 per year), 5 research assistantships with full and partial tuition reimbursements available (averaging $13,802 per year), 14 teaching assistantships with full and partial tuition reimbursements available (averaging $10,418 per year); career-related internships or fieldwork, Federal Work-Study, scholarships/ grants, unspecified assistantships, and health care benefits (full-time research or teaching assistantship recipients) also available. Financial award applicants required to submit FAFSA. *Faculty research:* Theoretical and multi-methodological promotion, disease prevention, quality of care, risk assessment, crisis management, consumer/provider relationships, health campaigns, communication policy. Total annual research expenditures: $572,734. *Unit head:* Gary Kreps, Chair, 703-993-1094, Fax: 703-993-1096, E-mail: gkreps@gmu.edu. *Application contact:* Maria Carabelli, Graduate Coordinator, 703-993-3552, E-mail: mverdino@gmu.edu.

Georgetown University, Graduate School of Arts and Sciences, Program in Communication, Culture, and Technology, Washington, DC 20057. Offers MA. Part-time and evening/weekend programs available. *Degree requirements:* For master's, thesis (for some programs). *Entrance requirements:* For master's, GRE General Test, 3 letters of recommendation, writing sample. Additional exam requirements/recommendations for international students: Required—TOEFL (minimum score 600 paper-based; 250 computer-based). Electronic applications accepted.

The George Washington University, Elliott School of International Affairs, Program in Global Communication, Washington, DC 20052. Offers MA. *Students:* 23 full-time (19 women), 13 part-time (10 women); includes 4 Black or African American, non-Hispanic/Latino; 2 Asian, non-Hispanic/Latino; 2 Hispanic/Latino, 3 international. Average age 26. 115 applicants, 50% accepted, 13 enrolled. In 2010, 4 master's awarded. *Application deadline:* For fall admission, 2/1 for domestic students; for spring admission, 10/1 for domestic students. *Financial support:* Application deadline: 1/15. *Unit head:* Sean Aday, Director, 202-994-4220, Fax: 202-994-5806, E-mail: seanaday@gwu.edu. *Application contact:* Jeff V. Miles, Director of Graduate Admissions, 202-994-7050, Fax: 202-994-9537, E-mail: esiagrad@gwu.edu.

Georgia State University, College of Arts and Sciences, Department of Communication, Atlanta, GA 30302-3083. Offers film/video/digital imaging (MA); human communication and social influence (MA); mass communication (MA); moving image studies (PhD); public communication (PhD). Part-time programs available. *Degree requirements:* For master's, one foreign language, thesis or alternative; for doctorate, comprehensive exam, thesis/dissertation. *Entrance requirements:* For master's and doctorate, GRE General Test. Additional exam requirements/recommendations for international students: Required—TOEFL (minimum score 80 computer-based). Electronic applications accepted. *Faculty research:* Critical/cultural studies, rhetoric studies, film/media studies, mass communications/journalism, audience studies.

Gonzaga University, School of Professional Studies, Program in Communication and Leadership Studies, Spokane, WA 99258. Offers MA. Postbaccalaureate distance learning degree programs offered.

Governors State University, College of Arts and Sciences, Program in Communication and Training, University Park, IL 60466-0975. Offers communication studies (MA); instructional and training technology (MA); media communication (MA). Part-time and evening/weekend programs available. *Degree requirements:* For master's, thesis or alternative. *Expenses:* Tuition, state resident: full-time $5400; part-time $225 per credit hour. Tuition, nonresident: full-time $16,200; part-time $675 per credit hour. Required fees: $1358; $46 per credit hour. $126 per term. Tuition and fees vary according to degree level and program.

Grand Valley State University, College of Liberal Arts and Sciences, School of Communications, Allendale, MI 49401-9403. Offers MS. Part-time and evening/weekend programs available. *Degree requirements:* For master's, thesis or alternative. *Entrance requirements:* For master's, minimum GPA of 3.0 in last 60 hours, 2 letters of recommendation. Additional exam requirements/ recommendations for international students: Required—TOEFL (minimum score 550 paper-based; 213 computer-based). Electronic applications accepted. *Faculty research:* Communication technology, databases, organizational communication, systems theory, public relations and advertising.

Harvard University, Extension School, Cambridge, MA 02138-3722. Offers applied sciences (CAS); biotechnology (ALM); educational technologies (ALM); educational technology (CET); English for graduate and professional studies (DGP); environmental management (ALM, CEM); information technology (ALM); journalism (ALM); liberal arts (ALM); management (ALM, CM); mathematics for teaching (ALM); museum studies (ALM); premedical studies (Diploma); publication and communication (CPC). Part-time and evening/weekend programs available. *Degree requirements:* For master's, thesis. *Entrance requirements:* For master's, 3 completed graduate courses with grade of B or higher. Additional exam requirements/recommendations for international students: Required—TOEFL (minimum score 600 paper-based; 250 computer-based), TWE (minimum score 5). *Expenses:* Contact institution.

Hawai'i Pacific University, College of Humanities and Social Sciences, Program in Communication, Honolulu, HI 96813. Offers MA. Part-time and evening/weekend programs available. *Degree requirements:* For master's, thesis. *Entrance requirements:* Additional exam requirements/ recommendations for international students: Recommended—TOEFL (minimum score 550 paper-based; 213 computer-based; 80 iBT), TWE (minimum score 5). Electronic applications accepted.

See Close-Up on page 725.

Hofstra University, School of Communication, Hempstead, NY 11549. Offers MA, MFA. Part-time and evening/weekend programs available. *Faculty:* 18 full-time (7 women), 2 part-time/adjunct (1 woman). *Students:* 37 full-time (25 women), 38 part-time (22 women); includes 23 minority (14 Black or African American, non-Hispanic/Latino; 1 American Indian or Alaska Native, non-Hispanic/Latino; 4 Asian, non-Hispanic/Latino; 4 Hispanic/Latino), 10 international. Average age 28. 79 applicants, 85% accepted, 30 enrolled. In 2010, 16 master's awarded. *Degree requirements:* For master's, thesis, thesis project. *Entrance requirements:* For master's, letters of recommendation, interview. Additional exam requirements/recommendations for international students: Required—TOEFL (minimum score 550 paper-based; 213 computer-based; 80 iBT). *Application deadline:* Applications are processed on a rolling basis. Application fee: $70 ($75 for international students). Electronic applications accepted. *Expenses:* Tuition: Full-time $18,000; part-time $1000 per credit hour. Required fees: $970; $145 per term. Tuition and fees vary according to program. *Financial support:* In 2010–11, 25 students received support, including 10 fellowships with full and partial tuition reimbursements available (averaging $2,450 per year), 2 research assistantships with full and partial tuition reimbursements available (averaging $10,502 per year); Federal Work-Study, institutionally sponsored loans, scholarships/ grants, tuition waivers (full and partial), and unspecified assistantships also available. Support available to part-time students. Financial award applicants required to submit FAFSA. *Faculty research:* Social impact of social media; media representations of difference (gender, race, sexual orientation); civic engagement and political participation; future of news/journalism; documentary film aesthetics, history, theory. Total annual research expenditures: $51,920. *Unit head:* Dr. Eric W. Cornog, Dean, 516-463-5215, Fax: 516-463-4866, E-mail: comewcj@hofstra.edu. *Application contact:* Carol Drummer, Dean of Graduate Admissions, 516-463-4876, Fax: 516-463-4664, E-mail: gradstudent@hofstra.edu.

Howard University, School of Communications, Washington, DC 20059-0002. Offers MA, MFA, MS, PhD. Part-time and evening/weekend programs available. Terminal master's awarded for partial completion of doctoral program. *Degree requirements:* For master's, comprehensive exam (for some programs), thesis optional; for doctorate, one foreign language, comprehensive exam, thesis/dissertation. *Entrance requirements:* For master's, GRE General Test, minimum GPA of 3.0; for doctorate, GRE General Test, minimum GPA of 3.2. Additional exam requirements/recommendations for international students: Required—TOEFL. Electronic applications accepted. *Expenses:* Contact institution. *Faculty research:* Communication disorders, intercultural communication, communication skills, race and media.

Illinois Institute of Technology, Graduate College, College of Science and Letters, Lewis Department of Humanities, Chicago, IL 60616-3793. Offers information architecture (MS); technical communication (PhD); technical communication and information design (MS). Part-time programs available. *Faculty:* 18 full-time (8 women), 16 part-time/adjunct (12 women). *Students:* 29 full-time (15 women), 16 part-time (12 women); includes 13 minority (10 Black or African American, non-Hispanic/Latino; 2 Asian, non-Hispanic/Latino; 1 Hispanic/Latino), 6 international. Average age 34. 34 applicants, 56% accepted, 11 enrolled. In 2010, 9 master's, 1 doctorate awarded. *Degree requirements:* For master's, comprehensive exam, thesis or alternative; for doctorate, comprehensive exam, thesis/dissertation. *Entrance requirements:* For master's and doctorate, GRE General Test (minimum score 500 Quantitative, 500 Verbal, and 3.0 Analytical Writing), minimum undergraduate GPA of 3.0. Additional exam requirements/recommendations for international students: Required—TOEFL (minimum score 523 paper-based; 70 iBT). *Application deadline:* For fall admission, 5/1 for domestic and international students; for spring admission, 10/15 for domestic and international students. Applications are processed on a rolling basis. Application fee: $50. Electronic applications accepted. *Expenses:* Tuition: Full-time $18,576; part-time $1032 per credit hour. Required fees: $583 per semester. One-time fee: $150. Tuition and fees vary according to program and student level. *Financial support:* In 2010–11, 4 research assistantships with partial tuition reimbursements (averaging $8,300 per year), 13 teaching assistantships with partial tuition reimbursements (averaging $7,553 per year) were awarded; fellowships with partial tuition reimbursements, career-related internships or fieldwork, Federal Work-Study, institutionally sponsored loans, scholarships/grants, health care benefits, tuition waivers (partial), and unspecified assistantships also available. Support available to part-time students. Financial award applicants required to submit FAFSA. *Faculty research:* Aesthetics, document and online design, ethics in the professions, history of art and architecture, humanizing technology. Total annual research expenditures: $180,587. *Unit head:* Dr. Maureen Flanagan, Professor and Chair, 312-567-3563, Fax: 312-567-5187, E-mail: maureen.flanagan@iit.edu. *Application contact:* Deborah Gibson, Director, Graduate Admission, 866-472-3448, Fax: 312-567-3138, E-mail: inquiry.grad@iit.edu.

Illinois State University, Graduate School, College of Arts and Sciences, School of Communication, Normal, IL 61790-2200. Offers MA, MS. *Degree requirements:* For master's, thesis or alternative. *Entrance requirements:* For master's, GRE General Test, minimum GPA of 2.8 in last 60 hours of course work. Additional exam requirements/recommendations for international students: Required—TOEFL. *Faculty research:* Corporation for public broadcasting, FY2007, community service grant for WGLT-FM, Illinois public broadcasting grant FY2007 for WGLT-FM; WGLT digital conversion fund.

Immaculata University, College of Graduate Studies, Program in Applied Communication, Immaculata, PA 19345. Offers MA. Part-time and evening/weekend programs available. *Faculty:* 2 full-time (both women). *Students:* 1 (woman) full-time, 9 part-time (8 women). 17 applicants, 82% accepted, 8 enrolled. *Entrance requirements:* For master's, GRE, MAT. Additional exam requirements/recommendations for international students: Required—TOEFL, IELTS. *Application deadline:* Applications are processed on a rolling basis. Application fee: $50. Electronic applications accepted. *Financial support:* Applicants required to submit FAFSA. *Unit head:* Dr. Stacy Skirvin, Program Director, 610-647-4400 Ext. 3488. *Application contact:* Sandra A. Rollison, Director of Graduate Admission, 610-647-4400 Ext. 3215, Fax: 610-993-8550, E-mail: srollison@immaculata.edu.

Indiana State University, College of Graduate and Professional Studies, College of Arts and Sciences, Department of Communication, Terre Haute, IN 47809. Offers communication studies (MA, MS); radio, television and film (MA, MS). Part-time programs available. *Degree requirements:* For master's, thesis (for some programs), oral and written exam. *Entrance requirements:* For master's, GRE General Test. Additional exam requirements/recommendations for international students: Required—TOEFL. *Faculty research:* Women in media, communication apprehension, media history.

Indiana University Bloomington, University Graduate School, College of Arts and Sciences, Department of Telecommunications, Bloomington, IN 47405-7000. Offers mass communications (PhD); telecommunications (MA, MS). *Faculty:* 11 full-time (4 women). *Students:* 50 full-time (29 women), 13 part-time (2 women); includes 7 minority (1 Black or African American, non-Hispanic/Latino; 2 Asian, non-Hispanic/Latino; 1 Hispanic/Latino; 3 Two or more races, non-Hispanic/Latino), 25 international. Average age 30. 61 applicants, 51% accepted, 19 enrolled. In 2010, 10 master's, 1 doctorate awarded. Terminal master's awarded for partial completion of doctoral program. *Degree requirements:* For master's, thesis (for some programs); for doctorate, thesis/dissertation. *Entrance requirements:* For master's and doctorate, GRE General Test. Additional exam requirements/recommendations for international students: Required—TOEFL. *Application deadline:* For fall admission, 1/15 priority date for domestic students, 12/15 for international students. Applications are processed on a rolling basis. Application fee: $55 ($65 for international students). *Financial support:* In 2010–11, 1 fellowship with full tuition reimbursement (averaging $18,000 per year) was awarded; research assistantships, teaching assistantships, tuition waivers (full) also available. *Faculty research:* Media processes and effects, media law and policy, media management, media design and production. *Unit head:* Tamera Theodore, Graduate Secretary, 812-855-2017, E-mail: ttheodor@indiana.edu. *Application contact:* Tamera Theodore, Graduate Secretary, 812-855-2017, E-mail: ttheodor@indiana.edu.

Indiana University of Pennsylvania, School of Graduate Studies and Research, College of Education and Educational Technology, Department of Communications Media, Indiana, PA 15705-1087. Offers adult education and communications technology (MA); communications media and instructional technology (PhD). Part-time and evening/weekend programs available. *Faculty:* 9 full-time (2 women). *Students:* 21 full-time (10 women), 30 part-time (14 women); includes 3 minority (2 Black or African American, non-Hispanic/Latino; 1 Asian, non-Hispanic/ Latino), 2 international. Average age 36. 42 applicants, 31% accepted, 13 enrolled.Application fee: $40. *Financial support:* In 2010–11, 2 fellowships with full tuition reimbursements (averaging $1,000 per year), 10 research assistantships with full and partial tuition reimbursements (averaging $5,428 per year), 3 teaching assistantships with partial tuition reimbursements (averaging $21,967 per year) were awarded; career-related internships or fieldwork, Federal Work-Study, scholarships/grants, and tuition waivers (full) also available. Support available to part-time students. Financial award application deadline: 3/15; financial award applicants required to submit FAFSA. *Unit head:* Dr. Mark Piwinsky, Chairperson, 724-357-3954, Fax: 724-357-5503, E-mail: mark.piwinsky@iup.edu. *Application contact:* Dr. Edward Nardi, Associate Dean, 724-357-2480, Fax: 724-357-5595, E-mail: ewnardi@iup.edu.

Indiana University–Purdue University Fort Wayne, College of Arts and Sciences, Department of Communication, Fort Wayne, IN 46805-1499. Offers professional communication (MA, MS). Part-time programs available. *Faculty:* 11 full-time (6 women). *Students:* 9 full-time (8 women), 33 part-time (18 women); includes 5 minority (3 Black or African American, non-Hispanic/ Latino; 1 Hispanic/Latino; 1 Two or more races, non-Hispanic/Latino), 2 international. Average age 34. 22 applicants, 100% accepted, 15 enrolled. In 2010, 4 master's awarded. *Entrance requirements:* For master's, minimum GPA of 3.0. Additional exam requirements/

Communication—General

Indiana University–Purdue University Fort Wayne (continued) recommendations for international students: Required—TOEFL (minimum score 550 paper-based; 213 computer-based; 77 iBT); Recommended—TWE. *Application deadline:* For fall admission, 4/15 priority date for domestic students, 2/15 priority date for international students; for spring admission, 11/30 priority date for domestic students, 9/15 priority date for international students. Applications are processed on a rolling basis. Application fee: $55 ($60 for international students). Electronic applications accepted. *Expenses:* Tuition, state resident: full-time $4824; part-time $268 per credit. Tuition, nonresident: full-time $11,625; part-time $646 per credit. Required fees: $555; $30.85 per credit. Tuition and fees vary according to course load. *Financial support:* In 2010–11, 10 teaching assistantships with partial tuition reimbursements (averaging $12,740 per year) were awarded; scholarships/grants also available. Support available to part-time students. Financial award application deadline: 3/1; financial award applicants required to submit FAFSA. *Faculty research:* Audience analysis, Bush vs. Gore motives and the Supreme Court. Total annual research expenditures: $1,952. *Unit head:* Dr. Marcia Dixson, Chair and Associate Professor, 260-481-6558, Fax: 260-481-6183, E-mail: dixson@ipfw.edu. *Application contact:* Dr. Steven Carr, Graduate Program Director, 260-481-6545, Fax: 260-481-6183, E-mail: carr@ipfw.edu.

Instituto Tecnologico de Santo Domingo, Graduate School, Area of Humanities and Social Sciences, Santo Domingo, Dominican Republic. Offers accounting (Certificate); adult education (Certificate); applied linguistics (MA); economics (MA); education (M Ed); educational psychology (MA, Certificate); gender and development (MA, Certificate); humanistic studies (MA); international marketing management (Certificate); international relations in the Caribbean basin (Certificate); intervention systems in family therapy (MA); linguistic and literary communication (Certificate); pedagogical support (MA); social science education (M Ed); sustainable human development (MA); terminal illness and death psychology (Certificate); youth and adult education (M Ed).

Instituto Tecnológico y de Estudios Superiores de Monterrey, Campus Ciudad Obregón, Programs in Education, Program in Communications, Ciudad Obregón, Mexico. Offers ME.

Instituto Tecnológico y de Estudios Superiores de Monterrey, Campus Monterrey, Graduate and Research Division, Program in Natural and Social Sciences, Monterrey, Mexico. Offers biotechnology (MS); chemistry (MS, PhD); communications (MS); education (MA). Part-time programs available. *Degree requirements:* For master's, one foreign language, thesis; for doctorate, one foreign language, thesis/dissertation. *Entrance requirements:* For master's, EXADEP; for doctorate, EXADEP, master's degree in related field. Additional exam requirements/recommendations for international students: Required—TOEFL. *Faculty research:* Cultural industries, mineral substances, bioremediation, food processing, CQ in industrial chemical processing.

Ithaca College, Division of Graduate and Professional Studies, Roy H. Park School of Communications, Program in Communications, Ithaca, NY 14850. Offers MS. Part-time programs available. *Faculty:* 6 full-time (1 woman). *Students:* 25 full-time (19 women), 16 part-time (10 women); includes 1 minority (American Indian or Alaska Native, non-Hispanic/Latino), 10 international. Average age 27. 45 applicants, 78% accepted, 19 enrolled. In 2010, 13 master's awarded. *Degree requirements:* For master's, thesis optional. *Entrance requirements:* For master's, minimum GPA of 3.0. Additional exam requirements/recommendations for international students: Required—TOEFL (minimum score 550 paper-based; 213 computer-based; 80 iBT). *Application deadline:* For fall admission, 7/5 for domestic and international students; for spring admission, 12/1 for domestic and international students. Applications are processed on a rolling basis. Application fee: $40. Electronic applications accepted. *Expenses:* Tuition: Full-time $19,890; part-time $663 per credit hour. *Financial support:* In 2010–11, 17 students received support, including 17 teaching assistantships (averaging $7,741 per year); career-related internships or fieldwork, Federal Work-Study, scholarships/grants, and unspecified assistantships also available. Support available to part-time students. Financial award application deadline: 3/1; financial award applicants required to submit CSS PROFILE or FAFSA. *Faculty research:* Managing corporate communication and learning, social systems design, crisis communication and diversity, social marketing, instructional design and interactive technologies. *Unit head:* Dr. Howard Kalman, Chairperson, 607-274-3527, Fax: 607-274-1263, E-mail: gps@ithaca.edu. *Application contact:* Rob Gearhart, Dean, Graduate and Professional Studies, 607-274-3527, Fax: 607-274-1263, E-mail: gps@ithaca.edu.

The Johns Hopkins University, Zanvyl Krieger School of Arts and Sciences, Advanced Academic Programs, Program in Communication, Baltimore, MD 21218-2699. Offers MA, MA/MBA. Part-time and evening/weekend programs available. *Faculty:* 4 full-time (all women), 18 part-time/adjunct (10 women). *Students:* 16 full-time (15 women), 203 part-time (166 women); includes 48 minority (23 Black or African American, non-Hispanic/Latino; 10 Asian, non-Hispanic/Latino; 9 Hispanic/Latino; 2 Native Hawaiian or other Pacific Islander, non-Hispanic/Latino; 4 Two or more races, non-Hispanic/Latino), 7 international. Average age 30. 211 applicants, 38% accepted, 42 enrolled. In 2010, 46 master's awarded. *Degree requirements:* For master's, thesis. *Entrance requirements:* For master's, minimum GPA of 3.0, strong writing skills. Additional exam requirements/recommendations for international students: Required—TOEFL (minimum score 250 computer-based; 100 iBT). *Application deadline:* For fall admission, 5/31 priority date for domestic students, 4/30 priority date for international students; for spring admission, 10/31 priority date for domestic and international students. Applications are processed on a rolling basis. Application fee: $75. Electronic applications accepted. *Financial support:* Applicants required to submit FAFSA. *Unit head:* Dr. Erika Falk, Associate Program Chair, 202-452-8711, E-mail: erikafalk@jhu.edu. *Application contact:* Valana M. McMickens, Admissions Manager, 202-452-1941, Fax: 202-452-1970, E-mail: aapadmissions@jhu.edu.

Kansas State University, Graduate School, College of Arts and Sciences, Department of Communication Studies, Theatre and Dance, Manhattan, KS 66505. Offers rhetoric/communication (MA); theatre (MA). *Degree requirements:* For master's, thesis or alternative. *Entrance requirements:* For master's, GRE General Test (recommended), minimum GPA of 3.0. Additional exam requirements/recommendations for international students: Required—TOEFL. Electronic applications accepted. *Faculty research:* Drama therapy, directing, costume design, scenic design, technical theatre mechanics and safety.

Kean University, College of Humanities and Social Sciences, Program in Communication Studies, Union, NJ 07083. Offers MA. Part-time and evening/weekend programs available. *Faculty:* 12 full-time (5 women). *Students:* 12 full-time (11 women), 4 part-time (3 women); includes 2 Black or African American, non-Hispanic/Latino; 1 Asian, non-Hispanic/Latino; 4 Hispanic/Latino, 2 international. Average age 26. 12 applicants, 92% accepted, 6 enrolled. In 2010, 7 master's awarded. *Degree requirements:* For master's, comprehensive exam, thesis optional. *Entrance requirements:* For master's, GRE General Test, minimum GPA of 3.0, 3 letters of recommendation, interview, transcripts, personal statement. *Application deadline:* For fall admission, 6/1 for domestic students; for spring admission, 11/1 for domestic students. Application fee: $75 ($150 for international students). Electronic applications accepted. *Expenses:* Tuition, state resident: full-time $10,872; part-time $500 per credit. Tuition, nonresident: full-time $14,736; part-time $614 per credit. Required fees: $2740.80; $125 per credit. Part-time tuition and fees vary according to course load and degree level. *Financial support:* In 2010–11, 6 research assistantships with full tuition reimbursements (averaging $3,263 per year) were awarded; unspecified assistantships also available. Financial award applicants required to submit FAFSA. *Unit head:* Dr. Wenli Yuan, Program Coordinator, 908-737-0471, E-mail: wyuan@kean.edu. *Application contact:* Steven Koch, Pre-Admissions Coordinator, 908-737-5924, Fax: 908-737-5925, E-mail: skoch@kean.edu.

Kent State University, College of Communication and Information, School of Communication Studies, Kent, OH 44242-0001. Offers MA, PhD. *Degree requirements:* For master's, thesis optional; for doctorate, variable foreign language requirement, thesis/dissertation. *Entrance requirements:* For master's and doctorate, GRE General Test, minimum GPA of 3.0. Additional exam requirements/recommendations for international students: Required—TOEFL (minimum

score 600 paper-based), TWE (minimum score 5). Electronic applications accepted. *Expenses:* Tuition, state resident: full-time $7866; part-time $437 per credit hour. Tuition, nonresident: full-time $14,022; part-time $779 per credit hour. *Faculty research:* Interpersonal communication, organizational communication, mass communication, new technologies and communication.

Lasell College, Graduate and Professional Studies in Communication, Newton, MA 02466-2709. Offers integrated marketing communication (MSC, Graduate Certificate); public relations (MSC, Graduate Certificate). Part-time and evening/weekend programs available. Postbaccalaureate distance learning degree programs offered (minimal on-campus study). *Faculty:* 2 full-time (both women), 2 part-time/adjunct (both women). *Students:* 8 full-time (all women), 25 part-time (22 women); includes 3 minority (all Black or African American, non-Hispanic/Latino), 2 international. Average age 28. 24 applicants, 83% accepted, 13 enrolled. In 2010, 10 master's awarded. *Entrance requirements:* For master's and Graduate Certificate, bachelor's degree from an accredited institution. Additional exam requirements/recommendations for international students: Required—TOEFL (minimum score 550 paper-based; 213 computer-based; 75 iBT), IELTS. *Application deadline:* For fall admission, 8/31 priority date for domestic students, 6/30 priority date for international students; for spring admission, 12/31 priority date for domestic students, 10/31 priority date for international students. Applications are processed on a rolling basis. Application fee: $40. Electronic applications accepted. *Expenses:* Tuition: Part-time $550 per credit hour. Required fees: $55 per semester. *Financial support:* In 2010–11, 2 students received support. Available to part-time students. Application deadline: 8/31. *Unit head:* Dr. Joan Dolamore, Dean of Graduate and Professional Studies, 617-243-2485, Fax: 617-243-2450, E-mail: gradinfo@lasell.edu. *Application contact:* Adrienne Franciosi, Director of Graduate Admission, 617-243-2214, Fax: 617-243-2450, E-mail: gradinfo@lasell.edu.

La Sierra University, College of Arts and Sciences, Department of English and Communication, Riverside, CA 92515. Offers communication (MA), including public relations/advertising, theory emphasis; English (MA), including literary emphasis, writing emphasis. Part-time programs available. *Degree requirements:* For master's, one foreign language. *Entrance requirements:* For master's, GRE General Test.

Liberty University, School of Communications, Lynchburg, VA 24502. Offers MA. Part-time programs available. *Students:* 70 full-time (53 women), 14 part-time (10 women); includes 10 minority (4 Black or African American, non-Hispanic/Latino; 1 American Indian or Alaska Native, non-Hispanic/Latino; 2 Asian, non-Hispanic/Latino; 3 Hispanic/Latino), 9 international. Average age 25. In 2010, 23 master's awarded. *Degree requirements:* For master's, thesis. *Entrance requirements:* For master's, minimum undergraduate GPA of 3.0, 2 faculty recommendations, written statement of purpose. Additional exam requirements/recommendations for international students: Required—TOEFL (minimum score 600 paper-based; 250 computer-based; 100 iBT). *Application deadline:* For fall admission, 6/1 priority date for domestic students; for spring admission, 11/1 priority date for domestic students. Application fee: $50. Electronic applications accepted. *Financial support:* Federal Work-Study and unspecified assistantships available. *Unit head:* Dr. William G. Gribbin, Dean, 434-582-2466, E-mail: wgribbin@liberty.edu. *Application contact:* Jay Bridge, Director of Graduate Admissions, 800-424-9595, Fax: 800-628-7977, E-mail: gradadmissions@liberty.edu.

Lindenwood University, Graduate Programs, College of Individualized Education, St. Charles, MO 63301-1695. Offers administration (MSA); business administration (MBA); communications (MA); criminal justice and administration (MS); gerontology (MA); health management (MS); human resource management (MS); information technology (MBA, Certificate); managing information technology (MS); writing (MFA). Part-time and evening/weekend programs available. *Faculty:* 15 full-time (8 women), 128 part-time/adjunct (53 women). *Students:* 828 full-time (527 women), 80 part-time (50 women); includes 284 minority (265 Black or African American, non-Hispanic/Latino; 3 American Indian or Alaska Native, non-Hispanic/Latino; 6 Asian, non-Hispanic/Latino; 10 Hispanic/Latino), 23 international. Average age 35. 223 applicants, 44% accepted, 87 enrolled. In 2010, 478 master's awarded. *Degree requirements:* For master's, thesis (for some programs), 1 colloquium per term. *Entrance requirements:* For master's, interview, minimum GPA of 3.0. Additional exam requirements/recommendations for international students: Required—TOEFL (minimum score 550 paper-based; 213 computer-based; 80 iBT). *Application deadline:* For fall admission, 10/2 priority date for domestic and international students; for winter admission, 1/8 priority date for domestic and international students; for spring admission, 4/8 priority date for domestic and international students. Applications are processed on a rolling basis. Application fee: $30 ($100 for international students). Electronic applications accepted. *Expenses:* Tuition: Full-time $13,260; part-time $380 per credit hour. Required fees: $340. One-time fee: $30. Tuition and fees vary according to course level and course load. *Financial support:* In 2010–11, 631 students received support. Career-related internships or fieldwork, institutionally sponsored loans, tuition waivers (partial), and unspecified assistantships available. Financial award application deadline: 6/30; financial award applicants required to submit FAFSA. *Unit head:* Dan Kemper, Dean, 636-949-4501, Fax: 636-949-4505, E-mail: dkemper@lindenwood.edu. *Application contact:* Brett Barger, Dean of Evening Admissions and Extension Campuses, 636-949-4934, Fax: 636-949-4109, E-mail: adultadmissions@lindenwood.edu.

Lindenwood University, Graduate Programs, School of Communications, St. Charles, MO 63301-1695. Offers MA. Part-time and evening/weekend programs available. *Faculty:* 5 full-time (0 women), 6 part-time/adjunct (2 women). *Students:* 12 full-time (4 women), 2 part-time (1 woman); includes 3 minority (all Black or African American, non-Hispanic/Latino), 1 international. Average age 26. 12 applicants, 5 enrolled. In 2010, 3 master's awarded. *Degree requirements:* For master's, thesis (for some programs). *Entrance requirements:* For master's, minimum GPA of 3.0, resume. Additional exam requirements/recommendations for international students: Required—TOEFL (minimum score 550 paper-based; 213 computer-based; 80 iBT). *Application deadline:* For fall admission, 8/27 priority date for domestic and international students; for spring admission, 1/28 priority date for domestic and international students. Applications are processed on a rolling basis. Application fee: $30 ($100 for international students). Electronic applications accepted. *Expenses:* Tuition: Full-time $13,260; part-time $380 per credit hour. Required fees: $340. One-time fee: $30. Tuition and fees vary according to course level and course load. *Financial support:* In 2010–11, 1 student received support. Career-related internships or fieldwork, institutionally sponsored loans, tuition waivers (partial), and unspecified assistantships available. Financial award application deadline: 6/30; financial award applicants required to submit FAFSA. *Unit head:* Mike Wall, Dean, 636-949-4880. *Application contact:* Brett Barger, Dean of Evening Admissions and Extension Campuses, 636-949-4934, Fax: 636-949-4109, E-mail: adultadmissions@lindenwood.edu.

Louisiana State University and Agricultural and Mechanical College, Graduate School, College of Humanities and Social Sciences, Department of Communication Studies, Baton Rouge, LA 70803. Offers MA, PhD. *Faculty:* 11 full-time (6 women). *Students:* 33 full-time (13 women), 8 part-time (5 women); includes 2 Black or African American, non-Hispanic/Latino, 1 international. Average age 32. 42 applicants, 60% accepted, 9 enrolled. In 2010, 3 master's, 4 doctorates awarded. *Degree requirements:* For master's, thesis; for doctorate, one foreign language, thesis/dissertation. *Entrance requirements:* For master's and doctorate, GRE General Test, minimum GPA of 3.0. Additional exam requirements/recommendations for international students: Required—TOEFL (minimum score 550 paper-based; 213 computer-based; 79 iBT) or IELTS (minimum score 6.5). *Application deadline:* For fall admission, 1/25 priority date for domestic students, 5/15 for international students; for spring admission, 10/15 for international students. Applications are processed on a rolling basis. Application fee: $50 ($70 for international students). Electronic applications accepted. *Financial support:* In 2010–11, 38 students received support, including 3 fellowships with full and partial tuition reimbursements available (averaging $20,023 per year), 1 research assistantship with full and partial tuition reimbursement available (averaging $13,000 per year), 23 teaching assistantships with full and partial tuition reimbursements available (averaging $11,348 per year); career-related internships or fieldwork, Federal Work-Study, institutionally sponsored loans, scholarships/grants, health care benefits, tuition waivers (full and partial), and unspecified assistantships also available. Support available to part-time students. Financial award applicants required to submit FAFSA. *Faculty research:* Rhetorical theory and criticism, performance studies, interpersonal communication. Total annual research expenditures: $125,783. *Unit head:* Dr. Renee Edwards, Chair, 225-578-4172, Fax: 225-578-4828, E-mail: edwards@lsu.edu. *Application contact:* Dr. Ruth Bowman, Graduate Adviser, 225-578-6812, Fax: 225-578-4828, E-mail: spbowm@lsu.edu.

Marquette University, Graduate School, College of Arts and Sciences, Department of Political Science/International Affairs, Milwaukee, WI 53201-1881. Offers international affairs (MA); political science (MA); political science/communication (MA); JD/MA; MA/MBA. Part-time programs available. *Faculty:* 16 full-time (4 women), 2 part-time/adjunct (both women). *Students:* 22 full-time (10 women), 4 part-time (all women); includes 1 minority (Asian, non-Hispanic/Latino), 4 international. Average age 27. 66 applicants, 65% accepted, 14 enrolled. In 2010, 11 master's awarded. *Degree requirements:* For master's, comprehensive exam, thesis optional. *Entrance requirements:* For master's, GRE General Test, official transcripts from all current and previous colleges/universities except Marquette, three letters of recommendation, statement of purpose. Additional exam requirements/recommendations for international students: Required—TOEFL (minimum score 530 paper-based; 78 computer-based). *Application deadline:* For fall admission, 2/15 for domestic and international students. Application fee: $50. Electronic applications accepted. *Expenses:* Tuition: Full-time $16,290; part-time $905 per credit hour. Tuition and fees vary according to program. *Financial support:* In 2010–11, 4 fellowships, 11 teaching assistantships were awarded; research assistantships, Federal Work-Study, institutionally sponsored loans, scholarships/grants, and tuition waivers (full and partial) also available. Support available to part-time students. Financial award application deadline: 2/15. *Faculty research:* Public opinion and electoral behavior, public policy analysis, Congress and the Presidency, judicial behavior, political system transitions. Total annual research expenditures: $187,654. *Unit head:* Dr. Barrett McCormick, Chair, 414-288-6842, Fax: 414-288-3360. *Application contact:* Dr. Lowell Barrington, Director of Graduate Studies, 414-288-5234, Fax: 414-288-3360.

Marquette University, Graduate School, College of Communication, Milwaukee, WI 53201-1881. Offers advertising and public relations (MA); broadcasting and electronic communications (MA); communications studies (MA); digital storytelling (Certificate); health, environment, science and sustainability (MA); journalism (MA); mass communications (MA). *Accreditation:* ACEJMC (one or more programs are accredited). Part-time and evening/weekend programs available. *Faculty:* 33 full-time (18 women), 30 part-time/adjunct (16 women). *Students:* 35 full-time (20 women), 31 part-time (25 women); includes 5 minority (2 Black or African American, non-Hispanic/Latino; 1 Hispanic/Latino; 2 Two or more races, non-Hispanic/Latino), 4 international. Average age 28. 97 applicants, 52% accepted, 21 enrolled. In 2010, 16 master's, 5 other advanced degrees awarded. *Degree requirements:* For master's, comprehensive exam, thesis or alternative. *Entrance requirements:* For master's, GRE, official transcripts from all current and previous colleges/universities except Marquette, three letters of recommendation, statement of academic and professional goals. Additional exam requirements/recommendations for international students: Required—TOEFL (minimum score 530 paper-based; 78 computer-based). *Application deadline:* Applications are processed on a rolling basis. Application fee: $50. Electronic applications accepted. *Expenses:* Tuition: Full-time $16,290; part-time $905 per credit hour. Tuition and fees vary according to program. *Financial support:* In 2010–11, 2 fellowships, 7 research assistantships, 12 teaching assistantships were awarded; career-related internships or fieldwork, Federal Work-Study, institutionally sponsored loans, scholarships/grants, and tuition waivers (full and partial) also available. Support available to part-time students. Financial award application deadline: 2/15. *Faculty research:* Urban journalism, gender and communication, intercultural communication, religious communication. Total annual research expenditures: $3,088. *Unit head:* Dr. Lori Bergen, Dean, 414-288-7133, Fax: 414-288-1578. *Application contact:* Erin Fox, Assistant Director for Recruitment, 414-288-5319, Fax: 414-288-1902, E-mail: erin.fox@marquette.edu.

Marshall University, Academic Affairs Division, College of Liberal Arts, Department of Communication Studies, Huntington, WV 25755. Offers MA. *Faculty:* 6 full-time (5 women). *Students:* 16 full-time (11 women), 3 part-time (0 women), 1 international. Average age 26. In 2010, 13 master's awarded. *Degree requirements:* For master's, thesis optional. Application fee: $40. *Financial support:* Fellowships available. *Unit head:* Dr. Robert Bookwalter, Interim Chair, 304-696-2815, E-mail: bookwalt@marshall.edu. *Application contact:* Dr. Edward Woods, Information Contact, 304-696-3104, Fax: 304-746-1902, E-mail: services@marshall.edu.

Marywood University, Academic Affairs, Insalaco College of Creative and Performing Arts, Department of Communication Arts, Program in Communication Arts, Scranton, PA 18509-1598. Offers interdisciplinary (MA); media management (MA); production (MA). *Entrance requirements:* Additional exam requirements/recommendations for international students: Required—TOEFL (minimum score 550 paper-based; 213 computer-based; 79 iBT). Electronic applications accepted. *Expenses:* Tuition: Part-time $735 per credit. Required fees: $470 per semester. Tuition and fees vary according to degree level and campus/location.

McGill University, Faculty of Graduate and Postdoctoral Studies, Faculty of Arts, Department of Art History and Communication Studies, Montréal, QC H3A 2T5, Canada. Offers MA, PhD.

Michigan State University, The Graduate School, College of Communication Arts and Sciences, Department of Communication, East Lansing, MI 48824. Offers MA, PhD. *Entrance requirements:* Additional exam requirements/recommendations for international students: Required—TOEFL (minimum score 580 paper-based; 237 computer-based). Electronic applications accepted.

Minnesota State University Mankato, College of Graduate Studies, College of Arts and Humanities, Department of Communication Studies, Mankato, MN 56001. Offers communication education (Certificate); communication studies (MA, MS); forensics (MFA); professional communication (Certificate). *Students:* 22 full-time (15 women), 22 part-time (8 women). *Degree requirements:* For master's, one foreign language, comprehensive exam, thesis. *Entrance requirements:* For master's, minimum GPA of 3.0 during previous 2 years, writing sample. *Application deadline:* For fall admission, 7/1 priority date for domestic students, 5/1 for international students; for spring admission, 11/1 for domestic students, 10/1 for international students. Applications are processed on a rolling basis. Application fee: $40. Electronic applications accepted. *Financial support:* Research assistantships, teaching assistantships with full tuition reimbursements, career-related internships or fieldwork, Federal Work-Study, and institutionally sponsored loans available. Support available to part-time students. Financial award application deadline: 3/15; financial award applicants required to submit FAFSA. *Unit head:* Dr. Kristen Cvancara, Chairperson, 507-389-2213. *Application contact:* 507-389-2321, E-mail: grad@mnsu.edu.

Mississippi College, Graduate School, College of Arts and Sciences, School of Christian Studies and the Arts, Department of Communication, Clinton, MS 39058. Offers applied communication (MSC); public relations and corporate communication (MSC). Part-time programs available. *Degree requirements:* For master's, comprehensive exam, thesis optional. *Entrance requirements:* For master's, GRE or NTE, minimum GPA of 2.5. Additional exam requirements/recommendations for international students: Recommended—IELTS. Electronic applications accepted.

Missouri State University, Graduate College, College of Arts and Letters, Department of Communication and Mass Media, Springfield, MO 65897. Offers MA. Part-time programs available. *Degree requirements:* For master's, comprehensive exam, thesis or alternative. *Entrance requirements:* For master's, GRE General Test, minimum GPA of 3.0. Additional exam requirements/recommendations for international students: Required—TOEFL (minimum score 550 paper-based; 213 computer-based; 79 iBT). Electronic applications accepted. *Expenses:* Tuition, state resident: full-time $3348; part-time $186 per credit hour. Tuition, nonresident: full-time $6696; part-time $372 per credit hour. Required fees: $238 per semester. Tuition and fees vary according to course level, course load and program. *Faculty research:* Conflict resolution, media analysis, intercultural communication, rhetorical criticism.

Missouri State University, Graduate College, Interdisciplinary Program in Administrative Studies, Springfield, MO 65897. Offers applied communication (MS); criminal justice (MS); environmental management (MS); project management (MS); sports management (MS). Part-time and evening/weekend programs available. Postbaccalaureate distance learning degree programs offered (no on-campus study). *Degree requirements:* For master's, comprehensive exam, thesis or alternative. *Entrance requirements:* For master's, GRE, GMAT, 3 years of work experience. Additional exam requirements/recommendations for international students: Required—TOEFL (minimum score 550 paper-based; 213 computer-based; 79 iBT). Electronic applications accepted. *Expenses:* Tuition, state resident: full-time $3348; part-time $186 per credit hour. Tuition, nonresident: full-time $6696; part-time $372 per credit hour. Required fees: $238 per semester. Tuition and fees vary according to course level, course load and program.

Monmouth University, The Graduate School, Department of Corporate and Public Communication, West Long Branch, NJ 07764-1898. Offers corporate and public communication (MA); human resources communication (Certificate); public relations (Certificate); public service communication specialist (Certificate). Part-time and evening/weekend programs available. *Faculty:* 8 full-time (5 women). *Students:* 11 full-time (9 women), 37 part-time (28 women); includes 2 Black or African American, non-Hispanic/Latino; 3 Hispanic/Latino; 1 Two or more races, non-Hispanic/Latino, 2 international. Average age 32. 28 applicants, 93% accepted, 15 enrolled. In 2010, 15 master's awarded. *Degree requirements:* For master's, comprehensive exam, project. *Entrance requirements:* For master's, GRE, minimum GPA of 3.0 in major, 2.75 overall. Additional exam requirements/recommendations for international students: Required—TOEFL (minimum score 550 paper-based; 213 computer-based; 79 iBT), IELTS (minimum score 5), Michigan English Language Assessment Battery (minimum score 77), Cambridge A, B, C. *Application deadline:* For fall admission, 7/15 priority date for domestic students, 6/1 for international students; for spring admission, 11/15 priority date for domestic students, 11/1 for international students. Applications are processed on a rolling basis. Application fee: $50. Electronic applications accepted. *Expenses:* Tuition: Full-time $19,572; part-time $816 per credit. Required fees: $628; $157 per semester. *Financial support:* In 2010–11, 24 students received support, including 23 fellowships (averaging $1,176 per year), 5 research assistantships (averaging $7,578 per year); scholarships/grants and unspecified assistantships also available. Support available to part-time students. Financial award applicants required to submit FAFSA. *Faculty research:* Service-learning, history of television, feminism and the media, executive communication, public relations pedagogy. *Unit head:* Dr. Shelia McAllister-Spooner, Program Director, 732-571-7553, Fax: 732-571-3609, E-mail: smcallis@monmouth.edu. *Application contact:* Kevin Roane, Director, Office of Graduate Admission, 732-571-3452, Fax: 732-263-5123, E-mail: gradadm@monmouth.edu.

Montana State University Billings, College of Arts and Sciences, Department of Communication and Theater, Billings, MT 59101-0298. Offers public relations (MS). Part-time programs available. Postbaccalaureate distance learning degree programs offered. *Degree requirements:* For master's, thesis optional. *Entrance requirements:* For master's, GRE General Test, minimum undergraduate GPA of 3.0, 3 letters of recommendation.

Montclair State University, The Graduate School, School of the Arts, Department of Communication Studies, Montclair, NJ 07043-1624. Offers public and organizational relations (MA). Part-time and evening/weekend programs available. *Faculty:* 6 full-time (2 women), 41 part-time/adjunct (23 women). *Students:* 16 full-time (14 women), 19 part-time (16 women); includes 3 Black or African American, non-Hispanic/Latino; 1 Asian, non-Hispanic/Latino; 4 Hispanic/Latino, 3 international. Average age 30. 26 applicants, 54% accepted, 9 enrolled. In 2010, 14 master's awarded. *Degree requirements:* For master's, comprehensive exam. *Entrance requirements:* For master's, GRE General Test, 2 letters of recommendation. Additional exam requirements/recommendations for international students: Required—TOEFL (minimum iBT score of 83) or IELTS. *Application deadline:* For fall admission, 6/1 for international students; for spring admission, 10/1 for international students. Applications are processed on a rolling basis. Application fee: $60. Electronic applications accepted. *Expenses:* Tuition, state resident: part-time $501.34 per credit. Tuition, nonresident: part-time $773.88 per credit. Required fees: $71.15 per credit. *Financial support:* In 2010–11, 3 research assistantships with full tuition reimbursements (averaging $7,000 per year) were awarded; Federal Work-Study, scholarships/grants, and unspecified assistantships also available. Support available to part-time students. Financial award application deadline: 3/1; financial award applicants required to submit FAFSA. *Unit head:* Dr. Harry Haines, Chair, 973-655-4200. *Application contact:* Amy Aiello, Director of Graduate Admissions and Operations, 973-655-5147, Fax: 973-655-7869, E-mail: graduate.school@montclair.edu.

Morehead State University, Graduate Programs, Caudill College of Arts, Humanities and Social Sciences, Department of Communication, Media and Leadership Studies, Morehead, KY 40351. Offers communication (MA). Part-time and evening/weekend programs available. *Degree requirements:* For master's, comprehensive exam, exit assessment, written examination, oral interview. *Entrance requirements:* For master's, GRE General Test, bachelor's degree in communications or closely related field. Additional exam requirements/recommendations for international students: Required—TOEFL (minimum score 500 paper-based; 173 computer-based). Electronic applications accepted. *Faculty research:* Mass media effects, organizational communications, advertising/public relations.

National University, Academic Affairs, School of Media and Communication, La Jolla, CA 92037-1011. Offers MA, MFA, MS. Part-time and evening/weekend programs available. Postbaccalaureate distance learning degree programs offered (no on-campus study). *Faculty:* 14 full-time (6 women), 89 part-time/adjunct (31 women). *Students:* 97 full-time (39 women), 173 part-time (85 women); includes 93 minority (42 Black or African American, non-Hispanic/Latino; 1 American Indian or Alaska Native, non-Hispanic/Latino; 8 Asian, non-Hispanic/Latino; 30 Hispanic/Latino; 2 Native Hawaiian or other Pacific Islander, non-Hispanic/Latino; 10 Two or more races, non-Hispanic/Latino), 10 international. Average age 39. 172 applicants, 100% accepted, 104 enrolled. In 2010, 60 master's awarded. *Degree requirements:* For master's, thesis (for some programs). *Entrance requirements:* For master's, interview, minimum GPA of 2.5. Additional exam requirements/recommendations for international students: Required—TOEFL (minimum score 550 paper-based; 213 computer-based; 79 iBT), IELTS (minimum score 6). *Application deadline:* Applications are processed on a rolling basis. Application fee: $60 ($65 for international students). Electronic applications accepted. *Expenses:* Tuition: Full-time $9450; part-time $350 per unit. Required fees: $350 per unit. One-time fee: $60. *Financial support:* Career-related internships or fieldwork, institutionally sponsored loans, scholarships/grants, and tuition waivers (partial). Support available to part-time students. Financial award application deadline: 6/30; financial award applicants required to submit FAFSA. *Faculty research:* Digital media, film, journalism. *Unit head:* Karla Berry, Dean, 858-309-3442, Fax: 858-309-3450, E-mail: kberry@nu.edu. *Application contact:* Dominick Giovanniello, Associate Regional Dean—San Diego, 800-NAT-UNIV, Fax: 858-541-7792, E-mail: dgiovann@nu.edu.

New Mexico State University, Graduate School, College of Arts and Sciences, Department of Communication Studies, Las Cruces, NM 88003-8001. Offers MA. Part-time programs available. *Faculty:* 5 full-time (2 women). *Students:* 34 full-time (21 women), 8 part-time (6 women); includes 14 minority (1 Black or African American, non-Hispanic/Latino; 2 American Indian or Alaska Native, non-Hispanic/Latino; 11 Hispanic/Latino), 7 international. Average age 30. 33 applicants, 100% accepted, 23 enrolled. In 2010, 17 master's awarded. *Degree requirements:* For master's, comprehensive exam (for some programs), thesis (for some programs). *Entrance requirements:* For master's, minimum GPA of 3.0. *Application deadline:* For fall admission, 7/1 priority date for domestic students; for spring admission, 4/1 priority date for domestic students. Applications are processed on a rolling basis. Application fee: $30 ($50 for international students). Electronic applications accepted. *Expenses:* Tuition, state resident: full-time $4536; part-time $242 per credit. Tuition, nonresident: full-time $15,816; part-time $712 per credit. Required fees: $636 per term. *Financial support:* In 2010–11, 1 research assistantship with tuition reimbursement (averaging $7,900 per year), 15 teaching assistantships with partial tuition reimbursements (averaging $7,770 per year) were awarded; fellowships, Federal Work-

Communication—General

New Mexico State University (continued)

Study and health care benefits also available. Financial award application deadline: 3/1. *Faculty research:* Interpersonal, organizational, intercultural, political, and health communication. *Unit head:* Dr. Anne P. Hubbell, Head, 575-646-2801, Fax: 575-646-1603, E-mail: ahubbell@nmsu.edu. *Application contact:* Dr. Anne P. Hubbell, Head, 575-646-2801, Fax: 575-646-1603, E-mail: ahubbell@nmsu.edu.

New York Institute of Technology, Graduate Division, School of Arts and Sciences, Program in Communication Arts, Old Westbury, NY 11568-8000. Offers MA. Part-time and evening/weekend programs available. *Students:* 98 full-time (70 women), 83 part-time (54 women); includes 46 minority (24 Black or African American, non-Hispanic/Latino; 7 Asian, non-Hispanic/Latino; 15 Hispanic/Latino), 62 international. Average age 27. In 2010, 100 master's awarded. *Degree requirements:* For master's, thesis or alternative. *Entrance requirements:* For master's, minimum QPA of 2.85. Additional exam requirements/recommendations for international students: Required—TOEFL (minimum score 550 paper-based; 213 computer-based). *Application deadline:* For fall admission, 7/1 priority date for domestic students; for spring admission, 12/1 priority date for domestic students. Applications are processed on a rolling basis. Application fee: $50. Electronic applications accepted. *Expenses:* Tuition: Part-time $835 per credit. *Financial support:* Research assistantships with partial tuition reimbursements, career-related internships or fieldwork, Federal Work-Study, institutionally sponsored loans, tuition waivers (partial), and unspecified assistantships available. Support available to part-time students. Financial award applicants required to submit FAFSA. *Faculty research:* Distance learning technology, computer animation, intercultural communication, multimedia technology. *Unit head:* Dr. Dena Winokur, Director, 212-261-1636, Fax: 516-686-7736, E-mail: dwinokur@nyit.edu. *Application contact:* Dr. Jacquelyn Nealon, Vice President for Enrollment Services, 516-686-7925, Fax: 516-686-7597, E-mail: jnealon@nyit.edu.

New York University, Steinhardt School of Culture, Education, and Human Development, Department of Media, Culture and Communication, New York, NY 10012-1019. Offers media, culture, and communication (MA, PhD). Part-time programs available. *Faculty:* 29 full-time (13 women), 88 part-time/adjunct (43 women). *Students:* 107 full-time (79 women), 65 part-time (42 women); includes 10 Black or African American, non-Hispanic/Latino; 8 Asian, non-Hispanic/Latino; 9 Hispanic/Latino, 47 international. Average age 27. 616 applicants, 24% accepted, 63 enrolled. In 2010, 44 master's, 2 doctorates awarded. Terminal master's awarded for partial completion of doctoral program. *Degree requirements:* For master's, thesis (for some programs); for doctorate, thesis/dissertation. *Entrance requirements:* For doctorate, GRE General Test, interview. Additional exam requirements/recommendations for international students: Required—TOEFL. *Application deadline:* For fall admission, 12/1 priority date for domestic and international students; for spring admission, 11/1 for domestic and international students. Applications are processed on a rolling basis. Application fee: $75. Electronic applications accepted. *Financial support:* Fellowships with full and partial tuition reimbursements, teaching assistantships with full and partial tuition reimbursements, career-related internships or fieldwork, Federal Work-Study, institutionally sponsored loans, scholarships/grants, tuition waivers (partial), and unspecified assistantships available. Support available to part-time students. Financial award application deadline: 2/1; financial award applicants required to submit FAFSA. *Faculty research:* Digital media and new technologies, media criticism, flow of media and culture transnationally and transculturally. *Unit head:* Dr. Marita Sturken, Chairperson, 212-992-9424, Fax: 212-995-4046, E-mail: marita.sturken@nyu.edu. *Application contact:* 212-998-5030, Fax: 212-995-4328, E-mail: steinhardt.gradadmissions@nyu.edu.

Norfolk State University, School of Graduate Studies, School of Liberal Arts, Department of Media and Communication, Norfolk, VA 23504. Offers MA. Part-time programs available. *Degree requirements:* For master's, thesis. *Entrance requirements:* For master's, GRE, minimum GPA of 2.5, letters of recommendation. Additional exam requirements/recommendations for international students: Required—TOEFL.

North Carolina State University, Graduate School, College of Humanities and Social Sciences, Department of Communication, Raleigh, NC 27695. Offers MS. Part-time programs available. *Degree requirements:* For master's, thesis optional. *Entrance requirements:* For master's, GRE, minimum undergraduate GPA of 3.0 during last 60 hours. Electronic applications accepted. *Faculty research:* Instructional communication, political communication, organizational conflict management, intercultural communication, communication technology.

North Dakota State University, College of Graduate and Interdisciplinary Studies, College of Arts, Humanities and Social Sciences, Department of Communication, Fargo, ND 58108. Offers communication (PhD); mass communication (MA, MS); speech communication (MA, MS). Part-time programs available. Postbaccalaureate distance learning degree programs offered (no on-campus study). *Faculty:* 11 full-time (5 women), 3 part-time/adjunct (1 woman). *Students:* 29 full-time (18 women), 27 part-time (17 women); includes 1 Black or African American, non-Hispanic/Latino; 2 Asian, non-Hispanic/Latino; 1 Hispanic/Latino, 3 international. Average age 27. 62 applicants, 40% accepted, 19 enrolled. In 2010, 15 master's, 8 doctorates awarded. Terminal master's awarded for partial completion of doctoral program. *Degree requirements:* For master's, thesis (for some programs); for doctorate, comprehensive exam, thesis/dissertation, 2-3 publications referred before comps. *Entrance requirements:* For master's, GRE, minimum undergraduate GPA of 3.25; for doctorate, GRE, minimum undergraduate GPA of 3.5. Additional exam requirements/recommendations for international students: Required—TOEFL (minimum score 600 paper-based; 250 computer-based; 100 iBT), IELTS (minimum score 7). *Application deadline:* For fall admission, 2/15 priority date for domestic students; for winter admission, 10/15 priority date for domestic students. Applications are processed on a rolling basis. Application fee: $45 ($60 for international students). Electronic applications accepted. *Financial support:* In 2010–11, 38 students received support, including 1 fellowship with full tuition reimbursement available (averaging $16,000 per year), 10 research assistantships with full tuition reimbursements available (averaging $12,000 per year), 10 teaching assistantships with full tuition reimbursements available (averaging $8,100 per year); career-related internships or fieldwork, Federal Work-Study, institutionally sponsored loans, tuition waivers (full), and unspecified assistantships also available. Financial award application deadline: 2/1. *Faculty research:* Communication and rhetorical theory, organizational communication, broadcast and print journalism, international communication, public relations and advertising. Total annual research expenditures: $148,496. *Unit head:* Dr. Paul E. Nelson, Chair, 701-231-7705, Fax: 701-231-7784, E-mail: paul.nelson.1@ndsu.edu. *Application contact:* Dr. Judy C. Pearson, Director of Graduate Studies, 701-231-6551, Fax: 701-231-1074, E-mail: judy.pearson@ndsu.edu.

Northeastern State University, Graduate College, College of Liberal Arts, Department of Communication, Tahlequah, OK 74464-2399. Offers MA. Part-time and evening/weekend programs available. *Students:* 16 full-time (8 women); includes 7 minority (all American Indian or Alaska Native, non-Hispanic/Latino). In 2010, 8 master's awarded. *Degree requirements:* For master's, comprehensive exam. *Entrance requirements:* For master's, GRE, MAT, minimum GPA of 2.5. Additional exam requirements/recommendations for international students: Required—TOEFL (minimum score 213 computer-based). *Application deadline:* For fall admission, 6/1 priority date for domestic students. Applications are processed on a rolling basis. Application fee: $0 ($25 for international students). Electronic applications accepted. *Expenses:* Tuition, state resident: part-time $144 per credit hour. Tuition, nonresident: part-time $384.05 per credit hour. Required fees: $34.90 per credit hour. Tuition and fees vary according to program. *Financial support:* Teaching assistantships, Federal Work-Study available. Financial award application deadline: 3/1. *Unit head:* Dr. Mike Chanselar, Chair, 918-456-5511 Ext. 3600, Fax: 918-458-2348. *Application contact:* Margie Railey, Administrative Assistant, 918-456-5511 Ext. 2093, Fax: 918-458-2061, E-mail: railey@nsouk.edu.

Northeastern University, College of Arts, Media and Design, Department of Communication Studies, Boston, MA 02115-5096. Offers communication, media, and cultural studies (MA). *Faculty:* 25 full-time (10 women), 6 part-time/adjunct (3 women). *Students:* 8 full-time (7 women), 1 part-time (0 women). 92 applicants, 36% accepted, 5 enrolled. In 2010, 1 master's awarded. *Degree requirements:* For master's, thesis (for some programs). *Entrance requirements:* For master's, GRE. Additional exam requirements/recommendations for international students: Required—TOEFL or IELTS. *Application deadline:* For fall admission, 2/1 priority date for domestic and international students. Applications are processed on a rolling basis. Application fee: $50. Electronic applications accepted. *Financial support:* Federal Work-Study and scholarships/grants available. *Unit head:* Dr. Joanne Morreale, Graduate Coordinator, 617-373-2506, E-mail: j.morreale@neu.edu. *Application contact:* Jo-Anne Dickinson, Admissions Contact, 617-373-5990, Fax: 617-373-7281, E-mail: gsas@neu.edu.

Northern Arizona University, Graduate College, College of Social and Behavioral Sciences, School of Communication, Flagstaff, AZ 86011. Offers applied communication (MA). Part-time programs available. *Faculty:* 39 full-time (18 women). *Students:* 14 full-time (6 women), 17 part-time (12 women); includes 6 minority (1 Black or African American, non-Hispanic/Latino; 1 American Indian or Alaska Native, non-Hispanic/Latino; 3 Hispanic/Latino; 1 Native Hawaiian or other Pacific Islander, non-Hispanic/Latino), 2 international. Average age 28. 21 applicants, 81% accepted, 11 enrolled. In 2010, 10 master's awarded. *Degree requirements:* For master's, thesis optional, thesis or project. *Entrance requirements:* For master's, GRE General Test. Additional exam requirements/recommendations for international students: Required—TOEFL (minimum score 550 paper-based; 213 computer-based; 80 iBT), IELTS (minimum score 7). *Application deadline:* For fall admission, 3/1 priority date for domestic and international students. Applications are processed on a rolling basis. Application fee: $65. Electronic applications accepted. *Financial support:* In 2010–11, 6 teaching assistantships with partial tuition reimbursements (averaging $10,439 per year) were awarded; Federal Work-Study, scholarships/grants, health care benefits, tuition waivers (full and partial), and unspecified assistantships also available. Support available to part-time students. Financial award applicants required to submit FAFSA. *Unit head:* Dr. Mark Neumann, Professor/Director, 928-523-8887, Fax: 928-523-1505, E-mail: mark.neumann@nau.edu. *Application contact:* Patricia Johnson, Administrative Associate, 928-523-0030, Fax: 928-523-1505, E-mail: comgrad@nau.edu.

Northern Illinois University, Graduate School, College of Liberal Arts and Sciences, Department of Communication, De Kalb, IL 60115-2854. Offers communication studies (MA). Part-time programs available. *Faculty:* 24 full-time (11 women), 1 part-time/adjunct (0 women). *Students:* 35 full-time (24 women), 21 part-time (13 women); includes 4 Black or African American, non-Hispanic/Latino; 1 American Indian or Alaska Native, non-Hispanic/Latino; 2 Hispanic/Latino, 2 international. Average age 26. 42 applicants, 67% accepted, 18 enrolled. In 2010, 19 master's awarded. *Degree requirements:* For master's, comprehensive exam, thesis optional. *Entrance requirements:* For master's, GRE General Test, minimum GPA of 2.75. Additional exam requirements/recommendations for international students: Required—TOEFL (minimum score 550 paper-based; 213 computer-based). *Application deadline:* For fall admission, 6/1 for domestic students, 5/1 for international students; for spring admission, 11/1 for domestic students, 10/1 for international students. Applications are processed on a rolling basis. Application fee: $30. Electronic applications accepted. *Expenses:* Tuition, state resident: full-time $7200; part-time $300 per credit hour. Tuition, nonresident: full-time $14,400; part-time $600 per credit hour. Required fees: $79 per credit hour. *Financial support:* In 2010–11, 31 teaching assistantships with full tuition reimbursements were awarded; fellowships with full tuition reimbursements, research assistantships with full tuition reimbursements, career-related internships or fieldwork, Federal Work-Study, scholarships/grants, tuition waivers (full), and unspecified assistantships also available. Support available to part-time students. Financial award applicants required to submit FAFSA. *Faculty research:* Journalism, history film studies, rhetoric or criticism, globalization, mass media law. *Unit head:* Dr. Jeffrey Chown, Chair, 815-753-7028, Fax: 815-753-7109, E-mail: jchown@niu.edu. *Application contact:* Dr. Jeffrey Chown, Director, Graduate Studies, 815-753-1711, E-mail: schown@niu.edu.

Northern Kentucky University, Office of Graduate Programs, College of Informatics, Program in Communication, Highland Heights, KY 41099. Offers communication (MA); communication teaching (Certificate); documentary studies (Certificate); public relations (Certificate); relationships (Certificate). Part-time and evening/weekend programs available. *Faculty:* 7 full-time (3 women), 1 part-time/adjunct (0 women). *Students:* 10 full-time (4 women), 36 part-time (15 women); includes 7 minority (3 Black or African American, non-Hispanic/Latino; 2 Asian, non-Hispanic/Latino; 2 Hispanic/Latino). Average age 29. 29 applicants, 62% accepted, 14 enrolled. In 2010, 11 master's, 2 other advanced degrees awarded. *Degree requirements:* For master's, thesis (for some programs), capstone experience, internship. *Entrance requirements:* For master's, GRE, minimum GPA of 3.0, 3 letters of recommendation, letter of intent. Additional exam requirements/recommendations for international students: Required—TOEFL (minimum score 550 paper-based; 213 computer-based; 79 iBT); Recommended—IELTS (minimum score 6.5). *Application deadline:* For fall admission, 2/1 for domestic students, 6/1 for international students; for spring admission, 7/1 for domestic students, 10/1 for international students. Applications are processed on a rolling basis. Application fee: $40. Electronic applications accepted. *Expenses:* Tuition, state resident: full-time $7254; part-time $403 per credit hour. Tuition, nonresident: full-time $12,492; part-time $694 per credit hour. Tuition and fees vary according to degree level and program. *Financial support:* Unspecified assistantships available. Financial award applicants required to submit FAFSA. *Faculty research:* Business/organizational communication, interpersonal/relational communication, public relations, communication teaching/pedagogy, media (production, criticism, popular culture). Total annual research expenditures: $29,000. *Unit head:* Dr. Jimmy Manning, Director, 859-572-1329, E-mail: manningj1@nku.edu. *Application contact:* Dr. Peg Griffin, Director of Graduate Programs, 859-572-6934, Fax: 859-572-6670, E-mail: griffinp@nku.edu.

Northwestern University, The Graduate School, School of Communication, Department of Communication Studies, Evanston, IL 60208. Offers communication studies (MA, PhD); communication systems strategy and management (MSC); managerial communication (MSC). MA and PhD admissions and degrees offered through The Graduate School. Terminal master's awarded for partial completion of doctoral program. *Degree requirements:* For doctorate, thesis/dissertation. *Entrance requirements:* For master's and doctorate, GRE General Test. Additional exam requirements/recommendations for international students: Required—TOEFL. Electronic applications accepted.

The Ohio State University, Graduate School, College of Arts and Sciences, School of Communication, Columbus, OH 43210. Offers MA, PhD. *Students:* 59 full-time (38 women), 9 part-time (3 women); includes 1 American Indian or Alaska Native, non-Hispanic/Latino; 3 Asian, non-Hispanic/Latino; 3 Hispanic/Latino, 7 international. Average age 28. In 2010, 55 master's, 1 doctorate awarded. *Entrance requirements:* Additional exam requirements/recommendations for international students: Required—TOEFL (minimum score 600 paper-based; 250 computer-based). *Application deadline:* For fall admission, 8/15 priority date for domestic students, 7/1 priority date for international students; for winter admission, 12/1 priority date for domestic students, 11/1 priority date for international students; for spring admission, 3/1 priority date for domestic students, 2/1 priority date for international students. Applications are processed on a rolling basis. Application fee: $40 ($50 for international students). Electronic applications accepted. *Expenses:* Tuition, state resident: full-time $10,605. Tuition, nonresident: full-time $26,535. Tuition and fees vary according to course load and program. *Unit head:* Carroll Glynn, Director, 614-292-3400, E-mail: glynn.14@osu.edu. *Application contact:* 614-292-9444, Fax: 614-292-3895, E-mail: domestic.grad@osu.edu.

Ohio University, Graduate College, Scripps College of Communication, Athens, OH 45701-2979. Offers MA, MCTP, MS, PhD. Part-time programs available. *Faculty:* 90 full-time (30 women), 10 part-time/adjunct (4 women). *Students:* 160 full-time (92 women), 74 part-time (50 women); includes 19 minority (11 Black or African American, non-Hispanic/Latino; 1 American Indian or Alaska Native, non-Hispanic/Latino; 2 Asian, non-Hispanic/Latino; 4 Hispanic/Latino; 1 Two or more races, non-Hispanic/Latino), 57 international. 362 applicants, 49% accepted, 100 enrolled. In 2010, 65 master's, 23 doctorates awarded. *Degree requirements:* For master's, comprehensive exam (for some programs), thesis or alternative; for doctorate, comprehensive exam, thesis/dissertation. *Entrance requirements:* For master's and doctorate, GRE General Test. Additional exam requirements/recommendations for international students: Required—

TOEFL or IELTS. Application fee: $50 ($55 for international students). Electronic applications accepted. *Expenses:* Contact institution. *Financial support:* Fellowships with tuition reimbursements, research assistantships with full and partial tuition reimbursements, teaching assistantships with full tuition reimbursements, career-related internships or fieldwork, Federal Work-Study, institutionally sponsored loans, tuition waivers (full and partial), and unspecified assistantships available. Financial award applicants required to submit FAFSA. *Unit head:* Dr. Gregory J. Shepherd, Dean, 740-593-4883, Fax: 740-593-0459, E-mail: shepherg@ohio.edu. *Application contact:* Dr. Eric Rothenbuhler, Associate Dean, 740-593-4885, Fax: 740-593-0459.

Our Lady of the Lake University of San Antonio, College of Arts and Sciences, Program in English, San Antonio, TX 78207-4689. Offers communication arts (MA); English and literature (MA); English education (MA); writing (MA). Program offered jointly with University of the Incarnate Word, St. Mary's University. Part-time and evening/weekend programs available. *Students:* 6 full-time (5 women), 18 part-time (14 women); includes 17 minority (1 Black or African American, non-Hispanic/Latino; 1 American Indian or Alaska Native, non-Hispanic/Latino; 15 Hispanic/Latino). Average age 35. In 2010, 8 master's awarded. *Degree requirements:* For master's, comprehensive exam, thesis optional. *Entrance requirements:* For master's, GRE General Test or MAT, minimum GPA of 3.0 in last 60 hours, 2.5 overall. Additional exam requirements/recommendations for international students: Required—TOEFL. *Application deadline:* Applications are processed on a rolling basis. Application fee: $25 ($50 for international students). Electronic applications accepted. *Expenses:* Tuition: Full-time $13,500; part-time $750 per contact hour. Required fees: $330. Tuition and fees vary according to course level, degree level and campus/location. *Financial support:* Research assistantships, teaching assistantships, career-related internships or fieldwork, Federal Work-Study, institutionally sponsored loans, and tuition waivers (partial) available. Financial award application deadline: 4/15. *Faculty research:* Writing theory and research, contemporary Southern literature, popular culture, poetry, literature of the Southwest. *Unit head:* Dr. Michael Lueker, Chair, 210-434-6711 Ext. 2242, E-mail: luekm@lake.ollusa.edu. *Application contact:* 210-434-6711, Fax: 210-431-4036, E-mail: gradadm@lake.ollusa.edu.

Penn State University Park, Graduate School, College of Communications, State College, University Park, PA 16802-1503. Offers MA, PhD. *Accreditation:* ACEJMC (one or more programs are accredited). *Students:* 71 full-time (44 women), 14 part-time (11 women). Average age 31. 201 applicants, 29% accepted, 18 enrolled. In 2010, 6 master's, 13 doctorates awarded. *Entrance requirements:* For master's and doctorate, GRE General Test. Additional exam requirements/recommendations for international students: Required—TOEFL (minimum score 550 paper-based; 213 computer-based; 80 iBT). *Application deadline:* Applications are processed on a rolling basis. Application fee: $65. Electronic applications accepted. *Financial support:* Fellowships, research assistantships, teaching assistantships available. Financial award applicants required to submit FAFSA. *Unit head:* Dr. Douglas A. Anderson, Dean, 814-863-1484, Fax: 814-863-8044, E-mail: doug-anderson@psu.edu. *Application contact:* Cynthia E. Nicosia, Director, Graduate Enrollment Services, 814-865-1834, E-mail: cey1@psu.edu.

Penn State University Park, Graduate School, College of the Liberal Arts, Department of Communication Arts and Sciences, State College, University Park, PA 16802-1503. Offers MA, PhD.

Pepperdine University, Seaver College, Division of Communication, Master of Science Program in Communication, Malibu, CA 90263. Offers MS. *Students:* 1 (woman) full-time, 4 part-time (3 women); includes 1 minority (Asian, non-Hispanic/Latino). In 2010, 3 master's awarded. *Entrance requirements:* For master's, GRE General Test, letters of recommendation, writing sample. *Application deadline:* For fall admission, 2/1 priority date for domestic students. Application fee: $55. *Unit head:* Dr. Kenneth E. Waters, Chair/Professor of Journalism, Communication Division, 310-506-4280, E-mail: ken.waters@pepperdine.edu. *Application contact:* Michael Truschke, Dean of Admission and Enrollment Management, 310-506-6165, Fax: 310-506-4861, E-mail: admission-seaver@pepperdine.edu.

Pittsburg State University, Graduate School, College of Arts and Sciences, Department of Communication, Pittsburg, KS 66762. Offers applied communication (MA); communication education (MA); theatre (MA). *Degree requirements:* For master's, thesis or alternative.

Point Park University, School of Communication, Pittsburgh, PA 15222-1984. Offers MA. Part-time and evening/weekend programs available. *Faculty:* 6 full-time, 10 part-time/adjunct. *Students:* 31 full-time (23 women), 33 part-time (25 women); includes 8 minority (5 Black or African American, non-Hispanic/Latino; 1 Asian, non-Hispanic/Latino; 2 Two or more races, non-Hispanic/Latino), 2 international. Average age 27. 103 applicants, 67% accepted, 32 enrolled. In 2010, 21 master's awarded. *Degree requirements:* For master's, comprehensive exam (for some programs), thesis or alternative. *Entrance requirements:* For master's, GRE (if GPA less than 2.75), minimum GPA of 2.75, 2 letters of recommendation, statement of intent. Additional exam requirements/recommendations for international students: Required—TOEFL (minimum score 570 paper-based; 88 iBT). *Application deadline:* Applications are processed on a rolling basis. Application fee: $30. Electronic applications accepted. *Expenses:* Tuition: Full-time $12,456; part-time $692 per credit. Required fees: $630; $35 per credit. *Financial support:* In 2010–11, 6 teaching assistantships with full tuition reimbursements (averaging $6,400 per year) were awarded; scholarships/grants and unspecified assistantships also available. Financial award application deadline: 4/15; financial award applicants required to submit FAFSA. *Unit head:* Dr. Tim Hudson, Chair, 412-392-4748, E-mail: thudson@pointpark.edu. *Application contact:* Marty M. Paonessa, Recruiter/Counselor, 412-392-3915, Fax: 412-392-6164, E-mail: mpaonessa@pointpark.edu.

Polytechnic Institute of NYU, Department of Electrical and Computer Engineering, Major in Wireless Communications, Brooklyn, NY 11201-2990. Offers Certificate. *Students:* 1 part-time (0 women), all international. Average age 45. 22 applicants, 59% accepted, 1 enrolled. *Entrance requirements:* Additional exam requirements/recommendations for international students: Required—TOEFL (minimum score 550 paper-based; 213 computer-based; 80 iBT); Recommended—IELTS (minimum score 6.5). *Application deadline:* For fall admission, 7/31 priority date for domestic students, 4/30 priority date for international students; for spring admission, 12/31 priority date for domestic students, 11/30 priority date for international students. Applications are processed on a rolling basis. Application fee: $75. Electronic applications accepted. *Expenses:* Tuition: Full-time $21,492; part-time $1194 per credit. Required fees: $385 per semester. Tuition and fees vary according to course load. *Unit head:* Dr. Jonathan Chao, Head, 718-860-3478, Fax: 718-260-3302, E-mail: chao@poly.edu. *Application contact:* JeanCarlo Bonilla, Director, Graduate Enrollment Management, 718-260-3182, Fax: 718-260-3624, E-mail: gradinfo@poly.edu.

Purdue University, Graduate School, College of Liberal Arts, Department of Communication, West Lafayette, IN 47907. Offers MA, MS, PhD. *Degree requirements:* For master's, comprehensive exams or thesis; for doctorate, thesis/dissertation. *Entrance requirements:* For master's, GRE General Test, writing sample; for doctorate, GRE General Test, master's degree, writing sample. Additional exam requirements/recommendations for international students: Required—TOEFL, TWE. Electronic applications accepted. *Faculty research:* Interpersonal communication, mass communication, organizational communication, public affairs and issue management, rhetorical studies.

Purdue University Calumet, Graduate Studies Office, School of Liberal Arts and Social Sciences, Department of Communication and Creative Arts, Hammond, IN 46323-2094. Offers communication (MA). Part-time and evening/weekend programs available. *Faculty:* 8 full-time (4 women). *Students:* 36 full-time (31 women), 16 part-time (13 women); includes 10 Black or African American, non-Hispanic/Latino; 1 Asian, non-Hispanic/Latino; 9 Hispanic/Latino. 12 applicants, 100% accepted. In 2010, 8 master's awarded. *Degree requirements:* For master's, comprehensive exam, thesis or extended course work. *Entrance requirements:* For master's, minimum GPA of 3.0. Additional exam requirements/recommendations for international students: Required—TOEFL. *Application deadline:* Applications are processed on a rolling basis. Application fee: $55. Electronic applications accepted. *Expenses:* Tuition, state resident: full-time $6867. Tuition, nonresident: full-time $14,157. *Financial support:* In 2010–11, teaching assistantships with full tuition reimbursements (averaging $3,000 per year). Financial award application deadline: 3/1. *Faculty research:* International communication, gender studies, political rhetoric, media effects, media accountability. *Unit head:* Dr. Yahya R. Kamalipour, Head, 219-989-2880, Fax: 219-989-2008, E-mail: kamaliyr@purduecal.edu. *Application contact:* Dr. Catherine M. Gillotti, Graduate Advisor, 219-989-2009, E-mail: gillotc@purduecal.edu.

Queen's University at Kingston, School of Graduate Studies and Research, Faculty of Arts and Sciences, Department of Sociology, Kingston, ON K7L 3N6, Canada. Offers communication and Information technology (MA, PhD); feminist sociology (MA, PhD); socio-legal studies (MA, PhD); sociological theory (MA, PhD). Part-time programs available. *Degree requirements:* For master's, thesis; for doctorate, comprehensive exam, thesis/dissertation. *Entrance requirements:* For master's, honors bachelors degree in sociology; for doctorate, honors bachelors degree, masters degree in sociology. Additional exam requirements/recommendations for international students: Required—TOEFL. *Faculty research:* Social change and modernization, social control, deviance and criminology, surveillance.

Quinnipiac University, School of Communications, Hamden, CT 06518-1940. Offers MS. Part-time and evening/weekend programs available. *Faculty:* 10 full-time (5 women), 23 part-time/adjunct (11 women). *Students:* 53 full-time (34 women), 101 part-time (63 women); includes 21 minority (14 Black or African American, non-Hispanic/Latino; 4 Asian, non-Hispanic/Latino; 3 Hispanic/Latino), 5 international. 79 applicants, 87% accepted, 49 enrolled. In 2010, 39 master's awarded. *Entrance requirements:* For master's, GRE (public relations), minimum GPA of 2.8, portfolio or writing sample. Additional exam requirements/recommendations for international students: Required—TOEFL (minimum score 575 paper-based; 233 computer-based; 90 iBT), IELTS (minimum score 6.5). *Application deadline:* For fall admission, 7/30 priority date for domestic students, 4/30 priority date for international students; for spring admission, 12/15 priority date for domestic students, 9/15 priority date for international students. Applications are processed on a rolling basis. Application fee: $45. Electronic applications accepted. *Expenses:* Tuition: Part-time $810 per credit. Required fees: $35 per credit. *Financial support:* In 2010–11, 1 fellowship with full tuition reimbursement was awarded; career-related internships or fieldwork, tuition waivers (partial), and unspecified assistantships also available. Support available to part-time students. Financial award application deadline: 4/30; financial award applicants required to submit FAFSA. *Unit head:* Graduate Admissions Office, 800-462-1944, Fax: 203-582-3443, E-mail: graduate@quinnipiac.edu. *Application contact:* Scott Farber, Information Contact, 203-582-8672, Fax: 203-582-3443, E-mail: graduate@quinnipiac.edu.

Regent University, Graduate School, School of Communication and the Arts, Virginia Beach, VA 23464-9800. Offers acting (MFA); cinema arts/television arts (MA); communication (MA, PhD); digital media (MA); directing for cinema/television (MA, MFA); editing for cinema/television (MA); journalism (MA); producing for cinema/television (MA, MFA); script and screenwriting (MFA); theatre (MA). Part-time programs available. Postbaccalaureate distance learning degree programs offered (minimal on-campus study). *Faculty:* 29 full-time (4 women), 25 part-time/adjunct (5 women). *Students:* 93 full-time (48 women), 167 part-time (80 women); includes 45 Black or African American, non-Hispanic/Latino; 2 American Indian or Alaska Native, non-Hispanic/Latino; 3 Asian, non-Hispanic/Latino; 9 Hispanic/Latino, 11 international. Average age 32. 247 applicants, 45% accepted, 65 enrolled. In 2010, 82 master's, 17 doctorates awarded. *Degree requirements:* For master's, thesis or alternative; for doctorate, thesis/dissertation. *Entrance requirements:* For master's, GRE General Test or MAT, minimum undergraduate GPA of 3.0, writing sample, computer literacy survey, recommendation, resume, interview, audition (MFA programs); for doctorate, GRE General Test, minimum graduate GPA of 3.0, writing sample, computer literacy survey, recommendation, interview, transcripts. Additional exam requirements/recommendations for international students: Required—TOEFL (minimum score 577 paper-based; 233 computer-based). *Application deadline:* For fall admission, 3/1 priority date for domestic students; for spring admission, 10/1 priority date for domestic students. Applications are processed on a rolling basis. Application fee: $50. Electronic applications accepted. *Expenses:* Contact institution. *Financial support:* Fellowships with full and partial tuition reimbursements, career-related internships or fieldwork, scholarships/grants, tuition waivers (full and partial), and unspecified assistantships available. Support available to part-time students. Financial award application deadline: 9/1; financial award applicants required to submit FAFSA. *Faculty research:* Southern gospel music, education and entertainment, celebrities and the media, journalism and ethics, C. S. Lewis. *Unit head:* Dr. Emmanuel Ayee, Interim Dean, 757-352-4945, Fax: 757-352-4291, E-mail: eayee@regent.edu. *Application contact:* Matthew Chadwick, Director of Enrollment Support Services, 800-373-5504, Fax: 757-352-4381, E-mail: admissions@regent.edu.

Regis University, College for Professional Studies, School of Humanities and Social Sciences, MA Program, Denver, CO 80221-1099. Offers communication (MA); fine arts (Certificate); interdisciplinary studies (MA); mediation and conflict resolution (Certificate); psychology (MA); social justice, peace, and reconciliation (Certificate); technical communication (Certificate). Program also offered in Henderson and Las Vegas (Summerlin), NV. Part-time and evening/weekend programs available. Postbaccalaureate distance learning degree programs offered (minimal on-campus study). *Degree requirements:* For master's, thesis, research project. *Entrance requirements:* For master's, resume, recommendations. Additional exam requirements/recommendations for international students: Required—TOEFL (minimum score 213 computer-based), TWE (minimum score 5). Electronic applications accepted. *Expenses:* Contact institution. *Faculty research:* Independent/nonresidential graduate study: new methods and models, adult learning and the capstone experience, Goal Setting, behavior of Adult students, Innovative Studies for Community Colleges.

Rochester Institute of Technology, Graduate Enrollment Services, College of Imaging Arts and Sciences, School of Print Media, Rochester, NY 14623-5603. Offers print media (MS). Part-time programs available. *Students:* 25 full-time (12 women), 6 part-time (1 woman); includes 1 Black or African American, non-Hispanic/Latino; 2 Asian, non-Hispanic/Latino, 20 international. Average age 27. 30 applicants, 60% accepted, 14 enrolled. In 2010, 10 master's awarded. *Entrance requirements:* For master's, minimum GPA of 3.0. Additional exam requirements/recommendations for international students: Required—TOEFL (minimum score 550 paper-based; 213 computer-based; 79 iBT) or IELTS (minimum score 6.5). *Application deadline:* For fall admission, 2/15 priority date for domestic and international students. Applications are processed on a rolling basis. Application fee: $50. Electronic applications accepted. *Expenses:* Tuition: Full-time $33,234; part-time $924 per credit hour. Required fees: $219. *Financial support:* In 2010–11, 14 students received support; research assistantships with partial tuition reimbursements available, teaching assistantships with partial tuition reimbursements available, career-related internships or fieldwork, institutionally sponsored loans, scholarships/grants, and unspecified assistantships available. Support available to part-time students. Financial award application deadline: 8/30; financial award applicants required to submit FAFSA. *Faculty research:* Printing Industry Center. *Unit head:* Dr. Patricia Sorce, Administrative Chair, 585-475-2728, Fax: 585-475-5336, E-mail: spminfo@rit.edu. *Application contact:* Diane Ellison, Assistant Vice President, Graduate Enrollment Services, 585-475-2229, Fax: 585-475-7164, E-mail: gradinfo@rit.edu.

Rochester Institute of Technology, Graduate Enrollment Services, College of Liberal Arts, Department of Communication, Program in Communication and Media Technologies, Rochester, NY 14623-5603. Offers MS. Part-time programs available. *Students:* 19 full-time (14 women), 30 part-time (24 women); includes 3 Black or African American, non-Hispanic/Latino; 1 Asian, non-Hispanic/Latino; 1 Hispanic/Latino; 1 Two or more races, non-Hispanic/Latino, 5 international. Average age 29. 42 applicants, 57% accepted, 20 enrolled. In 2010, 9 master's awarded. *Degree requirements:* For master's, thesis or project. *Entrance requirements:* For master's, minimum GPA of 3.0, writing sample. Additional exam requirements/recommendations for international students: Required—TOEFL (minimum score 600 paper-based; 250 computer-based; 100 iBT) or IELTS (minimum score 7). *Application deadline:* For

Communication—General

Rochester Institute of Technology (continued)
fall admission, 2/15 priority date for domestic and international students; for winter admission, 11/1 for domestic and international students; for spring admission, 2/1 for domestic and international students. Applications are processed on a rolling basis. Electronic applications accepted. *Expenses:* Tuition: Full-time $33,234; part-time $924 per credit hour. Required fees: $219. *Financial support:* In 2010–11, 17 students received support; research assistantships with partial tuition reimbursements available, teaching assistantships with partial tuition reimbursements available, career-related internships or fieldwork, scholarships/grants, and unspecified assistantships available. Support available to part-time students. Financial award applicants required to submit FAFSA. *Unit head:* Dr. Rudy Pugliese, Graduate Program Director, 585-475-5925, Fax: 585-475-7732, E-mail: rrpgsl@rit.edu. *Application contact:* Diane Ellison, Assistant Vice President, Graduate Enrollment Services, 585-475-2229, Fax: 585-475-7164, E-mail: gradinfo@rit.edu.

Roosevelt University, Graduate Division, College of Arts and Sciences, Department of Communication, Chicago, IL 60605. Offers integrated marketing communications (MSIMC); journalism (MSJ). Part-time and evening/weekend programs available.

Rutgers, The State University of New Jersey, New Brunswick, School of Communication, Information and Library Studies, Program in Communication, Library and Information Science and Media Studies, Piscataway, NJ 08854-8097. Offers PhD. Part-time programs available. *Faculty:* 43 full-time (21 women). *Students:* 37 full-time (30 women), 65 part-time (45 women); includes 7 Black or African American, non-Hispanic/Latino; 26 Asian, non-Hispanic/Latino; 1 Hispanic/Latino. Average age 35. 106 applicants, 68% accepted, 19 enrolled. In 2010, 11 doctorates awarded. *Degree requirements:* For doctorate, comprehensive exam, thesis/dissertation, qualifying exams. *Entrance requirements:* For doctorate, GRE General Test, proficiency in statistics. Additional exam requirements/recommendations for international students: Required—TOEFL (minimum score 600 paper-based; 250 computer-based). *Application deadline:* For fall admission, 1/15 priority date for domestic students, 1/15 for international students. Applications are processed on a rolling basis. Application fee: $50. Electronic applications accepted. *Expenses:* Tuition, state resident: full-time $7200; part-time $600 per credit. Tuition, nonresident: full-time $11,124; part-time $927 per credit. *Financial support:* In 2010–11, 2 fellowships with full tuition reimbursements (averaging $20,000 per year), 5 research assistantships with full tuition reimbursements (averaging $21,781 per year), 16 teaching assistantships with full tuition reimbursements (averaging $20,595 per year) were awarded; institutionally sponsored loans also available. Financial award application deadline: 2/1; financial award applicants required to submit FAFSA. *Faculty research:* Information science, media studies. Total annual research expenditures: $739,865. *Unit head:* Dr. Craig Scott, Director, 732-932-7500 Ext. 8142, Fax: 732-932-6916, E-mail: crscott@rci.rutgers.edu. *Application contact:* Linda J. Costa, Director of Graduate Admissions, 732-932-7711, Fax: 732-932-8231, E-mail: smeds@rci.rutgers.edu.

Saginaw Valley State University, College of Arts and Behavioral Sciences, Program in Communication and Digital Media Design, University Center, MI 48710. Offers MA. Part-time and evening/weekend programs available. *Degree requirements:* For master's, thesis. *Entrance requirements:* For master's, minimum GPA of 2.75. Additional exam requirements/recommendations for international students: Required—TOEFL. Electronic applications accepted. *Expenses:* Tuition, state resident: full-time $7902.

Saint Louis University, Graduate Education, College of Arts and Sciences and Graduate Education, Department of Communication, St. Louis, MO 63103-2097. Offers MA, MA-R. Part-time programs available. *Degree requirements:* For master's, thesis (for some programs), comprehensive oral and written exams. *Entrance requirements:* For master's, GRE General Test, letters of recommendation, resume, interview. Additional exam requirements/recommendations for international students: Required—TOEFL (minimum score 525 paper-based; 194 computer-based). Electronic applications accepted. *Faculty research:* Media studies, organizational communication, dialogue, intercultural communication, qualitative research methods.

St. Mary's University, Graduate School, Department of English and Communication Studies, Program in Communication Studies, San Antonio, TX 78228-8507. Offers MA. Part-time programs available. Postbaccalaureate distance learning degree programs offered (minimal on-campus study). *Degree requirements:* For master's, comprehensive exam. *Entrance requirements:* For master's, GRE General Test, MAT. Additional exam requirements/recommendations for international students: Required—TOEFL (minimum score 550 paper-based; 213 computer-based; 80 iBT). Electronic applications accepted. *Faculty research:* Persuasion and negotiation, group dynamics, language and communication, business communication, organizational communication.

St. Thomas University, School of Leadership Studies, Miami Gardens, FL 33054-6459. Offers MA, MPS, MS, Ed D, Certificate. Part-time and evening/weekend programs available. *Entrance requirements:* Additional exam requirements/recommendations for international students: Required—TOEFL (minimum score 550 paper-based; 213 computer-based; 79 iBT).

San Diego State University, Graduate and Research Affairs, College of Professional Studies and Fine Arts, School of Communication, San Diego, CA 92182. Offers advertising and public relations (MA); critical-cultural studies (MA); interaction studies (MA); intercultural and international studies (MA); new media studies (MA); news and information studies (MA); telecommunications and media management (MA). *Degree requirements:* For master's, thesis. *Entrance requirements:* For master's, GRE General Test, 3 letters of recommendation. Additional exam requirements/recommendations for international students: Required—TOEFL. Electronic applications accepted.

San Jose State University, Graduate Studies and Research, College of Social Sciences, Department of Communication Studies, San Jose, CA 95192-0001. Offers MA. *Degree requirements:* For master's, comprehensive exam, thesis or alternative, project. *Entrance requirements:* For master's, minimum GPA of 3.0. Electronic applications accepted.

Seton Hall University, College of Arts and Sciences, Department of Communication, South Orange, NJ 07079-2697. Offers corporate and professional communication (MA); intercultural communication (MA); organizational communication (MA); public relations (MA); strategic communication and leadership (MA); strategic communication planning (MA). Part-time and evening/weekend programs available. Postbaccalaureate distance learning degree programs offered (minimal on-campus study). *Degree requirements:* For master's, thesis. *Entrance requirements:* Additional exam requirements/recommendations for international students: Required—TOEFL. Electronic applications accepted. *Faculty research:* Managerial communication, communication consulting, communication and development.

Shippensburg University of Pennsylvania, School of Graduate Studies, College of Arts and Sciences, Department of Communication/Journalism, Shippensburg, PA 17257-2299. Offers communication studies (MS). Part-time and evening/weekend programs available. *Faculty:* 7 full-time (3 women). *Students:* 12 full-time (6 women), 14 part-time (11 women); includes 6 minority (4 Black or African American, non-Hispanic/Latino; 1 Asian, non-Hispanic/Latino; 1 Hispanic/Latino), 1 international. Average age 32. 22 applicants, 68% accepted, 10 enrolled. In 2010, 14 master's awarded. *Degree requirements:* For master's, 6-credit thesis or 3-credit professional project, candidacy. *Entrance requirements:* For master's, GRE or MAT (if GPA less than 2.75), 3 professional references, resume, essay. Additional exam requirements/recommendations for international students: Required—TOEFL (minimum score 580 paper-based; 237 computer-based); Recommended—IELTS (minimum score 6). *Application deadline:* For fall admission, 3/1 for international students; for spring admission, 7/1 for international students. Applications are processed on a rolling basis. Application fee: $30. Electronic applications accepted. *Expenses:* Contact institution. *Financial support:* In 2010–11, 6 research assistantships with full tuition reimbursements (averaging $5,000 per year) were awarded; career-related internships or fieldwork, scholarships/grants, unspecified assistantships, and resident hall director and student payroll positions also available. Support available to part-time students. Financial award application deadline: 3/1; financial award applicants required to submit FAFSA. *Unit head:* Dr. Joseph A. Borrell, Chairperson, 717-477-1521, Fax: 717-477-4013, E-mail: ajborr@ship.edu. *Application contact:* Jeremy R. Goshorn, Associate Dean of Graduate Admissions, 717-477-1231, Fax: 717-477-4016, E-mail: jrgoshorn@ship.edu.

Shippensburg University of Pennsylvania, School of Graduate Studies, College of Arts and Sciences, Department of Sociology and Anthropology, Shippensburg, PA 17257-2299. Offers organizational development and leadership (MS), including business, communications, education, environmental management, higher education, historical administration, individual and organizational development, public organizations, social structures and organizations. Part-time and evening/weekend programs available. *Faculty:* 3 full-time (all women). *Students:* 18 full-time (13 women), 46 part-time (33 women); includes 11 minority (6 Black or African American, non-Hispanic/Latino; 3 Asian, non-Hispanic/Latino; 2 Two or more races, non-Hispanic/Latino), 2 international. Average age 32. 56 applicants, 55% accepted, 20 enrolled. In 2010, 28 master's awarded. *Degree requirements:* For master's, capstone experience including internship. *Entrance requirements:* For master's, interview (if GPA less than 2.75), resume, personal goals statement. Additional exam requirements/recommendations for international students: Required—TOEFL (minimum score 580 paper-based; 237 computer-based); Recommended—IELTS (minimum score 6). *Application deadline:* For fall admission, 3/1 for international students; for spring admission, 7/1 for international students. Applications are processed on a rolling basis. Application fee: $30. Electronic applications accepted. *Expenses:* Tuition, state resident: full-time $6966. Tuition, nonresident: full-time $11,146. Required fees: $1802. *Financial support:* In 2010–11, 8 research assistantships with full tuition reimbursements (averaging $5,000 per year) were awarded; career-related internships or fieldwork, scholarships/grants, unspecified assistantships, and resident hall director and student payroll positions also available. Support available to part-time students. Financial award applicants required to submit FAFSA. *Unit head:* Dr. Barbara Denison, Chairperson, 717-477-1735, Fax: 717-477-4011, E-mail: bjdeni@ship.edu. *Application contact:* Jeremy R. Goshorn, Associate Dean of Graduate Admissions, 717-477-1231, Fax: 717-477-4016, E-mail: jrgoshorn@ship.edu.

Simon Fraser University, Graduate Studies, Faculty of Applied Sciences, School of Communication, Burnaby, BC V5A 1S6, Canada. Offers MA, PhD. *Degree requirements:* For master's, thesis optional; for doctorate, thesis/dissertation. *Entrance requirements:* For master's, minimum GPA of 3.0; for doctorate, minimum GPA of 3.5. Additional exam requirements/recommendations for international students: Required—TOEFL or IELTS. Electronic applications accepted. *Faculty research:* Theory and methodology, policy studies in communication media and telecommunication, international development, journalism studies, telelearning and telework.

South Dakota State University, Graduate School, College of Arts and Science, Department of Journalism and Mass Communication, Brookings, SD 57007. Offers communication studies and journalism (MS). Part-time and evening/weekend programs available. *Degree requirements:* For master's, thesis, oral exam. *Entrance requirements:* Additional exam requirements/recommendations for international students: Required—TOEFL (minimum score 550 paper-based; 213 computer-based; 79 iBT). *Faculty research:* Mass communication applications.

Southeastern Louisiana University, College of Arts, Humanities and Social Sciences, Department of Communication, Hammond, LA 70402. Offers organizational communication (MA). Part-time and evening/weekend programs available. *Faculty:* 4 full-time (all women). *Students:* 9 full-time (7 women), 19 part-time (15 women); includes 6 minority (all Black or African American, non-Hispanic/Latino). Average age 29. 31 applicants, 32% accepted, 7 enrolled. In 2010, 8 master's awarded. *Degree requirements:* For master's, comprehensive exam, thesis optional. *Entrance requirements:* For master's, GRE General Test (800 or better), bachelor's degree in communication or related field, minimum GPA of 3.0. Additional exam requirements/recommendations for international students: Required—TOEFL (minimum score 500 paper-based; 173 computer-based; 61 iBT). *Application deadline:* For fall admission, 7/15 priority date for domestic students, 6/1 priority date for international students; for spring admission, 12/1 priority date for domestic students, 10/1 priority date for international students. Applications are processed on a rolling basis. Application fee: $20 ($30 for international students). Electronic applications accepted. *Expenses:* Tuition, state resident: full-time $3533. Tuition, nonresident: full-time $12,002. Required fees: $907. Tuition and fees vary according to degree level. *Financial support:* In 2010–11, 8 students received support, including 5 research assistantships (averaging $9,880 per year); career-related internships or fieldwork, Federal Work-Study, institutionally sponsored loans, and administrative assistantships, professional services assistantship also available. Support available to part-time students. Financial award application deadline: 5/1; financial award applicants required to submit FAFSA. *Faculty research:* Cross-cultural communication in multi-national organizations, health communication among women, leadership communication, new media in organizations, crisis communication in organizations. *Unit head:* Dr. Lucia Guzzi Harrison, Interim Department Head, 985-549-2105, Fax: 985-549-5014, E-mail: lharrison@selu.edu. *Application contact:* Sandra Meyers, Graduate Admissions Analyst, 985-549-5620, Fax: 985-549-5632, E-mail: admissions@selu.edu.

Southern Illinois University Carbondale, Graduate School, College of Mass Communication and Media Arts, Carbondale, IL 62901-4701. Offers MA, MFA, PhD, MBA/MA. Part-time programs available. *Degree requirements:* For doctorate, thesis/dissertation. *Entrance requirements:* For doctorate, GRE General Test, minimum GPA of 3.25. Additional exam requirements/recommendations for international students: Required—TOEFL.

Southern Methodist University, Meadows School of the Arts, Division of Communication Arts, Dallas, TX 75275. Offers MA. Part-time and evening/weekend programs available. *Faculty:* 19 full-time (7 women), 11 part-time/adjunct (1 woman). *Students:* 34 full-time (25 women), 3 part-time (2 women); includes 1 Black or African American, non-Hispanic/Latino; 1 American Indian or Alaska Native, non-Hispanic/Latino; 6 Hispanic/Latino; 1 Two or more races, non-Hispanic/Latino, 3 international. Average age 27. 9 applicants, 78% accepted, 4 enrolled. In 2010, 6 master's awarded. *Degree requirements:* For master's, thesis or alternative. *Entrance requirements:* For master's, GRE General Test, minimum undergraduate GPA of 3.0 in major field during last 2 years. Additional exam requirements/recommendations for international students: Required—TOEFL (minimum score 550 paper-based; 213 computer-based; 80 iBT). *Application deadline:* For fall admission, 3/1 priority date for domestic and international students. Application fee: $75. *Financial support:* In 2010–11, 7 students received support, including 7 teaching assistantships (averaging $6,500 per year); research assistantships, scholarships/grants, tuition waivers (full), and unspecified assistantships also available. Financial award application deadline: 3/15. *Faculty research:* Digital sound, new technology, film and gender study, popular film and TV genres, Asian cinema. Total annual research expenditures: $10,000. *Unit head:* Rick Worland, Chair, 214-768-3708, Fax: 214-768-2784, E-mail: rworland@smu.edu. *Application contact:* Jean Cherry, Director of Graduate Admissions and Records, 214-768-3765, Fax: 214-768-3272, E-mail: jcherry@smu.edu.

Southern Polytechnic State University, School of Arts and Sciences, Department of English, Technical Communication, and Media Arts, Marietta, GA 30060-2896. Offers communications management (AGC); content development (AGC); information and instructional design (MSIID); information design and communication (MS); instructional design (AGC); technical communication (Graduate Certificate); visual communication and graphics (AGC). Part-time and evening/weekend programs available. Postbaccalaureate distance learning degree programs offered (no on-campus study). *Faculty:* 4 full-time (3 women), 1 (woman) part-time/adjunct. *Students:* 2 full-time (both women), 61 part-time (40 women); includes 19 Black or African American, non-Hispanic/Latino; 1 Two or more races, non-Hispanic/Latino, 3 international. Average age 38. 37 applicants, 100% accepted, 29 enrolled. In 2010, 6 master's, 5 other advanced degrees awarded. *Degree requirements:* For master's, thesis or internship; for other advanced degree, thesis optional, 18 hours completed through thesis option (6 hours), internship option (6 hours) or advanced coursework option (6 hours). *Entrance requirements:* For master's,

GRE, statement of purpose, writing sample, professional recommendations, timed essay; for other advanced degree, writing sample, professional recommendations. Additional exam requirements/recommendations for international students: Required—TOEFL (minimum score 550 paper-based; 213 computer-based; 79 iBT), IELTS (minimum score 6.5). *Application deadline:* For fall admission, 5/1 priority date for domestic students, 7/1 priority date for international students; for spring admission, 9/1 priority date for domestic students, 11/1 priority date for international students. Applications are processed on a rolling basis. Application fee: $20. Electronic applications accepted. *Expenses:* Tuition, state resident: full-time $3690; part-time $205 per semester hour. Tuition, nonresident: full-time $13,428; part-time $746 per semester hour. Required fees: $598 per semester. *Financial support:* Research assistantships with tuition reimbursements, teaching assistantships with tuition reimbursements, career-related internships or fieldwork, Federal Work-Study, scholarships/grants, and unspecified assistantships available. Support available to part-time students. Financial award application deadline: 5/1; financial award applicants required to submit FAFSA. *Faculty research:* Usability, user-centered design, instructional design, information architecture, information design. *Unit head:* Dr. Mark Nunes, Chair, 678-915-7202, Fax: 678-915-7425, E-mail: mnunes@spsu.edu. *Application contact:* Nikki Palamiotis, Director of Graduate Studies, 678-915-4276, Fax: 678-915-7292, E-mail: npalamio@spsu.edu.

Southern Utah University, College of Humanities and Social Sciences, Program in Communication, Cedar City, UT 84720-2498. Offers MA. *Faculty:* 8 full-time (1 woman). *Students:* 1 full-time (0 women), 51 part-time (25 women); includes 2 Asian, non-Hispanic/Latino; 1 Hispanic/Latino. 5 applicants, 100% accepted, 4 enrolled. In 2010, 9 master's awarded. *Application deadline:* Applications are processed on a rolling basis. Application fee: $50 ($65 for international students). Electronic applications accepted. *Financial support:* In 2010–11, 8 research assistantships with partial tuition reimbursements (averaging $500 per year), 10 teaching assistantships with partial tuition reimbursements (averaging $4,200 per year) were awarded. *Unit head:* Dr. James McDonald, Dean, 435-586-7898, Fax: 435-865-8193, E-mail: mcdonaldj@suu.edu. *Application contact:* Pam Halgren, Administrative Assistant, 435-586-7861, Fax: 435-865-8352, E-mail: halgren@suu.edu.

Spalding University, Graduate Studies, College of Business and Communication, Louisville, KY 40203-2188. Offers business communication (MS). Part-time and evening/weekend programs available. *Faculty:* 6 full-time (2 women), 7 part-time/adjunct (2 women). *Students:* 44 full-time (35 women), 41 part-time (32 women); includes 38 minority (27 Black or African American, non-Hispanic/Latino; 1 Asian, non-Hispanic/Latino; 1 Hispanic/Latino; 9 Two or more races, non-Hispanic/Latino). Average age 37. 41 applicants, 78% accepted, 31 enrolled. In 2010, 29 master's awarded. *Degree requirements:* For master's, project. *Entrance requirements:* For master's, GRE or GMAT, writing sample, interview, letters of recommendation, transcripts. Additional exam requirements/recommendations for international students: Required—TOEFL (minimum score 535 paper-based; 203 computer-based). *Application deadline:* Applications are processed on a rolling basis. Application fee: $30. *Financial support:* In 2010–11, 26 students received support. Application deadline: 3/15. *Faculty research:* Curriculum development, consumer behavior, interdisciplinary pedagogy. *Unit head:* Dr. Orville Blackman, Program Director, 502-585-9911 Ext. 2630, E-mail: cbc@spalding.edu. *Application contact:* Claire Rayburn, Administrative Assistant, 502-585-9911 Ext. 2120, E-mail: cbc@spalding.edu.

Spring Arbor University, School of Arts and Sciences, Spring Arbor, MI 49283-9799. Offers communication (MA); spiritual formation and leadership (MA). Part-time programs available. Postbaccalaureate distance learning degree programs offered (no on-campus study). *Faculty:* 6 full-time (1 woman), 9 part-time/adjunct (6 women). *Students:* 92 full-time (60 women), 75 part-time (57 women); includes 6 Black or African American, non-Hispanic/Latino; 1 Asian, non-Hispanic/Latino; 1 Hispanic/Latino. Average age 39. In 2010, 37 master's awarded. *Degree requirements:* For master's, thesis (for some programs). *Entrance requirements:* For master's, GRE (minimum score of 40th percentile and taken within last 5 years), bachelor's degree from regionally-accredited college or university, minimum GPA of 3.0 for at least the last two years of the bachelor's degree, at least two recommendations from professional/academic individuals. Additional exam requirements/recommendations for international students: Required—TOEFL (minimum score 600 paper-based; 220 computer-based). Application fee: $40. *Expenses:* Contact institution. *Financial support:* Applicants required to submit FAFSA. *Unit head:* Dr. Wally Metts, Chair of the Department of Communication, 517-750-1200 Ext. 1491, E-mail: wmetts@arbor.edu. *Application contact:* Dale Glinz, Lead Recruitment Specialist/Trainer, Graduate and Professional Studies, 517-750-6703, E-mail: dglinz@arbor.edu.

Stanford University, School of Humanities and Sciences, Department of Communication, Stanford, CA 94305-9991. Offers communication (journalism specialization) (MA); communication theory and research (PhD). *Faculty:* 10 full-time (1 woman). *Students:* 67 full-time (37 women). Average age 26. 162 applicants, 30% accepted, 35 enrolled. In 2010, 24 master's, 6 doctorates awarded. Terminal master's awarded for partial completion of doctoral program. *Degree requirements:* For master's, thesis, project; for doctorate, thesis/dissertation, qualifying examination, area examination, 2 projects. *Entrance requirements:* For master's and doctorate, GRE General Test. Additional exam requirements/recommendations for international students: Required—TOEFL (minimum score 650 paper-based; 280 computer-based; 115 iBT). *Application deadline:* For fall admission, 12/7 for domestic students, 12/1 for international students. Application fee: $125. Electronic applications accepted. *Expenses:* Tuition: Full-time $38,700; part-time $860 per unit. One-time fee: $200 full-time. *Financial support:* Fellowships, research assistantships, teaching assistantships available. *Unit head:* James S. Fishkin, Chair, 650-723-4611, E-mail: jfishkin@stanford.edu. *Application contact:* Student Services Manager, 650-723-2075, Fax: 650-725-2472, E-mail: comm-studentservices@stanford.edu.

State University of New York College at Potsdam, School of Arts and Sciences, Department of English and Communication, Potsdam, NY 13676. Offers English and communication (MA). Part-time and evening/weekend programs available. *Faculty:* 5 full-time (3 women). *Students:* 1 full-time (0 women), 14 part-time (9 women); includes 4 minority (3 Black or African American, non-Hispanic/Latino; 1 American Indian or Alaska Native, non-Hispanic/Latino). 6 applicants, 100% accepted, 5 enrolled. In 2010, 2 master's awarded. *Degree requirements:* For master's, one foreign language, thesis or alternative. *Entrance requirements:* For master's, minimum GPA of 3.0 in last 60 hours of undergraduate course work. Additional exam requirements/recommendations for international students: Required—TOEFL (minimum score 550 paper-based; 213 computer-based; 80 iBT), IELTS (minimum score 6). *Application deadline:* For fall admission, 4/1 for domestic students, 4/1 priority date for international students; for winter admission, 3/1 for domestic and international students; for spring admission, 10/15 for domestic students, 10/15 priority date for international students. Applications are processed on a rolling basis. Application fee: $50. *Financial support:* In 2010–11, 2 students received support; teaching assistantships with full tuition reimbursements available, Federal Work-Study and unspecified assistantships available. Support available to part-time students. Financial award application deadline: 3/1; financial award applicants required to submit FAFSA. *Unit head:* Dr. Sharmain van Blommestein, Director of Graduate Studies, 315-267-3158, Fax: 315-267-3256, E-mail: vanblos@potsdam.edu. *Application contact:* Peter Cutler, Graduate Admissions Counselor, 315-267-3154, Fax: 315-267-4802, E-mail: cutlerpj@potsdam.edu.

State University of New York College of Environmental Science and Forestry, Program in Environmental Science, Syracuse, NY 13210-2779. Offers environmental and community land planning (MPS, MS, PhD); environmental and natural resources policy (PhD); environmental communication and participatory processes (MPS, MS, PhD); environmental policy and democratic processes (MPS, MS, PhD); environmental systems and risk management (MPS, MS, PhD); water and wetland resource studies (MPS, MS, PhD). Part-time programs available. *Degree requirements:* For master's, thesis (for some programs); for doctorate, comprehensive exam, thesis/dissertation. *Entrance requirements:* For master's and doctorate, GRE General Test, minimum GPA of 3.0. Additional exam requirements/recommendations for international students: Required—TOEFL (minimum score 550 paper-based; 213 computer-based; 80 iBT), IELTS (minimum score 6). *Expenses:* Tuition, state resident: full-time $8370; part-time $349

per credit hour. Tuition, nonresident: full-time $13,780. Required fees: $30.30 per credit hour. $20 per year. *Faculty research:* Environmental education/communications, water resources, land resources, waste management.

Stephen F. Austin State University, Graduate School, College of Applied Arts and Science, Department of Communication, Nacogdoches, TX 75962. Offers communication (MA); mass communication (MA). Part-time programs available. *Degree requirements:* For master's, comprehensive exam, thesis optional. *Entrance requirements:* For master's, GRE General Test. Additional exam requirements/recommendations for international students: Required—TOEFL (minimum score 550 paper-based; 213 computer-based).

Stevens Institute of Technology, Graduate School, Charles V. Schaefer Jr. School of Engineering, Department of Electrical and Computer Engineering, Program in Electrical Engineering, Hoboken, NJ 07030. Offers computer architecture and digital systems (M Eng); electrical engineering (PhD); microelectronics and photonics science and technology (M Eng); signal processing for communications (M Eng); telecommunications systems engineering (M Eng); wireless communications (M Eng, Certificate). *Students:* 161 full-time (20 women), 54 part-time (4 women); includes 1 Black or African American, non-Hispanic/Latino; 28 Asian, non-Hispanic/Latino; 2 Hispanic/Latino, 140 international.. Average age 26. 177 applicants, 80% accepted. *Degree requirements:* For master's, thesis optional; for doctorate, variable foreign language requirement, thesis/dissertation. *Entrance requirements:* For master's, doctorate, and Certificate, GRE. Additional exam requirements/recommendations for international students: Required—TOEFL. *Application deadline:* Applications are processed on a rolling basis. Application fee: $50. Electronic applications accepted. *Unit head:* Prof. Yu-Dong Yao, Head, 201-216-5264. *Application contact:* Graduate Admissions, 800-496-4935, Fax: 201-216-8044, E-mail: gradadmissions@stevens.edu.

Suffolk University, College of Arts and Sciences, Department of Communication, Boston, MA 02108-2770. Offers communication studies (MAC); integrated marketing communication (MAC); organizational communication (MAC); public relations and advertising (MAC). Part-time and evening/weekend programs available. *Faculty:* 20 full-time (10 women), 1 part-time/adjunct (0 women). *Students:* 17 full-time (15 women), 18 part-time (13 women); includes 1 Asian, non-Hispanic/Latino, 3 international. Average age 26. 110 applicants, 54% accepted, 19 enrolled. In 2010, 23 master's awarded. *Degree requirements:* For master's, thesis optional. *Entrance requirements:* For master's, GRE General Test, MAT, or GMAT, 2 letters of recommendation, resume. Additional exam requirements/recommendations for international students: Required—TOEFL (minimum score 550 paper-based; 213 computer-based; 80 iBT). *Application deadline:* For fall admission, 6/15 priority date for domestic students, 6/15 for international students; for spring admission, 11/1 priority date for domestic students, 11/1 for international students. Applications are processed on a rolling basis. Application fee: $50. Electronic applications accepted. *Expenses:* Contact institution. *Financial support:* In 2010–11, 28 students received support, including 18 fellowships with partial tuition reimbursements available (averaging $5,403 per year); career-related internships or fieldwork, Federal Work-Study, and institutionally sponsored loans also available. Support available to part-time students. Financial award application deadline: 4/1; financial award applicants required to submit FAFSA. *Faculty research:* New media and new markets for advertising, First Amendment issues with the Internet, gender and intercultural communication, organizational development. *Unit head:* Dr. Robert Rosenthal, Chair, 617-573-8502, Fax: 617-742-6982, E-mail: rrosenth@suffolk.edu. *Application contact:* Judith Reynolds, Director of Graduate Admissions, 617-573-8302, Fax: 617-305-1733, E-mail: grad.admission@suffolk.edu.

Syracuse University, College of Visual and Performing Arts, Program in Communication and Rhetorical Studies, Syracuse, NY 13244. Offers MA. Part-time programs available. *Students:* 16 full-time (8 women), 3 part-time (2 women), 3 international. Average age 27. 28 applicants, 50% accepted, 7 enrolled. In 2010, 3 master's awarded. *Degree requirements:* For master's, thesis or alternative. *Entrance requirements:* For master's, GRE General Test, writing sample. Additional exam requirements/recommendations for international students: Required—TOEFL (minimum score 100 iBT). *Application deadline:* For fall admission, 2/1 priority date for domestic and international students. Application fee: $75. Electronic applications accepted. *Expenses:* Tuition: Part-time $1162 per credit. *Financial support:* In 2010–11, 9 students received support; fellowships with full tuition reimbursements available, teaching assistantships with full and partial tuition reimbursements available, tuition waivers (partial) available. Financial award application deadline: 1/1; financial award applicants required to submit FAFSA. *Unit head:* Dr. Kendall Phillips, Chair, 315-443-2883, E-mail: kphillip@syr.edu. *Application contact:* Harriett Conti, Assistant Dean for Recruitment and Admissions, 315-443-5755, E-mail: hmconti@syr.edu.

See Display on page 179 and Close-Up on page 227.

Syracuse University, S. I. Newhouse School of Public Communications, Syracuse, NY 13244. Offers MA, MS, PhD, JD/MA, JD/MS, MS/MA. *Accreditation:* ACEJMC (one or more programs are accredited). Postbaccalaureate distance learning degree programs offered (minimal on-campus study). *Faculty:* 65 full-time (23 women), 45 part-time/adjunct (18 women). *Students:* 271 full-time (185 women), 73 part-time (42 women); includes 83 minority (51 Black or African American, non-Hispanic/Latino; 1 American Indian or Alaska Native, non-Hispanic/Latino; 13 Asian, non-Hispanic/Latino; 15 Hispanic/Latino; 3 Two or more races, non-Hispanic/Latino), 67 international. Average age 28. 889 applicants, 55% accepted, 230 enrolled. In 2010, 161 master's, 3 doctorates awarded. *Degree requirements:* For master's, comprehensive exam (for some programs); for doctorate, thesis/dissertation, qualifying exams. *Entrance requirements:* For master's and doctorate, GRE General Test. Additional exam requirements/recommendations for international students: Required—TOEFL (minimum score 600 paper-based; 250 computer-based; 100 iBT), IELTS (minimum score 7). *Application deadline:* For fall admission, 2/1 priority date for domestic and international students. Application fee: $45. Electronic applications accepted. *Expenses:* Tuition: Part-time $1162 per credit. *Financial support:* Fellowships with full tuition reimbursements, research assistantships with partial tuition reimbursements, teaching assistantships with partial tuition reimbursements, career-related internships or fieldwork, Federal Work-Study, scholarships/grants, and tuition waivers (partial) available. Support available to part-time students. Financial award application deadline: 2/1; financial award applicants required to submit FAFSA. *Faculty research:* Media convergence, political reporting, interactive multimedia, popular television, advertising effectiveness. *Unit head:* Dr. Lorraine Branham, Dean, 315-443-3627, Fax: 315-443-3946. *Application contact:* Martha Coria, Graduate Records Office, 315-443-5749, Fax: 315-443-1834, E-mail: pcgrad@syr.edu.

Teachers College, Columbia University, Graduate Faculty of Education, Department of Math, Science and Technology, Program in Communication, New York, NY 10027. Offers Ed M, MA, Ed D. Part-time and evening/weekend programs available. *Faculty:* 12 full-time (5 women), 13 part-time/adjunct (7 women). *Students:* 6 full-time (5 women), 26 part-time (17 women); includes 10 minority (4 Black or African American, non-Hispanic/Latino; 1 Asian, non-Hispanic/Latino; 3 Hispanic/Latino; 2 Two or more races, non-Hispanic/Latino), 7 international. Average age 32. 25 applicants, 72% accepted, 8 enrolled. In 2010, 12 master's, 3 doctorates awarded. Terminal master's awarded for partial completion of doctoral program. *Degree requirements:* For master's, integrative project; for doctorate, comprehensive exam, thesis/dissertation. *Entrance requirements:* For doctorate, GRE General Test or MAT, writing sample; interview (recommended). *Application deadline:* For fall admission, 1/15 for domestic students; for spring admission, 11/1 for domestic students. Applications are processed on a rolling basis. Application fee: $65. Electronic applications accepted. *Expenses:* Tuition: Full-time $28,272; part-time $1178 per credit. Required fees: $756; $378 per semester. *Financial support:* Career-related internships or fieldwork, Federal Work-Study, institutionally sponsored loans, and tuition waivers (full and partial) available. Support available to part-time students. Financial award applicants required to submit FAFSA. *Faculty research:* Television and youth, application of digital technology to education reform. *Unit head:* Prof. Charles Kinzer, Program Coordinator, 212-678-3344, Fax: 212-678-8227, E-mail: tcccte@tc.edu. *Application contact:* Deanna Ghozati, Assistant Director of Admission, 212-678-4018, Fax: 212-678-4171, E-mail: ghozati@tc.edu.

Communication—General

Temple University, Health Sciences Center and Graduate School, College of Health Professions, Department of Communication Sciences, Philadelphia, PA 19122-6096. Offers communication sciences (PhD); linguistics (MA); speech-language-hearing (MA). *Accreditation:* ASHA. Part-time and evening/weekend programs available. *Faculty:* 9 full-time (3 women). *Students:* 61 full-time (60 women), 4 part-time (all women); includes 2 Asian, non-Hispanic/Latino; 2 Hispanic/Latino, 1 international. 363 applicants, 20% accepted, 28 enrolled. In 2010, 20 master's, 1 doctorate awarded. *Degree requirements:* For doctorate, thesis/dissertation. *Entrance requirements:* For master's and doctorate, GRE General Test, minimum GPA of 3.0. Additional exam requirements/recommendations for international students: Required—TOEFL (minimum score 550 paper-based; 213 computer-based; 79 iBT). Application fee: $50. Electronic applications accepted. *Financial support:* Fellowships, research assistantships, teaching assistantships with full tuition reimbursements, career-related internships or fieldwork, Federal Work-Study, institutionally sponsored loans, and tuition waivers (partial) available. Financial award application deadline: 1/15. *Faculty research:* Fluency, infants and families, multilingual/multicultural communication, geriatrics, conflict process, language, health communication. Total annual research expenditures: $1.1 million. *Unit head:* Dr. Carol Scheffner Hammer, Interim Chair, 215-204-7543, E-mail: cjhammer@temple.edu. *Application contact:* Dr. Carol Scheffner Hammer, Interim Chair, 215-204-7543, E-mail: cjhammer@temple.edu.

Temple University, School of Communications and Theater, Philadelphia, PA 19122-6096. Offers MA, MFA, MJ, MS, PhD. Part-time and evening/weekend programs available. *Faculty:* 61 full-time (24 women). *Students:* 146 full-time (83 women), 53 part-time (33 women); includes 15 Black or African American, non-Hispanic/Latino; 1 American Indian or Alaska Native, non-Hispanic/Latino; 4 Asian, non-Hispanic/Latino; 3 Hispanic/Latino; 2 Two or more races, non-Hispanic/Latino, 35 international. Average age 31. 314 applicants, 44% accepted, 54 enrolled. In 2010, 36 master's, 5 doctorates awarded. *Degree requirements:* For doctorate, one foreign language, thesis/dissertation. *Entrance requirements:* For master's, minimum GPA of 3.0; for doctorate, GRE General Test, minimum GPA of 3.0. Additional exam requirements/recommendations for international students: Required—TOEFL (minimum score 550 paper-based; 213 computer-based; 79 iBT). *Application deadline:* For fall admission, 12/15 for international students. Application fee: $50. Electronic applications accepted. *Financial support:* Fellowships, research assistantships with partial tuition reimbursements, teaching assistantships with partial tuition reimbursements, career-related internships or fieldwork, Federal Work-Study, institutionally sponsored loans, and tuition waivers (partial) available. Financial award application deadline: 1/15; financial award applicants required to submit FAFSA. *Unit head:* Dr. Thomas Jacobson, Interim Dean, 215-204-8422, Fax: 215-204-4811, E-mail: sct@temple.edu. *Application contact:* Nicole McKenna, Director, Office of Research & Graduate Studies, 215-204-1497, Fax: 215-204-0310, E-mail: nmckenna@temple.edu.

Texas A&M University, College of Liberal Arts, Department of Communication, College Station, TX 77843. Offers MA, PhD. *Faculty:* 16. *Students:* 44 full-time (23 women), 15 part-time (9 women); includes 4 Black or African American, non-Hispanic/Latino; 7 Hispanic/Latino, 12 international. Average age 27. In 2010, 6 master's, 12 doctorates awarded. *Degree requirements:* For master's, thesis or alternative; for doctorate, thesis/dissertation. *Entrance requirements:* For master's, GRE General Test. Additional exam requirements/recommendations for international students: Required—TOEFL. *Application deadline:* For fall admission, 2/15 priority date for domestic students; for spring admission, 10/15 for domestic students. Applications are processed on a rolling basis. Application fee: $50 ($75 for international students). Electronic applications accepted. *Financial support:* In 2010–11, fellowships with partial tuition reimbursements (averaging $12,000 per year), research assistantships with partial tuition reimbursements (averaging $11,000 per year), teaching assistantships with partial tuition reimbursements (averaging $11,000 per year) were awarded; institutionally sponsored loans also available. Financial award application deadline: 2/1; financial award applicants required to submit FAFSA. *Faculty research:* Rhetoric and public affairs, communication and health, communication and organizations. *Unit head:* Dr. Richard L. Street, Head, 979-845-0209, E-mail: r-street@tamu.edu. *Application contact:* Barbara F. Sharf, Director of Graduate Studies, 979-845-0625, Fax: 979-845-6594, E-mail: bsharf@tamu.edu.

Texas Southern University, Tavis Smiley School of Communication, Houston, TX 77004-4584. Offers MA. Part-time programs available. *Faculty:* 4 full-time (3 women), 1 part-time/adjunct (0 women). *Students:* 21 full-time (9 women), 45 part-time (36 women); includes 61 Black or African American, non-Hispanic/Latino; 1 Asian, non-Hispanic/Latino; 1 Hispanic/Latino, 2 international. Average age 30. 25 applicants, 100% accepted, 21 enrolled. In 2010, 6 master's awarded. *Degree requirements:* For master's, comprehensive exam, thesis. *Entrance requirements:* For master's, GRE General Test, minimum GPA of 2.5. Additional exam requirements/recommendations for international students: Required—TOEFL. *Application deadline:* For fall admission, 7/1 for domestic and international students; for spring admission, 11/1 for domestic and international students. Applications are processed on a rolling basis. Application fee: $50 ($75 for international students). Electronic applications accepted. *Expenses:* Tuition, state resident: full-time $1875; part-time $100 per credit hour. Tuition, nonresident: full-time $6641; part-time $343 per credit hour. Tuition and fees vary according to course level, course load and degree level. *Financial support:* In 2010–11, 5 teaching assistantships (averaging $3,500 per year) were awarded; unspecified assistantships also available. Financial award application deadline: 5/1. *Unit head:* Dr. James Ward, Dean, 713-313-7740, E-mail: ward_jw@tsu.edu. *Application contact:* Dr. Louis Browne, Graduate Advisor, 713-313-7024.

Texas State University–San Marcos, Graduate School, College of Fine Arts and Communication, San Marcos, TX 78666. Offers MA, MFA, MM. Part-time and evening/weekend programs available. *Faculty:* 72 full-time (31 women), 6 part-time/adjunct (3 women). *Students:* 140 full-time (76 women), 84 part-time (54 women); includes 6 Black or African American, non-Hispanic/Latino; 2 American Indian or Alaska Native, non-Hispanic/Latino; 5 Asian, non-Hispanic/Latino; 51 Hispanic/Latino; 3 Two or more races, non-Hispanic/Latino, 12 international. Average age 30. 134 applicants, 74% accepted, 73 enrolled. In 2010, 67 master's awarded. *Degree requirements:* For master's, comprehensive exam, thesis (for some programs). *Entrance requirements:* For master's, GRE General Test (for some programs), minimum GPA of 2.75 in last 60 hours of course work. Additional exam requirements/recommendations for international students: Required—TOEFL (minimum score 550 paper-based; 213 computer-based; 78 iBT). *Application deadline:* For fall admission, 6/15 priority date for domestic students, 6/1 for international students; for spring admission, 10/15 priority date for domestic students, 10/1 for international students. Applications are processed on a rolling basis. Application fee: $40 ($90 for international students). Electronic applications accepted. *Expenses:* Tuition, state resident: full-time $6024; part-time $251 per credit hour. Tuition, nonresident: full-time $13,536; part-time $564 per credit hour. Required fees: $1776; $50 per credit hour. $306 per semester. *Financial support:* In 2010–11, 109 students received support, including 4 research assistantships (averaging $5,154 per year), 80 teaching assistantships (averaging $3,716 per year); career-related internships or fieldwork, Federal Work-Study, institutionally sponsored loans, scholarships/grants, and unspecified assistantships also available. Support available to part-time students. Financial award application deadline: 4/1; financial award applicants required to submit FAFSA. *Faculty research:* AFRED survey-propane. Total annual research expenditures: $8,797. *Unit head:* Dr. Timothy Mottet, Dean, 512-245-2308, Fax: 512-245-8334, E-mail: tm15@txstate.edu. *Application contact:* Dr. J. Michael Willoughby, Dean of Graduate School, 512-245-2581, Fax: 512-245-8365, E-mail: gradcollege@txstate.edu.

Texas State University–San Marcos, Graduate School, College of Fine Arts and Communication, Department of Communication Studies, Program in Communication Studies, San Marcos, TX 78666. Offers MA. Part-time and evening/weekend programs available. *Faculty:* 7 full-time (4 women). *Students:* 29 full-time (19 women), 15 part-time (12 women); includes 2 Black or African American, non-Hispanic/Latino; 2 American Indian or Alaska Native, non-Hispanic/Latino; 9 Hispanic/Latino; 2 Two or more races, non-Hispanic/Latino, 1 international. Average age 26. 24 applicants, 83% accepted, 14 enrolled. In 2010, 16 master's awarded. *Degree requirements:* For master's, comprehensive exam, thesis optional. *Entrance requirements:* For master's, minimum GPA of 3.0 in last 60 hours. Additional exam requirements/recommendations for international students: Required—TOEFL (minimum score 550 paper-based; 213 computer-based; 78 iBT). *Application deadline:* For fall admission, 3/7 priority date for domestic students, 3/7 for international students; for spring admission, 10/15 priority date for domestic students, 10/15 for international students. Applications are processed on a rolling basis. Application fee: $40 ($90 for international students). Electronic applications accepted. *Expenses:* Tuition, state resident: full-time $6024; part-time $251 per credit hour. Tuition, nonresident: full-time $13,536; part-time $564 per credit hour. Required fees: $1776; $50 per credit hour. $306 per semester. *Financial support:* In 2010–11, 21 students received support, including 24 teaching assistantships (averaging $6,153 per year); research assistantships, career-related internships or fieldwork, Federal Work-Study, institutionally sponsored loans, scholarships/grants, and unspecified assistantships also available. Support available to part-time students. Financial award application deadline: 4/1; financial award applicants required to submit FAFSA. *Faculty research:* Speech education, rhetoric and criticism, interpersonal and group communication, communication theory, rhetoric of Sojourner Truth. *Unit head:* Dr. Phillip Salem, Graduate Adviser, 512-245-2165, Fax: 512-245-3138, E-mail: ps05@txstate.edu. *Application contact:* Dr. J. Michael Willoughby, Dean of Graduate School, 512-245-2581, Fax: 512-245-8365, E-mail: gradcollege@txstate.edu.

Texas Tech University, Graduate School, College of Arts and Sciences, Department of Communication Studies, Lubbock, TX 79409. Offers MA. Part-time programs available. *Faculty:* 7 full-time (3 women). *Students:* 20 full-time (10 women), 5 part-time (4 women); includes 2 Black or African American, non-Hispanic/Latino; 4 Hispanic/Latino, 1 international. Average age 24. 25 applicants, 40% accepted, 7 enrolled. In 2010, 9 master's awarded. *Degree requirements:* For master's, thesis. *Entrance requirements:* For master's, GRE General Test. Additional exam requirements/recommendations for international students: Required—TOEFL (minimum score 550 paper-based; 213 computer-based; 79 iBT). *Application deadline:* For fall admission, 6/1 priority date for domestic students, 1/15 priority date for international students; for spring admission, 9/1 priority date for domestic students, 6/15 priority date for international students. Applications are processed on a rolling basis. Application fee: $50 ($75 for international students). Electronic applications accepted. *Expenses:* Tuition, state resident: full-time $5495.76; part-time $228.99 per credit hour. Tuition, nonresident: full-time $12,936; part-time $538.99 per credit hour. Required fees: $2674; $36 per credit hour. $905 per semester. *Financial support:* In 2010–11, 21 students received support, including 1 research assistantship with partial tuition reimbursement available (averaging $4,596 per year), 11 teaching assistantships with partial tuition reimbursements available (averaging $5,326 per year). Financial award application deadline: 4/15; financial award applicants required to submit FAFSA. *Faculty research:* Computer mediated communication, intercultural communication, health communication, interpersonal communication, family communication. *Unit head:* Dr. Bolanle A. Olaniran, Chair, 806-742-3911, Fax: 806-742-1025, E-mail: b.olaniran@ttu.edu. *Application contact:* Dr. Juliann Scholl, Graduate Director, 806-742-1675, Fax: 806-742-1025, E-mail: juliann.scholl@ttu.edu.

Towson University, Program in Communications Management, Towson, MD 21252-0001. Offers MS. *Students:* 10 full-time (5 women), 28 part-time (23 women); includes 9 minority (all Black or African American, non-Hispanic/Latino), 1 international. Average age 29. In 2010, 8 master's awarded. *Degree requirements:* For master's, thesis. *Entrance requirements:* For master's, 24 credits in mass communications, public relations and/or advertising, writing and statistics; professional experience; minimum GPA of 3.0. *Application deadline:* For fall admission, 1/15 for domestic students. Application fee: $50. Electronic applications accepted. *Expenses:* Tuition, state resident: part-time $324 per credit. Tuition, nonresident: part-time $681 per credit. Required fees: $95 per term. *Financial support:* Application deadline: 4/1. *Unit head:* Theodora Carabas, Graduate Program Director, 410-704-4855, E-mail: tcarabas@towson.edu. *Application contact:* 410-704-2501, Fax: 410-704-4675, E-mail: grads@towson.edu.

Towson University, Program in Strategic Public Relations and Integrated Communications, Towson, MD 21252-0001. Offers Certificate. Evening/weekend programs available. Postbaccalaureate distance learning degree programs offered (no on-campus study). *Students:* 3 part-time (all women); includes 1 minority (Black or African American, non-Hispanic/Latino). In 2010, 6 Certificates awarded. *Entrance requirements:* For degree, 24 credits in related course work, minimum GPA of 3.0. *Application deadline:* For fall admission, 1/15 for domestic students. Application fee: $50. Electronic applications accepted. *Expenses:* Tuition, state resident: part-time $324 per credit. Tuition, nonresident: part-time $681 per credit. Required fees: $95 per term. *Financial support:* Fellowships, teaching assistantships, career-related internships or fieldwork, Federal Work-Study, and unspecified assistantships available. Support available to part-time students. Financial award application deadline: 4/1; financial award applicants required to submit FAFSA. *Unit head:* Theodora Carabas, Graduate Program Director, 410-704-4855, E-mail: tcarabas@towson.edu. *Application contact:* 410-704-2501, Fax: 410-704-4675, E-mail: grads@towson.edu.

Trinity International University, Trinity Graduate School, Deerfield, IL 60015-1284. Offers bioethics (MA); communication and culture (MA); counseling psychology (MA); instructional leadership (M Ed); teaching (MA). Part-time and evening/weekend programs available. Postbaccalaureate distance learning degree programs offered (minimal on-campus study). *Degree requirements:* For master's, comprehensive exam. *Entrance requirements:* For master's, GRE General Test or MAT, minimum undergraduate GPA of 3.0. Additional exam requirements/recommendations for international students: Required—TOEFL (minimum score 580 paper-based; 237 computer-based), TWE (minimum score 4). Electronic applications accepted.

Trinity (Washington) University, School of Professional Studies, Washington, DC 20017-1094. Offers business administration (MBA); communication (MA); international security studies (MA); organizational management (MSA), including federal program management, human resource management, nonprofit management, organizational development, public and community health. Part-time and evening/weekend programs available. *Degree requirements:* For master's, thesis (for some programs), capstone project (MSA). *Entrance requirements:* For master's, minimum GPA of 2.5. Additional exam requirements/recommendations for international students: Required—TOEFL (minimum score 550 paper-based; 213 computer-based).

Université de Montréal, Faculty of Arts and Sciences, Department of Communication, Montréal, QC H3C 3J7, Canada. Offers communication (PhD); communication sciences (M Sc). *Degree requirements:* For master's, thesis; for doctorate, one foreign language, thesis/dissertation, general exam. *Entrance requirements:* For doctorate, proficiency in French. Electronic applications accepted. *Faculty research:* Mass media/new communication technologies, organizational communication.

Université du Québec à Montréal, Graduate Programs, Program in Communications, Montréal, QC H3C 3P8, Canada. Offers MA, PhD. PhD offered jointly with Concordia University and Université de Montréal. Part-time programs available. *Degree requirements:* For master's, thesis; for doctorate, thesis/dissertation. *Entrance requirements:* For master's, appropriate bachelor's degree or equivalent, proficiency in French; for doctorate, appropriate master's degree or equivalent, proficiency in French.

Université du Québec à Trois-Rivières, Graduate Programs, Program in Social Communication, Trois-Rivières, QC G9A 5H7, Canada. Offers MA, DESS.

University at Albany, State University of New York, College of Arts and Sciences, Department of Communication, Albany, NY 12222-0001. Offers communication (MA); sociology and communication (PhD). Part-time programs available. *Degree requirements:* For master's, comprehensive exam, thesis or alternative; for doctorate, comprehensive exam, thesis/dissertation. *Entrance requirements:* For master's, minimum GPA of 3.0; for doctorate, GRE, minimum GPA of 3.0. Additional exam requirements/recommendations for international students: Required—TOEFL (minimum score 550 paper-based; 213 computer-based). Electronic applications accepted. *Faculty research:* Language and social interaction, campaign communication, media agenda-setting, high-speed management, organizational boundary-spanning.

University at Buffalo, the State University of New York, Graduate School, College of Arts and Sciences, Department of Communication, Buffalo, NY 14260. Offers MA, PhD. Part-time programs available. *Faculty:* 13 full-time (3 women), 13 part-time/adjunct (7 women). *Students:* 28 full-time (18 women), 29 part-time (14 women); includes 1 minority (Black or African American, non-Hispanic/Latino), 24 international. Average age 33. 93 applicants, 29% accepted, 16 enrolled. In 2010, 2 master's, 9 doctorates awarded. Terminal master's awarded for partial completion of doctoral program. *Degree requirements:* For master's, thesis; for doctorate, comprehensive exam, thesis/dissertation. *Entrance requirements:* For master's and doctorate, GRE General Test, minimum GPA of 3.0. Additional exam requirements/recommendations for international students: Required—TOEFL (minimum score 600 paper-based; 250 computer-based; 100 iBT); Recommended—TWE. *Application deadline:* For fall admission, 1/1 priority date for domestic and international students. Applications are processed on a rolling basis. Application fee: $75. Electronic applications accepted. *Financial support:* In 2010–11, 7 students received support, including 5 research assistantships with full tuition reimbursements available (averaging $12,500 per year), 13 teaching assistantships with full tuition reimbursements available (averaging $13,650 per year); career-related internships or fieldwork, institutionally sponsored loans, health care benefits, and unspecified assistantships also available. Financial award application deadline: 1/1; financial award applicants required to submit FAFSA. *Faculty research:* Technology, health, international, interpersonal. Total annual research expenditures: $231,588. *Unit head:* Dr. Thomas H. Feeley, Chairman, 716-645-1160, Fax: 716-645-2086, E-mail: thfeeley@buffalo.edu. *Application contact:* Rose Gryckiewicz, Graduate Secretary, 716-645-1505, Fax: 716-645-2086, E-mail: rfg@buffalo.edu.

The University of Akron, Graduate School, College of Creative and Professional Arts, School of Communication, Akron, OH 44325. Offers MA. Part-time and evening/weekend programs available. *Faculty:* 21 full-time (13 women), 45 part-time/adjunct (29 women). *Students:* 20 full-time (11 women), 18 part-time (11 women); includes 1 Black or African American, non-Hispanic/Latino; 1 Hispanic/Latino, 3 international. Average age 28. 30 applicants, 70% accepted, 14 enrolled. In 2010, 10 master's awarded. *Degree requirements:* For master's, thesis optional, thesis, project or written comprehensive exam. *Entrance requirements:* For master's, essay of no more than 500 words that outlines reasons for wanting to attend the program in communication at The University of Akron. Additional exam requirements/recommendations for international students: Required—TOEFL (minimum score 550 paper-based; 213 computer-based; 79 iBT). *Application deadline:* For fall admission, 5/1 for domestic students. Application fee: $30 ($40 for international students). Electronic applications accepted. *Expenses:* Tuition, state resident: full-time $6800; part-time $378 per credit hour. Tuition, nonresident: full-time $11,644; part-time $647 per credit hour. Required fees: $1265. One-time fee: $30 full-time. *Financial support:* In 2010–11, 1 research assistantship with full tuition reimbursement, 11 teaching assistantships with full tuition reimbursements were awarded; institutionally sponsored loans also available. *Faculty research:* Communications theory, business and organization communications, criticism of communications, film and video studies, interpersonal and intercultural communications. Total annual research expenditures: $22,535. *Unit head:* Dr. Elizabeth Graham, Director, 330-972-7600, E-mail: grahame@uakron.edu. *Application contact:* Dr. Heather Walter, Graduate Coordinator, 330-972-5741, E-mail: hlwalter@uakron.edu.

The University of Alabama, Graduate School, College of Communication and Information Sciences, Tuscaloosa, AL 35487-0172. Offers MA, MFA, MLIS, PhD. *Accreditation:* ACEJMC (one or more programs are accredited at the [master's] level). *Faculty:* 55 full-time (26 women), 3 part-time/adjunct (all women). *Students:* 204 full-time (137 women), 248 part-time (178 women); includes 49 minority (24 Black or African American, non-Hispanic/Latino; 3 American Indian or Alaska Native, non-Hispanic/Latino; 6 Asian, non-Hispanic/Latino; 12 Hispanic/Latino; 4 Two or more races, non-Hispanic/Latino), 18 international. Average age 33. 497 applicants, 47% accepted, 144 enrolled. In 2010, 169 master's, 12 doctorates awarded. *Degree requirements:* For master's, comprehensive exam, thesis or alternative; for doctorate, comprehensive exam, thesis/dissertation. *Entrance requirements:* For master's, GRE; for doctorate, GRE, minimum graduate GPA of 3.0, master's degree. Additional exam requirements/recommendations for international students: Required—TOEFL (minimum score 600 paper-based; 250 computer-based; 100 iBT). *Application deadline:* For fall admission, 2/15 priority date for domestic and international students; for winter admission, 11/1 priority date for international students; for spring admission, 11/1 priority date for domestic students. Applications are processed on a rolling basis. Application fee: $50 ($60 for international students). Electronic applications accepted. *Expenses:* Tuition, state resident: full-time $7900. Tuition, nonresident: full-time $20,500. *Financial support:* In 2010–11, 78 students received support, including 3 fellowships with tuition reimbursements available (averaging $15,000 per year), 34 research assistantships with tuition reimbursements available (averaging $13,045 per year), 38 teaching assistantships with tuition reimbursements available (averaging $13,045 per year); institutionally sponsored loans, health care benefits, and unspecified assistantships also available. Financial award application deadline: 2/15. *Faculty research:* Mass media research; media effects; information studies; cultural, critical, and rhetorical studies; electronic media; law and policy. Total annual research expenditures: $44,923. *Unit head:* Dr. Jennings Bryant, Associate Dean for Graduate Studies, 205-348-8593, Fax: 205-348-6774. *Application contact:* Diane Shaddix, Information Contact, 205-348-8593, Fax: 205-348-6774, E-mail: dshaddix@bama.ua.edu.

The University of Alabama at Birmingham, College of Arts and Sciences, Program in Communication Management, Birmingham, AL 35294. Offers MA. *Students:* 14 full-time (10 women), 10 part-time (6 women); includes 5 minority (2 Black or African American, non-Hispanic/Latino; 3 Hispanic/Latino), 5 international. Average age 28. 13 applicants, 77% accepted, 8 enrolled. In 2010, 9 master's awarded. *Expenses:* Tuition, state resident: full-time $5482. Tuition, nonresident: full-time $12,430. Tuition and fees vary according to program. *Unit head:* Dr. Claire Peel, Assistant Dean, 205-934-0513, Fax: 205-975-7677. *Application contact:* Julie Bryant, Director of Graduate Admissions, 205-934-8227, Fax: 205-934-8413, E-mail: jbryant@uab.edu.

University of Alaska Fairbanks, College of Liberal Arts, Department of Communications, Fairbanks, AK 99775-5680. Offers professional communications (MA). Part-time programs available. *Faculty:* 4 full-time (2 women). *Students:* 15 full-time (11 women), 6 part-time (5 women); includes 4 minority (1 Black or African American, non-Hispanic/Latino; 1 American Indian or Alaska Native, non-Hispanic/Latino; 1 Hispanic/Latino; 1 Two or more races, non-Hispanic/Latino), 2 international. Average age 34. 9 applicants, 67% accepted, 6 enrolled. In 2010, 9 master's awarded. *Degree requirements:* For master's, comprehensive exam, thesis, oral defense. *Entrance requirements:* Additional exam requirements/recommendations for international students: Required—TOEFL (minimum score 550 paper-based; 213 computer-based; 80 iBT). *Application deadline:* For fall admission, 6/1 for domestic students, 3/1 for international students; for spring admission, 10/15 for domestic students, 9/1 for international students. Applications are processed on a rolling basis. Application fee: $60. Electronic applications accepted. *Expenses:* Tuition, state resident: full-time $5688; part-time $316 per credit. Tuition, nonresident: full-time $11,628; part-time $646 per credit. Required fees: $289 per semester. Tuition and fees vary according to course load and reciprocity agreements. *Financial support:* In 2010–11, 12 teaching assistantships with tuition reimbursements (averaging $11,657 per year) were awarded; fellowships with tuition reimbursements, Federal Work-Study, scholarships/grants, tuition waivers, and unspecified assistantships also available. Support available to part-time students. Financial award application deadline: 7/1; financial award applicants required to submit FAFSA. *Faculty research:* Interpersonal communications, health communications, intercultural communications, politeness and face management in conversation, gender communication. *Unit head:* Dr. Robert Arundale, Department Chair, 907-474-6591, Fax: 907-474-5858, E-mail: fycomm@uaf.edu. *Application contact:* Dr. Robert Arundale, Department Chair, 907-474-6591, Fax: 907-474-5858, E-mail: fycomm@uaf.edu.

University of Alberta, Faculty of Extension, Edmonton, AB T6G 2E1, Canada. Offers communications and technology (MA).

University of Alberta, Faculty of Graduate Studies and Research, Program in Communications and Technology, Edmonton, AB T6G 2E1, Canada. Offers MACT.

The University of Arizona, College of Social and Behavioral Sciences, Department of Communication, Tucson, AZ 85721. Offers MA, PhD. Part-time programs available. *Faculty:* 7 full-time (2 women). *Students:* 17 full-time (12 women), 4 part-time (all women); includes 1 Black or African American, non-Hispanic/Latino; 1 Asian, non-Hispanic/Latino; 4 Hispanic/Latino, 3 international. Average age 28. 45 applicants, 18% accepted, 8 enrolled. In 2010, 3 master's, 2 doctorates awarded. Terminal master's awarded for partial completion of doctoral program. *Degree requirements:* For master's, thesis optional; for doctorate, comprehensive exam, thesis/dissertation. *Entrance requirements:* For master's, GRE General Test, minimum GPA of 3.25, writing sample, 3 letters of recommendation; for doctorate, GRE General Test, minimum GPA of 3.5, writing sample, 3 letters of recommendation, statement of purpose. Additional exam requirements/recommendations for international students: Required—TOEFL (minimum score 600 paper-based; 250 computer-based; 90 iBT). *Application deadline:* For fall admission, 2/1 for domestic and international students. Applications are processed on a rolling basis. Application fee: $65. Electronic applications accepted. *Expenses:* Tuition, state resident: full-time $7692. *Financial support:* In 2010–11, 2 research assistantships (averaging $20,937 per year), 19 teaching assistantships with full tuition reimbursements (averaging $19,331 per year) were awarded; career-related internships or fieldwork, Federal Work-Study, scholarships/grants, health care benefits, tuition waivers (full), and unspecified assistantships also available. *Faculty research:* Health communication, new communication technologies. Total annual research expenditures: $202,495. *Unit head:* Dr. Chris Segrin, Department Head, 520-621-1366, Fax: 520-621-5504, E-mail: segrin@email.arizona.edu. *Application contact:* Dr. Peggy Flyntz, Graduate Coordinator, 520-307-0695, Fax: 520-621-5504, E-mail: commgrad@email.arizona.edu.

University of Arkansas, Graduate School, J. William Fulbright College of Arts and Sciences, Department of Communication, Fayetteville, AR 72701-1201. Offers MA. Part-time programs available. *Students:* 9 full-time (7 women), 23 part-time (14 women); includes 4 minority (3 Black or African American, non-Hispanic/Latino; 1 Hispanic/Latino), 3 international. 15 applicants, 13% accepted. In 2010, 16 master's awarded. *Degree requirements:* For master's, thesis. *Entrance requirements:* For master's, GRE General Test. *Application deadline:* For fall admission, 4/1 for international students; for spring admission, 10/1 for international students. Applications are processed on a rolling basis. Application fee: $40 ($50 for international students). Electronic applications accepted. *Financial support:* In 2010–11, 22 teaching assistantships were awarded; fellowships, research assistantships, career-related internships or fieldwork and Federal Work-Study also available. Support available to part-time students. Financial award application deadline: 4/1; financial award applicants required to submit FAFSA. *Unit head:* Dr. Robert Brady, Department Chairperson, 479-575-3046, Fax: 479-575-6734, E-mail: rbrady@uark.edu. *Application contact:* Dr. Myria Allen, Graduate Coordinator, 479-575-5952, E-mail: myria@uark.edu.

University of Calgary, Faculty of Graduate Studies, Faculty of Communication and Culture, Calgary, AB T2N 1N4, Canada. Offers MA, MCS, PhD. Part-time and evening/weekend programs available. *Degree requirements:* For master's, project (MCS), thesis (MA); for doctorate, thesis/dissertation. *Entrance requirements:* For master's, minimum GPA of 3.0; for doctorate, master's degree, minimum GPA of 3.0, BA degree, min GPA of 3.0. Additional exam requirements/recommendations for international students: Required—TOEFL (minimum score 600 paper-based; 250 computer-based); Recommended—IELTS (minimum score 8). Electronic applications accepted. *Faculty research:* Science communications, structuration theory, organizational communication, communication theory, media law.

University of California, Davis, Graduate Studies, Program in Communication, Davis, CA 95616. Offers MA. *Degree requirements:* For master's, comprehensive exam (for some programs), thesis (for some programs). *Entrance requirements:* For master's, GRE. Additional exam requirements/recommendations for international students: Required—TOEFL (minimum score 550 paper-based; 213 computer-based).

University of California, San Diego, Office of Graduate Studies, Department of Communication, La Jolla, CA 92093. Offers MA, PhD. *Entrance requirements:* For doctorate, GRE General Test. Electronic applications accepted.

University of California, San Diego, Office of Graduate Studies, Interdisciplinary Program in Cognitive Science, La Jolla, CA 92093. Offers cognitive science/anthropology (PhD); cognitive science/communication (PhD); cognitive science/computer science and engineering (PhD); cognitive science/linguistics (PhD); cognitive science/neuroscience (PhD); cognitive science/philosophy (PhD); cognitive science/psychology (PhD); cognitive science/sociology (PhD). Admissions offered through affiliated departments. *Degree requirements:* For doctorate, thesis/dissertation. *Entrance requirements:* For doctorate, GRE General Test, acceptance into one of the eight participating departments. *Faculty research:* Language and cognition, philosophy of mind, visual perception, biological anthropology, sociolinguistics.

University of California, Santa Barbara, Graduate Division, College of Letters and Sciences, Division of Social Sciences, Department of Communication, Santa Barbara, CA 93106-4020. Offers cognitive science (PhD); feminist studies (PhD); quantitative methods in the social science (PhD); society and technology (PhD); MA/PhD. *Faculty:* 20 full-time (9 women). *Students:* 39 full-time (26 women); includes 3 Black or African American, non-Hispanic/Latino; 5 Asian, non-Hispanic/Latino; 6 Hispanic/Latino. Average age 30. 169 applicants, 6% accepted, 5 enrolled. In 2010, 3 doctorates awarded. Terminal master's awarded for partial completion of doctoral program. *Degree requirements:* For doctorate, comprehensive exam, thesis/dissertation. *Entrance requirements:* For doctorate, GRE. Additional exam requirements/recommendations for international students: Required—TOEFL (minimum score 550 paper-based; 80 iBT), IELTS (minimum score 7). *Application deadline:* For fall admission, 12/1 for domestic and international students. Application fee: $70 ($90 for international students). Electronic applications accepted. *Financial support:* In 2010–11, 39 students received support, including 39 fellowships with full and partial tuition reimbursements available (averaging $6,045 per year), 5 research assistantships with full and partial tuition reimbursements available (averaging $9,646 per year), 29 teaching assistantships with partial tuition reimbursements available (averaging $14,294 per year); career-related internships or fieldwork, health care benefits, and tuition waivers (full and partial) also available. Support available to part-time students. Financial award application deadline: 12/1. *Faculty research:* Interpersonal, intercultural, organizational, health, media. *Unit head:* Prof. Linda L. Putnam, Professor, 805-893-7935, Fax: 805-893-7102, E-mail: lputnam@comm.ucsb.edu. *Application contact:* Nancy Siris-Rawls, Graduate Program Assistant, 805-893-3046, Fax: 805-893-7102, E-mail: nsiris@comm.ucsb.edu.

University of California, Santa Cruz, Division of Graduate Studies, Division of Physical and Biological Sciences, Program in Science Communication, Santa Cruz, CA 95064. Offers Certificate. *Students:* 10 full-time (8 women); includes 1 minority (Asian, non-Hispanic/Latino), 1 international. Average age 31. 20 applicants, 65% accepted, 10 enrolled. In 2010, 9 Certificates awarded. *Entrance requirements:* For degree, GRE General Test, GRE Subject Test, bachelor's degree in science. Additional exam requirements/recommendations for international students: Required—TOEFL (minimum score 550 paper-based; 220 computer-based; 83 iBT); Recommended—IELTS (minimum score 8). *Application deadline:* For fall admission, 4/1 for domestic and international students. Application fee: $70 ($90 for international students). Electronic applications accepted. *Financial support:* Fellowships, research assistantships, teaching assistantships, institutionally sponsored loans and tuition waivers also available. Financial award applicants required to submit FAFSA. *Faculty research:* Science writing. *Unit head:* Andrea Michels, Graduate Program Coordinator, 831-459-4475, E-mail: amichels@ucsc.edu. *Application contact:* Andrea Michels, Graduate Program Coordinator, 831-459-4475, E-mail: amichels@ucsc.edu.

University of Central Florida, College of Sciences, Nicholson School of Communication, Orlando, FL 32816. Offers MA. Part-time and evening/weekend programs available. *Faculty:* 44 full-time (19 women), 23 part-time/adjunct (8 women). *Students:* 43 full-time (31 women), 33 part-time (26 women); includes 8 Black or African American, non-Hispanic/Latino; 2 American Indian or Alaska Native, non-Hispanic/Latino; 1 Asian, non-Hispanic/Latino; 5 Hispanic/Latino,

Communication—General

University of Central Florida (continued)
7 international. Average age 28. 64 applicants, 67% accepted, 19 enrolled. In 2010, 36 master's awarded. *Degree requirements:* For master's, thesis or comprehensive exam. *Entrance requirements:* For master's, GRE General Test, minimum GPA of 3.0 in last 60 hours of course work. Additional exam requirements/recommendations for international students: Required—TOEFL. *Application deadline:* For fall admission, 7/15 for domestic students; for spring admission, 12/7 for domestic students. Application fee: $30. Electronic applications accepted. *Expenses:* Tuition, state resident: part-time $256.56 per credit hour. Tuition, nonresident: part-time $1011.52 per credit hour. Part-time tuition and fees vary according to program. *Financial support:* In 2010–11, 17 students received support, including 4 fellowships with partial tuition reimbursements available (averaging $5,300 per year), 2 research assistantships with partial tuition reimbursements available (averaging $8,100 per year), 16 teaching assistantships with partial tuition reimbursements available (averaging $6,400 per year); career-related internships or fieldwork, Federal Work-Study, institutionally sponsored loans, tuition waivers (partial), and unspecified assistantships also available. Financial award application deadline: 3/1; financial award applicants required to submit FAFSA. *Faculty research:* Persuasion, communication apprehension, nonverbal communication, conflict resolution. *Unit head:* Dr. Robert Chandler, Director, 407-823-2683, Fax: 407-823-5216, E-mail: rcchandl@mail.ucf.edu. *Application contact:* Dr. Robert Chandler, Director, 407-823-2683, Fax: 407-823-5216, E-mail: rcchandl@mail.ucf.edu.

University of Cincinnati, Graduate School, McMicken College of Arts and Sciences, Department of Communication, Cincinnati, OH 45221. Offers MA. Part-time programs available. *Degree requirements:* For master's, comprehensive exam, thesis or alternative. *Entrance requirements:* For master's, GRE General Test, undergraduate course work in communication. Additional exam requirements/recommendations for international students: Required—TOEFL. Electronic applications accepted. *Faculty research:* Political communication, health communication, organizational communication, interpersonal communication.

University of Colorado at Colorado Springs, College of Letters, Arts and Sciences, Department of Communication, Colorado Springs, CO 80933-7150. Offers MA. Part-time programs available. *Faculty:* 15 full-time (11 women), 1 (woman) part-time/adjunct. *Students:* 23 full-time (12 women), 14 part-time (11 women); includes 2 Black or African American, non-Hispanic/Latino; 3 Hispanic/Latino, 1 international. Average age 34. 18 applicants, 78% accepted, 10 enrolled. In 2010, 11 master's awarded. *Degree requirements:* For master's, thesis optional. *Entrance requirements:* For master's, GRE General Test. *Application deadline:* Applications are processed on a rolling basis. Application fee: $60 ($75 for international students). *Expenses:* Tuition, state resident: full-time $7916. Tuition, nonresident: full-time $16,610. Tuition and fees vary according to course load, degree level, program, reciprocity agreements and student level. *Financial support:* Teaching assistantships, career-related internships or fieldwork, Federal Work-Study, and scholarships/grants available. Support available to part-time students. Financial award application deadline: 3/1; financial award applicants required to submit FAFSA. *Faculty research:* Organizational communication, interpersonal communication, communication education, oral communication, cultural diversity. *Unit head:* Dr. David Nelson, Chair, 719-255-4129, Fax: 719-255-4030, E-mail: drnelson@uccs.edu. *Application contact:* Debbie MacDonald, Program Assistant, 719-255-4114, Fax: 719-255-4030, E-mail: knorris@uccs.edu.

University of Colorado Boulder, Graduate School, College of Arts and Sciences, Department of Communication, Boulder, CO 80309. Offers MA, PhD. *Faculty:* 18 full-time (7 women). *Students:* 50 full-time (31 women), 5 part-time (3 women); includes 7 minority (1 Black or African American, non-Hispanic/Latino; 1 Asian, non-Hispanic/Latino; 5 Hispanic/Latino), 4 international. Average age 33. 98 applicants, 16 enrolled. In 2010, 8 master's, 8 doctorates awarded. *Degree requirements:* For master's, comprehensive exam, thesis optional; for doctorate, comprehensive exam, thesis/dissertation. *Entrance requirements:* For master's and doctorate, GRE General Test, minimum undergraduate GPA of 3.2. *Application deadline:* For fall admission, 12/31 priority date for domestic students, 12/15 for international students; for spring admission, 9/15 for domestic students, 8/15 for international students. Applications are processed on a rolling basis. Application fee: $50 ($60 for international students). *Financial support:* In 2010–11, 15 fellowships (averaging $860 per year), 29 research assistantships (averaging $12,099 per year) were awarded; tuition waivers (full) also available. Financial award application deadline: 12/15. *Faculty research:* Organizational communication, computer-mediated communication and new technology, critical cultural studies, rhetoric and civil discourse, interpersonal communication, language and social interaction.

University of Colorado Boulder, Graduate School, School of Journalism and Mass Communication, Boulder, CO 80309. Offers communication (PhD), including media studies; mass communication research (MA); newsgathering (MA). *Accreditation:* ACEJMC (one or more programs are accredited). Part-time programs available. *Faculty:* 22 full-time (11 women). *Students:* 78 full-time (49 women), 10 part-time (6 women); includes 4 minority (1 Black or African American, non-Hispanic/Latino; 2 Hispanic/Latino; 1 Two or more races, non-Hispanic/Latino), 11 international. Average age 30. 154 applicants, 35 enrolled. In 2010, 35 master's, 6 doctorates awarded. *Degree requirements:* For master's, comprehensive exam, thesis or alternative; for doctorate, comprehensive exam, thesis/dissertation. *Entrance requirements:* For master's, GRE General Test, minimum undergraduate GPA of 2.75; for doctorate, GRE General Test, minimum undergraduate GPA of 3.2, 3.5 graduate. *Application deadline:* For fall admission, 2/15 for domestic students, 12/1 for international students. Applications are processed on a rolling basis. Application fee: $50 ($60 for international students). *Financial support:* In 2010–11, 14 fellowships (averaging $1,807 per year), 21 research assistantships with tuition reimbursements (averaging $11,554 per year) were awarded; institutionally sponsored loans and unspecified assistantships also available. Financial award application deadline: 3/1. *Faculty research:* Writing on science and the environment, mass communication and public opinion, minority representation in the media, media and culture. Total annual research expenditures: $204,190.

University of Colorado Denver, College of Liberal Arts and Sciences, Department of Communication, Denver, CO 80217-3364. Offers academic track (MA); professional track/communication management (MA); technical communication (MS). Part-time and evening/weekend programs available. *Faculty:* 9 full-time (4 women), 3 part-time/adjunct (1 woman). *Students:* 15 full-time (12 women), 7 part-time (5 women); includes 2 Hispanic/Latino, 1 international. Average age 30. 21 applicants, 48% accepted, 5 enrolled. In 2010, 6 master's awarded. *Degree requirements:* For master's, thesis (for some programs), 33 credits. *Entrance requirements:* For master's, GRE General Test. Additional exam requirements/recommendations for international students: Required—TOEFL (minimum score 525 paper-based; 197 computer-based). *Application deadline:* For fall admission, 4/1 for domestic students; for spring admission, 10/1 for domestic students. Application fee: $50 ($75 for international students). Electronic applications accepted. *Expenses:* Tuition, state resident: full-time $7332; part-time $355 per credit hour. Tuition, nonresident: full-time $18,990; part-time $1055 per credit hour. Required fees: $998. Tuition and fees vary according to course level, course load, degree level, campus/location, program, reciprocity agreements and student level. *Financial support:* Fellowships, research assistantships, teaching assistantships, Federal Work-Study and scholarships/grants available. Financial award application deadline: 4/1; financial award applicants required to submit FAFSA. *Faculty research:* Diversity, difference, and intercultural communication; health communication/medical rhetoric; organizational communication; rhetoric and public affairs; social justice and civic engagement. *Unit head:* Dr. Lisa Keranen, Professor, 303-556-5668, E-mail: lisa.keranen@ucdenver.edu. *Application contact:* Michelle Medal, Program Assistant, 303-556-2591, E-mail: michelle.medal@ucdenver.edu.

University of Connecticut, Graduate School, College of Liberal Arts and Sciences, Department of Communication Sciences, Program in Communication Processes, Storrs, CT 06269. Offers MA. *Degree requirements:* For master's, comprehensive exam. *Entrance requirements:* For master's, GRE General Test. Additional exam requirements/recommendations for international students: Required—TOEFL (minimum score 550 paper-based; 213 computer-based). Electronic applications accepted.

University of Dayton, Graduate School, College of Arts and Sciences, Department of Communication, Dayton, OH 45469-1300. Offers MA. Part-time and evening/weekend programs available. *Faculty:* 8 full-time (5 women), 1 part-time/adjunct (0 women). *Students:* 16 full-time (14 women), 2 part-time (both women); includes 1 minority (Black or African American, non-Hispanic/Latino), 2 international. Average age 25. 28 applicants, 64% accepted, 10 enrolled. In 2010, 12 master's awarded. *Degree requirements:* For master's, comprehensive exam, thesis optional. *Entrance requirements:* For master's, GRE General Test, minimum undergraduate GPA of 3.0. Additional exam requirements/recommendations for international students: Required—TOEFL (minimum score 550 paper-based; 213 computer-based; 80 iBT). *Application deadline:* Applications are processed on a rolling basis. Application fee: $0 ($50 for international students). Electronic applications accepted. *Expenses:* Tuition: Full-time $7800; part-time $650 per credit hour. *Financial support:* In 2010–11, 8 teaching assistantships with full tuition reimbursements (averaging $10,048 per year) were awarded; institutionally sponsored loans, health care benefits, and unspecified assistantships also available. Financial award applicants required to submit FAFSA. *Faculty research:* Health communication, organizational communication, mass communication. *Unit head:* Dr. Jon Hess, Chair, 937-229-2028, E-mail: jonathan.hess@notes.udayton.edu. *Application contact:* Alexander Popovski, Associate Director of Graduate and International Admissions, 937-229-2357, Fax: 937-229-4729, E-mail: alex.popovski@notes.udayton.edu.

University of Delaware, College of Arts and Sciences, Department of Communication, Newark, DE 19716. Offers MA. Part-time and evening/weekend programs available. *Degree requirements:* For master's, comprehensive exam (for some programs), thesis (for some programs). *Entrance requirements:* For master's, GRE General Test, minimum GPA of 3.0. Additional exam requirements/recommendations for international students: Required—TOEFL (minimum score 600 paper-based; 270 computer-based). Electronic applications accepted. *Faculty research:* Politics and the media, online social interaction technologies, mass communication law, media and the perceptions of reality, the role of communication in public opinion processes, small group research, communication during resource dilemmas.

University of Dubuque, Program in Communication, Dubuque, IA 52001-5099. Offers information technologies communication (MAC); leadership and management (MAC); strategic and corporate communication (MAC). Part-time and evening/weekend programs available. *Degree requirements:* For master's, thesis optional. *Entrance requirements:* For master's, GRE, minimum GPA of 2.5, 3 recommendations. Additional exam requirements/recommendations for international students: Required—TOEFL (minimum score 550 paper-based; 213 computer-based). Electronic applications accepted. *Faculty research:* Intercultural communication, management communication.

University of Florida, Graduate School, College of Journalism and Communications, Gainesville, FL 32611. Offers advertising (M Adv); journalism (MAMC); mass communication (MAMC, PhD); public relations (MAMC); telecommunication (MAMC); JD/MAMC; JD/PhD. *Accreditation:* ACEJMC (one or more programs are accredited). Part-time programs available. *Faculty:* 36 full-time (17 women), 1 part-time/adjunct (0 women). *Students:* 164 full-time (123 women), 33 part-time (23 women); includes 15 Black or African American, non-Hispanic/Latino; 1 American Indian or Alaska Native, non-Hispanic/Latino; 14 Asian, non-Hispanic/Latino; 10 Hispanic/Latino, 82 international. Average age 29. 458 applicants, 35% accepted, 55 enrolled. In 2010, 63 master's, 12 doctorates awarded. *Degree requirements:* For master's, comprehensive exam (for some programs), thesis; for doctorate, comprehensive exam (for some programs), thesis/dissertation. *Entrance requirements:* For master's and doctorate, GRE General Test: 550 Verbal, 550 Quantitative (1100 total), minimum GPA of 3.0. Additional exam requirements/recommendations for international students: Required—TOEFL (minimum score 550 paper-based; 213 computer-based; 80 iBT), IELTS (minimum score 6). *Application deadline:* For fall admission, 1/15 for domestic and international students; for spring admission, 7/15 for domestic and international students. Applications are processed on a rolling basis. Application fee: $30. Electronic applications accepted. *Expenses:* Tuition, state resident: full-time $10,915.92. Tuition, nonresident: full-time $28,309. *Financial support:* In 2010–11, 69 students received support, including 11 fellowships with full and partial tuition reimbursements available, 11 research assistantships with full tuition reimbursements available (averaging $15,656 per year), 47 teaching assistantships with full tuition reimbursements available (averaging $15,518 per year); career-related internships or fieldwork, Federal Work-Study, institutionally sponsored loans, and unspecified assistantships also available. Support available to part-time students. Financial award application deadline: 3/15; financial award applicants required to submit FAFSA. *Faculty research:* Health communication, international/cross-cultural communication, political communication, ethics, persuasion/message development. Total annual research expenditures: $32,000. *Unit head:* Dr. John W. Wright, Dean, 352-392-0466, Fax: 352-392-1794, E-mail: dtreise@jou.ufl.edu. *Application contact:* Dr. Debbie M. Treise, Associate Dean for Graduate Programs, 352-392-6557.

University of Georgia, Grady School of Journalism and Mass Communication, Athens, GA 30602. Offers journalism and mass communication (MA); mass communication (PhD). *Accreditation:* ACEJMC (one or more programs are accredited). *Faculty:* 37 full-time (14 women). *Students:* 88 full-time (61 women), 24 part-time (16 women); includes 13 Black or African American, non-Hispanic/Latino; 4 Hispanic/Latino, 21 international. 297 applicants, 40% accepted, 48 enrolled. In 2010, 31 master's, 5 doctorates awarded. *Degree requirements:* For master's, comprehensive exam, thesis (MA); for doctorate, comprehensive exam, thesis/dissertation. *Entrance requirements:* For master's and doctorate, GRE General Test. Additional exam requirements/recommendations for international students: Required—TOEFL, TWE (for PhD). *Application deadline:* For spring admission, 2/15 for domestic students. Application fee: $50. Electronic applications accepted. *Expenses:* Tuition, state resident: full-time $7200; part-time $344 per credit hour. Tuition, nonresident: full-time $21,900; part-time $944 per credit hour. Tuition and fees vary according to course load and program. *Financial support:* Research assistantships, teaching assistantships, tuition waivers (full) and unspecified assistantships available. *Unit head:* Dr. E. Culpepper Clark, Dean, 706-542-1704, Fax: 706-542-2183, E-mail: cully@uga.edu. *Application contact:* Dr. Jeffrey K. Springston, Graduate Coordinator, 706-542-5030, Fax: 706-542-2183, E-mail: jspring@grady.uga.edu.

University of Hartford, College of Arts and Sciences, Program in Communication, West Hartford, CT 06117-1599. Offers MA. Part-time and evening/weekend programs available. *Degree requirements:* For master's, comprehensive exam, thesis optional. *Entrance requirements:* For master's, GRE, 3 letters of recommendation. Additional exam requirements/recommendations for international students: Required—TOEFL (minimum score 550 paper-based; 213 computer-based). Electronic applications accepted. *Expenses:* Contact institution. *Faculty research:* Communication reticence, relational communication, media literacy, journalism history, media audience attitude and behavior.

University of Hawaii at Manoa, Graduate Division, College of Social Sciences, School of Communications, Honolulu, HI 96822. Offers communication (MA); telecommunication and information resource management (Graduate Certificate). Part-time programs available. *Faculty:* 17 full-time (3 women), 5 part-time/adjunct (1 woman). *Students:* 13 full-time (9 women), 12 part-time (9 women); includes 14 minority (1 American Indian or Alaska Native, non-Hispanic/Latino; 6 Asian, non-Hispanic/Latino; 1 Hispanic/Latino; 2 Native Hawaiian or other Pacific Islander, non-Hispanic/Latino; 4 Two or more races, non-Hispanic/Latino), 7 international. Average age 32. 64 applicants, 45% accepted, 15 enrolled. In 2010, 4 master's awarded. *Degree requirements:* For master's, thesis optional. *Entrance requirements:* Additional exam requirements/recommendations for international students: Required—TOEFL (minimum score 600 paper-based; 250 computer-based; 100 iBT), IELTS (minimum score 7). *Application deadline:* For fall admission, 2/1 for domestic students, 1/15 for international students. Application fee: $60. *Financial support:* In 2010–11, 11 fellowships (averaging $3,100 per year), 1 teaching assistantship (averaging $14,382 per year) were awarded; career-related internships or fieldwork, institutionally sponsored loans, and tuition waivers (full) also available. Financial award application deadline: 2/1. *Faculty research:* Communication technology policy and development, intercultural communication, organizational communication. *Application contact:* Kevin Kawamoto, Chair, 808-956-8715, Fax: 808-956-5396, E-mail: kevinyk@hawaii.edu.

University of Houston, College of Liberal Arts and Social Sciences, School of Communication, Houston, TX 77204. Offers health communication (MA); mass communication studies (MA); public relations studies (MA); speech communication (MA). Part-time programs available. *Faculty:* 11 full-time (6 women), 2 part-time/adjunct (0 women). *Students:* 47 full-time (39 women), 46 part-time (36 women); includes 15 Black or African American, non-Hispanic/Latino; 2 American Indian or Alaska Native, non-Hispanic/Latino; 3 Asian, non-Hispanic/Latino; 16 Hispanic/Latino, 19 international. Average age 28. 54 applicants, 70% accepted, 24 enrolled. In 2010, 20 master's awarded. *Degree requirements:* For master's, comprehensive exam (for some programs), thesis (for some programs), 30-33 hours. *Entrance requirements:* For master's, GRE. Additional exam requirements/recommendations for international students: Required—TOEFL. *Application deadline:* For fall admission, 6/1 for domestic students, 4/1 for international students; for spring admission, 11/1 for domestic students, 10/1 for international students. Applications are processed on a rolling basis. Application fee: $50 ($100 for international students). Electronic applications accepted. *Expenses:* Tuition, state resident: full-time $8592; part-time $358 per credit hour. Tuition, nonresident: full-time $16,032; part-time $668 per credit hour. Required fees: $2889. Tuition and fees vary according to course load and program. *Financial support:* In 2010–11, 28 teaching assistantships with full tuition reimbursements (averaging $8,111 per year) were awarded; career-related internships or fieldwork, Federal Work-Study, institutionally sponsored loans, scholarships/grants, health care benefits, and unspecified assistantships also available. Support available to part-time students. Financial award application deadline: 2/1. *Unit head:* Dr. Beth Olson, Chairperson, 713-743-2873, Fax: 713-743-2876, E-mail: bolson@uh.edu. *Application contact:* Dr. Martha Haun, Director of Graduate Studies, 713-743-2886, E-mail: mhaun@uh.edu.

University of Illinois at Chicago, Graduate College, College of Liberal Arts and Sciences, Department of Communication, Chicago, IL 60607-7128. Offers MA, PhD. Evening/weekend programs available. *Degree requirements:* For master's, thesis. *Entrance requirements:* For master's, GRE General Test, minimum GPA of 3.0 in last 90 hours. Additional exam requirements/recommendations for international students: Required—TOEFL. Electronic applications accepted. *Faculty research:* Organizational, political, and interpersonal communication; public relations.

University of Illinois at Springfield, Graduate Programs, College of Liberal Arts and Sciences, Program in Communication, Springfield, IL 62703-5407. Offers MA. Part-time and evening/weekend programs available. *Degree requirements:* For master's, comprehensive exam, thesis, or project. *Entrance requirements:* For master's, in-house Graduate Admission Writing Exam, departmental writing proficiency exam, minimum undergraduate GPA of 3.0. Additional exam requirements/recommendations for international students: Required—TOEFL (minimum score 580 paper-based). Electronic applications accepted. *Expenses:* Tuition, state resident: full-time $6774; part-time $282.25 per credit hour. Tuition, nonresident: full-time $15,078; part-time $628.25 per credit hour. Required fees: $15.25 per credit hour. $492 per term.

University of Illinois at Urbana–Champaign, Graduate College, College of Liberal Arts and Sciences, Department of Communication, Champaign, IL 61820. Offers communication (MA). Postbaccalaureate distance learning degree programs offered (no on-campus study). *Faculty:* 21 full-time (10 women), 1 (woman) part-time/adjunct. *Students:* 43 full-time (32 women), 31 part-time (18 women); includes 8 Black or African American, non-Hispanic/Latino; 2 Asian, non-Hispanic/Latino; 2 Hispanic/Latino, 4 international. 252 applicants, 19% accepted, 30 enrolled. In 2010, 8 master's, 5 doctorates awarded. *Entrance requirements:* For master's and doctorate, GRE, minimum GPA of 3.0; writing sample. Additional exam requirements/recommendations for international students: Required—TOEFL (minimum score 611 paper-based; 245 computer-based; 103 iBT). *Application deadline:* Applications are processed on a rolling basis. Application fee: $75 ($90 for international students). Electronic applications accepted. *Financial support:* In 2010–11, 8 fellowships, 15 research assistantships, 50 teaching assistantships were awarded; tuition waivers (full and partial) also available. *Unit head:* Dale E. Brashers, Head, 217-333-2683, Fax: 217-244-1598, E-mail: dbrasher@illinois.edu. *Application contact:* Mary Strum, Office Support Specialist, 217-244-1595, Fax: 217-244-1598, E-mail: strum@illinois.edu.

University of Illinois at Urbana–Champaign, Graduate College, College of Media, Institute of Communications Research, Champaign, IL 61820. Offers communications and media (PhD). *Faculty:* 8 full-time (4 women). *Students:* 38 full-time (21 women), 13 part-time (6 women); includes 5 Black or African American, non-Hispanic/Latino; 4 Asian, non-Hispanic/Latino; 7 Hispanic/Latino, 22 international. 111 applicants, 8% accepted, 6 enrolled. In 2010, 7 doctorates awarded. *Entrance requirements:* For doctorate, GRE General Test, minimum GPA of 3.0. Additional exam requirements/recommendations for international students: Required—TOEFL (minimum score 550 paper-based). *Application deadline:* Applications are processed on a rolling basis. Application fee: $75 ($90 for international students). Electronic applications accepted. *Financial support:* In 2010–11, 7 fellowships, 12 research assistantships, 34 teaching assistantships were awarded; tuition waivers (full and partial) also available. *Faculty research:* Feminist cultural studies, media technology, international communications, Latino studies, economics of media. *Unit head:* Angharad N. Valdivia, Interim Director, 217-244-1422, Fax: 217-244-7695, E-mail: valdivia@illinois.edu. *Application contact:* M. Denise Davis, Office Support Specialist, 217-333-1549, Fax: 217-333-1549, E-mail: mddavis1@illinois.edu.

The University of Iowa, Graduate College, College of Liberal Arts and Sciences, Department of Communication Studies, Iowa City, IA 52242-1316. Offers communication research (MA, PhD); rhetorical studies (MA, PhD). *Degree requirements:* For master's, thesis optional, exam; for doctorate, comprehensive exam, thesis/dissertation. *Entrance requirements:* For master's and doctorate, GRE General Test, minimum GPA of 3.0. Additional exam requirements/recommendations for international students: Required—TOEFL (minimum score 550 paper-based; 213 computer-based; 81 iBT). Electronic applications accepted.

The University of Kansas, Graduate Studies, College of Liberal Arts and Sciences, Department of Communication Studies, Lawrence, KS 66045-7574. Offers MA, PhD. Evening/weekend programs available. *Faculty:* 19 full-time (12 women). *Students:* 58 full-time (28 women), 19 part-time (12 women); includes 4 minority (2 Black or African American, non-Hispanic/Latino; 1 Asian, non-Hispanic/Latino; 1 Hispanic/Latino), 6 international. Average age 32. 79 applicants, 46% accepted, 22 enrolled. In 2010, 12 master's, 8 doctorates awarded. *Degree requirements:* For master's, comprehensive exam (for some programs), thesis or alternative; for doctorate, comprehensive exam, thesis/dissertation. *Entrance requirements:* For master's, GRE General Test, minimum GPA of 3.1; for doctorate, GRE General Test, minimum GPA of 3.2 (undergraduate), 3.6 (graduate). Additional exam requirements/recommendations for international students: Required—TOEFL. *Application deadline:* For fall admission, 1/15 priority date for domestic and international students; for spring admission, 11/15 priority date for domestic and international students. Applications are processed on a rolling basis. Application fee: $55 ($65 for international students). Electronic applications accepted. *Expenses:* Tuition, state resident: full-time $7092; part-time $295.50 per credit hour. Tuition, nonresident: full-time $16,590; part-time $691.25 per credit hour. Required fees: $858; $71.49 per credit hour. Tuition and fees vary according to course load, campus/location and program. *Financial support:* Fellowships with tuition reimbursements, research assistantships, teaching assistantships with full and partial tuition reimbursements, unspecified assistantships available. Financial award application deadline: 1/15. *Faculty research:* Rhetoric, organizational communication, political communication, interpersonal communication, new technology. *Unit head:* Dr. Beth Innocenti, Associate Professor and Chair, 785-864-9018, Fax: 785-864-5203, E-mail: bimanole@ku.edu. *Application contact:* Dr. Robert C. Rowland, Professor and Director of Graduate Studies, 785-864-9868, Fax: 785-864-5203, E-mail: rrowland@ku.edu.

University of Kentucky, Graduate School, College of Communications and Information Studies, Program in Communication, Lexington, KY 40506-0032. Offers MA, PhD. *Degree requirements:* For master's, comprehensive exam, thesis optional; for doctorate, comprehensive exam, thesis/dissertation. *Entrance requirements:* For master's, GRE General Test, minimum undergraduate GPA of 2.75; for doctorate, GRE General Test, minimum graduate GPA of 3.0, undergraduate 2.75. Additional exam requirements/recommendations for international students: Required—TOEFL (minimum score 550 paper-based; 213 computer-based). Electronic applications accepted. *Faculty research:* Public service campaigns, health communication, mass media law and public policy, political communication, international and intercultural communication.

University of Louisiana at Lafayette, College of Liberal Arts, Department of Communication, Lafayette, LA 70504. Offers mass communications (MS). Part-time programs available. *Degree requirements:* For master's, thesis optional. *Entrance requirements:* For master's, GRE General Test, minimum GPA of 2.75. Additional exam requirements/recommendations for international students: Required—TOEFL (minimum score 550 paper-based; 213 computer-based). Electronic applications accepted. *Faculty research:* Mass media problems, issues and ethics, mass communication, historical studies, conflict of interest and law and ethics in journalism, contemporary issues and trends in publications.

University of Louisiana at Monroe, Graduate School, College of Arts and Sciences, Department of Communication, Monroe, LA 71209-0001. Offers MA. *Faculty:* 9 full-time (5 women). *Students:* 11 full-time (6 women), 1 (woman) part-time; includes 1 Black or African American, non-Hispanic/Latino, 1 international. Average age 25. In 2010, 7 master's awarded. *Degree requirements:* For master's, thesis. *Entrance requirements:* For master's, GRE (minimum verbal and quantitative score: 900), minimum GPA of 2.5. Additional exam requirements/recommendations for international students: Required—TOEFL (minimum score 500 paper-based; 173 computer-based; 61 iBT). *Application deadline:* For fall admission, 8/24 priority date for domestic students, 7/1 for international students; for winter admission, 12/14 priority date for domestic students; for spring admission, 1/19 priority date for domestic students, 11/1 for international students. Applications are processed on a rolling basis. Application fee: $20 ($30 for international students). Electronic applications accepted. *Expenses:* Tuition, state resident: full-time $2991; part-time $197 per credit hour. Tuition, nonresident: full-time $2991; part-time $197 per credit hour. International tuition: $10,288 full-time. *Financial support:* In 2010–11, 2 research assistantships (averaging $2,500 per year), 1 teaching assistantship with full and partial tuition reimbursement (averaging $2,500 per year) were awarded; career-related internships or fieldwork, Federal Work-Study, and unspecified assistantships also available. Financial award application deadline: 4/1; financial award applicants required to submit FAFSA. *Faculty research:* Interactive media, rhetoric progress, interpersonal, journalism history, gender/multicultural issues, forensics. *Unit head:* Dr. Carl L. Thameling, Interim Head, 318-342-1406, Fax: 318-342-1422, E-mail: thameling@ulm.edu. *Application contact:* Dr. Lesli K. Pace, Graduate Coordinator, 318-342-1165, Fax: 318-342-1422, E-mail: pace@ulm.edu.

University of Louisville, Graduate School, College of Arts and Sciences, Department of Communication, Louisville, KY 40292-0001. Offers MA. Part-time and evening/weekend programs available. Postbaccalaureate distance learning degree programs offered (no on-campus study). *Faculty:* 17 full-time (9 women). *Students:* 10 full-time (8 women), 17 part-time (13 women); includes 6 Black or African American, non-Hispanic/Latino. Average age 29. 25 applicants, 64% accepted, 9 enrolled. In 2010, 7 master's awarded. *Degree requirements:* For master's, comprehensive exam (for some programs), thesis or alternative. *Entrance requirements:* For master's, GRE. Additional exam requirements/recommendations for international students: Required—TOEFL (minimum score 550 paper-based; 213 computer-based). *Application deadline:* For fall admission, 7/1 for domestic students; for spring admission, 11/1 for domestic students. Applications are processed on a rolling basis. Application fee: $50. Electronic applications accepted. *Expenses:* Tuition, state resident: full-time $9144; part-time $508 per credit hour. Tuition, nonresident: full-time $19,026; part-time $1057 per credit hour. Tuition and fees vary according to program and reciprocity agreements. *Financial support:* In 2010–11, 1 research assistantship with full tuition reimbursement (averaging $11,000 per year), 2 teaching assistantships with full and partial tuition reimbursements (averaging $11,000 per year) were awarded; scholarships/grants, tuition waivers (partial), and unspecified assistantships also available. Support available to part-time students. Financial award applicants required to submit FAFSA. *Faculty research:* Health communication, interpersonal communication, computer-mediated communication, strategic communication, mass communication. *Unit head:* Dr. J. Blaine Hudson, Dean, 502-852-2234, Fax: 502-852-6888, E-mail: jbhuds01@louisville.edu. *Application contact:* Libby Leggett, Director, Graduate Admissions, 502-852-3101, Fax: 502-852-6536, E-mail: gradadm@louisville.edu.

University of Maine, Graduate School, College of Liberal Arts and Sciences, Department of Communication and Journalism, Orono, ME 04469. Offers communication (MA); mass communication (MA). Part-time programs available. *Faculty:* 8 full-time (3 women), 3 part-time/adjunct (1 woman). *Students:* 15 full-time (11 women), 2 part-time (0 women); includes 2 minority (both American Indian or Alaska Native, non-Hispanic/Latino), 1 international. Average age 29. 15 applicants, 60% accepted, 7 enrolled. In 2010, 10 master's awarded. *Degree requirements:* For master's, thesis or alternative. *Entrance requirements:* For master's, GRE General Test. Additional exam requirements/recommendations for international students: Required—TOEFL. *Application deadline:* For fall admission, 2/1 priority date for domestic students. Applications are processed on a rolling basis. Application fee: $65. Electronic applications accepted. *Expenses:* Tuition, state resident: full-time $400. Tuition, nonresident: full-time $1050. *Financial support:* In 2010–11, 15 teaching assistantships with tuition reimbursements (averaging $12,790 per year) were awarded; career-related internships or fieldwork, Federal Work-Study, institutionally sponsored loans, and tuition waivers (full and partial) also available. Support available to part-time students. Financial award application deadline: 3/1. *Faculty research:* Rhetorical theory, semiotics, discourse analysis, gender and communication, children's talk/communication disorders. *Unit head:* Dr. Paul Grosswiler, Chair, 207-581-1287, Fax: 207-581-1286. *Application contact:* Scott G. Delcourt, Associate Dean of the Graduate School, 207-581-3291, Fax: 207-581-3232, E-mail: graduate@maine.edu.

University of Maine, Graduate School, Interdisciplinary Doctoral Program, Orono, ME 04469. Offers communication (PhD); functional genomics (PhD); mass communication (PhD); ocean engineering (PhD). Part-time and evening/weekend programs available. *Students:* 22 full-time (13 women), 25 part-time (14 women); includes 2 minority (1 Black or African American, non-Hispanic/Latino; 1 Asian, non-Hispanic/Latino), 4 international. Average age 37. 17 applicants, 41% accepted, 7 enrolled. In 2010, 10 doctorates awarded. *Degree requirements:* For doctorate, comprehensive exam, thesis/dissertation. *Entrance requirements:* For doctorate, GRE General Test. Additional exam requirements/recommendations for international students: Required—TOEFL. *Application deadline:* For fall admission, 4/1 for domestic students; for spring admission, 11/1 for domestic students. Applications are processed on a rolling basis. Application fee: $65. Electronic applications accepted. *Expenses:* Tuition, state resident: full-time $400. Tuition, nonresident: full-time $1050. *Unit head:* Scott G. Delcourt, Associate Dean of the Graduate School, 207-581-3291, Fax: 207-581-3232, E-mail: graduate@maine.edu. *Application contact:* Scott G. Delcourt, Associate Dean of the Graduate School, 207-581-3291, Fax: 207-581-3232, E-mail: graduate@maine.edu.

University of Maryland, Baltimore County, Graduate School, College of Arts, Humanities and Social Sciences, Department of Modern Languages and Linguistics, Program in Intercultural Communication, Baltimore, MD 21250. Offers MA. Part-time and evening/weekend programs available. *Faculty:* 18 full-time (6 women), 3 part-time/adjunct (2 women). *Students:* 17 full-time (13 women), 12 part-time (10 women); includes 1 minority (Hispanic/Latino), 11 international. 24 applicants, 83% accepted, 15 enrolled. In 2010, 13 master's awarded. *Degree requirements:* For master's, one foreign language, comprehensive exam (for some programs), thesis (for some programs). *Entrance requirements:* For master's, GRE General Test, minimum GPA of 3.0, 3 letters of recommendation, self-evaluation and statement of support, resume. Additional exam requirements/recommendations for international students: Required—TOEFL (minimum score 550 paper-based; 213 computer-based; 80 iBT). *Application deadline:* For fall admission,

Communication—General

University of Maryland, Baltimore County *(continued)*
1/31 for domestic and international students. Application fee: $50. Electronic applications accepted. *Financial support:* In 2010–11, 8 students received support, including 5 teaching assistantships with full tuition reimbursements available (averaging $11,324 per year); tuition waivers also available. Financial award applicants required to submit FAFSA. *Faculty research:* Comparative television research-cross-cultural; cultural studies; social developments in Latin America; intercultural communication; French civilization and cultural studies; language, gender and sexuality; sociolinguistics; African linguistics; immigrants in U. S. and Latin American societies. *Unit head:* Dr. Denis Provencher, Director, 410-455-2109 Ext. 2636, Fax: 410-455-2636, E-mail: provench@umbc.edu. *Application contact:* Dr. Denis Provencher, Director, 410-455-2109 Ext. 2636, Fax: 410-455-2636, E-mail: provench@umbc.edu.

University of Maryland, College Park, Academic Affairs, College of Arts and Humanities, Department of Communication, College Park, MD 20742. Offers MA, PhD. *Faculty:* 25 full-time (15 women), 7 part-time/adjunct (4 women). *Students:* 61 full-time (45 women), 2 part-time (both women); includes 1 Black or African American, non-Hispanic/Latino; 5 Asian, non-Hispanic/Latino, 13 international. 232 applicants, 3% accepted, 7 enrolled. In 2010, 7 master's, 8 doctorates awarded. *Degree requirements:* For master's, thesis optional; for doctorate, comprehensive exam, thesis/dissertation. *Entrance requirements:* For master's, GRE General Test, minimum GPA of 3.0, sample of scholarly writing, 3 letters of recommendation; for doctorate, GRE General Test. Additional exam requirements/recommendations for international students: Required—TOEFL. *Application deadline:* For fall admission, 2/1 for domestic and international students. Applications are processed on a rolling basis. Application fee: $75. Electronic applications accepted. *Expenses:* Tuition, state resident: part-time $471 per credit hour. Tuition, nonresident: part-time $1016 per credit hour. Required fees: $337 per term. *Financial support:* In 2010–11, 3 fellowships with partial tuition reimbursements (averaging $8,000 per year), 46 teaching assistantships with tuition reimbursements (averaging $16,047 per year) were awarded; Federal Work-Study, scholarships/grants, and unspecified assistantships also available. Support available to part-time students. Financial award applicants required to submit FAFSA. *Faculty research:* Health communication, interpersonal communication, persuasion, intercultural communication, contemporary rhetoric theory. Total annual research expenditures: $30,560. *Unit head:* Dr. Elizabeth L. Toth, Chair, 301-405-0870, Fax: 301-314-9471, E-mail: eltoth@umd.edu. *Application contact:* Dean of Graduate School, 301-405-0376, Fax: 301-314-9305.

University of Massachusetts Amherst, Graduate School, College of Social and Behavioral Sciences, Department of Communication, Amherst, MA 01003. Offers MA, PhD. Part-time programs available. *Faculty:* 21 full-time (10 women). *Students:* 64 full-time (41 women), 14 part-time (7 women); includes 10 minority (2 Black or African American, non-Hispanic/Latino; 3 Asian, non-Hispanic/Latino; 4 Hispanic/Latino; 1 Two or more races, non-Hispanic/Latino), 34 international. Average age 35. 160 applicants, 14% accepted, 10 enrolled. In 2010, 3 master's, 2 doctorates awarded. Terminal master's awarded for partial completion of doctoral program. *Degree requirements:* For master's, thesis or alternative; for doctorate, comprehensive exam, thesis/dissertation. *Entrance requirements:* For master's and doctorate, GRE General Test, 3 letters of recommendation. Additional exam requirements/recommendations for international students: Required—TOEFL (minimum score 550 paper-based; 213 computer-based; 80 iBT), IELTS (minimum score 6.5). *Application deadline:* For fall admission, 1/2 for domestic and international students. Applications are processed on a rolling basis. Application fee: $50 ($65 for international students). Electronic applications accepted. *Expenses:* Tuition, state resident: full-time $2640. Required fees: $8282. One-time fee: $357 full-time. *Financial support:* In 2010–11, 17 research assistantships with full tuition reimbursements (averaging $5,224 per year), 51 teaching assistantships with full tuition reimbursements (averaging $4,297 per year) were awarded; fellowships, career-related internships or fieldwork, Federal Work-Study, scholarships/grants, traineeships, health care benefits, tuition waivers (full), and unspecified assistantships also available. Support available to part-time students. Financial award application deadline: 1/2; financial award applicants required to submit FAFSA. *Unit head:* Dr. Sut Jhally, Graduate Program Director, 413-545-2795, Fax: 413-545-6399. *Application contact:* Jean M. Ames, Supervisor of Admissions, 413-545-0722, Fax: 413-577-0010, E-mail: gradadm@grad.umass.edu.

University of Memphis, Graduate School, College of Communication and Fine Arts, Department of Communication, Memphis, TN 38152. Offers communication (MA); communication arts (PhD); film and video production (MA). Part-time programs available. *Faculty:* 12 full-time (6 women). *Students:* 51 full-time (38 women), 49 part-time (30 women); includes 27 minority (21 Black or African American, non-Hispanic/Latino; 1 American Indian or Alaska Native, non-Hispanic/Latino; 1 Asian, non-Hispanic/Latino; 3 Hispanic/Latino; 1 Two or more races, non-Hispanic/Latino), 2 international. Average age 35. 98 applicants, 48% accepted, 16 enrolled. In 2010, 6 master's, 4 doctorates awarded. *Degree requirements:* For master's, comprehensive exam, thesis or alternative; for doctorate, comprehensive exam, thesis/dissertation. *Entrance requirements:* For master's and doctorate, GRE General Test. Additional exam requirements/recommendations for international students: Required—TOEFL (minimum score 600 paper-based; 250 computer-based). *Application deadline:* For fall admission, 2/1 for domestic and international students. Application fee: $35 ($60 for international students). *Financial support:* In 2010–11, 27 students received support; research assistantships with full tuition reimbursements available, teaching assistantships with full tuition reimbursements available, Federal Work-Study, scholarships/grants, and unspecified assistantships available. Financial award application deadline: 2/15; financial award applicants required to submit FAFSA. *Faculty research:* Rhetoric, media studies, applied communication (health communication). *Unit head:* Dr. Sandra Sarkela, Chair, 901-678-3173, Fax: 901-678-4331, E-mail: ssarkela@memphis.edu. *Application contact:* Dr. Amanda Young, Coordinator of Graduate Studies, 901-678-3612, Fax: 901-678-4331, E-mail: ajyoung@memphis.edu.

University of Miami, Graduate School, School of Communication, Coral Gables, FL 33124. Offers communication (PhD); communication studies (MA); film studies (MA, PhD); motion pictures (MFA), including production, producing, and screenwriting; print journalism (MA); public relations (MA); Spanish language journalism (MA); television broadcast journalism (MA). Accreditation: ACEJMC. Part-time programs available. *Degree requirements:* For master's, comprehensive exam (for some programs), thesis (for some programs); for doctorate, comprehensive exam, thesis/dissertation. *Entrance requirements:* For master's, GRE General Test; for doctorate, GRE General Test, master's thesis or scholarly research. Additional exam requirements/recommendations for international students: Required—TOEFL (minimum score 600 paper-based; 250 computer-based; 100 iBT). Electronic applications accepted. *Faculty research:* Communication studies, mass communication, international/interpersonal communication, film studies, journalism.

University of Michigan, Horace H. Rackham School of Graduate Studies, College of Literature, Science, and the Arts, Department of Communication Studies, Ann Arbor, MI 48104-2523. Offers PhD. *Faculty:* 16 full-time (7 women). *Students:* 36 full-time (27 women); includes 6 minority (3 Black or African American, non-Hispanic/Latino; 2 Asian, non-Hispanic/Latino; 1 Hispanic/Latino), 10 international. Average age 29. 117 applicants, 8% accepted, 7 enrolled. In 2010, 1 doctorate awarded. *Degree requirements:* For doctorate, comprehensive exam, thesis/dissertation, first-year research project, 2 terms in student instructor position. *Entrance requirements:* For doctorate, GRE, U.S. bachelor's degree or its equivalent from accredited institution. Additional exam requirements/recommendations for international students: Required—TOEFL (minimum score 600 paper-based; 102 iBT). *Application deadline:* For fall admission, 12/1 for domestic and international students. Application fee: $65 ($75 for international students). Electronic applications accepted. *Expenses:* Tuition, state resident: full-time $17,784; part-time $1116 per credit hour. Tuition, nonresident: full-time $35,944; part-time $2125 per credit hour. International tuition: $35,994 full-time. Required fees: $95 per semester. Tuition and fees vary according to course load, degree level and program. *Financial support:* In 2010–11, 36 students received support, including 26 fellowships with full tuition reimbursements available (averaging $17,475 per year), research assistantships with full tuition reimbursements available (averaging $17,270 per year), 37 teaching assistantships with full tuition reimbursements available (averaging $17,270 per year); scholarships/grants, health care benefits, tuition waivers (full), and unspecified assistantships also available. Financial award application deadline: 4/30; financial award applicants required to submit FAFSA. *Faculty research:* Political communication; media, culture and society; media effects; race, gender, and the media; new media, media law and policy. *Unit head:* Prof. Susan J. Douglas, Professor and Chair, 734-764-0420, Fax: 734-764-3288, E-mail: sdoug@umich.edu. *Application contact:* Amy B. Eaton, Graduate Program Coordinator, 734-615-8974, Fax: 734-764-3288, E-mail: lsacommphd@umich.edu.

University of Minnesota, Twin Cities Campus, Graduate School, College of Design, Department of Design, Housing, and Apparel, Minneapolis, MN 55455-0213. Offers apparel (MA, MS, PhD); design communication (MA, MS, PhD); housing studies (MA, MS, PhD, Postbaccalaureate Certificate); interactive design (MFA); interior design (MA, MS, PhD). Part-time programs available. *Degree requirements:* For master's and Postbaccalaureate Certificate, comprehensive exam, thesis (for some programs); for doctorate, comprehensive exam, thesis/dissertation. *Entrance requirements:* For master's, GRE General Test, minimum GPA of 3.0 (preferred), portfolio, 3 letters of recommendation; for doctorate, GRE General Test, minimum GPA of 3.0 (preferred), portfolio, 3 letters of recommendation, writing sample; for Postbaccalaureate Certificate, GRE General Test, minimum GPA of 3.0 (preferred). Additional exam requirements/recommendations for international students: Required—TOEFL (minimum score 550 paper-based; 213 computer-based; 79 iBT). Electronic applications accepted. *Faculty research:* Housing policy and community development; consumer behavior; interactive design; design history; social, cultural, and behavioral issues related to designed environments.

University of Minnesota, Twin Cities Campus, Graduate School, College of Liberal Arts, Department of Communication Studies, Minneapolis, MN 55455-0213. Offers MA, PhD. *Degree requirements:* For master's, thesis or alternative; for doctorate, thesis/dissertation. *Entrance requirements:* For master's, GRE General Test, minimum GPA of 3.0; for doctorate, GRE General Test, minimum graduate GPA of 3.5. Additional exam requirements/recommendations for international students: Required—TOEFL. Electronic applications accepted. *Faculty research:* Rhetorical studies, communication theory, media studies, gender and communication, public address.

University of Missouri, Graduate School, College of Arts and Sciences, Department of Communication, Columbia, MO 65211. Offers MA, PhD. *Faculty:* 12 full-time (6 women), 1 (woman) part-time/adjunct. *Students:* 31 full-time (24 women), 10 part-time (5 women); includes 5 minority (3 Black or African American, non-Hispanic/Latino; 1 Asian, non-Hispanic/Latino; 1 Hispanic/Latino), 6 international. Average age 31. 93 applicants, 9% accepted, 6 enrolled. In 2010, 1 master's, 7 doctorates awarded. Terminal master's awarded for partial completion of doctoral program. *Degree requirements:* For doctorate, comprehensive exam, thesis/dissertation. *Entrance requirements:* For master's and doctorate, GRE General Test (minimum score 500 verbal, 500 quantitative, 4.0 analytical preferred), minimum GPA of 3.0. Additional exam requirements/recommendations for international students: Required—TOEFL (minimum score 600 paper-based; 250 computer-based; 100 iBT). *Application deadline:* For fall admission, 2/15 priority date for domestic students. Applications are processed on a rolling basis. Application fee: $45 ($60 for international students). Electronic applications accepted. *Financial support:* In 2010–11, 2 fellowships with full tuition reimbursements, 29 teaching assistantships with full tuition reimbursements were awarded; research assistantships with full tuition reimbursements, institutionally sponsored loans, health care benefits, and unspecified assistantships also available. *Unit head:* Dr. Michael Porter, Department Chair, 573-882-0525, E-mail: portermj@missouri.edu. *Application contact:* Martha Crump, Administrative Assistant, 573-882-4432, E-mail: crumpm@missouri.edu.

University of Missouri–St. Louis, College of Fine Arts and Communication, Department of Communication, St. Louis, MO 63121. Offers MA. Part-time and evening/weekend programs available. *Faculty:* 7 full-time (6 women). *Students:* 7 full-time (all women), 19 part-time (10 women); includes 7 minority (6 Black or African American, non-Hispanic/Latino; 1 Hispanic/Latino), 1 international. Average age 29. 26 applicants, 62% accepted, 9 enrolled. In 2010, 10 master's awarded. *Degree requirements:* For master's, thesis optional. *Entrance requirements:* For master's, 3 letters of recommendation, minimum GPA of 3.25. Additional exam requirements/recommendations for international students: Required—TOEFL (minimum score 600 paper-based; 233 computer-based). *Application deadline:* For fall admission, 7/1 for domestic and international students; for spring admission, 12/1 for domestic and international students. Application fee: $35 ($40 for international students). Electronic applications accepted. *Expenses:* Tuition, state resident: full-time $5522; part-time $306.80 per credit hour. Tuition, nonresident: full-time $14,253; part-time $792.10 per credit hour. Required fees: $658; $49 per credit hour. One-time fee: $12. Tuition and fees vary according to program. *Financial support:* In 2010–11, 6 teaching assistantships (averaging $12,000 per year) were awarded. Financial award application deadline: 4/1; financial award applicants required to submit FAFSA. *Faculty research:* Theory and methodology: intercultural, interpersonal, and mass organizational. *Unit head:* Dr. Alice Hall, Director of Graduate Studies, 314-516-5485, Fax: 314-516-5816, E-mail: halla@umsl.edu. *Application contact:* 314-516-5458, Fax: 314-516-6996, E-mail: gradadm@umsl.edu.

The University of Montana, Graduate School, College of Arts and Sciences, Department of Communication Studies, Missoula, MT 59812-0002. Offers MA. *Degree requirements:* For master's, thesis (for some programs). *Entrance requirements:* For master's, GRE General Test. Additional exam requirements/recommendations for international students: Required—TOEFL (minimum score 525 paper-based; 197 computer-based). *Faculty research:* Conflict management, organizational communication, language, personal relationships, rhetoric.

University of Nebraska at Omaha, Graduate Studies, College of Communication, Fine Arts and Media, School of Communication, Omaha, NE 68182. Offers MA. Part-time and evening/weekend programs available. *Faculty:* 19 full-time (10 women). *Students:* 5 full-time (3 women), 52 part-time (38 women); includes 9 minority (6 Black or African American, non-Hispanic/Latino; 3 Asian, non-Hispanic/Latino), 1 international. Average age 33. 220 applicants, 8% accepted, 16 enrolled. In 2010, 10 master's awarded. *Degree requirements:* For master's, comprehensive exam, thesis (for some programs). *Entrance requirements:* For master's, minimum GPA of 3.25, 15 undergraduate communication courses. Additional exam requirements/recommendations for international students: Required—TOEFL (minimum score 550 paper-based; 213 computer-based; 80 iBT). *Application deadline:* For fall admission, 6/1 priority date for domestic students; for spring admission, 11/1 priority date for domestic students. Applications are processed on a rolling basis. Application fee: $45. Electronic applications accepted. *Financial support:* In 2010–11, 29 students received support; fellowships, research assistantships with tuition reimbursements available, teaching assistantships with tuition reimbursements available, Federal Work-Study, institutionally sponsored loans, scholarships/grants, tuition waivers (partial), and unspecified assistantships available. Support available to part-time students. Financial award application deadline: 3/1; financial award applicants required to submit FAFSA. *Unit head:* Dr. Jeremy Lipschultz, Director, 402-554-2600. *Application contact:* Dr. Barbara Pickering, Student Contact, 402-554-2600.

University of Nebraska–Lincoln, Graduate College, College of Arts and Sciences, Department of Communication Studies, Lincoln, NE 68588. Offers instructional communication (MA, PhD); interpersonal communication (MA, PhD); marketing, communication studies, and advertising (MA, PhD); organizational communication (MA, PhD); rhetoric and culture (MA, PhD). *Degree requirements:* For master's, thesis optional; for doctorate, comprehensive exam, thesis/dissertation. *Entrance requirements:* For master's and doctorate, GRE General Test, writing sample. Additional exam requirements/recommendations for international students: Required—TOEFL (minimum score 600 paper-based; 250 computer-based). Electronic applications accepted. *Faculty research:* Message strategies, gender communication, political communication, organizational communication, instructional communication.

University of Nevada, Las Vegas, Graduate College, Greenspun College of Urban Affairs, Department of Communication Studies, Las Vegas, NV 89154-4052. Offers MA. Part-time

---

programs available. *Faculty:* 9 full-time (4 women). *Students:* 12 full-time (8 women), 5 part-time (4 women); includes 7 minority (1 Black or African American, non-Hispanic/Latino; 2 Hispanic/Latino; 4 Two or more races, non-Hispanic/Latino). Average age 26. 21 applicants, 81% accepted, 9 enrolled. In 2010, 7 master's awarded. *Degree requirements:* For master's, comprehensive exam (for some programs), thesis (for some programs). *Entrance requirements:* For master's, GRE General Test. Additional exam requirements/recommendations for international students: Required—TOEFL (minimum score 550 paper-based; 213 computer-based; 80 iBT), IELTS (minimum score 7). *Application deadline:* For fall admission, 1/15 priority date for domestic and international students. Applications are processed on a rolling basis. Application fee: $60 ($95 for international students). Electronic applications accepted. *Expenses:* Tuition, area resident: Part-time $239.50 per credit. Tuition, state resident: part-time $239.50 per credit. Tuition, nonresident: part-time $503 per credit. Required fees: $108 per semester. Tuition and fees vary according to course load, program and reciprocity agreements. *Financial support:* In 2010–11, 12 students received support, including 12 teaching assistantships with partial tuition reimbursements available (averaging $10,000 per year); institutionally sponsored loans, scholarships/grants, health care benefits, and unspecified assistantships also available. Financial award application deadline: 3/1. *Faculty research:* Rhetoric and persuasion, interpersonal communication, family and political communication, sex and gender, popular culture. Total annual research expenditures: $25,477. *Unit head:* Dr. Tom Burkholder, Chair/Associate Professor, 702-895-5125, Fax: 702-895-4805, E-mail: tom.burkholder@unlv.edu. *Application contact:* Graduate College Admissions Evaluator, 702-895-3320, Fax: 702-895-4180, E-mail: gradcollege@unlv.edu.

University of New Mexico, Graduate School, College of Arts and Sciences, Department of Communication and Journalism, Albuquerque, NM 87131-2039. Offers communication (MA, PhD). Part-time programs available. *Faculty:* 29 full-time (21 women), 55 part-time/adjunct (41 women). *Students:* 47 full-time (39 women), 16 part-time (13 women); includes 1 American Indian or Alaska Native, non-Hispanic/Latino; 1 Asian, non-Hispanic/Latino; 10 Hispanic/Latino; 2 Two or more races, non-Hispanic/Latino, 17 international. Average age 32. 82 applicants, 22% accepted, 16 enrolled. In 2010, 4 master's, 8 doctorates awarded. *Degree requirements:* For master's, 30 hours of class work and 6-hour thesis or project, or 36 hours of class work and comprehensive exam; for doctorate, 2 foreign languages, comprehensive exam, thesis/dissertation. *Entrance requirements:* For master's, GRE General Test, letters of recommendation, letter of intent, curriculum vitae, transcripts; for doctorate, GRE General Test, letters of recommendation, writing sample, letter of intent, curriculum vitae, transcripts. Additional exam requirements/recommendations for international students: Required—TOEFL (minimum score 550 paper-based; 213 computer-based). *Application deadline:* For fall admission, 1/15 for domestic students. Application fee: $50. Electronic applications accepted. *Expenses:* Tuition, state resident: full-time $5991; part-time $251 per credit hour. Tuition, nonresident: full-time $14,405; part-time $800.20 per credit hour. Tuition and fees vary according to course level, course load, program and reciprocity agreements. *Financial support:* In 2010–11, 46 students received support, including 2 fellowships with tuition reimbursements available (averaging $13,800 per year), 2 research assistantships (averaging $9,439 per year), 47 teaching assistantships with tuition reimbursements available (averaging $10,639 per year); career-related internships or fieldwork, scholarships/grants, health care benefits, and unspecified assistantships also available. Financial award application deadline: 3/1; financial award applicants required to submit FAFSA. *Faculty research:* Health communication, intercultural communication, interpersonal/organizational communication, mass communication. *Unit head:* Dr. Glenda Balas, Chair, 505-277-5305, Fax: 505-277-4206, E-mail: gbalas@unm.edu. *Application contact:* Gregoria Arienda Cavazos, Program Advisement Coordinator, 505-277-5305, Fax: 505-277-2068, E-mail: cjadvise@unm.edu.

The University of North Carolina at Chapel Hill, Graduate School, College of Arts and Sciences, Department of Communication Studies, Chapel Hill, NC 27599. Offers PhD. *Faculty:* 27 full-time (12 women), 2 part-time/adjunct (0 women). *Students:* 54 full-time (29 women), 1 (woman) part-time; includes 40 Black or African American, non-Hispanic/Latino; 1 Asian, non-Hispanic/Latino; 1 Hispanic/Latino, 3 international. Average age 33. 161 applicants, 14% accepted, 12 enrolled. In 2010, 5 doctorates awarded. *Degree requirements:* For doctorate, comprehensive exam, thesis/dissertation. *Entrance requirements:* For doctorate, GRE General Test, minimum GPA of 3.0. Additional exam requirements/recommendations for international students: Required—TOEFL (minimum score 550 paper-based; 79 iBT). *Application deadline:* For fall admission, 1/1 priority date for domestic students, 1/1 for international students. Applications are processed on a rolling basis. Application fee: $77. Electronic applications accepted. *Financial support:* In 2010–11, 9 fellowships with full tuition reimbursements (averaging $22,000 per year), 26 teaching assistantships with full tuition reimbursements (averaging $14,700 per year) were awarded; unspecified assistantships also available. Financial award application deadline: 1/1. *Unit head:* Dr. Dennis Keith Mumby, Chair, 919-843-3613, E-mail: mumby@email.unc.edu. *Application contact:* Vilma Berg, Student Services Manager, 919-962-4984, Fax: 919-962-3305, E-mail: vberg@email.unc.edu.

The University of North Carolina at Charlotte, Graduate School, College of Arts and Sciences, Department of Communication Studies, Charlotte, NC 28223-0001. Offers health communication (MA); media/rhetorical critical studies (MA); organizational communication (MA); public relations (MA). Part-time and evening/weekend programs available. *Faculty:* 12 full-time (5 women), 1 (woman) part-time/adjunct. *Students:* 6 full-time (5 women), 19 part-time (17 women); includes 7 minority (6 Black or African American, non-Hispanic/Latino; 1 Asian, non-Hispanic/Latino). Average age 27. 554 applicants, 4% accepted, 12 enrolled. In 2010, 12 master's awarded. Terminal master's awarded for partial completion of doctoral program. *Degree requirements:* For master's, project, thesis, or comprehensive exam. *Entrance requirements:* For master's, GRE General Test, minimum GPA of 2.75 overall. Additional exam requirements/recommendations for international students: Required—TOEFL (minimum score 557 paper-based; 220 computer-based; 83 iBT). *Application deadline:* For fall admission, 3/15 for domestic students, 5/1 for international students; for spring admission, 11/15 for domestic students, 10/1 for international students. Applications are processed on a rolling basis. Application fee: $55. Electronic applications accepted. *Expenses:* Tuition, state resident: full-time $3464. Tuition, nonresident: full-time $14,297. Required fees: $2094. Tuition and fees vary according to course load. *Financial support:* In 2010–11, 9 students received support, including 1 research assistantship (averaging $18,000 per year), 8 teaching assistantships (averaging $15,529 per year); career-related internships or fieldwork, institutionally sponsored loans, scholarships/grants, and unspecified assistantships also available. Support available to part-time students. Financial award application deadline: 4/1; financial award applicants required to submit FAFSA. *Faculty research:* Health literacy, systems of care and mental illness, the communication of emotions in gendered workplaces, international constructs of public relations managerial responsibilities, sports culture and the construction of social contracts, African-American oratory. Total annual research expenditures: $25,636. *Unit head:* Dr. Richard W. Leeman, Chair, 704-687-2086, Fax: 704-687-6900, E-mail: rwleeman@uncc.edu. *Application contact:* Kathy B. Giddings, Director of Graduate Admissions, 704-687-5503, Fax: 704-687-3279, E-mail: gradadm@uncc.edu.

The University of North Carolina at Greensboro, Graduate School, College of Arts and Sciences, Department of Communication, Greensboro, NC 27412-5001. Offers communication studies (MA). Part-time programs available. *Degree requirements:* For master's, thesis or alternative. *Entrance requirements:* For master's, GRE General Test, MAT, or PRAXIS. Additional exam requirements/recommendations for international students: Required—TOEFL. Electronic applications accepted.

University of North Dakota, Graduate School, College of Arts and Sciences, School of Communication, Grand Forks, ND 58202. Offers communication (MA); communication and public discourse (PhD). Part-time programs available. *Faculty:* 6 full-time (1 woman). *Students:* 10 full-time (5 women), 8 part-time (3 women); includes 1 minority (Hispanic/Latino), 1 international. Average age 32. 5 applicants, 0% accepted, 0 enrolled. In 2010, 3 master's, 5 doctorates awarded. *Degree requirements:* For master's, comprehensive exam, thesis or alternative; for doctorate, thesis/dissertation. *Entrance requirements:* For master's and doctorate, GRE General Test, minimum GPA of 3.0. Additional exam requirements/recommendations for international students: Required—TOEFL (minimum score 550 paper-based; 213 computer-based; 79 iBT), IELTS (minimum score 6.5). *Application deadline:* For fall admission, 3/15 for domestic and international students. Application fee: $35. Electronic applications accepted. *Expenses:* Tuition, state resident: full-time $5857; part-time $306.74 per credit. Tuition, nonresident: full-time $15,666; part-time $729.77 per credit. Required fees: $53.42 per credit. Tuition and fees vary according to course load, program and reciprocity agreements. *Financial support:* In 2010–11, 10 students received support, including 10 teaching assistantships with full and partial tuition reimbursements available (averaging $8,333 per year); fellowships with full and partial tuition reimbursements available, research assistantships with full and partial tuition reimbursements available, Federal Work-Study, institutionally sponsored loans, scholarships/grants, health care benefits, tuition waivers (full and partial), and unspecified assistantships also available. Support available to part-time students. Financial award application deadline: 3/15; financial award applicants required to submit FAFSA. *Faculty research:* Communication technologies, mass communication in diverse society, acculturation and socialization functions. Total annual research expenditures: $29,599. *Unit head:* Dr. Slavka Antonova, Graduate Director, 701-777-3232, Fax: 701-777-3090, E-mail: slavka.antonova@und.nodak.edu. *Application contact:* Matt Anderson, Admissions Associate, 701-777-2947, Fax: 701-777-3619, E-mail: matthew.anderson@gradschool.und.edu.

University of Northern Colorado, Graduate School, College of Humanities and Social Sciences, School of Communication, Program in Communication Studies, Greeley, CO 80639. Offers MA. Part-time programs available. *Faculty:* 6 full-time (3 women). *Students:* 11 full-time (7 women), 11 part-time (8 women); includes 2 Black or African American, non-Hispanic/Latino; 3 Asian, non-Hispanic/Latino; 2 Hispanic/Latino, 3 international. Average age 28. 8 applicants, 75% accepted, 6 enrolled. In 2010, 6 master's awarded. *Degree requirements:* For master's, comprehensive exam, thesis or alternative. *Entrance requirements:* For master's, GRE General Test, 3 letters of recommendation. *Application deadline:* Applications are processed on a rolling basis. Application fee: $50 ($60 for international students). Electronic applications accepted. *Expenses:* Tuition, state resident: full-time $6199; part-time $344 per credit hour. Tuition, nonresident: full-time $14,834; part-time $824 per credit hour. Required fees: $1091; $60.60 per credit hour. Tuition and fees vary according to course load, degree level and program. *Financial support:* In 2010–11, 1 research assistantship (averaging $11,529 per year), 7 teaching assistantships (averaging $10,119 per year) were awarded. Financial award application deadline: 3/1; financial award applicants required to submit FAFSA. *Unit head:* Dr. James Keaton, Program Coordinator, 970-351-2045, Fax: 970-351-2336. *Application contact:* Linda Sisson, Graduate Student Admission Coordinator, 970-351-1807, Fax: 970-351-2371, E-mail: linda.sisson@unco.edu.

University of Northern Iowa, Graduate College, College of Humanities and Fine Arts, Department of Communication Studies, Cedar Falls, IA 50614. Offers MA. Part-time and evening/weekend programs available. *Students:* 35 full-time (23 women), 15 part-time (12 women); includes 9 minority (5 Black or African American, non-Hispanic/Latino; 1 Asian, non-Hispanic/Latino; 3 Hispanic/Latino), 5 international. 36 applicants, 47% accepted, 15 enrolled. In 2010, 14 master's awarded. *Degree requirements:* For master's, comprehensive exam, thesis or alternative. *Entrance requirements:* For master's, minimum GPA of 3.0. Additional exam requirements/recommendations for international students: Required—TOEFL (minimum score 500 paper-based; 180 computer-based; 61 iBT). *Application deadline:* For fall admission, 8/1 priority date for domestic students. Applications are processed on a rolling basis. Application fee: $50 ($70 for international students). Electronic applications accepted. *Financial support:* Career-related internships or fieldwork, Federal Work-Study, scholarships/grants, and tuition waivers (full and partial) available. Support available to part-time students. Financial award application deadline: 2/1. *Unit head:* Dr. Christopher Martin, Interim Department Head, 319-273-6118, Fax: 319-273-7356, E-mail: martinc@uni.edu. *Application contact:* Laurie S. Russell, Record Analyst, 319-273-2623, Fax: 319-273-2885, E-mail: laurie.russell@uni.edu.

University of North Texas, Toulouse Graduate School, College of Arts and Sciences, Department of Communication Studies, Denton, TX 76203-5017. Offers MA, MS. Part-time programs available. *Degree requirements:* For master's, one foreign language, comprehensive exam, internship, problem, or thesis. *Entrance requirements:* For master's, GRE General Test, statement of purpose, curriculum vitae/resume, transcripts. Additional exam requirements/recommendations for international students: Recommended—TOEFL (minimum score 550 paper-based; 213 computer-based; 79 iBT). *Expenses:* Tuition, state resident: full-time $4298; part-time $239 per credit hour. Tuition, nonresident: full-time $10,782; part-time $549 per credit hour. Required fees: $1292; $270 per credit hour. *Financial support:* Teaching assistantships, career-related internships or fieldwork, Federal Work-Study, and institutionally sponsored loans available. Financial award application deadline: 4/15; financial award applicants required to submit FAFSA. *Faculty research:* Rhetoric, performance studies, interpersonal communication, organizational communication, health communication.

University of Oklahoma, College of Arts and Sciences, Department of Communication, Norman, OK 73019. Offers MA, PhD. Part-time programs available. Postbaccalaureate distance learning degree programs offered (no on-campus study). *Faculty:* 17 full-time (8 women), 4 part-time/adjunct (1 woman). *Students:* 42 full-time (22 women), 44 part-time (21 women); includes 11 minority (5 Black or African American, non-Hispanic/Latino; 4 American Indian or Alaska Native, non-Hispanic/Latino; 2 Asian, non-Hispanic/Latino), 12 international. Average age 34. 50 applicants, 70% accepted, 16 enrolled. In 2010, 13 master's, 10 doctorates awarded. *Degree requirements:* For master's, comprehensive exam, thesis or alternative; for doctorate, thesis/dissertation, general exam. *Entrance requirements:* For master's, GRE General Test, minimum undergraduate GPA of 3.0; for doctorate, GRE General Test, minimum graduate GPA of 3.5. Additional exam requirements/recommendations for international students: Required—TOEFL (minimum score 550 paper-based; 213 computer-based; 79 iBT). *Application deadline:* For fall admission, 4/1 priority date for domestic students, 4/1 for international students; for spring admission, 11/1 for domestic students, 9/1 for international students. Applications are processed on a rolling basis. Application fee: $40 ($90 for international students). Electronic applications accepted. *Expenses:* Tuition, state resident: full-time $3893; part-time $162.20 per credit hour. Tuition, nonresident: full-time $14,167; part-time $590.30 per credit hour. Required fees: $2523; $94.60 per credit hour. Tuition and fees vary according to course load and degree level. *Financial support:* In 2010–11, 44 students received support, including 1 research assistantship with partial tuition reimbursement available (averaging $9,586 per year), 22 teaching assistantships with partial tuition reimbursements available (averaging $13,707 per year); scholarships/grants, health care benefits, and unspecified assistantships also available. Financial award applicants required to submit FAFSA. *Faculty research:* Social influence, interpersonal/organization, health communication, intercultural/international, political/mass communication. Total annual research expenditures: $251,301. *Unit head:* Dr. Michael W. Kramer, Chair & Professor, 405-325-9503, Fax: 405-325-7625, E-mail: mkramer@ou.edu. *Application contact:* Kathy Martin, Academic Counselor, 405-325-7710, Fax: 405-325-7625, E-mail: kmartin@ou.edu.

University of Oregon, Graduate School, School of Journalism and Communication, Eugene, OR 97403. Offers MA, MS, PhD. *Accreditation:* ACEJMC (one or more programs are accredited); ASHA. Part-time programs available. *Degree requirements:* For master's, thesis or alternative. *Entrance requirements:* For master's, GRE General Test; for doctorate, master's degree. *Faculty research:* Impact of mass communication, media technology, media accountability, craft attitudes, media economics.

University of Ottawa, Faculty of Graduate and Postdoctoral Studies, Faculty of Arts, Department of Communication, Ottawa, ON K1N 6N5, Canada. Offers MA. Electronic applications accepted. *Faculty research:* Media studies, organizational communications.

University of Pennsylvania, Annenberg School for Communication, Philadelphia, PA 19104. Offers PhD. *Faculty:* 19 full-time (8 women), 3 part-time/adjunct (0 women). *Students:* 78 full-time (52 women), 3 part-time (0 women); includes 8 Black or African American, non-Hispanic/

Communication—General

University of Pennsylvania (continued)

Latino; 2 Asian, non-Hispanic/Latino; 1 Hispanic/Latino, 25 international. 537 applicants, 4% accepted, 13 enrolled. In 2010, 13 doctorates awarded. *Degree requirements:* For doctorate, thesis/dissertation. *Entrance requirements:* For doctorate, GRE General Test. *Application deadline:* For fall admission, 1/2 for domestic students. Application fee: $70. Electronic applications accepted. *Expenses:* Tuition: Full-time $25,660; part-time $4758 per course. Required fees: $2152; $270 per course. Tuition and fees vary according to course load, degree level and program. *Financial support:* In 2010–11, 86 students received support; fellowships, research assistantships, teaching assistantships, institutionally sponsored loans, scholarships/grants, traineeships, health care benefits, and unspecified assistantships available. Financial award application deadline: 12/15. *Unit head:* Dr. Michael X. Delli Carpini, Dean. *Application contact:* Beverly Henry, Graduate Studies Coordinator, 215-573-1091, Fax: 215-898-2024, E-mail: bhenry@asc.upenn.edu.

University of Pittsburgh, School of Arts and Sciences, Department of Communication, Pittsburgh, PA 15260. Offers MA, PhD. *Faculty:* 12 full-time (4 women), 1 (woman) part-time/adjunct. *Students:* 43 full-time (21 women); includes 5 Black or African American, non-Hispanic/Latino; 2 Asian, non-Hispanic/Latino; 2 Hispanic/Latino, 2 international. Average age 30. 110 applicants, 7% accepted, 8 enrolled. In 2010, 2 master's, 4 doctorates awarded. *Degree requirements:* For master's, comprehensive exam, thesis optional; for doctorate, comprehensive exam, thesis/dissertation. *Entrance requirements:* For master's and doctorate, GRE General Test, sample of written work. Additional exam requirements/recommendations for international students: Required—TOEFL (minimum score 550 paper-based; 213 computer-based; 80 iBT), IELTS (minimum score 6.5). *Application deadline:* For fall admission, 1/2 priority date for domestic and international students. Application fee: $50. Electronic applications accepted. *Expenses:* Tuition, state resident: full-time $17,304; part-time $701 per credit. Tuition, nonresident: full-time $29,554; part-time $1210 per credit. Required fees: $740; $214 per term. Tuition and fees vary according to program. *Financial support:* In 2010–11, 28 students received support, including 20 fellowships with full tuition reimbursements available (averaging $16,140 per year), 4 teaching assistantships with full tuition reimbursements available (averaging $15,520 per year); Federal Work-Study, scholarships/grants, health care benefits, tuition waivers (full), and unspecified assistantships also available. Financial award application deadline: 1/2; financial award applicants required to submit FAFSA. *Faculty research:* Media and cultural studies, public argument and discourse, rhetoric of science, history, criticism and theory of rhetoric. *Unit head:* Dr. Barbara Warnick, Department Chair, 412-624-1564, Fax: 412-624-1878, E-mail: bwarnick@pitt.edu. *Application contact:* Dr. Gordon R. Mitchell, Director of Graduate Studies, 412-624-8531, Fax: 412-624-1878, E-mail: gordonm@pitt.edu.

University of Portland, College of Arts and Sciences, Department of Communication Studies, Portland, OR 97203-5798. Offers communication (MA); management communication (MS). Part-time and evening/weekend programs available. *Faculty:* 5 full-time (3 women), 1 part-time/adjunct (0 women). *Students:* 4 full-time (1 woman), 10 part-time (8 women); includes 1 Black or African American, non-Hispanic/Latino; 1 Asian, non-Hispanic/Latino; 1 Two or more races, non-Hispanic/Latino, 2 international. Average age 33. In 2010, 4 master's awarded. *Degree requirements:* For master's, thesis optional. *Entrance requirements:* For master's, GRE General Test, minimum GPA of 3.25, 3 letters of recommendation, resume, statement of goals, official transcripts. Additional exam requirements/recommendations for international students: Required—TOEFL (minimum score 600 paper-based; 100 iBT), IELTS (minimum score 7.5). *Application deadline:* For fall admission, 7/15 priority date for domestic and international students; for spring admission, 12/15 priority date for domestic and international students. Applications are processed on a rolling basis. Application fee: $50. *Expenses:* Tuition: Part-time $940 per credit hour. Tuition and fees vary according to program. *Financial support:* Career-related internships or fieldwork, Federal Work-Study, scholarships/grants, and tuition waivers (partial) available. Financial award application deadline: 3/1; financial award applicants required to submit FAFSA. *Unit head:* Dr. Jeffrey Kerssen-Griep, Director, 503-943-7167, E-mail: kerssen@up.edu. *Application contact:* Chris James Olinger, Administrative Assistant, 503-943-7107, Fax: 503-943-7315, E-mail: olingerc@up.edu.

University of Puerto Rico, Río Piedras, School of Communication, Program in Communication Theory and Research, San Juan, PR 00931-3300. Offers MA.

University of Rhode Island, Graduate School, College of Arts and Sciences, Department of Communication Studies, Kingston, RI 02881. Offers MA. Part-time programs available. *Faculty:* 29 full-time (15 women), 3 part-time/adjunct (all women). *Students:* 12 full-time (7 women), 23 part-time (14 women); includes 2 minority (both Black or African American, non-Hispanic/Latino), 2 international. In 2010, 8 master's awarded. *Degree requirements:* For master's, comprehensive exam (for some programs), thesis optional. *Entrance requirements:* For master's, GRE, 2 letters of recommendation. Additional exam requirements/recommendations for international students: Required—TOEFL (minimum score 550 paper-based; 230 computer-based; 88 iBT). *Application deadline:* For fall admission, 7/15 for domestic students, 2/1 for international students. Application fee: $65. Electronic applications accepted. *Expenses:* Tuition, state resident: full-time $9588; part-time $533 per credit hour. Tuition, nonresident: full-time $22,968; part-time $1276 per credit hour. Required fees: $1282; $68 per semester. Tuition and fees vary according to program. *Financial support:* In 2010–11, 5 teaching assistantships with full tuition reimbursements (averaging $13,894 per year) were awarded. Financial award application deadline: 2/1; financial award applicants required to submit FAFSA. Total annual research expenditures: $18,189. *Unit head:* Dr. Lynne Derbyshire, Chair, 401-874-4732, Fax: 401-874-4722, E-mail: derbyshire@uri.edu. *Application contact:* Dr. Norbert Mundorf, Director of Graduate Studies, 401-874-4725, Fax: 401-874-4722, E-mail: mundorf@uri.edu.

University of South Africa, College of Human Sciences, Pretoria, South Africa. Offers adult education (M Ed); African languages (MA, PhD); African politics (MA, PhD); Afrikaans (MA, PhD); ancient history (MA, PhD); ancient Near Eastern studies (MA, PhD); anthropology (MA, PhD); applied linguistics (MA); Arabic (MA, PhD); archaeology (MA); art history (MA); Biblical archaeology (MA); Biblical studies (M Th, D Th, PhD); Christian spirituality (M Th, D Th); church history (M Th, D Th); classical studies (MA, PhD); clinical psychology (MA); communication (MA, PhD); comparative education (M Ed, Ed D); consulting psychology (D Admin, D Com, PhD); curriculum studies (M Ed, Ed D); development studies (M Admin, MA, D Admin, PhD); didactics (M Ed, Ed D); education (M Tech); education management (M Ed, Ed D); educational psychology (M Ed); English (MA); environmental education (M Ed); French (MA, PhD); German (MA, PhD); Greek (MA); guidance and counseling (M Ed); health studies (MA, PhD), including health sciences education (MA), health services management (MA), medical and surgical nursing science (critical care general) (MA), midwifery and neonatal nursing science (MA), trauma and emergency care (MA); history (MA, PhD); history of education (Ed D); inclusive education (M Ed, Ed D); information and communications technology policy and regulation (MA); information science (MA, MIS, PhD); international politics (MA, PhD); Islamic studies (MA, PhD); Italian (MA, PhD); Judaica (MA, PhD); linguistics (MA, PhD); mathematical education (M Ed); mathematics education (MA); missiology (M Th, D Th); modern Hebrew (MA, PhD); musicology (MA, MMus, D Mus, PhD); natural science education (M Ed); New Testament (M Th, D Th); Old Testament (D Th); pastoral therapy (M Th, D Th); philosophy (MA); philosophy of education (M Ed, Ed D); politics (MA, PhD); Portuguese (MA, PhD); practical theology (M Th, D Th); psychology (MA, MS, PhD); psychology of education (M Ed, Ed D); public health (MA); religious studies (MA, D Th, PhD); Romance languages (MA); Russian (MA, PhD); Semitic languages (MA, PhD); social behavior studies in HIV/AIDS (MA); social science (mental health) (MA); social science in development studies (MA); social science in psychology (MA); social science in social work (MA); social science in sociology (MA); social work (MSW, DSW, PhD); socio-education (M Ed, Ed D); sociolinguistics (MA); sociology (MA, PhD); Spanish (MA, PhD); systematic theology (M Th, D Th); TESOL (teaching English to speakers of other languages) (MA); theological ethics (M Th, D Th); theory of literature (MA, PhD); urban ministries (D Th); urban ministry (M Th).

University of South Alabama, Graduate School, College of Arts and Sciences, Department of Communication, Mobile, AL 36688-0002. Offers MA. *Faculty:* 10 full-time (4 women). *Students:* 24 full-time (17 women), 13 part-time (8 women); includes 4 Black or African American, non-Hispanic/Latino, 1 international. 21 applicants, 43% accepted, 8 enrolled. In 2010, 14 master's awarded. *Degree requirements:* For master's, comprehensive exam, thesis optional, completion of minimum of 34 semesters hours in approved 500 level course work, including 3 hours of thesis or project work; minimum of 25 semester hours in communication. *Entrance requirements:* For master's, GRE, GMAT, minimum GPA of 3.0, BA in communication or 36 semester hours. Additional exam requirements/recommendations for international students: Required—TOEFL (minimum score 525 paper-based). *Application deadline:* For fall admission, 7/15 priority date for domestic students, 6/15 priority date for international students; for spring admission, 12/1 priority date for domestic students, 11/1 priority date for international students. Applications are processed on a rolling basis. Application fee: $35. *Expenses:* Tuition, state resident: part-time $300 per credit hour. Tuition, nonresident: part-time $600 per credit hour. Required fees: $150 per semester. *Financial support:* Research assistantships available. Financial award application deadline: 4/1. *Unit head:* Dr. James Aucoin, Chair, 251-380-2800, Fax: 251-380-2850. *Application contact:* Dr. James Aucoin, Chair, 251-380-2800, Fax: 251-380-2850.

The University of South Dakota, Graduate School, College of Arts and Sciences, Department of Communication Studies, Vermillion, SD 57069-2390. Offers MA. Part-time programs available. *Degree requirements:* For master's, comprehensive exam (for some programs), thesis (for some programs). *Entrance requirements:* For master's, minimum GPA of 2.7. Additional exam requirements/recommendations for international students: Required—TOEFL (minimum score 575 paper-based; 213 computer-based; 79 iBT). Electronic applications accepted. *Faculty research:* Male/female communication, interpersonal communication, relational communication, rhetoric and public address, organizational communication.

University of Southern California, Graduate School, Annenberg School for Communication and Journalism, Los Angeles, CA 90089. Offers MA, MCM, MPD, PhD, JD/MCM, MA/M Sc, MCM/MAJCS. Part-time and evening/weekend programs available. *Faculty:* 74 full-time (24 women), 62 part-time/adjunct (18 women). *Students:* 605 full-time, 104 part-time; includes 219 minority (45 Black or African American, non-Hispanic/Latino; 3 American Indian or Alaska Native, non-Hispanic/Latino; 75 Asian, non-Hispanic/Latino; 77 Hispanic/Latino; 1 Native Hawaiian or other Pacific Islander, non-Hispanic/Latino; 18 Two or more races, non-Hispanic/Latino), 183 international. Average age 27. 1,325 applicants, 38% accepted, 255 enrolled. In 2010, 471 master's, 14 doctorates awarded. Terminal master's awarded for partial completion of doctoral program. *Degree requirements:* For master's, comprehensive exam (for some programs), thesis (for some programs); for doctorate, thesis/dissertation. *Entrance requirements:* For master's, GRE General Test (or GMAT for communication management program only), resume, writing samples, letters of recommendation, statement of purpose; for doctorate, GRE General Test, resume, writing samples, letters of recommendation, statement of purpose, interest survey. Additional exam requirements/recommendations for international students: Required—TOEFL (minimum score 280 computer-based; 114 iBT). *Application deadline:* For spring admission, 12/1 priority date for domestic students, 8/1 for international students. Applications are processed on a rolling basis. Application fee: $85. Electronic applications accepted. *Expenses:* Tuition: Full-time $31,240; part-time $1420 per unit. Required fees: $600. One-time fee: $35 full-time. Full-time tuition and fees vary according to degree level and program. *Financial support:* In 2010–11, 22 fellowships with full tuition reimbursements (averaging $24,845 per year), 33 research assistantships with full tuition reimbursements (averaging $23,939 per year), 41 teaching assistantships with full tuition reimbursements (averaging $21,253 per year) were awarded; career-related internships or fieldwork, Federal Work-Study, institutionally sponsored loans, scholarships/grants, health care benefits, tuition waivers (partial), and unspecified assistantships also available. Support available to part-time students. Financial award application deadline: 2/1; financial award applicants required to submit FAFSA. Total annual research expenditures: $5.6 million. *Unit head:* Dr. Ernest Wilson, Dean, 213-740-6180, Fax: 213-740-3772, E-mail: ascdean@usc.edu. *Application contact:* Allyson Hill, Assistant Dean, Admissions, 213-821-0770, Fax: 213-740-1933, E-mail: ascadm@usc.edu.

See Display on next page and Close-Up on page 727.

University of Southern California, Graduate School, Annenberg School for Communication and Journalism, School of Communication, Program in Communication, Los Angeles, CA 90089. Offers communication (MA, PhD), including information and society (PhD), interpersonal and health communication (PhD), media, culture and communication (PhD), organizational communication (PhD), rhetorical and political communication (PhD). *Students:* 97 full-time (64 women); includes 20 minority (4 Black or African American, non-Hispanic/Latino; 1 American Indian or Alaska Native, non-Hispanic/Latino; 8 Asian, non-Hispanic/Latino; 7 Hispanic/Latino), 30 international. Average age 31. 242 applicants, 9% accepted, 18 enrolled. In 2010, 14 doctorates awarded. *Degree requirements:* For doctorate, thesis/dissertation. *Entrance requirements:* For master's and doctorate, GRE General Test, resume, writing samples, 3 letters of recommendation, interest survey questionnaire, statement of purpose. Additional exam requirements/recommendations for international students: Required—TOEFL (minimum score 280 computer-based; 114 iBT); Recommended—TWE. *Application deadline:* For fall admission, 12/1 for domestic and international students. Application fee: $85. Electronic applications accepted. *Expenses:* Tuition: Full-time $31,240; part-time $1420 per unit. Required fees: $600. One-time fee: $35 full-time. Full-time tuition and fees vary according to degree level and program. *Financial support:* In 2010–11, 18 students received support, including 18 fellowships with full tuition reimbursements available (averaging $26,500 per year); research assistantships, teaching assistantships, Federal Work-Study, institutionally sponsored loans, scholarships/grants, health care benefits, and unspecified assistantships also available. Support available to part-time students. Financial award application deadline: 1/1; financial award applicants required to submit FAFSA. *Faculty research:* Computer-mediated communication, public health campaigns, communication democracy and the public sphere, new communication technologies in organizations, communication and community. *Unit head:* Dr. Thomas Goodnight, Director of the Ph.D. Program, 213-821-5384, E-mail: gtg@usc.edu. *Application contact:* Allyson Hill, Assistant Dean, Admissions, 213-821-0770, Fax: 213-740-1933, E-mail: ascadm@usc.edu.

See Display on next page and Close-Up on page 727.

University of Southern California, Graduate School, Annenberg School for Communication and Journalism, School of Communication, Program in Global Communication, Los Angeles, CA 90089. Offers MA/M Sc. Program offered jointly with London School of Economics. *Students:* 54 full-time, 1 part-time; includes 1 Black or African American, non-Hispanic/Latino; 2 Asian, non-Hispanic/Latino; 1 Hispanic/Latino, 15 international. Average age 24. 294 applicants, 21% accepted, 37 enrolled. *Entrance requirements:* Additional exam requirements/recommendations for international students: Required—TOEFL (minimum score 280 computer-based; 114 iBT), IELTS. *Application deadline:* For fall admission, 3/1 priority date for domestic and international students. Applications are processed on a rolling basis. Application fee: $85. Electronic applications accepted. *Expenses:* Tuition: Full-time $31,240; part-time $1420 per unit. Required fees: $600. One-time fee: $35 full-time. Full-time tuition and fees vary according to degree level and program. *Financial support:* In 2010–11, 16 research assistantships with full and partial tuition reimbursements (averaging $10,000 per year) were awarded; Federal Work-Study, institutionally sponsored loans, scholarships/grants, health care benefits, tuition waivers (partial), and unspecified assistantships also available. Support available to part-time students. Financial award application deadline: 1/15; financial award applicants required to submit FAFSA. *Faculty research:* New technology, audience analysis, globalization, entertainment industry, integrated communication. *Unit head:* Dr. Patricia Riley, Director, 213-740-3949, Fax: 213-740-0013, E-mail: priley@usc.edu. *Application contact:* Allyson Hill, Assistant Dean, Admissions, 213-821-0770, Fax: 213-740-1933, E-mail: ascadm@usc.edu.

See Display on next page and Close-Up on page 727.

University of Southern Indiana, Graduate Studies, College of Liberal Arts, Program in Communication, Evansville, IN 47712-3590. Offers MA. Part-time and evening/weekend programs available. *Faculty:* 1 full-time (0 women). *Students:* 4 full-time (3 women), 8 part-time (all women). Average age 32. 12 applicants, 83% accepted, 10 enrolled. *Entrance requirements:* For master's, GRE, written letter of intent, three positive professional letters of recommendation. Additional exam requirements/recommendations for international students: Required—TOEFL (minimum score 550 paper-based; 213 computer-based; 79 iBT), IELTS (minimum score 6). *Application deadline:* For fall admission, 8/1 for domestic students. Applications are processed on a rolling basis. Application fee: $25. Electronic applications accepted. *Expenses:* Tuition, state resident: full-time $4823; part-time $267.95 per credit hour. Tuition, nonresident: full-time $9515; part-time $528.62 per credit hour. Required fees: $220; $22.75 per term. Tuition and fees vary according to course load and reciprocity agreements. *Financial support:* Federal Work-Study, scholarships/grants, and unspecified assistantships available. Financial award application deadline: 3/1; financial award applicants required to submit FAFSA. *Unit head:* Dr. Wesley Durham, Director, 812-464-1739, E-mail: wdurham@usi.edu. *Application contact:* Dr. Wesley Durham, Director, 812-464-1739, E-mail: wdurham@usi.edu.

University of South Florida, Graduate School, College of Arts and Sciences, Department of Communication, Tampa, FL 33620-9951. Offers MA, PhD. Part-time programs available. *Faculty:* 5 full-time (1 woman). *Students:* 49 full-time (30 women), 14 part-time (7 women); includes 6 Black or African American, non-Hispanic/Latino; 1 Asian, non-Hispanic/Latino; 4 Hispanic/Latino; 1 Two or more races, non-Hispanic/Latino, 1 international. Average age 35. 103 applicants, 32% accepted, 21 enrolled. In 2010, 7 master's, 5 doctorates awarded. *Degree requirements:* For master's, comprehensive exam (for some programs), thesis (for some programs); for doctorate, comprehensive exam, thesis/dissertation. *Entrance requirements:* For master's, GRE General Test, minimum GPA of 3.0. Additional exam requirements/ recommendations for international students: Required—TOEFL (minimum score 550 paper-based; 213 computer-based). *Application deadline:* For fall admission, 1/15 for domestic students, 1/2 for international students; for spring admission, 11/1 for domestic students, 6/1 for international students. Applications are processed on a rolling basis. Application fee: $30. Electronic applications accepted. *Financial support:* In 2010–11, 3 students received support, including 1 research assistantship (averaging $17,629 per year), 37 teaching assistantships with full tuition reimbursements available (averaging $15,070 per year); unspecified assistantships also available. Financial award application deadline: 1/15; financial award applicants required to submit FAFSA. *Faculty research:* Organizational, interpersonal, and health communication; media and cultural studies; rhetoric; performance studies; qualitative research methods. Total annual research expenditures: $6,729. *Unit head:* Dr. Kenneth Cissna, Chairperson, 813-974-6820, Fax: 813-974-6817, E-mail: kcissna@usf.edu. *Application contact:* Stacy Holman Jones, Program Director, 813-974-6827, Fax: 813-974-6817, E-mail: holmanjo@usf.edu.

The University of Tennessee, Graduate School, College of Communication and Information, Knoxville, TN 37996. Offers advertising (MS, PhD); broadcasting (MS, PhD); communications (MS, PhD); information sciences (MS, PhD); journalism (MS, PhD); public relations (MS, PhD); speech communication (MS, PhD). *Accreditation:* ACEJMC (one or more programs are accredited at the [master's] level). Part-time and evening/weekend programs available. Post-baccalaureate distance learning degree programs offered (no on-campus study). *Degree requirements:* For master's, thesis or alternative; for doctorate, thesis/dissertation. *Entrance requirements:* For master's and doctorate, GRE General Test, minimum GPA of 2.7. Additional exam requirements/recommendations for international students: Required—TOEFL. Electronic applications accepted. *Expenses:* Tuition, state resident: full-time $7440; part-time $414 per credit hour. Tuition, nonresident: full-time $22,478; part-time $1250 per credit hour. Required fees: $922; $43 per credit hour. Tuition and fees vary according to program.

The University of Texas at Arlington, Graduate School, College of Liberal Arts, Department of Communication, Arlington, TX 76019. Offers MA. Part-time and evening/weekend programs available. *Faculty:* 7 full-time (2 women). *Students:* 13 full-time (7 women), 14 part-time (6 women); includes 8 minority (2 Black or African American, non-Hispanic/Latino; 2 Asian, non-Hispanic/Latino; 4 Hispanic/Latino), 7 international. 26 applicants, 69% accepted, 14

enrolled. In 2010, 6 master's awarded. *Degree requirements:* For master's, comprehensive exam (for some programs), thesis or alternative. *Entrance requirements:* For master's, GRE General Test. Additional exam requirements/recommendations for international students: Required—TOEFL (minimum score 550. paper-based; 213 computer-based). *Application deadline:* Applications are processed on a rolling basis. Application fee: $35 ($50 for international students). Electronic applications accepted. *Expenses:* Tuition, state resident: full-time $7500. Tuition, nonresident: full-time $13,080. International tuition: $13,250 full-time. *Financial support:* In 2010–11, 5 research assistantships (averaging $4,000 per year), 5 teaching assistantships (averaging $2,500 per year) were awarded. *Unit head:* Dr. Charla Markham-Shaw, Chair, 817-272-2163, E-mail: markham@uta.edu. *Application contact:* Dr. Tom Christie, Graduate Advisor, 817-272-2163, E-mail: christie@uta.edu.

The University of Texas at Austin, Graduate School, College of Communication, Austin, TX 78712-1111. Offers MA, MFA, Au D, PhD, MBA/MA, MP Aff/MA. Part-time programs available. *Entrance requirements:* For master's and doctorate, GRE General Test. Electronic applications accepted.

The University of Texas at Dallas, School of Behavioral and Brain Sciences, Program in Communication Sciences and Disorders, Richardson, TX 75080. Offers communication disorders (MS); communication sciences (PhD). Part-time and evening/weekend programs available. *Faculty:* 18 full-time (11 women). *Students:* 229 full-time (222 women), 14 part-time (12 women); includes 34 minority (4 Black or African American, non-Hispanic/Latino; 12 Asian, non-Hispanic/Latino; 17 Hispanic/Latino; 1 Two or more races, non-Hispanic/Latino), 10 international. Average age 26. 318 applicants, 26% accepted, 54 enrolled. In 2010, 98 master's, 4 doctorates awarded. *Degree requirements:* For doctorate, thesis/dissertation. *Entrance requirements:* For master's and doctorate, GRE General Test, minimum GPA of 3.0 in upper-level course work in field. Additional exam requirements/recommendations for international students: Required—TOEFL (minimum score 550 paper-based; 215 computer-based). *Application deadline:* For fall admission, 7/15 for domestic students, 5/1 priority date for international students; for spring admission, 11/15 for domestic students, 9/1 priority date for international students. Applications are processed on a rolling basis. Application fee: $50 ($100 for international students). Electronic applications accepted. *Expenses:* Tuition, state resident: full-time $10,248; part-time $569 per credit hour. Tuition, nonresident: full-time $18,544; part-time $1030 per credit hour. Tuition and fees vary according to course load. *Financial support:* In 2010–11, 151 students received support, including 3 research assistantships with partial tuition reimbursements available (averaging $16,782 per year), 9 teaching assistantships with partial tuition reimbursements available (averaging $11,778 per year); fellowships, Federal Work-Study, institutionally sponsored loans, scholarships/grants, and unspecified assistantships also available. Support available to part-time students. Financial award application deadline: 4/30; financial award applicants required to submit FAFSA. *Faculty research:* Developmental neurolinguistics, brain plasticity and biofeedback treatment, autism spectrum disorders, speech production, neurogenic speech and language disorders. *Unit head:* Dr. Robert D. Stillman, Program Head, 214-905-3106, Fax: 972-883-3022, E-mail: stillman@utdallas.edu. *Application contact:* Dr. Robert D. Stillman, Program Head, 214-905-3106, Fax: 972-883-3022, E-mail: stillman@utdallas.edu.

The University of Texas at El Paso, Graduate School, College of Liberal Arts, Department of Communication, El Paso, TX 79968-0001. Offers MA. Part-time and evening/weekend programs available. *Students:* 28 (18 women); includes 1 American Indian or Alaska Native, non-Hispanic/Latino; 1 Asian, non-Hispanic/Latino; 16 Hispanic/Latino, 3 international. Average age 34. In 2010, 6 master's awarded. *Degree requirements:* For master's, thesis optional. *Entrance requirements:* For master's, GRE General Test, minimum GPA of 3.0. Additional exam requirements/recommendations for international students: Required—TOEFL. *Application deadline:* For fall admission, 7/1 priority date for domestic students, 3/1 for international students; for spring admission, 11/1 priority date for domestic students, 9/1 for international students. Applications are processed on a rolling basis. Application fee: $15 ($65 for international students). Electronic applications accepted. *Financial support:* In 2010–11, 4 students

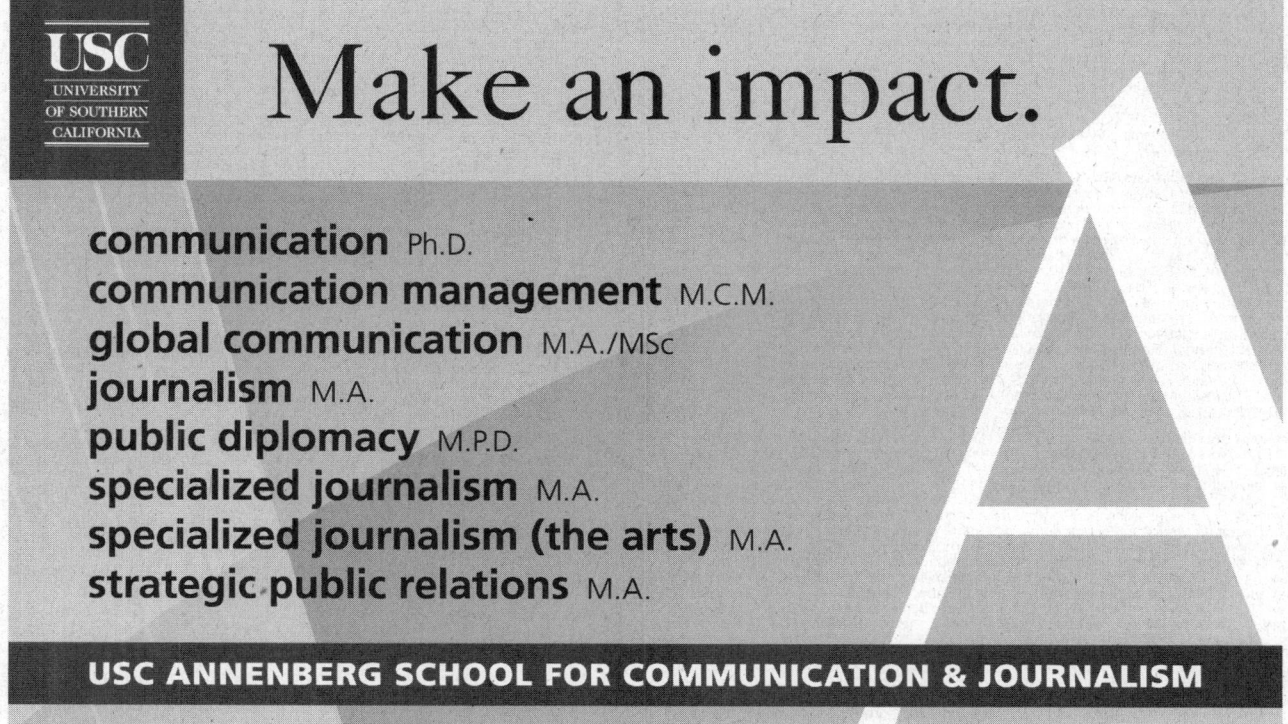

Communication—General

The University of Texas at El Paso (continued)
received support, including research assistantships with partial tuition reimbursements available (averaging $18,625 per year), 4 teaching assistantships with partial tuition reimbursements available (averaging $14,900 per year); career-related internships or fieldwork, Federal Work-Study, institutionally sponsored loans, scholarships/grants, and tuition waivers (partial) also available. Financial award application deadline: 3/15; financial award applicants required to submit FAFSA. *Faculty research:* Cross-cultural communication, information media, telecommunication technology, trans-border communication, human communication. *Unit head:* Dr. Patricia Witherspoon, Chairperson, 915-747-5129, Fax: 915-747-6515, E-mail: withersp@utep.edu. *Application contact:* Dr. Charles H. Ambler, Dean of the Graduate School, 915-747-5491 Ext. 7886, Fax: 915-747-5788, E-mail: cambler@utep.edu.

The University of Texas at San Antonio, College of Liberal and Fine Arts, Department of Communication, San Antonio, TX 78249-0617. Offers MA. Part-time and evening/weekend programs available. *Faculty:* 6 full-time (3 women), 1 (woman) part-time/adjunct. *Students:* 9 full-time (6 women), 21 part-time (12 women); includes 16 minority (2 Black or African American, non-Hispanic/Latino; 1 American Indian or Alaska Native, non-Hispanic/Latino; 13 Hispanic/Latino), 1 international. Average age 28. 31 applicants, 71% accepted, 15 enrolled. In 2010, 1 master's awarded. *Degree requirements:* For master's, comprehensive exam (for some programs), thesis (for some programs). *Entrance requirements:* For master's, GRE. Additional exam requirements/recommendations for international students: Required—TOEFL (minimum score 500 paper-based; 173 computer-based; 61 iBT), IELTS (minimum score 5). *Application deadline:* For fall admission, 7/1 for domestic students, 4/1 for international students; for spring admission, 11/1 for domestic students, 9/1 for international students. Applications are processed on a rolling basis. Application fee: $45 ($80 for international students). Electronic applications accepted. *Expenses:* Tuition, state resident: full-time $4172; part-time $231.75 per credit hour. Tuition, nonresident: full-time $15,332; part-time $851.75 per credit hour. *Financial support:* In 2010–11, 4 students received support, including 1 research assistantship (averaging $5,200 per year), 5 teaching assistantships (averaging $4,805 per year); career-related internships or fieldwork, scholarships/grants, tuition waivers, and unspecified assistantships also available. Support available to part-time students. *Unit head:* Dr. Paul LeBlanc, Department Chair, 210-458-5990, Fax: 210-458-5991, E-mail: paul.leblanc@utsa.edu. *Application contact:* Veronica Ramirez, Assistant Dean of the Graduate School, 210-458-4330, Fax: 210-458-4332, E-mail: graduatestudies@utsa.edu.

The University of Texas at Tyler, College of Arts and Sciences, Department of Communication, Tyler, TX 75799-0001. Offers communication (MA); interdisciplinary studies (MAIS, MSIS). Part-time programs available. *Degree requirements:* For master's, comprehensive exam. *Entrance requirements:* For master's, GRE General Test, minimum GPA of 2.5. Additional exam requirements/recommendations for international students: Required—TOEFL (minimum score 79 computer-based). Electronic applications accepted. *Faculty research:* Organizational communication, feminist criticism, religions communication, mass media.

The University of Texas–Pan American, College of Arts and Humanities, Department of Communications, Edinburg, TX 78539. Offers communication (MA); theatre (MA). *Accreditation:* NAST. Part-time and evening/weekend programs available. *Degree requirements:* For master's, comprehensive exam, thesis or alternative. *Entrance requirements:* For master's, minimum GPA of 3.0. Additional exam requirements/recommendations for international students: Required—TOEFL. *Faculty research:* Rhetorical theory, intercultural and mass communication, American theatre, multicultural theatre and drama, television and film.

University of the Incarnate Word, School of Graduate Studies and Research, H-E-B School of Business and Administration, Programs in Administration, San Antonio, TX 78209-6397. Offers adult education (MAA); applied administration (MAA); communication arts (MAA); healthcare administration (MAA); instructional technology (MAA); international business (Certificate); nutrition (MAA); organizational development (MAA, Certificate); project management (Certificate); sports management (MAA). Part-time and evening/weekend programs available. Postbaccalaureate distance learning degree programs offered (no on-campus study). *Students:* 30 full-time (20 women), 64 part-time (37 women); includes 10 Black or African American, non-Hispanic/Latino; 1 Asian, non-Hispanic/Latino; 48 Hispanic/Latino, 8 international. Average age 35. In 2010, 68 master's awarded. *Degree requirements:* For master's, capstone. *Entrance requirements:* For master's, GRE, GMAT, undergraduate degree, minimum GPA of 2.5. Additional exam requirements/recommendations for international students: Required—TOEFL (minimum score 560 paper-based; 220 computer-based; 83 iBT). *Application deadline:* Applications are processed on a rolling basis. Application fee: $20. Electronic applications accepted. *Expenses:* Tuition: Part-time $725 per contact hour. Required fees: $890 per semester. *Financial support:* Federal Work-Study and scholarships/grants available. Financial award applicants required to submit FAFSA. *Unit head:* Dr. Daniel Dominguez, MAA Programs Director, 210-829-3180, Fax: 210-805-3564, E-mail: domingue@uiwtx.edu. *Application contact:* Andrea Cyterski-Acosta, Dean of Enrollment, 210-829-6005, Fax: 210-829-3921, E-mail: admis@uiwtx.edu.

University of the Incarnate Word, School of Graduate Studies and Research, School of Interactive Media and Design, Program in Communication Arts, San Antonio, TX 78209-6397. Offers MA. Part-time and evening/weekend programs available. *Faculty:* 5 full-time (1 woman), 6 part-time/adjunct (all women). *Students:* 9 full-time (4 women), 39 part-time (21 women); includes 3 Black or African American, non-Hispanic/Latino; 30 Hispanic/Latino; 1 Two or more races, non-Hispanic/Latino, 2 international. Average age 31. In 2010, 8 master's awarded. *Degree requirements:* For master's, thesis or alternative. *Entrance requirements:* For master's, GMAT, GRE General Test, interview, writing sample. Additional exam requirements/recommendations for international students: Required—TOEFL (minimum score 560 paper-based; 220 computer-based; 83 iBT). *Application deadline:* Applications are processed on a rolling basis. Application fee: $20. Electronic applications accepted. *Expenses:* Tuition: Part-time $725 per contact hour. Required fees: $890 per semester. *Financial support:* Federal Work-Study and scholarships/grants available. Financial award applicants required to submit FAFSA. *Unit head:* Dr. Valerie Greenberg, 210-829-3891, Fax: 210-829-3196, E-mail: greenber@uiwtx.edu. *Application contact:* Andrea Cyterski-Acosta, Dean of Enrollment, 210-829-6005, Fax: 210-829-3921, E-mail: admis@uiwtx.edu.

University of the Pacific, College of the Pacific, Department of Communication, Stockton, CA 95211-0197. Offers MA. *Faculty:* 9 full-time (2 women), 3 part-time/adjunct (2 women). *Students:* 3 full-time (1 woman), 22 part-time (13 women); includes 1 Black or African American, non-Hispanic/Latino; 1 Asian, non-Hispanic/Latino; 1 Hispanic/Latino, 5 international. Average age 27. 30 applicants, 43% accepted, 6 enrolled. In 2010, 5 master's awarded. *Degree requirements:* For master's, thesis. *Entrance requirements:* For master's, GRE General Test. Additional exam requirements/recommendations for international students: Required—TOEFL (minimum score 475 paper-based; 150 computer-based). *Application deadline:* For fall admission, 3/1 priority date for domestic students; for spring admission, 10/1 for domestic students. Applications are processed on a rolling basis. Application fee: $75. *Financial support:* In 2010–11, 8 teaching assistantships were awarded. Support available to part-time students. Financial award application deadline: 3/1; financial award applicants required to submit FAFSA. *Unit head:* Dr. Qingwen Dong, Chairman, 209-946-2505, E-mail: qdong@pacific.edu. *Application contact:* Information Contact, 209-946-2261.

University of the Sacred Heart, Graduate Programs, Department of Communication, San Juan, PR 00914-0383. Offers contemporary culture and media (MA); digital journalism (MA, Certificate); editing for media (MA, Certificate); public relations (MA, Certificate); publicity (MA, Certificate); scriptwriting (MA, Certificate). Part-time and evening/weekend programs available. *Degree requirements:* For master's, thesis.

The University of Toledo, College of Graduate Studies, College of Language, Literature and Social Sciences, Department of Communication, Toledo, OH 43606-3390. Offers communication studies (Certificate). Part-time programs available. *Faculty:* 8. *Students:* 1 part-time (0 women). Average age 28. 2 applicants, 100% accepted, 1 enrolled. In 2010, 3 Certificates

awarded. *Entrance requirements:* For degree, 2.7 GPA on all prior academic work, transcripts from all prior institutions attended. *Application deadline:* For fall admission, 1/15 priority date for domestic and international students. Applications are processed on a rolling basis. Application fee: $45 ($75 for international students). Electronic applications accepted. *Expenses:* Tuition, state resident: full-time $11,426; part-time $476 per credit hour. Tuition, nonresident: full-time $21,660; part-time $903 per credit hour. One-time fee: $62. *Unit head:* Dr. Richard Knecht, Chair. *Application contact:* Graduate School Office, 419-530-4723, Fax: 419-530-4724, E-mail: grdsch@utnet.utoledo.edu.

University of Utah, Graduate School, College of Humanities, Department of Communication, Salt Lake City, UT 84112. Offers MA, MS, PhD. *Faculty:* 30 full-time (16 women), 1 part-time/adjunct (0 women). *Students:* 51 full-time (36 women), 35 part-time (19 women); includes 10 minority (4 Asian, non-Hispanic/Latino; 6 Hispanic/Latino), 3 international. Average age 33. 100 applicants, 48% accepted, 26 enrolled. In 2010, 7 master's, 5 doctorates awarded. *Degree requirements:* For master's, thesis or alternative; for doctorate, comprehensive exam, thesis/dissertation. *Entrance requirements:* For master's and doctorate, GRE General Test, minimum GPA of 3.0. Additional exam requirements/recommendations for international students: Required—TOEFL (minimum score 500 paper-based; 173 computer-based). *Application deadline:* For fall admission, 1/15 for domestic and international students. Application fee: $55 ($65 for international students). Electronic applications accepted. *Expenses:* Tuition, area resident: Part-time $179.19 per credit hour. Tuition, state resident: full-time $4384. Tuition, nonresident: full-time $16,684; part-time $630.67 per credit hour. Required fees: $350 per semester. Tuition and fees vary according to course load, degree level and program. *Financial support:* In 2010–11, 3 students received support, including 36 teaching assistantships with full tuition reimbursements available (averaging $13,500 per year); health care benefits also available. Financial award application deadline: 1/15; financial award applicants required to submit FAFSA. *Faculty research:* Communication theory and history, rhetoric, mass communications, journalism, public address and forensics. Total annual research expenditures: $87,414. *Unit head:* Dr. Ann L. Darling, Chair, 801-581-3912, Fax: 801-585-6255, E-mail: ann.darling@utah.edu. *Application contact:* Dr. Connie Bullis, Director of Graduate Studies, 801-581-6664, Fax: 801-585-6255, E-mail: connie.bullis@utah.edu.

University of Vermont, Graduate College, College of Arts and Sciences, Department of Communication Sciences, Burlington, VT 05405. Offers MS. *Accreditation:* ASHA. *Students:* 43 (40 women); includes 1 Hispanic/Latino, 1 international. 88 applicants, 32% accepted, 12 enrolled. In 2010, 9 master's awarded. *Entrance requirements:* For master's, GRE General Test. Additional exam requirements/recommendations for international students: Required—TOEFL (minimum score 550 paper-based; 213 computer-based; 80 iBT). *Application deadline:* For fall admission, 2/1 for domestic students. Application fee: $40. Electronic applications accepted. *Expenses:* Tuition, state resident: part-time $537 per credit hour. Tuition, nonresident: part-time $1355 per credit hour. *Financial support:* Fellowships available. Financial award application deadline: 3/1. *Unit head:* Prof. P. Prelock, Chair, 802-656-3861. *Application contact:* Prof. Barry Guitar, Coordinator, 802-656-3861.

University of Washington, Graduate School, College of Arts and Sciences, Department of Communication, Seattle, WA 98195. Offers MA, MC, PhD. Part-time programs available. Terminal master's awarded for partial completion of doctoral program. *Degree requirements:* For master's, thesis, project (MC); for doctorate, thesis/dissertation. *Entrance requirements:* For master's and doctorate, GRE, minimum GPA of 3.0, writing sample. Additional exam requirements/recommendations for international students: Required—TOEFL. Electronic applications accepted. *Faculty research:* Communication and culture, communication technology and society, international communication, political communication, rhetoric and critical studies.

University of Washington, Graduate School, College of Arts and Sciences, School of Art, Division of Design, Seattle, WA 98195. Offers industrial design (MFA); visual communication design (MFA).

University of West Florida, College of Arts and Sciences: Arts, Department of Communication Arts, Pensacola, FL 32514-5750. Offers MA. Part-time and evening/weekend programs available. *Faculty:* 6 full-time (2 women), 1 (woman) part-time/adjunct. *Students:* 11 full-time (8 women), 16 part-time (14 women); includes 2 Black or African American, non-Hispanic/Latino, 2 international. Average age 28. 21 applicants, 81% accepted, 8 enrolled. In 2010, 8 master's awarded. *Degree requirements:* For master's, thesis or alternative. *Entrance requirements:* For master's, GRE General Test, minimum GPA of 3.0. Additional exam requirements/recommendations for international students: Required—TOEFL (minimum score 550 paper-based; 213 computer-based). *Application deadline:* For fall admission, 6/1 for domestic students, 5/15 for international students; for spring admission, 10/1 for domestic and international students. Applications are processed on a rolling basis. Application fee: $30. *Expenses:* Tuition, state resident: full-time $4982; part-time $208 per credit hour. Tuition, nonresident: full-time $20,059; part-time $836 per credit hour. Required fees: $1365; $57 per credit hour. *Financial support:* In 2010–11, 5 fellowships with partial tuition reimbursements (averaging $904 per year), 6 research assistantships (averaging $3,280 per year), 5 teaching assistantships with partial tuition reimbursements (averaging $4,256 per year) were awarded; unspecified assistantships also available. Financial award application deadline: 4/15; financial award applicants required to submit FAFSA. *Faculty research:* Equity studies. *Unit head:* Dr. Brendan B. Kelly, Chairperson, 850-474-2332. *Application contact:* Terry McCray, Assistant Director of Graduate Admissions, 850-473-7718, Fax: 850-473-7714, E-mail: gradadmissions@uwf.edu.

University of Windsor, Faculty of Graduate Studies, Faculty of Arts and Social Sciences, Department of Communication Studies, Windsor, ON N9B 3P4, Canada. Offers communication and social justice (MA). *Degree requirements:* For master's, thesis. *Entrance requirements:* For master's, writing sample/media production or multimedia portfolio. Additional exam requirements/recommendations for international students: Required—TOEFL (minimum score 600 paper-based; 250 computer-based). Electronic applications accepted. *Faculty research:* Sociology of news, media ownership and control, communication networks and social movements, issues of media representation.

University of Wisconsin–Madison, Graduate School, College of Letters and Science, Department of Communication Arts, Madison, WI 53706-1380. Offers communication science (MA, PhD); film (MA, PhD); media and cultural studies (MA, PhD); rhetoric (MA, PhD). Terminal master's awarded for partial completion of doctoral program. *Degree requirements:* For master's, one foreign language, thesis (for some programs); for doctorate, one foreign language, thesis/dissertation. *Entrance requirements:* For master's and doctorate, GRE General Test, minimum GPA of 3.5. Electronic applications accepted. *Expenses:* Tuition, state resident: full-time $9887; part-time $617.96 per credit. Tuition, nonresident: full-time $24,054; part-time $1503.40 per credit. Required fees: $67.63 per credit. Tuition and fees vary according to reciprocity agreements.

University of Wisconsin–Madison, Graduate School, College of Letters and Science, School of Journalism and Mass Communication, Madison, WI 53706-1380. Offers family and consumer journalism (PhD); journalism and mass communication (MA); mass communication (PhD). Part-time programs available. *Degree requirements:* For master's, thesis (for some programs); for doctorate, thesis/dissertation. *Entrance requirements:* For master's, GRE General Test, minimum GPA of 3.0; for doctorate, GRE General Test, minimum GPA of 3.5. Additional exam requirements/recommendations for international students: Required—TOEFL. Electronic applications accepted. *Expenses:* Tuition, state resident: full-time $9887; part-time $617.96 per credit. Tuition, nonresident: full-time $24,054; part-time $1503.40 per credit. Required fees: $67.63 per credit. Tuition and fees vary according to reciprocity agreements. *Faculty research:* International/development communication; strategic mass communication; mass communication and the individual; science, technology, and environment communication; mass communication and societal institutions.

University of Wisconsin–Milwaukee, Graduate School, College of Letters and Sciences, Department of Communication, Milwaukee, WI 53201-0413. Offers communication (MA, PhD); mediation and negotiation (Certificate); rhetorical leadership (Certificate). Part-time programs available. *Faculty:* 20 full-time (12 women). *Students:* 20 full-time (14 women), 36 part-time (29 women); includes 1 Black or African American, non-Hispanic/Latino; 1 Asian, non-Hispanic/Latino; 1 Hispanic/Latino, 6 international. Average age 32. 68 applicants, 57% accepted, 11 enrolled. In 2010, 21 master's awarded. *Degree requirements:* For master's, thesis or alternative; for doctorate, comprehensive exam. *Entrance requirements:* For master's, GRE General Test, minimum GPA of 3.0. Additional exam requirements/recommendations for international students: Required—TOEFL (minimum score 550 paper-based; 79 iBT), IELTS (minimum score 6). *Application deadline:* For fall admission, 1/1 priority date for domestic students; for spring admission, 9/1 for domestic students. Applications are processed on a rolling basis. Application fee: $56. Electronic applications accepted. *Financial support:* In 2010–11, 3 fellowships, 34 teaching assistantships were awarded; research assistantships, career-related internships or fieldwork, unspecified assistantships, and project assistantships also available. Support available to part-time students. Financial award application deadline: 4/15; financial award applicants required to submit FAFSA. Total annual research expenditures: $106,365. *Unit head:* Mike R. Allen, Representative, 414-229-4261, Fax: 414-229-3859, E-mail: mikealle@uwm.edu. *Application contact:* General Information Contact, 414-229-4982, Fax: 414-229-6967, E-mail: gradschool@uwm.edu.

University of Wisconsin–Stevens Point, College of Fine Arts and Communication, Division of Communication, Stevens Point, WI 54481-3897. Offers interpersonal communication (MA); mass communication (MA); organizational communication (MA); public relations (MA). Part-time programs available. *Degree requirements:* For master's, thesis or alternative. *Entrance requirements:* For master's, GRE. Additional exam requirements/recommendations for international students: Required—TOEFL (minimum score 575 paper-based). *Faculty research:* Communication theory and research, film history.

University of Wisconsin–Superior, Graduate Division, Department of Communicating Arts, Superior, WI 54880-4500. Offers mass communication (MA); speech communication (MA); theater (MA). Part-time programs available. *Degree requirements:* For master's, comprehensive exam, thesis or alternative, position paper or project. *Entrance requirements:* For master's, minimum GPA of 2.75. *Faculty research:* Multimedia technology, ethics in journalism, diversity, electronic portfolio assessment.

University of Wisconsin–Whitewater, School of Graduate Studies, College of Arts and Communications, Department of Communication, Whitewater, WI 53190-1790. Offers corporate communication (MS); mass communication (MS). Part-time and evening/weekend programs available. Postbaccalaureate distance learning degree programs offered (no on-campus study). *Degree requirements:* For master's, thesis or alternative. *Entrance requirements:* For master's, 2 letters of recommendation. Additional exam requirements/recommendations for international students: Required—TOEFL (minimum score 550 paper-based; 213 computer-based). Electronic applications accepted.

University of Wyoming, College of Arts and Sciences, Department of Communication and Journalism, Laramie, WY 82070. Offers communication (MA). Part-time programs available. *Degree requirements:* For master's, thesis. *Entrance requirements:* For master's, GRE General Test, minimum GPA of 3.0. *Faculty research:* Personal relations, nonverbal behavior, media management, communication technology, conversation analysis.

Utah State University, School of Graduate Studies, College of Humanities, Arts and Social Sciences, Department of Journalism and Communication, Logan, UT 84322. Offers MA, MS. Part-time programs available. *Degree requirements:* For master's, comprehensive exam, thesis. *Entrance requirements:* For master's, GRE General Test or MAT, minimum GPA of 3.0. Additional exam requirements/recommendations for international students: Required—TOEFL. Electronic applications accepted. *Faculty research:* Race and gender and media, history of censorship, internet design and advertising, technology gap.

Valparaiso University, Graduate School, Program in Media and Communication, Valparaiso, IN 46383. Offers digital media (MS); sports media (MS, Certificate). Part-time and evening/weekend programs available. *Students:* 22 full-time (13 women), 10 part-time (2 women); includes 2 minority (both Black or African American, non-Hispanic/Latino), 18 international. Average age 26. In 2010, 7 master's awarded. *Entrance requirements:* For master's, minimum GPA of 3.0, undergraduate minor in communication. Additional exam requirements/recommendations for international students: Required—TOEFL (minimum score 550 paper-based; 213 computer-based; 80 iBT). *Application deadline:* Applications are processed on a rolling basis. Application fee: $30 ($50 for international students). Electronic applications accepted. *Expenses:* Tuition: Full-time $9540; part-time $530 per credit hour. Required fees: $292; $95 per semester. Tuition and fees vary according to program. *Financial support:* Available to part-time students. Applicants required to submit FAFSA. *Unit head:* Dr. David L. Rowland, Dean, Graduate School and Continuing Education/Associate Provost, 219-464-5313, Fax: 219-464-5381, E-mail: david.rowland@valpo.edu. *Application contact:* Laura Groth, Coordinator of Student Services and Support, 219-464-5313, Fax: 219-464-5381, E-mail: laura.groth@valpo.edu.

Villanova University, Graduate School of Liberal Arts and Sciences, Department of Communication, Villanova, PA 19085-1699. Offers MA. Part-time and evening/weekend programs available. *Faculty:* 7 full-time (2 women). *Students:* 30 full-time (20 women), 16 part-time (10 women); includes 6 minority (3 Black or African American, non-Hispanic/Latino; 1 Asian, non-Hispanic/Latino; 1 Hispanic/Latino; 1 Two or more races, non-Hispanic/Latino), 4 international. Average age 29. 34 applicants, 97% accepted, 16 enrolled. In 2010, 20 master's awarded. *Degree requirements:* For master's, comprehensive exam (for some programs), thesis optional. *Entrance requirements:* For master's, GRE or GMAT, minimum GPA of 3.0, writing sample, personal essay. Additional exam requirements/recommendations for international students: Required—TOEFL. *Application deadline:* For fall admission, 2/1 priority date for domestic and international students; for spring admission, 11/15 priority date for domestic and international students. Applications are processed on a rolling basis. Application fee: $50. Electronic applications accepted. *Expenses:* Tuition: Part-time $700 per credit. Part-time tuition and fees vary according to degree level and program. *Financial support:* Research assistantships, Federal Work-Study available. Financial award applicants required to submit FAFSA. *Unit head:* Dr. Emory Woodard, Director of Graduate Studies in Communication, 610-519-4780. *Application contact:* Dr. Emory Woodard, Director of Graduate Studies in Communication, 610-519-4780.

Virginia Commonwealth University, Graduate School, College of Humanities and Sciences, School of Mass Communications, Program in Media, Art, and Text, Richmond, VA 23284-9005. Offers PhD. *Students:* 20 full-time (15 women), 22 part-time (11 women); includes 10 minority (3 Black or African American, non-Hispanic/Latino; 1 American Indian or Alaska Native, non-Hispanic/Latino; 2 Asian, non-Hispanic/Latino; 3 Hispanic/Latino; 1 Two or more races, non-Hispanic/Latino), 1 international. 29 applicants, 31% accepted, 6 enrolled. In 2010, 1 doctorate awarded. *Entrance requirements:* For doctorate, GRE. Additional exam requirements/recommendations for international students: Required—TOEFL (minimum score 600 paper-based; 250 computer-based; 100 iBT); Recommended—IELTS (minimum score 6.5). *Application deadline:* For fall admission, 1/15 for domestic students. Application fee: $50. Electronic applications accepted. *Expenses:* Tuition, state resident: full-time $4308; part-time $479 per credit hour. Tuition, nonresident: full-time $8942; part-time $994 per credit hour. Required fees: $2000; $85 per credit hour. Tuition and fees vary according to course level, course load, degree level, campus/location and program. *Unit head:* Dr. Eric G. Garberson, Director, MATX Ph.D. Program, 804-828-7295, E-mail: eggarberson@vcu.edu. *Application contact:* Thom N. Didato, Graduate Programs Adviser, 804-828-1329, E-mail: tndidato@vcu.edu.

Virginia Polytechnic Institute and State University, Graduate School, College of Liberal Arts and Human Sciences, Department of Communication, Blacksburg, VA 24061. Offers MA. *Faculty:* 25 full-time (12 women). *Students:* 18 full-time (13 women), 2 part-time (both women); includes 1 Black or African American, non-Hispanic/Latino; 1 Asian, non-Hispanic/Latino, 1 international. Average age 25. 16 applicants, 94% accepted, 9 enrolled. In 2010, 9 master's awarded. *Degree requirements:* For master's, comprehensive exam (for some programs), thesis (for some programs). *Entrance requirements:* For master's, GRE. Additional exam requirements/recommendations for international students: Required—TOEFL (minimum score 550 paper-based; 213 computer-based). *Application deadline:* For fall admission, 7/1 for domestic and international students; for spring admission, 12/1 for domestic and international students. Applications are processed on a rolling basis. Application fee: $65. Electronic applications accepted. *Expenses:* Tuition, state resident: full-time $9399; part-time $488 per credit hour. Tuition, nonresident: full-time $17,854; part-time $957.75 per credit hour. Required fees: $1534. Full-time tuition and fees vary according to program. *Financial support:* In 2010–11, 13 teaching assistantships with full tuition reimbursements (averaging $11,894 per year) were awarded; career-related internships or fieldwork, Federal Work-Study, scholarships/grants, health care benefits, and unspecified assistantships also available. Financial award application deadline: 1/15. Total annual research expenditures: $2,587. *Unit head:* Dr. Robert E. Denton, UNIT HEAD, 540-231-7166, Fax: 540-231-9817, E-mail: rdenton@vt.edu. *Application contact:* Beth Waggenspack, Contact, 540-231-7625, Fax: 540-231-9817, E-mail: bwaggens@vt.edu.

Wake Forest University, Graduate School of Arts and Sciences, Department of Communication, Winston-Salem, NC 27109. Offers speech communication (MA). Part-time programs available. *Degree requirements:* For master's, one foreign language, thesis. *Entrance requirements:* For master's, GRE General Test, writing sample. Additional exam requirements/recommendations for international students: Required—TOEFL (minimum score 213 computer-based; 79 iBT). Electronic applications accepted.

Washington State University, Graduate School, The Edward R. Murrow College of Communication, Pullman, WA 99164-2520. Offers health communications (MA, PhD); intercultural and international communications (MA, PhD); media and society (MA, PhD); media process and effects (MA, PhD); organizational communications (MA, PhD). *Faculty:* 30. *Students:* 43 full-time (26 women), 6 part-time (4 women); includes 1 Asian, non-Hispanic/Latino; 1 Hispanic/Latino, 19 international. Average age 30. 120 applicants, 22% accepted, 19 enrolled. In 2010, 22 master's, 1 doctorate awarded. *Degree requirements:* For master's, comprehensive exam (for some programs), thesis optional, oral exam; for doctorate, comprehensive exam, thesis/dissertation. *Entrance requirements:* For master's, GRE General Test, minimum GPA of 3.25, 3 letters of recommendation; for doctorate, GRE General Test, minimum undergraduate GPA of 3.25, graduate 3.5; MA in communication; 3 letters of recommendation. Additional exam requirements/recommendations for international students: Required—TOEFL (minimum score 580 paper-based; 237 computer-based). *Application deadline:* For fall admission, 1/15 priority date for domestic students, 3/1 for international students. Applications are processed on a rolling basis. Application fee: $50. Electronic applications accepted. *Expenses:* Tuition, state resident: full-time $8552; part-time $443 per credit. Tuition, nonresident: full-time $21,650; part-time $1083 per credit. Required fees: $846. *Financial support:* In 2010–11, 46 students received support, including 2 fellowships (averaging $4,477 per year), 7 research assistantships with full and partial tuition reimbursements available (averaging $13,917 per year), 34 teaching assistantships with full and partial tuition reimbursements available (averaging $13,056 per year); career-related internships or fieldwork, Federal Work-Study, institutionally sponsored loans, tuition waivers (partial), and teaching associateships also available. Financial award application deadline: 4/1; financial award applicants required to submit FAFSA. *Faculty research:* Advocacy communication, mediated communication in decision making, communication technology policy and effects, multicultural and international psychology and physiology of communication. Total annual research expenditures: $550,455. *Unit head:* Dr. Erica Austin, Interim Director, 509-335-1556, E-mail: eaustin@wsu.edu. *Application contact:* Graduate School Admissions, 800-GRADWSU, Fax: 509-335-1949, E-mail: gradsch@wsu.edu.

Wayne State College, School of Education and Counseling, Department of Educational Foundations and Leadership, Program in Curriculum and Instruction, Wayne, NE 68787. Offers alternative education (MSE); business and information technology education (MSE); communication arts education (MSE); early childhood education (MSE); elementary education (MSE); English as a second language (MSE); English education (MSE); family and consumer sciences education (MSE); industrial technology and vocational education (MSE); learning communities (MSE); mathematics education (MSE); music education (MSE); science education (MSE); social science education (MSE). *Accreditation:* NCATE. Part-time and evening/weekend programs available. *Degree requirements:* For master's, comprehensive exam, thesis optional. *Entrance requirements:* For master's, GRE General Test. Additional exam requirements/recommendations for international students: Required—TOEFL (minimum score 550 paper-based; 213 computer-based).

Wayne State University, College of Fine, Performing and Communication Arts, Department of Communication, Detroit, MI 48202. Offers communication studies (MA, PhD); public relations and organizational communication (MA); radio-TV-film (MA, PhD); speech communication (MA, PhD). *Faculty:* 25 full-time (11 women), 4 part-time/adjunct (1 woman). *Students:* 64 full-time (43 women), 107 part-time (73 women); includes 44 minority (36 Black or African American, non-Hispanic/Latino; 2 American Indian or Alaska Native, non-Hispanic/Latino; 1 Asian, non-Hispanic/Latino; 5 Hispanic/Latino), 7 international. Average age 32. 65 applicants, 66% accepted, 31 enrolled. In 2010, 37 master's, 7 doctorates awarded. *Degree requirements:* For master's, thesis, essay, or comprehensive exam; for doctorate, thesis/dissertation. *Entrance requirements:* For master's, minimum GPA of 3.0, sample of academic writing; for doctorate, GRE, minimum GPA of 3.3, MA; letters of recommendation; personal statement; sample of written scholarship. Additional exam requirements/recommendations for international students: Required—TOEFL (minimum score 550 paper-based; 213 computer-based); Recommended—TWE (minimum score 6). *Application deadline:* For fall admission, 4/1 for domestic students, 6/1 for international students; for winter admission, 10/1 for international students; for spring admission, 2/1 for international students. Applications are processed on a rolling basis. Application fee: $30 ($50 for international students). Electronic applications accepted. *Expenses:* Tuition, state resident: full-time $7662; part-time $478.85 per credit hour. Tuition, nonresident: full-time $16,920; part-time $1057.55 per credit hour. Required fees: $571.20; $35.70 per credit hour. $188.05 per semester. Tuition and fees vary according to course load and program. *Financial support:* In 2010–11, 22 students received support, including 8 fellowships with tuition reimbursements available (averaging $14,956 per year), 1 research assistantship with tuition reimbursement available (averaging $23,000 per year), 19 teaching assistantships with tuition reimbursements available (averaging $14,620 per year); career-related internships or fieldwork also available. Financial award application deadline: 2/1. *Faculty research:* Rhetorical theory and criticism; mass media theory and research; argumentation; organizational communication; risk and crisis communication; interpersonal, family, and health communication. *Unit head:* Dr. Matthew Seeger, Chair, 313-577-2959, Fax: 313-577-6300, E-mail: aa4331@wayne.edu. *Application contact:* Hayg Oshagan, Associate Professor, 313-577-0429, E-mail: ad4570@wayne.edu.

Webster University, School of Communications, St. Louis, MO 63119-3194. Offers MA. Part-time and evening/weekend programs available. Postbaccalaureate distance learning degree programs offered. *Degree requirements:* For master's, thesis (for some programs). *Entrance requirements:* For master's, 36 hours of graduate course work. Additional exam requirements/recommendations for international students: Required—TOEFL. *Expenses:* Tuition: Part-time $585 per credit hour. Tuition and fees vary according to degree level, campus/location and program.

West Chester University of Pennsylvania, Office of Graduate Studies, College of Arts and Sciences, Department of Communication Studies, West Chester, PA 19383. Offers communication studies (MA). Part-time and evening/weekend programs available. *Students:* 16 full-time (14 women), 20 part-time (15 women); includes 7 minority (4 Black or African American, non-Hispanic/Latino; 2 Asian, non-Hispanic/Latino; 1 Hispanic/Latino), 1 international. Average age 30. 23 applicants, 78% accepted, 13 enrolled. In 2010, 7 master's awarded. *Degree*

Communication—General

West Chester University of Pennsylvania (continued)
requirements: For master's, comprehensive exam, thesis optional. *Entrance requirements:* For master's, GRE or MAT, minimum overall GPA of 2.8, 3.0 in major; writing sample; 3 letters of reference. Additional exam requirements/recommendations for international students: Required—TOEFL (minimum score 550 paper-based; 213 computer-based; 80 iBT). *Application deadline:* For fall admission, 4/15 priority date for domestic students, 3/15 for international students; for spring admission, 10/15 for domestic students, 9/1 for international students. Applications are processed on a rolling basis. Application fee: $35. Electronic applications accepted. *Expenses:* Tuition, state resident: full-time $6966; part-time $387 per credit. Tuition, nonresident: full-time $11,146; part-time $619 per credit. Required fees: $1614.40; $133.24 per credit. Part-time tuition and fees vary according to campus/location. *Financial support:* Unspecified assistantships available. Support available to part-time students. Financial award application deadline: 2/15; financial award applicants required to submit FAFSA. *Faculty research:* Leadership, rhetorical communication, social media, intercultural communication and conflict management. *Unit head:* Dr. Timothy Brown, Chair, 610-436-2500, E-mail: tbrown@wcupa.edu. *Application contact:* Dr. Denise Polk, Graduate Coordinator, 610-436-2180, E-mail: dpolk@wcupa.edu.

Western Illinois University, School of Graduate Studies, College of Fine Arts and Communication, Department of Communication, Macomb, IL 61455-1390. Offers MA. Part-time programs available. *Students:* 19 full-time (12 women), 8 part-time (6 women); includes 8 minority (4 Black or African American, non-Hispanic/Latino; 1 Asian, non-Hispanic/Latino; 2 Hispanic/Latino; 1 Two or more races, non-Hispanic/Latino), 3 international. Average age 28. 21 applicants, 71% accepted. In 2010, 13 master's awarded. *Degree requirements:* For master's, comprehensive exam (for some programs), thesis or alternative. *Entrance requirements:* Additional exam requirements/recommendations for international students: Required—TOEFL (minimum score 580 paper-based; 237 computer-based; 92 iBT). *Application deadline:* Applications are processed on a rolling basis. Application fee: $30. Electronic applications accepted. *Expenses:* Tuition, state resident: full-time $6370; part-time $265.40 per credit hour. Tuition, nonresident: full-time $12,740; part-time $530.80 per credit hour. Required fees: $75.67 per credit hour. *Financial support:* In 2010–11, 12 students received support, including 6 research assistantships with full tuition reimbursements available (averaging $7,280 per year), 6 teaching assistantships with full tuition reimbursements available (averaging $8,400 per year). Financial award applicants required to submit FAFSA. *Unit head:* Dr. Peter Jorgensen, Chairperson, 309-298-1507. *Application contact:* Evelyn Hoing, Assistant Director of Graduate Studies, 309-298-1806, Fax: 309-298-2345, E-mail: grad-office@wiu.edu.

Western Kentucky University, Graduate Studies, Potter College of Arts and Letters, Department of Communication, Bowling Green, KY 42101. Offers communication (MA); organizational communication (Graduate Certificate). Part-time and evening/weekend programs available. *Degree requirements:* For master's, comprehensive exam, thesis optional, final exam. *Entrance requirements:* For master's, GRE General Test, minimum GPA of 2.75. Additional exam requirements/recommendations for international students: Required—TOEFL (minimum score 555 paper-based; 213 computer-based; 79 iBT). *Faculty research:* Public rhetoric and public address organization communication, teamwork in communication, intercultural crisis communication.

Western Michigan University, Graduate College, College of Arts and Sciences, Department of Communication, Kalamazoo, MI 49008. Offers MA.

Westminster College, Program in Professional Communication, Salt Lake City, UT 84105-3697. Offers MPC. Part-time and evening/weekend programs available. *Faculty:* 7 full-time (3 women), 5 part-time/adjunct (3 women). *Students:* 14 full-time (8 women), 50 part-time (37 women); includes 1 Native Hawaiian or other Pacific Islander, non-Hispanic/Latino; 1 Two or more races, non-Hispanic/Latino, 2 international. Average age 32. 35 applicants, 66% accepted, 17 enrolled. In 2010, 15 master's awarded. *Degree requirements:* For master's, field project. *Entrance requirements:* For master's, resume, professional writing sample, 2 letters of recommendation, official transcripts. Additional exam requirements/recommendations for international students: Required—TOEFL (minimum score 600 paper-based; 250 computer-based; 100 iBT), IELTS (minimum score 7). *Application deadline:* For fall admission, 7/9 for domestic and international students. Applications are processed on a rolling basis. Application fee: $50. Electronic applications accepted. *Expenses:* Contact institution. *Financial support:* In 2010–11, 38 students received support. Career-related internships or fieldwork and tuition reimbursement, tuition remission available. Support available to part-time students. Financial award applicants required to submit FAFSA. *Faculty research:* Critical communication pedagogy, sexuality and gender, autoethnography, regulation of broadcast indecency, hypertext theory. *Unit head:* Dr. Helen Hodgson, Director, 801-832-2821, Fax: 801-832-3102, E-mail: hhodgson@westminstercollege.edu. *Application contact:* Joel Bauman, Vice President of Enrollment Services, 801-832-2200, Fax: 801-832-3101, E-mail: admission@westminstercollege.edu.

West Texas A&M University, College of Fine Arts and Humanities, Department of Art, Communication, and Theater, Program in Communication, Canyon, TX 79016-0001. Offers MA. Part-time programs available. *Degree requirements:* For master's, comprehensive exam, thesis optional. *Entrance requirements:* For master's, GRE General Test, 24 hours of undergraduate communications courses, 1 letter of recommendation, interview with communication advisor. Additional exam requirements/recommendations for international students: Required—TOEFL (minimum score 550 paper-based). Electronic applications accepted. *Faculty research:* Comparison student learning in basic public speaking in traditional versus online format, impact of supervisor immediacy and power on organizational outcomes, storytelling, gender, nonverbal.

West Virginia University, Eberly College of Arts and Sciences, Department of Communication Studies, Morgantown, WV 26506. Offers communication in instruction (MA); communication studies (PhD); communication theory and research (MA); corporate and organizational communication (MA). Part-time programs available. *Degree requirements:* For master's, comprehensive exam (for some programs), thesis (for some programs); for doctorate, comprehensive exam, thesis/dissertation. *Entrance requirements:* For master's and doctorate, minimum GPA of 3.0. Additional exam requirements/recommendations for international students: Required—TOEFL. Electronic applications accepted. *Faculty research:* Instructional communication, interpersonal communication, health communication, influence, instructional communication, social influence.

West Virginia University, Perley Isaac Reed School of Journalism, Program in Integrated Marketing Communications, Morgantown, WV 26506. Offers MS. Part-time programs available. Postbaccalaureate distance learning degree programs offered (no on-campus study). *Entrance requirements:* For master's, GRE or GMAT. Additional exam requirements/recommendations for international students: Required—TOEFL.

Wichita State University, Graduate School, Fairmount College of Liberal Arts and Sciences, Elliot School of Communication, Wichita, KS 67260. Offers MA. Part-time programs available. *Unit head:* Dr. Susan Huxman, Director, 316-978-3185, Fax: 316-978-3006, E-mail: susan.huxman@wichita.edu. *Application contact:* Dr. Patricia Dooley, Graduate Coordinator, 316-978-3185, E-mail: pat.dooley@wichita.edu.

Wilfrid Laurier University, Faculty of Graduate and Postdoctoral Studies, Faculty of Arts, Department of Communication Studies, Waterloo, ON N2L 3C5, Canada. Offers media, technology and culture (MA); visual communication and culture (MA). *Faculty:* 16 full-time (7 women). *Students:* 15 full-time (all women), 1 (woman) part-time, 1 international. 32 applicants, 56% accepted, 10 enrolled. In 2010, 7 master's awarded. *Degree requirements:* For master's, thesis optional. *Entrance requirements:* For master's, honours BA in communication studies or a cognate discipline from an approved university with a minimum B+ overall in last two years of study and in undergraduate major. Additional exam requirements/recommendations for international students: Required—TOEFL (minimum score 89 iBT). *Application deadline:* For fall admission, 2/1 priority date for domestic students, 2/1 for international students. Application fee: $100. Electronic applications accepted. Tuition and fees charges are reported in Canadian dollars. *Expenses:* Tuition, area resident: Full-time $15,300 Canadian dollars; part-time $1200 Canadian dollars per credit. International tuition: $21,300 Canadian dollars full-time. Required fees: $650 Canadian dollars; $100 Canadian dollars per credit. Tuition and fees vary according to course load, degree level, campus/location and program. *Financial support:* In 2010–11, 21 fellowships, 21 teaching assistantships were awarded; career-related internships or fieldwork, scholarships/grants, health care benefits, and unspecified assistantships also available. *Faculty research:* Visual communication and culture, media, technology and culture. *Unit head:* Dr. Martin Morris, Graduate Coordinator, 519-884-0710 Ext. 3015, E-mail: mmorris@wlu.ca. *Application contact:* Jennifer Williams, Graduate Admissions and Records Officer, 519-884-0710 Ext. 3536, Fax: 519-884-1020, E-mail: gradstudies@wlu.ca.

William Paterson University of New Jersey, College of the Arts and Communication, Wayne, NJ 07470-8420. Offers art (MFA); music (MM); professional communication (MA). *Accreditation:* NASAD. Part-time and evening/weekend programs available. *Entrance requirements:* For master's, minimum GPA of 2.75. Electronic applications accepted.

York University, Faculty of Graduate Studies, Program in Communication and Culture, Toronto, ON M3J 1P3, Canada. Offers MA, PhD. PhD, MA offered jointly with Ryerson University. *Degree requirements:* For master's, thesis or alternative; for doctorate, comprehensive exam, thesis/dissertation. Electronic applications accepted.

Arts Journalism

School of the Art Institute of Chicago, Graduate Division, Program in New Arts Journalism, Chicago, IL 60603-3103. Offers MA. *Entrance requirements:* Additional exam requirements/recommendations for international students: Required—TOEFL, IELTS.

See Close-Up on page 225.

Syracuse University, S. I. Newhouse School of Public Communications, Program in Arts Journalism, Syracuse, NY 13244. Offers MA. *Students:* 15 full-time (13 women); includes 2 minority (1 Black or African American, non-Hispanic/Latino; 1 Asian, non-Hispanic/Latino), 2 international. Average age 23. 39 applicants, 69% accepted, 15 enrolled. In 2010, 2 master's awarded. *Degree requirements:* For master's, capstone project. *Entrance requirements:* For master's, GRE General Test. Additional exam requirements/recommendations for international students: Required—TOEFL (minimum score 600 paper-based; 250 computer-based; 100 iBT). *Application deadline:* For fall admission, 2/1 priority date for domestic and international students. Application fee: $45. Electronic applications accepted. *Expenses:* Tuition: Part-time $1162 per credit. *Financial support:* Fellowships with full tuition reimbursements, research assistantships with partial tuition reimbursements, teaching assistantships with partial tuition reimbursements available. Financial award application deadline: 2/1; financial award applicants required to submit FAFSA. *Unit head:* Johanna Keller, Director, 315-443-9251, Fax: 315-443-3946, E-mail: pcgrad@syr.edu. *Application contact:* Martha Coria, Graduate Records Office, 315-443-5749, Fax: 315-443-1834, E-mail: pcgrad@syr.edu.

Broadcast Journalism

American University, School of Communication, Program in Journalism and Public Affairs, Washington, DC 20016-8001. Offers broadcast journalism (MA), including economic communication, international journalism, public policy journalism; interactive journalism (MA); print journalism (MA), including economic communication, international journalism, public policy journalism. *Accreditation:* ACEJMC. *Faculty:* 13 full-time (5 women), 4 part-time/adjunct (all women). *Students:* 39 full-time (29 women). 169 applicants, 74% accepted, 37 enrolled. In 2010, 40 master's awarded. *Degree requirements:* For master's, comprehensive exam, thesis or alternative. *Entrance requirements:* For master's, GRE General Test. Additional exam requirements/recommendations for international students: Required—TOEFL (minimum score 600 paper-based; 250 computer-based; 100 iBT), IELTS (minimum score 7). *Application deadline:* For fall admission, 2/1 priority date for domestic students, 4/1 priority date for international students. Applications are processed on a rolling basis. Application fee: $50. Electronic applications accepted. *Financial support:* In 2010–11, 3 fellowships with full and partial tuition reimbursements (averaging $27,000 per year), 14 research assistantships with partial tuition reimbursements (averaging $7,000 per year), 3 teaching assistantships with partial tuition reimbursements (averaging $7,000 per year) were awarded; career-related internships or fieldwork, Federal Work-Study, institutionally sponsored loans, scholarships/grants, tuition waivers (partial), and unspecified assistantships also available. Financial award application deadline: 2/1; financial award applicants required to submit FAFSA. *Faculty research:* Government and media effects of journalistic practices and policies, race and gender and the media, investigative reporting, computer assisted reporting. *Unit head:* Prof. Jill Olmsted, Division Director, 202-885-2010, E-mail: jolmste@american.edu. *Application contact:* Sharmeen Ahsan-Bracciale, Graduate Admissions Office, 202-885-2040, Fax: 202-885-2019, E-mail: sharmeen@american.edu.

The American University in Cairo, School of Global Affairs and Public Policy, Department of Journalism and Mass Communication, Cairo, Egypt. Offers journalism and mass communication (MA); television and digital journalism (MA). Part-time programs available. *Degree requirements:* For master's, thesis (for some programs). *Entrance requirements:* For master's, English entrance exam, GMAT. Electronic applications accepted. *Faculty research:* Mass media and national development/censorship, intercultural photo communication, comparative journalism/television.

Boston University, College of Communication, Department of Journalism, Boston, MA 02215. Offers broadcast journalism (MS); business and economics journalism (MS); photojournalism (MS); print journalism (MS); science journalism (MS). Part-time programs available. *Faculty:* 23 full-time, 26 part-time/adjunct. *Students:* 72 full-time (54 women), 7 part-time (3 women); includes 2 minority (both Asian, non-Hispanic/Latino), 12 international. Average age 25. In 2010, 62 master's awarded. *Degree requirements:* For master's, thesis. *Entrance requirements:* For master's, GRE General Test, sample of written work. Additional exam requirements/recommendations for international students: Required—TOEFL (minimum score 600 paper-based; 250 computer-based; 100 iBT). *Application deadline:* For fall admission, 2/1 for domestic and international students. Application fee: $70. Electronic applications accepted. *Expenses:* Tuition: Full-time $39,314; part-time $1228 per credit. Required fees: $40 per semester. *Financial support:* Teaching assistantships with partial tuition reimbursements, career-related internships or fieldwork, Federal Work-Study, institutionally sponsored loans, scholarships/grants, and unspecified assistantships available. Support available to part-time students. Financial award application deadline: 2/1; financial award applicants required to submit FAFSA. *Unit head:* William McKeen, Chairman, 617-353-3484, Fax: 617-353-1086, E-mail: wmckeen@bu.edu. *Application contact:* Jennifer Healey, Administrator of Graduate Services, 617-353-3481, Fax: 617-358-0399, E-mail: comgrad@bu.edu.

Emerson College, Graduate Studies, School of Communication, Department of Journalism, Boston, MA 02116-4624. Offers journalism (MA), including broadcast journalism, print/multimedia journalism. *Entrance requirements:* For master's, GRE General Test. Additional exam requirements/recommendations for international students: Required—TOEFL (minimum score 550 paper-based; 213 computer-based; 80 iBT), IELTS (minimum score 6.5). Electronic applications accepted. *Faculty research:* Journalism.

Northwestern University, Medill School of Journalism, Evanston, IL 60208. Offers broadcast journalism (MSJ); integrated marketing communications (MSIMC), including advertising/sales promotion, direct database and e-commerce marketing, general studies, public relations; magazine publishing (MSJ); new media (MSJ); reporting and writing (MSJ). *Accreditation:* ACEJMC (one or more programs are accredited). *Entrance requirements:* For master's, GRE General Test, GMAT or LSAT (MSJ). Additional exam requirements/recommendations for international students: Required—TOEFL. Electronic applications accepted. *Expenses:* Contact institution. *Faculty research:* Web business journalism, cultural stereotypes, voter apathy, digital television.

Syracuse University, S. I. Newhouse School of Public Communications, Program in Broadcast and Digital Journalism, Syracuse, NY 13244. Offers MS. *Students:* 33 full-time (20 women); includes 10 minority (8 Black or African American, non-Hispanic/Latino; 1 Hispanic/Latino; 1 Two or more races, non-Hispanic/Latino), 3 international. Average age 24. 43 applicants, 95% accepted, 31 enrolled. In 2010, 30 master's awarded. *Degree requirements:* For master's, capstone course. *Entrance requirements:* For master's, GRE General Test. Additional exam requirements/recommendations for international students: Required—TOEFL (minimum score 100 iBT). *Application deadline:* For fall admission, 2/1 priority date for domestic and international students. Application fee: $45. Electronic applications accepted. *Expenses:* Tuition: Part-time $1162 per credit. *Financial support:* Fellowships with full tuition reimbursements, research assistantships with partial tuition reimbursements, teaching assistantships with partial tuition reimbursements available. Financial award application deadline: 2/1. *Unit head:* Dona Hayes, Chair, 315-443-1944, Fax: 315-443-3946, E-mail: pcgrad@syr.edu. *Application contact:* Martha Coria, Graduate Records Office, 315-443-5749, Fax: 315-443-1834, E-mail: pcgrad@syr.edu.

University of Maryland, College Park, Academic Affairs, Phillip Merrill College of Journalism, College Park, MD 20742. Offers broadcast journalism (MA); journalism (MA); journalism and media studies (PhD); online news (MA); public affairs reporting (MA). *Accreditation:* ACEJMC (one or more programs are accredited). Part-time and evening/weekend programs available. *Faculty:* 18 full-time (10 women), 43 part-time/adjunct (18 women). *Students:* 76 full-time (46 women), 14 part-time (7 women); includes 20 minority (12 Black or African American, non-Hispanic/Latino; 5 Asian, non-Hispanic/Latino; 3 Hispanic/Latino), 11 international. 243 applicants, 37% accepted, 26 enrolled. In 2010, 26 master's, 5 doctorates awarded. *Degree requirements:* For doctorate, thesis/dissertation, preliminary written and oral comprehensive exams. *Entrance requirements:* For master's and doctorate, GRE General Test, minimum GPA of 3.0, 3 letters of recommendation. Additional exam requirements/recommendations for international students: Required—TOEFL. *Application deadline:* For fall admission, 1/15 for domestic and international students. Applications are processed on a rolling basis. Application fee: $75. Electronic applications accepted. *Expenses:* Tuition, state resident: part-time $471 per credit hour. Tuition, nonresident: part-time $1016 per credit hour. Required fees: $337 per term. *Financial support:* In 2010–11, 3 fellowships with full and partial tuition reimbursements (averaging $11,667 per year), 22 teaching assistantships with tuition reimbursements (averaging $16,647 per year) were awarded; research assistantships with tuition reimbursements, career-related internships or fieldwork, Federal Work-Study, and scholarships/grants also available. Support available to part-time students. Financial award applicants required to submit FAFSA. *Faculty research:* Mass communication theory, specialized journalism, new telecommunication technologies, press integration. Total annual research expenditures: $565,454. *Unit head:* Kevin Klose, Dean and Professor, 301-405-2383, E-mail: kklose@jmail.umd.edu. *Application contact:* Dr. Charles A. Caramello, Dean of Graduate School, 301-405-0358, Fax: 301-314-9305, E-mail: ccaramel@umd.edu.

University of Miami, Graduate School, School of Communication, Coral Gables, FL 33124. Offers communication (PhD); communication studies (MA); film studies (MA, PhD); motion pictures (MFA), including production, producing, and screenwriting; print journalism (MA); public relations (MA); Spanish language journalism (MA); television broadcast journalism (MA). *Accreditation:* ACEJMC. Part-time programs available. *Degree requirements:* For master's, comprehensive exam (for some programs), thesis (for some programs); for doctorate, comprehensive exam, thesis/dissertation. *Entrance requirements:* For master's, GRE General Test; for doctorate, GRE General Test, master's thesis or scholarly research. Additional exam requirements/recommendations for international students: Required—TOEFL (minimum score 600 paper-based; 250 computer-based; 100 iBT). Electronic applications accepted. *Faculty research:* Communication studies, mass communication, international/interpersonal communication, film studies, journalism.

University of Southern California, Graduate School, Annenberg School for Communication and Journalism, School of Journalism, Los Angeles, CA 90089. Offers journalism (MA); online journalism (MA); print journalism (MA); specialized journalism (MA), including specialized journalism, specialized journalism (the arts); strategic public relations (MA). Degree concentrations eliminated effective fall 2011; MA Journalism will replace broadcast, online and print concentrations. *Accreditation:* ACEJMC. *Faculty:* 28 full-time (10 women), 49 part-time/adjunct (14 women). *Students:* 215 full-time, 12 part-time; includes 73 minority (17 Black or African American, non-Hispanic/Latino; 22 Asian, non-Hispanic/Latino; 30 Hispanic/Latino; 1 Native Hawaiian or other Pacific Islander, non-Hispanic/Latino; 3 Two or more races, non-Hispanic/Latino), 33 international. Average age 26. 362 applicants, 61% accepted, 99 enrolled. In 2010, 114 master's awarded. *Degree requirements:* For master's, comprehensive exam (for some programs), thesis (for some programs). *Entrance requirements:* For master's, GRE General Test, resume, writing samples, letters of recommendation, statement of purpose. Additional exam requirements/recommendations for international students: Required—TOEFL (minimum score 280 computer-based; 114 iBT). *Application deadline:* For fall admission, 1/3 priority date for domestic students, 12/1 priority date for international students. Application fee: $85. Electronic applications accepted. *Expenses:* Tuition: Full-time $31,240; part-time $1420 per unit. Required fees: $600. One-time fee: $35 full-time. Full-time tuition and fees vary according to degree level and program. *Financial support:* In 2010–11, 4 fellowships with full tuition reimbursements, 4 research assistantships with full tuition reimbursements were awarded; career-related internships or fieldwork, Federal Work-Study, institutionally sponsored loans, scholarships/grants, health care benefits, and unspecified assistantships also available. Support available to part-time students. Financial award application deadline: 1/15; financial award applicants required to submit FAFSA. *Faculty research:* Image of the journalist in popular culture, diversity and the media, media and religion, immigration and demographic change, war and terrorism. *Unit head:* Geneva Overholser, Director, 213-740-3914, Fax: 213-740-8624, E-mail: jourbks@usc.edu. *Application contact:* Allyson Hill, Assistant Dean, Admissions, 213-821-0770, Fax: 213-740-1933, E-mail: ascadm@usc.edu.

University of the Sacred Heart, Graduate Programs, Department of Communication, San Juan, PR 00914-0383. Offers contemporary culture and media (MA); digital journalism (MA, Certificate); editing for media (MA, Certificate); public relations (MA, Certificate); publicity (MA, Certificate); scriptwriting (MA, Certificate). Part-time and evening/weekend programs available. *Degree requirements:* For master's, thesis.

Corporate and Organizational Communication

American International College, School of Business Administration, MBA Program, Springfield, MA 01109-3189. Offers accounting (MBA); corporate/public communication (MBA); finance (MBA); general business (MBA); hospitality, hotel and service management (MBA); international business (MBA); international business practice (MBA); management (MBA); management information systems (MBA); marketing (MBA). International business practice program developed in cooperation with the Mountbatten Institute.

The American University of Athens, School of Graduate Studies, Athens, Greece. Offers biomedical sciences (MS); business (MBA); business communication (MA); computer sciences (MS); engineering and applied sciences (MS); politics and policy making (MA); systems engineering (MS); telecommunications (MS). *Entrance requirements:* For master's, resume, 2 recommendation letters. Additional exam requirements/recommendations for international students: Required—TOEFL (minimum score 550 paper-based; 213 computer-based). *Faculty research:* Nanotechnology, environmental sciences, rock mechanics, human skin studies, Monte Carlo algorithms and software.

Antioch University Seattle, Graduate Programs, Center for Creative Change, Seattle, WA 98121-1814. Offers environment and community (MA); management (MS); organizational psychology (MA); strategic communications (MA); whole system design (MA). Evening/weekend programs available. Electronic applications accepted. *Expenses:* Contact institution.

Argosy University, Schaumburg, College of Business, Schaumburg, IL 60173-5403. Offers accounting (DBA, Adv C); customized professional concentration (MBA, DBA); finance (MBA, Certificate); fraud examination (MBA); global business sustainability (DBA); healthcare administration (MBA, Certificate); information systems (DBA, Adv C, Certificate); information systems management (MBA); international business (MBA, DBA, Adv C, Certificate); management (MBA, MSM, DBA, Adv C, Certificate); marketing (MBA, DBA, Adv C, Certificate); organizational leadership (Ed D); public administration (MBA); sustainable management (MBA).

Barry University, School of Arts and Sciences, Department of Communication, Miami Shores, FL 33161-6695. Offers broadcasting (Certificate); communication (MA), including broadcast communication, public relations and corporate communications; organizational communication (MS). Part-time and evening/weekend programs available. *Degree requirements:* For master's, thesis (for some programs). *Entrance requirements:* For master's, GRE General Test, MAT, minimum GPA of 3.0. Electronic applications accepted. *Faculty research:* Organizational communication, broadcast communication, intercultural communication, advertising, leadership.

Bernard M. Baruch College of the City University of New York, Weissman School of Arts and Sciences, Program in Corporate Communication, New York, NY 10010-5585. Offers MA.

Boston University, Metropolitan College, Program in Gastronomy, Boston, MA 02215. Offers business (MLA); communications (MLA); food policy (MLA); history and culture (MLA). Part-time and evening/weekend programs available. *Faculty:* 1 (woman) full-time, 11 part-time/adjunct (5 women). *Students:* 7 full-time (all women), 64 part-time (52 women); includes 13 minority (3 Black or African American, non-Hispanic/Latino; 1 American Indian or Alaska Native, non-Hispanic/Latino; 6 Asian, non-Hispanic/Latino; 1 Hispanic/Latino; 2 Two or more races, non-Hispanic/Latino), 2 international. Average age 29. 30 applicants, 93% accepted, 26 enrolled. In 2010, 9 master's awarded. *Degree requirements:* For master's, thesis optional. *Entrance requirements:* Additional exam requirements/recommendations for international students: Required—TOEFL. *Application deadline:* Applications are processed on a rolling basis. Application fee: $70. Electronic applications accepted. *Expenses:* Tuition: Full-time $39,314; part-time $1228 per credit. Required fees: $40 per semester. *Financial support:* In 2010–11, 4 research assistantships with partial tuition reimbursements (averaging $2,500 per year), 1 teaching assistantship (averaging $2,500 per year) were awarded; career-related internships or fieldwork, scholarships/grants, and unspecified assistantships also available. Support available to part-time students. Financial award applicants required to submit FAFSA. *Faculty research:* Food studies. *Unit head:* Dr. Rachel Black, Assistant Professor, 617-353-6291, Fax: 617-353-4130, E-mail: rblack@bu.edu. *Application contact:* Dr. Rachel Black, Assistant Professor, 617-353-6291, Fax: 617-353-4130, E-mail: rblack@bu.edu.

Bowie State University, Graduate Programs, Program in Organizational Communication, Bowie, MD 20715-9465. Offers MA, Certificate. Part-time and evening/weekend programs available. *Degree requirements:* For master's, comprehensive exam, thesis optional, research paper. *Entrance requirements:* For master's, minimum GPA of 2.5. Electronic applications accepted. *Expenses:* Tuition, state resident: full-time $4080; part-time $340 per credit. Tuition, nonresident: full-time $7752; part-time $646 per credit. Required fees: $2128; $340 per credit. *Faculty research:* International telecommunications, developmental communications.

California State University, San Bernardino, Graduate Studies, College of Arts and Letters, Department of Communication Studies, San Bernardino, CA 92407-2397. Offers communication studies (MA); integrated marketing communication (MA). *Degree requirements:* For master's, comprehensive exam, advancement to candidacy. *Entrance requirements:* Additional exam requirements/recommendations for international students: Required—TOEFL.

Corporate and Organizational Communication

Canisius College, Graduate Division, College of Arts and Sciences, Department of Communication Studies, Buffalo, NY 14208-1098. Offers communication and leadership (MS). Part-time and evening/weekend programs available. *Faculty:* 11 full-time (4 women), 3 part-time/adjunct (0 women). *Students:* 10 full-time (6 women), 32 part-time (20 women); includes 4 minority (2 Black or African American, non-Hispanic/Latino; 2 Hispanic/Latino), 1 international. Average age 28. 23 applicants, 61% accepted, 8 enrolled. In 2010, 12 master's awarded. *Degree requirements:* For master's, thesis. *Entrance requirements:* For master's, GRE, transcripts. Additional exam requirements/recommendations for international students: Required—TOEFL. *Application deadline:* For fall admission, 7/15 priority date for domestic students; for spring admission, 4/15 priority date for domestic students. Applications are processed on a rolling basis. Application fee: $25. Electronic applications accepted. *Expenses:* Tuition: Part-time $694 per credit hour. Required fees: $11 per credit hour. $90 per semester. *Financial support:* Career-related internships or fieldwork, Federal Work-Study, scholarships/grants, and unspecified assistantships available. Support available to part-time students. Financial award application deadline: 7/1; financial award applicants required to submit FAFSA. *Faculty research:* Conflict and communication, health and communication, leadership. *Unit head:* Dr. Rosanne L. Hartman, Graduate Program Director/Professor, Communication and Leadership, 716-888-2589, Fax: 716-888-3118, E-mail: hartmanr@canisius.edu. *Application contact:* Stephanie Q. Cattarin, Assistant Director, Graduate Programs, 716-888-2212, E-mail: cattaris@canisius.edu.

Carnegie Mellon University, College of Humanities and Social Sciences, Department of English, Program in Professional Writing, Pittsburgh, PA 15213-3891. Offers editing and publishing (MAPW); policy and non-profit communication (MAPW); public and media relations / corporate communications (MAPW); science or healthcare communication (MAPW); technical writing (MAPW); writing for new media (MAPW); writing for print media (MAPW). Part-time programs available. *Entrance requirements:* For master's, GRE General Test. Additional exam requirements/recommendations for international students: Required—TOEFL, TWE.

Central Connecticut State University, School of Graduate Studies, School of Arts and Sciences, Department of Communication, New Britain, CT 06050-4010. Offers organizational communication (MS); public relations/promotions (Certificate). Part-time and evening/weekend programs available. *Faculty:* 12 full-time (4 women), 8 part-time/adjunct (2 women). *Students:* 12 full-time (6 women), 17 part-time (12 women); includes 5 minority (2 Black or African American, non-Hispanic/Latino; 1 Asian, non-Hispanic/Latino; 2 Hispanic/Latino). Average age 28. 19 applicants, 42% accepted, 5 enrolled. In 2010, 16 master's awarded. *Degree requirements:* For master's, comprehensive exam, thesis or alternative; for Certificate, qualifying exam. *Entrance requirements:* For master's, minimum undergraduate GPA of 3.0. Additional exam requirements/recommendations for international students: Required—TOEFL. *Application deadline:* For fall admission, 7/1 for domestic students; for spring admission, 12/1 for domestic students. Applications are processed on a rolling basis. Application fee: $50. Electronic applications accepted. *Expenses:* Tuition, area resident: Full-time $5012; part-time $470 per credit. Tuition, state resident: full-time $7518; part-time $482 per credit. Tuition, nonresident: full-time $13,962; part-time $482 per credit. Required fees: $3772. One-time fee: $62 part-time. *Financial support:* In 2010–11, 4 students received support, including 2 research assistantships; career-related internships or fieldwork, Federal Work-Study, scholarships/grants, and unspecified assistantships also available. Support available to part-time students. Financial award application deadline: 2/15; financial award applicants required to submit FAFSA. *Faculty research:* Organizational communication, mass communication, intercultural communication, political communication, information management. *Unit head:* Dr. Serafin Mendez-Mendez, Chair, 860-832-2690. *Application contact:* Dr. Serafin Mendez-Mendez, Chair, 860-832-2690.

Central Michigan University, College of Graduate Studies, Interdisciplinary Administration Programs, Mount Pleasant, MI 48859. Offers acquisitions administration (MSA, Graduate Certificate); general administration (MSA, Graduate Certificate); health services administration (MSA, Graduate Certificate); human resource administration (Graduate Certificate); human resources administration (MSA); information resource management (MSA, Graduate Certificate); international administration (MSA, Graduate Certificate); leadership (MSA, Graduate Certificate); organizational communication (MSA, Graduate Certificate); public administration (MSA, Graduate Certificate); recreation and park administration (MSA); sport administration (MSA). *Accreditation:* AACSB. Part-time and evening/weekend programs available. Postbaccalaureate distance learning degree programs offered (no on-campus study). *Students:* 102 full-time (50 women), 77 part-time (51 women); includes 10 Black or African American, non-Hispanic/Latino; 3 American Indian or Alaska Native, non-Hispanic/Latino; 5 Asian, non-Hispanic/Latino, 65 international. Average age 29. *Degree requirements:* For master's, thesis or alternative. *Entrance requirements:* For master's, bachelor's degree with minimum GPA of 2.7. *Application deadline:* For fall admission, 6/1 for international students; for spring admission, 10/1 for international students. Applications are processed on a rolling basis. Application fee: $35 ($45 for international students). Electronic applications accepted. *Expenses:* Tuition, state resident: full-time $8208; part-time $456 per credit hour. Tuition, nonresident: full-time $13,788; part-time $766 per credit hour. One-time fee: $25. *Financial support:* Fellowships with tuition reimbursements, research assistantships with tuition reimbursements, career-related internships or fieldwork, Federal Work-Study, unspecified assistantships, and out-of-state merit awards, non-resident graduate awards available. *Faculty research:* Interdisciplinary studies in acquisitions administration, health services administration, sport administration, recreation and park administration, and international administration. *Unit head:* Dr. Nana Korash, Director, 989-774-6525, Fax: 989-774-2575, E-mail: msa@cmich.edu. *Application contact:* Denise Schafer, Coordinator, 989-774-4373, Fax: 989-774-2575, E-mail: schaf1dr@cmich.edu.

Columbia University, Graduate School of Business, MBA Program, New York, NY 10027. Offers accounting (MBA); decision, risk, and operations (MBA); entrepreneurship (MBA); finance and economics (MBA); healthcare and pharmaceutical management (MBA); human resource management (MBA); international business (MBA); leadership and ethics (MBA); management (MBA); marketing (MBA); media (MBA); private equity (MBA); real estate (MBA); social enterprise (MBA); value investing (MBA); DDS/MBA; JD/MBA; MBA/MIA; MBA/MPH; MBA/MS; MD/MBA. *Entrance requirements:* For master's, GMAT, 2 letters of recommendation. Additional exam requirements/recommendations for international students: Required—TOEFL. Electronic applications accepted. *Expenses:* Contact institution. *Faculty research:* Human decision making and behavioral research; real estate market and mortgage defaults; financial crisis and corporate governance; international business; security analysis and accounting.

Columbia University, School of Continuing Education, Program in Strategic Communications, New York, NY 10027. Offers MS. Part-time and evening/weekend programs available. *Entrance requirements:* For master's, minimum undergraduate GPA of 3.0. Additional exam requirements/recommendations for international students: Required—American Language Program placement test. Electronic applications accepted. *Faculty research:* Marketing communications, public relations, crisis management.

Concordia University, St. Paul, College of Arts and Sciences, St. Paul, MN 55104-5494. Offers strategic communication management (MA). Evening/weekend programs available. *Faculty:* 3 full-time (2 women), 3 part-time/adjunct (0 women). *Students:* 15 full-time (8 women); includes 1 Two or more races, non-Hispanic/Latino. Average age 32. 23 applicants, 83% accepted. *Application deadline:* Applications are processed on a rolling basis. Application fee: $50. Electronic applications accepted. *Expenses:* Tuition: Full-time $7500; part-time $460 per credit. Required fees: $460 per credit. Tuition and fees vary according to program. *Financial support:* Applicants required to submit FAFSA. *Unit head:* Dr. Marilyn Reineck, Dean, 651-641-8850, E-mail: reineck@csp.edu. *Application contact:* Kimberly Craig, Director of Graduate and Cohort Admission, 651-603-6223, Fax: 651-603-6320, E-mail: craig@csp.edu.

Concordia University Wisconsin, Graduate Programs, School of Business and Legal Studies, MBA Program, Mequon, WI 53097-2402. Offers finance (MBA); health care administration (MBA); human resource management (MBA); international business (MBA); international business-bilingual English/Chinese (MBA); management (MBA); management information systems (MBA); managerial communications (MBA); marketing (MBA); public administration (MBA); risk management (MBA). Postbaccalaureate distance learning degree programs offered (minimal on-campus study). *Degree requirements:* For master's, comprehensive exam, thesis or alternative. *Entrance requirements:* Additional exam requirements/recommendations for international students: Required—TOEFL. *Expenses:* Contact institution.

Dallas Baptist University, College of Business, Business Administration Program, Dallas, TX 75211-9299. Offers accounting (MBA); business communication (MBA); conflict resolution management (MBA); e-business (MBA); entrepreneurship (MBA); finance (MBA); health care management (MBA); international business (MBA); leading the non-profit organization (MBA); management (MBA); management information systems (MBA); marketing (MBA); project management (MBA); technology and engineering management (MBA). *Accreditation:* ACBSP. Part-time and evening/weekend programs available. *Entrance requirements:* For master's, GMAT, minimum GPA of 3.0. Additional exam requirements/recommendations for international students: Required—TOEFL, IELTS. Electronic applications accepted. *Expenses:* Tuition: Full-time $11,394; part-time $633 per credit hour. *Faculty research:* Sports management, services marketing, retailing, strategic management, financial planning/investments.

Dallas Baptist University, College of Business, Management Program, Dallas, TX 75211-9299. Offers business communication (MA); conflict resolution management (MA); general management (MA); health care management (MA); human resource management (MA); performance management (MA). Part-time and evening/weekend programs available. *Entrance requirements:* For master's, GRE General Test, minimum GPA of 3.0. Additional exam requirements/recommendations for international students: Required—TOEFL, IELTS. Electronic applications accepted. *Expenses:* Tuition: Full-time $11,394; part-time $633 per credit hour. *Faculty research:* Organizational behavior, conflict personalities.

Dallas Baptist University, Gary Cook School of Leadership, Program in Global Leadership, Dallas, TX 75211-9299. Offers business communication (MA); Christian education/missions (MA); ESL (MA); general studies (MA); global studies (MA); international business (MA); missions (MA); worship/missions (MA). Part-time and evening/weekend programs available. *Entrance requirements:* For master's, minimum GPA of 3.0. Additional exam requirements/recommendations for international students: Required—TOEFL, IELTS. *Expenses:* Tuition: Full-time $11,394; part-time $633 per credit hour.

DePaul University, College of Communication, Chicago, IL 60614. Offers journalism (MA); media, culture and society (MA); organizational and multicultural communication (MA); public relations and advertising (MA). Part-time and evening/weekend programs available. *Faculty:* 31 full-time (17 women), 15 part-time/adjunct (7 women). *Students:* 170 full-time (129 women), 70 part-time (52 women); includes 29 Black or African American, non-Hispanic/Latino; 9 Asian, non-Hispanic/Latino; 20 Hispanic/Latino; 7 Two or more races, non-Hispanic/Latino, 17 international. Average age 29. 354 applicants, 44% accepted, 79 enrolled. In 2010, 64 master's awarded. *Degree requirements:* For master's, comprehensive exam (for some programs), final exam or thesis/project. *Entrance requirements:* For master's, GRE General Test (public relations and advertising), minimum GPA of 3.0, writing sample, letters of recommendation, resume. Additional exam requirements/recommendations for international students: Required—TOEFL (minimum score 590 paper-based; 243 computer-based; 96 iBT). Application fee: $40. Electronic applications accepted. *Financial support:* In 2010–11, 8 students received support, including 4 research assistantships with partial tuition reimbursements available, 2 teaching assistantships with full tuition reimbursements available (averaging $12,000 per year); fellowships with full tuition reimbursements available, career-related internships or fieldwork, scholarships/grants, and tuition waivers (partial) also available. Support available to part-time students. Financial award applicants required to submit FAFSA. *Faculty research:* Intercultural communication, corporate culture, diversity in the working place, organizational socialization, critical cultural studies. *Unit head:* Dr. Jacqueline Taylor, Dean, 773-325-7216, Fax: 773-325-7584, E-mail: jtaylor@depaul.edu. *Application contact:* Ann Spittle, Director of Graduate Admission, 773-325-7315, Fax: 773-325-2395, E-mail: gradcom@depaul.edu.

Drexel University, College of Arts and Sciences, Department of Culture and Communication, Program in Communication, Philadelphia, PA 19104-2875. Offers public communication (MS); science communication (MS); technical communication (MS). Part-time and evening/weekend programs available. *Degree requirements:* For master's, internship, professional portfolio. *Entrance requirements:* For master's, GRE or minimum GPA of 3.0. Additional exam requirements/recommendations for international students: Required—TOEFL. Electronic applications accepted.

Emerson College, Graduate Studies, School of Communication, Department of Communication Studies, Program in Communication Management, Boston, MA 02116-4624. Offers MA. Part-time and evening/weekend programs available. *Entrance requirements:* For master's, GMAT or GRE General Test. Additional exam requirements/recommendations for international students: Required—TOEFL (minimum score 550 paper-based; 213 computer-based; 80 iBT), IELTS (minimum score 6.5). Electronic applications accepted. *Faculty research:* Organizational management, corporate and organizational communication.

Fairleigh Dickinson University, College at Florham, Maxwell Becton College of Arts and Sciences, Department of English, Communication and Philosophy, Program in Corporate and Organizational Communication, Madison, NJ 07940-1099. Offers MA, MA/MBA. *Students:* 16 full-time (14 women), 19 part-time (15 women), 2 international. Average age 29. 15 applicants, 67% accepted, 5 enrolled. In 2010, 8 master's awarded. *Entrance requirements:* For master's, GRE General Test. *Application deadline:* Applications are processed on a rolling basis. Application fee: $40. *Application contact:* Susan Brooman, University Director, Graduate Admissions, 973-443-8905, Fax: 973-443-8088, E-mail: grad@fdu.edu.

Florida Institute of Technology, Graduate Programs, College of Psychology and Liberal Arts, Department of Humanities and Communication, Melbourne, FL 32901-6975. Offers technical and professional communication (MS). Part-time and evening/weekend programs available. *Faculty:* 3 full-time (all women), 1 (woman) part-time/adjunct. *Students:* 11 full-time (7 women), 6 part-time (5 women); includes 5 minority (2 Black or African American, non-Hispanic/Latino; 1 American Indian or Alaska Native, non-Hispanic/Latino; 1 Asian, non-Hispanic/Latino; 1 Hispanic/Latino), 1 international. Average age 38. 5 applicants, 80% accepted, 3 enrolled. In 2010, 2 master's awarded. *Degree requirements:* For master's, comprehensive exam (for some programs), thesis optional. *Entrance requirements:* For master's, GRE (minimum score 1000 verbal and analytical), minimum GPA of 3.0, 2 letters of recommendation, discursive writing sample. Additional exam requirements/recommendations for international students: Required—TOEFL (minimum score 550 paper-based; 213 computer-based; 79 iBT). *Application deadline:* For fall admission, 4/1 for international students; for spring admission, 9/30 for international students. Applications are processed on a rolling basis. Application fee: $50. Electronic applications accepted. *Expenses:* Tuition: Part-time $1040 per credit hour. Tuition and fees vary according to campus/location. *Financial support:* Career-related internships or fieldwork and tuition remissions available. Support available to part-time students. Financial award application deadline: 3/1; financial award applicants required to submit FAFSA. *Faculty research:* Communication of astronomy in the seventeenth century, persuasion and patronage in seventeenth century work, technical and cross-cultural communication. Total annual research expenditures: $4,782. *Unit head:* Dr. Robert A. Taylor, Department Head, 321-674-7384, Fax: 321-674-8109, E-mail: rotaylor@fit.edu. *Application contact:* Cheryl A. Brown, Associate Director of Graduate Admissions, 321-674-7581, Fax: 321-723-9468, E-mail: cbrown@fit.edu.

Florida State University, The Graduate School, College of Communication and Information, School of Communication, Tallahassee, FL 32306. Offers corporate and public communication (MS); integrated marketing communication (MA, MS); mass communication (PhD); media and communication studies (MA, MS); speech communication (PhD). Part-time programs available. *Faculty:* 24 full-time (9 women), 6 part-time/adjunct (1 woman). *Students:* 147 full-time (94 women), 63 part-time (38 women); includes 92 minority (26 Black or African American, non-Hispanic/Latino; 2 American Indian or Alaska Native, non-Hispanic/Latino; 45 Asian, non-Hispanic/Latino; 16 Hispanic/Latino; 1 Native Hawaiian or other Pacific Islander, non-Hispanic/Latino; 2 Two or more races, non-Hispanic/Latino). Average age 24. 268 applicants, 57% accepted, 79 enrolled. In 2010, 103 master's, 4 doctorates awarded. *Degree requirements:* For master's, thesis (for some programs); for doctorate, comprehensive exam, thesis/dissertation. *Entrance requirements:* For master's, GRE General Test, minimum GPA of 3.0; for doctorate, GRE General Test, minimum GPA of 3.3 in graduate course work. Additional exam requirements/recommendations for international students: Required—TOEFL (minimum score 600 paper-based; 250 computer-based; 100 iBT). *Application deadline:* For fall admission, 7/1 priority date for domestic students, 5/1 priority date for international students; for spring admission, 11/1 priority date for domestic and international students. Applications are processed on a rolling basis. Application fee: $30. Electronic applications accepted. *Expenses:* Tuition, state resident: full-time $8238.24. *Financial support:* In 2010–11, 52 students received support, including 1 fellowship with full tuition reimbursement available, 8 research assistantships with full tuition reimbursements available (averaging $14,000 per year), 40 teaching assistantships with full tuition reimbursements available (averaging $5,000 per year); career-related internships or fieldwork, Federal Work-Study, institutionally sponsored loans, scholarships/grants, tuition waivers (partial), and unspecified assistantships also available. Support available to part-time students. Financial award application deadline: 2/1; financial award applicants required to submit FAFSA. *Faculty research:* Communication technology and policy, marketing communication, communication content and effect, new communication/information technologies. Total annual research expenditures: $400,000. *Unit head:* Dr. Stephen D. McDowell, Director, 850-644-2276, Fax: 850-644-8642, E-mail: steve.mcdowell@cci.fsu.edu. *Application contact:* Natashia Hinson-Turner, Graduate Coordinator, 850-644-8746, Fax: 850-644-8642, E-mail: natashia.turner@cci.fsu.edu.

Fordham University, Graduate School of Business, New York, NY 10023. Offers accounting (MBA); communications and media management (MBA); executive business administration (EMBA); finance (MBA, MS); information systems (MBA, MS); management systems (MBA); marketing (MBA); media management (MS); taxation (MS); taxation and accounting (MTA);); JD/MBA; MBA/MIM; MS/MBA. MBA/MIM offered jointly with Thunderbird School of Global Management. *Accreditation:* AACSB. Part-time and evening/weekend programs available. *Entrance requirements:* For master's, GMAT, 2 letters of recommendation, resume. Additional exam requirements/recommendations for international students: Required—TOEFL (minimum score 600 paper-based; 250 computer-based; 100 iBT). Electronic applications accepted. *Expenses:* Contact institution.

Franklin University, Marketing and Communications Program, Columbus, OH 43215-5399. Offers MS. Part-time and evening/weekend programs available. *Students:* 109 full-time (77 women), 37 part-time (28 women); includes 21 minority (17 Black or African American, non-Hispanic/Latino; 3 Asian, non-Hispanic/Latino; 1 Hispanic/Latino), 2 international. Average age 34. In 2010, 33 master's awarded. *Entrance requirements:* For master's, minimum undergraduate GPA of 2.75. Additional exam requirements/recommendations for international students: Required—TOEFL (minimum score 550 paper-based; 213 computer-based). *Application deadline:* For fall admission, 8/1 priority date for domestic students, 6/1 for international students; for winter admission, 12/1 priority date for domestic students, 10/1 for international students; for spring admission, 4/15 priority date for domestic students, 2/1 for international students. Applications are processed on a rolling basis. Application fee: $30. Electronic applications accepted. *Expenses:* Tuition: Full-time $9720; part-time $540 per credit hour. One-time fee: $30. Tuition and fees vary according to program. *Financial support:* Application deadline: 6/30. *Unit head:* Dr. Doug Ross, Program Chair, 614-947-6149. *Application contact:* Graduate Services Office, 614-797-4700, Fax: 614-224-7723, E-mail: gradschl@franklin.edu.

HEC Montreal, School of Business Administration, Diploma Programs in Administration, Program in Marketing Communication, Montréal, QC H3T 2A7, Canada. Offers Diploma. All courses are given in French. Program offered on part-time basis only. Part-time programs available. *Students:* 83 part-time (69 women). 82 applicants, 44% accepted, 32 enrolled. In 2010, 30 Diplomas awarded. *Degree requirements:* For Diploma, one foreign language. *Entrance requirements:* For degree, relevant work experience, letters of recommendation. *Application deadline:* For fall admission, 4/15 for domestic and international students. Application fee: $78 Canadian dollars. Electronic applications accepted. *Expenses:* Tuition, area resident: Part-time $68.93 per credit. Tuition, state resident: full-time $2481.48; part-time $188.92 per credit. Tuition, nonresident: full-time $6801; part-time $482.06 per course. International tuition: $17,354.16 full-time. Required fees: $1309.50; $30.28 per credit. $93.45 per term. Tuition and fees vary according to degree level and program. *Financial support:* Research assistantships, teaching assistantships, scholarships/grants available. Financial award application deadline: 9/2. *Unit head:* Silvia Ponce, Director, 514-340-6393, Fax: 514-340-6915, E-mail: silvia.ponce@hec.ca. *Application contact:* Marie Deshaies, Senior Student Advisor, 514-340-6135, Fax: 514-340-6411, E-mail: marie.deshaies@hec.ca.

High Point University, Norcross Graduate School, High Point, NC 27262-3598. Offers business administration (MBA); educational leadership (M Ed); elementary education (M Ed); history (MA); nonprofit management (MA); secondary math (M Ed); special education (M Ed); strategic communication (MA); teaching elementary education k-6 (MAT); teaching secondary mathematics 9-12 (MAT). *Accreditation:* ACBSP; NCATE. Part-time and evening/weekend programs available. *Faculty:* 30 full-time (11 women), 5 part-time/adjunct (1 woman). *Students:* 17 full-time (10 women), 292 part-time (198 women); includes 107 minority (100 Black or African American, non-Hispanic/Latino; 1 Asian, non-Hispanic/Latino; 6 Hispanic/Latino), 19 international. 249 applicants, 69% accepted, 141 enrolled. *Degree requirements:* For master's, comprehensive exam (for some programs), thesis (for some programs). *Entrance requirements:* For master's, GMAT (MBA), GRE, MAT, minimum GPA of 3.0. Additional exam requirements/recommendations for international students: Required—TOEFL (minimum score 550 paper-based). *Application deadline:* For fall admission, 4/15 priority date for domestic and international students; for spring admission, 10/15 priority date for domestic and international students. Applications are processed on a rolling basis. Application fee: $50. Electronic applications accepted. *Expenses:* Tuition: Full-time $11,520; part-time $640 per hour. Required fees: $90; $150 per semester. Part-time tuition and fees vary according to program. *Financial support:* Federal Work-Study available. Support available to part-time students. Financial award application deadline: 3/1; financial award applicants required to submit FAFSA. *Unit head:* Tracy Collum, Associate Dean, 336-767-4840, Fax: 336-841-9024, E-mail: tcollum@highpoint.edu. *Application contact:* Tracy Collum, Associate Dean, 336-767-4840, Fax: 336-841-9024, E-mail: tcollum@highpoint.edu.

Howard University, School of Communications, Department of Communication and Culture, Washington, DC 20059-0002. Offers intercultural communication (MA, PhD); organizational communication (MA, PhD). Offered through the Graduate School of Arts and Sciences. Part-time programs available. Terminal master's awarded for partial completion of doctoral program. *Degree requirements:* For master's, comprehensive exam or thesis; for doctorate, one foreign language, comprehensive exam, thesis/dissertation. *Entrance requirements:* For master's, English proficiency exam, GRE General Test, minimum GPA of 3.0; for doctorate, English proficiency exam, GRE General Test, master's degree in related field, minimum GPA of 3.5. Additional exam requirements/recommendations for international students: Required—TOEFL. *Faculty research:* Media effects, black discourse, development communication, African-American organizations.

Illinois Institute of Technology, Stuart School of Business, Program in Marketing Communication, Chicago, IL 60661. Offers MS, MBA/MS. Part-time and evening/weekend programs available. *Faculty:* 37 full-time (4 women), 21 part-time/adjunct (5 women). *Students:* 62 full-time (44 women), 3 part-time (2 women); includes 1 minority (Hispanic/Latino), 63 international. Average age 24. 198 applicants, 75% accepted, 32 enrolled. In 2010, 13 master's awarded. *Entrance requirements:* For master's, GRE (minimum score 1000) or GMAT (500). Additional exam requirements/recommendations for international students: Required—TOEFL (minimum score 600 paper-based; 85 iBT); Recommended—IELTS (minimum score 7). *Application deadline:* For fall admission, 8/1 for domestic students, 5/1 for international students; for spring admission, 12/15 for domestic students, 10/15 for international students. Applications are processed on a rolling basis. Application fee: $75. Electronic applications accepted. *Expenses:* Contact institution. *Financial support:* Career-related internships or fieldwork, Federal Work-Study, institutionally sponsored loans, scholarships/grants, traineeships, health care benefits, and tuition waivers (partial) available. Support available to part-time students. Financial award applicants required to submit FAFSA. *Unit head:* Dr. Krishna Erramilli, Professor, 312-906-6573, Fax: 312-906-6549, E-mail: krish@stuart.iit.edu. *Application contact:* Deborah Gibson, Director, Graduate Admission, 866-472-3448, Fax: 312-567-3138, E-mail: inquiry.grad@iit.edu.

Iowa State University of Science and Technology, Graduate College, College of Liberal Arts and Sciences, Department of English, Ames, IA 50011. Offers creative writing (MFA); English (MA); rhetoric and professional communication (PhD). *Faculty:* 46 full-time (21 women), 9 part-time/adjunct (8 women). *Students:* 118 full-time (77 women), 45 part-time (32 women); includes 2 Black or African American, non-Hispanic/Latino; 1 Asian, non-Hispanic/Latino; 6 Hispanic/Latino, 36 international. 135 applicants, 56% accepted, 48 enrolled. In 2010, 27 master's, 5 doctorates awarded. *Degree requirements:* For master's, thesis or alternative; for doctorate, thesis/dissertation. *Entrance requirements:* For master's, GRE General Test, sample of written work, resume, portfolio in creative writing; for doctorate, GRE General Test, sample of written work, resume. Additional exam requirements/recommendations for international students: Required—TOEFL (minimum score 600 paper-based; 100 iBT), IELTS (minimum score 7). *Application deadline:* For fall admission, 1/5 priority date for domestic and international students. Application fee: $40 ($90 for international students). Electronic applications accepted. *Financial support:* In 2010–11, 7 research assistantships with full and partial tuition reimbursements (averaging $10,211 per year), 86 teaching assistantships with full and partial tuition reimbursements (averaging $13,238 per year) were awarded; fellowships, scholarships/grants, health care benefits, and unspecified assistantships also available. *Faculty research:* Creative writing, literature, rhetoric, composition and professional communication, teaching English as a second language, applied linguistics. *Unit head:* Dr. Charles Kostelnick, Chair, 515-294-2477, Fax: 515-294-2125, E-mail: englgrad@iastate.edu. *Application contact:* Dr. Constance Post, Director of Graduate Education, 515-294-3175, E-mail: englgrad@iastate.edu.

John Carroll University, Graduate School, Department of Communications Management, University Heights, OH 44118-4581. Offers MA. Part-time and evening/weekend programs available. *Degree requirements:* For master's, comprehensive exam, thesis or project. *Entrance requirements:* For master's, GRE General Test, minimum GPA of 3.0. Additional exam requirements/recommendations for international students: Required—TOEFL. Electronic applications accepted. *Faculty research:* Communication law, media ethics, international studies, international broadcasting, media history.

Jones International University, School of Business, Centennial, CO 80112. Offers accounting (MBA); business communication (MABC); entrepreneurship (MABC, MBA); finance (MBA); global enterprise management (MBA); health care management (MBA); information security management (MBA); information technology management (MBA); leadership and influence (MABC); leading the customer-driven organization (MABC); negotiation and conflict management (MBA); project management (MABC, MBA). Program only offered online. Part-time and evening/weekend programs available. Postbaccalaureate distance learning degree programs offered (no on-campus study). *Degree requirements:* For master's, capstone project. *Entrance requirements:* For master's, minimum cumulative GPA of 2.5. Additional exam requirements/recommendations for international students: Recommended—TOEFL (minimum score 550 paper-based; 213 computer-based). Electronic applications accepted.

La Salle University, School of Arts and Sciences, Program in Professional Communication, Philadelphia, PA 19141-1199. Offers MA. Part-time and evening/weekend programs available. *Degree requirements:* For master's, exam or project. *Entrance requirements:* For master's, GRE or MAT. *Expenses:* Contact institution.

Lasell College, Graduate and Professional Studies in Communication, Newton, MA 02466-2709. Offers integrated marketing communication (MSC, Graduate Certificate); public relations (MSC, Graduate Certificate). Part-time and evening/weekend programs available. Postbaccalaureate distance learning degree programs offered (minimal on-campus study). *Faculty:* 2 full-time (both women), 2 part-time/adjunct (both women). *Students:* 8 full-time (all women), 25 part-time (22 women); includes 3 minority (all Black or African American, non-Hispanic/Latino), 2 international. Average age 28. 24 applicants, 83% accepted, 13 enrolled. In 2010, 10 master's awarded. *Entrance requirements:* For master's and Graduate Certificate, bachelor's degree from an accredited institution. Additional exam requirements/recommendations for international students: Required—TOEFL (minimum score 550 paper-based; 213 computer-based; 75 iBT), IELTS. *Application deadline:* For fall admission, 8/31 priority date for domestic students, 6/30 priority date for international students; for spring admission, 12/31 priority date for domestic students, 10/31 priority date for international students. Applications are processed on a rolling basis. Application fee: $40. Electronic applications accepted. *Expenses:* Tuition: Part-time $550 per credit hour. Required fees: $55 per semester. *Financial support:* In 2010–11, 2 students received support. Available to part-time students. Application deadline: 8/31. *Unit head:* Dr. Joan Dolamore, Dean of Graduate and Professional Studies, 617-243-2485, Fax: 617-243-2450, E-mail: gradinfo@lasell.edu. *Application contact:* Adrienne Franciosi, Director of Graduate Admission, 617-243-2214, Fax: 617-243-2450, E-mail: gradinfo@lasell.edu.

Lawrence Technological University, College of Arts and Sciences, Southfield, MI 48075-1058. Offers computer science (MS); educational technology (MS); integrated science (MSE); science education (MSE); technical and professional communication (MS). Part-time and evening/weekend programs available. *Faculty:* 14 full-time (6 women), 14 part-time/adjunct (4 women). *Students:* 1 full-time (0 women), 93 part-time (54 women); includes 17 Black or African American, non-Hispanic/Latino; 7 Asian, non-Hispanic/Latino; 1 Hispanic/Latino; 4 Two or more races, non-Hispanic/Latino, 10 international. Average age 36. 116 applicants, 61% accepted, 23 enrolled. In 2010, 40 master's awarded. *Degree requirements:* For master's, thesis (for some programs). *Entrance requirements:* For master's, GRE. Additional exam requirements/recommendations for international students: Required—TOEFL (minimum score 550 paper-based; 213 computer-based; 79 iBT). *Application deadline:* For fall admission, 6/30 priority date for domestic students, 6/30 for international students; for spring admission, 11/15 priority date for domestic students, 11/15 for international students. Applications are processed on a rolling basis. Application fee: $50. Electronic applications accepted. *Financial support:* In 2010–11, 22 students received support. Federal Work-Study available. Financial award application deadline: 4/1; financial award applicants required to submit FAFSA. *Unit head:* Dr. Hsiao-Ping Moore, Dean, 248-204-3500, Fax: 248-204-3518, E-mail: scidean@ltu.edu. *Application contact:* Jane Rohrback, Director of Admissions, 248-204-3160, Fax: 248-204-2228, E-mail: admissions@ltu.edu.

Loyola University Chicago, Graduate School of Business, Marketing Department, Chicago, IL 60660. Offers integrated marketing communications (MS); marketing (MSIMC). Part-time and evening/weekend programs available. *Entrance requirements:* For master's, GMAT, v. Additional exam requirements/recommendations for international students: Required—TOEFL (minimum score 550 paper-based; 213 computer-based; 80 iBT). Electronic applications accepted. *Expenses:* Contact institution. *Faculty research:* Web performance metrics, new venture marketing strategies over consumption, benefit segmentation strategies.

Marietta College, Program in Corporate Media, Marietta, OH 45750-4000. Offers MCM.

Marist College, Graduate Programs, School of Communication and the Arts, Poughkeepsie, NY 12601-1387. Offers organizational communication and leadership (MA). Part-time programs available. Postbaccalaureate distance learning degree programs offered (no on-campus study). *Degree requirements:* For master's, thesis or comprehensive exam. *Entrance requirements:* For master's, GRE, minimum undergraduate GPA of 3.0, resume, 3 letters of recommendation. Additional exam requirements/recommendations for international students: Required—TOEFL

Corporate and Organizational Communication

Marist College (continued)
(minimum score 550 paper-based; 213 computer-based; 80 iBT); Recommended—IELTS (minimum score 6.5). Electronic applications accepted.

Marywood University, Academic Affairs, Insalaco College of Creative and Performing Arts, Department of Communication Arts, Program in Information Sciences, Scranton, PA 18509-1598. Offers corporate communication (Certificate); e-business (Certificate); health communication (Certificate); information sciences (MS), including library science/information specialist; instructional technology (Certificate). *Entrance requirements:* Additional exam requirements/recommendations for international students: Required—TOEFL (minimum score 550 paper-based; 213 computer-based; 79 iBT). Electronic applications accepted. *Expenses:* Tuition: Part-time $735 per credit. Required fees: $470 per semester. Tuition and fees vary according to degree level and campus/location.

Metropolitan College of New York, Program in Media Management, New York, NY 10013. Offers MBA. Evening/weekend programs available. *Degree requirements:* For master's, thesis, 10 day study abroad. *Entrance requirements:* For master's, GMAT or GRE General Test, appropriate work experience, interview, minimum GPA of 2.7. Additional exam requirements/recommendations for international students: Required—TOEFL (minimum score 600 paper-based; 220 computer-based). Electronic applications accepted. *Expenses:* Contact institution.

Minnesota State University Mankato, College of Graduate Studies, College of Arts and Humanities, Department of Communication Studies, Mankato, MN 56001. Offers communication education (Certificate); communication studies (MA, MS); forensics (MFA); professional communication (Certificate). *Students:* 22 full-time (15 women), 22 part-time (8 women). *Degree requirements:* For master's, one foreign language, comprehensive exam, thesis. *Entrance requirements:* For master's, minimum GPA of 3.0 during previous 2 years, writing sample. *Application deadline:* For fall admission, 7/1 priority date for domestic students, 5/1 for international students; for spring admission, 11/1 for domestic students, 10/1 for international students. Applications are processed on a rolling basis. Application fee: $40. Electronic applications accepted. *Financial support:* Research assistantships, teaching assistantships with full tuition reimbursements, career-related internships or fieldwork, Federal Work-Study, and institutionally sponsored loans available. Support available to part-time students. Financial award application deadline: 3/15; financial award applicants required to submit FAFSA. *Unit head:* Dr. Kristen Cvancara, Chairperson, 507-389-2213. *Application contact:* 507-389-2321, E-mail: grad@mnsu.edu.

Mississippi College, Graduate School, College of Arts and Sciences, School of Christian Studies and the Arts, Department of Communication, Clinton, MS 39058. Offers applied communication (MSC); public relations and corporate communication (MSC). Part-time programs available. *Degree requirements:* For master's, comprehensive exam, thesis optional. *Entrance requirements:* For master's, GRE or NTE, minimum GPA of 2.5. Additional exam requirements/recommendations for international students: Recommended—IELTS. Electronic applications accepted.

Monmouth University, The Graduate School, Department of Corporate and Public Communication, West Long Branch, NJ 07764-1898. Offers corporate and public communication (MA); human resources communication (Certificate); public relations (Certificate); public service communication specialist (Certificate). Part-time and evening/weekend programs available. *Faculty:* 8 full-time (5 women). *Students:* 11 full-time (9 women), 37 part-time (28 women); includes 2 Black or African American, non-Hispanic/Latino; 3 Hispanic/Latino; 1 Two or more races, non-Hispanic/Latino, 2 international. Average age 32. 28 applicants, 93% accepted, 15 enrolled. In 2010, 15 master's awarded. *Degree requirements:* For master's, comprehensive exam, project. *Entrance requirements:* For master's, GRE, minimum GPA of 3.0 in major, 2.75 overall. Additional exam requirements/recommendations for international students: Required—TOEFL (minimum score 550 paper-based; 213 computer-based; 79 iBT), IELTS (minimum score 5), Michigan English Language Assessment Battery (minimum score 77), Cambridge A, B, C. *Application deadline:* For fall admission, 7/15 priority date for domestic students, 6/1 for international students; for spring admission, 11/15 priority date for domestic students, 11/1 for international students. Applications are processed on a rolling basis. Application fee: $50. Electronic applications accepted. *Expenses:* Tuition: Full-time $19,572; part-time $816 per credit. Required fees: $628; $157 per semester. *Financial support:* In 2010–11, 24 students received support, including 23 fellowships (averaging $1,176 per year), 5 research assistantships (averaging $7,578 per year); scholarships/grants and unspecified assistantships also available. Support available to part-time students. Financial award applicants required to submit FAFSA. *Faculty research:* Service-learning, history of television, feminism and the media, executive communication, public relations pedagogy. *Unit head:* Dr. Shelia McAllister-Spooner, Program Director, 732-571-7553, Fax: 732-571-3609, E-mail: smcallis@monmouth.edu. *Application contact:* Kevin Roane, Director, Office of Graduate Admission, 732-571-3452, Fax: 732-263-5123, E-mail: gradadm@monmouth.edu.

Montclair State University, The Graduate School, School of the Arts, Department of Communication Studies, Montclair, NJ 07043-1624. Offers public and organizational relations (MA). Part-time and evening/weekend programs available. *Faculty:* 6 full-time (2 women), 41 part-time/adjunct (23 women). *Students:* 16 full-time (14 women), 19 part-time (16 women); includes 3 Black or African American, non-Hispanic/Latino; 1 Asian, non-Hispanic/Latino; 4 Hispanic/Latino, 3 international. Average age 30. 26 applicants, 54% accepted, 9 enrolled. In 2010, 14 master's awarded. *Degree requirements:* For master's, comprehensive exam. *Entrance requirements:* For master's, GRE General Test, 2 letters of recommendation. Additional exam requirements/recommendations for international students: Required—TOEFL (minimum iBT score of 83) or IELTS. *Application deadline:* For fall admission, 6/1 for international students; for spring admission, 10/1 for international students. Applications are processed on a rolling basis. Application fee: $60. Electronic applications accepted. *Expenses:* Tuition, state resident: part-time $501.34 per credit. Tuition, nonresident: part-time $773.88 per credit. Required fees: $71.15 per credit. *Financial support:* In 2010–11, 3 research assistantships with full tuition reimbursements (averaging $7,000 per year) were awarded; Federal Work-Study, scholarships/grants, and unspecified assistantships also available. Support available to part-time students. Financial award application deadline: 3/1; financial award applicants required to submit FAFSA. *Unit head:* Dr. Harry Haines, Chair, 973-655-4200. *Application contact:* Amy Aiello, Director of Graduate Admissions and Operations, 973-655-5147, Fax: 973-655-7869, E-mail: graduate.school@montclair.edu.

Murray State University, College of Business and Public Affairs, Program in Organizational Communication, Murray, KY 42071. Offers MA, MS. Part-time programs available. *Degree requirements:* For master's, thesis (for some programs). *Entrance requirements:* For master's, minimum GPA of 2.5 for conditional admittance, 3.0 for unconditional admittance. Additional exam requirements/recommendations for international students: Required—TOEFL (minimum score 550 paper-based; 213 computer-based). *Faculty research:* Organizational learning, organizational culture, leadership, health communication, personality.

National University, Academic Affairs, School of Media and Communication, Department of Communication, La Jolla, CA 92037-1011. Offers strategic communication (MA). Part-time and evening/weekend programs available. Postbaccalaureate distance learning degree programs offered (no on-campus study). *Faculty:* 5 full-time (3 women), 28 part-time/adjunct (10 women). *Students:* 25 full-time (16 women), 42 part-time (22 women); includes 22 minority (11 Black or African American, non-Hispanic/Latino; 1 Asian, non-Hispanic/Latino; 7 Hispanic/Latino; 1 Native Hawaiian or other Pacific Islander, non-Hispanic/Latino; 2 Two or more races, non-Hispanic/Latino). Average age 33. 51 applicants, 100% accepted, 23 enrolled. In 2010, 13 master's awarded. *Degree requirements:* For master's, thesis. *Entrance requirements:* Additional exam requirements/recommendations for international students: Required—TOEFL (minimum score 550 paper-based; 213 computer-based; 79 iBT), IELTS (minimum score 6). *Application deadline:* For fall admission, 6/30 for international students. Applications are processed on a rolling basis. Application fee: $60 ($65 for international students). Electronic applications accepted. *Expenses:* Tuition: Full-time $9450; part-time $350 per unit. Required fees: $350 per unit. One-time fee: $60. *Financial support:* Application deadline: 6/30. *Unit head:* Dr. Joan Vas Tassel; Dean, 858-309-3446, Fax: 858-309-3450, E-mail: jvantassel@nu.edu. *Application contact:* Dominick Giovanniello, Associate Regional Dean—San Diego, 800-NAT-UNIV, Fax: 858-541-7792, E-mail: dgiovann@nu.edu.

New Mexico State University, Graduate School, College of Arts and Sciences, Department of English, Las Cruces, NM 88003-8001. Offers creative writing (MFA); English (MA); rhetoric and professional communication (PhD). Part-time programs available. *Faculty:* 22 full-time (13 women), 1 (woman) part-time/adjunct. *Students:* 71 full-time (39 women), 31 part-time (17 women); includes 22 minority (5 Black or African American, non-Hispanic/Latino; 2 Asian, non-Hispanic/Latino; 14 Hispanic/Latino; 1 Two or more races, non-Hispanic/Latino), 4 international. Average age 32. 109 applicants, 58% accepted, 27 enrolled. In 2010, 30 master's, 2 doctorates awarded. *Degree requirements:* For master's, one foreign language, thesis (for some programs); for doctorate, comprehensive exam, thesis/dissertation, internship. *Entrance requirements:* For master's and doctorate, sample of written work. Additional exam requirements/recommendations for international students: Required—TOEFL (minimum score 550 paper-based; 79 iBT), IELTS (minimum score 6.5). *Application deadline:* For fall admission, 2/1 for domestic and international students. Application fee: $30 ($50 for international students). Electronic applications accepted. *Expenses:* Tuition, state resident: full-time $4536; part-time $242 per credit. Tuition, nonresident: full-time $15,816; part-time $712 per credit. Required fees: $636 per term. *Financial support:* In 2010–11, 3 research assistantships (averaging $6,817 per year), 49 teaching assistantships (averaging $15,105 per year) were awarded; fellowships, career-related internships or fieldwork, Federal Work-Study, institutionally sponsored loans, scholarships/grants, health care benefits, and unspecified assistantships also available. Financial award application deadline: 2/1; financial award applicants required to submit FAFSA. *Faculty research:* Composition research, history and theory of rhetoric, technical/professional communication, creative writing, English and American literature. *Unit head:* Dr. Monica F. Torres, Head, 575-646-2319, Fax: 575-646-7725, E-mail: mftorres@nmsu.edu. *Application contact:* Dr. Elizabeth Schirmer, Director of Graduate Studies, 575-646-1733, E-mail: eschirme@nmsu.edu.

New York University, School of Continuing and Professional Studies, Division of Programs in Business, Program in Public Relations and Corporate Communication, New York, NY 10012-1019. Offers corporate and organizational communications (MS); public relations management (MS). Part-time and evening/weekend programs available. *Faculty:* 1 full-time (0 women), 44 part-time/adjunct (21 women). *Students:* 36 full-time (30 women), 74 part-time (60 women); includes 10 Black or African American, non-Hispanic/Latino; 8 Asian, non-Hispanic/Latino; 12 Hispanic/Latino. Average age 28. 199 applicants, 34% accepted, 35 enrolled. In 2010, 43 master's awarded. *Degree requirements:* For master's, thesis. *Entrance requirements:* For master's, GRE General Test or GMAT (for recent graduates), 2 letters of recommendation, resume, essay, professional experience. Additional exam requirements/recommendations for international students: Required—TOEFL (minimum score 600 paper-based; 250 computer-based; 100 iBT), TWE. *Application deadline:* For fall admission, 2/1 priority date for domestic and international students; for spring admission, 10/15 priority date for domestic students, 8/15 priority date for international students. Applications are processed on a rolling basis. Application fee: $75. Electronic applications accepted. *Financial support:* In 2010–11, 85 students received support, including 85 fellowships (averaging $2,490 per year); institutionally sponsored loans and scholarships/grants also available. Financial award application deadline: 3/1; financial award applicants required to submit FAFSA. *Unit head:* John Doorley, Director, 212-992-3221, Fax: 212-992-3676. *Application contact:* Angrand Fadia, Assistant Director, 212-992-3221, Fax: 212-992-3676, E-mail: fs20@nyu.edu.

Northwestern University, The Graduate School, School of Communication, Department of Communication Studies, Managerial Communication Program, Evanston, IL 60208. Offers MSC. *Entrance requirements:* For master's, GRE General Test.

Northwestern University, Medill School of Journalism, Integrated Marketing Communications Program, Evanston, IL 60208. Offers advertising/sales promotion (MSIMC); direct database and e-commerce marketing (MSIMC); general studies (MSIMC); public relations (MSIMC). Part-time programs available. *Entrance requirements:* For master's, GRE General Test or GMAT, full-time work experience (preferred). Additional exam requirements/recommendations for international students: Required—TOEFL. Electronic applications accepted. *Faculty research:* Data mining, business to business marketing, values in advertising, political advertising.

Ohio University, Graduate College, Scripps College of Communication, School of Communication Studies, Athens, OH 45701-2979. Offers health communication (PhD); organizational communication (MA); relating and organizing (PhD); rhetoric and public culture (PhD). Part-time programs available. Postbaccalaureate distance learning degree programs offered (minimal on-campus study). *Students:* 49 full-time (35 women), 42 part-time (33 women); includes 6 minority (4 Black or African American, non-Hispanic/Latino; 1 Hispanic/Latino; 1 Two or more races, non-Hispanic/Latino), 12 international. 104 applicants, 40% accepted, 31 enrolled. In 2010, 2 master's, 12 doctorates awarded. Terminal master's awarded for partial completion of doctoral program. *Degree requirements:* For master's, capstone; for doctorate, comprehensive exam, thesis/dissertation. *Entrance requirements:* For master's, GRE; for doctorate, GRE General Test, minimum GPA of 3.0. Additional exam requirements/recommendations for international students: Required—TOEFL (minimum score 550 paper-based; 80 iBT) or IELTS (minimum score 6.5). *Application deadline:* For fall admission, 1/15 priority date for domestic and international students. Application fee: $50 ($55 for international students). Electronic applications accepted. *Financial support:* In 2010–11, 12 students received support, including fellowships with full tuition reimbursements available (averaging $13,600 per year), research assistantships with full tuition reimbursements available (averaging $13,600 per year), teaching assistantships with full tuition reimbursements available (averaging $13,600 per year); career-related internships or fieldwork, Federal Work-Study, and institutionally sponsored loans also available. Financial award application deadline: 1/15. *Faculty research:* Rhetoric and public culture, relating and organizing, health communication. Total annual research expenditures: $200,000. *Unit head:* Dr. Scott Titsworth, Director, 740-593-9160, Fax: 740-593-4810, E-mail: titswort@ohio.edu. *Application contact:* Dr. Benjamin Bates, Associate Director for Graduate Studies, 740-593-9163, Fax: 740-593-4810, E-mail: batesb@ohio.edu.

Oklahoma City University, Meinders School of Business, Program in Business Administration, Oklahoma City, OK 73106-1402. Offers finance (MBA); health administration (MBA); information technology (MBA); integrated marketing communications (MBA); international business (MBA); marketing (MBA); JD/MBA. *Accreditation:* ACBSP. Part-time and evening/weekend programs available. *Degree requirements:* For master's, comprehensive exam. *Entrance requirements:* Additional exam requirements/recommendations for international students: Required—TOEFL (minimum score 560 paper-based; 220 computer-based; 83 iBT). *Faculty research:* Management information systems, international business strategies.

Queens University of Charlotte, School of Communication, Charlotte, NC 28274-0002. Offers organizational and strategic communication (MA). Part-time and evening/weekend programs available. *Degree requirements:* For master's, capstone course. *Entrance requirements:* Additional exam requirements/recommendations for international students: Required—TOEFL. *Expenses:* Contact institution.

Radford University, College of Graduate and Professional Studies, College of Humanities and Behavioral Sciences, School of Communication, Radford, VA 24142. Offers corporate and professional communication (MS). Part-time and evening/weekend programs available. *Faculty:* 9 full-time (4 women), 1 part-time/adjunct (0 women). *Students:* 18 full-time (10 women), 5 part-time (all women); includes 4 minority (2 Black or African American, non-Hispanic/Latino; 1 Hispanic/Latino; 1 Two or more races, non-Hispanic/Latino), 3 international. Average age 26. 17 applicants, 88% accepted, 7 enrolled. In 2010, 18 master's awarded. *Degree requirements:* For master's, comprehensive exam, thesis optional. *Entrance requirements:* For master's, GRE, minimum GPA of 2.75; short essay; 3 letters of reference. Additional exam requirements/

recommendations for international students: Required—TOEFL (minimum score 550 paper-based; 213 computer-based; 79 iBT). *Application deadline:* For fall admission, 2/15 priority date for domestic students, 12/1 for international students; for spring admission, 7/1 for international students. Applications are processed on a rolling basis. Application fee: $50. Electronic applications accepted. *Expenses:* Tuition, state resident: full-time $5746; part-time $239 per credit hour. Tuition, nonresident: full-time $14,174; part-time $591 per credit hour. Required fees: $2634; $111 per credit hour. *Financial support:* In 2010–11, 13 students received support, including 1 research assistantship with partial tuition reimbursement available (averaging $8,000 per year), 10 teaching assistantships with partial tuition reimbursements available (averaging $8,700 per year); career-related internships or fieldwork, Federal Work-Study, institutionally sponsored loans, and scholarships/grants also available. Financial award application deadline: 3/1; financial award applicants required to submit FAFSA. *Unit head:* Dr. Lynn Zoch, Director, 540-831-6553, Fax: 540-831-5883, E-mail: comm@radford.edu. *Application contact:* Rebecca Conner, Graduate Admissions, 540-831-5431, Fax: 540-831-6061, E-mail: gradcollege@radford.edu.

Regis College, Department of Organizational and Professional Communication, Weston, MA 02493. Offers MS. Part-time and evening/weekend programs available. *Degree requirements:* For master's, thesis. *Entrance requirements:* For master's, GRE or MAT. Additional exam requirements/recommendations for international students: Required—TOEFL (minimum score 550 paper-based; 213 computer-based). *Expenses:* Tuition: Part-time $765 per credit. Tuition and fees vary according to course load and degree level.

Roosevelt University, Graduate Division, College of Arts and Sciences, Department of Communication, Program in Integrated Marketing Communications, Chicago, IL 60605. Offers MSIMC. Part-time and evening/weekend programs available. *Faculty research:* Print journalism, urban high school journalism.

St. Bonaventure University, School of Graduate Studies, Russell J. Jandoli School of Journalism and Mass Communication, St. Bonaventure, NY 14778-2284. Offers integrated marketing communications (MA). Evening/weekend programs available. *Faculty:* 4 full-time (2 women). *Students:* 37 full-time (24 women), 7 part-time (3 women); includes 3 minority (2 Black or African American, non-Hispanic/Latino; 1 American Indian or Alaska Native, non-Hispanic/Latino). Average age 26. 42 applicants, 69% accepted, 20 enrolled. In 2010, 34 master's awarded. *Entrance requirements:* For master's, GRE, interview, writing sample, undergraduate transcript, letters of recommendation. Additional exam requirements/recommendations for international students: Required—TOEFL (minimum score 550 paper-based; 213 computer-based). *Application deadline:* For fall admission, 3/15 priority date for domestic students, 2/1 priority date for international students; for spring admission, 10/15 priority date for domestic students, 7/1 priority date for international students. Applications are processed on a rolling basis. Application fee: $30. Electronic applications accepted. *Expenses:* Tuition: Part-time $670 per credit hour. *Financial support:* In 2010–11, 1 research assistantship with full and partial tuition reimbursement was awarded; Federal Work-Study, scholarships/grants, health care benefits, tuition waivers (partial), and unspecified assistantships also available. Support available to part-time students. Financial award application deadline: 4/15; financial award applicants required to submit FAFSA. *Unit head:* Dr. Pauline Hoffmann, Program Director, 716-375-2578, E-mail: hoffmann@sbu.edu. *Application contact:* Dr. Pauline Hoffmann, Program Director, 716-375-2578, E-mail: hoffmann@sbu.edu.

Schiller International University, Graduate Programs, London, Program in Communications, London, United Kingdom. Offers business communication (MA).

Seton Hall University, College of Arts and Sciences, Department of Communication, South Orange, NJ 07079-2697. Offers corporate and professional communication (MA); intercultural communication (MA); organizational communication (MA); public relations (MA); strategic communication and leadership (MA); strategic communication planning (MA). Part-time and evening/weekend programs available. Postbaccalaureate distance learning degree programs offered (minimal on-campus study). *Degree requirements:* For master's, thesis. *Entrance requirements:* Additional exam requirements/recommendations for international students: Required—TOEFL. Electronic applications accepted. *Faculty research:* Managerial communication, communication consulting, communication and development.

Simmons College, College of Arts and Sciences Graduate Studies, Program in Communications Management, Boston, MA 02115. Offers MS, MS/MA. Part-time programs available. *Degree requirements:* For master's, thesis. *Entrance requirements:* For master's, GRE General Test, MAT, or GMAT, 2 years of professional experience. Additional exam requirements/recommendations for international students: Required—TOEFL (minimum score 600 paper-based; 250 computer-based; 100 iBT). Electronic applications accepted. *Faculty research:* Communications in non-profit management, online communications, communication across cultures.

Southern Illinois University Edwardsville, Graduate School, College of Arts and Sciences, Department of Speech Communication, Program in Corporate and Organizational Communication, Edwardsville, IL 62026-0001. Offers Postbaccalaureate Certificate. Part-time programs available. *Students:* 1 (woman) part-time. Average age 26. 8 applicants, 0% accepted. *Entrance requirements:* Additional exam requirements/recommendations for international students: Required—TOEFL (minimum score 550 paper-based; 213 computer-based; 79 iBT), IELTS (minimum score 6.5). *Application deadline:* For fall admission, 7/20 for domestic students, 6/1 for international students; for spring admission, 12/15 for domestic students, 10/1 for international students. Applications are processed on a rolling basis. Application fee: $30. Electronic applications accepted. *Expenses:* Tuition, state resident: full-time $6012; part-time $1503 per semester. Tuition, nonresident: full-time $15,030; part-time $3758 per semester. Required fees: $1711; $675 per semester. *Financial support:* Fellowships with full tuition reimbursements, research assistantships with full tuition reimbursements, teaching assistantships with full tuition reimbursements available. Financial award application deadline: 3/1; financial award applicants required to submit FAFSA. *Unit head:* Dr. Wai Hsien Cheah, Director, 618-650-5016, E-mail: wcheah@siue.edu. *Application contact:* Dr. Wai Hsien Cheah, Director, 618-650-5016, E-mail: wcheah@siue.edu.

Southern Illinois University Edwardsville, Graduate School, College of Arts and Sciences, Department of Speech Communication, Program in Organizational Communication, Edwardsville, IL 62026. Offers MA. Part-time and evening/weekend programs available. *Students:* 2 full-time (both women). Average age 26. *Degree requirements:* For master's, comprehensive exam (for some programs), thesis (for some programs). *Entrance requirements:* Additional exam requirements/recommendations for international students: Required—TOEFL (minimum score 550 paper-based; 213 computer-based; 79 iBT), IELTS (minimum score 6.5). *Application deadline:* For fall admission, 7/22 for domestic students, 6/1 for international students; for spring admission, 12/9 for domestic students, 10/1 for international students. Applications are processed on a rolling basis. Application fee: $30. Electronic applications accepted. *Expenses:* Tuition, state resident: full-time $6012; part-time $1503 per semester. Tuition, nonresident: full-time $15,030; part-time $3758 per semester. Required fees: $1711; $675 per semester. *Financial support:* Application deadline: 3/1. *Unit head:* Dr. Isaac Blankson, Chair, 618-650-3090, E-mail: iblanks@siue.edu. *Application contact:* Dr. Jocelyn DeGroot Brown, Director, 618-650-5828, E-mail: jocbrow@siue.edu.

Spalding University, Graduate Studies, College of Business and Communication, Louisville, KY 40203-2188. Offers business communication (MS). Part-time and evening/weekend programs available. *Faculty:* 6 full-time (2 women), 7 part-time/adjunct (2 women). *Students:* 44 full-time (35 women), 41 part-time (32 women); includes 38 minority (27 Black or African American, non-Hispanic/Latino; 1 Asian, non-Hispanic/Latino; 1 Hispanic/Latino; 9 Two or more races, non-Hispanic/Latino). Average age 37. 41 applicants, 78% accepted, 31 enrolled. In 2010, 29 master's awarded. *Degree requirements:* For master's, project. *Entrance requirements:* For master's, GRE or GMAT, writing sample, interview, letters of recommendation, transcripts. Additional exam requirements/recommendations for international students: Required—TOEFL (minimum score 535 paper-based; 203 computer-based). *Application deadline:* Applications are processed on a rolling basis. Application fee: $30. *Financial support:* In 2010–11, 26 students received support. Application deadline: 3/15. *Faculty research:* Curriculum development, consumer behavior, interdisciplinary pedagogy. *Unit head:* Dr. Orville Blackman, Program Director, 502-585-9911 Ext. 2630, E-mail: cbc@spalding.edu. *Application contact:* Claire Rayburn, Administrative Assistant, 502-585-9911 Ext. 2120, E-mail: cbc@spalding.edu.

Stevens Institute of Technology, Graduate School, Wesley J. Howe School of Technology Management, Program in Professional Communications, Hoboken, NJ 07030. Offers Certificate.

Suffolk University, College of Arts and Sciences, Department of Communication, Boston, MA 02108-2770. Offers communication studies (MAC); integrated marketing communication (MAC); organizational communication (MAC); public relations and advertising (MAC). Part-time and evening/weekend programs available. *Faculty:* 20 full-time (10 women), 1 part-time/adjunct (0 women). *Students:* 17 full-time (15 women), 18 part-time (13 women); includes 1 Asian, non-Hispanic/Latino, 3 international. Average age 26. 110 applicants, 54% accepted, 19 enrolled. In 2010, 23 master's awarded. *Degree requirements:* For master's, thesis optional. *Entrance requirements:* For master's, GRE General Test, MAT, or GMAT, 2 letters of recommendation, resume. Additional exam requirements/recommendations for international students: Required—TOEFL (minimum score 550 paper-based; 213 computer-based; 80 iBT). *Application deadline:* For fall admission, 6/15 priority date for domestic students, 6/15 for international students; for spring admission, 11/1 priority date for domestic students, 11/1 for international students. Applications are processed on a rolling basis. Application fee: $50. Electronic applications accepted. *Expenses:* Contact institution. *Financial support:* In 2010–11, 28 students received support, including 18 fellowships with partial tuition reimbursements available (averaging $5,403 per year); career-related internships or fieldwork, Federal Work-Study, and institutionally sponsored loans also available. Support available to part-time students. Financial award application deadline: 4/1; financial award applicants required to submit FAFSA. *Faculty research:* New media and new markets for advertising, First Amendment issues with the Internet, gender and intercultural communication, organizational development. *Unit head:* Dr. Robert Rosenthal, Chair, 617-573-8502, Fax: 617-742-6982, E-mail: rrosenth@suffolk.edu. *Application contact:* Judith Reynolds, Director of Graduate Admissions, 617-573-8302, Fax: 617-305-1733, E-mail: grad.admission@suffolk.edu.

Temple University, School of Communications and Theater, Department of Strategic and Organizational Communication, Philadelphia, PA 19122-6096. Offers communication management (MS). *Faculty:* 7 full-time (3 women). *Students:* 11 full-time (10 women), 18 part-time (12 women); includes 4 Black or African American, non-Hispanic/Latino; 1 Asian, non-Hispanic/Latino; 1 Two or more races, non-Hispanic/Latino, 7 international. 63 applicants, 49% accepted, 13 enrolled. In 2010, 7 master's awarded. *Entrance requirements:* Additional exam requirements/recommendations for international students: Required—TOEFL (minimum score 550 paper-based; 213 computer-based; 79 iBT). Application fee: $50. *Financial support:* Application deadline: 1/15. *Unit head:* Dr. Deborah Cai, Chair, 215-204-1882, E-mail: debcai@temple.edu. *Application contact:* Tara Schumacher, Coordinator of Outreach, 215-204-6575, Fax: 215-204-8781, E-mail: tara.schumacher@temple.edu.

Towson University, Program in Communications Management, Towson, MD 21252-0001. Offers MS. *Students:* 10 full-time (5 women), 28 part-time (23 women); includes 9 minority (all Black or African American, non-Hispanic/Latino), 1 international. Average age 29. In 2010, 8 master's awarded. *Degree requirements:* For master's, thesis. *Entrance requirements:* For master's, 24 credits in mass communications, public relations and/or advertising, writing and statistics; professional experience; minimum GPA of 3.0. *Application deadline:* For fall admission, 1/15 for domestic students. Application fee: $50. Electronic applications accepted. *Expenses:* Tuition, state resident: part-time $324 per credit. Tuition, nonresident: part-time $681 per credit. Required fees: $95 per term. *Financial support:* Application deadline: 4/1. *Unit head:* Theodora Carabas, Graduate Program Director, 410-704-4855, E-mail: tcarabas@towson.edu. *Application contact:* 410-704-2501, Fax: 410-704-4675, E-mail: grads@towson.edu.

Universidad Autonoma de Guadalajara, Graduate Programs, Guadalajara, Mexico. Offers administrative law and justice (LL M); advertising and corporate communications (MA); architecture (M Arch); business (MBA); computational science (MCC); education (Ed M, Ed D); English-Spanish translation (MA); entrepreneurship and management (MBA); integrated management of digital animation (MA); international business (MIB); international corporate law (LL M); internet technologies (MS); manufacturing systems (MMS); occupational health (MS); philosophy (MA, PhD); power electronics (MS); quality systems (MQS); renewable energy (MS); social evaluation of projects (MBA); strategic market research (MBA); tax law (MA); teaching mathematics (MA).

Université de Sherbrooke, Faculty of Administration, Program in Marketing Communications, Sherbrooke, QC J1K 1R1, Canada. Offers M Adm. *Faculty:* 3 full-time (0 women), 11 part-time/adjunct (1 woman). *Students:* 31 full-time (25 women). Average age 23. 91 applicants, 68% accepted, 22 enrolled. In 2010, 23 master's awarded. *Degree requirements:* For master's, one foreign language, thesis. *Entrance requirements:* For master's, bachelor degree in related field Minimum GPA 3/4.3. *Application deadline:* For fall admission, 4/30 for domestic students, 1/15 for international students. Applications are processed on a rolling basis. Application fee: $70. Electronic applications accepted. *Unit head:* Prof. Julien Bilodeau, Director, Graduate programs in business, 819-821-7311 Ext. 62355. *Application contact:* Marie-Claude Drouin, Programs director's assistant, 819-821-8000 Ext. 63301.

University of Alaska Fairbanks, College of Liberal Arts, Department of Communications, Fairbanks, AK 99775-5680. Offers professional communications (MA). Part-time programs available. *Faculty:* 4 full-time (2 women). *Students:* 15 full-time (11 women), 6 part-time (5 women); includes 4 minority (1 Black or African American, non-Hispanic/Latino; 1 American Indian or Alaska Native, non-Hispanic/Latino; 1 Hispanic/Latino; 1 Two or more races, non-Hispanic/Latino), 2 international. Average age 34. 9 applicants, 67% accepted, 6 enrolled. In 2010, 9 master's awarded. *Degree requirements:* For master's, comprehensive exam, thesis, oral defense. *Entrance requirements:* Additional exam requirements/recommendations for international students: Required—TOEFL (minimum score 550 paper-based; 213 computer-based; 80 iBT). *Application deadline:* For fall admission, 6/1 for domestic students, 3/1 for international students; for spring admission, 10/15 for domestic students, 9/1 for international students. Applications are processed on a rolling basis. Application fee: $60. Electronic applications accepted. *Expenses:* Tuition, state resident: full-time $5688; part-time $316 per credit. Tuition, nonresident: full-time $11,628; part-time $646 per credit. Required fees: $289 per semester. Tuition and fees vary according to course load and reciprocity agreements. *Financial support:* In 2010–11, 12 teaching assistantships with tuition reimbursements (averaging $11,657 per year) were awarded; fellowships with tuition reimbursements, Federal Work-Study, scholarships/grants, tuition waivers, and unspecified assistantships also available. Support available to part-time students. Financial award application deadline: 7/1; financial award applicants required to submit FAFSA. *Faculty research:* Interpersonal communications, health communications, intercultural communications, politeness and face management in conversation, gender communication. *Unit head:* Dr. Robert Arundale, Department Chair, 907-474-6591, Fax: 907-474-5858, E-mail: fycomm@uaf.edu. *Application contact:* Dr. Robert Arundale, Department Chair, 907-474-6591, Fax: 907-474-5858, E-mail: fycomm@uaf.edu.

University of Colorado Denver, Business School, Program in Management and Organization, Denver, CO 80217. Offers communications management (MS); enterprise technology management (MS); entrepreneurship and innovation (MS); global management (MS); human resources management (MS); leadership (MS); quantitative decision methods (MS); sports and entertainment management (MS); strategic management (MS); sustainability management (MS). *Accreditation:* AACSB. Part-time and evening/weekend programs available. Postbaccalaureate distance learning degree programs offered (no on-campus study). *Students:* 34 full-time (21 women), 9 part-time (2 women); includes 3 Asian, non-Hispanic/Latino; 5 Hispanic/Latino. Average age 33. 28 applicants, 61% accepted, 10 enrolled. In 2010, 20 master's awarded. *Degree requirements:* For master's, 30 semester hours (12 of required courses, 12

Corporate and Organizational Communication

University of Colorado Denver (continued)
of management electives, and 6 of free electives). *Entrance requirements:* For master's, GMAT. Additional exam requirements/recommendations for international students: Required—TOEFL (minimum score 525 paper-based; 197 computer-based; 71 iBT). *Application deadline:* For fall admission, 4/1 priority date for domestic students, 3/15 priority date for international students; for spring admission, 10/1 priority date for domestic and international students. Application fee: $50 ($75 for international students). Electronic applications accepted. *Expenses:* Contact institution. *Financial support:* Federal Work-Study and scholarships/grants available. Support available to part-time students. Financial award application deadline: 4/1; financial award applicants required to submit FAFSA. *Faculty research:* Human resource management, management of catastrophe, turnaround strategies. *Unit head:* Dr. Kenneth Bettenhausen, Associate Professor/Director, 303-315-8425, E-mail: kenneth.bettehausen@ucdenver.edu. *Application contact:* Shelly Townley, Admissions Director, Graduate Programs, 303-315-8202, E-mail: shelly.townley@ucdenver.edu.

University of Colorado Denver, Business School, Program in Marketing, Denver, CO 80217. Offers brand management and marketing communication (MS); global marketing (MS); high-tech/entrepreneurial marketing (MS); Internet marketing (MS); market research (MS); marketing and business intelligence (MS); marketing for sustainability (MS); marketing in nonprofit organizations (MS); sports and entertainment marketing (MS). Part-time and evening/weekend programs available. *Students:* 31 full-time (18 women), 8 part-time (4 women); includes 3 Hispanic/Latino, 5 international. Average age 29. 46 applicants, 63% accepted, 18 enrolled. In 2010, 11 master's awarded. *Degree requirements:* For master's, 30 semester hours (18 of marketing core courses, 12 of graduate marketing electives). *Entrance requirements:* For master's, GMAT. Additional exam requirements/recommendations for international students: Required—TOEFL (minimum score 525 paper-based; 197 computer-based; 71 iBT). *Application deadline:* For fall admission, 4/1 priority date for domestic students, 3/15 priority date for international students; for spring admission, 10/1 priority date for domestic and international students. Application fee: $50 ($75 for international students). Electronic applications accepted. *Expenses:* Contact institution. *Financial support:* Federal Work-Study and scholarships/grants available. Support available to part-time students. Financial award application deadline: 4/1; financial award applicants required to submit FAFSA. *Faculty research:* Marketing issues in the Chinese environment, impact of individual difference and contextual factors on the risk-taking behaviors of managers making new-business creation decisions, Attribution Theory perspective of conflict between marketers and engineers, organizational identity and identification, international market entry strategies. *Unit head:* Dr. David Forlani, Associate Professor/Director, 303-315-8420, E-mail: david.forlani@ucdenver.edu. *Application contact:* Shelly Townley, Admissions Director, Graduate Programs, 303-315-8202, E-mail: shelly.townley@ucdenver.edu.

University of Connecticut, Graduate School, College of Liberal Arts and Sciences, Department of Communication Sciences, Program in Communication Processes and Marketing Communication, Storrs, CT 06269. Offers PhD. *Degree requirements:* For doctorate, thesis/dissertation. *Entrance requirements:* For doctorate, GMAT or GRE General Test. Additional exam requirements/recommendations for international students: Required—TOEFL (minimum score 550 paper-based; 213 computer-based). Electronic applications accepted.

University of Denver, Division of Arts, Humanities and Social Sciences, Department of Media, Film and Journalism Studies, Denver, CO 80208. Offers advertising management (MS); digital media studies (MA); international and intercultural communication (MA); media, film, and journalism studies (MA); strategic communication (MS). Part-time programs available. *Faculty:* 14 full-time (7 women), 5 part-time/adjunct (3 women). *Students:* 28 full-time (24 women), 36 part-time (26 women); includes 12 minority (1 Black or African American, non-Hispanic/Latino; 3 Asian, non-Hispanic/Latino; 6 Hispanic/Latino; 2 Two or more races, non-Hispanic/Latino), 2 international. Average age 26. 155 applicants, 58% accepted, 32 enrolled. In 2010, 36 master's awarded. *Degree requirements:* For master's, thesis (for some programs). *Entrance requirements:* For master's, GRE General Test. Additional exam requirements/recommendations for international students: Required—TOEFL (minimum score 550 paper-based; 80 iBT). *Application deadline:* Applications are processed on a rolling basis. Application fee: $60. Electronic applications accepted. *Expenses:* Tuition: Full-time $35,604; part-time $29,670 per year. Required fees: $687 per year. Tuition and fees vary according to program. *Financial support:* In 2010–11, 4 teaching assistantships with full and partial tuition reimbursements (averaging $14,000 per year) were awarded; career-related internships or fieldwork, Federal Work-Study, institutionally sponsored loans, scholarships/grants, and unspecified assistantships also available. Support available to part-time students. Financial award application deadline: 3/1; financial award applicants required to submit FAFSA. *Faculty research:* Youth and civic engagement. *Unit head:* Dr. Renee Botta, Chair, 303-871-7918, Fax: 303-871-4949, E-mail: rbotta@du.edu. *Application contact:* Information Contact, 303-871-2166, E-mail: mfjs@du.edu.

University of Denver, University College, Denver, CO 80208. Offers arts and culture (MLS, Certificate), including art, literature, and culture, arts development and program management (Certificate), creative writing; environmental policy and management (MAS, Certificate), including energy and sustainability (Certificate), environmental assessment of nuclear power (Certificate), environmental health and safety (Certificate), environmental management, natural resource management (Certificate); geographic information systems (MAS, Certificate); global affairs (MLS, Certificate), including translation studies, world history and culture; healthcare leadership (MPH, Certificate), including healthcare policy, law, and ethics, medical and healthcare information technologies, strategic management of healthcare; information and communications technology (MCIS, Certificate), including database design and administration (Certificate), geographic information systems (MCIS), information security systems security (Certificate), information systems security (MCIS), project management (MCIS, MPS, Certificate), software design and administration (Certificate), software design and programming (MCIS), technology management, telecommunications technology (MCIS), Web design and development; leadership and organizations (MPS, Certificate), including human capital in organizations, philanthropic leadership, project management (MCIS, MPS, Certificate), strategic innovation and change; organizational and professional communication (MPS, Certificate), including alternative dispute resolution, organizational communication, organizational development and training, public relations and marketing; security management (MAS, Certificate), including emergency planning and response, information security (MAS), organizational security; strategic human resource management (MPS, Certificate), including global human resources (MPS), human resource management and development (MPS). Part-time and evening/weekend programs available. Postbaccalaureate distance learning degree programs offered (no on-campus study). *Faculty:* 7 full-time (2 women), 212 part-time/adjunct (83 women). *Students:* 52 full-time (19 women), 1,044 part-time (625 women); includes 196 minority (81 Black or African American, non-Hispanic/Latino; 7 American Indian or Alaska Native, non-Hispanic/Latino; 30 Asian, non-Hispanic/Latino; 66 Hispanic/Latino; 3 Native Hawaiian or other Pacific Islander, non-Hispanic/Latino; 9 Two or more races, non-Hispanic/Latino), 76 international. Average age 36. 488 applicants, 91% accepted, 339 enrolled. In 2010, 286 master's, 130 other advanced degrees awarded. *Entrance requirements:* Additional exam requirements/recommendations for international students: Required—TOEFL (minimum score 550 paper-based; 80 iBT). *Application deadline:* For fall admission, 6/22 priority date for domestic students, 6/10 priority date for international students; for winter admission, 9/15 priority date for domestic students, 9/6 priority date for international students; for spring admission, 2/3 priority date for domestic students, 12/15 priority date for international students. Applications are processed on a rolling basis. Application fee: $75. Electronic applications accepted. *Expenses:* Contact institution. *Financial support:* Applicants required to submit FAFSA. *Unit head:* Dr. James Davis, Dean, 303-871-2291, Fax: 303-871-4047, E-mail: jdavis@du.edu. *Application contact:* Information Contact, 303-871-3155, Fax: 303-871-4047, E-mail: ucolinfo@du.edu.

University of Nebraska–Lincoln, Graduate College, College of Arts and Sciences, Department of Communication Studies, Lincoln, NE 68588. Offers instructional communication (MA, PhD); interpersonal communication (MA, PhD); marketing, communication studies, and advertising (MA, PhD); organizational communication (MA, PhD); rhetoric and culture (MA, PhD). *Degree requirements:* For master's, thesis optional; for doctorate, comprehensive exam, thesis/dissertation. *Entrance requirements:* For master's and doctorate, GRE General Test, writing sample. Additional exam requirements/recommendations for international students: Required—TOEFL (minimum score 600 paper-based; 250 computer-based). Electronic applications accepted. *Faculty research:* Message strategies, gender communication, political communication, organizational communication, instructional communication.

The University of North Carolina at Charlotte, Graduate School, College of Arts and Sciences, Department of Communication Studies, Charlotte, NC 28223-0001. Offers health communication (MA); media/rhetorical critical studies (MA); organizational communication (MA); public relations (MA). Part-time and evening/weekend programs available. *Faculty:* 12 full-time (5 women), 1 (woman) part-time/adjunct. *Students:* 6 full-time (5 women), 19 part-time (17 women); includes 7 minority (6 Black or African American, non-Hispanic/Latino; 1 Asian, non-Hispanic/Latino). Average age 27. 554 applicants, 4% accepted, 12 enrolled. In 2010, 12 master's awarded. Terminal master's awarded for partial completion of doctoral program. *Degree requirements:* For master's, project, thesis, or comprehensive exam. *Entrance requirements:* For master's, GRE General Test, minimum GPA of 2.75 overall. Additional exam requirements/recommendations for international students: Required—TOEFL (minimum score 557 paper-based; 220 computer-based; 83 iBT). *Application deadline:* For fall admission, 3/15 for domestic students, 5/1 for international students; for spring admission, 11/15 for domestic students, 10/1 for international students. Applications are processed on a rolling basis. Application fee: $55. Electronic applications accepted. *Expenses:* Tuition, state resident: full-time $3464. Tuition, nonresident: full-time $14,297. Required fees: $2094. Tuition and fees vary according to course load. *Financial support:* In 2010–11, 9 students received support, including 1 research assistantship (averaging $18,000 per year), 8 teaching assistantships (averaging $15,529 per year); career-related internships or fieldwork, institutionally sponsored loans, scholarships/grants, and unspecified assistantships also available. Support available to part-time students. Financial award application deadline: 4/1; financial award applicants required to submit FAFSA. *Faculty research:* Health literacy, systems of care and mental illness, the communication of emotions in gendered workplaces, international constructs of public relations managerial responsibilities, sports culture and the construction of social contracts, African-American oratory. Total annual research expenditures: $25,636. *Unit head:* Dr. Richard W. Leeman, Chair, 704-687-2086, Fax: 704-687-6900, E-mail: rwleeman@uncc.edu. *Application contact:* Kathy B. Giddings, Director of Graduate Admissions, 704-687-5503, Fax: 704-687-3279, E-mail: gradadm@uncc.edu.

University of Portland, College of Arts and Sciences, Department of Communication Studies, Portland, OR 97203-5798. Offers communication (MA); management communication (MS). Part-time and evening/weekend programs available. *Faculty:* 5 full-time (3 women), 1 part-time/adjunct (0 women). *Students:* 4 full-time (1 woman), 10 part-time (8 women); includes 1 Black or African American, non-Hispanic/Latino; 1 Asian, non-Hispanic/Latino; 1 Two or more races, non-Hispanic/Latino, 2 international. Average age 33. In 2010, 4 master's awarded. *Degree requirements:* For master's, thesis optional. *Entrance requirements:* For master's, GRE General Test, minimum GPA of 3.25, 3 letters of recommendation, resume, statement of goals, official transcripts. Additional exam requirements/recommendations for international students: Required—TOEFL (minimum score 600 paper-based; 100 iBT), IELTS (minimum score 7.5). *Application deadline:* For fall admission, 7/15 priority date for domestic and international students; for spring admission, 12/15 priority date for domestic and international students. Applications are processed on a rolling basis. Application fee: $50. *Expenses:* Tuition: Part-time $940 per credit hour. Tuition and fees vary according to program. *Financial support:* Career-related internships or fieldwork, Federal Work-Study, scholarships/grants, and tuition waivers (partial) available. Financial award application deadline: 3/1; financial award applicants required to submit FAFSA. *Unit head:* Dr. Jeffrey Kerssen-Griep, Director, 503-943-7167, E-mail: kerssen@up.edu. *Application contact:* Chris James Olinger, Administrative Assistant, 503-943-7107, Fax: 503-943-7315, E-mail: olingerc@up.edu.

University of St. Thomas, Graduate Studies, Opus College of Business, Master of Business Communication Program, Minneapolis, MN 55403. Offers MBC. Part-time and evening/weekend programs available. *Students:* 83 part-time (64 women); includes 5 minority (1 American Indian or Alaska Native, non-Hispanic/Latino; 3 Asian, non-Hispanic/Latino; 1 Hispanic/Latino), 1 international. Average age 32. In 2010, 34 master's awarded. *Entrance requirements:* For master's, GMAT or GRE. Additional exam requirements/recommendations for international students: Required—TOEFL (minimum 80 iBT), IELTS (minimum 6.5), or Michigan English Language Assessment Battery. *Application deadline:* For fall admission, 8/1 priority date for domestic and international students; for spring admission, 1/3 priority date for domestic and international students. Application fee: $40. Electronic applications accepted. *Unit head:* Dr. Michael Porter, Director, 651-962-4380, Fax: 651-962-4020, E-mail: businesscom@stthomas.edu. *Application contact:* Leslie Krona, Program Manager/Advisor, 651-962-4380, Fax: 651-962-4020, E-mail: businesscom@stthomas.edu.

University of Southern California, Graduate School, Annenberg School for Communication and Journalism, School of Communication, Program in Communication, Los Angeles, CA 90089. Offers communication (MA, PhD), including information and society (PhD); interpersonal and health communication (PhD), media, culture and communication (PhD), organizational communication (PhD), rhetorical and political communication (PhD). *Students:* 97 full-time (64 women); includes 20 minority (4 Black or African American, non-Hispanic/Latino; 1 American Indian or Alaska Native, non-Hispanic/Latino; 8 Asian, non-Hispanic/Latino; 7 Hispanic/Latino), 30 international. Average age 31. 242 applicants, 9% accepted, 18 enrolled. In 2010, 14 doctorates awarded. *Degree requirements:* For doctorate, thesis/dissertation. *Entrance requirements:* For master's and doctorate, GRE General Test, resume, writing samples, 3 letters of recommendation, interest survey questionnaire, statement of purpose. Additional exam requirements/recommendations for international students: Required—TOEFL (minimum score 280 computer-based; 114 iBT); Recommended—TWE. *Application deadline:* For fall admission, 12/1 for domestic and international students. Application fee: $85. Electronic applications accepted. *Expenses:* Tuition: Full-time $31,240; part-time $1420 per unit. Required fees: $600. One-time fee: $35 full-time. Full-time tuition and fees vary according to degree level and program. *Financial support:* In 2010–11, 18 students received support, including 18 fellowships with full tuition reimbursements available (averaging $26,500 per year); research assistantships, teaching assistantships, Federal Work-Study, institutionally sponsored loans, scholarships/grants, health care benefits, and unspecified assistantships also available. Support available to part-time students. Financial award application deadline: 1/1; financial award applicants required to submit FAFSA. *Faculty research:* Computer-mediated communication, public health campaigns, communication democracy and the public sphere, new communication technologies in organizations, communication and community. *Unit head:* Dr. Thomas Goodnight, Director of the Ph.D. Program, 213-821-5384, E-mail: gtg@usc.edu. *Application contact:* Allyson Hill, Assistant Dean, Admissions, 213-821-0770, Fax: 213-740-1933, E-mail: ascadm@usc.edu.

See Display on page 675 and Close-Up on page 727.

University of Southern California, Graduate School, Annenberg School for Communication and Journalism, School of Communication, Program in Communication Management, Los Angeles, CA 90089. Offers MCM, JD/MCM, MCM/MAJCS. Part-time and evening/weekend programs available. Postbaccalaureate distance learning degree programs offered (no on-campus study). *Students:* 192 full-time, 89 part-time; includes 89 minority (18 Black or African American, non-Hispanic/Latino; 33 Asian, non-Hispanic/Latino; 32 Hispanic/Latino; 6 Two or more races, non-Hispanic/Latino), 90 international. Average age 31. 327 applicants, 52% accepted, 80 enrolled. In 2010, 117 master's awarded. *Degree requirements:* For master's, professional project. *Entrance requirements:* For master's, GRE General Test or GMAT, resume, writing samples, recommendation letters, statement of purpose. Additional exam requirements/recommendations for international students: Required—TOEFL (minimum score 280 computer-based; 114 iBT). *Application deadline:* For fall admission, 7/1 priority date for domestic students,

3/15 priority date for international students; for spring admission, 11/1 priority date for domestic students, 9/1 priority date for international students. Applications are processed on a rolling basis. Application fee: $85. Electronic applications accepted. *Expenses:* Tuition: Full-time $31,240; part-time $1420 per unit. Required fees: $600. One-time fee: $35 full-time. Full-time tuition and fees vary according to degree level and program. *Financial support:* Research assistantships with tuition reimbursements, Federal Work-Study, institutionally sponsored loans, scholarships/grants, health care benefits, and tuition waivers (partial) available. Support available to part-time students. Financial award application deadline: 2/1; financial award applicants required to submit FAFSA. *Faculty research:* Global communication, communication law and policy, entertainment management, marketing communication, strategic and corporate communication management. *Unit head:* Dr. Rebecca Weintraub, Director of the Communication Management Degree Program, 213-821-0764, Fax: 213-740-8036, E-mail: weintrau@usc.edu. *Application contact:* Allyson Hill, Assistant Dean, Admissions, 213-821-0770, Fax: 213-740-1933, E-mail: ascadm@usc.edu.

See Display on page 675 and Close-Up on page 727.

University of Wisconsin–Stevens Point, College of Fine Arts and Communication, Division of Communication, Stevens Point, WI 54481-3897. Offers interpersonal communication (MA); mass communication (MA); organizational communication (MA); public relations (MA). Part-time programs available. *Degree requirements:* For master's, thesis or alternative. *Entrance requirements:* For master's, GRE. Additional exam requirements/recommendations for international students: Required—TOEFL (minimum score 575 paper-based). *Faculty research:* Communication theory and research, film history.

University of Wisconsin–Whitewater, School of Graduate Studies, College of Arts and Communications, Department of Communication, Whitewater, WI 53190-1790. Offers corporate communication (MS); mass communication (MS). Part-time and evening/weekend programs available. Postbaccalaureate distance learning degree programs offered (no on-campus study). *Degree requirements:* For master's, thesis or alternative. *Entrance requirements:* For master's, 2 letters of recommendation. Additional exam requirements/recommendations for international students: Required—TOEFL (minimum score 550 paper-based; 213 computer-based). Electronic applications accepted.

Walsh University, Graduate Studies, MBA Program, North Canton, OH 44720-3396. Offers health care management (MBA); integrated marketing communications (MBA); management (MBA). Part-time and evening/weekend programs available. *Faculty:* 8 full-time (3 women), 21 part-time/adjunct (4 women). *Students:* 22 full-time (8 women), 132 part-time (68 women); includes 13 minority (10 Black or African American, non-Hispanic/Latino; 3 Hispanic/Latino). Average age 34. 60 applicants, 98% accepted, 49 enrolled. In 2010, 57 master's awarded. *Entrance requirements:* For master's, GMAT, minimum GPA of 3.0. Additional exam requirements/recommendations for international students: Required—TOEFL (minimum score 500 paper-based; 173 computer-based; 61 iBT). *Application deadline:* For fall admission, 7/15 priority date for domestic students. Applications are processed on a rolling basis. Application fee: $25. Electronic applications accepted. *Expenses:* Tuition: Full-time $13,080; part-time $545 per credit hour. *Financial support:* In 2010–11, 98 students received support, including 9 research assistantships with partial tuition reimbursements available (averaging $5,518 per year); tuition waivers (partial), unspecified assistantships, and tuition discounts also available. Financial award application deadline: 12/31. *Faculty research:* Patient and physician satisfaction, advancing and improving learning with information technology, consumer-driven healthcare, branding and the service industry, service provider training and customer satisfaction. *Unit head:* Dr. Michael A. Petrochuk, Director of the MBA Program and Assistant Professor, 330-244-4764, Fax: 330-490-7359, E-mail: mpetrochuk@walsh.edu. *Application contact:* Christine Haver, Assistant Director for Graduate and Transfer Admissions, 330-490-7177, Fax: 330-244-4925, E-mail: chaver@walsh.edu.

Washington State University, Graduate School, The Edward R. Murrow College of Communication, Pullman, WA 99164-2520. Offers health communications (MA, PhD); intercultural and international communications (MA, PhD); media and society (MA, PhD); media process and effects (MA, PhD); organizational communications (MA, PhD). *Faculty:* 30. *Students:* 43 full-time (26 women), 6 part-time (4 women); includes 1 Asian, non-Hispanic/Latino; 1 Hispanic/Latino, 19 international. Average age 30. 120 applicants, 22% accepted, 19 enrolled. In 2010, 22 master's, 1 doctorate awarded. *Degree requirements:* For master's, comprehensive exam (for some programs), thesis optional, oral exam; for doctorate, comprehensive exam, thesis/dissertation. *Entrance requirements:* For master's, GRE General Test, minimum GPA of 3.25, 3 letters of recommendation; for doctorate, GRE General Test, minimum undergraduate GPA of 3.25, graduate 3.5; MA in communication; 3 letters of recommendation. Additional exam requirements/recommendations for international students: Required—TOEFL (minimum score 580 paper-based; 237 computer-based). *Application deadline:* For fall admission, 1/15 priority date for domestic students, 3/1 for international students. Applications are processed on a rolling basis. Application fee: $50. Electronic applications accepted. *Expenses:* Tuition, state resident: full-time $8552; part-time $443 per credit. Tuition, nonresident: full-time $21,650; part-time $1083 per credit. Required fees: $846. *Financial support:* In 2010–11, 46 students received support, including 2 fellowships (averaging $4,477 per year), 7 research assistant-

ships with full and partial tuition reimbursements available (averaging $13,917 per year), 34 teaching assistantships with full and partial tuition reimbursements available (averaging $13,056 per year); career-related internships or fieldwork, Federal Work-Study, institutionally sponsored loans, tuition waivers (partial), and teaching associateships also available. Financial award application deadline: 4/1; financial award applicants required to submit FAFSA. *Faculty research:* Advocacy communication, mediated communication in decision making, communication technology policy and effects, multicultural and international psychology and physiology of communication. Total annual research expenditures: $550,455. *Unit head:* Dr. Erica Austin, Interim Director, 509-335-1556, E-mail: eaustin@wsu.edu. *Application contact:* Graduate School Admissions, 800-GRADWSU, Fax: 509-335-1949, E-mail: gradsch@wsu.edu.

Wayne State University, College of Fine, Performing and Communication Arts, Department of Communication, Detroit, MI 48202. Offers communication studies (MA, PhD); public relations and organizational communication (MA); radio-TV-film (MA, PhD); speech communication (MA, PhD). *Faculty:* 25 full-time (11 women), 4 part-time/adjunct (1 woman). *Students:* 64 full-time (43 women), 107 part-time (73 women); includes 44 minority (36 Black or African American, non-Hispanic/Latino; 2 American Indian or Alaska Native, non-Hispanic/Latino; 1 Asian, non-Hispanic/Latino; 5 Hispanic/Latino), 7 international. Average age 32. 65 applicants, 66% accepted, 31 enrolled. In 2010, 37 master's, 7 doctorates awarded. *Degree requirements:* For master's, thesis, essay, or comprehensive exam; for doctorate, thesis/dissertation. *Entrance requirements:* For master's, minimum GPA of 3.0, sample of academic writing; for doctorate, GRE, minimum GPA of 3.3, MA; letters of recommendation; personal statement; sample of written scholarship. Additional exam requirements/recommendations for international students: Required—TOEFL (minimum score 550 paper-based; 213 computer-based); Recommended—TWE (minimum score 6). *Application deadline:* For fall admission, 4/1 for domestic students, 6/1 for international students; for winter admission, 10/1 for international students; for spring admission, 2/1 for international students. Applications are processed on a rolling basis. Application fee: $30 ($50 for international students). Electronic applications accepted. *Expenses:* Tuition, state resident: full-time $7662; part-time $478.85 per credit hour. Tuition, nonresident: full-time $16,920; part-time $1057.55 per credit hour. Required fees: $571.20; $35.70 per credit hour. $188.05 per semester. Tuition and fees vary according to course load and program. *Financial support:* In 2010–11, 22 students received support, including 8 fellowships with tuition reimbursements available (averaging $14,956 per year), 1 research assistantship with tuition reimbursement available (averaging $23,000 per year), 19 teaching assistantships with tuition reimbursements available (averaging $14,620 per year); career-related internships or fieldwork also available. Financial award application deadline: 2/1. *Faculty research:* Rhetorical theory and criticism; mass media theory and research; argumentation; organizational communication; risk and crisis communication; interpersonal, family, and health communication. *Unit head:* Dr. Matthew Seeger, Chair, 313-577-2959, Fax: 313-577-6300, E-mail: aa4331@wayne.edu. *Application contact:* Hayg Oshagan, Associate Professor, 313-577-0429, E-mail: ad4570@wayne.edu.

Webster University, School of Communications, Program in Communications Management, St. Louis, MO 63119-3194. Offers MA. *Expenses:* Tuition: Part-time $585 per credit hour. Tuition and fees vary according to degree level, campus/location and program.

Western Kentucky University, Graduate Studies, Potter College of Arts and Letters, Department of Communication, Bowling Green, KY 42101. Offers communication (MA); organizational communication (Graduate Certificate). Part-time and evening/weekend programs available. *Degree requirements:* For master's, comprehensive exam, thesis optional, final exam. *Entrance requirements:* For master's, GRE General Test, minimum GPA of 2.75. Additional exam requirements/recommendations for international students: Required—TOEFL (minimum score 555 paper-based; 213 computer-based; 79 iBT). *Faculty research:* Public rhetoric and public address organization communication, teamwork in communication, intercultural crisis communication.

Western Michigan University, Graduate College, College of Arts and Sciences, Department of Communication, Kalamazoo, MI 49008. Offers MA.

West Virginia University, Eberly College of Arts and Sciences, Department of Communication Studies, Morgantown, WV 26506. Offers communication in instruction (MA); communication studies (PhD); communication theory and research (MA); corporate and organizational communication (MA). Part-time programs available. *Degree requirements:* For master's, comprehensive exam (for some programs), thesis (for some programs); for doctorate, comprehensive exam, thesis/dissertation. *Entrance requirements:* For master's and doctorate, minimum GPA of 3.0. Additional exam requirements/recommendations for international students: Required—TOEFL. Electronic applications accepted. *Faculty research:* Instructional communication, interpersonal communication, health communication, influence, instructional communication, social influence.

West Virginia University, Perley Isaac Reed School of Journalism, Program in Digital Marketing Communications, Morgantown, WV 26506. Offers Graduate Certificate. Postbaccalaureate distance learning degree programs offered (no on-campus study). *Entrance requirements:* For degree, resume. Electronic applications accepted.

Health Communication

Arkansas State University, Graduate School, College of Nursing and Health Professions, School of Nursing, Jonesboro, State University, AR 72467. Offers aging studies (Certificate); health care management (Certificate); health communications (Certificate); health sciences (MS); health sciences education (Certificate); nurse anesthesia (MSN); nursing (MSN). *Accreditation:* AANA/CANAEP (one or more programs are accredited); NLN. Part-time programs available. *Faculty:* 7 full-time (6 women), 5 part-time/adjunct (4 women). *Students:* 114 full-time (51 women), 109 part-time (97 women); includes 30 minority (23 Black or African American, non-Hispanic/Latino; 2 Asian, non-Hispanic/Latino; 1 Hispanic/Latino; 4 Two or more races, non-Hispanic/Latino), 3 international. Average age 33. 113 applicants, 42% accepted, 36 enrolled. In 2010, 87 master's awarded. *Degree requirements:* For master's, comprehensive exam, thesis or alternative. *Entrance requirements:* For master's, GRE General Test or MAT, appropriate bachelor's degree, current Arkansas nursing license, CPR certification, physical examination, professional liability insurance, critical care experience, ACLS Certification, PALS Certification, interview, immunization records, personal goal statement, health assessment. Additional exam requirements/recommendations for international students: Required—TOEFL (minimum score 550 paper-based; 213 computer-based; 79 iBT), IELTS (minimum score 6), PTE: Pearson Test of English Academic (56). *Application deadline:* Applications are processed on a rolling basis. Application fee: $30 ($40 for international students). Electronic applications accepted. *Expenses:* Contact institution. *Financial support:* In 2010–11, 8 students received support. Career-related internships or fieldwork, scholarships/grants, and unspecified assistantships available. Financial award application deadline: 7/1; financial award applicants required to submit FAFSA. *Unit head:* Dr. Sue McLarry, Chair, 870-972-3074, Fax: 870-972-2954, E-mail: smclarry@astate.edu. *Application contact:* Dr. Andrew Sustich, Dean of the Graduate School, 870-972-3029, Fax: 870-972-3857, E-mail: sustich@astate.edu.

Chapman University, Graduate Studies, Schmid College of Science, Health Communication Program, Orange, CA 92866. Offers MS. Part-time and evening/weekend programs available. *Faculty:* 1 (woman) full-time, 1 (woman) part-time/adjunct. *Students:* 6 full-time (all women), 4

part-time (all women); includes 4 minority (2 Asian, non-Hispanic/Latino; 2 Hispanic/Latino). Average age 27. 11 applicants, 73% accepted, 6 enrolled. In 2010, 5 master's awarded. *Entrance requirements:* For master's, GRE, minimum undergraduate GPA of 3.0. Additional exam requirements/recommendations for international students: Required—TOEFL (minimum score 550 paper-based; 213 computer-based; 80 iBT). *Application deadline:* Applications are processed on a rolling basis. Application fee: $60. Electronic applications accepted. *Financial support:* Fellowships, Federal Work-Study and scholarships/grants available. Financial award applicants required to submit FAFSA. *Unit head:* Dr. Lisa Sparks, Interim Dean, 714-997-6703, E-mail: sparks@chapman.edu. *Application contact:* Eva Yen, Admission Counselor, 714-997-6711, E-mail: eyen@chapman.edu.

Cleveland State University, College of Graduate Studies, College of Liberal Arts and Social Sciences, School of Communication, Cleveland, OH 44115. Offers applied communication theory and methodology (MA); culture, communication and health care (Certificate). Part-time and evening/weekend programs available. *Faculty:* 10 full-time (5 women). *Students:* 14 full-time (8 women), 22 part-time (13 women); includes 1 Black or African American, non-Hispanic/Latino, 3 international. Average age 30. 39 applicants, 41% accepted, 12 enrolled. In 2010, 14 master's awarded. *Degree requirements:* For master's, variable foreign language requirement, comprehensive exam (for some programs), thesis optional, thesis, project, comprehensive exam, or collaborative project. *Entrance requirements:* For master's, GRE or MAT, minimum undergraduate GPA of 2.75, 2 letters of recommendation. Additional exam requirements/recommendations for international students: Required—TOEFL (minimum score 525 paper-based; 197 computer-based; 65 iBT). *Application deadline:* For fall admission, 8/25 priority date for domestic students, 5/15 priority date for international students; for spring admission, 1/15 priority date for domestic students, 11/1 priority date for international students. Applications are processed on a rolling basis. Application fee: $30. Electronic applications accepted. *Expenses:* Tuition, state resident: full-time $8447; part-time $469 per credit hour. Tuition, nonresident: full-time $16,020; part-time $890 per credit hour. Required fees: $50.

Health Communication

Cleveland State University (continued)
Financial support: In 2010–11, 14 students received support, including 5 research assistantships with full and partial tuition reimbursements available (averaging $11,000 per year), 9 teaching assistantships with full and partial tuition reimbursements available (averaging $11,000 per year); tuition waivers (full) and unspecified assistantships also available. Financial award application deadline: 8/1. *Faculty research:* Interpersonal, organizational, and mass communication; health communication. *Unit head:* Dr. Richard M. Perloff, Director, 216-687-4631, Fax: 216-687-5435, E-mail: r.perloff@csuohio.edu. *Application contact:* Dr. George Ray, 216-687-5103, Fax: 216-687-5435, E-mail: g.ray@csuohio.edu.

East Carolina University, Graduate School, College of Fine Arts and Communication, School of Communication, Greenville, NC 27858-4353. Offers health communication (MA). *Entrance requirements:* For master's, GRE. *Expenses:* Tuition, state resident: full-time $3130; part-time $391.25 per credit hour. Tuition, nonresident: full-time $13,817; part-time $1727.13 per credit hour. Required fees: $1916; $239.50 per credit hour. Tuition and fees vary according to campus/location and program.

Emerson College, Graduate Studies, School of Communication, Department of Communication Sciences and Disorders, Program in Health Communication, Boston, MA 02116-4624. Offers MA. Program offered jointly with Tufts University. Part-time programs available. *Entrance requirements:* For master's, GMAT or GRE General Test. Additional exam requirements/recommendations for international students: Required—TOEFL (minimum score 550 paper-based; 213 computer-based; 80 iBT), IELTS (minimum score 6.5). Electronic applications accepted. *Faculty research:* Health promotion, health communications.

Fitchburg State University, Division of Graduate and Continuing Education, Program in Applied Communications, Fitchburg, MA 01420-2697. Offers applied communications (MS, Certificate); health communication (MS); library media (MS); technical and professional writing (MS). Part-time and evening/weekend programs available. *Students:* 2 full-time (1 woman), 18 part-time (11 women), 3 international. Average age 34. 4 applicants, 100% accepted, 1 enrolled. In 2010, 8 master's awarded. *Entrance requirements:* For master's, GRE General Test or MAT, minimum 2 years of related experience, letters of recommendation, resume. Additional exam requirements/recommendations for international students: Required—TOEFL (minimum score 550 paper-based; 213 computer-based; 79 iBT). *Application deadline:* Applications are processed on a rolling basis. Application fee: $25 ($50 for international students). *Expenses:* Tuition, area resident: Part-time $150 per credit. Tuition, state resident: part-time $150 per credit. Tuition, nonresident: part-time $150 per credit. Required fees: $127 per credit. *Financial support:* In 2010–11, research assistantships with partial tuition reimbursements (averaging $5,500 per year); Federal Work-Study, scholarships/grants, and unspecified assistantships also available. Support available to part-time students. Financial award application deadline: 3/1; financial award applicants required to submit FAFSA. *Unit head:* Dr. John Chetro-Szivos, Chair, 978-665-3261, Fax: 978-665-3658, E-mail: gce@fitchburgstate.edu. *Application contact:* Director of Admissions, 978-665-3144, Fax: 978-665-4540, E-mail: admissions@fsc.edu.

The Johns Hopkins University, Bloomberg School of Public Health, Department of Health, Behavior and Society, Baltimore, MD 21218-2699. Offers genetic counseling (Sc M); health education and health communication (MHS); social and behavioral sciences (Dr PH, PhD, Sc D); social factors in health (MHS). *Faculty:* 43 full-time (30 women), 59 part-time/adjunct (40 women). *Students:* 114 full-time (105 women), 5 part-time (all women); includes 43 minority (14 Black or African American, non-Hispanic/Latino; 15 Asian, non-Hispanic/Latino; 6 Hispanic/Latino; 8 Two or more races, non-Hispanic/Latino), 11 international. Average age 28. 227 applicants, 31% accepted, 26 enrolled. In 2010, 21 master's, 10 doctorates awarded. *Degree requirements:* For master's, comprehensive exam (for some programs), thesis (for some programs); for doctorate, comprehensive exam, thesis/dissertation. *Entrance requirements:* For master's, GRE, curriculum vitae, 3 letters of recommendation; for doctorate, GRE, transcripts, curriculum vitae, 3 recommendation letters. Additional exam requirements/recommendations for international students: Required—TOEFL (minimum score 600 paper-based; 250 computer-based; 100 iBT). *Application deadline:* For fall admission, 12/1 for domestic and international students. Applications are processed on a rolling basis. Application fee: $45. Electronic applications accepted. *Financial support:* In 2010–11, 96 students received support, including 17 fellowships with tuition reimbursements available (averaging $23,634 per year), 30 research assistantships (averaging $7,800 per year), 25 teaching assistantships (averaging $2,759 per year); career-related internships or fieldwork, Federal Work-Study, scholarships/grants, traineeships, health care benefits, unspecified assistantships, and stipends also available. Financial award application deadline: 3/15. *Faculty research:* Social determinants of health and structural and community-level inventions to improve health, communication and health education, behavioral and social aspects of genetic counseling. Total annual research expenditures: $6.3 million. *Unit head:* Georgean Smith, Administrator, 410-502-3715, Fax: 410-502-4333, E-mail: gcsmith@jhsph.edu. *Application contact:* Barbara W. Diehl, Senior Academic Program Coordinator, 410-502-4415, Fax: 410-502-4333, E-mail: bdiehl@jhsph.edu.

Marquette University, Graduate School, College of Communication, Milwaukee, WI 53201-1881. Offers advertising and public relations (MA); broadcasting and electronic communications (MA); communications studies (MA); digital storytelling (Certificate); health, environment, science and sustainability (MA); journalism (MA); mass communications (MA). *Accreditation:* ACEJMC (one or more programs are accredited). Part-time and evening/weekend programs available. *Faculty:* 33 full-time (18 women), 30 part-time/adjunct (16 women). *Students:* 35 full-time (20 women), 31 part-time (25 women); includes 5 minority (2 Black or African American, non-Hispanic/Latino; 1 Hispanic/Latino; 2 Two or more races, non-Hispanic/Latino), 4 international. Average age 28. 97 applicants, 52% accepted, 21 enrolled. In 2010, 16 master's, 5 other advanced degrees awarded. *Degree requirements:* For master's, comprehensive exam, thesis or alternative. *Entrance requirements:* For master's, GRE, official transcripts from all current and previous colleges/universities except Marquette, three letters of recommendation, statement of academic and professional goals. Additional exam requirements/recommendations for international students: Required—TOEFL (minimum score 530 paper-based; 78 computer-based). *Application deadline:* Applications are processed on a rolling basis. Application fee: $50. Electronic applications accepted. *Expenses:* Tuition: Full-time $16,290; part-time $905 per credit hour. Tuition and fees vary according to program. *Financial support:* In 2010–11, 2 fellowships, 7 research assistantships, 12 teaching assistantships were awarded; career-related internships or fieldwork, Federal Work-Study, institutionally sponsored loans, scholarships/grants, and tuition waivers (full and partial) also available. Support available to part-time students. Financial award application deadline: 2/15. *Faculty research:* Urban journalism, gender and communication, intercultural communication, religious communication. Total annual research expenditures: $3,088. *Unit head:* Dr. Lori Bergen, Dean, 414-288-7133, Fax: 414-288-1578. *Application contact:* Erin Fox, Assistant Director for Recruitment, 414-288-5319, Fax: 414-288-1902, E-mail: erin.fox@marquette.edu.

Marywood University, Academic Affairs, Insalaco College of Creative and Performing Arts, Department of Communication Arts, Program in Information Sciences, Scranton, PA 18509-1598. Offers corporate communication (Certificate); e-business (Certificate); health communication (Certificate); information sciences (MS), including library science/information specialist; instructional technology (Certificate). *Entrance requirements:* Additional exam requirements/recommendations for international students: Required—TOEFL (minimum score 550 paper-based; 213 computer-based; 79 iBT). Electronic applications accepted. *Expenses:* Tuition: Part-time $735 per credit. Required fees: $470 per semester. Tuition and fees vary according to degree level and campus/location.

Michigan State University, The Graduate School, College of Communication Arts and Sciences, Program in Health Communication, East Lansing, MI 48824. Offers MA. *Entrance requirements:* Additional exam requirements/recommendations for international students: Required—TOEFL. Electronic applications accepted. *Faculty research:* Mass communication and public health, health communication for diverse populations, descriptive and analytical epidemiology.

Ohio University, Graduate College, Scripps College of Communication, School of Communication Studies, Athens, OH 45701-2979. Offers health communication (PhD); organizational communication (MA); relating and organizing (PhD); rhetoric and public culture (PhD). Part-time programs available. Postbaccalaureate distance learning degree programs offered (minimal on-campus study). *Students:* 49 full-time (35 women), 42 part-time (33 women); includes 6 minority (4 Black or African American, non-Hispanic/Latino; 1 Hispanic/Latino; 1 Two or more races, non-Hispanic/Latino), 12 international. 104 applicants, 40% accepted, 31 enrolled. In 2010, 2 master's, 12 doctorates awarded. Terminal master's awarded for partial completion of doctoral program. *Degree requirements:* For master's, capstone; for doctorate, comprehensive exam, thesis/dissertation. *Entrance requirements:* For master's, GRE; for doctorate, GRE General Test, minimum GPA of 3.0. Additional exam requirements/recommendations for international students: Required—TOEFL (minimum score 550 paper-based; 80 iBT) or IELTS (minimum score 6.5). *Application deadline:* For fall admission, 1/15 priority date for domestic and international students. Application fee: $50 ($55 for international students). Electronic applications accepted. *Financial support:* In 2010–11, 12 students received support, including fellowships with full tuition reimbursements available (averaging $13,600 per year), research assistantships with full tuition reimbursements available (averaging $13,600 per year), teaching assistantships with full tuition reimbursements available (averaging $13,600 per year); career-related internships or fieldwork, Federal Work-Study, and institutionally sponsored loans also available. Financial award application deadline: 1/15. *Faculty research:* Rhetoric and public culture, relating and organizing, health communication. Total annual research expenditures: $200,000. *Unit head:* Dr. Scott Titsworth, Director, 740-593-9160, Fax: 740-593-4810, E-mail: titswort@ohio.edu. *Application contact:* Dr. Benjamin Bates, Associate Director for Graduate Studies, 740-593-9163, Fax: 740-593-4810, E-mail: batesb@ohio.edu.

Southern Illinois University Edwardsville, Graduate School, College of Arts and Sciences, Department of Speech Communication, Program in Health Communication, Edwardsville, IL 62026. Offers MA. Part-time and evening/weekend programs available. *Students:* 1 (woman) part-time; includes Native Hawaiian or other Pacific Islander, non-Hispanic/Latino. Average age 26. *Degree requirements:* For master's, comprehensive exam (for some programs), thesis (for some programs). *Entrance requirements:* Additional exam requirements/recommendations for international students: Required—TOEFL (minimum score 550 paper-based; 213 computer-based; 79 iBT), IELTS (minimum score 6.5). *Application deadline:* For fall admission, 7/22 for domestic students, 6/1 for international students; for spring admission, 12/9 for domestic students, 10/1 for international students. Applications are processed on a rolling basis. Application fee: $30. Electronic applications accepted. *Expenses:* Tuition, state resident: full-time $6012; part-time $1503 per semester. Tuition, nonresident: full-time $15,030; part-time $3758 per semester. Required fees: $1711; $675 per semester. *Financial support:* Application deadline: 3/1. *Unit head:* Dr. Isaac Blankson, Chair, 618-650-3090, E-mail: iblanks@siue.edu. *Application contact:* Dr. Jocelyn DeGroot Brown, Director, 618-650-5828, E-mail: jocbrow@siue.edu.

Tufts University, School of Medicine, Public Health and Professional Degree Programs, Boston, MA 02111. Offers biomedical sciences (MS); health communication (MS); pain research, education and policy (MS); public health (MPH). MS programs offered jointly with Emerson College. *Accreditation:* CEPH (one or more programs are accredited). Part-time and evening/weekend programs available. *Faculty:* 67 full-time (27 women), 42 part-time/adjunct (17 women). *Students:* 246 full-time (128 women), 84 part-time (68 women); includes 20 Black or African American, non-Hispanic/Latino; 2 American Indian or Alaska Native, non-Hispanic/Latino; 58 Asian, non-Hispanic/Latino; 20 Hispanic/Latino, 10 international. Average age 27. 913 applicants, 49% accepted, 175 enrolled. In 2010, 134 master's awarded. *Degree requirements:* For master's, thesis (for some programs). *Entrance requirements:* For master's, GRE General Test, MCAT, GMAT. Additional exam requirements/recommendations for international students: Required—TOEFL (minimum score 270 computer-based; 110 iBT). *Application deadline:* For fall admission, 3/15 priority date for domestic students, 3/15 for international students; for spring admission, 10/25 priority date for domestic students, 10/25 for international students. Applications are processed on a rolling basis. Application fee: $70. Electronic applications accepted. *Expenses:* Contact institution. *Financial support:* In 2010–11, 15 students received support, including 20 teaching assistantships (averaging $2,000 per year); Federal Work-Study and scholarships/grants also available. Support available to part-time students. Financial award application deadline: 2/28; financial award applicants required to submit FAFSA. *Faculty research:* Environmental and occupational health, nutrition, epidemiology, health communication, health services management and policy, biostatistics, protein interaction, mRNA processing, vascular pathology. *Unit head:* Dr. Aviva Must, Dean, Public Health and Professional Degree Programs, 617-636-0935, Fax: 617-636-0898, E-mail: aviva.must@tufts.edu. *Application contact:* Emily Keily, Director of Admissions, 617-636-6645, Fax: 617-636-0898, E-mail: med-phpd@tufts.edu.

Tulane University, School of Public Health and Tropical Medicine, Department of Community Health Sciences, Program in Health Education and Communication, New Orleans, LA 70118-5669. Offers MPH. *Accreditation:* CEPH; Teacher Education Accreditation Council. *Degree requirements:* For master's, comprehensive exam. *Entrance requirements:* For master's, GRE General Test. Additional exam requirements/recommendations for international students: Required—TOEFL.

University of Florida, Graduate School, College of Health and Human Performance, Department of Health Education and Behavior, Gainesville, FL 32611. Offers health behavior (PhD); health communication (Graduate Certificate); health education and behavior (MS). *Accreditation:* NCATE (one or more programs are accredited). Part-time programs available. *Students:* 42 full-time (32 women), 9 part-time (6 women); includes 5 Black or African American, non-Hispanic/Latino; 5 Asian, non-Hispanic/Latino; 11 Hispanic/Latino, 3 international. Average age 26. 25 applicants, 60% accepted, 12 enrolled. In 2010, 26 master's, 2 doctorates awarded. Terminal master's awarded for partial completion of doctoral program. *Degree requirements:* For master's, comprehensive exam, thesis (for some programs); for doctorate, comprehensive exam, thesis/dissertation. *Entrance requirements:* For master's and doctorate, GRE General Test, minimum GPA of 3.0. Additional exam requirements/recommendations for international students: Required—TOEFL (minimum score 550 paper-based; 213 computer-based; 80 iBT), IELTS (minimum score 6). *Application deadline:* For fall admission, 6/1 priority date for domestic students; for spring admission, 10/1 for domestic and international students. Applications are processed on a rolling basis. Application fee: $30. Electronic applications accepted. *Expenses:* Tuition, state resident: full-time $10,915.92. Tuition, nonresident: full-time $28,309. *Financial support:* In 2010–11, 22 students received support, including 9 fellowships, 7 research assistantships (averaging $14,960 per year), 6 teaching assistantships (averaging $16,396 per year); career-related internships or fieldwork and institutionally sponsored loans also available. Financial award application deadline: 2/1; financial award applicants required to submit FAFSA. *Faculty research:* Information technology and digital health for health promotion and disease prevention; prevention of high risk drinking among college students; scale development and measurement of youth prescription drug use; evaluation of state, regional, and community-based health education interventions. Total annual research expenditures: $1.5 million. *Unit head:* Dr. Robert M. Pigg, Chair & Graduate Coordinator, 352-392-0583 Ext. 1281, Fax: 352-392-1909, E-mail: rmpigg@hhp.ufl.edu. *Application contact:* Dr. Robert M. Pigg, Chair & Graduate Coordinator, 352-392-0583 Ext. 1281, Fax: 352-392-1909, E-mail: rmpigg@hhp.ufl.edu.

University of Houston, College of Liberal Arts and Social Sciences, School of Communication, Houston, TX 77204. Offers health communication (MA); mass communication studies (MA); public relations studies (MA); speech communication (MA). Part-time programs available. *Faculty:* 11 full-time (6 women), 2 part-time/adjunct (0 women). *Students:* 47 full-time (39 women), 46 part-time (36 women); includes 15 Black or African American, non-Hispanic/Latino; 2 American Indian or Alaska Native, non-Hispanic/Latino; 3 Asian, non-Hispanic/Latino; 16 Hispanic/Latino, 19 international. Average age 28. 54 applicants, 70% accepted, 24 enrolled.

In 2010, 20 master's awarded. *Degree requirements:* For master's, comprehensive exam (for some programs), thesis (for some programs), 30-33 hours. *Entrance requirements:* For master's, GRE. Additional exam requirements/recommendations for international students: Required—TOEFL. *Application deadline:* For fall admission, 6/1 for domestic students, 4/1 for international students; for spring admission, 11/1 for domestic students, 10/1 for international students. Applications are processed on a rolling basis. Application fee: $50 ($100 for international students). Electronic applications accepted. *Expenses:* Tuition, state resident: full-time $8592; part-time $358 per credit hour. Tuition, nonresident: full-time $16,032; part-time $668 per credit hour. Required fees: $2889. Tuition and fees vary according to course load and program. *Financial support:* In 2010–11, 28 teaching assistantships with full tuition reimbursements (averaging $8,111 per year) were awarded; career-related internships or fieldwork, Federal Work-Study, institutionally sponsored loans, scholarships/grants, health care benefits, and unspecified assistantships also available. Support available to part-time students. Financial award application deadline: 2/1. *Unit head:* Dr. Beth Olson, Chairperson, 713-743-2873, Fax: 713-743-2876, E-mail: bolson@uh.edu. *Application contact:* Dr. Martha Haun, Director of Graduate Studies, 713-743-2886, E-mail: mhaun@uh.edu.

The University of North Carolina at Charlotte, Graduate School, College of Arts and Sciences, Department of Communication Studies, Charlotte, NC 28223-0001. Offers health communication (MA); media/rhetorical critical studies (MA); organizational communication (MA); public relations (MA). Part-time and evening/weekend programs available. *Faculty:* 12 full-time (5 women), 1 (woman) part-time/adjunct. *Students:* 6 full-time (5 women), 19 part-time (17 women); includes 7 minority (6 Black or African American, non-Hispanic/Latino; 1 Asian, non-Hispanic/Latino). Average age 27. 554 applicants, 4% accepted, 12 enrolled. In 2010, 12 master's awarded. Terminal master's awarded for partial completion of doctoral program. *Degree requirements:* For master's, project, thesis, or comprehensive exam. *Entrance requirements:* For master's, GRE General Test, minimum GPA of 2.75 overall. Additional exam requirements/recommendations for international students: Required—TOEFL (minimum score 557 paper-based; 220 computer-based; 83 iBT). *Application deadline:* For fall admission, 3/15 for domestic students, 5/1 for international students; for spring admission, 11/15 for domestic students, 10/1 for international students. Applications are processed on a rolling basis. Application fee: $55. Electronic applications accepted. *Expenses:* Tuition, state resident: full-time $3464. Tuition, nonresident: full-time $14,297. Required fees: $2094. Tuition and fees vary according to course load. *Financial support:* In 2010–11, 9 students received support, including 1 research assistantship (averaging $18,000 per year), 8 teaching assistantships (averaging $15,529 per year); career-related internships or fieldwork, institutionally sponsored loans, scholarships/grants, and unspecified assistantships also available. Support available to part-time students. Financial award application deadline: 4/1; financial award applicants required to submit FAFSA. *Faculty research:* Health literacy, systems of care and mental illness, the communication of emotions in gendered workplaces, international constructs of public relations managerial responsibilities, sports culture and the construction of social contracts, African-American oratory. Total annual research expenditures: $25,636. *Unit head:* Dr. Richard W. Leeman, Chair, 704-687-2086, Fax: 704-687-6900, E-mail: rwleeman@uncc.edu. *Application contact:* Kathy B. Giddings, Director of Graduate Admissions, 704-687-5503, Fax: 704-687-3279, E-mail: gradadm@uncc.edu.

University of Southern California, Graduate School, Annenberg School for Communication and Journalism, School of Communication, Program in Communication, Los Angeles, CA 90089. Offers communication (MA, PhD), including information and society (PhD), interpersonal and health communication (PhD), media, culture and communication (PhD), organizational communication (PhD), rhetorical and political communication (PhD). *Students:* 97 full-time (64 women); includes 20 minority (4 Black or African American, non-Hispanic/Latino; 1 American Indian or Alaska Native, non-Hispanic/Latino; 8 Asian, non-Hispanic/Latino; 7 Hispanic/Latino), 30 international. Average age 31. 242 applicants, 9% accepted, 18 enrolled. In 2010, 14 doctorates awarded. *Degree requirements:* For doctorate, thesis/dissertation. *Entrance requirements:* For master's and doctorate, GRE General Test, resume, writing samples, 3 letters of recommendation, interest survey questionnaire, statement of purpose. Additional exam requirements/recommendations for international students: Required—TOEFL (minimum score 280 computer-based; 114 iBT); Recommended—TWE. *Application deadline:* For fall admission, 12/1 for domestic and international students. Application fee: $85. Electronic applications accepted. *Expenses:* Tuition: Full-time $31,240; part-time $1420 per unit. Required fees: $600. One-time fee: $35 full-time. Full-time tuition and fees vary according to degree level and program. *Financial support:* In 2010–11, 18 students received support, including 18 fellowships with full tuition reimbursements available (averaging $26,500 per year); research assistantships, teaching assistantships, Federal Work-Study, institutionally sponsored loans, scholarships/grants, health care benefits, and unspecified assistantships also available. Support available to part-time students. Financial award application deadline: 1/1; financial award applicants required to submit FAFSA. *Faculty research:* Computer-mediated communication, public health campaigns, communication democracy and the public sphere, new communication technologies in organizations, communication and community. *Unit head:* Dr. Thomas Goodnight, Director of the Ph.D. Program, 213-821-5384, E-mail: gtg@usc.edu. *Application contact:* Allyson Hill, Assistant Dean, Admissions, 213-821-0770, Fax: 213-740-1933, E-mail: ascadm@usc.edu.

See Display on page 675 and Close-Up on page 727.

University of Southern California, Keck School of Medicine and Graduate School, Graduate Programs in Medicine, Department of Preventive Medicine, Master of Public Health Program, Alhambra, CA 91803. Offers biostatistics/epidemiology (MPH); child and family health (MPH); global health leadership (MPH); health communication (MPH); health promotion (MPH). *Accreditation:* CEPH. Part-time programs available. *Faculty:* 22 full-time (12 women), 3 part-time/adjunct (0 women). *Students:* 208 full-time (152 women), 3 part-time (2 women); includes 15 Black or African American, non-Hispanic/Latino; 78 Asian, non-Hispanic/Latino; 14 Hispanic/Latino, 38 international. Average age 24. 218 applicants, 73% accepted, 88 enrolled. In 2010, 80 master's awarded. *Degree requirements:* For master's, practicum, final report, oral presentation. *Entrance requirements:* For master's, GRE General Test, MCAT, GMAT, minimum GPA of 3.0. Additional exam requirements/recommendations for international students: Required—TOEFL (minimum score 600 paper-based; 250 computer-based; 100 iBT). *Application deadline:* For fall admission, 6/1 priority date for domestic and international students; for spring admission, 11/1 priority date for domestic students, 10/1 priority date for international students. Applications are processed on a rolling basis. Application fee: $85. Electronic applications accepted. *Expenses:* Tuition: Full-time $31,240; part-time $1420 per unit. Required fees: $600. One-time fee: $35 full-time. Full-time tuition and fees vary according to degree level and program. *Financial support:* In 2010–11, 185 students received support. Career-related internships or fieldwork, Federal Work-Study, institutionally sponsored loans, and scholarships/grants available. Support available to part-time students. Financial award application deadline: 5/3; financial award applicants required to submit CSS PROFILE or FAFSA. *Faculty research:* Substance abuse prevention, cancer and heart disease prevention, mass media and health communication research, health promotion, treatment compliance. *Unit head:* Dr. Thomas W. Valente, Director, 626-457-4139, Fax: 626-457-6699, E-mail: tvalente@usc.edu. *Application contact:* Chrystal Romero, Admissions Counselor, 626-457-6676, Fax: 626-457-6699, E-mail: ccromero@usc.edu.

Washington State University, Graduate School, The Edward R. Murrow College of Communication, Pullman, WA 99164-2520. Offers health communications (MA, PhD); intercultural and international communications (MA, PhD); media and society (MA, PhD); media process and effects (MA, PhD); organizational communications (MA, PhD). *Faculty:* 30. *Students:* 43 full-time (26 women), 6 part-time (4 women); includes 1 Asian, non-Hispanic/Latino; 1 Hispanic/Latino, 19 international. Average age 30. 120 applicants, 22% accepted, 19 enrolled. In 2010, 22 master's, 1 doctorate awarded. *Degree requirements:* For master's, comprehensive exam (for some programs), thesis optional, oral exam; for doctorate, comprehensive exam, thesis/dissertation. *Entrance requirements:* For master's, GRE General Test, minimum GPA of 3.25, 3 letters of recommendation; for doctorate, GRE General Test, minimum undergraduate GPA of 3.25, graduate 3.5; MA in communication; 3 letters of recommendation. Additional exam requirements/recommendations for international students: Required—TOEFL (minimum score 580 paper-based; 237 computer-based). *Application deadline:* For fall admission, 1/15 priority date for domestic students, 3/1 for international students. Applications are processed on a rolling basis. Application fee: $50. Electronic applications accepted. *Expenses:* Tuition, state resident: full-time $8552; part-time $443 per credit. Tuition, nonresident: full-time $21,650; part-time $1083 per credit. Required fees: $846. *Financial support:* In 2010–11, 46 students received support, including 2 fellowships (averaging $4,477 per year), 7 research assistantships with full and partial tuition reimbursements available (averaging $13,917 per year), 34 teaching assistantships with full and partial tuition reimbursements available (averaging $13,056 per year); career-related internships or fieldwork, Federal Work-Study, institutionally sponsored loans, tuition waivers (partial), and teaching associateships also available. Financial award application deadline: 4/1; financial award applicants required to submit FAFSA. *Faculty research:* Advocacy communication, mediated communication in decision making, communication technology policy and effects, multicultural and international psychology and physiology of communication. Total annual research expenditures: $550,455. *Unit head:* Dr. Erica Austin, Interim Director, 509-335-1556, E-mail: eaustin@wsu.edu. *Application contact:* Graduate School Admissions, 800-GRADWSU, Fax: 509-335-1949, E-mail: gradsch@wsu.edu.

Internet and Interactive Multimedia

Academy of Art University, Graduate Program, School of Multimedia Communications, San Francisco, CA 94105-3410. Offers MA. Part-time programs available. Postbaccalaureate distance learning degree programs offered. *Faculty:* 3 full-time (1 woman), 24 part-time/adjunct (8 women). *Students:* 112 full-time (78 women), 38 part-time (25 women); includes 16 Black or African American, non-Hispanic/Latino; 1 American Indian or Alaska Native, non-Hispanic/Latino; 5 Asian, non-Hispanic/Latino; 7 Hispanic/Latino, 74 international. Average age 28. 77 applicants. In 2010, 4 master's awarded. *Degree requirements:* For master's, thesis, final review. *Application deadline:* For fall admission, 9/7 for domestic and international students; for spring admission, 2/2 for domestic and international students. Applications are processed on a rolling basis. Application fee: $100 ($500 for international students). Electronic applications accepted. *Expenses:* Tuition: Full-time $20,160; part-time $840 per semester hour. Required fees: $45 per semester. *Financial support:* Career-related internships or fieldwork and Federal Work-Study available. Support available to part-time students. Financial award applicants required to submit FAFSA.

Alfred University, Graduate School, New York State College of Ceramics, School of Art and Design, Alfred, NY 14802-1205. Offers ceramic art (MFA); electronic integrated arts (MFA); glass art (MFA); sculpture (MFA). *Accreditation:* NASAD. *Degree requirements:* For master's, exhibit. *Entrance requirements:* For master's, portfolio. Additional exam requirements/recommendations for international students: Required—TOEFL (minimum score 550 paper-based; 213 computer-based; 80 iBT), IELTS (minimum score 6). Electronic applications accepted. *Faculty research:* Ceramic sculpture, functional ceramics, wood, mixed media, hot and cold glass.

Brooklyn College of the City University of New York, Division of Graduate Studies, Program in Performance and Interactive Media Arts, Brooklyn, NY 11210-2889. Offers MFA, CAS. *Students:* 11 full-time (8 women), 17 part-time (10 women); includes 5 minority (3 Black or African American, non-Hispanic/Latino; 2 Hispanic/Latino), 3 international. Average age 32. 26 applicants, 69% accepted, 12 enrolled. In 2010, 8 master's awarded. *Entrance requirements:* For master's, 2 letters of recommendation, resume, portfolio, interview; for CAS, 2 letters of recommendation. Additional exam requirements/recommendations for international students: Required—TOEFL (minimum score 500 paper-based; 173 computer-based; 61 iBT). *Application deadline:* For fall admission, 2/15 priority date for domestic students, 2/1 priority date for international students. Applications are processed on a rolling basis. Application fee: $125. Electronic applications accepted. *Expenses:* Tuition, state resident: full-time $7360; part-time $310 per credit hour. Tuition, nonresident: full-time $13,800; part-time $575 per credit hour. Required fees: $190 per semester. *Financial support:* Application deadline: 5/1. *Unit head:* Dr. David Grubbs, Director, 718-951-4203, E-mail: dgrubbs@brooklyn.cuny.edu. *Application contact:* Hernan Sierra, Graduate Admissions Coordinator, 718-951-4536, Fax: 718-951-4506, E-mail: grads@brooklyn.cuny.edu.

California State University, East Bay, Office of Academic Programs and Graduate Studies, College of Letters, Arts, and Social Sciences, Multimedia Program, Hayward, CA 94542-3000. Offers MA. Part-time programs available. *Faculty:* 4 full-time (2 women). *Students:* 18 full-time (8 women), 13 part-time (6 women); includes 1 Black or African American, non-Hispanic/Latino; 4 Asian, non-Hispanic/Latino; 3 Hispanic/Latino; 2 Two or more races, non-Hispanic/Latino, 2 international. Average age 33. 31 applicants, 55% accepted, 10 enrolled. In 2010, 12 master's awarded. *Degree requirements:* For master's, multimedia project. *Entrance requirements:* For master's, minimum GPA of 2.5. Additional exam requirements/recommendations for international students: Required—TOEFL (minimum score 550 paper-based; 213 computer-based). *Application deadline:* For fall admission, 6/30 for domestic and international students. Application fee: $55. Electronic applications accepted. *Financial support:* Fellowships, teaching assistantships, Federal Work-Study, institutionally sponsored loans, and scholarships/grants available. Support available to part-time students. Financial award application deadline: 3/1; financial award applicants required to submit FAFSA. *Unit head:* Dr. Rafael Hernandez, Program Director, 510-885-3204, Fax: 510-885-4301, E-mail: rafael.hernandez@csueastbay.edu. *Application contact:* Dr. Donna Wiley, Interim Associate Director, 510-885-2928, Fax: 510-885-4777, E-mail: donna.wiley@csueastbay.edu.

Concordia University, School of Graduate Studies, Faculty of Engineering and Computer Science, Concordia Institute for Information Systems Engineering (CIISE), Montréal, QC H3G 1M8, Canada. Offers 3D graphics and game development (Certificate); information systems security (M Eng, MA Sc); quality systems engineering (M Eng, MA Sc); service engineering and network management (Certificate).

DePaul University, College of Computing and Digital Media, Chicago, IL 60604. Offers animation (MA, MFA); applied technology (MS); business information technology (MS); cinema (MFA); cinema production (MS); computational finance (MS); computer and information sciences (PhD); computer game development (MS); computer graphics and motion technology (MS); computer information and network security (MS); computer science (MS); e-commerce technology (MS); human-computer interaction (MS); information systems (MS); information technology (MA); information technology project management (MS); network engineering and

Internet and Interactive Multimedia

DePaul University (continued)
management (MS); predictive analytics (MS); screenwriting (MFA); software engineering (MS); JD/MA; JD/MS. Part-time and evening/weekend programs available. Postbaccalaureate distance learning degree programs offered (no on-campus study). *Faculty:* 51 full-time (11 women), 50 part-time/adjunct (9 women). *Students:* 952 full-time (230 women), 927 part-time (226 women); includes 557 minority (205 Black or African American, non-Hispanic/Latino; 2 American Indian or Alaska Native, non-Hispanic/Latino; 167 Asian, non-Hispanic/Latino; 136 Hispanic/Latino; 7 Native Hawaiian or other Pacific Islander, non-Hispanic/Latino; 40 Two or more races, non-Hispanic/Latino), 292 international. Average age 31. 896 applicants, 70% accepted, 324 enrolled. In 2010, 417 master's, 6 doctorates awarded. *Degree requirements:* For master's, thesis (for some programs); for doctorate, comprehensive exam, thesis/dissertation. *Entrance requirements:* For master's, GRE or GMAT (MS in computational finance only), bachelor's degree, resume (MS in predictive analytics only), IT experience (MS in information technology project management only), portfolio review (MFA); for doctorate, GRE, master's degree in computer science. Additional exam requirements/recommendations for international students: Required—TOEFL (minimum score 550 paper-based; 213 computer-based; 80 iBT), IELTS (minimum score 6.5), Pearson Test of English (minimum score 53). *Application deadline:* For fall admission, 8/15 priority date for domestic students, 6/1 priority date for international students; for winter admission, 12/15 priority date for domestic students, 9/15 priority date for international students; for spring admission, 3/1 priority date for domestic students, 12/15 priority date for international students. Applications are processed on a rolling basis. Application fee: $25. Electronic applications accepted. *Expenses:* Contact institution. *Financial support:* In 2010–11, 102 students received support, including 4 fellowships with full tuition reimbursements available (averaging $24,435 per year), 6 research assistantships (averaging $21,100 per year), 92 teaching assistantships with full and partial tuition reimbursements available (averaging $6,904 per year); Federal Work-Study, scholarships/grants, tuition waivers (full and partial), and unspecified assistantships also available. Support available to part-time students. Financial award application deadline: 4/30; financial award applicants required to submit FAFSA. *Faculty research:* Bioinformatics, visual computing, graphics and animation, high performance and scientific computing, databases. Total annual research expenditures: $1.4 million. *Unit head:* Dr. David Miller, Dean, 312-362-8381, Fax: 312-362-5185. *Application contact:* Dr. Liz Friedman, Assistant Dean of Student Services, 312-362-8714, Fax: 312-362-5179, E-mail: efriedm2@cdm.depaul.edu.

Duquesne University, Graduate School of Liberal Arts, Program in Multimedia Technology, Pittsburgh, PA 15282-0001. Offers MS, Certificate. Part-time and evening/weekend programs available. *Faculty:* 10 full-time (1 woman), 3 part-time/adjunct (0 women). *Students:* 45 full-time (24 women), 12 part-time (6 women); includes 1 Black or African American, non-Hispanic/Latino, 4 international. Average age 22. 24 applicants, 92% accepted, 20 enrolled. In 2010, 19 master's awarded. *Entrance requirements:* For master's, MAT or GRE General Test, portfolio. Additional exam requirements/recommendations for international students: Required—TOEFL. *Application deadline:* For fall admission, 8/1 for domestic students, 5/1 for international students; for spring admission, 11/1 for domestic students. Applications are processed on a rolling basis. Electronic applications accepted. *Expenses:* Tuition: Part-time $884 per credit. Required fees: $84 per credit. Tuition and fees vary according to course load. *Financial support:* In 2010–11, 5 research assistantships with full tuition reimbursements (averaging $8,400 per year) were awarded; Federal Work-Study also available. Support available to part-time students. Financial award application deadline: 5/1. *Unit head:* Dr. John Shepherd, Director, 412-396-5772. *Application contact:* Dr. John Shepherd, Assistant to the Dean, 412-396-5772, E-mail: shepherd@duq.edu.

Elon University, Program in Interactive Media, Elon, NC 27244-2010. Offers MA. *Faculty:* 16 full-time (5 women). *Students:* 37 full-time (25 women); includes 2 Black or African American, non-Hispanic/Latino; 1 Hispanic/Latino; 1 Two or more races, non-Hispanic/Latino, 1 international. Average age 25. 76 applicants, 86% accepted, 37 enrolled. In 2010, 36 master's awarded. *Degree requirements:* For master's, 6-hour capstone. *Entrance requirements:* For master's, GRE. Additional exam requirements/recommendations for international students: Required—TOEFL (minimum score 550 paper-based; 213 computer-based; 79 iBT). *Application deadline:* For fall admission, 5/1 priority date for domestic students. Applications are processed on a rolling basis. Application fee: $50. Electronic applications accepted. *Expenses:* Contact institution. *Financial support:* In 2010–11, 19 students received support. Federal Work-Study and scholarships/grants available. Financial award application deadline: 3/15; financial award applicants required to submit FAFSA. *Faculty research:* Effects of service-learning (local and international) on the quality of learning for interactive media students, pedagogy for visual communication, impact of reviewer comments on consumer product and news perceptions, visual communication, social media in pedagogy. *Unit head:* Dr. David Alan Copeland, Director, 336-278-5662, Fax: 336-278-5734, E-mail: dcopeland@elon.edu. *Application contact:* Art Fadde, Director of Graduate Admissions, 800-334-8448 Ext. 3, Fax: 336-278-7699, E-mail: afadde@elon.edu.

Full Sail University, Education Media Design and Technology Master of Science Program—Online, Winter Park, FL 32792-7437. Offers MS. Postbaccalaureate distance learning degree programs offered (no on-campus study). *Entrance requirements:* Additional exam requirements/recommendations for international students: Required—TOEFL (minimum score 550 paper-based; 213 computer-based; 79 iBT).

Full Sail University, Game Design Master of Science Program—Campus, Winter Park, FL 32792-7437. Offers MS.

Full Sail University, Internet Marketing Master of Science Program—Online, Winter Park, FL 32792-7437. Offers MS. Postbaccalaureate distance learning degree programs offered.

George Mason University, Volgenau School of Engineering, Department of Computer Science, Fairfax, VA 22030. Offers biometrics (Certificate); computer games technology (Certificate); computer networking (Certificate); computer science (MS, PhD); data mining (Certificate); database management (Certificate); electronic commerce (Certificate); foundations of information systems (Certificate); information engineering (Certificate); information security and assurance (MS, Certificate); information systems (MS); intelligent agents (Certificate); software architecture (Certificate); software engineering (MS, Certificate); systems engineering (MS); Web-based software engineering (Certificate). MS program offered jointly with Old Dominion University, University of Virginia, Virginia Commonwealth University, and Virginia Polytechnic Institute and State University. Part-time and evening/weekend programs available. Postbaccalaureate distance learning degree programs offered. *Faculty:* 42 full-time (9 women), 20 part-time/adjunct (1 woman). *Students:* 124 full-time (37 women), 453 part-time (103 women); includes 14 Black or African American, non-Hispanic/Latino; 66 Asian, non-Hispanic/Latino; 13 Hispanic/Latino; 3 Two or more races, non-Hispanic/Latino, 206 international. Average age 30. 904 applicants, 53% accepted, 150 enrolled. In 2010, 203 master's, 4 doctorates, 20 other advanced degrees awarded. *Degree requirements:* For master's, thesis optional; for doctorate, comprehensive exam, thesis/dissertation. *Entrance requirements:* For master's, GRE General Test, minimum GPA of 3.0 in last 60 hours, 3 letters of recommendation; for doctorate, GRE, 4-year BA, academic work in computer science, 3 letters of recommendation, statement of career goals and aspirations. Additional exam requirements/recommendations for international students: Required—TOEFL (minimum score 570 paper-based; 230 computer-based; 88 iBT). *Application deadline:* For fall admission, 4/15 priority date for domestic students, 1/15 for international students; for spring admission, 11/15 for domestic students. Application fee: $100. Electronic applications accepted. *Expenses:* Tuition, state resident: full-time $8192; part-time $440 per credit hour. Tuition, nonresident: full-time $22,952; part-time $1055 per credit hour. Required fees: $2364; $99 per credit hour. *Financial support:* In 2010–11, 101 students received support, including 3 fellowships (averaging $18,000 per year), 52 research assistantships (averaging $15,078 per year), 47 teaching assistantships (averaging $10,983 per year); career-related internships or fieldwork, Federal Work-Study, scholarships/grants, unspecified assistantships, and health care benefits (full-time research or teaching assistantship recipients) also available. Financial award application deadline: 3/1; financial award applicants required to submit FAFSA. *Faculty research:* Artificial intelligence, image processing/graphics, parallel/distributed systems, software engineering systems. Total annual research expenditures: $1.3 million. *Unit head:* Dr. Arun Sood, Director, 703-993-1524, Fax: 703-993-1710, E-mail: asood@gmu.edu. *Application contact:* Jay Shapiro, Professor, 703-993-1485, E-mail: jshapiro@gmu.edu.

Georgetown University, Graduate School of Arts and Sciences, Program in Communication, Culture, and Technology, Washington, DC 20057. Offers MA. Part-time and evening/weekend programs available. *Degree requirements:* For master's, thesis (for some programs). *Entrance requirements:* For master's, GRE General Test, 3 letters of recommendation, writing sample. Additional exam requirements/recommendations for international students: Required—TOEFL (minimum score 600 paper-based; 250 computer-based). Electronic applications accepted.

Georgia Institute of Technology, Graduate Studies and Research, Ivan Allen College of Policy and International Affairs, School of Literature, Communication and Culture, Atlanta, GA 30332-0001. Offers digital media (MS, PhD); human computer interaction (MSHCI). *Degree requirements:* For master's, thesis or alternative. *Entrance requirements:* Additional exam requirements/recommendations for international students: Required—TOEFL. Electronic applications accepted. *Faculty research:* New media studies.

Indiana University–Purdue University Indianapolis, School of Informatics, Indianapolis, IN 46202-2896. Offers informatics (PhD); media arts and science (MS). Part-time and evening/weekend programs available. *Faculty:* 3 full-time (0 women). *Students:* 43 full-time (15 women), 83 part-time (29 women); includes 21 minority (13 Black or African American, non-Hispanic/Latino; 5 Asian, non-Hispanic/Latino; 3 Hispanic/Latino), 32 international. Average age 34. 87 applicants, 54% accepted, 26 enrolled. In 2010, 39 master's awarded. *Degree requirements:* For master's, multimedia project. *Entrance requirements:* For master's, minimum undergraduate GPA of 3.0, graduate 3.2; interview; portfolio; BA with demonstrated media arts skills. Additional exam requirements/recommendations for international students: Required—TOEFL. *Application deadline:* For fall admission, 3/15 for domestic students; for spring admission, 11/15 for domestic students. Application fee: $55 ($65 for international students). *Financial support:* In 2010–11, 6 fellowships (averaging $17,447 per year), 13 teaching assistantships (averaging $9,392 per year) were awarded; career-related internships or fieldwork, Federal Work-Study, institutionally sponsored loans, and scholarships/grants also available. Support available to part-time students. *Unit head:* Darrell L. Bailey, Executive Associate Dean, 317-278-4636, Fax: 317-278-7769. *Application contact:* Dr. Sherry Queener, Director, Graduate Studies and Associate Dean, 317-274-1577, Fax: 317-278-2380.

Long Island University, C.W. Post Campus, School of Visual and Performing Arts, Department of Theatre, Film, Dance and Arts Management, Brookville, NY 11548-1300. Offers interactive multimedia (MA); theatre (MA). Part-time and evening/weekend programs available. *Degree requirements:* For master's, thesis. *Entrance requirements:* For master's, placement exam. Electronic applications accepted. *Faculty research:* Playwriting, intercultural dance and theatre, translation, Suzuki, set and costume design.

Marlboro College, Graduate School, Program in Teaching with Technology, Marlboro, VT 05344. Offers MAT. Part-time and evening/weekend programs available. Postbaccalaureate distance learning degree programs offered (minimal on-campus study). *Faculty:* 1 full-time (0 women), 4 part-time/adjunct (3 women). *Students:* 8 full-time (7 women), 30 part-time (15 women); includes 1 minority (American Indian or Alaska Native, non-Hispanic/Latino). Average age 44. 12 applicants, 100% accepted, 11 enrolled. In 2010, 2 master's awarded. *Degree requirements:* For master's, 30 credits including capstone project. *Entrance requirements:* For master's, letter of intent, 2 letters of recommendation, transcripts. *Application deadline:* For fall admission, 7/1 priority date for domestic students; for winter admission, 11/1 priority date for domestic students; for spring admission, 3/1 priority date for domestic students. Applications are processed on a rolling basis. Application fee: $0. Electronic applications accepted. *Expenses:* Tuition: Full-time $14,280; part-time $680 per credit. Tuition and fees vary according to course load and program. *Financial support:* Applicants required to submit FAFSA. *Unit head:* Caleb Clark, Director, 802-258-9207, E-mail: cclark@gradschool.marlboro.edu. *Application contact:* Joe Heslin, Associate Director of Admissions, 802-258-9209, Fax: 802-258-9201, E-mail: jheslin@gradcenter.marlboro.edu.

Mercy College, School of Liberal Arts, Program in Internet Business Systems, Dobbs Ferry, NY 10522-1189. Offers Web strategy and design (MS, Certificate). Part-time and evening/weekend programs available. Postbaccalaureate distance learning degree programs offered (no on-campus study). *Students:* 15 full-time (6 women), 3 part-time; includes 3 Black or African American, non-Hispanic/Latino; 1 Asian, non-Hispanic/Latino; 3 Hispanic/Latino, 3 international. Average age 35. 29 applicants, 52% accepted, 10 enrolled. In 2010, 7 master's awarded. *Entrance requirements:* For master's, interview, resume, 2 letters of recommendation, 2-page written personal statement. Additional exam requirements/recommendations for international students: Required—TOEFL (minimum score 600 paper-based; 250 computer-based; 100 iBT), IELTS (minimum score 8). *Application deadline:* For fall admission, 8/1 for international students. Applications are processed on a rolling basis. Application fee: $40. Electronic applications accepted. *Expenses:* Contact institution. *Financial support:* Career-related internships or fieldwork, Federal Work-Study, scholarships/grants, and unspecified assistantships available. Support available to part-time students. Financial award applicants required to submit FAFSA. *Faculty research:* Internet business systems, Internet marketing, Web design, Internet technologies. *Unit head:* John DiElsi, Program Director, 914-674-7306, E-mail: jdielsi@mercy.edu. *Application contact:* Allison Gurdineer, Senior Associate Director of Recruitment, 914-674-7601, E-mail: agurdineer@mercy.edu.

National University, Academic Affairs, School of Media and Communication, Department of Media, La Jolla, CA 92037-1011. Offers digital cinema (MFA); educational and instructional technology (MS); video game production and design (MFA). Part-time and evening/weekend programs available. Postbaccalaureate distance learning degree programs offered (no on-campus study). *Faculty:* 9 full-time (3 women), 61 part-time/adjunct (21 women). *Students:* 72 full-time (23 women), 131 part-time (63 women); includes 71 minority (31 Black or African American, non-Hispanic/Latino; 1 American Indian or Alaska Native, non-Hispanic/Latino; 7 Asian, non-Hispanic/Latino; 23 Hispanic/Latino; 1 Native Hawaiian or other Pacific Islander, non-Hispanic/Latino; 8 Two or more races, non-Hispanic/Latino), 10 international. Average age 39. 121 applicants, 100% accepted, 81 enrolled. In 2010, 47 master's awarded. *Degree requirements:* For master's, thesis. *Entrance requirements:* For master's, interview, minimum GPA of 2.5. Additional exam requirements/recommendations for international students: Required—TOEFL (minimum score 550 paper-based; 213 computer-based; 79 iBT), IELTS (minimum score 6). *Application deadline:* Applications are processed on a rolling basis. Application fee: $60 ($65 for international students). Electronic applications accepted. *Expenses:* Tuition: Full-time $9450; part-time $350 per unit. Required fees: $350 per unit. One-time fee: $60. *Financial support:* Career-related internships or fieldwork, institutionally sponsored loans, scholarships/grants, and tuition waivers (partial) available. Support available to part-time students. Financial award application deadline: 6/30; financial award applicants required to submit FAFSA. *Unit head:* Dr. Cynthia Sistek-Chandler, Department Chair, 858-309-3457, E-mail: cchandler@nu.edu. *Application contact:* Dominick Giovanniello, Associate Regional Dean—San Diego, 800-NAT-UNIV, Fax: 858-541-7792, E-mail: dgiovann@nu.edu.

New Mexico Highlands University, Graduate Studies, College of Arts and Sciences, Program in Media Arts and Computer Science, Las Vegas, NM 87701. Offers media arts and computer science (MS). *Faculty:* 7 full-time (2 women). *Students:* 9 full-time (5 women), 7 part-time (3 women); includes 7 Hispanic/Latino, 2 international. Average age 31. 17 applicants, 100% accepted, 4 enrolled. In 2010, 3 master's awarded. *Degree requirements:* For master's, comprehensive exam, thesis. *Entrance requirements:* For master's, minimum undergraduate GPA of 3.0. Additional exam requirements/recommendations for international students: Required—TOEFL (minimum score 540 paper-based; 270 computer-based). Application fee: $15. *Expenses:* Tuition, state resident: full-time $2544. Required fees: $624; $132 per credit hour. *Financial support:* In 2010–11, 7 students received support. Career-related internships or fieldwork, Federal Work-Study, institutionally sponsored loans, scholarships/grants, tuition waivers (full and partial), and unspecified assistantships available. Support available to part-time students. Financial award application deadline: 3/1; financial award applicants required to submit FAFSA. *Faculty research:* Advanced digital compositing, photographic installations and exhibition design, pattern recognition, parallel and distributed computing, computer security education. *Unit head:* Dr. Miriam Langer, Department Head, Visual and Performing Arts, 505-454-3390, E-mail: melanger@nmhu.edu. *Application contact:* Diane Trujillo, Administrative Assistant for Graduate Studies, 505-454-3266, Fax: 505-426-2117, E-mail: dtrujillo@nmhu.edu.

New York University, Tisch School of the Arts, Interactive Telecommunications Program, New York, NY 10012-1019. Offers MPS. *Faculty:* 9 full-time, 40 part-time/adjunct. *Students:* 197 full-time (80 women), 18 part-time (8 women); includes 7 Black or African American, non-Hispanic/Latino; 23 Asian, non-Hispanic/Latino; 12 Hispanic/Latino. Average age 29. 271 applicants, 74% accepted, 109 enrolled. In 2010, 102 master's awarded. *Degree requirements:* For master's, thesis. *Entrance requirements:* Additional exam requirements/recommendations for international students: Required—TOEFL (minimum score 600 paper-based; 250 computer-based; 100 iBT) or IELTS (minimum score 6). *Application deadline:* For fall admission, 12/1 priority date for domestic and international students. Application fee: $60. Electronic applications accepted. *Financial support:* In 2010–11, 90 students received support, including 24 fellowships with full and partial tuition reimbursements available; career-related internships or fieldwork, Federal Work-Study, institutionally sponsored loans, scholarships/grants, and tuition waivers (partial) also available. Financial award application deadline: 2/15; financial award applicants required to submit FAFSA. *Faculty research:* Interactive narrative/storytelling, interactive media, Web technology, physical computing, ubiquitous computing. *Unit head:* Red Burns, Chair, 212-998-1880, Fax: 212-998-1898, E-mail: itp.inquiries@nyu.edu. *Application contact:* Dan Sandford, Director of Graduate Admissions, 212-998-1918, Fax: 212-995-4060, E-mail: tisch.gradadmissions@nyu.edu.

North Central College, Graduate and Continuing Education Programs, Department of Computer Science, Naperville, IL 60566-7063. Offers Web and Internet applications (MS). Part-time and evening/weekend programs available. *Faculty:* 4 full-time (2 women). *Students:* 1 full-time (0 women), 10 part-time (3 women); includes 1 Black or African American, non-Hispanic/Latino, 1 international. Average age 30. In 2010, 4 master's awarded. *Degree requirements:* For master's, thesis optional, project. *Entrance requirements:* For master's, interview. Additional exam requirements/recommendations for international students: Required—TOEFL (minimum score 577 paper-based; 233 computer-based; 90 iBT). *Application deadline:* For fall admission, 8/15 for domestic students; for winter admission, 12/1 for domestic students; for spring admission, 2/1 for domestic students. Applications are processed on a rolling basis. Application fee: $25. *Expenses:* Contact institution. *Financial support:* Scholarships/grants available. Support available to part-time students. *Unit head:* Dr. Caroline St.Clair, Program Coordinator, 630-637-5171, Fax: 630-637-5172, E-mail: cstclair@noctrl.edu. *Application contact:* Wendy Kulpinski, Director and Graduate and Continuing Education Admission, 630-637-5808, Fax: 630-637-5819, E-mail: wekulpinski@noctrl.edu.

Northwestern University, School of Continuing Studies, Program in Information Systems, Evanston, IL 60208. Offers database and Internet technologies (MS); information systems management (MS); information systems security (MS); software project management and development (MS).

Pace University, Seidenberg School of Computer Science and Information Systems, New York, NY 10038. Offers computer communications and networks (Certificate); computer science (MS); computing studies (DPS); information systems (MS); Internet technologies for e-commerce (MS); Internet technology (MS); object-oriented programming (Certificate); security and information assurance (Certificate); software development and engineering (MS); telecommunications (MS, Certificate). Part-time and evening/weekend programs available. *Entrance requirements:* For master's, GRE General Test. Additional exam requirements/recommendations for international students: Required—TOEFL. Electronic applications accepted. *Expenses:* Contact institution.

Polytechnic Institute of NYU, Department of Humanities and Social Sciences, Major in Integrated Digital Media, Brooklyn, NY 11201-2990. Offers MS, Graduate Certificate. *Students:* 30 full-time (14 women), 4 part-time (3 women); includes 3 Black or African American, non-Hispanic/Latino; 1 American Indian or Alaska Native, non-Hispanic/Latino; 1 Asian, non-Hispanic/Latino, 19 international. Average age 28. 34 applicants, 65% accepted, 15 enrolled. In 2010, 4 master's awarded. *Entrance requirements:* Additional exam requirements/recommendations for international students: Required—TOEFL (minimum score 550 paper-based; 213 computer-based; 80 iBT); Recommended—IELTS (minimum score 6.5). *Application deadline:* For fall admission, 7/31 priority date for domestic students, 4/30 priority date for international students; for spring admission, 12/31 priority date for domestic students, 11/30 priority date for international students. Applications are processed on a rolling basis. Application fee: $75. Electronic applications accepted. *Expenses:* Tuition: Full-time $21,492; part-time $1194 per credit. Required fees: $385 per semester. Tuition and fees vary according to course load. *Financial support:* Institutionally sponsored loans, scholarships/grants, and unspecified assistantships available. Support available to part-time students. *Unit head:* Teresa Feroli, Head, 718-260-3422, E-mail: tferoli@poly.edu. *Application contact:* Jearcarlo Bonilla, Director, Graduate Enrollment Management, 718-260-3182, Fax: 718-260-3624, E-mail: gradinfo@poly.edu.

Pratt Institute, School of Art and Design, Program in Digital Arts, Brooklyn, NY 11205-3899. Offers MFA, MS/MFA. *Accreditation:* NASAD. *Faculty:* 6 full-time (1 woman), 17 part-time/adjunct (8 women). *Students:* 60 full-time (33 women); includes 2 Black or African American, non-Hispanic/Latino; 3 Asian, non-Hispanic/Latino; 4 Hispanic/Latino, 34 international. Average age 27. 126 applicants, 52% accepted, 27 enrolled. In 2010, 19 master's awarded. *Degree requirements:* For master's, thesis, exhibit. *Entrance requirements:* For master's, portfolio or video tape, letters of recommendation. Additional exam requirements/recommendations for international students: Required—TOEFL (minimum score 550 paper-based; 213 computer-based; 79 iBT). *Application deadline:* For fall admission, 1/5 for domestic and international students; for spring admission, 10/1 for domestic and international students. Applications are processed on a rolling basis. Application fee: $50 ($90 for international students). Electronic applications accepted. *Expenses:* Tuition: Full-time $22,734; part-time $1263 per credit. Required fees: $1280. *Financial support:* Career-related internships or fieldwork, Federal Work-Study, institutionally sponsored loans, scholarships/grants, health care benefits, and unspecified assistantships available. Support available to part-time students. Financial award application deadline: 2/1; financial award applicants required to submit FAFSA. *Unit head:* Peter Patchen, Chair, 718-636-3693, E-mail: ppatchen@pratt.edu. *Application contact:* Young Hah, Director of Graduate Admissions, 718-636-3683, Fax: 718-399-4242, E-mail: yhah@pratt.edu.

See Display on page 92 and Close-Up on page 131.

Quinnipiac University, School of Communications, Program in Interactive Communications, Hamden, CT 06518-1940. Offers MS. Part-time and evening/weekend programs available. *Faculty:* 4 full-time (2 women), 11 part-time/adjunct (4 women). *Students:* 17 full-time (9 women), 84 part-time (54 women); includes 9 Black or African American, non-Hispanic/Latino; 2 Asian, non-Hispanic/Latino; 3 Hispanic/Latino, 1 international. Average age 26. 22 applicants, 86% accepted, 14 enrolled. In 2010, 25 master's awarded. *Entrance requirements:* For master's, minimum GPA of 2.8, portfolio or writing sample. Additional exam requirements/recommendations for international students: Required—TOEFL (minimum score 575 paper-based; 233 computer-based; 90 iBT), IELTS (minimum score 6.5). *Application deadline:* For fall admission, 7/30 priority date for domestic students, 4/30 priority date for international students; for spring admission, 12/15 priority date for domestic students, 9/15 priority date for international students. Applications are processed on a rolling basis. Application fee: $45. Electronic applications accepted. *Expenses:* Tuition: Part-time $810 per credit. Required fees: $35 per credit. *Financial support:* Federal Work-Study, tuition waivers (partial), and unspecified assistantships available. Support available to part-time students. Financial award application deadline: 4/30; financial award applicants required to submit FAFSA. *Faculty research:* Technology and democracy, the role of computing in social change. *Unit head:* Phillip Simon, Director, 203-582-8274, Fax: 203-582-5310, E-mail: phillip.simon@quinnipiac.edu. *Application contact:* Scott Farber, Director of Graduate Admissions, 800-462-1944, Fax: 203-582-3443, E-mail: scott.farber@quinnipiac.edu.

Robert Morris University, Graduate Studies, School of Communications and Information Systems, Moon Township, PA 15108-1189. Offers communication and information systems (MS); competitive intelligence systems (MS); information security and assurance (MS); information systems and communications (D Sc); information systems management (MS); information technology project management (MS); Internet information systems (MS); organizational studies (MS). Part-time and evening/weekend programs available. *Degree requirements:* For doctorate, thesis/dissertation. *Entrance requirements:* For doctorate, employer letter of endorsement, interview. Additional exam requirements/recommendations for international students: Required—TOEFL (minimum score 550 paper-based; 213 computer-based; 79 iBT). Electronic applications accepted. *Expenses:* Contact institution.

Rochester Institute of Technology, Graduate Enrollment Services, B. Thomas Golisano College of Computing and Information Sciences, Department of Information Technology, Program in Interactive Multimedia Development, Rochester, NY 14623-5603. Offers AC. Part-time and evening/weekend programs available. *Students:* 7 part-time (3 women); includes 1 Hispanic/Latino. Average age 46. 2 applicants, 100% accepted, 2 enrolled. In 2010, 5 ACs awarded. *Entrance requirements:* For degree, GRE, minimum GPA of 3.0. Additional exam requirements/recommendations for international students: Required—TOEFL (minimum score 570 paper-based; 230 computer-based; 88 iBT) or IELTS (minimum score 6.5). *Application deadline:* For fall admission, 8/1 for domestic students, 7/1 for international students; for spring admission, 2/1 for domestic students. Applications are processed on a rolling basis. Electronic applications accepted. *Expenses:* Tuition: Full-time $33,234; part-time $924 per credit hour. Required fees: $219. *Financial support:* In 2010–11, 5 students received support. Career-related internships or fieldwork, scholarships/grants, and unspecified assistantships available. Support available to part-time students. Financial award applicants required to submit FAFSA. *Unit head:* Prof. Dianne Bills, Graduate Program Director, 585-475-2700, Fax: 585-475-6584, E-mail: informaticsgrad@rit.edu. *Application contact:* Diane Ellison, Assistant Vice President, Graduate Enrollment Services, 585-475-2229, Fax: 585-475-7164, E-mail: gradinfo@rit.edu.

Rochester Institute of Technology, Graduate Enrollment Services, B. Thomas Golisano College of Computing and Information Sciences, Department of Interactive Games and Media, Rochester, NY 14623-5603. Offers game design and development (MS). Part-time programs available. *Students:* 16 full-time (2 women), 1 part-time; includes 1 Black or African American, non-Hispanic/Latino; 2 Hispanic/Latino, 2 international. Average age 25. 26 applicants, 42% accepted, 7 enrolled. In 2010, 9 master's awarded. *Degree requirements:* For master's, thesis. *Entrance requirements:* For master's, GRE, minimum GPA of 3.25. Additional exam requirements/recommendations for international students: Required—TOEFL (minimum score 570 paper-based; 230 computer-based; 88 iBT) or IELTS (minimum score 6.5). *Application deadline:* For fall admission, 1/15 priority date for domestic students, 1/1 priority date for international students. Applications are processed on a rolling basis. Electronic applications accepted. *Expenses:* Tuition: Full-time $33,234; part-time $924 per credit hour. Required fees: $219. *Financial support:* Research assistantships with partial tuition reimbursements, teaching assistantships with partial tuition reimbursements, career-related internships or fieldwork, scholarships/grants, and unspecified assistantships available. Support available to part-time students. Financial award applicants required to submit FAFSA. *Faculty research:* Experimental game design and development; exploratory research in visualization environments and integrated media frameworks; outreach efforts that surround games and underlying technologies; support of STEM learning through games and interactive entertainment; the application of games and game technology to non-entertainment domains (Serious Games); small, discrete play experiences (Casual Games). *Unit head:* Andrew Phelps, Director, 585-475-6758, E-mail: andy@mail.rit.edu. *Application contact:* Diane Ellison, Assistant Vice President, Graduate Enrollment Services, 585-475-2229, Fax: 585-475-7164, E-mail: gradinfo@rit.edu.

Sacred Heart University, Graduate Programs, College of Arts and Sciences, Department of Computer Science and Information Technology, Fairfield, CT 06825-1000. Offers computer science (MS); database (CPS); information technology (MS, CPS); information technology and network security (CPS); interactive multimedia (CPS); Web development (CPS). Part-time and evening/weekend programs available. *Degree requirements:* For master's, thesis optional. *Entrance requirements:* Additional exam requirements/recommendations for international students: Required—TOEFL (minimum score 550 paper-based; 213 computer-based). Electronic applications accepted. *Faculty research:* Contemporary market software.

San Diego State University, Graduate and Research Affairs, College of Professional Studies and Fine Arts, School of Communication, San Diego, CA 92182. Offers advertising and public relations (MA); critical-cultural studies (MA); interaction studies (MA); intercultural and international studies (MA); new media studies (MA); news and information studies (MA); telecommunications and media management (MA). *Degree requirements:* For master's, thesis. *Entrance requirements:* For master's, GRE General Test, 3 letters of recommendation. Additional exam requirements/recommendations for international students: Required—TOEFL. Electronic applications accepted.

Savannah College of Art and Design, Graduate School, Program in Interactive Design and Game Development, Savannah, GA 31402-3146. Offers MA, MFA, Graduate Certificate. Part-time programs available. *Faculty:* 16 full-time (4 women), 4 part-time/adjunct (0 women). *Students:* 64 full-time (20 women), 34 part-time (15 women); includes 7 Black or African American, non-Hispanic/Latino; 3 Asian, non-Hispanic/Latino; 4 Hispanic/Latino, 19 international. Average age 29. In 2010, 19 master's, 1 other advanced degree awarded. *Degree requirements:* For master's, thesis, internships. *Entrance requirements:* For master's, interview, portfolio. Additional exam requirements/recommendations for international students: Required—TOEFL (minimum score 450 paper-based; 133 computer-based). *Application deadline:* For fall admission, 4/1 priority date for domestic and international students. Applications are processed on a rolling basis. Application fee: $35. Electronic applications accepted. *Expenses:* Tuition: Full-time $29,520; part-time $3280 per quarter. Tuition and fees vary according to campus/location. *Financial support:* Fellowships, career-related internships or fieldwork, Federal Work-Study, and scholarships/grants available. Financial award application deadline: 4/1; financial award applicants required to submit FAFSA. *Unit head:* Luis Cataldi, Chair, 912-525-8523, E-mail: lcataldi@scad.edu. *Application contact:* Elizabeth Mathis, Director of Graduate Recruitment, 912-525-5965, Fax: 912-525-5985, E-mail: emathis@scad.edu.

School of Visual Arts, Graduate Programs, Program in Photography, Video and Related Media, New York, NY 10010-3994. Offers MFA. *Accreditation:* NASAD. *Degree requirements:* For master's, final review, project or thesis. *Entrance requirements:* For master's, portfolio. Additional exam requirements/recommendations for international students: Required—TOEFL (minimum score 550 paper-based; 213 computer-based; 79 iBT). Electronic applications accepted.

Simon Fraser University, Graduate Studies, Faculty of Applied Sciences, School of Interactive Arts and Technology, Surrey, BC V3T 2W1, Canada. Offers information technology (M Sc, PhD); interactive arts (M Sc, PhD). *Degree requirements:* For master's, thesis; for doctorate, comprehensive exam, thesis/dissertation. *Entrance requirements:* For master's, 2 references, curriculum vitae; for doctorate, 3 references, curriculm vitae, minimum GPA of 3.0. Additional exam requirements/recommendations for international students: Required—TOEFL (minimum score 570 paper-based; 230 computer-based), TWE (minimum score 5). Electronic applications accepted.

Southern Polytechnic State University, School of Arts and Sciences, Department of English, Technical Communication, and Media Arts, Marietta, GA 30060-2896. Offers communications management (AGC); content development (AGC); information and instructional design (MSIID);

Internet and Interactive Multimedia

Southern Polytechnic State University (continued)
information design and communication (MS); instructional design (AGC); technical communication (Graduate Certificate); visual communication and graphics (AGC). Part-time and evening/weekend programs available. Postbaccalaureate distance learning degree programs offered (no on-campus study). *Faculty:* 4 full-time (3 women), 1 (woman) part-time/adjunct. *Students:* 2 full-time (both women), 61 part-time (40 women); includes 19 Black or African American, non-Hispanic/Latino; 1 Two or more races, non-Hispanic/Latino, 3 international. Average age 38. 37 applicants, 100% accepted, 29 enrolled. In 2010, 6 master's, 5 other advanced degrees awarded. *Degree requirements:* For master's, thesis or internship; for other advanced degree, thesis optional, 18 hours completed through thesis option (6 hours), internship option (6 hours) or advanced coursework option (6 hours). *Entrance requirements:* For master's, GRE, statement of purpose, writing sample, professional recommendations, timed essay; for other advanced degree, writing sample, professional recommendations. Additional exam requirements/recommendations for international students: Required—TOEFL (minimum score 550 paper-based; 213 computer-based; 79 iBT), IELTS (minimum score 6.5). *Application deadline:* For fall admission, 5/1 priority date for domestic students, 7/1 priority date for international students; for spring admission, 9/1 priority date for domestic students, 11/1 priority date for international students. Applications are processed on a rolling basis. Application fee: $20. Electronic applications accepted. *Expenses:* Tuition, state resident: full-time $3690; part-time $205 per semester hour. Tuition, nonresident: full-time $13,428; part-time $746 per semester hour. Required fees: $598 per semester. *Financial support:* Research assistantships with tuition reimbursements, teaching assistantships with tuition reimbursements, career-related internships or fieldwork, Federal Work-Study, scholarships/grants, and unspecified assistantships available. Support available to part-time students. Financial award application deadline: 5/1; financial award applicants required to submit FAFSA. *Faculty research:* Usability, user-centered design, instructional design, information architecture, information design. *Unit head:* Dr. Mark Nunes, Chair, 678-915-7202, Fax: 678-915-7425, E-mail: mnunes@spsu.edu. *Application contact:* Nikki Palamiotis, Director of Graduate Studies, 678-915-4276, Fax: 678-915-7292, E-mail: npalamio@spsu.edu.

Stevens Institute of Technology, Graduate School, Charles V. Schaefer Jr. School of Engineering, Department of Computer Science, Hoboken, NJ 07030. Offers computer graphics (Certificate); computer science (MS, PhD); computer systems (Certificate); database management systems (Certificate); distributed systems (Certificate); elements of computer science (Certificate); enterprise computing (Certificate); enterprise security and information assurance (Certificate); health informatics (Certificate); multimedia experience and management (Certificate); networks and systems administration (Certificate); security and privacy (Certificate); service oriented computing (Certificate); software design (Certificate); theoretical computer science (Certificate). Part-time and evening/weekend programs available. *Faculty:* 12 full-time (5 women). *Students:* 117 full-time (42 women), 88 part-time (17 women); includes 4 Black or African American, non-Hispanic/Latino; 21 Asian, non-Hispanic/Latino; 3 Hispanic/Latino, 99 international. Average age 28. 327 applicants, 57% accepted. In 2010, 72 master's, 2 doctorates awarded. Terminal master's awarded for partial completion of doctoral program. *Degree requirements:* For master's, thesis optional; for doctorate, variable foreign language requirement, comprehensive exam, thesis/dissertation. *Entrance requirements:* For master's and doctorate, GRE, minimum GPA of 3.0. Additional exam requirements/recommendations for international students: Required—TOEFL. *Application deadline:* Applications are processed on a rolling basis. Application fee: $50. Electronic applications accepted. *Financial support:* Fellowships, Federal Work-Study available. Financial award application deadline: 4/15. *Faculty research:* Semantics, reliability theory, programming language, cyber security. *Unit head:* Daniel Duchamp, Director, 201-216-5390, Fax: 201-216-8249, E-mail: djd@cs.stevens.edu. *Application contact:* Graduate Admissions, 800-496-4935, Fax: 201-216-8044, E-mail: gradadmissions@stevens.edu.

Towson University, Master's Program in Applied Information Technology, Towson, MD 21252-0001. Offers applied information technology (MS, PhD); database management systems (Postbaccalaureate Certificate); information security and assurance (Postbaccalaureate Certificate); information systems management (Graduate Certificate); Internet applications development (Postbaccalaureate Certificate); networking technologies (Postbaccalaureate Certificate); software engineering (Postbaccalaureate Certificate). *Students:* 111 full-time (25 women), 232 part-time (62 women); includes 122 minority (75 Black or African American, non-Hispanic/Latino; 4 American Indian or Alaska Native, non-Hispanic/Latino; 31 Asian, non-Hispanic/Latino; 11 Hispanic/Latino; 1 Native Hawaiian or other Pacific Islander, non-Hispanic/Latino), 85 international. In 2010, 75 master's, 9 doctorates, 74 other advanced degrees awarded. *Expenses:* Tuition, state resident: part-time $324 per credit. Tuition, nonresident: part-time $681 per credit. Required fees: $95 per term. *Unit head:* Mike O'Leary, Graduate Program Director, 410-704-4757, E-mail: moleary@towson.edu. *Application contact:* Mike O'Leary, Graduate Program Director, 410-704-4757, E-mail: moleary@towson.edu.

Towson University, Program in Interactive Media Design, Towson, MD 21252-0001. Offers Certificate. Postbaccalaureate distance learning degree programs offered (no on-campus study). *Students:* 1 (woman) full-time, 14 part-time (10 women); includes 5 minority (3 Black or African American, non-Hispanic/Latino; 1 American Indian or Alaska Native, non-Hispanic/Latino; 1 Asian, non-Hispanic/Latino), 1 international. Average age 43. In 2010, 1 Certificate awarded. *Entrance requirements:* For degree, minimum GPA of 3.0, resume, letter of intent, BA in art education, professional experience in graphic design or art education. Additional exam requirements/recommendations for international students: Required—TOEFL (minimum score 550 paper-based). *Expenses:* Tuition, state resident: part-time $324 per credit. Tuition, nonresident: part-time $681 per credit. Required fees: $95 per term. *Unit head:* Bridget Z. Sullivan, Director, 410-704-2802, E-mail: bsullivan@towson.edu. *Application contact:* Bridget Z. Sullivan, Director, 410-704-2802, E-mail: bsullivan@towson.edu.

Universidad Autonoma de Guadalajara, Graduate Programs, Guadalajara, Mexico. Offers administrative law and justice (LL M); advertising and corporate communications (MA); architecture (M Arch); business (MBA); computational science (MCC); education (Ed M, Ed D); English-Spanish translation (MA); entrepreneurship and management (MBA); integrated management of digital animation (MA); international business (MIB); international corporate law (LL M); internet technologies (MS); manufacturing systems (MMS); occupational health (MS); philosophy (MA, PhD); power electronics (MS); quality systems (MQS); renewable energy (MS); social evaluation of projects (MBA); strategic market research (MBA); tax law (MA); teaching mathematics (MA).

University of Advancing Technology, Master of Science Program in Technology, Tempe, AZ 85283-1042. Offers advancing computer science (MS); emerging technologies (MS); game production and management (MS); information assurance (MS); technology leadership (MS). *Faculty:* 9 full-time (3 women), 3 part-time/adjunct (1 woman). *Students:* 55 full-time (9 women), 4 part-time (1 woman). Average age 25. In 2010, 5 master's awarded. *Degree requirements:* For master's, project or thesis. *Entrance requirements:* Additional exam requirements/recommendations for international students: Required—TOEFL (minimum score 550 paper-based). *Application deadline:* For fall admission, 8/15 priority date for domestic students, 7/15 priority date for international students; for winter admission, 12/15 priority date for domestic students, 11/15 priority date for international students; for spring admission, 4/1 priority date for domestic students, 3/1 priority date for international students. Applications are processed on a rolling basis. Application fee: $100 ($250 for international students). Electronic applications accepted. *Expenses:* Tuition: Full-time $18,300. *Financial support:* Career-related internships or fieldwork, Federal Work-Study, and scholarships/grants available. Financial award applicants required to submit FAFSA. *Faculty research:* Artificial intelligence, fractals, organizational management. *Unit head:* Robert Marshall, Dean of Graduate Education, 602-383-8283, Fax: 602-383-8222, E-mail: rmarshall@uat.edu. *Application contact:* Information Contact, 800-658-5744, Fax: 602-383-8222.

University of Denver, University College, Denver, CO 80208. Offers arts and culture (MLS, Certificate), including art, literature, and culture, arts development and program management (Certificate), creative writing; environmental policy and management (MAS, Certificate), including energy and sustainability (Certificate), environmental assessment of nuclear power (Certificate), environmental health and safety (Certificate), environmental management, natural resource management (Certificate); geographic information systems (MAS, Certificate); global affairs (MLS, Certificate), including translation studies, world history and culture; healthcare leadership (MPH, Certificate), including healthcare policy, law, and ethics, medical and healthcare information technologies, strategic management of healthcare; information and communications technology (MCIS, Certificate), including database design and administration (Certificate), geographic information systems (MCIS), information security systems security (Certificate), information systems security (MCIS), project management (MCIS, MPS, Certificate), software design and administration (Certificate), software design and programming (MCIS), technology management, telecommunications technology (MCIS), Web design and development; leadership and organizations (MPS, Certificate), including human capital in organizations, philanthropic leadership, project management (MCIS, MPS, Certificate), strategic innovation and change; organizational and professional communication (MPS, Certificate), including alternative dispute resolution, organizational communication, organizational development and training, public relations and marketing; security management (MAS, Certificate), including emergency planning and response, information security (MAS), organizational security; strategic human resource management (MPS, Certificate), including global human resources (MPS), human resource management and development (MPS). Part-time and evening/weekend programs available. Postbaccalaureate distance learning degree programs offered (no on-campus study). *Faculty:* 7 full-time (2 women), 212 part-time/adjunct (83 women). *Students:* 52 full-time (19 women), 1,044 part-time (625 women); includes 196 minority (81 Black or African American, non-Hispanic/Latino; 7 American Indian or Alaska Native, non-Hispanic/Latino; 30 Asian, non-Hispanic/Latino; 66 Hispanic/Latino; 3 Native Hawaiian or other Pacific Islander, non-Hispanic/Latino; 9 Two or more races, non-Hispanic/Latino), 76 international. Average age 36. 488 applicants, 91% accepted, 339 enrolled. In 2010, 286 master's, 130 other advanced degrees awarded. *Entrance requirements:* Additional exam requirements/recommendations for international students: Required—TOEFL (minimum score 550 paper-based; 80 iBT). *Application deadline:* For fall admission, 6/22 priority date for domestic students, 6/10 priority date for international students; for winter admission, 9/15 priority date for domestic students, 9/6 priority date for international students; for spring admission, 2/3 priority date for domestic students, 12/15 priority date for international students. Applications are processed on a rolling basis. Application fee: $75. Electronic applications accepted. *Expenses:* Contact institution. *Financial support:* Applicants required to submit FAFSA. *Unit head:* Dr. James Davis, Dean, 303-871-2291, Fax: 303-871-4047, E-mail: jdavis@du.edu. *Application contact:* Information Contact, 303-871-3155, Fax: 303-871-4047, E-mail: ucolinfo@du.edu.

University of Florida, Graduate School, College of Fine Arts, School of Art and Art History, Gainesville, FL 32611. Offers art (MFA), including ceramics, creative photography, drawing, electronic intermedia, graphic design, painting, printmaking, sculpture; art education (MA); art history (MA, PhD); digital arts and sciences (MA); museology (museum studies) (MA). *Accreditation:* NASAD. Postbaccalaureate distance learning degree programs offered (minimal on-campus study). *Faculty:* 29 full-time (14 women). *Students:* 107 full-time (72 women), 57 part-time (52 women); includes 6 Black or African American, non-Hispanic/Latino; 1 American Indian or Alaska Native, non-Hispanic/Latino; 5 Asian, non-Hispanic/Latino; 13 Hispanic/Latino, 14 international. Average age 31. 282 applicants, 30% accepted, 61 enrolled. In 2010, 24 master's, 3 doctorates awarded. *Degree requirements:* For master's, thesis, project or thesis (MFA); 1 foreign language (MA in art history); for doctorate, 2 foreign languages, comprehensive exam, thesis/dissertation. *Entrance requirements:* For master's, GRE General Test, portfolio (MFA), writing sample (MA), minimum GPA of 3.0; for doctorate, GRE General Test, minimum GPA of 3.0. Additional exam requirements/recommendations for international students: Required—TOEFL (minimum score 550 paper-based; 213 computer-based; 80 iBT), IELTS (minimum score 6). *Application deadline:* For fall admission, 1/1 priority date for domestic students, 1/1 for international students; for spring admission, 11/1 for domestic and international students. Applications are processed on a rolling basis. Application fee: $30. Electronic applications accepted. *Expenses:* Tuition, state resident: full-time $10,915.92. Tuition, nonresident: full-time $28,309. *Financial support:* In 2010–11, 36 students received support, including 9 fellowships, 3 research assistantships with tuition reimbursements available (averaging $12,789 per year), 24 teaching assistantships with tuition reimbursements available (averaging $10,512 per year); Federal Work-Study, institutionally sponsored loans, and unspecified assistantships also available. Financial award applicants required to submit FAFSA. *Faculty research:* Studio production, art historical studies of style context. *Unit head:* Laura Robertsoon, SR Associate in Graduate Studies, 352-846-3425, E-mail: laurar@ufl.edu. *Application contact:* Lauren G. Lake, Coordinator, 352-273-3032, Fax: 352-392-8453, E-mail: lglake@arts.ufl.edu.

University of Georgia, Terry College of Business, Program in Internet Technology, Athens, GA 30602. Offers MIT. *Students:* 51 applicants, 61% accepted. *Application deadline:* For fall admission, 7/1 priority date for domestic students; for spring admission, 11/15 for domestic students. Application fee: $50. *Expenses:* Tuition, state resident: full-time $7200; part-time $344 per credit hour. Tuition, nonresident: full-time $21,900; part-time $944 per credit hour. Tuition and fees vary according to course load and program. *Unit head:* Director. *Application contact:* Dr. Craig A. Piercy, Graduate Coordinator, 706-542-3589, Fax: 706-543-0037, E-mail: cpiercy@terry.uga.edu.

University of Miami, Graduate School, College of Arts and Sciences, Department of Art and Art History, Coral Gables, FL 33124. Offers art history (MA); ceramics/glass (MFA); graphic design/multimedia (MFA); painting (MFA); photography/digital imaging (MFA); printmaking (MFA); sculpture (MFA). Part-time programs available. *Degree requirements:* For master's, variable foreign language requirement, thesis, exhibit (MFA), comprehensive exam (MA). *Entrance requirements:* For master's, GRE General Test (MA), research paper (MA), slide portfolio (MFA). Additional exam requirements/recommendations for international students: Required—TOEFL. Electronic applications accepted. *Faculty research:* Installation art, public art.

University of Phoenix–Madison Campus, School of Business, Madison, WI 53718-2416. Offers accounting (MBA); business and management (MBA); e-business (MBA); global management (MBA); human resources management (MBA, MM); management (MM); marketing (MBA); public administration (MBA).

University of San Francisco, College of Arts and Sciences, Department of Computer Science, Program in Web Science, San Francisco, CA 94117-1080. Offers MS. *Faculty:* 5 full-time (1 woman). *Students:* 15 full-time (3 women), 2 part-time (0 women); includes 2 minority (both Black or African American, non-Hispanic/Latino), 11 international. Average age 30. 20 applicants, 75% accepted, 5 enrolled. In 2010, 4 master's awarded. *Expenses:* Tuition: Full-time $20,070; part-time $1115 per credit hour. Tuition and fees vary according to course load, degree level and program. *Financial support:* In 2010–11, 7 students received support. *Unit head:* Terence Parr, Graduate Director, 415-422-6530, Fax: 415-422-5800. *Application contact:* Mark Landerghini, Graduate Adviser, 415-422-5135, E-mail: asgraduate@usfca.edu.

University of Southern California, Graduate School, Annenberg School for Communication and Journalism, School of Journalism, Program in Online Journalism, Los Angeles, CA 90089. Offers MA. Effective fall 2011, all journalism concentrations will be replaced by the M.A. in Journalism. Part-time programs available. *Students:* 25 full-time (14 women); includes 1 American Indian or Alaska Native, non-Hispanic/Latino; 4 Asian, non-Hispanic/Latino. Average age 25. 52 applicants, 75% accepted, 9 enrolled. In 2010, 14 master's awarded. *Degree requirements:* For master's, comprehensive exam, thesis. *Entrance requirements:* For master's, GRE General Test, resume, writing samples, letters of recommendation, statement of purpose. Additional exam requirements/recommendations for international students: Required—TOEFL (minimum score 280 computer-based; 114 iBT). *Application deadline:* For fall admission, 1/30 for domestic students, 12/1 for international students. Application fee: $85. Electronic applications accepted. *Expenses:* Tuition: Full-time $31,240; part-time $1420 per unit. Required fees:

$600. One-time fee: $35 full-time. Full-time tuition and fees vary according to degree level and program. *Financial support:* In 2010–11, 4 fellowships with full tuition reimbursements were awarded; Federal Work-Study and scholarships/grants also available. Support available to part-time students. Financial award application deadline: 2/1; financial award applicants required to submit FAFSA. *Application contact:* Allyson Hill, Assistant Dean, Admissions, 213-821-0770, Fax: 213-740-1933, E-mail: ascadm@usc.edu.

See Display on page 675 and Close-Up on page 727.

University of Southern California, Graduate School, School of Cinematic Arts, Interactive Media Division, Los Angeles, CA 90089. Offers interactive media (MFA); media arts and practice (PhD). *Faculty:* 10 full-time (2 women), 14 part-time/adjunct (2 women). *Students:* 40 full-time (12 women); includes 5 minority (4 Asian, non-Hispanic/Latino; 1 Hispanic/Latino), 8 international. 44 applicants, 45% accepted, 13 enrolled. In 2010, 10 master's awarded. *Degree requirements:* For master's, thesis, thesis project. *Entrance requirements:* Additional exam requirements/recommendations for international students: Required—TOEFL (minimum score 600 paper-based; 250 computer-based; 100 iBT). *Application deadline:* For fall admission, 12/1 for domestic and international students. Application fee: $85. Electronic applications accepted. *Expenses:* Contact institution. *Financial support:* In 2010–11, 29 students received support, including 6 fellowships with full tuition reimbursements available (averaging $20,000 per year), 5 research assistantships with full tuition reimbursements available (averaging $9,825 per year); career-related internships or fieldwork, Federal Work-Study, institutionally sponsored loans, scholarships/grants, health care benefits, unspecified assistantships, and research assistantships also available. Financial award application deadline: 5/3; financial award applicants required to submit CSS PROFILE or FAFSA. *Faculty research:* Immersive media, mobile media, stereoscopic, game design and development, serious games and games for health and learning, experiments in game play. Total annual research expenditures: $2 million. *Unit head:* Dr. Scott S. Fisher, Professor and Chair, Interactive Media Division and Associate Dean of Research, 213-821-4472, Fax: 213-821-2665, E-mail: sfisher@cinema.usc.edu. *Application contact:* Adrienne Capirchio, Graduate Program Coordinator, 213-821-2515, Fax: 213-821-2665, E-mail: acapirchio@cinema.usc.edu.

University of Southern California, Graduate School, Viterbi School of Engineering, Department of Computer Science, Los Angeles, CA 90089. Offers computer networks (MS); computer science (MS, PhD); computer security (MS); game development (MS); high performance computing and simulations (MS); human language technology (MS); intelligent robotics (MS); multimedia and creative technologies (MS); software engineering (MS). Part-time and evening/weekend programs available. Postbaccalaureate distance learning degree programs offered (no on-campus study). *Faculty:* 28 full-time (3 women), 56 part-time/adjunct (7 women). *Students:* 710 full-time (115 women), 302 part-time (59 women); includes 76 minority (1 Black or African American, non-Hispanic/Latino; 55 Asian, non-Hispanic/Latino; 14 Hispanic/Latino; 6 Two or more races, non-Hispanic/Latino), 819 international. 2,379 applicants, 30% accepted, 319 enrolled. In 2010, 332 master's, 32 doctorates awarded. *Entrance requirements:* For master's and doctorate, GRE General Test. Additional exam requirements/recommendations for international students: Required—TOEFL. *Application deadline:* For fall admission, 12/1 priority date for domestic and international students; for spring admission, 9/15 priority date for domestic and international students. Applications are processed on a rolling basis. Application fee: $85. Electronic applications accepted. *Expenses:* Tuition: Full-time $31,240; part-time $1420 per unit. Required fees: $600. One-time fee: $35 full-time. Full-time tuition and fees vary according to degree level and program. *Financial support:* In 2010–11, fellowships with full tuition reimbursements (averaging $30,000 per year), research assistantships with full tuition reimbursements (averaging $20,000 per year), teaching assistantships with full tuition reimbursements (averaging $20,000 per year) were awarded; career-related internships or fieldwork, scholarships/grants, health care benefits, and unspecified assistantships also available. Financial award application deadline: 12/1; financial award applicants required to submit CSS PROFILE or FAFSA. *Faculty research:* Databases, computer graphics and computer vision, software engineering, networks and security, robotics, multimedia and virtual reality. Total annual research expenditures: $11.8 million. *Unit head:* Dr. Shanghua Teng, Chair, 213-740-4494, E-mail: csdept@usc.edu. *Application contact:* Lizsl DeLeon, Director of Student Affairs, 213-740-4496, E-mail: ldeleon@usc.edu.

University of Southern California, Graduate School, Viterbi School of Engineering, Ming Hsieh Department of Electrical Engineering, Los Angeles, CA 90089. Offers computer engineering (MS, PhD); electric power (MS); electrical engineering (MS, PhD, Engr); engineering technology commercialization (Graduate Certificate); multimedia and creative technologies (MS); telecommunications (MS); VLSI design (MS); wireless health technology (MS). Part-time programs available. Postbaccalaureate distance learning degree programs offered (no on-campus study). *Faculty:* 56 full-time (3 women), 31 part-time/adjunct (1 woman). *Students:* 886 full-time (171 women), 605 part-time (100 women); includes 209 minority (20 Black or African American, non-Hispanic/Latino; 145 Asian, non-Hispanic/Latino; 36 Hispanic/Latino; 8 Two or more races, non-Hispanic/Latino), 1,003 international. 2,986 applicants, 36% accepted, 461 enrolled. In 2010, 351 master's, 41 doctorates, 2 other advanced degrees awarded. Terminal master's awarded for partial completion of doctoral program. *Degree requirements:* For master's, thesis optional; for doctorate, thesis/dissertation. *Entrance requirements:* For master's and doctorate, GRE General Test. *Application deadline:* For fall admission, 12/1 priority date for domestic and international students; for spring admission, 9/15 priority date for domestic and international students. Applications are processed on a rolling basis. Application fee: $85. Electronic applications accepted. *Expenses:* Tuition: Full-time $31,240; part-time $1420 per unit. Required fees: $600. One-time fee: $35 full-time. Full-time tuition and fees vary according to degree level and program. *Financial support:* In 2010–11, fellowships with full tuition reimbursements (averaging $30,000 per year), research assistantships with full tuition reimbursements (averaging $20,000 per year), teaching assistantships with full tuition reimbursements (averaging $20,000 per year) were awarded; career-related internships or fieldwork, scholarships/grants, health care benefits, and unspecified assistantships also available. Financial award application deadline: 12/1; financial award applicants required to submit CSS PROFILE or FAFSA. *Faculty research:* Communications, computer engineering and networks, control systems, integrated circuits and systems, electromagnetics and energy conversion, micro electro-mechanical systems and nanotechnology, photonics and quantum electronics, plasma research, signal and image processing. Total annual research expenditures: $18 million. *Unit head:* Dr. Alexander A. Sawchuk, Chair, 213-740-4447, E-mail: studentinfo@ee.usc.edu. *Application contact:* Diane Demetras, Director of Student Affairs, 213-740-4447, E-mail: studentinfo@ee.usc.edu.

The University of Texas at Dallas, School of Arts and Humanities, Program in Arts and Technology, Richardson, TX 75080. Offers arts and technology (MA, MFA, PhD); emerging media and communication (MA). *Faculty:* 19 full-time (9 women). *Students:* 98 full-time (34 women), 65 part-time (30 women); includes 41 minority (11 Black or African American, non-Hispanic/Latino; 1 American Indian or Alaska Native, non-Hispanic/Latino; 12 Asian, non-Hispanic/Latino; 15 Hispanic/Latino; 2 Two or more races, non-Hispanic/Latino), 15 international. Average age 31. 93 applicants, 55% accepted, 41 enrolled. In 2010, 39 master's awarded. *Degree requirements:* For master's and doctorate, portfolio, thesis, or capstone project. *Entrance requirements:* For master's and doctorate, minimum GPA of 3.3 in upper-level coursework in field. Additional exam requirements/recommendations for international students: Required—TOEFL (minimum score 550 paper-based; 215 computer-based). *Application deadline:* For fall admission, 7/15 for domestic students, 5/1 priority date for international students; for spring admission, 11/15 for domestic students, 9/1 priority date for international students. Applications are processed on a rolling basis. Application fee: $50 ($100 for international students). Electronic applications accepted. *Expenses:* Tuition, state resident: full-time $10,248; part-time $569 per credit hour. Tuition, nonresident: full-time $18,544; part-time $1030 per credit hour. Tuition and fees vary according to course load. *Financial support:* In 2010–11, 94 students received support, including 31 research assistantships with partial tuition reimbursements available (averaging $10,917 per year), 14 teaching assistantships with partial tuition reimbursements available (averaging $10,136 per year); career-related internships or fieldwork, Federal Work-Study, institutionally sponsored loans, scholarships/grants, and unspecified assistantships also available. Support available to part-time students. Financial award application deadline: 4/30; financial award applicants required to submit FAFSA. *Faculty research:* Motion capture, conversational/interactive robotics, simulations as modern teaching tools. *Unit head:* Dr. Thomas Linehan, Director, 972-883-4379, E-mail: thomas.linehan@utdallas.edu. *Application contact:* Dr. Michael Wilson, Associate Dean of Graduate Studies, 972-883-2756, Fax: 972-883-2989, E-mail: mwilson@utdallas.edu.

University of the Sacred Heart, Graduate Programs, Department of Communication, San Juan, PR 00914-0383. Offers contemporary culture and media (MA); digital journalism (MA, Certificate); editing for media (MA, Certificate); public relations (MA, Certificate); publicity (MA, Certificate); scriptwriting (MA, Certificate). Part-time and evening/weekend programs available. *Degree requirements:* For master's, thesis.

University of the Sacred Heart, Graduate Programs, Department of Education, San Juan, PR 00914-0383. Offers early childhood education (M Ed); information technology and multimedia (Certificate); instruction systems and education technology (M Ed), including English, information technology and multimedia, instructional design, mathematics, Spanish. Part-time and evening/weekend programs available. *Degree requirements:* For master's, thesis. *Entrance requirements:* For master's, EXADEP, minimum undergraduate GPA of 2.75, interview.

Virginia Commonwealth University, Graduate School, School of the Arts, Department of Graphic Design, Richmond, VA 23284-9005. Offers design/visual communications (MFA); interior environment (MFA). *Accreditation:* NASAD. *Faculty:* 15 full-time (3 women). *Students:* 35 full-time (27 women), 4 part-time (2 women); includes 3 minority (all Asian, non-Hispanic/Latino), 1 international. 212 applicants, 19% accepted, 25 enrolled. In 2010, 13 master's awarded. *Degree requirements:* For master's, thesis, exhibition. *Entrance requirements:* For master's, portfolio. Additional exam requirements/recommendations for international students: Required—TOEFL (minimum score 600 paper-based; 250 computer-based; 100 iBT). *Application deadline:* For fall admission, 2/1 for domestic students. Application fee: $50. Electronic applications accepted. *Expenses:* Tuition, state resident: full-time $4308; part-time $479 per credit hour. Tuition, nonresident: full-time $8942; part-time $994 per credit hour. Required fees: $2000; $85 per credit hour. Tuition and fees vary according to course level, course load, degree level, campus/location and program. *Financial support:* Fellowships, teaching assistantships, career-related internships or fieldwork, Federal Work-Study, institutionally sponsored loans, and tuition waivers (full and partial) available. Support available to part-time students. Financial award application deadline: 3/15. *Faculty research:* Conducting visual or theoretical research, and in investigating the intersection of function and expression in design problem solving. *Unit head:* John DeMao, Chair, 804-828-1709, E-mail: jdemao@vcu.edu. *Application contact:* John DeMao, Chair, 804-828-1709, E-mail: jdemao@vcu.edu.

Virginia Polytechnic Institute and State University, Graduate School, College of Architecture and Urban Studies, School of Visual Arts, Blacksburg, VA 24061. Offers creative technologies (MFA). *Expenses:* Tuition, state resident: full-time $9399; part-time $488 per credit hour. Tuition, nonresident: full-time $17,854; part-time $957.75 per credit hour. Required fees: $1534. Full-time tuition and fees vary according to program.

Western Illinois University, School of Graduate Studies, College of Education and Human Services, Department of Instructional Design and Technology, Macomb, IL 61455-1390. Offers distance learning (Certificate); educational technology specialist (Certificate); graphic applications (Certificate); instructional design and technology (MS); multimedia (Certificate); technology integration in education (Certificate); training development (Certificate). Part-time programs available. Postbaccalaureate distance learning degree programs offered (no on-campus study). *Students:* 18 full-time (12 women), 48 part-time (30 women); includes 7 minority (5 Black or African American, non-Hispanic/Latino; 2 American Indian or Alaska Native, non-Hispanic/Latino), 7 international. Average age 38. 23 applicants, 74% accepted. In 2010, 25 master's awarded. *Degree requirements:* For master's, thesis or alternative. *Entrance requirements:* Additional exam requirements/recommendations for international students: Required—TOEFL (minimum score 550 paper-based; 213 computer-based; 80 iBT). *Application deadline:* Applications are processed on a rolling basis. Application fee: $30. Electronic applications accepted. *Expenses:* Tuition, state resident: full-time $6370; part-time $265.40 per credit hour. Tuition, nonresident: full-time $12,740; part-time $530.80 per credit hour. Required fees: $75.67 per credit hour. *Financial support:* In 2010–11, 10 students received support, including 6 research assistantships with full tuition reimbursements available (averaging $7,280 per year), 4 teaching assistantships with full tuition reimbursements available (averaging $8,400 per year). Financial award applicants required to submit FAFSA. *Unit head:* Dr. Hoyet Hemphill, Chairperson, 309-298-1952. *Application contact:* Evelyn Hoing, Assistant Director of Graduate Studies, 309-298-1806, Fax: 309-298-2345, E-mail: grad-office@wiu.edu.

Wilmington University, College of Technology, New Castle, DE 19720-6491. Offers corporate training (MS); information assurance (MS); information systems technologies (MS); Internet web design (MS); management information systems (MS). Part-time and evening/weekend programs available. *Entrance requirements:* Additional exam requirements/recommendations for international students: Required—TOEFL (minimum score 500 paper-based; 173 computer-based). Electronic applications accepted. *Expenses:* Tuition: Full-time $7110; part-time $395 per credit hour. Tuition and fees vary according to campus/location.

Journalism

American University, School of Communication, Program in Journalism and Public Affairs, Washington, DC 20016-8001. Offers broadcast journalism (MA), including economic communication, international journalism, public policy journalism; interactive journalism (MA); print journalism (MA), including economic communication, international journalism, public policy journalism. *Accreditation:* ACEJMC. *Faculty:* 13 full-time (5 women), 4 part-time/adjunct (all women). *Students:* 39 full-time (29 women). 169 applicants, 74% accepted, 37 enrolled. In 2010, 40 master's awarded. *Degree requirements:* For master's, comprehensive exam, thesis or alternative. *Entrance requirements:* For master's, GRE General Test. Additional exam requirements/recommendations for international students: Required—TOEFL (minimum score 600 paper-based; 250 computer-based; 100 iBT), IELTS (minimum score 7). *Application deadline:* For fall admission, 2/1 priority date for domestic students, 4/1 priority date for international students. Applications are processed on a rolling basis. Application fee: $50. Electronic applications accepted. *Financial support:* In 2010–11, 3 fellowships with full and partial tuition reimbursements (averaging $27,000 per year), 14 research assistantships with

Journalism

American University (continued)
partial tuition reimbursements (averaging $7,000 per year), 3 teaching assistantships with partial tuition reimbursements (averaging $7,000 per year) were awarded; career-related internships or fieldwork, Federal Work-Study, institutionally sponsored loans, scholarships/grants, tuition waivers (partial), and unspecified assistantships also available. Financial award application deadline: 2/1; financial award applicants required to submit FAFSA. *Faculty research:* Government and media effects of journalistic practices and policies, race and gender and the media, investigative reporting, computer assisted reporting. *Unit head:* Prof. Jill Olmsted, Division Director, 202-885-2010, E-mail: jolmste@american.edu. *Application contact:* Sharmeen Ahsan-Bracciale, Graduate Admissions Office, 202-885-2040, Fax: 202-885-2019, E-mail: sharmeen@american.edu.

American University, School of Communication, Weekend Programs in Communication, Washington, DC 20016-8001. Offers interactive journalism (MA); news media studies (MA); producing for film and video (MA); public communication (MA). *Accreditation:* ACEJMC. Part-time and evening/weekend programs available. *Faculty:* 5 part-time/adjunct (2 women). *Students:* 113 part-time (64 women). 105 applicants, 72% accepted, 59 enrolled. In 2010, 15 master's awarded. *Degree requirements:* For master's, comprehensive exam, thesis or alternative. *Entrance requirements:* Additional exam requirements/recommendations for international students: Required—TOEFL (minimum score 600 paper-based; 250 computer-based; 100 iBT). *Application deadline:* For fall admission, 8/1 for domestic students. Applications are processed on a rolling basis. Application fee: $50. Electronic applications accepted. *Financial support:* In 2010–11, 3 fellowships (averaging $3,500 per year) were awarded; institutionally sponsored loans also available. Financial award applicants required to submit FAFSA. *Unit head:* Prof. Rose Ann Robertson, Associate Dean, 202-885-2002, E-mail: rrobert@american.edu. *Application contact:* Sharmeen Ahsan-Bracciale, Director of Graduate Services, 202-885-2040, Fax: 202-885-2019, E-mail: sharmeen@american.edu.

The American University in Cairo, School of Global Affairs and Public Policy, Department of Journalism and Mass Communication, Cairo, Egypt. Offers journalism and mass communication (MA); television and digital journalism (MA). Part-time programs available. *Degree requirements:* For master's, thesis (for some programs). *Entrance requirements:* For master's, English entrance exam, GMAT. Electronic applications accepted. *Faculty research:* Mass media and national development/censorship, intercultural photo communication, comparative journalism/television.

Angelo State University, College of Graduate Studies, College of Liberal and Fine Arts, Department of Communication, Mass Media and Theatre, San Angelo, TX 76909. Offers communication systems management (MA). Part-time and evening/weekend programs available. *Faculty:* 2 full-time (0 women). *Students:* 15 full-time (9 women), 8 part-time (3 women); includes 2 Black or African American, non-Hispanic/Latino; 4 Hispanic/Latino, 1 international. Average age 30. 10 applicants, 70% accepted, 6 enrolled. In 2010, 5 master's awarded. *Degree requirements:* For master's, comprehensive exam, thesis optional. *Entrance requirements:* Additional exam requirements/recommendations for international students: Required—TOEFL or IELTS. *Application deadline:* For fall admission, 7/15 priority date for domestic students, 6/10 for international students; for spring admission, 12/1 priority date for domestic students, 11/1 for international students. Applications are processed on a rolling basis. Application fee: $40 ($50 for international students). Electronic applications accepted. *Expenses:* Tuition, state resident: full-time $4560; part-time $152 per credit hour. Tuition, nonresident: full-time $13,860; part-time $462 per credit hour. Required fees: $2132. Tuition and fees vary according to course load. *Financial support:* In 2010–11, 5 students received support, including 3 teaching assistantships (averaging $10,251 per year); career-related internships or fieldwork, Federal Work-Study, scholarships/grants, and unspecified assistantships also available. Support available to part-time students. Financial award application deadline: 3/1; financial award applicants required to submit FAFSA. *Unit head:* Dr. Shawn T. Wahl, Department Head, 325-942-2031 Ext. 228, Fax: 325-942-2551, E-mail: swahl1@angelo.edu. *Application contact:* Dr. Lana Marlow, Graduate Advisor, 325-942-2032 Ext. 356, Fax: 325-942-2551, E-mail: lana.marlow@angelo.edu.

Arizona State University, Walter Cronkite School of Journalism and Mass Communication, Phoenix, AZ 85004. Offers journalism and mass communication (PhD); mass communication (MMC). *Accreditation:* ACEJMC. *Faculty:* 30 full-time (11 women), 1 part-time/adjunct (0 women). *Students:* 47 full-time (33 women), 1 (woman) part-time; includes 6 minority (2 Black or African American, non-Hispanic/Latino; 1 Native Hawaiian or other Pacific Islander, non-Hispanic/Latino; 3 Two or more races, non-Hispanic/Latino), 3 international. Average age 28. 170 applicants, 48% accepted, 28 enrolled. In 2010, 28 degrees awarded. Terminal master's awarded for partial completion of doctoral program. *Degree requirements:* For master's, 9-hour professional capstone experience; interactive Program of Study (iPOS) submitted before completing 50 percent of required credit hours; for doctorate, comprehensive exam, thesis/dissertation, interactive Program of Study (iPOS) submitted before completing 50 percent of required credit hours. *Entrance requirements:* For master's and doctorate, GRE, minimum GPA of 3.0 or equivalent in last 2 years of work leading to bachelor's degree. Additional exam requirements/recommendations for international students: Required—TOEFL, IELTS, or Pearson Test of English. *Application deadline:* For fall admission, 7/1 for domestic and international students; for spring admission, 12/1 for domestic and international students. Applications are processed on a rolling basis. Application fee: $70 ($90 for international students). Electronic applications accepted. *Expenses:* Contact institution. *Financial support:* In 2010–11, 17 teaching assistantships with full and partial tuition reimbursements (averaging $10,968 per year) were awarded; fellowships with full tuition reimbursements, research assistantships with full and partial tuition reimbursements, career-related internships or fieldwork, Federal Work-Study, institutionally sponsored loans, scholarships/grants, and tuition waivers (full and partial) also available. Financial award application deadline: 3/1; financial award applicants required to submit FAFSA. Total annual research expenditures: $3 million. *Unit head:* Christopher Callahan, Dean, 602-496-5012, Fax: 602-496-7041, E-mail: christopher.callahan@asu.edu. *Application contact:* Graduate Admissions, 480-965-6113.

Arkansas State University, Graduate School, College of Communications, Department of Journalism, Jonesboro, State University, AR 72467. Offers MSMC. Part-time programs available. *Faculty:* 4 full-time (2 women), 1 part-time/adjunct (0 women). *Students:* 8 full-time (6 women), 9 part-time (5 women); includes 5 minority (all Black or African American, non-Hispanic/Latino), 8 international. Average age 28. 22 applicants, 68% accepted, 6 enrolled. In 2010, 5 master's awarded. *Degree requirements:* For master's, comprehensive exam, thesis or alternative. *Entrance requirements:* For master's, GRE General Test, appropriate bachelor's degree, letters of reference, educational experience, professional experience, official transcripts, immunization records. Additional exam requirements/recommendations for international students: Required—TOEFL (minimum score 550 paper-based; 213 computer-based; 79 iBT), IELTS (minimum score 6), PTE: Pearson Test of English Academic (56). *Application deadline:* For fall admission, 7/1 for domestic and international students; for spring admission, 11/15 for domestic students, 11/14 for international students. Applications are processed on a rolling basis. Application fee: $30 ($40 for international students). Electronic applications accepted. *Expenses:* Tuition, state resident: full-time $3888; part-time $216 per credit hour. Tuition, nonresident: full-time $9918; part-time $551 per credit hour. International tuition: $8376 full-time. Required fees: $932; $49 per credit hour. $25 per term. One-time fee: $30. Tuition and fees vary according to course load and program. *Financial support:* In 2010–11, 6 students received support. Career-related internships or fieldwork, scholarships/grants, and unspecified assistantships available. Financial award application deadline: 7/1; financial award applicants required to submit FAFSA. *Unit head:* Dr. Gil Fowler, Chair, 870-972-3075, Fax: 870-910-8042, E-mail: gfowler@astate.edu. *Application contact:* Dr. Andrew Sustich, Dean of the Graduate School, 870-972-3029, Fax: 870-972-3857, E-mail: sustich@astate.edu.

Arkansas Tech University, Graduate College, College of Arts and Humanities, Russellville, AR 72801. Offers communication (MLA); English (M Ed, MA); fine arts (MLA); history (MA); multi-media journalism (MA); psychology (MS); social science (MLA); Spanish (MA, MLA); teaching English as a second language (MA, MLA). Part-time programs available. *Students:* 39 full-time (23 women), 87 part-time (69 women); includes 13 minority (3 Black or African American, non-Hispanic/Latino; 1 American Indian or Alaska Native, non-Hispanic/Latino; 1 Asian, non-Hispanic/Latino; 8 Hispanic/Latino), 14 international. Average age 32. In 2010, 54 master's awarded. *Degree requirements:* For master's, comprehensive exam (for some programs), thesis (for some programs), project. *Entrance requirements:* For master's, GRE General Test, MAT. Additional exam requirements/recommendations for international students: Required—TOEFL (minimum score 550 paper-based; 213 computer-based; 79 iBT), IELTS (minimum score 6). *Application deadline:* For fall admission, 3/1 priority date for domestic students, 5/1 priority date for international students; for spring admission, 10/1 priority date for domestic and international students. Applications are processed on a rolling basis. Application fee: $0 ($50 for international students). Electronic applications accepted. *Expenses:* Tuition, state resident: full-time $4680; part-time $195 per credit hour. Tuition, nonresident: full-time $9360; part-time $390 per credit hour. Required fees: $714; $14 per credit hour. One-time fee: $326 part-time. Tuition and fees vary according to course load. *Financial support:* In 2010–11, teaching assistantships with full tuition reimbursements (averaging $4,000 per year); research assistantships, career-related internships or fieldwork, Federal Work-Study, scholarships/grants, health care benefits, and unspecified assistantships also available. Support available to part-time students. Financial award application deadline: 4/15; financial award applicants required to submit FAFSA. *Unit head:* Dr. Micheal Tarver, Dean, 479-968-0274, Fax: 479-964-0812, E-mail: mtarver@atu.edu. *Application contact:* Dr. Mary B. Gunter, Dean of Graduate College, 479-968-0398, Fax: 479-964-0542, E-mail: graduate.school@atu.edu.

Ball State University, Graduate School, College of Communication, Information, and Media, Department of Journalism, Muncie, IN 47306-1099. Offers journalism (MA); public relations (MA). *Faculty:* 14. *Students:* 31 full-time (18 women), 32 part-time (23 women); includes 1 Black or African American, non-Hispanic/Latino, 14 international. Average age 26. 83 applicants, 54% accepted, 22 enrolled. In 2010, 35 master's awarded. *Entrance requirements:* For master's, resume. Application fee: $50. *Expenses:* Tuition, state resident: full-time $6160; part-time $299 per credit hour. Tuition, nonresident: full-time $16,020; part-time $783 per credit hour. Required fees: $2278; $95 per credit hour. *Financial support:* In 2010–11, 10 teaching assistantships with full tuition reimbursements (averaging $8,381 per year) were awarded; career-related internships or fieldwork also available. Financial award application deadline: 3/1. *Faculty research:* Image studies, readership surveys, audience perception studies. *Unit head:* William J. Willis, Chairperson, 765-285-8200, Fax: 765-285-7997. *Application contact:* Dan Waechter, Information Contact, 765-285-8200, Fax: 765-285-7997, E-mail: dwaechter@bsu.edu.

Baylor University, Graduate School, College of Arts and Sciences, Department of Journalism, Waco, TX 76798. Offers international journalism (MIJ); journalism (MA). *Students:* 8 full-time (6 women), 6 part-time (4 women); includes 1 minority (Asian, non-Hispanic/Latino), 3 international. Average age 24. In 2010, 8 master's awarded. *Degree requirements:* For master's, proficiency in 1 foreign language (MIJ). *Entrance requirements:* For master's, GRE General Test. *Application deadline:* Applications are processed on a rolling basis. Application fee: $25. *Financial support:* Research assistantships, teaching assistantships, career-related internships or fieldwork, Federal Work-Study, and institutionally sponsored loans available. Support available to part-time students. *Faculty research:* International politics, mass media and society, journalism history, editing practices. *Unit head:* Dr. Amanda Sturgill, Graduate Program Director, 254-710-6322, Fax: 254-710-3363, E-mail: amanda_sturgill@baylor.edu. *Application contact:* Jan Loosier, Administrative Assistant, 254-710-3261, Fax: 254-710-3870, E-mail: jan_loosier@baylor.edu.

Bob Jones University, Graduate Programs, Greenville, SC 29614. Offers accountancy (MS); Bible (MA); Bible translation (MA); Biblical studies (Certificate); broadcast management (MS); business administration (MBA); church history (MA, PhD); church ministries (MA); church music (MM); cinema and video production (MA); counseling (MS); curriculum and instruction (Ed D); divinity (M Div); dramatic production (MA); educational leadership (MS, Ed D, Ed S); elementary education (M Ed, MAT); English (M Ed, MA, MAT); fine arts (MA); graphic design (MA); history (M Ed, MA); illustration (MA); interpretative speech (MA); mathematics (M Ed, MAT); medical missions (Certificate); ministry (MM, D Min); multi-categorical special education (M Ed, MAT); music (M Ed); New Testament interpretation (PhD); Old Testament interpretation (PhD); orchestral instrument performance (MM); organ performance (MM); pastoral studies (MA); personnel services (MS, Ed S); piano pedagogy (MM); piano performance (MM); platform arts (MA); radio and television broadcasting (MS); rhetoric and public address (MA); secondary education (M Ed); studio art (MA); teaching Bible (MA); theology (MA, PhD); voice performance (MM); youth ministries (MA); M Div/MM.

Boston University, College of Communication, Department of Journalism, Boston, MA 02215. Offers broadcast journalism (MS); business and economics journalism (MS); photojournalism (MS); print journalism (MS); science journalism (MS). Part-time programs available. *Faculty:* 23 full-time, 26 part-time/adjunct. *Students:* 72 full-time (54 women), 7 part-time (3 women); includes 2 minority (both Asian, non-Hispanic/Latino), 12 international. Average age 25. In 2010, 62 master's awarded. *Degree requirements:* For master's, thesis. *Entrance requirements:* For master's, GRE General Test, sample of written work. Additional exam requirements/recommendations for international students: Required—TOEFL (minimum score 600 paper-based; 250 computer-based; 100 iBT). *Application deadline:* For fall admission, 2/1 for domestic and international students. Application fee: $70. Electronic applications accepted. *Expenses:* Tuition: Full-time $39,314; part-time $1228 per credit. Required fees: $40 per semester. *Financial support:* Teaching assistantships with partial tuition reimbursements, career-related internships or fieldwork, Federal Work-Study, institutionally sponsored loans, scholarships/grants, and unspecified assistantships available. Support available to part-time students. Financial award application deadline: 2/1; financial award applicants required to submit FAFSA. *Unit head:* William McKeen, Chairman, 617-353-3484, Fax: 617-353-1086, E-mail: wmckeen@bu.edu. *Application contact:* Jennifer Healey, Administrator of Graduate Services, 617-353-3481, Fax: 617-358-0399, E-mail: comgrad@bu.edu.

California State University, Fresno, Division of Graduate Studies, College of Arts and Humanities, Department of Mass Communication and Journalism, Fresno, CA 93740-8027. Offers MA. Part-time and evening/weekend programs available. *Degree requirements:* For master's, thesis. *Entrance requirements:* For master's, GRE General Test, minimum GPA of 3.0. Additional exam requirements/recommendations for international students: Required—TOEFL. Electronic applications accepted.

California State University, Fullerton, Graduate Studies, College of Communications, Department of Communications, Fullerton, CA 92834-9480. Offers advertising (MA); communications (MFA); entertainment and tourism (MA); journalism (MA); public relations (MA). Part-time programs available. *Students:* 24 full-time (15 women), 39 part-time (27 women); includes 2 Two or more races, non-Hispanic/Latino. Average age 29. 119 applicants, 40% accepted, 29 enrolled. In 2010, 30 master's awarded. *Degree requirements:* For master's, project or thesis. *Entrance requirements:* For master's, GRE General Test. Application fee: $55. *Financial support:* Teaching assistantships, career-related internships or fieldwork, Federal Work-Study, institutionally sponsored loans, and scholarships/grants available. Support available to part-time students. Financial award application deadline: 3/1; financial award applicants required to submit FAFSA. *Unit head:* Dr. Tony Fellow, Chair, 657-278-3517. *Application contact:* Coordinator, 657-278-3832.

California State University, Northridge, Graduate Studies, College of Arts, Media, and Communication, Department of Journalism, Northridge, CA 91330. Offers mass communication (MA). Part-time and evening/weekend programs available. *Degree requirements:* For master's, thesis. *Entrance requirements:* For master's, GRE General Test. Additional exam requirements/recommendations for international students: Required—TOEFL.

Carleton University, Faculty of Graduate Studies, Faculty of Public Affairs and Management, School of Journalism and Communication, Ottawa, ON K1S 5B6, Canada. Offers communication (MA, PhD); journalism (MJ). *Degree requirements:* For master's, thesis optional; for doctorate, comprehensive exam, thesis/dissertation. *Entrance requirements:* For master's, honors degree. Additional exam requirements/recommendations for international students: Required—TOEFL. *Faculty research:* Specialized print reporting, broadcast journalism, journalism studies.

Columbia College Chicago, Graduate School, Department of Journalism, Chicago, IL 60605-1996. Offers public affairs journalism (MA). *Students:* 20 full-time (13 women), 4 part-time (3 women); includes 5 Black or African American, non-Hispanic/Latino; 1 Asian, non-Hispanic/Latino; 2 Hispanic/Latino; 1 Two or more races, non-Hispanic/Latino, 2 international. Average age 30. 47 applicants, 79% accepted, 12 enrolled. In 2010, 15 master's awarded. *Degree requirements:* For master's, thesis. *Entrance requirements:* For master's, interview, minimum GPA of 3.0, writing sample. Additional exam requirements/recommendations for international students: Required—TOEFL (minimum score 550 paper-based; 213 computer-based). *Application deadline:* For fall admission, 1/15 for domestic and international students. Application fee: $55. Electronic applications accepted. *Expenses:* Tuition: Full-time $16,966; part-time $684 per credit. Required fees: $520; $113 per semester. One-time fee: $150 full-time. Tuition and fees vary according to course load and program. *Financial support:* Fellowships, career-related internships or fieldwork, Federal Work-Study, and scholarships/grants available. Support available to part-time students. Financial award application deadline: 8/13; financial award applicants required to submit FAFSA. *Unit head:* Norma Green, Program Director, 312-369-8920, E-mail: ngreen@colum.edu. *Application contact:* Cate Lagueux, Director of Graduate Admissions, 312-369-7260, Fax: 312-369-8047, E-mail: clagueux@colum.edu.

Columbia University, Fu Foundation School of Engineering and Applied Science, Department of Computer Science, New York, NY 10027. Offers computer science (MS, Eng Sc D, PhD, Engr); computer science and journalism (MS). PhD offered through the Graduate School of Arts and Sciences. Part-time programs available. Postbaccalaureate distance learning degree programs offered (no on-campus study). *Faculty:* 43 full-time (5 women), 21 part-time/adjunct (2 women). *Students:* 283 full-time (65 women), 107 part-time (20 women); includes 13 minority (1 Black or African American, non-Hispanic/Latino; 11 Asian, non-Hispanic/Latino; 1 Two or more races, non-Hispanic/Latino), 289 international. Average age 27. 974 applicants, 31% accepted, 170 enrolled. In 2010, 155 master's, 18 doctorates, 1 other advanced degree awarded. Terminal master's awarded for partial completion of doctoral program. *Degree requirements:* For master's and Engr, thesis optional; for doctorate, comprehensive exam, thesis/dissertation, candidacy exam. *Entrance requirements:* For master's and Engr, GRE General Test; for doctorate, GRE General Test, GRE Subject Test (computer science). Additional exam requirements/recommendations for international students: Required—TOEFL, IELTS. *Application deadline:* For fall admission, 12/1 priority date for domestic and international students; for spring admission, 10/1 priority date for domestic and international students. Application fee: $95. Electronic applications accepted. *Financial support:* In 2010–11, 134 students received support, including 11 fellowships with full tuition reimbursements available (averaging $28,405 per year), 95 research assistantships with full tuition reimbursements available (averaging $24,894 per year), 28 teaching assistantships with full and partial tuition reimbursements available (averaging $6,000 per year); health care benefits also available. Financial award application deadline: 12/1; financial award applicants required to submit FAFSA. *Faculty research:* Robotics, network security, graphics and user interfaces, computer vision, computational learning theory. *Unit head:* Dr. Shree K. Nayar, T.C. Chang Professor of Computer Science and Department Chairman, 212-939-7092, E-mail: nayar@cs.columbia.edu. *Application contact:* Remiko O. Moss, Assistant Director, 212-939-7000, Fax: 212-666-0140, E-mail: ms-admissions@cs.columbia.edu.

Columbia University, Graduate School of Journalism, New York, NY 10027. Offers MA, MS, PhD, JD/MS, MIA/MS, MS/MBA. *Accreditation:* ACEJMC. Part-time programs available. *Degree requirements:* For master's, thesis; for doctorate, thesis/dissertation. *Entrance requirements:* For master's, writing test, 2-3 samples of journalistic work, minimum typing speed of 50 words per minute; for doctorate, GRE. Additional exam requirements/recommendations for international students: Required—TOEFL. *Expenses:* Contact institution. *Faculty research:* International communication, communication technologies, ethics in journalism, journalism history.

Concordia University, School of Graduate Studies, Faculty of Arts and Science, Department of Journalism, Montréal, QC H3G 1M8, Canada. Offers Diploma. *Degree requirements:* For Diploma, one foreign language. *Entrance requirements:* Additional exam requirements/recommendations for international students: Required—departmental English test or TOEFL.

CUNY Graduate School of Journalism, Graduate Program, New York, NY 10018. Offers MA. *Faculty:* 10 full-time (3 women), 54 part-time/adjunct (26 women). *Students:* 163 full-time (101 women); includes 56 minority (18 Black or African American, non-Hispanic/Latino; 18 Asian, non-Hispanic/Latino; 20 Hispanic/Latino). Average age 27. 329 applicants, 50% accepted, 84 enrolled. In 2010, 58 master's awarded. *Degree requirements:* For master's, internship, final or capstone project. *Entrance requirements:* For master's, GRE, admissions exam, 3 letters of recommendation, resume, interview, 3 writing samples. Additional exam requirements/recommendations for international students: Required—TOEFL (minimum score 260 computer-based; 105 iBT). *Application deadline:* For fall admission, 12/15 for domestic students. Application fee: $65. Electronic applications accepted. *Expenses:* Tuition, state resident: full-time $7730. Required fees: $1795. *Financial support:* Career-related internships or fieldwork, Federal Work-Study, and scholarships/grants available. Financial award application deadline: 3/1; financial award applicants required to submit FAFSA. *Unit head:* Stephen B. Shepard, Dean, 646-758-7700. *Application contact:* Colleen Marshall, Admissions/Outreach Counselor, 646-758-7852, Fax: 646-758-7709, E-mail: colleen.marshall@journalism.cuny.edu.

DePaul University, College of Communication, Chicago, IL 60614. Offers journalism (MA); media, culture and society (MA); organizational and multicultural communication (MA); public relations and advertising (MA). Part-time and evening/weekend programs available. *Faculty:* 31 full-time (17 women), 15 part-time/adjunct (7 women). *Students:* 170 full-time (129 women), 70 part-time (52 women); includes 29 Black or African American, non-Hispanic/Latino; 9 Asian, non-Hispanic/Latino; 20 Hispanic/Latino; 7 Two or more races, non-Hispanic/Latino, 17 international. Average age 29. 354 applicants, 44% accepted, 79 enrolled. In 2010, 64 master's awarded. *Degree requirements:* For master's, comprehensive exam (for some programs), final exam or thesis/project. *Entrance requirements:* For master's, GRE General Test (public relations and advertising), minimum GPA of 3.0, writing sample, letters of recommendation, resume. Additional exam requirements/recommendations for international students: Required—TOEFL (minimum score 590 paper-based; 243 computer-based; 96 iBT). Application fee: $40. Electronic applications accepted. *Financial support:* In 2010–11, 8 students received support, including 4 research assistantships with partial tuition reimbursements available, 2 teaching assistantships with full tuition reimbursements available (averaging $12,000 per year); fellowships with full tuition reimbursements available, career-related internships or fieldwork, scholarships/grants, and tuition waivers (partial) also available. Support available to part-time students. Financial award applicants required to submit FAFSA. *Faculty research:* Intercultural communication, corporate culture, diversity in the working place, organizational socialization, critical cultural studies. *Unit head:* Dr. Jacqueline Taylor, Dean, 773-325-7216, Fax: 773-325-7584, E-mail: jtaylor@depaul.edu. *Application contact:* Ann Spittle, Director of Graduate Admission, 773-325-7315, Fax: 773-325-2395, E-mail: gradcom@depaul.edu.

Drexel University, School of Journalism, Philadelphia, PA 19104-2875. Offers MA. *Entrance requirements:* Additional exam requirements/recommendations for international students: Required—TOEFL.

Emerson College, Graduate Studies, School of Communication, Department of Journalism, Boston, MA 02116-4624. Offers journalism (MA), including broadcast journalism, print/multimedia journalism. *Entrance requirements:* For master's, GRE General Test. Additional exam requirements/recommendations for international students: Required—TOEFL (minimum score 550 paper-based; 213 computer-based; 80 iBT), IELTS (minimum score 6.5). Electronic applications accepted. *Faculty research:* Journalism.

Florida Agricultural and Mechanical University, Division of Graduate Studies, Research, and Continuing Education, School of Journalism and Graphic Communication, Tallahassee, FL 32307-3200. Offers journalism (MS). *Degree requirements:* For master's, comprehensive exam, thesis (for some programs). *Entrance requirements:* For master's, GRE General Test, minimum GPA of 3.0. Additional exam requirements/recommendations for international students: Required—TOEFL.

Florida Atlantic University, Dorothy F. Schmidt College of Arts and Letters, School of Communication and Multimedia Studies, Boca Raton, FL 33431-0991. Offers communication studies (MA); film and video (Certificate); film studies (MA); multimedia journalism studies (MA). Part-time programs available. *Faculty:* 28 full-time (10 women), 14 part-time/adjunct (3 women). *Students:* 19 full-time (15 women), 15 part-time (11 women); includes 8 minority (3 Black or African American, non-Hispanic/Latino; 1 American Indian or Alaska Native, non-Hispanic/Latino; 1 Asian, non-Hispanic/Latino; 1 Hispanic/Latino; 2 Two or more races, non-Hispanic/Latino), 6 international. Average age 28. 42 applicants, 26% accepted, 8 enrolled. In 2010, 3 master's awarded. *Degree requirements:* For master's, one foreign language, comprehensive exam (for some programs), thesis (for some programs). *Entrance requirements:* For master's, GRE General Test, minimum GPA of 3.0. *Application deadline:* For fall admission, 7/1 priority date for domestic students, 4/1 for international students; for spring admission, 11/1 for domestic students, 10/1 for international students. Applications are processed on a rolling basis. Application fee: $30. Electronic applications accepted. *Expenses:* Tuition, area resident: Part-time $319.96 per credit. Tuition, state resident: part-time $319.96 per credit. Tuition, nonresident: part-time $926.42 per credit. *Financial support:* Teaching assistantships with partial tuition reimbursements, Federal Work-Study and institutionally sponsored loans available. Support available to part-time students. Financial award application deadline: 3/1. *Faculty research:* Cultural studies, gender studies, film, communication theory, journalism, new media. *Unit head:* Dr. Susan S. Reilly, Director, 561-297-1095, Fax: 561-297-2615, E-mail: sreilly@fau.edu. *Application contact:* Dr. Eric M. Freedman, Graduate Coordinator, 561-297-2534, Fax: 561-297-2615, E-mail: efreedma@fau.edu.

Full Sail University, New Media Journalism Master of Arts Program—Online, Winter Park, FL 32792-7437. Offers MA.

Georgetown University, Graduate School of Arts and Sciences, School of Continuing Studies, Washington, DC 20057. Offers American studies (MALS); Catholic studies (MALS); classical civilizations (MALS); disability studies (MPS); ethics and the professions (MALS); human resources management (MPS); humanities (MALS); individualized study (MALS); international affairs (MALS); Islam and Muslim-Christian relations (MALS); journalism (MPS); liberal studies (DLS); literature and society (MALS); medieval and early modern European studies (MALS); public relations and corporate communications (MPS); real estate (MPS); religious studies (MALS); social and public policy (MALS); sports industry management (MPS); the theory and practice of American democracy (MALS); visual culture (MALS). *Entrance requirements:* Additional exam requirements/recommendations for international students: Required—TOEFL.

Harvard University, Extension School, Cambridge, MA 02138-3722. Offers applied sciences (CAS); biotechnology (ALM); educational technologies (ALM); educational technology (CET); English for graduate and professional studies (DGP); environmental management (ALM, CEM); information technology (ALM); journalism (ALM); liberal arts (ALM); management (ALM, CM); mathematics for teaching (ALM); museum studies (ALM); premedical studies (Diploma); publication and communication (CPC). Part-time and evening/weekend programs available. *Degree requirements:* For master's, thesis. *Entrance requirements:* For master's, 3 completed graduate courses with grade of B or higher. Additional exam requirements/recommendations for international students: Required—TOEFL (minimum score 600 paper-based; 250 computer-based), TWE (minimum score 5). *Expenses:* Contact institution.

Hofstra University, School of Communication, Program in Journalism, Hempstead, NY 11549. Offers MA. Part-time and evening/weekend programs available. *Faculty:* 5 full-time (3 women), 2 part-time/adjunct (1 woman). *Students:* 19 full-time (14 women), 14 part-time (7 women); includes 8 minority (4 Black or African American, non-Hispanic/Latino; 1 American Indian or Alaska Native, non-Hispanic/Latino; 3 Hispanic/Latino), 6 international. Average age 26. 39 applicants, 79% accepted, 14 enrolled. In 2010, 9 master's awarded. *Degree requirements:* For master's, thesis. *Entrance requirements:* For master's, minimum GPA of 2.75; bachelor's degree. Additional exam requirements/recommendations for international students: Required—TOEFL (minimum score 550 paper-based; 213 computer-based; 80 iBT). *Application deadline:* Applications are processed on a rolling basis. Application fee: $70 ($75 for international students). Electronic applications accepted. *Expenses:* Tuition: Full-time $18,000; part-time $1000 per credit hour. Required fees: $970; $145 per term. Tuition and fees vary according to program. *Financial support:* In 2010–11, 10 students received support, including 2 fellowships with full and partial tuition reimbursements available (averaging $2,750 per year); research assistantships with full and partial tuition reimbursements available, Federal Work-Study, institutionally sponsored loans, scholarships/grants, tuition waivers (full and partial), and unspecified assistantships also available. Support available to part-time students. Financial award applicants required to submit FAFSA. *Faculty research:* Media ethics/law; environmental, science, and health journalism; multimedia/future of news; race, gender, cultural issues, social justice; RTNDA/Hofstra University Annual Survey. *Unit head:* Dr. Kristal Zook, Program Director, 516-463-4304, Fax: 516-463-4873, E-mail: jrnkzb@hofstra.edu. *Application contact:* Carol Drummer, Dean of Graduate Admissions, 516-463-4876, Fax: 516-463-4664, E-mail: gradstudent@hofstra.edu.

Indiana University Bloomington, School of Journalism, Bloomington, IN 47405-7000. Offers journalism (MA, MAT); mass communication (PhD); MA/JD; MA/MA. *Faculty:* 11 full-time (5 women). *Students:* 62 full-time (37 women), 12 part-time (7 women); includes 2 Black or African American, non-Hispanic/Latino; 1 Asian, non-Hispanic/Latino; 1 Hispanic/Latino; 2 Two or more races, non-Hispanic/Latino, 33 international. Average age 30. 119 applicants, 57% accepted, 26 enrolled. In 2010, 24 master's, 4 doctorates awarded. Terminal master's awarded for partial completion of doctoral program. *Degree requirements:* For master's, thesis (for some programs); for doctorate, thesis/dissertation. *Entrance requirements:* For master's and doctorate, GRE General Test. Additional exam requirements/recommendations for international students: Required—TOEFL. *Application deadline:* For fall admission, 1/15 priority date for domestic students; for spring admission, 9/1 priority date for domestic students. Applications are processed on a rolling basis. Application fee: $55 ($65 for international students). *Financial support:* Fellowships, research assistantships with full tuition reimbursements, teaching assistantships with partial tuition reimbursements, career-related internships or fieldwork, Federal Work-Study, institutionally sponsored loans, and tuition waivers (full) available. Financial award application deadline: 1/15. *Faculty research:* Political communication, international communication, communication history, communication law, visual communication. Total annual research expenditures: $165,185. *Unit head:* Bradley Hamm, Dean, 812-855-9247. *Application contact:* Amy Reynolds, Associate Dean of Graduate Studies, 812-855-8111.

Iona College, School of Arts and Science, Department of Mass Communication, New Rochelle, NY 10801-1890. Offers journalism (MS); public relations (MA). *Accreditation:* ACEJMC (one or more programs are accredited). Part-time and evening/weekend programs available. *Faculty:* 6 full-time (2 women), 3 part-time/adjunct (2 women). *Students:* 6 full-time (5 women), 44 part-time (38 women); includes 11 minority (6 Black or African American, non-Hispanic/Latino; 1 Asian, non-Hispanic/Latino; 4 Hispanic/Latino), 3 international. Average age 27. 34 applicants, 59% accepted, 11 enrolled. In 2010, 16 master's awarded. *Degree requirements:* For master's, comprehensive exam or thesis. *Entrance requirements:* For master's, GRE General Test, minimum GPA of 3.0. Additional exam requirements/recommendations for international students: Required—TOEFL (minimum score 550 paper-based; 213 computer-based). *Application deadline:* Applications are processed on a rolling basis. Application fee: $50. Electronic applications accepted. *Expenses:* Contact institution. *Financial support:* Career-related internships or fieldwork, tuition waivers (partial), and unspecified assistantships available. Support available to part-time students. Financial award application deadline: 4/15; financial award

Journalism

Iona College (continued)

applicants required to submit FAFSA. *Faculty research:* Media ecology, new media, corporate communication, media images, organizational learning in public relations. *Unit head:* Br. Raymond Smith, Chair, 914-633-2354, E-mail: rrsmith@iona.edu. *Application contact:* Veronica Jarek-Prinz, Director of Graduate Admissions, 914-633-2420, Fax: 914-633-2277, E-mail: vjarekprinz@iona.edu.

Iowa State University of Science and Technology, Graduate College, College of Liberal Arts and Sciences, Greenlee School of Journalism and Mass Communication, Ames, IA 50011. Offers MS. *Faculty:* 18 full-time (6 women). *Students:* 25 full-time (19 women), 20 part-time (12 women); includes 4 Black or African American, non-Hispanic/Latino; 2 Hispanic/Latino, 27 international. 52 applicants, 54% accepted, 10 enrolled. In 2010, 11 master's awarded. *Degree requirements:* For master's, thesis or alternative. *Entrance requirements:* For master's, GRE General Test. Additional exam requirements/recommendations for international students: Required—TOEFL (minimum score 570 paper-based; 88 iBT), IELTS (minimum score 6.5). *Application deadline:* For fall admission, 4/1 priority date for international students; for spring admission, 11/1 priority date for international students. Applications are processed on a rolling basis. Application fee: $40 ($90 for international students). Electronic applications accepted. *Financial support:* In 2010–11, 11 research assistantships with full and partial tuition reimbursements (averaging $5,911 per year) were awarded; fellowships, teaching assistantships with partial tuition reimbursements, scholarships/grants, health care benefits, and unspecified assistantships also available. *Unit head:* Dr. Michael Bugeja, Chair, 515-294-0481, Fax: 515-294-5108, E-mail: greenlee@iastate.edu. *Application contact:* Dr. Eric Abbott, Director of Graduate Education, 515-294-0492, E-mail: masscomm@iastate.edu.

Kent State University, College of Communication and Information, School of Journalism and Mass Communication, Kent, OH 44242-0001. Offers MA. Part-time programs available. *Degree requirements:* For master's, thesis optional. *Entrance requirements:* For master's, GRE General Test, minimum GPA of 3.0. Additional exam requirements/recommendations for international students: Recommended—TOEFL (minimum score 600 paper-based; 250 computer-based). Electronic applications accepted. *Expenses:* Tuition, state resident: full-time $7866; part-time $437 per credit hour. Tuition, nonresident: full-time $14,022; part-time $779 per credit hour. *Faculty research:* Electronic tablet newspapers, accuracy and ethics in broadcast news, internet credibility, First Amendment, HDTV.

Marquette University, Graduate School, College of Communication, Milwaukee, WI 53201-1881. Offers advertising and public relations (MA); broadcasting and electronic communications (MA); communications studies (MA); digital storytelling (Certificate); health, environment, science and sustainability (MA); journalism (MA); mass communications (MA). *Accreditation:* ACEJMC (one or more programs are accredited). Part-time and evening/weekend programs available. *Faculty:* 33 full-time (18 women), 30 part-time/adjunct (16 women). *Students:* 35 full-time (20 women), 31 part-time (25 women); includes 5 minority (2 Black or African American, non-Hispanic/Latino; 1 Hispanic/Latino; 2 Two or more races, non-Hispanic/Latino), 4 international. Average age 28. 97 applicants, 52% accepted, 21 enrolled. In 2010, 16 master's, 5 other advanced degrees awarded. *Degree requirements:* For master's, comprehensive exam, thesis or alternative. *Entrance requirements:* For master's, GRE, official transcripts from all current and previous colleges/universities except Marquette, three letters of recommendation, statement of academic and professional goals. Additional exam requirements/recommendations for international students: Required—TOEFL (minimum score 530 paper-based; 78 computer-based). *Application deadline:* Applications are processed on a rolling basis. Application fee: $50. Electronic applications accepted. *Expenses:* Tuition: Full-time $16,290; part-time $905 per credit hour. Tuition and fees vary according to program. *Financial support:* In 2010–11, 2 fellowships, 7 research assistantships, 12 teaching assistantships were awarded; career-related internships or fieldwork, Federal Work-Study, institutionally sponsored loans, scholarships/grants, and tuition waivers (full and partial) also available. Support available to part-time students. Financial award application deadline: 2/15. *Faculty research:* Urban journalism, gender and communication, intercultural communication, religious communication. Total annual research expenditures: $3,088. *Unit head:* Dr. Lori Bergen, Dean, 414-288-7133, Fax: 414-288-1578. *Application contact:* Erin Fox, Assistant Director for Recruitment, 414-288-5319, Fax: 414-288-1902, E-mail: erin.fox@marquette.edu.

Marshall University, Academic Affairs Division, School of Journalism and Mass Communications, Huntington, WV 25755. Offers MAJ. *Faculty:* 5 full-time (2 women). *Students:* 24 full-time (18 women), 6 part-time (4 women); includes 1 Black or African American, non-Hispanic/Latino, 6 international. Average age 26. In 2010, 10 master's awarded. *Degree requirements:* For master's, thesis optional. *Entrance requirements:* For master's, GRE General Test. Application fee: $40. *Unit head:* Dr. Corley F. Dennison, Dean, 304-696-2809, E-mail: dennisoc@marshall.edu. *Application contact:* Janet Dooley, Assistant Dean, 304-696-2734, Fax: 304-746-1902, E-mail: dooley@marshall.edu.

Michigan State University, The Graduate School, College of Communication Arts and Sciences, School of Journalism, East Lansing, MI 48824. Offers MA. *Entrance requirements:* Additional exam requirements/recommendations for international students: Required—TOEFL. Electronic applications accepted.

New York University, Graduate School of Arts and Science, Arthur L. Carter Journalism Institute, New York, NY 10012-1019. Offers biomedical journalism (MS); cultural reporting and criticism (MA); French studies/journalism (MA); journalism (MA); Latin American and Caribbean studies/journalism (MA); Near Eastern studies/journalism (MA); science and environmental reporting (Advanced Certificate); MA/Advanced Certificate. *Accreditation:* ACEJMC. Part-time programs available. *Students:* 215 full-time (156 women), 41 part-time (28 women); includes 16 Black or African American, non-Hispanic/Latino; 1 American Indian or Alaska Native, non-Hispanic/Latino; 16 Asian, non-Hispanic/Latino; 14 Hispanic/Latino, 55 international. Average age 27. 490 applicants, 53% accepted, 135 enrolled. In 2010, 109 master's, 23 other advanced degrees awarded. *Degree requirements:* For master's, written projects. *Entrance requirements:* For master's, GRE General Test, sample of written work. Additional exam requirements/recommendations for international students: Required—TOEFL. *Application deadline:* For fall admission, 1/4 priority date for domestic students. Application fee: $90. *Financial support:* Fellowships with tuition reimbursements, teaching assistantships with tuition reimbursements, Federal Work-Study, institutionally sponsored loans, scholarships/grants, and tuition waivers (partial) available. Financial award application deadline: 1/4; financial award applicants required to submit FAFSA. *Faculty research:* Newspaper, magazine, and broadcast journalism; business and financial reporting; media studies. *Unit head:* Brooke Kroeger, Chair, 212-998-7980, Fax: 212-995-4148, E-mail: graduate.journalism@nyu.edu. *Application contact:* Perri Klass, Director of Graduate Studies, 212-998-7980, Fax: 212-995-4148, E-mail: graduate.journalism@nyu.edu.

New York University, Graduate School of Arts and Science, Department of Biology, New York, NY 10012-1019. Offers biology (PhD); biomedical journalism (MS); cancer and molecular biology (PhD); computational biology (PhD); computers in biological research (MS); developmental genetics (PhD); general biology (MS); immunology and microbiology (PhD); molecular genetics (PhD); neurobiology (PhD); oral biology (MS); plant biology (PhD); recombinant DNA technology (MS); MS/MBA. Part-time programs available. *Faculty:* 24 full-time (5 women). *Students:* 155 full-time (89 women), 38 part-time (24 women); includes 29 Asian, non-Hispanic/Latino; 7 Hispanic/Latino, 88 international. Average age 27. 324 applicants, 69% accepted, 63 enrolled. In 2010, 55 master's, 4 doctorates awarded. Terminal master's awarded for partial completion of doctoral program. *Degree requirements:* For master's, thesis or alternative, qualifying paper; for doctorate, comprehensive exam, thesis/dissertation. *Entrance requirements:* For master's, GRE General Test; for doctorate, GRE General Test, GRE Subject Test. Additional exam requirements/recommendations for international students: Required—TOEFL. *Application deadline:* For fall admission, 12/15 priority date for domestic students. Application fee: $90. *Financial support:* Fellowships with tuition reimbursements, research assistantships with tuition reimbursements, teaching assistantships with tuition reimbursements, career-related intern-

ships or fieldwork, Federal Work-Study, institutionally sponsored loans, scholarships/grants, health care benefits, and unspecified assistantships available. Financial award application deadline: 12/15; financial award applicants required to submit FAFSA. *Faculty research:* Genomics, molecular and cell biology, development and molecular genetics, molecular evolution of plants and animals. *Unit head:* Gloria Coruzzi, Chair, 212-998-8200, Fax: 212-995-4015, E-mail: biology@nyu.edu. *Application contact:* Justin Blau, Director of Graduate Studies, 212-998-8200, Fax: 212-995-4015, E-mail: biology@nyu.edu.

Northwestern University, Medill School of Journalism, Evanston, IL 60208. Offers broadcast journalism (MSJ); integrated marketing communications (MSIMC), including advertising/sales promotion, direct database and e-commerce marketing, general studies, public relations; magazine publishing (MSJ); new media (MSJ); reporting and writing (MSJ). *Accreditation:* ACEJMC (one or more programs are accredited). *Entrance requirements:* For master's, GRE General Test, GMAT or LSAT (MSJ). Additional exam requirements/recommendations for international students: Required—TOEFL. Electronic applications accepted. *Expenses:* Contact institution. *Faculty research:* Web business journalism, cultural stereotypes, voter apathy, digital television.

Ohio University, Graduate College, Scripps College of Communication, E. W. Scripps School of Journalism, Athens, OH 45701-2979. Offers MS, PhD. *Accreditation:* ACEJMC (one or more programs are accredited). Part-time programs available. *Students:* 29 full-time (12 women), 11 part-time (6 women); includes 2 minority (both Black or African American, non-Hispanic/Latino), 10 international. 109 applicants, 46% accepted, 19 enrolled. In 2010, 23 master's, 2 doctorates awarded. *Degree requirements:* For master's, thesis or alternative; for doctorate, comprehensive exam, thesis/dissertation. *Entrance requirements:* For master's and doctorate, GRE General Test, minimum GPA of 3.0. Additional exam requirements/recommendations for international students: Required—TOEFL (minimum score 550 paper-based; 80 iBT) or IELTS (minimum score 6.5). *Application deadline:* For fall admission, 2/1 for domestic and international students. Application fee: $50 ($55 for international students). Electronic applications accepted. *Financial support:* In 2010–11, 30 students received support, including fellowships (averaging $7,000 per year), research assistantships with full tuition reimbursements available (averaging $9,300 per year), teaching assistantships with full tuition reimbursements available (averaging $15,500 per year); career-related internships or fieldwork, Federal Work-Study, institutionally sponsored loans, and unspecified assistantships also available. Financial award application deadline: 2/1. *Faculty research:* Newspaper, magazine, broadcasting, public relations, advertising. *Unit head:* Thomas Hodson, Director, 740-593-2550, Fax: 740-593-2592, E-mail: hodson@ohio.edu. *Application contact:* Dr. Michael Sweeney, Associate Director, 740-593-2589 Ext. 740, Fax: 740-593-2592, E-mail: sweenem3@ohio.edu.

Point Park University, School of Communication, Pittsburgh, PA 15222-1984. Offers MA. Part-time and evening/weekend programs available. *Faculty:* 6 full-time, 10 part-time/adjunct. *Students:* 31 full-time (23 women), 33 part-time (25 women); includes 8 minority (5 Black or African American, non-Hispanic/Latino; 1 Asian, non-Hispanic/Latino; 2 Two or more races, non-Hispanic/Latino), 2 international. Average age 27. 103 applicants, 67% accepted, 32 enrolled. In 2010, 21 master's awarded. *Degree requirements:* For master's, comprehensive exam (for some programs), thesis or alternative. *Entrance requirements:* For master's, GRE (if GPA less than 2.75), minimum GPA of 2.75, 2 letters of recommendation, statement of intent. Additional exam requirements/recommendations for international students: Required—TOEFL (minimum score 570 paper-based; 88 iBT). *Application deadline:* Applications are processed on a rolling basis. Application fee: $30. Electronic applications accepted. *Expenses:* Tuition: Full-time $12,456; part-time $692 per credit. Required fees: $630; $35 per credit. *Financial support:* In 2010–11, 6 teaching assistantships with full tuition reimbursements (averaging $6,400 per year) were awarded; scholarships/grants and unspecified assistantships also available. Financial award application deadline: 4/15; financial award applicants required to submit FAFSA. *Unit head:* Dr. Tim Hudson, Chair, 412-392-4748, E-mail: thudson@pointpark.edu. *Application contact:* Marty M. Paonessa, Recruiter/Counselor, 412-392-3915, Fax: 412-392-6164, E-mail: mpaonessa@pointpark.edu.

Polytechnic Institute of NYU, Department of Humanities and Social Sciences, Major in Technical Writing and Specialized Journalism, Brooklyn, NY 11201-2990. Offers MS. *Students:* 1 (woman) full-time; minority (Black or African American, non-Hispanic/Latino). Average age 33. 2 applicants, 100% accepted, 0 enrolled. Application fee: $75. *Expenses:* Tuition: Full-time $21,492; part-time $1194 per credit. Required fees: $385 per semester. Tuition and fees vary according to course load. *Unit head:* Kristen Day, Head, 718-260-3899, E-mail: kday@poly.edu. *Application contact:* Kristen Day, Head, 718-260-3899, E-mail: kday@poly.edu.

Quinnipiac University, School of Communications, Program in Journalism, Hamden, CT 06518-1940. Offers MS. Part-time and evening/weekend programs available. *Faculty:* 1 full-time (0 women), 10 part-time/adjunct (5 women). *Students:* 22 full-time (11 women), 14 part-time (6 women); includes 5 minority (3 Black or African American, non-Hispanic/Latino; 2 Asian, non-Hispanic/Latino), 4 international. 32 applicants, 88% accepted, 20 enrolled. In 2010, 14 master's awarded. *Degree requirements:* For master's, project. *Entrance requirements:* For master's, minimum GPA of 2.8, portfolio or writing sample. Additional exam requirements/recommendations for international students: Required—TOEFL (minimum score 575 paper-based; 233 computer-based; 90 iBT), IELTS (minimum score 6.5). *Application deadline:* For fall admission, 7/30 priority date for domestic students, 4/30 priority date for international students; for spring admission, 12/15 priority date for domestic students, 9/15 priority date for international students. Applications are processed on a rolling basis. Application fee: $45. Electronic applications accepted. *Expenses:* Tuition: Part-time $810 per credit. Required fees: $35 per credit. *Financial support:* In 2010–11, 1 fellowship with full tuition reimbursement was awarded; career-related internships or fieldwork, Federal Work-Study, and unspecified assistantships also available. Support available to part-time students. Financial award application deadline: 4/15; financial award applicants required to submit FAFSA. *Faculty research:* Journalism history, media representation, media and politics, media influence. *Unit head:* Richard Hanley, Director, 203-582-8439, Fax: 203-582-5310, E-mail: rich.hanley@quinnipiac.edu. *Application contact:* Scott Farber, Director of Graduate Admissions, 800-462-1944, Fax: 203-582-3443, E-mail: scott.farber@quinnipiac.edu.

Regent University, Graduate School, School of Communication and the Arts, Virginia Beach, VA 23464-9800. Offers acting (MFA); cinema arts/television arts (MA); communication (MA, PhD); digital media (MA); directing for cinema/television (MA, MFA); editing for cinema/television (MA); journalism (MA); producing for cinema/television (MA, MFA); script and screenwriting (MFA); theatre (MA). Part-time programs available. Postbaccalaureate distance learning degree programs offered (minimal on-campus study). *Faculty:* 29 full-time (4 women), 25 part-time/adjunct (5 women). *Students:* 93 full-time (48 women), 167 part-time (80 women); includes 45 Black or African American, non-Hispanic/Latino; 2 American Indian or Alaska Native, non-Hispanic/Latino; 3 Asian, non-Hispanic/Latino; 9 Hispanic/Latino, 11 international. Average age 32. 247 applicants, 45% accepted, 65 enrolled. In 2010, 82 master's, 17 doctorates awarded. *Degree requirements:* For master's, thesis or alternative; for doctorate, thesis/dissertation. *Entrance requirements:* For master's, GRE General Test or MAT, minimum undergraduate GPA of 3.0, writing sample, computer literacy survey, recommendation, resume, interview, audition (MFA programs); for doctorate, GRE General Test, minimum graduate GPA of 3.0, writing sample, computer literacy survey, recommendation, interview, transcripts. Additional exam requirements/recommendations for international students: Required—TOEFL (minimum score 577 paper-based; 233 computer-based). *Application deadline:* For fall admission, 3/1 priority date for domestic students; for spring admission, 10/1 priority date for domestic students. Applications are processed on a rolling basis. Application fee: $50. Electronic applications accepted. *Expenses:* Contact institution. *Financial support:* Fellowships with full and partial tuition reimbursements, career-related internships or fieldwork, scholarships/grants, tuition waivers (full and partial), and unspecified assistantships available. Support available to part-time students. Financial award application deadline: 9/1; financial award applicants required to submit FAFSA. *Faculty research:* Southern gospel music, education and entertainment, celebrities and the media, journalism and ethics, C. S. Lewis. *Unit head:* Dr. Emmanuel Ayee,

Interim Dean, 757-352-4945, Fax: 757-352-4291, E-mail: eayee@regent.edu. *Application contact:* Matthew Chadwick, Director of Enrollment Support Services, 800-373-5504, Fax: 757-352-4381, E-mail: admissions@regent.edu.

Roosevelt University, Graduate Division, College of Arts and Sciences, Department of Communication, Program in Journalism, Chicago, IL 60605. Offers MSJ. Part-time and evening/weekend programs available.

School of the Art Institute of Chicago, Graduate Division, Program in New Arts Journalism, Chicago, IL 60603-3103. Offers MA. *Entrance requirements:* Additional exam requirements/recommendations for international students: Required—TOEFL, IELTS.

South Dakota State University, Graduate School, College of Arts and Science, Department of Journalism and Mass Communication, Brookings, SD 57007. Offers communication studies and journalism (MS). Part-time and evening/weekend programs available. *Degree requirements:* For master's, thesis, oral exam. *Entrance requirements:* Additional exam requirements/recommendations for international students: Required—TOEFL (minimum score 550 paper-based; 213 computer-based; 79 iBT). *Faculty research:* Mass communication applications.

Southern Illinois University Carbondale, Graduate School, College of Mass Communication and Media Arts, Department of Journalism, Carbondale, IL 62901-4701. Offers PhD.

Stanford University, School of Humanities and Sciences, Department of Communication, Stanford, CA 94305-9991. Offers communication (journalism specialization) (MA); communication theory and research (PhD). *Faculty:* 10 full-time (1 woman). *Students:* 67 full-time (37 women). Average age 26. 162 applicants, 30% accepted, 35 enrolled. In 2010, 24 master's, 6 doctorates awarded. Terminal master's awarded for partial completion of doctoral program. *Degree requirements:* For master's, thesis, project; for doctorate, thesis/dissertation, qualifying examination, area examination, 2 projects. *Entrance requirements:* For master's and doctorate, GRE General Test. Additional exam requirements/recommendations for international students: Required—TOEFL (minimum score 650 paper-based; 280 computer-based; 115 iBT). *Application deadline:* For fall admission, 12/7 for domestic students, 12/1 for international students. Application fee: $125. Electronic applications accepted. *Expenses:* Tuition: Full-time $38,700; part-time $860 per unit. One-time fee: $200 full-time. *Financial support:* Fellowships, research assistantships, teaching assistantships available. *Unit head:* James S. Fishkin, Chair, 650-723-4611, E-mail: jfishkin@stanford.edu. *Application contact:* Student Services Manager, 650-723-2075, Fax: 650-725-2472, E-mail: comm-studentservices@stanford.edu.

Syracuse University, S. I. Newhouse School of Public Communications, Program in Arts Journalism, Syracuse, NY 13244. Offers MA. *Students:* 15 full-time (13 women); includes 2 minority (1 Black or African American, non-Hispanic/Latino; 1 Asian, non-Hispanic/Latino), 2 international. Average age 23. 39 applicants, 69% accepted, 15 enrolled. In 2010, 2 master's awarded. *Degree requirements:* For master's, capstone project. *Entrance requirements:* For master's, GRE General Test. Additional exam requirements/recommendations for international students: Required—TOEFL (minimum score 600 paper-based; 250 computer-based; 100 iBT). *Application deadline:* For fall admission, 2/1 priority date for domestic and international students. Application fee: $45. Electronic applications accepted. *Expenses:* Tuition: Part-time $1162 per credit. *Financial support:* Fellowships with full tuition reimbursements, research assistantships with partial tuition reimbursements, teaching assistantships with partial tuition reimbursements available. Financial award application deadline: 2/1; financial award applicants required to submit FAFSA. *Unit head:* Johanna Keller, Director, 315-443-9251, Fax: 315-443-3946, E-mail: pcgrad@syr.edu. *Application contact:* Martha Coria, Graduate Records Office, 315-443-5749, Fax: 315-443-1834, E-mail: pcgrad@syr.edu.

Syracuse University, S. I. Newhouse School of Public Communications, Program in Broadcast and Digital Journalism, Syracuse, NY 13244. Offers MS. *Students:* 33 full-time (20 women); includes 10 minority (8 Black or African American, non-Hispanic/Latino; 1 Hispanic/Latino; 1 Two or more races, non-Hispanic/Latino), 3 international. Average age 24. 43 applicants, 95% accepted, 31 enrolled. In 2010, 30 master's awarded. *Degree requirements:* For master's, capstone course. *Entrance requirements:* For master's, GRE General Test. Additional exam requirements/recommendations for international students: Required—TOEFL (minimum score 100 iBT). *Application deadline:* For fall admission, 2/1 priority date for domestic and international students. Application fee: $45. Electronic applications accepted. *Expenses:* Tuition: Part-time $1162 per credit. *Financial support:* Fellowships with full tuition reimbursements, research assistantships with partial tuition reimbursements, teaching assistantships with partial tuition reimbursements available. Financial award application deadline: 2/1. *Unit head:* Dona Hayes, Chair, 315-443-1944, Fax: 315-443-3946, E-mail: pcgrad@syr.edu. *Application contact:* Martha Coria, Graduate Records Office, 315-443-5749, Fax: 315-443-1834, E-mail: pcgrad@syr.edu.

Syracuse University, S. I. Newhouse School of Public Communications, Program in Magazine, Newspaper and Online Journalism, Syracuse, NY 13244. Offers MA. *Students:* 34 full-time (20 women), 4 part-time (1 woman); includes 19 minority (9 Black or African American, non-Hispanic/Latino; 2 Asian, non-Hispanic/Latino; 7 Hispanic/Latino; 1 Two or more races, non-Hispanic/Latino), 2 international. Average age 24. 129 applicants, 81% accepted, 31 enrolled. In 2010, 13 master's awarded. *Degree requirements:* For master's, capstone course. *Entrance requirements:* For master's, GRE General Test. Additional exam requirements/recommendations for international students: Required—TOEFL (minimum score 600 paper-based; 250 computer-based; 100 iBT). *Application deadline:* For fall admission, 2/1 priority date for domestic and international students. Application fee: $45. Electronic applications accepted. *Expenses:* Tuition: Part-time $1162 per credit. *Financial support:* Fellowships with full tuition reimbursements, research assistantships with partial tuition reimbursements, teaching assistantships with partial tuition reimbursements available. Financial award application deadline: 2/1; financial award applicants required to submit FAFSA. *Unit head:* Melissa Chessher, Director, 315-443-4004, Fax: 315-443-3946, E-mail: pcgrad@syr.edu. *Application contact:* Martha Coria, Graduate Records Office, 315-443-5749, Fax: 315-443-1834, E-mail: pcgrad@syr.edu.

Temple University, School of Communications and Theater, Department of Journalism, Philadelphia, PA 19122-6096. Offers MJ. Part-time programs available. *Faculty:* 12 full-time (4 women). *Students:* 9 full-time (4 women), 10 part-time (7 women); includes 4 Black or African American, non-Hispanic/Latino. 39 applicants, 62% accepted, 4 enrolled. In 2010, 9 master's awarded. *Degree requirements:* For master's, written exam. *Entrance requirements:* For master's, GRE General Test, minimum GPA of 3.0. Additional exam requirements/recommendations for international students: Required—TOEFL (minimum score 550 paper-based; 213 computer-based; 79 iBT). *Application deadline:* For fall admission, 3/1 for domestic students, 12/15 for international students. Application fee: $50. Electronic applications accepted. *Financial support:* Research assistantships with partial tuition reimbursements, career-related internships or fieldwork, Federal Work-Study, and institutionally sponsored loans available. Financial award application deadline: 1/15; financial award applicants required to submit FAFSA. *Faculty research:* Journalism history, advertising research, media law, media institutions. *Unit head:* Dr. Andrew L. Mendelson, Chair, 215-204-8346, Fax: 215-204-1974, E-mail: amendels@temple.edu. *Application contact:* Dr. Andrew L. Mendelson, Chair, 215-204-8346, Fax: 215-204-1974, E-mail: amendels@temple.edu.

Texas A&M University, College of Veterinary Medicine and Biomedical Sciences, Department of Veterinary Integrative Biosciences, College Station, TX 77843. Offers epidemiology (MS); food safety/toxicology/environmental health (MS); science and technology journalism (MS); veterinary public health (MS). *Faculty:* 22. *Students:* 35 full-time (20 women), 13 part-time (8 women); includes 1 Asian, non-Hispanic/Latino; 1 Hispanic/Latino, 21 international. Average age 30. In 2010, 1 master's awarded. Terminal master's awarded for partial completion of doctoral program. *Degree requirements:* For master's, comprehensive exam, thesis. *Entrance requirements:* For master's, GRE General Test, minimum undergraduate GPA of 3.0. Additional exam requirements/recommendations for international students: Required—TOEFL. *Application deadline:* For fall admission, 7/15 priority date for domestic students, 4/1 priority date for international students; for spring admission, 10/1 priority date for domestic students, 9/15 priority date for international students. Applications are processed on a rolling basis. Application fee: $50 ($75 for international students). Electronic applications accepted. *Financial support:* In 2010–11, fellowships (averaging $18,000 per year), research assistantships (averaging $15,600 per year), teaching assistantships (averaging $15,600 per year) were awarded; institutionally sponsored loans, unspecified assistantships, and clinical associateships also available. Financial award application deadline: 7/15; financial award applicants required to submit FAFSA. *Faculty research:* Metal toxicology, reproductive biology, genetics of neural development, developmental biology, environmental toxicology. *Unit head:* Dr. Evelyn Tiffany-Castiglioni, Head, 979-458-1077, E-mail: ecastiglioni@cvm.tamu.edu. *Application contact:* Dr. Evelyn Tiffany-Castiglioni, Head, 979-458-1077, E-mail: ecastiglioni@cvm.tamu.edu.

Texas Christian University, College of Communication, Schieffer School of Journalism, Fort Worth, TX 76129-0002. Offers advertising/public relations (MS); news-editorial (MS). Part-time and evening/weekend programs available. *Degree requirements:* For master's, thesis optional, written exam. *Entrance requirements:* For master's, GRE General Test. Additional exam requirements/recommendations for international students: Required—TOEFL. *Application deadline:* For fall admission, 3/1 for domestic and international students; for spring admission, 10/1 for domestic and international students. Applications are processed on a rolling basis. Application fee: $50. *Expenses:* Tuition: Full-time $18,720; part-time $1040 per credit hour. Tuition and fees vary according to course load and program. *Financial support:* Tuition waivers (full and partial) and unspecified assistantships available. Financial award application deadline: 3/1. *Unit head:* John Lumpkin, Director, 817-257-4908, E-mail: j.lumpkin@tcu.edu. *Application contact:* Dr. John Tisdale, Associate Director, 817-257-7425, E-mail: j.tisdale@tcu.edu.

Université Laval, Faculty of Letters, Department of Information and Communication, Program in International Journalism, Québec, QC G1K 7P4, Canada. Offers Diploma. Offered jointly with École Supérieure De Journalisme De Lille (France). *Entrance requirements:* For degree, English exam, French exam, test on international current events, interview, knowledge of French, knowledge of English. Electronic applications accepted.

The University of Alabama, Graduate School, College of Communication and Information Sciences, Department of Journalism, Tuscaloosa, AL 35487-0172. Offers MA. *Faculty:* 9 full-time (3 women). *Students:* 10 full-time (5 women), 5 part-time (4 women); includes 2 minority (1 Hispanic/Latino; 1 Two or more races, non-Hispanic/Latino). Average age 26. 26 applicants, 54% accepted, 9 enrolled. In 2010, 10 master's awarded. Terminal master's awarded for partial completion of doctoral program. *Degree requirements:* For master's, comprehensive exam (for some programs), thesis or alternative. *Entrance requirements:* For master's, GRE or MAT, minimum GPA of 3.0. Additional exam requirements/recommendations for international students: Required—TOEFL (minimum score 550 paper-based; 213 computer-based; 79 iBT). *Application deadline:* For fall admission, 3/31 priority date for domestic students, 1/15 priority date for international students; for spring admission, 11/1 priority date for domestic students, 9/15 priority date for international students. Applications are processed on a rolling basis. Application fee: $50 ($60 for international students). Electronic applications accepted. *Expenses:* Tuition, state resident: full-time $7900. Tuition, nonresident: full-time $20,500. *Financial support:* In 2010–11, 7 students received support, including 8 fellowships with partial tuition reimbursements available, 3 research assistantships with full tuition reimbursements available (averaging $11,000 per year), 3 teaching assistantships with full tuition reimbursements available (averaging $11,000 per year); career-related internships or fieldwork, Federal Work-Study, institutionally sponsored loans, scholarships/grants, health care benefits, and unspecified assistantships also available. Financial award application deadline: 2/15; financial award applicants required to submit FAFSA. *Faculty research:* Journalistic processes, practices and ethics, media effects, media sociology, history, law. *Unit head:* Dr. Jennifer Greer, Chair, 205-348-6304, Fax: 205-348-2780, E-mail: jdgreer@ua.edu. *Application contact:* Dr. Wilson Lowrey, Graduate Coordinator, 205-348-8608, Fax: 205-348-2780, E-mail: wlowrey@ua.edu.

University of Arkansas, Graduate School, J. William Fulbright College of Arts and Sciences, Department of Journalism, Fayetteville, AR 72701-1201. Offers MA. *Students:* 6 full-time (4 women), 8 part-time (5 women), 3 international. 8 applicants, 88% accepted. In 2010, 3 master's awarded. Application fee: $40 ($50 for international students). *Financial support:* In 2010–11, 2 research assistantships, 3 teaching assistantships were awarded; fellowships with tuition reimbursements, career-related internships or fieldwork and Federal Work-Study also available. Support available to part-time students. Financial award application deadline: 4/1; financial award applicants required to submit FAFSA. *Unit head:* Dr. Dale Carpenter, Departmental Chairperson, 479-575-3601, Fax: 479-575-4314, E-mail: dcarpent@uark.edu. *Application contact:* Dr. Jan Wicks, Graduate Coordinator, 479-575-2006, Fax: 479-575-4314, E-mail: jwicks@uark.edu.

University of Arkansas at Little Rock, Graduate School, College of Professional Studies, School of Mass Communication, Little Rock, AR 72204-1099. Offers journalism (MA). Part-time and evening/weekend programs available. *Degree requirements:* For master's, comprehensive exam, thesis optional. *Entrance requirements:* For master's, GRE General Test, minimum GPA of 2.7. *Faculty research:* Theory and practice of mass communication, social role of the mass media.

The University of British Columbia, Faculty of Arts and Faculty of Graduate Studies, The School of Journalism, Vancouver, BC V6T 1Z2, Canada. Offers MJ. *Degree requirements:* For master's, thesis, 3 month internship. *Entrance requirements:* For master's, portfolio, resume with cover letter, letters of reference. Additional exam requirements/recommendations for international students: Required—TOEFL (minimum score 615 paper-based; 260 computer-based), IELTS (minimum score 7.5). Electronic applications accepted. *Expenses:* Contact institution. *Faculty research:* New media, media coverage, journalistic ethics, international journalism, multimedia.

University of California, Berkeley, Graduate Division, Graduate School of Journalism, Berkeley, CA 94720-1500. Offers MJ, JD/MJ, MJ/MA. *Accreditation:* ACEJMC. *Degree requirements:* For master's, project. *Entrance requirements:* For master's, GRE General Test, 3 work samples, minimum GPA of 3.0, 3 letters of recommendation. Additional exam requirements/recommendations for international students: Required—TOEFL (minimum score 600 paper-based; 250 computer-based). *Faculty research:* Documentary, new media, print (newspaper and magazine), broadcast (television and radio), photography.

University of Colorado Boulder, Graduate School, School of Journalism and Mass Communication, Boulder, CO 80309. Offers communication (PhD), including media studies; mass communication research (MA); newsgathering (MA). *Accreditation:* ACEJMC (one or more programs are accredited). Part-time programs available. *Faculty:* 22 full-time (11 women). *Students:* 78 full-time (49 women), 10 part-time (6 women); includes 4 minority (1 Black or African American, non-Hispanic/Latino; 2 Hispanic/Latino; 1 Two or more races, non-Hispanic/Latino), 11 international. Average age 30. 154 applicants, 35 enrolled. In 2010, 35 master's, 6 doctorates awarded. *Degree requirements:* For master's, comprehensive exam, thesis or alternative; for doctorate, comprehensive exam, thesis/dissertation. *Entrance requirements:* For master's, GRE General Test, minimum undergraduate GPA of 2.75; for doctorate, GRE General Test, minimum undergraduate GPA of 3.2, 3.5 graduate. *Application deadline:* For fall admission, 2/15 for domestic students, 12/1 for international students. Applications are processed on a rolling basis. Application fee: $50 ($60 for international students). *Financial support:* In 2010–11, 14 fellowships (averaging $1,807 per year), 21 research assistantships with tuition reimbursements (averaging $11,554 per year) were awarded; institutionally sponsored loans and unspecified assistantships also available. Financial award application deadline: 3/1. *Faculty research:* Writing on science and the environment, mass communication and public opinion, minority representation in the media, media and culture. Total annual research expenditures: $204,190.

Journalism

University of Florida, Graduate School, College of Journalism and Communications, Department of Journalism, Gainesville, FL 32611. Offers MAMC. *Faculty:* 19 full-time (9 women). *Entrance requirements:* For master's, GRE General Test, minimum GPA of 3.0. Additional exam requirements/recommendations for international students: Required—TOEFL (minimum score 550 paper-based; 213 computer-based; 80 iBT), IELTS (minimum score 6). Application fee: $30. *Expenses:* Tuition, state resident: full-time $10,915.92. Tuition, nonresident: full-time $28,309. *Unit head:* Dr. William McKeen, Chair, 352-392-0500, E-mail: wmckeen@jou.ufl.edu. *Application contact:* Clay Calvert, Graduate Coordinator, 352-273-1096, E-mail: ccalvert@jou.ufl.edu.

University of Georgia, Grady School of Journalism and Mass Communication, Athens, GA 30602. Offers journalism and mass communication (MA); mass communication (PhD). *Accreditation:* ACEJMC (one or more programs are accredited). *Faculty:* 37 full-time (14 women). *Students:* 88 full-time (61 women), 24 part-time (16 women); includes 13 Black or African American, non-Hispanic/Latino; 4 Hispanic/Latino, 21 international. 297 applicants, 40% accepted, 48 enrolled. In 2010, 31 master's, 5 doctorates awarded. *Degree requirements:* For master's, comprehensive exam, thesis (MA); for doctorate, comprehensive exam, thesis/dissertation. *Entrance requirements:* For master's and doctorate, GRE General Test. Additional exam requirements/recommendations for international students: Required—TOEFL, TWE (for PhD). *Application deadline:* For spring admission, 2/15 for domestic students. Application fee: $50. Electronic applications accepted. *Expenses:* Tuition, state resident: full-time $7200; part-time $344 per credit hour. Tuition, nonresident: full-time $21,900; part-time $944 per credit hour. Tuition and fees vary according to course load and program. *Financial support:* Research assistantships, teaching assistantships, tuition waivers (full) and unspecified assistantships available. *Unit head:* Dr. E. Culpepper Clark, Dean, 706-542-1704, Fax: 706-542-2183, E-mail: cully@uga.edu. *Application contact:* Dr. Jeffrey K. Springston, Graduate Coordinator, 706-542-5030, Fax: 706-542-2183, E-mail: jspring@grady.uga.edu.

University of Illinois at Springfield, Graduate Programs, College of Public Affairs and Administration, Public Affairs Reporting Program, Springfield, IL 62703-5407. Offers MA. Part-time and evening/weekend programs available. *Degree requirements:* For master's, internship, professional portfolio. *Entrance requirements:* For master's, literacy/competency writing test, interview, written work sample, 3 letters of reference. Additional exam requirements/recommendations for international students: Required—TOEFL (minimum score 500 paper-based; 176 computer-based; 61 iBT). Electronic applications accepted. *Expenses:* Tuition, state resident: full-time $6774; part-time $282.25 per credit hour. Tuition, nonresident: full-time $15,078; part-time $628.25 per credit hour. Required fees: $15.25 per credit hour. $492 per term.

University of Illinois at Urbana–Champaign, Graduate College, College of Media, Department of Journalism, Champaign, IL 61820. Offers MS, MS/JD, MS/MBA. *Accreditation:* ACEJMC. *Faculty:* 12 full-time (2 women). *Students:* 12 full-time (8 women), 8 part-time (5 women); includes 2 minority (1 Black or African American, non-Hispanic/Latino; 1 Asian, non-Hispanic/Latino), 2 international. 63 applicants, 19% accepted, 12 enrolled. In 2010, 20 master's awarded. *Entrance requirements:* For master's, GRE, minimum GPA of 3.0. Additional exam requirements/recommendations for international students: Required—TOEFL (minimum score 600 paper-based; 250 computer-based). *Application deadline:* Applications are processed on a rolling basis. Application fee: $75 ($90 for international students). Electronic applications accepted. *Financial support:* In 2010–11, 2 fellowships, 3 research assistantships, 11 teaching assistantships were awarded; tuition waivers (full and partial) also available. *Unit head:* Brian K. Johnson, Interim Head, 217-333-0709, Fax: 217-333-7931, E-mail: bkj@illinois.edu. *Application contact:* Diana King Schwanke, Office Administrator, 217-333-0709, Fax: 217-333-7931, E-mail: dking6@illinois.edu.

The University of Iowa, Graduate College, College of Liberal Arts and Sciences, School of Journalism and Mass Communication, Program in Professional Journalism, Iowa City, IA 52242-1316. Offers MA, JD/MA. *Degree requirements:* For master's, thesis optional, exam. *Entrance requirements:* For master's, GRE General Test, minimum GPA of 3.0. Additional exam requirements/recommendations for international students: Required—TOEFL (minimum score 637 paper-based; 270 computer-based; 110 iBT). Electronic applications accepted. *Faculty research:* Verbal and visual aspects of historical, legal, social, and cross-cultural communication.

The University of Kansas, Graduate Studies, School of Journalism and Mass Communications, Lawrence, KS 66045. Offers journalism (MS). *Accreditation:* ACEJMC. Part-time programs available. *Faculty:* 25 full-time (9 women), 7 part-time/adjunct (4 women). *Students:* 28 full-time (15 women), 56 part-time (35 women); includes 7 minority (3 Black or African American, non-Hispanic/Latino; 2 Asian, non-Hispanic/Latino; 1 Hispanic/Latino; 1 Two or more races, non-Hispanic/Latino), 7 international. Average age 30. 59 applicants, 69% accepted, 21 enrolled. In 2010, 28 master's awarded. *Degree requirements:* For master's, comprehensive exam, thesis. *Entrance requirements:* For master's, GRE General Test, minimum GPA of 3.0. Additional exam requirements/recommendations for international students: Required—TOEFL, TOEFL or IELTS. *Application deadline:* For fall admission, 2/1 priority date for domestic and international students; for spring admission, 11/1 priority date for domestic and international students. Application fee: $55 ($65 for international students). Electronic applications accepted. *Expenses:* Tuition, state resident: full-time $7092; part-time $295.50 per credit hour. Tuition, nonresident: full-time $16,590; part-time $691.25 per credit hour. Required fees: $858; $71.49 per credit hour. Tuition and fees vary according to course load, campus/location and program. *Financial support:* Fellowships, research assistantships, teaching assistantships with full and partial tuition reimbursements, career-related internships or fieldwork, scholarships/grants, and unspecified assistantships available. Support available to part-time students. Financial award application deadline: 2/1; financial award applicants required to submit FAFSA. *Faculty research:* Advertising, creativity, media economics, public relations, press law, online journalism, political journalism, marketing communication, new media, visual communication. *Unit head:* Ann Brill, Dean, 785-864-4755, Fax: 785-864-4396, E-mail: abrill@ku.edu. *Application contact:* Cindy Nesvarba, Graduate Records Coordinator, 785-864-7649, Fax: 785-864-5318, E-mail: cnesvarb@ku.edu.

University of Maryland, College Park, Academic Affairs, Phillip Merrill College of Journalism, College Park, MD 20742. Offers broadcast journalism (MA); journalism (MA); journalism and media studies (PhD); online news (MA); public affairs reporting (MA). *Accreditation:* ACEJMC (one or more programs are accredited). Part-time and evening/weekend programs available. *Faculty:* 18 full-time (10 women), 43 part-time/adjunct (18 women). *Students:* 76 full-time (46 women), 14 part-time (7 women); includes 20 minority (12 Black or African American, non-Hispanic/Latino; 5 Asian, non-Hispanic/Latino; 3 Hispanic/Latino), 11 international. 243 applicants, 37% accepted, 26 enrolled. In 2010, 26 master's, 5 doctorates awarded. *Degree requirements:* For doctorate, thesis/dissertation, preliminary written and oral comprehensive exams. *Entrance requirements:* For master's and doctorate, GRE General Test, minimum GPA of 3.0, 3 letters of recommendation. Additional exam requirements/recommendations for international students: Required—TOEFL. *Application deadline:* For fall admission, 1/15 for domestic and international students. Applications are processed on a rolling basis. Application fee: $75. Electronic applications accepted. *Expenses:* Tuition, state resident: part-time $471 per credit hour. Tuition, nonresident: part-time $1016 per credit hour. Required fees: $337 per term. *Financial support:* In 2010–11, 3 fellowships with full and partial tuition reimbursements (averaging $11,667 per year), 22 teaching assistantships with tuition reimbursements (averaging $16,647 per year) were awarded; research assistantships with tuition reimbursements, career-related internships or fieldwork, Federal Work-Study, and scholarships/grants also available. Support available to part-time students. Financial award applicants required to submit FAFSA. *Faculty research:* Mass communication theory, specialized journalism, new telecommunication technologies, press integration. Total annual research expenditures: $565,454. *Unit head:* Kevin Klose, Dean and Professor, 301-405-2383, E-mail: kklose@jmail.umd.edu. *Application contact:* Dr. Charles A. Caramello, Dean of Graduate School, 301-405-0358, Fax: 301-314-9305, E-mail: ccaramel@umd.edu.

University of Memphis, Graduate School, College of Communication and Fine Arts, Department of Journalism, Memphis, TN 38152. Offers general journalism (MA); journalism administration (MA). *Accreditation:* ACEJMC. Part-time and evening/weekend programs available. Post-baccalaureate distance learning degree programs offered (no on-campus study). *Faculty:* 6 full-time (3 women), 2 part-time/adjunct (1 woman). *Students:* 16 full-time (13 women), 29 part-time (17 women); includes 7 Black or African American, non-Hispanic/Latino; 1 Hispanic/Latino. Average age 34. 34 applicants, 79% accepted, 11 enrolled. In 2010, 9 master's awarded. *Degree requirements:* For master's, comprehensive exam, thesis (for some programs), culminating experience: project, thesis, or referred paper. *Entrance requirements:* For master's, GRE General Test, MAT, transcripts, resume, goal statement. Additional exam requirements/recommendations for international students: Required—TOEFL (minimum score 600 paper-based; 250 computer-based). *Application deadline:* For fall admission, 6/1 for domestic and international students; for spring admission, 10/1 for domestic and international students. Applications are processed on a rolling basis. Application fee: $35 ($60 for international students). *Financial support:* In 2010–11, 25 students received support; research assistantships with full tuition reimbursements available, teaching assistantships with full tuition reimbursements available, Federal Work-Study, scholarships/grants, and unspecified assistantships available. Support available to part-time students. Financial award application deadline: 2/15; financial award applicants required to submit FAFSA. *Faculty research:* Spirit of libel law, statistical software packages, college yearbooks, computer-assisted grammar project, newspaper in education. *Unit head:* Dr. David Arant, Chair, 901-678-2401, Fax: 901-678-4287, E-mail: darant@memphis.edu. *Application contact:* Dr. Rick Fischer, Coordinator of Graduate Studies, 901-678-2853, Fax: 901-678-4287, E-mail: rfischer@memphis.edu.

University of Miami, Graduate School, School of Communication, Coral Gables, FL 33124. Offers communication (PhD); communication studies (MA); film studies (MA, PhD); motion pictures (MFA), including production, producing, and screenwriting; print journalism (MA); public relations (MA); Spanish language journalism (MA); television broadcast journalism (MA). *Accreditation:* ACEJMC. Part-time programs available. *Degree requirements:* For master's, comprehensive exam (for some programs), thesis (for some programs); for doctorate, comprehensive exam, thesis/dissertation. *Entrance requirements:* For master's, GRE General Test; for doctorate, GRE General Test, master's thesis or scholarly research. Additional exam requirements/recommendations for international students: Required—TOEFL (minimum score 600 paper-based; 250 computer-based; 100 iBT). Electronic applications accepted. *Faculty research:* Communication studies, mass communication, international/interpersonal communication, film studies, journalism.

University of Mississippi, Graduate School, School of Journalism and New Media, Oxford, University, MS 38677. Offers journalism (MA). *Faculty:* 19 full-time (9 women), 4 part-time/adjunct (2 women). *Students:* 14 full-time (8 women), 6 part-time (3 women); includes 2 Black or African American, non-Hispanic/Latino. In 2010, 5 master's awarded. *Degree requirements:* For master's, thesis. *Unit head:* Dr. Will Norton, Dean, 662-915-7146. *Application contact:* Dr. Christy M. Wyandt, Associate Dean, 662-915-7474, Fax: 662-915-7577, E-mail: cwyandt@olemiss.edu.

University of Missouri, Graduate School, School of Journalism, Columbia, MO 65211. Offers MA, PhD. *Accreditation:* ACEJMC (one or more programs are accredited). Part-time programs available. Terminal master's awarded for partial completion of doctoral program. *Degree requirements:* For master's, thesis (for some programs); for doctorate, 2 foreign languages, thesis/dissertation. *Entrance requirements:* For master's and doctorate, GRE General Test, minimum GPA of 3.0. Additional exam requirements/recommendations for international students: Required—TOEFL (minimum score 600 paper-based; 250 computer-based; 100 iBT).

The University of Montana, Graduate School, School of Journalism, Missoula, MT 59812-0002. Offers MA. *Degree requirements:* For master's, thesis or alternative, professional project. *Entrance requirements:* For master's, GRE. Additional exam requirements/recommendations for international students: Required—TOEFL (minimum score 580 paper-based). Electronic applications accepted. *Faculty research:* Native American issues, natural resources, public affairs, economy, photojournalism, multimedia, media law.

University of Nebraska–Lincoln, Graduate College, College of Journalism and Mass Communications, Lincoln, NE 68588. Offers marketing, communication and advertising (MA); professional journalism (MA). Postbaccalaureate distance learning degree programs offered (no on-campus study). *Degree requirements:* For master's, thesis. *Entrance requirements:* For master's, samples of work. Additional exam requirements/recommendations for international students: Required—TOEFL (minimum score 600 paper-based; 250 computer-based). Electronic applications accepted. *Faculty research:* Interactive media and the Internet, community newspapers, children's radio, advertising involvement, telecommunications policy.

University of Nevada, Las Vegas, Graduate College, Greenspun College of Urban Affairs, School of Journalism and Media Studies, Las Vegas, NV 89154-5007. Offers MA. *Faculty:* 10 full-time (2 women). *Students:* 14 full-time (10 women), 13 part-time (7 women); includes 11 minority (3 Black or African American, non-Hispanic/Latino; 4 Hispanic/Latino; 1 Native Hawaiian or other Pacific Islander, non-Hispanic/Latino; 3 Two or more races, non-Hispanic/Latino), 1 international. Average age 30. 17 applicants, 82% accepted, 8 enrolled. In 2010, 7 master's awarded. *Entrance requirements:* For master's, GRE General Test. Additional exam requirements/recommendations for international students: Required—TOEFL (minimum score 550 paper-based; 213 computer-based; 80 iBT), IELTS (minimum score 7). *Application deadline:* For fall admission, 5/5 priority date for domestic and international students. Applications are processed on a rolling basis. Application fee: $60 ($95 for international students). Electronic applications accepted. *Expenses:* Tuition, area resident: Part-time $239.50 per credit. Tuition, state resident: part-time $239.50 per credit. Tuition, nonresident: part-time $503 per credit. Required fees: $108 per semester. Tuition and fees vary according to course load, program and reciprocity agreements. *Financial support:* In 2010–11, 8 students received support, including 4 research assistantships with partial tuition reimbursements available (averaging $10,000 per year), 4 teaching assistantships with partial tuition reimbursements available (averaging $10,000 per year); institutionally sponsored loans, scholarships/grants, health care benefits, and unspecified assistantships also available. Financial award application deadline: 3/1. *Faculty research:* Media and religion, science and communications, ethnic communities and journalism, journalism history, emerging technologies. *Unit head:* Dr. Ardyth Sohn, Director/Professor, 702-895-3270, Fax: 702-895-5189, E-mail: ardyth.sohn@unlv.edu. *Application contact:* Graduate College Admissions Evaluator, 702-895-3320, Fax: 702-895-4180, E-mail: gradcollege@unlv.edu.

University of Nevada, Reno, Graduate School, Donald W. Reynolds School of Journalism, Reno, NV 89557. Offers MA. *Degree requirements:* For master's, thesis. *Entrance requirements:* For master's, GRE General Test, minimum GPA of 2.75. Additional exam requirements/recommendations for international students: Required—TOEFL (minimum score 500 paper-based; 173 computer-based; 61 iBT), IELTS (minimum score 6). Electronic applications accepted. *Expenses:* Tuition, state resident: full-time $2219; part-time $246 per credit. Tuition, nonresident: part-time $510 per credit. International tuition: $9009 full-time. Required fees: $59 per term. One-time fee: $101. Tuition and fees vary according to course load. *Faculty research:* Interactive environmental journalism.

University of North Texas, Toulouse Graduate School, College of Arts and Sciences, Mayborn School of Journalism, Denton, TX 76203. Offers journalism (MA, MJ); narrative journalism (Graduate Certificate). *Accreditation:* ACEJMC (one or more programs are accredited). Part-time programs available. *Degree requirements:* For master's, variable foreign language requirement, comprehensive exam, thesis or alternative. *Entrance requirements:* For master's, GRE General Test, portfolio. Additional exam requirements/recommendations for international students: Recommended—TOEFL (minimum score 550 paper-based; 213 computer-based; 79 iBT). *Expenses:* Tuition, state resident: full-time $4298; part-time $239 per credit hour. Tuition, nonresident: full-time $10,782; part-time $549 per credit hour. Required fees: $1292; $270 per credit hour. *Financial support:* Research assistantships, teaching assistantships, career-related internships or fieldwork, Federal Work-Study, and institutionally sponsored loans available. Financial award application deadline: 4/1; financial award applicants required to submit FAFSA. *Faculty research:* Mass communication theory, public relations, advertising, mass communication technology, journalism ethics. *Application contact:* Graduate Adviser, 940-565-4564, Fax: 940-369-8959, E-mail: mland@unt.edu.

University of Oklahoma, Gaylord College of Journalism and Mass Communication, Program in Journalism and Mass Communication, Norman, OK 73019-0390. Offers advertising and public relations (MA); information gathering and distribution (MA); mass communication management and policy (MA); professional writing (MA); telecommunications and new technologies (MA). Part-time programs available. *Students:* 21 full-time (16 women), 26 part-time (13 women); includes 7 minority (4 Black or African American, non-Hispanic/Latino; 2 American Indian or Alaska Native, non-Hispanic/Latino; 1 Hispanic/Latino), 6 international. Average age 27. 29 applicants, 76% accepted, 10 enrolled. In 2010, 20 master's awarded. *Degree requirements:* For master's, thesis optional. *Entrance requirements:* For master's, GRE General Test, minimum GPA of 3.2, 9 hours of course work in journalism, course work in statistics. Additional exam requirements/recommendations for international students: Required—TOEFL (minimum score 600 paper-based; 250 computer-based; 100 iBT), TWE (minimum score 5). *Application deadline:* For fall admission, 2/1 for domestic students, 4/1 for international students; for spring admission, 11/1 for domestic students, 9/1 for international students. Application fee: $40 ($90 for international students). Electronic applications accepted. *Expenses:* Tuition, state resident: full-time $3893; part-time $162.20 per credit hour. Tuition, nonresident: full-time $14,167; part-time $590.30 per credit hour. Required fees: $2523; $94.60 per credit hour. Tuition and fees vary according to course load and degree level. *Financial support:* In 2010–11, 30 students received support. Career-related internships or fieldwork, scholarships/grants, health care benefits, and unspecified assistantships available. *Faculty research:* Organizational management, strategic communications, rhetorical theories and mass communication, interactive messaging and audience response; mass media history and law. *Unit head:* Dr. Joe Foote, Dean, 405-325-2721, Fax: 405-325-7565, E-mail: jfoote@ou.edu. *Application contact:* Kelly Storm, Graduate Advisor, 405-325-2722, Fax: 405-325-7565, E-mail: kstorm@ou.edu.

University of Oregon, Graduate School, School of Journalism and Communication, Eugene, OR 97403. Offers MA, MS, PhD. *Accreditation:* ACEJMC (one or more programs are accredited); ASHA. Part-time programs available. *Degree requirements:* For master's, thesis or alternative. *Entrance requirements:* For master's, GRE General Test; for doctorate, master's degree. *Faculty research:* Impact of mass communication, media technology, media accountability, craft attitudes, media economics.

University of Puerto Rico, Río Piedras, School of Communication, Program in Journalism, San Juan, PR 00931-3300. Offers MA.

University of South Carolina, The Graduate School, College of Mass Communications and Information Studies, School of Journalism and Mass Communications, Columbia, SC 29208. Offers MA, MMC, PhD. *Accreditation:* ACEJMC (one or more programs are accredited). Part-time programs available. *Degree requirements:* For master's, comprehensive exam, thesis (for some programs); for doctorate, one foreign language, comprehensive exam, thesis/dissertation. *Entrance requirements:* For master's and doctorate, GRE General Test, minimum GPA of 3.0. Additional exam requirements/recommendations for international students: Required—TOEFL (minimum score 600 paper-based; 250 computer-based; 75 iBT). Electronic applications accepted. *Faculty research:* Ethics, communications law, international communications, science/health/environmental/risk communications, convergent media.

University of Southern California, Graduate School, Annenberg School for Communication and Journalism, School of Journalism, MA Program in Journalism, Los Angeles, CA 90089. Offers MA. *Students:* 41 full-time, 2 part-time; includes 21 minority (4 Black or African American, non-Hispanic/Latino; 5 Asian, non-Hispanic/Latino; 10 Hispanic/Latino; 2 Two or more races, non-Hispanic/Latino), 2 international. Average age 25. 104 applicants, 52% accepted, 28 enrolled. In 2010, 23 master's awarded. *Degree requirements:* For master's, comprehensive exam, thesis. *Entrance requirements:* For master's, GRE General Test, resume, writing samples, letters of recommendation, statement of purpose. Additional exam requirements/recommendations for international students: Required—TOEFL (minimum score 280 computer-based; 114 iBT). *Application deadline:* For fall admission, 1/2 for domestic students, 12/1 for international students. Application fee: $85. Electronic applications accepted. *Expenses:* Tuition: Full-time $31,240; part-time $1420 per unit. Required fees: $600. One-time fee: $35 full-time. Full-time tuition and fees vary according to degree level and program. *Financial support:* Career-related internships or fieldwork, Federal Work-Study, institutionally sponsored loans, scholarships/grants, health care benefits, and unspecified assistantships available. Support available to part-time students. Financial award application deadline: 1/15; financial award applicants required to submit FAFSA. *Application contact:* Allyson Hill, Assistant Dean, Admissions, 213-821-0770, Fax: 213-740-1933, E-mail: ascadm@usc.edu.

See Display on page 675 and Close-Up on page 727.

University of Southern California, Graduate School, Annenberg School for Communication and Journalism, School of Journalism, Program in Print Journalism, Los Angeles, CA 90089. Offers MA. Effective fall 2011, concentrations will be discontinued and replaced by the M.A. in Journalism. *Students:* 26 full-time, 2 part-time; includes 3 Black or African American, non-Hispanic/Latino; 1 Asian, non-Hispanic/Latino; 3 Hispanic/Latino, 1 international. Average age 25. 64 applicants, 70% accepted, 7 enrolled. In 2010, 17 master's awarded. *Degree requirements:* For master's, comprehensive exam. *Entrance requirements:* For master's, GRE General Test, resume, writing samples, letters of recommendation. Additional exam requirements/recommendations for international students: Required—TOEFL (minimum score 280 computer-based; 114 iBT). *Application deadline:* For fall admission, 1/3 for domestic students, 12/1 for international students. Application fee: $85. Electronic applications accepted. *Expenses:* Tuition: Full-time $31,240; part-time $1420 per unit. Required fees: $600. One-time fee: $35 full-time. Full-time tuition and fees vary according to degree level and program. *Financial support:* In 2010–11, 4 fellowships with full tuition reimbursements were awarded; career-related internships or fieldwork, Federal Work-Study, institutionally sponsored loans, scholarships/grants, health care benefits, and unspecified assistantships also available. Support available to part-time students. Financial award application deadline: 2/1; financial award applicants required to submit FAFSA. *Application contact:* Allyson Hill, Assistant Dean, Admissions, 213-821-0770, Fax: 213-740-1933, E-mail: ascadm@usc.edu.

See Display on page 675 and Close-Up on page 727.

University of Southern California, Graduate School, Annenberg School for Communication and Journalism, School of Journalism, Program in Specialized Journalism, Los Angeles, CA 90089. Offers specialized journalism (MA); specialized journalism (the arts) (MA). Available in summer term only. *Students:* 9 full-time, 3 part-time; includes 1 Black or African American, non-Hispanic/Latino; 1 Hispanic/Latino, 1 international. Average age 31. 35 applicants, 66% accepted, 12 enrolled. In 2010, 15 master's awarded. *Degree requirements:* For master's, thesis. *Entrance requirements:* For master's, GRE General Test, resume, professional work samples, letters of recommendation, statement of purpose. Additional exam requirements/recommendations for international students: Required—TOEFL (minimum score 280 computer-based; 114 iBT). *Application deadline:* For fall admission, 3/1 priority date for domestic and international students. Applications are processed on a rolling basis. Application fee: $85. Electronic applications accepted. *Expenses:* Tuition: Full-time $31,240; part-time $1420 per unit. Required fees: $600. One-time fee: $35 full-time. Full-time tuition and fees vary according to degree level and program. *Financial support:* In 2010–11, 3 fellowships with full tuition reimbursements (averaging $20,000 per year) were awarded; Federal Work-Study, scholarships/grants, and health care benefits also available. Support available to part-time students. Financial award application deadline: 2/1; financial award applicants required to submit FAFSA. *Unit head:* Michael Parks, Director, 213-743-5324, E-mail: mparks@usc.edu. *Application contact:* Allyson Hill, Assistant Dean, Admissions, 213-821-0770, Fax: 213-740-1933, E-mail: ascadm@usc.edu.

See Display on page 675 and Close-Up on page 727.

The University of Tennessee, Graduate School, College of Communication and Information, Knoxville, TN 37996. Offers advertising (MS, PhD); broadcasting (MS, PhD); communications (MS, PhD); information sciences (MS, PhD); journalism (MS, PhD); public relations (MS, PhD); speech communication (MS, PhD). *Accreditation:* ACEJMC (one or more programs are accredited at the [master's] level). Part-time and evening/weekend programs available. Post-baccalaureate distance learning degree programs offered (no on-campus study). *Degree requirements:* For master's, thesis or alternative; for doctorate, thesis/dissertation. *Entrance requirements:* For master's and doctorate, GRE General Test, minimum GPA of 2.7. Additional exam requirements/recommendations for international students: Required—TOEFL. Electronic applications accepted. *Expenses:* Tuition, state resident: full-time $7440; part-time $414 per credit hour. Tuition, nonresident: full-time $22,478; part-time $1250 per credit hour. Required fees: $922; $43 per credit hour. Tuition and fees vary according to program.

The University of Texas at Austin, Graduate School, College of Communication, School of Journalism, Austin, TX 78712-1111. Offers MA, PhD. Part-time programs available. *Degree requirements:* For master's, thesis; for doctorate, one foreign language, thesis/dissertation. *Entrance requirements:* For master's and doctorate, GRE General Test. Electronic applications accepted. *Faculty research:* Politics of race, gender, and sexuality; visual ethics; media law and ethics; national television violence study; agenda setting and public opinion.

The University of Western Ontario, Faculty of Graduate Studies, Faculty of Information and Media Studies, Program in Journalism, London, ON N6A 5B8, Canada. Offers MA. *Degree requirements:* For master's, internship. *Entrance requirements:* For master's, honors degree, minimum B average during previous 2 years of course work. Additional exam requirements/recommendations for international students: Required—TOEFL (minimum score 640 paper-based; 273 computer-based), TWE (minimum score 5). Electronic applications accepted.

University of Wisconsin–Madison, Graduate School, College of Agricultural and Life Sciences, Department of Life Sciences Communication, Madison, WI 53706-1380. Offers life sciences communication (MPS, MS); mass communication (PhD). *Degree requirements:* For doctorate, thesis/dissertation. *Expenses:* Tuition, state resident: full-time $9887; part-time $617.96 per credit. Tuition, nonresident: full-time $24,054; part-time $1503.40 per credit. Required fees: $67.63 per credit. Tuition and fees vary according to reciprocity agreements.

University of Wisconsin–Madison, Graduate School, College of Letters and Science, School of Journalism and Mass Communication, Program in Journalism and Mass Communication, Madison, WI 53706-1380. Offers MA. *Expenses:* Tuition, state resident: full-time $9887; part-time $617.96 per credit. Tuition, nonresident: full-time $24,054; part-time $1503.40 per credit. Required fees: $67.63 per credit. Tuition and fees vary according to reciprocity agreements.

Virginia Commonwealth University, Graduate School, College of Humanities and Sciences, School of Mass Communications, Program in Mass Communications, Richmond, VA 23284-9005. Offers multimedia journalism (MS); strategic public relations (MS). *Students:* 62 applicants, 53% accepted, 26 enrolled. *Degree requirements:* For master's, comprehensive exam, thesis optional. *Entrance requirements:* For master's, GRE General Test. Additional exam requirements/recommendations for international students: Required—TOEFL (minimum score 600 paper-based; 250 computer-based; 100 iBT); Recommended—IELTS (minimum score 6.5). *Application deadline:* For fall admission, 3/15 for domestic students. Applications are processed on a rolling basis. Application fee: $50. Electronic applications accepted. *Expenses:* Tuition, state resident: full-time $4308; part-time $479 per credit hour. Tuition, nonresident: full-time $8942; part-time $994 per credit hour. Required fees: $2000; $85 per credit hour. Tuition and fees vary according to course level, course load, degree level, campus/location and program. *Financial support:* Teaching assistantships, career-related internships or fieldwork, Federal Work-Study, institutionally sponsored loans, and tuition waivers (full and partial) available. Support available to part-time students. Financial award applicants required to submit FAFSA. *Faculty research:* Multimedia journalism, strategic public relations. *Unit head:* Dr. Terry Oggel, Interim Director, School of Mass Communications, 804-828-2660, Fax: 804-828-9175, E-mail: masscomm@vcu.edu. *Application contact:* June O. Nicholson, Director of Graduate Studies, 804-827-0251, Fax: 804-828-9175, E-mail: jonichol@vcu.edu.

West Virginia University, Perley Isaac Reed School of Journalism, Morgantown, WV 26506. Offers digital marketing communications (Graduate Certificate); integrated marketing communications (MS); journalism (MSJ). MS program taught exclusively online. Part-time programs available. Postbaccalaureate distance learning degree programs offered (no on-campus study). *Degree requirements:* For master's, thesis or alternative. *Entrance requirements:* For master's, GRE General Test, minimum GPA of 3.0, writing samples. Additional exam requirements/recommendations for international students: Required—TOEFL. Electronic applications accepted. *Faculty research:* History, law, and women in media; press management; public opinion; advertising effectiveness; international advertising.

Mass Communication

American University, School of Communication, Program in International Media, Washington, DC 20016-8001. Offers MA. Part-time and evening/weekend programs available. *Students:* 13 full-time (11 women), 3 part-time (all women). 56 applicants, 54% accepted, 11 enrolled. *Degree requirements:* For master's, one foreign language, comprehensive exam, thesis or alternative. *Entrance requirements:* For master's, GRE General Test, bachelor's degree with minimum cumulative GPA of 3.3, 2 letters of reference. Additional exam requirements/recommendations for international students: Required—TOEFL (minimum score 600 paper-based; 250 computer-based; 100 iBT), IELTS (minimum score 7). *Application deadline:* For fall admission, 2/1 priority date for domestic students, 4/1 for international students; for spring admission, 11/15 for domestic and international students. Applications are processed on a rolling basis. Application fee: $50. *Financial support:* In 2010–11, 6 research assistantships with partial tuition reimbursements (averaging $8,000 per year) were awarded; career-related internships or fieldwork, Federal Work-Study, scholarships/grants, and unspecified assistantships also available. Financial award application deadline: 2/1; financial award applicants required to submit FAFSA. *Unit head:* Prof. Declan Fahy, Dean, 202-885-6486, Fax: 202-885-2099, E-mail: fahy@american.edu. *Application contact:* Sharmeen Ahsan-Bracciale, Graduate Admissions Office, 202-885-2040, Fax: 202-885-2019, E-mail: sharmeen@american.edu.

American University, School of Communication, Program in Public Communication, Washington, DC 20016-8001. Offers MA. *Accreditation:* ACEJMC. Part-time and evening/

Mass Communication

American University (continued)
weekend programs available. *Faculty:* 11 full-time (6 women), 6 part-time/adjunct (2 women). *Students:* 46 full-time (40 women), 17 part-time (16 women). 153 applicants, 68% accepted, 43 enrolled. In 2010, 61 master's awarded. *Degree requirements:* For master's, comprehensive exam, thesis or alternative. *Entrance requirements:* For master's, GRE General Test. Additional exam requirements/recommendations for international students: Required—TOEFL (minimum score 600 paper-based; 250 computer-based; 100 iBT), IELTS (minimum score 7). *Application deadline:* For fall admission, 2/1 priority date for domestic students, 4/1 priority date for international students. Applications are processed on a rolling basis. Application fee: $50. Electronic applications accepted. *Financial support:* In 2010–11, 10 research assistantships with partial tuition reimbursements (averaging $11,000 per year), 2 teaching assistantships with partial tuition reimbursements (averaging $11,000 per year) were awarded; career-related internships or fieldwork, Federal Work-Study, institutionally sponsored loans, scholarships/grants, tuition waivers (partial), and unspecified assistantships also available. Financial award application deadline: 2/1; financial award applicants required to submit FAFSA. *Faculty research:* Litigation and public relations, cross-cultural and intercultural communication, statistical public relations, African-Americans and women in public communication, international public relations. *Unit head:* Prof. Leonard Steinhorn, Director, Public Communication Division, 202-885-2031, E-mail: lsteinh@american.edu. *Application contact:* Sharmeen Ahsan-Bracciale, Director of Graduate Services, 202-885-2040, Fax: 202-885-2019, E-mail: sharmeen@american.edu.

American University, School of Communication, Weekend Programs in Communication, Washington, DC 20016-8001. Offers interactive journalism (MA); news media studies (MA); producing for film and video (MA); public communication (MA). *Accreditation:* ACEJMC. Part-time and evening/weekend programs available. *Faculty:* 5 part-time/adjunct (2 women). *Students:* 113 part-time (64 women). 105 applicants, 72% accepted, 59 enrolled. In 2010, 15 master's awarded. *Degree requirements:* For master's, comprehensive exam, thesis or alternative. *Entrance requirements:* Additional exam requirements/recommendations for international students: Required—TOEFL (minimum score 600 paper-based; 250 computer-based; 100 iBT). *Application deadline:* For fall admission, 8/1 for domestic students. Applications are processed on a rolling basis. Application fee: $50. Electronic applications accepted. *Financial support:* In 2010–11, 3 fellowships (averaging $3,500 per year) were awarded; institutionally sponsored loans also available. Financial award applicants required to submit FAFSA. *Unit head:* Prof. Rose Ann Robertson, Associate Dean, 202-885-2002, E-mail: rrobert@american.edu. *Application contact:* Sharmeen Ahsan-Bracciale, Director of Graduate Services, 202-885-2040, Fax: 202-885-2019, E-mail: sharmeen@american.edu.

American University, School of International Service, Washington, DC 20016-8071. Offers comparative and regional studies (Certificate); cross-cultural communication (Certificate); development management (MS); ethics, peace, and global affairs (MA); European studies (Certificate); global environmental policy (MA, Certificate); international affairs (MA), including comparative and regional studies, environmental policy, international economic policy, international politics, natural resources and sustainable development, U. S. foreign policy; international communication (MA, Certificate); international development (MA, Certificate); international development management (Certificate); international economic policy (Certificate); international economic relations (Certificate); international media (MA); international peace and conflict resolution (MA, Certificate); international relations (PhD); international service (MIS); peace building (Certificate); the Americas (Certificate); United States foreign policy (Certificate); JD/MA. Part-time and evening/weekend programs available. *Faculty:* 91 full-time (35 women), 48 part-time/adjunct (16 women). *Students:* 591 full-time (383 women), 367 part-time (229 women); includes 164 minority (51 Black or African American, non-Hispanic/Latino; 4 American Indian or Alaska Native, non-Hispanic/Latino; 42 Asian, non-Hispanic/Latino; 63 Hispanic/Latino; 4 Two or more races, non-Hispanic/Latino), 94 international. Average age 27. 2,115 applicants, 59% accepted, 360 enrolled. In 2010, 370 master's, 7 doctorates awarded. Terminal master's awarded for partial completion of doctoral program. *Degree requirements:* For master's, one foreign language, comprehensive exam, thesis or alternative; for doctorate, one foreign language, comprehensive exam, thesis/dissertation, research practicum; for Certificate, minimum 15 credit hours related course work. *Entrance requirements:* For master's, GRE, 24 credits of course work in related social sciences, minimum GPA of 3.5, 2 letters of recommendation, bachelor's degree, resume; for doctorate, GRE, 2 letters of recommendation, 24 credits in related social sciences; for Certificate, bachelor's degree. Additional exam requirements/recommendations for international students: Required—TOEFL (minimum score 600 paper-based; 250 computer-based; 100 iBT). *Application deadline:* For fall admission, 1/15 priority date for domestic students; for spring admission, 10/1 priority date for domestic students. Applications are processed on a rolling basis. Application fee: $50. *Financial support:* Career-related internships or fieldwork, Federal Work-Study, and institutionally sponsored loans available. Financial award application deadline: 1/15. *Faculty research:* International intellectual property, international environmental issues, international law and legal order, international telecommunications/technology, international sustainable development. *Unit head:* Dr. Louis W. Goodman, Dean, 202-885-1600, Fax: 202-885-2494. *Application contact:* Yasmin Quianzon, Director of Graduate Admissions and Financial Aid, 202-885-2496, Fax: 202-885-1109.

The American University in Cairo, School of Global Affairs and Public Policy, Department of Journalism and Mass Communication, Cairo, Egypt. Offers journalism and mass communication (MA); television and digital journalism (MA). Part-time programs available. *Degree requirements:* For master's, thesis (for some programs). *Entrance requirements:* For master's, English entrance exam, GMAT. Electronic applications accepted. *Faculty research:* Mass media and national development/censorship, intercultural photo communication, comparative journalism/television.

Arizona State University, Walter Cronkite School of Journalism and Mass Communication, Phoenix, AZ 85004. Offers journalism and mass communication (PhD); mass communication (MMC). *Accreditation:* ACEJMC. *Faculty:* 30 full-time (11 women), 1 part-time/adjunct (0 women). *Students:* 47 full-time (33 women), 1 (woman) part-time; includes 6 minority (2 Black or African American, non-Hispanic/Latino; 1 Native Hawaiian or other Pacific Islander, non-Hispanic/Latino; 3 Two or more races, non-Hispanic/Latino), 3 international. Average age 28. 170 applicants, 48% accepted, 28 enrolled. In 2010, 28 degrees awarded. Terminal master's awarded for partial completion of doctoral program. *Degree requirements:* For master's, 9-hour professional capstone experience; interactive Program of Study (iPOS) submitted before completing 50 percent of required credit hours; for doctorate, comprehensive exam, thesis/dissertation, interactive Program of Study (iPOS) submitted before completing 50 percent of required credit hours. *Entrance requirements:* For master's and doctorate, GRE, minimum GPA of 3.0 or equivalent in last 2 years of work leading to bachelor's degree. Additional exam requirements/recommendations for international students: Required—TOEFL, IELTS, or Pearson Test of English. *Application deadline:* For fall admission, 7/1 for domestic and international students; for spring admission, 12/1 for domestic and international students. Applications are processed on a rolling basis. Application fee: $70 ($90 for international students). Electronic applications accepted. *Expenses:* Contact institution. *Financial support:* In 2010–11, 17 teaching assistantships with full and partial tuition reimbursements (averaging $10,968 per year) were awarded; fellowships with full tuition reimbursements, research assistantships with full and partial tuition reimbursements, career-related internships or fieldwork, Federal Work-Study, institutionally sponsored loans, scholarships/grants, and tuition waivers (full and partial) also available. Financial award application deadline: 3/1; financial award applicants required to submit FAFSA. Total annual research expenditures: $3 million. *Unit head:* Christopher Callahan, Dean, 602-496-5012, Fax: 602-496-7041, E-mail: christopher.callahan@asu.edu. *Application contact:* Graduate Admissions, 480-965-6113.

Auburn University, Graduate School, College of Liberal Arts, Department of Communication and Journalism, Auburn University, AL 36849. Offers communication (MA); mass communications (MA). Part-time programs available. *Faculty:* 24 full-time (13 women), 10 part-time/adjunct (5 women). *Students:* 21 full-time (15 women), 6 part-time (4 women); includes 3 Black or African American, non-Hispanic/Latino; 1 Hispanic/Latino, 1 international. Average age 26. 26 applicants, 65% accepted, 13 enrolled. In 2010, 14 master's awarded. *Degree requirements:* For master's, thesis (for some programs). *Entrance requirements:* For master's, GRE General Test. *Application deadline:* For fall admission, 7/7 for domestic students; for spring admission, 11/24 for domestic students. Applications are processed on a rolling basis. Application fee: $50 ($60 for international students). Electronic applications accepted. *Expenses:* Tuition, state resident: full-time $7002. Tuition, nonresident: full-time $21,898. International tuition: $22,116 full-time. Required fees: $892. Tuition and fees vary according to course load and program. *Financial support:* Teaching assistantships, Federal Work-Study available. Support available to part-time students. Financial award application deadline: 3/15; financial award applicants required to submit FAFSA. *Unit head:* Dr. Mary Helen Brown, Acting Chair, 334-844-2727. *Application contact:* Dr. George Flowers, Dean of the Graduate School, 334-844-2125.

Boston University, College of Communication, Department of Mass Communication, Advertising, and Public Relations, Boston, MA 02215. Offers advertising (MS); communication research (MS); communication studies (MS); public relations (MS); JD/MS. Part-time programs available. *Faculty:* 21 full-time, 28 part-time/adjunct. *Students:* 91 full-time (75 women), 44 part-time (29 women); includes 13 minority (3 Black or African American, non-Hispanic/Latino; 4 Asian, non-Hispanic/Latino; 6 Hispanic/Latino), 23 international. Average age 25. In 2010, 18 master's awarded. *Degree requirements:* For master's, comprehensive exam (for some programs), thesis (for some programs). *Entrance requirements:* For master's, GRE General Test, samples of written work. Additional exam requirements/recommendations for international students: Required—TOEFL (minimum score 600 paper-based; 250 computer-based; 100 iBT). *Application deadline:* For fall admission, 2/1 for domestic and international students. Application fee: $70. Electronic applications accepted. *Expenses:* Tuition: Full-time $39,314; part-time $1228 per credit. Required fees: $40 per semester. *Financial support:* Research assistantships, teaching assistantships with partial tuition reimbursements, career-related internships or fieldwork, Federal Work-Study, institutionally sponsored loans, scholarships/grants, and unspecified assistantships available. Support available to part-time students. Financial award application deadline: 2/1; financial award applicants required to submit FAFSA. *Unit head:* T. Barton Carter, Chairman, 617-353-3482, E-mail: comlaw@bu.edu. *Application contact:* Jennifer Healey, Administrator of Graduate Services, 617-353-3481, Fax: 617-358-0399, E-mail: comgrad@bu.edu.

Brigham Young University, Graduate Studies, College of Fine Arts and Communications, Department of Communications, Provo, UT 84602. Offers mass communications (MA). *Faculty:* 19 full-time (3 women). *Students:* 17 full-time (13 women), 22 part-time (10 women); includes 2 minority (1 Black or African American, non-Hispanic/Latino; 1 Hispanic/Latino). Average age 30. 25 applicants, 36% accepted, 8 enrolled. In 2010, 8 master's awarded. *Degree requirements:* For master's, comprehensive exam, thesis. *Entrance requirements:* For master's, GRE, minimum GPA of 3.0 in last 60 hours of course work. Additional exam requirements/recommendations for international students: Required—TOEFL (minimum score 580 paper-based; 237 computer-based; 85 iBT). *Application deadline:* For fall admission, 2/28 for domestic and international students. Application fee: $50. Electronic applications accepted. *Expenses:* Tuition: Full-time $5580; part-time $310 per credit hour. Tuition and fees vary according to program and student's religious affiliation. *Financial support:* In 2010–11, 24 students received support, including 15 research assistantships with full and partial tuition reimbursements available (averaging $4,877 per year), 7 teaching assistantships with full and partial tuition reimbursements available (averaging $6,103 per year); career-related internships or fieldwork, institutionally sponsored loans, scholarships/grants, unspecified assistantships, and supplementary awards also available. Financial award application deadline: 4/15; financial award applicants required to submit FAFSA. *Faculty research:* Ethics, international, magazine, newspaper, media effects. *Unit head:* Dr. Bradley L. Rawlins, Chair, 801-422-2997, Fax: 801-422-0160, E-mail: comms_secretary@byu.edu. *Application contact:* Dr. Steven R. Thomsen, Graduate Coordinator, 801-422-2078, Fax: 801-422-0160, E-mail: steven_thomsen@byu.edu.

California State University, Fresno, Division of Graduate Studies, College of Arts and Humanities, Department of Mass Communication and Journalism, Fresno, CA 93740-8027. Offers MA. Part-time and evening/weekend programs available. *Degree requirements:* For master's, thesis. *Entrance requirements:* For master's, GRE General Test, minimum GPA of 3.0. Additional exam requirements/recommendations for international students: Required—TOEFL. Electronic applications accepted.

California State University, Northridge, Graduate Studies, College of Arts, Media, and Communication, Department of Journalism, Northridge, CA 91330. Offers mass communication (MA). Part-time and evening/weekend programs available. *Degree requirements:* For master's, thesis. *Entrance requirements:* For master's, GRE General Test. Additional exam requirements/recommendations for international students: Required—TOEFL.

Central Michigan University, College of Graduate Studies, College of Communication and Fine Arts, Department of Communication and Dramatic Arts, Mount Pleasant, MI 48859. Offers interpersonal and public communication (MA), including communication and dramatic arts. Part-time programs available. *Faculty:* 12 full-time (6 women). *Students:* 23 full-time (13 women), 5 part-time (2 women); includes 1 American Indian or Alaska Native, non-Hispanic/Latino; 2 Hispanic/Latino, 1 international. Average age 28. *Degree requirements:* For master's, thesis. *Application deadline:* For fall admission, 3/15 for domestic and international students; for winter admission, 10/15 for domestic and international students; for spring admission, 10/15 for domestic and international students. Applications are processed on a rolling basis. Application fee: $35 ($45 for international students). Electronic applications accepted. *Expenses:* Tuition, state resident: full-time $8208; part-time $456 per credit hour. Tuition, nonresident: full-time $13,788; part-time $766 per credit hour. One-time fee: $25. *Financial support:* Fellowships with tuition reimbursements, teaching assistantships with tuition reimbursements, career-related internships or fieldwork, Federal Work-Study, unspecified assistantships, and out-of-state merit awards, non-resident graduate awards available. *Faculty research:* Communication theory, interpersonal/nonverbal communication, organizational communication, family and interpersonal communication, political communication. *Unit head:* Dr. William O. Dailey, Chairperson, 989-774-3177, Fax: 989-774-2498, E-mail: daile1wo@cmich.edu. *Application contact:* Dr. Lesley Withers, Graduate Program Coordinator, 989-774-6673, Fax: 989-774-2498, E-mail: withe1la@cmich.edu.

The College of Saint Rose, Graduate Studies, School of Arts and Humanities, Department of Public Communications, Albany, NY 12203-1419. Offers MA. Part-time and evening/weekend programs available. *Degree requirements:* For master's, final project or thesis. *Entrance requirements:* For master's, minimum undergraduate GPA of 3.0, 2 writing samples. Additional exam requirements/recommendations for international students: Required—TOEFL (minimum score 550 paper-based; 213 computer-based). Electronic applications accepted.

Colorado State University, Graduate School, College of Liberal Arts, Department of Journalism and Technical Communication, Fort Collins, CO 80523-1785. Offers public communication and technology (MS, PhD); technical communication (MS). Part-time programs available. *Faculty:* 17 full-time (7 women), 1 (woman) part-time/adjunct. *Students:* 31 full-time (23 women), 34 part-time (23 women); includes 6 minority (4 Hispanic/Latino; 2 Two or more races, non-Hispanic/Latino), 2 international. Average age 33. 56 applicants, 50% accepted, 21 enrolled. In 2010, 14 master's awarded. *Degree requirements:* For master's, variable foreign language requirement, comprehensive exam (for some programs), thesis (for some programs); for doctorate, variable foreign language requirement, comprehensive exam (for some programs), thesis/dissertation (for some programs). *Entrance requirements:* For master's, GRE General Test, samples of written work, letters of recommendation, resume or curriculum vitae, 3 writing/communication projects; for doctorate, GRE General Test, master's degree, minimum GPA of 3.0, scholarly/professional work, letters of recommendation, statement of career plans, resume. Additional exam requirements/recommendations for international students: Required—TOEFL (minimum score 550 paper-based; 213 computer-based; 80 iBT). *Application deadline:* For fall admission, 2/15 priority date for domestic students, 12/15 priority date for international students; for spring admission, 6/15 priority date for domestic students. Applications are processed on a rolling basis. Application fee: $50. Electronic applications accepted. *Expenses:* Tuition, state resident: full-time $7434; part-time $413 per credit. Tuition, nonresident: full-time $19,022; part-time $1057 per credit. Required fees: $1729; $88 per credit. *Financial support:* In 2010–11, 35 students received support, including 2 research assistantships with full and partial tuition reimbursements available (averaging $9,269 per year), 33 teaching assistantships with partial tuition reimbursements available (averaging $10,636 per year); fellowships with partial tuition reimbursements available, career-related internships or fieldwork, Federal Work-Study, institutionally sponsored loans, scholarships/grants, traineeships, and unspecified assistantships also available. Support available to part-time students. Financial award application deadline: 3/1; financial award applicants required to submit FAFSA. *Faculty research:* Technical/science communication, public relations, health/risk communication, Web/new media technologies, environmental communication. Total annual research expenditures: $250,177. *Unit head:* Dr. Greg Luft, Chair, 970-491-1979, Fax: 970-491-2908, E-mail: greg.luft@colostate.edu. *Application contact:* Dr. Craig Trumbo, Graduate Program Coordinator, 970-491-2077, Fax: 970-491-2908, E-mail: craig.trumbo@colostate.edu.

Drexel University, College of Arts and Sciences, Department of Culture and Communication, Program in Communication, Philadelphia, PA 19104-2875. Offers public communication (MS); science communication (MS); technical communication (MS). Part-time and evening/weekend programs available. *Degree requirements:* For master's, internship, professional portfolio. *Entrance requirements:* For master's, GRE or minimum GPA of 3.0. Additional exam requirements/recommendations for international students: Required—TOEFL. Electronic applications accepted.

Florida International University, School of Journalism and Mass Communication, Miami, FL 33199. Offers mass communication (MS). *Accreditation:* ACEJMC. Part-time and evening/weekend programs available. *Faculty:* 21 full-time (13 women), 9 part-time/adjunct (7 women). *Students:* 94 full-time (71 women), 88 part-time (69 women); includes 26 Black or African American, non-Hispanic/Latino; 1 American Indian or Alaska Native, non-Hispanic/Latino; 6 Asian, non-Hispanic/Latino; 100 Hispanic/Latino, 21 international. Average age 27. 197 applicants, 30% accepted, 56 enrolled. In 2010, 57 master's awarded. *Degree requirements:* For master's, thesis optional. *Entrance requirements:* For master's, 2 letters of recommendation; minimum GPA of 3.0 during last 60 hours of upper-level work; resume. Additional exam requirements/recommendations for international students: Required—TOEFL (minimum score 550 paper-based; 80 iBT). *Application deadline:* For fall admission, 6/1 for domestic students, 4/1 for international students; for spring admission, 10/1 for domestic students, 9/1 for international students. Applications are processed on a rolling basis. Application fee: $30. Electronic applications accepted. *Financial support:* Institutionally sponsored loans and scholarships/grants available. Financial award application deadline: 3/1; financial award applicants required to submit FAFSA. *Faculty research:* Post-Hurricane Andrew population studies, Central American journalism, employment discrimination. *Unit head:* Dr. Lillian Kopenhaver, Dean, 305-919-5674, Fax: 305-919-5203, E-mail: kopenha@fiu.edu. *Application contact:* Nanett Rojas, Assistant Director of Graduate Admissions, 305-348-7442, Fax: 305-348-7441, E-mail: gradadm@fiu.edu.

Florida State University, The Graduate School, College of Communication and Information, School of Communication, Tallahassee, FL 32306. Offers corporate and public communication (MS); integrated marketing communication (MA, MS); mass communication (PhD); media and communication studies (MA, MS); speech communication (PhD). Part-time programs available. *Faculty:* 24 full-time (9 women), 6 part-time/adjunct (1 woman). *Students:* 147 full-time (94 women), 63 part-time (38 women); includes 92 minority (26 Black or African American, non-Hispanic/Latino; 2 American Indian or Alaska Native, non-Hispanic/Latino; 45 Asian, non-Hispanic/Latino; 16 Hispanic/Latino; 1 Native Hawaiian or other Pacific Islander, non-Hispanic/Latino; 2 Two or more races, non-Hispanic/Latino). Average age 24. 268 applicants, 57% accepted, 79 enrolled. In 2010, 103 master's, 4 doctorates awarded. *Degree requirements:* For master's, thesis (for some programs); for doctorate, comprehensive exam, thesis/dissertation. *Entrance requirements:* For master's, GRE General Test, minimum GPA of 3.0; for doctorate, GRE General Test, minimum GPA of 3.3 in graduate course work. Additional exam requirements/recommendations for international students: Required—TOEFL (minimum score 600 paper-based; 250 computer-based; 100 iBT). *Application deadline:* For fall admission, 7/1 priority date for domestic students, 5/1 priority date for international students; for spring admission, 11/1 priority date for domestic and international students. Applications are processed on a rolling basis. Application fee: $30. Electronic applications accepted. *Expenses:* Tuition, state resident: full-time $8238.24. *Financial support:* In 2010–11, 52 students received support, including 1 fellowship with full tuition reimbursement available, 8 research assistantships with full tuition reimbursements available (averaging $14,000 per year), 40 teaching assistantships with full tuition reimbursements available (averaging $5,000 per year); career-related internships or fieldwork, Federal Work-Study, institutionally sponsored loans, scholarships/grants, tuition waivers (partial), and unspecified assistantships also available. Support available to part-time students. Financial award application deadline: 2/1; financial award applicants required to submit FAFSA. *Faculty research:* Communication technology and policy, marketing communication, communication content and effect, new communication/information technologies. Total annual research expenditures: $400,000. *Unit head:* Dr. Stephen D. McDowell, Director, 850-644-2276, Fax: 850-644-8642, E-mail: steve.mcdowell@cci.fsu.edu. *Application contact:* Natashia Hinson-Turner, Graduate Coordinator, 850-644-8746, Fax: 850-644-8642, E-mail: natashia.turner@cci.fsu.edu.

Fordham University, Graduate School of Arts and Sciences, Department of Communication and Media Studies, New York, NY 10458. Offers public communications (MA). Part-time and evening/weekend programs available. *Faculty:* 11 full-time (3 women). *Students:* 16 full-time (15 women), 22 part-time (13 women); includes 6 minority (3 Black or African American, non-Hispanic/Latino; 1 Asian, non-Hispanic/Latino; 2 Hispanic/Latino), 9 international. Average age 26. 77 applicants, 44% accepted, 14 enrolled. In 2010, 24 master's awarded. *Degree requirements:* For master's, thesis, internship. *Entrance requirements:* For master's, GRE General Test. Additional exam requirements/recommendations for international students: Required—TOEFL (minimum score 600 paper-based; 250 computer-based). *Application deadline:* For fall admission, 1/4 priority date for domestic students; for spring admission, 11/1 for domestic students. Application fee: $70. Electronic applications accepted. *Financial support:* In 2010–11, 3 students received support, including 3 research assistantships with tuition reimbursements available (averaging $19,000 per year); fellowships, career-related internships or fieldwork, Federal Work-Study, institutionally sponsored loans, scholarships/grants, tuition waivers (full and partial), and unspecified assistantships also available. Financial award application deadline: 1/4. Total annual research expenditures: $80,000. *Unit head:* Dr. Paul Levinson, Chair, 718-817-4860, Fax: 718-817-4868, E-mail: levinson@fordham.edu. *Application contact:* Charlene Dundie, Director of Graduate Admissions, 718-817-4420, Fax: 718-817-3566, E-mail: dundie@fordham.edu.

The George Washington University, Columbian College of Arts and Sciences, School of Media and Public Affairs, Washington, DC 20052. Offers MA. *Faculty:* 24 full-time (7 women), 16 part-time/adjunct (5 women). *Students:* 22 full-time (14 women), 17 part-time (15 women); includes 1 Black or African American, non-Hispanic/Latino; 3 Asian, non-Hispanic/Latino; 1 Hispanic/Latino, 5 international. Average age 26. 119 applicants, 55% accepted, 21 enrolled. In 2010, 11 master's awarded. *Degree requirements:* For master's, thesis optional. *Entrance requirements:* For master's, GRE General Test. Additional exam requirements/recommendations for international students: Required—TOEFL (minimum score 550 paper-based; 213 computer-based; 80 iBT). *Application deadline:* For fall admission, 4/1 priority date for domestic students, 1/15 priority date for international students; for spring admission, 10/1 priority date for domestic students, 9/1 priority date for international students. Applications are processed on a rolling basis. Application fee: $75. Electronic applications accepted. *Financial support:* In 2010–11, fellowships with tuition reimbursements (averaging $10,000 per year), teaching assistantships with tuition reimbursements (averaging $5,000 per year) were awarded. Financial award application deadline: 1/15. *Unit head:* Lee W. Huebner, Director, 202-994-6227, E-mail:

huebner@gwu.edu. *Application contact:* Information Contact, 202-994-6227, Fax: 202-994-5806, E-mail: smpa@gwu.edu.

Georgia State University, College of Arts and Sciences, Department of Communication, Atlanta, GA 30302-3083. Offers film/video/digital imaging (MA); human communication and social influence (MA); mass communication (MA); moving image studies (PhD); public communication (PhD). Part-time programs available. *Degree requirements:* For master's, one foreign language, thesis or alternative; for doctorate, comprehensive exam, thesis/dissertation. *Entrance requirements:* For master's and doctorate, GRE General Test. Additional exam requirements/recommendations for international students: Required—TOEFL (minimum score 80 computer-based). Electronic applications accepted. *Faculty research:* Critical/cultural studies, rhetoric studies, film/media studies, mass communications/journalism, audience studies.

Grambling State University, School of Graduate Studies and Research, College of Professional Studies, Program in Mass Communication, Grambling, LA 71245. Offers MA. *Accreditation:* ACEJMC. Part-time programs available. *Degree requirements:* For master's, comprehensive exam, thesis optional. *Entrance requirements:* For master's, GRE, minimum GPA of 2.5 on last degree. Additional exam requirements/recommendations for international students: Required—TOEFL (minimum score 500 paper-based; 173 computer-based; 61 iBT). Electronic applications accepted.

Howard University, School of Communications, Division of Mass Communication and Media Studies, Washington, DC 20059-0002. Offers mass communication (MA, PhD); media studies (MA, PhD). Part-time and evening/weekend programs available. *Degree requirements:* For master's, comprehensive exam (for some programs), thesis optional; for doctorate, one foreign language, comprehensive exam, thesis/dissertation. *Entrance requirements:* For master's, GRE, minimum GPA of 3.0; for doctorate, GRE, minimum graduate GPA of 3.5. Additional exam requirements/recommendations for international students: Required—TOEFL. Electronic applications accepted. *Faculty research:* Advertising, public relations, journalism new media.

Indiana University Bloomington, School of Journalism, Bloomington, IN 47405-7000. Offers journalism (MA, MAT); mass communication (PhD); MA/JD; MA/MA. *Faculty:* 11 full-time (5 women). *Students:* 62 full-time (37 women), 12 part-time (7 women); includes 2 Black or African American, non-Hispanic/Latino; 1 Asian, non-Hispanic/Latino; 1 Hispanic/Latino; 2 Two or more races, non-Hispanic/Latino, 33 international. Average age 30. 119 applicants, 57% accepted, 26 enrolled. In 2010, 24 master's, 4 doctorates awarded. Terminal master's awarded for partial completion of doctoral program. *Degree requirements:* For master's, thesis (for some programs); for doctorate, thesis/dissertation. *Entrance requirements:* For master's and doctorate, GRE General Test. Additional exam requirements/recommendations for international students: Required—TOEFL. *Application deadline:* For fall admission, 1/15 priority date for domestic students; for spring admission, 9/1 priority date for domestic students. Applications are processed on a rolling basis. Application fee: $55 ($65 for international students). *Financial support:* Fellowships, research assistantships with full tuition reimbursements, teaching assistantships with partial tuition reimbursements, career-related internships or fieldwork, Federal Work-Study, institutionally sponsored loans, and tuition waivers (full) available. Financial award application deadline: 1/15. *Faculty research:* Political communication, international communication, communication history, communication law, visual communication. Total annual research expenditures: $165,185. *Unit head:* Bradley Hamm, Dean, 812-855-9247. *Application contact:* Amy Reynolds, Associate Dean of Graduate Studies, 812-855-8111.

Indiana University Bloomington, University Graduate School, College of Arts and Sciences, Department of Telecommunications, Program in Mass Communications, Bloomington, IN 47405-7000. Offers PhD. *Faculty:* 18 full-time (5 women). *Students:* 26 full-time (16 women); includes 1 minority (Asian, non-Hispanic/Latino), 13 international. Average age 32. 23 applicants, 35% accepted, 3 enrolled. In 2010, 1 doctorate awarded. *Degree requirements:* For doctorate, comprehensive exam, thesis/dissertation. *Entrance requirements:* For doctorate, GRE General Test, minimum graduate GPA of 3.5, 3 letters of recommendation. Additional exam requirements/recommendations for international students: Required—TOEFL (minimum score 600 paper-based; 250 computer-based; 100 iBT). *Application deadline:* For fall admission, 1/15 priority date for domestic students, 12/15 priority date for international students. Applications are processed on a rolling basis. Application fee: $55 ($65 for international students). Electronic applications accepted. *Financial support:* In 2010–11, 1 fellowship with full tuition reimbursement (averaging $18,000 per year), 1 research assistantship with full tuition reimbursement (averaging $15,000 per year), 15 teaching assistantships with full tuition reimbursements (averaging $11,860 per year) were awarded; scholarships/grants and health care benefits also available. Financial award application deadline: 1/15. *Faculty research:* Media management, media psychology, telecommunications law and policy, media processes and effects, media design and production (e.g., video games, virtual worlds, documentary, multi-media art). Total annual research expenditures: $152,000. *Unit head:* Tamera Theodore, Graduate Program Administrator, 812-855-2017, Fax: 812-855-7955, E-mail: ttheodor@indiana.edu. *Application contact:* Tamera Theodore, Graduate Program Administrator, 812-855-2017, Fax: 812-855-7955, E-mail: ttheodor@indiana.edu.

Iona College, School of Arts and Science, Department of Mass Communication, New Rochelle, NY 10801-1890. Offers journalism (MS); public relations (MA). *Accreditation:* ACEJMC (one or more programs are accredited). Part-time and evening/weekend programs available. *Faculty:* 6 full-time (2 women), 3 part-time/adjunct (2 women). *Students:* 6 full-time (5 women), 44 part-time (38 women); includes 11 minority (6 Black or African American, non-Hispanic/Latino; 1 Asian, non-Hispanic/Latino; 4 Hispanic/Latino), 3 international. Average age 27. 34 applicants, 59% accepted, 11 enrolled. In 2010, 16 master's awarded. *Degree requirements:* For master's, comprehensive exam or thesis. *Entrance requirements:* For master's, GRE General Test, minimum GPA of 3.0. Additional exam requirements/recommendations for international students: Required—TOEFL (minimum score 550 paper-based; 213 computer-based). *Application deadline:* Applications are processed on a rolling basis. Application fee: $50. Electronic applications accepted. *Expenses:* Contact institution. *Financial support:* Career-related internships or fieldwork, tuition waivers (partial), and unspecified assistantships available. Support available to part-time students. Financial award application deadline: 4/15; financial award applicants required to submit FAFSA. *Faculty research:* Media ecology, new media, corporate communication, media images, organizational learning in public relations. *Unit head:* Br. Raymond Smith, Chair, 914-633-2354, E-mail: rrsmith@iona.edu. *Application contact:* Veronica Jarek-Prinz, Director of Graduate Admissions, 914-633-2420, Fax: 914-633-2277, E-mail: vjarekprinz@iona.edu.

Iowa State University of Science and Technology, Graduate College, College of Liberal Arts and Sciences, Greenlee School of Journalism and Mass Communication, Ames, IA 50011. Offers MS. *Faculty:* 18 full-time (6 women). *Students:* 25 full-time (19 women), 20 part-time (12 women); includes 4 Black or African American, non-Hispanic/Latino; 2 Hispanic/Latino, 27 international. 52 applicants, 54% accepted, 10 enrolled. In 2010, 11 master's awarded. *Degree requirements:* For master's, thesis or alternative. *Entrance requirements:* For master's, GRE General Test. Additional exam requirements/recommendations for international students: Required—TOEFL (minimum score 570 paper-based; 88 iBT), IELTS (minimum score 6.5). *Application deadline:* For fall admission, 4/1 priority date for international students; for spring admission, 11/1 priority date for international students. Applications are processed on a rolling basis. Application fee: $40 ($90 for international students). Electronic applications accepted. *Financial support:* In 2010–11, 11 research assistantships with full and partial tuition reimbursements (averaging $5,911 per year) were awarded; fellowships, teaching assistantships with partial tuition reimbursements, scholarships/grants, health care benefits, and unspecified assistantships also available. *Unit head:* Dr. Michael Bugeja, Chair, 515-294-0481, Fax: 515-294-5108, E-mail: greenlee@iastate.edu. *Application contact:* Dr. Eric Abbott, Director of Graduate Education, 515-294-0492, E-mail: masscomm@iastate.edu.

Jackson State University, Graduate School, College of Liberal Arts, Department of Mass Communications, Jackson, MS 39217. Offers MS. Part-time and evening/weekend programs available. *Faculty:* 3 full-time (2 women). *Students:* 7 full-time (4 women), 26 part-time (16

Mass Communication

Jackson State University (continued)
women); includes 31 Black or African American, non-Hispanic/Latino. Average age 33. In 2010, 2 master's awarded. *Degree requirements:* For master's, comprehensive exam, thesis optional. *Entrance requirements:* For master's, GRE General Test. Additional exam requirements/recommendations for international students: Required—TOEFL (minimum score 520 paper-based; 195 computer-based; 67 iBT). *Application deadline:* For fall admission, 3/1 priority date for domestic students; for spring admission, 10/1 for domestic students. Applications are processed on a rolling basis. Application fee: $25. *Expenses:* Tuition, state resident: full-time $5050; part-time $281 per credit hour. Tuition, nonresident: full-time $12,380; part-time $689 per credit hour. *Financial support:* Career-related internships or fieldwork, Federal Work-Study, scholarships/grants, and unspecified assistantships available. Support available to part-time students. Financial award application deadline: 3/1; financial award applicants required to submit FAFSA. *Unit head:* Dr. Olorundare E. Aworuwa, Chair, 601-968-1352, Fax: 601-974-5800, E-mail: olorundare.aworuwa@jsums.edu. *Application contact:* Sharlene Wilson, Director of Graduate Admissions, 601-979-2455, Fax: 601-979-4325, E-mail: sharlene.f.wilson@jsums.edu.

Kansas State University, Graduate School, College of Arts and Sciences, A. Q. Miller School of Journalism and Mass Communications, Manhattan, KS 66506. Offers mass communications (MS). Part-time programs available. *Degree requirements:* For master's, thesis or alternative. *Entrance requirements:* For master's, GRE General Test, minimum GPA of 3.0. Additional exam requirements/recommendations for international students: Required—TOEFL (minimum score 600 paper-based). Electronic applications accepted. *Faculty research:* Synergistic effects of integrated marketing communications, risk and hazard communication, leadership in media coverage, political communication, advertising psycholinguistic effects.

Kent State University, College of Communication and Information, School of Journalism and Mass Communication, Kent, OH 44242-0001. Offers MA. Part-time programs available. *Degree requirements:* For master's, thesis optional. *Entrance requirements:* For master's, GRE General Test, minimum GPA of 3.0. Additional exam requirements/recommendations for international students: Recommended—TOEFL (minimum score 600 paper-based; 250 computer-based). Electronic applications accepted. *Expenses:* Tuition, state resident: full-time $7866; part-time $437 per credit hour. Tuition, nonresident: full-time $14,022; part-time $779 per credit hour. *Faculty research:* Electronic tablet newspapers, accuracy and ethics in broadcast news, internet credibility, First Amendment, HDTV.

Louisiana State University and Agricultural and Mechanical College, Graduate School, Manship School of Mass Communication, Baton Rouge, LA 70803. Offers MMC, PhD. *Accreditation:* ACEJMC. Part-time programs available. Postbaccalaureate distance learning degree programs offered (minimal on-campus study). *Faculty:* 26 full-time (14 women). *Students:* 53 full-time (32 women), 17 part-time (11 women); includes 10 Black or African American, non-Hispanic/Latino; 2 American Indian or Alaska Native, non-Hispanic/Latino; 2 Hispanic/Latino; 2 Two or more races, non-Hispanic/Latino, 4 international. Average age 30. 77 applicants, 40% accepted, 14 enrolled. In 2010, 20 master's, 1 doctorate awarded. *Degree requirements:* For master's, thesis; for doctorate, thesis/dissertation. *Entrance requirements:* For master's, GRE General Test, minimum GPA of 3.0. Additional exam requirements/recommendations for international students: Required—TOEFL (minimum score 550 paper-based; 213 computer-based; 79 iBT) or IELTS (minimum score 6.5). *Application deadline:* For fall admission, 1/25 priority date for domestic students, 5/15 for international students; for spring admission, 10/15 for international students. Applications are processed on a rolling basis. Application fee: $50 ($70 for international students). Electronic applications accepted. *Financial support:* In 2010–11, 57 students received support, including 2 fellowships (averaging $23,089 per year), 29 research assistantships with full and partial tuition reimbursements available (averaging $16,224 per year), 10 teaching assistantships with full and partial tuition reimbursements available (averaging $18,180 per year); career-related internships or fieldwork, Federal Work-Study, institutionally sponsored loans, scholarships/grants, health care benefits, tuition waivers (full and partial), and unspecified assistantships also available. Support available to part-time students. Financial award application deadline: 3/1; financial award applicants required to submit FAFSA. *Faculty research:* Media effects, political communication, new media technologies, persuasive communication, journalism processes and practice. Total annual research expenditures: $14,696. *Unit head:* Dr. John Maxwell Hamilton, Dean, 225-578-2002, Fax: 225-578-2125, E-mail: jhamilt@lsu.edu. *Application contact:* Dr. Amy L. Reynolds, Associate Dean of Graduate Studies and Research, 225-578-9294, Fax: 225-578-2125, E-mail: areynolds@lsu.edu.

Lynn University, College of Business and Management, Boca Raton, FL 33431-5598. Offers aviation management (MBA); financial valuation and investment management (MBA); hospitality management (MBA); international business (MBA); marketing (MBA); mass communication and media management (MBA); sports and athletics administration (MBA). Part-time and evening/weekend programs available. Postbaccalaureate distance learning degree programs offered. *Degree requirements:* For master's, project. *Entrance requirements:* For master's, GMAT or GRE, minimum undergraduate GPA of 3.0, resume, 2 letters of recommendation. Additional exam requirements/recommendations for international students: Required—TOEFL (minimum score 550 paper-based; 213 computer-based). Electronic applications accepted. *Faculty research:* Labor relations, dynamic balance in leisure-time skills, ethics in athletics, hotel development.

Lynn University, Eugene M. and Christine E. Lynn College of International Communication, Boca Raton, FL 33431-5598. Offers communication and media (MS). Part-time and evening/weekend programs available. *Entrance requirements:* For master's, GRE, resume, 2 letters of recommendation, minimum GPA of 3.0. Additional exam requirements/recommendations for international students: Required—TOEFL (minimum score 550 paper-based; 213 computer-based).

Marquette University, Graduate School, College of Communication, Milwaukee, WI 53201-1881. Offers advertising and public relations (MA); broadcasting and electronic communications (MA); communications studies (MA); digital storytelling (Certificate); health, environment, science and sustainability (MA); journalism (MA); mass communications (MA). *Accreditation:* ACEJMC (one or more programs are accredited). Part-time and evening/weekend programs available. *Faculty:* 33 full-time (18 women), 30 part-time/adjunct (16 women). *Students:* 35 full-time (20 women), 31 part-time (25 women); includes 5 minority (2 Black or African American, non-Hispanic/Latino; 1 Hispanic/Latino; 2 Two or more races, non-Hispanic/Latino), 4 international. Average age 28. 97 applicants, 52% accepted, 21 enrolled. In 2010, 16 master's, 5 other advanced degrees awarded. *Degree requirements:* For master's, comprehensive exam, thesis or alternative. *Entrance requirements:* For master's, GRE, official transcripts from all current and previous colleges/universities except Marquette, three letters of recommendation, statement of academic and professional goals. Additional exam requirements/recommendations for international students: Required—TOEFL (minimum score 530 paper-based; 78 computer-based). *Application deadline:* Applications are processed on a rolling basis. Application fee: $50. Electronic applications accepted. *Expenses:* Tuition: Full-time $16,290; part-time $905 per credit hour. Tuition and fees vary according to program. *Financial support:* In 2010–11, 2 fellowships, 7 research assistantships, 12 teaching assistantships were awarded; career-related internships or fieldwork, Federal Work-Study, institutionally sponsored loans, scholarships/grants, and tuition waivers (full and partial) also available. Support available to part-time students. Financial award application deadline: 2/15. *Faculty research:* Urban journalism, gender and communication, intercultural communication, religious communication. Total annual research expenditures: $3,088. *Unit head:* Dr. Lori Bergen, Dean, 414-288-7133, Fax: 414-288-1578. *Application contact:* Erin Fox, Assistant Director for Recruitment, 414-288-5319, Fax: 414-288-1902, E-mail: erin.fox@marquette.edu.

Marshall University, Academic Affairs Division, School of Journalism and Mass Communications, Huntington, WV 25755. Offers MAJ. *Faculty:* 5 full-time (2 women). *Students:* 24 full-time (18 women), 6 part-time (4 women); includes 1 Black or African American, non-Hispanic/Latino, 6 international. Average age 26. In 2010, 10 master's awarded. *Degree requirements:* For master's, thesis optional. *Entrance requirements:* For master's, GRE General Test. Application fee: $40. *Unit head:* Dr. Corley F. Dennison, Dean, 304-696-2809, E-mail: dennisoc@marshall.edu. *Application contact:* Janet Dooley, Assistant Dean, 304-696-2734, Fax: 304-746-1902, E-mail: dooley@marshall.edu.

Middle Tennessee State University, College of Graduate Studies, College of Mass Communication, Program in Mass Communication, Murfreesboro, TN 37132. Offers MS. Part-time and evening/weekend programs available. Postbaccalaureate distance learning degree programs offered. *Faculty:* 17 full-time (2 women). *Students:* 44 part-time (35 women); includes 4 Black or African American, non-Hispanic/Latino; 1 American Indian or Alaska Native, non-Hispanic/Latino; 5 Asian, non-Hispanic/Latino; 2 Hispanic/Latino; 1 Two or more races, non-Hispanic/Latino. Average age 28. 40 applicants, 78% accepted, 31 enrolled. In 2010, 12 master's awarded. *Degree requirements:* For master's, comprehensive exam, thesis optional. *Entrance requirements:* For master's, GRE. Additional exam requirements/recommendations for international students: Required—TOEFL (minimum score 525 paper-based; 195 computer-based; 71 iBT) or IELTS (minimum score 6). *Application deadline:* For fall admission, 6/1 for domestic and international students. Applications are processed on a rolling basis. Application fee: $25 ($30 for international students). *Expenses:* Tuition, state resident: full-time $4632. Tuition, nonresident: full-time $11,520. *Financial support:* In 2010–11, 8 students received support. Institutionally sponsored loans available. Support available to part-time students. Financial award application deadline: 5/1. *Faculty research:* Ethics of digital media, communication administration, international media issues. *Unit head:* Dr. Clare Bratten, Director, 615-898-2795. *Application contact:* Dr. Michael Allen, Dean and Vice Provost for Research, 615-898-2840, Fax: 615-904-8020, E-mail: mallen@mtsu.edu.

Murray State University, College of Business and Public Affairs, Program in Mass Communications, Murray, KY 42071. Offers MA, MS. Part-time programs available. *Entrance requirements:* Additional exam requirements/recommendations for international students: Required—TOEFL (minimum score 550 paper-based; 213 computer-based). *Faculty research:* AH media on the Internet, visual communication and learning, persuasion, media framing, history of radio and wireless technology.

North Dakota State University, College of Graduate and Interdisciplinary Studies, College of Arts, Humanities and Social Sciences, Department of Communication, Fargo, ND 58108. Offers communication (PhD); mass communication (MA, MS); speech communication (MA, MS). Part-time programs available. Postbaccalaureate distance learning degree programs offered (no on-campus study). *Faculty:* 11 full-time (5 women), 3 part-time/adjunct (1 woman). *Students:* 29 full-time (18 women), 27 part-time (17 women); includes 1 Black or African American, non-Hispanic/Latino; 2 Asian, non-Hispanic/Latino; 1 Hispanic/Latino, 3 international. Average age 27. 62 applicants, 40% accepted, 19 enrolled. In 2010, 15 master's, 8 doctorates awarded. Terminal master's awarded for partial completion of doctoral program. *Degree requirements:* For master's, thesis (for some programs); for doctorate, comprehensive exam, thesis/dissertation, 2-3 publications referred before comps. *Entrance requirements:* For master's, GRE, minimum undergraduate GPA of 3.25; for doctorate, GRE, minimum undergraduate GPA of 3.5. Additional exam requirements/recommendations for international students: Required—TOEFL (minimum score 600 paper-based; 250 computer-based; 100 iBT), IELTS (minimum score 7). *Application deadline:* For fall admission, 2/15 priority date for domestic students; for winter admission, 10/15 priority date for domestic students. Applications are processed on a rolling basis. Application fee: $45 ($60 for international students). Electronic applications accepted. *Financial support:* In 2010–11, 38 students received support, including 1 fellowship with full tuition reimbursement available (averaging $16,000 per year), 10 research assistantships with full tuition reimbursements available (averaging $12,000 per year), 10 teaching assistantships with full tuition reimbursements available (averaging $8,100 per year); career-related internships or fieldwork, Federal Work-Study, institutionally sponsored loans, tuition waivers (full), and unspecified assistantships also available. Financial award application deadline: 2/1. *Faculty research:* Communication and rhetorical theory, organizational communication, broadcast and print journalism, international communication, public relations and advertising. Total annual research expenditures: $148,496. *Unit head:* Dr. Paul E. Nelson, Chair, 701-231-7705, Fax: 701-231-7784, E-mail: paul.nelson.1@ndsu.edu. *Application contact:* Dr. Judy C. Pearson, Director of Graduate Studies, 701-231-6551, Fax: 701-231-1074, E-mail: judy.pearson@ndsu.edu.

Oklahoma City University, Petree College of Arts and Sciences, Program in Liberal Arts, Oklahoma City, OK 73106-1402. Offers art (MLA); general studies (MLA); leadership/management (MLA); literature (MLA); mass communications (MLA); philosophy (MLA); writing (MLA). Part-time and evening/weekend programs available. *Degree requirements:* For master's, comprehensive exam, thesis optional. *Entrance requirements:* Additional exam requirements/recommendations for international students: Required—TOEFL (minimum score 550 paper-based).

Oklahoma State University, College of Arts and Sciences, School of Media and Strategic Communications, Stillwater, OK 74078. Offers mass communication (MS). *Faculty:* 19 full-time (7 women), 5 part-time/adjunct (1 woman). *Students:* 14 full-time (9 women), 21 part-time (11 women); includes 2 Black or African American, non-Hispanic/Latino; 3 American Indian or Alaska Native, non-Hispanic/Latino; 1 Hispanic/Latino, 4 international. Average age 30. 27 applicants, 30% accepted, 8 enrolled. In 2010, 8 master's awarded. *Degree requirements:* For master's, thesis, project/creative component. *Entrance requirements:* For master's, GRE, minimum GPA of 3.0. Additional exam requirements/recommendations for international students: Required—TOEFL (minimum score 550 paper-based; 79 iBT). *Application deadline:* For fall admission, 3/1 priority date for international students; for spring admission, 8/1 priority date for international students. Applications are processed on a rolling basis. Application fee: $40 ($75 for international students). Electronic applications accepted. *Expenses:* Tuition, state resident: full-time $3716; part-time $154.85 per credit hour. Tuition, nonresident: full-time $14,892; part-time $621 per credit hour. Required fees: $2044; $85.20 per credit hour. One-time fee: $50. Tuition and fees vary according to course load and campus/location. *Financial support:* In 2010–11, 1 research assistantship (averaging $5,550 per year), 5 teaching assistantships (averaging $10,301 per year) were awarded; career-related internships or fieldwork, Federal Work-Study, scholarships/grants, health care benefits, tuition waivers (partial), and unspecified assistantships also available. Support available to part-time students. Financial award application deadline: 3/1; financial award applicants required to submit FAFSA. *Unit head:* Dr. Derina Holtzhausen, Director, 405-744-6354, Fax: 405-744-7104. *Application contact:* Dr. Gordon Emslie, Dean, 405-744-6368, Fax: 405-744-0355, E-mail: grad-i@okstate.edu.

Point Park University, School of Communication, Pittsburgh, PA 15222-1984. Offers MA. Part-time and evening/weekend programs available. *Faculty:* 6 full-time, 10 part-time/adjunct. *Students:* 31 full-time (23 women), 33 part-time (25 women); includes 8 minority (5 Black or African American, non-Hispanic/Latino; 1 Asian, non-Hispanic/Latino; 2 Two or more races, non-Hispanic/Latino), 2 international. Average age 27. 103 applicants, 67% accepted, 32 enrolled. In 2010, 21 master's awarded. *Degree requirements:* For master's, comprehensive exam (for some programs), thesis or alternative. *Entrance requirements:* For master's, GRE (if GPA less than 2.75), minimum GPA of 2.75, 2 letters of recommendation, statement of intent. Additional exam requirements/recommendations for international students: Required—TOEFL (minimum score 570 paper-based; 88 iBT). *Application deadline:* Applications are processed on a rolling basis. Application fee: $30. Electronic applications accepted. *Expenses:* Tuition: Full-time $12,456; part-time $692 per credit. Required fees: $630; $35 per credit. *Financial support:* In 2010–11, 6 teaching assistantships with full tuition reimbursements (averaging $6,400 per year) were awarded; scholarships/grants and unspecified assistantships also available. Financial award application deadline: 4/15; financial award applicants required to submit FAFSA. *Unit head:* Dr. Tim Hudson, Chair, 412-392-4748, E-mail: thudson@pointpark.edu. *Application contact:* Marty M. Paonessa, Recruiter/Counselor, 412-392-3915, Fax: 412-392-6164, E-mail: mpaonessa@pointpark.edu.

St. Cloud State University, School of Graduate Studies, College of Fine Arts and Humanities, Department of Mass Communication, St. Cloud, MN 56301-4498. Offers MS. *Accreditation:*

ACEJMC. *Degree requirements:* For master's, thesis or alternative. *Entrance requirements:* For master's, GRE General Test, minimum GPA of 2.75. Additional exam requirements/recommendations for international students: Required—Michigan English Language Assessment Battery; Recommended—TOEFL (minimum score 550 paper-based; 213 computer-based), IELTS (minimum score 6.5). Electronic applications accepted.

San Jose State University, Graduate Studies and Research, College of Applied Sciences and Arts, School of Journalism and Mass Communications, San Jose, CA 95192-0001. Offers mass communications (MS). *Accreditation:* ACEJMC. Part-time programs available. *Degree requirements:* For master's, thesis or alternative. *Entrance requirements:* For master's, GRE, minimum GPA of 3.0. Electronic applications accepted. *Faculty research:* Communications theory, mass media effects, public relations, international communications.

Southern Illinois University Carbondale, Graduate School, College of Mass Communication and Media Arts, Department of Mass Communication and Media Arts, Carbondale, IL 62901-4701. Offers MA, MFA.

Southern Illinois University Edwardsville, Graduate School, College of Arts and Sciences, Department of Mass Communications, Program in Mass Communications, Edwardsville, IL 62026-0001. Offers MS. Part-time programs available. *Faculty:* 8 full-time (3 women). *Students:* 8 full-time (4 women), 27 part-time (20 women); includes 7 minority (4 Black or African American, non-Hispanic/Latino; 1 American Indian or Alaska Native, non-Hispanic/Latino; 2 Hispanic/Latino), 6 international. Average age 26. 29 applicants, 55% accepted. In 2010, 6 master's awarded. *Degree requirements:* For master's, comprehensive exam (for some programs), thesis (for some programs). *Entrance requirements:* Additional exam requirements/recommendations for international students: Required—TOEFL (minimum score 550 paper-based; 213 computer-based; 79 iBT), IELTS (minimum score 6.5). *Application deadline:* For fall admission, 7/22 for domestic students, 6/1 for international students; for spring admission, 12/9 for domestic students, 10/1 for international students. Applications are processed on a rolling basis. Application fee: $30. Electronic applications accepted. *Expenses:* Tuition, state resident: full-time $6012; part-time $1503 per semester. Tuition, nonresident: full-time $15,030; part-time $3758 per semester. Required fees: $1711; $675 per semester. *Financial support:* In 2010–11, 1 fellowship with full tuition reimbursement (averaging $8,370 per year), 1 research assistantship with full tuition reimbursement (averaging $8,064 per year), 13 teaching assistantships with full tuition reimbursements (averaging $8,064 per year) were awarded; career-related internships or fieldwork, Federal Work-Study, institutionally sponsored loans, scholarships/grants, traineeships, and unspecified assistantships also available. Support available to part-time students. Financial award application deadline: 3/1; financial award applicants required to submit FAFSA. *Unit head:* Dr. Elza Ibroscheva, Director, 618-650-2242, E-mail: eibrosc@siue.edu. *Application contact:* Dr. Elza Ibroscheva, Director, 618-650-2242, E-mail: eibrosc@siue.edu.

Southern University and Agricultural and Mechanical College, Graduate School, College of Arts and Humanities, Department of Mass Communications, Baton Rouge, LA 70813. Offers MA. *Accreditation:* ACEJMC. *Degree requirements:* For master's, comprehensive exam, thesis. *Entrance requirements:* For master's, GRE General Test. Additional exam requirements/recommendations for international students: Required—TOEFL (minimum score 525 paper-based; 193 computer-based). *Faculty research:* Photojournalism, textbook on broadcast.

Stephen F. Austin State University, Graduate School, College of Applied Arts and Science, Department of Communication, Nacogdoches, TX 75962. Offers communication (MA); mass communication (MA). Part-time programs available. *Degree requirements:* For master's, comprehensive exam, thesis optional. *Entrance requirements:* For master's, GRE General Test. Additional exam requirements/recommendations for international students: Required—TOEFL (minimum score 550 paper-based; 213 computer-based).

Syracuse University, S. I. Newhouse School of Public Communications, Program in Communications Management, Syracuse, NY 13244. Offers MS. Part-time programs available. Postbaccalaureate distance learning degree programs offered (minimal on-campus study). *Students:* 47 part-time (30 women); includes 7 minority (3 Black or African American, non-Hispanic/Latino; 1 Asian, non-Hispanic/Latino; 3 Hispanic/Latino), 8 international. Average age 41. 120 applicants, 11% accepted, 11 enrolled. In 2010, 11 master's awarded. *Degree requirements:* For master's, comprehensive exam, internship. *Entrance requirements:* For master's, GRE General Test, 5 years minimum experience in public relations or related field; portfolio; 3 letters of recommendation including 1 from current employer, client, or business partner. Additional exam requirements/recommendations for international students: Required—TOEFL (minimum score 100 iBT). *Application deadline:* For fall admission, 5/15 priority date for domestic and international students. Application fee: $45. Electronic applications accepted. *Expenses:* Tuition: Part-time $1162 per credit. *Financial support:* Application deadline: 1/1. *Unit head:* Maria Russell, Academic Director, 315-443-3368. *Application contact:* Martha Coria, Graduate Contact, 315-443-5749, E-mail: pcgrad@syr.edu.

Syracuse University, S. I. Newhouse School of Public Communications, Program in Mass Communications, Syracuse, NY 13244. Offers PhD. *Students:* 17 full-time (11 women), 5 part-time (2 women); includes 3 minority (all Black or African American, non-Hispanic/Latino), 5 international. Average age 35. 70 applicants, 14% accepted, 7 enrolled. In 2010, 3 doctorates awarded. *Degree requirements:* For doctorate, thesis/dissertation, qualifying exams. *Entrance requirements:* For doctorate, GRE General Test. Additional exam requirements/recommendations for international students: Required—TOEFL (minimum score 100 iBT). *Application deadline:* For fall admission, 12/10 priority date for domestic and international students. Application fee: $45. Electronic applications accepted. *Expenses:* Tuition: Part-time $1162 per credit. *Financial support:* Fellowships with full tuition reimbursements, research assistantships with partial tuition reimbursements, teaching assistantships with partial tuition reimbursements, career-related internships or fieldwork and tuition waivers (partial) available. Financial award application deadline: 12/10. *Unit head:* Carol M. Liebler, Director, 315-443-3372, Fax: 315-443-3946, E-mail: masscomm@syr.edu. *Application contact:* Amy Arends, Doctoral Office, 315-443-3372, E-mail: masscomm@syr.edu.

Temple University, School of Communications and Theater, Program in Mass Media and Communication, Philadelphia, PA 19122-6096. Offers PhD. Part-time programs available. *Students:* 37 full-time (26 women), 10 part-time (6 women); includes 2 Black or African American, non-Hispanic/Latino; 1 American Indian or Alaska Native, non-Hispanic/Latino; 2 Asian, non-Hispanic/Latino; 1 Hispanic/Latino, 8 international. 49 applicants, 51% accepted, 11 enrolled. In 2010, 5 doctorates awarded. *Degree requirements:* For doctorate, one foreign language, thesis/dissertation. *Entrance requirements:* For doctorate, GRE General Test, minimum GPA of 3.0, sample of written work. Additional exam requirements/recommendations for international students: Required—TOEFL (minimum score 550 paper-based; 213 computer-based; 79 iBT). *Application deadline:* For fall admission, 1/15 for domestic students, 12/15 for international students. Application fee: $50. Electronic applications accepted. *Financial support:* Fellowships, research assistantships with partial tuition reimbursements, teaching assistantships with partial tuition reimbursements available. Financial award application deadline: 1/15; financial award applicants required to submit FAFSA. *Faculty research:* Aesthetics and criticism, media institutions, social theory and processes. *Unit head:* Dr. Mathew Lombard, Director, 215-204-1497, E-mail: mmc@temple.edu. *Application contact:* Dr. Mathew Lombard, Director, 215-204-1497, E-mail: mmc@temple.edu.

Texas State University–San Marcos, Graduate School, College of Fine Arts and Communication, School of Journalism and Mass Communication, San Marcos, TX 78666. Offers MA. *Faculty:* 13 full-time (7 women). *Students:* 33 full-time (21 women), 19 part-time (16 women); includes 17 minority (1 Black or African American, non-Hispanic/Latino; 16 Hispanic/Latino). Average age 29. 27 applicants, 89% accepted, 16 enrolled. In 2010, 16 master's awarded. *Degree requirements:* For master's, comprehensive exam, thesis optional. *Entrance requirements:* For master's, GRE General Test, departmental grammar test, minimum GPA of 3.0 in last 60 hours of course work. Additional exam requirements/recommendations for international students: Required—TOEFL (minimum score 550 paper-based; 213 computer-based; 78 iBT). *Application deadline:* For fall admission, 2/1 priority date for domestic students, 2/1 for international students; for spring admission, 10/15 priority date for domestic students, 10/1 for international students. Applications are processed on a rolling basis. Application fee: $40 ($90 for international students). Electronic applications accepted. *Expenses:* Tuition, state resident: full-time $6024; part-time $251 per credit hour. Tuition, nonresident: full-time $13,536; part-time $564 per credit hour. Required fees: $1776; $50 per credit hour. $306 per semester. *Financial support:* In 2010–11, 25 students received support, including 4 research assistantships (averaging $5,153 per year), 13 teaching assistantships (averaging $4,218 per year); career-related internships or fieldwork, Federal Work-Study, and institutionally sponsored loans also available. Support available to part-time students. Financial award application deadline: 4/1; financial award applicants required to submit FAFSA. *Faculty research:* AFRED survey-propane. Total annual research expenditures: $8,797. *Unit head:* Dr. Bruce Smith, Director, 512-245-2656, Fax: 512-245-7649, E-mail: bs20@txstate.edu. *Application contact:* Dr. Sandyha Rao, Graduate Adviser, 512-245-3790, Fax: 512-245-7649, E-mail: sr02@txstate.edu.

Texas Tech University, Graduate School, College of Mass Communications, Lubbock, TX 79409. Offers MA, PhD. Part-time programs available. *Faculty:* 11 full-time (3 women). *Students:* 47 full-time (19 women), 19 part-time (11 women); includes 5 Hispanic/Latino, 17 international. Average age 29. 72 applicants, 49% accepted, 20 enrolled. In 2010, 7 master's, 3 doctorates awarded. *Degree requirements:* For master's, thesis or alternative; for doctorate, thesis/dissertation. *Entrance requirements:* For master's and doctorate, GRE General Test. Additional exam requirements/recommendations for international students: Required—TOEFL (minimum score 550 paper-based; 213 computer-based; 79 iBT). *Application deadline:* For fall admission, 6/1 priority date for domestic students, 1/15 priority date for international students; for spring admission, 9/1 priority date for domestic students, 6/15 priority date for international students. Applications are processed on a rolling basis. Application fee: $50 ($75 for international students). Electronic applications accepted. *Expenses:* Tuition, state resident: full-time $5495.76; part-time $228.99 per credit hour. Tuition, nonresident: full-time $12,936; part-time $538.99 per credit hour. Required fees: $2674; $36 per credit hour. $905 per semester. *Financial support:* In 2010–11, 36 students received support, including 6 research assistantships with partial tuition reimbursements available (averaging $5,949 per year), 12 teaching assistantships with partial tuition reimbursements available (averaging $5,482 per year); career-related internships or fieldwork, Federal Work-Study, institutionally sponsored loans, scholarships/grants, traineeships, health care benefits, and unspecified assistantships also available. Support available to part-time students. Financial award application deadline: 4/15; financial award applicants required to submit FAFSA. *Faculty research:* Contemporary media use and structure, Hispanic media, characteristics of public relations spokesperson credibility, psychological measures of advertising effectiveness, media history and ethics. Total annual research expenditures: $117,273. *Unit head:* Dr. Jerry C. Hudson, Dean, 806-742-3385 Ext. 224, Fax: 806-742-1085, E-mail: jerry.hudson@ttu.edu. *Application contact:* Dr. Coy Callison, Associate Dean of Graduate Studies, 806-742-3385 Ext. 235, Fax: 806-742-1085, E-mail: coy.callison@ttu.edu.

Université Laval, Faculty of Letters, Department of Information and Communication, Program in Public Communication, Québec, QC G1K 7P4, Canada. Offers MA, PhD. Part-time programs available. *Degree requirements:* For master's, thesis (for some programs). *Entrance requirements:* For master's, knowledge of French, knowledge of English. Electronic applications accepted.

The University of Alabama, Graduate School, College of Communication and Information Sciences, Communication and Information Sciences Program, Tuscaloosa, AL 35487-0172. Offers PhD. *Faculty:* 1 full-time (0 women). *Students:* 40 full-time (18 women), 12 part-time (6 women); includes 8 minority (6 Black or African American, non-Hispanic/Latino; 1 American Indian or Alaska Native, non-Hispanic/Latino; 1 Two or more races, non-Hispanic/Latino), 9 international. Average age 35. 42 applicants, 29% accepted, 5 enrolled. In 2010, 12 doctorates awarded. *Degree requirements:* For doctorate, comprehensive exam, thesis/dissertation. *Entrance requirements:* For doctorate, GRE, master's degree, minimum undergraduate and graduate GPA of 3.0. Additional exam requirements/recommendations for international students: Required—TOEFL. *Application deadline:* For fall admission, 2/15 for domestic and international students; for winter admission, 11/1 for domestic and international students. Application fee: $50 ($60 for international students). *Expenses:* Tuition, state resident: full-time $7900. Tuition, nonresident: full-time $20,500. *Financial support:* In 2010–11, 4 fellowships with full tuition reimbursements (averaging $15,000 per year), 14 research assistantships with full tuition reimbursements (averaging $13,045 per year), 10 teaching assistantships with full tuition reimbursements (averaging $13,045 per year) were awarded; institutionally sponsored loans, health care benefits, and unspecified assistantships also available. Financial award application deadline: 2/15. *Faculty research:* Mass media; mass media effects; information studies; cultural, critical and rhetorical studies; policy and law; electronic media. Total annual research expenditures: $8,420. *Unit head:* Dr. Jennings Bryant, Associate Dean for Graduate Studies, 205-348-8593, Fax: 205-348-6774. *Application contact:* Diane Shaddix, Information Contact, 205-348-8593, Fax: 205-348-6774, E-mail: dshaddix@bama.ua.edu.

University of Arkansas at Little Rock, Graduate School, College of Professional Studies, School of Mass Communication, Little Rock, AR 72204-1099. Offers journalism (MA). Part-time and evening/weekend programs available. *Degree requirements:* For master's, comprehensive exam, thesis optional. *Entrance requirements:* For master's, GRE General Test, minimum GPA of 2.7. *Faculty research:* Theory and practice of mass communication, social role of the mass media.

University of Central Missouri, The Graduate School, College of Arts, Humanities and Social Sciences, Warrensburg, MO 64093. Offers English (MA); history (MA); mass communication (MA); music (MA); psychology (MS); speech communication (MA); teaching English as a second language (MA); theatre (MA). Part-time programs available. *Entrance requirements:* Additional exam requirements/recommendations for international students: Required—TOEFL (minimum score 550 paper-based; 79 computer-based). Electronic applications accepted.

University of Colorado Boulder, Graduate School, School of Journalism and Mass Communication, Boulder, CO 80309. Offers communication (PhD), including media studies; mass communication research (MA); newsgathering (MA). *Accreditation:* ACEJMC (one or more programs are accredited). Part-time programs available. *Faculty:* 22 full-time (11 women). *Students:* 78 full-time (49 women), 10 part-time (6 women); includes 4 minority (1 Black or African American, non-Hispanic/Latino; 2 Hispanic/Latino; 1 Two or more races, non-Hispanic/Latino), 11 international. Average age 30. 154 applicants, 35 enrolled. In 2010, 35 master's, 6 doctorates awarded. *Degree requirements:* For master's, comprehensive exam, thesis or alternative; for doctorate, comprehensive exam, thesis/dissertation. *Entrance requirements:* For master's, GRE General Test, minimum undergraduate GPA of 2.75; for doctorate, GRE General Test, minimum undergraduate GPA of 3.2, 3.5 graduate. *Application deadline:* For fall admission, 2/15 for domestic students, 12/1 for international students. Applications are processed on a rolling basis. Application fee: $50 ($60 for international students). *Financial support:* In 2010–11, 14 fellowships (averaging $1,807 per year), 21 research assistantships with tuition reimbursements (averaging $11,554 per year) were awarded; institutionally sponsored loans and unspecified assistantships also available. Financial award application deadline: 3/1. *Faculty research:* Writing on science and the environment, mass communication and public opinion, minority representation in the media, media and culture. Total annual research expenditures: $204,190.

University of Denver, Division of Arts, Humanities and Social Sciences, Department of Media, Film and Journalism Studies, Denver, CO 80208. Offers advertising management (MS); digital media studies (MA); international and intercultural communication (MA); media, film, and journalism studies (MA); strategic communication (MS). Part-time programs available. *Faculty:* 14 full-time (7 women), 5 part-time/adjunct (3 women). *Students:* 28 full-time (24

Mass Communication

University of Denver (continued)
women), 36 part-time (26 women); includes 12 minority (1 Black or African American, non-Hispanic/Latino; 3 Asian, non-Hispanic/Latino; 6 Hispanic/Latino; 2 Two or more races, non-Hispanic/Latino), 2 international. Average age 26. 155 applicants, 58% accepted, 32 enrolled. In 2010, 36 master's awarded. *Degree requirements:* For master's, thesis (for some programs). *Entrance requirements:* For master's, GRE General Test. Additional exam requirements/recommendations for international students: Required—TOEFL (minimum score 550 paper-based; 80 iBT). *Application deadline:* Applications are processed on a rolling basis. Application fee: $60. Electronic applications accepted. *Expenses:* Tuition: Full-time $35,604; part-time $29,670 per year. Required fees: $687 per year. Tuition and fees vary according to program. *Financial support:* In 2010–11, 4 teaching assistantships with full and partial tuition reimbursements (averaging $14,000 per year) were awarded; career-related internships or fieldwork, Federal Work-Study, institutionally sponsored loans, scholarships/grants, and unspecified assistantships also available. Support available to part-time students. Financial award application deadline: 3/1; financial award applicants required to submit FAFSA. *Faculty research:* Youth and civic engagement. *Unit head:* Dr. Renee Botta, Chair, 303-871-7918, Fax: 303-871-4949, E-mail: rbotta@du.edu. *Application contact:* Information Contact, 303-871-2166, E-mail: mfjs@du.edu.

University of Florida, Graduate School, College of Journalism and Communications, Gainesville, FL 32611. Offers advertising (M Adv); journalism (MAMC); mass communication (MAMC, PhD); public relations (MAMC); telecommunication (MAMC); JD/MAMC; JD/PhD. *Accreditation:* ACEJMC (one or more programs are accredited). Part-time programs available. *Faculty:* 36 full-time (17 women), 1 part-time/adjunct (0 women). *Students:* 164 full-time (123 women), 33 part-time (23 women); includes 15 Black or African American, non-Hispanic/Latino; 1 American Indian or Alaska Native, non-Hispanic/Latino; 14 Asian, non-Hispanic/Latino; 10 Hispanic/Latino, 82 international. Average age 29. 458 applicants, 35% accepted, 55 enrolled. In 2010, 63 master's, 12 doctorates awarded. *Degree requirements:* For master's, comprehensive exam (for some programs), thesis; for doctorate, comprehensive exam (for some programs), thesis/dissertation. *Entrance requirements:* For master's and doctorate, GRE General Test: 550 Verbal, 550 Quantitative (1100 total), minimum GPA of 3.0. Additional exam requirements/recommendations for international students: Required—TOEFL (minimum score 550 paper-based; 213 computer-based; 80 iBT), IELTS (minimum score 6). *Application deadline:* For fall admission, 1/15 for domestic and international students; for spring admission, 7/15 for domestic and international students. Applications are processed on a rolling basis. Application fee: $30. Electronic applications accepted. *Expenses:* Tuition, state resident: full-time $10,915.92. Tuition, nonresident: full-time $28,309. *Financial support:* In 2010–11, 69 students received support, including 11 fellowships with full and partial tuition reimbursements available, 11 research assistantships with full tuition reimbursements available (averaging $15,656 per year), 47 teaching assistantships with full tuition reimbursements available (averaging $15,518 per year); career-related internships or fieldwork, Federal Work-Study, institutionally sponsored loans, and unspecified assistantships also available. Support available to part-time students. Financial award application deadline: 3/15; financial award applicants required to submit FAFSA. *Faculty research:* Health communication, international/cross-cultural communication, political communication, ethics, persuasion/message development. Total annual research expenditures: $32,000. *Unit head:* Dr. John W. Wright, Dean, 352-392-0466, Fax: 352-392-1794, E-mail: dtreise@jou.ufl.edu. *Application contact:* Dr. Debbie M. Treise, Associate Dean for Graduate Programs, 352-392-6557.

University of Georgia, Grady School of Journalism and Mass Communication, Athens, GA 30602. Offers journalism and mass communication (MA); mass communication (PhD). *Accreditation:* ACEJMC (one or more programs are accredited). *Faculty:* 37 full-time (14 women). *Students:* 88 full-time (61 women), 24 part-time (16 women); includes 13 Black or African American, non-Hispanic/Latino; 4 Hispanic/Latino, 21 international. 297 applicants, 40% accepted, 48 enrolled. In 2010, 31 master's, 5 doctorates awarded. *Degree requirements:* For master's, comprehensive exam, thesis (MA); for doctorate, comprehensive exam, thesis/dissertation. *Entrance requirements:* For master's and doctorate, GRE General Test. Additional exam requirements/recommendations for international students: Required—TOEFL, TWE (for PhD). *Application deadline:* For spring admission, 2/15 for domestic students. Application fee: $50. Electronic applications accepted. *Expenses:* Tuition, state resident: full-time $7200; part-time $344 per credit hour. Tuition, nonresident: full-time $21,900; part-time $944 per credit hour. Tuition and fees vary according to course load and program. *Financial support:* Research assistantships, teaching assistantships, tuition waivers (full) and unspecified assistantships available. *Unit head:* Dr. E. Culpepper Clark, Dean, 706-542-1704, Fax: 706-542-2183, E-mail: cully@uga.edu. *Application contact:* Dr. Jeffrey K. Springston, Graduate Coordinator, 706-542-5030, Fax: 706-542-2183, E-mail: jspring@grady.uga.edu.

University of Houston, College of Liberal Arts and Social Sciences, School of Communication, Houston, TX 77204. Offers health communication (MA); mass communication studies (MA); public relations studies (MA); speech communication (MA). Part-time programs available. *Faculty:* 11 full-time (6 women), 2 part-time/adjunct (0 women). *Students:* 47 full-time (39 women), 46 part-time (36 women); includes 15 Black or African American, non-Hispanic/Latino; 2 American Indian or Alaska Native, non-Hispanic/Latino; 3 Asian, non-Hispanic/Latino; 16 Hispanic/Latino, 19 international. Average age 28. 54 applicants, 70% accepted, 24 enrolled. In 2010, 20 master's awarded. *Degree requirements:* For master's, comprehensive exam (for some programs), thesis (for some programs), 30-33 hours. *Entrance requirements:* For master's, GRE. Additional exam requirements/recommendations for international students: Required—TOEFL. *Application deadline:* For fall admission, 6/1 for domestic students, 4/1 for international students; for spring admission, 11/1 for domestic students, 10/1 for international students. Applications are processed on a rolling basis. Application fee: $50 ($100 for international students). Electronic applications accepted. *Expenses:* Tuition, state resident: full-time $8592; part-time $358 per credit hour. Tuition, nonresident: full-time $16,032; part-time $668 per credit hour. Required fees: $2889. Tuition and fees vary according to course load and program. *Financial support:* In 2010–11, 28 teaching assistantships with full tuition reimbursements (averaging $8,111 per year) were awarded; career-related internships or fieldwork, Federal Work-Study, institutionally sponsored loans, scholarships/grants, health care benefits, and unspecified assistantships also available. Support available to part-time students. Financial award application deadline: 2/1. *Unit head:* Dr. Beth Olson, Chairperson, 713-743-2873, Fax: 713-743-2876, E-mail: bolson@uh.edu. *Application contact:* Dr. Martha Haun, Director of Graduate Studies, 713-743-2886, E-mail: mhaun@uh.edu.

The University of Iowa, Graduate College, College of Liberal Arts and Sciences, School of Journalism and Mass Communication, Iowa City, IA 52242-1316. Offers mass communication (PhD); media communication (MA); professional journalism (MA); JD/MA. *Accreditation:* ACEJMC (one or more programs are accredited). *Degree requirements:* For master's, thesis optional, exam; for doctorate, comprehensive exam, thesis/dissertation. *Entrance requirements:* For master's and doctorate, GRE General Test, minimum GPA of 3.0. Additional exam requirements/recommendations for international students: Required—TOEFL (minimum score 637 paper-based; 270 computer-based; 110 iBT). Electronic applications accepted. *Faculty research:* Verbal and visual aspects of historical, legal, social, and cross-cultural communication.

University of Louisiana at Lafayette, College of Liberal Arts, Department of Communication, Lafayette, LA 70504. Offers mass communications (MS). Part-time programs available. *Degree requirements:* For master's, thesis optional. *Entrance requirements:* For master's, GRE General Test, minimum GPA of 2.75. Additional exam requirements/recommendations for international students: Required—TOEFL (minimum score 550 paper-based; 213 computer-based). Electronic applications accepted. *Faculty research:* Mass media problems, issues and ethics, mass communication, historical studies, conflict of interest and law and ethics in journalism, contemporary issues and trends in publications.

University of Maine, Graduate School, College of Liberal Arts and Sciences, Department of Communication and Journalism, Orono, ME 04469. Offers communication (MA); mass communication (MA). Part-time programs available. *Faculty:* 8 full-time (3 women), 3 part-time/adjunct (1 woman). *Students:* 15 full-time (11 women), 2 part-time (0 women); includes 2 minority (both American Indian or Alaska Native, non-Hispanic/Latino), 1 international. Average age 29. 15 applicants, 60% accepted, 7 enrolled. In 2010, 10 master's awarded. *Degree requirements:* For master's, thesis or alternative. *Entrance requirements:* For master's, GRE General Test. Additional exam requirements/recommendations for international students: Required—TOEFL. *Application deadline:* For fall admission, 2/1 priority date for domestic students. Applications are processed on a rolling basis. Application fee: $65. Electronic applications accepted. *Expenses:* Tuition, state resident: full-time $400. Tuition, nonresident: full-time $1050. *Financial support:* In 2010–11, 15 teaching assistantships with tuition reimbursements (averaging $12,790 per year) were awarded; career-related internships or fieldwork, Federal Work-Study, institutionally sponsored loans, and tuition waivers (full and partial) also available. Support available to part-time students. Financial award application deadline: 3/1. *Faculty research:* Rhetorical theory, semiotics, discourse analysis, gender and communication, children's talk/communication disorders. *Unit head:* Dr. Paul Grosswiler, Chair, 207-581-1287, Fax: 207-581-1286. *Application contact:* Scott G. Delcourt, Associate Dean of the Graduate School, 207-581-3291, Fax: 207-581-3232, E-mail: graduate@maine.edu.

University of Maine, Graduate School, Interdisciplinary Doctoral Program, Orono, ME 04469. Offers communication (PhD); functional genomics (PhD); mass communication (PhD); ocean engineering (PhD). Part-time and evening/weekend programs available. *Students:* 22 full-time (13 women), 25 part-time (14 women); includes 2 minority (1 Black or African American, non-Hispanic/Latino; 1 Asian, non-Hispanic/Latino), 4 international. Average age 37. 17 applicants, 41% accepted, 7 enrolled. In 2010, 10 doctorates awarded. *Degree requirements:* For doctorate, comprehensive exam, thesis/dissertation. *Entrance requirements:* For doctorate, GRE General Test. Additional exam requirements/recommendations for international students: Required—TOEFL. *Application deadline:* For fall admission, 4/1 for domestic students; for spring admission, 11/1 for domestic students. Applications are processed on a rolling basis. Application fee: $65. Electronic applications accepted. *Expenses:* Tuition, state resident: full-time $400. Tuition, nonresident: full-time $1050. *Unit head:* Scott G. Delcourt, Associate Dean of the Graduate School, 207-581-3291, Fax: 207-581-3232, E-mail: graduate@maine.edu. *Application contact:* Scott G. Delcourt, Associate Dean of the Graduate School, 207-581-3291, Fax: 207-581-3232, E-mail: graduate@maine.edu.

University of Michigan, Horace H. Rackham School of Graduate Studies, College of Literature, Science, and the Arts, Department of Communication Studies, Ann Arbor, MI 48104-2523. Offers PhD. *Faculty:* 16 full-time (7 women). *Students:* 36 full-time (27 women); includes 6 minority (3 Black or African American, non-Hispanic/Latino; 2 Asian, non-Hispanic/Latino; 1 Hispanic/Latino), 10 international. Average age 29. 117 applicants, 8% accepted, 7 enrolled. In 2010, 1 doctorate awarded. *Degree requirements:* For doctorate, comprehensive exam, thesis/dissertation, first-year research project, 2 terms in student instructor position. *Entrance requirements:* For doctorate, GRE, U.S. bachelor's degree or its equivalent from accredited institution. Additional exam requirements/recommendations for international students: Required—TOEFL (minimum score 600 paper-based; 102 iBT). *Application deadline:* For fall admission, 12/1 for domestic and international students. Application fee: $65 ($75 for international students). Electronic applications accepted. *Expenses:* Tuition, state resident: full-time $17,784; part-time $1116 per credit hour. Tuition, nonresident: full-time $35,944; part-time $2125 per credit hour. International tuition: $35,994 full-time. Required fees: $95 per semester. Tuition and fees vary according to course load, degree level and program. *Financial support:* In 2010–11, 36 students received support, including 26 fellowships with full tuition reimbursements available (averaging $17,475 per year), research assistantships with full tuition reimbursements available (averaging $17,270 per year), 37 teaching assistantships with full tuition reimbursements available (averaging $17,270 per year); scholarships/grants, health care benefits, tuition waivers (full), and unspecified assistantships also available. Financial award application deadline: 4/30; financial award applicants required to submit FAFSA. *Faculty research:* Political communication, media, culture and society; media effects; race, gender, and the media; new media, media law and policy. *Unit head:* Prof. Susan J. Douglas, Professor and Chair, 734-764-0420, Fax: 734-764-3288, E-mail: sdoug@umich.edu. *Application contact:* Amy B. Eaton, Graduate Program Coordinator, 734-615-8974, Fax: 734-764-3288, E-mail: lsa-commphd@umich.edu.

University of Minnesota, Twin Cities Campus, Graduate School, College of Liberal Arts, School of Journalism and Mass Communication, Minneapolis, MN 55455-0213. Offers mass communication (MA, PhD); strategic communication (professional program) (MA). *Degree requirements:* For master's, thesis; for doctorate, comprehensive exam, thesis/dissertation. *Entrance requirements:* For master's, GRE; GMAT (for strategic communications program), letters of recommendation, minimum undergraduate GPA of 3.0, writing sample; two years professional experience (for strategic communications program); for doctorate, GRE, letters of recommendation, minimum undergraduate GPA of 3.0, writing sample. Additional exam requirements/recommendations for international students: Required—TOEFL (minimum score 79 iBT). Electronic applications accepted. *Faculty research:* Communication law, regulation, and ethics; history; mass media effects; new media, health communication.

University of Nebraska–Lincoln, Graduate College, College of Journalism and Mass Communications, Lincoln, NE 68588. Offers marketing, communication and advertising (MA); professional journalism (MA). Postbaccalaureate distance learning degree programs offered (no on-campus study). *Degree requirements:* For master's, thesis. *Entrance requirements:* For master's, samples of work. Additional exam requirements/recommendations for international students: Required—TOEFL (minimum score 600 paper-based; 250 computer-based). Electronic applications accepted. *Faculty research:* Interactive media and the Internet, community newspapers, children's radio, advertising involvement, telecommunications policy.

The University of North Carolina at Chapel Hill, Graduate School, School of Journalism and Mass Communication, Chapel Hill, NC 27599. Offers mass communication (MA, PhD). *Accreditation:* ACEJMC (one or more programs are accredited). Part-time programs available. *Faculty:* 48 full-time (21 women). *Students:* 82 full-time (59 women), 1 (woman) part-time; includes 7 Black or African American, non-Hispanic/Latino; 8 Asian, non-Hispanic/Latino; 3 Hispanic/Latino. Average age 30. 278 applicants, 18% accepted, 33 enrolled. In 2010, 20 master's, 5 doctorates awarded. *Degree requirements:* For master's, comprehensive exam, thesis, http://jomc.unc.edu/graduate-studies-content-items/ma-in-mass-communication-program-info; for doctorate, comprehensive exam, thesis/dissertation, http://jomc.unc.edu/graduate-studies-content-items/phd-in-mass-communication-program-info. *Entrance requirements:* For master's and doctorate, GRE General Test, minimum GPA of 3.0. Additional exam requirements/recommendations for international students: Required—TOEFL (minimum score 620 paper-based; 260 computer-based; 105 iBT). *Application deadline:* For fall admission, 1/1 for domestic and international students. Application fee: $77. Electronic applications accepted. *Expenses:* Contact institution. *Financial support:* In 2010–11, 14 research assistantships with full tuition reimbursements (averaging $14,000 per year) were awarded; institutionally sponsored loans and health care benefits also available. Financial award application deadline: 3/1; financial award applicants required to submit FAFSA. *Faculty research:* Media processes and production, legal and regulatory issues, media effects, media history. *Unit head:* Dr. Jean Folkerts, Dean, 919-962-1204, Fax: 919-962-0620. *Application contact:* Graduate Program Administrator, 919-962-1204, E-mail: jomcgrad@unc.edu.

University of Oklahoma, Gaylord College of Journalism and Mass Communication, Program in Journalism and Mass Communication, Norman, OK 73019-0390. Offers advertising and public relations (MA); information gathering and distribution (MA); mass communication management and policy (MA); professional writing (MA); telecommunications and new technologies (MA). Part-time programs available. *Students:* 21 full-time (16 women), 26 part-time (13 women); includes 7 minority (4 Black or African American, non-Hispanic/Latino; 2 American Indian or Alaska Native, non-Hispanic/Latino; 1 Hispanic/Latino), 6 international. Average age 27. 29 applicants, 76% accepted, 10 enrolled. In 2010, 20 master's awarded. *Degree requirements:* For master's, thesis optional. *Entrance requirements:* For master's, GRE General

Test, minimum GPA of 3.2, 9 hours of course work in journalism, course work in statistics. Additional exam requirements/recommendations for international students: Required—TOEFL (minimum score 600 paper-based; 250 computer-based; 100 iBT), TWE (minimum score 5). *Application deadline:* For fall admission, 2/1 for domestic students, 4/1 for international students; for spring admission, 11/1 for domestic students, 9/1 for international students. Application fee: $40 ($90 for international students). Electronic applications accepted. *Expenses:* Tuition, state resident: full-time $3893; part-time $162.20 per credit hour. Tuition, nonresident: full-time $14,167; part-time $590.30 per credit hour. Required fees: $2523; $94.60 per credit hour. Tuition and fees vary according to course load and degree level. *Financial support:* In 2010–11, 30 students received support. Career-related internships or fieldwork, scholarships/grants, health care benefits, and unspecified assistantships available. *Faculty research:* Organizational management, strategic communications, rhetorical theories and mass communication, interactive messaging and audience response; mass media history and law. *Unit head:* Dr. Joe Foote, Dean, 405-325-2721, Fax: 405-325-7565, E-mail: jfoote@ou.edu. *Application contact:* Kelly Storm, Graduate Advisor, 405-325-2722, Fax: 405-325-7565, E-mail: kstorm@ou.edu.

University of Puerto Rico, Río Piedras, School of Communication, San Juan, PR 00931-3300. Offers MA. Part-time programs available. *Degree requirements:* For master's, comprehensive exam, thesis. *Entrance requirements:* For master's, GRE, PAEG, minimum GPA of 3.0, 2 letters of recommendation, interview.

University of Southern California, Graduate School, Annenberg School for Communication and Journalism, School of Communication, Program in Communication, Los Angeles, CA 90089. Offers communication (MA, PhD), including information and society (PhD), interpersonal and health communication (PhD), media, culture and communication (PhD), organizational communication (PhD), rhetorical and political communication (PhD). *Students:* 97 full-time (64 women); includes 20 minority (4 Black or African American, non-Hispanic/Latino; 1 American Indian or Alaska Native, non-Hispanic/Latino; 8 Asian, non-Hispanic/Latino; 7 Hispanic/Latino), 30 international. Average age 31. 242 applicants, 9% accepted, 18 enrolled. In 2010, 14 doctorates awarded. *Degree requirements:* For doctorate, thesis/dissertation. *Entrance requirements:* For master's and doctorate, GRE General Test, resume, writing samples, 3 letters of recommendation, interest survey questionnaire, statement of purpose. Additional exam requirements/recommendations for international students: Required—TOEFL (minimum score 280 computer-based; 114 iBT); Recommended—TWE. *Application deadline:* For fall admission, 12/1 for domestic and international students. Application fee: $85. Electronic applications accepted. *Expenses:* Tuition: Full-time $31,240; part-time $1420 per unit. Required fees: $600. One-time fee: $35 full-time. Full-time tuition and fees vary according to degree level and program. *Financial support:* In 2010–11, 18 students received support, including 18 fellowships with full tuition reimbursements available (averaging $26,500 per year); research assistantships, teaching assistantships, Federal Work-Study, institutionally sponsored loans, scholarships/grants, health care benefits, and unspecified assistantships also available. Support available to part-time students. Financial award application deadline: 1/1; financial award applicants required to submit FAFSA. *Faculty research:* Computer-mediated communication, public health campaigns, communication democracy and the public sphere, new communication technologies in organizations, communication and community. *Unit head:* Dr. Thomas Goodnight, Director of the Ph.D. Program, 213-821-5384, E-mail: gtg@usc.edu. *Application contact:* Allyson Hill, Assistant Dean, Admissions, 213-821-0770, Fax: 213-740-1933, E-mail: ascadm@usc.edu.

See Display on page 675 and Close-Up on page 727.

University of Southern Mississippi, Graduate School, College of Arts and Letters, School of Mass Communication and Journalism, Hattiesburg, MS 39406-0001. Offers mass communication (MA, MS, PhD); public relations (MS). Part-time programs available. *Faculty:* 10 full-time (3 women), 1 part-time/adjunct (0 women). *Students:* 28 full-time (21 women), 40 part-time (29 women); includes 12 Black or African American, non-Hispanic/Latino; 3 Hispanic/Latino; 4 Two or more races, non-Hispanic/Latino, 6 international. Average age 34. 37 applicants, 62% accepted, 13 enrolled. In 2010, 26 master's, 4 doctorates awarded. *Degree requirements:* For master's, comprehensive exam, thesis optional; for doctorate, comprehensive exam, thesis/dissertation. *Entrance requirements:* For master's, GRE General Test, minimum GPA of 3.0 in field of study, 2.75 in last 2 years; for doctorate, GRE General Test, minimum GPA of 3.5. Additional exam requirements/recommendations for international students: Required—TOEFL, IELTS. *Application deadline:* For fall admission, 3/1 priority date for domestic students, 3/1 for international students; for spring admission, 1/10 priority date for domestic and international students. Applications are processed on a rolling basis. Application fee: $50. *Financial support:* In 2010–11, 18 students received support, including 12 teaching assistantships with full tuition reimbursements available (averaging $8,000 per year); fellowships with full tuition reimbursements available, research assistantships with full tuition reimbursements available, career-related internships or fieldwork, Federal Work-Study, institutionally sponsored loans, scholarships/grants, health care benefits, and unspecified assistantships also available. Financial award application deadline: 3/15; financial award applicants required to submit FAFSA. *Unit head:* Dr. Christopher Campbell, Director, 601-266-5650, Fax: 601-266-4263. *Application contact:* Dr. Fei Xue, Graduate Coordinator, 601-266-5652, Fax: 601-266-6473, E-mail: fei.xue@usm.edu.

University of South Florida, Graduate School, College of Arts and Sciences, School of Mass Communications, Tampa, FL 33620-9951. Offers MA. Part-time and evening/weekend programs available. *Students:* 16 full-time (11 women), 20 part-time (14 women); includes 4 Black or African American, non-Hispanic/Latino; 1 Asian, non-Hispanic/Latino; 2 Hispanic/Latino; 1 Two or more races, non-Hispanic/Latino, 2 international. Average age 32. 39 applicants, 28% accepted, 4 enrolled. In 2010, 15 master's awarded. *Degree requirements:* For master's, comprehensive exam, thesis. *Entrance requirements:* For master's, GRE General Test, minimum GPA of 3.0 in last 60 hours of course work. Additional exam requirements/recommendations for international students: Required—TOEFL (minimum score 550 paper-based; 213 computer-based). *Application deadline:* For fall admission, 2/15 for domestic students, 1/2 for international students; for spring admission, 10/15 for domestic students, 6/1 for international students. Application fee: $30. Electronic applications accepted. *Financial support:* In 2010–11, 11 teaching assistantships with tuition reimbursements (averaging $10,085 per year) were awarded; unspecified assistantships also available. Financial award application deadline: 2/28. *Faculty research:* First Amendment analysis, civic journalism, public opinion, media ethics, public relation management. Total annual research expenditures: $58,210. *Unit head:* Dr. Edward Jay Friedlander, Chairperson, 813-974-6461, Fax: 813-974-2592, E-mail: efriedla@luna.cas.usf.edu. *Application contact:* Kelly Page Werder, Director, 813-974-6790, Fax: 813-974-2592, E-mail: kgpage@.cas.usf.edu.

University of Wisconsin–Madison, Graduate School, College of Letters and Science, School of Journalism and Mass Communication, Program in Journalism and Mass Communication, Madison, WI 53706-1380. Offers MA. *Expenses:* Tuition, state resident: full-time $9887; part-time $617.96 per credit. Tuition, nonresident: full-time $24,054; part-time $1503.40 per credit. Required fees: $67.63 per credit. Tuition and fees vary according to reciprocity agreements.

University of Wisconsin–Madison, Graduate School, College of Letters and Science, School of Journalism and Mass Communication, Program in Mass Communication, Madison, WI 53706-1380. Offers PhD. *Degree requirements:* For doctorate, thesis/dissertation. *Expenses:* Tuition, state resident: full-time $9887; part-time $617.96 per credit. Tuition, nonresident: full-time $24,054; part-time $1503.40 per credit. Required fees: $67.63 per credit. Tuition and fees vary according to reciprocity agreements.

University of Wisconsin–Stevens Point, College of Fine Arts and Communication, Division of Communication, Stevens Point, WI 54481-3897. Offers interpersonal communication (MA); mass communication (MA); organizational communication (MA); public relations (MA). Part-time programs available. *Degree requirements:* For master's, thesis or alternative. *Entrance requirements:* For master's, GRE. Additional exam requirements/recommendations for international students: Required—TOEFL (minimum score 575 paper-based). *Faculty research:* Communication theory and research, film history.

University of Wisconsin–Superior, Graduate Division, Department of Communicating Arts, Superior, WI 54880-4500. Offers mass communication (MA); speech communication (MA); theater (MA). Part-time programs available. *Degree requirements:* For master's, comprehensive exam, thesis or alternative, position paper or project. *Entrance requirements:* For master's, minimum GPA of 2.75. *Faculty research:* Multimedia technology, ethics in journalism, diversity, electronic portfolio assessment.

University of Wisconsin–Whitewater, School of Graduate Studies, College of Arts and Communications, Department of Communication, Whitewater, WI 53190-1790. Offers corporate communication (MS); mass communication (MS). Part-time and evening/weekend programs available. Postbaccalaureate distance learning degree programs offered (no on-campus study). *Degree requirements:* For master's, thesis or alternative. *Entrance requirements:* For master's, 2 letters of recommendation. Additional exam requirements/recommendations for international students: Required—TOEFL (minimum score 550 paper-based; 213 computer-based). Electronic applications accepted.

Virginia Commonwealth University, Graduate School, College of Humanities and Sciences, School of Mass Communications, Program in Mass Communications, Richmond, VA 23284-9005. Offers multimedia journalism (MS); strategic public relations (MS). *Students:* 62 applicants, 53% accepted, 26 enrolled. *Degree requirements:* For master's, comprehensive exam, thesis optional. *Entrance requirements:* For master's, GRE General Test. Additional exam requirements/recommendations for international students: Required—TOEFL (minimum score 600 paper-based; 250 computer-based; 100 iBT); Recommended—IELTS (minimum score 6.5). *Application deadline:* For fall admission, 3/15 for domestic students. Applications are processed on a rolling basis. Application fee: $50. Electronic applications accepted. *Expenses:* Tuition, state resident: full-time $4308; part-time $479 per credit hour. Tuition, nonresident: full-time $8942; part-time $994 per credit hour. Required fees: $2000; $85 per credit hour. Tuition and fees vary according to course level, course load, degree level, campus/location and program. *Financial support:* Teaching assistantships, career-related internships or fieldwork, Federal Work-Study, institutionally sponsored loans, and tuition waivers (full and partial) available. Support available to part-time students. Financial award applicants required to submit FAFSA. *Faculty research:* Multimedia journalism, strategic public relations. *Unit head:* Dr. Terry Oggel, Interim Director, School of Mass Communications, 804-828-2660, Fax: 804-828-9175, E-mail: masscomm@vcu.edu. *Application contact:* June O. Nicholson, Director of Graduate Studies, 804-827-0251, Fax: 804-828-9175, E-mail: jonichol@vcu.edu.

Media Studies

American University, School of Communication, Film and Electronic Media Program, Washington, DC 20016-8001. Offers MFA. Part-time and evening/weekend programs available. *Faculty:* 14 full-time (6 women). *Students:* 47 full-time (22 women), 40 part-time (23 women), 3 international. 74 applicants, 59% accepted, 26 enrolled. In 2010, 141 master's awarded. *Degree requirements:* For master's, comprehensive exam, thesis or alternative. *Entrance requirements:* For master's, GRE General Test. Additional exam requirements/recommendations for international students: Required—TOEFL (minimum score 600 paper-based; 250 computer-based; 100 iBT), IELTS. *Application deadline:* For fall admission, 2/1 priority date for domestic and international students; for spring admission, 11/15 for domestic and international students. Applications are processed on a rolling basis. Application fee: $50. Electronic applications accepted. *Financial support:* In 2010–11, 10 students received support, including 2 fellowships with partial tuition reimbursements available (averaging $13,000 per year), 2 research assistantships with partial tuition reimbursements available (averaging $11,000 per year), 4 teaching assistantships with partial tuition reimbursements available (averaging $11,000 per year); career-related internships or fieldwork, Federal Work-Study, institutionally sponsored loans, scholarships/grants, tuition waivers (partial), and unspecified assistantships also available. Financial award application deadline: 2/1; financial award applicants required to submit FAFSA. *Faculty research:* Documentary film production, social media, media and public policy, visual literacy, new technology. *Unit head:* Prof. John Douglass, Director, Film and Media Arts Division, 202-885-2045, Fax: 202-885-2019, E-mail: jdougla@american.edu. *Application contact:* Sharmeen Ahsan-Bracciale, Graduate Admissions Office, 202-885-2040, Fax: 202-885-2019, E-mail: sharmeen@american.edu.

American University, School of Communication, PhD Program in Communication, Washington, DC 20016-8001. Offers media industries and institutions (PhD); media, public issues, and engagement (PhD); media, technology, and culture (PhD). *Degree requirements:* For doctorate, comprehensive exam, thesis/dissertation. *Entrance requirements:* For doctorate, GRE General Test, MA with minimum cumulative GPA of 3.3. Additional exam requirements/recommendations for international students: Required—TOEFL (minimum score 600 paper-based; 250 computer-based; 100 iBT), IELTS (minimum score 7). *Application deadline:* For fall admission, 2/1 priority date for domestic students. Applications are processed on a rolling basis. Electronic applications accepted. *Financial support:* Fellowships, Federal Work-Study, scholarships/grants, and unspecified assistantships available. Financial award application deadline: 2/1; financial award applicants required to submit FAFSA. *Unit head:* Prof. Kathryn Montgomery, Director, PhD in Communication Program, 202-885-2680, Fax: 202-885-2099, E-mail: kcm@american.edu. *Application contact:* Sharmeen Ahsan-Bracciale, Director of Graduate Services, 202-885-2040, Fax: 202-885-2019, E-mail: sharmeen@american.edu.

Arizona State University, College of Liberal Arts and Sciences, Program in Film and Media Studies, Tempe, AZ 85287-0402. Offers American media and popular culture (MAS). Part-time and evening/weekend programs available. Postbaccalaureate distance learning degree programs offered (no on-campus study). *Faculty:* 10 full-time (3 women). *Students:* 5 full-time (all women), 12 part-time (4 women); includes 4 minority (all Hispanic/Latino). Average age 32. 20 applicants, 20% accepted, 3 enrolled. *Degree requirements:* For master's, integrated project. *Entrance requirements:* For master's, minimum GPA of 3.0 or equivalent in last 2 years of work leading to bachelor's degree. Additional exam requirements/recommendations for international students: Required—TOEFL, IELTS, or Pearson Test of English. *Application deadline:* For fall admission, 3/15 for domestic and international students; for spring admission, 10/15 for domestic and international students. Applications are processed on a rolling basis. Application fee: $70 ($90 for international students). Electronic applications accepted. *Expenses:* Contact institution. *Financial support:* In 2010–11, 1 teaching assistantship with full and partial tuition reimbursement (averaging $15,000 per year) was awarded; career-related internships or fieldwork, Federal Work-Study, institutionally sponsored loans, scholarships/grants, and tuition waivers (partial) also available. Financial award application deadline: 3/1; financial award

Media Studies

Arizona State University (continued)
applicants required to submit FAFSA. Total annual research expenditures: $198,441. *Unit head:* Dr. Bambi Haggins, Director, 480-965-6747, Fax: 480-965-9110, E-mail: bambi.haggins@asu.edu. *Application contact:* Graduate Admissions, 480-965-6113.

Arizona State University, Herberger Institute for Design and the Arts, School of Arts, Media and Engineering, Tempe, AZ 85287-8709. Offers media arts and sciences (PhD). *Faculty:* 9 full-time (2 women), 1 part-time/adjunct (0 women). *Students:* 13 full-time (8 women), 2 part-time (1 woman); includes 3 minority (1 Asian, non-Hispanic/Latino; 1 Hispanic/Latino; 1 Two or more races, non-Hispanic/Latino), 4 international. Average age 30. 18 applicants, 33% accepted, 3 enrolled. *Degree requirements:* For doctorate, comprehensive exam, thesis/dissertation, interactive Program of Study (iPOS) submitted before completing 50 percent of required credit hours. *Entrance requirements:* For doctorate, GRE, minimum GPA of 3.25 in last 2 years of work leading to bachelor's degree, portfolio of supporting material, statement of educational/career goals, 3 letters of recommendation, resume/curriculum vitae. Additional exam requirements/recommendations for international students: Required—TOEFL, IELTS, or Pearson Test of English. *Application deadline:* For fall admission, 2/1 for domestic and international students. Application fee: $70 ($90 for international students). Electronic applications accepted. *Expenses:* Tuition, state resident: full-time $8510; part-time $608 per credit. Tuition, nonresident: full-time $16,542; part-time $919 per credit. Required fees: $339; $110 per credit. Part-time tuition and fees vary according to course load. *Financial support:* In 2010–11, 3 research assistantships with full and partial tuition reimbursements (averaging $15,000 per year) were awarded; fellowships with full and partial tuition reimbursements, career-related internships or fieldwork, scholarships/grants, traineeships, and tuition waivers (full and partial) also available. Financial award application deadline: 3/1; financial award applicants required to submit FAFSA. Total annual research expenditures: $403,026. *Unit head:* Dr. Thanassis Rikakis, Director, 480-965-0972, Fax: 480-965—961, E-mail: thanassis.rikakis@asu.edu. *Application contact:* Graduate Admissions, 480-965-6113.

Arkansas State University, Graduate School, College of Communications, Department of Radio-Television, Jonesboro, State University, AR 72467. Offers MSMC. Part-time programs available. *Faculty:* 4 full-time (1 woman). *Students:* 20 full-time (12 women), 15 part-time (12 women); includes 16 minority (all Black or African American, non-Hispanic/Latino), 15 international. Average age 26. 26 applicants, 85% accepted, 15 enrolled. In 2010, 5 master's awarded. *Degree requirements:* For master's, comprehensive exam, thesis or alternative. *Entrance requirements:* For master's, GRE General Test or MAT, appropriate bachelor's degree, letters of reference, educational experience, professional experience, official transcripts, immunization records. Additional exam requirements/recommendations for international students: Required—TOEFL (minimum score 550 paper-based; 213 computer-based; 79 iBT), IELTS (minimum score 6), PTE: Pearson Test of English Academic (56). *Application deadline:* For fall admission, 7/1 for domestic and international students; for spring admission, 11/15 for domestic students, 11/14 for international students. Applications are processed on a rolling basis. Application fee: $30 ($40 for international students). Electronic applications accepted. *Expenses:* Tuition, state resident: full-time $3888; part-time $216 per credit hour. Tuition, nonresident: full-time $9918; part-time $551 per credit hour. International tuition: $8376 full-time. Required fees: $932; $49 per credit hour. $25 per term. One-time fee: $30. Tuition and fees vary according to course load and program. *Financial support:* In 2010–11, 12 students received support. Career-related internships or fieldwork, scholarships/grants, and unspecified assistantships available. Financial award application deadline: 7/1; financial award applicants required to submit FAFSA. *Unit head:* Dr. Mary Jackson-Pitts, Interim Chair, 870-972-3070, Fax: 870-972-2997, E-mail: mpitts@astate.edu. *Application contact:* Dr. Andrew Sustich, Dean of the Graduate School, 870-972-3029, Fax: 870-972-3857, E-mail: sustich@astate.edu.

Bob Jones University, Graduate Programs, Greenville, SC 29614. Offers accountancy (MS); Bible (MA); Bible translation (MA); Biblical studies (Certificate); broadcast management (MS); business administration (MBA); church history (MA, PhD); church ministries (MA); church music (MM); cinema and video production (MA); counseling (MS); curriculum and instruction (Ed D); divinity (M Div); dramatic production (MA); educational leadership (MS, Ed D, Ed S); elementary education (M Ed, MAT); English (M Ed, MA, MAT); fine arts (MA); graphic design (MA); history (M Ed, MA); illustration (MA); interpretative speech (MA); mathematics (M Ed, MAT); medical missions (Certificate); ministry (MM, D Min); multi-categorical special education (M Ed, MAT); music (M Ed); New Testament interpretation (PhD); Old Testament interpretation (PhD); orchestral instrument performance (MM); organ performance (MM); pastoral studies (MA); personnel services (MS, Ed S); piano pedagogy (MM); piano performance (MM); platform arts (MA); radio and television broadcasting (MS); rhetoric and public address (MA); secondary education (M Ed); studio art (MA); teaching Bible (MA); theology (MA, PhD); voice performance (MM); youth ministries (MA); M Div/MM.

Boston University, College of Communication, Department of Film and Television, Boston, MA 02215. Offers film production (MFA); film studies (MFA); media ventures (MS); screenwriting (MFA); television production (MS); MBA/MS. Part-time programs available. *Faculty:* 13 full-time, 27 part-time/adjunct. *Students:* 80 full-time (44 women), 11 part-time (4 women); includes 12 minority (7 Black or African American, non-Hispanic/Latino; 2 Asian, non-Hispanic/Latino; 2 Hispanic/Latino; 1 Two or more races, non-Hispanic/Latino), 17 international. Average age 26. In 2010, 54 master's awarded. *Degree requirements:* For master's, thesis. *Entrance requirements:* For master's, GRE General Test, sample of written or creative work. Additional exam requirements/recommendations for international students: Required—TOEFL (minimum score 600 paper-based; 250 computer-based; 100 iBT). *Application deadline:* For fall admission, 2/1 for domestic and international students. Application fee: $70. Electronic applications accepted. *Expenses:* Tuition: Full-time $39,314; part-time $1228 per credit. Required fees: $40 per semester. *Financial support:* Teaching assistantships with partial tuition reimbursements, career-related internships or fieldwork, Federal Work-Study, institutionally sponsored loans, scholarships/grants, and unspecified assistantships available. Support available to part-time students. Financial award application deadline: 2/1; financial award applicants required to submit FAFSA. *Unit head:* Paul Schneider, Chairman, 617-353-3483, Fax: 617-353-1084, E-mail: ftvchair@bu.edu. *Application contact:* Jennifer Healey, Administrator of Graduate Services, 617-353-3481, Fax: 617-358-0399, E-mail: comgrad@bu.edu.

Brooklyn College of the City University of New York, Division of Graduate Studies, Department of Television and Radio, Brooklyn, NY 11210-2889. Offers media studies (MS); television production (MFA). Part-time and evening/weekend programs available. *Students:* 14 full-time (8 women), 39 part-time (11 women); includes 16 minority (9 Black or African American, non-Hispanic/Latino; 1 Asian, non-Hispanic/Latino; 6 Hispanic/Latino), 15 international. Average age 29. 56 applicants, 71% accepted, 23 enrolled. In 2010, 23 master's awarded. *Degree requirements:* For master's, comprehensive exam. *Entrance requirements:* For master's, GRE General Test or MAT, 12 credits in television/radio with a minimum B average, 2 letters of recommendation. Additional exam requirements/recommendations for international students: Required—TOEFL (minimum score 580 paper-based; 237 computer-based; 92 iBT). *Application deadline:* For fall admission, 3/1 priority date for domestic students, 2/1 priority date for international students; for spring admission, 11/1 priority date for domestic students, 10/1 priority date for international students. Applications are processed on a rolling basis. Application fee: $125. Electronic applications accepted. *Expenses:* Tuition, state resident: full-time $7360; part-time $310 per credit hour. Tuition, nonresident: full-time $13,800; part-time $575 per credit hour. Required fees: $190 per semester. *Financial support:* Career-related internships or fieldwork, Federal Work-Study, and institutionally sponsored loans available. Support available to part-time students. Financial award application deadline: 5/1; financial award applicants required to submit FAFSA. *Faculty research:* Criticism, research methods, audience behavior, policy and regulation, program history, international television and radio. *Unit head:* Dr. Fred Wasser, Chairperson, 718-951-5555, E-mail: fwasser@brooklyn.cuny.edu. *Application contact:* Hernan Sierra, Graduate Admissions Coordinator, 718-951-4536, Fax: 718-951-4506, E-mail: grads@brooklyn.cuny.edu.

California State University, Fullerton, Graduate Studies, College of Communications, Department of Communications, Fullerton, CA 92834-9480. Offers advertising (MA); communications (MFA); entertainment and tourism (MA); journalism (MA); public relations (MA). Part-time programs available. *Students:* 24 full-time (15 women), 39 part-time (27 women); includes 2 Two or more races, non-Hispanic/Latino. Average age 29. 119 applicants, 40% accepted, 29 enrolled. In 2010, 30 master's awarded. *Degree requirements:* For master's, project or thesis. *Entrance requirements:* For master's, GRE General Test. Application fee: $55. *Financial support:* Teaching assistantships, career-related internships or fieldwork, Federal Work-Study, institutionally sponsored loans, and scholarships/grants available. Support available to part-time students. Financial award application deadline: 3/1; financial award applicants required to submit FAFSA. *Unit head:* Dr. Tony Fellow, Chair, 657-278-3517. *Application contact:* Coordinator, 657-278-3832.

Carnegie Mellon University, School of Computer Science and College of Fine Arts, Program in Entertainment Technology, Pittsburgh, PA 15213-3891. Offers MET.

Central Michigan University, College of Graduate Studies, College of Communication and Fine Arts, School of Broadcasting and Cinematic Arts, Mount Pleasant, MI 48859. Offers electronic media management (MA); electronic media production (MA); electronic media studies (MA); film theory and criticism (MA). Part-time programs available. *Faculty:* 11 full-time (2 women), 1 part-time/adjunct (0 women). *Students:* 15 full-time (4 women), 18 part-time (7 women); includes 2 Black or African American, non-Hispanic/Latino; 1 Asian, non-Hispanic/Latino; 1 Hispanic/Latino, 6 international. Average age 26. *Degree requirements:* For master's, thesis or alternative. *Entrance requirements:* For master's, undergraduate degree in broadcasting, film studies, or an associated discipline with minimum GPA of 2.7. *Application deadline:* For fall admission, 6/1 for international students; for spring admission, 10/1 for international students. Applications are processed on a rolling basis. Application fee: $35 ($45 for international students). Electronic applications accepted. *Expenses:* Tuition, state resident: full-time $8208; part-time $456 per credit hour. Tuition, nonresident: full-time $13,788; part-time $766 per credit hour. One-time fee: $25. *Financial support:* Fellowships with tuition reimbursements, teaching assistantships with tuition reimbursements, career-related internships or fieldwork, Federal Work-Study, unspecified assistantships, and out-of-state merit awards, non-resident graduate awards available. Financial award application deadline: 3/1. *Faculty research:* Multimedia production, film history and criticism, writing and promotions, international broadcasting and media systems, history of American broadcasting. *Unit head:* Dr. Peter B. Orlik, Chairperson, 989-774-3851, Fax: 989-774-2426, E-mail: peter.b.orlik@cmich.edu. *Application contact:* Dr. Patricia Williamson, Graduate Program Coordinator, 989-774-2561, Fax: 989-774-2426, E-mail: willi1pa@cmich.edu.

City College of the City University of New York, Graduate School, College of Liberal Arts and Science, Division of the Humanities and Arts, Department of Media Arts Production, New York, NY 10031-9198. Offers MFA. *Entrance requirements:* For master's, videotape portfolio. Additional exam requirements/recommendations for international students: Required—TOEFL (minimum score 575 paper-based; 90 iBT). Electronic applications accepted.

Claremont Graduate University, Graduate Programs, School of Arts and Humanities, Department of Cultural Studies, Claremont, CA 91711-6160. Offers Africana studies (Certificate); cultural studies (MA, PhD); media studies (MA, PhD); museum studies (MA). Part-time programs available. *Faculty:* 2 full-time (1 woman), 1 (woman) part-time/adjunct. *Students:* 57 full-time (36 women), 9 part-time (8 women); includes 12 Black or African American, non-Hispanic/Latino; 1 American Indian or Alaska Native, non-Hispanic/Latino; 3 Asian, non-Hispanic/Latino; 9 Hispanic/Latino; 5 Two or more races, non-Hispanic/Latino, 6 international. Average age 36. In 2010, 9 master's, 5 doctorates awarded. *Entrance requirements:* For master's and doctorate, GRE General Test. Additional exam requirements/recommendations for international students: Required—TOEFL (minimum score 550 paper-based; 213 computer-based; 80 iBT). *Application deadline:* For fall admission, 2/1 priority date for domestic students. Applications are processed on a rolling basis. Application fee: $60. Electronic applications accepted. *Expenses:* Tuition: Full-time $35,748; part-time $1554 per unit. Required fees: $215 per semester. *Financial support:* Fellowships, research assistantships, Federal Work-Study, institutionally sponsored loans, and scholarships/grants available. Support available to part-time students. Financial award application deadline: 2/15; financial award applicants required to submit FAFSA. *Unit head:* Eve Oishi, Chair, 909-607-7587, E-mail: eve.oishi@cgu.edu. *Application contact:* Susan Hampson, Admissions Coordinator, 909-607-1278, Fax: 909-607-1221, E-mail: humanities@cgu.edu.

College of Staten Island of the City University of New York, Graduate Programs, Program in Cinema and Media Studies, Staten Island, NY 10314-6600. Offers MA. Part-time and evening/weekend programs available. *Faculty:* 6 full-time (3 women). *Students:* 1 full-time (0 women), 19 part-time (7 women); includes 2 Hispanic/Latino, 3 international. Average age 27. 26 applicants, 31% accepted, 4 enrolled. In 2010, 5 master's awarded. *Degree requirements:* For master's, comprehensive exam, original film, media or production thesis or written examination. *Entrance requirements:* For master's, 10-12 page critical writing sample on film or media topic, 3 letters of recommendation. Additional exam requirements/recommendations for international students: Required—TOEFL (minimum score 550 paper-based; 213 computer-based; 79 iBT), IELTS (minimum score 6.5). *Application deadline:* For fall admission, 4/15 priority date for domestic and international students; for spring admission, 11/15 priority date for domestic and international students. Applications are processed on a rolling basis. Application fee: $125. Electronic applications accepted. *Expenses:* Tuition, state resident: full-time $7730; part-time $325 per credit. Tuition, nonresident: full-time $14,520; part-time $605 per credit. Required fees: $378. *Financial support:* In 2010–11, 4 teaching assistantships (averaging $1,250 per year) were awarded; career-related internships or fieldwork, Federal Work-Study, and scholarships/grants also available. Support available to part-time students. Financial award applicants required to submit FAFSA. *Unit head:* Dr. Matthew Solomon, Coordinator/Associate Professor, 718-982-2548, E-mail: cinemamasters@mail.csi.cuny.edu. *Application contact:* Sasha Spence, Assistant Director of Graduate Recruitment and Admissions, 718-982-2699, Fax: 718-982-2500, E-mail: sasha.spence@csi.cuny.edu.

Columbia College Chicago, Graduate School, Department of Arts, Entertainment and Media Management, Chicago, IL 60605-1996. Offers arts, entertainment and media management (MA), including media management, music business management, performing arts management, visual arts management. Evening/weekend programs available. *Students:* 68 full-time (53 women), 45 part-time (33 women); includes 44 minority (29 Black or African American, non-Hispanic/Latino; 1 American Indian or Alaska Native, non-Hispanic/Latino; 5 Asian, non-Hispanic/Latino; 9 Hispanic/Latino), 8 international. Average age 28. 252 applicants, 35% accepted, 31 enrolled. In 2010, 52 master's awarded. *Degree requirements:* For master's, thesis, internship. *Entrance requirements:* For master's, self-assessment essay. Additional exam requirements/recommendations for international students: Required—TOEFL (minimum score 550 paper-based; 213 computer-based). *Application deadline:* For fall admission, 1/15 for domestic and international students. Application fee: $55. Electronic applications accepted. *Expenses:* Tuition: Full-time $16,966; part-time $684 per credit. Required fees: $520; $113 per semester. One-time fee: $150 full-time. Tuition and fees vary according to course load and program. *Financial support:* Fellowships, career-related internships or fieldwork, Federal Work-Study, and scholarships/grants available. Support available to part-time students. Financial award application deadline: 8/13; financial award applicants required to submit FAFSA. *Unit head:* Prof. Dawn Larsen, Director of Graduate Studies, 312-369-7639, E-mail: dlarsen@colum.edu. *Application contact:* Cate Lagueux, Director of Graduate Admissions, 312-369-7260, Fax: 312-369-8047, E-mail: clagueux@colum.edu.

Concordia University, School of Graduate Studies, Faculty of Arts and Science, Department of Communication Studies, Montréal, QC H3G 1M8, Canada. Offers communication (PhD); communication studies (Diploma); media studies (MA). PhD program offered jointly with Université de Montréal and Université du Québec à Montréal. *Degree requirements:* For master's, thesis optional; for doctorate, one foreign language, comprehensive exam, thesis/

dissertation, research practicum, seminar. *Entrance requirements:* For master's, bachelor's degree in communications, 2 years of media-related experience; for doctorate, MA in communications. *Faculty research:* Communication and development, organizational communication, cultural studies, rhetoric, future studies.

Concordia University, School of Graduate Studies, Faculty of Fine Arts, Department of Studio Arts, Montréal, QC H3G 1M8, Canada. Offers studio arts (MFA), including film production, open media, painting, photography, print media, sculpture, ceramics and fibers. *Degree requirements:* For master's, thesis or alternative. *Entrance requirements:* For master's, portfolio.

Dallas Theological Seminary, Graduate Programs, Dallas, TX 75204-6499. Offers academic ministries (Th M); Bible translation (Th M); biblical and theological studies (CGS); biblical counseling (MA, Th M); biblical exegesis and linguistics (MA); biblical exposition (PhD); biblical studies (MA); Christian education (MA, D Min); cross-cultural ministries (MA, Th M); educational leadership (Th M); evangelism and discipleship (Th M); interdisciplinary studies (Th M); media and communication (MA); media arts in ministry (Th M); ministry (D Min); New Testament studies (Th M, PhD); Old Testament studies (PhD); parachurch ministries (Th M); pastoral ministries (Th M); sacred theology (STM); theological studies (PhD); women's ministry (Th M). *Accreditation:* ATS (one or more programs are accredited). Part-time and evening/weekend programs available. *Degree requirements:* For master's, variable foreign language requirement, thesis (for some programs); for doctorate, 2 foreign languages, thesis/dissertation. *Entrance requirements:* Additional exam requirements/recommendations for international students: Required—TOEFL, TWE. Electronic applications accepted.

DePaul University, College of Communication, Chicago, IL 60614. Offers journalism (MA); media, culture and society (MA); organizational and multicultural communication (MA); public relations and advertising (MA). Part-time and evening/weekend programs available. *Faculty:* 31 full-time (17 women), 15 part-time/adjunct (7 women). *Students:* 170 full-time (129 women), 70 part-time (52 women); includes 29 Black or African American, non-Hispanic/Latino; 9 Asian, non-Hispanic/Latino; 20 Hispanic/Latino; 7 Two or more races, non-Hispanic/Latino, 17 international. Average age 29. 354 applicants, 44% accepted, 79 enrolled. In 2010, 64 master's awarded. *Degree requirements:* For master's, comprehensive exam (for some programs), final exam or thesis/project. *Entrance requirements:* For master's, GRE General Test (public relations and advertising), minimum GPA of 3.0, writing sample, letters of recommendation, resume. Additional exam requirements/recommendations for international students: Required—TOEFL (minimum score 590 paper-based; 243 computer-based; 96 iBT). Application fee: $40. Electronic applications accepted. *Financial support:* In 2010–11, 8 students received support, including 4 research assistantships with partial tuition reimbursements available, 2 teaching assistantships with full tuition reimbursements available (averaging $12,000 per year); fellowships with full tuition reimbursements available, career-related internships or fieldwork, scholarships/grants, and tuition waivers (partial) also available. Support available to part-time students. Financial award applicants required to submit FAFSA. *Faculty research:* Intercultural communication, corporate culture, diversity in the working place, organizational socialization, critical cultural studies. *Unit head:* Dr. Jacqueline Taylor, Dean, 773-325-7216, Fax: 773-325-7584, E-mail: jtaylor@depaul.edu. *Application contact:* Ann Spittle, Director of Graduate Admission, 773-325-7315, Fax: 773-325-2395, E-mail: gradcom@depaul.edu.

Digital Media Arts College, Graduate Programs, Boca Raton, FL 33431. Offers graphic design (MFA); special FX animation (MFA).

Duke University, Graduate School, Center for Documentary Studies, Durham, NC 27708. Offers experimental and documentary arts (MFA). *Faculty:* 26 full-time. *Degree requirements:* For master's, thesis, final project. *Entrance requirements:* For master's, portfolio. Additional exam requirements/recommendations for international students: Required—TOEFL, IELTS. *Application deadline:* For fall admission, 1/30 priority date for domestic students. Applications are processed on a rolling basis. *Unit head:* Stanley Abe, Program Director, 919-660-3661, Fax: 919-681-7600, E-mail: stanley.abe@duke.edu. *Application contact:* Elizabeth Hutton, Director of Admissions, 919-684-3913, Fax: 919-684-2277, E-mail: grad-admissions@duke.edu.

Emerson College, Graduate Studies, School of the Arts, Department of Visual and Media Arts, Program in Media Art, Boston, MA 02116-4624. Offers MFA. *Entrance requirements:* For master's, creative portfolio. Additional exam requirements/recommendations for international students: Required—TOEFL (minimum score 550 paper-based; 213 computer-based; 80 iBT), IELTS (minimum score 6.5). Electronic applications accepted. *Faculty research:* Media studies.

Fairleigh Dickinson University, Metropolitan Campus, University College: Arts, Sciences, and Professional Studies, School of Art and Media Studies, Program in Media and Communications, Teaneck, NJ 07666-1914. Offers MA. *Students:* 14 full-time (9 women), 10 part-time (8 women), 5 international. Average age 29. 16 applicants, 81% accepted, 7 enrolled. In 2010, 16 master's awarded. Application fee: $40. *Application contact:* Susan Brooman, University Director of Graduate Admissions, 201-692-2554, Fax: 201-692-2560, E-mail: globaleducation@fdu.edu.

Florida State University, The Graduate School, College of Communication and Information, School of Communication, Tallahassee, FL 32306. Offers corporate and public communication (MS); integrated marketing communication (MA, MS); mass communication (PhD); media and communication studies (MA, MS); speech communication (PhD). Part-time programs available. *Faculty:* 24 full-time (9 women), 6 part-time/adjunct (1 woman). *Students:* 147 full-time (94 women), 63 part-time (38 women); includes 92 minority (26 Black or African American, non-Hispanic/Latino; 2 American Indian or Alaska Native, non-Hispanic/Latino; 45 Asian, non-Hispanic/Latino; 16 Hispanic/Latino; 1 Native Hawaiian or other Pacific Islander, non-Hispanic/Latino; 2 Two or more races, non-Hispanic/Latino). Average age 24. 268 applicants, 57% accepted, 79 enrolled. In 2010, 103 master's, 4 doctorates awarded. *Degree requirements:* For master's, thesis (for some programs); for doctorate, comprehensive exam, thesis/dissertation. *Entrance requirements:* For master's, GRE General Test, minimum GPA of 3.0; for doctorate, GRE General Test, minimum GPA of 3.3 in graduate course work. Additional exam requirements/recommendations for international students: Required—TOEFL (minimum score 600 paper-based; 250 computer-based; 100 iBT). *Application deadline:* For fall admission, 7/1 priority date for domestic students, 5/1 priority date for international students; for spring admission, 11/1 priority date for domestic and international students. Applications are processed on a rolling basis. Application fee: $30. Electronic applications accepted. *Expenses:* Tuition, state resident: full-time $8238.24. *Financial support:* In 2010–11, 52 students received support, including 1 fellowship with full tuition reimbursement available, 8 research assistantships with full tuition reimbursements available (averaging $14,000 per year), 40 teaching assistantships with full tuition reimbursements available (averaging $5,000 per year); career-related internships or fieldwork, Federal Work-Study, institutionally sponsored loans, scholarships/grants, tuition waivers (partial), and unspecified assistantships also available. Support available to part-time students. Financial award application deadline: 2/1; financial award applicants required to submit FAFSA. *Faculty research:* Communication technology and policy, marketing communication, communication content and effect, new communication/information technologies. Total annual research expenditures: $400,000. *Unit head:* Dr. Stephen D. McDowell, Director, 850-644-2276, Fax: 850-644-8642, E-mail: steve.mcdowell@cci.fsu.edu. *Application contact:* Natashia Hinson-Turner, Graduate Coordinator, 850-644-8746, Fax: 850-644-8642, E-mail: natashia.turner@cci.fsu.edu.

Fordham University, Graduate School of Business, New York, NY 10023. Offers accounting (MBA); communications and media management (MBA); executive business administration (EMBA); finance (MBA, MS); information systems (MBA, MS); management systems (MBA); marketing (MBA); media management (MS); taxation (MS); taxation and accounting (MTA);); JD/MBA; MBA/MIM; MS/MBA. MBA/MIM offered jointly with Thunderbird School of Global Management. *Accreditation:* AACSB. Part-time and evening/weekend programs available. *Entrance requirements:* For master's, GMAT, 2 letters of recommendation, resume. Additional exam requirements/recommendations for international students: Required—TOEFL (minimum score 600 paper-based; 250 computer-based; 100 iBT). Electronic applications accepted. *Expenses:* Contact institution.

Full Sail University, Media Design Master of Fine Arts Program—Online, Winter Park, FL 32792-7437. Offers MFA. Postbaccalaureate distance learning degree programs offered.

Georgetown University, Graduate School of Arts and Sciences, School of Continuing Studies, Washington, DC 20057. Offers American studies (MALS); Catholic studies (MALS); classical civilizations (MALS); disability studies (MPS); ethics and the professions (MALS); human resources management (MPS); humanities (MALS); individualized study (MALS); international affairs (MALS); Islam and Muslim-Christian relations (MALS); journalism (MPS); liberal studies (DLS); literature and society (MALS); medieval and early modern European studies (MALS); public relations and corporate communications (MPS); real estate (MPS); religious studies (MALS); social and public policy (MALS); sports industry management (MPS); the theory and practice of American democracy (MALS); visual culture (MALS). *Entrance requirements:* Additional exam requirements/recommendations for international students: Required—TOEFL.

Governors State University, College of Arts and Sciences, Program in Communication and Training, University Park, IL 60466-0975. Offers communication studies (MA); instructional and training technology (MA); media communication (MA). Part-time and evening/weekend programs available. *Degree requirements:* For master's, thesis or alternative. *Expenses:* Tuition, state resident: full-time $5400; part-time $225 per credit hour. Tuition, nonresident: full-time $16,200; part-time $675 per credit hour. Required fees: $1358; $46 per credit hour. $126 per term. Tuition and fees vary according to degree level and program.

Howard University, School of Communications, Division of Mass Communication and Media Studies, Washington, DC 20059-0002. Offers mass communication (MA, PhD); media studies (MA, PhD). Part-time and evening/weekend programs available. *Degree requirements:* For master's, comprehensive exam (for some programs), thesis optional; for doctorate, one foreign language, comprehensive exam, thesis/dissertation. *Entrance requirements:* For master's, GRE, minimum GPA of 3.0; for doctorate, GRE, minimum graduate GPA of 3.5. Additional exam requirements/recommendations for international students: Required—TOEFL. Electronic applications accepted. *Faculty research:* Advertising, public relations, journalism new media.

Hunter College of the City University of New York, Graduate School, School of Arts and Sciences, Department of Film and Media Studies, Program in Integrated Media Arts, New York, NY 10021-5085. Offers MA, MFA. Part-time and evening/weekend programs available. *Faculty:* 7 full-time (3 women), 2 part-time/adjunct (both women). *Students:* 14 full-time (12 women), 52 part-time (30 women); includes 9 Black or African American, non-Hispanic/Latino; 3 Asian, non-Hispanic/Latino; 6 Hispanic/Latino, 6 international. Average age 33. 105 applicants, 28% accepted, 15 enrolled. In 2010, 13 master's awarded. *Entrance requirements:* For master's, GRE General Test, 3 letters of recommendation, portfolio of media works, minimum GPA of 3.0. Additional exam requirements/recommendations for international students: Required—TOEFL, TWE. *Application deadline:* For fall admission, 2/1 for domestic students. Application fee: $125. *Financial support:* Federal Work-Study and tuition waivers (partial) available. Support available to part-time students. *Faculty research:* Nonfiction production, Internet as medium, public interest journalism, social and historical roots of media arts. *Unit head:* Kelly Anderson, Deputy Chair, 212-772-6008. *Application contact:* Mary Flanagan, New Media Advisor, 212-650-3219, E-mail: maryflanagan@hunter.cuny.edu.

Indiana State University, College of Graduate and Professional Studies, College of Arts and Sciences, Department of Communication, Terre Haute, IN 47809. Offers communication studies (MA, MS); radio, television and film (MA, MS). Part-time programs available. *Degree requirements:* For master's, thesis (for some programs), oral and written exam. *Entrance requirements:* For master's, GRE General Test. Additional exam requirements/recommendations for international students: Required—TOEFL. *Faculty research:* Women in media, communication apprehension, media history.

Indiana University Bloomington, University Graduate School, College of Arts and Sciences, Department of Communication and Culture, Bloomington, IN 47405-7000. Offers film and media studies (PhD); performance and ethnography (PhD); rhetoric and public culture (PhD). *Faculty:* 24 full-time (12 women). *Students:* 81 full-time (41 women), 3 part-time (all women); includes 10 minority (2 Black or African American, non-Hispanic/Latino; 8 Hispanic/Latino), 10 international. Average age 32. 187 applicants, 12% accepted, 11 enrolled. In 2010, 4 master's, 7 doctorates awarded. *Degree requirements:* For master's, comprehensive exam; for doctorate, one foreign language, comprehensive exam, thesis/dissertation, student teaching. *Entrance requirements:* For master's and doctorate, GRE General Test (recommended), minimum GPA of 3.0, 3 letters of recommendation, writing sample. Additional exam requirements/recommendations for international students: Required—TOEFL (minimum score 550 paper-based; 213 computer-based). *Application deadline:* For winter admission, 1/1 for domestic students, 12/1 for international students. Application fee: $55 ($65 for international students). Electronic applications accepted. *Financial support:* In 2010–11, 65 students received support, including 4 fellowships with full tuition reimbursements available (averaging $18,000 per year), 48 teaching assistantships with full tuition reimbursements available (averaging $13,257 per year). Financial award application deadline: 4/15. *Faculty research:* Rhetoric and public culture, film and media studies, performance ethnography. *Unit head:* Prof. Gregory A. Waller, Chair, 812-855-2367, Fax: 812-855-6014, E-mail: cmcl@indiana.edu. *Application contact:* Kathy P. Teige, Graduate Secretary, 812-855-6389, Fax: 812-855-6014, E-mail: kteige@indiana.edu.

Indiana University of Pennsylvania, School of Graduate Studies and Research, College of Education and Educational Technology, Department of Communications Media, Indiana, PA 15705-1087. Offers adult education and communications technology (MA); communications media and instructional technology (PhD). Part-time and evening/weekend programs available. *Faculty:* 9 full-time (2 women). *Students:* 21 full-time (10 women), 30 part-time (14 women); includes 3 minority (2 Black or African American, non-Hispanic/Latino; 1 Asian, non-Hispanic/Latino), 2 international. Average age 36. 42 applicants, 31% accepted, 13 enrolled.Application fee: $40. *Financial support:* In 2010–11, 2 fellowships with full tuition reimbursements (averaging $1,000 per year), 10 research assistantships with full and partial tuition reimbursements (averaging $5,428 per year), 3 teaching assistantships with partial tuition reimbursements (averaging $21,967 per year) were awarded; career-related internships or fieldwork, Federal Work-Study, scholarships/grants, and tuition waivers (full) also available. Support available to part-time students. Financial award application deadline: 3/15; financial award applicants required to submit FAFSA. *Unit head:* Dr. Mark Piwinsky, Chairperson, 724-357-3954, Fax: 724-357-5503, E-mail: mark.piwinsky@iup.edu. *Application contact:* Dr. Edward Nardi, Associate Dean, 724-357-2480, Fax: 724-357-5595, E-mail: ewnardi@iup.edu.

Kutztown University of Pennsylvania, College of Liberal Arts and Sciences, Program in Electronic Media, Kutztown, PA 19530-0730. Offers MS. Part-time and evening/weekend programs available. *Faculty:* 3 full-time (1 woman). *Students:* 5 full-time (1 woman), 12 part-time (6 women); includes 3 minority (all Black or African American, non-Hispanic/Latino), 1 international. Average age 28. 6 applicants, 50% accepted, 3 enrolled. In 2010, 10 master's awarded. *Degree requirements:* For master's, thesis. *Entrance requirements:* For master's, GRE General Test. Additional exam requirements/recommendations for international students: Required—TOEFL (minimum score 550 paper-based; 79 iBT). *Application deadline:* For fall admission, 8/15 priority date for domestic and international students; for spring admission, 12/15 priority date for domestic and international students. Applications are processed on a rolling basis. Application fee: $35. Electronic applications accepted. *Expenses:* Tuition, state resident: full-time $6966; part-time $387 per credit. Tuition, nonresident: full-time $11,146; part-time $619 per credit hour. Required fees: $1499; $54 per credit. $68 per year. *Financial support:* Career-related internships or fieldwork, Federal Work-Study, scholarships/grants, and unspecified assistantships available. Financial award application deadline: 3/1; financial award applicants required to submit FAFSA. *Unit head:* Dr. Joseph Chuk, Chairperson, 610-683-

Media Studies

Kutztown University of Pennsylvania (continued)
4492, Fax: 610-683-4659, E-mail: chuk@kutztown.edu. *Application contact:* Kelly D. Burr, Associate Director, Graduate Admissions, 610-683-4200, Fax: 610-683-1393, E-mail: graduate@kutztown.edu.

Louisiana State University and Agricultural and Mechanical College, Graduate School, Manship School of Mass Communication, Baton Rouge, LA 70803. Offers MMC, PhD. *Accreditation:* ACEJMC. Part-time programs available. Postbaccalaureate distance learning degree programs offered (minimal on-campus study). *Faculty:* 26 full-time (14 women). *Students:* 53 full-time (32 women), 17 part-time (11 women); includes 10 Black or African American, non-Hispanic/Latino; 2 American Indian or Alaska Native, non-Hispanic/Latino; 2 Hispanic/Latino; 2 Two or more races, non-Hispanic/Latino, 4 international. Average age 30. 77 applicants, 40% accepted, 14 enrolled. In 2010, 20 master's, 1 doctorate awarded. *Degree requirements:* For master's, thesis; for doctorate, thesis/dissertation. *Entrance requirements:* For master's, GRE General Test, minimum GPA of 3.0. Additional exam requirements/recommendations for international students: Required—TOEFL (minimum score 550 paper-based; 213 computer-based; 79 iBT) or IELTS (minimum score 6.5). *Application deadline:* For fall admission, 1/25 priority date for domestic students, 5/15 for international students; for spring admission, 10/15 for international students. Applications are processed on a rolling basis. Application fee: $50 ($70 for international students). Electronic applications accepted. *Financial support:* In 2010–11, 57 students received support, including 2 fellowships (averaging $23,089 per year), 29 research assistantships with full and partial tuition reimbursements available (averaging $16,224 per year), 10 teaching assistantships with full and partial tuition reimbursements available (averaging $18,180 per year); career-related internships or fieldwork, Federal Work-Study, institutionally sponsored loans, scholarships/grants, health care benefits, tuition waivers (full and partial), and unspecified assistantships also available. Support available to part-time students. Financial award application deadline: 3/1; financial award applicants required to submit FAFSA. *Faculty research:* Media effects, political communication, new media technologies, persuasive communication, journalism processes and practice. Total annual research expenditures: $14,696. *Unit head:* Dr. John Maxwell Hamilton, Dean, 225-578-2002, Fax: 225-578-2125, E-mail: jhamilt@lsu.edu. *Application contact:* Dr. Amy L. Reynolds, Associate Dean of Graduate Studies and Research, 225-578-9294, Fax: 225-578-2125, E-mail: areynolds@lsu.edu.

Lynn University, College of Business and Management, Boca Raton, FL 33431-5598. Offers aviation management (MBA); financial valuation and investment management (MBA); hospitality management (MBA); international business (MBA); marketing (MBA); mass communication and media management (MBA); sports and athletics administration (MBA). Part-time and evening/weekend programs available. Postbaccalaureate distance learning degree programs offered. *Degree requirements:* For master's, project. *Entrance requirements:* For master's, GMAT or GRE, minimum undergraduate GPA of 3.0, resume, 2 letters of recommendation. Additional exam requirements/recommendations for international students: Required—TOEFL (minimum score 550 paper-based; 213 computer-based). Electronic applications accepted. *Faculty research:* Labor relations, dynamic balance in leisure-time skills, ethics in athletics, hotel development.

Lynn University, Eugene M. and Christine E. Lynn College of International Communication, Boca Raton, FL 33431-5598. Offers communication and media (MS). Part-time and evening/weekend programs available. *Entrance requirements:* For master's, GRE, resume, 2 letters of recommendation, minimum GPA of 3.0. Additional exam requirements/recommendations for international students: Required—TOEFL (minimum score 550 paper-based; 213 computer-based).

Marquette University, Graduate School, College of Communication, Milwaukee, WI 53201-1881. Offers advertising and public relations (MA); broadcasting and electronic communications (MA); communications studies (MA); digital storytelling (Certificate); health, environment, science and sustainability (MA); journalism (MA); mass communications (MA). *Accreditation:* ACEJMC (one or more programs are accredited). Part-time and evening/weekend programs available. *Faculty:* 33 full-time (18 women), 30 part-time/adjunct (16 women). *Students:* 35 full-time (20 women), 31 part-time (25 women); includes 5 minority (2 Black or African American, non-Hispanic/Latino; 1 Hispanic/Latino; 2 Two or more races, non-Hispanic/Latino), 4 international. Average age 28. 97 applicants, 52% accepted, 21 enrolled. In 2010, 16 master's, 5 other advanced degrees awarded. *Degree requirements:* For master's, comprehensive exam, thesis or alternative. *Entrance requirements:* For master's, GRE, official transcripts from all current and previous colleges/universities except Marquette, three letters of recommendation, statement of academic and professional goals. Additional exam requirements/recommendations for international students: Required—TOEFL (minimum score 530 paper-based; 78 computer-based). *Application deadline:* Applications are processed on a rolling basis. Application fee: $50. Electronic applications accepted. *Expenses:* Tuition: Full-time $16,290; part-time $905 per credit hour. Tuition and fees vary according to program. *Financial support:* In 2010–11, 2 fellowships, 7 research assistantships, 12 teaching assistantships were awarded; career-related internships or fieldwork, Federal Work-Study, institutionally sponsored loans, scholarships/grants, and tuition waivers (full and partial) also available. Support available to part-time students. Financial award application deadline: 2/15. *Faculty research:* Urban journalism, gender and communication, intercultural communication, religious communication. Total annual research expenditures: $3,088. *Unit head:* Dr. Lori Bergen, Dean, 414-288-7133, Fax: 414-288-1578. *Application contact:* Erin Fox, Assistant Director for Recruitment, 414-288-5319, Fax: 414-288-1902, E-mail: erin.fox@marquette.edu.

Marywood University, Academic Affairs, Insalaco College of Creative and Performing Arts, Department of Communication Arts, Program in Communication Arts, Scranton, PA 18509-1598. Offers interdisciplinary (MA); media management (MA); production (MA). *Entrance requirements:* Additional exam requirements/recommendations for international students: Required—TOEFL (minimum score 550 paper-based; 213 computer-based; 79 iBT). Electronic applications accepted. *Expenses:* Tuition: Part-time $735 per credit. Required fees: $470 per semester. Tuition and fees vary according to degree level and campus/location.

Massachusetts Institute of Technology, School of Architecture and Planning, Program in Media Arts and Sciences, Cambridge, MA 02139-4307. Offers media arts and sciences (SM, PhD); media technology (SM). *Faculty:* 19 full-time (5 women). *Students:* 134 full-time (25 women), 3 part-time (1 woman); includes 22 minority (3 Black or African American, non-Hispanic/Latino; 2 American Indian or Alaska Native, non-Hispanic/Latino; 14 Asian, non-Hispanic/Latino; 2 Hispanic/Latino; 1 Two or more races, non-Hispanic/Latino), 48 international. Average age 28. 659 applicants, 9% accepted, 53 enrolled. In 2010, 31 master's, 4 doctorates awarded. Terminal master's awarded for partial completion of doctoral program. *Degree requirements:* For master's, thesis; for doctorate, comprehensive exam, thesis/dissertation. *Entrance requirements:* Additional exam requirements/recommendations for international students: Required—IELTS (minimum score 7). *Application deadline:* For fall admission, 12/15 for domestic and international students. Application fee: $75. Electronic applications accepted. *Expenses:* Tuition: Full-time $38,940; part-time $605 per unit. Required fees: $272. *Financial support:* In 2010–11, 133 students received support, including 9 fellowships with tuition reimbursements available (averaging $22,458 per year), 121 research assistantships with tuition reimbursements available (averaging $29,823 per year), 1 teaching assistantship (averaging $21,090 per year); Federal Work-Study, institutionally sponsored loans, scholarships/grants, health care benefits, and unspecified assistantships also available. *Faculty research:* Human machine interaction, communications technologies, new media technologies, physical computing, learning and creativity. Total annual research expenditures: $18.4 million. *Unit head:* Prof. Mitchel J. Resnick, Head, 617-253-5114, Fax: 617-253-8542. *Application contact:* Graduate Admissions, 617-253-5114, Fax: 617-253-8542, E-mail: mas@media.mit.edu.

Massachusetts Institute of Technology, School of Humanities, Arts, and Social Sciences, Program in Comparative Media Studies, Cambridge, MA 02139-4307. Offers SM. *Faculty:* 16 full-time (6 women). *Students:* 2 full-time (1 woman), 1 international. Average age 32. In 2010, 15 master's awarded. *Degree requirements:* For master's, thesis. *Entrance requirements:* For master's, GRE General Test. Additional exam requirements/recommendations for international students: Required—IELTS (minimum score 7). *Application deadline:* For fall admission, 1/15 for domestic and international students. Application fee: $75. Electronic applications accepted. *Expenses:* Tuition: Full-time $38,940; part-time $605 per unit. Required fees: $272. *Financial support:* In 2010–11, 1 student received support; fellowships with tuition reimbursements available, research assistantships with tuition reimbursements available, Federal Work-Study, institutionally sponsored loans, scholarships/grants, health care benefits, and unspecified assistantships available. *Faculty research:* Game design, learning games, and creative computing; civic media; digital humanities; mobile and location-based media; media history and theory. Total annual research expenditures: $2.8 million. *Unit head:* Prof. William Uricchio, Director, 617-253-3599, Fax: 617-258-5133, E-mail: cms@mit.edu. *Application contact:* Graduate Admissions, 617-253-3599, Fax: 617-258-5133, E-mail: cms-admissions@mit.edu.

Metropolitan College of New York, Program in Media Management, New York, NY 10013. Offers MBA. Evening/weekend programs available. *Degree requirements:* For master's, thesis, 10 day study abroad. *Entrance requirements:* For master's, GMAT or GRE General Test, appropriate work experience, interview, minimum GPA of 2.7. Additional exam requirements/recommendations for international students: Required—TOEFL (minimum score 600 paper-based; 220 computer-based). Electronic applications accepted. *Expenses:* Contact institution.

Michigan State University, The Graduate School, College of Communication Arts and Sciences, Department of Telecommunication, Information Studies, and Media, East Lansing, MI 48824. Offers digital media arts and technology (MA); information and telecommunication management (MA); information, policy and society (MA); serious game design (MA). *Entrance requirements:* Additional exam requirements/recommendations for international students: Required—TOEFL. Electronic applications accepted.

Michigan State University, The Graduate School, College of Communication Arts and Sciences, Program in Communication Arts and Sciences–Media and Information Studies, East Lansing, MI 48824. Offers PhD. *Entrance requirements:* Additional exam requirements/recommendations for international students: Required—TOEFL. Electronic applications accepted. *Faculty research:* Mass media, comparative media.

Missouri Western State University, Program in Integrated Media, St. Joseph, MO 64507-2294. Offers applied integrated media (MAS); convergent media (MAS). *Expenses:* Tuition, state resident: full-time $5544; part-time $308 per credit hour. Tuition, nonresident: full-time $10,206; part-time $567 per credit hour. Required fees: $30 per semester. One-time fee: $45 full-time.

National University, Academic Affairs, School of Media and Communication, Department of Media, La Jolla, CA 92037-1011. Offers digital cinema (MFA); educational and instructional technology (MS); video game production and design (MFA). Part-time and evening/weekend programs available. Postbaccalaureate distance learning degree programs offered (no on-campus study). *Faculty:* 9 full-time (3 women), 61 part-time/adjunct (21 women). *Students:* 72 full-time (23 women), 131 part-time (63 women); includes 71 minority (31 Black or African American, non-Hispanic/Latino; 1 American Indian or Alaska Native, non-Hispanic/Latino; 7 Asian, non-Hispanic/Latino; 23 Hispanic/Latino; 1 Native Hawaiian or other Pacific Islander, non-Hispanic/Latino; 8 Two or more races, non-Hispanic/Latino), 10 international. Average age 39. 121 applicants, 100% accepted, 81 enrolled. In 2010, 47 master's awarded. *Degree requirements:* For master's, thesis. *Entrance requirements:* For master's, interview, minimum GPA of 2.5. Additional exam requirements/recommendations for international students: Required—TOEFL (minimum score 550 paper-based; 213 computer-based; 79 iBT), IELTS (minimum score 6). *Application deadline:* Applications are processed on a rolling basis. Application fee: $60 ($65 for international students). Electronic applications accepted. *Expenses:* Tuition: Full-time $9450; part-time $350 per unit. Required fees: $350 per unit. One-time fee: $60. *Financial support:* Career-related internships or fieldwork, institutionally sponsored loans, scholarships/grants, and tuition waivers (partial) available. Support available to part-time students. Financial award application deadline: 6/30; financial award applicants required to submit FAFSA. *Unit head:* Dr. Cynthia Sistek-Chandler, Department Chair, 858-309-3457, E-mail: cchandler@nu.edu. *Application contact:* Dominick Giovanniello, Associate Regional Dean—San Diego, 800-NAT-UNIV, Fax: 858-541-7792, E-mail: dgiovann@nu.edu.

New Mexico Highlands University, Graduate Studies, College of Arts and Sciences, Program in Media Arts and Computer Science, Las Vegas, NM 87701. Offers media arts and computer science (MS). *Faculty:* 7 full-time (2 women). *Students:* 9 full-time (5 women), 7 part-time (3 women); includes 7 Hispanic/Latino, 2 international. Average age 31. 17 applicants, 100% accepted, 4 enrolled. In 2010, 3 master's awarded. *Degree requirements:* For master's, comprehensive exam, thesis. *Entrance requirements:* For master's, minimum undergraduate GPA of 3.0. Additional exam requirements/recommendations for international students: Required—TOEFL (minimum score 540 paper-based; 270 computer-based). Application fee: $15. *Expenses:* Tuition, state resident: full-time $2544. Required fees: $624; $132 per credit hour. *Financial support:* In 2010–11, 7 students received support. Career-related internships or fieldwork, Federal Work-Study, institutionally sponsored loans, scholarships/grants, tuition waivers (full and partial), and unspecified assistantships available. Support available to part-time students. Financial award application deadline: 3/1; financial award applicants required to submit FAFSA. *Faculty research:* Advanced digital compositing, photographic installations and exhibition design, pattern recognition, parallel and distributed computing, computer security education. *Unit head:* Dr. Miriam Langer, Department Head, Visual and Performing Arts, 505-454-3390, E-mail: melanger@nmhu.edu. *Application contact:* Diane Trujillo, Administrative Assistant for Graduate Studies, 505-454-3266, Fax: 505-426-2117, E-mail: dtrujillo@nmhu.edu.

The New School: A University, The New School for General Studies, Program in Media Studies, New York, NY 10011. Offers documentary media studies (Graduate Certificate); media management (Graduate Certificate); media studies (MA). Part-time and evening/weekend programs available. Postbaccalaureate distance learning degree programs offered (no on-campus study). *Degree requirements:* For master's, thesis optional. *Entrance requirements:* For master's, interview. Additional exam requirements/recommendations for international students: Required—TOEFL (minimum score 600 paper-based; 250 computer-based; 100 iBT). Electronic applications accepted. *Faculty research:* Effect of technology on society, effect of U. S. media on international affairs, effect of media on corporate affairs.

New York University, Graduate School of Arts and Science, Department of Anthropology, Program in Culture and Media, New York, NY 10012-1019. Offers MA/Advanced Certificate, PhD/Advanced Certificate. *Faculty:* 1 (woman) full-time. *Students:* 4 full-time (3 women), 2 part-time (both women); includes 1 American Indian or Alaska Native, non-Hispanic/Latino, 1 international. Average age 30. 37 applicants, 5% accepted, 2 enrolled. *Entrance requirements:* Additional exam requirements/recommendations for international students: Required—TOEFL. *Application deadline:* For fall admission, 1/4 priority date for domestic students. Application fee: $90. *Financial support:* Fellowships, research assistantships, teaching assistantships, career-related internships or fieldwork, institutionally sponsored loans, scholarships/grants, health care benefits, and unspecified assistantships available. Financial award application deadline: 1/4. *Faculty research:* Critical history of ethnographic film, ethnography of media, indigenous media, politics of reproduction and disability, social movements. *Unit head:* Faye Ginsburg, Co-Director, 212-998-3759, Fax: 212-995-4730, E-mail: anthropology@nyu.edu. *Application contact:* Susan Carol-Rogers, Co-Director, 212-998-3759, Fax: 212-995-4730, E-mail: anthropology@nyu.edu.

New York University, Steinhardt School of Culture, Education, and Human Development, Department of Media, Culture and Communication, New York, NY 10012-1019. Offers media, culture, and communication (MA, PhD). Part-time programs available. *Faculty:* 29 full-time (13 women), 88 part-time/adjunct (43 women). *Students:* 107 full-time (79 women), 65 part-time (42 women); includes 10 Black or African American, non-Hispanic/Latino; 8 Asian, non-Hispanic/Latino; 9 Hispanic/Latino, 47 international. Average age 27. 616 applicants, 24% accepted, 63 enrolled. In 2010, 44 master's, 2 doctorates awarded. Terminal master's awarded for partial completion of doctoral program. *Degree requirements:* For master's, thesis (for some programs); for doctorate, thesis/dissertation. *Entrance requirements:* For doctorate, GRE General Test, interview. Additional exam requirements/recommendations for international students: Required—TOEFL. *Application deadline:* For fall admission, 12/1 priority date for domestic and international students; for spring admission, 11/1 for domestic and international students. Applications are processed on a rolling basis. Application fee: $75. Electronic applications accepted. *Financial support:* Fellowships with full and partial tuition reimbursements, teaching assistantships with full and partial tuition reimbursements, career-related internships or fieldwork, Federal Work-Study, institutionally sponsored loans, scholarships/grants, tuition waivers (partial), and unspecified assistantships available. Support available to part-time students. Financial award application deadline: 2/1; financial award applicants required to submit FAFSA. *Faculty research:* Digital media and new technologies, media criticism, flow of media and culture transnationally and transculturally. *Unit head:* Dr. Marita Sturken, Chairperson, 212-992-9424, Fax: 212-995-4046, E-mail: marita.sturken@nyu.edu. *Application contact:* 212-998-5030, Fax: 212-995-4328, E-mail: steinhardt.gradadmissions@nyu.edu.

Norfolk State University, School of Graduate Studies, School of Liberal Arts, Department of Media and Communication, Norfolk, VA 23504. Offers MA. Part-time programs available. *Degree requirements:* For master's, thesis. *Entrance requirements:* For master's, GRE, minimum GPA of 2.5, letters of recommendation. Additional exam requirements/recommendations for international students: Required—TOEFL.

Northeastern University, College of Arts, Media and Design, Department of Communication Studies, Boston, MA 02115-5096. Offers communication, media, and cultural studies (MA). *Faculty:* 25 full-time (10 women), 6 part-time/adjunct (3 women). *Students:* 8 full-time (7 women), 1 part-time (0 women). 92 applicants, 36% accepted, 5 enrolled. In 2010, 1 master's awarded. *Degree requirements:* For master's, thesis (for some programs). *Entrance requirements:* For master's, GRE. Additional exam requirements/recommendations for international students: Required—TOEFL or IELTS. *Application deadline:* For fall admission, 2/1 priority date for domestic and international students. Applications are processed on a rolling basis. Application fee: $50. Electronic applications accepted. *Financial support:* Federal Work-Study and scholarships/grants available. *Unit head:* Dr. Joanne Morreale, Graduate Coordinator, 617-373-2506, E-mail: j.morreale@neu.edu. *Application contact:* Jo-Anne Dickinson, Admissions Contact, 617-373-5990, Fax: 617-373-7281, E-mail: gsas@neu.edu.

Northern Kentucky University, Office of Graduate Programs, College of Informatics, Program in Communication, Highland Heights, KY 41099. Offers communication (MA); communication teaching (Certificate); documentary studies (Certificate); public relations (Certificate); relationships (Certificate). Part-time and evening/weekend programs available. *Faculty:* 7 full-time (3 women), 1 part-time/adjunct (0 women). *Students:* 10 full-time (4 women), 36 part-time (15 women); includes 7 minority (3 Black or African American, non-Hispanic/Latino; 2 Asian, non-Hispanic/Latino; 2 Hispanic/Latino). Average age 29. 29 applicants, 62% accepted, 14 enrolled. In 2010, 11 master's, 2 other advanced degrees awarded. *Degree requirements:* For master's, thesis (for some programs), capstone experience, internship. *Entrance requirements:* For master's, GRE, minimum GPA of 3.0, 3 letters of recommendation, letter of intent. Additional exam requirements/recommendations for international students: Required—TOEFL (minimum score 550 paper-based; 213 computer-based; 79 iBT); Recommended—IELTS (minimum score 6.5). *Application deadline:* For fall admission, 2/1 for domestic students, 6/1 for international students; for spring admission, 7/1 for domestic students, 10/1 for international students. Applications are processed on a rolling basis. Application fee: $40. Electronic applications accepted. *Expenses:* Tuition, state resident: full-time $7254; part-time $403 per credit hour. Tuition, nonresident: full-time $12,492; part-time $694 per credit hour. Tuition and fees vary according to degree level and program. *Financial support:* Unspecified assistantships available. Financial award applicants required to submit FAFSA. *Faculty research:* Business/organizational communication, interpersonal/relational communication, public relations, communication teaching/pedagogy, media (production, criticism, popular culture). Total annual research expenditures: $29,000. *Unit head:* Dr. Jimmy Manning, Director, 859-572-1329, E-mail: manningj1@nku.edu. *Application contact:* Dr. Peg Griffin, Director of Graduate Programs, 859-572-6934, Fax: 859-572-6670, E-mail: griffinp@nku.edu.

Northwestern University, The Graduate School, School of Communication, Department of Radio/Television/Film, Evanston, IL 60208. Offers MA, MFA, PhD. Admissions and degrees offered through The Graduate School. Part-time programs available. Terminal master's awarded for partial completion of doctoral program. *Degree requirements:* For master's, comprehensive exam or thesis; for doctorate, thesis/dissertation, qualifying exam. *Entrance requirements:* For master's and doctorate, GRE General Test. Additional exam requirements/recommendations for international students: Required—TOEFL. Electronic applications accepted. *Faculty research:* Art and new media, media theory and criticism, gender, media history, documentary.

Northwestern University, Medill School of Journalism, Evanston, IL 60208. Offers broadcast journalism (MSJ); integrated marketing communications (MSIMC), including advertising/sales promotion, direct database and e-commerce marketing, general studies, public relations; magazine publishing (MSJ); new media (MSJ); reporting and writing (MSJ). *Accreditation:* ACEJMC (one or more programs are accredited). *Entrance requirements:* For master's, GRE General Test, GMAT or LSAT (MSJ). Additional exam requirements/recommendations for international students: Required—TOEFL. Electronic applications accepted. *Expenses:* Contact institution. *Faculty research:* Web business journalism, cultural stereotypes, voter apathy, digital television.

Ohio University, Graduate College, Scripps College of Communication, School of Media Arts and Studies, Athens, OH 45701-2979. Offers mass communication (PhD); media arts and studies (MA). *Students:* 29 full-time (24 women), 13 part-time (7 women); includes 6 minority (4 Black or African American, non-Hispanic/Latino; 1 American Indian or Alaska Native, non-Hispanic/Latino; 1 Hispanic/Latino), 14 international. 78 applicants, 32% accepted, 15 enrolled. In 2010, 7 master's, 7 doctorates awarded. *Degree requirements:* For master's, comprehensive exam (for some programs), thesis or alternative; for doctorate, comprehensive exam, thesis/dissertation. *Entrance requirements:* For master's, GRE General Test or MAT, minimum GPA of 3.0; for doctorate, GRE General Test or MAT. Additional exam requirements/recommendations for international students: Required—TOEFL (minimum score 600 paper-based; 100 iBT) or IELTS (minimum score 7). *Application deadline:* For fall admission, 1/31 priority date for domestic students, 12/31 priority date for international students. Application fee: $50 ($55 for international students). Electronic applications accepted. *Financial support:* Research assistantships with full tuition reimbursements, teaching assistantships with full tuition reimbursements, career-related internships or fieldwork, Federal Work-Study, institutionally sponsored loans, and unspecified assistantships available. Financial award application deadline: 1/31; financial award applicants required to submit FAFSA. *Faculty research:* Media and development communication, new media and society, industry studies. *Unit head:* Dr. Roger Cooper, Director, 740-593-4872, Fax: 740-593-9184, E-mail: cooperr@ohio.edu. *Application contact:* Dr. Gregory Newton, Interim Director for Graduate Studies, 740-593-4870, Fax: 740-593-9184, E-mail: newtong@ohio.edu.

Ohio University, Graduate College, Scripps College of Communication, School of Visual Communication, Athens, OH 45701-2979. Offers MA. *Accreditation:* NASAD. *Students:* 32 full-time (17 women), 4 part-time (2 women); includes 3 minority (1 Black or African American, non-Hispanic/Latino; 2 Hispanic/Latino), 5 international. 43 applicants, 91% accepted, 21 enrolled. In 2010, 21 master's awarded. *Entrance requirements:* For master's, minimum GPA of 2.5, portfolio. Additional exam requirements/recommendations for international students: Required—TOEFL (minimum score 600 paper-based; 100 iBT) or IELTS (minimum score 7). *Application deadline:* For fall admission, 2/1 for domestic students, 12/14 for international students. Application fee: $50 ($55 for international students). Electronic applications accepted. *Financial support:* Federal Work-Study, institutionally sponsored loans, and tuition waivers (partial) available. Financial award applicants required to submit FAFSA. *Faculty research:* Photojournalism (including documentary photography), commercial photography (including illustrative photography), picture editing, informational graphics/publication design, interactive multimedia, visual media management. *Unit head:* Terry Eiler, Director, 740-595-4895, Fax: 740-593-0190, E-mail: eiler@ohio.edu. *Application contact:* Stan Alost, Assistant Director, 740-597-1756, Fax: 740-593-0190, E-mail: alost@ohio.edu.

Rochester Institute of Technology, Graduate Enrollment Services, College of Liberal Arts, Department of Communications, Program in Communication and Media Technologies, Rochester, NY 14623-5603. Offers MS. Part-time programs available. *Students:* 19 full-time (14 women), 30 part-time (24 women); includes 3 Black or African American, non-Hispanic/Latino; 1 Asian, non-Hispanic/Latino; 1 Hispanic/Latino; 1 Two or more races, non-Hispanic/Latino, 5 international. Average age 29. 42 applicants, 57% accepted, 20 enrolled. In 2010, 9 master's awarded. *Degree requirements:* For master's, thesis or project. *Entrance requirements:* For master's, minimum GPA of 3.0, writing sample. Additional exam requirements/recommendations for international students: Required—TOEFL (minimum score 600 paper-based; 250 computer-based; 100 iBT) or IELTS (minimum score 7). *Application deadline:* For fall admission, 2/15 priority date for domestic and international students; for winter admission, 11/1 for domestic and international students; for spring admission, 2/1 for domestic and international students. Applications are processed on a rolling basis. Electronic applications accepted. *Expenses:* Tuition: Full-time $33,234; part-time $924 per credit hour. Required fees: $219. *Financial support:* In 2010–11, 17 students received support; research assistantships with partial tuition reimbursements available, teaching assistantships with partial tuition reimbursements available, career-related internships or fieldwork, scholarships/grants, and unspecified assistantships available. Support available to part-time students. Financial award applicants required to submit FAFSA. *Unit head:* Dr. Rudy Pugliese, Graduate Program Director, 585-475-5925, Fax: 585-475-7732, E-mail: rrpgsl@rit.edu. *Application contact:* Diane Ellison, Assistant Vice President, Graduate Enrollment Services, 585-475-2229, Fax: 585-475-7164, E-mail: gradinfo@rit.edu.

Rutgers, The State University of New Jersey, New Brunswick, School of Communication, Information and Library Studies, Program in Communication, Library and Information Science and Media Studies, Piscataway, NJ 08854-8097. Offers PhD. Part-time programs available. *Faculty:* 43 full-time (21 women). *Students:* 37 full-time (30 women), 65 part-time (45 women); includes 7 Black or African American, non-Hispanic/Latino; 26 Asian, non-Hispanic/Latino; 1 Hispanic/Latino. Average age 35. 106 applicants, 68% accepted, 19 enrolled. In 2010, 11 doctorates awarded. *Degree requirements:* For doctorate, comprehensive exam, thesis/dissertation, qualifying exams. *Entrance requirements:* For doctorate, GRE General Test, proficiency in statistics. Additional exam requirements/recommendations for international students: Required—TOEFL (minimum score 600 paper-based; 250 computer-based). *Application deadline:* For fall admission, 1/15 priority date for domestic students, 1/15 for international students. Applications are processed on a rolling basis. Application fee: $50. Electronic applications accepted. *Expenses:* Tuition, state resident: full-time $7200; part-time $600 per credit. Tuition, nonresident: full-time $11,124; part-time $927 per credit. *Financial support:* In 2010–11, 2 fellowships with full tuition reimbursements (averaging $20,000 per year), 5 research assistantships with full tuition reimbursements (averaging $21,781 per year), 16 teaching assistantships with full tuition reimbursements (averaging $20,595 per year) were awarded; institutionally sponsored loans also available. Financial award application deadline: 2/1; financial award applicants required to submit FAFSA. *Faculty research:* Information science, media studies. Total annual research expenditures: $739,865. *Unit head:* Dr. Craig Scott, Director, 732-932-7500 Ext. 8142, Fax: 732-932-6916, E-mail: crscott@rci.rutgers.edu. *Application contact:* Linda J. Costa, Director of Graduate Admissions, 732-932-7711, Fax: 732-932-8231, E-mail: smeds@rci.rutgers.edu.

Saginaw Valley State University, College of Arts and Behavioral Sciences, Program in Communication and Digital Media Design, University Center, MI 48710. Offers MA. Part-time and evening/weekend programs available. *Degree requirements:* For master's, thesis. *Entrance requirements:* For master's, minimum GPA of 2.75. Additional exam requirements/recommendations for international students: Required—TOEFL. Electronic applications accepted. *Expenses:* Tuition, state resident: full-time $7902.

St. Edward's University, School of Management and Business, Area of Digital Media Management, Austin, TX 78704. Offers MBA. *Students:* 46 full-time (18 women); includes 14 minority (1 Black or African American, non-Hispanic/Latino; 2 Asian, non-Hispanic/Latino; 11 Hispanic/Latino). Average age 27. 36 applicants, 72% accepted, 25 enrolled. In 2010, 12 master's awarded. *Entrance requirements:* For master's, GRE or GMAT, interview, 2 letters of recommendation, minimum GPA of 3.0 in last 60 hours of course work. Additional exam requirements/recommendations for international students: Required—TOEFL (minimum score 550 paper-based; 213 computer-based; 79 iBT) or IELTS (minimum score 6). *Application deadline:* For fall admission, 2/15 priority date for domestic and international students. Applications are processed on a rolling basis. Application fee: $45 ($50 for international students). Electronic applications accepted. *Expenses:* Contact institution. *Financial support:* Scholarships/grants available. *Unit head:* Russell Rains, Director, 512-428-1220, Fax: 512-448-8492, E-mail: russellr@stedwards.edu. *Application contact:* Kay L. Arnold, Assistant Director of Admissions, 512-233-1661, Fax: 512-428-1032, E-mail: kayla@stedwards.edu.

San Diego State University, Graduate and Research Affairs, College of Professional Studies and Fine Arts, School of Communication, San Diego, CA 92182. Offers advertising and public relations (MA); critical-cultural studies (MA); interaction studies (MA); intercultural and international studies (MA); new media studies (MA); news and information studies (MA); telecommunications and media management (MA). *Degree requirements:* For master's, thesis. *Entrance requirements:* For master's, GRE General Test, 3 letters of recommendation. Additional exam requirements/recommendations for international students: Required—TOEFL. Electronic applications accepted.

San Diego State University, Graduate and Research Affairs, College of Professional Studies and Fine Arts, School of Theater, Television and Film, Program in Television, Film, and New Media Production, San Diego, CA 92182. Offers MA. *Entrance requirements:* For master's, GRE General Test, 3 letters of recommendation, resume, sample reel, influential book list, influential films list, hobby list. Additional exam requirements/recommendations for international students: Required—TOEFL. Electronic applications accepted. *Faculty research:* Experimental film and television programs, documentary film, television research and production.

San Francisco State University, Division of Graduate Studies, College of Creative Arts, Department of Broadcast and Electronic Communication Arts, San Francisco, CA 94132-1722. Offers MA. *Unit head:* Dr. Scott Patterson, Chair, 415-338-1787, Fax: 415-338-1688. *Application contact:* Dr. Nancy Reist, Graduate Coordinator, 415-338-1787, E-mail: becagrad@sfsu.edu.

Savannah College of Art and Design, Graduate School, Program in Broadcast Design, Savannah, GA 31402-3146. Offers MA, MFA. Part-time programs available. Postbaccalaureate distance learning degree programs offered (no on-campus study). *Faculty:* 9 full-time (1 woman), 7 part-time/adjunct (2 women). *Students:* 38 full-time (14 women), 6 part-time (2 women); includes 1 Black or African American, non-Hispanic/Latino; 2 Asian, non-Hispanic/Latino; 2 Hispanic/Latino; 1 Native Hawaiian or other Pacific Islander, non-Hispanic/Latino, 13 international. Average age 30. In 2010, 24 master's awarded. *Degree requirements:* For master's, thesis, internships. *Entrance requirements:* For master's, interview, portfolio. Additional exam requirements/recommendations for international students: Required—TOEFL (minimum score 450 paper-based; 133 computer-based). *Application deadline:* For fall admission, 4/1 priority date for domestic and international students. Applications are processed on a rolling basis. Application fee: $35. Electronic applications accepted. *Expenses:* Tuition: Full-time $29,520; part-time $3280 per quarter. Tuition and fees vary according to campus/location. *Financial support:* Research assistantships, career-related internships or fieldwork, Federal Work-Study, and scholarships/grants available. Financial award application deadline: 4/1; financial award applicants required to submit FAFSA. *Unit head:* John Colette, Chair, 912-525-5000, E-mail: jcolette@scad.edu. *Application contact:* Elizabeth Mathis, Director of Graduate Recruitment, 912-525-5965, Fax: 912-525-5985, E-mail: emathis@scad.edu.

Media Studies

Savannah College of Art and Design, Graduate School, Program in Performing Arts, Savannah, GA 31402-3146. Offers MFA. *Faculty:* 11 full-time (5 women), 3 part-time/adjunct (2 women). *Students:* 17 full-time (11 women), 3 part-time (all women); includes 5 Black or African American, non-Hispanic/Latino. Average age 26. In 2010, 7 master's awarded. *Degree requirements:* For master's, thesis, internship. *Entrance requirements:* For master's, audition, interview. Additional exam requirements/recommendations for international students: Required—TOEFL (minimum score 450 paper-based; 133 computer-based). *Application deadline:* For fall admission, 4/1 priority date for domestic and international students. Applications are processed on a rolling basis. Application fee: $35. Electronic applications accepted. *Expenses:* Tuition: Full-time $29,520; part-time $3280 per quarter. Tuition and fees vary according to campus/location. *Financial support:* Fellowships, career-related internships or fieldwork, Federal Work-Study, and scholarships/grants available. Financial award application deadline: 4/1; financial award applicants required to submit FAFSA. *Unit head:* Michael Wainstein, Chair, 912-525-6933, Fax: 912-525-6935, E-mail: mwainste@scad.edu. *Application contact:* Elizabeth Mathis, Director of Graduate Recruitment, 912-525-5965, Fax: 912-525-5985, E-mail: emathis@scad.edu.

See Display on page 177 and Close-Up on page 223

Southern Illinois University Carbondale, Graduate School, College of Mass Communication and Media Arts, Department of Mass Communication and Media Arts, Carbondale, IL 62901-4701. Offers MA, MFA.

Southern Illinois University Carbondale, Graduate School, College of Mass Communication and Media Arts, Department of Professional Media and Media Management Studies, Carbondale, IL 62901-4701. Offers MA.

Southern Illinois University Carbondale, Graduate School, College of Mass Communication and Media Arts, Program in Media Theory and Research, Carbondale, IL 62901-4701. Offers MA.

Southern Illinois University Edwardsville, Graduate School, College of Arts and Sciences, Department of Mass Communications, Program in Media Literacy, Edwardsville, IL 62026-0001. Offers Postbaccalaureate Certificate. Part-time programs available. *Students:* 1 (woman) full-time. Average age 26. *Entrance requirements:* Additional exam requirements/recommendations for international students: Required—TOEFL (minimum score 550 paper-based; 213 computer-based; 79 iBT), IELTS (minimum score 6.5). *Application deadline:* For fall admission, 7/22 for domestic students, 6/1 for international students; for spring admission, 12/9 for domestic students, 10/1 for international students. Applications are processed on a rolling basis. Application fee: $30. Electronic applications accepted. *Expenses:* Tuition, state resident: full-time $6012; part-time $1503 per semester. Tuition, nonresident: full-time $15,030; part-time $3758 per semester. Required fees: $1711; $675 per semester. *Financial support:* Fellowships with full tuition reimbursements, research assistantships with full tuition reimbursements, teaching assistantships with full tuition reimbursements, career-related internships or fieldwork, Federal Work-Study, institutionally sponsored loans, scholarships/grants, traineeships, and unspecified assistantships available. Support available to part-time students. Financial award application deadline: 3/1; financial award applicants required to submit FAFSA. *Unit head:* Dr. Elza Ibroscheva, Director, 618-650-2242, E-mail: eibrosc@siue.edu. *Application contact:* Dr. Elza Ibroscheva, Director, 618-650-2242, E-mail: eibrosc@siue.edu.

Syracuse University, S. I. Newhouse School of Public Communications, Program in Media Management, Syracuse, NY 13244. Offers MS. *Students:* 25 full-time (17 women); includes 6 minority (5 Black or African American, non-Hispanic/Latino; 1 Asian, non-Hispanic/Latino), 11 international. Average age 24. 103 applicants, 43% accepted, 22 enrolled. In 2010, 10 master's awarded. *Degree requirements:* For master's, thesis optional, capstone course. *Entrance requirements:* For master's, GRE General Test or GMAT. Additional exam requirements/recommendations for international students: Required—TOEFL (minimum score 600 paper-based; 250 computer-based; 100 iBT). *Application deadline:* For fall admission, 2/1 priority date for domestic and international students. Application fee: $45. Electronic applications accepted. *Expenses:* Tuition: Part-time $1162 per credit. *Financial support:* Fellowships with full tuition reimbursements, research assistantships with partial tuition reimbursements, teaching assistantships with partial tuition reimbursements available. Financial award application deadline: 2/1. *Unit head:* Stephen Masiclat, Director, 315-443-9243, Fax: 315-443-3946, E-mail: pcgrad@syr.edu. *Application contact:* Martha Coria, Graduate Records Office, 315-443-5749, Fax: 315-334-1834, E-mail: pcgrad@syr.edu.

Syracuse University, S. I. Newhouse School of Public Communications, Program in Media Studies, Syracuse, NY 13244. Offers MA. *Students:* 23 full-time (17 women), 2 part-time (1 woman); includes 3 minority (all Black or African American, non-Hispanic/Latino), 5 international. Average age 25. 75 applicants, 48% accepted, 12 enrolled. In 2010, 9 master's awarded. *Degree requirements:* For master's, thesis. *Entrance requirements:* For master's, GRE General Test. Additional exam requirements/recommendations for international students: Required—TOEFL (minimum score 600 paper-based; 250 computer-based; 100 iBT). *Application deadline:* For fall admission, 2/1 priority date for domestic and international students. Application fee: $45. Electronic applications accepted. *Expenses:* Tuition: Part-time $1162 per credit. *Financial support:* Fellowships with full tuition reimbursements, research assistantships with partial tuition reimbursements, teaching assistantships with partial tuition reimbursements available. Financial award application deadline: 2/1. *Unit head:* Carol M. Liebler, Director, 315-443-3372, Fax: 315-443-3946, E-mail: pcgrad@syr.edu. *Application contact:* Martha Coria, 315-443-5749, E-mail: pcgrad@syr.edu.

Syracuse University, S. I. Newhouse School of Public Communications, Program in Television, Radio, and Film, Syracuse, NY 13244. Offers MA. *Students:* 41 full-time (24 women), 5 part-time (3 women); includes 8 minority (all Black or African American, non-Hispanic/Latino), 11 international. Average age 26. 102 applicants, 67% accepted, 39 enrolled. In 2010, 37 master's awarded. *Degree requirements:* For master's, comprehensive exam. *Entrance requirements:* For master's, GRE General Test. Additional exam requirements/recommendations for international students: Required—TOEFL (minimum score 600 paper-based; 250 computer-based; 100 iBT). *Application deadline:* For fall admission, 2/1 priority date for domestic and international students. Application fee: $45. Electronic applications accepted. *Expenses:* Tuition: Part-time $1162 per credit. *Financial support:* Fellowships with full tuition reimbursements, research assistantships with full tuition reimbursements, teaching assistantships with full tuition reimbursements available. Financial award application deadline: 2/1. *Unit head:* Michael Schoonmaker, Chair, 315-443-4004, Fax: 315-443-3946, E-mail: pcgrad@syr.edu. *Application contact:* Martha Coria, Graduate Records Office, 315-443-5749, Fax: 315-443-1834, E-mail: pcgrad@syr.edu.

Temple University, School of Communications and Theater, Department of Broadcasting, Telecommunications and Mass Media, Philadelphia, PA 19122-6096. Offers MA. Part-time programs available. *Faculty:* 14 full-time (5 women). *Students:* 17 full-time (11 women), 6 part-time (3 women); includes 1 Black or African American, non-Hispanic/Latino; 1 Asian, non-Hispanic/Latino, 2 international. 51 applicants, 55% accepted, 8 enrolled. In 2010, 8 master's awarded. *Degree requirements:* For master's, thesis optional, written exam. *Entrance requirements:* For master's, GRE General Test, minimum GPA of 3.0. Additional exam requirements/recommendations for international students: Required—TOEFL (minimum score 550 paper-based; 213 computer-based; 79 iBT). *Application deadline:* For fall admission, 2/15 for domestic students, 12/15 for international students. Application fee: $50. Electronic applications accepted. *Financial support:* Teaching assistantships with partial tuition reimbursements, career-related internships or fieldwork available. Financial award application deadline: 1/15; financial award applicants required to submit FAFSA. *Faculty research:* Media institutions, international communications, communication policy, media theory. *Unit head:* Dr. Patrick Murphy, Chair, 215-204-5401, Fax: 215-204-5402, E-mail: murphy.p@temple.edu. *Application contact:* Dr. Patrick Murphy, Chair, 215-204-5401, Fax: 215-204-5402, E-mail: murphy.p@temple.edu.

Temple University, School of Communications and Theater, Program in Mass Media and Communication, Philadelphia, PA 19122-6096. Offers PhD. Part-time programs available. *Students:* 37 full-time (26 women), 10 part-time (6 women); includes 2 Black or African American, non-Hispanic/Latino; 1 American Indian or Alaska Native, non-Hispanic/Latino; 2 Asian, non-Hispanic/Latino; 1 Hispanic/Latino, 8 international. 49 applicants, 51% accepted, 11 enrolled. In 2010, 5 doctorates awarded. *Degree requirements:* For doctorate, one foreign language, thesis/dissertation. *Entrance requirements:* For doctorate, GRE General Test, minimum GPA of 3.0, sample of written work. Additional exam requirements/recommendations for international students: Required—TOEFL (minimum score 550 paper-based; 213 computer-based; 79 iBT). *Application deadline:* For fall admission, 1/15 for domestic students, 12/15 for international students. Application fee: $50. Electronic applications accepted. *Financial support:* Fellowships, research assistantships with partial tuition reimbursements, teaching assistantships with partial tuition reimbursements available. Financial award application deadline: 1/15; financial award applicants required to submit FAFSA. *Faculty research:* Aesthetics and criticism, media institutions, social theory and processes. *Unit head:* Dr. Mathew Lombard, Director, 215-204-1497, E-mail: mmc@temple.edu. *Application contact:* Dr. Mathew Lombard, Director, 215-204-1497, E-mail: mmc@temple.edu.

University at Buffalo, the State University of New York, Graduate School, College of Arts and Sciences, Department of Media Study, Buffalo, NY 14260. Offers film studies (MAH); media arts production (MFA); media study (PhD); new media design (Certificate); M Arch/MFA. *Faculty:* 12 full-time (4 women), 10 part-time/adjunct (5 women). *Students:* 58 (22 women); includes 2 Black or African American, non-Hispanic/Latino; 7 Asian, non-Hispanic/Latino; 4 Hispanic/Latino, 6 international. 109 applicants, 32% accepted, 20 enrolled. In 2010, 12 master's awarded. *Degree requirements:* For master's, thesis. *Entrance requirements:* For master's, portfolio. Additional exam requirements/recommendations for international students: Required—TOEFL (minimum score 95 iBT). *Application deadline:* For fall admission, 1/15 priority date for domestic and international students. Applications are processed on a rolling basis. Application fee: $75. Electronic applications accepted. *Financial support:* In 2010–11, 16 students received support, including 2 fellowships (averaging $4,000 per year), 12 teaching assistantships with full tuition reimbursements available (averaging $13,387 per year); career-related internships or fieldwork, Federal Work-Study, scholarships/grants, and unspecified assistantships also available. Support available to part-time students. Financial award application deadline: 1/15; financial award applicants required to submit FAFSA. *Faculty research:* Digital arts, video, documentary, film, virtual reality, digital poetics, locative media. Total annual research expenditures: $63,000. *Unit head:* Dr. Royal Roussel, Chair, 716-645-6902, Fax: 716-645-6979, E-mail: roussel@buffalo.edu. *Application contact:* Dean Sanborn, Graduate Secretary, 716-645-0923, Fax: 716-645-6979, E-mail: deansanb@buffalo.edu.

The University of Alabama, Graduate School, College of Communication and Information Sciences, Department of Telecommunication and Film, Tuscaloosa, AL 35487-0152. Offers MA. *Faculty:* 10 full-time (3 women). *Students:* 9 full-time (5 women), 4 part-time (2 women); includes 2 minority (1 Black or African American, non-Hispanic/Latino; 1 Two or more races, non-Hispanic/Latino), 3 international. Average age 28. 13 applicants, 77% accepted, 7 enrolled. In 2010, 4 master's awarded. Terminal master's awarded for partial completion of doctoral program. *Degree requirements:* For master's, comprehensive exam, thesis or alternative. *Entrance requirements:* For master's, GRE, minimum GPA of 3.0. Additional exam requirements/recommendations for international students: Required—TOEFL (minimum score 600 paper-based; 79 iBT). *Application deadline:* For fall admission, 4/15 priority date for domestic students, 1/15 priority date for international students; for spring admission, 11/1 for domestic students, 10/1 priority date for international students. Applications are processed on a rolling basis. Application fee: $50 ($60 for international students). Electronic applications accepted. *Expenses:* Tuition, state resident: full-time $7900. Tuition, nonresident: full-time $20,500. *Financial support:* In 2010–11, 6 students received support, including 2 research assistantships with tuition reimbursements available (averaging $9,825 per year), 2 teaching assistantships with tuition reimbursements available (averaging $9,825 per year); institutionally sponsored loans also available. Financial award application deadline: 2/15. *Faculty research:* Entertainment theory, news and public affairs, effects of telecommunications, management, media law and policy. *Unit head:* Dr. Gary A. Copeland, Chair, 205-348-6350, Fax: 205-348-5162, E-mail: copeland@ua.edu. *Application contact:* Dr. Shuhua Zhou, Graduate Coordinator, 205-348-8653, Fax: 205-348-5162, E-mail: szhou@bama.ua.edu.

The University of Arizona, College of Fine Arts, School of Media Arts, Tucson, AZ 85721. Offers MA. Part-time programs available. *Faculty:* 8. *Students:* 8 full-time (5 women), 2 part-time (0 women); includes 1 Hispanic/Latino, 1 international. Average age 29. 34 applicants, 47% accepted, 10 enrolled. In 2010, 5 master's awarded. *Degree requirements:* For master's, comprehensive exam. *Entrance requirements:* For master's, GRE. Additional exam requirements/recommendations for international students: Required—TOEFL (minimum score 550 paper-based; 213 computer-based; 79 iBT). *Application deadline:* For fall admission, 2/15 for domestic students, 1/31 for international students. Applications are processed on a rolling basis. Application fee: $75. Electronic applications accepted. *Expenses:* Tuition, state resident: full-time $7692. *Financial support:* In 2010–11, 9 teaching assistantships with full tuition reimbursements (averaging $16,581 per year) were awarded; career-related internships or fieldwork, scholarships/grants, health care benefits, tuition waivers (full and partial), and unspecified assistantships also available. Financial award applicants required to submit FAFSA. *Unit head:* Beverly Seckinger, Interim Director, 520-621-1239, Fax: 520-621-9662, E-mail: bsecking@email.arizona.edu. *Application contact:* Sylvia Jo Miles, Administrative Secretary, 520-626-2847, Fax: 520-621-9662, E-mail: sjmiles@u.arizona.edu.

University of California, Santa Barbara, Graduate Division, College of Letters and Sciences, Division of Humanities and Fine Arts, Department of Media Arts and Technology, Santa Barbara, CA 93106-6065. Offers electronic music and sound design (MA); media arts and technology (PhD); multimedia engineering (MS); technology and society (PhD); visual and spatial arts (MA). *Faculty:* 19 full-time (4 women). *Students:* 35 full-time (5 women); includes 1 American Indian or Alaska Native, non-Hispanic/Latino; 5 Asian, non-Hispanic/Latino; 4 Hispanic/Latino. Average age 32. 57 applicants, 32% accepted, 6 enrolled. In 2010, 5 master's, 2 doctorates awarded. Terminal master's awarded for partial completion of doctoral program. *Degree requirements:* For master's, thesis; for doctorate, comprehensive exam, thesis/dissertation. *Entrance requirements:* For master's and doctorate, GRE. Additional exam requirements/recommendations for international students: Required—TOEFL (minimum score 550 paper-based; 80 iBT), IELTS (minimum score 7). *Application deadline:* For fall admission, 12/15 for domestic and international students. Application fee: $70 ($90 for international students). Electronic applications accepted. *Financial support:* In 2010–11, 28 students received support, including 11 fellowships with full tuition reimbursements available (averaging $7,399 per year), 8 research assistantships with full and partial tuition reimbursements available (averaging $12,014 per year), 16 teaching assistantships with partial tuition reimbursements available (averaging $9,358 per year); career-related internships or fieldwork and tuition waivers (full and partial) also available. Financial award application deadline: 12/15; financial award applicants required to submit FAFSA. *Faculty research:* Transarchitectures, and worldmaking, virtual and mixed reality, visualization, intelligent space and interactive installation, human-computer interaction. *Unit head:* Curtis Roads, Chair and Professor, 805-893-2932, Fax: 805-893-2930, E-mail: clang@create.ucsb.edu. *Application contact:* Yumi Kinoshita, Graduate Program Assistant, 805-893-2887, Fax: 805-893-2930, E-mail: yumi@mat.ucsb.edu.

University of Chicago, Division of the Humanities, Committee on Cinema and Media Studies, Chicago, IL 60637-1513. Offers AM, PhD. *Degree requirements:* For master's, one foreign language, thesis; for doctorate, 2 foreign languages, thesis/dissertation.

University of Colorado Boulder, Graduate School, ATLAS Institute (Alliance for Technology, Learning, and Society), Boulder, CO 80309. Offers technology, media, and society (PhD). *Students:* 17 full-time (12 women), 1 (woman) part-time; includes 3 minority (1 Black or African American, non-Hispanic/Latino; 1 American Indian or Alaska Native, non-Hispanic/Latino; 1 Asian, non-Hispanic/Latino), 1 international. Average age 33. 24 applicants, 10 enrolled.

Application deadline: For fall admission, 1/28 for domestic students, 12/1 for international students. *Financial support:* In 2010–11, 2 fellowships (averaging $33,692 per year), 5 research assistantships (averaging $13,970 per year) were awarded. Financial award application deadline: 1/15. *Faculty research:* Evaluation of the Dissector Tool based on the Visible Human Data Project, assessing student outcomes for SENCER (an NSF-sponsored program using civic engagement to increase the interest and learning in undergraduate science at over 300 U. S. universities).

University of Colorado Boulder, Graduate School, School of Journalism and Mass Communication, Program in Communication, Boulder, CO 80309. Offers media studies (PhD). *Students:* 23 full-time (13 women), 5 part-time (3 women); includes 2 minority (1 Black or African American, non-Hispanic/Latino; 1 Hispanic/Latino), 7 international. Average age 33. 42 applicants, 4 enrolled. In 2010, 6 doctorates awarded. *Entrance requirements:* For doctorate, GRE General Test, minimum undergraduate GPA of 3.25. Additional exam requirements/recommendations for international students: Required—TOEFL. *Application deadline:* For fall admission, 2/15 for domestic and international students. Application fee: $50 ($60 for international students). *Financial support:* In 2010–11, 5 fellowships (averaging $1,400 per year), 15 research assistantships (averaging $12,251 per year) were awarded; unspecified assistantships also available. Financial award application deadline: 3/1.

University of Denver, Division of Arts, Humanities and Social Sciences, Department of Media, Film and Journalism Studies, Denver, CO 80208. Offers advertising management (MS); digital media studies (MA); international and intercultural communication (MA); media, film, and journalism studies (MA); strategic communication (MS). Part-time programs available. *Faculty:* 14 full-time (7 women), 5 part-time/adjunct (3 women). *Students:* 28 full-time (24 women), 36 part-time (26 women); includes 12 minority (1 Black or African American, non-Hispanic/Latino; 3 Asian, non-Hispanic/Latino; 6 Hispanic/Latino; 2 Two or more races, non-Hispanic/Latino), 2 international. Average age 26. 155 applicants, 58% accepted, 32 enrolled. In 2010, 36 master's awarded. *Degree requirements:* For master's, thesis (for some programs). *Entrance requirements:* For master's, GRE General Test. Additional exam requirements/recommendations for international students: Required—TOEFL (minimum score 550 paper-based; 80 iBT). *Application deadline:* Applications are processed on a rolling basis. Application fee: $60. Electronic applications accepted. *Expenses:* Tuition: Full-time $35,604; part-time $29,670 per year. Required fees: $687 per year. Tuition and fees vary according to program. *Financial support:* In 2010–11, 4 teaching assistantships with full and partial tuition reimbursements (averaging $14,000 per year) were awarded; career-related internships or fieldwork, Federal Work-Study, institutionally sponsored loans, scholarships/grants, and unspecified assistantships also available. Support available to part-time students. Financial award application deadline: 3/1; financial award applicants required to submit FAFSA. *Faculty research:* Youth and civic engagement. *Unit head:* Dr. Renee Botta, Chair, 303-871-7918, Fax: 303-871-4949, E-mail: rbotta@du.edu. *Application contact:* Information Contact, 303-871-2166, E-mail: mfjs@du.edu.

University of Florida, Graduate School, College of Journalism and Communications, Department of Telecommunication, Gainesville, FL 32611. Offers MAMC. *Faculty:* 8 full-time (4 women). *Entrance requirements:* For master's, GRE General Test, minimum GPA of 3.0. Application fee: $30. *Expenses:* Tuition, state resident: full-time $10,915.92. Tuition, nonresident: full-time $28,309. *Unit head:* Dr. David H. Ostroff, Chair, 352-392-0436, Fax: 352-392-3919, E-mail: dostroff@jou.ufl.edu. *Application contact:* Lynda L. Kaid, Graduate Coordinator, 352-392-7922, Fax: 352-392-3919, E-mail: lkaid@jou.ufl.edu.

University of Illinois at Urbana–Champaign, Graduate College, College of Fine and Applied Arts, School of Art and Design, Program in Design and Media, Champaign, IL 61820. Offers art and design (MFA), including new media; graphic design (MFA); industrial design (MFA). *Accreditation:* NASAD. *Students:* 14 full-time (4 women), 3 part-time (1 woman); includes 1 Asian, non-Hispanic/Latino, 10 international. 156 applicants, 3% accepted, 5 enrolled. In 2010, 3 master's awarded. *Entrance requirements:* For master's, minimum GPA of 3.0. Additional exam requirements/recommendations for international students: Required—TOEFL (minimum score 550 paper-based; 213 computer-based; 79 iBT). *Application deadline:* Applications are processed on a rolling basis. Application fee: $75 ($90 for international students). Electronic applications accepted. *Financial support:* Fellowships, research assistantships, teaching assistantships, tuition waivers (full and partial) available. *Unit head:* Ernest Scott, Chair, 217-333-1579, E-mail: ernscott@illinois.edu. *Application contact:* Marsha Biddle, Coordinator of Graduate Academic Affairs, 217-333-0642, Fax: 217-244-7688, E-mail: mbiddle@illinois.edu.

University of Illinois at Urbana–Champaign, Graduate College, College of Media, Institute of Communications Research, Champaign, IL 61820. Offers communications and media (PhD). *Faculty:* 8 full-time (4 women). *Students:* 38 full-time (21 women), 13 part-time (6 women); includes 5 Black or African American, non-Hispanic/Latino; 4 Asian, non-Hispanic/Latino; 7 Hispanic/Latino, 22 international. 111 applicants, 8% accepted, 6 enrolled. In 2010, 7 doctorates awarded. *Entrance requirements:* For doctorate, GRE General Test, minimum GPA of 3.0. Additional exam requirements/recommendations for international students: Required—TOEFL (minimum score 550 paper-based). *Application deadline:* Applications are processed on a rolling basis. Application fee: $75 ($90 for international students). Electronic applications accepted. *Financial support:* In 2010–11, 7 fellowships, 12 research assistantships, 34 teaching assistantships were awarded; tuition waivers (full and partial) also available. *Faculty research:* Feminist cultural studies, media technology, international communications, Latino studies, economics of media. *Unit head:* Angharad N. Valdivia, Interim Director, 217-244-1422, Fax: 217-244-7695, E-mail: valdivia@illinois.edu. *Application contact:* M. Denise Davis, Office Support Specialist, 217-333-1549, Fax: 217-333-1549, E-mail: mddavis1@illinois.edu.

The University of Iowa, Graduate College, College of Liberal Arts and Sciences, School of Journalism and Mass Communication, Iowa City, IA 52242-1316. Offers mass communication (PhD); media communication (MA); professional journalism (MA); JD/MA. *Accreditation:* ACEJMC (one or more programs are accredited). *Degree requirements:* For master's, thesis optional, exam; for doctorate, comprehensive exam, thesis/dissertation. *Entrance requirements:* For master's and doctorate, GRE General Test, minimum GPA of 3.0. Additional exam requirements/recommendations for international students: Required—TOEFL (minimum score 637 paper-based; 270 computer-based; 110 iBT). Electronic applications accepted. *Faculty research:* Verbal and visual aspects of historical, legal, social, and cross-cultural communication.

The University of Kansas, Graduate Studies, College of Liberal Arts and Sciences, Department of Film and Media Studies, Lawrence, KS 66045. Offers MA, PhD. *Faculty:* 10 full-time (2 women). *Students:* 25 full-time (7 women), 2 part-time (1 woman); includes 4 minority (2 Asian, non-Hispanic/Latino; 2 Two or more races, non-Hispanic/Latino), 3 international. Average age 32. 23 applicants, 43% accepted, 7 enrolled. In 2010, 2 master's, 1 doctorate awarded. *Degree requirements:* For master's, thesis; for doctorate, one foreign language, comprehensive exam, thesis/dissertation. *Entrance requirements:* For master's, GRE General Test, minimum GPA of 3.2; for doctorate, GRE General Test, minimum GPA of 3.5; MA in film or related field. Additional exam requirements/recommendations for international students: Required—TOEFL. *Application deadline:* For fall admission, 2/15 for domestic and international students. Application fee: $55 ($65 for international students). Electronic applications accepted. *Expenses:* Tuition, state resident: full-time $7092; part-time $295.50 per credit hour. Tuition, nonresident: full-time $16,590; part-time $691.25 per credit hour. Required fees: $858; $71.49 per credit hour. Tuition and fees vary according to course load, campus/location and program. *Financial support:* Teaching assistantships with full and partial tuition reimbursements available. Financial award application deadline: 1/1; financial award applicants required to submit FAFSA. *Faculty research:* Film and media theory, film and media history, East Asian cinema, Latin American cinema, film and video production. *Unit head:* Dr. Tamara L. Falicov, Chair, 785-864-1353, Fax: 785-331-2671, E-mail: tfalicov@ku.edu. *Application contact:* Dr. Michael Baskett, Associate Professor, 785-864-1384, Fax: 785-331-2671, E-mail: eiga@ku.edu.

University of Lethbridge, School of Graduate Studies, Lethbridge, AB T1K 3M4, Canada. Offers accounting (MScM); addictions counseling (M Sc); agricultural biotechnology (M Sc); agricultural studies (M Sc, MA); anthropology (MA); archaeology (MA); art (MA, MFA); biochemistry (M Sc); biological sciences (M Sc); biomolecular science (PhD); biosystems and biodiversity (PhD); Canadian studies (MA); chemistry (M Sc); computer science (M Sc); computer science and geographical information science (M Sc); counseling psychology (M Ed); dramatic arts (MA); earth, space, and physical science (PhD); economics (MA); educational leadership (M Ed); English (MA); environmental science (M Sc); evolution and behavior (PhD); exercise science (M Sc); finance (MScM); French (MA); French/German (MA); French/Spanish (MA); general education (M Ed); general management (MScM); geography (M Sc, MA); German (MA); health science (M Sc); history (MA); human resource management and labour relations (MScM); individualized multidisciplinary (M Sc, MA); information systems (MScM); international management (MScM); kinesiology (M Sc, MA); management (M Sc, MA); marketing (MScM); mathematics (M Sc); music (M Mus, MA); Native American studies (MA); neuroscience (M Sc, PhD); new media (MA); nursing (M Sc); philosophy (MA); physics (M Sc); policy and strategy (MScM); political science (MA); psychology (M Sc, MA); religious studies (MA); social sciences (MA); sociology (MA); theatre and dramatic arts (MFA); theoretical and computational science (PhD); urban and regional studies (MA); women's studies (MA). Part-time and evening/weekend programs available. *Degree requirements:* For doctorate, comprehensive exam, thesis/dissertation. *Entrance requirements:* For master's, GMAT (M Sc in management), bachelor's degree in related field, minimum GPA of 3.0 during previous 20 graded semester courses, 2 years teaching or related experience (M Ed); for doctorate, master's degree, minimum graduate GPA of 3.5. Additional exam requirements/recommendations for international students: Required—TOEFL. *Faculty research:* Movement and brain plasticity, gibberellin physiology, photosynthesis, carbon cycling, molecular properties of main-group ring components.

University of Maine, Graduate School, Program in Liberal Studies, Orono, ME 04469. Offers Maine studies (MA); new media (MA); peace studies (MA). Part-time and evening/weekend programs available. *Students:* 2 full-time (both women), 19 part-time (13 women); includes 2 American Indian or Alaska Native, non-Hispanic/Latino, 1 international. Average age 47. 5 applicants, 40% accepted, 2 enrolled. In 2010, 6 master's awarded. *Degree requirements:* For master's, project. *Entrance requirements:* Additional exam requirements/recommendations for international students: Required—TOEFL. *Application deadline:* For fall admission, 4/1 for domestic students; for spring admission, 11/1 for domestic students. Applications are processed on a rolling basis. Application fee: $65. Electronic applications accepted. *Expenses:* Tuition, state resident: full-time $400. Tuition, nonresident: full-time $1050. *Financial support:* Federal Work-Study and institutionally sponsored loans available. Financial award application deadline: 3/1. *Unit head:* Amaranta Ruiz-Nelson, Coordinator, 207-581-3222, Fax: 207-581-3232, E-mail: graduate@maine.edu. *Application contact:* Amaranta Ruiz-Nelson, Coordinator, 207-581-3222, Fax: 207-581-3232, E-mail: graduate@maine.edu.

University of Maryland, College Park, Academic Affairs, Phillip Merrill College of Journalism, College Park, MD 20742. Offers broadcast journalism (MA); journalism (MA); journalism and media studies (PhD); online news (MA); public affairs reporting (MA). *Accreditation:* ACEJMC (one or more programs are accredited). Part-time and evening/weekend programs available. *Faculty:* 18 full-time (10 women), 43 part-time/adjunct (18 women). *Students:* 76 full-time (46 women), 14 part-time (7 women); includes 20 minority (12 Black or African American, non-Hispanic/Latino; 5 Asian, non-Hispanic/Latino; 3 Hispanic/Latino), 11 international. 243 applicants, 37% accepted, 26 enrolled. In 2010, 26 master's, 5 doctorates awarded. *Degree requirements:* For doctorate, thesis/dissertation, preliminary written and oral comprehensive exams. *Entrance requirements:* For master's and doctorate, GRE General Test, minimum GPA of 3.0, 3 letters of recommendation. Additional exam requirements/recommendations for international students: Required—TOEFL. *Application deadline:* For fall admission, 1/15 for domestic and international students. Applications are processed on a rolling basis. Application fee: $75. Electronic applications accepted. *Expenses:* Tuition, state resident: part-time $471 per credit hour. Tuition, nonresident: part-time $1016 per credit hour. Required fees: $337 per term. *Financial support:* In 2010–11, 3 fellowships with full and partial tuition reimbursements (averaging $11,667 per year), 22 teaching assistantships with tuition reimbursements (averaging $16,647 per year) were awarded; research assistantships with tuition reimbursements, career-related internships or fieldwork, Federal Work-Study, and scholarships/grants also available. Support available to part-time students. Financial award applicants required to submit FAFSA. *Faculty research:* Mass communication theory, specialized journalism, new telecommunication technologies, press integration. Total annual research expenditures: $565,454. *Unit head:* Kevin Klose, Dean and Professor, 301-405-2383, E-mail: kklose@jmail.umd.edu. *Application contact:* Dr. Charles A. Caramello, Dean of Graduate School, 301-405-0358, Fax: 301-314-9305, E-mail: ccaramel@umd.edu.

University of Michigan, Horace H. Rackham School of Graduate Studies, School of Music, Theatre, and Dance, Program in Media Arts, Ann Arbor, MI 48109-2085. Offers MA. *Entrance requirements:* For master's, GRE, portfolio. Additional exam requirements/recommendations for international students: Required—TOEFL (minimum score 600 paper-based; 250 computer-based; 100 iBT). *Expenses:* Tuition, state resident: full-time $17,784; part-time $1116 per credit hour. Tuition, nonresident: full-time $35,944; part-time $2125 per credit hour. International tuition: $35,994 full-time. Required fees: $95 per semester. Tuition and fees vary according to course load, degree level and program.

University of Missouri–Kansas City, College of Arts and Sciences, Department of English Language and Literature, Kansas City, MO 64110-2499. Offers creative writing and media arts (MFA); English (MA, PhD). PhD (interdisciplinary) offered through the School of Graduate Studies. Part-time and evening/weekend programs available. *Faculty:* 22 full-time (15 women), 21 part-time/adjunct (10 women). *Students:* 11 full-time (7 women), 47 part-time (23 women); includes 6 minority (5 Black or African American, non-Hispanic/Latino; 1 Asian, non-Hispanic/Latino). Average age 30. 75 applicants, 40% accepted, 22 enrolled. In 2010, 11 master's awarded. *Degree requirements:* For master's, one foreign language; for doctorate, 2 foreign languages, comprehensive exam, thesis/dissertation. *Entrance requirements:* For master's, GRE General Test, 3 letters of recommendation. Additional exam requirements/recommendations for international students: Required—TOEFL (minimum score 550 paper-based; 213 computer-based; 80 iBT). *Application deadline:* For fall admission, 1/15 for domestic students, 1/15 priority date for international students. Applications are processed on a rolling basis. Application fee: $45 ($50 for international students). Electronic applications accepted. *Expenses:* Tuition, state resident: full-time $5522.40; part-time $306.80 per credit hour. Tuition, nonresident: full-time $7128; part-time $792 per credit hour. Required fees: $261.15 per term. *Financial support:* In 2010–11, 12 teaching assistantships (averaging $13,358 per year) were awarded; career-related internships or fieldwork, Federal Work-Study, and institutionally sponsored loans also available. Support available to part-time students. Financial award application deadline: 3/1; financial award applicants required to submit FAFSA. *Faculty research:* Creative writing: poetry and prose, computational linguistics, rhetoric and composition, African-American and British literature, print culture. Total annual research expenditures: $13,729. *Unit head:* Dr. Jeff Rydberg-Cox, Co-Chair, 816-235-2560, Fax: 816-235-1308, E-mail: rydbergcoxj@umkc.edu. *Application contact:* Dr. Laurie Ellinghausen, Director of Graduate Studies, 816-235-6032, E-mail: ellinghausenl@umkc.edu.

University of Nevada, Las Vegas, Graduate College, Greenspun College of Urban Affairs, School of Journalism and Media Studies, Las Vegas, NV 89154-5007. Offers MA. *Faculty:* 10 full-time (2 women). *Students:* 14 full-time (10 women), 13 part-time (7 women); includes 11 minority (3 Black or African American, non-Hispanic/Latino; 4 Hispanic/Latino; 1 Native Hawaiian or other Pacific Islander, non-Hispanic/Latino; 3 Two or more races, non-Hispanic/Latino), 1 international. Average age 30. 17 applicants, 82% accepted, 8 enrolled. In 2010, 7 master's awarded. *Entrance requirements:* For master's, GRE General Test. Additional exam requirements/recommendations for international students: Required—TOEFL (minimum score 550 paper-based; 213 computer-based; 80 iBT), IELTS (minimum score 7). *Application deadline:* For fall admission, 5/5 priority date for domestic and international students. Applications are processed on a rolling basis. Application fee: $60 ($95 for international students). Electronic applications accepted. *Expenses:* Tuition, area resident: Part-time $239.50 per credit. Tuition, state resident: part-time $239.50 per credit. Tuition, nonresident: part-time $503 per credit.

Media Studies

University of Nevada, Las Vegas (continued)
Required fees: $108 per semester. Tuition and fees vary according to course load, program and reciprocity agreements. *Financial support:* In 2010–11, 8 students received support, including 4 research assistantships with partial tuition reimbursements available (averaging $10,000 per year), 4 teaching assistantships with partial tuition reimbursements available (averaging $10,000 per year); institutionally sponsored loans, scholarships/grants, health care benefits, and unspecified assistantships also available. Financial award application deadline: 3/1. *Faculty research:* Media and religion, science and communications, ethnic communities and journalism, journalism history, emerging technologies. *Unit head:* Dr. Ardyth Sohn, Director/Professor, 702-895-3270, Fax: 702-895-5189, E-mail: ardyth.sohn@unlv.edu. *Application contact:* Graduate College Admissions Evaluator, 702-895-3320, Fax: 702-895-4180, E-mail: gradcollege@unlv.edu.

The University of North Carolina at Charlotte, Graduate School, College of Arts and Sciences, Department of Communication Studies, Charlotte, NC 28223-0001. Offers health communication (MA); media/rhetorical critical studies (MA); organizational communication (MA); public relations (MA). Part-time and evening/weekend programs available. *Faculty:* 12 full-time (5 women), 1 (woman) part-time/adjunct. *Students:* 6 full-time (5 women), 19 part-time (17 women); includes 7 minority (6 Black or African American, non-Hispanic/Latino; 1 Asian, non-Hispanic/Latino). Average age 27. 554 applicants, 4% accepted, 12 enrolled. In 2010, 12 master's awarded. Terminal master's awarded for partial completion of doctoral program. *Degree requirements:* For master's, project, thesis, or comprehensive exam. *Entrance requirements:* For master's, GRE General Test, minimum GPA of 2.75 overall. Additional exam requirements/recommendations for international students: Required—TOEFL (minimum score 557 paper-based; 220 computer-based; 83 iBT). *Application deadline:* For fall admission, 3/15 for domestic students, 5/1 for international students; for spring admission, 11/15 for domestic students, 10/1 for international students. Applications are processed on a rolling basis. Application fee: $55. Electronic applications accepted. *Expenses:* Tuition, state resident: full-time $3464. Tuition, nonresident: full-time $14,297. Required fees: $2094. Tuition and fees vary according to course load. *Financial support:* In 2010–11, 9 students received support, including 1 research assistantship (averaging $18,000 per year), 8 teaching assistantships (averaging $15,529 per year); career-related internships or fieldwork, institutionally sponsored loans, scholarships/grants, and unspecified assistantships also available. Support available to part-time students. Financial award application deadline: 4/1; financial award applicants required to submit FAFSA. *Faculty research:* Health literacy, systems of care and mental illness, the communication of emotions in gendered workplaces, international constructs of public relations managerial responsibilities, sports culture and the construction of social contracts, African-American oratory. Total annual research expenditures: $25,636. *Unit head:* Dr. Richard W. Leeman, Chair, 704-687-2086, Fax: 704-687-6900, E-mail: rwleeman@uncc.edu. *Application contact:* Kathy B. Giddings, Director of Graduate Admissions, 704-687-5503, Fax: 704-687-3279, E-mail: gradadm@uncc.edu.

The University of North Carolina at Greensboro, Graduate School, College of Arts and Sciences, Department of Broadcasting and Cinema, Greensboro, NC 27412-5001. Offers film and video production (MFA).

University of Oregon, Graduate School, School of Architecture and Allied Arts, Program in Arts and Administration, Eugene, OR 97403. Offers arts management (MA, MS); media management (MA, MS). *Degree requirements:* For master's, summer internship, thesis/project. *Entrance requirements:* For master's, minimum GPA of 3.0; bachelor's degree in history, practice of visual, performing arts or other related degree. Additional exam requirements/recommendations for international students: Required—TOEFL. *Faculty research:* Museum education, arts program evaluation, community arts, information management, arts marketing.

University of Regina, Faculty of Graduate Studies and Research, Faculty of Fine Arts, Department of Media Production and Studies, Regina, SK S4S 0A2, Canada. Offers media production (MFA); media studies (MA). Part-time programs available. *Faculty:* 9 full-time (5 women). *Students:* 3 full-time (0 women). 2 applicants, 100% accepted. *Degree requirements:* For master's, thesis. *Entrance requirements:* For master's, proposal for research project. Additional exam requirements/recommendations for international students: Required—TOEFL (minimum score 580 paper-based; 80 iBT). *Application deadline:* For fall admission, 2/15 for domestic and international students. Application fee: $100. Electronic applications accepted. Tuition and fees charges are reported in Canadian dollars. *Expenses:* Tuition, area resident: Full-time $3244.50 Canadian dollars; part-time $180.25 Canadian dollars per credit hour. International tuition: $4744.50 Canadian dollars full-time. Required fees: $494 Canadian dollars; $115.25 Canadian dollars per credit hour. $115.25 Canadian dollars per semester. Tuition and fees vary according to program. *Financial support:* Fellowships, research assistantships, teaching assistantships, scholarships/grants available. Financial award application deadline: 6/15. *Faculty research:* Dramatic, documentary, and experimental film and video; new and interactive media; animation through a range of artistic, aesthetic, technical, and theoretical skills and knowledge; general and specialized study in media arts production; media arts theory. *Unit head:* Dr. Christine Ramsay, Head, 306-585-4948, Fax: 306-585-4439, E-mail: christine.ramsay@uregina.ca. *Application contact:* Dr. Christine Ramsay, Graduate Program Coordinator, 306-585-4948, Fax: 306-585-4439, E-mail: christine.ramsay@uregina.ca.

University of South Carolina, The Graduate School, College of Arts and Sciences, Department of Art, Division of Media Arts, Columbia, SC 29208. Offers MMA. *Degree requirements:* For master's, thesis. *Entrance requirements:* For master's, GRE General Test, interview, portfolio. Additional exam requirements/recommendations for international students: Required—TOEFL. Electronic applications accepted. *Faculty research:* Three dimensional imaging, script writing.

University of Southern California, Graduate School, Annenberg School for Communication and Journalism, School of Communication, Program in Communication, Los Angeles, CA 90089. Offers communication (MA, PhD), including information and society (PhD), interpersonal and health communication (PhD), media, culture and communication (PhD), organizational communication (PhD), rhetorical and political communication (PhD). *Students:* 97 full-time (64 women); includes 20 minority (4 Black or African American, non-Hispanic/Latino; 1 American Indian or Alaska Native, non-Hispanic/Latino; 8 Asian, non-Hispanic/Latino; 7 Hispanic/Latino), 30 international. Average age 31. 242 applicants, 9% accepted, 18 enrolled. In 2010, 14 doctorates awarded. *Degree requirements:* For doctorate, thesis/dissertation. *Entrance requirements:* For master's and doctorate, GRE General Test, resume, writing samples, 3 letters of recommendation, interest survey questionnaire, statement of purpose. Additional exam requirements/recommendations for international students: Required—TOEFL (minimum score 280 computer-based; 114 iBT); Recommended—TWE. *Application deadline:* For fall admission, 12/1 for domestic and international students. Application fee: $85. Electronic applications accepted. *Expenses:* Tuition: Full-time $31,240; part-time $1420 per unit. Required fees: $600. One-time fee: $35 full-time. Full-time tuition and fees vary according to degree level and program. *Financial support:* In 2010–11, 18 students received support, including 18 fellowships with full tuition reimbursements available (averaging $26,500 per year); research assistantships, teaching assistantships, Federal Work-Study, institutionally sponsored loans, scholarships/grants, health care benefits, and unspecified assistantships also available. Support available to part-time students. Financial award application deadline: 1/1; financial award applicants required to submit FAFSA. *Faculty research:* Computer-mediated communication, public health campaigns, communication democracy and the public sphere, new communication technologies in organizations, communication and community. *Unit head:* Dr. Thomas Goodnight, Director of the Ph.D. Program, 213-821-5384, E-mail: gtg@usc.edu. *Application contact:* Allyson Hill, Assistant Dean, Admissions, 213-821-0770, Fax: 213-740-1933, E-mail: ascadm@usc.edu.

See Display on page 675 and Close-Up on page 727.

University of Southern California, Graduate School, Annenberg School for Communication and Journalism, School of Communication, Program in Communication Management, Los Angeles, CA 90089. Offers MCM, JD/MCM, MCM/MAJCS. Part-time and evening/weekend programs available. Postbaccalaureate distance learning degree programs offered (no on-campus study). *Students:* 192 full-time, 89 part-time; includes 89 minority (18 Black or African American, non-Hispanic/Latino; 33 Asian, non-Hispanic/Latino; 32 Hispanic/Latino; 6 Two or more races, non-Hispanic/Latino), 90 international. Average age 31. 327 applicants, 52% accepted, 80 enrolled. In 2010, 117 master's awarded. *Degree requirements:* For master's, professional project. *Entrance requirements:* For master's, GRE General Test or GMAT, resume, writing samples, recommendation letters, statement of purpose. Additional exam requirements/recommendations for international students: Required—TOEFL (minimum score 280 computer-based; 114 iBT). *Application deadline:* For fall admission, 7/1 priority date for domestic students, 3/15 priority date for international students; for spring admission, 11/1 priority date for domestic students, 9/1 priority date for international students. Applications are processed on a rolling basis. Application fee: $85. Electronic applications accepted. *Expenses:* Tuition: Full-time $31,240; part-time $1420 per unit. Required fees: $600. One-time fee: $35 full-time. Full-time tuition and fees vary according to degree level and program. *Financial support:* Research assistantships with tuition reimbursements, Federal Work-Study, institutionally sponsored loans, scholarships/grants, health care benefits, and tuition waivers (partial) available. Support available to part-time students. Financial award application deadline: 2/1; financial award applicants required to submit FAFSA. *Faculty research:* Global communication, communication law and policy, entertainment management, marketing communication, strategic and corporate communication management. *Unit head:* Dr. Rebecca Weintraub, Director of the Communication Management Degree Program, 213-821-0764, Fax: 213-740-8036, E-mail: weintrau@usc.edu. *Application contact:* Allyson Hill, Assistant Dean, Admissions, 213-821-0770, Fax: 213-740-1933, E-mail: ascadm@usc.edu.

See Display on page 675 and Close-Up on page 727.

University of Southern California, Graduate School, Dana and David Dornsife College of Letters, Arts and Sciences, Comparative Studies in Literature and Culture Doctoral Program, Los Angeles, CA 90089. Offers comparative literature (PhD); comparative media and culture (PhD); Spanish and Latin American studies (PhD). *Faculty:* 16 full-time (7 women). *Students:* 27 full-time (17 women), 1 part-time (0 women); includes 6 minority (2 Black or African American, non-Hispanic/Latino; 2 Asian, non-Hispanic/Latino; 2 Hispanic/Latino), 6 international. In 2010, 1 doctorate awarded. *Median time to degree:* Of those who began their doctoral program in fall 2002, 50% received their degree in 8 years or less. *Degree requirements:* For doctorate, 2 foreign languages, comprehensive exam, thesis/dissertation. *Entrance requirements:* For doctorate, GRE, competence in language other than English (highly recommended). Additional exam requirements/recommendations for international students: Required—TOEFL. *Application deadline:* For fall admission, 12/1 priority date for domestic and international students. Application fee: $85. Electronic applications accepted. *Expenses:* Tuition: Full-time $31,240; part-time $1420 per unit. Required fees: $600. One-time fee: $35 full-time. Full-time tuition and fees vary according to degree level and program. *Financial support:* In 2010–11, 25 students received support, including 8 fellowships with full tuition reimbursements available (averaging $51,000 per year), 17 teaching assistantships with full tuition reimbursements available (averaging $51,000 per year). Financial award applicants required to submit FAFSA. *Faculty research:* Literary theory, Japanese film and contemporary fiction, Francophone literature and cinema, Latin American and Caribbean literature, Spanish literature and film, nineteenth and twentieth century British and American literature. *Unit head:* Prof. Peggy Kamuf, Director of Comparative Studies in Literature and Culture Doctoral Program, 213-740-0101, Fax: 213-740-8058, E-mail: kamuf@usc.edu. *Application contact:* Katherine Guevarra, Administrative Assistant, 213-740-0102, Fax: 213-740-0858, E-mail: kguevarr@usc.edu.

University of Southern California, Graduate School, School of Cinematic Arts, Interactive Media Division, Los Angeles, CA 90089. Offers interactive media (MFA); media arts and practice (PhD). *Faculty:* 10 full-time (2 women), 14 part-time/adjunct (2 women). *Students:* 40 full-time (12 women); includes 5 minority (4 Asian, non-Hispanic/Latino; 1 Hispanic/Latino), 8 international. 44 applicants, 45% accepted, 13 enrolled. In 2010, 10 master's awarded. *Degree requirements:* For master's, thesis, thesis project. *Entrance requirements:* Additional exam requirements/recommendations for international students: Required—TOEFL (minimum score 600 paper-based; 250 computer-based; 100 iBT). *Application deadline:* For fall admission, 12/1 for domestic and international students. Application fee: $85. Electronic applications accepted. *Expenses:* Contact institution. *Financial support:* In 2010–11, 29 students received support, including 6 fellowships with full tuition reimbursements available (averaging $20,000 per year), 5 research assistantships with full tuition reimbursements available (averaging $9,825 per year); career-related internships or fieldwork, Federal Work-Study, institutionally sponsored loans, scholarships/grants, health care benefits, unspecified assistantships, and research assistantships also available. Financial award application deadline: 5/3; financial award applicants required to submit CSS PROFILE or FAFSA. *Faculty research:* Immersive media, mobile media, stereoscopic, game design and development, serious games and games for health and learning, experiments in game play. Total annual research expenditures: $2 million. *Unit head:* Dr. Scott S. Fisher, Professor and Chair, Interactive Media Division and Associate Dean of Research, 213-821-4472, Fax: 213-821-2665, E-mail: sfisher@cinema.usc.edu. *Application contact:* Adrienne Capirchio, Graduate Program Coordinator, 213-821-2515, Fax: 213-821-2665, E-mail: acapirchio@cinema.usc.edu.

University of Southern California, Graduate School, School of Cinematic Arts, Interdivisional Program in Media Arts and Practice, Los Angeles, CA 90089. Offers PhD. *Faculty:* 11 full-time (5 women). *Students:* 12 full-time (9 women), 1 part-time (0 women); includes 4 minority (1 Asian, non-Hispanic/Latino; 2 Hispanic/Latino; 1 Two or more races, non-Hispanic/Latino), 2 international. 67 applicants, 4% accepted, 3 enrolled. *Degree requirements:* For doctorate, 2 foreign languages, thesis/dissertation. *Entrance requirements:* For doctorate, GRE, portfolio. Additional exam requirements/recommendations for international students: Required—TOEFL. *Application deadline:* For fall admission, 12/1 for domestic and international students. Application fee: $85. Electronic applications accepted. *Expenses:* Tuition: Full-time $31,240; part-time $1420 per unit. Required fees: $600. One-time fee: $35 full-time. Full-time tuition and fees vary according to degree level and program. *Financial support:* In 2010–11, 12 students received support, including 3 fellowships with full tuition reimbursements available (averaging $30,000 per year), 2 research assistantships with full tuition reimbursements available (averaging $30,000 per year), 4 teaching assistantships with full tuition reimbursements available (averaging $30,000 per year). *Faculty research:* Transmedia, theory and history of emerging technologies; documentary and experimental film and video; interactive media design; telepresence research and mobile media. Total annual research expenditures: $5 million. *Unit head:* Dr. Steve F. Anderson, Director. *Application contact:* Amanda Tasse, Program Coordinator, 213-743-1937, E-mail: imap@cinema.usc.edu.

The University of Tennessee, Graduate School, College of Communication and Information, Knoxville, TN 37996. Offers advertising (MS, PhD); broadcasting (MS, PhD); communications (MS, PhD); information sciences (MS, PhD); journalism (MS, PhD); public relations (MS, PhD); speech communication (MS, PhD). *Accreditation:* ACEJMC (one or more programs are accredited at the [master's] level). Part-time and evening/weekend programs available. Postbaccalaureate distance learning degree programs offered (no on-campus study). *Degree requirements:* For master's, thesis or alternative; for doctorate, thesis/dissertation. *Entrance requirements:* For master's and doctorate, GRE General Test, minimum GPA of 2.7. Additional exam requirements/recommendations for international students: Required—TOEFL. Electronic applications accepted. *Expenses:* Tuition, state resident: full-time $7440; part-time $414 per credit hour. Tuition, nonresident: full-time $22,478; part-time $1250 per credit hour. Required fees: $922; $43 per credit hour. Tuition and fees vary according to program.

The University of Texas at Austin, Graduate School, College of Communication, Department of Radio-Television-Film, Austin, TX 78712-1111. Offers film and video production (MFA); radio-television-film (MA, PhD); screenwriting (MFA). *Degree requirements:* For master's, thesis (for some programs); for doctorate, thesis/dissertation. *Entrance requirements:* For master's and doctorate, GRE General Test. Electronic applications accepted. *Faculty research:*

international communication, film studies, media and culture, telecommunication and new media, gender and sexuality.

The University of Western Ontario, Faculty of Graduate Studies, Faculty of Information and Media Studies, Programs in Media Studies, London, ON N6A 5B8, Canada. Offers MA, PhD. Part-time programs available. *Degree requirements:* For master's, thesis; for doctorate, comprehensive exam, thesis/dissertation. *Entrance requirements:* For master's, 2 letters of reference; for doctorate, MA in media studies, communications or related field. Additional exam requirements/recommendations for international students: Required—TOEFL (minimum score 625 paper-based), TWE (minimum score 5). Electronic applications accepted. *Faculty research:* Media cultures, media industries, media technologies.

University of Wisconsin–Madison, Graduate School, College of Letters and Science, Department of Communication Arts, Madison, WI 53706-1380. Offers communication science (MA, PhD); film (MA, PhD); media and cultural studies (MA, PhD); rhetoric (MA, PhD). Terminal master's awarded for partial completion of doctoral program. *Degree requirements:* For master's, one foreign language, thesis (for some programs); for doctorate, one foreign language, thesis/dissertation. *Entrance requirements:* For master's and doctorate, GRE General Test, minimum GPA of 3.5. Electronic applications accepted. *Expenses:* Tuition, state resident: full-time $9887; part-time $617.96 per credit. Tuition, nonresident: full-time $24,054; part-time $1503.40 per credit. Required fees: $67.63 per credit. Tuition and fees vary according to reciprocity agreements.

University of Wisconsin–Milwaukee, Graduate School, College of Letters and Sciences, Department of Media Studies, Milwaukee, WI 53201-0413. Offers media studies (MA); rhetorical leadership (Certificate). Part-time programs available. *Faculty:* 9 full-time (3 women). *Students:* 5 full-time (2 women), 18 part-time (8 women); includes 2 Black or African American, non-Hispanic/Latino, 6 international. Average age 29. 25 applicants, 48% accepted, 8 enrolled. In 2010, 11 master's awarded. *Degree requirements:* For master's, thesis or alternative. *Entrance requirements:* For master's, GRE General Test, minimum GPA of 3.0. Additional exam requirements/recommendations for international students: Required—TOEFL (minimum score 550 paper-based; 79 iBT), IELTS (minimum score 6.5). *Application deadline:* For fall admission, 1/1 priority date for domestic students; for spring admission, 9/1 for domestic students. Applications are processed on a rolling basis. Application fee: $56 ($96 for international students). Electronic applications accepted. *Financial support:* In 2010–11, 20 teaching assistantships were awarded; fellowships, research assistantships, career-related internships or fieldwork, health care benefits, and unspecified assistantships also available. Support available to part-time students. Financial award application deadline: 4/15; financial award applicants required to submit FAFSA. *Unit head:* Elana Levine, Representative, 414-229-4718, Fax: 414-229-2411, E-mail: ehlevine@uwm.edu. *Application contact:* General Information Contact, 414-229-4982, Fax: 414-229-6967, E-mail: gradschool@uwm.edu.

Valparaiso University, Graduate School, Program in Media and Communication, Valparaiso, IN 46383. Offers digital media (MS); sports media (MS, Certificate). Part-time and evening/weekend programs available. *Students:* 22 full-time (13 women), 10 part-time (2 women); includes 2 minority (both Black or African American, non-Hispanic/Latino), 18 international. Average age 26. In 2010, 7 master's awarded. *Entrance requirements:* For master's, minimum GPA of 3.0, undergraduate minor in communication. Additional exam requirements/recommendations for international students: Required—TOEFL (minimum score 550 paper-based; 213 computer-based; 80 iBT). *Application deadline:* Applications are processed on a rolling basis. Application fee: $30 ($50 for international students). Electronic applications accepted. *Expenses:* Tuition: Full-time $9540; part-time $530 per credit hour. Required fees: $292; $95 per semester. Tuition and fees vary according to program. *Financial support:* Available to part-time students. Applicants required to submit FAFSA. *Unit head:* Dr. David L. Rowland, Dean, Graduate School and Continuing Education/Associate Provost, 219-464-5313, Fax: 219-464-5381, E-mail: david.rowland@valpo.edu. *Application contact:* Laura Groth, Coordinator of Student Services and Support, 219-464-5313, Fax: 219-464-5381, E-mail: laura.groth@valpo.edu.

Virginia Commonwealth University, Graduate School, College of Humanities and Sciences, Department of English, Richmond, VA 23284-9005. Offers creative writing (MFA), including fiction, fictional poetry, poetry; English (MA), including literature, writing and rhetoric; media, art, and text (PhD). Part-time programs available. *Students:* 74 full-time (47 women), 54 part-time (32 women); includes 24 minority (10 Black or African American, non-Hispanic/Latino; 2 American Indian or Alaska Native, non-Hispanic/Latino; 4 Asian, non-Hispanic/Latino; 5 Hispanic/Latino; 3 Two or more races, non-Hispanic/Latino), 2 international. 176 applicants, 31% accepted, 30 enrolled. In 2010, 25 master's, 1 doctorate awarded. *Degree requirements:* For master's, thesis optional. *Entrance requirements:* For master's, GRE General Test, portfolio (MFA); for doctorate, GRE General Test. Additional exam requirements/recommendations for international students: Required—Either TOEFL (minimum score: paper-based 600, computer-based 250) or IELTS (6.5). *Application deadline:* Applications are processed on a rolling basis. Application fee: $50. Electronic applications accepted. *Expenses:* Tuition, state resident: full-time $4308; part-time $479 per credit hour. Tuition, nonresident: full-time $8942; part-time $994 per credit hour. Required fees: $2000; $85 per credit hour. Tuition and fees vary according to course level, course load, degree level, campus/location and program. *Financial support:* Fellowships, research assistantships, teaching assistantships, Federal Work-Study, institutionally sponsored loans, and tuition waivers (full and partial) available. Support available to part-time students. Financial award applicants required to submit FAFSA. *Unit head:* Dr. Terry Oggel, Chair, 804-828-1331, Fax: 804-828-2171, E-mail: toggel@vcu.edu. *Application contact:* Thom Didato, Director, 804-828-1329, E-mail: tndidato@vcu.edu.

Virginia Commonwealth University, Graduate School, College of Humanities and Sciences, School of Mass Communications, Program in Media, Art, and Text, Richmond, VA 23284-9005. Offers PhD. *Students:* 20 full-time (15 women), 22 part-time (11 women); includes 10 minority (3 Black or African American, non-Hispanic/Latino; 1 American Indian or Alaska Native, non-Hispanic/Latino; 2 Asian, non-Hispanic/Latino; 3 Hispanic/Latino; 1 Two or more races, non-Hispanic/Latino), 1 international. 29 applicants, 31% accepted, 6 enrolled. In 2010, 1 doctorate awarded. *Entrance requirements:* For doctorate, GRE. Additional exam requirements/recommendations for international students: Required—TOEFL (minimum score 600 paper-based; 250 computer-based; 100 iBT); Recommended—IELTS (minimum score 6.5). *Application deadline:* For fall admission, 1/15 for domestic students. Application fee: $50. Electronic applications accepted. *Expenses:* Tuition, state resident: full-time $4308; part-time $479 per credit hour. Tuition, nonresident: full-time $8942; part-time $994 per credit hour. Required fees: $2000; $85 per credit hour. Tuition and fees vary according to course level, course load, degree level, campus/location and program. *Unit head:* Dr. Eric G. Garberson, Director, MATX Ph.D. Program, 804-828-7295, E-mail: eggarberson@vcu.edu. *Application contact:* Thom N. Didato, Graduate Programs Adviser, 804-828-1329, E-mail: tndidato@vcu.edu.

Washington State University, Graduate School, The Edward R. Murrow College of Communication, Pullman, WA 99164-2520. Offers health communications (MA, PhD); intercultural and international communications (MA, PhD); media and society (MA, PhD); media process and effects (MA, PhD); organizational communications (MA, PhD). *Faculty:* 30. *Students:* 43 full-time (26 women), 6 part-time (4 women); includes 1 Asian, non-Hispanic/Latino; 1 Hispanic/Latino, 19 international. Average age 30. 120 applicants, 22% accepted, 19 enrolled. In 2010, 22 master's, 1 doctorate awarded. *Degree requirements:* For master's, comprehensive exam (for some programs), thesis optional, oral exam; for doctorate, comprehensive exam, thesis/dissertation. *Entrance requirements:* For master's, GRE General Test, minimum GPA of 3.25, 3 letters of recommendation; for doctorate, GRE General Test, minimum undergraduate GPA of 3.25, graduate 3.5; MA in communication; 3 letters of recommendation. Additional exam requirements/recommendations for international students: Required—TOEFL (minimum score 580 paper-based; 237 computer-based). *Application deadline:* For fall admission, 1/15 priority date for domestic students, 3/1 for international students. Applications are processed on a rolling basis. Application fee: $50. Electronic applications accepted. *Expenses:* Tuition, state resident: full-time $8552; part-time $443 per credit. Tuition, nonresident: full-time $21,650; part-time $1083 per credit. Required fees: $846. *Financial support:* In 2010–11, 46 students received support, including 2 fellowships (averaging $4,477 per year), 7 research assistantships with full and partial tuition reimbursements available (averaging $13,917 per year), 34 teaching assistantships with full and partial tuition reimbursements available (averaging $13,056 per year); career-related internships or fieldwork, Federal Work-Study, institutionally sponsored loans, tuition waivers (partial), and teaching associateships also available. Financial award application deadline: 4/1; financial award applicants required to submit FAFSA. *Faculty research:* Advocacy communication, mediated communication in decision making, communication technology policy and effects, multicultural and international psychology and physiology of communication. Total annual research expenditures: $550,455. *Unit head:* Dr. Erica Austin, Interim Director, 509-335-1556, E-mail: eaustin@wsu.edu. *Application contact:* Graduate School Admissions, 800-GRADWSU, Fax: 509-335-1949, E-mail: gradsch@wsu.edu.

Wayne State University, College of Fine, Performing and Communication Arts, Department of Communication, Detroit, MI 48202. Offers communication studies (MA, PhD); public relations and organizational communication (MA); radio-TV-film (MA, PhD); speech communication (MA, PhD). *Faculty:* 25 full-time (11 women), 4 part-time/adjunct (1 woman). *Students:* 64 full-time (43 women), 107 part-time (73 women); includes 44 minority (36 Black or African American, non-Hispanic/Latino; 2 American Indian or Alaska Native, non-Hispanic/Latino; 1 Asian, non-Hispanic/Latino; 5 Hispanic/Latino), 7 international. Average age 32. 65 applicants, 66% accepted, 31 enrolled. In 2010, 37 master's, 7 doctorates awarded. *Degree requirements:* For master's, thesis, essay, or comprehensive exam; for doctorate, thesis/dissertation. *Entrance requirements:* For master's, minimum GPA of 3.0, sample of academic writing; for doctorate, GRE, minimum GPA of 3.3, MA; letters of recommendation; personal statement; sample of written scholarship. Additional exam requirements/recommendations for international students: Required—TOEFL (minimum score 550 paper-based; 213 computer-based); Recommended—TWE (minimum score 6). *Application deadline:* For fall admission, 4/1 for domestic students, 6/1 for international students; for winter admission, 10/1 for international students; for spring admission, 2/1 for international students. Applications are processed on a rolling basis. Application fee: $30 ($50 for international students). Electronic applications accepted. *Expenses:* Tuition, state resident: full-time $7662; part-time $478.85 per credit hour. Tuition, nonresident: full-time $16,920; part-time $1057.55 per credit hour. Required fees: $571.20; $35.70 per credit hour. $188.05 per semester. Tuition and fees vary according to course load and program. *Financial support:* In 2010–11, 22 students received support, including 8 fellowships with tuition reimbursements available (averaging $14,956 per year), 1 research assistantship with tuition reimbursement available (averaging $23,000 per year), 19 teaching assistantships with tuition reimbursements available (averaging $14,620 per year); career-related internships or fieldwork also available. Financial award application deadline: 2/1. *Faculty research:* Rhetorical theory and criticism; mass media theory and research; argumentation; organizational communication; risk and crisis communication; interpersonal, family, and health communication. *Unit head:* Dr. Matthew Seeger, Chair, 313-577-2959, Fax: 313-577-6300, E-mail: aa4331@wayne.edu. *Application contact:* Hayg Oshagan, Associate Professor, 313-577-0429, E-mail: ad4570@wayne.edu.

Webster University, School of Communications, Program in Media Communications, St. Louis, MO 63119-3194. Offers MA. *Expenses:* Tuition: Part-time $585 per credit hour. Tuition and fees vary according to degree level, campus/location and program.

Webster University, School of Communications, Program in Media Literacy, St. Louis, MO 63119-3194. Offers MA. *Expenses:* Tuition: Part-time $585 per credit hour. Tuition and fees vary according to degree level, campus/location and program.

West Virginia State University, Graduate Programs, Institute, WV 25112-1000. Offers biotechnology (MA, MS); media studies (MA). *Entrance requirements:* For master's, GRE General Test, minimum GPA of 3.0, 3 letters of recommendation. Additional exam requirements/recommendations for international students: Required—TOEFL (minimum score 550 paper-based).

Wilfrid Laurier University, Faculty of Graduate and Postdoctoral Studies, Faculty of Arts, Department of Communication Studies, Waterloo, ON N2L 3C5, Canada. Offers media, technology and culture (MA); visual communication and culture (MA). *Faculty:* 16 full-time (7 women). *Students:* 15 full-time (all women), 1 (woman) part-time, 1 international. 32 applicants, 56% accepted, 10 enrolled. In 2010, 7 master's awarded. *Degree requirements:* For master's, thesis optional. *Entrance requirements:* For master's, honours BA in communication studies or a cognate discipline from an approved university with a minimum B+ overall in last two years of study and in undergraduate major. Additional exam requirements/recommendations for international students: Required—TOEFL (minimum score 89 iBT). *Application deadline:* For fall admission, 2/1 priority date for domestic students, 2/1 for international students. Application fee: $100. Electronic applications accepted. Tuition and fees charges are reported in Canadian dollars. *Expenses:* Tuition, area resident: Full-time $15,300 Canadian dollars; part-time $1200 Canadian dollars per credit. International tuition: $21,300 Canadian dollars full-time. Required fees: $650 Canadian dollars; $100 Canadian dollars per credit. Tuition and fees vary according to course load, degree level, campus/location and program. *Financial support:* In 2010–11, 21 fellowships, 21 teaching assistantships were awarded; career-related internships or fieldwork, scholarships/grants, health care benefits, and unspecified assistantships also available. *Faculty research:* Visual communication and culture, media, technology and culture. *Unit head:* Dr. Martin Morris, Graduate Coordinator, 519-884-0710 Ext. 3015, E-mail: mmorris@wlu.ca. *Application contact:* Jennifer Williams, Graduate Admissions and Records Officer, 519-884-0710 Ext. 3536, Fax: 519-884-1020, E-mail: gradstudies@wlu.ca.

Wilfrid Laurier University, Faculty of Graduate and Postdoctoral Studies, Faculty of Arts, Department of English and Film Studies, Waterloo, ON N2L 3C5, Canada. Offers gender and genre (MA, PhD); nation, diaspora, culture (PhD); textuality, media and print studies (PhD). *Faculty:* 22 full-time (14 women). *Students:* 29 full-time (16 women), 1 (woman) part-time. 71 applicants, 48% accepted, 18 enrolled. In 2010, 15 master's, 2 doctorates awarded. *Degree requirements:* For master's, thesis optional; for doctorate, thesis/dissertation. *Entrance requirements:* For master's, honours BA or the equivalent in English, minimum B+ in English courses above first year level; for doctorate, MA in English, minimum A- average in graduate work. Additional exam requirements/recommendations for international students: Recommended—TOEFL (minimum score 89 iBT). *Application deadline:* For fall admission, 2/1 priority date for domestic and international students. Application fee: $100. Electronic applications accepted. Tuition and fees charges are reported in Canadian dollars. *Expenses:* Tuition, area resident: Full-time $15,300 Canadian dollars; part-time $1200 Canadian dollars per credit. International tuition: $21,300 Canadian dollars full-time. Required fees: $650 Canadian dollars; $100 Canadian dollars per credit. Tuition and fees vary according to course load, degree level, campus/location and program. *Financial support:* In 2010–11, 44 fellowships, 44 teaching assistantships were awarded; career-related internships or fieldwork, scholarships/grants, health care benefits, and unspecified assistantships also available. *Faculty research:* Gender and genre, Canadian studies, early modern studies, postcolonial studies, nineteenth century studies. *Unit head:* Dr. Tanis MacDonald, Graduate Coordinator, 519-884-0710 Ext. 2931, Fax: 519-884-8307, E-mail: tmacdonald@wlu.ca. *Application contact:* Jennifer Williams, Graduate Admissions and Records Officer, 519-884-0710 Ext. 3536, Fax: 519-884-1020, E-mail: gradstudies@wlu.ca.

Publishing

Arizona State University, College of Liberal Arts and Sciences, School of Historical, Philosophical and Religious Studies, Tempe, AZ 85287-4301. Offers East/Southeast Asian history (MA, PhD); European history (MA, PhD); Latin American studies (MA, PhD); North American history (MA, PhD); philosophy (MA, PhD); public history (MA); religious studies (MA, PhD); scholarly publishing (Graduate Certificate). Part-time programs available. *Faculty:* 70 full-time (29 women), 2 part-time/adjunct (0 women). *Students:* 125 full-time (58 women), 68 part-time (37 women); includes 21 minority (5 Black or African American, non-Hispanic/Latino; 3 American Indian or Alaska Native, non-Hispanic/Latino; 1 Asian, non-Hispanic/Latino; 11 Hispanic/Latino; 1 Two or more races, non-Hispanic/Latino), 16 international. Average age 34. 221 applicants, 51% accepted, 41 enrolled. In 2010, 24 master's, 10 doctorates, 3 other advanced degrees awarded. Terminal master's awarded for partial completion of doctoral program. *Degree requirements:* For master's, thesis or alternative, interactive Program of Study (iPOS) submitted before completing 50 percent of required credit hours; for doctorate, variable foreign language requirement, comprehensive exam, thesis/dissertation, interactive Program of Study (iPOS) submitted before completing 50 percent of required credit hours. *Entrance requirements:* For master's and doctorate, GRE, minimum GPA of 3.0 or equivalent in last 2 years of work leading to bachelor's degree. Additional exam requirements/recommendations for international students: Required—TOEFL, IELTS, or Pearson Test of English. *Application deadline:* For fall admission, 1/1 for domestic and international students. Applications are processed on a rolling basis. Application fee: $70 ($90 for international students). Electronic applications accepted. *Expenses:* Tuition, state resident: full-time $8510; part-time $608 per credit. Tuition, nonresident: full-time $16,542; part-time $919 per credit. Required fees: $339; $110 per credit. Part-time tuition and fees vary according to course load. *Financial support:* In 2010–11, 26 research assistantships with full and partial tuition reimbursements (averaging $12,900 per year), 69 teaching assistantships with full and partial tuition reimbursements (averaging $11,771 per year) were awarded; fellowships with full tuition reimbursements, career-related internships or fieldwork, institutionally sponsored loans, scholarships/grants, and tuition waivers (partial) also available. Financial award application deadline: 3/1; financial award applicants required to submit FAFSA. Total annual research expenditures: $1.3 million. *Unit head:* Mark Von Hagen, Director, 480-965-4186, E-mail: mark.vonhagen@asu.edu. *Application contact:* Graduate Admissions, 480-965-6113.

Carnegie Mellon University, College of Humanities and Social Sciences, Department of English, Program in Professional Writing, Pittsburgh, PA 15213-3891. Offers editing and publishing (MAPW); policy and non-profit communication (MAPW); public and media relations / corporate communications (MAPW); science or healthcare communication (MAPW); technical writing (MAPW); writing for new media (MAPW); writing for print media (MAPW). Part-time programs available. *Entrance requirements:* For master's, GRE General Test. Additional exam requirements/recommendations for international students: Required—TOEFL, TWE.

DePaul University, College of Liberal Arts and Sciences, Department of English, Master of Arts in Writing and Publishing Program, Chicago, IL 60604-2287. Offers MA. *Students:* 103 full-time (70 women), 40 part-time (28 women); includes 8 Black or African American, non-Hispanic/Latino; 3 Asian, non-Hispanic/Latino; 6 Hispanic/Latino; 1 Native Hawaiian or other Pacific Islander, non-Hispanic/Latino. *Unit head:* Christine Tardy, Director, 773-325-4145. *Application contact:* Dr. Lesley Kordecki, Director, 773-325-1786, Fax: 773-325-8607, E-mail: lkordeck@depaul.edu.

Drexel University, College of Arts and Sciences, Department of Culture and Communication, Program in Publication Management, Philadelphia, PA 19104-2875. Offers MS. Part-time and evening/weekend programs available. *Degree requirements:* For master's, research project. *Entrance requirements:* Additional exam requirements/recommendations for international students: Required—TOEFL. Electronic applications accepted.

Emerson College, Graduate Studies, School of the Arts, Department of Writing, Literature and Publishing, Program in Publishing and Writing, Boston, MA 02116-4624. Offers MA. Part-time and evening/weekend programs available. *Degree requirements:* For master's, thesis or alternative. *Entrance requirements:* For master's, GRE General Test, 15 page writing sample. Additional exam requirements/recommendations for international students: Required—TOEFL (minimum score 550 paper-based; 213 computer-based; 80 iBT), IELTS (minimum score 6.5). Electronic applications accepted. *Faculty research:* Publishing.

The George Washington University, College of Professional Studies, Program in Publishing, Washington, DC 20052. Offers MPS. Program offered at Alexandria, VA education center. *Students:* 57 part-time (47 women); includes 7 Black or African American, non-Hispanic/Latino; 1 American Indian or Alaska Native, non-Hispanic/Latino; 1 Asian, non-Hispanic/Latino; 3 Hispanic/Latino; 1 Native Hawaiian or other Pacific Islander, non-Hispanic/Latino. Average age 30. 58 applicants, 93% accepted, 26 enrolled. In 2010, 24 master's awarded. *Entrance requirements:* For master's, minimum cumulative GPA of 3.0. *Application deadline:* For fall admission, 4/1 for domestic and international students. Electronic applications accepted. *Unit head:* Dr. Arnold Grossblatt, Director, 202-994-7220, E-mail: arnieg@gwu.edu. *Application contact:* Kristin Williams, Asst VP Gradpec Enrlmnt Mgmt, 202-994-0467, Fax: 202-994-0371, E-mail: ksw@gwu.edu.

New York University, School of Continuing and Professional Studies, Division for Media Industry Studies and Design, Center for Publishing, New York, NY 10012-1019. Offers publishing (MS), including book publishing, electronic publishing, magazine publishing. Part-time and evening/weekend programs available. *Faculty:* 1 (woman) full-time, 46 part-time/adjunct (23 women). *Students:* 30 full-time (26 women), 24 part-time (20 women); includes 1 Asian, non-Hispanic/Latino, 10 international. Average age 26. 109 applicants, 50% accepted, 32 enrolled. In 2010, 46 master's awarded. *Degree requirements:* For master's, thesis. *Entrance requirements:* For master's, GMAT or GRE General Test (for recent graduates), 2 letters of recommendation, resume, essay, professional experience. Additional exam requirements/recommendations for international students: Required—TOEFL (minimum score 600 paper-based; 250 computer-based; 100 iBT). *Application deadline:* For fall admission, 2/1 priority date for domestic and international students; for spring admission, 10/15 priority date for domestic students, 8/15 priority date for international students. Applications are processed on a rolling basis. Application fee: $75. Electronic applications accepted. *Financial support:* In 2010–11, 60 students received support, including 60 fellowships (averaging $2,613 per year); career-related internships or fieldwork, Federal Work-Study, institutionally sponsored loans, and scholarships/grants also available. Support available to part-time students. Financial award application deadline: 3/1; financial award applicants required to submit FAFSA. *Faculty research:* Digital publishing and marketing. *Unit head:* Andrea Chambers, Academic Director, 212-992-3232, Fax: 212-790-3233, E-mail: pub.center@nyu.edu. *Application contact:* Sara McCarthy, Associate Director, 212-792-3232, Fax: 212-790-3233, E-mail: sarah.mccarthy@nyu.edu.

Northwestern University, Medill School of Journalism, Evanston, IL 60208. Offers broadcast journalism (MSJ); integrated marketing communications (MSIMC), including advertising/sales promotion, direct database and e-commerce marketing, general studies, public relations; magazine publishing (MSJ); new media (MSJ); reporting and writing (MSJ). *Accreditation:* ACEJMC (one or more programs are accredited). *Entrance requirements:* For master's, GRE General Test, GMAT or LSAT (MSJ). Additional exam requirements/recommendations for international students: Required—TOEFL. Electronic applications accepted. *Expenses:* Contact institution. *Faculty research:* Web business journalism, cultural stereotypes, voter apathy, digital television.

Pace University, Dyson College of Arts and Sciences, Program in Publishing, New York, NY 10038. Offers book publishing (Certificate); business side of publishing (Certificate); magazine publishing (Certificate); publishing (MS). Part-time and evening/weekend programs available. Postbaccalaureate distance learning degree programs offered. *Degree requirements:* For master's, internship or thesis. *Entrance requirements:* For master's, GRE General Test. Additional exam requirements/recommendations for international students: Required—TOEFL. Electronic applications accepted.

Rosemont College, Schools of Graduate and Professional Studies, Program in English and Publishing and English Literature, Rosemont, PA 19010-1699. Offers English and publishing (MA); English literature (MA). Part-time programs available. *Degree requirements:* For master's, comprehensive exam (for some programs), thesis. *Entrance requirements:* For master's, 3 letters of recommendation. Additional exam requirements/recommendations for international students: Required—TOEFL. Electronic applications accepted. *Expenses:* Tuition: Full-time $11,700; part-time $650 per credit.

Simon Fraser University, Graduate Studies, Faculty of Arts and Social Sciences, Canadian Centre for Studies in Publishing, Burnaby, BC V5A 1S6, Canada. Offers M Pub. *Degree requirements:* For master's, internship, project report. *Entrance requirements:* For master's, minimum GPA of 3.0. Additional exam requirements/recommendations for international students: Required—TWE, TOEFL or IELTS. *Expenses:* Contact institution. *Faculty research:* History of publishing, electronic publishing, editing, multimedia, publication design.

University of Baltimore, Graduate School, The Yale Gordon College of Liberal Arts, Program in Creative Writing and Publishing Arts, Baltimore, MD 21201-5779. Offers MFA. Part-time and evening/weekend programs available. *Entrance requirements:* Additional exam requirements/recommendations for international students: Required—TOEFL.

University of Baltimore, Graduate School, The Yale Gordon College of Liberal Arts, Program in Publications Design, Baltimore, MD 21201-5779. Offers MA. Part-time and evening/weekend programs available. *Degree requirements:* For master's, seminar project. *Entrance requirements:* For master's, minimum GPA of 3.0, portfolio, interview. Additional exam requirements/recommendations for international students: Required—TOEFL (minimum score 550 paper-based; 213 computer-based). Electronic applications accepted. *Faculty research:* Communication theory, graphic design, media technology.

University of Houston–Victoria, School of Arts and Sciences, Program in Publishing, Victoria, TX 77901-4450. Offers MS. *Students:* 2 full-time (1 woman), 4 part-time (all women); includes 1 Black or African American, non-Hispanic/Latino; 1 Hispanic/Latino. Average age 42. 9 applicants, 78% accepted, 4 enrolled. *Entrance requirements:* For master's, GMAT or GRE, 2 letters of recommendation, writing sample. Additional exam requirements/recommendations for international students: Required—TOEFL. *Application deadline:* For fall admission, 6/1 for international students; for spring admission, 10/1 for international students. Applications are processed on a rolling basis. Electronic applications accepted. *Expenses:* Tuition, state resident: full-time $4050; part-time $225 per credit hour. Tuition, nonresident: full-time $8730; part-time $485 per credit hour. Required fees: $810; $54 per credit hour. Tuition and fees vary according to course load. *Financial support:* Career-related internships or fieldwork, Federal Work-Study, scholarships/grants, and unspecified assistantships available. Support available to part-time students. Financial award application deadline: 4/15; financial award applicants required to submit FAFSA. *Unit head:* Dr. Jeffrey Dileo, Dean, 361-570-4200, Fax: 361-570-4229, E-mail: dileoj@uhv.edu. *Application contact:* Tracey Fox, Director of Services, 361-570-4233, Fax: 361-580-5507, E-mail: foxt@uhv.edu.

Rhetoric

Abilene Christian University, Graduate School, College of Arts and Sciences, Department of English, Abilene, TX 79699-9100. Offers composition/rhetoric (MA); literature (MA); writing (MA). Part-time programs available. *Faculty:* 16 part-time/adjunct (7 women). *Students:* 15 full-time (8 women); includes 1 Two or more races, non-Hispanic/Latino, 1 international. 18 applicants, 72% accepted, 6 enrolled. In 2010, 5 master's awarded. *Degree requirements:* For master's, one foreign language, comprehensive exam (for some programs), thesis (for some programs). *Entrance requirements:* For master's, GRE General Test. Additional exam requirements/recommendations for international students: Required—TOEFL (minimum score 550 paper-based; 213 computer-based). *Application deadline:* For fall admission, 4/1 priority date for domestic students; for spring admission, 11/1 for domestic students. Applications are processed on a rolling basis. Application fee: $40. Electronic applications accepted. *Expenses:* Tuition: Full-time $12,906; part-time $717 per hour. Required fees: $1250; $61.50 per unit. *Financial support:* In 2010–11, 14 students received support; teaching assistantships, Federal Work-Study available. Support available to part-time students. Financial award application deadline: 4/1; financial award applicants required to submit FAFSA. *Faculty research:* Feminism, Shakespearean dimensions of new literature, poetic consciousness, deconstruction myths. *Unit head:* Dr. Dana McMichael, Graduate Adviser, 325-674-2083, Fax: 325-674-2408, E-mail: dana.mcmichael@acu.edu. *Application contact:* David Pittman, Graduate Admissions Counselor, 325-674-2656, Fax: 325-674-6717, E-mail: gradinfo@acu.edu.

Ball State University, Graduate School, College of Communication, Information, and Media, Department of Communication Studies, Muncie, IN 47306-1099. Offers speech, public address, forensics, and rhetoric (MA). *Faculty:* 5. *Students:* 22 full-time (13 women), 9 part-time (7 women); includes 3 Black or African American, non-Hispanic/Latino, 4 international. Average age 23. 28 applicants, 46% accepted, 10 enrolled. In 2010, 11 master's awarded. *Entrance requirements:* For master's, GRE General Test. Application fee: $50. *Expenses:* Tuition, state resident: full-time $6160; part-time $299 per credit hour. Tuition, nonresident: full-time $16,020; part-time $783 per credit hour. Required fees: $2278; $95 per credit hour. *Financial support:* In 2010–11, 27 teaching assistantships with full tuition reimbursements (averaging $8,549 per year) were awarded; research assistantships, career-related internships or fieldwork also available. Financial award application deadline: 3/1. *Unit head:* Glen Stamp, Chairperson, 765-285-1882, Fax: 765-285-2736. *Application contact:* Glen Stamp, Chairperson, 765-285-1882, Fax: 765-285-2736.

Bob Jones University, Graduate Programs, Greenville, SC 29614. Offers accountancy (MS); Bible (MA); Bible translation (MA); Biblical studies (Certificate); broadcast management (MS); business administration (MBA); church history (MA, PhD); church ministries (MA); church music (MM); cinema and video production (MA); counseling (MS); curriculum and instruction (Ed D); divinity (M Div); dramatic production (MA); educational leadership (MS, Ed D, Ed S); elementary education (M Ed, MAT); English (M Ed, MA, MAT); fine arts (MA); graphic design

(MA); history (M Ed, MA); illustration (MA); interpretative speech (MA); mathematics (M Ed, MAT); medical missions (Certificate); ministry (MM, D Min); multi-categorical special education (M Ed, MAT); music (M Ed); New Testament interpretation (PhD); Old Testament interpretation (PhD); orchestral instrument performance (MM); organ performance (MM); pastoral studies (MA); personnel services (MS, Ed S); piano pedagogy (MM); piano performance (MM); platform arts (MA); radio and television broadcasting (MS); rhetoric and public address (MS); secondary education (M Ed); studio art (MA); teaching Bible (MA); theology (MA, PhD); voice performance (MM); youth ministries (MA); M Div/MM.

Bowling Green State University, Graduate College, College of Arts and Sciences, Department of English, Program in English, Bowling Green, OH 43403. Offers English (MA, PhD); literature (MA); rhetoric and writing (PhD); scientific and technical communication (MA). Part-time programs available. *Degree requirements:* For master's, thesis or alternative; for doctorate, comprehensive exam, thesis/dissertation, foreign language or proficiency in Old English. *Entrance requirements:* For master's and doctorate, GRE General Test. Additional exam requirements/recommendations for international students: Required—TOEFL. Electronic applications accepted. *Faculty research:* Postmodern literary theory, rhetorical theory, ethnic American literature, literature and culture, composition pedagogy.

Brigham Young University, Graduate Studies, College of Humanities, Department of English, Provo, UT 84602-1001. Offers creative writing (MFA); literature (MA); rhetoric/composition (MA). *Faculty:* 50 full-time (16 women). *Students:* 63 full-time (44 women), 5 part-time (2 women); includes 1 Hispanic/Latino. Average age 24. 103 applicants, 34% accepted, 31 enrolled. In 2010, 30 master's awarded. *Degree requirements:* For master's, thesis. *Entrance requirements:* For master's, GRE General Test, creative portfolio (for MFA). Additional exam requirements/recommendations for international students: Required—TOEFL. *Application deadline:* For fall admission, 1/15 for domestic and international students. Application fee: $50. Electronic applications accepted. *Expenses:* Tuition: Full-time $5580; part-time $310 per credit hour. Tuition and fees vary according to program and student's religious affiliation. *Financial support:* In 2010–11, 79 students received support, including 10 research assistantships (averaging $3,000 per year), 62 teaching assistantships (averaging $6,000 per year); career-related internships or fieldwork, institutionally sponsored loans, scholarships/grants, and tuition waivers (partial) also available. Support available to part-time students. Financial award application deadline: 3/15. *Faculty research:* English literature, American literature, rhetoric, creative writing. *Unit head:* Prof. Ed Cutler, Head, 801-422-3581, Fax: 801-422-0221, E-mail: ed_cutler@byu.edu. *Application contact:* Lou Ann C. Crisler, Graduate Secretary, 801-422-8673, Fax: 801-422-0221, E-mail: louann_crisler@byu.edu.

California State University, Dominguez Hills, College of Arts and Humanities, Department of English, Carson, CA 90747-0001. Offers English (MA); rhetoric and composition (Certificate); teaching English as a second language (Certificate). Part-time and evening/weekend programs available. *Faculty:* 13 full-time (5 women). *Students:* 16 full-time (9 women), 67 part-time (42 women); includes 13 Black or African American, non-Hispanic/Latino; 5 Asian, non-Hispanic/Latino; 20 Hispanic/Latino; 1 Two or more races, non-Hispanic/Latino, 3 international. Average age 38. 64 applicants, 86% accepted, 24 enrolled. In 2010, 17 master's awarded. *Degree requirements:* For master's, comprehensive exam (for some programs), thesis or alternative. *Entrance requirements:* For master's, minimum GPA of 3.0 in last 60 units. Additional exam requirements/recommendations for international students: Required—TOEFL (minimum score 550 paper-based; 213 computer-based). *Application deadline:* Applications are processed on a rolling basis. Application fee: $55. Electronic applications accepted. *Faculty research:* Gender studies, transnationalism, discourse analysis, visual culture, Shakespeare. *Unit head:* Dr. Helen Oesterheld, Chair, 310-243-3322, E-mail: hoesterheld@csudh.edu. *Application contact:* 310-243-3600.

California State University, Northridge, Graduate Studies, College of Humanities, Department of English, Northridge, CA 91330. Offers creative writing (MA); literature (MA); rhetoric and composition theory (MA). Part-time and evening/weekend programs available. *Degree requirements:* For master's, thesis or alternative. *Entrance requirements:* For master's, writing proficiency test, GRE General Test or minimum GPA of 3.0. Additional exam requirements/recommendations for international students: Required—TOEFL. *Faculty research:* Reading improvement, professional writing, Dickens, Shaw, English as a second language.

California State University, Stanislaus, College of Humanities and Social Sciences, Program in English (MA), Turlock, CA 95382. Offers literature (Certificate); rhetoric and teaching writing (MA); teaching English to speakers of other languages (MA). Part-time programs available. *Faculty:* 21. *Students:* 10 full-time (7 women), 42 part-time (30 women); includes 19 minority (3 Black or African American, non-Hispanic/Latino; 1 Asian, non-Hispanic/Latino; 10 Hispanic/Latino; 1 Native Hawaiian or other Pacific Islander, non-Hispanic/Latino; 4 Two or more races, non-Hispanic/Latino), 1 international. Average age 35. 28 applicants, 68% accepted, 15 enrolled. In 2010, 19 master's awarded. *Degree requirements:* For master's, comprehensive exam, thesis or alternative. *Entrance requirements:* For master's, GRE, minimum GPA of 3.0, 2 letters of reference, personal statement. Additional exam requirements/recommendations for international students: Required—TOEFL (minimum score 575 paper-based; 233 computer-based), TWE (minimum score 4). *Application deadline:* For fall admission, 5/1 for domestic students; for spring admission, 9/15 for domestic students. Application fee: $55. Electronic applications accepted. Tuition and fees vary according to program. *Financial support:* Fellowships, research assistantships, teaching assistantships, career-related internships or fieldwork and Federal Work-Study available. Financial award application deadline: 3/1; financial award applicants required to submit FAFSA. *Faculty research:* Transnational literacies, Renaissance and medieval literature, abolition writings and slave narratives, qualitative writing. *Unit head:* Dr. Scott Davis, English Department Chair, 209-667-3361, Fax: 209-667-3720, E-mail: english@csustan.edu. *Application contact:* Graduate School, 209-667-3129, Fax: 209-664-7025, E-mail: graduate_school@csustan.edu.

Carnegie Mellon University, College of Humanities and Social Sciences, Department of English, Pittsburgh, PA 15213-3891. Offers communication planning and design (M Des); literary and cultural studies (MA, PhD); professional writing (MAPW), including editing and publishing, policy and non-profit communication, public and media relations / corporate communications, science or healthcare communication, technical writing, writing for new media, writing for print media; rhetoric (MA, PhD). Part-time programs available. Terminal master's awarded for partial completion of doctoral program. *Degree requirements:* For doctorate, 2 foreign languages, comprehensive exam, thesis/dissertation. *Entrance requirements:* For master's and doctorate, GRE General Test. Additional exam requirements/recommendations for international students: Required—TOEFL, TWE. *Faculty research:* Cognitive processes in discourse with emphasis on writing, testing, and evaluation.

The Catholic University of America, School of Arts and Sciences, Department of English Language and Literature, Washington, DC 20064. Offers English language and literature (MA, PhD); rhetoric (Certificate); MSLS/MA. Part-time programs available. *Faculty:* 12 full-time (5 women), 2 part-time/adjunct (0 women). *Students:* 17 full-time (14 women), 42 part-time (28 women), 2 international. Average age 29. 66 applicants, 41% accepted, 12 enrolled. In 2010, 8 master's, 3 doctorates awarded. *Degree requirements:* For master's, one foreign language, comprehensive exam; for doctorate, 2 foreign languages, comprehensive exam, thesis/dissertation. *Entrance requirements:* For master's and doctorate, GRE General Test, statement of purpose, official copies of academic transcripts, three letters of recommendation, writing sample. Additional exam requirements/recommendations for international students: Required—TOEFL (minimum score 580 paper-based; 237 computer-based). *Application deadline:* For fall admission, 8/1 priority date for domestic students, 7/15 for international students; for spring admission, 12/1 priority date for domestic students, 10/15 for international students. Applications are processed on a rolling basis. Application fee: $55. Electronic applications accepted. *Expenses:* Tuition: Full-time $33,580; part-time $1315 per credit hour. Required fees: $80; $40 per semester hour. One-time fee: $425. *Financial support:* Fellowships, research assistantships, teaching assistantships, Federal Work-Study, scholarships/grants, tuition waivers (full and partial), and unspecified assistantships available. Financial award application deadline: 2/1; financial award applicants required to submit FAFSA. *Faculty research:* Medieval literature, theory and history of rhetoric, Renaissance literature, religion and literature, English and American drama. *Unit head:* Dr. Ernest Suarez, Chair, 202-319-5488, Fax: 202-319-4188, E-mail: suarez@cua.edu. *Application contact:* Andrew Woodall, Director of Graduate Admissions, 202-319-5057, Fax: 202-319-6533, E-mail: cua-admissions@cua.edu.

Clemson University, Graduate School, College of Architecture, Arts, and Humanities, Program in Rhetorics, Communication and Information Design, Clemson, SC 29634. Offers PhD. *Students:* 20 full-time (8 women), 5 part-time (1 woman); includes 2 Black or African American, non-Hispanic/Latino; 1 Asian, non-Hispanic/Latino; 1 Hispanic/Latino; 1 Two or more races, non-Hispanic/Latino, 2 international. Average age 37. 13 applicants, 69% accepted, 4 enrolled. In 2010, 6 doctorates awarded. *Degree requirements:* For doctorate, thesis/dissertation (for some programs). *Entrance requirements:* For doctorate, GRE, master's degree in English, communications studies, art, professional communication or related field; portfolio; 3 letters of reference; minimum graduate GPA of 3.5. Additional exam requirements/recommendations for international students: Required—TOEFL (minimum score 550 paper-based; 213 computer-based). *Application deadline:* For fall admission, 2/1 priority date for domestic students, 4/15 for international students. Applications are processed on a rolling basis. Application fee: $70 ($80 for international students). Electronic applications accepted. *Expenses:* Tuition, state resident: full-time $6492; part-time $400 per credit hour. Tuition, nonresident: full-time $13,634; part-time $800 per credit hour. Required fees: $262 per semester. Part-time tuition and fees vary according to course load and program. *Financial support:* In 2010–11, 19 students received support, including 20 teaching assistantships with partial tuition reimbursements available (averaging $18,860 per year); career-related internships or fieldwork, institutionally sponsored loans, scholarships/grants, health care benefits, and unspecified assistantships also available. Support available to part-time students. *Faculty research:* Historiography and philology, multimodal writing, health communication, future of the book, readability studies, politics and rhetors. *Unit head:* Dr. Victor Vitanza, Director, 864-656-6411, Fax: 864-656-0599, E-mail: sophist@clemson.edu. *Application contact:* Dr. Victor Vitanza, Director, 864-656-6411, Fax: 864-656-0599, E-mail: sophist@clemson.edu.

Duquesne University, Graduate School of Liberal Arts, Department of Communication and Rhetorical Studies, Pittsburgh, PA 15282-0001. Offers communication (MA); rhetoric (PhD). Part-time and evening/weekend programs available. *Faculty:* 6 full-time (3 women), 5 part-time/adjunct (3 women). *Students:* 117 full-time (77 women), 20 part-time (16 women); includes 7 Black or African American, non-Hispanic/Latino; 1 Hispanic/Latino, 7 international. Average age 27. 66 applicants, 91% accepted, 34 enrolled. In 2010, 25 master's, 9 doctorates awarded. *Degree requirements:* For master's, thesis optional, practicum; for doctorate, 2 foreign languages, comprehensive exam, thesis/dissertation. *Entrance requirements:* For master's, GRE General Test, MAT or GMAT; for doctorate, GRE General Test. Additional exam requirements/recommendations for international students: Required—TOEFL. *Application deadline:* For fall admission, 2/1 priority date for domestic and international students; for spring admission, 11/1 priority date for domestic and international students. Applications are processed on a rolling basis. Electronic applications accepted. *Expenses:* Tuition: Part-time $884 per credit. Required fees: $84 per credit. Tuition and fees vary according to course load. *Financial support:* In 2010–11, 9 research assistantships with full tuition reimbursements (averaging $9,000 per year), 10 teaching assistantships with full tuition reimbursements (averaging $15,000 per year) were awarded; career-related internships or fieldwork, Federal Work-Study, institutionally sponsored loans, scholarships/grants, tuition waivers (full and partial), and unspecified assistantships also available. Financial award application deadline: 5/1. *Unit head:* Dr. Ronald Arnett, Chair, 412-396-5076. *Application contact:* Dr. Janie Fritz, Director, 412-396-6460.

Eastern Washington University, Graduate Studies, College of Arts and Letters, Department of English, Cheney, WA 99004-2431. Offers literature (MA); rhetoric, composition, and technical communication (MA); teaching English as a second language (MA). *Degree requirements:* For master's, comprehensive exam, thesis or alternative. *Entrance requirements:* For master's, GRE General Test, minimum GPA of 3.0.

Florida State University, The Graduate School, College of Arts and Sciences, Department of English, Tallahassee, FL 32312. Offers creative writing (MFA); English (PhD), including creative writing, literature, rhetoric and composition; literature (MA); rhetoric and composition (MA). Part-time programs available. *Faculty:* 48 full-time (23 women), 6 part-time/adjunct (1 woman). *Students:* 150 full-time (90 women), 20 part-time (10 women); includes 15 Black or African American, non-Hispanic/Latino; 1 American Indian or Alaska Native, non-Hispanic/Latino; 5 Asian, non-Hispanic/Latino; 10 Hispanic/Latino. Average age 30. 480 applicants, 21% accepted, 58 enrolled. In 2010, 22 master's, 14 doctorates awarded. *Degree requirements:* For master's, one foreign language, thesis or alternative; for doctorate, comprehensive exam, thesis/dissertation, 27 hours of coursework, 24 hours of dissertation work. *Entrance requirements:* For master's and doctorate, GRE General Test, GRE Subject Test (literature only), sample of written work, 3 letters of recommendation, resume. Additional exam requirements/recommendations for international students: Required—TOEFL. *Application deadline:* For fall admission, 1/1 priority date for domestic and international students. Application fee: $30. Electronic applications accepted. *Expenses:* Tuition, state resident: full-time $8238.24. *Financial support:* In 2010–11, 126 students received support, including 5 fellowships, teaching assistantships (averaging $11,375 per year); career-related internships or fieldwork, Federal Work-Study, and institutionally sponsored loans also available. Financial award application deadline: 1/1; financial award applicants required to submit FAFSA. *Faculty research:* British and Irish literature, American literature, creative writing, rhetoric and composition, multiethnic transnational literature. *Unit head:* Dr. Ralph Berry, Chairman, 850-644-4230, Fax: 850-644-0811, E-mail: rberry@fsu.edu. *Application contact:* Dr. Ralph Berry, Chairman, 850-644-4230, Fax: 850-644-0811, E-mail: rberry@fsu.edu.

Georgia State University, College of Arts and Sciences, Department of English, Atlanta, GA 30302-3083. Offers creative writing (MA, MFA, PhD), including fiction/poetry; English (MA, PhD); fiction (MFA); literary studies (MA, PhD); poetry (MFA); rhetoric and composition (MA, PhD). Part-time and evening/weekend programs available. *Degree requirements:* For master's, variable foreign language requirement, thesis; for doctorate, one foreign language, comprehensive exam, thesis/dissertation, second exam. *Entrance requirements:* For master's and doctorate, GRE General Test. Additional exam requirements/recommendations for international students: Required—TOEFL (minimum score 0 paper-based; 0 computer-based). Electronic applications accepted. *Faculty research:* Literature, theory, culture, rhetoric/composition, professional/technical writing.

Idaho State University, Office of Graduate Studies, College of Arts and Sciences, Department of Communication and Rhetorical Studies, Pocatello, ID 83209-8115. Offers communication and rhetorical studies (MA). Part-time programs available. *Degree requirements:* For master's, comprehensive exam, paper or thesis. *Entrance requirements:* For master's, GRE General Test, minimum GPA of 3.0 in all upper-level courses. Additional exam requirements/recommendations for international students: Required—TOEFL (minimum score 550 paper-based; 213 computer-based; 80 iBT). Electronic applications accepted. *Faculty research:* Metaphor and cognition in organizational groups and teams; rhetorical criticism of contemporary culture, including music, film, television, and advertising; communication pedagogy; the effect of language on organizational identification and commitment; risk communication and crisis communication.

Indiana University Bloomington, University Graduate School, College of Arts and Sciences, Department of Communication and Culture, Bloomington, IN 47405-7000. Offers film and media studies (PhD); performance and ethnography (PhD); rhetoric and public culture (PhD). *Faculty:* 24 full-time (12 women). *Students:* 81 full-time (41 women), 3 part-time (all women); includes 10 minority (2 Black or African American, non-Hispanic/Latino; 8 Hispanic/Latino), 10 international. Average age 32. 187 applicants, 12% accepted, 11 enrolled. In 2010, 4 master's, 7 doctorates awarded. *Degree requirements:* For master's, comprehensive exam; for doctorate,

Rhetoric

Indiana University Bloomington (continued)
one foreign language, comprehensive exam, thesis/dissertation, student teaching. *Entrance requirements:* For master's and doctorate, GRE General Test (recommended), minimum GPA of 3.0, 3 letters of recommendation, writing sample. Additional exam requirements/recommendations for international students: Required—TOEFL (minimum score 550 paper-based; 213 computer-based). *Application deadline:* For winter admission, 1/1 for domestic students, 12/1 for international students. Application fee: $55 ($65 for international students). Electronic applications accepted. *Financial support:* In 2010–11, 65 students received support, including 4 fellowships with full tuition reimbursements available (averaging $18,000 per year), 48 teaching assistantships with full tuition reimbursements available (averaging $13,257 per year). Financial award application deadline: 4/15. *Faculty research:* Rhetoric and public culture, film and media studies, performance ethnography. *Unit head:* Prof. Gregory A. Waller, Chair, 812-855-2367, Fax: 812-855-6014, E-mail: cmcl@indiana.edu. *Application contact:* Kathy P. Teige, Graduate Secretary, 812-855-6389, Fax: 812-855-6014, E-mail: kteige@indiana.edu.

Indiana University of Pennsylvania, School of Graduate Studies and Research, College of Humanities and Social Sciences, Department of English, Indiana, PA 15705-1087. Offers composition and teaching English to speakers of other languages (MA, MAT, PhD), including composition and teaching English to speakers of other languages (PhD), teaching English (MAT), teaching English to speakers of other languages (MA); literature and criticism (MA, PhD), including generalist (MA), literature (MA), literature and criticism (PhD); rhetoric and linguistics (PhD). Part-time programs available. *Faculty:* 30 full-time (12 women). *Students:* 113 full-time (71 women), 254 part-time (155 women); includes 25 minority (11 Black or African American, non-Hispanic/Latino; 1 American Indian or Alaska Native, non-Hispanic/Latino; 7 Asian, non-Hispanic/Latino; 5 Hispanic/Latino; 1 Two or more races, non-Hispanic/Latino), 99 international. Average age 35. 350 applicants, 37% accepted, 63 enrolled. In 2010, 31 master's, 36 doctorates awarded. *Degree requirements:* For master's, thesis optional; for doctorate, one foreign language, comprehensive exam, thesis/dissertation. *Entrance requirements:* For master's and doctorate, 2 letters of recommendation. Additional exam requirements/recommendations for international students: Required—TOEFL. *Application deadline:* For fall admission, 7/1 priority date for domestic students; for spring admission, 11/1 for domestic students. Applications are processed on a rolling basis. Application fee: $40. *Financial support:* In 2010–11, 8 fellowships (averaging $1,063 per year), 32 research assistantships with full and partial tuition reimbursements (averaging $6,053 per year), 21 teaching assistantships with partial tuition reimbursements (averaging $12,679 per year) were awarded. Financial award application deadline: 3/15; financial award applicants required to submit FAFSA. *Unit head:* Dr. Gail I. Berlin, Chairperson, 724-357-2261, E-mail: ivy@iup.edu. *Application contact:* Dr. Gail I. Berlin, Chairperson, 724-357-2261, E-mail: ivy@iup.edu.

Iowa State University of Science and Technology, Graduate College, College of Liberal Arts and Sciences, Department of English, Ames, IA 50011. Offers creative writing (MFA); English (MA); rhetoric and professional communication (PhD). *Faculty:* 46 full-time (21 women), 9 part-time/adjunct (8 women). *Students:* 118 full-time (77 women), 45 part-time (32 women); includes 2 Black or African American, non-Hispanic/Latino; 1 Asian, non-Hispanic/Latino; 6 Hispanic/Latino, 36 international. 135 applicants, 56% accepted, 48 enrolled. In 2010, 27 master's, 5 doctorates awarded. *Degree requirements:* For master's, thesis or alternative; for doctorate, thesis/dissertation. *Entrance requirements:* For master's, GRE General Test, sample of written work, resume, portfolio in creative writing; for doctorate, GRE General Test, sample of written work, resume. Additional exam requirements/recommendations for international students: Required—TOEFL (minimum score 600 paper-based; 100 iBT), IELTS (minimum score 7). *Application deadline:* For fall admission, 1/5 priority date for domestic and international students. Application fee: $40 ($90 for international students). Electronic applications accepted. *Financial support:* In 2010–11, 7 research assistantships with full and partial tuition reimbursements (averaging $10,211 per year), 86 teaching assistantships with full and partial tuition reimbursements (averaging $13,238 per year) were awarded; fellowships, scholarships/grants, health care benefits, and unspecified assistantships also available. *Faculty research:* Creative writing, literature, rhetoric, composition and professional communication, teaching English as a second language, applied linguistics. *Unit head:* Dr. Charles Kostelnick, Chair, 515-294-2477, Fax: 515-294-2125, E-mail: englgrad@iastate.edu. *Application contact:* Dr. Constance Post, Director of Graduate Education, 515-294-3175, E-mail: englgrad@iastate.edu.

Kansas State University, Graduate School, College of Arts and Sciences, Department of Communication Studies, Theatre and Dance, Manhattan, KS 66505. Offers rhetoric/communication (MA); theatre (MA). *Degree requirements:* For master's, thesis or alternative. *Entrance requirements:* For master's, GRE General Test (recommended), minimum GPA of 3.0. Additional exam requirements/recommendations for international students: Required—TOEFL. Electronic applications accepted. *Faculty research:* Drama therapy, directing, costume design, scenic design, technical theatre mechanics and safety.

Kent State University, College of Arts and Sciences, Department of English, Kent, OH 44242-0001. Offers comparative literature (MA); creative writing (MFA); English (PhD); English for teachers (MA); literature and writing (MA); rhetoric and composition (PhD); teaching English as a second language (MA). MFA program offered jointly with Cleveland State University, The University of Akron, and Youngstown State University. Part-time programs available. Terminal master's awarded for partial completion of doctoral program. *Degree requirements:* For master's, one foreign language, thesis optional; for doctorate, one foreign language, thesis/dissertation, qualifying exams. *Entrance requirements:* For master's and doctorate, GRE General Test, writing sample, letters of recommendation. Additional exam requirements/recommendations for international students: Required—TOEFL (minimum score 600 paper-based). Electronic applications accepted. *Expenses:* Tuition, state resident: full-time $7866; part-time $437 per credit hour. Tuition, nonresident: full-time $14,022; part-time $779 per credit hour. *Faculty research:* British and American literature, textual editing, rhetoric and composition, cultural studies, linguistic and critical theories.

Michigan State University, The Graduate School, College of Arts and Letters, Program in Rhetoric and Writing, East Lansing, MI 48824. Offers critical studies in literacy and pedagogy (MA); digital rhetoric and professional writing (MA); rhetoric and writing (PhD). *Entrance requirements:* Additional exam requirements/recommendations for international students: Required—TOEFL. Electronic applications accepted. *Faculty research:* Rhetoric, writing and communication studies; media studies; technical communication, writing for digital environments.

Michigan Technological University, Graduate School, College of Sciences and Arts, Department of Humanities, Program in Rhetoric and Technical Communication, Houghton, MI 49931. Offers MS, PhD. Part-time programs available. Terminal master's awarded for partial completion of doctoral program. *Degree requirements:* For master's, comprehensive exam; for doctorate, one foreign language, comprehensive exam, thesis/dissertation. *Entrance requirements:* Additional exam requirements/recommendations for international students: Required—TOEFL (minimum score 600 paper-based; 250 computer-based). Electronic applications accepted.

Missouri Western State University, Program in Assessment, St. Joseph, MO 64507-2294. Offers autism spectrum disorders (MAS); learning improvement (MAS); TESOL (MAS); writing (MAS). *Expenses:* Tuition, state resident: full-time $5544; part-time $308 per credit hour. Tuition, nonresident: full-time $10,206; part-time $567 per credit hour. Required fees: $30 per semester. One-time fee: $45 full-time.

Monmouth University, The Graduate School, Department of English, West Long Branch, NJ 07764-1898. Offers creative writing (MA); New Jersey studies (MA); rhetoric and writing (MA). Part-time and evening/weekend programs available. *Faculty:* 12 full-time (8 women). *Students:* 9 full-time (7 women), 30 part-time (21 women); includes 1 Black or African American, non-Hispanic/Latino; 1 Asian, non-Hispanic/Latino; 1 Hispanic/Latino. Average age 32. 30 applicants, 93% accepted, 14 enrolled. In 2010, 9 master's awarded. *Degree requirements:* For master's, comprehensive exam (for some programs), thesis (for some programs). *Entrance requirements:* For master's, minimum overall GPA of 2.75, at least 15 credits in literary studies. Additional exam requirements/recommendations for international students: Required—TOEFL (minimum score 550 paper-based; 213 computer-based; 79 iBT), IELTS (minimum score 5), Michigan English Language Assessment Battery (minimum score 77), Cambridge A, B, C. *Application deadline:* For fall admission, 7/15 for domestic students, 6/1 for international students; for spring admission, 11/15 for domestic students, 11/1 for international students. Application fee: $50. *Expenses:* Tuition: Full-time $19,572; part-time $816 per credit. Required fees: $628; $157 per semester. *Financial support:* In 2010–11, 28 students received support, including 28 fellowships (averaging $1,689 per year), 5 research assistantships (averaging $4,502 per year); career-related internships or fieldwork, scholarships/grants, and unspecified assistantships also available. Support available to part-time students. Financial award applicants required to submit FAFSA. *Faculty research:* Renaissance and medieval literature, nineteenth century American literature, eighteenth century British literature and women's studies, Old English and Middle English, African diaspora and African post-colonial literature. *Unit head:* Dr. Hiede Estes, Program Director, 732-571-7547, E-mail: hestes@monmouth.edu. *Application contact:* Kevin Roane, Director, Office of Graduate Admission, 732-571-3452, Fax: 732-263-5123, E-mail: gradadm@monmouth.edu.

New Mexico Highlands University, Graduate Studies, College of Arts and Sciences, Department of Humanities, Las Vegas, NM 87701. Offers English (MA), including creative writing, language, rhetoric and composition, literature. *Faculty:* 8 full-time (5 women). *Students:* 13 full-time (5 women), 2 part-time (both women); includes 1 Hispanic/Latino; 2 Two or more races, non-Hispanic/Latino. Average age 36. 10 applicants, 100% accepted, 7 enrolled. In 2010, 4 master's awarded. *Degree requirements:* For master's, comprehensive exam, thesis. *Entrance requirements:* For master's, minimum undergraduate GPA of 3.0. Additional exam requirements/recommendations for international students: Required—TOEFL (minimum score 540 paper-based; 207 computer-based). *Application deadline:* For fall admission, 8/1 priority date for domestic students. Applications are processed on a rolling basis. Application fee: $15. *Expenses:* Tuition, state resident: full-time $2544. Required fees: $624; $132 per credit hour. *Financial support:* In 2010–11, 11 students received support. Career-related internships or fieldwork, Federal Work-Study, institutionally sponsored loans, scholarships/grants, tuition waivers (full and partial), and unspecified assistantships available. Support available to part-time students. Financial award application deadline: 3/1; financial award applicants required to submit FAFSA. *Faculty research:* Twentieth century literature, life path writing in homeless shelters, native American philosophy, medieval intellectual and cultural history, creating pedagogical tools for teaching law. *Unit head:* Dr. Barbara Risch, Department Head, 505-454-3451, E-mail: barbararisch@nmhu.edu. *Application contact:* Diane Trujillo, Administrative Assistant, Graduate Studies, 505-454-3266, Fax: 505-426-2117, E-mail: dtrujillo@nmhu.edu.

New Mexico State University, Graduate School, College of Arts and Sciences, Department of English, Las Cruces, NM 88003-8001. Offers creative writing (MFA); English (MA); rhetoric and professional communication (PhD). Part-time programs available. *Faculty:* 22 full-time (13 women), 1 (woman) part-time/adjunct. *Students:* 71 full-time (39 women), 31 part-time (17 women); includes 22 minority (5 Black or African American, non-Hispanic/Latino; 2 Asian, non-Hispanic/Latino; 14 Hispanic/Latino; 1 Two or more races, non-Hispanic/Latino), 4 international. Average age 32. 109 applicants, 58% accepted, 27 enrolled. In 2010, 30 master's, 2 doctorates awarded. *Degree requirements:* For master's, one foreign language, thesis (for some programs); for doctorate, comprehensive exam, thesis/dissertation, internship. *Entrance requirements:* For master's and doctorate, sample of written work. Additional exam requirements/recommendations for international students: Required—TOEFL (minimum score 550 paper-based; 79 iBT), IELTS (minimum score 6.5). *Application deadline:* For fall admission, 2/1 for domestic and international students. Application fee: $30 ($50 for international students). Electronic applications accepted. *Expenses:* Tuition, state resident: full-time $4536; part-time $242 per credit. Tuition, nonresident: full-time $15,816; part-time $712 per credit. Required fees: $636 per term. *Financial support:* In 2010–11, 3 research assistantships (averaging $6,817 per year), 49 teaching assistantships (averaging $15,105 per year) were awarded; fellowships, career-related internships or fieldwork, Federal Work-Study, institutionally sponsored loans, scholarships/grants, health care benefits, and unspecified assistantships also available. Financial award application deadline: 2/1; financial award applicants required to submit FAFSA. *Faculty research:* Composition research, history and theory of rhetoric, technical/professional communication, creative writing, English and American literature. *Unit head:* Dr. Monica F. Torres, Head, 575-646-2319, Fax: 575-646-7725, E-mail: mftorres@nmsu.edu. *Application contact:* Dr. Elizabeth Schirmer, Director of Graduate Studies, 575-646-1733, E-mail: eschirme@nmsu.edu.

North Carolina State University, Graduate School, College of Humanities and Social Sciences, Program in Communication, Rhetoric, and Digital Media, Raleigh, NC 27695. Offers PhD.

Northern Kentucky University, Office of Graduate Programs, College of Arts and Sciences, Program in English, Highland Heights, KY 41099. Offers composition and rhetoric (Certificate); creative writing (Certificate); cultural studies (Certificate); English (MA); professional writing (Certificate). Part-time and evening/weekend programs available. *Faculty:* 11 full-time (6 women). *Students:* 8 full-time (5 women), 66 part-time (53 women); includes 6 minority (4 Black or African American, non-Hispanic/Latino; 1 Hispanic/Latino; 1 Two or more races, non-Hispanic/Latino). Average age 34. 36 applicants, 94% accepted, 32 enrolled. In 2010, 3 master's awarded. *Degree requirements:* For master's, comprehensive exam (for some programs), comprehensive exam, thesis, project, or portfolio. *Entrance requirements:* For master's, minimum GPA of 3.0, two letters of reference. Additional exam requirements/recommendations for international students: Required—TOEFL (minimum score 550 paper-based; 213 computer-based; 79 iBT); Recommended—IELTS (minimum score 6.5). *Application deadline:* For fall admission, 7/1 priority date for domestic students, 6/1 priority date for international students; for spring admission, 11/1 for domestic students, 10/1 for international students. Applications are processed on a rolling basis. Application fee: $40. Electronic applications accepted. *Expenses:* Tuition, state resident: full-time $7254; part-time $403 per credit hour. Tuition, nonresident: full-time $12,492; part-time $694 per credit hour. Tuition and fees vary according to degree level and program. *Financial support:* Unspecified assistantships available. Financial award applicants required to submit FAFSA. *Faculty research:* Composition and rhetoric, creative writing, English and American literature, professional writing, cultural studies. *Unit head:* Dr. Roxanne Kent-Drury, Coordinator, 859-572-6636, Fax: 859-572-6093, E-mail: rkdrury@nku.edu. *Application contact:* Dr. Peg Griffin, Director of Graduate Programs, 859-572-6934, Fax: 859-572-6670, E-mail: griffinp@nku.edu.

Ohio University, Graduate College, Scripps College of Communication, School of Communication Studies, Athens, OH 45701-2979. Offers health communication (PhD); organizational communication (MA); relating and organizing (PhD); rhetoric and public culture (PhD). Part-time programs available. Postbaccalaureate distance learning degree programs offered (minimal on-campus study). *Students:* 49 full-time (35 women), 42 part-time (33 women); includes 6 minority (4 Black or African American, non-Hispanic/Latino; 1 Hispanic/Latino; 1 Two or more races, non-Hispanic/Latino), 12 international. 104 applicants, 40% accepted, 31 enrolled. In 2010, 2 master's, 12 doctorates awarded. Terminal master's awarded for partial completion of doctoral program. *Degree requirements:* For master's, capstone; for doctorate, comprehensive exam, thesis/dissertation. *Entrance requirements:* For master's, GRE; for doctorate, GRE General Test, minimum GPA of 3.0. Additional exam requirements/recommendations for international students: Required—TOEFL (minimum score 550 paper-based; 80 iBT) or IELTS (minimum score 6.5). *Application deadline:* For fall admission, 1/15 priority date for domestic and international students. Application fee: $50 ($55 for international students). Electronic applications accepted. *Financial support:* In 2010–11, 12 students received support, including fellowships with full tuition reimbursements available (averaging $13,600 per year), research assistantships with full tuition reimbursements available (averaging $13,600 per year), teaching assistantships with full tuition reimbursements available (averaging $13,600 per year); career-related internships or fieldwork, Federal Work-Study, and institutionally sponsored loans also available. Financial award application deadline: 1/15. *Faculty research:* Rhetoric and public culture, relating and organizing, health communication. Total annual research expenditures: $200,000. *Unit head:* Dr. Scott Titsworth, Director, 740-593-9160, Fax: 740-593-4810, E-mail: titswort@ohio.edu. *Application contact:* Dr. Benjamin Bates, Associate Director for Graduate Studies, 740-593-9163, Fax: 740-593-4810, E-mail: batesb@ohio.edu.

Rensselaer Polytechnic Institute, Graduate School, School of Humanities, Arts, and Social Sciences, Programs in Communication and Rhetoric, Troy, NY 12180-3590. Offers MS, PhD. *Faculty:* 14 full-time (8 women), 1 part-time/adjunct (0 women). *Students:* 15 full-time (7 women), 1 part-time (0 women), 1 international. 38 applicants, 26% accepted, 2 enrolled. In 2010, 2 master's, 4 doctorates awarded. Terminal master's awarded for partial completion of doctoral program. *Degree requirements:* For master's, thesis optional; for doctorate, comprehensive exam, thesis/dissertation. *Entrance requirements:* For master's, GRE General Test, resume; for doctorate, GRE General Test, writing sample, resume or curriculum vitae. Additional exam requirements/recommendations for international students: Required—TOEFL (minimum score 570 paper-based; 230 computer-based; 89 iBT). *Application deadline:* For fall admission, 1/1 priority date for domestic and international students; for spring admission, 8/15 priority date for domestic students, 7/14 priority date for international students. Applications are processed on a rolling basis. *Application fee:* $75. Electronic applications accepted. *Expenses:* Tuition: Full-time $39,600; part-time $1650 per credit. Required fees: $1896. *Financial support:* In 2010–11, 3 fellowships with full tuition reimbursements (averaging $23,350 per year), 2 research assistantships with full tuition reimbursements (averaging $17,500 per year), 10 teaching assistantships with full tuition reimbursements (averaging $17,500 per year) were awarded; career-related internships or fieldwork, institutionally sponsored loans, and unspecified assistantships also available. Financial award application deadline: 1/15. *Faculty research:* Human-computer interaction (HCI) and usability design and analysis, media design and theory, rhetoric and culture, digital and visual rhetoric, communication in technologically-mediated contexts, technical/professional/cross- and inter-cultural communication. Total annual research expenditures: $73,438. *Unit head:* Prof. James P. Zappen, Head, 518-276-6468, Fax: 518-276-4092, E-mail: zappenj@rpi.edu. *Application contact:* Kathy A. Colman, Recruitment Coordinator, 518-276-6469, Fax: 518-276-4092, E-mail: colmak@rpi.edu.

San Diego State University, Graduate and Research Affairs, College of Arts and Letters, Department of Rhetoric and Writing, San Diego, CA 92182. Offers MA. Part-time programs available. *Degree requirements:* For master's, thesis. *Entrance requirements:* For master's, GRE General Test, writing sample, 3 letters of reference. Additional exam requirements/recommendations for international students: Required—TOEFL. Electronic applications accepted.

Southern Illinois University Carbondale, Graduate School, College of Liberal Arts, Department of English, Carbondale, IL 62901-4701. Offers composition (MA, PhD), including composition, literature, rhetoric; creative writing (MFA). *Degree requirements:* For master's, one foreign language, thesis; for doctorate, 2 foreign languages, thesis/dissertation. *Entrance requirements:* For master's, GRE General Test, GRE Subject Test, minimum GPA of 2.7; for doctorate, GRE General Test, GRE Subject Test, minimum GPA of 3.25. Additional exam requirements/recommendations for international students: Required—TOEFL. *Faculty research:* British literature, English literature, modern Continental literature, literary criticism and theory, film studies, Irish studies.

Syracuse University, College of Arts and Sciences, Program in Composition and Cultural Rhetoric, Syracuse, NY 13244. Offers PhD. *Students:* 29 full-time (19 women), 8 part-time (3 women); includes 6 minority (3 Black or African American, non-Hispanic/Latino; 2 Hispanic/Latino; 1 Two or more races, non-Hispanic/Latino), 1 international. Average age 36. 30 applicants, 17% accepted, 4 enrolled. In 2010, 4 doctorates awarded. *Degree requirements:* For doctorate, comprehensive exam, thesis/dissertation. *Entrance requirements:* For doctorate, GRE. Additional exam requirements/recommendations for international students: Required—TOEFL (minimum score 100 iBT). *Application deadline:* For fall admission, 2/1 priority date for domestic and international students. *Application fee:* $75. Electronic applications accepted. *Expenses:* Tuition: Part-time $1162 per credit. *Financial support:* Fellowships with full tuition reimbursements, teaching assistantships with full tuition reimbursements available. Financial award application deadline: 1/1; financial award applicants required to submit FAFSA. *Unit head:* Prof. Gwendolyn Pough, Graduate Director, 315-443-5146, E-mail: gdpough@syr.edu. *Application contact:* Velita Degraft, 315-443-5146, E-mail: vsdegraf@syr.edu.

Syracuse University, College of Visual and Performing Arts, Program in Communication and Rhetorical Studies, Syracuse, NY 13244. Offers MA. Part-time programs available. *Students:* 16 full-time (8 women), 3 part-time (2 women), 3 international. Average age 27. 28 applicants, 50% accepted, 7 enrolled. In 2010, 3 master's awarded. *Degree requirements:* For master's, thesis or alternative. *Entrance requirements:* For master's, GRE General Test, writing sample. Additional exam requirements/recommendations for international students: Required—TOEFL (minimum score 100 iBT). *Application deadline:* For fall admission, 2/1 priority date for domestic and international students. *Application fee:* $75. Electronic applications accepted. *Expenses:* Tuition: Part-time $1162 per credit. *Financial support:* In 2010–11, 9 students received support; fellowships with full tuition reimbursements available, teaching assistantships with full and partial tuition reimbursements available, tuition waivers (partial) available. Financial award application deadline: 1/1; financial award applicants required to submit FAFSA. *Unit head:* Dr. Kendall Phillips, Chair, 315-443-2883, E-mail: kphillip@syr.edu. *Application contact:* Harriett Conti, Assistant Dean for Recruitment and Admissions, 315-443-5755, E-mail: hmconti@syr.edu.

Texas Christian University, AddRan College of Liberal Arts, Department of English, Fort Worth, TX 76129-0002. Offers composition (MA); English (PhD), including rhetoric and/or literature; literature (MA); rhetoric (MA); rhetoric/composition (PhD). Part-time and evening/weekend programs available. In 2010, 3 master's, 2 doctorates awarded. *Degree requirements:* For master's, one foreign language, thesis, candidacy exam; for doctorate, one foreign language, comprehensive exam, thesis/dissertation, 66 hours, diagnostic exam, qualifying exam. *Entrance requirements:* For master's and doctorate, GRE General Test, 30 hours of English; 12 hours of foreign language study. Additional exam requirements/recommendations for international students: Required—TOEFL. *Application deadline:* For fall admission, 1/31 for domestic and international students; for winter admission, 1/10 for domestic and international students; for spring admission, 10/15 for domestic and international students. Applications are processed on a rolling basis. *Application fee:* $50. Electronic applications accepted. *Expenses:* Tuition: Full-time $18,720; part-time $1040 per credit hour. Tuition and fees vary according to course load and program. *Financial support:* In 2010–11, 39 students received support, including 2 fellowships with full tuition reimbursements available (averaging $17,500 per year), 29 teaching assistantships with full tuition reimbursements available (averaging $15,000 per year); research assistantships with full tuition reimbursements available, tuition waivers (full) and unspecified assistantships also available. Financial award application deadline: 1/10; financial award applicants required to submit FAFSA. *Unit head:* Dr. Brad Lucas, Chairperson, 817-257-7240, E-mail: b.e.lucas2@tcu.edu. *Application contact:* Dr. Mona Narain, Associate Professor/Director of Graduate Studies, 817-257-7284, E-mail: m.narain@tcu.edu.

Texas State University–San Marcos, Graduate School, College of Liberal Arts, Department of English, Program in Rhetoric and Composition, San Marcos, TX 78666. Offers MA. Part-time programs available. *Faculty:* 5 full-time (3 women). *Students:* 12 full-time (8 women), 11 part-time (7 women); includes 6 minority (1 American Indian or Alaska Native, non-Hispanic/Latino; 4 Hispanic/Latino; 1 Two or more races, non-Hispanic/Latino). Average age 33. 15 applicants, 100% accepted, 12 enrolled. In 2010, 3 master's awarded. *Degree requirements:* For master's, comprehensive exam, thesis optional. *Entrance requirements:* For master's, minimum GPA of 3.25 in minimum of 24 hours of undergraduate English, 6 hours of a foreign language. Additional exam requirements/recommendations for international students: Required—TOEFL (minimum score 550 paper-based; 213 computer-based; 78 iBT). *Application deadline:* For fall admission, 6/15 for domestic students, 6/1 for international students; for spring admission, 10/15 for domestic students, 10/1 for international students. Applications are processed on a rolling basis. *Application fee:* $40 ($90 for international students). Electronic applications accepted. *Expenses:* Tuition, state resident: full-time $6024; part-time $251 per credit hour.

Tuition, nonresident: full-time $13,536; part-time $564 per credit hour. Required fees: $1776; $50 per credit hour. $306 per semester. *Financial support:* In 2010–11, 12 students received support, including 4 research assistantships (averaging $5,727 per year), 4 teaching assistantships (averaging $5,385 per year); Federal Work-Study, institutionally sponsored loans, scholarships/grants, and unspecified assistantships also available. Support available to part-time students. Financial award application deadline: 4/1; financial award applicants required to submit FAFSA. *Unit head:* Dr. Rebecca Jackson, Graduate Advisor, 512-245-2163, E-mail: rj10@txstate.edu. *Application contact:* Dr. J. Michael Willoughby, Dean of Graduate School, 512-245-2581, Fax: 512-245-8365, E-mail: gradcollege@txstate.edu.

Texas Tech University, Graduate School, College of Arts and Sciences, Department of English, Lubbock, TX 79409. Offers English (MA, PhD); technical communication (MA); technical communication and rhetoric (PhD). Part-time programs available. *Faculty:* 38 full-time (16 women), 1 (woman) part-time/adjunct. *Students:* 106 full-time (62 women), 89 part-time (55 women); includes 4 Black or African American, non-Hispanic/Latino; 2 American Indian or Alaska Native, non-Hispanic/Latino; 7 Asian, non-Hispanic/Latino; 4 Hispanic/Latino, 18 international. Average age 34. 242 applicants, 21% accepted, 34 enrolled. In 2010, 25 master's, 11 doctorates awarded. *Degree requirements:* For master's, one foreign language, thesis (for some programs); for doctorate, one foreign language, thesis/dissertation (for some programs). *Entrance requirements:* For master's and doctorate, GRE General Test. Additional exam requirements/recommendations for international students: Required—TOEFL (minimum score 550 paper-based; 213 computer-based; 79 iBT). *Application deadline:* For fall admission, 6/1 priority date for domestic students, 1/15 priority date for international students; for spring admission, 9/1 priority date for domestic students, 6/15 priority date for international students. Applications are processed on a rolling basis. *Application fee:* $50 ($75 for international students). Electronic applications accepted. *Expenses:* Tuition, state resident: full-time $5495.76; part-time $228.99 per credit hour. Tuition, nonresident: full-time $12,936; part-time $538.99 per credit hour. Required fees: $2674; $36 per credit hour. $905 per semester. *Financial support:* In 2010–11, 110 students received support, including 10 research assistantships with partial tuition reimbursements available (averaging $8,815 per year), 48 teaching assistantships with partial tuition reimbursements available (averaging $6,362 per year). Financial award application deadline: 4/15; financial award applicants required to submit FAFSA. *Faculty research:* Computers and writing, technical communication and rhetoric, creative writing, nineteenth century studies, literature of social justice and the environment. *Unit head:* Dr. Sam Dragga, Chair, 806-742-2501, Fax: 806-742-0989, E-mail: sam.dragga@ttu.edu. *Application contact:* Dr. Brian McFadden, Director of Graduate Studies, 806-742-2501, Fax: 806-742-0989, E-mail: english.gradadvisor@ttu.edu.

Texas Woman's University, Graduate School, College of Arts and Sciences, Department of English, Speech, and Foreign Languages, Denton, TX 76201. Offers English (MA); rhetoric (PhD). Part-time programs available. *Faculty:* 13 full-time (7 women), 6 part-time/adjunct (0 women). *Students:* 11 full-time (8 women), 58 part-time (51 women); includes 5 Black or African American, non-Hispanic/Latino; 2 American Indian or Alaska Native, non-Hispanic/Latino; 4 Asian, non-Hispanic/Latino; 4 Hispanic/Latino, 1 international. Average age 37. 19 applicants, 68% accepted, 12 enrolled. In 2010, 7 master's, 5 doctorates awarded. *Degree requirements:* For master's, comprehensive exam, thesis; for doctorate, comprehensive exam, thesis/dissertation. *Entrance requirements:* For master's, GRE General Test (preferred minimum score 500 verbal, 350 quantitative), 3 letters of reference, interview (for graduate assistants), minimum GPA of 3.0 on previous upper division and graduate work; for doctorate, GRE General Test (preferred minimum score 500 verbal, 350 quantitative), writing sample, 3 letters of reference, interview (for graduate assistants), minimum GPA of 3.0 on previous upper-division and graduate work. Additional exam requirements/recommendations for international students: Recommended—TOEFL (minimum score 600 paper-based; 250 computer-based; 100 iBT). *Application deadline:* For fall admission, 7/1 priority date for domestic students, 3/1 for international students; for spring admission, 12/1 priority date for domestic students, 7/1 for international students. Applications are processed on a rolling basis. *Application fee:* $50 ($75 for international students). Electronic applications accepted. *Expenses:* Tuition, state resident: full-time $3834; part-time $213 per credit hour. Tuition, nonresident: full-time $9468; part-time $526 per credit hour. Required fees: $1247; $220 per credit hour. *Financial support:* In 2010–11, 16 students received support, including 6 research assistantships (averaging $12,942 per year), 15 teaching assistantships (averaging $12,942 per year); career-related internships or fieldwork, Federal Work-Study, institutionally sponsored loans, scholarships/grants, traineeships, health care benefits, and unspecified assistantships also available. Support available to part-time students. Financial award application deadline: 3/1; financial award applicants required to submit FAFSA. *Faculty research:* British and American literature, rhetoric: historical and applied, composition studies and technology, literary theory and criticism, women's literature and feminist rhetoric. *Unit head:* Dr. Genevieve West, Chair, 940-898-2324, Fax: 940-898-2297, E-mail: engspfl@twu.edu. *Application contact:* Dr. Samuel Wheeler, Assistant Director of Admissions, 940-898-3188, Fax: 940-898-3081, E-mail: wheelersr@twu.edu.

The University of Alabama, Graduate School, College of Arts and Sciences, Department of English, Tuscaloosa, AL 35487. Offers composition and rhetoric (PhD); creative writing (MFA), including fiction, poetry; literature (MA, PhD); rhetoric and composition (MA); teaching English as a second language (MATESOL). *Faculty:* 31 full-time (14 women). *Students:* 64 full-time (46 women), 75 part-time (44 women); includes 15 minority (11 Black or African American, non-Hispanic/Latino; 1 Asian, non-Hispanic/Latino; 1 Hispanic/Latino; 1 Native Hawaiian or other Pacific Islander, non-Hispanic/Latino; 1 Two or more races, non-Hispanic/Latino), 7 international. Average age 28. 364 applicants, 20% accepted, 46 enrolled. In 2010, 40 master's, 7 doctorates awarded. *Degree requirements:* For master's, one foreign language, comprehensive exam, thesis (for some programs); for doctorate, 2 foreign languages, comprehensive exam, thesis/dissertation. *Entrance requirements:* For master's and doctorate, GRE, minimum GPA of 3.0, critical writing sample. Additional exam requirements/recommendations for international students: Required—TOEFL. *Application deadline:* For fall admission, 1/15 priority date for domestic students, 1/15 for international students. *Application fee:* $50 ($60 for international students). Electronic applications accepted. *Expenses:* Tuition, state resident: full-time $7900. Tuition, nonresident: full-time $20,500. *Financial support:* In 2010–11, 7 fellowships with full tuition reimbursements (averaging $15,000 per year), 1 research assistantship (averaging $11,708 per year), 106 teaching assistantships with full tuition reimbursements (averaging $11,708 per year) were awarded; career-related internships or fieldwork, scholarships/grants, health care benefits, and unspecified assistantships also available. Financial award application deadline: 1/15. *Faculty research:* Critical theory; modern, Renaissance, and African-American literature. *Unit head:* Dr. Catherine E. Davies, Director of Graduate Studies, 205-348-8499, E-mail: cdavies@bama.ua.edu. *Application contact:* Vernita W. James, Office Assistant II, 205-348-0766, Fax: 205-348-1388, E-mail: vwjames@bama.ua.edu.

The University of Arizona, College of Humanities, Department of English, Rhetoric, Composition and the Teaching of English Program, Tucson, AZ 85721. Offers PhD. *Students:* 38 full-time (29 women), 14 part-time (11 women); includes 11 minority (4 Asian, non-Hispanic/Latino; 5 Hispanic/Latino; 2 Two or more races, non-Hispanic/Latino). Average age 35. 41 applicants, 15% accepted, 6 enrolled. In 2010, 17 doctorates awarded. *Degree requirements:* For doctorate, one foreign language, comprehensive exam, thesis/dissertation. *Entrance requirements:* For doctorate, GRE General Test, 3 letters of recommendation, writing sample. Additional exam requirements/recommendations for international students: Required—TOEFL (minimum score 550 paper-based; 213 computer-based; 79 iBT). *Application deadline:* Applications are processed on a rolling basis. *Application fee:* $75. Electronic applications accepted. *Expenses:* Tuition, state resident: full-time $7692. *Unit head:* Theresa Enos, Director, 520-621-3255, Fax: 520-621-7397, E-mail: enos@u.arizona.edu. *Application contact:* Alison Miller, Program Assistant, 520-621-7213, Fax: 520-621-7397, E-mail: admiller@u.arizona.edu.

University of Arkansas at Little Rock, Graduate School, College of Arts, Humanities, and Social Science, Department of Rhetoric and Writing, Little Rock, AR 72204-1099. Offers professional and technical writing (MA). Part-time and evening/weekend programs available. *Degree requirements:* For master's, thesis or alternative, oral defense of final project. *Entrance*

Rhetoric

University of Arkansas at Little Rock (continued)
requirements: For master's, GRE, minimum GPA of 3.0, writing portfolio. *Faculty research:* Writing for industry, science, business, and government; composition and rhetorical theory; writing nonfiction; teaching of writing.

University of California, Berkeley, Graduate Division, College of Letters and Science, Department of Rhetoric, Berkeley, CA 94720-1500. Offers PhD. *Degree requirements:* For doctorate, 2 foreign languages, thesis/dissertation, qualifying exam. *Entrance requirements:* For doctorate, GRE General Test, minimum GPA of 3.0, 3 letters of recommendation. *Faculty research:* History and theory of rhetoric, public discourse (law, politics, and science), literature and philosophy, film.

University of Colorado Denver, College of Liberal Arts and Sciences, Department of English, Denver, CO 80217. Offers applied linguistics (MA); literature (MA); rhetoric and teaching of writing (MA). Part-time and evening/weekend programs available. *Faculty:* 23 full-time (13 women). *Students:* 45 full-time (27 women), 22 part-time (15 women); includes 3 Hispanic/Latino, 3 international. Average age 30. 39 applicants, 77% accepted, 18 enrolled. In 2010, 18 master's awarded. *Degree requirements:* For master's, variable foreign language requirement, comprehensive exam (for some programs), thesis (for some programs), minimum of 33 credit hours (for literature), 30 (for rhetoric and teaching of writing and applied linguistics). *Entrance requirements:* For master's, GRE General Test, minimum GPA of 3.0, critical writing sample, letters of recommendation, completion of 24 semester hours in English courses (at least 16 at the upper-division). *Application deadline:* For fall admission, 4/1 for domestic students; for spring admission, 10/1 for domestic students. Application fee: $50 ($75 for international students). Electronic applications accepted. *Expenses:* Tuition, state resident: full-time $7332; part-time $355 per credit hour. Tuition, nonresident: full-time $18,990; part-time $1055 per credit hour. Required fees: $998. Tuition and fees vary according to course level, course load, degree level, campus/location, program, reciprocity agreements and student level. *Financial support:* Fellowships, teaching assistantships, Federal Work-Study, scholarships/grants, and unspecified assistantships available. Financial award application deadline: 4/1; financial award applicants required to submit FAFSA. *Faculty research:* Literature, rhetoric, teaching of writing, applied linguistics. *Unit head:* Prof. Nancy Ciccone, Chair, 303-556-8395, Fax: 303-556-2959, E-mail: nancy.ciccone@ucdenver.edu. *Application contact:* English Department, 303-556-2584, Fax: 303-556-2959.

University of Denver, Division of Arts, Humanities and Social Sciences, Department of English, Denver, CO 80208. Offers creative writing (PhD); literary studies (MA, PhD); rhetoric and theory (PhD). Part-time programs available. *Faculty:* 18 full-time (7 women), 1 (woman) part-time/adjunct. *Students:* 32 full-time (17 women), 10 part-time (9 women), 1 international. Average age 32. 195 applicants, 11% accepted, 18 enrolled. In 2010, 3 master's, 6 doctorates awarded. *Degree requirements:* For master's, one foreign language, comprehensive exam, thesis; for doctorate, 2 foreign languages, comprehensive exam, thesis/dissertation. *Entrance requirements:* For master's and doctorate, GRE General Test, GRE Subject Test. Additional exam requirements/recommendations for international students: Required—TOEFL (minimum score 570 paper-based; 88 iBT). *Application deadline:* Applications are processed on a rolling basis. Application fee: $60. Electronic applications accepted. *Expenses:* Tuition: Full-time $35,604; part-time $29,670 per year. Required fees: $687 per year. Tuition and fees vary according to program. *Financial support:* In 2010–11, 31 teaching assistantships with full and partial tuition reimbursements (averaging $16,910 per year) were awarded; Federal Work-Study, institutionally sponsored loans, scholarships/grants, and unspecified assistantships also available. Support available to part-time students. Financial award application deadline: 3/1; financial award applicants required to submit FAFSA. *Faculty research:* Cultural studies, creative nonfiction, eighteenth century colonial literature, multicultural literature, Cervantes. *Unit head:* Dr. Clark Davis, Chair, 303-871-2900, Fax: 303-871-2853, E-mail: cldavis@du.edu. *Application contact:* Niki Herrera, Graduate Student Services Assistant, 303-871-4313, Fax: 303-871-2853, E-mail: niki.herrera@du.edu.

The University of Iowa, Graduate College, College of Liberal Arts and Sciences, Department of Communication Studies, Iowa City, IA 52242-1316. Offers communication research (MA, PhD); rhetorical studies (MA, PhD). *Degree requirements:* For master's, thesis optional, exam; for doctorate, comprehensive exam, thesis/dissertation. *Entrance requirements:* For master's and doctorate, GRE General Test, minimum GPA of 3.0. Additional exam requirements/recommendations for international students: Required—TOEFL (minimum score 550 paper-based; 213 computer-based; 81 iBT). Electronic applications accepted.

The University of Iowa, Graduate College, College of Liberal Arts and Sciences, Department of English, Iowa City, IA 52242-1316. Offers English (PhD); literary criticism (PhD); literary history (PhD); literary studies (MA); nonfiction writing (MFA); rhetorical theory and stylistics (PhD); writer's workshop (MFA); JD/PhD. *Degree requirements:* For master's, thesis (for some programs), exam; for doctorate, comprehensive exam, thesis/dissertation. *Entrance requirements:* For master's and doctorate, GRE General Test, minimum GPA of 3.0. Additional exam requirements/recommendations for international students: Required—TOEFL (minimum score 640 paper-based; 273 computer-based; 111 iBT). Electronic applications accepted.

University of Louisiana at Lafayette, College of Liberal Arts, Department of English, Lafayette, LA 70504. Offers British and American literature (MA), including creative writing, folklore, rhetoric; creative writing (PhD); literature (PhD); rhetoric (PhD). Part-time programs available. Terminal master's awarded for partial completion of doctoral program. *Degree requirements:* For master's, one foreign language, thesis or alternative; for doctorate, 2 foreign languages, comprehensive exam, thesis/dissertation. *Entrance requirements:* For master's, GRE General Test, minimum GPA of 2.75; for doctorate, GRE General Test, minimum GPA of 3.0. Additional exam requirements/recommendations for international students: Required—TOEFL (minimum score 550 paper-based; 213 computer-based). Electronic applications accepted. *Faculty research:* Composition theory, Southern literature, medieval literature.

University of Louisville, Graduate School, College of Arts and Sciences, Department of English, Louisville, KY 40292. Offers English (MA), including creative writing, literature, rhetoric and composition (MA, PhD); English rhetoric and composition (PhD), including rhetoric and composition (MA, PhD). Part-time programs available. *Faculty:* 40 full-time (22 women). *Students:* 78 full-time (41 women), 25 part-time (12 women); includes 3 Black or African American, non-Hispanic/Latino; 1 American Indian or Alaska Native, non-Hispanic/Latino; 2 Asian, non-Hispanic/Latino; 2 Hispanic/Latino, 7 international. Average age 30. 97 applicants, 64% accepted, 38 enrolled. In 2010, 21 master's, 8 doctorates awarded. *Degree requirements:* For master's, one foreign language, thesis or culminating project; for doctorate, 2 foreign languages, comprehensive exam, thesis/dissertation. *Entrance requirements:* For master's, GRE General Test, 2 academic letters of recommendation; for doctorate, GRE General Test, 15-20 page critical writing sample, 1000-word statement of professional goals, 3 academic letters of recommendation, transcripts of all college work. Additional exam requirements/recommendations for international students: Required—TOEFL (minimum score 600 paper-based; 210 computer-based; 100 iBT). *Application deadline:* For fall admission, 8/1 for domestic students, 1/5 for international students; for spring admission, 12/1 for domestic students. Applications are processed on a rolling basis. Application fee: $50. Electronic applications accepted. *Expenses:* Tuition, state resident: full-time $9144; part-time $508 per credit hour. Tuition, nonresident: full-time $19,026; part-time $1057 per credit hour. Tuition and fees vary according to program and reciprocity agreements. *Financial support:* In 2010–11, 49 students received support, including 9 fellowships with full tuition reimbursements available, 40 teaching assistantships with full tuition reimbursements available; health care benefits and unspecified assistantships also available. Financial award application deadline: 1/5. *Faculty research:* American and English literatures and cultures, rhetoric and composition, critical theory and cultural studies, creative writing. Total annual research expenditures: $278,898. *Unit head:* Dr. Susan Griffin, Chair, 502-852-6801, Fax: 502-852-4182, E-mail: smgriff01@louisville.edu. *Application contact:* Libby Leggett, Director, Graduate Admissions, 502-852-3101, Fax: 502-852-6536, E-mail: gradadm@louisville.edu.

University of Nebraska–Lincoln, Graduate College, College of Arts and Sciences, Department of Communication Studies, Lincoln, NE 68588. Offers instructional communication (MA, PhD); interpersonal communication (MA, PhD); marketing, communication studies, and advertising (MA, PhD); organizational communication (MA, PhD); rhetoric and culture (MA, PhD). *Degree requirements:* For master's, thesis optional; for doctorate, comprehensive exam, thesis/dissertation. *Entrance requirements:* For master's and doctorate, GRE General Test, writing sample. Additional exam requirements/recommendations for international students: Required—TOEFL (minimum score 600 paper-based; 250 computer-based). Electronic applications accepted. *Faculty research:* Message strategies, gender communication, political communication, organizational communication, instructional communication.

University of Nebraska–Lincoln, Graduate College, College of Arts and Sciences, Department of English, Lincoln, NE 68588-0333. Offers composition and rhetoric (MA, PhD); creative writing (MA, PhD); literature studies (MA, PhD). *Degree requirements:* For master's, thesis optional; for doctorate, one foreign language, comprehensive exam, thesis/dissertation. *Entrance requirements:* For master's, writing sample; for doctorate, GRE General Test, writing sample. Additional exam requirements/recommendations for international students: Required—TOEFL (minimum score 600 paper-based; 250 computer-based). Electronic applications accepted. *Faculty research:* Creative writing, composition and rhetoric, women's studies, North American literature, medieval/Renaissance studies.

The University of North Carolina at Charlotte, Graduate School, College of Arts and Sciences, Department of Communication Studies, Charlotte, NC 28223-0001. Offers health communication (MA); media/rhetorical critical studies (MA); organizational communication (MA); public relations (MA). Part-time and evening/weekend programs available. *Faculty:* 12 full-time (5 women), 1 (woman) part-time/adjunct. *Students:* 6 full-time (5 women), 19 part-time (17 women); includes 7 minority (6 Black or African American, non-Hispanic/Latino; 1 Asian, non-Hispanic/Latino). Average age 27. 554 applicants, 4% accepted, 12 enrolled. In 2010, 12 master's awarded. Terminal master's awarded for partial completion of doctoral program. *Degree requirements:* For master's, project, thesis, or comprehensive exam. *Entrance requirements:* For master's, GRE General Test, minimum GPA of 2.75 overall. Additional exam requirements/recommendations for international students: Required—TOEFL (minimum score 557 paper-based; 220 computer-based; 83 iBT). *Application deadline:* For fall admission, 3/15 for domestic students, 5/1 for international students; for spring admission, 11/15 for domestic students, 10/1 for international students. Applications are processed on a rolling basis. Application fee: $55. Electronic applications accepted. *Expenses:* Tuition, state resident: full-time $3464. Tuition, nonresident: full-time $14,297. Required fees: $2094. Tuition and fees vary according to course load. *Financial support:* In 2010–11, 9 students received support, including 1 research assistantship (averaging $18,000 per year), 8 teaching assistantships (averaging $15,529 per year); career-related internships or fieldwork, institutionally sponsored loans, scholarships/grants, and unspecified assistantships also available. Support available to part-time students. Financial award application deadline: 4/1; financial award applicants required to submit FAFSA. *Faculty research:* Health literacy, systems of care and mental illness, the communication of emotions in gendered workplaces, international constructs of public relations managerial responsibilities, sports culture and the construction of social contracts, African-American oratory. Total annual research expenditures: $25,636. *Unit head:* Dr. Richard W. Leeman, Chair, 704-687-2086, Fax: 704-687-6900, E-mail: rwleeman@uncc.edu. *Application contact:* Kathy B. Giddings, Director of Graduate Admissions, 704-687-5503, Fax: 704-687-3279, E-mail: gradadm@uncc.edu.

The University of North Carolina at Greensboro, Graduate School, College of Arts and Sciences, Department of English, Program in English, Greensboro, NC 27412-5001. Offers American literature (PhD); English (M Ed, MA); English literature (PhD); rhetoric and composition (PhD). *Degree requirements:* For master's, comprehensive exam, thesis or alternative; for doctorate, variable foreign language requirement, thesis/dissertation, preliminary exam. *Entrance requirements:* For master's, GRE General Test, GRE Subject Test, minimum GPA of 3.0; for doctorate, GRE General Test, GRE Subject Test, critical writing sample, minimum GPA of 3.0. Additional exam requirements/recommendations for international students: Required—TOEFL. Electronic applications accepted.

The University of Tennessee at Chattanooga, Graduate School, College of Arts and Sciences, Department of English, Chattanooga, TN 37403. Offers creative writing (MA); literary study (MA); rhetoric and writing (MA, Graduate Certificate). Part-time and evening/weekend programs available. *Faculty:* 12 full-time (7 women). *Students:* 19 full-time (13 women), 26 part-time (15 women); includes 1 minority (Two or more races, non-Hispanic/Latino), 1 international. Average age 29. 33 applicants, 88% accepted, 23 enrolled. In 2010, 20 master's awarded. *Degree requirements:* For master's, one foreign language, comprehensive exam, thesis. *Entrance requirements:* For master's, GRE General Test or GRE Subject Test (literature), minimum GPA of 3.0 in English. Additional exam requirements/recommendations for international students: Required—TOEFL (minimum score 550 paper-based; 213 computer-based; 79 iBT), IELTS (minimum score 6). *Application deadline:* For fall admission, 8/1 priority date for domestic students, 6/1 for international students; for spring admission, 12/1 priority date for domestic students, 10/1 for international students. Applications are processed on a rolling basis. Application fee: $35. Electronic applications accepted. *Financial support:* In 2010–11, 6 research assistantships with full and partial tuition reimbursements (averaging $5,500 per year) were awarded; career-related internships or fieldwork, scholarships/grants, and unspecified assistantships also available. Support available to part-time students. *Faculty research:* Technical writing, African-American literature, Milton, creative writing and poetry, American modernism and gender theory. Total annual research expenditures: $74,953. *Unit head:* Dr. Verbie Prevost, Head, 423-425-4238, Fax: 423-785-2282, E-mail: verbie-prevost@utc.edu. *Application contact:* Dr. Jerald Ainsworth, Dean of Graduate Studies, 423-425-4478, Fax: 423-425-5223, E-mail: jerald-ainsworth@utc.edu.

The University of Texas at El Paso, Graduate School, College of Liberal Arts, Department of English, El Paso, TX 79968-0001. Offers bilingual professional writing (Certificate); English and American literature (MA); rhetoric and composition (PhD); rhetoric and writing studies (MA); teaching English (MAT). Part-time and evening/weekend programs available. *Students:* 68 (47 women); includes 1 Black or African American, non-Hispanic/Latino; 1 Asian, non-Hispanic/Latino; 36 Hispanic/Latino, 2 international. Average age 34. In 2010, 18 master's awarded. *Degree requirements:* For master's, thesis optional. *Entrance requirements:* For master's, GRE General Test, minimum GPA of 3.0. Additional exam requirements/recommendations for international students: Required—TOEFL. *Application deadline:* For fall admission, 7/1 priority date for domestic students, 3/1 for international students; for spring admission, 11/1 priority date for domestic students, 9/1 for international students. Applications are processed on a rolling basis. Application fee: $15 ($65 for international students). Electronic applications accepted. *Financial support:* In 2010–11, research assistantships with partial tuition reimbursements (averaging $20,555 per year), teaching assistantships with partial tuition reimbursements (averaging $16,444 per year) were awarded; Federal Work-Study, institutionally sponsored loans, scholarships/grants, and tuition waivers (partial) also available. Financial award application deadline: 3/15; financial award applicants required to submit FAFSA. *Faculty research:* Literature, creative writing, literary theory. *Unit head:* Evelyn Posey, Chair, 915-747-5731. *Application contact:* Dr. Charles H. Ambler, Dean of the Graduate School, 915-747-5491 Ext. 7886, Fax: 915-747-5788, E-mail: cambler@utep.edu.

University of Utah, Graduate School, College of Humanities, Department of English, Program in Creative Writing, Salt Lake City, UT 84112. Offers rhetoric/composition (MA, PhD). *Students:* 5 full-time (2 women), 5 part-time (3 women); includes 2 minority (1 Black or African American, non-Hispanic/Latino; 1 American Indian or Alaska Native, non-Hispanic/Latino). Average age 31. 58 applicants, 2% accepted, 1 enrolled. In 2010, 5 master's awarded. *Degree requirements:* For master's, variable foreign language requirement, comprehensive exam, thesis optional; for doctorate, variable foreign language requirement, comprehensive exam, thesis/dissertation. *Entrance requirements:* For master's and doctorate, GRE. *Application deadline:* For fall admission, 1/15 for domestic students. Application fee: $55 ($65 for international students).

Expenses: Tuition, area resident: Part-time $179.19 per credit hour. Tuition, state resident: full-time $4384. Tuition, nonresident: full-time $16,684; part-time $630.67 per credit hour. Required fees: $350 per semester. Tuition and fees vary according to course load, degree level and program. *Financial support:* In 2010–11, 9 teaching assistantships with full tuition reimbursements (averaging $12,430 per year) were awarded; institutionally sponsored loans, scholarships/grants, health care benefits, and unspecified assistantships also available. *Unit head:* Dr. Maureen Ann Mathison, Director, 801-581-7090, E-mail: maureen.mathison@hum.utah.edu. *Application contact:* Pauline Frances Light, Office Support Coordinator, 801-581-7098, E-mail: plight@utah.edu.

University of Wisconsin–Madison, Graduate School, College of Letters and Science, Department of Communication Arts, Madison, WI 53706-1380. Offers communication science (MA, PhD); film (MA, PhD); media and cultural studies (MA, PhD); rhetoric (MA, PhD). Terminal master's awarded for partial completion of doctoral program. *Degree requirements:* For master's, one foreign language, thesis (for some programs); for doctorate, one foreign language, thesis/dissertation. *Entrance requirements:* For master's and doctorate, GRE General Test, minimum GPA of 3.5. Electronic applications accepted. *Expenses:* Tuition, state resident: full-time $9887; part-time $617.96 per credit. Tuition, nonresident: full-time $24,054; part-time $1503.40 per credit. Required fees: $67.63 per credit. Tuition and fees vary according to reciprocity agreements.

University of Wisconsin–Milwaukee, Graduate School, College of Letters and Sciences, Department of Communication, Milwaukee, WI 53201-0413. Offers communication (MA, PhD); mediation and negotiation (Certificate); rhetorical leadership (Certificate). Part-time programs available. *Faculty:* 20 full-time (12 women). *Students:* 20 full-time (14 women), 36 part-time (29 women); includes 1 Black or African American, non-Hispanic/Latino; 1 Asian, non-Hispanic/Latino; 1 Hispanic/Latino, 6 international. Average age 32. 68 applicants, 57% accepted, 11 enrolled. In 2010, 21 master's awarded. *Degree requirements:* For master's, thesis or alternative; for doctorate, comprehensive exam. *Entrance requirements:* For master's, GRE General Test, minimum GPA of 3.0. Additional exam requirements/recommendations for international students: Required—TOEFL (minimum score 550 paper-based; 79 iBT), IELTS (minimum score 6). *Application deadline:* For fall admission, 1/1 priority date for domestic students; for spring admission, 9/1 for domestic students. Applications are processed on a rolling basis. Application fee: $56. Electronic applications accepted. *Financial support:* In 2010–11, 3 fellowships, 34 teaching assistantships were awarded; research assistantships, career-related internships or fieldwork, unspecified assistantships, and project assistantships also available. Support available to part-time students. Financial award application deadline: 4/15; financial award applicants required to submit FAFSA. Total annual research expenditures: $106,365. *Unit head:* Mike R. Allen, Representative, 414-229-4261, Fax: 414-229-3859, E-mail: mikealle@uwm.edu. *Application contact:* General Information Contact, 414-229-4982, Fax: 414-229-6967, E-mail: gradschool@uwm.edu.

University of Wisconsin–Milwaukee, Graduate School, College of Letters and Sciences, Department of English, Milwaukee, WI 53201-0413. Offers creative writing (PhD); English (MA); international technical communication (Certificate); linguistics (PhD); professional writing (PhD); professional writing and communication (Certificate); rhetoric and composition (PhD); MLIS/MA. *Faculty:* 40 full-time (19 women). *Students:* 106 full-time (62 women), 65 part-time (45 women); includes 4 Black or African American, non-Hispanic/Latino; 5 Asian, non-Hispanic/Latino, 17 international. Average age 34. 208 applicants, 54% accepted, 29 enrolled. In 2010, 19 master's, 14 doctorates awarded. *Degree requirements:* For master's, thesis or alternative; for doctorate, one foreign language, thesis/dissertation. *Entrance requirements:* For master's, GRE General Test, GRE Subject Test; for doctorate, GRE. Additional exam requirements/recommendations for international students: Required—TOEFL (minimum score 550 paper-based; 79 iBT), IELTS (minimum score 6.5). *Application deadline:* For fall admission, 1/1 priority date for domestic students; for spring admission, 9/1 for domestic students. Applications are processed on a rolling basis. Application fee: $56 ($96 for international students). Electronic applications accepted. *Financial support:* In 2010–11, 4 fellowships, 1 research assistantship, 84 teaching assistantships were awarded; career-related internships or fieldwork, unspecified assistantships, and project assistantships also available. Support available to part-time students. Financial award application deadline: 4/15; financial award applicants required to submit FAFSA. Total annual research expenditures: $36,259. *Unit head:* Tasha Oren, Representative, 414-229-6625, Fax: 414-229-2643, E-mail: tgoren@uwm.edu. *Application contact:* General Information Contact, 414-229-4982, Fax: 414-229-6967, E-mail: gradschool@uwm.edu.

Virginia Commonwealth University, Graduate School, College of Humanities and Sciences, Department of English, Program in English, Richmond, VA 23284-9005. Offers literature (MA); writing and rhetoric (MA). Part-time programs available. *Students:* 30 full-time (16 women), 28 part-time (18 women); includes 10 minority (5 Black or African American, non-Hispanic/Latino; 1 American Indian or Alaska Native, non-Hispanic/Latino; 1 Asian, non-Hispanic/Latino; 2 Hispanic/Latino; 1 Two or more races, non-Hispanic/Latino), 1 international. 39 applicants, 69% accepted, 15 enrolled. In 2010, 16 master's awarded. *Entrance requirements:* For master's, GRE General Test. Additional exam requirements/recommendations for international students: Required—TWE, Either TOEFL (minimum score: paper-based 600, computer-based 250) or IELTS (6.5). *Application deadline:* For fall admission, 3/1 for domestic students; for spring admission, 11/15 for domestic students. Applications are processed on a rolling basis. Application fee: $50. Electronic applications accepted. *Expenses:* Tuition, state resident: full-time $4308; part-time $479 per credit hour. Tuition, nonresident: full-time $8942; part-time $994 per credit hour. Required fees: $2000; $85 per credit hour. Tuition and fees vary according to course level, course load, degree level, campus/location and program. *Financial support:* Federal Work-Study, institutionally sponsored loans, and tuition waivers (full and partial) available. Support available to part-time students. Financial award applicants required to submit FAFSA. *Faculty research:* Literature, writing, rhetoric. *Unit head:* Dr. Katherine C. Bassard, Program Director, 804-828-1329, E-mail: kcbassar@vcu.edu. *Application contact:* Thom N. Didato, Director, 804-828-1329, E-mail: tndidato@vcu.edu.

Wright State University, School of Graduate Studies, College of Liberal Arts, Department of English Language and Literatures, Dayton, OH 45435. Offers composition and rhetoric (MA); English (MA); literature (MA); teaching English to speakers of other languages (MA). *Degree requirements:* For master's, thesis optional, portfolio. *Entrance requirements:* For master's, 20 hours in upper-level English. Additional exam requirements/recommendations for international students: Required—TOEFL. *Faculty research:* American literature, world literature in English, applied linguistics, writing theory and pedagogy.

Speech and Interpersonal Communication

Arkansas State University, Graduate School, College of Communications, Department of Communication Studies, Jonesboro, State University, AR 72467. Offers communication studies and theatre arts (MA); communication studies and theatre arts education (SCCT). Part-time programs available. *Faculty:* 5 full-time (2 women). *Students:* 5 full-time (2 women), 7 part-time (2 women); includes 6 minority (all Black or African American, non-Hispanic/Latino), 1 international. Average age 28. 15 applicants, 60% accepted, 8 enrolled. In 2010, 4 master's awarded. *Degree requirements:* For master's, one foreign language, comprehensive exam, thesis or alternative; for SCCT, comprehensive exam. *Entrance requirements:* For master's, GRE General Test or MAT, appropriate bachelor's degree, writing sample, letter of recommendation, official transcripts, immunization records; for SCCT, GRE or MAT, appropriate master's degree, interview, official transcript, immunization records. Additional exam requirements/recommendations for international students: Required—TOEFL (minimum score 550 paper-based; 213 computer-based; 79 iBT), IELTS (minimum score 6), PTE: Pearson Test of English Academic (56). *Application deadline:* For fall admission, 7/1 for domestic and international students; for spring admission, 11/15 for domestic students, 11/14 for international students. Applications are processed on a rolling basis. Application fee: $30 ($40 for international students). Electronic applications accepted. *Expenses:* Tuition, state resident: full-time $3888; part-time $216 per credit hour. Tuition, nonresident: full-time $9918; part-time $551 per credit hour. International tuition: $8376 full-time. Required fees: $932; $49 per credit hour. $25 per term. One-time fee: $30. Tuition and fees vary according to course load and program. *Financial support:* In 2010–11, 5 students received support; teaching assistantships, career-related internships or fieldwork, scholarships/grants, and unspecified assistantships available. Financial award application deadline: 7/1; financial award applicants required to submit FAFSA. *Unit head:* Dr. Thomas Bagland, Chair, 870-972-3091, Fax: 870-972-3856, E-mail: tbaglan@astate.edu. *Application contact:* Dr. Andrew Sustich, Dean of the Graduate School, 870-972-3029, Fax: 870-972-3857, E-mail: sustich@astate.edu.

Ball State University, Graduate School, College of Communication, Information, and Media, Department of Communication Studies, Muncie, IN 47306-1099. Offers speech, public address, forensics, and rhetoric (MA). *Faculty:* 5. *Students:* 22 full-time (13 women), 9 part-time (7 women); includes 3 Black or African American, non-Hispanic/Latino, 4 international. Average age 23. 28 applicants, 46% accepted, 10 enrolled. In 2010, 11 master's awarded. *Entrance requirements:* For master's, GRE General Test. Application fee: $50. *Expenses:* Tuition, state resident: full-time $6160; part-time $299 per credit hour. Tuition, nonresident: full-time $16,020; part-time $783 per credit hour. Required fees: $2278; $95 per credit hour. *Financial support:* In 2010–11, 27 teaching assistantships with full tuition reimbursements (averaging $8,549 per year) were awarded; research assistantships, career-related internships or fieldwork also available. Financial award application deadline: 3/1. *Unit head:* Glen Stamp, Chairperson, 765-285-1882, Fax: 765-285-2736. *Application contact:* Glen Stamp, Chairperson, 765-285-1882, Fax: 765-285-2736.

Bob Jones University, Graduate Programs, Greenville, SC 29614. Offers accountancy (MS); Bible (MA); Bible translation (MA); Biblical studies (Certificate); broadcast management (MS); business administration (MBA); church history (MA, PhD); church ministries (MA); church music (MM); cinema and video production (MA); counseling (MS); curriculum and instruction (Ed D); divinity (M Div); dramatic production (MA); educational leadership (MS, Ed D, Ed S); elementary education (M Ed, MAT); English (M Ed, MA, MAT); fine arts (MA); graphic design (MA); history (M Ed, MA); illustration (MA); interpretative speech (MA); mathematics (M Ed, MAT); medical missions (Certificate); ministry (MM, D Min); multi-categorical special education (M Ed, MAT); music (M Ed); New Testament interpretation (PhD); Old Testament interpretation (PhD); orchestral instrument performance (MM); organ performance (MM); pastoral studies (MA); personnel services (MS, Ed S); piano pedagogy (MM); piano performance (MM); platform arts (MA); radio and television broadcasting (MS); rhetoric and public address (MA); secondary education (M Ed); studio art (MA); teaching Bible (MA); theology (MA, PhD); voice performance (MM); youth ministries (MA); M Div/MM.

Bowling Green State University, Graduate College, College of Arts and Sciences, School of Communication Studies, Program of Communication Studies, Bowling Green, OH 43403. Offers MA, PhD. Terminal master's awarded for partial completion of doctoral program. *Degree requirements:* For master's, thesis or alternative; for doctorate, comprehensive exam, thesis/dissertation. *Entrance requirements:* For master's and doctorate, GRE General Test. Additional exam requirements/recommendations for international students: Required—TOEFL. Electronic applications accepted. *Faculty research:* Rhetorical theory and criticism, culture and communication, interpersonal/organizational communication.

Brooklyn College of the City University of New York, Division of Graduate Studies, Department of Speech Communication Arts and Sciences, Brooklyn, NY 11210-2889. Offers audiology (Au D); speech (MA), including public communication; speech and hearing sciences (PhD); speech pathology (MS). Au D offered jointly with Hunter College of the City University of New York. *Accreditation:* ASHA (one or more programs are accredited). Part-time programs available. *Students:* 40 full-time (39 women), 40 part-time (all women); includes 13 minority (3 Black or African American, non-Hispanic/Latino; 5 Asian, non-Hispanic/Latino; 5 Hispanic/Latino), 3 international. Average age 27. 372 applicants, 22% accepted, 38 enrolled. In 2010, 29 master's awarded. Terminal master's awarded for partial completion of doctoral program. *Degree requirements:* For master's, comprehensive exam, NTE. *Entrance requirements:* For master's, GRE, minimum GPA of 3.0, interview, essay. Additional exam requirements/recommendations for international students: Required—TOEFL (minimum score 500 paper-based; 173 computer-based; 61 iBT). *Application deadline:* For fall admission, 2/1 priority date for domestic and international students. Applications are processed on a rolling basis. Electronic applications accepted. *Expenses:* Tuition, state resident: full-time $7360; part-time $310 per credit hour. Tuition, nonresident: full-time $13,800; part-time $575 per credit hour. Required fees: $190 per semester. *Financial support:* Career-related internships or fieldwork, Federal Work-Study, institutionally sponsored loans, scholarships/grants, and traineeships available. Support available to part-time students. Financial award application deadline: 5/1; financial award applicants required to submit FAFSA. *Faculty research:* Language and learning disorders, aphasia, auditory disorders, public and business communication, voice and fluency disorders. *Unit head:* Dr. Timothy Gura, Acting Chairperson, 718-951-5225, Fax: 718-951-4167, E-mail: tgura@brooklyn.cuny.edu. *Application contact:* Hernan Sierra, Graduate Admissions Coordinator, 718-951-4536, Fax: 718-951-4506, E-mail: grads@brooklyn.cuny.edu.

California State University, Fullerton, Graduate Studies, College of Communications, Department of Human Communications, Fullerton, CA 92834-9480. Offers communicative disorders (MA); speech communication (MA). *Accreditation:* ASHA. Part-time programs available. *Students:* 69 full-time (59 women), 41 part-time (32 women); includes 8 Black or African American, non-Hispanic/Latino; 14 Asian, non-Hispanic/Latino; 22 Hispanic/Latino, 6 international. Average age 30. 391 applicants, 13% accepted, 39 enrolled. In 2010, 40 master's awarded. *Degree requirements:* For master's, comprehensive exam, thesis or alternative. *Entrance requirements:* For master's, minimum GPA of 3.0 in major. Application fee: $55. *Financial support:* Teaching assistantships, career-related internships or fieldwork, Federal Work-Study, institutionally sponsored loans, and scholarships/grants available. Support available to part-time students. Financial award application deadline: 3/1; financial award applicants required to submit FAFSA. *Faculty research:* Speech therapy. *Unit head:* Dr. John Reinard, Chair, 657-278-3617. *Application contact:* Dr. John Reinard, Chair, 657-278-3617.

California State University, Fullerton, Graduate Studies, College of Humanities and Social Sciences, Program in Linguistics, Fullerton, CA 92834-9480. Offers analysis of specific language structures (MA); anthropological linguistics (MA); applied linguistics (MA); communication and semantics (MA); disorders of communication (MA); experimental phonetics (MA). Part-time programs available. *Students:* 12 full-time (8 women), 11 part-time (5 women); includes 4 Asian, non-Hispanic/Latino; 3 Hispanic/Latino, 6 international. Average age 34. 33 applicants, 52% accepted, 7 enrolled. In 2010, 8 master's awarded. *Degree requirements:* For master's,

Speech and Interpersonal Communication

California State University, Fullerton (continued)
one foreign language, thesis or alternative, project. *Entrance requirements:* For master's, minimum GPA of 3.0, undergraduate major in linguistics or related field. Application fee: $55. *Financial support:* Career-related internships or fieldwork, Federal Work-Study, institutionally sponsored loans, and scholarships/grants available. Support available to part-time students. Financial award application deadline: 3/1; financial award applicants required to submit FAFSA. *Unit head:* Dr. Franz Muller-Gotama, Adviser, 657-278-2441. *Application contact:* Admissions/Applications, 657-278-2371.

California State University, Los Angeles, Graduate Studies, College of Arts and Letters, Department of Communication Studies, Los Angeles, CA 90032-8530. Offers speech communication (MA); television, film and theatre (MFA). Part-time and evening/weekend programs available. *Faculty:* 11 full-time (5 women), 3 part-time/adjunct (2 women). *Students:* 85 full-time (52 women), 57 part-time (41 women); includes 58 minority (20 Black or African American, non-Hispanic/Latino; 7 Asian, non-Hispanic/Latino; 26 Hispanic/Latino; 5 Two or more races, non-Hispanic/Latino), 29 international. Average age 32. 93 applicants, 100% accepted, 54 enrolled. In 2010, 19 master's awarded. *Degree requirements:* For master's, comprehensive exam or thesis. *Entrance requirements:* For master's, minimum GPA of 2.75 in last 90 units of course work. Additional exam requirements/recommendations for international students: Required—TOEFL (minimum score 500 paper-based; 173 computer-based). *Application deadline:* For fall admission, 5/1 for domestic and international students. Applications are processed on a rolling basis. Application fee: $55. Electronic applications accepted. *Financial support:* Career-related internships or fieldwork and Federal Work-Study available. Support available to part-time students. Financial award application deadline: 3/1. *Faculty research:* Organizational, interpersonal, intercultural, and instructional communication; rhetorical theories. *Unit head:* Dr. Bryant Keith Alexander, Chair, 323-343-4200, Fax: 323-343-6467, E-mail: abryant@calstatela.edu. *Application contact:* Dr. Alan Muchlinski, Dean of Graduate Studies, 323-343-3820, Fax: 323-343-5653, E-mail: amuchli@exchange.calstatela.edu.

California State University, Northridge, Graduate Studies, College of Arts, Media, and Communication, Department of Communication Studies, Northridge, CA 91330. Offers MA. *Entrance requirements:* For master's, GRE General Test. Additional exam requirements/recommendations for international students: Required—TOEFL.

Central Michigan University, College of Graduate Studies, College of Communication and Fine Arts, Department of Communication and Dramatic Arts, Mount Pleasant, MI 48859. Offers interpersonal and public communication (MA), including communication and dramatic arts. Part-time programs available. *Faculty:* 12 full-time (6 women). *Students:* 23 full-time (13 women), 5 part-time (2 women); includes 1 American Indian or Alaska Native, non-Hispanic/Latino; 2 Hispanic/Latino, 1 international. Average age 28. *Degree requirements:* For master's, thesis. *Application deadline:* For fall admission, 3/15 for domestic and international students; for winter admission, 10/15 for domestic and international students; for spring admission, 10/15 for domestic and international students. Applications are processed on a rolling basis. Application fee: $35 ($45 for international students). Electronic applications accepted. *Expenses:* Tuition, state resident: full-time $8208; part-time $456 per credit hour. Tuition, nonresident: full-time $13,788; part-time $766 per credit hour. One-time fee: $25. *Financial support:* Fellowships with tuition reimbursements, teaching assistantships with tuition reimbursements, career-related internships or fieldwork, Federal Work-Study, unspecified assistantships, and out-of-state merit awards, non-resident graduate awards available. *Faculty research:* Communication theory, interpersonal/nonverbal communication, organizational communication, family and interpersonal communication, political communication. *Unit head:* Dr. William O. Dailey, Chairperson, 989-774-3177, Fax: 989-774-2498, E-mail: daile1wo@cmich.edu. *Application contact:* Dr. Lesley Withers, Graduate Program Coordinator, 989-774-6673, Fax: 989-774-2498, E-mail: withe1la@cmich.edu.

Colorado State University, Graduate School, College of Liberal Arts, Department of Communication Studies, Fort Collins, CO 80523-1783. Offers MA. *Faculty:* 12 full-time (5 women), 1 part-time/adjunct (0 women). *Students:* 20 full-time (12 women), 7 part-time (5 women); includes 1 minority (Hispanic/Latino). Average age 25. 56 applicants, 27% accepted, 13 enrolled. In 2010, 8 master's awarded. *Entrance requirements:* For master's, GRE General Test, minimum GPA of 3.0; writing sample, letters of recommendation. Additional exam requirements/recommendations for international students: Required—TOEFL (minimum score 550 paper-based; 230 computer-based; 80 iBT). *Application deadline:* For fall admission, 1/31 priority date for domestic and international students. Applications are processed on a rolling basis. Application fee: $50. Electronic applications accepted. *Expenses:* Tuition, state resident: full-time $7434; part-time $413 per credit. Tuition, nonresident: full-time $19,022; part-time $1057 per credit. Required fees: $1729; $88 per credit. *Financial support:* In 2010–11, 19 students received support, including 19 teaching assistantships with full and partial tuition reimbursements available (averaging $12,110 per year); scholarships/grants and unspecified assistantships also available. Financial award application deadline: 3/1; financial award applicants required to submit FAFSA. *Faculty research:* Rhetorical theory and criticism, media and popular culture, intercultural communication, freedom of speech, communication theory. Total annual research expenditures: $17,456. *Unit head:* Dr. Sue Pendell, Head, 970-491-6140, Fax: 970-491-2160, E-mail: sue.pendell@colostate.edu. *Application contact:* Dr. Greg Dickinson, Director of Graduate Studies, 970-491-6893, Fax: 970-491-2160, E-mail: greg.dickinson@colostate.edu.

Eastern Illinois University, Graduate School, College of Arts and Humanities, Department of Communication Studies, Charleston, IL 61920-3099. Offers MA. Part-time programs available. *Degree requirements:* For master's, major paper.

Florida State University, The Graduate School, College of Communication and Information, School of Communication, Tallahassee, FL 32306. Offers corporate and public communication (MS); integrated marketing communication (MA, MS); mass communication (PhD); media and communication studies (MA, MS); speech communication (PhD). Part-time programs available. *Faculty:* 24 full-time (9 women), 6 part-time/adjunct (1 woman). *Students:* 147 full-time (94 women), 63 part-time (38 women); includes 92 minority (26 Black or African American, non-Hispanic/Latino; 2 American Indian or Alaska Native, non-Hispanic/Latino; 45 Asian, non-Hispanic/Latino; 16 Hispanic/Latino; 1 Native Hawaiian or other Pacific Islander, non-Hispanic/Latino; 2 Two or more races, non-Hispanic/Latino). Average age 24. 268 applicants, 57% accepted, 79 enrolled. In 2010, 103 master's, 4 doctorates awarded. *Degree requirements:* For master's, thesis (for some programs); for doctorate, comprehensive exam, thesis/dissertation. *Entrance requirements:* For master's, GRE General Test, minimum GPA of 3.0; for doctorate, GRE General Test, minimum GPA of 3.3 in graduate course work. Additional exam requirements/recommendations for international students: Required—TOEFL (minimum score 600 paper-based; 250 computer-based; 100 iBT). *Application deadline:* For fall admission, 7/1 priority date for domestic students, 5/1 priority date for international students; for spring admission, 11/1 priority date for domestic and international students. Applications are processed on a rolling basis. Application fee: $30. Electronic applications accepted. *Expenses:* Tuition, state resident: full-time $8238.24. *Financial support:* In 2010–11, 52 students received support, including 1 fellowship with full tuition reimbursement available, 8 research assistantships with full tuition reimbursements available (averaging $14,000 per year), 40 teaching assistantships with full tuition reimbursements available (averaging $5,000 per year); career-related internships or fieldwork, Federal Work-Study, institutionally sponsored loans, scholarships/grants, tuition waivers (partial), and unspecified assistantships also available. Support available to part-time students. Financial award application deadline: 2/1; financial award applicants required to submit FAFSA. *Faculty research:* Communication technology and policy, marketing communication, communication content and effect, new communication/information technologies. Total annual research expenditures: $400,000. *Unit head:* Dr. Stephen D. McDowell, Director, 850-644-2276, Fax: 850-644-8642, E-mail: steve.mcdowell@cci.fsu.edu. *Application contact:* Natashia Hinson-Turner, Graduate Coordinator, 850-644-8746, Fax: 850-644-8642, E-mail: natashia.turner@cci.fsu.edu.

Georgia State University, College of Arts and Sciences, Department of Communication, Atlanta, GA 30302-3083. Offers film/video/digital imaging (MA); human communication and social influence (MA); mass communication (MA); moving image studies (PhD); public communication (PhD). Part-time programs available. *Degree requirements:* For master's, one foreign language, thesis or alternative; for doctorate, comprehensive exam, thesis/dissertation. *Entrance requirements:* For master's and doctorate, GRE General Test. Additional exam requirements/recommendations for international students: Required—TOEFL (minimum score 80 computer-based). Electronic applications accepted. *Faculty research:* Critical/cultural studies, rhetoric studies, film/media studies, mass communications/journalism, audience studies.

Hofstra University, School of Communication, Program in Speech Communication and Rhetorical Studies, Hempstead, NY 11549. Offers MA. Part-time and evening/weekend programs available. *Faculty:* 5 full-time (2 women). *Students:* 5 full-time (3 women), 17 part-time (10 women); includes 12 minority (10 Black or African American, non-Hispanic/Latino; 1 Asian, non-Hispanic/Latino; 1 Hispanic/Latino). Average age 29. 18 applicants, 94% accepted, 8 enrolled. In 2010, 7 master's awarded. *Degree requirements:* For master's, thesis. *Entrance requirements:* For master's, 2 letters of recommendation, interview. Additional exam requirements/recommendations for international students: Required—TOEFL (minimum score 550 paper-based; 213 computer-based; 80 iBT). *Application deadline:* Applications are processed on a rolling basis. Application fee: $70 ($75 for international students). Electronic applications accepted. *Expenses:* Tuition: Full-time $18,000; part-time $1000 per credit hour. Required fees: $970; $145 per term. Tuition and fees vary according to program. *Financial support:* In 2010–11, 11 students received support, including 5 fellowships with full and partial tuition reimbursements available (averaging $2,600 per year), 1 research assistantship with full and partial tuition reimbursement available (averaging $10,474 per year); Federal Work-Study, institutionally sponsored loans, scholarships/grants, tuition waivers (full and partial), and unspecified assistantships also available. Support available to part-time students. Financial award applicants required to submit FAFSA. *Faculty research:* Performance of race and gender, public deliberation, civic engagement and political participation, popular culture, public memory. *Unit head:* Dr. Mary Anne Trasciatti, Chairperson, 516-463-5427, Fax: 516-463-7012, E-mail: sphmat@hofstra.edu. *Application contact:* Carol Drummer, Dean of Graduate Admissions, 516-463-4876, Fax: 516-463-4664, E-mail: gradstudent@hofstra.edu.

Idaho State University, Office of Graduate Studies, College of Arts and Sciences, Department of Communication and Rhetorical Studies, Pocatello, ID 83209-8115. Offers communication and rhetorical studies (MA). Part-time programs available. *Degree requirements:* For master's, comprehensive exam, paper or thesis. *Entrance requirements:* For master's, GRE General Test, minimum GPA of 3.0 in all upper-level courses. Additional exam requirements/recommendations for international students: Required—TOEFL (minimum score 550 paper-based; 213 computer-based; 80 iBT). Electronic applications accepted. *Faculty research:* Metaphor and cognition in organizational groups and teams; rhetorical criticism of contemporary culture, including music, film, television, and advertising; communication pedagogy; the effect of language on organizational identification and commitment; risk communication and crisis communication.

Indiana University Bloomington, University Graduate School, College of Arts and Sciences, Department of Communication and Culture, Bloomington, IN 47405-7000. Offers film and media studies (PhD); performance and ethnography (PhD); rhetoric and public culture (PhD). *Faculty:* 24 full-time (12 women). *Students:* 81 full-time (41 women), 3 part-time (all women); includes 10 minority (2 Black or African American, non-Hispanic/Latino; 8 Hispanic/Latino), 10 international. Average age 32. 187 applicants, 12% accepted, 11 enrolled. In 2010, 4 master's, 7 doctorates awarded. *Degree requirements:* For master's, comprehensive exam; for doctorate, one foreign language, comprehensive exam, thesis/dissertation, student teaching. *Entrance requirements:* For master's and doctorate, GRE General Test (recommended), minimum GPA of 3.0, 3 letters of recommendation, writing sample. Additional exam requirements/recommendations for international students: Required—TOEFL (minimum score 550 paper-based; 213 computer-based). *Application deadline:* For winter admission, 1/1 for domestic students, 12/1 for international students. Application fee: $55 ($65 for international students). Electronic applications accepted. *Financial support:* In 2010–11, 65 students received support, including 4 fellowships with full tuition reimbursements available (averaging $18,000 per year), 48 teaching assistantships with full tuition reimbursements available (averaging $13,257 per year). Financial award application deadline: 4/15. *Faculty research:* Rhetoric and public culture, film and media studies, performance ethnography. *Unit head:* Prof. Gregory A. Waller, Chair, 812-855-2367, Fax: 812-855-6014, E-mail: cmcl@indiana.edu. *Application contact:* Kathy P. Teige, Graduate Secretary, 812-855-6389, Fax: 812-855-6014, E-mail: kteige@indiana.edu.

Kansas State University, Graduate School, College of Arts and Sciences, Department of Communication Studies, Theatre and Dance, Manhattan, KS 66505. Offers rhetoric/communication (MA); theatre (MA). *Degree requirements:* For master's, thesis or alternative. *Entrance requirements:* For master's, GRE General Test (recommended), minimum GPA of 3.0. Additional exam requirements/recommendations for international students: Required—TOEFL. Electronic applications accepted. *Faculty research:* Drama therapy, directing, costume design, scenic design, technical theatre mechanics and safety.

Louisiana Tech University, Graduate School, College of Liberal Arts, Department of Speech, Ruston, LA 71272. Offers speech (MA); speech pathology and audiology (MA). *Accreditation:* ASHA. *Degree requirements:* For master's, thesis or alternative. *Entrance requirements:* For master's, GRE General Test.

Marquette University, Graduate School, College of Communication, Milwaukee, WI 53201-1881. Offers advertising and public relations (MA); broadcasting and electronic communications (MA); communications studies (MA); digital storytelling (Certificate); health, environment, science and sustainability (MA); journalism (MA); mass communications (MA). *Accreditation:* ACEJMC (one or more programs are accredited). Part-time and evening/weekend programs available. *Faculty:* 33 full-time (18 women), 30 part-time/adjunct (16 women). *Students:* 35 full-time (20 women), 31 part-time (25 women); includes 5 minority (2 Black or African American, non-Hispanic/Latino; 1 Hispanic/Latino; 2 Two or more races, non-Hispanic/Latino), 4 international. Average age 28. 97 applicants, 52% accepted, 21 enrolled. In 2010, 16 master's, 5 other advanced degrees awarded. *Degree requirements:* For master's, comprehensive exam, thesis or alternative. *Entrance requirements:* For master's, GRE, official transcripts from all current and previous colleges/universities except Marquette, three letters of recommendation, statement of academic and professional goals. Additional exam requirements/recommendations for international students: Required—TOEFL (minimum score 530 paper-based; 78 computer-based). *Application deadline:* Applications are processed on a rolling basis. Application fee: $50. Electronic applications accepted. *Expenses:* Tuition: Full-time $16,290; part-time $905 per credit hour. Tuition and fees vary according to program. *Financial support:* In 2010–11, 2 fellowships, 7 research assistantships, 12 teaching assistantships were awarded; career-related internships or fieldwork, Federal Work-Study, institutionally sponsored loans, scholarships/grants, and tuition waivers (full and partial) also available. Support available to part-time students. Financial award application deadline: 2/15. *Faculty research:* Urban journalism, gender and communication, intercultural communication, religious communication. Total annual research expenditures: $3,088. *Unit head:* Dr. Lori Bergen, Dean, 414-288-7133, Fax: 414-288-1578. *Application contact:* Erin Fox, Assistant Director for Recruitment, 414-288-5319, Fax: 414-288-1902, E-mail: erin.fox@marquette.edu.

New York University, Steinhardt School of Culture, Education, and Human Development, Department of Media, Culture and Communication, New York, NY 10012-1019. Offers media, culture, and communication (MA, PhD). Part-time programs available. *Faculty:* 29 full-time (13 women), 88 part-time/adjunct (43 women). *Students:* 107 full-time (79 women), 65 part-time (42 women); includes 10 Black or African American, non-Hispanic/Latino; 8 Asian, non-Hispanic/Latino; 9 Hispanic/Latino, 47 international. Average age 27. 616 applicants, 24% accepted, 63 enrolled. In 2010, 44 master's, 2 doctorates awarded. Terminal master's awarded for partial completion of doctoral program. *Degree requirements:* For master's, thesis (for some programs);

for doctorate, thesis/dissertation. *Entrance requirements:* For doctorate, GRE General Test, interview. Additional exam requirements/recommendations for international students: Required—TOEFL. *Application deadline:* For fall admission, 12/1 priority date for domestic and international students; for spring admission, 11/1 for domestic and international students. Applications are processed on a rolling basis. Application fee: $75. Electronic applications accepted. *Financial support:* Fellowships with full and partial tuition reimbursements, teaching assistantships with full and partial tuition reimbursements, career-related internships or fieldwork, Federal Work-Study, institutionally sponsored loans, scholarships/grants, tuition waivers (partial), and unspecified assistantships available. Support available to part-time students. Financial award application deadline: 2/1; financial award applicants required to submit FAFSA. *Faculty research:* Digital media and new technologies, media criticism, flow of media and culture transnationally and transculturally. *Unit head:* Dr. Marita Sturken, Chairperson, 212-992-9424, Fax: 212-995-4046, E-mail: marita.sturken@nyu.edu. *Application contact:* 212-998-5030, Fax: 212-995-4328, E-mail: steinhardt.gradadmissions@nyu.edu.

North Dakota State University, College of Graduate and Interdisciplinary Studies, College of Arts, Humanities and Social Sciences, Department of Communication, Fargo, ND 58108. Offers communication (PhD); mass communication (MA, MS); speech communication (MA, MS). Part-time programs available. Postbaccalaureate distance learning degree programs offered (no on-campus study). *Faculty:* 11 full-time (5 women), 3 part-time/adjunct (1 woman). *Students:* 29 full-time (18 women), 27 part-time (17 women); includes 1 Black or African American, non-Hispanic/Latino; 2 Asian, non-Hispanic/Latino; 1 Hispanic/Latino, 3 international. Average age 27. 62 applicants, 40% accepted, 19 enrolled. In 2010, 15 master's, 8 doctorates awarded. Terminal master's awarded for partial completion of doctoral program. *Degree requirements:* For master's, thesis (for some programs); for doctorate, comprehensive exam, thesis/dissertation, 2-3 publications referred before comps. *Entrance requirements:* For master's, GRE, minimum undergraduate GPA of 3.25; for doctorate, GRE, minimum undergraduate GPA of 3.5. Additional exam requirements/recommendations for international students: Required—TOEFL (minimum score 600 paper-based; 250 computer-based; 100 iBT), IELTS (minimum score 7). *Application deadline:* For fall admission, 2/15 priority date for domestic students; for winter admission, 10/15 priority date for domestic students. Applications are processed on a rolling basis. Application fee: $45 ($60 for international students). Electronic applications accepted. *Financial support:* In 2010–11, 38 students received support, including 1 fellowship with full tuition reimbursement available (averaging $16,000 per year), 10 research assistantships with full tuition reimbursements available (averaging $12,000 per year), 10 teaching assistantships with full tuition reimbursements available (averaging $8,100 per year); career-related internships or fieldwork, Federal Work-Study, institutionally sponsored loans, tuition waivers (full), and unspecified assistantships also available. Financial award application deadline: 2/1. *Faculty research:* Communication and rhetorical theory, organizational communication, broadcast and print journalism, international communication, public relations and advertising. Total annual research expenditures: $148,496. *Unit head:* Dr. Paul E. Nelson, Chair, 701-231-7705, Fax: 701-231-7784, E-mail: paul.nelson.1@ndsu.edu. *Application contact:* Dr. Judy C. Pearson, Director of Graduate Studies, 701-231-6551, Fax: 701-231-1074, E-mail: judy.pearson@ndsu.edu.

Northeastern Illinois University, Graduate College, College of Arts and Sciences, Department of Communication, Media and Theatre, Program in Communication, Media and Theatre, Chicago, IL 60625-4699. Offers MA. Part-time and evening/weekend programs available. *Faculty:* 12 full-time (6 women), 7 part-time/adjunct (2 women). *Students:* 3 full-time (2 women), 18 part-time (13 women); includes 8 minority (3 Black or African American, non-Hispanic/Latino; 1 Asian, non-Hispanic/Latino; 3 Hispanic/Latino; 1 Two or more races, non-Hispanic/Latino). Average age 34. 21 applicants, 48% accepted. In 2010, 9 master's awarded. *Degree requirements:* For master's, comprehensive exam, oral exams, thesis or 3 term papers. *Entrance requirements:* For master's, 15 undergraduate hours in speech and performing arts, minimum GPA of 2.75. Additional exam requirements/recommendations for international students: Required—TOEFL (minimum score 550 paper-based; 213 computer-based; 79 iBT). *Application deadline:* Applications are processed on a rolling basis. Application fee: $25. Electronic applications accepted. *Financial support:* In 2010–11, 10 students received support, including 1 research assistantship with full tuition reimbursement available (averaging $6,600 per year); career-related internships or fieldwork, Federal Work-Study, institutionally sponsored loans, scholarships/grants, tuition waivers (full and partial), and unspecified assistantships also available. Support available to part-time students. Financial award applicants required to submit FAFSA. *Faculty research:* Creative drama, family communication, fine arts and general education, playwriting techniques, interpersonal communications.

Northeastern University, Bouvé College of Health Sciences Graduate School, Department of Speech-Language Pathology, Program in Audiology, Boston, MA 02115-5096. Offers Au D. *Faculty:* 12 full-time (8 women), 6 part-time/adjunct (5 women). *Students:* 28 full-time (27 women). 89 applicants, 34% accepted, 8 enrolled. In 2010, 9 doctorates awarded. *Entrance requirements:* For doctorate, GRE, minimum GPA of 3.2. Additional exam requirements/recommendations for international students: Required—TOEFL (minimum score 100 iBT). *Application deadline:* For fall admission, 2/15 for domestic students. Application fee: $50. Electronic applications accepted. *Financial support:* Research assistantships, teaching assistantships, scholarships/grants, traineeships, and unspecified assistantships available. *Unit head:* Dr. Sandra Cleveland, Director, 617-373-2496, Fax: 617-373-8756, E-mail: sa.cleveland@neu.edu. *Application contact:* Margaret Schnabel, Director of Graduate Admissions, 617-373-2708, E-mail: bouvegrad@neu.edu.

Northwestern University, The Graduate School, School of Communication, Department of Performance Studies, Evanston, IL 60208. Offers MA, PhD. Admissions and degrees offered through The Graduate School. Part-time programs available. Terminal master's awarded for partial completion of doctoral program. *Degree requirements:* For master's, recital; for doctorate, one foreign language, thesis/dissertation, recital. *Entrance requirements:* For master's and doctorate, GRE General Test. Additional exam requirements/recommendations for international students: Required—TOEFL. *Faculty research:* Adaptation/performance of literature, ethnography of performance, critical cultural studies, performance theory, intercultural performance, gender studies.

Ohio University, Graduate College, Scripps College of Communication, School of Communication Studies, Athens, OH 45701-2979. Offers health communication (PhD); organizational communication (MA); relating and organizing (PhD); rhetoric and public culture (PhD). Part-time programs available. Postbaccalaureate distance learning degree programs offered (minimal on-campus study). *Students:* 49 full-time (35 women), 42 part-time (33 women); includes 6 minority (4 Black or African American, non-Hispanic/Latino; 1 Hispanic/Latino; 1 Two or more races, non-Hispanic/Latino), 12 international. 104 applicants, 40% accepted, 31 enrolled. In 2010, 2 master's, 12 doctorates awarded. Terminal master's awarded for partial completion of doctoral program. *Degree requirements:* For master's, capstone; for doctorate, comprehensive exam, thesis/dissertation. *Entrance requirements:* For master's, GRE; for doctorate, GRE General Test, minimum GPA of 3.0. Additional exam requirements/recommendations for international students: Required—TOEFL (minimum score 550 paper-based; 80 iBT) or IELTS (minimum score 6.5). *Application deadline:* For fall admission, 1/15 priority date for domestic and international students. Application fee: $50 ($55 for international students). Electronic applications accepted. *Financial support:* In 2010–11, 12 students received support, including fellowships with full tuition reimbursements available (averaging $13,600 per year), research assistantships with full tuition reimbursements available (averaging $13,600 per year), teaching assistantships with full tuition reimbursements available (averaging $13,600 per year); career-related internships or fieldwork, Federal Work-Study, and institutionally sponsored loans also available. Financial award application deadline: 1/15. *Faculty research:* Rhetoric and public culture, relating and organizing, health communication. Total annual research expenditures: $200,000. *Unit head:* Dr. Scott Titsworth, Director, 740-593-9160, Fax: 740-593-4810, E-mail: titswort@ohio.edu. *Application contact:* Dr. Benjamin Bates, Associate Director for Graduate Studies, 740-593-9163, Fax: 740-593-4810, E-mail: batesb@ohio.edu.

Old Dominion University, College of Arts and Letters, Program in Lifespan and Digital Communication, Norfolk, VA 23529. Offers MA. *Accreditation:* NASAD. Part-time programs available. *Faculty:* 15 full-time (5 women). *Degree requirements:* For master's, thesis optional, comprehensive exam (for non-thesis students of a project). *Entrance requirements:* For master's, GRE. *Expenses:* Tuition, state resident: full-time $8592; part-time $358 per credit. Tuition, nonresident: full-time $21,672; part-time $903 per credit. Required fees: $119 per semester. One-time fee: $50. *Faculty research:* Family communication, digital media studies, lifespan communication, social media, screenwriting. *Unit head:* Dr. Thomas J. Socha, Graduate Program Director, 757-683-3828, E-mail: tsocha@odu.edu. *Application contact:* Dr. Robert Wojtowicz, Associate Dean, 757-683-6077, Fax: 757-683-5746, E-mail: rwojtowi@odu.edu.

Portland State University, Graduate Studies, College of Liberal Arts and Sciences, Department of Communication, Portland, OR 97207-0751. Offers general speech communication (MA, MS, Certificate). Part-time programs available. *Faculty:* 12 full-time (8 women), 18 part-time/adjunct (10 women). *Students:* 25 full-time (17 women), 17 part-time (15 women); includes 12 minority (2 Black or African American, non-Hispanic/Latino; 1 American Indian or Alaska Native, non-Hispanic/Latino; 7 Asian, non-Hispanic/Latino; 2 Hispanic/Latino), 6 international. Average age 30. 21 applicants, 86% accepted, 12 enrolled. In 2010, 7 master's awarded. *Degree requirements:* For master's, thesis. *Entrance requirements:* For master's, GRE General Test, minimum GPA of 3.0 in upper-division course work or 2.75 overall, 3 letters of recommendation. Additional exam requirements/recommendations for international students: Required—TOEFL (minimum score 550 paper-based; 213 computer-based). *Application deadline:* For fall admission, 3/1 for domestic and international students. Application fee: $50. *Expenses:* Tuition, state resident: full-time $8505; part-time $315 per credit. Tuition, nonresident: full-time $13,284; part-time $492 per credit. Required fees: $1482; $21 per credit. $99 per term. One-time fee: $120. Part-time tuition and fees vary according to course load and program. *Financial support:* In 2010–11, 1 research assistantship with full tuition reimbursement (averaging $6,372 per year), 9 teaching assistantships with full tuition reimbursements (averaging $6,042 per year) were awarded; career-related internships or fieldwork, Federal Work-Study, scholarships/grants, and unspecified assistantships also available. Support available to part-time students. Financial award application deadline: 3/1; financial award applicants required to submit FAFSA. *Unit head:* Cynthia Coleman, Chair, 503-725-5384, Fax: 503-725-5385, E-mail: ccoleman@pdx.edu. *Application contact:* Kathleen Morgan, Office Coordinator, 503-725-5384, Fax: 503-725-5385, E-mail: morganbk@pdx.edu.

Rensselaer Polytechnic Institute, Graduate School, School of Humanities, Arts, and Social Sciences, Programs in Communication and Rhetoric, Troy, NY 12180-3590. Offers MS, PhD. *Faculty:* 14 full-time (8 women), 1 part-time/adjunct (0 women). *Students:* 15 full-time (7 women), 1 part-time (0 women), 1 international. 38 applicants, 26% accepted, 2 enrolled. In 2010, 2 master's, 4 doctorates awarded. Terminal master's awarded for partial completion of doctoral program. *Degree requirements:* For master's, thesis optional; for doctorate, comprehensive exam, thesis/dissertation. *Entrance requirements:* For master's, GRE General Test, resume; for doctorate, GRE General Test, writing sample, resume or curriculum vitae. Additional exam requirements/recommendations for international students: Required—TOEFL (minimum score 570 paper-based; 230 computer-based; 89 iBT). *Application deadline:* For fall admission, 1/1 priority date for domestic and international students; for spring admission, 8/15 priority date for domestic students, 7/14 priority date for international students. Applications are processed on a rolling basis. Application fee: $75. Electronic applications accepted. *Expenses:* Tuition: Full-time $39,600; part-time $1650 per credit. Required fees: $1896. *Financial support:* In 2010–11, 3 fellowships with full tuition reimbursements (averaging $23,350 per year), 2 research assistantships with full tuition reimbursements (averaging $17,500 per year), 10 teaching assistantships with full tuition reimbursements (averaging $17,500 per year) were awarded; career-related internships or fieldwork, institutionally sponsored loans, and unspecified assistantships also available. Financial award application deadline: 1/15. *Faculty research:* Human-computer interaction (HCI) and usability design and analysis, media design and theory, rhetoric and culture, digital and visual rhetoric, communication in technologically-mediated contexts, technical/professional/cross- and inter-cultural communication. Total annual research expenditures: $73,438. *Unit head:* Prof. James P. Zappen, Head, 518-276-6468, Fax: 518-276-4092, E-mail: zappenj@rpi.edu. *Application contact:* Kathy A. Colman, Recruitment Coordinator, 518-276-6469, Fax: 518-276-4092, E-mail: colmak@rpi.edu.

Sam Houston State University, College of Humanities and Social Sciences, Huntsville, TX 77341. Offers English and foreign languages (MA), including English; family and consumer sciences (MS), including dietetics, family and consumer sciences; history (MA); political science (MA, MPA), including political science (MA), public administration (MPA); psychology and philosophy (MA, PhD), including clinical psychology (PhD), psychology (MA); sociology (MA); speech communication (MA). *Faculty:* 60 full-time (30 women), 1 part-time/adjunct (0 women). *Students:* 123 full-time (92 women), 169 part-time (97 women); includes 12 Black or African American, non-Hispanic/Latino; 3 Asian, non-Hispanic/Latino; 16 Hispanic/Latino, 10 international. Average age 30. 216 applicants, 56% accepted, 96 enrolled. In 2010, 67 master's, 4 doctorates awarded. *Entrance requirements:* For master's, GRE General Test. Additional exam requirements/recommendations for international students: Required—TOEFL (minimum score 550 paper-based; 213 computer-based; 79 iBT). *Application deadline:* For fall admission, 8/1 for domestic students; for spring admission, 12/1 for domestic students. Application fee: $20. *Expenses:* Tuition, state resident: full-time $1363; part-time $163 per credit hour. Tuition, nonresident: full-time $3856; part-time $473 per credit hour. *Unit head:* Dr. John deCastro, Dean, 936-294-2200, Fax: 936-294-2207, E-mail: jmd018@shsu.edu. *Application contact:* Dr. Kandi Tayebi, Dean of Graduate Studies and Associate Vice President for Academic Affairs, 936-294-1971, Fax: 936-294-1271, E-mail: graduate@shsu.edu.

San Francisco State University, Division of Graduate Studies, College of Humanities, Department of Communication Studies, San Francisco, CA 94132-1722. Offers MA. Part-time programs available. *Application deadline:* Applications are processed on a rolling basis. *Financial support:* Teaching assistantships available. *Unit head:* Dr. Gerianne Merrigan, Chair, 415-338-1597, E-mail: merrigan@sfsu.edu. *Application contact:* Dr. Mercilee Jenkins, Graduate Coordinator, 415-338-1597, E-mail: leej@sfsu.edu.

San Jose State University, Graduate Studies and Research, College of Social Sciences, Department of History, San Jose, CA 95192-0001. Offers history (MA); history education (MA). *Degree requirements:* For master's, comprehensive exam, thesis or alternative. *Entrance requirements:* For master's, bachelor's degree or 15 units of course work in history, minimum GPA of 3.0. Electronic applications accepted.

Seton Hall University, School of Health and Medical Sciences, Program in Speech-Language Pathology, South Orange, NJ 07079-2697. Offers MS. *Accreditation:* ASHA. *Entrance requirements:* For master's, GRE, bachelor's degree, clinical experience; minimum GPA of 3.0, undergraduate preprofessional coursework in communication sciences and disorders. Electronic applications accepted. *Faculty research:* Child language disorders, motor speech control, voice disorders, dysphagia, early intervention/teaming.

Southern Illinois University Carbondale, Graduate School, College of Liberal Arts, Department of Speech Communication, Carbondale, IL 62901-4701. Offers speech communication (MA, MS, PhD); speech/theater (PhD). *Degree requirements:* For master's, one foreign language, thesis or alternative; for doctorate, one foreign language, thesis/dissertation. *Entrance requirements:* For master's, GRE General Test or MAT, minimum GPA of 2.7; for doctorate, GRE General Test or MAT, minimum GPA of 3.25. Additional exam requirements/recommendations for international students: Required—TOEFL.

Southern Illinois University Edwardsville, Graduate School, College of Arts and Sciences, Department of Speech Communication, Program in Interpersonal Communication, Edwardsville, IL 62026. Offers MA. Part-time and evening/weekend programs available. *Students:* 2 full-time, 2 part-time (both women); includes 1 Hispanic/Latino. Average age 26. In 2010, 1 master's awarded. *Degree requirements:* For master's, comprehensive exam (for some programs), thesis (for some programs). *Entrance requirements:* Additional exam requirements/

Speech and Interpersonal Communication

Southern Illinois University Edwardsville (continued) recommendations for international students: Required—TOEFL (minimum score 550 paper-based; 213 computer-based; 79 iBT), IELTS (minimum score 6.5). *Application deadline:* For fall admission, 7/22 for domestic students, 6/1 for international students; for spring admission, 12/9 for domestic students, 10/1 for international students. Applications are processed on a rolling basis. Application fee: $30. Electronic applications accepted. *Expenses:* Tuition, state resident: full-time $6012; part-time $1503 per semester. Tuition, nonresident: full-time $15,030; part-time $3758 per semester. Required fees: $1711; $675 per semester. *Financial support:* Application deadline: 3/1. *Unit head:* Dr. Isaac Blankson, Chair, 618-650-3090, E-mail: iblanks@siue.edu. *Application contact:* Dr. Jocelyn DeGroot Brown, Director, 618-650-5828, E-mail: jocbrow@siue.edu.

Southern Illinois University Edwardsville, Graduate School, College of Arts and Sciences, Department of Speech Communication, Program in Speech Communication, Edwardsville, IL 62026-0001. Offers MA. Part-time and evening/weekend programs available. *Faculty:* 9 full-time (6 women). *Students:* 17 full-time (14 women), 5 part-time (all women); includes 1 minority (Black or African American, non-Hispanic/Latino). Average age 26. 19 applicants, 63% accepted. In 2010, 7 master's awarded. *Degree requirements:* For master's, thesis (for some programs), final exam. *Entrance requirements:* Additional exam requirements/recommendations for international students: Required—TOEFL (minimum score 550 paper-based; 213 computer-based; 79 iBT), IELTS (minimum score 6.5). *Application deadline:* For fall admission, 7/22 for domestic students, 6/1 for international students; for spring admission, 12/9 for domestic students, 10/1 for international students. Applications are processed on a rolling basis. Application fee: $30. Electronic applications accepted. *Expenses:* Tuition, state resident: full-time $6012; part-time $1503 per semester. Tuition, nonresident: full-time $15,030; part-time $3758 per semester. Required fees: $1711; $675 per semester. *Financial support:* In 2010–11, 12 teaching assistantships with full tuition reimbursements (averaging $8,064 per year) were awarded; fellowships with full tuition reimbursements, research assistantships with full tuition reimbursements, career-related internships or fieldwork, Federal Work-Study, institutionally sponsored loans, scholarships/grants, traineeships, and unspecified assistantships also available. Support available to part-time students. Financial award application deadline: 3/1; financial award applicants required to submit FAFSA. *Unit head:* Dr. Jocelyn DeGroot Brown, Director, 618-650-5828, E-mail: jocbrow@siue.edu. *Application contact:* Dr. Jocelyn DeGroot Brown, Director, 618-650-5828, E-mail: jocbrow@siue.edu.

Texas A&M University–Commerce, Graduate School, College of Arts and Sciences, Department of Communication and Theatre, Commerce, TX 75429-3011. Offers theatre (MA, MS). Part-time programs available. *Degree requirements:* For master's, comprehensive exam, thesis (for some programs). *Entrance requirements:* For master's, GRE General Test. Electronic applications accepted. *Faculty research:* Theater history.

Texas Christian University, College of Communication, Department of Communication Studies, Fort Worth, TX 76129. Offers MS. Part-time programs available. *Faculty:* 10 full-time (3 women). *Students:* 13 full-time (11 women), 2 part-time (1 woman); includes 2 minority (1 Asian, non-Hispanic/Latino; 1 Hispanic/Latino). Average age 25. 18 applicants, 44% accepted, 7 enrolled. In 2010, 7 master's awarded. *Degree requirements:* For master's, comprehensive exam, thesis optional. *Entrance requirements:* For master's, GRE General Test. Additional exam requirements/recommendations for international students: Required—TOEFL. *Application deadline:* For spring admission, 3/1 for domestic and international students. Applications are processed on a rolling basis. Application fee: $50. *Expenses:* Tuition: Full-time $18,720; part-time $1040 per credit hour. Tuition and fees vary according to course load and program. *Financial support:* In 2010–11, 14 students received support, including 9 teaching assistantships with full tuition reimbursements available (averaging $8,000 per year); tuition waivers (full) and unspecified assistantships also available. Financial award application deadline: 3/1. *Faculty research:* Interpersonal and family communication, instructional communication, organizational communication, social media, public speaking anxiety. *Unit head:* Dr. Paul King, Chairperson, 817-257-7610, E-mail: p.king@tcu.edu. *Application contact:* Dr. Paul Schrodt, Director of Graduate Studies, 817-257-5674, Fax: 817-257-6580, E-mail: p.schrodt@tcu.edu.

The University of Alabama, Graduate School, College of Communication and Information Sciences, Department of Communication Studies, Tuscaloosa, AL 35487. Offers MA. *Faculty:* 11 full-time (9 women). *Students:* 25 full-time (16 women), 13 part-time (9 women); includes 13 minority (6 Black or African American, non-Hispanic/Latino; 1 American Indian or Alaska Native, non-Hispanic/Latino; 1 Asian, non-Hispanic/Latino; 5 Hispanic/Latino), 3 international. Average age 27. 38 applicants, 55% accepted, 12 enrolled. In 2010, 21 master's awarded. *Degree requirements:* For master's, comprehensive exam (for some programs), thesis optional, research colloquium presentation, final practicum report. *Entrance requirements:* For master's, GRE, MAT. Additional exam requirements/recommendations for international students: Required—TOEFL (minimum score 550 paper-based; 213 computer-based). *Application deadline:* For fall admission, 5/1 for domestic and international students; for spring admission, 11/1 for domestic and international students. Applications are processed on a rolling basis. Application fee: $50 ($60 for international students). Electronic applications accepted. *Expenses:* Tuition, state resident: full-time $7900. Tuition, nonresident: full-time $20,500. *Financial support:* In 2010–11, 7 students received support, including 12 teaching assistantships with full tuition reimbursements available (averaging $10,908 per year); health care benefits and unspecified assistantships also available. Financial award application deadline: 5/1. *Faculty research:* Rhetorical theory, organizational communication, interpersonal communication, rhetorical criticism, gender and communication, health communication. *Unit head:* Dr. Beth S. Bennett, Chair and Professor, 205-348-8073, Fax: 205-348-8080, E-mail: bbennett@ua.edu. *Application contact:* Dr. Mary M. Meares, Graduate Program Director and Assistant Professor, 205-348-8072, Fax: 205-348-8080, E-mail: mmmeares@ua.edu.

University of Arkansas at Little Rock, Graduate School, College of Professional Studies, Department of Speech Communication, Little Rock, AR 72204-1099. Offers applied communication studies (MA). Part-time and evening/weekend programs available. *Degree requirements:* For master's, comprehensive exam, internship, paper, or thesis. *Entrance requirements:* For master's, GRE General Test, MAT, minimum GPA of 2.7. *Faculty research:* Communication theory and applications, managerial communication, human resource training and development, relational communication.

University of California, Santa Barbara, Graduate Division, College of Letters and Sciences, Division of Humanities and Fine Arts, Department of Linguistics, Santa Barbara, CA 93106-9580. Offers applied linguistics (PhD); cognitive science (PhD); language, interaction, and social organizations (PhD); linguistics (PhD); translation studies (PhD); MA/PhD. *Faculty:* 9 full-time (5 women), 1 part-time/adjunct (0 women). *Students:* 28 full-time (14 women); includes 1 Asian, non-Hispanic/Latino. Average age 31. 62 applicants, 23% accepted, 8 enrolled. In 2010, 2 doctorates awarded. Terminal master's awarded for partial completion of doctoral program. *Degree requirements:* For doctorate, one foreign language, comprehensive exam, thesis/dissertation. *Entrance requirements:* For doctorate, GRE. Additional exam requirements/recommendations for international students: Required—TOEFL (minimum score 550 paper-based; 80 iBT), IELTS (minimum score 7). *Application deadline:* For fall admission, 12/1 for domestic and international students. Application fee: $70 ($90 for international students). Electronic applications accepted. *Financial support:* In 2010–11, 22 students received support, including 20 fellowships with full and partial tuition reimbursements available (averaging $16,513 per year), 2 research assistantships with full and partial tuition reimbursements available (averaging $12,185 per year), 10 teaching assistantships with full and partial tuition reimbursements available (averaging $6,586 per year). Financial award application deadline: 12/1; financial award applicants required to submit FAFSA. *Faculty research:* Sociolinguistics, linguistic theory, discourse, psycho-linguistics, anthropological linguistics. *Unit head:* Joni Schwartz, Director, 805-893-3237, Fax: 805-893-7492, E-mail: joni@hfa.ucsb.edu. *Application contact:* Cami Helmuth, Graduate Program Advisor, 805-893-7490, Fax: 805-893-7492, E-mail: helmuth@hfa.uscb.edu.

University of California, Santa Barbara, Graduate Division, College of Letters and Sciences, Division of Social Sciences, Department of Sociology, Santa Barbara, CA 93106-9430. Offers feminist studies (PhD); global studies (PhD); language, interaction and social organization (PhD); quantitative methods in the social sciences (PhD); technology and society (PhD); MA/PhD. *Faculty:* 35 full-time (14 women). *Students:* 71 full-time (44 women); includes 5 Black or African American, non-Hispanic/Latino; 4 Asian, non-Hispanic/Latino; 21 Hispanic/Latino. Average age 30. 162 applicants, 8% accepted, 6 enrolled. In 2010, 13 doctorates awarded. Terminal master's awarded for partial completion of doctoral program. *Degree requirements:* For doctorate, comprehensive exam, thesis/dissertation. *Entrance requirements:* For doctorate, GRE General Test. Additional exam requirements/recommendations for international students: Required—TOEFL (minimum score 550 paper-based; 80 iBT), IELTS (minimum score 7). *Application deadline:* For fall admission, 12/1 for domestic and international students. Application fee: $70 ($90 for international students). Electronic applications accepted. *Financial support:* In 2010–11, 60 students received support, including 40 fellowships with full and partial tuition reimbursements available (averaging $10,059 per year), 4 research assistantships with full and partial tuition reimbursements available (averaging $10,166 per year), 43 teaching assistantships with full and partial tuition reimbursements available (averaging $11,913 per year); career-related internships or fieldwork, Federal Work-Study, institutionally sponsored loans, scholarships/grants, health care benefits, tuition waivers (full and partial), and unspecified assistantships also available. Financial award application deadline: 12/1. *Faculty research:* Feminist studies/sexualities, race ethnicity, global, culture, conversation analysis. *Unit head:* Prof. Verta Taylor, Chair, 805-893-3118, Fax: 805-893-3324. *Application contact:* Sharon Applegate, Graduate Program Assistant, 805-893-3328, Fax: 805-893-3324, E-mail: grad-soc@soc.ucsb.edu.

University of Central Missouri, The Graduate School, College of Arts, Humanities and Social Sciences, Warrensburg, MO 64093. Offers English (MA); history (MA); mass communication (MA); music (MA); psychology (MS); speech communication (MA); teaching English as a second language (MA); theatre (MA). Part-time programs available. *Entrance requirements:* Additional exam requirements/recommendations for international students: Required—TOEFL (minimum score 550 paper-based; 79 computer-based). Electronic applications accepted.

University of Denver, Division of Arts, Humanities and Social Sciences, Department of Communication Studies, Denver, CO 80208. Offers MA, PhD. Part-time programs available. *Faculty:* 2 full-time (both women). *Students:* 25 full-time (17 women), 6 part-time (5 women); includes 2 Black or African American, non-Hispanic/Latino; 2 Hispanic/Latino, 5 international. Average age 32. 59 applicants, 68% accepted, 10 enrolled. In 2010, 3 master's, 4 doctorates awarded. *Degree requirements:* For master's, comprehensive exam or thesis; for doctorate, one foreign language, thesis/dissertation. *Entrance requirements:* For master's and doctorate, GRE General Test. Additional exam requirements/recommendations for international students: Required—TOEFL (minimum score 550 paper-based; 80 iBT). *Application deadline:* Applications are processed on a rolling basis. Application fee: $60. Electronic applications accepted. *Expenses:* Tuition: Full-time $35,604; part-time $29,670 per year. Required fees: $687 per year. Tuition and fees vary according to program. *Financial support:* In 2010–11, 13 teaching assistantships with full and partial tuition reimbursements (averaging $16,461 per year) were awarded; career-related internships or fieldwork, Federal Work-Study, institutionally sponsored loans, scholarships/grants, and unspecified assistantships also available. Support available to part-time students. Financial award application deadline: 2/10; financial award applicants required to submit FAFSA. *Faculty research:* Successful community collaborative efforts, long-term marriages, cross-ethnic friendships, public dialogue about environmental risk, women's international cooperation. *Unit head:* Dr. Roy Wood, Chair, 303-871-4325, Fax: 303-871-4316, E-mail: rwood@du.edu. *Application contact:* Information Contact, 303-871-2385, Fax: 303-871-4316, E-mail: hcom@du.edu.

University of Georgia, College of Arts and Sciences, Department of Speech Communication, Athens, GA 30602. Offers MA, PhD. *Faculty:* 13 full-time (9 women). *Students:* 29 full-time (14 women), 2 part-time (1 woman); includes 1 Black or African American, non-Hispanic/Latino; 1 Asian, non-Hispanic/Latino. 51 applicants, 37% accepted, 12 enrolled. In 2010, 6 master's, 4 doctorates awarded. *Degree requirements:* For master's, thesis; for doctorate, one foreign language, thesis/dissertation. *Entrance requirements:* For master's and doctorate, GRE General Test. *Application deadline:* For fall admission, 7/1 priority date for domestic students; for spring admission, 11/15 for domestic students. Application fee: $50. Electronic applications accepted. *Expenses:* Tuition, state resident: full-time $7200; part-time $344 per credit hour. Tuition, nonresident: full-time $21,900; part-time $944 per credit hour. Tuition and fees vary according to course load and program. *Financial support:* Fellowships, research assistantships, teaching assistantships, unspecified assistantships available. *Unit head:* Dr. Barbara Biesecker, Head, 706-542-4893, Fax: 706-542-3245, E-mail: bbieseck@uga.edu. *Application contact:* Dr. Jennifer A. Samp, Graduate Coordinator, 706-542-3246, E-mail: jasamp@uga.edu.

University of Hawaii at Manoa, Graduate Division, College of Arts and Humanities, Department of Speech, Honolulu, HI 96822. Offers MA. Part-time programs available. *Faculty:* 7 full-time (4 women), 6 part-time/adjunct (1 woman). *Students:* 10 full-time (all women), 2 part-time (both women); includes 4 Asian, non-Hispanic/Latino, 2 international. Average age 26. 12 applicants, 67% accepted, 7 enrolled. In 2010, 4 master's awarded. *Degree requirements:* For master's, thesis optional. *Entrance requirements:* For master's, GRE General Test. Additional exam requirements/recommendations for international students: Required—TOEFL (minimum score 600 paper-based; 250 computer-based; 100 iBT), IELTS (minimum score 7). *Application deadline:* For fall admission, 3/1 for domestic students, 1/15 for international students; for spring admission, 9/1 for domestic students, 8/1 for international students. Application fee: $60. *Financial support:* In 2010–11, 2 fellowships (averaging $2,600 per year), 7 teaching assistantships (averaging $14,547 per year) were awarded; tuition waivers (full) also available. *Faculty research:* Social influence, relational management, message processing, intercultural communication. *Application contact:* Amy Hubbard, Graduate Chairperson, 808-956-3316, Fax: 808-956-3947, E-mail: aebesu@hawaii.edu.

University of Houston, College of Liberal Arts and Social Sciences, School of Communication, Houston, TX 77204. Offers health communication (MA); mass communication studies (MA); public relations studies (MA); speech communication (MA). Part-time programs available. *Faculty:* 11 full-time (6 women), 2 part-time/adjunct (0 women). *Students:* 47 full-time (39 women), 46 part-time (36 women); includes 15 Black or African American, non-Hispanic/Latino; 2 American Indian or Alaska Native, non-Hispanic/Latino; 3 Asian, non-Hispanic/Latino; 16 Hispanic/Latino, 19 international. Average age 28. 54 applicants, 70% accepted, 24 enrolled. In 2010, 20 master's awarded. *Degree requirements:* For master's, comprehensive exam (for some programs), thesis (for some programs), 30-33 hours. *Entrance requirements:* For master's, GRE. Additional exam requirements/recommendations for international students: Required—TOEFL. *Application deadline:* For fall admission, 6/1 for domestic students, 4/1 for international students; for spring admission, 11/1 for domestic students, 10/1 for international students. Applications are processed on a rolling basis. Application fee: $50 ($100 for international students). Electronic applications accepted. *Expenses:* Tuition, state resident: full-time $8592; part-time $358 per credit hour. Tuition, nonresident: full-time $16,032; part-time $668 per credit hour. Required fees: $2889. Tuition and fees vary according to course load and program. *Financial support:* In 2010–11, 28 teaching assistantships with full tuition reimbursements (averaging $8,111 per year) were awarded; career-related internships or fieldwork, Federal Work-Study, institutionally sponsored loans, scholarships/grants, health care benefits, and unspecified assistantships also available. Support available to part-time students. Financial award application deadline: 2/1. *Unit head:* Dr. Beth Olson, Chairperson, 713-743-2873, Fax: 713-743-2876, E-mail: bolson@uh.edu. *Application contact:* Dr. Martha Haun, Director of Graduate Studies, 713-743-2886, E-mail: mhaun@uh.edu.

University of Maryland, College Park, Academic Affairs, College of Behavioral and Social Sciences, Department of Hearing and Speech Sciences, College Park, MD 20742. Offers audiology (MA, PhD); hearing and speech sciences (Au D); language pathology (MA, PhD); neuroscience (PhD); speech (MA, PhD). *Accreditation:* ASHA (one or more programs are accredited). *Faculty:* 22 full-time (20 women), 12 part-time/adjunct (9 women). *Students:* 68 full-time (62 women), 22 part-time (21 women); includes 19 minority (8 Black or African American, non-Hispanic/Latino; 5 Asian, non-Hispanic/Latino; 4 Hispanic/Latino; 1 Native Hawaiian or other Pacific Islander, non-Hispanic/Latino; 1 Two or more races, non-Hispanic/Latino), 2 international. 291 applicants, 32% accepted, 28 enrolled. In 2010, 20 master's, 11 doctorates awarded. *Degree requirements:* For master's, thesis optional; for doctorate, thesis/dissertation, written and oral exams. *Entrance requirements:* For master's, GRE General Test, minimum GPA of 3.5, 3 letters of recommendation; for doctorate, GRE General Test, minimum GPA of 3.5. Additional exam requirements/recommendations for international students: Required—TOEFL. *Application deadline:* For fall admission, 1/15 for domestic and international students. Applications are processed on a rolling basis. Application fee: $75. Electronic applications accepted. *Expenses:* Tuition, state resident: part-time $471 per credit hour. Tuition, nonresident: part-time $1016 per credit hour. Required fees: $337 per term. *Financial support:* In 2010–11, 5 fellowships with full and partial tuition reimbursements (averaging $14,722 per year), 22 research assistantships (averaging $15,396 per year), 16 teaching assistantships (averaging $14,171 per year) were awarded; career-related internships or fieldwork, Federal Work-Study, scholarships/grants, and health care benefits also available. Support available to part-time students. Financial award applicants required to submit FAFSA. *Faculty research:* Speech perception, language acquisition, bilingualism, hearing loss. Total annual research expenditures: $906,503. *Unit head:* Dr. Nan B. Bernstein-Ratner, Chair, 301-405-4217, Fax: 301-314-2023, E-mail: nratner@umd.edu. *Application contact:* Dean of Graduate School, 301-405-0358, Fax: 301-314-9305.

University of Nebraska–Lincoln, Graduate College, College of Arts and Sciences, Department of Communication Studies, Lincoln, NE 68588. Offers instructional communication (MA, PhD); interpersonal communication (MA, PhD); marketing, communication studies, and advertising (MA, PhD); organizational communication (MA, PhD); rhetoric and culture (MA, PhD). *Degree requirements:* For master's, thesis optional; for doctorate, comprehensive exam, thesis/dissertation. *Entrance requirements:* For master's and doctorate, GRE General Test, writing sample. Additional exam requirements/recommendations for international students: Required—TOEFL (minimum score 600 paper-based; 250 computer-based). Electronic applications accepted. *Faculty research:* Message strategies, gender communication, political communication, organizational communication, instructional communication.

University of Nevada, Reno, Graduate School, College of Liberal Arts, Department of Speech Communications, Reno, NV 89557. Offers MA. *Degree requirements:* For master's, thesis optional. *Entrance requirements:* For master's, GRE General Test, minimum GPA of 2.75. Additional exam requirements/recommendations for international students: Required—TOEFL (minimum score 500 paper-based; 173 computer-based; 61 iBT), IELTS (minimum score 6). Electronic applications accepted. *Expenses:* Tuition, state resident: full-time $2219; part-time $246 per credit. Tuition, nonresident: part-time $510 per credit. International tuition: $9009 full-time. Required fees: $59 per term. One-time fee: $101. Tuition and fees vary according to course load. *Faculty research:* Rhetorical theory and criticism; communications/sex roles; judicial, legal, contextual, and behavioral approaches to communication theory.

University of South Carolina, The Graduate School, College of Education, Department of Instruction and Teacher Education, Program in Secondary Education, Columbia, SC 29208. Offers art education (IMA, MAT); business education (IMA, MAT); English (MAT); foreign language (MAT); health education (MAT); mathematics (MAT); science (IMA, MAT); secondary (Ed D); secondary education (MT, PhD); social studies (MAT); theatre and speech (MAT). IMA and MT offered jointly with the subject areas. *Accreditation:* NCATE. *Degree requirements:* For master's, comprehensive exam, thesis (for some programs), foreign language (MA); for doctorate, one foreign language, comprehensive exam, thesis/dissertation. *Entrance requirements:* For master's, GRE General Test or MAT, teaching certificate (IMA, M Ed), interview; for doctorate, GRE General Test or MAT, interview. *Faculty research:* Middle school programs, professional development, school collaboration.

University of Southern California, Graduate School, Annenberg School for Communication and Journalism, School of Communication, Program in Communication, Los Angeles, CA 90089. Offers communication (MA, PhD), including information and society (PhD), interpersonal and health communication (PhD), media, culture and communication (PhD), organizational communication (PhD), rhetorical and political communication (PhD). *Students:* 97 full-time (64 women); includes 20 minority (4 Black or African American, non-Hispanic/Latino; 1 American Indian or Alaska Native, non-Hispanic/Latino; 8 Asian, non-Hispanic/Latino; 7 Hispanic/Latino), 30 international. Average age 31. 242 applicants, 9% accepted, 18 enrolled. In 2010, 14 doctorates awarded. *Degree requirements:* For doctorate, thesis/dissertation. *Entrance requirements:* For master's and doctorate, GRE General Test, resume, writing samples, 3 letters of recommendation, interest survey questionnaire, statement of purpose. Additional exam requirements/recommendations for international students: Required—TOEFL (minimum score 280 computer-based; 114 iBT); Recommended—TWE. *Application deadline:* For fall admission, 12/1 for domestic and international students. Application fee: $85. Electronic applications accepted. *Expenses:* Tuition: Full-time $31,240; part-time $1420 per unit. Required fees: $600. One-time fee: $35 full-time. Full-time tuition and fees vary according to degree level and program. *Financial support:* In 2010–11, 18 students received support, including 18 fellowships with full tuition reimbursements available (averaging $26,500 per year); research assistantships, teaching assistantships, Federal Work-Study, institutionally sponsored loans, scholarships/grants, health care benefits, and unspecified assistantships also available. Support available to part-time students. Financial award application deadline: 1/1; financial award applicants required to submit FAFSA. *Faculty research:* Computer-mediated communication, public health campaigns, communication democracy and the public sphere, new communication technologies in organizations, communication and community. *Unit head:* Dr. Thomas Goodnight, Director of the Ph.D. Program, 213-821-5384, E-mail: gtg@usc.edu. *Application contact:* Allyson Hill, Assistant Dean, Admissions, 213-821-0770, Fax: 213-740-1933, E-mail: ascadm@usc.edu.

See Display on page 675 and Close-Up on page 727.

University of Southern Mississippi, Graduate School, College of Arts and Letters, Department of Speech Communication, Hattiesburg, MS 39406-0001. Offers MA, MS, PhD. Part-time programs available. *Faculty:* 9 full-time (2 women). *Students:* 14 full-time (10 women), 8 part-time (3 women); includes 2 Black or African American, non-Hispanic/Latino; 1 Hispanic/Latino. Average age 32. 14 applicants, 14% accepted, 2 enrolled. In 2010, 1 master's, 3 doctorates awarded. *Degree requirements:* For master's, comprehensive exam, thesis optional; for doctorate, comprehensive exam, thesis/dissertation. *Entrance requirements:* For master's, GRE General Test, minimum GPA of 3.0 in last 60 hours and in major; for doctorate, GRE General Test, minimum GPA of 3.5. Additional exam requirements/recommendations for international students: Required—TOEFL, IELTS. *Application deadline:* For fall admission, 3/1 priority date for domestic students, 3/1 for international students; for spring admission, 1/10 priority date for domestic and international students. Application fee: $50. *Financial support:* In 2010–11, 1 fellowship with full tuition reimbursement (averaging $12,000 per year), 8 teaching assistantships with full tuition reimbursements (averaging $13,500 per year) were awarded; research assistantships, Federal Work-Study, institutionally sponsored loans, scholarships/grants, health care benefits, and unspecified assistantships also available. Financial award application deadline: 3/15; financial award applicants required to submit FAFSA. *Faculty research:* Persuasion and social influence, interpersonal communication, organizational communication, political communication, crisis communication, public advocacy. *Unit head:* Dr. Charles Tardy, Chair, 601-266-4271, Fax: 601-266-4275. *Application contact:* Dr. John Meyer, Director of Graduate Studies, 601-266-4271, Fax: 601-266-4275, E-mail: john.meyer@usm.edu.

The University of Tennessee, Graduate School, College of Communication and Information, Knoxville, TN 37996. Offers advertising (MS, PhD); broadcasting (MS, PhD); communications (MS, PhD); information sciences (MS, PhD); journalism (MS, PhD); public relations (MS, PhD); speech communication (MS, PhD). *Accreditation:* ACEJMC (one or more programs are accredited at the [master's] level). Part-time and evening/weekend programs available. Post-baccalaureate distance learning degree programs offered (no on-campus study). *Degree requirements:* For master's, thesis or alternative; for doctorate, thesis/dissertation. *Entrance requirements:* For master's and doctorate, GRE General Test, minimum GPA of 2.7. Additional exam requirements/recommendations for international students: Required—TOEFL. Electronic applications accepted. *Expenses:* Tuition, state resident: full-time $7440; part-time $414 per credit hour. Tuition, nonresident: full-time $22,478; part-time $1250 per credit hour. Required fees: $922; $43 per credit hour. Tuition and fees vary according to program.

University of Wisconsin–Madison, Graduate School, College of Letters and Science, Department of Communicative Disorders, Madison, WI 53706-1380. Offers normal aspects of speech, language and hearing (MS, PhD); speech-language pathology (MS, PhD); MS/PhD. *Accreditation:* ASHA (one or more programs are accredited). *Degree requirements:* For doctorate, thesis/dissertation. *Entrance requirements:* For master's and doctorate, GRE. Electronic applications accepted. *Expenses:* Tuition, state resident: full-time $9887; part-time $617.96 per credit. Tuition, nonresident: full-time $24,054; part-time $1503.40 per credit. Required fees: $67.63 per credit. Tuition and fees vary according to reciprocity agreements. *Faculty research:* Language disorders in children and adults, disorders of speech production, intelligibility, fluency, hearing impairment, deafness.

University of Wisconsin–Stevens Point, College of Fine Arts and Communication, Division of Communication, Stevens Point, WI 54481-3897. Offers interpersonal communication (MA); mass communication (MA); organizational communication (MA); public relations (MA). Part-time programs available. *Degree requirements:* For master's, thesis or alternative. *Entrance requirements:* For master's, GRE. Additional exam requirements/recommendations for international students: Required—TOEFL (minimum score 575 paper-based). *Faculty research:* Communication theory and research, film history.

University of Wisconsin–Superior, Graduate Division, Department of Communicating Arts, Superior, WI 54880-4500. Offers mass communication (MA); speech communication (MA); theater (MA). Part-time programs available. *Degree requirements:* For master's, comprehensive exam, thesis or alternative, position paper or project. *Entrance requirements:* For master's, minimum GPA of 2.75. *Faculty research:* Multimedia technology, ethics in journalism, diversity, electronic portfolio assessment.

Wake Forest University, Graduate School of Arts and Sciences, Department of Communication, Winston-Salem, NC 27109. Offers speech communication (MA). Part-time programs available. *Degree requirements:* For master's, one foreign language, thesis. *Entrance requirements:* For master's, GRE General Test, writing sample. Additional exam requirements/recommendations for international students: Required—TOEFL (minimum score 213 computer-based; 79 iBT). Electronic applications accepted.

Washington University in St. Louis, School of Medicine, Program in Audiology and Communication Sciences, Saint Louis, MO 63110. Offers audiology (Au D); deaf education (MS); speech and hearing sciences (PhD). *Accreditation:* ASHA (one or more programs are accredited). *Faculty:* 22 full-time (12 women), 18 part-time/adjunct (12 women). *Students:* 71 full-time (69 women). Average age 24. 120 applicants, 20% accepted, 24 enrolled. In 2010, 8 master's, 14 doctorates awarded. *Degree requirements:* For master's, comprehensive exam, thesis, independent study project, oral exam; for doctorate, comprehensive exam, thesis/dissertation, capstone project. *Entrance requirements:* For master's, GRE General Test, minimum B average in undergraduate course work; for doctorate, GRE General Test, minimum B average. Additional exam requirements/recommendations for international students: Required—TOEFL (minimum score 600 paper-based; 250 computer-based; 100 iBT). *Application deadline:* For fall admission, 2/15 for domestic and international students. Application fee: $60 ($80 for international students). Electronic applications accepted. *Expenses:* Contact institution. *Financial support:* In 2010–11, 71 students received support, including 71 fellowships with full and partial tuition reimbursements available (averaging $14,500 per year), 5 teaching assistantships with partial tuition reimbursements available (averaging $1,000 per year); career-related internships or fieldwork, Federal Work-Study, institutionally sponsored loans, scholarships/grants, traineeships, health care benefits, tuition waivers (partial), and unspecified assistantships also available. Financial award application deadline: 2/15; financial award applicants required to submit FAFSA. *Faculty research:* Audiology, deaf education, speech and hearing sciences, sensory neuroscience. *Unit head:* Dr. William W. Clark, Program Director, 314-747-0104, Fax: 314-747-0105. *Application contact:* Elizabeth A. Elliott, Manager, Financial Operations and Admissions, 314-747-0104, Fax: 314-747-0105, E-mail: elliottb@wustl.edu.

Wayne State University, College of Fine, Performing and Communication Arts, Department of Communication, Detroit, MI 48202. Offers communication studies (MA, PhD); public relations and organizational communication (MA); radio-TV-film (MA, PhD); speech communication (MA, PhD). *Faculty:* 25 full-time (11 women), 4 part-time/adjunct (1 woman). *Students:* 64 full-time (43 women), 107 part-time (73 women); includes 44 minority (36 Black or African American, non-Hispanic/Latino; 2 American Indian or Alaska Native, non-Hispanic/Latino; 1 Asian, non-Hispanic/Latino; 5 Hispanic/Latino), 7 international. Average age 32. 65 applicants, 66% accepted, 31 enrolled. In 2010, 37 master's, 7 doctorates awarded. *Degree requirements:* For master's, thesis, essay, or comprehensive exam; for doctorate, thesis/dissertation. *Entrance requirements:* For master's, minimum GPA of 3.0, sample of academic writing; for doctorate, GRE, minimum GPA of 3.3, MA; letters of recommendation; personal statement; sample of written scholarship. Additional exam requirements/recommendations for international students: Required—TOEFL (minimum score 550 paper-based; 213 computer-based); Recommended—TWE (minimum score 6). *Application deadline:* For fall admission, 4/1 for domestic students, 6/1 for international students; for winter admission, 10/1 for international students; for spring admission, 2/1 for international students. Applications are processed on a rolling basis. Application fee: $30 ($50 for international students). Electronic applications accepted. *Expenses:* Tuition, state resident: full-time $7662; part-time $478.85 per credit hour. Tuition, nonresident: full-time $16,920; part-time $1057.55 per credit hour. Required fees: $571.20; $35.70 per credit hour. $188.05 per semester. Tuition and fees vary according to course load and program. *Financial support:* In 2010–11, 22 students received support, including 8 fellowships with tuition reimbursements available (averaging $14,956 per year), 1 research assistantship with tuition reimbursement available (averaging $23,000 per year), 19 teaching assistantships with tuition reimbursements available (averaging $14,620 per year); career-related internships or fieldwork also available. Financial award application deadline: 2/1. *Faculty research:* Rhetorical theory and criticism; mass media theory and research; argumentation; organizational communication; risk and crisis communication; interpersonal, family, and health communication. *Unit head:* Dr. Matthew Seeger, Chair, 313-577-2959, Fax: 313-577-6300, E-mail: aa4331@wayne.edu. *Application contact:* Hayg Oshagan, Associate Professor, 313-577-0429, E-mail: ad4570@wayne.edu.

Technical Communication

Boise State University, Graduate College, College of Arts and Sciences, Department of English, Program in Technical Communication, Boise, ID 83725-0399. Offers MA. Part-time programs available. *Degree requirements:* For master's, thesis. *Entrance requirements:* For master's, minimum GPA of 3.0. Electronic applications accepted.

Bowling Green State University, Graduate College, College of Arts and Sciences, Department of English, Program in English, Bowling Green, OH 43403. Offers English (MA, PhD); literature (MA); rhetoric and writing (PhD); scientific and technical communication (MA). Part-time programs available. *Degree requirements:* For master's, thesis or alternative; for doctorate, comprehensive exam, thesis/dissertation, foreign language or proficiency in Old English. *Entrance requirements:* For master's and doctorate, GRE General Test. Additional exam requirements/recommendations for international students: Required—TOEFL. Electronic applications accepted. *Faculty research:* Postmodern literary theory, rhetorical theory, ethnic American literature, literature and culture, composition pedagogy.

Colorado State University, Graduate School, College of Liberal Arts, Department of Journalism and Technical Communication, Fort Collins, CO 80523-1785. Offers public communication and technology (MS, PhD); technical communication (MS). Part-time programs available. *Faculty:* 17 full-time (7 women), 1 (woman) part-time/adjunct. *Students:* 31 full-time (23 women), 34 part-time (23 women); includes 6 minority (4 Hispanic/Latino; 2 Two or more races, non-Hispanic/Latino), 2 international. Average age 33. 56 applicants, 50% accepted, 21 enrolled. In 2010, 14 master's awarded. *Degree requirements:* For master's, variable foreign language requirement, comprehensive exam (for some programs), thesis (for some programs); for doctorate, variable foreign language requirement, comprehensive exam (for some programs), thesis/dissertation (for some programs). *Entrance requirements:* For master's, GRE General Test, samples of written work, letters of recommendation, resume or curriculum vitae, 3 writing/communication projects; for doctorate, GRE General Test, master's degree, minimum GPA of 3.0, scholarly/professional work, letters of recommendation, statement of career plans, resume. Additional exam requirements/recommendations for international students: Required—TOEFL (minimum score 550 paper-based; 213 computer-based; 80 iBT). *Application deadline:* For fall admission, 2/15 priority date for domestic students, 12/15 priority date for international students; for spring admission, 6/15 priority date for domestic students. Applications are processed on a rolling basis. Application fee: $50. Electronic applications accepted. *Expenses:* Tuition, state resident: full-time $7434; part-time $413 per credit. Tuition, nonresident: full-time $19,022; part-time $1057 per credit. Required fees: $1729; $88 per credit. *Financial support:* In 2010–11, 35 students received support, including 2 research assistantships with full and partial tuition reimbursements available (averaging $9,269 per year), 33 teaching assistantships with partial tuition reimbursements available (averaging $10,636 per year); fellowships with partial tuition reimbursements available, career-related internships or fieldwork, Federal Work-Study, institutionally sponsored loans, scholarships/grants, traineeships, and unspecified assistantships also available. Support available to part-time students. Financial award application deadline: 3/1; financial award applicants required to submit FAFSA. *Faculty research:* Technical/science communication, public relations, health/risk communication, Web/new media technologies, environmental communication. Total annual research expenditures: $250,177. *Unit head:* Dr. Greg Luft, Chair, 970-491-1979, Fax: 970-491-2908, E-mail: greg.luft@colostate.edu. *Application contact:* Dr. Craig Trumbo, Graduate Program Coordinator, 970-491-2077, Fax: 970-491-2908, E-mail: craig.trumbo@colostate.edu.

Drexel University, College of Arts and Sciences, Department of Culture and Communication, Program in Communication, Philadelphia, PA 19104-2875. Offers public communication (MS); science communication (MS); technical communication (MS). Part-time and evening/weekend programs available. *Degree requirements:* For master's, internship, professional portfolio. *Entrance requirements:* For master's, GRE or minimum GPA of 3.0. Additional exam requirements/recommendations for international students: Required—TOEFL. Electronic applications accepted.

Eastern Michigan University, Graduate School, College of Arts and Sciences, Department of English Language and Literature, Program in Written Communication, Ypsilanti, MI 48197. Offers technical communications (MA, Graduate Certificate); written communications (MA). Part-time and evening/weekend programs available. Postbaccalaureate distance learning degree programs offered (minimal on-campus study). *Students:* 8 full-time (6 women), 38 part-time (30 women); includes 5 minority (4 Black or African American, non-Hispanic/Latino; 1 Hispanic/Latino), 1 international. Average age 34. In 2010, 11 master's awarded. *Entrance requirements:* Additional exam requirements/recommendations for international students: Required—TOEFL. *Application deadline:* Applications are processed on a rolling basis. Application fee: $35. *Financial support:* Fellowships, research assistantships with full tuition reimbursements, teaching assistantships with full tuition reimbursements, career-related internships or fieldwork, Federal Work-Study, institutionally sponsored loans, scholarships/grants, tuition waivers (partial), and unspecified assistantships available. Support available to part-time students. Financial award applicants required to submit FAFSA. *Application contact:* Prof. Steve Krause, Program Advisor, 734-487-3172, Fax: 734-483-9744, E-mail: skrause@emich.edu.

Eastern Washington University, Graduate Studies, College of Arts and Letters, Department of English, Cheney, WA 99004-2431. Offers literature (MA); rhetoric, composition, and technical communication (MA); teaching English as a second language (MA). *Degree requirements:* For master's, comprehensive exam, thesis or alternative. *Entrance requirements:* For master's, GRE General Test, minimum GPA of 3.0.

Florida Institute of Technology, Graduate Programs, College of Psychology and Liberal Arts, Department of Humanities and Communication, Melbourne, FL 32901-6975. Offers technical and professional communication (MS). Part-time and evening/weekend programs available. *Faculty:* 3 full-time (all women), 1 (woman) part-time/adjunct. *Students:* 11 full-time (7 women), 6 part-time (5 women); includes 5 minority (2 Black or African American, non-Hispanic/Latino; 1 American Indian or Alaska Native, non-Hispanic/Latino; 1 Asian, non-Hispanic/Latino; 1 Hispanic/Latino), 1 international. Average age 38. 5 applicants, 80% accepted, 3 enrolled. In 2010, 2 master's awarded. *Degree requirements:* For master's, comprehensive exam (for some programs), thesis optional. *Entrance requirements:* For master's, GRE (minimum score 1000 verbal and analytical), minimum GPA of 3.0, 2 letters of recommendation, discursive writing sample. Additional exam requirements/recommendations for international students: Required—TOEFL (minimum score 550 paper-based; 213 computer-based; 79 iBT). *Application deadline:* For fall admission, 4/1 for international students; for spring admission, 9/30 for international students. Applications are processed on a rolling basis. Application fee: $50. Electronic applications accepted. *Expenses:* Tuition: Part-time $1040 per credit hour. Tuition and fees vary according to campus/location. *Financial support:* Career-related internships or fieldwork and tuition remissions available. Support available to part-time students. Financial award application deadline: 3/1; financial award applicants required to submit FAFSA. *Faculty research:* Communication of astronomy in the seventeenth century, persuasion and patronage in seventeenth century work, technical and cross-cultural communication. Total annual research expenditures: $4,782. *Unit head:* Dr. Robert A. Taylor, Department Head, 321-674-7384, Fax: 321-674-8109, E-mail: rotaylor@fit.edu. *Application contact:* Cheryl A. Brown, Associate Director of Graduate Admissions, 321-674-7581, Fax: 321-723-9468, E-mail: cbrown@fit.edu.

Harvard University, Harvard Graduate School of Education, Master's Programs in Education, Cambridge, MA 02138. Offers arts in education (Ed M); education policy and management (Ed M); higher education (Ed M); human development and psychology (Ed M); international education policy (Ed M); language and literacy (Ed M); learning and teaching (Ed M); mid-career mathematics and science (teaching certificate) (Ed M); mind brain and education (Ed M); prevention science and practice (Ed M); school leadership (Ed M); special studies (Ed M); teaching and curriculum (teaching certificate) (Ed M); technology innovation and education (Ed M). Part-time programs available. *Faculty:* 79 full-time (42 women), 58 part-time/adjunct (24 women). *Students:* 601 full-time (453 women), 77 part-time (53 women); includes 198 minority (59 Black or African American, non-Hispanic/Latino; 3 American Indian or Alaska Native, non-Hispanic/Latino; 59 Asian, non-Hispanic/Latino; 48 Hispanic/Latino; 2 Native Hawaiian or other Pacific Islander, non-Hispanic/Latino; 27 Two or more races, non-Hispanic/Latino), 75 international. Average age 28. 1,667 applicants, 53% accepted, 633 enrolled. In 2010, 634 master's awarded. *Entrance requirements:* For master's, GRE General Test, statement of purpose, 3 letters of recommendation, resume, official transcripts. Additional exam requirements/recommendations for international students: Required—TOEFL (minimum score 600 paper-based; 250 computer-based; 100 iBT), TWE (minimum score 5). *Application deadline:* For fall admission, 1/3 for domestic and international students. Application fee: $85. Electronic applications accepted. *Expenses:* Contact institution. *Financial support:* In 2010–11, 422 students received support, including 24 fellowships with full and partial tuition reimbursements available (averaging $11,886 per year); career-related internships or fieldwork, Federal Work-Study, institutionally sponsored loans, scholarships/grants, health care benefits, tuition waivers (full and partial), and unspecified assistantships also available. Support available to part-time students. Financial award application deadline: 2/1; financial award applicants required to submit FAFSA. *Faculty research:* Learning and development, educational leadership and organizations, educational policy analysis. Total annual research expenditures: $23 million. *Unit head:* Jennifer L. Petrallia, Assistant Dean, 617-495-8445. *Application contact:* Information Contact, 617-495-3414, Fax: 617-496-3577, E-mail: gseadmissions@harvard.edu.

Lawrence Technological University, College of Arts and Sciences, Southfield, MI 48075-1058. Offers computer science (MS); educational technology (MS); integrated science (MSE); science education (MSE); technical and professional communication (MS). Part-time and evening/weekend programs available. *Faculty:* 14 full-time (6 women), 14 part-time/adjunct (4 women). *Students:* 1 full-time (0 women), 93 part-time (54 women); includes 17 Black or African American, non-Hispanic/Latino; 7 Asian, non-Hispanic/Latino; 1 Hispanic/Latino; 4 Two or more races, non-Hispanic/Latino, 10 international. Average age 36. 116 applicants, 61% accepted, 23 enrolled. In 2010, 40 master's awarded. *Degree requirements:* For master's, thesis (for some programs). *Entrance requirements:* For master's, GRE. Additional exam requirements/recommendations for international students: Required—TOEFL (minimum score 550 paper-based; 213 computer-based; 79 iBT). *Application deadline:* For fall admission, 6/30 priority date for domestic students, 6/30 for international students; for spring admission, 11/15 priority date for domestic students, 11/15 for international students. Applications are processed on a rolling basis. Application fee: $50. Electronic applications accepted. *Financial support:* In 2010–11, 22 students received support. Federal Work-Study available. Financial award application deadline: 4/1; financial award applicants required to submit FAFSA. *Unit head:* Dr. Hsiao-Ping Moore, Dean, 248-204-3500, Fax: 248-204-3518, E-mail: scidean@itu.edu. *Application contact:* Jane Rohrback, Director of Admissions, 248-204-3160, Fax: 248-204-2228, E-mail: admissions@ltu.edu.

Michigan Technological University, Graduate School, College of Sciences and Arts, Department of Humanities, Program in Rhetoric and Technical Communication, Houghton, MI 49931. Offers MS, PhD. Part-time programs available. Terminal master's awarded for partial completion of doctoral program. *Degree requirements:* For master's, comprehensive exam; for doctorate, one foreign language, comprehensive exam, thesis/dissertation. *Entrance requirements:* Additional exam requirements/recommendations for international students: Required—TOEFL (minimum score 600 paper-based; 250 computer-based). Electronic applications accepted.

Minnesota State University Mankato, College of Graduate Studies, College of Arts and Humanities, Department of English, Mankato, MN 56001. Offers creative writing (MFA); English (MAT); English studies (MA); teaching English as a second language (MA, Certificate); technical communication (MA, Certificate). Part-time programs available. *Students:* 46 full-time (28 women), 147 part-time (97 women). *Degree requirements:* For master's, one foreign language, comprehensive exam, thesis or alternative. *Entrance requirements:* For master's, minimum GPA of 3.0 during previous 2 years, writing sample (MFA). Additional exam requirements/recommendations for international students: Required—TOEFL (minimum score 500 paper-based; 61 iBT). *Application deadline:* For fall admission, 7/1 for domestic students, 5/1 for international students. Applications are processed on a rolling basis. Application fee: $40. Electronic applications accepted. *Financial support:* Research assistantships with full tuition reimbursements, teaching assistantships with full tuition reimbursements, career-related internships or fieldwork, Federal Work-Study, and unspecified assistantships available. Financial award application deadline: 3/15; financial award applicants required to submit FAFSA. *Faculty research:* Keats and Christianity. *Unit head:* Dr. John Banschbach, Chairperson, 507-389-2117. *Application contact:* 507-389-2321, E-mail: grad@mnsu.edu.

Missouri Western State University, Program in Written Communication, St. Joseph, MO 64507-2294. Offers technical communication (MAS); writing studies (MAS). *Expenses:* Tuition, state resident: full-time $5544; part-time $308 per credit hour. Tuition, nonresident: full-time $10,206; part-time $567 per credit hour. Required fees: $30 per semester. One-time fee: $45 full-time.

Montana Tech of The University of Montana, Graduate School, Department of Technical Communication, Butte, MT 59701-8997. Offers MS. Part-time programs available. *Faculty:* 6 full-time (4 women), 6 part-time/adjunct (2 women). *Students:* 7 full-time (4 women), 2 part-time (both women). 3 applicants, 67% accepted, 2 enrolled. In 2010, 4 master's awarded. *Degree requirements:* For master's, project or thesis. *Entrance requirements:* For master's, GRE General Test, minimum GPA of 3.0. Additional exam requirements/recommendations for international students: Required—TOEFL (minimum score 525 paper-based; 195 computer-based; 71 iBT). *Application deadline:* For fall admission, 4/1 priority date for domestic students, 3/1 priority date for international students; for spring admission, 10/1 priority date for domestic students, 7/1 priority date for international students. Applications are processed on a rolling basis. Application fee: $30. Electronic applications accepted. *Expenses:* Tuition, state resident: full-time $5084. Tuition, nonresident: full-time $15,104. *Financial support:* In 2010–11, 6 students received support, including 5 teaching assistantships with partial tuition reimbursements available (averaging $5,600 per year); research assistantships with partial tuition reimbursements available, career-related internships or fieldwork, tuition waivers (partial), and unspecified assistantships also available. Financial award application deadline: 4/1; financial award applicants required to submit FAFSA. *Faculty research:* Environmental concerns and the Big Hole River, history of Butte mining, African studies, multicultural communications. *Unit head:* Dr. Chad Okrusch, Head, 406-496-4297, Fax: 406-496-4510, E-mail: cokrusch@mtech.edu. *Application contact:* Fred Sullivan, Administrator, Graduate School, 406-496-4304, Fax: 406-496-4710, E-mail: fsullivan@mtech.edu.

New Jersey Institute of Technology, Office of Graduate Studies, College of Science and Liberal Arts, Department of Humanities and Social Sciences, Program in Professional and Technical Communication, Newark, NJ 07102. Offers MS. Part-time and evening/weekend programs available. *Students:* 5 full-time (4 women), 25 part-time (15 women); includes 3 Black or African American, non-Hispanic/Latino; 1 Hispanic/Latino, 1 international. Average age 39. 27 applicants, 63% accepted, 11 enrolled. In 2010, 9 master's awarded. Terminal master's awarded for partial completion of doctoral program. *Degree requirements:* For master's, thesis or alternative. *Entrance requirements:* For master's, GRE General Test. Additional exam requirements/recommendations for international students: Required—TOEFL (minimum score 550 paper-based; 213 computer-based). *Application deadline:* For fall admission, 6/5 priority date for domestic students, 4/1 for international students; for spring admission, 11/15 for domestic and international students. Applications are processed on a rolling basis. Application fee: $65. Electronic applications accepted. *Expenses:* Tuition, state resident: full-time $14,724; part-time $818 per credit. Tuition, nonresident: full-time $20,304; part-time $1128 per credit. Required fees: $2272; $209 per credit. $103 per semester. One-time fee: $312 full-time; $212 part-time. *Financial support:* Fellowships with full and partial tuition reimbursements, research assistantships with full and partial tuition reimbursements, teaching assistantships with full and partial tuition reimbursements, career-related internships or fieldwork, Federal Work-Study, institutionally sponsored loans, and unspecified assistantships available. Financial award application deadline: 3/15. *Faculty research:* Technology transfer, global sustainability, technology policy, professional ethics. *Unit head:* Dr. Robert S. Friedman, Chair, 973-596-5765, E-mail: robert.s.friedman@njit.edu. *Application contact:* Kathryn Kelly, Director of Admissions, 973-596-3300, Fax: 973-596-3461, E-mail: admissions@njit.edu.

North Carolina State University, Graduate School, College of Humanities and Social Sciences, Department of English, Program in Technical Communication, Raleigh, NC 27695. Offers MS. *Degree requirements:* For master's, thesis optional. *Entrance requirements:* For master's, GRE General Test. Electronic applications accepted. *Faculty research:* Workplace writing, organizational socialization and power, integrated and multimedia documentation systems, technical communication management, usability testing theories.

North Central College, Graduate and Continuing Education Programs, Department of Leadership Studies, Naperville, IL 60566-7063. Offers higher education leadership (MLS); professional leadership (MLS); social entrepreneurship (MLS); sports leadership (MLS). Part-time and evening/weekend programs available. *Faculty:* 7 full-time (1 woman), 7 part-time/adjunct (1 woman). *Students:* 28 full-time (15 women), 32 part-time (21 women); includes 5 Black or African American, non-Hispanic/Latino; 3 Hispanic/Latino; 1 Two or more races, non-Hispanic/Latino. Average age 28. In 2010, 2 master's awarded. *Degree requirements:* For master's, project. *Entrance requirements:* For master's, interview. Additional exam requirements/recommendations for international students: Required—TOEFL (minimum score 570 paper-based; 233 computer-based; 90 iBT). *Application deadline:* For fall admission, 8/15 for domestic students; for winter admission, 12/1 for domestic students; for spring admission, 2/1 for domestic students. Applications are processed on a rolling basis. Application fee: $25. *Expenses:* Contact institution. *Financial support:* Scholarships/grants available. Support available to part-time students. *Unit head:* Dr. Thomas Cavanagh, Head, 630-637-5285. *Application contact:* Wendy Kulpinski, Director of Graduate and Continuing Education Admissions, 630-637-5808, Fax: 630-637-5844, E-mail: wekulpinski@noctrl.edu.

Rensselaer Polytechnic Institute, Graduate School, School of Humanities, Arts, and Social Sciences, Program in Technical Communication, Troy, NY 12180-3590. Offers MS. Part-time programs available. *Faculty:* 14 full-time (8 women), 1 part-time/adjunct (0 women). *Students:* 2 full-time (1 woman); includes 1 minority (Black or African American, non-Hispanic/Latino). 2 applicants, 100% accepted, 2 enrolled. In 2010, 2 master's awarded. *Degree requirements:* For master's, thesis optional. *Entrance requirements:* For master's, GRE General Test, resume. Additional exam requirements/recommendations for international students: Required—TOEFL (minimum score 570 paper-based; 230 computer-based; 89 iBT). *Application deadline:* For fall admission, 1/1 priority date for domestic and international students; for spring admission, 8/15 priority date for domestic and international students. Applications are processed on a rolling basis. Application fee: $75. Electronic applications accepted. *Expenses:* Tuition: Full-time $39,600; part-time $1650 per credit. Required fees: $1896. *Financial support:* Fellowships, research assistantships, teaching assistantships, career-related internships or fieldwork and institutionally sponsored loans available. Financial award application deadline: 1/15. *Faculty research:* Human-computer interaction and usability; media design, theory and culture; visual communication and graphics; professional and technical communication; communication in technologically-mediated contexts. *Unit head:* Prof. James P. Zappen, Head, 518-276-6468, Fax: 518-276-4092, E-mail: zappenj@rpi.edu. *Application contact:* Kathy A. Colman, Recruitment Coordinator, 518-276-6469, Fax: 518-276-4092, E-mail: colmak@rpi.edu.

Rochester Institute of Technology, Graduate Enrollment Services, Center for Multidisciplinary Studies, Program in Technical Information Design, Rochester, NY 14623-5603. Offers AC. Part-time programs available. Postbaccalaureate distance learning degree programs offered (no on-campus study). *Students:* 1 (woman) part-time. 1 applicant, 100% accepted, 1 enrolled. *Entrance requirements:* Additional exam requirements/recommendations for international students: Required—TOEFL (minimum score 550 paper-based; 213 computer-based; 79 iBT) or IELTS (minimum score 6.5). *Application deadline:* For fall admission, 2/15 priority date for domestic and international students; for winter admission, 11/1 priority date for domestic students, 10/1 priority date for international students; for spring admission, 2/1 priority date for domestic students, 1/1 priority date for international students. Applications are processed on a rolling basis. Electronic applications accepted. *Expenses:* Tuition: Full-time $33,234; part-time $924 per credit hour. Required fees: $219. *Financial support:* Career-related internships or fieldwork and scholarships/grants available. Support available to part-time students. Financial award applicants required to submit FAFSA. *Unit head:* Thomas Moran, Program Chair, 585-475-4936, E-mail: tfmcad@rit.edu. *Application contact:* Diane Ellison, Assistant Vice President, Graduate Enrollment Services, 585-475-2229, Fax: 585-475-7164, E-mail: gradinfo@rit.edu.

Southern Polytechnic State University, School of Arts and Sciences, Department of English, Technical Communication, and Media Arts, Marietta, GA 30060-2896. Offers communications management (AGC); content development (AGC); information and instructional design (MSIID); information design and communication (MS); instructional design (AGC); technical communication (Graduate Certificate); visual communication and graphics (AGC). Part-time and evening/weekend programs available. Postbaccalaureate distance learning degree programs offered (no on-campus study). *Faculty:* 4 full-time (3 women), 1 (woman) part-time/adjunct. *Students:* 2 full-time (both women), 61 part-time (40 women); includes 19 Black or African American, non-Hispanic/Latino; 1 Two or more races, non-Hispanic/Latino, 3 international. Average age 38. 37 applicants, 100% accepted, 29 enrolled. In 2010, 6 master's, 5 other advanced degrees awarded. *Degree requirements:* For master's, thesis or internship; for other advanced degree, thesis optional, 18 hours completed through thesis option (6 hours), internship option (6 hours) or advanced coursework option (6 hours). *Entrance requirements:* For master's, GRE, statement of purpose, writing sample, professional recommendations, timed essay; for other advanced degree, writing sample, professional recommendations. Additional exam requirements/recommendations for international students: Required—TOEFL (minimum score 550 paper-based; 213 computer-based; 79 iBT), IELTS (minimum score 6.5). *Application deadline:* For fall admission, 5/1 priority date for domestic students, 7/1 priority date for international students; for spring admission, 9/1 priority date for domestic students, 11/1 priority date for international students. Applications are processed on a rolling basis. Application fee: $20. Electronic applications accepted. *Expenses:* Tuition, state resident: full-time $3690; part-time $205 per semester hour. Tuition, nonresident: full-time $13,428; part-time $746 per semester hour. Required fees: $598 per semester. *Financial support:* Research assistantships with tuition reimbursements, teaching assistantships with tuition reimbursements, career-related internships or fieldwork, Federal Work-Study, scholarships/grants, and unspecified assistantships available. Support available to part-time students. Financial award application deadline: 5/1; financial award applicants required to submit FAFSA. *Faculty research:* Usability, user-centered design, instructional design, information architecture, information design. *Unit head:* Dr. Mark Nunes, Chair, 678-915-7202, Fax: 678-915-7425, E-mail: mnunes@spsu.edu. *Application contact:* Nikki Palamiotis, Director of Graduate Studies, 678-915-4276, Fax: 678-915-7292, E-mail: npalamio@spsu.edu.

Texas State University–San Marcos, Graduate School, College of Liberal Arts, Department of English, Program in Technical Communication, San Marcos, TX 78666. Offers MA. *Faculty:* 6 full-time (4 women). *Students:* 8 full-time (7 women), 18 part-time (13 women); includes 1 Black or African American, non-Hispanic/Latino; 3 Hispanic/Latino; 2 Two or more races, non-Hispanic/Latino. Average age 32. 10 applicants, 100% accepted, 9 enrolled. In 2010, 11 master's awarded. *Degree requirements:* For master's, comprehensive exam, thesis or alternative. *Entrance requirements:* For master's, course work in English, 3 letters of reference, at least 2 non-fiction papers (15 typed, double-spaced pages), 1 academic research paper. Additional exam requirements/recommendations for international students: Required—TOEFL (minimum score 550 paper-based; 213 computer-based; 78 iBT). *Application deadline:* For fall admission, 6/15 priority date for domestic students, 6/1 for international students; for spring admission, 11/1 priority date for domestic students, 10/1 for international students. Applications are processed on a rolling basis. Application fee: $40 ($90 for international students). Electronic applications accepted. *Expenses:* Tuition, state resident: full-time $6024; part-time $251 per credit hour. Tuition, nonresident: full-time $13,536; part-time $564 per credit hour. Required fees: $1776; $50 per credit hour. $306 per semester. *Financial support:* In 2010–11, 7 students received support, including 1 teaching assistantship (averaging $6,289 per year); research assistantships, Federal Work-Study and institutionally sponsored loans also available. Support available to part-time students. Financial award application deadline: 4/1. *Unit head:* Dr. Libby Allison, Graduate Advisor, 512-245-2163, Fax: 512-245-8546, E-mail: ea10@txstate.edu. *Application contact:* Dr. J. Michael Willoughby, Dean of Graduate School, 512-245-2581, Fax: 512-245-8365, E-mail: gradcollege@txstate.edu.

University of Colorado Denver, College of Liberal Arts and Sciences, Department of Communication, Denver, CO 80217-3364. Offers academic track (MA); professional track/communication management (MA); technical communication (MS). Part-time and evening/weekend programs available. *Faculty:* 9 full-time (4 women), 3 part-time/adjunct (1 woman). *Students:* 15 full-time (12 women), 7 part-time (5 women); includes 2 Hispanic/Latino, 1 international. Average age 30. 21 applicants, 48% accepted, 5 enrolled. In 2010, 6 master's awarded. *Degree requirements:* For master's, thesis (for some programs), 33 credits. *Entrance requirements:* For master's, GRE General Test. Additional exam requirements/recommendations for international students: Required—TOEFL (minimum score 525 paper-based; 197 computer-based). *Application deadline:* For fall admission, 4/1 for domestic students; for spring admission, 10/1 for domestic students. Application fee: $50 ($75 for international students). Electronic applications accepted. *Expenses:* Tuition, state resident: full-time $7332; part-time $355 per credit hour. Tuition, nonresident: full-time $18,990; part-time $1055 per credit hour. Required fees: $998. Tuition and fees vary according to course level, course load, degree level, campus/location, program, reciprocity agreements and student level. *Financial support:* Fellowships, research assistantships, teaching assistantships, Federal Work-Study and scholarships/grants available. Financial award application deadline: 4/1; financial award applicants required to submit FAFSA. *Faculty research:* Diversity, difference, and intercultural communication; health communication/medical rhetoric; organizational communication; rhetoric and public affairs; social justice and civic engagement. *Unit head:* Dr. Lisa Keranen, Professor, 303-556-5668, E-mail: lisa.keranen@ucdenver.edu. *Application contact:* Michelle Medal, Program Assistant, 303-556-2591, E-mail: michelle.medal@ucdenver.edu.

University of Houston–Downtown, College of Humanities and Social Sciences, Department of English, Houston, TX 77002. Offers professional writing and technical communication (MS). Part-time and evening/weekend programs available. *Faculty:* 9 full-time (4 women). *Students:* 4 full-time (all women), 17 part-time (12 women); includes 4 Black or African American, non-Hispanic/Latino; 1 Asian, non-Hispanic/Latino; 2 Hispanic/Latino, 1 international. Average age 35. 6 applicants, 83% accepted, 4 enrolled. In 2010, 7 master's awarded. *Degree requirements:* For master's, thesis optional, graduation portfolio with oral defense. *Entrance requirements:* For master's, GRE (including Analytical Writing section), personal application statement, resume, writing sample, 3 letters of recommendation. Additional exam requirements/recommendations for international students: Required—TOEFL (minimum score 600 paper-based; 250 computer-based; 86 iBT). *Application deadline:* For fall admission, 3/15 for domestic and international students; for spring admission, 11/15 for domestic and international students. Application fee: $35 ($60 for international students). Electronic applications accepted. *Expenses:* Tuition, state resident: full-time $4280; part-time $183 per credit hour. Tuition, nonresident: full-time $9230; part-time $458 per credit hour. Required fees: $390 per term. *Financial support:* Applicants required to submit FAFSA. *Faculty research:* Environmental rhetoric, instructional design, usability, assessment, presentation slides. *Unit head:* Dr. Robert Jarrett, Chair, 713-221-8013, Fax: 713-226-5205, E-mail: jarrettr@uhd.edu. *Application contact:* Dr. Michelle Moosally, Coordinator of MS in Professional Writing and Technical Communication and Professor, Department of English, 713-221-8013, Fax: 713-226-5205, E-mail: mspwtc@uhd.edu.

University of Nebraska at Omaha, Graduate Studies, College of Arts and Sciences, Department of English, Omaha, NE 68182. Offers advanced writing (Certificate); English (MA); teaching English to speakers of other languages (Certificate); technical communication (Certificate). Part-time and evening/weekend programs available. *Faculty:* 16 full-time (8 women). *Students:* 22 full-time (9 women), 58 part-time (44 women); includes 3 minority (1 Asian, non-Hispanic/Latino; 2 Two or more races, non-Hispanic/Latino), 2 international. Average age 32. 48 applicants, 79% accepted, 27 enrolled. In 2010, 17 master's, 15 other advanced degrees awarded. *Degree requirements:* For master's, comprehensive exam, thesis (for some programs). *Entrance requirements:* For master's, minimum GPA of 3.0, 3 letters of recommendation, writing sample. Additional exam requirements/recommendations for international students: Required—TOEFL (minimum score 600 paper-based; 250 computer-based; 100 iBT). *Application deadline:* For fall admission, 8/1 priority date for domestic students; for spring admission, 12/1 priority date for domestic students. Applications are processed on a rolling basis. Application fee: $45. Electronic applications accepted. *Financial support:* In 2010–11, 46 students received support; fellowships, teaching assistantships with tuition reimbursements available, Federal Work-Study, institutionally sponsored loans, scholarships/grants, tuition waivers (partial), and unspecified assistantships available. Support available to part-time students. Financial award application deadline: 3/1; financial award applicants required to submit FAFSA. *Unit head:* Dr. Robert Darcy, Chairperson, 402-554-3636. *Application contact:* Dr. Tracy Bridgeford, Student Contact, 402-554-3636.

University of Washington, Graduate School, College of Engineering, Department of Human Centered Design and Engineering, Seattle, WA 98195-2315. Offers global technology and communication (MS, PhD); human centered design and engineering (MS, PhD); inter-engineering technical Japanese (MSE); technical communication (MS, PhD), including global technology and communication (MS), technical communication, user centered design; user centered design (MS, PhD). Part-time and evening/weekend programs available. Postbaccalaureate distance learning degree programs offered (no on-campus study). *Faculty:* 16 full-time (11 women), 8 part-time/adjunct (6 women). *Students:* 41 full-time (28 women), 99 part-time (49 women); includes 4 Black or African American, non-Hispanic/Latino; 15 Asian, non-Hispanic/Latino; 9 Hispanic/Latino, 6 international. Average age 34. 184 applicants, 54% accepted, 61 enrolled. In 2010, 32 master's, 3 doctorates awarded. *Degree requirements:* For master's, thesis or alternative; for doctorate, comprehensive exam, thesis/dissertation, preliminary, general, and final exams. *Entrance requirements:* For master's and doctorate, GRE General Test, minimum GPA of 3.0, transcripts, 3 letters of recommendation, curriculum vitae, personal statement of objectives. Additional exam requirements/recommendations for international students: Required—TOEFL (minimum score 600 paper-based; 237 computer-based; 92 iBT). *Application deadline:* For fall admission, 12/21 for domestic students, 11/15 priority date for international students. Applications are processed on a rolling basis. Application fee: $75. Electronic applications accepted. *Financial support:* In 2010–11, 1 student received support, including 1 fellowship with full tuition reimbursement available (averaging $22,500 per year), 14 research assistantships with full tuition reimbursements available (averaging $14,751 per year), 16 teaching assistantships with full tuition reimbursements available (averaging $13,725 per year); career-related internships or fieldwork, institutionally sponsored loans, and tuition waivers (full) also available. Financial award application deadline: 2/28; financial award applicants required to submit FAFSA. *Faculty research:* Human/computer interaction, communication design, user interface design and usability, new media design, comprehension processes. Total annual research expenditures: $1.5 million. *Unit head:* Dr. Jan Spyridakis, Professor and Chair, 206-685-1557, Fax: 206-543-8858, E-mail: jansp@u.washington.edu. *Application contact:* Gian Bruno, Academic Counselor, 206-543-1798, Fax: 206-543-8858, E-mail: gbruno@u.washington.edu.

University of Wisconsin–Milwaukee, Graduate School, College of Letters and Sciences, Department of English, Milwaukee, WI 53201-0413. Offers creative writing (PhD); English (MA); international technical communication (Certificate); linguistics (PhD); professional writing (PhD); professional writing and communication (Certificate); rhetoric and composition (PhD);

Technical Communication

University of Wisconsin–Milwaukee (continued)
MLIS/MA. *Faculty:* 40 full-time (19 women). *Students:* 106 full-time (62 women), 65 part-time (45 women); includes 4 Black or African American, non-Hispanic/Latino; 5 Asian, non-Hispanic/Latino, 17 international. Average age 34. 208 applicants, 54% accepted, 29 enrolled. In 2010, 19 master's, 14 doctorates awarded. *Degree requirements:* For master's, thesis or alternative; for doctorate, one foreign language, thesis/dissertation. *Entrance requirements:* For master's, GRE General Test, GRE Subject Test; for doctorate, GRE. Additional exam requirements/recommendations for international students: Required—TOEFL (minimum score 550 paper-based; 79 iBT), IELTS (minimum score 6.5). *Application deadline:* For fall admission, 1/1 priority date for domestic students; for spring admission, 9/1 for domestic students. Applications are processed on a rolling basis. Application fee: $56 ($96 for international students). Electronic applications accepted. *Financial support:* In 2010–11, 4 fellowships, 1 research assistantship, 84 teaching assistantships were awarded; career-related internships or fieldwork, unspecified assistantships, and project assistantships also available. Support available to part-time students. Financial award application deadline: 4/15; financial award applicants required to submit FAFSA. Total annual research expenditures: $36,259. *Unit head:* Tasha Oren, Representative, 414-229-6625, Fax: 414-229-2643, E-mail: tgoren@uwm.edu. *Application contact:* General Information Contact, 414-229-4982, Fax: 414-229-6967, E-mail: gradschool@uwm.edu.

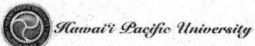

HAWAI'I PACIFIC UNIVERSITY

Program in Communication

Program of Study

The Master of Arts in Communication program (M.A./COM) provides students with an interdisciplinary approach integrating skills, theory, and knowledge. Students completing this Hawai'i Pacific University (HPU) program are prepared for careers ranging across the spectrum of business, marketing, advertising, mass media, public relations, entertainment, broadcast or print journalism, the Internet, or education. Technology is emphasized in each course so that graduates are prepared for rapid change in communication industries.

The M.A./COM requires a minimum of 39 semester hours of graduate work composed of 12 semester hours of core courses, 21 semester hours of electives, and 6 semester hours of writing a professional paper, project, or thesis. Assignments and internships use a pragmatic approach to develop marketable skills. Students apply what they learn in the classroom to actual problems faced by organizations and businesses.

Research Facilities

To support graduate studies, HPU's Meader and Atherton Libraries hold over 110,000 bound volumes, 350,000 microfiche items, and periodical subscriptions to 1,500 print titles and 30,000 electronic journals. Databases of public and state university libraries, legislative information, and business-oriented statistical data are also available in the library or online. Students can access HPU's library databases, course information, their academic information, and an e-mail account through Pipeline, the university's internal Web site for students. The University's accessible on-campus computer center houses more than 420 computers with specialized software to support graduate academic programs. HPU also provides free Wi-Fi so students can access Pipeline resources anywhere on campus using laptops. A significant number of online courses are available as well.

Financial Aid

The University participates in all federal financial aid programs designated for graduate students. These programs provide aid in the form of subsidized (need-based) and unsubsidized (non-need-based) Federal Stafford Student Loans. Through these loans, funds may be available to cover the student's entire cost of education. To apply for aid, students must submit the Free Application for Federal Student Aid (FAFSA) beginning January 1.

The University also offers institutional graduate scholarships to new full-time degree-seeking students. U.S. citizens, permanent residents, and international students who have a demonstrated financial need may apply. HPU's graduate scholarships include the Graduate Trustee Scholarship ($6000 for two semesters), the Graduate Dean Scholarship ($4000 for two semesters), and the Graduate Kokua Scholarship ($2000 for two semesters). Factors that may be considered when evaluating requests are previous academic record, community involvement and service, and professional work experience and achievement.

In order to be eligible for the best award package, students should apply by HPU's priority deadline of March 1. Applications received after the priority deadline will be awarded on a funds-available basis. Mailing of student award letters usually begins by the end of March. Applicants will be notified by mail as decisions are made.

Cost of Study

Tuition for graduate students enrolled in fall and spring semesters is determined on a per-credit basis; full-time status for a graduate student is 9 credits. Tuition for the optional winter and summer sessions is also determined on a per-credit basis. The estimated minimum funds needed for a nine-month academic year (September to May) is $28,650. For the 2011–12 academic year, full-time tuition is $13,230 for most graduate degree programs, including the M.A./COM program. Other expenses including books, personal expenses, fees, and a student bus pass are estimated at $3190.

Living and Housing Costs

Most graduate students live in off-campus housing. The cost of living in off-campus apartments is approximately $12,230 for a double-occupancy room.

Student Group

University enrollment currently stands at more than 8,200. HPU is one of the most culturally diverse universities in America, with students from all fifty U.S. states and more than 100 countries. HPU strives to maintain a student profile that is one third Hawai'i, one third mainland U.S.A., and one third global.

Location

Hawai'i Pacific University's urban campus in downtown Honolulu provides a fast-paced, exciting environment in the heart of the business community. The downtown campus comprises six buildings in the center of Honolulu's business district and is home to the College of Business Administration and the College of Humanities and Social Sciences.

Eight miles away, the 135-acre windward Hawai'i Loa campus, which is set in the lush foothills of the Ko'olau mountains, is home to the College of Nursing and Health Sciences and the College of Natural and Computational Sciences. The Hawai'i Loa campus has residence halls, dining commons, the Educational Technology Center, a student center, and outdoor recreational facilities, including a soccer field, tennis courts, a softball field, and an exercise room.

HPU is also affiliated with the Oceanic Institute, a 56-acre aquaculture research facility located at Makapu'u Point on the southeastern coast of O'ahu, Hawai'i. At the facility, undergraduate and graduate students are able to get hands-on experience in marine science. All three sites are linked by HPU shuttle as well as easily accessed by public transportation.

Notably, the downtown campus location is within walking distance of shopping and dining. Iolani Palace, the only palace in the U.S., is a few blocks away, as are the State Capitol, City Hall, and the Blaisdell Concert Hall. The Honolulu Academy of Arts, Museum of Contemporary Art, Waikiki Aquarium, Honolulu Zoo, and many other cultural attractions are located nearby.

The University

HPU is a private, nonprofit university with approximately 8,200 students. Founded in 1965, HPU prides itself on maintaining strong academic programs, small class sizes, individual attention to students, and a diverse faculty and student population. HPU is recognized as a "Best Western" college by the Princeton Review and a "Best Buy in College Education" by *Barron's* business magazine. HPU offers more than fifty acclaimed undergraduate programs and fourteen distinguished graduate programs. The University has a faculty of more than 500, a student-faculty ratio of 15:1, and an average class size of fewer than 25 students. A wide range of counseling and other student support services are available. There are more than sixty student organizations on campus, including the Graduate Student Organization.

Applying

Students must have a baccalaureate degree from an accredited college or university in the United States or an equivalent degree from another country. Applicants should complete and forward a graduate admissions application, send in the $50 nonrefundable application fee, have official transcripts sent from all colleges or universities previously attended, and forward two letters of recommendation. A personal statement about the applicant's academic and career goals is required; submitting a resume is optional. Applicants who have taken the Graduate Record Examination (GRE) should have their scores sent directly to the Graduate Admissions Office. International students should submit scores of a recognized English proficiency test such as TOEFL. Admissions decisions are made on a rolling basis, and applicants are notified between one and two weeks after all documents have been submitted. Applicants are encouraged to submit their applications online.

Correspondence and Information

Graduate Admissions
Hawai'i Pacific University
1164 Bishop Street, #911
Honolulu, Hawaii 96813
Phone: 808-544-1135
      866-GRAD-HPU (toll-free)
Fax: 808-544-0200
E-mail: graduate@hpu.edu
Web site: http://www.hpu.edu/hpumacom

Hawai'i Pacific University

THE FACULTY

John N. Barnum, Associate Professor of Communication; Ph.D., Texas at Austin.
Peter Britos, Associate Professor of Communication; Ph.D., USC.
Dale Burke, Instructor of Communication; D.Min., Ancilla Domini College.
Brian Cannon, Assistant Professor of Communication; Ph.D., Regent University (Virginia).
Katherine Clarke, Instructor of Communication; M.A., Denver.
Thomas Dowd, Instructor of Communication; M.A., California State, Northridge.
Steven Combs, Professor of Communication; Ph.D., USC.
Matthew George, Assistant Professor of Communication; Ph.D., Berkley.
John P. Hart, Professor of Communication; Ph.D., Kansas.
Serena Hashimoto, Associate Professor of Communication; Ph.D., European Graduate School (Switzerland).
Lowell Ing, Assistant Professor of Communication; M.F.A., CUNY, City College.
Anne Kennedy, Assistant Professor of Communication; Ph.D., Bowling Green State.
Laurence LeDoux, Assistant Professor of Communication; D.A., Oregon.
Marianne Luken, Instructor of Communication; M.I.A., School for International Training.
Malia Smith, Instructor of Communication; M.A., Hawai'i Pacific.
Penny Pence Smith, Assistant Professor of Communication; Ph.D., North Carolina at Chapel Hill.
Lewis Trusty, Instructor of Communication; M.A., USC.
James D. Whitfield, Professor of Communication; Ed.D., Texas Tech.
John Windrow, Instructor of Journalism; M.A., Missouri–Columbia.
Yanjun Zhao, Assistant Professor of Organizational Change; Ph.D., Nebraska–Lincoln.

UNIVERSITY OF SOUTHERN CALIFORNIA

Annenberg School for Communication & Journalism
School of Journalism
School of Communication
Programs In Communication, Journalism, Public Diplomacy, and Public Relations

Programs of Study
Through the School of Journalism and the School of Communication, the USC Annenberg School for Communication & Journalism offers master's degrees in communication management, global communication, journalism, public diplomacy, and strategic public relations and a Ph.D. in communication.

The School of Journalism, accredited by the Accrediting Council on Education of Journalism and Mass Communication (ACEJMC), places innovative multiplatform storytelling, pioneering digital and social networking opportunities, experimentation, and entrepreneurialism at the center of all that is taught. The School emphasizes hands-on training, writing, ethics, and professional practice. In the traditional two-year journalism programs, an innovative core curriculum teaches newswriting, reporting, and production across multiple media platforms. Students can choose from one of five tracks—long-form video, news video, audio, text, and digital. Student involvement is found in *Neon Tommy*, an online digital news site, *Annenberg TV News*, the award-winning day-of-air broadcasting operation; *Impact*, an outlet for long-form storytelling; and *Annenberg Radio News*, the day-of-air radio broadcast. The strategic public relations program focuses on advocacy communication and equips students with the skills to succeed in agency, corporate, and nonprofit work. In the summer after the first year, students in journalism and strategic public relations may study and intern in Cape Town, Hong Kong, Shanghai, or London. In the nine-month specialized journalism programs, students focus on journalism leadership and decision making while completing graduate course work in academic disciplines outside of journalism. In the specialized journalism (the arts) program, art practitioners and artists learn how to write for publications while advancing their academic exposure to the arts.

The School of Communication offers five master's degrees. Communication management students completing the on-campus program concentrate their studies in one of seven tracks: entertainment management, health and social change communication, marketing communication, information and communication technologies, international communication, organizational and strategic corporate communication, and communication law and policy. In addition, post-master's degree certificate programs are offered in the same tracks. Students in the online communication management degree concentrate their studies in marketing and strategic communication.Through the Charles Annenberg Weingarten Program on Online Communities (APOC), students explore the effects, impact, implementation, and management of social networking in different areas of society and business.

Global communication students live and study in two dynamic, multicultural media capitals of the world—first in London at the London School of Economics and Political Science (LSE) and the second year in Los Angeles at USC Annenberg.

Public diplomacy students study the impact of private activities—from popular culture to fashion to sports to news—on the national interests of organizations, corporations, and governments worldwide. As part of the degree program, students complete a summer field experience abroad or in the United States after completing their first year. In addition to the two-year program, a one-year master's degree is offered for mid-career professionals with five years or more of experience in public diplomacy, international relations, or international communication.

Students in the Ph.D. program in communication focus their critical studies of inquiry through concentrations in global and transitional communication; groups, organizations and networks; health communication and social dynamics; information, political economy and entertainment; media, culture and community; new media technology; and rhetoric, politics and publics. Students acquire and demonstrate humanistic and behavioral knowledge of communication while acquiring the skills requisite to scholarly research in the discipline.

Research Facilities
The School is home to the Annenberg Innovation Lab, Center on Communication Leadership and Policy, Center for the Digital Future, the Norman Lear Center, and the Annenberg Center for Online Communities. It is also a partner with the Schools of Cinema/Television and Engineering in USC's Integrated Media Systems Center, the nation's only university-based multimedia research center, which is funded by the National Science Foundation, and, in partnership with the Dornsife College of Letters, Arts, and Sciences, the USC Center on Public Diplomacy.

The Strategic Public Relations Center plays a leading role in bridging the substantial gap between the public relations profession and the academic community that studies it. A host of centers affiliated with the School of Journalism may be explored on the USC Annenberg Web site.

Financial Aid
Merit scholarships for master's degree students in communication management, journalism, public diplomacy, and strategic public relations are awarded competitively based on the graduate admission application. All U.S. citizens and permanent residents are encouraged to apply for need-based federal financial aid. International students are eligible for merit scholarship consideration, and are required to submit a confidential statement of financial support. Ph.D. students receive full support for five years.

Cost of Study
For the 2011–12 academic year, the estimated cost for a full-time master's degree student (tuition and fees) is $28,400. The costs of housing, board, books, supplies, and personal expenses vary. For part-time graduate student estimates, please refer to the USC financial aid Web site at http://www.usc.edu/admission/fa/applying_receiving/graduates2/costs/html.

Living and Housing Costs
USC maintains a number of apartment buildings for graduate students only. Housing applications are sent to admitted students only. Rates for privately owned apartments near USC and elsewhere in greater Los Angeles are comparable to those in other large metropolitan areas. For more information on University housing options and rates, prospective students should visit http://housing.usc.edu.

Student Group
USC Annenberg enrolls approximately 800 graduate students. Thirty percent are international students. Some students enter the programs directly after earning the bachelor's degree; however, the majority of students have had some professional work experience. The majority of Ph.D. students have completed a master's degree before enrolling at USC Annenberg. Most communication management students work or intern during the day, and many attend school part-time. Other master's degree and Ph.D. students attend daytime and evening classes. Graduate student organizations are active in this vibrant student-centered community.

Student Outcomes
School of Journalism graduates work at many of the nation's leading media and public relations organizations, such as ABC, CBS, NBC, CNN, Ketchum Public Relations, Manning Selvage & Lee, Weber Shandwick Worldwide, Ogilvy & Mather, EXPN, C-SPAN, CNBC, KMEX, Telemundo, KWHY, AOL, varity.com, LATimes.com, eCompanies, WashingtonPost.com, and the Associated Press. Communication management and global communication program graduates pursue careers in marketing communications and public relations, mass media, multimedia and interactive media management, media research and analysis, entertainment management, telecommunications, law and public policy, corporate communications, nonprofit management, and consulting. Graduates work at firms such as Warner Bros., FOXSports.com, GameSpot.com, AOL, McKinsey, KPMG, Nestlé USA, DIRECTV, MGM, Pacific Bell, and ABC TV.

The majority of Ph.D. graduates pursue careers in academia at such institutions as Georgetown University, Johns Hopkins University, Michigan State University, North Carolina State University, Northwestern University, City University of Hong Kong, Tokyo University, and the Universities of Illinois, Indiana, Texas at Austin, and Wisconsin. Ph.D. graduates also work in research, strategic analysis, and consulting with firms such as NuStats, the Pacific Telesis Group, Jet Propulsion Laboratory, and Frank Magid Associates.

Location
Los Angeles is a world capital of communication, entertainment, and multimedia. Many opportunities exist to contact and interact with alumni and other professionals and senior management, and for research in such areas as interactive media, radio/television/film, telecommunications, information systems, public and government policy, corporate communication, and marketing.

The School
Home to approximately 2,276 graduate and undergraduate students and 102 full-time faculty members, the USC Annenberg School is poised to tackle questions of our times with strategies and alternatives that serve the public good. The School's vibrant, intellectual community is enhanced by having Los Angeles as a neighborhood laboratory, providing critical exposure to new ideas, hands-on learning experiences, and professional opportunities. USC Annenberg offers professional academic advising, career development services, international programs, and a host of speaking series to compliment classroom instruction.

Applying
All applicants must complete the online USC Graduate Admission Application with required supplemental materials, including a professional resume, a statement of purpose, writing samples or scholarly writing, and letters of recommendation. Graduate Record Examinations (GRE) General Test scores are required for admission to all graduate degree programs, with two exceptions: the GRE is not required for admission to the global communication degree program, and the GMAT is accepted in lieu of the GRE for admission to the communication management degree program. Proof of English language proficiency is required if the student's native language or language of instruction for their bachelor's degree is not English. Students must refer to the USC Annenberg Web site for graduate admission application guidelines for instructions.

In addition to the online USC graduate admission application, applicants to the M.A./M.Sc. in global communication program must complete the online LSE application.

Correspondence and Information
Admissions Office
Annenberg School for Communication & Journalism
University of Southern California
3502 Watt Way, Suite 140
Los Angeles, California 90089-0281
Phone: 213-821-0770
Web site: http://annenberg.usc.edu

University of Southern California

THE FACULTY AND THEIR RESEARCH

School of Journalism

Alan Abrahamson, J.D., Lecturer. Former staff writer at *Los Angeles Times* and columnist at NBCOlympics.com, NBCSports.com, and UniversalSports.com.

Sasha Anawalt, B.A., Lecturer and Director of Arts Journalism Programs. Author of *The Joffrey Ballet: Robert Joffrey and the making of An American Dance.* Former dance critic for *Los Angeles Herald Examiner* and *LA Weekly.*

Daniel H. Birman, M.A., Professor of Professional Practice. Nonfiction/documentary producer, executive producer for USC Annenberg's *Impact.*

Laura Castañeda, Ed.D., Associate Professor of Professional Practice and Associate Director, School of Journalism. Former AP and business reporter, coeditor, coauthor.

William Celis, M.S., Associate Professor and Associate Director, School of Journalism. Author of *Battle Rock: The Struggle Over a One-Room School in America's Vanishing West.* Former education correspondent, reporter, columnist.

Serena Cha, M.S., Director and Faculty Adviser, Annenberg TV News. Former TV producer.

Dana Chinn, M.B.A., Lecturer. Senior consultant, Media Insight Group.

K. C. Cole, B.A., Professor. Science writer, columnist, editor, writer, author of seven books, including *The Universe and the Teacup: The Mathematics of Truth and Beauty.*

Marc Cooper Associate Professor of Professional Practice and Associate Director, Annenberg Digital News. Senior editor, contributing editor, contributing writer, author of 3 nonfiction books, codirects the News21 project.

Norman Corwin, B.A., Visiting Professor and Writer-in-Residence. Radio/television dramatist, writer of stage plays and books.

Geoffrey Cowan, L.L.B., University Professor and Annenberg Family Chair in Communication Leadership. Communication law attorney, Emmy Award–winning producer, playwright, newspaper columnist.

Ed Cray, B.A., Professor. Journalist, author of eighteen books.

Jennifer Floto, M.A., Associate Professor of Professional Practice. Former vice president/creative director of Ketchum Public Relations.

Félix Gutiérrez, Ph.D., Professor. Former senior vice president of Freedom Forum and Newseum, author/coauthor of chapters, scholarly articles, and books on Latinos and other racial/ethnic groups.

Jay T. Harris, B.A., Professor and Wallis Annenberg Chair in Journalism and Democracy. Formerly chairman and publisher of *San Jose Mercury News;* V.P. of operations, Knight-Ridder Inc.; executive editor, *Philadelphia Daily News.*

Robert Hernandez, B.A., Assistant Professor of Professional Practice. Former senior news director of development, *Seattle Times;* Web designer and consultant, El Salvador's *La Prensa Gráfica;* Web producer, *San Francisco Chronicle;* online editor, *San Francisco Examiner.*

Henry Jenkins, Ph.D., Provost's Professor of Communication, Journalism, and Cinematic Arts. Role of journalism in digital age, new media technologies in educational settings, transmedia storytelling.

Gabriel Kahn, B.A., Professor of Professional Practice. Former L.A. bureau chief, deputy bureau chief, Southern Europe, and Hong Kong for *Wall Street Journal.*

Jonathan Kotler, J.D., Associate Professor. Attorney, coauthor, former dean of USC Graduate School.

Josh Kun, Ph.D., Associate Professor. Author, director of the Popular Music Project at Norman Lear Center. Music, popular culture, U.S.-Mexico border, race.

Andrew Lih, M.S., Associate Professor. New media researcher, consultant, former video and multimedia journalist for *Wall Street Journal Online,* and author of *The Wikipedia Revolution: How a Bunch of Nobodies Created the World's Greatest Encyclopedia.*

Alan Mittelstaedt, B.A., Lecturer and Managing Editor of Annenberg Digital News. Former city editor, *Portland Press Herald* (Maine) and *Pasadena Star-News.*

Judy Muller, B.A., Associate Professor. Commentator, author, former *ABC News* and *CBS News* correspondent and radio anchor.

Mary Murphy, B.A., Senior Lecturer. Former reporter and news producer, *Entertainment Tonight,* contributing editor for *Los Angeles Times Magazine,* and coauthor.

Bryce Nelson, M. Phil., Professor. Former reporter, spokesman for Christopher Commission, and Director of School of Journalism.

Geneva Overholser, M.S., Professor and Director, School of Journalism. Award-winning journalist and media scholar, former editor, syndicated columnist, coeditor.

Tim Page, B.A., Professor. Chief music critic and culture writer for the *Washington Post,* Grammy Award nominee, author, winner of Pulitzer Prize in Criticism (1997).

Michael Parks, B.A., Professor. Former editor, executive vice president, vice president of Times Mirror Co., bureau chief, winner of Pulitzer Prize in International Reporting (1987).

Larry Pryor, M.S., Associate Professor. Founding editor of *Online Journalism Review;* former *Los Angeles Times* Web-site editor and newspaper writer, editor, and reporter. New media topics.

Richard Reeves, M.E., Senior Lecturer. Author of eleven books, syndicated columnist, former chief correspondent, national editor, magazine columnist, chief political correspondent.

Joe Saltzman, M.S., Professor. News and documentary writer/reporter/producer, author, director of the Image of the Journalist in Popular Culture project.

Stacy Scholder, B.A. Associate Director, *Annenberg TV News.* Former television producer, executive producer, news producer.

Philip Seib, J.D., Professor and Director of the USC Center on Public Diplomacy. Author of numerous books, coeditor. International communication issues related to new media technologies, democratization, war, terrorism.

Willa Seidenberg, B.A., Associate Professor of Professional Practice and Director, *Annenberg Radio News.* Former radio reporter, anchor, producer, TV news writer, coauthor.

Erna Smith, B.A., Professor of Professional Practice. Author of several studies on race and the media, former reporter and editor at several newspapers. Diversity issues in journalism, journalism education.

Roberto Suro, M.S., Professor. Newspaper print journalist in foreign, domestic, and Washington coverage; author; founding director, Pew Hispanic Center. Hispanic population.

Jerry Swerling, M.S., Professor of Professional Practice and Director, Strategic Public Relations Center. Principal of Swerling & Associates, Communications Management and Organizational Consulting.

Burghardt Tenderich, Ph.D., Associate Professor and Associate Director, Strategic Public Relations Center. Founding partner of TnT Initiatives, LLC; former vice president of public relations, Siebel Systems; senior V.P. and partner at Applied Communication.

Kjerstin Thorson, Ph.D., Assistant Professor. Effects of digital and social media on political engagement, activism and engagement.

Sandy Tolan, Associate Professor. Radio and print journalist, author, producer of radio documentaries and features.

Jian Wang, Ph.D., Associate Professor. Author, former senior communications specialist for McKinsey & Co., and former consultant for Ketchum Public Relations.

Diane Winston, Ph.D., Associate Professor and Knight Chair in Media and Religion. Author, columnist, coeditor. Former newspaper reporter, television news writer, independent documentary filmmaker.

School of Communication

Jonathan D. Aronson, Ph.D., Professor. Cofounded Annenberg Research Network on International Communication. Former director, USC School of International Relations. Communications policy, globalization, and international trade and trade negotiations.

Sandra Ball-Rokeach, Ph.D., Associate Professor. Rockefeller and Fulbright Fellow. On editorial boards of various journals, coeditor of *Communication Research.* Transformation of urban communities.

Anne Balsamo, Ph.D., Professor and Director of Learning, Annenberg Innovation Lab. Author. Relationship between culture and technology.

Sarah Banet-Weiser, Ph.D., Associate Professor. Author and coeditor. Popular culture, media and consumer culture, with focus on race, gender, and citizenship.

François Bar, Ph.D., Associate Professor and Director, Annenberg Research Network on International Communication. Continuing evolution of communication networks, including deployment, regulation, and business use.

Daniela Baroffio-Bota, Ph.D., Clinical Assistant Professor. How feminism, U.S. militarism, and race in post-9/11 portrayals of female soldiers consolidate traditional national ideologies and offer potential for resistance against patriarchal systems.

Ergin Bayrak, Ph.D., Lecturer. Economics of media and communication industries, economics of radio spectrum, economic literacy and entrepreneurship, and economics of innovation.

Manuel Castells, Ph.D., Professor and Wallis Annenberg Chair in Communication Technology and Society. Mass media, communication networks, and political power.

Peter Clarke, Ph.D., Professor. Author and former dean. Communication and health behavior; programs to improve public's well-being, especially among underserved groups.

Michael J. Cody, Ph.D., Professor. Author and editor. Interpersonal communication and persuasion.

Jeffrey Cole, Ph.D., Research Professor and Director, Annenberg Center for the Digital Future. Founder/director of the World Internet Project. Effects of media policy, violence, and computer and Internet technology on all aspects of society.

Geoffrey Cowan, L.L.B., University Professor and Annenberg Family Chair in Communication Leadership. Former director, *Voice of America;* communication law attorney; Emmy Award–winning producer, playwright, and newspaper columnist.

David Craig, M.A., Senior Lecturer. Film and television producer and former programming executive.

Nicholas Cull, Ph.D., Professor and Director, Master of Public Diplomacy Program. Author of numerous articles, including *Selling War.*

Matthew Curtis, Ph.D., Clinical Assistant Professor. How individuals and groups compare themselves to others to understand their role in work and social settings.

Daniel Durbin, Ph.D., Clinical Professor and Director of the Institute of Sports, Media, and Society. Rhetoric of sports, health, fitness, nutrition, and medicine; promotion of health, fitness, and medicine in popular-press advertising.

Robeson Taj P. Frazier, Ph.D., Assistant Professor. Race and ethnicity, comparative political economy, popular culture, sport, globalization, transnationalism and internationalism.

Janet Fulk, Ph.D., Professor. Author. Impact of communication systems on collaboration and knowledge distribution across boundaries of space, time, team, organization, and nation.

G. Thomas Goodnight, Ph.D., Professor and Director, Doctoral Studies. Deliberation and postwar society, science communication, argument and aesthetics, public discourse.

Jerrold Green, Ph.D., Research Professor. Formerly with RAND Corporation; partner, Best-Associates, merchant banking.

Larry Gross, Ph.D., Professor and Director, School of Communication. Author and editor. Media and culture, visual communication, media portrayals of minorities.

Thomas A. Hollihan, Ph.D., Professor. Arguments that shape public policy and political discourse; including issues of citizenship and community in postmodern age.

Andrea B. Hollingshead, Ph.D., Professor. Strategic communication, knowledge sharing, social influence, decision making in teams and online communities.

Yu Hong, Ph.D., Assistant Professor. ICTs and development, political economy of global communication, China's information and communications industry, information labor.

Lian Jian, Ph.D., Assistant Professor. Economics of online information systems.

Colleen Keough, Ph.D., Clinical Associate Professor. Strategic planning and financial management workshops in Central and Eastern Europe. Research: role of communications in conflict management.

Josh Kun, Ph.D., Associate Professor. Author of *Audiotopia;* directs the Popular Music Project at the Norman Lear Center. Music, popular culture, U.S.-Mexico border, race.

Randall Lake, Ph.D., Associate Professor. Writer. Contemporary rhetorical theory and practice, particularly political and public argumentation.

Andrew Lakoff, Ph.D., Associate Professor. Author. Global health and biosecurity.

Dorinne Lawrence-Hughes, J.D., Lecturer. Public speaking and debate.

Ben Lee, Ph.D., Clinical Associate Professor and Assistant Director, Communication Management Program. Sociologist and statistician. Human behavior in financial markets.

Kwan Min Lee, Ph.D., Assistant Professor. Author of "hot paper" in social sciences. Sociopsychological effects of new information and communication technologies, including human-computer and human-robot interaction.

James Maritato, M.A., Lecturer and Assistant Director of Public Debate and Forensics. Argumentation and rhetorical theory, mass media effects, impact of new media technologies on public understanding of social and political issues.

Doe Mayer, Professor and Mary Pickford Chair, School of Cinematic Arts. Coauthor of *Creative Filmmaking From the Inside Out.* Practical international application of communication campaign strategies and designs for social issues and health-defined organizations.

Margaret McLaughlin, Ph.D., Professor and Associate Dean of Faculty Affairs and Research. Key investigator at Integrated Media Systems Center. Use of virtual environments in delivery of health and social services.

Lynn C. Miller, Ph.D., Professor. Use of multidisciplinary approaches to create intelligent agents and virtual worlds for testing communication theory and enhancing health and educational outcomes.

Peter R. Monge, Ph.D., Professor. Coauthor and editor. Communication networks in a variety of social contexts, ecology of communication processes within organizational communities.

Sheila T. Murphy, Ph.D., Associate Professor. Emotion and cognition and their influence on judgments and beliefs, decision making, information processing, agenda setting, politics.

Stephen O'Leary, Ph.D., Associate Professor. Author. Religious communication, rhetorical theory, criticism.

Patricia Riley, Ph.D., Associate Professor and Director, M.A./M.Sc. in Global Communication Program. Author and consultant. Organizational communication and politics, culture change, knowledge management.

Robert Scheer, Clinical Professor. Journalist and nationally syndicated columnist, author, editor, radio host.

Kenneth K. Sereno, Ph.D., Associate Professor. Communication theory, persuasion, interpersonal and family communication, humor's role in intimate relationships, effect of "clicker" technology in classroom.

Paolo Sigismondi, Ph.D., Clinical Assistant Professor. Phenomena of globalization forged by new technologies and economic forces.

Christopher Smith, Ph.D., Clinical Associate Professor and Director, Johnson Communication Leadership Center. Modern financial markets and impact on everyday culture, entertainment's role in public diplomacy.

Stacy Smith, Ph.D., Associate Professor. Children's reactions to mass media—developmental differences in emotional and cognitive processing; content patterns and effects of media on youth.

Gordon Stables, Ph.D., Clinical Associate Professor and Director, USC Trojan Debate Squad. Rhetoric and argumentation, policy debate and forensics, public debate on global war on terrorism.

Kimberlie Stephens, Ph.D., Clinical Assistant Professor. Strategic communication, organizational design, interorganizational relationships.

Jonathan Taplin, Clinical Professor and Director, Annenberg Innovation Lab. TV and film producer.

Douglas Thomas, Ph.D., Associate Professor. Founding editor of *Games & Culture: A Journal of Interactive Media.*

Alison Trope, Ph.D., Clinical Associate Professor. Media history, media exhibition, popular culture, gender representation, and museum studies.

Rebecca Weintraub, Ph.D., Clinical Professor and Director of the Communication Management Program. Branding, interpersonal communication, marketing and organizational communication.

Susan Resnick West, Ph.D., Clinical Associate Professor. Author on performance appraisal, management of professional employees, and evaluation of strategic change efforts.

Dmitri Williams, Ph.D., Associate Professor. Social and economic impacts of new media, emphasis on video games and Internet.

Ernest J. Wilson III, Ph.D., Professor, Walter Annenberg Chair in Communication, and Dean of the Annenberg School. Politics of global sustainable innovation in high-tech industries, China-Africa relations, and role of culture in U.S. national security policy.

Section 17
Conflict Resolution and Mediation/
Peace Studies

This section contains a directory of institutions offering graduate work in conflict resolution and mediation/peace studies, followed by an in-depth entry submitted by an institution that chose to prepare a detailed program description. Additional information about programs listed in the directory but not augmented by an in-depth entry may be obtained by writing directly to the dean of a graduate school or chair of a department at the address given in the directory.

For programs offering related work, see also in this book *Political Science and International Affairs* and *Public, Regional, and Industrial Affairs*. In another guide in this series:

Graduate Programs in Business, Education, Health, Information Studies, Law & Social Work

See *Business Administration and Management* and *Law*

CONTENTS

Conflict Resolution and Mediation/ Peace Studies

Abilene Christian University, Graduate School, College of Arts and Sciences, Department of Conflict Resolution, Abilene, TX 79699-9100. Offers conflict resolution (Certificate); conflict resolution and reconciliation (MA); conflict resolution for educators (Certificate). Part-time and evening/weekend programs available. Postbaccalaureate distance learning degree programs offered (minimal on-campus study). *Faculty:* 2 full-time (0 women), 3 part-time/adjunct (1 woman). *Students:* 13 full-time (10 women), 101 part-time (66 women); includes 27 Black or African American, non-Hispanic/Latino; 1 Asian, non-Hispanic/Latino; 6 Hispanic/Latino; 2 Two or more races, non-Hispanic/Latino, 7 international. 154 applicants, 38% accepted, 57 enrolled. In 2010, 31 master's, 42 other advanced degrees awarded. *Degree requirements:* For master's, practicum. *Entrance requirements:* Additional exam requirements/recommendations for international students: Required—TOEFL (minimum score 550 paper-based; 213 computer-based). *Application deadline:* For fall admission, 4/1 priority date for domestic students; for spring admission, 10/1 for domestic students. Applications are processed on a rolling basis. Application fee: $100. Electronic applications accepted. *Expenses:* Tuition: Full-time $12,906; part-time $717 per hour. Required fees: $1250; $61.50 per unit. *Financial support:* Available to part-time students. Applicants required to submit FAFSA. *Unit head:* Dr. Garry P. Bailey, Graduate Adviser, 325-674-2015, Fax: 325-674-2427, E-mail: garrybailey@acu.edu. *Application contact:* David Pittman, Graduate Admissions Counselor, 325-674-2656, Fax: 325-674-6717, E-mail: gradinfo@acu.edu.

American Public University System, AMU/APU Graduate Programs, Charles Town, WV 25414. Offers accounting (MBA); administration and supervision (M Ed); air warfare (MA Military Studies); asymmetrical warfare (MA Military Studies); criminal justice (MA); emergency and disaster management (MA); entrepreneurship (MBA); environmental policy and management (MS); finance (MBA); general (MBA); global business management (MBA); guidance and counseling (M Ed); history (MA); homeland security (MA); homeland security resource allocation (MBA); humanities (MA); information technology (MS); information technology management (MBA); intelligence studies (MA); international relations and conflict resolution (MA); joint warfare (MA Military Studies); land warfare (MA Military Studies); legal studies (MA); management (MA), including defense mangement, general, human resource management, organizational leadership, public administration; marketing (MBA); military history (MA); national security studies (MA); naval warfare (MA Military Studies); nonprofit management (MBA); political science (MA); psychology (MA); public administration (MA); public health (MA); security management (MA); space studies (MS); sports management (MS); strategic leadership (MA Military Studies); teaching (M Ed), including elementary, secondary social sciences; transportation and logistics management (MA). Programs offered via distance learning only. Part-time and evening/weekend programs available. Postbaccalaureate distance learning degree programs offered (no on-campus study). *Faculty:* 253 full-time (134 women), 1,208 part-time/adjunct (570 women). *Students:* 956 full-time (422 women), 8,476 part-time (2,821 women); includes 2,511 minority (1,218 Black or African American, non-Hispanic/Latino; 68 American Indian or Alaska Native, non-Hispanic/Latino; 219 Asian, non-Hispanic/Latino; 705 Hispanic/Latino; 46 Native Hawaiian or other Pacific Islander, non-Hispanic/Latino; 255 Two or more races, non-Hispanic/Latino), 107 international. Average age 35. 9,550 applicants, 100% accepted. In 2010, 1,688 master's awarded. *Degree requirements:* For master's, comprehensive exam or practicum. *Entrance requirements:* For master's, official transcript showing earned bachelor's degree from institution accredited by recognized accrediting body. Additional exam requirements/recommendations for international students: Required—TOEFL (minimum score 550 paper-based; 213 computer-based), IELTS (minimum score 6.5). *Application deadline:* Applications are processed on a rolling basis. Application fee: $0. Electronic applications accepted. *Financial support:* Applicants required to submit FAFSA. *Faculty research:* Military history, criminal justice, management performance, national security. *Unit head:* Dr. Frank McCluskey, Provost, 877-468-6268, Fax: 304-724-3780. *Application contact:* Terry Grant, Director of Enrollment Management, 877-468-6268, Fax: 304-724-3780, E-mail: info@apus.edu.

American University, School of International Service, Washington, DC 20016-8071. Offers comparative and regional studies (Certificate); cross-cultural communication (Certificate); development management (MS); ethics, peace, and global affairs (MA); European studies (Certificate); global environmental policy (MA, Certificate); international affairs (MA), including comparative and regional studies, environmental policy, international economic policy, international politics, natural resources and sustainable development, U. S. foreign policy; international communication (MA, Certificate); international development (MA, Certificate); international development management (Certificate); international economic policy (Certificate); international economic relations (Certificate); international media (MA); international peace and conflict resolution (MA, Certificate); international relations (PhD); international service (MIS); peace building (Certificate); the Americas (Certificate); United States foreign policy (Certificate); JD/MA. Part-time and evening/weekend programs available. *Faculty:* 91 full-time (35 women), 48 part-time/adjunct (16 women). *Students:* 591 full-time (383 women), 367 part-time (229 women); includes 164 minority (51 Black or African American, non-Hispanic/Latino; 4 American Indian or Alaska Native, non-Hispanic/Latino; 42 Asian, non-Hispanic/Latino; 63 Hispanic/Latino; 4 Two or more races, non-Hispanic/Latino), 94 international. Average age 27. 2,115 applicants, 59% accepted, 360 enrolled. In 2010, 370 master's, 7 doctorates awarded. Terminal master's awarded for partial completion of doctoral program. *Degree requirements:* For master's, one foreign language, comprehensive exam, thesis or alternative; for doctorate, one foreign language, comprehensive exam, thesis/dissertation, research practicum; for Certificate, minimum 15 credit hours related course work. *Entrance requirements:* For master's, GRE, 24 credits of course work in related social sciences, minimum GPA of 3.5, 2 letters of recommendation, bachelor's degree, resume; for doctorate, GRE, 2 letters of recommendation, 24 credits in related social sciences; for Certificate, bachelor's degree. Additional exam requirements/recommendations for international students: Required—TOEFL (minimum score 600 paper-based; 250 computer-based; 100 iBT). *Application deadline:* For fall admission, 1/15 priority date for domestic students; for spring admission, 10/1 priority date for domestic students. Applications are processed on a rolling basis. Application fee: $50. *Financial support:* Career-related internships or fieldwork, Federal Work-Study, and institutionally sponsored loans available. Financial award application deadline: 1/15. *Faculty research:* International intellectual property, international environmental issues, international law and legal order, international telecommunications/technology, international sustainable development. *Unit head:* Dr. Louis W. Goodman, Dean, 202-885-1600, Fax: 202-885-2494. *Application contact:* Yasmin Quianzon, Director of Graduate Admissions and Financial Aid, 202-885-2496, Fax: 202-885-1109.

The American University of Paris, Graduate Programs, Paris, France. Offers cross-cultural and sustainable business management (MA); cultural translation (MA); global communications (MA); global communications and civil society (MA); international affairs, conflict resolution and civil society development (MA); Middle East and Islamic studies (MA); Middle East and Islamic studies and international affairs (MA); public policy and international affairs (MA); public policy and international law (MA). *Faculty:* 14 full-time (3 women). *Students:* 151 full-time (110 women), 56 part-time (43 women). 271 applicants, 83% accepted, 104 enrolled. In 2010, 67 master's awarded. *Degree requirements:* For master's, thesis. *Entrance requirements:* For master's, minimum undergraduate GPA of 3.0. Additional exam requirements/recommendations for international students: Recommended—IELTS. *Application deadline:* For fall admission, 4/15 priority date for international students; for spring admission, 11/15 priority date for international students. Applications are processed on a rolling basis. Application fee: $75. Electronic applications accepted. *Financial support:* Scholarships/grants available. Financial award applicants required to submit FAFSA. *Unit head:* Dr. Celeste Schenck, President,

33-1 40 62 06 59, E-mail: president@aup.fr. *Application contact:* International Admissions Counselor, 33-1 40 62 07 20, Fax: 33-1 47 05 34 32, E-mail: admissions@aup.edu.

Antioch University Midwest, Graduate Programs, Program in Conflict Analysis and Management, Yellow Springs, OH 45387-1609. Offers MA. Part-time and evening/weekend programs available. Postbaccalaureate distance learning degree programs offered (minimal on-campus study). *Faculty:* 2 full-time (0 women), 3 part-time/adjunct (all women). *Students:* 24 full-time (21 women), 22 part-time (16 women); includes 9 Black or African American, non-Hispanic/Latino; 1 American Indian or Alaska Native, non-Hispanic/Latino; 2 Asian, non-Hispanic/Latino; 1 Hispanic/Latino. Average age 40. 16 applicants, 100% accepted, 15 enrolled. In 2010, 6 master's awarded. *Degree requirements:* For master's, thesis or alternative. *Entrance requirements:* For master's, resume, goal statement, interview. *Application deadline:* For fall admission, 8/15 for domestic and international students; for winter admission, 12/10 for domestic and international students; for spring admission, 3/10 for domestic students, 3/8 for international students. Applications are processed on a rolling basis. Application fee: $50. Electronic applications accepted. *Expenses:* Contact institution. *Financial support:* Federal Work-Study available. Financial award applicants required to submit FAFSA. *Unit head:* Dr. Richard McGuigan, Chair, 937-769-1890, Fax: 937-769-1809, E-mail: rmcguigan@antioch.edu. *Application contact:* Rob McLaughlin, Enrollment Services Manager, 937-769-1816, Fax: 937-769-1804, E-mail: rmclaughlin@antioch.edu.

Arcadia University, Graduate Studies, Program in International Peace and Conflict Management, Glenside, PA 19038-3295. Offers MAIPCR. Part-time and evening/weekend programs available. *Faculty:* 13 full-time (6 women). *Students:* 57 full-time (43 women), 5 part-time (3 women); includes 14 minority (8 Black or African American, non-Hispanic/Latino; 2 Asian, non-Hispanic/Latino; 4 Two or more races, non-Hispanic/Latino), 5 international. Average age 26. In 2010, 19 master's awarded. *Degree requirements:* For master's, one foreign language. *Entrance requirements:* For master's, GRE. Additional exam requirements/recommendations for international students: Required—TOEFL. *Application deadline:* For fall admission, 4/1 priority date for domestic students. Application fee: $50. *Expenses:* Contact institution. *Unit head:* Dr. Warren Haffar, Director, 215-572-4094, Fax: 215-572-4049, E-mail: haffar@arcadia.edu. *Application contact:* 215-572-2910, Fax: 215-572-4049, E-mail: admiss@arcadia.edu.

See Display on next page and Close-Up on page 737.

Associated Mennonite Biblical Seminary, Graduate and Professional Programs, Elkhart, IN 46517-1999. Offers Christian formation (MA); divinity (M Div); mission and evangelism (MA); peace studies (MA); theological studies (MA, Certificate). *Accreditation:* ACIPE; ATS. Part-time programs available. *Degree requirements:* For master's, comprehensive exam, thesis optional; for M Div, integration paper. *Entrance requirements:* For M Div, master's, and Certificate, 3 letters of reference. Additional exam requirements/recommendations for international students: Required—TOEFL (minimum score 550 paper-based; 213 computer-based). Electronic applications accepted. *Faculty research:* Biblical studies, theology, church history, church leadership.

Baker University, School of Professional and Graduate Studies, Program in Conflict Management and Dispute Resolution, Baldwin City, KS 66006-0065. Offers MA. Part-time and evening/weekend programs available. *Students:* 34 full-time (27 women), 29 part-time (21 women); includes 13 Black or African American, non-Hispanic/Latino; 1 Asian, non-Hispanic/Latino; 4 Hispanic/Latino; 2 Two or more races, non-Hispanic/Latino. Average age 36. In 2010, 15 master's awarded. *Entrance requirements:* Additional exam requirements/recommendations for international students: Required—TOEFL (minimum score 600 paper-based; 250 computer-based; 100 iBT). Application fee: $45. *Financial support:* Applicants required to submit FAFSA. *Unit head:* Dr. Peggy Harris, Vice President and Dean, 785-594-8492, Fax: 785-594-8363, E-mail: peggy.harris@bakeru.edu. *Application contact:* Assistant Dean for Instruction and Curriculum.

Bethany Theological Seminary, Graduate and Professional Programs, Richmond, IN 47374-4019. Offers biblical studies (MA Th); ministry studies (M Div); peace studies (M Div, MA Th); theological studies (MA Th, CATS); youth ministry (M Div). *Accreditation:* ACIPE; ATS. Part-time programs available. Postbaccalaureate distance learning degree programs offered (minimal on-campus study). *Degree requirements:* For master's, thesis. *Entrance requirements:* For M Div, letters of reference, minimum GPA of 2.75; for master's, letters of reference, minimum GPA of 3.0. Additional exam requirements/recommendations for international students: Required—TOEFL (minimum score 550 paper-based; 218 computer-based).

Bethel University, Graduate Programs, McKenzie, TN 38201. Offers administration and supervision (MA Ed); business administration (MBA); conflict resolution (MA); physician assistant studies (MS). Part-time and evening/weekend programs available. *Faculty:* 7 full-time (4 women), 2 part-time/adjunct (both women). *Students:* 93 full-time (68 women), 27 part-time (18 women); includes 42 minority (27 Black or African American, non-Hispanic/Latino; 15 Asian, non-Hispanic/Latino). Average age 32. 120 applicants, 100% accepted, 120 enrolled. *Degree requirements:* For master's, thesis (for some programs). *Entrance requirements:* For master's, GRE General Test or MAT, minimum undergraduate GPA of 2.5. *Application deadline:* For fall admission, 8/23 priority date for domestic and international students; for spring admission, 1/11 priority date for domestic and international students. Applications are processed on a rolling basis. Application fee: $30. *Financial support:* In 2010–11, 61 students received support. Career-related internships or fieldwork available. Support available to part-time students. Financial award application deadline: 6/1; financial award applicants required to submit FAFSA. *Unit head:* J. Bentley Rawdon, Dean of Graduate Studies, 731-352-4028, Fax: 731-352-4097. *Application contact:* Dr. Ben G. McClure, Chair, Division of Education and Health Sciences, 731-352-4025, Fax: 731-352-4097.

California State University, Dominguez Hills, College of Arts and Humanities, Program in Negotiation, Conflict Resolution and Peacebuilding, Carson, CA 90747-0001. Offers MA. Part-time and evening/weekend programs available. Postbaccalaureate distance learning degree programs offered (no on-campus study). *Faculty:* 3 full-time (2 women), 7 part-time/adjunct (2 women). *Students:* 29 full-time (18 women), 182 part-time (123 women); includes 95 minority (62 Black or African American, non-Hispanic/Latino; 2 American Indian or Alaska Native, non-Hispanic/Latino; 5 Asian, non-Hispanic/Latino; 25 Hispanic/Latino; 1 Two or more races, non-Hispanic/Latino), 4 international. Average age 38. 125 applicants, 69% accepted, 44 enrolled. In 2010, 18 master's awarded. *Degree requirements:* For master's, portfolio. *Entrance requirements:* For master's, minimum GPA of 3.2, 3 letters of recommendation. *Application deadline:* For fall admission, 5/1 for domestic and international students; for spring admission, 12/1 for domestic and international students. Application fee: $55. Electronic applications accepted. *Faculty research:* Ethnic conflict, mediator ethics, teacher training, global conflict resolution (including role of ombuds), optimal multicultural process. *Unit head:* Dr. Nancy Erbe, Director, 310-243-2805, Fax: 310-516-4268, E-mail: nerbe@csudh.edu. *Application contact:* Penny Ann LaBaun, Administrative Coordinator, 310-243-3237, Fax: 310-516-4268, E-mail: plabaun@csudh.edu.

Cambridge College, School of Management, Cambridge, MA 02138-5304. Offers business negotiation and conflict resolution (M Mgt); general business (M Mgt); health care informatics (M Mgt); health care management (M Mgt); leadership in human and organizational dynamics (M Mgt); non-profit and public organization management (M Mgt); small business development (M Mgt); technology management (M Mgt). Part-time and evening/weekend programs available. *Faculty:* 6 full-time (3 women), 54 part-time/adjunct (26 women). *Students:* 222 full-time (121 women), 175 part-time (110 women); includes 127 minority (89 Black or African American, non-Hispanic/Latino; 2 American Indian or Alaska Native, non-Hispanic/Latino; 9 Asian, non-Hispanic/Latino; 25 Hispanic/Latino; 2 Two or more races, non-Hispanic/Latino), 125 international. Average age 37. In 2010, 221 master's awarded. *Degree requirements:* For master's, thesis, seminars. *Entrance requirements:* For master's, resume, 2 professional references. Additional exam requirements/recommendations for international students: Required—TOEFL (minimum score 550 paper-based; 213 computer-based; 79 iBT); Recommended—IELTS (minimum score 6). *Application deadline:* Applications are processed on a rolling basis. Application fee: $30. Electronic applications accepted. *Expenses:* Contact institution. *Financial support:* Career-related internships or fieldwork, Federal Work-Study, and scholarships/grants available. Financial award applicants required to submit FAFSA. *Faculty research:* Negotiation, mediation and conflict resolution; leadership; management of diverse organizations; case studies and simulation methodologies for management education, digital as a second language: social networking for digital immigrants, non-profit and public management. *Unit head:* Dr. Mary Ann Joseph, Acting Dean, 617-873-0227, E-mail: maryann.joseph@cambridgecollege.edu. *Application contact:* Elaine M. Lapomardo, Dean of Enrollment Management, 617-873-0274, Fax: 617-349-3561, E-mail: elaine.lapomardo@cambridgecollege.edu.

Carleton University, Faculty of Graduate Studies, Faculty of Public Affairs and Management, Department of Law, Ottawa, ON K1S 5B6, Canada. Offers conflict resolution (Certificate); legal studies (MA). *Degree requirements:* For master's, thesis. *Entrance requirements:* For master's, honors degree. Additional exam requirements/recommendations for international students: Required—TOEFL. *Faculty research:* Legal and social theory; women, law, and gender relations; law, crime, and social order; political economy of law; international law.

Chaminade University of Honolulu, Graduate Services, Program in Education, Honolulu, HI 96816-1578. Offers social science via peace education (M Ed). Part-time and evening/weekend programs available. Postbaccalaureate distance learning degree programs offered (minimal on-campus study). *Degree requirements:* For master's, thesis or alternative. *Entrance requirements:* For master's, minimum GPA of 2.75, 3 letters of recommendation. Additional exam requirements/recommendations for international students: Required—TOEFL (minimum score 550 paper-based). *Faculty research:* Peace and curriculum education.

Champlain College, Graduate Studies, Burlington, VT 05402-0670. Offers business (MBA); digital forensic management (MS); education (M Ed); emergent media (MFA); health care management (MS); law (MS); managing innovation and information technology (MS); mediation and applied conflict studies (MS). Part-time programs available. Postbaccalaureate distance learning degree programs offered (no on-campus study). *Faculty:* 14 full-time (0 women), 24 part-time/adjunct (9 women). *Students:* 304 full-time (144 women), 2 part-time (both women). Average age 30. 271 applicants, 90% accepted, 216 enrolled. In 2010, 8 master's awarded. *Degree requirements:* For master's, capstone project. *Entrance requirements:* Additional exam requirements/recommendations for international students: Required—TOEFL. *Application deadline:* For fall admission, 8/1 priority date for domestic and international students; for spring admission, 1/1 priority date for domestic and international students. Applications are processed on a rolling basis. Application fee: $50. Electronic applications accepted. *Expenses:* Tuition: Part-time $740 per credit hour. Part-time tuition and fees vary according to program. *Financial support:* Applicants required to submit FAFSA. *Unit head:* Dr. Donald Haggerty, Associate Provost, Graduate Studies, 802-865-6403, Fax: 802-865-6447. *Application contact:* Jon Walsh, Assistant Vice President, Graduate Admission, 800-570-5858, E-mail: walsh@champlain.edu.

Colorado Technical University Colorado Springs, Graduate Studies, Program in Management, Colorado Springs, CO 80907-3896. Offers accounting (MBA, MSA); business administration (MBA); finance (MBA); human resources management (MBA); logistics/supply chain management (MBA); management (DM); marketing (MBA); mediation and dispute resolution (MBA); operations management (MBA); project management (MBA); technology management (MBA). Part-time and evening/weekend programs available. Postbaccalaureate distance learning degree programs offered. *Degree requirements:* For master's, thesis or alternative; for doctorate, thesis/dissertation. *Entrance requirements:* For doctorate, minimum

graduate GPA of 3.0, 5 years of related work experience. *Faculty research:* Sexual harassment, performance evaluation, critical thinking.

Colorado Technical University Denver, Programs in Business Administration and Management, Greenwood Village, CO 80111. Offers accounting (MBA); business administration (MBA); business administration and management (EMBA); finance (MBA); human resource management (MBA); marketing (MBA); mediation and dispute resolution (MBA); operations management (MBA); project management (MBA); technology management (MBA). Part-time and evening/weekend programs available. *Degree requirements:* For master's, thesis or alternative. *Entrance requirements:* For master's, minimum undergraduate GPA of 3.0, resume.

Columbia College, Graduate Programs, Department of Human Relations, Columbia, SC 29203-5998. Offers human behavior and conflict management (MA); interpersonal relations/conflict management (Certificate); organizational behavior/conflict management (Certificate). Part-time and evening/weekend programs available. Postbaccalaureate distance learning degree programs offered (minimal on-campus study). *Degree requirements:* For master's, thesis, practicum. *Entrance requirements:* For master's, GRE General Test, MAT, 2 letters of recommendation, minimum GPA of 3.2. Additional exam requirements/recommendations for international students: Required—TOEFL. Electronic applications accepted. *Expenses:* Contact institution. *Faculty research:* Envisioning and the resolution of conflict, environmental conflict resolution, crisis negotiation.

Columbia University, School of Continuing Education, Program in Negotiation and Conflict Resolution, New York, NY 10027. Offers MS. Part-time programs available. *Entrance requirements:* For master's, 2 letters of recommendation, professional resume. Electronic applications accepted.

Cornell University, Graduate School, Graduate Fields of Architecture, Art and Planning, Field of Regional Science, Ithaca, NY 14853-0001. Offers environmental studies (MA, MS, PhD); international spatial problems (MA, MS, PhD); location theory (MA, MS, PhD); multiregional economic analysis (MA, MS, PhD); peace science (MA, MS, PhD); planning methods (MA, MS, PhD); urban and regional economics (MA, MS, PhD). *Faculty:* 22 full-time (6 women). *Students:* 20 full-time (6 women); includes 1 Black or African American, non-Hispanic/Latino, 18 international. Average age 31. 5 applicants, 80% accepted, 4 enrolled. In 2010, 3 doctorates awarded. Terminal master's awarded for partial completion of doctoral program. *Degree requirements:* For master's, thesis; for doctorate, comprehensive exam, thesis/dissertation. *Entrance requirements:* For master's and doctorate, GRE General Test, 2 letters of recommendation. Additional exam requirements/recommendations for international students: Required—TOEFL (minimum score 600 paper-based; 250 computer-based; 77 iBT). *Application deadline:* For fall admission, 1/15 priority date for domestic students. Application fee: $70. Electronic applications accepted. *Expenses:* Tuition: Full-time $29,500. Required fees: $76. Tuition and fees vary according to degree level and program. *Financial support:* In 2010–11, 1 research assistantship with full tuition reimbursement, 2 teaching assistantships with full tuition reimbursements were awarded; fellowships with full tuition reimbursements, institutionally sponsored loans, scholarships/grants, health care benefits, tuition waivers (full and partial), and unspecified assistantships also available. Financial award applicants required to submit FAFSA. *Faculty research:* Urban and regional growth, spatial economics, formation of spatial patterns by socioeconomic systems, non-linear dynamics and complex systems, environmental-economic systems. *Unit head:* Director of Graduate Studies, 607-255-6848, Fax: 607-255-1971. *Application contact:* Graduate Field Assistant, 607-255-6848, Fax: 607-255-1971, E-mail: regsci@cornell.edu.

Creighton University, School of Law, Program in Negotiation and Dispute Resolution, Omaha, NE 68178. Offers MS, Certificate. Part-time and evening/weekend programs available. Postbaccalaureate distance learning degree programs offered (minimal on-campus study). *Faculty:* 6 full-time (1 woman), 6 part-time/adjunct (4 women). *Students:* 66 full-time (41 women), 76 part-time (44 women); includes 23 minority (10 Black or African American, non-Hispanic/Latino; 6 Asian, non-Hispanic/Latino; 7 Hispanic/Latino), 1 international. Average age 35. In

Conflict Resolution and Mediation/Peace Studies

Creighton University *(continued)*
2010, 8 master's awarded. *Degree requirements:* For master's, thesis or alternative, practicum. *Entrance requirements:* For master's, GRE, MAT, or LSAT. Additional exam requirements/recommendations for international students: Required—TOEFL. *Application deadline:* Applications are processed on a rolling basis. Application fee: $50. Electronic applications accepted. *Expenses:* Tuition: Full-time $12,168; part-time $676 per credit hour. Required fees: $131 per semester. Tuition and fees vary according to program. *Financial support:* Institutionally sponsored loans available. Financial award applicants required to submit FAFSA. *Faculty research:* Nationalism/identity and conflict; complex adaptive items and conflict engagement; history, memory and conflict; culture and conflict. *Unit head:* Prof. Arthur Pearlstein, Director and Professor of Law, 402-280-3853. *Application contact:* Prof. Jacqueline Font, Associate Director and Assistant Professor, 402-280-3883, E-mail: jnfont@creighton.edu.

Dallas Baptist University, College of Business, Business Administration Program, Dallas, TX 75211-9299. Offers accounting (MBA); business communication (MBA); conflict resolution management (MBA); e-business (MBA); entrepreneurship (MBA); finance (MBA); health care management (MBA); international business (MBA); leading the non-profit organization (MBA); management (MBA); management information systems (MBA); marketing (MBA); project management (MBA); technology and engineering management (MBA). *Accreditation:* ACBSP. Part-time and evening/weekend programs available. *Entrance requirements:* For master's, GMAT, minimum GPA of 3.0. Additional exam requirements/recommendations for international students: Required—TOEFL, IELTS. Electronic applications accepted. *Expenses:* Tuition: Full-time $11,394; part-time $633 per credit hour. *Faculty research:* Sports management, services marketing, retailing, strategic management, financial planning/investments.

Dallas Baptist University, College of Business, Management Program, Dallas, TX 75211-9299. Offers business communication (MA); conflict resolution management (MA); general management (MA); health care management (MA); human resource management (MA); performance management (MA). Part-time and evening/weekend programs available. *Entrance requirements:* For master's, GRE General Test, minimum GPA of 3.0. Additional exam requirements/recommendations for international students: Required—TOEFL, IELTS. Electronic applications accepted. *Expenses:* Tuition: Full-time $11,394; part-time $633 per credit hour. *Faculty research:* Organizational behavior, conflict personalities.

Duquesne University, Graduate School of Liberal Arts, Graduate Center for Social and Public Policy, Pittsburgh, PA 15282-0001. Offers conflict resolution and peace studies (Certificate); social and public policy (MA, Certificate). Part-time and evening/weekend programs available. *Faculty:* 15 full-time (3 women), 1 (woman) part-time/adjunct. *Students:* 52 full-time (26 women), 9 part-time (4 women); includes 1 Black or African American, non-Hispanic/Latino, 5 international. Average age 27. 38 applicants, 95% accepted, 17 enrolled. In 2010, 11 master's awarded. *Degree requirements:* For master's, thesis. *Entrance requirements:* For master's, GRE General Test. Additional exam requirements/recommendations for international students: Required—TOEFL. *Application deadline:* For fall admission, 4/30 priority date for domestic and international students; for spring admission, 11/1 priority date for domestic and international students. Applications are processed on a rolling basis. Electronic applications accepted. *Expenses:* Tuition: Part-time $884 per credit. Required fees: $84 per credit. Tuition and fees vary according to course load. *Financial support:* In 2010–11, 20 students received support, including 12 research assistantships with full and partial tuition reimbursements available (averaging $9,000 per year), 4 teaching assistantships with full and partial tuition reimbursements available (averaging $9,000 per year); career-related internships or fieldwork, institutionally sponsored loans, scholarships/grants, tuition waivers (full and partial), and unspecified assistantships also available. Support available to part-time students. Financial award application deadline: 5/1. *Faculty research:* Program evaluation, environmental policy, criminal justice policy, health care policy. Total annual research expenditures: $30,000. *Unit head:* Dr. Joseph Yenerall, Director, 412-396-6485, Fax: 412-396-5265, E-mail: socialpolicy@duq.edu. *Application contact:* Dr. Joseph Yenerall, Assistant to the Dean, 412-396-6485.

Eastern Mennonite University, Program in Conflict Transformation, Harrisonburg, VA 22802-2462. Offers MA, Graduate Certificate. Part-time programs available. *Degree requirements:* For master's, practicum. *Entrance requirements:* For master's, minimum undergraduate GPA of 2.75. Additional exam requirements/recommendations for international students: Required—TOEFL (minimum score 550 paper-based; 213 computer-based). Electronic applications accepted. *Expenses:* Contact institution. *Faculty research:* Restorative justice, negotiation, security in an age of terror, trauma recovery, development, peace building.

Edinboro University of Pennsylvania, College of Arts and Sciences, Department of Communications and Media Studies, Edinboro, PA 16444. Offers communications studies (Certificate); conflict management (MA). Part-time and evening/weekend programs available. *Faculty:* 6 full-time (2 women). *Students:* 27 full-time (15 women), 16 part-time (9 women); includes 5 minority (3 Black or African American, non-Hispanic/Latino; 2 Asian, non-Hispanic/Latino). Average age 28. In 2010, 28 master's, 10 other advanced degrees awarded. *Degree requirements:* For master's, thesis or alternative, competency exam. *Entrance requirements:* For master's, GRE or MAT, minimum QPA of 2.5. *Application deadline:* Applications are processed on a rolling basis. Application fee: $30. Electronic applications accepted. *Expenses:* Tuition, state resident: full-time $6966; part-time $387 per credit. Tuition, nonresident: full-time $11,146; part-time $619 per credit. Required fees: $2401.70; $96.25 per credit. *Financial support:* In 2010–11, 13 research assistantships with full and partial tuition reimbursements (averaging $4,050 per year) were awarded; career-related internships or fieldwork, Federal Work-Study, scholarships/grants, and unspecified assistantships also available. Support available to part-time students. Financial award application deadline: 2/15; financial award applicants required to submit FAFSA. *Unit head:* Dr. Andrew Smith, Program Head, 814-732-2165, E-mail: arsmith@edinboro.edu. *Application contact:* Dr. Andrew Smith, Program Head, 814-732-2165, E-mail: arsmith@edinboro.edu.

Florida International University, College of Education, Department of Educational Leadership and Policy Studies, Miami, FL 33199. Offers adult education (MS); adult education in human resource development (Ed D); clinical mental health counseling (MS); conflict resolution and consensus building (Certificate); counselor education (MS); educational administration and supervision (Ed D); educational leadership (MS, Certificate, Ed S); higher education (Ed D); higher education administration (MS); human resource development (MS); instruction in urban settings (MS); international/intercultural education (MS); learning technologies (MS); multicultural-bilingual (MS); multicultural-TESOL (MS); recreation and sport management (MS); recreation therapy (MS); rehabilitation counseling (MS); school counseling (MS); school psychology (Ed S); urban education (MS). Part-time and evening/weekend programs available. *Students:* 164 full-time (124 women), 308 part-time (234 women); includes 107 Black or African American, non-Hispanic/Latino; 3 American Indian or Alaska Native, non-Hispanic/Latino; 8 Asian, non-Hispanic/Latino; 223 Hispanic/Latino, 12 international. Average age 31. 544 applicants, 41% accepted, 197 enrolled. In 2010, 123 master's, 5 doctorates, 16 other advanced degrees awarded. *Degree requirements:* For doctorate, thesis/dissertation. *Entrance requirements:* For master's, minimum GPA of 3.0; for doctorate and other advanced degree, GRE General Test. Additional exam requirements/recommendations for international students: Required—TOEFL (minimum score 550 paper-based; 213 computer-based; 80 iBT), IELTS (minimum score 6.3). *Application deadline:* For fall admission, 6/1 priority date for domestic students, 4/1 for international students; for winter admission, 10/1 priority date for domestic students, 9/1 for international students; for spring admission, 3/1 priority date for domestic students, 2/1 for international students. Applications are processed on a rolling basis. Application fee: $30. Electronic applications accepted. *Financial support:* Fellowships, research assistantships with full and partial tuition reimbursements, teaching assistantships with full and partial tuition reimbursements, Federal Work-Study and tuition waivers (full and partial) available. Support available to part-time students. Financial award applicants required to submit FAFSA. *Unit head:* Dr. Patricia Barbetta, Dean of Graduate Studies, 305-348-2835, Fax: 305-348-2081,

E-mail: barbetta@fiu.edu. *Application contact:* Nanett Rojas, Graduate Admission, 305-348-7442, Fax: 305-348-7441, E-mail: nanett.rojas@fiu.edu.

Fresno Pacific University, Graduate Programs, Program in Peacemaking and Conflict Studies, Fresno, CA 93702-4709. Offers MA. Part-time and evening/weekend programs available. *Degree requirements:* For master's, thesis. *Entrance requirements:* For master's, GMAT, MAT, GRE, interview, 2 writing samples. Additional exam requirements/recommendations for international students: Required—TOEFL (minimum score 550 paper-based; 213 computer-based). Electronic applications accepted.

George Mason University, School for Conflict Analysis and Resolution, Fairfax, VA 22030. Offers conflict analysis and resolution (MS, PhD); conflict analysis and resolution advanced skills (Certificate); conflict analysis and resolution for collaborative leadership in community planning (Certificate); conflict analysis and resolution for prevention, reconstruction, and stabilization contexts (Certificate); environmental conflict resolution and collaboration (Certificate); world religions, diplomacy, and conflict resolution (Certificate). Part-time and evening/weekend programs available. *Faculty:* 20 full-time (9 women), 14 part-time/adjunct (5 women). *Students:* 80 full-time (40 women), 196 part-time (113 women); includes 46 minority (27 Black or African American, non-Hispanic/Latino; 1 American Indian or Alaska Native, non-Hispanic/Latino; 6 Asian, non-Hispanic/Latino; 11 Hispanic/Latino; 1 Two or more races, non-Hispanic/Latino), 43 international. Average age 35. 398 applicants, 38% accepted, 76 enrolled. In 2010, 44 master's, 8 doctorates, 26 other advanced degrees awarded. *Degree requirements:* For master's, thesis optional; for doctorate, one foreign language, comprehensive exam, thesis/dissertation, oral defense of dissertation. *Entrance requirements:* For master's, 3 recommendation letters, resume; for doctorate, 3 recommendation letters, resume, expanded goals statement, writing sample. Additional exam requirements/recommendations for international students: Required—TOEFL (minimum score 570 paper-based; 230 computer-based; 88 iBT). *Application deadline:* For fall admission, 2/1 for domestic students. Application fee: $100. Electronic applications accepted. *Expenses:* Tuition, state resident: full-time $8192; part-time $440 per credit hour. Tuition, nonresident: full-time $22,952; part-time $1055 per credit hour. Required fees: $2364; $99 per credit hour. *Financial support:* In 2010–11, 24 students received support, including 3 fellowships with full tuition reimbursements available (averaging $18,000 per year), 15 research assistantships with full and partial tuition reimbursements available (averaging $13,674 per year), 7 teaching assistantships with full and partial tuition reimbursements available (averaging $9,523 per year); career-related internships or fieldwork, Federal Work-Study, scholarships/grants, unspecified assistantships, and health care benefits (full-time research or teaching assistantship recipients) also available. Financial award application deadline: 3/1; financial award applicants required to submit FAFSA. *Faculty research:* Preventive diplomacy, conflict/dispute resolution, peace/security, political violence, international terrorism. Total annual research expenditures: $419,929. *Unit head:* Andrea Bartoli, Director, 703-993-9716, Fax: 703-993-1302, E-mail: abartoli@gmu.edu. *Application contact:* Erin Ogilvie, Graduate Admissions and Student Services Director, 703-993-9683, E-mail: eogilvie@gmu.edu.

George Mason University, School of Public Policy, Program in Peace Operations, Arlington, VA 22201. Offers MS. Part-time programs available. *Faculty:* 66 full-time (24 women), 15 part-time/adjunct (3 women). *Students:* 25 full-time (16 women), 37 part-time (21 women); includes 3 Black or African American, non-Hispanic/Latino; 1 Asian, non-Hispanic/Latino; 2 Hispanic/Latino; 1 Two or more races, non-Hispanic/Latino, 2 international. Average age 32. 44 applicants, 73% accepted, 20 enrolled. In 2010, 25 master's awarded. *Degree requirements:* For master's, thesis or alternative. *Entrance requirements:* For master's, GRE (for students seeking merit-based scholarships), minimum undergraduate GPA of 3.0, 2 letters of recommendation, resume. Additional exam requirements/recommendations for international students: Required—TOEFL (minimum score 570 paper-based; 230 computer-based; 88 iBT). *Application deadline:* For fall admission, 6/1 priority date for domestic students, 5/1 priority date for international students; for spring admission, 12/1 priority date for domestic students, 11/1 priority date for international students. Applications are processed on a rolling basis. Application fee: $100. Electronic applications accepted. *Expenses:* Contact institution. *Financial support:* Career-related internships or fieldwork, Federal Work-Study, scholarships/grants, unspecified assistantships, and health care benefits (full-time research or teaching assistantship recipients) available. Financial award application deadline: 3/1; financial award applicants required to submit FAFSA. *Unit head:* Dr. Allison Frendak-Blume, Director, 703-993-8099, E-mail: spp@gmu.edu. *Application contact:* Tennille Haegele, Director of Graduate Admissions, 703-993-3183, Fax: 703-993-4876, E-mail: thaegele@gmu.edu.

Georgetown University, Graduate School of Arts and Sciences, Department of Government, Program in Conflict Resolution, Washington, DC 20057. Offers MA.

Georgetown University, Graduate School of Arts and Sciences, Edmund A. Walsh School of Foreign Service, Center for Peace and Security Studies, Washington, DC 20057. Offers security studies (MA); MA/JD; MA/PhD.

Hult International Business School, Program in International Relations—Hult London Campus, London, MA WC 1B 4JP, United Kingdom. Offers conflict resolution (MA); diplomacy (MA); international public law (MA); international relations (MA); Middle East international security (MA); politics (MA); security studies (MA); terrorism (MA); U.S. foreign policy (MA). Part-time programs available. *Entrance requirements:* Additional exam requirements/recommendations for international students: Required—TOEFL (minimum score 580 paper-based; 237 computer-based), TWE (minimum score 5). Electronic applications accepted. *Faculty research:* American foreign politics, Middle East, security studies.

Jones International University, School of Business, Centennial, CO 80112. Offers accounting (MBA); business communication (MABC); entrepreneurship (MABC, MBA); finance (MBA); global enterprise management (MBA); health care management (MBA); information security management (MBA); information technology management (MBA); leadership and influence (MABC); leading the customer-driven organization (MABC); negotiation and conflict management (MBA); project management (MABC, MBA). Program only offered online. Part-time and evening/weekend programs available. Postbaccalaureate distance learning degree programs offered (no on-campus study). *Degree requirements:* For master's, capstone project. *Entrance requirements:* For master's, minimum cumulative GPA of 2.5. Additional exam requirements/recommendations for international students: Recommended—TOEFL (minimum score 550 paper-based; 213 computer-based). Electronic applications accepted.

Kennesaw State University, College of Humanities and Social Sciences, PhD Program in International Conflict Management, Kennesaw, GA 30144-5591. Offers PhD. *Students:* 16 full-time (7 women); includes 1 minority (Black or African American, non-Hispanic/Latino), 10 international. Average age 37. 39 applicants, 51% accepted, 16 enrolled. *Degree requirements:* For doctorate, one foreign language, thesis/dissertation. *Entrance requirements:* For doctorate, GRE, portfolio of documents, copy of transcripts from all universities previously attended, resume, statement of goals and objectives, academic writing sample, three letters of recommendation. Additional exam requirements/recommendations for international students: Required—TOEFL (minimum score 90 iBT), IELTS (minimum score 7). *Application deadline:* For fall admission, 2/1 for domestic and international students. Application fee: $60. Electronic applications accepted. *Expenses:* Tuition, state resident: full-time $5500; part-time $225 per credit hour. Tuition, nonresident: full-time $16,100; part-time $813 per credit hour. Required fees: $673 per semester. *Financial support:* Fellowships, research assistantships, teaching assistantships, unspecified assistantships available. Financial award application deadline: 4/1; financial award applicants required to submit FAFSA. *Unit head:* Dr. Volker Franke, Director, 770-423-6127, Fax: 770-423-6705, E-mail: phdhss@kennesaw.edu. *Application contact:* Tamara Hutto, Admissions Counselor, 770-420-4377, Fax: 770-423-6885, E-mail: ksugrad@kennesaw.edu.

Kennesaw State University, College of Humanities and Social Sciences, Program in Conflict Management, Kennesaw, GA 30144-5591. Offers MSCM. Evening/weekend programs available. *Students:* 70 full-time (48 women), 1 part-time (0 women); includes 29 minority (25 Black or

African American, non-Hispanic/Latino; 1 Asian, non-Hispanic/Latino; 2 Hispanic/Latino; 1 Two or more races, non-Hispanic/Latino; 4 international. Average age 38. 36 applicants, 78% accepted, 24 enrolled. In 2010, 21 master's awarded. *Entrance requirements:* For master's, GMAT, GRE, LSAT. Additional exam requirements/recommendations for international students: Required—TOEFL (minimum score 550 paper-based; 213 computer-based; 80 iBT), IELTS (minimum score 6). *Application deadline:* For fall admission, 6/1 for domestic and international students. Applications are processed on a rolling basis. Application fee: $60. Electronic applications accepted. *Expenses:* Tuition, state resident: full-time $5500; part-time $225 per credit hour. Tuition, nonresident: full-time $16,100; part-time $813 per credit hour. Required fees: $673 per semester. *Financial support:* In 2010–11, 1 research assistantship with full tuition reimbursement (averaging $15,000 per year) was awarded; Federal Work-Study and unspecified assistantships also available. Support available to part-time students. Financial award application deadline: 6/15; financial award applicants required to submit FAFSA. *Unit head:* Dr. Susan Raines, Director, 770-423-6081, E-mail: sraines@kennesaw.edu. *Application contact:* Tamara Hutto, Admissions Counselor, 770-420-4377, Fax: 770-423-6885, E-mail: ksugrad@kennesaw.edu.

Lipscomb University, Institute for Conflict Management, Nashville, TN 37204-3951. Offers MA, Certificate. Part-time and evening/weekend programs available. *Faculty:* 2 full-time (0 women), 6 part-time/adjunct (3 women). *Students:* 15 full-time (9 women), 25 part-time (17 women); includes 9 Black or African American, non-Hispanic/Latino; 2 Hispanic/Latino. Average age 40. 16 applicants, 100% accepted, 11 enrolled. In 2010, 12 master's, 3 other advanced degrees awarded. *Degree requirements:* For master's, completion of externship. *Entrance requirements:* For master's, GRE, GMAT, LSAT or equivalent, 3 years work experience. *Application deadline:* Applications are processed on a rolling basis. Application fee: $50 ($75 for international students). *Expenses:* Contact institution. *Unit head:* Dr. Larry Bridgesmith, Executive Director, 615-966-7145, Fax: 615-966-7143, E-mail: larry.bridgesmith@lipscomb.edu. *Application contact:* Sherri Guenther, Administrative Assistant, 615-966-7140, Fax: 615-966-7143, E-mail: sherri.guenther@lipscomb.edu.

Lipscomb University, MBA Program, Nashville, TN 37204-3951. Offers accounting (MBA); business administration (general) (MBA); conflict management (MBA); financial services (MBA); healthcare management (MBA); leadership (MBA); nonprofit management (MBA); sports administration (MBA); sustainable practice (MBA). *Accreditation:* ACBSP. Part-time and evening/weekend programs available. *Faculty:* 17 full-time (5 women), 3 part-time/adjunct (0 women). *Students:* 52 full-time (30 women), 79 part-time (36 women); includes 20 Black or African American, non-Hispanic/Latino; 1 American Indian or Alaska Native, non-Hispanic/Latino; 1 Asian, non-Hispanic/Latino; 7 Hispanic/Latino. Average age 32. 151 applicants, 47% accepted, 45 enrolled. In 2010, 70 master's awarded. *Entrance requirements:* For master's, GMAT, interview, 2 references, resume. Additional exam requirements/recommendations for international students: Required—TOEFL (minimum score 570 paper-based; 230 computer-based). *Application deadline:* For fall admission, 2/1 for international students; for winter admission, 6/1 for international students. Applications are processed on a rolling basis. Application fee: $50 ($75 for international students). Electronic applications accepted. *Expenses:* Contact institution. *Financial support:* Career-related internships or fieldwork, Federal Work-Study, scholarships/grants, tuition waivers (partial), and unspecified assistantships available. Support available to part-time students. Financial award application deadline: 7/1; financial award applicants required to submit FAFSA. *Faculty research:* Impact of spirituality on organization commitment, leadership, psychological empowerment, training. *Unit head:* Dr. Mike Kendrick, Interim Chair of Graduate Business Studies, 615-966-1833, Fax: 615-966-1818, E-mail: mikekendrick@lipscomb.edu. *Application contact:* Emily Landsdell, 615-966-5284, E-mail: emily.lansdell@lipscomb.edu.

Marquette University, Graduate School, Program in Public Service, Milwaukee, WI 53201-1881. Offers criminal justice administration (MLS); dispute resolution (MDR, MLS); engineering (MLS); health care administration (MLS); law enforcement leadership and management (Certificate); leadership studies (Certificate); non-profit sector (MLS); public service (MAPS, MLS); sports leadership (MLS). Part-time and evening/weekend programs available. Post-baccalaureate distance learning degree programs offered (no on-campus study). *Faculty:* 3 full-time (2 women), 29 part-time/adjunct (11 women). *Students:* 27 full-time (13 women), 134 part-time (84 women); includes 29 minority (21 Black or African American, non-Hispanic/Latino; 1 American Indian or Alaska Native, non-Hispanic/Latino; 1 Asian, non-Hispanic/Latino; 6 Hispanic/Latino), 1 international. Average age 38. 108 applicants, 78% accepted, 36 enrolled. In 2010, 11 master's, 12 Certificates awarded. *Degree requirements:* For master's, comprehensive exam (for some programs). *Entrance requirements:* For master's, GRE General Test (preferred), GMAT, or LSAT, official transcripts from all current and previous colleges/universities except Marquette, three letters of recommendation, statement of purpose. Additional exam requirements/recommendations for international students: Required—TOEFL. *Application deadline:* Applications are processed on a rolling basis. Application fee: $50. Electronic applications accepted. *Expenses:* Tuition: Full-time $16,290; part-time $905 per credit hour. Tuition and fees vary according to program. *Financial support:* In 2010–11, 1 fellowship, 1 research assistantship were awarded; teaching assistantships. Financial award application deadline: 2/15. *Unit head:* Dr. Johnette Caulfield, Adjunct Assistant Professor and Director of Graduate Programs, 414-288-5556, E-mail: jay.caulfield@marquette.edu. *Application contact:* Erin Fox, Assistant Director for Recruitment, 414-288-5319, Fax: 414-288-1902, E-mail: erin.fox@marquette.edu.

Montclair State University, The Graduate School, College of Humanities and Social Sciences, Department of Political Science and Law, Montclair, NJ 07043-1624. Offers law and governance (MA), including conflict management and peace studies, governance, compliance and regulation, intellectual property, law and governance, legal management. Part-time and evening/weekend programs available. *Faculty:* 13 full-time (6 women), 25 part-time/adjunct (8 women). *Students:* 9 full-time (5 women), 26 part-time (15 women); includes 10 Black or African American, non-Hispanic/Latino; 4 Asian, non-Hispanic/Latino; 2 Hispanic/Latino, 2 international. Average age 30. 19 applicants, 68% accepted, 10 enrolled. In 2010, 16 master's, 3 other advanced degrees awarded. *Degree requirements:* For master's, thesis or comprehensive exam. *Entrance requirements:* For master's, GRE, minimum cumulative GPA of 2.75 for undergraduate work. Additional exam requirements/recommendations for international students: Required—TOEFL (minimum iBT score of 83) or IELTS. *Expenses:* Tuition, state resident: part-time $501.34 per credit. Tuition, nonresident: part-time $773.88 per credit. Required fees: $71.15 per credit. *Financial support:* In 2010–11, 1 research assistantship with full tuition reimbursement (averaging $7,000 per year) was awarded; Federal Work-Study, scholarships/grants, and unspecified assistantships also available. Support available to part-time students. Financial award application deadline: 3/1. *Unit head:* Dr. William Berlin, Chair, 973-655-7576, E-mail: berlinw@mail.montclair.edu. *Application contact:* Amy Aiello, Director of Graduate Admissions and Operations, 973-655-5147, Fax: 973-655-7869, E-mail: graduate.school@montclair.edu.

National Defense University, College of International Security Affairs, Washington, DC 20319-5066. Offers strategic security studies (MA), including conflict management, counterterrorism, homeland defense/ security, international security studies. Part-time and evening/weekend programs available. *Degree requirements:* For master's, thesis. *Entrance requirements:* Additional exam requirements/recommendations for international students: Required—TOEFL.

National University, Academic Affairs, College of Letters and Sciences, Department of Professional Studies, La Jolla, CA 92037-1011. Offers forensic science (MFS), including criminalistics and investigation; public administration (MPA), including alternative dispute resolution, human resource management, organizational leadership, public finance. Part-time and evening/weekend programs available. Postbaccalaureate distance learning degree programs offered (no on-campus study). *Faculty:* 10 full-time (3 women), 110 part-time/adjunct (22 women). *Students:* 189 full-time (117 women), 284 part-time (167 women); includes 259 minority (101 Black or African American, non-Hispanic/Latino; 2 American Indian or Alaska Native, non-Hispanic/Latino; 33 Asian, non-Hispanic/Latino; 104 Hispanic/Latino; 7 Native Hawaiian or other Pacific Islander, non-Hispanic/Latino; 12 Two or more races, non-Hispanic/Latino). Average

age 38. 305 applicants, 100% accepted, 192 enrolled. In 2010, 160 master's awarded. *Degree requirements:* For master's, thesis. *Entrance requirements:* For master's, interview, minimum GPA of 2.5. Additional exam requirements/recommendations for international students: Required—TOEFL (minimum score 550 paper-based; 213 computer-based; 79 iBT), IELTS (minimum score 6). *Application deadline:* Applications are processed on a rolling basis. Application fee: $60 ($65 for international students). Electronic applications accepted. *Expenses:* Tuition: Full-time $9450; part-time $350 per unit. Required fees: $350 per unit. One-time fee: $60. *Financial support:* Career-related internships or fieldwork, institutionally sponsored loans, scholarships/grants, and tuition waivers (partial) available. Support available to part-time students. Financial award application deadline: 6/30; financial award applicants required to submit FAFSA. *Unit head:* James G. Larsen, Associate Professor and Chair, 858-642-8418, Fax: 858-642-8715, E-mail: jlarson@nu.edu. *Application contact:* Dominick Giovanniello, Associate Regional Dean—San Diego, 800-NAT-UNIV, Fax: 858-541-7792, E-mail: dgiovann@nu.edu.

National University, Academic Affairs, School of Business and Management, Department of Leadership and Business Administration, La Jolla, CA 92037-1011. Offers alternative dispute resolution (MBA); e-business (MBA); financial management (MBA); human resource management (MBA); human resources management (MA); international business (MBA); knowledge management (MS); marketing (MBA); organizational leadership (MBA, MS); technology management (MBA). Part-time and evening/weekend programs available. Postbaccalaureate distance learning degree programs offered (no on-campus study). *Faculty:* 16 full-time (4 women), 126 part-time/adjunct (39 women). *Students:* 119 full-time (81 women), 410 part-time (202 women); includes 176 minority (81 Black or African American, non-Hispanic/Latino; 1 American Indian or Alaska Native, non-Hispanic/Latino; 31 Asian, non-Hispanic/Latino; 52 Hispanic/Latino; 4 Native Hawaiian or other Pacific Islander, non-Hispanic/Latino; 7 Two or more races, non-Hispanic/Latino), 183 international. Average age 38. 219 applicants, 100% accepted, 160 enrolled. In 2010, 95 master's awarded. *Degree requirements:* For master's, thesis. *Entrance requirements:* For master's, interview, minimum GPA of 2.5. Additional exam requirements/recommendations for international students: Required—TOEFL (minimum score 550 paper-based; 213 computer-based; 79 iBT), IELTS (minimum score 6). *Application deadline:* Applications are processed on a rolling basis. Application fee: $60 ($65 for international students). Electronic applications accepted. *Expenses:* Tuition: Full-time $9450; part-time $350 per unit. Required fees: $350 per unit. One-time fee: $60. *Financial support:* Career-related internships or fieldwork, institutionally sponsored loans, scholarships/grants, and tuition waivers (partial) available. Support available to part-time students. Financial award application deadline: 6/30; financial award applicants required to submit FAFSA. *Unit head:* Dr. Bruce Buchowicz, Chair, 858-642-8439, Fax: 858-642-8406, E-mail: bbuchowicz@nu.edu. *Application contact:* Dominick Giovanniello, Associate Regional Dean—San Diego, 800-NAT-UNIV, Fax: 858-541-7792, E-mail: dgiovann@nu.edu.

New York University, School of Continuing and Professional Studies, Center for Global Affairs, New York, NY 10012-1019. Offers global affairs (MS), including environment/energy policy, human rights and humanitarian assistance, international law, dispute settlement, and institutions, international relations, peace building, private sector: international business, economics, and development, transnational security. Part-time and evening/weekend programs available. *Faculty:* 10 full-time (3 women), 29 part-time/adjunct (14 women). *Students:* 92 full-time (62 women), 119 part-time (90 women); includes 12 Black or African American, non-Hispanic/Latino; 1 American Indian or Alaska Native, non-Hispanic/Latino; 14 Asian, non-Hispanic/Latino; 10 Hispanic/Latino, 32 international. Average age 30. 419 applicants, 58% accepted, 81 enrolled. In 2010, 113 master's awarded. *Degree requirements:* For master's, thesis. *Entrance requirements:* For master's, GRE General Test or GMAT (for recent graduates), 2 letters of recommendation, resume, essay, professional experience. Additional exam requirements/recommendations for international students: Required—TOEFL (minimum score 600 paper-based; 250 computer-based; 100 iBT). *Application deadline:* For fall admission, 2/1 priority date for domestic and international students; for spring admission, 10/15 priority date for domestic students, 8/15 priority date for international students. Applications are processed on a rolling basis. Application fee: $75. Electronic applications accepted. *Financial support:* In 2010–11, 163 students received support, including 163 fellowships (averaging $2,554 per year); institutionally sponsored loans, scholarships/grants, and tuition waivers (partial) also available. Support available to part-time students. Financial award application deadline: 3/1; financial award applicants required to submit FAFSA. *Unit head:* Dr. Vera Jelinek, Divisional Dean and Clinical Associate Professor, 212-992-8380, Fax: 212-995-4597, E-mail: vera.jelinek@nyu.edu. *Application contact:* Cori Epstein, Associate Director, 212-992-8380, Fax: 212-995-4597, E-mail: graduate.global.affairs@nyu.edu.

Norwich University, School of Graduate and Continuing Studies, Program in Diplomacy, Northfield, VT 05663. Offers international commerce (MA); international conflict management (MA); international terrorism (MA). Evening/weekend programs available. *Faculty:* 44 part-time/adjunct (8 women). *Students:* 168 full-time (62 women); includes 12 Black or African American, non-Hispanic/Latino; 4 Asian, non-Hispanic/Latino; 18 Hispanic/Latino. Average age 38. 273 applicants, 74% accepted, 168 enrolled. In 2010, 168 master's awarded. *Degree requirements:* For master's, comprehensive exam, thesis optional. *Entrance requirements:* For master's, minimum undergraduate GPA of 2.75. Additional exam requirements/recommendations for international students: Required—TOEFL. *Application deadline:* For fall admission, 8/10 for domestic and international students; for winter admission, 11/7 for domestic and international students; for spring admission, 2/6 for domestic and international students. Application fee: $50. Electronic applications accepted. *Expenses:* Tuition: Full-time $17,380; part-time $645 per credit. Tuition and fees vary according to program. *Financial support:* Scholarships/grants available. Financial award applicants required to submit FAFSA. *Unit head:* Dr. Harold Kearsley, Program Director, 802-485-2730, E-mail: hkearsley@norwich.edu. *Application contact:* Sally Burkart, Application Management Team Lead, 802-485-2096, Fax: 802-485-2533, E-mail: sburkart@norwich.edu.

Nova Southeastern University, Graduate School of Humanities and Social Sciences, Department of Conflict Analysis and Resolution, Doctor of Conflict Analysis and Resolution Program, Fort Lauderdale, FL 33314-7796. Offers PhD, PhD/JD. Part-time programs available. Postbaccalaureate distance learning degree programs offered (minimal on-campus study). *Faculty:* 11 full-time (6 women), 5 part-time/adjunct (1 woman). *Students:* 177 full-time (99 women), 117 part-time (69 women); includes 98 Black or African American, non-Hispanic/Latino; 2 American Indian or Alaska Native, non-Hispanic/Latino; 6 Asian, non-Hispanic/Latino; 36 Hispanic/Latino; 4 Two or more races, non-Hispanic/Latino, 27 international. Average age 41. 125 applicants, 58% accepted, 33 enrolled. In 2010, 8 doctorates awarded. *Degree requirements:* For doctorate, comprehensive exam, thesis/dissertation, qualifying exam. *Entrance requirements:* For doctorate, interview, minimum GPA of 3.5. Additional exam requirements/recommendations for international students: Required—TOEFL. *Application deadline:* For fall admission, 6/1 priority date for domestic and international students; for winter admission, 10/1 priority date for domestic and international students; for spring admission, 3/1 priority date for domestic and international students. Applications are processed on a rolling basis. Application fee: $50. Electronic applications accepted. *Financial support:* In 2010–11, 144 students received support, including 10 research assistantships with tuition reimbursements available (averaging $15,600 per year); teaching assistantships, career-related internships or fieldwork, Federal Work-Study, scholarships/grants, and unspecified assistantships also available. Financial award application deadline: 4/1; financial award applicants required to submit CSS PROFILE. *Faculty research:* International conflict, violence prevention, facilitation and mediation, communication and conflict. *Unit head:* Dr. Neil Katz, Chair, 954-262-3040, Fax: 954-262-3050, E-mail: kneil@nova.edu. *Application contact:* Marcia Arango, Student Recruitment Coordinator, 954-262-3006, Fax: 954-262-3968, E-mail: marango@nsu.nova.edu.

Nova Southeastern University, Graduate School of Humanities and Social Sciences, Department of Conflict Analysis and Resolution, Master's Program in Conflict Analysis and Resolution, Fort Lauderdale, FL 33314-7796. Offers MS, JD/MS. Part-time programs available. Postbaccalaureate distance learning degree programs offered (minimal on-campus study).

Conflict Resolution and Mediation/Peace Studies

Nova Southeastern University (continued)
Faculty: 11 full-time (6 women), 3 part-time/adjunct (2 women). *Students:* 36 full-time (28 women), 57 part-time (42 women); includes 26 Black or African American, non-Hispanic/Latino; 3 Asian, non-Hispanic/Latino; 20 Hispanic/Latino; 2 Two or more races, non-Hispanic/Latino, 6 international. Average age 34. 36 applicants, 47% accepted, 10 enrolled. In 2010, 14 master's awarded. *Degree requirements:* For master's, comprehensive exam, thesis optional. *Entrance requirements:* For master's, interview, minimum GPA of 3.0, writing sample. Additional exam requirements/recommendations for international students: Required—TOEFL. *Application deadline:* For fall admission, 6/1 priority date for domestic and international students; for winter admission, 10/1 priority date for domestic and international students; for spring admission, 3/1 priority date for domestic and international students. Applications are processed on a rolling basis. Application fee: $50. Electronic applications accepted. *Faculty research:* International conflict, violence prevention, communication and conflict facilitation, mediation. *Unit head:* Dr. Neil Katz, Chair, 954-262-3040, Fax: 954-262-3968, E-mail: kneil@nova.edu. *Application contact:* Marcia Arango, Student Recruitment Coordinator, 954-262-3006, Fax: 954-262-3968, E-mail: marango@nsu.nova.edu.

Pepperdine University, School of Law, Master of Dispute Resolution Program, Malibu, CA 90263. Offers MDR. *Faculty:* 35 full-time (12 women), 40 part-time/adjunct (5 women). *Students:* 5 full-time (3 women), 20 part-time (13 women); includes 4 minority (1 American Indian or Alaska Native, non-Hispanic/Latino; 1 Asian, non-Hispanic/Latino; 1 Hispanic/Latino; 1 Two or more races, non-Hispanic/Latino). 26 applicants, 69% accepted, 9 enrolled. In 2010, 34 master's awarded. *Entrance requirements:* For master's, GRE/LSAT, letters of recommendation. *Application deadline:* For fall admission, 2/15 for domestic students; for spring admission, 8/15 for domestic students. Application fee: $60. *Unit head:* Prof. Peter Robinson, Managing Director, Straus Institute for Dispute Resolution, 310-506-4655, E-mail: peter.robinson@pepperdine.edu. *Application contact:* Shellee Warnes, Associate Director, Straus Institute for Dispute Resolution, 310-506-7455, E-mail: shellee.warnes@pepperdine.edu.

Pepperdine University, School of Law, Master of Laws in Dispute Resolution Program, Malibu, CA 90263. Offers LL M. *Faculty:* 35 full-time (12 women), 40 part-time/adjunct (5 women). *Students:* 6 full-time (4 women), 20 part-time (12 women); includes 1 minority (Black or African American, non-Hispanic/Latino), 8 international. 30 applicants, 53% accepted, 8 enrolled. *Entrance requirements:* For master's, GRE General Test or LSAT, JD from ABA-accredited institution. *Application deadline:* For fall admission, 2/15 for domestic students; for spring admission, 8/15 for domestic students. Applications are processed on a rolling basis. Application fee: $60. Electronic applications accepted. *Expenses:* Contact institution. *Financial support:* Career-related internships or fieldwork, Federal Work-Study, institutionally sponsored loans, and scholarships/grants available. Support available to part-time students. Financial award application deadline: 4/1; financial award applicants required to submit FAFSA. *Unit head:* Dr. Peter Robinson, Director, Institute for Dispute Resolution, 310-506-4655, Fax: 310-506-4266, E-mail: peter.robinson@pepperdine.edu. *Application contact:* Shellee S. Warnes, Assistant Director, Academic Programs, 310-506-7455, Fax: 310-506-4266, E-mail: shellee.warnes@pepperdine.edu.

Portland State University, Graduate Studies, College of Liberal Arts and Sciences, Program in Conflict Resolution, Portland, OR 97207-0751. Offers MA, MS. *Faculty:* 6 full-time (2 women), 3 part-time/adjunct (all women). *Students:* 54 full-time (39 women), 52 part-time (36 women); includes 17 minority (6 Black or African American, non-Hispanic/Latino; 3 Asian, non-Hispanic/Latino; 6 Hispanic/Latino; 2 Two or more races, non-Hispanic/Latino), 10 international. Average age 33. 45 applicants, 91% accepted, 33 enrolled. In 2010, 45 master's awarded. *Degree requirements:* For master's, thesis or alternative, practicum. *Entrance requirements:* For master's, 3 letters of recommendation. Additional exam requirements/recommendations for international students: Required—TOEFL (minimum score 550 paper-based; 213 computer-based). *Application deadline:* For fall admission, 4/1 for domestic students, 3/1 for international students; for winter admission, 9/1 for domestic students, 8/1 for international students; for spring admission, 11/1 for domestic and international students. Application fee: $50. *Expenses:* Tuition, state resident: full-time $8505; part-time $315 per credit. Tuition, nonresident: full-time $13,284; part-time $492 per credit. Required fees: $1482; $21 per credit. $99 per term. One-time fee: $120. Part-time tuition and fees vary according to course load and program. *Financial support:* In 2010–11, 1 teaching assistantship with full tuition reimbursement (averaging $7,716 per year) was awarded; Federal Work-Study also available. Total annual research expenditures: $1,449. *Unit head:* Dr. Robert Gould, Director, 503-725-3502, E-mail: gouldr@pdx.edu. *Application contact:* Stephen Jahnke, Program Administrator, 503-725-9175, E-mail: jahnkes@pdx.edu.

Regis University, College for Professional Studies, School of Humanities and Social Sciences, MA Program, Denver, CO 80221-1099. Offers communication (MA); fine arts (Certificate); interdisciplinary studies (MA); mediation and conflict resolution (Certificate); psychology (MA); social justice, peace, and reconciliation (Certificate); technical communication (Certificate). Program also offered in Henderson and Las Vegas (Summerlin), NV. Part-time and evening/weekend programs available. Postbaccalaureate distance learning degree programs offered (minimal on-campus study). *Degree requirements:* For master's, thesis, research project. *Entrance requirements:* For master's, resume, recommendations. Additional exam requirements/recommendations for international students: Required—TOEFL (minimum score 213 computer-based), TWE (minimum score 5). Electronic applications accepted. *Expenses:* Contact institution. *Faculty research:* Independent/nonresidential graduate study: new methods and models, adult learning and the capstone experience, Goal Setting, behavior of Adult students, Innovative Studies for Community Colleges.

Royal Roads University, Graduate Studies, Peace and Conflict Studies Program, Victoria, BC V9B 5Y2, Canada. Offers conflict analysis (G Dip); conflict analysis and management (MA); disaster and emergency management (MA); human security and peacebuilding (MA). Postbaccalaureate distance learning degree programs offered (minimal on-campus study). *Degree requirements:* For master's, thesis. *Entrance requirements:* For master's, 5-7 years of related work experience. Additional exam requirements/recommendations for international students: Required—TOEFL (paper-based 570; computer-based 233) or IELTS (paper-based 7) (recommended). Electronic applications accepted. *Faculty research:* Conflict analysis, ethno-political conflict reconciliation, international relations, displaced persons.

St. Edward's University, School of Education, Program in Teaching, Austin, TX 78704. Offers curriculum leadership (Certificate); instructional technology (Certificate); mediation (Certificate); mentoring and supervision (Certificate); special education (Certificate); sports management (Certificate); teaching (MA), including conflict resolution, initial teacher certification, liberal arts, special education, sports management, teacher leadership. Part-time and evening/weekend programs available. *Students:* 7 full-time (6 women), 38 part-time (28 women); includes 13 minority (2 Black or African American, non-Hispanic/Latino; 10 Hispanic/Latino; 1 Two or more races, non-Hispanic/Latino). Average age 29. 25 applicants, 80% accepted, 17 enrolled. In 2010, 14 master's awarded. *Degree requirements:* For master's, minimum of 24 resident hours. *Entrance requirements:* For master's, GRE General Test, minimum GPA of 3.0 in last 60 hours or 2.75 overall. Additional exam requirements/recommendations for international students: Required—TOEFL (minimum score 550 paper-based; 213 computer-based; 79 iBT) or IELTS (minimum score 6). *Application deadline:* For fall admission, 7/1 for domestic and international students; for spring admission, 11/1 for domestic and international students. Applications are processed on a rolling basis. Application fee: $45 ($50 for international students). Electronic applications accepted. *Expenses:* Tuition: Full-time $16,200; part-time $900 per credit hour. Required fees: $50 per trimester. Full-time tuition and fees vary according to course load and program. *Financial support:* In 2010–11, 4 students received support. Scholarships/grants available. *Faculty research:* Assessment, school change and improvement, program change, curriculum evaluation in schools. *Unit head:* Dr. David Hollier, Director, 512-448-8666, Fax: 512-428-1372, E-mail: davidrh@stedwards.edu. *Application contact:* Carrie Martin, Graduate Admission Coordinator, 512-233-1694, Fax: 512-428-1032, E-mail: carriem@stedwards.edu.

Saint Paul University, Faculty of Human Sciences, Program in Conflict Studies, Ottawa, ON K1S 1C4, Canada. Offers MA. Part-time programs available. *Entrance requirements:* For master's, H=honors BA, B average.

Salisbury University, Graduate Division, Program in Conflict Analysis and Dispute Resolution, Salisbury, MD 21801-6837. Offers MA. *Faculty:* 3 full-time (0 women). *Students:* 33 full-time (18 women), 4 part-time (all women); includes 8 minority (4 Black or African American, non-Hispanic/Latino; 1 American Indian or Alaska Native, non-Hispanic/Latino; 1 Asian, non-Hispanic/Latino; 2 Two or more races, non-Hispanic/Latino), 2 international. Average age 34. 33 applicants, 67% accepted, 2 enrolled. *Entrance requirements:* Additional exam requirements/recommendations for international students: Required—TOEFL (minimum score 550 paper-based; 213 computer-based; 79 iBT). Application fee: $45. *Financial support:* In 2010–11, 10 students received support. *Unit head:* Rob LaChance, Program Director, 410-677-0231, E-mail: rmlachance@salisbury.edu. *Application contact:* Rob LaChance, Program Director, 410-677-0231, E-mail: rmlachance@salisbury.edu.

SIT Graduate Institute, Graduate Programs, Master's Programs in Intercultural Service, Leadership, and Management, Program in Conflict Transformation, Brattleboro, VT 05302-0676. Offers MA. *Expenses:* Tuition: Full-time $35,260; part-time $14,876 per year. Required fees: $1495; $1495 per year. Tuition and fees vary according to class time and campus/location.

Southern Methodist University, Annette Caldwell Simmons School of Education and Human Development, Department of Dispute Resolution and Counseling, Dallas, TX 75275. Offers counseling (MS); dispute resolution (MA, Certificate). Part-time programs available. *Faculty:* 8 full-time (3 women), 21 part-time/adjunct (11 women). *Students:* 5 full-time (3 women), 286 part-time (240 women); includes 73 minority (29 Black or African American, non-Hispanic/Latino; 11 Asian, non-Hispanic/Latino; 27 Hispanic/Latino; 1 Native Hawaiian or other Pacific Islander, non-Hispanic/Latino; 5 Two or more races, non-Hispanic/Latino), 7 international. Average age 34. 103 applicants, 50% accepted, 46 enrolled. In 2010, 93 master's, 14 other advanced degrees awarded. *Degree requirements:* For master's, practica experience, 2 internships (counseling). *Entrance requirements:* For master's, minimum undergraduate GPA of 2.75 (for dispute resolution), 3.0 (for counseling); 3 letters of recommendation. Additional exam requirements/recommendations for international students: Required—TOEFL. *Application deadline:* For fall admission, 5/1 for domestic students; for spring admission, 12/1 for domestic students. Applications are processed on a rolling basis. Application fee: $75. Electronic applications accepted. *Unit head:* Dr. Tony Picchioni, Department Chair, 972-473-3408, Fax: 972-473-3425. *Application contact:* Cynthia McIntyre, Program Manager, 972-473-3431, Fax: 972-473-3425, E-mail: adr@smu.edu.

Sullivan University, School of Business, Louisville, KY 40205. Offers business administration (MBA); collaborative leadership (MSCL); conflict management (MSCM); dispute resolution (MSDR); executive business administration (EMBA); human resource leadership (MSHRL); information technology (MSMIT); management (PhD); management and information technology (MBIT); pharmacy (Pharm D). Part-time programs available. Postbaccalaureate distance learning degree programs offered (no on-campus study). *Faculty:* 13 full-time (7 women), 11 part-time/adjunct (4 women). *Students:* 429 full-time (239 women), 322 part-time (198 women); includes 244 minority (152 Black or African American, non-Hispanic/Latino; 5 American Indian or Alaska Native, non-Hispanic/Latino; 5 Hispanic/Latino; 56 Native Hawaiian or other Pacific Islander, non-Hispanic/Latino; 26 Two or more races, non-Hispanic/Latino), 15 international. In 2010, 133 master's awarded. *Entrance requirements:* Additional exam requirements/recommendations for international students: Required—TOEFL. *Application deadline:* Applications are processed on a rolling basis. Application fee: $100. *Unit head:* Dr. Eric S. Harter, Dean of Graduate School, 502-456-6504, Fax: 502-456-0040, E-mail: eharter@sullivan.edu. *Application contact:* Beverly Horsley, Admissions Officer, 502-456-6505, Fax: 502-456-0040, E-mail: bhorsley@sullivan.edu.

Syracuse University, Maxwell School of Citizenship and Public Affairs, Program in Conflict Resolution, Syracuse, NY 13244. Offers CAS. Part-time programs available. *Students:* 15 applicants, 87% accepted, 0 enrolled. In 2010, 36 CASs awarded. Application fee: $75. Electronic applications accepted. *Expenses:* Tuition: Part-time $1162 per credit. *Unit head:* Catherine Gerard, Director, 315-443-2367, E-mail: parc@syr.edu. *Application contact:* Catherine Gerard, Director, 315-443-2367, E-mail: parc@syr.edu.

Syracuse University, Maxwell School of Citizenship and Public Affairs, Program in Post Conflict Reconstruction, Syracuse, NY 13244. Offers CAS. Part-time programs available. *Students:* 23 applicants, 100% accepted. *Entrance requirements:* For degree, matriculated graduate student status. *Expenses:* Tuition: Part-time $1162 per credit. *Application contact:* William Banks, Director, INSCT Office, 315-443-2284.

Tufts University, Fletcher School of Law and Diplomacy, Medford, MA 02155. Offers LL M, MA, MAHA, MALD, MIB, PhD, DVM/MA, JD/MALD, MALD/MA, MALD/MBA, MALD/MS, MD/MA. Postbaccalaureate distance learning degree programs offered (minimal on-campus study). *Faculty:* 37 full-time (10 women), 48 part-time/adjunct (14 women). *Students:* 541 full-time (278 women), 9 part-time (3 women); includes 73 minority (8 Black or African American, non-Hispanic/Latino; 30 Asian, non-Hispanic/Latino; 11 Hispanic/Latino; 24 Two or more races, non-Hispanic/Latino), 208 international. Average age 31. 1,875 applicants, 41% accepted, 296 enrolled. In 2010, 297 master's, 14 doctorates awarded. *Degree requirements:* For master's, one foreign language, thesis; for doctorate, one foreign language, comprehensive exam, thesis/dissertation, dissertation defense. *Entrance requirements:* For master's and doctorate, GMAT or GRE General Test. Additional exam requirements/recommendations for international students: Required—TOEFL (minimum score 600 paper-based; 250 computer-based; 100 iBT), IELTS (minimum score 7). *Application deadline:* For fall admission, 1/15 for domestic and international students; for spring admission, 10/15 for domestic and international students. Application fee: $70. Electronic applications accepted. *Expenses:* Contact institution. *Financial support:* Federal Work-Study, institutionally sponsored loans, scholarships/grants, and tuition waivers (partial) available. Financial award application deadline: 1/15; financial award applicants required to submit FAFSA. *Faculty research:* Negotiation and conflict resolution, international organizations, international business and economic law, security studies, development economics. *Unit head:* Stephen W. Bosworth, Dean, 617-627-3050, Fax: 617-627-3712. *Application contact:* Laurie A. Hurley, 617-627-3040, E-mail: fletcheradmissions@tufts.edu.

TUI University, College of Business Administration, Program in Business Administration, Cypress, CA 90630. Offers business administration (PhD); conflict and negotiation management (MBA); criminal justice administration (MBA); entrepreneurship (MBA); finance (MBA); general management (MBA); government accounting (MBA); human resource management (MBA); information security and digital assurance management (MBA); information technology management (MBA); international business (MBA); logistics management (MBA); marketing (MBA); project management (MBA); public management (MBA); quality management (MBA); strategic leadership (MBA). Part-time and evening/weekend programs available. Postbaccalaureate distance learning degree programs offered (no on-campus study). *Students:* 741 full-time (200 women), 1,585 part-time (410 women). 379 applicants, 81% accepted, 300 enrolled. In 2010, 752 master's, 28 doctorates awarded. *Degree requirements:* For doctorate, comprehensive exam, thesis/dissertation, defense of dissertation. *Entrance requirements:* For master's, minimum GPA of 2.5 (students with GPA 3.0 or greater may transfer up to 30% of graduate level credits); for doctorate, minimum GPA of 3.4, curriculum vitae, course work in research methods or statistics. Additional exam requirements/recommendations for international students: Required—TOEFL. *Application deadline:* For fall admission, 10/3 for domestic and international students; for winter admission, 12/22 for domestic and international students; for spring admission, 4/3 for domestic and international students. Applications are processed on a rolling basis. Application fee: $75. Electronic applications accepted. *Expenses:* Tuition: Full-time $11,040; part-time $345 per semester hour. *Unit head:* Paul Watkins, Dean, College of Business Administration, 800-375-9878, E-mail: pwatkins@tuiu.edu. *Application contact:* Wei Ren-Finaly, Registrar, 800-375-9878, Fax: 714-827-7407, E-mail: registration@tuiu.edu.

United States International University, School of Arts and Sciences, Nairobi, Kenya. Offers counseling psychology (MA), including chemical dependency, health psychology; international relations (MA), including development studies, diplomacy and foreign policy, peace and conflict studies. Part-time and evening/weekend programs available. *Faculty:* 43 full-time (14 women), 69 part-time/adjunct (28 women). *Students:* 94 full-time (60 women), 22 part-time (all women). Average age 30. 93 applicants, 80% accepted, 64 enrolled. In 2010, 33 master's awarded. *Degree requirements:* For master's, thesis, practicum. *Entrance requirements:* For master's, GRE General Test, 2 letters of recommendation, resume. Additional exam requirements/recommendations for international students: Required—TOEFL. *Application deadline:* For fall admission, 6/30 priority date for domestic and international students. Application fee: $50. *Financial support:* In 2010–11, 56 students received support, including 3 research assistantships (averaging $1,400 per year), 7 teaching assistantships (averaging $1,400 per year); career-related internships or fieldwork, scholarships/grants, and unspecified assistantships also available. Support available to part-time students. Financial award application deadline: 6/30; financial award applicants required to submit FAFSA. *Faculty research:* Trauma in children, African intellectualism, psychological assessment tools. *Unit head:* Prof. Mulinge Munyae, Dean, 254-02-3606-434, E-mail: mmulinge@usiu.ac.ke. *Application contact:* George Lumbasi, Director of Admissions, 254-02-3606563, Fax: 254-02-3606100, E-mail: glumbasi@usiu.ac.ke.

United Theological Seminary of the Twin Cities, Graduate Programs, New Brighton, MN 55112-2598. Offers advanced theological studies (Diploma); justice and peace studies (M Div, MA); leadership toward racial justice (M Div, MA, Certificate); Methodist studies (M Div, MA, Certificate); ministry (D Min); ministry renewal and professional development (Certificate); pastoral care and counseling (M Div, MA, MARL); religion and theology (MA); theological and religious studies (Certificate); theology and the arts (M Div, MA); urban ministry (M Div, MA, MARL); women's studies: religion, theology and ministry (M Div, MA). *Accreditation:* ACIPE; ATS. Part-time and evening/weekend programs available. *Faculty:* 8 full-time (5 women), 28 part-time/adjunct (16 women). *Students:* 57 full-time (41 women), 94 part-time (61 women); includes 6 minority (5 Black or African American, non-Hispanic/Latino; 1 Hispanic/Latino), 1 international. Average age 47. 49 applicants, 98% accepted, 41 enrolled. In 2010, 10 first professional degrees, 6 master's, 4 doctorates, 2 other advanced degrees awarded. *Degree requirements:* For master's, thesis; for doctorate, comprehensive exam, thesis/dissertation; for M Div, integrative notebook, spiritual chronicle. *Entrance requirements:* For M Div and master's, minimum GPA of 2.75; strong analytical, reflective thinking and writing skills; vocational and academic goals compatible with those of Seminary; for doctorate, M Div or equivalent, minimum GPA of 3.0, 3 years experience in professional ministry; for other advanced degree, BA or equivalent life experience; strong analytical, reflective thinking and writing skills (Certificate); proficiency in English language, previous study of theology at a theological school, recommendation of student's denomination (Diploma). Additional exam requirements/recommendations for international students: Required—TOEFL (minimum score 550 paper-based). *Application deadline:* For fall admission, 7/1 priority date for domestic students, 11/1 priority date for international students; for winter admission, 11/1 priority date for domestic students; for spring admission, 11/15 priority date for domestic students. Applications are processed on a rolling basis. Application fee: $50. *Expenses:* Tuition: Full-time $13,014; part-time $482 per credit hour. One-time fee: $170. Tuition and fees vary according to course load, degree level and program. *Financial support:* In 2010–11, 120 students received support. Career-related internships or fieldwork, institutionally sponsored loans, and scholarships/grants available. Support available to part-time students. Financial award application deadline: 5/1; financial award applicants required to submit FAFSA. *Unit head:* Prof. Susan K. Ebbers, Dean of the Seminary, 651-255-6143 Ext. 108, Fax: 651-633-4315, E-mail: sebbers@unitedseminary.edu. *Application contact:* Rev. Glen Herrington-Hall, Director of Admissions, 651-255-6107 Ext. 107, Fax: 651-633-4315, E-mail: gherrington-hall@unitedseminary.edu.

Universidad del Turabo, Graduate Programs, School of Social Sciences and Humanities, Programs in Public Affairs, Gurabo, PR 00778-3030. Offers arts administration (MPA); conflict and mediation studies (MPA); criminal justice studies (MPA); forensic science (MPA); human services administration (MPA). *Entrance requirements:* For master's, GRE, EXADEP, interview.

Université de Sherbrooke, Faculty of Law, Sherbrooke, QC J1K 2R1, Canada. Offers alternative dispute resolution (LL M, Diploma); biotechnology (LL B); business administration (LL B); business law (Diploma); health law (LL M, Diploma); law (LL B, LL D); legal management (Diploma); notarial law (DDN); transnational law (Diploma). Part-time and evening/weekend programs available. *Degree requirements:* For master's, thesis; for other advanced degree, one foreign language. *Entrance requirements:* For master's and other advanced degree, LL B. Electronic applications accepted.

University of Arkansas at Little Rock, Graduate School, College of Professional Studies, Program in Conflict Mediation, Little Rock, AR 72204-1099. Offers Graduate Certificate.

University of Baltimore, Graduate School, The Yale Gordon College of Liberal Arts, Program in Negotiations and Conflict Management, Baltimore, MD 21201-5779. Offers negotiations and conflict management (MS). Part-time and evening/weekend programs available. *Degree requirements:* For master's, thesis optional, internship. *Entrance requirements:* For master's, minimum GPA of 3.0. Additional exam requirements/recommendations for international students: Required—TOEFL (minimum score 550 paper-based; 213 computer-based). Electronic applications accepted. *Faculty research:* Communication and conflict, conflict management systems theory.

University of Bridgeport, International College, Bridgeport, CT 06604. Offers global development and peace (MA). Part-time and evening/weekend programs available. *Degree requirements:* For master's, thesis. *Entrance requirements:* Additional exam requirements/recommendations for international students: Recommended—TOEFL (minimum score 550 paper-based; 213 computer-based; 80 iBT), IELTS (minimum score 6.5). *Expenses:* Tuition: Full-time $22,000; part-time $575 per credit hour. Required fees: $90 per semester. Tuition and fees vary according to course level, course load and program.

University of Denver, Josef Korbel School of International Studies, Program in Conflict Resolution, Denver, CO 80208. Offers MA. Part-time programs available. *Degree requirements:* For master's, thesis, internship. *Entrance requirements:* For master's, GRE, GMAT, or LSAT, 3 letters of recommendation, personal statement. Additional exam requirements/recommendations for international students: Required—TOEFL. Electronic applications accepted. *Expenses:* Tuition: Full-time $35,604; part-time $29,670 per year. Required fees: $687 per year. Tuition and fees vary according to program.

University of Denver, University College, Denver, CO 80208. Offers arts and culture (MLS, Certificate), including art, literature, and culture, arts development and program management (Certificate), creative writing; environmental policy and management (MAS, Certificate), including energy and sustainability (Certificate), environmental assessment of nuclear power (Certificate), environmental health and safety (Certificate), environmental management, natural resource management (Certificate); geographic information systems (MAS, Certificate); global affairs (MLS, Certificate), including translation studies, world history and culture; healthcare leadership (MPH, Certificate), including healthcare policy, law, and ethics, medical and healthcare information technologies, strategic management of healthcare; information and communications technology (MCIS, Certificate), including database design and administration (Certificate), geographic information systems (MCIS), information security systems security (Certificate), information systems security (MCIS), project management (MCIS, MPS, Certificate), software design and administration (Certificate), software design and programming (MCIS), technology management, telecommunications technology (MCIS), Web design and development; leadership and organizations (MPS, Certificate), including human capital in organizations, philanthropic leadership, project management (MCIS, MPS, Certificate), strategic innovation and change; organizational and professional communication (MPS, Certificate), including alternative dispute resolution, organizational communication, organizational development and training, public relations and marketing; security management (MAS, Certificate), including emergency planning and response, information security (MAS), organizational security; strategic human resource management (MPS, Certificate), including global human resources (MPS), human resource management and development (MPS). Part-time and evening/weekend programs available. Postbaccalaureate distance learning degree programs offered (no on-campus study). *Faculty:* 7 full-time (2 women), 212 part-time/adjunct (83 women). *Students:* 52 full-time (19 women), 1,044 part-time (625 women); includes 196 minority (81 Black or African American, non-Hispanic/Latino; 7 American Indian or Alaska Native, non-Hispanic/Latino; 30 Asian, non-Hispanic/Latino; 66 Hispanic/Latino; 3 Native Hawaiian or other Pacific Islander, non-Hispanic/Latino; 9 Two or more races, non-Hispanic/Latino), 76 international. Average age 36. 488 applicants, 91% accepted, 339 enrolled. In 2010, 286 master's, 130 other advanced degrees awarded. *Entrance requirements:* Additional exam requirements/recommendations for international students: Required—TOEFL (minimum score 550 paper-based; 80 iBT). *Application deadline:* For fall admission, 6/22 priority date for domestic students, 6/10 priority date for international students; for winter admission, 9/15 priority date for domestic students, 9/6 priority date for international students; for spring admission, 2/3 priority date for domestic students, 12/15 priority date for international students. Applications are processed on a rolling basis. Application fee: $75. Electronic applications accepted. *Expenses:* Contact institution. *Financial support:* Applicants required to submit FAFSA. *Unit head:* Dr. James Davis, Dean, 303-871-2291, Fax: 303-871-4047, E-mail: jdavis@du.edu. *Application contact:* Information Contact, 303-871-3155, Fax: 303-871-4047, E-mail: ucolinfo@du.edu.

University of Hawaii at Manoa, Graduate Division, College of Social Sciences, Spark M. Matsunaga Institute for Peace, Honolulu, HI 96822. Offers conflict resolution (Graduate Certificate). Part-time programs available. *Faculty:* 9 full-time (3 women), 8 part-time/adjunct (2 women). *Students:* 14 full-time (10 women), 10 part-time (7 women); includes 4 minority (1 Asian, non-Hispanic/Latino; 1 Hispanic/Latino; 2 Two or more races, non-Hispanic/Latino), 12 international. Average age 36. 27 applicants, 78% accepted, 14 enrolled. In 2010, 11 Graduate Certificates awarded. *Entrance requirements:* For degree, GRE General Test. Additional exam requirements/recommendations for international students: Required—TOEFL (minimum score 540 paper-based; 207 computer-based; 76 iBT), IELTS (minimum score 5). *Application deadline:* For fall admission, 2/15 for domestic and international students; for spring admission, 9/30 for domestic and international students. Application fee: $60. *Financial support:* In 2010–11, 2 fellowships (averaging $1,960 per year), 2 research assistantships (averaging $17,160 per year), 3 teaching assistantships (averaging $14,574 per year) were awarded. *Application contact:* Dolores Foley, Chairperson, 808-956-6433, Fax: 808-956-9121, E-mail: dolores@hawaii.edu.

University of Maine, Graduate School, Program in Liberal Studies, Orono, ME 04469. Offers Maine studies (MA); new media (MA); peace studies (MA). Part-time and evening/weekend programs available. *Students:* 2 full-time (both women), 19 part-time (13 women); includes 2 American Indian or Alaska Native, non-Hispanic/Latino, 1 international. Average age 47. 5 applicants, 40% accepted, 2 enrolled. In 2010, 6 master's awarded. *Degree requirements:* For master's, project. *Entrance requirements:* Additional exam requirements/recommendations for international students: Required—TOEFL. *Application deadline:* For fall admission, 4/1 for domestic students; for spring admission, 11/1 for domestic students. Applications are processed on a rolling basis. Application fee: $65. Electronic applications accepted. *Expenses:* Tuition, state resident: full-time $400. Tuition, nonresident: full-time $1050. *Financial support:* Federal Work-Study and institutionally sponsored loans available. Financial award application deadline: 3/1. *Unit head:* Amaranta Ruiz-Nelson, Coordinator, 207-581-3222, Fax: 207-581-3232, E-mail: graduate@maine.edu. *Application contact:* Amaranta Ruiz-Nelson, Coordinator, 207-581-3222, Fax: 207-581-3232, E-mail: graduate@maine.edu.

The University of Manchester, School of Arts, Histories and Cultures, Manchester, United Kingdom. Offers anthropology, media and performance (PhD); applied theatre professional (PhD); archaeology (PhD); art history and visual studies (PhD); arts management and cultural policy (PhD); classics and ancient history (PhD); composition (PhD); creative writing (PhD); drama (PhD); economic and social history (PhD); electroacoustic composition (PhD); English and American studies (PhD); history (PhD); humanitarianism and conflict response (PhD); museology (PhD); music (PhD); musicology (PhD); religions and theology (PhD).

University of Massachusetts Amherst, Graduate School, College of Natural Sciences, Department of Psychology, Amherst, MA 01003. Offers clinical psychology (MS, PhD); cognitive psychology (MS, PhD); developmental science (MS, PhD); psychology of peace and violence (MS, PhD); social psychology (MS, PhD). *Accreditation:* APA (one or more programs are accredited). *Faculty:* 47 full-time (23 women). *Students:* 54 full-time (42 women), 6 part-time (4 women); includes 16 minority (3 Black or African American, non-Hispanic/Latino; 6 Asian, non-Hispanic/Latino; 4 Hispanic/Latino; 3 Two or more races, non-Hispanic/Latino), 3 international. Average age 29. 435 applicants, 4% accepted, 8 enrolled. In 2010, 12 master's, 16 doctorates awarded. Terminal master's awarded for partial completion of doctoral program. *Degree requirements:* For master's, thesis; for doctorate, comprehensive exam, thesis/dissertation. *Entrance requirements:* For master's and doctorate, GRE General Test, 3 letters of recommendation. Additional exam requirements/recommendations for international students: Required—TOEFL (minimum score 550 paper-based; 213 computer-based; 80 iBT), IELTS (minimum score 6.5). *Application deadline:* For fall admission, 12/1 for domestic and international students. Applications are processed on a rolling basis. Application fee: $50 ($65 for international students). Electronic applications accepted. *Expenses:* Tuition, state resident: full-time $2640. Required fees: $8282. One-time fee: $357 full-time. *Financial support:* In 2010–11, 8 fellowships with full tuition reimbursements (averaging $12,569 per year), 41 research assistantships with full tuition reimbursements (averaging $10,714 per year), 55 teaching assistantships with full tuition reimbursements (averaging $10,951 per year) were awarded; career-related internships or fieldwork, Federal Work-Study, scholarships/grants, traineeships, health care benefits, tuition waivers (full), and unspecified assistantships also available. Support available to part-time students. Financial award application deadline: 12/1; financial award applicants required to submit FAFSA. *Unit head:* Dr. Linda M. Isbell, Graduate Program Director, 413-545-2503, Fax: 413-545-0996. *Application contact:* Jean M. Ames, Supervisor of Admissions, 413-545-0722, Fax: 413-577-0010, E-mail: gradadm@grad.umass.edu.

University of Massachusetts Boston, Office of Graduate Studies, College of Public and Community Service, Program in Dispute Resolution, Boston, MA 02125-3393. Offers MA, Certificate. MA program accepts applications for fall admission only; Certificate program accepts applications for spring admission only. *Degree requirements:* For master's, practicum, final project. *Entrance requirements:* For master's, MAT or GRE, minimum GPA of 2.75; for Certificate, minimum GPA of 2.75. *Faculty research:* Mediation and negotiation, justice and conflict, cross-cultural mediation, environmental fairness, dispute resolution theory and ethics.

University of Missouri, Graduate School and School of Law, Program in Dispute Resolution, Columbia, MO 65211. Offers LL M. *Entrance requirements:* Additional exam requirements/recommendations for international students: Required—TOEFL (minimum score 600 paper-based; 250 computer-based; 100 iBT).

University of New Brunswick Fredericton, School of Graduate Studies, Policy Studies Program, Fredericton, NB E3B 5A3, Canada. Offers people, property and alternative dispute resolution (M Phil); philosophy politics and economics (M Phil); sustainable development (M Phil). Part-time programs available. *Faculty:* 7 full-time (4 women), 8 part-time/adjunct (4 women). *Students:* 4 full-time (2 women), 5 part-time (3 women). In 2010, 3 master's awarded. *Degree requirements:* For master's, thesis, report. *Entrance requirements:* For master's, minimum GPA of 3.5. Additional exam requirements/recommendations for international students: Required—TWE (minimum score 4), TOEFL (minimum score 600 paper-based; 250 computer-based; 100 iBT) or IELTS (minimum score 7). Application fee: $50 Canadian dollars. *Expenses:* Tuition, area resident: Full-time $3708; part-time $927 per term. International tuition: $6300 full-time. Required fees: $50 per term. *Financial support:* In 2010–11, 3 fellowships, research assistantships (averaging $5,600 per year), teaching assistantships (averaging $4,400 per

Conflict Resolution and Mediation/Peace Studies

University of New Brunswick Fredericton (continued)

year) were awarded. *Unit head:* Dr. Linda Eyre, Dean of Graduate Studies, 506-447-3044, Fax: 506-453-4817, E-mail: gradidst@unb.ca. *Application contact:* Janet Amurault, Graduate Secretary, 506-458-7558, Fax: 506-453-4817, E-mail: jamiraul@unb.ca.

University of New Haven, Graduate School, College of Arts and Sciences, Program in Industrial and Organizational Psychology, West Haven, CT 06516-1916. Offers conflict management (MA); human resource management (MA); industrial organizational psychology (MA); organizational development (MA); psychology of conflict management (Certificate). Part-time and evening/weekend programs available. *Students:* 75 full-time (54 women), 29 part-time (19 women); includes 7 Black or African American, non-Hispanic/Latino; 1 American Indian or Alaska Native, non-Hispanic/Latino; 1 Asian, non-Hispanic/Latino; 4 Hispanic/Latino, 13 international. Average age 28. 70 applicants, 100% accepted, 33 enrolled. In 2010, 44 master's, 1 other advanced degree awarded. *Degree requirements:* For master's, thesis or alternative. *Entrance requirements:* Additional exam requirements/recommendations for international students: Required—TOEFL (minimum score 520 paper-based; 190 computer-based; 70 iBT); Recommended—IELTS (minimum score 5.5). *Application deadline:* For fall admission, 5/31 for international students; for winter admission, 10/15 for international students; for spring admission, 1/15 for international students. Applications are processed on a rolling basis. Application fee: $50. Electronic applications accepted. *Expenses:* Contact institution. *Financial support:* Research assistantships with partial tuition reimbursements, teaching assistantships with partial tuition reimbursements, career-related internships or fieldwork, Federal Work-Study, scholarships/grants, tuition waivers, and unspecified assistantships available. Support available to part-time students. Financial award applicants required to submit FAFSA. *Unit head:* Dr. Stuart D. Sidle, Coordinator, 203-932-7341. *Application contact:* Eloise Gormley, Information Contact, 203-932-7449.

The University of North Carolina at Greensboro, Graduate School, Program in Conflict Resolution, Greensboro, NC 27412-5001. Offers MA, Certificate. Electronic applications accepted.

University of Notre Dame, Graduate School, College of Arts and Letters, Division of Social Science, Joan B. Kroc Institute for International Peace Studies, Notre Dame, IN 46556. Offers MA, PhD. *Degree requirements:* For master's, one foreign language, comprehensive exam, thesis optional; for doctorate, one foreign language, comprehensive exam, thesis/dissertation. *Entrance requirements:* For master's, GRE General Test. Additional exam requirements/recommendations for international students: Required—TOEFL (minimum score 600 paper-based; 250 computer-based; 80 iBT). Electronic applications accepted. *Faculty research:* The role of international norms and institutions in peacemaking; the impact of religious, philosophical, and cultural influences on peace; the dynamics of intergroup conflict and conflict transformation; the promotion of social, economic, and environmental justice.

University of San Diego, Joan B. Kroc School of Peace Studies, San Diego, CA 92110-2492. Offers peace and justice studies (MA). *Faculty:* 4 full-time (2 women), 1 part-time/adjunct (0 women). *Students:* 33 full-time (21 women), 1 (woman) part-time; includes 1 Black or African American, non-Hispanic/Latino; 3 Hispanic/Latino, 9 international. Average age 31. 100 applicants, 64% accepted, 26 enrolled. In 2010, 15 master's awarded. *Degree requirements:* For master's, capstone project. *Entrance requirements:* For master's, GRE General Test, minimum GPA of 3.0. Additional exam requirements/recommendations for international students: Required—TOEFL (minimum score 580 paper-based; 237 computer-based; 83 iBT), TWE. *Application deadline:* For fall admission, 2/15 for domestic and international students. Application fee: $45. Electronic applications accepted. *Expenses:* Tuition: Full-time $21,744; part-time $1208 per unit. Required fees: $224. Full-time tuition and fees vary according to course load and degree level. *Financial support:* In 2010–11, 20 students received support, including 9 fellowships; career-related internships or fieldwork, Federal Work-Study, institutionally sponsored loans, scholarships/grants, and unspecified assistantships also available. Support available to part-time students. Financial award application deadline: 4/1; financial award applicants required to submit FAFSA. *Faculty research:* Conflict analysis and resolution, human security and peacebuilding, human security-development-nexus, development and peacebuilding, human rights and transitional justice. *Unit head:* Fr. William Headley, Dean, 619-260-7919, E-mail: wheadley@sandiego.edu. *Application contact:* Stephen Pultz, Director of Admissions and Enrollment, 619-260-4506, Fax: 619-260-6836, E-mail: admissions@sandiego.edu.

University of the Sacred Heart, Graduate Programs, Program in Systems of Justice, San Juan, PR 00914-0383. Offers human rights and anti-discriminatory processes (MASJ); mediation and transformation of conflicts (MASJ).

University of Victoria, Faculty of Graduate Studies, Faculty of Human and Social Development, School of Public Administration, Victoria, BC V8W 2Y2, Canada. Offers dispute resolution (MADR); public administration (MPA, PhD); MPA/LL B. Part-time and evening/weekend programs available. Postbaccalaureate distance learning degree programs offered. *Degree requirements:* For master's, thesis (for some programs), report; for doctorate, thesis/dissertation, candidacy exam. *Entrance requirements:* For master's, GMAT or GRE General Test, professional resume; for doctorate, GMAT or GRE General Test. Additional exam requirements/recommendations for international students: Required—TOEFL (minimum score 610 paper-based; 255 computer-based). Electronic applications accepted. *Faculty research:* Policy analysis, local government, performance management, energy markets, labor markets.

University of Wisconsin–Milwaukee, Graduate School, College of Letters and Sciences, Department of Communication, Milwaukee, WI 53201-0413. Offers communication (MA, PhD); mediation and negotiation (Certificate); rhetorical leadership (Certificate). Part-time programs available. *Faculty:* 20 full-time (12 women). *Students:* 20 full-time (14 women), 36 part-time (29 women); includes 1 Black or African American, non-Hispanic/Latino; 1 Asian, non-Hispanic/Latino; 1 Hispanic/Latino, 6 international. Average age 32. 68 applicants, 57% accepted, 11 enrolled. In 2010, 21 master's awarded. *Degree requirements:* For master's, thesis or alternative; for doctorate, comprehensive exam. *Entrance requirements:* For master's, GRE General Test, minimum GPA of 3.0. Additional exam requirements/recommendations for international students: Required—TOEFL (minimum score 550 paper-based; 79 iBT), IELTS (minimum score 6). *Application deadline:* For fall admission, 1/1 priority date for domestic students; for spring admission, 9/1 for domestic students. Applications are processed on a rolling basis. Application fee: $56. Electronic applications accepted. *Financial support:* In 2010–11, 3 fellowships, 34 teaching assistantships were awarded; research assistantships, career-related internships or fieldwork, unspecified assistantships, and project assistantships also available. Support available to part-time students. Financial award application deadline: 4/15; financial award applicants required to submit FAFSA. Total annual research expenditures: $106,365. *Unit head:* Mike R. Allen, Representative, 414-229-4261, Fax: 414-229-3859, E-mail: mikealle@uwm.edu. *Application contact:* General Information Contact, 414-229-4982, Fax: 414-229-6967, E-mail: gradschool@uwm.edu.

University of Wisconsin–Milwaukee, Graduate School, College of Letters and Sciences, Interdepartmental Program in Human Resources and Labor Relations, Milwaukee, WI 53201-0413. Offers human resources and labor relations (MHRLR); international human resources and labor relations (Certificate); mediation and negotiation (Certificate). Part-time programs available. *Students:* 17 full-time (13 women), 30 part-time (23 women); includes 5 Black or African American, non-Hispanic/Latino; 1 American Indian or Alaska Native, non-Hispanic/Latino, 5 international. Average age 30. 38 applicants, 58% accepted, 8 enrolled. In 2010, 20 master's awarded. *Entrance requirements:* For master's, GMAT or GRE General Test. Additional exam requirements/recommendations for international students: Required—TOEFL (minimum score 550 paper-based; 79 iBT), IELTS (minimum score 6.5). *Application deadline:* For fall admission, 1/1 priority date for domestic students; for spring admission, 9/1 for domestic students. Applications are processed on a rolling basis. Application fee: $56 ($96 for international students). Electronic applications accepted. *Financial support:* Career-related internships or fieldwork available. Support available to part-time students. Financial award application deadline: 4/15; financial award applicants required to submit FAFSA. *Unit head:* Susan M. Donohue-Davies, Representative, 414-299-4009, Fax: 414-229-5915, E-mail: suedono@uwm.edu. *Application contact:* General Information Contact, 414-229-4982, Fax: 414-229-6967, E-mail: gradschool@uwm.edu.

Walden University, Graduate Programs, School of Public Policy and Administration, Minneapolis, MN 55401. Offers criminal justice (MPA); emergency management (MPA); government management (Postbaccalaureate Certificate); health policy (MPA); homeland security policy (MPA); homeland security policy and coordination (MPA); interdisciplinary policy studies (MPA); international nongovernmental organizations (ngos) (MPA); law and public policy (MPA); local government management for sustainable communities (MPA); nonprofit management (Postbaccalaureate Certificate); nonprofit management and leadership (MPA, MS); policy analysis (MPA); public management and leadership (MPA); public policy and administration (MPA, PhD), including criminal justice (PhD), emergency management (PhD), health policy (PhD), health services (PhD), homeland security policy (PhD), homeland security policy and coordination (PhD), interdisciplinary policy studies (PhD), international nongovernmental organizations (PhD), law and public policy (PhD), local government management for sustainable communities (PhD), nonprofit management and leadership (PhD), policy analysis (PhD), public management and leadership (PhD), terrorism, mediation, and peace (PhD); terrorism, mediation, and peace (MPA). Part-time and evening/weekend programs available. Postbaccalaureate distance learning degree programs offered (minimal on-campus study). *Faculty:* 10 full-time (5 women), 117 part-time/adjunct (49 women). *Students:* 1,408 full-time (901 women), 599 part-time (392 women); includes 1,022 Black or African American, non-Hispanic/Latino; 11 American Indian or Alaska Native, non-Hispanic/Latino; 37 Asian, non-Hispanic/Latino; 64 Hispanic/Latino; 26 Two or more races, non-Hispanic/Latino, 47 international. Average age 40. In 2010, 311 master's, 23 doctorates awarded. *Degree requirements:* For doctorate, thesis/dissertation, residency. *Entrance requirements:* For master's, bachelor's degree or equivalent in related field, minimum GPA of 2.5; for doctorate, master's degree or equivalent in related field; minimum GPA of 3.0; official transcripts; three years of related professional/academic experience (preferred); access to computer and Internet. Additional exam requirements/recommendations for international students: Required—TOEFL (minimum score 550 paper-based; 213 computer-based), IELTS (minimum score 6.5), TOEFL (minimum score 550 paper-based; 213 computer-based), IELTS (minimum score 6.5), or Michigan English Language Assessment Battery (minimum score 82). *Application deadline:* Applications are processed on a rolling basis. Application fee: $50. Electronic applications accepted. *Expenses:* Tuition: Full-time $10,274; part-time $445 per credit. Tuition and fees vary according to course load, degree level and program. *Financial support:* Fellowships with tuition reimbursements, Federal Work-Study, scholarships/grants, unspecified assistantships, and family tuition reduction, active duty/veteran tuition reduction, group tuition reduction, interest-free payment plans available. Support available to part-time students. Financial award applicants required to submit FAFSA. *Unit head:* Dr. Mark Gordon, Associate Dean, 800-925-3368. *Application contact:* Jennifer Hall, Vice President of Enrollment Management, 866-4-WALDEN, E-mail: info@waldenu.edu.

Wayne State University, College of Fine, Performing and Communication Arts, Interdisciplinary Program in Dispute Resolution, Detroit, MI 48202. Offers MADR, Certificate, JD/MADR. *Faculty:* 25 full-time (11 women), 4 part-time/adjunct (1 woman). *Students:* 1 full-time (0 women), 27 part-time (21 women); includes 17 minority (16 Black or African American, non-Hispanic/Latino; 1 Two or more races, non-Hispanic/Latino), 1 international. Average age 39. 8 applicants, 38% accepted, 3 enrolled. In 2010, 8 master's, 4 other advanced degrees awarded. *Entrance requirements:* For master's, GMAT, GRE General Test, or LSAT. Additional exam requirements/recommendations for international students: Required—TOEFL (minimum score 550 paper-based; 213 computer-based); Recommended—TWE (minimum score 6). *Application deadline:* For fall admission, 7/1 for domestic students, 6/1 for international students; for winter admission, 10/1 for international students; for spring admission, 2/1 for international students. Applications are processed on a rolling basis. Application fee: $30 ($50 for international students). Electronic applications accepted. *Expenses:* Tuition, state resident: full-time $7662; part-time $478.85 per credit hour. Tuition, nonresident: full-time $16,920; part-time $1057.55 per credit hour. Required fees: $571.20; $35.70 per credit hour. $188.05 per semester. Tuition and fees vary according to course load and program. *Faculty research:* Conflict resolution in higher education, workplace conflict and aggression, cultural diversity, domestic violence, intervention policies of major powers and small states. *Unit head:* Dr. Loraleigh Keashly, Academic Director, 313-577-3221, Fax: 313-577-8800, E-mail: l.keashly@wayne.edu. *Application contact:* John Vander Weg, Associate Dean, 313-577-5342.

Wilfrid Laurier University, Faculty of Graduate and Postdoctoral Studies, Faculty of Arts and School of Business and Economics, Global Governance Program, Waterloo, ON N2L 3C5, Canada. Offers conflict and security (PhD); global environment (PhD); global justice and human rights (PhD); global political economy (PhD); global social governance (PhD); multilateral institutions and diplomacy (PhD). *Faculty:* 27 full-time (7 women). *Students:* 14 full-time (7 women), 4 international. 83 applicants, 5% accepted, 3 enrolled. *Degree requirements:* For doctorate, thesis/dissertation. *Entrance requirements:* For doctorate, MA in political science, history, economics, international development studies, international peace studies, globalization studies, environmental studies or related field with minimum A-. Additional exam requirements/recommendations for international students: Required—TOEFL (minimum score 89 iBT). *Application deadline:* For fall admission, 1/31 priority date for domestic and international students. Application fee: $100. Electronic applications accepted. Tuition and fees charges are reported in Canadian dollars. *Expenses:* Tuition, area resident: Full-time $15,300 Canadian dollars; part-time $1200 Canadian dollars per credit. International tuition: $21,300 Canadian dollars full-time. Required fees: $650 Canadian dollars; $100 Canadian dollars per credit. Tuition and fees vary according to course load, degree level, campus/location and program. *Financial support:* In 2010–11, 4 fellowships, 4 teaching assistantships were awarded; career-related internships or fieldwork, scholarships/grants, health care benefits, and unspecified assistantships also available. *Faculty research:* Global political economy, global environment, conflict and security, global justice and human rights, multilateral institutions and diplomacy. *Unit head:* Dr. Randall Wigle, Associate Director, 519-884-1970 Ext. 2438, Fax: 519-884-8454, E-mail: rwigle@wlu.ca. *Application contact:* Jennifer Willaims, Student Contact, 519-884-0710 Ext. 3536, Fax: 519-884-1020, E-mail: gradstudies@wlu.ca.

Yeshiva University, Benjamin N. Cardozo School of Law, New York, NY 10003-4301. Offers comparative legal thought (LL M); dispute resolution and advocacy (LL M); general studies (LL M); intellectual property law (LL M); law (JD). *Accreditation:* ABA. Part-time programs available. *Faculty:* 59 full-time (19 women), 92 part-time/adjunct (31 women). *Students:* 1,122 full-time (585 women), 106 part-time (54 women); includes 54 Black or African American, non-Hispanic/Latino; 1 American Indian or Alaska Native, non-Hispanic/Latino; 101 Asian, non-Hispanic/Latino; 84 Hispanic/Latino, 75 international. Average age 24. 5,261 applicants, 26% accepted, 317 enrolled. In 2010, 354 first professional degrees, 68 master's awarded. *Entrance requirements:* LSAT, 2 letters of recommendation. *Application deadline:* For fall admission, 3/1 priority date for domestic students; for spring admission, 12/1 priority date for domestic students. Applications are processed on a rolling basis. Application fee: $75. Electronic applications accepted. *Expenses:* Contact institution. *Financial support:* In 2010–11, 919 students received support, including 111 research assistantships; career-related internships or fieldwork, Federal Work-Study, institutionally sponsored loans, scholarships/grants, health care benefits, and tuition waivers (full and partial) also available. Support available to part-time students. Financial award application deadline: 3/1; financial award applicants required to submit FAFSA. *Faculty research:* Corporate and commercial law, intellectual property law, criminal law and litigation, Constitutional law, legal theory and jurisprudence. *Unit head:* David G. Martinidez, Dean of Admissions, 212-790-0274, Fax: 212-790-0482, E-mail: lawinfo@yu.edu. *Application contact:* David G. Martinidez, Dean of Admissions, 212-790-0274, Fax: 212-790-0482, E-mail: lawinfo@yu.edu.

ARCADIA UNIVERSITY

Program in International Peace and Conflict Resolution

Programs of Study	Arcadia University's International Peace and Conflict Resolution (IPCR) master's degree program offers an innovative curriculum that allows students to develop an area of concentration within the discipline, build an international network of contacts, and gain practical experience.
	Conflict resolution skills are essential in everyday life. The IPCR program offers students opportunities to develop and apply these skills in an enterprising way as well as to explore many diverse career paths in both national and international settings. The program's strength lies in its interdisciplinary approach to the increasingly critical study of peace and conflict resolution. The off-campus courses and professional experience undertaken in the second year can be coordinated through Arcadia's College of Global Studies.
	Arcadia's program is one of the few graduate programs in the field of conflict resolution with a built-in overseas component—one that is founded on a long tradition of University-based international programs. Sites available for study abroad in the program include the following: the Nyerere Centre for Peace Research, operated by Arcadia and the East African Community in Arusha, Tanzania; the American Graduate School of International Relations and Diplomacy, Arcadia's affiliated program in Paris; the United Nations University for Peace in San Jose, Costa Rica; the M.A. program in ethnic conflict at Queens University in Belfast, Northern Ireland; and the M.A. program in peace and development studies at the University of Jaume I in Castellon, Spain. In addition to these programs, the second year of study and fieldwork experience abroad may be individually designed to reflect the IPCR student's specific area of interest. With the permission of the program director, M.A. candidates also have the option, based on their areas of interest, to fulfill second-year study and fieldwork credits within the United States.
	In addition to the second-year study-abroad component, IPCR students have the option of participating in a weeklong intensive field study in Northern Ireland during the first year of the program. Additional IPCR short-term field study courses include politics and ethnic conflict in Ukraine and sustainable development in Costa Rica.
Research Facilities	The Landman Library has 139,203 volumes, more than 57,000 units of microfilm, and 798 print periodical subscriptions. Students have access to several online bibliographical databases, and materials are made available through interlibrary loan and through membership in a cooperative group of academic libraries. For students of science and psychology, there are excellent laboratory facilities in Boyer Hall. Internet services for students include a campuswide wireless network, Telnet, file transfer protocol (FTP), and e-mail. All instructional buildings house PC-equipped teaching classrooms. Specialized library material is available in different programs' resource centers as well as an online medical library.
Financial Aid	Graduate students who have been accepted into a degree program and are enrolled for at least 6 credits per semester are eligible to apply for financial aid. Additional information, including required forms and documents, is available and can be submitted online at www.arcadia.edu/finaid. All students registered for at least 9 credits per semester (or those who have submitted a deposit and plan to be enrolled for at least 9 credits per semester) are eligible to apply for a graduate assistantship. Applications are available online at www.arcadia.edu/graduate (click on "forms"). Questions regarding graduate assistantships should be directed to the College of Graduate Studies at 215-572-2925.
Cost of Study	For 2011–12, tuition for the two-year full-time program is $26,688. Part-time IPCR students will be charged $1112 per credit ($6672 per semester if taking 6 credits). Parking, registration, and student liability insurance is $130 per year. Books and supplies are estimated at $1000. Expenses for travel vary by program. Dual degree IPCR/public health students should call 877-ARCADIA, #4034 for specific tuition rate information.
Living and Housing Costs	There are a variety of housing options in proximity to the University.
Location	The University is located in Glenside, Pennsylvania, a suburb of Philadelphia, 14 miles from the center of the city. Theaters, museums, and the Philadelphia Orchestra are a half hour away by train or car. On campus, there are always a variety of lectures, concerts, and plays.
The University	Arcadia University, founded in 1853, is a comprehensive university committed to providing an education that integrates liberal learning with career preparation. The University operates one of the country's largest campus-based centers for study abroad and supports a wide array of cultural, intellectual, and recreational activities.
Applying	Arcadia welcomes applications for this program from college graduates of all majors, especially those who have demonstrated scholastic excellence and a commitment to international peace and conflict resolution. Related experience and achievements, either domestic or international, also are desirable.
	In addition to the University's general admission requirements, the following program-specific requirements must be met. A graduate application, including personal statements, must be completed online at www.arcadia.edu/gradapp. A bachelor's degree from an accredited institution with a recommended GPA of 3.0 or better and a major in peace studies, political science, history, modern languages, economics, anthropology, sociology, psychology, philosophy, religion or another liberal arts discipline; students with undergraduate majors in biology and environmental education also are encouraged to apply. Applicants must submit one official transcript from each college, university or professional school attended. Transfer credits included on a transcript must include grades earned; if not, an official transcript from the original school must be submitted. Transcripts must be sent from the issuing school in a sealed envelope and contain the appropriate signatures and seals to be considered official. Three letters of recommendation from persons who are able to judge the applicant's qualifications to undertake graduate work abroad; at least one recommendation must be from a professor. A personal interview usually is required, but a phone interview may be substituted at the discretion of the program Director.
	GREs are not required for admission. In exceptional cases, after reviewing an applicant's academic record and nonacademic experience, the Director may waive one or more prerequisites.
	International applicants should visit www.arcadia.edu/international for detailed information on admission requirements and application procedures.
	Completed applications will be reviewed on a rolling basis starting February 1. Those received after February 1 will be reviewed based on availability of space in the attending class. Classes typically fill in early spring, so applicants are encouraged to apply by the February 1 deadline.
Correspondence and Information	Office of Enrollment Management Arcadia University 450 South Easton Road Glenside, Pennsylvania 19038-3295 Phone: 215-572-2910 877-272-2342 (toll-free) Fax: 215-572-4049 E-mail: admiss@arcadia.edu Web site: http://www.arcadia.edu

Arcadia University

THE FACULTY AND THEIR RESEARCH

The IPCR program includes a diverse range of full-time and adjunct faculty members that offer each student the personal attention that is the hallmark of an Arcadia education. They are committed to providing an education that ensures that students gain mastery of one field but are further able to bring multiple lenses to their endeavors upon graduation. The following is a select list of faculty members affiliated with the program:

Samer Abboud, Assistant Professor of History and International Studies; Ph.D., Exeter. Political economy, migration and mobility, citizenship.

Warren Haffar, Associate Professor, Director of the International Peace and Conflict Resolution program, and Dean of Internationalization; Ph.D., Pennsylvania. Mediation of environmental disputes, sources of environmental conflict, sustainable development strategies in post-conflict societies, research methods in conflict analysis.

Angela Kachuyevski, Assistant Professor of International Peace and Conflict Resolution; Ph.D., Tufts. Ethnic conflict management with particular focus on Eastern Europe.

Jennifer Riggan, Assistant Professor of International Studies and Director of the International Studies program; Ph.D., Pennsylvania. Nationalism, citizenship, the ethnography of the state, the anthropology of war and conflict, critical development studies, international education and globalization.

Section 18
Criminology and Forensics

This section contains a directory of institutions offering graduate work in criminology and forensics, followed by in-depth entries submitted by institutions that chose to prepare detailed program descriptions. Additional information about programs listed in the directory but not augmented by an in-depth entry may be obtained by writing directly to the dean of a graduate school or chair of a department at the address given in the directory.

For programs offering related work, see also in this book *Political Science and International Affairs, Psychology and Counseling,* and *Sociology, Anthropology, and Archaeology.* In another guide in this series:

Graduate Programs in Business, Education, Health, Information Studies, Law & Social Work

See *Law* and *Social Work*

CONTENTS

Program Directories

Close-Ups and Displays

Criminal Justice and Criminology

Adler School of Professional Psychology, Programs in Psychology, Chicago, IL 60602. Offers advanced Adlerian psychotherapy (Certificate); art therapy (MA); clinical neuropsychology (Certificate); clinical psychology (Psy D); community psychology (MA); counseling and organizational psychology (MA); counseling psychology (MA); forensic psychology (MA); gerontological counseling (MA); marriage and family counseling (MA); marriage and family therapy (Certificate); organizational psychology (MA); police psychology (MA); rehabilitation counseling (MA); sport and health psychology (MA); substance abuse counseling (Certificate); Psy D/Certificate; Psy D/MACAT; Psy D/MACP; Psy D/MAMFC; Psy D/MASAC. *Accreditation:* APA. Part-time and evening/weekend programs available. Postbaccalaureate distance learning degree programs offered (minimal on-campus study). *Faculty:* 40 full-time (18 women), 61 part-time/adjunct (31 women). *Students:* 688 full-time (532 women), 142 part-time (110 women). Average age 27.Terminal master's awarded for partial completion of doctoral program. *Degree requirements:* For master's, thesis or alternative, oral exam, practicum; for doctorate, thesis/dissertation, clinical exam, internship, oral exam, practicum, written qualifying exam. *Entrance requirements:* For master's, 12 semester hours in psychology, minimum GPA of 3.0; for doctorate, 18 semester hours in psychology, minimum GPA of 3.25; for Certificate, appropriate master's or doctoral degree. Additional exam requirements/recommendations for international students: Required—TOEFL (minimum score 550 paper-based; 213 computer-based; 79 iBT). *Application deadline:* For fall admission, 2/15 priority date for domestic students, 12/1 priority date for international students. Applications are processed on a rolling basis. Application fee: $50. Electronic applications accepted. *Financial support:* Career-related internships or fieldwork, Federal Work-Study, scholarships/grants, and tuition waivers (full and partial) available. Support available to part-time students. Financial award application deadline: 5/15; financial award applicants required to submit FAFSA. *Application contact:* Michelle Brice, Director of Admissions, 312-662-4113, Fax: 312-662-4199, E-mail: admissions@adler.edu.

Albany State University, College of Arts and Humanities, Program in Public Administration, Albany, GA 31705-2717. Offers community and economic development administration (MPA); criminal justice administration (MPA); fiscal management (MPA); general management (MPA); health administration and policy (MPA); human resources management (MPA); public policy (MPA); water resource management and policy (MPA). *Accreditation:* NASPAA. *Faculty:* 3 full-time (1 woman), 2 part-time/adjunct (0 women). *Students:* 13 full-time (7 women), 49 part-time (32 women); includes 60 Black or African American, non-Hispanic/Latino, 1 international. Average age 34. 18 applicants, 78% accepted, 12 enrolled. In 2010, 12 master's awarded. *Degree requirements:* For master's, professional public service internship, professional portfolio, capstone research project. *Entrance requirements:* For master's, GRE, MAT, or GMAT, baccalaureate degree from accredited college or university, two letters of recommendation, ASU medical and immunization form. *Application deadline:* For fall admission, 7/15 for domestic students, 5/15 for international students; for spring admission, 11/15 for domestic students, 9/15 for international students. Applications are processed on a rolling basis. Application fee: $20. Electronic applications accepted. *Expenses:* Tuition, state resident: full-time $3060; part-time $170 per credit hour. Tuition, nonresident: full-time $12,204; part-time $678 per credit hour. Required fees: $1160. Part-time tuition and fees vary according to course load. *Financial support:* Application deadline: 4/15. *Faculty research:* Public policy, strategic public human resources and human capital management, diversity management in the public sector and collective bargaining and labor relations in the public sector, e-government and public sector information systems, public administration pedagogy and business process modeling simulation, community development, nonprofit organizations, civic engagement and civic participation, healthcare disparities among minorities, poverty. Total annual research expenditures: $250. *Unit head:* Dr. Peter Ngwafu, Director, 229-430-4760, Fax: 229-430-7895, E-mail: peter.ngwafu@asurams.edu. *Application contact:* Dr. Rani George, Dean, Graduate School, 229-430-5118, Fax: 229-430-6398, E-mail: rani.george@asurams.edu.

Albany State University, College of Sciences and Health Professions, Department of Criminal Justice and Forensic Science, Albany, GA 31705-2717. Offers criminal justice (MS), including corrections, forensic science, law enforcement, public administration. Postbaccalaureate distance learning degree programs offered (no on-campus study). *Faculty:* 6 full-time (0 women), 2 part-time/adjunct (0 women). *Students:* 14 full-time (11 women), 41 part-time (30 women); includes 51 Black or African American, non-Hispanic/Latino. Average age 33. 20 applicants, 100% accepted, 14 enrolled. In 2010, 6 master's awarded. *Degree requirements:* For master's, comprehensive exam, thesis optional. *Entrance requirements:* For master's, GRE General Test or MAT. *Application deadline:* For fall admission, 7/15 for domestic students, 5/15 for international students; for spring admission, 11/15 for domestic students, 9/15 for international students. Applications are processed on a rolling basis. Application fee: $20. Electronic applications accepted. *Expenses:* Tuition, state resident: full-time $3060; part-time $170 per credit hour. Tuition, nonresident: full-time $12,204; part-time $678 per credit hour. Required fees: $1160. Part-time tuition and fees vary according to course load. *Financial support:* Application deadline: 4/15. *Faculty research:* Gang-related research, HIV-related research, behavioral-related research. Total annual research expenditures: $65,000. *Unit head:* Dr. Charles Ochie, Chair, 229-430-4864, Fax: 229-430-1676, E-mail: charles.ochie@asurams.edu. *Application contact:* Dr. Rani George, Dean, Graduate School, 229-430-5118, Fax: 229-430-6398, E-mail: rani.george@asurams.edu.

American Public University System, AMU/APU Graduate Programs, Charles Town, WV 25414. Offers accounting (MBA); administration and supervision (M Ed); air warfare (MA Military Studies); asymmetrical warfare (MA Military Studies); criminal justice (MA); emergency and disaster management (MA); entrepreneurship (MBA); environmental policy and management (MS); finance (MBA); general (MBA); global business management (MBA); guidance and counseling (M Ed); history (MA); homeland security (MA); homeland security resource allocation (MBA); humanities (MA); information technology (MS); information technology management (MBA); intelligence studies (MA); international relations and conflict resolution (MA); joint warfare (MA Military Studies); land warfare (MA Military Studies); legal studies (MA); management (MA), including defense mangement, general, human resource management, organizational leadership, public administration; marketing (MBA); military history (MA); national security studies (MA); naval warfare (MA Military Studies); nonprofit management (MBA); political science (MA); psychology (MA); public administration (MA); public health (MA); security management (MA); space studies (MS); sports management (MS); strategic leadership (MA Military Studies); teaching (M Ed), including elementary, secondary social sciences; transportation and logistics management (MA). Programs offered via distance learning only. Part-time and evening/weekend programs available. Postbaccalaureate distance learning degree programs offered (no on-campus study). *Faculty:* 253 full-time (134 women), 1,208 part-time/adjunct (570 women). *Students:* 956 full-time (422 women), 8,476 part-time (2,821 women); includes 2,511 minority (1,218 Black or African American, non-Hispanic/Latino; 68 American Indian or Alaska Native, non-Hispanic/Latino; 219 Asian, non-Hispanic/Latino; 705 Hispanic/Latino; 46 Native Hawaiian or other Pacific Islander, non-Hispanic/Latino; 255 Two or more races, non-Hispanic/Latino), 107 international. Average age 35. 9,550 applicants, 100% accepted. In 2010, 1,688 master's awarded. *Degree requirements:* For master's, comprehensive exam or practicum. *Entrance requirements:* For master's, official transcript showing earned bachelor's degree from institution accredited by recognized accrediting body. Additional exam requirements/recommendations for international students: Required—TOEFL (minimum score 550 paper-based; 213 computer-based), IELTS (minimum score 6.5). *Application deadline:* Applications are processed on a rolling basis. Application fee: $0. Electronic applications accepted. *Financial support:* Applicants required to submit FAFSA. *Faculty research:* Military history, criminal justice, management performance, national security. *Unit head:* Dr. Frank McCluskey, Provost, 877-468-6268, Fax: 304-724-3780. *Application contact:* Terry Grant, Director of Enrollment Management, 877-468-6268, Fax: 304-724-3780, E-mail: info@apus.edu.

American University, School of Public Affairs, Department of Justice, Law and Society, Washington, DC 20016-8043. Offers MS, PhD, JD/MS. Part-time and evening/weekend programs available. *Faculty:* 22 full-time (10 women), 22 part-time/adjunct (7 women). *Students:* 34 full-time (21 women), 28 part-time (18 women); includes 16 minority (10 Black or African American, non-Hispanic/Latino; 2 Asian, non-Hispanic/Latino; 4 Hispanic/Latino), 1 international. Average age 27. 83 applicants, 58% accepted, 20 enrolled. In 2010, 17 master's, 3 doctorates awarded. *Degree requirements:* For master's, comprehensive exam, research; for doctorate, comprehensive exam, thesis/dissertation. *Entrance requirements:* For master's, GRE, 2 recommendations; for doctorate, GRE, minimum GPA of 3.2. Additional exam requirements/recommendations for international students: Required—TOEFL. *Application deadline:* For fall admission, 2/1 for domestic students; for spring admission, 11/1 for domestic students. Application fee: $55. *Financial support:* Fellowships, research assistantships, teaching assistantships, career-related internships or fieldwork, Federal Work-Study, institutionally sponsored loans, and tuition waivers (full and partial) available. Financial award application deadline: 2/1. *Faculty research:* Mental health, court management. *Unit head:* Dr. Edward Maguire, Chair, 202-885-2769, E-mail: maguire@american.edu. *Application contact:* Dr. Edward Maguire, Chair, 202-885-2769, E-mail: maguire@american.edu.

American University of Puerto Rico, Program in Criminal Justice, Bayamón, PR 00960-2037. Offers MA. Evening/weekend programs available. *Faculty:* 9 part-time/adjunct (1 woman). *Students:* 3 full-time (0 women), 4 part-time (0 women); includes all Hispanic/Latino. *Application deadline:* For fall admission, 8/1 for domestic students; for winter admission, 10/15 for domestic students; for spring admission, 3/22 for domestic students. Applications are processed on a rolling basis. Application fee: $0. *Financial support:* Applicants required to submit FAFSA. *Application contact:* Information Contact, 787-620-2040, E-mail: oficnaadmisiones@aupr.edu.

Anderson University, Command College, Anderson, SC 29621-4035. Offers executive leadership (MA). Postbaccalaureate distance learning degree programs offered. *Entrance requirements:* For master's, minimum undergraduate GPA of 2.75, 5 years experience working in criminal justice field, resume. *Expenses:* Tuition: Part-time $320 per semester hour.

Andrew Jackson University, Jeffrey D. Rubenstein College of Criminal Justice, Program in Criminal Justice, Birmingham, AL 35244. Offers MS. Part-time and evening/weekend programs available. Postbaccalaureate distance learning degree programs offered (no on-campus study). *Entrance requirements:* For master's, course work in calculus, statistics. Additional exam requirements/recommendations for international students: Required—TOEFL (minimum score 550 paper-based; 213 computer-based).

Anna Maria College, Graduate Division, Program in Criminal Justice, Paxton, MA 01612. Offers criminal justice (MS). Part-time and evening/weekend programs available. *Degree requirements:* For master's, capstone project or thesis. *Entrance requirements:* For master's, bachelor's degree in related field, minimum GPA of 2.7. Additional exam requirements/recommendations for international students: Required—TOEFL (minimum score 500 paper-based). Electronic applications accepted.

Anna Maria College, Graduate Division, Program in Justice Administration, Paxton, MA 01612. Offers MS. Part-time and evening/weekend programs available. *Degree requirements:* For master's, capstone project. *Entrance requirements:* Additional exam requirements/recommendations for international students: Required—TOEFL (minimum score 500 paper-based). Electronic applications accepted.

Anna Maria College, Graduate Division, Program in Security Management, Paxton, MA 01612. Offers MA. *Degree requirements:* For master's, thesis.

Appalachian State University, Cratis D. Williams Graduate School, Department of Government and Justice Studies, Boone, NC 28608. Offers criminal justice (MS); political science (MA), including American government, environmental politics and policy analysis, international relations; public administration (MPA), including public management, town, city and county management. Part-time programs available. Postbaccalaureate distance learning degree programs offered (no on-campus study). *Faculty:* 24 full-time (5 women), 3 part-time/adjunct (2 women). *Students:* 72 full-time (29 women), 53 part-time (25 women); includes 6 Black or African American, non-Hispanic/Latino; 1 Asian, non-Hispanic/Latino; 3 Hispanic/Latino; 1 Two or more races, non-Hispanic/Latino. 86 applicants, 86% accepted, 58 enrolled. In 2010, 49 master's awarded. *Degree requirements:* For master's, variable foreign language requirement, comprehensive exam, thesis optional. *Entrance requirements:* For master's, GRE General Test, 3 letters of recommendation. Additional exam requirements/recommendations for international students: Required—TOEFL (minimum score 570 paper-based; 230 computer-based; 79 iBT), IELTS (minimum score 6.5). *Application deadline:* For fall admission, 7/1 for domestic students, 2/1 for international students; for spring admission, 11/1 for domestic students, 7/1 for international students. Applications are processed on a rolling basis. Application fee: $55. Electronic applications accepted. *Expenses:* Tuition, state resident: full-time $3428; part-time $428 per unit. Tuition, nonresident: full-time $14,518; part-time $1814 per unit. Required fees: $2320; $344 per unit. Tuition and fees vary according to campus/location. *Financial support:* In 2010–11, 20 research assistantships (averaging $8,000 per year) were awarded; fellowships, teaching assistantships, career-related internships or fieldwork, Federal Work-Study, scholarships/grants, and unspecified assistantships also available. Financial award application deadline: 4/1; financial award applicants required to submit FAFSA. *Faculty research:* Campaign finance, emerging democracies, bureaucratic politics, judicial behavior, administration of justice. Total annual research expenditures: $143,000. *Unit head:* Dr. Brian Ellison, Chairperson, 828-262-3085, E-mail: ellisonba@appstate.edu. *Application contact:* Sandy Krause, Director of Admissions and Recruiting, 828-262-2130, Fax: 828-262-2709, E-mail: krausesl@appstate.edu.

Arizona State University, College of Public Programs, School of Criminology and Criminal Justice, Phoenix, AZ 85004. Offers criminal justice (MA); criminology and criminal justice (MS, PhD). Part-time and evening/weekend programs available. Postbaccalaureate distance learning degree programs offered (minimal on-campus study). *Faculty:* 21 full-time (8 women), 1 part-time/adjunct (0 women). *Students:* 89 full-time (47 women), 87 part-time (44 women); includes 61 minority (15 Black or African American, non-Hispanic/Latino; 4 American Indian or Alaska Native, non-Hispanic/Latino; 5 Asian, non-Hispanic/Latino; 31 Hispanic/Latino; 2 Native Hawaiian or other Pacific Islander, non-Hispanic/Latino; 4 Two or more races, non-Hispanic/Latino), 2 international. Average age 30. 159 applicants, 68% accepted, 70 enrolled. In 2010, 24 master's awarded. Terminal master's awarded for partial completion of doctoral program. *Degree requirements:* For master's, thesis or alternative, policy analysis project, interactive Program of Study (iPOS) submitted before completing 50 percent of required credit hours; for doctorate, comprehensive exam, thesis/dissertation, interactive Program of Study (iPOS) submitted before completing 50 percent of required credit hours. *Entrance requirements:* For master's, GRE (MS), minimum GPA of 3.0 or equivalent in last 2 years of work leading to bachelor's degree; for doctorate, GRE, minimum GPA of 3.0 or equivalent in last 2 years of work leading to bachelor's degree, 2 letters of recommendation, resume, personal statement. Additional exam requirements/recommendations for international students: Required—TOEFL, IELTS, or Pearson Test of English. *Application deadline:* For fall admission, 2/1 for domestic and international students. Applications are processed on a rolling basis. Application fee: $50 ($90 for international students). Electronic applications accepted. *Expenses:* Tuition, state resident: full-time $8510; part-time $608 per credit. Tuition, nonresident: full-time $16,542; part-time $919 per credit. Required fees: $339; $110 per credit. Part-time tuition and fees vary according to course load. *Financial support:* In 2010–11, 27 research assistantships with full and partial tuition reimbursements (averaging $14,444 per year) were awarded; fellowships with full tuition reimbursements, teaching assistantships with full and partial tuition reimbursements, career-related internships or fieldwork, Federal Work-Study, institutionally sponsored loans, scholarships/grants, and tuition waivers (full and partial) also available. Financial award application deadline: 3/1; financial award applicants required to submit FAFSA. Total annual research expenditures: $526,714. *Unit head:* Dr. Scott Decker, Director, 602-496-2333, E-mail: scott.decker@asu.edu. *Application contact:* Graduate Admissions, 480-965-6113.

Arkansas State University, Graduate School, College of Humanities and Social Sciences, Department of Criminology, Sociology, and Geography, Jonesboro, State University, AR 72467. Offers criminal justice (MA, Certificate); sociology (MA); sociology education (SCCT). Part-time programs available. *Faculty:* 7 full-time (4 women). *Students:* 14 full-time (all women), 30 part-time (19 women); includes 14 minority (all Black or African American, non-Hispanic/Latino). Average age 33. 35 applicants, 69% accepted, 18 enrolled. In 2010, 10 master's awarded. *Degree requirements:* For master's, one foreign language, comprehensive exam, thesis or alternative; for other advanced degree, comprehensive exam. *Entrance requirements:* For master's, GRE General Test or MAT, appropriate bachelor's degree, letters of recommendation, official transcripts, immunization records; for other advanced degree, GRE General Test or MAT, interview, master's degree, official transcript, immunization records. Additional exam requirements/recommendations for international students: Required—TOEFL (minimum score 550 paper-based; 213 computer-based; 79 iBT), IELTS (minimum score 6), PTE: Pearson Test of English Academic (56). *Application deadline:* For fall admission, 7/1 for domestic and international students; for spring admission, 11/15 for domestic students, 11/14 for international students. Applications are processed on a rolling basis. Application fee: $30 ($40 for international students). Electronic applications accepted. *Expenses:* Tuition, state resident: full-time $3888; part-time $216 per credit hour. Tuition, nonresident: full-time $9918; part-time $551 per credit hour. International tuition: $8376 full-time. Required fees: $932; $49 per credit hour. $25 per term. One-time fee: $30. Tuition and fees vary according to course load and program. *Financial support:* In 2010–11, 14 students received support. Career-related internships or fieldwork, scholarships/grants, and unspecified assistantships available. Financial award application deadline: 7/1; financial award applicants required to submit FAFSA. *Unit head:* Dr. Gretchen Hill, Interim Chair, 870-972-3246, Fax: 870-972-3694, E-mail: ghill@astate.edu. *Application contact:* Dr. Andrew Sustich, Dean of the Graduate School, 870-972-3029, Fax: 870-972-3857, E-mail: sustich@astate.edu.

Armstrong Atlantic State University, School of Graduate Studies, Program in Criminal Justice, Savannah, GA 31419-1997. Offers MS. Part-time and evening/weekend programs available. *Degree requirements:* For master's, comprehensive exam, thesis optional. *Entrance requirements:* For master's, GRE General Test or MAT, minimum GPA of 2.5, 2 letters of recommendation. Additional exam requirements/recommendations for international students: Required—TOEFL (minimum score 523 paper-based; 193 computer-based). Electronic applications accepted.

Ashworth College, Graduate Programs, Norcross, GA 30092. Offers business administration (MBA); criminal justice (MS); health care administration (MBA, MS); human resource management (MBA, MS); international business (MBA); management (MS); marketing (MBA, MS). *Faculty:* 5 part-time/adjunct (1 woman). *Students:* 299. *Expenses:* Tuition: Full-time $9230; part-time $250 per credit hour. *Unit head:* Dr. Leslie A. Gargiulo, Vice President of Education, 770-729-8400, E-mail: lgargiulo@ashworthcollege.edu. *Application contact:* Dr. Leslie A. Gargiulo, Vice President of Education, 770-729-8400, E-mail: lgargiulo@ashworthcollege.edu.

Auburn University Montgomery, School of Sciences, Department of Justice and Public Safety, Montgomery, AL 36124-4023. Offers MSJPS. Part-time and evening/weekend programs available. *Degree requirements:* For master's, comprehensive exam, thesis optional. *Entrance requirements:* For master's, GRE General Test or MAT. Electronic applications accepted. *Faculty research:* Law enforcement, corrections, juvenile justice.

Aurora University, College of Professional Studies, Aurora, IL 60506-4892. Offers business (MBA); criminal justice (MS); nursing (MSN); social work (MSW, DSW). Part-time and evening/weekend programs available. *Faculty:* 22 full-time (7 women), 30 part-time/adjunct (15 women). *Students:* 275 full-time (220 women), 261 part-time (184 women); includes 75 Black or African American, non-Hispanic/Latino; 2 American Indian or Alaska Native, non-Hispanic/Latino; 4 Asian, non-Hispanic/Latino; 43 Hispanic/Latino. Average age 32. 274 applicants, 96% accepted, 197 enrolled. In 2010, 208 master's awarded. *Entrance requirements:* Additional exam requirements/recommendations for international students: Required—TOEFL (minimum score 550 paper-based; 213 computer-based). *Application deadline:* For fall admission, 8/15 priority date for domestic students, 3/1 for international students; for spring admission, 12/15 for domestic students, 7/1 for international students. Applications are processed on a rolling basis. Application fee: $25. Electronic applications accepted. *Financial support:* In 2010–11, 250 students received support; fellowships, research assistantships, teaching assistantships available. Financial award application deadline: 4/15; financial award applicants required to submit FAFSA. *Unit head:* Dr. Fred McKenzie, Dean, 630-844-5420, E-mail: mckenzie@aurora.edu. *Application contact:* Marcia Koenen, Director of Adult and Graduate Studies, 800-742-5281, Fax: 630-844-6854, E-mail: auadmission@aurora.edu.

Ball State University, Graduate School, College of Sciences and Humanities, Department of Political Science, Program in Public Administration, Muncie, IN 47306-1099. Offers criminal justice (MPA); public administration (MPA), including criminal justice. *Faculty:* 16. *Students:* 11 full-time (4 women), 20 part-time (11 women); includes 1 Black or African American, non-Hispanic/Latino, 1 international. Average age 28. 15 applicants, 73% accepted, 7 enrolled. In 2010, 11 master's awarded. *Entrance requirements:* For master's, GRE General Test. Application fee: $50. *Expenses:* Tuition, state resident: full-time $6160; part-time $299 per credit hour. Tuition, nonresident: full-time $16,020; part-time $783 per credit hour. Required fees: $2278; $95 per credit hour. *Financial support:* Career-related internships or fieldwork available. Financial award application deadline: 3/1. *Faculty research:* Employment training programs, personnel and labor relations, planning. *Unit head:* Dr. Joseph Losco, Director, 765-285-8800, Fax: 765-285-5345. *Application contact:* Dr. Gary Crawley, Associate Provost for Research and Dean of the Graduate School, 765-285-8785, E-mail: gcrawley@bsu.edu.

Bellevue University, Graduate School, Bellevue, NE 68005-3098. Offers acquisition and contract management (MS); business administration (MBA); clinical counseling (MS); computer information systems (MS); healthcare administration (MA, MHA, MS), including healthcare administration (MHA), human services (MA, MS); human capital management (MS, PhD); instructional design and development (MS); leadership (MA); management (MA); management information systems (MS); organizational performance (MS); public administration (MPA); public health (MPH); security management (MS). Part-time and evening/weekend programs available. Postbaccalaureate distance learning degree programs offered (no on-campus study). *Degree requirements:* For master's, thesis or project. *Entrance requirements:* For master's, minimum GPA of 2.5 in last 60 hours. Additional exam requirements/recommendations for international students: Required—TOEFL (minimum score 538 paper-based; 200 computer-based).

Boise State University, Graduate College, College of Social Sciences and Public Affairs, Program in Criminal Justice Administration, Boise, ID 83725-0399. Offers MA. *Degree requirements:* For master's, thesis. *Entrance requirements:* For master's, minimum GPA of 3.0. Electronic applications accepted.

Boston University, Metropolitan College, Program in Criminal Justice, Boston, MA 02215. Offers MCJ. Part-time and evening/weekend programs available. Postbaccalaureate distance learning degree programs offered (no on-campus study). *Faculty:* 5 full-time (1 woman), 4 part-time/adjunct (0 women). *Students:* 5 full-time (2 women), 387 part-time (237 women); includes 58 minority (21 Black or African American, non-Hispanic/Latino; 3 American Indian or Alaska Native, non-Hispanic/Latino; 8 Asian, non-Hispanic/Latino; 18 Hispanic/Latino; 2 Native Hawaiian or other Pacific Islander, non-Hispanic/Latino; 6 Two or more races, non-Hispanic/Latino), 11 international. Average age 31. 224 applicants, 97% accepted, 179 enrolled. In 2010, 190 degrees awarded. *Degree requirements:* For master's, comprehensive examination (for on-campus program only). *Entrance requirements:* Additional exam requirements/recommendations for international students: Required—TOEFL (minimum score 590 paper-based; 243 computer-based; 84 iBT). *Application deadline:* For fall admission, 7/15 for domestic students, 7/15 priority date for international students; for spring admission, 12/15 for domestic students, 11/15 priority date for international students. Applications are processed on a rolling basis. Application fee: $70. Electronic applications accepted. *Expenses:* Tuition: Full-time $39,314; part-time $1228 per credit. Required fees: $40 per semester. *Financial support:* In 2010–11, 2 research assistantships with partial tuition reimbursements (averaging $5,000 per year) were awarded; career-related internships or fieldwork, scholarships/grants, and unspecified assistantships also available. Support available to part-time students. Financial award application deadline: 6/15; financial award applicants required to submit FAFSA. *Faculty research:* Criminal justice administration and planning, criminology, police, corrections, collective violence, juvenile issues. *Unit head:* Dr. Daniel P. LeClair, Chair, 617-353-3025, Fax: 617-358-3595, E-mail: dleclair@bu.edu. *Application contact:* Dr. Mary Ellen Mastrorilli, Assistant Professor and Associate Chair, 617-353-3025, E-mail: memastro@bu.edu.

Bowling Green State University, Graduate College, College of Health and Human Services, Program in Criminal Justice, Bowling Green, OH 43403. Offers MSCJ. Part-time and evening/weekend programs available. Postbaccalaureate distance learning degree programs offered (no on-campus study). *Degree requirements:* For master's, thesis or alternative. *Entrance requirements:* For master's, GRE General Test. Additional exam requirements/recommendations for international students: Required—TOEFL. Electronic applications accepted.

Bridgewater State University, School of Graduate Studies, School of Arts and Sciences, Department of Sociology, Program in Criminal Justice, Bridgewater, MA 02325-0001. Offers MS. *Entrance requirements:* For master's, GRE General Test.

Buffalo State College, State University of New York, The Graduate School, Faculty of Applied Science and Education, Department of Criminal Justice, Buffalo, NY 14222-1095. Offers MS. Part-time and evening/weekend programs available. *Degree requirements:* For master's, comprehensive exam, project. *Entrance requirements:* For master's, minimum GPA of 3.0. Additional exam requirements/recommendations for international students: Required—TOEFL (minimum score 550 paper-based; 213 computer-based).

California Coast University, School of Criminal Justice, Santa Ana, CA 92701. Offers MS.

California State University, Fresno, Division of Graduate Studies, College of Social Sciences, Department of Criminology, Fresno, CA 93740-8027. Offers MS. Part-time and evening/weekend programs available. *Degree requirements:* For master's, thesis or alternative. *Entrance requirements:* For master's, GRE General Test, minimum GPA of 3.0. Additional exam requirements/recommendations for international students: Required—TOEFL. Electronic applications accepted. *Faculty research:* Substance abuse, gangs vs. law enforcement, needs of female offenders, battered women, crime victims.

California State University, Long Beach, Graduate Studies, College of Health and Human Services, Department of Criminal Justice, Long Beach, CA 90840. Offers criminal justice (MS); emergency services administration (MS). Part-time programs available. *Faculty:* 5 full-time (1 woman), 2 part-time/adjunct (0 women). *Students:* 17 full-time (11 women), 11 part-time (8 women); includes 2 Black or African American, non-Hispanic/Latino; 5 Asian, non-Hispanic/Latino; 4 Hispanic/Latino, 4 international. Average age 26. 66 applicants, 35% accepted, 12 enrolled. In 2010, 50 master's awarded. *Degree requirements:* For master's, comprehensive course or thesis. *Entrance requirements:* For master's, minimum GPA of 3.0. *Application deadline:* For fall admission, 5/1 for domestic students. Applications are processed on a rolling basis. Application fee: $55. Electronic applications accepted. *Financial support:* Federal Work-Study, institutionally sponsored loans, and scholarships/grants available. Financial award application deadline: 3/2. *Unit head:* Dr. Henry F. Fradella, Chair, 562-985-2669, Fax: 562-985-8086, E-mail: hfradell@csulb.edu. *Application contact:* Dr. Connie Estrada Ireland, Graduate Advisor, 562-985-8711, Fax: 562-985-8086, E-mail: cireland@csulb.edu.

California State University, Los Angeles, Graduate Studies, College of Health and Human Services, Department of Criminal Justice and Criminalistics, Los Angeles, CA 90032-8530. Offers criminal justice (MS); criminalistics (MS). Part-time and evening/weekend programs available. *Faculty:* 5 full-time (3 women), 1 part-time/adjunct (0 women). *Students:* 22 full-time (15 women), 27 part-time (20 women); includes 23 minority (1 Black or African American, non-Hispanic/Latino; 8 Asian, non-Hispanic/Latino; 13 Hispanic/Latino; 1 Two or more races, non-Hispanic/Latino), 1 international. Average age 27. 28 applicants, 100% accepted, 18 enrolled. In 2010, 36 master's awarded. *Degree requirements:* For master's, thesis. *Entrance requirements:* For master's, minimum GPA of 2.75. Additional exam requirements/recommendations for international students: Required—TOEFL (minimum score 500 paper-based; 173 computer-based). *Application deadline:* For fall admission, 5/1 for domestic and international students. Applications are processed on a rolling basis. Application fee: $55. *Financial support:* Federal Work-Study available. Support available to part-time students. Financial award application deadline: 3/1. *Unit head:* Dr. Joseph L. Peterson, Chair, 323-343-4610, Fax: 323-343-4646, E-mail: jpeters@calstatela.edu. *Application contact:* Dr. Alan Muchlinski, Dean of Graduate Studies, 323-343-3820, Fax: 323-343-5653, E-mail: amuchli@exchange.calstatela.edu.

California State University, Sacramento, Graduate Studies, College of Health and Human Services, Division of Criminal Justice, Sacramento, CA 95819. Offers MS. Part-time programs available. *Degree requirements:* For master's, thesis or alternative, writing proficiency exam. *Entrance requirements:* For master's, BA in criminal justice or equivalent, minimum GPA of 2.5 during previous 2 years of course work. Additional exam requirements/recommendations for international students: Required—TOEFL. Electronic applications accepted.

California State University, San Bernardino, Graduate Studies, College of Social and Behavioral Sciences, Department of Criminal Justice, San Bernardino, CA 92407-2397. Offers MA. Part-time programs available. *Degree requirements:* For master's, comprehensive exam or thesis, advancement to candidacy. *Entrance requirements:* For master's, GRE General Test, minimum GPA of 3.0. *Faculty research:* Crime seriousness, fear of crime, victimization, corrections management, crime correlates.

California State University, Stanislaus, College of Humanities and Social Sciences, Program in Criminal Justice (MA), Turlock, CA 95382. Offers MA. Part-time programs available. *Faculty:* 10. *Students:* 23 full-time (14 women), 13 part-time (8 women); includes 16 minority (1 Black or African American, non-Hispanic/Latino; 4 Asian, non-Hispanic/Latino; 10 Hispanic/Latino; 1 Two or more races, non-Hispanic/Latino), 1 international. Average age 29. 29 applicants, 79% accepted, 16 enrolled. In 2010, 9 master's awarded. *Degree requirements:* For master's, comprehensive exam, thesis or alternative. *Entrance requirements:* For master's, minimum GPA of 3.0, 3 letters of reference, personal statement. *Application deadline:* For fall admission, 5/1 for domestic students; for spring admission, 1/7 for domestic students. Application fee: $55. Electronic applications accepted. Tuition and fees vary according to program. *Financial support:* Fellowships available. Financial award application deadline: 3/1; financial award applicants required to submit FAFSA. *Faculty research:* Police gerontology services, hate crimes, juvenile justice, masculinities and modern society, nutrition and criminal behavior. *Unit head:* Dr. Peter Nelligan, Director of Graduate Studies (CJ), 209-667-3030, Fax: 209-664-7034, E-mail: pnelligan@csustan.edu. *Application contact:* Graduate School, 209-667-3129, Fax: 209-664-7025, E-mail: graduate_school@csustan.edu.

California University of Pennsylvania, School of Graduate Studies and Research, College of Liberal Arts, Department of Sociology/Criminal Justice, California, PA 15419-1394. Offers social science—criminal justice (MA). Part-time and evening/weekend programs available. *Degree requirements:* For master's, comprehensive exam, thesis optional. *Entrance requirements:* For master's, MAT, minimum GPA of 3.0. Additional exam requirements/recommendations for international students: Required—TOEFL (minimum score 550 paper-based; 213 computer-based; 80 iBT). Electronic applications accepted. *Faculty research:* Ethics and law, ethics in police practice, law and morality, police policy, St. Thomas Aquinas and crime.

Calumet College of Saint Joseph, Program in Public Safety Administration, Whiting, IN 46394-2195. Offers MS.

Criminal Justice and Criminology

Capella University, School of Human Services, Minneapolis, MN 55402. Offers addictions counseling (Certificate); counseling studies (MS, PhD); criminal justice (MS, PhD, Certificate); diversity studies (Certificate); general human services (MS, PhD); health care administration (MS, PhD, Certificate); management of nonprofit agencies (MS, PhD, Certificate); marital, couple and family counseling/therapy (MS); marriage and family services (Certificate); mental health counseling (MS); professional counseling (Certificate); social and community services (MS, PhD, Certificate). Part-time and evening/weekend programs available. Postbaccalaureate distance learning degree programs offered (minimal on-campus study). Terminal master's awarded for partial completion of doctoral program. *Degree requirements:* For master's, thesis optional, integrative project; for doctorate, comprehensive exam, thesis/dissertation. *Entrance requirements:* Additional exam requirements/recommendations for international students: Required—TOEFL (minimum score 550 paper-based; 213 computer-based), TWE (minimum score 4). Electronic applications accepted. *Expenses:* Tuition: Full-time $11,880; part-time $440 per credit hour. *Faculty research:* Compulsive and addictive behaviors, substance abuse, assessment of psychopathology and neuropsychology.

Capella University, School of Public Service Leadership, Minneapolis, MN 55402. Offers criminal justice (MS, PhD); emergency management (MS, PhD); general human services (MS, PhD); general public administration (MPA, DPA); gerontology (MS); health care administration (MS, PhD); health management and policy (MSPH); management of nonprofit agencies (MS, PhD); nurse educator (MS); public safety leadership (MS, PhD); social and community services (MS, PhD); social behavioral sciences (MSPH). *Expenses:* Tuition: Full-time $11,880; part-time $440 per credit hour.

Caribbean University, Graduate School, Bayamón, PR 00960-0493. Offers administration and supervision (MA Ed); criminal justice (MA); curriculum and instruction (MA Ed, PhD), including elementary education (MA Ed), English education (MA Ed), history education (MA Ed), mathematics education (MA Ed), primary education (MA Ed), science education (MA Ed), Spanish education (MA Ed); educational technology in instructional systems (MA Ed); gerontology (MSN); human resources (MBA); museology, archiving and art history (MA Ed); neonatal pediatrics (MSN); physical education (MA Ed); special education (MA Ed). *Entrance requirements:* For master's, interview, minimum GPA of 2.5.

Carnegie Mellon University, H. John Heinz III College, School of Information Systems and Management, Master of Science in Information Security Policy and Management Program, Pittsburgh, PA 15213-3891. Offers MSISPM. *Entrance requirements:* For master's, GRE or GMAT, college-level course in advanced algebra/pre-calculus; college-level courses in economics and statistics (recommended). Additional exam requirements/recommendations for international students: Required—TOEFL or IELTS.

Central Connecticut State University, School of Graduate Studies, School of Arts and Sciences, Department of Criminology and Criminal Justice, New Britain, CT 06050-4010. Offers criminal justice (MS). Part-time and evening/weekend programs available. *Faculty:* 11 full-time (5 women), 19 part-time/adjunct (5 women). *Students:* 6 full-time (5 women), 28 part-time (13 women); includes 12 minority (8 Black or African American, non-Hispanic/Latino; 3 Hispanic/Latino; 1 Two or more races, non-Hispanic/Latino). Average age 29. 32 applicants, 44% accepted, 8 enrolled. In 2010, 8 master's awarded. *Degree requirements:* For master's, comprehensive exam, thesis or alternative. *Entrance requirements:* For master's, minimum undergraduate GPA of 3.0. Additional exam requirements/recommendations for international students: Required—TOEFL. *Application deadline:* For fall admission, 5/1 for domestic students; for spring admission, 12/1 for domestic students. Applications are processed on a rolling basis. Application fee: $50. Electronic applications accepted. *Expenses:* Tuition, area resident: Full-time $5012; part-time $470 per credit. Tuition, state resident: full-time $7518; part-time $482 per credit. Tuition, nonresident: full-time $13,962; part-time $482 per credit. Required fees: $3772. One-time fee: $62 part-time. *Financial support:* In 2010–11, 4 students received support, including 2 research assistantships; career-related internships or fieldwork, Federal Work-Study, scholarships/grants, and unspecified assistantships also available. Support available to part-time students. Financial award application deadline: 2/15; financial award applicants required to submit FAFSA. *Unit head:* Dr. Raymond Tafrate, Chair, 860-832-3005. *Application contact:* Dr. Raymond Tafrate, Chair, 860-832-3005.

Chaminade University of Honolulu, Graduate Services, Program in Criminal Justice Administration, Honolulu, HI 96816-1578. Offers criminal justice administration (MSCJA); homeland security (Certificate). Part-time and evening/weekend programs available. Postbaccalaureate distance learning degree programs offered (no on-campus study). *Degree requirements:* For master's, thesis optional. *Entrance requirements:* For master's, minimum undergraduate GPA of 3.0, 3 letters of recommendation. Additional exam requirements/recommendations for international students: Required—TOEFL (minimum score 550 paper-based). Electronic applications accepted. *Faculty research:* Penology, juvenile delinquency, multicultural and ethnic diversity in criminology, law enforcement administration and training, homeland security.

Charleston Southern University, Department of Criminal Justice, Charleston, SC 29423-8087. Offers MSCJ. Part-time and evening/weekend programs available. *Degree requirements:* For master's, comprehensive exam, thesis optional. *Entrance requirements:* For master's, GRE or MAT, bachelor's degree in criminal justice. Additional exam requirements/recommendations for international students: Required—TOEFL (minimum score 550 paper-based; 213 computer-based; 79 iBT).

Chicago State University, School of Graduate and Professional Studies, College of Arts and Sciences, Department of Criminal Justice, Chicago, IL 60628. Offers MS. Part-time and evening/weekend programs available. *Entrance requirements:* For master's, minimum GPA of 2.75. *Faculty research:* Gang crime.

Clark Atlanta University, School of Arts and Sciences, Department of Criminal Justice, Atlanta, GA 30314. Offers MA. Part-time programs available. *Faculty:* 1 full-time (0 women), 2 part-time/adjunct (1 woman). *Students:* 13 full-time (10 women), 2 part-time (1 woman); includes 11 Black or African American, non-Hispanic/Latino; 1 American Indian or Alaska Native, non-Hispanic/Latino; 1 Hispanic/Latino. Average age 28. 13 applicants, 85% accepted, 6 enrolled. *Degree requirements:* For master's, one foreign language, comprehensive exam, thesis. *Entrance requirements:* For master's, GRE General Test, minimum GPA of 2.5. Additional exam requirements/recommendations for international students: Required—TOEFL (minimum score 500 paper-based; 173 computer-based; 61 iBT). *Application deadline:* For fall admission, 4/1 for domestic and international students; for spring admission, 11/1 for domestic and international students. Applications are processed on a rolling basis. Application fee: $40 ($55 for international students). *Expenses:* Tuition: Full-time $12,942; part-time $719 per credit hour. Required fees: $710; $355 per semester. *Financial support:* Career-related internships or fieldwork, Federal Work-Study, scholarships/grants, and unspecified assistantships available. Support available to part-time students. Financial award application deadline: 4/30; financial award applicants required to submit FAFSA. *Faculty research:* Race and crime, black ex-offenders in the labor market. *Unit head:* Dr. Sandra Taylor, Chairperson, 404-880-8681, E-mail: staylor@cau.edu. *Application contact:* Michelle Clark-Davis, Graduate Program Admissions, 404-880-6605, E-mail: cauadmissions@cau.edu.

College of Saint Elizabeth, Program in Justice Studies, Morristown, NJ 07960-6989. Offers justice administration and public service (MA). Part-time and evening/weekend programs available. *Faculty:* 1 full-time (0 women), 2 part-time/adjunct (both women). *Students:* 3 full-time (2 women), 13 part-time (9 women); includes 5 Black or African American, non-Hispanic/Latino; 2 Hispanic/Latino. Average age 33. 10 applicants, 80% accepted, 7 enrolled. In 2010, 1 master's awarded. *Degree requirements:* For master's, thesis or alternative. *Entrance requirements:* Additional exam requirements/recommendations for international students: Required—TOEFL (minimum score 550 paper-based). *Application deadline:* Applications are processed on a rolling basis. Application fee: $35. Electronic applications accepted. *Expenses:* Tuition: Part-time $857 per credit. Required fees: $70 per credit. *Financial support:* Unspecified assistantships available. Support available to part-time students. Financial award applicants required to submit FAFSA. *Unit head:* Dr. James Ford, Associate Professor, 973-290-4324, E-mail: jford@cse.edu. *Application contact:* Dean Donna Tatarka, Dean of Admission, 973-290-4705, Fax: 973-290-4710, E-mail: dtatarka@cse.edu.

Colorado Technical University Colorado Springs, Graduate Studies, Program in Criminal Justice, Colorado Springs, CO 80907-3896. Offers MSM. Postbaccalaureate distance learning degree programs offered.

Colorado Technical University Denver, Program in Computer Science, Greenwood Village, CO 80111. Offers computer systems security (MSCS); database systems (MSCS); software engineering (MSCS). Part-time and evening/weekend programs available. *Degree requirements:* For master's, thesis or alternative. *Entrance requirements:* For master's, minimum undergraduate GPA of 3.0, resume.

Colorado Technical University Sioux Falls, Program in Criminal Justice, Sioux Falls, SD 57108. Offers MSM.

Columbia College, Master of Science in Criminal Justice Program, Columbia, MO 65216-0002. Offers MSCJ. Evening/weekend programs available. Postbaccalaureate distance learning degree programs offered (no on-campus study). *Faculty:* 4 full-time (0 women); 15 part-time/adjunct (6 women). *Students:* 6 full-time (4 women), 117 part-time (62 women); includes 17 Black or African American, non-Hispanic/Latino; 1 American Indian or Alaska Native, non-Hispanic/Latino; 2 Asian, non-Hispanic/Latino; 6 Hispanic/Latino; 1 Two or more races, non-Hispanic/Latino. Average age 37. 48 applicants, 54% accepted, 21 enrolled. In 2010, 46 master's awarded. *Degree requirements:* For master's, final exams, culminating experience (intensive writing seminar). *Entrance requirements:* For master's, 3 letters of recommendation, minimum cumulative undergraduate GPA of 3.0, resume, goal statement. Additional exam requirements/recommendations for international students: Required—TOEFL (minimum score 550 paper-based; 213 computer-based; 79 iBT). *Application deadline:* For fall admission, 8/9 priority date for domestic and international students; for spring admission, 12/27 priority date for domestic and international students. Applications are processed on a rolling basis. Application fee: $55. Electronic applications accepted. *Expenses:* Tuition: Part-time $299 per credit hour. Tuition and fees vary according to course load. *Financial support:* In 2010–11, 1 student received support. Federal Work-Study and scholarships/grants available. Financial award applicants required to submit FAFSA. *Faculty research:* Organized crime, policing in America. *Unit head:* Dr. Mike Lyman, Coordinator, 573-875-7472, E-mail: mlyman@ccis.edu. *Application contact:* Samantha White, Director of Admissions, 573-875-7352, Fax: 573-875-7506, E-mail: sjwhite@ccis.edu.

Columbia Southern University, College of Safety and Emergency Services, Orange Beach, AL 36561. Offers criminal justice (MS); environmental management (MS); occupational safety and health (MS); occupational safety and health/environmental management (MS). Part-time and evening/weekend programs available. Postbaccalaureate distance learning degree programs offered (no on-campus study). *Entrance requirements:* For master's, bachelor's degree from accredited/approved institution. Additional exam requirements/recommendations for international students: Required—TOEFL. Electronic applications accepted.

Columbus State University, Graduate Studies, College of Letters and Sciences, Master of Public Administration Program, Columbus, GA 31907-5645. Offers justice administration (MPA). Part-time and evening/weekend programs available. *Faculty:* 6 full-time (1 woman), 13 part-time/adjunct (0 women). *Students:* 112 full-time (36 women), 204 part-time (56 women); includes 99 minority (86 Black or African American, non-Hispanic/Latino; 2 American Indian or Alaska Native, non-Hispanic/Latino; 7 Hispanic/Latino; 4 Two or more races, non-Hispanic/Latino), 2 international. Average age 40. 77 applicants, 79% accepted, 53 enrolled. In 2010, 116 master's awarded. *Entrance requirements:* For master's, GRE General Test, minimum GPA of 2.75. Additional exam requirements/recommendations for international students: Required—TOEFL (minimum score 550 paper-based; 213 computer-based; 79 iBT). *Application deadline:* For fall admission, 6/30 for domestic students, 5/1 for international students; for spring admission, 11/1 for domestic and international students. Applications are processed on a rolling basis. Application fee: $30. Electronic applications accepted. *Expenses:* Tuition, state resident: full-time $5573; part-time $232 per semester hour. Tuition, nonresident: full-time $13,968; part-time $582 per semester hour. Required fees: $1300; $650 per semester. Tuition and fees vary according to degree level and program. *Financial support:* In 2010–11, 66 students received support, including 6 research assistantships with partial tuition reimbursements available (averaging $3,000 per year); career-related internships or fieldwork, Federal Work-Study, institutionally sponsored loans, scholarships/grants, tuition waivers (partial), and unspecified assistantships also available. Support available to part-time students. Financial award application deadline: 5/1; financial award applicants required to submit FAFSA. *Unit head:* Dr. Tom Dolan, Director, 706-565-7875, E-mail: dolan_thomas@colstate.edu. *Application contact:* Katie Thornton, Graduate Admissions Specialist, 706-568-2035, Fax: 706-568-2462, E-mail: thornton_katie@colstate.edu.

Concordia University, St. Paul, College of Business and Organizational Leadership, St. Paul, MN 55104-5494. Offers business and organizational leadership (MBA); criminal justice leadership (MA); health care management (MBA); human resources management (MA); leadership and management (MA). *Accreditation:* ACBSP. Evening/weekend programs available. Postbaccalaureate distance learning degree programs offered (minimal on-campus study). *Faculty:* 14 full-time (6 women), 30 part-time/adjunct (8 women). *Students:* 338 full-time (203 women), 2 part-time (1 woman); includes 24 Black or African American, non-Hispanic/Latino; 3 American Indian or Alaska Native, non-Hispanic/Latino; 11 Asian, non-Hispanic/Latino; 3 Hispanic/Latino; 3 Two or more races, non-Hispanic/Latino. Average age 34. 191 applicants, 65% accepted, 117 enrolled. In 2010, 125 master's awarded. *Application deadline:* Applications are processed on a rolling basis. Application fee: $50. Electronic applications accepted. *Expenses:* Tuition: Full-time $7500; part-time $460 per credit. Required fees: $460 per credit. Tuition and fees vary according to program. *Financial support:* Applicants required to submit FAFSA. *Unit head:* Dr. Bruce Corrie, Dean, 651-641-8226, Fax: 651-641-8807, E-mail: corrie@csp.edu. *Application contact:* Kimberly Craig, Director of Graduate and Cohort Admission, 651-603-6223, Fax: 651-603-6320, E-mail: craig@csp.edu.

Coppin State University, Division of Graduate Studies, Division of Arts and Sciences, Department of Criminal Justice and Law Enforcement, Baltimore, MD 21216-3698. Offers criminal justice (MS). Part-time and evening/weekend programs available. *Degree requirements:* For master's, thesis optional. *Entrance requirements:* For master's, GRE, minimum GPA of 3.0.

Curry College, Graduate Studies, Program in Criminal Justice, Milton, MA 02186-9984. Offers MA. Part-time and evening/weekend programs available. *Faculty:* 5 full-time (1 woman), 5 part-time/adjunct (2 women). *Students:* 135 part-time (24 women). Average age 32. 32 applicants, 91% accepted, 29 enrolled. In 2010, 59 master's awarded. *Degree requirements:* For master's, thesis. *Entrance requirements:* For master's, resume, recommendations, interview. Additional exam requirements/recommendations for international students: Required—TOEFL (minimum score 550 paper-based; 213 computer-based; 80 iBT). *Application deadline:* For fall admission, 8/1 priority date for domestic students, 6/1 for international students; for winter admission, 10/1 for international students; for spring admission, 1/1 priority date for domestic students, 1/28 for international students. Applications are processed on a rolling basis. Application fee: $50. *Expenses:* Contact institution. *Unit head:* Dr. Rebecca Paynich, Director and Associate Professor, 617-333-2084, Fax: 617-979-3535. *Application contact:* John Bresnahan, Director of Graduate Enrollment and Student Services, 617-333-2243, Fax: 617-979-3535, E-mail: jbresnah0104@curry.edu.

Dallas Baptist University, College of Adult Education, Professional Development Program, Dallas, TX 75211-9299. Offers accounting (MA); church leadership (MA); counseling (MA); criminal justice (MA); English as a second language (MA); finance (MA); higher education

(MA); leadership studies (MA); management (MA); management information systems (MA); marketing (MA); missions (MA). Part-time and evening/weekend programs available. *Entrance requirements:* For master's, minimum GPA of 3.0. Additional exam requirements/ recommendations for international students: Required—TOEFL, IELTS. *Expenses:* Tuition: Full-time $11,394; part-time $633 per credit hour.

Defiance College, Program in Business Administration, Defiance, OH 43512-1610. Offers criminal justice (MBA); health care (MBA); leadership (MBA). Part-time and evening/weekend programs available. *Degree requirements:* For master's, thesis. *Entrance requirements:* For master's, minimum GPA of 2.5.

Delta State University, Graduate Programs, College of Arts and Sciences, Division of Social Sciences and History, Program in Social Justice and Criminology, Cleveland, MS 38733-0001. Offers MSJC. Part-time programs available. Postbaccalaureate distance learning degree programs offered. *Degree requirements:* For master's, thesis or alternative. *Expenses:* Tuition, state resident: full-time $4347; part-time $202 per credit hour. Tuition, nonresident: full-time $12,052; part-time $523 per credit hour. Required fees: $504.

DeSales University, Graduate Division, Program in Criminal Justice, Center Valley, PA 18034-9568. Offers criminal justice (MACJ); digital forensics (online) (MACJ); investigative forensics (online) (MACJ). Part-time programs available. Postbaccalaureate distance learning degree programs offered (no on-campus study). *Entrance requirements:* Additional exam requirements/ recommendations for international students: Required—TOEFL. *Application deadline:* Applications are processed on a rolling basis. Application fee: $35. Electronic applications accepted. *Expenses:* Tuition: Full-time $18,200; part-time $690 per credit. Required fees: $1200. *Unit head:* Dr. Patrick McGrain, Director, 610-282-1100 Ext. 1584, Fax: 610-282-0787, E-mail: patrick.mcgrain@desales.edu. *Application contact:* Caryn Stopper, Director of Graduate Admissions, 610-282-1100 Ext. 1768, Fax: 610-282-0525, E-mail: caryn.stopper@desales.edu.

Drury University, Program in Criminology/Criminal Justice, Springfield, MO 65802. Offers criminal justice (MS); criminology (MA). Part-time and evening/weekend programs available. *Degree requirements:* For master's, thesis (for some programs). *Entrance requirements:* For master's, GMAT or MAT. Additional exam requirements/recommendations for international students: Required—TOEFL. Electronic applications accepted. *Expenses:* Contact institution. *Faculty research:* Gangs, fear of crime, social justice, social change and law, drug laws in Iran.

East Carolina University, Graduate School, College of Human Ecology, Department of Criminal Justice, Greenville, NC 27858-4353. Offers MS. Part-time and evening/weekend programs available. Postbaccalaureate distance learning degree programs offered (no on-campus study). *Degree requirements:* For master's, thesis, internship. *Entrance requirements:* For master's, GRE or MAT, bachelor's degree in criminal justice or related field. Additional exam requirements/recommendations for international students: Required—TOEFL. *Expenses:* Tuition, state resident: full-time $3130; part-time $391.25 per credit hour. Tuition, nonresident: full-time $13,817; part-time $1727.13 per credit hour. Required fees: $1916; $239.50 per credit hour. Tuition and fees vary according to campus/location and program. *Faculty research:* Corrections, policing, international criminal justice, terrorism.

East Central University, School of Graduate Studies, Department of Human Resources, Ada, OK 74820-6899. Offers administration (MSHR); counseling (MSHR); criminal justice (MSHR); rehabilitation counseling (MSHR). *Accreditation:* CORE. Part-time and evening/weekend programs available. *Degree requirements:* For master's, thesis optional. *Entrance requirements:* For master's, GRE General Test, MAT, minimum GPA of 2.5. Electronic applications accepted.

Eastern Kentucky University, The Graduate School, College of Justice and Safety, Program in Correctional and Juvenile Justice Studies, Richmond, KY 40475-3102. Offers MS. *Degree requirements:* For master's, comprehensive exam (for some programs), thesis (for some programs). *Entrance requirements:* For master's, GRE.

Eastern Kentucky University, The Graduate School, College of Justice and Safety, Program in Criminal Justice and Police Studies, Richmond, KY 40475-3102. Offers criminal justice (MS); criminal justice education (MS); police studies (MS). Part-time programs available. *Degree requirements:* For master's, thesis optional. *Entrance requirements:* For master's, GRE General Test, minimum GPA of 3.0.

Eastern Kentucky University, The Graduate School, College of Justice and Safety, Program in Loss Prevention and Safety, Richmond, KY 40475-3102. Offers MS. *Entrance requirements:* For master's, GRE.

Eastern Michigan University, Graduate School, College of Arts and Sciences, Department of Sociology, Anthropology and Criminology, Program in Criminology and Criminal Justice, Ypsilanti, MI 48197. Offers MA. *Students:* 9 full-time (8 women), 30 part-time (18 women); includes 15 minority (11 Black or African American, non-Hispanic/Latino; 3 Hispanic/Latino; 1 Two or more races, non-Hispanic/Latino). Average age 30. In 2010, 6 master's awarded. Application fee: $35. *Application contact:* Dr. Marilyn Corsianos, Advisor, 734-487-0012, Fax: 734-487-9666, E-mail: mcorsiano@emich.edu.

East Tennessee State University, School of Graduate Studies, College of Arts and Sciences, Department of Criminal Justice and Criminology, Johnson City, TN 37614. Offers MA, Certificate. Part-time and evening/weekend programs available. *Faculty:* 8 full-time (2 women). *Students:* 28 full-time (15 women), 19 part-time (12 women); includes 3 minority (all Black or African American, non-Hispanic/Latino), 1 international. Average age 30. 36 applicants, 58% accepted, 12 enrolled. In 2010, 5 master's, 7 other advanced degrees awarded. *Degree requirements:* For master's, comprehensive exam, thesis optional. *Entrance requirements:* For master's, GRE General Test, minimum GPA of 3.0. Additional exam requirements/recommendations for international students: Required—TOEFL (minimum score 550 paper-based; 213 computer-based; 79 iBT). *Application deadline:* For fall admission, 6/1 priority date for domestic students, 4/30 for international students; for spring admission, 11/1 for domestic students, 9/30 for international students. Application fee: $25 ($35 for international students). Electronic applications accepted. *Financial support:* In 2010–11, 7 research assistantships with full tuition reimbursements (averaging $6,000 per year) were awarded; teaching assistantships with full tuition reimbursements, career-related internships or fieldwork, institutionally sponsored loans, scholarships/grants, and unspecified assistantships also available. Financial award application deadline: 7/1; financial award applicants required to submit FAFSA. *Faculty research:* Prisonization, peacemaking, sentencing decisions, family violence and sexual violence, juvenile justice. *Unit head:* Dr. John Whitehead, Chair, 423-439-5346, Fax: 423-439-4660, E-mail: whitehej@etsu.edu. *Application contact:* Admissions and Records Clerk, 423-439-4221, Fax: 423-439-5624, E-mail: gradsch@etsu.edu.

Everest University, Graduate Programs, Jacksonville, FL 32256. Offers business (MBA); criminal justice (MS).

Everest University, Program in Criminal Justice, Tampa, FL 33619. Offers MS. Part-time and evening/weekend programs available. Postbaccalaureate distance learning degree programs offered (minimal on-campus study). *Faculty:* 1 part-time/adjunct (0 women). *Students:* 4 full-time (3 women), 14 part-time (9 women); includes 12 minority (10 Black or African American, non-Hispanic/Latino; 2 Hispanic/Latino). Average age 41. In 2010, 1 master's awarded. *Degree requirements:* For master's, thesis optional, externship, research practicum. *Entrance requirements:* Additional exam requirements/recommendations for international students: Required—TOEFL (minimum score 550 paper-based; 213 computer-based). *Application deadline:* Applications are processed on a rolling basis. Application fee: $25. *Expenses:* Tuition: Full-time $12,120; part-time $55 per credit hour. Required fees: $60 per quarter. *Financial support:* Institutionally sponsored loans and scholarships/grants available. *Unit head:* Seth Kanowitz, Chair, 813-621-0041 Ext. 219, Fax: 813-623-5769, E-mail: skanowitz@cci.edu. *Application contact:* Shandretta Pointer, Admissions Office, 813-621-0041 Ext. 106, Fax: 813-628-0919, E-mail: spointer@cci.edu.

Everest University, Program in Criminal Justice, Lakeland, FL 33801. Offers MS.

Everest University, Program in Criminal Justice, Pompano Beach, FL 33062. Offers MS.

Fairleigh Dickinson University, Metropolitan Campus, University College: Arts, Sciences, and Professional Studies, School of Criminal Justice and Legal Studies, Program in Criminal Justice, Teaneck, NJ 07666-1914. Offers MA. *Unit head:* Dr. Robert F. Vodde, Director, 201-692-2465, E-mail: rvodde@fdu.edu. *Application contact:* Susan Brooman, University Director of Graduate Admissions, 201-692-2554, Fax: 201-692-2560, E-mail: globaleducation@fdu.edu.

Fairmont State University, Graduate Studies, Program in Criminal Justice, Fairmont, WV 26554. Offers MS. *Degree requirements:* For master's, thesis or comprehensive exam. *Entrance requirements:* For master's, GRE, minimum GPA of 3.0.

Faulkner University, Alabama Christian College of Arts and Sciences, Department of Criminal Justice and Legal Studies, Montgomery, AL 36109-3398. Offers criminal justice (MCJ). Postbaccalaureate distance learning degree programs offered (no on-campus study). *Degree requirements:* For master's, research project. *Entrance requirements:* For master's, MAT, GRE or GMAT, minimum overall GPA of 2.5, major 3.0; 3 letters of recommendation; letter of intent; resume.

Fayetteville State University, Graduate School, Program in Criminal Justice, Fayetteville, NC 28301-4298. Offers MA. *Faculty:* 11 full-time (7 women). *Students:* 12 full-time (10 women), 29 part-time (17 women); includes 18 minority (all Black or African American, non-Hispanic/Latino). Average age 34. 4 applicants, 100% accepted, 4 enrolled. In 2010, 3 master's awarded. *Application deadline:* For fall admission, 4/15 for domestic students; for spring admission, 10/15 for domestic students. Application fee: $35. *Unit head:* Dr. Miriam Delone, Interim Chair, 910-672-1478, Fax: 910-672-1908, E-mail: mdelone@uncfsu.edu. *Application contact:* Katrina Hoffman, Graduate Admissions Officer, 910-672-1374, Fax: 910-672-1470, E-mail: khoffma1@uncfsu.edu.

Ferris State University, College of Education and Human Services, School of Criminal Justice, Big Rapids, MI 49307. Offers criminal justice administration (MSCJ). Part-time and evening/weekend programs available. *Faculty:* 10 full-time (5 women). *Students:* 22 full-time (13 women), 49 part-time (24 women); includes 15 Black or African American, non-Hispanic/Latino; 2 American Indian or Alaska Native, non-Hispanic/Latino; 5 Hispanic/Latino; 2 Two or more races, non-Hispanic/Latino, 1 international. Average age 31. 18 applicants, 61% accepted, 11 enrolled. In 2010, 23 master's awarded. *Degree requirements:* For master's, thesis optional, comprehensive exam or thesis/dissertation. *Entrance requirements:* For master's, bachelor's degree in criminal justice or related field, minimum GPA of 3.0. Additional exam requirements/ recommendations for international students: Required—TOEFL (minimum score 500 paper-based; 173 computer-based; 61 iBT). *Application deadline:* For fall admission, 8/15 for domestic students; for winter admission, 12/15 for domestic students; for spring admission, 3/15 for domestic students. Applications are processed on a rolling basis. Application fee: $30. Electronic applications accepted. *Financial support:* In 2010–11, 2 research assistantships (averaging $4,850 per year) were awarded; Federal Work-Study and unspecified assistantships also available. Support available to part-time students. Financial award applicants required to submit FAFSA. *Faculty research:* Policy enactment, health and safety issues, criminological theory, juvenile justice, policy techniques, problem-based learning. *Unit head:* Dr. Nancy L. Hogan, Graduate Program Coordinator, 231-591-2664, Fax: 231-591-3792, E-mail: hogann@ferris.edu. *Application contact:* Dr. Nancy L. Hogan, Assistant Professor, 231-591-2664, Fax: 231-591-3792, E-mail: hogann@ferris.edu.

Florida Agricultural and Mechanical University, Division of Graduate Studies, Research, and Continuing Education, College of Arts and Sciences, Division of History and Political Sciences, Program in Applied Social Science, Tallahassee, FL 32307-3200. Offers African American history (MASS); criminal justice (MASS); economics (MASS); history (MASS); political science (MASS); public administration (MASS); public management (MASS); social work (MASS); sociology (MASS). Part-time programs available. *Degree requirements:* For master's, thesis optional. *Entrance requirements:* For master's, GRE General Test, minimum GPA of 3.0. *Faculty research:* Southern history, black history, election trends, presidential history.

Florida Atlantic University, College of Design and Social Inquiry, School of Criminology and Criminal Justice, Boca Raton, FL 33431-0991. Offers MS. Part-time and evening/weekend programs available. Postbaccalaureate distance learning degree programs offered. *Faculty:* 13 full-time (6 women), 12 part-time/adjunct (3 women). *Students:* 8 full-time (6 women), 22 part-time (13 women); includes 12 minority (6 Black or African American, non-Hispanic/Latino; 1 Asian, non-Hispanic/Latino; 5 Hispanic/Latino). Average age 28. 29 applicants, 59% accepted, 13 enrolled. In 2010, 6 master's awarded. *Degree requirements:* For master's, thesis optional. *Entrance requirements:* For master's, GRE General Test, minimum GPA of 3.0, undergraduate course work in statistics and criminology. Additional exam requirements/recommendations for international students: Required—TOEFL (minimum score 550 paper-based; 213 computer-based). *Application deadline:* For fall admission, 7/1 priority date for domestic students, 2/15 for international students; for spring admission, 11/1 priority date for domestic students, 7/15 for international students. Applications are processed on a rolling basis. Application fee: $30. Electronic applications accepted. *Expenses:* Tuition, area resident: Part-time $319.96 per credit. Tuition, state resident: part-time $319.96 per credit. Tuition, nonresident: part-time $926.42 per credit. *Financial support:* Research assistantships with partial tuition reimbursements, institutionally sponsored loans, scholarships/grants, and unspecified assistantships available. Financial award application deadline: 4/1. *Faculty research:* Restorative, justice corrections, logic modeling, criminal justice management, crime causation. *Unit head:* Dr. Gordon Bazemore, Chair, 561-297-3240. *Application contact:* Dr. Maria Schiff, Graduate Program Coordinator, 954-762-5638, Fax: 954-762-5673, E-mail: mschiff@fau.edu.

Florida Gulf Coast University, College of Professional Studies, Program in Criminal Justice Studies, Fort Myers, FL 33965-6565. Offers MS. *Faculty:* 35 full-time (15 women), 34 part-time/adjunct (12 women). *Students:* 12 full-time (4 women), 4 part-time (3 women); includes 1 Black or African American, non-Hispanic/Latino; 2 Hispanic/Latino. Average age 33. 12 applicants, 50% accepted, 5 enrolled. In 2010, 3 master's awarded. *Entrance requirements:* For master's, GRE General Test, minimum GPA of 3.0. Additional exam requirements/ recommendations for international students: Required—TOEFL (minimum score 550 paper-based; 213 computer-based). *Application deadline:* For fall admission, 3/1 for domestic students; for spring admission, 11/1 for domestic students. Applications are processed on a rolling basis. Application fee: $30. Electronic applications accepted. *Expenses:* Tuition, state resident: part-time $322.08 per credit hour. Tuition, nonresident: part-time $1117.08 per credit hour. *Unit head:* Tony Barringer, Chair, 239-590-7849, E-mail: tbarring@fgcu.edu. *Application contact:* Tony Barringer, Chair, 239-590-7849, E-mail: tbarring@fgcu.edu.

Florida Gulf Coast University, College of Professional Studies, Program in Public Administration, Fort Myers, FL 33965-6565. Offers criminal justice (MPA); environmental policy (MPA); general public administration (MPA); management (MPA). *Accreditation:* NASPAA. Part-time programs available. *Faculty:* 35 full-time (15 women), 34 part-time/adjunct (12 women). *Students:* 71 full-time (46 women), 20 part-time (11 women); includes 10 Black or African American, non-Hispanic/Latino; 1 American Indian or Alaska Native, non-Hispanic/ Latino; 7 Hispanic/Latino, 2 international. Average age 31. 46 applicants, 67% accepted, 26 enrolled. In 2010, 11 master's awarded. *Entrance requirements:* For master's, GRE General Test, MAT, minimum GPA of 3.0. Additional exam requirements/recommendations for international students: Required—TOEFL (minimum score 550 paper-based; 213 computer-based). *Application deadline:* For fall admission, 7/1 priority date for domestic students; for spring admission, 11/15 for domestic students. Applications are processed on a rolling basis. Application fee: $30. Electronic applications accepted. *Expenses:* Tuition, state resident: part-time $322.08 per credit hour. Tuition, nonresident: part-time $1117.08 per credit hour. *Financial support:* In 2010–11, 5 research assistantships were awarded; career-related intern-

Criminal Justice and Criminology

Florida Gulf Coast University (continued)

ships or fieldwork and tuition waivers (full and partial) also available. Support available to part-time students. *Faculty research:* Personnel, public policy, public finance, housing policy. *Unit head:* Terry Busson, Chair, 239-590-7704, E-mail: tbusson@fgcu.edu. *Application contact:* Roger Green, Information Contact, 239-590-7838, Fax: 239-590-7846.

Florida International University, College of Arts and Sciences, Department of Criminal Justice, Miami, FL 33199. Offers MS. Part-time and evening/weekend programs available. *Faculty:* 11 full-time (4 women), 10 part-time/adjunct (3 women). *Students:* 89 full-time (58 women), 119 part-time (74 women); includes 68 Black or African American, non-Hispanic/Latino; 4 Asian, non-Hispanic/Latino; 94 Hispanic/Latino, 2 international. Average age 29. 338 applicants, 44% accepted, 143 enrolled. In 2010, 36 master's awarded. *Degree requirements:* For master's, thesis optional. *Entrance requirements:* For master's, minimum undergraduate GPA of 3.0. Additional exam requirements/recommendations for international students: Required—TOEFL (minimum score 550 paper-based; 80 iBT). *Application deadline:* For fall admission, 6/1 for domestic students, 4/1 for international students; for spring admission, 10/1 for domestic students, 9/1 for international students. Applications are processed on a rolling basis. Application fee: $30. Electronic applications accepted. *Financial support:* Institutionally sponsored loans and scholarships/grants available. Financial award application deadline: 3/1; financial award applicants required to submit FAFSA. *Unit head:* Dr. Lisa Stolzenberg, Chair, 305-348-5890, Fax: 305-348-2503, E-mail: lisa.stolzenberg@fiu.edu. *Application contact:* Liga Replogle, Student Services Coordinator, 305-348-5890, Fax: 305-348-5848, E-mail: liga.replogle@fiu.edu.

Florida State University, The Graduate School, College of Criminology and Criminal Justice, Tallahassee, FL 32306-1127. Offers MA, MSC, PhD, MPA/MSC, MS/MSW. Part-time programs available. Postbaccalaureate distance learning degree programs offered (no on-campus study). *Faculty:* 19 full-time (4 women). *Students:* 93 full-time (56 women), 98 part-time (56 women); includes 40 minority (19 Black or African American, non-Hispanic/Latino; 2 American Indian or Alaska Native, non-Hispanic/Latino; 6 Asian, non-Hispanic/Latino; 13 Hispanic/Latino), 5 international. 192 applicants, 59% accepted, 58 enrolled. In 2010, 40 master's, 9 doctorates awarded. *Degree requirements:* For master's, thesis optional; for doctorate, comprehensive exam, thesis/dissertation. *Entrance requirements:* For master's, GRE General Test; for doctorate, GRE General Test, completed area paper or thesis. Additional exam requirements/recommendations for international students: Required—TOEFL (minimum score 600 paper-based; 260 computer-based; 100 iBT). *Application deadline:* For fall admission, 7/1 for domestic and international students; for spring admission, 11/1 for domestic and international students. Applications are processed on a rolling basis. Application fee: $30. Electronic applications accepted. *Expenses:* Tuition, state resident: full-time $8238.24. *Financial support:* In 2010–11, 1 fellowship with full tuition reimbursement (averaging $19,000 per year), 20 research assistantships with full tuition reimbursements (averaging $14,500 per year), 1 teaching assistantship with full tuition reimbursement (averaging $14,500 per year) were awarded; Federal Work-Study, institutionally sponsored loans, scholarships/grants, tuition waivers (partial), and unspecified assistantships also available. Financial award application deadline: 1/15; financial award applicants required to submit FAFSA. *Faculty research:* Criminological theory, criminal justice administration and planning, criminal justice policy and evaluation, law and social control, biosocial criminology. *Unit head:* Dr. Thomas G. Blomberg, Dean, 850-644-7365, Fax: 850-644-9614. *Application contact:* Margarita Frankeberger, Graduate Student Coordinator, 850-644-7373, Fax: 850-644-9614, E-mail: mfrankeberger@fsu.edu.

George Mason University, College of Humanities and Social Sciences, Administration of Justice Department, Fairfax, VA 22030. Offers criminology, law and society (MA, PhD). *Faculty:* 24 full-time (17 women), 13 part-time/adjunct (1 woman). *Students:* 9 full-time (6 women), 46 part-time (29 women); includes 3 Black or African American, non-Hispanic/Latino; 4 Asian, non-Hispanic/Latino; 3 Hispanic/Latino, 2 international. Average age 29. 73 applicants, 71% accepted, 8 enrolled. In 2010, 3 master's, 1 doctorate awarded. *Degree requirements:* For master's, thesis; for doctorate, comprehensive exam, thesis/dissertation. *Entrance requirements:* For master's, personal goal statement, transcripts, 2 letters of recommendation; for doctorate, 2 letters of recommendation. Additional exam requirements/recommendations for international students: Required—TOEFL (minimum score 570 paper-based; 230 computer-based; 88 iBT). *Application deadline:* For fall admission, 4/1 priority date for domestic students. Applications are processed on a rolling basis. Application fee: $100. Electronic applications accepted. *Expenses:* Tuition, state resident: full-time $8192; part-time $440 per credit hour. Tuition, nonresident: full-time $22,952; part-time $1055 per credit hour. Required fees: $2364; $99 per credit hour. *Financial support:* In 2010–11, 19 students received support, including 3 fellowships with full tuition reimbursements available (averaging $18,000 per year), 13 research assistantships with full and partial tuition reimbursements available (averaging $14,110 per year), 4 teaching assistantships with full and partial tuition reimbursements available (averaging $14,750 per year); career-related internships or fieldwork, Federal Work-Study, scholarships/grants, unspecified assistantships, and health care benefits (full-time research or teaching assistantship recipients) also available. Financial award application deadline: 3/1; financial award applicants required to submit FAFSA. *Faculty research:* Reducing violent crime in Trinidad and Tobago, wrongful convictions in capital cases, health and safety in incarcerated juveniles, impact of the war on terror on civil liberties. Total annual research expenditures: $4.8 million. *Unit head:* David Wilson, Chair, 703-993-8313, E-mail: dwilsonb@gmu.edu. *Application contact:* Crystal Harris, Graduate Academic Advisor, 703-993-9417, E-mail: charri4@gmu.edu.

The George Washington University, Columbian College of Arts and Sciences, Department of Forensic Sciences, Washington, DC 20052. Offers crime scene investigation (MFS); forensic chemistry (MFS); forensic molecular biology (MFS); forensic toxicology (MFS); high-technology crime investigation (MFS); security management (MFS). High-technology crime investigation and security management programs offered in Arlington, VA. Part-time and evening/weekend programs available. *Faculty:* 6 full-time (1 woman), 22 part-time/adjunct (5 women). *Students:* 80 full-time (61 women), 60 part-time (37 women); includes 8 Black or African American, non-Hispanic/Latino; 2 American Indian or Alaska Native, non-Hispanic/Latino; 7 Asian, non-Hispanic/Latino; 8 Hispanic/Latino, 7 international. Average age 27. 149 applicants, 91% accepted, 58 enrolled. In 2010, 57 master's awarded. *Degree requirements:* For master's, comprehensive exam. *Entrance requirements:* For master's, GRE General Test, minimum GPA of 3.0. Additional exam requirements/recommendations for international students: Required—TOEFL (minimum score 550 paper-based; 213 computer-based; 80 iBT). *Application deadline:* For fall admission, 1/16 priority date for international students; for spring admission, 10/1 priority date for domestic students, 9/1 priority date for international students. Applications are processed on a rolling basis. Application fee: $75. Electronic applications accepted. *Financial support:* In 2010–11, 19 students received support; fellowships with partial tuition reimbursements available, Federal Work-Study and tuition waivers available. *Unit head:* Dr. Walter F. Rowe, Chair, 202-994-1469, E-mail: wfrowe@gwu.edu. *Application contact:* Dr. Walter F. Rowe, Chair, 202-994-1469, E-mail: wfrowe@gwu.edu.

The George Washington University, Columbian College of Arts and Sciences, Department of Sociology, Program in Criminology, Washington, DC 20052. Offers MA. *Students:* 9 full-time (8 women), 6 part-time (all women); includes 2 Black or African American, non-Hispanic/Latino; 1 Asian, non-Hispanic/Latino; 1 Hispanic/Latino. Average age 26. 23 applicants, 39% accepted, 5 enrolled. In 2010, 1 master's awarded. *Degree requirements:* For master's, comprehensive exam. *Entrance requirements:* For master's, GRE General Test, minimum GPA of 3.0. Additional exam requirements/recommendations for international students: Required—TOEFL (minimum score 550 paper-based; 213 computer-based). *Application deadline:* For fall admission, 4/1 priority date for domestic and international students; for spring admission, 10/1 priority date for domestic and international students. Applications are processed on a rolling basis. Application fee: $75. Electronic applications accepted. *Financial support:* In 2010–11, fellowships with full tuition reimbursements (averaging $10,000 per year), teaching assistantships (averaging $5,000 per year) were awarded. Financial award application deadline: 2/1. *Unit head:* Ronald Weitzer, Director, 202-994-6895. *Application contact:* Information Contact, 202-994-6345, Fax: 202-994-3239, E-mail: soc@gwu.edu.

Georgia College & State University, Graduate School, College of Arts and Sciences, Department of Government and Sociology, Program in Criminal Justice, Milledgeville, GA 31061. Offers MS. Part-time and evening/weekend programs available. *Students:* 5 full-time (3 women), 12 part-time (8 women); includes 7 Black or African American, non-Hispanic/Latino. Average age 33. 9 applicants, 89% accepted, 5 enrolled. In 2010, 9 master's awarded. *Degree requirements:* For master's, comprehensive exam, thesis optional, capstone project. *Entrance requirements:* For master's, GRE or MAT. Additional exam requirements/recommendations for international students: Required—TOEFL (minimum score 550 paper-based; 213 computer-based; 79 iBT). *Application deadline:* For fall admission, 7/1 priority date for domestic students, 4/1 priority date for international students; for spring admission, 11/15 priority date for domestic students. Applications are processed on a rolling basis. Application fee: $40. Electronic applications accepted. *Expenses:* Tuition, state resident: full-time $4806; part-time $267 per hour. Tuition, nonresident: full-time $17,802; part-time $989 per hour. Tuition and fees vary according to course load. *Financial support:* In 2010–11, 1 research assistantship with full tuition reimbursement was awarded; unspecified assistantships also available. Financial award applicants required to submit FAFSA. *Unit head:* Dr. Gerald Fisher, Coordinator, 478-445-0940, E-mail: gerald.fisher@gcsu.edu. *Application contact:* Dr. Gerald Fisher, Coordinator, 478-445-0940, E-mail: gerald.fisher@gcsu.edu.

Georgia State University, Andrew Young School of Policy Studies, Department of Public Management and Policy, Atlanta, GA 30303. Offers disaster management (Certificate); nonprofit management (Certificate); planning and economic development (Certificate); public administration (MPA), including criminal justice, management and finance, nonprofit management, planning and economic development, policy analysis and evaluation, public health; public policy (MPP, PhD), including disaster policy (MPP), nonprofit policy (MPP), planning and economic development policy (MPP), public finance policy (MPP), social policy (MPP); JD/MPA. *Accreditation:* NASPAA (one or more programs are accredited). Part-time and evening/weekend programs available. Terminal master's awarded for partial completion of doctoral program. *Degree requirements:* For master's, thesis optional; for doctorate, comprehensive exam, thesis/dissertation. *Entrance requirements:* For master's and doctorate, GRE General Test. Additional exam requirements/recommendations for international students: Required—TOEFL. Electronic applications accepted. *Faculty research:* Public management, policy analysis, public finance, planning and economic development, nonprofit leadership and policy.

Georgia State University, College of Health and Human Sciences, Department of Criminal Justice, Atlanta, GA 30302-3083. Offers MS. Part-time and evening/weekend programs available. *Degree requirements:* For master's, thesis optional. *Entrance requirements:* For master's, GRE General Test. Additional exam requirements/recommendations for international students: Required—TOEFL (minimum score 550 paper-based; 213 computer-based). Electronic applications accepted. *Faculty research:* Urban violence, family violence, social support and adolescent crime, policing issues, active offender crime.

Graduate School and University Center of the City University of New York, Graduate Studies, Program in Criminal Justice, New York, NY 10016-4039. Offers PhD. *Degree requirements:* For doctorate, one foreign language, thesis/dissertation. *Entrance requirements:* For doctorate, GRE General Test, writing sample. Additional exam requirements/recommendations for international students: Required—TOEFL. Electronic applications accepted.

Grambling State University, School of Graduate Studies and Research, College of Professional Studies, Program in Criminal Justice, Grambling, LA 71245. Offers MS. Part-time programs available. *Degree requirements:* For master's, comprehensive exam, thesis optional. *Entrance requirements:* For master's, GRE, minimum GPA of 2.5 on last degree and in four core courses. Additional exam requirements/recommendations for international students: Required—TOEFL (minimum score 500 paper-based; 173 computer-based; 61 iBT). Electronic applications accepted. *Faculty research:* Corrections, terrorism, delinquency, complex organizations, post-modern theory.

Grand Valley State University, College of Community and Public Service, School of Criminal Justice, Allendale, MI 49401-9403. Offers MS. Part-time and evening/weekend programs available. *Degree requirements:* For master's, thesis or alternative. *Entrance requirements:* For master's, minimum GPA of 3.0. Additional exam requirements/recommendations for international students: Required—TOEFL. *Faculty research:* Correctional administration, juvenile justice issues/gangs, women's issues, leadership, program/policy evaluation.

Hodges University, Graduate Programs, Naples, FL 34119. Offers business administration (MBA); computer information technology (MS); criminal justice (MCJ); education (MPS); information systems management (MIS); interdisciplinary (MPS); legal studies (MS); management (MSM); mental health counseling (MS); psychology (MPS); public administration (MPA). Part-time and evening/weekend programs available. Postbaccalaureate distance learning degree programs offered (no on-campus study). *Faculty:* 25 full-time (9 women), 5 part-time/adjunct (4 women). *Students:* 27 full-time (15 women), 228 part-time (146 women); includes 76 minority (35 Black or African American, non-Hispanic/Latino; 5 Asian, non-Hispanic/Latino; 36 Hispanic/Latino). Average age 36. 92 applicants, 91% accepted, 81 enrolled. In 2010, 92 master's awarded. *Degree requirements:* For master's, comprehensive exam (for some programs), thesis (for some programs). *Entrance requirements:* For master's, in-house entrance exam. *Application deadline:* Applications are processed on a rolling basis. Application fee: $50. Electronic applications accepted. *Expenses:* Tuition: Full-time $16,605; part-time $615 per credit hour. Required fees: $190 per trimester. *Financial support:* In 2010–11, 200 students received support. Federal Work-Study and scholarships/grants available. Financial award application deadline: 7/9; financial award applicants required to submit FAFSA. *Unit head:* Terry McMahan, President, 239-513-1122, Fax: 239-598-6253, E-mail: tmcmahan@hodges.edu. *Application contact:* Rita Lampus, Vice President of Student Enrollment Management, 239-513-1122, Fax: 239-598-6253, E-mail: rlampus@hodges.edu.

Holy Family University, Graduate School, School of Arts and Sciences, Program in Criminal Justice, Philadelphia, PA 19114. Offers MA. Part-time and evening/weekend programs available. *Faculty:* 2 full-time (both women), 5 part-time/adjunct (2 women). *Students:* 24 part-time (7 women); includes 1 Hispanic/Latino. Average age 28. 44 applicants, 45% accepted, 6 enrolled. *Entrance requirements:* For master's, BS or BA, minimum GPA of 3.0, 2 letters of recommendation. *Application deadline:* For fall admission, 8/1 for domestic students; for winter admission, 1/1 for domestic students. Applications are processed on a rolling basis. Application fee: $25. Electronic applications accepted. *Expenses:* Tuition: Full-time $14,400; part-time $600 per credit hour. Required fees: $85 per term. *Financial support:* Application deadline: 5/1. *Unit head:* Dr. Leanne Owen, Director, 267-341-4791. *Application contact:* Gidget Marie Montelibans, Graduate Admissions Counselor, 267-341-3558, Fax: 215-637-1478, E-mail: gmontelibano@holyfamily.edu.

See Display on next page and Close-Up on page 769.

Husson University, School of Graduate and Professional Studies, Program in Criminal Justice Administration, Bangor, ME 04401-2999. Offers MS.

Illinois State University, Graduate School, College of Applied Science and Technology, Department of Criminal Justice Sciences, Normal, IL 61790-2200. Offers MA, MS. *Degree requirements:* For master's, thesis or alternative. *Entrance requirements:* For master's, GRE General Test, minimum GPA of 2.6 in last 60 hours of course work. *Faculty research:* Graduate practicum for victim assistance and advocacy, graduate practicum in adult probation cases, graduate practicum in youth intervention program.

Indiana State University, College of Graduate and Professional Studies, College of Arts and Sciences, Department of Criminology and Criminal Justice, Terre Haute, IN 47809. Offers MA, MS. Part-time programs available. Postbaccalaureate distance learning degree programs

Criminal Justice and Criminology

offered (no on-campus study). *Degree requirements:* For master's, thesis (for some programs). *Entrance requirements:* For master's, minimum GPA of 2.75 in undergraduate work, 3.0 in previous graduate work. Additional exam requirements/recommendations for international students: Required—TOEFL (minimum score 550 paper-based). Electronic applications accepted. *Faculty research:* Violent crime, rape attitudes, classification of offenders, substance abuse, domestic violence.

Indiana Tech, Program in Police Administration, Fort Wayne, IN 46803-1297. Offers MS. Part-time and evening/weekend programs available. Postbaccalaureate distance learning degree programs offered (no on-campus study). *Entrance requirements:* For master's, 2 letters of recommendation, bachelor's degree in criminal justice or related field with minimum GPA of 2.5. Electronic applications accepted.

Indiana University Bloomington, University Graduate School, College of Arts and Sciences, Department of Criminal Justice, Bloomington, IN 47405. Offers criminal justice (MA, PhD); criminology (MA, PhD); cross-cultural perspectives of crime and justice (MA, PhD); law and society (MA, PhD); psychology and the law (MA). Part-time programs available. *Faculty:* 15 full-time (5 women). *Students:* 39 full-time (23 women); includes 6 minority (4 Black or African American, non-Hispanic/Latino; 2 American Indian or Alaska Native, non-Hispanic/Latino), 3 international. Average age 31. 30 applicants, 30% accepted, 4 enrolled. In 2010, 3 master's, 2 doctorates awarded. Terminal master's awarded for partial completion of doctoral program. *Degree requirements:* For master's, thesis optional; for doctorate, thesis/dissertation, foreign language or research practicum. *Entrance requirements:* For master's and doctorate, GRE General Test. Additional exam requirements/recommendations for international students: Required—TOEFL (minimum score 600 paper-based; 250 computer-based; 100 iBT). *Application deadline:* For fall admission, 1/15 for domestic students, 12/1 for international students. Application fee: $55 ($65 for international students). Electronic applications accepted. *Expenses:* Contact institution. *Financial support:* In 2010–11, 4 fellowships with full tuition reimbursements (averaging $25,000 per year), 3 research assistantships with full tuition reimbursements (averaging $11,721 per year), 21 teaching assistantships with full tuition reimbursements (averaging $11,721 per year) were awarded; Federal Work-Study, health care benefits, tuition waivers (full), and unspecified assistantships also available. Financial award application deadline: 1/15. *Faculty research:* Violence, crime, juveniles, psychology and law, cross-cultural studies. *Unit head:* Dr. Roger J. R. Levesque, Chair, 812-856-1210, E-mail: rlevesqu@indiana.edu. *Application contact:* Ruth Cord, Graduate Secretary, 812-856-4675, Fax: 812-855-5522, E-mail: rkapusti@indiana.edu.

Indiana University Northwest, School of Public and Environmental Affairs, Gary, IN 46408-1197. Offers criminal justice (MPA); environmental affairs (Graduate Certificate); health services administration (MPA); human services administration (MPA); nonprofit management (Graduate Certificate); public management (MPA, Graduate Certificate). *Accreditation:* NASPAA (one or more programs are accredited). Part-time programs available. *Faculty:* 5 full-time (3 women). *Students:* 9 full-time (6 women), 127 part-time (96 women); includes 96 minority (81 Black or African American, non-Hispanic/Latino; 1 American Indian or Alaska Native, non-Hispanic/Latino; 2 Asian, non-Hispanic/Latino; 10 Hispanic/Latino; 2 Two or more races, non-Hispanic/Latino). Average age 38. 43 applicants, 95% accepted, 40 enrolled. In 2010, 37 master's, 24 other advanced degrees awarded. *Entrance requirements:* For master's, GRE General Test or GMAT, letters of recommendation. *Application deadline:* For fall admission, 8/15 priority date for domestic students. Applications are processed on a rolling basis. Application fee: $25. *Financial support:* Career-related internships or fieldwork, Federal Work-Study, and tuition waivers (partial) available. Support available to part-time students. Financial award application deadline: 3/1. *Faculty research:* Employment in income security policies, evidence in criminal justice, equal employment law, social welfare policy and welfare reform, public finance in developing countries. *Unit head:* George Assibey-Mensah, Interim Dean/Division Director, 219-980-6695, Fax: 219-980-6737. *Application contact:* Sandra Hall Smith, Secretary, 219-980-6695, Fax: 219-980-6737, E-mail: shsmith@iun.edu.

Indiana University of Pennsylvania, School of Graduate Studies and Research, College of Health and Human Services, Department of Criminology, Doctoral Program in Criminology, Indiana, PA 15705-1087. Offers PhD. Part-time programs available. *Faculty:* 14 full-time (9 women), 1 part-time/adjunct (0 women). *Students:* 20 full-time (6 women), 26 part-time (15 women); includes 4 minority (2 Black or African American, non-Hispanic/Latino; 2 Asian, non-Hispanic/Latino). Average age 31. 34 applicants, 41% accepted, 7 enrolled. In 2010, 10 doctorates awarded. *Degree requirements:* For doctorate, one foreign language, comprehensive exam, thesis/dissertation. *Entrance requirements:* For doctorate, GRE, 3 letters of recommendation, writing sample, interview. Additional exam requirements/recommendations for international students: Required—TOEFL. *Application deadline:* For fall admission, 7/1 priority date for domestic students; for spring admission, 11/1 for domestic students. Applications are processed on a rolling basis. Application fee: $40. *Financial support:* In 2010–11, 6 fellowships (averaging $917 per year), 11 research assistantships with full and partial tuition reimbursements (averaging $6,120 per year), 4 teaching assistantships with partial tuition reimbursements (averaging $19,167 per year) were awarded; Federal Work-Study also available. Support available to part-time students. Financial award application deadline: 3/15; financial award applicants required to submit FAFSA. *Unit head:* Dr. Jennifer Roberts, Graduate Coordinator, 724-357-5933, E-mail: jennifer.roberts@iup.edu. *Application contact:* Dr. Jacqueline Beck, Associate Dean, 724-357-2560, E-mail: jbeck@iup.edu.

Indiana University of Pennsylvania, School of Graduate Studies and Research, College of Health and Human Services, Department of Criminology, Master's Program in Criminology, Indiana, PA 15705-1087. Offers MA. Part-time and evening/weekend programs available. *Faculty:* 14 full-time (9 women), 1 part-time/adjunct (0 women). *Students:* 33 full-time (15 women), 63 part-time (29 women); includes 13 minority (9 Black or African American, non-Hispanic/Latino; 2 Asian, non-Hispanic/Latino; 2 Hispanic/Latino), 1 international. Average age 30. 71 applicants, 46% accepted, 27 enrolled. In 2010, 50 master's awarded. *Degree requirements:* For master's, thesis optional. *Entrance requirements:* For master's, 2 letters of recommendation. Additional exam requirements/recommendations for international students: Required—TOEFL. *Application deadline:* For fall admission, 7/1 priority date for domestic students; for spring admission, 11/1 for domestic students. Applications are processed on a rolling basis. Application fee: $40. *Financial support:* In 2010–11, 10 research assistantships with full and partial tuition reimbursements (averaging $2,296 per year) were awarded; fellowships, Federal Work-Study also available. Support available to part-time students. Financial award application deadline: 3/15; financial award applicants required to submit FAFSA. *Unit head:* Dr. Shannon Phaneuf, Graduate Coordinator, 724-357-5977, E-mail: shannon.phaneuf@iup.edu. *Application contact:* Dr. Jacqueline Beck, Associate Dean, 724-357-2560, E-mail: jbeck@iup.edu.

Indiana University–Purdue University Indianapolis, School of Public and Environmental Affairs, Indianapolis, IN 46202. Offers criminal justice and public safety (MSCJPS); public affairs (MPA), including criminal justice, nonprofit management, policy analysis, public management; public management (Graduate Certificate); JD/MPA; MATS/MM; MLS/NMC; MLS/PMC. *Accreditation:* CAHME (one or more programs are accredited); NASPAA. Part-time and evening/weekend programs available. Postbaccalaureate distance learning degree programs offered (no on-campus study). *Faculty:* 23 full-time (7 women). *Students:* 81 full-time (47 women), 205 part-time (142 women); includes 30 Black or African American, non-Hispanic/Latino; 6 Asian, non-Hispanic/Latino; 8 Hispanic/Latino, 9 international. Average age 31. 217 applicants, 73% accepted, 136 enrolled. In 2010, 77 degrees awarded. *Entrance requirements:* For master's, GRE General Test, GMAT or LSAT, minimum GPA of 3.0 (preferred). Additional exam requirements/recommendations for international students: Required—All international applicants to IUPUI whose native language is not English must demonstrate proficiency in English as a second language through an accepted examination and an accepted score. *Application deadline:* For fall admission, 5/15 priority date for domestic students; for spring admission, 2/15 priority date for domestic students. Applications are processed on a rolling basis. Application fee: $50 ($65 for international students). Electronic applications accepted. *Financial support:* In 2010–11, 1 fellowship with full tuition reimbursement (averaging $14,000 per year), 4 research assistantships with full tuition reimbursements (averaging $12,000 per year) were awarded; teaching assistantships, career-related internships or fieldwork, Federal

Criminal Justice and Criminology

Indiana University–Purdue University Indianapolis (continued)
Work-Study, institutionally sponsored loans, and scholarships/grants also available. Support available to part-time students. Financial award application deadline: 3/1; financial award applicants required to submit FAFSA. *Faculty research:* Nonprofit and public management, public policy, urban and environmental policy, disaster preparedness and recovery, vehicular safety, homicide, and offender rehabilitation and re-entry. Total annual research expenditures: $1.6 million. *Unit head:* Dr. Terry L. Baumer, Executive Associate Dean, 317-274-2016, Fax: 317-274-5153.

Inter American University of Puerto Rico, Aguadilla Campus, Graduate School, Aguadilla, PR 00605. Offers accounting (MBA); counseling psychology specializing in family (MS); criminal justice (MA); educative management and leadership (MA); elementary education (M Ed); finance (MBA); human resources (MBA); industrial management (MBA); management information systems (MBA); marketing (MBA). Part-time and evening/weekend programs available. *Degree requirements:* For master's, comprehensive exam. *Entrance requirements:* For master's, EXADEP, 2 letters of recommendation, minimum GPA of 2.5. Electronic applications accepted.

Inter American University of Puerto Rico, Metropolitan Campus, Graduate Programs, Program in Criminal Justice, San Juan, PR 00919-1293. Offers MA. Part-time and evening/weekend programs available. *Degree requirements:* For master's, comprehensive exam. *Entrance requirements:* For master's, GRE or EXADEP, interview. Electronic applications accepted.

Inter American University of Puerto Rico, Ponce Campus, Graduate School, Mercedita, PR 00715-1602. Offers accounting (MBA); biology (M Ed); chemistry (M Ed); criminal justice (MA); elementary education (M Ed); English as a Second Language (M Ed); finance (MBA); history (M Ed); human resources (MBA); marketing (MBA); mathematics (M Ed); Spanish (M Ed). *Entrance requirements:* For master's, minimum GPA of 2.5.

Iona College, School of Arts and Science, Program in Criminal Justice, New Rochelle, NY 10801-1890. Offers MS. Part-time and evening/weekend programs available. *Faculty:* 7 full-time (3 women), 4 part-time/adjunct (0 women). *Students:* 5 full-time (4 women), 21 part-time (13 women); includes 7 minority (2 Black or African American, non-Hispanic/Latino; 4 Hispanic/Latino; 1 Native Hawaiian or other Pacific Islander, non-Hispanic/Latino). Average age 31. 18 applicants, 83% accepted, 6 enrolled. In 2010, 10 master's awarded. *Degree requirements:* For master's, thesis. *Entrance requirements:* For master's, minimum GPA of 2.75. Additional exam requirements/recommendations for international students: Required—TOEFL (minimum score 550 paper-based; 213 computer-based). *Application deadline:* Applications are processed on a rolling basis. Application fee: $50. Electronic applications accepted. *Expenses:* Tuition: Part-time $830 per credit. Required fees: $225 per credit. *Financial support:* Unspecified assistantships available. Financial award application deadline: 4/15; financial award applicants required to submit FAFSA. *Faculty research:* Police administration, victimology and criminal justice program evaluation. *Unit head:* Dr. Cathryn Lavery, Chair, 914-633-2597, E-mail: clavery@iona.edu. *Application contact:* Veronica Jarek-Prinz, Director of Graduate Admissions, 914-633-2420, Fax: 914-633-2277, E-mail: vjarekprinz@iona.edu.

Jackson State University, Graduate School, College of Liberal Arts, Department of Sociology, Jackson, MS 39217. Offers criminology and justice services (MA); sociology (MA). Part-time and evening/weekend programs available. *Faculty:* 6 full-time (4 women), 1 part-time/adjunct (0 women). *Students:* 24 full-time (20 women), 49 part-time (38 women); includes 65 Black or African American, non-Hispanic/Latino. Average age 38. In 2010, 36 master's awarded. *Degree requirements:* For master's, comprehensive exam, thesis or alternative. *Entrance requirements:* For master's, GRE General Test. Additional exam requirements/recommendations for international students: Required—TOEFL (minimum score 520 paper-based; 195 computer-based; 67 iBT). *Application deadline:* For fall admission, 3/1 priority date for domestic students, 3/1 for international students; for spring admission, 10/1 for domestic students. Applications are processed on a rolling basis. Application fee: $25. *Expenses:* Tuition, state resident: full-time $5050; part-time $281 per credit hour. Tuition, nonresident: full-time $12,380; part-time $689 per credit hour. *Financial support:* Career-related internships or fieldwork, Federal Work-Study, scholarships/grants, and unspecified assistantships available. Support available to part-time students. Financial award application deadline: 3/1; financial award applicants required to submit FAFSA. *Unit head:* Dr. Etta F. Morgan, Interim Chair, 601-979-2626, E-mail: etta.faye.morgan@jsums.edu. *Application contact:* Sharlene Wilson, Director of Graduate Admissions, 601-979-2455, Fax: 601-979-4325, E-mail: sharlene.f.wilson@jsums.edu.

Jacksonville State University, College of Graduate Studies and Continuing Education, College of Arts and Sciences, Department of Criminal Justice, Jacksonville, AL 36265-1602. Offers MS. Part-time and evening/weekend programs available. *Degree requirements:* For master's, comprehensive exam, thesis (for some programs). *Entrance requirements:* For master's, GRE General Test or MAT. Electronic applications accepted.

John Jay College of Criminal Justice of the City University of New York, Graduate Studies, Program in Protection Management, New York, NY 10019-1093. Offers MS. Part-time and evening/weekend programs available. *Degree requirements:* For master's, thesis or alternative. *Entrance requirements:* For master's, minimum B average. Additional exam requirements/recommendations for international students: Required—TOEFL (minimum score 500 paper-based; 173 computer-based).

John Jay College of Criminal Justice of the City University of New York, Graduate Studies, Programs in Criminal Justice, New York, NY 10019-1093. Offers criminal justice (MA, PhD); criminology and deviance (PhD); forensic psychology (PhD); forensic science (PhD); law and philosophy (PhD); organizational behavior (PhD); public policy (PhD). Part-time and evening/weekend programs available. Terminal master's awarded for partial completion of doctoral program. *Degree requirements:* For master's, thesis or alternative; for doctorate, one foreign language, thesis/dissertation. *Entrance requirements:* For master's, GRE General Test, minimum B average; for doctorate, GRE General Test. Additional exam requirements/recommendations for international students: Required—TOEFL (minimum score 500 paper-based; 173 computer-based).

The Johns Hopkins University, School of Education, Division of Public Safety Leadership, Baltimore, MD 21218. Offers intelligence analysis (MS); management (MS). Part-time and evening/weekend programs available. *Faculty:* 10 full-time (3 women), 23 part-time/adjunct (7 women). *Students:* 131 full-time (39 women), 12 part-time (1 woman); includes 52 minority (35 Black or African American, non-Hispanic/Latino; 4 Asian, non-Hispanic/Latino; 12 Hispanic/Latino; 1 Two or more races, non-Hispanic/Latino). Average age 40. 81 applicants, 75% accepted, 54 enrolled. In 2010, 95 master's awarded. *Entrance requirements:* For master's, minimum undergraduate GPA of 3.0, curriculum vitae/resume, interview, professional experience, endorsement letter (MS in management). Additional exam requirements/recommendations for international students: Required—TOEFL (minimum score 600 paper-based; 250 computer-based; 100 iBT). *Application deadline:* For fall admission, 5/1 for international students; for spring admission, 10/15 for international students. Applications are processed on a rolling basis. Application fee: $0. Electronic applications accepted. *Financial support:* Scholarships/grants available. Support available to part-time students. Financial award application deadline: 6/1; financial award applicants required to submit FAFSA. *Faculty research:* Campus and school safety, prevention and effective response to violence against women, counterterrorism training, leadership development for public safety and homeland security executives. *Unit head:* Dr. Sheldon Greenberg, Associate Dean, 410-516-9900, Fax: 410-290-1061, E-mail: psl@jhu.edu. *Application contact:* Jennifer Shaffer, Director of Admissions, 410-516-9797, Fax: 410-516-9799, E-mail: educationinfo@jhu.edu.

Kaplan University, Davenport Campus, School of Criminal Justice, Davenport, IA 52807-2095. Offers corrections (MSCJ); global issues in criminal justice (MSCJ); law (MSCJ); leadership and executive management (MSCJ); policing (MSCJ). Part-time and evening/weekend programs available. Postbaccalaureate distance learning degree programs offered (no on-campus study). *Entrance requirements:* Additional exam requirements/recommendations for international students: Required—TOEFL (minimum score 550 paper-based; 218 computer-based; 80 iBT). Electronic applications accepted.

Kean University, College of Business and Public Management, Program in Criminal Justice, Union, NJ 07083. Offers MA. Part-time and evening/weekend programs available. *Faculty:* 6 full-time (2 women). *Students:* 1 (woman) full-time, 2 part-time (0 women); includes 1 Black or African American, non-Hispanic/Latino. Average age 30. 4 applicants, 75% accepted, 2 enrolled. *Degree requirements:* For master's, comprehensive exam or thesis. *Entrance requirements:* For master's, GRE (minimum Analytic Writing score of 3.5), 3 reference letters, minimum GPA of 3.0, writing sample, official transcripts from all institutions attended. *Application deadline:* For fall admission, 6/1 for domestic students; for spring admission, 11/1 for domestic students. Application fee: $75 ($150 for international students). Electronic applications accepted. *Expenses:* Tuition, state resident: full-time $10,872; part-time $500 per credit. Tuition, nonresident: full-time $14,736; part-time $614 per credit. Required fees: $2740.80; $125 per credit. Part-time tuition and fees vary according to course load and degree level. *Financial support:* In 2010–11, research assistantships with full tuition reimbursements (averaging $3,263 per year); unspecified assistantships also available. Financial award applicants required to submit FAFSA. *Unit head:* Dr. P. McManimon, Program Coordinator, 908-737-4309, E-mail: pmcmanim@kean.edu. *Application contact:* Steven Koch, Pre-Admissions Coordinator, 908-737-5924, Fax: 908-737-5925, E-mail: skoch@kean.edu.

Keiser University, MA in Criminal Justice Program, Fort Lauderdale, FL 33309. Offers MA. Part-time programs available. Postbaccalaureate distance learning degree programs offered (no on-campus study). *Faculty:* 1 (woman) full-time, 5 part-time/adjunct (all women). *Students:* 8 full-time (5 women), 14 part-time (9 women); includes 5 Black or African American, non-Hispanic/Latino; 1 American Indian or Alaska Native, non-Hispanic/Latino; 2 Hispanic/Latino. Average age 36. 19 applicants, 89% accepted, 13 enrolled. *Entrance requirements:* For master's, minimum GPA of 2.7 from an accredited college or university. Additional exam requirements/recommendations for international students: Required—TOEFL. *Application deadline:* Applications are processed on a rolling basis. Application fee: $50. Electronic applications accepted. *Financial support:* In 2010–11, 18 students received support. Federal Work-Study available. Financial award applicants required to submit FAFSA.

Kent State University, College of Arts and Sciences, Department of Justice Studies, Kent, OH 44242-0001. Offers MA. Part-time and evening/weekend programs available. *Degree requirements:* For master's, comprehensive exam, thesis optional. *Entrance requirements:* For master's, minimum GPA of 2.75. Additional exam requirements/recommendations for international students: Required—TOEFL. Electronic applications accepted. *Expenses:* Tuition, state resident: full-time $7866; part-time $437 per credit hour. Tuition, nonresident: full-time $14,022; part-time $779 per credit hour. *Faculty research:* School violence, community policing.

Keuka College, Program in Criminal Justice Administration, Keuka Park, NY 14478-0098. Offers MS. Part-time and evening/weekend programs available. *Faculty:* 6 part-time/adjunct (2 women). *Students:* 5 full-time (1 woman), 28 part-time (14 women); includes 6 Black or African American, non-Hispanic/Latino; 1 American Indian or Alaska Native, non-Hispanic/Latino; 1 Hispanic/Latino. 89 applicants, 100% accepted. In 2010, 9 master's awarded. *Application deadline:* For fall admission, 8/15 for domestic students; for winter admission, 12/15 for domestic students; for spring admission, 4/15 for domestic students. Application fee: $30. *Expenses:* Contact institution. *Unit head:* Dr. Tom Tremer, Program Director, 315-279-5672, E-mail: ttremer@mail.keuka.edu. *Application contact:* Fred Hoyle, Dean of Enrollment, 315-279-5413, Fax: 315-279-5386, E-mail: admissions@mail.keuka.edu.

Lamar University, College of Graduate Studies, College of Arts and Sciences, Department of Sociology, Social Work, and Criminal Justice, Beaumont, TX 77710. Offers applied criminology (MS). Part-time programs available. *Faculty:* 3 full-time (0 women), 1 part-time/adjunct (0 women). *Students:* 1 (woman) full-time, 10 part-time (5 women). Average age 28. 10 applicants, 40% accepted, 1 enrolled. In 2010, 3 master's awarded. *Degree requirements:* For master's, thesis or alternative, applied projects. *Entrance requirements:* For master's, GRE General Test. Additional exam requirements/recommendations for international students: Required—TOEFL. *Application deadline:* For fall admission, 8/1 priority date for domestic students; for spring admission, 12/1 priority date for domestic students. Applications are processed on a rolling basis. Application fee: $25 ($50 for international students). *Expenses:* Tuition, state resident: full-time $4160; part-time $208 per credit hour. Tuition, nonresident: full-time $10,360; part-time $518 per credit hour. *Financial support:* In 2010–11, 3 fellowships with partial tuition reimbursements (averaging $1,000 per year) were awarded; career-related internships or fieldwork, Federal Work-Study, and scholarships/grants also available. Support available to part-time students. Financial award application deadline: 4/1; financial award applicants required to submit FAFSA. *Faculty research:* Corrections, planning and evaluations, juveniles, terrorism, Mexican criminal justice. *Unit head:* Dr. Li-Chen J. Ma, Chair, 409-880-8545, Fax: 409-880-2324, E-mail: lma@lamar.edu. *Application contact:* Dr. J. Rick Altemose, Graduate Program Director, 409-880-8549, Fax: 409-880-2324, E-mail: altemosejr@hal.lamar.edu.

Lewis University, College of Arts and Sciences, Program in Criminal/Social Justice, Romeoville, IL 60446. Offers criminal/social justice (MS). Part-time and evening/weekend programs available. *Faculty:* 2 full-time (1 woman), 14 part-time/adjunct (2 women). *Students:* 14 full-time (10 women), 69 part-time (32 women); includes 25 Black or African American, non-Hispanic/Latino; 2 Asian, non-Hispanic/Latino; 13 Hispanic/Latino. Average age 31. In 2010, 37 master's awarded. *Entrance requirements:* For master's, bachelor's degree or a minimum of 12 related hours in criminal/social justice, 2 letters of recommendation, minimum GPA of 3.0, interview. Additional exam requirements/recommendations for international students: Required—TOEFL (minimum score 550 paper-based; 213 computer-based). *Application deadline:* For fall admission, 5/1 priority date for international students; for spring admission, 11/15 priority date for international students. Applications are processed on a rolling basis. Application fee: $40. Electronic applications accepted. *Expenses:* Tuition: Full-time $13,320; part-time $740 per credit hour. Tuition and fees vary according to program. *Financial support:* Federal Work-Study, scholarships/grants, tuition waivers (full and partial), and unspecified assistantships available. Financial award application deadline: 5/1; financial award applicants required to submit FAFSA. *Faculty research:* Community policing, management, terrorism, biological warfare, drugs. *Unit head:* Dr. Calvin Edwards, Chair of Justice, Law and Public Safety Studies, 815-838-0500, Fax: 815-836-5870, E-mail: koloshsa@lewisu.edu. *Application contact:* Sarah Wiegman, Coordinator, 815-838-0500 Ext. 5686, Fax: 815-836-5870, E-mail: wiegmasa@lewisu.edu.

Lincoln University, School of Graduate Studies and Continuing Education, Jefferson City, MO 65102. Offers business administration (MBA), including accounting, entrepreneurship, management, public administration and policy; educational leadership (Ed S), including elementary leadership, secondary leadership, superintendency; guidance and counseling (M Ed), including community/agency counseling, elementary school, secondary school; history (MA); school administration and supervision (M Ed), including elementary school administration, secondary school administration, special education administration; school teaching (M Ed), including elementary school teaching, secondary school teaching; social science (MA), including history, political science, sociology; sociology (MA); sociology/criminal justice (MA). Part-time and evening/weekend programs available. *Degree requirements:* For master's and Ed S, comprehensive exam, thesis optional. *Entrance requirements:* For master's and Ed S, GRE, MAT or GMAT, minimum GPA of 2.75 in major, 2.5 overall; 3 letters of recommendation; minimum C average in English composition; personal statement of purpose. Additional exam requirements/recommendations for international students: Required—TOEFL (minimum score 500 paper-based; 173 computer-based; 61 iBT). *Faculty research:* Suicide prevention.

Lindenwood University, Graduate Programs, College of Individualized Education, St. Charles, MO 63301-1695. Offers administration (MSA); business administration (MBA); communications (MA); criminal justice and administration (MS); gerontology (MA); health management (MS); human resource management (MS); information technology (MBA, Certificate); managing information technology (MS); writing (MFA). Part-time and evening/weekend programs available. *Faculty:* 15 full-time (8 women), 128 part-time/adjunct (53 women). *Students:* 828 full-time (527 women), 80 part-time (50 women); includes 284 minority (265 Black or African American, non-Hispanic/Latino; 3 American Indian or Alaska Native, non-Hispanic/Latino; 6 Asian, non-Hispanic/Latino; 10 Hispanic/Latino), 23 international. Average age 35. 223 applicants, 44% accepted, 87 enrolled. In 2010, 478 master's awarded. *Degree requirements:* For master's, thesis (for some programs), 1 colloquium per term. *Entrance requirements:* For master's, interview, minimum GPA of 3.0. Additional exam requirements/recommendations for international students: Required—TOEFL (minimum score 550 paper-based; 213 computer-based; 80 iBT). *Application deadline:* For fall admission, 10/2 priority date for domestic and international students; for winter admission, 1/8 priority date for domestic and international students; for spring admission, 4/8 priority date for domestic and international students. Applications are processed on a rolling basis. Application fee: $30 ($100 for international students). Electronic applications accepted. *Expenses:* Tuition: Full-time $13,260; part-time $380 per credit hour. Required fees: $340. One-time fee: $30. Tuition and fees vary according to course level and course load. *Financial support:* In 2010–11, 631 students received support. Career-related internships or fieldwork, institutionally sponsored loans, tuition waivers (partial), and unspecified assistantships available. Financial award application deadline: 6/30; financial award applicants required to submit FAFSA. *Unit head:* Dan Kemper, Dean, 636-949-4501, Fax: 636-949-4505, E-mail: dkemper@lindenwood.edu. *Application contact:* Brett Barger, Dean of Evening Admissions and Extension Campuses, 636-949-4934, Fax: 636-949-4109, E-mail: adultadmissions@lindenwood.edu.

Long Island University, Brentwood Campus, School of Public Service, Brentwood, NY 11717. Offers criminal justice (MS). Part-time and evening/weekend programs available.

Long Island University, C.W. Post Campus, College of Management, Department of Criminal Justice, Brookville, NY 11548-1300. Offers criminal justice (MS); fraud examination (MS); security administration (MS). Part-time and evening/weekend programs available. *Degree requirements:* For master's, thesis. *Entrance requirements:* For master's, minimum GPA of 3.0, background in criminal justice. Electronic applications accepted. *Faculty research:* Crime statistics, terrorism, women and law, policing.

Longwood University, Office of Graduate Studies, Department of Sociology, Anthropology, and Criminal Justice Studies, Farmville, VA 23909. Offers criminal justice (MS). Part-time and evening/weekend programs available. *Degree requirements:* For master's, comprehensive exam (for some programs), thesis (for some programs). *Entrance requirements:* For master's, minimum GPA of 2.75. Additional exam requirements/recommendations for international students: Required—TOEFL (minimum score 550 paper-based; 213 computer-based).

Loyola University Chicago, Graduate School, Department of Criminal Justice, Chicago, IL 60660. Offers MA. Part-time and evening/weekend programs available. *Faculty:* 8 full-time (1 woman), 12 part-time/adjunct (1 woman). *Students:* 17 full-time (12 women), 16 part-time (6 women); includes 15 minority (5 Black or African American, non-Hispanic/Latino; 2 Asian, non-Hispanic/Latino; 7 Hispanic/Latino; 1 Two or more races, non-Hispanic/Latino), 1 international. Average age 28. 35 applicants, 80% accepted, 14 enrolled. In 2010, 7 master's awarded. *Degree requirements:* For master's, thesis or alternative, comprehensive exams. *Entrance requirements:* For master's, GRE, minimum GPA of 3.0. Additional exam requirements/recommendations for international students: Required—TOEFL (minimum score 550 paper-based; 213 computer-based). *Application deadline:* For fall admission, 6/15 priority date for domestic students; for spring admission, 12/1 for domestic students. Applications are processed on a rolling basis. Application fee: $50. Electronic applications accepted. *Expenses:* Tuition: Full-time $14,940; part-time $830 per credit hour. Required fees: $87 per semester. Part-time tuition and fees vary according to course load and program. *Financial support:* In 2010–11, 1 student received support, including research assistantships with partial tuition reimbursements available (averaging $7,800 per year); career-related internships or fieldwork and scholarships/grants also available. Financial award application deadline: 2/1; financial award applicants required to submit FAFSA. *Faculty research:* Crime and delinquency causation, effectiveness and efficiency of criminal justice system. Total annual research expenditures: $120,000. *Unit head:* Dr. David Olson, Chair, 312-915-7563, Fax: 312-915-7650, E-mail: dolson1@luc.edu. *Application contact:* Dr. Loretta Stalans, Graduate Program Director, 312-915-7567, Fax: 312-915-7650, E-mail: lstalan@luc.edu.

Loyola University New Orleans, College of Social Sciences, Program in Criminal Justice, New Orleans, LA 70118-6195. Offers criminal justice (MCJ); criminal justice administration (MS); MCJ/MPS. Part-time and evening/weekend programs available. *Students:* 5 full-time (2 women), 22 part-time (14 women); includes 6 Black or African American, non-Hispanic/Latino; 1 Asian, non-Hispanic/Latino; 3 Hispanic/Latino. Average age 32. 12 applicants, 100% accepted, 12 enrolled. In 2010, 15 master's awarded. *Degree requirements:* For master's, comprehensive exam, research and practicum. *Entrance requirements:* For master's, GRE, resume, interview, letters of recommendation, work experience. Additional exam requirements/recommendations for international students: Required—TOEFL (minimum score 550 paper-based; 213 computer-based). *Application deadline:* For fall admission, 8/1 priority date for domestic and international students; for spring admission, 1/5 priority date for domestic and international students. Applications are processed on a rolling basis. Application fee: $20. Electronic applications accepted. *Expenses:* Contact institution. *Financial support:* In 2010–11, 4 research assistantships (averaging $4,000 per year) were awarded; scholarships/grants and unspecified assistantships also available. Financial award application deadline: 5/1; financial award applicants required to submit FAFSA. *Unit head:* Dr. William E. Thornton, Chair, 504-865-2134, Fax: 504-865-3883, E-mail: thornton@loyno.edu. *Application contact:* David M. Aplin, Assistant to the Director, 504-865-3323, Fax: 504-865-3883, E-mail: daplin@loyno.edu.

Lynn University, College of Liberal Education, Boca Raton, FL 33431-5598. Offers applied psychology (MS); criminal justice administration (MS); emergency planning and administration (MS, Certificate). Part-time and evening/weekend programs available. Postbaccalaureate distance learning degree programs offered. *Entrance requirements:* For master's, GRE, resume, 2 letters of recommendation, minimum undergraduate GPA of 3.0. Additional exam requirements/recommendations for international students: Required—TOEFL (minimum score 550 paper-based; 213 computer-based). *Faculty research:* Terrorism, criminological theory, corrections, emergency planning.

Madonna University, School of Business, Livonia, MI 48150-1173. Offers business administration (MBA); international business (MSBA); leadership studies (MSBA); leadership studies in criminal justice (MSBA); quality and operations management (MSBA). Part-time and evening/weekend programs available. Postbaccalaureate distance learning degree programs offered (minimal on-campus study). *Degree requirements:* For master's, thesis (for some programs), foreign language proficiency (international business). *Entrance requirements:* For master's, GMAT, GRE General Test, minimum GPA of 3.0. Electronic applications accepted. *Faculty research:* Management, women in management, future studies.

Marquette University, Graduate School, Program in Public Service, Milwaukee, WI 53201-1881. Offers criminal justice administration (MLS); dispute resolution (MDR, MLS); engineering (MLS); health care administration (MLS); law enforcement leadership and management (Certificate); leadership studies (Certificate); non-profit sector (MLS); public service (MAPS, MLS); sports leadership (MLS). Part-time and evening/weekend programs available. Postbaccalaureate distance learning degree programs offered (no on-campus study). *Faculty:* 3 full-time (2 women), 29 part-time/adjunct (11 women). *Students:* 27 full-time (13 women), 134 part-time (84 women); includes 29 minority (21 Black or African American, non-Hispanic/Latino; 1 American Indian or Alaska Native, non-Hispanic/Latino; 1 Asian, non-Hispanic/Latino; 6 Hispanic/Latino), 1 international. Average age 38. 108 applicants, 78% accepted, 36 enrolled. In 2010, 11 master's, 12 Certificates awarded. *Degree requirements:* For master's, comprehensive exam (for some programs). *Entrance requirements:* For master's, GRE General Test (preferred), GMAT, or LSAT, official transcripts from all current and previous colleges/universities except Marquette, three letters of recommendation, statement of purpose. Additional exam requirements/recommendations for international students: Required—TOEFL. *Application deadline:* Applications are processed on a rolling basis. Application fee: $50. Electronic applications accepted. *Expenses:* Tuition: Full-time $16,290; part-time $905 per credit hour. Tuition and fees vary according to program. *Financial support:* In 2010–11, 1 fellowship, 1 research assistantship were awarded; teaching assistantships. Financial award application deadline: 2/15. *Unit head:* Dr. Johnette Caulfield, Adjunct Assistant Professor and Director of Graduate Programs, 414-288-5556, E-mail: jay.caulfield@marquette.edu. *Application contact:* Erin Fox, Assistant Director for Recruitment, 414-288-5319, Fax: 414-288-1902, E-mail: erin.fox@marquette.edu.

Marshall University, Academic Affairs Division, College of Liberal Arts, Department of Criminal Justice, Huntington, WV 25755. Offers MS. Evening/weekend programs available. *Faculty:* 6 full-time (3 women), 2 part-time/adjunct (1 woman). *Students:* 13 full-time (6 women), 3 part-time (all women); includes 1 Black or African American, non-Hispanic/Latino. Average age 24. In 2010, 10 master's awarded. *Degree requirements:* For master's, thesis optional. *Entrance requirements:* For master's, GRE General Test. Application fee: $40. *Unit head:* Dr. Dru Bora, Chairperson, 304-696-3087, E-mail: bora@marshall.edu. *Application contact:* Dr. Dhruba Bora, Information Contact, 304-696-3087, Fax: 304-746-1902, E-mail: services@marshall.edu.

Marywood University, Academic Affairs, College of Liberal Arts and Sciences, Department of Social Sciences, Program in Criminal Justice, Scranton, PA 18509-1598. Offers MS. *Entrance requirements:* Additional exam requirements/recommendations for international students: Required—TOEFL (minimum score 550 paper-based; 213 computer-based; 79 iBT). Electronic applications accepted. *Expenses:* Tuition: Part-time $735 per credit. Required fees: $470 per semester. Tuition and fees vary according to degree level and campus/location.

Mercyhurst College, Graduate Program, Program in Administration of Justice, Erie, PA 16546. Offers administration of justice (MS). Part-time and evening/weekend programs available. *Degree requirements:* For master's, thesis optional. *Entrance requirements:* For master's, GRE General Test, MAT, or minimum GPA of 3.0. Additional exam requirements/recommendations for international students: Required—TOEFL. Electronic applications accepted. *Faculty research:* Research methods, criminal justice administration, juvenile justice.

Mercyhurst College, Graduate Program, Program in Applied Intelligence, Erie, PA 16546. Offers MS, Certificate. *Entrance requirements:* For master's, GRE or MAT, interview. Additional exam requirements/recommendations for international students: Required—TOEFL. Electronic applications accepted.

Methodist University, School of Graduate Studies, Program in Justice Administration, Fayetteville, NC 28311-1498. Offers MJA. Part-time and evening/weekend programs available. *Entrance requirements:* For master's, bachelor's degree in criminal justice or related discipline with minimum overall GPA of 3.0 from accredited institution. Additional exam requirements/recommendations for international students: Required—TOEFL (minimum score 500 paper-based; 173 computer-based; 60 iBT).

Michigan State University, The Graduate School, College of Social Science, School of Criminal Justice, East Lansing, MI 48824. Offers criminal justice (MS, PhD); forensic science (MS); law enforcement intelligence and analysis (MS). Postbaccalaureate distance learning degree programs offered. *Entrance requirements:* Additional exam requirements/recommendations for international students: Required—TOEFL. Electronic applications accepted.

Middle Tennessee State University, College of Graduate Studies, College of Behavioral and Health Sciences, Department of Criminal Justice Administration, Murfreesboro, TN 37132. Offers MCJ. Program offered jointly with Tennessee State University. Part-time and evening/weekend programs available. Postbaccalaureate distance learning degree programs offered. *Faculty:* 6 full-time (2 women). *Students:* 3 full-time (2 women), 49 part-time (29 women); includes 29 Black or African American, non-Hispanic/Latino; 1 Hispanic/Latino. Average age 31. 61 applicants, 67% accepted, 41 enrolled. In 2010, 8 master's awarded. *Degree requirements:* For master's, one foreign language, comprehensive exam, thesis. *Entrance requirements:* For master's, GRE or MAT. Additional exam requirements/recommendations for international students: Required—TOEFL (minimum score 525 paper-based; 195 computer-based; 71 iBT) or IELTS (minimum score 6). *Application deadline:* For fall admission, 6/1 for domestic and international students. Applications are processed on a rolling basis. Application fee: $25 ($30 for international students). Electronic applications accepted. *Expenses:* Tuition, state resident: full-time $4632. Tuition, nonresident: full-time $11,520. *Financial support:* In 2010–11, 1 student received support. Institutionally sponsored loans available. Support available to part-time students. Financial award application deadline: 5/1; financial award applicants required to submit FAFSA. *Unit head:* Dr. Deborah W. Newman, Chair, 615-898-2630, Fax: 615-898-5159, E-mail: dnewman@mtsu.edu. *Application contact:* Dr. Michael Allen, Dean and Vice Provost for Research, 615-898-2840, Fax: 615-904-8020, E-mail: mallen@mtsu.edu.

Midwestern State University, Graduate Studies, College of Health Sciences and Human Services, Program in Health Services and Public Administration, Wichita Falls, TX 76308. Offers health services administration (MHA); public administration (MPA); public administration (administrative justice) (MPA); public administration (health services administration) with certificate (MPA); public administration (health services) (MPA). Part-time and evening/weekend programs available. *Faculty:* 4 full-time (2 women), 1 (woman) part-time/adjunct. *Students:* 12 full-time (8 women), 46 part-time (21 women); includes 7 Black or African American, non-Hispanic/Latino; 2 Asian, non-Hispanic/Latino; 1 Hispanic/Latino, 18 international. Average age 32. 31 applicants, 52% accepted, 6 enrolled. In 2010, 12 master's awarded. *Degree requirements:* For master's, comprehensive exam, thesis. *Entrance requirements:* For master's, GRE. Additional exam requirements/recommendations for international students: Required—TOEFL (minimum score 550 paper-based; 213 computer-based). *Application deadline:* For fall admission, 7/1 priority date for domestic students, 4/1 for international students; for spring admission, 11/1 priority date for domestic students, 8/1 for international students. Applications are processed on a rolling basis. Application fee: $35 ($50 for international students). Electronic applications accepted. *Expenses:* Tuition, state resident: full-time $1620; part-time $90 per credit hour. Tuition, nonresident: full-time $2160; part-time $120 per credit hour. International tuition: $7200 full-time. *Financial support:* In 2010–11, 13 students received support; teaching assistantships with partial tuition reimbursements available, career-related internships or fieldwork, Federal Work-Study, institutionally sponsored loans, scholarships/grants, tuition waivers (partial), and unspecified assistantships available. Support available to part-time students. Financial award application deadline: 3/1; financial award applicants required to submit FAFSA. *Faculty research:* Universal service policy, telehealth, bullying, healthcare financial management, public health ethics. *Unit head:* Dr. Kirk Harlow, Acting Chair, 940-397-4745, Fax: 940-397-6291, E-mail: kirk.harlow@mwsu.edu. *Application contact:* 800-842-1922, Fax: 940-397-4672, E-mail: admissions@mwsu.edu.

Minot State University, Graduate School, Program in Criminal Justice, Minot, ND 58707-0002. Offers MS. *Degree requirements:* For master's, comprehensive exam, thesis. *Entrance requirements:* For master's, GRE General Test, bachelor's degree with a minor in criminal justice or related field, minimum GPA of 3.0. Additional exam requirements/recommendations for international students: Required—TOEFL. *Faculty research:* Sentencing, white-collar/organizational crime, juveniles, gender issues, policy analysis.

Mississippi College, Graduate School, College of Arts and Sciences, School of Humanities and Social Sciences, Department of History, Political Science, Administration of Justice, and Paralegal Studies, Clinton, MS 39058. Offers administration of justice (MSS); history (M Ed, MA, MSS); paralegal studies (Certificate); political science (MSS); social sciences (M Ed, MSS). Part-time programs available. *Degree requirements:* For master's, one foreign language, comprehensive exam, thesis (for some programs). *Entrance requirements:* For master's, GRE or NTE, minimum GPA of 2.5. Additional exam requirements/recommendations for international students: Recommended—IELTS. Electronic applications accepted.

Mississippi Valley State University, Department of Criminal Justice and Social Work, Itta Bena, MS 38941-1400. Offers criminal justice (MS). Part-time and evening/weekend programs

Criminal Justice and Criminology

Mississippi Valley State University (continued)
available. *Degree requirements:* For master's, thesis optional. *Entrance requirements:* For master's, minimum GPA of 2.5. Electronic applications accepted. *Faculty research:* Police in the criminal justice system, the United States and international terrorism.

Missouri Southern State University, Program in Criminal Justice Administration, Joplin, MO 64801-1595. Offers MS. Program offered jointly with Southeast Missouri State University. Postbaccalaureate distance learning degree programs offered. *Degree requirements:* For master's, thesis optional. *Entrance requirements:* For master's, minimum undergraduate GPA of 2.5.

Missouri State University, Graduate College, College of Humanities and Public Affairs, Department of Sociology, Anthropology, and Criminology, Springfield, MO 65897. Offers applied anthropology (MS); criminology (MS). Part-time programs available. *Degree requirements:* For master's, comprehensive exam. *Entrance requirements:* For master's, GRE, minimum GPA of 3.0. Additional exam requirements/recommendations for international students: Required—TOEFL (minimum score 550 paper-based; 213 computer-based; 79 iBT). Electronic applications accepted. *Expenses:* Tuition, state resident: full-time $3348; part-time $186 per credit hour. Tuition, nonresident: full-time $6696; part-time $372 per credit hour. Required fees: $238 per semester. Tuition and fees vary according to course level, course load and program. *Faculty research:* Youth delinquency, social theory, linguistic anthropology, forensic anthropology, homeland security.

Missouri State University, Graduate College, Interdisciplinary Program in Administrative Studies, Springfield, MO 65897. Offers applied communication (MS); criminal justice (MS); environmental management (MS); project management (MS); sports management (MS). Part-time and evening/weekend programs available. Postbaccalaureate distance learning degree programs offered (no on-campus study). *Degree requirements:* For master's, comprehensive exam, thesis or alternative. *Entrance requirements:* For master's, GRE, GMAT, 3 years of work experience. Additional exam requirements/recommendations for international students: Required—TOEFL (minimum score 550 paper-based; 213 computer-based; 79 iBT). Electronic applications accepted. *Expenses:* Tuition, state resident: full-time $3348; part-time $186 per credit hour. Tuition, nonresident: full-time $6696; part-time $372 per credit hour. Required fees: $238 per semester. Tuition and fees vary according to course level, course load and program.

Molloy College, Criminal Justice Program, Rockville Centre, NY 11571-5002. Offers MS. *Faculty:* 3 full-time (1 woman), 1 part-time/adjunct (0 women). *Students:* 16 full-time (11 women), 20 part-time (10 women); includes 5 Black or African American, non-Hispanic/Latino; 5 Hispanic/Latino. Average age 32. In 2010, 11 master's awarded. *Unit head:* Dr. John Eterno, Associate Dean/Director, 516-678-5000 Ext. 6135. *Application contact:* Alina Haitz, Interim Associate Dean/Director, 516-678-5000 Ext. 6399, Fax: 516-256-2247, E-mail: ahaitz@molloy.edu.

Monmouth University, The Graduate School, Department of Criminal Justice, West Long Branch, NJ 07764-1898. Offers criminal justice administration (MA, Certificate); homeland security (MA, Certificate). Part-time and evening/weekend programs available. *Faculty:* 4 full-time (0 women), 6 part-time/adjunct (3 women). *Students:* 26 full-time (11 women), 19 part-time (9 women); includes 3 Black or African American, non-Hispanic/Latino; 1 Asian, non-Hispanic/Latino; 6 Hispanic/Latino, 1 international. Average age 27. 35 applicants, 94% accepted, 20 enrolled. In 2010, 12 master's awarded. *Degree requirements:* For master's, comprehensive exam, thesis or alternative. *Entrance requirements:* For master's, minimum GPA of 3.0 in major, 2.5 overall. Additional exam requirements/recommendations for international students: Required—TOEFL (minimum score 550 paper-based; 213 computer-based; 79 iBT), IELTS (minimum score 6) or Michigan English Language Assessment Battery (minimum score 77), Cambridge A, B, C. *Application deadline:* For fall admission, 7/15 priority date for domestic students, 6/1 for international students; for spring admission, 11/15 priority date for domestic students, 11/1 for international students. Applications are processed on a rolling basis. Application fee: $50. Electronic applications accepted. *Expenses:* Tuition: Full-time $19,572; part-time $816 per credit. Required fees: $628; $157 per semester. *Financial support:* In 2010–11, 30 students received support, including 30 fellowships (averaging $1,840 per year), 2 research assistantships (averaging $422 per year); career-related internships or fieldwork, scholarships/grants, and unspecified assistantships also available. Support available to part-time students. Financial award applicants required to submit FAFSA. *Faculty research:* Violent crimes, criminal pathology, terrorism, computer crime, comparative criminal justice systems. *Unit head:* Dr. Gregory Coram, Director, 732-571-3448, Fax: 732-263-5148, E-mail: coram@monmouth.edu. *Application contact:* Kevin Roane, Director, Office of Graduate Admission, 732-571-3452, Fax: 732-263-5123, E-mail: gradadm@monmouth.edu.

Morehead State University, Graduate Programs, Caudill College of Arts, Humanities and Social Sciences, Department of Sociology, Social Work and Criminology, Morehead, KY 40351. Offers criminology (MA); general sociology (MA); gerontology (MA); sociology regional analysis (MA); sociology/chemical dependency (MA). Part-time and evening/weekend programs available. *Degree requirements:* For master's, comprehensive exam, thesis (for some programs). *Entrance requirements:* For master's, GRE General Test, minimum GPA of 3.0 in sociology, 2.75 overall; 18 hours of course work in sociology, writing sample. Additional exam requirements/recommendations for international students: Required—TOEFL (minimum score 500 paper-based; 173 computer-based). Electronic applications accepted. *Faculty research:* Death and dying; aging, drinking, and drugs; economic development; adult children of alcoholics.

Mountain State University, School of Graduate Studies, Program in Criminal Justice Administration, Beckley, WV 25802-9003. Offers MCJA. Part-time and evening/weekend programs available. Postbaccalaureate distance learning degree programs offered (no on-campus study). *Faculty:* 1 full-time (0 women), 2 part-time/adjunct (0 women). *Students:* 17 full-time (9 women), 9 part-time (5 women); includes 2 minority (1 Black or African American, non-Hispanic/Latino; 1 Hispanic/Latino). Average age 38. 40 applicants, 35% accepted, 10 enrolled. In 2010, 3 master's awarded. *Degree requirements:* For master's, thesis or alternative. *Entrance requirements:* Additional exam requirements/recommendations for international students: Required—TOEFL (minimum score 550 paper-based; 213 computer-based); Recommended—IELTS (minimum score 6.5). *Application deadline:* For fall admission, 5/31 priority date for domestic and international students. Applications are processed on a rolling basis. Application fee: $25 ($50 for international students). Electronic applications accepted. *Expenses:* Tuition: Full-time $4800; part-time $400 per credit hour. Required fees: $2250; $2250 per credit hour. Tuition and fees vary according to degree level and program. *Financial support:* Federal Work-Study, scholarships/grants, and unspecified assistantships available. Support available to part-time students. Financial award applicants required to submit FAFSA. *Unit head:* Dr. William White, Interim Dean, School of Graduate Studies/Dean, School of Leadership and Professional Development, 304-929-1658, Fax: 304-929-1637, E-mail: wwhite@mountainstate.edu. *Application contact:* Anita Diaz, Enrollment Coordinator of Graduate Studies, 304-929-1731, Fax: 304-929-1710, E-mail: adiaz@mountainstate.edu.

Mount Aloysius College, Criminal Justice Management in Correctional Administration Program, Cresson, PA 16630. Offers MA. *Entrance requirements:* For master's, GRE General Test. Electronic applications accepted.

National University, Academic Affairs, College of Letters and Sciences, Department of Professional Studies, La Jolla, CA 92037-1011. Offers forensic science (MFS), including criminalistics and investigation; public administration (MPA), including alternative dispute resolution, human resource management, organizational leadership, public finance. Part-time and evening/weekend programs available. Postbaccalaureate distance learning degree programs offered (no on-campus study). *Faculty:* 10 full-time (3 women), 110 part-time/adjunct (22 women). *Students:* 189 full-time (117 women), 284 part-time (167 women); includes 259 minority (101 Black or African American, non-Hispanic/Latino; 2 American Indian or Alaska Native, non-Hispanic/Latino; 33 Asian, non-Hispanic/Latino; 104 Hispanic/Latino; 7 Native Hawaiian or other Pacific Islander, non-Hispanic/Latino; 12 Two or more races, non-Hispanic/Latino). Average age 38. 305 applicants, 100% accepted, 192 enrolled. In 2010, 160 master's awarded. *Degree requirements:* For master's, thesis. *Entrance requirements:* For master's, interview, minimum GPA of 2.5. Additional exam requirements/recommendations for international students: Required—TOEFL (minimum score 550 paper-based; 213 computer-based; 79 iBT), IELTS (minimum score 6). *Application deadline:* Applications are processed on a rolling basis. Application fee: $60 ($65 for international students). Electronic applications accepted. *Expenses:* Tuition: Full-time $9450; part-time $350 per unit. Required fees: $350 per unit. One-time fee: $60. *Financial support:* Career-related internships or fieldwork, institutionally sponsored loans, scholarships/grants, and tuition waivers (partial) available. Support available to part-time students. Financial award application deadline: 6/30; financial award applicants required to submit FAFSA. *Unit head:* James G. Larsen, Associate Professor and Chair, 858-642-8418, Fax: 858-642-8715, E-mail: jlarson@nu.edu. *Application contact:* Dominick Giovanniello, Associate Regional Dean—San Diego, 800-NAT-UNIV, Fax: 858-541-7792, E-mail: dgiovann@nu.edu.

National University, Academic Affairs, School of Education, Department of Special Education, La Jolla, CA 92037-1011. Offers deaf and hard-of-hearing education (MS); juvenile justice special education (MS); special education (MS). Part-time and evening/weekend programs available. Postbaccalaureate distance learning degree programs offered (no on-campus study). *Faculty:* 16 full-time (14 women), 268 part-time/adjunct (181 women). *Students:* 1,044 full-time (762 women), 2,650 part-time (1,800 women); includes 1,232 minority (297 Black or African American, non-Hispanic/Latino; 23 American Indian or Alaska Native, non-Hispanic/Latino; 216 Asian, non-Hispanic/Latino; 641 Hispanic/Latino; 13 Native Hawaiian or other Pacific Islander, non-Hispanic/Latino; 42 Two or more races, non-Hispanic/Latino), 4 international. Average age 35. 2,002 applicants, 100% accepted, 1613 enrolled. In 2010, 139 master's awarded. *Degree requirements:* For master's, thesis (for some programs). *Entrance requirements:* For master's, interview, minimum GPA of 2.5. Additional exam requirements/recommendations for international students: Required—TOEFL (minimum score 550 paper-based; 213 computer-based; 79 iBT), IELTS (minimum score 6). *Application deadline:* Applications are processed on a rolling basis. Application fee: $60 ($65 for international students). Electronic applications accepted. *Expenses:* Tuition: Full-time $9450; part-time $350 per unit. Required fees: $350 per unit. One-time fee: $60. *Financial support:* Career-related internships or fieldwork, institutionally sponsored loans, scholarships/grants, and tuition waivers (partial) available. Support available to part-time students. Financial award application deadline: 6/30; financial award applicants required to submit FAFSA. *Unit head:* Dr. Britt Ferguson, Department Chair, 858-642-8346, Fax: 858-642-8729, E-mail: mferguson@nu.edu. *Application contact:* Dr. Britt Ferguson, Department Chair, 858-642-8346, Fax: 858-642-8729, E-mail: mferguson@nu.edu.

New Jersey City University, Graduate Studies and Continuing Education, College of Professional Studies, Department of Criminal Justice, Jersey City, NJ 07305-1597. Offers criminal justice (MS); law enforcement (MS). Part-time and evening/weekend programs available. *Degree requirements:* For master's, thesis or alternative. *Entrance requirements:* For master's, GRE General Test or MAT. Additional exam requirements/recommendations for international students: Required—TOEFL.

New Mexico State University, Graduate School, College of Arts and Sciences, Department of Criminal Justice, Las Cruces, NM 88003-8001. Offers MCJ. Part-time and evening/weekend programs available. Postbaccalaureate distance learning degree programs offered (no on-campus study). *Faculty:* 11 full-time (4 women), 4 part-time/adjunct (3 women). *Students:* 46 full-time (28 women), 63 part-time (38 women); includes 59 minority (4 Black or African American, non-Hispanic/Latino; 7 American Indian or Alaska Native, non-Hispanic/Latino; 48 Hispanic/Latino), 1 international. Average age 32. 52 applicants, 96% accepted, 37 enrolled. In 2010, 35 master's awarded. *Degree requirements:* For master's, comprehensive exam, thesis optional, oral and written exams. *Entrance requirements:* For master's, minimum GPA of 3.0. *Application deadline:* For fall admission, 4/1 priority date for domestic and international students; for spring admission, 11/1 priority date for domestic students, 10/1 priority date for international students. Applications are processed on a rolling basis. Application fee: $30 ($50 for international students). Electronic applications accepted. *Expenses:* Tuition, state resident: full-time $4536; part-time $242 per credit. Tuition, nonresident: full-time $15,816; part-time $712 per credit. Required fees: $636 per term. *Financial support:* In 2010–11, 8 research assistantships with partial tuition reimbursements (averaging $12,344 per year), 3 teaching assistantships with partial tuition reimbursements (averaging $10,270 per year) were awarded; fellowships with partial tuition reimbursements, career-related internships or fieldwork, health care benefits, and unspecified assistantships also available. Financial award application deadline: 4/1. *Faculty research:* Juvenile justice, jails and prison administration, courts and legal decision-making, victim studies, policy and evaluation research. *Unit head:* Dr. James R. Maupin, Head, 575-646-3316, Fax: 575-646-2827, E-mail: jmaupin@nmsu.edu. *Application contact:* Dr. Carlos Posadas, Assistant Professor/Program Director, 575-646-3316, Fax: 575-646-2827, E-mail: cposadas@nmsu.edu.

Niagara University, Graduate Division of Arts and Sciences, Department of Criminal Justice, Niagara Falls, Niagara University, NY 14109. Offers criminal justice administration (MS). Part-time programs available. *Faculty:* 6 full-time (2 women). *Students:* 21 full-time (12 women), 14 part-time (9 women); includes 3 Black or African American, non-Hispanic/Latino; 1 Hispanic/Latino, 2 international. Average age 27. In 2010, 17 master's awarded. *Entrance requirements:* For master's, GRE. Additional exam requirements/recommendations for international students: Required—TOEFL. *Application deadline:* For fall admission, 8/1 for domestic students. Applications are processed on a rolling basis. Application fee: $30. *Expenses:* Tuition: Full-time $13,230; part-time $735 per credit hour. Required fees: $50. One-time fee: $120 full-time. *Financial support:* Fellowships, career-related internships or fieldwork and Federal Work-Study available. Support available to part-time students. Financial award applicants required to submit FAFSA. *Unit head:* Ronald Winkley, Director, 716-286-8089, Fax: 716-286-8061, E-mail: rwinkley@niagara.edu. *Application contact:* Ronald Winkley, Director, 716-286-8089, Fax: 716-286-8061, E-mail: rwinkley@niagara.edu.

Nichols College, Graduate Program in Business Administration, Dudley, MA 01571-5000. Offers business administration (MBA, MOL); security management (MBA); sport management (MBA). Part-time and evening/weekend programs available. Postbaccalaureate distance learning degree programs offered (no on-campus study). *Entrance requirements:* For master's, 2 letters of recommendation. Additional exam requirements/recommendations for international students: Required—TOEFL (minimum score 500 paper-based; 213 computer-based). Electronic applications accepted.

Norfolk State University, School of Graduate Studies, School of Liberal Arts, Department of Sociology, Program in Criminal Justice, Norfolk, VA 23504. Offers MA.

North Carolina Central University, Division of Academic Affairs, College of Behavioral and Social Sciences, Department of Criminal Justice, Durham, NC 27707-3129. Offers MS. Part-time and evening/weekend programs available. *Degree requirements:* For master's, one foreign language, comprehensive exam, thesis or alternative. *Entrance requirements:* For master's, GRE, minimum GPA of 3.0 in major, 2.5 overall. Additional exam requirements/recommendations for international students: Required—TOEFL.

North Dakota State University, College of Graduate and Interdisciplinary Studies, College of Arts, Humanities and Social Sciences, Department of Criminal Justice and Political Science, Fargo, ND 58108. Offers criminal justice (MS, PhD). Part-time programs available. *Faculty:* 3 full-time (1 woman). *Students:* 6 full-time (4 women), 2 part-time (1 woman); includes 1 Hispanic/Latino. Average age 25. 5 applicants, 100% accepted, 1 enrolled. In 2010, 1 master's awarded. Terminal master's awarded for partial completion of doctoral program. *Degree requirements:* For master's, thesis; for doctorate, comprehensive exam, thesis/dissertation. *Entrance requirements:* For master's, minimum GPA of 3.0 in last 60 credit hours, approved bachelor's degree, course work in research methods and statistics; for doctorate, GRE General

Test, minimum GPA of 3.0 over last 60 credit hours, 3 letters of recommendation. Additional exam requirements/recommendations for international students: Required—TOEFL (minimum score 525 paper-based; 197 computer-based; 71 iBT). *Application deadline:* For spring admission, 4/1 priority date for domestic students, 4/1 for international students. Applications are processed on a rolling basis. Application fee: $45 ($60 for international students). *Financial support:* In 2010–11, 6 research assistantships with tuition reimbursements (averaging $12,000 per year), 3 teaching assistantships with tuition reimbursements (averaging $6,000 per year) were awarded; career-related internships or fieldwork, institutionally sponsored loans, tuition waivers (full), and unspecified assistantships also available. Financial award application deadline: 4/1. *Faculty research:* Corrections, policing, drugs and crime, gender and crime, criminology. Total annual research expenditures: $150,000. *Unit head:* Dr. Kevin Thompson, Chair, 701-231-8938, Fax: 701-231-5877, E-mail: kevin.thompson@ndsu.edu. *Application contact:* Dr. Kevin Thompson, Chair, 701-231-8938, Fax: 701-231-5877, E-mail: kevin.thompson@ndsu.edu.

Northeastern State University, Graduate College, College of Liberal Arts, Program in Criminal Justice and Legal Studies, Tahlequah, OK 74464-2399. Offers criminal justice (MS). Part-time and evening/weekend programs available. *Students:* 16 full-time (11 women), 25 part-time (12 women); includes 17 minority (7 Black or African American, non-Hispanic/Latino; 10 American Indian or Alaska Native, non-Hispanic/Latino). In 2010, 6 master's awarded. *Degree requirements:* For master's, thesis optional, oral exam. *Entrance requirements:* For master's, MAT or GRE, minimum GPA of 2.5. Additional exam requirements/recommendations for international students: Required—TOEFL (minimum score 213 computer-based). *Application deadline:* For fall admission, 6/1 priority date for domestic students. Applications are processed on a rolling basis. Application fee: $0 ($25 for international students). Electronic applications accepted. *Expenses:* Tuition, state resident: part-time $144 per credit hour. Tuition, nonresident: part-time $384.05 per credit hour. Required fees: $34.90 per credit hour. Tuition and fees vary according to program. *Financial support:* Teaching assistantships, Federal Work-Study available. Financial award application deadline: 3/1. *Unit head:* Dr. Frank Zeigler, Chair, 918-449-6595, E-mail: zeigler@nsuok.edu. *Application contact:* Margie Railey, Administrative Assistant, 918-456-5511 Ext. 2093, Fax: 918-458-2061, E-mail: railey@nsouk.edu.

Northeastern University, College of Social Sciences and Humanities, School of Criminology and Criminal Justice, Boston, MA 02115-5096. Offers MS, PhD. Part-time and evening/weekend programs available. *Faculty:* 17 full-time (6 women), 11 part-time/adjunct (5 women). *Students:* 77 full-time (52 women), 14 part-time (5 women); includes 7 Black or African American, non-Hispanic/Latino; 1 American Indian or Alaska Native, non-Hispanic/Latino; 1 Asian, non-Hispanic/Latino, 10 international. 108 applicants, 63% accepted, 29 enrolled. In 2010, 22 master's awarded. *Degree requirements:* For master's, comprehensive exam, thesis optional. *Entrance requirements:* For master's and doctorate, GRE General Test. Additional exam requirements/recommendations for international students: Required—TOEFL. *Application deadline:* For fall admission, 3/1 for domestic students; for spring admission, 10/1 for domestic students. Applications are processed on a rolling basis. Application fee: $50. Electronic applications accepted. *Financial support:* In 2010–11, 2 research assistantships with full and partial tuition reimbursements, 13 teaching assistantships with full tuition reimbursements (averaging $13,654 per year) were awarded; career-related internships or fieldwork, Federal Work-Study, and institutionally sponsored loans also available. Support available to part-time students. Financial award application deadline: 3/31; financial award applicants required to submit FAFSA. *Faculty research:* Juvenile justice, victimology, serial and mass murder, private security, criminology corrections, race and crime. *Unit head:* Jack McDevitt, Associate Dean, 617-373-2813, Fax: 617-373-8723. *Application contact:* Laurie A. Mastone, Assistant to the Director, 617-373-2813, Fax: 617-373-8723, E-mail: l.mastone@neu.edu.

Northern Arizona University, Graduate College, College of Social and Behavioral Sciences, Department of Criminology and Criminal Justice, Flagstaff, AZ 86011. Offers applied criminology (MS). Part-time programs available. Postbaccalaureate distance learning degree programs offered. *Faculty:* 17 full-time (10 women). *Students:* 21 full-time (17 women), 8 part-time (6 women); includes 5 minority (1 American Indian or Alaska Native, non-Hispanic/Latino; 3 Hispanic/Latino; 1 Two or more races, non-Hispanic/Latino), 2 international. Average age 30. 21 applicants, 67% accepted, 10 enrolled. In 2010, 11 master's awarded. *Degree requirements:* For master's, thesis, internship, comprehensive exam, or practicum. *Entrance requirements:* For master's, minimum GPA of 3.0. Additional exam requirements/recommendations for international students: Required—TOEFL (minimum score 550 paper-based; 213 computer-based; 80 iBT), IELTS (minimum score 7). *Application deadline:* For fall admission, 2/15 priority date for domestic and international students; for spring admission, 9/15 priority date for domestic and international students. Applications are processed on a rolling basis. Application fee: $65. Electronic applications accepted. *Financial support:* In 2010–11, 1 research assistantship with partial tuition reimbursement (averaging $5,220 per year), 5 teaching assistantships with partial tuition reimbursements (averaging $10,439 per year) were awarded; career-related internships or fieldwork, Federal Work-Study, scholarships/grants, health care benefits, tuition waivers (full and partial), and unspecified assistantships also available. Support available to part-time students. Financial award applicants required to submit FAFSA. *Unit head:* Dr. Cyndi Banks, Chair, 928-523-6522, Fax: 928-523-6777, E-mail: cyndi.banks@nau.edu. *Application contact:* Kara Stone, Administrative Assistant, 928-523-0605, Fax: 928-523-6777, E-mail: criminal.justice@nau.edu.

Northern Michigan University, College of Graduate Studies, College of Professional Studies, Department of Criminal Justice, Marquette, MI 49855-5301. Offers MS. Part-time and evening/weekend programs available. *Entrance requirements:* For master's, minimum GPA of 3.0.

Norwich University, School of Graduate and Continuing Studies, Program in Public Administration, Northfield, VT 05663. Offers continuity of government operations (MPA); criminal justice (MPA); fiscal management (MPA); leadership (MPA); organizational leadership (MPA); public works administration (MPA). Evening/weekend programs available. *Faculty:* 12 part-time/adjunct (5 women). *Students:* 64 full-time (21 women); includes 4 Black or African American, non-Hispanic/Latino; 2 Two or more races, non-Hispanic/Latino. Average age 37. 189 applicants, 81% accepted. In 2010, 64 master's awarded. *Entrance requirements:* Additional exam requirements/recommendations for international students: Required—TOEFL (minimum score 550 paper-based; 212 computer-based; 83 iBT). *Application deadline:* For fall admission, 8/10 for domestic and international students; for winter admission, 11/7 for domestic and international students; for spring admission, 2/6 for domestic and international students. Application fee: $50. *Expenses:* Tuition: Full-time $17,380; part-time $645 per credit. Tuition and fees vary according to program. *Financial support:* Scholarships/grants available. Financial award applicants required to submit FAFSA. *Unit head:* Donal Hartman, Program Director, 802-485-2567, Fax: 802-485-2533, E-mail: dhartman@norwich.edu. *Application contact:* Chris Ormsby, Associate Program Director, 802-249-7809, Fax: 802-485-2533, E-mail: cormsby@norwich.edu.

Nova Southeastern University, Criminal Justice Institute, Program in Criminal Justice, Fort Lauderdale, FL 33314-7796. Offers MS. Part-time programs available. Postbaccalaureate distance learning degree programs offered (no on-campus study). *Faculty:* 41 part-time/adjunct (7 women). *Students:* 57 full-time (48 women), 142 part-time (94 women); includes 84 Black or African American, non-Hispanic/Latino; 2 American Indian or Alaska Native, non-Hispanic/Latino; 2 Asian, non-Hispanic/Latino; 44 Hispanic/Latino. Average age 37. 65 applicants, 92% accepted, 57 enrolled. In 2010, 55 master's awarded. *Degree requirements:* For master's, thesis optional. *Entrance requirements:* For master's, 3 letters of recommendation, minimum GPA of 2.5. *Application deadline:* For fall admission, 8/4 for domestic and international students; for winter admission, 12/1 for domestic and international students; for spring admission, 4/12 for domestic and international students. Application fee: $50. *Financial support:* Applicants required to submit FAFSA. *Unit head:* Dr. Tammy Kushner, Executive Associate Dean, 954-262-7001, Fax: 954-262-7005, E-mail: kushner@nova.edu. *Application contact:* Russell Garner, Program Coordinator, 954-262-7001, E-mail: cji@nova.edu.

Oklahoma City University, Petree College of Arts and Sciences, Division of Sociology and Justice Studies, Oklahoma City, OK 73106-1402. Offers applied sociology (MA), including nonprofit leadership; criminal justice (MCJ). Part-time and evening/weekend programs available. *Degree requirements:* For master's, thesis optional. *Entrance requirements:* For master's, minimum GPA of 3.0, two letters of recommendation. Additional exam requirements/recommendations for international students: Required—TOEFL (minimum score 550 paper-based). *Expenses:* Contact institution. *Faculty research:* Victims, police, corrections, security, women and crime.

Old Dominion University, College of Arts and Letters, Program in Criminology and Criminal Justice, Norfolk, VA 23529. Offers PhD. Part-time and evening/weekend programs available. *Faculty:* 16 full-time (11 women). *Students:* 10 full-time (7 women), 6 part-time (3 women); includes 3 minority (1 Black or African American, non-Hispanic/Latino; 1 Asian, non-Hispanic/Latino; 1 Hispanic/Latino). Average age 33. 14 applicants, 57% accepted, 5 enrolled. *Degree requirements:* For doctorate, comprehensive exam, thesis/dissertation. *Entrance requirements:* For doctorate, GRE General Test, MA; minimum graduate GPA of 3.25; theory, methods, and statistics graduate coursework; letters of reference; writing sample. Additional exam requirements/recommendations for international students: Required—TOEFL. *Application deadline:* For fall admission, 2/15 for domestic and international students. Application fee: $40. Electronic applications accepted. *Expenses:* Tuition, state resident: full-time $8592; part-time $358 per credit. Tuition, nonresident: full-time $21,672; part-time $903 per credit. Required fees: $119 per semester. One-time fee: $50. *Financial support:* In 2010–11, 7 students received support, including 3 fellowships with full tuition reimbursements available (averaging $15,000 per year), 4 teaching assistantships with full tuition reimbursements available (averaging $15,000 per year). Financial award application deadline: 2/15. *Faculty research:* Inequality, crime and justice; domestic violence; community justice; criminological theory; methods; policing; courts and corrections; state crime. *Unit head:* Dr. Mona Danner, Graduate Program Director, 757-683-5931, Fax: 757-683-5634, E-mail: mdanner@odu.edu. *Application contact:* Dr. Robert Wojtowicz, Associate Dean, 757-683-6077, Fax: 757-683-5746, E-mail: rwojtowi@odu.edu.

Point Park University, School of Arts and Sciences, Department of Criminal Justice and Intelligence Studies, Pittsburgh, PA 15222-1984. Offers criminal justice administration (MS). Evening/weekend programs available. *Faculty:* 2 full-time, 3 part-time/adjunct. *Students:* 26 full-time (25 women), 4 part-time (2 women); includes 19 minority (14 Black or African American, non-Hispanic/Latino; 1 Asian, non-Hispanic/Latino; 3 Hispanic/Latino; 1 Two or more races, non-Hispanic/Latino). Average age 32. 33 applicants, 61% accepted, 16 enrolled. In 2010, 18 master's awarded. *Degree requirements:* For master's, comprehensive exam (for some programs), thesis or alternative. *Entrance requirements:* For master's, minimum GPA of 2.75, resume, 2 letters of recommendation. Additional exam requirements/recommendations for international students: Required—TOEFL (minimum score 550 paper-based; 79 iBT). *Application deadline:* Applications are processed on a rolling basis. Application fee: $30. Electronic applications accepted. *Expenses:* Tuition: Full-time $12,456; part-time $692 per credit. Required fees: $630; $35 per credit. *Financial support:* In 2010–11, 3 teaching assistantships with full tuition reimbursements (averaging $6,400 per year) were awarded; scholarships/grants also available. Financial award application deadline: 4/15; financial award applicants required to submit FAFSA. *Unit head:* Dr. Lorelei Stein, Program Director, 412-392-6169, Fax: 412-392-3925, E-mail: lstein@pointpark.edu. *Application contact:* Lynn Ribar, Associate Director of Graduate and Adult Enrollment, 412-392-3908, Fax: 412-392-6164, E-mail: lribar@pointpark.edu.

Polytechnic Institute of NYU, Department of Computer Science and Engineering, Brooklyn, NY 11201-2990. Offers computer science (MS, PhD); cyber security (Graduate Certificate); software engineering (Graduate Certificate). Part-time and evening/weekend programs available. *Faculty:* 18 full-time (1 woman), 12 part-time/adjunct (2 women). *Students:* 272 full-time (57 women), 134 part-time (17 women); includes 10 Black or African American, non-Hispanic/Latino; 26 Asian, non-Hispanic/Latino; 10 Hispanic/Latino, 261 international. Average age 27. 818 applicants, 52% accepted, 190 enrolled. In 2010, 121 master's, 3 doctorates awarded. *Degree requirements:* For master's, comprehensive exam (for some programs), thesis (for some programs); for doctorate, comprehensive exam, thesis/dissertation. *Entrance requirements:* For master's, BA or BS in computer science, mathematics, science, or engineering; working knowledge of a high-level program; for doctorate, GRE General Test, GRE Subject Test, qualifying exam, BA or BS in science, engineering, or management; MS or 1 year of graduate course work. Additional exam requirements/recommendations for international students: Required—TOEFL (minimum score 550 paper-based; 213 computer-based; 80 iBT); Recommended—IELTS (minimum score 6.5). *Application deadline:* For fall admission, 7/31 priority date for domestic students, 4/30 priority date for international students; for spring admission, 12/31 priority date for domestic students, 10/30 priority date for international students. Applications are processed on a rolling basis. Application fee: $75. Electronic applications accepted. *Expenses:* Tuition: Full-time $21,492; part-time $1194 per credit. Required fees: $385 per semester. Tuition and fees vary according to course load. *Financial support:* In 2010–11, 6 fellowships with partial tuition reimbursements (averaging $25,617 per year), 22 research assistantships with tuition reimbursements (averaging $26,693 per year), 1 teaching assistantship with tuition reimbursement (averaging $26,572 per year) were awarded; institutionally sponsored loans, scholarships/grants, and unspecified assistantships also available. Support available to part-time students. Financial award applicants required to submit FAFSA. Total annual research expenditures: $1.8 million. *Unit head:* Dr. Keith W. Ross, Head, 718-260-3859, Fax: 718-260-3609, E-mail: ross@poly.edu. *Application contact:* JeanCarlo Bonilla, Director, Graduate Center, 718-260-3182, Fax: 718-260-3624, E-mail: gradinfo@poly.edu.

Polytechnic Institute of NYU, Westchester Graduate Center, Graduate Programs, Department of Computer Science and Engineering, Major in Cyber Security, Hawthorne, NY 10532-1507. Offers MS. *Students:* 2 part-time (0 women). Average age 28. 3 applicants, 100% accepted. *Entrance requirements:* Additional exam requirements/recommendations for international students: Required—TOEFL (minimum score 550 paper-based; 213 computer-based; 80 iBT); Recommended—IELTS (minimum score 6.5). *Application deadline:* For fall admission, 7/31 priority date for domestic students, 4/30 priority date for international students; for spring admission, 12/31 priority date for domestic students, 11/30 priority date for international students. Applications are processed on a rolling basis. Application fee: $75. Electronic applications accepted. *Expenses:* Tuition: Full-time $21,492; part-time $1194 per credit. Required fees: $385 per semester. Tuition and fees vary according to course load. *Financial support:* Institutionally sponsored loans, scholarships/grants, and unspecified assistantships available. Support available to part-time students. *Unit head:* Dr. Keith W. Ross, Department Head, 718-260-3859, E-mail: ross@poly.edu. *Application contact:* JeanCarlo Bonilla, Director of Graduate Enrollment Management, 718-260-3182, Fax: 718-260-3624, E-mail: gradinfo@poly.edu.

Pontifical Catholic University of Puerto Rico, College of Graduate Studies in Behavioral Science and Community Affairs, Program in Criminology, Ponce, PR 00717-0777. Offers MA. Part-time and evening/weekend programs available. *Degree requirements:* For master's, thesis. *Entrance requirements:* For master's, EXADEP, 3 letters of recommendation, interview, minimum GPA of 2.75.

Pontificia Universidad Catolica Madre y Maestra, Graduate School, Faculty of Social and Administrative Sciences, Santiago, Dominican Republic. Offers business administration (MBA), including business development, finance, international business, management skills (M Mgmt, MBA), marketing, operations, strategic cost management, strategy, tourist destination planning and management; law (LL M), including civil law, corporate business law, criminal law, international relations, real estate law; management (M Mgmt), including higher financial management, insurance program administration, management skills (M Mgmt, MBA); psychology (MA), including clinical child and adolescent psychology, forensic psychology; strategic human resources (EMBA).

Portland State University, Graduate Studies, College of Urban and Public Affairs, Hatfield School of Government, Division of Criminology and Criminal Justice, Portland, OR 97207-0751. Offers MS, PhD. Part-time programs available. *Faculty:* 10 full-time (5 women), 9 part-time/adjunct (2 women). *Students:* 21 full-time (16 women), 6 part-time (4 women);

Criminal Justice and Criminology

Portland State University (continued)
includes 1 Black or African American, non-Hispanic/Latino; 1 Asian, non-Hispanic/Latino; 2 Two or more races, non-Hispanic/Latino. Average age 30. 18 applicants, 100% accepted, 14 enrolled. In 2010, 11 master's awarded. *Degree requirements:* For master's, thesis or alternative, comprehensive oral exam; for doctorate, comprehensive exam, thesis/dissertation, residency. *Entrance requirements:* For master's, minimum GPA of 3.0 in upper-division course work or 2.75 overall; for doctorate, GRE General Test. Additional exam requirements/recommendations for international students: Required—TOEFL (minimum score 550 paper-based; 213 computer-based). *Application deadline:* For fall admission, 3/15 priority date for domestic students, 3/1 priority date for international students. Application fee: $50. *Expenses:* Tuition, state resident: full-time $8505; part-time $315 per credit. Tuition, nonresident: full-time $13,284; part-time $492 per credit. Required fees: $1482; $21 per credit. $99 per term. One-time fee: $120. Part-time tuition and fees vary according to course load and program. *Financial support:* In 2010–11, 5 teaching assistantships with full tuition reimbursements (averaging $8,445 per year) were awarded; research assistantships with full tuition reimbursements, career-related internships or fieldwork, Federal Work-Study, scholarships/grants, and unspecified assistantships also available. Support available to part-time students. Financial award application deadline: 3/1; financial award applicants required to submit FAFSA. *Faculty research:* History of criminal justice, mental health issues, international terrorism, offender assessment, domestic violence. Total annual research expenditures: $532,682. *Unit head:* Dr. Brian C. Renauer, Chair, 503-725-4014, Fax: 503-725-5199, E-mail: renauer@pdx.edu. *Application contact:* Rod Johnson, Admissions Officer, 503-725-4044, Fax: 503-725-5199, E-mail: rod@pdx.edu.

Radford University, College of Graduate and Professional Studies, College of Humanities and Behavioral Sciences, Department of Criminal Justice, Radford, VA 24142. Offers MA, MS. Part-time programs available. *Faculty:* 10 full-time (5 women). *Students:* 25 full-time (13 women), 17 part-time (7 women); includes 4 Black or African American, non-Hispanic/Latino; 1 American Indian or Alaska Native, non-Hispanic/Latino; 1 Hispanic/Latino. Average age 27. 23 applicants, 87% accepted, 16 enrolled. In 2010, 16 master's awarded. *Degree requirements:* For master's, comprehensive exam, thesis optional. *Entrance requirements:* For master's, GRE, minimum GPA of 2.9; 2 letters of reference; original writing sample. Additional exam requirements/recommendations for international students: Required—TOEFL (minimum score 550 paper-based; 213 computer-based; 79 iBT). *Application deadline:* For fall admission, 2/15 priority date for domestic students, 12/1 for international students; for spring admission, 7/1 for international students. Applications are processed on a rolling basis. Application fee: $50. Electronic applications accepted. *Expenses:* Tuition, state resident: full-time $5746; part-time $239 per credit hour. Tuition, nonresident: full-time $14,174; part-time $591 per credit hour. Required fees: $2634; $111 per credit hour. *Financial support:* In 2010–11, 11 students received support, including 9 research assistantships with partial tuition reimbursements available (averaging $8,000 per year), 1 teaching assistantship (averaging $8,700 per year); career-related internships or fieldwork, Federal Work-Study, institutionally sponsored loans, scholarships/grants, and unspecified assistantships also available. Financial award application deadline: 3/1; financial award applicants required to submit FAFSA. *Faculty research:* Capital punishment, crime mapping and analysis, elder abuse, guns and gun control, rural crime. *Unit head:* Dr. Mary Atwell, Chair, 540-831-6339, Fax: 540-831-6075, E-mail: matwell@radford.edu. *Application contact:* Rebecca Conner, Graduate Admissions, 540-831-6431, Fax: 540-831-6061, E-mail: gradcollege@radford.edu.

Regis University, College for Professional Studies, School of Humanities and Social Sciences, Program in Criminology, Denver, CO 80221-1099. Offers M Sc.

The Richard Stockton College of New Jersey, School of Graduate and Continuing Studies, Program in Criminal Justice, Pomona, NJ 08240-0195. Offers MA. Part-time and evening/weekend programs available. *Faculty:* 6 full-time (2 women). *Students:* 12 full-time (9 women), 18 part-time (13 women); includes 5 minority (1 American Indian or Alaska Native, non-Hispanic/Latino; 1 Asian, non-Hispanic/Latino; 3 Hispanic/Latino). Average age 26. 17 applicants, 53% accepted, 7 enrolled. In 2010, 9 master's awarded. *Degree requirements:* For master's, comprehensive exam (for some programs), thesis, student portfolio project. *Entrance requirements:* For master's, GRE General Test, minimum GPA of 3.0. Additional exam requirements/recommendations for international students: Required—TOEFL. *Application deadline:* For fall admission, 7/1 for domestic and international students; for spring admission, 12/1 for domestic and international students. Applications are processed on a rolling basis. Application fee: $50. Electronic applications accepted. *Expenses:* Tuition, state resident: full-time $9310; part-time $517.25 per credit. Tuition, nonresident: full-time $14,332; part-time $796.23 per credit. Required fees: $2600; $144 per credit. $70 per semester. Tuition and fees vary according to degree level. *Financial support:* In 2010–11, 12 students received support, including 2 fellowships, 10 research assistantships with partial tuition reimbursements available; career-related internships or fieldwork, Federal Work-Study, scholarships/grants, and unspecified assistantships also available. Support available to part-time students. Financial award application deadline: 3/1; financial award applicants required to submit FAFSA. *Faculty research:* Homeland security, forensic psychology, corrections, sex crimes, violent crimes. *Unit head:* Dr. Christine Tartaro, Director, 609-626-6035, E-mail: christine.tartaro@stockton.edu. *Application contact:* Tara Williams, Assistant Director of Graduate Enrollment Management, 609-626-3640, Fax: 609-626-6050, E-mail: gradschools@stockton.edu.

Rochester Institute of Technology, Graduate Enrollment Services, College of Liberal Arts, Department of Criminal Justice, Rochester, NY 14623-5603. Offers MS. Part-time programs available. *Students:* 7 full-time (2 women), 2 part-time (both women); includes 1 Black or African American, non-Hispanic/Latino; 1 Asian, non-Hispanic/Latino. Average age 24. 11 applicants, 64% accepted, 7 enrolled. *Degree requirements:* For master's, thesis. *Entrance requirements:* For master's, GRE. Additional exam requirements/recommendations for international students: Required—TOEFL (minimum score 570 paper-based; 230 computer-based; 88 iBT) or IELTS (minimum score 6.5). *Expenses:* Tuition: Full-time $33,234; part-time $924 per credit hour. Required fees: $219. *Financial support:* In 2010–11, 4 students received support. Applicants required to submit FAFSA. *Faculty research:* Criminal justice policy; design, development of appropriate measures; collection and analysis of data using a wide range of methods. *Unit head:* Laverne McQuiller-Williams, Graduate Program Director, 585-475-2935, E-mail: llmgcj@rit.edu. *Application contact:* Diane Ellison, Assistant Vice President, Graduate Enrollment Services, 585-475-2229, Fax: 585-475-7164, E-mail: gradinfo@rit.edu.

Roger Williams University, School of Justice Studies, Bristol, RI 02809. Offers criminal justice (MS); MS/JD. Part-time and evening/weekend programs available. *Degree requirements:* For master's, comprehensive exam, thesis optional. *Entrance requirements:* For master's, 2 letters of recommendation. Additional exam requirements/recommendations for international students: Recommended—IELTS. Electronic applications accepted. *Expenses:* Contact institution.

Rowan University, Graduate School, College of Liberal Arts and Sciences, Program in Criminal Justice, Glassboro, NJ 08028-1701. Offers MA. Part-time and evening/weekend programs available. *Students:* 1 full-time (0 women), 7 part-time (4 women); includes 2 Black or African American, non-Hispanic/Latino. Average age 33. 7 applicants, 57% accepted, 3 enrolled. *Degree requirements:* For master's, thesis. *Entrance requirements:* For master's, GRE General Test. Additional exam requirements/recommendations for international students: Required—TOEFL. *Application deadline:* Applications are processed on a rolling basis. Application fee: $65 ($200 for international students). Electronic applications accepted. *Expenses:* Tuition, area resident: Part-time $602 per semester hour. Tuition, nonresident: part-time $602 per semester hour. Required fees: $100 per semester hour. One-time fee: $10 part-time. *Financial support:* Career-related internships or fieldwork, scholarships/grants, health care benefits, and unspecified assistantships available. *Unit head:* Dr. Horacio Sosa, Dean, College of Graduate and Continuing Education, 856-256-4747, Fax: 856-256-5638, E-mail: lalovic-hand@rowan.edu. *Application contact:* Karen Haynes, Graduate Coordinator, 856-256-4052, Fax: 856-256-4436, E-mail: haynes@rowan.edu.

Rutgers, The State University of New Jersey, Camden, Graduate School of Arts and Sciences, Program in Criminal Justice, Camden, NJ 08102. Offers MA, MPA/MA. Part-time and evening/weekend programs available. *Faculty:* 5 full-time (4 women). *Students:* 8 full-time (7 women), 26 part-time (13 women); includes 7 Black or African American, non-Hispanic/Latino; 3 Asian, non-Hispanic/Latino; 3 Hispanic/Latino, 2 international. Average age 30. 32 applicants, 72% accepted, 11 enrolled. In 2010, 3 master's awarded. *Degree requirements:* For master's, comprehensive exam, thesis optional, 30 credits. *Entrance requirements:* For master's, GRE, 3 letters of recommendation; statement of personal, professional, and academic goals. Additional exam requirements/recommendations for international students: Required—TOEFL, IELTS. *Application deadline:* For fall admission, 3/1 priority date for domestic students; for spring admission, 12/1 priority date for domestic students. Applications are processed on a rolling basis. Application fee: $65. Electronic applications accepted. *Expenses:* Tuition, state resident: full-time $4963; part-time $319 per credit. Tuition, nonresident: full-time $10,493; part-time $680 per credit. *Financial support:* In 2010–11, 23 students received support, including 5 fellowships with partial tuition reimbursements available (averaging $1,060 per year); Federal Work-Study, scholarships/grants, and tuition waivers (partial) also available. Financial award application deadline: 3/15; financial award applicants required to submit FAFSA. *Faculty research:* Criminal justice policy, public management, children in the criminal justice system, violence, gender and crime. *Unit head:* Dr. Jon'a F. Meyer, Director, 856-225-6470, Fax: 856-225-6435, E-mail: meyerj@rutgers.edu. *Application contact:* Dr. Jon'a F. Meyer, Director, 856-225-6470, Fax: 856-225-6435, E-mail: meyerj@rutgers.edu.

Rutgers, The State University of New Jersey, Newark, Graduate School, School of Criminal Justice, Doctoral Program in Criminal Justice, Newark, NJ 07102. Offers PhD. *Faculty:* 16 full-time (3 women). In 2010, 7 doctorates awarded. *Degree requirements:* For doctorate, thesis/dissertation. *Entrance requirements:* Additional exam requirements/recommendations for international students: Required—TOEFL. Application fee: $60. *Expenses:* Tuition, state resident: part-time $600 per credit. Tuition, nonresident: full-time $10,694. *Financial support:* Fellowships available. *Unit head:* Dr. James O. Finckenauer, Program Director, 973-353-3301, Fax: 973-353-5896, E-mail: finckena@andromeda.rutgers.edu. *Application contact:* Teresa Fontanez, Graduate Enrollment Coordinator, 973-353-3029, Fax: 973-353-1228, E-mail: tfontane@andromeda.rutgers.edu.

Rutgers, The State University of New Jersey, Newark, Graduate School, School of Criminal Justice, Master's Program in Criminal Justice, Newark, NJ 07102. Offers MA. *Faculty:* 16 full-time (3 women). *Students:* 57 full-time (29 women), 41 part-time (27 women); includes 12 Black or African American, non-Hispanic/Latino; 14 Asian, non-Hispanic/Latino; 4 Hispanic/Latino. In 2010, 17 master's awarded. *Entrance requirements:* For master's, GRE, minimum undergraduate B average. Additional exam requirements/recommendations for international students: Required—TOEFL. Application fee: $60. *Expenses:* Tuition, state resident: part-time $600 per credit. Tuition, nonresident: full-time $10,694. *Financial support:* In 2010–11, 10 teaching assistantships (averaging $19,815 per year) were awarded. *Unit head:* Dr. Marcus Felson, Program Director, 973-353-5237, E-mail: felson@andromeda.rutgers.edu. *Application contact:* Teresa Fontanez, Graduate Enrollment Coordinator, 973-353-3029, Fax: 973-353-1228, E-mail: tfontane@andromeda.rutgers.edu.

Sacred Heart University, Graduate Programs, College of Arts and Sciences, Department of Criminal Justice, Fairfield, CT 06825-1000. Offers MA. Part-time programs available. *Degree requirements:* For master's, thesis optional. *Entrance requirements:* Additional exam requirements/recommendations for international students: Required—TOEFL (minimum score 550 paper-based; 213 computer-based). Electronic applications accepted.

St. Ambrose University, College of Arts and Sciences, Program in Criminal Justice, Davenport, IA 52803-2898. Offers criminal justice (MCJ); juvenile justice education (MCJ). Part-time and evening/weekend programs available. *Faculty:* 4 full-time (3 women), 3 part-time/adjunct (0 women). *Students:* 10 full-time (5 women), 23 part-time (16 women); includes 7 minority (1 Black or African American, non-Hispanic/Latino; 2 American Indian or Alaska Native, non-Hispanic/Latino; 4 Hispanic/Latino). Average age 32. 13 applicants, 85% accepted, 11 enrolled. In 2010, 10 master's awarded. *Degree requirements:* For master's, thesis (for some programs), practicum or project. *Entrance requirements:* For master's, 2 years of work experience, 2 letters of recommendation, personal interview. Additional exam requirements/recommendations for international students: Required—TOEFL. *Application deadline:* For fall admission, 8/15 priority date for domestic students, 8/15 for international students; for spring admission, 11/1 for domestic and international students. Applications are processed on a rolling basis. Application fee: $25. Electronic applications accepted. *Expenses:* Tuition: Full-time $13,230; part-time $735 per credit hour. Required fees: $60 per semester. Tuition and fees vary according to degree level, program and reciprocity agreements. *Financial support:* In 2010–11, 29 students received support, including 5 research assistantships with partial tuition reimbursements available (averaging $2,670 per year); career-related internships or fieldwork, scholarships/grants, and unspecified assistantships also available. Financial award application deadline: 3/15; financial award applicants required to submit FAFSA. *Faculty research:* Community policing. *Unit head:* Dr. Christopher C. Barnum, Acting Head, 563-333-6157, Fax: 563-333-6243, E-mail: barnumchristopherc@sau.edu. *Application contact:* Vivian F. Force, Administrative Assistant, 563-333-6166, Fax: 563-333-6243, E-mail: forcevivianf@sau.edu.

St. Cloud State University, School of Graduate Studies, College of Social Sciences, Department of Criminal Justice, Program in Criminal Justice, St. Cloud, MN 56301-4498. Offers criminal justice administration (MS).

St. John's University, St. John's College of Liberal Arts and Sciences, Department of Sociology and Anthropology, Queens, NY 11439. Offers criminology and justice (MA); sociology (MA). Part-time and evening/weekend programs available. *Students:* 40 full-time (30 women), 30 part-time (17 women); includes 50 minority (24 Black or African American, non-Hispanic/Latino; 5 Asian, non-Hispanic/Latino; 19 Hispanic/Latino; 1 Native Hawaiian or other Pacific Islander, non-Hispanic/Latino; 1 Two or more races, non-Hispanic/Latino), 4 international. Average age 28. 76 applicants, 46% accepted, 28 enrolled. In 2010, 27 master's awarded. *Degree requirements:* For master's, comprehensive exam, thesis optional. *Entrance requirements:* For master's, 18 undergraduate credits in social services, minimum GPA of 3.0. Additional exam requirements/recommendations for international students: Required—TOEFL (minimum score 600 paper-based; 250 computer-based; 100 iBT), IELTS (minimum score 5.5). *Application deadline:* For fall admission, 5/1 priority date for domestic and international students; for spring admission, 11/1 priority date for domestic and international students. Applications are processed on a rolling basis. Application fee: $70. Electronic applications accepted. *Expenses:* Tuition: Full-time $17,100; part-time $950 per credit. Required fees: $340; $170 per semester. Tuition and fees vary according to program. *Financial support:* Research assistantships, career-related internships or fieldwork and scholarships/grants available. Support available to part-time students. Financial award application deadline: 3/1; financial award applicants required to submit FAFSA. *Faculty research:* Community studies and gentrification, global financial crisis, insurance fraud, globalization, immigration and human rights. *Unit head:* Dr. Dawn Esposito, Chair, 718-990-5667, E-mail: espositd@stjohns.edu. *Application contact:* Kathleen Davis, Director of Graduate Admission, 718-990-1601, Fax: 718-990-5686, E-mail: gradhelp@stjohns.edu.

Saint Joseph's University, College of Arts and Sciences, Department of Criminal Justice, Philadelphia, PA 19131-1395. Offers administration/police executive (MS); behavior analysis (MS, Post-Master's Certificate); criminal justice (MS, Post-Master's Certificate); criminology (MS); federal law (MS); intelligence and crime (MS); probation, parole, and corrections (MS). Part-time and evening/weekend programs available. Postbaccalaureate distance learning degree programs offered (no on-campus study). *Faculty:* 6 full-time (all women), 37 part-time/adjunct (26 women). *Students:* 50 full-time (35 women), 406 part-time (267 women). Average age 34. 193 applicants, 85% accepted, 140 enrolled. In 2010, 124 master's awarded. *Degree requirements:* For master's, thesis. *Entrance requirements:* For master's, GRE General Test or minimum GPA of 3.0, 2 letters of recommendation. Additional exam requirements/recommendations for international students: Required—TOEFL (minimum score 550 paper-based; 213 computer-based; 79 iBT). *Application deadline:* For fall admission, 7/15 priority date for domestic students, 4/15 for international students; for winter admission, 1/15 for international students; for spring admission, 11/15 priority date for domestic students, 10/15 for international students. Applications are processed on a rolling basis. Application fee: $35. Electronic applications accepted. *Expenses:* Tuition: Part-time $729 per credit. Tuition and fees vary according to course load, degree level and program. *Financial support:* Career-related internships or fieldwork and unspecified assistantships available. Financial award applicants required to submit FAFSA. *Unit head:* Patricia Griffin, Director, 610-660-1294, E-mail: pgriffin@sju.edu. *Application contact:* Kate McConnell, Director, Graduate College of Arts and Sciences Admissions and Retention, 610-660-3184, Fax: 610-660-3230, E-mail: kate.mconnell@sju.edu.

Saint Leo University, Graduate Studies in Criminal Justice, Saint Leo, FL 33574-6665. Offers criminal justice (MS); critical incident management (MS); forensic studies (MS). Part-time and evening/weekend programs available. Postbaccalaureate distance learning degree programs offered (minimal on-campus study). *Faculty:* 4 full-time (0 women), 11 part-time/adjunct (3 women). *Students:* 432 full-time (261 women), 5 part-time (1 woman); includes 195 minority (160 Black or African American, non-Hispanic/Latino; 4 American Indian or Alaska Native, non-Hispanic/Latino; 6 Asian, non-Hispanic/Latino; 20 Hispanic/Latino; 1 Native Hawaiian or other Pacific Islander, non-Hispanic/Latino; 4 Two or more races, non-Hispanic/Latino). Average age 38. In 2010, 75 master's awarded. *Degree requirements:* For master's, comprehensive project. *Entrance requirements:* For master's, bachelor's degree from regionally-accredited college or university with minimum GPA of 3.0. Additional exam requirements/recommendations for international students: Required—TOEFL (minimum score 550 paper-based; 213 computer-based; 80 iBT). *Application deadline:* For fall admission, 7/1 priority date for domestic and international students; for spring admission, 11/1 priority date for domestic and international students. Applications are processed on a rolling basis. Application fee: $75. Electronic applications accepted. *Expenses:* Tuition: Part-time $609 per semester hour. Required fees: $115 per course. Tuition and fees vary according to campus/location and program. *Financial support:* In 2010–11, 17 students received support. Federal Work-Study, scholarships/grants, and health care benefits available. *Unit head:* Dr. Robert Diemer, Director, 352-588-8974, Fax: 352-588-8289, E-mail: robert.diemer@saintleo.edu. *Application contact:* Jared Welling, Director, Graduate/Weekend and Evening Admission, 800-707-8846, Fax: 352-588-7873, E-mail: grad.admissions@saintleo.edu.

Saint Mary's University, Faculty of Arts, Program in Criminology, Halifax, NS B3H 3C3, Canada. Offers MA. Part-time programs available. *Degree requirements:* For master's, thesis. *Entrance requirements:* For master's, honors degree, official transcripts, sample of academic written work, 2 letters of recommendation. Electronic applications accepted. *Expenses:* Contact institution.

Saint Peter's College, Program in Criminal Justice Administration, Jersey City, NJ 07306-5997. Offers federal law enforcement administration (MA); police administration (MA). Part-time and evening/weekend programs available. *Entrance requirements:* Additional exam requirements/recommendations for international students: Required—TOEFL (minimum score 79 computer-based). *Application deadline:* Applications are processed on a rolling basis. Electronic applications accepted. *Financial support:* Applicants required to submit FAFSA. *Unit head:* Dr. Richard Cosgrove, Graduate Director, 201-761-6160, E-mail: rcosgrove@spc.edu. *Application contact:* Stephanie Autenrieth, Director, Graduate and Professional Studies Admission, 201-761-6474, Fax: 201-435-5270, E-mail: sautenrieth@spc.edu.

St. Thomas University, School of Business, Department of Management, Miami Gardens, FL 33054-6459. Offers accounting (MBA); general management (MSM, Certificate); health management (MBA, MSM, Certificate); human resource management (MBA, MSM, Certificate); international business (MBA, MIB, MSM, Certificate); justice administration (MSM, Certificate); management accounting (MSM, Certificate); public management (MSM, Certificate); sports administration (MS). Part-time and evening/weekend programs available. *Degree requirements:* For master's, comprehensive exam. *Entrance requirements:* For master's, interview, minimum GPA of 3.0 or GMAT. Additional exam requirements/recommendations for international students: Required—TOEFL (minimum score 550 paper-based; 213 computer-based; 79 iBT). Electronic applications accepted.

Salem State University, School of Graduate Studies, Program in Criminal Justice, Salem, MA 01970-5353. Offers MS. Part-time and evening/weekend programs available. *Students:* 3 full-time (2 women), 14 part-time (6 women); includes 1 Black or African American, non-Hispanic/Latino; 1 Asian, non-Hispanic/Latino. Average age 30. 5 applicants, 100% accepted, 5 enrolled. In 2010, 3 master's awarded. *Entrance requirements:* For master's, GRE or MAT. Additional exam requirements/recommendations for international students: Required—TOEFL (minimum score 550 paper-based; 80 iBT) or IELTS (minimum score 5.5). *Application deadline:* For fall admission, 5/1 for domestic students; for spring admission, 10/1 for domestic students. Applications are processed on a rolling basis. Application fee: $50. *Expenses:* Tuition, state resident: full-time $2520; part-time $290 per credit hour. Tuition, nonresident: full-time $4140; part-time $380 per credit hour. Required fees: $2700. *Financial support:* Career-related internships or fieldwork, Federal Work-Study, scholarships/grants, and unspecified assistantships available. Support available to part-time students. Financial award application deadline: 5/1; financial award applicants required to submit FAFSA. *Unit head:* Kristen Kuehnle, Associate Professor, 978-542-6075, E-mail: kkuehnle@salemstate.edu. *Application contact:* Dr. Lee A. Brossoit, Assistant Dean of Graduate Admissions, 978-542-6673, Fax: 978-542-7215, E-mail: lbrossoit@salemstate.edu.

Salve Regina University, Graduate Studies, Programs in Administration of Justice, Newport, RI 02840-4192. Offers justice and homeland security (MS); law enforcement leadership (MS). Part-time and evening/weekend programs available. *Entrance requirements:* For master's, GMAT, GRE General Test, or MAT. Additional exam requirements/recommendations for international students: Required—TOEFL (minimum score 600 paper-based; 250 computer-based; 100 iBT). Electronic applications accepted. *Expenses:* Tuition: Full-time $7740; part-time $430 per credit. Required fees: $40 per semester. Tuition and fees vary according to course level and degree level.

Sam Houston State University, College of Criminal Justice, Huntsville, TX 77341. Offers criminal justice (MS, PhD); criminal justice and criminology (MA); criminal justice management (MS); forensic science (MS); security studies (MS); victim services management (MS). *Faculty:* 22 full-time (4 women). *Students:* 91 full-time (55 women), 238 part-time (83 women); includes 25 Black or African American, non-Hispanic/Latino; 1 American Indian or Alaska Native, non-Hispanic/Latino; 6 Asian, non-Hispanic/Latino; 35 Hispanic/Latino, 33 international. Average age 34. 148 applicants, 88% accepted, 114 enrolled. In 2010, 46 master's, 6 doctorates awarded. *Degree requirements:* For master's, thesis (for some programs); for doctorate, comprehensive exam, thesis/dissertation. *Entrance requirements:* For master's, GRE General Test; for doctorate, GRE General Test, master's degree. Additional exam requirements/recommendations for international students: Required—TOEFL (minimum score 550 paper-based; 213 computer-based; 79 iBT). *Application deadline:* For fall admission, 8/1 for domestic students; for spring admission, 12/1 for domestic students. Applications are processed on a rolling basis. Application fee: $20. *Expenses:* Tuition, state resident: full-time $1363; part-time $163 per credit hour. Tuition, nonresident: full-time $3856; part-time $473 per credit hour. *Financial support:* Fellowships, research assistantships, teaching assistantships, career-related internships or fieldwork, Federal Work-Study, institutionally sponsored loans, and unspecified assistantships available. Support available to part-time students. Financial award application deadline: 5/31; financial award applicants required to submit FAFSA. *Unit head:* Dr. Vincent Webb, Dean, 936-294-1632, Fax: 936-294-1653, E-mail: vwebb@shsu.edu. *Application contact:* Doris Powell-Pratt, Advisor, 936-294-3637, Fax: 936-294-4055, E-mail: icc_dcp@shsu.edu.

San Diego State University, Graduate and Research Affairs, College of Professional Studies and Fine Arts, School of Public Affairs, Program in Criminal Justice Administration, San Diego, CA 92182. Offers MPA. Part-time programs available. *Entrance requirements:* For master's, GRE General Test, 2 letters of reference. Additional exam requirements/recommendations for international students: Required—TOEFL. Electronic applications accepted.

San Diego State University, Graduate and Research Affairs, College of Professional Studies and Fine Arts, School of Public Affairs, Program in Criminal Justice and Criminology, San Diego, CA 92182. Offers MS. *Entrance requirements:* For master's, GRE General Test, 2 letters of reference. Additional exam requirements/recommendations for international students: Required—TOEFL. Electronic applications accepted.

San Jose State University, Graduate Studies and Research, College of Applied Sciences and Arts, Department of Justice Studies, San Jose, CA 95192-0001. Offers MS. Part-time programs available. *Degree requirements:* For master's, thesis or alternative. *Entrance requirements:* For master's, GRE or LSAT, minimum GPA of 3.0. Additional exam requirements/recommendations for international students: Required—TOEFL. Electronic applications accepted. *Faculty research:* Employee stress, interagency cooperation, prison industries, application of death penalty sentences, sucrose ingestion and delinquency.

Seattle University, College of Arts and Sciences, Department of Criminal Justice, Seattle, WA 98122-1090. Offers MACJ.

Shippensburg University of Pennsylvania, School of Graduate Studies, College of Education and Human Services, Department of Criminal Justice, Shippensburg, PA 17257-2299. Offers administration of justice (MS), including administration of justice, juvenile justice. Part-time and evening/weekend programs available. *Faculty:* 4 full-time (2 women), 5 part-time/adjunct (3 women). *Students:* 12 full-time (2 women), 42 part-time (21 women); includes 14 minority (11 Black or African American, non-Hispanic/Latino; 3 Hispanic/Latino). Average age 31. 45 applicants, 78% accepted, 23 enrolled. In 2010, 19 master's awarded. *Degree requirements:* For master's, internship, practicum, or thesis. *Entrance requirements:* For master's, GRE or MAT (if GPA less than 2.75). Additional exam requirements/recommendations for international students: Required—TOEFL (minimum score 580 paper-based; 237 computer-based); Recommended—IELTS (minimum score 6). *Application deadline:* For fall admission, 3/1 for international students; for spring admission, 7/1 for international students. Applications are processed on a rolling basis. Application fee: $30. Electronic applications accepted. *Expenses:* Tuition, state resident: full-time $6966. Tuition, nonresident: full-time $11,146. Required fees: $1802. *Financial support:* In 2010–11, 5 research assistantships with full tuition reimbursements (averaging $5,000 per year) were awarded; career-related internships or fieldwork, scholarships/grants, unspecified assistantships, and resident hall director and student payroll positions also available. Support available to part-time students. Financial award application deadline: 3/1; financial award applicants required to submit FAFSA. *Unit head:* Dr. John Lemmon, Chairperson, 717-477-1558, Fax: 717-477-4087, E-mail: jhlemm@ship.edu. *Application contact:* Jeremy R. Goshorn, Associate Dean of Graduate Admissions, 717-477-1231, Fax: 717-477-4016, E-mail: jrgoshorn@ship.edu.

Simon Fraser University, Graduate Studies, Faculty of Arts and Social Sciences, School of Criminology, Burnaby, BC V5A 1S6, Canada. Offers MA, PhD. *Degree requirements:* For master's, thesis; for doctorate, thesis/dissertation. *Entrance requirements:* For master's, minimum GPA of 3.0; for doctorate, minimum GPA of 3.5. Additional exam requirements/recommendations for international students: Required—TOEFL or IELTS. *Faculty research:* Media and crime, feminist jurisprudence, policy evaluation, penology, terrorism.

Simpson College, Department of Social Sciences, Indianola, IA 50125-1297. Offers criminal justice (MACJ). Evening/weekend programs available.

Slippery Rock University of Pennsylvania, Graduate Studies (Recruitment), College of Business, Information and Social Sciences, Department of Criminology and Criminal Justice, Slippery Rock, PA 16057-1383. Offers criminal justice (MA). Part-time and evening/weekend programs available. Postbaccalaureate distance learning degree programs offered. *Faculty:* 3 full-time (2 women). *Students:* 20 full-time (12 women), 4 part-time (1 woman); includes 4 minority (all Black or African American, non-Hispanic/Latino). Average age 26. 41 applicants, 66% accepted, 24 enrolled. *Degree requirements:* For master's, comprehensive exam (for some programs), thesis (for some programs). *Entrance requirements:* For master's, GRE General Test or MAT, minimum GPA of 3.0, personal statement. Additional exam requirements/recommendations for international students: Required—TOEFL (minimum score 600 paper-based; 250 computer-based; 100 iBT). *Application deadline:* For fall admission, 3/1 priority date for domestic students, 5/1 priority date for international students; for spring admission, 11/1 priority date for domestic students, 9/1 priority date for international students. Applications are processed on a rolling basis. Application fee: $25 ($30 for international students). Electronic applications accepted. *Expenses:* Contact institution. *Financial support:* Career-related internships or fieldwork, scholarships/grants, and tuition waivers (partial) available. Support available to part-time students. Financial award application deadline: 5/1; financial award applicants required to submit FAFSA. *Unit head:* Dr. David Champion, Graduate Coordinator, 724-738-4462, E-mail: david.champion@sru.edu. *Application contact:* Angela Piverotto, Interim Director of Graduate Studies, 724-738-2051, Fax: 724-738-2146, E-mail: graduate.admissions@sru.edu.

Southeastern Louisiana University, College of Arts, Humanities and Social Sciences, Department of Sociology and Criminal Justice, Hammond, LA 70402. Offers applied sociology (MS), including criminal justice, globalization and social diversity, public policy. Part-time and evening/weekend programs available. *Faculty:* 7 full-time (2 women). *Students:* 23 full-time (17 women), 11 part-time (8 women); includes 11 minority (9 Black or African American, non-Hispanic/Latino; 2 Hispanic/Latino), 1 international. Average age 28. 18 applicants, 72% accepted, 12 enrolled. In 2010, 7 master's awarded. *Degree requirements:* For master's, comprehensive exam, thesis (for some programs), internship research (for those who select an internship track). *Entrance requirements:* For master's, GRE General Test (verbal and quantitative), bachelor's degree in sociology, social work, criminal justice or related social science; minimum GPA of 3.0. Additional exam requirements/recommendations for international students: Required—TOEFL (minimum score 500 paper-based; 173 computer-based; 61 iBT). *Application deadline:* For fall admission, 7/15 priority date for domestic students, 6/1 priority date for international students; for spring admission, 12/1 priority date for domestic students, 10/1 priority date for international students. Applications are processed on a rolling basis. Application fee: $20 ($30 for international students). Electronic applications accepted. *Expenses:* Tuition, state resident: full-time $3533. Tuition, nonresident: full-time $12,002. Required fees: $907. Tuition and fees vary according to degree level. *Financial support:* In 2010–11, 4 students received support, including 4 research assistantships (averaging $10,100 per year); Federal Work-Study, institutionally sponsored loans, and scholarships/grants also available. Support available to part-time students. Financial award application deadline: 5/1; financial award applicants required to submit FAFSA. *Faculty research:* Criminology, environmental sociology, globalization, public policy, race and ethnic relations. *Unit head:* Dr. Kenneth Bolton, Department Head, 985-549-2110, Fax: 985-549-5961, E-mail: kbolton@selu.edu. *Application contact:* Sandra Meyers, Graduate Admissions Analyst, 985-549-5620, Fax: 985-549-5632, E-mail: admissions@selu.edu.

Southeast Missouri State University, School of Graduate Studies, Department of Criminal Justice and Sociology, Cape Girardeau, MO 63701-4799. Offers criminal justice (MS). Postbaccalaureate distance learning degree programs offered (no on-campus study). *Faculty:* 6 full-time (3 women). *Students:* 6 full-time (4 women), 51 part-time (32 women); includes 13 minority (7 Black or African American, non-Hispanic/Latino; 5 American Indian or Alaska Native, non-Hispanic/Latino; 1 Asian, non-Hispanic/Latino). Average age 31. 35 applicants, 80% accepted, 19 enrolled. In 2010, 5 master's awarded. *Degree requirements:* For master's, comprehensive exam (for some programs), thesis (for some programs), internship, capstone seminar or additional course work. *Entrance requirements:* For master's, minimum undergraduate GPA of 2.5. Additional exam requirements/recommendations for international students: Required—TOEFL (minimum score 550 paper-based; 213 computer-based; 79 iBT);

Criminal Justice and Criminology

Southeast Missouri State University (continued)
Recommended—IELTS (minimum score 6). *Application deadline:* For fall admission, 8/1 for domestic students, 6/1 for international students; for spring admission, 11/21 for domestic students, 10/1 for international students. Applications are processed on a rolling basis. Application fee: $25 ($35 for international students). Electronic applications accepted. *Expenses:* Tuition, state resident: full-time $4698; part-time $261 per credit hour. Tuition, nonresident: full-time $8379; part-time $465.50 per credit hour. *Financial support:* In 2010–11, 7 students received support, including 4 teaching assistantships with full tuition reimbursements available (averaging $7,600 per year); career-related internships or fieldwork, Federal Work-Study, institutionally sponsored loans, scholarships/grants, tuition waivers (full), and unspecified assistantships also available. Financial award application deadline: 6/30; financial award applicants required to submit FAFSA. *Faculty research:* Drug courts, policing and higher education and issues in policing, family violence, program assessment, restorative justice. *Unit head:* Dr. Diana Bruns, Chairperson, 573-651-2541, E-mail: dbruns@semo.edu. *Application contact:* Gail Amick, Administrative Secretary, 573-651-2049, Fax: 573-651-2001, E-mail: gamick@semo.edu.

Southern Illinois University Carbondale, Graduate School, College of Liberal Arts, Administration of Justice Program, Carbondale, IL 62901-4701. Offers MA. *Degree requirements:* For master's, thesis optional. *Entrance requirements:* For master's, GRE General Test, minimum GPA of 2.7. Additional exam requirements/recommendations for international students: Required—TOEFL. *Faculty research:* Corrections, criminology, law enforcement, crime prevention, victims of crime.

Southern University and Agricultural and Mechanical College, Graduate School, Nelson Mandela School of Public Policy and Urban Affairs, Department of Criminal Justice, Baton Rouge, LA 70813. Offers MS. *Entrance requirements:* Additional exam requirements/recommendations for international students: Required—TOEFL (minimum score 525 paper-based; 193 computer-based).

South University, Graduate Programs, College of Business, Savannah, GA 31406. Offers corrections (MBA); entrepreneurship and small business (MBA); hospitality management (MBA); sustainability (MBA).

South University, Program in Criminal Justice, Columbia, SC 29203. Offers MS.

See Close-Up on page 771.

Southwestern College, Professional Studies Programs, Wichita, KS 67207. Offers business administration (MBA); leadership (MS); management (MS); security administration (MS); specialized ministries (MA); theological studies (MA). Part-time and evening/weekend programs available. Postbaccalaureate distance learning degree programs offered (minimal on-campus study). *Faculty:* 12 part-time/adjunct (5 women). *Students:* 154 part-time (62 women); includes 29 minority (20 Black or African American, non-Hispanic/Latino; 1 American Indian or Alaska Native, non-Hispanic/Latino; 4 Hispanic/Latino; 4 Two or more races, non-Hispanic/Latino). Average age 35. 91 applicants, 66% accepted, 52 enrolled. In 2010, 112 master's awarded. *Degree requirements:* For master's, practicum/capstone project. *Entrance requirements:* For master's, baccalaureate degree; minimum GPA of 2.5, 3.0 for MBA. Additional exam requirements/recommendations for international students: Required—TOEFL (minimum score 550 paper-based; 213 computer-based). *Application deadline:* For fall admission, 8/1 for domestic students; for spring admission, 12/1 for domestic students. Applications are processed on a rolling basis. Application fee: $0. Electronic applications accepted. *Expenses:* Tuition: Full-time $7470; part-time $415 per credit hour. Tuition and fees vary according to program. *Financial support:* In 2010–11, 6 students received support. Federal Work-Study, tuition waivers (partial), and unspecified assistantships available. Financial award application deadline: 4/1; financial award applicants required to submit FAFSA. *Unit head:* Gail Cullen, Director of Academic Affairs, 888-684-5335 Ext. 203, Fax: 316-688-5218, E-mail: gail.cullen@sckans.edu. *Application contact:* Gail Cullen, Director of Academic Affairs, 888-684-5335 Ext. 203, Fax: 316-688-5218, E-mail: gail.cullen@sckans.edu.

Southwest University, Program in Criminal Justice, Kenner, LA 70062. Offers MS.

Suffolk University, College of Arts and Sciences, Program in Crime and Justice Studies, Boston, MA 02108-2770. Offers MSCJS, MSCJS/JD, MSCJS/MPA, MSCJS/MSMHC. Part-time programs available. *Faculty:* 9 full-time (7 women), 4 part-time/adjunct (all women). *Students:* 37 full-time (25 women), 28 part-time (18 women); includes 3 Black or African American, non-Hispanic/Latino; 1 Asian, non-Hispanic/Latino; 1 Hispanic/Latino, 1 international. Average age 26. 66 applicants, 73% accepted, 26 enrolled. In 2010, 37 master's awarded. *Entrance requirements:* For master's, 2 letters of recommendation, resume. Additional exam requirements/recommendations for international students: Required—TOEFL (minimum score 550 paper-based; 213 computer-based; 80 iBT). *Application deadline:* For fall admission, 6/15 priority date for domestic students, 6/15 for international students; for spring admission, 11/1 priority date for domestic students, 11/1 for international students. Applications are processed on a rolling basis. Application fee: $50. Electronic applications accepted. *Expenses:* Contact institution. *Financial support:* In 2010–11, 54 students received support, including 41 fellowships with partial tuition reimbursements available (averaging $5,765 per year); career-related internships or fieldwork, Federal Work-Study, and institutionally sponsored loans also available. Support available to part-time students. Financial award application deadline: 4/1; financial award applicants required to submit FAFSA. *Faculty research:* Restorative justice, anti-gang initiative, healthcare for female ex-offenders, violence against women, juvenile justice and the courts. *Unit head:* Dr. Donald Morton, Chairperson, 617-305-1990, Fax: 617-720-0490, E-mail: mscjs@suffolk.edu. *Application contact:* Judith Reynolds, Director of Graduate Admissions, 617-573-8302, Fax: 617-305-1733, E-mail: grad.admission@suffolk.edu.

Sul Ross State University, School of Professional Studies, Department of Criminal Justice, Alpine, TX 79832. Offers MS. *Entrance requirements:* For master's, GRE General Test, minimum GPA of 2.5 in last 60 hours of undergraduate work.

Tarleton State University, College of Graduate Studies, College of Liberal and Fine Arts, Department of Social Work, Sociology, and Criminal Justice, Stephenville, TX 76402. Offers criminal justice (MCJ). Part-time and evening/weekend programs available. *Degree requirements:* For master's, comprehensive exam (for some programs), thesis optional. *Entrance requirements:* For master's, GRE General Test, minimum GPA of 3.0. Additional exam requirements/recommendations for international students: Required—TOEFL (minimum score 550 paper-based; 213 computer-based; 80 iBT). Electronic applications accepted.

Temple University, College of Liberal Arts, Department of Criminal Justice, Philadelphia, PA 19122-6096. Offers MA, PhD. Part-time programs available. *Faculty:* 17 full-time (6 women). *Students:* 36 full-time (22 women), 4 part-time (1 woman); includes 3 Black or African American, non-Hispanic/Latino; 2 Asian, non-Hispanic/Latino; 2 Hispanic/Latino, 2 international. 59 applicants, 44% accepted, 15 enrolled. In 2010, 6 master's, 4 doctorates awarded. Terminal master's awarded for partial completion of doctoral program. *Degree requirements:* For master's, thesis optional; for doctorate, thesis/dissertation, qualifying exams. *Entrance requirements:* For master's, GRE General Test, minimum GPA of 3.0; for doctorate, GRE General Test. Additional exam requirements/recommendations for international students: Required—TOEFL (minimum score 550 paper-based; 213 computer-based; 79 iBT). *Application deadline:* For fall admission, 1/15 for domestic students, 12/15 for international students. Applications are processed on a rolling basis. Application fee: $50. Electronic applications accepted. *Financial support:* Research assistantships with tuition reimbursements, teaching assistantships with tuition reimbursements, career-related internships or fieldwork and Federal Work-Study available. Financial award application deadline: 1/15. *Faculty research:* Criminal justice policy formulation, courts, correctional alternatives, community crime prevention, juvenile justice. Total annual research expenditures: $200,000. *Unit head:* Dr. Jerry Ratcliffe, Chair, 215-204-7918, Fax: 215-204-3872, E-mail: jhr@temple.edu. *Application contact:* Dr. Jerry Ratcliffe, Chair, 215-204-7918, Fax: 215-204-3872, E-mail: jhr@temple.edu.

Tennessee State University, The School of Graduate Studies and Research, College of Arts and Sciences, Department of Criminal Justice, Nashville, TN 37209-1561. Offers MCJ. Program offered jointly with Middle Tennessee State University. *Degree requirements:* For master's, thesis. *Entrance requirements:* For master's, GRE General Test or MAT. Electronic applications accepted.

Texas A&M International University, Office of Graduate Studies and Research, College of Arts and Sciences, Department of Behavioral Sciences, Laredo, TX 78041-1900. Offers counseling psychology (MACP); criminal justice (MS); psychology (MS); sociology (MA). *Faculty:* 9 full-time (5 women), 2 part-time/adjunct (1 woman). *Students:* 12 full-time (8 women), 116 part-time (80 women); includes 1 Black or African American, non-Hispanic/Latino; 1 Asian, non-Hispanic/Latino; 120 Hispanic/Latino, 1 international. Average age 29. 20 applicants, 90% accepted, 10 enrolled. In 2010, 16 master's awarded. *Degree requirements:* For master's, thesis (for some programs). *Entrance requirements:* For master's, GRE General Test. Additional exam requirements/recommendations for international students: Required—TOEFL (minimum score 550 paper-based; 213 computer-based; 79 iBT). *Application deadline:* For fall admission, 4/30 priority date for domestic students; for spring admission, 11/30 for domestic students. Applications are processed on a rolling basis. Application fee: $25. *Financial support:* In 2010–11, 17 students received support, including 2 fellowships, 6 research assistantships; teaching assistantships. Financial award application deadline: 11/1. *Unit head:* Dr. Frances P. Bernat, Chair, 956-326-2475, Fax: 956-326-2474, E-mail: gvillagran@tamiu.edu. *Application contact:* Suzanne Hansen-Alford, Director of Graduate Recruiting, 956-326-3023, Fax: 956-326-3021, E-mail: graduateschool@tamiu.edu.

Texas Southern University, School of Public Affairs, Program in Administration of Justice, Houston, TX 77004-4584. Offers MS, PhD. *Faculty:* 2 full-time (1 woman), 2 part-time/adjunct (0 women). *Students:* 45 full-time (31 women), 32 part-time (17 women); includes 70 Black or African American, non-Hispanic/Latino; 1 Asian, non-Hispanic/Latino; 4 Hispanic/Latino. Average age 36. 43 applicants, 98% accepted, 34 enrolled. In 2010, 7 master's awarded. *Application deadline:* For fall admission, 7/1 for domestic and international students; for spring admission, 11/1 for domestic and international students. Applications are processed on a rolling basis. Application fee: $50 ($75 for international students). Electronic applications accepted. *Expenses:* Tuition, state resident: full-time $1875; part-time $100 per credit hour. Tuition, nonresident: full-time $6641; part-time $343 per credit hour. Tuition and fees vary according to course level, course load and degree level. *Financial support:* In 2010–11, 18 research assistantships (averaging $10,120 per year) were awarded; teaching assistantships, scholarships/grants and unspecified assistantships also available. *Unit head:* Dr. Ihekwoaba Onwudiwe, Chair, 713-313-7445, E-mail: onwudiweid@tsu.edu. *Application contact:* Pinkie Cotton, Administrative Assistant, 713-313-7311, E-mail: cotton_pe@tsu.edu.

Texas State University–San Marcos, Graduate School, College of Applied Arts, Department of Criminal Justice, San Marcos, TX 78666. Offers MSCJ, PhD. Part-time and evening/weekend programs available. *Faculty:* 12 full-time (3 women). *Students:* 49 full-time (29 women), 68 part-time (38 women); includes 8 Black or African American, non-Hispanic/Latino; 2 Asian, non-Hispanic/Latino; 36 Hispanic/Latino; 3 Two or more races, non-Hispanic/Latino, 1 international. Average age 30. 79 applicants, 67% accepted, 35 enrolled. In 2010, 32 master's awarded. *Degree requirements:* For master's, comprehensive exam, thesis (for some programs); for doctorate, comprehensive exam, thesis/dissertation. *Entrance requirements:* For master's, bachelor's degree, minimum GPA of 3.0 in last 60 hours of course work; for doctorate, GRE (minimum combined Verbal and Quantitative score of 1000), master's degree in criminal justice or related field; minimum GPA of 3.5 in graduate courses; 3 letters of recommendation; personal/goals statement. Additional exam requirements/recommendations for international students: Required—TOEFL (minimum score 550 paper-based; 213 computer-based; 78 iBT). *Application deadline:* For fall admission, 6/15 priority date for domestic students, 6/1 for international students; for spring admission, 10/15 priority date for domestic students, 10/1 for international students. Applications are processed on a rolling basis. Application fee: $40 ($90 for international students). Electronic applications accepted. *Expenses:* Tuition, state resident: full-time $6024; part-time $251 per credit hour. Tuition, nonresident: full-time $13,536; part-time $564 per credit hour. Required fees: $1776; $50 per credit hour. $306 per semester. *Financial support:* In 2010–11, 55 students received support, including 11 research assistantships (averaging $5,608 per year), 19 teaching assistantships (averaging $4,652 per year); Federal Work-Study and institutionally sponsored loans also available. Support available to part-time students. Financial award application deadline: 4/1; financial award applicants required to submit FAFSA. *Faculty research:* Geographic profiling, illegal crossing, criminal hunt pattern, reducing inmate rape, counterterrorism, displaced residents, TYC classify systems. Total annual research expenditures: $2 million. *Unit head:* Dr. Quint C. Thurman, Chair, 512-245-2174, Fax: 512-245-8063, E-mail: qt10@txstate.edu. *Application contact:* Dr. Brian Withrow, Advisor, 512-245-2174, Fax: 512-245-8063, E-mail: bw32@txstate.edu.

Texas State University–San Marcos, Graduate School, College of Liberal Arts, Department of Sociology, Interdisciplinary Studies Program in Criminal Justice, San Marcos, TX 78666. Offers MSIS. Part-time and evening/weekend programs available. *Faculty:* 13 full-time (8 women), 1 part-time/adjunct (0 women). *Students:* 22 full-time (14 women), 29 part-time (20 women); includes 22 minority (9 Black or African American, non-Hispanic/Latino; 1 Asian, non-Hispanic/Latino; 10 Hispanic/Latino; 2 Two or more races, non-Hispanic/Latino). Average age 29. 30 applicants, 93% accepted, 19 enrolled. In 2010, 4 master's awarded. *Degree requirements:* For master's, comprehensive exam, thesis optional. *Entrance requirements:* For master's, minimum GPA of 2.75 in last 60 hours of undergraduate work. Additional exam requirements/recommendations for international students: Required—TOEFL (minimum score 550 paper-based; 213 computer-based; 78 iBT). *Application deadline:* For fall admission, 6/15 priority date for domestic students, 6/1 for international students; for spring admission, 10/15 priority date for domestic students, 10/1 for international students. Applications are processed on a rolling basis. Application fee: $40 ($90 for international students). Electronic applications accepted. *Expenses:* Tuition, state resident: full-time $6024; part-time $251 per credit hour. Tuition, nonresident: full-time $13,536; part-time $564 per credit hour. Required fees: $1776; $50 per credit hour. $306 per semester. *Financial support:* In 2010–11, 17 students received support, including 13 teaching assistantships (averaging $5,297 per year); research assistantships, Federal Work-Study, institutionally sponsored loans, scholarships/grants, health care benefits, and unspecified assistantships also available. Support available to part-time students. Financial award application deadline: 4/1; financial award applicants required to submit FAFSA. *Unit head:* Dr. Audwin Anderson, Graduate Advisor, 512-245-2174, Fax: 512-245-2174, E-mail: aa04@txstate.edu. *Application contact:* Dr. J. Michael Willoughby, Dean of Graduate School, 512-245-2581, Fax: 512-245-8365, E-mail: gradcollege@txstate.edu.

Tiffin University, Program in Criminal Justice, Tiffin, OH 44883-2161. Offers crime analysis (MSCJ); criminal behavior (MSCJ); forensic psychology (MSCJ); homeland security administration (MSCJ); justice administration (MSCJ). Part-time and evening/weekend programs available. Postbaccalaureate distance learning degree programs offered (no on-campus study). *Faculty:* 13 full-time (3 women), 20 part-time/adjunct (9 women). *Students:* 120 full-time (84 women), 312 part-time (205 women). Average age 31. 185 applicants, 58% accepted, 104 enrolled. In 2010, 340 master's awarded. *Degree requirements:* For master's, thesis optional. *Entrance requirements:* For master's, minimum undergraduate GPA of 2.5, work experience. Additional exam requirements/recommendations for international students: Required—TOEFL (minimum score 550 paper-based; 213 computer-based). *Application deadline:* For fall admission, 9/3 for domestic students, 8/1 for international students; for spring admission, 1/9 priority date for domestic students, 12/1 for international students. Applications are processed on a rolling basis. Application fee: $0. Electronic applications accepted. *Financial support:* In 2010–11, 64 students received support. Available to part-time students. Application deadline: 7/31. *Faculty research:* Terrorism, intelligence, homeland security, guns and crime. *Unit head:* Dr. Tim Shaw, Dean of Criminal Justice and Social Sciences, 419-448-3305, Fax: 419-443-5002, E-mail: shawta@tiffin.edu. *Application contact:* Kristi Krintzline, Director of Graduate Admissions, 800-968-6446 Ext. 3445, Fax: 419-443-5002, E-mail: krintzlineka@tiffin.edu.

Trine University, Program in Criminal Justice, Angola, IN 46703-1764. Offers MS.

Troy University, Graduate School, College of Arts and Sciences, Program in Criminal Justice, Troy, AL 36082. Offers MS. Part-time and evening/weekend programs available. *Students:* 81 full-time (45 women), 330 part-time (196 women); includes 270 minority (248 Black or African American, non-Hispanic/Latino; 4 American Indian or Alaska Native, non-Hispanic/Latino; 3 Asian, non-Hispanic/Latino; 14 Hispanic/Latino; 1 Two or more races, non-Hispanic/Latino). Average age 34. 188 applicants, 88% accepted. In 2010, 82 master's awarded. *Degree requirements:* For master's, comprehensive exam, research course, minimum GPA of 3.0, admission to candidacy. *Entrance requirements:* For master's, GRE (minimum score of 850) or MAT (minimum score of 385), minimum undergraduate GPA of 2.5. Additional exam requirements/recommendations for international students: Required—TOEFL (minimum score 523 paper-based; 193 computer-based; 70 iBT), IELTS (minimum score 6). *Application deadline:* Applications are processed on a rolling basis. Application fee: $50. Electronic applications accepted. *Expenses:* Tuition, state resident: full-time $4428; part-time $246 per credit hour. Tuition, nonresident: full-time $8856; part-time $492 per credit hour. Required fees: $432; $24 per credit hour. $50 per term. Tuition and fees vary according to program. *Financial support:* Available to part-time students. Applicants required to submit FAFSA. *Faculty research:* Crime victims, criminal justice personnel issues, disability issues in criminal justice. *Unit head:* Dr. Bill Grantham, Chairman, 334-670-3637, Fax: 334-670-3753, E-mail: bgranth@troy.edu. *Application contact:* Brenda K. Campbell, Director of Graduate Admissions, 334-670-3178, Fax: 334-670-3733, E-mail: bcamp@troy.edu.

Troy University, Graduate School, College of Arts and Sciences, Program in Public Administration, Troy, AL 36082. Offers education (MPA); environmental management (MPA); government contracting (MPA); health care administration (MPA); justice administration (MPA); national security affairs (MPA); nonprofit management (MPA); public human resources management (MPA); public management (MPA). *Accreditation:* NASPAA. Part-time and evening/weekend programs available. Postbaccalaureate distance learning degree programs offered (no on-campus study). *Degree requirements:* For master's, capstone course, research methodologies course. *Entrance requirements:* For master's, GRE, MAT or GMAT, minimum undergraduate GPA of 2.5, letter of recommendation, essay. Additional exam requirements/recommendations for international students: Required—TOEFL (minimum score 523 paper-based; 193 computer-based; 70 iBT), IELTS (minimum score 6). *Application deadline:* Applications are processed on a rolling basis. Application fee: $50. Electronic applications accepted. *Expenses:* Tuition, state resident: full-time $4428; part-time $246 per credit hour. Tuition, nonresident: full-time $8856; part-time $492 per credit hour. Required fees: $432; $24 per credit hour. $50 per term. Tuition and fees vary according to program. *Financial support:* Available to part-time students. Applicants required to submit FAFSA. *Unit head:* Dr. Ellen Rosell, Chairman, 334-670-3758, Fax: 334-670-5647, E-mail: erosell@troy.edu. *Application contact:* Brenda K. Campbell, Director of Graduate Admissions, 334-670-3178, Fax: 334-670-3733, E-mail: bcamp@troy.edu.

Troy University, Graduate School, College of Business, Program in Business Administration, Troy, AL 36082. Offers accounting (EMBA, MBA); criminal justice (EMBA); finance (MBA); general management (EMBA, MBA); healthcare management (EMBA); information systems (EMBA, MBA); international economic development (MBA). *Accreditation:* ACBSP. Part-time and evening/weekend programs available. *Students:* 351 full-time (198 women), 745 part-time (452 women); includes 589 minority (425 Black or African American, non-Hispanic/Latino; 13 American Indian or Alaska Native, non-Hispanic/Latino; 129 Asian, non-Hispanic/Latino; 21 Hispanic/Latino; 1 Two or more races, non-Hispanic/Latino). Average age 29. 748 applicants, 71% accepted. In 2010, 322 master's awarded. *Degree requirements:* For master's, minimum GPA 3.0, capstone course, research course. *Entrance requirements:* For master's, GMAT (minimum score 500) or GRE General Test (minimum score 900), minimum GPA of 2.5; letter of recommendation, bachelor's degree. Additional exam requirements/recommendations for international students: Required—TOEFL (minimum score 523 paper-based; 193 computer-based; 70 iBT), IELTS (minimum score 6), or ACT compass ESL (minimum Listening, Reading, and Grammar score: 270). *Application deadline:* Applications are processed on a rolling basis. Application fee: $50. *Expenses:* Tuition, state resident: full-time $4428; part-time $246 per credit hour. Tuition, nonresident: full-time $8856; part-time $492 per credit hour. Required fees: $432; $24 per credit hour. $50 per term. Tuition and fees vary according to program. *Unit head:* Dr. Henry M. Findley, Interim Chair/Professor, 334-670-3271, Fax: 334-670-3599, E-mail: hfindley@troy.edu. *Application contact:* Brenda K. Campbell, Director of Graduate Admissions, 334-670-3178, Fax: 334-670-3733, E-mail: bcamp@troy.edu.

Troy University, Graduate School, College of Education, Program in Counseling and Psychology, Troy, AL 36082. Offers agency counseling (Ed S); clinical mental health (MS); community counseling (MS, Ed S); corrections counseling (MS); rehabilitation counseling (MS); school psychology (MS, Ed S); school psychometry (MS); social service counseling (MS); student affairs counseling (MS); substance abuse counseling (MS). *Accreditation:* ACA; CORE; NCATE. Part-time and evening/weekend programs available. *Students:* 419 full-time (338 women), 720 part-time (603 women); includes 696 minority (592 Black or African American, non-Hispanic/Latino; 8 American Indian or Alaska Native, non-Hispanic/Latino; 4 Asian, non-Hispanic/Latino; 46 Hispanic/Latino; 46 Two or more races, non-Hispanic/Latino). Average age 33. 326 applicants, 90% accepted. In 2010, 198 master's, 1 other advanced degree awarded. *Degree requirements:* For master's, comprehensive exam, thesis. *Entrance requirements:* For master's, MAT, minimum GPA of 2.5. Additional exam requirements/recommendations for international students: Required—TOEFL (minimum score 523 paper-based; 193 computer-based; 70 iBT), IELTS (minimum score 6). *Application deadline:* Applications are processed on a rolling basis. Application fee: $50. Electronic applications accepted. *Expenses:* Tuition, state resident: full-time $4428; part-time $246 per credit hour. Tuition, nonresident: full-time $8856; part-time $492 per credit hour. Required fees: $432; $24 per credit hour. $50 per term. Tuition and fees vary according to program. *Unit head:* Dr. Andrew Creamer, Chair, 334-670-3350, Fax: 334-670-32961, E-mail: drcreamer@troy.edu. *Application contact:* Brenda K. Campbell, Director of Graduate Admissions, 334-670-3178, Fax: 334-670-3733, E-mail: bcamp@troy.edu.

Troy University, Graduate School, College of Education, Program in Postsecondary Education, Troy, AL 36082. Offers adult education (M Ed); biology (M Ed); criminal justice (M Ed); English (M Ed); foundations of education (M Ed); general science (M Ed); higher education administration (M Ed); history (M Ed); instructional technology (M Ed); mathematics (M Ed); music industry (M Ed); physical fitness (M Ed); political science (M Ed); public administration (M Ed); social science (M Ed); teaching English (M Ed). *Accreditation:* NCATE. Part-time and evening/weekend programs available. *Students:* 314 full-time (247 women), 153 part-time (122 women); includes 255 minority (242 Black or African American, non-Hispanic/Latino; 3 American Indian or Alaska Native, non-Hispanic/Latino; 5 Asian, non-Hispanic/Latino; 5 Hispanic/Latino). Average age 34. 223 applicants, 89% accepted. In 2010, 364 master's awarded. *Degree requirements:* For master's, comprehensive exam, thesis. *Entrance requirements:* For master's, MAT (minimum score 385), minimum GPA of 2.5. Additional exam requirements/recommendations for international students: Required—TOEFL (minimum score 523 paper-based; 193 computer-based; 70 iBT), IELTS, or ACT compass ESL (minimum Listening, Reading, and Grammar score: 270). *Application deadline:* Applications are processed on a rolling basis. Application fee: $50. Electronic applications accepted. *Expenses:* Tuition, state resident: full-time $4428; part-time $246 per credit hour. Tuition, nonresident: full-time $8856; part-time $492 per credit hour. Required fees: $432; $24 per credit hour. $50 per term. Tuition and fees vary according to program. *Financial support:* Available to part-time students. Applicants required to submit FAFSA. *Unit head:* Dr. Andrew Creamer, Chair, 334-670-3350, Fax: 334-670-3296, E-mail: drcreamer@troy.edu. *Application contact:* Brenda K. Campbell, Director of Graduate Admissions, 334-670-3178, Fax: 334-670-3733, E-mail: bcamp@troy.edu.

TUI University, College of Business Administration, Program in Business Administration, Cypress, CA 90630. Offers business administration (PhD); conflict and negotiation management (MBA); criminal justice administration (MBA); entrepreneurship (MBA); finance (MBA); general management (MBA); government accounting (MBA); human resource management (MBA); information security and digital assurance management (MBA); information technology management (MBA); international business (MBA); logistics management (MBA); marketing (MBA); project management (MBA); public management (MBA); quality management (MBA); strategic leadership (MBA). Part-time and evening/weekend programs available. Postbaccalaureate distance learning degree programs offered (no on-campus study). *Students:* 741 full-time (200 women), 1,585 part-time (410 women). 379 applicants, 81% accepted, 300 enrolled. In 2010, 752 master's, 28 doctorates awarded. *Degree requirements:* For doctorate, comprehensive exam, thesis/dissertation, defense of dissertation. *Entrance requirements:* For master's, minimum GPA of 2.5 (students with GPA 3.0 or greater may transfer up to 30% of graduate level credits); for doctorate, minimum GPA of 3.4, curriculum vitae, course work in research methods or statistics. Additional exam requirements/recommendations for international students: Required—TOEFL. *Application deadline:* For fall admission, 10/3 for domestic and international students; for winter admission, 12/22 for domestic and international students; for spring admission, 4/3 for domestic and international students. Applications are processed on a rolling basis. Application fee: $75. Electronic applications accepted. *Expenses:* Tuition: Full-time $11,040; part-time $345 per semester hour. *Unit head:* Paul Watkins, Dean, College of Business Administration, 800-375-9878, E-mail: pwatkins@tuiu.edu. *Application contact:* Wei Ren-Finaly, Registrar, 800-375-9878, Fax: 714-827-7407, E-mail: registration@tuiu.edu.

Universidad del Este, Graduate School, Carolina, PR 00984. Offers accounting (MBA); adult education (M Ed); agribusiness (MBA); criminal justice and criminology (MA); curriculum and instruction—early education (M Ed); curriculum and instruction—elementary (M Ed); curriculum and instruction—English (M Ed); curriculum and instruction—Spanish (M Ed); human resources (MBA); information security management (MBA); information technology and Web business development (MBA); management (MBA); public policy (MPA); social work (MA), including clinical social work; special education (M Ed); strategic leadership (MBA).

Universidad del Turabo, Graduate Programs, School of Social Sciences and Humanities, Programs in Public Affairs, Program in Criminal Justice Studies, Gurabo, PR 00778-3030. Offers MPA. *Entrance requirements:* For master's, GRE, EXADEP, interview.

Université de Montréal, Faculty of Arts and Sciences, School of Criminology, Montréal, QC H3C 3J7, Canada. Offers M Sc, PhD. Terminal master's awarded for partial completion of doctoral program. *Degree requirements:* For master's, thesis; for doctorate, thesis/dissertation, general exam. *Entrance requirements:* For master's, B Sc in criminology or the equivalent; for doctorate, M Sc in criminology or equivalent. Electronic applications accepted. *Faculty research:* Criminal behavior, criminality, prison population, victims of crime, female offenders.

University at Albany, State University of New York, School of Criminal Justice, Albany, NY 12222-0001. Offers MA, PhD, MSW/MA. Part-time programs available. *Degree requirements:* For doctorate, thesis/dissertation. *Entrance requirements:* For master's and doctorate, GRE General Test. Additional exam requirements/recommendations for international students: Required—TOEFL (minimum score 550 paper-based; 213 computer-based). Electronic applications accepted. *Faculty research:* Causes of delinquency, comparative policing, world crime data, correctional policy, family violence.

The University of Alabama, Graduate School, College of Arts and Sciences, Department of Criminal Justice, Tuscaloosa, AL 35487. Offers MS. Part-time programs available. *Faculty:* 6 full-time (4 women). *Students:* 18 full-time (12 women), 3 part-time (2 women); includes 5 minority (3 Black or African American, non-Hispanic/Latino; 1 Hispanic/Latino; 1 Two or more races, non-Hispanic/Latino). Average age 25. 24 applicants, 63% accepted, 10 enrolled. In 2010, 9 master's awarded. *Degree requirements:* For master's, comprehensive exam, thesis or policy and practice course. *Entrance requirements:* For master's, GRE. Additional exam requirements/recommendations for international students: Required—TOEFL. *Application deadline:* For fall admission, 3/1 priority date for domestic and international students; for winter admission, 11/1 priority date for domestic and international students. Applications are processed on a rolling basis. Application fee: $50 ($60 for international students). Electronic applications accepted. *Expenses:* Tuition, state resident: full-time $7900. Tuition, nonresident: full-time $20,500. *Financial support:* In 2010–11, 1 fellowship (averaging $1,500 per year), 11 teaching assistantships with partial tuition reimbursements (averaging $5,145 per year) were awarded; institutionally sponsored loans, health care benefits, and unspecified assistantships also available. Financial award application deadline: 3/15. *Faculty research:* Domestic violence, AIDS research, youth and violence, gender crime, drugs and alcohol abuse, crime prevention. Total annual research expenditures: $69,986. *Unit head:* Dr. Ida Johnson, Interim Chair and Professor, 205-348-7795, Fax: 205-348-7178, E-mail: ijohnson@ua.edu. *Application contact:* Dr. Celia Lo, Professor, 205-348-3162, Fax: 205-348-7178, E-mail: clo@bama.ua.edu.

The University of Alabama at Birmingham, College of Arts and Sciences, Program in Criminal Justice, Birmingham, AL 35294. Offers MSCJ. Evening/weekend programs available. *Students:* 3 full-time (2 women), 8 part-time (all women); includes 6 Black or African American, non-Hispanic/Latino. Average age 28. 8 applicants, 75% accepted, 4 enrolled. In 2010, 10 master's awarded. *Degree requirements:* For master's, thesis or alternative. *Entrance requirements:* For master's, GRE General Test or MAT. *Application deadline:* Applications are processed on a rolling basis. Electronic applications accepted. *Expenses:* Tuition, state resident: full-time $5482. Tuition, nonresident: full-time $12,430. Tuition and fees vary according to program. *Financial support:* Career-related internships or fieldwork available. *Unit head:* Dr. John J. Sloan, Chair, 205-934-2069. *Application contact:* Julie Bryant, Director of Graduate Admissions, 205-934-8227, Fax: 205-934-8413, E-mail: jbryant@uab.edu.

The University of Alabama in Huntsville, School of Graduate Studies, Interdisciplinary Studies, Interdisciplinary Program in Information Assurance and Cybersecurity, Huntsville, AL 35899. Offers MS, Certificate. Part-time and evening/weekend programs available. *Faculty:* 7 full-time (1 woman), 5 part-time/adjunct (0 women). *Students:* 1 full-time (0 women), 18 part-time (4 women); includes 4 minority (2 Black or African American, non-Hispanic/Latino; 1 American Indian or Alaska Native, non-Hispanic/Latino; 1 Asian, non-Hispanic/Latino). Average age 40. 21 applicants, 90% accepted, 16 enrolled. In 2010, 8 other advanced degrees awarded. *Degree requirements:* For master's, comprehensive exam, thesis or alternative, thesis: 24 hours course work plus 6 hour thesis. *Entrance requirements:* For master's, GRE General Test, minimum GPA of 3.0; for Certificate, GMAT, minimum GPA of 3.0. Additional exam requirements/recommendations for international students: Required—TOEFL (minimum score 550 paper-based; 213 computer-based; 62 iBT). *Application deadline:* For fall admission, 7/15 for domestic students, 4/1 for international students; for spring admission, 11/30 for domestic students, 9/1 for international students. Applications are processed on a rolling basis. Application fee: $40 ($50 for international students). Electronic applications accepted. *Expenses:* Tuition, state resident: full-time $7250; part-time $407.75 per credit hour. Tuition, nonresident: full-time $17,358; part-time $970.05 per credit hour. Required fees: $246.80 per semester. Tuition and fees vary according to course load and program. *Financial support:* Career-related internships or fieldwork, Federal Work-Study, institutionally sponsored loans, scholarships/grants, health care benefits, and unspecified assistantships available. Support available to part-time students. Financial award application deadline: 4/1; financial award applicants required to submit FAFSA. *Faculty research:* Service discovery, enterprise security, security metrics, cryptography, network security. *Unit head:* Dr. Rhonda Kay Gaede, Dean of Graduate Studies, 256-824-6002, Fax: 256-824-6405, E-mail: deangrad@uah.edu. *Application contact:* Jennifer Pettitt, College of Business Administration Director of Graduate Programs, 256-824-6681, Fax: 256-824-7572, E-mail: jennifer.pettitt@uah.edu.

University of Alaska Fairbanks, College of Liberal Arts, Department of Justice, Fairbanks, AK 99775-6120. Offers MA. Part-time programs available. Postbaccalaureate distance learning degree programs offered (no on-campus study). *Faculty:* 5 full-time (1 woman). *Students:* 1 (woman) full-time, 14 part-time (6 women). Average age 40. 13 applicants, 54% accepted, 6 enrolled. In 2010, 3 master's awarded. *Degree requirements:* For master's, comprehensive exam, thesis or alternative, oral defense. *Entrance requirements:* Additional exam requirements/recommendations for international students: Required—TOEFL (minimum score 550 paper-

Criminal Justice and Criminology

University of Alaska Fairbanks (continued)

based; 213 computer-based; 80 iBT). *Application deadline:* For fall admission, 6/1 for domestic students, 3/1 for international students; for spring admission, 10/15 for domestic students, 9/1 for international students. Applications are processed on a rolling basis. Application fee: $60. Electronic applications accepted. *Expenses:* Tuition, state resident: full-time $5688; part-time $316 per credit. Tuition, nonresident: full-time $11,628; part-time $646 per credit. Required fees: $289 per semester. Tuition and fees vary according to course load and reciprocity agreements. *Financial support:* Federal Work-Study, scholarships/grants, and health care benefits available. Support available to part-time students. Financial award application deadline: 7/1; financial award applicants required to submit FAFSA. *Faculty research:* Substantive and procedural law, native Alaskans imprisoned in the Alaska State Department of Corrections, school violence, substance abuse in juveniles, community justice. *Unit head:* Dr. David M. Blurton, Department Chair, 907-474-5500, Fax: 907-474-6510, E-mail: fyjust@uaf.edu. *Application contact:* Dr. David M. Blurton, Department Chair, 907-474-5500, Fax: 907-474-6510, E-mail: fyjust@uaf.edu.

University of Alberta, Faculty of Graduate Studies and Research, Department of Sociology, Edmonton, AB T6G 2E1, Canada. Offers criminal justice (MA); demography (MA, PhD); sociology (MA, PhD). Part-time programs available. *Degree requirements:* For master's, thesis (for some programs); for doctorate, thesis/dissertation. *Faculty research:* Criminology, knowledge and culture, methods and theory, population studies, stratification.

University of Arkansas at Little Rock, Graduate School, College of Professional Studies, Department of Criminal Justice, Little Rock, AR 72204-1099. Offers MA, MS, PhD. MS program is by distance education. Part-time and evening/weekend programs available. *Degree requirements:* For master's, thesis defense or written comprehensive exam; for doctorate, comprehensive exam, thesis/dissertation, research practicum. *Entrance requirements:* For master's, GRE General Test or MAT, interview, minimum GPA of 2.75; for doctorate, GRE General Test, minimum cumulative graduate GPA of 3.5; master's degree in criminology/criminal justice or closely related field; three courses in statistics and research methods at the master's level; transcripts; statement of purpose; career development plan; writing sample; two professional letters of recommendation. Additional exam requirements/recommendations for international students: Required—TOEFL (minimum score 550 paper-based; 213 computer-based; 79 iBT). *Faculty research:* Dissemination and analysis of behavioral science knowledge, leadership and managerial skills, philosophy of individual rights and humane treatment.

University of Baltimore, Graduate School, The Yale Gordon College of Liberal Arts, Division of Criminology, Criminal Justice, and Social Policy, Baltimore, MD 21201-5779. Offers criminal justice (MS); JD/MS. Part-time and evening/weekend programs available. *Degree requirements:* For master's, thesis or alternative. *Entrance requirements:* For master's, interview, minimum GPA of 2.8. Additional exam requirements/recommendations for international students: Required—TOEFL (minimum score 550 paper-based; 213 computer-based). Electronic applications accepted. *Faculty research:* Drugs and violence, police and community policing, women and crime, victimization, correction in community.

University of California, Irvine, School of Social Ecology, Department of Criminology, Law and Society, Irvine, CA 92697. Offers MAS, PhD. *Students:* 100 full-time (63 women), 26 part-time (12 women); includes 52 minority (8 Black or African American, non-Hispanic/Latino; 1 American Indian or Alaska Native, non-Hispanic/Latino; 14 Asian, non-Hispanic/Latino; 22 Hispanic/Latino; 7 Two or more races, non-Hispanic/Latino), 3 international. Average age 28. 141 applicants, 50% accepted, 51 enrolled. In 2010, 20 master's, 7 doctorates awarded. *Degree requirements:* For doctorate, thesis/dissertation, research project. *Entrance requirements:* For master's and doctorate, GRE General Test, minimum GPA of 3.0. Additional exam requirements/recommendations for international students: Required—TOEFL (minimum score 550 paper-based; 213 computer-based). *Application deadline:* For fall admission, 1/15 priority date for domestic and international students. Application fee: $80 ($100 for international students). Electronic applications accepted. *Financial support:* Fellowships, research assistantships with full tuition reimbursements, teaching assistantships, institutionally sponsored loans, traineeships, health care benefits, and unspecified assistantships available. Financial award application deadline: 3/1; financial award applicants required to submit FAFSA. *Faculty research:* White-collar and corporate crime; immigration, the poor, homelessness, and governmental regulation; sentencing, community corrections, and diversion; mathematical and scientific evidence in jury trials; legal and criminological theory development. *Unit head:* Prof. Simon A. Cole, Chair, 949-824-1437, Fax: 949-824-3001, E-mail: scole@uci.edu. *Application contact:* Maria Victoria Dela Cruz, Director, Graduate Services, 949-824-5918, Fax: 949-824-1845, E-mail: mvdelacr@uci.edu.

University of Central Florida, College of Health and Public Affairs, Department of Criminal Justice and Legal Studies, Orlando, FL 32816. Offers corrections leadership (Certificate); crime analysis (Certificate); criminal justice (MS); juvenile justice leadership (Certificate); police leadership (Certificate). Part-time and evening/weekend programs available. *Faculty:* 26 full-time (8 women), 12 part-time/adjunct (1 woman). *Students:* 83 full-time (53 women), 147 part-time (87 women); includes 70 minority (45 Black or African American, non-Hispanic/Latino; 2 American Indian or Alaska Native, non-Hispanic/Latino; 4 Asian, non-Hispanic/Latino; 18 Hispanic/Latino; 1 Two or more races, non-Hispanic/Latino). Average age 30. 165 applicants, 80% accepted, 87 enrolled. In 2010, 73 master's, 17 other advanced degrees awarded. *Degree requirements:* For master's, thesis or alternative. *Entrance requirements:* For master's, GRE General Test, minimum GPA of 3.0. Additional exam requirements/recommendations for international students: Required—TOEFL. *Application deadline:* For fall admission, 7/15 for domestic students; for spring admission, 4/15 for domestic students. Electronic applications accepted. *Expenses:* Tuition, state resident: part-time $256.56 per credit hour. Tuition, nonresident: part-time $1011.52 per credit hour. Part-time tuition and fees vary according to program. *Financial support:* In 2010–11, 6 students received support, including 2 fellowships with partial tuition reimbursements available (averaging $5,200 per year), 5 teaching assistantships with partial tuition reimbursements available (averaging $6,400 per year); career-related internships or fieldwork, Federal Work-Study, institutionally sponsored loans, tuition waivers (partial), and unspecified assistantships also available. Financial award application deadline: 3/1; financial award applicants required to submit FAFSA. *Unit head:* Dr. Robert Langworthy, Chair, 407-823-5929, E-mail: rlangwor@mail.ucf.edu. *Application contact:* Dr. Robert Langworthy, Chair, 407-823-5929, E-mail: rlangwor@mail.ucf.edu.

University of Central Missouri, The Graduate School, College of Health and Human Services, Warrensburg, MO 64093. Offers criminal justice (MS); industrial hygiene (MS); occupational safety management (MS); physical education/exercise and sport science (MS); rural family nursing (MS); social gerontology (MS); sociology (MA); speech language pathology and audiology (MS). *Accreditation:* NCATE. Part-time programs available. Postbaccalaureate distance learning degree programs offered. *Entrance requirements:* Additional exam requirements/recommendations for international students: Required—TOEFL (minimum score 550 paper-based; 79 computer-based). Electronic applications accepted.

University of Central Oklahoma, College of Graduate Studies and Research, College of Liberal Arts, Department of Sociology, Criminal Justice and Substance Abuse Studies, Edmond, OK 73034-5209. Offers criminal justice management and administration (MA). Part-time programs available. *Entrance requirements:* Additional exam requirements/recommendations for international students: Required—TOEFL (minimum score 550 paper-based; 213 computer-based). Electronic applications accepted. *Faculty research:* Gender issues, violent offenders.

University of Cincinnati, Graduate School, College of Education, Criminal Justice, and Human Services, Division of Criminal Justice, Cincinnati, OH 45221. Offers MS, PhD. Part-time programs available. Postbaccalaureate distance learning degree programs offered (no on-campus study). *Degree requirements:* For master's, thesis or alternative; for doctorate, thesis/dissertation. *Entrance requirements:* For master's, GRE or MAT, minimum GPA of 3.0; for doctorate, minimum GPA of 3.5. Additional exam requirements/recommendations for international students: Required—TOEFL (minimum score 550 paper-based), OEPT 3. Electronic applications accepted.

University of Colorado at Colorado Springs, Graduate School of Public Affairs, Colorado Springs, CO 80933-7150. Offers criminal justice (MCJ); public administration (MPA). Part-time and evening/weekend programs available. *Faculty:* 7 full-time (2 women). *Students:* 14 full-time (9 women), 3 part-time (1 woman); includes 1 Black or African American, non-Hispanic/Latino; 2 Asian, non-Hispanic/Latino; 4 Hispanic/Latino. Average age 34. 56 applicants, 88% accepted. In 2010, 18 master's awarded. *Degree requirements:* For master's, thesis optional, internship (if no experience), capstone project. *Entrance requirements:* For master's, GRE General Test, GMAT, LSAT, minimum GPA of 3.0. *Application deadline:* For fall admission, 6/1 priority date for domestic students; for spring admission, 11/1 priority date for domestic students. Applications are processed on a rolling basis. Application fee: $60 ($75 for international students). *Expenses:* Contact institution. *Financial support:* Career-related internships or fieldwork, Federal Work-Study, and scholarships/grants available. Support available to part-time students. Financial award application deadline: 3/1; financial award applicants required to submit FAFSA. Total annual research expenditures: $16,459. *Unit head:* Dr. Terry Schwartz, Dean, 719-255-4047, Fax: 719-255-4183, E-mail: tschwart@uccs.edu. *Application contact:* Mary Lou Kartis, Program Assistant, 719-255-4182, Fax: 719-255-4183, E-mail: mkartis@uccs.edu.

University of Colorado Denver, School of Public Affairs, Department of Criminology and Criminal Justice, Denver, CO 80217. Offers criminal justice (MCJ), including criminal justice, domestic violence, emergency management and homeland security. Part-time and evening/weekend programs available. *Faculty:* 7 full-time (4 women), 3 part-time/adjunct (2 women). *Students:* 35 full-time (23 women), 26 part-time (20 women); includes 3 Black or African American, non-Hispanic/Latino; 2 American Indian or Alaska Native, non-Hispanic/Latino; 3 Asian, non-Hispanic/Latino; 11 Hispanic/Latino, 1 international. Average age 31. 45 applicants, 80% accepted, 15 enrolled. In 2010, 28 master's awarded. *Degree requirements:* For master's, thesis or alternative, 36-39 semester credit hours. *Entrance requirements:* For master's, GRE, recommendations, official transcripts, current resume. Additional exam requirements/recommendations for international students: Required—TOEFL (minimum score 525 paper-based; 197 computer-based). *Application deadline:* For fall admission, 3/15 priority date for domestic students; for spring admission, 10/15 priority date for domestic students. Application fee: $50 ($75 for international students). Electronic applications accepted. *Expenses:* Contact institution. *Financial support:* Federal Work-Study and scholarships/grants available. Support available to part-time students. Financial award application deadline: 4/1; financial award applicants required to submit FAFSA. *Faculty research:* White collar crime, women and the criminal justice system, applied family violence issues, intimate partner violence and domestic violence interventions, juvenile delinquency. *Unit head:* Dr. Mary Dodge, Director, 303-315-2086, Fax: 303-315-2229, E-mail: mary.dodge@ucdenver.edu. *Application contact:* Brendan Hardy, Criminal Justice Coordinator, 303-315-2227, Fax: 303-315-2229, E-mail: brendan.hardy@ucdenver.edu.

University of Colorado Denver, School of Public Affairs, Program in Public Affairs and Administration, Denver, CO 80127. Offers public administration (MPA), including domestic violence, emergency management and homeland security, environmental policy, management and law, homeland security and defense, local government, nonprofit management, public administration; public affairs (PhD). *Accreditation:* NASPAA. Part-time and evening/weekend programs available. Postbaccalaureate distance learning degree programs offered (no on-campus study). *Faculty:* 19 full-time (9 women), 14 part-time/adjunct (5 women). *Students:* 317 full-time (181 women), 167 part-time (100 women); includes 15 Black or African American, non-Hispanic/Latino; 2 American Indian or Alaska Native, non-Hispanic/Latino; 18 Asian, non-Hispanic/Latino; 29 Hispanic/Latino; 1 Two or more races, non-Hispanic/Latino, 36 international. Average age 30. 270 applicants, 66% accepted, 118 enrolled. In 2010, 119 master's, 4 doctorates awarded. *Degree requirements:* For master's, thesis or alternative, 36-39 credit hours; for doctorate, comprehensive exam, thesis/dissertation, minimum of 66 semester hours, including at least 30 hours of doctoral dissertation credits. *Entrance requirements:* For master's and doctorate, GRE, resume, essay, transcripts, recommendations. Additional exam requirements/recommendations for international students: Required—TOEFL (minimum score 550 paper-based; 223 computer-based). *Application deadline:* For fall admission, 2/1 for domestic students; for spring admission, 10/15 priority date for domestic students. Application fee: $50 ($75 for international students). Electronic applications accepted. *Expenses:* Contact institution. *Financial support:* Fellowships with partial tuition reimbursements, research assistantships with partial tuition reimbursements, teaching assistantships with partial tuition reimbursements, Federal Work-Study and scholarships/grants available. Support available to part-time students. Financial award application deadline: 4/1; financial award applicants required to submit FAFSA. *Faculty research:* Housing, education and the social and economic issues of vulnerable populations; nonprofit governance and management; education finance, effectiveness and reform; P-20 (preschool through graduate school) education initiatives; municipal government accountability. *Unit head:* Dr. Mary Guy, Program Director, 303-315-2007, Fax: 303-315-2229, E-mail: mary.guy@ucdenver.edu. *Application contact:* Annie Davies, Director of Marketing, Community Outreach and Alumni Affairs, 303-315-2896, Fax: 303-315-2229, E-mail: annie.davies@ucdenver.edu.

University of Delaware, College of Arts and Sciences, Department of Sociology and Criminology, Newark, DE 19716. Offers criminology (MA, PhD); sociology (MA, PhD). *Degree requirements:* For master's, thesis; for doctorate, comprehensive exam, thesis/dissertation. *Entrance requirements:* For master's and doctorate, GRE, 3 letters of recommendation. Additional exam requirements/recommendations for international students: Required—TOEFL. Electronic applications accepted. *Faculty research:* Sex and gender, criminology/deviance, theory, methods, collective behavior.

University of Denver, University College, Denver, CO 80208. Offers arts and culture (MLS, Certificate), including art, literature, and culture, arts development and program management (Certificate), creative writing; environmental policy and management (MAS, Certificate), including energy and sustainability (Certificate), environmental assessment of nuclear power (Certificate), environmental health and safety (Certificate), environmental management, natural resource management (Certificate); geographic information systems (MAS, Certificate); global affairs (MLS, Certificate), including translation studies, world history and culture; healthcare leadership (MPH, Certificate), including healthcare policy, law, and ethics, medical and healthcare information technologies, strategic management of healthcare; information and communications technology (MCIS, Certificate), including database design and administration (Certificate), geographic information systems (MCIS), information security systems security (Certificate), information systems security (MCIS), project management (MCIS, MPS, Certificate), software design and administration (Certificate), software design and programming (MCIS), technology management, telecommunications technology (MCIS), Web design and development; leadership and organizations (MPS, Certificate), including human capital in organizations, philanthropic leadership, project management (MCIS, MPS, Certificate), strategic innovation and change; organizational and professional communication (MPS, Certificate), including alternative dispute resolution, organizational communication, organizational development and training, public relations and marketing; security management (MAS, Certificate), including emergency planning and response, information security (MAS), organizational security; strategic human resource management (MPS, Certificate), including global human resources (MPS), human resource management and development (MPS). Part-time and evening/weekend programs available. Postbaccalaureate distance learning degree programs offered (no on-campus study). *Faculty:* 7 full-time (2 women), 212 part-time/adjunct (83 women). *Students:* 52 full-time (19 women), 1,044 part-time (625 women); includes 196 minority (81 Black or African American, non-Hispanic/Latino; 7 American Indian or Alaska Native, non-Hispanic/Latino; 30 Asian, non-Hispanic/Latino; 66 Hispanic/Latino; 3 Native Hawaiian or other Pacific Islander, non-Hispanic/Latino; 9 Two or more races, non-Hispanic/Latino), 76 international. Average age 36. 488 applicants, 91% accepted, 339 enrolled. In 2010, 286 master's, 130 other advanced degrees awarded. *Entrance requirements:* Additional exam requirements/recommendations for international students: Required—TOEFL (minimum score 550 paper-based; 80 iBT). *Application deadline:*

For fall admission, 6/22 priority date for domestic students, 6/10 priority date for international students; for winter admission, 9/15 priority date for domestic students, 9/6 priority date for international students; for spring admission, 2/3 priority date for domestic students, 12/15 priority date for international students. Applications are processed on a rolling basis. Application fee: $75. Electronic applications accepted. *Expenses:* Contact institution. *Financial support:* Applicants required to submit FAFSA. *Unit head:* Dr. James Davis, Dean, 303-871-2291, Fax: 303-871-4047, E-mail: jdavis@du.edu. *Application contact:* Information Contact, 303-871-3155, Fax: 303-871-4047, E-mail: ucolinfo@du.edu.

University of Detroit Mercy, College of Liberal Arts and Education, Department of Criminal Justice and Human Services, Program in Criminal Justice Studies, Detroit, MI 48221. Offers MA. Part-time and evening/weekend programs available. *Degree requirements:* For master's, thesis or alternative. *Entrance requirements:* For master's, minimum GPA of 2.75. *Faculty research:* Socialization and social control, law and correction practices.

University of Detroit Mercy, College of Liberal Arts and Education, Department of Criminal Justice and Human Services, Program in Security Administration, Detroit, MI 48221. Offers MS. Part-time and evening/weekend programs available. *Degree requirements:* For master's, thesis or alternative. *Entrance requirements:* For master's, minimum GPA of 2.75. *Faculty research:* Physical information and personnel security.

University of Florida, Graduate School, College of Liberal Arts and Sciences, Department of Criminology, Law and Society, Gainesville, FL 32611. Offers MA, PhD, MA/JD, MA/PhD. Part-time programs available. *Faculty:* 18 full-time (9 women), 4 part-time/adjunct (1 woman). *Students:* 83 full-time (54 women), 18 part-time (14 women); includes 12 Black or African American, non-Hispanic/Latino; 3 Asian, non-Hispanic/Latino; 13 Hispanic/Latino, 13 international. Average age 29. 128 applicants, 25% accepted, 20 enrolled. In 2010, 7 master's, 8 doctorates awarded. Terminal master's awarded for partial completion of doctoral program. *Degree requirements:* For master's, thesis optional; for doctorate, comprehensive exam, thesis/dissertation. *Entrance requirements:* For master's and doctorate, GRE (minimum score of 1000), minimum GPA of 3.0. Additional exam requirements/recommendations for international students: Required—TOEFL (minimum score 550 paper-based; 213 computer-based; 80 iBT), IELTS (minimum score 6). *Application deadline:* For fall admission, 1/15 for domestic and international students; for spring admission, 6/1 for domestic and international students. Applications are processed on a rolling basis. Application fee: $30. Electronic applications accepted. *Expenses:* Tuition, state resident: full-time $10,915.92. Tuition, nonresident: full-time $28,309. *Financial support:* In 2010–11, 84 students received support, including 23 fellowships, 8 research assistantships (averaging $17,772 per year), 53 teaching assistantships (averaging $21,543 per year). Financial award application deadline: 1/15; financial award applicants required to submit FAFSA. *Faculty research:* Law and society, juvenile justice, criminal investigation procedures, deviance, biosocial criminology, environmental sociology, comparative race and ethnic studies, health and aging, families and gender. Total annual research expenditures: $187,795. *Unit head:* Dr. Constance L. Shehan, Chair, 352-392-0265 Ext. 254, Fax: 352-392-5065, E-mail: cshehan@ufl.edu. *Application contact:* Dr. Barbara Zsembik, Graduate Coordinator, 352-392-0265 Ext. 226, Fax: 352-392-6568, E-mail: zsembik@soc.ufl.edu.

University of Great Falls, Graduate Studies, Program in Criminal Justice, Great Falls, MT 59405. Offers MSM. Part-time and evening/weekend programs available. *Degree requirements:* For master's, thesis optional. *Entrance requirements:* For master's, GRE General Test or MAT, 3 letters of recommendation. Additional exam requirements/recommendations for international students: Required—TOEFL (minimum score 500 paper-based; 205 computer-based). Electronic applications accepted. *Faculty research:* Delinquency, domestic violence law.

University of Guelph, Graduate Studies, College of Social and Applied Human Sciences, Department of Criminology and Criminal Justice Policy, Guelph, ON N1G 2W1, Canada. Offers MA. *Degree requirements:* For master's, thesis or major paper. *Entrance requirements:* For master's, minimum B+ average during previous 2 years of coursework. Electronic applications accepted.

University of Guelph, Graduate Studies, College of Social and Applied Human Sciences, Department of Sociology and Anthropology, Guelph, ON N1G 2W1, Canada. Offers anthropology (MA); crime and criminal justice policy (MA); sociology (MA, PhD). *Degree requirements:* For master's, thesis or major paper; for doctorate, comprehensive exam, thesis/dissertation. *Entrance requirements:* For master's, minimum B+ average during previous 2 years of course work, honors BA or equivalent; for doctorate, must have an MA in Sociology, must have 80% or higher in graduate level studies. Additional exam requirements/recommendations for international students: Required—TOEFL (minimum score 550 paper-based; 213 computer-based; 89 iBT), IELTS (minimum score 6.5), TOEFL or IELTS. Electronic applications accepted. *Faculty research:* Rural and development sociology; education, employment, and the workplace; race, ethnicity, and native studies; criminology and deviance; social psychology.

University of Houston–Clear Lake, School of Human Sciences and Humanities, Programs in Human Sciences, Houston, TX 77058-1098. Offers behavioral sciences (MA), including criminology, cross cultural studies, general psychology, sociology; clinical psychology (MA); criminology (MA); cross cultural studies (MA); family therapy (MA); fitness and human performance (MA); school psychology (MA). *Accreditation:* AAMFT/COAMFTE. Part-time and evening/weekend programs available. Postbaccalaureate distance learning degree programs offered (minimal on-campus study). *Degree requirements:* For master's, thesis or alternative. *Entrance requirements:* For master's, GRE General Test. Additional exam requirements/recommendations for international students: Required—TOEFL (minimum score 550 paper-based; 213 computer-based). Electronic applications accepted. *Faculty research:* Smoking cessation, adolescent sexuality, white collar crime, serial murder, human factors/human computer interaction.

University of Houston–Downtown, College of Public Service, Department of Criminal Justice, Houston, TX 77002. Offers MS. Part-time and evening/weekend programs available. *Faculty:* 7 full-time (3 women). *Students:* 4 full-time (2 women), 60 part-time (28 women); includes 18 Black or African American, non-Hispanic/Latino; 5 Asian, non-Hispanic/Latino; 21 Hispanic/Latino. Average age 34. 20 applicants, 85% accepted, 16 enrolled. In 2010, 13 master's awarded. *Degree requirements:* For master's, thesis or project. *Entrance requirements:* For master's, GRE, MAT or GMAT, personal statement, 3 letters of recommendation. Additional exam requirements/recommendations for international students: Required—TOEFL (minimum score 550 paper-based; 213 computer-based; 80 iBT). *Application deadline:* For fall admission, 8/1 for domestic students, 5/1 for international students; for spring admission, 11/15 for domestic students, 10/1 for international students. Applications are processed on a rolling basis. Application fee: $35 ($60 for international students). Electronic applications accepted. *Expenses:* Tuition, state resident: full-time $4280; part-time $183 per credit hour. Tuition, nonresident: full-time $9230; part-time $458 per credit hour. Required fees: $390 per term. *Financial support:* Federal Work-Study and scholarships/grants available. Financial award applicants required to submit FAFSA. *Faculty research:* Criminal justice education, issues in law enforcement, issues in security, adult probation, legal issues in prisons. *Unit head:* Dr. Clete Snell, Chair, 713-221-8943, Fax: 713-221-2726, E-mail: snellc@uhd.edu. *Application contact:* Dr. Traqina Emeka, Assistant Professor and Graduate Coordinator, 713-221-8282, Fax: 713-221-2726, E-mail: emekat@uhd.edu.

University of Houston–Downtown, College of Public Service, Master of Security Management for Executives Program, Houston, TX 77002. Offers MSM. Part-time and evening/weekend programs available. *Faculty:* 3 full-time (1 woman), 1 part-time/adjunct (0 women). *Students:* 27 part-time (5 women); includes 5 Black or African American, non-Hispanic/Latino; 5 Hispanic/Latino. Average age 40. 19 applicants, 100% accepted, 18 enrolled. In 2010, 14 master's awarded. *Degree requirements:* For master's, capstone project. *Entrance requirements:* For master's, letter of intent, 3 letters of recommendation from supervisors indicating probability of applicant's success in program, proof of three years of paid work experience with supervisory or managerial responsibilities. Additional exam requirements/recommendations for international students: Required—TOEFL (minimum score 550 paper-based; 213 computer-based; 80 iBT). *Application deadline:* For fall admission, 8/10 for domestic students, 5/1 for international students. Applications are processed on a rolling basis. Application fee: $35 ($60 for international students). Electronic applications accepted. *Expenses:* Tuition, state resident: full-time $4280; part-time $183 per credit hour. Tuition, nonresident: full-time $9230; part-time $458 per credit hour. Required fees: $390 per term. *Financial support:* Federal Work-Study available. Financial award applicants required to submit FAFSA. *Unit head:* Dr. Beth Pelz, Dean, College of Public Service, 713-221-8194, Fax: 713-226-5274, E-mail: pelzb@uhd.edu. *Application contact:* John Presley, Executive Director, 713-221-5292, Fax: 713-226-5274, E-mail: presleyj@uhd.edu.

University of Illinois at Chicago, Graduate College, College of Liberal Arts and Sciences, Department of Criminal Justice, Chicago, IL 60607-7128. Offers MA, PhD. Evening/weekend programs available. *Degree requirements:* For master's, thesis. *Entrance requirements:* For master's, GRE General Test, minimum GPA of 3.0. Additional exam requirements/recommendations for international students: Required—TOEFL. Electronic applications accepted. *Faculty research:* Sentencing probation, police and court use of scientific evidence, community mediation and conflict resolution.

University of Louisiana at Monroe, Graduate School, College of Arts and Sciences, Program in Criminal Justice, Monroe, LA 71209-0001. Offers MA. Part-time and evening/weekend programs available. *Faculty:* 5 full-time (2 women). *Students:* 7 full-time (4 women), 12 part-time (7 women); includes 9 Black or African American, non-Hispanic/Latino. Average age 30. In 2010, 5 master's awarded. *Degree requirements:* For master's, thesis (for some programs). *Entrance requirements:* For master's, GRE General Test, minimum GPA of 2.5. Additional exam requirements/recommendations for international students: Required—TOEFL (minimum score 500 paper-based; 173 computer-based; 61 iBT). *Application deadline:* For fall admission, 8/24 priority date for domestic students, 7/1 for international students; for winter admission, 12/14 priority date for domestic students; for spring admission, 1/19 for domestic students, 11/1 for international students. Applications are processed on a rolling basis. Application fee: $20 ($30 for international students). Electronic applications accepted. *Expenses:* Tuition, state resident: full-time $2991; part-time $197 per credit hour. Tuition, nonresident: full-time $2991; part-time $197 per credit hour. International tuition: $10,288 full-time. *Financial support:* In 2010–11, 2 research assistantships with full tuition reimbursements (averaging $2,500 per year) were awarded; career-related internships or fieldwork, Federal Work-Study, and unspecified assistantships also available. Financial award application deadline: 4/1; financial award applicants required to submit FAFSA. *Unit head:* Dr. Robert D. Hanser, Department Head, 318-342-1440, Fax: 318-342-1431, E-mail: hanser@ulm.edu. *Application contact:* Dr. Robert D. Hanser, Department Head, 318-342-1440, Fax: 318-342-1431, E-mail: hanser@ulm.edu.

University of Louisville, Graduate School, College of Arts and Sciences, Department of Justice Administration, Louisville, KY 40292. Offers MS. Part-time and evening/weekend programs available. Postbaccalaureate distance learning degree programs offered (no on-campus study). *Faculty:* 13 full-time (4 women), 5 part-time/adjunct (2 women). *Students:* 23 full-time (11 women), 51 part-time (24 women); includes 13 Black or African American, non-Hispanic/Latino; 2 Two or more races, non-Hispanic/Latino. Average age 33. 35 applicants, 91% accepted, 25 enrolled. In 2010, 23 master's awarded. *Degree requirements:* For master's, comprehensive exam (for some programs), thesis (for some programs), professional paper. *Entrance requirements:* For master's, GRE General Test, 2 letters of recommendation. Additional exam requirements/recommendations for international students: Required—TOEFL (minimum score 550 paper-based; 213 computer-based; 79 iBT). *Application deadline:* For fall admission, 7/1 priority date for domestic and international students; for spring admission, 11/15 priority date for domestic and international students. Applications are processed on a rolling basis. Application fee: $50. Electronic applications accepted. *Expenses:* Tuition, state resident: full-time $9144; part-time $508 per credit hour. Tuition, nonresident: full-time $19,026; part-time $1057 per credit hour. Tuition and fees vary according to program and reciprocity agreements. *Financial support:* In 2010–11, 6 students received support, including 6 research assistantships with full tuition reimbursements available (averaging $13,622 per year); health care benefits also available. Financial award application deadline: 8/1; financial award applicants required to submit FAFSA. *Faculty research:* Applied research, program evaluation and policy analysis in criminal justice; juvenile sex offender research; theoretical criminology; crime analysis; organizational and leadership management. Total annual research expenditures: $137,442. *Unit head:* Dr. Deborah G. Keeling, Chair, 502-852-6567, Fax: 502-852-0065, E-mail: dgwilson@louisville.edu. *Application contact:* Libby Leggett, Director, Graduate Admissions, 502-852-3101, Fax: 502-852-6536, E-mail: gradadm@louisville.edu.

University of Management and Technology, Program in Criminal Justice, Arlington, VA 22209. Offers MS.

The University of Manchester, School of Law, Manchester, United Kingdom. Offers bioethics and medical jurisprudence (PhD); criminology (M Phil, PhD); law (M Phil, PhD).

University of Maryland, College Park, Academic Affairs, College of Behavioral and Social Sciences, Department of Criminology and Criminal Justice, College Park, MD 20742. Offers MA, PhD, JD/MA. Part-time and evening/weekend programs available. *Faculty:* 23 full-time (9 women), 18 part-time/adjunct (6 women). *Students:* 63 full-time (47 women), 21 part-time (12 women); includes 2 Black or African American, non-Hispanic/Latino; 2 Asian, non-Hispanic/Latino; 5 Hispanic/Latino; 1 Two or more races, non-Hispanic/Latino, 28 international. 108 applicants, 20% accepted, 10 enrolled. In 2010, 44 master's, 4 doctorates awarded. Terminal master's awarded for partial completion of doctoral program. *Degree requirements:* For master's, comprehensive exam, thesis optional; for doctorate, comprehensive exam, thesis/dissertation. *Entrance requirements:* For master's, GRE General Test, minimum GPA of 3.0, 3 letters of recommendation; for doctorate, GRE General Test. Additional exam requirements/recommendations for international students: Required—TOEFL. *Application deadline:* For fall admission, 12/1 for domestic and international students. Applications are processed on a rolling basis. Application fee: $75. Electronic applications accepted. *Expenses:* Tuition, state resident: part-time $471 per credit hour. Tuition, nonresident: part-time $1016 per credit hour. Required fees: $337 per term. *Financial support:* In 2010–11, 4 fellowships with full tuition reimbursements (averaging $19,250 per year), 2 research assistantships (averaging $15,992 per year), 31 teaching assistantships (averaging $15,820 per year) were awarded; Federal Work-Study and scholarships/grants also available. Support available to part-time students. Financial award applicants required to submit FAFSA. *Faculty research:* Theory, crime prevention, death penalty, criminal justice technology, policy. Total annual research expenditures: $930,777. *Unit head:* Dr. Sally Simpson, Chair, 301-405-4699, Fax: 301-405-4733, E-mail: ssimpson@umd.edu. *Application contact:* Dean of Graduate School, 301-405-0358, Fax: 301-314-9305.

University of Maryland Eastern Shore, Graduate Programs, Department of Criminal Justice, Princess Anne, MD 21853-1299. Offers criminology and criminal justice (MS). Part-time and evening/weekend programs available. *Degree requirements:* For master's, comprehensive exam, thesis optional. *Entrance requirements:* For master's, GRE General Test, interview. Additional exam requirements/recommendations for international students: Required—TOEFL (minimum score 213 computer-based; 80 iBT).

University of Massachusetts Lowell, College of Arts and Sciences, Department of Criminal Justice and Criminology, Lowell, MA 01854-2881. Offers MA. Part-time and evening/weekend programs available. *Degree requirements:* For master's, thesis optional. *Entrance requirements:* For master's, GRE General Test or MAT. Electronic applications accepted. *Faculty research:* Family violence, criminal justice management, corrections, policing, delinquency.

University of Memphis, Graduate School, College of Arts and Sciences, Department of Criminology and Criminal Justice, Memphis, TN 38152. Offers MA. Part-time programs available. *Faculty:* 3 full-time (1 woman), 2 part-time/adjunct (0 women). *Students:* 8 full-time (6 women),

Criminal Justice and Criminology

University of Memphis (continued)

10 part-time (4 women); includes 4 Black or African American, non-Hispanic/Latino. Average age 27. 11 applicants, 82% accepted, 5 enrolled. In 2010, 4 master's awarded. *Degree requirements:* For master's, comprehensive exam, thesis optional. *Entrance requirements:* For master's, GRE General Test, minimum GPA of 3.0. Additional exam requirements/recommendations for international students: Required—TOEFL. *Application deadline:* For fall admission, 6/1 for domestic students; for spring admission, 11/1 for domestic students. Application fee: $35 ($60 for international students). *Financial support:* In 2010–11, 11 students received support; research assistantships with full tuition reimbursements available, teaching assistantships with full tuition reimbursements available, career-related internships or fieldwork, Federal Work-Study, institutionally sponsored loans, scholarships/grants, tuition waivers (partial), and unspecified assistantships available. Financial award application deadline: 2/15; financial award applicants required to submit FAFSA. *Faculty research:* Violence, crime prevention, crime analysis, survey research, crisis intervention. *Unit head:* Prof. W. Randolph Dupont, Chair, 901-678-2737, Fax: 901-678-5279, E-mail: rdupont@memphis.edu. *Application contact:* Dr. K. B. Turner, Coordinator of Graduate Studies, 901-678-2737, Fax: 901-678-5279, E-mail: kbturner@memphis.edu.

University of Minnesota, Duluth, Graduate School, College of Liberal Arts, Department of Sociology/Anthropology, Program in Criminology, Duluth, MN 55812-2496. Offers MA. Part-time and evening/weekend programs available. *Degree requirements:* For master's, thesis or alternative. *Entrance requirements:* For master's, minimum GPA of 3.0, letter of recommendation, personal statement. Additional exam requirements/recommendations for international students: Required—TOEFL. *Faculty research:* Restorative justice, juvenile delinquency, social justice, program evaluation.

University of Missouri–Kansas City, College of Arts and Sciences, Department of Criminal Justice and Criminology, Kansas City, MO 64110-2499. Offers MS. Part-time and evening/weekend programs available. *Faculty:* 8 full-time (4 women). *Students:* 6 full-time (5 women), 25 part-time (16 women); includes 7 minority (3 Black or African American, non-Hispanic/Latino; 1 American Indian or Alaska Native, non-Hispanic/Latino; 1 Asian, non-Hispanic/Latino; 1 Hispanic/Latino; 1 Two or more races, non-Hispanic/Latino), 1 international. Average age 29. 21 applicants, 57% accepted, 10 enrolled. In 2010, 7 master's awarded. *Degree requirements:* For master's, thesis optional. *Entrance requirements:* For master's, GRE, minimum GPA of 3.0 in major, 2.7 overall. Additional exam requirements/recommendations for international students: Required—TOEFL (minimum score 550 paper-based; 213 computer-based; 80 iBT). *Application deadline:* For fall admission, 3/1 for domestic and international students; for spring admission, 11/1 for domestic and international students. Applications are processed on a rolling basis. Application fee: $45 ($50 for international students). Electronic applications accepted. *Expenses:* Tuition, state resident: full-time $5522.40; part-time $306.80 per credit hour. Tuition, nonresident: full-time $7128; part-time $792 per credit hour. Required fees: $261.15 per term. *Financial support:* In 2010–11, 1 research assistantship with full tuition reimbursement (averaging $10,667 per year), 3 teaching assistantships with full and partial tuition reimbursements (averaging $10,667 per year) were awarded; career-related internships or fieldwork, Federal Work-Study, institutionally sponsored loans, and tuition waivers (partial) also available. Support available to part-time students. Financial award application deadline: 3/1; financial award applicants required to submit FAFSA. *Faculty research:* Death penalty, community corrections, urban community and neighborhoods. Total annual research expenditures: $29,617. *Unit head:* Dr. Ken Novak, Chair, 816-235-1599, Fax: 816-235-5193, E-mail: novakk@umkc.edu. *Application contact:* Dr. Wayne L. Lucas, Graduate Advisor, 816-235-1598, Fax: 816-235-5193, E-mail: lucasw@umkc.edu.

University of Missouri–St. Louis, College of Arts and Sciences, Department of Criminology and Criminal Justice, St. Louis, MO 63121. Offers MA, PhD. *Faculty:* 12 full-time (5 women), 1 part-time/adjunct (0 women). *Students:* 29 full-time (19 women), 40 part-time (25 women); includes 8 Black or African American, non-Hispanic/Latino; 1 American Indian or Alaska Native, non-Hispanic/Latino; 2 Asian, non-Hispanic/Latino; 1 Hispanic/Latino, 3 international. Average age 29. In 2010, 11 master's, 3 doctorates awarded. *Degree requirements:* For doctorate, thesis/dissertation. *Entrance requirements:* For master's, essay; 2 letters of recommendation; for doctorate, GRE General Test, writing sample, 3 letters of recommendation. Additional exam requirements/recommendations for international students: Required—TOEFL (minimum score 550 paper-based; 213 computer-based). *Application deadline:* For fall admission, 4/1 priority date for domestic and international students. Applications are processed on a rolling basis. Application fee: $35 ($40 for international students). Electronic applications accepted. *Expenses:* Tuition, state resident: full-time $5522; part-time $306.80 per credit hour. Tuition, nonresident: full-time $14,253; part-time $792.10 per credit hour. Required fees: $658; $49 per credit hour. One-time fee: $12. Tuition and fees vary according to program. *Financial support:* In 2010–11, 14 research assistantships with full and partial tuition reimbursements (averaging $14,053 per year), 8 teaching assistantships with full and partial tuition reimbursements (averaging $13,500 per year) were awarded; fellowships with full tuition reimbursements, career-related internships or fieldwork also available. Financial award applicants required to submit FAFSA. *Faculty research:* Crime control, criminological theory, juvenile delinquency, violence, drugs. *Unit head:* Dr. Beth Huebner, Director of Graduate Studies, 314-516-5031, Fax: 314-516-5048, E-mail: huebner@umsl.edu. *Application contact:* 314-516-5458, Fax: 314-516-6996, E-mail: gradadm@umsl.edu.

The University of Montana, Graduate School, College of Arts and Sciences, Department of Sociology, Missoula, MT 59812-0002. Offers criminology (MA); rural and environmental change (MA); sociology (MA). *Entrance requirements:* For master's, GRE General Test. Additional exam requirements/recommendations for international students: Required—TOEFL. *Faculty research:* Housing, homelessness, hunger, infant mortality, work safety.

University of Nebraska at Omaha, Graduate Studies, College of Public Affairs and Community Service, Department of Criminal Justice, Omaha, NE 68182. Offers MA, MS, PhD. Part-time and evening/weekend programs available. *Faculty:* 19 full-time (10 women). *Students:* 22 full-time (13 women), 28 part-time (15 women); includes 5 minority (1 Black or African American, non-Hispanic/Latino; 1 Asian, non-Hispanic/Latino; 3 Hispanic/Latino), 4 international. Average age 31. 41 applicants, 54% accepted, 12 enrolled. In 2010, 13 master's, 2 doctorates awarded. Terminal master's awarded for partial completion of doctoral program. *Degree requirements:* For master's, comprehensive exam, thesis (for some programs); for doctorate, comprehensive exam, thesis/dissertation. *Entrance requirements:* For master's, GRE General Test or MAT, previous course work in criminal justice, statistics, and research methods; minimum GPA of 3.0; for doctorate, GRE General Test, letters of recommendation, statement of intent. Additional exam requirements/recommendations for international students: Required—TOEFL (minimum score 550 paper-based; 213 computer-based; 80 iBT). *Application deadline:* For fall admission, 2/15 for domestic students; for spring admission, 12/1 priority date for domestic students. Applications are processed on a rolling basis. Application fee: $45. Electronic applications accepted. *Financial support:* In 2010–11, 34 students received support; research assistantships with tuition reimbursements available, teaching assistantships with tuition reimbursements available, career-related internships or fieldwork, Federal Work-Study, institutionally sponsored loans, scholarships/grants, tuition waivers (partial), and unspecified assistantships available. Support available to part-time students. Financial award application deadline: 3/1; financial award applicants required to submit FAFSA. *Unit head:* Dr. Candice Batton, Head, 402-554-2610. *Application contact:* Dr. Lisa Sample, Student Contact, 402-554-2610.

University of Nevada, Las Vegas, Graduate College, Greenspun College of Urban Affairs, Department of Criminal Justice, Las Vegas, NV 89154-5009. Offers MA. Part-time programs available. *Faculty:* 12 full-time (5 women). *Students:* 26 full-time (14 women), 14 part-time (11 women); includes 21 minority (2 Black or African American, non-Hispanic/Latino; 2 Asian, non-Hispanic/Latino; 9 Hispanic/Latino; 8 Two or more races, non-Hispanic/Latino), 2 international. Average age 29. 35 applicants, 60% accepted, 17 enrolled. In 2010, 18 master's awarded. *Degree requirements:* For master's, comprehensive exam (for some programs), thesis (for some programs). *Entrance requirements:* Additional exam requirements/recommendations for international students: Required—TOEFL (minimum score 550 paper-based; 213 computer-based; 80 iBT), IELTS (minimum score 7). *Application deadline:* For fall admission, 8/1 priority date for domestic and international students. Applications are processed on a rolling basis. Application fee: $60 ($95 for international students). Electronic applications accepted. *Expenses:* Tuition, area resident: Part-time $239.50 per credit. Tuition, state resident: part-time $239.50 per credit. Tuition, nonresident: part-time $503 per credit. Required fees: $108 per semester. Tuition and fees vary according to course load, program and reciprocity agreements. *Financial support:* In 2010–11, 9 students received support, including 2 research assistantships with partial tuition reimbursements available (averaging $10,000 per year), 7 teaching assistantships with partial tuition reimbursements available (averaging $10,000 per year); institutionally sponsored loans, scholarships/grants, health care benefits, and unspecified assistantships also available. Financial award application deadline: 3/1. *Faculty research:* Risk assessment, drug courts, sex offender classification, correctional treatment programs and prisoner re-entry, youth gangs. Total annual research expenditures: $72,130. *Unit head:* Dr. Joel Lieberman, Chair/Associate Professor, 702-895-0013, Fax: 702-895-0252, E-mail: joel.lieberman@unlv.edu. *Application contact:* Graduate College Admissions Evaluator, 702-895-3320, Fax: 702-895-4180, E-mail: gradcollege@unlv.edu.

University of Nevada, Reno, Graduate School, College of Liberal Arts, School of Social Research and Justice Studies, Department of Criminal Justice, Reno, NV 89557. Offers MA. *Degree requirements:* For master's, comprehensive exam, thesis optional. *Entrance requirements:* For master's, GRE or LSAT, undergraduate degree in criminal justice with minimum GPA of 3.0. Additional exam requirements/recommendations for international students: Required—TOEFL (minimum score 500 paper-based; 173 computer-based; 61 iBT), IELTS (minimum score 6). Electronic applications accepted. *Expenses:* Tuition, state resident: full-time $2219; part-time $246 per credit. Tuition, nonresident: part-time $510 per credit. International tuition: $9009 full-time. Required fees: $59 per term. One-time fee: $101. Tuition and fees vary according to course load. *Faculty research:* Criminal justice system, social policy interaction.

University of Nevada, Reno, Graduate School, College of Liberal Arts, School of Social Research and Justice Studies, Program in Justice Management, Reno, NV 89557. Offers MJM. Part-time programs available. Postbaccalaureate distance learning degree programs offered (no on-campus study). *Degree requirements:* For master's, thesis optional. *Entrance requirements:* For master's, minimum GPA of 2.75. Additional exam requirements/recommendations for international students: Required—TOEFL (minimum score 500 paper-based; 173 computer-based; 61 iBT), IELTS (minimum score 6). Electronic applications accepted. *Expenses:* Tuition, state resident: full-time $2219; part-time $246 per credit. Tuition, nonresident: part-time $510 per credit. International tuition: $9009 full-time. Required fees: $59 per term. One-time fee: $101. Tuition and fees vary according to course load. *Faculty research:* Justice administration, adult justice management, juvenile justice management.

University of New Haven, Graduate School, Henry C. Lee College of Criminal Justice and Forensic Sciences, Program in Criminal Justice, West Haven, CT 06516-1916. Offers crime analysis (MS); criminal justice (PhD); criminal justice management (MS); forensic computer investigation (MS, Certificate); forensic psychology (MS); victim advocacy and services management (Certificate); victimology (MS). Part-time and evening/weekend programs available. *Students:* 47 full-time (29 women), 42 part-time (25 women); includes 17 Black or African American, non-Hispanic/Latino; 5 Hispanic/Latino, 6 international. Average age 29. 95 applicants, 96% accepted, 54 enrolled. In 2010, 12 master's, 12 other advanced degrees awarded. *Degree requirements:* For master's, thesis or alternative. *Entrance requirements:* Additional exam requirements/recommendations for international students: Required—TOEFL (minimum score 520 paper-based; 190 computer-based; 70 iBT), IELTS (minimum score 5.5). *Application deadline:* For fall admission, 5/31 for international students; for winter admission, 10/15 for international students; for spring admission, 1/15 for international students. Applications are processed on a rolling basis. Application fee: $50. Electronic applications accepted. *Financial support:* Research assistantships with partial tuition reimbursements, teaching assistantships with partial tuition reimbursements, career-related internships or fieldwork, Federal Work-Study, scholarships/grants, tuition waivers, and unspecified assistantships available. Support available to part-time students. Financial award applicants required to submit FAFSA. *Unit head:* Dr. James J. Cassidy, Coordinator, 203-932-7374. *Application contact:* Eloise Gormley, Director of Graduate Admissions, 203-932-7449, Fax: 203-932-7137, E-mail: gradinfo@newhaven.edu.

University of North Alabama, College of Arts and Sciences, Department of Criminal Justice, Florence, AL 35632-0001. Offers criminal justice (MSCJ). Part-time and evening/weekend programs available. *Faculty:* 1 full-time (0 women), 2 part-time/adjunct (0 women). *Students:* 17 full-time (9 women), 17 part-time (11 women); includes 12 minority (11 Black or African American, non-Hispanic/Latino; 1 Two or more races, non-Hispanic/Latino), 1 international. Average age 30. In 2010, 2 master's awarded. *Entrance requirements:* For master's, GRE General Test, MAT. *Application deadline:* For fall admission, 7/1 priority date for domestic students; for spring admission, 12/1 for domestic students. Applications are processed on a rolling basis. Application fee: $25. Electronic applications accepted. *Expenses:* Tuition, state resident: full-time $5472; part-time $228 per credit hour. Tuition, nonresident: full-time $10,944; part-time $456 per credit hour. Required fees: $986. Tuition and fees vary according to course load. *Unit head:* Dr. Phillip B. Bridgmon, Chair, 256-765-5045, E-mail: pbbridgmon@una.edu. *Application contact:* Kim Mauldin, Director of Admissions, 256-765-4608, Fax: 256-765-4960, E-mail: komauldin@una.edu.

The University of North Carolina at Charlotte, Graduate School, College of Arts and Sciences, Department of Criminal Justice, Charlotte, NC 28223-0001. Offers MS. Part-time and evening/weekend programs available. *Faculty:* 13 full-time (7 women). *Students:* 4 full-time (all women), 14 part-time (6 women); includes 3 minority (2 Black or African American, non-Hispanic/Latino; 1 Asian, non-Hispanic/Latino). Average age 29. 25 applicants, 40% accepted, 7 enrolled. In 2010, 5 master's awarded. *Degree requirements:* For master's, thesis or alternative, thesis or comprehensive exam. *Entrance requirements:* For master's, GRE General Test or MAT, minimum GPA of 3.0 in undergraduate major, 2.75 overall. Additional exam requirements/recommendations for international students: Required—TOEFL (minimum score 557 paper-based; 220 computer-based; 83 iBT). *Application deadline:* For fall admission, 7/1 for domestic students, 5/1 for international students; for spring admission, 11/1 for domestic students, 10/1 for international students. Applications are processed on a rolling basis. Application fee: $55. Electronic applications accepted. *Expenses:* Tuition, state resident: full-time $3464. Tuition, nonresident: full-time $14,297. Required fees: $2094. Tuition and fees vary according to course load. *Financial support:* In 2010–11, 5 students received support, including 4 teaching assistantships (averaging $9,125 per year); career-related internships or fieldwork, Federal Work-Study, institutionally sponsored loans, scholarships/grants, unspecified assistantships, and administrative assistantships also available. Support available to part-time students. Financial award application deadline: 4/1; financial award applicants required to submit FAFSA. *Faculty research:* Social psychology, terrorism, and identity; diminished capacity mitigation in death penalty proceedings; effects of prenatal problems, family functioning and neighborhood disadvantage in predicting violent offending; dynamic nature of the drug use/serious violence relationship; Chinese birth cohort: criminological implications. Total annual research expenditures: $199,904. *Unit head:* Dr. Vivian B. Lord, Chair, 704-687-2009, Fax: 704-687-3349, E-mail: vblord@uncc.edu. *Application contact:* Kathy B. Giddings, Director of Graduate Admissions, 704-687-5503, Fax: 704-687-3279, E-mail: gradadm@uncc.edu.

The University of North Carolina at Greensboro, Graduate School, College of Arts and Sciences, Department of Sociology, Greensboro, NC 27412-5001. Offers criminology (MA); sociology (MA). Part-time programs available. *Degree requirements:* For master's, comprehensive exam, thesis. *Entrance requirements:* For master's, GRE General Test. Additional exam requirements/recommendations for international students: Required—TOEFL. Electronic applications accepted.

The University of North Carolina Wilmington, College of Arts and Sciences, Department of Sociology and Criminology, Wilmington, NC 28403-3297. Offers criminology (MA); public sociology (MA). *Faculty:* 20 full-time (9 women). *Students:* 14 full-time (10 women), 6 part-time (4 women); includes 1 Black or African American, non-Hispanic/Latino. Average age 27. 24 applicants, 42% accepted, 7 enrolled. In 2010, 6 master's awarded. *Degree requirements:* For master's, comprehensive exam, thesis or internship. *Entrance requirements:* Additional exam requirements/recommendations for international students: Required—TOEFL (minimum score 550 paper-based; 217 computer-based; 79 iBT), IELTS (minimum score 6.5). *Application deadline:* For fall admission, 6/15 for domestic students. Application fee: $60. Electronic applications accepted. *Financial support:* In 2010–11, 5 teaching assistantships with full and partial tuition reimbursements (averaging $9,500 per year) were awarded; unspecified assistantships also available. *Unit head:* Dr. Kimberly J. Cook, Chair, 910-962-3785, E-mail: cookk@uncw.edu. *Application contact:* Dr. Michael Maume, Graduate Coordinator, 910-962-7749, E-mail: maumm@uncw.edu.

University of North Dakota, Graduate School, College of Arts and Sciences, Program in Criminal Justice, Grand Forks, ND 58202. Offers PhD. Part-time programs available. *Faculty:* 5 full-time (2 women), 2 part-time/adjunct (0 women). *Students:* 6 full-time (3 women), 7 part-time (4 women), 2 international. Average age 39. 10 applicants, 40% accepted, 3 enrolled. *Entrance requirements:* For doctorate, GRE General Test. Additional exam requirements/recommendations for international students: Required—TOEFL (minimum score 550 paper-based; 213 computer-based; 79 iBT), IELTS (minimum score 6.5). *Application deadline:* For fall admission, 3/31 for domestic and international students; for spring admission, 11/1 for domestic and international students. Application fee: $35. Electronic applications accepted. *Expenses:* Tuition, state resident: full-time $5857; part-time $306.74 per credit. Tuition, nonresident: full-time $15,666; part-time $729.77 per credit. Required fees: $53.42 per credit. Tuition and fees vary according to course load, program and reciprocity agreements. *Financial support:* In 2010–11, 6 students received support, including research assistantships with full and partial tuition reimbursements available (averaging $10,413 per year), 5 teaching assistantships with full and partial tuition reimbursements available (averaging $10,413 per year); fellowships with partial tuition reimbursements available, Federal Work-Study, scholarships/grants, health care benefits, and unspecified assistantships also available. Support available to part-time students. Financial award applicants required to submit FAFSA. Total annual research expenditures: $7,294. *Unit head:* Dr. Michael Meyer, Graduate Director, 701-777-4181, E-mail: michael_meyer2@und.nodak.edu. *Application contact:* Matt Anderson, Admissions Specialist, 701-777-2947, Fax: 701-777-3619, E-mail: matthew.anderson@gradschool.und.edu.

University of Northern Colorado, Graduate School, College of Humanities and Social Sciences, School of Sociology and Criminal Justice, Greeley, CO 80639. Offers criminal justice (MA); sociology (MA). *Faculty:* 11 full-time (6 women). *Students:* 6 full-time (2 women), 6 part-time (3 women); includes 2 Black or African American, non-Hispanic/Latino; 1 American Indian or Alaska Native, non-Hispanic/Latino; 1 Hispanic/Latino, 3 international. Average age 34. 13 applicants, 62% accepted, 0 enrolled. In 2010, 8 master's awarded. *Expenses:* Tuition, state resident: full-time $6199; part-time $344 per credit hour. Tuition, nonresident: full-time $14,834; part-time $824 per credit hour. Required fees: $1091; $60.60 per credit hour. Tuition and fees vary according to course load, degree level and program. *Financial support:* In 2010–11, 2 teaching assistantships (averaging $5,698 per year) were awarded. *Unit head:* Dr. Denise A. Battles, Dean, 970-351-2877, Fax: 970-351-2176. *Application contact:* Linda Sisson, Graduate Student Admission Coordinator, 970-351-1807, Fax: 970-351-2371, E-mail: linda.sisson@unco.edu.

University of Northern Iowa, Graduate College, College of Social and Behavioral Sciences, Department of Sociology, Anthropology and Criminology, Cedar Falls, IA 50614. Offers criminology (MA); sociology (MA). Part-time and evening/weekend programs available. *Students:* 14 full-time (8 women), 5 part-time (3 women); includes 2 minority (1 Black or African American, non-Hispanic/Latino; 1 American Indian or Alaska Native, non-Hispanic/Latino), 1 international. 27 applicants, 48% accepted, 9 enrolled. In 2010, 4 master's awarded. *Degree requirements:* For master's, thesis. *Entrance requirements:* For master's, minimum GPA of 3.0. Additional exam requirements/recommendations for international students: Required—TOEFL (minimum score 500 paper-based; 180 computer-based; 61 iBT). *Application deadline:* For fall admission, 8/1 priority date for domestic students. Applications are processed on a rolling basis. Application fee: $50 ($70 for international students). Electronic applications accepted. *Financial support:* Career-related internships or fieldwork, Federal Work-Study, scholarships/grants, and tuition waivers (full and partial) available. Support available to part-time students. Financial award application deadline: 2/1. *Unit head:* Dr. Kent Sandstrom, Head/Professor, 319-273-2786, Fax: 319-273-7104, E-mail: kent.sandstrom@uni.edu. *Application contact:* Laurie S. Russell, Record Analyst, 319-273-2623, Fax: 319-273-2885, E-mail: laurie.russell@uni.edu.

University of North Florida, College of Arts and Sciences, Department of Criminology and Criminal Justice, Jacksonville, FL 32224. Offers criminal justice (MSCJ). *Faculty:* 8 full-time (4 women). *Students:* 16 full-time (9 women), 15 part-time (12 women); includes 5 Black or African American, non-Hispanic/Latino, 1 international. Average age 28. 21 applicants, 38% accepted, 4 enrolled. In 2010, 15 master's awarded. *Degree requirements:* For master's, comprehensive exam, thesis optional. *Entrance requirements:* For master's, GRE General Test, minimum GPA of 3.0 in last 60 hours, letters of recommendation. Additional exam requirements/recommendations for international students: Required—TOEFL (minimum score 500 paper-based; 173 computer-based; 61 iBT). *Application deadline:* For fall admission, 7/1 priority date for domestic students, 5/1 for international students; for spring admission, 11/1 priority date for domestic students, 10/1 for international students. Applications are processed on a rolling basis. Application fee: $30. Electronic applications accepted. *Expenses:* Tuition, state resident: full-time $7646.40; part-time $318.60 per credit hour. Tuition, nonresident: full-time $23,502; part-time $979.24 per credit hour. Required fees: $1208.88; $50.37 per credit hour. Tuition and fees vary according to course load and program. *Financial support:* In 2010–11, 6 students received support, including 1 teaching assistantship (averaging $5,148 per year); Federal Work-Study, scholarships/grants, and unspecified assistantships also available. Financial award application deadline: 4/1; financial award applicants required to submit FAFSA. *Unit head:* Dr. Michael Hallett, Chair, 904-620-2850, E-mail: mhallett@unf.edu. *Application contact:* Lilith Richardson, Assistant Director, The Graduate School, 904-620-1360, Fax: 904-620-1362, E-mail: graduateschool@unf.edu.

University of North Texas, Toulouse Graduate School, College of Public Affairs and Community Service, Department of Criminal Justice, Denton, TX 76203-5017. Offers MS. Part-time and evening/weekend programs available. *Degree requirements:* For master's, comprehensive exam, thesis optional. *Entrance requirements:* For master's, GRE General Test, personal statement. Additional exam requirements/recommendations for international students: Recommended—TOEFL (minimum score 550 paper-based; 213 computer-based; 79 iBT). *Application deadline:* Applications are processed on a rolling basis. Electronic applications accepted. *Expenses:* Tuition, state resident: full-time $4298; part-time $239 per credit hour. Tuition, nonresident: full-time $10,782; part-time $549 per credit hour. Required fees: $1292; $270 per credit hour. *Financial support:* Applicants required to submit FAFSA. *Faculty research:* Law enforcement administration/strategy, juvenile justice/delinquency, violent crime/victimization, terrorism, correction administration/issues, capital punishment, criminalistics. *Application contact:* Graduate Adviser, 940-565-4954, Fax: 940-565-2548.

University of Ottawa, Faculty of Graduate and Postdoctoral Studies, Faculty of Social Sciences, Department of Criminology, Ottawa, ON K1N 6N5, Canada. Offers MA, MCA, PhD. *Degree requirements:* For master's, thesis or alternative. *Entrance requirements:* For master's, honors bachelor's degree or equivalent, minimum B average. Electronic applications accepted. *Faculty research:* Creation and reform of criminal policies in Canada.

University of Pennsylvania, School of Arts and Sciences, Graduate Group in Criminology, Philadelphia, PA 19104. Offers MA, MS, PhD. *Faculty:* 15 full-time (3 women), 2 part-time/

adjunct (1 woman). *Students:* 26 full-time (19 women), 5 part-time (3 women); includes 1 Black or African American, non-Hispanic/Latino; 3 Asian, non-Hispanic/Latino; 1 Hispanic/Latino, 3 international. 95 applicants, 40% accepted, 24 enrolled. In 2010, 27 master's, 3 doctorates awarded. Application fee: $70. *Expenses:* Tuition: Full-time $25,660; part-time $4758 per course. Required fees: $2152; $270 per course. Tuition and fees vary according to course load, degree level and program. *Financial support:* Institutionally sponsored loans, scholarships/grants, traineeships, health care benefits, and unspecified assistantships available. *Unit head:* Adrian Raine, Department Chair, Criminology, 215-573-9097, E-mail: araine@sas.upenn.edu. *Application contact:* Knakiya Hagans, Student Services Coordinator, 215-573-9097, E-mail: khagans@sas.upenn.edu.

University of Phoenix, College of Criminal Justice and Security, Phoenix, AZ 85034-7209. Offers administration of justice and security (MS). Programs are offered at the online campus. Evening/weekend programs available. Postbaccalaureate distance learning degree programs offered. *Students:* 1,855 full-time (1,247 women); includes 734 minority (562 Black or African American, non-Hispanic/Latino; 24 American Indian or Alaska Native, non-Hispanic/Latino; 15 Asian, non-Hispanic/Latino; 122 Hispanic/Latino; 6 Native Hawaiian or other Pacific Islander, non-Hispanic/Latino; 5 Two or more races, non-Hispanic/Latino), 24 international. Average age 38. *Entrance requirements:* For master's, minimum undergraduate GPA of 2.5 from accredited university, 3 years of work experience, citizen of the United States or have valid visa. Additional exam requirements/recommendations for international students: Required—TOEFL (minimum paper score 550, computer score 213, iBT 79), Test of English for International Communication, or IELTS. *Application deadline:* Applications are processed on a rolling basis. Application fee: $45. Electronic applications accepted. *Expenses:* Tuition: Full-time $16,440. One-time fee: $45 full-time. Full-time tuition and fees vary according to course load, degree level, campus/location and program. *Financial support:* Scholarships/grants available. Financial award applicants required to submit FAFSA. *Unit head:* James Ness, Dean, 602-557-7430, E-mail: james.ness@phoenix.edu. *Application contact:* James Ness, Dean, 602-557-7430, E-mail: james.ness@phoenix.edu.

University of Phoenix–Augusta Campus, College of Criminal Justice and Security, Augusta, GA 30909-4583. Offers administration of justice and security (MS).

University of Phoenix–Austin Campus, College of Criminal Justice and Security, Austin, TX 78759. Offers administration of justice and security (MS). Postbaccalaureate distance learning degree programs offered.

University of Phoenix–Birmingham Campus, College of Social and Behavioral Science, Birmingham, AL 35244. Offers administration of justice and security (MS); psychology (MS).

University of Phoenix–Cheyenne Campus, College of Criminal Justice and Security, Cheyenne, WY 82009. Offers administration of justice and security (MS). Postbaccalaureate distance learning degree programs offered.

University of Phoenix–Dallas Campus, College of Criminal Justice and Security, Dallas, TX 75251-2009. Offers administration of justice and security (MS). Postbaccalaureate distance learning degree programs offered. *Degree requirements:* For master's, thesis (for some programs). *Entrance requirements:* For master's, minimum undergraduate GPA of 2.5, 3 years of work experience. Additional exam requirements/recommendations for international students: Required—TOEFL (minimum score 550 paper-based; 213 computer-based; 79 iBT). Electronic applications accepted.

University of Phoenix–Des Moines Campus, College of Criminal Justice and Security, Des Moines, IA 50266. Offers administration of justice and security (MS). Postbaccalaureate distance learning degree programs offered.

University of Phoenix–Harrisburg Campus, College of Criminal Justice and Security, Harrisburg, PA 17112. Offers administration of justice and security (MS). Postbaccalaureate distance learning degree programs offered.

University of Phoenix–Jersey City Campus, College of Criminal Justice and Security, Jersey City, NJ 07310. Offers administration of justice and security (MS). Postbaccalaureate distance learning degree programs offered.

University of Phoenix–Kansas City Campus, College of Criminal Justice and Security, Kansas City, MO 64131-4517. Offers administration of justice and security (MS). Evening/weekend programs available. Postbaccalaureate distance learning degree programs offered. *Degree requirements:* For master's, thesis (for some programs). *Entrance requirements:* For master's, 3 years work experience, minimum undergraduate GPA of 2.5. Additional exam requirements/recommendations for international students: Required—TOEFL (minimum score 550 paper-based; 213 computer-based).

University of Phoenix–Memphis Campus, College of Criminal Justice and Security, Cordova, TN 38018. Offers administration of justice and security (MS).

University of Phoenix–Milwaukee Campus, College of Criminal Justice and Security, Milwaukee, WI 53045. Offers administration of justice and security (MS).

University of Phoenix–Northern Nevada Campus, College of Criminal Justice and Security, Reno, NV 89521-5862. Offers administration of justice and security (MS).

University of Phoenix–Northern Virginia Campus, College of Criminal Justice and Security, Reston, VA 20190. Offers administration of justice and security (MS). *Expenses:* Tuition: Full-time $16,440. One-time fee: $45 full-time. Full-time tuition and fees vary according to course load, degree level, campus/location and program.

University of Phoenix–Northwest Arkansas Campus, College of Criminal Justice and Security, Rogers, AR 72756-9615. Offers administration of justice and security (MS).

University of Phoenix–Omaha Campus, College of Criminal Justice and Security, Omaha, NE 68154-5240. Offers administration of justice and security (MS).

University of Phoenix–St. Louis Campus, College of Criminal Justice and Security, St. Louis, MO 63043-4828. Offers administration of justice and security (MS). Evening/weekend programs available. *Degree requirements:* For master's, thesis (for some programs). *Entrance requirements:* For master's, minimum undergraduate GPA of 2.5, 3 years work experience. Additional exam requirements/recommendations for international students: Required—TOEFL (minimum score 550 paper-based; 213 computer-based; 79 iBT). Electronic applications accepted.

University of Phoenix–San Antonio Campus, College of Criminal Justice and Security, San Antonio, TX 78230. Offers administration of justice and security (MS).

University of Phoenix–Savannah Campus, College of Criminal Justice and Security, Savannah, GA 31405-7400. Offers administration of justice and security (MS).

University of Phoenix–Southern California Campus, College of Social Sciences, Costa Mesa, CA 92626. Offers administration of justice and security (MS); community counseling (MSC); marriage, family and child therapy (MSC); mental health counseling (MSC); psychology (MS); school counseling (MSC). Evening/weekend programs available. *Degree requirements:* For master's, thesis (for some programs). *Entrance requirements:* For master's, minimum undergraduate GPA of 3.0, 3 years work experience. Additional exam requirements/recommendations for international students: Required—TOEFL (minimum score 550 paper-based; 213 computer-based; 79 iBT). Electronic applications accepted.

University of Phoenix–Springfield Campus, College of Criminal Justice and Security, Springfield, MO 65804-7211. Offers administration of justice and security (MS).

Criminal Justice and Criminology

University of Phoenix–Washington Campus, College of Criminal Justice and Security, Seattle, WA 98188-7500. Offers administration of justice and security (MS). Evening/weekend programs available. *Degree requirements:* For master's, thesis (for some programs). *Entrance requirements:* For master's, minimum undergraduate GPA of 2.5, 3 years of work experience. Additional exam requirements/recommendations for international students: Required—TOEFL (minimum score 550 paper-based; 213 computer-based; 79 iBT). Electronic applications accepted.

University of Phoenix–Washington D.C. Campus, College of Criminal Justice and Security, Washington, DC 20001. Offers administration of justice and security (MS).

University of Pittsburgh, Graduate School of Public and International Affairs, Doctoral Program in Public and International Affairs, Pittsburgh, PA 15260. Offers development policy (PhD); foreign and security policy (PhD); international political economy (PhD); public administration (PhD); public policy (PhD). *Accreditation:* NASPAA. Part-time programs available. *Faculty:* 30 full-time (12 women), 67 part-time/adjunct (25 women). *Students:* 43 full-time (18 women), 3 part-time (2 women); includes 3 minority (2 Black or African American, non-Hispanic/Latino; 1 Asian, non-Hispanic/Latino), 19 international. Average age 30. 105 applicants, 11% accepted, 6 enrolled. In 2010, 11 doctorates awarded. Terminal master's awarded for partial completion of doctoral program. *Degree requirements:* For doctorate, comprehensive exam, thesis/dissertation, mid-term evaluation, preliminary exam, annual review. *Entrance requirements:* For doctorate, GRE, 3 letters of recommendation, resume, minimum GPA of 3.0 (recommended), writing sample. Additional exam requirements/recommendations for international students: Required—TOEFL (minimum score 600 paper-based; 250 computer-based; 100 iBT), TWE (minimum score 4); Recommended—IELTS (minimum score 7). *Application deadline:* For fall admission, 2/1 for domestic students, 1/15 for international students. Application fee: $50. Electronic applications accepted. *Expenses:* Tuition, state resident: full-time $17,304; part-time $701 per credit. Tuition, nonresident: full-time $29,554; part-time $1210 per credit. Required fees: $740; $214 per term. Tuition and fees vary according to program. *Financial support:* In 2010–11, 10 students received support, including 10 fellowships (averaging $41,325 per year). Financial award application deadline: 2/1. *Faculty research:* International political economy, international development, public administration, public policy, foreign policy, international security policy. Total annual research expenditures: $893,349. *Unit head:* Dr. Kevin P. Kearns, Program Coordinator, 412-648-7621, Fax: 412-648-2605, E-mail: kkearns@pitt.edu. *Application contact:* Julie Korade, Program Administrator/Graduate Enrollment Counselor, 412-648-7640, Fax: 412-648-7641, E-mail: korade@pitt.edu.

University of Pittsburgh, School of Law, Master of Studies in Law Program, Pittsburgh, PA 15260. Offers business law (MSL), including commercial law, corporate law, general business law, international business, tax law; constitutional law (MSL); criminal law and justice (MSL); disabilities law (MSL); dispute resolution (MSL); education law (MSL); elder and estate planning law (MSL); employment and labor law (MSL); environment and real estate law (MSL); family law (MSL); general law and jurisprudence (MSL); health law (MSL); intellectual property and technology (MSL); international and comparative law (MSL); personal injury and civil litigation (MSL); regulatory law (MSL); self-designed (MSL); sports and entertainment law (MSL). Part-time programs available. *Faculty:* 43 full-time (16 women), 104 part-time/adjunct (30 women). *Students:* 3 full-time (2 women), 14 part-time (8 women); includes 3 Black or African American, non-Hispanic/Latino. Average age 31. 26 applicants, 58% accepted, 11 enrolled. In 2010, 9 master's awarded. *Entrance requirements:* Additional exam requirements/recommendations for international students: Required—TOEFL (minimum score 600 paper-based; 250 computer-based; 100 iBT). *Application deadline:* For fall admission, 6/30 for domestic students, 5/1 for international students. Applications are processed on a rolling basis. Application fee: $0. *Expenses:* Tuition, state resident: full-time $17,304; part-time $701 per credit. Tuition, nonresident: full-time $29,554; part-time $1210 per credit. Required fees: $740; $214 per term. Tuition and fees vary according to program. *Faculty research:* Law, health law, business law, contracts, intellectual property. *Unit head:* Prof. Alan Meisel, Director, 412-648-1384, Fax: 412-648-2649, E-mail: meisel@pitt.edu. *Application contact:* Bethann Pischke, Administrative Coordinator, 412-648-7120, Fax: 412-648-2649, E-mail: pischke@pitt.edu.

University of Regina, Faculty of Graduate Studies and Research, Faculty of Arts, Department of Justice Studies, Regina, SK S4S 0A2, Canada. Offers human justice (MA); justice studies (MA); police studies (MA). Part-time programs available. *Faculty:* 7 full-time (3 women). *Students:* 9 full-time (6 women), 13 part-time (7 women). 8 applicants, 88% accepted. In 2010, 3 master's awarded. *Degree requirements:* For master's, thesis. *Entrance requirements:* For master's, writing sample. Additional exam requirements/recommendations for international students: Required—TOEFL (minimum score 580 paper-based; 80 iBT). *Application deadline:* For fall admission, 3/31 for domestic students, 3/15 for international students. Application fee: $100. Electronic applications accepted. Tuition and fees charges are reported in Canadian dollars. *Expenses:* Tuition, area resident: Full-time $3244.50 Canadian dollars; part-time $180.25 Canadian dollars per credit hour. International tuition: $4744.50 Canadian dollars full-time. Required fees: $494 Canadian dollars; $115.25 Canadian dollars per credit hour. $115.25 Canadian dollars per semester. Tuition and fees vary according to program. *Financial support:* In 2010–11, 3 fellowships (averaging $18,000 per year), 1 research assistantship (averaging $16,500 per year), 4 teaching assistantships (averaging $6,759 per year) were awarded. Financial award application deadline: 6/15. *Faculty research:* Restorative and social justice, policing, public policy, social policy and planning. *Unit head:* Dr. Allan Patenaude, Head, 306-585-4035, Fax: 306-585-4815, E-mail: allan.patenaude@uregina.ca. *Application contact:* Dr. Nick Jones, Graduate Program Coordinator, 306-585-4862, Fax: 306-585-4815, E-mail: nick.jones@uregina.ca.

University of South Africa, College of Law, Pretoria, South Africa. Offers correctional services management (M Tech); criminology (MA, PhD); law (LL M, LL D); penology (MA, PhD); police science (MA, PhD); policing (M Tech); security risk management (M Tech); social science in criminology (MA).

University of South Carolina, The Graduate School, College of Arts and Sciences, Department of Criminology and Criminal Justice, Columbia, SC 29208. Offers MA, PhD, JD/MA. Part-time and evening/weekend programs available. *Degree requirements:* For master's, comprehensive exam, thesis; for doctorate, comprehensive exam, thesis/dissertation. *Entrance requirements:* For master's and doctorate, GRE. Additional exam requirements/recommendations for international students: Required—TOEFL. Electronic applications accepted. *Faculty research:* Juvenile delinquency, substance abuse, policy development, minority issues, law enforcement services.

University of Southern Mississippi, Graduate School, College of Science and Technology, Department of Administration of Justice, Hattiesburg, MS 39406-0001. Offers administration of justice (PhD); corrections (MA, MS); forensics (MS); juvenile justice (MA, MS); law enforcement (MA, MS). Part-time programs available. *Faculty:* 9 full-time (2 women), 2 part-time/adjunct (0 women). *Students:* 18 full-time (9 women), 19 part-time (12 women); includes 6 Black or African American, non-Hispanic/Latino; 1 Hispanic/Latino, 1 international. Average age 34. 20 applicants, 35% accepted, 4 enrolled. In 2010, 7 degrees awarded. *Degree requirements:* For master's, comprehensive exam, thesis; for doctorate, comprehensive exam, thesis/dissertation. *Entrance requirements:* For master's, GRE General Test, minimum GPA of 2.75 in last 60 hours, 3.0 in field of study; for doctorate, GRE General Test, minimum GPA of 3.5. Additional exam requirements/recommendations for international students: Required—TOEFL, IELTS. *Application deadline:* For fall admission, 3/15 priority date for domestic students, 3/15 for international students; for spring admission, 1/10 priority date for domestic and international students. Applications are processed on a rolling basis. Application fee: $50. *Financial support:* In 2010–11, 2 research assistantships with full tuition reimbursements (averaging $7,200 per year), 9 teaching assistantships with full tuition reimbursements (averaging $8,000 per year) were awarded; career-related internships or fieldwork, Federal Work-Study, institutionally sponsored loans, scholarships/grants, health care benefits, and unspecified assistantships also available. Financial award application deadline: 3/15; financial award applicants required to submit FAFSA. *Faculty research:* Crime in the family, police training models, humanities and criminal justice. *Unit head:* Dr. Lisa Nored, Chair, 601-266-4509, Fax: 601-266-4391. *Application contact:* Tera Wright, Manager of Graduate Admissions, 601-266-4509, Fax: 601-266-4391.

University of South Florida, Graduate School, College of Behavioral and Community Sciences, Department of Criminology, Tampa, FL 33620-9951. Offers criminal justice administration (MA); criminology (MA, PhD). *Faculty:* 4 full-time (2 women), 1 part-time/adjunct (0 women). *Students:* 35 full-time (21 women), 60 part-time (33 women); includes 12 Black or African American, non-Hispanic/Latino; 4 Asian, non-Hispanic/Latino; 10 Hispanic/Latino, 3 international. Average age 31. 130 applicants, 43% accepted, 36 enrolled. In 2010, 33 master's, 3 doctorates awarded. *Degree requirements:* For master's, comprehensive exam (for some programs), thesis (for some programs); for doctorate, comprehensive exam, thesis/dissertation. *Entrance requirements:* For master's, GRE General Test (criminology), 3 letters of recommendation, writing sample, minimum GPA of 3.0; for doctorate, GRE General Test, 3 letters of recommendation, statement of purpose, writing sample. Additional exam requirements/recommendations for international students: Required—TOEFL (minimum score 550 paper-based; 213 computer-based). *Application deadline:* For fall admission, 1/15 for domestic students, 1/2 for international students; for spring admission, 9/30 for domestic students, 6/1 for international students. Application fee: $30. Electronic applications accepted. *Financial support:* In 2010–11, 10 students received support, including 4 research assistantships (averaging $13,180 per year), 13 teaching assistantships with tuition reimbursements available (averaging $12,467 per year). *Faculty research:* Criminal theory, drug abuse, violence, policing. Total annual research expenditures: $511,767. *Application contact:* Lorie Fridell, Director, 813-974-6862, Fax: 813-974-2803, E-mail: lfridell@bcs.usf.edu.

The University of Tennessee, Graduate School, College of Arts and Sciences, Department of Sociology, Knoxville, TN 37996. Offers criminology (MA, PhD); energy, environment, and resource policy (MA, PhD); political economy (MA, PhD). Part-time programs available. *Degree requirements:* For master's, thesis or alternative; for doctorate, thesis/dissertation. *Entrance requirements:* For master's, GRE General Test, minimum GPA of 3.0; for doctorate, GRE General Test, minimum GPA of 3.5. Additional exam requirements/recommendations for international students: Required—TOEFL. Electronic applications accepted. *Expenses:* Tuition, state resident: full-time $7440; part-time $414 per credit hour. Tuition, nonresident: full-time $22,478; part-time $1250 per credit hour. Required fees: $922; $43 per credit hour. Tuition and fees vary according to program.

The University of Tennessee at Chattanooga, Graduate School, College of Arts and Sciences, Department of Criminal Justice, Chattanooga, TN 37403. Offers MSCJ. Part-time and evening/weekend programs available. *Faculty:* 4 full-time (2 women). *Students:* 20 full-time (15 women), 6 part-time (4 women); includes 4 minority (3 Black or African American, non-Hispanic/Latino; 1 Hispanic/Latino). Average age 32. 16 applicants, 100% accepted, 13 enrolled. In 2010, 7 master's awarded. *Degree requirements:* For master's, thesis optional, qualifying exams, internship. *Entrance requirements:* For master's, GRE General Test or MAT. Additional exam requirements/recommendations for international students: Required—TOEFL (minimum score 550 paper-based; 213 computer-based; 79 iBT), IELTS (minimum score 6). *Application deadline:* For fall admission, 8/1 priority date for domestic students, 6/1 for international students; for spring admission, 12/1 priority date for domestic students, 10/1 for international students. Applications are processed on a rolling basis. Application fee: $35. Electronic applications accepted. *Financial support:* In 2010–11, 3 research assistantships with full and partial tuition reimbursements (averaging $5,500 per year), 2 teaching assistantships with full and partial tuition reimbursements (averaging $5,500 per year) were awarded; career-related internships or fieldwork, scholarships/grants, and unspecified assistantships also available. Support available to part-time students. *Faculty research:* Violence against women, crime prevention, police accountability, criminal justice privatization, public policy. *Unit head:* Dr. Helen M. Eigenberg, Chair, 423-425-4135, Fax: 423-425-2228, E-mail: helen-eigenberg@utc.edu. *Application contact:* Dr. Jerald Ainsworth, Dean of Graduate Studies, 423-425-4478, Fax: 423-425-5223, E-mail: jerald-ainsworth@utc.edu.

The University of Texas at Arlington, Graduate School, College of Liberal Arts, Department of Criminology and Criminal Justice, Arlington, TX 76019. Offers MA. Part-time and evening/weekend programs available. *Faculty:* 9 full-time (3 women). *Students:* 18 full-time (9 women), 103 part-time (56 women); includes 57 minority (24 Black or African American, non-Hispanic/Latino; 1 American Indian or Alaska Native, non-Hispanic/Latino; 2 Asian, non-Hispanic/Latino; 30 Hispanic/Latino), 1 international. 58 applicants, 97% accepted, 43 enrolled. In 2010, 14 master's awarded. *Degree requirements:* For master's, comprehensive exam, thesis or alternative. *Entrance requirements:* For master's, GRE General Test, minimum GPA of 3.0 in last 60 hours of undergraduate course work, 3 letters of recommendation. Additional exam requirements/recommendations for international students: Required—TOEFL (minimum score 550 paper-based; 213 computer-based). *Application deadline:* For fall admission, 6/15 for domestic students. Applications are processed on a rolling basis. Application fee: $35 ($50 for international students). *Expenses:* Tuition, state resident: full-time $7500. Tuition, nonresident: full-time $13,080. International tuition: $13,250 full-time. *Financial support:* In 2010–11, 1 research assistantship (averaging $6,000 per year) was awarded; career-related internships or fieldwork also available. Financial award application deadline: 6/1; financial award applicants required to submit FAFSA. *Unit head:* Dr. Alejandro del Carmen, Chair, 817-272-3318, Fax: 817-272-5673, E-mail: adelcarmen@uta.edu. *Application contact:* Dr. Alejandro del Carmen, Chair, 817-272-3318, Fax: 817-272-5673, E-mail: adelcarmen@uta.edu.

The University of Texas at Dallas, School of Economic, Political and Policy Sciences, Program in Criminology, Richardson, TX 75080. Offers criminology (MS, PhD); justice administration and leadership (MS). Part-time and evening/weekend programs available. *Faculty:* 9 full-time (3 women), 2 part-time/adjunct (0 women). *Students:* 38 full-time (21 women), 27 part-time (12 women); includes 26 minority (14 Black or African American, non-Hispanic/Latino; 1 Asian, non-Hispanic/Latino; 11 Hispanic/Latino), 1 international. Average age 34. 42 applicants, 55% accepted, 15 enrolled. In 2010, 13 master's awarded. *Degree requirements:* For master's, thesis; for doctorate, thesis/dissertation. *Entrance requirements:* For master's, GRE General Test, minimum GPA of 3.0 in upper-level course work in field; for doctorate, GRE (minimum combined verbal and quantitative score of 1200), minimum GPA of 3.2 in upper-level course work in field. Additional exam requirements/recommendations for international students: Required—TOEFL (minimum score 550 paper-based; 215 computer-based). *Application deadline:* For fall admission, 7/15 for domestic students, 5/1 priority date for international students; for spring admission, 11/15 for domestic students, 9/1 priority date for international students. Applications are processed on a rolling basis. Application fee: $50 ($100 for international students). Electronic applications accepted. *Expenses:* Tuition, state resident: full-time $10,248; part-time $569 per credit hour. Tuition, nonresident: full-time $18,544; part-time $1030 per credit hour. Tuition and fees vary according to course load. *Financial support:* In 2010–11, 37 students received support, including 3 research assistantships with partial tuition reimbursements available (averaging $13,650 per year), 16 teaching assistantships with partial tuition reimbursements available (averaging $11,869 per year); career-related internships or fieldwork, Federal Work-Study, institutionally sponsored loans, scholarships/grants, and unspecified assistantships also available. Support available to part-time students. Financial award application deadline: 4/30; financial award applicants required to submit FAFSA. *Faculty research:* Developmental criminology, domestic violence, mental health and violence, the death penalty, corrections. *Unit head:* Dr. John L. Worrall, Program Head, 972-883-4893, Fax: 972-883-2735, E-mail: worrall@utdallas.edu. *Application contact:* Dr. Lynne M. Vieraitis, Associate Program Chair/Graduate Director, 972-883-6901, Fax: 972-883-2735, E-mail: lynnev@utdallas.edu.

The University of Texas at San Antonio, College of Public Policy, Department of Criminal Justice, San Antonio, TX 78249-0617. Offers justice policy (MS). Part-time and evening/weekend programs available. *Faculty:* 9 full-time (2 women). *Students:* 23 full-time (11 women), 40 part-time (23 women); includes 46 minority (4 Black or African American, non-Hispanic/Latino; 2 Asian, non-Hispanic/Latino; 37 Hispanic/Latino; 3 Two or more races, non-Hispanic/

Latino), 2 international. Average age 31. 32 applicants, 75% accepted, 23 enrolled. In 2010, 12 master's awarded. *Degree requirements:* For master's, comprehensive exam (for some programs), thesis (for some programs). *Entrance requirements:* For master's, GRE General Test, minimum GPA of 3.0 on last 60 hours. Additional exam requirements/recommendations for international students: Required—TOEFL (minimum score 500 paper-based; 173 computer-based; 61 iBT), IELTS (minimum score 5). *Application deadline:* For fall admission, 7/1 for domestic students, 4/1 for international students; for spring admission, 11/1 for domestic students, 9/1 for international students. Applications are processed on a rolling basis. Application fee: $45 ($80 for international students). Electronic applications accepted. *Expenses:* Tuition, state resident: full-time $4172; part-time $231.75 per credit hour. Tuition, nonresident: full-time $15,332; part-time $851.75 per credit hour. *Financial support:* In 2010–11, 9 students received support, including 15 research assistantships (averaging $10,019 per year); career-related internships or fieldwork, scholarships/grants, tuition waivers, and unspecified assistantships also available. Support available to part-time students. *Faculty research:* Drug control policy, neighborhood patterns of violence, white collar and corporate crime, crime prevention, Hispanic crime and delinquency. Total annual research expenditures: $26,782. *Unit head:* Roger Enriquez, Department Chair, 210-458-2535, Fax: 210-458-2680, E-mail: roger.enriquez@utsa.edu. *Application contact:* Veronica Ramirez, Assistant Dean of the Graduate School, 210-458-4330, Fax: 210-458-4332, E-mail: graduatestudies@utsa.edu.

The University of Texas at Tyler, College of Arts and Sciences, Department of Social Sciences, Tyler, TX 75799-0001. Offers criminal justice (MS); public administration (MPA); sociology (MS). Part-time and evening/weekend programs available. *Degree requirements:* For master's, comprehensive exam, thesis optional. *Entrance requirements:* For master's, GRE General Test, minimum GPA of 3.0. Additional exam requirements/recommendations for international students: Required—TOEFL (minimum score 79 computer-based). *Faculty research:* Urban segregation, minority business, violent crime, gender discrimination.

The University of Texas of the Permian Basin, Office of Graduate Studies, College of Arts and Sciences, Department of Social Sciences, Program in Criminal Justice Administration, Odessa, TX 79762-0001. Offers MS. Part-time and evening/weekend programs available. *Degree requirements:* For master's, comprehensive exam (for some programs), thesis (for some programs). *Entrance requirements:* For master's, GRE General Test, 3 letters of recommendation. Additional exam requirements/recommendations for international students: Required—TOEFL (minimum score 550 paper-based; 213 computer-based).

The University of Texas–Pan American, College of Social and Behavioral Sciences, Department of Criminal Justice, Edinburg, TX 78539. Offers MS. Part-time and evening/weekend programs available. Postbaccalaureate distance learning degree programs offered (no on-campus study). *Degree requirements:* For master's, comprehensive exam, applied project or thesis. *Entrance requirements:* For master's, minimum GPA of 2.75. *Faculty research:* Comparative criminal justice systems, death penalty, community policing, Hispanic women.

University of the Fraser Valley, Graduate Studies, Abbotsford, BC V2S 7M8, Canada. Offers criminal justice (MA). Evening/weekend programs available. *Degree requirements:* For master's, thesis optional, major research paper. *Entrance requirements:* For master's, bachelor's degree and work experience in related field. Additional exam requirements/recommendations for international students: Recommended—TOEFL (minimum score 88 iBT), IELTS (minimum score 6.5), TWE. Electronic applications accepted. *Expenses:* Contact institution. *Faculty research:* Human trafficking, illegal drug trade, criminal justice, criminology, safe schools.

University of the Pacific, McGeorge School of Law, Sacramento, CA 95817. Offers advocacy (JD); criminal justice (JD); experiential law teaching (LL M); intellectual property (JD); international legal studies (JD); international water resources law (LL M, JSD); law (JD); public law and policy (JD); public policy and law (LL M); tax (JD); transnational business practice (LL M); JD/MBA; JD/MPPA. *Accreditation:* ABA. Part-time and evening/weekend programs available. *Faculty:* 49 full-time (22 women), 45 part-time/adjunct (15 women). *Students:* 756 full-time (362 women), 303 part-time (148 women); includes 27 Black or African American, non-Hispanic/Latino; 19 American Indian or Alaska Native, non-Hispanic/Latino; 150 Asian, non-Hispanic/Latino; 60 Hispanic/Latino, 27 international. Average age 27. 3,209 applicants, 42% accepted, 344 enrolled. In 2010, 307 first professional degrees, 36 master's awarded. *Degree requirements:* For master's, thesis (for some programs); for doctorate, thesis/dissertation. *Entrance requirements:* For JD, LSAT; for master's, JD; for doctorate, LL M. Additional exam requirements/recommendations for international students: Required—TOEFL (minimum score 600 paper-based; 250 computer-based; 100 iBT). *Application deadline:* For fall admission, 3/15 priority date for domestic students. Applications are processed on a rolling basis. Application fee: $50. Electronic applications accepted. *Expenses:* Contact institution. *Financial support:* Fellowships, research assistantships, teaching assistantships, career-related internships or fieldwork, Federal Work-Study, institutionally sponsored loans, and scholarships/grants available. Support available to part-time students. Financial award applicants required to submit FAFSA. *Faculty research:* International legal studies, public policy and law, advocacy, intellectual property law, taxation, criminal law. *Unit head:* Elizabeth Rindskopf-Parker, Dean, 916-739-7151, E-mail: elizabeth@pacific.edu. *Application contact:* 916-739-7105, Fax: 916-739-7301, E-mail: mcgeorge@pacific.edu.

The University of Toledo, College of Graduate Studies, Judith Herb College of Education, Health Science and Human Service, Department of Criminal Justice and Social Work, Toledo, OH 43606-3390. Offers criminal justice (MA); elder law (Certificate); patient advocacy (Certificate); social work (MSW). *Accreditation:* CSWE. Part-time programs available. *Faculty:* 13. *Students:* 61 full-time (49 women), 59 part-time (49 women); includes 23 Black or African American, non-Hispanic/Latino; 1 American Indian or Alaska Native, non-Hispanic/Latino; 3 Asian, non-Hispanic/Latino; 5 Hispanic/Latino; 2 Two or more races, non-Hispanic/Latino, 1 international. Average age 32. 84 applicants, 60% accepted, 38 enrolled. In 2010, 52 master's, 3 other advanced degrees awarded. *Degree requirements:* For master's, comprehensive exam, thesis. *Entrance requirements:* For master's, GRE or other qualifying exams required vary by program. A minimum 2.70 cumulative GPA all previous academic work. Two/Three Letters of Recommendation (as required per program). ; for Certificate, A minimum 2.70 cumulative GPA all previous academic work. Two/Three Letters of Recommendation (as required per program). . Additional exam requirements/recommendations for international students: Required—TOEFL (minimum score 550 paper-based; 213 computer-based; 80 iBT), IELTS (minimum score 6.5). *Application deadline:* For fall admission, 1/15 priority date for domestic and international students. Applications are processed on a rolling basis. Application fee: $45 ($75 for international students). Electronic applications accepted. *Expenses:* Tuition, state resident: full-time $11,426; part-time $476 per credit hour. Tuition, nonresident: full-time $21,660; part-time $903 per credit hour. One-time fee: $62. *Financial support:* Research assistantships with tuition reimbursements, teaching assistantships with tuition reimbursements, Federal Work-Study, scholarships/grants, tuition waivers (full and partial), and unspecified assistantships available. *Unit head:* Dr. Morris Jenkins, Chair, 419-530-2313, Fax: 419-530-2153, E-mail: morris.jenkins@utoledo.edu. *Application contact:* Graduate School Office, 419-530-4723, Fax: 419-530-4724, E-mail: grdsch@utnet.utoledo.edu.

University of Toronto, School of Graduate Studies, Social Sciences Division, Centre for Criminology, Toronto, ON M5S 1A1, Canada. Offers MA, PhD. Part-time programs available. *Degree requirements:* For master's, research paper (optional); for doctorate, comprehensive exam, thesis/dissertation. *Entrance requirements:* For master's, 2 letters of reference, bachelor's degree in social science or humanities, minimum B+ average in last 2 years of undergraduate study; for doctorate, 2 letters of reference, MA in criminology or equivalent, minimum A– average. Additional exam requirements/recommendations for international students: Required—TOEFL (minimum score 580 paper-based; 237 computer-based), TWE (minimum score 5).

University of West Florida, College of Professional Studies, Department of Professional and Community Leadership, Program in Administration, Pensacola, FL 32514-5750. Offers acquisition and contract administration (MSA); biomedical/pharmaceutical (MSA); criminal justice administration (MSA); database administration (MSA); education leadership (MSA); healthcare administration (MSA); human performance technology (MSA); leadership (MSA); nursing administration (MSA); public administration (MSA); software engineering administration (MSA). Part-time and evening/weekend programs available. Postbaccalaureate distance learning degree programs offered (no on-campus study). *Students:* 26 full-time (24 women), 185 part-time (115 women); includes 30 Black or African American, non-Hispanic/Latino; 1 American Indian or Alaska Native, non-Hispanic/Latino; 5 Asian, non-Hispanic/Latino; 13 Hispanic/Latino; 1 Native Hawaiian or other Pacific Islander, non-Hispanic/Latino, 2 international. Average age 34. 139 applicants, 70% accepted, 80 enrolled. In 2010, 60 master's awarded. *Entrance requirements:* For master's, GRE General Test, letter of intent, names of references. Additional exam requirements/recommendations for international students: Required—TOEFL (minimum score 550 paper-based; 213 computer-based). *Application deadline:* For fall admission, 6/1 for domestic students, 5/15 for international students; for spring admission, 10/1 for domestic and international students. Applications are processed on a rolling basis. Application fee: $30. *Expenses:* Tuition, state resident: full-time $4982; part-time $208 per credit hour. Tuition, nonresident: full-time $20,059; part-time $836 per credit hour. Required fees: $1365; $57 per credit hour. *Financial support:* Unspecified assistantships available. Financial award application deadline: 4/15; financial award applicants required to submit FAFSA. *Unit head:* Dr. Karen Rasmussen, Chairperson, 850-474-2301, Fax: 850-474-2804, E-mail: krasmuss@uwf.edu. *Application contact:* Terry McCray, Assistant Director of Graduate Admissions, 850-473-7718, Fax: 850-473-7714, E-mail: gradadmissions@uwf.edu.

University of West Florida, College of Professional Studies, School of Justice Studies and Social Work, Department of Justice Studies, Pensacola, FL 32514-5750. Offers criminal justice (MS). Part-time and evening/weekend programs available. *Faculty:* 2 full-time (0 women), 2 part-time/adjunct (1 woman). *Students:* 5 full-time (4 women), 20 part-time (12 women); includes 3 Black or African American, non-Hispanic/Latino; 1 Asian, non-Hispanic/Latino; 2 Hispanic/Latino. Average age 33. 10 applicants, 40% accepted, 3 enrolled. In 2010, 2 master's awarded. *Degree requirements:* For master's, thesis optional. *Entrance requirements:* For master's, GRE or MAT, 3 letters of recommendation. Additional exam requirements/recommendations for international students: Required—TOEFL (minimum score 550 paper-based; 213 computer-based). *Application deadline:* For fall admission, 6/1 for domestic students, 5/1 for international students; for spring admission, 10/1 for domestic and international students. Applications are processed on a rolling basis. Electronic applications accepted. *Expenses:* Tuition, state resident: full-time $4982; part-time $208 per credit hour. Tuition, nonresident: full-time $20,059; part-time $836 per credit hour. Required fees: $1365; $57 per credit hour. *Financial support:* In 2010–11, 10 fellowships (averaging $319 per year), 4 research assistantships (averaging $3,280 per year), 2 teaching assistantships (averaging $3,760 per year) were awarded; unspecified assistantships also available. *Unit head:* Dr. Glenn Rohrer, Chair, 850-474-2154, E-mail: grohrer@uwf.edu. *Application contact:* Terry McCray, Assistant Director of Graduate Admissions, 850-473-7718, Fax: 850-473-7714, E-mail: gradadmissions@uwf.edu.

University of West Georgia, College of Arts and Sciences, Department of Sociology and Criminology, Carrollton, GA 30118. Offers criminology (MA); sociology (MA). Part-time and evening/weekend programs available. *Faculty:* 13 full-time (5 women), 5 part-time/adjunct (4 women). *Students:* 10 full-time (5 women), 8 part-time (4 women); includes 5 Black or African American, non-Hispanic/Latino; 1 Hispanic/Latino. Average age 28. 14 applicants, 29% accepted, 1 enrolled. In 2010, 8 master's awarded. *Degree requirements:* For master's, one foreign language, comprehensive exam (for some programs), thesis (for some programs). *Entrance requirements:* For master's, GRE General Test, minimum GPA of 2.5, references, intellectual biography. Additional exam requirements/recommendations for international students: Required—TOEFL. *Application deadline:* For fall admission, 7/17 for domestic students; for spring admission, 11/20 for domestic students. Applications are processed on a rolling basis. Application fee: $30. Electronic applications accepted. *Expenses:* Tuition, state resident: full-time $4130; part-time $173 per semester hour. Tuition, nonresident: full-time $16,524; part-time $689 per semester hour. Required fees: $1586; $44.01 per semester hour. $397 per semester. Tuition and fees vary according to program. *Financial support:* In 2010–11, 8 students received support, including 7 research assistantships with full tuition reimbursements available (averaging $6,000 per year); career-related internships or fieldwork, scholarships/grants, and unspecified assistantships also available. Financial award application deadline: 7/1; financial award applicants required to submit FAFSA. *Faculty research:* Criminology, gangs, courts, policing, ethics, women's studies, methods. *Unit head:* Dr. Laurel Holland, Interim Chair, 678-839-6505, Fax: 678-839-6506, E-mail: lholland@westga.edu. *Application contact:* Dr. Charles W. Clark, Dean, 678-839-6508, E-mail: cclark@westga.edu.

University of Windsor, Faculty of Graduate Studies, Faculty of Arts and Social Sciences, Department of Sociology and Anthropology, Windsor, ON N9B 3P4, Canada. Offers criminology (MA); sociology (MA); sociology-social justice (PhD). Part-time programs available. *Degree requirements:* For master's, thesis; for doctorate, comprehensive exam, thesis/dissertation. *Entrance requirements:* For master's, minimum B+ average; for doctorate, writing sample, minimum B+ average. Additional exam requirements/recommendations for international students: Required—TOEFL (minimum score 560 paper-based; 220 computer-based). Electronic applications accepted. *Faculty research:* Power and social change; criminology/deviance; social psychology; comparative development; race and ethnic relations; family, sex, and gender, social justice.

University of Wisconsin–Milwaukee, Graduate School, School of Social Welfare, Department of Criminal Justice, Milwaukee, WI 53201-0413. Offers administration (MS); corrections (MS); law enforcement (MS). Part-time programs available. *Faculty:* 7 full-time (2 women). *Students:* 20 full-time (12 women), 10 part-time (8 women); includes 1 Black or African American, non-Hispanic/Latino; 1 Asian, non-Hispanic/Latino. Average age 27. 35 applicants, 51% accepted, 13 enrolled. In 2010, 10 master's awarded. *Degree requirements:* For master's, thesis or alternative. *Entrance requirements:* For master's, GRE General Test, MAT. Additional exam requirements/recommendations for international students: Required—TOEFL (minimum score 550 paper-based; 79 iBT), IELTS (minimum score 6.5). *Application deadline:* For fall admission, 1/1 priority date for domestic students; for spring admission, 9/1 for domestic students. Applications are processed on a rolling basis. Application fee: $56 ($96 for international students). Electronic applications accepted. *Financial support:* In 2010–11, 2 teaching assistantships with full tuition reimbursements were awarded; fellowships, research assistantships, career-related internships or fieldwork, health care benefits, unspecified assistantships, and project assistantships also available. Support available to part-time students. Financial award application deadline: 4/15; financial award applicants required to submit FAFSA. *Unit head:* Steven Brandl, Representative, 414-229-5443, Fax: 414-229-5311, E-mail: sgb@uwm.edu. *Application contact:* General Information Contact, 414-229-4982, Fax: 414-229-6967, E-mail: gradschool@uwm.edu.

University of Wisconsin–Platteville, School of Graduate Studies, Distance Learning Center, Online Master of Science in Criminal Justice Program, Platteville, WI 53818-3099. Offers MS. Part-time and evening/weekend programs available. Postbaccalaureate distance learning degree programs offered (no on-campus study). *Students:* 1 (woman) full-time, 71 part-time (36 women); includes 8 minority (5 Black or African American, non-Hispanic/Latino; 2 American Indian or Alaska Native, non-Hispanic/Latino; 1 Hispanic/Latino), 5 international. 32 applicants, 72% accepted, 17 enrolled. In 2010, 18 master's awarded. *Degree requirements:* For master's, thesis or alternative. *Entrance requirements:* Additional exam requirements/recommendations for international students: Required—TOEFL (minimum score 500 paper-based; 173 computer-based; 61 iBT). *Application deadline:* For fall admission, 7/1 priority date for domestic students; for spring admission, 11/1 priority date for domestic students. Applications are processed on a rolling basis. Application fee: $56. Electronic applications accepted. *Expenses:* Contact institution. *Financial support:* Scholarships/grants available. Support available to part-time students. *Unit head:* Dr. Cheryl Banachowski-Fuller, Coordinator, 608-342-1652, Fax: 608-342-1986, E-mail: banachoc@uwplatt.edu. *Application contact:* 608-342-1652, Fax: 608-342-1986, E-mail: criminaljstc@uwplatt.edu.

Upper Iowa University, Online Master's Programs, Fayette, IA 52142-1857. Offers accounting (MBA); corporate financial management (MBA); global business (MBA); health and human

Criminal Justice and Criminology

Upper Iowa University *(continued)*

services (MPA); higher education administration (MHEA); homeland security (MPA); human resources management (MBA); justice administration (MPA); organizational development (MBA); public personnel management (MPA); quality management (MBA). MBA also available at Madison, WI campus. Part-time programs available. Postbaccalaureate distance learning degree programs offered (no on-campus study). *Degree requirements:* For master's, research project. *Entrance requirements:* For master's, GMAT, GRE, or minimum GPA of 2.7 during last 60 hours. Additional exam requirements/recommendations for international students: Required—TOEFL (minimum score 570 paper-based; 230 computer-based). Electronic applications accepted. *Faculty research:* Total quality management, CQI, teams, organization culture and climate, management.

Urbana University, College of Social and Behavioral Sciences, Urbana, OH 43078-2091. Offers criminal justice administration (MA). *Entrance requirements:* For master's, 3 letters of recommendation.

Utica College, Program in Economic Crime and Fraud Management, Utica, NY 13502-4892. Offers MBA. Part-time and evening/weekend programs available. Postbaccalaureate distance learning degree programs offered (minimal on-campus study). *Faculty:* 7 full-time (0 women). *Students:* 3 full-time (2 women), 95 part-time (65 women); includes 11 Black or African American, non-Hispanic/Latino; 3 Asian, non-Hispanic/Latino; 3 Hispanic/Latino, 1 international. Average age 33. In 2010, 41 master's awarded. *Entrance requirements:* For master's, BS, minimum GPA of 3.0. Additional exam requirements/recommendations for international students: Required—TOEFL (minimum score 525 paper-based; 195 computer-based). *Application deadline:* Applications are processed on a rolling basis. Application fee: $50. Electronic applications accepted. *Expenses:* Contact institution. *Financial support:* Career-related internships or fieldwork, scholarships/grants, tuition waivers (partial), and unspecified assistantships available. Support available to part-time students. Financial award application deadline: 3/15; financial award applicants required to submit FAFSA. *Unit head:* Dr. R. Bruce McBride, Director of Economic Crime Graduate Programs, 315-792-3808, E-mail: rmcbride@utica.edu. *Application contact:* John D. Rowe, Director of Graduate Admissions, 315-792-3824, Fax: 315-792-3003, E-mail: jrowe@utica.edu.

Utica College, Program in Economic Crime Management, Utica, NY 13502-4892. Offers MS. Part-time programs available. Postbaccalaureate distance learning degree programs offered (minimal on-campus study). *Faculty:* 4 full-time (0 women). *Students:* 1 (woman) full-time, 103 part-time (51 women); includes 7 Black or African American, non-Hispanic/Latino; 1 American Indian or Alaska Native, non-Hispanic/Latino; 2 Asian, non-Hispanic/Latino; 6 Hispanic/Latino, 1 international. Average age 36. In 2010, 35 master's awarded. *Degree requirements:* For master's, thesis. *Entrance requirements:* For master's, BS, minimum GPA of 3.0. Additional exam requirements/recommendations for international students: Required—TOEFL (minimum score 525 paper-based; 195 computer-based). *Application deadline:* Applications are processed on a rolling basis. Application fee: $50. Electronic applications accepted. *Expenses:* Contact institution. *Financial support:* Career-related internships or fieldwork, scholarships/grants, tuition waivers (partial), and unspecified assistantships available. Support available to part-time students. Financial award application deadline: 3/15; financial award applicants required to submit FAFSA. *Unit head:* Dr. R. Bruce McBride, Director of Economic Crime Graduate Programs, 315-792-3808, E-mail: rmcbride@utica.edu. *Application contact:* John D. Rowe, Director of Graduate Admissions, 315-792-3824, Fax: 315-792-3003, E-mail: jrowe@utica.edu.

Valdosta State University, Department of Sociology, Anthropology, and Criminal Justice, Valdosta, GA 31698. Offers criminal justice (MS); marriage and family therapy (MS); sociology (MS). *Accreditation:* AAMFT/COAMFTE. Part-time and evening/weekend programs available. *Faculty:* 18 full-time (9 women). *Students:* 3 full-time (2 women), 11 part-time (8 women); includes 6 minority (4 Black or African American, non-Hispanic/Latino; 1 American Indian or Alaska Native, non-Hispanic/Latino; 1 Asian, non-Hispanic/Latino). Average age 25. 6 applicants, 83% accepted, 5 enrolled. In 2010, 8 master's awarded. *Degree requirements:* For master's, thesis or alternative, comprehensive written and/or oral exams. *Entrance requirements:* For master's, GRE General Test or MAT (sociology, marriage and family therapy), minimum GPA of 2.5. Additional exam requirements/recommendations for international students: Required—TOEFL (minimum score 523 paper-based; 193 computer-based). *Application deadline:* For fall admission, 7/1 for domestic and international students; for spring admission, 11/15 for domestic and international students. Applications are processed on a rolling basis. Application fee: $35. Electronic applications accepted. *Expenses:* Tuition, state resident: full-time $5256; part-time $197 per credit hour. Tuition, nonresident: full-time $14,490; part-time $710 per credit hour. Required fees: $855 per semester. Tuition and fees vary according to course load and campus/location. *Financial support:* In 2010–11, 5 students received support, including 5 research assistantships with full tuition reimbursements available (averaging $3,652 per year); career-related internships or fieldwork, institutionally sponsored loans, scholarships/grants, and unspecified assistantships also available. Support available to part-time students. Financial award application deadline: 7/1; financial award applicants required to submit FAFSA. *Faculty research:* Police-civilian ride-along project. *Unit head:* Dr. Mike Capece, Acting Head, 229-333-5943, Fax: 229-333-5492. *Application contact:* Misty Lamb, Admissions Specialist, 229-333-5694, Fax: 229-245-3853, E-mail: mllamb@valdosta.edu.

Virginia College at Birmingham, Virginia College Online, Birmingham, AL 35209. Offers business administration (MBA); criminal justice (MCJ); cybersecurity (MC). Part-time and evening/weekend programs available. Postbaccalaureate distance learning degree programs offered (no on-campus study).

Virginia Commonwealth University, Graduate School, College of Humanities and Sciences, Wilder School of Government and Public Affairs, Department of Criminal Justice, Richmond, VA 23284-9005. Offers MS, CCJA. Part-time and evening/weekend programs available. *Students:* 34 full-time (25 women), 25 part-time (15 women); includes 12 minority (6 Black or African American, non-Hispanic/Latino; 1 Asian, non-Hispanic/Latino; 5 Hispanic/Latino), 1 international. 57 applicants, 75% accepted, 29 enrolled. In 2010, 28 master's, 8 other advanced degrees awarded. *Degree requirements:* For master's, thesis or comprehensive exam. *Entrance requirements:* For master's, GRE, LSAT or GMAT, minimum cumulative GPA of 3.0. Additional exam requirements/recommendations for international students: Required—TOEFL (minimum score 600 paper-based; 250 computer-based; 100 iBT); Recommended—IELTS (minimum score 6.5). *Application deadline:* For fall admission, 7/15 for domestic students; for spring admission, 10/1 for domestic students. Applications are processed on a rolling basis. Application fee: $50. Electronic applications accepted. *Expenses:* Tuition, state resident: full-time $4308; part-time $479 per credit hour. Tuition, nonresident: full-time $8942; part-time $994 per credit hour. Required fees: $2000; $85 per credit hour. Tuition and fees vary according to course level, course load, degree level, campus/location and program. *Financial support:* Federal Work-Study, institutionally sponsored loans, and tuition waivers (full and partial) available. Support available to part-time students. Financial award application deadline: 3/1. *Unit head:* Dr. Jill A. Gordon, Program Chair, 804-827-0901, E-mail: jagordon@vcu.edu. *Application contact:* Dr. Jill A. Gordon, Program Chair, 804-827-0901, Fax: 804-828-1253, E-mail: jagordon@vcu.edu.

Walden University, Graduate Programs, School of Counseling and Social Service, Minneapolis, MN 55401. Offers career counseling (MS); counselor education and supervision (PhD), including consultation, counseling and social change, forensic mental health counseling, general program, nonprofit management and leadership, trauma and crisis; human services (PhD), including clinical social work, counseling, criminal justice, disaster, crisis and intervention, family studies and intervention strategies, general program, human services administration, public health, self-designed, social policy analysis and planning; marriage, couple, and family counseling (MS), including forensic counseling, trauma and crisis counseling; mental health counseling (MS), including forensic counseling. Part-time and evening/weekend programs available. Postbaccalaureate distance learning degree programs offered (minimal on-campus study). *Faculty:* 25 full-time (17 women), 241 part-time/adjunct (162 women). *Students:* 2,687 full-time (2,269 women), 536 part-time (473 women); includes 1,582 minority (1,319 Black or African American, non-Hispanic/Latino; 34 American Indian or Alaska Native, non-Hispanic/Latino; 29 Asian, non-Hispanic/Latino; 142 Hispanic/Latino; 58 Two or more races, non-Hispanic/Latino), 47 international. Average age 38. In 2010, 182 master's, 8 doctorates awarded. *Degree requirements:* For master's, residency (for some programs); for doctorate, thesis/dissertation, residency. *Entrance requirements:* For master's, bachelor's degree or equivalent in related field, minimum GPA of 2.5; for doctorate, master's degree or equivalent in related field; minimum GPA of 3.0; official transcripts; three years' related professional/academic experience (preferred); access to computer and Internet. Additional exam requirements/recommendations for international students: Required—TOEFL (minimum score 550 paper-based; 213 computer-based), IELTS (minimum score 6.5), TOEFL (minimum score 550 paper-based; 213 computer-based), IELTS (minimum score 6.5), or Michigan English Language Assessment Battery (minimum score 82). *Application deadline:* Applications are processed on a rolling basis. Application fee: $50. Electronic applications accepted. *Expenses:* Tuition: Full-time $10,274; part-time $445 per credit. Tuition and fees vary according to course load, degree level and program. *Financial support:* Fellowships, Federal Work-Study, scholarships/grants, unspecified assistantships, and family tuition reduction, active duty/veteran tuition reduction, group tuition reduction, interest-free payment plans available. Support available to part-time students. Financial award applicants required to submit FAFSA. *Unit head:* Dr. Savitri Dixon-Saxon, Associate Dean, 800-925-3368. *Application contact:* Jennifer Hall, Vice President of Enrollment Management, 866-4-WALDEN, E-mail: info@waldenu.edu.

Walden University, Graduate Programs, School of Public Policy and Administration, Minneapolis, MN 55401. Offers criminal justice (MPA); emergency management (MPA); government management (Postbaccalaureate Certificate); health policy (MPA); homeland security policy (MPA); homeland security policy and coordination (MPA); interdisciplinary policy studies (MPA); international nongovernmental organizations (ngos) (MPA); law and public policy (MPA); local government management for sustainable communities (MPA); nonprofit management (Postbaccalaureate Certificate); nonprofit management and leadership (MPA, MS); policy analysis (MPA); public management and leadership (MPA); public policy and administration (MPA, PhD), including criminal justice (PhD), emergency management (PhD), health policy (PhD), health services (PhD), homeland security policy (PhD), homeland security policy and coordination (PhD), interdisciplinary policy studies (PhD), international nongovernmental organizations (PhD), law and public policy (PhD), local government management for sustainable communities (PhD), nonprofit management and leadership (PhD), policy analysis (PhD), public management and leadership (PhD), terrorism, mediation, and peace (PhD); terrorism, mediation, and peace (MPA). Part-time and evening/weekend programs available. Postbaccalaureate distance learning degree programs offered (minimal on-campus study). *Faculty:* 10 full-time (5 women), 117 part-time/adjunct (49 women). *Students:* 1,408 full-time (901 women), 599 part-time (392 women); includes 1,022 Black or African American, non-Hispanic/Latino; 11 American Indian or Alaska Native, non-Hispanic/Latino; 37 Asian, non-Hispanic/Latino; 64 Hispanic/Latino; 26 Two or more races, non-Hispanic/Latino, 47 international. Average age 40. In 2010, 311 master's, 23 doctorates awarded. *Degree requirements:* For doctorate, thesis/dissertation, residency. *Entrance requirements:* For master's, bachelor's degree or equivalent in related field, minimum GPA of 2.5; for doctorate, master's degree or equivalent in related field; minimum GPA of 3.0; official transcripts; three years of related professional/academic experience (preferred); access to computer and Internet. Additional exam requirements/recommendations for international students: Required—TOEFL (minimum score 550 paper-based; 213 computer-based), IELTS (minimum score 6.5), TOEFL (minimum score 550 paper-based; 213 computer-based), IELTS (minimum score 6.5), or Michigan English Language Assessment Battery (minimum score 82). *Application deadline:* Applications are processed on a rolling basis. Application fee: $50. Electronic applications accepted. *Expenses:* Tuition: Full-time $10,274; part-time $445 per credit. Tuition and fees vary according to course load, degree level and program. *Financial support:* Fellowships with tuition reimbursements, Federal Work-Study, scholarships/grants, unspecified assistantships, and family tuition reduction, active duty/veteran tuition reduction, group tuition reduction, interest-free payment plans available. Support available to part-time students. Financial award applicants required to submit FAFSA. *Unit head:* Dr. Mark Gordon, Associate Dean, 800-925-3368. *Application contact:* Jennifer Hall, Vice President of Enrollment Management, 866-4-WALDEN, E-mail: info@waldenu.edu.

Washburn University, School of Applied Studies, Department of Criminal Justice, Topeka, KS 66621. Offers MCJ. Part-time and evening/weekend programs available. Postbaccalaureate distance learning degree programs offered (minimal on-campus study). *Faculty:* 4 full-time (1 woman), 5 part-time/adjunct (2 women). *Students:* 20 full-time (10 women), 9 part-time (5 women); includes 5 Black or African American, non-Hispanic/Latino; 1 Asian, non-Hispanic/Latino; 2 Hispanic/Latino. Average age 27. 10 applicants, 80% accepted, 7 enrolled. In 2010, 7 master's awarded. *Degree requirements:* For master's, thesis or alternative, continuous enrollment each fall and spring semester, completion of all program requirements within seven years of entry (MCJ). *Entrance requirements:* For master's, GRE (may be waived in certain situations), 3 letters of reference, minimum GPA for undergraduate degree of 3.0, short biography, official transcripts. Additional exam requirements/recommendations for international students: Required—TOEFL (minimum score 79 iBT). *Application deadline:* For fall admission, 4/1 priority date for domestic and international students; for spring admission, 11/1 priority date for domestic and international students. Applications are processed on a rolling basis. Application fee: $35. Electronic applications accepted. *Expenses:* Tuition, state resident: full-time $5130; part-time $285 per credit hour. Tuition, nonresident: full-time $10,476; part-time $582 per credit hour. Required fees: $86; $43 per semester. Tuition and fees vary according to program. *Financial support:* Institutionally sponsored loans and scholarships/grants available. Support available to part-time students. Financial award application deadline: 3/1; financial award applicants required to submit FAFSA. *Faculty research:* Practitioner behavior, police management and training, field and institutional correction administration, terrorism, police training, sex slaves. *Unit head:* Dr. Gerald Bayens, Department Chair, 785-670-1411, Fax: 785-670-1027, E-mail: gerald.bayens@washburn.edu. *Application contact:* Dr. Phyllis E. Berry, MCJ Graduate Director, 785-670-2057, Fax: 785-670-1027, E-mail: phyllis.berry@washburn.edu.

Washington State University, Graduate School, College of Liberal Arts, Department of Political Science, Program in Criminal Justice, Pullman, WA 99164. Offers MA, PhD. *Faculty:* 8. *Students:* 24 full-time (11 women), 6 part-time (2 women); includes 1 Black or African American, non-Hispanic/Latino; 1 American Indian or Alaska Native, non-Hispanic/Latino; 1 Asian, non-Hispanic/Latino; 1 Hispanic/Latino, 3 international. Average age 32. 33 applicants, 58% accepted, 2 enrolled. In 2010, 15 master's, 5 doctorates awarded. *Degree requirements:* For master's, comprehensive exam (for some programs), thesis, oral exam; for doctorate, comprehensive exam, thesis/dissertation, oral or written exam. *Entrance requirements:* For master's, GRE General Test, major in criminal justice, sociology, psychology, liberal arts, or a related field; strong writing and analytical skills; minimum GPA of 3.0; for doctorate, GRE General Test, major in criminal justice, sociology, psychology, liberal arts, or a related field; strong writing and analytical skills. Additional exam requirements/recommendations for international students: Required—TOEFL, IELTS. *Application deadline:* For fall admission, 1/10 priority date for domestic and international students. Application fee: $50. Electronic applications accepted. *Expenses:* Tuition, state resident: full-time $8552; part-time $443 per credit. Tuition, nonresident: full-time $21,650; part-time $1083 per credit. Required fees: $846. *Financial support:* In 2010–11, 6 research assistantships with full and partial tuition reimbursements (averaging $13,917 per year), 7 teaching assistantships with full and partial tuition reimbursements (averaging $13,056 per year) were awarded; career-related internships or fieldwork, Federal Work-Study, institutionally sponsored loans, health care benefits, tuition waivers (partial), and teaching associateships also available. Financial award application deadline: 2/15; financial award applicants required to submit FAFSA. *Faculty research:* Community policing, community justice, corrections policy, crime prevention policy, criminal justice management. *Unit head:* Dr. Otwin Marenin, Interim Director, 509-335-2544, Fax: 509-335-7990, E-mail: siskeo@wsu.edu. *Application contact:* Graduate School Admissions, 800-GRADWSU, Fax: 509-335-1949, E-mail: gradsch@wsu.edu.

Washington State University Spokane, Graduate Programs, Program in Criminal Justice, Spokane, WA 99210. Offers MA, PhD. *Faculty:* 25. *Students:* 6 full-time (4 women), 4 part-time

(1 woman). Average age 42. *Degree requirements:* For master's, comprehensive exam, thesis (for some programs); for doctorate, comprehensive exam, thesis/dissertation. *Entrance requirements:* For master's, GRE, minimum GPA of 3.0. Additional exam requirements/recommendations for international students: Required—TOEFL (minimum score 550 paper-based). *Application deadline:* For fall admission, 1/10 priority date for domestic students, 1/10 for international students; for spring admission, 7/1 priority date for domestic students, 7/1 for international students. Application fee: $50. *Financial support:* In 2010–11, research assistantships (averaging $14,634 per year), teaching assistantships (averaging $13,383 per year) were awarded; fellowships also available. Financial award application deadline: 2/15. *Faculty research:* Community-oriented policing, crime, criminology theory, jury system, judicial evaluations, police performance. Total annual research expenditures: $443,591. *Unit head:* Dr. David Brody, Campus Academic Director, 509-358-7952, Fax: 509-358-7900, E-mail: brody@wsu.edu. *Application contact:* Graduate School Admissions, 800-GRADWSU, Fax: 509-335-1949, E-mail: gradsch@wsu.edu.

Wayland Baptist University, Graduate Programs, Program in Counseling, Plainview, TX 79072-6998. Offers counseling (MA); government administration (MPA); homeland security (MPA); justice administration (MPA). Part-time and evening/weekend programs available. Postbaccalaureate distance learning degree programs offered. *Degree requirements:* For master's, comprehensive exam. *Entrance requirements:* For master's, GRE, MAT. Additional exam requirements/recommendations for international students: Required—TOEFL (minimum score 500 paper-based; 173 computer-based; 61 iBT). Electronic applications accepted.

Wayne State University, College of Liberal Arts and Sciences, Department of Criminal Justice, Detroit, MI 48202. Offers MS. *Faculty:* 4 full-time (0 women), 3 part-time/adjunct (1 woman). *Students:* 19 full-time (15 women), 29 part-time (18 women); includes 20 minority (19 Black or African American, non-Hispanic/Latino; 1 Hispanic/Latino), 2 international. Average age 31. 33 applicants, 58% accepted, 11 enrolled. In 2010, 3 master's awarded. *Degree requirements:* For master's, comprehensive exam, essay. *Entrance requirements:* For master's, GRE (if GPA is between 2.75 and 2.99), minimum GPA of 3.0 (resume and writing sample if less than 3.0), 2 letters of recommendation. Additional exam requirements/recommendations for international students: Required—TOEFL (minimum score 550 paper-based; 213 computer-based); Recommended—TWE (minimum score 6). *Application deadline:* For fall admission, 7/1 for domestic students, 5/1 for international students; for winter admission, 11/1 for domestic students, 9/1 for international students. Applications are processed on a rolling basis. Application fee: $50. Electronic applications accepted. *Expenses:* Tuition, state resident: full-time $7662; part-time $478.85 per credit hour. Tuition, nonresident: full-time $16,920; part-time $1057.55 per credit hour. Required fees: $571.20; $35.70 per credit hour. $188.05 per semester. Tuition and fees vary according to course load and program. *Financial support:* In 2010–11, 2 students received support, including 1 teaching assistantship with tuition reimbursement available (averaging $15,181 per year); scholarships/grants also available. *Faculty research:* Criminology, juvenile delinquency and justice, law, policing, corrections, social deviance. *Unit head:* Marvin Zalman, Chair, 313-577-2705, Fax: 313-577-9977, E-mail: aa1887@wayne.edu. *Application contact:* Marvin Zalman, Chair, 313-577-2705, Fax: 313-577-9977, E-mail: aa1887@wayne.edu.

Wayne State University, College of Liberal Arts and Sciences, Department of Political Science, Program in Public Administration, Detroit, MI 48202. Offers criminal justice (MPA); public administration (MPA). *Accreditation:* NASPAA. Evening/weekend programs available. *Faculty:* 16 full-time (5 women), 2 part-time/adjunct (1 woman). *Students:* 15 full-time (9 women), 67 part-time (45 women); includes 27 minority (22 Black or African American, non-Hispanic/Latino; 1 American Indian or Alaska Native, non-Hispanic/Latino; 2 Asian, non-Hispanic/Latino; 2 Hispanic/Latino), 1 international. Average age 32. 47 applicants, 70% accepted, 22 enrolled. In 2010, 24 master's awarded. *Entrance requirements:* For master's, GRE General Test. Additional exam requirements/recommendations for international students: Required—TOEFL (minimum score 550 paper-based; 213 computer-based); Recommended—TWE (minimum score 6). *Application deadline:* For fall admission, 7/1 for domestic students, 6/1 for international students; for winter admission, 10/1 for international students; for spring admission, 2/1 for international students. Applications are processed on a rolling basis. Application fee: $30 ($50 for international students). Electronic applications accepted. *Expenses:* Tuition, state resident: full-time $7662; part-time $478.85 per credit hour. Tuition, nonresident: full-time $16,920; part-time $1057.55 per credit hour. Required fees: $571.20; $35.70 per credit hour. $188.05 per semester. Tuition and fees vary according to course load and program. *Faculty research:* Urban politics, urban education, state administration. *Unit head:* John Strate, Director, 313-577-2639, E-mail: jstrate@wayne.edu. *Application contact:* Ewa Golebiowska, Associate Professor, 313-577-2630, Fax: 313-993-3435, E-mail: ewa_golebiowska@wayne.edu.

Webber International University, Graduate School of Business, Babson Park, FL 33827-0096. Offers accounting (MBA); management (MBA); security management (MBA); sports management (MBA). Part-time and evening/weekend programs available. *Degree requirements:* For master's, thesis or alternative. *Entrance requirements:* For master's, previous course work in financial and managerial accounting. Additional exam requirements/recommendations for international students: Required—TOEFL. *Faculty research:* Finance strategy, market research, investments, intranet.

Webster University, George Herbert Walker School of Business and Technology, Department of Business, St. Louis, MO 63119-3194. Offers business (MA); business and organizational security management (MBA); computer resources and information management (MBA); environmental management (MBA); finance (MA, MBA); health services management (MBA); human resources development (MBA); human resources management (MBA); international business (MA, MBA); management and leadership (MBA); marketing (MBA); procurement and acquisitions management (MBA); telecommunications management (MBA). *Accreditation:* ACBSP. Part-time and evening/weekend programs available. Postbaccalaureate distance learning degree programs offered (no on-campus study). *Degree requirements:* For master's, comprehensive exam (for some programs), thesis (for some programs). *Entrance requirements:* Additional exam requirements/recommendations for international students: Required—TOEFL. *Expenses:* Tuition: Part-time $585 per credit hour. Tuition and fees vary according to degree level, campus/location and program.

Webster University, George Herbert Walker School of Business and Technology, Department of Management, St. Louis, MO 63119-3194. Offers business and organizational security management (MA); computer resources and information management (MA); environmental management (MS); government contracting (Certificate); health care management (MA); health services management (MA); human resources development (MA); human resources management (MA); management (DM); management and leadership (MA); marketing (MA); nonprofit management (Certificate); procurement and acquisitions management (MA); public administration (MA); quality management (MA); space systems operations management (MS); telecommunications management (MA). *Accreditation:* ACBSP. Part-time and evening/weekend programs available. Postbaccalaureate distance learning degree programs offered (no on-campus study). *Degree requirements:* For master's, thesis (for some programs); for doctorate, thesis/dissertation, written exam. *Entrance requirements:* For doctorate, GMAT, 3 years of work experience, MBA. Additional exam requirements/recommendations for international students: Required—TOEFL. *Expenses:* Tuition: Part-time $585 per credit hour. Tuition and fees vary according to degree level, campus/location and program.

West Chester University of Pennsylvania, Office of Graduate Studies, College of Business and Public Affairs, Department of Criminal Justice, West Chester, PA 19383. Offers criminal justice (MS). Part-time and evening/weekend programs available. *Students:* 31 full-time (18 women), 25 part-time (13 women); includes 10 minority (7 Black or African American, non-Hispanic/Latino; 3 Hispanic/Latino). Average age 26. 40 applicants, 73% accepted, 15 enrolled. In 2010, 19 master's awarded. *Degree requirements:* For master's, 15-credit core (law, research, ethics, theories, and capstone independent research project); 15 additional credits of criminal justice electives. *Entrance requirements:* For master's, MAT, minimum GPA of 3.0; two letters of recommendation. Additional exam requirements/recommendations for international students: Required—TOEFL (minimum score 550 paper-based; 213 computer-based; 80 iBT). *Application deadline:* For fall admission, 4/15 priority date for domestic students, 3/15 for international students; for spring admission, 10/15 for domestic students, 9/1 for international students. Applications are processed on a rolling basis. Application fee: $35. Electronic applications accepted. *Expenses:* Tuition, state resident: full-time $6966; part-time $387 per credit. Tuition, nonresident: full-time $11,146; part-time $619 per credit. Required fees: $1614.40; $133.24 per credit. Part-time tuition and fees vary according to campus/location. *Financial support:* Unspecified assistantships available. Support available to part-time students. Financial award application deadline: 2/15; financial award applicants required to submit FAFSA. *Faculty research:* Criminal law, criminal procedure, Constitutional interpretation, drug and alcohol prevention, drug courts, mental health courts, legislation related to sex offending, animal cruelty, pharmaceutical battery. *Unit head:* Jana Nestlerode, Chair, 610-436-2647, E-mail: jnestlerode@wcupa.edu. *Application contact:* Dr. Mary P. Brewster, Graduate Coordinator, 610-436-2630, E-mail: mbrewster@wcupa.edu.

Western Connecticut State University, Division of Graduate Studies and External Programs, Ancell School of Business, Program in Justice Administration, Danbury, CT 06810-6885. Offers MS. Part-time programs available. *Students:* 1 (woman) full-time, 9 part-time (4 women). Average age 31. In 2010, 4 master's awarded. *Degree requirements:* For master's, comprehensive exam or research project, completion of program within 6 years. *Entrance requirements:* For master's, GMAT, GRE, LSAT, or MAT. Additional exam requirements/recommendations for international students: Recommended—TOEFL (minimum score 550 paper-based; 213 computer-based; 79 iBT), IELTS (minimum score 6). *Application deadline:* For fall admission, 8/5 priority date for domestic students; for spring admission, 1/5 priority date for domestic students. Applications are processed on a rolling basis. Application fee: $50. *Expenses:* Tuition, state resident: full-time $5012; part-time $417 per credit hour. Tuition, nonresident: full-time $13,962; part-time $423 per credit hour. Required fees: $3886. Full-time tuition and fees vary according to course load, degree level and program. *Financial support:* Application deadline: 5/1. *Unit head:* Dr. George Kain, Coordinator, 203-837-8514, Fax: 203-837-8527. *Application contact:* Chris Shankle, Associate Director of Graduate Admissions, 203-837-9005, Fax: 203-837-8326, E-mail: shanklec@wcsu.edu.

Western Illinois University, School of Graduate Studies, College of Education and Human Services, School of Law Enforcement and Justice Administration, Macomb, IL 61455-1390. Offers law enforcement and justice administration (MA); police executive administration (Certificate). Part-time programs available. *Students:* 21 full-time (8 women), 30 part-time (11 women); includes 6 minority (2 Black or African American, non-Hispanic/Latino; 4 Hispanic/Latino). Average age 29. 20 applicants, 85% accepted. In 2010, 38 master's, 2 other advanced degrees awarded. *Degree requirements:* For master's, thesis or alternative. *Entrance requirements:* For master's, GRE or MAT, minimum GPA of 3.0. Additional exam requirements/recommendations for international students: Required—TOEFL (minimum score 520 paper-based; 190 computer-based; 68 iBT). *Application deadline:* Applications are processed on a rolling basis. Application fee: $30. Electronic applications accepted. *Expenses:* Tuition, state resident: full-time $6370; part-time $265.40 per credit hour. Tuition, nonresident: full-time $12,740; part-time $530.80 per credit hour. Required fees: $75.67 per credit hour. *Financial support:* In 2010–11, 8 students received support, including 7 research assistantships with full tuition reimbursements available (averaging $7,280 per year), 1 teaching assistantship with full tuition reimbursement available (averaging $8,400 per year). Financial award applicants required to submit FAFSA. *Unit head:* Dr. Terry Mors, Director, 309-298-1038. *Application contact:* Evelyn Hoing, Assistant Director of Graduate Studies, 309-298-1806, Fax: 309-298-2345, E-mail: grad-office@wiu.edu.

Western Kentucky University, Graduate Studies, Potter College of Arts and Letters, Department of Sociology, Bowling Green, KY 42101. Offers criminology (MA); sociology (MA). Postbaccalaureate distance learning degree programs offered. *Degree requirements:* For master's, comprehensive exam, thesis optional, final exam. *Entrance requirements:* For master's, GRE General Test, minimum GPA of 3.0. Additional exam requirements/recommendations for international students: Required—TOEFL (minimum score 555 paper-based; 213 computer-based; 79 iBT). *Faculty research:* Criminology/delinquency, quantitative and survey research methodology, occupations/professions, sex and gender, demography.

Western Oregon University, Graduate Programs, College of Liberal Arts and Sciences, Division of Social Science, Monmouth, OR 97361-1394. Offers criminal justice (MA, MS). Part-time and evening/weekend programs available. *Degree requirements:* For master's, thesis optional, written exams. *Entrance requirements:* For master's, minimum GPA of 3.0. Additional exam requirements/recommendations for international students: Required—TOEFL (minimum score 550 paper-based; 213 computer-based; 79 iBT), IELTS (minimum score 6.5). *Faculty research:* Prison to community transition of adult felons, community justice, restorative justice, parole and probation.

Westfield State University, Division of Graduate and Continuing Education, Department of Criminal Justice, Westfield, MA 01086. Offers MS. Part-time and evening/weekend programs available. *Degree requirements:* For master's, comprehensive exam, thesis (for some programs). *Entrance requirements:* For master's, GRE General Test or MAT, minimum undergraduate GPA of 2.7.

West Texas A&M University, College of Education and Social Sciences, Department of History and Political Science, Program in Criminal Justice, Canyon, TX 79016-0001. Offers MA. Part-time and evening/weekend programs available. *Degree requirements:* For master's, comprehensive exam, thesis optional. *Entrance requirements:* For master's, GRE General Test. Additional exam requirements/recommendations for international students: Required—TOEFL (minimum score 550 paper-based). Electronic applications accepted. *Faculty research:* Racial profiling, changing nature of prisons, campus police and parking services.

Wichita State University, Graduate School, Fairmount College of Liberal Arts and Sciences, School of Community Affairs, Wichita, KS 67260. Offers criminal justice (MA). Part-time programs available. *Unit head:* Dr. Michael Birzer, Director, 316-978-7200, Fax: 316-978-3626, E-mail: michael.birzer@wichita.edu. *Application contact:* Dr. Michael Birzer, Director, 316-978-7200, Fax: 316-978-3626, E-mail: michael.birzer@wichita.edu.

Widener University, College of Arts and Sciences, Program in Criminal Justice, Chester, PA 19013-5792. Offers MA, Psy D/MA. Part-time and evening/weekend programs available. *Faculty:* 1 full-time (0 women), 2 part-time/adjunct (0 women). *Students:* 15 part-time (9 women); includes 6 minority (all Black or African American, non-Hispanic/Latino). Average age 31. 21 applicants, 90% accepted. In 2010, 1 master's awarded. *Degree requirements:* For master's, project. *Entrance requirements:* For master's, interview, minimum undergraduate GPA of 3.0. *Application deadline:* For fall admission, 3/1 priority date for domestic students. Applications are processed on a rolling basis. Application fee: $25 ($300 for international students). *Expenses:* Contact institution. *Financial support:* Career-related internships or fieldwork and institutionally sponsored loans available. Support available to part-time students. Financial award application deadline: 5/1. *Faculty research:* Criminal law and procedure, corrections, domestic violence. *Unit head:* Dr. William E. Harver, Director, 610-499-4554, Fax: 510-499-4605, E-mail: william.e.harver@widener.edu. *Application contact:* Christine M. Weist, Assistant to Associate Provost for Graduate Studies, 610-499-4351, Fax: 610-499-4277, E-mail: christine.m.weist@widener.edu.

Wilfrid Laurier University, Laurier Brantford, Brantford, ON N3T 2Y3, Canada. Offers criminology (MA), including culture, crime and policy, international crime and justice, media criminology. *Faculty:* 13 full-time (6 women). *Degree requirements:* For master's, thesis. *Entrance requirements:* For master's, honours bachelor's degree with major in criminology or equivalent degree; minimum B+ average in final year and in all criminology courses. Additional exam requirements/recommendations for international students: Required—TOEFL (minimum score 89 iBT). *Application deadline:* For fall admission, 6/1 priority date for domestic students, 5/1 priority date for international students. Application fee: $100. Electronic applications accepted.

Criminal Justice and Criminology

Wilfrid Laurier University *(continued)*
Tuition and fees charges are reported in Canadian dollars. *Expenses:* Tuition, area resident: Full-time $15,300 Canadian dollars; part-time $1200 Canadian dollars per credit. International tuition: $21,300 Canadian dollars full-time. Required fees: $650 Canadian dollars; $100 Canadian dollars per credit. Tuition and fees vary according to course load, degree level, campus/location and program. *Financial support:* Career-related internships or fieldwork, scholarships/grants, health care benefits, and unspecified assistantships available. *Unit head:* Dr. Thomas Fleming, Graduate Coordinator, 519-756-8228 Ext. 5740, Fax: 519-759-2127, E-mail: tfleming@wlu.ca. *Application contact:* Jennifer Williams, Graduate Admissions and Records Officer, 519-884-0710 Ext. 3536, Fax: 519-884-1020, E-mail: gradstudies@wlu.ca.

Wilmington University, College of Social and Behavioral Sciences, New Castle, DE 19720-6491. Offers administration of human services (MS); administration of justice (MS); community counseling (MS). *Accreditation:* ACA. Part-time and evening/weekend programs available. *Entrance requirements:* Additional exam requirements/recommendations for international students: Required—TOEFL (minimum score 500 paper-based; 173 computer-based). Electronic applications accepted. *Expenses:* Tuition: Full-time $7110; part-time $395 per credit hour. Tuition and fees vary according to campus/location.

Wright State University, School of Graduate Studies, College of Liberal Arts, Program in Applied Behavioral Science, Dayton, OH 45435. Offers criminal justice and social problems (MA); international and comparative politics (MA). *Degree requirements:* For master's, thesis optional. *Entrance requirements:* Additional exam requirements/recommendations for international students: Required—TOEFL. *Faculty research:* Training and development, criminal justice and social problems, community systems, human factors, industrial/organizational psychology.

Xavier University, College of Social Sciences, Health and Education, Department of Criminal Justice, Cincinnati, OH 45207. Offers MS. Part-time and evening/weekend programs available. *Faculty:* 3 full-time (1 woman). *Students:* 4 full-time (1 woman), 6 part-time (3 women); includes 3 minority (2 Black or African American, non-Hispanic/Latino; 1 Asian, non-Hispanic/Latino). Average age 31. 17 applicants, 94% accepted, 5 enrolled. In 2010, 12 master's awarded. *Degree requirements:* For master's, comprehensive exam, thesis. *Entrance requirements:* For master's, MAT, GRE, or LSAT, minimum GPA of 2.7. Additional exam requirements/recommendations for international students: Required—TOEFL (minimum score 550 paper-based; 213 computer-based). *Application deadline:* For fall admission, 8/15 priority date for domestic students. Applications are processed on a rolling basis. Application fee: $35. Electronic applications accepted. *Expenses:* Tuition: Part-time $718 per credit hour. Tuition and fees vary according to degree level, campus/location and program. *Financial support:* In 2010–11, 6 students received support. Career-related internships or fieldwork, scholarships/grants, and unspecified assistantships available. Support available to part-time students. Financial award applicants required to submit FAFSA. *Faculty research:* Women and crime, crime policy, policing. *Unit head:* Dr. Y. Gail Hurst, Chair, 513-745-1070, Fax: 513-745-3220, E-mail: hurst@xavier.edu. *Application contact:* Roger Bosse, Graduate Services Director, 513-745-3357, Fax: 513-745-1048, E-mail: bosse@xavier.edu.

Youngstown State University, Graduate School, Bitonte College of Health and Human Services, Department of Criminal Justice, Youngstown, OH 44555-0001. Offers MS. Part-time and evening/weekend programs available. *Degree requirements:* For master's, thesis optional. *Entrance requirements:* For master's, minimum GPA of 2.7. Additional exam requirements/recommendations for international students: Required—TOEFL. *Faculty research:* Police human resource allocation, police administration, computerized test development, criminal law.

Forensic Sciences

Albany State University, College of Sciences and Health Professions, Department of Criminal Justice and Forensic Science, Albany, GA 31705-2717. Offers criminal justice (MS), including corrections, forensic science, law enforcement, public administration. Postbaccalaureate distance learning degree programs offered (no on-campus study). *Faculty:* 6 full-time (0 women), 2 part-time/adjunct (0 women). *Students:* 14 full-time (11 women), 41 part-time (30 women); includes 51 Black or African American, non-Hispanic/Latino. Average age 33. 20 applicants, 100% accepted, 14 enrolled. In 2010, 6 master's awarded. *Degree requirements:* For master's, comprehensive exam, thesis optional. *Entrance requirements:* For master's, GRE General Test or MAT. *Application deadline:* For fall admission, 7/15 for domestic students, 5/15 for international students; for spring admission, 11/15 for domestic students, 9/15 for international students. Applications are processed on a rolling basis. Application fee: $20. Electronic applications accepted. *Expenses:* Tuition, state resident: full-time $3060; part-time $170 per credit hour. Tuition, nonresident: full-time $12,204; part-time $678 per credit hour. Required fees: $1160. Part-time tuition and fees vary according to course load. *Financial support:* Application deadline: 4/15. *Faculty research:* Gang-related research, HIV-related research, behavioral-related research. Total annual research expenditures: $65,000. *Unit head:* Dr. Charles Ochie, Chair, 229-430-4864, Fax: 229-430-1676, E-mail: charles.ochie@asurams.edu. *Application contact:* Dr. Rani George, Dean, Graduate School, 229-430-5118, Fax: 229-430-6398, E-mail: rani.george@asurams.edu.

Alliant International University–Irvine, Center for Forensic Studies, Irvine, CA 92612. Offers Psy D.

Arcadia University, Graduate Studies, Program in Forensic Science, Glenside, PA 19038-3295. Offers MSFS. *Faculty:* 3 full-time (2 women), 12 part-time/adjunct (3 women). *Students:* 44 full-time (37 women), 3 part-time (1 woman); includes 2 minority (1 Asian, non-Hispanic/Latino; 1 Hispanic/Latino), 1 international. Average age 24. In 2010, 17 master's awarded. Application fee: $50. *Expenses:* Contact institution. *Unit head:* Heather Mazzanti, Director, 215-572-4140. *Application contact:* Office of Enrollment Management, 215-572-2910, Fax: 215-572-4049, E-mail: admiss@arcadia.edu.

See Display below and Close-Up on page 767.

Boston University, School of Medicine, Division of Graduate Medical Sciences, Program in Forensic Anthropology, Boston, MA 02215. Offers MS. *Faculty:* 10 full-time (3 women). *Students:* 22 full-time (16 women), 7 part-time (5 women); includes 2 Black or African American, non-Hispanic/Latino; 1 American Indian or Alaska Native, non-Hispanic/Latino; 4 Hispanic/Latino, 1 international. 42 applicants, 62% accepted, 15 enrolled. In 2010, 1 master's awarded. *Entrance requirements:* For master's, GRE. Additional exam requirements/recommendations for international students: Required—TOEFL. *Application deadline:* Applications are processed on a rolling basis. Application fee: $75. Electronic applications accepted. *Expenses:* Tuition:

Full-time $39,314; part-time $1228 per credit. Required fees: $40 per semester. *Financial support:* Applicants required to submit FAFSA. *Unit head:* Dr. Tara L. Moore, Co-Director, 617-638-4054, Fax: 617-638-4922, E-mail: tlmoore@bu.edu. *Application contact:* Patty Jones, Executive Financial Coordinator, 617-414-2315, E-mail: psterlin@bu.edu.

Cedar Crest College, Program in Forensic Science, Allentown, PA 18104-6196. Offers MS. *Degree requirements:* For master's, thesis. *Entrance requirements:* For master's, GRE. Electronic applications accepted. *Expenses:* Contact institution. *Faculty research:* Geotyping of low copy number DNA, presumptive and conformatory testing of GHB and GBL.

Chaminade University of Honolulu, Graduate Services, Program in Forensic Science, Honolulu, HI 96816-1578. Offers MSFS. Part-time programs available. *Degree requirements:* For master's, comprehensive exam, thesis or alternative. *Entrance requirements:* For master's, GRE, 2 letters of recommendation. Additional exam requirements/recommendations for international students: Required—TOEFL (minimum score 550 paper-based; 250 computer-based).

Champlain College, Graduate Studies, Burlington, VT 05402-0670. Offers business (MBA); digital forensic management (MS); education (M Ed); emergent media (MFA); health care management (MS); law (MS); managing innovation and information technology (MS); mediation and applied conflict studies (MS). Part-time programs available. Postbaccalaureate distance learning degree programs offered (no on-campus study). *Faculty:* 14 full-time (0 women), 24 part-time/adjunct (9 women). *Students:* 304 full-time (144 women), 2 part-time (both women). Average age 30. 271 applicants, 90% accepted, 216 enrolled. In 2010, 8 master's awarded. *Degree requirements:* For master's, capstone project. *Entrance requirements:* Additional exam requirements/recommendations for international students: Required—TOEFL. *Application deadline:* For fall admission, 8/1 priority date for domestic and international students; for spring admission, 1/1 priority date for domestic and international students. Applications are processed on a rolling basis. Application fee: $50. Electronic applications accepted. *Expenses:* Tuition: Part-time $740 per credit hour. Part-time tuition and fees vary according to program. *Financial support:* Applicants required to submit FAFSA. *Unit head:* Dr. Donald Haggerty, Associate Provost, Graduate Studies, 802-865-6403, Fax: 802-865-6447. *Application contact:* Jon Walsh, Assistant Vice President, Graduate Admission, 800-570-5858, E-mail: walsh@champlain.edu.

DeSales University, Graduate Division, Program in Criminal Justice, Center Valley, PA 18034-9568. Offers criminal justice (MACJ); digital forensics (online) (MACJ); investigative forensics (online) (MACJ). Part-time programs available. Postbaccalaureate distance learning degree programs offered (no on-campus study). *Entrance requirements:* Additional exam requirements/recommendations for international students: Required—TOEFL. *Application deadline:* Applications are processed on a rolling basis. Application fee: $35. Electronic applications accepted. *Expenses:* Tuition: Full-time $18,200; part-time $690 per credit. Required fees: $1200. *Unit head:* Dr. Patrick McGrain, Director, 610-282-1100 Ext. 1584, Fax: 610-282-0787, E-mail: patrick.mcgrain@desales.edu. *Application contact:* Caryn Stopper, Director of Graduate Admissions, 610-282-1100 Ext. 1768, Fax: 610-282-0525, E-mail: caryn.stopper@desales.edu.

Duquesne University, Bayer School of Natural and Environmental Sciences, Program in Forensic Science and Law, Pittsburgh, PA 15282-0001. Offers MS. *Faculty:* 4 full-time (2 women), 7 part-time/adjunct (4 women). *Students:* 14 full-time (7 women). Average age 23. 14 applicants, 100% accepted, 14 enrolled. In 2010, 19 master's awarded. *Degree requirements:* For master's, comprehensive exam. *Entrance requirements:* For master's, SAT or ACT, 1 recommendation form; minimum total QPA of 3.0, 2.5 in math and science. *Application deadline:* For fall admission, 7/1 for domestic and international students. Applications are processed on a rolling basis. Application fee: $50. Electronic applications accepted. *Expenses:* Tuition: Part-time $884 per credit. Required fees: $84 per credit. Tuition and fees vary according to course load. *Financial support:* In 2010–11, 1 student received support, including 1 research assistantship; career-related internships or fieldwork and unspecified assistantships also available. Financial award application deadline: 5/1. *Faculty research:* Extraction protocols, mass spectrometry, synthetic fiber analysis, synthetic polymer characterization, trace analysis, amplification of DNA, methods for labeling DNA, construction of a genetic profile, experiential exploration of mitochondrial DNA, the Y-chromosome, and amelogenin. *Unit head:* Dr. Federick W. Fochtman, Director, 412-396-6373, E-mail: fochtman@duq.edu. *Application contact:* Val Lijewski, Academic Advisor, 412-396-1084, Fax: 412-396-1402, E-mail: lijewski@duq.edu.

Florida Gulf Coast University, College of Professional Studies, Program in Criminal Forensic Studies, Fort Myers, FL 33965-6565. Offers MS. *Faculty:* 35 full-time (15 women), 34 part-time/adjunct (12 women). *Students:* 33 full-time (29 women), 18 part-time (16 women); includes 5 Black or African American, non-Hispanic/Latino; 2 American Indian or Alaska Native, non-Hispanic/Latino; 3 Hispanic/Latino, 1 international. Average age 29. 29 applicants, 79% accepted, 22 enrolled. In 2010, 20 master's awarded. *Entrance requirements:* For master's, GRE General Test, minimum GPA of 3.0. Additional exam requirements/recommendations for international students: Required—TOEFL (minimum score 550 paper-based; 213 computer-based). *Application deadline:* For fall admission, 4/1 for domestic students; for spring admission, 11/15 for domestic students. Applications are processed on a rolling basis. Application fee: $30. Electronic applications accepted. *Expenses:* Tuition, state resident: part-time $322.08 per credit hour. Tuition, nonresident: part-time $1117.08 per credit hour. *Financial support:* Research assistantships, career-related internships or fieldwork and tuition waivers (full and partial) available. Support available to part-time students. *Unit head:* Dr. Kenneth Millar, Dean, 239-590-7724, Fax: 239-590-7846, E-mail: kmillar@fgcu.edu. *Application contact:* Dr. Kenneth Millar, Dean, 239-590-7724, Fax: 239-590-7846, E-mail: kmillar@fgcu.edu.

Florida International University, College of Arts and Sciences, Department of Chemistry, Program in Forensic Science, Miami, FL 33199. Offers MS. Part-time programs available. *Degree requirements:* For master's, thesis optional. *Entrance requirements:* For master's, GRE, minimum GPA of 3.0, 3 letters of recommendation. Additional exam requirements/recommendations for international students: Required—TOEFL (minimum score 550 paper-based; 213 computer-based). *Application deadline:* For fall admission, 6/1 for domestic students, 4/1 for international students; for spring admission, 10/1 for domestic students, 9/1 for international students. Applications are processed on a rolling basis. Application fee: $30. Electronic applications accepted. *Financial support:* Research assistantships, teaching assistantships, institutionally sponsored loans and scholarships/grants available. Financial award application deadline: 3/1; financial award applicants required to submit FAFSA. *Unit head:* Dr. Stanislaw Wnuk, Chairperson, 305-348-2606, Fax: 305-348-3772, E-mail: stanislaw.wnuk@fiu.edu. *Application contact:* Nanett Rojas, Assistant Director of Graduate Admissions, 305-348-7442, Fax: 305-348-7441, E-mail: gradadm@fiu.edu.

George Mason University, College of Science, Fairfax, VA 22030. Offers advanced biomedical sciences (Certificate); bioinformatics and computational biology (MS, PhD, Certificate); biosciences (PhD); chemistry and biochemistry (MS, PhD), including chemistry (MS), chemistry and biochemistry (PhD); climate dynamics (PhD); computational and data sciences (MS, PhD, Certificate), including computational sciences (MS), computational sciences and informatics (PhD), computational techniques and applications (Certificate); environmental science and policy (MS, PhD, Certificate), including environmental management (Certificate), environmental science and policy (MS), environmental science and public policy (PhD); forensic science (MS); forensics (Certificate); geography and geoinformation science (MS, PhD, Certificate), including earth system science (MS), earth systems and geoinformation sciences (PhD), geographic and cartographic sciences (MS), geographic information sciences (Certificate), geoinformatics and geospatial intelligence (MS), geospatial intelligence (Certificate), remote sensing (Certificate); mathematical sciences (MS, PhD, Certificate), including actuarial sciences (Certificate), mathematics (MS, PhD); molecular and microbiology (MS, PhD), including biology (MS), biosciences (PhD); neuroscience (PhD); physical sciences (PhD); physics and astronomy (MS, PhD), including applied and engineering physics (MS), physics (PhD). Part-time and evening/weekend programs available. *Faculty:* 262 full-time (73 women), 62 part-time/adjunct (23 women). *Students:* 223 full-time (97 women), 716 part-time (305 women); includes 180 minority (36 Black or African American, non-Hispanic/Latino; 2 American Indian or Alaska Native, non-Hispanic/Latino; 90 Asian, non-Hispanic/Latino; 47 Hispanic/Latino; 1 Native Hawaiian or other Pacific Islander, non-Hispanic/Latino; 4 Two or more races, non-Hispanic/Latino), 144 international. Average age 33. 894 applicants, 59% accepted, 315 enrolled. In 2010, 95 master's, 32 doctorates, 27 other advanced degrees awarded. *Degree requirements:* For doctorate, comprehensive exam, thesis/dissertation. *Entrance requirements:* For master's and doctorate, GRE General Test, minimum GPA of 3.0 in last 60 hours. Additional exam requirements/recommendations for international students: Required—TOEFL (minimum score 570 paper-based; 230 computer-based; 88 iBT). *Application deadline:* For fall admission, 3/1 priority date for domestic students, 2/1 for international students; for spring admission, 11/1 priority date for domestic students. Applications are processed on a rolling basis. Application fee: $100. Electronic applications accepted. *Expenses:* Tuition, state resident: full-time $8192; part-time $440 per credit hour. Tuition, nonresident: full-time $22,952; part-time $1055 per credit hour. Required fees: $2364; $99 per credit hour. *Financial support:* In 2010–11, 233 students received support, including 26 fellowships with tuition reimbursements available (averaging $18,000 per year), 104 research assistantships with full tuition reimbursements available (averaging $15,616 per year), 107 teaching assistantships (averaging $12,215 per year); career-related internships or fieldwork, Federal Work-Study, scholarships/grants, and health care benefits (full time research or teaching assistantship recipients) also available. Support available to part-time students. Financial award application deadline: 2/1; financial award applicants required to submit FAFSA. *Faculty research:* Space sciences and astrophysics, fluid dynamics, materials modeling and simulation, bioinformatics, global changes and statistics. *Unit head:* Dr. Vikas E. Chandhoke, Director, 703-993-3622, Fax: 703-993-1993, E-mail: cosinfo@gmu.edu. *Application contact:* Dr. Tim Born, Associate Dean for Graduate Programs, 703-993-4171, Fax: 703-993-9034, E-mail: tborn@gmu.edu.

George Mason University, Volgenau School of Engineering, Department of Electrical and Computer Engineering, Fairfax, VA 22030. Offers advanced networking protocols for telecommunications (Certificate); communications and networking (Certificate); computer engineering (MS); computer forensics (MS); electrical and computer engineering (PhD); electrical engineering (MS); network technology and applications (Certificate); networks, system integration and testing (Certificate); signal processing (Certificate); telecom systems modeling (Certificate); telecommunications (MS); telecommunications forensics and security (Certificate); VLSI design/manufacturing (Certificate); wireless communication (Certificate). MS program offered jointly with Old Dominion University, University of Virginia, Virginia Commonwealth University, and Virginia Polytechnic Institute and State University. Part-time and evening/weekend programs available. *Faculty:* 33 full-time (4 women), 39 part-time/adjunct (4 women). *Students:* 106 full-time (27 women), 336 part-time (64 women); includes 24 Black or African American, non-Hispanic/Latino; 1 American Indian or Alaska Native, non-Hispanic/Latino; 54 Asian, non-Hispanic/Latino; 20 Hispanic/Latino; 1 Two or more races, non-Hispanic/Latino, 172 international. Average age 30. 506 applicants, 71% accepted, 142 enrolled. In 2010, 145 master's, 3 doctorates, 61 other advanced degrees awarded. *Degree requirements:* For master's, thesis optional; for doctorate, comprehensive exam, thesis or scholarly paper. *Entrance requirements:* For master's, GMAT or GRE General Test, letters of recommendation, resume; for doctorate, GRE/GMAT, personal goal statement, 2 transcripts, letter of recommendation. Additional exam requirements/recommendations for international students: Required—TOEFL (minimum score 570 paper-based; 230 computer-based; 88 iBT). *Application deadline:* For fall admission, 7/15 priority date for domestic and international students; for spring admission, 12/1 for domestic and international students. Applications are processed on a rolling basis. Application fee: $100. Electronic applications accepted. *Expenses:* Tuition, state resident: full-time $8192; part-time $440 per credit hour. Tuition, nonresident: full-time $22,952; part-time $1055 per credit hour. Required fees: $2364; $99 per credit hour. *Financial support:* In 2010–11, 74 students received support, including 2 fellowships with full tuition reimbursements available (averaging $18,000 per year), 26 research assistantships with full and partial tuition reimbursements available (averaging $14,648 per year), 46 teaching assistantships with full and partial tuition reimbursements available (averaging $10,946 per year); career-related internships or fieldwork, Federal Work-Study, scholarships/grants, unspecified assistantships, and health care benefits (full-time research or teaching assistantship recipients) also available. Financial award application deadline: 3/1; financial award applicants required to submit FAFSA. *Faculty research:* Communication networks, signal processing, system failure diagnosis, multiprocessors, material processing using microwave energy. Total annual research expenditures: $3.4 million. *Unit head:* Dr. Andre Manitius, Chairperson, 703-993-1569, Fax: 703-993-1601, E-mail: ece@gmu.edu. *Application contact:* Jessica Skinner, Associate Dean, 703-993-1569, E-mail: jskinne6@gmu.edu.

The George Washington University, Columbian College of Arts and Sciences, Department of Forensic Sciences, Washington, DC 20052. Offers crime scene investigation (MFS); forensic chemistry (MFS); forensic molecular biology (MFS); forensic toxicology (MFS); high-technology crime investigation (MFS); security management (MFS). High-technology crime investigation and security management programs offered in Arlington, VA. Part-time and evening/weekend programs available. *Faculty:* 6 full-time (1 woman), 22 part-time/adjunct (5 women). *Students:* 80 full-time (61 women), 60 part-time (37 women); includes 8 Black or African American, non-Hispanic/Latino; 2 American Indian or Alaska Native, non-Hispanic/Latino; 7 Asian, non-Hispanic/Latino; 8 Hispanic/Latino, 7 international. Average age 27. 149 applicants, 91% accepted, 58 enrolled. In 2010, 57 master's awarded. *Degree requirements:* For master's, comprehensive exam. *Entrance requirements:* For master's, GRE General Test, minimum GPA of 3.0. Additional exam requirements/recommendations for international students: Required—TOEFL (minimum score 550 paper-based; 213 computer-based; 80 iBT). *Application deadline:* For fall admission, 1/16 priority date for international students; for spring admission, 10/1 priority date for domestic students, 9/1 priority date for international students. Applications are processed on a rolling basis. Application fee: $75. Electronic applications accepted. *Financial support:* In 2010–11, 19 students received support; fellowships with partial tuition reimbursements available, Federal Work-Study and tuition waivers available. *Unit head:* Dr. Walter F. Rowe, Chair, 202-994-1469, E-mail: wfrowe@gwu.edu. *Application contact:* Dr. Walter F. Rowe, Chair, 202-994-1469, E-mail: wfrowe@gwu.edu.

Golden Gate University, School of Accounting, San Francisco, CA 94105-2968. Offers accounting (M Ac, Graduate Certificate); forensic (M Ac); forensic accounting (Graduate Certificate); taxation (M Ac). Part-time and evening/weekend programs available. *Faculty:* 5 full-time (2 women), 35 part-time/adjunct (12 women). *Students:* 129 full-time (84 women), 168 part-time (98 women); includes 127 minority (6 Black or African American, non-Hispanic/Latino; 1 American Indian or Alaska Native, non-Hispanic/Latino; 100 Asian, non-Hispanic/Latino; 15 Hispanic/Latino; 3 Native Hawaiian or other Pacific Islander, non-Hispanic/Latino; 2 Two or more races, non-Hispanic/Latino), 40 international. Average age 31. 132 applicants, 80% accepted, 52 enrolled. In 2010, 61 master's awarded. *Entrance requirements:* For master's, minimum GPA of 3.0. Additional exam requirements/recommendations for international students: Required—TOEFL. *Application deadline:* For fall admission, 5/15 for international students; for winter admission, 1/15 for international students; for spring admission, 9/15 for international students. Applications are processed on a rolling basis. Application fee: $70 ($110 for international students). Electronic applications accepted. *Financial support:* Career-related internships or fieldwork, Federal Work-Study, institutionally sponsored loans, and scholarships/grants available. Support available to part-time students. Financial award applicants required to submit FAFSA. *Faculty research:* Forensic accounting, audit, tax, CPA exam. *Unit head:* Mary Canning, 415-442-6559, Fax: 415-543-2607. *Application contact:* Angela Melero, Enrollment Services, 415-442-7800, Fax: 415-442-7807, E-mail: info@ggu.edu.

John Jay College of Criminal Justice of the City University of New York, Graduate Studies, Program in Forensic Computing, New York, NY 10019-1093. Offers MS. Part-time and evening/weekend programs available. *Degree requirements:* For master's, thesis or alternative. *Entrance requirements:* For master's, GRE General Test, minimum B average. Additional exam requirements/recommendations for international students: Required—TOEFL (minimum score 500 paper-based; 173 computer-based).

John Jay College of Criminal Justice of the City University of New York, Graduate Studies, Program in Forensic Science, New York, NY 10019-1093. Offers MS. Part-time and

Forensic Sciences

John Jay College of Criminal Justice of the City University of New York (continued)

evening/weekend programs available. *Degree requirements:* For master's, thesis. *Entrance requirements:* For master's, GRE, minimum B average. Additional exam requirements/recommendations for international students: Required—TOEFL (minimum score 500 paper-based; 173 computer-based).

John Jay College of Criminal Justice of the City University of New York, Graduate Studies, Programs in Criminal Justice, New York, NY 10019-1093. Offers criminal justice (MA, PhD); criminology and deviance (PhD); forensic psychology (PhD); forensic science (PhD); law and philosophy (PhD); organizational behavior (PhD); public policy (PhD). Part-time and evening/weekend programs available. Terminal master's awarded for partial completion of doctoral program. *Degree requirements:* For master's, thesis or alternative; for doctorate, one foreign language, thesis/dissertation. *Entrance requirements:* For master's, GRE General Test, minimum B average; for doctorate, GRE General Test. Additional exam requirements/recommendations for international students: Required—TOEFL (minimum score 500 paper-based; 173 computer-based).

Long Island University, C.W. Post Campus, School of Health Professions and Nursing, Master of Social Work Program, Brookville, NY 11548-1300. Offers alcohol and substance abuse (MSW); child and family welfare (MSW); forensic social work (MSW); gerontology (MSW); nonprofit management (MSW). *Accreditation:* CSWE.

McGill University, Faculty of Graduate and Postdoctoral Studies, Faculty of Dentistry, Montréal, QC H3A 2T5, Canada. Offers forensic dentistry (Certificate); oral and maxillofacial surgery (M Sc, PhD).

Mercyhurst College, Graduate Program, Program in Forensic and Biological Anthropology, Erie, PA 16546. Offers MS. *Entrance requirements:* For master's, GRE or MAT, undergraduate degree in related field, interview. Additional exam requirements/recommendations for international students: Required—TOEFL.

Michigan State University, The Graduate School, College of Social Science, School of Criminal Justice, East Lansing, MI 48824. Offers criminal justice (MS, PhD); forensic science (MS); law enforcement intelligence and analysis (MS). Postbaccalaureate distance learning degree programs offered. *Entrance requirements:* Additional exam requirements/recommendations for international students: Required—TOEFL. Electronic applications accepted.

Missouri Western State University, Program in Forensic Investigations, St. Joseph, MO 64507-2294. Offers MAS. *Expenses:* Tuition, state resident: full-time $5544; part-time $308 per credit hour. Tuition, nonresident: full-time $10,206; part-time $567 per credit hour. Required fees: $30 per semester. One-time fee: $45 full-time.

National University, Academic Affairs, College of Letters and Sciences, Department of Mathematics and Natural Sciences, La Jolla, CA 92037-1011. Offers forensic sciences (MFS). Part-time and evening/weekend programs available. Postbaccalaureate distance learning degree programs offered (no on-campus study). *Faculty:* 13 full-time (6 women), 163 part-time/adjunct (63 women). *Students:* 140 full-time (99 women), 252 part-time (173 women); includes 480 minority (70 Black or African American, non-Hispanic/Latino; 2 American Indian or Alaska Native, non-Hispanic/Latino; 25 Asian, non-Hispanic/Latino; 74 Hispanic/Latino; 303 Native Hawaiian or other Pacific Islander, non-Hispanic/Latino; 6 Two or more races, non-Hispanic/Latino), 2 international. Average age 32. 234 applicants, 100% accepted, 163 enrolled. In 2010, 75 master's awarded. *Degree requirements:* For master's, thesis (for some programs). *Entrance requirements:* For master's, interview, minimum GPA of 2.5. Additional exam requirements/recommendations for international students: Required—TOEFL (minimum score 550 paper-based; 213 computer-based; 79 iBT), IELTS (minimum score 6). *Application deadline:* Applications are processed on a rolling basis. Application fee: $60 ($65 for international students). Electronic applications accepted. *Expenses:* Tuition: Full-time $9450; part-time $350 per unit. Required fees: $350 per unit. One-time fee: $60. *Financial support:* Career-related internships or fieldwork, institutionally sponsored loans, scholarships/grants, and tuition waivers (partial) available. Support available to part-time students. Financial award application deadline: 6/30; financial award applicants required to submit FAFSA. *Unit head:* Dr. Michael R. Maxwell, Head, 858-642-8413, E-mail: mmaxwell@nu.edu. *Application contact:* Dominick Giovanniello, Associate Regional Dean—San Diego, 858-NAT-UNIV, Fax: 858-541-7792, E-mail: dgiovann@nu.edu.

National University, Academic Affairs, College of Letters and Sciences, Department of Professional Studies, La Jolla, CA 92037-1011. Offers forensic science (MFS), including criminalistics and investigation; public administration (MPA), including alternative dispute resolution, human resource management, organizational leadership, public finance. Part-time and evening/weekend programs available. Postbaccalaureate distance learning degree programs offered (no on-campus study). *Faculty:* 10 full-time (3 women), 110 part-time/adjunct (22 women). *Students:* 189 full-time (117 women), 284 part-time (167 women); includes 259 minority (101 Black or African American, non-Hispanic/Latino; 2 American Indian or Alaska Native, non-Hispanic/Latino; 33 Asian, non-Hispanic/Latino; 104 Hispanic/Latino; 7 Native Hawaiian or other Pacific Islander, non-Hispanic/Latino; 12 Two or more races, non-Hispanic/Latino). Average age 38. 305 applicants, 100% accepted, 192 enrolled. In 2010, 160 master's awarded. *Degree requirements:* For master's, thesis. *Entrance requirements:* For master's, interview, minimum GPA of 2.5. Additional exam requirements/recommendations for international students: Required—TOEFL (minimum score 550 paper-based; 213 computer-based; 79 iBT), IELTS (minimum score 6). *Application deadline:* Applications are processed on a rolling basis. Application fee: $60 ($65 for international students). Electronic applications accepted. *Expenses:* Tuition: Full-time $9450; part-time $350 per unit. Required fees: $350 per unit. One-time fee: $60. *Financial support:* Career-related internships or fieldwork, institutionally sponsored loans, scholarships/grants, and tuition waivers (partial) available. Support available to part-time students. Financial award application deadline: 6/30; financial award applicants required to submit FAFSA. *Unit head:* James G. Larsen, Associate Professor and Chair, 858-642-8418, Fax: 858-642-8715, E-mail: jlarson@nu.edu. *Application contact:* Dominick Giovanniello, Associate Regional Dean—San Diego, 800-NAT-UNIV, Fax: 858-541-7792, E-mail: dgiovann@nu.edu.

Nebraska Wesleyan University, University College, Program in Forensic Science, Lincoln, NE 68504-2796. Offers MFS. Part-time and evening/weekend programs available.

Oklahoma State University Center for Health Sciences, Graduate Program in Forensic Sciences, Tulsa, OK 74107-1898. Offers forensic DNA/molecular biology (MS); forensic examination of questioned documents (Certificate); forensic pathology (MS); forensic psychology (MS); forensic toxicology (MS). Part-time and evening/weekend programs available. Postbaccalaureate distance learning degree programs offered (no on-campus study). *Faculty:* 2 full-time (0 women), 14 part-time/adjunct (5 women). *Students:* 7 full-time (6 women), 21 part-time (12 women); includes 5 minority (2 Black or African American, non-Hispanic/Latino; 2 Asian, non-Hispanic/Latino; 1 Hispanic/Latino). Average age 34. 21 applicants, 57% accepted, 7 enrolled. In 2010, 6 master's awarded. *Degree requirements:* For master's, comprehensive exam (for some programs), thesis (for some programs). *Entrance requirements:* For master's, MAT (MFSA) or GRE General Test, professional experience (MFSA). Additional exam requirements/recommendations for international students: Required—TOEFL (minimum score 600 paper-based; 250 computer-based), TWE (minimum score 5). *Application deadline:* For fall admission, 3/1 for domestic and international students; for spring admission, 10/1 for domestic and international students. Application fee: $40 ($75 for international students). *Financial support:* In 2010–11, 10 students received support, including 10 research assistantships (averaging $29,000 per year); career-related internships or fieldwork, Federal Work-Study, and tuition waivers (partial) also available. Support available to part-time students. Financial award application deadline: 4/1; financial award applicants required to submit FAFSA. *Faculty research:* DNA typing, DNA polymorphism, identification through DNA, disease transmission, forensic dentistry, neurotoxicity of HIV, forensic toxicology method development, toxin detection and characterization. Total annual research expenditures: $58,000. *Unit head:* Dr. Robert T. Allen, Director, 918-561-1108, Fax: 918-561-8414. *Application contact:* Cathy Newsome, Coordinator, 918-561-1108, Fax: 918-561-8414, E-mail: cathy.newsome@okstate.edu.

Pace University, Dyson College of Arts and Sciences, Program in Forensic Science, New York, NY 10038. Offers MS. *Entrance requirements:* Additional exam requirements/recommendations for international students: Required—TOEFL. Electronic applications accepted.

Philadelphia College of Osteopathic Medicine, Graduate and Professional Programs, Program in Forensic Medicine, Philadelphia, PA 19131-1694. Offers MS. *Entrance requirements:* For master's, minimum GPA of 3.0; coursework in biology, chemistry, anatomy and physiology.

Saint Leo University, Graduate Studies in Criminal Justice, Saint Leo, FL 33574-6665. Offers criminal justice (MS); critical incident management (MS); forensic studies (MS). Part-time and evening/weekend programs available. Postbaccalaureate distance learning degree programs offered (minimal on-campus study). *Faculty:* 4 full-time (0 women), 11 part-time/adjunct (3 women). *Students:* 432 full-time (261 women), 5 part-time (1 woman); includes 195 minority (160 Black or African American, non-Hispanic/Latino; 4 American Indian or Alaska Native, non-Hispanic/Latino; 6 Asian, non-Hispanic/Latino; 20 Hispanic/Latino; 1 Native Hawaiian or other Pacific Islander, non-Hispanic/Latino; 4 Two or more races, non-Hispanic/Latino). Average age 38. In 2010, 75 master's awarded. *Degree requirements:* For master's, comprehensive project. *Entrance requirements:* For master's, bachelor's degree from regionally-accredited college or university with minimum GPA of 3.0. Additional exam requirements/recommendations for international students: Required—TOEFL (minimum score 550 paper-based; 213 computer-based; 80 iBT). *Application deadline:* For fall admission, 7/1 priority date for domestic and international students; for spring admission, 11/1 priority date for domestic and international students. Applications are processed on a rolling basis. Application fee: $75. Electronic applications accepted. *Expenses:* Tuition: Part-time $609 per semester hour. Required fees: $115 per course. Tuition and fees vary according to campus/location and program. *Financial support:* In 2010–11, 17 students received support. Federal Work-Study, scholarships/grants, and health care benefits available. *Unit head:* Dr. Robert Diemer, Director, 352-588-8974, Fax: 352-588-8289, E-mail: robert.diemer@saintleo.edu. *Application contact:* Jared Welling, Director, Graduate/Weekend and Evening Admission, 800-707-8846, Fax: 352-588-7873, E-mail: grad.admissions@saintleo.edu.

Sam Houston State University, College of Criminal Justice, Huntsville, TX 77341. Offers criminal justice (MS, PhD); criminal justice and criminology (MA); criminal justice management (MS); forensic science (MS); security studies (MS); victim services management (MS). *Faculty:* 22 full-time (4 women). *Students:* 91 full-time (55 women), 238 part-time (83 women); includes 25 Black or African American, non-Hispanic/Latino; 1 American Indian or Alaska Native, non-Hispanic/Latino; 6 Asian, non-Hispanic/Latino; 35 Hispanic/Latino, 33 international. Average age 34. 148 applicants, 88% accepted, 114 enrolled. In 2010, 46 master's, 6 doctorates awarded. *Degree requirements:* For master's, thesis (for some programs); for doctorate, comprehensive exam, thesis/dissertation. *Entrance requirements:* For master's, GRE General Test; for doctorate, GRE General Test, master's degree. Additional exam requirements/recommendations for international students: Required—TOEFL (minimum score 550 paper-based; 213 computer-based; 79 iBT). *Application deadline:* For fall admission, 8/1 for domestic students; for spring admission, 12/1 for domestic students. Applications are processed on a rolling basis. Application fee: $20. *Expenses:* Tuition, state resident: full-time $1363; part-time $163 per credit hour. Tuition, nonresident: full-time $3856; part-time $473 per credit hour. *Financial support:* Fellowships, research assistantships, teaching assistantships, career-related internships or fieldwork, Federal Work-Study, institutionally sponsored loans, and unspecified assistantships available. Support available to part-time students. Financial award application deadline: 5/31; financial award applicants required to submit FAFSA. *Unit head:* Dr. Vincent Webb, Dean, 936-294-1632, Fax: 936-294-1653, E-mail: vwebb@shsu.edu. *Application contact:* Doris Powell-Pratt, Advisor, 936-294-3637, Fax: 936-294-4055, E-mail: icc_dcp@shsu.edu.

Southern Utah University, College of Science, Program in Forensic Science, Cedar City, UT 84720-2498. Offers MS. In 2010, 4 master's awarded. *Application deadline:* Applications are processed on a rolling basis. Application fee: $50 ($65 for international students). Electronic applications accepted. *Unit head:* Dr. Robert Eves, Dean, 435-586-1934, Fax: 435-865-8550, E-mail: eves@suu.edu. *Application contact:* Barbara Rodriguez, Administrative Assistant, 435-586-7920, Fax: 435-865-8550, E-mail: rodriguez@suu.edu.

Stevenson University, Program in Forensic Science, Stevenson, MD 21153. Offers MS. Partnership program with Maryland State Police Forensic Sciences Division. *Students:* 18 full-time (17 women), 9 part-time (8 women); includes 3 Black or African American, non-Hispanic/Latino; 1 Asian, non-Hispanic/Latino, 1 international. In 2010, 7 master's awarded. *Entrance requirements:* For master's, bachelor's degree in chemistry, biology, physics, or a related science with a minimum cumulative and science/math GPA of 3.2; course/lab work in general biology, general chemistry, organic chemistry, physics, cell biology, molecular genetics, analytical chemistry, instrumental analysis, human anatomy and physiology, biotechniques, and biochemistry. *Expenses:* Tuition: Part-time $560 per credit. Required fees: $100 per semester. Part-time tuition and fees vary according to program. *Unit head:* John Tobin, Program Coordinator, Forensic Science, 443-352-4142, Fax: 443-392-0538, E-mail: jtobin@stevenson.edu. *Application contact:* Angela Scagliola, Director, Recruitment and Admissions, 443-352-4414, Fax: 443-352-4440, E-mail: ascagliola@stevenson.edu.

Stevenson University, Program in Forensic Studies, Stevenson, MD 21153. Offers forensic accounting (MS); forensic legal professional (MS); information technology (MS); interdisciplinary track (MS); investigations (MS). Postbaccalaureate distance learning degree programs offered (minimal on-campus study). *Students:* 36 full-time (26 women), 186 part-time (130 women); includes 76 Black or African American, non-Hispanic/Latino; 2 American Indian or Alaska Native, non-Hispanic/Latino; 4 Asian, non-Hispanic/Latino; 3 Hispanic/Latino; 1 Two or more races, non-Hispanic/Latino, 1 international. In 2010, 55 master's awarded. *Degree requirements:* For master's, capstone course. *Expenses:* Tuition: Part-time $560 per credit. Required fees: $100 per semester. Part-time tuition and fees vary according to program. *Unit head:* Thomas Coogan, Program Coordinator, Forensic Studies, 443-352-4075, Fax: 443-394-0538. *Application contact:* Angela Scagliola, Director, Recruitment and Admissions, 443-352-4414, Fax: 443-352-4440, E-mail: ascagliola@stevenson.edu.

Syracuse University, College of Arts and Sciences, Program in Forensic Science, Syracuse, NY 13244. Offers MS. Part-time programs available. *Students:* 11 full-time (5 women), 4 part-time (3 women); includes 5 minority (1 Black or African American, non-Hispanic/Latino; 2 Asian, non-Hispanic/Latino; 1 Hispanic/Latino; 1 Two or more races, non-Hispanic/Latino). Average age 25. 43 applicants, 91% accepted, 9 enrolled. *Entrance requirements:* For master's, GRE General Test. Additional exam requirements/recommendations for international students: Required—TOEFL (minimum score 100 iBT). *Application deadline:* For fall admission, 2/1 priority date for domestic and international students. Applications are processed on a rolling basis. Application fee: $75. Electronic applications accepted. *Expenses:* Tuition: Part-time $1162 per credit. *Financial support:* Application deadline: 1/1. *Unit head:* Dr. Michael Sponsler, Graduate Director, 315-443-4347, E-mail: sponsler@syr.edu. *Application contact:* Benjamin Zender, Information Contact, 315-443-0326, E-mail: brzender@syr.edu.

Towson University, Program in Forensic Science, Towson, MD 21252-0001. Offers MS. *Students:* 39 full-time (31 women), 9 part-time (7 women); includes 16 minority (12 Black or African American, non-Hispanic/Latino; 1 Asian, non-Hispanic/Latino; 2 Hispanic/Latino; 1 Two or more races, non-Hispanic/Latino), 2 international. Average age 26. In 2010, 12 master's awarded. *Entrance requirements:* For master's, minimum GPA of 3.0; bachelor's in chemistry, forensic chemistry, or related field. *Expenses:* Tuition, state resident: part-time $324 per credit. Tuition, nonresident: part-time $681 per credit. Required fees: $95 per term. *Unit head:* Mark

Profili, Graduate Program Director, 410-704-2668, E-mail: mprofili@towson.edu. *Application contact:* Mark Profili, Graduate Program Director, 410-704-2668, E-mail: mprofili@towson.edu.

Universidad del Turabo, Graduate Programs, School of Social Sciences and Humanities, Programs in Public Affairs, Program in Forensic Science, Gurabo, PR 00778-3030. Offers MPA.

University at Albany, State University of New York, College of Arts and Sciences, Department of Biological Sciences, Albany, NY 12222-0001. Offers biodiversity, conservation, and policy (MS); ecology, evolution, and behavior (MS, PhD); forensic molecular biology (MS); molecular, cellular, developmental, and neural biology (MS, PhD). *Degree requirements:* For master's, one foreign language; for doctorate, one foreign language, thesis/dissertation. *Entrance requirements:* For master's and doctorate, GRE General Test. Additional exam requirements/recommendations for international students: Required—TOEFL (minimum score 550 paper-based; 213 computer-based). Electronic applications accepted. *Faculty research:* Interferon, neural development, RNA self-splicing, behavioral ecology, DNA repair enzymes.

The University of Alabama at Birmingham, College of Arts and Sciences, Program in Computer Forensics and Security Management, Birmingham, AL 35294. Offers MS. *Expenses:* Tuition, state resident: full-time $5482. Tuition, nonresident: full-time $12,430. Tuition and fees vary according to program. *Unit head:* Dr. John J. Sloan, 205-934-2069. *Application contact:* Julie Bryant, Director of Graduate Admissions, 205-934-8227, Fax: 205-934-8413, E-mail: jbryant@uab.edu.

The University of Alabama at Birmingham, College of Arts and Sciences, Program in Forensic Science, Birmingham, AL 35294. Offers MSFS. *Students:* 17 full-time (16 women); includes 5 minority (3 Black or African American, non-Hispanic/Latino; 1 Asian, non-Hispanic/Latino; 1 Hispanic/Latino). Average age 24. 31 applicants, 48% accepted, 8 enrolled. In 2010, 10 master's awarded. *Expenses:* Tuition, state resident: full-time $5482. Tuition, nonresident: full-time $12,430. Tuition and fees vary according to program. *Unit head:* Dr. John Sloan, Director, 205-934-2069. *Application contact:* Julie Bryant, Director of Graduate Admissions, 205-934-8227, Fax: 205-934-8413, E-mail: jbryant@uab.edu.

University of California, Davis, Graduate Studies, Graduate Group in Forensic Science, Davis, CA 95616. Offers MS. *Degree requirements:* For master's, thesis. *Entrance requirements:* Additional exam requirements/recommendations for international students: Required—TOEFL (minimum score 550 paper-based; 213 computer-based), IELTS (minimum score 7). Electronic applications accepted.

University of Central Florida, College of Engineering and Computer Science, Department of Electrical Engineering and Computer Science, Program in Computer Science, Orlando, FL 32816. Offers computer science (MS, PhD); digital forensics (MS). Part-time and evening/weekend programs available. *Students:* 118 full-time (34 women), 164 part-time (30 women); includes 43 minority (12 Black or African American, non-Hispanic/Latino; 1 American Indian or Alaska Native, non-Hispanic/Latino; 12 Asian, non-Hispanic/Latino; 12 Hispanic/Latino; 1 Native Hawaiian or other Pacific Islander, non-Hispanic/Latino; 5 Two or more races, non-Hispanic/Latino), 63 international. Average age 30. 312 applicants, 58% accepted, 84 enrolled. In 2010, 51 master's, 16 doctorates awarded. *Degree requirements:* For master's, thesis or alternative; for doctorate, thesis/dissertation, candidacy exam, departmental qualifying exam. *Entrance requirements:* For master's, GRE General Test, GRE Subject Test, minimum GPA of 3.0 in last 60 hours; for doctorate, GRE Subject Test, minimum GPA of 3.0 in last 60 hours. Additional exam requirements/recommendations for international students: Required—TOEFL. *Application deadline:* For fall admission, 7/15 priority date for domestic students; for spring admission, 12/1 priority date for domestic students. Application fee: $30. Electronic applications accepted. *Expenses:* Tuition, state resident: part-time $256.56 per credit hour. Tuition, nonresident: part-time $1011.52 per credit hour. Part-time tuition and fees vary according to program. *Financial support:* In 2010–11, 62 students received support, including 13 fellowships with partial tuition reimbursements available (averaging $5,800 per year), 55 research assistantships with partial tuition reimbursements available (averaging $9,400 per year), 30 teaching assistantships with partial tuition reimbursements available (averaging $6,200 per year); career-related internships or fieldwork, Federal Work-Study, institutionally sponsored loans, tuition waivers (partial), and unspecified assistantships also available. Financial award application deadline: 3/1; financial award applicants required to submit FAFSA. *Faculty research:* Parallel processing, databases, algorithms, virtual reality.

University of Central Florida, College of Health and Public Affairs, Department of Criminal Justice and Legal Studies, Orlando, FL 32816. Offers corrections leadership (Certificate); crime analysis (Certificate); criminal justice (MS); juvenile justice leadership (Certificate); police leadership (Certificate). Part-time and evening/weekend programs available. *Faculty:* 26 full-time (8 women), 12 part-time/adjunct (1 woman). *Students:* 83 full-time (53 women), 147 part-time (87 women); includes 70 minority (45 Black or African American, non-Hispanic/Latino; 2 American Indian or Alaska Native, non-Hispanic/Latino; 4 Asian, non-Hispanic/Latino; 18 Hispanic/Latino; 1 Two or more races, non-Hispanic/Latino). Average age 30. 165 applicants, 80% accepted, 87 enrolled. In 2010, 73 master's, 17 other advanced degrees awarded. *Degree requirements:* For master's, thesis or alternative. *Entrance requirements:* For master's, GRE General Test, minimum GPA of 3.0. Additional exam requirements/recommendations for international students: Required—TOEFL. *Application deadline:* For fall admission, 7/15 for domestic students; for spring admission, 4/15 for domestic students. Electronic applications accepted. *Expenses:* Tuition, state resident: part-time $256.56 per credit hour. Tuition, nonresident: part-time $1011.52 per credit hour. Part-time tuition and fees vary according to program. *Financial support:* In 2010–11, 6 students received support, including 2 fellowships with partial tuition reimbursements available (averaging $5,200 per year), 5 teaching assistantships with partial tuition reimbursements available (averaging $6,400 per year); career-related internships or fieldwork, Federal Work-Study, institutionally sponsored loans, tuition waivers (partial), and unspecified assistantships also available. Financial award application deadline: 3/1; financial award applicants required to submit FAFSA. *Unit head:* Dr. Robert Langworthy, Chair, 407-823-5929, E-mail: rlangwor@mail.ucf.edu. *Application contact:* Dr. Robert Langworthy, Chair, 407-823-5929, E-mail: rlangwor@mail.ucf.edu.

University of Central Florida, College of Sciences, Department of Chemistry, Orlando, FL 32816. Offers chemistry (MS, PhD); computer forensics (Certificate). Part-time and evening/weekend programs available. *Faculty:* 24 full-time (1 woman), 7 part-time/adjunct (1 woman). *Students:* 75 full-time (32 women), 22 part-time (3 women); includes 20 minority (4 Black or African American, non-Hispanic/Latino; 1 American Indian or Alaska Native, non-Hispanic/Latino; 6 Asian, non-Hispanic/Latino; 9 Hispanic/Latino), 32 international. Average age 31. 103 applicants, 56% accepted, 28 enrolled. In 2010, 4 master's, 9 doctorates, 7 other advanced degrees awarded. *Degree requirements:* For master's, thesis, final exam. *Entrance requirements:* For master's, GRE General Test, minimum GPA of 3.0 in last 60 hours. Additional exam requirements/recommendations for international students: Required—TOEFL. *Application deadline:* For fall admission, 7/15 for domestic students; for spring admission, 12/1 for domestic students. Application fee: $30. Electronic applications accepted. *Expenses:* Tuition, state resident: part-time $256.56 per credit hour. Tuition, nonresident: part-time $1011.52 per credit hour. Part-time tuition and fees vary according to program. *Financial support:* In 2010–11, 65 students received support, including 7 fellowships with partial tuition reimbursements available (averaging $3,100 per year), 41 research assistantships with partial tuition reimbursements available (averaging $7,000 per year), 51 teaching assistantships with partial tuition reimbursements available (averaging $10,300 per year); career-related internships or fieldwork, Federal Work-Study, institutionally sponsored loans, tuition waivers (partial), and unspecified assistantships also available. Financial award application deadline: 3/1; financial award applicants required to submit FAFSA. *Faculty research:* Physical and synthetic organic chemistry, lasers, polymers, biochemical action of pesticides, environmental analysis. *Unit head:* Dr. Kevin D. Belfield, Chair, 407-823-2246, Fax: 407-823-2252, E-mail: kbelfield@mail.ucf.edu. *Application contact:* Dr. Kevin D. Belfield, Chair, 407-823-2246, Fax: 407-823-2252, E-mail: kbelfield@mail.ucf.edu.

University of Colorado Denver, Business School, Program in Accounting, Denver, CO 80217. Offers auditing and forensic accounting (MS); financial accounting (MS); information systems audit control (MS); taxation (MS). *Accreditation:* AACSB. Part-time and evening/weekend programs available. *Students:* 120 full-time (68 women), 33 part-time (21 women); includes 6 Black or African American, non-Hispanic/Latino; 13 Asian, non-Hispanic/Latino; 6 Hispanic/Latino, 18 international. Average age 30. 71 applicants, 66% accepted, 30 enrolled. In 2010, 46 master's awarded. *Degree requirements:* For master's, 30 semester hours. *Entrance requirements:* For master's, GMAT. Additional exam requirements/recommendations for international students: Required—TOEFL (minimum score 525 paper-based; 197 computer-based; 71 iBT). *Application deadline:* For fall admission, 4/1 for domestic students, 3/15 for international students; for spring admission, 10/1 for domestic and international students. Application fee: $50 ($75 for international students). Electronic applications accepted. *Expenses:* Contact institution. *Financial support:* Federal Work-Study and scholarships/grants available. Support available to part-time students. Financial award application deadline: 4/1; financial award applicants required to submit FAFSA. *Faculty research:* Transfer pricing, behavioral accounting, environmental accounting, health services, international auditing. *Unit head:* Bruce Neumann, Professor, 303-315-8473, E-mail: bruce.neumann@ucdenver.edu. *Application contact:* Shelly Townley, Admissions Coordinator, 303-315-8202, E-mail: shelly.townley@ucdenver.edu.

University of Florida, College of Pharmacy, Programs in Forensic Science, Gainesville, FL 32611. Offers clinical toxicology (Certificate); drug chemistry (Certificate); environmental forensics (Certificate); forensic death investigation (Certificate); forensic DNA and serology (MSP, Certificate); forensic drug chemistry (MSP); forensic science (MSP); forensic toxicology (Certificate). Postbaccalaureate distance learning degree programs offered (no on-campus study). *Faculty:* 7 full-time (2 women). *Students:* 35 full-time (24 women), 163 part-time (124 women); includes 14 Black or African American, non-Hispanic/Latino; 4 American Indian or Alaska Native, non-Hispanic/Latino; 5 Asian, non-Hispanic/Latino; 13 Hispanic/Latino, 6 international. Average age 28. In 2010, 88 master's awarded. *Degree requirements:* For master's, comprehensive exam. *Entrance requirements:* For master's, GRE general test minimum score 1000, minimum GPA of 3.0. Additional exam requirements/recommendations for international students: Required—TOEFL (minimum score 550 paper-based; 213 computer-based; 80 iBT), IELTS (minimum score 6). Application fee: $30. *Expenses:* Tuition, state resident: full-time $10,915.92. Tuition, nonresident: full-time $28,309. *Financial support:* In 2010–11, 2 students received support, including 2 research assistantships (averaging $14,076 per year). Financial award applicants required to submit FAFSA. *Unit head:* Dr. Ian Tibbett, Director, 352-273-6871, E-mail: itebbett@ufl.edu. *Application contact:* Dr. Ian Tibbett, Director, 352-273-6871; E-mail: itebbett@ufl.edu.

University of Illinois at Chicago, College of Pharmacy and Graduate College, Graduate Programs in Pharmacy, Program in Forensic Science, Chicago, IL 60607-7128. Offers MS. *Degree requirements:* For master's, thesis. *Entrance requirements:* For master's, GRE General Test. Additional exam requirements/recommendations for international students: Required—TOEFL. *Faculty research:* Interpretation of physical evidence, utilization of physical evidence, analytical toxicology of controlled substances, automated fingerprint systems, dye and ink characterizations.

University of Nevada, Las Vegas, Graduate College, Greenspun College of Urban Affairs, School of Social Work, Las Vegas, NV 89154-5032. Offers forensic social work (Advanced Certificate); social work (MSW). *Accreditation:* CSWE. *Faculty:* 14 full-time (11 women), 11 part-time/adjunct (7 women). *Students:* 129 full-time (105 women), 54 part-time (42 women); includes 88 minority (20 Black or African American, non-Hispanic/Latino; 13 Asian, non-Hispanic/Latino; 25 Hispanic/Latino; 3 Native Hawaiian or other Pacific Islander, non-Hispanic/Latino; 27 Two or more races, non-Hispanic/Latino), 5 international. Average age 33. 173 applicants, 55% accepted, 67 enrolled. In 2010, 62 master's, 1 other advanced degree awarded. *Degree requirements:* For master's, comprehensive exam, thesis optional. *Entrance requirements:* Additional exam requirements/recommendations for international students: Required—TOEFL (minimum score 550 paper-based; 231 computer-based; 80 iBT), IELTS (minimum score 7). *Application deadline:* For fall admission, 4/10 priority date for domestic and international students. Applications are processed on a rolling basis. Application fee: $60 ($95 for international students). Electronic applications accepted. *Expenses:* Tuition, area resident: Part-time $239.50 per credit. Tuition, state resident: part-time $239.50 per credit. Tuition, nonresident: part-time $503 per credit. Required fees: $108 per semester. Tuition and fees vary according to course load, program and reciprocity agreements. *Financial support:* In 2010–11, 4 students received support, including 4 teaching assistantships with partial tuition reimbursements available (averaging $10,000 per year); institutionally sponsored loans, scholarships/grants, health care benefits, and unspecified assistantships also available. Financial award application deadline: 3/1. *Faculty research:* Child welfare and juvenile justice, health and mental health, poverty and social justice, substance abuse, public policy. Total annual research expenditures: $588,105. *Unit head:* Dr. Joanne Thompson, Director/ Professor, 702-895-0521, Fax: 702-895-4079, E-mail: joanne.thompson@unlv.edu. *Application contact:* Graduate College Admissions Evaluator, 702-895-3320, Fax: 702-895-4180, E-mail: gradcollege@unlv.edu.

University of New Haven, Graduate School, Henry C. Lee College of Criminal Justice and Forensic Sciences, Program in Criminal Justice, West Haven, CT 06516-1916. Offers crime analysis (MS); criminal justice (PhD); criminal justice management (MS); forensic computer investigation (MS, Certificate); forensic psychology (MS); victim advocacy and services management (Certificate); victimology (MS). Part-time and evening/weekend programs available. *Students:* 47 full-time (29 women), 42 part-time (25 women); includes 17 Black or African American, non-Hispanic/Latino; 5 Hispanic/Latino, 6 international. Average age 29. 95 applicants, 96% accepted, 54 enrolled. In 2010, 12 master's, 12 other advanced degrees awarded. *Degree requirements:* For master's, thesis or alternative. *Entrance requirements:* Additional exam requirements/recommendations for international students: Required—TOEFL (minimum score 520 paper-based; 190 computer-based; 70 iBT), IELTS (minimum score 5.5). *Application deadline:* For fall admission, 5/31 for international students; for winter admission, 10/15 for international students; for spring admission, 1/15 for international students. Applications are processed on a rolling basis. Application fee: $50. Electronic applications accepted. *Financial support:* Research assistantships with partial tuition reimbursements, teaching assistantships with partial tuition reimbursements, career-related internships or fieldwork, Federal Work-Study, scholarships/grants, tuition waivers, and unspecified assistantships available. Support available to part-time students. Financial award applicants required to submit FAFSA. *Unit head:* Dr. James J. Cassidy, Coordinator, 203-932-7374. *Application contact:* Eloise Gormley, Director of Graduate Admissions, 203-932-7449, Fax: 203-932-7137, E-mail: gradinfo@newhaven.edu.

University of New Haven, Graduate School, Henry C. Lee College of Criminal Justice and Forensic Sciences, Program in Fire Science, West Haven, CT 06516-1916. Offers emergency management (Certificate); fire administration (MS); fire science technology (Certificate); fire/arson investigation (MS, Certificate); forensic science/fire science (Certificate); public safety management (MS, Certificate). Part-time and evening/weekend programs available. *Students:* 3 full-time (0 women), 15 part-time (3 women); includes 1 Black or African American, non-Hispanic/Latino, 1 international. Average age 38. 6 applicants, 100% accepted, 4 enrolled. In 2010, 4 master's, 3 other advanced degrees awarded. *Degree requirements:* For master's, thesis or alternative. *Entrance requirements:* Additional exam requirements/recommendations for international students: Required—TOEFL (minimum score 520 paper-based; 190 computer-based; 70 iBT). Recommended—IELTS (minimum score 5.5). *Application deadline:* For fall admission, 5/31 for international students; for winter admission, 10/15 for international students; for spring admission, 1/15 for international students. Applications are processed on a rolling basis. Application fee: $50. Electronic applications accepted. *Financial support:* Research assistantships with partial tuition reimbursements, teaching assistantships with partial tuition reimbursements, career-related internships or fieldwork, Federal Work-Study, scholarships/grants, tuition waivers, and unspecified assistantships available. Support available to part-time students. Financial award applicants required to submit FAFSA. *Unit head:* Robert E. Massicotte,

Forensic Sciences

University of New Haven (continued)

Director, 203-932-7424. *Application contact:* Eloise Gormley, Director of Graduate Admissions, 203-932-7449, Fax: 203-932-7137, E-mail: gradinfo@newhaven.edu.

University of New Haven, Graduate School, Henry C. Lee College of Criminal Justice and Forensic Sciences, Program in Forensic Science, West Haven, CT 06516-1916. Offers advanced investigation (MS, Certificate); criminalistics (MS, Certificate); fire science (MS). Part-time and evening/weekend programs available. *Students:* 78 full-time (64 women), 13 part-time (8 women); includes 5 Black or African American, non-Hispanic/Latino; 3 Asian, non-Hispanic/Latino; 5 Hispanic/Latino, 7 international. Average age 26. 89 applicants, 98% accepted, 42 enrolled. In 2010, 49 master's, 9 other advanced degrees awarded. *Degree requirements:* For master's, thesis or alternative. *Entrance requirements:* For master's, GRE. Additional exam requirements/recommendations for international students: Required—TOEFL (minimum score 520 paper-based; 70 iBT); Recommended—IELTS (minimum score 5.5). *Application deadline:* For fall admission, 5/31 for international students; for winter admission, 10/15 for international students; for spring admission, 1/15 for international students. Applications are processed on a rolling basis. Application fee: $50. Electronic applications accepted. *Financial support:* Research assistantships with partial tuition reimbursements, teaching assistantships with partial tuition reimbursements, career-related internships or fieldwork, Federal Work-Study, scholarships/grants, tuition waivers, and unspecified assistantships available. Support available to part-time students. Financial award applicants required to submit FAFSA. *Unit head:* Dr. Timothy M. Palmbach, Coordinator, 203-932-7116. *Application contact:* Dr. Timothy M. Palmbach, Coordinator, 203-932-7116.

University of North Texas Health Science Center at Fort Worth, Graduate School of Biomedical Sciences, Fort Worth, TX 76107-2699. Offers anatomy and cell biology (MS, PhD); biochemistry and molecular biology (MS, PhD); biomedical sciences (MS, PhD); biotechnology (MS); forensic genetics (MS); integrative physiology (MS, PhD); medical science (MS); microbiology and immunology (MS, PhD); pharmacology (MS, PhD); science education (MS); DO/MS; DO/PhD. Terminal master's awarded for partial completion of doctoral program. *Degree requirements:* For master's, thesis; for doctorate, thesis/dissertation. *Entrance requirements:* For master's and doctorate, GRE General Test. Additional exam requirements/recommendations for international students: Required—TOEFL. *Expenses:* Contact institution. *Faculty research:* Alzheimer's disease, aging, eye diseases, cancer, cardiovascular disease.

University of Rhode Island, Graduate School, College of Arts and Sciences, Department of Computer Science and Statistics, Kingston, RI 02881. Offers applied mathematics (PhD), including computer science, statistics; computer science (MS, PhD); digital forensics (Graduate Certificate); statistics (MS). Part-time programs available. *Faculty:* 10 full-time (3 women), 2 part-time/adjunct (0 women). *Students:* 39 full-time (10 women), 44 part-time (11 women); includes 16 minority (2 Black or African American, non-Hispanic/Latino; 2 American Indian or Alaska Native, non-Hispanic/Latino; 2 Asian, non-Hispanic/Latino; 2 Hispanic/Latino; 8 Native Hawaiian or other Pacific Islander, non-Hispanic/Latino), 8 international. In 2010, 5 master's awarded. *Degree requirements:* For master's, comprehensive exam (for some programs), thesis optional; for doctorate, comprehensive exam, thesis/dissertation. *Entrance requirements:* For master's and doctorate, GRE, 2 letters of recommendation. Additional exam requirements/recommendations for international students: Required—TOEFL (minimum score 550 paper-based; 213 computer-based). *Application deadline:* For fall admission, 7/15 for domestic students, 2/1 for international students; for spring admission, 11/15 for domestic students, 7/15 for international students. Application fee: $65. Electronic applications accepted. *Expenses:* Tuition, state resident: full-time $9588; part-time $533 per credit hour. Tuition, nonresident: full-time $22,968; part-time $1276 per credit hour. Required fees: $1282; $68 per semester. Tuition and fees vary according to program. *Financial support:* In 2010–11, 1 research assistantship (averaging $5,210 per year), 10 teaching assistantships with full and partial tuition reimbursements (averaging $10,456 per year) were awarded. Financial award application deadline: 2/1; financial award applicants required to submit FAFSA. *Faculty research:* Bioinformatics, computer and digital forensics, behavioral model of pedestrian dynamics, real-time distributed object computing, cryptography. Total annual research expenditures: $962,948. *Unit head:* Dr. James G. Kowalski, Chair, 401-874-2510, Fax: 401-874-4617, E-mail: kowalski@cs.uri.edu. *Application contact:* Dr. Victor Fay-Wolfe, Director of Graduate Studies, 401-874-2701, Fax: 401-874-4617, E-mail: wolfe@cs.uri.edu.

University of Southern Mississippi, Graduate School, College of Science and Technology, Department of Administration of Justice, Hattiesburg, MS 39406-0001. Offers administration of justice (PhD); corrections (MA, MS); forensics (MS); juvenile justice (MA, MS); law enforcement (MA, MS). Part-time programs available. *Faculty:* 9 full-time (2 women), 2 part-time/adjunct (0 women). *Students:* 18 full-time (9 women), 19 part-time (12 women); includes 6 Black or African American, non-Hispanic/Latino; 1 Hispanic/Latino, 1 international. Average age 34. 20 applicants, 35% accepted, 4 enrolled. In 2010, 7 degrees awarded. *Degree requirements:* For master's, comprehensive exam, thesis; for doctorate, comprehensive exam, thesis/dissertation. *Entrance requirements:* For master's, GRE General Test, minimum GPA of 2.75 in last 60 hours, 3.0 in field of study; for doctorate, GRE General Test, minimum GPA of 3.5. Additional exam requirements/recommendations for international students: Required—TOEFL, IELTS. *Application deadline:* For fall admission, 3/15 priority date for domestic students, 3/15 for international students; for spring admission, 1/10 priority date for domestic and international students. Applications are processed on a rolling basis. Application fee: $50. *Financial support:* In 2010–11, 2 research assistantships with full tuition reimbursements (averaging $7,200 per year), 9 teaching assistantships with full tuition reimbursements (averaging $8,000 per year) were awarded; career-related internships or fieldwork, Federal Work-Study, institutionally sponsored loans, scholarships/grants, health care benefits, and unspecified assistantships also available. Financial award application deadline: 3/15; financial award applicants required to submit FAFSA. *Faculty research:* Crime in the family, police training models, humanities and criminal justice. *Unit head:* Dr. Lisa Nored, Chair, 601-266-4509, Fax: 601-266-4391. *Application contact:* Tera Wright, Manager of Graduate Admissions, 601-266-4509, Fax: 601-266-4391.

Utica College, Program in Cybersecurity, Utica, NY 13502-4892. Offers MS. Part-time and evening/weekend programs available. Postbaccalaureate distance learning degree programs offered. *Students:* 58 part-time (19 women); includes 9 minority (4 Black or African American, non-Hispanic/Latino; 1 Asian, non-Hispanic/Latino; 4 Hispanic/Latino), 1 international. Average age 33. *Application deadline:* Applications are processed on a rolling basis. Electronic applications accepted. *Expenses:* Tuition: Full-time $26,100; part-time $580 per credit hour. Required fees: $400; $60 per course. Tuition and fees vary according to course load, degree level and program. *Financial support:* Applicants required to submit FAFSA. *Unit head:* Joseph Giordano, Chair, 315-792-2521. *Application contact:* John D. Rowe, Director of Graduate Admissions, 315-792-3824, Fax: 315-792-3003, E-mail: jrowe@utica.edu.

Virginia Commonwealth University, Graduate School, College of Humanities and Sciences, Department of Forensic Science, Richmond, VA 23284-9005. Offers forensic biology (MS); forensic chemistry/drugs and toxicology (MS); forensic chemistry/trace (MS); forensic physical evidence (MS). Part-time programs available. *Students:* 42 full-time (32 women), 3 part-time (all women); includes 8 minority (3 Black or African American, non-Hispanic/Latino; 1 American Indian or Alaska Native, non-Hispanic/Latino; 3 Asian, non-Hispanic/Latino; 1 Hispanic/Latino), 1 international. 95 applicants, 39% accepted, 23 enrolled. In 2010, 21 master's awarded. *Entrance requirements:* For master's, GRE General Test, bachelor's degree in a natural science discipline, including forensic science, or a degree with equivalent work. Additional exam requirements/recommendations for international students: Required—Either TOEFL (minimum score: paper-based 600, computer-based 250) or IELTS (6.5). *Application deadline:* For fall admission, 3/1 for domestic students. Application fee: $50. Electronic applications accepted. *Expenses:* Tuition, state resident: full-time $4308; part-time $479 per credit hour. Tuition, nonresident: full-time $8942; part-time $994 per credit hour. Required fees: $2000; $85 per credit hour. Tuition and fees vary according to course level, course load, degree level, campus/location and program. *Financial support:* Federal Work-Study, institutionally sponsored loans, and tuition waivers (full and partial) available. Support available to part-time students. Financial award applicants required to submit FAFSA. *Unit head:* Dr. Michelle R. Peace, Interim Chair, 804-828-8420, E-mail: mrpeace@vcu.edu. *Application contact:* Dr. Tracey Dawson Cruz, Graduate director of forensic science, 804-828-0642, E-mail: tcdawson@vcu.edu.

West Virginia University, Eberly College of Arts and Sciences, Department of Biology, Morgantown, WV 26506. Offers cell and molecular biology (MS, PhD); environmental and evolutionary biology (MS, PhD); forensic biology (MS, PhD); genomic biology (MS, PhD); neurobiology (MS, PhD). Terminal master's awarded for partial completion of doctoral program. *Degree requirements:* For master's, thesis, final exam; for doctorate, thesis/dissertation, preliminary and final exams. *Entrance requirements:* For master's, GRE General Test, GRE Subject Test, minimum GPA of 3.0; for doctorate, GRE General Test, minimum GPA of 3.0. Additional exam requirements/recommendations for international students: Required—TOEFL. *Faculty research:* Environmental biology, genetic engineering, developmental biology, global change, biodiversity.

ARCADIA UNIVERSITY

Program in Forensic Science

Programs of Study	Arcadia's Master of Science in Forensic Science (M.S.F.S.) program focuses primarily on the field of criminalistics, which includes forensic biology, chemistry, toxicology, and trace evidence analysis.
	The curriculum is unique in that it covers a variety of specialties, unlike other graduate programs that require a commitment to a single field of study, making for more well-rounded forensic practitioners. The curriculum involves classroom and laboratory exposure to the field of criminalistics, including forensic biology, chemistry and trace analysis, as well as forensic toxicology. Course work emphasizing the development of problem-solving abilities is designed to encourage a concentration in these forensic science specialty areas and expose students to both relevant laboratory techniques and relevant medico-legal developments.
	An emphasis on laboratory course work provides students with significant hands-on experiences. Students can reinforce their course work and hands-on experiences via internship arrangements with practicing forensic laboratories, including NMS Labs in Willow Grove, Pennsylvania. A comprehensive internal internship practicum at the Center for Forensic Science Research & Education is guaranteed for all students.
Research Facilities	Arcadia University has a partnership with the Center for Forensic Science Research & Education and NMS Labs, one of the nation's premier ASCLD-LAB ISO 17025 and ABFT-accredited laboratories. Both facilities are located about 10 minutes from Arcadia University in Willow Grove, Pennsylvania. A significant portion of M.S.F.S. course work is conducted at the Center for Forensic Science Research & Education facilities, and forensic practitioners from NMS Labs provide a substantial part of the instruction. Students also are guaranteed an internship at the Center for Forensic Science Research & Education. This highly desirable, comprehensive, and intensive 15-week internal internship program gives every student valuable real-world experience and career preparation in the following areas: forensic biology, forensic toxicology, forensic chemistry, and trace analysis.
Financial Aid	Qualified applicants are reviewed for merit scholarships by the Forensic Science Department during the application process. Graduate students who have been accepted into a degree program and are enrolled for at least 6 credits per semester are eligible to apply for financial aid. Students registered for at least 9 credits a semester may apply for a graduate assistantship provided they are matriculating in a degree program.
Cost of Study	Prospective students should visit www.arcadia.edu/tuition for the most current cost figures.
Living and Housing Costs	There are a variety of housing options in proximity to the University.
Student Outcomes	Arcadia's Forensic Science students continue to rank at the top of the class on the national Forensic Science Assessment test. In 2011, an Arcadia University master's student ranked No. 1 on the Forensic Science Assessment Test, marking the second time since 2009 where an Arcadia student took the top honor. Arcadia also made a clean sweep, taking the top five spots in the test.
	The success of any program is measured by the success of its graduates. Due to the excellent reputation of the program, Arcadia graduates are well received by the forensic science community. Alumni are employed in forensic laboratories at the state, private, and federal level. Employers include NMS Labs; Pennsylvania, Delaware, Wisconsin, and Maryland state crime labs; the Alaska Scientific Crime Detection Laboratory; the L.A. county Department of Coroner's office; the U.S. Army Expeditionary Forensics Division; New York Office of the Chief Medical Examiner's Office; the Philadelphia Medical Examiner's Office; the Armed Forces DNA Identification Laboratory; the U.S. Postal Inspection Service; Independent Forensics Inc.; the FBI Forensic Laboratory Services in Quantico; and the U.S. Customs and Border Protection Laboratory. Several alumni have gone on to become instructors in the field of forensics, and others have pursued professional degrees upon completion of the graduate degree.
Location	Arcadia University is a beautiful rolling campus built on the grounds of the historic landmark Grey Towers Castle in Glenside, Pennsylvania. Center City Philadelphia is just 25 minutes from campus and is easily accessed by car, bus, or train. Philadelphia offers a multitude of destinations and activities, including the National Constitution Center, Independence National Historic Park, Philadelphia Museum of Art, Franklin Institute, Philadelphia Zoo, South Street, and seven professional sports teams.
The University	Arcadia University is a top-ranked private university in metropolitan Philadelphia and a national leader in study abroad and international education. The 2010 Open Doors report ranked Arcadia University first in the nation in the percentage of undergraduate students studying abroad. *U.S. News & World Report* ranks Arcadia University among the top master's universities in the North, as one of the top study-abroad programs in the nation, and a "top up-and-coming school." The Physical Therapy program is ranked seventh in the nation. Arcadia University promises a distinctively global, integrative, and personal learning experience that prepares students to contribute and prosper in a diverse and dynamic world.
Applying	Prospective students should complete a Forensic Science application, including personal statements, online at www.arcadia.edu/gradapp. A bachelor's degree from an accredited institution with a GPA of 3.0 or better, with at least a 3.25 in the major, is required. It is expected that students have an undergraduate degree in the natural or physical sciences and have completed at least two semesters of general chemistry with laboratories, two semesters of organic chemistry with laboratories, and two semesters of general biology with laboratories. It is highly recommended that prospective undergraduate students have completed course work in genetics, molecular biology, biochemistry, statistics, and instrumental/analytical chemistry.
	Applicants also should submit one official transcript from each college, university, or professional school attended. Transfer credits included on a transcript must include grades earned; if not, an official transcript from the original school must be submitted. Transcripts must be sent from the issuing school in a sealed envelope and contain the appropriate signatures and seals to be considered official. Three letters of recommendation from persons familiar with the applicant's ability to study graduate-level science also are required as well as test scores for the Graduate Record Examination (GRE) or the Medical College Admission Test (MCAT), taken within the last five years.
Correspondence and Information	Office of Enrollment Management Arcadia University 450 S. Easton Road Glenside, Pennsylvania 19038 Phone: 877-ARCADIA (toll-free) 877-272-2342 (toll-free) E-mail: admiss@arcadia.edu Web site: http://www.arcadia.edu

Arcadia University

THE FACULTY AND THEIR RESEARCH

Arcadia's Forensic Science program is led by the renowned American Board of Criminalistics (ABC) and American Board of Forensic Toxicology (ABFT) certified faculty. Faculty members come from a diverse range of backgrounds, research interests, and career experiences, and they make sure each student receives the personal attention that is the hallmark of an Arcadia education.

HOLY FAMILY UNIVERSITY

Program in Criminal Justice

Program of Study	Holy Family University's Master of Arts (M.A.) in criminal justice program examines criminal behavior from a societal and multicultural perspective with a strong emphasis on ethics and social justice.
	Criminal justice is an interdisciplinary field of study that combines elements from psychology, sociology, social work, law, political science, history, philosophy, and business administration. Students in the criminal justice program learn the philosophical, political, and ideological basis for the criminalization of certain behaviors and the enforcement of those behaviors as unlawful. This learning comes through a curriculum that integrates theory and practice and sharpens students' writing, research, and communication skills. In Holy Family's program, doctoral-prepared faculty members explain how criminological theories relate to current social problems and present cutting-edge research in the discipline.
	The program is designed to develop and sharpen skills appropriate to beginning or continuing practitioners in the criminal justice system. Professionals in the fields of law enforcement, corrections, or the court system can utilize this degree to seek career advancement or personal enrichment. The mission of the program is to foster the development of professionals, scholars, and lifelong learners who can translate advanced study into effective problem solving skills; to facilitate the development of critical thinkers who can use their personal, professional, spiritual, and academic experiences in the analysis of current issues; to produce informed users of research capable of making significant contributions in their chosen fields; and to support and encourage scholarship, intellectual inquiry, and professional responsibility that nurtures the growth and development of others.
	The program consists of ten courses for a total of 30 credits. Core requirements include courses in the American criminal justice system, criminological theory, research methods, and ethics. The final course is a capstone scholarly research project.
Research Facilities	Holy Family University's Newtown Learning Resource Center (LRC) is an extension of the University's Northeast Philadelphia campus library. Staffed by library professionals, the LRC meets the research, information, and technology/audiovisual needs of students and faculty at the Newtown location. Staff members offer individualized research instruction as well as formal, in-depth research sessions.
	The LRC supports academic programs at Newtown through online research databases, print periodicals, books, and other media. Special collections include children's literature, curriculum materials, and an extensive collection of counseling psychology audiovisual materials. Holdings are supplemented by intercampus and interlibrary loan services.
Financial Aid	Holy Family is committed to helping adults further their education by consistently maintaining competitive tuition rates. Most graduate students are eligible for Federal Stafford Loans when attending with a half-time enrollment status (6 graduate credits) or greater. For more information, contact the Financial Aid Office at finaid@holyfamily.edu; phone: 267-341-3233.
Cost of Study	Tuition for Holy Family's traditional graduate programs is $630 per credit hour.
Living and Housing Costs	Holy Family University does not provide graduate student housing; however, there are numerous housing options available in the nearby area.
Student Group	Approximately 30 students, all studying part-time, are enrolled in the graduate program in criminal justice.
Student Outcomes	Future career opportunities in this growing field may include employment in juvenile justice, law enforcement, corrections, and court administration. The degree also prepares graduates for future doctoral study in the social sciences.
Location	Classes meet at the Newtown campus of Holy Family University, which occupies 79 acres in suburban Bucks County, Pennsylvania. The building contains the administrative service area; faculty offices; ten classrooms and laboratories, including two mixed-use labs, a science lab, and a nursing lab; the Learning Resource Center; the Center for Graduate Programs in Counseling Psychology; a chapel; the student services office; and a commons dining area.
The University	Holy Family University prides itself on programs that offer students real-world experience. This focus on preparedness and student outcomes is designed to help graduates stand out, with distinction.
	Respect for the individual, the dignity of the human person—these values are taught, lived, and form the foundation of Holy Family University. Concern for moral values and social justice guides the University's programs and enriches the student's education and experience.
Applying	Admissions are made on a rolling basis. Applicants must submit a statement of goals, official transcripts from every institution attended previously, two letters of recommendation, and a sample of scholarly writing, such as an undergraduate paper or article. Once all the admission materials have been received, the application will be forwarded to the Graduate Chair in Criminal Justice for review. Applicants will be considered based on their academic ability, expression of interests and goals, life experience, and personal interview.
Correspondence and Information	Graduate Admissions Office Holy Family University 9801 Frankford Avenue Philadelphia, Pennsylvania 19114 Phone: 267-341-3327 E-mail: gradstudy@holyfamily.edu Web site: http://my.holyfamily.edu/grad-programs/criminal_main.asp

Holy Family University

THE FACULTY AND THEIR RESEARCH

Leanne Owen, Associate Professor; Ph.D., Wales, 2004. Prosecutorial discretion, juvenile delinquency/school violence, assessment of pedagogical methods in criminology and criminal justice, institutional accreditation.

Michael Markowitz, Professor; Ph.D., Temple, 1994. Academic assessment and the impact of various demographic factors on patterns of criminality across the life course.

Danny Pirtle, Assistant Professor; Ph.D., Prairie View A&M, 2007. Female crime and delinquency, neighborhood disorder.

SouthUniversity℠

SOUTH UNIVERSITY

Columbia Campus
Criminal Justice Program

Program of Study

The Master of Science in criminal justice degree program at South University serves the growing number of individuals in the criminal justice system who desire post-baccalaureate education, as well as those in more traditional public and private employment who may wish to acquire further education in criminal justice. The program is primarily designed to prepare students for management, administrative, research, and teaching positions in order to foster a learning community of criminal justice professionals who can use their knowledge within law enforcement, correctional, political, and legal arenas. The delivery structure of the program gives students the ability to balance the rigors of work and home while pursuing their master's degree. Students can complete one or two courses each term, with each quarter lasting ten weeks.

The program has been designed with a limited prerequisite requirement to enable students with bachelor's degrees in related fields such as criminology, psychology, business or public administration, anthropology, political science, and sociology or related social sciences to enroll along with students who have already obtained undergraduate degrees in criminal justice. A general administration track as well as three specializations—Homeland Security, Corrections, and Cyber Crime—are available in order to meet student needs for more in-depth knowledge, skills, and applications in areas of great national and international interest.

Research Facilities

Along with classrooms and offices, the campus includes a bookstore, student lounge, and career services center. The South University Library provides in-library and remote access to electronic databases so that students may retrieve periodicals in paper or electronic form. Internet access is available on all computers throughout the campus.

Financial Aid

A wide range of financial aid options is available to students who qualify. The Columbia campus of South University offers access to federal and state programs, including grants, loans, and work-study programs. Eligible students may apply for veterans' educational benefits and are encouraged to investigate the availability of grants and scholarships through community resources. As a first step, students should complete the Free Application for Federal Student Aid (FAFSA). Students may apply electronically at http://www.fafsa.ed.gov or through the program. Applications should be submitted promptly to receive consideration for the maximum amount of aid.

Cost of Study

Tuition information for the professional counseling program may be obtained by contacting the Admissions Department at South University's Columbia campus.

Living and Housing Costs

South University does not offer or operate student housing. Students in the criminal justice program typically live in apartments in the Columbia area. Those who commute from long distances can arrange to stay at nearby hotels that offer long-term rates. More information may be obtained by contacting the Admissions Department.

Student Group

The Columbia campus of South University has a diverse student body enrolled in both day and evening classes. Students are primarily commuters who live within 50 miles of the city.

Student Outcomes

The South University Career Services Department has been established to assist currently enrolled students in developing their career plans and reaching their employment goals. Career services include, but are not limited to, one-on-one career counseling, special career-related workshops and programs, coaching for resume and cover letter development, and resume referral to employers.

Location

South University recently relocated its Columbia campus to the growing east side of Columbia, just minutes from downtown. The new campus is conveniently located off of I-77 at Farrow Road and Park Lane.

The campus surroundings are highlighted by a natural wooded landscape and vast green space featuring a tranquil campus courtyard. Convenient to malls, shopping, and the growing east side of Columbia, the new campus location provides easier access to students from throughout the greater Columbia area.

The University

South University is accredited by the Commission on Colleges of the Southern Association of Colleges and Schools (SACS) to award associate, baccalaureate, master's, and doctoral degrees. Students should contact the Commission on Colleges at 1866 Southern Lane, Decatur, Georgia 30033-4097 or call 404-679-4500 for questions about the accreditation of South University.

Applying

Students are accepted into the Master of Science in criminal justice degree program every academic quarter. Entrance into the program is gained through a formal application review and interview process. Acceptance is competitive and based on the admission committee's evaluation of the applicant's academic background and personal motivation. Application packets are available by contacting the South University Admissions Department (866-629-3031, toll-free) or visiting the University's Web site (http://www.southuniversity.edu).

Correspondence and Information

Applications for admission to the South University Master of Science in criminal justice program are available by contacting:

Criminal Justice Program
South University
9 Science Court
Columbia, South Carolina 29203

Phone: 803-799-9082
        866-629-3031 (toll-free)
Fax: 803-935-4382
E-mail: coladmis@southuniversity.edu
Web site: http://www.southuniversity.edu

See suprograms.info for program duration; tuition, fees, and other costs; median debt; federal salary data; alumni success; and other important information. (http://www.southuniversity.edu/programs-info/form/)

South University

THE FACULTY

One of the most outstanding aspects of South University's criminal justice program is the dedication of the faculty members and their ability to cultivate a supportive learning environment. Faculty members are committed to their roles as mentors, teachers, and co-learners. They are also dedicated to the training of students who can assume positions of leadership within the criminal justice field. A current list of program faculty members appears in the South University Web catalog, which is available on the South University Web site at http://www.southuniversity.edu.

South University is located on the fast-growing east side of Columbia, just minutes from downtown.

This section contains a directory of institutions offering graduate work in economics, followed by an in-depth entry submitted by an institution that chose to prepare a detailed program description. Additional information about programs listed in the directory but not augmented by an in-depth entry may be obtained by writing directly to the dean of a graduate school or chair of a department at the address given in the directory.

For programs offering related work, see also in this book *Family and Consumer Sciences, Political Science and International Affairs,* and *Public, Regional, and Industrial Affairs.* In the other guides in this series:

Graduate Programs in the Physical Sciences, Mathematics, Agricultural Sciences, the Environment & Natural Resources
See *Agricultural and Food Sciences* and *Mathematical Sciences*
Graduate Programs in Engineering & Applied Sciences
See *Computer Science and Information Technology; Geological, Mineral/Mining, and Petroleum Engineering;* and *Industrial Engineering*
Graduate Programs in Business, Education, Health, Information Studies, Law & Social Work
See *Business Administration and Management*

CONTENTS

Program Directories

Close-Ups

    See also:

Agricultural Economics and Agribusiness

Alabama Agricultural and Mechanical University, School of Graduate Studies, School of Agricultural and Environmental Sciences, Department of Agribusiness, Huntsville, AL 35811. Offers MS. Part-time programs available. *Degree requirements:* For master's, thesis (for some programs). *Entrance requirements:* For master's, GRE General Test. Additional exam requirements/recommendations for international students: Required—TOEFL (minimum score 500 paper-based; 173 computer-based; 61 iBT). Electronic applications accepted. *Faculty research:* Farm economics.

Alcorn State University, School of Graduate Studies, School of Agriculture and Applied Science, Alcorn State, MS 39096-7500. Offers agricultural economics (MS Ag); agronomy (MS Ag); animal science (MS Ag). *Degree requirements:* For master's, thesis optional. *Faculty research:* Aquatic systems, dairy herd improvement, fruit production, alternative farming practices.

American University of Beirut, Graduate Programs, Faculty of Agricultural and Food Sciences, Beirut, Lebanon. Offers agricultural economics (MS); animal sciences (MS); ecosystem management (MSES); food technology (MS); irrigation (MS); mechanization (MS); nutrition (MS); plant protection (MS); plant science (MS); poultry science (MS); soils (MS). Part-time programs available. *Faculty:* 22 full-time (6 women). *Students:* 6 full-time (3 women), 86 part-time (77 women). Average age 24. 94 applicants, 60% accepted, 15 enrolled. In 2010, 28 master's awarded. *Degree requirements:* For master's, one foreign language, comprehensive exam, thesis (for some programs). *Entrance requirements:* Additional exam requirements/recommendations for international students: Required—TOEFL (minimum score 600 paper-based; 250 computer-based; 100 iBT), IELTS (minimum score 7.5). *Application deadline:* For fall admission, 4/30 for domestic and international students; for spring admission, 11/1 for domestic and international students. Applications are processed on a rolling basis. Application fee: $50. Electronic applications accepted. *Expenses:* Tuition: Full-time $12,294; part-time $683 per credit. Required fees: $499; $499 per credit. Tuition and fees vary according to course load and program. *Financial support:* In 2010–11, 18 research assistantships with partial tuition reimbursements (averaging $13,132 per year), 42 teaching assistantships with full and partial tuition reimbursements (averaging $1,000 per year) were awarded; scholarships/grants, health care benefits, and unspecified assistantships also available. Financial award application deadline: 2/2. *Faculty research:* Community and therapeutic nutrition; food safety and food microbiology; landscape planning, nature and rural heritage conservation; pathology, immunology and control of poultry and animal diseases; agricultural economics and development. Total annual research expenditures: $900,000. *Unit head:* Prof. Nahla Hwalla, Dean, 961-134-3002 Ext. 4400, Fax: 961-174-4460, E-mail: nahla@aub.edu.lb. *Application contact:* Dr. Salim Kanaan, Director, Admissions Office, 961-135-0000 Ext. 2594, Fax: 961-175-0775, E-mail: sk00@aub.edu.lb.

Arizona State University, W. P. Carey School of Business, Morrison School of Agribusiness and Resource Management, Mesa, AZ 85212. Offers agribusiness (MS). Part-time and evening/weekend programs available. *Faculty:* 12 full-time (1 woman), 1 part-time/adjunct (0 women). *Students:* 8 full-time (3 women), 3 part-time (2 women); includes 3 minority (1 American Indian or Alaska Native, non-Hispanic/Latino; 2 Hispanic/Latino), 2 international. Average age 29. 6 applicants, 83% accepted, 3 enrolled. In 2010, 18 master's awarded. *Degree requirements:* For master's, thesis, oral defense, interactive Program of Study (iPOS) submitted before completing 50 percent of required credit hours. *Entrance requirements:* For master's, GMAT or GRE General Test, minimum GPA of 3.0 in last 2 years of work leading to bachelor's degree, 3 letters of recommendation, resume, official transcripts, statement of intent. Additional exam requirements/recommendations for international students: Required—TOEFL (minimum score 550 paper-based; 213 computer-based; 80 iBT), IELTS (minimum score 6.5); Recommended—TWE. *Application deadline:* For fall admission, 2/1 priority date for domestic and international students; for spring admission, 10/15 priority date for domestic and international students. Applications are processed on a rolling basis. Application fee: $70 ($90 for international students). Electronic applications accepted. *Expenses:* Tuition, state resident: full-time $8510; part-time $608 per credit. Tuition, nonresident: full-time $16,542; part-time $919 per credit. Required fees: $339; $110 per credit. Part-time tuition and fees vary according to course load. *Financial support:* In 2010–11, 2 research assistantships with partial tuition reimbursements (averaging $4,988 per year) were awarded; fellowships with full and partial tuition reimbursements, teaching assistantships with partial tuition reimbursements, career-related internships or fieldwork, institutionally sponsored loans, scholarships/grants, and tuition waivers (full and partial) also available. Financial award application deadline: 3/1; financial award applicants required to submit CSS PROFILE or FAFSA. *Faculty research:* Consumer behavior and marketing strategies in food markets, supply-chain management, derivatives and risk management, and international agricultural trade and policy. Total annual research expenditures: $365,322. *Unit head:* Dr. Timothy Richards, Chair, 480-727-1488, Fax: 480-727-1186, E-mail: trichards@asu.edu. *Application contact:* Graduate Admissions, 480-965-6113.

Arizona State University, W. P. Carey School of Business, Program in Business Administration, Tempe, AZ 85287-4906. Offers accountancy (PhD); agribusiness (PhD); business administration (MBA); finance (PhD); financial management and markets (MBA); information management (MBA); information systems (PhD); management (PhD); marketing (PhD); strategic marketing and services leadership (MBA); supply chain financial management (MBA); supply chain management (MBA, PhD); JD/MBA; MBA/M Acc; MBA/M Arch. *Accreditation:* AACSB. Part-time and evening/weekend programs available. Postbaccalaureate distance learning degree programs offered (minimal on-campus study). *Faculty:* 84 full-time (22 women), 7 part-time/adjunct (2 women). *Students:* 1,302 full-time (379 women), 86 part-time (26 women); includes 241 minority (37 Black or African American, non-Hispanic/Latino; 11 American Indian or Alaska Native, non-Hispanic/Latino; 103 Asian, non-Hispanic/Latino; 76 Hispanic/Latino; 4 Native Hawaiian or other Pacific Islander, non-Hispanic/Latino; 10 Two or more races, non-Hispanic/Latino), 171 international. Average age 31. 1,795 applicants, 44% accepted, 525 enrolled. In 2010, 734 master's, 9 doctorates awarded. Terminal master's awarded for partial completion of doctoral program. *Degree requirements:* For master's, thesis or alternative, internship, interactive Program of Study (iPOS) submitted before completing 50 percent of required credit hours; for doctorate, comprehensive exam, thesis/dissertation, interactive Program of Study (iPOS) submitted before completing 50 percent of required credit hours. *Entrance requirements:* For master's, GMAT, minimum GPA of 3.0 in last 2 years of work leading to bachelor's degree, 2 letters of recommendation, professional resume, official transcripts, 3 essays; for doctorate, GMAT or GRE, minimum GPA of 3.0 in last 2 years of work leading to bachelor's degree, 3 letters of recommendation, resume, personal statement/essay. Additional exam requirements/recommendations for international students: Required—TOEFL (minimum score 550 paper-based; 213 computer-based; 80 iBT), IELTS (minimum score 6.5). Application fee: $70 ($90 for international students). Electronic applications accepted. *Expenses:* Contact institution. *Financial support:* In 2010–11, 17 research assistantships with full and partial tuition reimbursements (averaging $18,121 per year), 153 teaching assistantships with full and partial tuition reimbursements (averaging $9,176 per year) were awarded; fellowships with full and partial tuition reimbursements, career-related internships or fieldwork, institutionally sponsored loans, scholarships/grants, and tuition waivers (full and partial) also available. Support available to part-time students. Financial award application deadline: 3/1; financial award applicants required to submit FAFSA. Total annual research expenditures: $540,779. *Unit head:* Dr. Robert E. Mittelstaedt, Dean, 480-965-2468, Fax: 480-965-5539, E-mail: mittelsr@asu.edu. *Application contact:* Graduate Admissions, 480-965-6113.

Auburn University, Graduate School, College of Agriculture, Department of Agricultural Economics and Rural Sociology, Auburn University, AL 36849. Offers agricultural economics (M Ag, MS); applied economics (PhD). Part-time programs available. *Faculty:* 18 full-time (3 women). *Students:* 28 full-time (9 women), 7 part-time (3 women); includes 1 Black or African American, non-Hispanic/Latino; 1 Asian, non-Hispanic/Latino, 24 international. Average age 31. 55 applicants, 55% accepted, 9 enrolled. In 2010, 5 master's awarded. *Degree requirements:* For master's, thesis (for some programs); for doctorate, thesis/dissertation. *Entrance requirements:* For master's and doctorate, GRE General Test. *Application deadline:* For fall admission, 7/7 for domestic students; for spring admission, 11/24 for domestic students. Applications are processed on a rolling basis. Application fee: $50 ($60 for international students). Electronic applications accepted. *Expenses:* Tuition, state resident: full-time $7002. Tuition, nonresident: full-time $21,898. International tuition: $22,116 full-time. Required fees: $892. Tuition and fees vary according to course load and program. *Financial support:* Research assistantships, teaching assistantships, Federal Work-Study available. Support available to part-time students. Financial award application deadline: 3/15; financial award applicants required to submit FAFSA. *Faculty research:* Farm management, agricultural marketing, production economics, resource economics, agricultural finance. *Unit head:* Dr. Curtis M. Jolly, Chair, 334-844-4800. *Application contact:* Dr. George Flowers, Dean of the Graduate School, 334-844-2125.

California Polytechnic State University, San Luis Obispo, College of Agriculture, Food and Environmental Sciences, Department of Agribusiness, San Luis Obispo, CA 93407. Offers MS. Part-time programs available. *Students:* 6 full-time (3 women), 2 part-time (1 woman); includes 1 minority (Hispanic/Latino). Average age 27. 11 applicants, 64% accepted, 5 enrolled. In 2010, 2 master's awarded. *Degree requirements:* For master's, comprehensive exam, thesis. *Entrance requirements:* For master's, GRE General Test (50th percentile), minimum GPA of 2.75 in last 90 quarter units of course work. Additional exam requirements/recommendations for international students: Required—TOEFL (minimum score 550 paper-based; 213 computer-based) or IELTS (minimum score 6). *Application deadline:* For fall admission, 4/1 for domestic students, 11/30 for international students; for winter admission, 10/1 for domestic students, 6/30 for international students; for spring admission, 10/1 for domestic students. Applications are processed on a rolling basis. Application fee: $55. Electronic applications accepted. *Expenses:* Tuition, state resident: full-time $5386; part-time $3124 per year. Tuition, nonresident: full-time $11,160; part-time $248 per unit. Required fees: $2250; $614 per term. One-time fee: $2250 full-time; $1842 part-time. *Financial support:* Fellowships, research assistantships, teaching assistantships, career-related internships or fieldwork, Federal Work-Study, institutionally sponsored loans, scholarships/grants, and unspecified assistantships available. Support available to part-time students. Financial award application deadline: 3/2; financial award applicants required to submit FAFSA. *Faculty research:* Agribusiness management, commodity marketing, international and domestic agribusiness. *Unit head:* Dr. James Ahern, Graduate Coordinator, 805-756-5030, Fax: 805-756-5040, E-mail: jahern@calpoly.edu. *Application contact:* Dr. Mark Shelton, Associate Dean/Graduate Coordinator, 805-756-2161, Fax: 805-756-6577, E-mail: mshelton@calpoly.edu.

Colorado State University, Graduate School, College of Agricultural Sciences, Department of Agricultural and Resource Economics, Fort Collins, CO 80523-1172. Offers MS, PhD. Part-time programs available. *Faculty:* 16 full-time (3 women). *Students:* 26 full-time (8 women), 18 part-time (11 women); includes 3 Hispanic/Latino; 1 Two or more races, non-Hispanic/Latino, 14 international. Average age 29. 92 applicants, 80% accepted, 16 enrolled. In 2010, 4 master's, 2 doctorates awarded. Terminal master's awarded for partial completion of doctoral program. *Degree requirements:* For master's, comprehensive exam (for some programs), thesis (for some programs); for doctorate, comprehensive exam, thesis/dissertation. *Entrance requirements:* For master's, minimum GPA of 3.0, bachelor's degree, 3 letters of recommendation; for doctorate, minimum GPA of 3.0, bachelor's degree, 3 letters of recommendation, statement of purpose. Additional exam requirements/recommendations for international students: Required—TOEFL (minimum score 550 paper-based; 213 computer-based; 80 iBT). *Application deadline:* For fall admission, 2/1 priority date for domestic students, 2/1 for international students; for spring admission, 7/1 priority date for domestic students, 7/1 for international students. Application fee: $50. Electronic applications accepted. *Expenses:* Tuition, state resident: full-time $7434; part-time $413 per credit. Tuition, nonresident: full-time $19,022; part-time $1057 per credit. Required fees: $1729; $88 per credit. *Financial support:* In 2010–11, 16 students received support, including 10 research assistantships with full tuition reimbursements available (averaging $14,555 per year), 6 teaching assistantships with full tuition reimbursements available (averaging $12,019 per year); fellowships with partial tuition reimbursements available, Federal Work-Study, scholarships/grants, and unspecified assistantships also available. Financial award application deadline: 2/1; financial award applicants required to submit FAFSA. *Faculty research:* Agricultural production and finance economics, agricultural business and marketing economics, community and international development economics, natural resource and environmental economics. Total annual research expenditures: $1.5 million. *Unit head:* Dr. Stephen P. Davies, Chair, 970-491-6955, Fax: 970-491-2067, E-mail: stephen.davies@colostate.edu. *Application contact:* Barbara A. Brown, Program Assistant, 970-491-6955, Fax: 970-491-2067, E-mail: barbara.brown@colostate.edu.

Cornell University, Graduate School, Graduate Fields of Agriculture and Life Sciences, Field of International Agriculture and Rural Development, Ithaca, NY 14853-0001. Offers international agriculture and development (MPS). *Faculty:* 44 full-time (9 women). *Students:* 31 full-time (12 women); includes 1 Black or African American, non-Hispanic/Latino; 1 Hispanic/Latino, 4 international. Average age 29. 45 applicants, 76% accepted, 29 enrolled. In 2010, 15 master's awarded. *Degree requirements:* For master's, project paper. *Entrance requirements:* For master's, GRE General Test (recommended), 2 years of development experience, 2 letters of recommendation. Additional exam requirements/recommendations for international students: Required—TOEFL (minimum score 550 paper-based; 213 computer-based; 77 iBT). *Application deadline:* For fall admission, 3/1 for domestic students. Application fee: $70. Electronic applications accepted. *Expenses:* Tuition: Full-time $29,500. Required fees: $76. Tuition and fees vary according to degree level and program. *Financial support:* In 2010–11, 12 fellowships with full tuition reimbursements, 1 teaching assistantship with full tuition reimbursement were awarded; research assistantships with full tuition reimbursements, institutionally sponsored loans, scholarships/grants, health care benefits, tuition waivers (full and partial), and unspecified assistantships also available. Financial award applicants required to submit FAFSA. *Unit head:* Director of Graduate Studies, 607-255-3037, Fax: 607-255-1005. *Application contact:* Graduate Field Assistant, 607-255-3035, Fax: 607-255-1005, E-mail: mpsiard@cornell.edu.

Delaware Valley College, MBA Program, Doylestown, PA 18901-2697. Offers accounting (MBA); food and agribusiness (MBA); general business (MBA); online global executive leadership (MBA). Part-time and evening/weekend programs available. Postbaccalaureate distance learning degree programs offered (no on-campus study). *Entrance requirements:* For master's, minimum undergraduate GPA of 3.0. *Expenses:* Contact institution.

Florida Agricultural and Mechanical University, Division of Graduate Studies, Research, and Continuing Education, College of Engineering Science, Technology, and Agriculture, Division of Agricultural Sciences, Tallahassee, FL 32307-3200. Offers agribusiness (MS); animal science (MS); engineering technology (MS); entomology (MS); food science (MS); international programs (MS); plant science (MS). *Degree requirements:* For master's, thesis. *Entrance requirements:* For master's, GRE General Test, minimum GPA of 3.0. Additional exam requirements/recommendations for international students: Required—TOEFL (minimum score 500 paper-based).

Illinois State University, Graduate School, College of Applied Science and Technology, Department of Agriculture, Normal, IL 61790-2200. Offers agribusiness (MS). *Degree requirements:* For master's, thesis optional. *Entrance requirements:* For master's, GRE General Test, minimum GPA of 3.0 in last 60 hours. *Faculty research:* Engineering-economic system models for rural ethanol production facilities, development and evaluation of a propane-fueled, production scale, on-site thermal destruction system C-FAR 2007; field scale evaluation and technology transfer of economically, ecologically sound liquid swine manure treatment and application.

Instituto Centroamericano de Administración de Empresas, Graduate Programs, La Garita, Costa Rica. Offers agribusiness management (MIAM); business administration (EMBA); finance (MBA); real estate management (MGREM); sustainable development (MBA); technology (MBA). *Degree requirements:* For master's, comprehensive exam, essay. *Entrance requirements:* For master's, GMAT or GRE General Test, fluency in Spanish, interview, letters of recommendation, minimum 1 year of work experience. Electronic applications accepted. *Faculty research:* Competitiveness, production.

Iowa State University of Science and Technology, Graduate College, College of Liberal Arts and Sciences, Department of Economics and College of Agriculture, Program in Agricultural Economics, Ames, IA 50011. Offers MS, PhD. *Faculty:* 29 full-time (3 women), 3 part-time/adjunct (all women). *Students:* 32 full-time (9 women), 14 part-time (8 women); includes 1 Asian, non-Hispanic/Latino, 30 international. 69 applicants, 10% accepted, 7 enrolled. In 2010, 2 master's, 1 doctorate awarded. *Degree requirements:* For master's, thesis or alternative; for doctorate, thesis/dissertation. *Entrance requirements:* For master's and doctorate, GRE General Test. Additional exam requirements/recommendations for international students: Required—TOEFL (minimum score 570 paper-based; 88 iBT), IELTS (minimum score 6.5). *Application deadline:* For fall admission, 1/31 priority date for domestic and international students. Application fee: $40 ($90 for international students). Electronic applications accepted. *Financial support:* In 2010–11, 15 research assistantships with full and partial tuition reimbursements (averaging $10,898 per year), 18 teaching assistantships with full and partial tuition reimbursements (averaging $10,762 per year) were awarded; fellowships, scholarships/grants, health care benefits, and unspecified assistantships also available. *Unit head:* Section Leader, 515-294-2702. *Application contact:* Dr. John Schroeter, Information Contact, 515-294-2702, E-mail: grad@econ.iastate.edu.

Iowa State University of Science and Technology, Graduate College, Interdisciplinary Programs, Program in Seed Technology and Business, Ames, IA 50011. Offers MS. Part-time and evening/weekend programs available. Postbaccalaureate distance learning degree programs offered (no on-campus study). *Students:* 38 part-time (8 women); includes 1 Asian, non-Hispanic/Latino; 1 Hispanic/Latino, 6 international. *Degree requirements:* For master's, thesis or alternative. *Entrance requirements:* For master's, resume, 3 letters of recommendation. Additional exam requirements/recommendations for international students: Required—TOEFL (minimum score 570 paper-based; 85 iBT), IELTS (minimum score 6.5). *Application deadline:* For fall admission, 4/15 priority date for domestic students, 4/15 for international students. Application fee: $40 ($90 for international students). Electronic applications accepted. *Unit head:* Dr. Gary Munkvold, Supervisory Committee Chair, 515-294-8745. *Application contact:* Information Contact, 515-294-5836, Fax: 515-294-2592, E-mail: grad_admissions@iastate.edu.

Kansas State University, Graduate School, College of Agriculture, Department of Agricultural Economics, Manhattan, KS 66506. Offers MAB, MS, PhD. Part-time programs available. Postbaccalaureate distance learning degree programs offered (minimal on-campus study). Terminal master's awarded for partial completion of doctoral program. *Degree requirements:* For master's, thesis or alternative, oral exam; for doctorate, thesis/dissertation, preliminary exams. *Entrance requirements:* For master's and doctorate, GRE General Test. Additional exam requirements/recommendations for international students: Required—TOEFL (minimum score 550 paper-based; 213 computer-based). Electronic applications accepted. *Faculty research:* Livestock marketing, biofuels research, natural resources, agribusiness industry, international development and trade.

Louisiana State University and Agricultural and Mechanical College, Graduate School, College of Agriculture, Department of Agricultural Economics and Agribusiness, Baton Rouge, LA 70803. Offers MS, PhD. *Faculty:* 20 full-time (0 women). *Students:* 30 full-time (13 women), 9 part-time (1 woman); includes 1 Black or African American, non-Hispanic/Latino; 1 Asian, non-Hispanic/Latino, 27 international. Average age 31. 24 applicants, 50% accepted, 1 enrolled. In 2010, 15 master's, 3 doctorates awarded. *Degree requirements:* For master's, thesis (for some programs); for doctorate, thesis/dissertation. *Entrance requirements:* For master's and doctorate, GRE General Test, minimum GPA of 3.0. Additional exam requirements/recommendations for international students: Required—TOEFL (minimum score 550 paper-based; 213 computer-based; 79 iBT) or IELTS (minimum score 6.5). *Application deadline:* For fall admission, 1/25 priority date for domestic students, 5/15 for international students; for spring admission, 10/15 for international students. Applications are processed on a rolling basis. Application fee: $50 ($70 for international students). Electronic applications accepted. *Financial support:* In 2010–11, 37 students received support, including 28 research assistantships with partial tuition reimbursements available (averaging $16,232 per year); teaching assistantships with partial tuition reimbursements available, Federal Work-Study, institutionally sponsored loans, scholarships/grants, health care benefits, tuition waivers (full and partial), and unspecified assistantships also available. Support available to part-time students. Financial award applicants required to submit FAFSA. *Faculty research:* Natural and environmental economics, agribusiness, marketing, production economics, community economics, rural development. Total annual research expenditures: $67,102. *Unit head:* Dr. Gail L. Cramer, Head, 225-578-3282, Fax: 225-578-2716, E-mail: gcramer@agctr.lsu.edu. *Application contact:* Dr. Richard Kaemierczak, Graduate Coordinator, 225-578-2712, Fax: 225-578-2716, E-mail: rkazmierczak@agcenter.lsu.edu.

McGill University, Faculty of Graduate and Postdoctoral Studies, Faculty of Agricultural and Environmental Sciences, Department of Agricultural Economics, Montréal, QC H3A 2T5, Canada. Offers M Sc.

Michigan State University, The Graduate School, College of Agriculture and Natural Resources, Department of Agricultural, Food, and Resource Economics, East Lansing, MI 48824. Offers agricultural economics (MS, PhD); agricultural, food, and resource economics (MS, PhD). *Entrance requirements:* Additional exam requirements/recommendations for international students: Required—TOEFL (minimum score 550 paper-based; 213 computer-based), Michigan State University ELT (minimum score 85), Michigan English Language Assessment Battery (minimum score 83). Electronic applications accepted.

Mississippi State University, College of Agriculture and Life Sciences, Department of Agricultural Economics, Mississippi State, MS 39762. Offers agribusiness management (MABM); agriculture (MS), including agricultural economics. Part-time programs available. *Faculty:* 12 full-time (0 women). *Students:* 16 full-time (6 women), 3 part-time (1 woman); includes 1 minority (Asian, non-Hispanic/Latino), 5 international. Average age 27. 16 applicants, 63% accepted, 6 enrolled. In 2010, 3 master's awarded. *Degree requirements:* For master's, thesis (for some programs), comprehensive oral or written exam, thesis defense. *Entrance requirements:* For master's, GRE, GMAT, minimum GPA of 3.0. Additional exam requirements/recommendations for international students: Required—TOEFL (minimum score 575 paper-based; 233 computer-based; 84 iBT); Recommended—IELTS (minimum score 7). *Application deadline:* For fall admission, 7/1 for domestic students, 5/1 for international students; for spring admission, 11/1 for domestic students, 9/1 for international students. Applications are processed on a rolling basis. Application fee: $40. Electronic applications accepted. *Expenses:* Tuition, state resident: full-time $2730.50; part-time $304 per credit hour. Tuition, nonresident: full-time $6901; part-time $767 per credit hour. *Financial support:* In 2010–11, 9 research assistantships with full tuition reimbursements (averaging $12,270 per year) were awarded; career-related internships or fieldwork, Federal Work-Study, institutionally sponsored loans, and unspecified assistantships also available. Financial award application deadline: 4/1; financial award applicants required to submit FAFSA. *Faculty research:* Production economics, policy, resource economics, international trade, agribusiness management. *Unit head:* Dr. Steven C. Turner, Professor and Head, 662-325-2049, Fax: 662-325-8777, E-mail: turner@aegcon.msstate.edu. *Application contact:* Dr. Barry Barnett, Professor and Graduate Coordinator, 662-325-0128, Fax: 662-325-8777, E-mail: bjb11@msstate.edu.

New Mexico State University, Graduate School, College of Agricultural, Consumer and Environmental Sciences, Department of Agricultural Economics and Agricultural Business, Las Cruces, NM 88003-8001. Offers agribusiness (M Ag, MBA); agricultural economics (MS); economics (MA). Part-time programs available. *Faculty:* 7 full-time (1 woman). *Students:* 13 full-time (5 women), 7 part-time (4 women); includes 3 minority (1 Asian, non-Hispanic/Latino; 2 Hispanic/Latino), 7 international. Average age 27. 14 applicants, 93% accepted, 10 enrolled. In 2010, 4 master's awarded. *Degree requirements:* For master's, thesis (for some programs). *Entrance requirements:* For master's, previous course work in intermediate microeconomics, intermediate macroeconomics, college-level calculus, statistics. Additional exam requirements/recommendations for international students: Required—TOEFL. *Application deadline:* For fall admission, 7/1 priority date for domestic and international students; for spring admission, 11/1 priority date for domestic and international students. Applications are processed on a rolling basis. Application fee: $30 ($50 for international students). Electronic applications accepted. *Expenses:* Tuition, state resident: full-time $4536; part-time $242 per credit. Tuition, nonresident: full-time $15,816; part-time $712 per credit. Required fees: $636 per term. *Financial support:* In 2010–11, 8 research assistantships (averaging $16,300 per year), 1 teaching assistantship (averaging $7,900 per year) were awarded; career-related internships or fieldwork and health care benefits also available. Financial award application deadline: 3/1. *Faculty research:* Natural resource policy, production economics and farm/ranch management, agribusiness and marketing, international marketing and trade, agricultural risk management. *Unit head:* Dr. Terry Crawford, Head, 575-646-3215, Fax: 575-646-3808, E-mail: crawford@nmsu.edu. *Application contact:* Dr. L. Allen Torell, Professor, 575-646-4732, Fax: 575-646-3808, E-mail: atorell@nmsu.edu.

North Carolina Agricultural and Technical State University, Graduate School, School of Agriculture and Environmental Sciences, Department of Agribusiness, Applied Economics, and Agriscience Education, Greensboro, NC 27411. Offers agricultural economics (MS); agricultural education (MS). *Accreditation:* NCATE. Part-time and evening/weekend programs available. *Degree requirements:* For master's, comprehensive exam, thesis or alternative, qualifying exam. *Entrance requirements:* For master's, GRE General Test, minimum GPA of 3.0. *Faculty research:* Aid for small farmers, agricultural technology resources, labor force mobility, agrology.

North Carolina State University, Graduate School, College of Agriculture and Life Sciences, Program in Agricultural and Resource Economics, Raleigh, NC 27695. Offers MS. Part-time programs available. *Degree requirements:* For master's, thesis. *Entrance requirements:* Additional exam requirements/recommendations for international students: Required—TOEFL. Electronic applications accepted. *Faculty research:* Resource economics, international economics, labor economics, econometrics, environmental economics.

North Dakota State University, College of Graduate and Interdisciplinary Studies, College of Agriculture, Food Systems, and Natural Resources, Department of Agribusiness and Applied Economics, Fargo, ND 58108. Offers agribusiness and applied economics (MS); international agribusiness (MS); natural resource management (MS). Part-time programs available. *Faculty:* 16 full-time (3 women), 5 part-time/adjunct (1 woman). *Students:* 10 full-time (5 women), 4 part-time (0 women); includes 3 Black or African American, non-Hispanic/Latino; 1 Hispanic/Latino. Average age 24. 28 applicants, 68% accepted, 12 enrolled. In 2010, 13 master's awarded. *Degree requirements:* For master's, thesis. *Entrance requirements:* For master's, minimum GPA of 3.0. Additional exam requirements/recommendations for international students: Required—TOEFL (minimum score 525 paper-based; 225 computer-based; 71 iBT). *Application deadline:* For fall admission, 2/1 priority date for domestic students, 3/1 priority date for international students. Applications are processed on a rolling basis. Application fee: $45 ($60 for international students). Electronic applications accepted. *Financial support:* In 2010–11, 8 research assistantships with tuition reimbursements (averaging $14,520 per year) were awarded; Federal Work-Study and institutionally sponsored loans also available. Financial award application deadline: 4/15. *Faculty research:* Agribusiness, transportation, marketing, microeconomics, trade. Total annual research expenditures: $1 million. *Unit head:* Dr. Thomas I. Wahl, Chair, 701-231-7470, Fax: 701-231-7400. *Application contact:* Dr. Thomas I. Wahl, Chair, 701-231-7470, Fax: 701-231-7400.

Northwest Missouri State University, Graduate School, Melvin and Valorie Booth College of Business and Professional Studies, Department of Agriculture, Program in Agricultural Economics, Maryville, MO 64468-6001. Offers MBA. *Faculty:* 7 full-time (2 women). *Students:* 1 full-time (0 women), 1 part-time (0 women). 2 applicants, 100% accepted, 1 enrolled. In 2010, 2 master's awarded. *Degree requirements:* For master's, comprehensive exam. *Entrance requirements:* For master's, GMAT, GRE, minimum GPA of 2.5. Additional exam requirements/recommendations for international students: Required—TOEFL (minimum score 550 paper-based; 213 computer-based). *Application deadline:* For fall admission, 7/1 for domestic and international students; for spring admission, 12/1 for domestic students, 11/15 for international students. Applications are processed on a rolling basis. Application fee: $0 ($50 for international students). *Financial support:* Application deadline: 4/1. *Unit head:* Naveen Musunuru, Program Director, 660-562-1341. *Application contact:* Dr. Gregory Haddock, Dean of Graduate School, 660-562-1145, Fax: 660-562-1096, E-mail: gradsch@nwmissouri.edu.

The Ohio State University, Graduate School, College of Food, Agricultural, and Environmental Sciences, Department of Agricultural, Environmental, and Development Economics, Columbus, OH 43210. Offers agricultural economics and rural sociology (MS, PhD). *Faculty:* 32. *Students:* 64 full-time (28 women), 18 part-time (8 women); includes 2 Black or African American, non-Hispanic/Latino; 7 Asian, non-Hispanic/Latino, 39 international. Average age 28. In 2010, 15 master's, 8 doctorates awarded. *Degree requirements:* For master's, thesis optional; for doctorate, thesis/dissertation. *Entrance requirements:* For master's and doctorate, GRE General Test. Additional exam requirements/recommendations for international students: Required—TOEFL (minimum score 550 paper-based; 213 computer-based), IELTS (minimum score 7), or Michigan English Language Assessment Battery (minimum score 92). *Application deadline:* For fall admission, 8/15 priority date for domestic students, 7/1 priority date for international students; for winter admission, 12/1 priority date for domestic students, 11/1 priority date for international students; for spring admission, 3/1 priority date for domestic students, 2/1 priority date for international students. Applications are processed on a rolling basis. Application fee: $40 ($50 for international students). Electronic applications accepted. *Expenses:* Tuition, state resident: full-time $10,605. Tuition, nonresident: full-time $26,535. Tuition and fees vary according to course load and program. *Financial support:* Fellowships, research assistantships, teaching assistantships, Federal Work-Study and institutionally sponsored loans available. Support available to part-time students. *Unit head:* Tim Haab, Graduate Studies Committee Chair, 614-292-6237, E-mail: haab.1@osu.edu. *Application contact:* Graduate Admissions, 614-292-9444, Fax: 614-292-3895, E-mail: domestic.grad@osu.edu.

Oklahoma State University, College of Agricultural Science and Natural Resources, Department of Agricultural Economics, Stillwater, OK 74078. Offers M Ag, MS, PhD. *Faculty:* 33 full-time (8 women), 2 part-time/adjunct (0 women). *Students:* 46 full-time (16 women), 24 part-time (9 women); includes 1 American Indian or Alaska Native, non-Hispanic/Latino; 1 Asian, non-Hispanic/Latino, 34 international. Average age 29. 99 applicants, 56% accepted, 22 enrolled. In 2010, 12 master's, 6 doctorates awarded. *Degree requirements:* For master's, thesis or report, oral exam; for doctorate, comprehensive exam, thesis/dissertation. *Entrance requirements:* For master's and doctorate, GRE or GMAT. Additional exam requirements/recommendations for international students: Required—TOEFL (minimum score 550 paper-based; 79 iBT). *Application deadline:* For fall admission, 3/1 priority date for international students; for spring admission, 8/1 priority date for international students. Applications are processed on a rolling basis. Application fee: $40 ($75 for international students). Electronic applications accepted. *Expenses:* Tuition, state resident: full-time $3716; part-time $154.85 per credit hour. Tuition, nonresident: full-time $14,892; part-time $621 per credit hour. Required fees: $2044; $85.20 per credit hour. One-time fee: $50. Tuition and fees vary according to course load and campus/location. *Financial support:* In 2010–11, 42 research assistantships (averaging $15,518 per year), 2 teaching assistantships (averaging $16,008 per year) were awarded; career-related internships or fieldwork, Federal Work-Study, scholarships/grants, health care benefits, tuition waivers (partial), and unspecified assistantships also available. Support available to part-time students. Financial award application deadline: 3/1; financial award applicants required

Agricultural Economics and Agribusiness

Oklahoma State University (continued)
to submit FAFSA. *Faculty research:* Marketing and agribusiness, production and farm management, policy and natural resources, community and rural development, international trade and development. *Unit head:* Dr. Mike Woods, Head, 405-744-6161, Fax: 405-744-8210. *Application contact:* Dr. Gordon Emslie, Dean, 405-744-6368, Fax: 405-744-0355, E-mail: grad-i@okstate.edu.

Oregon State University, Graduate School, College of Agricultural Sciences, Department of Agricultural and Resource Economics, Corvallis, OR 97331. Offers agricultural and resource economics (M Agr, MAIS, MS, PhD); economics (MS, PhD). MS and PhD in economics offered through the University Graduate Faculty of Economics. Part-time programs available. Terminal master's awarded for partial completion of doctoral program. *Degree requirements:* For master's, thesis (for some programs); for doctorate, thesis/dissertation. *Entrance requirements:* For master's and doctorate, GRE General Test, minimum GPA of 3.0 in last 90 hours. Additional exam requirements/recommendations for international students: Required—TOEFL. *Faculty research:* Marine economics, environmental economics, effects of global climate change on agriculture, efficiency of agricultural markets, analysis of aquaculture development.

Penn State University Park, Graduate School, College of Agricultural Sciences, Department of Agricultural Economics and Rural Sociology, State College, University Park, PA 16802-1503. Offers MS, PhD.

Prairie View A&M University, College of Agriculture and Human Sciences, Prairie View, TX 77446-0519. Offers agricultural economics (MS); animal sciences (MS); interdisciplinary human sciences (MS); soil science (MS). Part-time and evening/weekend programs available. *Faculty:* 11 full-time (2 women). *Students:* 47 full-time (33 women), 34 part-time (26 women); includes 62 Black or African American, non-Hispanic/Latino; 2 Asian, non-Hispanic/Latino; 2 Hispanic/Latino, 5 international. Average age 30. 147 applicants, 100% accepted. In 2010, 21 master's awarded. *Degree requirements:* For master's, comprehensive exam, thesis (for some programs), field placement. *Entrance requirements:* For master's, GRE General Test, minimum GPA of 2.45. Additional exam requirements/recommendations for international students: Required—TOEFL (minimum score 550 paper-based). *Application deadline:* For fall admission, 6/1 for domestic and international students; for spring admission, 10/1 for domestic and international students. Applications are processed on a rolling basis. Application fee: $50. *Expenses:* Tuition, state resident: full-time $3586.14; part-time $119.06 per credit hour. Tuition, nonresident: part-time $511.23 per credit hour. *Financial support:* In 2010–11, 57 students received support, including 8 fellowships with tuition reimbursements available (averaging $12,000 per year), 10 research assistantships with tuition reimbursements available (averaging $15,000 per year); career-related internships or fieldwork, Federal Work-Study, institutionally sponsored loans, scholarships/grants, tuition waivers (partial), and unspecified assistantships also available. Support available to part-time students. Financial award application deadline: 4/1; financial award applicants required to submit FAFSA. *Faculty research:* Domestic violence prevention, water quality, food growth regulators, wetland dynamics, biochemistry, obesity and nutrition, family therapy. Total annual research expenditures: $4 million. *Unit head:* Dr. Freddie Richards, Dean, 936-261-2528, Fax: 936-261-5143, E-mail: flrichards@pvamu.edu. *Application contact:* Dr. Richard W. Griffin, Interim Department Head, 936-261-5019, Fax: 936-261-5148, E-mail: rwgriffin@pvamu.edu.

Purdue University, Graduate School, College of Agriculture, Department of Agricultural Economics, West Lafayette, IN 47907. Offers agricultural economics (MS, PhD); food and agricultural business (EMBA). Part-time programs available. Terminal master's awarded for partial completion of doctoral program. *Degree requirements:* For master's, thesis (for some programs); for doctorate, thesis/dissertation. *Entrance requirements:* For master's and doctorate, GRE General Test. Additional exam requirements/recommendations for international students: Required—TOEFL, TWE (minimum score 4). Electronic applications accepted. *Faculty research:* Marketing, international trade, policy and development, production, resources.

Rutgers, The State University of New Jersey, New Brunswick, Graduate School-New Brunswick, Program in Food and Business Economics, Piscataway, NJ 08854-8097. Offers MS. *Degree requirements:* For master's, comprehensive exam, thesis or alternative. *Entrance requirements:* Additional exam requirements/recommendations for international students: Required—TOEFL. Electronic applications accepted. *Expenses:* Tuition, state resident: full-time $7200; part-time $600 per credit. Tuition, nonresident: full-time $11,124; part-time $927 per credit. *Faculty research:* Science policy, land use, nutrition policy, food industry, international development.

Santa Clara University, Leavey School of Business, Program in Business Administration, Santa Clara, CA 95053. Offers accounting (MBA); entrepreneurship (MBA); executive business administration (EMBA); finance (MBA); food and agribusiness (MBA); international business (MBA); leading people and organizations (MBA); managing technology and innovation (MBA); marketing management (MBA); supply chain management (MBA). *Accreditation:* AACSB. Part-time and evening/weekend programs available. *Students:* 229 full-time (80 women), 748 part-time (244 women); includes 354 minority (14 Black or African American, non-Hispanic/Latino; 1 American Indian or Alaska Native, non-Hispanic/Latino; 287 Asian, non-Hispanic/Latino; 42 Hispanic/Latino; 5 Native Hawaiian or other Pacific Islander, non-Hispanic/Latino; 5 Two or more races, non-Hispanic/Latino), 209 international. Average age 32. 334 applicants, 76% accepted, 191 enrolled. In 2010, 307 master's awarded. *Degree requirements:* For master's, thesis or alternative. *Entrance requirements:* For master's, GMAT, GRE. Additional exam requirements/recommendations for international students: Required—TOEFL (minimum score 600 paper-based; 250 computer-based; 100 iBT). *Application deadline:* For fall admission, 6/1 for domestic and international students; for spring admission, 1/19 for domestic students, 1/17 for international students. Applications are processed on a rolling basis. Application fee: $75 ($100 for international students). Electronic applications accepted. *Expenses:* Contact institution. *Financial support:* In 2010–11, 350 students received support; fellowships with partial tuition reimbursements available, research assistantships with partial tuition reimbursements available, career-related internships or fieldwork, Federal Work-Study, institutionally sponsored loans, scholarships/grants, health care benefits, and unspecified assistantships available. Support available to part-time students. Financial award application deadline: 6/1; financial award applicants required to submit FAFSA. *Unit head:* Elizabeth B. Ford, Senior Assistant Dean, 408-554-2752, Fax: 408-554-4571, E-mail: eford@scu.edu. *Application contact:* Molly Mulally, Assistant Director, Graduate Business Admissions, 408-554-4539, Fax: 408-554-4571, E-mail: mbaadmissions@scu.edu.

South Carolina State University, School of Graduate Studies, Department of Accounting, Agribusiness and Economics, Orangeburg, SC 29117-0001. Offers agribusiness (MS); agribusiness and entrepreneurship (MBA). Part-time and evening/weekend programs available. *Degree requirements:* For master's, comprehensive exam, business plan. *Entrance requirements:* For master's, GMAT, minimum GPA of 2.8. Additional exam requirements/recommendations for international students: Required—TOEFL. Electronic applications accepted. *Faculty research:* Small farm income and profitability, agricultural credit, aquaculture, low-input sustainable agriculture, rural development.

Southern Illinois University Carbondale, Graduate School, College of Agriculture, Department of Agribusiness Economics, Carbondale, IL 62901-4701. Offers MS, MBA/MS. Part-time programs available. *Degree requirements:* For master's, thesis. *Entrance requirements:* For master's, minimum GPA of 2.7. Additional exam requirements/recommendations for international students: Required—TOEFL. *Faculty research:* Agricultural finance and credit, agribusiness management, resource use, rural area economic development, marketing and price analysis.

Texas A&M University, College of Agriculture and Life Sciences, Department of Agricultural Economics, College Station, TX 77843. Offers agribusiness (MAB); agribusiness and managerial economics (PhD); agricultural economics (MS, PhD). Part-time programs available. *Faculty:* 29. *Students:* 167 full-time (66 women), 21 part-time (6 women); includes 11 minority (2 Black or African American, non-Hispanic/Latino; 2 Asian, non-Hispanic/Latino; 7 Hispanic/Latino), 111 international. Average age 29. In 2010, 8 master's, 13 doctorates awarded. Terminal master's awarded for partial completion of doctoral program. *Degree requirements:* For master's, comprehensive exam (for some programs), thesis (for some programs); for doctorate, comprehensive exam, thesis/dissertation. *Entrance requirements:* For master's and doctorate, GRE General Test. Additional exam requirements/recommendations for international students: Required—TOEFL. *Application deadline:* For fall admission, 3/1 for domestic students; for spring admission, 8/1 for domestic students. Applications are processed on a rolling basis. Application fee: $50 ($75 for international students). Electronic applications accepted. *Financial support:* Fellowships, research assistantships, teaching assistantships, career-related internships or fieldwork, Federal Work-Study, institutionally sponsored loans, and unspecified assistantships available. Financial award application deadline: 3/1; financial award applicants required to submit FAFSA. *Faculty research:* Production economics, agricultural finance, resources, marketing and policy, agribusiness. *Unit head:* John P. Nichols, Head, 979-845-2116, Fax: 979-862-1563, E-mail: jpn@tamu.edu. *Application contact:* Vicki L. Heard, Graduate Admissions Supervisor, 979-845-5222, Fax: 979-862-1563, E-mail: vheard@tamu.edu.

Texas A&M University–Kingsville, College of Graduate Studies, College of Agriculture and Home Economics, Program in Agribusiness, Kingsville, TX 78363. Offers MS. *Degree requirements:* For master's, comprehensive exam, thesis or alternative. *Entrance requirements:* For master's, GRE General Test, minimum GPA of 3.0. Additional exam requirements/recommendations for international students: Required—TOEFL.

Texas Tech University, Graduate School, College of Agricultural Sciences and Natural Resources, Department of Agricultural and Applied Economics, Lubbock, TX 79409. Offers agribusiness (MAB); agricultural and applied economics (MS, PhD); JD/MS. Part-time programs available. *Faculty:* 13 full-time (0 women). *Students:* 37 full-time (14 women), 8 part-time (1 woman); includes 1 Black or African American, non-Hispanic/Latino; 1 Hispanic/Latino, 29 international. Average age 29. 39 applicants, 51% accepted, 12 enrolled. In 2010, 11 master's, 4 doctorates awarded. *Degree requirements:* For master's, thesis or alternative; for doctorate, thesis/dissertation. *Entrance requirements:* For master's and doctorate, GRE General Test, formal approval from departmental committee. Additional exam requirements/recommendations for international students: Required—TOEFL (minimum score 550 paper-based; 213 computer-based; 79 iBT). *Application deadline:* For fall admission, 6/1 priority date for domestic students, 1/15 priority date for international students; for spring admission, 9/1 priority date for domestic students, 6/15 priority date for international students. Applications are processed on a rolling basis. Application fee: $50 ($75 for international students). Electronic applications accepted. *Expenses:* Tuition, state resident: full-time $5495.76; part-time $228.99 per credit hour. Tuition, nonresident: full-time $12,936; part-time $538.99 per credit hour. Required fees: $2674; $36 per credit hour. $905 per semester. *Financial support:* In 2010–11, 32 students received support, including 9 research assistantships with partial tuition reimbursements available (averaging $7,828 per year), 1 teaching assistantship with partial tuition reimbursement available (averaging $16,457 per year). Financial award application deadline: 4/15; financial award applicants required to submit FAFSA. *Faculty research:* Economics of the United States cotton and textile industries, natural resource management in semi-arid climates, commodity policy analysis, international trade in agricultural products, agribusiness analysis. Total annual research expenditures: $1.4 million. *Unit head:* Dr. Eduardo Segarra, Chair, 806-742-2821, Fax: 806-742-1099, E-mail: eduardo.segarra@ttu.edu. *Application contact:* Dr. Tom Knight, Graduate Adviser, 806-742-2821, Fax: 806-742-1099, E-mail: tom.knight@ttu.edu.

Texas Tech University, Graduate School, Jerry S. Rawls College of Business Administration, Programs in Business Administration, Lubbock, TX 79409. Offers agricultural business (MBA); business administration (IMBA); business statistics (MBA); entrepreneurship and innovation (MBA); general business (MBA); health organization management (MBA); international business (MBA); management and leadership skills (MBA); management information systems (MBA); marketing (MBA); real estate (MBA); JD/MBA; MBA/M Arch; MBA/MA; MBA/MD; MBA/MS; MBA/Pharm D. Part-time and evening/weekend programs available. *Faculty:* 47 full-time (8 women), 5 part-time/adjunct (0 women). *Students:* 52 full-time (13 women), 531 part-time (152 women); includes 121 minority (28 Black or African American, non-Hispanic/Latino; 3 American Indian or Alaska Native, non-Hispanic/Latino; 31 Asian, non-Hispanic/Latino; 53 Hispanic/Latino; 6 Two or more races, non-Hispanic/Latino), 49 international. Average age 30. 437 applicants, 77% accepted, 258 enrolled. In 2010, 228 master's awarded. *Degree requirements:* For master's, capstone course. *Entrance requirements:* For master's, GMAT, holistic review of academic credentials. Additional exam requirements/recommendations for international students: Required—TOEFL (minimum score 550 paper-based; 213 computer-based; 79 iBT). *Application deadline:* For fall admission, 4/1 priority date for domestic students, 1/15 for international students; for spring admission, 9/1 priority date for domestic students, 6/15 for international students. Applications are processed on a rolling basis. Application fee: $50 ($75 for international students). Electronic applications accepted. *Expenses:* Tuition, state resident: full-time $5495.76; part-time $228.99 per credit hour. Tuition, nonresident: full-time $12,936; part-time $538.99 per credit hour. Required fees: $2674; $36 per credit hour. $905 per semester. *Financial support:* In 2010–11, 25 research assistantships (averaging $8,800 per year) were awarded; teaching assistantships, career-related internships or fieldwork, Federal Work-Study, scholarships/grants, health care benefits, and unspecified assistantships also available. Support available to part-time students. Financial award applicants required to submit FAFSA. *Unit head:* Dr. W. Jay Conover, Director, 806-742-1546, Fax: 806-742-3958, E-mail: jay.conover@ttu.edu. *Application contact:* Cynthia D. Barnes, Director, Graduate Services Center, 806-742-3184, Fax: 806-742-3958, E-mail: ba_grad@ttu.edu.

Tropical Agriculture Research and Higher Education Center, Graduate School, Turrialba, Costa Rica. Offers agribusiness management (MS); agroforestry systems (PhD); development practices (MS); ecological agriculture (MS); environmental socioeconomics (MS); forestry in tropical and subtropical zones (PhD); integrated watershed management (MS); international sustainable tourism (MS); management and conservation of tropical rainforests and biodiversity (MS); tropical agriculture (PhD); tropical agroforestry (MS). *Entrance requirements:* For master's, GRE, 2 years of related professional experience, letters of recommendation; for doctorate, GRE, 4 letters of recommendation, letter of support from employing organization, master's degree in agronomy, biological sciences, forestry, natural resources or related field. Additional exam requirements/recommendations for international students: Required—TOEFL (minimum score 550 paper-based; 213 computer-based). Electronic applications accepted. *Faculty research:* Biodiversity in fragmented landscapes, ecosystem management, integrated pest management, environmental livestock production, biotechnology carbon balances in diverse land uses.

Tuskegee University, Graduate Programs, College of Agricultural, Environmental and Natural Sciences, Department of Agricultural Sciences, Program in Agricultural and Resource Economics, Tuskegee, AL 36088. Offers MS. *Faculty:* 13 full-time (1 woman), 2 part-time/adjunct (1 woman). *Students:* 13 full-time (6 women); includes 7 Black or African American, non-Hispanic/Latino, 5 international. Average age 32. In 2010, 3 master's awarded. *Degree requirements:* For master's, thesis. *Entrance requirements:* For master's, GRE General Test. Additional exam requirements/recommendations for international students: Required—TOEFL (minimum score 500 paper-based; 69 computer-based). *Application deadline:* For fall admission, 7/15 for domestic students. Applications are processed on a rolling basis. Application fee: $25 ($35 for international students). *Expenses:* Tuition: Full-time $16,100; part-time $665 per credit hour. Required fees: $650. *Financial support:* Application deadline: 4/15. *Unit head:* Dr. P. K. Biswas, Head, 334-727-8446. *Application contact:* Dr. Robert L. Laney, Vice President/Director of Admissions and Enrollment Management, 334-727-8580, Fax: 334-727-5750, E-mail: planey@tuskegee.edu.

Universidad del Este, Graduate School, Carolina, PR 00984. Offers accounting (MBA); adult education (M Ed); agribusiness (MBA); criminal justice and criminology (MA); curriculum and instruction—early education (M Ed); curriculum and instruction—elementary (M Ed); curriculum and instruction—English (M Ed); curriculum and instruction—Spanish (M Ed); human resources (MBA); information security management (MBA); information technology and Web business development (MBA); management (MBA); public policy (MPA); social work (MA), including clinical social work; special education (M Ed); strategic leadership (MBA).

Université Laval, Faculty of Agricultural and Food Sciences, Department of Agricultural Economics and Consumer Sciences, Program in Agricultural Economics, Québec, QC G1K 7P4, Canada. Offers M Sc. Part-time programs available. *Degree requirements:* For master's, thesis (for some programs). *Entrance requirements:* For master's, knowledge of French. Electronic applications accepted.

University of Alberta, Faculty of Graduate Studies and Research, Department of Rural Economy, Edmonton, AB T6G 2E1, Canada. Offers agricultural economics (M Ag, M Sc, PhD); forest economics (M Ag, M Sc, PhD); rural sociology (M Ag, M Sc); MBA/M Ag. Part-time programs available. *Degree requirements:* For doctorate, thesis/dissertation. *Entrance requirements:* Additional exam requirements/recommendations for international students: Required—TOEFL. *Faculty research:* Agroforestry, development, extension education, marketing and trade, natural resources and environment, policy, production economics.

The University of Arizona, College of Agriculture and Life Sciences, Department of Agricultural and Resource Economics, Tucson, AZ 85721. Offers MS. *Faculty:* 8 full-time (1 woman). *Students:* 21 full-time (9 women), 2 part-time (0 women); includes 1 Black or African American, non-Hispanic/Latino; 1 Asian, non-Hispanic/Latino; 3 Hispanic/Latino, 8 international. Average age 29. 28 applicants, 29% accepted, 8 enrolled. In 2010, 15 master's awarded. *Degree requirements:* For master's, thesis or alternative. *Entrance requirements:* For master's, GRE General Test, 3 letters of recommendation, minimum GPA of 3.0. Additional exam requirements/recommendations for international students: Required—TOEFL. *Application deadline:* For fall admission, 2/1 for domestic and international students. Applications are processed on a rolling basis. Application fee: $75. Electronic applications accepted. *Expenses:* Tuition, state resident: full-time $7692. *Financial support:* In 2010–11, 12 research assistantships (averaging $20,293 per year), 9 teaching assistantships (averaging $19,575 per year) were awarded; career-related internships or fieldwork, institutionally sponsored loans, scholarships/grants, traineeships, health care benefits, tuition waivers (partial), and unspecified assistantships also available. Financial award application deadline: 3/1. *Faculty research:* Natural resources, international development trade, production and marketing, agricultural policy, rural development. Total annual research expenditures: $297,634. *Unit head:* Dr. Gary D. Thompson, Head, 520-621-6249, E-mail: garyt@ag.arizona.edu. *Application contact:* Nancy Smith, Graduate Coordinator, 520-621-2421, E-mail: garec@ag.arizona.edu.

University of Arkansas, Graduate School, Dale Bumpers College of Agricultural, Food and Life Sciences, Department of Agricultural Economics, Fayetteville, AR 72701-1201. Offers MS. *Students:* 28 full-time (14 women), 9 part-time (5 women); includes 4 minority (all Black or African American, non-Hispanic/Latino), 15 international. 28 applicants, 100% accepted. In 2010, 18 master's awarded. *Degree requirements:* For master's, thesis optional. *Application deadline:* For fall admission, 4/1 for international students; for spring admission, 10/1 for international students. Applications are processed on a rolling basis. Application fee: $40 ($50 for international students). Electronic applications accepted. *Financial support:* In 2010–11, 5 fellowships with tuition reimbursements, 9 research assistantships, 1 teaching assistantship were awarded; career-related internships or fieldwork and Federal Work-Study also available. Support available to part-time students. Financial award application deadline: 4/1; financial award applicants required to submit FAFSA. *Unit head:* Dr. Steve A. Halbrook, Chair, 479-575-2281, E-mail: halbrook@uark.edu. *Application contact:* Dr. Lucas Parsch, Graduate Coordinator, 479-575-2323, E-mail: lparsch@uark.edu.

The University of British Columbia, Faculty of Land and Food Systems, Agricultural Economics Program, Vancouver, BC V6T 1Z1, Canada. Offers M Sc. Part-time programs available. *Degree requirements:* For master's, thesis. *Entrance requirements:* Additional exam requirements/recommendations for international students: Required—TOEFL (minimum score 577 paper-based; 233 computer-based; 90 iBT), IELTS (minimum score 6.5). Electronic applications accepted. Tuition charges are reported in Canadian dollars. *Expenses:* Tuition, area resident: Full-time $4179 Canadian dollars. International tuition: $7344 Canadian dollars full-time. *Faculty research:* International development, natural resources and environmental economics, marketing and trade, agribusiness, food market analysis, applied econometrics.

University of California, Berkeley, Graduate Division, College of Natural Resources, Department of Agricultural and Resource Economics, Berkeley, CA 94720-1500. Offers PhD. *Degree requirements:* For doctorate, thesis/dissertation, qualifying exam. *Entrance requirements:* For doctorate, GRE General Test, minimum GPA of 3.0, 3 letters of recommendation. *Faculty research:* Agricultural economics and policy, environmental and resource economics and policy, international agricultural development and trade.

University of California, Davis, Graduate Studies, Program in Agricultural and Resource Economics, Davis, CA 95616. Offers MS, PhD, MBA/MS. Terminal master's awarded for partial completion of doctoral program. *Degree requirements:* For master's, thesis optional; for doctorate, thesis/dissertation. *Entrance requirements:* For master's, GRE General Test, minimum GPA of 3.0; for doctorate, GRE General Test, minimum GPA of 3.3. Additional exam requirements/recommendations for international students: Required—TOEFL (minimum score 550 paper-based; 213 computer-based). Electronic applications accepted. *Faculty research:* Applied microeconomics, international trade, development, econometrics, environmental economics.

University of California, Santa Barbara, Graduate Division, Donald Bren School of Environmental Science and Management, Santa Barbara, CA 93106-5131. Offers economics and environmental science (PhD); environmental science and management (MESM, PhD); technology and society (PhD). *Faculty:* 17 full-time (3 women), 2 part-time/adjunct (0 women). *Students:* 219 full-time (128 women); includes 1 Black or African American, non-Hispanic/Latino; 1 American Indian or Alaska Native, non-Hispanic/Latino; 33 Asian, non-Hispanic/Latino; 11 Hispanic/Latino. Average age 28. 521 applicants, 40% accepted, 82 enrolled. In 2010, 75 master's awarded. *Degree requirements:* For master's, thesis; for doctorate, thesis/dissertation. *Entrance requirements:* For master's and doctorate, GRE. Additional exam requirements/recommendations for international students: Required—TOEFL (minimum score 550 paper-based; 80 iBT), IELTS (minimum score 7). *Application deadline:* For fall admission, 12/15 priority date for domestic and international students. Application fee: $70 ($90 for international students). Electronic applications accepted. *Financial support:* In 2010–11, 105 students received support, including 83 fellowships with full and partial tuition reimbursements available (averaging $6,929 per year), 27 research assistantships with full and partial tuition reimbursements available (averaging $8,918 per year), 32 teaching assistantships with partial tuition reimbursements available (averaging $8,112 per year); career-related internships or fieldwork and tuition waivers (full and partial) also available. Financial award application deadline: 12/15; financial award applicants required to submit FAFSA. *Faculty research:* Coastal marine resources management, conservation planning, corporate environmental management, economics and politics of the environment, energy and climate, pollution prevention and remediation, water resources management. *Unit head:* Bryant Wieneke, Assistant Dean, Planning and Administration, 805-893-2212, Fax: 805-893-7612, E-mail: bryant@bren.ucsb.edu. *Application contact:* Graduate Advisor, 805-893-7611, Fax: 805-893-7612, E-mail: admissions@bren.ucsb.edu.

University of Connecticut, Graduate School, College of Agriculture and Natural Resources, Department of Agricultural and Resource Economics, Storrs, CT 06269. Offers MS, PhD. Terminal master's awarded for partial completion of doctoral program. *Degree requirements:* For master's, comprehensive exam; for doctorate, thesis/dissertation. *Entrance requirements:* For master's and doctorate, GRE General Test. Additional exam requirements/recommendations for international students: Required—TOEFL (minimum score 550 paper-based; 213 computer-based). Electronic applications accepted. *Faculty research:* Food marketing, international agricultural development.

University of Delaware, College of Agriculture and Natural Resources, Department of Food and Resource Economics, Newark, DE 19716. Offers agricultural economics (MS); agriculture and technical education (MA); bioresources engineering (MS). Part-time programs available. *Degree requirements:* For master's, thesis. *Entrance requirements:* For master's, GRE General Test, 3 letters of recommendation. Additional exam requirements/recommendations for international students: Required—TOEFL (minimum score 550 paper-based; 213 computer-based). Electronic applications accepted. *Faculty research:* Experimental economics, environmental and resource economics, land use, law and economics.

University of Florida, Graduate School, College of Agricultural and Life Sciences, Department of Food and Resource Economics, Gainesville, FL 32611. Offers MAB, MS, PhD. Part-time programs available. *Faculty:* 21 full-time (5 women), 1 (woman) part-time/adjunct. *Students:* 75 full-time (24 women), 19 part-time (11 women); includes 4 Black or African American, non-Hispanic/Latino; 7 Asian, non-Hispanic/Latino; 8 Hispanic/Latino, 31 international. Average age 27. 75 applicants, 67% accepted, 25 enrolled. In 2010, 48 master's, 5 doctorates awarded. *Degree requirements:* For master's, comprehensive exam (for some programs), thesis optional; for doctorate, comprehensive exam, thesis/dissertation. *Entrance requirements:* For master's and doctorate, GRE General Test, minimum GPA of 3.0. Additional exam requirements/recommendations for international students: Required—TOEFL (minimum score 550 paper-based; 213 computer-based; 80 iBT), IELTS (minimum score 6). *Application deadline:* For fall admission, 6/1 priority date for domestic students, 6/1 for international students. Applications are processed on a rolling basis. Application fee: $30. Electronic applications accepted. *Expenses:* Tuition, state resident: full-time $10,915.92. Tuition, nonresident: full-time $28,309. *Financial support:* In 2010–11, 34 students received support, including 9 fellowships, 22 research assistantships (averaging $16,422 per year), 3 teaching assistantships (averaging $17,321 per year); unspecified assistantships also available. Financial award application deadline: 2/1; financial award applicants required to submit FAFSA. *Faculty research:* Agribusiness management, production, environmental economics, international trade, economic development. *Unit head:* Dr. Ray G. Huffaker, Chair, 352-392-1826 Ext. 204, E-mail: rhuffaker@ufl.edu. *Application contact:* Dr. Charles B. Moss, Graduate Coordinator, 352-392-1845 Ext. 404, Fax: 352-846-0988, E-mail: cbmoss@ufl.edu.

University of Georgia, College of Agricultural and Environmental Sciences, Department of Agricultural and Applied Economics, Athens, GA 30602. Offers agricultural economics (MAE, MS, PhD); environmental economics (MS). *Faculty:* 24 full-time (4 women). *Students:* 43 full-time (20 women), 8 part-time (4 women); includes 4 Black or African American, non-Hispanic/Latino; 1 Hispanic/Latino, 25 international. 54 applicants, 63% accepted, 18 enrolled. In 2010, 3 master's, 4 doctorates awarded. *Degree requirements:* For master's, thesis (MS); for doctorate, thesis/dissertation. *Entrance requirements:* For master's and doctorate, GRE General Test. *Application deadline:* For fall admission, 7/1 priority date for domestic students; for spring admission, 11/15 for domestic students. Application fee: $50. Electronic applications accepted. *Expenses:* Tuition, state resident: full-time $7200; part-time $344 per credit hour. Tuition, nonresident: full-time $21,900; part-time $944 per credit hour. Tuition and fees vary according to course load and program. *Financial support:* Fellowships, research assistantships, teaching assistantships, career-related internships or fieldwork and unspecified assistantships available. *Unit head:* Dr. Octavio A. Ramirez, Interim Head, 706-542-2481, Fax: 706-542-0739, E-mail: oramirez@agecon.uga.edu. *Application contact:* Dr. Michael E. Wetzstein, Graduate Coordinator, 706-543-0758, Fax: 706-542-0739, E-mail: mwetz@uga.edu.

University of Guelph, Graduate Studies, College of Management and Economics, MBA Program, Guelph, ON N1G 2W1, Canada. Offers food and agribusiness management (MBA); hospitality and tourism management (MBA). Part-time and evening/weekend programs available. Postbaccalaureate distance learning degree programs offered (minimal on-campus study). *Entrance requirements:* For master's, minimum B-average, minimum of 3 years of relevant work experience. Additional exam requirements/recommendations for international students: Required—TOEFL (minimum score 550 paper-based; 213 computer-based). Electronic applications accepted. *Faculty research:* Marketing, operations management, business policy, financial management, organizational behavior.

University of Guelph, Graduate Studies, Ontario Agricultural College, Department of Food, Agricultural and Resource Economics, Guelph, ON N1G 2W1, Canada. Offers agricultural economics (M Sc, PhD); collaborative international development studies (MA/M Sc); MA/M Sc. Part-time programs available. *Degree requirements:* For master's, thesis; for doctorate, comprehensive exam, thesis/dissertation. *Entrance requirements:* For master's, minimum B-average during previous 2 years of course work; for doctorate, minimum B standing in recognized master's degree. Additional exam requirements/recommendations for international students: Required—TOEFL (minimum score 550 paper-based; 213 computer-based), IELTS (minimum score 6.5). Electronic applications accepted. *Faculty research:* Agricultural policy, agribusiness, environmental economics, agricultural marketing, production economics.

University of Idaho, College of Graduate Studies, College of Agricultural and Life Sciences, Department of Agricultural Economics and Rural Sociology, Moscow, ID 83844-2282. Offers agricultural economics (MS); applied economics (MS), including agribusiness emphasis, agricultural economics emphasis, applied economics. *Faculty:* 8 full-time. *Students:* 13 full-time, 6 part-time. Average age 25. In 2010, 3 master's awarded. *Entrance requirements:* For master's, minimum GPA of 2.8. *Application deadline:* For fall admission, 8/1 for domestic students; for spring admission, 12/15 for domestic students. Applications are processed on a rolling basis. Application fee: $60. Electronic applications accepted. *Expenses:* Tuition, nonresident: part-time $580 per credit. Required fees: $306 per credit. *Financial support:* Research assistantships, teaching assistantships available. Financial award applicants required to submit FAFSA. *Faculty research:* Crops: potatoes, blue grass; livestock: beef, dairy; rural and community development; natural resources and the environment; farm and ranch management. *Unit head:* Dr. Larry Makus, Interim Department Head, 208-885-6262, Fax: 208-885-5759, E-mail: cdarby@uidaho.edu. *Application contact:* Dr. Larry Makus, Interim Department Head, 208-885-6262, Fax: 208-885-5759, E-mail: cdarby@uidaho.edu.

University of Illinois at Urbana–Champaign, Graduate College, College of Agricultural, Consumer and Environmental Sciences, Department of Agricultural and Consumer Economics, Champaign, IL 61820. Offers agricultural and applied economics (MS, PhD). *Faculty:* 31 full-time (11 women). *Students:* 65 full-time (26 women), 15 part-time (8 women); includes 3 Black or African American, non-Hispanic/Latino; 3 Asian, non-Hispanic/Latino, 49 international. 117 applicants, 23% accepted, 15 enrolled. In 2010, 10 master's, 10 doctorates awarded. *Entrance requirements:* For master's, GRE, minimum GPA of 3.0; for doctorate, GRE, writing sample. Additional exam requirements/recommendations for international students: Required—TOEFL (minimum score 570 paper-based; 230 computer-based; 88 iBT) or IELTS (minimum score 6.5). *Application deadline:* Applications are processed on a rolling basis. Application fee: $75 ($90 for international students). Electronic applications accepted. *Financial support:* In 2010–11, 16 fellowships, 47 research assistantships, 32 teaching assistantships were awarded; tuition waivers (full and partial) also available. *Unit head:* Paul N. Ellinger, Head, 217-333-5503, Fax: 217-333-5538, E-mail: pellinge@illinois.edu. *Application contact:* Pamela S. Splittstoesser, Administrative Assistant, 217-333-1830, Fax: 217-244-7088, E-mail: splttsts@illinois.edu.

University of Kentucky, Graduate School, College of Agriculture, Program in Agricultural Economics, Lexington, KY 40506-0032. Offers MS, PhD. *Degree requirements:* For master's, comprehensive exam, thesis optional; for doctorate, comprehensive exam, thesis/dissertation. *Entrance requirements:* For master's, GRE General Test, minimum undergraduate GPA of 2.75; for doctorate, GRE General Test, minimum graduate GPA of 3.0. Additional exam requirements/recommendations for international students: Required—TOEFL (minimum score 550 paper-based; 213 computer-based). Electronic applications accepted. *Faculty research:*

Agricultural Economics and Agribusiness

University of Kentucky (continued)
Food and agricultural marketing, agricultural and food policy, natural resources and environment, rural economic development.

University of Maine, Graduate School, College of Natural Sciences, Forestry, and Agriculture, Department of Resource Economics and Policy, Orono, ME 04469. Offers resource economics and policy (MS); resource utilization (MS). Part-time programs available. *Faculty:* 15 full-time (3 women), 5 part-time/adjunct (2 women). *Students:* 19 full-time (9 women), 5 part-time (2 women), 6 international. Average age 29. 35 applicants, 34% accepted, 9 enrolled. In 2010, 12 degrees awarded. *Degree requirements:* For master's, thesis (for some programs). *Entrance requirements:* For master's, GRE General Test. Additional exam requirements/recommendations for international students: Required—TOEFL. *Application deadline:* For fall admission, 2/1 priority date for domestic students. Applications are processed on a rolling basis. Application fee: $65. Electronic applications accepted. *Expenses:* Tuition, state resident: full-time $400. Tuition, nonresident: full-time $1050. *Financial support:* In 2010–11, 3 teaching assistantships with tuition reimbursements (averaging $12,790 per year) were awarded; career-related internships or fieldwork, Federal Work-Study, institutionally sponsored loans, scholarships/grants, and tuition waivers (full and partial) also available. Support available to part-time students. Financial award application deadline: 3/1. *Faculty research:* International trade, agricultural marketing, nonmarketing valuation, livestock health economics. *Unit head:* Dr. George Criner, Chair, 207-581-3151, Fax: 207-581-4278. *Application contact:* Scott G. Delcourt, Associate Dean of the Graduate School, 207-581-3291, Fax: 207-581-3232, E-mail: graduate@maine.edu.

University of Manitoba, Faculty of Graduate Studies, Faculty of Agricultural and Food Sciences, Department of Agribusiness and Agricultural Economics, Winnipeg, MB R3T 2N2, Canada. Offers agribusiness (M Sc, PhD). *Degree requirements:* For master's, thesis or alternative; for doctorate, thesis/dissertation.

University of Maryland, College Park, Academic Affairs, College of Agriculture and Natural Resources, Department of Agricultural and Resource Economics, College Park, MD 20742. Offers agriculture economics (MS, PhD); resource economics (MS, PhD). Part-time and evening/weekend programs available. *Faculty:* 22 full-time (6 women). *Students:* 60 full-time (23 women), 6 part-time (2 women); includes 4 Asian, non-Hispanic/Latino; 1 Hispanic/Latino; 2 Two or more races, non-Hispanic/Latino, 36 international. 206 applicants, 17% accepted, 9 enrolled. In 2010, 10 master's, 10 doctorates awarded. *Degree requirements:* For master's, variable foreign language requirement, thesis optional, oral exam; for doctorate, variable foreign language requirement, oral dissertation defense. *Entrance requirements:* For master's, GRE General Test, minimum GPA of 3.0, course work in microeconomics and calculus, 3 letters of recommendation; for doctorate, GRE General Test. Additional exam requirements/recommendations for international students: Required—TOEFL. *Application deadline:* For fall admission, 1/15 for domestic students, 2/1 for international students; for spring admission, 6/1 for international students. Applications are processed on a rolling basis. Application fee: $75. Electronic applications accepted. *Expenses:* Tuition, state resident: part-time $471 per credit hour. Tuition, nonresident: part-time $1016 per credit hour. Required fees: $337 per term. *Financial support:* In 2010–11, 1 fellowship (averaging $23,407 per year), 34 research assistantships with tuition reimbursements (averaging $17,892 per year) were awarded; teaching assistantships with tuition reimbursements, Federal Work-Study and scholarships/grants also available. Support available to part-time students. Financial award applicants required to submit FAFSA. *Faculty research:* Agricultural development, international trade, agricultural marketing, econometrics, farm management and production economics. Total annual research expenditures: $1.8 million. *Unit head:* Lars Olson, Chair, 301-405-7180, E-mail: ljolson@umd.edu. *Application contact:* Dr. Charles A. Caramello, Dean of Graduate School, 301-405-0358, Fax: 301-314-9305, E-mail: ccaramel@umd.edu.

University of Massachusetts Amherst, Graduate School, Isenberg School of Management, Department of Resource Economics, Amherst, MA 01003. Offers MS, PhD. Part-time programs available. *Faculty:* 17 full-time (5 women). *Students:* 19 full-time (7 women), 4 part-time (3 women); includes 2 minority (1 Black or African American, non-Hispanic/Latino; 1 Asian, non-Hispanic/Latino, 8 international. Average age 28. 36 applicants, 53% accepted, 11 enrolled. In 2010, 5 master's awarded. Terminal master's awarded for partial completion of doctoral program. *Degree requirements:* For master's, thesis or alternative; for doctorate, comprehensive exam, thesis/dissertation. *Entrance requirements:* For master's and doctorate, GRE General Test. Additional exam requirements/recommendations for international students: Required—TOEFL (minimum score 550 paper-based; 213 computer-based; 80 iBT), IELTS (minimum score 6.5). *Application deadline:* For fall admission, 2/1 for domestic and international students. Applications are processed on a rolling basis. Application fee: $50 ($65 for international students). Electronic applications accepted. *Expenses:* Tuition, state resident: full-time $2640. Required fees: $8282. One-time fee: $357 full-time. *Financial support:* In 2010–11, 16 research assistantships with full tuition reimbursements (averaging $8,479 per year), 11 teaching assistantships with full tuition reimbursements (averaging $12,509 per year) were awarded; fellowships, career-related internships or fieldwork, Federal Work-Study, scholarships/grants, traineeships, health care benefits, tuition waivers (full), and unspecified assistantships also available. Support available to part-time students. Financial award application deadline: 2/1; financial award applicants required to submit FAFSA. *Unit head:* Dr. Nathalie Lavoie, Graduate Program Director, 413-545-5732, Fax: 413-545-5853. *Application contact:* Jean M. Ames, Supervisor of Admissions, 413-545-0722, Fax: 413-577-0010, E-mail: gradadm@grad.umass.edu.

University of Missouri, Graduate School, College of Agriculture, Food and Natural Resources, Department of Agricultural Economics, Columbia, MO 65211. Offers MS, PhD. *Faculty:* 26 full-time (5 women), 2 part-time/adjunct (1 woman). *Students:* 31 full-time (16 women), 10 part-time (5 women); includes 2 Asian, non-Hispanic/Latino; 1 Hispanic/Latino, 19 international. Average age 31. 56 applicants, 30% accepted, 6 enrolled. In 2010, 6 master's, 2 doctorates awarded. *Degree requirements:* For doctorate, comprehensive exam, thesis/dissertation. *Entrance requirements:* For master's and doctorate, GRE General Test, minimum GPA of 3.0. Additional exam requirements/recommendations for international students: Required—TOEFL (minimum score 550 paper-based; 80 iBT). *Application deadline:* For fall admission, 2/15 priority date for domestic students; for winter admission, 9/15 for domestic students. Applications are processed on a rolling basis. Application fee: $45 ($60 for international students). Electronic applications accepted. *Financial support:* Fellowships, research assistantships with tuition reimbursements, teaching assistantships with tuition reimbursements, Federal Work-Study, institutionally sponsored loans, scholarships/grants, health care benefits, and unspecified assistantships available. *Faculty research:* Agribusiness management, contracting and strategy; collective action and cooperative theory; econometrics and price analysis; entrepreneurship; environmental and natural resource economics; food, biofuel and agricultural policy and regulation; international development; regional economics and rural development policy; science policy and innovation; sustainable agriculture and applied ethics. *Unit head:* Dr. Michael Monson, Department Chair, 573-882-0153, E-mail: monsonm@missouri.edu. *Application contact:* Jody Pestle, Administrative Assistant, 573-882-3747, E-mail: pestlej@missouri.edu.

University of Nebraska–Lincoln, Graduate College, College of Agricultural Sciences and Natural Resources, Department of Agricultural Economics, Lincoln, NE 68588. Offers agribusiness (MBA); agricultural economics (MS, PhD); community development (M Ag). *Degree requirements:* For master's, thesis optional; for doctorate, comprehensive exam, thesis/dissertation. *Entrance requirements:* For master's and doctorate, GRE General Test. Additional exam requirements/recommendations for international students: Required—TOEFL (minimum score 550 paper-based; 213 computer-based). Electronic applications accepted. *Faculty research:* Marketing and agribusiness, production economics, resource law, international trade and development, rural policy and revitalization.

University of Nevada, Reno, Graduate School, College of Agriculture, Biotechnology and Natural Resources, Department of Resource Economics, Reno, NV 89557. Offers MS, PhD. Terminal master's awarded for partial completion of doctoral program. *Degree requirements:* For master's, thesis optional; for doctorate, thesis/dissertation. *Entrance requirements:* For

master's, GRE General Test, minimum GPA of 2.75; for doctorate, GRE General Test, minimum GPA of 3.0. Additional exam requirements/recommendations for international students: Required—TOEFL (minimum score 500 paper-based; 173 computer-based; 61 iBT), IELTS (minimum score 6). Electronic applications accepted. *Expenses:* Tuition, state resident: full-time $2219; part-time $246 per credit. Tuition, nonresident: part-time $510 per credit. International tuition: $9009 full-time. Required fees: $59 per term. One-time fee: $101. Tuition and fees vary according to course load. *Faculty research:* Econometrics, environmental valuation, natural resource and environmental policy analysis, public lands management.

University of Puerto Rico, Mayagüez Campus, Graduate Studies, College of Agricultural Sciences, Department of Agricultural Economics, Mayagüez, PR 00681-9000. Offers MS. Part-time programs available. *Students:* 9 full-time (3 women); includes all Hispanic/Latino. 6 applicants, 83% accepted, 0 enrolled. In 2010, 1 master's awarded. *Degree requirements:* For master's, comprehensive exam, thesis. *Entrance requirements:* For master's, bachelor's degree in agricultural economics or its equivalent. *Application deadline:* For fall admission, 2/15 for domestic and international students; for spring admission, 9/15 for domestic and international students. Applications are processed on a rolling basis. Application fee: $25. *Expenses:* Tuition, state resident: full-time $1188. Tuition, nonresident: full-time $1188. International tuition: $6126 full-time. Tuition and fees vary according to course level and course load. *Financial support:* In 2010–11, 8 students received support, including 6 research assistantships with tuition reimbursements available (averaging $15,000 per year), 3 teaching assistantships with tuition reimbursements available (averaging $8,500 per year); Federal Work-Study and institutionally sponsored loans also available. *Faculty research:* Farm management, agricultural development, agrimarketing, natural resource economics. *Unit head:* Dr. Jorge Gonzalez, Director, 787-265-3860 Ext. 2471, Fax: 787-265-3860. *Application contact:* Margarita Olivencia, Secretary, 787-832-4040 Ext. 2471, Fax: 787-265-3860, E-mail: molivencia@uprm.edu.

University of Saskatchewan, College of Graduate Studies and Research, College of Agriculture, Department of Agricultural Economics, Saskatoon, SK S7N 5A2, Canada. Offers M Ag, M Sc, MA, PhD, PGD. *Degree requirements:* For master's, thesis; for doctorate, comprehensive exam (for some programs), thesis/dissertation. *Entrance requirements:* Additional exam requirements/recommendations for international students: Required—TOEFL (minimum score 80 iBT); Recommended—IELTS (minimum score 6.5).

University of Saskatchewan, College of Graduate Studies and Research, Edwards School of Business, Program in Business Administration, Saskatoon, SK S7N 5A2, Canada. Offers agribusiness management (MBA); biotechnology management (MBA); health services management (MBA); indigenous management (MBA); international business management (MBA).

University of Vermont, Graduate College, College of Agriculture and Life Sciences, Department of Community Development and Applied Economics, Burlington, VT 05405. Offers community development and applied economics (MS); public administration (MPA). *Students:* 28 (17 women); includes 2 Asian, non-Hispanic/Latino, 3 international. 39 applicants, 77% accepted, 7 enrolled. In 2010, 3 master's awarded. *Degree requirements:* For master's, thesis. *Entrance requirements:* For master's, GRE General Test. Additional exam requirements/recommendations for international students: Required—TOEFL (minimum score 550 paper-based; 213 computer-based; 80 iBT). *Application deadline:* For fall admission, 4/1 priority date for domestic students; for spring admission, 11/15 for domestic students. Applications are processed on a rolling basis. Application fee: $40. Electronic applications accepted. *Expenses:* Tuition, state resident: part-time $537 per credit hour. Tuition, nonresident: part-time $1355 per credit hour. *Financial support:* Fellowships, research assistantships, teaching assistantships, career-related internships or fieldwork available. Financial award application deadline: 3/1. *Faculty research:* Agricultural production and marketing. *Unit head:* Dr. J. Kolodinsky, Chairperson, 802-656-2001. *Application contact:* Dr. J. Kolodinsky, Chairperson, 802-656-2001.

University of Wisconsin–Madison, Graduate School, College of Agricultural and Life Sciences, Department of Agricultural and Applied Economics, Madison, WI 53706. Offers MA, MS, PhD. Part-time programs available. *Faculty:* 23 full-time (3 women). *Students:* 52 full-time (24 women), 1 part-time (0 women); includes 2 Asian, non-Hispanic/Latino, 22 international. Average age 25. 205 applicants, 25% accepted, 10 enrolled. In 2010, 8 master's, 4 doctorates awarded. *Degree requirements:* For doctorate, thesis/dissertation, preliminary exams. *Entrance requirements:* For master's and doctorate, GRE General Test. Additional exam requirements/recommendations for international students: Required—TOEFL (minimum score 580 paper-based; 237 computer-based; 92 iBT). *Application deadline:* For fall admission, 2/1 priority date for domestic and international students. Application fee: $56. Electronic applications accepted. *Expenses:* Tuition, state resident: full-time $9887; part-time $617.96 per credit. Tuition, nonresident: full-time $24,054; part-time $1503.40 per credit. Required fees: $67.63 per credit. Tuition and fees vary according to reciprocity agreements. *Financial support:* In 2010–11, 41 students received support, including 3 fellowships with full tuition reimbursements available (averaging $18,760 per year), 42 research assistantships with full tuition reimbursements available (averaging $20,400 per year), 8 teaching assistantships with full tuition reimbursements available (averaging $14,100 per year); career-related internships or fieldwork, Federal Work-Study, traineeships, health care benefits, and unspecified assistantships also available. Support available to part-time students. Financial award application deadline: 12/15. *Faculty research:* Environmental and resource economics, international development, community economics, energy economics, agricultural technology, food systems, markets and trade. Total annual research expenditures: $35.8 million. *Unit head:* Prof. Kenneth Shapiro, Chair, 608-262-8966, Fax: 608-262-4376. *Application contact:* Barbara Forrest, Academic Programs Coordinator, 608-262-9489, Fax: 608-262-4376, E-mail: admissions@aae.wisc.edu.

University of Wyoming, College of Agriculture and Natural Resources, Department of Agricultural and Applied Economics, Laramie, WY 82070. Offers MS. Part-time programs available. *Degree requirements:* For master's, thesis (for some programs). *Entrance requirements:* For master's, GRE General Test, minimum GPA of 3.0. Additional exam requirements/recommendations for international students: Required—TOEFL. Electronic applications accepted. *Faculty research:* Farm management, agricultural markets, water economics, community development, agricultural business.

Virginia Polytechnic Institute and State University, Graduate School, College of Agriculture and Life Sciences, Department of Agricultural and Applied Economics, Blacksburg, VA 24061. Offers MS, PhD. *Faculty:* 20 full-time (3 women). *Students:* 36 full-time (27 women), 2 part-time (1 woman); includes 2 Asian, non-Hispanic/Latino, 19 international. Average age 27. 58 applicants, 59% accepted, 11 enrolled. In 2010, 9 master's, 3 doctorates awarded. *Degree requirements:* For master's, comprehensive exam (for some programs), thesis (for some programs); for doctorate, comprehensive exam (for some programs), thesis/dissertation (for some programs). *Entrance requirements:* For master's and doctorate, GRE. Additional exam requirements/recommendations for international students: Required—TOEFL (minimum score 550 paper-based; 213 computer-based). *Application deadline:* For fall admission, 7/1 for domestic and international students; for spring admission, 12/1 for domestic and international students. Applications are processed on a rolling basis. Application fee: $65. Electronic applications accepted. *Expenses:* Tuition, state resident: full-time $9399; part-time $488 per credit hour. Tuition, nonresident: full-time $17,854; part-time $957.75 per credit hour. Required fees: $1534. Full-time tuition and fees vary according to program. *Financial support:* In 2010–11, 1 fellowship with full tuition reimbursement (averaging $20,000 per year), 25 research assistantships with full tuition reimbursements (averaging $20,332 per year), 8 teaching assistantships with full tuition reimbursements (averaging $15,387 per year) were awarded; career-related internships or fieldwork, Federal Work-Study, scholarships/grants, health care benefits, and unspecified assistantships also available. Financial award application deadline: 1/15. *Faculty research:* Rural development. Total annual research expenditures: $2.2 million. *Unit head:* Dr. Kevin Boyle, Unit Head, 540-231-6301, Fax: 540-231-7417, E-mail: kjboyle@vt.edu. *Application contact:* Bradford Mills, Contact, 540-231-6461, Fax: 540-231-7417, E-mail: bfmills@vt.edu.

Washington State University, Graduate School, College of Agricultural, Human, and Natural Resource Sciences, School of Economic Sciences, Pullman, WA 99164. Offers agribusiness (MA, Certificate); agricultural economics (MA, PhD); applied economics (MA); economics (MA, PhD, Certificate), including applied economics (MA), economics (MA, PhD), international business economics (Certificate). *Faculty:* 26. *Students:* 68 full-time (20 women), 9 part-time (5 women); includes 4 minority (1 Black or African American, non-Hispanic/Latino; 1 American Indian or Alaska Native, non-Hispanic/Latino; 1 Asian, non-Hispanic/Latino; 1 Hispanic/Latino), 39 international. Average age 28. 224 applicants, 21% accepted, 27 enrolled. In 2010, 9 master's, 9 doctorates awarded. Terminal master's awarded for partial completion of doctoral program. *Degree requirements:* For master's, comprehensive exam (for some programs), thesis (for some programs), oral exam; for doctorate, comprehensive exam, thesis/dissertation, oral exam, written exam, qualifying exams. *Entrance requirements:* For master's and doctorate, minimum GPA of 3.0, 3 letters of recommendation. Additional exam requirements/recommendations for international students: Required—TOEFL (minimum score 550 paper-based; 213 computer-based). *Application deadline:* For fall admission, 2/15 priority date for domestic students, 2/1 priority date for international students. Applications are processed on a rolling basis. Application fee: $50. Electronic applications accepted. *Expenses:* Tuition, state resident: full-time $8552; part-time $443 per credit. Tuition, nonresident: full-time $21,650; part-time $1083 per credit. Required fees: $846. *Financial support:* In 2010–11, 59 students received support, including 13 research assistantships with full and partial tuition reimbursements available (averaging $18,204 per year), 7 teaching assistantships with full and partial tuition reimbursements available (averaging $18,204 per year); career-related internships or fieldwork, Federal Work-Study, institutionally sponsored loans, tuition waivers (partial), and teaching associateships also available. Financial award application deadline: 4/1; financial award applicants required to submit FAFSA. *Faculty research:* Marketing, natural resources, production economics. Total annual research expenditures: $1.1 million. *Unit head:* Dr. Ron Mittelhammer, Director, 509-335-5555, E-mail: mittleha@wsu.edu. *Application contact:* Graduate School Admissions, 800-GRADWSU, Fax: 509-335-1949, E-mail: gradsch@wsu.edu.

West Texas A&M University, College of Agriculture, Nursing, and Natural Sciences, Division of Agriculture, Emphasis in Agricultural Business and Economics, Canyon, TX 79016-0001. Offers MS. Part-time programs available. *Degree requirements:* For master's, comprehensive exam, thesis optional. *Entrance requirements:* For master's, GRE General Test. Additional exam requirements/recommendations for international students: Required—TOEFL (minimum score 550 paper-based). Electronic applications accepted. *Faculty research:* Utilizing expected revenue in selecting optimal marketing alternatives for fixed resource cow/calf operators in the Texas panhandle.

West Virginia University, Davis College of Agriculture, Forestry and Consumer Sciences, Division of Resource Management and Sustainable Development, Program in Agricultural and Resource Economics, Morgantown, WV 26506. Offers MS. Part-time programs available. *Degree requirements:* For master's, thesis optional. *Entrance requirements:* For master's, GRE General Test, minimum GPA of 2.5, 1 calculus course. Additional exam requirements/recommendations for international students: Required—TOEFL. *Faculty research:* Agricultural production and marketing, rural development, mineral and energy economics, economic development.

William Woods University, Graduate and Adult Studies, Fulton, MO 65251-1098. Offers administration (Ed S); agriculture (MBA); athletic/activities administration (M Ed); curriculum and instruction (M Ed); curriculum leadership (Ed S); elementary administration (M Ed); health management (MBA); human resources (MBA); principalship (Ed S); secondary administration (M Ed); special education director (M Ed). Evening/weekend programs available. *Degree requirements:* For master's, capstone course (MBA), action research (M Ed); for Ed S, field experience. *Entrance requirements:* For master's, 2 recommendations, resumé, BA/BS; teaching certification (M Ed); course work in economics and accounting (MBA); for Ed S, M Ed, 2 letters of recommendation, resume, teaching certification. Additional exam requirements/recommendations for international students: Required—TOEFL (minimum score 550 paper-based). Electronic applications accepted.

Applied Economics

American University, College of Arts and Sciences, Department of Economics, Washington, DC 20016-8029. Offers applied microeconomics (Certificate); economics (MA, PhD); international economic relations (Certificate). Part-time and evening/weekend programs available. *Faculty:* 26 full-time (9 women). *Students:* 48 full-time (20 women), 71 part-time (26 women); includes 12 minority (7 Black or African American, non-Hispanic/Latino; 3 Asian, non-Hispanic/Latino; 2 Hispanic/Latino), 44 international. Average age 30. 186 applicants, 68% accepted, 32 enrolled. In 2010, 15 master's, 10 doctorates, 1 other advanced degree awarded. Terminal master's awarded for partial completion of doctoral program. *Degree requirements:* For master's, comprehensive exam, thesis or alternative; for doctorate, comprehensive exam, thesis/dissertation, 2 research seminars, field work. *Entrance requirements:* For master's and doctorate, GRE; for Certificate, bachelor's degree. Additional exam requirements/recommendations for international students: Required—TOEFL. *Application deadline:* For spring admission, 10/1 for domestic students. Applications are processed on a rolling basis. Application fee: $80. *Financial support:* Fellowships, research assistantships with full and partial tuition reimbursements, teaching assistantships with full and partial tuition reimbursements, career-related internships or fieldwork, Federal Work-Study, institutionally sponsored loans, and tuition waivers (full and partial) available. Financial award application deadline: 2/1. *Faculty research:* Political economy, development, labor, gender. *Unit head:* Robert A. Blecker, Chair, 202-885-3767, Fax: 202-885-3790, E-mail: blecker@american.edu. *Application contact:* Kathleen Clowery, Director of Graduate Admissions, 202-885-3621, Fax: 202-885-1505, E-mail: clowery@american.edu.

Auburn University, Graduate School, College of Agriculture, Department of Agricultural Economics and Rural Sociology, Auburn University, AL 36849. Offers agricultural economics (M Ag, MS); applied economics (PhD). Part-time programs available. *Faculty:* 18 full-time (3 women). *Students:* 28 full-time (9 women), 7 part-time (3 women); includes 1 Black or African American, non-Hispanic/Latino; 1 Asian, non-Hispanic/Latino, 24 international. Average age 31. 55 applicants, 55% accepted, 9 enrolled. In 2010, 5 master's awarded. *Degree requirements:* For master's, thesis (for some programs); for doctorate, thesis/dissertation. *Entrance requirements:* For master's and doctorate, GRE General Test. *Application deadline:* For fall admission, 7/7 for domestic students; for spring admission, 11/24 for domestic students. Applications are processed on a rolling basis. Application fee: $50 ($60 for international students). Electronic applications accepted. *Expenses:* Tuition, state resident: full-time $7002. Tuition, nonresident: full-time $21,898. International tuition: $22,116 full-time. Required fees: $892. Tuition and fees vary according to course load and program. *Financial support:* Research assistantships, teaching assistantships, Federal Work-Study available. Support available to part-time students. Financial award application deadline: 3/15; financial award applicants required to submit FAFSA. *Faculty research:* Farm management, agricultural marketing, production economics, resource economics, agricultural finance. *Unit head:* Dr. Curtis M. Jolly, Chair, 334-844-4800. *Application contact:* Dr. George Flowers, Dean of the Graduate School, 334-844-2125.

Buffalo State College, State University of New York, The Graduate School, Faculty of Natural and Social Sciences, Department of Economics and Finance, Buffalo, NY 14222-1095. Offers applied economics (MA). *Degree requirements:* For master's, project. *Entrance requirements:* Additional exam requirements/recommendations for international students: Required—TOEFL (minimum score 550 paper-based; 213 computer-based).

Clemson University, Graduate School, College of Business and Behavioral Science, Department of Economics, Program in Applied Economics and Statistics, Clemson, SC 29634. Offers MS, PhD. *Faculty:* 20 full-time (5 women). *Students:* 34 full-time (14 women), 6 part-time (1 woman); includes 1 minority (Asian, non-Hispanic/Latino), 7 international. Average age 30. 127 applicants, 65% accepted, 17 enrolled. In 2010, 1 master's, 14 doctorates awarded. *Degree requirements:* For master's, thesis optional. *Entrance requirements:* For master's, GRE General Test, minimum GPA of 3.0. Additional exam requirements/recommendations for international students: Required—TOEFL. *Application deadline:* For fall admission, 5/1 for domestic students, 4/15 for international students; for spring admission, 10/1 for domestic students, 9/15 for international students. Applications are processed on a rolling basis. Application fee: $70 ($80 for international students). Electronic applications accepted. *Expenses:* Contact institution. *Financial support:* In 2010–11, 27 students received support, including 7 research assistantships with partial tuition reimbursements available (averaging $13,268 per year), 25 teaching assistantships with partial tuition reimbursements available (averaging $16,379 per year); fellowships with full and partial tuition reimbursements available, institutionally sponsored loans, scholarships/grants, and unspecified assistantships also available. Financial award application deadline: 3/1; financial award applicants required to submit FAFSA. *Faculty research:* Agricultural policy, agricultural production, agricultural marketing, natural resource economics, regional economic development. Total annual research expenditures: $489,768. *Unit head:* Dr. Hoke Hill, Chair, 864-656-3225, E-mail: hhill@clemson.edu. *Application contact:* Ellen Reneke, Staff Assistant for Graduate Programs, 864-656-5791, Fax: 864-656-5776, E-mail: ereneke@clemson.edu.

Cornell University, Graduate School, Graduate Fields of Agriculture and Life Sciences, Graduate Field of Applied Economics and Management, Ithaca, NY 14853-0001. Offers MPS, MS, PhD. *Faculty:* 42 full-time (8 women). *Students:* 88 full-time (40 women); includes 7 Asian, non-Hispanic/Latino, 54 international. Average age 27. 350 applicants, 16% accepted, 24 enrolled. In 2010, 11 master's, 3 doctorates awarded. *Entrance requirements:* For master's and doctorate, GRE. Additional exam requirements/recommendations for international students: Required—TOEFL. Application fee: $70. *Expenses:* Tuition: Full-time $29,500. Required fees: $76. Tuition and fees vary according to degree level and program. *Financial support:* In 2010–11, 4 fellowships, 29 research assistantships, 22 teaching assistantships were awarded. *Application contact:* Graduate School Application Requests, Caldwell Hall, 607-255-5820.

Cornell University, Graduate School, Graduate Fields of Arts and Sciences, Field of Economics, Ithaca, NY 14853-0001. Offers applied economics (PhD); basic analytical economics (PhD); econometrics and economic statistics (PhD); economic development and planning (PhD); economic theory (PhD); industrial organization and control (PhD); international economics (PhD); labor economics (PhD); monetary and macroeconomics (PhD); public finance (PhD). *Faculty:* 78 full-time (10 women). *Students:* 100 full-time (40 women); includes 1 Black or African American, non-Hispanic/Latino; 4 Asian, non-Hispanic/Latino; 1 Hispanic/Latino, 61 international. Average age 27. 742 applicants, 10% accepted, 20 enrolled. In 2010, 21 doctorates awarded. *Degree requirements:* For doctorate, comprehensive exam, thesis/dissertation. *Entrance requirements:* For doctorate, GRE General Test, 3 letters of recommendation. Additional exam requirements/recommendations for international students: Required—TOEFL (minimum score 550 paper-based; 213 computer-based; 77 iBT). *Application deadline:* For fall admission, 1/15 priority date for domestic students. Application fee: $80. Electronic applications accepted. *Expenses:* Tuition: Full-time $29,500. Required fees: $76. Tuition and fees vary according to degree level and program. *Financial support:* In 2010–11, 20 fellowships with full tuition reimbursements, 16 research assistantships with full tuition reimbursements, 50 teaching assistantships with full tuition reimbursements were awarded; institutionally sponsored loans, scholarships/grants, health care benefits, tuition waivers (full and partial), and unspecified assistantships also available. Financial award applicants required to submit FAFSA. *Faculty research:* Learning and games, economics of education, political economy, transfer payments, time series and nonparametrics. *Unit head:* Director of Graduate Studies, 607-255-4893, Fax: 607-255-2818. *Application contact:* Graduate Field Assistant, 607-255-4893, Fax: 607-255-2818, E-mail: econ_phd@cornell.edu.

Eastern Michigan University, Graduate School, College of Arts and Sciences, Department of Economics, Ypsilanti, MI 48197. Offers applied economics (MA); economics (MA); health economics (MA); international economics and development (MA); trade and development (MA). Part-time and evening/weekend programs available. Postbaccalaureate distance learning degree programs offered (minimal on-campus study). *Faculty:* 11 full-time (2 women). *Students:* 25 full-time (5 women), 32 part-time (7 women); includes 19 minority (10 Black or African American, non-Hispanic/Latino; 1 American Indian or Alaska Native, non-Hispanic/Latino; 4 Asian, non-Hispanic/Latino; 4 Hispanic/Latino), 7 international. Average age 29. 50 applicants, 74% accepted, 19 enrolled. In 2010, 18 master's awarded. *Degree requirements:* For master's, thesis or alternative. *Entrance requirements:* Additional exam requirements/recommendations for international students: Required—TOEFL. *Application deadline:* Applications are processed on a rolling basis. Application fee: $35. *Financial support:* Fellowships, research assistantships with full tuition reimbursements, teaching assistantships with full tuition reimbursements, career-related internships or fieldwork, Federal Work-Study, institutionally sponsored loans, scholarships/grants, tuition waivers (partial), and unspecified assistantships available. Support available to part-time students. Financial award applicants required to submit FAFSA. *Unit head:* Dr. Raouf S. Hanna, Department Head, 734-487-3395, Fax: 734-487-9666, E-mail: rhanna@emich.edu. *Application contact:* Dr. David Crary, Advisor, 734-487-0001, Fax: 734-487-9666, E-mail: dcrary@emich.edu.

Georgia Southern University, Jack N. Averitt College of Graduate Studies, College of Business Administration, School of Economic Development, Statesboro, GA 30460. Offers applied economics (MS). Part-time and evening/weekend programs available. Postbaccalaureate distance learning degree programs offered (no on-campus study). *Students:* 8 full-time (3 women), 57 part-time (12 women); includes 7 Black or African American, non-Hispanic/Latino; 1 American Indian or Alaska Native, non-Hispanic/Latino; 3 Asian, non-Hispanic/Latino; 3 Hispanic/Latino; 3 Two or more races, non-Hispanic/Latino, 1 international. Average age 34. 50 applicants, 88% accepted, 31 enrolled. In 2010, 1 master's awarded. *Entrance requirements:* For master's, GRE or GMAT, minimum GPA of 3.0. Additional exam requirements/recommendations for international students: Required—TOEFL (minimum score 550 paper-based; 213 computer-based; 80 iBT). *Application deadline:* For fall admission, 3/1 for domestic and international students; for spring admission, 10/1 priority date for domestic students, 10/1 for international students. Applications are processed on a rolling basis. Application fee: $50. Electronic applications accepted. *Expenses:* Tuition, state resident: full-time $6000; part-time $250 per semester hour. Tuition, nonresident: full-time $23,976; part-time $999 per semester hour. Required fees: $1644. *Financial support:* In 2010–11, 24 students received support. Application deadline: 4/15. *Unit head:* Dr. Godfrey Gibbison, Director, 912-478-0086, Fax: 912-478-0710, E-mail: ggibbso@georgiasouthern.edu. *Application contact:* Dr. Charles Ziglar, Coordinator of Graduate Student Recruitment, 912-478-5635, Fax: 912-478-0740, E-mail: gradadmissions@georgiasouthern.edu.

Applied Economics

HEC Montreal, School of Business Administration, Master of Science Programs in Administration, Program in Applied Economics, Montréal, QC H3T 2A7, Canada. Offers M Sc. All courses are given in French. Part-time programs available. *Students:* 20 full-time (9 women), 2 part-time (1 woman). 16 applicants, 69% accepted, 7 enrolled. In 2010, 14 master's awarded. *Degree requirements:* For master's, one foreign language, thesis. *Application deadline:* For fall admission, 3/15 for domestic and international students; for winter admission, 9/15 for domestic and international students. Application fee: $78 Canadian dollars. Electronic applications accepted. *Expenses:* Tuition, area resident: Part-time $68.93 per credit. Tuition, state resident: full-time $2481.48; part-time $188.92 per credit. Tuition, nonresident: full-time $6801; part-time $482.06 per course. International tuition: $17,354.16 full-time. Required fees: $1309.50; $30.28 per credit. $93.45 per term. Tuition and fees vary according to degree level and program. *Financial support:* Fellowships, research assistantships, teaching assistantships, scholarships/grants available. Financial award application deadline: 9/2. *Unit head:* Dr. Claude Laurin, Director, 514-340-6485, Fax: 514-340-6880, E-mail: claude.laurin@hec.ca. *Application contact:* Francine Blais, Administrative Director, 514-340-6112, Fax: 514-340-6411, E-mail: francine.blais@hec.ca.

The Johns Hopkins University, Zanvyl Krieger School of Arts and Sciences, Advanced Academic Programs, Program in Applied Economics, Baltimore, MD 21218-2699. Offers MA. Part-time and evening/weekend programs available. *Faculty:* 1 full-time (0 women), 32 part-time/adjunct (4 women). *Students:* 41 full-time (16 women), 354 part-time (133 women); includes 96 minority (26 Black or African American, non-Hispanic/Latino; 38 Asian, non-Hispanic/Latino; 24 Hispanic/Latino; 8 Two or more races, non-Hispanic/Latino), 47 international. Average age 28. 198 applicants, 58% accepted, 88 enrolled. In 2010, 83 master's awarded. *Degree requirements:* For master's, thesis (for some programs). *Entrance requirements:* For master's, minimum GPA of 3.0, coursework in microeconomics and macroeconomics. Additional exam requirements/recommendations for international students: Required—TOEFL (minimum score 250 computer-based; 100 iBT). *Application deadline:* For fall admission, 5/31 priority date for domestic students, 4/30 priority date for international students; for spring admission, 10/31 priority date for domestic and international students. Applications are processed on a rolling basis. Application fee: $75. Electronic applications accepted. *Financial support:* Applicants required to submit FAFSA. *Unit head:* Dr. Frank Weiss, Associate Program Chair, 202-452-0769, E-mail: fdweiss@jhu.edu. *Application contact:* Valana M. McMickens, Admissions Manager, 202-452-1941, Fax: 202-452-1970, E-mail: aapadmissions@jhu.edu.

Mississippi State University, College of Business, Department of Finance and Economics, Mississippi State, MS 39762. Offers applied economics (PhD); business administration (PhD), including finance; economics (MA); finance (MSBA). Part-time programs available. *Faculty:* 10 full-time (2 women). *Students:* 14 full-time (3 women), 3 part-time (1 woman); includes 1 minority (Black or African American, non-Hispanic/Latino), 10 international. Average age 31. 63 applicants, 11% accepted, 6 enrolled. In 2010, 1 master's, 2 doctorates awarded. Terminal master's awarded for partial completion of doctoral program. *Degree requirements:* For master's, comprehensive exam, thesis optional; for doctorate, comprehensive exam, thesis/dissertation. *Entrance requirements:* For master's and doctorate, GMAT, GRE General Test. Additional exam requirements/recommendations for international students: Required—TOEFL (minimum score 575 paper-based; 233 computer-based; 90 iBT); Recommended—IELTS (minimum score 6.5). *Application deadline:* For fall admission, 7/1 for domestic students, 5/1 for international students; for spring admission, 11/1 for domestic students, 10/1 for international students. Applications are processed on a rolling basis. Application fee: $40. Electronic applications accepted. *Expenses:* Tuition, state resident: full-time $2730.50; part-time $304 per credit hour. Tuition, nonresident: full-time $6901; part-time $767 per credit hour. *Financial support:* In 2010–11, 3 teaching assistantships with tuition reimbursements (averaging $14,677 per year) were awarded; Federal Work-Study, scholarships/grants, health care benefits, and unspecified assistantships also available. Financial award application deadline: 4/1; financial award applicants required to submit FAFSA. *Faculty research:* Economics development, mergers, event studies, economic education, bank performance. Total annual research expenditures: $961,000. *Unit head:* Dr. Mike Highfield, Department Head, 662-325-1984, Fax: 662-325-1977, E-mail: m.highfield@msstate.edu. *Application contact:* Dr. Benjamin F. Blair, Associate Professor/Graduate Coordinator, 662-325-1980, Fax: 662-325-1977, E-mail: bblair@cobilan.msstate.edu.

New York University, Graduate School of Arts and Science, Department of Economics, New York, NY 10012-1019. Offers applied economic analysis (Advanced Certificate); economics (MA, PhD); JD/MA; MD/PhD. Part-time and evening/weekend programs available. *Faculty:* 35 full-time (2 women). *Students:* 225 full-time (77 women), 38 part-time (10 women); includes 19 Asian, non-Hispanic/Latino; 2 Hispanic/Latino, 176 international. Average age 27. 1,650 applicants, 14% accepted, 90 enrolled. In 2010, 77 master's, 15 doctorates, 2 other advanced degrees awarded. Terminal master's awarded for partial completion of doctoral program. *Degree requirements:* For master's, thesis; for doctorate, one foreign language, thesis/dissertation, 4 qualifying exams. *Entrance requirements:* For master's and doctorate, GRE General Test; for Advanced Certificate, master's degree. Additional exam requirements/recommendations for international students: Required—TOEFL. *Application deadline:* For fall admission, 12/15 priority date for domestic students. Application fee: $90. *Financial support:* Fellowships with tuition reimbursements, research assistantships with tuition reimbursements, teaching assistantships with tuition reimbursements, Federal Work-Study, institutionally sponsored loans, scholarships/grants, health care benefits, and unspecified assistantships available. Financial award application deadline: 12/15; financial award applicants required to submit FAFSA. *Faculty research:* Economic theory, experimental economics, growth and development, macroeconomics and finance, international trade and international finance. *Unit head:* Nicola Persico, Chair, 212-998-8900, Fax: 212-995-4186, E-mail: admissions@econ.nyu.edu. *Application contact:* Debraj Ray, Director of Graduate Studies, 212-998-8900, Fax: 212-995-4186, E-mail: admissions@econ.nyu.edu.

North Carolina Agricultural and Technical State University, Graduate School, School of Agriculture and Environmental Sciences, Department of Agribusiness, Applied Economics, and Agriscience Education, Greensboro, NC 27411. Offers agricultural economics (MS); agricultural education (MS). *Accreditation:* NCATE. Part-time and evening/weekend programs available. *Degree requirements:* For master's, comprehensive exam, thesis or alternative, qualifying exam. *Entrance requirements:* For master's, GRE General Test, minimum GPA of 3.0. *Faculty research:* Aid for small farmers, agricultural technology resources, labor force mobility, agrology.

Northeastern University, College of Social Sciences and Humanities, Department of Economics, Boston, MA 02115-5096. Offers MA, PhD. Part-time and evening/weekend programs available. *Faculty:* 17 full-time (2 women), 11 part-time/adjunct (6 women). *Students:* 79 full-time (38 women), 2 part-time (0 women). 219 applicants, 51% accepted, 26 enrolled. In 2010, 19 master's awarded. *Degree requirements:* For master's and doctorate, comprehensive exam. *Entrance requirements:* For master's, GRE. Additional exam requirements/recommendations for international students: Required—TOEFL. *Application deadline:* For fall admission, 8/1 for domestic students, 5/1 priority date for international students; for spring admission, 12/1 for domestic and international students. Applications are processed on a rolling basis. Application fee: $50. *Financial support:* In 2010–11, 13 teaching assistantships (averaging $15,667 per year) were awarded; Federal Work-Study, institutionally sponsored loans, tuition waivers (full and partial), and unspecified assistantships also available. Financial award application deadline: 2/1; financial award applicants required to submit FAFSA. *Faculty research:* U. S. labor markets, applied economics, microeconomic theory, macroeconomic theory, econometrics. *Unit head:* Dr. Steven Morrison, Chair, 617-373-2872, Fax: 617-373-3640, E-mail: econ@neu.edu. *Application contact:* Dr. Gregory Wassall, Graduate Coordinator, 617-373-2882, Fax: 617-373-3640, E-mail: econ@neu.edu.

Ohio University, Graduate College, College of Arts and Sciences, Department of Economics, Athens, OH 45701-2979. Offers applied economics (MA); financial economics (MFE). Part-time and evening/weekend programs available. *Students:* 65 full-time (16 women), 18 part-time (10 women); includes 10 minority (6 Black or African American, non-Hispanic/Latino; 3 Asian, non-Hispanic/Latino; 1 Two or more races, non-Hispanic/Latino), 46 international. 55 applicants, 42% accepted, 11 enrolled. In 2010, 42 master's awarded. *Degree requirements:* For master's, thesis or alternative. *Entrance requirements:* For master's, GRE or GMAT (recommended), minimum GPA of 3.0. Additional exam requirements/recommendations for international students: Required—TOEFL (minimum score 550 paper-based; 80 iBT) or IELTS (minimum score 6.5). *Application deadline:* For fall admission, 2/15 priority date for domestic and international students; for winter admission, 12/1 for domestic students, 10/1 priority date for international students. Application fee: $50 ($55 for international students). Electronic applications accepted. *Financial support:* Research assistantships with full and partial tuition reimbursements, Federal Work-Study, tuition waivers (partial), and unspecified assistantships available. Financial award application deadline: 2/15. *Faculty research:* Macroeconomics, public finance, international economics and finance, monetary theory, healthcare economics. *Unit head:* Dr. Rosmary Rossiter, Chair, 740-593-2040, E-mail: rossiter@ohio.edu. *Application contact:* Dr. K. Doroodian, Graduate Chair, 740-593-2046, E-mail: doroodia@ohio.edu.

Old Dominion University, College of Business and Public Administration, MBA Program, Norfolk, VA 23529. Offers business and economic forecasting (MBA); financial analysis and valuation (MBA); information technology and enterprise integration (MBA); international business (MBA); maritime and port management (MBA); public administration (MBA). *Accreditation:* AACSB. Part-time and evening/weekend programs available. *Faculty:* 66 full-time (15 women), 6 part-time/adjunct (1 woman). *Students:* 74 full-time (32 women), 166 part-time (62 women); includes 45 minority (21 Black or African American, non-Hispanic/Latino; 1 American Indian or Alaska Native, non-Hispanic/Latino; 8 Asian, non-Hispanic/Latino; 10 Hispanic/Latino; 1 Native Hawaiian or other Pacific Islander, non-Hispanic/Latino; 4 Two or more races, non-Hispanic/Latino), 19 international. Average age 31. 169 applicants, 52% accepted, 61 enrolled. In 2010, 100 master's awarded. *Entrance requirements:* For master's, GMAT, letter of reference, resume, coursework in calculus, essay. Additional exam requirements/recommendations for international students: Required—TOEFL (minimum score 550 paper-based; 213 computer-based; 80 iBT). *Application deadline:* For fall admission, 6/1 priority date for domestic students, 4/15 priority date for international students; for spring admission, 11/1 priority date for domestic students, 10/1 priority date for international students. Applications are processed on a rolling basis. Application fee: $50. Electronic applications accepted. *Expenses:* Tuition, state resident: full-time $8592; part-time $358 per credit. Tuition, nonresident: full-time $21,672; part-time $903 per credit. Required fees: $119 per semester. One-time fee: $50. *Financial support:* In 2010–11, 44 students received support, including 90 research assistantships with partial tuition reimbursements available (averaging $3,200 per year); career-related internships or fieldwork, scholarships/grants, and unspecified assistantships also available. Support available to part-time students. Financial award application deadline: 2/15; financial award applicants required to submit FAFSA. *Faculty research:* International business, buyer behavior, financial markets, strategy, operations research. *Unit head:* Dr. Larry Filer, Graduate Program Director, 757-683-3585, Fax: 757-683-5750, E-mail: mbainfo@odu.edu. *Application contact:* Shanna Wood, MBA Program Manager, 757-683-3585, Fax: 757-683-5750, E-mail: mbainfo@odu.edu.

Portland State University, Graduate Studies, College of Liberal Arts and Sciences, Department of Economics, Portland, OR 97207-0751. Offers applied economics (MA, MS); economics (PhD); general economics (MA, MS). Part-time programs available. *Faculty:* 15 full-time (5 women), 3 part-time/adjunct (1 woman). *Students:* 13 full-time (3 women), 6 part-time (0 women); includes 2 Asian, non-Hispanic/Latino; 1 Native Hawaiian or other Pacific Islander, non-Hispanic/Latino, 4 international. Average age 28. 18 applicants, 50% accepted, 4 enrolled. In 2010, 10 master's awarded. *Degree requirements:* For master's, thesis optional; for doctorate, one foreign language, thesis/dissertation. *Entrance requirements:* For master's, minimum GPA of 3.0 in upper-division course work or 2.75 overall, course work in calculus. Additional exam requirements/recommendations for international students: Required—TOEFL (minimum score 550 paper-based; 213 computer-based). *Application deadline:* For fall admission, 4/1 for domestic students, 3/1 for international students; for spring admission, 11/1 for domestic and international students. Applications are processed on a rolling basis. Application fee: $50. *Expenses:* Tuition, state resident: full-time $8505; part-time $315 per credit. Tuition, nonresident: full-time $13,284; part-time $492 per credit. Required fees: $1482; $21 per credit. $99 per term. One-time fee: $120. Part-time tuition and fees vary according to course load and program. *Financial support:* In 2010–11, 4 research assistantships with full tuition reimbursements (averaging $6,372 per year), 1 teaching assistantship (averaging $8,820 per year) were awarded; career-related internships or fieldwork, Federal Work-Study, and unspecified assistantships also available. Support available to part-time students. Financial award application deadline: 3/1; financial award applicants required to submit FAFSA. *Faculty research:* NAFTA, economies of transition, economics of Eastern Europe, artificial intelligence, comparative economic systems. Total annual research expenditures: $130,434. *Unit head:* Dr. Randy Bluffstone, Chair, 503-725-3938, Fax: 503-725-3945, E-mail: bluffsto@pdx.edu. *Application contact:* Rita Spears, Office Specialist, 503-725-3941, Fax: 503-725-3945, E-mail: spearsr@pdx.edu.

Roosevelt University, Graduate Division, College of Arts and Sciences, Department of Economics, Chicago, IL 60605. Offers applied economics (MA); economics (MA). Part-time and evening/weekend programs available. *Degree requirements:* For master's, thesis or alternative. *Entrance requirements:* For master's, minimum GPA of 2.7. *Faculty research:* Labor, gender issues, international trade and development, entrepreneurship, political economy and money.

St. Cloud State University, School of Graduate Studies, College of Social Sciences, Department of Economics, Program in Applied Economics, St. Cloud, MN 56301-4498. Offers MS.

San Jose State University, Graduate Studies and Research, College of Social Sciences, Department of Economics, San Jose, CA 95192-0001. Offers applied economics (MA); economics (MA). Part-time programs available. *Degree requirements:* For master's, comprehensive exam, thesis optional. *Entrance requirements:* For master's, GRE, minimum GPA of 3.0. Electronic applications accepted.

Southern Methodist University, Dedman College, Department of Economics, Dallas, TX 75205. Offers applied economics (MA); economics (MA, PhD); JD/MA. Part-time and evening/weekend programs available. *Faculty:* 18 full-time (4 women), 19 part-time/adjunct (9 women). *Students:* 63 full-time (29 women), 14 part-time (6 women); includes 3 Black or African American, non-Hispanic/Latino; 7 Asian, non-Hispanic/Latino; 7 Hispanic/Latino, 32 international. Average age 26. 139 applicants, 63% accepted, 28 enrolled. In 2010, 21 master's, 6 doctorates awarded. Terminal master's awarded for partial completion of doctoral program. *Degree requirements:* For master's, thesis, oral qualifying exam; for doctorate, thesis/dissertation, written exams. *Entrance requirements:* For master's, GRE General Test or GMAT, 12 hours course work in economics, minimum GPA of 3.0, previous course work in calculus and statistics; for doctorate, GRE General Test, minimum GPA of 3.0; 3 semesters of course work in calculus; 1 semester each of course work in statistics and linear algebra. Additional exam requirements/recommendations for international students: Required—TOEFL (minimum score 550 paper-based; 213 computer-based). *Application deadline:* For fall admission, 2/1 priority date for domestic students; for spring admission, 11/30 priority date for domestic students. Applications are processed on a rolling basis. Application fee: $75. Electronic applications accepted. *Financial support:* In 2010–11, 23 students received support, including 1 fellowship with full tuition reimbursement available (averaging $16,000 per year), 1 research assistantship with full tuition reimbursement available (averaging $16,000 per year), 16 teaching assistantships with full tuition reimbursements available (averaging $16,000 per year). Financial award application deadline: 2/1; financial award applicants required to submit FAFSA. *Faculty research:* Economic theory, game theory, econometrics, international trade, labor. *Unit head:* Dr. Nathan Balke, Chair, 214-768-2693, Fax: 214-768-3911, E-mail: nbalke@smu.edu. *Application contact:* Stephanie Hall, Information Contact, 214-768-2694, E-mail: eco@smu.edu.

Texas Tech University, Graduate School, College of Agricultural Sciences and Natural Resources, Department of Agricultural and Applied Economics, Lubbock, TX 79409. Offers agribusiness (MAB); agricultural and applied economics (MS, PhD); JD/MS. Part-time programs available. *Faculty:* 13 full-time (0 women). *Students:* 37 full-time (14 women), 8 part-time (1 woman); includes 1 Black or African American, non-Hispanic/Latino; 1 Hispanic/Latino, 29 international. Average age 29. 39 applicants, 51% accepted, 12 enrolled. In 2010, 11 master's, 4 doctorates awarded. *Degree requirements:* For master's, thesis or alternative; for doctorate, thesis/dissertation. *Entrance requirements:* For master's and doctorate, GRE General Test, formal approval from departmental committee. Additional exam requirements/recommendations for international students: Required—TOEFL (minimum score 550 paper-based; 213 computer-based; 79 iBT). *Application deadline:* For fall admission, 6/1 priority date for domestic students, 1/15 priority date for international students; for spring admission, 9/1 priority date for domestic students, 6/15 priority date for international students. Applications are processed on a rolling basis. Application fee: $50 ($75 for international students). Electronic applications accepted. *Expenses:* Tuition, state resident: full-time $5495.76; part-time $228.99 per credit hour. Tuition, nonresident: full-time $12,936; part-time $538.99 per credit hour. Required fees: $2674; $36 per credit hour. $905 per semester. *Financial support:* In 2010–11, 32 students received support, including 9 research assistantships with partial tuition reimbursements available (averaging $7,828 per year), 1 teaching assistantship with partial tuition reimbursement available (averaging $16,457 per year). Financial award application deadline: 4/15; financial award applicants required to submit FAFSA. *Faculty research:* Economics of the United States cotton and textile industries, natural resource management in semi-arid climates, commodity policy analysis, international trade in agricultural products, agribusiness analysis. Total annual research expenditures: $1.4 million. *Unit head:* Dr. Eduardo Segarra, Chair, 806-742-2821, Fax: 806-742-1099, E-mail: eduardo.segarra@ttu.edu. *Application contact:* Dr. Tom Knight, Graduate Adviser, 806-742-2821, Fax: 806-742-1099, E-mail: tom.knight@ttu.edu.

University of California, Santa Cruz, Division of Graduate Studies, Division of Social Sciences, Program in Applied Economics and Finance, Santa Cruz, CA 95064. Offers MS. *Students:* 32 full-time (11 women); includes 7 Asian, non-Hispanic/Latino; 4 Hispanic/Latino, 12 international. Average age 25. 112 applicants, 65% accepted, 24 enrolled. In 2010, 12 master's awarded. *Degree requirements:* For master's, thesis or alternative, project. *Entrance requirements:* For master's, GRE General Test, GRE Subject Test. Additional exam requirements/recommendations for international students: Required—TOEFL (minimum score 550 paper-based; 220 computer-based; 83 iBT); Recommended—IELTS (minimum score 8). *Application deadline:* For fall admission, 12/15 for domestic and international students. Application fee: $70 ($90 for international students). Electronic applications accepted. *Financial support:* Research assistantships, teaching assistantships, institutionally sponsored loans and tuition waivers available. Financial award applicants required to submit FAFSA. *Faculty research:* Economic decision-making skills for the design and operation of complex institutional systems. *Unit head:* Sandra Reebie, Graduate Program Coordinator, 831-459-2219, E-mail: screebie@ucsc.edu. *Application contact:* Sandra Reebie, Graduate Program Coordinator, 831-459-2219, E-mail: screebie@ucsc.edu.

University of Georgia, College of Agricultural and Environmental Sciences, Department of Agricultural and Applied Economics, Athens, GA 30602. Offers agricultural economics (MAE, MS, PhD); environmental economics (MS). *Faculty:* 24 full-time (4 women). *Students:* 43 full-time (20 women), 8 part-time (4 women); includes 4 Black or African American, non-Hispanic/Latino; 1 Hispanic/Latino, 25 international. 54 applicants, 63% accepted, 18 enrolled. In 2010, 3 master's, 4 doctorates awarded. *Degree requirements:* For master's, thesis (MS); for doctorate, thesis/dissertation. *Entrance requirements:* For master's and doctorate, GRE General Test. *Application deadline:* For fall admission, 7/1 priority date for domestic students; for spring admission, 11/15 for domestic students. Application fee: $50. Electronic applications accepted. *Expenses:* Tuition, state resident: full-time $7200; part-time $344 per credit hour. Tuition, nonresident: full-time $21,900; part-time $944 per credit hour. Tuition and fees vary according to course load and program. *Financial support:* Fellowships, research assistantships, teaching assistantships, career-related internships or fieldwork and unspecified assistantships available. *Unit head:* Dr. Octavio A. Ramirez, Interim Head, 706-542-2481, Fax: 706-542-0739, E-mail: oramirez@agecon.uga.edu. *Application contact:* Dr. Michael E. Wetzstein, Graduate Coordinator, 706-543-0758, Fax: 706-542-0739, E-mail: mwetz@uga.edu.

University of Houston, College of Liberal Arts and Social Sciences, Department of Economics, Houston, TX 77204. Offers applied economics (MA); economics (MA, PhD). *Faculty:* 12 full-time (5 women), 3 part-time/adjunct (2 women). *Students:* 60 full-time (26 women), 5 part-time (4 women); includes 2 Black or African American, non-Hispanic/Latino; 6 Asian, non-Hispanic/Latino; 3 Hispanic/Latino, 35 international. Average age 26. 103 applicants, 38% accepted, 15 enrolled. In 2010, 23 master's, 4 doctorates awarded. Terminal master's awarded for partial completion of doctoral program. *Degree requirements:* For master's, thesis optional; for doctorate, comprehensive exam, thesis/dissertation. *Entrance requirements:* For master's and doctorate, GRE General Test, minimum GPA of 3.0, statement of purpose, three letters of recommendation. Additional exam requirements/recommendations for international students: Required—TOEFL (minimum score 550 paper-based; 79 iBT), IELTS (minimum score 6.5). *Application deadline:* For fall admission, 2/1 for domestic and international students. Applications are processed on a rolling basis. Electronic applications accepted. *Expenses:* Tuition, state resident: full-time $8592; part-time $358 per credit hour. Tuition, nonresident: full-time $16,032; part-time $668 per credit hour. Required fees: $2889. Tuition and fees vary according to course load and program. *Financial support:* In 2010–11, 12 fellowships with full tuition reimbursements (averaging $4,600 per year), 29 teaching assistantships with full tuition reimbursements (averaging $10,800 per year) were awarded; career-related internships or fieldwork, Federal Work-Study, institutionally sponsored loans, scholarships/grants, health care benefits, and unspecified assistantships also available. Support available to part-time students. Financial award application deadline: 2/1. *Faculty research:* Econometrics, labor economics, international economics. *Unit head:* Dr. David Papell, Chairperson, 713-743-3800, Fax: 713-743-3798, E-mail: dpapell@uh.edu. *Application contact:* Rebecca Thornton, Director, 713-743-3820, E-mail: rthornton@uh.edu.

University of Idaho, College of Graduate Studies, College of Agricultural and Life Sciences, Department of Agricultural Economics and Rural Sociology, Moscow, ID 83844-2282. Offers agricultural economics (MS); applied economics (MS), including agribusiness emphasis, agricultural economics emphasis, applied economics. *Faculty:* 8 full-time. *Students:* 13 full-time, 6 part-time. Average age 25. In 2010, 3 master's awarded. *Entrance requirements:* For master's, minimum GPA of 2.8. *Application deadline:* For fall admission, 8/1 for domestic students; for spring admission, 12/15 for domestic students. Applications are processed on a rolling basis. Application fee: $60. Electronic applications accepted. *Expenses:* Tuition, nonresident: part-time $580 per credit. Required fees: $306 per credit. *Financial support:* Research assistantships, teaching assistantships available. Financial award applicants required to submit FAFSA. *Faculty research:* Crops: potatoes, blue grass; livestock: beef, dairy; rural and community development; natural resources and the environment; farm and ranch management. *Unit head:* Dr. Larry Makus, Interim Department Head, 208-885-6262, Fax: 208-885-5759, E-mail: cdarby@uidaho.edu. *Application contact:* Dr. Larry Makus, Interim Department Head, 208-885-6262, Fax: 208-885-5759, E-mail: cdarby@uidaho.edu.

University of Illinois at Urbana–Champaign, Graduate College, College of Agricultural, Consumer and Environmental Sciences, Department of Agricultural and Consumer Economics, Champaign, IL 61820. Offers agricultural and applied economics (MS, PhD). *Faculty:* 31 full-time (11 women). *Students:* 65 full-time (26 women), 15 part-time (8 women); includes 3 Black or African American, non-Hispanic/Latino; 3 Asian, non-Hispanic/Latino, 49 international. 117 applicants, 23% accepted, 15 enrolled. In 2010, 10 master's, 10 doctorates awarded. *Entrance requirements:* For master's, GRE, minimum GPA of 3.0; for doctorate, GRE, writing sample. Additional exam requirements/recommendations for international students: Required—TOEFL (minimum score 570 paper-based; 230 computer-based; 88 iBT) or IELTS (minimum score 6.5). *Application deadline:* Applications are processed on a rolling basis. Application fee: $75 ($90 for international students). Electronic applications accepted. *Financial support:* In 2010–11, 16 fellowships, 47 research assistantships, 32 teaching assistantships were awarded; tuition waivers (full and partial) also available. *Unit head:* Paul N. Ellinger, Head, 217-333-5503, Fax: 217-333-5538, E-mail: pellinge@illinois.edu. *Application contact:* Pamela S. Splittstoesser, Administrative Assistant, 217-333-1830, Fax: 217-244-7088, E-mail: splttsts@illinois.edu.

University of Michigan, Horace H. Rackham School of Graduate Studies, College of Literature, Science, and the Arts, Department of Economics, Program in Applied Economics, Ann Arbor, MI 48109. Offers AM. Part-time programs available. *Faculty:* 49 full-time (6 women). *Students:* 73 full-time (27 women); includes 53 Asian, non-Hispanic/Latino; 1 Hispanic/Latino. 279 applicants, 31% accepted, 31 enrolled. In 2010, 48 master's awarded. *Entrance requirements:* For master's, GRE General Test. Additional exam requirements/recommendations for international students: Required—TOEFL (minimum score 600 paper-based; 250 computer-based). *Application deadline:* For fall admission, 2/5 for domestic and international students. Application fee: $65 ($75 for international students). *Expenses:* Tuition, state resident: full-time $17,784; part-time $1116 per credit hour. Tuition, nonresident: full-time $35,944; part-time $2125 per credit hour. International tuition: $35,994 full-time. Required fees: $95 per semester. Tuition and fees vary according to course load, degree level and program. *Faculty research:* Econometric analysis transition, macro. *Unit head:* John Laitner, Director, 734-763-5316, Fax: 734-764-2769. *Application contact:* LaRue Cochran, Student Services Assistant, 734-763-5316, Fax: 734-764-2769, E-mail: larue@umich.edu.

University of Minnesota, Twin Cities Campus, Graduate School, College of Food, Agricultural and Natural Resource Sciences, Applied Economics Graduate Program, Saint Paul, MN 55108. Offers MS, PhD. *Faculty:* 59 full-time (15 women). *Students:* 79 full-time (29 women), 14 part-time (4 women); includes 3 minority (1 Black or African American, non-Hispanic/Latino; 1 Asian, non-Hispanic/Latino; 1 Two or more races, non-Hispanic/Latino), 42 international. Average age 30. 224 applicants, 17% accepted, 29 enrolled. In 2010, 12 master's, 9 doctorates awarded. *Degree requirements:* For master's, comprehensive exam, thesis; for doctorate, comprehensive exam, thesis/dissertation. *Entrance requirements:* For master's and doctorate, GRE, minimum GPA of 3.0 preferred. Additional exam requirements/recommendations for international students: Required—TOEFL (minimum score 550 paper-based; 213 computer-based; 79 iBT). *Application deadline:* For fall admission, 12/15 for domestic and international students; for spring admission, 10/15 for domestic and international students. Applications are processed on a rolling basis. Application fee: $75 ($95 for international students). Electronic applications accepted. *Financial support:* In 2010–11, fellowships with full tuition reimbursements (averaging $23,500 per year), research assistantships with full tuition reimbursements (averaging $19,000 per year), teaching assistantships with full tuition reimbursements (averaging $19,000 per year) were awarded; scholarships/grants, health care benefits, tuition waivers (full and partial), unspecified assistantships, and stipends also available. Financial award application deadline: 12/15. *Faculty research:* Consumer behavior, household and labor, policy analysis and health, production and marketing, resource and environmental, trade and development. Total annual research expenditures: $1.4 million. *Unit head:* Dr. Elizabeth Davis, Director of Graduate Studies, 612-625-7028, Fax: 612-625-6245, E-mail: edavis@umn.edu. *Application contact:* Gary Cooper, Program Coordinator, 612-625-0213, Fax: 612-625-6245, E-mail: coope056@umn.edu.

University of Nevada, Reno, Graduate School, College of Agriculture, Biotechnology and Natural Resources, Department of Resource Economics, Reno, NV 89557. Offers MS, PhD. Terminal master's awarded for partial completion of doctoral program. *Degree requirements:* For master's, thesis optional; for doctorate, thesis/dissertation. *Entrance requirements:* For master's, GRE General Test, minimum GPA of 2.75; for doctorate, GRE General Test, minimum GPA of 3.0. Additional exam requirements/recommendations for international students: Required—TOEFL (minimum score 500 paper-based; 173 computer-based; 61 iBT), IELTS (minimum score 6). Electronic applications accepted. *Expenses:* Tuition, state resident: full-time $2219; part-time $246 per credit. Tuition, nonresident: part-time $510 per credit. International tuition: $9009 full-time. Required fees: $59 per term. One-time fee: $101. Tuition and fees vary according to course load. *Faculty research:* Econometrics, environmental valuation, natural resource and environmental policy analysis, public lands management.

University of New Brunswick Fredericton, School of Graduate Studies, Faculty of Arts, Department of Economics, Fredericton, NB E3B 5A3, Canada. Offers applied economics and finance (M Sc); economics (MA). M Sc offered on Saint John campus. *Faculty:* 11 full-time (1 woman). *Students:* 9 full-time (4 women), 3 part-time (1 woman). In 2010, 3 master's awarded. *Entrance requirements:* For master's, GRE, minimum GPA of 3.0. Additional exam requirements/recommendations for international students: Required—TWE, TOEFL (minimum score 550 paper-based) or IELTS. *Application deadline:* 1/31 for domestic and international students. Applications are processed on a rolling basis. Application fee: $50 Canadian dollars. *Expenses:* Tuition, area resident: Full-time $3708; part-time $927 per term. International tuition: $6300 full-time. Required fees: $50 per term. *Financial support:* In 2010–11, 5 research assistantships (averaging $16,000 per year) were awarded; scholarships/grants, health care benefits, and unspecified assistantships also available. Financial award application deadline: 1/31. *Faculty research:* Epidemiology and population health, micro/macro economics, economics of transportation, regional development. *Unit head:* Dr. Yuri Yevdokimov, Director of Graduate Studies, 506-447-3221, Fax: 506-453-4514, E-mail: yuri@unb.ca. *Application contact:* Lucina MacDonald, Graduate Secretary, 506-453-4828, Fax: 506-453-4514, E-mail: lmacdona@unb.ca.

The University of North Carolina at Greensboro, Graduate School, Bryan School of Business and Economics, Department of Economics, Program in Applied Economics, Greensboro, NC 27412-5001. Offers MA, MA/PhD. *Degree requirements:* For master's, comprehensive exam, thesis or alternative. *Entrance requirements:* For master's, GRE. Additional exam requirements/recommendations for international students: Required—TOEFL. Electronic applications accepted.

University of North Dakota, Graduate School, College of Business and Public Administration, Applied Economics Program, Grand Forks, ND 58202. Offers MSAE. Part-time programs available. Postbaccalaureate distance learning degree programs offered (minimal on-campus study). *Faculty:* 9 full-time (0 women). *Students:* 8 full-time (0 women), 26 part-time (6 women); includes 4 minority (2 Asian, non-Hispanic/Latino; 1 Hispanic/Latino; 1 Two or more races, non-Hispanic/Latino), 1 international. Average age 30. 25 applicants, 28% accepted, 7 enrolled. In 2010, 5 master's awarded. *Degree requirements:* For master's, comprehensive exam, thesis or alternative. *Entrance requirements:* For master's, GRE General Test. Additional exam requirements/recommendations for international students: Required—TOEFL (minimum score 550 paper-based; 213 computer-based; 79 iBT), IELTS (minimum score 6.5). *Application deadline:* For fall admission, 8/1 priority date for domestic and international students; for spring admission, 12/1 priority date for domestic and international students. Applications are processed on a rolling basis. Application fee: $35. Electronic applications accepted. *Expenses:* Tuition, state resident: full-time $5857; part-time $306.74 per credit. Tuition, nonresident: full-time $15,666; part-time $729.77 per credit. Required fees: $53.42 per credit. Tuition and fees vary according to course load, program and reciprocity agreements. *Financial support:* In 2010–11, 2 students received support, including 1 teaching assistantship with full and partial tuition reimbursement available; fellowships with full and partial tuition reimbursements available, research assistantships with full and partial tuition reimbursements available, Federal Work-Study, scholarships/grants, health care benefits, tuition waivers (full and partial), and unspecified assistantships also available. Support available to part-time students. Financial award applicants required to submit FAFSA. Total annual research expenditures: $9,894. *Unit head:* Dr. Cullen Goenner, Graduate Director, 701-777-3353, E-mail: cullen.goenner@mail.business.und.edu. *Application contact:* Matt Anderson, Admissions Specialist, 701-777-2947, Fax: 701-777-3619, E-mail: matthew.anderson@gradschool.und.edu.

University of North Texas, Toulouse Graduate School, College of Public Affairs and Community Service, Institute of Applied Economics, Denton, TX 76203. Offers MS. Part-time programs available. *Degree requirements:* For master's, comprehensive exam, thesis or alternative. *Entrance requirements:* For master's, GRE General Test or GMAT, minimum B average in last 60 hours of course work. Additional exam requirements/recommendations for

Applied Economics

University of North Texas (continued)

international students: Recommended—TOEFL (minimum score 550 paper-based; 213 computer-based; 79 iBT). *Application deadline:* Applications are processed on a rolling basis. Electronic applications accepted. *Expenses:* Tuition, state resident: full-time $4298; part-time $239 per credit hour. Tuition, nonresident: full-time $10,782; part-time $549 per credit hour. Required fees: $1292; $270 per credit hour. *Financial support:* Research assistantships, career-related internships or fieldwork, Federal Work-Study, and tuition waivers (partial) available. Financial award applicants required to submit FAFSA. *Faculty research:* Economic/focal impact of sports and entertainment venues, economic development potential of stem cell research, state and local incentive programs, city and metropolitan area industrial targeting dispute resolution. *Application contact:* Graduate Adviser, 940-565-3437, Fax: 940-565-4658.

University of Oklahoma, College of Arts and Sciences, Department of Economics, Norman, OK 73019. Offers applied economics (MA); economics (PhD); managerial economics (MA). *Faculty:* 19 full-time (7 women), 3 part-time/adjunct (2 women). *Students:* 41 full-time (17 women), 68 part-time (14 women); includes 23 minority (8 Black or African American, non-Hispanic/Latino; 1 American Indian or Alaska Native, non-Hispanic/Latino; 8 Asian, non-Hispanic/Latino; 6 Hispanic/Latino), 20 international. Average age 30. 62 applicants, 63% accepted, 25 enrolled. In 2010, 48 master's, 2 doctorates awarded. Terminal master's awarded for partial completion of doctoral program. *Degree requirements:* For doctorate, 2 foreign languages, thesis/dissertation, general exams. *Entrance requirements:* For master's, GRE General Test, minimum GPA of 3.0 in last 60 hours of course work; for doctorate, GRE General Test. Additional exam requirements/recommendations for international students: Required—TOEFL (minimum score 550 paper-based; 213 computer-based; 79 iBT). *Application deadline:* For fall admission, 1/15 for domestic and international students; for spring admission, 9/1 for domestic and international students. Applications are processed on a rolling basis. Application fee: $40 ($90 for international students). Electronic applications accepted. *Expenses:* Tuition, state resident: full-time $3893; part-time $162.20 per credit hour. Tuition, nonresident: full-time $14,167; part-time $590.30 per credit hour. Required fees: $2523; $94.60 per credit hour. Tuition and fees vary according to course load and degree level. *Financial support:* In 2010–11, 31 students received support, including 1 research assistantship with partial tuition reimbursement available (averaging $13,765 per year), 21 teaching assistantships with partial tuition reimbursements available (averaging $13,138 per year); scholarships/grants and unspecified assistantships also available. Financial award applicants required to submit FAFSA. *Faculty research:* Industrial organization, international economics, growth and development, public economics. Total annual research expenditures: $49,396. *Unit head:* Dr. Lex Holmes, Chair, 405-325-2861, Fax: 405-325-5842, E-mail: aholmes@ou.edu. *Application contact:* Cynthia Rogers, Graduate Program Director, 405-235-5843, Fax: 405-325-5842, E-mail: crogers@ou.edu.

University of Pennsylvania, Wharton School, Program in Applied Economics, Philadelphia, PA 19104. Offers PhD. *Expenses:* Tuition: Full-time $25,660; part-time $4758 per course. Required fees: $2152; $270 per course. Tuition and fees vary according to course load, degree level and program.

University of Vermont, Graduate College, College of Agriculture and Life Sciences, Department of Community Development and Applied Economics, Burlington, VT 05405. Offers community development and applied economics (MS); public administration (MPA). *Students:* 28 (17 women); includes 2 Asian, non-Hispanic/Latino, 3 international. 39 applicants, 77% accepted, 7 enrolled. In 2010, 3 master's awarded. *Degree requirements:* For master's, thesis. *Entrance requirements:* For master's, GRE General Test. Additional exam requirements/recommendations for international students: Required—TOEFL (minimum score 550 paper-based; 213 computer-based; 80 iBT). *Application deadline:* For fall admission, 4/1 priority date for domestic students; for spring admission, 11/15 for domestic students. Applications are processed on a rolling basis. Application fee: $40. Electronic applications accepted. *Expenses:* Tuition, state resident: part-time $537 per credit hour. Tuition, nonresident: part-time $1355 per credit hour. *Financial support:* Fellowships, research assistantships, teaching assistantships, career-related internships or fieldwork available. Financial award application deadline: 3/1. *Faculty research:* Agricultural production and marketing. *Unit head:* Dr. J. Kolodinsky, Chairperson, 802-656-2001. *Application contact:* Dr. J. Kolodinsky, Chairperson, 802-656-2001.

University of Wisconsin–Madison, Graduate School, College of Agricultural and Life Sciences, Department of Agricultural and Applied Economics, Madison, WI 53706. Offers MA, MS, PhD. Part-time programs available. *Faculty:* 23 full-time (3 women). *Students:* 52 full-time (24 women), 1 part-time (0 women); includes 2 Asian, non-Hispanic/Latino, 22 international. Average age 25. 205 applicants, 25% accepted, 10 enrolled. In 2010, 8 master's, 4 doctorates awarded. *Degree requirements:* For doctorate, thesis/dissertation, preliminary exams. *Entrance requirements:* For master's and doctorate, GRE General Test. Additional exam requirements/recommendations for international students: Required—TOEFL (minimum score 580 paper-based; 237 computer-based; 92 iBT). *Application deadline:* For fall admission, 2/1 priority date for domestic and international students. Application fee: $56. Electronic applications accepted. *Expenses:* Tuition, state resident: full-time $9887; part-time $617.96 per credit. Tuition, nonresident: full-time $24,054; part-time $1503.40 per credit. Required fees: $67.63 per credit. Tuition and fees vary according to reciprocity agreements. *Financial support:* In 2010–11, 41 students received support, including 3 fellowships with full tuition reimbursements available (averaging $18,760 per year), 42 research assistantships with full tuition reimbursements available (averaging $20,400 per year), 8 teaching assistantships with full tuition reimbursements available (averaging $14,100 per year); career-related internships or fieldwork, Federal Work-Study, traineeships, health care benefits, and unspecified assistantships also available. Support available to part-time students. Financial award application deadline: 12/15. *Faculty research:* Environmental and resource economics, international development, community economics, energy economics, agricultural technology, food systems, markets and trade. Total annual research expenditures: $35.8 million. *Unit head:* Prof. Kenneth Shapiro, Chair, 608-262-8966, Fax: 608-262-4376. *Application contact:* Barbara Forrest, Academic Programs Coordinator, 608-262-9489, Fax: 608-262-4376, E-mail: admissions@aae.wisc.edu.

University of Wyoming, College of Agriculture and Natural Resources, Department of Agricultural and Applied Economics, Laramie, WY 82070. Offers MS. Part-time programs available. *Degree requirements:* For master's, thesis (for some programs). *Entrance requirements:* For master's, GRE General Test, minimum GPA of 3.0. Additional exam requirements/recommendations for international students: Required—TOEFL. Electronic applications accepted. *Faculty research:* Farm management, agricultural markets, water economics, community development, agricultural business.

Utah State University, School of Graduate Studies, College of Business and College of Agriculture, Department of Economics, Program in Applied Economics, Logan, UT 84322. Offers MS. Part-time programs available. *Degree requirements:* For master's, thesis optional. *Entrance requirements:* For master's, GRE General Test, minimum GPA of 3.0.

Virginia Polytechnic Institute and State University, Graduate School, College of Agriculture and Life Sciences, Department of Agricultural and Applied Economics, Blacksburg, VA 24061. Offers MS, PhD. *Faculty:* 20 full-time (3 women). *Students:* 36 full-time (27 women), 2 part-time (1 woman); includes 2 Asian, non-Hispanic/Latino, 19 international. Average age 27. 58 applicants, 59% accepted, 11 enrolled. In 2010, 9 master's, 3 doctorates awarded. *Degree requirements:* For master's, comprehensive exam (for some programs), thesis (for some programs); for doctorate, comprehensive exam (for some programs), thesis/dissertation (for some programs). *Entrance requirements:* For master's and doctorate, GRE. Additional exam requirements/recommendations for international students: Required—TOEFL (minimum score 550 paper-based; 213 computer-based). *Application deadline:* For fall admission, 7/1 for domestic and international students; for spring admission, 12/1 for domestic and international students. Applications are processed on a rolling basis. Application fee: $65. Electronic applications accepted. *Expenses:* Tuition, state resident: full-time $9399; part-time $488 per credit hour. Tuition, nonresident: full-time $17,854; part-time $957.75 per credit hour. Required fees: $1534. Full-time tuition and fees vary according to program. *Financial support:* In 2010–11, 1 fellowship with full tuition reimbursement (averaging $20,000 per year), 25 research assistantships with full tuition reimbursements (averaging $20,332 per year), 8 teaching assistantships with full tuition reimbursements (averaging $15,387 per year) were awarded; career-related internships or fieldwork, Federal Work-Study, scholarships/grants, health care benefits, and unspecified assistantships also available. Financial award application deadline: 1/15. *Faculty research:* Rural development. Total annual research expenditures: $2.2 million. *Unit head:* Dr. Kevin Boyle, UNIT HEAD, 540-231-6301, Fax: 540-231-7417, E-mail: kjboyle@vt.edu. *Application contact:* Bradford Mills, Contact, 540-231-6461, Fax: 540-231-7417, E-mail: bfmills@vt.edu.

Washington State University, Graduate School, College of Agricultural, Human, and Natural Resource Sciences, School of Economic Sciences, Department of Economics, Pullman, WA 99164. Offers applied economics (MA); economics (MA, PhD); international business economics (Certificate). *Faculty:* 26. *Students:* 48 full-time (12 women), 2 part-time (1 woman); includes 3 minority (1 American Indian or Alaska Native, non-Hispanic/Latino; 1 Asian, non-Hispanic/Latino; 1 Hispanic/Latino), 26 international. Average age 30. 97 applicants, 21% accepted, 15 enrolled. In 2010, 8 doctorates awarded. *Degree requirements:* For master's, comprehensive exam (for some programs), thesis (for some programs), oral exam; for doctorate, comprehensive exam, thesis/dissertation, oral exam, written exam, field exams. *Entrance requirements:* For master's, GRE General Test, statement of purpose, three letters of reference, copies of all transcripts; for doctorate, GRE General Test or GMAT, statement of purpose, three letters of reference, copies of all transcripts. Additional exam requirements/recommendations for international students: Required—TOEFL, IELTS. *Application deadline:* For fall admission, 1/10 priority date for domestic students, 1/10 for international students. Applications are processed on a rolling basis. Application fee: $50. *Expenses:* Tuition, state resident: full-time $8552; part-time $443 per credit. Tuition, nonresident: full-time $21,650; part-time $1083 per credit. Required fees: $846. *Financial support:* In 2010–11, 16 research assistantships (averaging $18,204 per year), 7 teaching assistantships (averaging $18,204 per year) were awarded; career-related internships or fieldwork, Federal Work-Study, institutionally sponsored loans, tuition waivers (partial), and teaching associateships also available. Financial award application deadline: 4/1; financial award applicants required to submit FAFSA. *Faculty research:* Economic theory and quantitative methods, applied microeconomics. Total annual research expenditures: $1 million. *Unit head:* Dr. Ron C. Mittelhammer, Director, 509-335-1706, Fax: 509-335-1173, E-mail: mittelha@wsu.edu. *Application contact:* Graduate School Admissions, 800-GRADWSU, Fax: 509-335-1949, E-mail: gradsch@wsu.edu.

Western Kentucky University, Graduate Studies, Gordon Ford College of Business, Program in Applied Economics, Bowling Green, KY 42101. Offers MA.

Western Michigan University, Graduate College, College of Arts and Sciences, Department of Economics, Kalamazoo, MI 49008. Offers applied economics (MA, PhD). *Degree requirements:* For master's, thesis, oral or written exams; for doctorate, thesis/dissertation, oral exam, internship. *Entrance requirements:* For doctorate, GRE General Test.

Wright State University, School of Graduate Studies, Raj Soin College of Business, Department of Economics, Program in Social and Applied Economics, Dayton, OH 45435. Offers MS.

Economic Development

Albany State University, College of Arts and Humanities, Program in Public Administration, Albany, GA 31705-2717. Offers community and economic development administration (MPA); criminal justice administration (MPA); fiscal management (MPA); general management (MPA); health administration and policy (MPA); human resources management (MPA); public policy (MPA); water resource management and policy (MPA). *Accreditation:* NASPAA. *Faculty:* 3 full-time (1 woman), 2 part-time/adjunct (0 women). *Students:* 13 full-time (7 women), 49 part-time (32 women); includes 60 Black or African American, non-Hispanic/Latino, 1 international. Average age 34. 18 applicants, 78% accepted, 12 enrolled. In 2010, 12 master's awarded. *Degree requirements:* For master's, professional public service internship, professional portfolio, capstone research project. *Entrance requirements:* For master's, GRE, MAT, or GMAT, baccalaureate degree from accredited college or university, two letters of recommendation, ASU medical and immunization form. *Application deadline:* For fall admission, 7/15 for domestic students, 5/15 for international students; for spring admission, 11/15 for domestic students, 9/15 for international students. Applications are processed on a rolling basis. Application fee: $20. Electronic applications accepted. *Expenses:* Tuition, state resident: full-time $3060; part-time $170 per credit hour. Tuition, nonresident: full-time $12,204; part-time $678 per credit hour. Required fees: $1160. Part-time tuition and fees vary according to course load. *Financial support:* Application deadline: 4/15. *Faculty research:* Public policy, strategic public human resources and human capital management, diversity management in the public sector and collective bargaining and labor relations in the public sector, e-government and public sector information systems, public administration pedagogy and business process modeling simulation, community development, nonprofit organizations, civic engagement and civic participation, healthcare disparities among minorities, poverty. Total annual research expenditures: $250. *Unit head:* Dr. Peter Ngwafu, Director, 229-430-4760, Fax: 229-430-7895, E-mail: peter.ngwafu@asurams.edu. *Application contact:* Dr. Rani George, Dean, Graduate School, 229-430-5118, Fax: 229-430-6398, E-mail: rani.george@asurams.edu.

Boston University, Metropolitan College, Department of Administrative Sciences, Boston, MA 02215. Offers banking and financial management (MSM); business continuity in emergency management (MSM); economics development and tourism management (MSAS); electronic commerce, systems, and technology (MSAS); financial economics (MSAS); innovation and technology (MSAS); insurance management (MSM); international market management (MSM); multinational commerce (MSAS); project management (MSM). *Accreditation:* AACSB. Part-time and evening/weekend programs available. Postbaccalaureate distance learning degree programs offered (no on-campus study). *Faculty:* 14 full-time (2 women), 22 part-time/adjunct (2 women). *Students:* 107 full-time (51 women), 786 part-time (356 women); includes 130 minority (55 Black or African American, non-Hispanic/Latino; 1 American Indian or Alaska Native, non-Hispanic/Latino; 30 Asian, non-Hispanic/Latino; 36 Hispanic/Latino; 1 Native Hawaiian or other Pacific Islander, non-Hispanic/Latino; 7 Two or more races, non-Hispanic/Latino), 175 international. Average age 33. 398 applicants, 87% accepted, 180 enrolled. In 2010, 154 master's awarded. *Degree requirements:* For master's, thesis optional. *Entrance requirements:* For master's, 1 year of work experience, minimum GPA of 3.0. Additional exam requirements/recommendations for international students: Required—TOEFL (minimum score 560 paper-based; 220 computer-based; 84 iBT). *Application deadline:* Applications are processed on a rolling basis. Application fee: $70. Electronic applications accepted. *Expenses:* Tuition: Full-time $39,314; part-time $1228 per credit. Required fees: $40 per semester. *Financial support:* In 2010–11, 15 students received support, including 7 research assistantships with partial tuition reimbursements available (averaging $10,000 per year); career-related internships or fieldwork, Federal Work-Study, and unspecified assistantships also available. *Faculty research:* International business, innovative process. *Unit head:* Dr. Kip Becker, Chairman, 617-353-3016, E-mail: adminsc@bu.edu. *Application contact:* Lucille Dicker, Administrative Sciences Department, 617-353-3016, E-mail: adminsc@bu.edu.

Chicago State University, School of Graduate and Professional Studies, College of Arts and Sciences, Department of Geography, Sociology, Economics, and Anthropology, Chicago, IL 60628. Offers geography and economic development (MA). *Entrance requirements:* For master's, minimum GPA of 2.75.

Claremont Graduate University, Graduate Programs, School of Politics and Economics, Department of Economics, Claremont, CA 91711-6160. Offers business and financial economics (MA, PhD); economic development (Certificate); economics (PhD); industrial organization (PhD); international and development economics (PhD); international economics policy and development (MA); international money and finance (PhD); neuroeconomics (PhD); political economy and public policy (MA); public choice and public economics (PhD); MBA/PhD. Part-time programs available. *Faculty:* 8 full-time (0 women), 1 (woman) part-time/adjunct. *Students:* 128 full-time (39 women), 14 part-time (5 women); includes 3 Black or African American, non-Hispanic/Latino; 13 Asian, non-Hispanic/Latino; 5 Hispanic/Latino; 4 Two or more races, non-Hispanic/Latino, 73 international. Average age 32. In 2010, 13 master's, 8 doctorates awarded. *Entrance requirements:* For master's and doctorate, GRE General Test or GMAT. Additional exam requirements/recommendations for international students: Required—TOEFL (minimum score 550 paper-based; 213 computer-based; 80 iBT). *Application deadline:* For fall admission, 2/1 priority date for domestic students. Applications are processed on a rolling basis. Application fee: $60. Electronic applications accepted. *Expenses:* Tuition: Full-time $35,748; part-time $1554 per unit. Required fees: $215 per semester. *Financial support:* Fellowships, research assistantships, teaching assistantships, Federal Work-Study, institutionally sponsored loans, and scholarships/grants available. Support available to part-time students. Financial award application deadline: 2/15; financial award applicants required to submit FAFSA. *Faculty research:* International and financial economics, law and economics, regulation, public choice economics. *Unit head:* Paul Zak, Chair, 909-621-8788, Fax: 909-621-8545, E-mail: paul.zak@cgu.edu. *Application contact:* Lesa Hiben, Admissions Coordinator, 909-621-8699, Fax: 909-621-7545, E-mail: lesa.hiben@cga.edu.

Cleveland State University, College of Graduate Studies, Maxine Goodman Levin College of Urban Affairs, Program in Nonprofit Administration and Leadership, Cleveland, OH 44115. Offers geographic information systems (Certificate); local and urban management (Certificate); nonprofit administration and leadership (MNAL); nonprofit management (Certificate); urban economic development (Certificate). Part-time and evening/weekend programs available. *Faculty:* 10 full-time (9 women), 8 part-time/adjunct (4 women). *Students:* 11 full-time (10 women), 20 part-time (17 women); includes 7 Black or African American, non-Hispanic/Latino; 2 Asian, non-Hispanic/Latino. Average age 35. 35 applicants, 57% accepted, 14 enrolled. *Degree requirements:* For master's, thesis or alternative, capstone course. *Entrance requirements:* For master's, GRE (minimum 40th percentile verbal and quantitative, 4.0 analytical writing), minimum GPA of 3.0. Additional exam requirements/recommendations for international students: Required—TOEFL (minimum score 525 paper-based; 197 computer-based; 65 iBT). *Application deadline:* For fall admission, 7/15 priority date for domestic students, 5/15 for international students; for spring admission, 11/1 for international students. Applications are processed on a rolling basis. Application fee: $30. Electronic applications accepted. *Expenses:* Tuition, state resident: full-time $8447; part-time $469 per credit hour. Tuition, nonresident: full-time $16,020; part-time $890 per credit hour. Required fees: $50. *Financial support:* In 2010–11, 5 students received support, including research assistantships with full and partial tuition reimbursements available (averaging $6,960 per year); career-related internships or fieldwork, Federal Work-Study, scholarships/grants, tuition waivers (full and partial), and unspecified assistantships also available. Support available to part-time students. Financial award application deadline: 3/1; financial award applicants required to submit FAFSA. *Faculty research:* Human resource management, volunteerism, performance measurement in nonprofits, government-nonprofit partnerships. *Unit head:* Dr. Jennifer Alexander, Director, 216-687-5011, Fax: 216-687-2013, E-mail: j.k.alexander@csuohio.edu. *Application contact:* Joan Demko, Graduate Academic Support Specialist, 216-523-7522, Fax: 216-687-5398, E-mail: urbanprograms@csuohio.edu.

Cleveland State University, College of Graduate Studies, Maxine Goodman Levin College of Urban Affairs, Program in Urban Planning, Design, and Development, Cleveland, OH 44115. Offers geographic information systems (Certificate); local and urban management (Certificate); urban economic development (Certificate); urban planning, design, and development (MUPDD); urban real estate development and finance (Certificate); JD/MUPDD. *Accreditation:* ACSP. Part-time and evening/weekend programs available. *Faculty:* 32 full-time (19 women), 8 part-time/adjunct (4 women). *Students:* 30 full-time (10 women), 28 part-time (17 women); includes 6 Black or African American, non-Hispanic/Latino; 3 Hispanic/Latino, 5 international. Average age 38. 72 applicants, 56% accepted, 21 enrolled. In 2010, 24 master's, 9 Certificates awarded. *Degree requirements:* For master's, thesis or alternative, project or thesis. *Entrance requirements:* For master's, GRE General Test (minimum 50th percentile verbal and quantitative, 4.0 analytical writing), minimum GPA of 3.0. Additional exam requirements/recommendations for international students: Required—TOEFL (minimum score 525 paper-based; 197 computer-based; 65 iBT). *Application deadline:* For fall admission, 7/15 priority date for domestic students, 5/15 for international students; for spring admission, 11/1 for international students. Applications are processed on a rolling basis. Application fee: $30. Electronic applications accepted. *Expenses:* Tuition, state resident: full-time $8447; part-time $469 per credit hour. Tuition, nonresident: full-time $16,020; part-time $890 per credit hour. Required fees: $50. *Financial support:* In 2010–11, 15 students received support, including 10 research assistantships with full and partial tuition reimbursements available (averaging $6,960 per year), 5 teaching assistantships with full and partial tuition reimbursements available (averaging $6,960 per year); career-related internships or fieldwork, Federal Work-Study, tuition waivers (full and partial), and unspecified assistantships also available. Support available to part-time students. Financial award application deadline: 3/1. *Faculty research:* Housing and neighborhood development, urban housing policy, environmental sustainability, economic development, metropolitan change, GIS and planning decision support, PPGIS. *Unit head:* Dr. Dennis Keating, Director, 216-687-2298, Fax: 216-687-2013, E-mail: w.keating@csuohio.edu. *Application contact:* Joan Demkow, Graduate Program Coordinator, 216-523-7522, Fax: 216-687-5398, E-mail: urbanprograms@csuohio.edu.

Cleveland State University, College of Graduate Studies, Maxine Goodman Levin College of Urban Affairs, Program in Urban Studies, Cleveland, OH 44115. Offers geographic information systems (Certificate); local and urban management (Certificate); nonprofit management (Certificate); urban economic development (Certificate); urban real estate development and finance (Certificate); urban studies (MS); urban studies and public affairs (PhD). PhD program offered jointly with The University of Akron. Part-time and evening/weekend programs available. *Faculty:* 26 full-time (10 women), 20 part-time/adjunct (11 women). *Students:* 16 full-time (10 women), 35 part-time (18 women); includes 7 Black or African American, non-Hispanic/Latino, 17 international. Average age 37. 90 applicants, 38% accepted, 18 enrolled. In 2010, 6 master's, 7 doctorates, 6 other advanced degrees awarded. *Degree requirements:* For master's, thesis or alternative, exit project, capstone course; for doctorate, comprehensive exam, thesis/dissertation. *Entrance requirements:* For master's, GRE General Test, minimum GPA of 3.0; for doctorate, GRE General Test, minimum GPA of 3.5. Additional exam requirements/recommendations for international students: Required—TOEFL (minimum score 525 paper-based; 197 computer-based; 65 iBT). *Application deadline:* For fall admission, 7/15 priority date for domestic students, 5/15 for international students; for spring admission, 11/1 for international students. Applications are processed on a rolling basis. Application fee: $30.

Electronic applications accepted. *Expenses:* Tuition, state resident: full-time $8447; part-time $469 per credit hour. Tuition, nonresident: full-time $16,020; part-time $890 per credit hour. Required fees: $50. *Financial support:* In 2010–11, 15 students received support, including 11 research assistantships with full tuition reimbursements available (averaging $7,000 per year), 4 teaching assistantships with full and partial tuition reimbursements available (averaging $7,000 per year); career-related internships or fieldwork, Federal Work-Study, institutionally sponsored loans, scholarships/grants, tuition waivers (full and partial), and unspecified assistantships also available. Support available to part-time students. Financial award application deadline: 3/1; financial award applicants required to submit FAFSA. *Faculty research:* Environmental issues, economic development, urban and public policy, public management. *Unit head:* Dr. Sugie Lee, Director, 216-687-2381, Fax: 216-687-9342, E-mail: s.lee56@csuohio.edu. *Application contact:* Joan Demko, Graduate Academic Support Specialist, 216-523-7522, Fax: 216-687-5398, E-mail: urbanprograms@csuohio.edu.

Concordia University, School of Graduate Studies, Faculty of Arts and Science, School of Community and Public Affairs, Montréal, QC H3G 1M8, Canada. Offers community economic development (Diploma).

Cornell University, Graduate School, Graduate Fields of Architecture, Art and Planning, Field of City and Regional Planning, Ithaca, NY 14853-0001. Offers city and regional planning (MRP, PhD); environmental planning and design (MRP, PhD); historic preservation planning (MA); international development planning (MRP, PhD); planning theory and systems analysis (MRP, PhD); regional economics and development planning (MRP, PhD); regional science (MRP, PhD); social and health systems planning (MRP, PhD); urban and regional theory (MRP, PhD); urban planning history (MRP, PhD). *Accreditation:* ACSP (one or more programs are accredited). *Faculty:* 31 full-time (10 women). *Students:* 136 full-time (66 women); includes 6 Black or African American, non-Hispanic/Latino; 10 Asian, non-Hispanic/Latino; 9 Hispanic/Latino, 20 international. Average age 27. 452 applicants, 32% accepted, 64 enrolled. In 2010, 42 master's, 4 doctorates awarded. *Degree requirements:* For master's, thesis (MA); for doctorate, comprehensive exam, thesis/dissertation. *Entrance requirements:* For master's and doctorate, GRE General Test, 2 letters of recommendation. Additional exam requirements/recommendations for international students: Required—TOEFL (minimum score 600 paper-based; 250 computer-based; 77 iBT). *Application deadline:* For fall admission, 1/10 for domestic students. Application fee: $70. Electronic applications accepted. *Expenses:* Tuition: Full-time $29,500. Required fees: $76. Tuition and fees vary according to degree level and program. *Financial support:* In 2010–11, 9 fellowships with full tuition reimbursements, 2 research assistantships with full tuition reimbursements, 13 teaching assistantships with full tuition reimbursements were awarded; institutionally sponsored loans, scholarships/grants, health care benefits, tuition waivers (full and partial), and unspecified assistantships also available. Financial award applicants required to submit FAFSA. *Faculty research:* Land use planning, economic development, international development, historic preservation, community development. *Unit head:* Director of Graduate Studies, 607-255-6848, Fax: 607-255-1971. *Application contact:* Graduate Field Assistant, 607-255-6848, Fax: 607-255-1971, E-mail: crp_admissions@cornell.edu.

Cornell University, Graduate School, Graduate Fields of Arts and Sciences, Field of Economics, Ithaca, NY 14853-0001. Offers applied economics (PhD); basic analytical economics (PhD); econometrics and economic statistics (PhD); economic development and planning (PhD); economic theory (PhD); industrial organization and control (PhD); international economics (PhD); labor economics (PhD); monetary and macroeconomics (PhD); public finance (PhD). *Faculty:* 78 full-time (10 women). *Students:* 100 full-time (40 women); includes 1 Black or African American, non-Hispanic/Latino; 4 Asian, non-Hispanic/Latino; 1 Hispanic/Latino, 61 international. Average age 27. 742 applicants, 10% accepted, 20 enrolled. In 2010, 21 doctorates awarded. *Degree requirements:* For doctorate, comprehensive exam, thesis/dissertation. *Entrance requirements:* For doctorate, GRE General Test, 3 letters of recommendation. Additional exam requirements/recommendations for international students: Required—TOEFL (minimum score 550 paper-based; 213 computer-based; 77 iBT). *Application deadline:* For fall admission, 1/15 priority date for domestic students. Application fee: $80. Electronic applications accepted. *Expenses:* Tuition: Full-time $29,500. Required fees: $76. Tuition and fees vary according to degree level and program. *Financial support:* In 2010–11, 20 fellowships with full tuition reimbursements, 16 research assistantships with full tuition reimbursements, 50 teaching assistantships with full tuition reimbursements were awarded; institutionally sponsored loans, scholarships/grants, health care benefits, tuition waivers (full and partial), and unspecified assistantships also available. Financial award applicants required to submit FAFSA. *Faculty research:* Learning and games, economics of education, political economy, transfer payments, time series and nonparametrics. *Unit head:* Director of Graduate Studies, 607-255-4893, Fax: 607-255-2818. *Application contact:* Graduate Field Assistant, 607-255-4893, Fax: 607-255-2818, E-mail: econ_phd@cornell.edu.

Eastern Michigan University, Graduate School, College of Arts and Sciences, Department of Economics, Ypsilanti, MI 48197. Offers applied economics (MA); economics (MA); health economics (MA); international economics and development (MA); trade and development (MA). Part-time and evening/weekend programs available. Postbaccalaureate distance learning degree programs offered (minimal on-campus study). *Faculty:* 11 full-time (2 women). *Students:* 25 full-time (5 women), 32 part-time (7 women); includes 19 minority (10 Black or African American, non-Hispanic/Latino; 1 American Indian or Alaska Native, non-Hispanic/Latino; 4 Asian, non-Hispanic/Latino; 4 Hispanic/Latino), 7 international. Average age 29. 50 applicants, 74% accepted, 19 enrolled. In 2010, 18 master's awarded. *Degree requirements:* For master's, thesis or alternative. *Entrance requirements:* Additional exam requirements/recommendations for international students: Required—TOEFL. *Application deadline:* Applications are processed on a rolling basis. Application fee: $35. *Financial support:* Fellowships, research assistantships with full tuition reimbursements, teaching assistantships with full tuition reimbursements, career-related internships or fieldwork, Federal Work-Study, institutionally sponsored loans, scholarships/grants, tuition waivers (partial), and unspecified assistantships available. Support available to part-time students. Financial award applicants required to submit FAFSA. *Unit head:* Dr. Raouf S. Hanna, Department Head, 734-487-3395, Fax: 734-487-9666, E-mail: rhanna@emich.edu. *Application contact:* Dr. David Crary, Advisor, 734-487-0001, Fax: 734-487-9666, E-mail: dcrary@emich.edu.

Eastern University, School of Leadership and Development, St. Davids, PA 19087-3696. Offers economic development (MBA), including international development, urban development (MA, MBA); international development (MA), including global development, urban development (MA, MBA); nonprofit management (MS); organizational leadership (MA); M Div/MBA. Part-time and evening/weekend programs available. *Degree requirements:* For master's, thesis (for some programs). *Entrance requirements:* For master's, GMAT (MBA), minimum GPA of 2.5. *Expenses:* Contact institution. *Faculty research:* Micro-level economic development, China welfare and economic development, macroethics, micro- and macro-level economic development in transitional economics, organizational effectiveness.

Florida Atlantic University, College of Design and Social Inquiry, School of Urban and Regional Planning, Boca Raton, FL 33431-0991. Offers economic development and tourism (Certificate); environmental planning (Certificate); sustainable community planning (Certificate); urban and regional planning (MURP); visual planning technology (Certificate). *Accreditation:* ACSP. Part-time and evening/weekend programs available. *Faculty:* 8 full-time (5 women), 2 part-time/adjunct (1 woman). *Students:* 24 full-time (18 women), 12 part-time (1 woman); includes 17 minority (4 Black or African American, non-Hispanic/Latino; 1 American Indian or Alaska Native, non-Hispanic/Latino; 12 Hispanic/Latino), 2 international. Average age 30. 55 applicants, 35% accepted, 12 enrolled. In 2010, 13 master's awarded. *Entrance requirements:* For master's, GRE General Test, minimum GPA of 3.0. Additional exam requirements/recommendations for international students: Required—TOEFL. *Application deadline:* For fall admission, 7/1 priority date for domestic students, 2/15 for international students; for spring admission, 11/1 priority date for domestic students, 7/15 for international students. Applications are processed on a rolling basis. Application fee: $30. *Expenses:* Tuition, area resident: Part-time $319.96 per credit. Tuition, state resident: part-time $319.96 per credit. Tuition,

Economic Development

Florida Atlantic University (continued)
nonresident: part-time $926.42 per credit. *Financial support:* Fellowships with full tuition reimbursements, research assistantships, career-related internships or fieldwork, Federal Work-Study, institutionally sponsored loans, and tuition waivers (partial) available. Financial award application deadline: 4/1. *Faculty research:* Growth management, urban design, computer applications/geographical information systems, environmental planning. *Unit head:* Dr. Jaap Vos, Chair, 954-762-5653, Fax: 954-762-5673, E-mail: jvos@fau.edu. *Application contact:* Dr. Jaap Vos, Chair, 954-762-5653, Fax: 954-762-5673, E-mail: jvos@fau.edu.

Fordham University, Graduate School of Arts and Sciences, Program in International Political Economy and Development, New York, NY 10458. Offers MA, Certificate. Part-time and evening/weekend programs available. *Students:* 44 full-time (22 women), 27 part-time (11 women); includes 1 American Indian or Alaska Native, non-Hispanic/Latino; 1 Asian, non-Hispanic/Latino; 4 Hispanic/Latino, 19 international. Average age 28. 213 applicants, 37% accepted, 36 enrolled. In 2010, 28 master's awarded. *Degree requirements:* For master's, comprehensive exam. *Entrance requirements:* For master's, GRE General Test. Additional exam requirements/recommendations for international students: Required—TOEFL (minimum score 600 paper-based; 250 computer-based). *Application deadline:* For fall admission, 1/4 priority date for domestic students; for spring admission, 11/1 for domestic students. Application fee: $70. Electronic applications accepted. *Financial support:* In 2010–11, 16 students received support, including 16 research assistantships with tuition reimbursements available (averaging $18,400 per year); career-related internships or fieldwork, institutionally sponsored loans, tuition waivers (full and partial), and unspecified assistantships also available. Financial award application deadline: 1/4; financial award applicants required to submit FAFSA. *Faculty research:* International economics, comparative international politics, international banking and finance, international development, emerging markets and country risk analysis. *Unit head:* Dr. Henry Schwalbenberg, Chair, 718-817-3866, Fax: 718-817-3518. *Application contact:* Charlene Dundie, Director of Graduate Admissions, 718-817-4420, Fax: 718-817-3566, E-mail: dundie@fordham.edu.

Georgetown University, Graduate School of Arts and Sciences, Department of Economics, Washington, DC 20057. Offers econometrics (PhD); economic development (PhD); economic theory (PhD); industrial organization (PhD); international macro and finance (PhD); international trade (PhD); labor economics (PhD); macroeconomics (PhD); public economics and political economics (PhD); MA/PhD; MS/MA. *Degree requirements:* For doctorate, comprehensive exam, thesis/dissertation. *Entrance requirements:* For doctorate, GRE General Test. Additional exam requirements/recommendations for international students: Required—TOEFL. *Faculty research:* International economics, economic development.

Georgia Institute of Technology, Graduate Studies and Research, College of Architecture, City and Regional Planning Program, Atlanta, GA 30332-0001. Offers city and regional planning (PhD); economic development (MCRP); environmental planning and management (MCRP); geographic information systems (MCRP); land and community development (MCRP); land use planning (MCRP); transportation (MCRP); urban design (MCRP); MCP/MSCE. *Accreditation:* ACSP. *Degree requirements:* For master's, thesis, internship. *Entrance requirements:* For master's, GRE General Test, minimum GPA of 2.7. Additional exam requirements/recommendations for international students: Required—TOEFL. Electronic applications accepted.

Georgia State University, Andrew Young School of Policy Studies, Department of Public Management and Policy, Atlanta, GA 30303. Offers disaster management (Certificate); nonprofit management (Certificate); planning and economic development (Certificate); public administration (MPA), including criminal justice, management and finance, nonprofit management, planning and economic development, policy analysis and evaluation, public health; public policy (MPP, PhD), including disaster policy (MPP), nonprofit policy (MPP), planning and economic development policy (MPP), public finance policy (MPP), social policy (MPP); JD/MPA. *Accreditation:* NASPAA (one or more programs are accredited). Part-time and evening/weekend programs available. Terminal master's awarded for partial completion of doctoral program. *Degree requirements:* For master's, thesis optional; for doctorate, comprehensive exam, thesis/dissertation. *Entrance requirements:* For master's and doctorate, GRE General Test. Additional exam requirements/recommendations for international students: Required—TOEFL. Electronic applications accepted. *Faculty research:* Public management, policy analysis, public finance, planning and economic development, nonprofit leadership and policy.

Indiana University Bloomington, School of Public and Environmental Affairs, Public Affairs Programs, Bloomington, IN 47405-7000. Offers comparative and international affairs (MPA); economic development (MPA); energy (MPA); environmental policy (PhD); environmental policy and natural resource management (MPA); information systems (MPA); local government management (MPA); nonprofit management (MPA, Certificate); policy analysis (MPA); public finance (PhD); public financial administration (MPA); public management (MPA, PhD); public policy analysis (PhD); specialized public affairs (MPA); sustainability and sustainable development (MPA); JD/MPA; MPA/MIS; MPA/MLS; MSES/MPA. *Accreditation:* NASPAA (one or more programs are accredited). Part-time programs available. *Faculty:* 31 full-time, 15 part-time/adjunct. *Students:* 466 full-time (261 women); includes 11 Black or African American, non-Hispanic/Latino; 2 American Indian or Alaska Native, non-Hispanic/Latino; 42 Asian, non-Hispanic/Latino; 1 Hispanic/Latino, 65 international. Average age 26. 650 applicants, 218 enrolled. In 2010, 166 master's, 10 doctorates awarded. *Degree requirements:* For master's, core classes, capstone; for doctorate, comprehensive exam, thesis/dissertation. *Entrance requirements:* For master's, GRE General Test or GMAT, official transcripts, 3 letters of recommendation, resume, personal statement, departmental questions; for doctorate, GRE General Test or LSAT, official transcripts, 3 letters of recommendation, resume or curriculum vitae, statement of purpose. Additional exam requirements/recommendations for international students: Required—TOEFL (minimum score 600 paper-based; 96 iBT); Recommended—IELTS (minimum score 7). *Application deadline:* For fall admission, 5/1 priority date for domestic students, 12/1 priority date for international students. Applications are processed on a rolling basis. Application fee: $55 ($65 for international students). Electronic applications accepted. *Financial support:* Fellowships with partial tuition reimbursements, research assistantships with partial tuition reimbursements, teaching assistantships with partial tuition reimbursements, career-related internships or fieldwork, Federal Work-Study, scholarships/grants, health care benefits, unspecified assistantships, and Service Corps programs available. Financial award application deadline: 2/1; financial award applicants required to submit FAFSA. *Faculty research:* Comparative and international affairs, environmental policy and resource management, policy analysis, public finance, public management, urban management, nonprofit management, energy policy, social policy, public finance. *Unit head:* Jennifer Forney, Director of Graduate Student Services, 812-855-9485, Fax: 812-856-3665, E-mail: speampo@indiana.edu. *Application contact:* Audrey Whitaker, Admissions Assistant, 812-855-2840, E-mail: speaapps@indiana.edu.

See Close-Up on page 1271.

New Mexico State University, Graduate School, College of Business, Department of Economics, Applied Statistics and International Business, Las Cruces, NM 88003. Offers applied statistics (MS); economic development (DED); economics (MA). Part-time programs available. *Faculty:* 12 full-time (2 women), 2 part-time/adjunct (1 woman). *Students:* 64 full-time (21 women), 16 part-time (5 women); includes 22 minority (3 Black or African American, non-Hispanic/Latino; 2 Asian, non-Hispanic/Latino; 17 Hispanic/Latino), 37 international. Average age 31. 84 applicants, 83% accepted, 34 enrolled. In 2010, 16 master's awarded. Terminal master's awarded for partial completion of doctoral program. *Degree requirements:* For master's, comprehensive exam, thesis or alternative; for doctorate, comprehensive exam, thesis/dissertation, internship, written project. *Entrance requirements:* For master's, minimum GPA of 3.0; for doctorate, appropriate master's degree, minimum GPA of 3.0. Additional exam requirements/recommendations for international students: Required—TOEFL (minimum score 530 paper-based; 71 computer-based), IELTS. *Application deadline:* Applications are processed on a rolling basis. Application fee: $30 ($50 for international students). Electronic applications accepted. *Expenses:* Tuition, state resident: full-time $4536; part-time $242 per credit. Tuition, nonresident: full-time $15,816; part-time $712 per credit. Required fees: $636 per term. *Financial support:* In 2010–11, 34 students received support, including 14 research assistantships (averaging $11,225 per year), 29 teaching assistantships (averaging $6,846 per year); fellowships, career-related internships or fieldwork, Federal Work-Study, and health care benefits also available. Support available to part-time students. Financial award application deadline: 3/1. *Faculty research:* Public utilities, environment, linear models, biological sampling, public policy, economic development, energy. *Unit head:* Dr. Richard V. Adkisson, Head, 575-646-4988, Fax: 575-646-1915, E-mail: radkisso@nmsu.edu. *Application contact:* Dr. Richard V. Adkisson, Head, 575-646-4988, Fax: 575-646-1915, E-mail: radkisso@nmsu.edu.

Southern New Hampshire University, School of Community Economic Development, Manchester, NH 03106-1045. Offers MA, MBA, MS, PhD. Part-time and evening/weekend programs available. *Degree requirements:* For master's, thesis or alternative, community project; for doctorate, comprehensive exam, thesis/dissertation, community project. *Entrance requirements:* For master's, 2 years of work experience, minimum GPA of 3.0, 2 letters of recommendation, review; for doctorate, 2 years of work experience, minimum GPA of 3.5, 3 letters of recommendation, research samples. Additional exam requirements/recommendations for international students: Required—TOEFL (minimum score 550 paper-based; 300 computer-based; 70 iBT). Electronic applications accepted. *Expenses:* Contact institution.

Troy University, Graduate School, College of Business, Program in Business Administration, Troy, AL 36082. Offers accounting (EMBA, MBA); criminal justice (EMBA); finance (MBA); general management (EMBA, MBA); healthcare management (EMBA); information systems (EMBA, MBA); international economic development (MBA). *Accreditation:* ACBSP. Part-time and evening/weekend programs available. *Students:* 351 full-time (198 women), 745 part-time (452 women); includes 589 minority (425 Black or African American, non-Hispanic/Latino; 13 American Indian or Alaska Native, non-Hispanic/Latino; 129 Asian, non-Hispanic/Latino; 21 Hispanic/Latino; 1 Two or more races, non-Hispanic/Latino). Average age 29. 748 applicants, 71% accepted. In 2010, 322 master's awarded. *Degree requirements:* For master's, minimum GPA 3.0, capstone course, research course. *Entrance requirements:* For master's, GMAT (minimum score 500) or GRE General Test (minimum score 900), minimum GPA of 2.5; letter of recommendation, bachelor's degree. Additional exam requirements/recommendations for international students: Required—TOEFL (minimum score 523 paper-based; 193 computer-based; 70 iBT), IELTS (minimum score 6), or ACT compass ESL (minimum Listening, Reading, and Grammar score: 270). *Application deadline:* Applications are processed on a rolling basis. Application fee: $50. *Expenses:* Tuition, state resident: full-time $4428; part-time $246 per credit hour. Tuition, nonresident: full-time $8856; part-time $492 per credit hour. Required fees: $432; $24 per credit hour. $50 per term. Tuition and fees vary according to program. *Unit head:* Dr. Henry M. Findley, Interim Chair/Professor, 334-670-3271, Fax: 334-670-3599, E-mail: hfindley@troy.edu. *Application contact:* Brenda K. Campbell, Director of Graduate Admissions, 334-670-3178, Fax: 334-670-3733, E-mail: bcamp@troy.edu.

Université de Sherbrooke, Faculty of Administration, PhD Program in Economic Development, Sherbrooke, QC J1K 2R1, Canada. Offers PhD. *Faculty:* 21 full-time (11 women). *Degree requirements:* For doctorate, one foreign language, comprehensive exam, thesis/dissertation, advanced English as a second language. *Application deadline:* For fall admission, 4/30 for domestic students, 1/15 for international students. Application fee: $70. *Faculty research:* Impact analysis of economical policies; productivity, competitivity and international commerce; macroeconometric modelisation; environmental economy. *Unit head:* Dorothe Boccanfuso, Director of the program, 819-821-8000 Ext. 65169, Fax: 819-821-7934, E-mail: dorothee.boccanfuso@usherbrooke.ca. *Application contact:* Marie-Claude Drouin, Assistant to the director, 819-821-8000 Ext. 63301, Fax: 819-819-7364, E-mail: marie-claude.drouin@usherbrooke.ca.

University of Central Arkansas, Graduate School, College of Liberal Arts, Department of Geography, Conway, AR 72035-0001. Offers community and economic development (MS); geographic information systems (MGIS, Certificate). Part-time programs available. Postbaccalaureate distance learning degree programs offered (minimal on-campus study). *Faculty:* 3 full-time (0 women). *Students:* 4 full-time (1 woman), 11 part-time (1 woman); includes 1 minority (Black or African American, non-Hispanic/Latino). Average age 30. 6 applicants, 100% accepted, 5 enrolled. *Entrance requirements:* Additional exam requirements/recommendations for international students: Required—TOEFL (minimum score 550 paper-based; 213 computer-based). *Application deadline:* For fall admission, 3/1 priority date for domestic and international students; for spring admission, 10/1 priority date for domestic and international students. Applications are processed on a rolling basis. Application fee: $25 ($50 for international students). *Financial support:* Applicants required to submit FAFSA. *Unit head:* Dr. Brooks Green, Chairperson, 501-450-5636, Fax: 501-450-5185, E-mail: brooksg@uca.edu. *Application contact:* Susan Wood, Admissions Assistant, 501-450-3124, Fax: 501-450-5678, E-mail: swood@uca.edu.

University of Central Arkansas, Graduate School, College of Liberal Arts, Program in Community and Economic Development, Conway, AR 72035-0001. Offers MS. *Students:* 7 full-time (1 woman), 17 part-time (5 women); includes 8 minority (5 Black or African American, non-Hispanic/Latino; 2 Hispanic/Latino; 1 Two or more races, non-Hispanic/Latino), 2 international. Average age 31. 14 applicants, 100% accepted, 11 enrolled. In 2010, 9 master's awarded. *Degree requirements:* For master's, comprehensive exam, thesis. *Entrance requirements:* For master's, GRE General Test, minimum GPA of 2.7. Additional exam requirements/recommendations for international students: Required—TOEFL (minimum score 550 paper-based; 213 computer-based). *Application deadline:* For fall admission, 3/1 priority date for domestic students; for spring admission, 10/1 priority date for domestic students. Applications are processed on a rolling basis. Application fee: $25 ($40 for international students). *Expenses:* Contact institution. *Financial support:* Career-related internships or fieldwork, Federal Work-Study, and unspecified assistantships available. Financial award applicants required to submit FAFSA. *Unit head:* Dr. Lauren Maxwell, Coordinator, 501-450-5349. *Application contact:* Brenda Herring, Admissions Assistant, 501-450-5065, Fax: 501-450-5678, E-mail: bherring@uca.edu.

University of Colorado Denver, College of Architecture and Planning, Program in Urban and Regional Planning, Denver, CO 80217-3364. Offers economic and community development planning (MURP); land use and environmental planning (MURP); urban place making (MURP). *Accreditation:* ACSP. Part-time programs available. *Students:* 125 full-time (57 women), 5 part-time (3 women); includes 1 Black or African American, non-Hispanic/Latino; 2 American Indian or Alaska Native, non-Hispanic/Latino; 3 Asian, non-Hispanic/Latino; 8 Hispanic/Latino, 9 international. Average age 30. 145 applicants, 68% accepted, 38 enrolled. In 2010, 47 master's awarded. *Degree requirements:* For master's, thesis optional, minimum of 51 semester hours. *Entrance requirements:* For master's, GRE if GPA below 3.0, writing sample. Additional exam requirements/recommendations for international students: Required—TOEFL (minimum score 550 paper-based; 213 computer-based). *Application deadline:* For fall admission, 2/15 for domestic students; for spring admission, 10/1 for domestic students. Application fee: $50 ($75 for international students). Electronic applications accepted. *Expenses:* Contact institution. *Financial support:* Career-related internships or fieldwork, Federal Work-Study, and scholarships/grants available. Financial award application deadline: 4/1; financial award applicants required to submit FAFSA. *Faculty research:* Physical planning, environmental planning, economic development planning. *Unit head:* Brian Muller, Associate Professor and Chair, 303-556-5967, E-mail: brian.muller@ucdenver.edu. *Application contact:* Brian Muller, Associate Professor and Chair, 303-556-5967, E-mail: brian.muller@ucdenver.edu.

University of Houston–Victoria, School of Business Administration, Victoria, TX 77901-4450. Offers accounting (MBA); economic development and entrepreneurship (MS); finance (GMBA, MBA); general business (MBA); international business (MBA); management (GMBA, MBA); marketing (MBA). *Accreditation:* AACSB. Part-time and evening/weekend programs available. Postbaccalaureate distance learning degree programs offered (minimal on-campus study). *Faculty:* 37 full-time (11 women). *Students:* 234 full-time (108 women), 714 part-time (303 women); includes 542 minority (215 Black or African American, non-Hispanic/Latino; 1

American Indian or Alaska Native, non-Hispanic/Latino; 197 Asian, non-Hispanic/Latino; 124 Hispanic/Latino; 1 Native Hawaiian or other Pacific Islander, non-Hispanic/Latino; 4 Two or more races, non-Hispanic/Latino), 115 international. Average age 34. 362 applicants, 65% accepted, 147 enrolled. In 2010, 181 master's awarded. *Entrance requirements:* For master's, GMAT. Additional exam requirements/recommendations for international students: Required—TOEFL (minimum score 550 paper-based; 213 computer-based). *Application deadline:* For fall admission, 6/1 for international students; for spring admission, 10/1 for international students. Applications are processed on a rolling basis. Application fee: $0. Electronic applications accepted. *Expenses:* Tuition, state resident: full-time $4050; part-time $225 per credit hour. Tuition, nonresident: full-time $8730; part-time $485 per credit hour. Required fees: $810; $54 per credit hour. Tuition and fees vary according to course load. *Financial support:* In 2010–11, research assistantships with partial tuition reimbursements (averaging $2,000 per year), teaching assistantships with partial tuition reimbursements (averaging $2,000 per year) were awarded; Federal Work-Study, scholarships/grants, and unspecified assistantships also available. Support available to part-time students. Financial award application deadline: 4/15; financial award applicants required to submit FAFSA. *Faculty research:* Economic development, marketing, finance. *Unit head:* Dr. Farhang Niroomand, Dean, 361-570-4230, Fax: 361-580-5599, E-mail: niroomandf@uhv.edu. *Application contact:* Jane Mims, Assistant Dean, 361-570-4639, Fax: 361-580-5529, E-mail: mims@uhv.edu.

University of Massachusetts Lowell, College of Arts and Sciences, Department of Regional Economic and Social Development, Lowell, MA 01854-2881. Offers MA, Graduate Certificate. Part-time programs available. *Entrance requirements:* For master's, GRE. Electronic applications accepted.

University of Miami, Graduate School, School of Business Administration, Department of Economics, Coral Gables, FL 33124. Offers economic development (MA, PhD); environmental economics (PhD); human resource economics (MA, PhD); international economics (MA, PhD); macroeconomics (PhD). Students admitted every two years in the fall semester. Terminal master's awarded for partial completion of doctoral program. *Degree requirements:* For master's, comprehensive exam; for doctorate, comprehensive exam, thesis/dissertation. *Entrance requirements:* For master's and doctorate, GRE General Test, minimum GPA of 3.0. Additional exam requirements/recommendations for international students: Required—TOEFL (minimum score 550 paper-based). *Faculty research:* International economics/trade, applied microeconomics, development.

University of Minnesota, Twin Cities Campus, Graduate School, Hubert H. Humphrey School of Public Affairs, Program in Public Policy, Minneapolis, MN 55455-0213. Offers advanced policy analysis methods (MPP); economic and community development (MPP); foreign policy (MPP); public and nonprofit leadership and management (MPP); science technology and environmental policy (MPP); social policy (MPP); women and public policy (MPP); JD/MPP; MPP/MS; MSW/MPP. Part-time programs available. *Degree requirements:* For master's, thesis or alternative, internship or equivalent work experience. *Entrance requirements:* For master's, GRE General Test, minimum undergraduate GPA of 3.0. Additional exam requirements/recommendations for international students: Required—TOEFL (minimum score 600 paper-based; 250 computer-based; 100 iBT). Electronic applications accepted. *Faculty research:* Social policy, public and non-profit management and leadership, community and economic development, foreign policy and international affairs, women and public policy.

University of Minnesota, Twin Cities Campus, Graduate School, Hubert H. Humphrey School of Public Affairs, Program in Urban and Regional Planning, Minneapolis, MN 55455-0213. Offers environmental planning (MURP); housing and community development (MURP); land use and urban design (MURP); regional, economic and workforce development (MURP); transportation planning (MURP); JD/MURP; MURP/MLA; MURP/MS. *Accreditation:* ACSP (one or more programs are accredited). Part-time programs available. *Degree requirements:* For master's, thesis or alternative, internship or equivalent work experience. *Entrance requirements:* For master's, GRE General Test, minimum undergraduate GPA of 3.0. Additional exam requirements/recommendations for international students: Required—TOEFL (minimum score 600 paper-based; 250 computer-based; 100 iBT). Electronic applications accepted. *Faculty research:* Policy planning, resource allocation planning, regulatory planning, program planning, project planning.

The University of North Carolina at Greensboro, Graduate School, College of Arts and Sciences, Department of Geography, Greensboro, NC 27412-5001. Offers applied geography (MA); geographic information science (Certificate); geography (PhD); urban and economic development (Certificate). *Degree requirements:* For master's, comprehensive exam, thesis or alternative. *Entrance requirements:* For master's, GRE General Test. Additional exam requirements/recommendations for international students: Required—TOEFL. Electronic applications accepted.

The University of North Carolina at Greensboro, Graduate School, College of Arts and Sciences, Department of Political Science, Greensboro, NC 27412-5001. Offers nonprofit management (Certificate); public affairs (MPA); urban and economic development (Certificate). *Accreditation:* NASPAA. *Degree requirements:* For master's, comprehensive exam. *Entrance requirements:* For master's, GRE General Test. Additional exam requirements/recommendations for international students: Required—TOEFL. Electronic applications accepted. *Faculty research:* U.S. Constitution, Canadian parliament, public management, ethical challenge of public service.

University of Puerto Rico, Río Piedras, Graduate School of Planning, San Juan, PR 00931-3300. Offers economic planning systems (MP); environmental planning (MP); social policy and planning (MP); urban and territorial planning (MP). *Accreditation:* ACSP. Part-time programs available. *Degree requirements:* For master's, comprehensive exam, thesis, planning project defense. *Entrance requirements:* For master's, PAEG, GRE, minimum GPA of 3.0, 2 letters of recommendation. *Faculty research:* Municipalities, historic Atlas, Puerto Rico, economic future.

University of Southern California, Graduate School, Dana and David Dornsife College of Letters, Arts and Sciences, Department of Economics, Los Angeles, CA 90089. Offers economic development programming (MA, PhD); mathematical finance (MS); M Pl/MA; MA/JD. *Faculty:* 20 full-time (2 women), 9 part-time/adjunct (0 women). *Students:* 106 full-time (41 women), 6 part-time (0 women); includes 7 minority (5 Asian, non-Hispanic/Latino; 2 Two or more races, non-Hispanic/Latino), 89 international. 417 applicants, 19% accepted, 40 enrolled. In 2010, 34 master's, 9 doctorates awarded. Terminal master's awarded for partial completion of doctoral program. *Degree requirements:* For master's, comprehensive exam; for doctorate, comprehensive exam, thesis/dissertation. *Entrance requirements:* For master's and doctorate, GRE. Additional exam requirements/recommendations for international students: Required—TOEFL (minimum score 93 iBT). *Application deadline:* For fall admission, 12/1 priority date for domestic and international students. Application fee: $85. Electronic applications accepted. *Expenses:* Tuition: Full-time $31,240; part-time $1420 per unit. Required fees: $600. One-time fee: $35 full-time. Full-time tuition and fees vary according to degree level and program. *Financial support:* In 2010–11, 53 students received support, including 24 fellowships with full tuition reimbursements available (averaging $21,000 per year), 3 research assistantships with full tuition reimbursements available (averaging $21,000 per year), 27 teaching assistantships with full tuition reimbursements available (averaging $21,000 per year). Financial award application deadline: 12/1. *Faculty research:* Macro theory, development economics, econometrics. *Unit head:* Prof. Simon Wilkie, Chair, 213-740-8335, Fax: 213-740-8543, E-mail: swilkie@usc.edu. *Application contact:* Morgan Ponder, Assistant Director, 213-740-3507, Fax: 213-740-8543, E-mail: ponder@dornsife.usc.edu.

University of Southern Mississippi, Graduate School, College of Science and Technology, Department of Economic and Workforce Development, Hattiesburg, MS 39406-0001. Offers economic development (MS); human capital development (PhD); workforce training and development (MS). Part-time and evening/weekend programs available. *Faculty:* 6 full-time (3 women). *Students:* 37 full-time (14 women), 50 part-time (31 women); includes 22 Black or African American, non-Hispanic/Latino; 1 Asian, non-Hispanic/Latino; 1 Hispanic/Latino; 1 Two or more races, non-Hispanic/Latino. Average age 41. 27 applicants, 74% accepted, 17 enrolled. In 2010, 17 master's, 2 doctorates awarded. *Degree requirements:* For master's, comprehensive exam, thesis optional, internships; for doctorate, comprehensive exam, thesis/dissertation. *Entrance requirements:* For master's, GMAT or GRE General Test, minimum GPA of 2.75 in last 60 hours; for doctorate, GMAT or GRE General Test, minimum GPA of 3.5. Additional exam requirements/recommendations for international students: Required—TOEFL, IELTS. *Application deadline:* For fall admission, 8/1 for domestic students, 3/1 for international students; for spring admission, 1/3 for domestic and international students. Applications are processed on a rolling basis. Application fee: $50. Electronic applications accepted. *Financial support:* In 2010–11, 11 students received support, including 2 research assistantships with full tuition reimbursements available (averaging $13,000 per year), 6 teaching assistantships with full tuition reimbursements available (averaging $7,200 per year); career-related internships or fieldwork, Federal Work-Study, scholarships/grants, health care benefits, and unspecified assistantships also available. Financial award application deadline: 3/1; financial award applicants required to submit FAFSA. *Faculty research:* Economic development, international studies, geography. *Unit head:* Dr. Brent Hales, Interim Chair, 601-266-4736, Fax: 601-266-6071. *Application contact:* Dr. Chad Miller, Director, Graduate Studies, 601-266-6666, Fax: 601-266-6071.

University of Waterloo, Graduate Studies, Faculty of Environmental Studies, Program in Local Economic Development, Waterloo, ON N2L 3G1, Canada. Offers MAES. Part-time programs available. *Degree requirements:* For master's, internship, research paper. Electronic applications accepted.

Vanderbilt University, Graduate School, Department of Economics, Nashville, TN 37240-1001. Offers economic development (MA); economics (MA, MAT, PhD); JD/PhD. *Faculty:* 31 full-time (6 women). *Students:* 123 full-time (47 women), 6 part-time (4 women); includes 2 Asian, non-Hispanic/Latino; 3 Hispanic/Latino; 2 Two or more races, non-Hispanic/Latino. Average age 27. 371 applicants, 7% accepted, 19 enrolled. In 2010, 29 master's, 6 doctorates awarded. Terminal master's awarded for partial completion of doctoral program. *Degree requirements:* For master's, thesis or alternative; for doctorate, thesis/dissertation, final and qualifying exams. *Entrance requirements:* For master's and doctorate, GRE General Test, GRE Subject Test (recommended). Additional exam requirements/recommendations for international students: Required—TOEFL (minimum score 570 paper-based; 230 computer-based; 88 iBT). *Application deadline:* For fall admission, 1/15 for domestic and international students; for spring admission, 11/1 for domestic students. Applications are processed on a rolling basis. Application fee: $0. Electronic applications accepted. *Financial support:* Fellowships with full and partial tuition reimbursements, teaching assistantships with full and partial tuition reimbursements, career-related internships or fieldwork, Federal Work-Study, institutionally sponsored loans, scholarships/grants, and health care benefits available. Financial award application deadline: 1/15; financial award applicants required to submit CSS PROFILE or FAFSA. *Faculty research:* Economic theory, applied fields, developmental economics, environmental economics, health economics and policy. *Unit head:* Dr. Tong Li, Chair, 615-322-3582, Fax: 615-343-8495, E-mail: tong.li@vanderbilt.edu. *Application contact:* Dr. Bill Collins, Director of Graduate Studies, 615-322-3428, Fax: 615-343-8495, E-mail: william.collins@vanderbilt.edu.

Virginia Polytechnic Institute and State University, Graduate School, College of Architecture and Urban Studies, School of Public and International Affairs, Blacksburg, VA 24061. Offers economic development (Certificate); government and international affairs (MPIA, PhD); homeland security policy (Certificate); local government management (Certificate); nonprofit and nongovernmental organization management (Certificate); planning, governance and globalization (PhD); public administration and public affairs (MPA, PhD); urban and regional planning (MURPL). *Accreditation:* ACSP. *Faculty:* 31 full-time (9 women). *Students:* 114 full-time (66 women), 105 part-time (54 women); includes 11 Black or African American, non-Hispanic/Latino; 1 American Indian or Alaska Native, non-Hispanic/Latino; 7 Asian, non-Hispanic/Latino; 8 Hispanic/Latino, 19 international. Average age 31. 166 applicants, 67% accepted, 53 enrolled. In 2010, 41 master's, 3 doctorates awarded. *Degree requirements:* For master's, comprehensive exam (for some programs), thesis (for some programs); for doctorate, comprehensive exam (for some programs), thesis/dissertation (for some programs). *Entrance requirements:* For master's and doctorate, GRE. Additional exam requirements/recommendations for international students: Required—TOEFL (minimum score 550 paper-based; 213 computer-based). *Application deadline:* For fall admission, 7/1 for domestic and international students; for spring admission, 12/1 for domestic and international students. Applications are processed on a rolling basis. Application fee: $65. Electronic applications accepted. *Expenses:* Tuition, state resident: full-time $9399; part-time $488 per credit hour. Tuition, nonresident: full-time $17,854; part-time $957.75 per credit hour. Required fees: $1534. Full-time tuition and fees vary according to program. *Financial support:* In 2010–11, 1 teaching assistantship with full tuition reimbursement (averaging $21,395 per year) was awarded; career-related internships or fieldwork, Federal Work-Study, scholarships/grants, health care benefits, and unspecified assistantships also available. Financial award application deadline: 1/15. *Faculty research:* Design theory, environmental planning, town planning, transportation planning. Total annual research expenditures: $610,749. *Unit head:* Dr. Karen M. Hult, UNIT HEAD, 540-231-5351, Fax: 540-231-9938, E-mail: khult@vt.edu. *Application contact:* Krystal D. Wright, Contact, 540-231-2291, Fax: 540-231-9938, E-mail: garch@vt.edu.

Western Illinois University, School of Graduate Studies, College of Business and Technology, Department of Economics and Decision Sciences, Macomb, IL 61455-1390. Offers community development (Certificate); economics (MA). Part-time programs available. *Students:* 25 full-time (5 women), 1 part-time (0 women); includes 1 minority (Black or African American, non-Hispanic/Latino), 19 international. Average age 27. 32 applicants, 78% accepted. In 2010, 19 master's awarded. *Degree requirements:* For master's, thesis or alternative. *Entrance requirements:* Additional exam requirements/recommendations for international students: Required—TOEFL (minimum score 550 paper-based; 213 computer-based; 80 iBT). *Application deadline:* Applications are processed on a rolling basis. Application fee: $30. Electronic applications accepted. *Expenses:* Tuition, state resident: full-time $6370; part-time $265.40 per credit hour. Tuition, nonresident: full-time $12,740; part-time $530.80 per credit hour. Required fees: $75.67 per credit hour. *Financial support:* In 2010–11, 6 students received support, including 6 research assistantships with full tuition reimbursements available (averaging $7,280 per year). Financial award applicants required to submit FAFSA. *Unit head:* Dr. Tej Kaul, Chairperson, 309-298-1153. *Application contact:* Evelyn Hoing, Assistant Director of Graduate Studies, 309-298-1806, Fax: 309-298-2345, E-mail: grad-office@wiu.edu.

West Virginia University, College of Business and Economics, Division of Economics and Finance, Morgantown, WV 26506. Offers business analysis (MA); developmental financial economics (PhD); environmental and resource economics (PhD); international economics (PhD); mathematical economics (MA); monetary economics (PhD); public finance (PhD); public policy (MA); regional and urban economics (PhD); statistics and economics (MA). Terminal master's awarded for partial completion of doctoral program. *Degree requirements:* For master's, thesis optional; for doctorate, comprehensive exam, thesis/dissertation. *Entrance requirements:* For master's and doctorate, GRE General Test, minimum GPA of 3.0; course work in intermediate microeconomics, intermediate macroeconomics, calculus, and statistics. Additional exam requirements/recommendations for international students: Required—TOEFL. Electronic applications accepted. *Faculty research:* Financial economics, regional/urban development, public economics, international trade/international finance/development economics, monetary economics.

Yale University, Graduate School of Arts and Sciences, Department of Economics, Program in International and Development Economics, New Haven, CT 06520. Offers MA. *Entrance requirements:* For master's, GRE General Test.

Economics

Albany State University, College of Arts and Humanities, Program in Public Administration, Albany, GA 31705-2717. Offers community and economic development administration (MPA); criminal justice administration (MPA); fiscal management (MPA); general management (MPA); health administration and policy (MPA); human resources management (MPA); public policy (MPA); water resource management and policy (MPA). *Accreditation:* NASPAA. *Faculty:* 3 full-time (1 woman), 2 part-time/adjunct (0 women). *Students:* 13 full-time (7 women), 49 part-time (32 women); includes 60 Black or African American, non-Hispanic/Latino, 1 international. Average age 34. 18 applicants, 78% accepted, 12 enrolled. In 2010, 12 master's awarded. *Degree requirements:* For master's, professional public service internship, professional portfolio, capstone research project. *Entrance requirements:* For master's, GRE, MAT, or GMAT, baccalaureate degree from accredited college or university, two letters of recommendation, ASU medical and immunization form. *Application deadline:* For fall admission, 7/15 for domestic students, 5/15 for international students; for spring admission, 11/15 for domestic students, 9/15 for international students. Applications are processed on a rolling basis. Application fee: $20. Electronic applications accepted. *Expenses:* Tuition, state resident: full-time $3060; part-time $170 per credit hour. Tuition, nonresident: full-time $12,204; part-time $678 per credit hour. Required fees: $1160. Part-time tuition and fees vary according to course load. *Financial support:* Application deadline: 4/15. *Faculty research:* Public policy, strategic public human resources and human capital management, diversity management in the public sector and collective bargaining and labor relations in the public sector, e-government and public sector information systems, public administration pedagogy and business process modeling simulation, community development, nonprofit organizations, civic engagement and civic participation, healthcare disparities among minorities, poverty. Total annual research expenditures: $250. *Unit head:* Dr. Peter Ngwafu, Director, 229-430-4760, Fax: 229-430-7895, E-mail: peter.ngwafu@asurams.edu. *Application contact:* Dr. Rani George, Dean, Graduate School, 229-430-5118, Fax: 229-430-6398, E-mail: rani.george@asurams.edu.

American University, College of Arts and Sciences, Department of Economics, Washington, DC 20016-8029. Offers applied microeconomics (Certificate); economics (MA, PhD); international economic relations (Certificate). Part-time and evening/weekend programs available. *Faculty:* 26 full-time (9 women). *Students:* 48 full-time (20 women), 71 part-time (26 women); includes 12 minority (7 Black or African American, non-Hispanic/Latino; 3 Asian, non-Hispanic/Latino; 2 Hispanic/Latino), 44 international. Average age 30. 186 applicants, 68% accepted, 32 enrolled. In 2010, 15 master's, 10 doctorates, 1 other advanced degree awarded. Terminal master's awarded for partial completion of doctoral program. *Degree requirements:* For master's, comprehensive exam, thesis or alternative; for doctorate, comprehensive exam, thesis/dissertation, 2 research seminars, field work. *Entrance requirements:* For master's and doctorate, GRE; for Certificate, bachelor's degree. Additional exam requirements/recommendations for international students: Required—TOEFL. *Application deadline:* For spring admission, 10/1 for domestic students. Applications are processed on a rolling basis. Application fee: $80. *Financial support:* Fellowships, research assistantships with full and partial tuition reimbursements, teaching assistantships with full and partial tuition reimbursements, career-related internships or fieldwork, Federal Work-Study, institutionally sponsored loans, and tuition waivers (full and partial) available. Financial award application deadline: 2/1. *Faculty research:* Political economy, development, labor, gender. *Unit head:* Robert A. Blecker, Chair, 202-885-3767, Fax: 202-885-3790, E-mail: blecker@american.edu. *Application contact:* Kathleen Clowery, Director of Graduate Admissions, 202-885-3621, Fax: 202-885-1505, E-mail: clowery@american.edu.

The American University in Cairo, School of Business, Economics and Communication, Department of Economics, Cairo, Egypt. Offers MA. Part-time programs available. *Degree requirements:* For master's, thesis or alternative. *Entrance requirements:* For master's, GMAT. Additional exam requirements/recommendations for international students: Required—English entrance exam. Electronic applications accepted. *Faculty research:* Macro-economic policies, agricultural growth and rural credit markets, alleviation of poverty in Egypt.

American University of Beirut, Graduate Programs, Faculty of Arts and Sciences, Beirut, Lebanon. Offers anthropology (MA); Arabic language and literature (MA); archaeology (MA); biology (MS); chemistry (MS); computational science (MS); computer science (MS); economics (MA); education (MA); English language (MA); English literature (MA); environmental policy planning (MSES); financial economics (MAFE); geology (MS); history (MA); mathematics (MA, MS); Middle Eastern studies (MA); philosophy (MA); physics (MS); political studies (MA); psychology (MA); public administration (MA); sociology (MA); statistics (MA, MS). Part-time programs available. *Faculty:* 229 full-time (98 women), 136 part-time/adjunct (79 women). *Students:* 158 full-time (104 women), 263 part-time (171 women). Average age 25. 356 applicants, 59% accepted, 127 enrolled. In 2010, 57 master's awarded. *Degree requirements:* For master's, one foreign language, comprehensive exam, thesis (for some programs). *Entrance requirements:* For master's, GRE, letter of recommendation. Additional exam requirements/recommendations for international students: Required—TOEFL (minimum score 600 paper-based; 250 computer-based; 97 iBT), IELTS (minimum score 7). *Application deadline:* For fall admission, 4/30 for domestic and international students; for spring admission, 11/1 for domestic and international students. Application fee: $50. *Expenses:* Tuition: Full-time $12,294; part-time $683 per credit. Required fees: $499; $499 per credit. Tuition and fees vary according to course load and program. *Financial support:* In 2010–11, 33 students received support. Career-related internships or fieldwork, institutionally sponsored loans, scholarships/grants, health care benefits, and unspecified assistantships available. Financial award application deadline: 2/4; financial award applicants required to submit FAFSA. *Faculty research:* Modern and contemporary world theatre; mineralogy, petrology, and geochemistry; cell differentiation and transformation; combinatorial technologies; philosophy of action; continental philosophy; Phoenician epigraphy; nascent complex societies and urbanism; the economies of the Arab world; environmental economics; tectonophysics; host-parasite interactions; innate immunity; insect-plant interactions; history of the Ottoman archives; decentralization; transparency and corruption. Total annual research expenditures: $622,243. *Unit head:* Dr. Patrick McGreevy, Dean, 961-137-4374 Ext. 3800, Fax: 961-174-4461, E-mail: pm07@aub.edu.lb. *Application contact:* Dr. Salim Kanaan, Director, Admissions Office, 961-135-0000 Ext. 2594, Fax: 961-175-0775, E-mail: sk00@aub.edu.lb.

Andrews University, School of Graduate Studies, School of Business, Graduate Programs in Business, Berrien Springs, MI 49104. Offers MBA, MSA. *Entrance requirements:* For master's, GMAT. Additional exam requirements/recommendations for international students: Required—TOEFL (minimum score 550 paper-based).

Arizona State University, W. P. Carey School of Business, Department of Economics, Tempe, AZ 85287-9801. Offers PhD. *Faculty:* 41 full-time (8 women), 3 part-time/adjunct (0 women). *Students:* 43 full-time (9 women), 3 part-time (1 woman); includes 3 minority (1 Asian, non-Hispanic/Latino; 1 Hispanic/Latino; 1 Two or more races, non-Hispanic/Latino), 34 international. Average age 26. 178 applicants, 25% accepted, 22 enrolled. In 2010, 5 degrees awarded. *Median time to degree:* Of those who began their doctoral program in fall 2002, 70% received their degree in 8 years or less. *Degree requirements:* For doctorate, comprehensive exam, thesis/dissertation, interactive Program of Study (iPOS) submitted before completing 50 percent of required credit hours. *Entrance requirements:* For doctorate, GRE, minimum GPA of 3.0 in last 2 years of work leading to bachelor's degree, 3 letters of recommendation, resume/curriculum vitae, letter of intent, thesis (if applicable), official university transcripts, personal statement. Additional exam requirements/recommendations for international students: Required—TOEFL (minimum score 550 paper-based; 213 computer-based; 80 iBT), IELTS (minimum score 6.5). *Application deadline:* For fall admission, 1/15 for domestic and international students. Application fee: $70 ($90 for international students). Electronic applications accepted. *Expenses:* Tuition, state resident: full-time $8510; part-time $608 per credit. Tuition, nonresident: full-time $16,542; part-time $919 per credit. Required fees: $339; $110 per credit. Part-time tuition and fees vary according to course load. *Financial support:* In 2010–11, 45 teaching assistantships with full and partial tuition reimbursements (averaging $18,674 per year) were awarded; fellowships with full and partial tuition reimbursements, research assistantships with full and partial tuition reimbursements, institutionally sponsored loans, scholarships/grants, and tuition waivers (full and partial) also available. Financial award application deadline: 3/1; financial award applicants required to submit FAFSA. *Faculty research:* Macroeconomics, general equilibrium, business cycles, monetary policy, environmental economics, applied econometrics, economic theory, game theory, procurement and auctions, industrial organization, labor economics, marketing, consumer choice behavior. Total annual research expenditures: $235,572. *Unit head:* Dr. Arthur E. Blakemore, Chair, 480-965-8432, Fax: 480-965-0748, E-mail: asuecn@asu.edu. *Application contact:* Graduate Admissions, 480-965-6113.

Assumption College, Graduate School, Department of Business Studies, Worcester, MA 01609-1296. Offers accounting (MBA); business administration (CAGS); finance/economics (MBA); general business (MBA); human resources (MBA); international business (MBA); management (MBA); marketing (MBA); nonprofit leadership (MBA). Part-time and evening/weekend programs available. *Faculty:* 3 full-time (0 women), 13 part-time/adjunct (3 women). *Students:* 20 full-time (9 women), 135 part-time (70 women); includes 24 minority (19 Black or African American, non-Hispanic/Latino; 2 Asian, non-Hispanic/Latino; 3 Hispanic/Latino), 4 international. Average age 26. 85 applicants, 95% accepted. In 2010, 40 master's, 2 other advanced degrees awarded. *Entrance requirements:* For master's and CAGS, 3 letters of recommendation, resume, essay. Additional exam requirements/recommendations for international students: Required—TOEFL (minimum score 540 paper-based; 200 computer-based; 76 iBT), IELTS (minimum score 6). *Application deadline:* For fall admission, 6/1 priority date for domestic students, 5/1 priority date for international students; for spring admission, 11/1 priority date for domestic students, 9/1 priority date for international students. Applications are processed on a rolling basis. Application fee: $30. Electronic applications accepted. *Expenses:* Tuition: Part-time $503 per credit. Required fees: $20 per semester. One-time fee: $100. Part-time tuition and fees vary according to campus/location. *Financial support:* Application deadline: 6/1. *Faculty research:* Workplace diversity, dynamics of team interaction, utilization of leased employees. *Unit head:* Michael Lewis, Director, 508-767-7372, Fax: 508-767-7252, E-mail: milewis@assumption.edu. *Application contact:* Daniel Provost, Assistant Director of Graduate Student Services, 508-767-7426, Fax: 508-767-7030, E-mail: dprovost@assumption.edu.

Auburn University, Graduate School, College of Liberal Arts, Department of Economics, Auburn University, AL 36849. Offers MS. Part-time programs available. *Faculty:* 10 full-time (1 woman), 4 part-time/adjunct (0 women). *Students:* 15 full-time (3 women), 5 part-time (0 women), 2 international. Average age 26. 58 applicants, 45% accepted, 13 enrolled. In 2010, 11 master's awarded. *Degree requirements:* For master's, thesis. *Entrance requirements:* For master's, GMAT, GRE General Test. Additional exam requirements/recommendations for international students: Required—TOEFL. *Application deadline:* For fall admission, 7/7 for domestic students; for spring admission, 11/24 for domestic students. Applications are processed on a rolling basis. Application fee: $50 ($60 for international students). Electronic applications accepted. *Expenses:* Tuition, state resident: full-time $7002. Tuition, nonresident: full-time $21,898. International tuition: $22,116 full-time. Required fees: $892. Tuition and fees vary according to course load and program. *Financial support:* Teaching assistantships, career-related internships or fieldwork and Federal Work-Study available. Support available to part-time students. Financial award application deadline: 3/15; financial award applicants required to submit FAFSA. *Unit head:* Dr. Barry Burkhart, Interim Chair, 334-844-6476. *Application contact:* Dr. George Flowers, Dean of the Graduate School, 334-844-2125.

Baylor University, Graduate School, Hankamer School of Business, Department of Economics, Waco, TX 76798. Offers economics (MS Eco); international economics (MA, MS). *Students:* 12 full-time (7 women), 4 international. In 2010, 12 master's awarded. *Entrance requirements:* For master's, GMAT or GRE General Test. *Application deadline:* For fall admission, 8/1 for domestic students; for spring admission, 12/1 for domestic students. Applications are processed on a rolling basis. Application fee: $25. *Financial support:* Research assistantships, Federal Work-Study and institutionally sponsored loans available. Financial award application deadline: 4/1. *Faculty research:* Econometrics, international economics, private enterprise, comparative economic systems. *Unit head:* Dr. Tom Kelly, Chair, 254-710-4146, Fax: 254-710-3265, E-mail: tom_kelly@baylor.edu. *Application contact:* Susan Armstrong, Administrative Assistant, 254-710-6177, Fax: 254-710-1066, E-mail: susan_armstrong@baylor.edu.

Bernard M. Baruch College of the City University of New York, Zicklin School of Business, Department of Economics and Finance, Program in Economics, New York, NY 10010-5585. Offers MBA. Part-time and evening/weekend programs available. *Entrance requirements:* For master's, GMAT, 2 letters of recommendation, resume, 2 years of work experience. Additional exam requirements/recommendations for international students: Required—TOEFL (minimum score 590 paper-based; 243 computer-based), TWE (minimum score 5).

Boston College, Graduate School of Arts and Sciences, Department of Economics, Chestnut Hill, MA 02467-3800. Offers PhD. *Degree requirements:* For doctorate, comprehensive exam, thesis/dissertation. *Entrance requirements:* For doctorate, GRE General Test, GRE Subject Test. Additional exam requirements/recommendations for international students: Required—TOEFL (minimum score 600 paper-based; 250 computer-based; 100 iBT). Electronic applications accepted. *Faculty research:* Econometrics, international economics, public sector economics, monetary economics, urban economics.

Boston University, Graduate School of Arts and Sciences, Department of Economics, Boston, MA 02215. Offers economic policy (MAEP); economics (MA, PhD); political economy (MAPE); MBA/MA. *Students:* 288 full-time (122 women), 16 part-time (5 women); includes 27 minority (1 Black or African American, non-Hispanic/Latino; 18 Asian, non-Hispanic/Latino; 5 Hispanic/Latino; 3 Two or more races, non-Hispanic/Latino), 218 international. Average age 26. 1,029 applicants, 26% accepted, 117 enrolled. In 2010, 100 master's, 17 doctorates awarded. Terminal master's awarded for partial completion of doctoral program. *Degree requirements:* For master's, one foreign language, comprehensive exam; for doctorate, one foreign language, comprehensive exam, thesis/dissertation, qualifying exam. *Entrance requirements:* For master's and doctorate, GRE General Test, 3 letters of recommendation. Additional exam requirements/recommendations for international students: Required—TOEFL (minimum score 550 paper-based; 213 computer-based). *Application deadline:* For fall admission, 3/1 for domestic and international students. Application fee: $70. Electronic applications accepted. *Expenses:* Tuition: Full-time $39,314; part-time $1228 per credit. Required fees: $40 per semester. *Financial support:* In 2010–11, 91 students received support, including 9 fellowships with full tuition reimbursements available (averaging $19,300 per year), 17 research assistantships with full and partial tuition reimbursements available (averaging $18,800 per year), 27 teaching assistantships with full tuition reimbursements available (averaging $18,800 per year); Federal Work-Study and scholarships/grants also available. Support available to part-time students. Financial award application deadline: 1/2; financial award applicants required to submit FAFSA. *Unit head:* Robert Margo, Chairman, 617-353-6819, Fax: 617-353-4449, E-mail: margora@bu.edu. *Application contact:* Andrew Campolieto, Graduate Program Administrator, 617-353-4454, Fax: 617-353-4449, E-mail: acamp@bu.edu.

Boston University, Metropolitan College, Department of Administrative Sciences, Boston, MA 02215. Offers banking and financial management (MSM); business continuity in emergency management (MSM); economics development and tourism management (MSAS); electronic commerce, systems, and technology (MSAS); financial economics (MSAS); innovation and technology (MSAS); insurance management (MSM); international market management (MSM); multinational commerce (MSAS); project management (MSM). *Accreditation:* AACSB. Part-time and evening/weekend programs available. Postbaccalaureate distance learning degree programs offered (no on-campus study). *Faculty:* 14 full-time (2 women), 22 part-time/adjunct (2 women). *Students:* 107 full-time (51 women), 786 part-time (356 women); includes 130 minority (55

Black or African American, non-Hispanic/Latino; 1 American Indian or Alaska Native, non-Hispanic/Latino; 30 Asian, non-Hispanic/Latino; 36 Hispanic/Latino; 1 Native Hawaiian or other Pacific Islander, non-Hispanic/Latino; 7 Two or more races, non-Hispanic/Latino), 175 international. Average age 33. 398 applicants, 87% accepted, 180 enrolled. In 2010, 154 master's awarded. *Degree requirements:* For master's, thesis optional. *Entrance requirements:* For master's, 1 year of work experience, minimum GPA of 3.0. Additional exam requirements/recommendations for international students: Required—TOEFL (minimum score 560 paper-based; 220 computer-based; 84 iBT). *Application deadline:* Applications are processed on a rolling basis. Application fee: $70. Electronic applications accepted. *Expenses:* Tuition: Full-time $39,314; part-time $1228 per credit. Required fees: $40 per semester. *Financial support:* In 2010–11, 15 students received support, including 7 research assistantships with partial tuition reimbursements available (averaging $10,000 per year); career-related internships or fieldwork, Federal Work-Study, and unspecified assistantships also available. *Faculty research:* International business, innovative process. *Unit head:* Dr. Kip Becker, Chairman, 617-353-3016, E-mail: adminsc@bu.edu. *Application contact:* Lucille Dicker, Administrative Sciences Department, 617-353-3016, E-mail: adminsc@bu.edu.

Bowling Green State University, Graduate College, College of Business Administration, Department of Economics, Bowling Green, OH 43403. Offers MA. Part-time programs available. *Degree requirements:* For master's, thesis or alternative. *Entrance requirements:* For master's, GRE General Test. Additional exam requirements/recommendations for international students: Required—TOEFL. Electronic applications accepted. *Faculty research:* Labor economics, monetary economics, economic education, mathematical economics.

Brandeis University, International Business School, Program in International Economics and Finance, Waltham, MA 02454-9110. Offers MA. *Entrance requirements:* For master's, GRE.

Brock University, Faculty of Graduate Studies, Faculty of Social Sciences, Program in Business Economics, St. Catharines, ON L2S 3A1, Canada. Offers MBE. *Degree requirements:* For master's, thesis or alternative. *Entrance requirements:* For master's, honours degree. Additional exam requirements/recommendations for international students: Required—TOEFL (minimum score 550 paper-based; 213 computer-based; 80 iBT), IELTS (minimum score 6.5), TWE (minimum score 4). Electronic applications accepted. *Faculty research:* Microeconomic theory, macroeconomics, econometrics, applied econometrics, economic development.

Brooklyn College of the City University of New York, Division of Graduate Studies, Department of Economics, Brooklyn, NY 11210-2889. Offers accounting (MS); business economics (MS), including economic analysis, global business and finance; economics (MA). Part-time and evening/weekend programs available. *Students:* 27 full-time (16 women), 163 part-time (76 women); includes 84 minority (60 Black or African American, non-Hispanic/Latino; 18 Asian, non-Hispanic/Latino; 6 Hispanic/Latino), 42 international. Average age 32. 184 applicants, 76% accepted, 68 enrolled. In 2010, 44 master's awarded. *Degree requirements:* For master's, comprehensive exam, thesis or alternative. *Entrance requirements:* For master's, GMAT (for MS), 2 letters of recommendation. Additional exam requirements/recommendations for international students: Required—TOEFL (minimum score 550 paper-based; 213 computer-based; 79 iBT). *Application deadline:* For fall admission, 3/1 priority date for domestic students, 2/1 priority date for international students; for spring admission, 11/1 priority date for domestic students, 10/1 priority date for international students. Applications are processed on a rolling basis. Application fee: $125. Electronic applications accepted. *Expenses:* Tuition, state resident: full-time $7360; part-time $310 per credit hour. Tuition, nonresident: full-time $13,800; part-time $575 per credit hour. Required fees: $190 per semester. *Financial support:* Career-related internships or fieldwork, Federal Work-Study, institutionally sponsored loans, and scholarships/grants available. Support available to part-time students. Financial award application deadline: 5/1; financial award applicants required to submit FAFSA. *Faculty research:* Econometrics, environmental economics, microeconomics, macroeconomics, taxation. *Unit head:* Dr. Emmanuel Thorne, Chairperson, 718-951-5317, E-mail: ethorne@brooklyn.cuny.edu. *Application contact:* Hernan Sierra, Graduate Admissions Coordinator, 718-951-4536, Fax: 718-951-4506, E-mail: grads@brooklyn.cuny.edu.

Brown University, Graduate School, Department of Economics, Providence, RI 02912. Offers PhD. Terminal master's awarded for partial completion of doctoral program. *Degree requirements:* For doctorate, thesis/dissertation. *Entrance requirements:* For doctorate, GRE General Test.

Buffalo State College, State University of New York, The Graduate School, Faculty of Natural and Social Sciences, Department of Economics and Finance, Buffalo, NY 14222-1095. Offers applied economics (MA). *Degree requirements:* For master's, project. *Entrance requirements:* Additional exam requirements/recommendations for international students: Required—TOEFL (minimum score 550 paper-based; 213 computer-based).

California Lutheran University, Graduate Studies, School of Management, Thousand Oaks, CA 91360-2787. Offers business (IMBA); computer science (MS); econometrics (MBA); economics (MS); entrepreneurship (MBA, Certificate); finance (MBA, Certificate); financial planning (MBA, Certificate); information systems and technology (MS); information technology management (MBA, Certificate); international business (MBA, Certificate); management and organization behavior (MBA); management and organizational behavior (Certificate); marketing (MBA, Certificate); microeconomics (MBA); nonprofit and social enterprise (MBA). Part-time and evening/weekend programs available. Postbaccalaureate distance learning degree programs offered (no on-campus study). *Faculty:* 12 full-time (3 women), 27 part-time/adjunct (6 women). *Students:* 350 full-time (162 women), 262 part-time (99 women); includes 21 Black or African American, non-Hispanic/Latino; 44 Asian, non-Hispanic/Latino; 56 Hispanic/Latino; 4 Native Hawaiian or other Pacific Islander, non-Hispanic/Latino; 12 Two or more races, non-Hispanic/Latino, 185 international. Average age 32. 379 applicants, 74% accepted, 138 enrolled. In 2010, 231 master's awarded. *Entrance requirements:* For master's, GMAT, interview, minimum GPA of 3.0. *Application deadline:* Applications are processed on a rolling basis. Application fee: $50. *Expenses:* Contact institution. *Unit head:* Dr. Charles Maxey, Dean, 805-493-3360. *Application contact:* 805-493-3127, Fax: 805-493-3542, E-mail: clugrad@clunet.edu.

California State Polytechnic University, Pomona, Academic Affairs, College of Letters, Arts, and Social Sciences, Program in Economics, Pomona, CA 91768-2557. Offers MS. Part-time programs available. *Students:* 13 full-time (5 women), 52 part-time (19 women); includes 39 minority (4 Black or African American, non-Hispanic/Latino; 1 American Indian or Alaska Native, non-Hispanic/Latino; 19 Asian, non-Hispanic/Latino; 14 Hispanic/Latino; 1 Two or more races, non-Hispanic/Latino), 10 international. Average age 29. 86 applicants, 58% accepted, 28 enrolled. In 2010, 10 master's awarded. *Degree requirements:* For master's, thesis or alternative. *Entrance requirements:* For master's, GRE General Test. *Application deadline:* For fall admission, 5/1 priority date for domestic students; for winter admission, 10/15 priority date for domestic students; for spring admission, 1/20 priority date for domestic students. Applications are processed on a rolling basis. Application fee: $55. Electronic applications accepted. *Expenses:* Tuition, state resident: full-time $5386; part-time $2850 per year. Tuition, nonresident: full-time $12,082; part-time $248 per credit. Required fees: $577; $248 per credit. $577 per year. Tuition and fees vary according to course load and program. *Financial support:* In 2010–11, 9 students received support. Federal Work-Study and institutionally sponsored loans available. Support available to part-time students. Financial award application deadline: 3/2; financial award applicants required to submit FAFSA. *Unit head:* Dr. Carsten Lange, Graduate Coordinator, 909-869-3843, E-mail: clange@csupomona.edu. *Application contact:* Scott J. Duncan, Director, Admissions, 909-869-3258, Fax: 909-869-4529, E-mail: sjduncan@csupomona.edu.

California State University, East Bay, Office of Academic Programs and Graduate Studies, College of Business and Economics, Department of Economics, Hayward, CA 94542-3000. Offers economics (MA). Part-time and evening/weekend programs available. *Faculty:* 5 full-time (0 women), 1 part-time/adjunct (0 women). *Students:* 6 full-time (4 women), 34 part-time (14 women); includes 18 minority (3 Black or African American, non-Hispanic/Latino; 8 Asian, non-Hispanic/Latino; 4 Hispanic/Latino; 1 Native Hawaiian or other Pacific Islander, non-

Hispanic/Latino; 2 Two or more races, non-Hispanic/Latino), 12 international. Average age 29. 330 applicants, 22% accepted, 20 enrolled. In 2010, 6 master's awarded. *Degree requirements:* For master's, comprehensive exam, project or thesis. *Entrance requirements:* For master's, GMAT, minimum GPA of 2.75 during previous 2 years of course work. Additional exam requirements/recommendations for international students: Required—TOEFL (minimum score 580 paper-based; 237 computer-based; 92 iBT). *Application deadline:* For fall admission, 6/30 for domestic and international students. Applications are processed on a rolling basis. Application fee: $55. Electronic applications accepted. *Financial support:* Career-related internships or fieldwork, Federal Work-Study, and institutionally sponsored loans available. Support available to part-time students. Financial award application deadline: 3/2; financial award applicants required to submit FAFSA. *Unit head:* Prof. James Ahiakpor, Interim Chair, 510-885-3265, Fax: 510-885-4699, E-mail: james.ahiakpor@csueastbay.edu. *Application contact:* Dr. Donna Wiley, Interim Associate Director, 510-885-2928, Fax: 510-885-4777, E-mail: donna.wiley@csueastbay.edu.

California State University, Fullerton, Graduate Studies, College of Business and Economics, Department of Economics, Fullerton, CA 92834-9480. Offers business economics (MBA); economics (MA). Part-time programs available. *Students:* 41 full-time (14 women), 16 part-time (3 women); includes 1 Black or African American, non-Hispanic/Latino; 8 Asian, non-Hispanic/Latino; 9 Hispanic/Latino; 2 Two or more races, non-Hispanic/Latino, 13 international. Average age 28. 71 applicants, 44% accepted, 26 enrolled. In 2010, 9 master's awarded. *Degree requirements:* For master's, thesis. *Entrance requirements:* For master's, GMAT, GRE General Test. Application fee: $55. *Financial support:* Career-related internships or fieldwork, Federal Work-Study, institutionally sponsored loans, and scholarships/grants available. Support available to part-time students. Financial award application deadline: 3/1; financial award applicants required to submit FAFSA. *Faculty research:* Environmental and natural resource issues. *Unit head:* Dr. Morteza Rahmatian, Chair, 657-278-2228. *Application contact:* Admissions/Applications, 657-278-2371.

California State University, Long Beach, Graduate Studies, College of Liberal Arts, Department of Economics, Long Beach, CA 90840. Offers economics (MA); global logistics (MA). Part-time programs available. *Faculty:* 5 full-time (2 women), 1 part-time/adjunct (0 women). *Students:* 13 full-time (5 women), 17 part-time (11 women); includes 1 Black or African American, non-Hispanic/Latino; 5 Asian, non-Hispanic/Latino; 2 Hispanic/Latino, 8 international. Average age 29. 101 applicants, 57% accepted, 17 enrolled. In 2010, 22 master's awarded. *Degree requirements:* For master's, comprehensive exam or thesis. *Entrance requirements:* For master's, GRE General Test, GRE Subject Test, minimum GPA of 3.0. *Application deadline:* For fall admission, 4/1 for domestic students. Applications are processed on a rolling basis. Application fee: $55. Electronic applications accepted. *Financial support:* Federal Work-Study, institutionally sponsored loans, and scholarships/grants available. Financial award application deadline: 3/2. *Faculty research:* Trade and development, economic forecasting, resource economics. *Unit head:* Dr. Joseph P. Magaddino, Chair, 562-985-5061, Fax: 562-985-5804, E-mail: magaddin@csulb.edu. *Application contact:* Dr. Alejandra C. Edwards, Graduate Advisor, 562-985-5969, Fax: 562-985-5804, E-mail: acoxedwa@csulb.edu.

California State University, Los Angeles, Graduate Studies, College of Business and Economics, Department of Economics and Statistics, Los Angeles, CA 90032-8530. Offers analytical quantitative economics (MA); business economics (MA, MBA, MS); economics (MA). Part-time and evening/weekend programs available. *Faculty:* 2 full-time (1 woman), 4 part-time/adjunct (2 women). *Students:* 7 full-time (3 women), 15 part-time (4 women); includes 6 minority (5 Asian, non-Hispanic/Latino; 1 Hispanic/Latino), 5 international. Average age 28. 7 applicants, 100% accepted, 3 enrolled. In 2010, 10 master's awarded. *Degree requirements:* For master's, comprehensive exam or thesis. *Entrance requirements:* For master's, GMAT, minimum GPA of 2.5 during previous 2 years of course work. Additional exam requirements/recommendations for international students: Required—TOEFL (minimum score 550 paper-based; 213 computer-based). *Application deadline:* For fall admission, 5/1 for domestic and international students. Applications are processed on a rolling basis. Application fee: $55. Electronic applications accepted. *Financial support:* Career-related internships or fieldwork and Federal Work-Study available. Support available to part-time students. Financial award application deadline: 3/1. *Unit head:* Dr. Dang Tran, Chair, 323-343-2930, Fax: 323-343-5462, E-mail: dtran@calstatela.edu. *Application contact:* Dr. Alan Muchlinski, Dean of Graduate Studies, 323-343-3820, Fax: 323-343-5653, E-mail: amuchli@exchange.calstatela.edu.

Carleton University, Faculty of Graduate Studies, Faculty of Public Affairs and Management, Department of Economics, Ottawa, ON K1S 5B6, Canada. Offers MA, PhD. PhD program offered jointly with University of Ottawa. *Degree requirements:* For master's, thesis optional; for doctorate, comprehensive exam, thesis/dissertation. *Entrance requirements:* For master's, honors degree; for doctorate, master's degree. Additional exam requirements/recommendations for international students: Required—TOEFL. *Faculty research:* Monetary economics, economic development, public economics, industrial organization, international trade.

Carleton University, Faculty of Graduate Studies, Faculty of Public Affairs and Management, Institute of Political Economy, Ottawa, ON K1S 5B6, Canada. Offers MA, PhD. *Degree requirements:* For master's, thesis optional. *Entrance requirements:* For master's, honors degree. Additional exam requirements/recommendations for international students: Required—TOEFL. *Faculty research:* Relationships between economy and politics as they affect the political, social and cultural life of societies; historical processes whereby social change is located in the interaction of the economic, political and cultural, and ideological moments of social life.

Carnegie Mellon University, Tepper School of Business, Program in Economics, Pittsburgh, PA 15213-3891. Offers PhD. *Degree requirements:* For doctorate, thesis/dissertation. *Entrance requirements:* For doctorate, GMAT, GRE General Test. *Faculty research:* Research allocation under asymmetric information, monetary theory, estimation of rational expectations models.

Case Western Reserve University, Weatherhead School of Management, Department of Economics, Cleveland, OH 44106. Offers MBA. Part-time and evening/weekend programs available. *Entrance requirements:* For master's, GMAT. *Faculty research:* Public finance and public choice, direct foreign investment, employment relationships, technical and institutional change, regional economics.

The Catholic University of America, School of Arts and Sciences, Department of Business and Economics, Washington, DC 20064. Offers international political economics (MA). Part-time programs available. *Faculty:* 10 full-time (4 women), 15 part-time/adjunct (4 women). *Students:* 16 full-time (12 women); includes 1 Black or African American, non-Hispanic/Latino; 1 Asian, non-Hispanic/Latino; 1 Hispanic/Latino, 1 international. Average age 23. 19 applicants, 84% accepted, 16 enrolled. *Degree requirements:* For master's, comprehensive exam. *Entrance requirements:* For master's, GRE General Test, statement of purpose, official copies of academic transcripts, three letters of recommendation. Additional exam requirements/recommendations for international students: Required—TOEFL (minimum score 580 paper-based; 237 computer-based). *Application deadline:* For fall admission, 8/1 priority date for domestic students, 7/15 for international students; for spring admission, 12/1 priority date for domestic students, 10/15 for international students. Applications are processed on a rolling basis. Application fee: $55. Electronic applications accepted. *Expenses:* Tuition: Full-time $33,580; part-time $1315 per credit hour. Required fees: $80; $40 per semester hour. One-time fee: $425. *Financial support:* Fellowships, research assistantships, teaching assistantships, Federal Work-Study, scholarships/grants, tuition waivers (full and partial), and unspecified assistantships available. Financial award application deadline: 2/1; financial award applicants required to submit FAFSA. *Faculty research:* Integrity of the marketing process, economics of energy and the environment, emerging markets, social change, international finance and economic development. Total annual research expenditures: $6,459. *Unit head:* Dr. Andrew V. Abela, Chair, 202-319-5235, Fax: 202-319-4426, E-mail: abela@cua.edu. *Application contact:* Andrew Woodall, Director of Graduate Admissions, 202-319-5057, Fax: 202-319-6533, E-mail: cua-admissions@cua.edu.

Economics

Central European University, Graduate Studies, Department of Legal Studies, Budapest, Hungary. Offers comparative Constitutional law (LL M); economic and legal studies (LL M, MA); human rights (LL M, MA); international business law (LL M); legal studies (SJD). *Faculty:* 8 full-time (2 women), 1 (woman) part-time/adjunct. *Students:* 94 full-time (53 women). Average age 28. 503 applicants, 23% accepted, 88 enrolled. In 2010, 62 master's, 5 doctorates awarded. Terminal master's awarded for partial completion of doctoral program. *Degree requirements:* For master's, one foreign language, thesis; for doctorate, one foreign language, comprehensive exam, thesis/dissertation. *Entrance requirements:* For master's and doctorate, LSAT, CEU admissions exams. Additional exam requirements/recommendations for international students: Required—TOEFL (minimum score 570 paper-based; 230 computer-based). *Application deadline:* For fall admission, 1/5 for domestic and international students. Application fee: $0. Electronic applications accepted. *Expenses:* Contact institution. *Financial support:* In 2010–11, 88 students received support, including 88 fellowships with full and partial tuition reimbursements available (averaging $6,000 per year); career-related internships or fieldwork, institutionally sponsored loans, scholarships/grants, and tuition waivers (full and partial) also available. Financial award application deadline: 1/5. *Faculty research:* Institutional, constitutional and human rights in European Union law; biomedical law and reproductive rights; data protection law; Islamic banking and finance. *Unit head:* Dr. Stefan Messmann, Head, 361-327-3274, Fax: 361-327-3198, E-mail: legalst@ceu.hu. *Application contact:* Maria Balla, Coordinator, 361-327-3204, Fax: 361-327-3198, E-mail: ballam@ceu.hu.

Central European University, Graduate Studies, School of Social Sciences and Humanities, Budapest, Hungary. Offers economics (MA, PhD); gender studies (MA, PhD); international relations and European studies (MA, PhD); mathematics and its applications (MS, PhD); medieval studies (MA, PhD); nationalism studies (MA, PhD); philosophy (MA, PhD); political science (MA, PhD); public policy (MA, PhD); sociology and social anthropology (MA, PhD). *Faculty:* 90 full-time (29 women), 13 part-time/adjunct (7 women). *Students:* 732 full-time (404 women). Average age 28. 3,639 applicants, 22% accepted, 416 enrolled. In 2010, 278 master's, 16 doctorates awarded. Terminal master's awarded for partial completion of doctoral program. *Degree requirements:* For master's, one foreign language, thesis; for doctorate, one foreign language, comprehensive exam, thesis/dissertation. *Entrance requirements:* For master's, interview; for doctorate, GRE, CEU subject test, interview. Additional exam requirements/recommendations for international students: Required—TOEFL (minimum score 570 paper-based; 230 computer-based); Recommended—IELTS (minimum score 6.5). *Application deadline:* For fall admission, 1/15 priority date for domestic and international students. Application fee: $0. Electronic applications accepted. Tuition and fees charges are reported in euros. *Expenses:* Tuition: Full-time 11,000 euros. Required fees: 250 euros. One-time fee: 200 euros full-time. Tuition and fees vary according to degree level, program, reciprocity agreements and student level. *Financial support:* In 2010–11, 402 students received support, including 416 fellowships with full and partial tuition reimbursements available (averaging $6,200 per year); career-related internships or fieldwork, institutionally sponsored loans, and scholarships/grants also available. Financial award application deadline: 1/5. *Faculty research:* Civil society, fiscal decentralization, party politics, political philosophy (especially liberalism, theory of democracy). Total annual research expenditures: $35,000. *Unit head:* Dr. Katalin Farkas, Provost/Academic Pro Rector, 361-327-3000 Ext. 2227, E-mail: farkask@ceu.hu. *Application contact:* Zsuzsanna Jaszberenyi, Admissions Officer, 361-327-3009, Fax: 361-327-3211, E-mail: admissions@ceu.hu.

Central Michigan University, College of Graduate Studies, College of Business Administration, Department of Economics, Mount Pleasant, MI 48859. Offers MA. Part-time programs available. *Faculty:* 8 full-time (1 woman), 1 part-time/adjunct (0 women). *Students:* 29 full-time (10 women), 9 part-time (4 women); includes 1 Black or African American, non-Hispanic/Latino, 21 international. Average age 26. *Degree requirements:* For master's, thesis or alternative. *Application deadline:* For fall admission, 6/1 for international students; for spring admission, 10/1 for international students. Applications are processed on a rolling basis. Application fee: $35 ($45 for international students). Electronic applications accepted. *Expenses:* Tuition, state resident: full-time $8208; part-time $456 per credit hour. Tuition, nonresident: full-time $13,788; part-time $766 per credit hour. One-time fee: $25. *Financial support:* Fellowships with tuition reimbursements, research assistantships with tuition reimbursements, teaching assistantships with tuition reimbursements, Federal Work-Study, unspecified assistantships, and out-of-state merit awards, non-resident graduate awards available. *Faculty research:* Economic development, industrial organization, international trade, monetary theory, public choice/labor. *Unit head:* Dr. Paul Natke, Chairperson, 989-774-3870, Fax: 989-774-2040, E-mail: natke1pa@cmich.edu. *Application contact:* Dr. Bharati Basu, Graduate Student Coordinator, 989-774-3730, Fax: 989-774-2040, E-mail: basu1b@cmich.edu.

Chapman University, Graduate Studies, School of Law, Orange, CA 92866. Offers advocacy and dispute resolution (JD); entertainment law (JD); environmental, land use, and real estate (JD); international law (JD); law (LL M), including business law and economics, entertainment and media law, international and comparative law; prosecutorial science (LL M); tax law (JD); taxation (LL M); JD/MBA; JD/MFA. *Accreditation:* ABA. Part-time and evening/weekend programs available. *Faculty:* 57 full-time (25 women), 26 part-time/adjunct (4 women). *Students:* 580 full-time (283 women), 64 part-time (22 women); includes 132 minority (5 Black or African American, non-Hispanic/Latino; 1 American Indian or Alaska Native, non-Hispanic/Latino; 77 Asian, non-Hispanic/Latino; 37 Hispanic/Latino; 1 Native Hawaiian or other Pacific Islander, non-Hispanic/Latino; 11 Two or more races, non-Hispanic/Latino), 8 international. Average age 27. 2,779 applicants, 28% accepted, 212 enrolled. In 2010, 173 first professional degrees, 19 master's awarded. *Entrance requirements:* LSAT, minimum undergraduate GPA of 2.75. Additional exam requirements/recommendations for international students: Required—TOEFL (minimum score 600 paper-based; 213 computer-based; 80 iBT). *Application deadline:* For fall admission, 4/15 priority date for domestic students. Applications are processed on a rolling basis. Application fee: $65. Electronic applications accepted. *Expenses:* Contact institution. *Financial support:* Fellowships, Federal Work-Study and scholarships/grants available. Financial award applicants required to submit FAFSA. *Unit head:* Dr. Tom Campbell, Dean, 714-628-2500. *Application contact:* Marissa Vargas, Assistant Director of Admission and Financial Aid, 877-CHAPLAW, E-mail: mvargas@chapman.edu.

City College of the City University of New York, Graduate School, College of Liberal Arts and Science, Division of Social Science, Department of Economics, New York, NY 10031-9198. Offers MA. Part-time programs available. *Degree requirements:* For master's, comprehensive exam, proficiency in a foreign language or advanced statistics. *Entrance requirements:* Additional exam requirements/recommendations for international students: Required—TOEFL (minimum score 550 paper-based; 79 iBT). Electronic applications accepted. *Faculty research:* International economics, health, banking.

Claremont Graduate University, Graduate Programs, School of Politics and Economics, Department of Economics, Claremont, CA 91711-6160. Offers business and financial economics (MA, PhD); economic development (Certificate); economics (PhD); industrial organization (PhD); international and development economics (PhD); international economics policy and development (MA); international money and finance (PhD); neuroeconomics (PhD); political economy and public policy (MA); public choice and public economics (PhD); MBA/PhD. Part-time programs available. *Faculty:* 8 full-time (0 women), 1 (woman) part-time/adjunct. *Students:* 128 full-time (39 women), 14 part-time (5 women); includes 3 Black or African American, non-Hispanic/Latino; 13 Asian, non-Hispanic/Latino; 5 Hispanic/Latino; 4 Two or more races, non-Hispanic/Latino, 73 international. Average age 32. In 2010, 13 master's, 8 doctorates awarded. *Entrance requirements:* For master's and doctorate, GRE General Test or GMAT. Additional exam requirements/recommendations for international students: Required—TOEFL (minimum score 550 paper-based; 213 computer-based; 80 iBT). *Application deadline:* For fall admission, 2/1 priority date for domestic students. Applications are processed on a rolling basis. Application fee: $60. Electronic applications accepted. *Expenses:* Tuition: Full-time $35,748; part-time $1554 per unit. Required fees: $215 per semester. *Financial support:* Fellowships, research assistantships, teaching assistantships, Federal Work-Study, institutionally sponsored loans, and scholarships/grants available. Support available to part-time students. Financial award application deadline: 2/15; financial award applicants required to submit FAFSA. *Faculty research:* International and financial economics, law and economics, regulation, public choice economics. *Unit head:* Paul Zak, Chair, 909-621-8788, Fax: 909-621-8545, E-mail: paul.zak@cgu.edu. *Application contact:* Lesa Hiben, Admissions Coordinator, 909-621-8699, Fax: 909-621-7545, E-mail: lesa.hiben@cga.edu.

Claremont Graduate University, Graduate Programs, School of Politics and Economics, Department of Politics and Policy, Claremont, CA 91711-6160. Offers American politics (MA, PhD); comparative politics (PhD); international political economy (MA); international studies (MA); political philosophy (PhD); political science (PhD); politics, economics and business (MA); public policy (MA, PhD); world politics (PhD); MBA/PhD. Part-time programs available. *Faculty:* 8 full-time (5 women), 3 part-time/adjunct (0 women). *Students:* 155 full-time (59 women), 15 part-time (6 women); includes 35 minority (5 Black or African American, non-Hispanic/Latino; 9 Asian, non-Hispanic/Latino; 17 Hispanic/Latino; 3 Native Hawaiian or other Pacific Islander, non-Hispanic/Latino; 1 Two or more races, non-Hispanic/Latino), 36 international. Average age 32. In 2010, 16 master's, 21 doctorates awarded. Terminal master's awarded for partial completion of doctoral program. *Entrance requirements:* For master's and doctorate, GRE General Test. Additional exam requirements/recommendations for international students: Required—TOEFL (minimum score 550 paper-based; 213 computer-based; 80 iBT). *Application deadline:* For fall admission, 2/1 priority date for domestic students. Applications are processed on a rolling basis. Application fee: $60. Electronic applications accepted. *Expenses:* Tuition: Full-time $35,748; part-time $1554 per unit. Required fees: $215 per semester. *Financial support:* Fellowships, research assistantships, teaching assistantships, Federal Work-Study, institutionally sponsored loans, and scholarships/grants available. Support available to part-time students. Financial award application deadline: 2/15; financial award applicants required to submit FAFSA. *Faculty research:* Environmental policy, international debt, global democratization, Third World development, public sector discrimination. *Unit head:* Jennifer Merolla, Chair, 909-621-8696, Fax: 909-621-8545, E-mail: jennifer.merolla@cgu.edu. *Application contact:* Lesa Hiben, Admissions Coordinator, 909-621-8699, Fax: 909-621-7545, E-mail: lesa.hiben@cga.edu.

Clark Atlanta University, School of Business Administration, Department of Economics, Atlanta, GA 30314. Offers MA. Part-time programs available. *Faculty:* 2 full-time (0 women). *Degree requirements:* For master's, thesis optional. *Entrance requirements:* For master's, GRE General Test, minimum GPA of 2.5. Additional exam requirements/recommendations for international students: Required—TOEFL (minimum score 500 paper-based; 173 computer-based; 61 iBT). *Application deadline:* For fall admission, 4/1 for domestic and international students; for spring admission, 11/1 for domestic and international students. Applications are processed on a rolling basis. Application fee: $40 ($55 for international students). Electronic applications accepted. *Expenses:* Tuition: Full-time $12,942; part-time $719 per credit hour. Required fees: $710; $355 per semester. *Financial support:* Career-related internships or fieldwork, Federal Work-Study, scholarships/grants, and unspecified assistantships available. Support available to part-time students. Financial award application deadline: 4/30; financial award applicants required to submit FAFSA. *Faculty research:* Minority energy demand. *Unit head:* Dr. Ajamu Nyomba, Chairperson, 404-880-6286, E-mail: anyomba@cau.edu. *Application contact:* Michelle Clark-Davis, Graduate Program Admissions, 404-880-6605, E-mail: cauadmissions@cau.edu.

Clark University, Graduate School, Department of Economics, Worcester, MA 01610-1477. Offers PhD. *Faculty:* 8 full-time (3 women), 1 (woman) part-time/adjunct. *Students:* 41 full-time (16 women), 1 (woman) part-time; includes 3 minority (1 Black or African American, non-Hispanic/Latino; 1 Hispanic/Latino; 1 Two or more races, non-Hispanic/Latino), 31 international. Average age 29. 52 applicants, 46% accepted, 7 enrolled. In 2010, 5 doctorates awarded. *Degree requirements:* For doctorate, thesis/dissertation. *Entrance requirements:* For doctorate, GRE General Test. Additional exam requirements/recommendations for international students: Required—TOEFL. *Application deadline:* For fall admission, 2/1 priority date for domestic students. Applications are processed on a rolling basis. Application fee: $50. *Expenses:* Tuition: Full-time $37,000; part-time $1156 per credit hour. Required fees: $30; $1156 per credit hour. *Financial support:* In 2010–11, fellowships with full and partial tuition reimbursements (averaging $12,000 per year), 2 research assistantships with full and partial tuition reimbursements (averaging $12,000 per year), 9 teaching assistantships with full and partial tuition reimbursements (averaging $12,000 per year) were awarded; career-related internships or fieldwork, institutionally sponsored loans, and tuition waivers (full and partial) also available. *Faculty research:* Public finance, economic development, industrial organization, international finance and trade, environmental regulation. Total annual research expenditures: $365,000. *Unit head:* Dr. Wayne Gray, Chair, 508-793-7226. *Application contact:* Cindy Rice, Department Secretary, 508-793-7226, Fax: 508-793-8849, E-mail: economics@clarku.edu.

Clemson University, Graduate School, College of Business and Behavioral Science, Department of Economics, Clemson, SC 29634. Offers applied economics and statistics (MS, PhD); economics (MA, PhD). *Faculty:* 20 full-time (0 women), 6 part-time/adjunct (1 woman). *Students:* 94 full-time (28 women), 9 part-time (0 women); includes 9 minority (4 Black or African American, non-Hispanic/Latino; 4 Asian, non-Hispanic/Latino; 1 Hispanic/Latino), 43 international. Average age 28. 273 applicants, 66% accepted, 58 enrolled. In 2010, 35 master's, 4 doctorates awarded. *Degree requirements:* For doctorate, thesis/dissertation. *Entrance requirements:* For master's and doctorate, GRE General Test. Additional exam requirements/recommendations for international students: Required—TOEFL. *Application deadline:* For fall admission, 4/15 for international students; for spring admission, 9/15 for international students. Application fee: $70 ($80 for international students). Electronic applications accepted. *Expenses:* Contact institution. *Financial support:* In 2010–11, 78 students received support, including 19 fellowships (averaging $4,814 per year), 7 research assistantships with partial tuition reimbursements available (averaging $7,830 per year), 71 teaching assistantships with partial tuition reimbursements available (averaging $22,738 per year); career-related internships or fieldwork, institutionally sponsored loans, scholarships/grants, health care benefits, and unspecified assistantships also available. Support available to part-time students. Financial award applicants required to submit FAFSA. *Faculty research:* Applied price theory, financial economics, industrial economics, labor economics, monetary economics, agricultural policy, agricultural production, agricultural marketing, natural resource economics, regional economic development. Total annual research expenditures: $429,919. *Unit head:* Dr. Raymond Sauer, Interim Chair, 864-656-3969, Fax: 864-656-4192, E-mail: sauerr@clemson.edu. *Application contact:* Dr. Michael T. Maloney, Director of Graduate Programs, 864-656-3430, Fax: 864-656-4192, E-mail: maloney@clemson.edu.

Cleveland State University, College of Graduate Studies, College of Liberal Arts and Social Sciences, Department of Economics, Cleveland, OH 44115. Offers MA. Part-time and evening/weekend programs available. *Faculty:* 7 full-time (1 woman), 4 part-time/adjunct (0 women). *Students:* 13 full-time (6 women), 12 part-time (3 women); includes 1 Black or African American, non-Hispanic/Latino; 2 Asian, non-Hispanic/Latino, 4 international. Average age 29. 41 applicants, 51% accepted, 13 enrolled. In 2010, 10 master's awarded. *Entrance requirements:* For master's, minimum GPA of 2.75; coursework in micro theory, macro theory, statistics, and calculus. Additional exam requirements/recommendations for international students: Required—TOEFL (minimum score 515 paper-based; 197 computer-based). *Application deadline:* For fall admission, 8/20 priority date for domestic students, 5/20 priority date for international students. Applications are processed on a rolling basis. Application fee: $30. Electronic applications accepted. *Expenses:* Tuition, state resident: full-time $8447; part-time $469 per credit hour. Tuition, nonresident: full-time $16,020; part-time $890 per credit hour. Required fees: $50. *Financial support:* In 2010–11, 4 research assistantships with full tuition reimbursements (averaging $3,780 per year) were awarded; teaching assistantships with full tuition reimbursements, scholarships/grants and unspecified assistantships also available. *Faculty research:* Labor economics, health economics, energy, environment, economics of law, organization theory, industrial organization. *Unit head:* Dr. Myong-Hun Chang, Chairperson, 216-687-4523, Fax: 216-687-9206, E-mail: m.chang@csuohio.edu. *Application contact:* Glenda Carbaugh, Administrative Secretary, 216-687-4520, Fax: 216-687-9206, E-mail: g.carbaugh@csuohio.edu.

Cleveland State University, College of Graduate Studies, Maxine Goodman Levin College of Urban Affairs, Program in Nonprofit Administration and Leadership, Cleveland, OH 44115. Offers geographic information systems (Certificate); local and urban management (Certificate); nonprofit administration and leadership (MNAL); nonprofit management (Certificate); urban economic development (Certificate). Part-time and evening/weekend programs available. *Faculty:* 10 full-time (9 women), 8 part-time/adjunct (4 women). *Students:* 11 full-time (10 women), 20 part-time (17 women); includes 7 Black or African American, non-Hispanic/Latino; 2 Asian, non-Hispanic/Latino. Average age 35. 35 applicants, 57% accepted, 14 enrolled. *Degree requirements:* For master's, thesis or alternative, capstone course. *Entrance requirements:* For master's, GRE (minimum 40th percentile verbal and quantitative, 4.0 analytical writing), minimum GPA of 3.0. Additional exam requirements/recommendations for international students: Required—TOEFL (minimum score 525 paper-based; 197 computer-based; 65 iBT). *Application deadline:* For fall admission, 7/15 priority date for domestic students, 5/15 for international students; for spring admission, 11/1 for international students. Applications are processed on a rolling basis. Application fee: $30. Electronic applications accepted. *Expenses:* Tuition, state resident: full-time $8447; part-time $469 per credit hour. Tuition, nonresident: full-time $16,020; part-time $890 per credit hour. Required fees: $50. *Financial support:* In 2010–11, 5 students received support, including research assistantships with full and partial tuition reimbursements available (averaging $6,960 per year); career-related internships or fieldwork, Federal Work-Study, scholarships/grants, tuition waivers (full and partial), and unspecified assistantships also available. Support available to part-time students. Financial award application deadline: 3/1; financial award applicants required to submit FAFSA. *Faculty research:* Human resource management, volunteerism, performance measurement in nonprofits, government-nonprofit partnerships. *Unit head:* Dr. Jennifer Alexander, Director, 216-687-5011, Fax: 216-687-2013, E-mail: j.k.alexander@csuohio.edu. *Application contact:* Joan Demko, Graduate Academic Support Specialist, 216-523-7522, Fax: 216-687-5398, E-mail: urbanprograms@csuohio.edu.

Cleveland State University, College of Graduate Studies, Maxine Goodman Levin College of Urban Affairs, Program in Urban Planning, Design, and Development, Cleveland, OH 44115. Offers geographic information systems (Certificate); local and urban management (Certificate); urban economic development (Certificate); urban planning, design, and development (MUPDD); urban real estate development and finance (Certificate); JD/MUPDD. *Accreditation:* ACSP. Part-time and evening/weekend programs available. *Faculty:* 32 full-time (19 women), 8 part-time/adjunct (4 women). *Students:* 30 full-time (10 women), 28 part-time (17 women); includes 6 Black or African American, non-Hispanic/Latino; 3 Hispanic/Latino, 5 international. Average age 38. 72 applicants, 56% accepted, 21 enrolled. In 2010, 24 master's, 9 Certificates awarded. *Degree requirements:* For master's, thesis or alternative, project or thesis. *Entrance requirements:* For master's, GRE General Test (minimum 50th percentile verbal and quantitative, 4.0 analytical writing), minimum GPA of 3.0. Additional exam requirements/recommendations for international students: Required—TOEFL (minimum score 525 paper-based; 197 computer-based; 65 iBT). *Application deadline:* For fall admission, 7/15 priority date for domestic students, 5/15 for international students; for spring admission, 11/1 for international students. Applications are processed on a rolling basis. Application fee: $30. Electronic applications accepted. *Expenses:* Tuition, state resident: full-time $8447; part-time $469 per credit hour. Tuition, nonresident: full-time $16,020; part-time $890 per credit hour. Required fees: $50. *Financial support:* In 2010–11, 15 students received support, including 10 research assistantships with full and partial tuition reimbursements available (averaging $6,960 per year), 5 teaching assistantships with full and partial tuition reimbursements available (averaging $6,960 per year); career-related internships or fieldwork, Federal Work-Study, tuition waivers (full and partial), and unspecified assistantships also available. Support available to part-time students. Financial award application deadline: 3/1. *Faculty research:* Housing and neighborhood development, urban housing policy, environmental sustainability, economic development, metropolitan change, GIS and planning decision support, PPGIS. *Unit head:* Dr. Dennis Keating, Director, 216-687-2298, Fax: 216-687-2013, E-mail: w.keating@csuohio.edu. *Application contact:* Joan Demkow, Graduate Program Coordinator, 216-523-7522, Fax: 216-687-5398, E-mail: urbanprograms@csuohio.edu.

Cleveland State University, College of Graduate Studies, Maxine Goodman Levin College of Urban Affairs, Program in Urban Studies, Cleveland, OH 44115. Offers geographic information systems (Certificate); local and urban management (Certificate); nonprofit management (Certificate); urban economic development (Certificate); urban real estate development and finance (Certificate); urban studies (MS); urban studies and public affairs (PhD). PhD program offered jointly with The University of Akron. Part-time and evening/weekend programs available. *Faculty:* 26 full-time (10 women), 20 part-time/adjunct (11 women). *Students:* 16 full-time (10 women), 35 part-time (18 women); includes 7 Black or African American, non-Hispanic/Latino, 17 international. Average age 37. 90 applicants, 38% accepted, 18 enrolled. In 2010, 6 master's, 7 doctorates, 6 other advanced degrees awarded. *Degree requirements:* For master's, thesis or alternative, exit project, capstone course; for doctorate, comprehensive exam, thesis/dissertation. *Entrance requirements:* For master's, GRE General Test, minimum GPA of 3.0; for doctorate, GRE General Test, minimum GPA of 3.5. Additional exam requirements/recommendations for international students: Required—TOEFL (minimum score 525 paper-based; 197 computer-based; 65 iBT). *Application deadline:* For fall admission, 7/15 priority date for domestic students, 5/15 for international students; for spring admission, 11/1 for international students. Applications are processed on a rolling basis. Application fee: $30. Electronic applications accepted. *Expenses:* Tuition, state resident: full-time $8447; part-time $469 per credit hour. Tuition, nonresident: full-time $16,020; part-time $890 per credit hour. Required fees: $50. *Financial support:* In 2010–11, 15 students received support, including 11 research assistantships with full tuition reimbursements available (averaging $7,000 per year), 4 teaching assistantships with full and partial tuition reimbursements available (averaging $7,000 per year); career-related internships or fieldwork, Federal Work-Study, institutionally sponsored loans, scholarships/grants, tuition waivers (full and partial), and unspecified assistantships also available. Support available to part-time students. Financial award application deadline: 3/1; financial award applicants required to submit FAFSA. *Faculty research:* Environmental issues, economic development, urban and public policy, public management. *Unit head:* Dr. Sugie Lee, Director, 216-687-2381, Fax: 216-687-9342, E-mail: s.lee56@csuohio.edu. *Application contact:* Joan Demko, Graduate Academic Support Specialist, 216-523-7522, Fax: 216-687-5398, E-mail: urbanprograms@csuohio.edu.

Colorado State University, Graduate School, College of Liberal Arts, Department of Economics, Fort Collins, CO 80523-1771. Offers MA, PhD. Part-time programs available. *Faculty:* 13 full-time (5 women), 2 part-time/adjunct (1 woman). *Students:* 34 full-time (7 women), 32 part-time (8 women); includes 3 minority (all Hispanic/Latino), 23 international. Average age 31. 92 applicants, 79% accepted, 21 enrolled. In 2010, 5 master's, 6 doctorates awarded. Terminal master's awarded for partial completion of doctoral program. *Degree requirements:* For master's, variable foreign language requirement, thesis or alternative; for doctorate, variable foreign language requirement, comprehensive exam, thesis/dissertation. *Entrance requirements:* For master's, GRE General Test (minimum score 1000 verbal and quantitative, 600 quantitative), minimum GPA of 3.0, letters of recommendation; for doctorate, GRE General Test (combined score of 1000 on Verbal and Quantitative sections with at least 600 on Quantitative section), minimum GPA of 3.0, letters of recommendation, statement of purpose. Additional exam requirements/recommendations for international students: Required—TOEFL. *Application deadline:* For fall admission, 1/31 priority date for domestic students. Applications are processed on a rolling basis. Application fee: $50. Electronic applications accepted. *Expenses:* Tuition, state resident: full-time $7434; part-time $413 per credit. Tuition, nonresident: full-time $19,022; part-time $1057 per credit. Required fees: $1729; $88 per credit. *Financial support:* In 2010–11, 20 students received support, including 20 teaching assistantships with full tuition reimbursements available (averaging $14,637 per year); fellowships, research assistantships, career-related internships or fieldwork, Federal Work-Study, institutionally sponsored loans, scholarships/grants, traineeships, and unspecified assistantships also available. Financial award application deadline: 3/1; financial award applicants required to submit FAFSA. *Faculty research:* Regional and development economics, political economy, international trade and investment, public finance, labor markets. Total annual research expenditures: $94,350. *Unit head:* Dr. Steven J. Shulman, Chair, 970-491-6940, Fax: 970-491-2925, E-mail: steven.shulman@colostate.edu. *Application contact:* Barbara Alldredge, Graduate Contact, 970-491-6566, Fax: 970-491-2925, E-mail: barbara.alldredge@colostate.edu.

Columbia University, Graduate School of Arts and Sciences, Division of Social Sciences, Department of Economics, New York, NY 10027. Offers M Phil, MA, PhD, JD/MA, JD/PhD. *Degree requirements:* For master's, thesis or alternative; for doctorate, thesis/dissertation. *Entrance requirements:* For master's and doctorate, GRE General Test, GRE Subject Test, previous course work in mathematics. Additional exam requirements/recommendations for international students: Required—TOEFL. *Faculty research:* International trade.

Columbia University, Graduate School of Business, Doctoral Program in Business, New York, NY 10027. Offers business (PhD), including accounting, decision, risk, and operations, finance and economics, management, marketing. *Accreditation:* AACSB. *Degree requirements:* For doctorate, comprehensive exam, thesis/dissertation, major field exam, research paper, thesis proposal. *Entrance requirements:* For doctorate, GMAT or GRE (finance), 2 letters of reference, resume. Additional exam requirements/recommendations for international students: Required—TOEFL. Electronic applications accepted. *Expenses:* Contact institution. *Faculty research:* Human decision making and behavioral research; real estate market and mortgage defaults; financial crisis and corporate governance; international business; security analysis and accounting.

Columbia University, Graduate School of Business, MBA Program, New York, NY 10027. Offers accounting (MBA); decision, risk, and operations (MBA); entrepreneurship (MBA); finance and economics (MBA); healthcare and pharmaceutical management (MBA); human resource management (MBA); international business (MBA); leadership and ethics (MBA); management (MBA); marketing (MBA); media (MBA); private equity (MBA); real estate (MBA); social enterprise (MBA); value investing (MBA); DDS/MBA; JD/MBA; MBA/MIA; MBA/MPH; MBA/MS; MD/MBA. *Entrance requirements:* For master's, GMAT, 2 letters of recommendation. Additional exam requirements/recommendations for international students: Required—TOEFL. Electronic applications accepted. *Expenses:* Contact institution. *Faculty research:* Human decision making and behavioral research; real estate market and mortgage defaults; financial crisis and corporate governance; international business; security analysis and accounting.

Concordia University, School of Graduate Studies, Faculty of Arts and Science, Department of Economics, Montréal, QC H3G 1M8, Canada. Offers MA, PhD, Diploma. *Degree requirements:* For master's, thesis or alternative, research paper; for doctorate, one foreign language, comprehensive exam, thesis/dissertation, research seminar. *Entrance requirements:* For master's and doctorate, honors degree in economics or equivalent. *Faculty research:* Trade and industrial adjustment, tax policy and reform, environmental policy, economics of migration, economics of telecommunications.

Cornell University, Graduate School, Graduate Fields of Architecture, Art and Planning, Field of Regional Science, Ithaca, NY 14853-0001. Offers environmental studies (MA, MS, PhD); international spatial problems (MA, MS, PhD); location theory (MA, MS, PhD); multiregional economic analysis (MA, MS, PhD); peace science (MA, MS, PhD); planning methods (MA, MS, PhD); urban and regional economics (MA, MS, PhD). *Faculty:* 22 full-time (6 women). *Students:* 20 full-time (6 women); includes 1 Black or African American, non-Hispanic/Latino, 18 international. Average age 31. 5 applicants, 80% accepted, 4 enrolled. In 2010, 3 doctorates awarded. Terminal master's awarded for partial completion of doctoral program. *Degree requirements:* For master's, thesis; for doctorate, comprehensive exam, thesis/dissertation. *Entrance requirements:* For master's and doctorate, GRE General Test, 2 letters of recommendation. Additional exam requirements/recommendations for international students: Required—TOEFL (minimum score 600 paper-based; 250 computer-based; 77 iBT). *Application deadline:* For fall admission, 1/15 priority date for domestic students. Application fee: $70. Electronic applications accepted. *Expenses:* Tuition: Full-time $29,500. Required fees: $76. Tuition and fees vary according to degree level and program. *Financial support:* In 2010–11, 1 research assistantship with full tuition reimbursement, 2 teaching assistantships with full tuition reimbursements were awarded; fellowships with full tuition reimbursements, institutionally sponsored loans, scholarships/grants, health care benefits, tuition waivers (full and partial), and unspecified assistantships also available. Financial award applicants required to submit FAFSA. *Faculty research:* Urban and regional growth, spatial economics, formation of spatial patterns by socioeconomic systems, non-linear dynamics and complex systems, environmental-economic systems. *Unit head:* Director of Graduate Studies, 607-255-6848, Fax: 607-255-1971. *Application contact:* Graduate Field Assistant, 607-255-6848, Fax: 607-255-1971, E-mail: regsci@cornell.edu.

Cornell University, Graduate School, Graduate Fields of Arts and Sciences, Field of Economics, Ithaca, NY 14853-0001. Offers applied economics (PhD); basic analytical economics (PhD); econometrics and economic statistics (PhD); economic development and planning (PhD); economic theory (PhD); industrial organization and control (PhD); international economics (PhD); labor economics (PhD); monetary and macroeconomics (PhD); public finance (PhD). *Faculty:* 78 full-time (10 women). *Students:* 100 full-time (40 women); includes 1 Black or African American, non-Hispanic/Latino; 4 Asian, non-Hispanic/Latino; 1 Hispanic/Latino, 61 international. Average age 27. 742 applicants, 10% accepted, 20 enrolled. In 2010, 21 doctorates awarded. *Degree requirements:* For doctorate, comprehensive exam, thesis/dissertation. *Entrance requirements:* For doctorate, GRE General Test, 3 letters of recommendation. Additional exam requirements/recommendations for international students: Required—TOEFL (minimum score 550 paper-based; 213 computer-based; 77 iBT). *Application deadline:* For fall admission, 1/15 priority date for domestic students. Application fee: $80. Electronic applications accepted. *Expenses:* Tuition: Full-time $29,500. Required fees: $76. Tuition and fees vary according to degree level and program. *Financial support:* In 2010–11, 20 fellowships with full tuition reimbursements, 16 research assistantships with full tuition reimbursements, 50 teaching assistantships with full tuition reimbursements were awarded; institutionally sponsored loans, scholarships/grants, health care benefits, tuition waivers (full and partial), and unspecified assistantships also available. Financial award applicants required to submit FAFSA. *Faculty research:* Learning and games, economics of education, political economy, transfer payments, time series and nonparametrics. *Unit head:* Director of Graduate Studies, 607-255-4893, Fax: 607-255-2818. *Application contact:* Graduate Field Assistant, 607-255-4893, Fax: 607-255-2818, E-mail: econ_phd@cornell.edu.

Dalhousie University, Faculty of Science, Department of Economics, Halifax, NS B3H 4R2, Canada. Offers MA, MDE, PhD. *Degree requirements:* For master's, thesis; for doctorate, thesis/dissertation. *Entrance requirements:* For master's and doctorate, GRE (recommended). Additional exam requirements/recommendations for international students: Required—TOEFL, IELTS, CANTEST, CAEL, or Michigan English Language Assessment Battery. Electronic applications accepted. *Faculty research:* Applied econometrics, industrial organization, labor and income distribution, economic theory (micro and macro), resource economics (fishing, forestry).

DePaul University, Charles H. Kellstadt Graduate School of Business and College of Liberal Arts and Sciences, Department of Economics, Chicago, IL 60604-2287. Offers applied economics (MBA); business strategy (MBA); economics and policy analysis (MA); international business (MBA). Part-time and evening/weekend programs available. *Faculty:* 26 full-time (5 women), 21 part-time/adjunct (5 women). *Students:* 80 full-time (30 women), 31 part-time (12 women); includes 18 minority (8 Black or African American, non-Hispanic/Latino; 7 Asian, non-Hispanic/Latino; 3 Hispanic/Latino), 8 international. In 2010, 7 master's awarded. *Degree requirements:* For master's, thesis optional. *Entrance requirements:* For master's, GMAT (MBA), GRE (MS). Additional exam requirements/recommendations for international students: Required—TOEFL. *Application deadline:* For fall admission, 7/1 for domestic students; for winter admission, 10/1 for domestic students; for spring admission, 2/1 for domestic students. Applications are processed on a rolling basis. Application fee: $40. Electronic applications accepted. *Financial support:* In 2010–11, 3 students received support, including 2 research assistantships with partial tuition reimbursements available (averaging $9,999 per year). Support available to

Economics

DePaul University (continued)

part-time students. *Faculty research:* Forensic economics, game theory sports, economics of education, banking in Poland and Thailand. *Unit head:* Dr. Thomas D. Donley, Chairperson, 312-362-8887, Fax: 312-362-5452, E-mail: tdonley@depaul.edu. *Application contact:* Gabriella Bucci, Director of Graduate Program in Economics, 773-362-6787, Fax: 312-362-5452, E-mail: gbucci@depaul.edu.

Drexel University, LeBow College of Business, Program in Business Administration, Philadelphia, PA 19104-2875. Offers business administration (MBA, PhD, APC), including accounting (MBA, PhD), decision sciences (PhD), economics (MBA, PhD), finance (MBA, PhD), legal studies (MBA), management (MBA), marketing (MBA, PhD), organizational sciences (PhD), quantitative methods (MBA), strategic management (PhD). *Accreditation:* AACSB. Part-time and evening/weekend programs available. Postbaccalaureate distance learning degree programs offered (minimal on-campus study). Terminal master's awarded for partial completion of doctoral program. *Entrance requirements:* For master's, GMAT, minimum GPA of 2.75; for doctorate, GMAT. Additional exam requirements/recommendations for international students: Required—TOEFL. Electronic applications accepted. *Faculty research:* Decision support systems, individual and group behavior, operations research, techniques and strategy.

Duke University, Graduate School, Department of Economics, Durham, NC 27708. Offers AM, PhD, JD/AM. *Faculty:* 49 full-time. *Students:* 202 full-time (87 women); includes 4 Black or African American, non-Hispanic/Latino; 6 Asian, non-Hispanic/Latino; 7 Hispanic/Latino, 119 international. 985 applicants, 17% accepted, 72 enrolled. In 2010, 54 master's, 7 doctorates awarded. *Degree requirements:* For doctorate, thesis/dissertation. *Entrance requirements:* For master's and doctorate, GRE General Test. Additional exam requirements/recommendations for international students: Required—TOEFL (minimum score 550 paper-based; 213 computer-based; 83 iBT), IELTS (minimum score 7). *Application deadline:* For fall admission, 12/8 priority date for domestic and international students; for spring admission, 10/15 for domestic and international students. Application fee: $75. Electronic applications accepted. *Financial support:* Fellowships, research assistantships, teaching assistantships, Federal Work-Study available. Financial award application deadline: 12/8. *Unit head:* Barbara Rossi, Director of Graduate Studies, 919-660-1891, Fax: 919-660-1879, E-mail: jennifer.counts@duke.edu. *Application contact:* Elizabeth Hutton, Director, Graduate Admissions, 919-684-3913, Fax: 919-684-2277, E-mail: grad-admissions@duke.edu.

East Carolina University, Graduate School, Thomas Harriot College of Arts and Sciences, Department of Economics, Greenville, NC 27858-4353. Offers applied resource economics (MS). Part-time programs available. *Degree requirements:* For master's, one foreign language, comprehensive exam. *Entrance requirements:* For master's, GRE General Test. Additional exam requirements/recommendations for international students: Required—TOEFL. *Expenses:* Tuition, state resident: full-time $3130; part-time $391.25 per credit hour. Tuition, nonresident: full-time $13,817; part-time $1727.13 per credit hour. Required fees: $1916; $239.50 per credit hour. Tuition and fees vary according to campus/location and program.

Eastern Illinois University, Graduate School, College of Sciences, Department of Economics, Charleston, IL 61920-3099. Offers MA.

Eastern Michigan University, Graduate School, College of Arts and Sciences, Department of Economics, Ypsilanti, MI 48197. Offers applied economics (MA); economics (MA); health economics (MA); international economics and development (MA); trade and development (MA). Part-time and evening/weekend programs available. Postbaccalaureate distance learning degree programs offered (minimal on-campus study). *Faculty:* 11 full-time (2 women). *Students:* 25 full-time (5 women), 32 part-time (7 women); includes 19 minority (10 Black or African American, non-Hispanic/Latino; 1 American Indian or Alaska Native, non-Hispanic/Latino; 4 Asian, non-Hispanic/Latino; 4 Hispanic/Latino), 7 international. Average age 29. 50 applicants, 74% accepted, 19 enrolled. In 2010, 18 master's awarded. *Degree requirements:* For master's, thesis or alternative. *Entrance requirements:* Additional exam requirements/recommendations for international students: Required—TOEFL. *Application deadline:* Applications are processed on a rolling basis. Application fee: $35. *Financial support:* Fellowships, research assistantships with full tuition reimbursements, teaching assistantships with full tuition reimbursements, career-related internships or fieldwork, Federal Work-Study, institutionally sponsored loans, scholarships/grants, tuition waivers (partial), and unspecified assistantships available. Support available to part-time students. Financial award applicants required to submit FAFSA. *Unit head:* Dr. Raouf S. Hanna, Department Head, 734-487-3395, Fax: 734-487-9666, E-mail: rhanna@emich.edu. *Application contact:* Dr. David Crary, Advisor, 734-487-0001, Fax: 734-487-9666, E-mail: dcrary@emich.edu.

East Tennessee State University, School of Graduate Studies, College of Arts and Sciences, Department of Economics, Finance, and Urban Studies, Johnson City, TN 37614. Offers city management (MCM); not-for-profit (MPA); planning and development (MPA); public financial management (MPA). Part-time programs available. *Faculty:* 1 full-time (0 women). *Students:* 15 full-time (5 women), 8 part-time (4 women); includes 1 Black or African American, non-Hispanic/Latino, 2 international. Average age 30. 19 applicants, 42% accepted, 7 enrolled. In 2010, 14 master's awarded. *Degree requirements:* For master's, comprehensive exam, internship, capstone, research report. *Entrance requirements:* For master's, GRE General Test, minimum GPA of 2.5. Additional exam requirements/recommendations for international students: Required—TOEFL (minimum score 550 paper-based; 213 computer-based; 79 iBT). *Application deadline:* For fall admission, 6/1 priority date for domestic students, 4/30 for international students; for spring admission, 11/1 for domestic students, 9/30 for international students. Application fee: $25 ($35 for international students). Electronic applications accepted. *Financial support:* In 2010–11, 9 research assistantships with full tuition reimbursements (averaging $5,500 per year) were awarded; career-related internships or fieldwork, institutionally sponsored loans, scholarships/grants, and unspecified assistantships also available. Financial award application deadline: 7/1; financial award applicants required to submit FAFSA. Total annual research expenditures: $6,519. *Unit head:* Dr. Weixing Chen, Chair, 423-439-6632, Fax: 423-439-4348, E-mail: chen@etsu.edu. *Application contact:* Dr. Weixing Chen, Chair, 423-439-6632, Fax: 423-439-4348, E-mail: chen@etsu.edu.

Emory University, Laney Graduate School, Department of Economics, Atlanta, GA 30322-1100. Offers PhD. *Degree requirements:* For doctorate, comprehensive exam, thesis/dissertation. *Entrance requirements:* For doctorate, GRE General Test. Electronic applications accepted. *Expenses:* Tuition: Full-time $33,800. Required fees: $1300. *Faculty research:* Applied microeconomics, econometrics, public choice, macroeconomics, law and economics.

Florida Agricultural and Mechanical University, Division of Graduate Studies, Research, and Continuing Education, College of Arts and Sciences, Division of History and Political Sciences, Program in Applied Social Science, Tallahassee, FL 32307-3200. Offers African American history (MASS); criminal justice (MASS); economics (MASS); history (MASS); political science (MASS); public administration (MASS); public management (MASS); social work (MASS); sociology (MASS). Part-time programs available. *Degree requirements:* For master's, thesis optional. *Entrance requirements:* For master's, GRE General Test, minimum GPA of 3.0. *Faculty research:* Southern history, black history, election trends, presidential history.

Florida Atlantic University, College of Business, Department of Economics, Boca Raton, FL 33431-0991. Offers MS. Part-time and evening/weekend programs available. *Faculty:* 14 full-time (3 women), 7 part-time/adjunct (1 woman). *Students:* 23 full-time (7 women), 17 part-time (3 women); includes 12 minority (1 Black or African American, non-Hispanic/Latino; 5 Asian, non-Hispanic/Latino; 6 Hispanic/Latino), 7 international. Average age 32. 33 applicants, 45% accepted, 11 enrolled. In 2010, 6 master's awarded. *Degree requirements:* For master's, thesis optional. *Entrance requirements:* For master's, GMAT, GRE General Test, minimum GPA of 3.0. Additional exam requirements/recommendations for international students: Required—TOEFL (minimum score 600 paper-based; 250 computer-based). *Application deadline:* For fall admission, 7/1 priority date for domestic students, 2/15 priority date for

international students; for winter admission, 11/1 priority date for domestic students, 8/15 priority date for international students; for spring admission, 4/1 priority date for domestic students, 1/15 priority date for international students. Applications are processed on a rolling basis. Application fee: $30. *Expenses:* Tuition, area resident: Part-time $319.96 per credit. Tuition, state resident: part-time $319.96 per credit. Tuition, nonresident: part-time $926.42 per credit. *Financial support:* Teaching assistantships with tuition reimbursements, tuition waivers (partial) and unspecified assistantships available. Financial award application deadline: 3/1. *Faculty research:* International trade and finance, decision-making, monetary conditions, economic fluctuations and growth. *Unit head:* Dr. Charles Register, Chair, 561-297-4176, Fax: 561-297-2542, E-mail: register@fau.edu. *Application contact:* Dr. Eric P. Chiang, Graduate Director, 561-297-2947, Fax: 561-297-1315, E-mail: chiang@fau.edu.

Florida International University, College of Arts and Sciences, Department of Economics, Miami, FL 33199. Offers MA, PhD. Part-time and evening/weekend programs available. *Faculty:* 11 full-time (3 women), 5 part-time/adjunct (2 women). *Students:* 25 full-time (7 women), 3 part-time (1 woman); includes 1 Asian, non-Hispanic/Latino; 3 Hispanic/Latino, 18 international. Average age 26. 77 applicants, 3% accepted, 2 enrolled. In 2010, 4 master's, 3 doctorates awarded. *Degree requirements:* For master's, thesis or alternative; for doctorate, comprehensive exam, thesis/dissertation. *Entrance requirements:* For master's, GRE, minimum GPA of 3.0, letters of recommendation; for doctorate, GRE General Test, 3 letters of recommendation, minimum GPA of 3.0. Additional exam requirements/recommendations for international students: Required—TOEFL (minimum score 550 paper-based; 80 iBT). *Application deadline:* For fall admission, 4/1 for domestic and international students. Application fee: $30. Electronic applications accepted. *Financial support:* Federal Work-Study, institutionally sponsored loans, and scholarships/grants available. Financial award application deadline: 3/1; financial award applicants required to submit FAFSA. *Faculty research:* Economic development, international economics, urban/regional economics, Latin American economics. *Unit head:* Dr. Peter Thompson, Chair, 305-348-2316, Fax: 305-348-1524, E-mail: peter.thompson2@fiu.edu. *Application contact:* Dr. Cem Karayalcin, Graduate Director, 305-348-3285, Fax: 305-348-1524, E-mail: karayalc@fiu.edu.

Florida State University, The Graduate School, College of Social Sciences and Public Policy, Department of Economics, Tallahassee, FL 32306-2180. Offers MS, PhD, JD/MS. Part-time programs available. *Faculty:* 32 full-time (9 women), 2 part-time/adjunct (both women). *Students:* 57 full-time (10 women), 8 part-time (3 women); includes 1 Black or African American, non-Hispanic/Latino; 2 Asian, non-Hispanic/Latino; 3 Hispanic/Latino, 10 international. Average age 27. 162 applicants, 69% accepted, 32 enrolled. In 2010, 21 master's, 9 doctorates awarded. Terminal master's awarded for partial completion of doctoral program. *Degree requirements:* For master's, thesis or alternative; for doctorate, thesis/dissertation, 2 comprehensive exams, workshops. *Entrance requirements:* For master's, GRE General Test, minimum GPA of 3.0, 3.4 on graduate work; minimum 1 course each in statistics and calculus; for doctorate, GRE General Test, minimum graduate GPA of 3.4; minimum 1 course each in statistics and linear algebra, 2 in calculus. Additional exam requirements/recommendations for international students: Required—TOEFL (minimum score 550 paper-based; 213 computer-based; 80 iBT), IELTS (minimum score 6.5). *Application deadline:* For fall admission, 7/1 priority date for domestic students, 5/1 priority date for international students; for spring admission, 11/1 priority date for domestic students, 9/1 priority date for international students. Applications are processed on a rolling basis. Application fee: $30. Electronic applications accepted. *Expenses:* Tuition, state resident: full-time $8238.24. *Financial support:* In 2010–11, 40 students received support, including 7 fellowships with full tuition reimbursements available (averaging $22,000 per year), 7 research assistantships with full tuition reimbursements available (averaging $16,000 per year), 22 teaching assistantships with full tuition reimbursements available (averaging $16,000 per year); scholarships/grants and tuition waivers also available. Financial award application deadline: 1/31; financial award applicants required to submit FAFSA. *Faculty research:* Industrial organization, international, experimental/behavioral, public, law and economics. Total annual research expenditures: $400,000. *Unit head:* Dr. Bruce L. Benson, Chairman, 850-644-5001, Fax: 850-644-4535, E-mail: bbenson@fsu.edu. *Application contact:* Dr. Thomas W. Zuehlke, Graduate Director, 850-644-7206, Fax: 850-644-4535, E-mail: tzuehlke@fsu.edu.

Fordham University, Graduate School of Arts and Sciences, Department of Economics, New York, NY 10458. Offers MA, PhD. Part-time and evening/weekend programs available. *Faculty:* 22 full-time (4 women). *Students:* 24 full-time (7 women), 54 part-time (21 women); includes 1 Black or African American, non-Hispanic/Latino; 1 American Indian or Alaska Native, non-Hispanic/Latino; 4 Asian, non-Hispanic/Latino; 3 Hispanic/Latino, 26 international. Average age 30. 158 applicants, 42% accepted, 30 enrolled. In 2010, 22 master's, 6 doctorates awarded. Terminal master's awarded for partial completion of doctoral program. *Degree requirements:* For master's, comprehensive exam; for doctorate, comprehensive exam, thesis/dissertation. *Entrance requirements:* For master's and doctorate, GRE General Test. Additional exam requirements/recommendations for international students: Required—TOEFL (minimum score 600 paper-based; 250 computer-based). *Application deadline:* For fall admission, 1/4 priority date for domestic students; for spring admission, 11/1 for domestic students. Application fee: $70. Electronic applications accepted. *Financial support:* In 2010–11, 29 students received support, including 2 fellowships with tuition reimbursements available (averaging $22,225 per year), 10 research assistantships with tuition reimbursements available (averaging $16,290 per year), 17 teaching assistantships with tuition reimbursements available (averaging $12,593 per year); career-related internships or fieldwork, institutionally sponsored loans, tuition waivers (full and partial), and unspecified assistantships also available. Financial award application deadline: 1/4; financial award applicants required to submit FAFSA. *Faculty research:* Developmental economics, econometrics. Total annual research expenditures: $25,000. *Unit head:* Dr. Henry Schwalbenberg, Chair, 718-817-3866, Fax: 718-817-3518. *Application contact:* Charlene Dundie, Director of Graduate Admissions, 718-817-4420, Fax: 718-817-3566, E-mail: dundie@fordham.edu.

Fordham University, Graduate School of Arts and Sciences, Program in International Political Economy and Development, New York, NY 10458. Offers MA, Certificate. Part-time and evening/weekend programs available. *Students:* 44 full-time (22 women), 27 part-time (11 women); includes 1 American Indian or Alaska Native, non-Hispanic/Latino; 1 Asian, non-Hispanic/Latino; 4 Hispanic/Latino, 19 international. Average age 28. 213 applicants, 37% accepted, 36 enrolled. In 2010, 28 master's awarded. *Degree requirements:* For master's, comprehensive exam. *Entrance requirements:* For master's, GRE General Test. Additional exam requirements/recommendations for international students: Required—TOEFL (minimum score 600 paper-based; 250 computer-based). *Application deadline:* For fall admission, 1/4 priority date for domestic students; for spring admission, 11/1 for domestic students. Application fee: $70. Electronic applications accepted. *Financial support:* In 2010–11, 16 students received support, including 16 research assistantships with tuition reimbursements available (averaging $18,400 per year); career-related internships or fieldwork, institutionally sponsored loans, tuition waivers (full and partial), and unspecified assistantships also available. Financial award application deadline: 1/4; financial award applicants required to submit FAFSA. *Faculty research:* International economics, comparative international politics, international banking and finance, international development, emerging markets and country risk analysis. *Unit head:* Dr. Henry Schwalbenberg, Chair, 718-817-3866, Fax: 718-817-3518. *Application contact:* Charlene Dundie, Director of Graduate Admissions, 718-817-4420, Fax: 718-817-3566, E-mail: dundie@fordham.edu.

George Mason University, College of Humanities and Social Sciences, Department of Economics, Fairfax, VA 22030. Offers economic systems design (Graduate Certificate); economics (MA, PhD). *Faculty:* 33 full-time (2 women), 8 part-time/adjunct (1 woman). *Students:* 98 full-time (25 women), 103 part-time (19 women); includes 1 Black or African American, non-Hispanic/Latino; 6 Asian, non-Hispanic/Latino; 5 Hispanic/Latino; 1 Two or more races, non-Hispanic/Latino, 35 international. Average age 30. 335 applicants, 45% accepted, 63 enrolled. In 2010, 50 master's, 19 doctorates awarded. *Degree requirements:* For master's, thesis optional, 2 comprehensive exams; for doctorate, comprehensive exam, thesis/dissertation,

2 preliminary exams, field exams. *Entrance requirements:* For master's, GRE, course work in microeconomics and macroeconomics through intermediate level; for doctorate, GRE, 1 year each of coursework in calculus and statistics; 1 semester each of matrix algebra and econometrics. Additional exam requirements/recommendations for international students: Required—TOEFL (minimum score 570 paper-based; 230 computer-based). *Application deadline:* For fall admission, 2/1 priority date for domestic students. Application fee: $100. Electronic applications accepted. *Expenses:* Tuition, state resident: full-time $8192; part-time $440 per credit hour. Tuition, nonresident: full-time $22,952; part-time $1055 per credit hour. Required fees: $2364; $99 per credit hour. *Financial support:* In 2010–11, 52 students received support, including 3 fellowships with full tuition reimbursements available (averaging $18,000 per year), 33 research assistantships with full and partial tuition reimbursements available (averaging $14,027 per year), 19 teaching assistantships with full and partial tuition reimbursements available (averaging $7,825 per year); career-related internships or fieldwork, Federal Work-Study, scholarships/grants, unspecified assistantships, and health care benefits (full-time research or teaching assistantship recipients) also available. Support available to part-time students. Financial award applicants required to submit FAFSA. *Faculty research:* Neuroeconomics, experimental economics (computer-based). Total annual research expenditures: $1.7 million. *Unit head:* Dr. Donald Boudreaux, Chairman, 703-993-1157, Fax: 703-993-1133, E-mail: dboudrea@gmu.edu. *Application contact:* Mary Jackson, Graduate Coordinator, 703-993-1135, E-mail: mjacksoq@gmu.edu.

Georgetown University, Graduate School of Arts and Sciences, Department of Economics, Washington, DC 20057. Offers econometrics (PhD); economic development (PhD); economic theory (PhD); industrial organization (PhD); international macro and finance (PhD); international trade (PhD); labor economics (PhD); macroeconomics (PhD); public economics and political economics (PhD); MA/PhD; MS/MA. *Degree requirements:* For doctorate, comprehensive exam, thesis/dissertation. *Entrance requirements:* For doctorate, GRE General Test. Additional exam requirements/recommendations for international students: Required—TOEFL. *Faculty research:* International economics, economic development.

The George Washington University, Columbian College of Arts and Sciences, Department of Economics, Washington, DC 20052. Offers MA, PhD. Part-time and evening/weekend programs available. *Faculty:* 22 full-time (7 women). *Students:* 57 full-time (25 women), 65 part-time (29 women); includes 3 Black or African American, non-Hispanic/Latino; 6 Asian, non-Hispanic/Latino; 3 Hispanic/Latino, 72 international. Average age 30. 389 applicants, 51% accepted, 33 enrolled. In 2010, 11 master's, 5 doctorates awarded. Terminal master's awarded for partial completion of doctoral program. *Degree requirements:* For master's, comprehensive exam, thesis or alternative; for doctorate, thesis/dissertation, general exam. *Entrance requirements:* For master's and doctorate, GRE General Test, minimum GPA of 3.0. Additional exam requirements/recommendations for international students: Required—TOEFL (minimum score 550 paper-based; 213 computer-based; 80 iBT). *Application deadline:* For fall admission, 1/15 priority date for domestic and international students; for spring admission, 9/1 for international students. Applications are processed on a rolling basis. Application fee: $75. Electronic applications accepted. *Financial support:* In 2010–11, 25 students received support; fellowships with full tuition reimbursements available, teaching assistantships with tuition reimbursements available, Federal Work-Study available. Financial award application deadline: 1/15. *Unit head:* Robert F. Phillips, Chair, 202-994-8619, E-mail: rphil@gwu.edu. *Application contact:* Information Contact, 202-994-6150, Fax: 202-994-6147, E-mail: econgrad@gwu.edu.

Georgia Institute of Technology, Graduate Studies and Research, Ivan Allen College of Policy and International Affairs, School of Economics, Atlanta, GA 30332-0001. Offers MS. *Degree requirements:* For master's, thesis. *Entrance requirements:* For master's, GRE. Additional exam requirements/recommendations for international students: Required—TOEFL. *Faculty research:* Land use patterns in developing countries, office automation and productivity, dynamic modeling of financial markets.

Georgia State University, Andrew Young School of Policy Studies, Department of Economics, Atlanta, GA 30302-3083. Offers MA, PhD. MA offered through the College of Arts and Sciences. Part-time and evening/weekend programs available. Terminal master's awarded for partial completion of doctoral program. *Degree requirements:* For master's, thesis optional; for doctorate, comprehensive exam, thesis/dissertation. *Entrance requirements:* For master's, GRE; for doctorate, GRE General Test. Additional exam requirements/recommendations for international students: Required—TOEFL. Electronic applications accepted. *Faculty research:* Tax policy, economic growth and development, environmental economics, urban and regional economics, economics of science.

Georgia State University, J. Mack Robinson College of Business, Program in General Business Administration, Atlanta, GA 30302-3083. Offers accounting/information systems (MBA); economics (MBA, MS); enterprise risk management (MBA); general business (MBA); general business administration (EMBA, PMBA); information systems consulting (MBA); information systems risk management (MBA); international business and information technology (MBA); international entrepreneurship (MBA); MBA/JD. *Accreditation:* AACSB. Part-time and evening/weekend programs available. *Entrance requirements:* For master's, GMAT. Additional exam requirements/recommendations for international students: Required—TOEFL (minimum score 610 paper-based; 255 computer-based; 101 iBT). Electronic applications accepted.

Graduate School and University Center of the City University of New York, Graduate Studies, Program in Economics, New York, NY 10016-4039. Offers PhD. *Degree requirements:* For doctorate, thesis/dissertation. *Entrance requirements:* For doctorate, GRE General Test. Additional exam requirements/recommendations for international students: Required—TOEFL. Electronic applications accepted.

Harvard University, Graduate School of Arts and Sciences, Committee on Business Economics, Cambridge, MA 02138. Offers PhD. *Degree requirements:* For doctorate, thesis/dissertation. *Entrance requirements:* For doctorate, GMAT or GRE General Test. Additional exam requirements/recommendations for international students: Required—TOEFL. *Expenses:* Tuition: Full-time $34,976. Required fees: $1166. Full-time tuition and fees vary according to program.

Harvard University, Graduate School of Arts and Sciences, Department of Economics, Cambridge, MA 02138. Offers PhD. *Degree requirements:* For doctorate, thesis/dissertation, oral exam. *Entrance requirements:* For doctorate, GRE General Test, GRE Subject Test. Additional exam requirements/recommendations for international students: Required—TOEFL. *Expenses:* Tuition: Full-time $34,976. Required fees: $1166. Full-time tuition and fees vary according to program. *Faculty research:* Industrial organization, macromonetary issues, international economics.

Hawai'i Pacific University, College of Business Administration, Honolulu, HI 96813. Offers accounting/CPA (MBA); e-business (MBA); economics (MBA); finance (MBA); human resource management (MA, MBA); information systems (MBA, MSIS), including knowledge management (MSIS), software engineering (MSIS), telecommunications security (MSIS); international business (MBA); management (MBA); marketing (MBA); organizational change (MA, MBA); travel industry management (MBA). Part-time and evening/weekend programs available. *Degree requirements:* For master's, thesis. *Entrance requirements:* For master's, GMAT. Additional exam requirements/recommendations for international students: Recommended—TOEFL (minimum score 550 paper-based; 213 computer-based; 80 iBT), TWE (minimum score 5). Electronic applications accepted. *Faculty research:* Statistical control process as used by management, studies in comparative cross-cultural management styles, not-for-profit management.

Howard University, Graduate School, Department of Economics, Washington, DC 20059-0002. Offers MA, PhD. Part-time programs available. *Degree requirements:* For master's, comprehensive exam, thesis optional; for doctorate, one foreign language, comprehensive exam, thesis/dissertation. *Entrance requirements:* For master's, GRE General Test, minimum GPA of 3.0; for doctorate, GRE General Test, master's degree in economics or related field, minimum GPA of 3.0. Electronic applications accepted. *Faculty research:* Economic development, international trade, urban rentalization.

Hunter College of the City University of New York, Graduate School, School of Arts and Sciences, Department of Economics, New York, NY 10021-5085. Offers accounting (MS); economics (MA). Part-time and evening/weekend programs available. *Faculty:* 5 full-time (1 woman), 4 part-time/adjunct (0 women). *Students:* 25 full-time (9 women), 50 part-time (24 women); includes 8 Black or African American, non-Hispanic/Latino; 19 Asian, non-Hispanic/Latino; 5 Hispanic/Latino, 24 international. Average age 29. 109 applicants, 51% accepted, 29 enrolled. In 2010, 19 master's awarded. *Degree requirements:* For master's, research paper or thesis. *Entrance requirements:* For master's, GMAT or GRE General Test, minimum GPA of 3.0, 18 credits of undergraduate course work in economics (9 in mathematics), 2 letters of recommendation (1 from member of Department of Economics). Additional exam requirements/recommendations for international students: Required—TOEFL. *Application deadline:* For fall admission, 4/1 for domestic students, 2/1 for international students; for spring admission, 11/1 for domestic students, 9/1 for international students. Application fee: $125. *Financial support:* Fellowships, research assistantships, teaching assistantships, career-related internships or fieldwork, Federal Work-Study, institutionally sponsored loans, and tuition waivers (partial) available. Support available to part-time students. *Faculty research:* Earnings of immigrants and minority groups, taxation and the regional economy. *Unit head:* Dr. Marjorie P. Honig, Chairperson, 212-772-5400, Fax: 212-772-5398, E-mail: mhonig@hunter.cuny.edu. *Application contact:* Randall Filer, Professor/Advisor, 212-772-5399, Fax: 212-772-5398, E-mail: grad.econadvisor@hunter.cuny.edu.

Illinois State University, Graduate School, College of Arts and Sciences, Department of Economics, Normal, IL 61790-2200. Offers MA, MS. *Degree requirements:* For master's, thesis or alternative. *Entrance requirements:* For master's, GRE General Test, minimum GPA of 2.6 in last 60 hours of course work. *Faculty research:* Stevenson Center Graduate Assistantship in Community/Economic Development; the social, economic and educational correlates of rural school closure; Stevenson Center Americorps project.

Indiana University Bloomington, University Graduate School, College of Arts and Sciences, Department of Economics, Bloomington, IN 47405-7104. Offers MA, PhD. *Faculty:* 20 full-time (3 women). *Students:* 68 full-time (21 women); includes 4 minority (1 Black or African American, non-Hispanic/Latino; 2 Asian, non-Hispanic/Latino; 1 Hispanic/Latino), 49 international. Average age 29. 235 applicants, 14% accepted, 14 enrolled. In 2010, 12 master's, 16 doctorates awarded. Terminal master's awarded for partial completion of doctoral program. *Degree requirements:* For master's, thesis optional, tool skill classes; for doctorate, comprehensive exam, thesis/dissertation, field exam, 3rd year paper, tool skill classes, dissertation proposal presentation, oral defense of dissertation. *Entrance requirements:* For master's and doctorate, GRE General Test, minimum one year of calculus, semester of linear algebra. Additional exam requirements/recommendations for international students: Required—TOEFL (minimum score 600 paper-based; 250 computer-based; 100 iBT); Recommended—IELTS (minimum score 6.5). *Application deadline:* For fall admission, 1/15 priority date for domestic students, 12/1 priority date for international students. Applications are processed on a rolling basis. Application fee: $55 ($65 for international students). Electronic applications accepted. *Financial support:* In 2010–11, 54 students received support, including 3 fellowships with full tuition reimbursements available (averaging $18,000 per year), 3 research assistantships with full tuition reimbursements available (averaging $15,000 per year), 48 teaching assistantships with full tuition reimbursements available (averaging $14,500 per year); institutionally sponsored loans and health care benefits also available. Financial award application deadline: 1/15. *Faculty research:* Games, experiments and organization, transition economics, growth and development, macroeconomics, econometrics. *Unit head:* Prof. Gerhard Glomm, Chair, 812-855-6160, Fax: 812-855-3736, E-mail: gglomm@indiana.edu. *Application contact:* Chris Cunningham, Graduate Services Assistant, 812-855-8453, Fax: 812-855-3736, E-mail: rcunning@indiana.edu.

Indiana University–Purdue University Indianapolis, School of Liberal Arts, Department of Economics, Indianapolis, IN 46202-2896. Offers MA, MA/MA. *Faculty:* 16 full-time (3 women). *Students:* 10 full-time (5 women), 9 part-time (3 women); includes 1 minority (Hispanic/Latino), 9 international. Average age 27. 49 applicants, 43% accepted, 13 enrolled. In 2010, 10 master's awarded. *Entrance requirements:* For master's, GRE, minimum GPA of 3.0; courses in economic theory, statistics, calculus. Additional exam requirements/recommendations for international students: Required—TOEFL (minimum score 600 paper-based). *Application deadline:* For fall admission, 2/1 priority date for domestic and international students. Application fee: $55 ($65 for international students). *Financial support:* In 2010–11, 1 fellowship with partial tuition reimbursement (averaging $10,000 per year), 7 teaching assistantships (averaging $9,586 per year) were awarded; research assistantships with partial tuition reimbursements, career-related internships or fieldwork and health care benefits also available. *Faculty research:* Charitable giving. *Unit head:* Paul Carlin, Chair, 317-278-9236, E-mail: pcarlin@iupui.edu. *Application contact:* Natalie Harvey, Information Contact, 317-274-4756, Fax: 317-274-0097.

Instituto Tecnologico de Santo Domingo, Graduate School, Area of Humanities and Social Sciences, Santo Domingo, Dominican Republic. Offers accounting (Certificate); adult education (Certificate); applied linguistics (MA); economics (MA); education (M Ed); educational psychology (MA, Certificate); gender and development (MA, Certificate); humanistic studies (MA); international marketing management (Certificate); international relations in the Caribbean basin (Certificate); intervention systems in family therapy (MA); linguistic and literary communication (Certificate); pedagogical support (MA); social science education (M Ed); sustainable human development (MA); terminal illness and death psychology (Certificate); youth and adult education (M Ed).

Instituto Tecnológico y de Estudios Superiores de Monterrey, Campus Ciudad de México, Division of Business, Ciudad de Mexico, Mexico. Offers business administration (EMBA, MBA, PhD); economy (MBA); finance (MBA). EMBA program offered jointly with The University of Texas at Austin. Part-time and evening/weekend programs available. Postbaccalaureate distance learning degree programs offered (minimal on-campus study). *Entrance requirements:* For master's and doctorate, Instituto entrance exam. Additional exam requirements/recommendations for international students: Required—TOEFL.

Iowa State University of Science and Technology, Graduate College, College of Liberal Arts and Sciences, Department of Economics, Ames, IA 50011. Offers agricultural economics (MS, PhD); economics (MS, PhD); JD/MS; JD/PhD. JD/MS and JD/PhD offered jointly with Drake University and The University of Iowa. *Faculty:* 53 full-time (7 women), 4 part-time/adjunct (3 women). *Students:* 73 full-time (26 women), 29 part-time (14 women); includes 1 Asian, non-Hispanic/Latino, 72 international. 300 applicants, 6% accepted, 18 enrolled. In 2010, 12 master's, 10 doctorates awarded. *Degree requirements:* For master's, thesis or alternative; for doctorate, thesis/dissertation. *Entrance requirements:* For master's and doctorate, GRE General Test. Additional exam requirements/recommendations for international students: Required—TOEFL (minimum score 570 paper-based; 88 iBT), IELTS (minimum score 6.5). *Application deadline:* For fall admission, 1/31 priority date for domestic and international students. Application fee: $40 ($90 for international students). Electronic applications accepted. *Financial support:* In 2010–11, 6 research assistantships with full and partial tuition reimbursements (averaging $6,577 per year), 30 teaching assistantships with full and partial tuition reimbursements (averaging $10,880 per year) were awarded; fellowships, scholarships/grants, health care benefits, and unspecified assistantships also available. *Unit head:* Dr. GianCarlo Moschini, Chair, 515-294-6741, Fax: 515-294-7755, E-mail: grad@econ.iastate.edu. *Application contact:* Dr. John Schroeter, Information Contact, 515-294-2702, E-mail: grad@econ.iastate.edu.

The Johns Hopkins University, Zanvyl Krieger School of Arts and Sciences, Department of Economics, Baltimore, MD 21218-2699. Offers PhD. *Faculty:* 20 full-time (4 women), 1 part-time/adjunct (0 women). *Students:* 61 full-time (30 women); includes 4 minority (2 Asian, non-Hispanic/Latino; 1 Hispanic/Latino; 1 Two or more races, non-Hispanic/Latino), 43 international. Average age 27. 393 applicants, 3% accepted, 12 enrolled. In 2010, 11 doctorates

Economics

The Johns Hopkins University (continued)

awarded. Terminal master's awarded for partial completion of doctoral program. *Degree requirements:* For doctorate, comprehensive exam, thesis/dissertation. *Entrance requirements:* For doctorate, GRE General Test. Additional exam requirements/recommendations for international students: Required—TOEFL (minimum score 600 paper-based; 250 computer-based), IELTS. *Application deadline:* For fall admission, 1/2 priority date for domestic and international students. Applications are processed on a rolling basis. Application fee: $75. Electronic applications accepted. *Financial support:* In 2010–11, 7 fellowships (averaging $20,500 per year), 3 research assistantships (averaging $17,850 per year), 39 teaching assistantships (averaging $15,000 per year) were awarded. Financial award application deadline: 4/15; financial award applicants required to submit FAFSA. *Faculty research:* General economic theory, econometrics and mathematical economics, trade and development, game theory, urban economics. Total annual research expenditures: $521,538. *Unit head:* Prof. Joseph Harrington, Chair, 410-516-7615, Fax: 410-516-7600, E-mail: joe.harrington@jhu.edu. *Application contact:* Karen Allen, Graduate Admissions Coordinator, 410-516-7601, Fax: 410-516-7600, E-mail: econadmissions@jhu.edu.

Kansas State University, Graduate School, College of Arts and Sciences, Department of Economics, Manhattan, KS 66506. Offers MA, PhD. Part-time programs available. Terminal master's awarded for partial completion of doctoral program. *Degree requirements:* For master's, thesis optional; for doctorate, comprehensive exam, thesis/dissertation. *Entrance requirements:* For master's, GRE (highly recommended), minimum GPA of 3.0; course work in microeconomics, macroeconomics, calculus and statistics; for doctorate, GRE (highly recommended), course work in microeconomics, macroeconomics, and calculus. Additional exam requirements/recommendations for international students: Required—TOEFL (minimum score 550 paper-based; 213 computer-based). Electronic applications accepted. *Faculty research:* Macroeconomics, microeconomics and labor economics, development and growth, international economics, industrial organization.

Kent State University, Graduate School of Management, Master's Program in Economics, Kent, OH 44242-0001. Offers MA. Part-time programs available. *Faculty:* 10 full-time (2 women), 2 part-time/adjunct (both women). *Students:* 21 full-time (15 women), 6 part-time (0 women); includes 2 Hispanic/Latino, 17 international. Average age 23. 24 applicants, 96% accepted, 11 enrolled. In 2010, 16 master's awarded. *Entrance requirements:* For master's, GMAT or GRE General Test, minimum GPA of 2.75. Additional exam requirements/recommendations for international students: Required—TOEFL (minimum score 550 paper-based; 213 computer-based; 79 iBT). *Application deadline:* For fall admission, 4/1 priority date for domestic students, 3/1 for international students; for spring admission, 12/1 for domestic students. Applications are processed on a rolling basis. Application fee: $30 ($60 for international students). Electronic applications accepted. *Expenses:* Tuition, state resident: full-time $7866; part-time $437 per credit hour. Tuition, nonresident: full-time $14,022; part-time $779 per credit hour. *Financial support:* In 2010–11, 10 students received support, including 10 research assistantships with full tuition reimbursements available (averaging $5,025 per year); fellowships, Federal Work-Study also available. Financial award application deadline: 4/1; financial award applicants required to submit FAFSA. *Faculty research:* Macro and microeconomic theory, labor economics, international economics, quantitative methods. *Unit head:* Dr. Richard J. Kent, Chair and Professor, 330-672-2366, Fax: 330-672-9808, E-mail: rkent@kent.edu. *Application contact:* Louise M. Ditchey, Administrative Director, 330-672-2282, Fax: 330-672-7303, E-mail: gradbus@kent.edu.

Lakehead University, Graduate Studies, Faculty of Social Sciences and Humanities, Department of Economics, Thunder Bay, ON P7B 5E1, Canada. Offers MA. Part-time and evening/weekend programs available. *Degree requirements:* For master's, thesis or comprehensive exams, research papers. *Entrance requirements:* For master's, minimum B average. Additional exam requirements/recommendations for international students: Required—TOEFL. *Faculty research:* Public finance, economic history, mathematical economics, quantitative economics.

Lehigh University, College of Business and Economics, Department of Economics, Bethlehem, PA 18015. Offers economics (MS, PhD); health and bio-pharmaceutical economics (MS). *Faculty:* 12 full-time (3 women), 2 part-time/adjunct (0 women). *Students:* 45 full-time (23 women), 4 part-time (2 women); includes 3 minority (all Asian, non-Hispanic/Latino), 21 international. Average age 24. 112 applicants, 57% accepted, 26 enrolled. In 2010, 22 master's, 3 doctorates awarded. Terminal master's awarded for partial completion of doctoral program. *Degree requirements:* For master's, thesis optional; for doctorate, comprehensive exam, thesis/dissertation, proposal defense. *Entrance requirements:* For master's and doctorate, GMAT or GRE General Test. Additional exam requirements/recommendations for international students: Required—TOEFL (minimum score 600 paper-based; 250 computer-based; 94 iBT). *Application deadline:* For fall admission, 7/15 for domestic students, 5/1 for international students; for spring admission, 12/1 for domestic students. Applications are processed on a rolling basis. Application fee: $100. Electronic applications accepted. *Expenses:* Contact institution. *Financial support:* In 2010–11, 18 students received support, including 2 fellowships with full tuition reimbursements available (averaging $16,000 per year), 1 research assistantship with full tuition reimbursement available (averaging $16,000 per year), 13 teaching assistantships with full tuition reimbursements available (averaging $16,000 per year); scholarships/grants, health care benefits, tuition waivers (full and partial), and unspecified assistantships also available. Financial award application deadline: 1/15. *Faculty research:* Public finance, investments, applied econometrics, labor economics. Total annual research expenditures: $17,360. *Unit head:* Dr. James Dearden, 610-758-5129, Fax: 610-758-4677, E-mail: jad8@lehigh.edu. *Application contact:* Corinn McBride, Director of Recruitment and Admissions, 610-758-3418, Fax: 610-758-5283, E-mail: com207@lehigh.edu.

Long Island University, Brooklyn Campus, Richard L. Conolly College of Liberal Arts and Sciences, Department of Economics, Brooklyn, NY 11201-8423. Offers MA. Part-time and evening/weekend programs available. *Degree requirements:* For master's, thesis or alternative. *Entrance requirements:* For master's, 2 letters of recommendation. Additional exam requirements/recommendations for international students: Required—TOEFL (minimum score 550 paper-based; 173 computer-based). Electronic applications accepted.

Louisiana State University and Agricultural and Mechanical College, Graduate School, E. J. Ourso College of Business, Department of Economics, Baton Rouge, LA 70803. Offers MS, PhD. *Faculty:* 14 full-time (1 woman). *Students:* 27 full-time (10 women), 5 part-time (0 women); includes 1 Black or African American, non-Hispanic/Latino, 22 international. Average age 29. 77 applicants, 21% accepted, 5 enrolled. In 2010, 7 master's, 2 doctorates awarded. Terminal master's awarded for partial completion of doctoral program. *Degree requirements:* For doctorate, thesis/dissertation. *Entrance requirements:* For master's and doctorate, GRE General Test, minimum GPA of 3.0. Additional exam requirements/recommendations for international students: Required—TOEFL (minimum score 550 paper-based; 213 computer-based; 79 iBT) or IELTS (minimum score 6.5). *Application deadline:* For fall admission, 1/25 priority date for domestic students, 5/15 for international students; for spring admission, 10/15 for international students. Applications are processed on a rolling basis. Application fee: $50 ($70 for international students). *Financial support:* In 2010–11, 30 students received support, including 2 fellowships (averaging $19,885 per year), 16 research assistantships with full and partial tuition reimbursements available (averaging $17,644 per year), 9 teaching assistantships with full and partial tuition reimbursements available (averaging $16,433 per year); Federal Work-Study, scholarships/grants, health care benefits, and unspecified assistantships also available. Support available to part-time students. Financial award application deadline: 6/15; financial award applicants required to submit FAFSA. *Faculty research:* Microeconomics, macroeconomics, econometrics, industrial organization, public finance, labor. Total annual research expenditures: $1.1 million. *Unit head:* Dr. Robert Newman, Chair, 225-578-3794, Fax: 225-578-3807, E-mail: eonewm@lsu.edu. *Application contact:* Dr. Arrendam Chanda, Graduate Director, 225-578-5211, Fax: 225-578-3807, E-mail: sarangi@lsu.edu.

Louisiana Tech University, Graduate School, College of Business, Department of Finance and Economics, Ruston, LA 71272. Offers business economics (MBA, DBA); finance (MBA, DBA). Part-time programs available. *Degree requirements:* For doctorate, thesis/dissertation. *Entrance requirements:* For master's and doctorate, GMAT.

Marquette University, Graduate School of Management, Department of Economics, Milwaukee, WI 53201-1881. Offers business economics (MSAE); financial economics (MSAE); international economics (MSAE); marketing research (MSAE); real estate economics (MSAE). Part-time and evening/weekend programs available. *Faculty:* 13 full-time (4 women), 3 part-time/adjunct (0 women). *Students:* 29 full-time (11 women), 33 part-time (8 women); includes 5 minority (2 Black or African American, non-Hispanic/Latino; 1 Asian, non-Hispanic/Latino; 1 Hispanic/Latino; 1 Two or more races, non-Hispanic/Latino), 17 international. Average age 25. 96 applicants, 73% accepted, 27 enrolled. In 2010, 15 master's awarded. *Degree requirements:* For master's, comprehensive exam, professional project. *Entrance requirements:* For master's, GMAT or GRE General Test. Additional exam requirements/recommendations for international students: Required—TOEFL (minimum score 530 paper-based; 78 computer-based). *Application deadline:* Applications are processed on a rolling basis. Application fee: $50. Electronic applications accepted. *Expenses:* Tuition: Full-time $16,290; part-time $905 per credit hour. Tuition and fees vary according to program. *Financial support:* In 2010–11, 2 fellowships, 7 teaching assistantships were awarded; research assistantships, Federal Work-Study, institutionally sponsored loans, scholarships/grants, and tuition waivers (full and partial) also available. Support available to part-time students. Financial award application deadline: 2/15. *Faculty research:* Monetary and fiscal policy in open economy, housing and regional migration, political economy of taxation and state/local government. Total annual research expenditures: $15,656. *Unit head:* Dr. Abdur Chowdhury, Chair, 414-288-6915, Fax: 414-288-5757. *Application contact:* Farrokh Nourzad, Information Contact, 414-288-3570.

Marquette University, Graduate School of Management, Executive MBA Program, Milwaukee, WI 53201-1881. Offers economics (MBA); finance (MBA); human resources (MBA); international business (MBA); management information systems (MBA); marketing (MBA); operations and supply chain management (MBA); sports business (MBA). *Accreditation:* AACSB. *Faculty:* 3 full-time (1 woman), 2 part-time/adjunct (0 women). *Students:* 43 full-time (11 women); includes 6 minority (1 Black or African American, non-Hispanic/Latino; 4 Asian, non-Hispanic/Latino; 1 Hispanic/Latino), 3 international. Average age 37. 47 applicants, 74% accepted, 29 enrolled. In 2010, 13 master's awarded. *Degree requirements:* For master's, international trip. *Entrance requirements:* For master's, GMAT, two letters of recommendation, official transcripts from current and previous colleges/universities. Additional exam requirements/recommendations for international students: Required—TOEFL (minimum score 530 paper-based; 78 computer-based). *Application deadline:* Applications are processed on a rolling basis. Application fee: $50. Electronic applications accepted. *Expenses:* Contact institution. *Financial support:* Application deadline: 2/15. *Faculty research:* International trade and finance, customer relationship management, consumer satisfaction, customer service. *Unit head:* Dr. Jeanne Simmons, Graduate Director, 414-288-7145, Fax: 414-288-1660, E-mail: jeanne.simmons@marquette.edu. *Application contact:* Erin Fox, Assistant Director for Recruitment, 414-288-5319, Fax: 414-288-1902, E-mail: erin.fox@marquette.edu.

Marquette University, Graduate School of Management, Program in Business Administration, Milwaukee, WI 53201-1881. Offers business administration (MBA); economics (MBA); finance (MBA); human resources (MBA); international business (MBA); management information systems (MBA); marketing (MBA); operations and supply chain management (MBA); sports business (MBA); JD/MBA; MBA/MA; MBA/MSN. *Accreditation:* AACSB. Part-time and evening/weekend programs available. *Faculty:* 38 full-time (9 women), 24 part-time/adjunct (8 women). *Students:* 44 full-time (17 women), 368 part-time (105 women); includes 36 minority (4 Black or African American, non-Hispanic/Latino; 2 American Indian or Alaska Native, non-Hispanic/Latino; 20 Asian, non-Hispanic/Latino; 10 Hispanic/Latino), 30 international. Average age 31. 256 applicants, 60% accepted, 98 enrolled. In 2010, 117 master's awarded. *Entrance requirements:* For master's, GMAT, letters of recommendation. Additional exam requirements/recommendations for international students: Required—TOEFL (minimum score 530 paper-based; 78 computer-based). *Application deadline:* Applications are processed on a rolling basis. Application fee: $50. Electronic applications accepted. *Expenses:* Tuition: Full-time $16,290; part-time $905 per credit hour. Tuition and fees vary according to program. *Financial support:* In 2010–11, 4 fellowships, 11 teaching assistantships were awarded; research assistantships, Federal Work-Study, institutionally sponsored loans, scholarships/grants, and tuition waivers (full and partial) also available. Support available to part-time students. Financial award application deadline: 2/15. *Faculty research:* Ethics in the professions, services marketing, technology impact on decision-making, mentoring. *Unit head:* Dr. Jeanne Simmons, Graduate Director, 414-288-7145, Fax: 414-288-1660, E-mail: jeanne.simmons@marquette.edu. *Application contact:* Debra Leutermann, Admissions Coordinator, 414-288-8064, Fax: 414-288-1902, E-mail: debra.leutermann@marquette.edu.

Massachusetts Institute of Technology, School of Humanities, Arts, and Social Sciences, Department of Economics, Cambridge, MA 02139. Offers SM, PhD. *Faculty:* 32 full-time (5 women), 3 part-time/adjunct (0 women). *Students:* 116 full-time (41 women); includes 13 minority (3 Black or African American, non-Hispanic/Latino; 8 Asian, non-Hispanic/Latino; 1 Hispanic/Latino; 1 Two or more races, non-Hispanic/Latino), 55 international. Average age 27. 795 applicants, 6% accepted, 24 enrolled. In 2010, 1 master's, 20 doctorates awarded. Terminal master's awarded for partial completion of doctoral program. *Degree requirements:* For doctorate, comprehensive exam, thesis/dissertation. *Entrance requirements:* For doctorate, GRE General Test. Additional exam requirements/recommendations for international students: Required—TOEFL (minimum score 600 paper-based; 250 computer-based; 100 iBT), IELTS (minimum score 7). *Application deadline:* For fall admission, 12/15 for domestic and international students. Application fee: $75. Electronic applications accepted. *Expenses:* Tuition: Full-time $38,940; part-time $605 per unit. Required fees: $272. *Financial support:* In 2010–11, 109 students received support, including 44 fellowships with tuition reimbursements available (averaging $35,636 per year), 2 research assistantships with tuition reimbursements available (averaging $32,626 per year), 37 teaching assistantships with tuition reimbursements available (averaging $38,572 per year); Federal Work-Study, institutionally sponsored loans, scholarships/grants, health care benefits, and unspecified assistantships also available. *Faculty research:* Macroeconomics, international economics and political economy; economic theory; econometrics and statistical methods; labor and development economics; public finance. Total annual research expenditures: $1.4 million. *Unit head:* Prof. Ricardo Caballero, Department Head, 617-253-3361, Fax: 617-253-1330. *Application contact:* Peter Hoagland, Graduate Administrator, 617-253-8787, Fax: 617-253-1330, E-mail: econ-admit@mit.edu.

McGill University, Faculty of Graduate and Postdoctoral Studies, Faculty of Arts, Department of Economics, Montréal, QC H3A 2T5, Canada. Offers economics (MA, PhD); social statistics (MA).

McMaster University, School of Graduate Studies, Faculty of Social Sciences, Department of Economics, Hamilton, ON L8S 4M2, Canada. Offers MA, PhD. Part-time programs available. *Degree requirements:* For doctorate, comprehensive exam, thesis/dissertation. *Entrance requirements:* For master's, GRE (recommended), honors BA in economics; for doctorate, GRE (recommended), B+ average in a master's degree. Additional exam requirements/recommendations for international students: Required—TOEFL (minimum score 580 paper-based; 237 computer-based). *Faculty research:* Applied microeconomics, econometrics, health economics, labor economics, public finance.

Memorial University of Newfoundland, School of Graduate Studies, Department of Economics, St. John's, NL A1C 5S7, Canada. Offers MA. *Degree requirements:* For master's, thesis optional. *Entrance requirements:* For master's, honors degree (minimum 2nd class standing). *Faculty research:* Public sector economics, natural resource economics.

Miami University, Graduate School, Farmer School of Business, Department of Economics, Oxford, OH 45056. Offers MA. Part-time programs available. *Students:* 11 full-time (3 women);

includes 1 minority (Two or more races, non-Hispanic/Latino), 3 international. Average age 23. In 2010, 10 master's awarded. *Entrance requirements:* For master's, GMAT, minimum undergraduate GPA of 3.0 during previous 2 years or 2.75 overall. Additional exam requirements/recommendations for international students: Required—TOEFL. Application fee: $50. *Expenses:* Tuition, state resident: full-time $11,616; part-time $484 per credit hour. Tuition, nonresident: full-time $25,656; part-time $1069 per credit hour. Required fees: $528. *Financial support:* Fellowships with full tuition reimbursements, research assistantships, teaching assistantships, Federal Work-Study, health care benefits, tuition waivers (full), and unspecified assistantships available. Financial award application deadline: 3/1. *Unit head:* George Davis, Chair, 513-529-2836, Fax: 513-529-8047, E-mail: miamieco@muohio.edu. *Application contact:* Dr. Barnali Gupta, Director of Graduate Studies, 513-529-2856, E-mail: miamieco@muohio.edu.

Michigan State University, The Graduate School, College of Social Science, Department of Economics, East Lansing, MI 48824. Offers MA, PhD. *Entrance requirements:* Additional exam requirements/recommendations for international students: Required—TOEFL. Electronic applications accepted.

Middle Tennessee State University, College of Graduate Studies, Jennings A. Jones College of Business, Department of Economics and Finance, Murfreesboro, TN 37132. Offers economics (MA, PhD). Part-time and evening/weekend programs available. Postbaccalaureate distance learning degree programs offered. *Faculty:* 20 full-time (3 women). *Students:* 10 full-time (1 woman), 45 part-time (10 women); includes 12 Black or African American, non-Hispanic/Latino; 9 Asian, non-Hispanic/Latino; 4 Hispanic/Latino; 3 Two or more races, non-Hispanic/Latino. Average age 29. 30 applicants, 50% accepted, 15 enrolled. In 2010, 10 master's, 5 doctorates awarded. *Degree requirements:* For master's, thesis optional; for doctorate, comprehensive exam, thesis/dissertation. *Entrance requirements:* For master's and doctorate, GRE or MAT. Additional exam requirements/recommendations for international students: Required—TOEFL (minimum score 525 paper-based; 195 computer-based; 71 iBT) or IELTS (minimum score 6). *Application deadline:* For fall admission, 6/1 for domestic and international students. Applications are processed on a rolling basis. Application fee: $25 ($30 for international students). Electronic applications accepted. *Expenses:* Tuition, state resident: full-time $4632. Tuition, nonresident: full-time $11,520. *Financial support:* In 2010–11, 21 students received support. Institutionally sponsored loans available. Support available to part-time students. Financial award application deadline: 5/1; financial award applicants required to submit FAFSA. *Unit head:* Dr. Charles L. Baum, Chair, 615-898-2520, Fax: 615-898-5596, E-mail: cbaum@mtsu.edu. *Application contact:* Dr. Michael Allen, Dean and Vice Provost for Research, 615-898-2840, Fax: 615-904-8020, E-mail: mallen@mtsu.edu.

Mississippi State University, College of Business, Department of Finance and Economics, Mississippi State, MS 39762. Offers applied economics (PhD); business administration (PhD), including finance; economics (MA); finance (MSBA). Part-time programs available. *Faculty:* 10 full-time (2 women). *Students:* 14 full-time (3 women), 3 part-time (1 woman); includes 1 minority (Black or African American, non-Hispanic/Latino), 10 international. Average age 31. 63 applicants, 11% accepted, 6 enrolled. In 2010, 1 master's, 2 doctorates awarded. Terminal master's awarded for partial completion of doctoral program. *Degree requirements:* For master's, comprehensive exam, thesis optional; for doctorate, comprehensive exam, thesis/dissertation. *Entrance requirements:* For master's and doctorate, GMAT, GRE General Test. Additional exam requirements/recommendations for international students: Required—TOEFL (minimum score 575 paper-based; 233 computer-based; 90 iBT); Recommended—IELTS (minimum score 6.5). *Application deadline:* For fall admission, 7/1 for domestic students, 5/1 for international students; for spring admission, 11/1 for domestic students, 10/1 for international students. Applications are processed on a rolling basis. Application fee: $40. Electronic applications accepted. *Expenses:* Tuition, state resident: full-time $2730.50; part-time $304 per credit hour. Tuition, nonresident: full-time $6901; part-time $767 per credit hour. *Financial support:* In 2010–11, 3 teaching assistantships with tuition reimbursements (averaging $14,677 per year) were awarded; Federal Work-Study, scholarships/grants, health care benefits, and unspecified assistantships also available. Financial award application deadline: 4/1; financial award applicants required to submit FAFSA. *Faculty research:* Economics development, mergers, event studies, economic education, bank performance. Total annual research expenditures: $961,000. *Unit head:* Dr. Mike Highfield, Department Head, 662-325-1984, Fax: 662-325-1977, E-mail: m.highfield@msstate.edu. *Application contact:* Dr. Benjamin F. Blair, Associate Professor/Graduate Coordinator, 662-325-1980, Fax: 662-325-1977, E-mail: bblair@cobilan.msstate.edu.

Morgan State University, School of Graduate Studies, College of Liberal Arts, Department of Economics, Baltimore, MD 21251. Offers MA. *Degree requirements:* For master's, comprehensive exam. *Entrance requirements:* For master's, GRE. Additional exam requirements/recommendations for international students: Required—TOEFL (minimum score 550 paper-based; 213 computer-based).

Murray State University, College of Business and Public Affairs, Program in Economics, Murray, KY 42071. Offers MS. Part-time programs available. *Entrance requirements:* For master's, GRE General Test or GMAT, economics minor or equivalent, students may be conditionally admitted and fulfill undergraduate requirements. Additional exam requirements/recommendations for international students: Required—TOEFL. *Faculty research:* Economic education, public finance, economic development, banking, telecommunications systems management.

National University, Academic Affairs, School of Business and Management, Department of Accounting and Finance, La Jolla, CA 92037-1011. Offers accountancy (MS); corporate and international finance (MS). Part-time and evening/weekend programs available. Postbaccalaureate distance learning degree programs offered (no on-campus study). *Faculty:* 15 full-time (2 women), 149 part-time/adjunct (39 women). *Students:* 171 full-time (76 women), 410 part-time (202 women); includes 201 minority (40 Black or African American, non-Hispanic/Latino; 1 American Indian or Alaska Native, non-Hispanic/Latino; 67 Asian, non-Hispanic/Latino; 86 Hispanic/Latino; 1 Native Hawaiian or other Pacific Islander, non-Hispanic/Latino; 6 Two or more races, non-Hispanic/Latino), 147 international. Average age 33. 727 applicants, 100% accepted, 466 enrolled. In 2010, 58 master's awarded. *Degree requirements:* For master's, thesis. *Entrance requirements:* For master's, interview, minimum GPA of 2.5. Additional exam requirements/recommendations for international students: Required—TOEFL (minimum score 550 paper-based; 213 computer-based; 79 iBT), IELTS (minimum score 6). *Application deadline:* Applications are processed on a rolling basis. Application fee: $60 ($65 for international students). Electronic applications accepted. *Expenses:* Tuition: Full-time $9450; part-time $350 per unit. Required fees: $350 per unit. One-time fee: $60. *Financial support:* Career-related internships or fieldwork, institutionally sponsored loans, scholarships/grants, and tuition waivers (partial) available. Support available to part-time students. Financial award application deadline: 6/30; financial award applicants required to submit FAFSA. *Unit head:* Prof. Donald A. Schwartz, Chair and Associate Professor, 858-642-8420, Fax: 858-642-8740, E-mail: dschwartz@nu.edu. *Application contact:* Dominick Giovanniello, Associate Regional Dean—San Diego, 800-NAT-UNIV, Fax: 858-541-7792, E-mail: dgiovann@nu.edu.

New Mexico State University, Graduate School, College of Agricultural, Consumer and Environmental Sciences, Department of Agricultural Economics and Agricultural Business, Las Cruces, NM 88003-8001. Offers agribusiness (M Ag, MBA); agricultural economics (MS); economics (MA). Part-time programs available. *Faculty:* 7 full-time (1 woman). *Students:* 13 full-time (5 women), 7 part-time (4 women); includes 3 minority (1 Asian, non-Hispanic/Latino; 2 Hispanic/Latino), 7 international. Average age 27. 14 applicants, 93% accepted, 10 enrolled. In 2010, 4 master's awarded. *Degree requirements:* For master's, thesis (for some programs). *Entrance requirements:* For master's, previous course work in intermediate microeconomics, intermediate macroeconomics, college-level calculus, statistics. Additional exam requirements/recommendations for international students: Required—TOEFL. *Application deadline:* For fall admission, 7/1 priority date for domestic and international students; for spring admission, 11/1 priority date for domestic and international students. Applications are processed on a rolling basis. Application fee: $30 ($50 for international students). Electronic applications accepted. *Expenses:* Tuition, state resident: full-time $4536; part-time $242 per credit. Tuition, nonresident: full-time $15,816; part-time $712 per credit. Required fees: $636 per term. *Financial support:* In 2010–11, 8 research assistantships (averaging $16,300 per year), 1 teaching assistantship (averaging $7,900 per year) were awarded; career-related internships or fieldwork and health care benefits also available. Financial award application deadline: 3/1. *Faculty research:* Natural resource policy, production economics and farm/ranch management, agribusiness and marketing, international marketing and trade, agricultural risk management. *Unit head:* Dr. Terry Crawford, Head, 575-646-3215, Fax: 575-646-3808, E-mail: crawford@nmsu.edu. *Application contact:* Dr. L. Allen Torell, Professor, 575-646-4732, Fax: 575-646-3808, E-mail: atorell@nmsu.edu.

New Mexico State University, Graduate School, College of Business, Department of Economics, Applied Statistics and International Business, Las Cruces, NM 88003. Offers applied statistics (MS); economic development (DED); economics (MA). Part-time programs available. *Faculty:* 12 full-time (2 women), 2 part-time/adjunct (1 woman). *Students:* 64 full-time (21 women), 16 part-time (5 women); includes 22 minority (3 Black or African American, non-Hispanic/Latino; 2 Asian, non-Hispanic/Latino; 17 Hispanic/Latino), 37 international. Average age 31. 84 applicants, 83% accepted, 34 enrolled. In 2010, 16 master's awarded. Terminal master's awarded for partial completion of doctoral program. *Degree requirements:* For master's, comprehensive exam, thesis or alternative; for doctorate, comprehensive exam, thesis/dissertation, internship, written project. *Entrance requirements:* For master's, minimum GPA of 3.0; for doctorate, appropriate master's degree, minimum GPA of 3.0. Additional exam requirements/recommendations for international students: Required—TOEFL (minimum score 530 paper-based; 71 computer-based), IELTS. *Application deadline:* Applications are processed on a rolling basis. Application fee: $30 ($50 for international students). Electronic applications accepted. *Expenses:* Tuition, state resident: full-time $4536; part-time $242 per credit. Tuition, nonresident: full-time $15,816; part-time $712 per credit. Required fees: $636 per term. *Financial support:* In 2010–11, 34 students received support, including 14 research assistantships (averaging $11,225 per year), 29 teaching assistantships (averaging $6,846 per year); fellowships, career-related internships or fieldwork, Federal Work-Study, and health care benefits also available. Support available to part-time students. Financial award application deadline: 3/1. *Faculty research:* Public utilities, environment, linear models, biological sampling, public policy, economic development, energy. *Unit head:* Dr. Richard V. Adkisson, Head, 575-646-4988, Fax: 575-646-1915, E-mail: radkisso@nmsu.edu. *Application contact:* Dr. Richard V. Adkisson, Head, 575-646-4988, Fax: 575-646-1915, E-mail: radkisso@nmsu.edu.

The New School: A University, The New School for Social Research, Department of Economics, New York, NY 10003. Offers economics (M Phil, MA, MS, DS Sc, PhD); global finance (MS); global political economy and finance (MA). Part-time and evening/weekend programs available. Terminal master's awarded for partial completion of doctoral program. *Degree requirements:* For master's, exam; for doctorate, one foreign language, thesis/dissertation, qualifying exam. *Entrance requirements:* For master's, GRE General Test; for doctorate, GRE General Test, MA. Additional exam requirements/recommendations for international students: Required—TOEFL (minimum score 600 paper-based; 250 computer-based; 100 iBT). Electronic applications accepted. *Faculty research:* Heterodox, history of economic thought, post-Keynesian, global political economy and finance.

New York University, Graduate School of Arts and Science, Department of Economics, New York, NY 10012-1019. Offers applied economic analysis (Advanced Certificate); economics (MA, PhD); JD/MA; MD/PhD. Part-time and evening/weekend programs available. *Faculty:* 35 full-time (2 women). *Students:* 225 full-time (77 women), 38 part-time (10 women); includes 19 Asian, non-Hispanic/Latino; 2 Hispanic/Latino, 176 international. Average age 27. 1,650 applicants, 14% accepted, 90 enrolled. In 2010, 77 master's, 15 doctorates, 2 other advanced degrees awarded. Terminal master's awarded for partial completion of doctoral program. *Degree requirements:* For master's, thesis; for doctorate, one foreign language, thesis/dissertation, 4 qualifying exams. *Entrance requirements:* For master's and doctorate, GRE General Test; for Advanced Certificate, master's degree. Additional exam requirements/recommendations for international students: Required—TOEFL. *Application deadline:* For fall admission, 12/15 priority date for domestic students. Application fee: $90. *Financial support:* Fellowships with tuition reimbursements, research assistantships with tuition reimbursements, teaching assistantships with tuition reimbursements, Federal Work-Study, institutionally sponsored loans, scholarships/grants, health care benefits, and unspecified assistantships available. Financial award application deadline: 12/15; financial award applicants required to submit FAFSA. *Faculty research:* Economic theory, experimental economics, growth and development, macroeconomics and finance, international trade and international finance. *Unit head:* Nicola Persico, Chair, 212-998-8900, Fax: 212-995-4186, E-mail: admissions@econ.nyu.edu. *Application contact:* Debraj Ray, Director of Graduate Studies, 212-998-8900, Fax: 212-995-4186, E-mail: admissions@econ.nyu.edu.

New York University, Leonard N. Stern School of Business, Department of Economics, New York, NY 10012-1019. Offers MBA, PhD. *Faculty research:* Applied macroeconomics, macroeconomics and macroeconomic policy, international financial markets, international trade and business, game theory.

North Carolina State University, Graduate School, College of Management and College of Agriculture and Life Sciences, Program in Economics, Raleigh, NC 27695. Offers M Econ, MA, PhD. Part-time programs available. Terminal master's awarded for partial completion of doctoral program. *Degree requirements:* For master's, thesis (for some programs); for doctorate, thesis/dissertation. *Entrance requirements:* For master's and doctorate, GRE General Test. Additional exam requirements/recommendations for international students: Required—TOEFL. Electronic applications accepted. *Faculty research:* Endogenous growth modeling, generalized methods of moments estimation, integration and trade, agricultural policy, path dependence and network externalities.

Northeastern University, College of Social Sciences and Humanities, Department of Economics, Boston, MA 02115-5096. Offers MA, PhD. Part-time and evening/weekend programs available. *Faculty:* 17 full-time (2 women), 11 part-time/adjunct (6 women). *Students:* 79 full-time (38 women), 2 part-time (0 women). 219 applicants, 51% accepted, 26 enrolled. In 2010, 19 master's awarded. *Degree requirements:* For master's and doctorate, comprehensive exam. *Entrance requirements:* For master's, GRE. Additional exam requirements/recommendations for international students: Required—TOEFL. *Application deadline:* For fall admission, 8/1 for domestic students, 5/1 priority date for international students; for spring admission, 12/1 for domestic and international students. Applications are processed on a rolling basis. Application fee: $50. *Financial support:* In 2010–11, 13 teaching assistantships (averaging $15,667 per year) were awarded; Federal Work-Study, institutionally sponsored loans, tuition waivers (full and partial), and unspecified assistantships also available. Financial award application deadline: 2/1; financial award applicants required to submit FAFSA. *Faculty research:* U. S. labor markets, applied economics, microeconomic theory, macroeconomic theory, econometrics. *Unit head:* Dr. Steven Morrison, Chair, 617-373-2872, Fax: 617-373-3640, E-mail: econ@neu.edu. *Application contact:* Dr. Gregory Wassall, Graduate Coordinator, 617-373-2882, Fax: 617-373-3640, E-mail: econ@neu.edu.

Northern Illinois University, Graduate School, College of Liberal Arts and Sciences, Department of Economics, De Kalb, IL 60115-2854. Offers MA, PhD. Part-time programs available. *Faculty:* 15 full-time (3 women). *Students:* 33 full-time (10 women), 9 part-time (6 women); includes 4 Black or African American, non-Hispanic/Latino; 2 Asian, non-Hispanic/Latino, 28 international. Average age 28. 86 applicants, 45% accepted, 11 enrolled. In 2010, 11 master's, 1 doctorate awarded. Terminal master's awarded for partial completion of doctoral program. *Degree requirements:* For master's, comprehensive exam, thesis or alternative; for doctorate, thesis/dissertation, candidacy exam, dissertation defense, research seminar. *Entrance requirements:* For master's, GRE General Test, minimum GPA of 2.75; for doctorate, GRE General Test, minimum GPA of 2.75 (undergraduate), 3.2 (graduate). Additional exam requirements/recommendations for international students: Required—TOEFL (minimum score

Economics

Northern Illinois University (continued)
550 paper-based; 213 computer-based). *Application deadline:* For fall admission, 6/1 for domestic students, 5/1 for international students; for spring admission, 11/1 for domestic students, 10/1 for international students. Applications are processed on a rolling basis. Application fee: $30. Electronic applications accepted. *Expenses:* Tuition, state resident: full-time $7200; part-time $300 per credit hour. Tuition, nonresident: full-time $14,400; part-time $600 per credit hour. Required fees: $79 per credit hour. *Financial support:* In 2010–11, 4 research assistantships with full tuition reimbursements, 26 teaching assistantships with full tuition reimbursements were awarded; fellowships with full tuition reimbursements, career-related internships or fieldwork, Federal Work-Study, scholarships/grants, tuition waivers (full), and unspecified assistantships also available. Support available to part-time students. Financial award applicants required to submit FAFSA. *Faculty research:* Unemployment, behavior under uncertainty, effect of debt on compensation and capital utilization, racial inequality of earnings. *Unit head:* Dr. Carl M. Campbell, Chair, 815-753-6974, Fax: 815-753-1019, E-mail: carlcamp@niu.edu. *Application contact:* Dr. Ardeshir Dalal, Director, Graduate Studies, 815-753-6966.

Northwestern University, The Graduate School, Judd A. and Marjorie Weinberg College of Arts and Sciences, Department of Economics, Evanston, IL 60208. Offers MA, PhD, JD/PhD. Admissions and degrees offered through The Graduate School. *Degree requirements:* For doctorate, thesis/dissertation, preliminary written exam. *Entrance requirements:* For doctorate, GRE General Test. Additional exam requirements/recommendations for international students: Required—TOEFL. *Faculty research:* Organization of industry, behavior of labor markets, effects of monetary policy, theory of markets.

Northwestern University, The Graduate School, Kellogg School of Management, Program in Managerial Economics and Strategy, Evanston, IL 60208. Offers PhD. Admissions and degree offered through The Graduate School. *Degree requirements:* For doctorate, comprehensive exam, thesis/dissertation. *Entrance requirements:* For doctorate, GMAT or GRE General Test. Additional exam requirements/recommendations for international students: Required—TOEFL. Electronic applications accepted. *Faculty research:* Competitive strategy and organization, managerial economics, decision sciences, game theory, operations management.

Oakland University, Graduate Study and Lifelong Learning, School of Business Administration, Department of Economics, Rochester, MI 48309-4401. Offers Certificate.

The Ohio State University, Graduate School, College of Arts and Sciences, Division of Social and Behavioral Sciences, Department of Economics, Columbus, OH 43210. Offers MA, PhD. *Faculty:* 38. *Students:* 75 full-time (25 women), 27 part-time (8 women); includes 4 Asian, non-Hispanic/Latino; 3 Hispanic/Latino, 77 international. Average age 28. In 2010, 30 master's, 15 doctorates awarded. *Degree requirements:* For doctorate, thesis/dissertation. *Entrance requirements:* Additional exam requirements/recommendations for international students: Required—TOEFL (minimum score 600 paper-based; 250 computer-based). *Application deadline:* For fall admission, 8/15 priority date for domestic students, 7/1 priority date for international students; for winter admission, 12/1 priority date for domestic students, 11/1 priority date for international students; for spring admission, 3/1 priority date for domestic students, 2/1 priority date for international students. Applications are processed on a rolling basis. Application fee: $40 ($50 for international students). Electronic applications accepted. *Expenses:* Tuition, state resident: full-time $10,605. Tuition, nonresident: full-time $26,535. Tuition and fees vary according to course load and program. *Financial support:* Fellowships, research assistantships, teaching assistantships, Federal Work-Study and institutionally sponsored loans available. Support available to part-time students. *Unit head:* Donald Haurin, Chair, 614-292-6809, Fax: 614-292-3906, E-mail: haurin.2@osu.edu. *Application contact:* 614-292-9444, Fax: 614-292-3895, E-mail: domestic.grad@osu.edu.

Ohio University, Graduate College, College of Arts and Sciences, Department of Economics, Athens, OH 45701-2979. Offers applied economics (MA); financial economics (MFE). Part-time and evening/weekend programs available. *Students:* 65 full-time (16 women), 18 part-time (10 women); includes 10 minority (6 Black or African American, non-Hispanic/Latino; 3 Asian, non-Hispanic/Latino; 1 Two or more races, non-Hispanic/Latino), 46 international. 55 applicants, 42% accepted, 11 enrolled. In 2010, 42 master's awarded. *Degree requirements:* For master's, thesis or alternative. *Entrance requirements:* For master's, GRE or GMAT (recommended), minimum GPA of 3.0. Additional exam requirements/recommendations for international students: Required—TOEFL (minimum score 550 paper-based; 80 iBT) or IELTS (minimum score 6.5). *Application deadline:* For fall admission, 2/15 priority date for domestic and international students; for winter admission, 12/1 for domestic students, 10/1 priority date for international students. Application fee: $50 ($55 for international students). Electronic applications accepted. *Financial support:* Research assistantships with full and partial tuition reimbursements, Federal Work-Study, tuition waivers (partial), and unspecified assistantships available. Financial award application deadline: 2/15. *Faculty research:* Macroeconomics, public finance, international economics and finance, monetary theory, healthcare economics. *Unit head:* Dr. Rosmary Rossiter, Chair, 740-593-2040, E-mail: rossiter@ohio.edu. *Application contact:* Dr. K. Doroodian, Graduate Chair, 740-593-2046, E-mail: doroodia@ohio.edu.

Oklahoma State University, Spears School of Business, Department of Economics and Legal Studies in Business, Stillwater, OK 74078. Offers MS, PhD. Part-time programs available. *Faculty:* 20 full-time (5 women), 3 part-time/adjunct (2 women). *Students:* 22 full-time (10 women), 19 part-time (7 women); includes 1 Black or African American, non-Hispanic/Latino; 1 American Indian or Alaska Native, non-Hispanic/Latino, 30 international. Average age 31. 54 applicants, 26% accepted, 8 enrolled. In 2010, 4 master's, 4 doctorates awarded. *Degree requirements:* For master's, thesis or alternative; for doctorate, comprehensive exam, thesis/dissertation. *Entrance requirements:* For master's and doctorate, GRE or GMAT. Additional exam requirements/recommendations for international students: Required—TOEFL (minimum score 550 paper-based; 79 iBT). *Application deadline:* For fall admission, 3/1 priority date for international students; for spring admission, 8/1 priority date for international students. Applications are processed on a rolling basis. Application fee: $40 ($75 for international students). Electronic applications accepted. *Expenses:* Tuition, state resident: full-time $3716; part-time $154.85 per credit hour. Tuition, nonresident: full-time $14,892; part-time $621 per credit hour. Required fees: $2044; $85.20 per credit hour. One-time fee: $50. Tuition and fees vary according to course load and campus/location. *Financial support:* In 2010–11, 22 teaching assistantships (averaging $17,388 per year) were awarded; career-related internships or fieldwork, Federal Work-Study, scholarships/grants, health care benefits, tuition waivers (partial), and unspecified assistantships also available. Support available to part-time students. Financial award application deadline: 3/1; financial award applicants required to submit FAFSA. *Faculty research:* Economics and legal studies in business regional economic modeling/econometrics, urban/regional economics, monetary economics, international trade/finance/development, environmental economics. *Unit head:* Dr. Jim Fain, Head, 405-744-5195, Fax: 405-744-5180. *Application contact:* Dr. Gordon Emslie, Dean, 405-744-6368, Fax: 405-744-0355, E-mail: grad-i@okstate.edu.

Oklahoma State University, Spears School of Business, Department of Finance, Stillwater, OK 74078. Offers finance (PhD); quantitative financial economics (MS). Part-time programs available. *Faculty:* 13 full-time (1 woman), 5 part-time/adjunct (0 women). *Students:* 20 full-time (8 women), 9 part-time (2 women); includes 1 Black or African American, non-Hispanic/Latino; 1 Asian, non-Hispanic/Latino, 14 international. Average age 29. 59 applicants, 32% accepted, 8 enrolled. In 2010, 9 master's, 1 doctorate awarded. *Degree requirements:* For master's, thesis or alternative; for doctorate, comprehensive exam, thesis/dissertation. *Entrance requirements:* For master's and doctorate, GRE or GMAT. Additional exam requirements/recommendations for international students: Required—TOEFL (minimum score 550 paper-based; 79 iBT). *Application deadline:* For fall admission, 3/1 priority date for international students; for spring admission, 8/1 priority date for international students. Applications are processed on a rolling basis. Application fee: $40 ($75 for international students). Electronic applications accepted. *Expenses:* Tuition, state resident: full-time $3716; part-time $154.85 per credit hour. Tuition, nonresident: full-time $14,892; part-time $621 per credit hour. Required fees: $2044; $85.20 per credit hour. One-time fee: $50. Tuition and fees vary according to course load and campus/location. *Financial support:* In 2010–11, 13 research assistantships (averaging $8,749 per year), 5 teaching assistantships (averaging $21,587 per year) were awarded; career-related internships or fieldwork, Federal Work-Study, scholarships/grants, health care benefits, tuition waivers (partial), and unspecified assistantships also available. Support available to part-time students. Financial award application deadline: 3/1; financial award applicants required to submit FAFSA. *Faculty research:* Corporate risk management, derivatives banking, investments and securities issuance, corporate governance, banking. *Unit head:* Dr. John Polonchek, Head, 405-744-5199, Fax: 405-744-5180. *Application contact:* Dr. Gordon Emslie, Dean, 405-744-6368, Fax: 405-744-0355, E-mail: grad-i@okstate.edu.

Old Dominion University, College of Business and Public Administration, Program in Economics, Norfolk, VA 23529. Offers MA. Part-time and evening/weekend programs available. *Faculty:* 11 full-time (1 woman). *Students:* 17 full-time (4 women), 19 part-time (2 women); includes 8 minority (3 Black or African American, non-Hispanic/Latino; 2 Asian, non-Hispanic/Latino; 2 Hispanic/Latino; 1 Two or more races, non-Hispanic/Latino), 6 international. Average age 30. 32 applicants, 44% accepted, 14 enrolled. In 2010, 9 master's awarded. *Degree requirements:* For master's, comprehensive exam, thesis optional, independent research. *Entrance requirements:* For master's, GMAT or GRE General Test, minimum GPA of 2.5. Additional exam requirements/recommendations for international students: Required—TOEFL (minimum score 520 paper-based; 213 computer-based; 79 iBT). *Application deadline:* For fall admission, 8/1 priority date for domestic students; for spring admission, 10/1 priority date for domestic students. Applications are processed on a rolling basis. Application fee: $50. Electronic applications accepted. *Expenses:* Tuition, state resident: full-time $8592; part-time $358 per credit. Tuition, nonresident: full-time $21,672; part-time $903 per credit. Required fees: $119 per semester. One-time fee: $50. *Financial support:* In 2010–11, 6 students received support, including 7 research assistantships with partial tuition reimbursements available (averaging $3,200 per year); unspecified assistantships also available. Financial award application deadline: 8/1; financial award applicants required to submit FAFSA. *Faculty research:* International economics, transportation, monetary economics, immigration, econometrics. *Unit head:* Dr. David Duden Selover, Graduate Program Director, 757-683-3541, Fax: 757-638-5639, E-mail: dselover@odu.edu. *Application contact:* Dr. Ali Ardalan, Associate Dean, 757-683-3520, Fax: 757-683-4076, E-mail: aardalan@odu.edu.

Oregon State University, Graduate School, College of Agricultural Sciences, Department of Agricultural and Resource Economics, Corvallis, OR 97331. Offers agricultural and resource economics (M Agr, MAIS, MS, PhD); economics (MS, PhD). MS and PhD in economics offered through the University Graduate Faculty of Economics. Part-time programs available. Terminal master's awarded for partial completion of doctoral program. *Degree requirements:* For master's, thesis (for some programs); for doctorate, thesis/dissertation. *Entrance requirements:* For master's and doctorate, GRE General Test, minimum GPA of 3.0 in last 90 hours. Additional exam requirements/recommendations for international students: Required—TOEFL. *Faculty research:* Marine economics, environmental economics, effects of global climate change on agriculture, efficiency of agricultural markets, analysis of aquaculture development.

Oregon State University, Graduate School, College of Liberal Arts, Department of Economics, Corvallis, OR 97331. Offers MA, MS, PhD. Part-time programs available. Terminal master's awarded for partial completion of doctoral program. *Degree requirements:* For master's, thesis or alternative; for doctorate, thesis/dissertation. *Entrance requirements:* For master's and doctorate, GRE General Test, minimum GPA of 3.0 in last 90 hours. Additional exam requirements/recommendations for international students: Required—TOEFL. *Faculty research:* Applied microeconomics, applied econometrics.

Pace University, Lubin School of Business, Program in Business Economics, New York, NY 10038. Offers corporate economic planning (MBA); financial economics (MBA); international economics (MBA). Part-time and evening/weekend programs available. *Entrance requirements:* For master's, GMAT. Additional exam requirements/recommendations for international students: Required—TOEFL. Electronic applications accepted.

Penn State University Park, Graduate School, College of the Liberal Arts, Department of Economics, State College, University Park, PA 16802-1503. Offers MA, PhD.

Pepperdine University, School of Public Policy, Malibu, CA 90263. Offers American politics (MPP); economics (MPP); international relations (MPP); public policy (MPP); state and local policy (MPP). *Faculty:* 7 full-time (2 women), 10 part-time/adjunct (0 women). *Students:* 123 full-time (72 women), 4 part-time (all women); includes 36 minority (11 Black or African American, non-Hispanic/Latino; 2 American Indian or Alaska Native, non-Hispanic/Latino; 11 Asian, non-Hispanic/Latino; 9 Hispanic/Latino; 3 Two or more races, non-Hispanic/Latino), 13 international. 168 applicants, 93% accepted, 66 enrolled. In 2010, 50 master's awarded. *Entrance requirements:* For master's, GRE or GMAT, 2 letters of recommendation, resume, two essays. Additional exam requirements/recommendations for international students: Required—TOEFL. *Application deadline:* For fall admission, 5/1 for domestic students. Applications are processed on a rolling basis. Application fee: $50. Electronic applications accepted. *Financial support:* Institutionally sponsored loans and scholarships/grants available. Financial award application deadline: 5/1; financial award applicants required to submit FAFSA. *Unit head:* Dr. James R. Wilburn, Dean, 310-506-7490, Fax: 310-506-7494, E-mail: james.wilburn@pepperdine.edu. *Application contact:* Melinda E. van Hemert, Director of Recruitment and Career Services, 310-506-7492, Fax: 310-506-7494, E-mail: melinda.vanhemert@pepperdine.edu.

Peru State College, Graduate Programs, Program in Organizational Management, Peru, NE 68421. Offers MS. Program offered online only. Part-time programs available. *Degree requirements:* For master's, thesis (for some programs). *Expenses:* Contact institution. *Faculty research:* Emotional intelligence.

Portland State University, Graduate Studies, College of Liberal Arts and Sciences, Department of Economics, Portland, OR 97207-0751. Offers applied economics (MA, MS); economics (PhD); general economics (MA, MS). Part-time programs available. *Faculty:* 15 full-time (5 women), 3 part-time/adjunct (1 woman). *Students:* 13 full-time (3 women), 6 part-time (0 women); includes 2 Asian, non-Hispanic/Latino; 1 Native Hawaiian or other Pacific Islander, non-Hispanic/Latino, 4 international. Average age 28. 18 applicants, 50% accepted, 4 enrolled. In 2010, 10 master's awarded. *Degree requirements:* For master's, thesis optional; for doctorate, one foreign language, thesis/dissertation. *Entrance requirements:* For master's, minimum GPA of 3.0 in upper-division course work or 2.75 overall, course work in calculus. Additional exam requirements/recommendations for international students: Required—TOEFL (minimum score 550 paper-based; 213 computer-based). *Application deadline:* For fall admission, 4/1 for domestic students, 3/1 for international students; for spring admission, 11/1 for domestic and international students. Applications are processed on a rolling basis. Application fee: $50. *Expenses:* Tuition, state resident: full-time $8505; part-time $315 per credit. Tuition, nonresident: full-time $13,284; part-time $492 per credit. Required fees: $1482; $21 per credit. $99 per term. One-time fee: $120. Part-time tuition and fees vary according to course load and program. *Financial support:* In 2010–11, 4 research assistantships with full tuition reimbursements (averaging $6,372 per year), 1 teaching assistantship (averaging $8,820 per year) were awarded; career-related internships or fieldwork, Federal Work-Study, and unspecified assistantships also available. Support available to part-time students. Financial award application deadline: 3/1; financial award applicants required to submit FAFSA. *Faculty research:* NAFTA, economies of transition, economics of Eastern Europe, artificial intelligence, comparative economic systems. Total annual research expenditures: $130,434. *Unit head:* Dr. Randy Bluffstone, Chair, 503-725-3938, Fax: 503-725-3945, E-mail: bluffsto@pdx.edu. *Application contact:* Rita Spears, Office Specialist, 503-725-3941, Fax: 503-725-3945, E-mail: spearsr@pdx.edu.

Portland State University, Graduate Studies, Systems Science Program, Portland, OR 97207-0751. Offers computational intelligence (Certificate); computer modeling and simulation (Certificate); systems science (MS); systems science/anthropology (PhD); systems science/business administration (PhD); systems science/civil engineering (PhD); systems science/economics (PhD); systems science/engineering management (PhD); systems science/general (PhD); systems science/mathematical sciences (PhD); systems science/mechanical engineering (PhD); systems science/psychology (PhD); systems science/sociology (PhD). *Faculty:* 4 full-time (0 women), 1 part-time/adjunct (0 women). *Students:* 15 full-time (4 women), 35 part-time (11 women); includes 1 American Indian or Alaska Native, non-Hispanic/Latino; 1 Asian, non-Hispanic/Latino; 1 Two or more races, non-Hispanic/Latino, 4 international. Average age 39. 8 applicants, 88% accepted, 5 enrolled. In 2010, 2 master's, 4 doctorates awarded. *Degree requirements:* For doctorate, variable foreign language requirement, thesis/dissertation. *Entrance requirements:* For master's, 2 letters of recommendation; for doctorate, GMAT, GRE General Test, minimum undergraduate GPA of 3.0. Additional exam requirements/recommendations for international students: Required—TOEFL. *Application deadline:* For fall admission, 2/1 for domestic students; for spring admission, 11/1 for domestic students. Application fee: $50. *Expenses:* Tuition, state resident: full-time $8505; part-time $315 per credit. Tuition, nonresident: full-time $13,284; part-time $492 per credit. Required fees: $1482; $21 per credit. $99 per term. One-time fee: $120. Part-time tuition and fees vary according to course load and program. *Financial support:* In 2010–11, 1 research assistantship with full tuition reimbursement (averaging $7,704 per year) was awarded; teaching assistantships with full tuition reimbursements, career-related internships or fieldwork, Federal Work-Study, scholarships/grants, and unspecified assistantships also available. Support available to part-time students. Financial award application deadline: 3/1; financial award applicants required to submit FAFSA. *Faculty research:* Systems theory and methodology, artificial intelligence neural networks, information theory, nonlinear dynamics/chaos, modeling and simulation. *Unit head:* George Lendaris, Acting Director, 503-725-4960. *Application contact:* Dawn Sharafi, Administrative Assistant, 503-725-4960, E-mail: dawn@sysc.pdx.edu.

Princeton University, Graduate School, Department of Economics, Princeton, NJ 08544-1019. Offers PhD. *Degree requirements:* For doctorate, thesis/dissertation. *Entrance requirements:* For doctorate, GRE General Test, GRE Subject Test (recommended), working knowledge of multivariate calculus and matrix algebra. Additional exam requirements/recommendations for international students: Required—TOEFL (minimum score 600 paper-based; 250 computer-based). Electronic applications accepted.

Princeton University, Graduate School, Program in Population Studies, Princeton, NJ 08544-1019. Offers demography (PhD, Certificate); economics and demography (PhD); public affairs and demography (PhD); sociology and demography (PhD). *Degree requirements:* For doctorate, thesis/dissertation. *Entrance requirements:* For doctorate, GRE General Test. Additional exam requirements/recommendations for international students: Required—TOEFL (minimum score 600 paper-based; 250 computer-based). Electronic applications accepted. *Faculty research:* Models, fertility, infant and child mortality, migration.

Purdue University, Graduate School, Krannert School of Management, Doctoral Program in Economics, West Lafayette, IN 47907-2056. Offers PhD. *Students:* 35 full-time (13 women); includes 1 Asian, non-Hispanic/Latino; 1 Hispanic/Latino, 19 international. Average age 26. 400 applicants, 3% accepted, 12 enrolled. In 2010, 7 doctorates awarded. *Degree requirements:* For doctorate, comprehensive exam, thesis/dissertation, dissertation proposal in 3rd year of study. *Entrance requirements:* For doctorate, GRE, two semesters of calculus, one semester of linear algebra. Additional exam requirements/recommendations for international students: Required—TOEFL (minimum score 575 paper-based; 233 computer-based); Recommended—TWE. *Application deadline:* For fall admission, 2/15 priority date for domestic and international students. Application fee: $55. Electronic applications accepted. *Financial support:* In 2010–11, 30 students received support, including 1 fellowship with full and partial tuition reimbursement available (averaging $25,000 per year), 22 research assistantships with partial tuition reimbursements available (averaging $18,000 per year), 12 teaching assistantships with partial tuition reimbursements available (averaging $18,000 per year); institutionally sponsored loans, scholarships/grants, health care benefits, tuition waivers (partial), unspecified assistantships, and travel funds to present at a major conference also available. Financial award application deadline: 2/15. *Faculty research:* Econometrics, experimental economics, international economics, macroeconomic theory, industrial organization. *Unit head:* Dr. Gerald J. Lynch, Dean, 765-494-4366. *Application contact:* Krannert Ph.D. Admissions, 765-494-4375, E-mail: krannertphd@purdue.edu.

Rice University, Graduate Programs, School of Social Sciences, Department of Economics, Houston, TX 77251-1892. Offers MA, PhD. *Degree requirements:* For doctorate, comprehensive exam, thesis/dissertation. *Entrance requirements:* For doctorate, GRE. Additional exam requirements/recommendations for international students: Required—TOEFL (minimum score 600 paper-based; 90 iBT). Electronic applications accepted.

Roosevelt University, Graduate Division, College of Arts and Sciences, Department of Economics, Chicago, IL 60605. Offers applied economics (MA); economics (MA). Part-time and evening/weekend programs available. *Degree requirements:* For master's, thesis or alternative. *Entrance requirements:* For master's, minimum GPA of 2.7. *Faculty research:* Labor, gender issues, international trade and development, entrepreneurship, political economy and money.

Rutgers, The State University of New Jersey, Newark, Graduate School, Program in Economics, Newark, NJ 07102. Offers MA. *Faculty:* 11 full-time (2 women). *Students:* 16 full-time (2 women), 23 part-time (7 women); includes 9 Black or African American, non-Hispanic/Latino; 10 Asian, non-Hispanic/Latino; 3 Hispanic/Latino. 51 applicants, 35% accepted, 15 enrolled. In 2010, 9 master's awarded. *Entrance requirements:* For master's, GRE, minimum undergraduate B average. Application fee: $60. *Expenses:* Tuition, state resident: part-time $600 per credit. Tuition, nonresident: full-time $10,694. *Unit head:* Sara Markowitz, Program Director, 973-353-5350, E-mail: smarkow@newark.rutgers.edu. *Application contact:* Jason Hand, Director of Admissions, 973-353-5205, Fax: 973-353-1440.

Rutgers, The State University of New Jersey, Newark, Rutgers Business School–Newark and New Brunswick, Doctoral Programs in Management, Newark, NJ 07102. Offers accounting (PhD); accounting information systems (PhD); economics (PhD); finance (PhD); individualized study (PhD); information technology (PhD); international business (PhD); management science (PhD); marketing science (PhD); organizational management (PhD); science, technology and management (PhD); supply chain management (PhD). *Faculty:* 143 full-time (36 women), 2 part-time/adjunct (0 women). *Students:* 117 full-time (42 women), 1 (woman) part-time; includes 8 Black or African American, non-Hispanic/Latino; 14 Asian, non-Hispanic/Latino; 3 Hispanic/Latino, 68 international. Average age 33. 355 applicants, 14% accepted, 35 enrolled. In 2010, 8 doctorates awarded. *Degree requirements:* For doctorate, comprehensive exam, thesis/dissertation. *Entrance requirements:* For doctorate, GRE or GMAT. Additional exam requirements/recommendations for international students: Required—TOEFL (minimum score 550 paper-based; 213 computer-based; 79 iBT). *Application deadline:* For fall admission, 3/1 for domestic and international students; for spring admission, 10/15 for domestic and international students. Application fee: $65. Electronic applications accepted. *Expenses:* Tuition, state resident: part-time $600 per credit. Tuition, nonresident: full-time $10,694. *Financial support:* In 2010–11, 52 students received support, including 7 fellowships (averaging $18,000 per year), 4 research assistantships with tuition reimbursements available (averaging $23,112 per year), 41 teaching assistantships with tuition reimbursements available (averaging $23,112 per year); health care benefits also available. Financial award application deadline: 3/1. *Unit head:* Dr. Glenn Shafer, Director, 973-353-1604, Fax: 973-353-5691, E-mail: gshafer@rbs.rutgers.edu. *Application contact:* Information Contact, 973-353-5371, Fax: 973-353-5691, E-mail: phdinfo@andromeda.rutgers.edu.

Rutgers, The State University of New Jersey, New Brunswick, Graduate School-New Brunswick, Program in Economics, Piscataway, NJ 08854-8097. Offers MA, PhD. Terminal

master's awarded for partial completion of doctoral program. *Degree requirements:* For master's, comprehensive exam (for some programs), thesis or alternative; for doctorate, comprehensive exam, thesis/dissertation. *Entrance requirements:* For master's and doctorate, GRE General Test. Additional exam requirements/recommendations for international students: Required—TOEFL. Electronic applications accepted. *Expenses:* Tuition, state resident: full-time $7200; part-time $600 per credit. Tuition, nonresident: full-time $11,124; part-time $927 per credit. *Faculty research:* Econometrics, microeconomics, macroeconomics, economichistory.

St. Cloud State University, School of Graduate Studies, College of Social Sciences, Department of Economics, St. Cloud, MN 56301-4498. Offers applied economics (MS); public and nonprofit institutions (MS). Part-time programs available. *Degree requirements:* For master's, thesis or alternative. *Entrance requirements:* For master's, GRE General Test, minimum GPA of 2.75. Additional exam requirements/recommendations for international students: Recommended—TOEFL (minimum score 550 paper-based; 213 computer-based), IELTS (minimum score 6.5). Electronic applications accepted.

San Diego State University, Graduate and Research Affairs, College of Arts and Letters, Department of Economics, San Diego, CA 92182. Offers MA. *Entrance requirements:* For master's, GRE General Test, 2 letters of recommendation. Additional exam requirements/recommendations for international students: Required—TOEFL. Electronic applications accepted. *Faculty research:* Financing public education, demand for alternative fuel vehicles, economics of the Gold Rush, interdependence of equity and economic efficiency, economics of welfare.

San Francisco State University, Division of Graduate Studies, College of Behavioral and Social Sciences, Department of Economics, San Francisco, CA 94132-1722. Offers MA. *Unit head:* Dr. Sudip Chattopadhyay, Chair, 415-338-1839. *Application contact:* Dr. Lisa Takeyama, Graduate Coordinator, 415-338-1839, E-mail: takeyama@sfsu.edu.

San Jose State University, Graduate Studies and Research, College of Social Sciences, Department of Economics, San Jose, CA 95192-0001. Offers applied economics (MA); economics (MA). Part-time programs available. *Degree requirements:* For master's, comprehensive exam, thesis optional. *Entrance requirements:* For master's, GRE, minimum GPA of 3.0. Electronic applications accepted.

Simon Fraser University, Graduate Studies, Faculty of Arts and Social Sciences, Department of Economics, Burnaby, BC V5A 1S6, Canada. Offers MA, PhD. Evening/weekend programs available. *Degree requirements:* For doctorate, comprehensive exam, thesis/dissertation. *Entrance requirements:* For master's, GRE, minimum GPA of 3.0; for doctorate, GRE, minimum GPA of 3.5. Additional exam requirements/recommendations for international students: Required—TWE or IELTS. *Faculty research:* Industrial organization, public economics, econometrics, labor, macroeconomics.

South Dakota State University, Graduate School, College of Agriculture and Biological Sciences, Department of Economics, Brookings, SD 57007. Offers MS. *Degree requirements:* For master's, comprehensive exam, thesis (for some programs), oral exam. *Entrance requirements:* For master's, minimum GPA of 2.75. Additional exam requirements/recommendations for international students: Required—TOEFL (minimum score 550 paper-based; 213 computer-based; 79 iBT). *Faculty research:* Sustainable agriculture, rural finance, grain and livestock marketing, agricultural policy, applied economics.

Southern Illinois University Carbondale, Graduate School, College of Liberal Arts, Department of Economics, Carbondale, IL 62901-4701. Offers MA, MS, PhD. *Degree requirements:* For master's, thesis; for doctorate, thesis/dissertation. *Entrance requirements:* For master's, GRE General Test, minimum GPA of 2.7; for doctorate, GRE General Test, minimum GPA of 3.25. Additional exam requirements/recommendations for international students: Required—TOEFL. *Faculty research:* Advanced economic theory, applied microeconomics, economic development, finance, international economics, monetary theory and policy.

Southern Illinois University Edwardsville, Graduate School, School of Business, Department of Economics and Finance, Edwardsville, IL 62026. Offers MA, MS. Part-time and evening/weekend programs available. *Faculty:* 13 full-time (3 women). *Students:* 22 full-time (5 women), 12 part-time (3 women); includes 1 minority (Black or African American, non-Hispanic/Latino), 10 international. Average age 26. 36 applicants, 72% accepted. In 2010, 14 master's awarded. *Degree requirements:* For master's, thesis or alternative, final exam, portfolio. *Entrance requirements:* For master's, GMAT or GRE. Additional exam requirements/recommendations for international students: Required—TOEFL (minimum score 550 paper-based; 213 computer-based; 79 iBT), IELTS (minimum score 6.5). *Application deadline:* For fall admission, 7/22 for domestic students, 6/1 for international students; for spring admission, 12/10 for domestic students, 10/1 for international students. Applications are processed on a rolling basis. Application fee: $30. Electronic applications accepted. *Expenses:* Tuition, state resident: full-time $6012; part-time $1503 per semester. Tuition, nonresident: full-time $15,030; part-time $3758 per semester. Required fees: $1711; $675 per semester. *Financial support:* In 2010–11, 1 fellowship with full tuition reimbursement (averaging $8,370 per year), 16 teaching assistantships with full tuition reimbursements (averaging $8,064 per year) were awarded; research assistantships with full tuition reimbursements, career-related internships or fieldwork, Federal Work-Study, institutionally sponsored loans, scholarships/grants, traineeships, and unspecified assistantships also available. Support available to part-time students. Financial award application deadline: 3/1; financial award applicants required to submit FAFSA. *Unit head:* Dr. Rik Hafer, Chair, 618-650-2542, E-mail: rhafer@siue.edu. *Application contact:* Dr. Ali Kutan, Director, 618-650-3473, E-mail: akutan@siue.edu.

Southern Methodist University, Dedman College, Department of Economics, Dallas, TX 75205. Offers applied economics (MA); economics (MA, PhD); JD/MA. Part-time and evening/weekend programs available. *Faculty:* 18 full-time (4 women), 19 part-time/adjunct (9 women). *Students:* 63 full-time (29 women), 14 part-time (6 women); includes 3 Black or African American, non-Hispanic/Latino; 7 Asian, non-Hispanic/Latino; 7 Hispanic/Latino, 32 international. Average age 26. 139 applicants, 63% accepted, 28 enrolled. In 2010, 21 master's, 6 doctorates awarded. Terminal master's awarded for partial completion of doctoral program. *Degree requirements:* For master's, thesis, oral qualifying exam; for doctorate, thesis/dissertation, written exams. *Entrance requirements:* For master's, GRE General Test or GMAT, 12 hours course work in economics, minimum GPA of 3.0, previous course work in calculus and statistics; for doctorate, GRE General Test, minimum GPA of 3.0; 3 semesters of course work in calculus; 1 semester each of course work in statistics and linear algebra. Additional exam requirements/recommendations for international students: Required—TOEFL (minimum score 550 paper-based; 213 computer-based). *Application deadline:* For fall admission, 2/1 priority date for domestic students; for spring admission, 11/30 priority date for domestic students. Applications are processed on a rolling basis. Application fee: $75. Electronic applications accepted. *Financial support:* In 2010–11, 23 students received support, including 1 fellowship with full tuition reimbursement available (averaging $16,000 per year), 1 research assistantship with full tuition reimbursement available (averaging $16,000 per year), 16 teaching assistantships with full tuition reimbursements available (averaging $16,000 per year). Financial award application deadline: 2/1; financial award applicants required to submit FAFSA. *Faculty research:* Economic theory, game theory, econometrics, international trade, labor. *Unit head:* Dr. Nathan Balke, Chair, 214-768-2693, Fax: 214-768-3911, E-mail: nbalke@smu.edu. *Application contact:* Stephanie Hall, Information Contact, 214-768-2694, E-mail: eco@smu.edu.

Stanford University, School of Humanities and Sciences, Department of Economics, Stanford, CA 94305-9991. Offers PhD. *Degree requirements:* For doctorate, thesis/dissertation, oral exam. *Entrance requirements:* For doctorate, GRE General Test. Additional exam requirements/recommendations for international students: Required—TOEFL. Electronic applications accepted. *Expenses:* Tuition: Full-time $38,700; part-time $860 per unit. One-time fee: $200 full-time.

State University of New York at Binghamton, Graduate School, School of Arts and Sciences, Department of Economics, Binghamton, NY 13902-6000. Offers economics (MA, PhD); economics and finance (MA, PhD). *Faculty:* 20 full-time (5 women), 2 part-time/adjunct (0

Economics

State University of New York at Binghamton (continued)
women). *Students:* 45 full-time (20 women), 33 part-time (11 women); includes 1 Black or African American, non-Hispanic/Latino; 4 Asian, non-Hispanic/Latino; 1 Hispanic/Latino, 58 international. Average age 28. 152 applicants, 48% accepted, 29 enrolled. In 2010, 12 master's, 5 doctorates awarded. Terminal master's awarded for partial completion of doctoral program. *Degree requirements:* For doctorate, thesis/dissertation. *Entrance requirements:* For master's and doctorate, GRE General Test. Additional exam requirements/recommendations for international students: Required—TOEFL (minimum score 550 paper-based; 213 computer-based; 80 iBT). *Application deadline:* For fall admission, 8/1 priority date for domestic and international students. Applications are processed on a rolling basis. Application fee: $60. Electronic applications accepted. *Financial support:* In 2010–11, 29 students received support, including 8 fellowships with full tuition reimbursements available (averaging $14,500 per year), 27 teaching assistantships with full tuition reimbursements available (averaging $14,500 per year); career-related internships or fieldwork, Federal Work-Study, institutionally sponsored loans, scholarships/grants, health care benefits, tuition waivers (full and partial), and unspecified assistantships also available. Financial award application deadline: 2/15; financial award applicants required to submit FAFSA. *Unit head:* Dr. Susan Wolcott, Chairperson, 607-777-2339, E-mail: swolcott@binghamton.edu. *Application contact:* Catherine Smith, Recruiting and Admissions Coordinator, 607-777-2151, Fax: 607-777-2501, E-mail: cmsmith@binghamton.edu.

Stony Brook University, State University of New York, Graduate School, College of Arts and Sciences, Department of Economics, Stony Brook, NY 11794. Offers MA, PhD. *Faculty:* 11 full-time (1 woman), 4 part-time/adjunct (0 women). *Students:* 55 full-time (36 women); includes 1 Black or African American, non-Hispanic/Latino, 48 international. Average age 28. 169 applicants, 30% accepted, 14 enrolled. In 2010, 1 master's, 4 doctorates awarded. *Degree requirements:* For doctorate, comprehensive exam, thesis/dissertation. *Entrance requirements:* For master's and doctorate, GRE General Test. Additional exam requirements/recommendations for international students: Required—TOEFL. *Application deadline:* For fall admission, 1/15 for domestic students. Application fee: $100. *Expenses:* Tuition, state resident: full-time $8370; part-time $349 per credit. Tuition, nonresident: full-time $13,780; part-time $574 per credit. Required fees: $994. *Financial support:* In 2010–11, 1 research assistantship, 29 teaching assistantships were awarded; fellowships also available. *Faculty research:* Economic theory, game theory, econometrics, macroeconomics, applied microeconomics. Total annual research expenditures: $114,580. *Unit head:* Dr. William Dawes, Co-Chair, 631-632-7530. *Application contact:* Dr. Sandro Brusco, Director of Graduate Studies, 631-632-7548, E-mail: sbrusco@notes.cc.sunysb.edu.

Suffolk University, College of Arts and Sciences, Department of Economics, Boston, MA 02108-2770. Offers economic policy (MSEP); economics (MSE, PhD); international economics (MSIE); JD/MSIE. Part-time and evening/weekend programs available. *Faculty:* 13 full-time (3 women). *Students:* 25 full-time (5 women), 16 part-time (5 women); includes 3 Asian, non-Hispanic/Latino; 1 Hispanic/Latino, 16 international. Average age 27. 108 applicants, 56% accepted, 17 enrolled. In 2010, 9 master's, 3 doctorates awarded. *Degree requirements:* For doctorate, comprehensive exam, thesis/dissertation. *Entrance requirements:* For master's, GRE General Test or GMAT, 2 letters of recommendation, resume; for doctorate, GRE General Test, 3 letters of recommendation. Additional exam requirements/recommendations for international students: Required—TOEFL (minimum score 550 paper-based; 213 computer-based; 80 iBT). *Application deadline:* For fall admission, 6/15 priority date for domestic students, 6/15 for international students; for spring admission, 11/1 priority date for domestic students, 11/1 for international students. Applications are processed on a rolling basis. Application fee: $50. Electronic applications accepted. *Expenses:* Contact institution. *Financial support:* In 2010–11, 34 students received support, including 27 fellowships with full and partial tuition reimbursements available (averaging $15,298 per year); career-related internships or fieldwork, Federal Work-Study, and institutionally sponsored loans also available. Support available to part-time students. Financial award application deadline: 4/1; financial award applicants required to submit FAFSA. *Faculty research:* Trade demands, fair tax, smoking, multinational firms, charitable giving, fair tax. *Unit head:* Dr. David Tuerck, Chairperson, 617-573-8259, Fax: 617-994-4216, E-mail: dtuerck@suffolk.edu. *Application contact:* Judith Reynolds, Director of Graduate Admissions, 617-573-8302, Fax: 617-305-1733, E-mail: grad.admission@suffolk.edu.

Syracuse University, Maxwell School of Citizenship and Public Affairs, Joint Program in Economics and International Relations, Syracuse, NY 13244. Offers MA/MA. *Students:* 11 full-time (8 women); includes 4 minority (all Two or more races, non-Hispanic/Latino), 6 international. Average age 26. 16 applicants, 56% accepted, 3 enrolled. *Entrance requirements:* Additional exam requirements/recommendations for international students: Required—TOEFL (minimum score 100 iBT). *Application deadline:* For fall admission, 2/1 priority date for domestic and international students. Application fee: $75. Electronic applications accepted. *Expenses:* Tuition: Part-time $1162 per credit. *Financial support:* Fellowships with full tuition reimbursements, research assistantships with full and partial tuition reimbursements, teaching assistantships with full and partial tuition reimbursements available. Financial award application deadline: 1/1. *Unit head:* Dr. Stuart Brown, Program Contact, 315-443-7097, Fax: 315-443-3385, E-mail: ssbrown@maxwell.syr.edu. *Application contact:* Dr. Stuart Brown, Program Contact, 315-443-7097, Fax: 315-443-3385, E-mail: ssbrown@maxwell.syr.edu.

Syracuse University, Maxwell School of Citizenship and Public Affairs, Program in Econometrics, Syracuse, NY 13244. Offers CAS. Part-time programs available. *Entrance requirements:* Additional exam requirements/recommendations for international students: Required—TOEFL (minimum score 100 iBT). *Application deadline:* For fall admission, 2/1 priority date for domestic and international students. Application fee: $75. *Expenses:* Tuition: Part-time $1162 per credit. *Unit head:* Dr. Devashish Mitra, Chair, 315-443-3612, Fax: 315-443-3385, E-mail: dmitra@syr.edu. *Application contact:* Laura Sauta, Program Contact, 315-443-2414, E-mail: llsauta@maxwell.syr.edu.

Syracuse University, Maxwell School of Citizenship and Public Affairs, Program in Economics, Syracuse, NY 13244. Offers MA, PhD. *Students:* 58 full-time (29 women), 6 part-time (0 women); includes 7 minority (2 Black or African American, non-Hispanic/Latino; 4 Asian, non-Hispanic/Latino; 1 Two or more races, non-Hispanic/Latino), 49 international. Average age 27. 310 applicants, 20% accepted, 20 enrolled. In 2010, 21 master's, 5 doctorates awarded. *Degree requirements:* For doctorate, comprehensive exam, thesis/dissertation. *Entrance requirements:* For master's and doctorate, GRE General Test. Additional exam requirements/recommendations for international students: Required—TOEFL (minimum score 100 iBT). *Application deadline:* For fall admission, 2/1 priority date for domestic and international students. Applications are processed on a rolling basis. Application fee: $75. Electronic applications accepted. *Expenses:* Tuition: Part-time $1162 per credit. *Financial support:* Fellowships with full tuition reimbursements, research assistantships with full and partial tuition reimbursements, teaching assistantships with full and partial tuition reimbursements available. Financial award application deadline: 1/1. *Faculty research:* International economics, labor economics, public finance, urban economics. *Unit head:* Dr. Chihwa Kao, Chair, 315-443-3612, Fax: 315-443-3717. *Application contact:* Laura Sauta, Recruiting Contact, 315-443-2414, E-mail: lsauta@maxwell.syr.edu.

Tarleton State University, College of Graduate Studies, College of Business Administration, Department of Accounting, Finance and Economics, Stephenville, TX 76402. Offers business administration (MBA). Part-time and evening/weekend programs available. *Degree requirements:* For master's, comprehensive exam. *Entrance requirements:* For master's, GRE or GMAT, minimum GPA of 3.0. Additional exam requirements/recommendations for international students: Required—TOEFL (minimum score 550 paper-based; 213 computer-based; 80 iBT). Electronic applications accepted.

Teachers College, Columbia University, Graduate Faculty of Education, Department of International and Transcultural Studies, Program in Economics and Education, New York, NY 10027. Offers Ed M, MA, PhD. *Faculty:* 5 full-time (1 woman), 3 part-time/adjunct (0 women). *Students:* 25 full-time (9 women), 50 part-time (32 women); includes 18 minority (4 Black or

African American, non-Hispanic/Latino; 6 Asian, non-Hispanic/Latino; 8 Hispanic/Latino), 40 international. Average age 30. 57 applicants, 70% accepted, 16 enrolled. In 2010, 10 master's, 7 doctorates awarded. *Degree requirements:* For master's, thesis; for doctorate, one foreign language, comprehensive exam, thesis/dissertation. *Entrance requirements:* For doctorate, GRE. *Application deadline:* For fall admission, 12/15 for domestic students; for spring admission, 11/1 for domestic students. Applications are processed on a rolling basis. Application fee: $65. Electronic applications accepted. *Expenses:* Tuition: Full-time $28,272; part-time $1178 per credit. Required fees: $756; $378 per semester. *Financial support:* Career-related internships or fieldwork, Federal Work-Study, institutionally sponsored loans, and tuition waivers (full and partial) available. Support available to part-time students. Financial award application deadline: 2/1; financial award applicants required to submit FAFSA. *Faculty research:* Education and economic growth, efficiency in education, training in education, labor and education policy, economic status of immigrant groups. *Unit head:* Prof. Francisco Rivera-Batiz, Program Coordinator, 212-678-3152, E-mail: flr9@columbia.edu. *Application contact:* Deanna Ghozati, Assistant Director of Admission, 212-678-4018, Fax: 212-678-4171, E-mail: ghozati@tc.edu.

Temple University, College of Liberal Arts, Department of Economics, Philadelphia, PA 19122-6096. Offers MA, PhD. Part-time and evening/weekend programs available. *Faculty:* 18 full-time (2 women). *Students:* 41 full-time (10 women), 21 part-time (8 women); includes 3 Black or African American, non-Hispanic/Latino; 1 American Indian or Alaska Native, non-Hispanic/Latino; 6 Asian, non-Hispanic/Latino; 1 Hispanic/Latino, 13 international. 97 applicants, 75% accepted, 25 enrolled. In 2010, 8 master's, 1 doctorate awarded. *Entrance requirements:* Additional exam requirements/recommendations for international students: Required—TOEFL (minimum score 550 paper-based; 213 computer-based; 79 iBT). *Application deadline:* For fall admission, 12/15 for international students; for spring admission, 8/1 for international students. Application fee: $50. Electronic applications accepted. *Financial support:* Application deadline: 1/15. *Unit head:* Dr. Michael L. Bognanno, Chair, 215-204-1680, E-mail: bognanno@temple.edu. *Application contact:* Dr. Michael L. Bognanno, Chair, 215-204-1680, E-mail: bognanno@temple.edu.

Texas A&M University, College of Liberal Arts, Department of Economics, College Station, TX 77843. Offers MS, PhD. Part-time programs available. *Faculty:* 17. *Students:* 101 full-time (33 women), 9 part-time (3 women); includes 1 Asian, non-Hispanic/Latino; 2 Hispanic/Latino, 90 international. Average age 31. In 2010, 24 master's, 7 doctorates awarded. Terminal master's awarded for partial completion of doctoral program. *Degree requirements:* For master's, comprehensive exam, thesis optional; for doctorate, comprehensive exam, thesis/dissertation. *Entrance requirements:* For master's and doctorate, GRE General Test. Additional exam requirements/recommendations for international students: Required—TOEFL. *Application deadline:* For fall admission, 3/1 priority date for domestic students; for winter admission, 8/1 priority date for domestic students; for spring admission, 11/1 priority date for domestic students. Applications are processed on a rolling basis. Application fee: $50 ($75 for international students). Electronic applications accepted. *Financial support:* In 2010–11, fellowships (averaging $14,850 per year), research assistantships (averaging $12,380 per year), teaching assistantships (averaging $10,062 per year) were awarded; scholarships/grants, tuition waivers, and unspecified assistantships also available. Financial award application deadline: 2/1; financial award applicants required to submit FAFSA. *Faculty research:* Tax policy, state tax, labor, international economics, macroeconomics. *Unit head:* Dr. Timothy Gronberg, Head, 979-845-7351. *Application contact:* Korey Glanz, Senior Office Associate, 979-845-7376, Fax: 979-847-8557, E-mail: kglanz@econmail.tamu.edu.

Texas A&M University–Commerce, Graduate School, College of Business and Technology, Department of Economics and Finance, Commerce, TX 75429-3011. Offers economics (MA, MS). Part-time programs available. *Degree requirements:* For master's, comprehensive exam, thesis (for some programs). *Entrance requirements:* For master's, GMAT or GRE General Test. Electronic applications accepted. *Faculty research:* Economic activity, forensic economics, volatility and finance, international economics.

Texas Tech University, Graduate School, College of Arts and Sciences, Department of Economics, Lubbock, TX 79409. Offers economics (MA, PhD); MPA/MA. Part-time programs available. *Faculty:* 13 full-time (3 women), 1 part-time/adjunct (0 women). *Students:* 36 full-time (7 women), 4 part-time (2 women); includes 1 Black or African American, non-Hispanic/Latino; 2 Hispanic/Latino, 29 international. Average age 29. 37 applicants, 65% accepted, 7 enrolled. In 2010, 8 master's, 2 doctorates awarded. *Degree requirements:* For master's, comprehensive exam (for some programs), thesis (for some programs); for doctorate, comprehensive exam, thesis/dissertation. *Entrance requirements:* For master's and doctorate, GRE General Test. Additional exam requirements/recommendations for international students: Required—TOEFL (minimum score 550 paper-based; 213 computer-based; 79 iBT). *Application deadline:* For fall admission, 6/1 priority date for domestic students, 1/15 priority date for international students; for spring admission, 9/1 priority date for domestic students, 6/15 priority date for international students. Applications are processed on a rolling basis. Application fee: $50 ($75 for international students). Electronic applications accepted. *Expenses:* Tuition, state resident: full-time $5495.76; part-time $228.99 per credit hour. Tuition, nonresident: full-time $12,936; part-time $538.99 per credit hour. Required fees: $2674; $36 per credit hour. $905 per semester. *Financial support:* In 2010–11, 28 students received support, including 14 teaching assistantships with partial tuition reimbursements available (averaging $8,452 per year). Financial award application deadline: 4/15; financial award applicants required to submit FAFSA. *Faculty research:* Monetary and international economics, labor economics, industrial organization, environmental economics, public finance. Total annual research expenditures: $53,420. *Unit head:* Dr. Klaus G. Becker, Chair, 806-742-2201 Ext. 231, Fax: 806-742-1137, E-mail: klaus.becker@ttu.edu. *Application contact:* Dr. Rashid Al-Hmoud, Graduate Advisor, 806-742-2201 Ext. 223, Fax: 806-742-1137, E-mail: rashid.al-hmoud@ttu.edu.

Trinity College, Graduate Programs, Department of Economics, Hartford, CT 06106-3100. Offers MA. Part-time and evening/weekend programs available. *Degree requirements:* For master's, thesis optional, qualifying exam. *Entrance requirements:* For master's, minimum GPA of 3.0.

Tufts University, Graduate School of Arts and Sciences, Department of Economics, Medford, MA 02155. Offers MS. Part-time programs available. *Degree requirements:* For master's, thesis optional. *Entrance requirements:* For master's, GRE General Test. Additional exam requirements/recommendations for international students: Required—TOEFL (minimum score 550 paper-based; 213 computer-based; 80 iBT). Electronic applications accepted. *Expenses:* Tuition: Full-time $39,624; part-time $3962 per course. Required fees: $40 per year. Full-time tuition and fees vary according to degree level, program and student level. Part-time tuition and fees vary according to course load.

Tulane University, School of Liberal Arts, Department of Economics, New Orleans, LA 70118-5669. Offers MA, PhD. *Degree requirements:* For master's, thesis or alternative; for doctorate, one foreign language, thesis/dissertation. *Entrance requirements:* For master's, GRE General Test, minimum B average in undergraduate course work; for doctorate, GRE General Test. Additional exam requirements/recommendations for international students: Required—TOEFL. Electronic applications accepted. *Faculty research:* Economic development, public finance, labor economics, international and regional economics, industrial organization.

Universidad de las Américas–Puebla, Division of Graduate Studies, School of Social Sciences, Program in Economics, Puebla, Mexico. Offers economics (MA); finance (M Adm). Part-time and evening/weekend programs available. *Degree requirements:* For master's, one foreign language, thesis. *Faculty research:* Economic models (mathematics), industrial organization, assets and values market.

Université de Moncton, Faculty of Arts and Social Sciences, Department of Economics, Moncton, NB E1A 3E9, Canada. Offers MA. *Degree requirements:* For master's, one foreign language, thesis. *Entrance requirements:* For master's, minimum GPA of 3.0. *Faculty research:*

Free trade, public finance, small and medium size businesses, regional development, demography and development.

Université de Montréal, Faculty of Arts and Sciences, Department of Economic Sciences, Montréal, QC H3C 3J7, Canada. Offers economics (M Sc, PhD); mathematical and computational finance (M Sc). *Degree requirements:* For master's, one foreign language, thesis; for doctorate, one foreign language, thesis/dissertation, general exam. Electronic applications accepted. *Faculty research:* Applied and economic theory, public choice, international trade, labor economics, industrial organization.

Université de Sherbrooke, Faculty of Administration, Program in Economics, Sherbrooke, QC J1K 2R1, Canada. Offers M Sc. *Faculty:* 4 full-time (2 women), 3 part-time/adjunct (0 women). *Students:* 26 full-time (11 women). Average age 24. 117 applicants, 83% accepted, 26 enrolled. In 2010, 11 master's awarded. Terminal master's awarded for partial completion of doctoral program. *Degree requirements:* For master's, one foreign language, thesis. *Entrance requirements:* For master's, Bachelor in related degree Minimum GPA 3/4.3. *Application deadline:* For fall admission, 4/30 for domestic students, 1/15 for international students. Applications are processed on a rolling basis. Application fee: $70. Electronic applications accepted. *Faculty research:* Poverty and inequality analysis, wellbeing analysis, international trade, econometrics. *Unit head:* Prof. Julien Bilodeau, Director, Graduate programs in business, 819-821-8000 Ext. 62355. *Application contact:* Marie-Claude Drouin, Programs director assistant, 819-821-8000 Ext. 63301.

Université de Sherbrooke, Faculty of Letters and Human Sciences, Department of Economics, Sherbrooke, QC J1K 2R1, Canada. Offers MA. *Degree requirements:* For master's, thesis. *Faculty research:* Economic development, public finance, macroeconomics.

Université du Québec à Montréal, Graduate Programs, Program in Economics, Montréal, QC H3C 3P8, Canada. Offers M Sc, PhD. Part-time programs available. *Degree requirements:* For master's, thesis; for doctorate, thesis/dissertation. *Entrance requirements:* For master's, appropriate bachelor's degree or equivalent, proficiency in French; for doctorate, appropriate master's degree or equivalent, proficiency in French.

Université Laval, Faculty of Social Sciences, Department of Economics, Programs in Economics, Québec, QC G1K 7P4, Canada. Offers MA, PhD. Terminal master's awarded for partial completion of doctoral program. *Degree requirements:* For master's, thesis (for some programs); for doctorate, comprehensive exam, thesis/dissertation. *Entrance requirements:* For master's and doctorate, knowledge of French. Electronic applications accepted.

University at Albany, State University of New York, College of Arts and Sciences, Department of Economics, Albany, NY 12222-0001. Offers economics (MA, PhD); regulatory economics (Certificate). Part-time programs available. Terminal master's awarded for partial completion of doctoral program. *Degree requirements:* For doctorate, one foreign language, thesis/dissertation. *Entrance requirements:* For doctorate, GRE General Test, GRE Subject Test. Additional exam requirements/recommendations for international students: Required—TOEFL (minimum score 550 paper-based; 213 computer-based). Electronic applications accepted. *Faculty research:* Expectations of inflation and interest rates, diffusion of new technology, labor markets in developing countries, government deficits and international exchange markets.

University at Buffalo, the State University of New York, Graduate School, College of Arts and Sciences, Department of Economics, Buffalo, NY 14260. Offers economics (MA, MS, PhD); financial economics (Certificate); health services (Certificate); information and Internet economics (Certificate); international economics (Certificate); law and regulation (Certificate); urban and regional economics (Certificate). Part-time programs available. *Faculty:* 19 full-time (3 women), 7 part-time/adjunct (2 women). *Students:* 264 full-time (124 women); includes 23 minority (3 Black or African American, non-Hispanic/Latino; 1 American Indian or Alaska Native, non-Hispanic/Latino; 16 Asian, non-Hispanic/Latino; 3 Hispanic/Latino), 177 international. Average age 24. 483 applicants, 48% accepted, 99 enrolled. In 2010, 82 master's, 7 doctorates, 3 other advanced degrees awarded. Terminal master's awarded for partial completion of doctoral program. *Degree requirements:* For master's, comprehensive exam; for doctorate, comprehensive exam, thesis/dissertation, field and theory exams. *Entrance requirements:* For master's, GRE or GMAT Test; for doctorate, GRE General Test. Additional exam requirements/recommendations for international students: Required—TOEFL (minimum score 550 paper-based; 213 computer-based; 79 iBT), TWE. *Application deadline:* For fall admission, 1/15 priority date for domestic and international students; for spring admission, 11/1 priority date for domestic and international students. Applications are processed on a rolling basis. Application fee: $75. Electronic applications accepted. *Financial support:* In 2010–11, 24 students received support, including 10 fellowships with full tuition reimbursements available (averaging $2,200 per year), 1 research assistantship with full tuition reimbursement available (averaging $13,500 per year), 12 teaching assistantships with full tuition reimbursements available (averaging $13,500 per year); Federal Work-Study, health care benefits, and unspecified assistantships also available. Financial award application deadline: 2/1; financial award applicants required to submit FAFSA. *Faculty research:* Human capital, international economics, econometrics, applied economics, urban economics, economic growth and development. *Unit head:* Dr. Isaac Ehrlich, Chair, 716-645-8670, Fax: 716-645-2127, E-mail: mgtehrl@buffalo.edu. *Application contact:* Dr. Nagesh Revankar, Director of Graduate Studies, 716-645-2121 Ext. 428, Fax: 716-645-2127, E-mail: ecorevan@buffalo.edu.

The University of Akron, Graduate School, Buchtel College of Arts and Sciences, Department of Economics, Akron, OH 44325. Offers economics (MA). Part-time programs available. *Faculty:* 9 full-time (3 women), 3 part-time/adjunct (2 women). *Students:* 21 full-time (3 women), 2 part-time (1 woman); includes 2 Black or African American, non-Hispanic/Latino, 6 international. Average age 25. 24 applicants, 67% accepted, 6 enrolled. In 2010, 12 master's awarded. *Degree requirements:* For master's, thesis optional. *Entrance requirements:* For master's, minimum GPA of 2.75, three letters of recommendation (preferably from academics), statement of purpose. Additional exam requirements/recommendations for international students: Required—TOEFL (minimum score 550 paper-based; 213 computer-based; 79 iBT), GRE. *Application deadline:* For fall admission, 2/15 for domestic and international students; for spring admission, 10/15 for domestic and international students. Application fee: $30 ($40 for international students). *Expenses:* Tuition, state resident: full-time $6800; part-time $378 per credit hour. Tuition, nonresident: full-time $11,644; part-time $647 per credit hour. Required fees: $1265. One-time fee: $30 full-time. *Financial support:* In 2010–11, 1 research assistantship with full tuition reimbursement, 19 teaching assistantships with full tuition reimbursements were awarded; institutionally sponsored loans also available. *Faculty research:* Regional economic performance, effects of addiction on labor market outcomes, programmatic assessment, regional trading arrangements, agriculture production in early twentieth century South. Total annual research expenditures: $77,232. *Unit head:* Dr. Michael Nelson, Chair, 330-972-7939, E-mail: nelson2@uakron.edu. *Application contact:* Dr. Sucharita Ghosh, Director of Graduate Studies, 330-972-7549, E-mail: sghosh@uakron.edu.

The University of Alabama, Graduate School, Manderson Graduate School of Business, Economics, Finance and Legal Studies Department, Tuscaloosa, AL 35487. Offers economics (MA, PhD); finance (MS, PhD). *Faculty:* 28 full-time (2 women). *Students:* 89 full-time (24 women), 7 part-time (3 women); includes 17 minority (9 Black or African American, non-Hispanic/Latino; 3 Asian, non-Hispanic/Latino; 3 Hispanic/Latino; 2 Two or more races, non-Hispanic/Latino), 19 international. Average age 27. 252 applicants, 34% accepted, 32 enrolled. In 2010, 46 master's, 7 doctorates awarded. Terminal master's awarded for partial completion of doctoral program. *Degree requirements:* For master's, comprehensive exam (MA), thesis (MS); for doctorate, comprehensive exam, thesis/dissertation. *Entrance requirements:* For master's, GMAT, GRE; for doctorate, GRE or GMAT. Additional exam requirements/recommendations for international students: Required—TOEFL (minimum score 550 paper-based; 213 computer-based). *Application deadline:* For fall admission, 7/1 priority date for domestic students, 1/15 for international students; for spring admission, 11/1 priority date for domestic students, 6/1 for international students. Applications are processed on a rolling basis. Application fee: $50 ($60 for international students). Electronic applications accepted. *Expenses:* Tuition, state resident: full-time $7900. Tuition, nonresident: full-time $20,500. *Financial support:* In 2010–11, 10 fellowships (averaging $10,000 per year), 21 research assistantships with full and partial tuition reimbursements (averaging $12,000 per year), 15 teaching assistantships with full and partial tuition reimbursements (averaging $12,000 per year) were awarded; Federal Work-Study, institutionally sponsored loans, and unspecified assistantships also available. *Faculty research:* Taxation, futures market, monetary theory and policy, income distribution. *Unit head:* Prof. Billy P. Helms, Head, 205-348-8067, E-mail: bhelms@cba.ua.edu. *Application contact:* Debra F. Wheatley, 205-348-6683, Fax: 205-348-0590, E-mail: dwheatle@cba.ua.edu.

University of Alaska Fairbanks, School of Management, Department of Economics, Fairbanks, AK 99775-6080. Offers resource and applied economics (MS). Part-time programs available. *Faculty:* 7 full-time (2 women). *Students:* 8 full-time (1 woman), 7 part-time (2 women); includes 3 minority (1 Asian, non-Hispanic/Latino; 1 Hispanic/Latino; 1 Two or more races, non-Hispanic/Latino), 1 international. Average age 30. 13 applicants, 69% accepted, 6 enrolled. In 2010, 2 master's awarded. *Degree requirements:* For master's, comprehensive exam, thesis or alternative. *Entrance requirements:* Additional exam requirements/recommendations for international students: Required—TOEFL (minimum score 550 paper-based; 213 computer-based). *Application deadline:* For fall admission, 6/1 priority date for domestic students, 3/1 for international students; for spring admission, 10/15 priority date for domestic students, 9/1 for international students. Applications are processed on a rolling basis. Application fee: $60. Electronic applications accepted. *Expenses:* Tuition, state resident: full-time $5688; part-time $316 per credit. Tuition, nonresident: full-time $11,628; part-time $646 per credit. Required fees: $289 per semester. Tuition and fees vary according to course load and reciprocity agreements. *Financial support:* In 2010–11, 1 research assistantship with tuition reimbursement (averaging $4,962 per year), 5 teaching assistantships with tuition reimbursements (averaging $14,083 per year) were awarded; fellowships with tuition reimbursements, career-related internships or fieldwork, Federal Work-Study, scholarships/grants, health care benefits, and unspecified assistantships also available. Support available to part-time students. Financial award application deadline: 2/15; financial award applicants required to submit FAFSA. *Faculty research:* Statistics; resource and agriculture economics; oil, gas, and energy; sustainability; public land management. Total annual research expenditures: $11,233. *Unit head:* Gregory Goering, Program Director, 907-474-5572, Fax: 907-474-5219, E-mail: gegoering@alaska.edu. *Application contact:* Gregory Goering, Program Director, 907-474-5572, Fax: 907-474-5219, E-mail: gegoering@alaska.edu.

University of Alberta, Faculty of Graduate Studies and Research, Department of Economics, Edmonton, AB T6G 2E1, Canada. Offers economics (MA, PhD); economics and finance (MA); environmental and natural resource economics (PhD). Part-time programs available. *Degree requirements:* For doctorate, thesis/dissertation. *Entrance requirements:* For master's and doctorate, GRE. Additional exam requirements/recommendations for international students: Required—TOEFL. *Faculty research:* Public finance, international trade, industrial organization, Pacific Rim economics, monetary economics.

The University of Arizona, Eller College of Management, Department of Economics, Tucson, AZ 85721. Offers MA, PhD, JD/MA, JD/PhD. *Faculty:* 15 full-time (2 women), 2 part-time/adjunct (0 women). *Students:* 55 full-time (20 women), 4 part-time (1 woman); includes 4 minority (1 Black or African American, non-Hispanic/Latino; 1 Hispanic/Latino; 2 Two or more races, non-Hispanic/Latino), 28 international. Average age 29. 237 applicants, 16% accepted, 21 enrolled. In 2010, 10 master's, 5 doctorates awarded. Terminal master's awarded for partial completion of doctoral program. *Degree requirements:* For master's, comprehensive exam; for doctorate, thesis/dissertation. *Entrance requirements:* For doctorate, GRE General Test, 3 letters of recommendation. Additional exam requirements/recommendations for international students: Required—TOEFL (minimum score 550 paper-based; 213 computer-based; 79 iBT). *Application deadline:* For fall admission, 2/1 for domestic and international students. Applications are processed on a rolling basis. Application fee: $75. Electronic applications accepted. *Expenses:* Tuition, state resident: full-time $7692. *Financial support:* In 2010–11, 9 research assistantships with full tuition reimbursements (averaging $19,805 per year), 32 teaching assistantships with full tuition reimbursements (averaging $19,805 per year) were awarded; Federal Work-Study, scholarships/grants, health care benefits, tuition waivers (partial), and unspecified assistantships also available. Financial award application deadline: 2/1. *Faculty research:* Applied microeconomics, experimental economics, economic history, microeconomic theory, property rights, industrial organization. Total annual research expenditures: $260,644. *Unit head:* Dr. Mark Walker, Head, 520-621-2821, Fax: 520-621-8450, E-mail: mwalker@eller.arizona.edu. *Application contact:* Lana Sooter, Information Contact, 520-621-2821, Fax: 520-621-8450, E-mail: lsooter@email.arizona.edu.

University of Arkansas, Graduate School, Sam M. Walton College of Business Administration, Department of Economics, Fayetteville, AR 72701-1201. Offers MA, PhD. *Students:* 9 full-time (1 woman), 5 part-time (1 woman), 7 international. 7 applicants, 29% accepted. In 2010, 5 master's awarded. *Degree requirements:* For doctorate, variable foreign language requirement, thesis/dissertation. *Entrance requirements:* For master's and doctorate, GRE General Test. Application fee: $40 ($50 for international students). *Financial support:* In 2010–11, 4 fellowships with tuition reimbursements, 8 research assistantships, 5 teaching assistantships were awarded; career-related internships or fieldwork and Federal Work-Study also available. Support available to part-time students. Financial award application deadline: 4/1; financial award applicants required to submit FAFSA. *Unit head:* Dr. Gary Ferrier, Chair, 479-575-3266, E-mail: gferrier@uark.edu. *Application contact:* Dr. Cary Deck, Graduate Coordinator, 479-575-6226, E-mail: cdeck@uark.edu.

The University of British Columbia, Faculty of Arts and Faculty of Graduate Studies, Department of Economics, Vancouver, BC V6T 1Z1, Canada. Offers MA, PhD. *Degree requirements:* For master's, thesis (for some programs); for doctorate, comprehensive exam, thesis/dissertation. *Entrance requirements:* For master's and doctorate, GRE General Test. Additional exam requirements/recommendations for international students: Required—TOEFL (minimum score 550 paper-based; 213 computer-based; 80 iBT). Electronic applications accepted. Tuition charges are reported in Canadian dollars. *Expenses:* Tuition, area resident: Full-time $4179 Canadian dollars. International tuition: $7344 Canadian dollars full-time. *Faculty research:* Economic theory, international economics, labor economics, public finance, economic development.

University of Calgary, Faculty of Graduate Studies, Faculty of Social Sciences, Department of Economics, Calgary, AB T2N 1N4, Canada. Offers M Ec, MA, PhD. Part-time and evening/weekend programs available. *Degree requirements:* For master's, thesis (for some programs); for doctorate, thesis/dissertation, candidacy exam. *Entrance requirements:* Additional exam requirements/recommendations for international students: Required—TOEFL. *Faculty research:* Energy economics, public finance/public choice, resource economics, international trade, monetary economics.

University of California, Berkeley, Graduate Division, College of Letters and Science, Department of Economics, Berkeley, CA 94720-1500. Offers PhD, JD/MA. *Degree requirements:* For doctorate, thesis/dissertation, field exams, oral qualifying exam. *Entrance requirements:* For doctorate, GRE General Test, minimum GPA of 3.0, 3 letters of recommendation. Additional exam requirements/recommendations for international students: Required—TOEFL.

University of California, Davis, Graduate Studies, Program in Economics, Davis, CA 95616. Offers MA, PhD. Terminal master's awarded for partial completion of doctoral program. *Degree requirements:* For master's, comprehensive exam (for some programs), thesis (for some programs); for doctorate, thesis/dissertation. *Entrance requirements:* For master's, GRE General Test, minimum GPA of 3.0; for doctorate, GRE General Test, minimum GPA of 3.25. Additional exam requirements/recommendations for international students: Required—TOEFL (minimum

Economics

University of California, Davis (continued)
score 550 paper-based; 213 computer-based). Electronic applications accepted. *Faculty research:* Applied microeconomics, macroeconomics, international studies, economic theory, economic history.

University of California, Irvine, School of Social Sciences, Department of Economics, Irvine, CA 92697. Offers economics (MA, PhD); public choice (MA, PhD); transportation economics (MA, PhD). *Students:* 74 full-time (18 women); includes 18 minority (15 Asian, non-Hispanic/Latino; 2 Hispanic/Latino; 1 Two or more races, non-Hispanic/Latino), 20 international. Average age 28. 244 applicants, 23% accepted, 27 enrolled. In 2010, 10 master's, 5 doctorates awarded. *Degree requirements:* For doctorate, thesis/dissertation. *Entrance requirements:* For master's and doctorate, GRE General Test, minimum GPA of 3.0. Additional exam requirements/recommendations for international students: Required—TOEFL (minimum score 550 paper-based; 213 computer-based). *Application deadline:* For fall admission, 1/15 priority date for domestic and international students. Applications are processed on a rolling basis. Application fee: $80 ($100 for international students). Electronic applications accepted. *Financial support:* Fellowships, research assistantships with full tuition reimbursements, teaching assistantships, institutionally sponsored loans, traineeships, health care benefits, and unspecified assistantships available. Financial award application deadline: 3/1; financial award applicants required to submit FAFSA. *Faculty research:* Econometrics, urban economics, applied microeconomics. *Unit head:* Prof. Jan L. Brueckner, Chair, 949-824-0083, Fax: 949-824-2182, E-mail: jkbrueck@uci.edu. *Application contact:* Prof. Dale J. Pirier, Professor, 949-824-3186, Fax: 949-824-2182, E-mail: dpoirier@uci.edu.

University of California, Los Angeles, Graduate Division, College of Letters and Science, Department of Economics, Los Angeles, CA 90034. Offers MA, PhD. *Faculty:* 37 full-time (10 women). *Students:* 117 full-time (28 women); includes 14 minority (2 Black or African American, non-Hispanic/Latino; 10 Asian, non-Hispanic/Latino; 2 Hispanic/Latino), 69 international. Average age 27. 491 applicants, 20% accepted, 34 enrolled. In 2010, 23 master's, 13 doctorates awarded. Terminal master's awarded for partial completion of doctoral program. *Degree requirements:* For master's, comprehensive exam; for doctorate, thesis/dissertation, oral and written qualifying exams. *Entrance requirements:* For master's, GRE General Test; for doctorate, GRE General Test, minimum undergraduate GPA of 3.0. *Application deadline:* For fall admission, 12/1 for domestic and international students. Application fee: $70 ($90 for international students). Electronic applications accepted. *Financial support:* In 2010–11, 82 fellowships with full and partial tuition reimbursements, 45 research assistantships with full and partial tuition reimbursements, 68 teaching assistantships with full and partial tuition reimbursements were awarded; Federal Work-Study, institutionally sponsored loans, scholarships/grants, health care benefits, tuition waivers (full and partial), and unspecified assistantships also available. Financial award application deadline: 3/1; financial award applicants required to submit FAFSA. *Unit head:* Dr. Roger Farmer, Chair, 310-825-6547, E-mail: rfarmer@econ.ucla.edu. *Application contact:* Sara S. Lee, Department Office, 310-206-1413, E-mail: slee@econ.ucla.edu.

University of California, Los Angeles, Graduate Division, UCLA Anderson School of Management, Los Angeles, CA 90095-1481. Offers accounting (PhD); business administration (MBA); decisions, operations and technology management (PhD); finance (PhD); financial engineering (MFE); global economics and management (PhD); human resources and organizational behavior (PhD); marketing (PhD); strategy and policy (PhD); DDS/MBA; MBA/JD; MBA/MD; MBA/MLAS; MBA/MLIS; MBA/MPH; MBA/MPP; MBA/MSCS; MBA/MSN; MBA/MUP. *Accreditation:* AACSB. Part-time programs available. *Faculty:* 102 full-time (17 women), 43 part-time/adjunct (6 women). *Students:* 833 full-time (270 women), 1,052 part-time (271 women); includes 592 minority (25 Black or African American, non-Hispanic/Latino; 3 American Indian or Alaska Native, non-Hispanic/Latino; 482 Asian, non-Hispanic/Latino; 60 Hispanic/Latino; 6 Native Hawaiian or other Pacific Islander, non-Hispanic/Latino; 16 Two or more races, non-Hispanic/Latino), 445 international. In 2010, 735 master's, 10 doctorates awarded. *Degree requirements:* For master's, comprehensive exam, field study consulting project (for MBA); thesis/dissertation (for MFE); for doctorate, comprehensive exam, thesis/dissertation, oral and written qualifying exams. *Entrance requirements:* For master's, GMAT (MBA); GMAT or GRE General Test (MFE), minimum undergraduate GPA of 3.0; for doctorate, GMAT or GRE General Test, minimum undergraduate GPA of 3.0. Additional exam requirements/recommendations for international students: Required—TOEFL (minimum score 560 paper-based; 220 computer-based; 87 iBT), IELTS (minimum score 7). *Application deadline:* For fall admission, 10/20 for domestic and international students; for winter admission, 1/5 for domestic and international students; for spring admission, 4/13 for domestic and international students. Application fee: $200. Electronic applications accepted. *Expenses:* Contact institution. *Financial support:* Fellowships, research assistantships, teaching assistantships, career-related internships or fieldwork, institutionally sponsored loans, scholarships/grants, health care benefits, and tuition waivers (partial) available. Financial award application deadline: 3/2; financial award applicants required to submit FAFSA. *Unit head:* Judy D. Olian, Dean, UCLA Anderson School of Management, 310-825-7982, Fax: 310-206-2073. *Application contact:* Mae Jennifer Shores, Assistant Dean and Director of Full-time MBA Admissions and Financial Aid, 310-825-6944, Fax: 310-825-8582, E-mail: mba.admissions@anderson.ucla.edu.

University of California, Riverside, Graduate Division, Department of Economics, Riverside, CA 92521-0102. Offers MA, PhD. *Faculty:* 20 full-time (4 women). *Students:* 58 full-time (25 women); includes 2 Black or African American, non-Hispanic/Latino; 5 Asian, non-Hispanic/Latino; 2 Hispanic/Latino, 40 international. Average age 29. 134 applicants, 19% accepted, 13 enrolled. In 2010, 5 master's, 8 doctorates awarded. Terminal master's awarded for partial completion of doctoral program. *Degree requirements:* For master's, comprehensive exam; for doctorate, thesis/dissertation, qualifying exams. *Entrance requirements:* For master's and doctorate, GRE General Test, minimum GPA of 3.2. Additional exam requirements/recommendations for international students: Required—TOEFL (minimum score 550 paper-based; 213 computer-based; 80 iBT). *Application deadline:* For fall admission, 5/1 for domestic students, 2/1 for international students. Applications are processed on a rolling basis. Application fee: $85 ($100 for international students). Electronic applications accepted. *Financial support:* In 2010–11, fellowships with partial tuition reimbursements (averaging $12,000 per year), teaching assistantships with partial tuition reimbursements (averaging $16,500 per year) were awarded; research assistantships, career-related internships or fieldwork, institutionally sponsored loans, and tuition waivers (full and partial) also available. Financial award application deadline: 1/15; financial award applicants required to submit FAFSA. *Faculty research:* Advanced political economy; resource and environmental economics; advanced econometrics; labor economics; advanced microeconomics theory; advanced macroeconomics theory; development economics; economic history; international trade theory; money, credit and business cycles; public economics. *Unit head:* Dr. Aman Ullah, Chair, 951-827-1474, Fax: 951-827-5685, E-mail: econgrad@ucr.edu. *Application contact:* Amanda Labagnara, Graduate Program Assistant, 951-827-1474, Fax: 951-827-5685, E-mail: econgrad@ucr.edu.

University of California, San Diego, Office of Graduate Studies, Department of Economics, La Jolla, CA 92093. Offers economics (PhD); economics and international affairs (PhD). *Degree requirements:* For doctorate, thesis/dissertation. *Entrance requirements:* For doctorate, GRE General Test. Electronic applications accepted. *Faculty research:* Microfoundations of macroeconomics, econometric model specification and testing, industrial organization.

University of California, San Diego, Office of Graduate Studies, Graduate School of International Relations and Pacific Studies, La Jolla, CA 92093. Offers economics and international affairs (PhD); Pacific international affairs (MPIA); political science and international affairs (PhD). *Degree requirements:* For master's, one foreign language; for doctorate, thesis/dissertation. *Entrance requirements:* For master's, GMAT or GRE General Test; for doctorate, GRE General Test. Additional exam requirements/recommendations for international students: Required—TOEFL (minimum score 550 paper-based; 213 computer-based). Electronic applications accepted. *Faculty research:* Pacific Rim as system and placement in global relations; studies in international economics, management and finance; analysis of patterns of policymaking in countries of the Pacific.

University of California, Santa Barbara, Graduate Division, College of Letters and Sciences, Division of Social Sciences, Department of Economics, Santa Barbara, CA 93106-9210. Offers economics (MA, PhD); economics and environmental science (PhD); MA/PhD. *Faculty:* 30 full-time (4 women), 14 part-time/adjunct (4 women). *Students:* 104 full-time (41 women); includes 31 Asian, non-Hispanic/Latino; 11 Hispanic/Latino. Average age 26. 318 applicants, 55% accepted, 57 enrolled. In 2010, 34 master's, 10 doctorates awarded. Terminal master's awarded for partial completion of doctoral program. *Degree requirements:* For master's, comprehensive exam, thesis; for doctorate, comprehensive exam, thesis/dissertation. *Entrance requirements:* For master's, GRE General Test, 3 letters of recommendation, resume/curriculum vitae; for doctorate, GRE General Test, 3 letters of recommendation, statement of purpose, personal achievements/contributions statement, resume/curriculum vitae, transcripts for post-secondary institutions attended. Additional exam requirements/recommendations for international students: Required—TOEFL (minimum score 550 paper-based; 80 iBT), IELTS (minimum score 7). *Application deadline:* For fall admission, 12/1 priority date for domestic and international students. Application fee: $70 ($90 for international students). Electronic applications accepted. *Financial support:* In 2010–11, 65 students received support, including 24 fellowships with full and partial tuition reimbursements available (averaging $12,105 per year), 7 research assistantships with full and partial tuition reimbursements available (averaging $9,616 per year), 56 teaching assistantships with partial tuition reimbursements available (averaging $12,114 per year); Federal Work-Study, institutionally sponsored loans, scholarships/grants, health care benefits, tuition waivers (full and partial), and unspecified assistantships also available. Support available to part-time students. Financial award application deadline: 12/1; financial award applicants required to submit FAFSA. *Faculty research:* Labor economics, econometrics, macroeconomic theory and policy, environmental and natural resources economics (EES), experimental and behavioral economics. *Unit head:* Prof. Perry Shapiro, Chair, 805-893-2253, Fax: 805-893-8830, E-mail: pxshap@econ.ucsb.edu. *Application contact:* Mark Patterson, Staff Graduate Advisor, 805-893-2205, Fax: 805-893-8830, E-mail: mark@econ.ucsb.edu.

University of California, Santa Barbara, Graduate Division, College of Letters and Sciences, Division of Social Sciences, Department of Global and International Studies, Santa Barbara, CA 93106-7065. Offers global culture and religion (MA); global government and human rights (MA); political economy, sustainable development, and the environment (MA). *Faculty:* 14 full-time (5 women), 4 part-time/adjunct (1 woman). *Students:* 37 full-time (25 women); includes 6 Asian, non-Hispanic/Latino; 2 Hispanic/Latino; 1 Native Hawaiian or other Pacific Islander, non-Hispanic/Latino. Average age 28. 55 applicants, 42% accepted, 12 enrolled. In 2010, 14 master's awarded. *Degree requirements:* For master's, one foreign language, thesis or alternative, 2 years of a second language. *Entrance requirements:* For master's, GRE, 2 years of a second language with minimum B grade, 3 letters of recommendation, resume/curriculum vitae. Additional exam requirements/recommendations for international students: Required—TOEFL (minimum score 600 paper-based; 80 iBT), IELTS (minimum score 7). *Application deadline:* For fall admission, 12/15 for domestic and international students. Application fee: $70 ($90 for international students). Electronic applications accepted. *Financial support:* In 2010–11, 36 students received support, including 29 fellowships with partial tuition reimbursements available (averaging $6,805 per year), 31 teaching assistantships with partial tuition reimbursements available (averaging $8,175 per year); career-related internships or fieldwork also available. Financial award application deadline: 12/15; financial award applicants required to submit FAFSA. *Faculty research:* Global culture religion, global governance human rights, political economy, environment, sustainable development. Total annual research expenditures: $240,000. *Unit head:* Prof. Giles Gunn, Chair, 805-893-4299, Fax: 805-893-8003, E-mail: ggunn@global.ucsb.edu. *Application contact:* Jessea Gay Marie, Graduate Program Advisor/Internship Assistance Officer, 805-893-4668, Fax: 805-893-8003, E-mail: gd-global@global.ucsb.edu.

University of California, Santa Barbara, Graduate Division, Donald Bren School of Environmental Science and Management, Santa Barbara, CA 93106-5131. Offers economics and environmental science (PhD); environmental science and management (MESM, PhD); technology and society (PhD). *Faculty:* 17 full-time (3 women), 2 part-time/adjunct (0 women). *Students:* 219 full-time (128 women); includes 1 Black or African American, non-Hispanic/Latino; 1 American Indian or Alaska Native, non-Hispanic/Latino; 33 Asian, non-Hispanic/Latino; 11 Hispanic/Latino. Average age 28. 521 applicants, 40% accepted, 82 enrolled. In 2010, 75 master's awarded. *Degree requirements:* For master's, thesis; for doctorate, thesis/dissertation. *Entrance requirements:* For master's and doctorate, GRE. Additional exam requirements/recommendations for international students: Required—TOEFL (minimum score 550 paper-based; 80 iBT), IELTS (minimum score 7). *Application deadline:* For fall admission, 12/15 priority date for domestic and international students. Application fee: $70 ($90 for international students). Electronic applications accepted. *Financial support:* In 2010–11, 105 students received support, including 83 fellowships with full and partial tuition reimbursements available (averaging $6,929 per year), 27 research assistantships with full and partial tuition reimbursements available (averaging $8,918 per year), 32 teaching assistantships with partial tuition reimbursements available (averaging $8,112 per year); career-related internships or fieldwork and tuition waivers (full and partial) also available. Financial award application deadline: 12/15; financial award applicants required to submit FAFSA. *Faculty research:* Coastal marine resources management, conservation planning, corporate environmental management, economics and politics of the environment, energy and climate, pollution prevention and remediation, water resources management. *Unit head:* Bryant Wieneke, Assistant Dean, Planning and Administration, 805-893-2212, Fax: 805-893-7612, E-mail: bryant@bren.ucsb.edu. *Application contact:* Graduate Advisor, 805-893-7611, Fax: 805-893-7612, E-mail: admissions@bren.ucsb.edu.

University of California, Santa Cruz, Division of Graduate Studies, Division of Social Sciences, Program in International Economics, Santa Cruz, CA 95064. Offers PhD. *Students:* 62 full-time (24 women), 1 (woman) part-time; includes 12 minority (1 Black or African American, non-Hispanic/Latino; 4 Asian, non-Hispanic/Latino; 7 Hispanic/Latino), 31 international. Average age 32. 133 applicants, 47% accepted, 15 enrolled. In 2010, 9 doctorates awarded. *Degree requirements:* For doctorate, thesis/dissertation, 4 field exams, field papers, econometrics project, qualifying exams. *Entrance requirements:* For doctorate, GRE General Test. Additional exam requirements/recommendations for international students: Required—TOEFL (minimum score 550 paper-based; 220 computer-based; 83 iBT); Recommended—IELTS (minimum score 8). *Application deadline:* For fall admission, 1/15 for domestic and international students. Application fee: $70 ($90 for international students). Electronic applications accepted. *Financial support:* Fellowships, research assistantships, teaching assistantships, institutionally sponsored loans and tuition waivers (partial) available. Financial award applicants required to submit FAFSA. *Faculty research:* Current and emerging issues in taxation, industrial policy, environmental regulation, market structure, labor economics focus on behavior and adjustment in an interdependent world economy. *Unit head:* Sandra Reebie, Graduate Program Coordinator, 831-459-2219, E-mail: screebie@ucsc.edu. *Application contact:* Sandra Reebie, Graduate Program Coordinator, 831-459-2219, E-mail: screebie@ucsc.edu.

University of Central Arkansas, Graduate School, College of Liberal Arts, Program in Community and Economic Development, Conway, AR 72035-0001. Offers MS. *Students:* 7 full-time (1 woman), 17 part-time (5 women); includes 8 minority (5 Black or African American, non-Hispanic/Latino; 2 Hispanic/Latino; 1 Two or more races, non-Hispanic/Latino), 2 international. Average age 31. 14 applicants, 100% accepted, 11 enrolled. In 2010, 9 master's awarded. *Degree requirements:* For master's, comprehensive exam, thesis. *Entrance requirements:* For master's, GRE General Test, minimum GPA of 2.7. Additional exam requirements/recommendations for international students: Required—TOEFL (minimum score 550 paper-based; 213 computer-based). *Application deadline:* For fall admission, 3/1 priority date for domestic students; for spring admission, 10/1 priority date for domestic students. Applications are processed on a rolling basis. Application fee: $25 ($40 for international students). *Expenses:* Contact institution. *Financial support:* Career-related internships or fieldwork, Federal Work-Study, and unspecified assistantships available. Financial award applicants required to submit FAFSA. *Unit head:* Dr. Lauren Maxwell, Coordinator, 501-450-5349. *Application contact:* Brenda Herring, Admissions Assistant, 501-450-5065, Fax: 501-450-5678, E-mail: bherring@uca.edu.

University of Chicago, Booth School of Business, Full-Time MBA Program, Chicago, IL 60637. Offers accounting (MBA); analytic finance (MBA); analytic management (MBA); econometrics and statistics (MBA); economics (MBA); entrepreneurship (MBA); finance (MBA); general management (MBA); human resource management (MBA); international business (MBA); managerial and organizational behavior (MBA); marketing management (MBA); operations management (MBA); strategic management (MBA); MBA/AM; MBA/JD; MBA/MA; MBA/MD; MBA/MPP. *Accreditation:* AACSB. Part-time and evening/weekend programs available. *Faculty:* 157 full-time, 35 part-time/adjunct. *Students:* 1,177 full-time (417 women); includes 301 minority (62 Black or African American, non-Hispanic/Latino; 1 American Indian or Alaska Native, non-Hispanic/Latino; 164 Asian, non-Hispanic/Latino; 55 Hispanic/Latino; 19 Two or more races, non-Hispanic/Latino), 403 international. Average age 28. 4,299 applicants, 22% accepted, 579 enrolled. In 2010, 1,374 master's awarded. *Entrance requirements:* For master's, GMAT, 2 letters of recommendation, 3 essays, resume, interview, transcripts. Additional exam requirements/recommendations for international students: Required—TOEFL (minimum score 600 paper-based; 250 computer-based), IELTS. *Application deadline:* For fall admission, 10/10 priority date for domestic students, 10/13 priority date for international students; for winter admission, 1/5 for domestic and international students; for spring admission, 4/13 for domestic and international students. Application fee: $200. Electronic applications accepted. *Expenses:* Contact institution. *Financial support:* Fellowships available. Financial award applicants required to submit FAFSA. *Faculty research:* Finance, economics, entrepreneurship, strategy, management. *Unit head:* Stacey Kole, Deputy Dean, 773-702-7121. *Application contact:* Kurt Ahlm, Associate Dean of Admissions and Financial Aid, 773-702-7369, Fax: 773-702-9085, E-mail: admissions@chicagobooth.edu.

University of Chicago, Division of Social Sciences, Department of Economics, Chicago, IL 60637-1513. Offers PhD. *Degree requirements:* For doctorate, one foreign language, thesis/dissertation, written exams in 2 fields. *Entrance requirements:* For doctorate, GRE General Test. Additional exam requirements/recommendations for international students: Required—TOEFL, IELTS (minimum score 7). Electronic applications accepted.

University of Cincinnati, Graduate School, McMicken College of Arts and Sciences, Department of Economics, Program in Applied Economics, Cincinnati, OH 45221. Offers MA. Part-time and evening/weekend programs available. *Degree requirements:* For master's, thesis optional. *Entrance requirements:* For master's, GRE General Test or GMAT, intermediate micro, macro theory, statistics, calculus. Additional exam requirements/recommendations for international students: Required—TOEFL. Electronic applications accepted. *Faculty research:* Econometrics, labor markets, pollution markets, transportation.

University of Colorado Boulder, Graduate School, College of Arts and Sciences, Department of Economics, Boulder, CO 80309. Offers MA, PhD. *Faculty:* 27 full-time (6 women). *Students:* 82 full-time (31 women), 2 part-time (0 women); includes 5 minority (1 American Indian or Alaska Native, non-Hispanic/Latino; 3 Asian, non-Hispanic/Latino; 1 Hispanic/Latino), 43 international. Average age 30. 158 applicants, 15 enrolled. In 2010, 10 master's, 11 doctorates awarded. Terminal master's awarded for partial completion of doctoral program. *Degree requirements:* For master's, comprehensive exam, thesis or alternative; for doctorate, comprehensive exam, thesis/dissertation, preliminary exam. *Entrance requirements:* For master's, GRE General Test, minimum undergraduate GPA of 2.75; for doctorate, GRE General Test. Additional exam requirements/recommendations for international students: Required—TOEFL. *Application deadline:* For fall admission, 2/1 priority date for domestic students, 12/1 for international students. Applications are processed on a rolling basis. Application fee: $50 ($60 for international students). *Financial support:* In 2010–11, 17 fellowships with full tuition reimbursements (averaging $5,083 per year), 29 research assistantships with full tuition reimbursements (averaging $12,252 per year) were awarded; tuition waivers (full) also available. Financial award application deadline: 2/1; financial award applicants required to submit FAFSA. *Faculty research:* International, econometrics, public economics and natural resources and environmental economics, urban and regional economics, development economics, labor economics and demography, economic history. Total annual research expenditures: $389,942.

University of Colorado Denver, College of Liberal Arts and Sciences, Department of Economics, Denver, CO 80217. Offers MA. Part-time and evening/weekend programs available. *Faculty:* 10 full-time (1 woman), 3 part-time/adjunct (2 women). *Students:* 43 full-time (11 women), 11 part-time (6 women); includes 3 Black or African American, non-Hispanic/Latino; 5 Asian, non-Hispanic/Latino; 4 Hispanic/Latino, 11 international. Average age 29. 61 applicants, 41% accepted, 19 enrolled. In 2010, 21 master's awarded. *Degree requirements:* For master's, thesis or alternative, 30 credit hours, including 21 of core courses and 9 of electives. *Entrance requirements:* For master's, GRE General Test, 15 hours of course work in economics, minimum GPA of 2.5. Additional exam requirements/recommendations for international students: Required—TOEFL (minimum score 525 paper-based; 197 computer-based). *Application deadline:* For fall admission, 6/1 priority date for domestic students; for spring admission, 11/1 priority date for domestic students. Application fee: $50 ($75 for international students). Electronic applications accepted. *Expenses:* Tuition, state resident: full-time $7332; part-time $355 per credit hour. Tuition, nonresident: full-time $18,990; part-time $1055 per credit hour. Required fees: $998. Tuition and fees vary according to course level, course load, degree level, campus/location, program, reciprocity agreements and student level. *Financial support:* Fellowships, research assistantships, teaching assistantships, Federal Work-Study, scholarships/grants, and unspecified assistantships available. Financial award application deadline: 4/1; financial award applicants required to submit FAFSA. *Faculty research:* Economic/income inequality, poverty and mobility measurement; international finance and monetary policy; economics of philanthropy; history of economic thought; health and labor economics. *Unit head:* Dr. Laura Argys, Chair, 303-556-3949, Fax: 303-556-3547, E-mail: laura.argys@ucdenver.edu. *Application contact:* Brian Duncan, Graduate Admissions Advisor, 303-315-2030, E-mail: brian.duncan@ucdenver.edu.

University of Connecticut, Graduate School, College of Liberal Arts and Sciences, Department of Economics, Storrs, CT 06269-1063. Offers MA, PhD. Terminal master's awarded for partial completion of doctoral program. *Degree requirements:* For master's, comprehensive exam; for doctorate, thesis/dissertation. *Entrance requirements:* For master's and doctorate, GRE General Test, GRE Subject Test. Additional exam requirements/recommendations for international students: Required—TOEFL (minimum score 550 paper-based; 213 computer-based). Electronic applications accepted.

University of Delaware, Alfred Lerner College of Business and Economics, Department of Economics, Newark, DE 19716. Offers economic education (PhD); economics (MA, MS, PhD); economics for entrepreneurship and educators (MA); MA/MBA. Part-time programs available. *Degree requirements:* For master's, comprehensive exam, thesis (for some programs), mathematics review exam, research project; for doctorate, comprehensive exam, thesis/dissertation, field exam. *Entrance requirements:* For master's, GMAT or GRE General Test, minimum GPA of 2.5; for doctorate, GRE General Test, minimum GPA of 3.5 in graduate economics course work. Additional exam requirements/recommendations for international students: Required—TOEFL (minimum score 550 paper-based; 225 computer-based). Electronic applications accepted. *Faculty research:* Applied quantitative economics, industrial organization, resource economics, monetary economics, labor economics.

University of Denver, Division of Arts, Humanities and Social Sciences, Department of Economics, Denver, CO 80208. Offers MA. Part-time programs available. *Faculty:* 9 full-time (4 women), 2 part-time/adjunct (0 women). *Students:* 14 full-time (5 women), 5 part-time (0 women); includes 4 minority (1 American Indian or Alaska Native, non-Hispanic/Latino; 1 Asian, non-Hispanic/Latino; 2 Hispanic/Latino), 3 international. Average age 26. 59 applicants,

68% accepted, 12 enrolled. In 2010, 3 master's awarded. *Degree requirements:* For master's, thesis. *Entrance requirements:* For master's, GRE General Test. Additional exam requirements/recommendations for international students: Required—TOEFL (minimum score 550 paper-based; 80 iBT). *Application deadline:* Applications are processed on a rolling basis. Application fee: $60. Electronic applications accepted. *Expenses:* Tuition: Full-time $35,604; part-time $29,670 per year. Required fees: $687 per year. Tuition and fees vary according to program. *Financial support:* In 2010–11, 5 teaching assistantships with full and partial tuition reimbursements (averaging $5,600 per year) were awarded; career-related internships or fieldwork, Federal Work-Study, scholarships/grants, and unspecified assistantships also available. Support available to part-time students. Financial award application deadline: 3/1; financial award applicants required to submit FAFSA. *Unit head:* Dr. Tracy Mott, Chair, 303-871-2569, E-mail: tmott@du.edu. *Application contact:* Information Contact, 303-871-2685, E-mail: econ04@denver.du.edu.

University of Florida, Graduate School, Warrington College of Business Administration, Hough Graduate School of Business, Department of Economics, Gainesville, FL 32611. Offers MA, PhD. *Faculty:* 16 full-time (2 women). *Students:* 21 full-time (8 women), 4 part-time (1 woman); includes 1 Asian, non-Hispanic/Latino; 3 Hispanic/Latino, 7 international. Average age 28. 51 applicants, 0% accepted, 0 enrolled. In 2010, 2 master's, 7 doctorates awarded. Terminal master's awarded for partial completion of doctoral program. *Degree requirements:* For master's, thesis optional; for doctorate, comprehensive exam, thesis/dissertation. *Entrance requirements:* For master's and doctorate, GMAT or GRE General Test, Minimum GPA of 3.0. Additional exam requirements/recommendations for international students: Required—TOEFL (minimum score 550 paper-based; 213 computer-based; 80 iBT), IELTS (minimum score 6). *Application deadline:* For fall admission, 2/1 for domestic and international students. Applications are processed on a rolling basis. Application fee: $30. Electronic applications accepted. *Expenses:* Tuition, state resident: full-time $10,915.92. Tuition, nonresident: full-time $28,309. *Financial support:* In 2010–11, 6 students received support, including 4 fellowships, 1 research assistantship (averaging $20,600 per year), 1 teaching assistantship (averaging $24,092 per year); unspecified assistantships also available. Financial award applicants required to submit FAFSA. *Faculty research:* Econometrics, international economics, industrial organization, public finance, economic theory. *Unit head:* Dr. Roger D. Blair, Chair, 352-392-0179, Fax: 352-392-7860, E-mail: blair@warrington.ufl.edu. *Application contact:* Dr. Steve Slutsky, Graduate Coordinator, 352-392-8106, Fax: 352-392-7860, E-mail: slutsky@ufl.edu.

University of Georgia, Terry College of Business, Department of Economics, Athens, GA 30602. Offers MA, PhD. *Faculty:* 16 full-time (2 women). *Students:* 20 full-time (6 women), 8 part-time (2 women); includes 2 Asian, non-Hispanic/Latino; 3 Hispanic/Latino; 1 Two or more races, non-Hispanic/Latino, 7 international. 67 applicants, 22% accepted, 6 enrolled. In 2010, 3 master's, 5 doctorates awarded. *Degree requirements:* For master's, thesis; for doctorate, thesis/dissertation. *Entrance requirements:* For master's and doctorate, GRE General Test. *Application deadline:* For fall admission, 7/1 priority date for domestic students; for spring admission, 11/15 for domestic students. Application fee: $50. Electronic applications accepted. *Expenses:* Tuition, state resident: full-time $7200; part-time $344 per credit hour. Tuition, nonresident: full-time $21,900; part-time $944 per credit hour. Tuition and fees vary according to course load and program. *Financial support:* Fellowships, research assistantships, teaching assistantships available. *Unit head:* Dr. Christopher M. Cornwell, Head, 706-542-3670, Fax: 706-542-3376, E-mail: cornwl@terry.uga.edu. *Application contact:* Dr. Santanu Chatterjee, Graduate Coordinator, 706-542-3696, Fax: 706-542-3376, E-mail: econgc@terry.uga.edu.

University of Guelph, Graduate Studies, College of Management and Economics, Department of Economics, Guelph, ON N1G 2W1, Canada. Offers MA, PhD. Part-time programs available. *Degree requirements:* For master's, thesis or alternative; for doctorate, comprehensive exam, thesis/dissertation. *Entrance requirements:* For master's, minimum B+ average during previous 2 years of course work; for doctorate, minimum A- average, MA in economics. Additional exam requirements/recommendations for international students: Required—TOEFL (minimum score 550 paper-based; 213 computer-based; 89 iBT), IELTS (minimum score 6.5). Electronic applications accepted. *Faculty research:* Resource and environmental economics, econometrics, labor economics, micro and macro economics.

University of Hawaii at Manoa, Graduate Division, College of Social Sciences, Department of Economics, Honolulu, HI 96822. Offers MA, PhD. Part-time programs available. *Faculty:* 24 full-time (5 women), 8 part-time/adjunct (1 woman). *Students:* 46 full-time (24 women), 5 part-time (2 women); includes 9 minority (7 Asian, non-Hispanic/Latino; 1 Native Hawaiian or other Pacific Islander, non-Hispanic/Latino; 1 Two or more races, non-Hispanic/Latino), 34 international. Average age 30. 79 applicants, 62% accepted, 16 enrolled. In 2010, 6 master's, 5 doctorates awarded. Terminal master's awarded for partial completion of doctoral program. *Degree requirements:* For master's, thesis optional; for doctorate, comprehensive exam, thesis/dissertation. *Entrance requirements:* For master's and doctorate, GRE General Test. Additional exam requirements/recommendations for international students: Required—TOEFL (minimum score 500 paper-based; 173 computer-based; 61 iBT), IELTS (minimum score 5). *Application deadline:* For fall admission, 1/15 for domestic and international students; for spring admission, 8/1 for domestic and international students. Application fee: $60. *Financial support:* In 2010–11, 6 fellowships (averaging $8,537 per year), 16 research assistantships (averaging $18,002 per year), 10 teaching assistantships (averaging $15,088 per year) were awarded. *Faculty research:* Trade, development, demography, labor, resource economics. Total annual research expenditures: $35,000. *Application contact:* Nori Tarui, Graduate Chair, 808-956-2321, Fax: 808-956-4347, E-mail: nori@hawaii.edu.

University of Houston, College of Liberal Arts and Social Sciences, Department of Economics, Houston, TX 77204. Offers applied economics (MA); economics (MA, PhD). *Faculty:* 12 full-time (5 women), 3 part-time/adjunct (2 women). *Students:* 60 full-time (26 women), 5 part-time (4 women); includes 2 Black or African American, non-Hispanic/Latino; 6 Asian, non-Hispanic/Latino; 3 Hispanic/Latino, 35 international. Average age 26. 103 applicants, 38% accepted, 15 enrolled. In 2010, 23 master's, 4 doctorates awarded. Terminal master's awarded for partial completion of doctoral program. *Degree requirements:* For master's, thesis optional; for doctorate, comprehensive exam, thesis/dissertation. *Entrance requirements:* For master's and doctorate, GRE General Test, minimum GPA of 3.0, statement of purpose, three letters of recommendation. Additional exam requirements/recommendations for international students: Required—TOEFL (minimum score 550 paper-based; 79 iBT), IELTS (minimum score 6.5). *Application deadline:* For fall admission, 2/1 for domestic and international students. Applications are processed on a rolling basis. Electronic applications accepted. *Expenses:* Tuition, state resident: full-time $8592; part-time $358 per credit hour. Tuition, nonresident: full-time $16,032; part-time $668 per credit hour. Required fees: $2889. Tuition and fees vary according to course load and program. *Financial support:* In 2010–11, 12 fellowships with full tuition reimbursements (averaging $4,600 per year), 29 teaching assistantships with full tuition reimbursements (averaging $10,800 per year) were awarded; career-related internships or fieldwork, Federal Work-Study, institutionally sponsored loans, scholarships/grants, health care benefits, and unspecified assistantships also available. Support available to part-time students. Financial award application deadline: 2/1. *Faculty research:* Econometrics, labor economics, international economics. *Unit head:* Dr. David Papell, Chairperson, 713-743-3800, Fax: 713-743-3798, E-mail: dpapell@uh.edu. *Application contact:* Rebecca Thornton, Director, 713-743-3820, E-mail: rthornton@uh.edu.

University of Idaho, College of Graduate Studies, College of Business and Economics, Department of Business and Economics, Moscow, ID 83844-2282. Offers economics (MS); general management (MBA). *Faculty:* 8 full-time, 1 part-time/adjunct. *Students:* 9 full-time, 7 part-time. Average age 41. In 2010, 9 master's awarded. *Application deadline:* For fall admission, 8/1 for domestic students; for spring admission, 12/15 for domestic students. Applications are processed on a rolling basis. Application fee: $60. Electronic applications accepted. *Expenses:* Tuition, nonresident: part-time $580 per credit. Required fees: $306 per credit. *Financial support:* Applicants required to submit FAFSA. *Unit head:* Dr. Mario Reyes, Associate Dean,

Economics

University of Idaho (continued)

208-885-6478, E-mail: cbe@uidaho.edu. *Application contact:* Dr. Mario Reyes, Associate Dean, 208-885-6478, E-mail: cbe@uidaho.edu.

University of Illinois at Chicago, Graduate College, College of Liberal Arts and Sciences, Department of Economics, Chicago, IL 60607-7128. Offers MA, PhD, MBA/MA. Terminal master's awarded for partial completion of doctoral program. *Degree requirements:* For master's, comprehensive exam; for doctorate, thesis/dissertation. *Entrance requirements:* For master's and doctorate, GRE General Test, minimum GPA of 2.75. Additional exam requirements/recommendations for international students: Required—TOEFL. Electronic applications accepted. *Faculty research:* International, labor, and urban economics.

University of Illinois at Urbana–Champaign, Graduate College, College of Liberal Arts and Sciences, Department of Economics, Champaign, IL 61820. Offers economics (MS, PhD); policy economics (MS). *Faculty:* 26 full-time (3 women). *Students:* 241 full-time (95 women), 14 part-time (1 woman); includes 9 Asian, non-Hispanic/Latino; 2 Hispanic/Latino; 1 Two or more races, non-Hispanic/Latino, 223 international. 634 applicants, 19% accepted, 108 enrolled. In 2010, 57 master's, 10 doctorates awarded. Terminal master's awarded for partial completion of doctoral program. *Entrance requirements:* For master's, minimum GPA of 3.0; for doctorate, GRE General Test, minimum GPA of 3.3. Additional exam requirements/recommendations for international students: Required—TOEFL (minimum score 550 paper-based; 213 computer-based; 79 iBT). *Application deadline:* Applications are processed on a rolling basis. Application fee: $75 ($90 for international students). Electronic applications accepted. *Financial support:* In 2010–11, 23 fellowships, 7 research assistantships, 78 teaching assistantships were awarded; tuition waivers (full and partial) also available. *Unit head:* Dr. Geoffrey J. D. Hewings, Interim Head, 217-333-4740, Fax: 217-244-6678, E-mail: hewings@illinois.edu. *Application contact:* Toni Wendler, Office Support Specialist, 217-333-0120, Fax: 217-244-6678, E-mail: twendler@illinois.edu.

The University of Iowa, Henry B. Tippie College of Business, Department of Economics, Iowa City, IA 52242-1316. Offers PhD. *Faculty:* 20 full-time (4 women), 1 part-time/adjunct (0 women). *Students:* 32 full-time (6 women), 2 part-time (1 woman); includes 2 minority (both Asian, non-Hispanic/Latino), 22 international. Average age 28. 190 applicants, 11% accepted, 11 enrolled. In 2010, 7 doctorates awarded. *Degree requirements:* For doctorate, comprehensive exam, thesis/dissertation, thesis defense. *Entrance requirements:* For doctorate, GRE General Test. Additional exam requirements/recommendations for international students: Required—TOEFL (minimum score 600 paper-based; 250 computer-based; 100 iBT). *Application deadline:* For fall admission, 1/15 priority date for domestic and international students. Applications are processed on a rolling basis. Application fee: $60 ($100 for international students). Electronic applications accepted. *Financial support:* In 2010–11, 32 students received support, including 3 fellowships with full tuition reimbursements available (averaging $16,600 per year), 1 research assistantship with full tuition reimbursement available (averaging $16,600 per year), 28 teaching assistantships with full tuition reimbursements available (averaging $16,600 per year); institutionally sponsored loans, scholarships/grants, health care benefits, and unspecified assistantships also available. Financial award application deadline: 1/15. *Faculty research:* Political economy, macroeconomics, econometrics, game theory, economic development. *Unit head:* Prof. John Solow, Director/Executive Officer, 319-335-0829, Fax: 319-335-1956, E-mail: john-solow@uiowa.edu. *Application contact:* Renea L. Jay, PhD Program Coordinator, 319-335-0830, Fax: 319-335-1956, E-mail: renea-jay@uiowa.edu.

The University of Kansas, Graduate Studies, College of Liberal Arts and Sciences, Department of Economics, Lawrence, KS 66045. Offers MA, PhD, JD/MA. Part-time programs available. *Faculty:* 18 full-time (2 women). *Students:* 84 full-time (35 women), 5 part-time (2 women); includes 6 minority (2 Black or African American, non-Hispanic/Latino; 1 American Indian or Alaska Native, non-Hispanic/Latino; 1 Asian, non-Hispanic/Latino; 1 Hispanic/Latino; 1 Two or more races, non-Hispanic/Latino), 66 international. Average age 28. 147 applicants, 54% accepted, 21 enrolled. In 2010, 21 master's, 5 doctorates awarded. Terminal master's awarded for partial completion of doctoral program. *Degree requirements:* For master's, comprehensive exam, thesis optional; for doctorate, thesis/dissertation, qualifying exams. *Entrance requirements:* For doctorate, GRE. Additional exam requirements/recommendations for international students: Required—TOEFL, IELTS, We go by part scores, not total scores. TOEFL—R, W, L = 23 part; IELTS R, W, L = 6.0. *Application deadline:* For fall admission, 2/1 priority date for domestic and international students; for winter admission, 5/1 priority date for domestic and international students; for spring admission, 11/1 priority date for domestic and international students. Applications are processed on a rolling basis. Application fee: $55 ($65 for international students). Electronic applications accepted. *Expenses:* Tuition, state resident: full-time $7092; part-time $295.50 per credit hour. Tuition, nonresident: full-time $16,590; part-time $691.25 per credit hour. Required fees: $858; $71.49 per credit hour. Tuition and fees vary according to course load, campus/location and program. *Financial support:* Fellowships with full tuition reimbursements, research assistantships with full tuition reimbursements, teaching assistantships with full tuition reimbursements, institutionally sponsored loans, scholarships/grants, health care benefits, and unspecified assistantships available. Financial award application deadline: 2/1. *Faculty research:* Macroeconomics, econometrics, industrial organization, microeconomics, economic development, international economics, financial economics. *Unit head:* Joseph Sicilian, Chair, 785-864-3501, Fax: 785-864-5270, E-mail: jsic@ku.edu. *Application contact:* Teri Chambers, Graduate Secretary, 785-864-3501, Fax: 785-864-5270, E-mail: econgrad@ku.edu.

University of Kentucky, Graduate School, Gatton College of Business and Economics, Program in Economics, Lexington, KY 40506-0032. Offers MS, PhD. *Degree requirements:* For master's, comprehensive exam; for doctorate, comprehensive exam, thesis/dissertation. *Entrance requirements:* For master's, GMAT, minimum undergraduate GPA of 2.75; for doctorate, GMAT, minimum undergraduate GPA of 3.0. Additional exam requirements/recommendations for international students: Required—TOEFL (minimum score 550 paper-based; 213 computer-based). Electronic applications accepted. *Faculty research:* Public economics, international economics and economic development, labor economics, environmental economics, industrial economics.

University of Lethbridge, School of Graduate Studies, Lethbridge, AB T1K 3M4, Canada. Offers accounting (MScM); addictions counseling (M Sc); agricultural biotechnology (M Sc); agricultural studies (M Sc, MA); anthropology (MA); archaeology (MA); art (MA, MFA); biochemistry (M Sc); biological sciences (M Sc); biomolecular science (PhD); biosystems and biodiversity (PhD); Canadian studies (MA); chemistry (M Sc); computer science (M Sc); computer science and geographical information science (M Sc); counseling psychology (M Ed); dramatic arts (MA); earth, space, and physical science (PhD); economics (MA); educational leadership (M Ed); English (MA); environmental science (M Sc); evolution and behavior (PhD); exercise science (M Sc); finance (MScM); French (MA); French/German (MA); French/Spanish (MA); general education (M Ed); general management (MScM); geography (M Sc, MA); German (MA); health science (M Sc); history (MA); human resource management and labour relations (MScM); individualized multidisciplinary (M Sc, MA); information systems (MScM); international management (MScM); kinesiology (M Sc, MA); management (M Sc, MA); marketing (MScM); mathematics (M Sc); music (M Mus, MA); Native American studies (MA); neuroscience (M Sc, PhD); new media (MA); nursing (M Sc); philosophy (MA); physics (M Sc); policy and strategy (MScM); political science (MA); psychology (M Sc, MA); religious studies (MA); social sciences (MA); sociology (MA); theatre and dramatic arts (MFA); theoretical and computational science (PhD); urban and regional studies (MA); women's studies (MA). Part-time and evening/weekend programs available. *Degree requirements:* For doctorate, comprehensive exam, thesis/dissertation. *Entrance requirements:* For master's, GMAT (M Sc in management), bachelor's degree in related field, minimum GPA of 3.0 during previous 20 graded semester courses, 2 years teaching or related experience (M Ed); for doctorate, master's degree, minimum graduate GPA of 3.5. Additional exam requirements/recommendations for international students: Required—TOEFL. *Faculty research:* Movement and brain plasticity, gibberellin physiology, photosynthesis, carbon cycling, molecular properties of main-group ring components.

The University of Manchester, School of Arts, Histories and Cultures, Manchester, United Kingdom. Offers anthropology, media and performance (PhD); applied theatre professional (PhD); archaeology (PhD); art history and visual studies (PhD); arts management and cultural policy (PhD); classics and ancient history (PhD); composition (PhD); creative writing (PhD); drama (PhD); economic and social history (PhD); electroacoustic composition (PhD); English and American studies (PhD); history (PhD); humanitarianism and conflict response (PhD); museology (PhD); music (PhD); musicology (PhD); religions and theology (PhD).

University of Manitoba, Faculty of Graduate Studies, Faculty of Arts, Department of Economics, Winnipeg, MB R3T 2N2, Canada. Offers MA, PhD. *Degree requirements:* For master's, thesis or alternative; for doctorate, one foreign language, thesis/dissertation.

University of Maryland, Baltimore County, Graduate School, College of Arts, Humanities and Social Sciences, Department of Economics, Program in Economic Policy Analysis, Baltimore, MD 21250. Offers MA. Part-time and evening/weekend programs available. *Faculty:* 25 full-time (9 women), 2 part-time/adjunct (0 women). *Students:* 13 full-time (6 women), 8 part-time (1 woman); includes 4 minority (1 American Indian or Alaska Native, non-Hispanic/Latino; 3 Asian, non-Hispanic/Latino), 3 international. Average age 27. 26 applicants, 62% accepted, 9 enrolled. In 2010, 9 master's awarded. *Degree requirements:* For master's, comprehensive exam, capstone research project. *Entrance requirements:* For master's, GRE General Test, undergraduate coursework in economic theory, econometrics, calculus. Additional exam requirements/recommendations for international students: Required—TOEFL (minimum score 80 computer-based). *Application deadline:* For fall admission, 7/1 priority date for domestic students, 3/1 priority date for international students; for spring admission, 1/1 priority date for domestic students, 9/15 priority date for international students. Applications are processed on a rolling basis. Application fee: $45. Electronic applications accepted. *Financial support:* In 2010–11, 5 students received support, including 5 research assistantships with full and partial tuition reimbursements available (averaging $11,324 per year); Federal Work-Study, health care benefits, tuition waivers (full and partial), and unspecified assistantships also available. Support available to part-time students. Financial award application deadline: 4/15; financial award applicants required to submit FAFSA. *Faculty research:* International trade policy analysis, health and hospital policy evaluation, environmental policy analysis, economics of education, economic growth and development. Total annual research expenditures: $70,000. *Unit head:* Prof. David F. Mitch, Professor of Economics and Graduate Director, 410-455-2157, Fax: 410-455-1054, E-mail: mitch@umbc.edu. *Application contact:* Prof. David F. Mitch, Professor of Economics and Graduate Director, 410-455-2157, Fax: 410-455-1054, E-mail: mitch@umbc.edu.

University of Maryland, Baltimore County, Graduate School, College of Arts, Humanities and Social Sciences, Department of Public Policy, Program in Public Policy, Baltimore, MD 21250. Offers economics (PhD); education (MPP, PhD); evaluation (MPP); health (MPP, PhD); management (MPP, PhD); policy history (PhD); urban (MPP, PhD). Part-time and evening/weekend programs available. *Faculty:* 10 full-time (3 women), 2 part-time/adjunct (0 women). *Students:* 62 full-time (37 women), 94 part-time (54 women); includes 39 minority (25 Black or African American, non-Hispanic/Latino; 6 Asian, non-Hispanic/Latino; 2 Hispanic/Latino; 1 Native Hawaiian or other Pacific Islander, non-Hispanic/Latino; 5 Two or more races, non-Hispanic/Latino), 10 international. Average age 36. 102 applicants, 65% accepted, 28 enrolled. In 2010, 20 master's, 8 doctorates awarded. Terminal master's awarded for partial completion of doctoral program. *Degree requirements:* For master's, thesis optional, public analysis paper, internship for pre-service; for doctorate, comprehensive exam, thesis/dissertation, comprehensive and field qualifying exams. *Entrance requirements:* For master's, GRE General Test, 3 academic letters of reference, transcripts, resume; for doctorate, GRE General Test, 3 academic letters of reference, transcripts, resume, research paper. Additional exam requirements/recommendations for international students: Required—TOEFL (minimum score 550 paper-based; 213 computer-based; 80 iBT). *Application deadline:* For fall admission, 1/15 priority date for domestic students, 1/1 priority date for international students; for spring admission, 11/1 priority date for domestic students, 5/1 priority date for international students. Applications are processed on a rolling basis. Application fee: $50. Electronic applications accepted. *Financial support:* In 2010–11, 26 students received support, including fellowships (averaging $3,000 per year), 21 research assistantships with full tuition reimbursements available (averaging $17,400 per year); career-related internships or fieldwork, Federal Work-Study, scholarships/grants, health care benefits, and unspecified assistantships also available. Support available to part-time students. Financial award application deadline: 1/15; financial award applicants required to submit FAFSA. *Faculty research:* Health policy, education policy, urban policy, public management, evaluation and analytical methods. *Unit head:* Dr. Donald Norris, Chair, 410-455-1455, E-mail: norris@umbc.edu. *Application contact:* Sally F. Helms, Administrator of Academic Affairs, 410-455-3202, Fax: 410-455-1172, E-mail: gradposi@umbc.edu.

University of Maryland, College Park, Academic Affairs, College of Behavioral and Social Sciences, Department of Economics, College Park, MD 20742. Offers MA, PhD. Part-time and evening/weekend programs available. *Faculty:* 55 full-time (23 women), 15 part-time/adjunct (3 women). *Students:* 125 full-time (44 women); includes 1 Black or African American, non-Hispanic/Latino; 3 Asian, non-Hispanic/Latino; 2 Hispanic/Latino; 2 Two or more races, non-Hispanic/Latino, 88 international. 858 applicants, 5% accepted, 19 enrolled. In 2010, 14 master's, 18 doctorates awarded. Terminal master's awarded for partial completion of doctoral program. *Degree requirements:* For master's, comprehensive exam, thesis optional; for doctorate, comprehensive exam, thesis/dissertation, exams. *Entrance requirements:* For master's, GRE General Test, minimum GPA of 3.0, course work in calculus and mathematics, 3 letters of recommendation; for doctorate, GRE General Test, calculus background. Additional exam requirements/recommendations for international students: Required—TOEFL. *Application deadline:* For fall admission, 1/15 for domestic and international students. Applications are processed on a rolling basis. Application fee: $75. Electronic applications accepted. *Expenses:* Tuition, state resident: part-time $471 per credit hour. Tuition, nonresident: part-time $1016 per credit hour. Required fees: $337 per term. *Financial support:* In 2010–11, 2 fellowships with partial tuition reimbursements (averaging $9,821 per year), 1 research assistantship (averaging $18,446 per year), 90 teaching assistantships (averaging $18,156 per year) were awarded; Federal Work-Study and scholarships/grants also available. Support available to part-time students. Financial award applicants required to submit FAFSA. *Faculty research:* International economics, natural resource and environmental economics, forecasting and policy analysis, economic growth, demography of inequality. Total annual research expenditures: $775,016. *Unit head:* Dr. Peter Murrell, Chairman, 301-405-3506, Fax: 301-405-4733, E-mail: pmurrell@umd.edu. *Application contact:* Dean of Graduate School, 301-405-0358, Fax: 301-314-9305.

University of Maryland, College Park, Academic Affairs, College of Behavioral and Social Sciences, Department of Government and Politics, College Park, MD 20742. Offers American politics (PhD); comparative politics (PhD); international relations (PhD); political economy (PhD); political theory (PhD). Part-time and evening/weekend programs available. *Faculty:* 46 full-time (14 women), 14 part-time/adjunct (4 women). *Students:* 131 full-time (58 women), 16 part-time (4 women); includes 5 Black or African American, non-Hispanic/Latino; 2 American Indian or Alaska Native, non-Hispanic/Latino; 8 Asian, non-Hispanic/Latino; 4 Hispanic/Latino, 23 international. 283 applicants, 14% accepted, 23 enrolled. In 2010, 12 doctorates awarded. *Degree requirements:* For doctorate, comprehensive exam, thesis/dissertation, written exams in 2 fields. *Entrance requirements:* For doctorate, GRE General Test, minimum GPA of 3.5, writing sample. Additional exam requirements/recommendations for international students: Required—TOEFL. *Application deadline:* For fall admission, 2/1 for domestic and international students. Applications are processed on a rolling basis. Application fee: $75. Electronic applications accepted. *Expenses:* Tuition, state resident: part-time $471 per credit hour. Tuition, nonresident: part-time $1016 per credit hour. Required fees: $337 per term. *Financial support:* In 2010–11, 6 fellowships with full and partial tuition reimbursements (averaging $19,085 per year), 73 teaching assistantships (averaging $15,935 per year) were awarded; research assistantships, career-related internships or fieldwork, Federal Work-Study, scholarships/grants, and unspecified assistantships also available. Support available to part-time students. Financial award applicants required to submit FAFSA. *Faculty research:* International development/conflict, international security, post-communist society, public service, dynamics of conflict and conflict resolution. Total annual research expenditures: $1.9 million. *Unit head:* Dr. Mark Lichbach, Chairman, 301-405-4156, Fax: 301-314-9690, E-mail: mlichbac@umd.edu. *Application contact:* Dean of Graduate School, 301-405-0358, Fax: 301-314-9305.

University of Massachusetts Amherst, Graduate School, College of Social and Behavioral Sciences, Department of Economics, Amherst, MA 01003. Offers MA, PhD. Part-time programs available. *Faculty:* 25 full-time (5 women). *Students:* 74 full-time (37 women), 9 part-time (2 women); includes 9 minority (1 Black or African American, non-Hispanic/Latino; 1 Asian, non-Hispanic/Latino; 6 Hispanic/Latino; 1 Two or more races, non-Hispanic/Latino), 42 international. Average age 31. 149 applicants, 13% accepted, 14 enrolled. In 2010, 9 master's, 9 doctorates awarded. Terminal master's awarded for partial completion of doctoral program. *Degree requirements:* For master's, thesis or alternative; for doctorate, comprehensive exam, thesis/dissertation. *Entrance requirements:* For master's and doctorate, GRE General Test. Additional exam requirements/recommendations for international students: Required—TOEFL (minimum score 550 paper-based; 213 computer-based; 80 iBT), IELTS (minimum score 6.5). *Application deadline:* For fall admission, 1/15 for domestic and international students. Applications are processed on a rolling basis. Application fee: $50 ($65 for international students). Electronic applications accepted. *Expenses:* Tuition, state resident: full-time $2640. Required fees: $8282. One-time fee: $357 full-time. *Financial support:* In 2010–11, 6 fellowships with full tuition reimbursements (averaging $6,500 per year), 4 research assistantships with full tuition reimbursements (averaging $12,616 per year), 57 teaching assistantships with full tuition reimbursements (averaging $9,981 per year) were awarded; career-related internships or fieldwork, Federal Work-Study, scholarships/grants, traineeships, health care benefits, tuition waivers (full), and unspecified assistantships also available. Support available to part-time students. Financial award application deadline: 1/15; financial award applicants required to submit FAFSA. *Unit head:* Dr. David M. Kotz, Graduate Program Director, 413-545-6352, Fax: 413-545-2921, E-mail: gradinfo@econs.umass.edu. *Application contact:* Jean M. Ames, Supervisor of Admissions, 413-545-0722, Fax: 413-577-0010, E-mail: gradadm@grad.umass.edu.

University of Massachusetts Lowell, College of Arts and Sciences, Department of Regional Economic and Social Development, Lowell, MA 01854-2881. Offers MA, Graduate Certificate. Part-time programs available. *Entrance requirements:* For master's, GRE. Electronic applications accepted.

University of Memphis, Graduate School, Fogelman College of Business and Economics, Department of Economics, Memphis, TN 38152. Offers MA, PhD. Part-time programs available. *Faculty:* 10 full-time (1 woman). *Students:* 2 full-time (1 woman), 3 part-time (0 women); includes 1 Asian, non-Hispanic/Latino, 1 international. Average age 28. 6 applicants, 83% accepted, 0 enrolled. In 2010, 3 master's awarded. *Degree requirements:* For master's, comprehensive exam, thesis or alternative; for doctorate, comprehensive exam, thesis/dissertation. *Entrance requirements:* For master's, GMAT or GRE General Test, previous course work in statistics, intermediate micro and macro theory; for doctorate, GMAT, interview, minimum GPA of 3.4. *Application deadline:* For fall admission, 8/1 for domestic students; for spring admission, 12/1 for domestic students. Application fee: $35 ($60 for international students). *Financial support:* In 2010–11, 3 students received support; research assistantships with full tuition reimbursements available, teaching assistantships with full tuition reimbursements available, Federal Work-Study, scholarships/grants, and unspecified assistantships available. Financial award application deadline: 2/15; financial award applicants required to submit FAFSA. *Faculty research:* Tax research, medical economics, law and economics, labor economics, U. S. and Japanese economic relations. *Unit head:* Dr. William Smith, Interim Chair, 901-678-2785, E-mail: wtsmith@memphis.edu. *Application contact:* Dr. Pinaki Bose, Master's Program Coordinator, 901-678-5528, Fax: 901-678-4705, E-mail: psbose@memphis.edu.

University of Memphis, Graduate School, Fogelman College of Business and Economics, Program in Business Administration, Memphis, TN 38152. Offers accounting (MBA, PhD); economics (MBA, PhD); executive business administration (MBA); finance (PhD); finance, insurance, and real estate (MBA, MS); international business administration (IMBA); management (MBA, MS, PhD); management information systems (MBA, MS, PhD); management science (MBA); marketing (MBA, MS); marketing and supply chain management (PhD); real estate development (MS); JD/MBA. *Accreditation:* AACSB. *Faculty:* 44 full-time (9 women), 5 part-time/adjunct (0 women). *Students:* 263 full-time (106 women), 181 part-time (66 women); includes 46 Black or African American, non-Hispanic/Latino; 3 American Indian or Alaska Native, non-Hispanic/Latino; 16 Asian, non-Hispanic/Latino; 5 Hispanic/Latino, 109 international. Average age 31. 374 applicants, 73% accepted, 119 enrolled. In 2010, 140 master's, 17 doctorates awarded. *Degree requirements:* For master's, comprehensive exam; for doctorate, comprehensive exam, thesis/dissertation. *Entrance requirements:* For master's, GMAT, resume; for doctorate, GMAT, interview, minimum GPA of 3.4, resume, letter of recommendation. Additional exam requirements/recommendations for international students: Required—TOEFL (minimum score 550 paper-based; 220 computer-based). *Application deadline:* For fall admission, 8/1 for domestic students; for spring admission, 12/1 for domestic students. Application fee: $35 ($60 for international students). *Financial support:* In 2010–11, 164 students received support; research assistantships with full tuition reimbursements available, teaching assistantships with full tuition reimbursements available, career-related internships or fieldwork, Federal Work-Study, scholarships/grants, and unspecified assistantships available. Financial award application deadline: 2/15; financial award applicants required to submit FAFSA. *Faculty research:* Competitive business strategy, finance microstructures, supply chain management innovations, health care economics, litigation risks and corporate audits. *Unit head:* Rajiv Grover, Dean, 901-678-3759, E-mail: rgrover@memphis.edu. *Application contact:* Dr. Carol V. Danehower, Associate Dean, 901-678-5402, Fax: 901-678-3579, E-mail: fcbegp@memphis.edu.

University of Miami, Graduate School, School of Business Administration, Department of Economics, Coral Gables, FL 33124. Offers economic development (MA, PhD); environmental economics (PhD); human resource economics (MA, PhD); international economics (MA, PhD); macroeconomics (PhD). Students admitted every two years in the fall semester. Terminal master's awarded for partial completion of doctoral program. *Degree requirements:* For master's, comprehensive exam; for doctorate, comprehensive exam, thesis/dissertation. *Entrance requirements:* For master's and doctorate, GRE General Test, minimum GPA of 3.0. Additional exam requirements/recommendations for international students: Required—TOEFL (minimum score 550 paper-based). *Faculty research:* International economics/trade, applied microeconomics, development.

University of Michigan, Horace H. Rackham School of Graduate Studies, College of Literature, Science, and the Arts, Department of Economics, Ann Arbor, MI 48109. Offers applied economics (AM); economics (AM, PhD); public policy and economics (PhD); social work and economics (PhD); JD/PhD; MPP/AM. Terminal master's awarded for partial completion of doctoral program. *Degree requirements:* For doctorate, oral defense of dissertation, preliminary exam. *Entrance requirements:* For master's and doctorate, GRE General Test. Additional exam requirements/recommendations for international students: Required—TOEFL (minimum score 600 paper-based; 250 computer-based; 100 iBT). Electronic applications accepted. *Expenses:* Tuition, state resident: full-time $17,784; part-time $1116 per credit hour. Tuition, nonresident: full-time $35,944; part-time $2125 per credit hour. International tuition: $35,994 full-time. Required fees: $95 per semester. Tuition and fees vary according to course load, degree level and program. *Faculty research:* Economic and econometrical analysis, industrial organization, international trade, public finance, development, health, labor, population standard, macro, theory.

University of Minnesota, Twin Cities Campus, Graduate School, College of Liberal Arts, Department of Economics, Minneapolis, MN 55455. Offers PhD. *Faculty:* 22 full-time (3 women), 5 part-time/adjunct (1 woman). *Students:* 104 full-time (26 women), 6 part-time (3 women); includes 6 Asian, non-Hispanic/Latino; 2 Hispanic/Latino, 67 international. Average age 27. 468 applicants, 13% accepted, 20 enrolled. In 2010, 19 doctorates awarded. *Degree requirements:* For doctorate, thesis/dissertation, preliminary exams. *Entrance requirements:* For doctorate, GRE General Test. Additional exam requirements/recommendations for international students: Required—TOEFL (minimum score 600 paper-based; 250 computer-based; 100 iBT), IELTS (minimum score 7). *Application deadline:* For fall admission, 12/15 priority date for domestic and international students. Application fee: $75 ($95 for international students). Electronic applications accepted. *Financial support:* In 2010–11, 85 students received support, including fellowships with full tuition reimbursements available (averaging $21,000 per year), research assistantships with full tuition reimbursements available (averaging $15,500 per year), teaching assistantships with full tuition reimbursements available (averaging $15,300 per year); scholarships/grants and unspecified assistantships also available. Financial award application deadline: 12/15. *Faculty research:* Econometrics, macro and monetary economics, mathematical economics, industrial organization, applied micro theory. *Unit head:* Larry Jones, Chair, 612-625-6353, Fax: 612-624-0209. *Application contact:* Christopher Phelan, Director of Graduate Studies, 612-625-6833, Fax: 612-624-0209, E-mail: econdgs@econ.umn.edu.

University of Mississippi, Graduate School, College of Liberal Arts, Department of Economics, Oxford, University, MS 38677. Offers MA, PhD. *Students:* 21 full-time (7 women), 1 part-time (0 women); includes 5 Black or African American, non-Hispanic/Latino; 1 American Indian or Alaska Native, non-Hispanic/Latino; 4 Asian, non-Hispanic/Latino; 1 Hispanic/Latino; 2 Two or more races, non-Hispanic/Latino. In 2010, 1 master's, 2 doctorates awarded. *Application deadline:* For fall admission, 4/1 for domestic students; for spring admission, 10/1 for domestic students. Applications are processed on a rolling basis. Electronic applications accepted. *Financial support:* Scholarships/grants available. Financial award applicants required to submit FAFSA. *Unit head:* Dr. Jon Moen, Interim Chair, 662-915-6942, Fax: 662-915-6943, E-mail: jmoen@olemiss.edu. *Application contact:* Dr. Christy M. Wyandt, Associate Dean, 662-915-7474, Fax: 662-915-7577, E-mail: cwyandt@olemiss.edu.

University of Missouri, Graduate School, College of Arts and Sciences, Department of Economics, Columbia, MO 65211. Offers MA, PhD, JD/MA. *Faculty:* 25 full-time (7 women), 3 part-time/adjunct (1 woman). *Students:* 58 full-time (23 women), 9 part-time (5 women); includes 1 minority (Hispanic/Latino), 57 international. Average age 28. 115 applicants, 38% accepted, 21 enrolled. In 2010, 13 master's, 8 doctorates awarded. Terminal master's awarded for partial completion of doctoral program. *Degree requirements:* For doctorate, comprehensive exam, thesis/dissertation. *Entrance requirements:* For master's, GRE General Test (minimum score 700 quantitative, 400 verbal), minimum GPA of 3.0; bachelor's degree in any field; for doctorate, GRE General Test (minimum score 700 quantitative, 400 verbal), minimum GPA of 3.0. Additional exam requirements/recommendations for international students: Required—TOEFL (minimum score 550 paper-based; 213 computer-based; 79 iBT), IELTS (minimum score 6). *Application deadline:* For fall admission, 1/15 priority date for domestic students; for winter admission, 11/1 priority date for domestic students; for spring admission, 3/1 priority date for domestic students. Application fee: $45 ($60 for international students). Electronic applications accepted. *Financial support:* In 2010–11, 2 fellowships with full and partial tuition reimbursements, 6 research assistantships with full tuition reimbursements, 51 teaching assistantships with full tuition reimbursements were awarded; institutionally sponsored loans, health care benefits, and unspecified assistantships also available. *Faculty research:* Monetary economics, econometrics, macroeconomics, public economics, industrial organization, game theory, labor economics, microeconomic theory, teacher labor markets, international trade. *Unit head:* Dr. David Mandy, Department Chair, 573-882-1763, E-mail: mandyd@missouri.edu. *Application contact:* Lynne Riddell, 573-884-7989, E-mail: riddelll@missouri.edu.

University of Missouri–Kansas City, College of Arts and Sciences, Department of Economics, Kansas City, MO 64110-2499. Offers MA, PhD. PhD (interdisciplinary) offered through the School of Graduate Studies. Part-time and evening/weekend programs available. *Faculty:* 12 full-time (1 woman), 2 part-time/adjunct (0 women). *Students:* 37 full-time (9 women), 26 part-time (1 woman); includes 14 minority (6 Black or African American, non-Hispanic/Latino; 1 American Indian or Alaska Native, non-Hispanic/Latino; 3 Asian, non-Hispanic/Latino; 3 Hispanic/Latino; 1 Native Hawaiian or other Pacific Islander, non-Hispanic/Latino), 17 international. Average age 31. 60 applicants, 72% accepted, 28 enrolled. In 2010, 6 master's awarded. *Degree requirements:* For doctorate, comprehensive exam, thesis/dissertation. *Entrance requirements:* For master's, GRE or minimum undergraduate GPA of 2.5; for doctorate, GRE, master's degree in economics or equivalent. Additional exam requirements/recommendations for international students: Required—TOEFL (minimum score 550 paper-based; 213 computer-based; 80 iBT). *Application deadline:* For fall admission, 2/1 priority date for domestic and international students; for spring admission, 9/1 priority date for domestic and international students. Applications are processed on a rolling basis. Application fee: $45 ($50 for international students). Electronic applications accepted. *Expenses:* Tuition, state resident: full-time $5522.40; part-time $306.80 per credit hour. Tuition, nonresident: full-time $7128; part-time $792 per credit hour. Required fees: $261.15 per term. *Financial support:* In 2010–11, 1 research assistantship with partial tuition reimbursement (averaging $13,332 per year), 27 teaching assistantships with partial tuition reimbursements (averaging $13,036 per year) were awarded; fellowships with partial tuition reimbursements, career-related internships or fieldwork, Federal Work-Study, institutionally sponsored loans, and tuition waivers (full and partial) also available. Support available to part-time students. Financial award application deadline: 3/1; financial award applicants required to submit FAFSA. *Faculty research:* International trade, general theory, institutions/utilities, forensic economics, human resources. Total annual research expenditures: $186,444. *Unit head:* James Sturgeon, Chair, 816-235-2837, Fax: 816-238-2836, E-mail: sturgeonj@umkc.edu. *Application contact:* Fred Lee, Graduate Advisor, 816-235-2543, Fax: 816-238-2836, E-mail: leefs@umkc.edu.

University of Missouri–St. Louis, College of Arts and Sciences, Department of Economics, St. Louis, MO 63121. Offers general economics (MA), including business economics. Part-time and evening/weekend programs available. *Faculty:* 9 full-time (3 women), 4 part-time/adjunct (2 women). *Students:* 15 full-time (7 women), 13 part-time (3 women), 6 international. Average age 27. 15 applicants, 47% accepted, 4 enrolled. In 2010, 6 master's awarded. *Entrance requirements:* For master's, GRE General Test, 2 letters of recommendation. Additional exam requirements/recommendations for international students: Required—TOEFL (minimum score 550 paper-based; 213 computer-based). *Application deadline:* For fall admission, 7/1 priority date for domestic and international students; for spring admission, 12/1 priority date for domestic and international students. Applications are processed on a rolling basis. Application fee: $35 ($40 for international students). Electronic applications accepted. *Expenses:* Tuition, state resident: full-time $5522; part-time $306.80 per credit hour. Tuition, nonresident: full-time $14,253; part-time $792.10 per credit hour. Required fees: $658; $49 per credit hour. One-time fee: $12. Tuition and fees vary according to program. *Financial support:* In 2010–11, 6 research assistantships with full and partial tuition reimbursements (averaging $5,000 per year) were awarded. Financial award applicants required to submit FAFSA. *Faculty research:* Health economics, public policy analysis, econometrics, public choice, telecommunications and forensic economics. *Unit head:* Dr. Donald Kridel, Director of Graduate Studies, 314-516-5351, Fax: 314-516-5562, E-mail: kridel@umsl.edu. *Application contact:* 314-516-5458, Fax: 314-516-6996, E-mail: gradadm@umsl.edu.

The University of Montana, Graduate School, College of Arts and Sciences, Department of Economics, Missoula, MT 59812-0002. Offers MA. *Degree requirements:* For master's, thesis. *Entrance requirements:* For master's, GRE General Test. Additional exam requirements/recommendations for international students: Required—TOEFL (minimum score 525 paper-based; 197 computer-based). *Faculty research:* Resource economics, public policy, environmental economics, economic development, regional economics.

University of Nebraska at Omaha, Graduate Studies, College of Business Administration, Department of Economics, Omaha, NE 68182. Offers MA, MS. Part-time and evening/

Economics

University of Nebraska at Omaha (continued)

weekend programs available. *Faculty:* 9 full-time (1 woman). *Students:* 30 full-time (17 women), 31 part-time (8 women); includes 13 minority (8 Black or African American, non-Hispanic/Latino; 4 Asian, non-Hispanic/Latino; 1 Hispanic/Latino), 27 international. Average age 29. 58 applicants, 52% accepted, 20 enrolled. In 2010, 18 master's awarded. *Degree requirements:* For master's, comprehensive exam, thesis (for some programs). *Entrance requirements:* For master's, minimum GPA of 3.0. Additional exam requirements/recommendations for international students: Required—TOEFL (minimum score 530 paper-based; 197 computer-based; 71 iBT). *Application deadline:* For fall admission, 7/1 priority date for domestic students; for spring admission, 12/15 priority date for domestic students. Applications are processed on a rolling basis. Application fee: $45. Electronic applications accepted. *Financial support:* In 2010–11, 35 students received support; research assistantships with tuition reimbursements available, Federal Work-Study, institutionally sponsored loans, scholarships/grants, and unspecified assistantships available. Support available to part-time students. Financial award application deadline: 3/1; financial award applicants required to submit FAFSA. *Faculty research:* Labor, economics of science, international development, monetary economics, econometrics. *Unit head:* Dr. Donald Baum, Graduate Chair, 402-554-2570. *Application contact:* Dr. Donald Baum.

University of Nebraska–Lincoln, Graduate College, College of Business Administration, Department of Economics, Lincoln, NE 68588. Offers MA, PhD, JD/MA. *Degree requirements:* For master's, thesis optional; for doctorate, comprehensive exam, thesis/dissertation. *Entrance requirements:* For master's and doctorate, GRE General Test. Additional exam requirements/recommendations for international students: Required—TOEFL (minimum score 550 paper-based; 213 computer-based). Electronic applications accepted. *Faculty research:* Applied microeconomics, economic education, international trade and finance, public finance, regional and institutional economics.

University of Nevada, Las Vegas, Graduate College, College of Business, Department of Economics, Las Vegas, NV 89154-6005. Offers MA. Part-time and evening/weekend programs available. *Faculty:* 16 full-time (1 woman), 1 part-time/adjunct (0 women). *Students:* 14 full-time (6 women), 11 part-time (4 women); includes 8 minority (1 Asian, non-Hispanic/Latino; 7 Two or more races, non-Hispanic/Latino), 7 international. Average age 26. 31 applicants, 87% accepted, 12 enrolled. In 2010, 6 master's awarded. *Degree requirements:* For master's, thesis, oral defense of thesis. *Entrance requirements:* For master's, GRE General Test or GMAT. Additional exam requirements/recommendations for international students: Required—TOEFL (minimum score 550 paper-based; 213 computer-based; 80 iBT), IELTS (minimum score 7). *Application deadline:* For fall admission, 6/15 priority date for domestic students, 6/15 for international students; for spring admission, 11/15 priority date for domestic students, 11/15 for international students. Applications are processed on a rolling basis. Application fee: $60 ($95 for international students). Electronic applications accepted. *Expenses:* Tuition, area resident: Part-time $239.50 per credit. Tuition, state resident: part-time $239.50 per credit. Tuition, nonresident: part-time $503 per credit. Required fees: $108 per semester. Tuition and fees vary according to course load, program and reciprocity agreements. *Financial support:* In 2010–11, 7 students received support, including 7 research assistantships with partial tuition reimbursements available (averaging $10,000 per year); institutionally sponsored loans, scholarships/grants, health care benefits, and unspecified assistantships also available. Financial award application deadline: 3/1. *Faculty research:* Asymmetric information: adverse selection, moral hazard; housing markets: hedonic prices, forecasting, foreclosures, discrimination; central bank decision making and commercial bank performance, failure and structure; economic effects of regulation and international and regional price convergence; economic effects on wages, benefits and economic effects of risk, uncertainty. *Unit head:* Dr. Stephen Miller, Chair/Professor, 702-895-3969, Fax: 702-895-1354, E-mail: stephen.miller@unlv.edu. *Application contact:* Graduate College Admissions Evaluator, 702-895-3320, Fax: 702-895-4180, E-mail: gradcollege@unlv.edu.

University of Nevada, Reno, Graduate School, College of Business Administration, Department of Economics, Reno, NV 89557. Offers MA, MS. *Degree requirements:* For master's, thesis. *Entrance requirements:* For master's, GMAT or GRE, minimum GPA of 2.75. Additional exam requirements/recommendations for international students: Required—TOEFL (minimum score 500 paper-based; 173 computer-based; 61 iBT), IELTS (minimum score 6). Electronic applications accepted. *Expenses:* Tuition, state resident: full-time $2219; part-time $246 per credit. Tuition, nonresident: part-time $510 per credit. International tuition: $9009 full-time. Required fees: $59 per term. One-time fee: $101. Tuition and fees vary according to course load. *Faculty research:* Applied microeconomics, public finance, development, labor.

University of New Brunswick Fredericton, School of Graduate Studies, Faculty of Arts, Department of Economics, Fredericton, NB E3B 5A3, Canada. Offers applied economics and finance (M Sc); economics (MA). M Sc offered on Saint John campus. *Faculty:* 11 full-time (1 woman). *Students:* 9 full-time (4 women), 3 part-time (1 woman). In 2010, 3 master's awarded. *Entrance requirements:* For master's, GRE, minimum GPA of 3.0. Additional exam requirements/recommendations for international students: Required—TWE, TOEFL (minimum score 550 paper-based) or IELTS. *Application deadline:* 1/31 for domestic and international students. Applications are processed on a rolling basis. Application fee: $50 Canadian dollars. *Expenses:* Tuition, area resident: Full-time $3708; part-time $927 per term. International tuition: $6300 full-time. Required fees: $50 per term. *Financial support:* In 2010–11, 5 research assistantships (averaging $16,000 per year) were awarded; scholarships/grants, health care benefits, and unspecified assistantships also available. Financial award application deadline: 1/31. *Faculty research:* Epidemiology and population health, micro/macro economics, economics of transportation, regional development. *Unit head:* Dr. Yuri Yevdokimov, Director of Graduate Studies, 506-447-3221, Fax: 506-453-4514, E-mail: yuri@unb.ca. *Application contact:* Lucina MacDonald, Graduate Secretary, 506-453-4828, Fax: 506-453-4514, E-mail: lmacdona@unb.ca.

University of New Brunswick Fredericton, School of Graduate Studies, Policy Studies Program, Fredericton, NB E3B 5A3, Canada. Offers people, property and alternative dispute resolution (M Phil); philosophy politics and economics (M Phil); sustainable development (M Phil). Part-time programs available. *Faculty:* 7 full-time (4 women), 8 part-time/adjunct (4 women). *Students:* 4 full-time (2 women), 5 part-time (3 women). In 2010, 3 master's awarded. *Degree requirements:* For master's, thesis, report. *Entrance requirements:* For master's, minimum GPA of 3.5. Additional exam requirements/recommendations for international students: Required—TWE (minimum score 4), TOEFL (minimum score 600 paper-based; 250 computer-based; 100 iBT) or IELTS (minimum score 7). Application fee: $50 Canadian dollars. *Expenses:* Tuition, area resident: Full-time $3708; part-time $927 per term. International tuition: $6300 full-time. Required fees: $50 per term. *Financial support:* In 2010–11, 3 fellowships, research assistantships (averaging $5,600 per year), teaching assistantships (averaging $4,400 per year) were awarded. *Unit head:* Dr. Linda Eyre, Dean of Graduate Studies, 506-447-3044, Fax: 506-453-4817, E-mail: gradidst@unb.ca. *Application contact:* Janet Amurault, Graduate Secretary, 506-458-7558, Fax: 506-453-4817, E-mail: jamiraul@unb.ca.

University of New Hampshire, Graduate School, Whittemore School of Business and Economics, Department of Economics, Durham, NH 03824. Offers MA, PhD. Part-time programs available. *Faculty:* 13 full-time (4 women). *Students:* 32 full-time (15 women); includes 1 Hispanic/Latino, 14 international. Average age 29. 75 applicants, 45% accepted, 19 enrolled. In 2010, 14 master's, 2 doctorates awarded. Terminal master's awarded for partial completion of doctoral program. *Degree requirements:* For master's, thesis or alternative; for doctorate, one foreign language, thesis/dissertation. *Entrance requirements:* For master's and doctorate, GRE General Test. Additional exam requirements/recommendations for international students: Required—TOEFL (minimum score 550 paper-based; 213 computer-based; 80 iBT). *Application deadline:* For fall admission, 6/1 priority date for domestic students, 4/1 for international students; for spring admission, 11/1 for domestic students. Applications are processed on a rolling basis. Application fee: $65. Electronic applications accepted. *Financial support:* In 2010–11, 28 students received support, including 1 fellowship, 1 research assistantship, 25 teaching assistantships; career-related internships or fieldwork, Federal Work-Study, scholarships/grants, and tuition waivers (full and partial) also available. Support available to part-time students. Financial award application deadline: 2/15. *Faculty research:* Labor economics, international development, econometrics, finance, political economy. *Unit head:* Dr. Bruce Elmslie, Chair, 603-862-3357. *Application contact:* Sinthy Kounlasa, Administrative Assistant, 603-862-3457, E-mail: wsbe.grad@unh.edu.

University of New Mexico, Graduate School, College of Arts and Sciences, Department of Economics, Albuquerque, NM 87131-2039. Offers environmental/natural resources (MA, PhD); international/development (MA, PhD); labor/human resources (MA, PhD); public finance (MA, PhD). Part-time programs available. *Faculty:* 26 full-time (9 women), 7 part-time/adjunct (1 woman). *Students:* 47 full-time (14 women), 17 part-time (5 women); includes 2 American Indian or Alaska Native, non-Hispanic/Latino; 2 Asian, non-Hispanic/Latino; 8 Hispanic/Latino, 18 international. Average age 34. 75 applicants, 51% accepted, 15 enrolled. In 2010, 14 master's, 1 doctorate awarded. Terminal master's awarded for partial completion of doctoral program. *Degree requirements:* For master's, comprehensive exam, thesis (for some programs); for doctorate, comprehensive exam, thesis/dissertation. *Entrance requirements:* For master's and doctorate, GRE General Test, 3 letters of recommendation, letter of intent. Additional exam requirements/recommendations for international students: Required—TOEFL (minimum score 520 paper-based; 190 computer-based; 68 iBT). *Application deadline:* For fall admission, 3/1 priority date for domestic students, 3/1 for international students. Applications are processed on a rolling basis. Application fee: $50. Electronic applications accepted. *Expenses:* Tuition, state resident: full-time $5991; part-time $251 per credit hour. Tuition, nonresident: full-time $14,405; part-time $800.20 per credit hour. Tuition and fees vary according to course level, course load, program and reciprocity agreements. *Financial support:* In 2010–11, 47 students received support, including 3 fellowships with tuition reimbursements available (averaging $3,611 per year), 14 research assistantships with tuition reimbursements available (averaging $7,791 per year), 15 teaching assistantships (averaging $7,467 per year); career-related internships or fieldwork, Federal Work-Study, scholarships/grants, health care benefits, and unspecified assistantships also available. Support available to part-time students. Financial award application deadline: 3/1; financial award applicants required to submit FAFSA. *Faculty research:* Core theory, econometrics, public finance, international/development economics, labor/human resource economics, environmental/natural resource economics. Total annual research expenditures: $1.8 million. *Unit head:* Dr. Robert Berrens, Chair, 505-277-5304, Fax: 505-277-9445, E-mail: rberrens@unm.edu. *Application contact:* Shoshana Handel, Academic Advisor, 505-277-3056, Fax: 505-277-9445, E-mail: shandel@unm.edu.

University of New Orleans, Graduate School, College of Business Administration, Department of Economics and Finance, Program in Financial Economics, New Orleans, LA 70148. Offers PhD. Terminal master's awarded for partial completion of doctoral program. *Degree requirements:* For doctorate, one foreign language, comprehensive exam, thesis/dissertation, general exams. *Entrance requirements:* For doctorate, GRE General Test, minimum GPA of 3.0. Additional exam requirements/recommendations for international students: Required—TOEFL (minimum score 550 paper-based; 213 computer-based; 79 iBT). Electronic applications accepted. *Faculty research:* Urban and regional economics, economic development, monetary theory and policy, international finance.

The University of North Carolina at Chapel Hill, Graduate School, College of Arts and Sciences, Department of Economics, Chapel Hill, NC 27599. Offers MS, PhD. Terminal master's awarded for partial completion of doctoral program. *Degree requirements:* For master's, comprehensive exam, thesis or alternative; for doctorate, comprehensive exam, thesis/dissertation. *Entrance requirements:* For master's, GRE General Test, minimum GPA of 3.0; for doctorate, GRE General Test, minimum GPA of 3.5. Additional exam requirements/recommendations for international students: Required—TOEFL (minimum score 550 paper-based; 213 computer-based). Electronic applications accepted. *Faculty research:* Health economics, micro theory/IO, labor economics, economic history, financial econometrics.

The University of North Carolina at Charlotte, Graduate School, Belk College of Business, Department of Economics, Charlotte, NC 28223-0001. Offers MS. Part-time and evening/weekend programs available. *Faculty:* 16 full-time (4 women), 1 part-time/adjunct (0 women). *Students:* 22 full-time (7 women), 36 part-time (11 women); includes 14 minority (6 Black or African American, non-Hispanic/Latino; 5 Asian, non-Hispanic/Latino; 3 Hispanic/Latino), 19 international. Average age 28. 67 applicants, 93% accepted, 2 enrolled. In 2010, 12 master's awarded. *Degree requirements:* For master's, thesis or alternative, thesis or project. *Entrance requirements:* For master's, GRE General Test, minimum undergraduate GPA of 3.0 in major, 2.8 overall. Additional exam requirements/recommendations for international students: Required—TOEFL (minimum score 557 paper-based; 220 computer-based; 83 iBT). *Application deadline:* For fall admission, 7/15 for domestic students, 5/1 for international students; for spring admission, 11/15 for domestic students, 10/1 for international students. Applications are processed on a rolling basis. Application fee: $55. Electronic applications accepted. *Expenses:* Tuition, state resident: full-time $3464. Tuition, nonresident: full-time $14,297. Required fees: $2094. Tuition and fees vary according to course load. *Financial support:* Career-related internships or fieldwork, institutionally sponsored loans, scholarships/grants, and unspecified assistantships available. Support available to part-time students. Financial award application deadline: 4/1; financial award applicants required to submit FAFSA. *Faculty research:* Health care, taxation, energy, economic growth, monetary policy. *Unit head:* Dr. Rob Roy McGregor, Program Director, 704-687-7639, Fax: 704-687-6442, E-mail: rrmcgreg@uncc.edu. *Application contact:* Kathy B. Giddings, Director of Graduate Admissions, 704-687-5503, Fax: 704-687-3279, E-mail: gradadm@uncc.edu.

The University of North Carolina at Greensboro, Graduate School, Bryan School of Business and Economics, Department of Economics, Program in Economics, Greensboro, NC 27412-5001. Offers PhD. *Degree requirements:* For doctorate, comprehensive exam, thesis/dissertation. *Entrance requirements:* Additional exam requirements/recommendations for international students: Required—TOEFL. Electronic applications accepted.

University of North Florida, Coggin College of Business, MBA Program, Jacksonville, FL 32224. Offers accounting (MBA); construction management (MBA); e-commerce (MBA); economics (MBA); finance (MBA); human resource management (MBA); international business (MBA); logistics (MBA); management applications (MBA). *Accreditation:* AACSB. Part-time and evening/weekend programs available. *Faculty:* 17 full-time (5 women), 1 part-time/adjunct (0 women). *Students:* 137 full-time (56 women), 268 part-time (112 women); includes 17 Black or African American, non-Hispanic/Latino; 21 Asian, non-Hispanic/Latino; 12 Hispanic/Latino; 3 Two or more races, non-Hispanic/Latino, 29 international. Average age 30. 250 applicants, 57% accepted, 94 enrolled. In 2010, 173 master's awarded. *Entrance requirements:* For master's, GMAT or GRE, U.S. bachelor's degree from regionally-accredited university or equivalent foreign degree. Additional exam requirements/recommendations for international students: Required—TOEFL (minimum score 550 paper-based; 213 computer-based; 79 iBT). *Application deadline:* For fall admission, 7/1 priority date for domestic students, 5/1 for international students; for spring admission, 11/1 priority date for domestic students, 10/1 for international students. Applications are processed on a rolling basis. Application fee: $30. *Expenses:* Tuition, state resident: full-time $7646.40; part-time $318.60 per credit hour. Tuition, nonresident: full-time $23,502; part-time $979.24 per credit hour. Required fees: $1208.88; $50.37 per credit hour. Tuition and fees vary according to course load and program. *Financial support:* In 2010–11, 40 students received support; research assistantships, teaching assistantships, Federal Work-Study and tuition waivers (partial) available. Support available to part-time students. Financial award application deadline: 4/1; financial award applicants required to submit FAFSA. *Faculty research:* Performance measures, costing, and inventory issues in logistics and supply chain management; inter-organizational systems; international management and marketing practices; e-commerce; organizational learning and socialization processes. Total annual research expenditures: $9,024. *Unit head:* Dr. C. Bruce Kavan, Chair, 904-620-

2780, Fax: 904-620-2832. *Application contact:* Cheryl Campbell, Graduate Advisor, 904-620-2575, Fax: 904-620-2832, E-mail: ccampbell@unf.edu.

University of North Texas, Toulouse Graduate School, College of Arts and Sciences, Department of Economics, Denton, TX 76203. Offers economic research (MS); economics (MA, MS); labor and industrial relations (MS). Part-time and evening/weekend programs available. *Degree requirements:* For master's, comprehensive exam, thesis (for some programs). *Entrance requirements:* For master's, GMAT, GRE General Test, minimum GPA of 3.0, 2 letters of recommendation, 500-word essay. Additional exam requirements/recommendations for international students: Recommended—TOEFL (minimum score 550 paper-based; 213 computer-based). *Expenses:* Tuition, state resident: full-time $4298; part-time $239 per credit hour. Tuition, nonresident: full-time $10,782; part-time $549 per credit hour. Required fees: $1292; $270 per credit hour. *Financial support:* Fellowships with partial tuition reimbursements, research assistantships with partial tuition reimbursements, teaching assistantships with partial tuition reimbursements, career-related internships or fieldwork, Federal Work-Study, and institutionally sponsored loans available. Support available to part-time students. Financial award application deadline: 4/1. *Faculty research:* Econometrics, international trade and development, immigration, telecommunications, micro enterprise development. *Application contact:* Graduate Adviser, 940-565-3442, Fax: 940-565-4426, E-mail: tieslau@unt.edu.

University of Notre Dame, Graduate School, College of Arts and Letters, Division of Social Science, Department of Economics and Econometrics, Notre Dame, IN 46556. Offers MA, PhD. Terminal master's awarded for partial completion of doctoral program. *Degree requirements:* For master's, comprehensive exam (for some programs), thesis optional; for doctorate, thesis/dissertation, candidacy exam. *Entrance requirements:* For doctorate, GRE General Test. Additional exam requirements/recommendations for international students: Required—TOEFL (minimum score 600 paper-based; 250 computer-based; 80 iBT). Electronic applications accepted.

University of Oklahoma, College of Arts and Sciences, Department of Economics, Norman, OK 73019. Offers applied economics (MA); economics (PhD); managerial economics (MA). *Faculty:* 19 full-time (7 women), 3 part-time/adjunct (2 women). *Students:* 41 full-time (17 women), 68 part-time (14 women); includes 23 minority (8 Black or African American, non-Hispanic/Latino; 1 American Indian or Alaska Native, non-Hispanic/Latino; 8 Asian, non-Hispanic/Latino; 6 Hispanic/Latino), 20 international. Average age 30. 62 applicants, 63% accepted, 25 enrolled. In 2010, 48 master's, 2 doctorates awarded. Terminal master's awarded for partial completion of doctoral program. *Degree requirements:* For doctorate, 2 foreign languages, thesis/dissertation, general exams. *Entrance requirements:* For master's, GRE General Test, minimum GPA of 3.0 in last 60 hours of course work; for doctorate, GRE General Test. Additional exam requirements/recommendations for international students: Required—TOEFL (minimum score 550 paper-based; 213 computer-based; 79 iBT). *Application deadline:* For fall admission, 1/15 for domestic and international students; for spring admission, 9/1 for domestic and international students. Applications are processed on a rolling basis. Application fee: $40 ($90 for international students). Electronic applications accepted. *Expenses:* Tuition, state resident: full-time $3893; part-time $162.20 per credit hour. Tuition, nonresident: full-time $14,167; part-time $590.30 per credit hour. Required fees: $2523; $94.60 per credit hour. Tuition and fees vary according to course load and degree level. *Financial support:* In 2010–11, 31 students received support, including 1 research assistantship with partial tuition reimbursement available (averaging $13,765 per year), 21 teaching assistantships with partial tuition reimbursements available (averaging $13,138 per year); scholarships/grants and unspecified assistantships also available. Financial award applicants required to submit FAFSA. *Faculty research:* Industrial organization, international economics, growth and development, public economics. Total annual research expenditures: $49,396. *Unit head:* Dr. Lex Holmes, Chair, 405-325-2861, Fax: 405-325-5842, E-mail: aholmes@ou.edu. *Application contact:* Cynthia Rogers, Graduate Program Director, 405-235-5843, Fax: 405-325-5842, E-mail: crogers@ou.edu.

University of Oregon, Graduate School, College of Arts and Sciences, Department of Economics, Eugene, OR 97403. Offers MA, MS, PhD. Terminal master's awarded for partial completion of doctoral program. *Degree requirements:* For master's, thesis or alternative; for doctorate, thesis/dissertation, qualifying exam. *Entrance requirements:* For master's and doctorate, GRE General Test, minimum GPA of 3.0. Additional exam requirements/recommendations for international students: Required—TOEFL. *Faculty research:* Labor economics, macroeconomics, international economics, industrial organization, public finance.

University of Ottawa, Faculty of Graduate and Postdoctoral Studies, Faculty of Social Sciences, Department of Economics, Ottawa, ON K1N 6N5, Canada. Offers MA, PhD. PhD offered jointly with Carleton University. Part-time programs available. *Degree requirements:* For master's, thesis or alternative; for doctorate, comprehensive exam, thesis/dissertation. *Entrance requirements:* For master's, honors bachelor's degree or equivalent, minimum B average; for doctorate, master's degree, minimum B+ average. Electronic applications accepted. *Faculty research:* Public economics, industrial organizations, monetary economics, international economics, economic development.

University of Pennsylvania, School of Arts and Sciences, Graduate Group in Economics, Philadelphia, PA 19104. Offers AM, PhD, JD/AM, JD/PhD. *Faculty:* 39 full-time (6 women), 3 part-time/adjunct (0 women). *Students:* 120 full-time (38 women), 2 part-time (1 woman); includes 7 Asian, non-Hispanic/Latino, 87 international. 873 applicants, 11% accepted, 30 enrolled. In 2010, 14 master's, 20 doctorates awarded. *Degree requirements:* For doctorate, thesis/dissertation. *Entrance requirements:* For doctorate, GRE General Test. Additional exam requirements/recommendations for international students: Required—TOEFL. *Application deadline:* For fall admission, 12/1 priority date for domestic students. Application fee: $70. Electronic applications accepted. *Expenses:* Tuition: Full-time $25,660; part-time $4758 per course. Required fees: $2152; $270 per course. Tuition and fees vary according to course load, degree level and program. *Financial support:* Institutionally sponsored loans, scholarships/grants, traineeships, health care benefits, and unspecified assistantships available. Financial award application deadline: 12/15. *Faculty research:* Economic theory, econometrics, international economics, monetary/macroeconomics, applied microeconomics, empirical microeconomics.

University of Pittsburgh, Graduate School of Public and International Affairs, Doctoral Program in Public and International Affairs, Pittsburgh, PA 15260. Offers development policy (PhD); foreign and security policy (PhD); international political economy (PhD); public administration (PhD); public policy (PhD). *Accreditation:* NASPAA. Part-time programs available. *Faculty:* 30 full-time (12 women), 67 part-time/adjunct (25 women). *Students:* 43 full-time (18 women), 3 part-time (2 women); includes 3 minority (2 Black or African American, non-Hispanic/Latino; 1 Asian, non-Hispanic/Latino), 19 international. Average age 30. 105 applicants, 11% accepted, 6 enrolled. In 2010, 11 doctorates awarded. Terminal master's awarded for partial completion of doctoral program. *Degree requirements:* For doctorate, comprehensive exam, thesis/dissertation, mid-term evaluation, preliminary exam, annual review. *Entrance requirements:* For doctorate, GRE, 3 letters of recommendation, resume, minimum GPA of 3.0 (recommended), writing sample. Additional exam requirements/recommendations for international students: Required—TOEFL (minimum score 600 paper-based; 250 computer-based; 100 iBT), TWE (minimum score 4); Recommended—IELTS (minimum score 7). *Application deadline:* For fall admission, 2/1 for domestic students, 1/15 for international students. Application fee: $50. Electronic applications accepted. *Expenses:* Tuition, state resident: full-time $17,304; part-time $701 per credit. Tuition, nonresident: full-time $29,554; part-time $1210 per credit. Required fees: $740; $214 per term. Tuition and fees vary according to program. *Financial support:* In 2010–11, 10 students received support, including 10 fellowships (averaging $41,325 per year). Financial award application deadline: 2/1. *Faculty research:* International political economy, international development, public administration, public policy, foreign policy, international security policy. Total annual research expenditures: $893,349. *Unit head:* Dr. Kevin P. Kearns, Program Coordinator, 412-648-7621, Fax: 412-648-2605, E-mail: kkearns@pitt.edu. *Application contact:* Julie Korade, Program Administrator/Graduate Enrollment Counselor, 412-648-7640, Fax: 412-648-7641, E-mail: korade@pitt.edu.

University of Pittsburgh, Graduate School of Public and International Affairs, International Affairs Division, Pittsburgh, PA 15260. Offers global political economy (MPIA); human security (MPIA); security and intelligence studies (MPIA); JD/MPIA; MBA/MPIA; MID/MPIA; MPA/MPIA; MSIS/MPIA. Part-time and evening/weekend programs available. *Faculty:* 30 full-time (12 women), 67 part-time/adjunct (25 women). *Students:* 187 full-time (93 women), 26 part-time (7 women); includes 17 minority (9 Black or African American, non-Hispanic/Latino; 1 American Indian or Alaska Native, non-Hispanic/Latino; 4 Asian, non-Hispanic/Latino; 3 Hispanic/Latino), 17 international. Average age 25. 325 applicants, 73% accepted, 100 enrolled. In 2010, 92 master's awarded. *Degree requirements:* For master's, thesis optional, internship, capstone seminar. *Entrance requirements:* For master's, GRE General Test, 3 letters of recommendation, resume; minimum GPA of 3.2 (recommended). Additional exam requirements/recommendations for international students: Required—TOEFL (minimum score 550 paper-based; 213 computer-based), TWE (minimum score 4); Recommended—IELTS (minimum score 7). *Application deadline:* For fall admission, 3/1 for domestic students, 1/15 for international students; for spring admission, 11/1 for domestic students, 8/1 for international students. Application fee: $50. Electronic applications accepted. *Expenses:* Tuition, state resident: full-time $17,304; part-time $701 per credit. Tuition, nonresident: full-time $29,554; part-time $1210 per credit. Required fees: $740; $214 per term. Tuition and fees vary according to program. *Financial support:* In 2010–11, 44 students received support. Scholarships/grants, tuition waivers (full and partial), unspecified assistantships, and student employment available. Financial award application deadline: 2/1. *Faculty research:* International political economy, international security and intelligence, transnational organized crime, international trade, international finance, globalization, terrorism, multinational corporations and the global economy. Total annual research expenditures: $892,349. *Unit head:* Dr. Martin Staniland, Director, International Affairs and International Development Divisions, 412-648-7656, Fax: 412-648-2605, E-mail: mstan@pitt.edu. *Application contact:* Kelly C. McDevitt, Graduate Enrollment Counselor, 412-648-7640, Fax: 412-648-7641, E-mail: mcdevitt@pitt.edu.

University of Pittsburgh, School of Arts and Sciences, Department of Economics, Pittsburgh, PA 15260. Offers PhD. *Faculty:* 22 full-time (4 women). *Students:* 55 full-time (18 women); includes 19 Asian, non-Hispanic/Latino; 6 Hispanic/Latino. Average age 26. 383 applicants, 23% accepted, 19 enrolled. In 2010, 5 doctorates awarded. Terminal master's awarded for partial completion of doctoral program. *Degree requirements:* For doctorate, comprehensive exam, thesis/dissertation, comprehensive research paper. *Entrance requirements:* For doctorate, GRE, 3 letters of recommendation. Additional exam requirements/recommendations for international students: Required—TOEFL (minimum score 550 paper-based; 213 computer-based; 80 iBT), IELTS (minimum score 6.5). *Application deadline:* For fall admission, 1/15 for domestic and international students. Application fee: $50. Electronic applications accepted. *Expenses:* Tuition, state resident: full-time $17,304; part-time $701 per credit. Tuition, nonresident: full-time $29,554; part-time $1210 per credit. Required fees: $740; $214 per term. Tuition and fees vary according to program. *Financial support:* In 2010–11, 39 students received support, including 12 fellowships with full tuition reimbursements available (averaging $18,546 per year), 4 research assistantships with full tuition reimbursements available (averaging $16,140 per year), 23 teaching assistantships with full tuition reimbursements available (averaging $16,140 per year); institutionally sponsored loans, scholarships/grants, traineeships, health care benefits, and unspecified assistantships also available. Financial award application deadline: 1/15. *Faculty research:* Game theory, experimental economics, econometrics, labor, international trade. Total annual research expenditures: $1.8 million. *Unit head:* Dr. Jean-Francois Richard, Department Chair, 412-648-1750, Fax: 412-648-7038, E-mail: fantin@pitt.edu. *Application contact:* Amy M. Linn, Graduate Program Administrator, 412-648-1399, Fax: 412-648-1793, E-mail: amlinn@pitt.edu.

University of Puerto Rico, Río Piedras, College of Social Sciences, Department of Economics, San Juan, PR 00931-3300. Offers MA. Part-time programs available. *Degree requirements:* For master's, comprehensive exam, thesis. *Entrance requirements:* For master's, GRE, PAEG, interview, minimum GPA of 3.0, letter of recommendation.

University of Regina, Faculty of Graduate Studies and Research, Johnson-Shoyama Graduate School of Public Policy, Regina, SK S4S 0A2, Canada. Offers economic analysis for public policy (Master's Certificate); health systems management (Master's Certificate); health systems research (MPP); non-profit management (Master's Certificate); public management (MPA, Master's Certificate); public policy (MPA, MPP, PhD); public policy analysis (Master's Certificate). Part-time programs available. *Faculty:* 7 full-time (3 women). *Students:* 60 full-time (28 women), 71 part-time (36 women). 101 applicants, 72% accepted. In 2010, 48 master's awarded. *Degree requirements:* For master's, thesis; for doctorate, thesis/dissertation. *Entrance requirements:* For doctorate, master's degree, intended research program in an area of public policy. Additional exam requirements/recommendations for international students: Required—TOEFL (minimum score 580 paper-based; 80 iBT), GRE. *Application deadline:* For fall admission, 2/1 for domestic and international students. Application fee: $100. Electronic applications accepted. *Expenses:* Contact institution. *Financial support:* In 2010–11, 11 fellowships (averaging $18,000 per year), 2 research assistantships (averaging $16,500 per year), 15 teaching assistantships (averaging $6,759 per year) were awarded; scholarships/grants also available. Financial award application deadline: 6/15. *Faculty research:* Governance and administration, public finance, public policy analysis, non-governmental organizations and alternative service delivery, micro-economics for policy analysis. *Unit head:* Dr. Michael Atkinson, Director, 306-996-1984, Fax: 306-585-5461, E-mail: michael.atkinson@usask.ca. *Application contact:* Elaine Groenendyk, Program Advisor, 306-585-5462, Fax: 306-585-5461, E-mail: elaine.groenendyk@uregina.ca.

University of Rhode Island, Graduate School, College of the Environment and Life Sciences, Department of Environmental and Natural Resource Economics, Kingston, RI 02881. Offers MESM, MS, PhD. Part-time programs available. *Faculty:* 6 full-time (2 women), 3 part-time/adjunct (1 woman). *Students:* 37 full-time (17 women), 4 part-time (2 women); includes 3 minority (1 Asian, non-Hispanic/Latino; 2 Hispanic/Latino), 13 international. In 2010, 4 master's, 4 doctorates awarded. *Degree requirements:* For master's, comprehensive exam (for some programs), thesis optional; for doctorate, comprehensive exam, thesis/dissertation. *Entrance requirements:* For master's, GRE, 2 letters of recommendation; for doctorate, GRE, 3 letters of recommendation. Additional exam requirements/recommendations for international students: Required—TOEFL (minimum score 550 paper-based; 213 computer-based). *Application deadline:* For fall admission, 7/15 for domestic students, 2/1 for international students; for spring admission, 11/15 for domestic students, 7/15 for international students. Application fee: $65. Electronic applications accepted. *Expenses:* Tuition, state resident: full-time $9588; part-time $533 per credit hour. Tuition, nonresident: full-time $22,968; part-time $1276 per credit hour. Required fees: $1282; $68 per semester. Tuition and fees vary according to program. *Financial support:* In 2010–11, 10 research assistantships with partial tuition reimbursements (averaging $12,990 per year), 2 teaching assistantships with full and partial tuition reimbursements (averaging $6,985 per year) were awarded. Financial award application deadline: 7/15; financial award applicants required to submit FAFSA. *Faculty research:* Policy Simulation Laboratory: utilizes computer technologies to help understand the consequences of policy actions, experimental economics. Total annual research expenditures: $637,583. *Unit head:* Dr. James Opaluch, Chair, 401-874-4590, Fax: 401-874-4766, E-mail: jimo@uri.edu. *Application contact:* Dr. James Opaluch, Graduate Admission Committee, 401-874-4590, Fax: 401-874-4766, E-mail: jimo@uri.edu.

University of Rochester, School of Arts and Sciences, Department of Economics, Rochester, NY 14627. Offers MA, PhD. *Degree requirements:* For doctorate, thesis/dissertation, qualifying exam. *Entrance requirements:* For doctorate, GRE General Test, GRE Subject Test (strongly recommended). Additional exam requirements/recommendations for international students: Required—TOEFL.

Economics

University of San Francisco, College of Arts and Sciences, Department of Economics, San Francisco, CA 94117-1080. Offers economics (MA); financial analysis (MS); international and development economics (MA); MS/MBA. Part-time and evening/weekend programs available. *Faculty:* 8 full-time (2 women), 9 part-time/adjunct (3 women). *Students:* 204 full-time (100 women), 19 part-time (9 women); includes 48 minority (2 Black or African American, non-Hispanic/Latino; 35 Asian, non-Hispanic/Latino; 6 Hispanic/Latino; 5 Two or more races, non-Hispanic/Latino), 119 international. Average age 27. 712 applicants, 42% accepted, 112 enrolled. In 2010, 124 master's awarded. *Degree requirements:* For master's, comprehensive exam, thesis or alternative. *Entrance requirements:* For master's, GRE General Test (recommended), BA in economics (preferred). Additional exam requirements/recommendations for international students: Required—TOEFL. *Application deadline:* For fall admission, 7/15 priority date for domestic students; for spring admission, 12/15 for domestic students. Applications are processed on a rolling basis. Application fee: $55 ($65 for international students). *Expenses:* Tuition: Full-time $20,070; part-time $1115 per credit hour. Tuition and fees vary according to course load, degree level and program. *Financial support:* In 2010–11, 125 students received support; fellowships, teaching assistantships, career-related internships or fieldwork available. Financial award application deadline: 3/2; financial award applicants required to submit FAFSA. *Faculty research:* Economic development, forecasting and planning, labor markets, Pacific Rim, financial markets. *Unit head:* Man-lui Lau, Chair, 415-422-2765, Fax: 415-422-5784. *Application contact:* Information Contact, 415-422-5135, Fax: 415-422-2217, E-mail: asgraduate@usfca.edu.

University of San Francisco, School of Business and Professional Studies, Masagung Graduate School of Management, Program in Business Administration, San Francisco, CA 94117-1080. Offers business economics (MBA); e-business (MBA); entrepreneurship (MBA); finance (MBA); international business (MBA); management (MBA); marketing (MBA); telecommunications management and policy (MBA); JD/MBA; MSN/MBA. *Accreditation:* AACSB. *Faculty:* 17 full-time (4 women), 16 part-time/adjunct (7 women). *Students:* 263 full-time (130 women), 11 part-time (6 women); includes 98 minority (3 Black or African American, non-Hispanic/Latino; 65 Asian, non-Hispanic/Latino; 18 Hispanic/Latino; 3 Native Hawaiian or other Pacific Islander, non-Hispanic/Latino; 9 Two or more races, non-Hispanic/Latino), 43 international. Average age 29. 503 applicants, 60% accepted, 80 enrolled. In 2010, 115 master's awarded. *Entrance requirements:* For master's, GMAT, minimum undergraduate GPA of 3.2. Additional exam requirements/recommendations for international students: Required—TOEFL. *Application deadline:* For fall admission, 7/1 priority date for domestic students; for spring admission, 11/30 for domestic students. Applications are processed on a rolling basis. Application fee: $55 ($65 for international students). *Expenses:* Tuition: Full-time $20,070; part-time $1115 per credit hour. Tuition and fees vary according to course load, degree level and program. *Financial support:* In 2010–11, 156 students received support; fellowships available. Financial award application deadline: 3/2; financial award applicants required to submit FAFSA. *Faculty research:* International financial markets, technology transfer licensing, international marketing, strategic planning. Total annual research expenditures: $50,000. *Unit head:* Kelly Brookes, Director, 415-422-2221, Fax: 415-422-6315. *Application contact:* Director, MBA Program, 415-422-2221, Fax: 415-422-6315, E-mail: mba@usfca.edu.

University of Saskatchewan, College of Graduate Studies and Research, College of Arts and Sciences, Department of Economics, Saskatoon, SK S7N 5A2, Canada. Offers MA, Diploma. *Degree requirements:* For master's, thesis (for some programs). *Entrance requirements:* Additional exam requirements/recommendations for international students: Required—TOEFL (minimum score 80 iBT); Recommended—IELTS (minimum score 6.5). Electronic applications accepted.

University of South Africa, College of Economic and Management Sciences, Pretoria, South Africa. Offers accounting (D Admin, D Com); accounting science (DA); auditing (D Admin, D Com); business administration (M Tech); business economics (D Admin); business leadership (DBL); business management (D Admin, D Com); economic management analysis (M Tech); economics (D Admin, D Com, PhD); human resource development (M Tech); industrial psychology (D Admin, D Com, PhD); logistics (D Com); marketing (M Tech); public administration (D Admin, D Com, DPA, PhD); public management (M Tech); quantitative management (D Admin, D Com); real estate (M Tech); statistics (D Admin, PhD); tourism management (D Admin, D Com); transport economics (D Admin, D Com).

University of South Carolina, The Graduate School, Darla Moore School of Business, Master of Arts in Economics Program, Columbia, SC 29208. Offers MA, PhD, JD/MA. *Faculty:* 99 full-time (23 women), 10 part-time/adjunct (2 women). *Students:* 23 full-time (8 women); includes 2 Black or African American, non-Hispanic/Latino; 1 Hispanic/Latino, 4 international. Average age 24. 32 applicants, 81% accepted, 11 enrolled. In 2010, 6 master's awarded. *Degree requirements:* For master's, thesis optional. *Entrance requirements:* For master's, GMAT or GRE General Test. Additional exam requirements/recommendations for international students: Required—TOEFL (minimum score 250 computer-based; 100 iBT); Recommended—IELTS. *Application deadline:* Applications are processed on a rolling basis. Application fee: $100. Electronic applications accepted. *Financial support:* Fellowships, Federal Work-Study, scholarships/grants, and unspecified assistantships available. *Faculty research:* Monetary theory, labor economics, international economics, industrial organization. *Unit head:* Christine LaCola, Assistant Dean & Director, Graduate Division, 803-777-2730, Fax: 803-777-0414, E-mail: christine.lacola@moore.sc.edu. *Application contact:* Scott King, Director, Graduate Admissions, 803-777-6087, Fax: 803-777-0414, E-mail: mcinnes@moore.sc.edu.

University of Southern California, Graduate School, Dana and David Dornsife College of Letters, Arts and Sciences, Department of Economics, Los Angeles, CA 90089. Offers economic development programming (MA, PhD); mathematical finance (MS); M Pl/MA; MA/JD. *Faculty:* 20 full-time (2 women), 9 part-time/adjunct (0 women). *Students:* 106 full-time (41 women), 6 part-time (0 women); includes 7 minority (5 Asian, non-Hispanic/Latino; 2 Two or more races, non-Hispanic/Latino), 89 international. 417 applicants, 19% accepted, 40 enrolled. In 2010, 34 master's, 9 doctorates awarded. Terminal master's awarded for partial completion of doctoral program. *Degree requirements:* For master's, comprehensive exam; for doctorate, comprehensive exam, thesis/dissertation. *Entrance requirements:* For master's and doctorate, GRE. Additional exam requirements/recommendations for international students: Required—TOEFL (minimum score 93 iBT). *Application deadline:* For fall admission, 12/1 priority date for domestic and international students. Application fee: $85. Electronic applications accepted. *Expenses:* Tuition: Full-time $31,240; part-time $1420 per unit. Required fees: $600. One-time fee: $35 full-time. Full-time tuition and fees vary according to degree level and program. *Financial support:* In 2010–11, 53 students received support, including 24 fellowships with full tuition reimbursements available (averaging $21,000 per year), 3 research assistantships with full tuition reimbursements available (averaging $21,000 per year), 27 teaching assistantships with full tuition reimbursements available (averaging $21,000 per year). Financial award application deadline: 12/1. *Faculty research:* Macro theory, development economics, econometrics. *Unit head:* Prof. Simon Wilkie, Chair, 213-740-8335, Fax: 213-740-8543, E-mail: swilkie@usc.edu. *Application contact:* Morgan Ponder, Assistant Director, 213-740-3507, Fax: 213-740-8543, E-mail: ponder@dornsife.usc.edu.

University of Southern Mississippi, Graduate School, College of Science and Technology, Department of Economic and Workforce Development, Hattiesburg, MS 39406-0001. Offers economic development (MS); human capital development (PhD); workforce training and development (MS). Part-time and evening/weekend programs available. *Faculty:* 6 full-time (3 women). *Students:* 37 full-time (14 women), 50 part-time (31 women); includes 22 Black or African American, non-Hispanic/Latino; 1 Asian, non-Hispanic/Latino; 1 Hispanic/Latino; 1 Two or more races, non-Hispanic/Latino. Average age 41. 27 applicants, 74% accepted, 17 enrolled. In 2010, 17 master's, 2 doctorates awarded. *Degree requirements:* For master's, comprehensive exam, thesis optional, internships; for doctorate, comprehensive exam, thesis/dissertation. *Entrance requirements:* For master's, GMAT or GRE General Test, minimum GPA of 2.75 in last 60 hours; for doctorate, GMAT or GRE General Test, minimum GPA of 3.5. Additional exam requirements/recommendations for international students: Required—TOEFL, IELTS. *Application deadline:* For fall admission, 8/1 for domestic students, 3/1 for international students; for spring admission, 1/3 for domestic and international students. Applications are processed on a rolling basis. Application fee: $50. Electronic applications accepted. *Financial support:* In 2010–11, 11 students received support, including 2 research assistantships with full tuition reimbursements available (averaging $13,000 per year), 6 teaching assistantships with full tuition reimbursements available (averaging $7,200 per year); career-related internships or fieldwork, Federal Work-Study, scholarships/grants, health care benefits, and unspecified assistantships also available. Financial award application deadline: 3/1; financial award applicants required to submit FAFSA. *Faculty research:* Economic development, international studies, geography. *Unit head:* Dr. Brent Hales, Interim Chair, 601-266-4736, Fax: 601-266-6071. *Application contact:* Dr. Chad Miller, Director, Graduate Studies, 601-266-6666, Fax: 601-266-6071.

University of South Florida, Graduate School, College of Arts and Sciences, Department of Economics, Tampa, FL 33620-9951. Offers MA, PhD. Part-time and evening/weekend programs available. *Faculty:* 1 (woman) full-time, 1 part-time/adjunct (0 women). *Students:* 23 full-time (5 women), 15 part-time (5 women); includes 5 Black or African American, non-Hispanic/Latino; 4 Asian, non-Hispanic/Latino, 5 international. Average age 30. 50 applicants, 56% accepted, 18 enrolled. In 2010, 16 master's awarded. *Degree requirements:* For master's, comprehensive exam; for doctorate, comprehensive exam, thesis/dissertation. *Entrance requirements:* For master's, GMAT, minimum GPA of 3.0 in last 60 hours of course work. Additional exam requirements/recommendations for international students: Required—TOEFL (minimum score 550 paper-based; 213 computer-based). *Application deadline:* For fall admission, 6/1 for domestic students, 1/2 for international students; for spring admission, 10/15 for domestic students, 6/1 for international students. Applications are processed on a rolling basis. Application fee: $30. *Financial support:* In 2010–11, 1 research assistantship (averaging $13,082 per year), 15 teaching assistantships with tuition reimbursements (averaging $12,987 per year) were awarded; unspecified assistantships also available. Financial award application deadline: 2/1; financial award applicants required to submit FAFSA. Total annual research expenditures: $78,325. *Unit head:* Dr. Kwabena Gyimah-Brempong, Chairperson, 813-974-4252, Fax: 813-974-6510, E-mail: kgyimah@coba.usf.edu. *Application contact:* Michael Loewy, Program Director, 813-974-4653, Fax: 813-974-6510, E-mail: mloewy@coba.usf.edu.

The University of Tennessee, Graduate School, College of Arts and Sciences, Department of Sociology, Knoxville, TN 37996. Offers criminology (MA, PhD); energy, environment, and resource policy (MA, PhD); political economy (MA, PhD). Part-time programs available. *Degree requirements:* For master's, thesis or alternative; for doctorate, thesis/dissertation. *Entrance requirements:* For master's, GRE General Test, minimum GPA of 3.0; for doctorate, GRE General Test, minimum GPA of 3.5. Additional exam requirements/recommendations for international students: Required—TOEFL. Electronic applications accepted. *Expenses:* Tuition, state resident: full-time $7440; part-time $414 per credit hour. Tuition, nonresident: full-time $22,478; part-time $1250 per credit hour. Required fees: $922; $43 per credit hour. Tuition and fees vary according to program.

The University of Tennessee, Graduate School, College of Business Administration, Department of Economics, Knoxville, TN 37996. Offers MA, PhD. *Degree requirements:* For master's, thesis or alternative; for doctorate, thesis/dissertation. *Entrance requirements:* For master's and doctorate, GRE General Test or GMAT, minimum GPA of 2.7. Additional exam requirements/recommendations for international students: Required—TOEFL. Electronic applications accepted. *Expenses:* Tuition, state resident: full-time $7440; part-time $414 per credit hour. Tuition, nonresident: full-time $22,478; part-time $1250 per credit hour. Required fees: $922; $43 per credit hour. Tuition and fees vary according to program.

The University of Texas at Arlington, Graduate School, College of Business, Economics Department, Arlington, TX 76019. Offers MA. Part-time and evening/weekend programs available. *Faculty:* 9 full-time (1 woman). *Students:* 15 full-time (4 women), 15 part-time (2 women); includes 9 minority (2 Black or African American, non-Hispanic/Latino; 2 Asian, non-Hispanic/Latino; 4 Hispanic/Latino; 1 Two or more races, non-Hispanic/Latino), 5 international. 20 applicants, 95% accepted, 6 enrolled. In 2010, 8 master's awarded. *Degree requirements:* For master's, thesis optional. *Entrance requirements:* For master's, GMAT or GRE General Test. Additional exam requirements/recommendations for international students: Required—TOEFL (minimum score 550 paper-based; 213 computer-based; 79 iBT). *Application deadline:* For fall admission, 6/1 for domestic students, 4/1 for international students; for spring admission, 10/15 for domestic students, 9/15 for international students. Applications are processed on a rolling basis. Application fee: $35 ($50 for international students). *Expenses:* Tuition, state resident: full-time $7500. Tuition, nonresident: full-time $13,080. International tuition: $13,250 full-time. *Financial support:* In 2010–11, 10 teaching assistantships (averaging $10,000 per year) were awarded; career-related internships or fieldwork, scholarships/grants, and unspecified assistantships also available. Support available to part-time students. Financial award application deadline: 6/1; financial award applicants required to submit FAFSA. *Unit head:* Dr. Daniel Himarios, Chair, 817-272-2881, Fax: 817-272-2073, E-mail: himarios@uta.edu. *Application contact:* Dr. Leo Krasnozhon, Graduate Advisor, 817-272-3202, Fax: 817-272-3145, E-mail: krasnozhon@uta.edu.

The University of Texas at Austin, Graduate School, College of Liberal Arts, Department of Economics, Austin, TX 78712-1111. Offers MA, MS Econ, PhD. Part-time programs available. *Degree requirements:* For master's, thesis; for doctorate, comprehensive exam, thesis/dissertation. *Entrance requirements:* For master's and doctorate, GRE General Test, minimum GPA of 3.5 (based on upper-division undergraduate and graduate course work). Additional exam requirements/recommendations for international students: Required—TOEFL. Electronic applications accepted. *Faculty research:* Industrial organization, game theory, monetary economics, labor economics, public economics.

The University of Texas at Dallas, School of Economic, Political and Policy Sciences, Program in Economics, Richardson, TX 75080. Offers MS, PhD. Part-time and evening/weekend programs available. *Faculty:* 12 full-time (3 women), 1 (woman) part-time/adjunct. *Students:* 65 full-time (28 women), 15 part-time (1 woman); includes 13 minority (4 Black or African American, non-Hispanic/Latino; 6 Asian, non-Hispanic/Latino; 2 Hispanic/Latino; 1 Two or more races, non-Hispanic/Latino), 34 international. Average age 29. 123 applicants, 63% accepted, 29 enrolled. In 2010, 10 master's, 4 doctorates awarded. *Degree requirements:* For master's, internship; for doctorate, thesis/dissertation. *Entrance requirements:* For master's, GRE (minimum combined verbal and quantitative score of 1200), minimum GPA of 3.0 in upper-level course work in field; for doctorate, GRE (minimum combined verbal and quantitative score of 1200, writing 4.5), minimum GPA of 3.25 in upper-level and graduate course work in field. Additional exam requirements/recommendations for international students: Required—TOEFL (minimum score 550 paper-based; 215 computer-based). *Application deadline:* For fall admission, 7/15 for domestic students, 5/1 priority date for international students; for spring admission, 11/15 for domestic students, 9/1 priority date for international students. Applications are processed on a rolling basis. Application fee: $50 ($100 for international students). Electronic applications accepted. *Expenses:* Tuition, state resident: full-time $10,248; part-time $569 per credit hour. Tuition, nonresident: full-time $18,544; part-time $1030 per credit hour. Tuition and fees vary according to course load. *Financial support:* In 2010–11, 40 students received support, including 10 research assistantships with partial tuition reimbursements available (averaging $11,748 per year), 21 teaching assistantships with partial tuition reimbursements available (averaging $11,291 per year); career-related internships or fieldwork, Federal Work-Study, institutionally sponsored loans, scholarships/grants, and unspecified assistantships also available. Support available to part-time students. Financial award application deadline: 4/30; financial award applicants required to submit FAFSA. *Faculty research:* Bargaining and negotiation, experimental economics, judgment and decision making, game theory, terrorism. *Unit head:* Dr. Daniel Arce, Program Head, 972-883-6857, Fax: 972-883-2735, E-mail: darce@utdallas.edu. *Application contact:* Dr. Nathan Berg, Associate Program Head, 972-883-2088, Fax: 972-883-2735, E-mail: nberg@utdallas.edu.

See Close-Up on page 811.

The University of Texas at Dallas, School of Economic, Political and Policy Sciences, Program in Public Policy and Political Economy, Richardson, TX 75080. Offers international political economy (MS); public policy (MPP); public policy and political economy (PhD). Part-time and evening/weekend programs available. *Faculty:* 19 full-time (5 women), 1 (woman) part-time/adjunct. *Students:* 59 full-time (28 women), 41 part-time (17 women); includes 30 minority (14 Black or African American, non-Hispanic/Latino; 8 Asian, non-Hispanic/Latino; 8 Hispanic/Latino), 17 international. Average age 35. 84 applicants, 48% accepted, 24 enrolled. In 2010, 9 master's, 11 doctorates awarded. *Degree requirements:* For doctorate, thesis/dissertation. *Entrance requirements:* For master's and doctorate, GRE General Test, minimum GPA of 3.0 in upper-level course work in field. Additional exam requirements/recommendations for international students: Required—TOEFL (minimum score 550 paper-based; 215 computer-based). *Application deadline:* For fall admission, 7/15 for domestic students, 5/1 priority date for international students; for spring admission, 11/15 for domestic students, 9/1 priority date for international students. Applications are processed on a rolling basis. Application fee: $50 ($100 for international students). Electronic applications accepted. *Expenses:* Tuition, state resident: full-time $10,248; part-time $569 per credit hour. Tuition, nonresident: full-time $18,544; part-time $1030 per credit hour. Tuition and fees vary according to course load. *Financial support:* In 2010–11, 45 students received support, including 6 research assistantships with partial tuition reimbursements available (averaging $14,850 per year), 14 teaching assistantships with partial tuition reimbursements available (averaging $11,517 per year); career-related internships or fieldwork, Federal Work-Study, institutionally sponsored loans, scholarships/grants, and unspecified assistantships also available. Support available to part-time students. Financial award application deadline: 4/30; financial award applicants required to submit FAFSA. *Faculty research:* Ethnicity, community and local public good provision; community mental health policy; Texas Schools Project; biological and chemical arms control; cross-disciplinary applications of quantitative methodology. *Unit head:* Dr. Paul Jargowski, Program Head, 972-883-2992, Fax: 972-883-6297, E-mail: jargo@utdallas.edu. *Application contact:* Dr. Marie I. Chevrier, Associate Program Head, 972-883-2727, Fax: 972-883-6297, E-mail: chevrier@utdallas.edu.

See Close-Up on page 811.

The University of Texas at El Paso, Graduate School, College of Business Administration, Department of Economics and Finance, El Paso, TX 79968-0001. Offers economics (MS). Part-time and evening/weekend programs available. *Students:* Average age 34. In 2010, 1 master's awarded. *Degree requirements:* For master's, thesis optional. *Entrance requirements:* For master's, GMAT, minimum GPA of 2.7. Additional exam requirements/recommendations for international students: Required—TOEFL. *Application deadline:* For fall admission, 7/1 priority date for domestic students, 3/1 for international students; for spring admission, 11/1 priority date for domestic students, 9/1 for international students. Applications are processed on a rolling basis. Application fee: $15 ($65 for international students). Electronic applications accepted. *Financial support:* In 2010–11, research assistantships with partial tuition reimbursements (averaging $18,750 per year), teaching assistantships with partial tuition reimbursements (averaging $15,000 per year) were awarded; Federal Work-Study and institutionally sponsored loans also available. Support available to part-time students. Financial award application deadline: 3/15; financial award applicants required to submit FAFSA. *Unit head:* Dr. Timothy Roth, Chairperson, 915-747-7779, Fax: 915-747-6282, E-mail: troth@utep.edu. *Application contact:* Dr. Charles H. Ambler, Director, Graduate Student Services, 915-747-5491, Fax: 915-747-5778, E-mail: sjordan@utep.edu.

The University of Texas at San Antonio, College of Business, Department of Economics, San Antonio, TX 78249-0617. Offers business economics (MBA); economics (MA). Part-time and evening/weekend programs available. *Faculty:* 7 full-time (2 women), 2 part-time/adjunct (0 women). *Students:* 9 full-time (5 women), 7 part-time (3 women); includes 4 minority (2 Asian, non-Hispanic/Latino; 2 Hispanic/Latino), 3 international. Average age 33. 20 applicants, 40% accepted, 4 enrolled. In 2010, 6 master's awarded. *Degree requirements:* For master's, comprehensive exam (for some programs), thesis (for some programs). *Entrance requirements:* For master's, GMAT or GRE, minimum GPA of 3.0. Additional exam requirements/recommendations for international students: Required—TOEFL (minimum score 500 paper-based; 173 computer-based; 61 iBT), IELTS (minimum score 5). *Application deadline:* For fall admission, 7/1 for domestic students, 4/1 for international students; for spring admission, 11/1 for domestic students, 9/1 for international students. Application fee: $45 ($80 for international students). *Expenses:* Tuition, state resident: full-time $4172; part-time $231.75 per credit hour. Tuition, nonresident: full-time $15,332; part-time $851.75 per credit hour. *Financial support:* In 2010–11, 4 students received support, including 4 research assistantships (averaging $10,511 per year), 13 teaching assistantships (averaging $6,929 per year); career-related internships or fieldwork, Federal Work-Study, scholarships/grants, and unspecified assistantships also available. Support available to part-time students. *Faculty research:* International economics, macroeconomics, microeconomics, econometrics, forecasting. Total annual research expenditures: $67,632. *Unit head:* Dr. Kenneth E. Weiher, Chair, 210-458-5315, Fax: 210-458-5837, E-mail: kweiher@utsa.edu. *Application contact:* Veronica Ramirez, Assistant Dean of the Graduate School, 210-458-4330, Fax: 210-458-4332, E-mail: graduatestudies@utsa.edu.

The University of Texas–Pan American, College of Business Administration, Program in International Business, Edinburg, TX 78539. Offers computer information systems (PhD); economics (PhD); finance (PhD); management (PhD); marketing (PhD). *Degree requirements:* For doctorate, comprehensive exam, thesis/dissertation. *Entrance requirements:* For doctorate, GMAT or GRE. Additional exam requirements/recommendations for international students: Required—TOEFL, IELTS. Electronic applications accepted. *Expenses:* Contact institution.

The University of Toledo, College of Graduate Studies, College of Language, Literature and Social Sciences, Department of Economics, Toledo, OH 43606-3390. Offers MA. Part-time programs available. *Faculty:* 8. *Students:* 7 full-time (3 women), 1 part-time (0 women), 5 international. Average age 27. 26 applicants, 69% accepted, 7 enrolled. In 2010, 10 master's awarded. *Degree requirements:* For master's, comprehensive exam, paper or thesis. *Entrance requirements:* For master's, GRE General Test, minimum cumulative GPA of 2.7 on all previous academic work, three letters of recommendation, statement of purpose, transcripts from all prior institutions attended. Additional exam requirements/recommendations for international students: Required—TOEFL (minimum score 550 paper-based; 213 computer-based; 80 iBT), IELTS (minimum score 6.5). *Application deadline:* For fall admission, 1/15 priority date for domestic and international students. Applications are processed on a rolling basis. Application fee: $45 ($75 for international students). Electronic applications accepted. *Expenses:* Tuition, state resident: full-time $11,426; part-time $476 per credit hour. Tuition, nonresident: full-time $21,660; part-time $903 per credit hour. One-time fee: $62. *Financial support:* Teaching assistantships with full tuition reimbursements, career-related internships or fieldwork, Federal Work-Study, institutionally sponsored loans, scholarships/grants, tuition waivers (full and partial), and unspecified assistantships available. Support available to part-time students. *Faculty research:* Economic development. *Unit head:* Dr. Michael Dowd, Chair, 419-530-4603, Fax: 419-530-7844, E-mail: michael.dowd@utoledo.edu. *Application contact:* Graduate School Office, 419-530-4723, Fax: 419-530-4724, E-mail: grdsch@utnet.utoledo.edu.

The University of Toledo, College of Graduate Studies, Judith Herb College of Education, Health Science and Human Service, Department of Curriculum and Instruction, Toledo, OH 43606-3390. Offers art education (ME); career and technical education (ME, Ed S); curriculum and instruction (ME, DE, PhD, Ed S); early childhood education (ME, Ed S); education and biology (MES); education and chemistry (MES); education and economics (MAE); education and English (MAE); education and French (MAE); education and geography (MAE); education and geology (MES); education and German (MAE); education and history (MAE); education and mathematics (MAE, MES); education and physics (MES); education and political science (MAE); education and sociology (MAE); education and Spanish (MAE); educational media (DE, PhD, Ed S); educational technology (ME); elementary education (DE, PhD); English as a second language (MAE); gifted and talented (DE, PhD); health education (ME); middle childhood education (ME); music education (MME); secondary education (ME, DE, PhD, Ed S); special education (DE, PhD, Ed S). *Accreditation:* NCATE. Part-time and evening/weekend programs available. *Faculty:* 21. *Students:* 134 full-time (87 women), 182 part-time (136 women); includes 22 Black or African American, non-Hispanic/Latino; 1 American Indian or Alaska Native, non-Hispanic/Latino; 1 Asian, non-Hispanic/Latino; 6 Hispanic/Latino; 2 Two or more races, non-Hispanic/Latino, 16 international. Average age 35. 115 applicants, 73% accepted, 74 enrolled. In 2010, 99 master's, 8 doctorates, 3 other advanced degrees awarded. *Degree requirements:* For master's, comprehensive exam, thesis or alternative; for doctorate, comprehensive exam, thesis/dissertation; for Ed S, thesis optional. *Entrance requirements:* For master's, GRE or other qualifying exams required vary by program , A minimum 2.70 cumulative GPA all previous academic work. Two/Three Letters of Recommendation (as required per program). ; for doctorate, GRE or other qualifying exams required vary by program, A minimum 2.70 cumulative GPA all previous academic work. Two/Three Letters of Recommendation (as required per program). ; for Ed S, GRE or other qualifying exams required vary by program, A minimum 2.70 cumulative GPA all previous academic work. Two/Three Letters of Recommendation (as required per program). . Additional exam requirements/recommendations for international students: Required—TOEFL (minimum score 550 paper-based; 213 computer-based; 80 iBT), IELTS (minimum score 6.5). *Application deadline:* For fall admission, 1/15 priority date for domestic and international students. Applications are processed on a rolling basis. Application fee: $45 ($75 for international students). Electronic applications accepted. *Expenses:* Tuition, state resident: full-time $11,426; part-time $476 per credit hour. Tuition, nonresident: full-time $21,660; part-time $903 per credit hour. One-time fee: $62. *Financial support:* Research assistantships with full tuition reimbursements, teaching assistantships with full tuition reimbursements, career-related internships or fieldwork, Federal Work-Study, institutionally sponsored loans, scholarships/grants, tuition waivers (full and partial), unspecified assistantships, and administrative assistantships available. Support available to part-time students. *Unit head:* Dr. Leigh Chiarelott, Chair, 419-530-5371, E-mail: eigh.chiarelott@utoledo.edu. *Application contact:* Graduate School Office, 419-530-4723, Fax: 419-530-4724, E-mail: grdsch@utnet.utoledo.edu.

University of Toronto, School of Graduate Studies, Social Sciences Division, Department of Economics, Toronto, ON M5S 1A1, Canada. Offers MA, MFE, PhD. Part-time programs available. *Degree requirements:* For doctorate, comprehensive exam, thesis/dissertation. *Entrance requirements:* For master's, GRE (for applicants without a degree from a Canadian university), minimum B average in final year, 2 letters of reference; for doctorate, GRE (for applicants without a degree from a Canadian university), master's degree in economics, minimum B+ average, 3 letters of reference. Additional exam requirements/recommendations for international students: Required—TOEFL (minimum score 580 paper-based; 237 computer-based), TWE (minimum score 5), IELTS (minimum score: 7) or Michigan English Language Assessment Battery (minimum score: 85).

University of Utah, Graduate School, College of Social and Behavioral Science, Department of Economics, Salt Lake City, UT 84112-1107. Offers econometrics (M Stat); economics (M Phil, MA, MS, PhD). Part-time programs available. *Faculty:* 20 full-time (4 women), 1 (woman) part-time/adjunct. *Students:* 61 full-time (16 women), 48 part-time (14 women); includes 11 minority (5 Asian, non-Hispanic/Latino; 6 Hispanic/Latino), 39 international. Average age 33. 149 applicants, 40% accepted, 28 enrolled. In 2010, 14 master's, 8 doctorates awarded. Terminal master's awarded for partial completion of doctoral program. *Degree requirements:* For master's, thesis or alternative, exam, oral presentation, research project; for doctorate, comprehensive exam, thesis/dissertation, qualifying exams. *Entrance requirements:* For master's, GRE General Test, undergraduate course work in economics; for doctorate, GRE General Test, GRE Subject Test, minimum GPA of 3.0, course work in calculus and statistics. Additional exam requirements/recommendations for international students: Required—TOEFL (minimum score 500 paper-based; 173 computer-based) or IELTS (minimum score 6). *Application deadline:* For fall admission, 2/1 priority date for domestic and international students. Application fee: $55 ($65 for international students). Electronic applications accepted. *Expenses:* Tuition, area resident: Part-time $179.19 per credit hour. Tuition, state resident: full-time $4384. Tuition, nonresident: full-time $16,684; part-time $630.67 per credit hour. Required fees: $350 per semester. Tuition and fees vary according to course load, degree level and program. *Financial support:* In 2010–11, 41 students received support, including 19 fellowships with full tuition reimbursements available (averaging $12,000 per year), 22 teaching assistantships (averaging $12,000 per year); career-related internships or fieldwork, Federal Work-Study, institutionally sponsored loans, health care benefits, tuition waivers (full and partial), and unspecified assistantships also available. Financial award application deadline: 2/1. *Faculty research:* Economic doctrines, economic history, labor and gender, development, international, environmental and natural resources, health economics. Total annual research expenditures: $151,964. *Unit head:* Dr. Thomas Maloney, Chair, 801-581-7481, Fax: 801-585-5649, E-mail: maloney@economics.utah.edu. *Application contact:* Tracey Farnsworth, Academic Advisor, 801-581-7481, Fax: 801-585-5649, E-mail: tracey.farnsworth@economics.utah.edu.

University of Utah, Graduate School, Interdepartmental Program in Statistics, Salt Lake City, UT 84112-1107. Offers biostatistics (M Stat); econometrics (M Stat); educational psychology (M Stat); mathematics (M Stat); sociology (M Stat); statistics (M Stat). Part-time programs available. *Students:* 28 full-time (11 women), 17 part-time (9 women); includes 2 Black or African American, non-Hispanic/Latino; 2 Asian, non-Hispanic/Latino; 2 Hispanic/Latino, 10 international. Average age 30. 59 applicants, 44% accepted, 12 enrolled. In 2010, 15 master's awarded. *Degree requirements:* For master's, comprehensive exam, projects. *Entrance requirements:* For master's, GRE General Test (sociology and educational psychology), minimum GPA of 3.0; course work in calculus, matrix theory, statistics. Additional exam requirements/recommendations for international students: Required—TOEFL (minimum score 500 paper-based; 173 computer-based). *Application deadline:* For fall admission, 7/1 for domestic students, 4/1 for international students. Applications are processed on a rolling basis. Application fee: $55 ($65 for international students). *Expenses:* Tuition, area resident: Part-time $179.19 per credit hour. Tuition, state resident: full-time $4384. Tuition, nonresident: full-time $16,684; part-time $630.67 per credit hour. Required fees: $350 per semester. Tuition and fees vary according to course load, degree level and program. *Financial support:* Career-related internships or fieldwork available. *Faculty research:* Biostatistics, management, economics, educational psychology, mathematics. *Unit head:* Tariq Mughal, Chair, University Statistics Committee, 801-585-9547, E-mail: tariaq.mughal@business.utah.edu. *Application contact:* Laura Egbert, MSTAT Program Coordinator, 801-585-6853, E-mail: laura.demattia@utah.edu.

University of Victoria, Faculty of Graduate Studies, Faculty of Social Sciences, Department of Economics, Victoria, BC V8W 2Y2, Canada. Offers MA, PhD. Part-time programs available. *Degree requirements:* For master's, comprehensive exam (for some programs), thesis optional; for doctorate, comprehensive exam, thesis/dissertation, candidacy exam. *Entrance requirements:* For master's and doctorate, GRE. Additional exam requirements/recommendations for international students: Required—TOEFL (minimum score 575 paper-based; 233 computer-based), IELTS (minimum score 7). Electronic applications accepted. *Faculty research:* Industrial organization, cost/benefit, applied economics, econometrics, airline economics, health economics.

University of Virginia, College and Graduate School of Arts and Sciences, Department of Economics, Charlottesville, VA 22903. Offers MA, PhD, JD/MA. *Faculty:* 29 full-time (3 women), 3 part-time/adjunct (0 women). *Students:* 96 full-time (35 women); includes 2 Asian, non-Hispanic/Latino; 1 Hispanic/Latino; 1 Two or more races, non-Hispanic/Latino, 54 international. Average age 27. 550 applicants, 15% accepted, 28 enrolled. In 2010, 21 master's, 8 doctorates awarded. *Degree requirements:* For master's, comprehensive exam (for some programs), thesis (for some programs), thesis or comprehensive exam; for doctorate, comprehensive exam, thesis/dissertation. *Entrance requirements:* For master's and doctorate, GRE General Test. Additional exam requirements/recommendations for international students: Required—TOEFL (minimum score 600 paper-based; 250 computer-based; 90 iBT), IELTS (minimum score 7). *Application deadline:* For fall admission, 4/1 for domestic and international students. Applications are processed on a rolling basis. Application fee: $60. Electronic applications accepted. *Financial support:* Fellowships, research assistantships, teaching assistantships,

Economics

University of Virginia (continued)
tuition waivers (full and partial) available. Financial award application deadline: 2/1; financial award applicants required to submit FAFSA. *Faculty research:* Macroeconomics, public economics, labor, industrial organization, economic history. *Unit head:* Charlie Holt, Chair, 434-924-3177, Fax: 434-982-2904, E-mail: econ@virginia.edu. *Application contact:* Leora Friedburg, Director of Graduate Studies, 434-924-3225, E-mail: lfriedberg@virginia.edu.

University of Washington, Graduate School, College of Arts and Sciences, Department of Economics, Seattle, WA 98195. Offers PhD. Terminal master's awarded for partial completion of doctoral program. *Degree requirements:* For doctorate, comprehensive exam, thesis/dissertation. *Entrance requirements:* For doctorate, GRE General Test, minimum GPA of 3.0. Additional exam requirements/recommendations for international students: Required—TOEFL. Electronic applications accepted. *Faculty research:* Microeconomic theory; macroeconomic theory; econometrics; natural resource economics; international, development, and industrial organization.

University of Washington, Graduate School, School of Public Health, Department of Health Services, Seattle, WA 98195. Offers bioinformatics (PhD); cancer prevention and control (PhD); clinical research (MS); community oriented public health practice (MPH); economics or finance (PhD); evaluation sciences (PhD); executive program (MHA); health behavior and health promotion (PhD); health care and population health research (MPH); health policy analysis and process (PhD); health policy and analysis and process (MPH); health services (MS, PhD); health services administration (EMHA, MHA); in residence program (MHA); maternal and child health (MPH, PhD); occupational health (PhD); population health and social determinants (PhD); social and behavioral sciences (MPH); sociology and demography (PhD); JD/MHA; MHA/MBA; MHA/MD; MHA/MPA; MPH/JD; MPH/MD; MPH/MN; MPH/MPA; MPH/MS; MPH/MSD; MPH/MSW; MPH/PhD. Part-time and evening/weekend programs available. Post-baccalaureate distance learning degree programs offered (minimal on-campus study). *Faculty:* 36 full-time (18 women), 59 part-time/adjunct (26 women). *Students:* 107 full-time (82 women), 101 part-time (82 women); includes 1 Black or African American, non-Hispanic/Latino; 1 American Indian or Alaska Native, non-Hispanic/Latino; 27 Asian, non-Hispanic/Latino; 10 Hispanic/Latino, 4 international. Average age 34. 426 applicants, 41% accepted, 106 enrolled. In 2010, 37 master's, 11 doctorates awarded. Terminal master's awarded for partial completion of doctoral program. *Degree requirements:* For master's, thesis (for some programs), practicum (MPH); for doctorate, comprehensive exam, thesis/dissertation. *Entrance requirements:* For master's and doctorate, GRE General Test, minimum GPA of 3.0. Additional exam requirements/recommendations for international students: Required—TOEFL (minimum score 580 paper-based; 237 computer-based; 92 iBT), IELTS (minimum score 7). *Application deadline:* For fall admission, 1/1 for domestic students, 11/1 for international students. Application fee: 75 Albanian leks. Electronic applications accepted. *Financial support:* In 2010–11, 47 students received support, including 10 fellowships with full and partial tuition reimbursements available (averaging $22,000 per year), 10 research assistantships with full and partial tuition reimbursements available (averaging $18,700 per year), 3 teaching assistantships with full and partial tuition reimbursements available (averaging $4,575 per year); institutionally sponsored loans, traineeships, and health care benefits also available. Financial award application deadline: 2/28; financial award applicants required to submit FAFSA. *Faculty research:* Public health practice, health promotion and disease prevention, maternal and child health, organizational behavior and culture, health policy. *Unit head:* Dr. Larry Kessler, Chair, 206-543-2930. *Application contact:* Kitty A. Andert, MPH/MS/PhD Program Manager, 206-616-2926, Fax: 206-543-3964, E-mail: kitander@u.washington.edu.

University of Waterloo, Graduate Studies, Faculty of Arts, Department of Economics, Waterloo, ON N2L 3G1, Canada. Offers MA, PhD. Part-time programs available. *Entrance requirements:* For master's, honors degree, minimum B average. Additional exam requirements/recommendations for international students: Required—TOEFL, TWE. Electronic applications accepted. *Faculty research:* Applied microeconomics, applied macroeconomics, public finance, international trade and finance, wage inflation and consumer problems.

The University of Western Ontario, Faculty of Graduate Studies, Social Sciences Division, Department of Economics, London, ON N6A 5B8, Canada. Offers MA, PhD. *Degree requirements:* For doctorate, thesis/dissertation. *Entrance requirements:* For master's, GRE, honours BA with B+ average. Additional exam requirements/recommendations for international students: Required—TOEFL.

University of Windsor, Faculty of Graduate Studies, Faculty of Science, Department of Economics, Windsor, ON N9B 3P4, Canada. Offers MA. Part-time programs available. *Degree requirements:* For master's, thesis or alternative. *Entrance requirements:* For master's, minimum B average. Additional exam requirements/recommendations for international students: Required—TOEFL (minimum score 560 paper-based; 220 computer-based). Electronic applications accepted. *Faculty research:* International trade, economic growth, microeconomic theory.

University of Wisconsin–Madison, Graduate School, College of Letters and Science, Department of Economics, Madison, WI 53706-1380. Offers PhD. *Degree requirements:* For doctorate, thesis/dissertation. *Entrance requirements:* For doctorate, GRE General Test, 3 semesters of course work in calculus, 1 semester of course work in algebra and mathematics/statistics. Electronic applications accepted. *Expenses:* Tuition, state resident: full-time $9887; part-time $617.96 per credit. Tuition, nonresident: full-time $24,054; part-time $1503.40 per credit, Required fees: $67.63 per credit. Tuition and fees vary according to reciprocity agreements.

University of Wisconsin–Milwaukee, Graduate School, College of Letters and Sciences, Department of Economics, Milwaukee, WI 53201-0413. Offers MA, PhD. *Faculty:* 21 full-time (2 women). *Students:* 70 full-time (26 women), 19 part-time (3 women); includes 4 Black or African American, non-Hispanic/Latino; 2 Asian, non-Hispanic/Latino, 46 international. Average age 30. 112 applicants, 76% accepted, 28 enrolled. In 2010, 20 master's, 8 doctorates awarded. *Degree requirements:* For master's, comprehensive exam; for doctorate, comprehensive exam, thesis/dissertation. *Entrance requirements:* For master's, GRE General Test; for doctorate, GRE General Test, GRE Subject Test, minimum GPA of 3.0. Additional exam requirements/recommendations for international students: Required—TOEFL (minimum score 550 paper-based; 79 iBT), IELTS (minimum score 6.5). *Application deadline:* For fall admission, 1/1 priority date for domestic students; for spring admission, 9/1 for domestic students. Applications are processed on a rolling basis. Application fee: $56 ($96 for international students). *Financial support:* In 2010–11, 28 teaching assistantships were awarded; career-related internships or fieldwork and unspecified assistantships also available. Support available to part-time students. Financial award application deadline: 4/15; financial award applicants required to submit FAFSA. Total annual research expenditures: $12,709. *Unit head:* Scott Adams, Representative, 414-229-4212, E-mail: sjadams@uwm.edu. *Application contact:* General Information Contact, 414-229-4982, Fax: 414-229-6967, E-mail: gradschool@uwm.edu.

University of Wyoming, College of Business, Department of Economics and Finance, Program in Economics, Laramie, WY 82070. Offers MS, PhD. Part-time programs available. *Degree requirements:* For master's, thesis; for doctorate, comprehensive exam, thesis/dissertation. *Entrance requirements:* For master's, GRE General Test or GMAT, minimum GPA of 3.0; for doctorate, GRE General Test, minimum GPA of 3.0. Additional exam requirements/recommendations for international students: Required—TOEFL (minimum score 525 paper-based; 197 computer-based). *Faculty research:* Resource and environmental economics, industrial organization, regulation.

University of Wyoming, College of Business, Department of Economics and Finance, Program in Economics and Finance, Laramie, WY 82070. Offers MS. *Degree requirements:* For master's, thesis. *Entrance requirements:* For master's, GRE, minimum GPA of 3.0. Additional exam requirements/recommendations for international students: Required—TOEFL (minimum score 540 paper-based; 207 computer-based; 76 iBT). *Faculty research:* Financial economics.

Utah State University, School of Graduate Studies, College of Business and College of Agriculture, Department of Economics, Logan, UT 84322. Offers applied economics (MS); economics (MA, MS, PhD). Terminal master's awarded for partial completion of doctoral program. *Degree requirements:* For master's, thesis (for some programs); for doctorate, comprehensive exam, thesis/dissertation. *Entrance requirements:* For master's, GRE General Test, GMAT, minimum GPA of 3.0, TOEFL for international; for doctorate, GRE General Test, minimum GPA of 3.0, TOEFL. Additional exam requirements/recommendations for international students: Required—TOEFL. Electronic applications accepted. *Faculty research:* Resource economics, economic theory, international trade, industrial organization, development.

Vanderbilt University, Graduate School, Department of Economics, Nashville, TN 37240-1001. Offers economic development (MA); economics (MA, MAT, PhD); JD/PhD. *Faculty:* 31 full-time (6 women). *Students:* 123 full-time (47 women), 6 part-time (4 women); includes 2 Asian, non-Hispanic/Latino; 3 Hispanic/Latino; 2 Two or more races, non-Hispanic/Latino. Average age 27. 371 applicants, 7% accepted, 19 enrolled. In 2010, 29 master's, 6 doctorates awarded. Terminal master's awarded for partial completion of doctoral program. *Degree requirements:* For master's, thesis or alternative; for doctorate, thesis/dissertation, final and qualifying exams. *Entrance requirements:* For master's and doctorate, GRE General Test, GRE Subject Test (recommended). Additional exam requirements/recommendations for international students: Required—TOEFL (minimum score 570 paper-based; 230 computer-based; 88 iBT). *Application deadline:* For fall admission, 1/15 for domestic and international students; for spring admission, 11/1 for domestic students. Applications are processed on a rolling basis. Application fee: $0. Electronic applications accepted. *Financial support:* Fellowships with full and partial tuition reimbursements, teaching assistantships with full and partial tuition reimbursements, career-related internships or fieldwork, Federal Work-Study, institutionally sponsored loans, scholarships/grants, and health care benefits available. Financial award application deadline: 1/15; financial award applicants required to submit CSS PROFILE or FAFSA. *Faculty research:* Economic theory, applied fields, developmental economics, environmental economics, health economics and policy. *Unit head:* Dr. Tong Li, Chair, 615-322-3582, Fax: 615-343-8495, E-mail: tong.li@vanderbilt.edu. *Application contact:* Dr. Bill Collins, Director of Graduate Studies, 615-322-3428, Fax: 615-343-8495, E-mail: william.collins@vanderbilt.edu.

Vanderbilt University, Vanderbilt University Law School, Nashville, TN 37203. Offers law (JD, LL M); law and economics (PhD); JD/M Div; JD/MA; JD/MBA; JD/MD; JD/MPP; JD/MTS; JD/PhD; LL M/MA. *Accreditation:* ABA. *Faculty:* 47 full-time (20 women), 71 part-time/adjunct (22 women). *Students:* 612 full-time (289 women); includes 54 Black or African American, non-Hispanic/Latino; 3 American Indian or Alaska Native, non-Hispanic/Latino; 24 Asian, non-Hispanic/Latino; 28 Hispanic/Latino, 46 international. Average age 23. 4,885 applicants, 22% accepted, 193 enrolled. In 2010, 204 first professional degrees, 28 master's awarded. *Degree requirements:* For doctorate, comprehensive exam, thesis/dissertation, 72 hours of coursework and research. *Entrance requirements:* For JD, LSAT; for master's, foreign law degree; for doctorate, GRE, LSAT, advanced undergraduate economics. Additional exam requirements/recommendations for international students: Required—TOEFL. *Application deadline:* For fall admission, 3/15 for domestic and international students. Applications are processed on a rolling basis. Application fee: $50. Electronic applications accepted. *Expenses:* Contact institution. *Financial support:* In 2010–11, 433 students received support. Career-related internships or fieldwork, Federal Work-Study, institutionally sponsored loans, scholarships/grants, and health care benefits available. Financial award application deadline: 2/15; financial award applicants required to submit FAFSA. *Unit head:* G. Todd Morton, Assistant Dean and Dean of Admissions, 615-322-6452, Fax: 615-322-1531, E-mail: admissions@law.vanderbilt.edu. *Application contact:* Admissions Office, 615-322-6452, Fax: 615-322-1531, E-mail: admissions@law.vanderbilt.edu.

Virginia Commonwealth University, Graduate School, School of Business, Program in Economics, Richmond, VA 23284-9005. Offers MA. *Faculty:* 12 full-time (3 women). *Students:* 9 full-time (1 woman), 7 part-time (0 women); includes 1 minority (Asian, non-Hispanic/Latino), 2 international. 24 applicants, 79% accepted, 12 enrolled. In 2010, 10 master's awarded. *Degree requirements:* For master's, thesis optional. *Entrance requirements:* For master's, GRE General Test (preferred) or GMAT. Additional exam requirements/recommendations for international students: Required—TOEFL (minimum score 600 paper-based; 250 computer-based; 100 iBT). *Application deadline:* For fall admission, 7/15 for domestic students; for spring admission, 11/15 for domestic students. Applications are processed on a rolling basis. Application fee: $50. Electronic applications accepted. *Expenses:* Tuition, state resident: full-time $4308; part-time $479 per credit hour. Tuition, nonresident: full-time $8942; part-time $994 per credit hour. Required fees: $2000; $85 per credit hour. Tuition and fees vary according to course level, course load, degree level, campus/location and program. *Financial support:* Fellowships, research assistantships, teaching assistantships, Federal Work-Study, institutionally sponsored loans, and tuition waivers (full and partial) available. Financial award application deadline: 3/15; financial award applicants required to submit FAFSA. *Unit head:* Dr. Edward L. Millner, Chair, Department of Economics, 804-828-1717, Fax: 804-828-1719, E-mail: elmillne@vcu.edu. *Application contact:* Jana P. McQuaid, Assistant Dean, Masters Programs, 804-828-4622, Fax: 804-828-7174, E-mail: jpmcquaid@vcu.edu.

Virginia Polytechnic Institute and State University, Graduate School, College of Science, Department of Economics, Blacksburg, VA 24061. Offers PhD. *Faculty:* 13 full-time (2 women). *Students:* 25 full-time (10 women), 1 part-time (0 women); includes 1 Hispanic/Latino, 21 international. Average age 30. 87 applicants, 13% accepted, 6 enrolled. In 2010, 2 doctorates awarded. *Degree requirements:* For doctorate, comprehensive exam (for some programs), thesis/dissertation (for some programs). *Entrance requirements:* For doctorate, GRE. Additional exam requirements/recommendations for international students: Required—TOEFL (minimum score 500 paper-based; 213 computer-based). *Application deadline:* For fall admission, 7/1 for domestic and international students; for spring admission, 12/1 for domestic and international students. Applications are processed on a rolling basis. Application fee: $65. Electronic applications accepted. *Expenses:* Tuition, state resident: full-time $9399; part-time $488 per credit hour. Tuition, nonresident: full-time $17,854; part-time $957.75 per credit hour. Required fees: $1534. Full-time tuition and fees vary according to program. *Financial support:* In 2010–11, 1 research assistantship with full tuition reimbursement (averaging $14,467 per year), 21 teaching assistantships with full tuition reimbursements (averaging $13,775 per year) were awarded; career-related internships or fieldwork, Federal Work-Study, scholarships/grants, health care benefits, and unspecified assistantships also available. Financial award application deadline: 1/15. Total annual research expenditures: $15,396. *Unit head:* Dr. Aris Spanos, UNIT HEAD, 540-231-7981, Fax: 540-231-5097, E-mail: aris@vt.edu. *Application contact:* Richard Ashley, Contact, 540-231-6220, Fax: 540-231-5097, E-mail: ashleyr@vt.edu.

Virginia State University, School of Graduate Studies, Research, and Outreach, School of Liberal Arts and Education, Department of Economics, Petersburg, VA 23806-0001. Offers MA. *Degree requirements:* For master's, thesis optional. *Entrance requirements:* For master's, GRE General Test. *Expenses:* Tuition, state resident: full-time $5576; part-time $335 per credit hour. Tuition, nonresident: full-time $13,402; part-time $670 per credit hour.

Washington State University, Graduate School, College of Agricultural, Human, and Natural Resource Sciences, School of Economic Sciences, Department of Economics, Pullman, WA 99164. Offers applied economics (MA); economics (MA, PhD); international business economics (Certificate). *Faculty:* 26. *Students:* 48 full-time (12 women), 2 part-time (1 woman); includes 3 minority (1 American Indian or Alaska Native, non-Hispanic/Latino; 1 Asian, non-Hispanic/Latino; 1 Hispanic/Latino), 26 international. Average age 30. 97 applicants, 21% accepted, 15 enrolled. In 2010, 8 doctorates awarded. *Degree requirements:* For master's, comprehensive exam (for some programs), thesis (for some programs), oral exam; for doctorate, comprehensive exam, thesis/dissertation, oral exam, written exam, field exams. *Entrance requirements:* For master's, GRE General Test, statement of purpose, three letters of reference, copies of all transcripts; for doctorate, GRE General Test or GMAT, statement of purpose, three letters of reference, copies of all transcripts. Additional exam requirements/recommendations for international students: Required—TOEFL, IELTS. *Application deadline:* For fall admission, 1/10 priority date for domestic students, 1/10 for international students. Applications are processed on a rolling basis. Application fee: $50. *Expenses:* Tuition, state resident: full-time $8552; part-time $443 per credit. Tuition, nonresident: full-time $21,650; part-time $1083 per credit. Required fees: $846. *Financial support:* In 2010–11, 16 research assistantships (averaging $18,204 per year), 7 teaching assistantships (averaging $18,204 per year) were awarded; career-related internships or fieldwork, Federal Work-Study, institutionally sponsored loans, tuition waivers (partial), and teaching associateships also available. Financial award application deadline: 4/1; financial award applicants required to submit FAFSA. *Faculty research:* Economic theory and quantitative methods, applied microeconomics. Total annual research expenditures: $1 million. *Unit head:* Dr. Ron C. Mittelhammer, Director, 509-335-1706, Fax: 509-335-1173, E-mail: mittelha@wsu.edu. *Application contact:* Graduate School Admissions, 800-GRADWSU, Fax: 509-335-1949, E-mail: gradsch@wsu.edu.

Washington University in St. Louis, Graduate School of Arts and Sciences, Department of Economics, St. Louis, MO 63130-4899. Offers PhD. Terminal master's awarded for partial completion of doctoral program. *Degree requirements:* For doctorate, one foreign language, thesis/dissertation. *Entrance requirements:* For doctorate, GRE General Test, GRE Subject Test. Electronic applications accepted.

Wayne State University, College of Liberal Arts and Sciences, Department of Economics, Detroit, MI 48202. Offers MA, PhD, JD/MA. *Faculty:* 24 full-time (4 women), 4 part-time/adjunct (0 women). *Students:* 49 full-time (18 women), 22 part-time (9 women); includes 13 minority (8 Black or African American, non-Hispanic/Latino; 5 Asian, non-Hispanic/Latino), 24 international. Average age 32. 72 applicants, 51% accepted, 19 enrolled. In 2010, 13 master's, 9 doctorates awarded. *Degree requirements:* For master's, thesis optional; for doctorate, thesis/dissertation. *Entrance requirements:* For master's, minimum GPA of 3.0; for doctorate, GRE, minimum GPA of 3.0. Additional exam requirements/recommendations for international students: Required—TOEFL (minimum score 550 paper-based; 213 computer-based); Recommended—TWE (minimum score 6). *Application deadline:* For fall admission, 7/1 for domestic students, 6/1 for international students; for winter admission, 10/1 for international students; for spring admission, 2/1 for international students. Applications are processed on a rolling basis. Application fee: $30 ($50 for international students). Electronic applications accepted. *Expenses:* Tuition, state resident: full-time $7662; part-time $478.85 per credit hour. Tuition, nonresident: full-time $16,920; part-time $1057.55 per credit hour. Required fees: $571.20; $35.70 per credit hour. $188.05 per semester. Tuition and fees vary according to course load and program. *Financial support:* In 2010–11, 2 fellowships with tuition reimbursements (averaging $17,875 per year), 2 research assistantships (averaging $21,078 per year), 20 teaching assistantships with tuition reimbursements (averaging $15,181 per year) were awarded; institutionally sponsored loans and tuition waivers (full and partial) also available. Support available to part-time students. Financial award application deadline: 3/1. *Faculty research:* Health economics, international economics, macro economics, urban and labor economics, econometrics. *Unit head:* Li Way Lee, Chair, 313-577-3345, Fax: 313-577-0149, E-mail: aa1313@wayne.edu. *Application contact:* Allen Goodman, Director, 313-577-3235, E-mail: allen.goodman@wayne.edu.

Western Illinois University, School of Graduate Studies, College of Business and Technology, Department of Economics and Decision Sciences, Macomb, IL 61455-1390. Offers community development (Certificate); economics (MA). Part-time programs available. *Students:* 25 full-time (5 women), 1 part-time (0 women); includes 1 minority (Black or African American, non-Hispanic/Latino), 19 international. Average age 27. 32 applicants, 78% accepted. In 2010, 19 master's awarded. *Degree requirements:* For master's, thesis or alternative. *Entrance requirements:* Additional exam requirements/recommendations for international students: Required—TOEFL (minimum score 550 paper-based; 213 computer-based; 80 iBT). *Application deadline:* Applications are processed on a rolling basis. Application fee: $30. Electronic applications accepted. *Expenses:* Tuition, state resident: full-time $6370; part-time $265.40 per credit hour. Tuition, nonresident: full-time $12,740; part-time $530.80 per credit hour. Required fees: $75.67 per credit hour. *Financial support:* In 2010–11, 6 students received support, including 6 research assistantships with full tuition reimbursements available (averaging $7,280 per year). Financial award applicants required to submit FAFSA. *Unit head:* Dr. Tej Kaul, Chairperson, 309-298-1153. *Application contact:* Evelyn Hoing, Assistant Director of Graduate Studies, 309-298-1806, Fax: 309-298-2345, E-mail: grad-office@wiu.edu.

Western Michigan University, Graduate College, College of Arts and Sciences, Department of Economics, Kalamazoo, MI 49008. Offers applied economics (MA, PhD). *Degree requirements:* For master's, thesis, oral or written exams; for doctorate, thesis/dissertation, oral exam, internship. *Entrance requirements:* For doctorate, GRE General Test.

West Texas A&M University, College of Business, Department of Accounting, Economics, and Finance, Program in Finance and Economics, Canyon, TX 79016-0001. Offers MS. Part-time and evening/weekend programs available. Postbaccalaureate distance learning degree programs offered (minimal on-campus study). *Degree requirements:* For master's, comprehensive exam, thesis optional. *Entrance requirements:* For master's, GMAT. Additional exam requirements/recommendations for international students: Required—TOEFL (minimum score 550 paper-based). Electronic applications accepted. *Faculty research:* International trade composition, cycle of poverty, trade effects in Asian countries, structural problems in Japanese economy, reform and the US sugar program-Nebraska.

West Virginia University, College of Business and Economics, Division of Economics and Finance, Morgantown, WV 26506. Offers business analysis (MA); developmental financial economics (PhD); environmental and resource economics (PhD); international economics (PhD); mathematical economics (MA); monetary economics (PhD); public finance (PhD); public policy (MA); regional and urban economics (PhD); statistics and economics (MA). Terminal master's awarded for partial completion of doctoral program. *Degree requirements:* For master's, thesis optional; for doctorate, comprehensive exam, thesis/dissertation. *Entrance requirements:* For master's and doctorate, GRE General Test, minimum GPA of 3.0; course work in intermediate microeconomics, intermediate macroeconomics, calculus, and statistics. Additional exam requirements/recommendations for international students: Required—TOEFL. Electronic applications accepted. *Faculty research:* Financial economics, regional/urban development, public economics, international trade/international finance/development economics, monetary economics.

Wichita State University, Graduate School, W. Frank Barton School of Business, Department of Economics, Wichita, KS 67260. Offers business economics (MA); economic analysis (MA). Part-time and evening/weekend programs available. *Unit head:* Dr. Jen-Chi Cheng, Chair, 316-978-3220, Fax: 316-978-3845, E-mail: jenchi.cheng@wichita.edu. *Application contact:* Dr. Philip Hersch, Graduate Coordinator, 316-978-3220, Fax: 316-978-3845, E-mail: philip.hersch@wichita.edu.

Wilfrid Laurier University, Faculty of Graduate and Postdoctoral Studies, Faculty of Arts and School of Business and Economics, Global Governance Program, Waterloo, ON N2L 3C5, Canada. Offers conflict and security (PhD); global environment (PhD); global justice and human rights (PhD); global political economy (PhD); global social governance (PhD); multilateral institutions and diplomacy (PhD). *Faculty:* 27 full-time (7 women). *Students:* 14 full-time (7 women), 4 international. 83 applicants, 5% accepted, 3 enrolled. *Degree requirements:* For doctorate, thesis/dissertation. *Entrance requirements:* For doctorate, MA in political science, history, economics, international development studies, international peace studies, globalization studies, environmental studies or related field with minimum A-. Additional exam requirements/recommendations for international students: Required—TOEFL (minimum score 89 iBT). *Application deadline:* For fall admission, 1/31 priority date for domestic and international students. Application fee: $100. Electronic applications accepted. Tuition and fees charges are reported in Canadian dollars. *Expenses:* Tuition, area resident: Full-time $15,300 Canadian dollars; part-time $1200 Canadian dollars per credit. International tuition: $21,300 Canadian dollars full-time. Required fees: $650 Canadian dollars; $100 Canadian dollars per credit. Tuition and fees vary according to course load, degree level, campus/location and program. *Financial support:* In 2010–11, 4 fellowships, 4 teaching assistantships were awarded; career-related internships or fieldwork, scholarships/grants, health care benefits, and unspecified assistantships also available. *Faculty research:* Global political economy, global environment, conflict and security, global justice and human rights, multilateral institutions and diplomacy. *Unit head:* Dr. Randall Wigle, Associate Director, 519-884-1970 Ext. 2438, Fax: 519-884-8454, E-mail: rwigle@wlu.ca. *Application contact:* Jennifer Willaims, Student Contact, 519-884-0710 Ext. 3536, Fax: 519-884-1020, E-mail: gradstudies@wlu.ca.

Wilfrid Laurier University, Faculty of Graduate and Postdoctoral Studies, School of Business and Economics, Department of Business, Waterloo, ON N2L 3C5, Canada. Offers accounting (PhD); finance (M Fin); financial economics (PhD); marketing (PhD); operations and supply chain management (PhD); organizational behavior and human resource management (M Sc); organizational behaviour and human resource management (PhD); supply chain management (M Sc); technology management (EMTM). Part-time and evening/weekend programs available. *Faculty:* 67 full-time (20 women), 12 part-time/adjunct (4 women). *Students:* 20 full-time (11 women), 1 part-time (0 women), 5 international. 80 applicants, 28% accepted, 3 enrolled. In 2010, 6 master's, 1 doctorate awarded. *Degree requirements:* For master's, thesis optional; for doctorate, comprehensive exam, thesis/dissertation. *Entrance requirements:* For master's, GMAT, 4-year honors degree with minimum B+ average; for doctorate, GMAT, master's degree, minimum B+ average. Additional exam requirements/recommendations for international students: Required—TOEFL (minimum score 89 iBT). *Application deadline:* For fall admission, 1/15 priority date for domestic and international students. Application fee: $125. Electronic applications accepted. Tuition and fees charges are reported in Canadian dollars. *Expenses:* Tuition, area resident: Full-time $15,300 Canadian dollars; part-time $1200 Canadian dollars per credit. International tuition: $21,300 Canadian dollars full-time. Required fees: $650 Canadian dollars; $100 Canadian dollars per credit. Tuition and fees vary according to course load, degree level, campus/location and program. *Financial support:* In 2010–11, 27 fellowships, 1 research assistantship, 27 teaching assistantships were awarded; career-related internships or fieldwork, scholarships/grants, health care benefits, and unspecified assistantships also available. *Faculty research:* Financial economics, management and organizational behavior, operations and supply chain management. *Unit head:* Dr. Hamid Noori, Director, 519-884-0710 Ext. 2571, Fax: 519-884-2357, E-mail: sbephdmasters@wlu.ca. *Application contact:* Jennifer Williams, Graduate Admission and Records Officer, 519-884-0710 Ext. 3536, Fax: 519-884-1020, E-mail: gradstudies@wlu.ca.

Wilfrid Laurier University, Faculty of Graduate and Postdoctoral Studies, School of Business and Economics, Department of Economics, Waterloo, ON N2L 3C5, Canada. Offers MA. *Faculty:* 19 full-time (7 women), 2 part-time/adjunct (0 women). *Students:* 28 full-time (12 women), 5 international. 68 applicants, 49% accepted, 16 enrolled. In 2010, 13 master's awarded. *Entrance requirements:* For master's, honors BA or the equivalent in economics, minimum B average in undergraduate course work. Additional exam requirements/recommendations for international students: Required—TOEFL (minimum score 89 iBT). *Application deadline:* For fall admission, 2/1 priority date for domestic and international students. Application fee: $100. Electronic applications accepted. Tuition and fees charges are reported in Canadian dollars. *Expenses:* Tuition, area resident: Full-time $15,300 Canadian dollars; part-time $1200 Canadian dollars per credit. International tuition: $21,300 Canadian dollars full-time. Required fees: $650 Canadian dollars; $100 Canadian dollars per credit. Tuition and fees vary according to course load, degree level, campus/location and program. *Financial support:* In 2010–11, 34 fellowships, 34 teaching assistantships were awarded; career-related internships or fieldwork, scholarships/grants, health care benefits, and unspecified assistantships also available. *Faculty research:* Economic forecasting, economic policy analysis, industry and market studies, financial economics, strategic planning, public policy and business. *Unit head:* Dr. Steffan Ziss, Chairperson, 519-884-1970 Ext. 2776, E-mail: sziss@wlu.ca. *Application contact:* Jennifer Williams, Graduate Admissions and Records Officer, 519-884-0710 Ext. 3536, Fax: 519-884-1020, E-mail: gradstudies@wlu.ca.

Wright State University, School of Graduate Studies, Raj Soin College of Business, Department of Economics, Dayton, OH 45435. Offers business economics (MBA); social and applied economics (MS); MBA/MS. *Entrance requirements:* For master's, GRE General Test. Additional exam requirements/recommendations for international students: Required—TOEFL.

Yale University, Graduate School of Arts and Sciences, Department of Economics, New Haven, CT 06520. Offers economics (PhD); international and development economics (MA). *Degree requirements:* For doctorate, thesis/dissertation. *Entrance requirements:* For master's, GRE General Test; for doctorate, GRE General Test, GRE Subject Test. *Faculty research:* Economic history of Western Europe, environmental economics, economic growth and development.

Yorktown University, School of Government, Denver, CO 80246. Offers American culture and the life of the citizen (MA); foundations of democracy in America and Western Europe (MA); political economy (MA); political theory (MA).

York University, Faculty of Graduate Studies, Faculty of Arts, Program in Economics, Toronto, ON M3J 1P3, Canada. Offers MA, PhD. Part-time programs available. *Degree requirements:* For doctorate, comprehensive exam, thesis/dissertation. Electronic applications accepted.

Youngstown State University, Graduate School, College of Liberal Arts and Social Sciences, Department of Economics, Youngstown, OH 44555-0001. Offers economics (MA); financial economics (MA). Part-time programs available. *Degree requirements:* For master's, comprehensive exam, thesis optional. *Entrance requirements:* For master's, minimum GPA of 2.7, 21 hours in economics. Additional exam requirements/recommendations for international students: Required—TOEFL. *Faculty research:* Forecasting, applied econometrics, labor economics, applied macroeconomics, industrial organization.

International Economics

Claremont Graduate University, Graduate Programs, School of Politics and Economics, Department of Economics, Claremont, CA 91711-6160. Offers business and financial economics (MA, PhD); economic development (Certificate); economics (PhD); industrial organization (PhD); international and development economics (PhD); international economics policy and development (MA); international money and finance (PhD); neuroeconomics (PhD); political economy and public policy (MA); public choice and public economics (PhD); MBA/PhD. Part-time programs available. *Faculty:* 8 full-time (0 women), 1 (woman) part-time/adjunct. *Students:* 128 full-time (39 women), 14 part-time (5 women); includes 3 Black or African American, non-Hispanic/Latino; 13 Asian, non-Hispanic/Latino; 5 Hispanic/Latino; 4 Two or more races, non-Hispanic/Latino, 73 international. Average age 32. In 2010, 13 master's, 8 doctorates awarded. *Entrance requirements:* For master's and doctorate, GRE General Test or GMAT. Additional exam requirements/recommendations for international students: Required—TOEFL (minimum score 550 paper-based; 213 computer-based; 80 iBT). *Application deadline:* For fall admission, 2/1 priority date for domestic students. Applications are processed on a rolling basis. Application fee: $60. Electronic applications accepted. *Expenses:* Tuition: Full-time $35,748; part-time $1554 per unit. Required fees: $215 per semester. *Financial support:* Fellowships, research assistantships, teaching assistantships, Federal Work-Study, institutionally sponsored loans, and scholarships/grants available. Support available to part-time students. Financial award application deadline: 2/15; financial award applicants required to submit FAFSA. *Faculty research:* International and financial economics, law and economics, regulation, public choice economics. *Unit head:* Paul Zak, Chair, 909-621-8788, Fax: 909-621-8545, E-mail: paul.zak@cgu.edu. *Application contact:* Lesa Hiben, Admissions Coordinator, 909-621-8699, Fax: 909-621-7545, E-mail: lesa.hiben@cga.edu.

Eastern Michigan University, Graduate School, College of Arts and Sciences, Department of Economics, Ypsilanti, MI 48197. Offers applied economics (MA); economics (MA); health economics (MA); international economics and development (MA); trade and development (MA). Part-time and evening/weekend programs available. Postbaccalaureate distance learning degree programs offered (minimal on-campus study). *Faculty:* 11 full-time (2 women). *Students:* 25 full-time (5 women), 32 part-time (7 women); includes 19 minority (10 Black or African American, non-Hispanic/Latino; 1 American Indian or Alaska Native, non-Hispanic/Latino; 4 Asian, non-Hispanic/Latino; 4 Hispanic/Latino), 7 international. Average age 29. 50 applicants, 74% accepted, 19 enrolled. In 2010, 18 master's awarded. *Degree requirements:* For master's, thesis or alternative. *Entrance requirements:* Additional exam requirements/recommendations for international students: Required—TOEFL. *Application deadline:* Applications are processed on a rolling basis. Application fee: $35. *Financial support:* Fellowships, research assistantships with full tuition reimbursements, teaching assistantships with full tuition reimbursements, career-related internships or fieldwork, Federal Work-Study, institutionally sponsored loans, scholarships/grants, tuition waivers (partial), and unspecified assistantships available. Support available to part-time students. Financial award applicants required to submit FAFSA. *Unit head:* Dr. Raouf S. Hanna, Department Head, 734-487-3395, Fax: 734-487-9666, E-mail: rhanna@emich.edu. *Application contact:* Dr. David Crary, Advisor, 734-487-0001, Fax: 734-487-9666, E-mail: dcrary@emich.edu.

Fordham University, Graduate School of Arts and Sciences, Program in International Political Economy and Development, New York, NY 10458. Offers MA, Certificate. Part-time and evening/weekend programs available. *Students:* 44 full-time (22 women), 27 part-time (11 women); includes 1 American Indian or Alaska Native, non-Hispanic/Latino; 1 Asian, non-Hispanic/Latino; 4 Hispanic/Latino, 19 international. Average age 28. 213 applicants, 37% accepted, 36 enrolled. In 2010, 28 master's awarded. *Degree requirements:* For master's, comprehensive exam. *Entrance requirements:* For master's, GRE General Test. Additional exam requirements/recommendations for international students: Required—TOEFL (minimum score 600 paper-based; 250 computer-based). *Application deadline:* For fall admission, 1/4 priority date for domestic students; for spring admission, 11/1 for domestic students. Application fee: $70. Electronic applications accepted. *Financial support:* In 2010–11, 16 students received support, including 16 research assistantships with tuition reimbursements available (averaging $18,400 per year); career-related internships or fieldwork, institutionally sponsored loans, tuition waivers (full and partial), and unspecified assistantships also available. Financial award application deadline: 1/4; financial award applicants required to submit FAFSA. *Faculty research:* International economics, comparative international politics, international banking and finance, international development, emerging markets and country risk analysis. *Unit head:* Dr. Henry Schwalbenberg, Chair, 718-817-3866, Fax: 718-817-3518. *Application contact:* Charlene Dundie, Director of Graduate Admissions, 718-817-4420, Fax: 718-817-3566, E-mail: dundie@fordham.edu.

The Johns Hopkins University, Paul H. Nitze School of Advanced International Studies, Washington, DC 20036. Offers international development (MA, Certificate), including international economics (MA); international public policy (MIPP); international relations (PhD); international studies (Certificate); Japan studies (MA), including international economics; Korea Studies (MA), including international economics; South Asia studies (MA), including international economics; Southeast Asia studies (MA), including international economics; JD/MA; MBA/MA; MHS/MA. *Faculty:* 57 full-time (18 women), 125 part-time/adjunct (40 women). *Students:* 627 full-time (305 women), 39 part-time (24 women); includes 127 minority (18 Black or African American, non-Hispanic/Latino; 60 Asian, non-Hispanic/Latino; 32 Hispanic/Latino; 1 Native Hawaiian or other Pacific Islander, non-Hispanic/Latino; 16 Two or more races, non-Hispanic/Latino), 176 international. Average age 27. 1,753 applicants, 42% accepted, 307 enrolled. In 2010, 441 master's, 10 doctorates awarded. Terminal master's awarded for partial completion of doctoral program. *Degree requirements:* For master's, one foreign language, 4-6 International Economics courses, 5-6 functional or regional concentration courses, 2 core examinations, proficiency in a language other than native language, and capstone project; for doctorate, 2 foreign languages, thesis/dissertation, 3 comprehensive exams, economics, quantitative and qualitative course, dissertation prospectus and defense. *Entrance requirements:* For master's, GMAT or GRE General Test, previous course work in economics, foreign language, undergraduate degree; for doctorate, GRE General Test, master's degree. Additional exam requirements/recommendations for international students: Required—TOEFL (minimum score 600 paper-based; 250 computer-based; 100 iBT) or IELTS (minimum score 7). *Application deadline:* For fall admission, 1/7 for domestic and international students. Application fee: $85. Electronic applications accepted. *Expenses:* Contact institution. *Financial support:* In 2010–11, 450 students received support, including 450 fellowships (averaging $12,000 per year), 32 teaching assistantships (averaging $3,906 per year); career-related internships or fieldwork, Federal Work-Study, and scholarships/grants also available. Financial award application deadline: 2/15; financial award applicants required to submit FAFSA. *Faculty research:* Regional studies, international relations, international economics, energy and environment, international development. Total annual research expenditures: $8.1 million. *Unit head:* Sidney Jackson, Director of Admissions, 202-663-5700, Fax: 202-663-7788. *Application contact:* Admissions, 202-663-5700, Fax: 202-663-7788, E-mail: admissions.sais@jhu.edu.

The New School: A University, The New School for Social Research, Department of Economics, New York, NY 10003. Offers economics (M Phil, MA, MS, DS Sc, PhD); global finance (MS); global political economy and finance (MA). Part-time and evening/weekend programs available. Terminal master's awarded for partial completion of doctoral program. *Degree requirements:* For master's, exam; for doctorate, one foreign language, thesis/dissertation, qualifying exam. *Entrance requirements:* For master's, GRE General Test; for doctorate, GRE General Test, MA. Additional exam requirements/recommendations for international students: Required—TOEFL (minimum score 600 paper-based; 250 computer-based; 100 iBT). Electronic applications accepted. *Faculty research:* Heterodox, history of economic thought, post-Keynesian, global political economy and finance.

University of Denver, Josef Korbel School of International Studies, Denver, CO 80208. Offers conflict resolution (MA); development practice (MDP); global finance, trade and economic integration (MA); global health affairs (Certificate); homeland security (Certificate); humanitarian assistance (Certificate); international development (MA); international human rights (MA); international security (MA); international studies (MA, PhD). Part-time programs available. *Faculty:* 33 full-time (13 women), 38 part-time/adjunct (11 women). *Students:* 461 full-time (279 women), 52 part-time (27 women); includes 71 minority (8 Black or African American, non-Hispanic/Latino; 3 American Indian or Alaska Native, non-Hispanic/Latino; 25 Asian, non-Hispanic/Latino; 25 Hispanic/Latino; 2 Native Hawaiian or other Pacific Islander, non-Hispanic/Latino; 8 Two or more races, non-Hispanic/Latino), 42 international. Average age 28. 1,056 applicants, 69% accepted, 259 enrolled. In 2010, 230 master's, 5 doctorates, 42 other advanced degrees awarded. *Degree requirements:* For master's, one foreign language, thesis; for doctorate, one foreign language, thesis/dissertation. *Entrance requirements:* For master's and doctorate, GRE General Test. Additional exam requirements/recommendations for international students: Required—TOEFL (minimum score 587 paper-based; 95 iBT). *Application deadline:* For fall admission, 1/15 priority date for domestic students, 12/15 priority date for international students; for winter admission, 10/15 priority date for domestic and international students. Applications are processed on a rolling basis. Application fee: $60. Electronic applications accepted. *Expenses:* Tuition: Full-time $35,604; part-time $29,670 per year. Required fees: $687 per year. Tuition and fees vary according to program. *Financial support:* In 2010–11, 1 teaching assistantship with partial tuition reimbursement (averaging $9,999 per year) was awarded; career-related internships or fieldwork, Federal Work-Study, institutionally sponsored loans, scholarships/grants, and unspecified assistantships also available. Support available to part-time students. Financial award applicants required to submit FAFSA. *Faculty research:* Human rights and international security, international politics and economics, economic-social and political development, international technology analysis and management. *Unit head:* Ambassador Christopher R. Hill, Dean, 303-871-2539, Fax: 303-871-2124, E-mail: christopher.r.hill@du.edu. *Application contact:* Brad Miller, Director of Graduate Admissions and Financial Aid, 303-871-2989, Fax: 303-871-2124, E-mail: korbeladm@du.edu.

University of Miami, Graduate School, School of Business Administration, Department of Economics, Coral Gables, FL 33124. Offers economic development (MA, PhD); environmental economics (PhD); human resource economics (MA, PhD); international economics (MA, PhD); macroeconomics (PhD). Students admitted every two years in the fall semester. Terminal master's awarded for partial completion of doctoral program. *Degree requirements:* For master's, comprehensive exam; for doctorate, comprehensive exam, thesis/dissertation. *Entrance requirements:* For master's and doctorate, GRE General Test, minimum GPA of 3.0. Additional exam requirements/recommendations for international students: Required—TOEFL (minimum score 550 paper-based). *Faculty research:* International economics/trade, applied microeconomics, development.

University of New Mexico, Graduate School, College of Arts and Sciences, Department of Economics, Albuquerque, NM 87131-2039. Offers environmental/natural resources (MA, PhD); international/development (MA, PhD); labor/human resources (MA, PhD); public finance (MA, PhD). Part-time programs available. *Faculty:* 26 full-time (9 women), 7 part-time/adjunct (1 woman). *Students:* 47 full-time (14 women), 17 part-time (5 women); includes 2 American Indian or Alaska Native, non-Hispanic/Latino; 2 Asian, non-Hispanic/Latino; 8 Hispanic/Latino, 18 international. Average age 34. 75 applicants, 51% accepted, 15 enrolled. In 2010, 14 master's, 1 doctorate awarded. Terminal master's awarded for partial completion of doctoral program. *Degree requirements:* For master's, comprehensive exam, thesis (for some programs); for doctorate, comprehensive exam, thesis/dissertation. *Entrance requirements:* For master's and doctorate, GRE General Test, 3 letters of recommendation, letter of intent. Additional exam requirements/recommendations for international students: Required—TOEFL (minimum score 520 paper-based; 190 computer-based; 68 iBT). *Application deadline:* For fall admission, 3/1 priority date for domestic students, 3/1 for international students. Applications are processed on a rolling basis. Application fee: $50. Electronic applications accepted. *Expenses:* Tuition, state resident: full-time $5991; part-time $251 per credit hour. Tuition, nonresident: full-time $14,405; part-time $800.20 per credit hour. Tuition and fees vary according to course level, course load, program and reciprocity agreements. *Financial support:* In 2010–11, 47 students received support, including 3 fellowships with tuition reimbursements available (averaging $3,611 per year), 14 research assistantships with tuition reimbursements available (averaging $7,791 per year), 15 teaching assistantships (averaging $7,467 per year); career-related internships or fieldwork, Federal Work-Study, scholarships/grants, health care benefits, and unspecified assistantships also available. Support available to part-time students. Financial award application deadline: 3/1; financial award applicants required to submit FAFSA. *Faculty research:* Core theory, econometrics, public finance, international/development economics, labor/human resource economics, environmental/natural resource economics. Total annual research expenditures: $1.8 million. *Unit head:* Dr. Robert Berrens, Chair, 505-277-5304, Fax: 505-277-9445, E-mail: rberrens@unm.edu. *Application contact:* Shoshana Handel, Academic Advisor, 505-277-3056, Fax: 505-277-9445, E-mail: shandel@unm.edu.

Valparaiso University, Graduate School, Program in International Economics and Finance, Valparaiso, IN 46383. Offers MS. Part-time and evening/weekend programs available. *Students:* 31 full-time (15 women), 11 part-time (2 women); includes 2 minority (1 Asian, non-Hispanic/Latino; 1 Hispanic/Latino), 35 international. Average age 23. In 2010, 9 master's awarded. *Entrance requirements:* For master's, 1 semester of college level calculus; 1 statistics or quantitative methods class; 2 semesters of introductory economics; 1 introductory accounting course; minimum undergraduate GPA of 3.0; 2 letters of recommendation. Additional exam requirements/recommendations for international students: Required—TOEFL (minimum score 550 paper-based; 213 computer-based; 80 iBT). Application fee: $30 ($50 for international students). *Expenses:* Tuition: Full-time $9540; part-time $530 per credit hour. Required fees: $292; $95 per semester. Tuition and fees vary according to program. *Financial support:* Available to part-time students. Applicants required to submit FAFSA. *Unit head:* Dr. David L. Rowland, Dean, Graduate School and Continuing Education/Associate Provost, 219-464-5313, Fax: 219-464-5381, E-mail: david.rowland@valpo.edu. *Application contact:* Laura Groth, Coordinator of Student Services and Support, 219-464-5313, Fax: 219-464-5381, E-mail: laura.groth@valpo.edu.

West Virginia University, College of Business and Economics, Division of Economics and Finance, Morgantown, WV 26506. Offers business analysis (MA); developmental financial economics (PhD); environmental and resource economics (PhD); international economics (PhD); mathematical economics (MA); monetary economics (PhD); public finance (PhD); public policy (MA); regional and urban economics (PhD); statistics and economics (MA). Terminal master's awarded for partial completion of doctoral program. *Degree requirements:* For master's, thesis optional; for doctorate, comprehensive exam, thesis/dissertation. *Entrance requirements:* For master's and doctorate, GRE General Test, minimum GPA of 3.0; course work in intermediate microeconomics, intermediate macroeconomics, calculus, and statistics. Additional exam requirements/recommendations for international students: Required—TOEFL. Electronic applications accepted. *Faculty research:* Financial economics, regional/urban development, public economics, international trade/international finance/development economics, monetary economics.

Wilfrid Laurier University, Faculty of Graduate and Postdoctoral Studies, Faculty of Arts and School of Business and Economics, International Public Policy Program, Waterloo, ON N2L 3C5, Canada. Offers global governance (MIPP); human security (MIPP); international economic relations (MIPP); international environmental policy (MIPP). *Faculty:* 17 full-time (8 women). *Students:* 16 full-time (9 women), 2 international. 90 applicants, 30% accepted, 14 enrolled. In 2010, 15 master's awarded. *Entrance requirements:* For master's, honours BA with minimum B average. Additional exam requirements/recommendations for international students: Required—TOEFL (minimum score 89 iBT). *Application deadline:* For fall admission, 2/1 priority date for domestic and international students. Application fee: $100. Electronic applications accepted. Tuition and fees charges are reported in Canadian dollars. *Expenses:* Tuition, area resident: Full-time $15,300 Canadian dollars; part-time $1200 Canadian dollars per credit. International tuition: $21,300 Canadian dollars full-time. Required fees: $650 Canadian dollars; $100 Canadian dollars per credit. Tuition and fees vary according to course load, degree level, campus/location and program. *Financial support:* In 2010–11, 5 fellowships, 5 teaching assistantships were awarded; career-related internships or fieldwork, scholarships/grants, health care benefits, and unspecified assistantships also available. *Faculty research:* International environmental policy, international economic relations, human security, global

governance. *Unit head:* Dr. Terry Snodden, Graduate Coordinator, 519-884-0710 Ext. 2945, Fax: 519-884-8854, E-mail: tlevesque@wlu.ca. *Application contact:* Jennifer Williams, Graduate Admissions and Records Officer, 519-884-0710 Ext. 3536, Fax: 519-884-1020, E-mail: gradstudies@wlu.ca.

Yale University, Graduate School of Arts and Sciences, Department of Economics, Program in International and Development Economics, New Haven, CT 06520. Offers MA. *Entrance requirements:* For master's, GRE General Test.

Mineral Economics

Colorado School of Mines, Graduate School, Division of Economics and Business, Golden, CO 80401. Offers engineering and technology management (MS); mineral economics (MS, PhD). Part-time programs available. *Faculty:* 12 full-time (3 women), 8 part-time/adjunct (1 woman). *Students:* 121 full-time (22 women), 23 part-time (5 women); includes 1 Black or African American, non-Hispanic/Latino; 2 American Indian or Alaska Native, non-Hispanic/Latino; 1 Asian, non-Hispanic/Latino; 6 Hispanic/Latino, 31 international. Average age 29. 179 applicants, 72% accepted, 63 enrolled. In 2010, 70 master's, 3 doctorates awarded. *Degree requirements:* For master's, thesis (for some programs); for doctorate, comprehensive exam, thesis/dissertation. *Entrance requirements:* For master's and doctorate, GRE General Test. Additional exam requirements/recommendations for international students: Required—TOEFL (minimum score 550 paper-based; 213 computer-based; 80 iBT). *Application deadline:* For fall admission, 1/15 priority date for domestic and international students; for spring admission, 10/15 priority date for domestic and international students. Application fee: $50 ($70 for international students). Electronic applications accepted. *Expenses:* Tuition, state resident: full-time $11,550; part-time $641 per credit. Tuition, nonresident: full-time $25,980; part-time $1444 per credit. Required fees: $1874; $937 per semester. *Financial support:* In 2010–11, 45 students received support, including 6 fellowships with full tuition reimbursements available (averaging $20,000 per year), 11 research assistantships with full tuition reimbursements available (averaging $20,000 per year), 28 teaching assistantships with full tuition reimburse-

ments available (averaging $20,000 per year); scholarships/grants, health care benefits, and unspecified assistantships also available. Financial award application deadline: 1/15; financial award applicants required to submit FAFSA. *Faculty research:* International trade, resource and environmental economics, energy economics, operations research. Total annual research expenditures: $137,815. *Unit head:* Dr. Rod Eggert, Division Head, 303-273-3981, Fax: 303-273-3416, E-mail: reggert@mines.edu. *Application contact:* Kathleen A. Feighny, Administrative Faculty, 303-273-3979, Fax: 303-273-3416, E-mail: kfeighny@mines.edu.

Michigan Technological University, Graduate School, School of Business and Economics, Program in Applied Natural Resource Economics, Houghton, MI 49931. Offers MS. Part-time programs available. *Degree requirements:* For master's, GRE. Additional exam requirements/recommendations for international students: Required—TOEFL (minimum score 550 paper-based; 213 computer-based). Electronic applications accepted.

The University of Texas at Austin, Graduate School, Cockrell School of Engineering, Department of Petroleum and Geosystems Engineering, Program in Energy and Earth Resources, Austin, TX 78712-1111. Offers MA. *Degree requirements:* For master's, thesis, seminar. *Entrance requirements:* For master's, GRE General Test. Additional exam requirements/recommendations for international students: Required—TOEFL. Electronic applications accepted.

THE UNIVERSITY OF TEXAS AT DALLAS

School of Economic, Political, and Policy Sciences

Programs of Study

The School of Economic, Political, and Policy Sciences (EPPS) at the University of Texas at Dallas (UT Dallas) offers Ph.D.'s in criminology, economics, geospatial information sciences, political science, public affairs, and public policy and political economy (PPPE). It also offers master's degrees in applied sociology, criminology, economics, geospatial information sciences (in conjunction with the School of Natural Sciences), international political economy, public affairs, and public policy. Students receive education through lecture, internships, and workshop courses; a basic knowledge of statistics and computer skills is considered crucial.

The 30-hour Master of Arts in political science offers advanced instruction in the social science literature and theories regarding citizenship and governance. This program overlaps with the Ph.D. program extensively, so students who wish to continue on for that degree are able to do so without duplication in curriculum. For more information, students should contact Cheryl Berry (clb092000@utdallas.edu) or Dr. Linda Camp Keith (linda.keith@utdallas.edu).

The 30-hour Master of Arts in political science–legislative studies is a preprofessional degree for students interested in careers as staff members for state or national legislatures, political consultants, or other careers in professional politics. Students take courses on campaigns, elections, survey research, governing, and research and management skills. For more information, students should contact Cheryl Berry (clb092000@utdallas.edu) or Dr. Linda Camp Keith (linda.keith@utdallas.edu).

The 30-hour Master of Arts in political science–constitutional law studies is a degree for students interested in understanding the technical rules of law, legal practices and policies, and law more generally as a social phenomenon. This curriculum is also useful for students interested in going to law school or for students who wish to pursue a career in law that does not involve being an attorney. For more information, students should contact Cheryl Berry (clb092000@utdallas.edu) or Dr. Linda Camp Keith (linda.keith@utdallas.edu).

EPPS offers a 36-hour M.S. program in applied sociology. This includes 12 hours of core courses in applied sociology, 15 hours of core courses, and 3 hours of internship. The program is designed for students interested in areas such as nonprofit organizations and federal, state, and local government philosophy. For more information, students should contact Betsy Albritton (betsy.albritton@utdallas.edu) or Dr. Sheryl Skaggs (slskagges@utdallas.edu).

The 36-hour Master of Science in criminology provides students with a coherent and intellectually challenging degree that prepares them to conduct interdisciplinary research on various aspects of criminology and/or criminal justice, depending on their specific areas of specialty. Students will be well prepared for analytical and administrative posts in international and domestic research and policy institutions, criminal justice organizations, and the private sector. For more information, students should contact Dr. John Worrall (worrall@utdallas.edu).

The 36-hour M.S. in economics is aimed at students seeking to learn advanced economic theory and apply advanced economic tools to real socioeconomic problems. For more information, students should contact Judy Du (judy.du@utdallas.edu) or Dr. Nathan Berg (nberg@utdallas.edu).

In addition, EPPS offers a 30-hour M.S. in geospatial information sciences (GIS). Offered jointly by the School of Economic, Political, and Policy Sciences and the School of Natural Sciences and Mathematics, it focuses on the use of geographic information systems. For more information, students should contact Rita Medford (rmedford@utdallas.edu) or Dr. Denis Dean (Denis.Dean@utdallas.edu).

The School also offers a 36-hour Master of Science in international political economy (IPE) that consists of three components, including required course work (18 hours), prescribed electives (12 hours), and free electives (6 hours). Moreover, students must demonstrate a foreign language proficiency equivalent to two years of study in one foreign language before graduation. For more information, students should contact Dr. Jennifer Holmes (jholmes@utdallas.edu).

The Master of Public Affairs (M.P.A.) degree is a 42-hour, interdisciplinary program that includes 21 hours of core courses and 18 hours of directed electives as well as an internship or workshop. It explores the interrelationship between economic, political, and social institutions. Students may emphasize course work in management, policy analysis, or applied technology. The curriculum places strong emphasis upon the development of computer and statistical skills that are necessary for successful performance in both the public and private sectors in the twenty-first century. For more information, students should contact Suzzane Potts (suzanne.e.potts@utdallas.edu) or Dr. Paul Battaglio (battaglio@utdallas.edu).

The M.S. in public policy is an interdisciplinary 36-hour graduate degree designed to develop those skill sets critical for a career in which a solid understanding of the public policy process and the analysis and evaluation of public policies are essential. Specific skills include knowledge of the policy process and related ethical concerns, rigorous research skills that provide students with an essential grounding in statistical and data analysis and research design, and effective communication skills. Students will be prepared for analytical and administrative positions and responsibilities in a wide array of professional settings in the public, non-profit, and private sectors. For more information, students should contact Dr. Marie Chevrier (chevrier@utdallas.edu).

The Ph.D. degree in criminology is an interdisciplinary, research-oriented program that provides students with a coherent and intellectually challenging research degree that prepares them for an academic appointment as a university professor or an administrative appointment with oversight of research and development within criminal justice organizations. Graduates of the program will be competent to teach and conduct interdisciplinary research at both graduate and undergraduate levels in aspects of criminology and/or criminal justice, depending on their specific areas of specialty. They also will be well prepared for analytical and administrative posts in international and domestic research and policy institutions and in the private sector. For more information, students should contact Dr. John Worrall (worrall@utdallas.edu).

The Ph.D. program in economics prepares students for careers in academics as well as research-oriented positions in the private and public sector. It provides cutting-edge education in micro and macroeconomic theory, rigorous training in mathematical and econometric techniques, and extensive exposure to various research areas in economics. Students complete a set of core courses, pass comprehensive exams in microeconomic and macroeconomic theory as well as econometrics, are certified in two research areas in economics, and submit and defend a dissertation. For more information, students should contact Judy Du (judy.du@utdallas.edu) or Dr. Nathan Berg (nberg@utdallas.edu).

The Ph.D. program in geospatial information sciences, offered with the Schools of Natural Sciences and Mathematics as well as Engineering and Computer Science, offers advanced training in geographic information sciences and related fields. Students complete core courses and pass a qualifying exam before proceeding to the dissertation. For more information, students should contact Rita Medford (rmedford@utdallas.edu) or Dr. Denis Dean (Denis.Dean@utdallas.edu).

The Ph.D. in political science provides a rigorous, student-focused disciplinary program with multidisciplinary links. Students receive state-of-the-science graduate education in political methodology and the fields of democratization, globalization and international relations, institutions and processes, and public management and decision making. Students complete a set of core courses, course work in their designated major and minor fields, and examinations in the core courses and major and minor fields; students also write and defend a dissertation. For more information, students should contact Cheryl Berry (clb092000@utdallas.edu) or Dr. Linda Camp Keith (linda.keith@utdallas.edu).

The Ph.D. in public affairs is an interdisciplinary program that prepares graduates to assume positions in academe, research-producing organizations, or positions of administrative authority in public organizations. The degree is nontraditional in that it requires all students to conduct applied, field-based research as the foundation for the production of their dissertations. The Ph.D. program in public affairs is a cohort program, with entering cohorts beginning each fall semester. For more information, students should contact Suzanne Potts (suzanne.e.potts@utdallas.edu) or Dr. Richard Scotch (richard.scotch@utdallas.edu).

The Ph.D. in public policy and political economy is centered in critical thought and interdisciplinary research that explores the interaction of institutions, markets, and public policies. Students are expected to complete a set of core courses in topics related to public policy, including rigorous training in statistics and research design; students must also complete course work in two fields and a specialization and defend a dissertation. For more information, students should contact Betsy Albritton (betsy.albritton@utdallas.edu) or Dr. Paul Jargowsky (jargo@utdallas.edu).

Research Facilities

The University of Texas at Dallas has advanced computing facilities. The School of Economic, Political, and Policy Sciences also houses the Bruton Center for Development Studies and the Center for Educational Studies and is affiliated with the Cecil and Ida Green Center for Science and Society. Students have access to the computing facilities in the School of Economic, Political, and Policy Sciences and the University's Computing Center. The School's two computing laboratories house over 30 computers that are network linked and equipped with major social science software packages, including E-Views, R, RATS, SPSS, and STATA. A computerized geographic information system, the LexisNexis Database, and WestLaw are also available for student use. The University's Computing Center provides personal computers and UNIX workstations. Many important data and reference materials are available online from professional associations or at UT–D via the Library's and School's memberships in the Inter-University Consortium for Political and Social Research (ICPSR), the Roper Center, the University Consortium for Geographic Information Science (UCGIS), and other organizations. The library has a substantial number of social science journals.

Financial Aid

The School of Economic, Political, and Policy Sciences (EPPS) provides teaching assistantships that range from $1100 to $1400, depending on experience. Students who are awarded a full-time, 20-hour assistantship receive in-state tuition waivers. The School also offers tuition waivers that cover all tuition for up to 12 credit hours. Teaching assistantships and graduate studies scholarships are competitive, with GRE scores and grades being important criteria in the selection process.

Cost of Study

Tuition and fees can be expected to be in the range of $8000 to $10,000 per year for full-time in-state students taking 9 hours per semester, including summers. Costs might be higher for international and out-of-state students. Students are eligible for teaching assistantships and graduate-studies scholarships, as detailed above.

Living and Housing Costs

On-campus housing is available at Waterview Park Apartments, with rents varying from $800 to $1200 per month.

Student Group

There are 6,000 graduate students and more than 8,000 undergraduates studying at UT Dallas. UT Dallas also has a varied international student body in both graduate and undergraduate programs of study.

Location

Richardson is located just north of Dallas and south of Plano in a pleasant suburban setting. It is near the high-technology corridor that is home to Ericsson, Nortel, and numerous other telecommunications companies.

The University

UT Dallas was created in September 1969 by Act of the Sixty-First Texas Legislature, which provided for transfer of the privately funded Southwest Center for Advanced Studies (SCAS) to the state of Texas. Undergraduate and graduate programs grew rapidly. Today, UT Dallas has a distinguished faculty that includes numerous members of the National Academy of Sciences and National Academy of Engineering.

Applying

Application for admission to the graduate school can be made for fall, spring, or summer. GRE scores are required for degree-seeking students, although applicants may be admitted provisionally as nondegree students. A combined verbal and quantitative GRE score of at least 1100 is recommended for doctoral students, and a combined score of at least 1000 is recommended for master's degree students.

Correspondence and Information

Thomas Brunell, Senior Associate Dean for Academic Programs
School of Economic, Political, and Policy Sciences
800 W. Campbell Road, GR 31
The University of Texas at Dallas
Richardson, Texas 75080

E-mail: tbrunell@utdallas.edu
Web site: http://epps.utdallas.edu/

The University of Texas at Dallas

THE FACULTY AND THEIR RESEARCH

Bobby C. Alexander, Associate Professor of Sociology; Ph.D. (religious studies/social-scientific study of religion), Columbia, 1985. Religious studies.

Rodney Andrews, Assistant Professor of Economis; Ph.D. (economics), Michigan, 2007. Economics of education, labor economics.

Sheila Amin Gutiérrez de Piñeres, Professor of Economics; Ph.D. (economics), Duke, 1992. Latin American development, trade policy.

Donald R. Arbuckle, Clinical Research Professor; Ph.D. (American civilizations), Pennsylvania. Public management, bureaucratic behavior, policymaking.

Daniel Arce, Professor of Economics; Ph.D. (economics), Illinois at Urbana-Champaign, 1992. Economics, defense economics.

Philip K. Armour, Associate Professor of Sociology; Ph.D. (sociology), Berkeley, 1979. Sociology of religion, medical sociology.

James C. Barnes, Assistant Professor of Criminology; Ph.D. (criminology), Florida State, 2010. Biosocial factors that influence antisocial behavior.

Brian A. Bearry, Senior Lecturer of Political Science; Ph.D. (political science), North Texas, 2006. American political thought.

Paul Battaglio, Assistant Professor of Public Affairs; Ph.D. (public administration), Georgia, 2005. Comparative policy and administration, public human resource management, comparative political attitudes.

Ted Benavides, Senior Lecturer; M.P.A., SMU, 1994. Public management, human resources management.

Nathan Berg, Associate Professor of Economics; Ph.D. (economics), Kansas, 2001. Finance, behavioral economics.

Kurt J. Beron, Professor of Economics and Political Economy; Ph.D. (economics), North Carolina at Chapel Hill, 1985. Education policy, tax compliance, Internet economics.

Brian J. L. Berry, Lloyd Viel Berkner Regental Professor, Professor of Political Economy, and Dean; Ph.D. (geography), Washington (Seattle), 1958. Urban economics and geography, development, cycles of growth and decline..

Denise Paquette Boots, Assistant Professor; Ph.D. (criminology), South Florida, 2006. American correction systems, family and interpersonal violence, juvenile delinquency.

Patrick T. Brandt, Assistant Professor of Political Science; Ph.D. (political science), Indiana, 2001. Presidency, congressional behavior, time series analysis, Bayesian econometrics.

Timothy Bray, Clinical Assistant Professor of Criminology and Sociology; Ph.D. (criminology), Missouri–St. Louis, 2002. Criminology.

Thomas Brunell, Professor of Political Science; Ph.D. (political science), California, Irvine, 1997. Representation, congressional elections, redistricting.

Anthony Champagne, Professor of Political Science; Ph.D. (political science), Illinois, 1973. Law and public policy, judicial politics.

Marie Isabelle Chevrier, Professor of Public Policy and Political Economy; Ph.D. (public policy), Harvard, 1991. Arms control, international negotiation.

Yongwan Chun, Clinical Assistant Professor of GIS; Ph.D. (GIS), Ohio State, 2007. Spatial analysis and modeling, spatial statistics.

Harold D. Clarke, Professor of Political Science and Program Head for Political Science; Ph.D. (political science), Duke, 1971. Electoral behavior, public opinion and political support.

Rachel Croson, Professor of Economics; Ph.D. (economics), Harvard, 1994. Economics, experimental economics, behavioral economics.

Kruti R. Dholakia, Clinical Assistant Professor of Political Economy; Ph.D. (public policy and political economy), Texas at Dallas, 2006. Methodology, global economy, development economics, health policy.

Lloyd J. Dumas, Professor of Public Policy and Political Economy; Ph.D. (economics), Columbia, 1972. International security, economic conversion, human and technical reliability.

Catherine C. Eckel, Professor of Economics; Ph.D. (economics), Virginia, 1983. Experimental economics, risk and decision making, economic education.

Euel Elliott, Professor of Public Policy and Political Economy, Senior Associate Dean, and Director of Graduate Studies; Ph.D. (political science), Duke, 1987. Public policy (general), regulatory policy, electoral behavior, nonlinear dynamics.

Simon Fass, Associate Professor of Public Policy and Political Economy; Ph.D. (urban planning), UCLA, 1978. Economic and political development.

Doug Goodman, Associate Professor of Public Affairs; Ph.D. (political science), Utah, 2002. Public human resource management.

Daniel Griffith, Ashbel Smith Professor of Geography and Geospatial Sciences; Ph.D. (geography), Toronto, 1978. Spatial statistics, quantitative urban-economic geography, applied statistics.

Jeremy Hall, Assistant Professor of Public Affairs; Ph.D. (public administration), Kentucky, 2005. Human resource management, public budgeting.

Edward J. Harpham, Professor of Political Science and Political Economy and Director of Collegium V Honors Program; Ph.D. (government), Cornell, 1980. Political theory, public policy.

Wendy L. Hassett, Clinical Associate Professor; Ph.D. (public administration and public policy), Auburn, 2003. Public management, human resource development.

Jennifer S. Holmes, Associate Professor of Political Economy; Ph.D. (political science), Minnesota, 1998. Political violence, terrorism, and political development.

Donald A. Hicks, Professor of Public Policy and Political Economy and Vice Chairman, Bruton Center for Development Studies; Ph.D. (sociology), North Carolina at Chapel Hill, 1976. Urban and regional policy, technology innovation and diffusion.

Bruce Jacobs, Professor of Sociology and Criminology; Ph.D. (sociology), USC, 1994. Street offenders, drugs and crime, qualitative methods.

Paul A. Jargowsky, Professor of Sociology and of Public Policy and Political Economy; Ph.D. (public policy), Harvard, 1991. Welfare policy.

Linda Camp Keith, Associate Professor of Political Science; Ph.D. (political science), North Texas, 1999. Public law/judicial process, human rights.

L. Douglas Kiel, Professor of Public Administration; Ph.D. (political science), Oklahoma, 1986. Public administration, organizational change, productivity improvement, nonlinear dynamics.

Brandon Kinne, Assistant Professor of Political Science; Ph.D. (political science), Yale, 2009. International conflict and social networks.

Tom Kovandzic, Associate Professor of Criminology; Ph.D. (criminal justice and criminology), Florida State, 1999. Firearms and violence, criminal justice policy, quantitative methods, inequality and crime, and policing, with particular interest in use of econometric methods as a tool to evaluate criminal justice policy initiatives.

Murray Leaf, Professor of Public Policy and Political Economy; Ph.D. (social anthropology), Chicago, 1966. Comparative social and economic development.

Xin Li, Assistant Professor of Economics; Ph.D. (economics), Michigan, 2006. Public economics, labor economics, experimental economics, economics of the Internet.

Robert Lowry, Professor of Political Science and of Public Policy and Political Economy and Program Head for Political Science; Ph.D. (political science), Harvard, 1993. Institutions and organizations, methodology.

Sarah Maxwell, Clinical Assistant Professor and Assistant Dean for Undergraduate Education; Ph.D. (public policy), George Mason, 2004. Youth, crime prevention, and public policy.

James W. Marquart, Professor of Criminology and Program Head for Criminology; Ph.D. (sociology), Texas A&M, 1983. Criminology, legal reform, victimology, health issues in prison populations, community-based corrections.

Susan McElroy, Associate Professor of Economics and Political Economy; Ph.D. (economics of education), Stanford, 1996. Education policy.

Banks Miller, Assistant Professor of Political Science; Ph.D. (political science), Ohio State, 2009. Judicial behavior, state supreme courts.

Robert Morris, Assistant Professor of Criminology; Ph.D. (criminology), Sam Houston State, 2007. White-collar offending over the life course, computer crime and computer deviance, identity theft, quantitative methods.

Stuart B. Murchison, Clinical Associate Professor of Geospatial Sciences and Geography; Ph.D. (geography), Utah, 1989. Remote sensing, global positioning systems.

James C. Murdoch, Professor of Economics and Program Head for Economics; Ph.D. (economics), Wyoming, 1982. Environmental policy, public goods provision, coalition theory.

Clint W. Peinhardt, Assistant Professor of Political Science; Ph.D. (political science), Michigan, 2004. International political economy, economic development and transition, formal modeling.

Fang Qiu, Associate Professor of Geospatial Sciences and Political Economy; Ph.D. (geography), South Carolina, 2000. Geographic information sciences (GIS), remote sensing.

Todd Sandler, Professor of Economics and Political Science; Ph.D. (economics), SUNY at Binghamton, 1971. International relations, public economics, collective action, theories of terrorism.

Richard K. Scotch, Professor of Sociology and of Public Policy and Political Economy; Ph.D. (sociology), Harvard, 1982. Social policy, health policy, disabilities policy.

Barry J. Seldon, Professor of Economics; Ph.D. (economics), Duke, 1985. Microeconomics, industrial organization, advertising.

Kevin Siqueira, Associate Professor of Economics; Ph.D. (economics), Iowa State, 1998. Public economics, environmental economics, microeconomic theory, game theory.

Sheryl Skaggs, Associate Professor of Sociology; Ph.D. (sociology), North Carolina State, 2001. Work, organizations and industry, social inequality.

Donggyu Sul, Professor of Economics; Ph.D. (economics), Ohio State, 1992. Econometrics and international finance.

Marianne C. Stewart, Professor of Political Science; Ph.D. (political science), Duke, 1986. Comparative politics, Anglo-American voting behavior, political participation.

Robert Taylor, Professor of Public Affairs; Ph.D. (urban affairs), Portland State, 1981. Law enforcement, policing, anti-terrorism.

Gregory S. Thielemann, Associate Professor of Political Economy; Ph.D. (political science), Rice, 1988. Southern politics, gay and lesbian politics.

Michael Tiefelsdorf, Associate Professor of Geography and Geospatial Sciences; Ph.D. (geography), Free University of Berlin, 1988. Spatial processes, spatial statistics, quantitative geography.

Lynne Vieraitis, Associate Professor of Criminology; Ph.D. (criminal justice and criminology), Florida State, 2000. Inequality and crime, gender and crime, violence against women, theoretical criminology.

John L. Worrall, Professor of Criminology; Ph.D. (political science), Washington State, 1999. Crime central policy, legal issues in policing, methodology.

Section 20
Family and Consumer Sciences

This section contains a directory of institutions offering graduate work in family and consumer sciences. Additional information about programs listed in the directory may be obtained by writing directly to the dean of a graduate school or chair of a department at the address given in the directory.

For programs offering related work, see also in this book *Economics, Psychology and Counseling,* and *Sociology, Anthropology, and Archaeology.* In another guide in this series:

Graduate Programs in Business, Education, Health, Information Studies, Law & Social Work

See *Social Work*

CONTENTS

Program Directories

Close-Up and Display

See:

Family and Consumer Sciences—General

Alabama Agricultural and Mechanical University, School of Graduate Studies, School of Agricultural and Environmental Sciences, Department of Family and Consumer Sciences, Huntsville, AL 35811. Offers family and consumer sciences (MS); food science (MS, PhD). Part-time and evening/weekend programs available. *Degree requirements:* For master's, comprehensive exam, thesis optional; for doctorate, one foreign language, thesis/dissertation. *Entrance requirements:* For master's, GRE General Test; for doctorate, GRE General Test, MS. Additional exam requirements/recommendations for international students: Required—TOEFL (minimum score 500 paper-based; 173 computer-based; 61 iBT). Electronic applications accepted. *Faculty research:* Food biotechnology, nutrition, food microbiology, food engineering, food chemistry.

Ball State University, Graduate School, College of Applied Science and Technology, Department of Family and Consumer Sciences, Muncie, IN 47306-1099. Offers MA, MS. *Faculty:* 23. *Students:* 20 full-time (15 women), 107 part-time (97 women); includes 5 minority (2 Black or African American, non-Hispanic/Latino; 1 Hispanic/Latino; 2 Two or more races, non-Hispanic/Latino), 10 international. Average age 25. 82 applicants, 82% accepted, 21 enrolled. In 2010, 14 master's awarded. *Entrance requirements:* For master's, resume. Application fee: $25 ($35 for international students). *Expenses:* Tuition, state resident: full-time $6160; part-time $299 per credit hour. Tuition, nonresident: full-time $16,020; part-time $783 per credit hour. Required fees: $2278; $95 per credit hour. *Financial support:* In 2010–11, 1 research assistantship with full tuition reimbursement (averaging $9,033 per year), 13 teaching assistantships with full tuition reimbursements (averaging $9,033 per year) were awarded; career-related internships or fieldwork also available. Financial award application deadline: 3/1. *Faculty research:* Maternal and infant nutrition, nutrition education. *Unit head:* Dr. Jay Kandiah, Head, 765-285-5932, Fax: 765-285-2314, E-mail: aspangler@bsu.edu. *Application contact:* Dr. Robert Morris, Associate Provost for Research and Dean of the Graduate School, 765-285-5723, Fax: 765-285-1328, E-mail: rmorris@bsu.edu.

Bowling Green State University, Graduate College, College of Education and Human Development, School of Family and Consumer Sciences, Bowling Green, OH 43403. Offers food and nutrition (MFCS); human development and family studies (MFCS). Part-time programs available. *Degree requirements:* For master's, thesis. *Entrance requirements:* For master's, GRE General Test, minimum GPA of 3.0. Additional exam requirements/recommendations for international students: Required—TOEFL. Electronic applications accepted. *Faculty research:* Public health, wellness, social issues and policies, ethnic foods, nutrition and aging.

California State University, Fresno, Division of Graduate Studies, College of Agricultural Sciences and Technology, Department of Child, Family and Consumer Sciences, Fresno, CA 93740-8027. Offers family and consumer sciences (MS). Currently not accepting applications. Part-time and evening/weekend programs available. *Degree requirements:* For master's, thesis (for some programs). *Entrance requirements:* For master's, GRE General Test, minimum GPA of 3.0 in last 60 hours. Additional exam requirements/recommendations for international students: Required—TOEFL. Electronic applications accepted

California State University, Long Beach, Graduate Studies, College of Health and Human Services, Department of Family and Consumer Sciences, Long Beach, CA 90840. Offers family and consumer sciences (MA); nutritional science (MS), including food science, hospitality foodservice and hotel management, nutritional science. Part-time and evening/weekend programs available. *Faculty:* 6 full-time (4 women). *Students:* 31 full-time (all women), 21 part-time (20 women); includes 1 Black or African American, non-Hispanic/Latino; 7 Asian, non-Hispanic/Latino; 4 Hispanic/Latino, 1 international. Average age 26. 129 applicants, 37% accepted, 24 enrolled. In 2010, 16 master's awarded. *Degree requirements:* For master's, comprehensive exam or thesis. *Entrance requirements:* For master's, GRE (MS), minimum GPA of 3.0. *Application deadline:* For fall admission, 5/1 for domestic students. Applications are processed on a rolling basis. Application fee: $55. Electronic applications accepted. *Financial support:* Federal Work-Study, institutionally sponsored loans, and scholarships/grants available. Financial award application deadline: 3/2. *Faculty research:* School uniforms, consumer complaining behavior, nutrition and fitness education and behavior change, curriculum change, teaching experience of interns. *Unit head:* Dr. Wendy Reiboldt, Chair, 562-985-8250, Fax: 562-985-4414, E-mail: reiboldt@csulb.edu. *Application contact:* Dr. Jacqueline Lee, Graduate Coordinator, 562-985-4545, Fax: 562-985-4414, E-mail: jjlee@csulb.edu.

California State University, Northridge, Graduate Studies, College of Health and Human Development, Department of Family and Consumer Sciences, Northridge, CA 91330. Offers MS. Part-time and evening/weekend programs available. *Degree requirements:* For master's, thesis, project, or comprehensive exam. *Entrance requirements:* For master's, GRE General Test or minimum GPA of 3.0. Additional exam requirements/recommendations for international students: Required—TOEFL.

Central Michigan University, College of Graduate Studies, College of Education and Human Services, Department of Human Environmental Studies, Mount Pleasant, MI 48859. Offers apparel product development and merchandising technology (MS); gerontology (Graduate Certificate); human development and family studies (MA); nutrition and dietetics (MS). Part-time and evening/weekend programs available. *Faculty:* 15 full-time (11 women), 1 (woman) part-time/adjunct. *Students:* 6 full-time (4 women), 24 part-time (22 women); includes 2 Black or African American, non-Hispanic/Latino, 4 international. *Degree requirements:* For master's, thesis or alternative. *Application deadline:* Applications are processed on a rolling basis. Application fee: $35 ($45 for international students). Electronic applications accepted. *Expenses:* Tuition, state resident: full-time $8208; part-time $456 per credit hour. Tuition, nonresident: full-time $13,788; part-time $766 per credit hour. One-time fee: $25. *Financial support:* Fellowships with tuition reimbursements, research assistantships, career-related internships or fieldwork, Federal Work-Study, unspecified assistantships, and out-of-state merit awards, non-resident graduate awards available. *Faculty research:* Human growth and development, family studies and human sexuality, human nutrition and dietetics, apparel and textile retailing, computer-aided design for apparel. *Unit head:* Dr. Megan P. Goodwin, Chairperson, 989-774-3218, Fax: 989-774-2435, E-mail: goodw1mp@cmich.edu. *Application contact:* Dr. Candace Maylee, Assistant Coordinator of Graduate Programs, 989-774-2613, Fax: 989-774-2435, E-mail: mayle1ce@cmich.edu.

Central Washington University, Graduate Studies and Research, College of Education and Professional Studies, Department of Family and Consumer Sciences, Ellensburg, WA 98926. Offers family and consumer sciences education (MS); family studies (MS). Part-time programs available. *Degree requirements:* For master's, thesis or alternative. *Entrance requirements:* For master's, minimum GPA of 3.0. Additional exam requirements/recommendations for international students: Required—TOEFL (minimum score 550 paper-based; 213 computer-based; 79 iBT). Electronic applications accepted.

Eastern Illinois University, Graduate School, Lumpkin College of Business and Applied Sciences, School of Family and Consumer Sciences, Charleston, IL 61920-3099. Offers dietetics (MS); family and consumer sciences (MS). Part-time programs available. *Degree requirements:* For master's, comprehensive exam.

Florida State University, The Graduate School, College of Human Sciences, Tallahassee, FL 32306-1490. Offers MS, PhD. *Accreditation:* AAMFT/COAMFTE. Part-time programs available. *Faculty:* 41 full-time (27 women). *Students:* 135 full-time (87 women), 35 part-time (27 women); includes 20 Black or African American, non-Hispanic/Latino; 4 Asian, non-Hispanic/Latino; 10 Hispanic/Latino; 1 Two or more races, non-Hispanic/Latino, 31 international. 198 applicants, 47% accepted, 44 enrolled. In 2010, 45 master's, 18 doctorates awarded. *Degree requirements:* For master's, comprehensive exam (for some programs), thesis optional; for doctorate, thesis/dissertation. *Entrance requirements:* For master's, GRE General Test, minimum upper-division GPA of 3.0; for doctorate, GRE General Test, minimum upper-division GPA of 3.0, master's

degree. Additional exam requirements/recommendations for international students: Required—TOEFL (minimum score 570 paper-based; 80 iBT). *Application deadline:* For fall admission, 7/1 for domestic and international students; for spring admission, 11/1 for domestic and international students. Applications are processed on a rolling basis. Application fee: $30. Electronic applications accepted. *Expenses:* Tuition, state resident: full-time $8238.24. *Financial support:* In 2010–11, 105 students received support, including 2 fellowships with partial tuition reimbursements available (averaging $12,650 per year), 30 research assistantships with partial tuition reimbursements available (averaging $6,980 per year), 70 teaching assistantships with partial tuition reimbursements available (averaging $10,051 per year); career-related internships or fieldwork, Federal Work-Study, institutionally sponsored loans, scholarships/grants, and unspecified assistantships also available. Financial award application deadline: 1/15; financial award applicants required to submit FAFSA. *Faculty research:* Body composition, functional food, chronic disease and aging response; food safety, food allergy, and safety/quality detection methods; sports nutrition, energy balance and human performance; families at risk and relational interventions; parenting, martial process and family therapy. Total annual research expenditures: $1.6 million. *Unit head:* Dr. Billie J. Collier, Dean, 850-644-1281, Fax: 850-644-0700, E-mail: bcollier@fsu.edu. *Application contact:* Tara L. Hartman, Academic Program Specialist, 850-644-7221, Fax: 850-644-0700, E-mail: thartman@fsu.edu.

Fontbonne University, Graduate Programs, Department of Human Environmental Sciences, St. Louis, MO 63105-3098. Offers family and consumer sciences (MA). *Faculty:* 4 full-time (all women), 3 part-time/adjunct (all women). *Students:* 6 full-time (all women), 4 part-time (all women); includes 1 Black or African American, non-Hispanic/Latino. Average age 33. In 2010, 3 master's awarded. *Degree requirements:* For master's, action paper/presentation portfolio. *Entrance requirements:* For master's, minimum GPA of 3.0. *Application deadline:* For fall admission, 8/8 priority date for domestic students; for spring admission, 1/8 priority date for domestic students. Application fee: $25. *Expenses:* Tuition: Full-time $11,328. Full-time tuition and fees vary according to program. *Financial support:* Application deadline: 4/1. *Faculty research:* Early intervention, public policy: children and families, program designer. *Unit head:* Cheryl Houston, Chairperson, 314-719-8020, Fax: 314-719-8615. *Application contact:* Dr. Janine Duncan, Program Director, 314-719-3639, Fax: 314-719-8015.

Hofstra University, School of Education, Health, and Human Services, Programs in Teaching K-12, Hempstead, NY 11549. Offers bilingual education (MS Ed); bilingual extension (CAS); including education/speech language pathology, intensive teacher institute; family and consumer science (MS Ed); fine art and music education (Advanced Certificate); fine arts education (MA, MS Ed); middle childhood extension (Advanced Certificate), including grades 5-6 or 7-9; music education (MA, MS Ed); teaching languages other than English and TESOL (MS Ed); TESOL (MS Ed); wind conducting (MA). Part-time and evening/weekend programs available. *Students:* 65 full-time (55 women), 67 part-time (52 women); includes 8 Black or African American, non-Hispanic/Latino; 8 Asian, non-Hispanic/Latino; 16 Hispanic/Latino; 1 Two or more races, non-Hispanic/Latino, 1 international. Average age 30. 102 applicants, 87% accepted, 41 enrolled. In 2010, 56 master's, 24 other advanced degrees awarded. *Degree requirements:* For master's, one foreign language, thesis (for some programs), completion of electronic and Tk20 portfolios. *Entrance requirements:* For master's, 2 letters of recommendation, portfolio, teacher certification (MA), essay; for other advanced degree, 2 letters of recommendation, interview, teaching certificate, essay. Additional exam requirements/recommendations for international students: Required—TOEFL (minimum score 550 paper-based; 213 computer-based; 80 iBT). *Application deadline:* Applications are processed on a rolling basis. Application fee: $70 ($75 for international students). Electronic applications accepted. *Expenses:* Tuition: Full-time $18,000; part-time $1000 per credit hour. Required fees: $970; $145 per term. Tuition and fees vary according to program. *Financial support:* In 2010–11, 49 students received support, including 14 fellowships with full and partial tuition reimbursements available (averaging $2,750 per year), 2 research assistantships with full and partial tuition reimbursements available (averaging $9,091 per year); career-related internships or fieldwork, Federal Work-Study, institutionally sponsored loans, scholarships/grants, tuition waivers (full and partial), unspecified assistantships, and scholarships also available. Support available to part-time students. Financial award applicants required to submit FAFSA. *Faculty research:* The teacher/artist, interdisciplinary curriculum, applied linguistics, structural inequalities, creativity. *Unit head:* Dr. Esther Fusco, Chairperson, 516-463-7704, Fax: 516-463-6196, E-mail: catezf@hofstra.edu. *Application contact:* Carol Drummer, Dean of Graduate Admissions, 516-463-4876, Fax: 516-463-4664, E-mail: gradstudent@hofstra.edu.

Illinois State University, Graduate School, College of Applied Science and Technology, Department of Family and Consumer Sciences, Normal, IL 61790-2200. Offers MA, MS. *Degree requirements:* For master's, thesis or alternative. *Entrance requirements:* For master's, GRE General Test, minimum GPA of 2.8 in last 60 hours of course work. *Faculty research:* Graduate practicum assistantships, startup for Jump Start of McLean County grant, providing low-income preschool children with early literacy experiences, generations of Hope-ICI replication.

Indiana State University, College of Graduate and Professional Studies, College of Arts and Sciences, Department of Family and Consumer Sciences, Terre Haute, IN 47809. Offers dietetics (MS); family and consumer sciences education (MS); inter-area option (MS). *Accreditation:* ADtA. Part-time programs available. *Degree requirements:* For master's, thesis optional. Electronic applications accepted.

Iowa State University of Science and Technology, Graduate College, College of Human Sciences, Program in Family and Consumer Sciences, Ames, IA 50011. Offers MFCS. *Students:* 8 full-time (6 women), 42 part-time (35 women); includes 3 Black or African American, non-Hispanic/Latino, 2 international. 18 applicants, 89% accepted, 11 enrolled. In 2010, 19 master's awarded. *Degree requirements:* For master's, thesis or alternative. *Entrance requirements:* For master's, GRE General Test. Additional exam requirements/recommendations for international students: Required—TOEFL (minimum score 550 paper-based; 79 iBT), IELTS (minimum score 6.5). *Application deadline:* For fall admission, 4/15 priority date for domestic and international students; for spring admission, 10/15 priority date for domestic and international students. Application fee: $40 ($90 for international students). Electronic applications accepted. *Financial support:* In 2010–11, 1 research assistantship with full and partial tuition reimbursement, 3 teaching assistantships with full and partial tuition reimbursements (averaging $1,122 per year) were awarded; scholarships/grants, health care benefits, and unspecified assistantships also available. *Unit head:* Dr. Carla Peterson, Supervisory Committee Chair, 515-294-7804, E-mail: mfcsinfo@iastate.edu. *Application contact:* Dr. Carla Peterson, Supervisory Committee Chair, 515-294-7804, E-mail: mfcsinfo@iastate.edu.

Kansas State University, Graduate School, College of Human Ecology, Manhattan, KS 66506. Offers MS, PhD. Part-time programs available. Postbaccalaureate distance learning degree programs offered. *Degree requirements:* For master's, residency; for doctorate, thesis/dissertation, residency. Electronic applications accepted. *Faculty research:* Apparel and textiles, food service and hospitality management, life span human development, family life education and consultation, marriage and family therapy.

Lamar University, College of Graduate Studies, College of Education and Human Development, Department of Family and Consumer Sciences, Beaumont, TX 77710. Offers family and consumer science (MS); vocational home economics (Certificate). Part-time and evening/weekend programs available. *Faculty:* 6 full-time (5 women), 1 (woman) part-time/adjunct. *Students:* 14 full-time (13 women), 6 part-time (5 women); includes 1 Black or African American, non-Hispanic/Latino; 1 American Indian or Alaska Native, non-Hispanic/Latino; 2 Asian, non-Hispanic/Latino. Average age 27. 11 applicants, 73% accepted, 8 enrolled. In 2010, 7 master's awarded. *Degree requirements:* For master's, thesis optional. *Entrance requirements:* For master's, GRE General Test. Additional exam requirements/recommendations for international students: Required—TOEFL. *Application deadline:* For fall admission, 8/1 for domestic students; for spring admission, 12/1 for domestic students. Applications are processed on a rolling basis. Application fee: $25 ($50 for international students). *Expenses:* Tuition, state resident: full-time $4160; part-time $208 per credit hour. Tuition, nonresident: full-time $10,360; part-time $518 per credit hour. *Financial support:* In 2010–11, 3 students received support, including 3 teaching assistantships (averaging $5,000 per year); fellowships, research assistantships, career-related internships or fieldwork, Federal Work-Study, and institutionally sponsored loans also available. Support available to part-time students. Financial award application deadline: 4/1. *Faculty research:* Maternal and infant nutrition, eating disorders, sports nutrition, human sexuality, family violence. *Unit head:* Dr. Connie Ruiz, Chair, 409-880-8663, Fax: 409-880-8666. *Application contact:* Sandy Drane, Coordinator of Graduate Admissions, 409-880-8356, Fax: 409-880-8414, E-mail: gradmissions@hal.lamar.edu.

Louisiana State University and Agricultural and Mechanical College, Graduate School, College of Agriculture, School of Human Ecology, Baton Rouge, LA 70803. Offers MS, PhD. Part-time programs available. *Faculty:* 26 full-time (16 women). *Students:* 36 full-time (33 women), 18 part-time (15 women); includes 9 Black or African American, non-Hispanic/Latino; 1 Asian, non-Hispanic/Latino; 2 Hispanic/Latino, 12 international. Average age 31. 19 applicants, 63% accepted, 2 enrolled. In 2010, 9 master's, 4 doctorates awarded. *Degree requirements:* For master's, thesis; for doctorate, thesis/dissertation. *Entrance requirements:* For master's and doctorate, GRE General Test, minimum GPA of 3.0. Additional exam requirements/recommendations for international students: Required—TOEFL (minimum score 550 paper-based; 213 computer-based; 79 iBT) or IELTS (minimum score 6.5). *Application deadline:* For fall admission, 1/25 priority date for domestic students, 5/15 for international students; for spring admission, 10/15 for international students. Applications are processed on a rolling basis. Application fee: $50 ($70 for international students). Electronic applications accepted. *Financial support:* In 2010–11, 41 students received support, including 1 fellowship with full and partial tuition reimbursement available (averaging $15,426 per year), 16 research assistantships with full and partial tuition reimbursements available (averaging $15,366 per year), 10 teaching assistantships with full and partial tuition reimbursements available (averaging $10,220 per year); career-related internships or fieldwork, Federal Work-Study, institutionally sponsored loans, scholarships/grants, health care benefits, and unspecified assistantships also available. Support available to part-time students. Financial award application deadline: 4/15; financial award applicants required to submit FAFSA. *Faculty research:* Nutrition for optimum health, textile and apparel production development, children's relationships with parents and caregivers, contextual influences on families. Total annual research expenditures: $77,664. *Unit head:* Dr. Karen Overstreet, 225-578-2282, Fax: 225-578-2697, E-mail: koverstreet@agcenter.lsu.edu. *Application contact:* Dr. Karen Overstreet, 225-578-2282, Fax: 225-578-2697, E-mail: koverstreet@agcenter.lsu.edu.

Louisiana Tech University, Graduate School, College of Applied and Natural Sciences, School for Human Ecology, Ruston, LA 71272. Offers dietetics (MS); human ecology (MS). Part-time programs available. *Degree requirements:* For master's, thesis or alternative, Registered Dietician Exam eligibility. *Entrance requirements:* For master's, GRE General Test.

Marshall University, Academic Affairs Division, College of Education and Human Services, Division of Human Development and Allied Technology, Department of Family and Consumer Sciences, Huntington, WV 25755. Offers MA. *Students:* 1 (woman) part-time. Average age 34. *Degree requirements:* For master's, thesis optional, comprehensive assessment. Application fee: $40. *Unit head:* Prof. Mary Mhango, Program Coordinator, 304-696-3535, E-mail: mhango@marshall.edu. *Application contact:* Information Contact, 304-746-1900, Fax: 304-746-1902, E-mail: services@marshall.edu.

Missouri State University, Graduate College, College of Natural and Applied Sciences, Department of Fashion and Interior Design, Springfield, MO 65897. Offers secondary education (MS Ed), including consumer sciences. Part-time programs available. *Degree requirements:* For master's, comprehensive exam, thesis or alternative. *Entrance requirements:* For master's, 9-12 teaching certification (MS Ed), minimum GPA of 3.0 (MNAS). Additional exam requirements/recommendations for international students: Required—TOEFL (minimum score 550 paper-based; 213 computer-based; 79 iBT). Electronic applications accepted. *Expenses:* Tuition, state resident: full-time $3348; part-time $186 per credit hour. Tuition, nonresident: full-time $6696; part-time $372 per credit hour. Required fees: $238 per semester. Tuition and fees vary according to course level, course load and program.

New Mexico State University, Graduate School, College of Agricultural, Consumer and Environmental Sciences, Department of Family and Consumer Sciences, Las Cruces, NM 88003-8001. Offers MS. Part-time programs available. *Faculty:* 9 full-time (7 women). *Students:* 31 full-time (27 women), 19 part-time (16 women); includes 24 minority (1 Black or African American, non-Hispanic/Latino; 2 American Indian or Alaska Native, non-Hispanic/Latino; 2 Asian, non-Hispanic/Latino; 19 Hispanic/Latino), 8 international. Average age 32. 35 applicants, 94% accepted, 25 enrolled. In 2010, 21 master's awarded. *Degree requirements:* For master's, comprehensive exam (for some programs), thesis (for some programs), oral exam. *Entrance requirements:* For master's, GRE, 3 letters of reference, resume. Additional exam requirements/recommendations for international students: Required—TOEFL. *Application deadline:* For fall admission, 6/30 priority date for domestic students, 3/1 priority date for international students; for spring admission, 11/30 for domestic and international students. Applications are processed on a rolling basis. Application fee: $30 ($50 for international students). Electronic applications accepted. *Expenses:* Tuition, state resident: full-time $4536; part-time $242 per credit. Tuition, nonresident: full-time $15,816; part-time $712 per credit. Required fees: $636 per term. *Financial support:* In 2010–11, 4 research assistantships (averaging $9,100 per year), 13 teaching assistantships (averaging $12,398 per year) were awarded; career-related internships or fieldwork, Federal Work-Study, scholarships/grants, health care benefits, and unspecified assistantships also available. Support available to part-time students. Financial award application deadline: 3/1; financial award applicants required to submit FAFSA. *Faculty research:* Work, stress, and family functioning; youth at risk; food product analysis; diet and health. Total annual research expenditures: $750,000. *Unit head:* Dr. Esther Devall, Head, 575-646-3936, Fax: 575-646-1889, E-mail: edevall@nmsu.edu. *Application contact:* Dr. Roselyn Smitley, Coordinator, 575-646-1183, Fax: 575-646-1889, E-mail: rosmite@nmsu.edu.

North Carolina Central University, Division of Academic Affairs, College of Behavioral and Social Sciences, Department of Human Sciences, Durham, NC 27707-3129. Offers family and consumer sciences (MS). Part-time and evening/weekend programs available. *Degree requirements:* For master's, one foreign language, comprehensive exam, thesis. *Entrance requirements:* For master's, GRE, minimum GPA of 3.0 in major, 2.5 overall. Additional exam requirements/recommendations for international students: Required—TOEFL.

North Dakota State University, College of Graduate and Interdisciplinary Studies, College of Human Development and Education, School of Education, Program in Family and Consumer Sciences Education, Fargo, ND 58108. Offers M Ed, MS. *Accreditation:* NCATE. Part-time programs available. *Faculty:* 1 (woman) full-time. *Students:* 6 full-time (all women), 2 part-time (both women). Average age 40. *Degree requirements:* For master's, comprehensive exam, thesis or alternative. *Entrance requirements:* For master's, MAT. Additional exam requirements/recommendations for international students: Required—TOEFL. *Application deadline:* Applications are processed on a rolling basis. Application fee: $45 ($60 for international students). *Financial support:* Teaching assistantships, career-related internships or fieldwork and institutionally sponsored loans available. Financial award application deadline: 4/15. *Faculty research:* Needs of beginning teachers, learning styles and achievement, school-level variables and curriculum change. *Unit head:* Dr. William Martin, Chair, 701-231-7202, Fax: 701-231-7416, E-mail: william.martin@ndsu.edu. *Application contact:* Dr. Mari Borr, Assistant Professor, 701-231-7968, Fax: 701-231-9685, E-mail: mari.borr@ndsu.edu.

Ohio University, Graduate College, Gladys W. and David H. Patton College of Education and Human Services, Department of Human and Consumer Sciences Education, Athens, OH 45701-2979. Offers apparel, textiles, and merchandising (MS). Part-time programs available.

Students: 6 full-time (5 women), 1 (woman) part-time; includes 2 minority (1 Asian, non-Hispanic/Latino; 1 Hispanic/Latino). 5 applicants, 80% accepted, 3 enrolled. In 2010, 8 master's awarded. *Degree requirements:* For master's, comprehensive exam (for some programs), thesis. *Entrance requirements:* For master's, GRE. Additional exam requirements/recommendations for international students: Required—TOEFL (minimum score 550 paper-based; 80 iBT) or IELTS (minimum score 6.5). *Application deadline:* For fall admission, 3/1 priority date for domestic and international students. Applications are processed on a rolling basis. Application fee: $50 ($55 for international students). Electronic applications accepted. *Financial support:* Research assistantships, teaching assistantships, career-related internships or fieldwork, Federal Work-Study, institutionally sponsored loans, and unspecified assistantships available. Financial award application deadline: 3/15. *Unit head:* Dr. V. Ann Paulins, Chair, 740-593-2880, Fax: 740-593-0289, E-mail: paulins@ohio.edu. *Application contact:* Dr. V. Ann Paulins, Chair, 740-593-2880, Fax: 740-593-0289, E-mail: paulins@ohio.edu.

Oklahoma State University, College of Human Sciences, Department of Human Development and Family Science, Programs in Human Development and Family Science, Stillwater, OK 74078. Offers family financial planning (MS); human environmental sciences (PhD). Part-time programs available. Postbaccalaureate distance learning degree programs offered. *Faculty:* 1 full-time (0 women). *Students:* 1 (woman) full-time, 21 part-time (13 women); includes 1 American Indian or Alaska Native, non-Hispanic/Latino; 1 Asian, non-Hispanic/Latino; 1 Hispanic/Latino. Average age 37. 54 applicants, 35% accepted, 13 enrolled. In 2010, 2 master's awarded. *Degree requirements:* For master's, thesis or alternative, creative component; for doctorate, comprehensive exam, thesis/dissertation. *Entrance requirements:* For master's and doctorate, GRE or GMAT. Additional exam requirements/recommendations for international students: Required—TOEFL (minimum score 550 paper-based; 79 iBT). *Application deadline:* For fall admission, 3/1 priority date for international students; for spring admission, 8/1 priority date for international students. Applications are processed on a rolling basis. Application fee: $40 ($75 for international students). Electronic applications accepted. *Expenses:* Tuition, state resident: full-time $3716; part-time $154.85 per credit hour. Tuition, nonresident: full-time $14,892; part-time $621 per credit hour. Required fees: $2044; $85.20 per credit hour. One-time fee: $50. Tuition and fees vary according to course load and campus/location. *Financial support:* Career-related internships or fieldwork, Federal Work-Study, scholarships/grants, health care benefits, tuition waivers (partial), and unspecified assistantships available. Support available to part-time students. Financial award application deadline: 3/1; financial award applicants required to submit FAFSA. *Unit head:* Dr. Stephan Wilson, Dean, 405-744-5053, Fax: 405-744-7113. *Application contact:* Dr. Gordon Emslie, Dean, 405-744-6368, Fax: 405-744-0355, E-mail: grad-i@okstate.edu.

Oregon State University, Graduate School, College of Education, Program in Family and Consumer Sciences Education, Corvallis, OR 97331. Offers MAT, MS. Part-time programs available. *Degree requirements:* For master's, thesis (for some programs). *Entrance requirements:* For master's, NTE, California Basic Educational Skills Test, minimum GPA of 3.0 in last 90 hours of course work. Additional exam requirements/recommendations for international students: Required—TOEFL. *Faculty research:* Economy of time and methods.

Prairie View A&M University, College of Agriculture and Human Sciences, Prairie View, TX 77446-0519. Offers agricultural economics (MS); animal sciences (MS); interdisciplinary human sciences (MS); soil science (MS). Part-time and evening/weekend programs available. *Faculty:* 11 full-time (2 women). *Students:* 47 full-time (33 women), 34 part-time (26 women); includes 62 Black or African American, non-Hispanic/Latino; 2 Asian, non-Hispanic/Latino; 2 Hispanic/Latino, 5 international. Average age 30. 147 applicants, 100% accepted. In 2010, 21 master's awarded. *Degree requirements:* For master's, comprehensive exam, thesis (for some programs), field placement. *Entrance requirements:* For master's, GRE General Test, minimum GPA of 2.45. Additional exam requirements/recommendations for international students: Required—TOEFL (minimum score 550 paper-based). *Application deadline:* For fall admission, 6/1 for domestic and international students; for spring admission, 10/1 for domestic and international students. Applications are processed on a rolling basis. Application fee: $50. *Expenses:* Tuition, state resident: full-time $3586.14; part-time $119.06 per credit hour. Tuition, nonresident: part-time $511.23 per credit hour. *Financial support:* In 2010–11, 57 students received support, including 8 fellowships with tuition reimbursements available (averaging $12,000 per year), 10 research assistantships with tuition reimbursements available (averaging $15,000 per year); career-related internships or fieldwork, Federal Work-Study, institutionally sponsored loans, scholarships/grants, tuition waivers (partial), and unspecified assistantships also available. Support available to part-time students. Financial award application deadline: 4/1; financial award applicants required to submit FAFSA. *Faculty research:* Domestic violence prevention, water quality, food growth regulators, wetland dynamics, biochemistry, obesity and nutrition, family therapy. Total annual research expenditures: $4 million. *Unit head:* Dr. Freddie Richards, Dean, 936-261-2528, Fax: 936-261-5143, E-mail: flrichards@pvamu.edu. *Application contact:* Dr. Richard W. Griffin, Interim Department Head, 936-261-5019, Fax: 936-261-5148, E-mail: rwgriffin@pvamu.edu.

Purdue University, Graduate School, College of Consumer and Family Sciences, West Lafayette, IN 47907. Offers MS, PhD. Part-time programs available. *Degree requirements:* For doctorate, thesis/dissertation. *Entrance requirements:* Additional exam requirements/recommendations for international students: Required—TOEFL. Electronic applications accepted.

Queens College of the City University of New York, Division of Graduate Studies, Mathematics and Natural Sciences Division, Department of Family, Nutrition and Exercise Sciences, Flushing, NY 11367-1597. Offers home economics (MS Ed); physical education and exercise sciences (MS Ed). Part-time and evening/weekend programs available. *Faculty:* 12 full-time (7 women). *Students:* 17 full-time (12 women), 63 part-time (42 women); includes 8 Black or African American, non-Hispanic/Latino; 17 Asian, non-Hispanic/Latino; 10 Hispanic/Latino, 3 international. 58 applicants, 78% accepted, 25 enrolled. In 2010, 57 master's awarded. *Degree requirements:* For master's, research project. *Entrance requirements:* For master's, minimum GPA of 3.0. Additional exam requirements/recommendations for international students: Required—TOEFL. *Application deadline:* For fall admission, 4/1 for domestic students; for spring admission, 11/1 for domestic students. Applications are processed on a rolling basis. Application fee: $125. *Financial support:* Career-related internships or fieldwork, Federal Work-Study, institutionally sponsored loans, and tuition waivers (partial) available. Support available to part-time students. Financial award application deadline: 4/1; financial award applicants required to submit FAFSA. *Faculty research:* Exercise and environmental physiology, interdisciplinary approaches to school curricula using outdoor education, program development in cardiac rehabilitation and adult fitness, nutrition education. *Unit head:* Dr. Elizabeth Lowe, Chairperson, 718-997-4168. *Application contact:* Mario Caruso, Director of Graduate Admissions, 718-997-5200, Fax: 718-997-5193, E-mail: graduate_admissions@qc.edu.

Sam Houston State University, College of Humanities and Social Sciences, Department of Family and Consumer Sciences, Huntsville, TX 77341. Offers dietetics (MS); family and consumer sciences (MS). Part-time and evening/weekend programs available. *Faculty:* 5 full-time (all women). *Students:* 20 full-time (18 women), 2 part-time (both women); includes 1 Hispanic/Latino. Average age 24. 15 applicants, 93% accepted, 12 enrolled. In 2010, 9 master's awarded. *Entrance requirements:* For master's, GRE General Test, minimum GPA of 2.5. Additional exam requirements/recommendations for international students: Required—TOEFL (minimum score 550 paper-based; 213 computer-based; 79 iBT). *Application deadline:* For fall admission, 8/1 for domestic students; for spring admission, 12/1 for domestic students. Application fee: $20. *Expenses:* Tuition, state resident: full-time $1363; part-time $163 per credit hour. Tuition, nonresident: full-time $3856; part-time $473 per credit hour. *Financial support:* Teaching assistantships available. Financial award application deadline: 5/31; financial award applicants required to submit FAFSA. *Unit head:* Dr. Janis White, Chair, 936-294-1242, Fax: 936-294-4204, E-mail: jwhite@shsu.edu. *Application contact:* Dr. Claudia Sealey-Potts, Advisor, 936-294-1250, E-mail: clapotts@shsu.edu.

San Francisco State University, Division of Graduate Studies, College of Health and Human Services, Department of Consumer and Family Studies/Dietetics, San Francisco, CA 94132-

Family and Consumer Sciences—General

San Francisco State University (continued)
1722. Offers family and consumer sciences (MA). Part-time programs available. *Application deadline:* Applications are processed on a rolling basis. *Unit head:* Nancy Rabolt, Chair, 415-338-2060, E-mail: nrabolt@sfsu.edu. *Application contact:* Nancy Rabolt, Chair, 415-338-2060, E-mail: nrabolt@sfsu.edu.

South Carolina State University, School of Graduate Studies, Department of Family and Consumer Sciences, Orangeburg, SC 29117-0001. Offers individual and family development (MS); nutritional sciences (MS). Part-time and evening/weekend programs available. *Degree requirements:* For master's, comprehensive exam, thesis optional, departmental qualifying exam. *Entrance requirements:* For master's, GRE, MAT, or NTE, minimum GPA of 2.7. Electronic applications accepted. *Faculty research:* Societal competence, relationship of parent-child interaction to adult, quality of well-being of rural elders.

South Dakota State University, Graduate School, College of Education and Human Sciences, Department of Human Development, Consumer and Family Sciences, Brookings, SD 57007. Offers MFCS. *Entrance requirements:* For master's, resume. Additional exam requirements/recommendations for international students: Required—TOEFL (minimum score 525 paper-based).

State University of New York College at Oneonta, Graduate Education, Division of Education, Department of Secondary Education, Oneonta, NY 13820-4015. Offers adolescence education (MS Ed); family and consumer science education (MS Ed). *Accreditation:* NCATE. Part-time and evening/weekend programs available. *Students:* 3 full-time (2 women), 4 part-time (3 women). Average age 27. 7 applicants, 100% accepted, 7 enrolled. *Entrance requirements:* For master's, GRE General Test. *Application deadline:* For fall admission, 3/25 priority date for domestic students; for spring admission, 10/1 priority date for domestic students. Applications are processed on a rolling basis. Application fee: $50. *Expenses:* Tuition, state resident: full-time $8370; part-time $349 per credit hour. Tuition, nonresident: full-time $13,780; part-time $558 per credit hour. Required fees: $899; $22 per credit hour. *Unit head:* Dr. Dennis Banks, Chair, 607-436-3391, Fax: 607-436-2554, E-mail: banksdn@oneonta.edu. *Application contact:* Patrick J. Mente, Director of Graduate Studies, 607-436-2523, Fax: 607-436-3084, E-mail: gradstudies@oneonta.edu.

Stephen F. Austin State University, Graduate School, College of Education, Department of Human Sciences, Nacogdoches, TX 75962. Offers MS. *Degree requirements:* For master's, comprehensive exam, thesis or alternative. *Entrance requirements:* For master's, GRE General Test. Additional exam requirements/recommendations for international students: Required—TOEFL. *Faculty research:* Consumer economics, nutrition education, clothing and textiles, family, interior design.

Tennessee State University, The School of Graduate Studies and Research, School of Agriculture and Consumer Sciences, Nashville, TN 37209-1561. Offers agricultural sciences (MS), including agribusiness, agricultural education, animal science, plant science. Part-time and evening/weekend programs available. *Degree requirements:* For master's, thesis. *Entrance requirements:* For master's, GRE General Test, GRE Subject Test, MAT. *Faculty research:* Small farm economics, ornamental horticulture, beef cattle production, rural elderly.

Texas A&M University–Kingsville, College of Graduate Studies, College of Agriculture and Home Economics, Department of Human Sciences, Kingsville, TX 78363. Offers MS. Part-time and evening/weekend programs available. *Degree requirements:* For master's, comprehensive exam, thesis or alternative. *Entrance requirements:* For master's, GRE General Test, minimum GPA of 3.0. Additional exam requirements/recommendations for international students: Required—TOEFL. *Faculty research:* Mexican-American families, abuse in families, nontraditional students.

Texas Southern University, College of Liberal Arts and Behavioral Sciences, Department of Human Services and Consumer Sciences, Houston, TX 77004-4584. Offers MS. Part-time and evening/weekend programs available. *Faculty:* 2 full-time (both women). *Students:* 11 full-time (9 women), 21 part-time (19 women); includes all Black or African American, non-Hispanic/Latino. Average age 34. 8 applicants, 100% accepted, 6 enrolled. In 2010, 14 master's awarded. *Degree requirements:* For master's, comprehensive exam, thesis (for some programs). *Entrance requirements:* For master's, GRE General Test, minimum GPA of 2.5. Additional exam requirements/recommendations for international students: Required—TOEFL. *Application deadline:* For fall admission, 7/1 for domestic and international students; for spring admission, 11/1 for domestic and international students. Applications are processed on a rolling basis. Application fee: $50 ($75 for international students). Electronic applications accepted. *Expenses:* Tuition, state resident: full-time $1875; part-time $100 per credit hour. Tuition, nonresident: full-time $6641; part-time $343 per credit hour. Tuition and fees vary according to course level, course load and degree level. *Financial support:* Teaching assistantships, scholarships/grants and unspecified assistantships available. Financial award application deadline: 5/1. *Faculty research:* Food radiation/food for space travel, adolescent parenting, gerontology/grandparenting. *Unit head:* Dr. Shirley R. Nealy, Chair, 713-313-7638, Fax: 713-313-7228, E-mail: nealy_sr@tsu.edu. *Application contact:* Dr. Gregory Maddox, Dean of the Graduate School, 713-313-7011 Ext. 4410, Fax: 713-639-1876, E-mail: maddox_gh@tsu.edu.

Texas Tech University, Graduate School, College of Human Sciences, Lubbock, TX 79409. Offers MS, PhD, JD/MS, MS/MBA, MS/MS. Part-time and evening/weekend programs available. Postbaccalaureate distance learning degree programs offered (minimal on-campus study). *Faculty:* 53 full-time (35 women), 3 part-time/adjunct (2 women). *Students:* 272 full-time (174 women), 97 part-time (47 women); includes 11 Black or African American, non-Hispanic/Latino; 4 American Indian or Alaska Native, non-Hispanic/Latino; 4 Asian, non-Hispanic/Latino; 33 Hispanic/Latino, 88 international. Average age 29. 321 applicants, 60% accepted, 111 enrolled. In 2010, 88 master's, 28 doctorates awarded. Terminal master's awarded for partial completion of doctoral program. *Degree requirements:* For master's, thesis (for some programs); for doctorate, thesis/dissertation. *Entrance requirements:* For master's, GRE; for doctorate, GRE General Test. Additional exam requirements/recommendations for international students: Required—TOEFL (minimum score 550 paper-based; 213 computer-based; 79 iBT). *Application deadline:* For fall admission, 6/1 priority date for domestic students, 1/15 priority date for international students; for spring admission, 9/1 priority date for domestic students, 6/15 priority date for international students. Applications are processed on a rolling basis. Application fee: $50 ($75 for international students). Electronic applications accepted. *Expenses:* Contact institution. *Financial support:* In 2010–11, 151 students received support, including 26 research assistantships with partial tuition reimbursements available (averaging $2,966 per year), 50 teaching assistantships with partial tuition reimbursements available (averaging $3,480 per year); career-related internships or fieldwork, Federal Work-Study, institutionally sponsored loans, scholarships/grants, traineeships, health care benefits, and unspecified assistantships also available. Support available to part-time students. Financial award application deadline: 4/15; financial award applicants required to submit FAFSA. *Faculty research:* Substance abuse and recovery, the role of nutrition in the prevention of obesity, cancer and illness, the role of family factors in children's treatment response to cancer and serious illness, financial planning and credit management. Total annual research expenditures: $2.4 million. *Unit head:* Dr. Linda C. Hoover, Dean, 806-742-3031, Fax: 806-742-1849. *Application contact:* Dr. Lynn Huffman, Executive Associate Dean, 806-742-3031, Fax: 806-742-1849, E-mail: lynn.huffman@ttu.edu.

Tufts University, Graduate School of Arts and Sciences, Department of Child Development, Medford, MA 02155. Offers child development (MA, PhD, CAGS); early childhood education (MAT). Part-time programs available. *Degree requirements:* For master's, thesis (for some programs); for doctorate, thesis/dissertation. *Entrance requirements:* For master's and doctorate, GRE General Test. Additional exam requirements/recommendations for international students: Required—TOEFL (minimum score 550 paper-based; 213 computer-based; 80 iBT). Electronic applications accepted. *Expenses:* Tuition: Full-time $39,624; part-time $3962 per course.

Required fees: $40 per year. Full-time tuition and fees vary according to degree level, program and student level. Part-time tuition and fees vary according to course load.

The University of Alabama, Graduate School, College of Human Environmental Sciences, Tuscaloosa, AL 35487. Offers MA, MS, MSHES, PhD. Part-time and evening/weekend programs available. Postbaccalaureate distance learning degree programs offered (no on-campus study). *Faculty:* 39 full-time (26 women), 2 part-time/adjunct (1 woman). *Students:* 168 full-time (118 women), 281 part-time (197 women); includes 117 minority (95 Black or African American, non-Hispanic/Latino; 2 American Indian or Alaska Native, non-Hispanic/Latino; 3 Asian, non-Hispanic/Latino; 7 Hispanic/Latino; 10 Two or more races, non-Hispanic/Latino), 4 international. Average age 32. 333 applicants, 79% accepted, 172 enrolled. In 2010, 174 master's, 5 doctorates awarded. *Degree requirements:* For doctorate, thesis/dissertation. *Entrance requirements:* For master's, GRE General Test or MAT (minimum score: 50th percentile), minimum GPA of 3.0; for doctorate, GRE General Test or MAT, minimum GPA of 3.0. *Application deadline:* For fall admission, 7/6 for domestic students. Applications are processed on a rolling basis. Application fee: $50 ($60 for international students). Electronic applications accepted. *Expenses:* Tuition, state resident: full-time $7900. Tuition, nonresident: full-time $20,500. *Financial support:* In 2010–11, 2 research assistantships with full tuition reimbursements (averaging $9,000 per year) were awarded; fellowships with tuition reimbursements, teaching assistantships with full tuition reimbursements, career-related internships or fieldwork, Federal Work-Study, institutionally sponsored loans, and scholarships/grants also available. *Faculty research:* Students' use of credit, determinants of income differential: comparing Asians with blacks and whites, expenditure patterns of Chinese, racial and ethnic differences in the likelihood of charitable contributions, health insurance coverage and precautionary behavior savings. Total annual research expenditures: $807,775. *Unit head:* Dr. Milla D. Boschung, Dean, 205-348-6250, Fax: 205-348-1786, E-mail: mboschun@ches.ua.edu. *Application contact:* Dr. Milla D. Boschung, Dean, 205-348-6250, Fax: 205-348-1786, E-mail: mboschun@ches.ua.edu.

University of Alberta, Faculty of Graduate Studies and Research, Department of Human Ecology, Edmonton, AB T6G 2E1, Canada. Offers family ecology and practice (M Sc, PhD); textiles and clothing (M Sc, MA, PhD). Postbaccalaureate distance learning degree programs offered (no on-campus study). *Degree requirements:* For master's, thesis (for some programs); for doctorate, comprehensive exam, thesis/dissertation. *Entrance requirements:* For master's and doctorate, minimum GPA of 7.0 on a 9.0 scale. Additional exam requirements/recommendations for international students: Required—TOEFL (minimum score 580 paper-based; 237 computer-based). *Faculty research:* Families and aging, family and child poverty, paid and unpaid work of families, textiles and clothing, parent-child relationships.

The University of Arizona, College of Agriculture and Life Sciences, School of Family and Consumer Sciences, Tucson, AZ 85721. Offers MS, PhD. Part-time programs available. *Faculty:* 16 full-time (12 women). *Students:* 33 full-time (21 women), 3 part-time (2 women); includes 2 Black or African American, non-Hispanic/Latino; 4 Hispanic/Latino; 1 Two or more races, non-Hispanic/Latino, 10 international. Average age 33. 25 applicants, 44% accepted, 8 enrolled. In 2010, 1 master's, 3 doctorates awarded. *Entrance requirements:* For master's and doctorate, GRE General Test, minimum GPA of 3.0. Additional exam requirements/recommendations for international students: Required—TOEFL. *Application deadline:* Applications are processed on a rolling basis. Application fee: $75. *Expenses:* Tuition, state resident: full-time $7692. *Financial support:* In 2010–11, 19 research assistantships with full and partial tuition reimbursements (averaging $13,821 per year), 8 teaching assistantships with full and partial tuition reimbursements (averaging $13,778 per year) were awarded; fellowships, career-related internships or fieldwork, Federal Work-Study, institutionally sponsored loans, scholarships/grants, health care benefits, tuition waivers (full), and unspecified assistantships also available. Financial award application deadline: 3/1. *Faculty research:* Interpersonal relationships, human development, retailing management, consumer behaviors. Total annual research expenditures: $928,549. *Unit head:* Dr. Soyeon Shim, Director, 520-621-1075, Fax: 520-621-9445, E-mail: shim@ag.arizona.edu. *Application contact:* Mary Helen Scott, Program Coordinator, 520-621-5884, Fax: 520-621-9445, E-mail: mhscott@ag.arizona.edu.

University of Arkansas, Graduate School, Dale Bumpers College of Agricultural, Food and Life Sciences, School of Human Environmental Sciences, Fayetteville, AR 72701-1201. Offers MS. Part-time programs available. Postbaccalaureate distance learning degree programs offered (minimal on-campus study). *Students:* 12 full-time (9 women), 12 part-time (all women); includes 1 minority (Black or African American, non-Hispanic/Latino). 10 applicants, 80% accepted. In 2010, 9 master's awarded. *Degree requirements:* For master's, comprehensive exam, thesis (for some programs). *Application deadline:* For fall admission, 4/1 for international students; for spring admission, 10/1 for international students. Applications are processed on a rolling basis. Application fee: $40 ($50 for international students). Electronic applications accepted. *Financial support:* In 2010–11, 7 research assistantships, 1 teaching assistantship were awarded; fellowships, Federal Work-Study also available. Support available to part-time students. Financial award application deadline: 4/1; financial award applicants required to submit FAFSA. *Unit head:* Dr. Mary Warnock, Department Head, 479-575-4305, E-mail: hesc@uark.edu. *Application contact:* Dr. Mary Warnock, Department Head, 479-575-4305, E-mail: hesc@uark.edu.

University of Central Arkansas, Graduate School, College of Health and Behavioral Sciences, Department of Family and Consumer Sciences, Conway, AR 72035-0001. Offers MS. *Faculty:* 1 (woman) full-time. *Students:* 38 full-time (37 women), 27 part-time (26 women); includes 11 minority (10 Black or African American, non-Hispanic/Latino; 1 Hispanic/Latino). Average age 28. 30 applicants, 97% accepted, 24 enrolled. In 2010, 32 master's awarded. *Degree requirements:* For master's, comprehensive exam, thesis optional. *Entrance requirements:* For master's, GRE General Test, minimum GPA of 2.7. Additional exam requirements/recommendations for international students: Required—TOEFL (minimum score 550 paper-based; 213 computer-based). *Application deadline:* For fall admission, 3/1 priority date for domestic students; for spring admission, 10/1 for domestic students. Applications are processed on a rolling basis. Application fee: $25 ($40 for international students). *Expenses:* Contact institution. *Financial support:* Career-related internships or fieldwork, scholarships/grants, and unspecified assistantships available. Support available to part-time students. Financial award application deadline: 2/15. *Faculty research:* Neurology, developmental disabilities, diet consequences. *Unit head:* Dr. Mary Harlan, Chairperson, 501-450-5950, Fax: 501-450-5958, E-mail: maryh@uca.edu. *Application contact:* Susan Wood, Administrative Assistant, 501-450-3124, Fax: 501-450-5678, E-mail: swood@uca.edu.

University of Central Oklahoma, College of Graduate Studies and Research, College of Education, Department of Human Environmental Sciences, Edmond, OK 73034-5209. Offers family and child studies (MS); family and consumer science education (MS); interior design (MS); nutrition-food management (MS). Part-time programs available. *Entrance requirements:* Additional exam requirements/recommendations for international students: Required—TOEFL (minimum score 550 paper-based; 213 computer-based). Electronic applications accepted. *Faculty research:* Dietetics and food science.

University of Florida, Graduate School, College of Agricultural and Life Sciences, Department of Family, Youth, and Community Sciences, Gainesville, FL 32611. Offers M Ag, MFYCS, MS. Part-time programs available. *Faculty:* 17 full-time (10 women). *Students:* 21 full-time (17 women), 9 part-time (7 women); includes 3 Black or African American, non-Hispanic/Latino; 2 American Indian or Alaska Native, non-Hispanic/Latino; 2 Hispanic/Latino. Average age 26. 18 applicants, 78% accepted, 11 enrolled. In 2010, 11 master's awarded. *Degree requirements:* For master's, comprehensive exam (for some programs), thesis (for some programs). *Entrance requirements:* For master's, GRE general test, minimum score 1000, minimum GPA 3.0. Additional exam requirements/recommendations for international students: Required—TOEFL (minimum score 550 paper-based; 213 computer-based; 80 iBT), IELTS (minimum score 6). *Application deadline:* For fall admission, 7/1 for domestic students, 11/1 for international students; for spring admission, 11/1 for domestic and international students. Applications are processed on a rolling basis. Application fee: $30. Electronic applications accepted. *Expenses:* Tuition, state resident: full-time $10,915.92. Tuition, nonresident: full-time $28,309. *Financial support:* Applicants required to submit FAFSA. *Faculty research:* Family financial management, family nutrition and wellness, community-based interventions, family and youth relations, nonprofit organizations. *Unit head:* Dr. Nayda I. Torres, Department Chair, 352-273-3541, E-mail: nitorres@ufl.edu. *Application contact:* Jennifer Gove-Cooper, Coordinator of Academic Programs, 352-273-3551, Fax: 352-392-8196, E-mail: jennerg@ufl.edu.

University of Georgia, College of Family and Consumer Sciences, Athens, GA 30602. Offers MAT, MFCS, MS, PhD. *Faculty:* 54 full-time (33 women). *Students:* 113 full-time (92 women), 41 part-time (37 women); includes 19 Black or African American, non-Hispanic/Latino; 2 Asian, non-Hispanic/Latino; 3 Hispanic/Latino, 20 international. 184 applicants, 44% accepted, 37 enrolled. In 2010, 40 master's, 4 doctorates awarded. *Degree requirements:* For doctorate, thesis/dissertation. *Entrance requirements:* For master's and doctorate, GRE General Test. *Application deadline:* For fall admission, 7/1 priority date for domestic students; for spring admission, 11/15 for domestic students. Application fee: $50. Electronic applications accepted. *Expenses:* Tuition, state resident: full-time $7200; part-time $344 per credit hour. Tuition, nonresident: full-time $21,900; part-time $944 per credit hour. Tuition and fees vary according to course load and program. *Financial support:* Fellowships, research assistantships, teaching assistantships, unspecified assistantships available. *Unit head:* Dr. Laura Dunn Jolly, Dean, 706-542-4879, Fax: 706-542-4862, E-mail: dean@fcs.uga.edu. *Application contact:* Director of Enrolled Student Services.

University of Houston, College of Technology, Department of Human Development and Consumer Science, Houston, TX 77204. Offers future studies in commerce (MS); human resources development (MS). Part-time programs available. *Faculty:* 3 full-time (2 women), 6 part-time/adjunct (3 women). *Students:* 45 full-time (33 women), 54 part-time (36 women); includes 16 Black or African American, non-Hispanic/Latino; 1 American Indian or Alaska Native, non-Hispanic/Latino; 9 Asian, non-Hispanic/Latino; 11 Hispanic/Latino, 20 international. Average age 32. 47 applicants, 89% accepted, 30 enrolled. In 2010, 22 master's awarded. *Degree requirements:* For master's, project or thesis. *Entrance requirements:* For master's, GMAT, MAT. Additional exam requirements/recommendations for international students: Required—TOEFL (minimum score 550 paper-based; 79 iBT). *Application deadline:* For fall admission, 7/1 for domestic students, 4/1 for international students; for spring admission, 12/1 for domestic students, 10/1 for international students. Applications are processed on a rolling basis. Application fee: $75 ($150 for international students). Electronic applications accepted. *Expenses:* Tuition, state resident: full-time $8592; part-time $358 per credit hour. Tuition, nonresident: full-time $16,032; part-time $668 per credit hour. Required fees: $2889. Tuition and fees vary according to course load and program. *Financial support:* In 2010–11, 11 teaching assistantships with partial tuition reimbursements (averaging $8,400 per year) were awarded. *Unit head:* Carole Goodson, Chairperson, 713-743-4046, Fax: 713-743-4033, E-mail: cgoodson@uh.edu. *Application contact:* Tiffany Roosa, Academic Advisor, 713-743-4100, Fax: 713-743-4151, E-mail: troosa@uh.edu.

University of Manitoba, Faculty of Graduate Studies, Faculty of Human Ecology, Winnipeg, MB R3T 2N2, Canada. Offers M Sc. *Degree requirements:* For master's, thesis.

University of Maryland, College Park, Academic Affairs, School of Public Health, Department of Family Science, College Park, MD 20742. Offers family studies (PhD); marriage and family therapy (MS); maternal and child health (PhD). *Accreditation:* AAMFT/COAMFTE. Part-time and evening/weekend programs available. *Faculty:* 22 full-time (17 women), 14 part-time/adjunct (13 women). *Students:* 51 full-time (45 women), 1 (woman) part-time; includes 15 minority (10 Black or African American, non-Hispanic/Latino; 2 Asian, non-Hispanic/Latino; 3 Hispanic/Latino), 6 international. 150 applicants, 11% accepted, 16 enrolled. In 2010, 12 master's, 2 doctorates awarded. *Degree requirements:* For master's, thesis or alternative; for doctorate, comprehensive exam, thesis/dissertation, oral defense. *Entrance requirements:* For master's, GRE General Test, minimum GPA of 3.0, 3 letters of recommendation; for doctorate, GRE General Test, minimum GPA of 3.0, 3 letters of recommendation, research sample. *Application deadline:* For fall admission, 12/15 for domestic and international students. Applications are processed on a rolling basis. Application fee: $75. Electronic applications accepted. *Expenses:* Tuition, state resident: part-time $471 per credit hour. Tuition, nonresident: part-time $1016 per credit hour. Required fees: $337 per term. *Financial support:* In 2010–11, 2 fellowships with full and partial tuition reimbursements (averaging $18,673 per year), 1 research assistantship (averaging $15,878 per year), 36 teaching assistantships (averaging $16,148 per year) were awarded; career-related internships or fieldwork, Federal Work-Study, and scholarships/grants also available. Support available to part-time students. Financial award applicants required to submit FAFSA. *Faculty research:* Family life quality, interracial couples, child support, homeless families, family and child well-being. Total annual research expenditures: $1.1 million. *Unit head:* Elaine Anderson, Chairman, 301-405-4009, Fax: 301-314-9161, E-mail: eanders@umd.edu. *Application contact:* Dr. Charles A. Caramello, Dean of Graduate School, 301-405-0358, Fax: 301-314-9305.

University of Memphis, Graduate School, University College, Memphis, TN 38152. Offers liberal studies (MALS); merchandising and consumer science (MS), including consumer science and education; strategic leadership (MPS). Part-time and evening/weekend programs available. *Faculty:* 3 full-time (2 women), 3 part-time/adjunct (1 woman). *Students:* 30 full-time (19 women), 122 part-time (93 women); includes 88 Black or African American, non-Hispanic/Latino; 1 American Indian or Alaska Native, non-Hispanic/Latino; 1 Asian, non-Hispanic/Latino; 1 Hispanic/Latino, 1 international. Average age 40. 89 applicants, 74% accepted, 8 enrolled. In 2010, 41 master's awarded. *Degree requirements:* For master's, comprehensive exam, thesis (for some programs). *Entrance requirements:* For master's, MAT, GRE General Test (MS), interview (MALS). Additional exam requirements/recommendations for international students: Required—TOEFL (minimum score 550 paper-based; 210 computer-based). *Application deadline:* For fall admission, 7/1 for domestic students, 5/1 for international students; for spring admission, 11/1 for domestic students, 9/15 for international students. Applications are processed on a rolling basis. Application fee: $35 ($60 for international students). Electronic applications accepted. *Financial support:* In 2010–11, 123 students received support; research assistantships with full tuition reimbursements available, teaching assistantships with tuition reimbursements available, Federal Work-Study, scholarships/grants, and unspecified assistantships available. Financial award application deadline: 2/15; financial award applicants required to submit FAFSA. *Faculty research:* Media ethics, history of psychiatry, public relations. *Unit head:* Dr. Dan Lattimore, Dean, 901-678-2991. *Application contact:* Dr. Herbert McCree, Coordinator of Graduate Studies, 901-678-4171, Fax: 901-678-3363, E-mail: hmccree@memphis.edu.

University of Mississippi, Graduate School, School of Applied Sciences, Department of Family and Consumer Sciences, Oxford, University, MS 38677. Offers MS. *Students:* 14 full-time (12 women), 11 part-time (all women); includes 2 minority (1 Black or African American, non-Hispanic/Latino; 1 Two or more races, non-Hispanic/Latino), 1 international. In 2010, 1 master's awarded. *Unit head:* Dr. Mary Roseman, Chair, 662-915-7371, Fax: 662-915-7039, E-mail: fcs@olemiss.edu. *Application contact:* Dr. Christy M. Wyandt, Associate Dean, 662-915-7474, Fax: 662-915-7577, E-mail: cwyandt@olemiss.edu.

University of Missouri, Graduate School, College of Human Environmental Science, Columbia, MO 65211. Offers MA, MS, PhD. Part-time programs available. *Degree requirements:* For doctorate, thesis/dissertation. *Entrance requirements:* For master's and doctorate, GRE General Test, minimum GPA of 3.0. Additional exam requirements/recommendations for international students: Required—TOEFL.

University of Nebraska–Lincoln, Graduate College, College of Education and Human Sciences, Department of Child, Youth and Family Studies, Lincoln, NE 68588. Offers child development/early childhood education (MS, PhD); child, youth and family studies (MS); family and consumer sciences education (MS, PhD); family financial planning (MS); family science (MS, PhD); gerontology (PhD); human sciences (PhD), including child, youth and family studies, gerontology, medical family therapy; marriage and family therapy (MS); medical family therapy (PhD); youth development (MS). *Accreditation:* AAMFT/COAMFTE (one or more programs are accredited). Postbaccalaureate distance learning degree programs offered. *Degree requirements:* For master's, thesis optional. *Entrance requirements:* For master's, GRE. Additional exam requirements/recommendations for international students: Required—TOEFL (minimum score 550 paper-based; 213 computer-based). Electronic applications accepted. *Faculty research:* Marriage and family therapy, child development/early childhood education, family financial management.

The University of North Carolina at Greensboro, Graduate School, School of Human Environmental Sciences, Greensboro, NC 27412-5001. Offers M Ed, MS, MSW, PhD, Certificate. *Degree requirements:* For master's, thesis (for some programs); for doctorate, thesis/dissertation. *Entrance requirements:* For master's and doctorate, GRE General Test. Additional exam requirements/recommendations for international students: Required—TOEFL. Electronic applications accepted. *Faculty research:* Impact of phosphate removal, protective clothing for pesticide workers, adolescent mothers, cancer prevention, immuno-stimulant effects.

University of Puerto Rico, Río Piedras, College of Education, Program in Family Ecology and Nutrition, San Juan, PR 00931-3300. Offers M Ed. Part-time programs available. *Degree requirements:* For master's, thesis. *Entrance requirements:* For master's, PAEG or GRE, minimum GPA of 3.0, letter of recommendation.

University of South Africa, College of Agriculture and Environmental Sciences, Pretoria, South Africa. Offers agriculture (MS); consumer science (MCS); environmental management (MA, MS, PhD); environmental science (MA, MS, PhD); geography (MA, MS, PhD); horticulture (M Tech); human ecology (MHE); life sciences (MS); nature conservation (M Tech).

The University of Tennessee, Graduate School, College of Education, Health and Human Sciences, Program in Human Ecology, Knoxville, TN 37996. Offers child and family studies (PhD); community health (PhD); nutrition science (PhD); retailing and consumer sciences (PhD); textile science (PhD). *Degree requirements:* For doctorate, thesis/dissertation. *Entrance requirements:* For doctorate, GRE General Test, minimum GPA of 2.7. Additional exam requirements/recommendations for international students: Required—TOEFL. Electronic applications accepted. *Expenses:* Tuition, state resident: full-time $7440; part-time $414 per credit hour. Tuition, nonresident: full-time $22,478; part-time $1250 per credit hour. Required fees: $922; $43 per credit hour. Tuition and fees vary according to program.

The University of Tennessee at Martin, Graduate Programs, College of Agriculture and Applied Sciences, Department of Family and Consumer Sciences, Martin, TN 38238-1000. Offers dietetics (MSFCS); general family and consumer sciences (MSFCS). Part-time programs available. Postbaccalaureate distance learning degree programs offered (minimal on-campus study). *Faculty:* 8. *Students:* 40 (38 women); includes 6 Black or African American, non-Hispanic/Latino; 2 Hispanic/Latino; 1 Two or more races, non-Hispanic/Latino, 1 international. 45 applicants, 69% accepted, 12 enrolled. In 2010, 10 master's awarded. *Degree requirements:* For master's, comprehensive exam, thesis optional. *Entrance requirements:* For master's, GRE General Test, minimum GPA of 2.5. Additional exam requirements/recommendations for international students: Required—TOEFL (minimum score 525 paper-based; 197 computer-based; 71 iBT). *Application deadline:* For fall admission, 8/1 priority date for domestic students, 6/15 priority date for international students; for spring admission, 12/15 priority date for domestic students, 12/1 priority date for international students. Applications are processed on a rolling basis. Application fee: $30 ($130 for international students). Electronic applications accepted. *Expenses:* Tuition, state resident: full-time $7164; part-time $400 per credit hour. Tuition, nonresident: full-time $19,574; part-time $1090 per credit hour. Required fees: $1044; $60 per credit hour. *Financial support:* In 2010–11, 2 students received support, including 2 research assistantships with full tuition reimbursements available (averaging $7,893 per year); scholarships/grants and unspecified assistantships also available. Support available to part-time students. Financial award application deadline: 2/15; financial award applicants required to submit FAFSA. *Faculty research:* Children with developmental disabilities, regional food product development and marketing, parent education. *Unit head:* Dr. Lisa LeBleu, Coordinator, 731-881-7116, Fax: 731-881-7106, E-mail: llebleu@utm.edu. *Application contact:* Linda S. Arant, Student Services Specialist, 731-881-7012, Fax: 731-881-7499, E-mail: larant@utm.edu.

The University of Texas at Austin, Graduate School, College of Natural Sciences, School of Human Ecology, Austin, TX 78712-1111. Offers human development and family sciences (MA, PhD); nutritional sciences (MA, PhD), including nutrition (MA), nutritional sciences (PhD); textile and apparel technology (MS). *Degree requirements:* For master's, thesis; for doctorate, thesis/dissertation. *Entrance requirements:* For master's and doctorate, GRE General Test. Electronic applications accepted.

University of Wisconsin–Madison, Graduate School, School of Human Ecology, Madison, WI 53706. Offers consumer behavior and family economics (MS, PhD); design studies (MFA, MS, PhD); human development and family studies (MS, PhD). *Faculty:* 31 full-time (21 women). *Students:* 55 full-time (46 women), 9 part-time (8 women); includes 1 Black or African American, non-Hispanic/Latino; 4 Asian, non-Hispanic/Latino; 4 Hispanic/Latino. Average age 32. 118 applicants, 17% accepted, 16 enrolled. In 2010, 7 master's, 7 doctorates awarded. Terminal master's awarded for partial completion of doctoral program. *Degree requirements:* For master's, thesis (for some programs); for doctorate, comprehensive exam, thesis/dissertation. *Entrance requirements:* For master's, GRE General Test, portfolio (design studies), 3 letters of recommendation; for doctorate, GRE General Test. Additional exam requirements/recommendations for international students: Required—TOEFL (minimum score 580 paper-based; 237 computer-based; 92 iBT). *Application deadline:* For fall admission, 1/3 for domestic and international students. Application fee: $56. Electronic applications accepted. *Expenses:* Tuition, state resident: full-time $9887; part-time $617.96 per credit. Tuition, nonresident: full-time $24,054; part-time $1503.40 per credit. Required fees: $67.63 per credit. Tuition and fees vary according to reciprocity agreements. *Financial support:* Fellowships with full tuition reimbursements, research assistantships with full tuition reimbursements, teaching assistantships with full tuition reimbursements, institutionally sponsored loans, scholarships/grants, health care benefits, and unspecified assistantships available. *Unit head:* Robin A. Douthitt, Dean, 608-262-4847. *Application contact:* Allison Murray, Student Academic Affairs, 608-262-1138, Fax: 608-265-3616, E-mail: armurray@wisc.edu.

University of Wisconsin–Stevens Point, College of Professional Studies, School of Health Promotion and Human Development, Program in Human and Community Resources, Stevens Point, WI 54481-3897. Offers MS. Part-time programs available. *Degree requirements:* For master's, thesis or alternative. *Entrance requirements:* For master's, minimum GPA of 2.75.

Utah State University, School of Graduate Studies, College of Education and Human Services, Department of Family, Consumer, and Human Development, Logan, UT 84322. Offers family and human development (MFHD); family, consumer, and human development (MS, PhD), including adolescence/youth (MS), adult development/aging (MS), consumer science (MS), infancy/childhood (MS), marriage and family relations (MS), marriage and family therapy (MS). *Accreditation:* AAMFT/COAMFTE (one or more programs are accredited). Part-time and evening/weekend programs available. Postbaccalaureate distance learning degree programs offered (minimal on-campus study). *Degree requirements:* For master's, thesis; for doctorate, comprehensive exam, thesis/dissertation, competencies. *Entrance requirements:* For master's, GRE General Test or MAT, minimum GPA of 3.0, 3 letters of recommendation; for doctorate,

Family and Consumer Sciences—General

Utah State University (continued)
GRE, minimum GPA of 3.0, 3 letters of recommendation. Additional exam requirements/recommendations for international students: Required—TOEFL. Electronic applications accepted. *Faculty research:* Marriage and family relations, adolescent problem behavior, family financial management, early literacy, mental health in the elderly, parent child attachment.

Western Michigan University, Graduate College, College of Education and Human Development, Department of Family and Consumer Sciences, Program in Family and Consumer Sciences, Kalamazoo, MI 49008. Offers MA. *Faculty research:* Parenting education, kinship care, entrepreneurship, textiles and dress, nutrition.

Child and Family Studies

Arizona State University, College of Liberal Arts and Sciences, School of Social and Family Dynamics, Tempe, AZ 85287-3701. Offers family and human development (MS, PhD); infant-family practice (MAS); marriage and family therapy (MAS); sociology (MA, PhD). *Faculty:* 60 full-time (39 women), 2 part-time/adjunct (both women). *Students:* 91 full-time (82 women), 32 part-time (27 women); includes 28 minority (3 Black or African American, non-Hispanic/Latino; 2 American Indian or Alaska Native, non-Hispanic/Latino; 4 Asian, non-Hispanic/Latino; 17 Hispanic/Latino; 1 Native Hawaiian or other Pacific Islander, non-Hispanic/Latino; 1 Two or more races, non-Hispanic/Latino), 10 international. Average age 27. 186 applicants, 38% accepted, 44 enrolled. In 2010, 32 master's, 7 doctorates awarded. Terminal master's awarded for partial completion of doctoral program. *Degree requirements:* For master's, thesis or alternative, interactive Program of Study (iPOS) submitted before completing 50 percent of required credit hours; for doctorate, thesis/dissertation, interactive Program of Study (iPOS) submitted before completing 50 percent of required credit hours. *Entrance requirements:* For master's and doctorate, GRE, minimum GPA of 3.0 or equivalent in last 2 years of work leading to bachelor's degree. Additional exam requirements/recommendations for international students: Required—TOEFL, IELTS, or Pearson Test of English. *Application deadline:* For fall admission, 1/15 for domestic and international students. Application fee: $70 ($90 for international students). Electronic applications accepted. *Expenses:* Contact institution. *Financial support:* In 2010–11, 22 research assistantships with full and partial tuition reimbursements (averaging $14,111 per year), 27 teaching assistantships with full and partial tuition reimbursements (averaging $12,750 per year) were awarded; fellowships with full tuition reimbursements, career-related internships or fieldwork, Federal Work-Study, institutionally sponsored loans, scholarships/grants, and tuition waivers (full and partial) also available. Financial award application deadline: 3/1; financial award applicants required to submit FAFSA. Total annual research expenditures: $4.2 million. *Unit head:* Dr. Richard Fabes, Director, 480-965-4892, E-mail: rf@asu.edu. *Application contact:* Graduate Admissions, 480-965-6113.

Asbury University, School of Graduate and Professional Studies, Master of Social Work Program, Wilmore, KY 40390-1198. Offers child and family services (MSW). *Accreditation:* CSWE. *Degree requirements:* For master's, comprehensive exam, 954 praticum hours completed in agency. *Entrance requirements:* For master's, prerequisite courses in psychology, sociology, and statistics. Additional exam requirements/recommendations for international students: Required—TOEFL. Electronic applications accepted. *Expenses:* Contact institution. *Faculty research:* Integration of faith and practice, survivors of family violence, program evaluation, cross-cultural counseling.

Assumption College, Graduate School, Counseling Psychology Program, Worcester, MA 01609-1296. Offers child and family interventions (MA); cognitive-behavioral therapies (MA); counseling psychology (CAGS); general psychology (MA). Part-time and evening/weekend programs available. *Faculty:* 4 full-time (1 woman), 8 part-time/adjunct (2 women). *Students:* 74 full-time (66 women), 35 part-time (33 women); includes 18 minority (5 Black or African American, non-Hispanic/Latino; 2 Asian, non-Hispanic/Latino; 8 Hispanic/Latino; 3 Two or more races, non-Hispanic/Latino). Average age 24. 100 applicants, 78% accepted. In 2010, 20 master's, 2 other advanced degrees awarded. *Degree requirements:* For master's, comprehensive exam, internship, practicum, oral exam; for CAGS, comprehensive exam, oral exam. *Entrance requirements:* For master's, 3 letters of recommendation, resume, essay; for CAGS, 3 letters of recommendation, resume, interview, essay. Additional exam requirements/recommendations for international students: Required—TOEFL (minimum score 540 paper-based; 200 computer-based; 76 iBT), IELTS (minimum score 6). *Application deadline:* For fall admission, 6/1 priority date for domestic students, 5/1 priority date for international students; for spring admission, 11/1 priority date for domestic students, 9/1 priority date for international students. Applications are processed on a rolling basis. Application fee: $30. Electronic applications accepted. *Expenses:* Tuition: Part-time $503 per credit. Required fees: $20 per semester. One-time fee: $100. Part-time tuition and fees vary according to campus/location. *Financial support:* In 2010–11, 21 students received support, including 19 fellowships with partial tuition reimbursements available (averaging $8,206 per year), 2 teaching assistantships with full tuition reimbursements available (averaging $7,575 per year). Financial award application deadline: 3/1; financial award applicants required to submit FAFSA. *Faculty research:* Mood disorders, adjustment to life-threatening illness, perception of movement, socioemotional development of young children, discovery versus disclosure. *Unit head:* Dr. Leonard A. Doerfler, Director, 508-767-7549, Fax: 508-767-7263, E-mail: doerfler@assumption.edu. *Application contact:* Daniel Provost, Director of Graduate Enrollment Management and Services, 508-767-7426, Fax: 508-767-7030, E-mail: dprovost@assumption.edu.

Auburn University, Graduate School, College of Human Sciences, Department of Human Development and Family Studies, Auburn University, AL 36849. Offers MS, PhD. *Accreditation:* AAMFT/COAMFTE (one or more programs are accredited). Part-time programs available. *Faculty:* 20 full-time (12 women), 1 (woman) part-time/adjunct. *Students:* 28 full-time (24 women), 26 part-time (22 women); includes 10 Black or African American, non-Hispanic/Latino; 6 Asian, non-Hispanic/Latino; 2 Hispanic/Latino, 6 international. Average age 28. 56 applicants, 55% accepted, 18 enrolled. In 2010, 15 master's, 2 doctorates awarded. *Degree requirements:* For master's, thesis, oral exam; for doctorate, thesis/dissertation. *Entrance requirements:* For master's, GRE General Test; for doctorate, GRE General Test, master's degree. *Application deadline:* For fall admission, 7/7 for domestic students; for spring admission, 11/24 for domestic students. Applications are processed on a rolling basis. Application fee: $50 ($60 for international students). *Expenses:* Tuition, state resident: full-time $7002. Tuition, nonresident: full-time $21,898. International tuition: $22,116 full-time. Required fees: $892. Tuition and fees vary according to course load and program. *Financial support:* Research assistantships, teaching assistantships, Federal Work-Study available. Support available to part-time students. Financial award application deadline: 3/15; financial award applicants required to submit FAFSA. *Faculty research:* Family influences on personality and social development, parent-child relations, infancy, day care, parent education. *Unit head:* Dr. Leanne K. Lamke, Head, 334-844-3231, E-mail: mbradbar@humsci.auburn.edu. *Application contact:* Dr. George Flowers, Dean of the Graduate School, 334-844-2125.

Bank Street College of Education, Graduate School, Program in Child Life, New York, NY 10025. Offers MS. *Students:* 22 full-time (all women), 7 part-time (all women); includes 4 minority (1 Black or African American, non-Hispanic/Latino; 1 Asian, non-Hispanic/Latino; 2 Two or more races, non-Hispanic/Latino). Average age 27. 32 applicants, 47% accepted, 11 enrolled. In 2010, 10 master's awarded. *Degree requirements:* For master's, thesis. *Entrance requirements:* For master's, interview, 100 hours of volunteer experience in a child life setting. Additional exam requirements/recommendations for international students: Required—TOEFL (minimum score 600 paper-based; 250 computer-based; 100 iBT), IELTS (minimum score 7). *Application deadline:* For fall admission, 2/15 priority date for domestic and international students; for spring admission, 11/1 priority date for domestic and international students. Applications are processed on a rolling basis. Application fee: $65. *Financial support:* Career-related internships or fieldwork, Federal Work-Study, scholarships/grants, and unspecified assistantships available. Support available to part-time students. Financial award application deadline: 4/15; financial award applicants required to submit FAFSA. *Faculty research:* Therapeutic play in child life setting, child advocacy, psychosocial and educational intervention with care of sick children. *Unit head:* Troy Pinkney-Ragsdale, Director, 212-875-4473, Fax: 212-875-4753, E-mail: tpinkneyragsdale@bankstreet.edu. *Application contact:* Seena Berg, Associate Director of Graduate Admissions, 212-875-4402, Fax: 212-875-4678, E-mail: sberg@bankstreet.edu.

Bank Street College of Education, Graduate School, Program in Infant and Family Development and Early Intervention, New York, NY 10025. Offers infant and family development (MS Ed); infant and family early childhood special and general education (MS Ed); infant and family/early childhood special education (Ed M). *Students:* 9 full-time (all women), 22 part-time (all women); includes 8 minority (4 Black or African American, non-Hispanic/Latino; 2 Asian, non-Hispanic/Latino; 2 Two or more races, non-Hispanic/Latino), 1 international. Average age 29. 21 applicants, 76% accepted, 9 enrolled. In 2010, 23 master's awarded. *Degree requirements:* For master's, thesis. *Entrance requirements:* For master's, interview. Additional exam requirements/recommendations for international students: Required—TOEFL (minimum score 600 paper-based; 250 computer-based; 100 iBT), IELTS (minimum score 7). *Application deadline:* For fall admission, 2/15 priority date for domestic and international students; for spring admission, 11/1 priority date for domestic and international students. Applications are processed on a rolling basis. Application fee: $65. Electronic applications accepted. *Financial support:* Career-related internships or fieldwork, Federal Work-Study, scholarships/grants, and unspecified assistantships available. Support available to part-time students. Financial award application deadline: 4/15; financial award applicants required to submit FAFSA. *Faculty research:* Early intervention, early attachment practice in infant and toddler childcare, parenting skills in adolescents. *Unit head:* Sue Cabary, Director, 212-875-4509, Fax: 212-875-4753, E-mail: scarbary@bankstreet.edu. *Application contact:* Ann Morgan, Director of Graduate Admissions, 212-875-4403, Fax: 212-875-4678, E-mail: amorgan@bankstreet.edu.

Bowling Green State University, Graduate College, College of Education and Human Development, School of Family and Consumer Sciences, Bowling Green, OH 43403. Offers food and nutrition (MFCS); human development and family studies (MFCS). Part-time programs available. *Degree requirements:* For master's, thesis. *Entrance requirements:* For master's, GRE General Test, minimum GPA of 3.0. Additional exam requirements/recommendations for international students: Required—TOEFL. Electronic applications accepted. *Faculty research:* Public health, wellness, social issues and policies, ethnic foods, nutrition and aging.

Brandeis University, The Heller School for Social Policy and Management, Program in Public Policy, Waltham, MA 02454-9110. Offers aging (MPP); behavioral health (MPP); children, youth and families (MPP); general social policy (MPP); health (MPP); poverty alleviation and development (MPP); MPP/MA. *Faculty:* 36 full-time, 107 part-time/adjunct. *Students:* 45 full-time (36 women); includes 2 Black or African American, non-Hispanic/Latino; 5 Asian, non-Hispanic/Latino; 4 Hispanic/Latino. Average age 26. 136 applicants, 61% accepted, 26 enrolled. In 2010, 18 master's awarded. *Degree requirements:* For master's, thesis. *Entrance requirements:* For master's, GRE, 3 letters of recommendation, statement of purpose, 3 to 5 years of professional experience. Additional exam requirements/recommendations for international students: Required—TOEFL (minimum score 600 paper-based; 250 computer-based; 100 iBT). *Application deadline:* For fall admission, 3/15 for domestic and international students. Applications are processed on a rolling basis. Application fee: $55. Electronic applications accepted. *Financial support:* Scholarships/grants and tuition waivers (full and partial) available. Financial award application deadline: 3/15; financial award applicants required to submit FAFSA. *Faculty research:* Health and behavioral health, children and families, disabilities, aging policy, substance abuse, work, inequality and social change, women/gender, poverty alleviation. *Unit head:* Dr. Michael Doonan, Program Director, 781-736-4831, E-mail: doonan@brandeis.edu. *Application contact:* Shana Mongan, Admissions Officer, 781-736-4229, E-mail: mongan@brandeis.edu.

Brandeis University, The Heller School for Social Policy and Management, Program in Social Policy, Waltham, MA 02454-9110. Offers assets and inequalities (PhD); children, youth and families (PhD); global health and development (PhD); health and behavioral health (PhD). *Faculty:* 36 full-time, 107 part-time/adjunct. *Students:* 64 full-time (34 women), 82 part-time (72 women), 17 international. Average age 32. 105 applicants, 51% accepted, 23 enrolled. In 2010, 8 doctorates awarded. *Degree requirements:* For doctorate, thesis/dissertation, qualifying paper, 2-year residency. *Entrance requirements:* For doctorate, GRE General Test, 3 letters of recommendation, statement of purpose, writing sample, at least 3-5 years of professional experience. Additional exam requirements/recommendations for international students: Required—TOEFL (minimum score 600 paper-based; 250 computer-based; 100 iBT). *Application deadline:* For fall admission, 1/2 for domestic and international students. Application fee: $55. Electronic applications accepted. *Financial support:* In 2010–11, 15 fellowships with full tuition reimbursements (averaging $20,000 per year) were awarded; scholarships/grants, traineeships, health care benefits, tuition waivers (full and partial), and unspecified assistantships also available. Financial award application deadline: 1/2. *Faculty research:* Health; mental health; substance abuse; children, youth, and families; aging; international and community development; disabilities; work and inequality; and hunger and poverty. *Unit head:* Dr. Christine Bishop, Program Director, 781-736-3942, E-mail: bishop@brandeis.edu. *Application contact:* Elizabeth Cole, Assistant Director for Admissions and Financial Aid, 781-736-2647, E-mail: elcole@brandeis.edu.

Brigham Young University, Graduate Studies, College of Family, Home, and Social Sciences, Program in Marriage, Family and Human Development, Provo, UT 84602. Offers MS, PhD. *Accreditation:* AAMFT/COAMFTE. *Faculty:* 23 full-time (4 women). *Students:* 22 full-time (18 women), 4 international. Average age 33. 18 applicants, 61% accepted, 9 enrolled. In 2010, 8 master's, 2 doctorates awarded. *Degree requirements:* For master's, thesis; for doctorate, comprehensive exam, thesis/dissertation, 2 publishable papers. *Entrance requirements:* For master's and doctorate, GRE General Test, minimum GPA of 3.0 in last 60 semester hours, letters of recommendation. Additional exam requirements/recommendations for international students: Required—TOEFL (minimum score 580 paper-based; 237 computer-based; 85 iBT), IELTS (minimum score 7). *Application deadline:* For fall admission, 1/10 for domestic and international students. Application fee: $50. Electronic applications accepted. *Expenses:* Tuition: Full-time $5580; part-time $310 per credit hour. Tuition and fees vary according to program and student's religious affiliation. *Financial support:* In 2010–11, 18 students received support, including 18 research assistantships with full and partial tuition reimbursements available (averaging $5,800 per year), 3 teaching assistantships with full and partial tuition reimbursements available (averaging $5,800 per year); scholarships/grants and unspecified assistantships also available. Financial award application deadline: 3/27. *Faculty research:*

Family studies and family process, marriage, adolescence and emerging adulthood, adult development and aging, child development. *Unit head:* Dr. Richard Miller, Director, School of Life, 801-422-2069, Fax: 801-422-0230, E-mail: rick_miller@byu.edu. *Application contact:* Graduate Secretary, 801-422-2060, E-mail: mfhdgrad@byu.edu.

Brock University, Faculty of Graduate Studies, Faculty of Social Sciences, Program in Child and Youth Studies, St. Catharines, ON L2S 3A1, Canada. Offers MA. Part-time programs available. *Degree requirements:* For master's, thesis. *Entrance requirements:* For master's, honors BA. Additional exam requirements/recommendations for international students: Required—TOEFL (minimum score 550 paper-based; 213 computer-based; 80 iBT), IELTS (minimum score 6.5), TWE (minimum score 4). Electronic applications accepted. *Faculty research:* Cognitive mechanisms, youth resilience, developmental disabilities, parent-child interactions and communication.

California State University, Los Angeles, Graduate Studies, College of Health and Human Services, Department of Child and Family Studies, Los Angeles, CA 90032-8530. Offers child development (MA). Part-time and evening/weekend programs available. *Faculty:* 3 full-time (all women), 2 part-time/adjunct (both women). *Students:* 4 full-time (2 women), 23 part-time (21 women); includes 16 minority (6 Asian, non-Hispanic/Latino; 10 Hispanic/Latino), 1 international. Average age 29. 13 applicants, 100% accepted, 12 enrolled. In 2010, 6 master's awarded. *Degree requirements:* For master's, comprehensive exam, project or thesis. *Entrance requirements:* Additional exam requirements/recommendations for international students: Required—TOEFL (minimum score 500 paper-based; 173 computer-based). *Application deadline:* For fall admission, 5/1 for domestic and international students. Applications are processed on a rolling basis. Application fee: $55. *Financial support:* Career-related internships or fieldwork and Federal Work-Study available. Support available to part-time students. Financial award application deadline: 3/1. *Faculty research:* Nutrition education, laundry product and fabric durability, computer usage in public school home economics. *Unit head:* Dr. Rita Ledesma, Chair, 323-343-4590, Fax: 323-343-5019, E-mail: rledesm@calstatela.edu. *Application contact:* Dr. Alan Muchlinski, Dean of Graduate Studies, 323-343-3820, Fax: 323-343-5653, E-mail: amuchli@exchange.calstatela.edu.

Capella University, Harold Abel School of Psychology, Minneapolis, MN 55402. Offers child and adolescent development (MS); clinical psychology (MS, Psy D); counseling psychology (MS); educational psychology (MS, PhD); evaluation, research, and measurement (MS); general psychology (MS, PhD); industrial/organizational psychology (MS, PhD); leadership coaching psychology (MS); organizational leader development (MS); school psychology (MS); sport psychology (MS). Part-time and evening/weekend programs available. Postbaccalaureate distance learning degree programs offered (minimal on-campus study). Terminal master's awarded for partial completion of doctoral program. *Degree requirements:* For master's, thesis optional, project; for doctorate, thesis/dissertation. *Entrance requirements:* For degree, master's degree in school psychology. Additional exam requirements/recommendations for international students: Required—TOEFL (minimum score 550 paper-based; 213 computer-based), TWE (minimum score 4); Recommended—IELTS. Electronic applications accepted. *Expenses:* Tuition: Full-time $11,880; part-time $440 per credit hour.

Capella University, School of Human Services, Minneapolis, MN 55402. Offers addictions counseling (Certificate); counseling studies (MS, PhD); criminal justice (MS, PhD, Certificate); diversity studies (Certificate); general human services (MS, PhD); health care administration (MS, PhD, Certificate); management of nonprofit agencies (MS, PhD, Certificate); marital, couple and family counseling/therapy (MS); marriage and family services (Certificate); mental health counseling (MS); professional counseling (Certificate); social and community services (MS, PhD, Certificate). Part-time and evening/weekend programs available. Postbaccalaureate distance learning degree programs offered (minimal on-campus study). Terminal master's awarded for partial completion of doctoral program. *Degree requirements:* For master's, thesis optional, integrative project; for doctorate, comprehensive exam, thesis/dissertation. *Entrance requirements:* Additional exam requirements/recommendations for international students: Required—TOEFL (minimum score 550 paper-based; 213 computer-based), TWE (minimum score 4). Electronic applications accepted. *Expenses:* Tuition: Full-time $11,880; part-time $440 per credit hour. *Faculty research:* Compulsive and addictive behaviors, substance abuse, assessment of psychopathology and neuropsychology.

Central Michigan University, College of Graduate Studies, College of Education and Human Services, Department of Human Environmental Studies, Mount Pleasant, MI 48859. Offers apparel product development and merchandising technology (MS); gerontology (Graduate Certificate); human development and family studies (MA); nutrition and dietetics (MS). Part-time and evening/weekend programs available. *Faculty:* 15 full-time (11 women), 1 (woman) part-time/adjunct. *Students:* 6 full-time (4 women), 24 part-time (22 women); includes 2 Black or African American, non-Hispanic/Latino, 4 international. *Degree requirements:* For master's, thesis or alternative. *Application deadline:* Applications are processed on a rolling basis. Application fee: $35 ($45 for international students). Electronic applications accepted. *Expenses:* Tuition, state resident: full-time $8208; part-time $456 per credit hour. Tuition, nonresident: full-time $13,788; part-time $766 per credit hour. One-time fee: $25. *Financial support:* Fellowships with tuition reimbursements, research assistantships, career-related internships or fieldwork, Federal Work-Study, unspecified assistantships, and out-of-state merit awards, non-resident graduate awards available. *Faculty research:* Human growth and development, family studies and human sexuality, human nutrition and dietetics, apparel and textile retailing, computer-aided design for apparel. *Unit head:* Dr. Megan P. Goodwin, Chairperson, 989-774-3218, Fax: 989-774-2435, E-mail: goodw1mp@cmich.edu. *Application contact:* Dr. Candace Maylee, Assistant Coordinator of Graduate Programs, 989-774-2613, Fax: 989-774-2435, E-mail: mayle1ce@cmich.edu.

Central Washington University, Graduate Studies and Research, College of Education and Professional Studies, Department of Family and Consumer Sciences, Ellensburg, WA 98926. Offers family and consumer sciences education (MS); family studies (MS). Part-time programs available. *Degree requirements:* For master's, thesis or alternative. *Entrance requirements:* For master's, minimum GPA of 3.0. Additional exam requirements/recommendations for international students: Required—TOEFL (minimum score 550 paper-based; 213 computer-based; 79 iBT). Electronic applications accepted.

Colorado State University, Graduate School, College of Applied Human Sciences, Department of Human Development and Family Studies, Fort Collins, CO 80523-1570. Offers MS, PhD. *Accreditation:* AAMFT/COAMFTE. Part-time programs available. *Faculty:* 14 full-time (10 women). *Students:* 30 full-time (28 women), 6 part-time (5 women); includes 1 minority (Black or African American, non-Hispanic/Latino), 4 international. Average age 28. 108 applicants, 29% accepted, 16 enrolled. In 2010, 10 master's awarded. Terminal master's awarded for partial completion of doctoral program. *Degree requirements:* For master's, thesis or alternative; for doctorate, comprehensive exam (for some programs), thesis/dissertation, competency exams. *Entrance requirements:* For master's, GRE General Test, minimum GPA of 3.0; course work in human development, family studies, and statistics; letters of recommendation; interview; BS/BA in human development and family studies or related field; for doctorate, GRE General Test (50th percentile on Verbal and Quantitative sections and 4.5 on Analytical Writing section), minimum GPA of 3.0; coursework in human development, family studies, and statistics; letters of recommendation; departmental application; interview; BS/BA or master's degree in related field. Additional exam requirements/recommendations for international students: Required—TOEFL (minimum score 550 paper-based; 213 computer-based; 80 iBT). *Application deadline:* For fall admission, 1/2 for domestic and international students. Application fee: $50. Electronic applications accepted. *Expenses:* Tuition, state resident: full-time $7434; part-time $413 per credit. Tuition, nonresident: full-time $19,022; part-time $1057 per credit. Required fees: $1729; $88 per credit. *Financial support:* In 2010–11, 32 students received support, including 1 fellowship (averaging $37,368 per year), 11 research assistantships with full and partial tuition reimbursements available (averaging $7,481 per year), 20 teaching assistantships with full and partial tuition reimbursements available (averaging $8,405 per year); career-related

internships or fieldwork, Federal Work-Study, institutionally sponsored loans, scholarships/grants, health care benefits, and unspecified assistantships also available. Financial award application deadline: 2/15; financial award applicants required to submit FAFSA. *Faculty research:* Promoting resiliency and optimal development; gender, culture and diversity; gerontology/aging; child and adolescent health; disabilities. Total annual research expenditures: $824,524. *Unit head:* Dr. Lise Youngblade, Department Head, 970-491-5558, Fax: 970-491-7975, E-mail: lise.youngblade@colostate.edu. *Application contact:* Dr. Karen C. Barrett, Graduate Chair, 970-491-7382, Fax: 970-491-7975, E-mail: karen.barrett@colostate.edu.

Concordia University, School of Graduate Studies, Faculty of Arts and Science, Department of Education, Program in Child Study, Montréal, QC H3G 1M8, Canada. Offers MA. *Degree requirements:* For master's, one foreign language, thesis optional. *Entrance requirements:* For master's, minimum B average in undergraduate course work. *Faculty research:* Development and family relations, children and technology, cooperative learning strategies, exceptional children, second language acquisition.

Concordia University, St. Paul, College of Education, St. Paul, MN 55104-5494. Offers curriculum and instruction (MA Ed), including K-12 reading endorsement; differentiated instruction (MA Ed); early childhood education (MA Ed); educational leadership (MA Ed); family life education (MA); K-12 reading endorsement (Certificate); special education (Certificate); sports management (MA). *Accreditation:* NCATE. Evening/weekend programs available. Postbaccalaureate distance learning degree programs offered (minimal on-campus study). *Faculty:* 11 full-time (7 women), 69 part-time/adjunct (47 women). *Students:* 699 full-time (566 women), 1 (woman) part-time; includes 26 Black or African American, non-Hispanic/Latino; 2 American Indian or Alaska Native, non-Hispanic/Latino; 20 Asian, non-Hispanic/Latino; 7 Hispanic/Latino; 8 Two or more races, non-Hispanic/Latino. Average age 36. 311 applicants, 78% accepted, 230 enrolled. In 2010, 172 master's, 83 other advanced degrees awarded. *Application deadline:* Applications are processed on a rolling basis. Application fee: $50. Electronic applications accepted. *Expenses:* Tuition: Full-time $7500; part-time $460 per credit. Required fees: $460 per credit. Tuition and fees vary according to program. *Financial support:* Applicants required to submit FAFSA. *Unit head:* Dr. Donald Helmstetter, Dean, 651-641-8227, Fax: 651-641-8807, E-mail: helmstetter@csp.edu. *Application contact:* Kimberly Craig, Director of Graduate and Cohort Admission, 651-603-6223, Fax: 651-603-6320, E-mail: craig@csp.edu.

Concordia University Wisconsin, Graduate Programs, Department of Education, Program in Family Studies, Mequon, WI 53097-2402. Offers MS Ed. *Degree requirements:* For master's, comprehensive exam, thesis or alternative. *Entrance requirements:* For master's, minimum GPA of 3.0. Additional exam requirements/recommendations for international students: Required—TOEFL.

Cornell University, Graduate School, Graduate Fields of Human Ecology, Field of Human Development, Ithaca, NY 14853-0001. Offers developmental psychology (PhD), including cognitive development, developmental psychopathology, ecology of human development, social and personality development; human development and family studies (PhD), including ecology of human development, family studies and the life course. *Faculty:* 32 full-time (16 women). *Students:* 44 full-time (29 women); includes 1 Asian, non-Hispanic/Latino; 1 Hispanic/Latino, 12 international. Average age 27. 110 applicants, 26% accepted, 19 enrolled. In 2010, 2 doctorates awarded. *Degree requirements:* For doctorate, comprehensive exam, thesis/dissertation, pre-doctoral research project, teaching experience. *Entrance requirements:* For doctorate, GRE General Test, 2 letters of recommendation. Additional exam requirements/recommendations for international students: Required—TOEFL (minimum score 550 paper-based; 213 computer-based; 77 iBT). *Application deadline:* For fall admission, 1/15 for domestic students. Application fee: $70. Electronic applications accepted. *Expenses:* Tuition: Full-time $29,500. Required fees: $76. Tuition and fees vary according to degree level and program. *Financial support:* In 2010–11, 26 students received support, including 4 fellowships with full tuition reimbursements available, 9 research assistantships with full tuition reimbursements available, 18 teaching assistantships with full tuition reimbursements available; institutionally sponsored loans, scholarships/grants, health care benefits, tuition waivers (full and partial), and unspecified assistantships also available. Financial award applicants required to submit FAFSA. *Faculty research:* Cognitive development, developmental psychopathology, ecology of human development, family studies and the life course, social and personality development. *Unit head:* Director of Graduate Studies, 607-255-3181, Fax: 607-255-9856. *Application contact:* Graduate Field Assistant, 607-255-3181, Fax: 607-255-9856, E-mail: hdfs@cornell.edu.

East Carolina University, Graduate School, College of Human Ecology, Department of Child Development and Family Relations, Greenville, NC 27858-4353. Offers child development and family relations (MS); marriage and family therapy (MS). *Accreditation:* AAMFT/COAMFTE. Part-time programs available. *Degree requirements:* For master's, comprehensive exam, thesis optional. *Expenses:* Tuition, state resident: full-time $3130; part-time $391.25 per credit hour. Tuition, nonresident: full-time $13,817; part-time $1727.13 per credit hour. Required fees: $1916; $239.50 per credit hour. Tuition and fees vary according to campus/location and program. *Faculty research:* Child care quality, mental health delivery systems for children, family violence.

Eastern Michigan University, Graduate School, College of Health and Human Services, School of Social Work, Ypsilanti, MI 48197. Offers family and children's services (MSW); mental health and chemical dependency (MSW); services to the aging (MSW). *Accreditation:* CSWE. Part-time and evening/weekend programs available. *Faculty:* 19 full-time (15 women). *Students:* 20 full-time (18 women), 201 part-time (181 women); includes 89 minority (81 Black or African American, non-Hispanic/Latino; 1 American Indian or Alaska Native, non-Hispanic/Latino; 1 Asian, non-Hispanic/Latino; 4 Hispanic/Latino; 2 Two or more races, non-Hispanic/Latino), 1 international. Average age 36. 300 applicants, 33% accepted, 89 enrolled. In 2010, 76 master's awarded. *Entrance requirements:* Additional exam requirements/recommendations for international students: Required—TOEFL. *Application deadline:* For fall admission, 1/15 priority date for domestic students. Applications are processed on a rolling basis. Application fee: $35. *Financial support:* Fellowships, research assistantships with full tuition reimbursements, teaching assistantships with full tuition reimbursements, career-related internships or fieldwork, Federal Work-Study, institutionally sponsored loans, scholarships/grants, tuition waivers (partial), and unspecified assistantships available. Support available to part-time students. Financial award applicants required to submit FAFSA. *Unit head:* Dr. Ann Alvarez, Director, 734-487-0393, Fax: 734-487-6832, E-mail: aalvare4@emich.edu. *Application contact:* Julie Harkema, Admissions Director, 734-487-4206, Fax: 734-487-6832, E-mail: jharkema@emich.edu.

Fairfield University, Graduate School of Education and Allied Professions, Department of Marriage and Family Therapy, Fairfield, CT 06824-5195. Offers family studies (MA); marriage and family therapy (MA). *Accreditation:* AAMFT/COAMFTE. Part-time and evening/weekend programs available. *Faculty:* 3 full-time (all women), 5 part-time/adjunct (3 women). *Students:* 28 full-time (23 women), 55 part-time (51 women); includes 1 Black or African American, non-Hispanic/Latino; 3 Hispanic/Latino. Average age 39. 38 applicants, 53% accepted, 8 enrolled. In 2010, 17 master's awarded. *Degree requirements:* For master's, comprehensive exam. *Entrance requirements:* For master's, minimum QPA of 3.0, 2 recommendations, resume. Additional exam requirements/recommendations for international students: Required—TOEFL (minimum score 550 paper-based; 213 computer-based; 84 iBT). *Application deadline:* For fall admission, 4/15 for domestic and international students; for spring admission, 10/1 for domestic and international students. Application fee: $60. Electronic applications accepted. *Expenses:* Tuition: Part-time $600 per hour. Part-time tuition and fees vary according to degree level and program. *Financial support:* Unspecified assistantships available. Financial award applicants required to submit FAFSA. *Faculty research:* Diversity and multiculturalism, accreditation, professional ethics, program development and alumni engagement, international family therapy. *Unit head:* Dr. Rona Preli, Chair, 203-254-4000 Ext. 2475, Fax: 203-254-4047, E-mail: rpreli@fairfield.edu. *Application contact:* Marianne Gumpper, Director of Graduate and Continuing Studies Admissions, 203-254-4184, Fax: 203-254-4073, E-mail: gradadmis@fairfield.edu.

Child and Family Studies

Florida State University, The Graduate School, College of Human Sciences, Department of Family and Child Sciences, Tallahassee, FL 32306. Offers family and child sciences (MS); family relations (PhD); marriage and family therapy (PhD). *Accreditation:* AAMFT/COAMFTE. Part-time programs available. *Faculty:* 13 full-time (8 women). *Students:* 36 full-time (27 women), 15 part-time (13 women); includes 12 Black or African American, non-Hispanic/Latino; 1 Asian, non-Hispanic/Latino; 4 Hispanic/Latino, 1 international. 43 applicants, 28% accepted, 10 enrolled. In 2010, 6 master's, 9 doctorates awarded. *Degree requirements:* For master's, comprehensive exam, thesis optional; for doctorate, thesis/dissertation, preliminary examination; clinical examination (for marriage and family therapy). *Entrance requirements:* For master's and doctorate, GRE General Test, minimum GPA of 3.0. Additional exam requirements/recommendations for international students: Required—TOEFL (minimum score 80 iBT). *Application deadline:* For fall admission, 7/1 for domestic students, 5/1 for international students; for spring admission, 11/1 priority date for domestic students, 10/1 priority date for international students. Application fee: $30. Electronic applications accepted. *Expenses:* Tuition, state resident: full-time $8238.24. *Financial support:* In 2010–11, 33 students received support, including 2 fellowships with full tuition reimbursements available (averaging $15,000 per year), 6 research assistantships with full tuition reimbursements available (averaging $16,000 per year), 31 teaching assistantships with full tuition reimbursements available (averaging $16,000 per year); career-related internships or fieldwork, Federal Work-Study, institutionally sponsored loans, scholarships/grants, health care benefits, and unspecified assistantships also available. Financial award application deadline: 1/5; financial award applicants required to submit FAFSA. *Faculty research:* Family therapy, parent-child relations, distressed families and foster care, marital processes, relational interventions. *Unit head:* Dr. Kay Pasley, Chair, 850-644-3217, Fax: 850-644-3439, E-mail: kpasley@admin.fsu.edu. *Application contact:* Bethany Lowe, Academic Support Assistant, 850-644-3217, Fax: 850-644-3439, E-mail: blowe@fsu.edu.

Indiana University Bloomington, School of Health, Physical Education and Recreation, Department of Applied Health Science, Bloomington, IN 47405-7000. Offers health behavior (PhD); health promotion (MS); human development/family studies (MS); nutrition science (MS); public health (MPH); safety management (MS); school and college health programs (MS). *Accreditation:* CEPH (one or more programs are accredited). *Faculty:* 24 full-time (12 women). *Students:* 143 full-time (105 women), 32 part-time (20 women); includes 36 Black or African American, non-Hispanic/Latino; 2 American Indian or Alaska Native, non-Hispanic/Latino; 2 Asian, non-Hispanic/Latino; 7 Hispanic/Latino; 1 Two or more races, non-Hispanic/Latino, 28 international. Average age 30. 135 applicants, 80% accepted, 73 enrolled. In 2010, 49 master's, 7 doctorates awarded. *Degree requirements:* For master's, thesis optional; for doctorate, thesis/dissertation. *Entrance requirements:* For master's, GRE (MS in nutrition science), 3 recommendations; for doctorate, GRE, 3 recommendations. Additional exam requirements/recommendations for international students: Required—TOEFL (minimum score 550 paper-based; 213 computer-based; 79 iBT). *Application deadline:* For fall admission, 4/30 priority date for domestic students, 12/1 priority date for international students; for spring admission, 11/15 priority date for domestic students, 9/1 priority date for international students. Application fee: $55 ($65 for international students). *Financial support:* Fellowships, research assistantships with full and partial tuition reimbursements, teaching assistantships with full and partial tuition reimbursements, career-related internships or fieldwork, Federal Work-Study, institutionally sponsored loans, scholarships/grants, tuition waivers (partial), and fee remissions available. Financial award application deadline: 3/1. *Faculty research:* Cancer education, HIV/AIDS and drug education, public health, parent-child interactions, safety education. Total annual research expenditures: $2.8 million. *Unit head:* Dr. Mohammad R. Torabi, Chair, 812-855-4808, Fax: 812-855-3936, E-mail: torabi@indiana.edu. *Application contact:* Dr. Mohammad R. Torabi, Chair, 812-855-4808, Fax: 812-855-3936, E-mail: torabi@indiana.edu.

Indiana University–Purdue University Indianapolis, School of Liberal Arts, Department of Sociology, Indianapolis, IN 46202-2896. Offers family/gender studies (MA); medical sociology (MA); work/occupations (MA). *Faculty:* 17 full-time (8 women). *Students:* 13 full-time (8 women), 9 part-time (5 women); includes 1 minority (Black or African American, non-Hispanic/Latino), 2 international. Average age 30. 16 applicants, 75% accepted, 10 enrolled. In 2010, 9 master's awarded. Application fee: $55 ($65 for international students). *Financial support:* In 2010–11, 2 fellowships (averaging $9,500 per year), 2 teaching assistantships (averaging $6,309 per year) were awarded. *Unit head:* Carrie Foote, Director of Graduate Studies, 317-274-8981, E-mail: sociology@iupui.edu. *Application contact:* Director of Research and Graduate Programs, 317-274-8305.

Iowa State University of Science and Technology, Graduate College, College of Human Sciences, Department of Human Development and Family Studies, Ames, IA 50011. Offers human development and family studies (MFCS, MS, PhD). *Accreditation:* AAMFT/COAMFTE. *Faculty:* 19 full-time (15 women), 6 part-time/adjunct (5 women). *Students:* 62 full-time (55 women), 21 part-time (17 women); includes 2 Black or African American, non-Hispanic/Latino; 1 Asian, non-Hispanic/Latino; 4 Hispanic/Latino, 10 international. 34 applicants, 74% accepted, 11 enrolled. In 2010, 11 master's, 9 doctorates awarded. *Degree requirements:* For master's, thesis; for doctorate, thesis/dissertation. *Entrance requirements:* For master's and doctorate, GRE General Test. Additional exam requirements/recommendations for international students: Required—TOEFL (minimum score 550 paper-based; 79 iBT), IELTS (minimum score 6.5). *Application deadline:* For fall admission, 1/15 priority date for domestic and international students. Application fee: $40 ($90 for international students). Electronic applications accepted. *Financial support:* In 2010–11, 36 research assistantships with full and partial tuition reimbursements (averaging $12,375 per year), 11 teaching assistantships with full and partial tuition reimbursements (averaging $11,066 per year) were awarded; fellowships, scholarships/grants also available. *Faculty research:* Child development, early childhood education, family resource management and housing, life span studies. *Unit head:* Dr. Dianne Draper, Interim Chair, 515-294-6316, Fax: 515-294-2502, E-mail: hdfs-grad-adm@iastate.edu. *Application contact:* Dr. Dianne Draper, Interim Chair, 515-294-6316, Fax: 515-294-2502, E-mail: hdfs-grad-adm@iastate.edu.

Kansas State University, Graduate School, College of Human Ecology, Program in Human Ecology, Manhattan, KS 66506. Offers apparel and textiles (PhD); family life education and consultation (PhD); food service and hospitality management (PhD); lifespan and human development (PhD); marriage and family therapy (PhD); personal financial planning (PhD). *Degree requirements:* For doctorate, thesis/dissertation. Electronic applications accepted.

Kansas State University, Graduate School, College of Human Ecology, School of Family Studies and Human Services, Manhattan, KS 66506. Offers communication sciences and disorders (MS); early childhood education (MS); family studies (MS); life span human development (MS); marriage and family therapy (MS). *Accreditation:* AAMFT/COAMFTE; ASHA. Part-time programs available. *Degree requirements:* For master's, thesis or alternative, oral exam, residency. *Entrance requirements:* For master's, GRE, minimum GPA of 3.0 in last 2 years of undergraduate study. Additional exam requirements/recommendations for international students: Required—TOEFL (minimum score 600 paper-based; 250 computer-based). Electronic applications accepted. *Faculty research:* Health and security of military families, personal and family risk assessment and evaluation, disorders of communication and swallowing, families and health.

Kent State University, Graduate School of Education, Health, and Human Services, School of Lifespan Development and Educational Sciences, Program in Family Studies, Kent, OH 44242-0001. Offers gerontology (MA); human development and family studies (MA). *Faculty:* 8 full-time (6 women), 12 part-time/adjunct (11 women). *Students:* 3 full-time (all women), 12 part-time (11 women); includes 2 Black or African American, non-Hispanic/Latino. 10 applicants, 70% accepted. In 2010, 4 master's awarded. Application fee: $30 ($60 for international students). *Expenses:* Tuition, state resident: full-time $7866; part-time $437 per credit hour. Tuition, nonresident: full-time $14,022; part-time $779 per credit hour. *Financial support:* In 2010–11, research assistantships (averaging $8,313 per year); 2 administrative assistantships (averaging $8,313 per year) also available. *Unit head:* Dr. Rhonda Richardson, Coordinator,

330-672-2026, E-mail: rrichard@kent.edu. *Application contact:* Nancy Miller, Academic Program Coordinator, 330-672-2576, Fax: 330-672-9162, E-mail: ogs@kent.edu.

Loma Linda University, School of Science and Technology, Department of Counseling and Family Science, Loma Linda, CA 92350. Offers MA, MS, DMFT, PhD, Certificate, MA/Certificate. *Degree requirements:* For master's, comprehensive exam, thesis optional; for doctorate, comprehensive exam, thesis/dissertation (for some programs). *Entrance requirements:* For master's, minimum GPA of 3.0; for doctorate, GRE. Additional exam requirements/recommendations for international students: Required—TOEFL (minimum score 550 paper-based; 213 computer-based), MTELP. Electronic applications accepted.

Miami University, Graduate School, School of Education and Allied Professions, Department of Family Studies and Social Work, Oxford, OH 45056. Offers child and family studies (MS). Part-time programs available. *Students:* 11 full-time (9 women), 5 part-time (all women); includes 3 minority (2 Black or African American, non-Hispanic/Latino; 1 Hispanic/Latino), 4 international. Average age 32. In 2010, 7 master's awarded. *Entrance requirements:* For master's, minimum undergraduate GPA of 3.0 during previous 2 years or 2.75 overall. Application fee: $50. *Expenses:* Tuition, state resident: full-time $11,616; part-time $484 per credit hour. Tuition, nonresident: full-time $25,656; part-time $1069 per credit hour. Required fees: $528. *Financial support:* Fellowships, research assistantships, teaching assistantships, career-related internships or fieldwork, Federal Work-Study, health care benefits, tuition waivers (full), and unspecified assistantships available. Financial award application deadline: 3/1. *Unit head:* Dr. Gary Peterson, Chair, 513-529-2323, E-mail: petersgw@muohio.edu. *Application contact:* Dr. Charles Hennon, Director of Graduate Studies, 513-529-2323, Fax: 513-529-6468, E-mail: hennoncb@mushio.edu.

Michigan State University, The Graduate School, College of Social Science, Department of Family and Child Ecology, East Lansing, MI 48824. Offers child development (MA); community services (MS); family and child ecology (PhD); family studies (MA); marriage and family therapy (MA); youth development (MA). *Accreditation:* AAMFT/COAMFTE (one or more programs are accredited). *Entrance requirements:* For master's, GRE General Test, minimum GPA of 3.0 in last 2 years of undergraduate course work, 3 letters of recommendation; for doctorate, GRE General Test, minimum GPA of 3.0, 3 letters of recommendation, background in behavioral sciences. Additional exam requirements/recommendations for international students: Required—TOEFL. Electronic applications accepted.

Middle Tennessee State University, College of Graduate Studies, College of Behavioral and Health Sciences, Department of Human Sciences, Murfreesboro, TN 37132. Offers child development and family studies (MS); nutrition and food science (MS). Part-time and evening/weekend programs available. Postbaccalaureate distance learning degree programs offered. *Faculty:* 7 full-time (all women). *Students:* 24 part-time (23 women); includes 4 Black or African American, non-Hispanic/Latino; 2 Asian, non-Hispanic/Latino; 1 Hispanic/Latino. Average age 31. 22 applicants, 82% accepted, 18 enrolled. In 2010, 5 master's awarded. *Degree requirements:* For master's, comprehensive exam, thesis. *Entrance requirements:* For master's, GRE or MAT. Additional exam requirements/recommendations for international students: Required—TOEFL (minimum score 525 paper-based; 195 computer-based; 71 iBT) or IELTS (minimum score 6). *Application deadline:* For fall admission, 6/1 for domestic and international students. Applications are processed on a rolling basis. Application fee: $25 ($30 for international students). Electronic applications accepted. *Expenses:* Tuition, state resident: full-time $4632. Tuition, nonresident: full-time $11,520. *Financial support:* In 2010–11, 5 students received support. Application deadline: 5/1. *Faculty research:* Courtship relationships, feminist methodology and epistemology in family studies, school uniforms, body fat in elderly, asynchronous distance education. *Unit head:* Dr. Deborah G. Belcher, Interim Chair, 615-898-2884, Fax: 615-898-5130, E-mail: dbelcher@mtsu.edu. *Application contact:* Dr. Michael Allen, Dean and Vice Provost for Research, 615-898-2840, Fax: 615-904-8020, E-mail: mallen@mtsu.edu.

Missouri State University, Graduate College, College of Education, Department of Childhood Education and Family Studies, Program in Early Childhood and Family Development, Springfield, MO 65897. Offers MS. Part-time programs available. Postbaccalaureate distance learning degree programs offered. *Entrance requirements:* For master's, GRE, minimum GPA of 3.0. Additional exam requirements/recommendations for international students: Required—TOEFL (minimum score 550 paper-based; 213 computer-based; 79 iBT). Electronic applications accepted. *Expenses:* Tuition, state resident: full-time $3348; part-time $186 per credit hour. Tuition, nonresident: full-time $6696; part-time $372 per credit hour. Required fees: $238 per semester. Tuition and fees vary according to course level, course load and program.

Mount Saint Vincent University, Graduate Programs, Department of Child and Youth Study, Halifax, NS B3M 2J6, Canada. Offers MA. Part-time and evening/weekend programs available. *Degree requirements:* For master's, thesis. *Entrance requirements:* For master's, bachelor's degree in related field, minimum B+ average, professional experience. Electronic applications accepted.

Mount Saint Vincent University, Graduate Programs, Department of Family Studies and Gerontology, Halifax, NS B3M 2J6, Canada. Offers MA. Part-time programs available. Postbaccalaureate distance learning degree programs offered (minimal on-campus study). *Degree requirements:* For master's, thesis. *Entrance requirements:* For master's, minimum GPA of 3.0; course work in statistics, research methods, family and social theories.

North Dakota State University, College of Graduate and Interdisciplinary Studies, College of Human Development and Education, Department of Child Development and Family Science, Fargo, ND 58108. Offers child development and family science (MS); couple and family therapy (MS); family financial planning (MS); gerontology (MS, PhD). *Accreditation:* AAMFT/COAMFTE. Part-time and evening/weekend programs available. Postbaccalaureate distance learning degree programs offered (no on-campus study). *Faculty:* 12 full-time (7 women). *Students:* 30 full-time (27 women), 20 part-time (19 women); includes 2 Black or African American, non-Hispanic/Latino, 2 international. 26 applicants, 62% accepted, 13 enrolled. *Degree requirements:* For master's, thesis or alternative; for doctorate, thesis/dissertation. *Entrance requirements:* Additional exam requirements/recommendations for international students: Required—TOEFL (minimum score 525 paper-based; 197 computer-based; 71 iBT). *Application deadline:* For fall admission, 2/1 for domestic and international students; for spring admission, 10/1 for domestic and international students. Application fee: $45 ($60 for international students). *Financial support:* In 2010–11, 17 students received support, including research assistantships with full tuition reimbursements available (averaging $3,000 per year), 17 teaching assistantships with full tuition reimbursements available (averaging $3,000 per year); career-related internships or fieldwork, Federal Work-Study, institutionally sponsored loans, and tuition waivers (full) also available. Financial award application deadline: 4/1. *Faculty research:* Family therapy, resilience, parenting, adolescent development, mental health. Total annual research expenditures: $333,582. *Unit head:* Dr. James Deal, Head, 701-231-7568, Fax: 701-231-9645, E-mail: jim_deal@ndsu.edu. *Application contact:* Theresa Anderson, Administrative Assistant, 701-231-8628, Fax: 701-231-9645, E-mail: theresa.anderson@ndsu.edu.

Northern Illinois University, Graduate School, College of Health and Human Sciences, School of Family, Consumer and Nutrition Sciences, De Kalb, IL 60115-2854. Offers applied family and child studies (MS); nutrition and dietetics (MS). *Accreditation:* AAMFT/COAMFTE. Part-time programs available. *Faculty:* 16 full-time (14 women), 2 part-time/adjunct (1 woman). *Students:* 56 full-time (42 women), 28 part-time (27 women); includes 8 Black or African American, non-Hispanic/Latino; 3 Asian, non-Hispanic/Latino; 3 Hispanic/Latino; 2 Two or more races, non-Hispanic/Latino, 5 international. Average age 27. In 2010, 35 master's awarded. *Degree requirements:* For master's, comprehensive exam, internship, thesis (nutrition and dietetics). *Entrance requirements:* For master's, GRE General Test, minimum GPA of 2.75. Additional exam requirements/recommendations for international students: Required—TOEFL (minimum score 550 paper-based; 213 computer-based). *Application deadline:* For fall admission, 6/1 for domestic students, 5/1 for international students; for spring admission, 11/1 for domestic students, 10/1 for international students. Applications are processed on a rolling basis. Application fee: $30. Electronic applications accepted. *Expenses:* Tuition, state resident: full-time $7200; part-time $300 per credit hour. Tuition, nonresident: full-time $14,400; part-time $600 per credit hour. Required fees: $79 per credit hour. *Financial support:* In 2010–11, 8 research assistantships with full tuition reimbursements, 30 teaching assistantships with full tuition reimbursements were awarded; fellowships with full tuition reimbursements, career-related internships or fieldwork, Federal Work-Study, scholarships/grants, tuition waivers (full), and staff assistantships also available. Support available to part-time students. Financial award applicants required to submit FAFSA. *Faculty research:* Preliminary child development, hospitality administration in Asia, sports nutrition, eating disorders. *Unit head:* Dr. Laura Smart, Acting Chair, 815-753-1960, Fax: 815-753-1321, E-mail: lsmart@niu.edu. *Application contact:* Dr. Laura Smart, Acting Chair, 815-753-1960, Fax: 815-753-1321, E-mail: lsmart@niu.edu.

Nova Southeastern University, Fischler School of Education and Human Services, Programs in Human Services, Fort Lauderdale, FL 33314-7796. Offers child and youth studies (Ed D); child protection (MHS); education (MS), including human services; health professions education (MS); substance abuse counseling and education (MS). Part-time and evening/weekend programs available. *Students:* 1,867 full-time (1,442 women), 1,273 part-time (976 women); includes 1,545 Black or African American, non-Hispanic/Latino; 16 American Indian or Alaska Native, non-Hispanic/Latino; 48 Asian, non-Hispanic/Latino; 257 Hispanic/Latino, 27 international. In 2010, 118 doctorates awarded. *Degree requirements:* For master's, thesis, practicum; for doctorate, thesis/dissertation, practicum. *Entrance requirements:* For master's, GRE or MAT, work experience in field, minimum GPA of 2.5; for doctorate, GRE or MAT, master's degree, minimum GPA of 3.0, work experience. Additional exam requirements/recommendations for international students: Recommended—TOEFL (minimum score 550 paper-based; 213 computer-based), IELTS (minimum score 6). *Application deadline:* Applications are processed on a rolling basis. Application fee: $50. Electronic applications accepted. *Expenses:* Contact institution. *Financial support:* Career-related internships or fieldwork and Federal Work-Study available. Support available to part-time students. Financial award application deadline: 4/15; financial award applicants required to submit FAFSA. *Unit head:* Dr. H. Wells Singleton, Dean, 800-986-3223 Ext. 28730, Fax: 954-262-3894, E-mail: singlew@nova.edu. *Application contact:* Lenny Jacobskind, Director of School-Wide Recruiting, 800-986-3223 Ext. 28538, Fax: 954-262-2914, E-mail: lenny@nova.edu.

The Ohio State University, Graduate School, College of Education and Human Ecology, Department of Human Development and Family Science, Columbus, OH 43210. Offers M Ed, MS, PhD. *Faculty:* 24. *Students:* 23 full-time (20 women), 17 part-time (13 women); includes 2 Black or African American, non-Hispanic/Latino; 1 American Indian or Alaska Native, non-Hispanic/Latino; 1 Asian, non-Hispanic/Latino, 9 international. Average age 28. In 2010, 9 master's, 3 doctorates awarded. *Degree requirements:* For master's, thesis optional; for doctorate, thesis/dissertation. *Entrance requirements:* For master's and doctorate, GRE General Test. Additional exam requirements/recommendations for international students: Required—TOEFL (minimum score 577 paper-based; 233 computer-based). *Application deadline:* For fall admission, 8/15 priority date for domestic students, 7/1 priority date for international students; for winter admission, 12/1 priority date for domestic students, 11/1 priority date for international students; for spring admission, 3/1 priority date for domestic students, 2/1 priority date for international students. Applications are processed on a rolling basis. Application fee: $40 ($50 for international students). Electronic applications accepted. *Expenses:* Tuition, state resident: full-time $10,605. Tuition, nonresident: full-time $26,535. Tuition and fees vary according to course load and program. *Financial support:* Fellowships, research assistantships, teaching assistantships, Federal Work-Study and institutionally sponsored loans available. Support available to part-time students. *Unit head:* Julianne Serovich, Chair, 614-292-5685, Fax: 614-292-4365, E-mail: jserovich@ehe.osu.edu. *Application contact:* 614-292-9444, Fax: 614-292-3895, E-mail: domestic.grad@osu.edu.

Ohio University, Graduate College, College of Health Sciences and Professions, Department of Social and Public Health, Athens, OH 45701-2979. Offers early child development and family life (MS); family studies (MS); health administration (MHA); public health (MPH). *Accreditation:* CEPH. Part-time and evening/weekend programs available. Postbaccalaureate distance learning degree programs offered (no on-campus study). *Students:* 15 full-time (11 women), 304 part-time (211 women); includes 42 minority (25 Black or African American, non-Hispanic/Latino; 1 American Indian or Alaska Native, non-Hispanic/Latino; 11 Asian, non-Hispanic/Latino; 3 Hispanic/Latino; 2 Two or more races, non-Hispanic/Latino), 11 international. 125 applicants, 85% accepted, 75 enrolled. In 2010, 12 master's awarded. *Degree requirements:* For master's, capstone (MPH). *Entrance requirements:* For master's, GMAT, GRE General Test, previous course work in accounting, management, and statistics, previous public health background (MHA, MPH). Additional exam requirements/recommendations for international students: Required—TOEFL (minimum score 550 paper-based; 80 iBT) or IELTS (minimum score 6.5). *Application deadline:* Applications are processed on a rolling basis. Application fee: $50 ($55 for international students). Electronic applications accepted. *Expenses:* Contact institution. *Financial support:* Research assistantships with full tuition reimbursements, career-related internships or fieldwork, Federal Work-Study, institutionally sponsored loans, and unspecified assistantships available. Financial award applicants required to submit FAFSA. *Faculty research:* Health care management, health policy, managed care, health behavior, disease prevention. *Unit head:* Dr. Matthew Adeyanju, School Director, 740-593-1849, Fax: 740-593-0555, E-mail: adeyanju@ohio.edu. *Application contact:* Dr. Ruth Ann Althaus, Graduate Coordinator, Master of Health Administration Program, 740-597-2981, E-mail: althaus@ohio.edu.

Oklahoma State University, College of Human Sciences, Department of Human Development and Family Science, Stillwater, OK 74078. Offers human development and family science (MS, PhD), including family financial planning (MS), human environmental sciences (PhD); marriage and family therapy (MS). *Accreditation:* AAMFT/COAMFTE (one or more programs are accredited). Postbaccalaureate distance learning degree programs offered. *Faculty:* 29 full-time (20 women), 4 part-time/adjunct (all women). *Students:* 35 full-time (30 women), 33 part-time (26 women); includes 5 Black or African American, non-Hispanic/Latino; 3 American Indian or Alaska Native, non-Hispanic/Latino; 2 Hispanic/Latino, 7 international. Average age 31. 78 applicants, 31% accepted, 19 enrolled. In 2010, 21 master's, 4 doctorates awarded. *Degree requirements:* For master's, thesis (for some programs); for doctorate, comprehensive exam, thesis/dissertation. *Entrance requirements:* For master's and doctorate, GRE or GMAT. Additional exam requirements/recommendations for international students: Required—TOEFL (minimum score 550 paper-based; 79 iBT). *Application deadline:* For fall admission, 3/1 priority date for international students; for spring admission, 8/1 priority date for international students. Applications are processed on a rolling basis. Application fee: $40 ($75 for international students). Electronic applications accepted. *Expenses:* Tuition, state resident: full-time $3716; part-time $154.85 per credit hour. Tuition, nonresident: full-time $14,892; part-time $621 per credit hour. Required fees: $2044; $85.20 per credit hour. One-time fee: $50. Tuition and fees vary according to course load and campus/location. *Financial support:* In 2010–11, 26 research assistantships (averaging $8,826 per year), 21 teaching assistantships (averaging $8,143 per year) were awarded; career-related internships or fieldwork, Federal Work-Study, scholarships/grants, health care benefits, tuition waivers (partial), and unspecified assistantships also available. Support available to part-time students. Financial award application deadline: 3/1; financial award applicants required to submit FAFSA. *Faculty research:* Family relations and child development, consequences of adolescent parenting, family stress and coping, impacts of sexual abuse on families, children's social cognition and self-competence, gerontology and health care. *Unit head:* Dr. Sue Williams, Head, 405-744-5057, Fax: 405-744-2800. *Application contact:* Dr. Gordon Emslie, Dean, 405-744-6368, Fax: 405-744-0355, E-mail: grad-i@okstate.edu.

Oregon State University, Graduate School, College of Health and Human Sciences, Department of Human Development and Family Sciences, Corvallis, OR 97331. Offers gerontology (MAIS); human development and family studies (MS, PhD). *Degree requirements:*

For doctorate, thesis/dissertation. *Entrance requirements:* For master's and doctorate, GRE, minimum GPA of 3.0 in last 90 hours. Additional exam requirements/recommendations for international students: Required—TOEFL.

Oxford Graduate School, Graduate Programs, Dayton, TN 37321-6736. Offers family life education (M Litt); organizational leadership (M Litt); sociological integration of religion and society (D Phil). *Faculty:* 10 full-time (2 women), 22 part-time/adjunct (7 women). *Students:* 105 full-time (40 women). *Application contact:* Joanne Phillips, Information Contact, 423-775-6596, Fax: 423-775-6599, E-mail: oxfordgraduateschool@ogs.edu.

Penn State University Park, Graduate School, College of Health and Human Development, Department of Human Development and Family Studies, State College, University Park, PA 16802-1503. Offers MS, PhD. *Unit head:* Dr. Steven H. Zarit, Head, 814-865-5260, Fax: 814-863-7963, E-mail: z67@psu.edu. *Application contact:* Dr. Douglas M. Teti, Professor/Graduate Program Director, 814-865-2644, E-mail: dmt16@psu.edu.

Purdue University, Graduate School, College of Consumer and Family Sciences, Department of Child Development and Family Studies, West Lafayette, IN 47907. Offers developmental studies (MS, PhD); family studies (MS, PhD); marriage and family therapy (MS, PhD). *Accreditation:* AAMFT/COAMFTE (one or more programs are accredited). Part-time programs available. Terminal master's awarded for partial completion of doctoral program. *Degree requirements:* For master's, thesis; for doctorate, thesis/dissertation. *Entrance requirements:* For master's and doctorate, GRE General Test. Additional exam requirements/recommendations for international students: Required—TWE. Electronic applications accepted. *Faculty research:* Inclusion of children with special needs, families as learning environments, relationships in child care, work-family relations, AIDS prevention.

Purdue University Calumet, Graduate Studies Office, School of Liberal Arts and Social Sciences, Department of Behavioral Sciences, Hammond, IN 46323-2094. Offers child development and family studies (MS); marriage and family therapy (MS). *Accreditation:* AAMFT/COAMFTE. Part-time programs available. *Faculty:* 3 full-time (1 woman), 2 part-time/adjunct (0 women). *Students:* 18 full-time (16 women), 2 part-time (both women); includes 1 Black or African American, non-Hispanic/Latino; 1 Hispanic/Latino. 35 applicants, 26% accepted, 9 enrolled. In 2010, 4 master's awarded. *Degree requirements:* For master's, thesis. *Entrance requirements:* For master's, GRE, interview. Additional exam requirements/recommendations for international students: Required—TOEFL. *Application deadline:* For fall admission, 1/28 for domestic and international students. Application fee: $50. *Expenses:* Tuition, state resident: full-time $6867. Tuition, nonresident: full-time $14,157. *Financial support:* In 2010–11, 3 research assistantships with full tuition reimbursements (averaging $3,500 per year), 20 teaching assistantships with full tuition reimbursements (averaging $3,500 per year) were awarded; career-related internships or fieldwork and unspecified assistantships also available. Financial award application deadline: 3/1. *Faculty research:* Substance abuse, sexual abuse, couple therapy, professional issues, adolescent therapy. *Unit head:* Dr. Anne Edwards, Interim Head, 219-989-2863, E-mail: edwardsa@purduecal.edu. *Application contact:* Dr. Joseph Wetchler, Program Director, 219-989-2587, E-mail: wetchler@purduecal.edu.

Roberts Wesleyan College, Division of Social Work, Rochester, NY 14624-1997. Offers child and family practice (MSW); congregational and community practice (MSW); mental health practice (MSW). *Accreditation:* CSWE. *Entrance requirements:* For master's, minimum GPA of 2.75. *Faculty research:* Religion and social work, family studies, values and ethics.

Sage Graduate School, Graduate School, School of Health Sciences, Department of Psychology, Program in Community Psychology, Troy, NY 12180-4115. Offers child care and children's services (MA). Part-time and evening/weekend programs available. *Faculty:* 3 full-time (all women), 8 part-time/adjunct (7 women). *Students:* 9 full-time (8 women), 12 part-time (11 women); includes 4 minority (3 Black or African American, non-Hispanic/Latino; 1 Hispanic/Latino). Average age 29. 10 applicants, 60% accepted, 4 enrolled. In 2010, 5 master's awarded. *Degree requirements:* For master's, thesis or alternative. *Entrance requirements:* For master's, minimum GPA of 2.75; 2 letters of reference; undergraduate courses in statistics, history, and systems of psychology; 3 other courses in behavioral science; resume. Additional exam requirements/recommendations for international students: Required—TOEFL (minimum score 550 paper-based; 213 computer-based). *Application deadline:* Applications are processed on a rolling basis. Application fee: $40. *Expenses:* Tuition: Full-time $10,980; part-time $610 per credit hour. Tuition and fees vary according to course load, degree level and program. *Financial support:* Fellowships, research assistantships, teaching assistantships, Federal Work-Study, scholarships/grants, and unspecified assistantships available. Support available to part-time students. Financial award application deadline: 3/1; financial award applicants required to submit FAFSA. *Unit head:* Dr. Esther Haskevitz, Interim Dean, School of Health Sciences, 518-244-2296, Fax: 518-244-4571, E-mail: haskve@sage.edu. *Application contact:* Dr. Bronna Romanoff, Director, 518-244-2260, Fax: 518-244-4545, E-mail: romanb@sage.edu.

St. Cloud State University, School of Graduate Studies, College of Education, Department of Child and Family Studies, St. Cloud, MN 56301-4498. Offers MS. *Degree requirements:* For master's, thesis or alternative. *Entrance requirements:* For master's, GRE General Test, minimum GPA of 2.75. Additional exam requirements/recommendations for international students: Required—Michigan English Language Assessment Battery; Recommended—TOEFL (minimum score 550 paper-based; 213 computer-based), IELTS (minimum score 6.5). Electronic applications accepted.

San Diego State University, Graduate and Research Affairs, College of Education, Department of Child and Family Development, San Diego, CA 92182. Offers child development (MS). Part-time programs available. *Degree requirements:* For master's, thesis. *Entrance requirements:* For master's, GRE General Test, 3 letters of recommendation, interview. Additional exam requirements/recommendations for international students: Required—TOEFL. Electronic applications accepted.

San Jose State University, Graduate Studies and Research, Connie L. Lurie College of Education, Department of Child and Adolescent Development, San Jose, CA 95192-0001. Offers MA. Electronic applications accepted.

South Carolina State University, School of Graduate Studies, Department of Family and Consumer Sciences, Orangeburg, SC 29117-0001. Offers individual and family development (MS); nutritional sciences (MS). Part-time and evening/weekend programs available. *Degree requirements:* For master's, comprehensive exam, thesis optional, departmental qualifying exam. *Entrance requirements:* For master's, GRE, MAT, or NTE, minimum GPA of 2.7. Electronic applications accepted. *Faculty research:* Societal competence, relationship of parent-child interaction to adult, quality of well-being of rural elders.

Spring Arbor University, School of Graduate and Professional Studies, Spring Arbor, MI 49283-9799. Offers counseling (MAC); family studies (MAFS); nursing (MSN); organizational management (MAOM). Part-time and evening/weekend programs available. Postbaccalaureate distance learning degree programs offered (no on-campus study). *Faculty:* 16 full-time (7 women), 100 part-time/adjunct (56 women). *Students:* 407 full-time (324 women), 357 part-time (293 women); includes 171 Black or African American, non-Hispanic/Latino; 3 American Indian or Alaska Native, non-Hispanic/Latino; 9 Asian, non-Hispanic/Latino; 19 Hispanic/Latino, 2 international. Average age 39. In 2010, 279 master's awarded. *Entrance requirements:* For master's, bachelor's degree from regionally-accredited college or university, minimum GPA of 3.0 for at least the last two years of the bachelor's degree, at least two recommendations from professional/academic individuals. Additional exam requirements/recommendations for international students: Required—TOEFL (minimum score 600 paper-based; 220 computer-based). *Application deadline:* Applications are processed on a rolling basis. Application fee: $40. Electronic applications accepted. *Expenses:* Tuition: Full-time $6300; part-time $525 per credit hour. Required fees: $240; $120 per semester. Tuition and fees vary according to course load and program. *Financial support:* Scholarships/grants available. Support available to part-time students. Financial award applicants required to submit FAFSA. *Unit head:* Natalie

Child and Family Studies

Spring Arbor University (continued)
Gianetti, Dean, 517-750-1200 Ext. 1343, Fax: 517-750-6602, E-mail: gianetti@arbor.edu. *Application contact:* Greg Bentle, Coordinator of Graduate Recruitment, 517-750-6763, Fax: 517-750-6624, E-mail: gbentle@arbor.edu.

Stanford University, School of Education, Program in Psychological Studies in Education, Stanford, CA 94305-9991. Offers child and adolescent development (PhD); counseling psychology (PhD); educational psychology (PhD). *Degree requirements:* For doctorate, thesis/dissertation. *Entrance requirements:* For doctorate, GRE General Test. Electronic applications accepted. *Expenses:* Tuition: Full-time $38,700; part-time $860 per unit. One-time fee: $200 full-time.

State University of New York at Oswego, Graduate Studies, School of Education, Department of Vocational Teacher Preparation, Oswego, NY 13126. Offers agriculture (MS Ed); business and marketing (MS Ed); family and consumer sciences (MS Ed); health careers (MS Ed); technical education (MS Ed); trade education (MS Ed). *Accreditation:* NCATE. Part-time and evening/weekend programs available. *Faculty:* 5 full-time (2 women), 4 part-time/adjunct (all women). *Students:* 25 full-time (19 women), 40 part-time (25 women); includes 6 minority (3 Black or African American, non-Hispanic/Latino; 2 Asian, non-Hispanic/Latino; 1 Hispanic/Latino). Average age 37. 38 applicants, 100% accepted. In 2010, 24 master's awarded. *Degree requirements:* For master's, comprehensive exam, thesis or alternative. *Entrance requirements:* Additional exam requirements/recommendations for international students: Required—TOEFL (minimum score 560 paper-based; 220 computer-based). *Application deadline:* For fall admission, 4/1 for domestic students; for spring admission, 10/1 for domestic students. Applications are processed on a rolling basis. Application fee: $50. *Expenses:* Tuition, state resident: full-time $8370; part-time $349 per credit hour. Tuition, nonresident: full-time $13,780; part-time $574 per credit hour. Required fees: $853; $22.59 per credit hour. *Financial support:* In 2010–11, 2 students received support, including fellowships with full tuition reimbursements available (averaging $5,100 per year), 2 teaching assistantships with partial tuition reimbursements available (averaging $3,800 per year); career-related internships or fieldwork, Federal Work-Study, institutionally sponsored loans, health care benefits, and unspecified assistantships also available. Support available to part-time students. Financial award application deadline: 4/1; financial award applicants required to submit FAFSA. *Unit head:* Dr. Margaret Martin, Chair, 315-312-2480. *Application contact:* Dr. David W. King, Dean of Graduate Studies, 315-312-3152, Fax: 315-312-3228, E-mail: david.king@oswego.edu.

Syracuse University, College of Human Ecology, Program in Child and Family Studies, Syracuse, NY 13244. Offers MA, MS, PhD. *Accreditation:* AAMFT/COAMFTE (one or more programs are accredited). Part-time programs available. *Students:* 42 full-time (38 women), 11 part-time (10 women); includes 9 minority (5 Black or African American, non-Hispanic/Latino; 1 American Indian or Alaska Native, non-Hispanic/Latino; 2 Asian, non-Hispanic/Latino; 1 Hispanic/Latino), 17 international. Average age 37. 32 applicants, 59% accepted, 9 enrolled. In 2010, 4 master's, 3 doctorates awarded. *Degree requirements:* For master's, comprehensive exam (for some programs); for doctorate, thesis/dissertation. *Entrance requirements:* For master's and doctorate, GRE General Test. Additional exam requirements/recommendations for international students: Required—TOEFL (minimum score 100 iBT). *Application deadline:* For fall admission, 3/15 priority date for domestic and international students. Application fee: $75. Electronic applications accepted. *Expenses:* Tuition: Part-time $1162 per credit. *Financial support:* Fellowships with full tuition reimbursements, research assistantships with full and partial tuition reimbursements, teaching assistantships with full and partial tuition reimbursements, tuition waivers (partial) available. Financial award application deadline: 1/1. *Unit head:* Dr. Ambika Krishnakumar, Chair, 315-443-4293, Fax: 315-443-9402. *Application contact:* Kathy Pitts, Information Contact, 315-443-5555, E-mail: inquire@hshp.syr.edu.

Texas State University–San Marcos, Graduate School, College of Applied Arts, Department of Family and Consumer Science, Program in Family and Child Studies, San Marcos, TX 78666. Offers MS. Part-time programs available. *Faculty:* 5 full-time (all women), 1 (woman) part-time/adjunct. *Students:* 25 full-time (24 women), 18 part-time (all women); includes 2 Black or African American, non-Hispanic/Latino; 1 Asian, non-Hispanic/Latino; 7 Hispanic/Latino; 1 Two or more races, non-Hispanic/Latino. Average age 26. 44 applicants, 77% accepted, 19 enrolled. In 2010, 9 master's awarded. *Degree requirements:* For master's, thesis (for some programs). *Entrance requirements:* For master's, minimum GPA of 3.0, three letters of reference, statement of interest and goals. Additional exam requirements/recommendations for international students: Required—TOEFL (minimum score 550 paper-based; 213 computer-based; 78 iBT). *Application deadline:* For fall admission, 6/15 priority date for domestic students, 6/1 for international students; for spring admission, 10/15 for domestic students, 10/1 for international students. Applications are processed on a rolling basis. Application fee: $40 ($90 for international students). *Expenses:* Tuition, state resident: full-time $6024; part-time $251 per credit hour. Tuition, nonresident: full-time $13,536; part-time $564 per credit hour. Required fees: $1776; $50 per credit hour. $306 per semester. *Financial support:* In 2010–11, 17 students received support, including 5 research assistantships (averaging $3,046 per year), 13 teaching assistantships (averaging $3,319 per year). Financial award application deadline: 4/1. *Faculty research:* Healthy marriage. Total annual research expenditures: $513,572. *Unit head:* Dr. Michelle Toews, Graduate Adviser, 512-245-2155, Fax: 512-245-3829, E-mail: mt15@txstate.edu. *Application contact:* Dr. Michelle Toews, Graduate Adviser, 512-245-2155, Fax: 512-245-3829, E-mail: mt15@txstate.edu.

Texas Tech University, Graduate School, College of Human Sciences, Department of Human Development and Family Studies, Lubbock, TX 79409. Offers gerontology (MS); human development and family studies (MS, PhD). *Accreditation:* AAMFT/COAMFTE (one or more programs are accredited). Part-time programs available. *Faculty:* 17 full-time (13 women), 2 part-time/adjunct (both women). *Students:* 42 full-time (38 women), 14 part-time (6 women); includes 1 American Indian or Alaska Native, non-Hispanic/Latino; 1 Asian, non-Hispanic/Latino; 3 Hispanic/Latino, 14 international. Average age 32. 46 applicants, 43% accepted, 10 enrolled. In 2010, 6 master's, 3 doctorates awarded. *Degree requirements:* For master's, thesis; for doctorate, comprehensive exam, thesis/dissertation. *Entrance requirements:* For master's and doctorate, GRE General Test. Additional exam requirements/recommendations for international students: Required—TOEFL (minimum score 550 paper-based; 213 computer-based; 79 iBT). *Application deadline:* For fall admission, 6/1 priority date for domestic students, 1/15 priority date for international students; for spring admission, 9/1 priority date for domestic students, 6/15 priority date for international students. Applications are processed on a rolling basis. Application fee: $50 ($75 for international students). Electronic applications accepted. *Expenses:* Tuition, state resident: full-time $5495.76; part-time $228.99 per credit hour. Tuition, nonresident: full-time $12,936; part-time $538.99 per credit hour. Required fees: $2674; $36 per credit hour. $905 per semester. *Financial support:* In 2010–11, 40 students received support, including 8 research assistantships with partial tuition reimbursements available (averaging $3,281 per year), 14 teaching assistantships with partial tuition reimbursements available (averaging $3,551 per year). Financial award application deadline: 4/15; financial award applicants required to submit FAFSA. *Faculty research:* Parenting, marital and premarital relationships, adolescent risky behaviors, life span; child development. Total annual research expenditures: $509,694. *Unit head:* Dr. Jean Pearson Scott, Chairperson, 806-742-3000 Ext. 271, Fax: 806-742-0285, E-mail: jean.scott@ttu.edu. *Application contact:* Monya Castle, Graduate Secretary, 806-742-3000 Ext. 250, Fax: 806-742-0285, E-mail: monya.castle@ttu.edu.

Texas Woman's University, Graduate School, College of Professional Education, Department of Family Sciences, Denton, TX 76201. Offers child development (MS); counseling and development (MS); early childhood development and education (PhD); early childhood education (M Ed, MA, MS); family studies (MS, PhD); family therapy (MS, PhD). *Accreditation:* ACA (one or more programs are accredited). Part-time and evening/weekend programs available. *Faculty:* 22 full-time (17 women). *Students:* 106 full-time (103 women), 327 part-time (303 women); includes 118 Black or African American, non-Hispanic/Latino; 2 American Indian or Alaska Native, non-Hispanic/Latino; 12 Asian, non-Hispanic/Latino; 50 Hispanic/Latino, 20 international. Average age 36. 243 applicants, 58% accepted, 109 enrolled. In 2010, 86 master's, 14 doctorates awarded. Terminal master's awarded for partial completion of doctoral program. *Degree requirements:* For master's, portfolio; for doctorate, comprehensive exam, thesis/dissertation. *Entrance requirements:* For master's, interview, letter of intent, curriculum vitae, minimum GPA of 3.25 on last 60 hours (MS in family therapy); for doctorate, interview, minimum GPA of 3.5 in last 60 hours of course work (family therapy), letter of intent, curriculum vitae. Additional exam requirements/recommendations for international students: Required—TOEFL (minimum score 550 paper-based; 213 computer-based; 79 iBT). *Application deadline:* For fall admission, 2/15 priority date for domestic students, 3/1 for international students; for spring admission, 9/15 priority date for domestic students, 8/1 for international students. Applications are processed on a rolling basis. Application fee: $50 ($75 for international students). Electronic applications accepted. *Expenses:* Tuition, state resident: full-time $3834; part-time $213 per credit hour. Tuition, nonresident: full-time $9468; part-time $526 per credit hour. Required fees: $1247; $220 per credit hour. *Financial support:* In 2010–11, 100 students received support, including 21 research assistantships (averaging $12,942 per year), 2 teaching assistantships (averaging $12,942 per year); career-related internships or fieldwork, Federal Work-Study, institutionally sponsored loans, scholarships/grants, traineeships, health care benefits, and unspecified assistantships also available. Support available to part-time students. Financial award application deadline: 3/1; financial award applicants required to submit FAFSA. *Faculty research:* Parenting/parent education, military families, play therapy, family sexuality, diversity, healthy relationships/healthy marriages, childhood obesity, male communication. Total annual research expenditures: $26,116. *Unit head:* Dr. Larry LeFlore, Chair, 940-898-2685, Fax: 940-898-2676, E-mail: famsci@twu.edu. *Application contact:* Dr. Samuel Wheeler, Assistant Director of Admissions, 940-898-3188, Fax: 940-898-3081, E-mail: wheelersr@twu.edu.

Towson University, Program in Child Life, Administration and Family Collaboration, Towson, MD 21252-0001. Offers MS. *Students:* 13 full-time (all women), 2 part-time (both women); includes 2 minority (1 Black or African American, non-Hispanic/Latino; 1 Hispanic/Latino), 1 international. *Expenses:* Tuition, state resident: part-time $324 per credit. Tuition, nonresident: part-time $681 per credit. Required fees: $95 per term. *Unit head:* Lisa Martinelli Beasley, Dean, 410-704-3766, E-mail: lmartinelli@towson.edu. *Application contact:* Lisa Martinelli Beasley, Dean, 410-704-3766, E-mail: lmartinelli@towson.edu.

Towson University, Program in Family-Professional Collaboration, Towson, MD 21252-0001. Offers Certificate. *Students:* 13 full-time (all women), 5 part-time (all women); includes 2 minority (1 Black or African American, non-Hispanic/Latino; 1 Hispanic/Latino), 2 international. Average age 25.Application fee: $50. *Expenses:* Tuition, state resident: part-time $324 per credit. Tuition, nonresident: part-time $681 per credit. Required fees: $95 per term. *Unit head:* Karen Eskow, Graduate Program Director, 410-704-5851, E-mail: keskow@towson.edu. *Application contact:* The Graduate School, 410-704-2501, Fax: 410-704-4675, E-mail: grads@towson.edu.

Tufts University, Graduate School of Arts and Sciences, Department of Child Development, Medford, MA 02155. Offers child development (MA, PhD, CAGS); early childhood education (MAT). Part-time programs available. *Degree requirements:* For master's, thesis (for some programs); for doctorate, thesis/dissertation. *Entrance requirements:* For master's and doctorate, GRE General Test. Additional exam requirements/recommendations for international students: Required—TOEFL (minimum score 550 paper-based; 213 computer-based; 80 iBT). Electronic applications accepted. *Expenses:* Tuition: Full-time $39,624; part-time $3962 per course. Required fees: $40 per year. Full-time tuition and fees vary according to degree level, program and student level. Part-time tuition and fees vary according to course load.

The University of Akron, Graduate School, College of Health Sciences and Human Services, School of Family and Consumer Sciences, Program in Child and Family Development, Akron, OH 44325. Offers child development (MA); family development (MA). *Students:* 3 full-time (all women). Average age 35. 5 applicants, 40% accepted, 0 enrolled. *Degree requirements:* For master's, comprehensive exam, project or thesis. *Entrance requirements:* For master's, GRE, minimum GPA of 2.75, three letters of recommendation, statement of purpose, resume. Additional exam requirements/recommendations for international students: Required—TOEFL (minimum score 550 paper-based; 213 computer-based; 79 iBT). *Application deadline:* For fall admission, 3/1 for domestic and international students; for spring admission, 10/1 for domestic and international students. Application fee: $30 ($40 for international students). Electronic applications accepted. *Expenses:* Tuition, state resident: full-time $6800; part-time $378 per credit hour. Tuition, nonresident: full-time $11,644; part-time $647 per credit hour. Required fees: $1265. One-time fee: $30 full-time. *Unit head:* Dr. Susan M. Witt, Coordinator, 330-972-7729, E-mail: susan8@uakron.edu. *Application contact:* Dr. Susan M. Witt, Coordinator, 330-972-7729, E-mail: susan8@uakron.edu.

The University of Akron, Graduate School, College of Health Sciences and Human Services, School of Family and Consumer Sciences, Program in Child Life, Akron, OH 44325. Offers MA. *Students:* 5 full-time (all women); includes 1 Black or African American, non-Hispanic/Latino. Average age 29. 9 applicants, 56% accepted, 3 enrolled. In 2010, 1 master's awarded. *Degree requirements:* For master's, comprehensive exam, project or thesis. *Entrance requirements:* For master's, GRE, minimum GPA of 2.75, three letters of recommendation, statement of purpose, resume. Additional exam requirements/recommendations for international students: Required—TOEFL (minimum score 550 paper-based; 213 computer-based; 79 iBT). *Application deadline:* For fall admission, 3/1 for domestic and international students; for spring admission, 10/1 for domestic and international students. Application fee: $30 ($40 for international students). Electronic applications accepted. *Expenses:* Tuition, state resident: full-time $6800; part-time $378 per credit hour. Tuition, nonresident: full-time $11,644; part-time $647 per credit hour. Required fees: $1265. One-time fee: $30 full-time. *Unit head:* Rose Resler, Coordinator, 330-972-8040, E-mail: rresler@uakron.edu. *Application contact:* Rose Resler, Coordinator, 330-972-8040, E-mail: rresler@uakron.edu.

The University of Alabama, Graduate School, College of Human Environmental Sciences, Department of Human Development and Family Studies, Tuscaloosa, AL 35487. Offers MSHES. *Faculty:* 8 full-time (5 women). *Students:* 25 full-time (24 women), 15 part-time (14 women); includes 12 minority (9 Black or African American, non-Hispanic/Latino; 1 Asian, non-Hispanic/Latino; 2 Two or more races, non-Hispanic/Latino). Average age 27. 27 applicants, 70% accepted, 13 enrolled. In 2010, 14 master's awarded. *Degree requirements:* For master's, thesis (for some programs). *Entrance requirements:* For master's, GRE General Test or MAT, minimum GPA of 3.0. Additional exam requirements/recommendations for international students: Required—TOEFL. *Application deadline:* For fall admission, 2/1 priority date for domestic and international students. Applications are processed on a rolling basis. Application fee: $50 ($60 for international students). Electronic applications accepted. *Expenses:* Tuition, state resident: full-time $7900. Tuition, nonresident: full-time $20,500. *Financial support:* In 2010–11, 10 students received support, including 1 fellowship with full tuition reimbursement available (averaging $15,000 per year), 4 research assistantships with full tuition reimbursements available (averaging $10,908 per year), 5 teaching assistantships (averaging $10,000 per year); career-related internships or fieldwork, Federal Work-Study, scholarships/grants, health care benefits, and unspecified assistantships also available. Financial award application deadline: 2/15. *Faculty research:* Parent/child relationships, preschool curricula and quality measures for child care programs, family strengths and adolescent behaviors, depression in mothers and infants, word association and word learning in young children. *Unit head:* Dr. Carroll M. Tingle, Chair, 205-348-6158, Fax: 205-348-8153, E-mail: ctingle@ches.ua.edu. *Application contact:* Dr. Maria Hernandez-Reif, Associate Professor, 205-348-5894, Fax: 205-348-8153, E-mail: mhernandez-reif@ches.ua.edu.

The University of Arizona, College of Education, Department of Disability and Psychoeducational Studies, Division of Family Studies and Human Development, Tucson, AZ 85721. Offers M Ed. *Faculty:* 17 full-time (9 women). *Students:* 62 full-time (48 women), 39 part-time (34 women);

includes 3 Black or African American, non-Hispanic/Latino; 1 Asian, non-Hispanic/Latino; 9 Hispanic/Latino; 11 Two or more races, non-Hispanic/Latino, 9 international. Average age 36. 30 applicants, 70% accepted, 14 enrolled. In 2010, 25 master's awarded. Terminal master's awarded for partial completion of doctoral program. *Entrance requirements:* Additional exam requirements/recommendations for international students: Required—TOEFL (minimum score 600 paper-based). *Application deadline:* For fall admission, 2/1 for domestic students. Applications are processed on a rolling basis. Application fee: $65. *Expenses:* Tuition, state resident: full-time $7692. *Financial support:* In 2010–11, 4 research assistantships with full tuition reimbursements (averaging $12,828 per year), 4 teaching assistantships with full tuition reimbursements (averaging $12,378 per year) were awarded. *Unit head:* Dr. Ron Marx, Dean, 520-621-1081, E-mail: ronmarx@email.arizona.edu. *Application contact:* Cecilia Carlon, Administrative Assistant, 520-626-1248, E-mail: ccarlon@email.arizona.edu.

University of California, Santa Barbara, Graduate Division, Gevirtz Graduate School of Education, Santa Barbara, CA 93106-9490. Offers counseling, clinical and school psychology (PhD), including clinical psychology, counseling psychology, school psychology; education (M Ed, MA, PhD), including child and adolescent development (MA, PhD), cultural perspectives and comparative education (MA, PhD), educational leadership and organizations (MA, PhD), research methodology (MA, PhD), special education disabilities and risk studies (MA), special education, disabilities and risk studies (PhD), teaching (M Ed), teaching and learning (MA, PhD); educational leadership (Ed D); school psychology (M Ed); MA/PhD. *Accreditation:* APA (one or more programs are accredited). Postbaccalaureate distance learning degree programs offered (minimal on-campus study). *Faculty:* 40 full-time (22 women), 5 part-time/adjunct (1 woman). *Students:* 411 full-time (325 women); includes 19 Black or African American, non-Hispanic/Latino; 3 American Indian or Alaska Native, non-Hispanic/Latino; 59 Asian, non-Hispanic/Latino; 67 Hispanic/Latino. Average age 29. 683 applicants, 38% accepted, 154 enrolled. In 2010, 128 master's, 58 doctorates awarded. Terminal master's awarded for partial completion of doctoral program. *Degree requirements:* For master's, comprehensive exam (for some programs), thesis (for some programs); for doctorate, comprehensive exam (for some programs), thesis/dissertation. *Entrance requirements:* For master's and doctorate, GRE. Additional exam requirements/recommendations for international students: Required—TOEFL (minimum score 550 paper-based; 80 iBT), IELTS (minimum score 7). Application fee: $70 ($90 for international students). Electronic applications accepted. *Financial support:* In 2010–11, 269 students received support, including 222 fellowships with partial tuition reimbursements available (averaging $5,615 per year), 75 research assistantships with full tuition reimbursements available (averaging $6,470 per year), 65 teaching assistantships with partial tuition reimbursements available (averaging $7,059 per year); career-related internships or fieldwork also available. Financial award applicants required to submit FAFSA. *Faculty research:* Needs of diverse students, school accountability and leadership, school violence, language learning and literacy, science/math education. Total annual research expenditures: $3.1 million. *Unit head:* Carol North Dixon, Graduate Advisor, 805-893-2185, E-mail: dixon@education.ucsb.edu. *Application contact:* Kathryn Marie Tucciarone, Student Affairs Officer, 805-893-2137, Fax: 805-893-2588, E-mail: katiet@education.ucsb.edu.

University of Central Florida, College of Health and Public Affairs, School of Social Work, Orlando, FL 32816. Offers aging studies (Certificate); children's services (Certificate); social work (MSW); social work administration (Certificate). *Accreditation:* CSWE. Part-time and evening/weekend programs available. *Faculty:* 20 full-time (16 women), 23 part-time/adjunct (18 women). *Students:* 190 full-time (176 women), 169 part-time (138 women); includes 78 Black or African American, non-Hispanic/Latino; 2 American Indian or Alaska Native, non-Hispanic/Latino; 6 Asian, non-Hispanic/Latino; 38 Hispanic/Latino; 4 Two or more races, non-Hispanic/Latino, 3 international. Average age 32. 337 applicants, 82% accepted, 207 enrolled. In 2010, 88 master's, 5 other advanced degrees awarded. *Degree requirements:* For master's, thesis or alternative, field education. *Entrance requirements:* For master's, resume. Additional exam requirements/recommendations for international students: Required—TOEFL. *Application deadline:* For fall admission, 3/1 for domestic students. Application fee: $30. Electronic applications accepted. *Expenses:* Tuition, state resident: part-time $256.56 per credit hour. Tuition, nonresident: part-time $1011.52 per credit hour. Part-time tuition and fees vary according to program. *Financial support:* In 2010–11, 4 students received support, including 3 fellowships with partial tuition reimbursements available (averaging $10,000 per year), 1 research assistantship with partial tuition reimbursement available (averaging $7,100 per year); career-related internships or fieldwork, Federal Work-Study, institutionally sponsored loans, and unspecified assistantships also available. Financial award application deadline: 3/1; financial award applicants required to submit FAFSA. *Unit head:* Dr. John Ronnau, Director, 407-823-2114, Fax: 407-823-5697, E-mail: jronnau@mail.ucf.edu. *Application contact:* Dr. John Ronnau, Director, 407-823-2114, Fax: 407-823-5697, E-mail: jronnau@mail.ucf.edu.

University of Connecticut, Graduate School, College of Liberal Arts and Sciences, Department of Human Development and Family Studies, Storrs, CT 06269. Offers culture, health and human development (Graduate Certificate); human development and family studies (MA, PhD). *Accreditation:* AAMFT/COAMFTE (one or more programs are accredited). Terminal master's awarded for partial completion of doctoral program. *Degree requirements:* For master's, comprehensive exam; for doctorate, thesis/dissertation. *Entrance requirements:* For doctorate, GRE General Test. Additional exam requirements/recommendations for international students: Required—TOEFL (minimum score 550 paper-based; 213 computer-based). Electronic applications accepted.

University of Delaware, College of Human Services, Education and Public Policy, Department of Individual and Family Studies, Newark, DE 19716. Offers human development and family studies (MS, PhD). Part-time programs available. Terminal master's awarded for partial completion of doctoral program. *Degree requirements:* For master's, thesis or alternative; for doctorate, comprehensive exam, thesis/dissertation. *Entrance requirements:* For master's and doctorate, GRE General Test, 3 letters of recommendation. Additional exam requirements/recommendations for international students: Required—TOEFL. Electronic applications accepted. *Faculty research:* Early childhood inclusive education, relationships, family risk and resilience, disability issues, program development and evaluation.

University of Denver, Morgridge College of Education, Denver, CO 80208. Offers counseling psychology (MA, PhD); curriculum and instruction (MA, PhD, Certificate), including curriculum leadership (MA, PhD); educational administration and policy studies (Certificate); educational psychology (MA, PhD, Ed S), including child and family studies (MA, PhD), quantitative research methods (MA, PhD), school psychology (PhD, Ed S); higher education and adult studies (MA, PhD); library and information science (MLIS); library and information sciences (Certificate); school administration (PhD). *Accreditation:* ALA; APA (one or more programs are accredited). Part-time and evening/weekend programs available. Postbaccalaureate distance learning degree programs offered (no on-campus study). *Faculty:* 48 full-time (33 women), 68 part-time/adjunct (52 women). *Students:* 405 full-time (311 women), 423 part-time (326 women); includes 171 minority (53 Black or African American, non-Hispanic/Latino; 5 American Indian or Alaska Native, non-Hispanic/Latino; 17 Asian, non-Hispanic/Latino; 88 Hispanic/Latino; 8 Two or more races, non-Hispanic/Latino), 19 international. Average age 33. 934 applicants, 66% accepted, 381 enrolled. In 2010, 203 master's, 59 doctorates, 108 other advanced degrees awarded. Terminal master's awarded for partial completion of doctoral program. *Degree requirements:* For master's, comprehensive exam; for doctorate, 2 foreign languages, comprehensive exam, thesis/dissertation. *Entrance requirements:* For master's and doctorate, GRE General Test or GMAT. Additional exam requirements/recommendations for international students: Required—TOEFL (minimum score 550 paper-based; 80 iBT). *Application deadline:* Applications are processed on a rolling basis. Application fee: $60. Electronic applications accepted. *Expenses:* Tuition: Full-time $35,604; part-time $29,670 per year. Required fees: $687 per year. Tuition and fees vary according to program. *Financial support:* In 2010–11, 1 research assistantship with full and partial tuition reimbursement (averaging $18,297 per year), 26 teaching assistantships with full and partial tuition reimbursements (averaging $12,341 per year) were awarded; career-related internships or fieldwork, Federal Work-Study, institutionally sponsored loans, scholarships/grants, and unspecified assistantships also available. Support available to part-time students. Financial award application deadline: 3/1; financial award applicants required to submit FAFSA. *Faculty research:* Parkinson's disease, personnel training, development and assessments, gifted education, service-learning, transportation, public schools. *Unit head:* Dr. Gregory M. Anderson, Dean, 303-871-3665, E-mail: gregory.m.anderson@du.edu. *Application contact:* Janet Erickson, Director of Graduate Admission, 303-871-2485, E-mail: edinfo@du.edu.

University of Georgia, College of Education, Department of Elementary and Social Studies Education, Athens, GA 30602. Offers early childhood education (M Ed, MAT, PhD, Ed S), including child and family development (MAT); elementary education (PhD); middle school education (M Ed, PhD, Ed S); social studies education (M Ed, Ed D, PhD, Ed S). *Faculty:* 14 full-time (9 women). *Students:* 132 full-time (108 women), 130 part-time (110 women); includes 24 Black or African American, non-Hispanic/Latino; 1 American Indian or Alaska Native, non-Hispanic/Latino; 16 Asian, non-Hispanic/Latino; 7 Hispanic/Latino; 2 Two or more races, non-Hispanic/Latino, 9 international. 122 applicants, 59% accepted, 48 enrolled. In 2010, 78 master's, 8 doctorates, 16 other advanced degrees awarded. *Entrance requirements:* For master's and Ed S, GRE General Test or MAT; for doctorate, GRE General Test. *Application deadline:* For fall admission, 7/1 priority date for domestic students; for spring admission, 11/15 for domestic students. Application fee: $50. Electronic applications accepted. *Expenses:* Tuition, state resident: full-time $7200; part-time $344 per credit hour. Tuition, nonresident: full-time $21,900; part-time $944 per credit hour. Tuition and fees vary according to course load and program. *Financial support:* Fellowships, research assistantships, teaching assistantships, unspecified assistantships available. *Unit head:* Dr. Ronald Butchart, Interim Head, 706-542-6490, E-mail: butchart@uga.edu. *Application contact:* Dr. Stephanie R. Jones, Graduate Coordinator, 706-542-4283, Fax: 706-542-8996, E-mail: essegrad@uga.edu.

University of Georgia, College of Family and Consumer Sciences, Department of Child and Family Development, Athens, GA 30602. Offers child and family development (MS, PhD); early childhood education (MAT), including child and family development. *Accreditation:* AAMFT/COAMFTE (one or more programs are accredited). *Faculty:* 15 full-time (8 women). *Students:* 40 full-time (37 women), 21 part-time (19 women); includes 7 Black or African American, non-Hispanic/Latino; 2 Asian, non-Hispanic/Latino; 1 Hispanic/Latino, 8 international. 80 applicants, 30% accepted, 12 enrolled. In 2010, 10 master's, 1 doctorate awarded. *Degree requirements:* For master's, thesis (MS); for doctorate, thesis/dissertation. *Entrance requirements:* For master's and doctorate, GRE General Test. *Application deadline:* For fall admission, 7/1 priority date for domestic students; for spring admission, 11/15 for domestic students. Application fee: $50. Electronic applications accepted. *Expenses:* Tuition, state resident: full-time $7200; part-time $344 per credit hour. Tuition, nonresident: full-time $21,900; part-time $944 per credit hour. Tuition and fees vary according to course load and program. *Financial support:* Fellowships, research assistantships, teaching assistantships, unspecified assistantships available. *Unit head:* Dr. Jay Mancini, Head, 706-542-4844, Fax: 706-542-4389, E-mail: mancini@fcs.uga.edu. *Application contact:* Dr. Leslie G. Simons, Graduate Coordinator, 706-542-4588, E-mail: lgsimons@fcs.uga.edu.

University of Guelph, Graduate Studies, College of Social and Applied Human Sciences, Department of Family Relations and Applied Nutrition, Guelph, ON N1G 2W1, Canada. Offers applied nutrition (MAN); family relations and human development (M Sc, PhD), including applied human nutrition, couple and family therapy (M Sc), family relations and human development. *Accreditation:* AAMFT/COAMFTE (one or more programs are accredited). Part-time programs available. *Degree requirements:* For master's, thesis (for some programs); for doctorate, comprehensive exam, thesis/dissertation. *Entrance requirements:* For master's, minimum B+ average; for doctorate, master's degree in family relations and human development or related field with a minimum B+ average or master's degree in applied human nutrition. Additional exam requirements/recommendations for international students: Required—TOEFL (minimum score 600 paper-based; 250 computer-based). Electronic applications accepted. *Faculty research:* Child and adolescent development, social gerontology, family roles and relations, couple and family therapy, applied human nutrition.

University of Illinois at Springfield, Graduate Programs, College of Education and Human Services, Program in Human Services, Springfield, IL 62703-5407. Offers alcoholism and substance abuse (MA); child and family services (MA); gerontology (MA); social services administration (MA). Part-time and evening/weekend programs available. Postbaccalaureate distance learning degree programs offered (no on-campus study). *Degree requirements:* For master's, internship; project or thesis. *Entrance requirements:* For master's, minimum undergraduate GPA of 3.0, 2 letters of recommendation. Additional exam requirements/recommendations for international students: Required—TOEFL (minimum score 500 paper-based; 176 computer-based; 61 iBT). Electronic applications accepted. *Expenses:* Tuition, state resident: full-time $6774; part-time $282.25 per credit hour. Tuition, nonresident: full-time $15,078; part-time $628.25 per credit hour. Required fees: $15.25 per credit hour. $492 per term.

University of Kentucky, Graduate School, College of Agriculture, Program in Family Studies, Human Development, and Resource Management, Lexington, KY 40506-0032. Offers MSFAM, PhD. *Accreditation:* AAMFT/COAMFTE. *Degree requirements:* For master's, comprehensive exam, thesis optional. *Entrance requirements:* For master's, GRE General Test, minimum undergraduate GPA of 2.75; for doctorate, GRE General Test, minimum undergraduate GPA of 3.0. Additional exam requirements/recommendations for international students: Required—TOEFL (minimum score 550 paper-based; 213 computer-based). Electronic applications accepted. *Faculty research:* Early childhood education, family therapy, family resource management and consumer studies, human development.

University of La Verne, College of Education and Organizational Leadership, Programs in Child Development/Child Life, La Verne, CA 91750-4443. Offers child development (MS); child life (MS). Part-time programs available. *Faculty:* 31 full-time (22 women), 39 part-time/adjunct (30 women). *Students:* 37 full-time (35 women), 36 part-time (34 women); includes 6 Black or African American, non-Hispanic/Latino; 10 Asian, non-Hispanic/Latino; 18 Hispanic/Latino, 1 international. Average age 30. In 2010, 32 master's awarded. *Entrance requirements:* For master's, minimum GPA of 3.0, 3 letters of reference, writing sample. Additional exam requirements/recommendations for international students: Required—TOEFL (minimum score 550 paper-based; 213 computer-based). *Application deadline:* Applications are processed on a rolling basis. Application fee: $50. *Expenses:* Contact institution. *Financial support:* Institutionally sponsored loans, scholarships/grants, and unspecified assistantships available. Financial award application deadline: 3/2; financial award applicants required to submit FAFSA. *Unit head:* Dr. Barbara Nicoll, Chairperson, 909-593-3511 Ext. 4632, Fax: 909-392-2710, E-mail: bnicoll@laverne.edu. *Application contact:* Christy Ranells, Program and Admission Specialist, 909-593-3511 Ext. 4644, Fax: 909-392-2761, E-mail: cranells@laverne.edu.

University of Manitoba, Faculty of Graduate Studies, Faculty of Human Ecology, Department of Family Social Sciences, Winnipeg, MB R3T 2N2, Canada. Offers M Sc. *Degree requirements:* For master's, thesis.

University of Maryland, College Park, Academic Affairs, School of Public Health, Department of Family Science, College Park, MD 20742. Offers family studies (PhD); marriage and family therapy (MS); maternal and child health (PhD). *Accreditation:* AAMFT/COAMFTE. Part-time and evening/weekend programs available. *Faculty:* 22 full-time (17 women), 14 part-time/adjunct (13 women). *Students:* 51 full-time (45 women), 1 (woman) part-time; includes 15 minority (10 Black or African American, non-Hispanic/Latino; 2 Asian, non-Hispanic/Latino; 3 Hispanic/Latino), 6 international. 150 applicants, 11% accepted, 16 enrolled. In 2010, 12 master's, 2 doctorates awarded. *Degree requirements:* For master's, thesis or alternative; for doctorate, comprehensive exam, thesis/dissertation, oral defense. *Entrance requirements:* For master's, GRE General Test, minimum GPA of 3.0, 3 letters of recommendation; for doctorate, GRE General Test, minimum GPA of 3.0, 3 letters of recommendation, research sample. *Application deadline:* For fall admission, 12/15 for domestic and international students. Applications are processed on a rolling basis. Application fee: $75. Electronic applications accepted.

Child and Family Studies

University of Maryland, College Park (continued)

Expenses: Tuition, state resident: part-time $471 per credit hour. Tuition, nonresident: part-time $1016 per credit hour. Required fees: $337 per term. *Financial support:* In 2010–11, 2 fellowships with full and partial tuition reimbursements (averaging $18,673 per year), 1 research assistantship (averaging $15,878 per year), 36 teaching assistantships (averaging $16,148 per year) were awarded; career-related internships or fieldwork, Federal Work-Study, and scholarships/grants also available. Support available to part-time students. Financial award applicants required to submit FAFSA. *Faculty research:* Family life quality, interracial couples, child support, homeless families, family and child well-being. Total annual research expenditures: $1.1 million. *Unit head:* Elaine Anderson, Chairman, 301-405-4009, Fax: 301-314-9161, E-mail: eanders@umd.edu. *Application contact:* Dr. Charles A. Caramello, Dean of Graduate School, 301-405-0358, Fax: 301-314-9305.

University of Massachusetts Amherst, Graduate School, School of Education, Program in Education, Amherst, MA 01003. Offers bilingual, English as a second language, and multicultural education (M Ed, CAGS); child study and early education (M Ed); children, families and schools (Ed D, CAGS); early childhood and elementary teacher education (M Ed); education policy and leadership (CAGS); educational administration (CAGS); educational leadership (M Ed); educational policy and leadership (Ed D); higher education (M Ed, CAGS); international education (M Ed); language, literacy and culture (Ed D); learning, media and technology (M Ed, CAGS); mathematics, science, and learning technologies (Ed D); policy studies (M Ed); policy studies in education (CAGS); reading and writing (M Ed); research and evaluation methods (Ed D); school counselor education (M Ed, CAGS); science education (CAGS); secondary teacher education (M Ed); social justice education (M Ed, Ed D, CAGS); special education (M Ed, Ed D, CAGS). *Accreditation:* NCATE. Part-time programs available. Postbaccalaureate distance learning degree programs offered (minimal on-campus study). *Faculty:* 75 full-time (41 women). *Students:* 374 full-time (261 women), 338 part-time (229 women); includes 112 minority (42 Black or African American, non-Hispanic/Latino; 1 American Indian or Alaska Native, non-Hispanic/Latino; 15 Asian, non-Hispanic/Latino; 43 Hispanic/Latino; 11 Two or more races, non-Hispanic/Latino), 93 international. Average age 35. 779 applicants, 60% accepted, 249 enrolled. In 2010, 217 master's, 38 doctorates awarded. Terminal master's awarded for partial completion of doctoral program. *Degree requirements:* For doctorate, comprehensive exam, thesis/dissertation. *Entrance requirements:* Additional exam requirements/recommendations for international students: Required—TOEFL (minimum score 550 paper-based; 213 computer-based; 80 iBT), IELTS (minimum score 6.5). *Application deadline:* For fall admission, 1/15 for domestic and international students. Applications are processed on a rolling basis. Application fee: $50 ($65 for international students). Electronic applications accepted. *Expenses:* Tuition, state resident: full-time $2640. Required fees: $8282. One-time fee: $357 full-time. *Financial support:* In 2010–11, 1 fellowship with full tuition reimbursement (averaging $8,036 per year), 92 research assistantships with full tuition reimbursements (averaging $8,555 per year), 83 teaching assistantships with full tuition reimbursements (averaging $4,661 per year) were awarded; career-related internships or fieldwork, Federal Work-Study, scholarships/grants, traineeships, health care benefits, tuition waivers (full), and unspecified assistantships also available. Support available to part-time students. Financial award application deadline: 1/15; financial award applicants required to submit FAFSA. *Unit head:* Dr. Linda L. Griffin, Graduate Program Director, 413-545-6984, Fax: 413-545-2873. *Application contact:* Jean M. Ames, Supervisor of Admissions, 413-545-0722, Fax: 413-577-0010, E-mail: gradadm@grad.umass.edu.

University of Minnesota, Twin Cities Campus, Graduate School, College of Education and Human Development, Department of Family Social Science, Minneapolis, MN 55455-0213. Offers marriage and family therapy (MA, PhD). *Accreditation:* AAMFT/COAMFTE (one or more programs are accredited). *Faculty:* 15 full-time (11 women). *Students:* 54 full-time (44 women), 13 part-time (10 women); includes 3 Black or African American, non-Hispanic/Latino; 2 American Indian or Alaska Native, non-Hispanic/Latino; 1 Hispanic/Latino, 13 international. Average age 34. 35 applicants, 49% accepted, 10 enrolled. In 2010, 3 master's, 9 doctorates awarded. *Degree requirements:* For master's, thesis; for doctorate, thesis/dissertation. *Entrance requirements:* For master's and doctorate, GRE General Test, minimum undergraduate GPA of 3.0 (preferred). Additional exam requirements/recommendations for international students: Required—TOEFL. *Application deadline:* For fall admission, 12/15 for domestic students. Application fee: $55 ($75 for international students). *Financial support:* In 2010–11, 2 fellowships (averaging $22,500 per year), 43 research assistantships (averaging $26,645 per year), 17 teaching assistantships (averaging $26,645 per year) were awarded; career-related internships or fieldwork, Federal Work-Study, institutionally sponsored loans, and tuition waivers (partial) also available. Financial award application deadline: 6/30; financial award applicants required to submit FAFSA. *Faculty research:* Families and diversity, families and health, families and economic well-being, individuals and relationships across the lifespan. Total annual research expenditures: $795,206. *Unit head:* Dr. Jan McCulloch, Head, 612-624-1208, Fax: 612-625-4227, E-mail: jmccullo@che.umn.edu. *Application contact:* Roberta Daigle, Information Contact, 612-625-3116, E-mail: rdaigle@che.umn.edu.

University of Missouri, Graduate School, College of Human Environmental Science, Department of Human Development and Family Studies, Columbia, MO 65211. Offers MA, MS, PhD. *Entrance requirements:* For master's, GRE General Test, minimum GPA of 3.0. Additional exam requirements/recommendations for international students: Required—TOEFL (minimum score 550 paper-based; 213 computer-based; 80 iBT).

University of Nebraska–Lincoln, Graduate College, College of Education and Human Sciences, Department of Child, Youth and Family Studies, Lincoln, NE 68588. Offers child development/early childhood education (MS, PhD); child, youth and family studies (MS); family and consumer sciences education (MS, PhD); family financial planning (MS); family science (MS, PhD); gerontology (PhD); human sciences (PhD), including child, youth and family studies, gerontology, medical family therapy; marriage and family therapy (MS); medical family therapy (PhD); youth development (MS). *Accreditation:* AAMFT/COAMFTE (one or more programs are accredited). Postbaccalaureate distance learning degree programs offered. *Degree requirements:* For master's, thesis optional. *Entrance requirements:* For master's, GRE. Additional exam requirements/recommendations for international students: Required—TOEFL (minimum score 550 paper-based; 213 computer-based). Electronic applications accepted. *Faculty research:* Marriage and family therapy, child development/early childhood education, family financial management.

University of Nevada, Reno, Graduate School, College of Education, Department of Human Development and Family Studies, Reno, NV 89557. Offers MS. *Degree requirements:* For master's, thesis optional. *Entrance requirements:* For master's, GRE General Test, minimum GPA of 2.75. Additional exam requirements/recommendations for international students: Required—TOEFL (minimum score 500 paper-based; 173 computer-based; 61 iBT), IELTS (minimum score 6). Electronic applications accepted. *Expenses:* Tuition, state resident: full-time $2219; part-time $246 per credit. Tuition, nonresident: part-time $510 per credit. International tuition: $9009 full-time. Required fees: $59 per term. One-time fee: $101. Tuition and fees vary according to course load. *Faculty research:* Early childhood/adolescent development, family studies.

University of New Hampshire, Graduate School, School of Health and Human Services, Department of Family Studies, Durham, NH 03824. Offers family studies (MS); marriage and family therapy (MS). Program offered in fall only. *Accreditation:* AAMFT/COAMFTE. Part-time programs available. *Faculty:* 9 full-time (6 women). *Students:* 17 full-time (15 women), 6 part-time (5 women); includes 1 Hispanic/Latino, 1 international. Average age 30. 26 applicants, 65% accepted, 12 enrolled. In 2010, 10 master's awarded. *Degree requirements:* For master's, thesis or alternative. *Entrance requirements:* For master's, GRE General Test. Additional exam requirements/recommendations for international students: Required—TOEFL (minimum score 550 paper-based; 213 computer-based; 80 iBT). *Application deadline:* For fall admission, 5/15 priority date for domestic students, 4/1 for international students. Applications are processed on a rolling basis. Application fee: $65. Electronic applications accepted. *Financial support:* In 2010–11, 11 students received support, including 5 teaching assistantships; fellowships, research assistantships, career-related internships or fieldwork, Federal Work-Study, scholarships/grants, and tuition waivers (full and partial) also available. Support available to part-time students. Financial award application deadline: 2/15. *Unit head:* Dr. Kerry Kazura, Chairperson, 603-862-2135. *Application contact:* Matty Leighton, Administrative Assistant, 603-862-5021, E-mail: family.studies@unh.edu.

University of New Mexico, Graduate School, College of Education, Department of Individual, Family and Community Education, Program in Family Studies, Albuquerque, NM 87131-2039. Offers MA, PhD. Part-time and evening/weekend programs available. *Students:* 15 full-time (11 women), 15 part-time (14 women); includes 15 minority (2 Black or African American, non-Hispanic/Latino; 3 American Indian or Alaska Native, non-Hispanic/Latino; 2 Asian, non-Hispanic/Latino; 8 Hispanic/Latino), 2 international. Average age 36. 20 applicants, 55% accepted, 9 enrolled. In 2010, 2 master's awarded. *Degree requirements:* For master's, comprehensive exam, thesis (for some programs); for doctorate, comprehensive exam, thesis/dissertation. *Entrance requirements:* For master's, written paper, 3 letters of recommendation, personal statement, departmental application; for doctorate, GRE General Test, written paper, 3 letters of recommendation, personal statement, departmental application, interview. Additional exam requirements/recommendations for international students: Required—TOEFL (minimum score 550 paper-based; 213 computer-based). *Application deadline:* For fall admission, 3/15 priority date for domestic and international students; for spring admission, 10/15 priority date for domestic and international students. Applications are processed on a rolling basis. Application fee: $50. Electronic applications accepted. *Expenses:* Tuition, state resident: full-time $5991; part-time $251 per credit hour. Tuition, nonresident: full-time $14,405; part-time $800.20 per credit hour. Tuition and fees vary according to course level, course load, program and reciprocity agreements. *Financial support:* In 2010–11, 20 students received support, including 1 fellowship (averaging $7,200 per year), 1 research assistantship (averaging $18,106 per year), 1 teaching assistantship with full and partial tuition reimbursement available (averaging $3,698 per year); scholarships/grants also available. Financial award application deadline: 3/1; financial award applicants required to submit FAFSA. *Faculty research:* Home, community and school relations; multicultural issues; parent-child interactions; grandparents as primary caretakers for grandchildren; fathering, early childhood evaluation, early childhood development, globalization and indigenous cultures. *Unit head:* Dr. Ziarat Hossain, Program Coordinator, 505-277-4162, Fax: 505-277-8361, E-mail: zhossain@unm.edu. *Application contact:* Cynthia Salas, Department Administrator, 505-277-4535, Fax: 505-277-8361, E-mail: divbse@unm.edu.

The University of North Carolina at Greensboro, Graduate School, School of Human Environmental Sciences, Department of Human Development and Family Studies, Greensboro, NC 27412-5001. Offers M Ed, MS, PhD. *Degree requirements:* For master's, one foreign language; for doctorate, one foreign language, thesis/dissertation. *Entrance requirements:* For master's and doctorate, GRE General Test. Additional exam requirements/recommendations for international students: Required—TOEFL. Electronic applications accepted. *Expenses:* Contact institution. *Faculty research:* Adolescent mothers, multi-handicapped, older adults.

University of North Texas, Toulouse Graduate School, College of Education, Department of Educational Psychology, Program in Development and Family Studies, Denton, TX 76203. Offers MS, Certificate. Evening/weekend programs available. *Degree requirements:* For master's, comprehensive exam, thesis optional. *Entrance requirements:* For master's, GRE General Test, resume, references. Additional exam requirements/recommendations for international students: Recommended—TOEFL (minimum score 550 paper-based; 213 computer-based). *Application deadline:* Applications are processed on a rolling basis. Electronic applications accepted. *Expenses:* Tuition, state resident: full-time $4298; part-time $239 per credit hour. Tuition, nonresident: full-time $10,782; part-time $549 per credit hour. Required fees: $1292; $270 per credit hour. *Financial support:* Teaching assistantships, career-related internships or fieldwork, Federal Work-Study, and institutionally sponsored loans available. Financial award applicants required to submit FAFSA. *Faculty research:* Parent-child issues, cognitive development, social development. *Application contact:* Becky Glover, Graduate Advisor, 940-565-4876, E-mail: becky.glover@unt.edu.

University of Oklahoma, College of Arts and Sciences, Department of Human Relations, Norman, OK 73019-0390. Offers human relations (MHR), including affirmative action, chemical addictions counseling, family relations, general, human resources, juvenile justice; human relations licensure (Graduate Certificate). Part-time and evening/weekend programs available. Postbaccalaureate distance learning degree programs offered (minimal on-campus study). *Faculty:* 25 full-time (16 women), 27 part-time/adjunct (13 women). *Students:* 315 full-time (216 women), 499 part-time (312 women); includes 258 minority (159 Black or African American, non-Hispanic/Latino; 39 American Indian or Alaska Native, non-Hispanic/Latino; 14 Asian, non-Hispanic/Latino; 24 Hispanic/Latino; 2 Native Hawaiian or other Pacific Islander, non-Hispanic/Latino; 20 Two or more races, non-Hispanic/Latino), 24 international. Average age 34. 262 applicants, 89% accepted, 151 enrolled. In 2010, 384 master's awarded. *Degree requirements:* For master's, thesis optional. *Entrance requirements:* For master's, minimum GPA of 3.0 in last 60 hours of undergraduate course work, resume, 3 letters of reference. Additional exam requirements/recommendations for international students: Required—TOEFL (minimum score 550 paper-based; 213 computer-based; 79 iBT). *Application deadline:* For fall admission, 4/1 priority date for domestic students, 4/1 for international students; for spring admission, 11/1 for domestic students, 9/1 for international students. Applications are processed on a rolling basis. Application fee: $40 ($90 for international students). Electronic applications accepted. *Expenses:* Tuition, state resident: full-time $3893; part-time $162.20 per credit hour. Tuition, nonresident: full-time $14,167; part-time $590.30 per credit hour. Required fees: $2523; $94.60 per credit hour. Tuition and fees vary according to course load and degree level. *Financial support:* In 2010–11, 201 students received support, including 12 research assistantships with partial tuition reimbursements available (averaging $10,699 per year), 1 teaching assistantship (averaging $10,800 per year); career-related internships or fieldwork, scholarships/grants, and unspecified assistantships also available. Financial award applicants required to submit FAFSA. *Faculty research:* Non-profit organizations, high risk youth, trauma, women's studies, impact of war on women and children. Total annual research expenditures: $30,549. *Unit head:* Dr. Susan Marcus-Mendoza, Dept Chair, 405-325-1756, Fax: 405-325-4402, E-mail: smmendoza@ou.edu. *Application contact:* Lawana Miller, Admissions Coordinator, 405-325-1756, Fax: 405-325-4402, E-mail: lmiller@ou.edu.

University of Rhode Island, Graduate School, College of Human Science and Services, Department of Human Development and Family Studies, Kingston, RI 02881. Offers college student personnel (MS); human development and family studies (MS); marriage and family therapy (MS). *Accreditation:* AAMFT/COAMFTE. Part-time programs available. *Faculty:* 12 full-time (9 women), 3 part-time/adjunct (all women). *Students:* 38 full-time (30 women), 16 part-time (11 women); includes 6 minority (2 Black or African American, non-Hispanic/Latino; 4 Hispanic/Latino). In 2010, 23 master's awarded. *Degree requirements:* For master's, comprehensive exam (for some programs), thesis optional. *Entrance requirements:* For master's, GRE or MAT, 2 letters of recommendation. Additional exam requirements/recommendations for international students: Required—TOEFL (minimum score 550 paper-based; 213 computer-based). Application fee: $65. Electronic applications accepted. *Expenses:* Tuition, state resident: full-time $9588; part-time $533 per credit hour. Tuition, nonresident: full-time $22,968; part-time $1276 per credit hour. Required fees: $1282; $68 per semester. Tuition and fees vary according to program. *Financial support:* In 2010–11, 3 research assistantships with full and partial tuition reimbursements (averaging $11,578 per year), 4 teaching assistantships with full and partial tuition reimbursements (averaging $8,105 per year) were awarded. Financial award applicants required to submit FAFSA. Total annual research expenditures: $1.2 million. *Unit head:* Dr. Jerome Adams, Chair, 401-874-5962, Fax: 401-874-4020, E-mail: jadams@uri.edu. *Application contact:* Dr. Jerome Adams, Chair, 401-874-5962, Fax: 401-874-4020, E-mail: jadams@uri.edu.

University of Southern California, Graduate School, School of Social Work, Los Angeles, CA 90089. Offers community organization, planning and administration (MSW); families and children (MSW); health (MSW); mental health (MSW); military social work and veterans services (MSW); older adults (MSW); public child welfare (MSW); school settings (MSW); social work (MSW, PhD); systems of mental illness recovery (MSW); work and life (MSW); JD/MSW; M Pl/MSW; MPA/MSW; MSW/MAJCS; MSW/MBA; MSW/MS. *Accreditation:* CSWE (one or more programs are accredited). *Faculty:* 68 full-time (43 women), 67 part-time/adjunct (49 women). *Students:* 924 full-time (786 women), 162 part-time (128 women); includes 730 minority (137 Black or African American, non-Hispanic/Latino; 2 American Indian or Alaska Native, non-Hispanic/Latino; 120 Asian, non-Hispanic/Latino; 445 Hispanic/Latino; 4 Native Hawaiian or other Pacific Islander, non-Hispanic/Latino; 22 Two or more races, non-Hispanic/Latino), 34 international. 1,627 applicants, 50% accepted, 477 enrolled. In 2010, 288 master's, 7 doctorates awarded. *Degree requirements:* For doctorate, comprehensive exam, thesis/dissertation, qualifying exam/publishable paper. *Entrance requirements:* For doctorate, GRE Standard Test. Additional exam requirements/recommendations for international students: Required—TOEFL (minimum score 600 paper-based; 250 computer-based; 100 iBT), ESL Exam. *Application deadline:* For fall admission, 12/1 for domestic and international students. Electronic applications accepted. *Expenses:* Tuition: Full-time $31,240; part-time $1420 per unit. Required fees: $600. One-time fee: $35 full-time. Full-time tuition and fees vary according to degree level and program. *Financial support:* In 2010–11, 32 students received support, including 29 fellowships with full tuition reimbursements available (averaging $35,000 per year), 1 research assistantship with full tuition reimbursement available (averaging $30,000 per year), 2 teaching assistantships with full tuition reimbursements available (averaging $35,000 per year); scholarships/grants, traineeships, health care benefits, and unspecified assistantships also available. Financial award applicants required to submit FAFSA. *Faculty research:* Department of Defense Educational Activity, detection/treatment of depression among older adults, health/aging, psychosocial adaptation to extreme environments/man made disasters; mental health needs of older adults. Total annual research expenditures: $7.3 million. *Unit head:* Janine Luzano, Director of Admissions and Financial Aid, 213-740-2017, Fax: 213-821-1235, E-mail: janinelu@usc.edu. *Application contact:* Necole Yaacoub, Admissions and Operations Manager, 213-740-3595, Fax: 213-821-1235, E-mail: naanouh@usc.edu.

University of Southern Mississippi, Graduate School, College of Education and Psychology, Department of Child and Family Studies, Hattiesburg, MS 39406-0001. Offers child and family studies (MS); marriage and family therapy (MS). *Accreditation:* AAMFT/COAMFTE. Part-time programs available. *Faculty:* 7 full-time (3 women). *Students:* 26 full-time (all women), 32 part-time (31 women); includes 12 Black or African American, non-Hispanic/Latino; 2 Asian, non-Hispanic/Latino. Average age 29. 61 applicants, 48% accepted, 29 enrolled. In 2010, 17 master's awarded. *Degree requirements:* For master's, comprehensive exam, thesis optional. *Entrance requirements:* For master's, GRE General Test, minimum GPA of 2.75 on last 60 hours. Additional exam requirements/recommendations for international students: Required—TOEFL. *Application deadline:* For fall admission, 3/1 priority date for domestic students, 3/1 for international students; for spring admission, 1/1 priority date for domestic and international students. Applications are processed on a rolling basis. Application fee: $50. Electronic applications accepted. *Financial support:* In 2010–11, 21 students received support, including 3 research assistantships with full tuition reimbursements available (averaging $7,200 per year); fellowships, career-related internships or fieldwork, Federal Work-Study, institutionally sponsored loans, scholarships/grants, health care benefits, and unspecified assistantships also available. Financial award application deadline: 3/15; financial award applicants required to submit FAFSA. *Faculty research:* School food service, teen pregnancy, diet and cholesterol metabolism. *Unit head:* Dr. Jeff Hinton, Interim Chair, 601-266-4679, Fax: 601-266-4680, E-mail: jeff.hinton@usm.edu. *Application contact:* Dr. Jeff Hinton, Interim Chair, 601-266-4679, Fax: 601-266-4680, E-mail: jeff.hinton@usm.edu.

The University of Tennessee, Graduate School, College of Education, Health and Human Sciences, Department of Child and Family Studies, Knoxville, TN 37996. Offers child and family studies (MS); early childhood education (MS). Part-time programs available. *Degree requirements:* For master's, thesis or alternative. *Entrance requirements:* For master's, GRE General Test, minimum GPA of 2.7. Additional exam requirements/recommendations for international students: Required—TOEFL. Electronic applications accepted. *Expenses:* Tuition, state resident: full-time $7440; part-time $414 per credit hour. Tuition, nonresident: full-time $22,478; part-time $1250 per credit hour. Required fees: $922; $43 per credit hour. Tuition and fees vary according to program.

The University of Tennessee, Graduate School, College of Education, Health and Human Sciences, Program in Human Ecology, Knoxville, TN 37996. Offers child and family studies (PhD); community health (PhD); nutrition science (PhD); retailing and consumer sciences (PhD); textile science (PhD). *Degree requirements:* For doctorate, thesis/dissertation. *Entrance requirements:* For doctorate, GRE General Test, minimum GPA of 2.7. Additional exam requirements/recommendations for international students: Required—TOEFL. Electronic applications accepted. *Expenses:* Tuition, state resident: full-time $7440; part-time $414 per credit hour. Tuition, nonresident: full-time $22,478; part-time $1250 per credit hour. Required fees: $922; $43 per credit hour. Tuition and fees vary according to program.

The University of Tennessee at Martin, Graduate Programs, College of Agriculture and Applied Sciences, Department of Family and Consumer Sciences, Martin, TN 38238-1000. Offers dietetics (MSFCS); general family and consumer sciences (MSFCS). Part-time programs available. Postbaccalaureate distance learning degree programs offered (minimal on-campus study). *Faculty:* 8. *Students:* 40 (38 women); includes 6 Black or African American, non-Hispanic/Latino; 2 Hispanic/Latino; 1 Two or more races, non-Hispanic/Latino, 1 international. 45 applicants, 69% accepted, 12 enrolled. In 2010, 10 master's awarded. *Degree requirements:* For master's, comprehensive exam, thesis optional. *Entrance requirements:* For master's, GRE General Test, minimum GPA of 2.5. Additional exam requirements/recommendations for international students: Required—TOEFL (minimum score 525 paper-based; 197 computer-based; 71 iBT). *Application deadline:* For fall admission, 8/1 priority date for domestic students, 6/15 priority date for international students; for spring admission, 12/15 priority date for domestic students, 12/1 priority date for international students. Applications are processed on a rolling basis. Application fee: $30 ($130 for international students). Electronic applications accepted. *Expenses:* Tuition, state resident: full-time $7164; part-time $400 per credit hour. Tuition, nonresident: full-time $19,574; part-time $1090 per credit hour. Required fees: $1044; $60 per credit hour. *Financial support:* In 2010–11, 2 students received support, including 2 research assistantships with full tuition reimbursements available (averaging $7,893 per year); scholarships/grants and unspecified assistantships also available. Support available to part-time students. Financial award application deadline: 2/15; financial award applicants required to submit FAFSA. *Faculty research:* Children with developmental disabilities, regional food product development and marketing, parent education. *Unit head:* Dr. Lisa LeBleu, Coordinator, 731-881-7116, Fax: 731-881-7106, E-mail: llebleu@utm.edu. *Application contact:* Linda S. Arant, Student Services Specialist, 731-881-7012, Fax: 731-881-7499, E-mail: larant@utm.edu.

The University of Texas at Austin, Graduate School, College of Natural Sciences, School of Human Ecology, Program in Human Development and Family Sciences, Austin, TX 78712-1111. Offers MA, PhD. *Degree requirements:* For master's, thesis; for doctorate, thesis/dissertation. *Entrance requirements:* For master's and doctorate, GRE General Test. Additional exam requirements/recommendations for international students: Required—TOEFL. Electronic applications accepted. *Faculty research:* Marriage and family relationships, parenting, impact of television on children, courtship, family policy.

The University of Texas at Dallas, School of Behavioral and Brain Sciences, Program in Psychological Sciences, Richardson, TX 75080. Offers early childhood disorders (MS); psychological sciences (MS, PhD). Part-time and evening/weekend programs available. *Faculty:* 12 full-time (7 women). *Students:* 52 full-time (42 women), 18 part-time (16 women); includes 23 minority (7 Black or African American, non-Hispanic/Latino; 5 Asian, non-Hispanic/Latino; 10 Hispanic/Latino; 1 Two or more races, non-Hispanic/Latino), 8 international. Average age 29. 97 applicants, 34% accepted, 22 enrolled. In 2010, 21 master's, 4 doctorates awarded. *Degree requirements:* For master's, directed project or internship; for doctorate, thesis/dissertation. *Entrance requirements:* For master's and doctorate, GRE General Test, minimum GPA of 3.0 in upper-level course work. Additional exam requirements/recommendations for international students: Required—TOEFL (minimum score 550 paper-based; 215 computer-based). *Application deadline:* For fall admission, 7/15 for domestic students, 5/1 priority date for international students; for spring admission, 11/15 for domestic students, 9/1 priority date for international students. Applications are processed on a rolling basis. Application fee: $50 ($100 for international students). Electronic applications accepted. *Expenses:* Tuition, state resident: full-time $10,248; part-time $569 per credit hour. Tuition, nonresident: full-time $18,544; part-time $1030 per credit hour. Tuition and fees vary according to course load. *Financial support:* In 2010–11, 35 students received support, including 4 research assistantships with partial tuition reimbursements available (averaging $10,242 per year), 14 teaching assistantships with partial tuition reimbursements available (averaging $12,025 per year); career-related internships or fieldwork, Federal Work-Study, scholarships/grants, and unspecified assistantships also available. Support available to part-time students. Financial award application deadline: 4/30; financial award applicants required to submit FAFSA. *Faculty research:* Neurocognitive development in young adulthood, infant learning, infant and toddler eye tracking, social aggression. *Unit head:* Dr. Marion K. Underwood, Program Head, 972-883-2470, Fax: 972-883-2491, E-mail: undrwd@utdallas.edu. *Application contact:* Dr. Robert D. Stillman, Associate Dean of Graduate Programs, 972-883-3630, Fax: 972-883-2491, E-mail: stillman@utdallas.edu.

University of Utah, Graduate School, College of Social and Behavioral Science, Department of Family and Consumer Studies, Salt Lake City, UT 84112-0080. Offers early childhood education (M Ed); human development and social policy (MS). Part-time and evening/weekend programs available. *Faculty:* 17 full-time (8 women). *Students:* 18 full-time (17 women), 9 part-time (6 women); includes 1 minority (Native Hawaiian or other Pacific Islander, non-Hispanic/Latino), 1 international. Average age 31. 25 applicants, 80% accepted, 17 enrolled. In 2010, 9 master's awarded. *Degree requirements:* For master's, comprehensive exam (for some programs), thesis or alternative. *Entrance requirements:* For master's, GRE General Test, minimum undergraduate GPA of 3.0, courses in research methods and statistics. Additional exam requirements/recommendations for international students: Required—TOEFL (minimum score 500 paper-based; 173 computer-based). *Application deadline:* For fall admission, 3/1 priority date for domestic and international students. Application fee: $55 ($65 for international students). Electronic applications accepted. *Expenses:* Tuition, area resident: Part-time $179.19 per credit hour. Tuition, state resident: full-time $4384. Tuition, nonresident: full-time $16,684; part-time $630.67 per credit hour. Required fees: $350 per semester. Tuition and fees vary according to course load, degree level and program. *Financial support:* In 2010–11, 10 students received support, including 9 teaching assistantships with partial tuition reimbursements available (averaging $5,500 per year). Financial award application deadline: 2/1. *Faculty research:* Social, physical, educational and economic contexts of families and communities. Total annual research expenditures: $20,724. *Unit head:* Dr. Russell A. Isabella, Chair, 801-581-7712, Fax: 801-581-5156, E-mail: russ@fcs.utah.edu. *Application contact:* Dr. Marissa Diener, Graduate Director, 801-581-6521, E-mail: marissa.diener@fcs.utah.edu.

University of Victoria, Faculty of Graduate Studies, Faculty of Human and Social Development, School of Child and Youth Care, Victoria, BC V8W 2Y2, Canada. Offers MA, PhD. Part-time programs available. *Degree requirements:* For master's, thesis. *Entrance requirements:* For master's, resume, professional references, sample of academic writing. Additional exam requirements/recommendations for international students: Required—TOEFL (minimum score 575 paper-based; 233 computer-based), IELTS (minimum score 7). Electronic applications accepted.

University of Wisconsin–Madison, Graduate School, School of Human Ecology, Program in Human Development and Family Studies, Madison, WI 53706-1380. Offers MS, PhD. Part-time programs available. *Faculty:* 12 full-time (9 women). *Students:* 19 full-time (18 women), 4 part-time (all women); includes 1 Black or African American, non-Hispanic/Latino; 2 Asian, non-Hispanic/Latino; 3 Hispanic/Latino. Average age 31. 64 applicants, 8% accepted, 5 enrolled. In 2010, 3 master's, 6 doctorates awarded. Terminal master's awarded for partial completion of doctoral program. *Degree requirements:* For master's, thesis; for doctorate, comprehensive exam, thesis/dissertation. *Entrance requirements:* For master's, GRE General Test, 3 letters of recommendation; for doctorate, GRE General Test, MS or MA, 3 letters of recommendation. Additional exam requirements/recommendations for international students: Required—TOEFL (minimum score 580 paper-based; 237 computer-based; 92 iBT). *Application deadline:* For fall admission, 1/3 for domestic and international students. Application fee: $56. Electronic applications accepted. *Expenses:* Tuition, state resident: full-time $9887; part-time $617.96 per credit. Tuition, nonresident: full-time $24,054; part-time $1503.40 per credit. Required fees: $67.63 per credit. Tuition and fees vary according to reciprocity agreements. *Financial support:* Fellowships with full tuition reimbursements, research assistantships with full tuition reimbursements, teaching assistantships with full tuition reimbursements, institutionally sponsored loans, scholarships/grants, health care benefits, and unspecified assistantships available. *Faculty research:* Human development, adolescence, adulthood, prevention, intervention. *Unit head:* Linda J. Roberts, Chair, 608-263-2290, E-mail: ljroberts@wisc.edu. *Application contact:* Jane A. Weier, Program Assistant, 608-263-2381, Fax: 608-265-1172, E-mail: jaweier@wisc.edu.

University of Wisconsin–Stout, Graduate School, College of Human Development, Program in Family Studies and Human Development, Menomonie, WI 54751. Offers MS. Part-time programs available. *Degree requirements:* For master's, thesis. *Entrance requirements:* For master's, minimum GPA of 2.75. Additional exam requirements/recommendations for international students: Required—TOEFL (minimum score 500 paper-based; 173 computer-based; 61 iBT). Electronic applications accepted. *Faculty research:* Diversity, work and family medical ethics, family policy, dementia and families.

Utah State University, School of Graduate Studies, College of Education and Human Services, Department of Family, Consumer, and Human Development, Logan, UT 84322. Offers family and human development (MFHD); family, consumer, and human development (MS, PhD), including adolescence/youth (MS), adult development/aging (MS), consumer science (MS), infancy/childhood (MS), marriage and family relations (MS), marriage and family therapy (MS). *Accreditation:* AAMFT/COAMFTE (one or more programs are accredited). Part-time and evening/weekend programs available. Postbaccalaureate distance learning degree programs offered (minimal on-campus study). *Degree requirements:* For master's, thesis; for doctorate, comprehensive exam, thesis/dissertation, competencies. *Entrance requirements:* For master's, GRE General Test or MAT, minimum GPA of 3.0, 3 letters of recommendation; for doctorate, GRE, minimum GPA of 3.0, 3 letters of recommendation. Additional exam requirements/recommendations for international students: Required—TOEFL. Electronic applications accepted. *Faculty research:* Marriage and family relations, adolescent problem behavior, family financial management, early literacy, mental health in the elderly, parent child attachment.

Vanderbilt University, Peabody College, Department of Psychology and Human Development, Nashville, TN 37240-1001. Offers child studies (M Ed). *Accreditation:* APA. Part-time programs available. *Faculty:* 36 full-time (18 women), 2 part-time/adjunct (0 women). *Students:* 17 full-time (all women), 2 part-time (both women); includes 5 minority (3 Black or African American, non-Hispanic/Latino; 1 Asian, non-Hispanic/Latino; 1 Hispanic/Latino). Average age 25. 46 applicants, 37% accepted, 10 enrolled. In 2010, 8 master's awarded. *Degree requirements:* For master's, comprehensive exam, thesis optional. *Entrance requirements:* For master's, GRE General Test. Additional exam requirements/recommendations for international students: Required—TOEFL (minimum score 550 paper-based; 213 computer-based). *Application deadline:* For fall admission, 12/31 for domestic and international students; for spring admission, 11/1 for domestic and international students. Applications are processed on a rolling basis. Application fee: $0. Electronic applications accepted. *Financial support:* In 2010–11, 17 students received support, including 6 research assistantships with full and partial tuition reimbursements available, 7 teaching assistantships with full and partial tuition reimbursements available; fellowships with full and partial tuition reimbursements available, Federal

Child and Family Studies

Vanderbilt University (continued)

Work-Study, institutionally sponsored loans, scholarships/grants, tuition waivers (partial), and unspecified assistantships also available. Financial award application deadline: 2/1; financial award applicants required to submit FAFSA. *Faculty research:* Child clinical psychology and developmental psychopathology; cognitive psychology, language and social development; educational and developmental neuroscience; quantitative methods and evaluation. *Unit head:* Dr. David Cole, Acting Chair, 615-322-8141, Fax: 615-343-9494, E-mail: david.cole@vanderbilt.edu. *Application contact:* Sharone Hall, Educational Coordinator, 615-343-4963, Fax: 615-343-9494, E-mail: sharone.k.hall@vanderbilt.edu.

Walden University, Graduate Programs, School of Counseling and Social Service, Minneapolis, MN 55401. Offers career counseling (MS); counselor education and supervision (PhD), including consultation, counseling and social change, forensic mental health counseling, general program, nonprofit management and leadership, trauma and crisis; human services (PhD), including clinical social work, counseling, criminal justice, disaster, crisis and intervention, family studies and intervention strategies, general program, human services administration, public health, self-designed, social policy analysis and planning; marriage, couple, and family counseling (MS), including forensic counseling, trauma and crisis counseling; mental health counseling (MS), including forensic counseling. Part-time and evening/weekend programs available. Postbaccalaureate distance learning degree programs offered (minimal on-campus study). *Faculty:* 25 full-time (17 women), 241 part-time/adjunct (162 women). *Students:* 2,687 full-time (2,269 women), 536 part-time (473 women); includes 1,582 minority (1,319 Black or African American, non-Hispanic/Latino; 34 American Indian or Alaska Native, non-Hispanic/Latino; 29 Asian, non-Hispanic/Latino; 142 Hispanic/Latino; 58 Two or more races, non-Hispanic/Latino), 47 international. Average age 38. In 2010, 182 master's, 8 doctorates awarded. *Degree requirements:* For master's, residency (for some programs); for doctorate, thesis/dissertation, residency. *Entrance requirements:* For master's, bachelor's degree or equivalent in related field, minimum GPA of 2.5; for doctorate, master's degree or equivalent in related field; minimum GPA of 3.0; official transcripts; three years' related professional/academic experience (preferred); access to computer and Internet. Additional exam requirements/recommendations for international students: Required—TOEFL (minimum score 550 paper-based; 213 computer-based), IELTS (minimum score 6.5), TOEFL (minimum score 550 paper-based; 213 computer-based), IELTS (minimum score 6.5), or Michigan English Language Assessment Battery (minimum score 82). *Application deadline:* Applications are processed on a rolling basis. Application fee: $50. Electronic applications accepted. *Expenses:* Tuition: Full-time $10,274; part-time $445 per credit. Tuition and fees vary according to course load, degree level and program. *Financial support:* Fellowships, Federal Work-Study, scholarships/grants, unspecified assistantships, and family tuition reduction, active duty/veteran tuition reduction, group tuition reduction, interest-free payment plans available. Support available to part-time students. Financial award applicants required to submit FAFSA. *Unit head:* Dr. Savitri Dixon-Saxon, Associate Dean, 800-925-3368. *Application contact:* Jennifer Hall, Vice President of Enrollment Management, 866-4-WALDEN, E-mail: info@waldenu.edu.

West Virginia University, College of Human Resources and Education, Department of Technology, Learning and Culture, Program in Child Development and Family Studies, Morgantown, WV 26506. Offers MA. Part-time programs available. *Degree requirements:* For master's, thesis. *Entrance requirements:* For master's, GRE General Test, minimum GPA of 3.0, interview. Additional exam requirements/recommendations for international students: Required—TOEFL. Electronic applications accepted.

Wheelock College, Graduate Programs, Division of Child and Family Studies, Boston, MA 02215-4176. Offers family studies (MS); family support and parent education (MS); family, culture, and society (MS). Part-time programs available. Postbaccalaureate distance learning degree programs offered (minimal on-campus study). *Degree requirements:* For master's, comprehensive exam. Electronic applications accepted. *Faculty research:* Cross-cultural studies of parenting, effects of chronic illness on families, parenting education.

Child Development

Arcadia University, Graduate Studies, Department of Education, Glenside, PA 19038-3295. Offers art education (M Ed, MA Ed); biology education (MA Ed); chemistry education (MA Ed); child development (CAS); computer education (M Ed, CAS); computer education 7-12 (MA Ed); early childhood education (M Ed, CAS), including individualized (M Ed), master teacher (M Ed), research in child development (M Ed); educational leadership (M Ed, CAS); educational psychology (CAS); elementary education (M Ed, CAS); English education (MA Ed); environmental education (MA Ed, CAS); history education (MA Ed); language arts (M Ed, CAS); mathematics education (M Ed, MA Ed, CAS); music education (MA Ed); psychology (MA Ed); pupil personnel services (CAS); reading (M Ed, CAS); school library science (M Ed); science education (M Ed, CAS); secondary education (M Ed, CAS); special education (M Ed, Ed D, CAS); theater arts (MA Ed); written communication (MA Ed). *Accreditation:* NASAD. Part-time and evening/weekend programs available. Postbaccalaureate distance learning degree programs offered (minimal on-campus study). *Faculty:* 12 full-time (8 women), 38 part-time/adjunct (26 women). *Students:* 101 full-time (80 women), 667 part-time (508 women); includes 85 Black or African American, non-Hispanic/Latino; 10 Asian, non-Hispanic/Latino; 9 Hispanic/Latino; 5 Two or more races, non-Hispanic/Latino, 1 international. Average age 32. In 2010, 211 master's, 6 doctorates awarded. *Application deadline:* Applications are processed on a rolling basis. Application fee: $50. Electronic applications accepted. *Expenses:* Contact institution. *Financial support:* Career-related internships or fieldwork, tuition waivers (partial), and unspecified assistantships available. *Unit head:* Dr. Steven P. Gulkus. *Application contact:* 215-572-2925, Fax: 215-572-2126, E-mail: grad@arcadia.edu.

California State University, Los Angeles, Graduate Studies, College of Health and Human Services, Department of Child and Family Studies, Los Angeles, CA 90032-8530. Offers child development (MA). Part-time and evening/weekend programs available. *Faculty:* 3 full-time (all women), 2 part-time/adjunct (both women). *Students:* 4 full-time (2 women), 23 part-time (21 women); includes 16 minority (6 Asian, non-Hispanic/Latino; 10 Hispanic/Latino), 1 international. Average age 29. 13 applicants, 100% accepted, 12 enrolled. In 2010, 6 master's awarded. *Degree requirements:* For master's, comprehensive exam, project or thesis. *Entrance requirements:* Additional exam requirements/recommendations for international students: Required—TOEFL (minimum score 500 paper-based; 173 computer-based). *Application deadline:* For fall admission, 5/1 for domestic and international students. Applications are processed on a rolling basis. Application fee: $55. *Financial support:* Career-related internships or fieldwork and Federal Work-Study available. Support available to part-time students. Financial award application deadline: 3/1. *Faculty research:* Nutrition education, laundry product and fabric durability, computer usage in public school home economics. *Unit head:* Dr. Rita Ledesma, Chair, 323-343-4590, Fax: 323-343-5019, E-mail: rledesm@calstatela.edu. *Application contact:* Dr. Alan Muchlinski, Dean of Graduate Studies, 323-343-3820, Fax: 323-343-5653, E-mail: amuchli@exchange.calstatela.edu.

California State University, San Bernardino, Graduate Studies, College of Social and Behavioral Sciences, Department of Psychology, San Bernardino, CA 92407-2397. Offers child development (MA), including psychology-life span; clinical/counseling psychology (MS), including clinical psychology; general/experimental psychology (MA), including psychology; industrial/organizational psychology (MS), including organizational psychology. *Degree requirements:* For master's, comprehensive exam, thesis (for some programs), advancement to candidacy. *Entrance requirements:* For master's, writing exam, minimum GPA of 3.0 in major. *Faculty research:* Perceptual development, human memory, psychopharmacology, psychology of women, language acquisition.

East Carolina University, Graduate School, College of Human Ecology, Department of Child Development and Family Relations, Greenville, NC 27858-4353. Offers child development and family relations (MS); marriage and family therapy (MS). *Accreditation:* AAMFT/COAMFTE. Part-time programs available. *Degree requirements:* For master's, comprehensive exam, thesis optional. *Expenses:* Tuition, state resident: full-time $3130; part-time $391.25 per credit hour. Tuition, nonresident: full-time $13,817; part-time $1727.13 per credit hour. Required fees: $1916; $239.50 per credit hour. Tuition and fees vary according to campus/location and program. *Faculty research:* Child care quality, mental health delivery systems for children, family violence.

Erikson Institute, Academic Programs, Program in Child Development, Chicago, IL 60654. Offers MS. *Degree requirements:* For master's, comprehensive exam, internship. *Entrance requirements:* For master's, 3 letters of recommendation, minimum GPA of 2.75. Additional exam requirements/recommendations for international students: Required—TOEFL. *Expenses:* Tuition: Part-time $810 per credit. Required fees: $420 per year.

Lee University, Graduate Studies in Counseling, Cleveland, TN 37320-3450. Offers college student development (MS); holistic child development (MS); marriage and family therapy (MS); school counseling (MS). Part-time programs available. *Faculty:* 7 full-time (3 women), 6 part-time/adjunct (2 women). *Students:* 74 full-time (64 women), 36 part-time (30 women); includes 2 Black or African American, non-Hispanic/Latino; 2 American Indian or Alaska Native, non-Hispanic/Latino; 1 Asian, non-Hispanic/Latino; 2 Hispanic/Latino; 1 Native Hawaiian or other Pacific Islander, non-Hispanic/Latino, 4 international. Average age 27. 53 applicants, 91% accepted, 34 enrolled. In 2010, 19 master's awarded. *Degree requirements:* For master's, variable foreign language requirement, comprehensive exam, thesis, internship. *Entrance requirements:* For master's, GRE General Test or MAT, minimum undergraduate GPA of 3.0, 3 letters of recommendation, interview. Additional exam requirements/recommendations for international students: Required—TOEFL (minimum score 450 paper-based; 45 computer-based). *Application deadline:* For fall admission, 4/1 priority date for domestic and international students; for spring admission, 10/1 priority date for domestic and international students. Applications are processed on a rolling basis. Application fee: $25. *Expenses:* Tuition: Full-time $12,120; part-time $506 per credit hour. Required fees: $560; $305 per semester. Part-time tuition and fees vary according to course load and campus/location. *Financial support:* Teaching assistantships, career-related internships or fieldwork, Federal Work-Study, institutionally sponsored loans, scholarships/grants, and unspecified assistantships available. Financial award application deadline: 3/1; financial award applicants required to submit FAFSA. *Unit head:* Dr. Trevor Milliron, Director, 423-614-8126, Fax: 423-614-8129, E-mail: tmilliron@leeuniversity.edu. *Application contact:* Vicki Glasscock, Graduate Admissions Director, 423-614-8059, E-mail: vglasscock@leeuniversity.edu.

Michigan State University, The Graduate School, College of Social Science, Department of Family and Child Ecology, East Lansing, MI 48824. Offers child development (MA); community services (MS); family and child ecology (PhD); family studies (MA); marriage and family therapy (MA); youth development (MA). *Accreditation:* AAMFT/COAMFTE (one or more programs are accredited). *Entrance requirements:* For master's, GRE General Test, minimum GPA of 3.0 in last 2 years of undergraduate course work, 3 letters of recommendation; for doctorate, GRE General Test, minimum GPA of 3.0, 3 letters of recommendation, background in behavioral sciences. Additional exam requirements/recommendations for international students: Required—TOEFL. Electronic applications accepted.

Middle Tennessee State University, College of Graduate Studies, College of Behavioral and Health Sciences, Department of Human Sciences, Murfreesboro, TN 37132. Offers child development and family studies (MS); nutrition and food science (MS). Part-time and evening/weekend programs available. Postbaccalaureate distance learning degree programs offered. *Faculty:* 7 full-time (all women). *Students:* 24 part-time (23 women); includes 4 Black or African American, non-Hispanic/Latino; 2 Asian, non-Hispanic/Latino; 1 Hispanic/Latino. Average age 31. 22 applicants, 82% accepted, 18 enrolled. In 2010, 5 master's awarded. *Degree requirements:* For master's, comprehensive exam, thesis. *Entrance requirements:* For master's, GRE or MAT. Additional exam requirements/recommendations for international students: Required—TOEFL (minimum score 525 paper-based; 195 computer-based; 71 iBT) or IELTS (minimum score 6). *Application deadline:* For fall admission, 6/1 for domestic and international students. Applications are processed on a rolling basis. Application fee: $25 ($30 for international students). Electronic applications accepted. *Expenses:* Tuition, state resident: full-time $4632. Tuition, nonresident: full-time $11,520. *Financial support:* In 2010–11, 5 students received support. Application deadline: 5/1. *Faculty research:* Courtship relationships, feminist methodology and epistemology in family studies, school uniforms, body fat in elderly, asynchronous distance education. *Unit head:* Dr. Deborah G. Belcher, Interim Chair, 615-898-2884, Fax: 615-898-5130, E-mail: dbelcher@mtsu.edu. *Application contact:* Dr. Michael Allen, Dean and Vice Provost for Research, 615-898-2840, Fax: 615-904-8020, E-mail: mallen@mtsu.edu.

North Dakota State University, College of Graduate and Interdisciplinary Studies, College of Human Development and Education, Department of Child Development and Family Science, Fargo, ND 58108. Offers child development and family science (MS); couple and family therapy (MS); family financial planning (MS); gerontology (MS, PhD). *Accreditation:* AAMFT/COAMFTE. Part-time and evening/weekend programs available. Postbaccalaureate distance learning degree programs offered (no on-campus study). *Faculty:* 12 full-time (7 women). *Students:* 30 full-time (27 women), 20 part-time (19 women); includes 2 Black or African American, non-Hispanic/Latino, 2 international. 26 applicants, 62% accepted, 13 enrolled. *Degree requirements:* For master's, thesis or alternative; for doctorate, thesis/dissertation. *Entrance requirements:* Additional exam requirements/recommendations for international students: Required—TOEFL (minimum score 525 paper-based; 197 computer-based; 71 iBT). *Application deadline:* For fall admission, 2/1 for domestic and international students; for spring admission, 10/1 for domestic and international students. Application fee: $45 ($60 for international students). *Financial support:* In 2010–11, 17 students received support, including research assistantships with full tuition reimbursements available (averaging $3,000 per year), 17 teaching assistantships with full tuition reimbursements available (averaging $3,000 per year); career-related internships or fieldwork, Federal Work-Study, institutionally sponsored loans, and tuition waivers (full) also available. Financial award application deadline: 4/1. *Faculty research:* Family therapy, resilience, parenting, adolescent development, mental health. Total annual research expenditures: $333,582. *Unit head:* Dr. James Deal, Head, 701-231-7568, Fax: 701-231-9645, E-mail: jim_deal@ndsu.edu. *Application contact:* Theresa Anderson, Administrative Assistant, 701-231-8628, Fax: 701-231-9645, E-mail: theresa.anderson@ndsu.edu.

Ohio University, Graduate College, College of Health Sciences and Professions, Department of Social and Public Health, Athens, OH 45701-2979. Offers early child development and family life (MS); family studies (MS); health administration (MHA); public health (MPH). *Accreditation:* CEPH. Part-time and evening/weekend programs available. Postbaccalaureate distance learning degree programs offered (no on-campus study). *Students:* 15 full-time (11 women), 304 part-time (211 women); includes 42 minority (25 Black or African American, non-Hispanic/Latino; 1 American Indian or Alaska Native, non-Hispanic/Latino; 11 Asian, non-Hispanic/Latino; 3 Hispanic/Latino; 2 Two or more races, non-Hispanic/Latino), 11 international. 125 applicants, 85% accepted, 75 enrolled. In 2010, 12 master's awarded. *Degree requirements:* For master's, capstone (MPH). *Entrance requirements:* For master's, GMAT, GRE General Test, previous course work in accounting, management, and statistics, previous public health background (MHA, MPH). Additional exam requirements/recommendations for international students: Required—TOEFL (minimum score 550 paper-based; 80 iBT) or IELTS (minimum score 6.5). *Application deadline:* Applications are processed on a rolling basis. Application fee: $50 ($55 for international students). Electronic applications accepted. *Expenses:* Contact institution. *Financial support:* Research assistantships with full tuition reimbursements, career-related internships or fieldwork, Federal Work-Study, institutionally sponsored loans, and unspecified assistantships available. Financial award applicants required to submit FAFSA. *Faculty research:* Health care management, health policy, managed care, health behavior, disease prevention. *Unit head:* Dr. Matthew Adeyanju, School Director, 740-593-1849, Fax: 740-593-0555, E-mail: adeyanju@ohio.edu. *Application contact:* Dr. Ruth Ann Althaus, Graduate Coordinator, Master of Health Administration Program, 740-597-2981, E-mail: althaus@ohio.edu.

Purdue University, Graduate School, College of Consumer and Family Sciences, Department of Child Development and Family Studies, West Lafayette, IN 47907. Offers developmental studies (MS, PhD); family studies (MS, PhD); marriage and family therapy (MS, PhD). *Accreditation:* AAMFT/COAMFTE (one or more programs are accredited). Part-time programs available. Terminal master's awarded for partial completion of doctoral program. *Degree requirements:* For master's, thesis; for doctorate, thesis/dissertation. *Entrance requirements:* For master's and doctorate, GRE General Test. Additional exam requirements/recommendations for international students: Required—TWE. Electronic applications accepted. *Faculty research:* Inclusion of children with special needs, families as learning environments, relationships in child care, work-family relations, AIDS prevention.

Purdue University Calumet, Graduate Studies Office, School of Liberal Arts and Social Sciences, Department of Behavioral Sciences, Hammond, IN 46323-2094. Offers child development and family studies (MS); marriage and family therapy (MS). *Accreditation:* AAMFT/COAMFTE. Part-time programs available. *Faculty:* 3 full-time (1 woman), 2 part-time/adjunct (0 women). *Students:* 18 full-time (16 women), 2 part-time (both women); includes 1 Black or African American, non-Hispanic/Latino; 1 Hispanic/Latino. 35 applicants, 26% accepted, 9 enrolled. In 2010, 4 master's awarded. *Degree requirements:* For master's, thesis. *Entrance requirements:* For master's, GRE, interview. Additional exam requirements/recommendations for international students: Required—TOEFL. *Application deadline:* For fall admission, 1/28 for domestic and international students. Application fee: $50. *Expenses:* Tuition, state resident: full-time $6867. Tuition, nonresident: full-time $14,157. *Financial support:* In 2010–11, 3 research assistantships with full tuition reimbursements (averaging $3,500 per year), 20 teaching assistantships with full tuition reimbursements (averaging $3,500 per year) were awarded; career-related internships or fieldwork and unspecified assistantships also available. Financial award application deadline: 3/1. *Faculty research:* Substance abuse, sexual abuse, couple therapy, professional issues, adolescent therapy. *Unit head:* Dr. Anne Edwards, Interim Head, 219-989-2863, E-mail: edwardsa@purduecal.edu. *Application contact:* Dr. Joseph Wetchler, Program Director, 219-989-2587, E-mail: wetchler@purduecal.edu.

Rutgers, The State University of New Jersey, Camden, Graduate School of Arts and Sciences, Program in Childhood Studies, Camden, NJ 08102. Offers MA, PhD. Part-time and evening/weekend programs available. *Faculty:* 26 full-time (16 women). *Students:* 11 full-time (8 women), 14 part-time (11 women); includes 5 Black or African American, non-Hispanic/Latino, 2 international. Average age 38. 23 applicants, 65% accepted, 10 enrolled. In 2010, 1 master's awarded. *Degree requirements:* For master's, comprehensive exam, thesis (for some programs), 30 credits; for doctorate, comprehensive exam, thesis/dissertation, 60 credits. *Entrance requirements:* For master's and doctorate, GRE, 3 letters of recommendation; statement of personal, professional and academic goals. Additional exam requirements/recommendations for international students: Required—TOEFL, IELTS. *Application deadline:* For fall admission, 1/5 for domestic students. Application fee: $65. Electronic applications accepted. *Expenses:* Tuition, state resident: full-time $4963; part-time $319 per credit. Tuition, nonresident: full-time $10,493; part-time $680 per credit. *Financial support:* In 2010–11, 14 fellowships with partial tuition reimbursements (averaging $430 per year), 9 research assistantships with full tuition reimbursements (averaging $26,000 per year) were awarded; Federal Work-Study, scholarships/grants, and tuition waivers (partial) also available. Financial award application deadline: 3/15; financial award applicants required to submit FAFSA. *Faculty research:* Children's consumer culture, moral development, development of personality and social relations, children's literature, commodification of childhood. Total annual research expenditures: $562,419. *Unit head:* Dr. Daniel Cook, Chair, 856-225-6741, E-mail: cstudies@camden.rutgers.edu. *Application contact:* Dr. Daniel Cook, Chair, 856-225-6741, E-mail: cstudies@camden.rutgers.edu.

San Diego State University, Graduate and Research Affairs, College of Education, Department of Child and Family Development, San Diego, CA 92182. Offers child development (MS). Part-time programs available. *Degree requirements:* For master's, thesis. *Entrance requirements:* For master's, GRE General Test, 3 letters of recommendation, interview. Additional exam requirements/recommendations for international students: Required—TOEFL. Electronic applications accepted.

Sarah Lawrence College, Graduate Studies, Program in Child Development, Bronxville, NY 10708-5999. Offers MA. Part-time programs available. *Degree requirements:* For master's, thesis, fieldwork. *Entrance requirements:* For master's, minimum B average in undergraduate coursework.

Southern New Hampshire University, School of Education, Manchester, NH 03106-1045. Offers business education (MS); child development (M Ed); computer technology education (Certificate); curriculum and instruction (M Ed); education (M Ed, CAS); elementary education (M Ed); general special education (Certificate); school business administrator (Certificate); secondary education (M Ed); training and development (Certificate). Part-time and evening/weekend programs available. Postbaccalaureate distance learning degree programs offered (no on-campus study). *Degree requirements:* For master's, comprehensive exam (for some programs), thesis or alternative. *Entrance requirements:* For master's, PRAXIS I, minimum GPA of 2.75. Additional exam requirements/recommendations for international students: Required—TOEFL (minimum score 550 paper-based; 213 computer-based). Electronic applications accepted. *Expenses:* Contact institution.

Texas Woman's University, Graduate School, College of Professional Education, Department of Family Sciences, Denton, TX 76201. Offers child development (MS); counseling and development (MS); early childhood development and education (PhD); early childhood education (M Ed, MA, MS); family studies (MS, PhD); family therapy (MS, PhD). *Accreditation:* ACA (one or more programs are accredited). Part-time and evening/weekend programs available. *Faculty:* 22 full-time (17 women). *Students:* 106 full-time (103 women), 327 part-time (303 women); includes 118 Black or African American, non-Hispanic/Latino; 2 American Indian or Alaska Native, non-Hispanic/Latino; 12 Asian, non-Hispanic/Latino; 50 Hispanic/Latino, 20 international. Average age 36. 243 applicants, 58% accepted, 109 enrolled. In 2010, 86 master's, 14 doctorates awarded. Terminal master's awarded for partial completion of doctoral program. *Degree requirements:* For master's, portfolio; for doctorate, comprehensive exam, thesis/dissertation. *Entrance requirements:* For master's, interview, letter of intent, curriculum vitae, minimum GPA of 3.25 on last 60 hours (MS in family therapy); for doctorate, interview, minimum GPA of 3.5 in last 60 hours of course work (family therapy), letter of intent, curriculum vitae. Additional exam requirements/recommendations for international students: Required—TOEFL (minimum score 550 paper-based; 213 computer-based; 79 iBT). *Application deadline:* For fall admission, 2/15 priority date for domestic students, 3/1 for international students; for spring admission, 9/15 priority date for domestic students, 8/1 for international students. Applications are processed on a rolling basis. Application fee: $50 ($75 for international students). Electronic applications accepted. *Expenses:* Tuition, state resident: full-time $3834; part-time $213 per credit hour. Tuition, nonresident: full-time $9468; part-time $526 per credit hour. Required fees: $1247; $220 per credit hour. *Financial support:* In 2010–11, 100 students received support, including 21 research assistantships (averaging $12,942 per year), 2 teaching assistantships (averaging $12,942 per year); career-related internships or fieldwork, Federal Work-Study, institutionally sponsored loans, scholarships/grants, traineeships, health care benefits, and unspecified assistantships also available. Support available to part-time students. Financial award application deadline: 3/1; financial award applicants required to submit FAFSA. *Faculty research:* Parenting/parent education, military families, play therapy, family sexuality, diversity, healthy relationships/healthy marriages, childhood obesity, male communication. Total annual research expenditures: $26,116. *Unit head:* Dr. Larry LeFlore, Chair, 940-898-2685, Fax: 940-898-2676, E-mail: famsci@twu.edu. *Application contact:* Dr. Samuel Wheeler, Assistant Director of Admissions, 940-898-3188, Fax: 940-898-3081, E-mail: wheelersr@twu.edu.

Tufts University, Graduate School of Arts and Sciences, Department of Child Development, Medford, MA 02155. Offers child development (MA, PhD, CAGS); early childhood education (MAT). Part-time programs available. *Degree requirements:* For master's, thesis (for some programs); for doctorate, thesis/dissertation. *Entrance requirements:* For master's and doctorate, GRE General Test. Additional exam requirements/recommendations for international students: Required—TOEFL (minimum score 550 paper-based; 213 computer-based; 80 iBT). Electronic applications accepted. *Expenses:* Tuition: Full-time $39,624; part-time $3962 per course. Required fees: $40 per year. Full-time tuition and fees vary according to degree level, program and student level. Part-time tuition and fees vary according to course load.

The University of Akron, Graduate School, College of Health Sciences and Human Services, School of Family and Consumer Sciences, Program in Child and Family Development, Akron, OH 44325. Offers child development (MA); family development (MA). *Students:* 3 full-time (all women). Average age 35. 5 applicants, 40% accepted, 0 enrolled. *Degree requirements:* For master's, comprehensive exam, project or thesis. *Entrance requirements:* For master's, GRE, minimum GPA of 2.75, three letters of recommendation, statement of purpose, resume. Additional exam requirements/recommendations for international students: Required—TOEFL (minimum score 550 paper-based; 213 computer-based; 79 iBT). *Application deadline:* For fall admission, 3/1 for domestic and international students; for spring admission, 10/1 for domestic and international students. Application fee: $30 ($40 for international students). Electronic applications accepted. *Expenses:* Tuition, state resident: full-time $6800; part-time $378 per credit hour. Tuition, nonresident: full-time $11,644; part-time $647 per credit hour. Required fees: $1265. One-time fee: $30 full-time. *Unit head:* Dr. Susan M. Witt, Coordinator, 330-972-7729, E-mail: susan8@uakron.edu. *Application contact:* Dr. Susan M. Witt, Coordinator, 330-972-7729, E-mail: susan8@uakron.edu.

University of California, Davis, Graduate Studies, Graduate Group in Child Development, Davis, CA 95616. Offers MS. *Degree requirements:* For master's, comprehensive exam (for some programs), thesis (for some programs). *Entrance requirements:* For master's, GRE General Test, minimum GPA of 3.0. Additional exam requirements/recommendations for international students: Required—TOEFL (minimum score 550 paper-based; 213 computer-based). Electronic applications accepted. *Faculty research:* Cognitive development, socio-emotional development, early childhood.

University of La Verne, College of Education and Organizational Leadership, Programs in Child Development/Child Life, La Verne, CA 91750-4443. Offers child development (MS); child life (MS). Part-time programs available. *Faculty:* 31 full-time (22 women), 39 part-time/adjunct (30 women). *Students:* 37 full-time (35 women), 36 part-time (34 women); includes 6 Black or African American, non-Hispanic/Latino; 10 Asian, non-Hispanic/Latino; 18 Hispanic/Latino, 1 international. Average age 30. In 2010, 32 master's awarded. *Entrance requirements:* For master's, minimum GPA of 3.0, 3 letters of reference, writing sample. Additional exam requirements/recommendations for international students: Required—TOEFL (minimum score 550 paper-based; 213 computer-based). *Application deadline:* Applications are processed on a rolling basis. Application fee: $50. *Expenses:* Contact institution. *Financial support:* Institutionally sponsored loans, scholarships/grants, and unspecified assistantships available. Financial award application deadline: 3/2; financial award applicants required to submit FAFSA. *Unit head:* Dr. Barbara Nicoll, Chairperson, 909-593-3511 Ext. 4632, Fax: 909-392-2710, E-mail: bnicoll@laverne.edu. *Application contact:* Christy Ranells, Program and Admission Specialist, 909-593-3511 Ext. 4644, Fax: 909-392-2761, E-mail: cranells@laverne.edu.

University of Minnesota, Twin Cities Campus, Graduate School, College of Education and Human Development, Institute of Child Development, Minneapolis, MN 55455-0213. Offers child psychology (MA, PhD); early childhood education (M Ed, MA, PhD); school psychology (MA, PhD). *Faculty:* 17 full-time (8 women). *Students:* 94 full-time (87 women), 28 part-time (26 women); includes 2 Black or African American, non-Hispanic/Latino; 3 American Indian or Alaska Native, non-Hispanic/Latino; 3 Asian, non-Hispanic/Latino; 5 Hispanic/Latino, 12 international. Average age 30. 133 applicants, 32% accepted, 29 enrolled. In 2010, 38 master's, 12 doctorates awarded. *Financial support:* In 2010–11, 20 fellowships (averaging $22,273 per year), 24 research assistantships with full tuition reimbursements (averaging $26,645 per year), 32 teaching assistantships with full tuition reimbursements (averaging $28,128 per year) were awarded. *Faculty research:* Developmental affective and cognitive neuroscience; developmental psychopathology; intervention and prevention science; social and emotional development; cognitive, language, and perceptual development. Total annual research expenditures: $5.2 million. *Unit head:* Dr. Megan Gunnar, Director, 612-624-2846, Fax: 612-624-6373, E-mail: gunnar@umn.edu. *Application contact:* Dr. Jennifer Engler, Assistant Dean, 612-626-2887, Fax: 612-626-7496, E-mail: engle009@umn.edu.

University of Nebraska–Lincoln, Graduate College, College of Education and Human Sciences, Department of Child, Youth and Family Studies, Lincoln, NE 68588. Offers child development/early childhood education (MS, PhD); child, youth and family studies (MS); family and consumer sciences education (MS, PhD); family financial planning (MS); family science (MS, PhD); gerontology (PhD); human sciences (PhD), including child, youth and family studies, gerontology, medical family therapy; marriage and family therapy (MS); medical family therapy (PhD); youth development (MS). *Accreditation:* AAMFT/COAMFTE (one or more programs are accredited). Postbaccalaureate distance learning degree programs offered. *Degree requirements:* For master's, thesis optional. *Entrance requirements:* For master's, GRE. Additional exam requirements/recommendations for international students: Required—TOEFL (minimum score 550 paper-based; 213 computer-based). Electronic applications accepted. *Faculty research:* Marriage and family therapy, child development/early childhood education, family financial management.

The University of North Carolina at Charlotte, Graduate School, College of Education, Department of Special Education and Child Development, Charlotte, NC 28223-0001. Offers child and family studies (M Ed); special education (M Ed, PhD), including academically gifted (M Ed), behavioral—emotional handicaps (M Ed), cross-categorical disabilities (M Ed), learning disabilities (M Ed), mental handicaps (M Ed), severe and profound handicaps (M Ed). Part-time programs available. *Faculty:* 24 full-time (16 women), 6 part-time/adjunct (all women). *Students:* 20 full-time (19 women), 197 part-time (178 women); includes 36 minority (29 Black or African American, non-Hispanic/Latino; 3 American Indian or Alaska Native, non-Hispanic/Latino; 1 Asian, non-Hispanic/Latino; 2 Hispanic/Latino; 1 Two or more races, non-Hispanic/Latino), 1 international. Average age 35. 96 applicants, 90% accepted, 66 enrolled. In 2010, 41 master's, 6 doctorates awarded. *Degree requirements:* For master's, thesis or alternative; for doctorate, comprehensive exam, thesis/dissertation, portfolio, qualifying exam. *Entrance requirements:*

Child Development

The University of North Carolina at Charlotte (continued)

For master's, GRE or MAT; for doctorate, GRE or MAT, 3 letters of reference, resume or curriculum vitae, minimum GPA of 3.5, master's degree in special education or related field, 3 years of teaching experience. Additional exam requirements/recommendations for international students: Required—TOEFL (minimum score 557 paper-based; 220 computer-based; 83 iBT). *Application deadline:* For fall admission, 7/15 for domestic students, 5/1 for international students; for spring admission, 11/15 for domestic students, 10/1 for international students. Application fee: $55. *Expenses:* Tuition, state resident: full-time $3464. Tuition, nonresident: full-time $14,297. Required fees: $2094. Tuition and fees vary according to course load. *Financial support:* In 2010–11, 12 students received support, including 7 research assistantships (averaging $12,161 per year), 5 teaching assistantships (averaging $14,621 per year). Financial award application deadline: 4/1; financial award applicants required to submit FAFSA. *Faculty research:* Transition to adulthood and self-determination, teaching reading and other academic skills to students with disabilities, alternate assessment, early intervention, preschool education. Total annual research expenditures: $3.4 million. *Unit head:* David Gilmore, Unit Head, 704-687-8186, Fax: 704-687-2916. *Application contact:* Kathy B. Giddings, Director of Graduate Admissions, 704-687-5503, Fax: 704-687-3279, E-mail: gradadm@uncc.edu.

The University of Tennessee at Martin, Graduate Programs, College of Agriculture and Applied Sciences, Department of Family and Consumer Sciences, Martin, TN 38238-1000. Offers dietetics (MSFCS); general family and consumer sciences (MSFCS). Part-time programs available. Postbaccalaureate distance learning degree programs offered (minimal on-campus study). *Faculty:* 8. *Students:* 40 (38 women); includes 6 Black or African American, non-Hispanic/Latino; 2 Hispanic/Latino; 1 Two or more races, non-Hispanic/Latino, 1 international. 45 applicants, 69% accepted, 12 enrolled. In 2010, 10 master's awarded. *Degree requirements:* For master's, comprehensive exam, thesis optional. *Entrance requirements:* For master's, GRE General Test, minimum GPA of 2.5. Additional exam requirements/recommendations for international students: Required—TOEFL (minimum score 525 paper-based; 197 computer-based; 71 iBT). *Application deadline:* For fall admission, 8/1 priority date for domestic students, 6/15 priority date for international students; for spring admission, 12/15 priority date for domestic students, 12/1 priority date for international students. Applications are processed on a rolling basis. Application fee: $30 ($130 for international students). Electronic applications accepted. *Expenses:* Tuition, state resident: full-time $7164; part-time $400 per credit hour. Tuition, nonresident: full-time $19,574; part-time $1090 per credit hour. Required fees: $1044; $60 per credit hour. *Financial support:* In 2010–11, 2 students received support, including 2 research assistantships with full tuition reimbursements available (averaging $7,893 per year); scholarships/grants and unspecified assistantships also available. Support available to part-time students. Financial award application deadline: 2/15; financial award applicants required to submit FAFSA. *Faculty research:* Children with developmental disabilities, regional food product development and marketing, parent education. *Unit head:* Dr. Lisa LeBleu, Coordinator, 731-881-7116, Fax: 731-881-7106, E-mail: llebleu@utm.edu. *Application contact:* Linda S. Arant, Student Services Specialist, 731-881-7012, Fax: 731-881-7499, E-mail: larant@utm.edu.

The University of Texas at Austin, Graduate School, College of Natural Sciences, School of Human Ecology, Austin, TX 78712-1111. Offers human development and family sciences (MA, PhD); nutritional sciences (MA, PhD), including nutrition (MA), nutritional sciences (PhD); textile and apparel technology (MS). *Degree requirements:* For master's, thesis; for doctorate, thesis/dissertation. *Entrance requirements:* For master's and doctorate, GRE General Test. Electronic applications accepted.

University of Wyoming, College of Agriculture and Natural Resources, Department of Family and Consumer Sciences, Laramie, WY 82070. Offers early childhood development (MS); family and consumer sciences (MS); food science and human nutrition (MS). Part-time programs available. *Degree requirements:* For master's, thesis, project. *Entrance requirements:* For master's, GRE General Test or MCAT, minimum GPA of 3.0. Additional exam requirements/recommendations for international students: Required—TOEFL (minimum score 540 paper-based; 207 computer-based; 76 iBT). Electronic applications accepted. *Faculty research:* Asthma, obesity and healthy weights, nutrition concerns of children with special health care needs, food product development, food safety, postpartum health, exercise nutrition.

Whittier College, Graduate Programs, Department of Education and Child Development, Whittier, CA 90608-0634. Offers educational administration (MA Ed); elementary education (MA Ed); secondary education (MA Ed). Part-time and evening/weekend programs available. *Degree requirements:* For master's, thesis. *Entrance requirements:* For master's, GRE General Test, MAT, minimum GPA of 3.5, academic writing sample.

Clothing and Textiles

Academy of Art University, Graduate Program, School of Fashion, San Francisco, CA 94105-3410. Offers fashion design (MFA); fashion merchandising (MFA); fashion textiles (MFA); knitwear (MFA). Part-time programs available. Postbaccalaureate distance learning degree programs offered (no on-campus study). *Faculty:* 23 full-time (13 women), 110 part-time/adjunct (87 women). *Students:* 487 full-time (445 women), 260 part-time (237 women); includes 73 Black or African American, non-Hispanic/Latino; 6 American Indian or Alaska Native, non-Hispanic/Latino; 45 Asian, non-Hispanic/Latino; 35 Hispanic/Latino, 310 international. Average age 29. 218 applicants. In 2010, 107 master's awarded. *Degree requirements:* For master's, thesis, final review. *Entrance requirements:* For master's, minimum GPA of 3.0, portfolio. *Application deadline:* For fall admission, 9/7 for domestic and international students; for spring admission, 2/2 for domestic and international students. Applications are processed on a rolling basis. Application fee: $100 ($500 for international students). Electronic applications accepted. *Expenses:* Tuition: Full-time $20,160; part-time $840 per semester hour. Required fees: $45 per semester. *Financial support:* Career-related internships or fieldwork and Federal Work-Study available. Support available to part-time students. Financial award application deadline: 8/10; financial award applicants required to submit FAFSA. *Application contact:* Prospective Student Services, 800-544-ARTS, Fax: 415-263-4130, E-mail: info@academyart.edu.

Auburn University, Graduate School, College of Human Sciences, Department of Consumer Affairs, Auburn University, AL 36849. Offers apparel and textiles (MS). Part-time programs available. *Faculty:* 14 full-time (all women), 1 (woman) part-time/adjunct. *Students:* 5 full-time (4 women), 7 part-time (6 women); includes 2 Black or African American, non-Hispanic/Latino; 1 Hispanic/Latino, 5 international. Average age 28. 16 applicants, 69% accepted, 3 enrolled. In 2010, 8 master's awarded. *Degree requirements:* For master's, thesis (for some programs). *Entrance requirements:* For master's, GRE General Test. *Application deadline:* For fall admission, 7/7 for domestic students; for spring admission, 11/24 for domestic students. Applications are processed on a rolling basis. Application fee: $50 ($60 for international students). Electronic applications accepted. *Expenses:* Tuition, state resident: full-time $7002. Tuition, nonresident: full-time $21,898. International tuition: $22,116 full-time. Required fees: $892. Tuition and fees vary according to course load and program. *Financial support:* Fellowships, research assistantships, teaching assistantships, career-related internships or fieldwork and Federal Work-Study available. Support available to part-time students. Financial award application deadline: 3/15; financial award applicants required to submit FAFSA. *Faculty research:* Merchandising, consumer behavior, international marketing of textiles and apparel, apparel product development. Total annual research expenditures: $875,000. *Unit head:* Dr. Carol L. Warfield, Head, 334-844-1329, E-mail: cwarfiel@humsci.auburn.edu. *Application contact:* Dr. George Flowers, Dean of the Graduate School, 334-844-2125.

Central Michigan University, College of Graduate Studies, College of Education and Human Services, Department of Human Environmental Studies, Mount Pleasant, MI 48859. Offers apparel product development and merchandising technology (MS); gerontology (Graduate Certificate); human development and family studies (MA); nutrition and dietetics (MS). Part-time and evening/weekend programs available. *Faculty:* 15 full-time (11 women), 1 (woman) part-time/adjunct. *Students:* 6 full-time (4 women), 24 part-time (22 women); includes 2 Black or African American, non-Hispanic/Latino, 4 international. *Degree requirements:* For master's, thesis or alternative. *Application deadline:* Applications are processed on a rolling basis. Application fee: $35 ($45 for international students). Electronic applications accepted. *Expenses:* Tuition, state resident: full-time $8208; part-time $456 per credit hour. Tuition, nonresident: full-time $13,788; part-time $766 per credit hour. One-time fee: $25. *Financial support:* Fellowships with tuition reimbursements, research assistantships, career-related internships or fieldwork, Federal Work-Study, unspecified assistantships, and out-of-state merit awards, non-resident graduate awards available. *Faculty research:* Human growth and development, family studies and human sexuality, human nutrition and dietetics, apparel and textile retailing, computer-aided design for apparel. *Unit head:* Dr. Megan P. Goodwin, Chairperson, 989-774-3218, Fax: 989-774-2435, E-mail: goodw1mp@cmich.edu. *Application contact:* Dr. Candace Maylee, Assistant Coordinator of Graduate Programs, 989-774-2613, Fax: 989-774-2435, E-mail: mayle1ce@cmich.edu.

Cornell University, Graduate School, Graduate Fields of Human Ecology, Field of Textiles, Ithaca, NY 14853. Offers apparel design (MA, MPS); fiber science (MS, PhD); polymer science (MS, PhD); textile science (MS, PhD). *Faculty:* 19 full-time (7 women). *Students:* 20 full-time (15 women); includes 1 Black or African American, non-Hispanic/Latino; 1 Asian, non-Hispanic/Latino, 9 international. Average age 28. 41 applicants, 29% accepted, 9 enrolled. In 2010, 5 master's, 3 doctorates awarded. *Degree requirements:* For master's, thesis (MA, MS), project paper (MPS); for doctorate, comprehensive exam, thesis/dissertation. *Entrance requirements:* For master's, GRE General Test, 2 letters of recommendation, portfolio (functional apparel design); for doctorate, GRE General Test, 2 letters of recommendation. Additional exam requirements/recommendations for international students: Required—TOEFL (minimum score 600 paper-based; 250 computer-based; 77 iBT). *Application deadline:* For fall admission, 3/1 for domestic students; for spring admission, 10/1 for domestic students. Application fee: $70. Electronic applications accepted. *Expenses:* Tuition: Full-time $29,500. Required fees: $76. Tuition and fees vary according to degree level and program. *Financial support:* In 2010–11, 19 students received support, including 2 fellowships with full tuition reimbursements available, 7 research assistantships with full tuition reimbursements available, 8 teaching assistantships with full tuition reimbursements available; institutionally sponsored loans, scholarships/grants, health care benefits, tuition waivers (full and partial), and unspecified assistantships also available. Financial award applicants required to submit FAFSA. *Faculty research:* Apparel design, consumption, mass customization, 3-D body scanning. *Unit head:* Director of Graduate Studies, 607-255-3151, Fax: 607-255-1093. *Application contact:* Graduate Field Assistant, 607-255-3151, Fax: 607-255-1093, E-mail: textiles_grad@cornell.edu.

Eastern Michigan University, Graduate School, College of Technology, School of Technology Studies, Program in Apparel, Textile Merchandising, Ypsilanti, MI 48197. Offers MS. Part-time and evening/weekend programs available. Postbaccalaureate distance learning degree programs offered (minimal on-campus study). *Students:* 1 (woman) full-time, 15 part-time (11 women); includes 5 minority (all Black or African American, non-Hispanic/Latino), 7 international. Average age 30. In 2010, 6 master's awarded. *Entrance requirements:* Additional exam requirements/recommendations for international students: Required—TOEFL. *Application deadline:* Applications are processed on a rolling basis. Application fee: $35. *Financial support:* Fellowships, research assistantships with full tuition reimbursements, teaching assistantships with full tuition reimbursements, career-related internships or fieldwork, Federal Work-Study, institutionally sponsored loans, scholarships/grants, tuition waivers (partial), and unspecified assistantships available. Support available to part-time students. Financial award applicants required to submit FAFSA. *Unit head:* Dr. Subhas Ghosh, Program Coordinator, 734-487-2476, Fax: 734-487-7690, E-mail: sghosh@emich.edu. *Application contact:* Dr. Subhas Ghosh, Program Coordinator, 734-487-2476, Fax: 734-487-7690, E-mail: sghosh@emich.edu.

Fashion Institute of Technology, School of Graduate Studies, Programs in Fashion and Textile Studies: History, Theory, Museum Practice, New York, NY 10001-5992. Offers MA. *Accreditation:* NASAD. *Degree requirements:* For master's, one foreign language, thesis, internship. *Entrance requirements:* For master's, GRE General Test or GRE Subject Test, previous course work in art history and chemistry, 4 semesters of a foreign language. Additional exam requirements/recommendations for international students: Required—TOEFL (minimum score 550 paper-based; 213 computer-based). Electronic applications accepted.

See Display on page 209 and Close-Up on page 219.

Iowa State University of Science and Technology, Graduate College, College of Human Sciences, Department of Apparel, Education Studies, and Hospitality Management, Program in Textiles and Clothing, Ames, IA 50011. Offers MFCS, MS, PhD. *Students:* 29 full-time (21 women), 2 part-time (both women); includes 3 Black or African American, non-Hispanic/Latino; 1 Asian, non-Hispanic/Latino; 1 Hispanic/Latino, 21 international. In 2010, 4 master's, 1 doctorate awarded. *Degree requirements:* For master's, thesis; for doctorate, thesis/dissertation. *Application deadline:* For fall admission, 2/1 priority date for domestic and international students. Applications are processed on a rolling basis. Application fee: $40 ($90 for international students). Electronic applications accepted. *Financial support:* In 2010–11, 7 research assistantships with full and partial tuition reimbursements (averaging $7,461 per year), 11 teaching assistantships with full and partial tuition reimbursements (averaging $7,334 per year) were awarded; scholarships/grants also available. *Unit head:* Dr. Ann Marie Fiore, Director of Graduate Education, 515-294-9303, E-mail: amfiore@iastate.edu. *Application contact:* Dr. Ann Marie Fiore, Director of Graduate Education, 515-294-9303, E-mail: amfiore@iastate.edu.

Kansas State University, Graduate School, College of Human Ecology, Department of Apparel, Textiles, and Interior Design, Manhattan, KS 66506. Offers design (MS); general apparel and textile (MS); marketing (MS); merchandising (MS); product development (MS). *Degree requirements:* For master's, thesis optional, residency. *Entrance requirements:* For master's, GRE General Test, minimum undergraduate GPA of 3.0. Additional exam requirements/recommendations for international students: Required—TOEFL (minimum score 600 paper-based; 250 computer-based). Electronic applications accepted. *Faculty research:* Apparel marketing and consumer behavior, protective and functional clothing and textiles, social and environmental responsibility, apparel design, new product development.

Kansas State University, Graduate School, College of Human Ecology, Program in Human Ecology, Manhattan, KS 66506. Offers apparel and textiles (PhD); family life education and consultation (PhD); food service and hospitality management (PhD); lifespan and human development (PhD); marriage and family therapy (PhD); personal financial planning (PhD). *Degree requirements:* For doctorate, thesis/dissertation. Electronic applications accepted.

Clothing and Textiles

North Carolina State University, Graduate School, College of Textiles, Program in Textile Technology Management, Raleigh, NC 27695. Offers PhD. *Degree requirements:* For doctorate, one foreign language, thesis/dissertation, cumulative exams. *Entrance requirements:* For doctorate, GRE or GMAT. Electronic applications accepted. *Faculty research:* Niche markets, supply chain, globalization, logistics.

The Ohio State University, Graduate School, College of Education and Human Ecology, Department of Consumer Sciences, Columbus, OH 43210. Offers family resource management (MS, PhD); fashion and retail studies (MS, PhD); hospitality management (MS, PhD). *Students:* 22 full-time (17 women), 6 part-time (5 women); includes 2 Asian, non-Hispanic/Latino, 19 international. Average age 31. In 2010, 4 master's, 6 doctorates awarded. *Entrance requirements:* Additional exam requirements/recommendations for international students: Required—TOEFL. *Application deadline:* Applications are processed on a rolling basis. Application fee: $40 ($50 for international students). Electronic applications accepted. *Expenses:* Tuition, state resident: full-time $10,605. Tuition, nonresident: full-time $26,535. Tuition and fees vary according to course load and program. *Unit head:* Jonathan Fox, Interim Chair, 614-292-4561, E-mail: jfox@ehe.osu.edu. *Application contact:* Jonathan Fox, Interim Chair, 614-292-4561, E-mail: jfox@ehe.osu.edu.

Ohio University, Graduate College, Gladys W. and David H. Patton College of Education and Human Services, Department of Human and Consumer Sciences Education, Athens, OH 45701-2979. Offers apparel, textiles, and merchandising (MS). Part-time programs available. *Students:* 6 full-time (5 women), 1 (woman) part-time; includes 2 minority (1 Asian, non-Hispanic/Latino; 1 Hispanic/Latino). 5 applicants, 80% accepted, 3 enrolled. In 2010, 8 master's awarded. *Degree requirements:* For master's, comprehensive exam (for some programs), thesis. *Entrance requirements:* For master's, GRE. Additional exam requirements/recommendations for international students: Required—TOEFL (minimum score 550 paper-based; 80 iBT) or IELTS (minimum score 6.5). *Application deadline:* For fall admission, 3/1 priority date for domestic and international students. Applications are processed on a rolling basis. Application fee: $50 ($55 for international students). Electronic applications accepted. *Financial support:* Research assistantships, teaching assistantships, career-related internships or fieldwork, Federal Work-Study, institutionally sponsored loans, and unspecified assistantships available. Financial award application deadline: 3/15. *Unit head:* Dr. V. Ann Paulins, Chair, 740-593-2880, Fax: 740-593-0289, E-mail: paulins@ohio.edu. *Application contact:* Dr. V. Ann Paulins, Chair, 740-593-2880, Fax: 740-593-0289, E-mail: paulins@ohio.edu.

Oklahoma State University, College of Human Sciences, Department of Design, Housing and Merchandising, Stillwater, OK 74078. Offers MS, PhD. *Faculty:* 16 full-time (12 women). *Students:* 10 full-time (9 women), 17 part-time (15 women); includes 1 Black or African American, non-Hispanic/Latino; 1 Asian, non-Hispanic/Latino; 1 Hispanic/Latino, 6 international. Average age 31. 21 applicants, 38% accepted, 4 enrolled. In 2010, 7 master's, 6 doctorates awarded. *Degree requirements:* For master's, thesis (for some programs); for doctorate, comprehensive exam, thesis/dissertation. *Entrance requirements:* For master's and doctorate, GRE or GMAT. Additional exam requirements/recommendations for international students: Required—TOEFL (minimum score 550 paper-based; 79 iBT). *Application deadline:* For fall admission, 3/1 priority date for international students; for spring admission, 8/1 priority date for international students. Applications are processed on a rolling basis. Application fee: $40 ($75 for international students). Electronic applications accepted. *Expenses:* Tuition, state resident: full-time $3716; part-time $154.85 per credit hour. Tuition, nonresident: full-time $14,892; part-time $621 per credit hour. Required fees: $2044; $85.20 per credit hour. One-time fee: $50. Tuition and fees vary according to course load and campus/location. *Financial support:* In 2010–11, 8 research assistantships (averaging $10,343 per year), 10 teaching assistantships (averaging $11,369 per year) were awarded; career-related internships or fieldwork, Federal Work-Study, scholarships/grants, health care benefits, tuition waivers (partial), and unspecified assistantships also available. Support available to part-time students. Financial award application deadline: 3/1; financial award applicants required to submit FAFSA. *Faculty research:* Environmental sciences design, housing and merchandising; creativity and physical environment; product development, production and evaluation; experimental learning and critical thinking; technology strategies and assessment; customer expectation and satisfaction. *Unit head:* Dr. Randall Russ, Interim Head, 405-744-5049, Fax: 405-744-6910. *Application contact:* Dr. Gordon Emslie, Dean, 405-744-6368, Fax: 405-744-0355, E-mail: grad-i@okstate.edu.

Oregon State University, Graduate School, College of Health and Human Sciences, Department of Design and Human Environment, Corvallis, OR 97331. Offers MA, MAIS, MS, PhD. Terminal master's awarded for partial completion of doctoral program. *Degree requirements:* For master's, thesis or alternative; for doctorate, thesis/dissertation. *Entrance requirements:* For master's and doctorate, GRE General Test, minimum GPA of 3.0 in last 90 hours. Additional exam requirements/recommendations for international students: Required—TOEFL.

Philadelphia University, School of Engineering and Textiles, Program in Fashion Apparel Studies, Philadelphia, PA 19144. Offers MS. Part-time programs available. *Entrance requirements:* For master's, GRE or GMAT, minimum GPA of 2.8. Additional exam requirements/recommendations for international students: Required—TOEFL (minimum score 550 paper-based; 213 computer-based; 79 iBT). Electronic applications accepted.

Purdue University, Graduate School, College of Consumer and Family Sciences, Department of Consumer Sciences and Retailing, West Lafayette, IN 47907. Offers consumer behavior (MS, PhD); family and consumer economics (MS, PhD); retail management (MS, PhD); textile science (MS, PhD). Part-time programs available. *Degree requirements:* For master's, thesis; for doctorate, thesis/dissertation. *Entrance requirements:* For master's and doctorate, GMAT or GRE General Test. Additional exam requirements/recommendations for international students: Required—TOEFL. Electronic applications accepted. *Faculty research:* Family financial resources, retail management and patronage, chemical analysis of textile dyes and finishes.

Savannah College of Art and Design, Graduate School, Savannah, GA 31402-3146. Offers accessory design (MA, MFA); advertising design (MA, MFA); animation (MA, MFA); architectural history (MA, MFA); architecture (M Arch); art history (MA); arts administration (MA); broadcast design (MA, MFA); cinema studies (MA); commercial photography (MA); digital photography (MA); documentary photography (MA); fashion (MA, MFA); fibers (MA, MFA); film and television (MA, MFA); furniture design (MA, MFA); graphic design (MA, MFA); historic preservation (MA, MFA, Graduate Certificate); illustration (MA, MFA); illustration design (MA); industrial design (MA, MFA); interactive design and game development (MA, MFA, Graduate Certificate); interior design (MA, MFA); international preservation (MA); luxury and fashion management (MA, MFA); metals and jewelry (MA, MFA); painting (MA, MFA); performing arts (MFA); photography (MA, MFA); printmaking (MA, MFA); production design (MA, MFA); professional education (MAT), including art, drama; professional writing (MFA); sculpture (MA, MFA); sequential art (MA, MFA); service design (MFA); sound design (MA, MFA); urban design and development (MUD); visual effects (MA, MFA). Part-time programs available. Postbaccalaureate distance learning degree programs offered (no on-campus study). *Students:* 1,576 full-time (898 women), 407 part-time (240 women); includes 208 minority (115 Black or African American, non-Hispanic/Latino; 8 American Indian or Alaska Native, non-Hispanic/Latino; 29 Asian, non-Hispanic/Latino; 45 Hispanic/Latino; 2 Native Hawaiian or other Pacific Islander, non-Hispanic/Latino; 9 Two or more races, non-Hispanic/Latino), 435 international. Average age 28. 2,826 applicants, 36% accepted, 642 enrolled. In 2010, 534 master's, 8 other advanced degrees awarded. *Degree requirements:* For master's, thesis, internship. *Entrance requirements:* For master's, interview, 3 letters of recommendation. Additional exam requirements/recommendations for international students: Required—TOEFL (minimum score 550 paper-based; 133 computer-based). *Application deadline:* For fall admission, 4/1 priority date for domestic and international students. Applications are processed on a rolling basis. Application fee: $35. Electronic applications accepted. *Expenses:* Tuition: Full-time $29,520; part-time $3280 per quarter. Tuition and fees vary according to campus/location. *Financial support:* Fellowships, career-related internships or fieldwork, Federal Work-Study, and scholarships/grants available. Financial award application deadline: 4/1; financial award applicants required to submit FAFSA. *Unit head:* Edward Dupuy, Dean of Graduate Studies, 912-525-5838, E-mail: edupuy@scad.edu. *Application contact:* Elizabeth Mathis, Director of Graduate Recruitment, 912-525-5965, Fax: 912-525-5985, E-mail: emathis@scad.edu.

South Dakota State University, Graduate School, College of Education and Human Sciences, Department of Apparel Merchandising and Interior Design, Brookings, SD 57007. Offers MFCS. Part-time and evening/weekend programs available. Postbaccalaureate distance learning degree programs offered. *Entrance requirements:* Additional exam requirements/recommendations for international students: Required—TOEFL (minimum score 550 paper-based; 213 computer-based; 79 iBT). *Faculty research:* Rural internet shopping, professional development in apparel merchandising, gender, aesthetics.

The University of Akron, Graduate School, College of Health Sciences and Human Services, School of Family and Consumer Sciences, Program in Clothing, Textiles and Interiors, Akron, OH 44325. Offers MA. *Students:* 4 full-time (3 women), 2 part-time (both women); includes 1 Black or African American, non-Hispanic/Latino, 1 international. Average age 34. 2 applicants, 100% accepted, 0 enrolled. *Degree requirements:* For master's, comprehensive exam, thesis or project. *Entrance requirements:* For master's, GRE, minimum GPA of 2.75, three letters of recommendation, statement of purpose, resume. Additional exam requirements/recommendations for international students: Required—TOEFL (minimum score 550 paper-based; 213 computer-based; 79 iBT). *Application deadline:* For fall admission, 3/1 for domestic and international students; for spring admission, 10/1 for domestic and international students. Application fee: $30 ($40 for international students). Electronic applications accepted. *Expenses:* Tuition, state resident: full-time $6800; part-time $378 per credit hour. Tuition, nonresident: full-time $11,644; part-time $647 per credit hour. Required fees: $1265. One-time fee: $30 full-time. *Unit head:* Dr. Teena Jennings-Rentenaar, Associate Professor, 330-972-8313, E-mail: tjenn@uakron.edu. *Application contact:* Dr. Teena Jennings-Rentenaar, Associate Professor, 330-972-8313, E-mail: tjenn@uakron.edu.

The University of Alabama, Graduate School, College of Human Environmental Sciences, Department of Clothing, Textiles, and Interior Design, Tuscaloosa, AL 35487. Offers MSHES. *Faculty:* 6 full-time (all women), 1 (woman) part-time/adjunct. *Students:* 3 full-time (all women), 1 (woman) part-time. Average age 31. 3 applicants, 100% accepted, 2 enrolled. *Degree requirements:* For master's, comprehensive exam, thesis optional. *Entrance requirements:* For master's, GRE General Test or MAT, minimum GPA of 3.0. *Application deadline:* For fall admission, 7/6 for domestic students. Applications are processed on a rolling basis. Application fee: $50 ($60 for international students). *Expenses:* Tuition, state resident: full-time $7900. Tuition, nonresident: full-time $20,500. *Financial support:* In 2010–11, 1 research assistantship with full tuition reimbursement (averaging $8,100 per year), 2 teaching assistantships with full tuition reimbursements (averaging $8,100 per year) were awarded; fellowships, career-related internships or fieldwork, Federal Work-Study, and scholarships/grants also available. Financial award application deadline: 3/15. *Faculty research:* Archeological textiles, textile science, material culture, social psychology, international trade. *Unit head:* Dr. Carolyn Callis, Chair and Associate Professor, 205-348-6176, Fax: 205-348-0022, E-mail: ccallis@ches.ua.edu. *Application contact:* Dr. Carolyn Callis, Chair and Associate Professor, 205-348-6176, Fax: 205-348-0022, E-mail: ccallis@ches.ua.edu.

University of Alberta, Faculty of Graduate Studies and Research, Department of Human Ecology, Edmonton, AB T6G 2E1, Canada. Offers family ecology and practice (M Sc, PhD); textiles and clothing (M Sc, MA, PhD). Postbaccalaureate distance learning degree programs offered (no on-campus study). *Degree requirements:* For master's, thesis (for some programs); for doctorate, comprehensive exam, thesis/dissertation. *Entrance requirements:* For master's and doctorate, minimum GPA of 7.0 on a 9.0 scale. Additional exam requirements/recommendations for international students: Required—TOEFL (minimum score 580 paper-based; 237 computer-based). *Faculty research:* Families and aging, family and child poverty, paid and unpaid work of families, textiles and clothing, parent-child relationships.

University of California, Davis, Graduate Studies, Graduate Group in Textiles, Davis, CA 95616. Offers MS. *Degree requirements:* For master's, comprehensive exam (for some programs), thesis (for some programs). *Entrance requirements:* For master's, GRE General Test, minimum GPA of 3.0. Additional exam requirements/recommendations for international students: Required—TOEFL (minimum score 550 paper-based; 213 computer-based). Electronic applications accepted. *Faculty research:* Fiber science, social psychology, consumer psychology, chemical and physical properties of fibrous and polymeric materials.

University of Delaware, College of Arts and Sciences, Department of Fashion and Apparel Studies, Newark, DE 19716. Offers MS.

University of Georgia, College of Family and Consumer Sciences, Department of Textiles, Merchandising, and Interiors, Athens, GA 30602. Offers historic costume and textiles (MS); merchandising/international trade (MS); textile analysis (PhD); textile chemical processes (PhD); textile products and standards (PhD); textile science (MS). *Faculty:* 13 full-time (9 women). *Students:* 18 full-time (16 women), 2 part-time (both women); includes 2 Black or African American, non-Hispanic/Latino; 1 Hispanic/Latino, 8 international. 23 applicants, 52% accepted, 5 enrolled. In 2010, 8 master's awarded. *Degree requirements:* For master's, thesis; for doctorate, thesis/dissertation. *Entrance requirements:* For master's and doctorate, GRE General Test. *Application deadline:* For fall admission, 7/1 priority date for domestic students; for spring admission, 11/15 for domestic students. Application fee: $50. Electronic applications accepted. *Expenses:* Tuition, state resident: full-time $7200; part-time $344 per credit hour. Tuition, nonresident: full-time $21,900; part-time $944 per credit hour. Tuition and fees vary according to course load and program. *Financial support:* Fellowships, research assistantships, teaching assistantships, unspecified assistantships available. *Unit head:* Dr. Patricia K. Hunt-Hurst, Department Head, 706-542-4891, Fax: 706-542-4862, E-mail: phunt@fcs.uga.edu. *Application contact:* Dr. Soyoung Kim, Graduate Coordinator, 706-542-4887, E-mail: skim@fcs.uga.edu.

University of Kentucky, Graduate School, College of Design, Program in Interior Design, Merchandising, and Textiles, Lexington, KY 40506-0032. Offers MAIDM, MSIDM. *Degree requirements:* For master's, comprehensive exam, thesis optional. *Entrance requirements:* For master's, GRE General Test, minimum undergraduate GPA of 2.75. Additional exam requirements/recommendations for international students: Required—TOEFL (minimum score 550 paper-based; 213 computer-based). Electronic applications accepted. *Faculty research:* Interior design, apparel merchandising, textile evaluation, creativity in design, social-psychological aspects of dress and interiors.

The University of Manchester, School of Materials, Manchester, United Kingdom. Offers advanced aerospace materials engineering (M Sc); advanced metallic systems (PhD); biomedical materials (M Phil, M Sc, PhD); ceramics and glass (M Phil, M Sc, PhD); composite materials (M Sc, PhD); corrosion and protection (M Phil, M Sc, PhD); materials (M Phil, PhD); metallic materials (M Phil, M Sc, PhD); nanostructural materials (M Phil, M Sc, PhD); paper science (M Phil, M Sc, PhD); polymer science and engineering (M Phil, M Sc, PhD); technical textiles (M Sc); textile design, fashion and management (M Phil, M Sc, PhD); textile science and technology (M Phil, M Sc, PhD); textiles (M Phil, PhD); textiles and fashion (M Ent).

University of Manitoba, Faculty of Graduate Studies, Faculty of Human Ecology, Department of Textile Sciences, Winnipeg, MB R3T 2N2, Canada. Offers M Sc. *Degree requirements:* For master's, thesis.

University of Minnesota, Twin Cities Campus, Graduate School, College of Design, Department of Design, Housing, and Apparel, Minneapolis, MN 55455-0213. Offers apparel (MA, MS, PhD); design communication (MA, MS, PhD); housing studies (MA, MS, PhD, Postbaccalaureate Certificate); interactive design (MFA); interior design (MA, MS, PhD). Part-time programs available. *Degree requirements:* For master's and Postbaccalaureate Certificate, comprehensive exam, thesis (for some programs); for doctorate, comprehensive exam, thesis/dissertation. *Entrance requirements:* For master's, GRE General Test, minimum GPA of 3.0

Clothing and Textiles

University of Minnesota, Twin Cities Campus (continued)
(preferred), portfolio, 3 letters of recommendation; for doctorate, GRE General Test, minimum GPA of 3.0 (preferred), portfolio, 3 letters of recommendation, writing sample; for Postbaccalaureate Certificate, GRE General Test, minimum GPA of 3.0 (preferred). Additional exam requirements/recommendations for international students: Required—TOEFL (minimum score 550 paper-based; 213 computer-based; 79 iBT). Electronic applications accepted. *Faculty research:* Housing policy and community development; consumer behavior; interactive design; design history; social, cultural, and behavioral issues related to designed environments.

University of Missouri, Graduate School, College of Human Environmental Science, Department of Textile and Apparel Management, Columbia, MO 65211. Offers MA, MS. *Entrance requirements:* For master's, GRE General Test, minimum GPA of 3.0. Additional exam requirements/recommendations for international students: Required—TOEFL (minimum score 550 paper-based; 213 computer-based; 79 iBT).

University of Nebraska–Lincoln, Graduate College, College of Education and Human Sciences, Department of Textiles, Clothing and Design, Lincoln, NE 68588. Offers human sciences (PhD), including textiles, clothing and design (MS, PhD); merchandising (MS); textile history/quilt studies (MA); textile science (MS); textile-apparel (MA); textiles, clothing and design (MA, MS), including textiles, clothing and design (MS, PhD). Part-time programs available. Postbaccalaureate distance learning degree programs offered (minimal on-campus study). *Degree requirements:* For master's, thesis optional. *Entrance requirements:* For master's, GRE General Test. Additional exam requirements/recommendations for international students: Required—TOEFL (minimum score 550 paper-based; 213 computer-based). Electronic applications accepted. *Faculty research:* Merchandising, textile science, fiber arts, textile history, quilt studies.

University of North Texas, Toulouse Graduate School, School of Merchandising and Hospitality Management, Denton, TX 76203. Offers hospitality management (MS); merchandising (MS). Part-time programs available. Postbaccalaureate distance learning degree programs offered (no on-campus study). *Degree requirements:* For master's, comprehensive exam, thesis or alternative. *Entrance requirements:* For master's, GRE General Test or GMAT, minimum GPA of 2.8, course work in major area, 3 references, resume. Additional exam requirements/recommendations for international students: Recommended—TOEFL (minimum score 550 paper-based; 213 computer-based; 79 iBT). *Application deadline:* Applications are processed on a rolling basis. Electronic applications accepted. *Expenses:* Tuition, state resident: full-time $4298; part-time $239 per credit hour. Tuition, nonresident: full-time $10,782; part-time $549 per credit hour. Required fees: $1292; $270 per credit hour. *Financial support:* Fellowships, research assistantships, teaching assistantships, career-related internships or fieldwork, Federal Work-Study, and institutionally sponsored loans available. Financial award application deadline: 4/1; financial award applicants required to submit FAFSA. *Faculty research:* Management, hospitality, merchandising, globalization, consumer behavior and experiences. *Application contact:* Coordinator, 940-565-4757, Fax: 940-565-4348, E-mail: kennon@smhm.unt.edu.

University of Rhode Island, Graduate School, College of Human Science and Services, Department of Textiles, Fashion Merchandising and Design, Kingston, RI 02881. Offers MS. Part-time programs available. *Faculty:* 8 full-time (6 women). *Students:* 10 full-time (9 women), 4 part-time (all women); includes 2 minority (both Asian, non-Hispanic/Latino), 2 international. In 2010, 9 master's awarded. *Degree requirements:* For master's, comprehensive exam (for some programs), thesis optional. *Entrance requirements:* For master's, GRE, 2 letters of recommendation. Additional exam requirements/recommendations for international students: Required—TOEFL (minimum score 550 paper-based; 213 computer-based). *Application deadline:* For fall admission, 7/15 for domestic students, 2/1 for international students; for spring admission, 11/15 for domestic students, 7/15 for international students. Application fee: $65. Electronic applications accepted. *Expenses:* Tuition, state resident: full-time $9588; part-time $533 per credit hour. Tuition, nonresident: full-time $22,968; part-time $1276 per credit hour. Required fees: $1282; $68 per semester. Tuition and fees vary according to program. *Financial support:* In 2010–11, 2 teaching assistantships with partial tuition reimbursements (averaging $6,947 per year) were awarded. Financial award application deadline: 7/15; financial award applicants required to submit FAFSA. Total annual research expenditures: $38,523. *Unit head:* Dr. Martin Bide, Chair, 401-874-2276, Fax: 401-874-2581, E-mail: mbide@uri.edu. *Application contact:* Dr. Martin Bide, Chair, 401-874-2276, Fax: 401-874-2581, E-mail: mbide@uri.edu.

The University of Tennessee, Graduate School, College of Education, Health and Human Sciences, Department of Consumer and Industry Services Management, Program in Consumer Services Management, Knoxville, TN 37996. Offers retail and consumer sciences (MS); textile science (MS). Part-time programs available. *Degree requirements:* For master's, thesis or alternative. *Entrance requirements:* For master's, GRE General Test, minimum GPA of 2.7. Additional exam requirements/recommendations for international students: Required—TOEFL. Electronic applications accepted. *Expenses:* Tuition, state resident: full-time $7440; part-time $414 per credit hour. Tuition, nonresident: full-time $22,478; part-time $1250 per credit hour. Required fees: $922; $43 per credit hour. Tuition and fees vary according to program.

The University of Tennessee, Graduate School, College of Education, Health and Human Sciences, Program in Human Ecology, Knoxville, TN 37996. Offers child and family studies (PhD); community health (PhD); nutrition science (PhD); retailing and consumer sciences (PhD); textile science (PhD). *Degree requirements:* For doctorate, thesis/dissertation. *Entrance requirements:* For doctorate, GRE General Test, minimum GPA of 2.7. Additional exam requirements/recommendations for international students: Required—TOEFL. Electronic applications accepted. *Expenses:* Tuition, state resident: full-time $7440; part-time $414 per credit hour. Tuition, nonresident: full-time $22,478; part-time $1250 per credit hour. Required fees: $922; $43 per credit hour. Tuition and fees vary according to program.

Virginia Polytechnic Institute and State University, Graduate School, College of Liberal Arts and Human Sciences, Department of Apparel, Housing, and Resource Management, Blacksburg, VA 24061. Offers apparel business and economics (MS, PhD); apparel product design and analysis (MS, PhD); apparel quality analysis (MS, PhD); consumer studies (MS, PhD); family financial management (MS, PhD); household equipment (MS, PhD); housing (MS, PhD); interior design (MS, PhD); resource management (MS, PhD). *Faculty:* 13 full-time (all women). *Students:* 7 full-time (all women), 2 part-time (both women); includes 1 Black or African American, non-Hispanic/Latino; 1 Asian, non-Hispanic/Latino; 1 Hispanic/Latino, 4 international. Average age 39. In 2010, 3 master's, 2 doctorates awarded. *Degree requirements:* For master's, comprehensive exam (for some programs), thesis (for some programs); for doctorate, comprehensive exam (for some programs), thesis/dissertation (for some programs). *Entrance requirements:* For master's and doctorate, GRE. Additional exam requirements/recommendations for international students: Required—TOEFL (minimum score 550 paper-based; 213 computer-based). *Application deadline:* For fall admission, 7/1 for domestic and international students; for spring admission, 12/1 for domestic and international students. Applications are processed on a rolling basis. Application fee: $65. Electronic applications accepted. *Expenses:* Tuition, state resident: full-time $9399; part-time $488 per credit hour. Tuition, nonresident: full-time $17,854; part-time $957.75 per credit hour. Required fees: $1534. Full-time tuition and fees vary according to program. *Financial support:* In 2010–11, 6 teaching assistantships with full tuition reimbursements (averaging $12,561 per year) were awarded; career-related internships or fieldwork, Federal Work-Study, scholarships/grants, health care benefits, and unspecified assistantships also available. Financial award application deadline: 1/15. *Faculty research:* Housing for elderly, affordable housing, household time use, phosphate laundry study, economic well-living. Total annual research expenditures: $11,651. *Unit head:* Dr. LuAnn R. Gaskill, UNIT HEAD, 540-231-4781, Fax: 540-231-3250, E-mail: lagaskil@vt.edu. *Application contact:* Julia Beemish, Contact, 540-231-8881, Fax: 540-231-3250, E-mail: jbeamish@vt.edu.

Washington State University, Graduate School, College of Agricultural, Human, and Natural Resource Sciences, Department of Apparel, Merchandising, Design, and Textiles, Pullman, WA 99164. Offers apparel, merchandising, design and textiles (MA); interdisciplinary (PhD); interior design (MA). Part-time programs available. *Faculty:* 8. *Students:* 7 full-time (6 women), 2 part-time (both women); includes 2 minority (1 Asian, non-Hispanic/Latino; 1 Native Hawaiian or other Pacific Islander, non-Hispanic/Latino), 2 international. Average age 33. 16 applicants, 31% accepted, 5 enrolled. In 2010, 6 master's awarded. *Degree requirements:* For master's, comprehensive exam (for some programs), thesis, oral exam; for doctorate, comprehensive exam, thesis/dissertation. *Entrance requirements:* For master's, GRE, minimum GPA of 3.0, 3 writing samples, 3 letters of recommendation, portfolio. Additional exam requirements/recommendations for international students: Required—TOEFL, IELTS. *Application deadline:* For fall admission, 1/11 priority date for domestic students, 1/10 for international students; for spring admission, 7/1 for domestic and international students. Applications are processed on a rolling basis. Application fee: $50. Electronic applications accepted. *Expenses:* Tuition, state resident: full-time $8552; part-time $443 per credit. Tuition, nonresident: full-time $21,650; part-time $1083 per credit. Required fees: $846. *Financial support:* In 2010–11, research assistantships with full and partial tuition reimbursements (averaging $18,204 per year), 5 teaching assistantships with full and partial tuition reimbursements (averaging $18,204 per year) were awarded; career-related internships or fieldwork, Federal Work-Study, institutionally sponsored loans, and scholarships/grants also available. Financial award application deadline: 2/15; financial award applicants required to submit FAFSA. *Faculty research:* Product development, design theory, cultural diversity, computer design accessibility. Total annual research expenditures: $26,000. *Unit head:* Dr. Karen K. Leonas, Department Chair, 509-335-1233, Fax: 509-355-7299, E-mail: kleonas@wsu.edu. *Application contact:* Graduate School Admissions, 800-GRADWSU, Fax: 509-335-1949, E-mail: gradsch@wsu.edu.

Consumer Economics

California State University, Long Beach, Graduate Studies, College of Health and Human Services, Department of Family and Consumer Sciences, Long Beach, CA 90840. Offers family and consumer sciences (MA); nutritional science (MS), including food science, hospitality foodservice and hotel management, nutritional science. Part-time and evening/weekend programs available. *Faculty:* 6 full-time (4 women). *Students:* 31 full-time (all women), 21 part-time (20 women); includes 1 Black or African American, non-Hispanic/Latino; 7 Asian, non-Hispanic/Latino; 4 Hispanic/Latino, 1 international. Average age 26. 129 applicants, 37% accepted, 24 enrolled. In 2010, 16 master's awarded. *Degree requirements:* For master's, comprehensive exam or thesis. *Entrance requirements:* For master's, GRE (MS), minimum GPA of 3.0. *Application deadline:* For fall admission, 5/1 for domestic students. Applications are processed on a rolling basis. Application fee: $55. Electronic applications accepted. *Financial support:* Federal Work-Study, institutionally sponsored loans, and scholarships/grants available. Financial award application deadline: 3/2. *Faculty research:* School uniforms, consumer complaining behavior, nutrition and fitness education and behavior change, curriculum change, teaching experience of interns. *Unit head:* Dr. Wendy Reiboldt, Chair, 562-985-8250, Fax: 562-985-4414, E-mail: reiboldt@csulb.edu. *Application contact:* Dr. Jacqueline Lee, Graduate Coordinator, 562-985-4545, Fax: 562-985-4414, E-mail: jjlee@csulb.edu.

Colorado State University, Graduate School, College of Applied Human Sciences, Department of Design and Merchandising, Fort Collins, CA 80523-1574. Offers MS. Part-time programs available. Postbaccalaureate distance learning degree programs offered (no on-campus study). *Faculty:* 13 full-time (10 women). *Students:* 19 full-time (all women), 19 part-time (18 women); includes 8 minority (2 Black or African American, non-Hispanic/Latino; 4 Hispanic/Latino; 1 Native Hawaiian or other Pacific Islander, non-Hispanic/Latino; 1 Two or more races, non-Hispanic/Latino), 3 international. Average age 31. 28 applicants, 71% accepted, 6 enrolled. In 2010, 8 master's awarded. *Degree requirements:* For master's, thesis (for some programs). *Entrance requirements:* For master's, GRE General Test (if GPA is less than 3.5 and professional experience is less than 5 years), minimum GPA of 3.0, resume, portfolio (if applicable to area of study), letters of recommendation. Additional exam requirements/recommendations for international students: Required—TOEFL (minimum score 550 paper-based; 213 computer-based; 80 iBT). *Application deadline:* For fall admission, 4/1 priority date for domestic and international students; for spring admission, 11/1 priority date for domestic and international students. Applications are processed on a rolling basis. Application fee: $50. Electronic applications accepted. *Expenses:* Tuition, state resident: full-time $7434; part-time $413 per credit. Tuition, nonresident: full-time $19,022; part-time $1057 per credit. Required fees: $1729; $88 per credit. *Financial support:* In 2010–11, 10 students received support, including 10 teaching assistantships with full and partial tuition reimbursements available (averaging $6,551 per year); fellowships, research assistantships with partial tuition reimbursements available, career-related internships or fieldwork, Federal Work-Study, institutionally sponsored loans, scholarships/grants, traineeships, and unspecified assistantships also available. Support available to part-time students. Financial award application deadline: 2/15; financial award applicants required to submit FAFSA. *Faculty research:* Consumer and textile end use, apparel design, consumer behavior, interior design, historic costume and textiles. Total annual research expenditures: $51,777. *Unit head:* Dr. Mary A. Littrell, Head, 970-491-7890, Fax: 970-491-4855, E-mail: mary.littrell@colostate.edu. *Application contact:* Norma Bulera, Graduate Coordinator, 970-491-7890, Fax: 970-491-4855, E-mail: norma.bulera@colostate.edu.

Cornell University, Graduate School, Graduate Fields of Human Ecology, Field of Policy Analysis and Management, Ithaca, NY 14853-0001. Offers consumer policy (PhD); evaluation (PhD); family and social welfare policy (PhD); health administration (MHA); health management and policy (PhD). *Faculty:* 34 full-time (15 women). *Students:* 73 full-time (39 women); includes 6 Black or African American, non-Hispanic/Latino; 1 American Indian or Alaska Native, non-Hispanic/Latino; 9 Asian, non-Hispanic/Latino; 2 Hispanic/Latino, 9 international. Average age 24. 157 applicants, 43% accepted, 46 enrolled. In 2010, 18 master's, 3 doctorates awarded. *Degree requirements:* For master's, thesis; for doctorate, thesis/dissertation. *Entrance requirements:* For master's, GRE General Test or GMAT, 2 letters of recommendation; for doctorate, GRE General Test, 2 letters of recommendation. Additional exam requirements/recommendations for international students: Required—TOEFL (minimum score 550 paper-based; 213 computer-based; 77 iBT). *Application deadline:* For fall admission, 1/15 for domestic students. Application fee: $70. Electronic applications accepted. *Expenses:* Tuition: Full-time $29,500. Required fees: $76. Tuition and fees vary according to degree level and program. *Financial support:* In 2010–11, 17 students received support, including 4 fellowships with full and partial tuition reimbursements available, 6 research assistantships with full and partial tuition reimbursements available, 11 teaching assistantships with full and partial tuition reimbursements available; institutionally sponsored loans, scholarships/grants, health care benefits, tuition waivers (full and partial), and unspecified assistantships also available. Financial award applicants required to submit FAFSA. *Faculty research:* Health policy, family policy, social welfare policy, program evaluation, consumer policy. *Unit head:* Director of Graduate Studies, 607-255-7772. *Application contact:* Graduate Field Assistant, 607-255-7772, Fax: 607-255-4071, E-mail: pam_phd@cornell.edu.

Eastern Illinois University, Graduate School, Lumpkin College of Business and Applied Sciences, School of Family and Consumer Sciences, Charleston, IL 61920-3099. Offers dietetics (MS); family and consumer sciences (MS). Part-time programs available. *Degree requirements:* For master's, comprehensive exam.

Indiana State University, College of Graduate and Professional Studies, College of Arts and Sciences, Department of Family and Consumer Sciences, Terre Haute, IN 47809. Offers dietetics (MS); family and consumer sciences education (MS); inter-area option (MS). *Accreditation:* ADtA. Part-time programs available. *Degree requirements:* For master's, thesis optional. Electronic applications accepted.

Iowa State University of Science and Technology, Graduate College, College of Human Sciences, Department of Apparel, Education Studies, and Hospitality Management, Program in Family and Consumer Sciences Education and Studies, Ames, IA 50011. Offers M Ed, MS, PhD. *Students:* 15 part-time (13 women); includes 3 Black or African American, non-Hispanic/Latino, 1 international. In 2010, 5 doctorates awarded. *Degree requirements:* For master's, thesis (for some programs); for doctorate, thesis/dissertation. Application fee: $40 ($90 for international students). *Financial support:* Research assistantships with full and partial tuition reimbursements, teaching assistantships with full and partial tuition reimbursements, scholarships/grants available. *Unit head:* Dr. Robert Bosselman, Director of Graduate Education, 515-294-7474. *Application contact:* Dr. Robert Bosselman, Director of Graduate Education, 515-294-7474.

Kansas State University, Graduate School, College of Human Ecology, Program in Human Ecology, Manhattan, KS 66506. Offers apparel and textiles (PhD); family life education and consultation (PhD); food service and hospitality management (PhD); lifespan and human development (PhD); marriage and family therapy (PhD); personal financial planning (PhD). *Degree requirements:* For doctorate, thesis/dissertation. Electronic applications accepted.

North Dakota State University, College of Graduate and Interdisciplinary Studies, College of Human Development and Education, Department of Child Development and Family Science, Fargo, ND 58108. Offers child development and family science (MS); couple and family therapy (MS); family financial planning (MS); gerontology (MS, PhD). *Accreditation:* AAMFT/COAMFTE. Part-time and evening/weekend programs available. Postbaccalaureate distance learning degree programs offered (no on-campus study). *Faculty:* 12 full-time (7 women). *Students:* 30 full-time (27 women), 20 part-time (19 women); includes 2 Black or African American, non-Hispanic/Latino, 2 international. 26 applicants, 62% accepted, 13 enrolled. *Degree requirements:* For master's, thesis or alternative; for doctorate, thesis/dissertation. *Entrance requirements:* Additional exam requirements/recommendations for international students: Required—TOEFL (minimum score 525 paper-based; 197 computer-based; 71 iBT). *Application deadline:* For fall admission, 2/1 for domestic and international students; for spring admission, 10/1 for domestic and international students. Application fee: $45 ($60 for international students). *Financial support:* In 2010–11, 17 students received support, including research assistantships with full tuition reimbursements available (averaging $3,000 per year), 17 teaching assistantships with full tuition reimbursements available (averaging $3,000 per year); career-related internships or fieldwork, Federal Work-Study, institutionally sponsored loans, and tuition waivers (full) also available. Financial award application deadline: 4/1. *Faculty research:* Family therapy, resilience, parenting, adolescent development, mental health. Total annual research expenditures: $333,582. *Unit head:* Dr. James Deal, Head, 701-231-7568, Fax: 701-231-9645, E-mail: jim_deal@ndsu.edu. *Application contact:* Theresa Anderson, Administrative Assistant, 701-231-8628, Fax: 701-231-9645, E-mail: theresa.anderson@ndsu.edu.

The Ohio State University, Graduate School, College of Education and Human Ecology, Department of Consumer Sciences, Columbus, OH 43210. Offers family resource management (MS, PhD); fashion and retail studies (MS, PhD); hospitality management (MS, PhD). *Students:* 22 full-time (17 women), 6 part-time (5 women); includes 2 Asian, non-Hispanic/Latino, 19 international. Average age 31. In 2010, 4 master's, 6 doctorates awarded. *Entrance requirements:* Additional exam requirements/recommendations for international students: Required—TOEFL. *Application deadline:* Applications are processed on a rolling basis. Application fee: $40 ($50 for international students). Electronic applications accepted. *Expenses:* Tuition, state resident: full-time $10,605. Tuition, nonresident: full-time $26,535. Tuition and fees vary according to course load and program. *Unit head:* Jonathan Fox, Interim Chair, 614-292-4561, E-mail: jfox@ehe.osu.edu. *Application contact:* Jonathan Fox, Interim Chair, 614-292-4561, E-mail: jfox@ehe.osu.edu.

Oklahoma State University, College of Human Sciences, Department of Human Development and Family Science, Programs in Human Development and Family Science, Stillwater, OK 74078. Offers family financial planning (MS); human environmental sciences (PhD). Part-time programs available. Postbaccalaureate distance learning degree programs offered. *Faculty:* 1 full-time (0 women). *Students:* 1 (woman) full-time, 21 part-time (13 women); includes 1 American Indian or Alaska Native, non-Hispanic/Latino; 1 Asian, non-Hispanic/Latino; 1 Hispanic/Latino. Average age 37. 54 applicants, 35% accepted, 13 enrolled. In 2010, 2 master's awarded. *Degree requirements:* For master's, thesis or alternative, creative component; for doctorate, comprehensive exam, thesis/dissertation. *Entrance requirements:* For master's and doctorate, GRE or GMAT. Additional exam requirements/recommendations for international students: Required—TOEFL (minimum score 550 paper-based; 79 iBT). *Application deadline:* For fall admission, 3/1 priority date for international students; for spring admission, 8/1 priority date for international students. Applications are processed on a rolling basis. Application fee: $40 ($75 for international students). Electronic applications accepted. *Expenses:* Tuition, state resident: full-time $3716; part-time $154.85 per credit hour. Tuition, nonresident: full-time $14,892; part-time $621 per credit hour. Required fees: $2044; $85.20 per credit hour. One-time fee: $50. Tuition and fees vary according to course load and campus/location. *Financial support:* Career-related internships or fieldwork, Federal Work-Study, scholarships/grants, health care benefits, tuition waivers (partial), and unspecified assistantships available. Support available to part-time students. Financial award application deadline: 3/1; financial award applicants required to submit FAFSA. *Unit head:* Dr. Stephan Wilson, Dean, 405-744-5053, Fax: 405-744-7113. *Application contact:* Dr. Gordon Emslie, Dean, 405-744-6368, Fax: 405-744-0355, E-mail: grad-i@okstate.edu.

Purdue University, Graduate School, College of Consumer and Family Sciences, Department of Consumer Sciences and Retailing, West Lafayette, IN 47907. Offers consumer behavior (MS, PhD); family and consumer economics (MS, PhD); retail management (MS, PhD); textile science (MS, PhD). Part-time programs available. *Degree requirements:* For master's, thesis; for doctorate, thesis/dissertation. *Entrance requirements:* For master's and doctorate, GMAT or GRE General Test. Additional exam requirements/recommendations for international students: Required—TOEFL. Electronic applications accepted. *Faculty research:* Family financial resources, retail management and patronage, chemical analysis of textile dyes and finishes.

State University of New York at Oswego, Graduate Studies, School of Education, Department of Vocational Teacher Preparation, Oswego, NY 13126. Offers agriculture (MS Ed); business and marketing (MS Ed); family and consumer sciences (MS Ed); health careers (MS Ed); technical education (MS Ed); trade education (MS Ed). *Accreditation:* NCATE. Part-time and evening/weekend programs available. *Faculty:* 5 full-time (2 women), 4 part-time/adjunct (all women). *Students:* 25 full-time (19 women), 40 part-time (25 women); includes 6 minority (3 Black or African American, non-Hispanic/Latino; 2 Asian, non-Hispanic/Latino; 1 Hispanic/Latino). Average age 37. 38 applicants, 100% accepted. In 2010, 24 master's awarded. *Degree requirements:* For master's, comprehensive exam, thesis or alternative. *Entrance requirements:* Additional exam requirements/recommendations for international students: Required—TOEFL (minimum score 560 paper-based; 220 computer-based). *Application deadline:* For fall admission, 4/1 for domestic students; for spring admission, 10/1 for domestic students. Applications are processed on a rolling basis. Application fee: $50. *Expenses:* Tuition, state resident: full-time $8370; part-time $349 per credit hour. Tuition, nonresident: full-time $13,780; part-time $574 per credit hour. Required fees: $853; $22.59 per credit hour. *Financial support:* In 2010–11, 2 students received support, including fellowships with full tuition reimbursements available (averaging $5,100 per year), 2 teaching assistantships with partial tuition reimbursements available (averaging $3,800 per year); career-related internships or fieldwork, Federal Work-Study, institutionally sponsored loans, health care benefits, and unspecified assistantships also available. Support available to part-time students. Financial award application deadline: 4/1; financial award applicants required to submit FAFSA. *Unit head:* Dr. Margaret Martin, Chair, 315-312-2480. *Application contact:* Dr. David W. King, Dean of Graduate Studies, 315-312-3152, Fax: 315-312-3228, E-mail: david.king@oswego.edu.

Texas Tech University, Graduate School, College of Human Sciences, Department of Applied and Professional Studies, Division of Personal Financial Planning, Lubbock, TX 79409. Offers MS, PhD, JD/MS, MS/MBA, MS/MS. Part-time programs available. *Students:* 75 full-time (27 women), 30 part-time (6 women); includes 7 Black or African American, non-Hispanic/Latino; 2 American Indian or Alaska Native, non-Hispanic/Latino; 1 Asian, non-Hispanic/Latino; 12 Hispanic/Latino, 18 international. Average age 29. 76 applicants, 71% accepted, 32 enrolled. In 2010, 46 master's, 4 doctorates awarded. *Degree requirements:* For master's, thesis or alternative; for doctorate, comprehensive exam, thesis/dissertation. *Entrance requirements:* For master's, GRE General Test; for doctorate, GRE General Test, GMAT. Additional exam requirements/recommendations for international students: Required—TOEFL (minimum score 550 paper-based; 213 computer-based; 79 iBT). *Application deadline:* For fall admission, 6/1 priority date for domestic students, 1/15 priority date for international students; for spring admission, 9/1 priority date for domestic students, 6/15 priority date for international students. Applications are processed on a rolling basis. Application fee: $50 ($75 for international students). Electronic applications accepted. *Expenses:* Tuition, state resident: full-time $5495.76; part-time $228.99 per credit hour. Tuition, nonresident: full-time $12,936; part-time $538.99 per credit hour. Required fees: $2674; $36 per credit hour. $905 per semester. *Financial support:* Research assistantships, teaching assistantships available. Financial award application deadline: 4/15; financial award applicants required to submit FAFSA. *Faculty research:* Financial literacy, the value of financial advisors, charitable financial planning, financial risk tolerance, retirement planning. *Unit head:* Dr. Vickie Hampton, Director, 806-742-5050 Ext. 272, Fax: 806-742-5033, E-mail: vickie.hampton@ttu.edu. *Application contact:* Dr. Vickie Hampton, Director, 806-742-5050 Ext. 272, Fax: 806-742-5033, E-mail: vickie.hampton@ttu.edu.

Université Laval, Faculty of Agricultural and Food Sciences, Department of Agricultural Economics and Consumer Sciences, Program in Consumer Sciences, Québec, QC G1K 7P4, Canada. Offers Diploma. Part-time programs available. *Entrance requirements:* For degree, knowledge of French and English. Electronic applications accepted.

The University of Alabama, Graduate School, College of Human Environmental Sciences, Department of Consumer Sciences, Tuscaloosa, AL 35487-0158. Offers MS. Part-time and evening/weekend programs available. Postbaccalaureate distance learning degree programs offered (minimal on-campus study). *Faculty:* 10 full-time (5 women). *Students:* 15 full-time (10 women), 38 part-time (18 women); includes 18 minority (17 Black or African American, non-Hispanic/Latino; 1 American Indian or Alaska Native, non-Hispanic/Latino). Average age 34. 32 applicants, 91% accepted, 20 enrolled. In 2010, 14 master's awarded. *Degree requirements:* For master's, capstone. *Entrance requirements:* For master's, minimum GPA of 3.0. Additional exam requirements/recommendations for international students: Required—TOEFL. *Application deadline:* For fall admission, 7/1 priority date for domestic and international students; for winter admission, 1/1 priority date for domestic and international students. Applications are processed on a rolling basis. Application fee: $50 ($60 for international students). Electronic applications accepted. *Expenses:* Tuition, state resident: full-time $7900. Tuition, nonresident: full-time $20,500. *Financial support:* In 2010–11, 1 research assistantship (averaging $8,100 per year), 1 teaching assistantship (averaging $8,100 per year) were awarded; fellowships also available. Financial award application deadline: 3/15. *Faculty research:* Consumer economics, financial planning. *Unit head:* Dr. Milla Dailey Boschung, Chair, 205-348-6250, Fax: 205-348-3789, E-mail: mboschun@ches.ua.edu. *Application contact:* Dr. Cliff A. Robb, Assistant Professor, 205-348-6178, Fax: 205-348-8721, E-mail: crobb@ches.ua.edu.

University of Georgia, College of Family and Consumer Sciences, Department of Housing and Consumer Economics, Athens, GA 30602. Offers MS, PhD. Part-time programs available. *Faculty:* 16 full-time (8 women). *Students:* 18 full-time (11 women), 12 part-time (5 women); includes 7 Black or African American, non-Hispanic/Latino; 1 Asian, non-Hispanic/Latino. 16 applicants, 63% accepted, 6 enrolled. In 2010, 3 master's, 2 doctorates awarded. *Degree requirements:* For master's, thesis; for doctorate, thesis/dissertation. *Entrance requirements:* For master's and doctorate, GRE General Test. Additional exam requirements/recommendations for international students: Required—TOEFL (minimum score 575 paper-based; 230 computer-based). *Application deadline:* For fall admission, 7/1 for domestic students, 2/1 for international students; for spring admission, 11/15 for domestic students. Application fee: $50. Electronic applications accepted. *Expenses:* Tuition, state resident: full-time $7200; part-time $344 per credit hour. Tuition, nonresident: full-time $21,900; part-time $944 per credit hour. Tuition and fees vary according to course load and program. *Financial support:* In 2010–11, 10 students received support; fellowships, research assistantships, teaching assistantships, unspecified assistantships available. Financial award application deadline: 2/1. *Faculty research:* Demographics, consumer decision making, home ownership counseling, financial management, economics of divorce and poverty. *Unit head:* Dr. Anne L. Sweaney, Head, 706-542-4877, Fax: 706-542-0313, E-mail: asweaney@fcs.uga.edu. *Application contact:* Dr. Andrew T. Carswell, Graduate Coordinator, 706-542-4867, E-mail: carswell@fcs.uga.edu.

University of Guelph, Graduate Studies, College of Management and Economics, Department of Marketing and Consumer Studies, Guelph, ON N1G 2W1, Canada. Offers M Sc. *Degree requirements:* For master's, thesis. *Entrance requirements:* For master's, GMAT or GRE General Test, minimum B average during previous 2 years of course work. Additional exam requirements/recommendations for international students: Required—TOEFL (minimum score 575 paper-based; 213 computer-based). Electronic applications accepted. *Faculty research:* Marketing, quality management, consumer economics, housing and real estate management, problem gambling.

University of Idaho, College of Graduate Studies, College of Agricultural and Life Sciences, Margaret Ritchie School of Family and Consumer Sciences, Moscow, ID 83844-3183. Offers MS. *Faculty:* 8 full-time (all women). *Students:* 10 full-time, 17 part-time. Average age 36. In 2010, 2 master's awarded. *Degree requirements:* For master's, thesis. *Entrance requirements:* For master's, minimum GPA of 2.8. *Application deadline:* For fall admission, 8/1 for domestic students; for spring admission, 12/15 for domestic students. Application fee: $60. *Expenses:* Tuition, nonresident: part-time $580 per credit. Required fees: $306 per credit. *Financial support:* Research assistantships, teaching assistantships available. Financial award application deadline: 2/15. *Faculty research:* Food and nutrition; clothing, textiles and design; child, family and consumer studies; early childhood development. *Unit head:* Dr. Sandra Evenson, Interim Chair, 208-885-6546. *Application contact:* Dr. Sandra Evenson, Interim Chair, 208-885-6546.

University of Illinois at Urbana–Champaign, Graduate College, College of Agricultural, Consumer and Environmental Sciences, Department of Agricultural and Consumer Economics, Champaign, IL 61820. Offers agricultural and applied economics (MS, PhD). *Faculty:* 31 full-time (11 women). *Students:* 65 full-time (26 women), 15 part-time (8 women); includes 3 Black or African American, non-Hispanic/Latino; 3 Asian, non-Hispanic/Latino, 49 international. 117 applicants, 23% accepted, 15 enrolled. In 2010, 10 master's, 10 doctorates awarded. *Entrance requirements:* For master's, GRE, minimum GPA of 3.0; for doctorate, GRE, writing sample. Additional exam requirements/recommendations for international students: Required—TOEFL (minimum score 570 paper-based; 230 computer-based; 88 iBT) or IELTS (minimum

Consumer Economics

University of Illinois at Urbana–Champaign (continued)
score 6.5). *Application deadline:* Applications are processed on a rolling basis. Application fee: $75 ($90 for international students). Electronic applications accepted. *Financial support:* In 2010–11, 16 fellowships, 47 research assistantships, 32 teaching assistantships were awarded; tuition waivers (full and partial) also available. *Unit head:* Paul N. Ellinger, Head, 217-333-5503, Fax: 217-333-5538, E-mail: pellinge@illinois.edu. *Application contact:* Pamela S. Splittstoesser, Administrative Assistant, 217-333-1830, Fax: 217-244-7088, E-mail: splttsts@illinois.edu.

University of Missouri, Graduate School, College of Human Environmental Science, Department of Personal Financial Planning, Columbia, MO 65211. Offers MS. *Entrance requirements:* For master's, GRE General Test, minimum GPA of 3.0. Additional exam requirements/recommendations for international students: Required—TOEFL (minimum score 550 paper-based; 213 computer-based; 79 iBT).

University of Nebraska–Lincoln, Graduate College, College of Education and Human Sciences, Department of Child, Youth and Family Studies, Lincoln, NE 68588. Offers child development/early childhood education (MS, PhD); child, youth and family studies (MS); family and consumer sciences education (MS, PhD); family financial planning (MS); family science (MS, PhD); gerontology (PhD); human sciences (PhD), including child, youth and family studies, gerontology, medical family therapy; marriage and family therapy (MS); medical family therapy (PhD); youth development (MS). *Accreditation:* AAMFT/COAMFTE (one or more programs are accredited). Postbaccalaureate distance learning degree programs offered. *Degree requirements:* For master's, thesis optional. *Entrance requirements:* For master's, GRE. Additional exam requirements/recommendations for international students: Required—TOEFL (minimum score 550 paper-based; 213 computer-based). Electronic applications accepted. *Faculty research:* Marriage and family therapy, child development/early childhood education, family financial management.

University of South Carolina, The Graduate School, College of Hospitality, Retail, and Sport Management, Department of Retailing, Columbia, SC 29208. Offers MR. Part-time programs available. *Degree requirements:* For master's, comprehensive exam, internship or thesis. *Entrance requirements:* For master's, GMAT or GRE General Test, minimum GPA of 3.0. Additional exam requirements/recommendations for international students: Required—TOEFL (minimum score 80 iBT). Electronic applications accepted. *Faculty research:* Retail technology, retail strategy, international retailing.

The University of Tennessee, Graduate School, College of Education, Health and Human Sciences, Department of Consumer and Industry Services Management, Program in Consumer Services Management, Knoxville, TN 37996. Offers retail and consumer sciences (MS); textile science (MS). Part-time programs available. *Degree requirements:* For master's, thesis or alternative. *Entrance requirements:* For master's, GRE General Test, minimum GPA of 2.7. Additional exam requirements/recommendations for international students: Required—TOEFL. Electronic applications accepted. *Expenses:* Tuition, state resident: full-time $7440; part-time $414 per credit hour. Tuition, nonresident: full-time $22,478; part-time $1250 per credit hour. Required fees: $922; $43 per credit hour. Tuition and fees vary according to program.

The University of Tennessee, Graduate School, College of Education, Health and Human Sciences, Program in Human Ecology, Knoxville, TN 37996. Offers child and family studies (PhD); community health (PhD); nutrition science (PhD); retailing and consumer sciences (PhD); textile science (PhD). *Degree requirements:* For doctorate, thesis/dissertation. *Entrance requirements:* For doctorate, GRE General Test, minimum GPA of 2.7. Additional exam requirements/recommendations for international students: Required—TOEFL. Electronic applications accepted. *Expenses:* Tuition, state resident: full-time $7440; part-time $414 per credit hour. Tuition, nonresident: full-time $22,478; part-time $1250 per credit hour. Required fees: $922; $43 per credit hour. Tuition and fees vary according to program.

University of Utah, Graduate School, College of Social and Behavioral Science, Department of Family and Consumer Studies, Salt Lake City, UT 84112-0080. Offers early childhood education (M Ed); human development and social policy (MS). Part-time and evening/weekend programs available. *Faculty:* 17 full-time (8 women). *Students:* 18 full-time (17 women), 9 part-time (6 women); includes 1 minority (Native Hawaiian or other Pacific Islander, non-Hispanic/Latino), 1 international. Average age 31. 25 applicants, 80% accepted, 17 enrolled. In 2010, 9 master's awarded. *Degree requirements:* For master's, comprehensive exam (for some programs), thesis or alternative. *Entrance requirements:* For master's, GRE General Test, minimum undergraduate GPA of 3.0, courses in research methods and statistics. Additional exam requirements/recommendations for international students: Required—TOEFL (minimum score 500 paper-based; 173 computer-based). *Application deadline:* For fall admission, 3/1 priority date for domestic and international students. Application fee: $55 ($65 for international students). Electronic applications accepted. *Expenses:* Tuition, area resident: Part-time $179.19 per credit hour. Tuition, state resident: full-time $4384. Tuition, nonresident: full-time $16,684; part-time $630.67 per credit hour. Required fees: $350 per semester. Tuition and fees vary according to course load, degree level and program. *Financial support:* In 2010–11, 10 students received support, including 9 teaching assistantships with partial tuition reimbursements available (averaging $5,500 per year). Financial award application deadline: 2/1. *Faculty research:* Social, physical, educational and economic contexts of families and communities. Total annual research expenditures: $20,724. *Unit head:* Dr. Russell A. Isabella, Chair, 801-581-7712, Fax: 801-581-5156, E-mail: russ@fcs.utah.edu. *Application contact:* Dr. Marissa Diener, Graduate Director, 801-581-6521, E-mail: marissa.diener@fcs.utah.edu.

University of Wisconsin–Madison, Graduate School, School of Human Ecology, Program in Consumer Behavior and Family Economics, Madison, WI 53706-1380. Offers MS, PhD. *Faculty:* 8 full-time (6 women). *Students:* 14 full-time (9 women), 3 part-time (2 women); includes 2 Asian, non-Hispanic/Latino; 1 Hispanic/Latino. Average age 28. 26 applicants, 46% accepted, 9 enrolled. In 2010, 4 master's, 1 doctorate awarded. Terminal master's awarded for partial completion of doctoral program. *Degree requirements:* For master's, thesis optional; for doctorate, comprehensive exam, thesis/dissertation. *Entrance requirements:* For master's and doctorate, GRE General Test, 3 letters of recommendation. Additional exam requirements/recommendations for international students: Required—TOEFL (minimum score 580 paper-based; 237 computer-based; 92 iBT). *Application deadline:* For fall admission, 1/3 for domestic and international students. Application fee: $56. Electronic applications accepted. *Expenses:* Tuition, state resident: full-time $9887; part-time $617.96 per credit. Tuition, nonresident: full-time $24,054; part-time $1503.40 per credit. Required fees: $67.63 per credit. Tuition and fees vary according to reciprocity agreements. *Financial support:* Fellowships with full tuition reimbursements, research assistantships with full tuition reimbursements, teaching assistantships with full tuition reimbursements, institutionally sponsored loans, scholarships/grants, health care benefits, and unspecified assistantships available. *Faculty research:* Economic well-being of elderly, finance, financial planning, health care policy, consumer behavior. *Unit head:* Nancy Wong, Graduate Program Coordinator, 608-265-5954, E-mail: nywong@wisc.edu. *Application contact:* Nancy Wong, Graduate Program Coordinator, 608-265-5954, E-mail: nywong@wisc.edu.

University of Wyoming, College of Agriculture and Natural Resources, Department of Family and Consumer Sciences, Laramie, WY 82070. Offers early childhood development (MS); family and consumer sciences (MS); food science and human nutrition (MS). Part-time programs available. *Degree requirements:* For master's, thesis, project. *Entrance requirements:* For master's, GRE General Test or MCAT, minimum GPA of 3.0. Additional exam requirements/recommendations for international students: Required—TOEFL (minimum score 540 paper-based; 207 computer-based; 76 iBT). Electronic applications accepted. *Faculty research:* Asthma, obesity and healthy weights, nutrition concerns of children with special health care needs, food product development, food safety, postpartum health, exercise nutrition.

Utah State University, School of Graduate Studies, College of Agriculture, Department of Agricultural Systems Technology and Education, Logan, UT 84322. Offers agricultural systems technology (MS), including agricultural extension education, agricultural mechanization, international agricultural extension, secondary and postsecondary agricultural education; family and consumer sciences education (MS). Part-time programs available. Postbaccalaureate distance learning degree programs offered (minimal on-campus study). *Degree requirements:* For master's, comprehensive exam (for some programs), thesis (for some programs). *Entrance requirements:* For master's, GRE General Test, MAT, BS in agricultural education, agricultural extension, or related agricultural or science discipline; minimum GPA of 3.0. Additional exam requirements/recommendations for international students: Required—TOEFL. *Faculty research:* Extension and adult education; structures and environment; low-input agriculture; farm safety, systems, and mechanizations.

Virginia Polytechnic Institute and State University, Graduate School, College of Liberal Arts and Human Sciences, Department of Apparel, Housing, and Resource Management, Blacksburg, VA 24061. Offers apparel business and economics (MS, PhD); apparel product design and analysis (MS, PhD); apparel quality analysis (MS, PhD); consumer studies (MS, PhD); family financial management (MS, PhD); household equipment (MS, PhD); housing (MS, PhD); interior design (MS, PhD); resource management (MS, PhD). *Faculty:* 13 full-time (all women). *Students:* 7 full-time (all women), 2 part-time (both women); includes 1 Black or African American, non-Hispanic/Latino; 1 Asian, non-Hispanic/Latino; 1 Hispanic/Latino, 4 international. Average age 39. In 2010, 3 master's, 2 doctorates awarded. *Degree requirements:* For master's, comprehensive exam (for some programs), thesis (for some programs); for doctorate, comprehensive exam (for some programs), thesis/dissertation (for some programs). *Entrance requirements:* For master's and doctorate, GRE. Additional exam requirements/recommendations for international students: Required—TOEFL (minimum score 550 paper-based; 213 computer-based). *Application deadline:* For fall admission, 7/1 for domestic and international students; for spring admission, 12/1 for domestic and international students. Applications are processed on a rolling basis. Application fee: $65. Electronic applications accepted. *Expenses:* Tuition, state resident: full-time $9399; part-time $488 per credit hour. Tuition, nonresident: full-time $17,854; part-time $957.75 per credit hour. Required fees: $1534. Full-time tuition and fees vary according to program. *Financial support:* In 2010–11, 6 teaching assistantships with full tuition reimbursements (averaging $12,561 per year) were awarded; career-related internships or fieldwork, Federal Work-Study, scholarships/grants, health care benefits, and unspecified assistantships also available. Financial award application deadline: 1/15. *Faculty research:* Housing for elderly, affordable housing, household time use, phosphate laundry study, economic well-living. Total annual research expenditures: $11,651. *Unit head:* Dr. LuAnn R. Gaskill, UNIT HEAD, 540-231-4781, Fax: 540-231-3250, E-mail: lagaskil@vt.edu. *Application contact:* Julia Beemish, Contact, 540-231-8881, Fax: 540-231-3250, E-mail: jbeamish@vt.edu.

Gerontology

Adelphi University, School of Education, Program in Physical Education and Human Performance Science, Garden City, NY 11530-0701. Offers aging (Certificate); physical/educational human performance science (MA). Part-time and evening/weekend programs available. *Students:* 39 full-time (15 women), 81 part-time (39 women); includes 6 Black or African American, non-Hispanic/Latino; 1 Asian, non-Hispanic/Latino; 9 Hispanic/Latino, 2 international. Average age 28. In 2010, 65 master's awarded. *Degree requirements:* For master's, internship. *Entrance requirements:* For master's, 3 letters of recommendation, resume. Additional exam requirements/recommendations for international students: Required—TOEFL (minimum score 550 paper-based; 213 computer-based; 80 iBT). *Application deadline:* For fall admission, 4/1 for international students; for spring admission, 11/1 for international students. Applications are processed on a rolling basis. Application fee: $50. Electronic applications accepted. *Financial support:* Fellowships, research assistantships with full and partial tuition reimbursements, teaching assistantships, career-related internships or fieldwork, Federal Work-Study, institutionally sponsored loans, and tuition waivers (full) available. Support available to part-time students. Financial award application deadline: 2/15; financial award applicants required to submit FAFSA. *Faculty research:* Physical education for the handicapped, sport sociology, sport pedagogy. *Unit head:* Dr. Ronald S. Feingold, Chair, 516-877-4764, E-mail: feingold@adelphi.edu. *Application contact:* Christine Murphy, Director of Admissions, 516-877-3050, Fax: 516-877-3039, E-mail: graduateadmissions@adelphi.edu.

Adler School of Professional Psychology, Programs in Psychology, Chicago, IL 60602. Offers advanced Adlerian psychotherapy (Certificate); art therapy (MA); clinical neuropsychology (Certificate); clinical psychology (Psy D); community psychology (MA); counseling and organizational psychology (MA); counseling psychology (MA); forensic psychology (MA); gerontological counseling (MA); marriage and family counseling (MA); marriage and family therapy (Certificate); organizational psychology (MA); police psychology (MA); rehabilitation counseling (MA); sport and health psychology (MA); substance abuse counseling (Certificate); Psy D/Certificate; Psy D/MACAT; Psy D/MACP; Psy D/MAMFC; Psy D/MASAC. *Accreditation:* APA. Part-time and evening/weekend programs available. Postbaccalaureate distance learning degree programs offered (minimal on-campus study). *Faculty:* 40 full-time (18 women), 61 part-time/adjunct (31 women). *Students:* 688 full-time (532 women), 142 part-time (110 women). Average age 27.Terminal master's awarded for partial completion of doctoral program. *Degree requirements:* For master's, thesis or alternative, oral exam, practicum; for doctorate, thesis/dissertation, clinical exam, internship, oral exam, practicum, written qualifying exam. *Entrance requirements:* For master's, 12 semester hours in psychology, minimum GPA of 3.0; for doctorate, 18 semester hours in psychology, minimum GPA of 3.25; for Certificate, appropriate master's or doctoral degree. Additional exam requirements/recommendations for international students: Required—TOEFL (minimum score 550 paper-based; 213 computer-based; 79 iBT). *Application deadline:* For fall admission, 2/15 priority date for domestic students, 12/1 priority date for international students. Applications are processed on a rolling basis. Application fee: $50. Electronic applications accepted. *Financial support:* Career-related internships or fieldwork, Federal Work-Study, scholarships/grants, and tuition waivers (full and partial) available. Support available to part-time students. Financial award application deadline: 5/15; financial award applicants required to submit FAFSA. *Application contact:* Michelle Brice, Director of Admissions, 312-662-4113, Fax: 312-662-4199, E-mail: admissions@adler.edu.

Alliant International University–Los Angeles, California School of Professional Psychology, Program in Marital and Family Therapy, Alhambra, CA 91803-1360. Offers biofeedback (MA); chemical dependency (MA); gerontology (MA); Latin American family therapy (MA). *Accreditation:* AAMFT/COAMFTE.

Arizona State University, College of Public Programs, School of Social Work, Phoenix, AZ 85004-0689. Offers assessment of integrative health modalities (Graduate Certificate);

gerontology and geriatric care (Graduate Certificate); Latino cultural competency (Graduate Certificate); social work (PhD); social work (advanced direct practice) (MSW); social work (planning, administration and community practice) (MSW); trauma and bereavement (Graduate Certificate); MPA/MSW. *Accreditation:* CSWE (one or more programs are accredited). Part-time programs available. *Faculty:* 40 full-time (29 women), 1 (woman) part-time/adjunct. *Students:* 596 full-time (508 women), 126 part-time (99 women); includes 217 minority (46 Black or African American, non-Hispanic/Latino; 17 American Indian or Alaska Native, non-Hispanic/Latino; 21 Asian, non-Hispanic/Latino; 123 Hispanic/Latino; 1 Native Hawaiian or other Pacific Islander, non-Hispanic/Latino; 9 Two or more races, non-Hispanic/Latino), 4 international. Average age 32. 702 applicants, 77% accepted, 358 enrolled. In 2010, 278 master's, 4 doctorates, 9 other advanced degrees awarded. Terminal master's awarded for partial completion of doctoral program. *Degree requirements:* For master's, thesis or alternative, capstone project, interactive Program of Study (iPOS) submitted before completing 50 percent of required credit hours; for doctorate, comprehensive exam, thesis/dissertation, interactive Program of Study (iPOS) submitted before completing 50 percent of required credit hours. *Entrance requirements:* For master's, GRE or MAT, minimum GPA of 3.2 or equivalent in last 2 years of work leading to bachelor's degree; for doctorate, GRE, minimum GPA of 3.0 or equivalent in last 2 years of work leading to bachelor's degree, 3 letters of recommendation, resume, samples of professional writing, personal statement. Additional exam requirements/recommendations for international students: Required—TOEFL, IELTS, or Pearson Test of English. *Application deadline:* For fall admission, 2/1 for domestic and international students. Application fee: $70 ($90 for international students). Electronic applications accepted. *Expenses:* Contact institution. *Financial support:* In 2010–11, 13 research assistantships with full and partial tuition reimbursements (averaging $13,295 per year) were awarded; fellowships with full tuition reimbursements, teaching assistantships with full and partial tuition reimbursements, career-related internships or fieldwork, Federal Work-Study, institutionally sponsored loans, scholarships/grants, and tuition waivers (full and partial) also available. Financial award application deadline: 3/1; financial award applicants required to submit FAFSA. Total annual research expenditures: $4.9 million. *Unit head:* Dr. Steven G. Anderson, Director, 602-496-0800, Fax: 602-496-0960, E-mail: steven.anderson.2@asu.edu. *Application contact*» Graduate Admissions, 480-965-6113.

Arkansas State University, Graduate School, College of Nursing and Health Professions, School of Nursing, Jonesboro, State University, AR 72467. Offers aging studies (Certificate); health care management (Certificate); health communications (Certificate); health sciences (MS); health sciences education (Certificate); nurse anesthesia (MSN); nursing (MSN). *Accreditation:* AANA/CANAEP (one or more programs are accredited); NLN. Part-time programs available. *Faculty:* 7 full-time (6 women), 5 part-time/adjunct (4 women). *Students:* 114 full-time (51 women), 109 part-time (97 women); includes 30 minority (23 Black or African American, non-Hispanic/Latino; 2 Asian, non-Hispanic/Latino; 1 Hispanic/Latino; 4 Two or more races, non-Hispanic/Latino), 3 international. Average age 33. 113 applicants, 42% accepted, 36 enrolled. In 2010, 87 master's awarded. *Degree requirements:* For master's, comprehensive exam, thesis or alternative. *Entrance requirements:* For master's, GRE General Test or MAT, appropriate bachelor's degree, current Arkansas nursing license, CPR certification, physical examination, professional liability insurance, critical care experience, ACLS Certification, PALS Certification, interview, immunization records, personal goal statement, health assessment. Additional exam requirements/recommendations for international students: Required—TOEFL (minimum score 550 paper-based; 213 computer-based; 79 iBT), IELTS (minimum score 6), PTE: Pearson Test of English Academic (56). *Application deadline:* Applications are processed on a rolling basis. Application fee: $30 ($40 for international students). Electronic applications accepted. *Expenses:* Contact institution. *Financial support:* In 2010–11, 8 students received support. Career-related internships or fieldwork, scholarships/grants, and unspecified assistantships available. Financial award application deadline: 7/1; financial award applicants required to submit FAFSA. *Unit head:* Dr. Sue McLarry, Chair, 870-972-3074, Fax: 870-972-2954, E-mail: smclarry@astate.edu. *Application contact:* Dr. Andrew Sustich, Dean of the Graduate School, 870-972-3029, Fax: 870-972-3857, E-mail: sustich@astate.edu.

A.T. Still University of Health Sciences, School of Health Management, Kirksville, MO 63501. Offers dental emphasis (MPH); geriatric healthcare (MGH); health administration (MHA); health education (MH Ed, DH Ed); public health (MPH). Part-time and evening/weekend programs available. Postbaccalaureate distance learning degree programs offered (minimal on-campus study). *Faculty:* 12 full-time (6 women), 65 part-time/adjunct (29 women). *Students:* 87 full-time (59 women), 503 part-time (340 women); includes 147 minority (74 Black or African American, non-Hispanic/Latino; 7 American Indian or Alaska Native, non-Hispanic/Latino; 38 Asian, non-Hispanic/Latino; 26 Hispanic/Latino; 1 Native Hawaiian or other Pacific Islander, non-Hispanic/Latino; 1 Two or more races, non-Hispanic/Latino). Average age 34. 121 applicants, 100% accepted, 105 enrolled. In 2010, 141 master's, 40 doctorates awarded. *Degree requirements:* For master's, thesis (for some programs), integrated terminal project; for doctorate, thesis/dissertation. *Entrance requirements:* For master's, minimum GPA of 3.0, bachelor's degree or equivalent from U.S. institution; for doctorate, minimum GPA of 3.0, master's or terminal degree, employment. Additional exam requirements/recommendations for international students: Required—TOEFL (minimum score 550 paper-based; 213 computer-based; 80 iBT). *Application deadline:* For fall admission, 7/9 for domestic and international students; for winter admission, 10/23 for domestic students, 10/1 for international students; for spring admission, 1/15 for domestic students, 1/14 for international students. Applications are processed on a rolling basis. Application fee: $60. Electronic applications accepted. *Expenses:* Contact institution. *Financial support:* In 2010–11, 10 students received support. Scholarships/grants available. Financial award application deadline: 5/1; financial award applicants required to submit FAFSA. *Faculty research:* Curriculum and educational technologies, QI in on-line programming. *Unit head:* Dr. Kimberly O'Reilly, Interim Dean, 660-626-2820, Fax: 660-626-2826, E-mail: koreilley@atsu.edu. *Application contact:* Sarah Spencer, Director of Recruitment, 660-626-2820 Ext. 2669, Fax: 660-626-2826, E-mail: sbartlett@atsu.edu.

Ball State University, Graduate School, College of Applied Science and Technology, Fisher Institute for Wellness and Gerontology, Program in Applied Gerontology, Muncie, IN 47306-1099. Offers MA. *Faculty:* 1. *Students:* 2 full-time (both women), 10 part-time (8 women); includes 3 minority (all Black or African American, non-Hispanic/Latino), 2 international. Average age 23. 5 applicants, 100% accepted, 4 enrolled. In 2010, 11 master's awarded. Application fee: $25 ($35 for international students). *Expenses:* Tuition, state resident: full-time $6160; part-time $299 per credit hour. Tuition, nonresident: full-time $16,020; part-time $783 per credit hour. Required fees: $2278; $95 per credit hour. *Financial support:* In 2010–11, 7 teaching assistantships (averaging $8,431 per year) were awarded. Financial award application deadline: 3/1. *Unit head:* Dr. Kathryn Segrist, Information Contact, 765-285-1296. *Application contact:* Dr. Kathryn Segrist, Information Contact, 765-285-8259, Fax: 765-285-8237, E-mail: ksegrist@gw.bsu.edu.

Bethel University, Graduate School, Program in Gerontology, St. Paul, MN 55112-6999. Offers gerontology (MA). Part-time and evening/weekend programs available. *Faculty:* 5 full-time (2 women), 3 part-time/adjunct (all women). *Students:* 23 full-time (21 women), 6 part-time (all women); includes 1 Black or African American, non-Hispanic/Latino; 1 Asian, non-Hispanic/Latino; 1 Hispanic/Latino. Average age 45. 15 applicants, 93% accepted, 12 enrolled. In 2010, 9 master's awarded. *Degree requirements:* For master's, thesis or alternative, project, practicum. *Entrance requirements:* For master's, interview, 3 years of work experience, minimum GPA of 3.0, letters of reference. Additional exam requirements/recommendations for international students: Required—TOEFL (minimum score 550 paper-based; 213 computer-based; 80 iBT). *Application deadline:* For fall admission, 7/15 priority date for domestic students; for spring admission, 5/1 priority date for domestic students. Applications are processed on a rolling basis. Electronic applications accepted. *Expenses:* Tuition: Full-time $5400; part-time $450 per credit. Tuition and fees vary according to course level, course load, degree level and program. *Financial support:* Applicants required to submit FAFSA. *Unit head:* Dr. Diane L. Dahl, Assistant Dean, 651-635-8000, Fax: 651-635-8004, E-mail: diane-dahl@bethel.edu. *Application contact:* Paul Ives, Director of Admissions, 651-635-8000, Fax: 651-635-8004, E-mail: gs@bethel.edu.

California State University, Fullerton, Graduate Studies, College of Humanities and Social Sciences, Program in Gerontology, Fullerton, CA 92834-9480. Offers MS. Part-time programs available. *Students:* 10 full-time (8 women), 25 part-time (23 women); includes 6 Asian, non-Hispanic/Latino; 7 Hispanic/Latino; 1 Two or more races, non-Hispanic/Latino. Average age 37. 27 applicants, 70% accepted, 16 enrolled. In 2010, 14 master's awarded. *Financial support:* Career-related internships or fieldwork, Federal Work-Study, institutionally sponsored loans, and scholarships/grants available. Financial award application deadline: 3/1; financial award applicants required to submit FAFSA. *Unit head:* Dr. Joseph Weber, Coordinator, 657-278-7057. *Application contact:* Admissions/Applications, 657-278-2371.

California State University, Long Beach, Graduate Studies, College of Health and Human Services, Program in Gerontology, Long Beach, CA 90840. Offers MS. Part-time programs available. *Faculty:* 5 full-time (4 women). *Students:* 5 full-time (all women), 14 part-time (11 women). Average age 33. 21 applicants, 67% accepted, 9 enrolled. In 2010, 2 master's awarded. *Degree requirements:* For master's, thesis optional. *Application deadline:* For fall admission, 7/1 for domestic students. Applications are processed on a rolling basis. Application fee: $55. Electronic applications accepted. *Financial support:* Federal Work-Study, institutionally sponsored loans, and scholarships/grants available. Financial award application deadline: 3/2. *Unit head:* Dr. Barbara White, Director, 562-985-1582, Fax: 562-985-4414, E-mail: bwhite@csulb.edu. *Application contact:* Dr. Barbara White, Director, 562-985-1582, Fax: 562-985-4414, E-mail: bwhite@csulb.edu.

Capella University, School of Public Service Leadership, Minneapolis, MN 55402. Offers criminal justice (MS, PhD); emergency management (MS, PhD); general human services (MS, PhD); general public administration (MPA, DPA); gerontology (MS); health care administration (MS, PhD); health management and policy (MSPH); management of nonprofit agencies (MS, PhD); nurse educator (MS); public safety leadership (MS, PhD); social and community services (MS, PhD); social behavioral sciences (MSPH). *Expenses:* Tuition: Full-time $11,880; part-time $440 per credit hour.

Central Michigan University, College of Graduate Studies, College of Education and Human Services, Department of Human Environmental Studies, Mount Pleasant, MI 48859. Offers apparel product development and merchandising technology (MS); gerontology (Graduate Certificate); human development and family studies (MA); nutrition and dietetics (MS). Part-time and evening/weekend programs available. *Faculty:* 15 full-time (11 women), 1 (woman) part-time/adjunct. *Students:* 6 full-time (4 women), 24 part-time (22 women); includes 2 Black or African American, non-Hispanic/Latino, 4 international. *Degree requirements:* For master's, thesis or alternative. *Application deadline:* Applications are processed on a rolling basis. Application fee: $35 ($45 for international students). Electronic applications accepted. *Expenses:* Tuition, state resident: full-time $8208; part-time $456 per credit hour. Tuition, nonresident: full-time $13,788; part-time $766 per credit hour. One-time fee: $25. *Financial support:* Fellowships with tuition reimbursements, research assistantships, career-related internships or fieldwork, Federal Work-Study, unspecified assistantships, and out-of-state merit awards, non-resident graduate awards available. *Faculty research:* Human growth and development, family studies and human sexuality, human nutrition and dietetics, apparel and textile retailing, computer-aided design for apparel. *Unit head:* Dr. Megan P. Goodwin, Chairperson, 989-774-3218, Fax: 989-774-2435, E-mail: goodw1mp@cmich.edu. *Application contact:* Dr. Candace Maylee, Assistant Coordinator of Graduate Programs, 989-774-2613, Fax: 989-774-2435, E-mail: mayle1ce@cmich.edu.

Cleveland State University, College of Graduate Studies, College of Sciences and Health Professions, Department of Psychology, Cleveland, OH 44115. Offers adult development and aging (PhD); clinical psychology (MA); consumer/industrial research (MA); diversity management (MA); experimental research psychology (MA); school psychology (Psy S). *Accreditation:* APA. *Faculty:* 20 full-time (7 women), 16 part-time/adjunct (8 women). *Students:* 63 full-time (45 women), 43 part-time (27 women); includes 15 Black or African American, non-Hispanic/Latino; 1 American Indian or Alaska Native, non-Hispanic/Latino; 3 Asian, non-Hispanic/Latino; 3 Hispanic/Latino, 1 international. Average age 30. 164 applicants, 44% accepted, 62 enrolled. In 2010, 39 master's, 8 other advanced degrees awarded. Terminal master's awarded for partial completion of doctoral program. *Degree requirements:* For master's, comprehensive exam (for some programs), thesis (for some programs); for doctorate, comprehensive exam, thesis/dissertation; for Psy S, internship. *Entrance requirements:* For master's and doctorate, GRE General Test. Additional exam requirements/recommendations for international students: Required—TOEFL (minimum score 525 paper-based; 197 computer-based). *Application deadline:* For fall admission, 2/1 priority date for domestic and international students. Application fee: $30. Electronic applications accepted. *Expenses:* Tuition, state resident: full-time $8447; part-time $469 per credit hour. Tuition, nonresident: full-time $16,020; part-time $890 per credit hour. Required fees: $50. *Financial support:* In 2010–11, 45 students received support. Career-related internships or fieldwork, Federal Work-Study, scholarships/grants, tuition waivers (partial), and unspecified assistantships available. Financial award applicants required to submit FAFSA. *Faculty research:* Cognitive and social psychology, consumer psychology, clinical psychology, school psychology, aging. Total annual research expenditures: $112,607. *Unit head:* Dr. Kathleen M. McNamara, Chairperson, 216-687-2545, Fax: 216-687-9294, E-mail: k.mcnamara@csuohio.edu. *Application contact:* Karen R. Colston, Administrative Coordinator, 216-687-2552, Fax: 216-687-9294, E-mail: k.colston@csuohio.edu.

The College of New Rochelle, Graduate School, Division of Human Services, Program in Gerontology, New Rochelle, NY 10805-2308. Offers MS, Certificate. Part-time and evening/weekend programs available. *Degree requirements:* For master's, fieldwork, internship. *Entrance requirements:* For master's, interview, minimum GPA of 3.0, writing sample.

Concordia University Chicago, College of Graduate and Innovative Programs, Program in Gerontology, River Forest, IL 60305-1499. Offers MA. Part-time and evening/weekend programs available. *Degree requirements:* For master's, comprehensive exam, thesis. *Entrance requirements:* For master's, minimum GPA of 2.9. Additional exam requirements/recommendations for international students: Required—TOEFL (minimum score 550 paper-based; 195 computer-based). Electronic applications accepted.

Eastern Illinois University, Graduate School, Lumpkin College of Business and Applied Sciences, Program in Gerontology, Charleston, IL 61920-3099. Offers MA.

Eastern Michigan University, Graduate School, College of Arts and Sciences, Department of Sociology, Anthropology and Criminology, Ypsilanti, MI 48197. Offers criminology and criminal justice (MA); gerontology-dementia (Graduate Certificate); sociology (MA), including schools, society and violence, sociology, sociology—family specialty. Part-time and evening/weekend programs available. Postbaccalaureate distance learning degree programs offered (minimal on-campus study). *Faculty:* 18 full-time (8 women). *Students:* 15 full-time (11 women), 47 part-time (34 women); includes 23 minority (18 Black or African American, non-Hispanic/Latino; 1 Asian, non-Hispanic/Latino; 3 Hispanic/Latino; 1 Two or more races, non-Hispanic/Latino). Average age 30. 43 applicants, 65% accepted, 20 enrolled. In 2010, 13 master's awarded. *Degree requirements:* For master's, thesis optional. *Entrance requirements:* Additional exam requirements/recommendations for international students: Required—TOEFL. *Application deadline:* Applications are processed on a rolling basis. Application fee: $35. *Financial support:* Fellowships, research assistantships with full tuition reimbursements, teaching assistantships with full tuition reimbursements, career-related internships or fieldwork, Federal Work-Study, institutionally sponsored loans, scholarships/grants, tuition waivers (partial), and unspecified assistantships available. Support available to part-time students. Financial award applicants required to submit FAFSA. *Unit head:* Dr. David Woike, Interim Head, 734-487-0012, Fax: 734-487-9666, E-mail: dwoike@emich.edu. *Application contact:* Dr. David Woike, Interim Head, 734-487-0012, Fax: 734-487-9666, E-mail: dwoike@emich.edu.

East Tennessee State University, School of Graduate Studies, College of Public Health, Department of Public Health, Johnson City, TN 37614. Offers biostatistics (MPH); community health (MPH, DPH); environmental health sciences (MPH); epidemiology (MPH, Certificate);

Gerontology

East Tennessee State University (continued)
gerontology (Certificate); health care management (Certificate); health services administration (MPH); rural health (Certificate). *Accreditation:* CEPH. Part-time programs available. Post-baccalaureate distance learning degree programs offered (no on-campus study). *Faculty:* 9 full-time (3 women). *Students:* 49 full-time (29 women), 32 part-time (22 women); includes 15 minority (10 Black or African American, non-Hispanic/Latino; 4 Asian, non-Hispanic/Latino; 1 Hispanic/Latino), 17 international. Average age 32. 151 applicants, 38% accepted, 32 enrolled. In 2010, 38 master's, 6 other advanced degrees awarded. Terminal master's awarded for partial completion of doctoral program. *Degree requirements:* For master's, comprehensive exam, thesis optional, field experience; for doctorate, comprehensive exam, thesis/dissertation, culminating experience/practicum. *Entrance requirements:* For master's, GRE General Test, minimum GPA of 2.75; for doctorate, GRE General Test, MPH or equivalent. Additional exam requirements/recommendations for international students: Required—TOEFL (minimum score 550 paper-based; 213 computer-based; 79 iBT). *Application deadline:* For fall admission, 3/1 for domestic and international students. Application fee: $25 ($35 for international students). Electronic applications accepted. *Financial support:* In 2010–11, 6 research assistantships with full tuition reimbursements (averaging $6,000 per year), 4 teaching assistantships with full tuition reimbursements (averaging $6,000 per year) were awarded; career-related internships or fieldwork, institutionally sponsored loans, scholarships/grants, tuition waivers (full), and unspecified assistantships also available. Financial award application deadline: 7/1; financial award applicants required to submit FAFSA. *Faculty research:* Rural health issues, youth and adolescent health, health of the elderly, environmental epidemiology, spatial analysis of data. Total annual research expenditures: $616,124. *Unit head:* Dr. Rob Pack, Assistant Dean, 423-439-4243, Fax: 423-439-5238, E-mail: packr@etsu.edu. *Application contact:* Admissions and Records Clerk, 423-439-4221, Fax: 423-439-5624, E-mail: gradsch@etsu.edu.

Emory University, Nell Hodgson Woodruff School of Nursing, Atlanta, GA 30322-1100. Offers adult and elder health advanced practice nursing (MSN), including acute care, adult nurse practitioner, gerontological nurse practitioner; emergency nurse practitioner (MSN); family nurse practitioner (MSN); family nurse-midwife (MSN); nurse midwifery (MSN); pediatric nurse practitioner acute and primary care (MSN); public health nursing leadership (MSN); women's health nurse practitioner (MSN); women's health title x (MSN); women's health/adult health nurse practitioner (MSN); MSN/MPH. *Accreditation:* AACN; ACNM/DOA (one or more programs are accredited). Part-time programs available. *Entrance requirements:* For master's, GRE General Test or MAT, minimum GPA of 3.0, BS in nursing from an accredited institution, RN license and additional course work, 3 letters of recommendation. Additional exam requirements/recommendations for international students: Required—TOEFL (minimum score 600 paper-based; 100 iBT). Electronic applications accepted. *Expenses:* Contact institution. *Faculty research:* Older adult falls and injuries, minority health issues, cardiac symptoms and quality of life, bio-ethics and decision making, menopausal issues.

Gannon University, School of Graduate Studies, College of Humanities, Education, and Social Sciences, School of Humanities, Program in Gerontology, Erie, PA 16541-0001. Offers Certificate. Part-time and evening/weekend programs available. *Students:* 1 applicant, 100% accepted, 0 enrolled. *Entrance requirements:* For degree, interview. Additional exam requirements/recommendations for international students: Required—TOEFL (minimum score 79 iBT). *Application deadline:* Applications are processed on a rolling basis. Application fee: $25. Electronic applications accepted. *Expenses:* Tuition: Full-time $14,670; part-time $815 per credit. Required fees: $430; $18 per credit. Tuition and fees vary according to class time, course load, degree level, campus/location and program. *Financial support:* Career-related internships or fieldwork available. Financial award application deadline: 7/1; financial award applicants required to submit FAFSA. *Unit head:* Parris Baker, Director, 814-871-7781, E-mail: baker002@gannon.edu. *Application contact:* Kara Morgan, Assistant Director of Graduate Admissions, 814-871-5831, Fax: 814-871-5827, E-mail: graduate@gannon.edu.

George Mason University, College of Health and Human Services, Department of Global and Community Health, Fairfax, VA 22030. Offers biostatistics (Certificate); epidemiology (Certificate); epidemiology and biostatistics (MS); gerontology (Certificate); global health (MS, Certificate); nutrition (Certificate); public health (MPH, Certificate); rehabilitation science (Certificate). *Faculty:* 15 full-time (10 women), 21 part-time/adjunct (17 women). *Students:* 99 full-time (80 women), 158 part-time (126 women); includes 110 minority (66 Black or African American, non-Hispanic/Latino; 1 American Indian or Alaska Native, non-Hispanic/Latino; 30 Asian, non-Hispanic/Latino; 11 Hispanic/Latino; 2 Two or more races, non-Hispanic/Latino), 23 international. Average age 32. 202 applicants, 41% accepted, 41 enrolled. In 2010, 29 master's, 11 other advanced degrees awarded. *Degree requirements:* For master's, comprehensive exam (for some programs), thesis or practicum. *Entrance requirements:* For master's, GRE, BA with minimum GPA of 3.0, 2 letters of recommendation. Additional exam requirements/recommendations for international students: Required—TOEFL (minimum score 570 paper-based; 230 computer-based; 88 iBT). *Application deadline:* For fall admission, 4/1 priority date for domestic students, 4/1 for international students; for spring admission, 11/1 for domestic and international students. Applications are processed on a rolling basis. Application fee: $100. Electronic applications accepted. *Expenses:* Tuition, state resident: full-time $8192; part-time $440 per credit hour. Tuition, nonresident: full-time $22,952; part-time $1055 per credit hour. Required fees: $2364; $99 per credit hour. *Financial support:* In 2010–11, 15 students received support, including 13 research assistantships with full and partial tuition reimbursements available (averaging $13,006 per year), 3 teaching assistantships with full and partial tuition reimbursements available (averaging $15,000 per year); career-related internships or fieldwork, Federal Work-Study, scholarships/grants, health care benefits, unspecified assistantships, and research awards also available. Financial award application deadline: 3/1; financial award applicants required to submit FAFSA. *Faculty research:* Providing introductory and advanced degrees in health-related disciplines centered in global and community issues, health issues and the needs of affected populations at the regional and global level. Total annual research expenditures: $13,285. *Unit head:* Dr. Shirley S. Travis, Dean, 703-993-1918. *Application contact:* Allan Weiss, Office Manager, 703-993-3126, E-mail: aweiss2@gmu.edu.

Georgia State University, College of Arts and Sciences, Gerontology Institute, Atlanta, GA 30302-3083. Offers MA. Part-time programs available. *Degree requirements:* For master's, thesis, internship. *Entrance requirements:* For master's, GRE, 3 letters of reference, resume. Additional exam requirements/recommendations for international students: Required—TOEFL, TWE. Electronic applications accepted. *Faculty research:* Long-term care; assisted living; aging families and grandparenting; mental health, caregiving and well-being; health, exercise and rehabilitation; images of aging; and work, retirement, and economics of aging.

Hofstra University, School of Education, Health, and Human Services, Programs in Counseling, Hempstead, NY 11549. Offers counseling (MS Ed, PD); creative arts therapy (MA); gerontology (MS, Advanced Certificate); marriage and family therapy (MA); mental health counseling (MA); rehabilitation counseling (MS Ed, CAS, PD); rehabilitation counseling in mental health (MS Ed, CAS); school counselor-bilingual extension (Advanced Certificate). Part-time and evening/weekend programs available. *Students:* 145 full-time (132 women), 80 part-time (74 women); includes 41 minority (23 Black or African American, non-Hispanic/Latino; 5 Asian, non-Hispanic/Latino; 11 Hispanic/Latino; 1 Native Hawaiian or other Pacific Islander, non-Hispanic/Latino; 1 Two or more races, non-Hispanic/Latino), 8 international. Average age 30. 187 applicants, 63% accepted, 67 enrolled. In 2010, 79 master's, 1 other advanced degree awarded. *Degree requirements:* For master's, comprehensive exam (for some programs), thesis (for some programs), internship, practicum, student teaching, seminars. *Entrance requirements:* For master's, GRE, interview, letters of recommendation, portfolio, essay, professional experience, certification; for other advanced degree, GRE, interview, letters of recommendation, essay, professional experience, resume, master's degree. Additional exam requirements/recommendations for international students: Required—TOEFL (minimum score 550 paper-based; 213 computer-based; 80 iBT). *Application deadline:* Applications are processed on a rolling basis. Application fee: $70 ($75 for international students). Electronic applications accepted. *Expenses:* Tuition: Full-time $18,000; part-time $1000 per credit hour. Required fees: $970; $145 per term. Tuition and fees vary according to program. *Financial support:* In 2010–11, 102 students received support, including 27 fellowships with full and partial tuition reimbursements available (averaging $2,466 per year), 4 research assistantships with full and partial tuition reimbursements available (averaging $14,567 per year); career-related internships or fieldwork, Federal Work-Study, institutionally sponsored loans, scholarships/grants, tuition waivers (full and partial), unspecified assistantships, and scholarships also available. Support available to part-time students. Financial award applicants required to submit FAFSA. *Faculty research:* Bereavement, loss, and trauma counseling, creativity for non-artists. *Unit head:* Dr. Darra Pace, Chairperson, 516-463-6476, Fax: 516-463-6415, E-mail: cprdzp@hofstra.edu. *Application contact:* Carol Drummer, Dean of Graduate Admissions, 516-463-4876, Fax: 516-463-4664, E-mail: gradstudent@hofstra.edu.

Kent State University, Graduate School of Education, Health, and Human Services, School of Lifespan Development and Educational Sciences, Program in Family Studies, Kent, OH 44242-0001. Offers gerontology (MA); human development and family studies (MA). *Faculty:* 8 full-time (6 women), 12 part-time/adjunct (11 women). *Students:* 3 full-time (all women), 12 part-time (11 women); includes 2 Black or African American, non-Hispanic/Latino. 10 applicants, 70% accepted. In 2010, 4 master's awarded. Application fee: $30 ($60 for international students). *Expenses:* Tuition, state resident: full-time $7866; part-time $437 per credit hour. Tuition, nonresident: full-time $14,022; part-time $779 per credit hour. *Financial support:* In 2010–11, research assistantships (averaging $8,313 per year); 2 administrative assistantships (averaging $8,313 per year) also available. *Unit head:* Dr. Rhonda Richardson, Coordinator, 330-672-2026, E-mail: rrichard@kent.edu. *Application contact:* Nancy Miller, Academic Program Coordinator, 330-672-2576, Fax: 330-672-9162, E-mail: ogs@kent.edu.

Lakehead University, Graduate Studies, Department of History, Thunder Bay, ON P7B 5E1, Canada. Offers gerontology (MA); history (MA); women's studies (MA). Part-time programs available. *Degree requirements:* For master's, one foreign language, thesis. *Entrance requirements:* For master's, minimum B average. Additional exam requirements/recommendations for international students: Required—TOEFL. *Faculty research:* Canadian history, British history, Russian/German history, women's studies.

Lakehead University, Graduate Studies, Faculty of Education, Thunder Bay, ON P7B 5E1, Canada. Offers educational studies (PhD); gerontology (M Ed); women's studies (M Ed). Part-time and evening/weekend programs available. *Degree requirements:* For master's, project or thesis. *Entrance requirements:* For master's, minimum B average. Additional exam requirements/recommendations for international students: Required—TOEFL. *Faculty research:* Art education, AIDS education, language arts education, gerontology, women's studies.

Lakehead University, Graduate Studies, Faculty of Social Sciences and Humanities, Department of Sociology, Thunder Bay, ON P7B 5E1, Canada. Offers gerontology (MA); health services and policy research (MA); sociology (MA); women's studies (MA). Part-time and evening/weekend programs available. *Degree requirements:* For master's, research project or thesis. *Entrance requirements:* For master's, minimum B average. Additional exam requirements/recommendations for international students: Required—TOEFL. *Faculty research:* Sociology of medicine, cultural and social change, health human resources, gerontology, women's studies.

Lakehead University, Graduate Studies, Gerontology Collaborative Program-Northern Educational Center for Aging and Health, Thunder Bay, ON P7B 5E1, Canada. Offers gerontology (M Ed, M Sc, MA, MSW). Part-time programs available. *Degree requirements:* For master's, thesis (for some programs). *Entrance requirements:* Additional exam requirements/recommendations for international students: Required—TOEFL. *Faculty research:* Integrated health information systems.

Lakehead University, Graduate Studies, School of Kinesiology, Thunder Bay, ON P7B 5E1, Canada. Offers kinesiology (M Sc); kinesiology and gerontology (M Sc). Part-time programs available. *Degree requirements:* For master's, thesis. *Entrance requirements:* For master's, minimum B average. Additional exam requirements/recommendations for international students: Required—TOEFL. *Faculty research:* Social psychology and physical education, sport history, sports medicine, exercise physiology, gerontology.

Lakehead University, Graduate Studies, School of Social Work, Thunder Bay, ON P7B 5E1, Canada. Offers gerontology (MSW); social work (MSW); women's studies (MSW). Part-time programs available. *Degree requirements:* For master's, thesis or project. *Entrance requirements:* For master's, minimum B average. Additional exam requirements/recommendations for international students: Required—TOEFL. *Faculty research:* Clinical psychology, social work and practice theory, long-term care, health care for frail elderly, women's studies.

Lindenwood University, Graduate Programs, College of Individualized Education, St. Charles, MO 63301-1695. Offers administration (MSA); business administration (MBA); communications (MA); criminal justice and administration (MS); gerontology (MA); health management (MS); human resource management (MS); information technology (MBA, Certificate); managing information technology (MS); writing (MFA). Part-time and evening/weekend programs available. *Faculty:* 15 full-time (8 women), 128 part-time/adjunct (53 women). *Students:* 828 full-time (527 women), 80 part-time (50 women); includes 284 minority (265 Black or African American, non-Hispanic/Latino; 3 American Indian or Alaska Native, non-Hispanic/Latino; 6 Asian, non-Hispanic/Latino; 10 Hispanic/Latino), 23 international. Average age 35. 223 applicants, 44% accepted, 87 enrolled. In 2010, 478 master's awarded. *Degree requirements:* For master's, thesis (for some programs), 1 colloquium per term. *Entrance requirements:* For master's, interview, minimum GPA of 3.0. Additional exam requirements/recommendations for international students: Required—TOEFL (minimum score 550 paper-based; 213 computer-based; 80 iBT). *Application deadline:* For fall admission, 10/2 priority date for domestic and international students; for winter admission, 1/8 priority date for domestic and international students; for spring admission, 4/8 priority date for domestic and international students. Applications are processed on a rolling basis. Application fee: $30 ($100 for international students). Electronic applications accepted. *Expenses:* Tuition: Full-time $13,260; part-time $380 per credit hour. Required fees: $340. One-time fee: $30. Tuition and fees vary according to course level and course load. *Financial support:* In 2010–11, 631 students received support. Career-related internships or fieldwork, institutionally sponsored loans, tuition waivers (partial), and unspecified assistantships available. Financial award application deadline: 6/30; financial award applicants required to submit FAFSA. *Unit head:* Dan Kemper, Dean, 636-949-4501, Fax: 636-949-4505, E-mail: dkemper@lindenwood.edu. *Application contact:* Brett Barger, Dean of Evening Admissions and Extension Campuses, 636-949-4934, Fax: 636-949-4109, E-mail: adultadmissions@lindenwood.edu.

Long Island University, C.W. Post Campus, College of Management, Department of Health Care and Public Administration, Brookville, NY 11548-1300. Offers gerontology (Certificate); health care administration (MPA); health care administration/gerontology (MPA); nonprofit management (MPA, Certificate); public administration (MPA). *Accreditation:* NASPAA (one or more programs are accredited). Part-time and evening/weekend programs available. *Degree requirements:* For master's, thesis. *Entrance requirements:* For master's, GMAT, minimum GPA of 2.5; for Certificate, minimum GPA of 2.5. Electronic applications accepted. *Faculty research:* Critical issues in sexuality, social work in religious communities, gerontological social work.

Long Island University, C.W. Post Campus, School of Health Professions and Nursing, Master of Social Work Program, Brookville, NY 11548-1300. Offers alcohol and substance abuse (MSW); child and family welfare (MSW); forensic social work (MSW); gerontology (MSW); nonprofit management (MSW). *Accreditation:* CSWE.

Long Island University, Rockland Graduate Campus, Graduate School, Programs in Health and Public Administration, Orangeburg, NY 10962. Offers gerontology (Advanced Certificate); health administration (MPA); public administration (MPA). Part-time and evening/weekend programs available. *Faculty:* 1 full-time (0 women), 5 part-time/adjunct (3 women). *Students:* 2

full-time (both women), 22 part-time (16 women). In 2010, 9 master's awarded. *Degree requirements:* For master's, thesis. *Entrance requirements:* For master's, college transcripts, letters of recommendation, personal statement, resume. *Application deadline:* Applications are processed on a rolling basis. Application fee: $30. *Expenses:* Tuition: Part-time $1028 per credit. Required fees: $340 per semester. *Financial support:* Applicants required to submit FAFSA. *Unit head:* Prof. Patricia Latona, Program Director, 845-359-7200 Ext. 5410, Fax: 845-359-7248, E-mail: patricia.latona@liu.edu. *Application contact:* Carolyn Reiter, Admissions Manager, 845-359-7200 Ext. 5417, Fax: 845-359-7248, E-mail: carolyn.reiter@liu.edu.

Marywood University, Academic Affairs, College of Health and Human Services, Department of Nursing and Public Administration, Program in Gerontology, Scranton, PA 18509-1598. Offers MS. *Entrance requirements:* Additional exam requirements/recommendations for international students: Required—TOEFL (minimum score 550 paper-based; 213 computer-based; 79 iBT). Electronic applications accepted. *Expenses:* Tuition: Part-time $735 per credit. Required fees: $470 per semester. Tuition and fees vary according to degree level and campus/location. *Faculty research:* Dementia.

Miami University, Graduate School, College of Arts and Science, Department of Sociology and Gerontology, Oxford, OH 45056. Offers gerontology (MGS); social gerontology (PhD). Part-time programs available. *Students:* 31 full-time (22 women), 9 part-time (8 women); includes 2 minority (1 Asian, non-Hispanic/Latino; 1 Two or more races, non-Hispanic/Latino), 11 international. Average age 35. In 2010, 7 master's, 1 doctorate awarded. *Entrance requirements:* For master's, GRE General Test, minimum undergraduate GPA of 3.0 during previous 2 years or 2.75 overall; for doctorate, GRE, minimum undergraduate GPA of 3.0 during previous 2 years or 2.75 overall. Additional exam requirements/recommendations for international students: Required—TOEFL. Application fee: $50. *Expenses:* Tuition, state resident: full-time $11,616; part-time $484 per credit hour. Tuition, nonresident: full-time $25,656; part-time $1069 per credit hour. Required fees: $528. *Financial support:* Fellowships, research assistantships, teaching assistantships, career-related internships or fieldwork, Federal Work-Study, institutionally sponsored loans, health care benefits, tuition waivers (full), and unspecified assistantships available. Financial award application deadline: 3/1; financial award applicants required to submit FAFSA. *Unit head:* Dr. Suzanne R. Kunkel, Director, Scripps Gerontology Center, 513-529-2914, Fax: 513-529-1476, E-mail: scripps@muohio.edu. *Application contact:* Dr. Lisa Groger, Director of Graduate Programs, 513-529-2914, Fax: 513-529-1476, E-mail: scripps@muohio.edu.

Middle Tennessee State University, College of Graduate Studies, College of Liberal Arts, Program in Gerontology, Murfreesboro, TN 37132. Offers Graduate Certificate. Part-time and evening/weekend programs available. Postbaccalaureate distance learning degree programs offered. *Students:* 6 part-time (5 women); includes 5 Black or African American, non-Hispanic/Latino. In 2010, 2 Graduate Certificates awarded. *Entrance requirements:* Additional exam requirements/recommendations for international students: Required—TOEFL (minimum score 525 paper-based; 195 computer-based; 71 iBT) or IELTS (minimum score 6). *Expenses:* Tuition, state resident: full-time $4632. Tuition, nonresident: full-time $11,520. *Financial support:* Application deadline: 5/1. *Unit head:* Dr. Brandon Wallace, Program Director, 615-898-5976, E-mail: jbwallae@mtsu.edu. *Application contact:* Dr. Michael Allen, Dean and Vice Provost for Research, 615-898-2840, Fax: 615-904-8020, E-mail: mallen@mtsu.edu.

Minnesota State University Mankato, College of Graduate Studies, College of Social and Behavioral Sciences, Program in Gerontology, Mankato, MN 56001. Offers MS, Certificate. *Students:* 10 part-time (9 women). *Degree requirements:* For master's, comprehensive exam, thesis. *Entrance requirements:* For master's, GRE, minimum GPA of 3.0 during previous 2 years, letters of recommendation. Additional exam requirements/recommendations for international students: Required—TOEFL. *Application deadline:* For fall admission, 7/1 priority date for domestic students; for spring admission, 11/1 for domestic students. Applications are processed on a rolling basis. Application fee: $40. Electronic applications accepted. *Financial support:* Federal Work-Study and unspecified assistantships available. Support available to part-time students. Financial award application deadline: 3/15; financial award applicants required to submit FAFSA. *Unit head:* Dr. Don Ebel, Director, 507-389-5188. *Application contact:* 507-389-2321, E-mail: grad@mnsu.edu.

Morehead State University, Graduate Programs, Caudill College of Arts, Humanities and Social Sciences, Department of Sociology, Social Work and Criminology, Morehead, KY 40351. Offers criminology (MA); general sociology (MA); gerontology (MA); sociology regional analysis (MA); sociology/chemical dependency (MA). Part-time and evening/weekend programs available. *Degree requirements:* For master's, comprehensive exam, thesis (for some programs). *Entrance requirements:* For master's, GRE General Test, minimum GPA of 3.0 in sociology, 2.75 overall; 18 hours of course work in sociology, writing sample. Additional exam requirements/recommendations for international students: Required—TOEFL (minimum score 500 paper-based; 173 computer-based). Electronic applications accepted. *Faculty research:* Death and dying; aging, drinking, and drugs; economic development; adult children of alcoholics.

Mount Saint Vincent University, Graduate Programs, Department of Family Studies and Gerontology, Halifax, NS B3M 2J6, Canada. Offers MA. Part-time programs available. Postbaccalaureate distance learning degree programs offered (minimal on-campus study). *Degree requirements:* For master's, thesis. *Entrance requirements:* For master's, minimum GPA of 3.0; course work in statistics, research methods, family and social theories.

New York University, College of Nursing, Doctor of Nursing Practice Program, New York, NY 10012-1019. Offers advanced practice nursing (DNP), including adult acute care, adult nurse practitioner/holistic nursing, adult nurse practitioner/palliative care nursing, adult primary care, adult primary care/geriatrics, geriatrics, mental health nursing, nurse-midwifery, pediatrics. Part-time and evening/weekend programs available. *Faculty:* 7 full-time (all women). *Students:* 22 full-time (18 women); includes 4 Black or African American, non-Hispanic/Latino; 1 Asian, non-Hispanic/Latino. Average age 47. 18 applicants, 83% accepted, 14 enrolled. *Entrance requirements:* Additional exam requirements/recommendations for international students: Required—TOEFL, IELTS. *Application deadline:* For fall admission, 4/1 priority date for domestic students, 4/1 for international students. Applications are processed on a rolling basis. Application fee: $75. *Financial support:* In 2010–11, 15 students received support; fellowships with full and partial tuition reimbursements available, institutionally sponsored loans, scholarships/grants, and tuition waivers (partial) available. Support available to part-time students. Financial award application deadline: 2/1; financial award applicants required to submit FAFSA. *Faculty research:* Elderly black diabetics, families and illness, oral systemic connection. *Unit head:* Dr. Jamesetta A. Newland, Director, 212-998-5319, Fax: 212-995-3143, E-mail: jan7@nyu.edu. *Application contact:* Amy Knowles, Assistant Dean for Student Affairs and Admissions, 212-998-5333, Fax: 212-995-4302, E-mail: ak96@nyu.edu.

North Dakota State University, College of Graduate and Interdisciplinary Studies, College of Human Development and Education, Department of Child Development and Family Science, Fargo, ND 58108. Offers child development and family science (MS); couple and family therapy (MS); family financial planning (MS); gerontology (MS, PhD). *Accreditation:* AAMFT/COAMFTE. Part-time and evening/weekend programs available. Postbaccalaureate distance learning degree programs offered (no on-campus study). *Faculty:* 12 full-time (7 women). *Students:* 30 full-time (27 women), 20 part-time (19 women); includes 2 Black or African American, non-Hispanic/Latino, 2 international. 26 applicants, 62% accepted, 13 enrolled. *Degree requirements:* For master's, thesis or alternative; for doctorate, thesis/dissertation. *Entrance requirements:* Additional exam requirements/recommendations for international students: Required—TOEFL (minimum score 525 paper-based; 197 computer-based; 71 iBT). *Application deadline:* For fall admission, 2/1 for domestic and international students; for spring admission, 10/1 for domestic and international students. Application fee: $45 ($60 for international students). *Financial support:* In 2010–11, 17 students received support, including research assistantships with full tuition reimbursements available (averaging $3,000 per year), 17 teaching assistantships with full tuition reimbursements available (averaging $3,000 per year); career-related internships or fieldwork, Federal Work-Study, institutionally sponsored loans, and tuition waivers (full) also available. Financial award application deadline: 4/1. *Faculty research:* Family therapy, resilience, parenting, adolescent development, mental health. Total annual research expenditures: $333,582. *Unit head:* Dr. James Deal, Head, 701-231-7568, Fax: 701-231-9645, E-mail: jim_deal@ndsu.edu. *Application contact:* Theresa Anderson, Administrative Assistant, 701-231-8628, Fax: 701-231-9645, E-mail: theresa.anderson@ndsu.edu.

Northeastern Illinois University, Graduate College, College of Arts and Sciences, Department of Gerontology, Program in Gerontology, Chicago, IL 60625-4699. Offers MA. Part-time and evening/weekend programs available. *Faculty:* 13 full-time (9 women), 6 part-time/adjunct (5 women). *Students:* 2 full-time (both women), 22 part-time (18 women); includes 9 minority (3 Black or African American, non-Hispanic/Latino; 4 Asian, non-Hispanic/Latino; 2 Hispanic/Latino), 1 international. Average age 44. 7 applicants, 43% accepted. In 2010, 1 master's awarded. *Degree requirements:* For master's, comprehensive exam, paper and project or thesis, practicum. *Entrance requirements:* For master's, 15 hours in social sciences (3 hours in gerontology), 1 course in research methods or statistics, minimum GPA of 2.75. Additional exam requirements/recommendations for international students: Required—TOEFL (minimum score 550 paper-based; 213 computer-based; 79 iBT). *Application deadline:* For fall admission, 4/1 priority date for domestic students; for spring admission, 8/15 for domestic students. Applications are processed on a rolling basis. Application fee: $30. Electronic applications accepted. *Financial support:* In 2010–11, 12 students received support, including 1 research assistantship with full tuition reimbursement available (averaging $6,600 per year); career-related internships or fieldwork, Federal Work-Study, institutionally sponsored loans, scholarships/grants, tuition waivers (full and partial), and unspecified assistantships also available. Support available to part-time students. Financial award applicants required to submit FAFSA. *Faculty research:* Later life development, cultural diversity, humanities and aging, elder abuse, AIDS and aging, computer training. *Unit head:* Dr. Saba Ayman-Nolley, Department Chair. *Application contact:* Dr. Saba Ayman-Nolley, Department Chair.

Oregon Health & Science University, School of Nursing, Program in Nursing Education, Portland, OR 97239-3098. Offers MN, MS, Post Master's Certificate.

Oregon State University, Graduate School, College of Health and Human Sciences, Department of Human Development and Family Sciences, Program in Gerontology, Corvallis, OR 97331. Offers MAIS. *Degree requirements:* For master's, thesis optional. *Entrance requirements:* For master's, GRE, minimum GPA of 3.0 in last 90 hours. Additional exam requirements/recommendations for international students: Required—TOEFL. *Faculty research:* Aging/families, social/psychological aspects of aging, osteoporosis, nutrition, disease and aging.

Portland State University, Graduate Studies, College of Urban and Public Affairs, School of Community Health, Institute on Aging, Portland, OR 97207-0751. Offers Certificate. Part-time programs available. *Faculty:* 3 full-time (2 women). *Students:* 1 (woman) full-time, 6 part-time (3 women). Average age 41. 5 applicants, 100% accepted, 4 enrolled. *Application deadline:* For fall admission, 2/1 for domestic and international students. Application fee: $50. *Expenses:* Tuition, state resident: full-time $8505; part-time $315 per credit. Tuition, nonresident: full-time $13,284; part-time $492 per credit. Required fees: $1482; $21 per credit. $99 per term. One-time fee: $120. Part-time tuition and fees vary according to course load and program. *Financial support:* In 2010–11, 3 research assistantships with full tuition reimbursements (averaging $9,456 per year) were awarded; teaching assistantships, career-related internships or fieldwork and Federal Work-Study also available. Support available to part-time students. Financial award application deadline: 3/1; financial award applicants required to submit FAFSA. Total annual research expenditures: $536,905. *Unit head:* Dr. Margaret Neal, Director, 503-725-3952, Fax: 503-725-5199, E-mail: nealm@pdx.edu. *Application contact:* Dr. Margaret Neal, Director, 503-725-3952, Fax: 503-725-5199, E-mail: nealm@pdx.edu.

Rochester Institute of Technology, Graduate Enrollment Services, College of Applied Science and Technology, Department of Hospitality and Service Management, Rochester, NY 14623-5603. Offers health systems administration (MS, AC), including elements of health care leadership (AC), health information resources (AC), health systems administration (MS), health systems administration executive leader (MS), health systems-finance (AC), senior living management (AC); hospitality-tourism management (MS); human resources development (MS); service leadership and innovation (MS). Part-time and evening/weekend programs available. Postbaccalaureate distance learning degree programs offered (no on-campus study). *Students:* 56 full-time (38 women), 117 part-time (64 women); includes 11 Black or African American, non-Hispanic/Latino; 1 American Indian or Alaska Native, non-Hispanic/Latino; 1 Asian, non-Hispanic/Latino; 2 Hispanic/Latino, 43 international. Average age 31. 201 applicants, 58% accepted, 56 enrolled. In 2010, 64 master's, 2 other advanced degrees awarded. *Degree requirements:* For master's, thesis or alternative. *Entrance requirements:* For master's and AC, minimum GPA of 3.0. Additional exam requirements/recommendations for international students: Required—TOEFL (minimum score 550 paper-based; 213 computer-based; 79 iBT) or IELTS (minimum score 6.5). *Application deadline:* For fall admission, 2/15 priority date for domestic and international students; for winter admission, 11/1 priority date for domestic students, 10/1 priority date for international students; for spring admission, 2/1 priority date for domestic students, 1/1 priority date for international students. Applications are processed on a rolling basis. Electronic applications accepted. *Expenses:* Tuition: Full-time $33,234; part-time $924 per credit hour. Required fees: $219. *Financial support:* In 2010–11, 82 students received support; research assistantships with partial tuition reimbursements available, teaching assistantships with partial tuition reimbursements available, career-related internships or fieldwork, scholarships/grants, and unspecified assistantships available. Support available to part-time students. Financial award applicants required to submit FAFSA. *Faculty research:* Investment criterion in hotel development, legal impacts on meeting/conference planning, tourism marketing systems, computers in the food industry. *Unit head:* Dr. Linda Underhill, Program Chair, 585-475-2867, Fax: 585-475-5099, E-mail: lmuism@rit.edu. *Application contact:* Diane Ellison, Assistant Vice President, Graduate Enrollment Services, 585-475-2229, Fax: 585-475-7164, E-mail: gradinfo@rit.edu.

Sacred Heart University, Graduate Programs, College of Education and Health Professions, Program in Geriatric Health and Wellness, Fairfield, CT 06825-1000. Offers MS. Part-time and evening/weekend programs available. Postbaccalaureate distance learning degree programs offered. *Entrance requirements:* Additional exam requirements/recommendations for international students: Required—TOEFL (minimum score 550 paper-based; 213 computer-based; 75 iBT). Electronic applications accepted. *Expenses:* Contact institution.

Sage Graduate School, Graduate School, School of Management, Program in Health Services Administration, Troy, NY 12180-4115. Offers dietetic internship (Certificate); gerontology (MS). Part-time and evening/weekend programs available. *Faculty:* 4 full-time (2 women), 8 part-time/adjunct (3 women). *Students:* 7 full-time (6 women), 24 part-time (18 women); includes 6 Black or African American, non-Hispanic/Latino; 1 Asian, non-Hispanic/Latino; 2 Hispanic/Latino. Average age 30. 18 applicants, 39% accepted, 3 enrolled. In 2010, 4 master's awarded. *Entrance requirements:* For master's, minimum GPA of 2.75, resume, 2 letters of recommendation. Additional exam requirements/recommendations for international students: Required—TOEFL (minimum score 550 paper-based; 213 computer-based). Application fee: $40. *Expenses:* Tuition: Full-time $10,980; part-time $610 per credit hour. Tuition and fees vary according to course load, degree level and program. *Financial support:* Fellowships, research assistantships, Federal Work-Study, scholarships/grants, and unspecified assistantships available. Support available to part-time students. Financial award application deadline: 3/1; financial award applicants required to submit FAFSA. *Unit head:* Dr. Kimberly Fredricks, Program Director, 518-292-1782, Fax: 518-292-1964, E-mail: fredek1@sage.edu. *Application contact:* Wendy D. Diefendorf, Director of Graduate and Adult Admission, 518-244-2443, Fax: 518-244-6880, E-mail: diefew@sage.edu.

St. Cloud State University, School of Graduate Studies, College of Social Sciences, Program in Gerontology, St. Cloud, MN 56301-4498. Offers MS. Part-time programs available. *Degree*

Gerontology

St. Cloud State University (continued)
requirements: For master's, thesis or alternative. *Entrance requirements:* For master's, GRE General Test, minimum GPA of 2.75. Additional exam requirements/recommendations for international students: Required—Michigan English Language Assessment Battery; Recommended—TOEFL (minimum score 550 paper-based; 213 computer-based), IELTS (minimum score 6.5). Electronic applications accepted.

Saint Joseph College, Department of Gerontology, West Hartford, CT 06117-2700. Offers human development/gerontology (MA, Certificate). Part-time and evening/weekend programs available. *Students:* 17 part-time (all women). *Entrance requirements:* For master's, 2 letters of recommendation. *Application deadline:* Applications are processed on a rolling basis. Application fee: $50. Electronic applications accepted. *Expenses:* Tuition: Full-time $11,340; part-time $630 per credit. Required fees: $540; $30 per credit. Tuition and fees vary according to course load, campus/location and program. *Financial support:* Career-related internships or fieldwork and unspecified assistantships available. Support available to part-time students. Financial award applicants required to submit FAFSA. *Application contact:* Graduate Admissions Office, 860-231-5261, E-mail: graduate@sjc.edu.

Saint Joseph's University, College of Arts and Sciences, Program in Gerontological Services, Philadelphia, PA 19131-1395. Offers gerontological counseling (MS); gerontological services (Post-Master's Certificate); human services administration (MS). Part-time and evening/weekend programs available. *Faculty:* 1 (woman) full-time, 4 part-time/adjunct (1 woman). *Students:* 3 full-time (all women), 16 part-time (15 women); includes 8 minority (all Black or African American, non-Hispanic/Latino), 2 international. Average age 34. 14 applicants, 79% accepted, 5 enrolled. In 2010, 5 master's awarded. *Entrance requirements:* For master's, 2 letters of recommendation. Additional exam requirements/recommendations for international students: Required—TOEFL (minimum score 550 paper-based; 213 computer-based; 79 iBT). *Application deadline:* For fall admission, 7/15 priority date for domestic students, 4/15 for international students; for winter admission, 1/15 for international students; for spring admission, 11/15 priority date for domestic students, 10/15 for international students. Applications are processed on a rolling basis. Application fee: $35. Electronic applications accepted. *Expenses:* Tuition: Part-time $729 per credit. Tuition and fees vary according to course load, degree level and program. *Financial support:* Fellowships available. Financial award applicants required to submit FAFSA. *Unit head:* Dr. Catherine Murray, Director, 610-660-1805, E-mail: cmurray@sju.edu. *Application contact:* Kate McConnell, Director, Graduate College of Arts and Sciences Admissions and Retention, 610-660-3184, Fax: 610-660-3230, E-mail: kate.mcconnell@sju.edu.

San Diego State University, Graduate and Research Affairs, College of Health and Human Services, Department of Gerontology, San Diego, CA 92182. Offers MS. Part-time and evening/weekend programs available. *Degree requirements:* For master's, thesis. *Entrance requirements:* For master's, GRE General Test. Additional exam requirements/recommendations for international students: Required—TOEFL. Electronic applications accepted.

San Francisco State University, Division of Graduate Studies, College of Health and Human Services, Gerontology Program, San Francisco, CA 94132-1722. Offers geriatric care management (MA); health, wellness and aging (MA); long-term care administration (MA). Part-time programs available. *Application deadline:* Applications are processed on a rolling basis. *Financial support:* Career-related internships or fieldwork and unspecified assistantships available. *Unit head:* Dr. Anabel Pelham, Director, 415-338-3557, Fax: 415-338-6378, E-mail: apelham@sfsu.edu. *Application contact:* Darlene Yee-Melichar, Coordinator, 415-338-3558, E-mail: dyee@sfsu.edu.

San Jose State University, Graduate Studies and Research, College of Applied Sciences and Arts, Department of Health Science, San Jose, CA 95192-0001. Offers applied social gerontology (Certificate); community health education (MPH). *Accreditation:* CEPH (one or more programs are accredited). Postbaccalaureate distance learning degree programs offered. *Entrance requirements:* For master's, GRE General Test. Electronic applications accepted. *Faculty research:* Behavioral science in occupational and health care settings, epidemiology in health care settings.

Shippensburg University of Pennsylvania, School of Graduate Studies, College of Education and Human Services, Department of Social Work and Gerontology, Shippensburg, PA 17257-2299. Offers aging (Certificate); social work (MSW). *Accreditation:* CSWE. Part-time and evening/weekend programs available. *Faculty:* 7 full-time (5 women), 1 part-time/adjunct (0 women). *Students:* 26 full-time (23 women), 26 part-time (22 women); includes 11 minority (9 Black or African American, non-Hispanic/Latino; 2 Two or more races, non-Hispanic/Latino). Average age 33. 66 applicants, 64% accepted, 27 enrolled. In 2010, 21 master's awarded. *Degree requirements:* For master's, thesis, practicum. *Entrance requirements:* For master's, GRE or MAT (if GPA is below 2.8), 3 letters of reference; resume; personal statement; course work in human biology, economics, government/political science, psychology, sociology/anthropology and statistics. Additional exam requirements/recommendations for international students: Required—TOEFL (minimum score 580 paper-based; 237 computer-based); Recommended—IELTS (minimum score 6). *Application deadline:* For fall admission, 3/1 for international students. Applications are processed on a rolling basis. Application fee: $30. Electronic applications accepted. *Expenses:* Tuition, state resident: full-time $6966. Tuition, nonresident: full-time $11,146. Required fees: $1802. *Financial support:* In 2010–11, 5 research assistantships with full tuition reimbursements (averaging $5,000 per year) were awarded; career-related internships or fieldwork, scholarships/grants, unspecified assistantships, and resident hall director and student payroll positions also available. Support available to part-time students. Financial award application deadline: 3/1; financial award applicants required to submit FAFSA. *Unit head:* Dr. Marita Flagler, Co-Director, MU-SU Master of Social Work Program, 717-477-1717, Fax: 717-477-4051, E-mail: mnflagler@ship.edu. *Application contact:* Jeremy R. Goshorn, Associate Dean of Graduate Admissions, 717-477-1231, Fax: 717-477-4016, E-mail: jrgoshorn@ship.edu.

Simon Fraser University, Graduate Studies, Faculty of Arts and Social Sciences, Department of Gerontology, Burnaby, BC V5A 1S6, Canada. Offers MA, PhD. *Degree requirements:* For master's, thesis (for some programs). *Entrance requirements:* For master's, minimum GPA of 3.5. Additional exam requirements/recommendations for international students: Required—TOEFL or IELTS. *Faculty research:* Aging and the built environment, health promotion and aging.

Texas A&M University–Kingsville, College of Graduate Studies, College of Arts and Sciences, Department of Psychology and Sociology, Kingsville, TX 78363. Offers gerontology (MS); psychology (MA, MS); sociology (MA, MS). Part-time and evening/weekend programs available. *Degree requirements:* For master's, comprehensive exam, thesis or alternative. *Entrance requirements:* For master's, GRE General Test, minimum GPA of 2.5. Additional exam requirements/recommendations for international students: Required—TOEFL. *Faculty research:* Hispanic female voting behavior, attitudes toward criminal justice, immigration of aged into south Texas, folk medicine.

Texas Tech University, Graduate School, College of Human Sciences, Department of Human Development and Family Studies, Lubbock, TX 79409. Offers gerontology (MS); human development and family studies (MS, PhD). *Accreditation:* AAMFT/COAMFTE (one or more programs are accredited). Part-time programs available. *Faculty:* 17 full-time (13 women), 2 part-time/adjunct (both women). *Students:* 42 full-time (38 women), 14 part-time (6 women); includes 1 American Indian or Alaska Native, non-Hispanic/Latino; 1 Asian, non-Hispanic/Latino; 3 Hispanic/Latino, 14 international. Average age 32. 46 applicants, 43% accepted, 10 enrolled. In 2010, 6 master's, 3 doctorates awarded. *Degree requirements:* For master's, thesis; for doctorate, comprehensive exam, thesis/dissertation. *Entrance requirements:* For master's and doctorate, GRE General Test. Additional exam requirements/recommendations for international students: Required—TOEFL (minimum score 550 paper-based; 213 computer-based; 79 iBT). *Application deadline:* For fall admission, 6/1 priority date for domestic students, 1/15 priority date for international students; for spring admission, 9/1 priority date for domestic students, 6/15 priority date for international students. Applications are processed on a rolling basis. Application fee: $50 ($75 for international students). Electronic applications accepted. *Expenses:* Tuition, state resident: full-time $5495.76; part-time $228.99 per credit hour. Tuition, nonresident: full-time $12,936; part-time $538.99 per credit hour. Required fees: $2674; $36 per credit hour. $905 per semester. *Financial support:* In 2010–11, 40 students received support, including 8 research assistantships with partial tuition reimbursements available (averaging $3,281 per year), 14 teaching assistantships with partial tuition reimbursements available (averaging $3,551 per year). Financial award application deadline: 4/15; financial award applicants required to submit FAFSA. *Faculty research:* Parenting, marital and premarital relationships, adolescent risky behaviors, life span; child development. Total annual research expenditures: $509,694. *Unit head:* Dr. Jean Pearson Scott, Chairperson, 806-742-3000 Ext. 271, Fax: 806-742-0285, E-mail: jean.scott@ttu.edu. *Application contact:* Monya Castle, Graduate Secretary, 806-742-3000 Ext. 250, Fax: 806-742-0285, E-mail: monya.castle@ttu.edu.

Towson University, Program in Applied Gerontology, Towson, MD 21252-0001. Offers MS, Certificate. *Students:* 6 full-time (all women), 7 part-time (6 women); includes 4 minority (2 Black or African American, non-Hispanic/Latino; 2 Hispanic/Latino), 2 international. Average age 36. In 2010, 6 master's awarded. *Entrance requirements:* For master's, minimum of 9 credits of upper-level related coursework, 2 letters of recommendation; for Certificate, minimum of 9 credits of upper-level related coursework. *Application deadline:* Applications are processed on a rolling basis. Application fee: $50. Electronic applications accepted. *Expenses:* Tuition, state resident: part-time $324 per credit. Tuition, nonresident: part-time $681 per credit. Required fees: $95 per term. *Financial support:* Application deadline: 4/1. *Unit head:* Mary McSweeney-Feld, Graduate Program Director, 410-704-4219, E-mail: mmcsweeneyfeld@towson.edu. *Application contact:* 410-704-2501, Fax: 410-704-4675, E-mail: grads@towson.edu.

Université de Sherbrooke, Faculty of Letters and Human Sciences, Department of Psychology, Sherbrooke, QC J1K 2R1, Canada. Offers gerontology (MA). *Degree requirements:* For master's, thesis. *Faculty research:* Human relations.

Université Laval, Faculty of Medicine, Post-Professional Programs in Medical Studies, Québec, QC G1K 7P4, Canada. Offers anatomy–pathology (DESS); anesthesiology (DESS); cardiology (DESS); care of older people (Diploma); clinical research (DESS); community health (DESS); dermatology (DESS); diagnostic radiology (DESS); emergency medicine (Diploma); family medicine (DESS); general surgery (DESS); geriatrics (DESS); hematology (DESS); internal medicine (DESS); maternal and fetal medicine (Diploma); medical biochemistry (DESS); medical microbiology and infectious diseases (DESS); medical oncology (DESS); nephrology (DESS); neurology (DESS); neurosurgery (DESS); obstetrics and gynecology (DESS); ophthalmology (DESS); orthopedic surgery (DESS); oto-rhino-laryngology (DESS); palliative medicine (Diploma); pediatrics (DESS); plastic surgery (DESS); psychiatry (DESS); pulmonary medicine (DESS); radiology–oncology (DESS); thoracic surgery (DESS); urology (DESS). *Degree requirements:* For other advanced degree, comprehensive exam. *Entrance requirements:* For degree, knowledge of French. Electronic applications accepted.

University of Arkansas at Little Rock, Graduate School, College of Arts, Humanities, and Social Science, Program in Gerontology, Little Rock, AR 72204-1099. Offers Graduate Certificate.

University of Central Florida, College of Health and Public Affairs, School of Social Work, Orlando, FL 32816. Offers aging studies (Certificate); children's services (Certificate); social work (MSW); social work administration (Certificate). *Accreditation:* CSWE. Part-time and evening/weekend programs available. *Faculty:* 20 full-time (16 women), 23 part-time/adjunct (18 women). *Students:* 190 full-time (176 women), 169 part-time (138 women); includes 78 Black or African American, non-Hispanic/Latino; 2 American Indian or Alaska Native, non-Hispanic/Latino; 6 Asian, non-Hispanic/Latino; 38 Hispanic/Latino; 4 Two or more races, non-Hispanic/Latino, 3 international. Average age 32. 337 applicants, 82% accepted, 207 enrolled. In 2010, 88 master's, 5 other advanced degrees awarded. *Degree requirements:* For master's, thesis or alternative, field education. *Entrance requirements:* For master's, resume. Additional exam requirements/recommendations for international students: Required—TOEFL. *Application deadline:* For fall admission, 3/1 for domestic students. Application fee: $30. Electronic applications accepted. *Expenses:* Tuition, state resident: part-time $256.56 per credit hour. Tuition, nonresident: part-time $1011.52 per credit hour. Part-time tuition and fees vary according to program. *Financial support:* In 2010–11, 4 students received support, including 3 fellowships with partial tuition reimbursements available (averaging $10,000 per year), 1 research assistantship with partial tuition reimbursement available (averaging $7,100 per year); career-related internships or fieldwork, Federal Work-Study, institutionally sponsored loans, and unspecified assistantships also available. Financial award application deadline: 3/1; financial award applicants required to submit FAFSA. *Unit head:* Dr. John Ronnau, Director, 407-823-2114, Fax: 407-823-5697, E-mail: jronnau@mail.ucf.edu. *Application contact:* Dr. John Ronnau, Director, 407-823-2114, Fax: 407-823-5697, E-mail: jronnau@mail.ucf.edu.

University of Central Missouri, The Graduate School, College of Health and Human Services, Warrensburg, MO 64093. Offers criminal justice (MS); industrial hygiene (MS); occupational safety management (MS); physical education/exercise and sport science (MS); rural family nursing (MS); social gerontology (MS); sociology (MA); speech language pathology and audiology (MS). *Accreditation:* NCATE. Part-time programs available. Postbaccalaureate distance learning degree programs offered. *Entrance requirements:* Additional exam requirements/recommendations for international students: Required—TOEFL (minimum score 550 paper-based; 79 computer-based). Electronic applications accepted.

University of Central Oklahoma, College of Graduate Studies and Research, College of Education, Department of Occupational and Technical Education, Program in Adult Education, Edmond, OK 73034-5209. Offers community services (M Ed); gerontology (M Ed). *Accreditation:* NCATE. Part-time programs available. *Entrance requirements:* For master's, GRE General Test. Additional exam requirements/recommendations for international students: Required—TOEFL (minimum score 550 paper-based; 213 computer-based). Electronic applications accepted.

University of Georgia, College of Public Health, Institute of Gerontology, Athens, GA 30602. Offers Certificate. *Faculty:* 2 full-time (1 woman). *Students:* 3 part-time (all women). 3 applicants, 67% accepted. *Expenses:* Tuition, state resident: full-time $7200; part-time $344 per credit hour. Tuition, nonresident: full-time $21,900; part-time $944 per credit hour. Tuition and fees vary according to course load and program. *Unit head:* Dr. Leonard W. Poon, Director, 706-425-3222, E-mail: lpoon@geron.uga.edu. *Application contact:* Dr. Anne H. Glass, Graduate Coordinator, 706-425-3222, E-mail: aglass@geron.uga.edu.

University of Illinois at Springfield, Graduate Programs, College of Education and Human Services, Program in Human Services, Springfield, IL 62703-5407. Offers alcoholism and substance abuse (MA); child and family services (MA); gerontology (MA); social services administration (MA). Part-time and evening/weekend programs available. Postbaccalaureate distance learning degree programs offered (no on-campus study). *Degree requirements:* For master's, internship; project or thesis. *Entrance requirements:* For master's, minimum undergraduate GPA of 3.0, 2 letters of recommendation. Additional exam requirements/recommendations for international students: Required—TOEFL (minimum score 500 paper-based; 176 computer-based; 61 iBT). Electronic applications accepted. *Expenses:* Tuition, state resident: full-time $6774; part-time $282.25 per credit hour. Tuition, nonresident: full-time $15,078; part-time $628.25 per credit hour. Required fees: $15.25 per credit hour. $492 per term.

University of Indianapolis, Graduate Programs, Center for Aging and Community, Indianapolis, IN 46227-3697. Offers gerontology (MS, Certificate). Part-time and evening/weekend programs available. Postbaccalaureate distance learning degree programs offered. *Students:* 1 (woman) full-time, 24 part-time (22 women); includes 2 minority (both Black or African American, non-Hispanic/Latino). Average age 39. *Degree requirements:* For master's, capstone course. *Entrance requirements:* For master's, 3 letters of recommendation. Additional exam requirements/recommendations for international students: Required—TOEFL (minimum score 550 paper-based; 213 computer-based). *Application deadline:* Applications are processed on a rolling basis. Application fee: $50. Tuition and fees vary according to course load, degree level and program. *Financial support:* Career-related internships or fieldwork, Federal Work-Study, scholarships/grants, and tuition waivers (full and partial) available. Support available to part-time students. *Unit head:* Dr. Ellen Miller, Executive Director, 317-791-5930, Fax: 317-791-5945, E-mail: emiller@uindy.edu. *Application contact:* Tamora Wolske, Academic Program Director, 317-791-5930, Fax: 317-791-5945, E-mail: wolsketl@uindy.edu.

University of Indianapolis, Graduate Programs, School of Nursing, Indianapolis, IN 46227-3697. Offers family practice (post-RN) (MSN); gerontological nurse practitioner (MSN); nurse-midwifery (MSN); nursing (MSN); nursing administration (MSN); nursing education (MSN); MBA/MSN. *Accreditation:* AACN; ACNM. *Faculty:* 4 full-time (3 women), 2 part-time/adjunct (both women). *Students:* 25 full-time (23 women), 134 part-time (125 women); includes 13 minority (6 Black or African American, non-Hispanic/Latino; 1 American Indian or Alaska Native, non-Hispanic/Latino; 2 Asian, non-Hispanic/Latino; 3 Hispanic/Latino; 1 Two or more races, non-Hispanic/Latino), 5 international. Average age 38. In 2010, 26 master's awarded. *Entrance requirements:* For master's, minimum GPA of 3.0, interview, letters of recommendation, resume, IN nursing license, 1 year professional practice. Additional exam requirements/recommendations for international students: Required—TOEFL (minimum score 550 paper-based; 213 computer-based). *Application deadline:* For fall admission, 8/1 for domestic students; for winter admission, 12/15 for domestic students; for spring admission, 4/15 for domestic students. Applications are processed on a rolling basis. Application fee: $50. Tuition and fees vary according to course load, degree level and program. *Financial support:* Federal Work-Study available. *Unit head:* Dr. Anne Thomas, Dean, 317-788-3206, E-mail: athomas@uindy.edu. *Application contact:* T. C. Crum, Information Contact, 317-788-2128, Fax: 317-788-3542, E-mail: tcrum@uindy.edu.

The University of Kansas, Graduate Studies, College of Liberal Arts and Sciences, Program in Gerontology, Lawrence, KS 66045. Offers MA, PhD, Graduate Certificate. *Faculty:* 4 full-time (2 women). *Students:* 1 (woman) full-time, 1 (woman) part-time. Average age 29. 8 applicants, 50% accepted, 2 enrolled. *Degree requirements:* For master's, thesis; for doctorate, comprehensive exam, thesis/dissertation, written preliminary exam. *Entrance requirements:* For master's and doctorate, GRE, 3 letters of reference. Additional exam requirements/recommendations for international students: Required—TOEFL. *Application deadline:* For fall admission, 2/1 priority date for domestic and international students. Applications are processed on a rolling basis. Application fee: $55 ($65 for international students). Electronic applications accepted. *Expenses:* Tuition, state resident: full-time $7092; part-time $295.50 per credit hour. Tuition, nonresident: full-time $16,590; part-time $691.25 per credit hour. Required fees: $858; $71.49 per credit hour. Tuition and fees vary according to course load, campus/location and program. *Financial support:* Fellowships with full tuition reimbursements, research assistantships with full tuition reimbursements, career-related internships or fieldwork, traineeships, and unspecified assistantships available. Financial award application deadline: 1/15. *Faculty research:* Communication and aging, work and retirement, family studies, cognitive aging, exercise and disability. *Unit head:* David J. Ekerdt, Center Director, 785-864-4130, Fax: 785-864-2666, E-mail: gerontology@ku.edu. *Application contact:* Susan Kemper, Graduate Adviser, 785-864-0748, E-mail: skemper@ku.edu.

University of Kentucky, Graduate School, College of Public Health, Program in Gerontology, Lexington, KY 40506-0032. Offers PhD. *Degree requirements:* For doctorate, comprehensive exam, thesis/dissertation. *Entrance requirements:* For doctorate, GRE General Test, minimum undergraduate GPA of 2.75, graduate 3.0. Additional exam requirements/recommendations for international students: Required—TOEFL (minimum score 550 paper-based; 213 computer-based). Electronic applications accepted.

University of La Verne, College of Business and Public Management, Program in Gerontology, La Verne, CA 91750-4443. Offers gerontology (Certificate); gerontology administration (MS). Part-time programs available. *Faculty:* 34 full-time (12 women), 36 part-time/adjunct (9 women). *Students:* 14 full-time (13 women), 20 part-time (18 women); includes 7 Black or African American, non-Hispanic/Latino; 3 Asian, non-Hispanic/Latino; 9 Hispanic/Latino. Average age 39. In 2010, 7 master's awarded. *Entrance requirements:* For master's, minimum GPA of 2.5. Additional exam requirements/recommendations for international students: Required—TOEFL (minimum score 550 paper-based; 213 computer-based). *Application deadline:* Applications are processed on a rolling basis. Application fee: $50. *Expenses:* Contact institution. *Financial support:* Institutionally sponsored loans available. Financial award application deadline: 3/2; financial award applicants required to submit FAFSA. *Unit head:* Joan Branin, Chairperson, 909-593-3511 Ext. 4247, E-mail: jbranin@laverne.edu. *Application contact:* Barbara Cox, Program and Admissions Specialist, 909-593-3511 Ext. 4004, Fax: 909-392-2761, E-mail: bcox@laverne.edu.

University of Louisiana at Monroe, Graduate School, College of Arts and Sciences, Program in Gerontology, Monroe, LA 71209-0001. Offers MA, CGS. *Faculty:* 1 (woman) full-time, 3 part-time/adjunct (2 women). *Students:* 8 full-time (all women), 26 part-time (22 women); includes 13 Black or African American, non-Hispanic/Latino. Average age 37. In 2010, 2 master's awarded. *Degree requirements:* For master's, thesis (for some programs), internship. *Entrance requirements:* For master's, GRE General Test, minimum GPA of 2.75. Additional exam requirements/recommendations for international students: Required—TOEFL (minimum score 500 paper-based; 173 computer-based; 61 iBT). *Application deadline:* For fall admission, 8/24 priority date for domestic students, 7/1 for international students; for winter admission, 12/14 priority date for domestic students; for spring admission, 1/19 for domestic students, 11/1 for international students. Applications are processed on a rolling basis. Application fee: $20 ($30 for international students). Electronic applications accepted. *Expenses:* Tuition, state resident: full-time $2991; part-time $197 per credit hour. Tuition, nonresident: full-time $2991; part-time $197 per credit hour. International tuition: $10,288 full-time. *Financial support:* In 2010–11, 4 research assistantships with full tuition reimbursements (averaging $2,500 per year) were awarded; career-related internships or fieldwork, Federal Work-Study, and unspecified assistantships also available. Financial award application deadline: 4/1; financial award applicants required to submit FAFSA. *Unit head:* Dr. James Bulot, Unit Head, 318-342-1465, Fax: 318-342-1431, E-mail: bulot@ulm.edu. *Application contact:* Paul Karlowitz, Assistant Dean, 318-342-1758, Fax: 318-342-1755, E-mail: karlowitz@ulm.edu.

University of Louisville, Graduate School, Raymond A. Kent School of Social Work, Louisville, KY 40292-0001. Offers marriage and family therapy (PMC), including mental health; social work (MSSW, PhD), including alcohol and drug counseling (MSSW), gerontology (MSSW), marriage and family (PhD), school social work (MSSW). *Accreditation:* AAMFT/COAMFTE; CSWE (one or more programs are accredited). Part-time and evening/weekend programs available. *Faculty:* 23 full-time (15 women), 38 part-time/adjunct (21 women). *Students:* 259 full-time (209 women), 71 part-time (60 women); includes 84 minority (66 Black or African American, non-Hispanic/Latino; 1 American Indian or Alaska Native, non-Hispanic/Latino; 3 Asian, non-Hispanic/Latino; 6 Hispanic/Latino; 8 Two or more races, non-Hispanic/Latino), 7 international. Average age 32. 249 applicants, 78% accepted, 141 enrolled. In 2010, 141 master's, 7 doctorates awarded. *Degree requirements:* For doctorate, comprehensive exam, thesis/dissertation. *Entrance requirements:* For master's, GRE or minimum GPA of 2.75; for doctorate, GRE General Test, interview, writing sample. Additional exam requirements/recommendations for international students: Required—TOEFL (minimum score 550 paper-based; 213 computer-based; 79 iBT). *Application deadline:* For fall admission, 7/31 for domestic and international students. Applications are processed on a rolling basis. Application fee: $50. Electronic applications accepted. *Expenses:* Tuition, state resident: full-time $9144; part-time $508 per credit hour. Tuition, nonresident: full-time $19,026; part-time $1057 per credit hour. Tuition and fees vary according to program and reciprocity agreements. *Financial support:* In 2010–11, 70 students received support, including 9 research assistantships with full tuition reimbursements available (averaging $19,000 per year), 1 teaching assistantship (averaging $19,000 per year); Federal Work-Study, institutionally sponsored loans, scholarships/grants, health care benefits, and unspecified assistantships also available. Support available to part-time students. Financial award application deadline: 5/15; financial award applicants required to submit FAFSA. *Faculty research:* Child welfare, substance abuse, gerontology, family functioning, health behavior. Total annual research expenditures: $2.8 million. *Unit head:* Dr. Terry Singer, Dean, 502-852-6402, Fax: 502-852-0422, E-mail: terry.singer@louisville.edu. *Application contact:* Libby Leggett, Director, Graduate Admissions, 502-852-3101, Fax: 502-852-6536, E-mail: gradadm@louisville.edu.

University of Maryland, Baltimore, Graduate School, Graduate Program in Life Sciences, Program in Gerontology, Baltimore, MD 21201. Offers PhD. *Degree requirements:* For doctorate, comprehensive exam, thesis/dissertation. *Entrance requirements:* For doctorate, GRE General Test. Additional exam requirements/recommendations for international students: Required—TOEFL (minimum score 550 paper-based; 80 iBT) or IELTS (minimum score 7). Electronic applications accepted. Part-time tuition and fees vary according to course load, degree level and program.

University of Maryland, Baltimore, School of Medicine, Department of Epidemiology and Preventive Medicine, Baltimore, MD 21201. Offers biostatistics (MS); clinical research (MS); epidemiology and preventive medicine (PhD); epidemiology and preventive medicine (MPH, MS); gerontology (PhD); human genetics and genomic (PhD); human genetics and genomic medicine (MS); molecular epidemiology (MS, PhD); toxicology (MS, PhD); JD/MS; MD/PhD; MS/PhD. *Accreditation:* CEPH. Part-time programs available. *Students:* 84 full-time (57 women), 64 part-time (46 women); includes 17 Black or African American, non-Hispanic/Latino; 23 Asian, non-Hispanic/Latino; 4 Hispanic/Latino, 18 international. Average age 32. In 2010, 21 master's, 10 doctorates awarded. *Entrance requirements:* For master's and doctorate, GRE General Test. Additional exam requirements/recommendations for international students: Required—TOEFL (minimum score 550 paper-based; 213 computer-based; 80 iBT); Recommended—IELTS. *Application deadline:* For fall admission, 1/15 for domestic and international students. Electronic applications accepted. *Expenses:* Contact institution. *Financial support:* In 2010–11, research assistantships with partial tuition reimbursements (averaging $25,000 per year); fellowships, Federal Work-Study, scholarships/grants, and unspecified assistantships also available. Financial award application deadline: 3/1; financial award applicants required to submit FAFSA. *Unit head:* Dr. Patricia Langenberg, Program Director, 410-706-3251, Fax: 410-706-8013. *Application contact:* Danielle Fitzpatrick, Program Coordinator, 410-706-8492, Fax: 410-706-4225, E-mail: dfitzpatrick@epi.umaryland.edu.

University of Maryland, Baltimore County, Graduate School, Erickson School of Aging Studies, Baltimore, MD 21228. Offers management of aging services (MA). *Faculty:* 3 full-time (0 women), 5 part-time/adjunct (1 woman). *Students:* 30 full-time (18 women); includes 4 Black or African American, non-Hispanic/Latino; 1 Asian, non-Hispanic/Latino; 1 Hispanic/Latino. Average age 39. 50 applicants, 84% accepted, 30 enrolled. In 2010, 30 master's awarded. *Degree requirements:* For master's, thesis or alternative. *Entrance requirements:* For master's, essays. *Application deadline:* Applications are processed on a rolling basis. Application fee: $50. Electronic applications accepted. *Expenses:* Contact institution. *Financial support:* In 2010–11, 8 students received support, including 1 teaching assistantship with tuition reimbursement available (averaging $21,600 per year). Financial award applicants required to submit FAFSA. *Faculty research:* Policy implications of entitlement programs, demographic impact of aging population, person-centered care for dementia, changing culture in long-term care. *Unit head:* Dr. Joseph Gribbin, Graduate Program Director, 443-543-5603, E-mail: gribbin@umbc.edu. *Application contact:* Megan Risavi, Administrative Assistant, 443-543-5633, E-mail: meganr2@umbc.edu.

University of Maryland, Baltimore County, Graduate School, Program in Gerontology, Baltimore, MD 21201. Offers aging policy for the elderly (PhD); epidemiology of aging (PhD); social, cultural, and behavioral sciences (PhD); MA/PhD; MS/PhD. Part-time programs available. *Faculty:* 19 part-time/adjunct (13 women). *Students:* 12 full-time (10 women), 14 part-time (12 women); includes 4 Black or African American, non-Hispanic/Latino; 1 Asian, non-Hispanic/Latino; 1 Hispanic/Latino, 1 international. Average age 34. 24 applicants, 33% accepted, 5 enrolled. In 2010, 3 doctorates awarded. *Degree requirements:* For doctorate, comprehensive exam, thesis/dissertation. *Entrance requirements:* For doctorate, GRE General Test. Additional exam requirements/recommendations for international students: Required—TOEFL, TWE. *Application deadline:* For spring admission, 1/15 for domestic and international students. Application fee: $45. Electronic applications accepted. *Financial support:* In 2010–11, 4 fellowships with full tuition reimbursements (averaging $21,180 per year), 7 research assistantships with full tuition reimbursements (averaging $21,000 per year), 1 teaching assistantship with full tuition reimbursement (averaging $20,000 per year) were awarded; career-related internships or fieldwork, scholarships/grants, traineeships, health care benefits, tuition waivers (partial), and unspecified assistantships also available. Financial award application deadline: 2/1; financial award applicants required to submit FAFSA. *Faculty research:* Aging and health policy, behavioral aspects of aging, caregiving, epidemiology of aging. Total annual research expenditures: $32.5 million. *Unit head:* Dr. Leslie Morgan, Co-Director, 410-455-2074, Fax: 410-455-1154, E-mail: lmorgan@umbc.edu. *Application contact:* Justine Golden, Academic Coordinator, 410-706-4926, Fax: 410-706-4433, E-mail: jgold002@umaryland.edu.

University of Massachusetts Boston, Office of Graduate Studies, John W. McCormack Graduate School of Policy Studies, Program in Gerontology, Boston, MA 02125-3393. Offers gerontology (MS, PhD, Certificate); gerontology research (MA); management in aging services (MA). Part-time programs available. *Degree requirements:* For doctorate, comprehensive exam, thesis/dissertation. *Entrance requirements:* For doctorate, GRE General Test, minimum GPA of 3.0. *Faculty research:* Aging with a chronic disability, pension policy and social security system, elderly minorities, health services research, living arrangements.

University of Missouri–St. Louis, College of Arts and Sciences, Program in Gerontology, St. Louis, MO 63121. Offers gerontology (MS, Certificate); long term care administration (Certificate). Part-time and evening/weekend programs available. *Faculty:* 10 full-time (8 women), 6 part-time/adjunct (all women). *Students:* 7 full-time (all women), 16 part-time (13 women); includes 5 minority (3 Black or African American, non-Hispanic/Latino; 1 Asian, non-Hispanic/Latino; 1 Hispanic/Latino), 2 international. Average age 37. In 2010, 10 master's, 3 other advanced degrees awarded. *Entrance requirements:* For master's, 3 letters of recommendation. Additional exam requirements/recommendations for international students: Required—TOEFL (minimum score 550 paper-based; 213 computer-based). *Application deadline:* For fall admission, 7/1 priority date for domestic and international students; for spring admission, 12/1 priority date for domestic and international students. Applications are processed on a rolling basis. Application fee: $35 ($40 for international students). Electronic applications accepted. *Expenses:* Tuition, state resident: full-time $5522; part-time $306.80 per credit hour. Tuition, nonresident: full-time $14,253; part-time $792.10 per credit hour. Required fees: $658; $49 per credit hour. One-time fee: $12. Tuition and fees vary according to program. *Financial support:* Career-related internships or fieldwork and Federal Work-Study available. Financial award applicants required to submit FAFSA. *Faculty research:* Health care policy, social support and stress, retirement policy health behavior, ethnic differences in aging. *Unit head:* Thomas Meuser, Director, 314-516-5421, Fax: 314-516-5210, E-mail: meusert@umsl.edu. *Application contact:* 314-516-5458, Fax: 314-516-6996, E-mail: gradadm@umsl.edu.

University of Missouri–St. Louis, College of Arts and Sciences, School of Social Work, St. Louis, MO 63121. Offers gerontology (MS, Certificate), including gerontology, long term care administration (Certificate); nonprofit organization management and leadership (Certificate); social work (MSW). *Accreditation:* CSWE. *Faculty:* 10 full-time (8 women), 5 part-time/adjunct (3 women). *Students:* 66 full-time (60 women), 69 part-time (62 women); includes 18 minority (16 Black or African American, non-Hispanic/Latino; 1 Asian, non-Hispanic/Latino; 1 Hispanic/Latino), 2 international. Average age 31. In 2010, 50 master's, 3 other advanced degrees

Gerontology

University of Missouri–St. Louis *(continued)*
awarded. *Entrance requirements:* For master's, 3 letters of recommendation. Additional exam requirements/recommendations for international students: Required—TOEFL (minimum score 550 paper-based; 213 computer-based). *Application deadline:* For fall admission, 2/15 for domestic and international students. *Application fee:* $35 ($40 for international students). Electronic applications accepted. *Expenses:* Tuition, state resident: full-time $5522; part-time $306.80 per credit hour. Tuition, nonresident: full-time $14,253; part-time $792.10 per credit hour. Required fees: $658; $49 per credit hour. One-time fee: $12. Tuition and fees vary according to program. *Financial support:* In 2010–11, 1 research assistantship with full and partial tuition reimbursement (averaging $9,900 per year), 7 teaching assistantships with full and partial tuition reimbursements (averaging $8,360 per year) were awarded. Financial award applicants required to submit FAFSA. *Faculty research:* Family violence, child abuse/neglect, immigration, community economic development. *Unit head:* Dr. Lois Pierce, Graduate Program Director, 314-516-6364, Fax: 314-516-5816, E-mail: socialwork@umsl.edu. *Application contact:* 314-516-5458, Fax: 314-516-6996, E-mail: gradadm@umsl.edu.

University of Nebraska at Omaha, Graduate Studies, College of Education, Department of Counseling, Omaha, NE 68182. Offers community counseling (MA, MS); counseling gerontology (MA, MS); school counseling (MA, MS); student affairs practice in higher education (MA, MS). *Accreditation:* ACA (one or more programs are accredited); NCATE. Part-time and evening/weekend programs available. *Faculty:* 4 full-time (1 woman). *Students:* 43 full-time (37 women), 116 part-time (92 women); includes 9 minority (7 Black or African American, non-Hispanic/Latino; 2 Hispanic/Latino). Average age 29. 48 applicants, 52% accepted, 22 enrolled. In 2010, 44 master's awarded. *Degree requirements:* For master's, comprehensive exam, thesis (for some programs). *Entrance requirements:* For master's, GRE General Test, MAT, department test, interview, minimum GPA of 3.0. Additional exam requirements/recommendations for international students: Required—TOEFL (minimum score 550 paper-based; 213 computer-based; 80 iBT). *Application deadline:* For fall admission, 3/1 for domestic students; for spring admission, 10/1 for domestic students. Applications are processed on a rolling basis. Application fee: $45. Electronic applications accepted. *Financial support:* In 2010–11, 100 students received support, including 2 research assistantships with tuition reimbursements available; fellowships, Federal Work-Study, institutionally sponsored loans, scholarships/grants, tuition waivers (partial), and unspecified assistantships also available. Support available to part-time students. Financial award application deadline: 3/1; financial award applicants required to submit FAFSA. *Unit head:* Dr. Paul Barnes, Chairperson, 402-554-2727. *Application contact:* Dr. Paul Barnes, 402-554-2341, Fax: 402-554-3143, E-mail: graduate@unomaha.edu.

University of Nebraska at Omaha, Graduate Studies, College of Public Affairs and Community Service, Department of Gerontology, Omaha, NE 68182. Offers gerontology (Certificate); social gerontology (MA). Part-time and evening/weekend programs available. *Faculty:* 5 full-time (2 women). *Students:* 8 part-time (all women). Average age 36. 8 applicants, 25% accepted, 1 enrolled. In 2010, 1 master's, 8 other advanced degrees awarded. *Degree requirements:* For master's, comprehensive exam, thesis. *Entrance requirements:* For master's, GRE General Test, MAT, minimum GPA of 3.0, writing sample, letters of recommendation. Additional exam requirements/recommendations for international students: Required—TOEFL (minimum score 550 paper-based; 213 computer-based; 80 iBT). *Application deadline:* For fall admission, 7/1 priority date for domestic students; for spring admission, 12/1 priority date for domestic students. Applications are processed on a rolling basis. Application fee: $45. Electronic applications accepted. *Financial support:* In 2010–11, 2 students received support; fellowships, career-related internships or fieldwork, Federal Work-Study, institutionally sponsored loans, scholarships/grants, and tuition waivers (partial) available. Support available to part-time students. Financial award application deadline: 3/1; financial award applicants required to submit FAFSA. *Unit head:* Dr. Julie Masters, Chairperson, 402-554-2272. *Application contact:* Dr. Karl Kosloski, Student Contact, 402-554-2341, Fax: 402-554-3143, E-mail: graduate@unomaha.edu.

University of Nebraska–Lincoln, Graduate College, College of Education and Human Sciences, Department of Child, Youth and Family Studies, Lincoln, NE 68588. Offers child development/early childhood education (MS, PhD); child, youth and family studies (MS); family and consumer sciences education (MS, PhD); family financial planning (MS); family science (MS, PhD); gerontology (PhD); human sciences (PhD), including child, youth and family studies, gerontology, medical family therapy; marriage and family therapy (MS); medical family therapy (PhD); youth development (MS). *Accreditation:* AAMFT/COAMFTE (one or more programs are accredited). Postbaccalaureate distance learning degree programs offered. *Degree requirements:* For master's, thesis optional. *Entrance requirements:* For master's, GRE. Additional exam requirements/recommendations for international students: Required—TOEFL (minimum score 550 paper-based; 213 computer-based). Electronic applications accepted. *Faculty research:* Marriage and family therapy, child development/early childhood education, family financial management.

University of New England, Westbrook College of Health Professions, School of Social Work, Biddeford, ME 04005-9526. Offers addictions counseling (Certificate); gerontology (Certificate); social work (MSW). *Accreditation:* CSWE. Part-time programs available. *Students:* 361 full-time (323 women), 61 part-time (57 women); includes 83 minority (48 Black or African American, non-Hispanic/Latino; 3 American Indian or Alaska Native, non-Hispanic/Latino; 5 Asian, non-Hispanic/Latino; 16 Hispanic/Latino; 2 Native Hawaiian or other Pacific Islander, non-Hispanic/Latino; 9 Two or more races, non-Hispanic/Latino). 276 applicants, 75% accepted, 181 enrolled. In 2010, 44 master's awarded. *Degree requirements:* For master's, field internships. *Entrance requirements:* Additional exam requirements/recommendations for international students: Required—TOEFL (minimum score 550 paper-based; 213 computer-based). *Application deadline:* For fall admission, 1/15 priority date for domestic students; for spring admission, 3/31 priority date for domestic students, 3/31 for international students. Applications are processed on a rolling basis. Application fee: $40. Electronic applications accepted. *Financial support:* In 2010–11, 40 students received support. Scholarships/grants and tuition waivers (partial) available. Financial award application deadline: 5/1; financial award applicants required to submit FAFSA. *Faculty research:* Domestic violence, solution-focused practice, empowerment models, adverse childhood experiences. *Unit head:* Martha Wilson, Director, 207-221-4513, E-mail: mwilson@une.edu. *Application contact:* Stacy Gato, Assistant Director of Graduate Admissions, 207-221-4225, Fax: 207-221-4898, E-mail: gradadmissions@une.edu.

The University of North Carolina at Charlotte, Graduate School, College of Arts and Sciences, Program in Interdisciplinary Studies, Charlotte, NC 28223-0001. Offers gerontology (MA, Certificate); Latin American studies (MA); liberal studies (MA); women's studies (Certificate). *Faculty:* 2 full-time (1 woman), 2 part-time/adjunct (both women). *Students:* 15 full-time (14 women), 53 part-time (39 women); includes 20 minority (11 Black or African American, non-Hispanic/Latino; 8 Hispanic/Latino; 1 Two or more races, non-Hispanic/Latino), 5 international. Average age 30. 24 applicants, 96% accepted, 15 enrolled. In 2010, 16 master's awarded. *Degree requirements:* For master's, thesis optional, comprehensive exam or project. *Entrance requirements:* For master's, GRE General Test or MAT, minimum GPA of 3.0 during previous 2 years, 2.75 overall. Additional exam requirements/recommendations for international students: Required—TOEFL (minimum score 557 paper-based; 220 computer-based; 83 iBT). *Application deadline:* For fall admission, 7/1 for domestic students, 5/1 for international students; for spring admission, 11/1 for domestic students, 10/1 for international students. Applications are processed on a rolling basis. Application fee: $55. Electronic applications accepted. *Expenses:* Tuition, state resident: full-time $3464. Tuition, nonresident: full-time $14,297. Required fees: $2094. Tuition and fees vary according to course load. *Financial support:* In 2010–11, 7 students received support, including 2 research assistantships (averaging $3,025 per year), 5 teaching assistantships (averaging $7,950 per year); career-related internships or fieldwork, institutionally sponsored loans, scholarships/grants, and unspecified assistantships also available. Support available to part-time students. Financial award application deadline: 4/1; financial award applicants required to submit FAFSA. *Unit head:* Dr. Paula Eckard, Interim Director, 704-687-

4309, Fax: 704-687-4347, E-mail: pgeckard@uncc.edu. *Application contact:* Kathy B. Giddings, Director of Graduate Admissions, 704-687-5503, Fax: 704-687-3279, E-mail: gradadm@uncc.edu.

The University of North Carolina at Greensboro, Graduate School, Program in Gerontology, Greensboro, NC 27412-5001. Offers MS, Certificate, MS/MBA. Electronic applications accepted.

The University of North Carolina Wilmington, College of Arts and Sciences, Department of Health and Applied Human Sciences, Wilmington, NC 28403-3297. Offers applied gerontology (MS). Part-time programs available. Postbaccalaureate distance learning degree programs offered. *Faculty:* 8 full-time (3 women). *Students:* 3 full-time (2 women), 4 part-time (3 women); includes 2 Black or African American, non-Hispanic/Latino. Average age 40. 5 applicants, 80% accepted, 4 enrolled. In 2010, 6 master's awarded. *Degree requirements:* For master's, comprehensive exam, thesis or alternative. *Entrance requirements:* For master's, GRE, minimum undergraduate B average. Additional exam requirements/recommendations for international students: Required—TOEFL (minimum score 550 paper-based; 217 computer-based; 79 iBT), IELTS (minimum score 6.5). *Application deadline:* For fall admission, 3/15 for domestic students. Application fee: $60. *Financial support:* In 2010–11, 6 teaching assistantships with full and partial tuition reimbursements (averaging $9,500 per year) were awarded; scholarships/grants and unspecified assistantships also available. Support available to part-time students. *Unit head:* Dr. Terry Kinney, Interim Department Chair, 910-962-7570, Fax: 910-962-7906, E-mail: kinneyt@uncw.edu. *Application contact:* Dr. Eleanor Covan, Graduate Coordinator, 910-962-3435, Fax: 910-962-7906, E-mail: covane@uncw.edu.

University of Northern Colorado, Graduate School, College of Natural and Health Sciences, School of Human Sciences, Program in Gerontology, Greeley, CO 80639. Offers MA. Part-time programs available. *Faculty:* 3 full-time (all women). *Students:* 2 full-time (both women), 5 part-time (all women); includes 1 minority (Hispanic/Latino). Average age 38. 5 applicants, 100% accepted, 1 enrolled. In 2010, 2 master's awarded. *Degree requirements:* For master's, comprehensive exam. *Entrance requirements:* For master's, GRE General Test or MAT, 2 letters of recommendation. *Application deadline:* Applications are processed on a rolling basis. Application fee: $50 ($60 for international students). Electronic applications accepted. *Expenses:* Tuition, state resident: full-time $6199; part-time $344 per credit hour. Tuition, nonresident: full-time $14,834; part-time $824 per credit hour. Required fees: $1091; $60.60 per credit hour. Tuition and fees vary according to course load, degree level and program. *Financial support:* Fellowships, research assistantships, teaching assistantships, unspecified assistantships available. Financial award application deadline: 3/1; financial award applicants required to submit FAFSA. *Unit head:* Dr. Susan Collins, Program Coordinator, 970-351-2403. *Application contact:* Linda Sisson, Graduate Student Admission Coordinator, 970-351-1807, Fax: 970-351-2371, E-mail: linda.sisson@unco.edu.

University of North Florida, Brooks College of Health, Department of Public Health, Jacksonville, FL 32224. Offers aging services (Certificate); community health (MPH); geriatric management (MSH); health administration (MHA); rehabilitation counseling (MS). *Accreditation:* CEPH. Part-time and evening/weekend programs available. *Faculty:* 17 full-time (10 women), 3 part-time/adjunct (1 woman). *Students:* 108 full-time (84 women), 77 part-time (50 women); includes 13 Black or African American, non-Hispanic/Latino; 2 American Indian or Alaska Native, non-Hispanic/Latino; 9 Asian, non-Hispanic/Latino; 10 Hispanic/Latino; 2 Two or more races, non-Hispanic/Latino, 8 international. Average age 32. 219 applicants, 37% accepted, 54 enrolled. In 2010, 43 master's awarded. *Degree requirements:* For master's, thesis optional. *Entrance requirements:* For master's, GRE General Test (MSH, MS, MPH); GMAT or GRE General Test (MHA), minimum GPA of 3.0 in last 60 hours. Additional exam requirements/recommendations for international students: Required—TOEFL (minimum score 500 paper-based; 173 computer-based). *Application deadline:* For fall admission, 7/1 priority date for domestic students, 5/1 for international students; for spring admission, 11/1 priority date for domestic students, 10/1 for international students. Applications are processed on a rolling basis. Application fee: $30. Electronic applications accepted. *Expenses:* Tuition, state resident: full-time $7646.40; part-time $318.60 per credit hour. Tuition, nonresident: full-time $23,502; part-time $979.24 per credit hour. Required fees: $1208.88; $50.37 per credit hour. Tuition and fees vary according to course load and program. *Financial support:* In 2010–11, 39 students received support, including 1 teaching assistantship (averaging $1,004 per year); research assistantships, career-related internships or fieldwork, Federal Work-Study, scholarships/grants, and tuition waivers (partial) also available. Support available to part-time students. Financial award application deadline: 4/1; financial award applicants required to submit FAFSA. *Faculty research:* Dietary supplements; alcohol, tobacco, and other drug use prevention; turnover among health professionals; aging; psychosocial aspects of disabilities. Total annual research expenditures: $225,351. *Unit head:* Dr. JoAnn Nolin, Chair, 904-620-2840, Fax: 904-620-2848, E-mail: jnolin@unf.edu. *Application contact:* Heather Kenney, Director of Advising, 904-620-2810, Fax: 904-620-1030, E-mail: heather.kenney@unf.edu.

University of North Texas, Toulouse Graduate School, College of Public Affairs and Community Service, Department of Applied Gerontology, Denton, TX 76203-5017. Offers aging (Certificate); applied gerontology (PhD); general studies in aging (MA, MS); long term care, senior housing, and aging services (MA, MS). Part-time and evening/weekend programs available. Postbaccalaureate distance learning degree programs offered (minimal on-campus study). *Degree requirements:* For master's, comprehensive exam (for some programs), thesis, internship; capstone; for doctorate, one foreign language, comprehensive exam, thesis/dissertation. *Entrance requirements:* For master's and doctorate, GRE General Test. Additional exam requirements/recommendations for international students: Recommended—TOEFL (minimum score 550 paper-based; 213 computer-based; 79 iBT). *Application deadline:* For fall admission, 7/15 for domestic students; for spring admission, 11/15 for domestic students. Applications are processed on a rolling basis. *Expenses:* Tuition, state resident: full-time $4298; part-time $239 per credit hour. Tuition, nonresident: full-time $10,782; part-time $549 per credit hour. Required fees: $1292; $270 per credit hour. *Financial support:* Fellowships, research assistantships, teaching assistantships, career-related internships or fieldwork, Federal Work-Study, institutionally sponsored loans, and scholarships/grants available. Financial award application deadline: 6/1; financial award applicants required to submit FAFSA. *Faculty research:* Minority aging, housing for the elderly, aging and developmental disability, caregiving, public policy and aging. *Unit head:* Dr. Keith W. Turner, Chair, 940-565-2765, Fax: 940-565-4370, E-mail: keith.turner@unt.edu. *Application contact:* Keith Turner, Graduate Advisor, 940-565-2765, Fax: 940-565-4370, E-mail: gerontology@unt.edu.

University of Phoenix, College of Natural Sciences, Phoenix, AZ 85034-7209. Offers gerontology (MHA); health administration (MHA); health administration education (MHA); informatics (MHA). Programs are offered at the online campus. Evening/weekend programs available. Postbaccalaureate distance learning degree programs offered. *Students:* 2,644 full-time (2,223 women); includes 947 minority (728 Black or African American, non-Hispanic/Latino; 20 American Indian or Alaska Native, non-Hispanic/Latino; 61 Asian, non-Hispanic/Latino; 119 Hispanic/Latino; 11 Native Hawaiian or other Pacific Islander, non-Hispanic/Latino; 8 Two or more races, non-Hispanic/Latino), 81 international. Average age 39. *Entrance requirements:* For master's, minimum undergraduate GPA of 2.5 from accredited university, 3 years of work experience, citizen of the United States or have valid visa. Additional exam requirements/recommendations for international students: Required—TOEFL (minimum paper score 550, computer score 213, iBT 79), Test of English for International Communication, or IELTS. *Application deadline:* Applications are processed on a rolling basis. Application fee: $45. Electronic applications accepted. *Expenses:* Tuition: Full-time $16,440. One-time fee: $45 full-time. Full-time tuition and fees vary according to course load, degree level, campus/location and program. *Financial support:* Scholarships/grants available. Financial award applicants required to submit FAFSA. *Unit head:* Dr. Hinrich Eylers, Dean/Executive Director, 602-557-7428, Fax: 602-794-8454, E-mail: hinrich.eylers@phoenix.edu. *Application contact:* Dr. Hinrich Eylers, Dean/Executive Director, 602-557-7428, Fax: 602-794-8454, E-mail: hinrich.eylers@phoenix.edu.

University of Phoenix–Birmingham Campus, College of Health and Human Services, Birmingham, AL 35244. Offers education (MHA); gerontology (MHA); health administration (MHA); health care management (MBA); informatics (MHA); nursing (MSN); nursing/health care education (MSN); MSN/MBA; MSN/MHA.

University of Phoenix–Central Valley Campus, College of Nursing, Fresno, CA 93720-1562. Offers education (MHA); gerontology (MHA); health administration (MHA); nursing (MSN); MSN/MBA.

University of Phoenix–Charlotte Campus, College of Nursing, Charlotte, NC 28273-3409. Offers education (MHA); gerontology (MHA); health administration (MHA); informatics (MHA, MSN); nursing (MSN); nursing/health care education (MSN). Evening/weekend programs available. *Degree requirements:* For master's, thesis (for some programs). *Entrance requirements:* For master's, minimum undergraduate GPA of 2.5, 3 years work experience. Additional exam requirements/recommendations for international students: Required—TOEFL (minimum score 550 paper-based; 213 computer-based; 79 iBT). Electronic applications accepted.

University of Phoenix–Chattanooga Campus, College of Nursing, Chattanooga, TN 37421-3707. Offers education (MHA); gerontology (MHA); health administration (MHA).

University of Phoenix–Des Moines Campus, College of Nursing, Des Moines, IA 50266. Offers education (MHA); gerontology (MHA); health administration (MHA, DHA); informatics (MHA, MSN); nursing (MSN, PhD); nursing/health care education (MSN).

University of Phoenix–Hawaii Campus, College of Nursing, Honolulu, HI 96813-4317. Offers education (MHA); family nurse practitioner (MSN); gerontology (MHA); health administration (MHA); nursing (MSN); nursing/health care education (MSN); MSN/MBA. Evening/weekend programs available. *Degree requirements:* For master's, thesis (for some programs). *Entrance requirements:* For master's, minimum undergraduate GPA of 2.5, 3 years of work experience, RN license. Additional exam requirements/recommendations for international students: Required—TOEFL (minimum score 550 paper-based; 213 computer-based; 79 iBT). Electronic applications accepted.

University of Phoenix–Louisville Campus, College of Nursing, Louisville, KY 40223-3839. Offers education (MHA); gerontology (MHA); health administration (MHA); informatics (MHA, MSN); nursing (MSN); nursing/health care education (MSN). Postbaccalaureate distance learning degree programs offered.

University of Phoenix–Milwaukee Campus, College of Nursing, Milwaukee, WI 53045. Offers education (MHA); gerontology (MHA); health administration (MHA, DHA); informatics (MHA, MSN); nursing (MSN, PhD); nursing/health care education (MSN); MSN/MBA; MSN/MHA.

University of Phoenix–Raleigh Campus, College of Nursing, Raleigh, NC 27606. Offers education (MHA); gerontology (MHA); health administration (MHA, DHA); informatics (MHA, MSN); nursing (MSN, PhD); nursing/health care education (MSN).

University of Phoenix–Southern Colorado Campus, College of Nursing, Colorado Springs, CO 80919-2335. Offers education (MHA); gerontology (MHA); health administration (MHA); nursing (MSN); MSN/MBA. Evening/weekend programs available. *Degree requirements:* For master's, thesis (for some programs). *Entrance requirements:* For master's, minimum undergraduate GPA of 2.5, 3 years of work experience, RN license. Additional exam requirements/recommendations for international students: Required—TOEFL (minimum score 550 paper-based; 213 computer-based; 79 iBT). Electronic applications accepted.

University of Phoenix–Washington D.C. Campus, College of Nursing, Washington, DC 20001. Offers education (MHA); gerontology (MHA); health administration (MHA, DHA); informatics (MHA, MSN); nursing (MSN, PhD); nursing/health care education (MSN); MSN/MBA; MSN/MHA.

University of Pittsburgh, Graduate School of Public Health, Department of Behavioral and Community Health Science, Pittsburgh, PA 15260. Offers behavioral and community health sciences (MPH, Dr PH); community-based participatory research and practice (Certificate); lesbian, gay, bisexual and transgender health and wellness (Certificate); minority health and health disparities (Certificate); program evaluation (Certificate); public health and aging (Certificate); public health preparedness (Certificate); MID/MPH; MPH/MPA; MPH/MSW; MPH/PhD. *Accreditation:* CAHME (one or more programs are accredited). Part-time programs available. *Faculty:* 15 full-time (7 women), 38 part-time/adjunct (15 women). *Students:* 77 full-time (63 women), 56 part-time (44 women); includes 18 Black or African American, non-Hispanic/Latino; 1 American Indian or Alaska Native, non-Hispanic/Latino; 3 Asian, non-Hispanic/Latino; 4 Hispanic/Latino; 2 Two or more races, non-Hispanic/Latino, 6 international. Average age 30. 303 applicants, 72% accepted, 37 enrolled. In 2010, 39 master's, 3 doctorates awarded. *Degree requirements:* For master's, thesis; for doctorate, comprehensive exam, thesis/dissertation, preliminary exams. *Entrance requirements:* For master's and Certificate, GRE; for doctorate, GRE, master's degree in public health or related field. Additional exam requirements/recommendations for international students: Required—TOEFL (minimum score 550 paper-based; 213 computer-based; 80 iBT). *Application deadline:* For fall admission, 5/1 priority date for domestic students, 4/1 for international students; for winter admission, 9/1 for international students; for spring admission, 10/1 priority date for domestic students, 2/1 for international students. Applications are processed on a rolling basis. Application fee: $115. Electronic applications accepted. *Expenses:* Tuition, state resident: full-time $17,304; part-time $701 per credit. Tuition, nonresident: full-time $29,554; part-time $1210 per credit. Required fees: $740; $214 per term. Tuition and fees vary according to program. *Financial support:* In 2010–11, 21 students received support, including 3 fellowships with full tuition reimbursements available (averaging $3,000 per year), 12 research assistantships with full and partial tuition reimbursements available (averaging $20,813 per year), 6 teaching assistantships with full tuition reimbursements available (averaging $9,567 per year); unspecified assistantships also available. *Faculty research:* Maternal and child health, program evaluation, community-based participatory research, minority health and health disparities, aging. Total annual research expenditures: $2.5 million. *Unit head:* Dr. Ronald D. Stall, Chairman, 412-624-7933, Fax: 412-648-5975, E-mail: rstall@pitt.edu. *Application contact:* Natalie C. Arnold, Recruitment and Academic Affairs Administrator, 412-624-3107, Fax: 412-624-5510, E-mail: narnold@pitt.edu.

University of Pittsburgh, School of Social Work, Pittsburgh, PA 15260. Offers gerontology (Certificate); social work (MSW, PhD); M Div/MSW; MPA/MSW; MPH/PhD; MPIA/MSW; MSW/JD; MSW/MAJCS; MSW/MPH. *Accreditation:* CSWE (one or more programs are accredited). Part-time programs available. *Faculty:* 20 full-time (12 women), 39 part-time/adjunct (29 women). *Students:* 406 full-time (346 women), 218 part-time (178 women); includes 121 minority (74 Black or African American, non-Hispanic/Latino; 1 American Indian or Alaska Native, non-Hispanic/Latino; 19 Asian, non-Hispanic/Latino; 13 Hispanic/Latino; 1 Native Hawaiian or other Pacific Islander, non-Hispanic/Latino; 13 Two or more races, non-Hispanic/Latino). Average age 28. 603 applicants, 83% accepted, 293 enrolled. In 2010, 227 master's, 8 doctorates awarded. *Degree requirements:* For master's, practicum; for doctorate, comprehensive exam, thesis/dissertation; for Certificate, thesis. *Entrance requirements:* For master's, minimum QPA of 3.0, course work in statistics; for doctorate, GRE, MSW or related degree, course work in statistics. Additional exam requirements/recommendations for international students: Required—TOEFL (minimum score 550 paper-based; 213 computer-based; 80 iBT). *Application deadline:* For fall admission, 5/1 for domestic and international students. Applications are processed on a rolling basis. Application fee: $40. Electronic applications accepted. *Expenses:* Tuition, state resident: full-time $17,304; part-time $701 per credit. Tuition, nonresident: full-time $29,554; part-time $1210 per credit. Required fees: $740; $214 per term. Tuition and fees vary according to program. *Financial support:* In 2010–11, 234 students received support, including 1 research assistantship with full tuition reimbursement available (averaging $12,670 per year), 3 teaching assistantships with full tuition reimbursements available (averaging $15,520 per year); fellowships, career-related internships or fieldwork, institutionally sponsored loans, scholarships/grants, traineeships, tuition waivers (full), and unspecified assistantships also available. Financial award application deadline: 3/31; financial award applicants required to submit FAFSA. *Faculty research:* Mental health services research, child abuse and neglect, geriatrics, criminal justice race issues. *Unit head:* Dr. Larry E. Davis, Dean, 412-624-6304, Fax: 412-624-6323, E-mail: ledavis@pitt.edu. *Application contact:* Philip Mack, Director of Admissions, 412-624-6346, Fax: 412-624-6323, E-mail: psm8@pitt.edu.

University of Puerto Rico, Medical Sciences Campus, Graduate School of Public Health, Department of Human Development, Program in Gerontology, San Juan, PR 00936-5067. Offers MPH, Certificate. Part-time and evening/weekend programs available. *Entrance requirements:* For master's, GRE, previous course work in social sciences, biology, psychology, and algebra.

University of Regina, Faculty of Graduate Studies and Research, Faculty of Arts, Program in Gerontology, Regina, SK S4S 0A2, Canada. Offers M Sc, MA. Part-time programs available. *Faculty:* 14 full-time (5 women). *Students:* 3 full-time (2 women), 4 part-time (3 women). 3 applicants, 0% accepted. *Degree requirements:* For master's, thesis. *Entrance requirements:* Additional exam requirements/recommendations for international students: Required—TOEFL (minimum score 580 paper-based; 80 iBT). *Application deadline:* For fall admission, 3/31 for domestic and international students. Application fee: $100. Electronic applications accepted. Tuition and fees charges are reported in Canadian dollars. *Expenses:* Tuition, area resident: Full-time $3244.50 Canadian dollars; part-time $180.25 Canadian dollars per credit hour. International tuition: $4744.50 Canadian dollars full-time. Required fees: $494 Canadian dollars; $115.25 Canadian dollars per credit hour. $115.25 Canadian dollars per semester. Tuition and fees vary according to program. *Financial support:* In 2010–11, 2 teaching assistantships (averaging $6,759 per year) were awarded; fellowships, research assistantships, scholarships/grants also available. Financial award application deadline: 6/15. *Faculty research:* Health economics and policy; aging, society, and human service work; end-of-life issues for human service workers; physiology of aging; ethical decision making in kinesiology and health care administration. *Unit head:* Dr. Darren Candow, Program Coordinator, 306-585-4906, Fax: 306-337-3204, E-mail: darren.candow@uregina.ca. *Application contact:* Dr. Darren Candow, Graduate Program Coordinator, 306-585-4906, Fax: 306-337-3204, E-mail: darren.candow@uregina.ca.

University of Rhode Island, Graduate School, College of Nursing, Kingston, RI 02881. Offers administration (MS); clinical nurse leader (MS); clinical specialist in gerontology (MS); clinical specialist in psychiatric/mental health (MS); family nurse practitioner (MS); gerontological nurse practitioner (MS); nursing (DNP, PhD); nursing education (MS). *Accreditation:* AACN; ACNM/DOA (one or more programs are accredited). Part-time programs available. *Faculty:* 27 full-time (26 women), 2 part-time/adjunct (1 woman). *Students:* 25 full-time (all women), 76 part-time (71 women); includes 2 minority (both Black or African American, non-Hispanic/Latino), 5 international. In 2010, 26 master's, 1 doctorate awarded. *Degree requirements:* For master's, comprehensive exam; for doctorate, comprehensive exam, thesis/dissertation. *Entrance requirements:* For master's, GRE or MAT, 2 letters of recommendation, scholarly papers; for doctorate, GRE, 3 letters of recommendation, scholarly papers. Additional exam requirements/recommendations for international students: Required—TOEFL (minimum score 550 paper-based; 213 computer-based). *Application deadline:* For fall admission, 4/15 for domestic students, 2/1 for international students; for spring admission, 11/15 for domestic students, 7/15 for international students. Application fee: $65. Electronic applications accepted. *Expenses:* Tuition, state resident: full-time $9588; part-time $533 per credit hour. Tuition, nonresident: full-time $22,968; part-time $1276 per credit hour. Required fees: $1282; $68 per semester. Tuition and fees vary according to program. *Financial support:* In 2010–11, 4 teaching assistantships with full and partial tuition reimbursements (averaging $9,817 per year) were awarded. Financial award application deadline: 4/15; financial award applicants required to submit FAFSA. *Faculty research:* Group intervention for grieving women in prison, translating Best Practice in non-drug interventions for postoperative pain management, further development and testing of the pain assessment inventory, preschool motor and functional performance of two cohorts, neuroactivation of brain motor areas in preterm children. Total annual research expenditures: $1.2 million. *Unit head:* Dr. Dayle Joseph, Dean, 401-874-2766, Fax: 401-874-2061, E-mail: dayle@uri.edu. *Application contact:* Dr. Mary C. Sullivan, Director of Graduate Studies, 401-874-5339, Fax: 401-874-2061, E-mail: mcsullivan@uri.edu.

University of South Alabama, Graduate School, College of Arts and Sciences, Program in Gerontology, Mobile, AL 36688-0002. Offers Certificate. Part-time programs available. In 2010, 1 Certificate awarded. *Entrance requirements:* For degree, GRE General Test. *Application deadline:* For fall admission, 7/15 priority date for domestic students, 6/15 priority date for international students; for spring admission, 12/1 priority date for domestic students, 11/1 priority date for international students. Applications are processed on a rolling basis. Application fee: $25 ($35 for international students). *Expenses:* Tuition, state resident: part-time $300 per credit hour. Tuition, nonresident: part-time $600 per credit hour. Required fees: $150 per semester. *Financial support:* Application deadline: 4/1. *Unit head:* Dr. Roma Hanks, Chair, 251-460-6347. *Application contact:* Dr. Roma Hanks, Chair, 251-460-6347.

University of South Carolina, The Graduate School, Program in Gerontology, Columbia, SC 29208. Offers Certificate. Part-time programs available. *Degree requirements:* For Certificate, practicum. Electronic applications accepted.

University of Southern California, Graduate School, Davis School of Gerontology, Los Angeles, CA 90089. Offers gerontology/social work (MS/MSW); DDS/MS; JD/MS; M Pl/MS; MBA/MS; MHA/MS; MPA/MS; MS/MA; MS/MSW; Pharm D/MS. Part-time programs available. Postbaccalaureate distance learning degree programs offered (no on-campus study). *Faculty:* 18 full-time (7 women), 7 part-time/adjunct (3 women). *Students:* 102 full-time (83 women), 30 part-time (23 women); includes 40 minority (4 Black or African American, non-Hispanic/Latino; 17 Asian, non-Hispanic/Latino; 15 Hispanic/Latino; 4 Two or more races, non-Hispanic/Latino), 7 international. 83 applicants, 80% accepted, 57 enrolled. In 2010, 24 master's, 4 doctorates, 7 other advanced degrees awarded. Terminal master's awarded for partial completion of doctoral program. *Degree requirements:* For master's, thesis or alternative; for doctorate, comprehensive exam, thesis/dissertation. *Entrance requirements:* For master's, GRE (recommended); for doctorate, GRE. *Application deadline:* For fall admission, 2/1 priority date for domestic and international students; for spring admission, 10/1 priority date for domestic and international students. Applications are processed on a rolling basis. Application fee: $85. Electronic applications accepted. *Expenses:* Tuition: Full-time $31,240; part-time $1420 per unit. Required fees: $600. One-time fee: $35 full-time. Full-time tuition and fees vary according to degree level and program. *Financial support:* In 2010–11, 90 students received support, including 4 fellowships with full tuition reimbursements available (averaging $30,000 per year), 14 research assistantships with full tuition reimbursements available (averaging $19,000 per year), 2 teaching assistantships (averaging $19,000 per year); Federal Work-Study and scholarships/grants also available. Financial award application deadline: 3/15. *Faculty research:* Sex steroids and Alzheimer's disease, memory, cognition and brain plasticity, environment and injury prevention, antioxidants, stress and aging, inflammation and aging, euthanasia, caloric restriction and chemotherapy, biodemographic of aging, health outcomes research, families and intergenerational relatives, care-giving of elderly, biology, psychology, sociology, policy. *Unit head:* Maria Henke, Assistant Dean, 213-740-5156, Fax: 213-740-7069, E-mail: ldsgero@usc.edu. *Application contact:* Whitney Fountas, Admission Counselor, 213-740-5156, E-mail: ldsgero@usc.edu.

University of Southern California, Graduate School, School of Social Work, Los Angeles, CA 90089. Offers community organization, planning and administration (MSW); families and children (MSW); health (MSW); mental health (MSW); military social work and veterans services (MSW); older adults (MSW); public child welfare (MSW); school settings (MSW); social work (MSW, PhD); systems of mental illness recovery (MSW); work and life (MSW); JD/MSW; M Pl/MSW; MPA/MSW; MSW/MAJCS; MSW/MBA; MSW/MS. *Accreditation:* CSWE (one or more programs are accredited). *Faculty:* 68 full-time (43 women), 67 part-time/adjunct

Gerontology

University of Southern California (continued)
(49 women). *Students:* 924 full-time (786 women), 162 part-time (128 women); includes 730 minority (137 Black or African American, non-Hispanic/Latino; 2 American Indian or Alaska Native, non-Hispanic/Latino; 120 Asian, non-Hispanic/Latino; 445 Hispanic/Latino; 4 Native Hawaiian or other Pacific Islander, non-Hispanic/Latino; 22 Two or more races, non-Hispanic/Latino), 34 international. 1,627 applicants, 50% accepted, 477 enrolled. In 2010, 288 master's, 7 doctorates awarded. *Degree requirements:* For doctorate, comprehensive exam, thesis/dissertation, qualifying exam/publishable paper. *Entrance requirements:* For doctorate, GRE Standard Test. Additional exam requirements/recommendations for international students: Required—TOEFL (minimum score 600 paper-based; 250 computer-based; 100 iBT), ESL Exam. *Application deadline:* For fall admission, 12/1 for domestic and international students. Electronic applications accepted. *Expenses:* Tuition: Full-time $31,240; part-time $1420 per unit. Required fees: $600. One-time fee: $35 full-time. Full-time tuition and fees vary according to degree level and program. *Financial support:* In 2010–11, 32 students received support, including 29 fellowships with full tuition reimbursements available (averaging $35,000 per year), 1 research assistantship with full tuition reimbursement available (averaging $30,000 per year), 2 teaching assistantships with full tuition reimbursements available (averaging $35,000 per year); scholarships/grants, traineeships, health care benefits, and unspecified assistantships also available. Financial award applicants required to submit FAFSA. *Faculty research:* Department of Defense Educational Activity, detection/treatment of depression among older adults, health/aging, psychosocial adaptation to extreme environments/man made disasters; mental health needs of older adults. Total annual research expenditures: $7.3 million. *Unit head:* Janine Luzano, Director of Admissions and Financial Aid, 213-740-2017, Fax: 213-821-1235, E-mail: janinelu@usc.edu. *Application contact:* Necole Yaacoub, Admissions and Operations Manager, 213-740-3595, Fax: 213-821-1235, E-mail: naanouh@usc.edu.

University of South Florida, Graduate School, College of Behavioral and Community Sciences, Department of Aging Studies, Tampa, FL 33620-9951. Offers aging studies (PhD); gerontology (MA). Part-time and evening/weekend programs available. *Faculty:* 9 full-time (5 women). *Students:* 29 full-time (27 women), 12 part-time (10 women); includes 1 Black or African American, non-Hispanic/Latino; 4 Hispanic/Latino, 4 international. Average age 31. 34 applicants, 50% accepted, 12 enrolled. In 2010, 6 master's, 3 doctorates awarded. *Degree requirements:* For master's, comprehensive exam, thesis; for doctorate, comprehensive exam, thesis/dissertation. *Entrance requirements:* For master's, GRE General Test, minimum GPA of 3.0 in last 60 hours; for doctorate, GRE General Test, minimum GPA of 3.25, letter of recommendation. Additional exam requirements/recommendations for international students: Required—TOEFL (minimum score 550 paper-based; 213 computer-based). *Application deadline:* For fall admission, 2/1 priority date for domestic students, 1/2 priority date for international students. Application fee: $30. Electronic applications accepted. *Financial support:* In 2010–11, 4 research assistantships with tuition reimbursements (averaging $27,892 per year), 16 teaching assistantships with tuition reimbursements (averaging $14,535 per year) were awarded. Financial award application deadline: 2/3. *Faculty research:* Minorities, care giving, guardianship, Alzheimer's disease, cognitive aging. Total annual research expenditures: $693,872. *Unit head:* Cathy L. McEvoy, Director, 813-974-2414, Fax: 813-974-9754, E-mail: cmcevoy@cas.usf.edu. *Application contact:* Amy Woodberry, Staff Assistant, 813-974-2419, Fax: 813-974-9754, E-mail: amwoodbu@chuma1.cas.usf.edu.

The University of Tennessee, Graduate School, College of Education, Health and Human Sciences, Program in Public Health, Knoxville, TN 37996. Offers community health education (MPH); gerontology (MPH); health planning/administration (MPH); MS/MPH. *Accreditation:* CEPH. *Degree requirements:* For master's, thesis optional. *Entrance requirements:* For master's, minimum GPA of 2.7. Additional exam requirements/recommendations for international students: Required—TOEFL. Electronic applications accepted. *Expenses:* Tuition, state resident: full-time $7440; part-time $414 per credit hour. Tuition, nonresident: full-time $22,478; part-time $1250 per credit hour. Required fees: $922; $43 per credit hour. Tuition and fees vary according to program.

The University of Toledo, College of Graduate Studies, College of Medicine and Life Sciences, Department of Public Health and Preventative Medicine, Toledo, OH 43606-3390. Offers biostatistics and epidemiology (Certificate); contemporary gerontological practice (Certificate); environmental and occupational health and safety (MPH), including public health; epidemiology (MPH, Certificate); health administration (MPH); health promotion (MPH); nutrition (MPH); occupational health (MSOH, Certificate); MD/MPH. Part-time programs available. *Faculty:* 5. *Students:* 98 full-time (69 women), 42 part-time (28 women); includes 20 Black or African American, non-Hispanic/Latino; 8 Asian, non-Hispanic/Latino; 4 Hispanic/Latino, 3 international. Average age 29. 132 applicants, 75% accepted, 70 enrolled. In 2010, 44 master's, 28 other advanced degrees awarded. *Degree requirements:* For master's, thesis or alternative. *Entrance requirements:* For master's, GRE (international applicants only), Minimum undergraduate GPA of 3.0. Three letters of recommendation, a statement of purpose and transcripts from all prior institutions attended; for Certificate, GRE, Minimum undergraduate GPA of 3.0. Three letters of recommendation, a statement of purpose and transcripts from all prior institutions attended. Additional exam requirements/recommendations for international students: Required—TOEFL (minimum score 550 paper-based; 213 computer-based; 80 iBT), IELTS (minimum score 6.5). *Application deadline:* For fall admission, 6/15 for domestic students, 3/15 for international students; for spring admission, 10/15 for domestic students, 2/15 for international students. Applications are processed on a rolling basis. Application fee: $45 ($75 for international students). Electronic applications accepted. *Expenses:* Tuition, state resident: full-time $11,426; part-time $476 per credit hour. Tuition, nonresident: full-time $21,660; part-time $903 per credit hour. One-time fee: $62. *Financial support:* In 2010–11, 14 research assistantships with full tuition reimbursements (averaging $10,000 per year) were awarded; Federal Work-Study, institutionally sponsored loans, scholarships/grants, tuition waivers (full and partial), and unspecified assistantships also available. *Unit head:* Dr. Sheryl A. Milz, Chair, 419-383-3976, Fax: 419-383-6140, E-mail: sheryl.milz@utoledo.edu. *Application contact:* Joan Mulligan, Admissions Analyst, 419-383-4186, Fax: 419-383-6140, E-mail: joan.mulligan@utoledo.edu.

University of Utah, Graduate School, College of Nursing, Gerontology Interdisciplinary Program, Salt Lake City, UT 84112. Offers MS, Certificate. *Accreditation:* AACN. Part-time programs available. *Faculty:* 2 full-time (0 women), 1 (woman) part-time/adjunct. *Students:* 6 full-time (all women), 6 part-time (all women); includes 2 minority (1 Asian, non-Hispanic/Latino; 1 Hispanic/Latino), 4 international. Average age 38. 7 applicants, 100% accepted, 5 enrolled. In 2010, 4 master's awarded. *Degree requirements:* For master's, thesis optional, thesis or project. *Entrance requirements:* For master's, GRE General Test (if cumulative GPA is less that 3.2), minimum undergraduate GPA of 3.0. Additional exam requirements/recommendations for international students: Required—TOEFL (minimum score 500 paper-based; 173 computer-based). *Application deadline:* For fall admission, 4/1 priority date for domestic and international students. Application fee: $55 ($65 for international students). Electronic applications accepted. *Expenses:* Contact institution. *Financial support:* In 2010–11, 12 students received support, including 12 fellowships with partial tuition reimbursements available (averaging $1,500 per year); scholarships/grants also available. Support available to part-time students. Financial award application deadline: 4/1; financial award applicants required to submit FAFSA. *Faculty research:* Spousal bereavement, family caregiving, healthy promotion and self-care, environmental issues, geriatric care management, technology and aging. Total annual research expenditures: $104,232. *Unit head:* Dr. Scott D. Wright, Director, 801-793-5752, E-mail: scott.wright@nurs.utah.edu. *Application contact:* Mirela Rankovic, Administrative Assistant, 801-581-8273, Fax: 801-581-4642, E-mail: mirela.rankovic@nurs.utah.edu.

University of West Florida, College of Professional Studies, Department of Health, Leisure, and Exercise Science, Community Health Education Program, Pensacola, FL 32514-5750. Offers aging studies (MS); health promotion and worksite wellness (MS); psychosocial (MS). Part-time and evening/weekend programs available. *Faculty:* 1 (woman) part-time/adjunct. *Students:* 11 full-time (all women), 4 part-time (2 women); includes 2 Black or African American, non-Hispanic/Latino; 1 Asian, non-Hispanic/Latino; 1 Hispanic/Latino. Average age 33. 10 applicants, 90% accepted, 6 enrolled. In 2010, 5 master's awarded. *Degree requirements:* For master's, thesis or alternative. *Entrance requirements:* For master's, GRE General Test, minimum GPA of 3.0. Additional exam requirements/recommendations for international students: Required—TOEFL (minimum score 550 paper-based; 213 computer-based). *Application deadline:* For fall admission, 6/1 for domestic students, 5/15 for international students; for spring admission, 10/1 for domestic and international students. Applications are processed on a rolling basis. Application fee: $30. *Expenses:* Tuition, state resident: full-time $4982; part-time $208 per credit hour. Tuition, nonresident: full-time $20,059; part-time $836 per credit hour. Required fees: $1365; $57 per credit hour. *Financial support:* Research assistantships, teaching assistantships, unspecified assistantships available. *Unit head:* Dr. John Todorovich, Chairperson, 850-473-7248, Fax: 850-474-2106. *Application contact:* Terry McCray, Assistant Director of Graduate Admissions, 850-473-7718, Fax: 850-473-7714, E-mail: gradadmissions@uwf.edu.

University of Wisconsin–Milwaukee, Graduate School, School of Social Welfare, Department of Social Work, Milwaukee, WI 53201-0413. Offers applied gerontology (Certificate); marriage and family therapy (Certificate); non-profit management (Certificate); social work (MSW, PhD). *Accreditation:* CSWE. Part-time programs available. *Faculty:* 19 full-time (10 women). *Students:* 214 full-time (196 women), 109 part-time (97 women); includes 35 Black or African American, non-Hispanic/Latino; 1 American Indian or Alaska Native, non-Hispanic/Latino; 6 Asian, non-Hispanic/Latino; 5 Hispanic/Latino. Average age 30. 351 applicants, 55% accepted, 95 enrolled. In 2010, 105 master's awarded. *Degree requirements:* For master's, thesis or alternative. *Entrance requirements:* For doctorate, GRE, bachelor's degree. Additional exam requirements/recommendations for international students: Required—TOEFL (minimum score 550 paper-based; 79 iBT), IELTS (minimum score 6.5). *Application deadline:* For fall admission, 1/1 priority date for domestic students; for spring admission, 9/1 for domestic students. Applications are processed on a rolling basis. Application fee: $56 ($96 for international students). Electronic applications accepted. *Financial support:* In 2010–11, 5 fellowships, 4 research assistantships, 3 teaching assistantships were awarded; career-related internships or fieldwork, health care benefits, unspecified assistantships, and project assistantships also available. Support available to part-time students. Financial award application deadline: 4/15; financial award applicants required to submit FAFSA. *Unit head:* Deborah Padgett, Representative—MSW, 414-229-4851, Fax: 414-229-5311, E-mail: dpadgett@uwm.edu. *Application contact:* Steve McMurtry, Representative—PhD, 414-229-2249, Fax: 414-229-6967, E-mail: mcmurtry@uwm.edu.

Valparaiso University, Graduate School, Programs in Liberal Studies, Concentration in Gerontology, Valparaiso, IN 46383. Offers MALS, Post-Master's Certificate, JD/MALS. Part-time and evening/weekend programs available. *Students:* 1 (woman) part-time. Average age 50. *Entrance requirements:* For master's, minimum GPA of 3.0. Additional exam requirements/recommendations for international students: Required—TOEFL (minimum score 550 paper-based; 213 computer-based; 80 iBT). *Application deadline:* Applications are processed on a rolling basis. Application fee: $30 ($50 for international students). Electronic applications accepted. *Expenses:* Tuition: Full-time $9540; part-time $530 per credit hour. Required fees: $292; $95 per semester. Tuition and fees vary according to program. *Financial support:* Available to part-time students. Applicants required to submit FAFSA. *Unit head:* Dr. David L. Rowland, Dean, Graduate School and Continuing Education/Associate Provost, 219-464-5313, Fax: 219-464-5381, E-mail: david.rowland@valpo.edu. *Application contact:* Laura Groth, Coordinator of Student Services and Support, 219-464-5313, Fax: 219-464-5381, E-mail: laura.groth@valpo.edu.

Virginia Commonwealth University, Graduate School, School of Allied Health Professions, Department of Gerontology, Richmond, VA 23284-9005. Offers aging studies (CAS); gerontology (MS). *Students:* 8 full-time (7 women), 21 part-time (18 women); includes 9 minority (7 Black or African American, non-Hispanic/Latino; 2 Two or more races, non-Hispanic/Latino). 29 applicants, 76% accepted, 13 enrolled. In 2010, 11 master's, 8 other advanced degrees awarded. *Entrance requirements:* For master's, GRE General Test or MAT. Additional exam requirements/recommendations for international students: Required—TOEFL (minimum score 600 paper-based; 250 computer-based; 100 iBT); Recommended—IELTS (minimum score 6.5). Application fee: $50. Electronic applications accepted. *Expenses:* Tuition, state resident: full-time $4308; part-time $479 per credit hour. Tuition, nonresident: full-time $8942; part-time $994 per credit hour. Required fees: $2000; $85 per credit hour. Tuition and fees vary according to course level, course load, degree level, campus/location and program. *Financial support:* Career-related internships or fieldwork available. Financial award applicants required to submit FAFSA. *Faculty research:* Alzheimer's disease, age-related alcoholism and suicide, pain perception, curriculum development and evaluation in gerontology/geriatrics. *Unit head:* Dr. E. Ayn Welleford, Chair, Department of Gerontology, 804-828-1565, E-mail: ewellefo@vcu.edu. *Application contact:* Monica L. White, Director of Student Services, 804-828-3273, Fax: 804-828-8656, E-mail: mlwhite1@vcu.edu.

Virginia Commonwealth University, Graduate School, School of Allied Health Professions, Department of Health Administration, Doctoral Program in Health Related Sciences, Richmond, VA 23284-9005. Offers clinical laboratory sciences (PhD); gerontology (PhD); health administration (PhD); nurse anesthesia (PhD); occupational therapy (PhD); physical therapy (PhD); radiation sciences (PhD); rehabilitation leadership (PhD). *Faculty:* 2 full-time (1 woman). *Students:* 21 full-time (13 women), 35 part-time (21 women); includes 5 minority (all Black or African American, non-Hispanic/Latino). 26 applicants, 31% accepted, 7 enrolled. In 2010, 10 doctorates awarded. *Entrance requirements:* For doctorate, GRE (minimum score 1100), MAT (minimum score 425), minimum GPA of 3.3 in master's degree. Additional exam requirements/recommendations for international students: Required—TOEFL (minimum score 600 paper-based; 250 computer-based; 100 iBT); Recommended—IELTS (minimum score 6.5). *Application deadline:* For fall admission, 3/15 for domestic students. Application fee: $50. Electronic applications accepted. *Expenses:* Tuition, state resident: full-time $4308; part-time $479 per credit hour. Tuition, nonresident: full-time $8942; part-time $994 per credit hour. Required fees: $2000; $85 per credit hour. Tuition and fees vary according to course level, course load, degree level, campus/location and program. *Unit head:* Dr. J. James Cotter, Associate Professor and Assistant Dean, School of Allied Health Professions, 804-828-7247, E-mail: jcotter@vcu.edu. *Application contact:* Monica L. White, Director of Student Services, 804-828-3273, Fax: 804-828-8656, E-mail: mlwhite1@vcu.edu.

Webster University, College of Arts and Sciences, Department of Behavioral and Social Sciences, Program in Gerontology, St. Louis, MO 63119-3194. Offers MA. Part-time programs available. *Entrance requirements:* Additional exam requirements/recommendations for international students: Required—TOEFL. *Expenses:* Tuition: Part-time $585 per credit hour. Tuition and fees vary according to degree level, campus/location and program.

West Chester University of Pennsylvania, Office of Graduate Studies, College of Arts and Sciences, Department of Anthropology and Sociology, West Chester, PA 19383. Offers gerontology (Certificate); long term health care (MPA, MSA). Part-time and evening/weekend programs available. *Students:* 2 full-time (both women), 4 part-time (all women); includes 3 minority (all Black or African American, non-Hispanic/Latino). Average age 39. 3 applicants, 100% accepted, 1 enrolled. In 2010, 1 other advanced degree awarded. *Degree requirements:* For master's, comprehensive exam. *Entrance requirements:* For master's, MAT, GRE, or GMAT, interview, resume, 2 letters of reference. Additional exam requirements/recommendations for international students: Required—TOEFL (minimum score 550 paper-based; 213 computer-based; 80 iBT). *Application deadline:* For fall admission, 4/15 priority date for domestic students, 3/15 for international students; for spring admission, 10/15 for domestic students, 9/1 for international students. Applications are processed on a rolling basis. Application fee: $35. Electronic applications accepted. *Expenses:* Tuition, state resident: full-time $6966; part-time $387 per credit. Tuition, nonresident: full-time $11,146; part-time $619 per credit. Required fees: $1614.40; $133.24 per credit. Part-time tuition and fees vary according to campus/location. *Financial support:* Unspecified assistantships available. Support available to part-time students. Financial award application deadline: 2/15; financial award applicants required to submit FAFSA. *Faculty research:* West African communities in the U. S., life-long learning and distance education, comparative religions. *Unit head:* Dr. Douglas McConatha, Chair and Graduate Coordinator, 610-436-2556, E-mail: dmcconatha@wcupa.edu. *Application contact:* Dr. Douglas McConatha, Chair and Graduate Coordinator, 610-436-2556, E-mail: dmcconatha@wcupa.edu.

Wichita State University, Graduate School, College of Health Professions, Department of Public Health Sciences, Wichita, KS 67260. Offers gerontology (MA). *Unit head:* Dr. Jean Brickell, Interim Chairperson, 316-978-3060, Fax: 316-978-3072, E-mail: jean.brickell@wichita.edu. *Application contact:* Dr. Jean Brickell, Interim Chairperson, 316-978-3060, Fax: 316-978-3072, E-mail: jean.brickell@wichita.edu.

Wilmington University, College of Health Professions, New Castle, DE 19720-6491. Offers adult nurse practitioner (MSN); family nurse practitioner (MSN); gerontology (MSN); leadership (MSN); nursing (MSN); women's nurse practitioner (MSN). *Accreditation:* AACN. Part-time programs available. *Degree requirements:* For master's, thesis. *Entrance requirements:* For master's, BSN, RN license, interview, 3 letters of recommendation. Additional exam requirements/recommendations for international students: Required—TOEFL (minimum score 500 paper-based; 173 computer-based). Electronic applications accepted. *Expenses:* Tuition: Full-time $7110; part-time $395 per credit hour. Tuition and fees vary according to campus/location. *Faculty research:* Outcomes assessment, student writing ability.

Section 21
Geography

This section contains a directory of institutions offering graduate work in geography, followed by an in-depth entry submitted by an institution that chose to prepare a detailed program description. Additional information about programs listed in the directory but not augmented by an in-depth entry may be obtained by writing directly to the dean of a graduate school or chair of a department at the address given in the directory.

For programs offering related work, see also in this book *Area and Cultural Studies* and *Humanities.* In another guide in this series:
Graduate Programs in the Physical Sciences, Mathematics, Agricultural Sciences, the Environment & Natural Resources
See *Geosciences*

CONTENTS

Program Directories

Close-Up

Geographic Information Systems

Acadia University, Faculty of Pure and Applied Science, Program in Applied Geomatics, Wolfville, NS B4P 2R6, Canada. Offers M Sc. Program jointly offered with Nova Scotia Community College. *Students:* 5 full-time (4 women), 3 part-time (0 women). 5 applicants, 100% accepted, 5 enrolled. In 2010, 3 master's awarded. *Degree requirements:* For master's, thesis optional. *Entrance requirements:* Additional exam requirements/recommendations for international students: Required—TOEFL (minimum score 580 paper-based; 237 computer-based; 93 iBT), IELTS (minimum score 6.5). *Application deadline:* For fall admission, 2/1 for domestic and international students. Applications are processed on a rolling basis. Application fee: $50. *Financial support:* Research assistantships, teaching assistantships, scholarships/grants and unspecified assistantships available. Financial award application deadline: 2/1. *Unit head:* Dr. Ian Spooner, Coordinator, 902-585-1312, E-mail: ian.spooner@acadiau.ca. *Application contact:* Dr. Ian Spooner, Coordinator, 902-585-1312, E-mail: ian.spooner@acadiau.ca.

Appalachian State University, Cratis D. Williams Graduate School, Department of Geography and Planning, Boone, NC 28608. Offers geography (MA), including GIS, planning. Part-time programs available. Postbaccalaureate distance learning degree programs offered (no on-campus study). *Faculty:* 18 full-time (5 women), 1 part-time/adjunct (0 women). *Students:* 21 full-time (9 women), 21 part-time (13 women); includes 1 Hispanic/Latino. 52 applicants, 73% accepted, 25 enrolled. In 2010, 26 master's awarded. *Degree requirements:* For master's, comprehensive exam, thesis or alternative. *Entrance requirements:* For master's, GRE General Test, 3 letters of recommendation. Additional exam requirements/recommendations for international students: Required—TOEFL (minimum score 570 paper-based; 230 computer-based; 79 iBT), IELTS (minimum score 6.5). *Application deadline:* For fall admission, 7/1 for domestic students, 2/1 for international students; for spring admission, 11/1 for domestic students, 7/1 for international students. Applications are processed on a rolling basis. Application fee: $55. Electronic applications accepted. *Expenses:* Tuition, state resident: full-time $3428; part-time $428 per unit. Tuition, nonresident: full-time $14,518; part-time $1814 per unit. Required fees: $2320; $344 per unit. Tuition and fees vary according to campus/location. *Financial support:* In 2010–11, 10 research assistantships (averaging $8,000 per year) were awarded; fellowships, teaching assistantships, career-related internships or fieldwork, Federal Work-Study, scholarships/grants, and unspecified assistantships also available. Financial award application deadline: 4/1; financial award applicants required to submit FAFSA. *Faculty research:* Global change, climatology, production cartography, geographic information systems, North Carolina geography, Latin America. Total annual research expenditures: $273,000. *Unit head:* Dr. James Young, Chairperson, 828-262-3000, Fax: 828-262-3067. *Application contact:* Dr. Kathleen Schroeder, Graduate Program Director, 828-262-3000.

Arizona State University, College of Liberal Arts and Sciences, School of Geographical Sciences, Tempe, AZ 85287-5302. Offers atmospheric science (Graduate Certificate); geographic education (MAS); geographic information systems (MAS); geographical information science (Graduate Certificate); geography (MA, PhD); transportation systems (Graduate Certificate); urban and environmental planning (MUEP). *Faculty:* 34 full-time (9 women), 2 part-time/adjunct (both women). *Students:* 125 full-time (40 women), 47 part-time (25 women); includes 24 minority (4 Black or African American, non-Hispanic/Latino; 1 American Indian or Alaska Native, non-Hispanic/Latino; 1 Asian, non-Hispanic/Latino; 16 Hispanic/Latino; 2 Two or more races, non-Hispanic/Latino), 34 international. Average age 30. 261 applicants, 56% accepted, 79 enrolled. In 2010, 76 master's, 3 doctorates, 13 other advanced degrees awarded. Terminal master's awarded for partial completion of doctoral program. *Degree requirements:* For master's, thesis, interactive Program of Study (iPOS) submitted before completing 50 percent of required credit hours; for doctorate, comprehensive exam, thesis/dissertation, interactive Program of Study (iPOS) submitted before completing 50 percent of required credit hours. *Entrance requirements:* For master's and doctorate, GRE, minimum GPA of 3.0 or equivalent in last 2 years of work leading to bachelor's degree. Additional exam requirements/recommendations for international students: Required—TOEFL, IELTS, or Pearson Test of English. *Application deadline:* For fall admission, 1/15 for domestic and international students. Applications are processed on a rolling basis. Application fee: $70 ($90 for international students). Electronic applications accepted. *Expenses:* Contact institution. *Financial support:* In 2010–11, 25 research assistantships with full and partial tuition reimbursements (averaging $15,546 per year), 50 teaching assistantships with full and partial tuition reimbursements (averaging $10,686 per year) were awarded; fellowships with full tuition reimbursements, career-related internships or fieldwork, Federal Work-Study, institutionally sponsored loans, scholarships/grants, and tuition waivers (full and partial) also available. Financial award application deadline: 3/1; financial award applicants required to submit FAFSA. Total annual research expenditures: $2.6 million. *Unit head:* Dr. Luc Anselin, Chair and Director, 480-965-7533, E-mail: luc.anselin@asu.edu. *Application contact:* Graduate Admissions, 480-965-6113.

Boston University, Graduate School of Arts and Sciences, Department of Geography and Environment, Boston, MA 02215. Offers energy and environmental analysis (MA); environmental remote sensing and GIs (MA); geography (MA); geography and environment (PhD); international relations and environmental policy (MA). *Students:* 55 full-time (23 women), 10 part-time (3 women); includes 3 minority (1 Asian, non-Hispanic/Latino; 1 Hispanic/Latino; 1 Two or more races, non-Hispanic/Latino), 17 international. Average age 28. 64 applicants, 23% accepted, 5 enrolled. In 2010, 1 master's, 2 doctorates awarded. Terminal master's awarded for partial completion of doctoral program. *Degree requirements:* For master's, one foreign language, comprehensive exam, thesis; for doctorate, one foreign language, comprehensive exam, thesis/dissertation. *Entrance requirements:* For master's and doctorate, GRE General Test, GRE Subject Test, 3 letters of recommendation. Additional exam requirements/recommendations for international students: Required—TOEFL (minimum score 600 paper-based; 250 computer-based). *Application deadline:* For fall admission, 7/1 for domestic and international students; for spring admission, 11/15 for domestic and international students. Application fee: $70. Electronic applications accepted. *Expenses:* Tuition: Full-time $39,314; part-time $1228 per credit. Required fees: $40 per semester. *Financial support:* In 2010–11, 33 students received support, including 2 fellowships with full tuition reimbursements available (averaging $19,300 per year), 20 research assistantships with full tuition reimbursements available (averaging $18,800 per year), 11 teaching assistantships with full tuition reimbursements available (averaging $18,800 per year); Federal Work-Study and unspecified assistantships also available. Support available to part-time students. Financial award application deadline: 1/15; financial award applicants required to submit FAFSA. Total annual research expenditures: $1.2 million. *Unit head:* Robert Kaufmann, Chairman, 617-353-3940, Fax: 617-353-8399, E-mail: kaufmann@bu.edu. *Application contact:* Christopher DeVits, Graduate Program Coordinator, 617-353-7554, Fax: 617-353-8399, E-mail: cdevits@bu.edu.

Clark University, Graduate School, Department of Geography, Program in Geographic Information Science, Worcester, MA 01610-1477. Offers MA. *Students:* 5 full-time (2 women). Average age 22. 4 applicants, 100% accepted, 4 enrolled. In 2010, 3 master's awarded. *Application deadline:* For fall admission, 12/31 priority date for domestic students. Application fee: $50. *Expenses:* Tuition: Full-time $37,000; part-time $1156 per credit hour. Required fees: $30; $1156 per credit hour. *Unit head:* Dr. Anthony Lee Bebbington, Director, 508-793-7336. *Application contact:* Christine Silva, Admission Coordinator, 508-793-7337, Fax: 508-793-8881, E-mail: geography@clarku.edu.

Clark University, Graduate School, Department of International Development, Community, and Environment, Program in Geographic Information Science for Development and Environment, Worcester, MA 01610-1477. Offers MA. *Students:* 41 full-time (19 women), 1 part-time (0 women); includes 2 minority (1 Asian, non-Hispanic/Latino; 1 Hispanic/Latino), 22 international. Average age 26. 80 applicants, 44% accepted, 19 enrolled. In 2010, 7 master's awarded. *Degree requirements:* For master's, thesis. *Entrance requirements:* For master's, 3 references, resume or curriculum vitae. Additional exam requirements/recommendations for international students: Required—TOEFL (minimum score 575 paper-based; 233 computer-based; 90 iBT) or IELTS (minimum score 6.5). *Application deadline:* For fall admission, 1/15 for domestic students. Application fee: $50. *Expenses:* Tuition: Full-time $37,000; part-time $1156 per credit hour. Required fees: $30; $1156 per credit hour. *Financial support:* In 2010–11, research assistantships with partial tuition reimbursements (averaging $5,000 per year), teaching assistantships with partial tuition reimbursements (averaging $5,000 per year) were awarded; fellowships with partial tuition reimbursements, institutionally sponsored loans and scholarships/grants also available. *Faculty research:* Land-use change, the effects of environmental influences on child health and development, quantitative methods, watershed management, brownfields redevelopment, human/environment interactions, biodiversity conservation, climate change. *Unit head:* IDCE, 508-793-7201, Fax: 508-793-8820. *Application contact:* Paula Hall, IDCE Graduate Admissions Office, 508-793-7205, E-mail: idce@clarku.edu.

Cleveland State University, College of Graduate Studies, Maxine Goodman Levin College of Urban Affairs, Program in Environmental Studies, Cleveland, OH 44115. Offers environmental studies (MAES); geographic information systems (Certificate); urban real estate development and finance (Certificate); JD/MAES. Part-time and evening/weekend programs available. *Faculty:* 26 full-time (10 women), 3 part-time/adjunct (0 women). *Students:* 12 full-time (5 women), 23 part-time (12 women); includes 1 Asian, non-Hispanic/Latino, 4 international. 16 applicants, 50% accepted, 6 enrolled. In 2010, 7 master's awarded. *Degree requirements:* For master's, thesis or alternative, exit project. *Entrance requirements:* For master's, GRE General Test (minimum score: verbal and quantitative 40th percentile, analytical writing 4.0), minimum GPA of 3.0. Additional exam requirements/recommendations for international students: Required—TOEFL (minimum score 525 paper-based; 197 computer-based; 65 iBT). *Application deadline:* For fall admission, 7/15 priority date for domestic students, 5/15 for international students; for spring admission, 11/1 for international students. Applications are processed on a rolling basis. Application fee: $30. Electronic applications accepted. *Expenses:* Tuition, state resident: full-time $8447; part-time $469 per credit hour. Tuition, nonresident: full-time $16,020; part-time $890 per credit hour. Required fees: $50. *Financial support:* In 2010–11, 1 student received support, including 1 research assistantship with full and partial tuition reimbursement available (averaging $6,960 per year); career-related internships or fieldwork, Federal Work-Study, scholarships/grants, tuition waivers (full and partial), and unspecified assistantships also available. Support available to part-time students. Financial award application deadline: 3/1; financial award applicants required to submit FAFSA. *Faculty research:* Environmental policy and administration, environmental planning, geographic information systems (GIS), urban sustainability planning and management, energy policy, land re-use. *Unit head:* Dr. Sanda Kaufman, Director, 216-687-2367, Fax: 216-687-9342, E-mail: s.kaufman@csuohio.edu. *Application contact:* Joan Demko, Graduate Academic Support Specialist, 216-523-7522, Fax: 216-687-5398, E-mail: urbanprograms@csuohio.edu.

Cleveland State University, College of Graduate Studies, Maxine Goodman Levin College of Urban Affairs, Program in Nonprofit Administration and Leadership, Cleveland, OH 44115. Offers geographic information systems (Certificate); local and urban management (Certificate); nonprofit administration and leadership (MNAL); nonprofit management (Certificate); urban economic development (Certificate). Part-time and evening/weekend programs available. *Faculty:* 10 full-time (9 women), 8 part-time/adjunct (4 women). *Students:* 11 full-time (10 women), 20 part-time (17 women); includes 7 Black or African American, non-Hispanic/Latino; 2 Asian, non-Hispanic/Latino. Average age 35. 35 applicants, 57% accepted, 14 enrolled. *Degree requirements:* For master's, thesis or alternative, capstone course. *Entrance requirements:* For master's, GRE (minimum 40th percentile verbal and quantitative, 4.0 analytical writing), minimum GPA of 3.0. Additional exam requirements/recommendations for international students: Required—TOEFL (minimum score 525 paper-based; 197 computer-based; 65 iBT). *Application deadline:* For fall admission, 7/15 priority date for domestic students, 5/15 for international students; for spring admission, 11/1 for international students. Applications are processed on a rolling basis. Application fee: $30. Electronic applications accepted. *Expenses:* Tuition, state resident: full-time $8447; part-time $469 per credit hour. Tuition, nonresident: full-time $16,020; part-time $890 per credit hour. Required fees: $50. *Financial support:* In 2010–11, 5 students received support, including research assistantships with full and partial tuition reimbursements available (averaging $6,960 per year); career-related internships or fieldwork, Federal Work-Study, scholarships/grants, tuition waivers (full and partial), and unspecified assistantships also available. Support available to part-time students. Financial award application deadline: 3/1; financial award applicants required to submit FAFSA. *Faculty research:* Human resource management, volunteerism, performance measurement in nonprofits, government-nonprofit partnerships. *Unit head:* Dr. Jennifer Alexander, Director, 216-687-5011, Fax: 216-687-2013, E-mail: j.k.alexander@csuohio.edu. *Application contact:* Joan Demko, Graduate Academic Support Specialist, 216-523-7522, Fax: 216-687-5398, E-mail: urbanprograms@csuohio.edu.

Cleveland State University, College of Graduate Studies, Maxine Goodman Levin College of Urban Affairs, Program in Public Administration, Cleveland, OH 44115. Offers geographic information systems (Certificate); local and urban management (Certificate); non-profit management (Certificate); public administration (MPA); urban real estate development (Certificate); JD/MPA. *Accreditation:* NASPAA. Part-time and evening/weekend programs available. *Faculty:* 26 full-time (10 women), 14 part-time/adjunct (8 women). *Students:* 36 full-time (22 women), 70 part-time (41 women); includes 26 Black or African American, non-Hispanic/Latino; 1 American Indian or Alaska Native, non-Hispanic/Latino; 1 Asian, non-Hispanic/Latino; 2 Hispanic/Latino; 1 Two or more races, non-Hispanic/Latino, 4 international. Average age 36. 82 applicants, 41% accepted, 15 enrolled. In 2010, 37 master's, 8 other advanced degrees awarded. *Degree requirements:* For master's, thesis or alternative, capstone course. *Entrance requirements:* For master's, GRE General Test (minimum 40th percentile verbal and quantitative, 4.0 writing), minimum GPA of 3.0. Additional exam requirements/recommendations for international students: Required—TOEFL (minimum score 525 paper-based; 197 computer-based; 65 iBT). *Application deadline:* For fall admission, 7/15 priority date for domestic students, 5/15 for international students; for spring admission, 11/1 for international students. Applications are processed on a rolling basis. Application fee: $30. Electronic applications accepted. *Expenses:* Tuition, state resident: full-time $8447; part-time $469 per credit hour. Tuition, nonresident: full-time $16,020; part-time $890 per credit hour. Required fees: $50. *Financial support:* In 2010–11, 10 students received support, including 7 research assistantships with full and partial tuition reimbursements available (averaging $6,960 per year), 3 teaching assistantships with full and partial tuition reimbursements available (averaging $6,960 per year); career-related internships or fieldwork, institutionally sponsored loans, tuition waivers (full and partial), and unspecified assistantships also available. Financial award application deadline: 3/1; financial award applicants required to submit FAFSA. *Faculty research:* Health care administration, public management, economic development, city management, nonprofit management. *Unit head:* Dr. Jennifer Alexander, Director, 216-687-5011, Fax: 216-687-2013, E-mail: j.k.alexander@csuohio.edu. *Application contact:* Joan Demko, Graduate Academic Support Specialist, 216-523-7522, Fax: 216-687-5398, E-mail: urbanprograms@csuohio.edu.

Cleveland State University, College of Graduate Studies, Maxine Goodman Levin College of Urban Affairs, Program in Urban Planning, Design, and Development, Cleveland, OH 44115. Offers geographic information systems (Certificate); local and urban management (Certificate); urban economic development (Certificate); urban planning, design, and development (MUPDD); urban real estate development and finance (Certificate); JD/MUPDD. *Accreditation:* ACSP. Part-time and evening/weekend programs available. *Faculty:* 32 full-time (19 women), 8 part-time/adjunct (4 women). *Students:* 30 full-time (10 women), 28 part-time (17 women); includes 6 Black or African American, non-Hispanic/Latino; 3 Hispanic/Latino, 5 international. Average age 38. 72 applicants, 56% accepted, 21 enrolled. In 2010, 24 master's, 9 Certificates awarded. *Degree requirements:* For master's, thesis or alternative, project or thesis. *Entrance requirements:* For master's, GRE General Test (minimum 50th percentile verbal and quantitative, 4.0 analytical writing), minimum GPA of 3.0. Additional exam requirements/recommendations for international students: Required—TOEFL (minimum score 525 paper-based; 197 computer-based; 65 iBT). *Application deadline:* For fall admission, 7/15 priority date for domestic students, 5/15 for international students; for spring admission, 11/1 for international students. Applications are processed on a rolling basis. Application fee: $30. Electronic applications accepted. *Expenses:* Tuition, state resident: full-time $8447; part-time $469 per credit hour. Tuition, nonresident: full-time $16,020; part-time $890 per credit hour. Required fees: $50. *Financial support:* In 2010–11, 15 students received support, including 10 research assistantships with full and partial tuition reimbursements available (averaging $6,960 per year), 5 teaching assistantships with full and partial tuition reimbursements available (averaging $6,960 per year); career-related internships or fieldwork, Federal Work-Study, tuition waivers (full and partial), and unspecified assistantships also available. Support available to part-time students. Financial award application deadline: 3/1. *Faculty research:* Housing and neighborhood development, urban housing policy, environmental sustainability, economic development, metropolitan change, GIS and planning decision support, PPGIS. *Unit head:* Dr. Dennis Keating, Director, 216-687-2298, Fax: 216-687-2013, E-mail: w.keating@csuohio.edu. *Application contact:* Joan Demkow, Graduate Program Coordinator, 216-523-7522, Fax: 216-687-5398, E-mail: urbanprograms@csuohio.edu.

Cleveland State University, College of Graduate Studies, Maxine Goodman Levin College of Urban Affairs, Program in Urban Studies, Cleveland, OH 44115. Offers geographic information systems (Certificate); local and urban management (Certificate); nonprofit management (Certificate); urban economic development (Certificate); urban real estate development and finance (Certificate); urban studies (MS); urban studies and public affairs (PhD). PhD program offered jointly with The University of Akron. Part-time and evening/weekend programs available. *Faculty:* 26 full-time (10 women), 20 part-time/adjunct (11 women). *Students:* 16 full-time (10 women), 35 part-time (18 women); includes 7 Black or African American, non-Hispanic/Latino, 17 international. Average age 37. 90 applicants, 38% accepted, 18 enrolled. In 2010, 6 master's, 7 doctorates, 6 other advanced degrees awarded. *Degree requirements:* For master's, thesis or alternative, exit project, capstone course; for doctorate, comprehensive exam, thesis/dissertation. *Entrance requirements:* For master's, GRE General Test, minimum GPA of 3.0; for doctorate, GRE General Test, minimum GPA of 3.5. Additional exam requirements/recommendations for international students: Required—TOEFL (minimum score 525 paper-based; 197 computer-based; 65 iBT). *Application deadline:* For fall admission, 7/15 priority date for domestic students, 5/15 for international students; for spring admission, 11/1 for international students. Applications are processed on a rolling basis. Application fee: $30. Electronic applications accepted. *Expenses:* Tuition, state resident: full-time $8447; part-time $469 per credit hour. Tuition, nonresident: full-time $16,020; part-time $890 per credit hour. Required fees: $50. *Financial support:* In 2010–11, 15 students received support, including 11 research assistantships with full tuition reimbursements available (averaging $7,000 per year), 4 teaching assistantships with full and partial tuition reimbursements available (averaging $7,000 per year); career-related internships or fieldwork, Federal Work-Study, institutionally sponsored loans, scholarships/grants, tuition waivers (full and partial), and unspecified assistantships also available. Support available to part-time students. Financial award application deadline: 3/1; financial award applicants required to submit FAFSA. *Faculty research:* Environmental issues, economic development, urban and public policy, public management. *Unit head:* Dr. Sugie Lee, Director, 216-687-2381, Fax: 216-687-9342, E-mail: s.lee56@csuohio.edu. *Application contact:* Joan Demko, Graduate Academic Support Specialist, 216-523-7522, Fax: 216-687-5398, E-mail: urbanprograms@csuohio.edu.

Eastern Michigan University, Graduate School, College of Arts and Sciences, Department of Geography and Geology, Program in Geographic Information Systems, Ypsilanti, MI 48197. Offers geographic information systems (MS); GIS educator (Graduate Certificate); GIS professional (Graduate Certificate); GIS-planning (MS). *Students:* 21 full-time (6 women), 28 part-time (13 women); includes 1 minority (Black or African American, non-Hispanic/Latino), 23 international. Average age 29. In 2010, 16 master's, 2 other advanced degrees awarded. Application fee: $35. *Application contact:* Dr. Hugh Semple, Program Advisor, 734-487-8169, Fax: 734-487-6979, E-mail: hsemple@emich.edu.

Florida State University, The Graduate School, College of Social Sciences and Public Policy, Department of Geography, Tallahassee, FL 32306. Offers geographic information science (MS); geography (MA, MS, PhD). *Faculty:* 9 full-time (2 women), 8 part-time/adjunct (2 women). *Students:* 58 full-time (26 women), 29 part-time (15 women); includes 2 Black or African American, non-Hispanic/Latino; 1 American Indian or Alaska Native, non-Hispanic/Latino; 4 Asian, non-Hispanic/Latino; 3 Hispanic/Latino, 7 international. Average age 29. 44 applicants, 73% accepted, 26 enrolled. In 2010, 29 master's, 4 doctorates awarded. Terminal master's awarded for partial completion of doctoral program. *Degree requirements:* For master's, thesis (for some programs); for doctorate, comprehensive exam, thesis/dissertation. *Entrance requirements:* For master's and doctorate, GRE General Test, minimum GPA of 3.0. Additional exam requirements/recommendations for international students: Required—TOEFL. *Application deadline:* For fall admission, 1/15 priority date for domestic students, 12/15 priority date for international students; for spring admission, 11/1 priority date for domestic students, 9/15 priority date for international students. Applications are processed on a rolling basis. Application fee: $30. Electronic applications accepted. *Expenses:* Tuition, state resident: full-time $8238.24. *Financial support:* In 2010–11, 23 students received support, including 3 research assistantships with full tuition reimbursements available (averaging $13,000 per year), 20 teaching assistantships with full tuition reimbursements available (averaging $13,000 per year); fellowships with full tuition reimbursements available, career-related internships or fieldwork, Federal Work-Study, institutionally sponsored loans, scholarships/grants, health care benefits, and unspecified assistantships also available. Financial award application deadline: 1/15; financial award applicants required to submit FAFSA. *Faculty research:* Society-nature interactions, geographic information science, environmental studies, hurricanes, remote sensing, urban, transportation. Total annual research expenditures: $177,712. *Unit head:* Dr. Victor Mesev, Chair, 850-645-2498, Fax: 850-644-5913, E-mail: vmesev@fsu.edu. *Application contact:* Dr. Mark Horner, Graduate Director, 850-644-8377, Fax: 850-644-5193, E-mail: mhorner@fsu.edu.

George Mason University, College of Science, Department of Geography and Geoinformation Science, Fairfax, VA 22030. Offers earth system science (MS); earth systems and geoinformation sciences (PhD); geographic and cartographic sciences (MS); geographic information sciences (Certificate); geoinformatics and geospatial intelligence (MS); geospatial intelligence (Certificate); remote sensing (Certificate). *Faculty:* 31 full-time (7 women), 7 part-time/adjunct (0 women). *Students:* 32 full-time (8 women), 194 part-time (69 women); includes 23 minority (4 Black or African American, non-Hispanic/Latino; 1 American Indian or Alaska Native, non-Hispanic/Latino; 6 Asian, non-Hispanic/Latino; 8 Hispanic/Latino; 1 Native Hawaiian or other Pacific Islander, non-Hispanic/Latino; 3 Two or more races, non-Hispanic/Latino), 27 international. Average age 35. 156 applicants, 74% accepted, 82 enrolled. In 2010, 23 master's, 1 doctorate, 24 other advanced degrees awarded. *Degree requirements:* For master's, thesis optional. *Entrance requirements:* For master's, GRE General Test, minimum GPA of 3.0 in last 60 hours; BS or BA in geography, cartography, or related field. Additional exam requirements/recommendations for international students: Required—TOEFL (minimum score 570 paper-based; 230 computer-based; 88 iBT). *Application deadline:* For fall admission, 5/1 for domestic students; for spring admission, 11/1 for domestic students. Application fee: $100. Electronic applications accepted. *Expenses:* Tuition, state resident: full-time $8192; part-time $440 per credit hour. Tuition, nonresident: full-time $22,952; part-time $1055 per credit hour. Required fees: $2364; $99 per credit hour. *Financial support:* In 2010–11, 23 students received support, including 2 fellowships with full tuition reimbursements available (averaging $18,000 per year), 17 research assistantships with full and partial tuition reimbursements available (averaging $16,244 per year), 4 teaching assistantships with full and partial tuition reimbursements available (averaging $10,345 per year); career-related internships or fieldwork, Federal Work-Study, scholarships/grants, unspecified assistantships, and health care benefits (full-time research or teaching assistantship recipients) also available. Support available to part-time students. Financial award application deadline: 3/1; financial award applicants required to submit FAFSA. *Faculty research:* Gender and earth science, earth science education, remote

sensing, planetary geology, hydrology. Total annual research expenditures: $912,752. *Unit head:* Agouris Peggy, Chair, 703-993-9265, Fax: 703-993-9230, E-mail: pagouris@gmu.edu. *Application contact:* Tim Born, Associate Dean of Academic and Student Affairs, 703-993-4171, Fax: 703-993-9034, E-mail: tborn@gmu.edu.

Georgia Institute of Technology, Graduate Studies and Research, College of Architecture, City and Regional Planning Program, Atlanta, GA 30332-0001. Offers city and regional planning (PhD); economic development (MCRP); environmental planning and management (MCRP); geographic information systems (MCRP); land and community development (MCRP); land use planning (MCRP); transportation (MCRP); urban design (MCRP); MCP/MSCE. *Accreditation:* ACSP. *Degree requirements:* For master's, thesis, internship. *Entrance requirements:* For master's, GRE General Test, minimum GPA of 2.7. Additional exam requirements/recommendations for international students: Required—TOEFL. Electronic applications accepted.

Georgia State University, College of Arts and Sciences, Department of Geosciences, Program in Geographic Information Systems, Atlanta, GA 30302-3083. Offers Certificate. Part-time programs available. *Entrance requirements:* Additional exam requirements/recommendations for international students: Required—TOEFL. Electronic applications accepted. *Faculty research:* Cartography, remote sensing.

Hunter College of the City University of New York, Graduate School, School of Arts and Sciences, Department of Geography, New York, NY 10021-5085. Offers analytical geography (MA); earth system science (MA); environmental and social issues (MA); geographic information science (Certificate); geographic information systems (MA); teaching earth science (MA). Part-time and evening/weekend programs available. *Faculty:* 13 full-time (7 women), 8 part-time/adjunct (1 woman). *Students:* 2 full-time (both women), 50 part-time (23 women); includes 5 Black or African American, non-Hispanic/Latino; 4 Asian, non-Hispanic/Latino; 5 Hispanic/Latino. Average age 31. 22 applicants, 82% accepted, 12 enrolled. In 2010, 15 master's, 3 other advanced degrees awarded. *Degree requirements:* For master's, comprehensive exam or thesis. *Entrance requirements:* For master's, GRE General Test, minimum B average in major, B- overall; 18 credits of course work in geography; 2 letters of recommendation; for Certificate, minimum B average in major, B- overall. Additional exam requirements/recommendations for international students: Required—TOEFL. *Application deadline:* For fall admission, 4/1 for domestic students; for spring admission, 11/1 for domestic students. Applications are processed on a rolling basis. Application fee: $125. *Financial support:* In 2010–11, 1 fellowship (averaging $3,000 per year), 2 research assistantships (averaging $10,000 per year), 10 teaching assistantships (averaging $6,000 per year) were awarded; career-related internships or fieldwork, Federal Work-Study, institutionally sponsored loans, and unspecified assistantships also available. Financial award application deadline: 3/1. *Faculty research:* Urban geography, economic geography, geographic information science, demographic methods, climate change. *Unit head:* Prof. William Solecki, Chair, 212-772-4536, Fax: 212-772-5268, E-mail: wsolecki@hunter.cuny.edu. *Application contact:* Prof. Marianna Pavlovskaya, Graduate Adviser, 212-772-5320, Fax: 212-772-5268, E-mail: mpavlov@geo.hunter.cuny.edu.

Idaho State University, Office of Graduate Studies, College of Arts and Sciences, Department of Geosciences, Pocatello, ID 83209-8072. Offers geographic information science (MS); geology (MNS, MS); geology with emphasis in environmental geoscience (MS); geophysics/hydrology/geology (MS); geotechnology (Postbaccalaureate Certificate). Part-time programs available. *Degree requirements:* For master's, comprehensive exam, thesis, oral colloquium; for Postbaccalaureate Certificate, thesis optional, minimum 19 credits. *Entrance requirements:* For master's, GRE General Test (minimum 50th percentile in 2 sections), 3 letters of recommendation; for Postbaccalaureate Certificate, GRE General Test, 3 letters of recommendation, bachelor's degree, statement of goals. Additional exam requirements/recommendations for international students: Required—TOEFL (minimum score 550 paper-based; 213 computer-based; 80 iBT). Electronic applications accepted. *Faculty research:* Quantitative field mapping and sampling: microscopic, geochemical, and isotopic analysis of rocks, minerals and water; remote sensing, geographic information systems, and global positioning systems: environmental and watershed management; surficial and fluvial processes: landscape change; regional tectonics, structural geology; planetary geology.

Indiana University–Purdue University Indianapolis, School of Liberal Arts, Department of Geography, Indianapolis, IN 46202-2896. Offers geographic information systems (MS, Certificate). *Students:* 3 full-time (all women), 11 part-time (3 women); includes 1 Asian, non-Hispanic/Latino, 1 international. Average age 35. 9 applicants, 67% accepted, 4 enrolled. In 2010, 3 master's awarded. *Entrance requirements:* For master's, GRE, minimum GPA of 3.0. Application fee: $55 ($65 for international students). *Financial support:* In 2010–11, 2 fellowships (averaging $9,000 per year), 1 teaching assistantship (averaging $7,067 per year) were awarded. *Unit head:* Robert W. White, Dean, School of Liberal Arts, 317-274-8448. *Application contact:* Joyce Haibe, Department Secretary, 317-274-8877, E-mail: geogdept@iupui.edu.

Minnesota State University Mankato, College of Graduate Studies, College of Social and Behavioral Sciences, Department of Geography, Mankato, MN 56001. Offers geography (MS); GIS (Certificate). Part-time programs available. *Students:* 3 full-time (0 women), 20 part-time (9 women). *Degree requirements:* For master's, one foreign language, comprehensive exam. *Entrance requirements:* For master's, GRE General Test (if GPA less than 2.8 for the last 2 years), minimum GPA of 3.0 during previous 2 years. *Application deadline:* For fall admission, 7/1 priority date for domestic students; for spring admission, 11/1 for domestic students. Applications are processed on a rolling basis. Application fee: $40. Electronic applications accepted. *Financial support:* Research assistantships, teaching assistantships with full tuition reimbursements, career-related internships or fieldwork, Federal Work-Study, institutionally sponsored loans, and unspecified assistantships available. Support available to part-time students. Financial award application deadline: 3/15; financial award applicants required to submit FAFSA. *Unit head:* Dr. Donald Friend, Chairperson, 507-389-2617. *Application contact:* 507-389-2321, E-mail: grad@mnsu.edu.

Montclair State University, The Graduate School, College of Science and Mathematics, Department of Earth and Environmental Studies, Montclair, NJ 07043-1624. Offers earth science (Certificate); environmental management (MA, PhD); environmental studies (MS), including environmental education, environmental management, environmental science; geographic information science (Certificate); geoscience (MS), including geoscience. Part-time and evening/weekend programs available. *Faculty:* 16 full-time (2 women), 20 part-time/adjunct (7 women). *Students:* 39 full-time (19 women), 59 part-time (29 women); includes 3 Black or African American, non-Hispanic/Latino; 1 Asian, non-Hispanic/Latino; 4 Hispanic/Latino, 17 international. Average age 34. 43 applicants, 65% accepted, 21 enrolled. In 2010, 23 master's, 1 doctorate, 2 other advanced degrees awarded. *Degree requirements:* For master's, comprehensive exam, thesis or alternative; for doctorate, thesis/dissertation. *Entrance requirements:* For master's, GRE General Test, 2 letters of recommendation; for doctorate, GRE General Test, 3 letters of recommendation. Additional exam requirements/recommendations for international students: Required—TOEFL (minimum score: 83 iBT) or IELTS. *Application deadline:* For fall admission, 6/1 for international students; for spring admission, 10/1 for international students. Applications are processed on a rolling basis. Application fee: $60. Electronic applications accepted. *Expenses:* Tuition, state resident: part-time $501.34 per credit. Tuition, nonresident: part-time $773.88 per credit. Required fees: $71.15 per credit. *Financial support:* In 2010–11, 3 fellowships (averaging $15,000 per year), 9 research assistantships with full tuition reimbursements (averaging $7,000 per year), 13 teaching assistantships with full tuition reimbursements (averaging $15,000 per year) were awarded; Federal Work-Study, scholarships/grants, and unspecified assistantships also available. Support available to part-time students. Financial award application deadline: 3/1; financial award applicants required to submit FAFSA. *Faculty research:* Antarctica, carbon pools, contaminated sediments, wetlands. Total annual research expenditures: $712,648. *Unit head:* Dr. Matthew Goring, Chairperson, 973-655-5409. *Application contact:* Amy Aiello, Director of Graduate Admissions and Operations, 973-655-5147, Fax: 973-655-7869, E-mail: graduate.school@montclair.edu.

Geographic Information Systems

North Carolina State University, Graduate School, College of Natural Resources, Department of Parks, Recreation and Tourism Management, Raleigh, NC 27695. Offers natural resource management (MPRTM, MS); park and recreation management (MPRTM, MS); parks, recreation and tourism management (PhD); recreational sport management (MPRTM, MS); spatial information science (MPRTM, MS); tourism policy and development (MPRTM, MS). *Degree requirements:* For master's, thesis (for some programs); for doctorate, thesis/dissertation. *Entrance requirements:* For master's and doctorate, GRE General Test. Additional exam requirements/recommendations for international students: Required—TOEFL. Electronic applications accepted. *Faculty research:* Tourism policy and development, spatial information systems, natural resource management, recreational sports management, park and recreation management.

Northern Arizona University, Graduate College, College of Social and Behavioral Sciences, Department of Geography, Planning, and Recreation, Flagstaff, AZ 86011. Offers applied geospatial sciences (MS); geographic information systems (Certificate). Postbaccalaureate distance learning degree programs offered. *Faculty:* 13 full-time (5 women). *Students:* 16 full-time (8 women), 16 part-time (4 women); includes 4 minority (2 Asian, non-Hispanic/Latino; 2 Hispanic/Latino), 3 international. Average age 32. 19 applicants, 79% accepted, 9 enrolled. In 2010, 6 master's, 4 other advanced degrees awarded. *Degree requirements:* For master's, thesis optional. *Entrance requirements:* For master's, GRE General Test. Additional exam requirements/recommendations for international students: Required—TOEFL (minimum score 550 paper-based; 213 computer-based; 80 iBT), IELTS (minimum score 7). *Application deadline:* For fall admission, 2/15 priority date for domestic students, 2/15 for international students; for spring admission, 10/15 priority date for domestic students, 10/15 for international students. Applications are processed on a rolling basis. Application fee: $65. Electronic applications accepted. *Financial support:* In 2010–11, 1 fellowship (averaging $10,774 per year), 5 teaching assistantships with partial tuition reimbursements (averaging $9,625 per year) were awarded; career-related internships or fieldwork, Federal Work-Study, scholarships/grants, health care benefits, tuition waivers (full and partial), and unspecified assistantships also available. Financial award applicants required to submit FAFSA. *Unit head:* Dr. Pamela Foti, Chair, 928-523-6196, Fax: 928-523-2275, E-mail: pam.foti@nau.edu. *Application contact:* Nicole Harris, Administrative Associate, 928-523-2650, Fax: 928-523-2275, E-mail: geog@nau.edu.

Northern Kentucky University, Office of Graduate Programs, College of Informatics, Department of Computer Science, Highland Heights, KY 41099. Offers computer science (MSCS); geographic information systems (Certificate); secure software engineering (Certificate). Part-time and evening/weekend programs available. *Faculty:* 6 full-time (1 woman). *Students:* 3 full-time (1 woman), 18 part-time (3 women); includes 7 minority (3 Black or African American, non-Hispanic/Latino; 3 Asian, non-Hispanic/Latino; 1 Hispanic/Latino), 5 international. Average age 34. 23 applicants, 52% accepted, 7 enrolled. In 2010, 8 master's, 6 Certificates awarded. *Degree requirements:* For master's, thesis optional. *Entrance requirements:* For master's, minimum GPA of 3.0, at least 4 semesters of undergraduate study in computer science including intermediate computer programming and data structures, one year of calculus, one course in discrete mathematics. Additional exam requirements/recommendations for international students: Required—TOEFL (minimum score 550 paper-based; 213 computer-based; 79 iBT); Recommended—IELTS (minimum score 6.5). *Application deadline:* For fall admission, 8/1 for domestic students, 6/1 for international students; for spring admission, 12/1 for domestic students, 10/1 for international students. Applications are processed on a rolling basis. Application fee: $40. Electronic applications accepted. *Expenses:* Tuition, state resident: full-time $7254; part-time $403 per credit hour. Tuition, nonresident: full-time $12,492; part-time $694 per credit hour. Tuition and fees vary according to degree level and program. *Financial support:* Scholarships/grants and unspecified assistantships available. Financial award applicants required to submit FAFSA. *Faculty research:* Data privacy, data mining, wireless security, secure software engineering, secure networking. *Unit head:* Dr. Maureen Doyle, Program Director, 859-572-5468, Fax: 859-572-6097, E-mail: doylem3@nku.edu. *Application contact:* Dr. Peg Griffin, Director of Graduate Programs, 859-572-6934, Fax: 859-572-6670, E-mail: griffinp@nku.edu.

Northwest Missouri State University, Graduate School, College of Arts and Sciences, Department of Geology/Geography, Program in Geographic Information Sciences, Maryville, MO 64468-6001. Offers MS, Certificate. Part-time programs available. *Faculty:* 11 full-time (3 women). *Students:* 5 full-time (1 woman, 104 part-time (37 women); includes 1 Black or African American, non-Hispanic/Latino; 4 Asian, non-Hispanic/Latino; 1 Hispanic/Latino. 14 applicants, 79% accepted, 8 enrolled. In 2010, 10 master's awarded. *Degree requirements:* For master's, comprehensive exam, thesis. *Entrance requirements:* For master's, GRE General Test, 2 letters of recommendation, writing sample, minimum undergraduate GPA of 2.5. Additional exam requirements/recommendations for international students: Required—TOEFL (minimum score 550 paper-based; 213 computer-based). *Application deadline:* For fall admission, 4/15 for domestic and international students. Application fee: $0 ($50 for international students). *Financial support:* In 2010–11, 2 research assistantships with full tuition reimbursements (averaging $6,000 per year) were awarded. Financial award application deadline: 4/1; financial award applicants required to submit FAFSA. *Unit head:* Dr. Patricia Drews, Head, 660-562-1273, E-mail: drews@nwmissouri.edu. *Application contact:* Dr. Gregory Haddock, Dean of Graduate School, 660-562-1145, Fax: 660-562-1096, E-mail: gradsch@nwmissouri.edu.

Saint Louis University, Graduate Education, College of Education and Public Service, Department of Public Policy Studies, St. Louis, MO 63103-2097. Offers geographic information systems (Certificate); organizational development (Certificate); public administration (MAPA); public policy analysis (PhD); urban affairs (MAUA); urban planning and real estate development (MUPRED). *Accreditation:* NASPAA. Part-time programs available. *Degree requirements:* For master's, comprehensive exam (for some programs), thesis (for some programs); for doctorate, comprehensive exam, thesis/dissertation, preliminary exams. *Entrance requirements:* For master's, GMAT, GRE General Test, or LSAT, letters of recommendation, resume; for doctorate, GMAT, GRE General Test, or LSAT, letters of recommendation, resumé, interview, transcripts, goal statement. Additional exam requirements/recommendations for international students: Required—TOEFL (minimum score 525 paper-based; 194 computer-based). Electronic applications accepted. *Faculty research:* Urban politics, brown fields, e-government, and administration, evaluation research, community development, electronic government and governance.

Saint Mary's University of Minnesota, Schools of Graduate and Professional Programs, Graduate School of Business and Technology, Geographic Information Science Program, Winona, MN 55987-1399. Offers MS, Certificate. *Unit head:* Dr. David McConville, Director, 507-457-1542, Fax: 507-457-1633, E-mail: dmcconvi@smumn.edu. *Application contact:* Jami Spitzer, Information Contact, 507-457-7500, E-mail: jspitzer@smumn.edu.

Salisbury University, Graduate Division, Master of Science in Geographic Information Systems Management Program, Salisbury, MD 21801-6837. Offers MS. Part-time programs available. Postbaccalaureate distance learning degree programs offered (minimal on-campus study). *Faculty:* 2 full-time (0 women). *Students:* 5 full-time (2 women), 10 part-time (4 women); includes 1 minority (Black or African American, non-Hispanic/Latino). Average age 32. 15 applicants, 87% accepted, 11 enrolled. In 2010, 3 master's awarded. *Degree requirements:* For master's, cooperative project. *Entrance requirements:* For master's, GRE (for recent graduates), GIS and administration experience. Additional exam requirements/recommendations for international students: Required—TOEFL (minimum score 550 paper-based; 213 computer-based; 79 iBT). *Application deadline:* For fall admission, 2/15 for domestic students. Application fee: $45. Electronic applications accepted. *Financial support:* In 2010–11, 5 students received support. *Faculty research:* GIS in local governments, parallel applications of GIS, GIS and vulnerability, GIS and crime analysis. *Unit head:* Dr. Michael Scott, Director, 410-543-6456, Fax: 410-548-4506, E-mail: msscott@salisbury.edu. *Application contact:* Susan Parks, Program Management Specialist, 410-543-6460, Fax: 410-548-4506, E-mail: slparks@salisbury.edu.

San Francisco State University, Division of Graduate Studies, College of Behavioral and Social Sciences, Department of Geography and Human Environmental Studies, San Francisco, CA 94132-1722. Offers geographic information science (MS); geography (MA), including resource management and environmental planning. *Unit head:* Dr. Jerry Davis, Chair, 415-338-2049, E-mail: jerry@sfsu.edu. *Application contact:* Nancy Wilkinson, Graduate Coordinator, 415-338-2049.

San Jose State University, Graduate Studies and Research, College of Social Sciences, Department of Geography, San Jose, CA 95192-0001. Offers geographic information science (Certificate); geography (MA). *Entrance requirements:* For master's, minimum GPA of 3.0. Electronic applications accepted.

State University of New York College of Environmental Science and Forestry, Department of Environmental Resources Engineering, Syracuse, NY 13210-2779. Offers ecological engineering (MS, PhD); environmental and resources engineering (MPS, MS, PhD); environmental management (MPS); geospatial information science and engineering (MS, PhD); mapping sciences (MPS); water resources engineering (MS, PhD). *Degree requirements:* For master's, thesis (for some programs); for doctorate, comprehensive exam, thesis/dissertation. *Entrance requirements:* For master's and doctorate, GRE General Test, minimum GPA of 3.0. Additional exam requirements/recommendations for international students: Required—TOEFL (minimum score 550 paper-based; 213 computer-based; 80 iBT), IELTS (minimum score 6). *Expenses:* Tuition, state resident: full-time $8370; part-time $349 per credit hour. Tuition, nonresident: full-time $13,780. Required fees: $30.30 per credit hour. $20 per year. *Faculty research:* Forest engineering, paper science and engineering, wood products engineering.

Texas State University–San Marcos, Graduate School, College of Liberal Arts, Department of Geography, Program in Environmental Geography, Geography Education, and Geography Information Science, San Marcos, TX 78666. Offers environmental geography (PhD); geography education (PhD); information science (PhD). Part-time programs available. *Faculty:* 24 full-time (6 women), 1 part-time/adjunct (0 women). *Students:* 46 full-time (22 women), 28 part-time (13 women); includes 7 minority (6 Hispanic/Latino; 1 Two or more races, non-Hispanic/Latino), 12 international. Average age 39. 23 applicants, 83% accepted, 8 enrolled. In 2010, 7 doctorates awarded. *Degree requirements:* For doctorate, thesis/dissertation. *Entrance requirements:* For doctorate, GRE General Test, minimum GPA of 3.5, master's degree in geography, demonstrated scholarly research. Additional exam requirements/recommendations for international students: Required—TOEFL (minimum score 550 paper-based; 213 computer-based; 78 iBT). *Application deadline:* For fall admission, 6/15 priority date for domestic students, 6/1 for international students; for spring admission, 10/15 priority date for domestic students, 10/1 for international students. Applications are processed on a rolling basis. Application fee: $40 ($90 for international students). Electronic applications accepted. *Expenses:* Tuition, state resident: full-time $6024; part-time $251 per credit hour. Tuition, nonresident: full-time $13,536; part-time $564 per credit hour. Required fees: $1776; $50 per credit hour. $306 per semester. *Financial support:* In 2010–11, 24 students received support, including 16 research assistantships (averaging $1,274 per year), 32 teaching assistantships (averaging $785 per year); career-related internships or fieldwork, Federal Work-Study, and institutionally sponsored loans also available. Support available to part-time students. Financial award application deadline: 4/1; financial award applicants required to submit FAFSA. *Faculty research:* Water and food production, geography education, watershed education. Total annual research expenditures: $530,310. *Unit head:* Dr. David Butler, Graduate Adviser, 512-245-2170, Fax: 512-245-8353, E-mail: db25@txstate.edu. *Application contact:* Dr. J. Michael Willoughby, Dean of Graduate School, 512-245-2581, Fax: 512-245-8365, E-mail: gradcollege@txstate.edu.

Texas State University–San Marcos, Graduate School, College of Liberal Arts, Department of Geography, Program in Geographic Information Science, San Marcos, TX 78666. Offers MAG. Part-time and evening/weekend programs available. *Faculty:* 6 full-time (2 women). *Students:* 7 full-time (4 women), 8 part-time (4 women); includes 2 minority (both Hispanic/Latino). Average age 30. 7 applicants, 100% accepted, 4 enrolled. In 2010, 1 master's awarded. *Degree requirements:* For master's, comprehensive exam. *Entrance requirements:* For master's, GRE General Test, minimum GPA of 3.0 in last 60 hours of course work, letter of interest, 2 letters of recommendation, curriculum vitae/resume. Additional exam requirements/recommendations for international students: Required—TOEFL (minimum score 550 paper-based; 213 computer-based; 78 iBT). *Application deadline:* For fall admission, 5/1 priority date for domestic students, 4/15 for international students. Applications are processed on a rolling basis. Application fee: $40 ($90 for international students). Electronic applications accepted. *Expenses:* Tuition, state resident: full-time $6024; part-time $251 per credit hour. Tuition, nonresident: full-time $13,536; part-time $564 per credit hour. Required fees: $1776; $50 per credit hour. $306 per semester. *Financial support:* In 2010–11, 7 students received support, including 1 teaching assistantship (averaging $5,387 per year); research assistantships, career-related internships or fieldwork, Federal Work-Study, institutionally sponsored loans, and scholarships/grants also available. Support available to part-time students. Financial award application deadline: 4/1; financial award applicants required to submit FAFSA. *Faculty research:* Holocaust history, special methods hotspots, residential proximity. Total annual research expenditures: $89,398. *Unit head:* Dr. David Butler, Graduate Adviser, 512-245-2170, Fax: 512-245-8353, E-mail: db25@txstate.edu. *Application contact:* Dr. J. Michael Willoughby, Dean of Graduate School, 512-245-2581, Fax: 512-245-8365, E-mail: gradcollege@txstate.edu.

Université du Québec à Montréal, Graduate Programs, Program in Geographical Information Systems, Montréal, QC H3C 3P8, Canada. Offers Diploma. Part-time programs available. *Entrance requirements:* For degree, appropriate bachelor's degree or equivalent, proficiency in French.

Université Laval, Faculty of Administrative Sciences, Programs in Business Administration, Québec, QC G1K 7P4, Canada. Offers accounting (MBA); agri-food management (MBA); electronic business (MBA, Diploma); factory management and logistics (MBA); finance (MBA); firm management (MBA); geomatic management (MBA); information technology management (MBA); international management (MBA); management (MBA); management accounting (MBA, Diploma); marketing (MBA); modeling and organizational decision (MBA); occupational health and safety management (MBA); pharmacy management (MBA); social and environmental responsibility (MBA); technological entrepreneurship (Diploma). *Accreditation:* AACSB. Part-time and evening/weekend programs available. Postbaccalaureate distance learning degree programs offered (no on-campus study). *Entrance requirements:* For master's and Diploma, knowledge of French and English. Electronic applications accepted.

University at Albany, State University of New York, College of Arts and Sciences, Department of Geography and Planning, Program in Geography, Albany, NY 12222-0001. Offers geographic information systems and spatial analysis (Certificate); geography (MA). *Degree requirements:* For master's, thesis or alternative. *Entrance requirements:* Additional exam requirements/recommendations for international students: Required—TOEFL (minimum score 550 paper-based; 213 computer-based). Electronic applications accepted. *Faculty research:* Remote sensing, cultural/social geography, urban geography.

University at Buffalo, the State University of New York, Graduate School, College of Arts and Sciences, Department of Geography, Buffalo, NY 14260. Offers earth systems science (MA); economic geography and international business and world trade (MA); environmental and earth systems science (MS); environmental modeling and analysis (MA); geographic information science (MA, Certificate); geographic information systems and science (MS); geography (MA, PhD); urban and regional geography (MA); MA/MBA. *Faculty:* 14 full-time (6 women), 1 part-time/adjunct (0 women). *Students:* 60 full-time (24 women), 49 part-time (13 women); includes 1 Black or African American, non-Hispanic/Latino; 46 Asian, non-Hispanic/Latino; 4 Hispanic/Latino, 1 international. 162 applicants, 46% accepted, 38 enrolled. In 2010, 21 master's, 5 doctorates awarded. Terminal master's awarded for partial completion of doctoral program. *Degree requirements:* For master's, thesis (for some programs), project; for doctorate, thesis/dissertation. *Entrance requirements:* For master's, GRE General Test, minimum GPA of 2.9; for doctorate, GRE General Test, minimum GPA of 3.0. Additional exam requirements/recommendations for international students: Required—TOEFL (minimum score 550 paper-based; 213 computer-based; 79 iBT). *Application deadline:* For fall admission, 7/1 priority date for domestic students, 1/10 priority date for international students; for spring admission, 12/1 priority date for domestic students, 10/1 priority date for international students. Applications are processed on a rolling basis. Application fee: $75. Electronic applications accepted. *Financial support:* In 2010–11, 19 students received support, including 7 fellowships with full tuition reimbursements available (averaging $5,714 per year), 14 teaching assistantships with full tuition reimbursements available (averaging $13,520 per year); research assistantships with full tuition reimbursements available, career-related internships or fieldwork, Federal Work-Study, institutionally sponsored loans, traineeships, health care benefits, and unspecified assistantships also available. Financial award application deadline: 1/10. *Faculty research:* International business and world trade, geographic information systems and cartography, transportation, urban and regional analysis, physical and environmental geography. Total annual research expenditures: $944,614. *Unit head:* Dr. Sharmistha Bagchi-Sen, Chairman, 716-645-0473, Fax: 716-645-2329, E-mail: geosbs@buffalo.edu. *Application contact:* Betsy Abraham, Graduate Secretary, 716-645-0471, Fax: 716-645-2329, E-mail: babraham@buffalo.edu.

The University of Akron, Graduate School, Buchtel College of Arts and Sciences, Department of Geography and Planning, Program in Geographic Information Science, Akron, OH 44325. Offers MS. *Students:* 13 full-time (5 women), 4 part-time (2 women); includes 1 Black or African American, non-Hispanic/Latino; 1 Asian, non-Hispanic/Latino; 2 Hispanic/Latino, 2 international. Average age 28. 17 applicants, 100% accepted, 3 enrolled. In 2010, 10 master's awarded. *Degree requirements:* For master's, thesis optional. *Entrance requirements:* For master's, two letters of recommendation; statement of purpose. Additional exam requirements/recommendations for international students: Required—TOEFL (minimum score 550 paper-based; 213 computer-based; 79 iBT). *Application deadline:* Applications are processed on a rolling basis. Electronic applications accepted. *Expenses:* Tuition, state resident: full-time $6800; part-time $378 per credit hour. Tuition, nonresident: full-time $11,644; part-time $647 per credit hour. Required fees: $1265. One-time fee: $30 full-time. *Unit head:* Dr. Linda Barrett, Graduate Director, 330-972-6120, E-mail: barrettr@uakron.edu. *Application contact:* Dr. Linda Barrett, Graduate Director, 330-972-6120, E-mail: barrettr@uakron.edu.

University of Central Arkansas, Graduate School, College of Liberal Arts, Department of Geography, Conway, AR 72035-0001. Offers community and economic development (MS); geographic information systems (MGIS, Certificate). Part-time programs available. Postbaccalaureate distance learning degree programs offered (minimal on-campus study). *Faculty:* 3 full-time (0 women). *Students:* 4 full-time (1 woman), 11 part-time (1 woman); includes 1 minority (Black or African American, non-Hispanic/Latino). Average age 30. 6 applicants, 100% accepted, 5 enrolled. *Entrance requirements:* Additional exam requirements/recommendations for international students: Required—TOEFL (minimum score 550 paper-based; 213 computer-based). *Application deadline:* For fall admission, 3/1 priority date for domestic and international students; for spring admission, 10/1 priority date for domestic and international students. Applications are processed on a rolling basis. Application fee: $25 ($50 for international students). *Financial support:* Applicants required to submit FAFSA. *Unit head:* Dr. Brooks Green, Chairperson, 501-450-5636, Fax: 501-450-5185, E-mail: brooksg@uca.edu. *Application contact:* Susan Wood, Admissions Assistant, 501-450-3124, Fax: 501-450-5678, E-mail: swood@uca.edu.

University of Colorado Denver, College of Engineering and Applied Science, Department of Civil Engineering, Denver, CO 80217-3364. Offers civil engineering (PhD); environmental and sustainability engineering (MS); geographic information systems (MS); geotechnical engineering (MS); hydrology and hydraulics (MS); structural engineering (MS); transportation engineering (MS). Part-time and evening/weekend programs available. *Faculty:* 14 full-time (1 woman), 6 part-time/adjunct (0 women). *Students:* 66 full-time (13 women), 72 part-time (16 women); includes 9 Black or African American, non-Hispanic/Latino; 8 Asian, non-Hispanic/Latino; 11 Hispanic/Latino, 15 international. Average age 32. 72 applicants, 54% accepted, 29 enrolled. In 2010, 14 master's, 3 doctorates awarded. *Degree requirements:* For master's, comprehensive exam, thesis or alternative; for doctorate, comprehensive exam, thesis/dissertation. *Entrance requirements:* For master's, GRE, statement of purpose, transcripts, references; for doctorate, GRE, statement of purpose, transcripts, references, letter of support from faculty stating willingness to serve as dissertation advisor and outlining plan for financial support. Additional exam requirements/recommendations for international students: Required—TOEFL (minimum score 525 paper-based; 197 computer-based). *Application deadline:* For fall admission, 7/15 for domestic students, 6/15 for international students; for spring admission, 12/1 for domestic students, 11/1 for international students. Applications are processed on a rolling basis. Application fee: $50 ($75 for international students). Electronic applications accepted. *Expenses:* Contact institution. *Financial support:* Research assistantships, teaching assistantships, career-related internships or fieldwork and Federal Work-Study available. Financial award application deadline: 4/1; financial award applicants required to submit FAFSA. *Faculty research:* Environmental engineering and sustainable systems, geosynthetics, hydrologic and hydraulic engineering, structural engineering, transportation, transportation energy use and greenhouse gas emissions. *Unit head:* Dr. Nien-Yin Chang, Acting Chair, 303-556-2810, Fax: 303-556-2368, E-mail: nien.chang@ucdenver.edu. *Application contact:* Mindy Gewuerz, Program Assistant, 303-556-6712, Fax: 303-556-2368, E-mail: mindy.gewuerz@ucdenver.edu.

University of Colorado Denver, College of Liberal Arts and Sciences, Department of Geography and Environmental Sciences, Denver, CO 80217. Offers environmental sciences (MS), including air quality, ecosystems, environmental health, environmental science education, environmental sciences, geo-spatial analysis, hazardous waste, water quality. Part-time and evening/weekend programs available. *Students:* 48 full-time (28 women), 4 part-time (3 women); includes 2 Black or African American, non-Hispanic/Latino; 2 Asian, non-Hispanic/Latino; 3 Hispanic/Latino, 8 international. Average age 29. 44 applicants, 52% accepted, 14 enrolled. In 2010, 17 master's awarded. *Degree requirements:* For master's, thesis or alternative. *Entrance requirements:* For master's, GRE General Test, BA in one of the natural/physical sciences or engineering (or equivalent background); prerequisite coursework in calculus and physics (one semester each), general chemistry with lab and general biology with lab (two semesters each). Additional exam requirements/recommendations for international students: Required—TOEFL (minimum score 525 paper-based; 197 computer-based). *Application deadline:* For fall admission, 4/1 for domestic students; for spring admission, 10/1 for domestic students. Application fee: $50 ($75 for international students). Electronic applications accepted. *Expenses:* Tuition, state resident: full-time $7332; part-time $355 per credit hour. Tuition, nonresident: full-time $18,990; part-time $1055 per credit hour. Required fees: $998. Tuition and fees vary according to course level, course load, degree level, campus/location, program, reciprocity agreements and student level. *Financial support:* Research assistantships, teaching assistantships, Federal Work-Study available. Financial award application deadline: 4/1; financial award applicants required to submit FAFSA. *Faculty research:* Air quality, environmental health, ecosystems, hazardous waste, water quality, geo-spatial analysis and environmental science education. *Unit head:* Dr. John Wyckoff, Director, 303-556-2590, Fax: 303-556-6197, E-mail: john.wyckoff@cudenver.edu. *Application contact:* Dr. John Wyckoff, Director, 303-556-2590, Fax: 303-556-6197, E-mail: john.wyckoff@cudenver.edu.

University of Connecticut, Graduate School, College of Liberal Arts and Sciences, Department of Geography, Storrs, CT 06269. Offers geographic information systems (Certificate); geography (MS, PhD). *Degree requirements:* For master's, comprehensive exam; for doctorate, thesis/dissertation. *Entrance requirements:* For master's and doctorate, GRE General Test. Additional exam requirements/recommendations for international students: Required—TOEFL (minimum score 550 paper-based; 213 computer-based). Electronic applications accepted.

University of Denver, Faculty of Natural Sciences and Mathematics, Department of Geography, Denver, CO 80208. Offers geographic information science (MS); geography (MA, PhD). Part-time programs available. *Faculty:* 15 full-time (6 women), 1 part-time/adjunct (0 women). *Students:* 11 full-time (4 women), 44 part-time (20 women); includes 5 minority (1 Black or African American, non-Hispanic/Latino; 1 Asian, non-Hispanic/Latino; 3 Hispanic/Latino), 2 international. Average age 32. 66 applicants, 80% accepted, 28 enrolled. In 2010, 19 master's, 3 doctorates awarded. Terminal master's awarded for partial completion of doctoral program. *Degree requirements:* For master's, comprehensive exam (for some programs), thesis or project; for doctorate, one foreign language, comprehensive exam, thesis/dissertation. *Entrance requirements:* For master's, GRE General Test; for doctorate, GRE General Test, MA. Additional exam requirements/recommendations for international students: Required—TOEFL (minimum score 570 paper-based; 88 iBT). *Application deadline:* Applications are processed on a rolling basis. Application fee: $60. Electronic applications accepted. *Expenses:* Tuition: Full-time $35,604; part-time $29,670 per year. Required fees: $687 per year. Tuition and fees vary according to program. *Financial support:* In 2010–11, 15 teaching assistantships with full and partial tuition reimbursements (averaging $18,300 per year) were awarded; career-related internships or fieldwork, Federal Work-Study, institutionally sponsored loans, scholarships/grants, and unspecified assistantships also available. Support available to part-time students. Financial award application deadline: 3/1; financial award applicants required to submit FAFSA. *Faculty research:* Transportation and land use, fluvial geography and water resources, climatology, geographic information systems, biogeography. Total annual research expenditures: $158,000. *Unit head:* Dr. Andrew Goetz, Chair, 303-871-2201, Fax: 303-871-2201, E-mail: agoetz@du.edu. *Application contact:* Karen Escobar, Assistant to the Chair, 303-871-2201, Fax: 303-871-2201, E-mail: kescobar@du.edu.

University of Denver, University College, Denver, CO 80208. Offers arts and culture (MLS, Certificate), including art, literature, and culture, arts development and program management (Certificate), creative writing; environmental policy and management (MAS, Certificate), including energy and sustainability (Certificate), environmental assessment of nuclear power (Certificate), environmental health and safety (Certificate), environmental management, natural resource management (Certificate); geographic information systems (MAS, Certificate); global affairs (MLS, Certificate), including translation studies, world history and culture; healthcare leadership (MPH, Certificate), including healthcare policy, law, and ethics, medical and healthcare information technologies, strategic management of healthcare; information and communications technology (MCIS, Certificate), including database design and administration (Certificate), geographic information systems (MCIS), information security systems security (Certificate), information systems security (MCIS), project management (MCIS, MPS, Certificate), software design and administration (Certificate), software design and programming (MCIS), technology management, telecommunications technology (MCIS), Web design and development; leadership and organizations (MPS, Certificate), including human capital in organizations, philanthropic leadership, project management (MCIS, MPS, Certificate), strategic innovation and change; organizational and professional communication (MPS, Certificate), including alternative dispute resolution, organizational communication, organizational development and training, public relations and marketing; security management (MAS, Certificate), including emergency planning and response, information security (MAS), organizational security; strategic human resource management (MPS, Certificate), including global human resources (MPS), human resource management and development (MPS). Part-time and evening/weekend programs available. Postbaccalaureate distance learning degree programs offered (no on-campus study). *Faculty:* 7 full-time (2 women), 212 part-time/adjunct (83 women). *Students:* 52 full-time (19 women), 1,044 part-time (625 women); includes 196 minority (81 Black or African American, non-Hispanic/Latino; 7 American Indian or Alaska Native, non-Hispanic/Latino; 30 Asian, non-Hispanic/Latino; 66 Hispanic/Latino; 3 Native Hawaiian or other Pacific Islander, non-Hispanic/Latino; 9 Two or more races, non-Hispanic/Latino), 76 international. Average age 36. 488 applicants, 91% accepted, 339 enrolled. In 2010, 286 master's, 130 other advanced degrees awarded. *Entrance requirements:* Additional exam requirements/recommendations for international students: Required—TOEFL (minimum score 550 paper-based; 80 iBT). *Application deadline:* For fall admission, 6/22 priority date for domestic students, 6/10 priority date for international students; for winter admission, 9/15 priority date for domestic students, 9/6 priority date for international students; for spring admission, 2/3 priority date for domestic students, 12/15 priority date for international students. Applications are processed on a rolling basis. Application fee: $75. Electronic applications accepted. *Expenses:* Contact institution. *Financial support:* Applicants required to submit FAFSA. *Unit head:* Dr. James Davis, Dean, 303-871-2291, Fax: 303-871-4047, E-mail: jdavis@du.edu. *Application contact:* Information Contact, 303-871-3155, Fax: 303-871-4047, E-mail: ucolinfo@du.edu.

University of Lethbridge, School of Graduate Studies, Lethbridge, AB T1K 3M4, Canada. Offers accounting (MScM); addictions counseling (M Sc); agricultural biotechnology (M Sc); agricultural studies (M Sc, MA); anthropology (MA); archaeology (MA); art (MA, MFA); biochemistry (M Sc); biological sciences (M Sc); biomolecular science (PhD); biosystems and biodiversity (PhD); Canadian studies (MA); chemistry (M Sc); computer science (M Sc); computer science and geographical information science (M Sc); counseling psychology (M Ed); dramatic arts (MA); earth, space, and physical science (PhD); economics (MA); educational leadership (M Ed); English (MA); environmental science (M Sc); evolution and behavior (PhD); exercise science (M Sc); finance (MScM); French (MA); French/German (MA); French/Spanish (MA); general education (M Ed); general management (MScM); geography (M Sc, MA); German (MA); health science (M Sc); history (MA); human resource management and labour relations (MScM); individualized multidisciplinary (M Sc, MA); information systems (MScM); international management (MScM); kinesiology (M Sc, MA); management (M Sc, MA); marketing (MScM); mathematics (M Sc); music (M Mus, MA); Native American studies (MA); neuroscience (M Sc, PhD); new media (MA); nursing (M Sc); philosophy (MA); physics (M Sc); policy and strategy (MScM); political science (MA); psychology (M Sc, MA); religious studies (MA); social sciences (MA); sociology (MA); theatre and dramatic arts (MFA); theoretical and computational science (PhD); urban and regional studies (MA); women's studies (MA). Part-time and evening/weekend programs available. *Degree requirements:* For doctorate, comprehensive exam, thesis/dissertation. *Entrance requirements:* For master's, GMAT (M Sc in management), bachelor's degree in related field, minimum GPA of 3.0 during previous 20 graded semester courses, 2 years teaching or related experience (M Ed); for doctorate, master's degree, minimum graduate GPA of 3.5. Additional exam requirements/recommendations for international students: Required—TOEFL. *Faculty research:* Movement and brain plasticity, gibberellin physiology, photosynthesis, carbon cycling, molecular properties of main-group ring components.

University of Maryland, Baltimore County, Graduate School, College of Arts, Humanities and Social Sciences, Department of Geography and Environmental Systems, Program in Geographic Information Systems, Baltimore, MD 21250. Offers MPS, Certificate. Part-time and evening/weekend programs available. *Faculty:* 10 part-time/adjunct (3 women). *Students:* 15 full-time (10 women), 26 part-time (2 women); includes 6 Black or African American, non-Hispanic/Latino; 3 Asian, non-Hispanic/Latino; 3 Hispanic/Latino, 1 international. Average age 35. 22 applicants, 86% accepted, 13 enrolled. *Entrance requirements:* Additional exam requirements/recommendations for international students: Required—TOEFL. *Application deadline:* For fall admission, 6/1 for domestic and international students; for spring admission, 11/1 for domestic and international students. Applications are processed on a rolling basis. Application fee: $50. Electronic applications accepted. *Faculty research:* Enterprise GIS. *Unit head:* Dr. Sandy Parker, Chair, 410-455-2002, E-mail: eparker@umbc.edu. *Application contact:* Kathryn Nee, Coordinator of Domestic Admissions, 410-455-2944, E-mail: nee@umbc.edu.

University of Memphis, Graduate School, College of Arts and Sciences, Department of Earth Sciences, Memphis, TN 38152. Offers archaeology (MS); earth sciences (PhD); geographic information systems (Graduate Certificate); geography (MA, MS); geology (MS); geophysics (MS); interdisciplinary (MS). Part-time and evening/weekend programs available. *Faculty:* 15 full-time (3 women), 6 part-time/adjunct (2 women). *Students:* 35 full-time (7 women), 28 part-time (13 women); includes 5 Black or African American, non-Hispanic/Latino; 1 Asian, non-Hispanic/Latino, 15 international. Average age 33. 48 applicants, 69% accepted, 18 enrolled. In 2010, 2 master's, 2 doctorates, 1 other advanced degree awarded. Terminal master's awarded for partial completion of doctoral program. *Degree requirements:* For master's, comprehensive exam, thesis, seminar presentation; for doctorate, thesis/dissertation. *Entrance requirements:* For master's, GRE General Test, 3 letters of recommendation, statement of research interests; for doctorate, GRE General Test, 2 letters of recommendation, resume, personal statement. Additional exam requirements/recommendations for international students:

Geographic Information Systems

University of Memphis (continued)

Required—TOEFL (minimum score 550 paper-based; 210 computer-based). *Application deadline:* For fall admission, 1/31 for domestic students; for spring admission, 11/1 for domestic students. Applications are processed on a rolling basis. Application fee: $35 ($60 for international students). Electronic applications accepted. *Financial support:* In 2010–11, 18 students received support; fellowships with full tuition reimbursements available, research assistantships with full tuition reimbursements available, teaching assistantships with full tuition reimbursements available, Federal Work-Study, scholarships/grants, and unspecified assistantships available. Financial award application deadline: 2/15; financial award applicants required to submit FAFSA. *Faculty research:* Hazards, active tectonics, geophysics, hydrology and water resources, spatial analysis. *Unit head:* Dr. M. Jerry Bartholomew, Chair, 901-678-4536, Fax: 901-678-4467, E-mail: jbrthlm1@memphis.edu. *Application contact:* Dr. Arlene Hill, Associate Professor and Graduate Program Coordinator, 901-678-4358, Fax: 901-678-2178, E-mail: dlarsen@memphis.edu.

University of Minnesota, Twin Cities Campus, Graduate School, College of Liberal Arts, Program in Geographic Information Science, Minneapolis, MN 55455-0213. Offers MGIS. Part-time programs available. *Degree requirements:* For master's, comprehensive exam, capstone project. *Entrance requirements:* For master's, minimum GPA of 3.0; course work in college-level math, statistics, and computer programming. Additional exam requirements/recommendations for international students: Required—TOEFL (minimum score 600 paper-based; 250 computer-based; 100 iBT). *Expenses:* Contact institution. *Faculty research:* Geographic information science and society, spatial analysis and modeling, spatial databases, remote sensing, geovisualization.

The University of Montana, Graduate School, College of Arts and Sciences, Department of Geography, Missoula, MT 59812-0002. Offers geography (MA), including cartography and GIS, community and environmental planning. *Entrance requirements:* For master's, GRE General Test. Additional exam requirements/recommendations for international students: Required—TOEFL.

University of New Haven, Graduate School, College of Arts and Sciences, Program in Environmental Sciences, West Haven, CT 06516-1916. Offers environmental ecology (Certificate); environmental geoscience (MS); environmental health and management (MS); environmental science (MS); geographical information systems (Certificate). Part-time and evening/weekend programs available. *Students:* 13 full-time (5 women), 24 part-time (10 women); includes 2 Black or African American, non-Hispanic/Latino; 1 American Indian or Alaska Native, non-Hispanic/Latino; 1 Asian, non-Hispanic/Latino; 1 Hispanic/Latino, 4 international. Average age 27. 29 applicants, 100% accepted, 14 enrolled. In 2010, 13 master's, 1 other advanced degree awarded. *Degree requirements:* For master's, thesis or alternative. *Application deadline:* For fall admission, 5/31 for international students; for winter admission, 10/15 for international students; for spring admission, 1/15 for international students. Applications are processed on a rolling basis. Application fee: $50. Electronic applications accepted. *Financial support:* Research assistantships with partial tuition reimbursements, teaching assistantships with partial tuition reimbursements, career-related internships or fieldwork, Federal Work-Study, scholarships/grants, tuition waivers, and unspecified assistantships available. Support available to part-time students. Financial award applicants required to submit FAFSA. *Faculty research:* Mapping and assessing geological and living resources in Long Island Sound, geology, San Salvador Island, Bahamas. *Unit head:* Dr. Roman Zajac, Coordinator, 203-932-7108. *Application contact:* Eloise Gormley, Director of Graduate Admissions, 203-932-7449, Fax: 203-932-7137, E-mail: gradinfo@newhaven.edu.

The University of North Carolina at Charlotte, Graduate School, College of Arts and Sciences, Department of Geography and Earth Sciences, Charlotte, NC 28223-0001. Offers earth sciences (MS); geography (MA), including community planning, geographic location science and technologies, location analysis, transportation studies, urban regional analysis; geography and urban regional analysis (PhD). Part-time and evening/weekend programs available. *Faculty:* 27 full-time (9 women), 2 part-time/adjunct (1 woman). *Students:* 57 full-time (26 women), 38 part-time (12 women); includes 5 minority (3 Black or African American, non-Hispanic/Latino; 1 Hispanic/Latino; 1 Native Hawaiian or other Pacific Islander, non-Hispanic/Latino), 17 international. Average age 30. 46 applicants, 72% accepted, 17 enrolled. In 2010, 18 master's awarded. *Degree requirements:* For master's, comprehensive exam, thesis or alternative, project. *Entrance requirements:* For master's, GRE General Test or MAT, Doppelt Mathematical Reasoning Test, minimum GPA of 3.0 in undergraduate major, 2.75 overall. Additional exam requirements/recommendations for international students: Required—TOEFL (minimum score 557 paper-based; 220 computer-based; 83 iBT). *Application deadline:* For fall admission, 7/1 for domestic students, 5/1 for international students; for spring admission, 11/1 for domestic students, 10/1 for international students. Applications are processed on a rolling basis. Application fee: $55. Electronic applications accepted. *Expenses:* Tuition, state resident: full-time $3464. Tuition, nonresident: full-time $14,297. Required fees: $2094. Tuition and fees vary according to course load. *Financial support:* In 2010–11, 48 students received support, including 2 fellowships (averaging $17,876 per year), 23 research assistantships (averaging $10,760 per year), 23 teaching assistantships (averaging $9,449 per year); career-related internships or fieldwork, institutionally sponsored loans, scholarships/grants, and unspecified assistantships also available. Support available to part-time students. Financial award application deadline: 4/1; financial award applicants required to submit FAFSA. *Faculty research:* Location analysis, applications of GIS technology, community planning and development, regional economic modeling, retail geography. Total annual research expenditures: $755,074. *Unit head:* Dr. Harrison Campbell, Graduate Coordinator, 704-687-5997, Fax: 704-687-3182, E-mail: hscampbe@uncc.edu. *Application contact:* Kathy B. Giddings, Director of Graduate Admissions, 704-687-5503, Fax: 704-687-3279, E-mail: gradadm@uncc.edu.

The University of North Carolina at Greensboro, Graduate School, College of Arts and Sciences, Department of Geography, Greensboro, NC 27412-5001. Offers applied geography (MA); geographic information science (Certificate); geography (PhD); urban and economic development (Certificate). *Degree requirements:* For master's, comprehensive exam, thesis or alternative. *Entrance requirements:* For master's, GRE General Test. Additional exam requirements/recommendations for international students: Required—TOEFL. Electronic applications accepted.

University of Pittsburgh, School of Arts and Sciences, Department of Geology and Planetary Science, Pittsburgh, PA 15260-3332. Offers geographical information systems (PM Sc); geology and planetary science (MS, PhD). Part-time programs available. *Faculty:* 9 full-time (1 woman), 4 part-time/adjunct (1 woman). *Students:* 26 full-time (13 women), 9 part-time (4 women); includes 1 Asian, non-Hispanic/Latino, 1 international. Average age 30. 56 applicants, 36% accepted, 8 enrolled. In 2010, 3 master's, 2 doctorates awarded. *Degree requirements:* For master's, thesis, oral thesis defense; for doctorate, comprehensive exam, thesis/dissertation, oral dissertation defense. *Entrance requirements:* For master's and doctorate, GRE General Test. Additional exam requirements/recommendations for international students: Required—TOEFL (minimum score 550 paper-based; 213 computer-based; 80 iBT). *Application deadline:* For fall admission, 2/1 priority date for domestic students, 2/1 for international students. Application fee: $50. Electronic applications accepted. *Expenses:* Tuition, state resident: full-time $17,304; part-time $701 per credit. Tuition, nonresident: full-time $29,554; part-time $1210 per credit. Required fees: $740; $214 per term. Tuition and fees vary according to program. *Financial support:* In 2010–11, 25 students received support, including 3 fellowships with full tuition reimbursements available (averaging $16,140 per year), 10 research assistantships with full and partial tuition reimbursements available (averaging $14,400 per year), 9 teaching assistantships with full and partial tuition reimbursements available (averaging $15,830 per year); career-related internships or fieldwork, Federal Work-Study, institutionally sponsored loans, scholarships/grants, and tuition waivers (full and partial) also available. Support available to part-time students. Financial award application deadline: 2/1; financial award applicants required to submit FAFSA. *Faculty research:* Geographical information systems, hydrology, low temperature geochemistry, volcanology, paleoclimatology. Total annual research expenditures: $1.5 million. *Unit head:* Dr. William Harbert, Chair, 412-624-8783, Fax: 412-624-3914, E-mail: harbert@pitt.edu. *Application contact:* Dr. Michael Ramsey, Director of Graduate Studies, 412-624-8772, Fax: 412-624-3914, E-mail: mramsey@pitt.edu.

University of Redlands, College of Arts and Sciences, Program in Geographic Information Systems, Redlands, CA 92373-0999. Offers MS. *Entrance requirements:* For master's, 2 years of professional experience using GIS or 2 university-level GIS courses plus internship, minimum undergraduate GPA of 3.0, 2 letters of recommendation. Additional exam requirements/recommendations for international students: Required—TOEFL (minimum score 550 paper-based; 210 computer-based); Recommended—IELTS (minimum score 5.5). Electronic applications accepted. *Expenses:* Contact institution.

University of Southern California, Graduate School, Dana and David Dornsife College of Letters, Arts and Sciences, Spatial Sciences Institute, Los Angeles, CA 90089. Offers geographic information science and technology (MS, Graduate Certificate). Part-time and evening/weekend programs available. Postbaccalaureate distance learning degree programs offered (minimal on-campus study). *Faculty:* 3 full-time (2 women), 3 part-time/adjunct (0 women). *Students:* 53 full-time (26 women), 21 part-time (7 women); includes 22 minority (2 Black or African American, non-Hispanic/Latino; 2 American Indian or Alaska Native, non-Hispanic/Latino; 9 Asian, non-Hispanic/Latino; 7 Hispanic/Latino; 2 Two or more races, non-Hispanic/Latino), 5 international. 49 applicants, 88% accepted, 35 enrolled. In 2010, 22 other advanced degrees awarded. Terminal master's awarded for partial completion of doctoral program. *Degree requirements:* For master's, thesis. *Entrance requirements:* For master's, GRE. Additional exam requirements/recommendations for international students: Required—TOEFL. *Application deadline:* For fall admission, 8/1 priority date for domestic students; for spring admission, 11/1 priority date for domestic students. Applications are processed on a rolling basis. Application fee: $85. Electronic applications accepted. *Expenses:* Tuition: Full-time $31,240; part-time $1420 per unit. Required fees: $600. One-time fee: $35 full-time. Full-time tuition and fees vary according to degree level and program. *Financial support:* In 2010–11, 5 students received support, including 5 fellowships with full tuition reimbursements available (averaging $19,250 per year), 1 research assistantship with full tuition reimbursement available (averaging $19,250 per year), 8 teaching assistantships with full tuition reimbursements available (averaging $19,250 per year); health care benefits and unspecified assistantships also available. Financial award applicants required to submit FAFSA. *Faculty research:* Geocoding, geocomputation, GIS, environmental exposure estimation, spatial data accuracy and uncertainty. *Unit head:* Dr. John P. Wilson, Professor, Director of Spatial Sciences Institute, 213-740-1908, Fax: 213-740-9687, E-mail: jpwilson@usc.edu. *Application contact:* Kate A. Kelsey, Student Advisor, 213-740-8298, Fax: 213-740-9687, E-mail: kkelsey@usc.edu.

The University of Texas at Dallas, School of Economic, Political and Policy Sciences, Program in Geospatial Sciences, Richardson, TX 75080. Offers MS, PhD. Part-time and evening/weekend programs available. *Faculty:* 7 full-time (1 woman), 1 part-time/adjunct (0 women). *Students:* 19 full-time (5 women), 10 part-time (5 women); includes 3 minority (1 Black or African American, non-Hispanic/Latino; 1 Asian, non-Hispanic/Latino; 1 Hispanic/Latino), 13 international. Average age 33. 50 applicants, 46% accepted, 8 enrolled. In 2010, 19 master's, 2 doctorates awarded. *Degree requirements:* For master's, thesis (for some programs), project or thesis; internship; for doctorate, comprehensive exam, thesis/dissertation. *Entrance requirements:* For master's and doctorate, GRE General Test, minimum GPA of 3.0 in upper-level coursework in field. Additional exam requirements/recommendations for international students: Required—TOEFL (minimum score 550 paper-based; 215 computer-based). *Application deadline:* For fall admission, 7/15 for domestic students, 5/1 priority date for international students; for spring admission, 11/15 for domestic students, 9/1 priority date for international students. Applications are processed on a rolling basis. Application fee: $50 ($100 for international students). Electronic applications accepted. *Expenses:* Tuition, state resident: full-time $10,248; part-time $569 per credit hour. Tuition, nonresident: full-time $18,544; part-time $1030 per credit hour. Tuition and fees vary according to course load. *Financial support:* In 2010–11, 13 students received support, including 3 research assistantships with partial tuition reimbursements available (averaging $15,900 per year), 9 teaching assistantships with partial tuition reimbursements available (averaging $11,100 per year); career-related internships or fieldwork, Federal Work-Study, institutionally sponsored loans, scholarships/grants, and unspecified assistantships also available. Support available to part-time students. Financial award application deadline: 4/30; financial award applicants required to submit FAFSA. *Faculty research:* Urban and regional development, artificial intelligence techniques for geospatial investigation, improvement of current spatial analysis and modeling techniques, demographic studies. *Unit head:* Dr. Denis Dean, Program Head, 972-883-6852, Fax: 972-883-2735, E-mail: denis.dean@utdallas.edu. *Application contact:* Dr. Daniel A. Griffith, Associate Program Head, 972-883-4950, Fax: 972-883-2735, E-mail: dagriffith@utdallas.edu.

See Close-Up on page 811.

The University of Toledo, College of Graduate Studies, College of Language, Literature and Social Sciences, Department of Geography and Planning, Toledo, OH 43606-3390. Offers geographic information systems and applied geographics (Certificate); geography (MA); planning (MA); spatially-integrated social sciences (PhD). Part-time programs available. *Faculty:* 10. *Students:* 18 full-time (8 women), 9 part-time (5 women), 10 international. Average age 29. 32 applicants, 66% accepted, 18 enrolled. In 2010, 7 master's, 4 other advanced degrees awarded. *Degree requirements:* For master's, comprehensive exam, thesis; for doctorate, thesis/dissertation. *Entrance requirements:* For master's and doctorate, GRE General Test, A minimum 2.7 cumulative point-hour ratio (on a 4.0 scale) for all previous academic work. Three Letters of Recommendation; for Certificate, A minimum 2.7 cumulative point-hour ratio (on a 4.0 scale) for all previous academic work. Three Letters of Recommendation. Additional exam requirements/recommendations for international students: Required—TOEFL (minimum score 550 paper-based; 213 computer-based; 80 iBT), IELTS (minimum score 6.5). *Application deadline:* For fall admission, 1/15 priority date for domestic and international students. Applications are processed on a rolling basis. Application fee: $45 ($75 for international students). Electronic applications accepted. *Expenses:* Tuition, state resident: full-time $11,426; part-time $476 per credit hour. Tuition, nonresident: full-time $21,660; part-time $903 per credit hour. One-time fee: $62. *Financial support:* Research assistantships with full tuition reimbursements, teaching assistantships with full tuition reimbursements, career-related internships or fieldwork, institutionally sponsored loans, scholarships/grants, tuition waivers (full), and unspecified assistantships available. Support available to part-time students. *Unit head:* Dr. Patrick Lawrence, Chair, 419-530-4128, Fax: 419-530-7919, E-mail: patrick.lawrence@utoledo.edu. *Application contact:* Graduate School Office, 419-530-4723, Fax: 419-530-4724, E-mail: grdsch@utnet.utoledo.edu.

University of Wisconsin–Madison, Graduate School, College of Letters and Science, Department of Geography, Madison, WI 53706-1380. Offers cartography and geographic information systems (MS); geographic information systems (Certificate); geography (MS, PhD). Part-time programs available. *Degree requirements:* For master's, thesis; for doctorate, thesis/dissertation; for Certificate, internship. *Entrance requirements:* For master's and doctorate, GRE General Test, minimum GPA of 3.25. Electronic applications accepted. *Expenses:* Tuition, state resident: full-time $9887; part-time $617.96 per credit. Tuition, nonresident: full-time $24,054; part-time $1503.40 per credit. Required fees: $67.63 per credit. Tuition and fees vary according to reciprocity agreements. *Faculty research:* Physical geography, urban/historical geography, people-environment, history of cartography, GIS.

University of Wisconsin–Milwaukee, Graduate School, School of Architecture and Urban Planning, Department of Urban Planning, Milwaukee, WI 53201-0413. Offers geographic information systems (Certificate); real estate development (Certificate); urban planning (MUP); M Arch/MUP; MPA/MUP; MUP/MS. *Accreditation:* ACSP. Part-time programs available. *Faculty:* 5 full-time (2 women). *Students:* 40 full-time (14 women), 28 part-time (11 women); includes 3 Black or African American, non-Hispanic/Latino; 1 American Indian or Alaska Native, non-

Hispanic/Latino; 3 Asian, non-Hispanic/Latino; 1 Hispanic/Latino, 3 international. Average age 29. 75 applicants, 72% accepted, 28 enrolled. In 2010, 21 master's awarded. *Degree requirements:* For master's, comprehensive exam, thesis or alternative. *Entrance requirements:* For master's, GRE General Test. Additional exam requirements/recommendations for international students: Required—TOEFL (minimum score 550 paper-based; 213 computer-based; 79 iBT), IELTS (minimum score 6.5). *Application deadline:* For fall admission, 1/1 priority date for domestic students; for spring admission, 9/1 for domestic students. Applications are processed on a rolling basis. Application fee: $56 ($96 for international students). Electronic applications accepted. *Financial support:* Fellowships, research assistantships, teaching assistantships, career-related internships or fieldwork, health care benefits, and unspecified assistantships available. Support available to part-time students. Financial award application deadline: 4/15; financial award applicants required to submit FAFSA. *Unit head:* Joan Simuncak, Representative, 414-229-4015, Fax: 414-229-6976, E-mail: joanarch@uwm.edu. *Application contact:* General Information Contact, 414-229-4982, Fax: 414-229-6967, E-mail: gradschool@uwm.edu.

Virginia Commonwealth University, Graduate School, College of Humanities and Sciences, Wilder School of Government and Public Affairs, Department of Urban Studies and Planning, Program in Geographic Information Systems, Richmond, VA 23284-9005. Offers Certificate. *Students:* 7 part-time (2 women); includes 1 minority (Black or African American, non-Hispanic/Latino). 14 applicants, 100% accepted. In 2010, 22 Certificates awarded. *Entrance requirements:* Additional exam requirements/recommendations for international students: Required—TOEFL (minimum score 600 paper-based; 250 computer-based; 100 iBT); Recommended—IELTS (minimum score 6.5). *Application deadline:* Applications are processed on a rolling basis. Application fee: $50. Electronic applications accepted. *Expenses:* Tuition, state resident: full-time $4308; part-time $479 per credit hour. Tuition, nonresident: full-time $8942; part-time $994 per credit hour. Required fees: $2000; $85 per credit hour. Tuition and fees vary according to course level, course load, degree level, campus/location and program. *Unit head:* Dr. I-Shian Suen, Program Chair, 804-828-2721, E-mail: isuen@vcu.edu. *Application contact:* Dr. I-Shian Suen, Program Chair, 804-828-2721, E-mail: isuen@vcu.edu.

Virginia Polytechnic Institute and State University, Graduate School, College of Natural Resources and Environment, Department of Geography, Program in Geospatial and Environmental Analysis, Blacksburg, VA 24061. Offers PhD. *Expenses:* Tuition, state resident: full-time $9399; part-time $488 per credit hour. Tuition, nonresident: full-time $17,854; part-time $957.75 per credit hour. Required fees: $1534. Full-time tuition and fees vary according to program.

Virginia Polytechnic Institute and State University, Graduate School, Intercollege, Certificate Programs, Blacksburg, VA 24061. Offers collaborative community leadership (Certificate); future professoriate (Certificate); geospatial information technology (Certificate); international research and development (Certificate); macromolecular interfaces with life sciences (Certificate); qualitative resource assessment (Certificate). *Students:* 61 part-time (29 women); includes 9 Black or African American, non-Hispanic/Latino; 2 Asian, non-Hispanic/Latino; 1 Hispanic/Latino, 2 international. Average age 40. 51 applicants, 96% accepted, 32 enrolled. In 2010, 135 Certificates awarded. *Entrance requirements:* Additional exam requirements/recommendations for international students: Required—TOEFL (minimum score 550 paper-based; 213 computer-based). *Application deadline:* For fall admission, 7/1 for domestic and international students; for spring admission, 12/1 for domestic and international students. Application fee: $65. *Expenses:* Tuition, state resident: full-time $9399; part-time $488 per credit hour. Tuition, nonresident: full-time $17,854; part-time $957.75 per credit hour. Required fees: $1534. Full-time tuition and fees vary according to program. *Financial support:* Career-related internships or fieldwork, Federal Work-Study, scholarships/grants, health care benefits, and unspecified assistantships available. *Unit head:* By Program. *Application contact:* By Program.

West Chester University of Pennsylvania, Office of Graduate Studies, College of Business and Public Affairs, Department of Geography and Planning, West Chester, PA 19383. Offers geographic technology (Certificate); geography (MA); regional planning (MPA, MSA); urban regional planning (Certificate). Part-time and evening/weekend programs available. *Students:* 18 full-time (8 women), 18 part-time (6 women); includes 7 minority (6 Black or African American, non-Hispanic/Latino; 1 Hispanic/Latino), 2 international. Average age 28. 18 applicants, 89% accepted, 11 enrolled. In 2010, 8 master's, 6 other advanced degrees awarded. *Degree requirements:* For master's, comprehensive exam, thesis optional. *Entrance requirements:* For master's, GRE, GMAT, or MAT, minimum GPA of 2.8, resume, two letters of recommendation; for Certificate, minimum GPA of 2.8, resume, two letters of recommendation. Additional exam requirements/recommendations for international students: Required—TOEFL (minimum score 550 paper-based; 213 computer-based; 80 iBT). *Application deadline:* For fall admission, 4/15 priority date for domestic students, 3/15 for international students; for spring admission, 10/15 for domestic students, 9/1 for international students. Applications are processed on a rolling basis. Application fee: $35. Electronic applications accepted. *Expenses:* Tuition, state resident: full-time $6966; part-time $387 per credit. Tuition, nonresident: full-time $11,146; part-time $619 per credit. Required fees: $1614.40; $133.24 per credit. Part-time tuition and fees vary according to campus/location. *Financial support:* Unspecified assistantships available. Support available to part-time students. Financial award application deadline: 2/15; financial award applicants required to submit FAFSA. *Faculty research:* Environmental education, land use/suburban planning, landscapes of Catalunya, transportation planning, housing, environmental planning. *Unit head:* Dr. Joan Welch, Chair and Graduate Coordinator for the Geography Programs, 610-436-2940, E-mail: jwelch@wcupa.edu. *Application contact:* Dr. Dottie Ives Dewey, Graduate Coordinator for the Urban and Regional Planning Programs, 610-436-2746, E-mail: divesdewey@wcupa.edu.

Western Illinois University, School of Graduate Studies, College of Arts and Sciences, Department of Biological Sciences, Macomb, IL 61455-1390. Offers biological sciences (MS); environmental geographic information systems (Certificate); zoo and aquarium studies (Certificate). Part-time programs available. *Students:* 64 full-time (41 women), 31 part-time (22 women); includes 10 minority (4 Black or African American, non-Hispanic/Latino; 1 Asian, non-Hispanic/Latino; 4 Hispanic/Latino; 1 Two or more races, non-Hispanic/Latino), 7 international. Average age 26. 60 applicants, 67% accepted. In 2010, 23 master's, 15 other advanced degrees awarded. *Degree requirements:* For master's, thesis or alternative. *Entrance requirements:* Additional exam requirements/recommendations for international students: Required—TOEFL (minimum score 550 paper-based; 213 computer-based; 80 iBT); Recommended—IELTS. *Application deadline:* Applications are processed on a rolling basis. Application fee: $30. Electronic applications accepted. *Expenses:* Tuition, state resident: full-time $6370; part-time $265.40 per credit hour. Tuition, nonresident: full-time $12,740; part-time $530.80 per credit hour. Required fees: $75.67 per credit hour. *Financial support:* In 2010–11, 28 students received support, including 10 research assistantships with full tuition reimbursements available (averaging $7,280 per year), 18 teaching assistantships with full tuition reimbursements available (averaging $8,400 per year). Financial award applicants required to submit FAFSA. *Unit head:* Dr. Michael Romano, Chairperson, 309-298-1546. *Application contact:* Evelyn Hoing, Assistant Director of Graduate Studies, 309-298-1806, Fax: 309-298-2345, E-mail: grad-office@wiu.edu.

Western Illinois University, School of Graduate Studies, College of Arts and Sciences, Department of Geography, Macomb, IL 61455-1390. Offers community development (Certificate); environmental GIS (Certificate); geography (MA). Part-time programs available. *Students:* 13 full-time (3 women), 5 part-time (4 women); includes 3 minority (1 Black or African American, non-Hispanic/Latino; 1 Asian, non-Hispanic/Latino; 1 Hispanic/Latino), 1 international. Average age 32. 9 applicants, 78% accepted. In 2010, 7 master's, 7 other advanced degrees awarded. *Degree requirements:* For master's, thesis or alternative. *Entrance requirements:* Additional exam requirements/recommendations for international students: Required—TOEFL (minimum score 550 paper-based; 213 computer-based; 80 iBT). *Application deadline:* Applications are processed on a rolling basis. Application fee: $30. Electronic applications accepted. *Expenses:* Tuition, state resident: full-time $6370; part-time $265.40 per credit hour. Tuition, nonresident: full-time $12,740; part-time $530.80 per credit hour. Required fees: $75.67 per credit hour. *Financial support:* In 2010–11, 11 students received support, including 11 research assistantships with full tuition reimbursements available (averaging $7,280 per year). Financial award applicants required to submit FAFSA. *Unit head:* Dr. Sam Thompson, Chairperson, 309-298-1648. *Application contact:* Evelyn Hoing, Assistant Director of Graduate Studies, 309-298-1806, Fax: 309-298-2345, E-mail: grad-office@wiu.edu.

Western Michigan University, Graduate College, College of Arts and Sciences, Department of Geography, Kalamazoo, MI 49008. Offers geographic information science (Graduate Certificate); geography (MA). *Degree requirements:* For master's, thesis, internship.

West Virginia University, Eberly College of Arts and Sciences, Department of Geology and Geography, Program in Geography, Morgantown, WV 26506. Offers energy and environmental resources (MA); geographic information systems (PhD); geography-regional development (PhD); GIS/cartographic analysis (MA); regional development (MA). Part-time programs available. *Degree requirements:* For master's, thesis, oral and written exams; for doctorate, comprehensive exam, thesis/dissertation, oral and written exams. *Entrance requirements:* For master's and doctorate, GRE General Test, minimum GPA of 3.0. Additional exam requirements/recommendations for international students: Required—TOEFL. Electronic applications accepted. *Faculty research:* Space, place and development, geographic information science, environmental geography.

Geography

Appalachian State University, Cratis D. Williams Graduate School, Department of Geography and Planning, Boone, NC 28608. Offers geography (MA), including GIS, planning. Part-time programs available. Postbaccalaureate distance learning degree programs offered (no on-campus study). *Faculty:* 18 full-time (5 women), 1 part-time/adjunct (0 women). *Students:* 21 full-time (9 women), 21 part-time (13 women); includes 1 Hispanic/Latino. 52 applicants, 73% accepted, 25 enrolled. In 2010, 26 master's awarded. *Degree requirements:* For master's, comprehensive exam, thesis or alternative. *Entrance requirements:* For master's, GRE General Test, 3 letters of recommendation. Additional exam requirements/recommendations for international students: Required—TOEFL (minimum score 570 paper-based; 230 computer-based; 79 iBT), IELTS (minimum score 6.5). *Application deadline:* For fall admission, 7/1 for domestic students, 2/1 for international students; for spring admission, 11/1 for domestic students, 7/1 for international students. Applications are processed on a rolling basis. Application fee: $55. Electronic applications accepted. *Expenses:* Tuition, state resident: full-time $3428; part-time $428 per unit. Tuition, nonresident: full-time $14,518; part-time $1814 per unit. Required fees: $2320; $344 per unit. Tuition and fees vary according to campus/location. *Financial support:* In 2010–11, 10 research assistantships (averaging $8,000 per year) were awarded; fellowships, teaching assistantships, career-related internships or fieldwork, Federal Work-Study, scholarships/grants, and unspecified assistantships also available. Financial award application deadline: 4/1; financial award applicants required to submit FAFSA. *Faculty research:* Global change, climatology, production cartography, geographic information systems, North Carolina geography, Latin America. Total annual research expenditures: $273,000. *Unit head:* Dr. James Young, Chairperson, 828-262-3000, Fax: 828-262-3067. *Application contact:* Dr. Kathleen Schroeder, Graduate Program Director, 828-262-3000.

Arizona State University, College of Liberal Arts and Sciences, School of Geographical Sciences, Tempe, AZ 85287-5302. Offers atmospheric science (Graduate Certificate); geographic education (MAS); geographic information systems (MAS); geographical information science (Graduate Certificate); geography (MA, PhD); transportation systems (Graduate Certificate); urban and environmental planning (MUEP). *Faculty:* 34 full-time (9 women), 2 part-time/adjunct (both women). *Students:* 125 full-time (40 women), 47 part-time (25 women); includes 24 minority (4 Black or African American, non-Hispanic/Latino; 1 American Indian or Alaska Native, non-Hispanic/Latino; 1 Asian, non-Hispanic/Latino; 16 Hispanic/Latino; 2 Two or more races, non-Hispanic/Latino), 34 international. Average age 30. 261 applicants, 56% accepted, 79 enrolled. In 2010, 76 master's, 3 doctorates, 13 other advanced degrees awarded. Terminal master's awarded for partial completion of doctoral program. *Degree requirements:* For master's, thesis, interactive Program of Study (iPOS) submitted before completing 50 percent of required credit hours; for doctorate, comprehensive exam, thesis/dissertation, interactive Program of Study (iPOS) submitted before completing 50 percent of required credit hours. *Entrance requirements:* For master's and doctorate, GRE, minimum GPA of 3.0 or equivalent in last 2 years of work leading to bachelor's degree. Additional exam requirements/recommendations for international students: Required—TOEFL, IELTS, or Pearson Test of English. *Application deadline:* For fall admission, 1/15 for domestic and international students. Applications are processed on a rolling basis. Application fee: $70 ($90 for international students). Electronic applications accepted. *Expenses:* Contact institution. *Financial support:* In 2010–11, 25 research assistantships with full and partial tuition reimbursements (averaging $15,546 per year), 50 teaching assistantships with full and partial tuition reimbursements (averaging $10,686 per year) were awarded; fellowships with full tuition reimbursements, career-related internships or fieldwork, Federal Work-Study, institutionally sponsored loans, scholarships/grants, and tuition waivers (full and partial) also available. Financial award application deadline: 3/1; financial award applicants required to submit FAFSA. Total annual research expenditures: $2.6 million. *Unit head:* Dr. Luc Anselin, Chair and Director, 480-965-7533, E-mail: luc.anselin@asu.edu. *Application contact:* Graduate Admissions, 480-965-6113.

Auburn University, Graduate School, College of Sciences and Mathematics, Department of Geology and Geography, Auburn University, AL 36849. Offers geography (MS); geology (MS). Part-time programs available. *Faculty:* 14 full-time (2 women), 1 part-time/adjunct (0 women). *Students:* 13 full-time (3 women), 8 part-time (3 women), 4 international. Average age 28. 25 applicants, 56% accepted, 7 enrolled. In 2010, 5 master's awarded. *Degree requirements:* For master's, computer language or geographic information systems, field camp. *Entrance requirements:* For master's, GRE General Test. *Application deadline:* For fall admission, 7/7 for domestic students; for spring admission, 11/24 for domestic students. Applications are processed on a rolling basis. Application fee: $50 ($60 for international students). Electronic applications accepted. *Expenses:* Tuition, state resident: full-time $7002. Tuition, nonresident: full-time $21,898. International tuition: $22,116 full-time. Required fees: $892. Tuition and fees vary according to course load and program. *Financial support:* Research assistantships, teaching assistantships, Federal Work-Study available. Support available to part-time students. Financial award application deadline: 3/15; financial award applicants required to submit FAFSA. *Faculty research:* Empirical magma dynamics and melt migration, ore mineralogy, role of terrestrial plant biomass in deposition, metamorphic petrology and isotope geochemistry, reef development, crinoid topology. *Unit head:* Dr. Charles E. Savrda, Professor/Interim Dean,

Geography

Auburn University (continued)

334-844-4282. *Application contact:* Dr. George Flowers, Dean of the Graduate School, 334-844-2125.

Ball State University, Graduate School, College of Sciences and Humanities, Department of Geography, Muncie, IN 47306-1099. Offers MS. *Faculty:* 8. *Students:* 12 full-time (7 women), 3 part-time (1 woman), 2 international. Average age 29. 12 applicants, 75% accepted, 5 enrolled.Application fee: $50. *Expenses:* Tuition, state resident: full-time $6160; part-time $299 per credit hour. Tuition, nonresident: full-time $16,020; part-time $783 per credit hour. Required fees: $2278; $95 per credit hour. *Financial support:* In 2010–11, 7 teaching assistantships with full tuition reimbursements (averaging $9,103 per year) were awarded. Financial award application deadline: 3/1. *Faculty research:* Remote sensing, tourism and recreation, Latin American urbanization. *Unit head:* Dr. Gopalan Venugopal, Chairman, 765-285-1776. *Application contact:* Dr. Christopher Airriess, Associate Provost for Research and Dean of the Graduate School, 765-285-1614, E-mail: cairriess@bsu.edu.

Boston University, Graduate School of Arts and Sciences, Department of Geography and Environment, Boston, MA 02215. Offers energy and environmental analysis (MA); environmental remote sensing and GIs (MA); geography (MA); geography and environment (PhD); international relations and environmental policy (MA). *Students:* 55 full-time (23 women), 10 part-time (3 women); includes 3 minority (1 Asian, non-Hispanic/Latino; 1 Hispanic/Latino; 1 Two or more races, non-Hispanic/Latino), 17 international. Average age 28. 64 applicants, 23% accepted, 5 enrolled. In 2010, 1 master's, 2 doctorates awarded. Terminal master's awarded for partial completion of doctoral program. *Degree requirements:* For master's, one foreign language, comprehensive exam, thesis; for doctorate, one foreign language, comprehensive exam, thesis/dissertation. *Entrance requirements:* For master's and doctorate, GRE General Test, GRE Subject Test, 3 letters of recommendation. Additional exam requirements/recommendations for international students: Required—TOEFL (minimum score 600 paper-based; 250 computer-based). *Application deadline:* For fall admission, 7/1 for domestic and international students; for spring admission, 11/15 for domestic and international students. Application fee: $70. Electronic applications accepted. *Expenses:* Tuition: Full-time $39,314; part-time $1228 per credit. Required fees: $40 per semester. *Financial support:* In 2010–11, 33 students received support, including 2 fellowships with full tuition reimbursements available (averaging $19,300 per year), 20 research assistantships with full tuition reimbursements available (averaging $18,800 per year), 11 teaching assistantships with full tuition reimbursements available (averaging $18,800 per year); Federal Work-Study and unspecified assistantships also available. Support available to part-time students. Financial award application deadline: 1/15; financial award applicants required to submit FAFSA. Total annual research expenditures: $1.2 million. *Unit head:* Robert Kaufmann, Chairman, 617-353-3940, Fax: 617-353-8399, E-mail: kaufmann@bu.edu. *Application contact:* Christopher DeVits, Graduate Program Coordinator, 617-353-7554, Fax: 617-353-8399, E-mail: cdevits@bu.edu.

Brigham Young University, Graduate Studies, College of Family, Home, and Social Sciences, Department of Geography, Provo, UT 84602-1001. Offers MS. *Faculty:* 4 full-time (0 women). *Students:* 1 (woman) full-time. Average age 26. In 2010, 3 master's awarded. *Expenses:* Tuition: Full-time $5580; part-time $310 per credit hour. Tuition and fees vary according to program and student's religious affiliation. *Faculty research:* Global studies, physical environment, urban planning, travel and tourism, geospatial intelligence, geographic information systems. *Unit head:* Dr. J. Matthew Shumway, Chair, 801-422-2707, Fax: 801-422-0266, E-mail: jms7@byu.edu. *Application contact:* Adviser, 801-422-4541, Fax: 801-378-5238, E-mail: gradstudies@byu.edu.

Brock University, Faculty of Graduate Studies, Faculty of Social Sciences, Program in Geography, St. Catharines, ON L2S 3A1, Canada. Offers MA. Part-time programs available. *Degree requirements:* For master's, thesis optional. *Entrance requirements:* For master's, honors degree. Additional exam requirements/recommendations for international students: Required—TOEFL (minimum score 550 paper-based; 213 computer-based; 80 iBT), IELTS (minimum score 6.5), TWE (minimum score 4).

California State University, Chico, Graduate School, College of Behavioral and Social Sciences, Department of Geography and Planning, Program in Geography, Chico, CA 95929-0722. Offers MA. Part-time programs available. *Students:* 2 full-time (1 woman), 5 part-time (4 women); includes 1 American Indian or Alaska Native, non-Hispanic/Latino; 1 Hispanic/Latino. Average age 40. 6 applicants, 83% accepted, 3 enrolled. In 2010, 1 master's awarded. *Entrance requirements:* For master's, GRE General Test, 2 letters of recommendation. Additional exam requirements/recommendations for international students: Required—TOEFL (minimum score 550 paper-based; 213 computer-based; 80 iBT), IELTS (minimum score 6.5). *Application deadline:* For fall admission, 3/1 priority date for domestic students, 3/1 for international students; for spring admission, 9/15 priority date for domestic students, 9/15 for international students. Applications are processed on a rolling basis. Application fee: $55. Electronic applications accepted. *Unit head:* Dr. Dean Fairbanks, Graduate Coordinator, 530-898-5780. *Application contact:* Dr. Paul Melcon, Graduate Coordinator, 530-898-6871.

California State University, East Bay, Office of Academic Programs and Graduate Studies, College of Letters, Arts, and Social Sciences, Department of Geography and Environmental Studies, Hayward, CA 94542-3000. Offers geography (MA). Part-time programs available. *Faculty:* 6 full-time (1 woman). *Students:* 6 full-time (2 women), 14 part-time (11 women); includes 1 Black or African American, non-Hispanic/Latino; 1 Asian, non-Hispanic/Latino; 2 Two or more races, non-Hispanic/Latino. Average age 39. 20 applicants, 65% accepted, 2 enrolled. In 2010, 3 master's awarded. *Degree requirements:* For master's, variable foreign language requirement, project or thesis. *Entrance requirements:* For master's, GRE, minimum GPA of 3.0 in field. Additional exam requirements/recommendations for international students: Required—TOEFL (minimum score 550 paper-based; 213 computer-based). *Application deadline:* For fall admission, 6/30 for domestic and international students. Applications are processed on a rolling basis. Application fee: $55. Electronic applications accepted. *Financial support:* Fellowships, teaching assistantships, career-related internships or fieldwork, Federal Work-Study, institutionally sponsored loans, and scholarships/grants available. Support available to part-time students. Financial award application deadline: 3/2; financial award applicants required to submit FAFSA. *Unit head:* Dr. David Larson, Chair, 510-885-3193 Ext. 3193, Fax: 510-885-2353, E-mail: david.larson@csueastbay.edu. *Application contact:* Dr. Donna Wiley, Interim Associate Director, 510-885-2928, Fax: 510-885-4777, E-mail: donna.wiley@csueastbay.edu.

California State University, Fullerton, Graduate Studies, College of Humanities and Social Sciences, Department of Geography, Fullerton, CA 92834-9480. Offers MA. Part-time programs available. *Students:* 9 full-time (2 women), 18 part-time (5 women); includes 1 Asian, non-Hispanic/Latino; 4 Hispanic/Latino; 1 Two or more races, non-Hispanic/Latino. Average age 31. 23 applicants, 83% accepted, 11 enrolled. In 2010, 10 master's awarded. *Degree requirements:* For master's, comprehensive exam or thesis. *Entrance requirements:* For master's, minimum GPA of 3.0, 18 undergraduate credits in field. Application fee: $55. *Financial support:* Career-related internships or fieldwork, Federal Work-Study, institutionally sponsored loans, and scholarships/grants available. Support available to part-time students. Financial award application deadline: 3/1; financial award applicants required to submit FAFSA. *Faculty research:* Human geography, physical geography. *Unit head:* Dr. John Carroll, Chair, 657-278-3161. *Application contact:* Admissions/Applications, 657-278-2371.

California State University, Long Beach, Graduate Studies, College of Liberal Arts, Department of Geography, Long Beach, CA 90840. Offers MA. Part-time programs available. *Faculty:* 10 full-time (5 women). *Students:* 9 full-time (3 women), 21 part-time (13 women); includes 2 Asian, non-Hispanic/Latino; 3 Hispanic/Latino, 1 international. Average age 32. 22 applicants, 64% accepted, 7 enrolled. In 2010, 3 master's awarded. *Degree requirements:* For master's, thesis. *Application deadline:* For fall admission, 4/15 for domestic students; for spring admission, 10/15 for domestic students. Applications are processed on a rolling basis. Application fee: $55. Electronic applications accepted. *Financial support:* Career-related internships or fieldwork, Federal Work-Study, institutionally sponsored loans, and scholarships/grants available. Financial award application deadline: 3/2. *Faculty research:* Demography, geographic information systems, world landforms and societies. *Unit head:* Dr. Vincent J. Del Casino, Chair, 562-985-4977, Fax: 562-985-8993, E-mail: vdelcasi@csulb.edu. *Application contact:* Dr. Christine Rodrigue, Graduate Advisor, 562-985-2358, Fax: 562-985-8993, E-mail: rodrigue@csulb.edu.

California State University, Los Angeles, Graduate Studies, College of Natural and Social Sciences, Department of Geography and Urban Analysis, Los Angeles, CA 90032-8530. Offers geography (MA). Part-time and evening/weekend programs available. *Faculty:* 2 full-time (1 woman), 1 part-time/adjunct (0 women). *Students:* 4 full-time (1 woman), 19 part-time (7 women); includes 11 minority (1 Black or African American, non-Hispanic/Latino; 3 Asian, non-Hispanic/Latino; 7 Hispanic/Latino), 3 international. Average age 34. 14 applicants, 100% accepted, 7 enrolled. In 2010, 10 master's awarded. *Degree requirements:* For master's, one foreign language, comprehensive exam or thesis. *Entrance requirements:* Additional exam requirements/recommendations for international students: Required—TOEFL (minimum score 500 paper-based; 173 computer-based). *Application deadline:* For fall admission, 5/1 for domestic and international students. Applications are processed on a rolling basis. Application fee: $55. Electronic applications accepted. *Financial support:* Career-related internships or fieldwork and Federal Work-Study available. Support available to part-time students. Financial award application deadline: 3/1. *Faculty research:* Technique focus-air photography, cartography, locational analysis. *Unit head:* Dr. Ali Modarres, Chair, 323-343-2220, Fax: 323-343-6494, E-mail: amodarr@calstatela.edu. *Application contact:* Dr. Alan Muchlinski, Dean of Graduate Studies, 323-343-3820, Fax: 323-343-5653, E-mail: amuchli@exchange.calstatela.edu.

California State University, Northridge, Graduate Studies, College of Social and Behavioral Sciences, Department of Geography, Northridge, CA 91330. Offers MA. Part-time programs available. *Degree requirements:* For master's, one foreign language, thesis. *Entrance requirements:* For master's, GRE General Test or minimum GPA of 3.0. Additional exam requirements/recommendations for international students: Required—TOEFL.

Carleton University, Faculty of Graduate Studies, Faculty of Arts and Social Sciences, Department of Geography and Environmental Studies, Ottawa, ON K1S 5B6, Canada. Offers geography (M Sc, MA, PhD). *Degree requirements:* For master's, thesis, seminar; for doctorate, one foreign language, thesis/dissertation, 2 comprehensive exams. *Entrance requirements:* For master's, honors degree; for doctorate, master's degree in geography. Additional exam requirements/recommendations for international students: Required—TOEFL. *Faculty research:* Human dimensions of global environmental change, winter environments, population studies, historical geography, globalization.

Central Connecticut State University, School of Graduate Studies, School of Arts and Sciences, Department of Geography, New Britain, CT 06050-4010. Offers MS. Part-time and evening/weekend programs available. *Faculty:* 11 full-time (3 women), 8 part-time/adjunct (1 woman). *Students:* 10 full-time (5 women), 16 part-time (8 women); includes 4 minority (2 Hispanic/Latino; 2 Two or more races, non-Hispanic/Latino), 2 international. Average age 30. 20 applicants, 70% accepted, 9 enrolled. In 2010, 3 master's awarded. *Degree requirements:* For master's, comprehensive exam, thesis or alternative. *Entrance requirements:* For master's, minimum undergraduate GPA of 2.7. Additional exam requirements/recommendations for international students: Required—TOEFL. *Application deadline:* For fall admission, 7/1 for domestic students; for spring admission, 12/1 for domestic students. Applications are processed on a rolling basis. Application fee: $50. Electronic applications accepted. *Expenses:* Tuition, area resident: Full-time $5012; part-time $470 per credit. Tuition, state resident: full-time $7518; part-time $482 per credit. Tuition, nonresident: full-time $13,962; part-time $482 per credit. Required fees: $3772. One-time fee: $62 part-time. *Financial support:* In 2010–11, 7 students received support, including 1 research assistantship; career-related internships or fieldwork, Federal Work-Study, scholarships/grants, and unspecified assistantships also available. Support available to part-time students. Financial award application deadline: 2/15; financial award applicants required to submit FAFSA. *Faculty research:* Regional planning, environmental protection, tourism, computer mapping and geographic information systems. *Unit head:* Dr. Peter Kyem, Chair, 860-832-2785. *Application contact:* Dr. Peter Kyem, Chair, 860-832-2785.

Chicago State University, School of Graduate and Professional Studies, College of Arts and Sciences, Department of Geography, Sociology, Economics, and Anthropology, Chicago, IL 60628. Offers geography and economic development (MA). *Entrance requirements:* For master's, minimum GPA of 2.75.

Clark University, Graduate School, Department of Geography, Worcester, MA 01610-1477. Offers geographic information science (MA); geography (PhD). *Faculty:* 16 full-time (5 women), 1 part-time/adjunct (0 women). *Students:* 45 full-time (20 women), 21 international. Average age 29. 98 applicants, 21% accepted, 15 enrolled. In 2010, 9 master's, 9 doctorates awarded. *Degree requirements:* For doctorate, thesis/dissertation. *Entrance requirements:* For doctorate, GRE General Test. Additional exam requirements/recommendations for international students: Required—TOEFL. *Application deadline:* For fall admission, 12/31 priority date for domestic students. Applications are processed on a rolling basis. Application fee: $50. *Expenses:* Tuition: Full-time $37,000; part-time $1156 per credit hour. Required fees: $30; $1156 per credit hour. *Financial support:* In 2010–11, 3 fellowships with full tuition reimbursements (averaging $15,700 per year), 14 research assistantships with full tuition reimbursements (averaging $15,700 per year), 13 teaching assistantships with full tuition reimbursements (averaging $15,700 per year) were awarded; career-related internships or fieldwork and tuition waivers (full) also available. *Faculty research:* Global environmental change, geographic information systems, natural and technological hazards, water resources, urbanization. Total annual research expenditures: $2 million. *Unit head:* Dr. Anthony Bebbington, Director, 508-793-7336. *Application contact:* Christine Silva, Admission Coordinator, 508-793-7337, Fax: 508-793-8881, E-mail: geography@clarku.edu.

Concordia University, School of Graduate Studies, Faculty of Arts and Science, Department of Geography, Planning and Environment, Montréal, QC H3G 1M8, Canada. Offers environmental impact assessment (Diploma); geography, urban and environmental studies (M Sc).

Concordia University, School of Graduate Studies, Faculty of Arts and Science, Department of Political Science, Montréal, QC H3G 1M8, Canada. Offers political science (PhD); public policy and public administration (MA), including geography. *Degree requirements:* For master's, one foreign language, comprehensive exam, thesis optional, internship. *Entrance requirements:* For master's, honors degree or equivalent. Additional exam requirements/recommendations for international students: Required—TOEFL. *Faculty research:* International public policy and administration, Quebec public administration, public policy and social/political theory, geography and public policy, public administration and decision making.

Concord University, Graduate Studies, Athens, WV 24712-1000. Offers educational leadership and supervision (M Ed); geography (M Ed); health promotion (M Ed); reading specialist (M Ed). Part-time and evening/weekend programs available. Postbaccalaureate distance learning degree programs offered (no on-campus study). *Faculty:* 16 full-time (7 women). *Students:* 2 full-time (both women), 247 part-time (173 women); includes 6 Black or African American, non-Hispanic/Latino; 1 American Indian or Alaska Native, non-Hispanic/Latino; 2 Asian, non-Hispanic/Latino. Average age 36. 124 applicants, 71% accepted, 88 enrolled. In 2010, 27 master's awarded. *Entrance requirements:* For master's, GRE or MAT, baccalaureate degree with minimum GPA of 2.5 from regionally-accredited institution; teaching license; 2 letters of recommendation; completed disposition assessment form. *Application deadline:* Applications are processed on a rolling basis. Application fee: $25. Electronic applications accepted. *Expenses:* Tuition, state resident: full-time $2674; part-time $297 per credit hour. Tuition, nonresident: full-time $4697; part-time $522 per credit hour. Required fees: $18 per term. One-time fee: $25. Tuition and fees vary according to course load. *Financial support:* Tuition waivers and unspecified assistantships available. *Unit head:* Dr. Cheryl Barnes, Interim Director, 304-384-5148, E-mail: ctrull@concord.edu. *Application contact:* Wendy Bailey, 304-384-6223, E-mail: baileyw@concord.edu.

East Carolina University, Graduate School, Thomas Harriot College of Arts and Sciences, Department of Geography, Greenville, NC 27858-4353. Offers MA. Part-time and evening/weekend programs available. *Degree requirements:* For master's, one foreign language, comprehensive exam, thesis optional. *Entrance requirements:* For master's, GRE General Test. Additional exam requirements/recommendations for international students: Required—TOEFL. *Expenses:* Tuition, state resident: full-time $3130; part-time $391.25 per credit hour. Tuition, nonresident: full-time $13,817; part-time $1727.13 per credit hour. Required fees: $1916; $239.50 per credit hour. Tuition and fees vary according to campus/location and program.

Eastern Michigan University, Graduate School, College of Arts and Sciences, Department of Geography and Geology, Programs in Geography and Geology, Ypsilanti, MI 48197. Offers geography (MA, MS); water resources (Graduate Certificate). Part-time and evening/weekend programs available. Postbaccalaureate distance learning degree programs offered (minimal on-campus study). *Students:* 1 full-time (0 women). Average age 27. *Degree requirements:* For master's, thesis optional. *Entrance requirements:* Additional exam requirements/recommendations for international students: Required—TOEFL. *Application deadline:* Applications are processed on a rolling basis. Application fee: $35. *Financial support:* Fellowships, research assistantships with full tuition reimbursements, teaching assistantships with full tuition reimbursements, career-related internships or fieldwork, Federal Work-Study, institutionally sponsored loans, traineeships, and unspecified assistantships available. Support available to part-time students. Financial award applicants required to submit FAFSA. *Application contact:* Dr. Andrew Nazzaro, Program Advisor, 734-487-8486, Fax: 734-487-6979, E-mail: andrew.nazzaro@emich.edu.

Florida Atlantic University, Charles E. Schmidt College of Science, Department of Geosciences, Boca Raton, FL 33431-0991. Offers geography (MA); geology (MS); geosciences (PhD). Part-time programs available. *Faculty:* 14 full-time (3 women), 1 part-time/adjunct (0 women). *Students:* 24 full-time (14 women), 12 part-time (5 women); includes 5 minority (1 Asian, non-Hispanic/Latino; 4 Hispanic/Latino), 3 international. Average age 34. 25 applicants, 52% accepted, 11 enrolled. In 2010, 6 master's awarded. *Degree requirements:* For master's, thesis (for some programs). *Entrance requirements:* For master's, GRE General Test, minimum GPA of 3.0. *Application deadline:* For fall admission, 3/15 for domestic and international students; for spring admission, 10/15 for domestic and international students. Applications are processed on a rolling basis. Application fee: $30. Electronic applications accepted. *Expenses:* Tuition, area resident: Part-time $319.96 per credit. Tuition, state resident: part-time $319.96 per credit. Tuition, nonresident: part-time $926.42 per credit. *Financial support:* Research assistantships with partial tuition reimbursements, teaching assistantships with partial tuition reimbursements, career-related internships or fieldwork, Federal Work-Study, institutionally sponsored loans, and unspecified assistantships available. *Faculty research:* GIS applications, paleontology, hydrogeology, economic development. *Unit head:* Dr. Russell Ivy, Chair, 561-297-3295, Fax: 561-297-2745, E-mail: ivy@fau.edu. *Application contact:* Dr. David Warburton, Graduate Coordinator, 561-297-3312, Fax: 561-297-2745, E-mail: warburto@fau.edu.

Florida State University, The Graduate School, College of Social Sciences and Public Policy, Department of Geography, Tallahassee, FL 32306. Offers geographic information science (MS); geography (MA, MS, PhD). *Faculty:* 9 full-time (2 women), 8 part-time/adjunct (2 women). *Students:* 58 full-time (26 women), 29 part-time (15 women); includes 2 Black or African American, non-Hispanic/Latino; 1 American Indian or Alaska Native, non-Hispanic/Latino; 4 Asian, non-Hispanic/Latino; 3 Hispanic/Latino, 7 international. Average age 29. 44 applicants, 73% accepted, 26 enrolled. In 2010, 29 master's, 4 doctorates awarded. Terminal master's awarded for partial completion of doctoral program. *Degree requirements:* For master's, thesis (for some programs); for doctorate, comprehensive exam, thesis/dissertation. *Entrance requirements:* For master's and doctorate, GRE General Test, minimum GPA of 3.0. Additional exam requirements/recommendations for international students: Required—TOEFL. *Application deadline:* For fall admission, 1/15 priority date for domestic students, 12/15 priority date for international students; for spring admission, 11/1 priority date for domestic students, 9/15 priority date for international students. Applications are processed on a rolling basis. Application fee: $30. Electronic applications accepted. *Expenses:* Tuition, state resident: full-time $8238.24. *Financial support:* In 2010–11, 23 students received support, including 3 research assistantships with full tuition reimbursements available (averaging $13,000 per year), 20 teaching assistantships with full tuition reimbursements available (averaging $13,000 per year); fellowships with full tuition reimbursements available, career-related internships or fieldwork, Federal Work-Study, institutionally sponsored loans, scholarships/grants, health care benefits, and unspecified assistantships also available. Financial award application deadline: 1/15; financial award applicants required to submit FAFSA. *Faculty research:* Society-nature interactions, geographic information science, environmental studies, hurricanes, remote sensing, urban, transportation. Total annual research expenditures: $177,712. *Unit head:* Dr. Victor Mesev, Chair, 850-645-2498, Fax: 850-644-5913, E-mail: vmesev@fsu.edu. *Application contact:* Dr. Mark Horner, Graduate Director, 850-644-8377, Fax: 850-644-5193, E-mail: mhorner@fsu.edu.

Fort Hays State University, Graduate School, College of Arts and Sciences, Department of Geosciences, Program in Geosciences, Hays, KS 67601-4099. Offers geography (MS); geology (MS). *Degree requirements:* For master's, comprehensive exam, thesis. *Entrance requirements:* For master's, GRE General Test. Additional exam requirements/recommendations for international students: Required—TOEFL (minimum score 550 paper-based; 213 computer-based). Electronic applications accepted. *Faculty research:* Cretaceous and late Cenozoic stratigraphy, sedimentation, paleontology.

George Mason University, College of Science, Department of Geography and Geoinformation Science, Fairfax, VA 22030. Offers earth system science (MS); earth systems and geoinformation sciences (PhD); geographic and cartographic sciences (MS); geographic information sciences (Certificate); geoinformatics and geospatial intelligence (MS); geospatial intelligence (Certificate); remote sensing (Certificate). *Faculty:* 31 full-time (7 women), 7 part-time/adjunct (0 women). *Students:* 32 full-time (8 women), 194 part-time (69 women); includes 23 minority (4 Black or African American, non-Hispanic/Latino; 1 American Indian or Alaska Native, non-Hispanic/Latino; 6 Asian, non-Hispanic/Latino; 8 Hispanic/Latino; 1 Native Hawaiian or other Pacific Islander, non-Hispanic/Latino; 3 Two or more races, non-Hispanic/Latino), 27 international. Average age 35. 156 applicants, 74% accepted, 82 enrolled. In 2010, 23 master's, 1 doctorate, 24 other advanced degrees awarded. *Degree requirements:* For master's, thesis optional. *Entrance requirements:* For master's, GRE General Test, minimum GPA of 3.0 in last 60 hours; BS or BA in geography, cartography, or related field. Additional exam requirements/recommendations for international students: Required—TOEFL (minimum score 570 paper-based; 230 computer-based; 88 iBT). *Application deadline:* For fall admission, 5/1 for domestic students; for spring admission, 11/1 for domestic students. Application fee: $100. Electronic applications accepted. *Expenses:* Tuition, state resident: full-time $8192; part-time $440 per credit hour. Tuition, nonresident: full-time $22,952; part-time $1055 per credit hour. Required fees: $2364; $99 per credit hour. *Financial support:* In 2010–11, 23 students received support, including 2 fellowships with full tuition reimbursements available (averaging $18,000 per year), 17 research assistantships with full and partial tuition reimbursements available (averaging $16,244 per year), 4 teaching assistantships with full and partial tuition reimbursements available (averaging $10,345 per year); career-related internships or fieldwork, Federal Work-Study, scholarships/grants, unspecified assistantships, and health care benefits (full-time research or teaching assistantship recipients) also available. Support available to part-time students. Financial award application deadline: 3/1; financial award applicants required to submit FAFSA. *Faculty research:* Gender and earth science, earth science education, remote sensing, planetary geology, hydrology. Total annual research expenditures: $912,752. *Unit head:* Agouris Peggy, Chair, 703-993-9265, Fax: 703-993-9230, E-mail: pagouris@gmu.edu. *Application contact:* Tim Born, Associate Dean of Academic and Student Affairs, 703-993-4171, Fax: 703-993-9034, E-mail: tborn@gmu.edu.

The George Washington University, Columbian College of Arts and Sciences, Department of Geography, Washington, DC 20052. Offers MA. *Faculty:* 7 full-time (4 women), 12 part-time/adjunct (3 women). *Students:* 11 full-time (7 women), 12 part-time (4 women); includes 1 American Indian or Alaska Native, non-Hispanic/Latino, 1 international. Average age 28. 33 applicants, 85% accepted, 13 enrolled. In 2010, 10 master's awarded. *Degree requirements:* For master's, comprehensive exam, thesis or alternative. *Entrance requirements:* For master's, GRE General Test, BA in geography or related field, minimum GPA of 3.0. Additional exam requirements/recommendations for international students: Required—TOEFL (minimum score 550 paper-based; 213 computer-based; 80 iBT). *Application deadline:* For fall admission, 4/1 priority date for domestic students, 1/15 priority date for international students; for spring admission, 10/1 priority date for domestic students, 9/1 priority date for international students. Applications are processed on a rolling basis. Application fee: $75. Electronic applications accepted. *Financial support:* In 2010–11, 10 students received support; fellowships with tuition reimbursements available, teaching assistantships with tuition reimbursements available, Federal Work-Study, institutionally sponsored loans, and tuition waivers available. Financial award application deadline: 1/15. *Unit head:* Dr. Marie Price, Chair, 202-994-6187. *Application contact:* Information Contact, 202-994-6185, Fax: 202-994-2484.

Georgia State University, College of Arts and Sciences, Department of Geosciences, Program in Geography, Atlanta, GA 30302-3083. Offers MA. Part-time programs available. *Degree requirements:* For master's, one foreign language, thesis or alternative, written and oral exams. *Entrance requirements:* For master's, GRE General Test. Additional exam requirements/recommendations for international students: Required—TOEFL. Electronic applications accepted. *Faculty research:* Urban economics, biogeography, cartography, GIS, environmental.

Hunter College of the City University of New York, Graduate School, School of Arts and Sciences, Department of Geography, New York, NY 10021-5085. Offers analytical geography (MA); earth system science (MA); environmental and social issues (MA); geographic information science (Certificate); geographic information systems (MA); teaching earth science (MA). Part-time and evening/weekend programs available. *Faculty:* 13 full-time (7 women), 8 part-time/adjunct (1 woman). *Students:* 2 full-time (both women), 50 part-time (23 women); includes 5 Black or African American, non-Hispanic/Latino; 4 Asian, non-Hispanic/Latino; 5 Hispanic/Latino. Average age 31. 22 applicants, 82% accepted, 12 enrolled. In 2010, 15 master's, 3 other advanced degrees awarded. *Degree requirements:* For master's, comprehensive exam or thesis. *Entrance requirements:* For master's, GRE General Test, minimum B average in major, B- overall; 18 credits of course work in geography; 2 letters of recommendation; for Certificate, minimum B average in major, B- overall. Additional exam requirements/recommendations for international students: Required—TOEFL. *Application deadline:* For fall admission, 4/1 for domestic students; for spring admission, 11/1 for domestic students. Applications are processed on a rolling basis. Application fee: $125. *Financial support:* In 2010–11, 1 fellowship (averaging $3,000 per year), 2 research assistantships (averaging $10,000 per year), 10 teaching assistantships (averaging $6,000 per year) were awarded; career-related internships or fieldwork, Federal Work-Study, institutionally sponsored loans, and unspecified assistantships also available. Financial award application deadline: 3/1. *Faculty research:* Urban geography, economic geography, geographic information science, demographic methods, climate change. *Unit head:* Prof. William Solecki, Chair, 212-772-4536, Fax: 212-772-5268, E-mail: wsolecki@hunter.cuny.edu. *Application contact:* Prof. Marianna Pavlovskaya, Graduate Adviser, 212-772-5320, Fax: 212-772-5268, E-mail: mpavlov@geo.hunter.cuny.edu.

Indiana State University, College of Graduate and Professional Studies, College of Arts and Sciences, Department of Geography, Geology and Anthropology, Terre Haute, IN 47809. Offers geography (MA); geology (MS); physical geography (PhD). *Degree requirements:* For master's, thesis or alternative; for doctorate, comprehensive exam, thesis/dissertation, departmental qualifying exam. *Entrance requirements:* For doctorate, GRE General Test. Additional exam requirements/recommendations for international students: Required—TOEFL (minimum score 550 paper-based). Electronic applications accepted.

Indiana University Bloomington, University Graduate School, College of Arts and Sciences, Department of Geography, Bloomington, IN 47405-7000. Offers MA, MAT, MS, PhD, MSES/MA, MSES/MS. *Faculty:* 11 full-time (5 women), 14 part-time/adjunct (1 woman). *Students:* 20 full-time (10 women), 2 part-time (0 women); includes 1 minority (Asian, non-Hispanic/Latino), 6 international. Average age 32. 25 applicants, 48% accepted, 7 enrolled. In 2010, 5 master's, 4 doctorates awarded. *Degree requirements:* For master's, comprehensive exam, thesis; for doctorate, comprehensive exam, thesis/dissertation. *Entrance requirements:* For master's and doctorate, GRE General Test, minimum GPA of 3.0. Additional exam requirements/recommendations for international students: Required—TOEFL (minimum score 620 paper-based; 260 computer-based; 105 iBT). *Application deadline:* For fall admission, 2/15 priority date for domestic students, 12/15 priority date for international students; for spring admission, 11/15 priority date for domestic students, 11/1 priority date for international students. Application fee: $55 ($65 for international students). Electronic applications accepted. *Financial support:* In 2010–11, 17 students received support, including 2 fellowships with full tuition reimbursements available (averaging $15,000 per year), 1 research assistantship with full tuition reimbursement available (averaging $12,901 per year), 14 teaching assistantships with full tuition reimbursements available (averaging $12,901 per year); health care benefits also available. Financial award application deadline: 2/15; financial award applicants required to submit FAFSA. *Faculty research:* Synoptic climatology, urban and regional modeling, regional development, hydrology and statistical climatology, migration, atmospheric science, GIS human environment interaction, human geography. Total annual research expenditures: $2 million. *Unit head:* Dr. Scott Robeson, Chair and Professor, 812-855-6303, Fax: 812-855-1661, E-mail: srobeson@indiana.edu. *Application contact:* Susan White, Graduate Secretary, 812-855-6303, Fax: 812-855-1661, E-mail: suswhite@indiana.edu.

Indiana University of Pennsylvania, School of Graduate Studies and Research, College of Humanities and Social Sciences, Department of Geography and Regional Planning, Program in Geography, Indiana, PA 15705-1087. Offers MA, MS. Part-time programs available. *Faculty:* 8 full-time (0 women). *Students:* 24 full-time (4 women), 3 part-time (0 women); includes 2 minority (1 Asian, non-Hispanic/Latino; 1 Two or more races, non-Hispanic/Latino), 2 international. Average age 27. 32 applicants, 53% accepted, 9 enrolled. In 2010, 8 master's awarded. *Degree requirements:* For master's, thesis optional. *Entrance requirements:* For master's, GRE, 2 letters of recommendation. Additional exam requirements/recommendations for international students: Required—TOEFL. *Application deadline:* For fall admission, 7/1 priority date for domestic students; for spring admission, 11/1 for domestic students. Applications are processed on a rolling basis. Application fee: $40. *Financial support:* In 2010–11, 15 research assistantships with full and partial tuition reimbursements (averaging $5,544 per year) were awarded; Federal Work-Study also available. Support available to part-time students. Financial award application deadline: 3/15; financial award applicants required to submit FAFSA. *Unit head:* Dr. Kevin Patrick, 724-357-3767, E-mail: kevin.patrick@iup.edu. *Application contact:* Dr. John E. Benhart, Chairperson, 724-357-2250, E-mail: jbenhart@iup.edu.

The Johns Hopkins University, G. W. C. Whiting School of Engineering, Department of Geography and Environmental Engineering, Baltimore, MD 21218-2699. Offers MA, MS, MSE, PhD. *Faculty:* 15 full-time (4 women), 4 part-time/adjunct (0 women). *Students:* 69 full-time (35 women), 7 part-time (4 women); includes 13 minority (2 Black or African American, non-Hispanic/Latino; 4 Asian, non-Hispanic/Latino; 6 Hispanic/Latino; 1 Two or more races, non-Hispanic/Latino), 37 international. Average age 25. 151 applicants, 74% accepted, 35 enrolled. In 2010, 19 master's, 5 doctorates awarded. Terminal master's awarded for partial completion of doctoral program. *Median time to degree:* Of those who began their doctoral program in fall 2002, 100% received their degree in 8 years or less. *Degree requirements:* For master's, thesis (for some programs), 1 year full-time residency; for doctorate, comprehensive exam, thesis/dissertation, oral exam, 2 year full-time residency. *Entrance requirements:* For master's

Geography

The Johns Hopkins University (continued)
and doctorate, GRE General Test. Additional exam requirements/recommendations for international students: Required—TOEFL (minimum score 670 paper-based; 300 computer-based; 120 iBT); Recommended—IELTS. *Application deadline:* For fall admission, 1/15 priority date for domestic and international students. Applications are processed on a rolling basis. Application fee: $75. Electronic applications accepted. *Financial support:* In 2010–11, 12 fellowships with full tuition reimbursements (averaging $24,600 per year), 19 research assistantships with full tuition reimbursements (averaging $24,600 per year), 1 teaching assistantship with full tuition reimbursement (averaging $18,000 per year) were awarded; Federal Work-Study, institutionally sponsored loans, scholarships/grants, health care benefits, tuition waivers (partial), and unspecified assistantships also available. *Faculty research:* Environmental engineering; environmental chemistry; water resources engineering; systems analysis and economics for public decision-making; geomorphology, hydrology and ecology. Total annual research expenditures: $1.4 million. *Unit head:* Dr. Edward J. Bouwer, Chair, 410-516-7102, Fax: 410-516-8996, E-mail: bouwer@jhu.edu. *Application contact:* Dr. Edward J. Bouwer, Chair, 410-516-7102, Fax: 410-516-8996, E-mail: bouwer@jhu.edu.

Kansas State University, Graduate School, College of Arts and Sciences, Department of Geography, Manhattan, KS 66506. Offers MA, PhD. *Degree requirements:* For master's, thesis optional, oral exam; for doctorate, one foreign language, thesis/dissertation. *Entrance requirements:* For master's and doctorate, GRE General Test, minimum GPA of 3.0. Electronic applications accepted. *Faculty research:* Human environment interaction, health and population, culture and landscape, physical geography, geospatial analysis and applications.

Kent State University, College of Arts and Sciences, Department of Geography, Kent, OH 44242-0001. Offers MA, PhD. Part-time programs available. *Degree requirements:* For master's, thesis optional; for doctorate, comprehensive exam, thesis/dissertation. *Entrance requirements:* For master's and doctorate, GRE, minimum GPA of 3.0. Additional exam requirements/recommendations for international students: Required—TOEFL. Electronic applications accepted. *Expenses:* Tuition, state resident: full-time $7866; part-time $437 per credit hour. Tuition, nonresident: full-time $14,022; part-time $779 per credit hour.

Louisiana State University and Agricultural and Mechanical College, Graduate School, College of Humanities and Social Sciences, Department of Geography and Anthropology, Baton Rouge, LA 70803. Offers anthropology (MA); geography (MA, MS, PhD). Part-time programs available. *Faculty:* 30 full-time (11 women), 1 part-time/adjunct (0 women). *Students:* 75 full-time (40 women), 24 part-time (12 women); includes 1 Black or African American, non-Hispanic/Latino; 1 Hispanic/Latino; 2 Two or more races, non-Hispanic/Latino, 24 international. Average age 31. 84 applicants, 67% accepted, 18 enrolled. In 2010, 13 master's, 7 doctorates awarded. Terminal master's awarded for partial completion of doctoral program. *Degree requirements:* For master's, 2 foreign languages, thesis (for some programs); for doctorate, 2 foreign languages, thesis/dissertation. *Entrance requirements:* For master's and doctorate, GRE General Test, minimum GPA of 3.0. Additional exam requirements/recommendations for international students: Required—TOEFL (minimum score 550 paper-based; 213 computer-based; 79 iBT) or IELTS (minimum score 6.5). *Application deadline:* For fall admission, 1/25 priority date for domestic students, 5/15 for international students; for spring admission, 10/15 for international students. Applications are processed on a rolling basis. Application fee: $50 ($70 for international students). Electronic applications accepted. *Financial support:* In 2010–11, 72 students received support, including 3 fellowships with full tuition reimbursements available (averaging $20,126 per year), 29 research assistantships with full and partial tuition reimbursements available (averaging $18,220 per year), 25 teaching assistantships with full and partial tuition reimbursements available (averaging $12,636 per year); career-related internships or fieldwork, health care benefits, and unspecified assistantships also available. Financial award application deadline: 3/1; financial award applicants required to submit FAFSA. *Faculty research:* Cultural, coastal, climate, geographic information systems-geography, cultural, linguistics, archaeology-anthropology. Total annual research expenditures: $731,204. *Unit head:* Dr. Kevin Robbins, Chair, 225-578-5942, Fax: 225-578-4420, E-mail: gachair@lsu.edu. *Application contact:* Dr. Barry Keim, Graduate Adviser, 225-578-6170, Fax: 225-578-4420, E-mail: bkeim@lsu.edu.

Marshall University, Academic Affairs Division, College of Liberal Arts, Department of Geography, Huntington, WV 25755. Offers MA, MS. *Faculty:* 5 full-time (1 woman). *Students:* 13 full-time (8 women), 3 part-time (all women); includes 1 Black or African American, non-Hispanic/Latino. Average age 29. In 2010, 2 master's awarded. *Degree requirements:* For master's, thesis optional. Application fee: $40. *Unit head:* Dr. Joshua Hagen, Chairperson, 304-696-2505, E-mail: hagenj@marshall.edu. *Application contact:* Information Contact, 304-746-1907, Fax: 304-746-1902, E-mail: services@marshall.edu.

McGill University, Faculty of Graduate and Postdoctoral Studies, Faculty of Science, Department of Geography, Montréal, QC H3A 2T5, Canada. Offers geography (M Sc, MA, PhD); neo-tropical environment (MA, PhD); social statistics (MA).

McMaster University, School of Graduate Studies, Faculty of Science, School of Geography and Earth Sciences, Hamilton, ON L8S 4M2, Canada. Offers geochemistry (PhD); geology (M Sc, PhD); human geography (MA, PhD); physical geography (M Sc, PhD). Part-time programs available. Terminal master's awarded for partial completion of doctoral program. *Degree requirements:* For master's, thesis; for doctorate, comprehensive exam, thesis/dissertation. *Entrance requirements:* For master's, minimum B+ average. Additional exam requirements/recommendations for international students: Required—TOEFL (minimum score 550 paper-based; 213 computer-based).

Memorial University of Newfoundland, School of Graduate Studies, Department of Geography, St. John's, NL A1C 5S7, Canada. Offers M Sc, MA, PhD. *Degree requirements:* For master's, thesis; for doctorate, comprehensive exam, thesis/dissertation, seminar, oral defense of thesis. *Entrance requirements:* For master's, 2nd class degree; for doctorate, master's degree. Electronic applications accepted. *Faculty research:* Cultural/historical geography, physical geography, economic geography, cartography, geographical information systems.

Miami University, Graduate School, College of Arts and Science, Department of Geography, Oxford, OH 45056. Offers MA. Part-time programs available. *Students:* 11 full-time (6 women); includes 1 minority (Black or African American, non-Hispanic/Latino), 2 international. Average age 26. In 2010, 10 master's awarded. *Entrance requirements:* For master's, minimum undergraduate GPA of 3.0 during previous 2 years or 2.75 overall. Additional exam requirements/recommendations for international students: Required—TOEFL. Application fee: $50. *Expenses:* Tuition, state resident: full-time $11,616; part-time $484 per credit hour. Tuition, nonresident: full-time $25,656; part-time $1069 per credit hour. Required fees: $528. *Financial support:* Fellowships with full tuition reimbursements, research assistantships, teaching assistantships, career-related internships or fieldwork, Federal Work-Study, institutionally sponsored loans, health care benefits, tuition waivers (full), and unspecified assistantships available. Financial award application deadline: 3/1; financial award applicants required to submit FAFSA. *Unit head:* Dr. Bill Renwick, Chair, 513-529-5010, Fax: 513-529-1948, E-mail: renwicwh@muohio.edu. *Application contact:* Department of Geography, 513-529-5010, Fax: 513-529-1949, E-mail: geography@muohio.edu.

Michigan State University, The Graduate School, College of Social Science, Department of Geography, East Lansing, MI 48824. Offers geographic information science (MS); geography (MS, PhD). *Degree requirements:* For master's, comprehensive exam, thesis (for some programs), presentation of poster/paper or oral defense of thesis; for doctorate, comprehensive exam, thesis/dissertation, presentation of poster/paper, presentation and defense of dissertation proposal, oral exam in defense of dissertation. *Entrance requirements:* Additional exam requirements/recommendations for international students: Required—TOEFL (minimum score 600 paper-based; 250 computer-based). Electronic applications accepted.

Minnesota State University Mankato, College of Graduate Studies, College of Social and Behavioral Sciences, Department of Geography, Mankato, MN 56001. Offers geography (MS); GIS (Certificate). Part-time programs available. *Students:* 3 full-time (0 women), 20 part-time (9 women). *Degree requirements:* For master's, one foreign language, comprehensive exam. *Entrance requirements:* For master's, GRE General Test (if GPA less than 2.8 for the last 2 years), minimum GPA of 3.0 during previous 2 years. *Application deadline:* For fall admission, 7/1 priority date for domestic students; for spring admission, 11/1 for domestic students. Applications are processed on a rolling basis. Application fee: $40. Electronic applications accepted. *Financial support:* Research assistantships, teaching assistantships with full tuition reimbursements, career-related internships or fieldwork, Federal Work-Study, institutionally sponsored loans, and unspecified assistantships available. Support available to part-time students. Financial award application deadline: 3/15; financial award applicants required to submit FAFSA. *Unit head:* Dr. Donald Friend, Chairperson, 507-389-2617. *Application contact:* 507-389-2321, E-mail: grad@mnsu.edu.

Missouri State University, Graduate College, College of Natural and Applied Sciences, Department of Geography, Geology, and Planning, Springfield, MO 65897. Offers geospatial sciences (MS); natural and applied science (MNAS), including geography, geology and planning; secondary education (MS Ed), including earth science, geography. Part-time and evening/weekend programs available. *Degree requirements:* For master's, comprehensive exam, thesis (for some programs). *Entrance requirements:* For master's, GRE General Test (MS, MNAS), minimum undergraduate GPA of 3.0 (MS, MNAS), 9-12 teacher certification (MS Ed). Additional exam requirements/recommendations for international students: Required—TOEFL (minimum score 550 paper-based; 213 computer-based; 79 iBT). Electronic applications accepted. *Expenses:* Tuition, state resident: full-time $3348; part-time $186 per credit hour. Tuition, nonresident: full-time $6696; part-time $372 per credit hour. Required fees: $238 per semester. Tuition and fees vary according to course level, course load and program. *Faculty research:* Stratigraphy and ancient meteorite impacts, environmental geochemistry of karst, hyper-spectral image processing, water quality, small town planning.

New Mexico State University, Graduate School, College of Arts and Sciences, Department of Geography, Las Cruces, NM 88003-8001. Offers MAG. Part-time programs available. *Faculty:* 5 full-time (2 women). *Students:* 15 full-time (4 women), 13 part-time (6 women); includes 6 minority (all Hispanic/Latino), 1 international. Average age 35. 12 applicants, 92% accepted, 5 enrolled. In 2010, 3 master's awarded. *Degree requirements:* For master's, thesis or alternative. *Entrance requirements:* For master's, GRE General Test. Additional exam requirements/recommendations for international students: Required—TOEFL. *Application deadline:* Applications are processed on a rolling basis. Application fee: $30 ($50 for international students). Electronic applications accepted. *Expenses:* Tuition, state resident: full-time $4536; part-time $242 per credit. Tuition, nonresident: full-time $15,816; part-time $712 per credit. Required fees: $636 per term. *Financial support:* In 2010–11, 7 teaching assistantships (averaging $8,057 per year) were awarded; research assistantships, career-related internships or fieldwork and health care benefits also available. Financial award application deadline: 3/1. *Faculty research:* Landscape ecology, land use, geomorphology, Latin America and the U. S.-Mexico border, geographic information systems, geographic education. *Unit head:* Dr. Christopher Brown, Head, 575-646-3509, Fax: 575-646-7430, E-mail: brownchr@nmsu.edu. *Application contact:* Dr. Daniel Dugas, Assistant Professor, 575-646-3509, Fax: 575-646-7430, E-mail: ddugas@nmsu.edu.

Northeastern Illinois University, Graduate College, College of Arts and Sciences, Department of Geography, Environmental Studies and Economics, Program in Geography and Environmental Studies, Chicago, IL 60625-4699. Offers MA. Part-time and evening/weekend programs available. *Faculty:* 6 full-time (0 women), 3 part-time/adjunct (2 women). *Students:* 13 full-time (6 women), 31 part-time (18 women); includes 7 minority (3 Black or African American, non-Hispanic/Latino; 1 Asian, non-Hispanic/Latino; 2 Hispanic/Latino; 1 Two or more races, non-Hispanic/Latino), 1 international. Average age 34. 14 applicants, 86% accepted, 8 enrolled. In 2010, 8 master's awarded. *Degree requirements:* For master's, comprehensive exam, thesis optional. *Entrance requirements:* For master's, undergraduate minor in geography or environmental studies, minimum GPA of 2.75. Additional exam requirements/recommendations for international students: Required—TOEFL (minimum score 550 paper-based; 213 computer-based; 79 iBT). *Application deadline:* For fall admission, 4/1 priority date for domestic students; for spring admission, 8/15 for domestic students. Applications are processed on a rolling basis. Application fee: $30. Electronic applications accepted. *Financial support:* In 2010–11, 2 research assistantships with full tuition reimbursements (averaging $6,600 per year) were awarded; career-related internships or fieldwork, Federal Work-Study, institutionally sponsored loans, scholarships/grants, tuition waivers (full and partial), and unspecified assistantships also available. Support available to part-time students. Financial award applicants required to submit FAFSA. *Faculty research:* Segregation and urbanization of minority groups in the Chicago area, scale dependence and parameterization in nonpoint source pollution modeling, ecological land classification and mapping, ecosystem restoration, soil-vegetation relationships. *Unit head:* Dr. Dennis Grammenos, Department Chair. *Application contact:* Dr. Dennis Grammenos, Department Chair.

Northern Arizona University, Graduate College, College of Social and Behavioral Sciences, Department of Geography, Planning, and Recreation, Flagstaff, AZ 86011. Offers applied geospatial sciences (MS); geographic information systems (Certificate). Postbaccalaureate distance learning degree programs offered. *Faculty:* 13 full-time (5 women). *Students:* 16 full-time (8 women), 16 part-time (4 women); includes 4 minority (2 Asian, non-Hispanic/Latino; 2 Hispanic/Latino), 3 international. Average age 32. 19 applicants, 79% accepted, 9 enrolled. In 2010, 6 master's, 4 other advanced degrees awarded. *Degree requirements:* For master's, thesis optional. *Entrance requirements:* For master's, GRE General Test. Additional exam requirements/recommendations for international students: Required—TOEFL (minimum score 550 paper-based; 213 computer-based; 80 iBT), IELTS (minimum score 7). *Application deadline:* For fall admission, 2/15 priority date for domestic students, 2/15 for international students; for spring admission, 10/15 priority date for domestic students, 10/15 for international students. Applications are processed on a rolling basis. Application fee: $65. Electronic applications accepted. *Financial support:* In 2010–11, 1 fellowship (averaging $10,774 per year), 5 teaching assistantships with partial tuition reimbursements (averaging $9,625 per year) were awarded; career-related internships or fieldwork, Federal Work-Study, scholarships/grants, health care benefits, tuition waivers (full and partial), and unspecified assistantships also available. Financial award applicants required to submit FAFSA. *Unit head:* Dr. Pamela Foti, Chair, 928-523-6196, Fax: 928-523-2275, E-mail: pam.foti@nau.edu. *Application contact:* Nicole Harris, Administrative Associate, 928-523-2650, Fax: 928-523-2275, E-mail: geog@nau.edu.

Northern Illinois University, Graduate School, College of Liberal Arts and Sciences, Department of Geography, De Kalb, IL 60115-2854. Offers MS, PhD. Part-time programs available. *Faculty:* 8 full-time (2 women). *Students:* 24 full-time (10 women), 10 part-time (5 women); includes 1 Black or African American, non-Hispanic/Latino; 1 Asian, non-Hispanic/Latino; 1 Hispanic/Latino, 3 international. Average age 28. 28 applicants, 75% accepted, 12 enrolled. In 2010, 17 master's awarded. *Degree requirements:* For master's, comprehensive exam, thesis optional, research seminar. *Entrance requirements:* For master's, GRE General Test, minimum GPA of 2.75; for doctorate, master's degree. Additional exam requirements/recommendations for international students: Required—TOEFL (minimum score 550 paper-based; 213 computer-based). *Application deadline:* For fall admission, 2/1 priority date for domestic students, 5/1 for international students; for spring admission, 10/1 priority date for domestic students, 10/1 for international students. Applications are processed on a rolling basis. Application fee: $30. Electronic applications accepted. *Expenses:* Tuition, state resident: full-time $7200; part-time $300 per credit hour. Tuition, nonresident: full-time $14,400; part-time $600 per credit hour. Required fees: $79 per credit hour. *Financial support:* In 2010–11, 10 research assistantships with full tuition reimbursements, 15 teaching assistantships with full tuition reimbursements were awarded; fellowships with full tuition reimbursements, career-related internships or fieldwork, Federal Work-Study, scholarships/grants, tuition waivers (full), and unspecified assistantships also available. Support available to part-time students. Financial award applicants required to submit FAFSA. *Faculty research:* Synoptic meteorology, human impacts on soil properties, plant-soil relationships, hydrological cycle, climate variability. *Unit head:* Dr. Andrew Krmenec, Chair, 815-753-6826, Fax: 815-753-6872, E-mail: akrmenec@niu.edu. *Application contact:* Dr. Fahui Wang, Coordinator of Graduate Studies, 815-753-6842, E-mail: fwang@niu.edu.

Northwest Missouri State University, Graduate School, College of Arts and Sciences, Department of Geology/Geography, Maryville, MO 64468-6001. Offers geographic information sciences (MS, Certificate). Part-time programs available. *Faculty:* 11 full-time (3 women). *Students:* 5 full-time (1 woman), 104 part-time (37 women); includes 1 Black or African American, non-Hispanic/Latino; 4 Asian, non-Hispanic/Latino; 1 Hispanic/Latino. 24 applicants, 83% accepted, 16 enrolled. In 2010, 10 master's awarded. *Degree requirements:* For master's, comprehensive exam, thesis. *Entrance requirements:* For master's, GRE General Test, 2 letters of recommendation, writing sample, minimum undergraduate GPA of 2.5. *Application deadline:* For fall admission, 4/15 for domestic and international students. Application fee: $0 ($50 for international students). *Financial support:* In 2010–11, 2 research assistantships with full tuition reimbursements (averaging $6,000 per year) were awarded. Financial award application deadline: 4/1; financial award applicants required to submit FAFSA. *Unit head:* Renee Rohs, Chairperson, 660-562-1719. *Application contact:* Dr. Gregory Haddock, Dean of Graduate School, 660-562-1145, Fax: 660-562-1096, E-mail: gradsch@nwmissouri.edu.

The Ohio State University, Graduate School, College of Arts and Sciences, Division of Social and Behavioral Sciences, Department of Geography, Columbus, OH 43210. Offers atmospheric sciences (MS, PhD); geography (MA, PhD). *Faculty:* 24. *Students:* 47 full-time (17 women), 26 part-time (9 women); includes 1 Asian, non-Hispanic/Latino, 21 international. Average age 29. In 2010, 14 master's, 10 doctorates awarded. *Degree requirements:* For doctorate, variable foreign language requirement, thesis/dissertation. *Entrance requirements:* Additional exam requirements/recommendations for international students: Recommended—TOEFL (minimum score 600 paper-based; 250 computer-based). *Application deadline:* For fall admission, 8/15 priority date for domestic students, 7/1 priority date for international students; for winter admission, 12/1 priority date for domestic students, 11/1 priority date for international students; for spring admission, 3/1 priority date for domestic students, 2/1 priority date for international students. Applications are processed on a rolling basis. Application fee: $40 ($50 for international students). Electronic applications accepted. *Expenses:* Tuition, state resident: full-time $10,605. Tuition, nonresident: full-time $26,535. Tuition and fees vary according to course load and program. *Financial support:* Fellowships, research assistantships, teaching assistantships, Federal Work-Study and institutionally sponsored loans available. Support available to part-time students. *Unit head:* Morton O'Kelly, Chair, 614-292-8744, Fax: 614-292-6213, E-mail: okelly.1@osu.edu. *Application contact:* 614-292-9444, Fax: 614-292-3895, E-mail: domestic.grad@osu.edu.

Ohio University, Graduate College, College of Arts and Sciences, Department of Geography, Athens, OH 45701-2979. Offers MA. Part-time programs available. *Students:* 20 full-time (12 women), 1 part-time (0 women); includes 1 minority (American Indian or Alaska Native, non-Hispanic/Latino), 5 international. 25 applicants, 56% accepted, 10 enrolled. In 2010, 15 master's awarded. *Degree requirements:* For master's, thesis or alternative. *Entrance requirements:* For master's, GRE General Test, minimum GPA of 3.0. Additional exam requirements/recommendations for international students: Required—TOEFL (minimum score 600 paper-based; 100 iBT) or IELTS (minimum score 8). *Application deadline:* For fall admission, 2/15 priority date for domestic and international students. Application fee: $50 ($55 for international students). Electronic applications accepted. *Financial support:* Research assistantships with full tuition reimbursements, teaching assistantships with full tuition reimbursements, Federal Work-Study, institutionally sponsored loans, tuition waivers (partial), and unspecified assistantships available. Financial award application deadline: 2/15. *Faculty research:* Environmental geography, cartography and geographic information systems, cultural ecology, area studies, historical geography. Total annual research expenditures: $81,622. *Unit head:* Dr. Timothy G. Anderson, Graduate Chair, 740-593-1138, Fax: 740-593-1139, E-mail: anderstl@ohio.edu. *Application contact:* Dr. James Dyer, Graduate Chair, 740-593-1142, Fax: 740-593-1139, E-mail: dyer@ohio.edu.

Oklahoma State University, College of Arts and Sciences, Department of Geography, Stillwater, OK 74078. Offers MS, PhD. *Faculty:* 14 full-time (4 women). *Students:* 6 full-time (3 women), 25 part-time (8 women); includes 1 Asian, non-Hispanic/Latino; 1 Hispanic/Latino, 9 international. Average age 31. 29 applicants, 34% accepted, 4 enrolled. In 2010, 2 master's, 2 doctorates awarded. *Degree requirements:* For master's, thesis or alternative; for doctorate, comprehensive exam, thesis/dissertation. *Entrance requirements:* For master's and doctorate, GRE. Additional exam requirements/recommendations for international students: Required—TOEFL (minimum score 550 paper-based; 79 iBT). *Application deadline:* For fall admission, 3/1 priority date for international students; for spring admission, 8/1 priority date for international students. Applications are processed on a rolling basis. Application fee: $40 ($75 for international students). Electronic applications accepted. *Expenses:* Tuition, state resident: full-time $3716; part-time $154.85 per credit hour. Tuition, nonresident: full-time $14,892; part-time $621 per credit hour. Required fees: $2044; $85.20 per credit hour. One-time fee: $50. Tuition and fees vary according to course load and campus/location. *Financial support:* In 2010–11, 9 research assistantships (averaging $12,115 per year), 20 teaching assistantships (averaging $15,073 per year) were awarded; career-related internships or fieldwork, Federal Work-Study, scholarships/grants, health care benefits, tuition waivers (partial), and unspecified assistantships also available. Support available to part-time students. Financial award application deadline: 3/1; financial award applicants required to submit FAFSA. *Faculty research:* Cultural ecology, resource management, historical/cultural geography, central Asia, geographic information systems. *Unit head:* Dr. Dale R. Lightfoot, Head, 405-744-6250, Fax: 405-744-5620. *Application contact:* Dr. Gordon Emslie, Dean, 405-744-6368, Fax: 405-744-0355, E-mail: grad-i@okstate.edu.

Oregon State University, Graduate School, College of Science, Department of Geosciences, Program in Geography, Corvallis, OR 97331. Offers MA, MAIS, MS, PhD. Part-time programs available. Terminal master's awarded for partial completion of doctoral program. *Degree requirements:* For master's, variable foreign language requirement, thesis optional; for doctorate, one foreign language, thesis/dissertation. *Entrance requirements:* For master's and doctorate, GRE General Test, GRE Subject Test, minimum GPA of 3.0 in last 90 hours. Additional exam requirements/recommendations for international students: Required—TOEFL. *Faculty research:* Resources, physical geography, cartography, remote sensing.

Penn State University Park, Graduate School, College of Earth and Mineral Sciences, Department of Geography, State College, University Park, PA 16802-1503. Offers MS, PhD.

Portland State University, Graduate Studies, College of Liberal Arts and Sciences, Department of Geography, Portland, OR 97207-0751. Offers MA, MAT, MS, MST, PhD. Part-time programs available. *Faculty:* 10 full-time (3 women), 5 part-time/adjunct (0 women). *Students:* 37 full-time (16 women), 48 part-time (20 women); includes 1 Asian, non-Hispanic/Latino; 3 Hispanic/Latino. Average age 33. 66 applicants, 82% accepted, 38 enrolled. In 2010, 9 master's awarded. *Degree requirements:* For master's, thesis (for some programs). *Entrance requirements:* For master's, GRE General Test, minimum GPA of 3.0 in upper-division course work or 2.75 overall, 3 letters of recommendation. Additional exam requirements/recommendations for international students: Required—TOEFL (minimum score 550 paper-based; 213 computer-based). *Application deadline:* For fall admission, 4/1 for domestic students, 3/1 for international students. Applications are processed on a rolling basis. Application fee: $50. *Expenses:* Tuition, state resident: full-time $8505; part-time $315 per credit. Tuition, nonresident: full-time $13,284; part-time $492 per credit. Required fees: $1482; $21 per credit. $99 per term. One-time fee: $120. Part-time tuition and fees vary according to course load and program. *Financial support:* In 2010–11, 4 research assistantships with full tuition reimbursements (averaging $5,778 per year), 8 teaching assistantships with full tuition reimbursements (averaging $5,778 per year) were awarded; career-related internships or fieldwork, Federal Work-Study, scholarships/grants, and unspecified assistantships also available. Support available to part-time students. Financial award application deadline: 3/1; financial award applicants required to submit FAFSA. *Faculty research:* Geographic information systems, natural lands, Latin American subsistence farming, climatic change, urban perspectives. Total annual research expenditures: $321,158. *Unit head:* Dr. Thomas Harvey, Chair, 503-725-3164, Fax: 503-725-3166, E-mail: harveyt@pdx.edu. *Application contact:* Karin Waller, Office Coordinator, 503-725-3916, Fax: 503-725-3166, E-mail: geog@pdx.edu.

Queen's University at Kingston, School of Graduate Studies and Research, Faculty of Arts and Sciences, Department of Geography, Kingston, ON K7L 3N6, Canada. Offers M Sc, MA, PhD. *Degree requirements:* For master's, thesis; for doctorate, comprehensive exam, thesis/dissertation. *Entrance requirements:* Additional exam requirements/recommendations for international students: Required—TOEFL. *Faculty research:* Urban and economic geography, historical-cultural geography, earth system science.

Rutgers, The State University of New Jersey, New Brunswick, Graduate School-New Brunswick, Program in Geography, Piscataway, NJ 08854-8097. Offers MA, MS, PhD. Terminal master's awarded for partial completion of doctoral program. *Degree requirements:* For master's, thesis or alternative; for doctorate, comprehensive exam, thesis/dissertation. *Entrance requirements:* For master's and doctorate, GRE General Test. Additional exam requirements/recommendations for international students: Required—TOEFL. *Expenses:* Tuition, state resident: full-time $7200; part-time $600 per credit. Tuition, nonresident: full-time $11,124; part-time $927 per credit. *Faculty research:* Urban social theory, climate, political biology, hazards, economic development.

St. Cloud State University, School of Graduate Studies, College of Social Sciences, Department of Geography, St. Cloud, MN 56301-4498. Offers MS. *Degree requirements:* For master's, comprehensive exam (for some programs), thesis or alternative. *Entrance requirements:* For master's, GRE General Test, minimum GPA of 2.75. Additional exam requirements/recommendations for international students: Required—Michigan English Language Assessment Battery; Recommended—TOEFL (minimum score 550 paper-based; 213 computer-based), IELTS (minimum score 6.5). Electronic applications accepted.

Salem State University, School of Graduate Studies, Program in Geo-Information Science, Salem, MA 01970-5353. Offers geo-information science (MS). Part-time and evening/weekend programs available. *Students:* 1 (woman) full-time, 12 part-time (2 women), 3 international. Average age 34. 3 applicants, 100% accepted, 3 enrolled. In 2010, 5 master's awarded. *Degree requirements:* For master's, thesis optional. *Entrance requirements:* For master's, GRE or MAT. Additional exam requirements/recommendations for international students: Required—TOEFL (minimum score 550 paper-based; 80 iBT) or IELTS (minimum score 5.5). *Application deadline:* For fall admission, 5/1 for domestic students; for spring admission, 10/1 for domestic students. Applications are processed on a rolling basis. Application fee: $50. *Expenses:* Tuition, state resident: full-time $2520; part-time $290 per credit hour. Tuition, nonresident: full-time $4140; part-time $380 per credit hour. Required fees: $2700. *Financial support:* Career-related internships or fieldwork, Federal Work-Study, scholarships/grants, and unspecified assistantships available. Support available to part-time students. Financial award application deadline: 5/1; financial award applicants required to submit FAFSA. *Unit head:* Dr. Keith Ratner, Coordinator, 978-542-6075, E-mail: kratner@salemstate.edu. *Application contact:* Dr. Lee A. Brossoit, Assistant Dean of Graduate Admissions, 978-542-6675, Fax: 978-542-7215, E-mail: lbrossoit@salemstate.edu.

San Diego State University, Graduate and Research Affairs, College of Arts and Letters, Department of Geography, San Diego, CA 92182. Offers MA, PhD. PhD offered jointly with University of California, Santa Barbara. *Degree requirements:* For master's, thesis; for doctorate, thesis/dissertation. *Entrance requirements:* For master's, GRE General Test, bachelor's degree in related field, 3 letters of recommendation. Additional exam requirements/recommendations for international students: Required—TOEFL. Electronic applications accepted. *Faculty research:* Physical geography, human geography, biogeography, environmental resources, geographic analysis.

San Francisco State University, Division of Graduate Studies, College of Behavioral and Social Sciences, Department of Geography and Human Environmental Studies, San Francisco, CA 94132-1722. Offers geographic information science (MS); geography (MA), including resource management and environmental planning. *Unit head:* Dr. Jerry Davis, Chair, 415-338-2049, E-mail: jerry@sfsu.edu. *Application contact:* Nancy Wilkinson, Graduate Coordinator, 415-338-2049.

San Jose State University, Graduate Studies and Research, College of Social Sciences, Department of Geography, San Jose, CA 95192-0001. Offers geographic information science (Certificate); geography (MA). *Entrance requirements:* For master's, minimum GPA of 3.0. Electronic applications accepted.

Shippensburg University of Pennsylvania, School of Graduate Studies, College of Education and Human Services, Department of Teacher Education, Shippensburg, PA 17257-2299. Offers curriculum and instruction (M Ed), including biology, early childhood education, elementary education, English, geography/earth science, history, mathematics, middle school education, modern languages; reading (M Ed). *Accreditation:* NCATE. Part-time and evening/weekend programs available. *Faculty:* 15 full-time (13 women), 11 part-time/adjunct (9 women). *Students:* 15 full-time (11 women), 170 part-time (158 women); includes 10 minority (7 Black or African American, non-Hispanic/Latino; 2 Hispanic/Latino; 1 Two or more races, non-Hispanic/Latino), 2 international. Average age 30. 74 applicants, 68% accepted, 31 enrolled. In 2010, 66 master's awarded. *Degree requirements:* For master's, comprehensive exam (for some programs), thesis optional, practicum or internship; capstone seminar (for some programs). *Entrance requirements:* For master's, MAT (if GPA less than 2.75), interview, 3 letters of reference, questionnaire of teaching background and future goals. Additional exam requirements/recommendations for international students: Required—TOEFL (minimum score 580 paper-based; 237 computer-based); Recommended—IELTS (minimum score 6). *Application deadline:* For fall admission, 6/1 priority date for domestic students, 3/1 for international students; for spring admission, 9/1 priority date for domestic students, 7/1 for international students. Applications are processed on a rolling basis. Application fee: $30. Electronic applications accepted. *Expenses:* Tuition, state resident: full-time $6966. Tuition, nonresident: full-time $11,146. Required fees: $1802. *Financial support:* In 2010–11, 3 research assistantships with full tuition reimbursements (averaging $5,000 per year) were awarded; career-related internships or fieldwork, scholarships/grants, unspecified assistantships, and resident hall director and student payroll positions also available. Support available to part-time students. Financial award application deadline: 3/1; financial award applicants required to submit FAFSA. *Unit head:* Dr. Christine A. Royce, Chairperson, 717-477-1688, Fax: 717-477-4046, E-mail: caroyc@ship.edu. *Application contact:* Jeremy R. Goshorn, Associate Dean of Graduate Admissions, 717-477-1231, Fax: 717-477-4016, E-mail: jrgoshorn@ship.edu.

Simon Fraser University, Graduate Studies, Faculty of Arts and Social Sciences, Department of Geography, Burnaby, BC V5A 1S6, Canada. Offers M Sc, MA, PhD. *Degree requirements:* For master's, one foreign language, thesis or alternative; for doctorate, one foreign language, thesis/dissertation, qualifying exams. *Entrance requirements:* For master's, minimum GPA of 3.0; for doctorate, minimum GPA of 3.5. Additional exam requirements/recommendations for international students: Required—TOEFL or IELTS. Electronic applications accepted. *Faculty research:* Theoretical and systematic aspects of geography, ginseng research, geographic information sciences, tourism and community planning, geomorphology.

South Dakota State University, Graduate School, College of Arts and Science, Department of Geography, Brookings, SD 57007. Offers MS. Part-time programs available. *Degree requirements:* For master's, thesis, oral exam. *Entrance requirements:* Additional exam requirements/recommendations for international students: Required—TOEFL (minimum score 525 paper-based; 197 computer-based; 71 iBT). *Faculty research:* Contemporary agriculture

Geography

South Dakota State University *(continued)*
and rural land use, geography of Indian casino gambling, geography of illegal drug trade, geography of crop circles.

Southern Illinois University Carbondale, Graduate School, College of Liberal Arts, Department of Geography, Carbondale, IL 62901-4701. Offers MS, PhD. *Degree requirements:* For master's, thesis; for doctorate, thesis/dissertation. *Entrance requirements:* For master's, minimum GPA of 2.7; for doctorate, minimum GPA of 3.25. Additional exam requirements/recommendations for international students: Required—TOEFL. *Faculty research:* Natural resources management emphasizing water resources and environmental quality of air, water, and land systems.

Southern Illinois University Edwardsville, Graduate School, College of Arts and Sciences, Department of Geography, Edwardsville, IL 62026. Offers MS. Part-time and evening/weekend programs available. *Faculty:* 13 full-time (5 women). *Students:* 12 full-time (7 women), 22 part-time (11 women); includes 3 minority (1 Black or African American, non-Hispanic/Latino; 1 Hispanic/Latino; 1 Two or more races, non-Hispanic/Latino), 3 international. Average age 26. 21 applicants, 67% accepted. In 2010, 3 master's awarded. *Degree requirements:* For master's, thesis (for some programs), final exam. *Entrance requirements:* For master's, GRE for applicants with a GPA less than 2.8. Additional exam requirements/recommendations for international students: Required—TOEFL (minimum score 550 paper-based; 213 computer-based; 79 iBT), IELTS (minimum score 6.5). *Application deadline:* For fall admission, 7/22 for domestic students, 6/1 for international students; for spring admission, 12/9 for domestic students, 10/1 for international students. Applications are processed on a rolling basis. Application fee: $30. Electronic applications accepted. *Expenses:* Tuition, state resident: full-time $6012; part-time $1503 per semester. Tuition, nonresident: full-time $15,030; part-time $3758 per semester. Required fees: $1711; $675 per semester. *Financial support:* In 2010–11, fellowships with full tuition reimbursements (averaging $8,370 per year), 13 teaching assistantships with full tuition reimbursements (averaging $8,064 per year) were awarded; research assistantships with full tuition reimbursements, career-related internships or fieldwork, Federal Work-Study, institutionally sponsored loans, scholarships/grants, traineeships, and unspecified assistantships also available. Support available to part-time students. Financial award application deadline: 3/1; financial award applicants required to submit FAFSA. *Unit head:* Dr. Randall Pearson, Chair, 618-650-2090, E-mail: rapears@siue.edu. *Application contact:* Dr. Michael Starr, Director, 618-650-2492, E-mail: mstarr@siue.edu.

State University of New York at Binghamton, Graduate School, School of Arts and Sciences, Department of Geography, Binghamton, NY 13902-6000. Offers MA. *Faculty:* 8 full-time (2 women). *Students:* 28 full-time (12 women), 4 part-time (2 women); includes 3 Asian, non-Hispanic/Latino; 6 Hispanic/Latino, 10 international. Average age 26. 38 applicants, 76% accepted, 17 enrolled. In 2010, 5 master's awarded. *Degree requirements:* For master's, one foreign language, thesis (for some programs), oral and written exams. *Entrance requirements:* For master's, GRE General Test, GRE Subject Test. Additional exam requirements/recommendations for international students: Required—TOEFL (minimum score 550 paper-based; 213 computer-based; 80 iBT). *Application deadline:* For fall admission, 5/15 priority date for domestic and international students; for spring admission, 10/15 priority date for domestic and international students. Applications are processed on a rolling basis. Application fee: $60. Electronic applications accepted. *Financial support:* In 2010–11, 16 students received support, including 3 fellowships with full tuition reimbursements available (averaging $10,000 per year), 10 teaching assistantships with full tuition reimbursements available (averaging $10,000 per year); career-related internships or fieldwork, Federal Work-Study, institutionally sponsored loans, scholarships/grants, health care benefits, tuition waivers (full and partial), and unspecified assistantships also available. Financial award application deadline: 2/15; financial award applicants required to submit FAFSA. *Unit head:* Dr. Norah Henry, Chairperson, 607-777-2615, E-mail: nhenry@binghamton.edu. *Application contact:* Catherine Smith, Recruiting and Admissions Coordinator, 607-777-2151, Fax: 607-777-2501, E-mail: cmsmith@binghamton.edu.

Syracuse University, Maxwell School of Citizenship and Public Affairs, Program in Geography, Syracuse, NY 13244. Offers MA, PhD. Part-time and evening/weekend programs available. *Students:* 30 full-time (16 women), 6 part-time (4 women); includes 6 minority (3 Black or African American, non-Hispanic/Latino; 1 Asian, non-Hispanic/Latino; 2 Hispanic/Latino), 8 international. Average age 31. 76 applicants, 39% accepted, 8 enrolled. In 2010, 2 master's, 2 doctorates awarded. *Degree requirements:* For master's, thesis or alternative; for doctorate, thesis/dissertation. *Entrance requirements:* For master's and doctorate, GRE General Test. Additional exam requirements/recommendations for international students: Required—TOEFL (minimum score 100 iBT). *Application deadline:* For fall admission, 2/1 priority date for domestic and international students. Application fee: $75. Electronic applications accepted. *Expenses:* Tuition: Part-time $1162 per credit. *Financial support:* Fellowships with full tuition reimbursements, research assistantships with full and partial tuition reimbursements, teaching assistantships with full and partial tuition reimbursements available. Financial award application deadline: 1/1. *Unit head:* Dr. Tod Rutherford, Chair, 315-443-2605, Fax: 315-443-4227, E-mail: trutherf@syr.edu. *Application contact:* Chris Chapman, Recruiting Contact, 315-443-2605, E-mail: cmchapma@maxwell.syr.edu.

Temple University, College of Liberal Arts, Department of Geography and Urban Studies, Philadelphia, PA 19122-6096. Offers geography (MA); geography and urban studies (MA); urban studies (MA, PhD). *Faculty:* 25 full-time (16 women). *Students:* 19 full-time (11 women), 12 part-time (6 women); includes 3 Black or African American, non-Hispanic/Latino; 2 Asian, non-Hispanic/Latino; 1 Hispanic/Latino, 3 international. 69 applicants, 41% accepted, 11 enrolled. In 2010, 13 master's awarded. *Degree requirements:* For master's, comprehensive exam, thesis or alternative. *Entrance requirements:* For master's, GRE General Test, minimum GPA of 3.0. Additional exam requirements/recommendations for international students: Required—TOEFL (minimum score 550 paper-based; 213 computer-based; 79 iBT). *Application deadline:* For fall admission, 1/15 for domestic students, 12/15 for international students; for spring admission, 10/15 for domestic students, 8/1 for international students. Applications are processed on a rolling basis. Application fee: $50. Electronic applications accepted. *Financial support:* Fellowships, teaching assistantships, career-related internships or fieldwork, Federal Work-Study, and tuition waivers (partial) available. Financial award application deadline: 1/15; financial award applicants required to submit FAFSA. *Faculty research:* Environmental issues, urban political economy, poverty and unemployment, neighborhood development, African and Asian urbanization, housing, computer cartography. Total annual research expenditures: $400,000. *Unit head:* Dr. Michele Masucci, Chair, 215-204-7692, Fax: 215-204-7833, E-mail: masucci@temple.edu. *Application contact:* Dr. Michele Masucci, Chair, 215-204-7692, Fax: 215-204-7833, E-mail: masucci@temple.edu.

Texas A&M University, College of Geosciences, Department of Geography, College Station, TX 77843. Offers MS, PhD. Part-time programs available. *Faculty:* 16. *Students:* 65 full-time (25 women), 18 part-time (8 women); includes 9 minority (1 Black or African American, non-Hispanic/Latino; 4 Asian, non-Hispanic/Latino; 4 Hispanic/Latino), 27 international. Average age 34. In 2010, 6 master's, 3 doctorates awarded. *Degree requirements:* For master's, thesis optional; for doctorate, thesis/dissertation. *Entrance requirements:* For master's and doctorate, GRE General Test. Additional exam requirements/recommendations for international students: Required—TOEFL. *Application deadline:* For fall admission, 3/1 priority date for domestic students; for spring admission, 10/1 for domestic students. Applications are processed on a rolling basis. Application fee: $50 ($75 for international students). Electronic applications accepted. *Financial support:* Fellowships, research assistantships, teaching assistantships, career-related internships or fieldwork, Federal Work-Study, and institutionally sponsored loans available. Financial award application deadline: 3/1; financial award applicants required to submit FAFSA. *Faculty research:* Geomorphology, historical geography, urban-economic geography, geographic education and technology, human-environment interaction. *Unit head:* Vatche P. Tchakerian, Interim Head, 979-845-7141. *Application contact:* Gail Rowe, Academic Advisor II, 979-458-0895, Fax: 979-862-4487, E-mail: growe@geog.tamu.edu.

Texas State University–San Marcos, Graduate School, College of Liberal Arts, Department of Geography, Program in Environmental Geography, Geography Education, and Geography Information Science, San Marcos, TX 78666. Offers environmental geography (PhD); geography education (PhD); information science (PhD). Part-time programs available. *Faculty:* 24 full-time (6 women), 1 part-time/adjunct (0 women). *Students:* 46 full-time (22 women), 28 part-time (13 women); includes 7 minority (6 Hispanic/Latino; 1 Two or more races, non-Hispanic/Latino), 12 international. Average age 39. 23 applicants, 83% accepted, 8 enrolled. In 2010, 7 doctorates awarded. *Degree requirements:* For doctorate, thesis/dissertation. *Entrance requirements:* For doctorate, GRE General Test, minimum GPA of 3.5, master's degree in geography, demonstrated scholarly research. Additional exam requirements/recommendations for international students: Required—TOEFL (minimum score 550 paper-based; 213 computer-based; 78 iBT). *Application deadline:* For fall admission, 6/15 priority date for domestic students, 6/1 for international students; for spring admission, 10/15 priority date for domestic students, 10/1 for international students. Applications are processed on a rolling basis. Application fee: $40 ($90 for international students). Electronic applications accepted. *Expenses:* Tuition, state resident: full-time $6024; part-time $251 per credit hour. Tuition, nonresident: full-time $13,536; part-time $564 per credit hour. Required fees: $1776; $50 per credit hour. $306 per semester. *Financial support:* In 2010–11, 24 students received support, including 16 research assistantships (averaging $1,274 per year), 32 teaching assistantships (averaging $785 per year); career-related internships or fieldwork, Federal Work-Study, and institutionally sponsored loans also available. Support available to part-time students. Financial award application deadline: 4/1; financial award applicants required to submit FAFSA. *Faculty research:* Water and food production, geography education, watershed education. Total annual research expenditures: $530,310. *Unit head:* Dr. David Butler, Graduate Adviser, 512-245-2170, Fax: 512-245-8353, E-mail: db25@txstate.edu. *Application contact:* Dr. J. Michael Willoughby, Dean of Graduate School, 512-245-2581, Fax: 512-245-8365, E-mail: gradcollege@txstate.edu.

Texas State University–San Marcos, Graduate School, College of Liberal Arts, Department of Geography, Program in Geography, San Marcos, TX 78666. Offers applied geography (MAG); geography (MS). Part-time and evening/weekend programs available. *Faculty:* 5 full-time (1 woman), 2 part-time/adjunct (0 women). *Students:* 31 full-time (13 women), 36 part-time (15 women); includes 2 minority (1 Asian, non-Hispanic/Latino; 1 Hispanic/Latino). Average age 32. 26 applicants, 85% accepted, 22 enrolled. In 2010, 25 master's awarded. *Degree requirements:* For master's, comprehensive exam, thesis (for some programs). *Entrance requirements:* For master's, GRE General Test, minimum GPA of 3.0 in last 60 hours of course work, letter of interest, 2 letters of recommendation, curriculum vitae/resume. Additional exam requirements/recommendations for international students: Required—TOEFL (minimum score 550 paper-based; 213 computer-based; 78 iBT). *Application deadline:* For fall admission, 5/1 priority date for domestic students, 4/15 for international students; for spring admission, 10/15 priority date for domestic students, 10/1 for international students. Applications are processed on a rolling basis. Application fee: $40 ($90 for international students). Electronic applications accepted. *Expenses:* Tuition, state resident: full-time $6024; part-time $251 per credit hour. Tuition, nonresident: full-time $13,536; part-time $564 per credit hour. Required fees: $1776; $50 per credit hour. $306 per semester. *Financial support:* In 2010–11, 29 students received support, including 7 research assistantships (averaging $5,342 per year), 11 teaching assistantships (averaging $5,387 per year); career-related internships or fieldwork, Federal Work-Study, and institutionally sponsored loans also available. Support available to part-time students. Financial award application deadline: 4/1; financial award applicants required to submit FAFSA. *Faculty research:* Applied cartography and geographic information systems, physical and environmental studies, land/area development and management. Total annual research expenditures: $473,028. *Unit head:* Dr. David Butler, Graduate Adviser, 512-245-2170, Fax: 512-245-8353, E-mail: db25@txstate.edu. *Application contact:* Dr. J. Michael Willoughby, Dean of Graduate School, 512-245-2581, Fax: 512-245-8365, E-mail: gradcollege@txstate.edu.

Texas State University–San Marcos, Graduate School, College of Liberal Arts, Department of Geography, Program in Land/Area Studies, San Marcos, TX 78666. Offers MAG. Part-time and evening/weekend programs available. *Faculty:* 5 full-time (0 women), 1 part-time/adjunct (0 women). *Students:* 4 full-time (1 woman), 12 part-time (4 women); includes 2 Hispanic/Latino. Average age 29. 6 applicants, 100% accepted, 5 enrolled. In 2010, 3 master's awarded. *Degree requirements:* For master's, comprehensive exam. *Entrance requirements:* For master's, GRE General Test, minimum GPA of 3.0 in last 60 hours of course work, letter of interest, 2 letters of recommendation, curriculum vitae/resume. Additional exam requirements/recommendations for international students: Required—TOEFL (minimum score 550 paper-based; 213 computer-based; 78 iBT). *Application deadline:* For fall admission, 6/15 priority date for domestic students, 6/1 for international students; for spring admission, 10/15 priority date for domestic students, 10/1 for international students. Applications are processed on a rolling basis. Application fee: $40 ($90 for international students). Electronic applications accepted. *Expenses:* Tuition, state resident: full-time $6024; part-time $251 per credit hour. Tuition, nonresident: full-time $13,536; part-time $564 per credit hour. Required fees: $1776; $50 per credit hour. $306 per semester. *Financial support:* In 2010–11, 3 students received support; research assistantships, teaching assistantships, career-related internships or fieldwork, Federal Work-Study, institutionally sponsored loans, and scholarships/grants available. Support available to part-time students. Financial award application deadline: 4/1; financial award applicants required to submit FAFSA. *Unit head:* Dr. David Butler, Graduate Adviser, 512-245-2170, Fax: 512-245-8353, E-mail: db25@txstate.edu. *Application contact:* Dr. J. Michael Willoughby, Dean of Graduate School, 512-245-2581, Fax: 512-245-8365, E-mail: gradcollege@txstate.edu.

Towson University, Program in Geography and Environmental Planning, Towson, MD 21252-0001. Offers MA. Part-time and evening/weekend programs available. *Students:* 8 full-time (4 women), 26 part-time (17 women); includes 2 minority (both Black or African American, non-Hispanic/Latino), 1 international. Average age 30. In 2010, 3 master's awarded. *Degree requirements:* For master's, thesis optional. *Entrance requirements:* For master's, 9 credits of course work in geography, minimum GPA of 3.0 in geography, 2 narrative letters of recommendation. Additional exam requirements/recommendations for international students: Required—TOEFL. *Application deadline:* Applications are processed on a rolling basis. Application fee: $50. Electronic applications accepted. *Expenses:* Tuition, state resident: part-time $324 per credit. Tuition, nonresident: part-time $681 per credit. Required fees: $95 per term. *Financial support:* In 2010–11, 1 teaching assistantship with full tuition reimbursement (averaging $4,000 per year) was awarded; Federal Work-Study and unspecified assistantships also available. Financial award application deadline: 4/1; financial award applicants required to submit FAFSA. *Faculty research:* Geographic information systems, regional planning, hazards, development issues, urban fluvial systems. *Unit head:* Martin Roberge, Graduate Program Director, 410-704-5011, Fax: 410-704-3880, E-mail: mroberge@towson.edu. *Application contact:* 410-704-2501, Fax: 410-704-4675, E-mail: grads@towson.edu.

Trent University, Graduate Studies, Program in Applications of Modeling in the Natural and Social Sciences, Peterborough, ON K9J 7B8, Canada. Offers applications of modeling in the natural and social sciences (MA); biology (M Sc, PhD); chemistry (M Sc); computer studies (M Sc); geography (M Sc, PhD); physics (M Sc). Part-time programs available. *Degree requirements:* For master's, thesis. *Entrance requirements:* For master's, honours degree. *Faculty research:* Computation of heat transfer, atmospheric physics, statistical mechanics, stress and coping, evolutionary ecology.

Trent University, Graduate Studies, Program in Environmental and Life Sciences and Program in Applications of Modeling in the Natural and Social Sciences, Department of Geography, Peterborough, ON K9J 7B8, Canada. Offers M Sc, PhD. Part-time programs available. *Degree requirements:* For master's, thesis; for doctorate, thesis/dissertation. *Entrance requirements:* For master's, honors degree; for doctorate, master's degree. *Faculty research:* Hydrometeorology, snow and ice, urban hydrology, fluvial geomorphology.

Université de Montréal, Faculty of Arts and Sciences, Department of Geography, Montréal, QC H3C 3J7, Canada. Offers environment and durable development (DESS); geography

(M Sc, PhD, DESS). *Degree requirements:* For master's, 2 foreign languages, thesis (for some programs); for doctorate, 3 foreign languages, thesis/dissertation, general exam. *Entrance requirements:* For master's, bachelor's degree in related field; for doctorate, MA in geography or related field. Electronic applications accepted. *Faculty research:* Cartography, palynology, geomorphology, economic geography, regional and urban development.

Université de Sherbrooke, Faculty of Letters and Human Sciences, Department of Geography and Remote Sensing, Sherbrooke, QC J1K 2R1, Canada. Offers M Sc, PhD. *Degree requirements:* For master's, one foreign language, thesis; for doctorate, thesis/dissertation. *Faculty research:* Cartography.

Université du Québec à Montréal, Graduate Programs, Program in Geography, Montréal, QC H3C 3P8, Canada. Offers M Sc. Part-time programs available. *Degree requirements:* For master's, thesis optional. *Entrance requirements:* For master's, appropriate bachelor's degree or equivalent and proficiency in French.

Université Laval, Faculty of Forestry and Geomatics, Department of Geography, Program in Geographical Sciences, Québec, QC G1K 7P4, Canada. Offers M Sc Geogr, PhD. Terminal master's awarded for partial completion of doctoral program. *Degree requirements:* For master's, thesis; for doctorate, comprehensive exam, thesis/dissertation. *Entrance requirements:* For master's, knowledge of French; for doctorate, knowledge of French, knowledge of a second language. Electronic applications accepted.

University at Albany, State University of New York, College of Arts and Sciences, Department of Geography and Planning, Program in Geography, Albany, NY 12222-0001. Offers geographic information systems and spatial analysis (Certificate); geography (MA). *Degree requirements:* For master's, thesis or alternative. *Entrance requirements:* Additional exam requirements/recommendations for international students: Required—TOEFL (minimum score 550 paper-based; 213 computer-based). Electronic applications accepted. *Faculty research:* Remote sensing, cultural/social geography, urban geography.

University at Buffalo, the State University of New York, Graduate School, College of Arts and Sciences, Department of Geography, Buffalo, NY 14260. Offers earth systems science (MA); economic geography and international business and world trade (MA); environmental and earth systems science (MS); environmental modeling and analysis (MA); geographic information science (MA, Certificate); geographic information systems and science (MS); geography (MA, PhD); urban and regional geography (MA); MA/MBA. *Faculty:* 14 full-time (6 women), 1 part-time/adjunct (0 women). *Students:* 60 full-time (24 women), 49 part-time (13 women); includes 1 Black or African American, non-Hispanic/Latino; 46 Asian, non-Hispanic/Latino; 4 Hispanic/Latino, 1 international. 162 applicants, 46% accepted, 38 enrolled. In 2010, 21 master's, 5 doctorates awarded. Terminal master's awarded for partial completion of doctoral program. *Degree requirements:* For master's, thesis (for some programs), project; for doctorate, thesis/dissertation. *Entrance requirements:* For master's, GRE General Test, minimum GPA of 2.9; for doctorate, GRE General Test, minimum GPA of 3.0. Additional exam requirements/recommendations for international students: Required—TOEFL (minimum score 550 paper-based; 213 computer-based; 79 iBT). *Application deadline:* For fall admission, 7/1 priority date for domestic students, 1/10 priority date for international students; for spring admission, 12/1 priority date for domestic students, 10/1 priority date for international students. Applications are processed on a rolling basis. Application fee: $75. Electronic applications accepted. *Financial support:* In 2010–11, 19 students received support, including 7 fellowships with full tuition reimbursements available (averaging $5,714 per year), 14 teaching assistantships with full tuition reimbursements available (averaging $13,520 per year); research assistantships with full tuition reimbursements available, career-related internships or fieldwork, Federal Work-Study, institutionally sponsored loans, traineeships, health care benefits, and unspecified assistantships also available. Financial award application deadline: 1/10. *Faculty research:* International business and world trade, geographic information systems and cartography, transportation, urban and regional analysis, physical and environmental geography. Total annual research expenditures: $944,614. *Unit head:* Dr. Sharmistha Bagchi-Sen, Chairman, 716-645-0473, Fax: 716-645-2329, E-mail: geosbs@buffalo.edu. *Application contact:* Betsy Abraham, Graduate Secretary, 716-645-0471, Fax: 716-645-2329, E-mail: babraham@buffalo.edu.

The University of Akron, Graduate School, Buchtel College of Arts and Sciences, Department of Geography and Planning, Akron, OH 44325. Offers geographic information science (MS); urban planning (MA). Part-time and evening/weekend programs available. *Faculty:* 7 full-time (3 women), 9 part-time/adjunct (1 woman). *Students:* 31 full-time (13 women), 9 part-time (3 women); includes 3 Black or African American, non-Hispanic/Latino; 2 Asian, non-Hispanic/Latino; 3 Hispanic/Latino, 9 international. Average age 28. 40 applicants, 95% accepted, 16 enrolled. In 2010, 17 master's awarded. *Degree requirements:* For master's, thesis optional. *Entrance requirements:* For master's, minimum GPA of 2.75, two letters of recommendation, statement of purpose. Additional exam requirements/recommendations for international students: Required—TOEFL (minimum score 550 paper-based; 213 computer-based; 79 iBT). *Application deadline:* Applications are processed on a rolling basis. Application fee: $30 ($40 for international students). Electronic applications accepted. *Expenses:* Tuition, state resident: full-time $6800; part-time $378 per credit hour. Tuition, nonresident: full-time $11,644; part-time $647 per credit hour. Required fees: $1265. One-time fee: $30 full-time. *Financial support:* In 2010–11, 25 teaching assistantships with full and partial tuition reimbursements were awarded; career-related internships or fieldwork, Federal Work-Study, institutionally sponsored loans, scholarships/grants, and unspecified assistantships also available. *Faculty research:* Geographic information sciences; urban and regional planning; human geography especially cultural, political, and urban; regional geography, especially Native America, Asia, and Middle East. Total annual research expenditures: $154,978. *Unit head:* Dr. Raymond Cox, Interim Chair, 330-972-7622, E-mail: rcox@uakron.edu. *Application contact:* Dr. Linda Barrett, Director of Graduate Studies, 330-972-6120, Fax: 330-972-6080, E-mail: barrett@uakron.edu.

The University of Alabama, Graduate School, College of Arts and Sciences, Department of Geography, Tuscaloosa, AL 35487. Offers MS. Part-time programs available. *Faculty:* 11 full-time (1 woman). *Students:* 20 full-time (11 women), 13 part-time (5 women); includes 2 minority (1 Black or African American, non-Hispanic/Latino; 1 Two or more races, non-Hispanic/Latino), 3 international. Average age 26. 21 applicants, 81% accepted, 13 enrolled. In 2010, 6 master's awarded. *Degree requirements:* For master's, comprehensive exam, thesis or alternative. *Entrance requirements:* For master's, GRE, minimum GPA of 3.0. Additional exam requirements/recommendations for international students: Required—TOEFL. *Application deadline:* For fall admission, 2/15 priority date for domestic students, 2/1 priority date for international students; for spring admission, 10/1 priority date for domestic and international students. Applications are processed on a rolling basis. Application fee: $50 ($60 for international students). Electronic applications accepted. *Expenses:* Tuition, state resident: full-time $7900. Tuition, nonresident: full-time $20,500. *Financial support:* In 2010–11, 16 students received support, including fellowships (averaging $12,500 per year), 3 research assistantships with full tuition reimbursements available (averaging $10,908 per year), 15 teaching assistantships with full tuition reimbursements available (averaging $10,908 per year); career-related internships or fieldwork, health care benefits, and unspecified assistantships also available. Financial award application deadline: 2/15. *Faculty research:* Land use, regional and urban planning, geographic information systems, forest ecology, environmental management, geomorphology, climatology. Total annual research expenditures: $3,975. *Unit head:* Prof. Bobby Wilson, Chair, 205-348-5047, Fax: 205-348-2278, E-mail: bmwilson@bama.ua.edu. *Application contact:* Information Contact, 205-348-5047, Fax: 205-348-2278.

University of Alaska Fairbanks, School of Natural Resources and Agricultural Sciences, Fairbanks, AK 99775-7140. Offers natural resource and sustainability (PhD); natural resource management (MS); natural resource management and geography (MNRM, MS). Part-time programs available. *Faculty:* 37 full-time (12 women), 5 part-time/adjunct (4 women). *Students:* 31 full-time (22 women), 24 part-time (10 women); includes 5 minority (2 American Indian or Alaska Native, non-Hispanic/Latino; 1 Hispanic/Latino; 2 Two or more races, non-Hispanic/

Latino), 6 international. Average age 33. 42 applicants, 26% accepted, 8 enrolled. In 2010, 3 master's, 2 doctorates awarded. *Degree requirements:* For master's, comprehensive exam, thesis or alternative. *Entrance requirements:* For master's, GRE General Test. Additional exam requirements/recommendations for international students: Required—TOEFL (minimum score 550 paper-based; 213 computer-based). *Application deadline:* For fall admission, 6/1 for domestic students, 3/1 for international students; for spring admission, 10/15 for domestic students, 9/1 for international students. Applications are processed on a rolling basis. Application fee: $60. Electronic applications accepted. *Expenses:* Tuition, state resident: full-time $5688; part-time $316 per credit. Tuition, nonresident: full-time $11,628; part-time $646 per credit. Required fees: $289 per semester. Tuition and fees vary according to course load and reciprocity agreements. *Financial support:* In 2010–11, 17 research assistantships (averaging $11,187 per year), 4 teaching assistantships (averaging $8,943 per year) were awarded; fellowships, career-related internships or fieldwork, Federal Work-Study, scholarships/grants, health care benefits, and unspecified assistantships also available. Support available to part-time students. Financial award application deadline: 2/15; financial award applicants required to submit FAFSA. *Faculty research:* Conservation biology, soil/water conservation, land use policy and planning in the arctic and subarctic, forest ecosystem management, subarctic agricultural production. Total annual research expenditures: $5.6 million. *Unit head:* Dr. Carol E. Lewis, Dean, 907-474-7083, Fax: 907-474-6567, E-mail: fysnras@uaf.edu. *Application contact:* Veazey David, Director of Enrollment Management, 907-474-5276, Fax: 907-474-6567, E-mail: dave.veazey@alaska.edu.

The University of Arizona, College of Social and Behavioral Sciences, Department of Geography and Regional Development, Tucson, AZ 85721. Offers geography (MA, PhD). Part-time programs available. *Faculty:* 14 full-time (7 women). *Students:* 89 full-time (42 women), 27 part-time (17 women); includes 1 Black or African American, non-Hispanic/Latino; 1 Asian, non-Hispanic/Latino; 8 Hispanic/Latino; 4 Two or more races, non-Hispanic/Latino, 11 international. Average age 34. 107 applicants, 29% accepted, 14 enrolled. In 2010, 7 master's, 4 doctorates awarded. Terminal master's awarded for partial completion of doctoral program. *Degree requirements:* For master's, thesis or additional course work; for doctorate, variable foreign language requirement, thesis/dissertation. *Entrance requirements:* For master's, GRE General Test, 2 letters of recommendation; for doctorate, GRE General Test, statement of purpose, 2 letters of recommendation, master's degree. Additional exam requirements/recommendations for international students: Required—TOEFL (minimum score 550 paper-based; 213 computer-based; 79 iBT). *Application deadline:* For fall admission, 1/15 for domestic and international students. Application fee: $65. Electronic applications accepted. *Expenses:* Tuition, state resident: full-time $7692. *Financial support:* In 2010–11, 8 research assistantships with full tuition reimbursements (averaging $19,566 per year), 28 teaching assistantships with full tuition reimbursements (averaging $19,492 per year) were awarded; career-related internships or fieldwork, scholarships/grants, health care benefits, and unspecified assistantships also available. Financial award application deadline: 2/1. *Faculty research:* Population, Latin America, Anglo America, the former Soviet Union, Middle East. Total annual research expenditures: $514,629. *Unit head:* Dr. John Paul Jones, Department Head, 520-621-1652, Fax: 520-621-2889, E-mail: jpjones@email.arizona.edu. *Application contact:* Linda Koski, Information Contact, 520-621-1652, Fax: 520-621-2889, E-mail: lkoski@email.arizona.edu.

University of Arkansas, Graduate School, J. William Fulbright College of Arts and Sciences, Department of Geosciences, Program in Geography, Fayetteville, AR 72701-1201. Offers MA. Part-time programs available. *Students:* 8 full-time (1 woman), 12 part-time (4 women), 2 international. 11 applicants, 100% accepted. In 2010, 5 master's awarded. *Degree requirements:* For master's, thesis. *Application deadline:* For fall admission, 4/1 for international students; for spring admission, 10/1 for international students. Applications are processed on a rolling basis. Application fee: $40 ($50 for international students). Electronic applications accepted. *Financial support:* In 2010–11, 3 research assistantships, 6 teaching assistantships were awarded; fellowships, career-related internships or fieldwork and Federal Work-Study also available. Support available to part-time students. Financial award application deadline: 4/1; financial award applicants required to submit FAFSA. *Unit head:* Dr. Ralph Davis, Chair, 479-575-3355, Fax: 479-575-3469, E-mail: ralphd@uark.edu. *Application contact:* Dr. Tom Graff, Graduate Coordinator, 479-575-3878, E-mail: tgraff@uark.edu.

The University of British Columbia, Faculty of Arts and Faculty of Graduate Studies, Department of Geography, Vancouver, BC V6T 1Z2, Canada. Offers M Sc, MA, PhD. Part-time programs available. Terminal master's awarded for partial completion of doctoral program. *Degree requirements:* For master's, thesis; for doctorate, comprehensive exam, thesis/dissertation. *Entrance requirements:* For master's and doctorate, minimum B average, 2nd class honors, upper division (class II, division I). Additional exam requirements/recommendations for international students: Required—TOEFL (minimum score 600 paper-based; 250 computer-based; 100 iBT). Electronic applications accepted. Tuition charges are reported in Canadian dollars. *Expenses:* Tuition, area resident: Full-time $4179 Canadian dollars. International tuition: $7344 Canadian dollars full-time. *Faculty research:* Earth system science, environmental geography, historical geography, social geography, urban geography.

University of Calgary, Faculty of Graduate Studies, Faculty of Social Sciences, Department of Geography, Calgary, AB T2N 1N4, Canada. Offers M Sc, MA, MGIS, PhD. Part-time programs available. *Degree requirements:* For master's, thesis, departmental conference; for doctorate, thesis/dissertation, candidacy exam, departmental conference. *Entrance requirements:* For master's, minimum undergraduate GPA of 3.0 during last 2 years; for doctorate, minimum GPA of 3.0 during previous 2 years, master's degree. Additional exam requirements/recommendations for international students: Required—TOEFL (minimum score 550 paper-based; 213 computer-based). Electronic applications accepted. *Faculty research:* Geographic information systems, remote sensing, geomorphology, earth system processes, urban and required environmental health research.

University of California, Berkeley, Graduate Division, College of Letters and Science, Department of Geography, Berkeley, CA 94720-1500. Offers PhD. *Degree requirements:* For doctorate, thesis/dissertation, qualifying exam. *Entrance requirements:* For doctorate, GRE General Test, minimum GPA of 3.0, 3 letters of recommendation. Electronic applications accepted.

University of California, Davis, Graduate Studies, Graduate Group in Geography, Davis, CA 95616. Offers MA, PhD. Terminal master's awarded for partial completion of doctoral program. *Degree requirements:* For master's, comprehensive exam (for some programs), thesis (for some programs); for doctorate, thesis/dissertation. *Entrance requirements:* For master's, GRE General Test, minimum GPA of 3.0; for doctorate, GRE General Test, master's degree, minimum GPA of 3.0. Additional exam requirements/recommendations for international students: Required—TOEFL (minimum score 550 paper-based; 213 computer-based). Electronic applications accepted. *Faculty research:* Cultural agrosystems, mountain society habitat and South Asia.

University of California, Los Angeles, Graduate Division, College of Letters and Science, Department of Geography, Los Angeles, CA 90095. Offers MA, PhD. *Faculty:* 21 full-time (5 women). *Students:* 40 full-time (19 women); includes 6 Asian, non-Hispanic/Latino; 2 Hispanic/Latino, 6 international. Average age 30. 53 applicants, 26% accepted, 8 enrolled. In 2010, 11 master's, 9 doctorates awarded. Terminal master's awarded for partial completion of doctoral program. *Degree requirements:* For master's, thesis; for doctorate, thesis/dissertation, oral and written qualifying exams. *Entrance requirements:* For master's, GRE General Test, minimum GPA of 3.3; for doctorate, GRE General Test, minimum undergraduate GPA of 3.3, sample of research writing or thesis. *Application deadline:* For fall admission, 12/31 for domestic and international students. Application fee: $70 ($90 for international students). Electronic applications accepted. *Financial support:* In 2010–11, 40 fellowships with full and partial tuition reimbursements, 10 research assistantships with full and partial tuition reimbursements, 27 teaching assistantships with full and partial tuition reimbursements were awarded; Federal Work-Study, institutionally sponsored loans, scholarships/grants, health care benefits, tuition

Geography

University of California, Los Angeles (continued)
waivers (full and partial), and unspecified assistantships also available. Financial award application deadline: 3/1; financial award applicants required to submit FAFSA. *Unit head:* Dr. Marilyn N. Raphael, Chair, 310-206-4590, E-mail: raphael@geog.ucla.edu. *Application contact:* Department Office, 310-825-1071, E-mail: gradapps@geog.ucla.edu.

University of California, Santa Barbara, Graduate Division, College of Letters and Sciences, Division of Mathematics, Life, and Physical Sciences, Department of Geography, Santa Barbara, CA 93106-4060. Offers cognitive science (PhD); geography (MA, PhD); quantitative methods in the social sciences (PhD); transportation (PhD); MA/PhD. *Faculty:* 23 full-time (4 women), 11 part-time/adjunct (4 women). *Students:* 71 full-time (32 women); includes 2 Black or African American, non-Hispanic/Latino; 14 Asian, non-Hispanic/Latino; 6 Hispanic/Latino. Average age 31. 82 applicants, 33% accepted, 18 enrolled. In 2010, 3 master's, 13 doctorates awarded. Terminal master's awarded for partial completion of doctoral program. *Degree requirements:* For master's, comprehensive exam (for some programs), thesis or alternative; for doctorate, comprehensive exam, thesis/dissertation. *Entrance requirements:* For master's and doctorate, GRE (minimum verbal/quantitative score 1100). Additional exam requirements/recommendations for international students: Required—TOEFL (minimum score 550 paper-based; 80 iBT), IELTS (minimum score 7). *Application deadline:* For fall admission, 2/1 for domestic and international students. Application fee: $70 ($90 for international students). Electronic applications accepted. *Financial support:* In 2010–11, 61 students received support, including 49 fellowships with full and partial tuition reimbursements available (averaging $8,958 per year), 32 research assistantships with full and partial tuition reimbursements available (averaging $10,335 per year), 29 teaching assistantships with partial tuition reimbursements available (averaging $9,384 per year). Financial award applicants required to submit FAFSA. *Faculty research:* Earth system science, human environment relations, modeling, measurement and computation. *Unit head:* Dr. Dar Alexander Roberts, Professor/Chair, 805-880-2531, Fax: 805-893-2578, E-mail: dar@geog.ucsb.edu. *Application contact:* Jose Luis Saleta, Student Programs Manager, 805-456-2829, Fax: 805-893-2578, E-mail: saleta@geog.ucsb.edu.

University of Central Arkansas, Graduate School, College of Liberal Arts, Department of Geography, Conway, AR 72035-0001. Offers community and economic development (MS); geographic information systems (MGIS, Certificate). Part-time programs available. Post-baccalaureate distance learning degree programs offered (minimal on-campus study). *Faculty:* 3 full-time (0 women). *Students:* 4 full-time (1 woman), 11 part-time (1 woman); includes 1 minority (Black or African American, non-Hispanic/Latino). Average age 30. 6 applicants, 100% accepted, 5 enrolled. *Entrance requirements:* Additional exam requirements/recommendations for international students: Required—TOEFL (minimum score 550 paper-based; 213 computer-based). *Application deadline:* For fall admission, 3/1 priority date for domestic and international students; for spring admission, 10/1 priority date for domestic and international students. Applications are processed on a rolling basis. Application fee: $25 ($50 for international students). *Financial support:* Applicants required to submit FAFSA. *Unit head:* Dr. Brooks Green, Chairperson, 501-450-5636, Fax: 501-450-5185, E-mail: brooksg@uca.edu. *Application contact:* Susan Wood, Admissions Assistant, 501-450-3124, Fax: 501-450-5678, E-mail: swood@uca.edu.

University of Cincinnati, Graduate School, McMicken College of Arts and Sciences, Department of Geography, Cincinnati, OH 45221. Offers MA, PhD. Terminal master's awarded for partial completion of doctoral program. *Degree requirements:* For master's, thesis optional; for doctorate, one foreign language, comprehensive exam, thesis/dissertation. *Entrance requirements:* For master's and doctorate, GRE General Test. Additional exam requirements/recommendations for international students: Required—TOEFL. Electronic applications accepted. *Faculty research:* Urban-economics, GIS, physical-environmental.

University of Colorado at Colorado Springs, College of Letters, Arts and Sciences, Department of Geography and Environmental Studies, Colorado Springs, CO 80933-7150. Offers MA. Part-time programs available. *Faculty:* 11 full-time (2 women). *Students:* 14 full-time (5 women), 4 part-time (2 women); includes 1 Hispanic/Latino. Average age 36. 13 applicants, 77% accepted, 6 enrolled. In 2010, 7 master's awarded. *Degree requirements:* For master's, comprehensive exam (for some programs), thesis (for some programs). *Entrance requirements:* For master's, GRE. *Application deadline:* For fall admission, 4/1 priority date for domestic students. Applications are processed on a rolling basis. Application fee: $60 ($75 for international students). *Expenses:* Tuition, state resident: full-time $7916. Tuition, nonresident: full-time $16,610. Tuition and fees vary according to course load, degree level, program, reciprocity agreements and student level. *Financial support:* Federal Work-Study and scholarships/grants available. Support available to part-time students. Financial award application deadline: 3/1; financial award applicants required to submit FAFSA. *Faculty research:* Natural hazard mitigation and policy issues, applied geography, geographic information systems, population geography. Total annual research expenditures: $106,415. *Unit head:* Dr. Emily Skop, Associate Professor, 719-255-3789, Fax: 719-255-4066, E-mail: eskop@uccs.edu. *Application contact:* Mary McGill, Program Assistant, 719-255-3016, E-mail: mmcgill@uccs.edu.

University of Colorado Boulder, Graduate School, College of Arts and Sciences, Department of Geography, Boulder, CO 80309. Offers MA, PhD. Part-time programs available. *Faculty:* 24 full-time (7 women). *Students:* 79 full-time (37 women), 10 part-time (5 women); includes 1 minority (Hispanic/Latino), 11 international. Average age 31. 163 applicants, 26 enrolled. In 2010, 13 master's, 7 doctorates awarded. Terminal master's awarded for partial completion of doctoral program. *Degree requirements:* For master's, thesis; for doctorate, one foreign language, comprehensive exam, thesis/dissertation. *Entrance requirements:* For master's, GRE General Test, minimum undergraduate GPA of 3.0; for doctorate, GRE General Test. *Application deadline:* For fall admission, 1/15 priority date for domestic students, 12/1 for international students. Application fee: $50 ($60 for international students). *Financial support:* In 2010–11, 19 fellowships (averaging $11,176 per year), 14 research assistantships with tuition reimbursements (averaging $15,971 per year) were awarded. Financial award application deadline: 1/15. *Faculty research:* Physical geography, human geography, environmental society relations, technical geography, GIS and cartography. Total annual research expenditures: $33.4 million.

University of Connecticut, Graduate School, College of Liberal Arts and Sciences, Department of Geography, Storrs, CT 06269. Offers geographic information systems (Certificate); geography (MS, PhD). *Degree requirements:* For master's, comprehensive exam; for doctorate, thesis/dissertation. *Entrance requirements:* For master's and doctorate, GRE General Test. Additional exam requirements/recommendations for international students: Required—TOEFL (minimum score 550 paper-based; 213 computer-based). Electronic applications accepted.

University of Delaware, College of Earth, Ocean, and Environment, Department of Geography, Newark, DE 19716. Offers MA, MS, PhD. *Degree requirements:* For master's, thesis; for doctorate, thesis/dissertation. *Entrance requirements:* For master's and doctorate, GRE General Test. Additional exam requirements/recommendations for international students: Required—TOEFL. Electronic applications accepted. *Faculty research:* Permafrost, Glaciers, Climatology, Physical Geography, Human Geography.

University of Denver, Faculty of Natural Sciences and Mathematics, Department of Geography, Denver, CO 80208. Offers geographic information science (MS); geography (MA, PhD). Part-time programs available. *Faculty:* 15 full-time (6 women), 1 part-time/adjunct (0 women). *Students:* 11 full-time (4 women), 44 part-time (20 women); includes 5 minority (1 Black or African American, non-Hispanic/Latino; 1 Asian, non-Hispanic/Latino; 3 Hispanic/Latino), 2 international. Average age 32. 66 applicants, 80% accepted, 28 enrolled. In 2010, 19 master's, 3 doctorates awarded. Terminal master's awarded for partial completion of doctoral program. *Degree requirements:* For master's, comprehensive exam (for some programs), thesis or project; for doctorate, one foreign language, comprehensive exam, thesis/dissertation. *Entrance requirements:* For master's, GRE General Test; for doctorate, GRE General Test, MA. Additional exam requirements/recommendations for international students: Required—TOEFL (minimum score 570 paper-based; 88 iBT). *Application deadline:* Applications are processed on a rolling basis. Application fee: $60. Electronic applications accepted. *Expenses:* Tuition: Full-time $35,604; part-time $29,670 per year. Required fees: $687 per year. Tuition and fees vary according to program. *Financial support:* In 2010–11, 15 teaching assistantships with full and partial tuition reimbursements (averaging $18,300 per year) were awarded; career-related internships or fieldwork, Federal Work-Study, institutionally sponsored loans, scholarships/grants, and unspecified assistantships also available. Support available to part-time students. Financial award application deadline: 3/1; financial award applicants required to submit FAFSA. *Faculty research:* Transportation and land use, fluvial geography and water resources, climatology, geographic information systems, biogeography. Total annual research expenditures: $158,000. *Unit head:* Dr. Andrew Goetz, Chair, 303-871-2201, Fax: 303-871-2201, E-mail: agoetz@du.edu. *Application contact:* Karen Escobar, Assistant to the Chair, 303-871-2201, Fax: 303-871-2201, E-mail: kescobar@du.edu.

University of Florida, Graduate School, College of Liberal Arts and Sciences, Department of Geography, Gainesville, FL 32611. Offers MA, MS, PhD. *Faculty:* 15 full-time (3 women), 2 part-time/adjunct (1 woman). *Students:* 39 full-time (19 women), 9 part-time (4 women); includes 1 Black or African American, non-Hispanic/Latino; 1 American Indian or Alaska Native, non-Hispanic/Latino; 2 Asian, non-Hispanic/Latino; 2 Hispanic/Latino, 18 international. Average age 30. 34 applicants, 38% accepted, 8 enrolled. In 2010, 12 master's, 3 doctorates awarded. *Degree requirements:* For master's, thesis; for doctorate, comprehensive exam, thesis/dissertation. *Entrance requirements:* For master's and doctorate, GRE General Test, minimum GPA of 3.0. Additional exam requirements/recommendations for international students: Required—TOEFL (minimum score 550 paper-based; 213 computer-based; 80 iBT), IELTS (minimum score 6). *Application deadline:* For fall admission, 6/1 priority date for domestic students. Applications are processed on a rolling basis. Application fee: $30. Electronic applications accepted. *Expenses:* Tuition, state resident: full-time $10,915.92. Tuition, nonresident: full-time $28,309. *Financial support:* In 2010–11, 42 students received support, including 22 fellowships, 6 research assistantships (averaging $18,730 per year), 14 teaching assistantships (averaging $19,821 per year); career-related internships or fieldwork and unspecified assistantships also available. Financial award applicants required to submit FAFSA. *Faculty research:* Economic development, physical geography, hydrology, climatology, tropical agriculture. *Unit head:* Dr. Peter R. Waylen, Chair, 352-392-0494, Fax: 352-392-8855, E-mail: prwaylen@ufl.edu. *Application contact:* Dr. Jane Southworth, Graduate Coordinator, 352-392-0494, Fax: 352-392-8855, E-mail: jsouthwo@ufl.edu.

University of Georgia, College of Arts and Sciences, Department of Geography, Athens, GA 30602. Offers MA, MS, PhD. *Faculty:* 20 full-time (7 women), 1 part-time/adjunct (0 women). *Students:* 61 full-time (22 women), 7 part-time (3 women); includes 4 Black or African American, non-Hispanic/Latino, 14 international. 89 applicants, 49% accepted, 22 enrolled. In 2010, 10 master's, 4 doctorates awarded. *Degree requirements:* For master's, one foreign language, thesis; for doctorate, one foreign language, thesis/dissertation. *Entrance requirements:* For master's and doctorate, GRE General Test. *Application deadline:* For fall admission, 7/1 priority date for domestic students; for spring admission, 11/15 for domestic students. Application fee: $50. Electronic applications accepted. *Expenses:* Tuition, state resident: full-time $7200; part-time $344 per credit hour. Tuition, nonresident: full-time $21,900; part-time $944 per credit hour. Tuition and fees vary according to course load and program. *Financial support:* Fellowships, research assistantships, teaching assistantships, unspecified assistantships available. *Unit head:* Dr. George A. Brook, Head, 706-542-2856, Fax: 706-542-2388, E-mail: gabrook@uga.edu. *Application contact:* Dr. Steven Holloway, Graduate Coordinator, 706-542-4109, Fax: 706-542-2388, E-mail: holloway@uga.edu.

University of Guelph, Graduate Studies, College of Social and Applied Human Sciences, Department of Geography, Guelph, ON N1G 2W1, Canada. Offers M Sc, MA, PhD. Part-time programs available. *Degree requirements:* For master's, thesis (for some programs); for doctorate, comprehensive exam, thesis/dissertation. *Entrance requirements:* For master's, minimum B average during previous 2 years of course work; for doctorate, minimum A-average. Additional exam requirements/recommendations for international students: Required—TOEFL (minimum score 550 paper-based; 213 computer-based). Electronic applications accepted. *Faculty research:* Rural resource evaluation, environmental analysis, biophysical process, rural settlement and land use, resource assessment.

University of Hawaii at Manoa, Graduate Division, College of Social Sciences, Department of Geography, Honolulu, HI 96822. Offers geography (MA, PhD); ocean policy (Graduate Certificate). Part-time programs available. *Faculty:* 23 full-time (7 women), 5 part-time/adjunct (1 woman). *Students:* 36 full-time (19 women), 9 part-time (4 women); includes 10 minority (4 Asian, non-Hispanic/Latino; 1 Hispanic/Latino; 3 Native Hawaiian or other Pacific Islander, non-Hispanic/Latino; 2 Two or more races, non-Hispanic/Latino), 9 international. Average age 34. 34 applicants, 38% accepted, 12 enrolled. In 2010, 5 master's, 4 doctorates awarded. *Degree requirements:* For master's, one foreign language, comprehensive exam, thesis; for doctorate, one foreign language, comprehensive exam, thesis/dissertation. *Entrance requirements:* For master's, GRE General Test; for doctorate, GRE General Test, sample of written work. Additional exam requirements/recommendations for international students: Required—TOEFL (minimum score 500 paper-based; 173 computer-based; 61 iBT), IELTS (minimum score 5). *Application deadline:* For fall admission, 1/15 for domestic and international students. Applications are processed on a rolling basis. Application fee: $60. *Financial support:* In 2010–11, 1 student received support, including 20 fellowships (averaging $1,652 per year), 9 research assistantships (averaging $18,480 per year), 8 teaching assistantships (averaging $14,529 per year); career-related internships or fieldwork, Federal Work-Study, institutionally sponsored loans, and tuition waivers (full) also available. Financial award application deadline: 3/1. *Faculty research:* Physical geography, human geography, methodology. Total annual research expenditures: $740,000. *Application contact:* Matthew McGranaghan, Graduate Chair, 808-956-7018, Fax: 808-956-3512, E-mail: matt@hawaii.edu.

University of Idaho, College of Graduate Studies, College of Science, Department of Geography, Moscow, ID 83844-2282. Offers MS, PhD. *Faculty:* 10 full-time, 1 part-time/adjunct. *Students:* 16 full-time, 7 part-time. Average age 33. In 2010, 2 master's, 1 doctorate awarded. *Degree requirements:* For doctorate, one foreign language, thesis/dissertation. *Entrance requirements:* For master's, minimum GPA of 2.8; for doctorate, minimum undergraduate GPA of 2.8, graduate 3.0. *Application deadline:* For fall admission, 8/1 for domestic students; for spring admission, 12/15 for domestic students. Applications are processed on a rolling basis. Application fee: $60. Electronic applications accepted. *Expenses:* Tuition, nonresident: part-time $580 per credit. Required fees: $306 per credit. *Financial support:* Research assistantships, teaching assistantships available. Financial award applicants required to submit FAFSA. *Faculty research:* Land cover land use changes, rural development, geographic trade models, climate change and effects on ecosystems, migration and regional development. *Unit head:* Dr. Harley E. Johansen, Head, 208-885-6216, E-mail: geog@uidaho.edu. *Application contact:* Dr. Harley E. Johansen, Head, 208-885-6216, E-mail: geog@uidaho.edu.

University of Illinois at Chicago, Graduate College, College of Liberal Arts and Sciences, Department of Anthropology, Program in Environmental and Urban Geography, Chicago, IL 60607-7128. Offers environmental studies (MA); urban geography (MA). Part-time programs available. *Degree requirements:* For master's, thesis. *Entrance requirements:* For master's, GRE General Test, minimum GPA of 2.75. Additional exam requirements/recommendations for international students: Required—TOEFL. Electronic applications accepted.

University of Illinois at Urbana–Champaign, Graduate College, College of Liberal Arts and Sciences, School of Earth, Society and Environment, Department of Geography, Champaign, IL 61820. Offers MA, MS, PhD. *Faculty:* 12 full-time (2 women). *Students:* 32 full-time (12 women), 13 part-time (5 women); includes 6 minority (3 Black or African American, non-Hispanic/Latino; 1 Asian, non-Hispanic/Latino; 1 Hispanic/Latino; 1 Two or more races, non-Hispanic/Latino), 15 international. 78 applicants, 15% accepted, 8 enrolled. In 2010, 5 master's, 2 doctorates awarded. *Entrance requirements:* For master's, GRE, minimum GPA of 3.0; for doctorate, GRE, minimum GPA of 3.5. Additional exam requirements/recommendations for international students: Required—TOEFL. *Application deadline:* Applications are processed on a rolling basis. Application fee: $75 ($90 for international students). Electronic applications accepted. *Financial support:* In 2010–11, 14 fellowships, 20 research assistantships, 18 teaching assistantships were awarded; tuition waivers (full and partial) also available. *Unit head:* Bruce Rhoads, Head, 217-333-1322, Fax: 217-244-1785, E-mail: brhoads@illinois.edu. *Application contact:* Susan Etter, Office Support Specialist, 217-244-3488, Fax: 217-244-1785, E-mail: etter1@illinois.edu.

The University of Iowa, Graduate College, College of Liberal Arts and Sciences, Department of Geography, Iowa City, IA 52242-1316. Offers MA, PhD. *Degree requirements:* For master's, thesis optional, exam; for doctorate, comprehensive exam, thesis/dissertation. *Entrance requirements:* For master's and doctorate, GRE General Test, minimum GPA of 3.0. Additional exam requirements/recommendations for international students: Required—TOEFL (minimum score 550 paper-based; 213 computer-based; 81 iBT). Electronic applications accepted.

The University of Kansas, Graduate Studies, College of Liberal Arts and Sciences, Department of Geography, Lawrence, KS 66045-7613. Offers atmospheric science (MS); geography (MA, PhD); MUP/MA. Part-time programs available. *Faculty:* 23 full-time (4 women). *Students:* 75 full-time (28 women), 12 part-time (3 women); includes 5 minority (1 Black or African American, non-Hispanic/Latino; 3 American Indian or Alaska Native, non-Hispanic/Latino; 1 Hispanic/Latino), 12 international. Average age 32. 71 applicants, 49% accepted, 20 enrolled. In 2010, 9 master's, 9 doctorates awarded. *Degree requirements:* For master's, comprehensive exam, thesis, thesis defense; for doctorate, one foreign language, comprehensive exam, thesis/dissertation, dissertation defense. *Entrance requirements:* For master's and doctorate, GRE General Test, 3 letters of reference, transcripts, statement of interests. Additional exam requirements/recommendations for international students: Required—TOEFL. *Application deadline:* For fall admission, 1/15 priority date for domestic and international students; for spring admission, 11/1 for domestic students, 10/1 for international students. Applications are processed on a rolling basis. Application fee: $55 ($65 for international students). Electronic applications accepted. *Expenses:* Tuition, state resident: full-time $7092; part-time $295.50 per credit hour. Tuition, nonresident: full-time $16,590; part-time $691.25 per credit hour. Required fees: $858; $71.49 per credit hour. Tuition and fees vary according to course load, campus/location and program. *Financial support:* Fellowships with full tuition reimbursements, research assistantships with full tuition reimbursements, teaching assistantships with full and partial tuition reimbursements, unspecified assistantships available. Financial award application deadline: 1/15. *Faculty research:* Physical geography, techniques (cartography, GIS, remote sensing), cultural/regional geography, atmospheric science. *Unit head:* Terry Slocum, Chair, 785-864-5146, Fax: 785-864-5378, E-mail: t-slocum@ku.edu. *Application contact:* Stephen Egbert, Graduate Director, 785-864-4252, Fax: 785-864-5378, E-mail: s-egbert@ku.edu.

University of Kentucky, Graduate School, College of Arts and Sciences, Program in Geography, Lexington, KY 40506-0032. Offers MA, PhD. *Degree requirements:* For master's, comprehensive exam, thesis optional; for doctorate, one foreign language, comprehensive exam, thesis/dissertation. *Entrance requirements:* For master's, GRE General Test, minimum undergraduate GPA of 2.75; for doctorate, GRE General Test, minimum graduate GPA of 3.0. Additional exam requirements/recommendations for international students: Required—TOEFL (minimum score 550 paper-based; 213 computer-based). Electronic applications accepted. *Faculty research:* Cultural, industrial, medical, political, social, population, and transportation geography; geographic analysis; Third World (especially Southeast Asia theory); Eastern Europe.

University of Lethbridge, School of Graduate Studies, Lethbridge, AB T1K 3M4, Canada. Offers accounting (MScM); addictions counseling (M Sc); agricultural biotechnology (M Sc); agricultural studies (M Sc, MA); anthropology (MA); archaeology (MA); art (MA, MFA); biochemistry (M Sc); biological sciences (M Sc); biomolecular science (PhD); biosystems and biodiversity (PhD); Canadian studies (MA); chemistry (M Sc); computer science (M Sc); computer science and geographical information science (M Sc); counseling psychology (M Ed); dramatic arts (MA); earth, space, and physical science (PhD); economics (MA); educational leadership (M Ed); English (MA); environmental science (M Sc); evolution and behavior (PhD); exercise science (M Sc); finance (MScM); French (MA); French/German (MA); French/Spanish (MA); general education (M Ed); general management (MScM); geography (M Sc, MA); German (MA); health science (M Sc); history (MA); human resource management and labour relations (MScM); individualized multidisciplinary (M Sc, MA); information systems (MScM); international management (MScM); kinesiology (M Sc, MA); management (M Sc, MA); marketing (MScM); mathematics (M Sc); music (M Mus, MA); Native American studies (MA); neuroscience (M Sc, PhD); new media (MA); nursing (M Sc); philosophy (MA); physics (M Sc); policy and strategy (MScM); political science (MA); psychology (M Sc, MA); religious studies (MA); social sciences (MA); sociology (MA); theatre and dramatic arts (MFA); theoretical and computational science (PhD); urban and regional studies (MA); women's studies (MA). Part-time and evening/weekend programs available. *Degree requirements:* For doctorate, comprehensive exam, thesis/dissertation. *Entrance requirements:* For master's, GMAT (M Sc in management), bachelor's degree in related field, minimum GPA of 3.0 during previous 20 graded semester courses, 2 years teaching or related experience (M Ed); for doctorate, master's degree, minimum graduate GPA of 3.5. Additional exam requirements/recommendations for international students: Required—TOEFL. *Faculty research:* Movement and brain plasticity, gibberellin physiology, photosynthesis, carbon cycling, molecular properties of main-group ring components.

University of Louisville, Graduate School, College of Arts and Sciences, Department of Geography and Geosciences, Louisville, KY 40292-0001. Offers applied geography (MS). Part-time programs available. *Faculty:* 9 full-time (4 women). *Students:* 7 full-time (2 women), 4 part-time (2 women); includes 1 Black or African American, non-Hispanic/Latino; 1 Hispanic/Latino. Average age 30. 10 applicants, 100% accepted, 6 enrolled. *Degree requirements:* For master's, thesis. *Entrance requirements:* For master's, GRE (combined score of 1000), BA/BS with minimum cumulative GPA of 3.0. Additional exam requirements/recommendations for international students: Required—TOEFL (minimum score 550 paper-based; 213 computer-based; 79 iBT). *Application deadline:* For fall admission, 11/1 priority date for domestic students, 11/1 for international students; for spring admission, 4/1 priority date for domestic students, 4/1 for international students. Application fee: $50. Electronic applications accepted. *Expenses:* Tuition, state resident: full-time $9144; part-time $508 per credit hour. Tuition, nonresident: full-time $19,026; part-time $1057 per credit hour. Tuition and fees vary according to program and reciprocity agreements. *Financial support:* Departmental scholarships available. Financial award application deadline: 4/1. *Faculty research:* Climatology and global climate change, physical geography, human geography, medical and population geography, GIS, remote sensing and spatial statistics. Total annual research expenditures: $197,106. *Unit head:* Dr. Keith R. Mountain, Chair, 502-852-2692, E-mail: krmoun01@gwise.louisville.edu. *Application contact:* Dr. Carol L. Hanchette, Director, Graduate Admissions, 502-852-2699, Fax: 502-852-4560, E-mail: carol.hanchette@louisville.edu.

The University of Manchester, School of Environment and Development, Manchester, United Kingdom. Offers architecture (M Phil, PhD); development policy and management (M Phil, PhD); human geography (M Phil, PhD); physical geography (M Phil, PhD); planning and landscape (M Phil, PhD).

The University of Manchester, School of Nursing, Midwifery and Social Work, Manchester, United Kingdom. Offers nursing (M Phil, PhD); social work (M Phil, PhD).

University of Manitoba, Faculty of Graduate Studies, Clayton H. Riddell Faculty of Environment, Earth, and Resources, Department of Environment and Geography, Winnipeg, MB R3T 2N2, Canada. Offers environment (M Env); environment and geography (M Sc); geography (MA, PhD). *Degree requirements:* For master's, thesis; for doctorate, one foreign language, thesis/dissertation.

University of Maryland, Baltimore County, Graduate School, College of Arts, Humanities and Social Sciences, Department of Geography and Environmental Systems, Program in Geography and Environmental Systems, Baltimore, MD 21250. Offers MS, PhD. *Faculty:* 11 full-time (4 women), 6 part-time/adjunct (1 woman). *Students:* 19 full-time (12 women), 5 part-time (4 women); includes 2 Black or African American, non-Hispanic/Latino, 2 international. Average age 32. 25 applicants, 56% accepted, 6 enrolled.Terminal master's awarded for partial completion of doctoral program. *Degree requirements:* For master's, thesis optional, annual faculty evaluation, research paper; for doctorate, comprehensive exam, thesis/dissertation, annual faculty evaluation, qualifying exams, proposal and dissertation defense. *Entrance requirements:* For master's and doctorate, GRE, minimum GPA of 3.0 overall, 3.3 in major. Additional exam requirements/recommendations for international students: Required—TOEFL (minimum score 550 paper-based; 213 computer-based; 80 iBT). *Application deadline:* For fall admission, 2/1 for domestic and international students. Application fee: $50. Electronic applications accepted. *Financial support:* In 2010–11, 15 students received support, including 1 fellowship with full tuition reimbursement available (averaging $30,000 per year), 8 research assistantships with full tuition reimbursements available (averaging $18,392 per year), 6 teaching assistantships with full tuition reimbursements available (averaging $18,392 per year); scholarships/grants, traineeships, and unspecified assistantships also available. Financial award application deadline: 2/1. *Faculty research:* Watershed processes, climate and weather systems; ecology and biogeography; landscape ecology and land-use change; human geography, urban sustainability and environmental health; environmental policy; geographic information science and remote sensing. *Unit head:* Dr. Christopher M. Swan, Graduate Program Director, 410-455-2002, E-mail: gpd.ges@umbc.edu. *Application contact:* Kathryn Nee, Coordinator of Domestic Admissions, 410-455-2944, E-mail: nee@umbc.edu.

University of Maryland, College Park, Academic Affairs, College of Behavioral and Social Sciences, Department of Geography, College Park, MD 20742. Offers MA, PhD, MA/MLS. Part-time and evening/weekend programs available. *Faculty:* 60 full-time (19 women), 8 part-time/adjunct (5 women). *Students:* 66 full-time (38 women), 7 part-time (3 women); includes 6 Black or African American, non-Hispanic/Latino; 4 Asian, non-Hispanic/Latino; 2 Hispanic/Latino; 1 Two or more races, non-Hispanic/Latino, 27 international. 70 applicants, 33% accepted, 21 enrolled. In 2010, 12 master's, 9 doctorates awarded. Terminal master's awarded for partial completion of doctoral program. *Degree requirements:* For master's, thesis, oral exam; for doctorate, comprehensive exam, thesis/dissertation. *Entrance requirements:* For master's, GRE General Test, minimum GPA of 3.0, 3 letters of recommendation; for doctorate, GRE General Test. Additional exam requirements/recommendations for international students: Required—TOEFL, TWE. *Application deadline:* For fall admission, 1/15 for domestic students, 2/1 for international students. Applications are processed on a rolling basis. Application fee: $75. Electronic applications accepted. *Expenses:* Tuition, state resident: part-time $471 per credit hour. Tuition, nonresident: part-time $1016 per credit hour. Required fees: $337 per term. *Financial support:* In 2010–11, 7 fellowships with full and partial tuition reimbursements (averaging $16,817 per year), 14 research assistantships (averaging $16,617 per year), 41 teaching assistantships (averaging $16,574 per year) were awarded; Federal Work-Study and scholarships/grants also available. Support available to part-time students. Financial award applicants required to submit FAFSA. *Faculty research:* Cartography and automated mapping, environmental systems analysis, metropolitan analysis and planning, historical and human geography, coastal geomorphology. Total annual research expenditures: $8 million. *Unit head:* Chris Justice, Chair, 301-405-2270, E-mail: cjustice@umd.edu. *Application contact:* Dean of Graduate School, 301-405-0358, Fax: 301-314-9305.

University of Maryland, College Park, Academic Affairs, Program in Geography, Library, and Information Services, College Park, MD 20742. Offers MA/MLS. *Application deadline:* For fall admission, 1/15 for domestic and international students. Applications are processed on a rolling basis. Application fee: $60. Electronic applications accepted. *Expenses:* Tuition, state resident: part-time $471 per credit hour. Tuition, nonresident: part-time $1016 per credit hour. Required fees: $337 per term. *Financial support:* Fellowships, research assistantships, teaching assistantships available. Financial award application deadline: 2/1; financial award applicants required to submit FAFSA. *Unit head:* Dr. Diane Barlow, Associate Dean, 301-405-2042, Fax: 301-314-9145, E-mail: dbarlow@umd.edu. *Application contact:* Dean of Graduate School, 301-405-0376, Fax: 301-314-9305.

University of Massachusetts Amherst, Graduate School, College of Natural Sciences, Department of Geosciences, Program in Geography, Amherst, MA 01003. Offers MS. Part-time programs available. *Students:* 6 full-time (3 women), 3 part-time (1 woman); includes 2 minority (1 Hispanic/Latino; 1 Two or more races, non-Hispanic/Latino), 1 international. Average age 33. 15 applicants, 53% accepted, 2 enrolled. In 2010, 2 master's awarded. *Degree requirements:* For master's, thesis or alternative. *Entrance requirements:* For master's, GRE General Test. Additional exam requirements/recommendations for international students: Required—TOEFL (minimum score 550 paper-based; 213 computer-based; 80 iBT), IELTS (minimum score 6.5). *Application deadline:* For fall admission, 2/1 for domestic and international students; for spring admission, 10/1 for domestic and international students. Applications are processed on a rolling basis. Application fee: $50 ($65 for international students). Electronic applications accepted. *Expenses:* Tuition, state resident: full-time $2640. Required fees: $8282. One-time fee: $357 full-time. *Financial support:* Fellowships, research assistantships, teaching assistantships, career-related internships or fieldwork, Federal Work-Study, scholarships/grants, traineeships, health care benefits, tuition waivers (full), and unspecified assistantships available. Support available to part-time students. Financial award application deadline: 2/1; financial award applicants required to submit FAFSA. *Unit head:* Dr. Piper R. Gaubatz, Graduate Program Director, 413-545-2286, Fax: 413-545-1200. *Application contact:* Jean M. Ames, Supervisor of Admissions, 413-545-0722, Fax: 413-577-0010, E-mail: gradadm@grad.umass.edu.

University of Memphis, Graduate School, College of Arts and Sciences, Department of Earth Sciences, Memphis, TN 38152. Offers archaeology (MS); earth sciences (PhD); geographic information systems (Graduate Certificate); geography (MA, MS); geology (MS); geophysics (MS); interdisciplinary (MS). Part-time and evening/weekend programs available. *Faculty:* 15 full-time (3 women), 6 part-time/adjunct (2 women). *Students:* 35 full-time (7 women), 28 part-time (13 women); includes 5 Black or African American, non-Hispanic/Latino; 1 Asian, non-Hispanic/Latino, 15 international. Average age 33. 48 applicants, 69% accepted, 18 enrolled. In 2010, 2 master's, 2 doctorates, 1 other advanced degree awarded. Terminal master's awarded for partial completion of doctoral program. *Degree requirements:* For master's, comprehensive exam, thesis, seminar presentation; for doctorate, thesis/dissertation. *Entrance requirements:* For master's, GRE General Test, 3 letters of recommendation, statement of research interests; for doctorate, GRE General Test, 2 letters of recommendation, resume, personal statement. Additional exam requirements/recommendations for international students: Required—TOEFL (minimum score 550 paper-based; 210 computer-based). *Application deadline:* For fall admission, 1/31 for domestic students; for spring admission, 11/1 for domestic students. Applications are processed on a rolling basis. Application fee: $35 ($60 for international students). Electronic applications accepted. *Financial support:* In 2010–11, 18 students received support; fellowships with full tuition reimbursements available, research assistantships with full tuition reimbursements available, teaching assistantships with full tuition reimbursements available, Federal Work-Study, scholarships/grants, and unspecified assistantships available. Financial award application deadline: 2/15; financial award applicants required to submit FAFSA. *Faculty research:* Hazards, active tectonics, geophysics, hydrology and water resources, spatial analysis. *Unit head:* Dr. M. Jerry Bartholomew, Chair, 901-678-4536, Fax: 901-678-4467, E-mail: jbrthlm1@memphis.edu. *Application contact:* Dr. Arlene Hill, Associate Professor and Graduate Program Coordinator, 901-678-4358, Fax: 901-678-2178, E-mail: dlarsen@memphis.edu.

University of Miami, Graduate School, College of Arts and Sciences, Department of Geography and Regional Studies, Coral Gables, FL 33124. Offers geography (MA). Part-time programs available. *Degree requirements:* For master's, thesis. *Entrance requirements:* For master's, GRE, 3 letters of recommendation, official transcripts. Additional exam requirements/

Geography

University of Miami *(continued)*
recommendations for international students: Required—TOEFL. Electronic applications accepted. *Faculty research:* Urbanization, globalization, environmental change.

University of Missouri, Graduate School, College of Arts and Sciences, Department of Geography, Columbia, MO 65211. Offers MA. *Faculty:* 12 full-time (3 women). *Students:* 16 full-time (10 women), 4 part-time (2 women); includes 1 minority (Asian, non-Hispanic/Latino), 4 international. Average age 29. 18 applicants, 67% accepted, 9 enrolled. In 2010, 6 master's awarded. *Degree requirements:* For master's, thesis or alternative. *Entrance requirements:* For master's, GRE General Test (minimum score 1000 verbal and quantitative), minimum GPA of 3.0. Additional exam requirements/recommendations for international students: Required—TOEFL (minimum score 500 paper-based; 173 computer-based; 61 iBT). *Application deadline:* For fall admission, 2/15 priority date for domestic students; for winter admission, 10/1 priority date for domestic students; for spring admission, 4/1 priority date for domestic students. Applications are processed on a rolling basis. Application fee: $45 ($60 for international students). Electronic applications accepted. *Financial support:* In 2010–11, 3 fellowships with full tuition reimbursements, 2 research assistantships with full tuition reimbursements, 6 teaching assistantships with full tuition reimbursements were awarded; institutionally sponsored loans, health care benefits, and unspecified assistantships also available. *Faculty research:* Human geography, nature/society relationships, the physical environment, application of geographic information sciences. *Unit head:* Dr. Joseph Hobbs, Department Chair, 573-529-2013, E-mail: hobbsj@missouri.edu. *Application contact:* Dina Weaver, 573-882-8370, E-mail: weaverdr@missouri.edu.

The University of Montana, Graduate School, College of Arts and Sciences, Department of Geography, Missoula, MT 59812-0002. Offers geography (MA), including cartography and GIS, community and environmental planning. *Entrance requirements:* For master's, GRE General Test. Additional exam requirements/recommendations for international students: Required—TOEFL.

University of Nebraska at Omaha, Graduate Studies, College of Arts and Sciences, Department of Geography and Geology, Omaha, NE 68182. Offers geographic information science (Certificate); geography (MA). Part-time programs available. *Faculty:* 11 full-time (2 women). *Students:* 6 full-time (1 woman), 20 part-time (6 women); includes 5 minority (3 Black or African American, non-Hispanic/Latino; 2 Hispanic/Latino), 2 international. Average age 37. 13 applicants, 77% accepted, 10 enrolled. In 2010, 7 master's awarded. *Degree requirements:* For master's, comprehensive exam, thesis (for some programs). *Entrance requirements:* For master's, GRE, minimum GPA of 3.0, 15 undergraduate geography hours, resume. Additional exam requirements/recommendations for international students: Required—TOEFL (minimum score 550 paper-based; 213 computer-based; 80 iBT). *Application deadline:* For fall admission, 3/1 priority date for domestic students; for spring admission, 12/1 priority date for domestic students. Applications are processed on a rolling basis. Application fee: $45. Electronic applications accepted. *Financial support:* In 2010–11, 14 students received support; fellowships, research assistantships with tuition reimbursements available, teaching assistantships with tuition reimbursements available, Federal Work-Study, institutionally sponsored loans, scholarships/grants, tuition waivers (partial), and unspecified assistantships available. Support available to part-time students. Financial award application deadline: 3/1; financial award applicants required to submit FAFSA. *Unit head:* Dr. Jeffrey Peake, Chairperson, 402-554-2662. *Application contact:* Christina Dando, Student Contact, 402-554-2341, Fax: 402-554-3143, E-mail: graduate@unomaha.edu.

University of Nebraska–Lincoln, Graduate College, College of Arts and Sciences, Department of Anthropology and Geography, Program in Geography, Lincoln, NE 68588. Offers MA, PhD. *Degree requirements:* For master's, thesis optional; for doctorate, comprehensive exam, thesis/dissertation. *Entrance requirements:* For master's and doctorate, GRE General Test. Additional exam requirements/recommendations for international students: Required—TOEFL (minimum score 550 paper-based; 213 computer-based). Electronic applications accepted. *Faculty research:* Climatology, historical-cultural geography, geographic information systems/cartography/remote sensing, human geography, Great Plains studies.

University of Nevada, Reno, Graduate School, College of Science, Mackay School of Earth Sciences and Engineering, Department of Geography, Program in Geography, Reno, NV 89557. Offers MS, PhD. Terminal master's awarded for partial completion of doctoral program. *Degree requirements:* For master's, comprehensive exam, thesis; for doctorate, comprehensive exam, thesis/dissertation. *Entrance requirements:* For master's and doctorate, GRE General Test, minimum GPA of 2.75. Additional exam requirements/recommendations for international students: Required—TOEFL (minimum score 500 paper-based; 173 computer-based; 61 iBT), IELTS (minimum score 6). Electronic applications accepted. *Expenses:* Tuition, state resident: full-time $2219; part-time $246 per credit. Tuition, nonresident: part-time $510 per credit. International tuition: $9009 full-time. Required fees: $59 per term. One-time fee: $101. Tuition and fees vary according to course load. *Faculty research:* Natural resources, education, climatology, biogeography, ethnic/cultural geography.

University of New Mexico, Graduate School, College of Arts and Sciences, Department of Geography, Albuquerque, NM 87131-2039. Offers MS. Part-time programs available. *Faculty:* 13 full-time (3 women), 7 part-time/adjunct (4 women). *Students:* 7 full-time (5 women), 8 part-time (2 women); includes 2 minority (both Hispanic/Latino). Average age 33. 13 applicants, 54% accepted, 3 enrolled. In 2010, 4 master's awarded. *Degree requirements:* For master's, comprehensive exam (for some programs), thesis (for some programs). *Entrance requirements:* For master's, GRE. Additional exam requirements/recommendations for international students: Required—TOEFL. *Application deadline:* For fall admission, 2/1 priority date for domestic students, 1/1 priority date for international students; for spring admission, 11/15 for domestic and international students. Application fee: $50. Electronic applications accepted. *Expenses:* Tuition, state resident: full-time $5991; part-time $251 per credit hour. Tuition, nonresident: full-time $14,405; part-time $800.20 per credit hour. Tuition and fees vary according to course level, course load, program and reciprocity agreements. *Financial support:* In 2010–11, 10 students received support, including 4 research assistantships with full tuition reimbursements available (averaging $10,993 per year), 5 teaching assistantships with full tuition reimbursements available (averaging $10,034 per year); health care benefits and tuition waivers (full and partial) also available. Financial award applicants required to submit FAFSA. *Faculty research:* Geographic information science, environmental management. Total annual research expenditures: $94,525. *Unit head:* Dr. Scott M. Freundschuh, Chair, 505-277-0058, Fax: 505-277-3614, E-mail: sfreunds@unm.edu. *Application contact:* Dr. Paul A. Zandbergen, Department Administrator, 505-277-3105, Fax: 505-277-3614, E-mail: zandberg@unm.edu.

University of New Orleans, Graduate School, College of Liberal Arts, Department of Geography, New Orleans, LA 70148. Offers MA. *Entrance requirements:* For master's, GRE General Test. Additional exam requirements/recommendations for international students: Required—TOEFL (minimum score 550 paper-based; 213 computer-based; 79 iBT). Electronic applications accepted.

The University of North Carolina at Chapel Hill, Graduate School, College of Arts and Sciences, Department of Geography, Chapel Hill, NC 27599. Offers MA, PhD. *Degree requirements:* For master's, one foreign language, comprehensive exam, thesis; for doctorate, 2 foreign languages, comprehensive exam, thesis/dissertation. *Entrance requirements:* For master's and doctorate, GRE General Test, minimum GPA of 3.0. *Faculty research:* Geographic information systems, climatology, hydrology, population research, Latino immigration.

The University of North Carolina at Charlotte, Graduate School, College of Arts and Sciences, Department of Geography and Earth Sciences, Charlotte, NC 28223-0001. Offers earth sciences (MS); geography (MA), including community planning, geographic location science and technologies, location analysis, transportation studies, urban regional analysis; geography and urban regional analysis (PhD). Part-time and evening/weekend programs

available. *Faculty:* 27 full-time (9 women), 2 part-time/adjunct (1 woman). *Students:* 57 full-time (26 women), 38 part-time (12 women); includes 5 minority (3 Black or African American, non-Hispanic/Latino; 1 Hispanic/Latino; 1 Native Hawaiian or other Pacific Islander, non-Hispanic/Latino), 17 international. Average age 30. 46 applicants, 72% accepted, 17 enrolled. In 2010, 18 master's awarded. *Degree requirements:* For master's, comprehensive exam, thesis or alternative, project. *Entrance requirements:* For master's, GRE General Test or MAT, Doppelt Mathematical Reasoning Test, minimum GPA of 3.0 in undergraduate major, 2.75 overall. Additional exam requirements/recommendations for international students: Required—TOEFL (minimum score 557 paper-based; 220 computer-based; 83 iBT). *Application deadline:* For fall admission, 7/1 for domestic students, 5/1 for international students; for spring admission, 11/1 for domestic students, 10/1 for international students. Applications are processed on a rolling basis. Application fee: $55. Electronic applications accepted. *Expenses:* Tuition, state resident: full-time $3464. Tuition, nonresident: full-time $14,297. Required fees: $2094. Tuition and fees vary according to course load. *Financial support:* In 2010–11, 48 students received support, including 2 fellowships (averaging $17,876 per year), 23 research assistantships (averaging $10,760 per year), 23 teaching assistantships (averaging $9,449 per year); career-related internships or fieldwork, institutionally sponsored loans, scholarships/grants, and unspecified assistantships also available. Support available to part-time students. Financial award application deadline: 4/1; financial award applicants required to submit FAFSA. *Faculty research:* Location analysis, applications of GIS technology, community planning and development, regional economic modeling, retail geography. Total annual research expenditures: $755,074. *Unit head:* Dr. Harrison Campbell, Graduate Coordinator, 704-687-5997, Fax: 704-687-3182, E-mail: hscampbe@uncc.edu. *Application contact:* Kathy B. Giddings, Director of Graduate Admissions, 704-687-5503, Fax: 704-687-3279, E-mail: gradadm@uncc.edu.

The University of North Carolina at Greensboro, Graduate School, College of Arts and Sciences, Department of Geography, Greensboro, NC 27412-5001. Offers applied geography (MA); geographic information science (Certificate); geography (PhD); urban and economic development (Certificate). *Degree requirements:* For master's, comprehensive exam, thesis or alternative. *Entrance requirements:* For master's, GRE General Test. Additional exam requirements/recommendations for international students: Required—TOEFL. Electronic applications accepted.

University of North Dakota, Graduate School, College of Arts and Sciences, Department of Geography, Grand Forks, ND 58202. Offers MA, MS. Part-time programs available. *Faculty:* 7 full-time (1 woman), 1 (woman) part-time/adjunct. *Students:* 8 full-time (5 women), 32 part-time (13 women); includes 5 minority (1 Black or African American, non-Hispanic/Latino; 2 American Indian or Alaska Native, non-Hispanic/Latino; 1 Asian, non-Hispanic/Latino; 1 Hispanic/Latino). Average age 32. 12 applicants, 67% accepted, 8 enrolled. In 2010, 6 master's awarded. *Degree requirements:* For master's, comprehensive exam, thesis or alternative. *Entrance requirements:* For master's, minimum GPA of 3.0. Additional exam requirements/recommendations for international students: Required—TOEFL (minimum score 550 paper-based; 213 computer-based; 79 iBT), IELTS (minimum score 6.5). *Application deadline:* For fall admission, 8/1 priority date for domestic students, 5/1 priority date for international students; for spring admission, 12/1 priority date for domestic students, 9/1 priority date for international students. Applications are processed on a rolling basis. Application fee: $35. Electronic applications accepted. *Expenses:* Tuition, state resident: full-time $5857; part-time $306.74 per credit. Tuition, nonresident: full-time $15,666; part-time $729.77 per credit. Required fees: $53.42 per credit. Tuition and fees vary according to course load, program and reciprocity agreements. *Financial support:* In 2010–11, 9 students received support, including 2 research assistantships with full and partial tuition reimbursements available (averaging $10,728 per year), 6 teaching assistantships with full and partial tuition reimbursements available (averaging $10,413 per year); fellowships with full and partial tuition reimbursements available, Federal Work-Study, institutionally sponsored loans, scholarships/grants, health care benefits, tuition waivers (full and partial), and unspecified assistantships also available. Support available to part-time students. Financial award application deadline: 3/15; financial award applicants required to submit FAFSA. *Faculty research:* Regional and urban development, environmental geography, geographic education, geographic techniques. Total annual research expenditures: $40,597. *Unit head:* Dr. Douglas Munski, Graduate Director, 701-777-6195, Fax: 701-777-6195, E-mail: douglas_munski@und.nodak.edu. *Application contact:* Matt Anderson, Admissions Specialist, 701-777-2947, Fax: 701-777-3619, E-mail: matthew.anderson@gradschool.und.edu.

University of Northern Iowa, Graduate College, College of Social and Behavioral Sciences, Department of Geography, Cedar Falls, IA 50614. Offers MA. Part-time programs available. *Students:* 8 full-time (1 woman), 4 part-time (1 woman); includes 1 minority (Black or African American, non-Hispanic/Latino), 2 international. 7 applicants, 71% accepted, 5 enrolled. In 2010, 2 master's awarded. *Degree requirements:* For master's, thesis or alternative. *Entrance requirements:* For master's, minimum GPA of 3.0; 2 letters of recommendation; brief statement about professional interests and career objectives. Additional exam requirements/recommendations for international students: Required—TOEFL (minimum score 500 paper-based; 180 computer-based; 61 iBT). *Application deadline:* For fall admission, 8/1 priority date for domestic students. Applications are processed on a rolling basis. Application fee: $50 ($70 for international students). Electronic applications accepted. *Financial support:* Career-related internships or fieldwork, Federal Work-Study, scholarships/grants, and tuition waivers (full and partial) available. Support available to part-time students. Financial award application deadline: 2/1. *Unit head:* Dr. Patrick P. Pease, Department Head/Associate Professor, 319-273-2772, Fax: 319-273-7103, E-mail: patrick.pease@uni.edu. *Application contact:* Laurie S. Russell, Record Analyst, 319-273-2623, Fax: 319-273-2885, E-mail: laurie.russell@uni.edu.

University of North Texas, Toulouse Graduate School, College of Arts and Sciences, Department of Geography, Denton, TX 76203. Offers MS. Part-time programs available. *Degree requirements:* For master's, comprehensive exam (for some programs), thesis (for some programs). *Entrance requirements:* For master's, GRE General Test, BA/BS. Additional exam requirements/recommendations for international students: Recommended—TOEFL (minimum score 550 paper-based; 213 computer-based; 79 iBT). Electronic applications accepted. *Expenses:* Tuition, state resident: full-time $4298; part-time $239 per credit hour. Tuition, nonresident: full-time $10,782; part-time $549 per credit hour. Required fees: $1292; $270 per credit hour. *Financial support:* Fellowships with full and partial tuition reimbursements, teaching assistantships, career-related internships or fieldwork, health care benefits, and tuition waivers (partial) available. Financial award application deadline: 4/15; financial award applicants required to submit FAFSA. *Faculty research:* Environmental monitoring and modeling, health and economic geography, environmental archaeology. *Application contact:* Graduate Adviser/Coordinator, 940-565-2721, Fax: 940-369-7550.

University of Oklahoma, College of Atmospheric and Geographic Sciences, Department of Geography, Norman, OK 73019. Offers MA, PhD. Part-time programs available. *Faculty:* 13 full-time (3 women), 1 (woman) part-time/adjunct. *Students:* 28 full-time (14 women), 14 part-time (5 women); includes 2 minority (both American Indian or Alaska Native, non-Hispanic/Latino), 10 international. Average age 32. 20 applicants, 65% accepted, 7 enrolled. In 2010, 3 master's, 4 doctorates awarded. Terminal master's awarded for partial completion of doctoral program. *Degree requirements:* For master's, thesis, oral and written exams; for doctorate, one foreign language, thesis/dissertation, general exams. *Entrance requirements:* For master's, GRE, minimum GPA of 3.0, writing sample, 3 letters of recommendation. Additional exam requirements/recommendations for international students: Required—TOEFL (minimum score 550 paper-based; 213 computer-based; 79 iBT). *Application deadline:* For fall admission, 2/1 for domestic students, 4/1 for international students; for spring admission, 12/1 for domestic students, 9/1 for international students. Applications are processed on a rolling basis. Application fee: $40 ($90 for international students). Electronic applications accepted. *Expenses:* Tuition, state resident: full-time $3893; part-time $162.20 per credit hour. Tuition, nonresident: full-time $14,167; part-time $590.30 per credit hour. Required fees: $2523; $94.60 per credit hour. Tuition and fees vary according to course load and degree level. *Financial support:* In 2010–11, 33 students received support, including 4 fellowships with full tuition reimbursements available (averaging $5,000 per year), 2 research assistantships with partial tuition reimbursements available (averaging $17,630 per year), 13 teaching assistantships with partial tuition reimbursements available (averaging $15,526 per year); Federal Work-Study, scholarships/grants, health care benefits, and unspecified assistantships also available. Financial award application deadline: 2/1; financial award applicants required to submit FAFSA. *Faculty research:* Human/cultural geography, physical geography, remote sensing/geographic information systems, environmental sustainability. Total annual research expenditures: $894,133. *Unit head:* Aondover Tarhule, Acting Chair, 405-325-5325, Fax: 405-325-6090, E-mail: atarhule@ou.edu. *Application contact:* Fred M. Shelley, Professor & Graduate Liaison, 405-325-5325, Fax: 405-325-6090, E-mail: fshelley@ou.edu.

University of Oregon, Graduate School, College of Arts and Sciences, Department of Geography, Eugene, OR 97403. Offers MA, MS, PhD. *Degree requirements:* For master's, one foreign language, thesis; for doctorate, one foreign language, thesis/dissertation. *Entrance requirements:* For master's and doctorate, GRE General Test, minimum GPA of 3.0. Additional exam requirements/recommendations for international students: Required—TOEFL. *Faculty research:* Place-name research, past climates, quaternary environments, plant diffusions, population redistributions.

University of Ottawa, Faculty of Graduate and Postdoctoral Studies, Faculty of Arts, Department of Geography, Ottawa, ON K1N 6N5, Canada. Offers M Geog, M Sc, MA, PhD. *Degree requirements:* For master's, one foreign language, thesis; for doctorate, one foreign language, comprehensive exam, thesis/dissertation. *Entrance requirements:* For master's, honors degree or equivalent, minimum B average; for doctorate, master's degree, minimum B+ average. Electronic applications accepted. *Faculty research:* The physical geography of cold environment; space, place and society, environmental change.

University of Prince Edward Island, Faculty of Arts, Charlottetown, PE C1A 4P3, Canada. Offers island studies (MA). Part-time programs available. *Degree requirements:* For master's, thesis. *Entrance requirements:* Additional exam requirements/recommendations for international students: Required—TOEFL (minimum score 550 paper-based; 213 computer-based; 80 iBT), Canadian Academic English Language Assessment, Michigan English Language Assessment Battery, Canadian Test of English for Scholars and Trainees. *Faculty research:* International island studies.

University of Regina, Faculty of Graduate Studies and Research, Faculty of Arts, Department of Geography, Regina, SK S4S 0A2, Canada. Offers M Sc, MA. Part-time programs available. *Faculty:* 10 full-time (3 women). *Students:* 2 full-time (1 woman), 1 part-time (0 women). 9 applicants, 78% accepted. *Degree requirements:* For master's, thesis. *Entrance requirements:* Additional exam requirements/recommendations for international students: Required—TOEFL (minimum score 580 paper-based; 80 iBT). *Application deadline:* Applications are processed on a rolling basis. Application fee: $100. Electronic applications accepted. Tuition and fees charges are reported in Canadian dollars. *Expenses:* Tuition, area resident: Full-time $3244.50 Canadian dollars; part-time $180.25 Canadian dollars per credit hour. International tuition: $4744.50 Canadian dollars full-time. Required fees: $494 Canadian dollars; $115.25 Canadian dollars per credit hour. $115.25 Canadian dollars per semester. Tuition and fees vary according to program. *Financial support:* In 2010–11, 1 research assistantship (averaging $16,500 per year), 1 teaching assistantship (averaging $6,759 per year) were awarded; fellowships, scholarships/grants also available. Financial award application deadline: 6/15. *Faculty research:* Cultural, historical, economic, rural, urban, population, and prairie geography; thematic and atlas cartography; climatology and meteorology; geomorphology; biogeography. *Unit head:* Dr. Ulrike Hardenbicker, Acting Head, 306-585-4679, Fax: 306-585-4815, E-mail: ulrike.hardenbicker@uregina.ca. *Application contact:* Dr. Joe Piwowar, Graduate Program Coordinator, 306-585-5273, Fax: 306-585-4815, E-mail: joe.piwowar@uregina.ca.

University of Saskatchewan, College of Graduate Studies and Research, College of Arts and Sciences, Department of Geography, Saskatoon, SK S7N 5A2, Canada. Offers M Sc, MA, PhD. *Degree requirements:* For master's, thesis; for doctorate, comprehensive exam (for some programs), thesis/dissertation. *Entrance requirements:* Additional exam requirements/recommendations for international students: Required—TOEFL (minimum score 80 iBT); Recommended—IELTS (minimum score 6.5). Electronic applications accepted.

University of South Africa, College of Agriculture and Environmental Sciences, Pretoria, South Africa. Offers agriculture (MS); consumer science (MCS); environmental management (MA, MS, PhD); environmental science (MA, MS, PhD); geography (MA, MS, PhD); horticulture (M Tech); human ecology (MHE); life sciences (MS); nature conservation (M Tech).

University of South Carolina, The Graduate School, College of Arts and Sciences, Department of Geography, Columbia, SC 29208. Offers geography (MA, MS, PhD); geography education (IMA). IMA and MAT offered in cooperation with the College of Education. Part-time programs available. *Degree requirements:* For master's, comprehensive exam, thesis (for some programs); for doctorate, comprehensive exam, thesis/dissertation. *Entrance requirements:* For master's, GRE General Test; for doctorate, GRE General Test, master's degree. Electronic applications accepted. *Faculty research:* Geographic information processing; economic, cultural, physical, and environmental geography.

University of Southern California, Graduate School, Dana and David Dornsife College of Letters, Arts and Sciences, Spatial Sciences Institute, Los Angeles, CA 90089. Offers geographic information science and technology (MS, Graduate Certificate). Part-time and evening/weekend programs available. Postbaccalaureate distance learning degree programs offered (minimal on-campus study). *Faculty:* 3 full-time (2 women), 3 part-time/adjunct (0 women). *Students:* 53 full-time (26 women), 21 part-time (7 women); includes 22 minority (2 Black or African American, non-Hispanic/Latino; 2 American Indian or Alaska Native, non-Hispanic/Latino; 9 Asian, non-Hispanic/Latino; 7 Hispanic/Latino; 2 Two or more races, non-Hispanic/Latino), 5 international. 49 applicants, 88% accepted, 35 enrolled. In 2010, 22 other advanced degrees awarded. Terminal master's awarded for partial completion of doctoral program. *Degree requirements:* For master's, thesis. *Entrance requirements:* For master's, GRE. Additional exam requirements/recommendations for international students: Required—TOEFL. *Application deadline:* For fall admission, 8/1 priority date for domestic students; for spring admission, 11/1 priority date for domestic students. Applications are processed on a rolling basis. Application fee: $85. Electronic applications accepted. *Expenses:* Tuition: Full-time $31,240; part-time $1420 per unit. Required fees: $600. One-time fee: $35 full-time. Full-time tuition and fees vary according to degree level and program. *Financial support:* In 2010–11, 5 students received support, including 5 fellowships with full tuition reimbursements available (averaging $19,250 per year), 1 research assistantship with full tuition reimbursement available (averaging $19,250 per year), 8 teaching assistantships with full tuition reimbursements available (averaging $19,250 per year); health care benefits and unspecified assistantships also available. Financial award applicants required to submit FAFSA. *Faculty research:* Geocoding, geocomputation, GIS, environmental exposure estimation, spatial data accuracy and uncertainty. *Unit head:* Dr. John P. Wilson, Professor, Director of Spatial Sciences Institute, 213-740-1908, Fax: 213-740-9687, E-mail: jpwilson@usc.edu. *Application contact:* Kate A. Kelsey, Student Advisor, 213-740-8298, Fax: 213-740-9687, E-mail: kkelsey@usc.edu.

University of Southern Mississippi, Graduate School, College of Science and Technology, Department of Geography and Geology, Hattiesburg, MS 39406-0001. Offers geography (MS, PhD); geology (MS). Part-time programs available. *Faculty:* 11 full-time (2 women), 1 part-time/adjunct (0 women). *Students:* 20 full-time (3 women), 11 part-time (5 women). Average age 34. 18 applicants, 44% accepted, 7 enrolled. In 2010, 7 master's awarded. *Degree requirements:* For master's, comprehensive exam, thesis (for some programs), internships; for doctorate, comprehensive exam, thesis/dissertation. *Entrance requirements:* For master's, GMAT, GRE General Test, minimum GPA of 3.0 for last 60 hours; for doctorate, GRE, minimum GPA of 3.5. Additional exam requirements/recommendations for international students: Required—TOEFL, IELTS. *Application deadline:* For fall admission, 3/15 for domestic and international students; for spring admission, 1/3 for domestic students. Applications are processed on a rolling basis. Application fee: $50. Electronic applications accepted. *Financial support:* In 2010–11, 1 research assistantship with tuition reimbursement (averaging $18,000 per year), 8 teaching assistantships with full tuition reimbursements (averaging $8,700 per year) were awarded; fellowships with full tuition reimbursements, career-related internships or fieldwork, Federal Work-Study, scholarships/grants, health care benefits, and unspecified assistantships also available. Financial award application deadline: 3/15; financial award applicants required to submit FAFSA. *Faculty research:* City and regional planning, geographic techniques, physical geography, human geography. *Unit head:* Dr. Clifton Dixon, Chair, 601-266-4729, Fax: 601-266-6219, E-mail: c.dixon@usm.edu. *Application contact:* Dr. Clifton Dixon, Director, Graduate Studies, 601-266-4729, Fax: 601-266-6219.

University of South Florida, Graduate School, College of Arts and Sciences, Department of Geography, Tampa, FL 33620-9951. Offers MA, PhD. Part-time and evening/weekend programs available. *Faculty:* 9 full-time (5 women). *Students:* 26 full-time (11 women), 12 part-time (1 woman); includes 1 Black or African American, non-Hispanic/Latino; 1 American Indian or Alaska Native, non-Hispanic/Latino; 1 Asian, non-Hispanic/Latino; 2 Hispanic/Latino; 1 Two or more races, non-Hispanic/Latino, 1 international. Average age 32. 40 applicants, 63% accepted, 14 enrolled. In 2010, 6 master's awarded. *Degree requirements:* For master's, comprehensive exam, thesis; for doctorate, comprehensive exam, thesis/dissertation. *Entrance requirements:* For master's, GRE General Test, minimum GPA of 3.0 in last 60 hours of course work. Additional exam requirements/recommendations for international students: Required—TOEFL (minimum score 550 paper-based; 213 computer-based). *Application deadline:* For fall admission, 2/15 for domestic students, 1/2 for international students; for spring admission, 10/15 for domestic students, 6/1 for international students. Application fee: $30. *Financial support:* In 2010–11, 2 research assistantships (averaging $14,080 per year), 23 teaching assistantships with tuition reimbursements (averaging $15,203 per year) were awarded; unspecified assistantships also available. Financial award application deadline: 3/1. *Faculty research:* Natural hazards, geographic information systems models, soil contamination, urban geography and social theory. Total annual research expenditures: $58,164. *Unit head:* Dr. Robert Brinkmann, Associate Professor/Chair, 813-974-4939, Fax: 813-974-4808, E-mail: rbrinkmann@cas.usf.edu. *Application contact:* Philip Van Beynen, Program Director, 813-974-3026, Fax: 813-974-4808, E-mail: vanbeynen@cas.usf.edu.

The University of Tennessee, Graduate School, College of Arts and Sciences, Department of Geography, Knoxville, TN 37996. Offers MS, PhD. *Degree requirements:* For master's, thesis or alternative; for doctorate, thesis/dissertation. *Entrance requirements:* For master's and doctorate, GRE General Test, minimum GPA of 2.7. Additional exam requirements/recommendations for international students: Required—TOEFL. Electronic applications accepted. *Expenses:* Tuition, state resident: full-time $7440; part-time $414 per credit hour. Tuition, nonresident: full-time $22,478; part-time $1250 per credit hour. Required fees: $922; $43 per credit hour. Tuition and fees vary according to program.

The University of Texas at Austin, Graduate School, College of Liberal Arts, Department of Geography and the Environment, Austin, TX 78712-1111. Offers MA, PhD, MSCRP/PhD. *Degree requirements:* For master's, thesis or alternative; for doctorate, thesis/dissertation. *Entrance requirements:* For master's and doctorate, GRE General Test. Additional exam requirements/recommendations for international students: Required—TOEFL. Electronic applications accepted. *Faculty research:* Cultural and historical geography, environmental and physical geography, human-environment interactions, electronic technology and hypermedia, international area studies.

The University of Toledo, College of Graduate Studies, College of Language, Literature and Social Sciences, Department of Geography and Planning, Toledo, OH 43606-3390. Offers geographic information systems and applied geographics (Certificate); geography (MA); planning (MA); spatially-integrated social sciences (PhD). Part-time programs available. *Faculty:* 10. *Students:* 18 full-time (8 women), 9 part-time (5 women), 10 international. Average age 29. 32 applicants, 66% accepted, 18 enrolled. In 2010, 7 master's, 4 other advanced degrees awarded. *Degree requirements:* For master's, comprehensive exam, thesis; for doctorate, thesis/dissertation. *Entrance requirements:* For master's and doctorate, GRE General Test, A minimum 2.7 cumulative point-hour ratio (on a 4.0 scale) for all previous academic work. Three Letters of Recommendation; for Certificate, A minimum 2.7 cumulative point-hour ratio (on a 4.0 scale) for all previous academic work. Three Letters of Recommendation. Additional exam requirements/recommendations for international students: Required—TOEFL (minimum score 550 paper-based; 213 computer-based; 80 iBT), IELTS (minimum score 6.5). *Application deadline:* For fall admission, 1/15 priority date for domestic and international students. Applications are processed on a rolling basis. Application fee: $45 ($75 for international students). Electronic applications accepted. *Expenses:* Tuition, state resident: full-time $11,426; part-time $476 per credit hour. Tuition, nonresident: full-time $21,660; part-time $903 per credit hour. One-time fee: $62. *Financial support:* Research assistantships with full tuition reimbursements, teaching assistantships with full tuition reimbursements, career-related internships or fieldwork, institutionally sponsored loans, scholarships/grants, tuition waivers (full), and unspecified assistantships available. Support available to part-time students. *Unit head:* Dr. Patrick Lawrence, Chair, 419-530-4128, Fax: 419-530-7919, E-mail: patrick.lawrence@utoledo.edu. *Application contact:* Graduate School Office, 419-530-4723, Fax: 419-530-4724, E-mail: grdsch@utnet.utoledo.edu.

The University of Toledo, College of Graduate Studies, Judith Herb College of Education, Health Science and Human Service, Department of Curriculum and Instruction, Toledo, OH 43606-3390. Offers art education (ME); career and technical education (ME, Ed S); curriculum and instruction (ME, DE, PhD, Ed S); early childhood education (ME, Ed S); education and biology (MES); education and chemistry (MES); education and economics (MAE); education and English (MAE); education and French (MAE); education and geography (MAE); education and geology (MES); education and German (MAE); education and history (MAE); education and mathematics (MAE, MES); education and physics (MES); education and political science (MAE); education and sociology (MAE); education and Spanish (MAE); educational media (DE, PhD, Ed S); educational technology (ME); elementary education (DE, PhD); English as a second language (MAE); gifted and talented (DE, PhD); health education (ME); middle childhood education (ME); music education (MME); secondary education (ME, DE, PhD, Ed S); special education (DE, PhD, Ed S). *Accreditation:* NCATE. Part-time and evening/weekend programs available. *Faculty:* 21. *Students:* 134 full-time (87 women), 182 part-time (136 women); includes 22 Black or African American, non-Hispanic/Latino; 1 American Indian or Alaska Native, non-Hispanic/Latino; 1 Asian, non-Hispanic/Latino; 6 Hispanic/Latino; 2 Two or more races, non-Hispanic/Latino, 16 international. Average age 35. 115 applicants, 73% accepted, 74 enrolled. In 2010, 99 master's, 8 doctorates, 3 other advanced degrees awarded. *Degree requirements:* For master's, comprehensive exam, thesis or alternative; for doctorate, comprehensive exam, thesis/dissertation; for Ed S, thesis optional. *Entrance requirements:* For master's, GRE or other qualifying exams required vary by program , A minimum 2.70 cumulative GPA all previous academic work. Two/Three Letters of Recommendation (as required per program). ; for doctorate, GRE or other qualifying exams required vary by program, A minimum 2.70 cumulative GPA all previous academic work. Two/Three Letters of Recommendation (as required per program). ; for Ed S, GRE or other qualifying exams required vary by program, A minimum 2.70 cumulative GPA all previous academic work. Two/Three Letters of Recommendation (as required per program). . Additional exam requirements/recommendations for international students: Required—TOEFL (minimum score 550 paper-based; 213 computer-based; 80 iBT), IELTS (minimum score 6.5). *Application deadline:* For fall admission, 1/15 priority date for domestic and international students. Applications are processed on a rolling basis. Application fee: $45 ($75 for international students). Electronic applications accepted. *Expenses:* Tuition, state resident: full-time $11,426; part-time $476 per credit hour. Tuition, nonresident: full-time $21,660; part-time $903 per credit hour. One-time fee: $62. *Financial support:* Research assistantships with full tuition reimbursements, teaching assistantships with full tuition reimbursements, career-related internships or fieldwork, Federal Work-Study, institutionally sponsored loans, scholarships/grants, tuition waivers (full and partial), unspecified assistantships, and administrative assistantships available. Support available to part-time students. *Unit head:* Dr. Leigh Chiarelott, Chair, 419-530-5371,

Geography

The University of Toledo (continued)

E-mail: eigh.chiarelott@utoledo.edu. *Application contact:* Graduate School Office, 419-530-4723, Fax: 419-530-4724, E-mail: grdsch@utnet.utoledo.edu.

University of Toronto, School of Graduate Studies, Social Sciences Division, Department of Geography, Toronto, ON M5S 1A1, Canada. Offers geography (M Sc, MA, PhD); planning (M Sc Pl); urban design studies (MUD). Part-time programs available. *Degree requirements:* For master's, thesis optional; for doctorate, thesis/dissertation. *Entrance requirements:* For master's, bachelor's degree or equivalent in geography or a closely related field, minimum B+ average in each of 2 final years of degree, 3 letters of reference; for doctorate, master of geography degree, minimum A–average.

University of Utah, Graduate School, College of Social and Behavioral Science, Department of Geography, Salt Lake City, UT 84112-9155. Offers MA, MS, PhD. Part-time programs available. *Faculty:* 10 full-time (2 women), 3 part-time/adjunct (2 women). *Students:* 29 full-time (12 women), 15 part-time (4 women); includes 3 minority (1 Asian, non-Hispanic/Latino; 2 Hispanic/Latino), 13 international. Average age 33. 48 applicants, 54% accepted, 12 enrolled. In 2010, 5 master's, 2 doctorates awarded. *Degree requirements:* For master's, variable foreign language requirement, thesis or alternative, 6 research hours; for doctorate, comprehensive exam, thesis/dissertation, 14 research hours. *Entrance requirements:* For master's and doctorate, GRE General Test, minimum undergraduate GPA of 3.0. Additional exam requirements/recommendations for international students: Required—TOEFL (minimum score 500 paper-based; 173 computer-based; 61 iBT), IELTS (minimum score 6). *Application deadline:* For fall admission, 12/15 priority date for domestic and international students. Application fee: $55 ($65 for international students). Electronic applications accepted. *Expenses:* Tuition, area resident: Part-time $179.19 per credit hour. Tuition, state resident: full-time $4384. Tuition, nonresident: full-time $16,684; part-time $630.67 per credit hour. Required fees: $350 per semester. Tuition and fees vary according to course load, degree level and program. *Financial support:* In 2010–11, 27 students received support, including 1 fellowship with full tuition reimbursement available (averaging $15,000 per year), 11 research assistantships with full tuition reimbursements available (averaging $13,000 per year), 11 teaching assistantships with full tuition reimbursements available (averaging $13,000 per year); career-related internships or fieldwork, Federal Work-Study, scholarships/grants, health care benefits, and unspecified assistantships also available. Financial award application deadline: 2/15; financial award applicants required to submit FAFSA. *Faculty research:* Urban geography, earth system science, geographic information systems, remote sensing, hazards. Total annual research expenditures: $1 million. *Unit head:* Dr. George F. Hepner, Chair, 801-581-8218, Fax: 801-581-8219, E-mail: george.hepner@geog.utah.edu. *Application contact:* Dr. Harvey J. Miller, Director of Graduate Studies, 801-581-8218, Fax: 801-581-8219, E-mail: harvey.miller@geog.utah.edu.

University of Victoria, Faculty of Graduate Studies, Faculty of Social Sciences, Department of Geography, Victoria, BC V8W 2Y2, Canada. Offers M Sc, MA, PhD. Part-time programs available. *Degree requirements:* For master's, thesis; for doctorate, comprehensive exam, thesis/dissertation, candidacy exam. *Entrance requirements:* For master's, minimum B+ average in undergraduate course work; for doctorate, master's degree. Additional exam requirements/recommendations for international students: Required—TOEFL (minimum score 575 paper-based; 233 computer-based), IELTS (minimum score 7). Electronic applications accepted. *Faculty research:* Resources and protected areas, remote sensing and forestry, geographic information systems and cartography, urban regional planning, physical climatology.

University of Washington, Graduate School, College of Arts and Sciences, Department of Geography, Seattle, WA 98195. Offers MA, PhD. *Degree requirements:* For master's, thesis; for doctorate, thesis/dissertation. *Entrance requirements:* For master's and doctorate, GRE General Test. Additional exam requirements/recommendations for international students: Required—TOEFL. Electronic applications accepted. *Faculty research:* Globalization and social theory, nature and society, regional economic development, urban patterns and processes, geographic information systems.

University of Waterloo, Graduate Studies, Faculty of Environmental Studies, Department of Geography, Waterloo, ON N2L 3G1, Canada. Offers MA, PhD. MA, PhD offered jointly with Wilfrid Laurier University. *Degree requirements:* For master's, thesis optional; for doctorate, one foreign language, comprehensive exam, thesis/dissertation. *Entrance requirements:* For master's, honors degree, minimum B average; for doctorate, master's degree, minimum A-average. Additional exam requirements/recommendations for international students: Required—TOEFL, TWE. Electronic applications accepted. *Faculty research:* Urban economic geography; physical geography; resource management; cultural, regional, historical geography; spatial data.

The University of Western Ontario, Faculty of Graduate Studies, Social Sciences Division, Department of Geography, London, ON N6A 5B8, Canada. Offers M Sc, MA, PhD. *Degree requirements:* For master's, thesis; for doctorate, thesis/dissertation. *Entrance requirements:* For master's, GRE, honors degree, minimum B average; for doctorate, honors degree, minimum B average. Additional exam requirements/recommendations for international students: Required—TOEFL.

University of Wisconsin–Madison, Graduate School, College of Letters and Science, Department of Geography, Madison, WI 53706-1380. Offers cartography and geographic information systems (MS); geographic information systems (Certificate); geography (MS, PhD). Part-time programs available. *Degree requirements:* For master's, thesis; for doctorate, thesis/dissertation; for Certificate, internship. *Entrance requirements:* For master's and doctorate, GRE General Test, minimum GPA of 3.25. Electronic applications accepted. *Expenses:* Tuition, state resident: full-time $9887; part-time $617.96 per credit. Tuition, nonresident: full-time $24,054; part-time $1503.40 per credit. Required fees: $67.63 per credit. Tuition and fees vary according to reciprocity agreements. *Faculty research:* Physical geography, urban/historical geography, people-environment, history of cartography, GIS.

University of Wisconsin–Milwaukee, Graduate School, College of Letters and Sciences, Department of Geography, Milwaukee, WI 53201-0413. Offers MA, MS, PhD. *Faculty:* 13 full-time (6 women). *Students:* 16 full-time (5 women), 11 part-time (4 women); includes 2 Asian, non-Hispanic/Latino; 1 Hispanic/Latino, 7 international. Average age 32. 24 applicants, 46% accepted, 6 enrolled. In 2010, 4 master's, 4 doctorates awarded. *Degree requirements:* For master's, comprehensive exam, thesis; for doctorate, thesis/dissertation. *Entrance requirements:* For master's and doctorate, GRE. Additional exam requirements/recommendations for international students: Required—TOEFL (minimum score 550 paper-based; 79 iBT), IELTS (minimum score 6.5). *Application deadline:* For fall admission, 1/1 priority date for domestic students; for spring admission, 9/1 for domestic students. Applications are processed on a rolling basis. Application fee: $56 ($96 for international students). Electronic applications accepted. *Financial support:* In 2010–11, 2 research assistantships, 19 teaching assistantships were awarded; fellowships, career-related internships or fieldwork, unspecified assistantships, and project assistantships also available. Support available to part-time students. Financial award application deadline: 4/15; financial award applicants required to submit FAFSA. Total annual research expenditures: $249,087. *Unit head:* Changshan Wu, Representative, 414-229-4860, Fax: 414-229-3981, E-mail: cswu@uwm.edu. *Application contact:* General Information Contact, 414-229-4982, Fax: 414-229-6967, E-mail: gradschool@uwm.edu.

University of Wyoming, College of Arts and Sciences, Department of Geography, Laramie, WY 82070. Offers geography (MA, MP, MST); geography/water resources (MA); rural planning and natural resources (MP), including community and regional planning and natural resources. Postbaccalaureate distance learning degree programs offered (minimal on-campus study). *Degree requirements:* For master's, thesis optional. *Entrance requirements:* For master's, GRE General Test, minimum GPA of 3.0. Additional exam requirements/recommendations for international students: Required—TOEFL. Electronic applications accepted. *Faculty research:* Landscape ecology, landscape change, public land management, rural and small town planning, GIS.

Utah State University, School of Graduate Studies, College of Natural Resources, Department of Environment and Society, Logan, UT 84322. Offers bioregional planning (MS); geography (MA, MS); human dimensions of ecosystem science and management (MS, PhD); recreation resource management (MS, PhD). *Degree requirements:* For master's, comprehensive exam, thesis (for some programs). *Entrance requirements:* For master's and doctorate, GRE General Test, minimum GPA of 3.0. Additional exam requirements/recommendations for international students: Required—TOEFL. Electronic applications accepted. *Faculty research:* Geographic information systems/geographic and environmental education, bioregional planning, natural resource and environmental policy, outdoor recreation and tourism, natural resource and environmental management.

Virginia Polytechnic Institute and State University, Graduate School, College of Natural Resources and Environment, Department of Geography, Blacksburg, VA 24061. Offers geography (MS, PhD); geospatial and environmental analysis (PhD). *Faculty:* 8 full-time (3 women). *Students:* 11 full-time (5 women), 2 part-time, 2 international. Average age 27. 18 applicants, 33% accepted, 4 enrolled. In 2010, 4 master's awarded. *Degree requirements:* For master's, comprehensive exam (for some programs), thesis (for some programs); for doctorate, comprehensive exam (for some programs), thesis/dissertation (for some programs). *Entrance requirements:* For master's and doctorate, GRE. Additional exam requirements/recommendations for international students: Required—TOEFL (minimum score 550 paper-based; 213 computer-based). *Application deadline:* For fall admission, 7/1 for domestic and international students; for spring admission, 12/1 for domestic and international students. Applications are processed on a rolling basis. Application fee: $65. Electronic applications accepted. *Expenses:* Tuition, state resident: full-time $9399; part-time $488 per credit hour. Tuition, nonresident: full-time $17,854; part-time $957.75 per credit hour. Required fees: $1534. Full-time tuition and fees vary according to program. *Financial support:* In 2010–11, 1 research assistantship with full tuition reimbursement (averaging $16,606 per year), 7 teaching assistantships with full tuition reimbursements (averaging $13,971 per year) were awarded; career-related internships or fieldwork, Federal Work-Study, scholarships/grants, health care benefits, and unspecified assistantships also available. Financial award application deadline: 1/15. *Faculty research:* Third world development, geographical information systems, remote sensing, critical geopolitics, medical geography. Total annual research expenditures: $221,869. *Unit head:* Dr. Laurence W. Carstensen, UNIT HEAD, 540-231-5116, Fax: 540-231-7557, E-mail: carstens@vt.edu. *Application contact:* Karen Bland, Contact, 540-231-6886, Fax: 540-231-7557, E-mail: kbland@vt.edu.

Wayne State University, College of Liberal Arts and Sciences, Program in Geography, Detroit, MI 48202. Offers MA. *Entrance requirements:* For master's, GRE General Test. Additional exam requirements/recommendations for international students: Required—TOEFL (minimum score 550 paper-based; 213 computer-based); Recommended—TWE (minimum score 6). *Application deadline:* For fall admission, 7/1 for domestic students, 6/1 for international students; for winter admission, 10/1 for international students; for spring admission, 2/1 for international students. Applications are processed on a rolling basis. Application fee: $30 ($50 for international students). Electronic applications accepted. *Expenses:* Tuition, state resident: full-time $7662; part-time $478.85 per credit hour. Tuition, nonresident: full-time $16,920; part-time $1057.55 per credit hour. Required fees: $571.20; $35.70 per credit hour. $188.05 per semester. Tuition and fees vary according to course load and program. *Unit head:* Robert Thomas, Dean, 313-577-2519, Fax: 313-577-8971, E-mail: aa0817@wayne.edu. *Application contact:* Janet Hankin, Professor, 313-577-0841, E-mail: janet.hankin@wayne.edu.

West Chester University of Pennsylvania, Office of Graduate Studies, College of Business and Public Affairs, Department of Geography and Planning, West Chester, PA 19383. Offers geographic technology (Certificate); geography (MA); regional planning (MPA, MSA); urban regional planning (Certificate). Part-time and evening/weekend programs available. *Students:* 18 full-time (8 women), 18 part-time (6 women); includes 7 minority (6 Black or African American, non-Hispanic/Latino; 1 Hispanic/Latino), 2 international. Average age 28. 18 applicants, 89% accepted, 11 enrolled. In 2010, 8 master's, 6 other advanced degrees awarded. *Degree requirements:* For master's, comprehensive exam, thesis optional. *Entrance requirements:* For master's, GRE, GMAT, or MAT, minimum GPA of 2.8, resume, two letters of recommendation; for Certificate, minimum GPA of 2.8, resume, two letters of recommendation. Additional exam requirements/recommendations for international students: Required—TOEFL (minimum score 550 paper-based; 213 computer-based; 80 iBT). *Application deadline:* For fall admission, 4/15 priority date for domestic students, 3/15 for international students; for spring admission, 10/15 for domestic students, 9/1 for international students. Applications are processed on a rolling basis. Application fee: $35. Electronic applications accepted. *Expenses:* Tuition, state resident: full-time $6966; part-time $387 per credit. Tuition, nonresident: full-time $11,146; part-time $619 per credit. Required fees: $1614.40; $133.24 per credit. Part-time tuition and fees vary according to campus/location. *Financial support:* Unspecified assistantships available. Support available to part-time students. Financial award application deadline: 2/15; financial award applicants required to submit FAFSA. *Faculty research:* Environmental education, land use/suburban planning, landscapes of Catalunya, transportation planning, housing, environmental planning. *Unit head:* Dr. Joan Welch, Chair and Graduate Coordinator for the Geography Programs, 610-436-2940, E-mail: jwelch@wcupa.edu. *Application contact:* Dr. Dottie Ives Dewey, Graduate Coordinator for the Urban and Regional Planning Programs, 610-436-2746, E-mail: divesdewey@wcupa.edu.

Western Illinois University, School of Graduate Studies, College of Arts and Sciences, Department of Geography, Macomb, IL 61455-1390. Offers community development (Certificate); environmental GIS (Certificate); geography (MA). Part-time programs available. *Students:* 13 full-time (3 women), 5 part-time (4 women); includes 3 minority (1 Black or African American, non-Hispanic/Latino; 1 Asian, non-Hispanic/Latino; 1 Hispanic/Latino), 1 international. Average age 32. 9 applicants, 78% accepted. In 2010, 7 master's, 7 other advanced degrees awarded. *Degree requirements:* For master's, thesis or alternative. *Entrance requirements:* Additional exam requirements/recommendations for international students: Required—TOEFL (minimum score 550 paper-based; 213 computer-based; 80 iBT). *Application deadline:* Applications are processed on a rolling basis. Application fee: $30. Electronic applications accepted. *Expenses:* Tuition, state resident: full-time $6370; part-time $265.40 per credit hour. Tuition, nonresident: full-time $12,740; part-time $530.80 per credit hour. Required fees: $75.67 per credit hour. *Financial support:* In 2010–11, 11 students received support, including 11 research assistantships with full tuition reimbursements available (averaging $7,280 per year). Financial award applicants required to submit FAFSA. *Unit head:* Dr. Sam Thompson, Chairperson, 309-298-1648. *Application contact:* Evelyn Hoing, Assistant Director of Graduate Studies, 309-298-1806, Fax: 309-298-2345, E-mail: grad-office@wiu.edu.

Western Michigan University, Graduate College, College of Arts and Sciences, Department of Geography, Kalamazoo, MI 49008. Offers geographic information science (Graduate Certificate); geography (MA). *Degree requirements:* For master's, thesis, internship.

Western Washington University, Graduate School, Huxley College of the Environment, Department of Environmental Studies, Program in Geography, Bellingham, WA 98225-5996. Offers MS. *Entrance requirements:* Additional exam requirements/recommendations for international students: Required—TOEFL (minimum score 567 paper-based; 227 computer-based). Electronic applications accepted.

West Virginia University, Eberly College of Arts and Sciences, Department of Geology and Geography, Program in Geography, Morgantown, WV 26506. Offers energy and environmental resources (MA); geographic information systems (PhD); geography-regional development (PhD); GIS/cartographic analysis (MA); regional development (MA). Part-time programs available. *Degree requirements:* For master's, thesis, oral and written exams; for doctorate, comprehensive exam, thesis/dissertation, oral and written exams. *Entrance requirements:* For master's and

Geography

doctorate, GRE General Test, minimum GPA of 3.0. Additional exam requirements/recommendations for international students: Required—TOEFL. Electronic applications accepted. *Faculty research:* Space, place and development, geographic information science, environmental geography.

Wilfrid Laurier University, Faculty of Graduate and Postdoctoral Studies, Faculty of Arts, Department of Geography and Environmental Studies, Waterloo, ON N2L 3C5, Canada. Offers environmental and resource management (MA, MES, PhD); environmental science (M Sc, MES, PhD); geomatics (M Sc, MES, PhD); human geography (MES, PhD). Part-time programs available. *Faculty:* 17 full-time (5 women). *Students:* 47 full-time (20 women), 12 part-time (6 women), 4 international. 78 applicants, 40% accepted, 18 enrolled. In 2010, 11 master's, 7 doctorates awarded. *Degree requirements:* For master's, thesis optional; for doctorate, thesis/dissertation. *Entrance requirements:* For master's, honors BA in geography, minimum B average in undergraduate course work; honors BSc with minimum B+ or honors BES or BA in physical geography, environmental or earth sciences or the equivalent; for doctorate, MA in geography, minimum A- average. Additional exam requirements/recommendations for international students: Required—TOEFL (minimum score 89 iBT). *Application deadline:* For fall admission, 2/1 priority date for domestic and international students.

Application fee: $100. Electronic applications accepted. Tuition and fees charges are reported in Canadian dollars. *Expenses:* Tuition, area resident: Full-time $15,300 Canadian dollars; part-time $1200 Canadian dollars per credit. International tuition: $21,300 Canadian dollars full-time. Required fees: $650 Canadian dollars; $100 Canadian dollars per credit. Tuition and fees vary according to course load, degree level, campus/location and program. *Financial support:* In 2010–11, 51 fellowships, 8 research assistantships, 51 teaching assistantships were awarded; career-related internships or fieldwork, scholarships/grants, health care benefits, and unspecified assistantships also available. *Faculty research:* Resources management, urban, economic, physical, cultural, earth surfaces, geomatics, historical, regional, spatial data handling. *Unit head:* Dr. Houston Saunderson, Graduate Coordinator, 519-884-0710 Ext. 2573, Fax: 519-725-1342, E-mail: hsaunderson@wlu.ca. *Application contact:* Jennifer Williams, Graduate Admissions and Records Officer, 519-884-0710 Ext. 3536, Fax: 519-884-1020, E-mail: gradstudies@wlu.ca.

York University, Faculty of Graduate Studies, Faculty of Arts and Faculty of Science and Engineering, Program in Geography, Toronto, ON M3J 1P3, Canada. Offers M Sc, MA, PhD. Part-time programs available. *Degree requirements:* For master's, thesis or alternative; for doctorate, comprehensive exam, thesis/dissertation. Electronic applications accepted.

Section 22
Military and Defense Studies

This section contains a directory of institutions offering graduate work in military and defense studies, followed by an in-depth entry submitted by an institution that chose to prepare a detailed program description. Additional information about programs listed in the directory but not augmented by an in-depth entry may be obtained by writing directly to the dean of a graduate school or chair of a department at the address given in the directory.

For programs offering related work, see also in this book *History* and *Political Science and International Affairs*.

CONTENTS

Program Directories

Close-Up

Military and Defense Studies

American Public University System, AMU/APU Graduate Programs, Charles Town, WV 25414. Offers accounting (MBA); administration and supervision (M Ed); air warfare (MA Military Studies); asymmetrical warfare (MA Military Studies); criminal justice (MA); emergency and disaster management (MA); entrepreneurship (MBA); environmental policy and management (MS); finance (MBA); general (MBA); global business management (MBA); guidance and counseling (M Ed); history (MA); homeland security (MA); homeland security resource allocation (MBA); humanities (MA); information technology (MS); information technology management (MBA); intelligence studies (MA); international relations and conflict resolution (MA); joint warfare (MA Military Studies); land warfare (MA Military Studies); legal studies (MA); management (MA), including defense mangement, general, human resource management, organizational leadership, public administration; marketing (MBA); military history (MA); national security studies (MA); naval warfare (MA Military Studies); nonprofit management (MBA); political science (MA); psychology (MA); public administration (MA); public health (MA); security management (MA); space studies (MS); sports management (MS); strategic leadership (MA Military Studies); teaching (M Ed), including elementary, secondary social sciences; transportation and logistics management (MA). Programs offered via distance learning only. Part-time and evening/weekend programs available. Postbaccalaureate distance learning degree programs offered (no on-campus study). *Faculty:* 253 full-time (134 women), 1,208 part-time/adjunct (570 women). *Students:* 956 full-time (422 women), 8,476 part-time (2,821 women); includes 2,511 minority (1,218 Black or African American, non-Hispanic/Latino; 68 American Indian or Alaska Native, non-Hispanic/Latino; 219 Asian, non-Hispanic/Latino; 705 Hispanic/Latino; 46 Native Hawaiian or other Pacific Islander, non-Hispanic/Latino; 255 Two or more races, non-Hispanic/Latino), 107 international. Average age 35. 9,550 applicants, 100% accepted. In 2010, 1,688 master's awarded. *Degree requirements:* For master's, comprehensive exam or practicum. *Entrance requirements:* For master's, official transcript showing earned bachelor's degree from institution accredited by recognized accrediting body. Additional exam requirements/recommendations for international students: Required—TOEFL (minimum score 550 paper-based; 213 computer-based), IELTS (minimum score 6.5). *Application deadline:* Applications are processed on a rolling basis. Application fee: $0. Electronic applications accepted. *Financial support:* Applicants required to submit FAFSA. *Faculty research:* Military history, criminal justice, management performance, national security. *Unit head:* Dr. Frank McCluskey, Provost, 877-468-6268, Fax: 304-724-3780. *Application contact:* Terry Grant, Director of Enrollment Management, 877-468-6268, Fax: 304-724-3780, E-mail: info@apus.edu.

Austin Peay State University, College of Graduate Studies, College of Arts and Letters, Department of History and Philosophy, Clarksville, TN 37044. Offers military history (MA). Part-time programs available. Postbaccalaureate distance learning degree programs offered (minimal on-campus study). *Faculty:* 10 full-time (2 women), 3 part-time/adjunct (1 woman). *Students:* 16 full-time (2 women), 30 part-time (7 women); includes 5 minority (1 Black or African American, non-Hispanic/Latino; 3 Native Hawaiian or other Pacific Islander, non-Hispanic/Latino; 1 Two or more races, non-Hispanic/Latino), 1 international. Average age 36. 33 applicants, 97% accepted, 17 enrolled. In 2010, 9 master's awarded. *Degree requirements:* For master's, comprehensive exam, thesis optional. *Entrance requirements:* For master's, GRE General Test, minimum undergraduate GPA of 2.75, 3 letters of recommendation, bachelor's degree. Additional exam requirements/recommendations for international students: Required—TOEFL (minimum score 500 paper-based; 173 computer-based). *Application deadline:* For fall admission, 7/27 priority date for domestic students; for spring admission, 12/17 priority date for domestic students. Applications are processed on a rolling basis. Application fee: $25. Electronic applications accepted. *Expenses:* Tuition, state resident: full-time $6480; part-time $324 per credit hour. Tuition, nonresident: full-time $17,960; part-time $898 per credit hour. Required fees: $1244; $61.20 per credit hour. *Financial support:* In 2010–11, research assistantships with full tuition reimbursements (averaging $5,174 per year); career-related internships or fieldwork, Federal Work-Study, institutionally sponsored loans, scholarships/grants, and unspecified assistantships also available. Support available to part-time students. Financial award application deadline: 3/1; financial award applicants required to submit FAFSA. *Unit head:* Dr. Dewey Browder, Chair, 931-221-7919, Fax: 931-221-9917, E-mail: browderd@apsu.edu. *Application contact:* Dr. Dixie Dennis, Dean, College of Graduate Studies, 931-221-7662, Fax: 931-221-7641, E-mail: dennisdi@apsu.edu.

Columbia College, Master of Arts in Military Studies Program, Columbia, MO 65216-0002. Offers MA. Postbaccalaureate distance learning degree programs offered (no on-campus study). *Degree requirements:* For master's, thesis. *Expenses:* Tuition: Part-time $299 per credit hour. Tuition and fees vary according to course load. *Application contact:* Samantha White, Director of Admissions, 573-875-7343, Fax: 573-875-7506, E-mail: sjwhite@ccis.edu.

The George Washington University, Elliott School of International Affairs, Program in Security Policy Studies, Washington, DC 20052. Offers MA, JD/MA. Part-time and evening/weekend programs available. *Students:* 51 full-time (15 women), 41 part-time (16 women); includes 1 Black or African American, non-Hispanic/Latino; 7 Asian, non-Hispanic/Latino; 1 Hispanic/Latino, 4 international. Average age 27. 284 applicants, 40% accepted, 25 enrolled. In 2010, 52 master's awarded. *Degree requirements:* For master's, one foreign language, capstone project. *Entrance requirements:* For master's, GRE General Test, 2 semesters of introductory economics, 2 years of a modern foreign language or 1 semester of statistics. Additional exam requirements/recommendations for international students: Required—TOEFL. *Application deadline:* For fall admission, 2/1 for domestic students; for spring admission, 10/1 for domestic students. Application fee: $75. Electronic applications accepted. *Financial support:* In 2010–11, 22 students received support; fellowships with tuition reimbursements available, research assistantships with tuition reimbursements available, career-related internships or fieldwork, Federal Work-Study, institutionally sponsored loans, and tuition waivers (full) available. Financial award application deadline: 1/15; financial award applicants required to submit FAFSA. *Faculty research:* U. S. arms transfer policies, military balance in the Third World, U. S. foreign policy, technology and security policy. *Unit head:* Joanna Spear, Director, 202-994-1088, E-mail: jspear@gwu.edu. *Application contact:* Jeff V. Miles, Director of Graduate Admissions, 202-994-7050, Fax: 202-994-9537, E-mail: esiagrad@gwu.edu.

Hawai'i Pacific University, College of Humanities and Social Sciences, Program in Diplomacy and Military Studies, Honolulu, HI 96813. Offers MA.

See Close-Up on page 869.

Henley-Putnam University, Program in Intelligence Management, San Jose, CA 95110. Offers MS. Part-time programs available. Postbaccalaureate distance learning degree programs offered.

The Institute of World Politics, Graduate Programs in National Security, Intelligence, and International Affairs, Washington, DC 20036. Offers American foreign policy (Certificate); comparative political culture (Certificate); counterintelligence (Certificate); democracy building (Certificate); intelligence (Certificate); international politics (Certificate); national security affairs (Certificate); public diplomacy and political warfare (Certificate); statecraft and national security affairs (MA); statecraft and world politics (MA); strategic intelligence studies (MA). Part-time and evening/weekend programs available. *Degree requirements:* For master's, comprehensive exam, thesis optional. *Entrance requirements:* For master's, GRE General Test. Additional exam requirements/recommendations for international students: Required—TOEFL. Electronic applications accepted. *Faculty research:* Intelligence, national security, statecraft.

The Johns Hopkins University, School of Education, Division of Public Safety Leadership, Baltimore, MD 21218. Offers intelligence analysis (MS); management (MS). Part-time and evening/weekend programs available. *Faculty:* 10 full-time (3 women), 23 part-time/adjunct (7 women). *Students:* 131 full-time (39 women), 12 part-time (1 woman); includes 52 minority (35 Black or African American, non-Hispanic/Latino; 4 Asian, non-Hispanic/Latino; 12 Hispanic/Latino; 1 Two or more races, non-Hispanic/Latino). Average age 40. 81 applicants, 75% accepted, 54 enrolled. In 2010, 95 master's awarded. *Entrance requirements:* For master's, minimum undergraduate GPA of 3.0, curriculum vitae/resume, interview, professional experience, endorsement letter (MS in management). Additional exam requirements/recommendations for international students: Required—TOEFL (minimum score 600 paper-based; 250 computer-based; 100 iBT). *Application deadline:* For fall admission, 5/1 for international students; for spring admission, 10/15 for international students. Applications are processed on a rolling basis. Application fee: $0. Electronic applications accepted. *Financial support:* Scholarships/grants available. Support available to part-time students. Financial award application deadline: 6/1; financial award applicants required to submit FAFSA. *Faculty research:* Campus and school safety, prevention and effective response to violence against women, counterterrorism training, leadership development for public safety and homeland security executives. *Unit head:* Dr. Sheldon Greenberg, Associate Dean, 410-516-9900, Fax: 410-290-1061, E-mail: psl@jhu.edu. *Application contact:* Jennifer Shaffer, Director of Admissions, 410-516-9797, Fax: 410-516-9799, E-mail: educationinfo@jhu.edu.

The Judge Advocate General's School, U.S. Army, Graduate Programs, Charlottesville, VA 22903-1781. Offers military law (LL M). Only active duty military lawyers attend this school. *Accreditation:* ABA. *Degree requirements:* For master's, thesis optional. *Entrance requirements:* For master's, active duty military lawyer, international military officer, or DOD civilian attorney, JD or LL B. *Faculty research:* Criminal law, administrative and civil law, contract law, international law, legal research and writing.

Missouri State University, Graduate College, College of Humanities and Public Affairs, Department of Defense and Strategic Studies, Fairfax, VA 22031. Offers MS. Part-time programs available. *Degree requirements:* For master's, comprehensive exam, thesis or alternative. *Entrance requirements:* For master's, GRE, minimum GPA of 2.75, 3 letters of recommendation. Additional exam requirements/recommendations for international students: Required—TOEFL (minimum score 550 paper-based; 213 computer-based; 79 iBT). Electronic applications accepted. *Expenses:* Tuition, state resident: full-time $3348; part-time $186 per credit hour. Tuition, nonresident: full-time $6696; part-time $372 per credit hour. Required fees: $238 per semester. Tuition and fees vary according to course level, course load and program. *Faculty research:* Middle East, terrorism, arms control, U.S.-Soviet military balance, Strategic Defense Initiative.

National Defense Intelligence College, Graduate Program, Washington, DC 20340-5100. Offers MSSI. Open only to federal government employees. Part-time and evening/weekend programs available. *Degree requirements:* For master's, thesis. *Entrance requirements:* For master's, MAT, authorized nomination. *Faculty research:* Law and intelligence, intelligence and higher education, low-intensity conflict, intelligence information systems.

National Defense University, Industrial College of the Armed Forces, Washington, DC 20319-5066. Offers national resource strategy (MS). Open only to Department of Defense employees and specific federal agencies. *Degree requirements:* For master's, comprehensive exam. *Entrance requirements:* Additional exam requirements/recommendations for international students: Required—TOEFL. *Faculty research:* Industrial base and relation to national security, acquisition and relation to national security, resourcing the national security strategy.

National Defense University, Joint Advanced Warfighting School, Norfolk, AB 23511. Offers joint campaign planning and strategy (MS). Open only to Department of Defense employees and specific federal agencies. *Degree requirements:* For master's, thesis. *Entrance requirements:* For master's, Phase 1 JPME. *Faculty research:* Irregular warfare, national policy and strategy, international organizations and policies, modern military history and applications of lessons learned, historical military leadership relating to present-day environments.

National Defense University, National War College, Washington, DC 20319-5066. Offers national security strategy (MS). Open only to Department of Defense employees and specific federal agencies. *Degree requirements:* For master's, comprehensive exam. *Entrance requirements:* Additional exam requirements/recommendations for international students: Required—TOEFL. *Faculty research:* National security policy, regional security, US national security strategy, US military, strategy.

Naval Postgraduate School, Graduate Programs, Department of Computer Science, Program in Modeling of Virtual Environments and Simulations, Monterey, CA 93943. Offers MS, PhD. Program only open to commissioned officers of the United States and friendly nations and selected United States federal civilian employees. Part-time programs available. *Degree requirements:* For master's, thesis; for doctorate, one foreign language, thesis/dissertation.

Naval Postgraduate School, Graduate Programs, Department of Defense Analysis, Monterey, CA 93943. Offers defense analysis (MS); joint information operations (MS); special operations (MS). Program only open to commissioned officers of the United States and friendly nations and selected United States federal civilian employees. Part-time programs available. *Degree requirements:* For master's, thesis.

Naval Postgraduate School, Graduate Programs, Program in Undersea Warfare, Monterey, CA 93943. Offers applied science (MS); electrical engineering (MS); engineering acoustics (MS); operations research (MS); physical oceanography (MS). Program only open to commissioned officers of the United States and friendly nations and selected United States federal civilian employees. Part-time programs available. *Degree requirements:* For master's, thesis.

Naval Postgraduate School, Graduate Programs, School of Business and Public Policy, Monterey, CA 93943. Offers contract management (MS); defense-focused business administration (MBA); executive business administration (MBA); leadership and human resource development (MS); management (MS); program management (MS); systems engineering management (MS). Program only open to commissioned officers of the United States and friendly nations and selected United States federal civilian employees. *Accreditation:* AACSB; NASPAA. Part-time programs available. Postbaccalaureate distance learning degree programs offered (minimal on-campus study). *Degree requirements:* For master's, thesis.

Norwich University, School of Graduate and Continuing Studies, Program in Military History, Northfield, VT 05663. Offers race and gender in military history (MA); total war (MA); U. S. military history (MA). Evening/weekend programs available. *Faculty:* 33 part-time/adjunct (2 women). *Students:* 127 full-time (23 women); includes 2 Black or African American, non-Hispanic/Latino; 7 Hispanic/Latino. Average age 42. 157 applicants, 96% accepted, 127 enrolled. In 2010, 127 master's awarded. *Entrance requirements:* For master's, minimum undergraduate GPA of 2.75. Additional exam requirements/recommendations for international students: Required—TOEFL (minimum score 550 paper-based; 212 computer-based; 83 iBT). *Application deadline:* For fall admission, 8/10 for domestic and international students; for winter admission, 11/7 for domestic and international students; for spring admission, 2/6 for domestic and international students. Application fee: $50. Electronic applications accepted. *Expenses:* Tuition: Full-time $17,380; part-time $645 per credit. Tuition and fees vary according to program. *Financial support:* Scholarships/grants available. Financial award applicants required to submit FAFSA. *Unit head:* Dr. James Erhman, Program Director, 802-485-2567, Fax: 802-485-2533. *Application contact:* Lars Nielsen, Administrative Director, 802-485-2853, Fax: 802-485-2533, E-mail: lnielsen@norwich.edu.

Royal Military College of Canada, Division of Graduate Studies and Research, Continuing Studies, Department of History, Kingston, ON K7K 7B4, Canada. Offers defense management and policy (MA); history (PhD); war studies (MA). *Degree requirements:* For master's, thesis. *Entrance requirements:* For master's, honours degree with second-class standing; for doctorate, master's degree. Electronic applications accepted.

School of Advanced Air and Space Studies, Program in Airpower Art and Science, Maxwell AFB, AL 36112-6424. Offers MA. Available to active duty military officers only. *Degree requirements:* For master's, comprehensive exam, thesis. *Entrance requirements:* For master's, less than 16 years total of active commissioned service; master's degree or undergraduate degree with a minimum GPA of 2.75. Additional exam requirements/recommendations for international students: Required—TOEFL. *Faculty research:* Military history, political science, international relations, social history, technology.

United States Army Command and General Staff College, Graduate Program, Fort Leavenworth, KS 66027-2301. Offers military art and science (MMAS). Only career military officers are selected to attend United States Army Command and General Staff College; Graduate Program is voluntary for first-year students, but mandatory for second-year students.

University of Calgary, Faculty of Graduate Studies, Centre for Military and Strategic Studies, Calgary, AB T2N 1N4, Canada. Offers MSS, PhD. PhD offered in special cases only. Part-time programs available. *Degree requirements:* For master's, thesis; for doctorate, comprehensive exam, thesis/dissertation. *Entrance requirements:* For master's, minimum GPA of 3.4. Additional exam requirements/recommendations for international students: Recommended—TOEFL (minimum score 550 paper-based). *Faculty research:* Military history, Israeli studies, strategic studies, int'l relations, Arctic security.

University of Colorado Denver, School of Public Affairs, Program in Public Affairs and Administration, Denver, CO 80127. Offers public administration (MPA), including domestic violence, emergency management and homeland security, environmental policy, management and law, homeland security and defense, local government, nonprofit management, public administration; public affairs (PhD). *Accreditation:* NASPAA. Part-time and evening/weekend programs available. Postbaccalaureate distance learning degree programs offered (no on-campus study). *Faculty:* 19 full-time (9 women), 14 part-time/adjunct (5 women). *Students:* 317 full-time (181 women), 167 part-time (100 women); includes 15 Black or African American, non-Hispanic/Latino; 2 American Indian or Alaska Native, non-Hispanic/Latino; 18 Asian, non-Hispanic/Latino; 29 Hispanic/Latino; 1 Two or more races, non-Hispanic/Latino, 36 international. Average age 30. 270 applicants, 66% accepted, 118 enrolled. In 2010, 119 master's, 4 doctorates awarded. *Degree requirements:* For master's, thesis or alternative, 36-39 credit hours; for doctorate, comprehensive exam, thesis/dissertation, minimum of 66 semester hours, including at least 30 hours of doctoral dissertation credits. *Entrance requirements:* For master's and doctorate, GRE, resume, essay, transcripts, recommendations. Additional exam requirements/recommendations for international students: Required—TOEFL (minimum score 550 paper-based; 223 computer-based). *Application deadline:* For fall admission, 2/1 for domestic students; for spring admission, 10/15 priority date for domestic students. Application fee: $50 ($75 for international students). Electronic applications accepted. *Expenses:* Contact institution. *Financial support:* Fellowships with partial tuition reimbursements, research assistantships with partial tuition reimbursements, teaching assistantships with partial tuition reimbursements, Federal Work-Study and scholarships/grants available. Support available to part-time students. Financial award application deadline: 4/1; financial award applicants required to submit FAFSA. *Faculty research:* Housing, education and the social and economic issues of vulnerable populations; nonprofit governance and management; education finance, effectiveness and reform; P-20 (preschool through graduate school) education initiatives; municipal government accountability. *Unit head:* Dr. Mary Guy, Program Director, 303-315-2007, Fax: 303-315-2229, E-mail: mary.guy@ucdenver.edu. *Application contact:* Annie Davies, Director of Marketing, Community Outreach and Alumni Affairs, 303-315-2896, Fax: 303-315-2229, E-mail: annie.davies@ucdenver.edu.

University of Detroit Mercy, College of Liberal Arts and Education, Department of Criminal Justice and Human Services, Detroit, MI 48221. Offers criminal justice (MA); intelligence analysis (MS); security administration (MS).

University of Pittsburgh, Graduate School of Public and International Affairs, International Affairs Division, Pittsburgh, PA 15260. Offers global political economy (MPIA); human security (MPIA); security and intelligence studies (MPIA); JD/MPIA; MBA/MPIA; MID/MPIA; MPA/MPIA; MSIS/MPIA. Part-time and evening/weekend programs available. *Faculty:* 30 full-time (12 women), 67 part-time/adjunct (25 women). *Students:* 187 full-time (93 women), 26 part-time (7 women); includes 17 minority (9 Black or African American, non-Hispanic/Latino; 1 American Indian or Alaska Native, non-Hispanic/Latino; 4 Asian, non-Hispanic/Latino; 3 Hispanic/Latino), 17 international. Average age 25. 325 applicants, 73% accepted, 100 enrolled. In 2010, 92 master's awarded. *Degree requirements:* For master's, thesis optional, internship, capstone seminar. *Entrance requirements:* For master's, GRE General Test, 3 letters of recommendation, resume; minimum GPA of 3.2 (recommended). Additional exam requirements/recommendations for international students: Required—TOEFL (minimum score 550 paper-based; 213 computer-based), TWE (minimum score 4); Recommended—IELTS (minimum score 7). *Application deadline:* For fall admission, 3/1 for domestic students, 1/15 for international students; for spring admission, 11/1 for domestic students, 8/1 for international students. Application fee: $50. Electronic applications accepted. *Expenses:* Tuition, state resident: full-time $17,304; part-time $701 per credit. Tuition, nonresident: full-time $29,554; part-time $1210 per credit. Required fees: $740; $214 per term. Tuition and fees vary according to program. *Financial support:* In 2010–11, 44 students received support. Scholarships/grants, tuition waivers (full and partial), unspecified assistantships, and student employment available. Financial award application deadline: 2/1. *Faculty research:* International political economy, international security and intelligence, transnational organized crime, international trade, international finance, globalization, terrorism, multinational corporations and the global economy. Total annual research expenditures: $892,349. *Unit head:* Dr. Martin Staniland, Director, International Affairs and International Development Divisions, 412-648-7656, Fax: 412-648-2605, E-mail: mstan@pitt.edu. *Application contact:* Kelly C. McDevitt, Graduate Enrollment Counselor, 412-648-7640, Fax: 412-648-7641, E-mail: mcdevitt@pitt.edu.

The University of Texas at El Paso, Graduate School, Institute for Policy and Economic Development, El Paso, TX 79968-0001. Offers border administration (Certificate); homeland security (Certificate); intelligence and national security (MS, Certificate); leadership studies (MA); public administration (MPA). *Accreditation:* NASPAA. Part-time and evening/weekend programs available. *Students:* 187 (57 women); includes 19 Black or African American, non-Hispanic/Latino; 1 American Indian or Alaska Native, non-Hispanic/Latino; 5 Asian, non-Hispanic/Latino; 99 Hispanic/Latino, 5 international. 142 applicants, 77% accepted. In 2010, 76 master's awarded. *Degree requirements:* For master's, thesis optional. *Entrance requirements:* For master's, GRE, statement of purpose, letters of recommendation. Additional exam requirements/recommendations for international students: Required—TOEFL; Recommended—IELTS. *Application deadline:* For fall admission, 8/1 for domestic students, 3/1 for international students; for spring admission, 10/1 for domestic students, 9/1 for international students. Applications are processed on a rolling basis. Application fee: $45 ($80 for international students). Electronic applications accepted. *Financial support:* Fellowships with partial tuition reimbursements, research assistantships with partial tuition reimbursements, teaching assistantships with partial tuition reimbursements, institutionally sponsored loans, scholarships/grants, health care benefits, tuition waivers (partial), and unspecified assistantships available. Support available to part-time students. Financial award application deadline: 3/15; financial award applicants required to submit FAFSA. *Unit head:* Dr. Dennis Soden, Director, 915-747-7974, Fax: 915-747-7948, E-mail: desoden@utep.edu. *Application contact:* Dr. Patricia D. Witherspoon, Dean of the Graduate School, 915-747-5491, Fax: 915-747-5788, E-mail: withersp@utep.edu.

University of West Florida, College of Arts and Sciences: Arts, Department of History, Pensacola, FL 32514-5750. Offers history (MA); military history (MA); public history (MA). Part-time and evening/weekend programs available. *Faculty:* 8 full-time (2 women). *Students:* 10 full-time (7 women), 33 part-time (19 women); includes 1 Black or African American, non-Hispanic/Latino; 1 Asian, non-Hispanic/Latino; 2 Hispanic/Latino. Average age 30. 25 applicants, 52% accepted, 11 enrolled. In 2010, 10 master's awarded. *Degree requirements:* For master's, thesis or alternative. *Entrance requirements:* For master's, GRE General Test, minimum GPA of 3.0, minimum 15 hours of upper-level history courses. Additional exam requirements/recommendations for international students: Required—TOEFL (minimum score 550 paper-based; 213 computer-based). *Application deadline:* For fall admission, 6/1 for domestic students, 5/15 for international students; for spring admission, 10/1 for domestic and international students. Applications are processed on a rolling basis. Application fee: $30. *Expenses:* Tuition, state resident: full-time $4982; part-time $208 per credit hour. Tuition, nonresident: full-time $20,059; part-time $836 per credit hour. Required fees: $1365; $57 per credit hour. *Financial support:* In 2010–11, 20 fellowships with partial tuition reimbursements (averaging $377 per year), 13 research assistantships with partial tuition reimbursements (averaging $3,280 per year) were awarded; unspecified assistantships also available. Financial award application deadline: 4/15; financial award applicants required to submit FAFSA. *Unit head:* Dr. John J. Clune, Chairperson, 850-474-2680. *Application contact:* Terry McCray, Assistant Director of Graduate Admissions, 850-473-7718, Fax: 850-473-7714, E-mail: gradadmissions@uwf.edu.

National Security

American Public University System, AMU/APU Graduate Programs, Charles Town, WV 25414. Offers accounting (MBA); administration and supervision (M Ed); air warfare (MA Military Studies); asymmetrical warfare (MA Military Studies); criminal justice (MA); emergency and disaster management (MA); entrepreneurship (MBA); environmental policy and management (MS); finance (MBA); general (MBA); global business management (MBA); guidance and counseling (M Ed); history (MA); homeland security (MA); homeland security resource allocation (MBA); humanities (MA); information technology (MS); information technology management (MBA); intelligence studies (MA); international relations and conflict resolution (MA); joint warfare (MA Military Studies); land warfare (MA Military Studies); legal studies (MA); management (MA), including defense mangement, general, human resource management, organizational leadership, public administration; marketing (MBA); military history (MA); national security studies (MA); naval warfare (MA Military Studies); nonprofit management (MBA); political science (MA); psychology (MA); public administration (MA); public health (MA); security management (MA); space studies (MS); sports management (MS); strategic leadership (MA Military Studies); teaching (M Ed), including elementary, secondary social sciences; transportation and logistics management (MA). Programs offered via distance learning only. Part-time and evening/weekend programs available. Postbaccalaureate distance learning degree programs offered (no on-campus study). *Faculty:* 253 full-time (134 women), 1,208 part-time/adjunct (570 women). *Students:* 956 full-time (422 women), 8,476 part-time (2,821 women); includes 2,511 minority (1,218 Black or African American, non-Hispanic/Latino; 68 American Indian or Alaska Native, non-Hispanic/Latino; 219 Asian, non-Hispanic/Latino; 705 Hispanic/Latino; 46 Native Hawaiian or other Pacific Islander, non-Hispanic/Latino; 255 Two or more races, non-Hispanic/Latino), 107 international. Average age 35. 9,550 applicants, 100% accepted. In 2010, 1,688 master's awarded. *Degree requirements:* For master's, comprehensive exam or practicum. *Entrance requirements:* For master's, official transcript showing earned bachelor's degree from institution accredited by recognized accrediting body. Additional exam requirements/recommendations for international students: Required—TOEFL (minimum score 550 paper-based; 213 computer-based), IELTS (minimum score 6.5). *Application deadline:* Applications are processed on a rolling basis. Application fee: $0. Electronic applications accepted. *Financial support:* Applicants required to submit FAFSA. *Faculty research:* Military history, criminal justice, management performance, national security. *Unit head:* Dr. Frank McCluskey, Provost, 877-468-6268, Fax: 304-724-3780. *Application contact:* Terry Grant, Director of Enrollment Management, 877-468-6268, Fax: 304-724-3780, E-mail: info@apus.edu.

California State University, San Bernardino, Graduate Studies, College of Social and Behavioral Sciences, National Security Studies Program, San Bernardino, CA 92407-2397. Offers MA. Part-time and evening/weekend programs available. *Degree requirements:* For master's, comprehensive exam. *Entrance requirements:* For master's, minimum GPA of 2.5. *Faculty research:* Strategy, arms control, defense policy, terrorism, U.S. foreign policy, operations analysis.

George Mason University, School of Public Policy, Arlington, VA 22201. Offers culture and values in social policy (Certificate); global medical policy (Certificate); global trade management (Certificate); health and medical policy (MS); international commerce and policy (MA); national security and public policy (Certificate); organization development and knowledge management (MS); peace operations (MS); public policy (EMPP, MPP, PhD); transportation and logistics policy (Certificate); transportation policy, operations and logistics (MA). Part-time and evening/weekend programs available. *Faculty:* 66 full-time (24 women), 15 part-time/adjunct (3 women). *Students:* 344 full-time (199 women), 607 part-time (310 women); includes 55 Black or African American, non-Hispanic/Latino; 1 American Indian or Alaska Native, non-Hispanic/Latino; 33 Asian, non-Hispanic/Latino; 55 Hispanic/Latino; 5 Two or more races, non-Hispanic/Latino, 106 international. Average age 31. 842 applicants, 62% accepted, 280 enrolled. In 2010, 291 master's, 15 doctorates, 12 other advanced degrees awarded. *Degree requirements:* For master's, thesis or alternative; for doctorate, comprehensive exam, thesis/dissertation. *Entrance requirements:* For master's, GRE (for students seeking merit-based scholarships), minimum undergraduate GPA of 3.0, resume, 2 letters of recommendation; for doctorate, GMAT or GRE General Test, résume, writing sample, master's degree, goals statement, 2 letters of recommendation; for Certificate, minimum undergraduate GPA of 3.0, resume, 2 letters of recommendation, goals statement. Additional exam requirements/recommendations for international students: Required—TOEFL (minimum score 570 paper-based; 230 computer-based; 88 iBT). *Application deadline:* Applications are processed on a rolling basis. Application fee: $100. Electronic applications accepted. *Expenses:* Contact institution. *Financial support:* In 2010–11, 43 students received support, including 2 fellowships with full tuition reimbursements available (averaging $18,000 per year), 41 research assistantships with full and partial tuition reimbursements available (averaging $18,104 per year), 2 teaching assistantships (averaging $10,408 per year); career-related internships or fieldwork, Federal Work-Study, scholarships/grants, unspecified assistantships, and health care benefits (full-time research or teaching assistantship recipients) also available. Financial award application deadline: 3/1; financial award applicants required to submit FAFSA. *Faculty research:* Governance, regional and economic development, international commerce and policy, science and technology policy, entrepreneurship, culture and values. Total annual research expenditures: $8 million. *Unit head:* Dr. Edward Rhodes, Dean, 703-993-2280, Fax: 703-993-8215, E-mail: edrhodes@gmu.edu. *Application contact:* Tennille Haegele, Director of Graduate Admissions, School of Public Policy, 703-993-3183, Fax: 703-993-4876, E-mail: thaegele@gmu.edu.

Henley-Putnam University, Program in Strategic Security, San Jose, CA 95110. Offers PhD.

National Security

Hult International Business School, Program in International Relations—Hult London Campus, London, MA WC 1B 4JP, United Kingdom. Offers conflict resolution (MA); diplomacy (MA); international public law (MA); international relations (MA); Middle East international security (MA); politics (MA); security studies (MA); terrorism (MA); U.S. foreign policy (MA). Part-time programs available. *Entrance requirements:* Additional exam requirements/recommendations for international students: Required—TOEFL (minimum score 580 paper-based; 237 computer-based), TWE (minimum score 5). Electronic applications accepted. *Faculty research:* American foreign politics, Middle East, security studies.

The Institute of World Politics, Graduate Programs in National Security, Intelligence, and International Affairs, Washington, DC 20036. Offers American foreign policy (Certificate); comparative political culture (Certificate); counterintelligence (Certificate); democracy building (Certificate); intelligence (Certificate); international politics (Certificate); national security affairs (Certificate); public diplomacy and political warfare (Certificate); statecraft and national security affairs (MA); statecraft and world politics (MA); strategic intelligence studies (MA). Part-time and evening/weekend programs available. *Degree requirements:* For master's, comprehensive exam, thesis optional. *Entrance requirements:* For master's, GRE General Test. Additional exam requirements/recommendations for international students: Required—TOEFL. Electronic applications accepted. *Faculty research:* Intelligence, national security, statecraft.

Kansas State University, Graduate School, College of Arts and Sciences, Department of History, Manhattan, KS 66506. Offers history (MA); security studies (MA, PhD). Part-time programs available. *Degree requirements:* For master's, thesis (for some programs); for doctorate, one foreign language, thesis/dissertation, qualifying exam. *Entrance requirements:* For master's, GRE General Test or MAT, minimum undergraduate GPA of 3.0; for doctorate, GRE General Test or MAT. Additional exam requirements/recommendations for international students: Required—TOEFL (minimum score 600 paper-based). Electronic applications accepted. *Faculty research:* Environmental history, history of Christianity, American social history, history of war and society, history of international relations and diplomacy.

National Defense University, College of International Security Affairs, Washington, DC 20319-5066. Offers strategic security studies (MA), including conflict management, counterterrorism, homeland defense/ security, international security studies. Part-time and evening/weekend programs available. *Degree requirements:* For master's, thesis. *Entrance requirements:* Additional exam requirements/recommendations for international students: Required—TOEFL.

National Defense University, National War College, Washington, DC 20319-5066. Offers national security strategy (MS). Open only to Department of Defense employees and specific federal agencies. *Degree requirements:* For master's, comprehensive exam. *Entrance requirements:* Additional exam requirements/recommendations for international students: Required—TOEFL. *Faculty research:* National security policy, regional security, US national security strategy, US military, strategy.

Naval Postgraduate School, Graduate Programs, Department of National Security Affairs, Monterey, CA 93943. Offers intelligence (MA); international relations (MA); political science (MA); regional security education (MA); security building (MA); security studies (MA). Program only open to commissioned officers of the United States and friendly nations and select U.S. federal civilian employees. Part-time programs available. *Degree requirements:* For master's, thesis.

Naval War College, Program in National Security and Strategic Studies, Newport, RI 02841-1207. Offers MA. Program open only to full-time military personnel.

New York University, School of Continuing and Professional Studies, Center for Global Affairs, New York, NY 10012-1019. Offers global affairs (MS), including environment/energy policy, human rights and humanitarian assistance, international law, dispute settlement, and institutions, international relations, peace building, private sector: international business, economics, and development, transnational security. Part-time and evening/weekend programs available. *Faculty:* 10 full-time (3 women), 29 part-time/adjunct (14 women). *Students:* 92 full-time (62 women), 119 part-time (90 women); includes 12 Black or African American, non-Hispanic/Latino; 1 American Indian or Alaska Native, non-Hispanic/Latino; 14 Asian, non-Hispanic/Latino; 10 Hispanic/Latino, 32 international. Average age 30. 419 applicants, 58% accepted, 81 enrolled. In 2010, 113 master's awarded. *Degree requirements:* For master's, thesis. *Entrance requirements:* For master's, GRE General Test or GMAT (for recent graduates), 2 letters of recommendation, resume, essay, professional experience. Additional exam requirements/recommendations for international students: Required—TOEFL (minimum score 600 paper-based; 250 computer-based; 100 iBT). *Application deadline:* For fall admission, 2/1 priority date for domestic and international students; for spring admission, 10/15 priority date for domestic students, 8/15 priority date for international students. Applications are processed on a rolling basis. Application fee: $75. Electronic applications accepted. *Financial support:* In 2010–11, 163 students received support, including 163 fellowships (averaging $2,554 per year); institutionally sponsored loans, scholarships/grants, and tuition waivers (partial) also available. Support available to part-time students. Financial award application deadline: 3/1; financial award applicants required to submit FAFSA. *Unit head:* Dr. Vera Jelinek, Divisional Dean and Clinical Associate Professor, 212-992-8380, Fax: 212-995-4597, E-mail: vera.jelinek@nyu.edu. *Application contact:* Cori Epstein, Associate Director, 212-992-8380, Fax: 212-995-4597, E-mail: graduate.global.affairs@nyu.edu.

Nova Southeastern University, Graduate School of Humanities and Social Sciences, Department of Multi-Disciplinary Studies, Fort Lauderdale, FL 33314-7796. Offers college student affairs (MS); college student personnel administration (Certificate); cross-disciplinary studies (MA); national security affairs (MS); qualitative methods (Certificate). Part-time programs available. Postbaccalaureate distance learning degree programs offered (minimal on-campus study). *Faculty:* 1 (woman) full-time, 52 part-time/adjunct (30 women). *Students:* 50 full-time (34 women), 65 part-time (52 women); includes 34 Black or African American, non-Hispanic/Latino; 3 Asian, non-Hispanic/Latino; 25 Hispanic/Latino; 1 Two or more races, non-Hispanic/Latino, 6 international. Average age 32. 76 applicants, 66% accepted, 40 enrolled. In 2010, 27 master's awarded. *Degree requirements:* For master's, comprehensive exam, thesis optional, portfolio. *Entrance requirements:* For master's, interview, minimum GPA of 3.0. Additional exam requirements/recommendations for international students: Required—TOEFL. *Application deadline:* For fall admission, 7/1 priority date for domestic and international students; for winter admission, 11/1 priority date for domestic and international students; for spring admission, 3/1 priority date for domestic and international students. Applications are processed on a rolling basis. Application fee: $50. Electronic applications accepted. *Financial support:* In 2010–11, 1 research assistantship (averaging $15,000 per year) was awarded; career-related internships or fieldwork, Federal Work-Study, institutionally sponsored loans, and scholarships/grants also available. Financial award applicants required to submit CSS PROFILE. *Unit head:* Dr. Judith McKay, Chair, 954-262-3060, Fax: 954-262-3893, E-mail: mckayj@nsu.nova.edu. *Application contact:* Marcia Arango, Student Recruitment Coordinator, 954-262-3006, Fax: 954-262-3968, E-mail: marango@nsu.nova.edu.

Texas A&M University, Bush School of Government and Public Service, College Station, TX 77843. Offers advanced international affairs (Certificate); China studies (Certificate); homeland security (Certificate); international affairs (MPIA); national security affairs (Certificate); nonprofit management (Certificate); public service and administration (MPSA). *Accreditation:* NASPAA. *Faculty:* 45. *Students:* 215 full-time (98 women), 93 part-time (32 women); includes 20 Black or African American, non-Hispanic/Latino; 2 American Indian or Alaska Native, non-Hispanic/Latino; 14 Asian, non-Hispanic/Latino; 30 Hispanic/Latino, 15 international. Average age 24. In 2010, 93 master's awarded. *Degree requirements:* For master's, summer internship. *Entrance requirements:* For master's, GRE (preferred) or GMAT. *Application deadline:* For fall admission, 1/24 for domestic and international students. Application fee: $50 ($75 for international students). Electronic applications accepted. *Financial support:* In 2010–11, fellowships (averaging $11,000 per year), research assistantships (averaging $11,250 per year) were awarded; career-related internships or fieldwork, Federal Work-Study, and institutionally sponsored loans also available. Financial award application deadline: 2/1; financial award applicants required to submit FAFSA. *Faculty research:* Public policy, presidential studies, public leadership, economic policy, social policy. *Unit head:* Ryan C. Crocker, Dean, 979-862-8007, E-mail: rcrocker@bushschool.tamu.edu. *Application contact:* Kathryn Meyer, Director of Recruiting, 979-458-4767, Fax: 979-845-4155, E-mail: kmeyer@bushschool.tamu.edu.

Trinity (Washington) University, School of Professional Studies, Washington, DC 20017-1094. Offers business administration (MBA); communication (MA); international security studies (MA); organizational management (MSA), including federal program management, human resource management, nonprofit management, organizational development, public and community health. Part-time and evening/weekend programs available. *Degree requirements:* For master's, thesis (for some programs), capstone project (MSA). *Entrance requirements:* For master's, minimum GPA of 2.5. Additional exam requirements/recommendations for international students: Required—TOEFL (minimum score 550 paper-based; 213 computer-based).

Troy University, Graduate School, College of Arts and Sciences, Program in International Relations, Troy, AL 36082. Offers national security affairs (MS), including global studies, national security affairs, regional affairs. Part-time and evening/weekend programs available. Postbaccalaureate distance learning degree programs offered (no on-campus study). *Students:* 72 full-time (29 women), 281 part-time (109 women); includes 99 minority (38 Black or African American, non-Hispanic/Latino; 5 American Indian or Alaska Native, non-Hispanic/Latino; 26 Asian, non-Hispanic/Latino; 27 Hispanic/Latino; 2 Native Hawaiian or other Pacific Islander, non-Hispanic/Latino; 1 Two or more races, non-Hispanic/Latino). Average age 32. 279 applicants, 83% accepted, 74 enrolled. In 2010, 212 master's awarded. *Degree requirements:* For master's, comprehensive exam or thesis, minimum GPA of 3.0, admission to candidacy. *Entrance requirements:* For master's, GRE (minimum score of 920), MAT (minimum score of 390), or GMAT (minimum score of 490), minimum undergraduate GPA of 2.5. Additional exam requirements/recommendations for international students: Required—TOEFL (minimum score 523 paper-based; 193 computer-based; 70 iBT), IELTS (minimum score 6). *Application deadline:* Applications are processed on a rolling basis. Application fee: $50. Electronic applications accepted. *Expenses:* Tuition, state resident: full-time $4428; part-time $246 per credit hour. Tuition, nonresident: full-time $8856; part-time $492 per credit hour. Required fees: $432; $24 per credit hour. $50 per term. Tuition and fees vary according to program. *Financial support:* Available to part-time students. Applicants required to submit FAFSA. *Faculty research:* Elections, religion and world politics, terrorism. *Unit head:* Dr. Charles Krupnick, Department Chairman, 334-670-5968, Fax: 334-670-5647, E-mail: ckrupnick@troy.edu. *Application contact:* Brenda K. Campbell, Director of Graduate Admissions, 334-670-3178, Fax: 334-670-3733, E-mail: bcamp@troy.edu.

Troy University, Graduate School, College of Arts and Sciences, Program in Public Administration, Troy, AL 36082. Offers education (MPA); environmental management (MPA); government contracting (MPA); health care administration (MPA); justice administration (MPA); national security affairs (MPA); nonprofit management (MPA); public human resources management (MPA); public management (MPA). *Accreditation:* NASPAA. Part-time and evening/weekend programs available. Postbaccalaureate distance learning degree programs offered (no on-campus study). *Degree requirements:* For master's, capstone course, research methodologies course. *Entrance requirements:* For master's, GRE, MAT or GMAT, minimum undergraduate GPA of 2.5, letter of recommendation, essay. Additional exam requirements/recommendations for international students: Required—TOEFL (minimum score 523 paper-based; 193 computer-based; 70 iBT), IELTS (minimum score 6). *Application deadline:* Applications are processed on a rolling basis. Application fee: $50. Electronic applications accepted. *Expenses:* Tuition, state resident: full-time $4428; part-time $246 per credit hour. Tuition, nonresident: full-time $8856; part-time $492 per credit hour. Required fees: $432; $24 per credit hour. $50 per term. Tuition and fees vary according to program. *Financial support:* Available to part-time students. Applicants required to submit FAFSA. *Unit head:* Dr. Ellen Rosell, Chairman, 334-670-3758, Fax: 334-670-5647, E-mail: erosell@troy.edu. *Application contact:* Brenda K. Campbell, Director of Graduate Admissions, 334-670-3178, Fax: 334-670-3733, E-mail: bcamp@troy.edu.

University of Denver, Josef Korbel School of International Studies, Denver, CO 80208. Offers conflict resolution (MA); development practice (MDP); global finance, trade and economic integration (MA); global health affairs (Certificate); homeland security (Certificate); humanitarian assistance (Certificate); international development (MA); international human rights (MA); international security (MA); international studies (MA, PhD). Part-time programs available. *Faculty:* 33 full-time (13 women), 38 part-time/adjunct (11 women). *Students:* 461 full-time (279 women), 52 part-time (27 women); includes 71 minority (8 Black or African American, non-Hispanic/Latino; 3 American Indian or Alaska Native, non-Hispanic/Latino; 25 Asian, non-Hispanic/Latino; 25 Hispanic/Latino; 2 Native Hawaiian or other Pacific Islander, non-Hispanic/Latino; 8 Two or more races, non-Hispanic/Latino), 42 international. Average age 28. 1,056 applicants, 69% accepted, 259 enrolled. In 2010, 230 master's, 5 doctorates, 42 other advanced degrees awarded. *Degree requirements:* For master's, one foreign language, thesis; for doctorate, one foreign language, thesis/dissertation. *Entrance requirements:* For master's and doctorate, GRE General Test. Additional exam requirements/recommendations for international students: Required—TOEFL (minimum score 587 paper-based; 95 iBT). *Application deadline:* For fall admission, 1/15 priority date for domestic students, 12/15 priority date for international students; for winter admission, 10/15 priority date for domestic and international students. Applications are processed on a rolling basis. Application fee: $60. Electronic applications accepted. *Expenses:* Tuition: Full-time $35,604; part-time $29,670 per year. Required fees: $687 per year. Tuition and fees vary according to program. *Financial support:* In 2010–11, 1 teaching assistantship with partial tuition reimbursement (averaging $9,999 per year) was awarded; career-related internships or fieldwork, Federal Work-Study, institutionally sponsored loans, scholarships/grants, and unspecified assistantships also available. Support available to part-time students. Financial award applicants required to submit FAFSA. *Faculty research:* Human rights and international security, international politics and economics, economic-social and political development, international technology analysis and management. *Unit head:* Ambassador Christopher R. Hill, Dean, 303-871-2539, Fax: 303-871-2124, E-mail: christopher.r.hill@du.edu. *Application contact:* Brad Miller, Director of Graduate Admissions and Financial Aid, 303-871-2989, Fax: 303-871-2124, E-mail: korbeladm@du.edu.

University of New Haven, Graduate School, Henry C. Lee College of Criminal Justice and Forensic Sciences, National Security and Public Safety Program, West Haven, CT 06516-1916. Offers information protection and security (MS); national security (Certificate); national security administration (Certificate). Part-time and evening/weekend programs available. *Students:* 36 full-time (15 women), 38 part-time (17 women); includes 7 Black or African American, non-Hispanic/Latino; 2 American Indian or Alaska Native, non-Hispanic/Latino; 2 Asian, non-Hispanic/Latino; 10 Hispanic/Latino, 6 international. Average age 32. 27 applicants, 96% accepted, 19 enrolled. In 2010, 28 master's awarded. *Entrance requirements:* Additional exam requirements/recommendations for international students: Required—TOEFL (minimum score 520 paper-based; 190 computer-based; 70 iBT); Recommended—IELTS (minimum score 5.5). *Application deadline:* For fall admission, 5/31 for international students; for winter admission, 10/15 for international students; for spring admission, 1/15 for international students. Applications are processed on a rolling basis. Application fee: $50. Electronic applications accepted. *Financial support:* Research assistantships with partial tuition reimbursements, teaching assistantships with partial tuition reimbursements, career-related internships or fieldwork, Federal Work-Study, scholarships/grants, tuition waivers, and unspecified assistantships available. Support available to part-time students. Financial award applicants required to submit FAFSA. *Unit head:* Dr. William L. Tafoya, Dean, 203-932-7260. *Application contact:* Eloise Gormley, Director of Graduate Admissions, 203-932-7449, Fax: 203-932-7137, E-mail: gradinfo@newhaven.edu.

University of Pittsburgh, Graduate School of Public and International Affairs, Public Policy and Management Program for Mid-Career Professionals, Pittsburgh, PA 15260. Offers development planning (MPPM); international development (MPPM); international political economy (MPPM); international security studies (MPPM); management of non profit organizations (MPPM); metropolitan management and regional development (MPPM); policy analysis and evaluation (MPPM). Part-time programs available. *Faculty:* 30 full-time (12 women), 67 part-time/adjunct (25 women). *Students:* 14 full-time (1 woman), 34 part-time (17 women), 8 international. Average age 38. 31 applicants, 74% accepted, 15 enrolled. In 2010, 14 master's awarded. *Degree requirements:* For master's, thesis optional, capstone seminar. *Entrance requirements:* For master's, 2 letters of recommendation, resume, 5 years of supervisory or budgetary experience. Additional exam requirements/recommendations for international students: Required—TOEFL (minimum score 600 paper-based; 250 computer-based; 100 iBT), TWE (minimum score 4); Recommended—IELTS (minimum score 7). *Application deadline:* For fall admission, 6/1 priority date for domestic students, 2/15 for international students; for spring admission, 1/1 priority date for domestic students, 8/1 for international students. Applications are processed on a rolling basis. Application fee: $50. Electronic applications accepted. *Expenses:* Tuition, state resident: full-time $17,304; part-time $701 per credit. Tuition, nonresident: full-time $29,554; part-time $1210 per credit. Required fees: $740; $214 per term. Tuition and fees vary according to program. *Financial support:* In 2010–11, 14 students received support. Scholarships/grants and tuition waivers (partial) available. Support available to part-time students. Financial award application deadline: 2/1. *Faculty research:* Nonprofit management, urban and regional affairs, policy analysis and evaluation, security and intelligence studies, global political economy, nongovernmental organizations, civil society, development planning and environmental sustainability, human security. Total annual research expenditures: $892,349. *Unit head:* Dr. George Dougherty, Director, Executive Education, 412-648-7603, Fax: 412-648-2605, E-mail: gwdjr@pitt.edu. *Application contact:* Michael T. Rizzi, Associate Director of Student Services, 412-648-7640, Fax: 412-648-7641, E-mail: rizzim@pitt.edu.

The University of Texas at El Paso, Graduate School, Institute for Policy and Economic Development, El Paso, TX 79968-0001. Offers border administration (Certificate); homeland security (Certificate); intelligence and national security (MS, Certificate); leadership studies (MA); public administration (MPA). *Accreditation:* NASPAA. Part-time and evening/weekend programs available. *Students:* 187 (57 women); includes 19 Black or African American, non-Hispanic/Latino; 1 American Indian or Alaska Native, non-Hispanic/Latino; 5 Asian, non-Hispanic/Latino; 99 Hispanic/Latino, 5 international. 142 applicants, 77% accepted. In 2010, 76 master's awarded. *Degree requirements:* For master's, thesis optional. *Entrance requirements:* For master's, GRE, statement of purpose, letters of recommendation. Additional exam requirements/recommendations for international students: Required—TOEFL; Recommended—IELTS. *Application deadline:* For fall admission, 8/1 for domestic students, 3/1 for international students; for spring admission, 10/1 for domestic students, 9/1 for international students. Applications are processed on a rolling basis. Application fee: $45 ($80 for international students). Electronic applications accepted. *Financial support:* Fellowships with partial tuition reimbursements, research assistantships with partial tuition reimbursements, teaching assistantships with partial tuition reimbursements, institutionally sponsored loans, scholarships/grants, health care benefits, tuition waivers (partial), and unspecified assistantships available. Support available to part-time students. Financial award application deadline: 3/15; financial award applicants required to

submit FAFSA. *Unit head:* Dr. Dennis Soden, Director, 915-747-7974, Fax: 915-747-7948, E-mail: desoden@utep.edu. *Application contact:* Dr. Patricia D. Witherspoon, Dean of the Graduate School, 915-747-5491, Fax: 915-747-5788, E-mail: withersp@utep.edu.

Virginia Polytechnic Institute and State University, Graduate School, College of Liberal Arts and Human Sciences, Department of Political Science, Blacksburg, VA 24061. Offers environmental politics and policy (Certificate); foundations of political analysis (Certificate); information policy and society (Certificate); political science (MA); security studies (Certificate). *Faculty:* 22 full-time (6 women), 1 (woman) part-time/adjunct. *Students:* 40 full-time (15 women), 49 part-time (19 women); includes 1 Black or African American, non-Hispanic/Latino; 1 American Indian or Alaska Native, non-Hispanic/Latino; 3 Asian, non-Hispanic/Latino; 4 Hispanic/Latino, 10 international. Average age 32. 49 applicants, 47% accepted, 13 enrolled. In 2010, 12 master's awarded. *Degree requirements:* For master's, comprehensive exam (for some programs), thesis (for some programs). *Entrance requirements:* For master's, GRE. Additional exam requirements/recommendations for international students: Required—TOEFL (minimum score 550 paper-based; 213 computer-based). *Application deadline:* For fall admission, 7/1 for domestic and international students; for spring admission, 12/1 for domestic and international students. Applications are processed on a rolling basis. Application fee: $65. Electronic applications accepted. *Expenses:* Tuition, state resident: full-time $9399; part-time $488 per credit hour. Tuition, nonresident: full-time $17,854; part-time $957.75 per credit hour. Required fees: $1534. Full-time tuition and fees vary according to program. *Financial support:* In 2010–11, 12 teaching assistantships with full tuition reimbursements (averaging $12,972 per year) were awarded; career-related internships or fieldwork, Federal Work-Study, scholarships/grants, health care benefits, and unspecified assistantships also available. Financial award application deadline: 1/15. *Faculty research:* Comparative politics, international relations, American government and politics, research methods. Total annual research expenditures: $24,854. *Unit head:* Dr. Ilja A. Luciak, UNIT HEAD, 540-231-6571, Fax: 540-231-6078, E-mail: iluciak@vt.edu. *Application contact:* Tim Luke, Contact, 540-231-6633, Fax: 540-231-6078, E-mail: twluke@vt.edu.

Virginia Polytechnic Institute and State University, VT Online, Blacksburg, VA 24061. Offers aerospace engineering (MS); business information systems (Graduate Certificate); career and technical education (MS); computer engineering (M Eng, MS); decision support systems (Graduate Certificate); eLearning leadership (MA); electrical engineering (M Eng, MS); engineering administration (MEA); environmental politics and policy (Graduate Certificate); foundations of political analysis (Graduate Certificate); health product risk management (Graduate Certificate); information policy and society (Graduate Certificate); information security (Graduate Certificate); instructional technology (MA); liberal arts (Graduate Certificate); life sciences: health product risk management (MS); natural resources (MNR, Graduate Certificate); networking (Graduate Certificate); nonprofit and nongovernmental organization management (Graduate Certificate); ocean engineering (MS); political science (MA); security studies (Graduate Certificate); software development (Graduate Certificate). *Expenses:* Tuition, state resident: full-time $9399; part-time $488 per credit hour. Tuition, nonresident: full-time $17,854; part-time $957.75 per credit hour. Required fees: $1534. Full-time tuition and fees vary according to program.

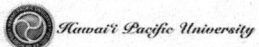

HAWAI'I PACIFIC UNIVERSITY

Diplomacy and Military Studies Program

Program of Study	Hawai'i Pacific University's (HPU's) Master of Arts in Diplomacy and Military Studies (M.A./DMS) is designed to provide students with an interdisciplinary view of the role of diplomacy and the military in world affairs from both historical and contemporary perspectives. The program combines courses in history, art history, literature, philosophy, anthropology, international relations, strategic studies, and political science to acquaint students with different approaches and methods in the study of diplomacy and the military.
	The M.A./DMS program is an excellent opportunity for those wishing to explore the complex relationships of politics, society, and the military. It is a useful degree for those who are either professional military officers or those who work in a variety of government positions. It is also outstanding preparation for more advanced graduate studies in history, political science, or international relations.
	The M.A./DMS requires a minimum of 42 semester hours of graduate work: 12 semester hours of core courses, 12 semester hours of electives in diplomatic and military history, 12 semester hours of supporting field electives, and 6 semester hours of capstone courses. HPU's M.A./DMS program is unique in its global perspective; it not only considers the United States and Europe, but integrates a variety of courses in Asia and the Pacific, as well as other courses of a comparative nature.
	The core classes are drawn from the disciplines of history, interdisciplinary humanities, philosophy, and political science and provide students with the historical, ethical, and practical background necessary to understand fully the multifaceted character of the military. They are also intended to give students a sound introduction to the fundamental literature dealing with the history of foreign relations and the military.
Research Facilities	To support graduate studies, HPU's Meader and Atherton Libraries hold more than 110,000 bound volumes, 350,000 microfiche items, and periodical subscriptions to 1,500 print titles and 30,000 electronic journals. Databases of public and state university libraries, legislative information, and business-oriented statistical data are also available in the library or online. Students can access HPU's library databases, course information, their academic information, and an e-mail account through Pipeline, the university's internal Web site for students. The University's accessible on-campus computer center houses more than 420 computers with specialized software to support graduate academic programs. HPU also provides free Wi-Fi so that students can access Pipeline resources anywhere on campus using laptops. A significant number of online courses are available.
Financial Aid	The University participates in all federal financial aid programs designated for graduate students. These programs provide aid in the form of subsidized (need-based) and unsubsidized (non-need-based) Federal Stafford Student Loans. Through these loans, funds may be available to cover a student's entire cost of education. To apply for aid, students must submit the Free Application for Federal Student Aid (FAFSA) beginning January 1.
	The University also offers several types of institutional graduate scholarships to new full-time, degree-seeking students. U.S. citizens, permanent residents, and international students who have a demonstrated financial need may apply. HPU's graduate scholarships include the Graduate Trustee Scholarship ($6000 for two semesters), the Graduate Dean Scholarship ($4000 for two semesters), and the Graduate Kokua Scholarship ($2000 for two semesters). Factors that may be considered when evaluating requests are previous academic record, community involvement and service, and professional work experience and achievement.
	In order to be eligible for the best award package, students should apply by HPU's priority deadline of March 1. Applications received after the priority deadline will be awarded on a funds-available basis. Mailing of student award letters usually begins by the end of March. Applicants will be notified by mail as decisions are made.
Cost of Study	Tuition for graduate students enrolled in fall and spring semesters is determined on a per-credit basis; full-time status for a graduate student is 9 credits. Tuition for the optional winter and summer sessions is also determined on a per-credit basis. The estimated minimum funds needed for a nine-month academic year (September to May) is $28,650. For the 2011–12 academic year, full-time tuition is $13,230 for most graduate degree programs, including the M.A./DMS program. Other expenses, including books, personal expenses, fees, and a student bus pass is estimated at $3190.
Living and Housing Costs	Most graduate students live in off-campus housing. The cost of living in off-campus apartments is approximately $12,230 for a double-occupancy room.
Student Group	University enrollment currently stands at more than 8,200. HPU is one of the most culturally diverse universities in America, with students from all fifty U.S. states and more than 100 countries. HPU strives to maintain a student profile that is one third Hawai'I, one third mainland U.S.A., and one third global.
Location	Hawai'i Pacific combines the excitement of an urban, downtown campus with the serenity of a residential campus. The urban campus is ideally located in downtown Honolulu, the business and financial center of the Pacific. The downtown campus comprises six buildings in the center of Honolulu's business district and is home to the College of Business Administration and the College of Humanities and Social Sciences.
	Eight miles away, situated on 135 acres in Kaneohe, the windward Hawai'i Loa campus is the site of the College of Nursing and Health Sciences and the College of Natural and Computational Sciences. The Hawai'i Loa campus has residence halls, dining commons, the Educational Technology Center, a student center, and outdoor recreational facilities, including a soccer field, tennis courts, a softball field, and an exercise room.
	HPU is affiliated with the Oceanic Institute, an applied aquaculture research facility located on a 56-acre site at Makapu'u Point on the windward coast of Oahu, Hawaii. All three sites are linked by HPU shuttle as well as easily accessed by public transportation.
	Notably, the downtown campus location is within walking distance of shopping and dining. Iolani Palace, the only palace in the U.S., is a few blocks away, as are the State Capitol, City Hall, and the Blaisdell Concert Hall. The Honolulu Academy of Arts, Museum of Contemporary Art, Waikiki Aquarium, Honolulu Zoo, and many other cultural attractions are located nearby.
The University	HPU is a private, nonprofit university with approximately 8,200 students. Founded in 1965, HPU prides itself on maintaining strong academic programs, small class sizes, individual attention to students, and a diverse faculty and student population. HPU is recognized as a "Best Western" college by the Princeton Review and a "Best Buy in College Education" by *Barron's* business magazine. HPU offers more than fifty acclaimed undergraduate programs and fourteen distinguished graduate programs. The University has a faculty of more than 500, a student-faculty ratio of 15:1, and an average class size of fewer than 25 students. A wide range of counseling and other student support services are available. There are more than sixty student organizations on campus, including the Graduate Student Organization.
Applying	Students must have a baccalaureate degree from an accredited college or university in the United States or an equivalent degree from another country. Applicants should complete and forward a graduate admissions application, send in the $50 nonrefundable application fee, have official transcripts sent from all colleges or universities previously attended, and forward two letters of recommendation. A personal statement about the applicant's academic and career goals is required; submitting a resume is optional. Applicants who have taken the Graduate Record Examination (GRE) should have their scores sent directly to the Graduate Admissions Office. International students should submit scores of a recognized English proficiency test such as TOEFL. Admissions decisions are made on a rolling basis, and applicants are notified between one and two weeks after all documents have been submitted. Applicants are encouraged to submit their applications online.
Correspondence and Information	Graduate Admissions Hawai'i Pacific University 1164 Bishop Street, #911 Honolulu, Hawaii 96813 Phone: 808-544-1135 866-GRAD-HPU (toll-free) Fax: 808-544-0280 E-mail: graduate@hpu.edu Web site: http://www.hpu.edu/hpumadms

Hawai'i Pacific University

THE FACULTY

Pierre Asselin, Associate Professor of History; Ph.D., Hawai'i at Manoa.
Patrick Bratton, Assistant Professor of Political Science; Ph.D., Catholic University.
Grace Cheng, Associate Professor of Political Science; Ph.D., Hawai'i.
Allison Gough, Associate Professor of History; Ph.D., Ohio State.
Russell Hart, Associate Professor of History; Ph.D., Ohio State.
Carlos Juarez, Professor of Political Science; Ph.D., UCLA.
James Primm, Associate Professor of Political Science; Ph.D., Hawai'i.
George Satterfield, Associate Professor of History; Ph.D., Illinois at Urbana-Champaign.

Section 23
Political Science and International Affairs

This section contains a directory of institutions offering graduate work in political science and international affairs. Additional information about programs listed in the directory may be obtained by writing directly to the dean of a graduate school or chair of a department at the address given in the directory.

For programs offering related work, see also in this book *Area and Cultural Studies, History, Language and Literature,* and *Public, Regional, and Industrial Affairs.* In another guide in this series:
Graduate Programs in Business, Education, Health, Information Studies, Law & Social Work
See *International Business*

CONTENTS

Program Directories

Close-Ups and Display

International Affairs

Alliant International University–México City, International Studies Division, Mexico City, Mexico. Offers international relations (MA).

Alliant International University–México City, Marshall Goldsmith School of Management, Mexico City, Mexico. Offers international business administration (MIBA); international relations (MA). Part-time and evening/weekend programs available. *Entrance requirements:* For master's, GMAT, minimum GPA of 3.0. Additional exam requirements/recommendations for international students: Required—TOEFL (minimum score 550 paper-based; 213 computer-based), TWE (minimum score 5). Electronic applications accepted. *Faculty research:* Environmental impact and business in Mexico.

Alliant International University–México City, Programs in Arts and Science, Mexico City, Mexico. Offers counseling psychology (MA); international relations (MA). Part-time programs available. *Degree requirements:* For master's, thesis optional. *Entrance requirements:* For master's, GRE General Test, letters of recommendation. Additional exam requirements/recommendations for international students: Required—TOEFL. Electronic applications accepted.

Alliant International University–San Diego, Marshall Goldsmith School of Management, International Studies Division, San Diego, CA 92131-1799. Offers international relations (MA). Part-time programs available. *Degree requirements:* For master's, thesis. *Entrance requirements:* For master's, GRE, minimum GPA of 2.5, letters of recommendation. Additional exam requirements/recommendations for international students: Required—TOEFL (minimum score 550 paper-based).

American Graduate School in Paris, Program in International Relations and Diplomacy, Paris, France. Offers MA, PhD.

American Public University System, AMU/APU Graduate Programs, Charles Town, WV 25414. Offers accounting (MBA); administration and supervision (M Ed); air warfare (MA Military Studies); asymmetrical warfare (MA Military Studies); criminal justice (MA); emergency and disaster management (MA); entrepreneurship (MBA); environmental policy and management (MS); finance (MBA); general (MBA); global business management (MBA); guidance and counseling (M Ed); history (MA); homeland security (MA); homeland security resource allocation (MBA); humanities (MA); information technology (MS); information technology management (MBA); intelligence studies (MA); international relations and conflict resolution (MA); joint warfare (MA Military Studies); land warfare (MA Military Studies); legal studies (MA); management (MA), including defense mangement, general, human resource management, organizational leadership, public administration; marketing (MBA); military history (MA); national security studies (MA); naval warfare (MA Military Studies); nonprofit management (MBA); political science (MA); psychology (MA); public administration (MA); public health (MA); security management (MA); space studies (MS); sports management (MS); strategic leadership (MA Military Studies); teaching (M Ed), including elementary, secondary social sciences; transportation and logistics management (MA). Programs offered via distance learning only. Part-time and evening/weekend programs available. Postbaccalaureate distance learning degree programs offered (no on-campus study). *Faculty:* 253 full-time (134 women), 1,208 part-time/adjunct (570 women). *Students:* 956 full-time (422 women), 8,476 part-time (2,821 women); includes 2,511 minority (1,218 Black or African American, non-Hispanic/Latino; 68 American Indian or Alaska Native, non-Hispanic/Latino; 219 Asian, non-Hispanic/Latino; 705 Hispanic/Latino; 46 Native Hawaiian or other Pacific Islander, non-Hispanic/Latino; 255 Two or more races, non-Hispanic/Latino), 107 international. Average age 35. 9,550 applicants, 100% accepted. In 2010, 1,688 master's awarded. *Degree requirements:* For master's, comprehensive exam or practicum. *Entrance requirements:* For master's, official transcript showing earned bachelor's degree from institution accredited by recognized accrediting body. Additional exam requirements/recommendations for international students: Required—TOEFL (minimum score 550 paper-based; 213 computer-based), IELTS (minimum score 6.5). *Application deadline:* Applications are processed on a rolling basis. Application fee: $0. Electronic applications accepted. *Financial support:* Applicants required to submit FAFSA. *Faculty research:* Military history, criminal justice, management performance, national security. *Unit head:* Dr. Frank McCluskey, Provost, 877-468-6268, Fax: 304-724-3780. *Application contact:* Terry Grant, Director of Enrollment Management, 877-468-6268, Fax: 304-724-3780, E-mail: info@apus.edu.

American University, College of Arts and Sciences, Department of Economics, Washington, DC 20016-8029. Offers applied microeconomics (Certificate); economics (MA, PhD); international economic relations (Certificate). Part-time and evening/weekend programs available. *Faculty:* 26 full-time (9 women). *Students:* 48 full-time (20 women), 71 part-time (26 women); includes 12 minority (7 Black or African American, non-Hispanic/Latino; 3 Asian, non-Hispanic/Latino; 2 Hispanic/Latino), 44 international. Average age 30. 186 applicants, 68% accepted, 32 enrolled. In 2010, 15 master's, 10 doctorates, 1 other advanced degree awarded. Terminal master's awarded for partial completion of doctoral program. *Degree requirements:* For master's, comprehensive exam, thesis or alternative; for doctorate, comprehensive exam, thesis/dissertation, 2 research seminars, field work. *Entrance requirements:* For master's and doctorate, GRE; for Certificate, bachelor's degree. Additional exam requirements/recommendations for international students: Required—TOEFL. *Application deadline:* For spring admission, 10/1 for domestic students. Applications are processed on a rolling basis. Application fee: $80. *Financial support:* Fellowships, research assistantships with full and partial tuition reimbursements, teaching assistantships with full and partial tuition reimbursements, career-related internships or fieldwork, Federal Work-Study, institutionally sponsored loans, and tuition waivers (full and partial) available. Financial award application deadline: 2/1. *Faculty research:* Political economy, development, labor, gender. *Unit head:* Robert A. Blecker, Chair, 202-885-3767, Fax: 202-885-3790, E-mail: blecker@american.edu. *Application contact:* Kathleen Clowery, Director of Graduate Admissions, 202-885-3621, Fax: 202-885-1505, E-mail: clowery@american.edu.

American University, School of International Service, Washington, DC 20016-8071. Offers comparative and regional studies (Certificate); cross-cultural communication (Certificate); development management (MS); ethics, peace, and global affairs (MA); European studies (Certificate); global environmental policy (MA, Certificate); international affairs (MA), including comparative and regional studies, environmental policy, international economic policy, international politics, natural resources and sustainable development, U. S. foreign policy; international communication (MA, Certificate); international development (MA, Certificate); international development management (Certificate); international economic policy (Certificate); international economic relations (Certificate); international media (MA); international peace and conflict resolution (MA, Certificate); international relations (PhD); international service (MIS); peace building (Certificate); the Americas (Certificate); United States foreign policy (Certificate); JD/MA. Part-time and evening/weekend programs available. *Faculty:* 91 full-time (35 women), 48 part-time/adjunct (16 women). *Students:* 591 full-time (383 women), 367 part-time (229 women); includes 164 minority (51 Black or African American, non-Hispanic/Latino; 4 American Indian or Alaska Native, non-Hispanic/Latino; 42 Asian, non-Hispanic/Latino; 63 Hispanic/Latino; 4 Two or more races, non-Hispanic/Latino), 94 international. Average age 27. 2,115 applicants, 59% accepted, 360 enrolled. In 2010, 370 master's, 7 doctorates awarded. Terminal master's awarded for partial completion of doctoral program. *Degree requirements:* For master's, one foreign language, comprehensive exam, thesis or alternative; for doctorate, one foreign language, comprehensive exam, thesis/dissertation, research practicum; for Certificate, minimum 15 credit hours related course work. *Entrance requirements:* For master's, GRE, 24 credits of course work in related social sciences, minimum GPA of 3.5, 2 letters of recommendation, bachelor's degree, resume; for doctorate, GRE, 2 letters of recommendation, 24 credits in related social sciences; for Certificate, bachelor's degree. Additional exam requirements/recommendations for international students: Required—TOEFL (minimum score 600 paper-based; 250 computer-based; 100 iBT). *Application deadline:* For fall admission, 1/15 priority date for domestic students; for spring admission, 10/1 priority date

for domestic students. Applications are processed on a rolling basis. Application fee: $50. *Financial support:* Career-related internships or fieldwork, Federal Work-Study, and institutionally sponsored loans available. Financial award application deadline: 1/15. *Faculty research:* International intellectual property, international environmental issues, international law and legal order, international telecommunications/technology, international sustainable development. *Unit head:* Dr. Louis W. Goodman, Dean, 202-885-1600, Fax: 202-885-2494. *Application contact:* Yasmin Quianzon, Director of Graduate Admissions and Financial Aid, 202-885-2496, Fax: 202-885-1109.

The American University of Paris, Graduate Programs, Paris, France. Offers cross-cultural and sustainable business management (MA); cultural translation (MA); global communications (MA); global communications and civil society (MA); international affairs, conflict resolution and civil society development (MA); Middle East and Islamic studies (MA); Middle East and Islamic studies and international affairs (MA); public policy and international affairs (MA); public policy and international law (MA). *Faculty:* 14 full-time (3 women). *Students:* 151 full-time (110 women), 56 part-time (43 women). 271 applicants, 83% accepted, 104 enrolled. In 2010, 67 master's awarded. *Degree requirements:* For master's, thesis. *Entrance requirements:* For master's, minimum undergraduate GPA of 3.0. Additional exam requirements/recommendations for international students: Recommended—IELTS. *Application deadline:* For fall admission, 4/15 priority date for international students; for spring admission, 11/15 priority date for international students. Applications are processed on a rolling basis. Application fee: $75. Electronic applications accepted. *Financial support:* Scholarships/grants available. Financial award applicants required to submit FAFSA. *Unit head:* Dr. Celeste Schenck, President, 33-1 40 62 06 59, E-mail: president@aup.fr. *Application contact:* International Admissions Counselor, 33-1 40 62 07 20, Fax: 33-1 47 05 34 32, E-mail: admissions@aup.edu.

Appalachian State University, Cratis D. Williams Graduate School, Department of Government and Justice Studies, Boone, NC 28608. Offers criminal justice (MS); political science (MA), including American government, environmental politics and policy analysis, international relations; public administration (MPA), including public management, town, city and county management. Part-time programs available. Postbaccalaureate distance learning degree programs offered (no on-campus study). *Faculty:* 24 full-time (5 women), 3 part-time/adjunct (2 women). *Students:* 72 full-time (29 women), 53 part-time (25 women); includes 6 Black or African American, non-Hispanic/Latino; 1 Asian, non-Hispanic/Latino; 3 Hispanic/Latino; 1 Two or more races, non-Hispanic/Latino. 86 applicants, 86% accepted, 58 enrolled. In 2010, 49 master's awarded. *Degree requirements:* For master's, variable foreign language requirement, comprehensive exam, thesis optional. *Entrance requirements:* For master's, GRE General Test, 3 letters of recommendation. Additional exam requirements/recommendations for international students: Required—TOEFL (minimum score 570 paper-based; 230 computer-based; 79 iBT), IELTS (minimum score 6.5). *Application deadline:* For fall admission, 7/1 for domestic students, 2/1 for international students; for spring admission, 11/1 for domestic students, 7/1 for international students. Applications are processed on a rolling basis. Application fee: $55. Electronic applications accepted. *Expenses:* Tuition, state resident: full-time $3428; part-time $428 per unit. Tuition, nonresident: full-time $14,518; part-time $1814 per unit. Required fees: $2320; $344 per unit. Tuition and fees vary according to campus/location. *Financial support:* In 2010–11, 20 research assistantships (averaging $8,000 per year) were awarded; fellowships, teaching assistantships, career-related internships or fieldwork, Federal Work-Study, scholarships/grants, and unspecified assistantships also available. Financial award application deadline: 4/1; financial award applicants required to submit FAFSA. *Faculty research:* Campaign finance, emerging democracies, bureaucratic politics, judicial behavior, administration of justice. Total annual research expenditures: $143,000. *Unit head:* Dr. Brian Ellison, Chairperson, 828-262-3085, E-mail: ellisonba@appstate.edu. *Application contact:* Sandy Krause, Director of Admissions and Recruiting, 828-262-2130, Fax: 828-262-2709, E-mail: krausesl@appstate.edu.

Azusa Pacific University, School of Behavioral and Applied Sciences, Department of Higher Education and Organizational Leadership, Azusa, CA 91702-7000. Offers college student affairs (M Ed); global leadership (MA); organizational leadership (MA). *Faculty:* 5 full-time (4 women), 1 part-time/adjunct (0 women). *Students:* 12 full-time (5 women), 64 part-time (33 women); includes 11 minority (6 Black or African American, non-Hispanic/Latino; 1 Asian, non-Hispanic/Latino; 4 Hispanic/Latino), 3 international. Average age 39. Application fee: $45 ($65 for international students). *Unit head:* Dr. Laurie Schreiner, Chair, 626-815-5349. *Application contact:* Linda Witte, Graduate Admissions Office, 626-969-3434.

Baylor University, Graduate School, College of Arts and Sciences, Department of Political Science, Waco, TX 76798. Offers international studies (MA); political science (MA, PhD); public policy and administration (MPPA); JD/MPPA. *Students:* 29 full-time (8 women), 1 part-time (0 women), 3 international. In 2010, 6 master's, 3 doctorates awarded. *Entrance requirements:* For master's, GRE General Test. *Application deadline:* Applications are processed on a rolling basis. Application fee: $25. *Financial support:* Research assistantships, career-related internships or fieldwork, Federal Work-Study, and institutionally sponsored loans available. Financial award application deadline: 3/1. *Unit head:* Dr. David Corey, Graduate Program Director, 254-710-3161, Fax: 254-710-3122, E-mail: david_d_corey@baylor.edu. *Application contact:* Jenice Langston, Administrative Assistant, 254-710-3161, Fax: 254-710-3870, E-mail: jenice_langston@baylor.edu.

Baylor University, Graduate School, Hankamer School of Business, Department of Economics, Waco, TX 76798. Offers economics (MS Eco); international economics (MA, MS). *Students:* 12 full-time (7 women), 4 international. In 2010, 12 master's awarded. *Entrance requirements:* For master's, GMAT or GRE General Test. *Application deadline:* For fall admission, 8/1 for domestic students; for spring admission, 12/1 for domestic students. Applications are processed on a rolling basis. Application fee: $25. *Financial support:* Research assistantships, Federal Work-Study and institutionally sponsored loans available. Financial award application deadline: 4/1. *Faculty research:* Econometrics, international economics, private enterprise, comparative economic systems. *Unit head:* Dr. Tom Kelly, Chair, 254-710-4146, Fax: 254-710-3265, E-mail: tom_kelly@baylor.edu. *Application contact:* Susan Armstrong, Administrative Assistant, 254-710-6177, Fax: 254-710-1066, E-mail: susan_armstrong@baylor.edu.

Boston University, Graduate School of Arts and Sciences, Department of Geography and Environment, Boston, MA 02215. Offers energy and environmental analysis (MA); environmental remote sensing and GIs (MA); geography (MA); geography and environment (PhD); international relations and environmental policy (MA). *Students:* 55 full-time (23 women), 10 part-time (3 women); includes 3 minority (1 Asian, non-Hispanic/Latino; 1 Hispanic/Latino; 1 Two or more races, non-Hispanic/Latino), 17 international. Average age 28. 64 applicants, 23% accepted, 5 enrolled. In 2010, 1 master's, 2 doctorates awarded. Terminal master's awarded for partial completion of doctoral program. *Degree requirements:* For master's, one foreign language, comprehensive exam, thesis; for doctorate, one foreign language, comprehensive exam, thesis/dissertation. *Entrance requirements:* For master's and doctorate, GRE General Test, GRE Subject Test, 3 letters of recommendation. Additional exam requirements/recommendations for international students: Required—TOEFL (minimum score 600 paper-based; 250 computer-based). *Application deadline:* For fall admission, 7/1 for domestic and international students; for spring admission, 11/15 for domestic and international students. Application fee: $70. Electronic applications accepted. *Expenses:* Tuition: Full-time $39,314; part-time $1228 per credit. Required fees: $40 per semester. *Financial support:* In 2010–11, 33 students received support, including 2 fellowships with full tuition reimbursements available (averaging $19,300 per year), 20 research assistantships with full tuition reimbursements available (averaging $18,800 per year), 11 teaching assistantships with full tuition reimbursements available (averaging $18,800 per year); Federal Work-Study and unspecified assistantships also available. Support available to part-time students. Financial award application deadline: 1/15; financial award applicants required to submit FAFSA. Total annual research expenditures: $1.2 million. *Unit head:* Robert Kaufmann, Chairman, 617-353-3940, Fax: 617-

353-8399, E-mail: kaufmann@bu.edu. *Application contact:* Christopher DeVits, Graduate Program Coordinator, 617-353-7554, Fax: 617-353-8399, E-mail: cdevits@bu.edu.

Boston University, Graduate School of Arts and Sciences, Department of International Relations, Boston, MA 02215. Offers African studies (Certificate); international relations (MA); international relations and environmental policy management (MA); international relations and international communication (MA); JD/MA; MBA/MA. *Students:* 49 full-time (36 women), 12 part-time (7 women); includes 10 minority (2 Black or African American, non-Hispanic/Latino; 5 Asian, non-Hispanic/Latino; 1 Hispanic/Latino; 2 Two or more races, non-Hispanic/Latino), 10 international. Average age 26. 417 applicants, 59% accepted, 50 enrolled. In 2010, 41 master's awarded. *Degree requirements:* For master's, one foreign language, comprehensive exam, thesis. *Entrance requirements:* For master's, GRE General Test, 3 letters of recommendation; for Certificate, GRE General Test. Additional exam requirements/recommendations for international students: Required—TOEFL (minimum score 600 paper-based; 250 computer-based). *Application deadline:* For fall admission, 4/15 for domestic and international students; for spring admission, 10/15 for domestic and international students. Application fee: $70. Electronic applications accepted. *Expenses:* Tuition: Full-time $39,314; part-time $1228 per credit. Required fees: $40 per semester. *Financial support:* In 2010–11, 19 students received support. Federal Work-Study, scholarships/grants, and unspecified assistantships available. Support available to part-time students. Financial award application deadline: 1/15; financial award applicants required to submit FAFSA. *Unit head:* William Grimes, Chairman, 617-353-9420, Fax: 617-353-9290, E-mail: wgrimes@bu.edu. *Application contact:* Michael Williams, Graduate Program Administrator, 617-353-9349, Fax: 617-353-9290, E-mail: mawillia@bu.edu.

Brandeis University, Graduate School of Arts and Sciences, Graduate Program in Global Studies, Waltham, MA 02454-9110. Offers MA. Part-time programs available. *Faculty:* 8 full-time (3 women). *Students:* 11 full-time (6 women), 1 part-time (0 women); includes 1 Asian, non-Hispanic/Latino; 2 Hispanic/Latino, 2 international. 44 applicants, 52% accepted, 9 enrolled. In 2010, 5 master's awarded. *Degree requirements:* For master's, thesis. *Entrance requirements:* For master's, GRE, official transcript(s), 2 recommendation letters, curriculum vitae or resume, statement of purpose, writing sample. Additional exam requirements/recommendations for international students: Required—TOEFL (minimum score 600 paper-based; 250 computer-based; 100 iBT); Recommended—IELTS (minimum score 7). *Application deadline:* Applications are processed on a rolling basis. Application fee: $75. Electronic applications accepted. *Financial support:* In 2010–11, 7 teaching assistantships (averaging $3,200 per year) were awarded; scholarships/grants and unspecified assistantships also available. Support available to part-time students. Financial award application deadline: 4/15; financial award applicants required to submit FAFSA. *Faculty research:* Globalization, civil society and human rights, communications and media, culture and globalization, global and regional governance, global environment, global health, immigration, social justice and gender. *Unit head:* Prof. Richard J. Parmentier, Director, 781-736-2220, Fax: 781-736-2232, E-mail: rparmentier@brandeis.edu. *Application contact:* Mangok Bol, Department Administrator, 781-736-2234, Fax: 781-736-2232, E-mail: mbol@brandeis.edu.

Brandeis University, International Business School, Waltham, MA 02454-9110. Offers finance (MSF); international business (MBAi); international economics and finance (MA, PhD); international finance/international economics (MBAi). Part-time and evening/weekend programs available. Terminal master's awarded for partial completion of doctoral program. *Degree requirements:* For master's, one foreign language, semester abroad; for doctorate, thesis/dissertation. *Entrance requirements:* For master's, GMAT or GRE General Test (MA), GMAT (MBAi, MSF); for doctorate, GRE General Test. Additional exam requirements/recommendations for international students: Required—TOEFL (minimum score 600 paper-based; 250 computer-based), IELTS (minimum score 7). Electronic applications accepted. *Faculty research:* International finance and business, trade policy, macroeconomics, Asian economic issues, developmental economics.

Brock University, Faculty of Graduate Studies, Faculty of Social Sciences, Program in Political Science, St. Catharines, ON L2S 3A1, Canada. Offers Canadian politics (MA); comparative politics (MA); international relations (MA); political theory or philosophy (MA); public policy (MA). Part-time programs available. *Degree requirements:* For master's, thesis optional. *Entrance requirements:* For master's, honors degree. Additional exam requirements/recommendations for international students: Required—TOEFL (minimum score 550 paper-based; 213 computer-based; 80 iBT), IELTS (minimum score 6.5), TWE (minimum score 4). Electronic applications accepted. *Faculty research:* Public administration reform, economic and social justice, politics of societies, Canadian politics, international relations.

Brooklyn College of the City University of New York, Division of Graduate Studies, Department of Political Science, Brooklyn, NY 11210-2889. Offers international affairs (MA); political science (MA, PhD); political science, urban policy and administration (MA). Part-time and evening/weekend programs available. *Students:* 23 full-time (13 women), 219 part-time (124 women); includes 119 minority (92 Black or African American, non-Hispanic/Latino; 12 Asian, non-Hispanic/Latino; 15 Hispanic/Latino), 28 international. Average age 30. 155 applicants, 80% accepted, 88 enrolled. In 2010, 49 master's awarded. *Degree requirements:* For master's, comprehensive exam (for some programs), thesis or alternative, foreign language exam (for international affairs program). *Entrance requirements:* For master's, 2 letters of recommendation, personal statement. Additional exam requirements/recommendations for international students: Required—TOEFL (minimum score 500 paper-based; 173 computer-based; 61 iBT). *Application deadline:* For fall admission, 5/1 for domestic and international students; for spring admission, 12/15 for domestic students, 11/1 for international students. *Expenses:* Tuition, state resident: full-time $7360; part-time $310 per credit hour. Tuition, nonresident: full-time $13,800; part-time $575 per credit hour. Required fees: $190 per semester. *Financial support:* Career-related internships or fieldwork and Federal Work-Study available. Support available to part-time students. Financial award application deadline: 5/1; financial award applicants required to submit FAFSA. *Faculty research:* Ethics and politics, politics of criminal justice, Western Europe, international law and politics, labor politics. *Unit head:* Dr. Paisley Currah, Acting Chairperson, 718-951-5306, E-mail: pcurrah@brooklyn.cuny.edu. *Application contact:* Hernan Sierra, Graduate Admissions Coordinator, 718-951-4536, Fax: 718-951-4506, E-mail: grads@brooklyn.cuny.edu.

California State University, Fresno, Division of Graduate Studies, College of Social Sciences, Department of Political Science, Program in International Relations, Fresno, CA 93740-8027. Offers MA. Part-time and evening/weekend programs available. *Degree requirements:* For master's, one foreign language, thesis or alternative. *Entrance requirements:* For master's, GRE General Test, minimum GPA of 3.0. Additional exam requirements/recommendations for international students: Required—TOEFL. Electronic applications accepted.

California State University, Sacramento, Graduate Studies, College of Social Sciences and Interdisciplinary Studies, International Affairs Graduate Program, Sacramento, CA 95819. Offers MA. Part-time programs available. *Degree requirements:* For master's, one foreign language, thesis or alternative, writing proficiency exam. *Entrance requirements:* For master's, GRE General Test, appropriate bachelor's degree, minimum GPA of 3.0 in last 2 years of course work. Additional exam requirements/recommendations for international students: Required—TOEFL. Electronic applications accepted.

California State University, Stanislaus, College of Humanities and Social Sciences, Program in History (MA), Turlock, CA 95382. Offers history (MA); international relations (MA); secondary school teachers (MA). Part-time programs available. *Faculty:* 7. *Students:* 8 full-time (4 women), 17 part-time (5 women); includes 7 minority (1 Asian, non-Hispanic/Latino; 3 Hispanic/Latino; 1 Native Hawaiian or other Pacific Islander, non-Hispanic/Latino; 2 Two or more races, non-Hispanic/Latino). Average age 35. 10 applicants, 70% accepted, 5 enrolled. In 2010, 9 master's awarded. *Degree requirements:* For master's, comprehensive exam, thesis or alternative. *Entrance requirements:* For master's, GRE, minimum GPA of 3.0, personal statement. Additional exam requirements/recommendations for international students: Required—TOEFL (minimum score 575 paper-based; 233 computer-based). *Application deadline:* For fall admission, 5/1 for domestic students; for spring admission, 1/7 for domestic students. Application fee: $55. Electronic applications accepted. Tuition and fees vary according to program. *Financial support:* Fellowships, Federal Work-Study available. Financial award application deadline: 3/1; financial award applicants required to submit FAFSA. *Faculty research:* History of Ancient Greece, history and ecology of the central valley, acculturation and gender. *Unit head:* Dr. Bret Carroll, History Department Chair, 209-667-3238, Fax: 209-667-3132, E-mail: bcarroll@csustan.edu. *Application contact:* Graduate School, 209-667-3129, Fax: 209-664-7025.

Carleton University, Faculty of Graduate Studies, Faculty of Public Affairs and Management, Norman Paterson School of International Affairs, Ottawa, ON K1S 5B6, Canada. Offers MA, PhD. Part-time programs available. *Degree requirements:* For master's, one foreign language, comprehensive exam, thesis optional. *Entrance requirements:* For master's, honors degree. Additional exam requirements/recommendations for international students: Required—TOEFL. *Faculty research:* International conflict, development, political economy, conflict analysis.

The Catholic University of America, School of Arts and Sciences, Department of Business and Economics, Washington, DC 20064. Offers international political economics (MA). Part-time programs available. *Faculty:* 10 full-time (4 women), 15 part-time/adjunct (4 women). *Students:* 16 full-time (12 women); includes 1 Black or African American, non-Hispanic/Latino; 1 Asian, non-Hispanic/Latino; 1 Hispanic/Latino, 1 international. Average age 23. 19 applicants, 84% accepted, 16 enrolled. *Degree requirements:* For master's, comprehensive exam. *Entrance requirements:* For master's, GRE General Test, statement of purpose, official copies of academic transcripts, three letters of recommendation. Additional exam requirements/recommendations for international students: Required—TOEFL (minimum score 580 paper-based; 237 computer-based). *Application deadline:* For fall admission, 8/1 priority date for domestic students, 7/15 for international students; for spring admission, 12/1 priority date for domestic students, 10/15 for international students. Applications are processed on a rolling basis. Application fee: $55. Electronic applications accepted. *Expenses:* Tuition: Full-time $33,580; part-time $1315 per credit hour. Required fees: $80; $40 per semester hour. One-time fee: $425. *Financial support:* Fellowships, research assistantships, teaching assistantships, Federal Work-Study, scholarships/grants, tuition waivers (full and partial), and unspecified assistantships available. Financial award application deadline: 2/1; financial award applicants required to submit FAFSA. *Faculty research:* Integrity of the marketing process, economics of energy and the environment, emerging markets, social change, international finance and economic development. Total annual research expenditures: $6,459. *Unit head:* Dr. Andrew V. Abela, Chair, 202-319-5235, Fax: 202-319-4426, E-mail: abela@cua.edu. *Application contact:* Andrew Woodall, Director of Graduate Admissions, 202-319-5057, Fax: 202-319-6533, E-mail: cua-admissions@cua.edu.

The Catholic University of America, School of Arts and Sciences, Department of Politics, Washington, DC 20064. Offers American government (MA, PhD); Congressional and presidential studies (MA); international affairs (MA); international political economics (MA); political theory (MA, PhD); world politics (MA, PhD); MA/JD. Part-time programs available. *Faculty:* 13 full-time (1 woman), 8 part-time/adjunct (0 women). *Students:* 28 full-time (8 women), 76 part-time (19 women); includes 4 Black or African American, non-Hispanic/Latino; 5 Asian, non-Hispanic/Latino; 5 Hispanic/Latino, 6 international. Average age 30. 111 applicants, 59% accepted, 25 enrolled. In 2010, 23 master's, 4 doctorates awarded. *Degree requirements:* For master's, one foreign language, comprehensive exam, thesis or alternative; for doctorate, variable foreign language requirement, comprehensive exam, thesis/dissertation. *Entrance requirements:* For master's, GRE General Test, statement of purpose, official copies of academic transcripts, three letters of recommendation, minimum GPA of 3.0; for doctorate, GRE General Test, statement of purpose, official copies of academic transcripts, three letters of recommendation. Additional exam requirements/recommendations for international students: Required—TOEFL (minimum score 580 paper-based; 237 computer-based). *Application deadline:* For fall admission, 8/1 priority date for domestic students, 7/15 for international students; for spring admission, 12/1 priority date for domestic students, 10/15 for international students. Applications are processed on a rolling basis. Application fee: $55. Electronic applications accepted. *Expenses:* Tuition: Full-time $33,580; part-time $1315 per credit hour. Required fees: $80; $40 per semester hour. One-time fee: $425. *Financial support:* Fellowships, research assistantships, teaching assistantships, Federal Work-Study, scholarships/grants, tuition waivers (full and partial), and unspecified assistantships available. Financial award application deadline: 2/1; financial award applicants required to submit FAFSA. *Faculty research:* Political philosophy, American political institutions and processes, political economy, international relations, U. S. political leadership since 1789. *Unit head:* Dr. Philip Henderson, Chair, 202-319-5128, Fax: 202-319-6289, E-mail: hendersp@cua.edu. *Application contact:* Andrew Woodall, Director of Graduate Admissions, 202-319-5057, Fax: 202-319-6533, E-mail: cua-admissions@cua.edu.

Central Connecticut State University, School of Graduate Studies, School of Arts and Sciences, Program in International Area Studies, New Britain, CT 06050-4010. Offers international studies (MS). Part-time and evening/weekend programs available. *Students:* 14 full-time (8 women), 23 part-time (9 women); includes 8 minority (5 Black or African American, non-Hispanic/Latino; 1 American Indian or Alaska Native, non-Hispanic/Latino; 1 Asian, non-Hispanic/Latino; 1 Hispanic/Latino), 1 international. Average age 33. 17 applicants, 71% accepted, 8 enrolled. In 2010, 8 master's awarded. *Degree requirements:* For master's, comprehensive exam, thesis or alternative. *Entrance requirements:* For master's, minimum undergraduate GPA of 2.7. Additional exam requirements/recommendations for international students: Required—TOEFL. *Application deadline:* For fall admission, 5/1 for domestic students; for spring admission, 12/1 for domestic students. Applications are processed on a rolling basis. Application fee: $50. Electronic applications accepted. *Expenses:* Tuition, area resident: Full-time $5012; part-time $470 per credit. Tuition, state resident: full-time $7518; part-time $482 per credit. Tuition, nonresident: full-time $13,962; part-time $482 per credit. Required fees: $3772. One-time fee: $62 part-time. *Financial support:* In 2010–11, 5 students received support. Career-related internships or fieldwork, Federal Work-Study, scholarships/grants, and unspecified assistantships available. Support available to part-time students. Financial award application deadline: 2/15; financial award applicants required to submit FAFSA. *Unit head:* Dr. Evelyn Newman Phillips, Program Director, 860-832-2617. *Application contact:* Dr. Evelyn Newman Phillips, Program Director, 860-832-2617.

Central European University, Graduate Studies, School of Social Sciences and Humanities, Budapest, Hungary. Offers economics (MA, PhD); gender studies (MA, PhD); international relations and European studies (MA, PhD); mathematics and its applications (MS, PhD); medieval studies (MA, PhD); nationalism studies (MA, PhD); philosophy (MA, PhD); political science (MA, PhD); public policy (MA, PhD); sociology and social anthropology (MA, PhD). *Faculty:* 90 full-time (29 women), 13 part-time/adjunct (7 women). *Students:* 732 full-time (404 women). Average age 28. 3,639 applicants, 22% accepted, 416 enrolled. In 2010, 278 master's, 16 doctorates awarded. Terminal master's awarded for partial completion of doctoral program. *Degree requirements:* For master's, one foreign language, thesis; for doctorate, one foreign language, comprehensive exam, thesis/dissertation. *Entrance requirements:* For master's, interview; for doctorate, GRE, CEU subject test, interview. Additional exam requirements/recommendations for international students: Required—TOEFL (minimum score 570 paper-based; 230 computer-based); Recommended—IELTS (minimum score 6.5). *Application deadline:* For fall admission, 1/15 priority date for domestic and international students. Application fee: $0. Electronic applications accepted. Tuition and fees charges are reported in euros. *Expenses:* Tuition: Full-time 11,000 euros. Required fees: 250 euros. One-time fee: 200 euros full-time. Tuition and fees vary according to degree level, program, reciprocity agreements and student level. *Financial support:* In 2010–11, 402 students received support, including 416 fellowships with full and partial tuition reimbursements available (averaging $6,200 per year); career-related internships or fieldwork, institutionally sponsored loans, and scholarships/grants also available. Financial award application deadline: 1/5. *Faculty research:* Civil society, fiscal decentralization, party politics, political philosophy (especially liberalism, theory of democracy). Total annual research expenditures: $35,000. *Unit head:* Dr. Katalin Farkas, Provost/Academic Pro Rector, 361-327-3000 Ext. 2227, E-mail: farkask@ceu.hu. *Application contact:* Zsuzsanna Jaszberenyi, Admissions Officer, 361-327-3009, Fax: 361-327-3211, E-mail: admissions@ceu.hu.

International Affairs

Central Michigan University, Central Michigan University Off-Campus Programs, Program in Administration, Mount Pleasant, MI 48859. Offers acquisitions administration (MSA, Certificate); general administration (MSA, Certificate); health services administration (MSA, Certificate); human resources administration (MSA, Certificate); information resource management (MSA, Certificate); international administration (MSA, Certificate); leadership (MSA, Certificate); public administration (MSA, Certificate); vehicle design and manufacturing administration (Certificate). Part-time and evening/weekend programs available. Postbaccalaureate distance learning degree programs offered (no on-campus study). *Students:* Average age 38. *Entrance requirements:* For master's, minimum GPA of 2.7 in major. *Application deadline:* Applications are processed on a rolling basis. Application fee: $50. Electronic applications accepted. *Expenses:* Tuition, state resident: full-time $8208; part-time $456 per credit hour. Tuition, nonresident: full-time $13,788; part-time $766 per credit hour. One-time fee: $25. *Financial support:* Scholarships/grants available. Support available to part-time students. Financial award applicants required to submit FAFSA. *Unit head:* Dr. Nana Korsah, Director, MSA Programs, 989-774-6525, E-mail: korsa1na@cmich.edu. *Application contact:* 877-268-4636, E-mail: cmuoffcampus@cmich.edu.

Chapman University, Graduate Studies, Wilkinson College of Humanities and Social Sciences, International Studies Program, Orange, CA 92866. Offers MA. Part-time and evening/weekend programs available. *Faculty:* 16 full-time (7 women), 3 part-time/adjunct (1 woman). *Students:* 22 full-time (13 women); includes 12 minority (2 Black or African American, non-Hispanic/Latino; 3 Asian, non-Hispanic/Latino; 7 Hispanic/Latino), 3 international. Average age 25. 45 applicants, 53% accepted, 12 enrolled. *Entrance requirements:* For master's, GRE, minimum undergraduate GPA of 2.5. Additional exam requirements/recommendations for international students: Required—TOEFL (minimum score 550 paper-based; 213 computer-based; 80 iBT). *Application deadline:* Applications are processed on a rolling basis. Application fee: $60. Electronic applications accepted. *Financial support:* Fellowships, Federal Work-Study and scholarships/grants available. Financial award applicants required to submit FAFSA. *Unit head:* Dr. Lynn Horton, Director, 714-997-6976, E-mail: horton@chapman.edu. *Application contact:* Allison Tritch, Administrative Assistant, 714-997-6752, E-mail: tritch@chapman.edu.

City College of the City University of New York, Graduate School, College of Liberal Arts and Science, Division of Social Science, Program in International Relations, New York, NY 10031-9198. Offers MA. Part-time programs available. *Degree requirements:* For master's, one foreign language, thesis. *Entrance requirements:* For master's, GRE, 3 letters of recommendation. Additional exam requirements/recommendations for international students: Required—TOEFL (minimum score 600 paper-based; 100 iBT). Electronic applications accepted. *Faculty research:* International finance, international economics, European diplomatic history, area studies, international politics and diplomacy.

Claremont Graduate University, Graduate Programs, School of Politics and Economics, Department of Politics and Policy, Claremont, CA 91711-6160. Offers American politics (MA, PhD); comparative politics (PhD); international political economy (MA); international studies (MA); political philosophy (PhD); political science (PhD); politics, economics and business (MA); public policy (MA, PhD); world politics (PhD); MBA/PhD. Part-time programs available. *Faculty:* 8 full-time (5 women), 3 part-time/adjunct (0 women). *Students:* 155 full-time (59 women), 15 part-time (6 women); includes 35 minority (5 Black or African American, non-Hispanic/Latino; 9 Asian, non-Hispanic/Latino; 17 Hispanic/Latino; 3 Native Hawaiian or other Pacific Islander, non-Hispanic/Latino; 1 Two or more races, non-Hispanic/Latino), 36 international. Average age 32. In 2010, 16 master's, 21 doctorates awarded. Terminal master's awarded for partial completion of doctoral program. *Entrance requirements:* For master's and doctorate, GRE General Test. Additional exam requirements/recommendations for international students: Required—TOEFL (minimum score 550 paper-based; 213 computer-based; 80 iBT). *Application deadline:* For fall admission, 2/1 priority date for domestic students. Applications are processed on a rolling basis. Application fee: $60. Electronic applications accepted. *Expenses:* Tuition: Full-time $35,748; part-time $1554 per unit. Required fees: $215 per semester. *Financial support:* Fellowships, research assistantships, teaching assistantships, Federal Work-Study, institutionally sponsored loans, and scholarships/grants available. Support available to part-time students. Financial award application deadline: 2/15; financial award applicants required to submit FAFSA. *Faculty research:* Environmental policy, international debt, global democratization, Third World development, public sector discrimination. *Unit head:* Jennifer Merolla, Chair, 909-621-8696, Fax: 909-621-8545, E-mail: jennifer.merolla@cgu.edu. *Application contact:* Lesa Hiben, Admissions Coordinator, 909-621-8699, Fax: 909-621-7545, E-mail: lesa.hiben@cga.edu.

Colorado School of Mines, Graduate School, Division of Liberal Arts and International Studies, Golden, CO 80401. Offers international political economy (Graduate Certificate); liberal arts and international studies (MIPER); science and technology policy (Graduate Certificate). Part-time programs available. *Faculty:* 20 full-time (9 women), 18 part-time/adjunct (8 women). *Students:* 17 full-time (6 women), 2 part-time (1 woman); includes 2 Asian, non-Hispanic/Latino; 1 Hispanic/Latino, 4 international. Average age 28. 16 applicants, 88% accepted, 11 enrolled. In 2010, 7 master's awarded. *Degree requirements:* For master's, thesis (for some programs). *Entrance requirements:* For master's, GRE. Additional exam requirements/recommendations for international students: Required—TOEFL (minimum score 550 paper-based; 213 computer-based; 80 iBT). *Application deadline:* For fall admission, 1/15 priority date for domestic and international students; for spring admission, 10/15 priority date for domestic and international students. Application fee: $50 ($70 for international students). Electronic applications accepted. *Expenses:* Tuition, state resident: full-time $11,550; part-time $641 per credit. Tuition, nonresident: full-time $25,980; part-time $1444 per credit. Required fees: $1874; $937 per semester. *Financial support:* In 2010–11, 11 students received support, including fellowships with full tuition reimbursements available (averaging $20,000 per year), research assistantships with full tuition reimbursements available (averaging $20,000 per year), 11 teaching assistantships with full tuition reimbursements available (averaging $20,000 per year); scholarships/grants, health care benefits, and unspecified assistantships also available. Financial award application deadline: 1/15. Total annual research expenditures: $75,288. *Unit head:* Dr. Elizabeth Davis, Director, 303-273-3567, Fax: 303-273-3751, E-mail: edavis@mines.edu. *Application contact:* Connie Warren, Program Assistant, 303-273-3590, Fax: 303-273-3751, E-mail: cwarren@mines.edu.

Columbia University, School of International and Public Affairs, Program in International Affairs, New York, NY 10027. Offers MIA, JD/MIA, MBA/MIA, MIA/MS, MPH/MIA, MSJ/MIA. *Degree requirements:* For master's, one foreign language. *Entrance requirements:* For master's, GRE General Test. Additional exam requirements/recommendations for international students: Required—TOEFL (minimum score 600 paper-based; 250 computer-based; 100 iBT). Electronic applications accepted.

Concordia University, School of Business and Professional Studies, Irvine, CA 92612-3299. Offers business administration: business practice (MBA); international studies (MA). Part-time and evening/weekend programs available. *Faculty:* 3 full-time (0 women), 19 part-time/adjunct (3 women). *Students:* 80 full-time (37 women), 48 part-time (22 women); includes 28 minority (6 Black or African American, non-Hispanic/Latino; 12 Asian, non-Hispanic/Latino; 10 Hispanic/Latino), 8 international. Average age 30. 52 applicants, 44% accepted, 15 enrolled. In 2010, 66 master's awarded. *Degree requirements:* For master's, capstone project or thesis. *Entrance requirements:* For master's, official college transcript(s), signed statement of intent, resume, two references, interview (MBA); passport photo, photocopies of valid U.S. passport, and college diploma (MAIS). Additional exam requirements/recommendations for international students: Required—TOEFL. *Application deadline:* For fall admission, 8/1 for domestic students, 6/1 for international students; for spring admission, 1/1 for domestic students, 11/1 for international students. Application fee: $50 ($125 for international students). Electronic applications accepted. *Expenses:* Contact institution. *Financial support:* In 2010–11, 107 students received support. Tuition waivers (full and partial) and unspecified assistantships available. Financial award applicants required to submit FAFSA. *Unit head:* Dr. Timothy Peters, Dean, 949-214-3363, E-mail: tim.peters@cui.edu. *Application contact:* Sherry Powers, MBA Admissions Coordinator, 949-214-3032, Fax: 949-854-6894, E-mail: sherry.powers@cui.edu.

Cornell University, Graduate School, Graduate Fields of Arts and Sciences, Field of Government, Ithaca, NY 14853-0001. Offers American politics (PhD); comparative politics (PhD); international relations (PhD); political methodology (PhD); political thought (PhD); public policy (PhD). *Faculty:* 45 full-time (14 women). *Students:* 74 full-time (40 women); includes 1 Black or African American, non-Hispanic/Latino; 5 Asian, non-Hispanic/Latino; 4 Hispanic/Latino, 22 international. Average age 28. 394 applicants, 9% accepted, 20 enrolled. In 2010, 12 doctorates awarded. *Degree requirements:* For doctorate, comprehensive exam, thesis/dissertation. *Entrance requirements:* For doctorate, GRE General Test, sample of written work, 3 letters of recommendation. Additional exam requirements/recommendations for international students: Required—TOEFL (minimum score 550 paper-based; 213 computer-based; 77 iBT). *Application deadline:* For fall admission, 1/15 for domestic students. Application fee: $80. Electronic applications accepted. *Expenses:* Tuition: Full-time $29,500. Required fees: $76. Tuition and fees vary according to degree level and program. *Financial support:* In 2010–11, 29 fellowships with full tuition reimbursements, 2 research assistantships with full tuition reimbursements, 29 teaching assistantships with full tuition reimbursements were awarded; institutionally sponsored loans, scholarships/grants, health care benefits, tuition waivers (full and partial), and unspecified assistantships also available. Financial award applicants required to submit FAFSA. *Faculty research:* Political theory, American politics, comparative politics, international relations, methodology. *Unit head:* Director of Graduate Studies, 607-255-3567, Fax: 607-255-4530. *Application contact:* Graduate Field Assistant, 607-255-3567, Fax: 607-255-4530, E-mail: cu_govt@cornell.edu.

Creighton University, Graduate School, College of Arts and Sciences, Program in International Relations, Omaha, NE 68178-0001. Offers MA. Part-time and evening/weekend programs available. *Faculty:* 10 full-time (3 women). *Students:* 11 full-time (6 women), 19 part-time (7 women); includes 1 minority (Hispanic/Latino), 2 international. Average age 28. 13 applicants, 62% accepted, 7 enrolled. In 2010, 3 master's awarded. *Degree requirements:* For master's, comprehensive exam, thesis optional. *Entrance requirements:* For master's, GRE General Test, 3 letters of recommendation. Additional exam requirements/recommendations for international students: Required—TOEFL (minimum score 550 paper-based; 213 computer-based; 80 iBT). *Application deadline:* For fall admission, 3/1 priority date for domestic and international students; for winter admission, 12/1 priority date for domestic students, 7/1 priority date for international students; for spring admission, 4/1 priority date for domestic students, 9/1 priority date for international students. Applications are processed on a rolling basis. Application fee: $50. Electronic applications accepted. *Expenses:* Tuition: Full-time $12,168; part-time $676 per credit hour. Required fees: $131 per semester. Tuition and fees vary according to program. *Financial support:* In 2010–11, 4 fellowships with full and partial tuition reimbursements (averaging $10,698 per year) were awarded; health care benefits also available. Support available to part-time students. Financial award application deadline: 5/1; financial award applicants required to submit FAFSA. *Unit head:* Dr. Terry Clark, Chair, 402-280-4712, E-mail: tclark@creighton.edu. *Application contact:* Taunya Plater, Senior Program Coordinator, 402-280-2870, Fax: 402-280-2899, E-mail: taunyaplater@creighton.edu.

East Carolina University, Graduate School, Thomas Harriot College of Arts and Sciences, Program in International Studies, Greenville, NC 27858-4353. Offers MA. Part-time programs available. *Degree requirements:* For master's, comprehensive exam. *Entrance requirements:* For master's, GRE General Test. Additional exam requirements/recommendations for international students: Required—TOEFL. *Expenses:* Tuition, state resident: full-time $3130; part-time $391.25 per credit hour. Tuition, nonresident: full-time $13,817; part-time $1727.13 per credit hour. Required fees: $1916; $239.50 per credit hour. Tuition and fees vary according to campus/location and program.

Fairleigh Dickinson University, Metropolitan Campus, University College: Arts, Sciences, and Professional Studies, School of History, Political and International Studies, Program in International Studies, Teaneck, NJ 07666-1914. Offers MA. *Students:* 4 full-time (3 women), 4 part-time (1 woman), 3 international. Average age 27. 10 applicants, 50% accepted, 4 enrolled. In 2010, 1 master's awarded. *Application deadline:* Applications are processed on a rolling basis. Application fee: $40. *Application contact:* Susan Brooman, University Director of Graduate Admissions, 201-692-2554, Fax: 201-692-2560, E-mail: globaleducation@fdu.edu.

Florida Agricultural and Mechanical University, Division of Graduate Studies, Research, and Continuing Education, College of Engineering Science, Technology, and Agriculture, Division of Agricultural Sciences, Tallahassee, FL 32307-3200. Offers agribusiness (MS); animal science (MS); engineering technology (MS); entomology (MS); food science (MS); international programs (MS); plant science (MS). *Degree requirements:* For master's, thesis. *Entrance requirements:* For master's, GRE General Test, minimum GPA of 3.0. Additional exam requirements/recommendations for international students: Required—TOEFL (minimum score 500 paper-based).

Florida International University, College of Arts and Sciences, Department of Politics and International Relations, Program in International Relations, Miami, FL 33199. Offers international studies (MA). PhD is fall admission only. Part-time and evening/weekend programs available. *Students:* 38 full-time (19 women), 26 part-time (12 women); includes 6 Black or African American, non-Hispanic/Latino; 5 Asian, non-Hispanic/Latino; 11 Hispanic/Latino, 19 international. Average age 28. 130 applicants, 14% accepted, 18 enrolled. In 2010, 12 master's, 9 doctorates awarded. *Degree requirements:* For master's, one foreign language, thesis optional; for doctorate, comprehensive exam, thesis/dissertation. *Entrance requirements:* For master's, GRE General Test, 2 letters of recommendation; for doctorate, GRE General Test, letter of intent; 2 letters of recommendation; minimum undergraduate GPA of 3.2 or equivalent, 3.5 for all combined graduate work. Additional exam requirements/recommendations for international students: Required—TOEFL (minimum score 550 paper-based; 80 iBT). *Application deadline:* For fall admission, 3/15 for domestic and international students; for spring admission, 8/15 for domestic and international students. Application fee: $30. Electronic applications accepted. *Financial support:* Institutionally sponsored loans and scholarships/grants available. Financial award application deadline: 3/1; financial award applicants required to submit FAFSA. *Unit head:* Dr. Richard Olsen, Chair, Politics and International Relations, 305-348-2556, Fax: 305-348-6138, E-mail: pir@fiu.edu. *Application contact:* Dr. Ronald Çox, Director of Graduate Studies, 305-348-2556, Fax: 305-348-6138, E-mail: pir@fiu.edu.

Florida State University, The Graduate School, College of Social Sciences and Public Policy, Program in International Affairs, Tallahassee, FL 32306. Offers MA, MS, JD/MA, JD/MS. Part-time programs available. *Students:* 33 full-time (20 women), 74 part-time (37 women); includes 12 Black or African American, non-Hispanic/Latino; 11 Asian, non-Hispanic/Latino; 13 Hispanic/Latino. Average age 25. 130 applicants, 97% accepted, 55 enrolled. In 2010, 36 master's awarded. *Degree requirements:* For master's, one foreign language, comprehensive exam, thesis optional. *Entrance requirements:* For master's, GRE General Test, minimum GPA of 3.0. Additional exam requirements/recommendations for international students: Required—TOEFL (minimum score 550 paper-based; 213 computer-based; 80 iBT). *Application deadline:* For fall admission, 7/1 for domestic students; for spring admission, 7/1 for domestic students. Applications are processed on a rolling basis. Application fee: $30. *Expenses:* Tuition, state resident: full-time $8238.24. *Financial support:* In 2010–11, 5 students received support, including 5 research assistantships with full tuition reimbursements available (averaging $5,000 per year); career-related internships or fieldwork, Federal Work-Study, institutionally sponsored loans, and unspecified assistantships also available. Financial award application deadline: 2/1; financial award applicants required to submit FAFSA. *Unit head:* Dr. Lee K. Metcalf, Director, 850-644-7327, Fax: 850-645-4981, E-mail: lmetcalf@fsu.edu. *Application contact:* Kaley Boggs, Academic Program Specialist, 850-644-4418, Fax: 850-645-4981, E-mail: plollis@fsu.edu.

Fordham University, Graduate School of Arts and Sciences, Program in International Political Economy and Development, New York, NY 10458. Offers MA, Certificate. Part-time and evening/weekend programs available. *Students:* 44 full-time (22 women), 27 part-time (11 women); includes 1 American Indian or Alaska Native, non-Hispanic/Latino; 1 Asian, non-Hispanic/Latino; 4 Hispanic/Latino, 19 international. Average age 28. 213 applicants, 37% accepted, 36 enrolled. In 2010, 28 master's awarded. *Degree requirements:* For master's, comprehensive exam. *Entrance requirements:* For master's, GRE General Test. Additional exam requirements/recommendations for international students: Required—TOEFL (minimum score 600 paper-based; 250 computer-based). *Application deadline:* For fall admission, 1/4 priority date for domestic students; for spring admission, 11/1 for domestic students. Application fee: $70. Electronic applications accepted. *Financial support:* In 2010–11, 16 students received support, including 16 research assistantships with tuition reimbursements available (averaging $18,400 per year); career-related internships or fieldwork, institutionally sponsored loans, tuition waivers (full and partial), and unspecified assistantships also available. Financial award application deadline: 1/4; financial award applicants required to submit FAFSA. *Faculty research:* International economics, comparative international politics, international banking and finance, international development, emerging markets and country risk analysis. *Unit head:* Dr. Henry Schwalbenberg, Chair, 718-817-3866, Fax: 718-817-3518. *Application contact:* Charlene Dundie, Director of Graduate Admissions, 718-817-4420, Fax: 718-817-3566, E-mail: dundie@fordham.edu.

George Mason University, School of Public Policy, Program in International Commerce and Policy, Fairfax, VA 22030. Offers MA. Part-time programs available. *Faculty:* 66 full-time (24 women), 15 part-time/adjunct (3 women). *Students:* 90 full-time (50 women), 147 part-time (81 women); includes 11 Black or African American, non-Hispanic/Latino; 8 Asian, non-Hispanic/Latino; 22 Hispanic/Latino; 1 Two or more races, non-Hispanic/Latino, 29 international. Average age 28. 172 applicants, 63% accepted, 71 enrolled. In 2010, 84 master's awarded. *Degree requirements:* For master's, thesis or alternative. *Entrance requirements:* For master's, GRE (for students seeking merit-based scholarships), minimum undergraduate GPA of 3.0, 2 letters of recommendation, resume. Additional exam requirements/recommendations for international students: Required—TOEFL (minimum score 570 paper-based; 230 computer-based; 88 iBT). *Application deadline:* For fall admission, 6/1 priority date for domestic students, 5/1 priority date for international students; for spring admission, 12/1 priority date for domestic students, 11/1 priority date for international students. Applications are processed on a rolling basis. Application fee: $100. Electronic applications accepted. *Expenses:* Contact institution. *Financial support:* Career-related internships or fieldwork, Federal Work-Study, scholarships/grants, unspecified assistantships, and health care benefits (full-time research or teaching assistantship recipients) available. Financial award application deadline: 3/1; financial award applicants required to submit FAFSA. *Unit head:* Dr. Kenneth Reinert, Director, 703-993-8099, E-mail: spp@gmu.edu. *Application contact:* Tennille Haegele, Director, Graduate Admissions, 703-993-3183, Fax: 703-993-4876, E-mail: thaegele@gmu.edu.

Georgetown University, Graduate School of Arts and Sciences, BMW Center for German and European Studies, Washington, DC 20057. Offers MA, MA/JD, MA/PhD. *Degree requirements:* For master's, 2 foreign languages, comprehensive exam. *Entrance requirements:* For master's, GRE General Test. Additional exam requirements/recommendations for international students: Required—TOEFL. *Faculty research:* Trans-Atlantic relations, European Union, German and European Studies.

Georgetown University, Graduate School of Arts and Sciences, Department of Government, Washington, DC 20057. Offers American government (MA, PhD); comparative government (PhD); conflict resolution (MA); democracy and governance (MA); international law and government (MA); international relations (PhD); political theory (PhD); MA/PhD. Terminal master's awarded for partial completion of doctoral program. *Degree requirements:* For master's, one foreign language, comprehensive exam; for doctorate, one foreign language, comprehensive exam, thesis/dissertation. *Entrance requirements:* For master's, GRE General Test, minimum B average; for doctorate, GRE General Test, MA. Additional exam requirements/recommendations for international students: Required—TOEFL. *Faculty research:* Western Europe, Latin America, the Middle East, political theory, international relations and law, methodology, American politics and institutions.

Georgetown University, Graduate School of Arts and Sciences, Edmund A. Walsh School of Foreign Service, Washington, DC 20057. Offers international affairs (MS); JD/MS; MA/JD; MA/PhD; MBA/MS. *Faculty:* 32 full-time (7 women), 42 part-time/adjunct (7 women). *Students:* 207 full-time (93 women), 78 international. Average age 28. 1,173 applicants. In 2010, 96 master's awarded. *Degree requirements:* For master's, one foreign language, comprehensive exam, internship. *Entrance requirements:* For master's, GRE General Test or GMAT (for students with undergraduate degree from English-speaking institution), one semester each of micro and macroeonomics with minimum B grade. Additional exam requirements/recommendations for international students: Required—TOEFL (minimum iBT score 100) or IELTS (7). *Application deadline:* For fall admission, 1/15 for domestic students. Application fee: $75. Electronic applications accepted. *Financial support:* Career-related internships or fieldwork and tuition waivers (full and partial) available. Financial award application deadline: 1/15. *Faculty research:* International business diplomacy, political risk analysis, foreign policy decision making, intercultural perspectives on contemporary issues. *Unit head:* Dr. Anthony Arend, Director, MSFS, 202-687-5763. *Application contact:* Information, 202-687-5763, E-mail: msfsinfo@georgetown.edu.

Georgetown University, Graduate School of Arts and Sciences, School of Continuing Studies, Washington, DC 20057. Offers American studies (MALS); Catholic studies (MALS); classical civilizations (MALS); disability studies (MPS); ethics and the professions (MALS); human resources management (MPS); humanities (MALS); individualized study (MALS); international affairs (MALS); Islam and Muslim-Christian relations (MALS); journalism (MPS); liberal studies (DLS); literature and society (MALS); medieval and early modern European studies (MALS); public relations and corporate communications (MPS); real estate (MPS); religious studies (MALS); social and public policy (MALS); sports industry management (MPS); the theory and practice of American democracy (MALS); visual culture (MALS). *Entrance requirements:* Additional exam requirements/recommendations for international students: Required—TOEFL.

Georgetown University, Law Center, Washington, DC 20001. Offers general (LL M); global health law (LL M); international and comparative law (LL M); international business and economic law (LL M); international legal studies (LL M); law (JD, SJD); securities and financial regulation (LL M); taxation (LL M); JD/LL M; JD/MA; JD/MBA; JD/MPH; JD/PhD. *Accreditation:* ABA. Part-time and evening/weekend programs available. *Degree requirements:* For master's, thesis; for doctorate, thesis/dissertation. *Entrance requirements:* For JD, LSAT; for master's and doctorate, JD, LL B, or first law degree earned in country of origin. Additional exam requirements/recommendations for international students: Required—TOEFL. *Expenses:* Contact institution. *Faculty research:* Constitutional law, legal history, jurisprudence.

The George Washington University, Elliott School of International Affairs, Program in International Affairs, Washington, DC 20052. Offers MA, JD/MA, MBA/MA, MPH/MA. Part-time and evening/weekend programs available. *Students:* 215 full-time (116 women), 113 part-time (78 women); includes 3 Black or African American, non-Hispanic/Latino; 19 Asian, non-Hispanic/Latino; 15 Hispanic/Latino; 1 Two or more races, non-Hispanic/Latino, 51 international. Average age 26. 781 applicants, 47% accepted, 110 enrolled. In 2010, 141 master's awarded. *Degree requirements:* For master's, one foreign language, capstone project. *Entrance requirements:* For master's, GRE General Test, 2 years of a modern foreign language, 2 semesters of introductory economics. Additional exam requirements/recommendations for international students: Required—TOEFL. *Application deadline:* For fall admission, 2/1 for domestic students; for spring admission, 10/1 for domestic students. Application fee: $75. Electronic applications accepted. *Financial support:* In 2010–11, 61 students received support; fellowships with tuition reimbursements available, research assistantships with tuition reimbursements available, career-related internships or fieldwork, Federal Work-Study, institutionally sponsored loans, and tuition waivers (full) available. Financial award application deadline: 1/15; financial award applicants required to submit FAFSA. *Faculty research:* Area studies, international economics, national security policy studies, international economic development, Sino-Soviet studies. *Unit head:* Dr. Karl F. Inderfurth, Director, 202-994-2619, E-mail: ambkfi@gwu.edu. *Application contact:* Jeff V. Miles, Director of Graduate Admissions, 202-994-7050, Fax: 202-994-9537, E-mail: esiagrad@gwu.edu.

The George Washington University, Elliott School of International Affairs, Program in International Policy and Practice, Washington, DC 20052. Offers MIPP. Part-time and evening/weekend programs available. *Students:* 13 full-time (6 women), 25 part-time (11 women); includes 3 Black or African American, non-Hispanic/Latino; 3 Asian, non-Hispanic/Latino, 9 international. Average age 40. 54 applicants, 74% accepted, 15 enrolled. In 2010, 18 master's awarded. *Degree requirements:* For master's, one foreign language, capstone project. *Entrance requirements:* For master's, GRE (recommended), advanced degree or 8 years experience plus BA. Additional exam requirements/recommendations for international students: Required—TOEFL. *Application deadline:* For fall admission, 2/1 for domestic students; for spring admission, 10/1 for domestic students. Application fee: $75. Electronic applications accepted. *Financial support:* In 2010–11, 13 students received support; fellowships with tuition reimbursements available, research assistantships with tuition reimbursements available, career-related internships or fieldwork, Federal Work-Study, institutionally sponsored loans, and tuition waivers available. Financial award application deadline: 1/15; financial award applicants required to submit FAFSA. *Unit head:* Dr. Chris Kojm, Director, 202-994-7969, E-mail: ckojm@gwu.edu. *Application contact:* Jeff V. Miles, Director of Graduate Admissions, 202-994-7050, Fax: 202-994-9537, E-mail: esiagrad@gwu.edu.

The George Washington University, Elliott School of International Affairs, Program in International Studies, Washington, DC 20052. Offers MIS.

Georgia Institute of Technology, Graduate Studies and Research, Ivan Allen College of Policy and International Affairs, Sam Nunn School of International Affairs, Atlanta, GA 30332-0001. Offers MS Int A; PhD. *Degree requirements:* For master's, one foreign language. *Entrance requirements:* Additional exam requirements/recommendations for international students: Required—TOEFL. Electronic applications accepted. *Faculty research:* International political economy, international security, Asian and European studies.

Harvard University, Graduate School of Arts and Sciences, Department of Government, Cambridge, MA 02138. Offers political science (PhD), including American politics, comparative politics, international relations, political thought, quantitative methods. *Degree requirements:* For doctorate, one foreign language, thesis/dissertation, general exams. *Entrance requirements:* For doctorate, GRE General Test. Additional exam requirements/recommendations for international students: Required—TOEFL. *Expenses:* Tuition: Full-time $34,976. Required fees: $1166. Full-time tuition and fees vary according to program.

Harvard University, Law School, Professional Programs in Law, Cambridge, MA 02138. Offers international and comparative law (JD); law and business (JD); law and government (JD); law and social change (JD); law, science and technology (JD); JD/MALD; JD/MBA; JD/MPH; JD/MPP; JD/PhD. *Accreditation:* ABA. *Degree requirements:* For JD, 3rd year paper. *Entrance requirements:* LSAT. *Expenses:* Tuition: Full-time $34,976. Required fees: $1166. Full-time tuition and fees vary according to program. *Faculty research:* Constitutional law, voting rights law, cyber law.

Hult International Business School, Program in International Relations—Hult London Campus, London, MA WC 1B 4JP, United Kingdom. Offers conflict resolution (MA); diplomacy (MA); international public law (MA); international relations (MA); Middle East international security (MA); politics (MA); security studies (MA); terrorism (MA); U.S. foreign policy (MA). Part-time programs available. *Entrance requirements:* Additional exam requirements/recommendations for international students: Required—TOEFL (minimum score 580 paper-based; 237 computer-based), TWE (minimum score 5). Electronic applications accepted. *Faculty research:* American foreign politics, Middle East, security studies.

Hult International Business School, Program in International Relations—Hult San Francisco Campus, San Francisco, CA 94133. Offers MA.

Indiana University Bloomington, School of Public and Environmental Affairs, Public Affairs Programs, Bloomington, IN 47405-7000. Offers comparative and international affairs (MPA); economic development (MPA); energy (MPA); environmental policy (PhD); environmental policy and natural resource management (MPA); information systems (MPA); local government management (MPA); nonprofit management (MPA, Certificate); policy analysis (MPA); public finance (PhD); public financial administration (MPA); public management (MPA, PhD); public policy analysis (PhD); specialized public affairs (MPA); sustainability and sustainable development (MPA); JD/MPA; MPA/MIS; MPA/MLS; MSES/MPA. *Accreditation:* NASPAA (one or more programs are accredited). Part-time programs available. *Faculty:* 31 full-time, 15 part-time/adjunct. *Students:* 466 full-time (261 women); includes 11 Black or African American, non-Hispanic/Latino; 2 American Indian or Alaska Native, non-Hispanic/Latino; 42 Asian, non-Hispanic/Latino; 1 Hispanic/Latino, 65 international. Average age 26. 650 applicants, 218 enrolled. In 2010, 166 master's, 10 doctorates awarded. *Degree requirements:* For master's, core classes, capstone; for doctorate, comprehensive exam, thesis/dissertation. *Entrance requirements:* For master's, GRE General Test or GMAT, official transcripts, 3 letters of recommendation, resume, personal statement, departmental questions; for doctorate, GRE General Test or LSAT, official transcripts, 3 letters of recommendation, resume or curriculum vitae, statement of purpose. Additional exam requirements/recommendations for international students: Required—TOEFL (minimum score 600 paper-based; 96 iBT); Recommended—IELTS (minimum score 7). *Application deadline:* For fall admission, 5/1 priority date for domestic students, 12/1 priority date for international students. Applications are processed on a rolling basis. Application fee: $55 ($65 for international students). Electronic applications accepted. *Financial support:* Fellowships with partial tuition reimbursements, research assistantships with partial tuition reimbursements, teaching assistantships with partial tuition reimbursements, career-related internships or fieldwork, Federal Work-Study, scholarships/grants, health care benefits, unspecified assistantships, and Service Corps programs available. Financial award application deadline: 2/1; financial award applicants required to submit FAFSA. *Faculty research:* Comparative and international affairs, environmental policy and resource management, policy analysis, public finance, public management, urban management, nonprofit management, energy policy, social policy, public finance. *Unit head:* Jennifer Forney, Director of Graduate Student Services, 812-855-9485, Fax: 812-856-3665, E-mail: speampo@indiana.edu. *Application contact:* Audrey Whitaker, Admissions Assistant, 812-855-2840, E-mail: speaapps@indiana.edu.

See Close-Up on page 1271.

Instituto Tecnologico de Santo Domingo, Graduate School, Area of Humanities and Social Sciences, Santo Domingo, Dominican Republic. Offers accounting (Certificate); adult education (Certificate); applied linguistics (MA); economics (MA); education (M Ed); educational psychology (MA, Certificate); gender and development (MA, Certificate); humanistic studies (MA); international marketing management (Certificate); international relations in the Caribbean basin (Certificate); intervention systems in family therapy (MA); linguistic and literary communication (Certificate); pedagogical support (MA); social science education (M Ed); sustainable human development (MA); terminal illness and death psychology (Certificate); youth and adult education (M Ed).

Instituto Tecnológico y de Estudios Superiores de Monterrey, Campus Ciudad Obregón, Program in International Relations, Ciudad Obregón, Mexico. Offers MIR.

The Johns Hopkins University, Paul H. Nitze School of Advanced International Studies, Washington, DC 20036. Offers international development (MA, Certificate), including international economics (MA); international public policy (MIPP); international relations (PhD); international studies (Certificate); Japan studies (MA), including international economics; Korea Studies (MA), including international economics; South Asia studies (MA), including international economics; Southeast Asia studies (MA), including international economics; JD/MA; MBA/MA; MHS/MA. *Faculty:* 57 full-time (18 women), 125 part-time/adjunct (40 women).

International Affairs

The Johns Hopkins University (continued)

Students: 627 full-time (305 women), 39 part-time (24 women); includes 127 minority (18 Black or African American, non-Hispanic/Latino; 60 Asian, non-Hispanic/Latino; 32 Hispanic/Latino; 1 Native Hawaiian or other Pacific Islander, non-Hispanic/Latino; 16 Two or more races, non-Hispanic/Latino), 176 international. Average age 27. 1,753 applicants, 42% accepted, 307 enrolled. In 2010, 441 master's, 10 doctorates awarded. Terminal master's awarded for partial completion of doctoral program. *Degree requirements:* For master's, one foreign language, 4-6 International Economics courses, 5-6 functional or regional concentration courses, 2 core examinations, proficiency in a language other than native language, and capstone project; for doctorate, 2 foreign languages, thesis/dissertation, 3 comprehensive exams, economics, quantitative and qualitative course, dissertation prospectus and defense. *Entrance requirements:* For master's, GMAT or GRE General Test, previous course work in economics, foreign language, undergraduate degree; for doctorate, GRE General Test, master's degree. Additional exam requirements/recommendations for international students: Required—TOEFL (minimum score 600 paper-based; 250 computer-based; 100 iBT) or IELTS (minimum score 7). *Application deadline:* For fall admission, 1/7 for domestic and international students. Application fee: $85. Electronic applications accepted. *Expenses:* Contact institution. *Financial support:* In 2010–11, 450 students received support, including 450 fellowships (averaging $12,000 per year), 32 teaching assistantships (averaging $3,906 per year); career-related internships or fieldwork, Federal Work-Study, and scholarships/grants also available. Financial award application deadline: 2/15; financial award applicants required to submit FAFSA. *Faculty research:* Regional studies, international relations, international economics, energy and environment, international development. Total annual research expenditures: $8.1 million. *Unit head:* Sidney Jackson, Director of Admissions, 202-663-5700, Fax: 202-663-7788. *Application contact:* Admissions, 202-663-5700, Fax: 202-663-7788, E-mail: admissions.sais@jhu.edu.

Kansas State University, Graduate School, College of Arts and Sciences, Department of Political Science, Manhattan, KS 66506. Offers political science (MA), including international service, political science; public administration (MPA). Part-time programs available. *Degree requirements:* For master's, thesis or alternative. *Entrance requirements:* For master's, GRE (recommended), minimum GPA of 3.0. Additional exam requirements/recommendations for international students: Required—TOEFL (minimum score 550 paper-based; 213 computer-based). Electronic applications accepted. *Faculty research:* Armed conflict, civil military relations, comparative public administration and policy, electoral competition, legislative studies.

Kennesaw State University, College of Humanities and Social Sciences, Program in International Policy Management, Kennesaw, GA 30144-5591. Offers MS. Postbaccalaureate distance learning degree programs offered (minimal on-campus study). *Students:* 25 full-time (9 women); includes 4 Asian, non-Hispanic/Latino; 4 Hispanic/Latino. Average age 30. 39 applicants, 77% accepted, 25 enrolled. *Degree requirements:* For master's, practicum or thesis. *Entrance requirements:* For master's, GRE, resume, letters of recommendation, writing sample, application letter. Additional exam requirements/recommendations for international students: Required—TOEFL (minimum score 550 paper-based; 80 iBT), IELTS (minimum score 6). *Application deadline:* For fall admission, 6/1 for domestic and international students. Application fee: $60. *Expenses:* Tuition, state resident: full-time $5500; part-time $225 per credit hour. Tuition, nonresident: full-time $16,100; part-time $813 per credit hour. Required fees: $673 per semester. *Financial support:* In 2010–11, 2 research assistantships with full tuition reimbursements (averaging $4,000 per year) were awarded. Financial award application deadline: 4/1; financial award applicants required to submit FAFSA. *Unit head:* Dr. Michele Zebich-Knos, Director, 770-423-6631, E-mail: msipm@kennesaw.edu. *Application contact:* Tamara Hutto, Admissions Counselor, 770-420-4377, Fax: 770-423-6885, E-mail: ksugrad@kennesaw.edu.

Kentucky State University, College of Professional Studies, Frankfort, KY 40601. Offers business administration (MBA), including accounting, finance, management, marketing; public administration (MPA), including human resource management, international administration and development, management information systems, nonprofit management; special education (MA). Part-time and evening/weekend programs available. Postbaccalaureate distance learning degree programs offered (minimal on-campus study). *Faculty:* 12 full-time (4 women), 2 part-time/adjunct (both women). *Students:* 88 full-time (57 women), 79 part-time (42 women); includes 104 minority (101 Black or African American, non-Hispanic/Latino; 1 Asian, non-Hispanic/Latino; 2 Hispanic/Latino), 2 international. Average age 34. 124 applicants, 62% accepted, 45 enrolled. In 2010, 38 master's awarded. *Degree requirements:* For master's, comprehensive exam, thesis optional. *Entrance requirements:* For master's, GMAT, GRE. Additional exam requirements/recommendations for international students: Required—TOEFL (minimum score 525 paper-based; 173 computer-based). *Application deadline:* Applications are processed on a rolling basis. Application fee: $30 ($100 for international students). Electronic applications accepted. *Expenses:* Tuition, state resident: full-time $5886; part-time $352 per credit hour. Tuition, nonresident: full-time $9054; part-time $528 per credit hour. Required fees: $450; $26 per credit hour. *Financial support:* In 2010–11, 46 students received support, including 4 research assistantships (averaging $10,975 per year); career-related internships or fieldwork, scholarships/grants, tuition waivers (partial), and unspecified assistantships also available. Financial award application deadline: 4/15; financial award applicants required to submit FAFSA. *Unit head:* Dr. Gashaw Lake, Dean, 502-597-6105, Fax: 502-597-6715, E-mail: gashaw.lake@kysu.edu. *Application contact:* Dr. Titilayo Ufomata, Acting Director of Graduate Studies, 502-597-6443, E-mail: titilayo.ufomata@kysu.edu.

Lebanese American University, School of Arts and Sciences, Beirut, Lebanon. Offers computer science (MS); international affairs (MA).

Lesley University, Graduate School of Arts and Social Sciences, Program in Intercultural Relations, Cambridge, MA 02138-2790. Offers MA, CAGS. Part-time and evening/weekend programs available. *Degree requirements:* For master's, one foreign language, internship, practicum; for CAGS, one foreign language, thesis. *Entrance requirements:* For master's, interview; for CAGS, interview, master's degree. Additional exam requirements/recommendations for international students: Required—TOEFL (minimum score 550 paper-based; 213 computer-based; 80 iBT). *Faculty research:* Sociolinguistics, cross-cultural feminist theory, immigration and diaspora, intercultural business training.

Lindenwood University, Graduate Programs, School of Humanities, St. Charles, MO 63301-1695. Offers American studies (MA); international studies (MA). Part-time programs available. *Faculty:* 4 full-time (2 women), 5 part-time/adjunct (1 woman). *Students:* 18 full-time (13 women), 2 part-time (1 woman); includes 1 minority (Black or African American, non-Hispanic/Latino), 10 international. Average age 26. 8 applicants, 6 enrolled. In 2010, 2 master's awarded. *Degree requirements:* For master's, minimum cumulative GPA of 3.0. *Entrance requirements:* For master's, minimum GPA of 2.5, 2 letters of recommendation. Additional exam requirements/recommendations for international students: Required—TOEFL (minimum score 550 paper-based; 213 computer-based; 80 iBT). *Application deadline:* For fall admission, 8/27 priority date for domestic and international students; for spring admission, 1/28 for domestic students, 1/28 priority date for international students. Applications are processed on a rolling basis. Application fee: $30 ($100 for international students). Electronic applications accepted. *Expenses:* Tuition: Full-time $13,260; part-time $380 per credit hour. Required fees: $340. One-time fee: $30. Tuition and fees vary according to course level and course load. *Financial support:* In 2010–11, 19 students received support. Career-related internships or fieldwork, institutionally sponsored loans, tuition waivers (partial), and unspecified assistantships available. Financial award application deadline: 6/30; financial award applicants required to submit FAFSA. *Unit head:* Dr. Ana Schnellmann, Dean, 636-949-4873, E-mail: aschnellmann@lindenwood.edu. *Application contact:* Brett Barger, Dean of Evening Admissions and Extension Campuses, 636-949-4934, Fax: 636-949-4109, E-mail: adultadmissions@lindenwood.edu.

Long Island University, Brooklyn Campus, Richard L. Conolly College of Liberal Arts and Sciences, Program in Social Science, Brooklyn, NY 11201-8423. Offers history (MS); United Nations studies (Certificate). Part-time and evening/weekend programs available. *Entrance requirements:* For master's, 2 letters of recommendation. Additional exam requirements/recommendations for international students: Required—TOEFL (minimum score 500 paper-based; 173 computer-based). Electronic applications accepted.

Long Island University, C.W. Post Campus, College of Liberal Arts and Sciences, Department of Political Science/International Studies, Brookville, NY 11548-1300. Offers MA. Part-time and evening/weekend programs available. *Degree requirements:* For master's, comprehensive exam, thesis or alternative. *Entrance requirements:* For master's, GRE. Electronic applications accepted. *Faculty research:* International relations, Middle Eastern politics, political philosophy.

Marquette University, Graduate School, College of Arts and Sciences, Department of History, Milwaukee, WI 53201-1881. Offers European history (MA, PhD); global studies (MA); United States history (MA, PhD). Part-time programs available. *Faculty:* 23 full-time (6 women), 1 part-time/adjunct (0 women). *Students:* 32 full-time (15 women), 5 part-time (2 women); includes 1 minority (Two or more races, non-Hispanic/Latino), 1 international. Average age 30. 49 applicants, 57% accepted, 13 enrolled. In 2010, 6 master's, 3 doctorates awarded. Terminal master's awarded for partial completion of doctoral program. *Degree requirements:* For master's, comprehensive exam, essay, 2 classes of research seminars (6 hours); for doctorate, one foreign language, comprehensive exam, thesis/dissertation, 2 research seminars, dissertation seminar. *Entrance requirements:* For master's, GRE General Test, official transcripts from all current and previous colleges/universities except Marquette, one-page statement of purpose, three letters of recommendation from former teachers; for doctorate, GRE General Test, official transcripts from all current and previous colleges/universities except Marquette, one-page statement of purpose, three letters of recommendation from former teachers, writing sample. Additional exam requirements/recommendations for international students: Required—TOEFL (minimum score 530 paper-based; 78 computer-based). *Application deadline:* For fall admission, 12/31 for domestic and international students. Application fee: $50. Electronic applications accepted. *Expenses:* Tuition: Full-time $16,290; part-time $905 per credit hour. Tuition and fees vary according to program. *Financial support:* In 2010–11, 3 fellowships, 7 research assistantships, 14 teaching assistantships were awarded; Federal Work-Study, institutionally sponsored loans, scholarships/grants, and tuition waivers (full and partial) also available. Support available to part-time students. Financial award application deadline: 2/15. *Faculty research:* Children's history, Soviet and post-Soviet history, modern Ireland and Britain, Japan and martial arts, American Catholicism. Total annual research expenditures: $5,905. *Unit head:* James Marten, Chair, 414-288-7901, Fax: 414-288-1578. *Application contact:* Erin Fox, Assistant Director for Recruitment, 414-288-5319, Fax: 414-288-1902, E-mail: erin.fox@marquette.edu.

Marquette University, Graduate School, College of Arts and Sciences, Department of Political Science/International Affairs, Milwaukee, WI 53201-1881. Offers international affairs (MA); political science (MA); political science/communication (MA); JD/MA; MA/MBA. Part-time programs available. *Faculty:* 16 full-time (4 women), 2 part-time/adjunct (both women). *Students:* 22 full-time (10 women), 4 part-time (all women); includes 1 minority (Asian, non-Hispanic/Latino), 4 international. Average age 27. 66 applicants, 65% accepted, 14 enrolled. In 2010, 11 master's awarded. *Degree requirements:* For master's, comprehensive exam, thesis optional. *Entrance requirements:* For master's, GRE General Test, official transcripts from all current and previous colleges/universities except Marquette, three letters of recommendation, statement of purpose. Additional exam requirements/recommendations for international students: Required—TOEFL (minimum score 530 paper-based; 78 computer-based). *Application deadline:* For fall admission, 2/15 for domestic and international students. Application fee: $50. Electronic applications accepted. *Expenses:* Tuition: Full-time $16,290; part-time $905 per credit hour. Tuition and fees vary according to program. *Financial support:* In 2010–11, 4 fellowships, 11 teaching assistantships were awarded; research assistantships, Federal Work-Study, institutionally sponsored loans, scholarships/grants, and tuition waivers (full and partial) also available. Support available to part-time students. Financial award application deadline: 2/15. *Faculty research:* Public opinion and electoral behavior, public policy analysis, Congress and the Presidency, judicial behavior, political system transitions. Total annual research expenditures: $187,654. *Unit head:* Dr. Barrett McCormick, Chair, 414-288-6842, Fax: 414-288-3360. *Application contact:* Dr. Lowell Barrington, Director of Graduate Studies, 414-288-5234, Fax: 414-288-3360.

McMaster University, School of Graduate Studies, Faculty of Humanities and Faculty of Social Sciences, Institute on Globalization and the Human Condition, Hamilton, ON L8S 4M2, Canada. Offers globalization studies (MA).

McMaster University, School of Graduate Studies, Faculty of Social Sciences, Department of Political Science, Hamilton, ON L8S 4M2, Canada. Offers international relations (PhD); political science (MA); public and the global economy (MA); public policy (PhD); public policy and administration (MA). MA program in public policy and administration offered jointly with University of Guelph. Part-time programs available. *Degree requirements:* For master's, thesis or alternative. *Entrance requirements:* For master's, minimum B+ average. Additional exam requirements/recommendations for international students: Required—TOEFL (minimum score 580 paper-based; 237 computer-based). *Faculty research:* Organizational theory, internationalization of public policy, water resource policies, political interest intermediation, comparative politics.

Missouri State University, Graduate College, College of Humanities and Public Affairs, Department of Political Science, Program in Global Studies, Springfield, MO 65897. Offers MGS. Part-time programs available. *Degree requirements:* For master's, 2 foreign languages, comprehensive exam, thesis or alternative. *Entrance requirements:* For master's, GRE, minimum GPA of 3.0. Additional exam requirements/recommendations for international students: Required—TOEFL (minimum score 550 paper-based; 213 computer-based; 79 iBT). Electronic applications accepted. *Expenses:* Tuition, state resident: full-time $3348; part-time $186 per credit hour. Tuition, nonresident: full-time $6696; part-time $372 per credit hour. Required fees: $238 per semester. Tuition and fees vary according to course level, course load and program. *Faculty research:* U.S.-China policy, Eastern European politics, South American political reform, landmine use policy.

Monterey Institute of International Studies, Graduate School of International Policy and Management, Program in International Policy Studies, Monterey, CA 93940-2691. Offers MA. *Degree requirements:* For master's, one foreign language. *Entrance requirements:* For master's, minimum GPA of 3.0, proficiency in a foreign language. Additional exam requirements/recommendations for international students: Required—TOEFL (minimum score 550 paper-based; 213 computer-based; 80 iBT). Electronic applications accepted. *Expenses:* Tuition: Full-time $32,000; part-time $1525 per credit hour. Required fees: $56.

Morgan State University, School of Graduate Studies, College of Liberal Arts, Department of World Languages and International Studies, Baltimore, MD 21251. Offers international studies (MA). Part-time and evening/weekend programs available. *Degree requirements:* For master's, one foreign language, comprehensive exam, thesis. *Entrance requirements:* For master's, GRE. Additional exam requirements/recommendations for international students: Required—TOEFL (minimum score 550 paper-based; 213 computer-based).

Naval Postgraduate School, Graduate Programs, Department of National Security Affairs, Monterey, CA 93943. Offers intelligence (MA); international relations (MA); political science (MA); regional security education (MA); security building (MA); security studies (MA). Program only open to commissioned officers of the United States and friendly nations and select U.S. federal civilian employees. Part-time programs available. *Degree requirements:* For master's, thesis.

New England College, Program in Management, Henniker, NH 03242-3293. Offers accounting (MSA); healthcare administration (MS); international relations (MA); marketing management (MS); nonprofit leadership (MS); project management (MS); strategic leadership (MS). Part-time and evening/weekend programs available. *Degree requirements:* For master's, independent research project. Electronic applications accepted.

The New School: A University, The New School for General Studies, Program in International Affairs, New York, NY 10011. Offers MA, MS. Part-time and evening/weekend programs available. *Degree requirements:* For master's, thesis or practicum. *Entrance requirements:* Additional exam requirements/recommendations for international students: Required—TOEFL (minimum score 600 paper-based; 250 computer-based; 100 iBT). Electronic applications accepted.

New York University, Graduate School of Arts and Science, Department of Politics, New York, NY 10012-1019. Offers political campaign management (MA); politics (MA, PhD); JD/MA; MBA/MA. Part-time programs available. *Faculty:* 30 full-time (4 women). *Students:* 183 full-time (92 women), 54 part-time (29 women); includes 2 Black or African American, non-Hispanic/Latino; 14 Asian, non-Hispanic/Latino; 6 Hispanic/Latino, 111 international. Average age 28. 747 applicants, 34% accepted, 78 enrolled. In 2010, 78 master's, 9 doctorates awarded. Terminal master's awarded for partial completion of doctoral program. *Degree requirements:* For master's, one foreign language, thesis or alternative; for doctorate, 2 foreign languages, comprehensive exam, thesis/dissertation. *Entrance requirements:* For master's, GRE General Test; for doctorate, GRE General Test, master's degree in political science, minimum GPA of 2.5. Additional exam requirements/recommendations for international students: Required—TOEFL. *Application deadline:* For fall admission, 12/15 priority date for domestic students. Application fee: $90. *Financial support:* Fellowships with tuition reimbursements, teaching assistantships with tuition reimbursements, career-related internships or fieldwork, Federal Work-Study, and institutionally sponsored loans available. Financial award application deadline: 12/15; financial award applicants required to submit FAFSA. *Faculty research:* Comparative politics, democratic theory and practice, rational choice, political economy, international relations. *Unit head:* Michael Gilligan, Director of PhD Program, 212-998-8500, Fax: 212-995-4184, E-mail: politics.phd@nyu.edu. *Application contact:* Shinasi Rama, Director of Master's Program, 212-998-8500, Fax: 212-995-4184, E-mail: politics.masters@nyu.edu.

New York University, Robert F. Wagner Graduate School of Public Service, Program in Public Administration, New York, NY 10012-1019. Offers public administration (PhD); public and nonprofit management and policy (MPA, Advanced Certificate), including developmental administration (Advanced Certificate), financial management and public finance, human resources management (Advanced Certificate), international administration (Advanced Certificate), management (MPA), management for public and nonprofit organizations (Advanced Certificate), public policy analysis, quantitative analysis and computer applications (Advanced Certificate), urban public policy (Advanced Certificate); JD/MPA; MBA/MPA; MPA/MA. *Accreditation:* NASPAA (one or more programs are accredited). Part-time and evening/weekend programs available. *Faculty:* 32 full-time (13 women), 41 part-time/adjunct (22 women). *Students:* 400 full-time (301 women), 206 part-time (156 women); includes 43 Black or African American, non-Hispanic/Latino; 58 Asian, non-Hispanic/Latino; 36 Hispanic/Latino, 65 international. Average age 28. 1,230 applicants, 54% accepted, 219 enrolled. In 2010, 210 master's, 5 doctorates awarded. *Degree requirements:* For master's, thesis or alternative, capstone end event; for doctorate, one foreign language, thesis/dissertation. *Entrance requirements:* For master's, minimum undergraduate GPA of 3.0; for doctorate, GMAT or GRE General Test, minimum GPA of 3.5. Additional exam requirements/recommendations for international students: Required—TOEFL (minimum score 600 paper-based; 250 computer-based; 100 iBT), IELTS (minimum score 7.5), TWE (minimum score 4). *Application deadline:* For fall admission, 1/15 for domestic students, 1/4 for international students; for spring admission, 11/15 for domestic students, 10/1 for international students. Applications are processed on a rolling basis. Application fee: $80. Electronic applications accepted. *Expenses:* Contact institution. *Financial support:* In 2010–11, 176 students received support, including 171 fellowships (averaging $14,022 per year), 5 research assistantships with full tuition reimbursements available (averaging $22,440 per year); career-related internships or fieldwork, Federal Work-Study, institutionally sponsored loans, scholarships/grants, health care benefits, and unspecified assistantships also available. Support available to part-time students. Financial award application deadline: 1/5; financial award applicants required to submit FAFSA. *Unit head:* Katty Jones, Director, Program Services, 212-998-7411, Fax: 212-995-4164, E-mail: katty.jones@nyu.edu. *Application contact:* Christopher Alexander, Administrative Aide, Enrollment, 212-998-7414, Fax: 212-995-4611, E-mail: wagner.admissions@nyu.edu.

New York University, School of Continuing and Professional Studies, Center for Global Affairs, New York, NY 10012-1019. Offers global affairs (MS), including environment/energy policy, human rights and humanitarian assistance, international law, dispute settlement, and institutions, international relations, peace building, private sector: international business, economics, and development, transnational security. Part-time and evening/weekend programs available. *Faculty:* 10 full-time (3 women), 29 part-time/adjunct (14 women). *Students:* 92 full-time (62 women), 119 part-time (90 women); includes 12 Black or African American, non-Hispanic/Latino; 1 American Indian or Alaska Native, non-Hispanic/Latino; 14 Asian, non-Hispanic/Latino; 10 Hispanic/Latino, 32 international. Average age 30. 419 applicants, 58% accepted, 81 enrolled. In 2010, 113 master's awarded. *Degree requirements:* For master's, thesis. *Entrance requirements:* For master's, GRE General Test or GMAT (for recent graduates), 2 letters of recommendation, resume, essay, professional experience. Additional exam requirements/recommendations for international students: Required—TOEFL (minimum score 600 paper-based; 250 computer-based; 100 iBT). *Application deadline:* For fall admission, 2/1 priority date for domestic and international students; for spring admission, 10/15 priority date for domestic students, 8/15 priority date for international students. Applications are processed on a rolling basis. Application fee: $75. Electronic applications accepted. *Financial support:* In 2010–11, 163 students received support, including 163 fellowships (averaging $2,554 per year); institutionally sponsored loans, scholarships/grants, and tuition waivers (partial) also available. Support available to part-time students. Financial award application deadline: 3/1; financial award applicants required to submit FAFSA. *Unit head:* Dr. Vera Jelinek, Divisional Dean and Clinical Associate Professor, 212-992-8380, Fax: 212-995-4597, E-mail: vera.jelinek@nyu.edu. *Application contact:* Cori Epstein, Associate Director, 212-992-8380, Fax: 212-995-4597, E-mail: graduate.global.affairs@nyu.edu.

North Carolina State University, Graduate School, College of Humanities and Social Sciences, School of Public and International Affairs, Program in International Studies, Raleigh, NC 27695. Offers MIS. *Degree requirements:* For master's, thesis optional. *Entrance requirements:* For master's, GRE General Test, minimum GPA of 3.0 during previous 2 years. Electronic applications accepted. *Faculty research:* Global environmental policy and climate change, drug policy and the Caribbean, U.S. national security politics, local responses to globalization, the political economy of the European Union.

Northeastern University, College of Social Sciences and Humanities, Department of Political Science, Boston, MA 02115-5096. Offers political science (MA); public administration (MPA, Certificate), including development administration (MPA), health administration and policy (MPA), state and local government (MPA), urban studies (Certificate); public and international affairs (PhD). Part-time and evening/weekend programs available. *Faculty:* 22 full-time (4 women), 10 part-time/adjunct (1 woman). *Students:* 64 full-time (30 women), 12 part-time (7 women). Average age 30. 132 applicants, 47% accepted, 23 enrolled. In 2010, 21 master's, 3 doctorates awarded. *Degree requirements:* For master's, thesis optional; for doctorate, thesis/dissertation. *Entrance requirements:* For master's, GRE General Test. Additional exam requirements/recommendations for international students: Required—TOEFL. *Application deadline:* Applications are processed on a rolling basis. Application fee: $50. *Financial support:* In 2010–11, 12 fellowships, 1 research assistantship with tuition reimbursement, 17 teaching assistantships with tuition reimbursements (averaging $14,035 per year) were awarded; career-related internships or fieldwork, Federal Work-Study, tuition waivers (full and partial), and unspecified assistantships also available. Support available to part-time students. Financial award application deadline: 2/1; financial award applicants required to submit FAFSA. *Faculty research:* Presidency, public opinion, Congress, democratization, national identity. *Unit head:* Dr. John Portz, Chair, 617-373-2796, Fax: 617-373-5311, E-mail: gradpolisci@neu.edu. *Application contact:* Brynn Thompson, Graduate Programs Assistant, 617-373-4404, Fax: 617-373-5311, E-mail: gradpolisci@neu.edu.

Northwestern University, The Graduate School, Center for International and Comparative Studies, Evanston, IL 60208. Offers Certificate.

Northwestern University, Law School, Chicago, IL 60611-3069. Offers executive (LL M); international human rights (LL M); law (JD, LL M); tax (LL M in Tax); two-year accelerated (JD); JD/LL M; JD/MBA; JD/PhD; LL M/Certificate. *Accreditation:* ABA. *Entrance requirements:* For JD, LSAT, 1 letter of recommendation, resume; for master's, law degree or equivalent, letter of recommendation, resume. Additional exam requirements/recommendations for international students: Required—TOEFL. Electronic applications accepted. *Expenses:* Contact institution. *Faculty research:* Constitutional law, corporate law, international law, law and social policy, ethical studies.

Norwich University, School of Graduate and Continuing Studies, Program in Diplomacy, Northfield, VT 05663. Offers international commerce (MA); international conflict management (MA); international terrorism (MA). Evening/weekend programs available. *Faculty:* 44 part-time/adjunct (8 women). *Students:* 168 full-time (62 women); includes 12 Black or African American, non-Hispanic/Latino; 4 Asian, non-Hispanic/Latino; 18 Hispanic/Latino. Average age 38. 273 applicants, 74% accepted, 168 enrolled. In 2010, 168 master's awarded. *Degree requirements:* For master's, comprehensive exam, thesis optional. *Entrance requirements:* For master's, minimum undergraduate GPA of 2.75. Additional exam requirements/recommendations for international students: Required—TOEFL. *Application deadline:* For fall admission, 8/10 for domestic and international students; for winter admission, 11/7 for domestic and international students; for spring admission, 2/6 for domestic and international students. Application fee: $50. Electronic applications accepted. *Expenses:* Tuition: Full-time $17,380; part-time $645 per credit. Tuition and fees vary according to program. *Financial support:* Scholarships/grants available. Financial award applicants required to submit FAFSA. *Unit head:* Dr. Harold Kearsley, Program Director, 802-485-2730, E-mail: hkearsley@norwich.edu. *Application contact:* Sally Burkart, Application Management Team Lead, 802-485-2096, Fax: 802-485-2533, E-mail: sburkart@norwich.edu.

Ohio University, Graduate College, Center for International Studies, Program in Communications and Development Studies, Athens, OH 45701-2979. Offers MA. Part-time programs available. *Students:* 27 full-time (15 women), 2 part-time (both women); includes 3 minority (all Black or African American, non-Hispanic/Latino), 20 international. Average age 30. 50 applicants, 52% accepted, 15 enrolled. In 2010, 17 master's awarded. *Degree requirements:* For master's, one foreign language, thesis optional, internship. *Entrance requirements:* For master's, minimum GPA of 3.0. Additional exam requirements/recommendations for international students: Required—TOEFL (minimum score 550 paper-based; 213 computer-based; 80 iBT), IELTS (minimum score 6.5). *Application deadline:* For fall admission, 1/1 for domestic and international students. Application fee: $50 ($55 for international students). Electronic applications accepted. *Financial support:* In 2010–11, 19 students received support, including research assistantships with full tuition reimbursements available (averaging $11,499 per year); Federal Work-Study, institutionally sponsored loans, and tuition waivers (partial) also available. Financial award application deadline: 1/1. *Faculty research:* National development processes, public relations and participatory research, audio and video production, health communication, urban development. *Unit head:* Dr. Rafael Obregon, Director, 740-593-1833, E-mail: obregon@ohio.edu. *Application contact:* Joan Kraynanski, Administrative Assistant, 740-593-1840, Fax: 740-593-1837, E-mail: kraynans@ohio.edu.

Oklahoma State University, Graduate College, Stillwater, OK 74078. Offers environmental science (MS); international studies (MS); natural and applied science (MS); photonics (PhD); plant science (PhD). Programs are interdisciplinary. *Faculty:* 2 full-time (1 woman). *Students:* 69 full-time (40 women), 131 part-time (68 women); includes 13 Black or African American, non-Hispanic/Latino; 15 American Indian or Alaska Native, non-Hispanic/Latino; 8 Asian, non-Hispanic/Latino; 8 Hispanic/Latino, 70 international. Average age 30. 690 applicants, 74% accepted, 75 enrolled. In 2010, 66 master's, 7 doctorates awarded. *Degree requirements:* For master's, thesis (for some programs); for doctorate, comprehensive exam, thesis/dissertation. *Entrance requirements:* For master's and doctorate, GRE or GMAT. Additional exam requirements/recommendations for international students: Required—TOEFL (minimum score 550 paper-based; 79 iBT). *Application deadline:* For fall admission, 3/1 priority date for international students; for spring admission, 8/1 priority date for international students. Applications are processed on a rolling basis. Application fee: $40 ($75 for international students). Electronic applications accepted. *Expenses:* Tuition, state resident: full-time $3716; part-time $154.85 per credit hour. Tuition, nonresident: full-time $14,892; part-time $621 per credit hour. Required fees: $2044; $85.20 per credit hour. One-time fee: $50. Tuition and fees vary according to course load and campus/location. *Financial support:* In 2010–11, 2 research assistantships (averaging $12,900 per year) were awarded; career-related internships or fieldwork, Federal Work-Study, scholarships/grants, health care benefits, tuition waivers (partial), and unspecified assistantships also available. Support available to part-time students. Financial award application deadline: 3/1; financial award applicants required to submit FAFSA. *Unit head:* Dr. Gordon Emslie, Dean, 405-744-6368, Fax: 405-744-0355, E-mail: grad-i@okstate.edu. *Application contact:* Dr. Susan Mathew, Coordinator of Admissions, 405-744-6368, Fax: 405-744-0355, E-mail: grad-i@okstate.edu.

Old Dominion University, College of Arts and Letters, Graduate Program in International Studies, Norfolk, VA 23529. Offers modeling and simulation (MA); women's studies (PhD). Part-time programs available. *Faculty:* 14 full-time (3 women). *Students:* 54 full-time (23 women), 40 part-time (16 women); includes 11 minority (5 Black or African American, non-Hispanic/Latino; 3 Asian, non-Hispanic/Latino; 3 Hispanic/Latino), 28 international. Average age 31. 99 applicants, 54% accepted, 30 enrolled. In 2010, 14 master's, 7 doctorates awarded. Terminal master's awarded for partial completion of doctoral program. *Degree requirements:* For master's, one foreign language, comprehensive exam, thesis optional; for doctorate, one foreign language, comprehensive exam, thesis/dissertation. *Entrance requirements:* For master's, GRE General Test, sample of written work, 2 letters of recommendation; for doctorate, GRE General Test, sample of written work, 3 letters of recommendation. Additional exam requirements/recommendations for international students: Required—TOEFL (minimum score 570 paper-based; 230 computer-based). *Application deadline:* For fall admission, 1/15 for domestic and international students; for spring admission, 10/15 for domestic and international students. Application fee: $40. Electronic applications accepted. *Expenses:* Tuition, state resident: full-time $8592; part-time $358 per credit. Tuition, nonresident: full-time $21,672; part-time $903 per credit. Required fees: $119 per semester. One-time fee: $50. *Financial support:* In 2010–11, 20 students received support, including 2 fellowships (averaging $13,000 per year), 5 research assistantships with tuition reimbursements available (averaging $15,000 per year), 7 teaching assistantships with tuition reimbursements available (averaging $15,000 per year); career-related internships or fieldwork, institutionally sponsored loans, scholarships/grants, and unspecified assistantships also available. Support available to part-time students. Financial award application deadline: 2/15; financial award applicants required to submit FAFSA. *Faculty research:* U. S. foreign policy, international security, transatlantic and transpacific relations, transnational issues, IPE and development. Total annual research expenditures: $330,391. *Unit head:* Dr. Regina Karp, Graduate Program Director, 757-683-5700, Fax: 757-683-5701, E-mail: rkarp@odu.edu. *Application contact:* Dr. Regina Karp, Graduate Program Director, 757-683-5700, Fax: 757-683-5701, E-mail: rkarp@odu.edu.

Pepperdine University, School of Public Policy, Malibu, CA 90263. Offers American politics (MPP); economics (MPP); international relations (MPP); public policy (MPP); state and local policy (MPP). *Faculty:* 7 full-time (2 women), 10 part-time/adjunct (0 women). *Students:* 123 full-time (72 women), 4 part-time (all women); includes 36 minority (11 Black or African American, non-Hispanic/Latino; 2 American Indian or Alaska Native, non-Hispanic/Latino; 11 Asian, non-Hispanic/Latino; 9 Hispanic/Latino; 3 Two or more races, non-Hispanic/Latino), 13 international. 168 applicants, 93% accepted, 66 enrolled. In 2010, 50 master's awarded. *Entrance requirements:* For master's, GRE or GMAT, 2 letters of recommendation, resume, two essays. Additional exam requirements/recommendations for international students: Required—TOEFL. *Application deadline:* For fall admission, 5/1 for domestic students. Applica-

International Affairs

Pepperdine University (continued)
tions are processed on a rolling basis. Application fee: $50. Electronic applications accepted. *Financial support:* Institutionally sponsored loans and scholarships/grants available. Financial award application deadline: 5/1; financial award applicants required to submit FAFSA. *Unit head:* Dr. James R. Wilburn, Dean, 310-506-7490, Fax: 310-506-7494, E-mail: james.wilburn@pepperdine.edu. *Application contact:* Melinda E. van Hemert, Director of Recruitment and Career Services, 310-506-7492, Fax: 310-506-7494, E-mail: melinda.vanhemert@pepperdine.edu.

Pontificia Universidad Catolica Madre y Maestra, Graduate School, Faculty of Social and Administrative Sciences, Santiago, Dominican Republic. Offers business administration (MBA), including business development, finance, international business, management skills (M Mgmt, MBA), marketing, operations, strategic cost management, strategy, tourist destination planning and management; law (LL M), including civil law, corporate business law, criminal law, international relations, real estate law; management (M Mgmt), including higher financial management, insurance program administration, management skills (M Mgmt, MBA); psychology (MA), including clinical child and adolescent psychology, forensic psychology; strategic human resources (EMBA).

Princeton University, Graduate School, Woodrow Wilson School of Public and International Affairs, Princeton, NJ 08544-1019. Offers public affairs (MPA, PhD); public policy (MPP); JD/MPA. JD/MPA offered jointly with Columbia University, New York University, Stanford University. Terminal master's awarded for partial completion of doctoral program. *Degree requirements:* For master's, internship; for doctorate, one foreign language, thesis/dissertation. *Entrance requirements:* For master's, GRE General Test, original policy memo; for doctorate, GRE General Test. Additional exam requirements/recommendations for international students: Required—TOEFL (minimum score 600 paper-based; 250 computer-based). Electronic applications accepted.

Queen's University at Kingston, School of Graduate Studies and Research, Faculty of Arts and Sciences, Department of Political Studies, Kingston, ON K7L 3N6, Canada. Offers Canadian politics (PhD); comparative politics (PhD); gender and politics (PhD); international relations (PhD); political theory (PhD). *Degree requirements:* For master's, thesis or alternative; for doctorate, one foreign language, thesis/dissertation, qualifying exams. *Entrance requirements:* Additional exam requirements/recommendations for international students: Required—TOEFL (minimum score 600 paper-based; 250 computer-based). *Faculty research:* Canadian politics, comparative politics, political thought, international politics, women and politics.

Regent's American College London, Webster Graduate School, London, United Kingdom. Offers business (MBA); finance (MS); human resources (MA); information technology management (MA); international business (MA); international non-governmental organizations (MA); international relations (MA); management and leadership (MA); marketing (MA). Part-time programs available.

Richmond, The American International University in London, MA in International Relations Program, Richmond, United Kingdom. Offers MA. Part-time programs available. *Entrance requirements:* Additional exam requirements/recommendations for international students: Required—TOEFL, IELTS. Electronic applications accepted.

Rutgers, The State University of New Jersey, Camden, Graduate School of Arts and Sciences, Department of Public Policy and Administration, Camden, NJ 08102. Offers education policy and leadership (MPA); international public service and development (MPA); public management (MPA); JD/MPA; MPA/MA. *Accreditation:* NASPAA. Part-time and evening/weekend programs available. *Faculty:* 17 full-time (7 women), 3 part-time/adjunct (1 woman). *Students:* 75 full-time (45 women), 49 part-time (26 women); includes 38 Black or African American, non-Hispanic/Latino; 1 American Indian or Alaska Native, non-Hispanic/Latino; 5 Asian, non-Hispanic/Latino; 11 Hispanic/Latino. Average age 32. 132 applicants, 73% accepted, 58 enrolled. In 2010, 44 master's awarded. *Degree requirements:* For master's, directed study, research workshop, 42 credits. *Entrance requirements:* For master's, GRE General Test, GMAT or LSAT, 3 letters of recommendation; resume. Additional exam requirements/recommendations for international students: Required—TOEFL (minimum score 550 paper-based; 213 computer-based), IELTS. *Application deadline:* For fall admission, 5/1 priority date for domestic students; for spring admission, 12/1 priority date for domestic students. Applications are processed on a rolling basis. Application fee: $65. Electronic applications accepted. *Expenses:* Tuition, state resident: full-time $4963; part-time $319 per credit. Tuition, nonresident: full-time $10,493; part-time $680 per credit. *Financial support:* In 2010–11, 97 students received support, including 3 fellowships with partial tuition reimbursements available (averaging $3,500 per year), 1 research assistantship with full tuition reimbursement available (averaging $26,000 per year); career-related internships or fieldwork, Federal Work-Study, scholarships/grants, and tuition waivers (partial) also available. Financial award application deadline: 3/15; financial award applicants required to submit FAFSA. *Faculty research:* Nonprofit management, county and municipal administration, health and human services, government communication, administrative law, educational finance. Total annual research expenditures: $8.8 million. *Unit head:* Dr. Robyne Turner, Chair, 856-225-2982, Fax: 856-225-6559, E-mail: rsturner@camden.rutgers.edu. *Application contact:* Sandra J. Cheesman, Department Administrator, 856-225-6860, Fax: 856-225-6559, E-mail: scheesma@camden.rutgers.edu.

Rutgers, The State University of New Jersey, Newark, Graduate School, Division of Global Affairs, Newark, NJ 07102. Offers MS, PhD. Part-time and evening/weekend programs available. *Faculty:* 35 full-time (7 women). *Students:* 62 full-time (30 women), 92 part-time (46 women); includes 24 Black or African American, non-Hispanic/Latino; 22 Asian, non-Hispanic/Latino; 11 Hispanic/Latino. 199 applicants, 62% accepted, 50 enrolled. In 2010, 23 master's, 9 doctorates awarded. *Degree requirements:* For master's, one foreign language, thesis optional. *Entrance requirements:* For master's and doctorate, GRE General Test, minimum B average. *Application deadline:* Applications are processed on a rolling basis. Application fee: $60. Electronic applications accepted. *Expenses:* Tuition, state resident: part-time $600 per credit. Tuition, nonresident: full-time $10,694. *Financial support:* In 2010–11, 2 fellowships (averaging $18,000 per year), 9 teaching assistantships with full and partial tuition reimbursements (averaging $23,112 per year) were awarded; research assistantships, career-related internships or fieldwork, Federal Work-Study, institutionally sponsored loans, and tuition waivers (full and partial) also available. Support available to part-time students. Financial award application deadline: 3/7; financial award applicants required to submit FAFSA. *Faculty research:* International organizations, diplomacy, world history, international political economy, global environment. *Unit head:* Dr. Alex Motyl, Director, 973-353-3285, Fax: 973-353-5074, E-mail: ajmotyl@andromeda.rutgers.edu. *Application contact:* Jason Hand, Director of Admissions, 973-353-5205, Fax: 973-353-1440.

Rutgers, The State University of New Jersey, Newark, Graduate School, Program in Political Science, Newark, NJ 07102. Offers American political system (MA); international relations (MA); JD/MA. Part-time and evening/weekend programs available. *Faculty:* 8 full-time (4 women), 2 part-time/adjunct (both women). *Students:* 7 full-time (3 women), 22 part-time (11 women); includes 6 Black or African American, non-Hispanic/Latino; 2 Asian, non-Hispanic/Latino; 2 Hispanic/Latino. 44 applicants, 61% accepted, 7 enrolled. In 2010, 10 master's awarded. *Degree requirements:* For master's, comprehensive exam, thesis optional. *Entrance requirements:* For master's, GRE, minimum undergraduate B average. *Application deadline:* For fall admission, 8/1 priority date for domestic students; for spring admission, 12/1 for domestic students. Applications are processed on a rolling basis. Application fee: $60. Electronic applications accepted. *Expenses:* Tuition, state resident: part-time $600 per credit. Tuition, nonresident: full-time $10,694. *Financial support:* Federal Work-Study and tuition waivers (full and partial) available. Support available to part-time students. Financial award application deadline: 3/1. *Faculty research:* Policymaking and policy evaluation in the United States; government and politics in Europe, Middle East, Asia, Africa, and Latin America. *Unit head:* Dr. Mara Sidney, Director, 973-353-5105, E-mail: msidney@andromeda.rutgers.edu. *Application contact:* Jason Hand, Director of Admissions, 973-353-5205, Fax: 973-353-1440.

Rutgers, The State University of New Jersey, New Brunswick, Graduate School-New Brunswick, Department of Political Science, Piscataway, NJ 08854-8097. Offers American politics (PhD); comparative politics (PhD); international relations (PhD); political theory (PhD); public law (PhD); women and politics (PhD). *Degree requirements:* For doctorate, one foreign language, comprehensive exam, thesis/dissertation. *Entrance requirements:* For doctorate, GRE General Test. Additional exam requirements/recommendations for international students: Required—TOEFL. *Expenses:* Tuition, state resident: full-time $7200; part-time $600 per credit. Tuition, nonresident: full-time $11,124; part-time $927 per credit.

St. John Fisher College, School of Arts and Sciences, Program in International Studies, Rochester, NY 14618-3597. Offers MS. Part-time and evening/weekend programs available. *Faculty:* 5 full-time (0 women), 2 part-time/adjunct (0 women). *Students:* 9 full-time (5 women), 18 part-time (11 women); includes 4 minority (2 Black or African American, non-Hispanic/Latino; 1 Asian, non-Hispanic/Latino; 1 Hispanic/Latino). Average age 28. 13 applicants, 85% accepted, 7 enrolled. In 2010, 20 master's awarded. *Degree requirements:* For master's, research project. *Entrance requirements:* For master's, 2 letters of recommendation, personal statement, current resume. Additional exam requirements/recommendations for international students: Required—TOEFL (minimum score 575 paper-based; 233 computer-based; 80 iBT). *Application deadline:* Applications are processed on a rolling basis. Application fee: $30. Electronic applications accepted. *Expenses:* Tuition: Part-time $705 per credit hour. Required fees: $25 per semester. *Financial support:* In 2010–11, 22 students received support. Scholarships/grants available. Financial award applicants required to submit FAFSA. *Faculty research:* International relations, international affairs, international economics, Chinese politics. *Unit head:* Dr. David Baronov, Program Director, 585-385-8220, E-mail: dbaronov@sjfc.edu. *Application contact:* Jose Perales, Director of Graduate Admissions, 585-385-8067, E-mail: jperales@sjfc.edu.

St. John's University, College of Professional Studies, Department of Mass Communications, Queens, NY 11439. Offers international communications (MS). *Students:* 23 full-time (19 women), 12 part-time (5 women); includes 25 minority (5 Black or African American, non-Hispanic/Latino; 1 Asian, non-Hispanic/Latino; 18 Hispanic/Latino; 1 Two or more races, non-Hispanic/Latino), 2 international. Average age 26. 33 applicants, 73% accepted, 12 enrolled. *Degree requirements:* For master's, one foreign language, thesis optional. *Entrance requirements:* For master's, GRE, official transcript showing conferral of bachelor's degree, 2 letters of recommendation, proficiency in a foreign language. Additional exam requirements/recommendations for international students: Required—TOEFL (minimum score 600 paper-based; 250 computer-based; 100 iBT), IELTS (minimum score 5.5). *Application deadline:* For fall admission, 5/1 priority date for domestic and international students; for spring admission, 11/1 priority date for domestic and international students. Applications are processed on a rolling basis. Application fee: $70. Electronic applications accepted. *Expenses:* Tuition: Full-time $17,100; part-time $950 per credit. Required fees: $340; $170 per semester. Tuition and fees vary according to program. *Unit head:* Dr. Basilio Monteiro, Chair, 718-990-7339, E-mail: monteirb@stjohns.edu. *Application contact:* Kathleen Davis, Director of Graduate Admission, 718-990-1601, Fax: 718-990-5686, E-mail: gradhelp@stjohns.edu.

St. Mary's University, Graduate School, Department of Political Science, Interdisciplinary Program in International Relations, San Antonio, TX 78228-8507. Offers MA, JD/MA. Part-time programs available. Postbaccalaureate distance learning degree programs offered (no on-campus study). *Degree requirements:* For master's, one foreign language, comprehensive exam. *Entrance requirements:* For master's, GRE General Test. Additional exam requirements/recommendations for international students: Required—TOEFL (minimum score 550 paper-based; 213 computer-based; 80 iBT). Electronic applications accepted. *Faculty research:* Eastern Europe, Soviet Union, Balkans, modern Asia, Latin America.

Salve Regina University, Graduate Studies, Program in International Relations, Newport, RI 02840-4192. Offers homeland security (Certificate); international relations (MA, Certificate). Part-time and evening/weekend programs available. Postbaccalaureate distance learning degree programs offered (minimal on-campus study). *Entrance requirements:* For master's, GMAT, GRE General Test, MAT or LSAT. Additional exam requirements/recommendations for international students: Required—TOEFL (minimum score 600 paper-based; 250 computer-based; 100 iBT) or IELTS. Electronic applications accepted. *Expenses:* Tuition: Full-time $7740; part-time $430 per credit. Required fees: $40 per semester. Tuition and fees vary according to course level and degree level.

San Francisco State University, Division of Graduate Studies, College of Behavioral and Social Sciences, Department of International Relations, San Francisco, CA 94132-1722. Offers MA. *Unit head:* Dr. Sanjoy Banerjee, Chair, 415-338-1105, E-mail: banerjee@sfsu.edu. *Application contact:* Dr. Jean-Marc Blanchard, Graduate Coordinator, 415-338-2654, E-mail: irgrad@sfsu.edu.

Schiller International University, Graduate Programs, London, Program in International Relations and Diplomacy, London, United Kingdom. Offers MA. Part-time programs available. *Degree requirements:* For master's, thesis optional, GMAT before graduation. *Entrance requirements:* For master's, 1 year of undergraduate economics, 1 foreign language. Additional exam requirements/recommendations for international students: Required—TOEFL (minimum score 550 paper-based; 213 computer-based).

Schiller International University, Program in International Relations and Diplomacy, Paris, France. Offers MA. Part-time and evening/weekend programs available. *Degree requirements:* For master's, one foreign language, final comprehensive exam or thesis. *Entrance requirements:* For master's, undergraduate mathematics (strongly advised). Additional exam requirements/recommendations for international students: Required—TOEFL (minimum score 550 paper-based; 213 computer-based).

Seton Hall University, Whitehead School of Diplomacy and International Relations, South Orange, NJ 07079-2697. Offers MA, JD/MA, MA/MA, MBA/MA, MPA/MA. Part-time and evening/weekend programs available. *Faculty:* 16 full-time (5 women), 16 part-time/adjunct (5 women). *Students:* 250. Average age 26. In 2010, 80 master's awarded. *Degree requirements:* For master's, thesis (for some programs), research project, internship. *Entrance requirements:* For master's, GMAT, GRE, or LSAT, minimum GPA of 3.2. Additional exam requirements/recommendations for international students: Required—TOEFL (minimum: 600 paper, 250 computer, 10 iBT) or IELTS (minimum: 6.5). *Application deadline:* For fall admission, 5/1 priority date for domestic students. Applications are processed on a rolling basis. Application fee: $50. Electronic applications accepted. *Financial support:* Research assistantships with full and partial tuition reimbursements, career-related internships or fieldwork, scholarships/grants, tuition waivers (full and partial), and unspecified assistantships available. *Faculty research:* International economics and development, global health, United Nations, conflict negotiation and conflict management, international security. *Unit head:* Dr. Ursula Sanjamino, Associate Dean, 973-313-6210, Fax: 973-275-2519, E-mail: ursula.sanjamino@shu.edu. *Application contact:* Dr. Catherine Ruby, Director of Graduate Admissions, 973-275-2142, Fax: 973-275-2519, E-mail: catherine.ruby@shu.edu.

SIT Graduate Institute, Graduate Programs, Master's Programs in Intercultural Service, Leadership, and Management, Brattleboro, VT 05302-0676. Offers conflict transformation (MA); intercultural service, leadership, and management (MA); international education (MA); sustainable development (MA). Postbaccalaureate distance learning degree programs offered (minimal on-campus study). *Degree requirements:* For master's, one foreign language, thesis. *Entrance requirements:* For master's, 3 letters of reference. Additional exam requirements/recommendations for international students: Required—TOEFL. *Expenses:* Tuition: Full-time $35,260; part-time $14,876 per year. Required fees: $1495; $1495 per year. Tuition and fees vary according to class time and campus/location. *Faculty research:* Intercultural communication, conflict resolution, advising and training, world issues, international business.

Stanford University, School of Humanities and Sciences, Program in International Policy Studies, Stanford, CA 94305-9991. Offers MA. *Degree requirements:* For master's, thesis optional. *Entrance requirements:* For master's, GRE General Test. Additional exam requirements/recommendations for international students: Required—TOEFL. Electronic applications accepted. *Expenses:* Tuition: Full-time $38,700; part-time $860 per unit. One-time fee: $200 full-time.

Syracuse University, Maxwell School of Citizenship and Public Affairs, Executive Master in International Relations Program, Syracuse, NY 13244. Offers MA. Part-time programs available. *Entrance requirements:* Additional exam requirements/recommendations for international students: Required—TOEFL (minimum score 100 iBT). *Application deadline:* For fall admission, 2/1 priority date for domestic and international students; for spring admission, 8/15 priority date for domestic and international students. Applications are processed on a rolling basis. Application fee: $75. Electronic applications accepted. *Expenses:* Tuition: Part-time $1162 per credit. *Financial support:* Application deadline: 2/1. *Application contact:* Margaret Lane, Assistant Director, 315-443-8708, E-mail: melane@syr.edu.

Syracuse University, Maxwell School of Citizenship and Public Affairs, International Relations/Public Administration Joint Program, Syracuse, NY 13244. Offers MPA/MA. *Students:* 32 full-time (19 women), 2 part-time (1 woman); includes 6 minority (2 Black or African American, non-Hispanic/Latino; 4 Asian, non-Hispanic/Latino), 2 international. Average age 26. 66 applicants, 65% accepted, 19 enrolled. *Entrance requirements:* Additional exam requirements/recommendations for international students: Required—TOEFL (minimum score 100 iBT). *Application deadline:* For fall admission, 2/1 priority date for domestic and international students. Application fee: $75. Electronic applications accepted. *Expenses:* Tuition: Part-time $1162 per credit. *Financial support:* Fellowships with full tuition reimbursements, research assistantships with full and partial tuition reimbursements, teaching assistantships with full and partial tuition reimbursements available. Financial award application deadline: 1/1; financial award applicants required to submit FAFSA. *Unit head:* Donald Planty, Chair and Ambassador, 315-443-2306. *Application contact:* Nell Silva Bartkowiak, Director, International Relations, 315-443-9340, E-mail: nsbartko@syr.edu.

Syracuse University, Maxwell School of Citizenship and Public Affairs, Joint Program in Economics and International Relations, Syracuse, NY 13244. Offers MA/MA. *Students:* 11 full-time (8 women); includes 4 minority (all Two or more races, non-Hispanic/Latino), 6 international. Average age 26. 16 applicants, 56% accepted, 3 enrolled. *Entrance requirements:* Additional exam requirements/recommendations for international students: Required—TOEFL (minimum score 100 iBT). *Application deadline:* For fall admission, 2/1 priority date for domestic and international students. Application fee: $75. Electronic applications accepted. *Expenses:* Tuition: Part-time $1162 per credit. *Financial support:* Fellowships with full tuition reimbursements, research assistantships with full and partial tuition reimbursements, teaching assistantships with full and partial tuition reimbursements available. Financial award application deadline: 1/1. *Unit head:* Dr. Stuart Brown, Program Contact, 315-443-7097, Fax: 315-443-3385, E-mail: ssbrown@maxwell.syr.edu. *Application contact:* Dr. Stuart Brown, Program Contact, 315-443-7097, Fax: 315-443-3385, E-mail: ssbrown@maxwell.syr.edu.

Syracuse University, Maxwell School of Citizenship and Public Affairs, Program in Public Diplomacy, Syracuse, NY 13244. Offers MS/MA. *Students:* 35 full-time (24 women), 2 part-time (1 woman); includes 7 minority (1 Black or African American, non-Hispanic/Latino; 3 Asian, non-Hispanic/Latino; 3 Hispanic/Latino), 6 international. Average age 26. 67 applicants, 52% accepted, 19 enrolled. *Entrance requirements:* Additional exam requirements/recommendations for international students: Required—TOEFL (minimum score 100 iBT). *Application deadline:* For fall admission, 2/1 for domestic students, 2/1 priority date for international students. Application fee: $75. Electronic applications accepted. *Expenses:* Tuition: Part-time $1162 per credit. *Financial support:* Fellowships with full tuition reimbursements available. Financial award application deadline: 1/1. *Unit head:* Dr. Dennis Kinsey, Director, 315-443-1944, E-mail: publicdiplomacy@syr.edu. *Application contact:* Martha Coria, Program Contact, 315-443-5749, Fax: 315-443-1834, E-mail: pcgrad@syr.edu.

Syracuse University, S. I. Newhouse School of Public Communications, Program in Public Diplomacy, Syracuse, NY 13244. Offers MS/MA. *Students:* 35 full-time (24 women), 2 part-time (1 woman); includes 7 minority (1 Black or African American, non-Hispanic/Latino; 3 Asian, non-Hispanic/Latino; 3 Hispanic/Latino), 6 international. Average age 25. 67 applicants, 52% accepted, 19 enrolled. *Entrance requirements:* Additional exam requirements/recommendations for international students: Required—TOEFL (minimum score 100 iBT). *Application deadline:* For fall admission, 2/1 priority date for domestic and international students. Application fee: $45. Electronic applications accepted. *Expenses:* Tuition: Part-time $1162 per credit. *Financial support:* Fellowships with full tuition reimbursements, research assistantships with partial tuition reimbursements, teaching assistantships with partial tuition reimbursements available. Financial award application deadline: 2/1. *Unit head:* Dr. Dennis Kinsey, Director, 315-443-1944, E-mail: publicdiplomacy@syr.edu. *Application contact:* Martha Coria, Graduate Records Office, 315-443-5749, Fax: 315-443-1834, E-mail: pcgrad@syr.edu.

Texas A&M University, Bush School of Government and Public Service, College Station, TX 77843. Offers advanced international affairs (Certificate); China studies (Certificate); homeland security (Certificate); international affairs (MPIA); national security affairs (Certificate); nonprofit management (Certificate); public service and administration (MPSA). *Accreditation:* NASPAA. *Faculty:* 45. *Students:* 215 full-time (98 women), 93 part-time (32 women); includes 20 Black or African American, non-Hispanic/Latino; 2 American Indian or Alaska Native, non-Hispanic/Latino; 14 Asian, non-Hispanic/Latino; 30 Hispanic/Latino, 15 international. Average age 24. In 2010, 93 master's awarded. *Degree requirements:* For master's, summer internship. *Entrance requirements:* For master's, GRE (preferred) or GMAT. *Application deadline:* For fall admission, 1/24 for domestic and international students. Application fee: $50 ($75 for international students). Electronic applications accepted. *Financial support:* In 2010–11, fellowships (averaging $11,000 per year), research assistantships (averaging $11,250 per year) were awarded; career-related internships or fieldwork, Federal Work-Study, and institutionally sponsored loans also available. Financial award application deadline: 2/1; financial award applicants required to submit FAFSA. *Faculty research:* Public policy, presidential studies, public leadership, economic policy, social policy. *Unit head:* Ryan C. Crocker, Dean, 979-862-8007, E-mail: rcrocker@bushschool.tamu.edu. *Application contact:* Kathryn Meyer, Director of Recruiting, 979-458-4767, Fax: 979-845-4155, E-mail: kmeyer@bushschool.tamu.edu.

Texas State University–San Marcos, Graduate School, Program in International Studies, San Marcos, TX 78666. Offers MA. *Students:* 32 full-time (18 women), 25 part-time (14 women); includes 13 minority (3 Asian, non-Hispanic/Latino; 10 Hispanic/Latino), 1 international. Average age 29. 24 applicants, 92% accepted, 18 enrolled. In 2010, 7 master's awarded. *Degree requirements:* For master's, comprehensive exam, thesis optional. *Entrance requirements:* For master's, minimum GPA of 3.0 on last 60 hours of undergraduate work, 2- to 5-page essay, 2 letters of reference. Additional exam requirements/recommendations for international students: Required—TOEFL (minimum score 550 paper-based; 213 computer-based; 78 iBT). *Application deadline:* For fall admission, 6/15 priority date for domestic students, 6/1 for international students; for spring admission, 10/15 priority date for domestic students, 10/1 for international students. Applications are processed on a rolling basis. Application fee: $40 ($90 for international students). *Expenses:* Tuition, state resident: full-time $6024; part-time $251 per credit hour. Tuition, nonresident: full-time $13,536; part-time $564 per credit hour. Required fees: $1776; $50 per credit hour. $306 per semester. *Financial support:* In 2010–11, 27 students received support, including 5 research assistantships (averaging $4,987 per year), 1 teaching assistantship (averaging $5,076 per year); Federal Work-Study, institutionally sponsored loans, scholarships/grants, health care benefits, and unspecified assistantships also available. Support available to part-time students. Financial award application deadline: 4/1; financial award applicants required to submit FAFSA. *Unit head:* Dr. Dennis Dunn, Head, 512-245-2339,

E-mail: dd05@txstate.edu. *Application contact:* Dr. J. Michael Willoughby, Dean of Graduate School, 512-245-2581, Fax: 512-245-8365, E-mail: gradcollege@txstate.edu.

Troy University, Graduate School, College of Arts and Sciences, Program in International Relations, Troy, AL 36082. Offers national security affairs (MS), including global studies, national security affairs, regional affairs. Part-time and evening/weekend programs available. Postbaccalaureate distance learning degree programs offered (no on-campus study). *Students:* 72 full-time (29 women), 281 part-time (109 women); includes 99 minority (38 Black or African American, non-Hispanic/Latino; 5 American Indian or Alaska Native, non-Hispanic/Latino; 26 Asian, non-Hispanic/Latino; 27 Hispanic/Latino; 2 Native Hawaiian or other Pacific Islander, non-Hispanic/Latino; 1 Two or more races, non-Hispanic/Latino). Average age 32. 279 applicants, 83% accepted, 74 enrolled. In 2010, 212 master's awarded. *Degree requirements:* For master's, comprehensive exam or thesis, minimum GPA of 3.0, admission to candidacy. *Entrance requirements:* For master's, GRE (minimum score of 920), MAT (minimum score of 390), or GMAT (minimum score of 490), minimum undergraduate GPA of 2.5. Additional exam requirements/recommendations for international students: Required—TOEFL (minimum score 523 paper-based; 193 computer-based; 70 iBT), IELTS (minimum score 6). *Application deadline:* Applications are processed on a rolling basis. Application fee: $50. Electronic applications accepted. *Expenses:* Tuition, state resident: full-time $4428; part-time $246 per credit hour. Tuition, nonresident: full-time $8856; part-time $492 per credit hour. Required fees: $432; $24 per credit hour. $50 per term. Tuition and fees vary according to program. *Financial support:* Available to part-time students. Applicants required to submit FAFSA. *Faculty research:* Elections, religion and world politics, terrorism. *Unit head:* Dr. Charles Krupnick, Department Chairman, 334-670-5968, Fax: 334-670-5647, E-mail: ckrupnick@troy.edu. *Application contact:* Brenda K. Campbell, Director of Graduate Admissions, 334-670-3178, Fax: 334-670-3733, E-mail: bcamp@troy.edu.

Tufts University, Fletcher School of Law and Diplomacy, Medford, MA 02155. Offers LL M, MA, MAHA, MALD, MIB, PhD, DVM/MA, JD/MALD, MALD/MA, MALD/MBA, MALD/MS, MD/MA. Postbaccalaureate distance learning degree programs offered (minimal on-campus study). *Faculty:* 37 full-time (10 women), 48 part-time/adjunct (14 women). *Students:* 541 full-time (278 women), 9 part-time (3 women); includes 73 minority (8 Black or African American, non-Hispanic/Latino; 30 Asian, non-Hispanic/Latino; 11 Hispanic/Latino; 24 Two or more races, non-Hispanic/Latino), 208 international. Average age 31. 1,875 applicants, 41% accepted, 296 enrolled. In 2010, 297 master's, 14 doctorates awarded. *Degree requirements:* For master's, one foreign language, thesis; for doctorate, one foreign language, comprehensive exam, thesis/dissertation, dissertation defense. *Entrance requirements:* For master's and doctorate, GMAT or GRE General Test. Additional exam requirements/recommendations for international students: Required—TOEFL (minimum score 600 paper-based; 250 computer-based; 100 iBT), IELTS (minimum score 7). *Application deadline:* For fall admission, 1/15 for domestic and international students; for spring admission, 10/15 for domestic and international students. Application fee: $70. Electronic applications accepted. *Expenses:* Contact institution. *Financial support:* Federal Work-Study, institutionally sponsored loans, scholarships/grants, and tuition waivers (partial) available. Financial award application deadline: 1/15; financial award applicants required to submit FAFSA. *Faculty research:* Negotiation and conflict resolution, international organizations, international business and economic law, security studies, development economics. *Unit head:* Stephen W. Bosworth, Dean, 617-627-3050, Fax: 617-627-3712. *Application contact:* Laurie A. Hurley, 617-627-3040, E-mail: fletcheradmissions@tufts.edu.

United States International University, School of Arts and Sciences, Nairobi, Kenya. Offers counseling psychology (MA), including chemical dependency, health psychology; international relations (MA), including development studies, diplomacy and foreign policy, peace and conflict studies. Part-time and evening/weekend programs available. *Faculty:* 43 full-time (14 women), 69 part-time/adjunct (28 women). *Students:* 94 full-time (60 women), 22 part-time (all women). Average age 30. 93 applicants, 80% accepted, 64 enrolled. In 2010, 33 master's awarded. *Degree requirements:* For master's, thesis, practicum. *Entrance requirements:* For master's, GRE General Test, 2 letters of recommendation, resume. Additional exam requirements/recommendations for international students: Required—TOEFL. *Application deadline:* For fall admission, 6/30 priority date for domestic and international students. Application fee: $50. *Financial support:* In 2010–11, 56 students received support, including 3 research assistantships (averaging $1,400 per year), 7 teaching assistantships (averaging $1,400 per year); career-related internships or fieldwork, scholarships/grants, and unspecified assistantships also available. Support available to part-time students. Financial award application deadline: 6/30; financial award applicants required to submit FAFSA. *Faculty research:* Trauma in children, African intellectualism, psychological assessment tools. *Unit head:* Prof. Mulinge Munyae, Dean, 254-02-3606-434, E-mail: mmulinge@usiu.ac.ke. *Application contact:* George Lumbasi, Director of Admissions, 254-02-3606563, Fax: 254-02-3606100, E-mail: glumbasi@usiu.ac.ke.

Universidad de las Americas, A.C., Program in International Organizations and Institutions, Mexico City, Mexico. Offers MA.

Universidad Nacional Pedro Henriquez Urena, Graduate School, Santo Domingo, Dominican Republic. Offers agricultural diversity (MS), including horticultural/fruit production, tropical animal production; conservation of monuments and cultural assets (M Arch); ecology and environment (MS); environmental engineering (MEE); international relations (MA); natural resource management (MS); political science (MA); project optimization (MPM); project feasibility (MPM); project management (MPM); sanitation engineering (ME); science for teachers (MS); tropical Caribbean architecture (M Arch).

Université de Montréal, Faculty of Arts and Sciences, Programs in International Studies, Montréal, QC H3C 3J7, Canada. Offers M Sc, DESS.

Université Laval, Québec Institute for Advanced International Studies, Program in International Relations, Québec, QC G1K 7P4, Canada. Offers MA, PhD. *Degree requirements:* For master's, thesis (for some programs). *Entrance requirements:* For master's, English exam, French exam. Electronic applications accepted.

University of Bridgeport, International College, Bridgeport, CT 06604. Offers global development and peace (MA). Part-time and evening/weekend programs available. *Degree requirements:* For master's, thesis. *Entrance requirements:* Additional exam requirements/recommendations for international students: Recommended—TOEFL (minimum score 550 paper-based; 213 computer-based; 80 iBT), IELTS (minimum score 6.5). *Expenses:* Tuition: Full-time $22,000; part-time $575 per credit hour. Required fees: $90 per semester. Tuition and fees vary according to course level, course load and program.

The University of British Columbia, Institute of Asian Research, Vancouver, BC V6T 1Z2, Canada. Offers MAPPS. *Degree requirements:* For master's, thesis optional. *Entrance requirements:* Additional exam requirements/recommendations for international students: Required—TOEFL (minimum score 600 paper-based; 250 computer-based; 100 iBT), GRE (recommended). Electronic applications accepted. Tuition charges are reported in Canadian dollars. *Expenses:* Tuition, area resident: full-time $4179 Canadian dollars. International tuition: $7344 Canadian dollars full-time. *Faculty research:* Social cohesion, globalization, social safety nets, policy research, research and development alliances, knowledge-based workshops on Asia-Pacific studies.

University of California, Berkeley, Graduate Division, Group in International and Area Studies, Berkeley, CA 94720-1500. Offers MA, PhD, JD/MA, MBA/MA, MJ/MA.

University of California, Berkeley, Graduate Division, Haas School of Business and Group in International and Area Studies, MBA/MA Program in International and Area Studies, Berkeley, CA 94720-1500. Offers MBA/MA. *Accreditation:* AACSB. *Entrance requirements:* Additional exam requirements/recommendations for international students: Required—TOEFL. *Application fee:* $200. *Financial support:* Fellowships with full tuition reimbursements, research assistantships, teaching assistantships with partial tuition reimbursements, career-related internships or

International Affairs

University of California, Berkeley (continued)
fieldwork, scholarships/grants, and unspecified assistantships available. Financial award application deadline: 3/1; financial award applicants required to submit FAFSA. *Unit head:* Julia Hwang, Director, MBA Program, 510-642-1405, Fax: 510-643-6659, E-mail: julia_hwang@haas.berkeley.edu. *Application contact:* 510-642-1405, Fax: 510-643-6659.

University of California, San Diego, Office of Graduate Studies, Department of Economics, La Jolla, CA 92093. Offers economics (PhD); economics and international affairs (PhD). *Degree requirements:* For doctorate, thesis/dissertation. *Entrance requirements:* For doctorate, GRE General Test. Electronic applications accepted. *Faculty research:* Microfoundations of macroeconomics, econometric model specification and testing, industrial organization.

University of California, San Diego, Office of Graduate Studies, Department of Political Science, La Jolla, CA 92093. Offers Latin American studies (MA); political science (PhD); political science and international affairs (PhD). *Entrance requirements:* For master's and doctorate, GRE General Test. Electronic applications accepted.

University of California, San Diego, Office of Graduate Studies, Graduate School of International Relations and Pacific Studies, La Jolla, CA 92093. Offers economics and international affairs (PhD); Pacific international affairs (MPIA); political science and international affairs (PhD). *Degree requirements:* For master's, one foreign language; for doctorate, thesis/dissertation. *Entrance requirements:* For master's, GMAT or GRE General Test; for doctorate, GRE General Test. Additional exam requirements/recommendations for international students: Required—TOEFL (minimum score 550 paper-based; 213 computer-based). Electronic applications accepted. *Faculty research:* Pacific Rim as system and placement in global relations; studies in international economics, management and finance; analysis of patterns of policymaking in countries of the Pacific.

University of California, Santa Barbara, Graduate Division, College of Letters and Sciences, Division of Humanities and Fine Arts, Department of English, Santa Barbara, CA 93106-3170. Offers English (PhD); European medieval studies (PhD); feminist studies (PhD); global studies (PhD); technology and society (PhD); MA/PhD. *Faculty:* 26 full-time (13 women), 17 part-time/adjunct (12 women). *Students:* 68 full-time (37 women); includes 2 Black or African American, non-Hispanic/Latino; 5 Asian, non-Hispanic/Latino; 2 Hispanic/Latino. Average age 30. 173 applicants, 12% accepted, 8 enrolled. In 2010, 4 doctorates awarded. Terminal master's awarded for partial completion of doctoral program. *Degree requirements:* For doctorate, one foreign language, comprehensive exam, thesis/dissertation. *Entrance requirements:* For doctorate, GRE General Test, GRE Subject Test (English). Additional exam requirements/recommendations for international students: Required—TOEFL (minimum score 550 paper-based; 80 iBT), IELTS (minimum score 7). *Application deadline:* For fall admission, 12/15 priority date for domestic and international students. Application fee: $70 ($90 for international students). Electronic applications accepted. *Financial support:* In 2010–11, 68 students received support, including 38 fellowships with full and partial tuition reimbursements available (averaging $9,204 per year), 3 research assistantships with full and partial tuition reimbursements available (averaging $10,512 per year), 50 teaching assistantships with full and partial tuition reimbursements available (averaging $13,031 per year); career-related internships or fieldwork and tuition waivers (full and partial) also available. Financial award application deadline: 12/15; financial award applicants required to submit FAFSA. *Faculty research:* Medieval, Romantic, and Victorian studies; gender studies and feminist theory; literature and the mind; American literature; literature and new media/information culture. Total annual research expenditures: $25,000. *Unit head:* Prof. Ken Hiltner, Graduate Program Chair, 805-564-2304, Fax: 805-893-7492, E-mail: hiltner@english.ucsb.edu. *Application contact:* Mary Rae Staton, Graduate Program Staff Advisor, 805-893-2639, Fax: 805-893-7492, E-mail: staton@hfa.ucsb.edu.

University of California, Santa Barbara, Graduate Division, College of Letters and Sciences, Division of Humanities and Fine Arts, Department of Film and Media Studies, Santa Barbara, CA 93106-4010. Offers film and media studies (PhD); global studies (PhD); technology and society (PhD); MA/PhD. *Faculty:* 28 full-time (15 women). *Students:* 29 full-time (16 women); includes 4 Asian, non-Hispanic/Latino; 1 Hispanic/Latino. Average age 27. 106 applicants, 9% accepted, 5 enrolled. In 2010, 1 doctorate awarded. Terminal master's awarded for partial completion of doctoral program. *Degree requirements:* For doctorate, one foreign language, comprehensive exam, thesis/dissertation. *Entrance requirements:* For doctorate, GRE. Additional exam requirements/recommendations for international students: Required—TOEFL (minimum score 600 paper-based; 100 iBT), IELTS (minimum score 7). *Application deadline:* For fall admission, 12/1 priority date for domestic and international students. Application fee: $70 ($90 for international students). Electronic applications accepted. *Financial support:* In 2010–11, 23 students received support, including 10 fellowships with full tuition reimbursements available (averaging $17,143 per year), 3 research assistantships with full and partial tuition reimbursements available (averaging $11,893 per year), 17 teaching assistantships with partial tuition reimbursements available (averaging $11,254 per year). Financial award application deadline: 12/1; financial award applicants required to submit FAFSA. *Faculty research:* Classical film theory, film and television history, historiography, cultural studies, global media, media industries, regulation and policy. *Unit head:* Prof. Lisa Parks, Chair, 805-893-2120, Fax: 805-893-8630, E-mail: parks@filmandmedia.ucsb.edu. *Application contact:* Melany J. Miners, Graduate Program Assistant, 805-893-8535, Fax: 805-893-8630, E-mail: mminers@filmandmedia.ucsb.edu.

University of California, Santa Barbara, Graduate Division, College of Letters and Sciences, Division of Humanities and Fine Arts, Department of History, Santa Barbara, CA 93106-9410. Offers ancient Mediterranean studies (PhD); European medieval studies (PhD); feminist studies (PhD); global studies (PhD); history (PhD); public history (PhD); technology and society (PhD); MA/PhD. *Faculty:* 42 full-time (18 women), 10 part-time/adjunct (6 women). *Students:* 92 full-time (50 women); includes 1 Black or African American, non-Hispanic/Latino; 6 Asian, non-Hispanic/Latino; 11 Hispanic/Latino. Average age 34. 124 applicants, 19% accepted, 8 enrolled. In 2010, 20 doctorates awarded. *Degree requirements:* For doctorate, variable foreign language requirement, comprehensive exam, thesis/dissertation. *Entrance requirements:* For doctorate, GRE. Additional exam requirements/recommendations for international students: Required—TOEFL (minimum score 550 paper-based; 80 iBT), IELTS (minimum score 7). *Application deadline:* For fall admission, 12/5 priority date for domestic and international students. Application fee: $70 ($90 for international students). Electronic applications accepted. *Financial support:* In 2010–11, 92 students received support, including 68 fellowships with full and partial tuition reimbursements available (averaging $6,583 per year), 4 research assistantships with full and partial tuition reimbursements available (averaging $5,862 per year), 57 teaching assistantships with full and partial tuition reimbursements available (averaging $12,123 per year); tuition waivers (partial) also available. Financial award application deadline: 12/5; financial award applicants required to submit FAFSA. *Faculty research:* Europe, U. S., Latin America, Africa, Middle East, East Asia. *Unit head:* John Majewski, Chair, 805-893-2837, E-mail: majewski@history.ucrb.edu. *Application contact:* Sharon Farmer, Director of Graduate Studies, 805-893-3398, E-mail: farmer@history.ucsb.edu.

University of California, Santa Barbara, Graduate Division, College of Letters and Sciences, Division of Humanities and Fine Arts, Department of Religious Studies, Santa Barbara, CA 93106-3130. Offers ancient Mediterranean studies (PhD); European medieval studies (PhD); feminist studies (PhD); global studies (PhD); religious studies (MA, PhD); translation studies (PhD); MA/PhD. *Faculty:* 19 full-time (9 women), 8 part-time/adjunct (3 women). *Students:* 79 full-time (29 women); includes 2 Black or African American, non-Hispanic/Latino; 1 American Indian or Alaska Native, non-Hispanic/Latino; 9 Asian, non-Hispanic/Latino; 5 Hispanic/Latino. Average age 31. 139 applicants, 22% accepted, 10 enrolled. In 2010, 11 master's, 10 doctorates awarded. *Degree requirements:* For master's, one foreign language, comprehensive exam (for some programs), thesis (for some programs), colloquium; for doctorate, one foreign language, thesis/dissertation, methodology, colloquium. *Entrance requirements:* For master's and doctorate, GRE General Test. Additional exam requirements/recommendations for international students: Required—TOEFL (minimum score 550 paper-based; 80 iBT), IELTS (minimum score 7). *Application deadline:* For fall admission, 12/1 for domestic and international students. Application fee: $70 ($90 for international students). Electronic applications accepted. *Financial support:* In 2010–11, 64 students received support, including 31 fellowships with full tuition reimbursements available (averaging $12,351 per year), 4 research assistantships with full and partial tuition reimbursements available (averaging $4,147 per year), 37 teaching assistantships with partial tuition reimbursements available (averaging $9,573 per year); career-related internships or fieldwork, scholarships/grants, tuition waivers (full and partial), and associateships also available. Financial award application deadline: 12/1; financial award applicants required to submit FAFSA. *Faculty research:* Area studies; religious traditions; theory and method in the study of religion; religion, culture, and politics; spirituality and religious experience. *Unit head:* Prof. Jose I. Cabezon, Professor and Chair, 805-893-3564, Fax: 805-893-7671, E-mail: jcabezon@religion.ucsb.edu. *Application contact:* Sally J. Lombrozo, Graduate Program Assistant, 805-893-2744, Fax: 805-893-7671, E-mail: lombrozo@hfa.ucsb.edu.

University of California, Santa Barbara, Graduate Division, College of Letters and Sciences, Division of Humanities and Fine Arts, Program in Comparative Literature, Santa Barbara, CA 93106-4130. Offers comparative literature (PhD); East Asian literatures (PhD); feminist studies (PhD); French (PhD); global studies (PhD); translation studies (PhD); MA/PhD. *Faculty:* 63 full-time (31 women). *Students:* 21 full-time (14 women); includes 3 Asian, non-Hispanic/Latino; 2 Hispanic/Latino. Average age 31. 41 applicants, 12% accepted, 2 enrolled. In 2010, 1 doctorate awarded. *Degree requirements:* For doctorate, 2 foreign languages, comprehensive exam, thesis/dissertation. *Entrance requirements:* For doctorate, GRE. Additional exam requirements/recommendations for international students: Required—TOEFL (minimum score 550 paper-based; 80 iBT), IELTS (minimum score 7). *Application deadline:* For fall admission, 12/15 for domestic and international students. Application fee: $70 ($90 for international students). Electronic applications accepted. *Financial support:* In 2010–11, 19 students received support, including 14 fellowships with full and partial tuition reimbursements available (averaging $16,232 per year), 12 teaching assistantships with partial tuition reimbursements available (averaging $12,826 per year); research assistantships, Federal Work-Study, institutionally sponsored loans, scholarships/grants, health care benefits, and tuition waivers (full and partial) also available. Financial award application deadline: 12/15; financial award applicants required to submit FAFSA. *Faculty research:* Comparative literary studies in global context, critical theory, translation studies, mediatechnological studies, trauma studies. *Unit head:* Prof. Susan Derwin, Chair, 805-893-4399, Fax: 805-893-8341, E-mail: derwin@gss.ucsb.edu. *Application contact:* Ashley Bradbury, Graduate Program Assistant, 805-893-2131, Fax: 805-893-8341, E-mail: ashley@hfa.ucsb.edu.

University of California, Santa Barbara, Graduate Division, College of Letters and Sciences, Division of Social Sciences, Department of Global and International Studies, Santa Barbara, CA 93106-7065. Offers global culture and religion (MA); global government and human rights (MA); political economy, sustainable development, and the environment (MA). *Faculty:* 14 full-time (5 women), 4 part-time/adjunct (1 woman). *Students:* 37 full-time (25 women); includes 6 Asian, non-Hispanic/Latino; 2 Hispanic/Latino; 1 Native Hawaiian or other Pacific Islander, non-Hispanic/Latino. Average age 28. 55 applicants, 42% accepted, 12 enrolled. In 2010, 14 master's awarded. *Degree requirements:* For master's, one foreign language, thesis or alternative, 2 years of a second language. *Entrance requirements:* For master's, GRE, 2 years of a second language with minimum B grade, 3 letters of recommendation, resume/curriculum vitae. Additional exam requirements/recommendations for international students: Required—TOEFL (minimum score 600 paper-based; 80 iBT), IELTS (minimum score 7). *Application deadline:* For fall admission, 12/15 for domestic and international students. Application fee: $70 ($90 for international students). Electronic applications accepted. *Financial support:* In 2010–11, 36 students received support, including 29 fellowships with partial tuition reimbursements available (averaging $6,805 per year), 31 teaching assistantships with partial tuition reimbursements available (averaging $8,175 per year); career-related internships or fieldwork also available. Financial award application deadline: 12/15; financial award applicants required to submit FAFSA. *Faculty research:* Global culture religion, global governance human rights, political economy, environment, sustainable development. Total annual research expenditures: $240,000. *Unit head:* Prof. Giles Gunn, Chair, 805-893-4299, Fax: 805-893-8003, E-mail: ggunn@global.ucsb.edu. *Application contact:* Jessea Gay Marie, Graduate Program Advisor/Internship Assistance Officer, 805-893-4668, Fax: 805-893-8003, E-mail: gd-global@global.ucsb.edu.

University of California, Santa Barbara, Graduate Division, College of Letters and Sciences, Division of Social Sciences, Department of Sociology, Santa Barbara, CA 93106-9430. Offers feminist studies (PhD); global studies (PhD); language, interaction and social organization (PhD); quantitative methods in the social sciences (PhD); technology and society (PhD); MA/PhD. *Faculty:* 35 full-time (14 women). *Students:* 71 full-time (44 women); includes 5 Black or African American, non-Hispanic/Latino; 4 Asian, non-Hispanic/Latino; 21 Hispanic/Latino. Average age 30. 162 applicants, 8% accepted, 6 enrolled. In 2010, 13 doctorates awarded. Terminal master's awarded for partial completion of doctoral program. *Degree requirements:* For doctorate, comprehensive exam, thesis/dissertation. *Entrance requirements:* For doctorate, GRE General Test. Additional exam requirements/recommendations for international students: Required—TOEFL (minimum score 550 paper-based; 80 iBT), IELTS (minimum score 7). *Application deadline:* For fall admission, 12/1 for domestic and international students. Application fee: $70 ($90 for international students). Electronic applications accepted. *Financial support:* In 2010–11, 60 students received support, including 40 fellowships with full and partial tuition reimbursements available (averaging $10,059 per year), 4 research assistantships with full and partial tuition reimbursements available (averaging $10,166 per year), 43 teaching assistantships with full and partial tuition reimbursements available (averaging $11,913 per year); career-related internships or fieldwork, Federal Work-Study, institutionally sponsored loans, scholarships/grants, health care benefits, tuition waivers (full and partial), and unspecified assistantships also available. Financial award application deadline: 12/1. *Faculty research:* Feminist studies/sexualities, race ethnicity, global, culture, conversation analysis. *Unit head:* Prof. Verta Taylor, Chair, 805-893-3118, Fax: 805-893-3324. *Application contact:* Sharon Applegate, Graduate Program Assistant, 805-893-3328, Fax: 805-893-3324, E-mail: grad-soc@soc.ucsb.edu.

University of California, Santa Cruz, Division of Graduate Studies, Division of Social Sciences, Program in International Economics, Santa Cruz, CA 95064. Offers PhD. *Students:* 62 full-time (24 women), 1 (woman) part-time; includes 12 minority (1 Black or African American, non-Hispanic/Latino; 4 Asian, non-Hispanic/Latino; 7 Hispanic/Latino), 31 international. Average age 32. 133 applicants, 47% accepted, 15 enrolled. In 2010, 9 doctorates awarded. *Degree requirements:* For doctorate, thesis/dissertation, 4 field exams, field papers, econometrics project, qualifying exams. *Entrance requirements:* For doctorate, GRE General Test. Additional exam requirements/recommendations for international students: Required—TOEFL (minimum score 550 paper-based; 220 computer-based; 83 iBT); Recommended—IELTS (minimum score 8). *Application deadline:* For fall admission, 1/15 for domestic and international students. Application fee: $70 ($90 for international students). Electronic applications accepted. *Financial support:* Fellowships, research assistantships, teaching assistantships, institutionally sponsored loans and tuition waivers (partial) available. Financial award applicants required to submit FAFSA. *Faculty research:* Current and emerging issues in taxation, industrial policy, environmental regulation, market structure, labor economics focus on behavior and adjustment in an interdependent world economy. *Unit head:* Sandra Reebie, Graduate Program Coordinator, 831-459-2219, E-mail: screebie@ucsc.edu. *Application contact:* Sandra Reebie, Graduate Program Coordinator, 831-459-2219, E-mail: screebie@ucsc.edu.

University of Central Oklahoma, College of Graduate Studies and Research, College of Liberal Arts, Department of Political Science, Program in International Affairs, Edmond, OK 73034-5209. Offers MA. Part-time programs available. *Entrance requirements:* Additional exam requirements/recommendations for international students: Required—TOEFL (minimum score 550 paper-based; 213 computer-based). Electronic applications accepted. *Faculty research:* Korean and Japanese politics.

University of Chicago, Division of Social Sciences, Committee on International Relations, Chicago, IL 60637-1513. Offers AM, MBA/AM. Part-time programs available. *Degree* *requirements:* For master's, thesis. *Entrance requirements:* For master's, GRE General Test. Additional exam requirements/recommendations for international students: Required—TOEFL. Electronic applications accepted.

University of Colorado Boulder, Graduate School, College of Arts and Sciences, Department of Political Science, Boulder, CO 80309. Offers international affairs (MA); political science (MA, PhD); public policy (MA). *Faculty:* 27 full-time (9 women). *Students:* 65 full-time (31 women), 2 part-time (0 women); includes 7 minority (2 American Indian or Alaska Native, non-Hispanic/Latino; 2 Asian, non-Hispanic/Latino; 3 Hispanic/Latino), 7 international. Average age 30. 184 applicants, 15 enrolled. In 2010, 23 master's, 6 doctorates awarded. Terminal master's awarded for partial completion of doctoral program. *Degree requirements:* For master's, comprehensive exam, thesis; for doctorate, one foreign language, thesis/dissertation. *Entrance requirements:* For master's, GRE General Test, minimum undergraduate GPA of 3.0; for doctorate, GRE General Test, minimum GPA of 3.5 (undergraduate), 3.0 (graduate). *Application deadline:* For fall admission, 12/31 priority date for domestic students, 12/31 for international students. Application fee: $50 ($60 for international students). *Financial support:* In 2010–11, 10 fellowships (averaging $2,060 per year), 41 research assistantships (averaging $12,087 per year) were awarded; Federal Work-Study also available. Financial award application deadline: 12/31. *Faculty research:* American government and politics, comparative politics, international relations, public policy, law and politics, political philosophy, empirical theory and methodology. Total annual research expenditures: $92,305.

University of Colorado Denver, College of Liberal Arts and Sciences, Program in Humanities, Denver, CO 80217-3364. Offers community health science (MSS); humanities (MH); international studies (MSS); social science (MSS); society and the environment (MSS); women's and gender studies (MSS). Part-time and evening/weekend programs available. *Students:* 53 full-time (39 women), 35 part-time (22 women); includes 4 Black or African American, non-Hispanic/Latino; 1 American Indian or Alaska Native, non-Hispanic/Latino; 3 Asian, non-Hispanic/Latino; 7 Hispanic/Latino, 1 international. Average age 33. 41 applicants, 54% accepted, 19 enrolled. In 2010, 29 master's awarded. *Degree requirements:* For master's, thesis or alternative, 36 credit hours, project or thesis. *Entrance requirements:* For master's, writing sample, statement of purpose/letter of intent. Additional exam requirements/recommendations for international students: Required—TOEFL (minimum score 525 paper-based). *Application deadline:* For fall admission, 5/15 priority date for domestic students; for spring admission, 10/15 priority date for domestic students. Application fee: $50 ($75 for international students). Electronic applications accepted. *Expenses:* Tuition, state resident: full-time $7332; part-time $355 per credit hour. Tuition, nonresident: full-time $18,990; part-time $1055 per credit hour. Required fees: $998. Tuition and fees vary according to course level, course load, degree level, campus/location, program, reciprocity agreements and student level. *Financial support:* Federal Work-Study and scholarships/grants available. Financial award application deadline: 4/1; financial award applicants required to submit FAFSA. *Faculty research:* Women and gender in the classical Mediterranean, communication theory and democracy, relationship between psychology and philosophy. *Unit head:* Myra Bookman, Associate Director of Humanities and Social Science, 303-556-2496, Fax: 303-556-8100, E-mail: myra.bookman@ucdenver.edu. *Application contact:* Catherine Osmundson, Program Assistant, 303-556-2305, E-mail: catherine.osmundson@ucdenver.edu.

University of Connecticut, Graduate School, College of Liberal Arts and Sciences, Field of International Studies, Program in International Studies, Storrs, CT 06269. Offers MA. *Degree requirements:* For master's, comprehensive exam. *Entrance requirements:* For master's, GRE General Test. Additional exam requirements/recommendations for international students: Required—TOEFL (minimum score 550 paper-based; 213 computer-based). Electronic applications accepted.

University of Delaware, College of Arts and Sciences, Department of Political Science and International Relations, Newark, DE 19716. Offers MA, PhD. Terminal master's awarded for partial completion of doctoral program. *Degree requirements:* For master's, research paper; for doctorate, one foreign language, comprehensive exam, thesis/dissertation. *Entrance requirements:* For master's and doctorate, GRE General Test, minimum GPA of 3.2 in major, 3.0 overall. Additional exam requirements/recommendations for international students: Required—TOEFL (minimum score 600 paper-based). Electronic applications accepted. *Faculty research:* Social constructivism. international migration, international security, democratization, human rights.

University of Denver, Division of Arts, Humanities and Social Sciences, Department of Media, Film and Journalism Studies, Denver, CO 80208. Offers advertising management (MS); digital media studies (MA); international and intercultural communication (MA); media, film, and journalism studies (MA); strategic communication (MS). Part-time programs available. *Faculty:* 14 full-time (7 women), 5 part-time/adjunct (3 women). *Students:* 28 full-time (24 women), 36 part-time (26 women); includes 12 minority (1 Black or African American, non-Hispanic/Latino; 3 Asian, non-Hispanic/Latino; 6 Hispanic/Latino; 2 Two or more races, non-Hispanic/Latino), 2 international. Average age 26. 155 applicants, 58% accepted, 32 enrolled. In 2010, 36 master's awarded. *Degree requirements:* For master's, thesis (for some programs). *Entrance requirements:* For master's, GRE General Test. Additional exam requirements/recommendations for international students: Required—TOEFL (minimum score 550 paper-based; 80 iBT). *Application deadline:* Applications are processed on a rolling basis. Application fee: $60. Electronic applications accepted. *Expenses:* Tuition: Full-time $35,604; part-time $29,670 per year. Required fees: $687 per year. Tuition and fees vary according to program. *Financial support:* In 2010–11, 4 teaching assistantships with full and partial tuition reimbursements (averaging $14,000 per year) were awarded; career-related internships or fieldwork, Federal Work-Study, institutionally sponsored loans, scholarships/grants, and unspecified assistantships also available. Support available to part-time students. Financial award application deadline: 3/1; financial award applicants required to submit FAFSA. *Faculty research:* Youth and civic engagement. *Unit head:* Dr. Renee Botta, Chair, 303-871-7918, Fax: 303-871-4949, E-mail: rbotta@du.edu. *Application contact:* Information Contact, 303-871-2166, E-mail: mfjs@du.edu.

University of Denver, Josef Korbel School of International Studies, Denver, CO 80208. Offers conflict resolution (MA); development practice (MDP); global finance, trade and economic integration (MA); global health affairs (Certificate); homeland security (Certificate); humanitarian assistance (Certificate); international development (MA); international human rights (MA); international security (MA); international studies (MA, PhD). Part-time programs available. *Faculty:* 33 full-time (13 women), 38 part-time/adjunct (11 women). *Students:* 461 full-time (279 women), 52 part-time (27 women); includes 71 minority (8 Black or African American, non-Hispanic/Latino; 3 American Indian or Alaska Native, non-Hispanic/Latino; 25 Asian, non-Hispanic/Latino; 25 Hispanic/Latino; 2 Native Hawaiian or other Pacific Islander, non-Hispanic/Latino; 8 Two or more races, non-Hispanic/Latino), 42 international. Average age 28. 1,056 applicants, 69% accepted, 259 enrolled. In 2010, 230 master's, 5 doctorates, 42 other advanced degrees awarded. *Degree requirements:* For master's, one foreign language, thesis; for doctorate, one foreign language, thesis/dissertation. *Entrance requirements:* For master's and doctorate, GRE General Test. Additional exam requirements/recommendations for international students: Required—TOEFL (minimum score 587 paper-based; 95 iBT). *Application deadline:* For fall admission, 1/15 priority date for domestic students, 12/15 priority date for international students; for winter admission, 10/15 priority date for domestic and international students. Applications are processed on a rolling basis. Application fee: $60. Electronic applications accepted. *Expenses:* Tuition: Full-time $35,604; part-time $29,670 per year. Required fees: $687 per year. Tuition and fees vary according to program. *Financial support:* In 2010–11, 1 teaching assistantship with partial tuition reimbursement (averaging $9,999 per year) was awarded; career-related internships or fieldwork, Federal Work-Study, institutionally sponsored loans, scholarships/grants, and unspecified assistantships also available. Support available to part-time students. Financial award applicants required to submit FAFSA. *Faculty research:* Human rights and international security, international politics and economics, economic-social and political development, international technology analysis and management. *Unit head:* Ambassador Christopher R. Hill, Dean, 303-871-2539, Fax: 303-871-2124, E-mail: christopher.r.hill@du.edu. *Application contact:* Brad Miller, Director of Graduate Admissions and Financial Aid, 303-871-2989, Fax: 303-871-2124, E-mail: korbeladm@du.edu.

University of Denver, University College, Denver, CO 80208. Offers arts and culture (MLS, Certificate), including art, literature, and culture, arts development and program management (Certificate), creative writing; environmental policy and management (MAS, Certificate), including energy and sustainability (Certificate), environmental assessment of nuclear power (Certificate), environmental health and safety (Certificate), environmental management, natural resource management (Certificate); geographic information systems (MAS, Certificate); global affairs (MLS, Certificate), including translation studies, world history and culture; healthcare leadership (MPH, Certificate), including healthcare policy, law, and ethics, medical and healthcare information technologies, strategic management of healthcare; information and communications technology (MCIS, Certificate), including database design and administration (Certificate), geographic information systems (MCIS), information security systems security (Certificate), information systems security (MCIS), project management (MCIS, MPS, Certificate), software design and administration (Certificate), software design and programming (MCIS), technology management, telecommunications technology (MCIS), Web design and development; leadership and organizations (MPS, Certificate), including human capital in organizations, philanthropic leadership, project management (MCIS, MPS, Certificate), strategic innovation and change; organizational and professional communication (MPS, Certificate), including alternative dispute resolution, organizational communication, organizational development and training, public relations and marketing; security management (MAS, Certificate), including emergency planning and response, information security (MAS), organizational security; strategic human resource management (MPS, Certificate), including global human resources (MPS), human resource management and development (MPS). Part-time and evening/weekend programs available. Postbaccalaureate distance learning degree programs offered (no on-campus study). *Faculty:* 7 full-time (2 women), 212 part-time/adjunct (83 women). *Students:* 52 full-time (19 women), 1,044 part-time (625 women); includes 196 minority (81 Black or African American, non-Hispanic/Latino; 7 American Indian or Alaska Native, non-Hispanic/Latino; 30 Asian, non-Hispanic/Latino; 66 Hispanic/Latino; 3 Native Hawaiian or other Pacific Islander, non-Hispanic/Latino; 9 Two or more races, non-Hispanic/Latino), 76 international. Average age 36. 488 applicants, 91% accepted, 339 enrolled. In 2010, 286 master's, 130 other advanced degrees awarded. *Entrance requirements:* Additional exam requirements/recommendations for international students: Required—TOEFL (minimum score 550 paper-based; 80 iBT). *Application deadline:* For fall admission, 6/22 priority date for domestic students, 6/10 priority date for international students; for winter admission, 9/15 priority date for domestic students, 9/6 priority date for international students; for spring admission, 2/3 priority date for domestic students, 12/15 priority date for international students. Applications are processed on a rolling basis. Application fee: $75. Electronic applications accepted. *Expenses:* Contact institution. *Financial support:* Applicants required to submit FAFSA. *Unit head:* Dr. James Davis, Dean, 303-871-2291, Fax: 303-871-4047, E-mail: jdavis@du.edu. *Application contact:* Information Contact, 303-871-3155, Fax: 303-871-4047, E-mail: ucolinfo@du.edu.

University of Florida, Graduate School, College of Liberal Arts and Sciences, Department of Political Science, Program in International Relations, Gainesville, FL 32611. Offers MA, MAT. *Students:* 7 full-time (3 women), 1 part-time (0 women); includes 1 Black or African American, non-Hispanic/Latino; 1 Asian, non-Hispanic/Latino; 1 Hispanic/Latino. Average age 26. 48 applicants, 21% accepted, 4 enrolled. In 2010, 1 master's awarded. *Degree requirements:* For master's, comprehensive exam (for some programs), thesis optional. *Entrance requirements:* For master's, GRE General Test, minimum GPA of 3.0. Additional exam requirements/recommendations for international students: Required—TOEFL (minimum score 550 paper-based; 213 computer-based; 80 iBT), IELTS (minimum score 6). *Application deadline:* For fall admission, 3/1 priority date for domestic students, 3/1 for international students. Applications are processed on a rolling basis. Application fee: $30. Electronic applications accepted. *Expenses:* Tuition, state resident: full-time $10,915.92. Tuition, nonresident: full-time $28,309. *Faculty research:* International relations theory, international political economy, feminist international relations, international security, international organization. *Unit head:* Dr. Michael D. Martinez, Chair, 352-273-2363, Fax: 352-392-8127, E-mail: martinez@ufl.edu. *Application contact:* Dr. Scott K. Griffiths, Graduate Coordinator, 352-273-3725, Fax: 352-392-8127, E-mail: sgriff@ufl.edu.

University of Hawaii at Manoa, Graduate Division, International Cultural Studies Graduate Certificate Program, Honolulu, HI 96822. Offers Graduate Certificate. Part-time programs available. *Students:* 15 full-time (10 women), 3 part-time (0 women); includes 7 minority (1 American Indian or Alaska Native, non-Hispanic/Latino; 1 Asian, non-Hispanic/Latino; 1 Hispanic/Latino; 2 Native Hawaiian or other Pacific Islander, non-Hispanic/Latino; 2 Two or more races, non-Hispanic/Latino), 5 international. Average age 34. 20 applicants, 70% accepted, 8 enrolled. In 2010, 10 Graduate Certificates awarded. *Entrance requirements:* For degree, GRE General Test. Additional exam requirements/recommendations for international students: Required—TOEFL (minimum score 540 paper-based; 207 computer-based; 76 iBT), IELTS (minimum score 5). *Application deadline:* For fall admission, 3/1 for domestic and international students; for spring admission, 9/1 for domestic and international students. Application fee: $50. *Financial support:* In 2010–11, 3 fellowships (averaging $1,325 per year), 3 research assistantships (averaging $17,496 per year), 5 teaching assistantships (averaging $15,438 per year) were awarded. *Application contact:* Wimal Dissanayake, Graduate Chairperson, 808-944-7593, Fax: 808-956-4733, E-mail: ddissa@yahoo.edu.

University of Indianapolis, Graduate Programs, College of Arts and Sciences, Department of History and Political Science, Indianapolis, IN 46227-3697. Offers history (MA); international relations (MA). Part-time and evening/weekend programs available. *Faculty:* 5 full-time (2 women). *Students:* 5 full-time (1 woman), 25 part-time (15 women); includes 3 minority (2 Black or African American, non-Hispanic/Latino; 1 Hispanic/Latino), 3 international. Average age 29. In 2010, 7 master's awarded. *Degree requirements:* For master's, thesis optional. *Entrance requirements:* For master's, GRE Subject Test, minimum GPA of 3.0, 3 letters of recommendation. Additional exam requirements/recommendations for international students: Required—TOEFL (minimum score 550 paper-based; 213 computer-based). *Application deadline:* Applications are processed on a rolling basis. Application fee: $30. Electronic applications accepted. Tuition and fees vary according to course load, degree level and program. *Financial support:* Federal Work-Study, scholarships/grants, and tuition waivers (full and partial) available. Support available to part-time students. Financial award application deadline: 5/1; financial award applicants required to submit FAFSA. *Unit head:* Dr. Lawrence Sondhaus, Chairperson, 317-788-2196, Fax: 317-788-3480, E-mail: sondhaus@uindy.edu. *Application contact:* Dr. Lawrence Sondhaus, Chairperson, 317-788-2196, Fax: 317-788-3480, E-mail: sondhaus@uindy.edu.

The University of Kansas, Graduate Studies, College of Liberal Arts and Sciences, Global and International Studies Program, Lawrence, KS 66045. Offers MA. Part-time and evening/weekend programs available. *Faculty:* 3 full-time (1 woman), 4 part-time/adjunct (1 woman). *Students:* 11 full-time (4 women), 55 part-time (19 women); includes 13 minority (5 Asian, non-Hispanic/Latino; 5 Hispanic/Latino; 3 Two or more races, non-Hispanic/Latino), 3 international. Average age 33. 47 applicants, 68% accepted, 29 enrolled. In 2010, 4 master's awarded. *Degree requirements:* For master's, one foreign language, thesis or exam. *Entrance requirements:* For master's, GRE, minimum GPA of 3.0, 3 letters of reference, curriculum vitae. Additional exam requirements/recommendations for international students: Required—TOEFL. *Application deadline:* For fall admission, 4/1 priority date for domestic and international students; for spring admission, 10/1 priority date for domestic and international students. Applications are processed on a rolling basis. Application fee: $55 ($65 for international students). Electronic applications accepted. *Expenses:* Tuition, state resident: full-time $7092; part-time $295.50 per credit hour. Tuition, nonresident: full-time $16,590; part-time $691.25 per credit hour. Required fees: $858; $71.49 per credit hour. Tuition and fees vary according to course load, campus/location and program. *Financial support:* Scholarships/grants available. *Faculty research:* Globalization, environmental sociology, economic development,

International Affairs

The University of Kansas (continued)
comparative government, international relations. *Unit head:* Dr. Eric Hanley, Program Director, 785-864-1120, E-mail: hanley@ku.edu. *Application contact:* Lesley Owens, Graduate Advisor, 913-897-8510, Fax: 913-897-8491, E-mail: laowens@ku.edu.

University of Kentucky, Graduate School, Patterson School of Diplomacy and International Commerce, Lexington, KY 40506-0027. Offers MA. *Degree requirements:* For master's, one foreign language, comprehensive exam, statistics. *Entrance requirements:* For master's, GRE General Test, minimum undergraduate GPA of 3.0. Additional exam requirements/recommendations for international students: Required—TOEFL (minimum score 550 paper-based; 213 computer-based; 79 iBT). Electronic applications accepted. *Faculty research:* International relations, foreign and defense policy, cross-cultural negotiation, international science and technology, diplomacy, international economics and development, geopolitical modeling.

The University of Manchester, School of Arts, Histories and Cultures, Manchester, United Kingdom. Offers anthropology, media and performance (PhD); applied theatre professional (PhD); archaeology (PhD); art history and visual studies (PhD); arts management and cultural policy (PhD); classics and ancient history (PhD); composition (PhD); creative writing (PhD); drama (PhD); economic and social history (PhD); electroacoustic composition (PhD); English and American studies (PhD); history (PhD); humanitarianism and conflict response (PhD); museology (PhD); music (PhD); musicology (PhD); religions and theology (PhD).

University of Miami, Graduate School, College of Arts and Sciences, Department of International Studies, Coral Gables, FL 33124. Offers MA, PhD. *Degree requirements:* For master's, one foreign language, comprehensive exam; for doctorate, one foreign language, comprehensive exam, thesis/dissertation. *Entrance requirements:* For master's, GRE General Test, minimum GPA of 3.0; for doctorate, GRE General Test. Additional exam requirements/recommendations for international students: Required—TOEFL. Electronic applications accepted. *Faculty research:* Latin American studies, international economics, international security and conflict, comparative development, international health policy.

University of Miami, Graduate School, Program in International Administration, Coral Gables, FL 33124. Offers MAIA. Part-time and evening/weekend programs available. *Degree requirements:* For master's, practicum. *Entrance requirements:* For master's, GRE General Test. Additional exam requirements/recommendations for international students: Required—TOEFL (minimum score 550 paper-based; 213 computer-based), IELTS (minimum score 6.5). Electronic applications accepted.

University of Northern British Columbia, Office of Graduate Studies, Prince George, BC V2N 4Z9, Canada. Offers business administration (Diploma); community health science (M Sc); disability management (MA); education (M Ed); first nations studies (MA); gender studies (MA); history (MA); interdisciplinary studies (MA); international studies (MA); mathematical, computer and physical sciences (M Sc); natural resources and environmental studies (M Sc, MA, MNRES, PhD); political science (MA); psychology (M Sc, PhD); social work (MSW). Part-time and evening/weekend programs available. Postbaccalaureate distance learning degree programs offered (no on-campus study). *Degree requirements:* For master's, thesis; for doctorate, thesis/dissertation. *Entrance requirements:* For master's, GRE, minimum B average in undergraduate course work; for doctorate, candidacy exam, minimum A average in graduate course work.

University of Oklahoma, College of International Studies, Norman, OK 73019-0390. Offers area studies (MAIS, Graduate Certificate); global studies (MAIS, Graduate Certificate), including global economics and development, global security studies. Part-time programs available. *Faculty:* 17 full-time (5 women). *Students:* 14 full-time (4 women), 5 part-time (4 women); includes 1 minority (Asian, non-Hispanic/Latino), 2 international. Average age 26. 17 applicants, 47% accepted, 4 enrolled. In 2010, 6 master's awarded. *Degree requirements:* For master's, one foreign language, thesis optional. *Entrance requirements:* For master's, GMAT or GRE. Additional exam requirements/recommendations for international students: Required—TOEFL (minimum score 550 paper-based; 213 computer-based; 79 iBT). *Application deadline:* For fall admission, 2/15 for domestic students, 4/1 for international students; for spring admission, 10/15 for domestic students, 9/1 for international students. Applications are processed on a rolling basis. Application fee: $40 ($90 for international students). Electronic applications accepted. *Expenses:* Tuition, state resident: full-time $3893; part-time $162.20 per credit hour. Tuition, nonresident: full-time $14,167; part-time $590.30 per credit hour. Required fees: $2523; $94.60 per credit hour. Tuition and fees vary according to course load and degree level. *Financial support:* In 2010–11, 4 research assistantships (averaging $11,611 per year), 7 teaching assistantships with partial tuition reimbursements (averaging $13,616 per year) were awarded; career-related internships or fieldwork, scholarships/grants, health care benefits, tuition waivers (full), and unspecified assistantships also available. Financial award applicants required to submit FAFSA. *Faculty research:* International security studies, global economics and development, Asian studies, European studies, Latin American studies, Middle Eastern studies. Total annual research expenditures: $585,293. *Unit head:* Mark Fraizer, Director, 405-325-1584, Fax: 405-325-7738, E-mail: markfrazier@ou.edu. *Application contact:* Eric Heinze, Director of Graduate Studies, 405-325-5802, Fax: 405-325-7738, E-mail: eheinze@ou.edu.

University of Oregon, Graduate School, College of Arts and Sciences, Program in International Studies, Eugene, OR 97403. Offers MA. Part-time programs available. *Degree requirements:* For master's, one foreign language, thesis, internship. *Entrance requirements:* For master's, minimum GPA of 3.0. Additional exam requirements/recommendations for international students: Required—TOEFL. *Faculty research:* International development studies; environmental studies; cross-cultural communications; planning, public policy, and management; several world regions.

University of Pennsylvania, School of Arts and Sciences, Graduate Group in International Studies, Philadelphia, PA 19104. Offers AM. *Students:* 10 full-time (3 women), 2 part-time (1 woman); includes 1 Black or African American, non-Hispanic/Latino; 2 Asian, non-Hispanic/Latino, 2 international. In 2010, 61 master's awarded. Application fee: $70. *Expenses:* Tuition: Full-time $25,660; part-time $4758 per course. Required fees: $2152; $270 per course. Tuition and fees vary according to course load, degree level and program.

University of Pittsburgh, Graduate School of Public and International Affairs, Doctoral Program in Public and International Affairs, Pittsburgh, PA 15260. Offers development policy (PhD); foreign and security policy (PhD); international political economy (PhD); public administration (PhD); public policy (PhD). *Accreditation:* NASPAA. Part-time programs available. *Faculty:* 30 full-time (12 women), 67 part-time/adjunct (25 women). *Students:* 43 full-time (18 women), 3 part-time (2 women); includes 3 minority (2 Black or African American, non-Hispanic/Latino; 1 Asian, non-Hispanic/Latino), 19 international. Average age 30. 105 applicants, 11% accepted, 6 enrolled. In 2010, 11 doctorates awarded. Terminal master's awarded for partial completion of doctoral program. *Degree requirements:* For doctorate, comprehensive exam, thesis/dissertation, mid-term evaluation, preliminary exam, annual review. *Entrance requirements:* For doctorate, GRE, 3 letters of recommendation, resume, minimum GPA of 3.0 (recommended), writing sample. Additional exam requirements/recommendations for international students: Required—TOEFL (minimum score 600 paper-based; 250 computer-based; 100 iBT), TWE (minimum score 4); Recommended—IELTS (minimum score 7). *Application deadline:* For fall admission, 2/1 for domestic students, 1/15 for international students. Application fee: $50. Electronic applications accepted. *Expenses:* Tuition, state resident: full-time $17,304; part-time $701 per credit. Tuition, nonresident: full-time $29,554; part-time $1210 per credit. Required fees: $740; $214 per term. Tuition and fees vary according to program. *Financial support:* In 2010–11, 10 students received support, including 10 fellowships (averaging $41,325 per year). Financial award application deadline: 2/1. *Faculty research:* International political economy, international development, public administration, public policy, foreign policy, international security policy. Total annual research expenditures: $893,349. *Unit head:* Dr. Kevin P. Kearns, Program Coordinator, 412-648-7621, Fax: 412-648-2605, E-mail: kkearns@pitt.edu. *Application contact:* Julie Korade, Program Administrator/Graduate Enrollment Counselor, 412-648-7640, Fax: 412-648-7641, E-mail: korade@pitt.edu.

University of Pittsburgh, Graduate School of Public and International Affairs, International Affairs Division, Pittsburgh, PA 15260. Offers global political economy (MPIA); human security (MPIA); security and intelligence studies (MPIA); JD/MPIA; MBA/MPIA; MID/MPIA; MPA/MPIA; MSIS/MPIA. Part-time and evening/weekend programs available. *Faculty:* 30 full-time (12 women), 67 part-time/adjunct (25 women). *Students:* 187 full-time (93 women), 26 part-time (7 women); includes 17 minority (9 Black or African American, non-Hispanic/Latino; 1 American Indian or Alaska Native, non-Hispanic/Latino; 4 Asian, non-Hispanic/Latino; 3 Hispanic/Latino), 17 international. Average age 25. 325 applicants, 73% accepted, 100 enrolled. In 2010, 92 master's awarded. *Degree requirements:* For master's, thesis optional, internship, capstone seminar. *Entrance requirements:* For master's, GRE General Test, 3 letters of recommendation, resume; minimum GPA of 3.2 (recommended). Additional exam requirements/recommendations for international students: Required—TOEFL (minimum score 550 paper-based; 213 computer-based), TWE (minimum score 4); Recommended—IELTS (minimum score 7). *Application deadline:* For fall admission, 3/1 for domestic students, 1/15 for international students; for spring admission, 11/1 for domestic students, 8/1 for international students. Application fee: $50. Electronic applications accepted. *Expenses:* Tuition, state resident: full-time $17,304; part-time $701 per credit. Tuition, nonresident: full-time $29,554; part-time $1210 per credit. Required fees: $740; $214 per term. Tuition and fees vary according to program. *Financial support:* In 2010–11, 44 students received support. Scholarships/grants, tuition waivers (full and partial), unspecified assistantships, and student employment available. Financial award application deadline: 2/1. *Faculty research:* International political economy, international security and intelligence, transnational organized crime, international trade, international finance, globalization, terrorism, multinational corporations and the global economy. Total annual research expenditures: $892,349. *Unit head:* Dr. Martin Staniland, Director, International Affairs and International Development Divisions, 412-648-7656, Fax: 412-648-2605, E-mail: mstan@pitt.edu. *Application contact:* Kelly C. McDevitt, Graduate Enrollment Counselor, 412-648-7640, Fax: 412-648-7641, E-mail: mcdevitt@pitt.edu.

University of Pittsburgh, Katz Graduate School of Business, MBA/Master of Public and International Affairs Dual-Degree Program, Pittsburgh, PA 15260. Offers MBA/MPIA. *Accreditation:* AACSB. Part-time and evening/weekend programs available. *Faculty:* 60 full-time (18 women), 22 part-time/adjunct (5 women). *Students:* 2 full-time (0 women), 1 (woman) part-time. Average age 27. 2 applicants, 0% accepted, 0 enrolled. *Entrance requirements:* Additional exam requirements/recommendations for international students: Required—TOEFL (minimum 600 paper, 250 computer, 100 iBT) or IELTS. *Application deadline:* For fall admission, 4/1 priority date for domestic students, 2/1 priority date for international students. Application fee: $50. Electronic applications accepted. *Expenses:* Tuition, state resident: full-time $17,304; part-time $701 per credit. Tuition, nonresident: full-time $29,554; part-time $1210 per credit. Required fees: $740; $214 per term. Tuition and fees vary according to program. *Financial support:* Career-related internships or fieldwork and scholarships/grants available. Financial award application deadline: 3/1; financial award applicants required to submit FAFSA. *Faculty research:* Transitional economies; incentives and governance; corporate finance, mergers and acquisitions; global information systems and structures, consumer behavior and marketing models, entrepreneurship and globalization. *Unit head:* William T. Valenta, Assistant Dean, Director of MBA Programs, 412-648-1610, Fax: 412-648-1659, E-mail: wtvalenta@katz.pitt.edu. *Application contact:* Cliff McCormick, Director MBA Admissions, 412-648-1700, Fax: 412-648-1659, E-mail: mba@katz.pitt.edu.

University of Pittsburgh, University Center for International Studies, Pittsburgh, PA 15260. Offers African studies (Certificate); Asian studies (Certificate); European Union studies (Certificate); global studies (Certificate); Latin American studies (Certificate); Russian and East European studies (Certificate); West European studies (Certificate). *Students:* 322 full-time (192 women), 19 part-time (14 women); includes 22 minority (8 Black or African American, non-Hispanic/Latino; 3 Asian, non-Hispanic/Latino; 6 Hispanic/Latino; 5 Two or more races, non-Hispanic/Latino), 134 international. In 2010, 61 Certificates awarded. *Degree requirements:* For Certificate, one foreign language, study abroad. *Application deadline:* Applications are processed on a rolling basis. *Expenses:* Tuition, state resident: full-time $17,304; part-time $701 per credit. Tuition, nonresident: full-time $29,554; part-time $1210 per credit. Required fees: $740; $214 per term. Tuition and fees vary according to program. *Unit head:* Dr. Lawrence F. Feick, Director, University Center for International Studies, 412-648-7374, Fax: 412-624-4672, E-mail: feick@pitt.edu. *Application contact:* Information Contact, 412-624-4141, E-mail: graduate@pitt.edu.

University of Rhode Island, Graduate School, College of Arts and Sciences, Department of Political Science, Kingston, RI 02881. Offers political science (MA), including American politics, comparative government, international relations, public policy; public policy and administration (MPA); MLIS/MPA. Part-time programs available. *Faculty:* 10 full-time (4 women). *Students:* 17 full-time (10 women), 31 part-time (19 women); includes 10 minority (4 Black or African American, non-Hispanic/Latino; 1 Asian, non-Hispanic/Latino; 5 Hispanic/Latino). In 2010, 22 master's awarded. *Degree requirements:* For master's, comprehensive exam (for some programs), thesis optional. *Entrance requirements:* For master's, GRE, GMAT or MAT, 2 letters of recommendation. Additional exam requirements/recommendations for international students: Required—TOEFL (minimum score 550 paper-based; 213 computer-based). *Application deadline:* For fall admission, 2/1 for international students; for spring admission, 7/15 for international students. Application fee: $65. Electronic applications accepted. *Expenses:* Tuition, state resident: full-time $9588; part-time $533 per credit hour. Tuition, nonresident: full-time $22,968; part-time $1276 per credit hour. Required fees: $1282; $68 per semester. Tuition and fees vary according to program. *Financial support:* In 2010–11, 4 teaching assistantships with full tuition reimbursements (averaging $9,263 per year) were awarded. Financial award applicants required to submit FAFSA. *Unit head:* Dr. Gerry Tyler, Department Chair, 401-874-4053, Fax: 401-874-4072, E-mail: gtyler@uri.edu. *Application contact:* Dr. Gerry Tyler, Department Chair, 401-874-4053, Fax: 401-874-4072, E-mail: gtyler@uri.edu.

University of San Diego, College of Arts and Sciences, Department of Political Science and International Relations, San Diego, CA 92110-2492. Offers international relations (MA); JD/MA. Part-time and evening/weekend programs available. *Faculty:* 4 part-time/adjunct (1 woman). *Students:* 13 full-time (8 women), 7 part-time (3 women); includes 4 Hispanic/Latino; 1 Two or more races, non-Hispanic/Latino, 2 international. Average age 27. 45 applicants, 56% accepted, 10 enrolled. In 2010, 13 master's awarded. *Degree requirements:* For master's, comprehensive exam. *Entrance requirements:* For master's, GRE General Test, minimum GPA of 3.1. Additional exam requirements/recommendations for international students: Required—TOEFL (minimum score 580 paper-based; 237 computer-based; 83 iBT), TWE. *Application deadline:* For fall admission, 8/31 for domestic and international students; for spring admission, 1/15 for domestic students, 11/15 for international students. Applications are processed on a rolling basis. Application fee: $45. Electronic applications accepted. *Expenses:* Tuition: Full-time $21,744; part-time $1208 per unit. Required fees: $224. Full-time tuition and fees vary according to course load and degree level. *Financial support:* In 2010–11, 13 students received support. Federal Work-Study, institutionally sponsored loans, and unspecified assistantships available. Support available to part-time students. Financial award application deadline: 4/1; financial award applicants required to submit FAFSA. *Faculty research:* International security, U.S.-Mexican border politics, Latin American politics, African politics, Soviet politics. *Unit head:* Dr. Emily Edmonds-Poli, Graduate Program Director, 619-260-7802, Fax: 619-260-6840, E-mail: edmonds@sandiego.edu. *Application contact:* Stephen Pultz, Director of Admissions and Enrollment, 619-260-4506, Fax: 619-260-6836, E-mail: admissions@sandiego.edu.

University of San Francisco, College of Arts and Sciences, Department of Economics, San Francisco, CA 94117-1080. Offers economics (MA); financial analysis (MS); international and development economics (MA); MS/MBA. Part-time and evening/weekend programs available. *Faculty:* 8 full-time (2 women), 9 part-time/adjunct (3 women). *Students:* 204 full-time (100 women), 19 part-time (9 women); includes 48 minority (2 Black or African American, non-Hispanic/Latino; 35 Asian, non-Hispanic/Latino; 6 Hispanic/Latino; 5 Two or more races, non-Hispanic/Latino), 119 international. Average age 27. 712 applicants, 42% accepted, 112 enrolled. In 2010, 124 master's awarded. *Degree requirements:* For master's, comprehensive exam, thesis or alternative. *Entrance requirements:* For master's, GRE General Test (recommended), BA in economics (preferred). Additional exam requirements/recommendations for international students: Required—TOEFL. *Application deadline:* For fall admission, 7/15 priority date for domestic students; for spring admission, 12/15 for domestic students. Applications are processed on a rolling basis. Application fee: $55 ($65 for international students). *Expenses:* Tuition: Full-time $20,070; part-time $1115 per credit hour. Tuition and fees vary according to course load, degree level and program. *Financial support:* In 2010–11, 125 students received support; fellowships, teaching assistantships, career-related internships or fieldwork available. Financial award application deadline: 3/2; financial award applicants required to submit FAFSA. *Faculty research:* Economic development, forecasting and planning, labor markets, Pacific Rim, financial markets. *Unit head:* Man-lui Lau, Chair, 415-422-2765, Fax: 415-422-5784. *Application contact:* Information Contact, 415-422-5135, Fax: 415-422-2217, E-mail: asgraduate@usfca.edu.

University of San Francisco, College of Arts and Sciences, International Studies Program, San Francisco, CA 94117-1080. Offers MA. *Faculty:* 3 full-time (2 women). *Students:* 42 full-time (28 women), 18 part-time (12 women); includes 18 minority (2 Black or African American, non-Hispanic/Latino; 2 American Indian or Alaska Native, non-Hispanic/Latino; 4 Asian, non-Hispanic/Latino; 8 Hispanic/Latino; 2 Two or more races, non-Hispanic/Latino), 6 international. Average age 28. 225 applicants, 35% accepted, 41 enrolled. In 2010, 13 master's awarded. *Expenses:* Tuition: Full-time $20,070; part-time $1115 per credit hour. Tuition and fees vary according to course load, degree level and program. *Financial support:* In 2010–11, 45 students received support. *Unit head:* Prof. Anne Bartlett, Program Director, 415-422-5101. *Application contact:* Information Contact, 415-422-5135, Fax: 415-422-2217, E-mail: asgraduate@usfca.edu.

University of South Carolina, The Graduate School, College of Arts and Sciences, Department of Political Science, Program in International Studies, Columbia, SC 29208. Offers MA, PhD. Part-time programs available. Terminal master's awarded for partial completion of doctoral program. *Degree requirements:* For master's, one foreign language, thesis or alternative; for doctorate, one foreign language, comprehensive exam, thesis/dissertation. *Entrance requirements:* For master's, GRE General Test, minimum GPA of 3.3; for doctorate, GRE General Test, minimum GPA of 3.5. Additional exam requirements/recommendations for international students: Required—TOEFL. Electronic applications accepted. *Faculty research:* International relations, international organization, foreign policy, comparative politics.

University of Southern California, Graduate School, Annenberg School for Communication and Journalism, School of Communication, Program in Public Diplomacy, Los Angeles, CA 90089. Offers MPD. *Students:* 47 full-time, 2 part-time; includes 15 minority (2 Black or African American, non-Hispanic/Latino; 5 Hispanic/Latino; 7 Native Hawaiian or other Pacific Islander, non-Hispanic/Latino; 1 Two or more races, non-Hispanic/Latino), 11 international. Average age 26. 100 applicants, 51% accepted, 21 enrolled. In 2010, 23 master's awarded. *Degree requirements:* For master's, thesis. *Entrance requirements:* For master's, GRE, resume, writing samples, recommendation letters. Additional exam requirements/recommendations for international students: Required—TOEFL (minimum score 280 computer-based; 114 iBT). *Application deadline:* For fall admission, 12/15 priority date for domestic and international students. Application fee: $85. Electronic applications accepted. *Expenses:* Tuition: Full-time $31,240; part-time $1420 per unit. Required fees: $600. One-time fee: $35 full-time. Full-time tuition and fees vary according to degree level and program. *Financial support:* Career-related internships or fieldwork, Federal Work-Study, scholarships/grants, and tuition waivers available. Support available to part-time students. Financial award application deadline: 1/15; financial award applicants required to submit FAFSA. *Unit head:* Dr. Nicholas Cull, Director of Public Diplomacy Degree Program, 213-821-4080, E-mail: cull@usc.edu. *Application contact:* Allyson Hill, Assistant Dean, Admissions, 213-821-0770, Fax: 213-740-1933, E-mail: ascadm@usc.edu.

See Display on page 675 and Close-Up on page 727.

University of Southern California, Graduate School, Dana and David Dornsife College of Letters, Arts and Sciences, Political Science and International Relations (Joint PhD Program), Los Angeles, CA 90089. Offers PhD. *Faculty:* 29 full-time (12 women). *Students:* 53 full-time (25 women); includes 14 minority (3 Asian, non-Hispanic/Latino; 8 Hispanic/Latino; 3 Two or more races, non-Hispanic/Latino), 20 international. 117 applicants, 13% accepted, 8 enrolled. In 2010, 14 doctorates awarded. *Degree requirements:* For doctorate, variable foreign language requirement, comprehensive exam, thesis/dissertation. *Entrance requirements:* For doctorate, GRE (minimum score 1000). Additional exam requirements/recommendations for international students: Required—TOEFL (minimum score 600 paper-based; 250 computer-based; 100 iBT). *Application deadline:* For fall admission, 12/1 priority date for domestic and international students. Application fee: $85. Electronic applications accepted. *Expenses:* Tuition: Full-time $31,240; part-time $1420 per unit. Required fees: $600. One-time fee: $35 full-time. Full-time tuition and fees vary according to degree level and program. *Financial support:* In 2010–11, 37 students received support, including 14 fellowships with full tuition reimbursements available (averaging $23,000 per year), 1 research assistantship with full tuition reimbursement available (averaging $20,000 per year), 30 teaching assistantships with full tuition reimbursements available (averaging $20,000 per year); health care benefits also available. Financial award application deadline: 12/1. *Faculty research:* American politics, foreign policy analysis, international political economy, race/ethics politics, security studies. *Unit head:* Prof. Saori Katada, Director POIR Program, 213-740-8542, E-mail: skatada@usc.edu. *Application contact:* Veridiana Chavarin, Graduate Advisor, 213-740-1695, E-mail: vchavari@usc.edu.

University of Southern California, Graduate School, School of Policy, Planning, and Development, Master of International Public Policy and Management Program, Los Angeles, CA 90089. Offers MPPM. Part-time programs available. *Faculty:* 51 full-time (12 women), 100 part-time/adjunct (30 women). *Students:* 41 full-time (21 women), 17 part-time (15 women); includes 10 minority (1 Black or African American, non-Hispanic/Latino; 5 Asian, non-Hispanic/Latino; 4 Hispanic/Latino), 48 international. 115 applicants, 55% accepted, 39 enrolled. In 2010, 39 master's awarded. *Entrance requirements:* Additional exam requirements/recommendations for international students: Required—TOEFL (minimum score 71 iBT). *Application deadline:* For fall admission, 4/1 for domestic and international students. Applications are processed on a rolling basis. Application fee: $85. Electronic applications accepted. *Expenses:* Contact institution. *Faculty research:* International development, economic development, social policy problems, issues of developing countries, international and comparative. Total annual research expenditures: $6.2 million. *Unit head:* Dr. Joyce Mann, Director, International Education Programs, 213-740-0547, Fax: 213-821-1331, E-mail: joyceman@usc.edu. *Application contact:* Marisol R. Gonzalez, Director of Recruitment and Admission, 213-740-0550, Fax: 213-740-7573, E-mail: marisolr@usc.edu.

University of Southern Mississippi, Graduate School, College of Arts and Letters, Department of Political Science, International Development, and International Affairs, Hattiesburg, MS 39406-0001. Offers international development (PhD); political science (MA, MS). Part-time and evening/weekend programs available. Postbaccalaureate distance learning degree programs offered. *Faculty:* 14 full-time (2 women). *Students:* 33 full-time (14 women), 65 part-time (28 women); includes 19 Black or African American, non-Hispanic/Latino; 1 American Indian or Alaska Native, non-Hispanic/Latino; 2 Asian, non-Hispanic/Latino; 6 Hispanic/Latino, 7 international. Average age 36. 44 applicants, 64% accepted, 22 enrolled. In 2010, 10 master's, 2 doctorates awarded. *Degree requirements:* For master's, comprehensive exam, thesis (for some programs); for doctorate, comprehensive exam, thesis/dissertation. *Entrance requirements:* For master's, GRE General Test, minimum GPA of 2.75 in last 2 years, 3.0 in field of study; for doctorate, GRE General Test, minimum GPA of 3.5. Additional exam requirements/recommendations for international students: Required—TOEFL, IELTS. *Application deadline:* For fall admission, 3/1 priority date for domestic students, 3/1 for international students. Applications are processed on a rolling basis. Application fee: $50. *Financial support:* In 2010–11, 4 research assistantships with full and partial tuition reimbursements (averaging $9,000 per year), 8 teaching assistantships with full tuition reimbursements (averaging $7,000 per year) were awarded; career-related internships or fieldwork, Federal Work-Study, scholarships/grants, health care benefits, and unspecified assistantships also available. Financial award application deadline: 3/15; financial award applicants required to submit FAFSA. *Faculty research:* American politics, international politics, political theory, comparative politics, public law. *Unit head:* Dr. Allan McBride, Chair, 601-266-4310. *Application contact:* Dr. Mark Stedman, Director, Graduate Studies, 601-266-4310, Fax: 601-266-4172.

University of South Florida, Graduate School, College of Arts and Sciences, Department of Government and International Affairs, Tampa, FL 33620-9951. Offers government (PhD); Latin American Caribbean and Latino Studies (MA); political science (MA); public administration (MPA). Part-time and evening/weekend programs available. *Faculty:* 5 full-time (1 woman), 1 part-time/adjunct (0 women). *Students:* 57 full-time (35 women), 84 part-time (42 women); includes 23 Black or African American, non-Hispanic/Latino; 1 American Indian or Alaska Native, non-Hispanic/Latino; 4 Asian, non-Hispanic/Latino; 18 Hispanic/Latino, 2 international. Average age 32. 151 applicants, 38% accepted, 41 enrolled. In 2010, 31 master's awarded. *Degree requirements:* For master's, comprehensive exam, thesis; for doctorate, comprehensive exam, thesis/dissertation. *Entrance requirements:* For master's, GRE (minimum score 470 verbal, 470 quantitative), minimum GPA of 3.0 in last 60 hours of course work. Additional exam requirements/recommendations for international students: Required—TOEFL (minimum score 550 paper-based; 213 computer-based). *Application deadline:* For fall admission, 2/15 for domestic students, 1/2 for international students; for spring admission, 10/15 for domestic students, 6/1 for international students. Applications are processed on a rolling basis. Application fee: $30. Electronic applications accepted. *Financial support:* In 2010–11, 12 teaching assistantships with tuition reimbursements (averaging $15,000 per year) were awarded; unspecified assistantships also available. Financial award application deadline: 4/1. *Unit head:* Dr. Mohsen Milani, Chairperson, 813-974-2384, Fax: 813-974-0832, E-mail: milani@chuma1.cas.usf.edu. *Application contact:* Dr. Stephen Tauber, Graduate Coordinator, 813-974-0781, Fax: 813-974-0832, E-mail: stauber@chuma1.cas.usf.edu.

University of the Pacific, McGeorge School of Law, Sacramento, CA 95817. Offers advocacy (JD); criminal justice (JD); experiential law teaching (LL M); intellectual property (JD); international legal studies (JD); international water resources law (LL M, JSD); law (JD); public law and policy (JD); public policy and law (LL M); tax (JD); transnational business practice (LL M); JD/MBA; JD/MPPA. *Accreditation:* ABA. Part-time and evening/weekend programs available. *Faculty:* 49 full-time (22 women), 45 part-time/adjunct (15 women). *Students:* 756 full-time (362 women), 303 part-time (148 women); includes 27 Black or African American, non-Hispanic/Latino; 19 American Indian or Alaska Native, non-Hispanic/Latino; 150 Asian, non-Hispanic/Latino; 60 Hispanic/Latino, 27 international. Average age 27. 3,209 applicants, 42% accepted, 344 enrolled. In 2010, 307 first professional degrees, 36 master's awarded. *Degree requirements:* For master's, thesis (for some programs); for doctorate, thesis/dissertation. *Entrance requirements:* For JD, LSAT; for master's, JD; for doctorate, LL M. Additional exam requirements/recommendations for international students: Required—TOEFL (minimum score 600 paper-based; 250 computer-based; 100 iBT). *Application deadline:* For fall admission, 3/15 priority date for domestic students. Applications are processed on a rolling basis. Application fee: $50. Electronic applications accepted. *Expenses:* Contact institution. *Financial support:* Fellowships, research assistantships, teaching assistantships, career-related internships or fieldwork, Federal Work-Study, institutionally sponsored loans, and scholarships/grants available. Support available to part-time students. Financial award applicants required to submit FAFSA. *Faculty research:* International legal studies, public policy and law, advocacy, intellectual property law, taxation, criminal law. *Unit head:* Elizabeth Rindskopf Parker, Dean, 916-739-7151, E-mail: elizabeth@pacific.edu. *Application contact:* 916-739-7105, Fax: 916-739-7301, E-mail: mcgeorge@pacific.edu.

University of the Pacific, School of International Studies, Program in Intercultural Relations, Stockton, CA 95211-0197. Offers MA. *Faculty:* 8 full-time (4 women), 1 part-time/adjunct (0 women). In 2010, 6 master's awarded. *Entrance requirements:* Additional exam requirements/recommendations for international students: Required—TOEFL (minimum score 475 paper-based; 150 computer-based). Application fee: $75. *Financial support:* Application deadline: 3/1. *Unit head:* Dr. Cynthia Weick, Dean, 209-946-2650, E-mail: mensign@pacific.edu. *Application contact:* Office of Graduate Admissions, 209-946-2344.

University of Toronto, School of Graduate Studies, Social Sciences Division, Munk School of Global Affairs, Toronto, ON M5S 1A1, Canada. Offers MGA. *Entrance requirements:* For master's, GRE General Test, GMAT, or LSAT.

University of Utah, Graduate School, College of Social and Behavioral Science, Program in International Affairs and Global Enterprise, Salt Lake City, UT 84112-1107. Offers MS. Part-time programs available. *Faculty:* 1 part-time/adjunct (0 women). *Students:* 8 full-time (2 women), 10 part-time (4 women); includes 2 minority (both Hispanic/Latino), 2 international. Average age 29. 16 applicants, 56% accepted, 5 enrolled. In 2010, 4 master's awarded. *Degree requirements:* For master's, one foreign language, comprehensive exam, thesis optional, major research paper. *Entrance requirements:* For master's, GMAT, LSAT, or GRE, completed undergraduate coursework in statistics, microeconomics theory and macroeconomics theory. Additional exam requirements/recommendations for international students: Required—TOEFL (minimum score 233 computer-based; 90 iBT). *Application deadline:* For fall admission, 3/1 for domestic and international students; for spring admission, 9/1 for domestic and international students. Applications are processed on a rolling basis. Application fee: $55 ($65 for international students). *Expenses:* Tuition, area resident: Part-time $179.19 per credit hour. Tuition, state resident: full-time $4384. Tuition, nonresident: full-time $16,684; part-time $630.67 per credit hour. Required fees: $350 per semester. Tuition and fees vary according to course load, degree level and program. *Financial support:* In 2010–11, 2 students received support. Unspecified assistantships available. *Faculty research:* East Asian economies. *Unit head:* Stephen Reynolds, Program DIrector, 801-581-8620, Fax: 801-585-5081, E-mail: stephen.reynolds@csbs.utah.edu. *Application contact:* Tricia Baker, Program Advisor, 801-581-7722, Fax: 801-585-5081, E-mail: tricia.baker@cppa.utah.edu.

University of Virginia, College and Graduate School of Arts and Sciences, Department of Politics, Program in Foreign Affairs, Charlottesville, VA 22903. Offers MA, PhD. *Students:* 51 full-time (22 women), 4 part-time (1 woman); includes 1 Black or African American, non-Hispanic/Latino; 5 Asian, non-Hispanic/Latino, 11 international. Average age 30. 133 applicants, 23% accepted, 13 enrolled. In 2010, 6 master's, 9 doctorates awarded. *Degree requirements:* For master's, one foreign language, 2 research/statistics courses or thesis; for doctorate, variable foreign language requirement, thesis/dissertation, 2 research/statistics courses. *Entrance requirements:* For master's and doctorate, GRE General Test, long writing sample; 2 letters of recommendation. Additional exam requirements/recommendations for international students: Required—TOEFL (minimum score 600 paper-based; 250 computer-based; 90 iBT), IELTS (minimum score 7). *Application deadline:* For fall admission, 12/4 for domestic and international students. Applications are processed on a rolling basis. Application fee: $60. Electronic applications accepted. *Financial support:* Fellowships, teaching assistantships available. Financial award application deadline: 12/4; financial award applicants required to submit FAFSA. *Unit head:* David Leblang, Chair, 434-924-3192, Fax: 434-924-3359. *Application contact:* David Leblang, Chair, 434-924-3192, Fax: 434-924-3359.

University of Washington, Graduate School, College of Arts and Sciences, Henry M. Jackson School of International Studies, Seattle, WA 98195. Offers China studies (MAIS); comparative religion (MAIS); international studies (MAIS); Japan studies (MAIS); Korea studies (MAIS); Middle East studies (MAIS); Russian, East European and Central Asian studies (MAIS), including Central Asian studies, East European studies, Russian studies; South Asian studies (MAIS); Southeast Asian studies (MAIS); JD/MAIS; MBA/MAIS; MFR/MAIS; MMA/MAIS; MPA/

International Affairs

University of Washington (continued)

MAIS; MPH/MAIS. *Students:* 163 full-time (79 women); includes 2 Black or African American, non-Hispanic/Latino; 1 American Indian or Alaska Native, non-Hispanic/Latino; 25 Asian, non-Hispanic/Latino; 2 Hispanic/Latino, 20 international. 333 applicants, 55% accepted, 70 enrolled. In 2010, 45 master's awarded. *Degree requirements:* For master's, variable foreign language requirement, thesis (for some programs). *Entrance requirements:* For master's, GRE General Test, minimum GPA of 3.00 (last two years). Additional exam requirements/ recommendations for international students: Required—TOEFL (minimum score 500 paper-based; 213 computer-based; 92 iBT) or IELTS (minimum score 7). *Application deadline:* For fall admission, 1/5 for domestic and international students. Application fee: $75. Electronic applications accepted. *Financial support:* Fellowships with full and partial tuition reimbursements, research assistantships with full and partial tuition reimbursements, teaching assistantships with full and partial tuition reimbursements, career-related internships or fieldwork, Federal Work-Study, institutionally sponsored loans, scholarships/grants, tuition waivers (full and partial), and summer language study awards available. Financial award application deadline: 1/5; financial award applicants required to submit FAFSA. *Unit head:* Prof. Resat Kasaba, Director, 206-543-4373. *Application contact:* 206-543-6001, Fax: 206-616-3170, E-mail: jsisinfo@uw.edu.

University of Waterloo, Graduate Studies, Faculty of Arts, Department of Political Science, Global Governance Program, Waterloo, ON N2L 3G1, Canada. Offers MA, PhD. *Entrance requirements:* For doctorate, MA. Additional exam requirements/recommendations for international students: Required—TOEFL. Electronic applications accepted. *Faculty research:* Global political economy, global environment, peace and security, global justice and human rights, multilateral institutions and diplomacy.

University of Wyoming, College of Arts and Sciences, Program in International Studies, Laramie, WY 82070. Offers international peace corps (MA); international studies (MA). Part-time programs available. *Degree requirements:* For master's, one foreign language, thesis. *Entrance requirements:* For master's, GRE General Test, minimum GPA of 3.0. Additional exam requirements/recommendations for international students: Required—TOEFL (minimum score 525 paper-based; 195 computer-based). Electronic applications accepted. *Faculty research:* International political economy, comparative social institutions, foreign policy, economic development.

Virginia Polytechnic Institute and State University, Graduate School, College of Architecture and Urban Studies, School of Public and International Affairs, Blacksburg, VA 24061. Offers economic development (Certificate); government and international affairs (MPIA, PhD); homeland security policy (Certificate); local government management (Certificate); nonprofit and nongovernmental organization management (Certificate); planning, governance and globalization (PhD); public administration and public affairs (MPA, PhD); urban and regional planning (MURPL). *Accreditation:* ACSP. *Faculty:* 31 full-time (9 women). *Students:* 114 full-time (66 women), 105 part-time (54 women); includes 11 Black or African American, non-Hispanic/ Latino; 1 American Indian or Alaska Native, non-Hispanic/Latino; 7 Asian, non-Hispanic/Latino; 8 Hispanic/Latino, 19 international. Average age 31. 166 applicants, 67% accepted, 53 enrolled. In 2010, 41 master's, 3 doctorates awarded. *Degree requirements:* For master's, comprehensive exam (for some programs), thesis (for some programs); for doctorate, comprehensive exam (for some programs), thesis/dissertation (for some programs). *Entrance requirements:* For master's and doctorate, GRE. Additional exam requirements/recommendations for international students: Required—TOEFL (minimum score 550 paper-based; 213 computer-based). *Application deadline:* For fall admission, 7/1 for domestic and international students; for spring admission, 12/1 for domestic and international students. Applications are processed on a rolling basis. Application fee: $65. Electronic applications accepted. *Expenses:* Tuition, state resident: full-time $9399; part-time $488 per credit hour. Tuition, nonresident: full-time $17,854; part-time $957.75 per credit hour. Required fees: $1534. Full-time tuition and fees vary according to program. *Financial support:* In 2010–11, 1 teaching assistantship with full tuition reimbursement (averaging $21,395 per year) was awarded; career-related internships or fieldwork, Federal Work-Study, scholarships/grants, health care benefits, and unspecified assistantships also available. Financial award application deadline: 1/15. *Faculty research:* Design theory, environmental planning, town planning, transportation planning. Total annual research expenditures: $610,749. *Unit head:* Dr. Karen M. Hult, UNIT HEAD, 540-231-5351, Fax: 540-231-9938, E-mail: khult@vt.edu. *Application contact:* Krystal D. Wright, Contact, 540-231-2291, Fax: 540-231-9938, E-mail: garch@vt.edu.

Walden University, Graduate Programs, School of Public Policy and Administration, Minneapolis, MN 55401. Offers criminal justice (MPA); emergency management (MPA); government management (Postbaccalaureate Certificate); health policy (MPA); homeland security policy (MPA); homeland security policy and coordination (MPA); interdisciplinary policy studies (MPA); international nongovernmental organizations (ngos) (MPA); law and public policy (MPA); local government management for sustainable communities (MPA); nonprofit management (Postbaccalaureate Certificate); nonprofit management and leadership (MPA, MS); policy analysis (MPA); public management and leadership (MPA); public policy and administration (MPA, PhD), including criminal justice (PhD), emergency management (PhD), health policy (PhD), health services (PhD), homeland security policy (PhD), homeland security policy and coordination (PhD), interdisciplinary policy studies (PhD), international nongovernmental organizations (PhD), law and public policy (PhD), local government management for sustainable communities (PhD), nonprofit management and leadership (PhD), policy analysis (PhD), public management and leadership (PhD), terrorism, mediation, and peace (PhD); terrorism, mediation, and peace (MPA). Part-time and evening/weekend programs available. Postbaccalaureate distance learning degree programs offered (minimal on-campus study). *Faculty:* 10 full-time (5 women), 117 part-time/adjunct (49 women). *Students:* 1,408 full-time (901 women), 599 part-time (392 women); includes 1,022 Black or African American, non-Hispanic/Latino; 11 American Indian or Alaska Native, non-Hispanic/Latino; 37 Asian, non-Hispanic/Latino; 64 Hispanic/Latino; 26 Two or more races, non-Hispanic/Latino, 47 international. Average age 40. In 2010, 311 master's, 23 doctorates awarded. *Degree requirements:* For doctorate, thesis/dissertation, residency. *Entrance requirements:* For master's, bachelor's degree or equivalent in related field, minimum GPA of 2.5; for doctorate, master's degree or equivalent in related field; minimum GPA of 3.0; official transcripts; three years of related professional/academic experience (preferred); access to computer and Internet. Additional exam requirements/recommendations for international students: Required—TOEFL (minimum score 550 paper-based; 213 computer-based), IELTS (minimum score 6.5), TOEFL (minimum score 550 paper-based; 213 computer-based), IELTS (minimum score 6.5), or Michigan English Language Assessment Battery (minimum score 82). *Application deadline:* Applications are processed on a rolling basis. Application fee: $50. Electronic applications accepted. *Expenses:* Tuition: Full-time $10,274; part-time $445 per credit. Tuition and fees vary according to course load, degree level and program. *Financial support:* Fellowships with tuition reimbursements, Federal Work-Study, scholarships/grants, unspecified assistantships, and family tuition reduction, active duty/ veteran tuition reduction, group tuition reduction, interest-free payment plans available. Support available to part-time students. Financial award applicants required to submit FAFSA. *Unit head:* Dr. Mark Gordon, Associate Dean, 800-925-3368. *Application contact:* Jennifer Hall, Vice President of Enrollment Management, 866-4-WALDEN, E-mail: info@waldenu.edu.

Washington State University, Graduate School, The Edward R. Murrow College of Communication, Pullman, WA 99164-2520. Offers health communications (MA, PhD); intercultural and international communications (MA, PhD); media and society (MA, PhD); media process and effects (MA, PhD); organizational communications (MA, PhD). *Faculty:* 30. *Students:* 43 full-time (26 women), 6 part-time (4 women); includes 1 Asian, non-Hispanic/Latino; 1 Hispanic/ Latino, 19 international. Average age 30. 120 applicants, 22% accepted, 19 enrolled. In 2010, 22 master's, 1 doctorate awarded. *Degree requirements:* For master's, comprehensive exam (for some programs), thesis optional, oral exam; for doctorate, comprehensive exam, thesis/ dissertation. *Entrance requirements:* For master's, GRE General Test, minimum GPA of 3.25, 3 letters of recommendation; for doctorate, GRE General Test, minimum undergraduate GPA of 3.25, graduate 3.5; MA in communication; 3 letters of recommendation. Additional exam requirements/recommendations for international students: Required—TOEFL (minimum score 580 paper-based; 237 computer-based). *Application deadline:* For fall admission, 1/15 priority date for domestic students, 3/1 for international students. Applications are processed on a rolling basis. Application fee: $50. Electronic applications accepted. *Expenses:* Tuition, state resident: full-time $8552; part-time $443 per credit. Tuition, nonresident: full-time $21,650; part-time $1083 per credit. Required fees: $846. *Financial support:* In 2010–11, 46 students received support, including 2 fellowships (averaging $4,477 per year), 7 research assistantships with full and partial tuition reimbursements available (averaging $13,917 per year), 34 teaching assistantships with full and partial tuition reimbursements available (averaging $13,056 per year); career-related internships or fieldwork, Federal Work-Study, institutionally sponsored loans, tuition waivers (partial), and teaching associateships also available. Financial award application deadline: 4/1; financial award applicants required to submit FAFSA. *Faculty research:* Advocacy communication, mediated communication in decision making, communication technology policy and effects, multicultural and international psychology and physiology of communication. Total annual research expenditures: $550,455. *Unit head:* Dr. Erica Austin, Interim Director, 509-335-1556, E-mail: eaustin@wsu.edu. *Application contact:* Graduate School Admissions, 800-GRADWSU, Fax: 509-335-1949, E-mail: gradsch@wsu.edu.

Webster University, College of Arts and Sciences, Department of History, Politics and International Relations, Program in International Relations, St. Louis, MO 63119-3194. Offers MA. Part-time and evening/weekend programs available. *Degree requirements:* For master's, thesis optional. *Expenses:* Tuition: Part-time $585 per credit hour. Tuition and fees vary according to degree level, campus/location and program. *Faculty research:* International organizations, international political economy, politics of development, environmental law, Latin American law.

Western Michigan University, Graduate College, College of Arts and Sciences, Department of Political Science, Program in International Development Administration, Kalamazoo, MI 49008. Offers MDA.

West Virginia University, Eberly College of Arts and Sciences, Department of Political Science, Morgantown, WV 26506. Offers American public policy and politics (MA); international and comparative public policy and politics (MA); political science (PhD); public policy analysis (PhD). Terminal master's awarded for partial completion of doctoral program. *Degree requirements:* For master's, thesis optional; for doctorate, comprehensive exam, thesis/ dissertation. *Entrance requirements:* For master's, GRE General Test, minimum GPA of 2.75; for doctorate, GRE General Test, minimum GPA of 3.0. Additional exam requirements/ recommendations for international students: Required—TOEFL. *Faculty research:* Public policy, research methods, foreign policy analysis, judicial politics, environmental and energy policy.

Wilfrid Laurier University, Faculty of Graduate and Postdoctoral Studies, Faculty of Arts, Department of Political Science, Waterloo, ON N2L 3C5, Canada. Offers Canadian political studies (MA); comparative politics/international relations (MA). Part-time programs available. *Faculty:* 20 full-time (6 women). *Students:* 18 full-time (7 women), 3 part-time (1 woman), 1 international. 68 applicants, 49% accepted, 13 enrolled. In 2010, 13 master's awarded. *Degree requirements:* For master's, thesis optional. *Entrance requirements:* For master's, honors bachelor's degree or the equivalent in political science, minimum B average in undergraduate course work. Additional exam requirements/recommendations for international students: Required—TOEFL (minimum score 89 iBT). *Application deadline:* For fall admission, 2/1 priority date for domestic and international students. Application fee: $100. Electronic applications accepted. Tuition and fees charges are reported in Canadian dollars. *Expenses:* Tuition, area resident: Full-time $15,300 Canadian dollars; part-time $1200 Canadian dollars per credit. International tuition: $21,300 Canadian dollars full-time. Required fees: $650 Canadian dollars; $100 Canadian dollars per credit. Tuition and fees vary according to course load, degree level, campus/location and program. *Financial support:* In 2010–11, 26 fellowships, 5 research assistantships, 26 teaching assistantships were awarded; career-related internships or fieldwork, scholarships/grants, health care benefits, and unspecified assistantships also available. *Faculty research:* Political behavior/political psychology, Canadian political studies, comparative, politics/relations, public opinion and electoral studies, international. *Unit head:* Dr. Andrea Perella, Graduate Coordinator, 519-884-0710 Ext. 2719, Fax: 519-746-3655, E-mail: aperrella@wlu.ca. *Application contact:* Jennifer Williams, Graduate Admission and Records Officer, 519-884-0710 Ext. 3536, Fax: 519-884-1020, E-mail: gradstudies@wlu.ca.

Wilfrid Laurier University, Faculty of Graduate and Postdoctoral Studies, Faculty of Arts and School of Business and Economics, Global Governance Program, Waterloo, ON N2L 3C5, Canada. Offers conflict and security (PhD); global environment (PhD); global justice and human rights (PhD); global political economy (PhD); global social governance (PhD); multilateral institutions and diplomacy (PhD). *Faculty:* 27 full-time (7 women). *Students:* 14 full-time (7 women), 4 international. 83 applicants, 5% accepted, 3 enrolled. *Degree requirements:* For doctorate, thesis/dissertation. *Entrance requirements:* For doctorate, MA in political science, history, economics, international development studies, international peace studies, globalization studies, environmental studies or related field with minimum A-. Additional exam requirements/ recommendations for international students: Required—TOEFL (minimum score 89 iBT). *Application deadline:* For fall admission, 1/31 priority date for domestic and international students. Application fee: $100. Electronic applications accepted. Tuition and fees charges are reported in Canadian dollars. *Expenses:* Tuition, area resident: Full-time $15,300 Canadian dollars; part-time $1200 Canadian dollars per credit. International tuition: $21,300 Canadian dollars full-time. Required fees: $650 Canadian dollars; $100 Canadian dollars per credit. Tuition and fees vary according to course load, degree level, campus/location and program. *Financial support:* In 2010–11, 4 fellowships, 4 teaching assistantships were awarded; career-related internships or fieldwork, scholarships/grants, health care benefits, and unspecified assistantships also available. *Faculty research:* Global political economy, global environment, conflict and security, global justice and human rights, multilateral institutions and diplomacy. *Unit head:* Dr. Randall Wigle, Associate Director, 519-884-1970 Ext. 2438, Fax: 519-884-8454, E-mail: rwigle@wlu.ca. *Application contact:* Jennifer Willaims, Student Contact, 519-884-0710 Ext. 3536, Fax: 519-884-1020, E-mail: gradstudies@wlu.ca.

Wilfrid Laurier University, Faculty of Graduate and Postdoctoral Studies, Faculty of Arts and School of Business and Economics, International Public Policy Program, Waterloo, ON N2L 3C5, Canada. Offers global governance (MIPP); human security (MIPP); international economic relations (MIPP); international environmental policy (MIPP). *Faculty:* 17 full-time (8 women). *Students:* 16 full-time (9 women), 2 international. 90 applicants, 30% accepted, 14 enrolled. In 2010, 15 master's awarded. *Entrance requirements:* For master's, honours BA with minimum B average. Additional exam requirements/recommendations for international students: Required—TOEFL (minimum score 89 iBT). *Application deadline:* For fall admission, 2/1 priority date for domestic and international students. Application fee: $100. Electronic applications accepted. Tuition and fees charges are reported in Canadian dollars. *Expenses:* Tuition, area resident: Full-time $15,300 Canadian dollars; part-time $1200 Canadian dollars per credit. International tuition: $21,300 Canadian dollars full-time. Required fees: $650 Canadian dollars; $100 Canadian dollars per credit. Tuition and fees vary according to course load, degree level, campus/location and program. *Financial support:* In 2010–11, 5 fellowships, 5 teaching assistantships were awarded; career-related internships or fieldwork, scholarships/ grants, health care benefits, and unspecified assistantships also available. *Faculty research:* International environmental policy, international economic relations, human security, global governance. *Unit head:* Dr. Terry Snodden, Graduate Coordinator, 519-884-0710 Ext. 2945, Fax: 519-884-8854, E-mail: tlevesque@wlu.ca. *Application contact:* Jennifer Williams, Graduate Admissions and Records Officer, 519-884-0710 Ext. 3536, Fax: 519-884-1020, E-mail: gradstudies@wlu.ca.

Wilfrid Laurier University, Laurier Brantford, Brantford, ON N3T 2Y3, Canada. Offers criminology (MA), including culture, crime and policy, international crime and justice, media criminology. *Faculty:* 13 full-time (6 women). *Degree requirements:* For master's, thesis. *Entrance requirements:* For master's, honours bachelor's degree with major in criminology or equivalent degree; minimum B+ average in final year and in all criminology courses. Additional exam requirements/recommendations for international students: Required—TOEFL (minimum score 89 iBT). *Application deadline:* For fall admission, 6/1 priority date for domestic students, 5/1 priority date for international students. Application fee: $100. Electronic applications accepted. Tuition and fees charges are reported in Canadian dollars. *Expenses:* Tuition, area resident: Full-time $15,300 Canadian dollars; part-time $1200 Canadian dollars per credit. International tuition: $21,300 Canadian dollars full-time. Required fees: $650 Canadian dollars; $100 Canadian dollars per credit. Tuition and fees vary according to course load, degree level, campus/location and program. *Financial support:* Career-related internships or fieldwork, scholarships/grants, health care benefits, and unspecified assistantships available. *Unit head:* Dr. Thomas Fleming, Graduate Coordinator, 519-756-8228 Ext. 5740, Fax: 519-759-2127, E-mail: tfleming@wlu.ca. *Application contact:* Jennifer Williams, Graduate Admissions and Records Officer, 519-884-0710 Ext. 3536, Fax: 519-884-1020, E-mail: gradstudies@wlu.ca.

Yale University, Graduate School of Arts and Sciences, Department of Economics, Program in International and Development Economics, New Haven, CT 06520. Offers MA. *Entrance requirements:* For master's, GRE General Test.

Yale University, Graduate School of Arts and Sciences, Graduate Program in International Relations, New Haven, CT 06520. Offers MA, JD/MA, M E Sc/MA, MBA/MA, ME Sc/MA, MEM/MA, MF/MA, MFS/MA, MPH/MA. *Faculty:* 184. *Students:* 46 full-time (25 women); includes 7 minority (3 Asian, non-Hispanic/Latino; 1 Native Hawaiian or other Pacific Islander,

non-Hispanic/Latino; 3 Two or more races, non-Hispanic/Latino), 16 international. 334 applicants, 19% accepted, 22 enrolled. In 2010, 26 master's awarded. *Degree requirements:* For master's, one foreign language, research paper, summer project. *Entrance requirements:* For master's, GRE General Test, previous course work in microeconomics and macroeconomics, professional experience (preferred). Additional exam requirements/recommendations for international students: Required—TOEFL (minimum score 610 paper-based, 253 computer-based, 102 iBT) or IELTS (7.5). *Application deadline:* For fall admission, 1/2 for domestic and international students. Application fee: $100. Electronic applications accepted. *Financial support:* In 2010–11, 29 students received support, including 3 fellowships with full and partial tuition reimbursements available (averaging $15,000 per year), 48 teaching assistantships (averaging $7,740 per year); research assistantships, career-related internships or fieldwork, institutionally sponsored loans, scholarships/grants, tuition waivers (full and partial), unspecified assistantships, and competitive fellowships for summer research also available. Financial award application deadline: 1/2. *Faculty research:* International security studies, global health, international economic development, political economy, policy studies. *Unit head:* Prof. Cheryl Doss, Director of Graduate Studies, 203-432-3418, Fax: 203-432-9886, E-mail: international.relations@yale.edu. *Application contact:* Alice J. Kustenbauder, Registrar, 203-432-3418, Fax: 203-432-9886, E-mail: international.relations@yale.edu.

York University, Faculty of Graduate Studies, Glendon College, Program in Public and International Affairs, Toronto, ON M3J 1P3, Canada. Offers MA.

International Development

American University, School of International Service, Washington, DC 20016-8071. Offers comparative and regional studies (Certificate); cross-cultural communication (Certificate); development management (MS); ethics, peace, and global affairs (MA); European studies (Certificate); global environmental policy (MA, Certificate); international affairs (MA), including comparative and regional studies, environmental policy, international economic policy, international politics, natural resources and sustainable development, U. S. foreign policy; international communication (MA, Certificate); international development (MA, Certificate); international development management (Certificate); international economic policy (Certificate); international economic relations (Certificate); international media (MA); international peace and conflict resolution (MA, Certificate); international relations (PhD); international service (MIS); peace building (Certificate); the Americas (Certificate); United States foreign policy (Certificate); JD/MA. Part-time and evening/weekend programs available. *Faculty:* 91 full-time (35 women), 48 part-time/adjunct (16 women). *Students:* 591 full-time (383 women), 367 part-time (229 women); includes 164 minority (51 Black or African American, non-Hispanic/Latino; 4 American Indian or Alaska Native, non-Hispanic/Latino; 42 Asian, non-Hispanic/Latino; 63 Hispanic/Latino; 4 Two or more races, non-Hispanic/Latino), 94 international. Average age 27. 2,115 applicants, 59% accepted, 360 enrolled. In 2010, 370 master's, 7 doctorates awarded. Terminal master's awarded for partial completion of doctoral program. *Degree requirements:* For master's, one foreign language, comprehensive exam, thesis or alternative; for doctorate, one foreign language, comprehensive exam, thesis/dissertation, research practicum; for Certificate, minimum 15 credit hours related course work. *Entrance requirements:* For master's, GRE, 24 credits of course work in related social sciences, minimum GPA of 3.5, 2 letters of recommendation, bachelor's degree, resume; for doctorate, GRE, 2 letters of recommendation, 24 credits in related social sciences; for Certificate, bachelor's degree. Additional exam requirements/recommendations for international students: Required—TOEFL (minimum score 600 paper-based; 250 computer-based; 100 iBT). *Application deadline:* For fall admission, 1/15 priority date for domestic students; for spring admission, 10/1 priority date for domestic students. Applications are processed on a rolling basis. Application fee: $50. *Financial support:* Career-related internships or fieldwork, Federal Work-Study, and institutionally sponsored loans available. Financial award application deadline: 1/15. *Faculty research:* International intellectual property, international environmental issues, international law and legal order, international telecommunications/technology, international sustainable development. *Unit head:* Dr. Louis W. Goodman, Dean, 202-885-1600, Fax: 202-885-2494. *Application contact:* Yasmin Quianzon, Director of Graduate Admissions and Financial Aid, 202-885-2496, Fax: 202-885-1109.

Andrews University, School of Graduate Studies, College of Arts and Sciences, Department of Behavioral Science, Program in International Development, Berrien Springs, MI 49104. Offers MSA. Postbaccalaureate distance learning degree programs offered. *Entrance requirements:* For master's, GRE General Test. Additional exam requirements/recommendations for international students: Required—TOEFL (minimum score 550 paper-based).

Athabasca University, Centre for Integrated Studies, Athabasca, AB T9S 3A3, Canada. Offers adult education (MA); community studies (MA); cultural studies (MA); educational studies (MA); global change (MA); work, organization, and leadership (MA). Part-time and evening/weekend programs available. Postbaccalaureate distance learning degree programs offered (no on-campus study). *Degree requirements:* For master's, project. *Entrance requirements:* Additional exam requirements/recommendations for international students: Required—TOEFL (minimum score 560 paper-based; 220 computer-based). Electronic applications accepted. *Faculty research:* Women's history, literature and culture studies, sustainable development, labor and education.

Brandeis University, The Heller School for Social Policy and Management, Program in Sustainable International Development, Waltham, MA 02454-9110. Offers international development (MA); sustainable development (MA); MA/JD; MA/MA; MBA/MA. MA/JD program offered in conjunction with Northeastern University School of Law. *Faculty:* 36 full-time, 107 part-time/adjunct. *Students:* 246 full-time (148 women); includes 7 Black or African American, non-Hispanic/Latino; 5 Asian, non-Hispanic/Latino; 7 Hispanic/Latino, 148 international. Average age 30. 772 applicants, 47% accepted, 106 enrolled. In 2010, 68 master's awarded. *Degree requirements:* For master's, 2nd year fieldwork or internship. *Entrance requirements:* For master's, 3 letters of recommendation, curriculum vitae or resume, 3 years of development experience (international experience preferred). Additional exam requirements/recommendations for international students: Required—TOEFL (minimum score 600 paper-based; 250 computer-based; 100 iBT). *Application deadline:* For fall admission, 3/15 for domestic and international students. Applications are processed on a rolling basis. Application fee: $55. Electronic applications accepted. *Expenses:* Contact institution. *Financial support:* In 2010–11, 2 fellowships with full and partial tuition reimbursements (averaging $10,000 per year) were awarded; scholarships/grants and tuition waivers (full and partial) also available. Financial award application deadline: 3/15; financial award applicants required to submit FAFSA. *Faculty research:* Water resource management, human rights, biosphere management, rural development, public policy and governance, gender, conservation, civil society, poverty eradication, project planning and implementation, evaluation, organizational management. *Unit head:* Dr. Laurence R. Simon, Director, 781-736-2770, Fax: 781-736-2774, E-mail: sid@brandeis.edu. *Application contact:* Jamie McCarthy, Admissions Officer, 781-736-3923, E-mail: jamiemcc@brandeis.edu.

Clark University, Graduate School, Department of International Development, Community, and Environment, Program in International Development and Social Change, Worcester, MA 01610-1477. Offers MA. *Students:* 58 full-time (38 women), 14 part-time (7 women); includes 12 minority (9 Black or African American, non-Hispanic/Latino; 3 Hispanic/Latino), 25 international. Average age 29. 221 applicants, 78% accepted, 44 enrolled. In 2010, 27 master's

awarded. *Degree requirements:* For master's, thesis. *Entrance requirements:* For master's, 3 references, resume or curriculum vitae. Additional exam requirements/recommendations for international students: Required—TOEFL (minimum score 575 paper-based; 233 computer-based; 90 iBT) or IELTS (minimum score 6.5). *Application deadline:* For fall admission, 1/15 for domestic students. Application fee: $50. *Expenses:* Tuition: Full-time $37,000; part-time $1156 per credit hour. Required fees: $30; $1156 per credit hour. *Financial support:* In 2010–11, research assistantships with partial tuition reimbursements (averaging $5,000 per year), teaching assistantships with partial tuition reimbursements (averaging $5,000 per year) were awarded; fellowships with partial tuition reimbursements, institutionally sponsored loans and scholarships/grants also available. *Faculty research:* Community action research, gender analysis, land-use planning, geographic information systems, HIV and AIDS, global health and social justice, environmental health, climate change and sustainability. *Unit head:* IDCE, 508-793-7201, Fax: 508-793-8820. *Application contact:* Paula Hall, IDCE Graduate Admissions Office, 508-793-7205, E-mail: idce@clarku.edu.

Cornell University, Graduate School, Graduate Fields of Arts and Sciences, Field of International Development, Ithaca, NY 14853-0001. Offers development policy (MPS); international nutrition (MPS); international planning (MPS); international population (MPS); science and technology policy (MPS). *Faculty:* 41 full-time (14 women). *Students:* 7 full-time (3 women), 5 international. Average age 28. 36 applicants, 22% accepted, 4 enrolled. In 2010, 7 master's awarded. *Degree requirements:* For master's, project paper. *Entrance requirements:* For master's, GRE General Test (recommended), 2 academic recommendations, 2 years of development experience. Additional exam requirements/recommendations for international students: Required—TOEFL (minimum score 77 iBT). *Application deadline:* Applications are processed on a rolling basis. Application fee: $80. Electronic applications accepted. *Expenses:* Tuition: Full-time $29,500. Required fees: $76. Tuition and fees vary according to degree level and program. *Financial support:* In 2010–11, 1 fellowship with full tuition reimbursement was awarded; research assistantships with full tuition reimbursements, teaching assistantships with full tuition reimbursements, institutionally sponsored loans, scholarships/grants, health care benefits, tuition waivers (full and partial), and unspecified assistantships also available. Financial award applicants required to submit FAFSA. *Faculty research:* Development policy, international nutrition, international planning, science and technology policy, international population. *Unit head:* Director of Graduate Studies, 607-255-3037, Fax: 607-255-1005. *Application contact:* Graduate Field Assistant, 607-255-0831, Fax: 607-255-1005, E-mail: mpsid@cornell.edu.

Dalhousie University, Faculty of Arts and Social Science, Department of International Development Studies, Halifax, NS B3H 4R2, Canada. Offers MA. *Entrance requirements:* Additional exam requirements/recommendations for international students: Required—TOEFL, IELTS, CANTEST, CAEL, or Michigan English Language Assessment Battery. Electronic applications accepted.

Duke University, Graduate School, Duke Sanford Institute of Public Policy, Master of International Development Policy Program, Durham, NC 27708-0237. Offers AM, Certificate. *Degree requirements:* For master's, internship, project. *Entrance requirements:* For master's, minimum 3 years of professional experience in a development-related field. Additional exam requirements/recommendations for international students: Required—TOEFL (minimum score 550 paper-based; 213 computer-based; 83 iBT), IELTS (minimum score 7). Electronic applications accepted. *Expenses:* Contact institution.

Eastern University, School of Leadership and Development, St. Davids, PA 19087-3696. Offers economic development (MBA), including international development, urban development (MA, MBA); international development (MA), including global development, urban development (MA, MBA); nonprofit management (MS); organizational leadership (MA); M Div/MBA. Part-time and evening/weekend programs available. *Degree requirements:* For master's, thesis (for some programs). *Entrance requirements:* For master's, GMAT (MBA), minimum GPA of 2.5. *Expenses:* Contact institution. *Faculty research:* Micro-level economic development, China welfare and economic development, macroethics, micro- and macro-level economic development in transitional economics, organizational effectiveness.

Fordham University, Graduate School of Arts and Sciences, Program in International Political Economy and Development, New York, NY 10458. Offers MA, Certificate. Part-time and evening/weekend programs available. *Students:* 44 full-time (22 women), 27 part-time (11 women); includes 1 American Indian or Alaska Native, non-Hispanic/Latino; 1 Asian, non-Hispanic/Latino; 4 Hispanic/Latino, 19 international. Average age 28. 213 applicants, 37% accepted, 36 enrolled. In 2010, 28 master's awarded. *Degree requirements:* For master's, comprehensive exam. *Entrance requirements:* For master's, GRE General Test. Additional exam requirements/recommendations for international students: Required—TOEFL (minimum score 600 paper-based; 250 computer-based). *Application deadline:* For fall admission, 1/4 priority date for domestic students; for spring admission, 11/1 for domestic students. Application fee: $70. Electronic applications accepted. *Financial support:* In 2010–11, 16 students received support, including 16 research assistantships with tuition reimbursements available (averaging $18,400 per year); career-related internships or fieldwork, institutionally sponsored loans, tuition waivers (full and partial), and unspecified assistantships also available. Financial award application deadline: 1/4; financial award applicants required to submit FAFSA. *Faculty research:* International economics, comparative international politics, international banking and finance, international development, emerging markets and country risk analysis. *Unit head:* Dr. Henry Schwalbenberg, Chair, 718-817-3866, Fax: 718-817-3518. *Application contact:* Charlene Dundie, Director of Graduate Admissions, 718-817-4420, Fax: 718-817-3566, E-mail: dundie@fordham.edu.

International Development

The George Washington University, Columbian College of Arts and Sciences, Department of Anthropology, Concentration in International Development, Washington, DC 20052. Offers MA. *Unit head:* Prof. Barbara Miller, Director, 202-994-6075, E-mail: barbar@gwu.edu. *Application contact:* Information Contact, 202-994-6075, E-mail: anth@gwu.edu.

The George Washington University, Elliott School of International Affairs, Program in International Development Studies, Washington, DC 20052. Offers MA, JD/MA, MPH/MA. *Students:* 64 full-time (46 women), 25 part-time (21 women); includes 4 Asian, non-Hispanic/Latino; 2 Hispanic/Latino; 1 Two or more races, non-Hispanic/Latino, 6 international. Average age 27. 424 applicants, 33% accepted, 40 enrolled. In 2010, 37 master's awarded. *Degree requirements:* For master's, one foreign language, capstone project. *Entrance requirements:* For master's, GRE General Test, 2 years (or the equivalent) of a modern foreign language, introductory course in microeconomics, 1 semester of statistics. Additional exam requirements/recommendations for international students: Required—TOEFL. *Application deadline:* For fall admission, 2/1 for domestic students; for spring admission, 10/1 for domestic students. Application fee: $75. Electronic applications accepted. *Financial support:* In 2010–11, 27 students received support; fellowships with tuition reimbursements available, research assistantships with tuition reimbursements available, career-related internships or fieldwork, Federal Work-Study, institutionally sponsored loans, and tuition waivers available. Financial award application deadline: 1/15; financial award applicants required to submit FAFSA. *Faculty research:* Development, anthropology, health and development, political science, education. *Unit head:* Sean Roberts, 202-994-7739, E-mail: seanrr@gwu.edu. *Application contact:* Jeff V. Miles, Director of Graduate Admissions, 202-994-7050, Fax: 202-994-9537, E-mail: esiagrad@gwu.edu.

Harvard University, John F. Kennedy School of Government, Master in Public Administration/International Development Program, Cambridge, MA 02138. Offers MPAID. *Students:* 130 full-time (58 women), 2 part-time (both women); includes 1 Black or African American, non-Hispanic/Latino; 9 Asian, non-Hispanic/Latino, 87 international. Average age 29. 371 applicants, 26% accepted, 69 enrolled. In 2010, 58 master's awarded. *Entrance requirements:* For master's, GMAT or GRE General Test (for joint Business School applicants), one course each in microeconomics and macroeconomics; two college-level calculus courses (one must contain multivariable calculus); bachelor's degree; 2-3 years of professional experience in development (strongly encouraged). Additional exam requirements/recommendations for international students: Required—TOEFL (minimum score 600 paper-based; 250 computer-based; 100 iBT). *Application deadline:* For fall admission, 12/2 for domestic students. Application fee: $100. Electronic applications accepted. *Expenses:* Tuition: Full-time $34,976. Required fees: $1166. Full-time tuition and fees vary according to program. *Financial support:* Fellowships, research assistantships, teaching assistantships, career-related internships or fieldwork, Federal Work-Study, institutionally sponsored loans, scholarships/grants, health care benefits, and unspecified assistantships available. Financial award application deadline: 2/6; financial award applicants required to submit CSS PROFILE or FAFSA. *Unit head:* Carol Finney, Director, 617-495-7799, E-mail: carol_finney@harvard.edu. *Application contact:* 617-495-2133, E-mail: mpaid_program@hks.harvard.edu.

Hope International University, School of Graduate and Professional Studies, Program in Business Administration, Fullerton, CA 92831-3138. Offers business administration (MBA); educational administration (MSM); international development (MBA, MSM); management (MBA); nonprofit management (MBA). Part-time programs available. Postbaccalaureate distance learning degree programs offered (no on-campus study). *Degree requirements:* For master's, comprehensive exam (for some programs), thesis (for some programs), project. *Entrance requirements:* For master's, minimum GPA of 3.0; 2 references. Additional exam requirements/recommendations for international students: Required—TOEFL (minimum score 550 paper-based; 213 computer-based; 86 iBT); Recommended—IELTS (minimum score 6.5). Electronic applications accepted. *Expenses:* Contact institution.

John Brown University, Graduate Business Programs, Siloam Springs, AR 72761-2121. Offers business administration (MBA), including international business, leadership and ethics; international community development leadership (MS); leadership and ethics (MS); leadership and higher education (MS). Part-time and evening/weekend programs available. Postbaccalaureate distance learning degree programs offered (minimal on-campus study). *Entrance requirements:* For master's, MAT, GMAT or GRE if undergraduate GPA is less than 3.0, recommendation forms from three people, 200-word essay describing professional plans and reason for seeking acceptance. Additional exam requirements/recommendations for international students: Required—TOEFL (minimum score 550 paper-based; 173 computer-based; 70 iBT). Electronic applications accepted.

The Johns Hopkins University, Paul H. Nitze School of Advanced International Studies, Washington, DC 20036. Offers international development (MA, Certificate), including international economics (MA); international public policy (MIPP); international relations (PhD); international studies (Certificate); Japan studies (MA), including international economics; Korea Studies (MA), including international economics; South Asia studies (MA), including international economics; Southeast Asia studies (MA), including international economics; JD/MA; MBA/MA; MHS/MA. *Faculty:* 57 full-time (18 women), 125 part-time/adjunct (40 women). *Students:* 627 full-time (305 women), 39 part-time (24 women); includes 127 minority (18 Black or African American, non-Hispanic/Latino; 60 Asian, non-Hispanic/Latino; 32 Hispanic/Latino; 1 Native Hawaiian or other Pacific Islander, non-Hispanic/Latino; 16 Two or more races, non-Hispanic/Latino), 176 international. Average age 27. 1,753 applicants, 42% accepted, 307 enrolled. In 2010, 441 master's, 10 doctorates awarded. Terminal master's awarded for partial completion of doctoral program. *Degree requirements:* For master's, one foreign language, 4-6 International Economics courses, 5-6 functional or regional concentration courses, 2 core examinations, proficiency in a language other than native language, and capstone project; for doctorate, 2 foreign languages, thesis/dissertation, 3 comprehensive exams, economics, quantitative and qualitative course, dissertation prospectus and defense. *Entrance requirements:* For master's, GMAT or GRE General Test, previous course work in economics, foreign language, undergraduate degree; for doctorate, GRE General Test, master's degree. Additional exam requirements/recommendations for international students: Required—TOEFL (minimum score 600 paper-based; 250 computer-based; 100 iBT) or IELTS (minimum score 7). *Application deadline:* For fall admission, 1/7 for domestic and international students. Application fee: $85. Electronic applications accepted. *Expenses:* Contact institution. *Financial support:* In 2010–11, 450 students received support, including 450 fellowships (averaging $12,000 per year), 32 teaching assistantships (averaging $3,906 per year); career-related internships or fieldwork, Federal Work-Study, and scholarships/grants also available. Financial award application deadline: 2/15; financial award applicants required to submit FAFSA. *Faculty research:* Regional studies, international relations, international economics, energy and environment, international development. Total annual research expenditures: $8.1 million. *Unit head:* Sidney Jackson, Director of Admissions, 202-663-5700, Fax: 202-663-7788. *Application contact:* Admissions, 202-663-5700, Fax: 202-663-7788, E-mail: admissions.sais@jhu.edu.

Lehigh University, College of Education, Program in Comparative and International Education, Bethlehem, PA 18015. Offers comparative and international education (MA); globalization and educational change (M Ed); international counseling (Certificate); international development in education (Certificate); special education (Certificate); TESOL (Certificate). Part-time programs available. Postbaccalaureate distance learning degree programs offered (no on-campus study). *Faculty:* 2 full-time (1 woman), 3 part-time/adjunct (all women). *Students:* 24 full-time (12 women), 50 part-time (39 women); includes 3 minority (all Asian, non-Hispanic/Latino), 13 international. Average age 33. 61 applicants, 62% accepted, 38 enrolled. In 2010, 19 master's awarded. *Degree requirements:* For master's, thesis (MA). *Entrance requirements:* For master's, 2 letters of recommendation. Additional exam requirements/recommendations for international students: Required—TOEFL (minimum score 600 paper-based; 250 computer-based; 93 iBT). *Application deadline:* For fall admission, 5/15 for domestic and international students; for spring admission, 11/1 for domestic and international students. Applications are processed on a rolling basis. Application fee: $65. Electronic applications accepted. *Financial support:* In 2010–11, 6 students received support, including 4 research assistantships with full and partial tuition reimbursements available (averaging $13,000 per year). Financial award application deadline: 3/15. *Faculty research:* Gender equity in education, post-socialist education transformation, educational borrowing, comparing education systems, education policy and globalization. *Unit head:* Dr. Alexander W. Wiseman, Coordinator, 610-758-5740, Fax: 610-758-6223, E-mail: aww207@lehigh.edu. *Application contact:* Donna M. Johnson, Coordinator, 610-758-3231, Fax: 610-758-6223, E-mail: dmj4@lehigh.edu.

McGill University, Faculty of Graduate and Postdoctoral Studies, Desautels Faculty of Management, Montréal, QC H3A 2T5, Canada. Offers administration (PhD); entrepreneurial studies (MBA); finance (MBA); general management (Post Master's Certificate); information systems (MBA); international business (exchange program) (MBA); international Master's program in practicing management (MM); management (MBA); management for development (MBA); manufacturing management (MMM); marketing (MBA); operations management (MBA); public accountancy (Diploma); strategic management (MBA); MBA/LL B; MD/MBA. MMM offered jointly with Faculty of Engineering; PhD with Concordia University, HEC Montreal, Université de Montréal, Université du Québec à Montréal.

Ohio University, Graduate College, Center for International Studies, Program in International Development Studies, Athens, OH 45701-2979. Offers MA. Part-time programs available. *Students:* 31 full-time (18 women), 1 (woman) part-time; includes 3 minority (2 Black or African American, non-Hispanic/Latino; 1 Two or more races, non-Hispanic/Latino), 20 international. Average age 29. 90 applicants, 57% accepted, 18 enrolled. In 2010, 16 master's awarded. *Degree requirements:* For master's, one foreign language, thesis optional. *Entrance requirements:* For master's, minimum GPA of 3.0. Additional exam requirements/recommendations for international students: Required—TOEFL (minimum score 550 paper-based; 213 computer-based; 80 iBT), IELTS (minimum score 6.5). *Application deadline:* For fall admission, 1/1 for domestic and international students. Application fee: $50 ($55 for international students). Electronic applications accepted. *Financial support:* In 2010–11, 21 students received support; research assistantships with full tuition reimbursements available, career-related internships or fieldwork, Federal Work-Study, institutionally sponsored loans, tuition waivers (partial), and unspecified assistantships available. Financial award application deadline: 1/1. *Faculty research:* Problems and issues in social, economic, political, health and environmental development. *Unit head:* Dr. Tom Smucker, Director, 740-593-1152, E-mail: smucker@ohio.edu. *Application contact:* Joan Kraynanski, Administrative Assistant, 740-593-1840, Fax: 740-593-1837, E-mail: kraynans@ohio.edu.

Rutgers, The State University of New Jersey, Camden, Graduate School of Arts and Sciences, Department of Public Policy and Administration, Camden, NJ 08102. Offers education policy and leadership (MPA); international public service and development (MPA); public management (MPA); JD/MPA; MPA/MA. *Accreditation:* NASPAA. Part-time and evening/weekend programs available. *Faculty:* 17 full-time (7 women), 3 part-time/adjunct (1 woman). *Students:* 75 full-time (45 women), 49 part-time (26 women); includes 38 Black or African American, non-Hispanic/Latino; 1 American Indian or Alaska Native, non-Hispanic/Latino; 5 Asian, non-Hispanic/Latino; 11 Hispanic/Latino. Average age 32. 132 applicants, 73% accepted, 58 enrolled. In 2010, 44 master's awarded. *Degree requirements:* For master's, directed study, research workshop, 42 credits. *Entrance requirements:* For master's, GRE General Test, GMAT or LSAT, 3 letters of recommendation; resume. Additional exam requirements/recommendations for international students: Required—TOEFL (minimum score 550 paper-based; 213 computer-based), IELTS. *Application deadline:* For fall admission, 5/1 priority date for domestic students; for spring admission, 12/1 priority date for domestic students. Applications are processed on a rolling basis. Application fee: $65. Electronic applications accepted. *Expenses:* Tuition, state resident: full-time $4963; part-time $319 per credit. Tuition, nonresident: full-time $10,493; part-time $680 per credit. *Financial support:* In 2010–11, 97 students received support, including 3 fellowships with partial tuition reimbursements available (averaging $3,500 per year), 1 research assistantship with full tuition reimbursement available (averaging $26,000 per year); career-related internships or fieldwork, Federal Work-Study, scholarships/grants, and tuition waivers (partial) also available. Financial award application deadline: 3/15; financial award applicants required to submit FAFSA. *Faculty research:* Nonprofit management, county and municipal administration, health and human services, government communication, administrative law, educational finance. Total annual research expenditures: $8.8 million. *Unit head:* Dr. Robyne Turner, Chair, 856-225-2982, Fax: 856-225-6559, E-mail: rsturner@camden.rutgers.edu. *Application contact:* Sandra J. Cheesman, Department Administrator, 856-225-6860, Fax: 856-225-6559, E-mail: scheesma@camden.rutgers.edu.

Saint Mary's University, Faculty of Arts, International Development Studies Program, Halifax, NS B3H 3C3, Canada. Offers MA, Graduate Diploma. Part-time programs available. *Degree requirements:* For master's, thesis. *Entrance requirements:* For master's, honors degree. *Faculty research:* Dynamics of global development, gender and development, policy analysis, models and strategies for development, Latin American and Caribbean development.

Tufts University, Fletcher School of Law and Diplomacy, Medford, MA 02155. Offers LL M, MA, MAHA, MALD, MIB, PhD, DVM/MA, JD/MALD, MALD/MA, MALD/MBA, MALD/MS, MD/MA. Postbaccalaureate distance learning degree programs offered (minimal on-campus study). *Faculty:* 37 full-time (10 women), 48 part-time/adjunct (14 women). *Students:* 541 full-time (278 women), 9 part-time (3 women); includes 73 minority (8 Black or African American, non-Hispanic/Latino; 30 Asian, non-Hispanic/Latino; 11 Hispanic/Latino; 24 Two or more races, non-Hispanic/Latino), 208 international. Average age 31. 1,875 applicants, 41% accepted, 296 enrolled. In 2010, 297 master's, 14 doctorates awarded. *Degree requirements:* For master's, one foreign language, thesis; for doctorate, one foreign language, comprehensive exam, thesis/dissertation, dissertation defense. *Entrance requirements:* For master's and doctorate, GMAT or GRE General Test. Additional exam requirements/recommendations for international students: Required—TOEFL (minimum score 600 paper-based; 250 computer-based; 100 iBT), IELTS (minimum score 7). *Application deadline:* For fall admission, 1/15 for domestic and international students; for spring admission, 10/15 for domestic and international students. Application fee: $70. Electronic applications accepted. *Expenses:* Contact institution. *Financial support:* Federal Work-Study, institutionally sponsored loans, scholarships/grants, and tuition waivers (partial) available. Financial award application deadline: 1/15; financial award applicants required to submit FAFSA. *Faculty research:* Negotiation and conflict resolution, international organizations, international business and economic law, security studies, development economics. *Unit head:* Stephen W. Bosworth, Dean, 617-627-3050, Fax: 617-627-3712. *Application contact:* Laurie A. Hurley, 617-627-3040, E-mail: fletcheradmissions@tufts.edu.

Tufts University, Graduate School of Arts and Sciences, Department of Urban and Environmental Policy and Planning, Medford, MA 02155. Offers community development (MA); environmental policy (MA); health and human welfare (MA); housing policy (MA); international environment/development policy (MA); public policy (MPP); MA/MS; MALD/MA. *Accreditation:* ACSP (one or more programs are accredited). Part-time programs available. *Degree requirements:* For master's, thesis, internship. *Entrance requirements:* For master's, GRE General Test. Additional exam requirements/recommendations for international students: Required—TOEFL (minimum score 550 paper-based; 213 computer-based; 80 iBT). Electronic applications accepted. *Expenses:* Contact institution.

Tulane University, School of Liberal Arts, The Payson Center for International Development and Technology Transfer, New Orleans, LA 70118-5669. Offers international development (MS, PhD). Part-time programs available. *Degree requirements:* For master's, comprehensive exam (for some programs), thesis optional; for doctorate, comprehensive exam, thesis/dissertation. *Entrance requirements:* For master's, GRE General Test, minimum B average in undergraduate course work. Additional exam requirements/recommendations for international students: Required—TOEFL. Electronic applications accepted. *Faculty research:* Third World development.

University of Denver, Josef Korbel School of International Studies, Denver, CO 80208. Offers conflict resolution (MA); development practice (MDP); global finance, trade and economic integration (MA); global health affairs (Certificate); homeland security (Certificate); humanitarian assistance (Certificate); international development (MA); international human rights (MA); international security (MA); international studies (MA, PhD). Part-time programs available. *Faculty:* 33 full-time (13 women), 38 part-time/adjunct (11 women). *Students:* 461 full-time (279 women), 52 part-time (27 women); includes 71 minority (8 Black or African American, non-Hispanic/Latino; 3 American Indian or Alaska Native, non-Hispanic/Latino; 25 Asian, non-Hispanic/Latino; 25 Hispanic/Latino; 2 Native Hawaiian or other Pacific Islander, non-Hispanic/Latino; 8 Two or more races, non-Hispanic/Latino), 42 international. Average age 28. 1,056 applicants, 69% accepted, 259 enrolled. In 2010, 230 master's, 5 doctorates, 42 other advanced degrees awarded. *Degree requirements:* For master's, one foreign language, thesis; for doctorate, one foreign language, thesis/dissertation. *Entrance requirements:* For master's and doctorate, GRE General Test. Additional exam requirements/recommendations for international students: Required—TOEFL (minimum score 587 paper-based; 95 iBT). *Application deadline:* For fall admission, 1/15 priority date for domestic students, 12/15 priority date for international students; for winter admission, 10/15 priority date for domestic and international students. Applications are processed on a rolling basis. Application fee: $60. Electronic applications accepted. *Expenses:* Tuition: Full-time $35,604; part-time $29,670 per year. Required fees: $687 per year. Tuition and fees vary according to program. *Financial support:* In 2010–11, 1 teaching assistantship with partial tuition reimbursement (averaging $9,999 per year) was awarded; career-related internships or fieldwork, Federal Work-Study, institutionally sponsored loans, scholarships/grants, and unspecified assistantships also available. Support available to part-time students. Financial award applicants required to submit FAFSA. *Faculty research:* Human rights and international security, international politics and economics, economic-social and political development, international technology analysis and management. *Unit head:* Ambassador Christopher R. Hill, Dean, 303-871-2539, Fax: 303-871-2124, E-mail: christopher.r.hill@du.edu. *Application contact:* Brad Miller, Director of Graduate Admissions and Financial Aid, 303-871-2989, Fax: 303-871-2124, E-mail: korbeladm@du.edu.

University of Florida, Graduate School, College of Liberal Arts and Sciences, Department of Political Science, Gainesville, FL 32611. Offers international development policy and administration (MA, Certificate); international relations (MA, MAT); political campaigning (MA, Certificate); political science (MA, MAT, PhD); public affairs (MA, Certificate); JD/MA. *Faculty:* 27 full-time (9 women), 3 part-time/adjunct (1 woman). *Students:* 115 full-time (43 women), 23 part-time (13 women); includes 6 Black or African American, non-Hispanic/Latino; 3 Asian, non-Hispanic/Latino; 10 Hispanic/Latino, 25 international. Average age 27. 185 applicants, 48% accepted, 35 enrolled. In 2010, 28 master's, 11 doctorates awarded. Terminal master's awarded for partial completion of doctoral program. *Degree requirements:* For master's, variable foreign language requirement, comprehensive exam (for some programs), thesis or alternative, internship (for some programs); for doctorate, variable foreign language requirement, comprehensive exam, thesis/dissertation. *Entrance requirements:* For master's and doctorate, GRE General Test, minimum GPA of 3.0. Additional exam requirements/recommendations for international students: Required—TOEFL (minimum score 550 paper-based; 213 computer-based; 80 iBT), IELTS (minimum score 6). *Application deadline:* For fall admission, 1/1 priority date for domestic students, 1/1 for international students. Applications are processed on a rolling basis. Application fee: $30. Electronic applications accepted. *Expenses:* Tuition, state resident: full-time $10,915.92. Tuition, nonresident: full-time $28,309. *Financial support:* In 2010–11, 104 students received support, including 50 fellowships, 13 research assistantships (averaging $15,878 per year), 41 teaching assistantships (averaging $16,099 per year); career-related internships or fieldwork, Federal Work-Study, institutionally sponsored loans, and unspecified assistantships also available. Financial award application deadline: 1/15; financial award applicants required to submit FAFSA. *Faculty research:* American political institutions, comparative democratization, political theory and judgment, religion and politics, theories of international relations. *Unit head:* Dr. Michael D. Martinez, Chair, 352-273-2363, Fax: 352-392-8127, E-mail: martinez@ufl.edu. *Application contact:* Dr. Dan O'Neill, Interim Graduate Coordinator, 352-273-2386, Fax: 352-392-8127, E-mail: doneill@ufl.edu.

University of Guelph, Graduate Studies, Collaborative International Development Studies, Guelph, ON N1G 2W1, Canada. Offers M Eng, M Sc, MA, MBA, PhD. Part-time programs available. *Degree requirements:* For master's, thesis (for some programs), seminar; for doctorate, comprehensive exam (for some programs), thesis/dissertation. *Entrance requirements:* For master's, honour's degree with courses in economics, social science, and empirical methods. *Faculty research:* Transformation of developing societies, regional differences, national and international processes of development, long-term change.

The University of Manchester, School of Environment and Development, Manchester, United Kingdom. Offers architecture (M Phil, PhD); development policy and management (M Phil, PhD); human geography (M Phil, PhD); physical geography (M Phil, PhD); planning and landscape (M Phil, PhD).

University of Minnesota, Twin Cities Campus, Graduate School, Hubert H. Humphrey School of Public Affairs, Master of Development Practice in International Development Program, Minneapolis, MN 55455-0213. Offers MDP. Program offered jointly with Interdisciplinary Center for the Study of Global Change (ICGC). *Students:* 16 full-time (11 women); includes 5 minority (2 Black or African American, non-Hispanic/Latino; 1 American Indian or Alaska Native, non-Hispanic/Latino; 2 Asian, non-Hispanic/Latino), 2 international. Average age 26. 117 applicants, 42% accepted, 16 enrolled. *Degree requirements:* For master's, thesis or alternative, International field experience. *Entrance requirements:* For master's, Graduate Record Exam. Additional exam requirements/recommendations for international students: Required—TOEFL (minimum score 600 paper-based; 200 computer-based; 100 iBT). *Application deadline:* For fall admission, 1/15 for domestic and international students. Application fee: $75 ($95 for international students). Electronic applications accepted. *Financial support:* In 2010–11, 6 students received support. Application deadline: 12/15. *Unit head:* Greg Lindsey, Dean, 612-624-3800, Fax: 612-626-0002, E-mail: hhhadmit@umn.edu. *Application contact:* Julie Harrold, Director of Admissions, 612-624-3800, Fax: 612-626-0002, E-mail: hhhadmit@umn.edu.

University of New Hampshire, Graduate School, Interdisciplinary Programs, Durham, NH 03824. Offers college teaching (MST); development policy and practice (MA); environmental education (MA); interdisciplinary studies (Postbaccalaureate Certificate); natural resources and earth system science (PhD), including earth and environmental science, natural resources and environmental studies. Part-time programs available. *Faculty:* 104 full-time. *Students:* 66 full-time (39 women), 24 part-time (15 women); includes 5 Asian, non-Hispanic/Latino, 12 international. Average age 35. 49 applicants, 37% accepted, 7 enrolled. In 2010, 8 master's, 8 doctorates, 1 other advanced degree awarded. *Degree requirements:* For master's, thesis (for some programs); for doctorate, thesis/dissertation (for some programs). *Entrance requirements:* For doctorate, GRE (if from a non-US university). Additional exam requirements/recommendations for international students: Required—TOEFL (minimum score 550 paper-based; 213 computer-based; 80 iBT). *Application deadline:* For fall admission, 7/1 priority date for domestic students, 4/1 for international students; for winter admission, 12/1 priority date for domestic students. Applications are processed on a rolling basis. Application fee: $65. Electronic applications accepted. *Financial support:* In 2010–11, 47 students received support, including 10 fellowships, 21 research assistantships, 10 teaching assistantships. Financial award application deadline: 3/1. *Unit head:* Dr. Harry J. Richards, Dean, 603-862-3005, Fax: 603-862-0275, E-mail: harry.richards@unh.edu. *Application contact:* Sharon Andrews, Senior Administrative Assistant, 603-862-3005, E-mail: college.teaching@unh.edu.

University of New Mexico, Graduate School, College of Arts and Sciences, Department of Economics, Albuquerque, NM 87131-2039. Offers environmental/natural resources (MA, PhD); international/development (MA, PhD); labor/human resources (MA, PhD); public finance (MA, PhD). Part-time programs available. *Faculty:* 26 full-time (9 women), 7 part-time/adjunct (1 woman). *Students:* 47 full-time (14 women), 17 part-time (5 women); includes 2 American Indian or Alaska Native, non-Hispanic/Latino; 2 Asian, non-Hispanic/Latino; 8 Hispanic/Latino, 18 international. Average age 34. 75 applicants, 51% accepted, 15 enrolled. In 2010, 14 master's, 1 doctorate awarded. Terminal master's awarded for partial completion of doctoral program. *Degree requirements:* For master's, comprehensive exam, thesis (for some programs); for doctorate, comprehensive exam, thesis/dissertation. *Entrance requirements:* For master's and doctorate, GRE General Test, 3 letters of recommendation, letter of intent. Additional exam requirements/recommendations for international students: Required—TOEFL (minimum score 520 paper-based; 190 computer-based; 68 iBT). *Application deadline:* For fall admission, 3/1 priority date for domestic students, 3/1 for international students. Applications are processed on a rolling basis. Application fee: $50. Electronic applications accepted. *Expenses:* Tuition, state resident: full-time $5991; part-time $251 per credit hour. Tuition, nonresident: full-time $14,405; part-time $800.20 per credit hour. Tuition and fees vary according to course level, course load, program and reciprocity agreements. *Financial support:* In 2010–11, 47 students received support, including 3 fellowships with tuition reimbursements available (averaging $3,611 per year), 14 research assistantships with tuition reimbursements available (averaging $7,791 per year), 15 teaching assistantships (averaging $7,467 per year); career-related internships or fieldwork, Federal Work-Study, scholarships/grants, health care benefits, and unspecified assistantships also available. Support available to part-time students. Financial award application deadline: 3/1; financial award applicants required to submit FAFSA. *Faculty research:* Core theory, econometrics, public finance, international/development economics, labor/human resource economics, environmental/natural resource economics. Total annual research expenditures: $1.8 million. *Unit head:* Dr. Robert Berrens, Chair, 505-277-5304, Fax: 505-277-9445, E-mail: rberrens@unm.edu. *Application contact:* Shoshana Handel, Academic Advisor, 505-277-3056, Fax: 505-277-9445, E-mail: shandel@unm.edu.

University of Ottawa, Faculty of Graduate and Postdoctoral Studies, Program in Globalization and International Development, Ottawa, ON K1N 6N5, Canada. Offers MA. *Degree requirements:* For master's, thesis or alternative. *Entrance requirements:* For master's, honours bachelor's degree or equivalent, minimum B average.

University of Pittsburgh, Graduate School of Public and International Affairs, Division of International Development, Pittsburgh, PA 15260. Offers development planning and environmental sustainability (MID); human security (MID); nongovernmental organizations and civil society (MID); MID/JD; MID/MBA; MID/MPH; MID/MPIA; MID/MSIS; MID/MSW. Part-time programs available. *Faculty:* 30 full-time (12 women), 67 part-time/adjunct (25 women). *Students:* 66 full-time (46 women), 7 part-time (5 women); includes 7 minority (1 Black or African American, non-Hispanic/Latino; 3 Asian, non-Hispanic/Latino; 3 Hispanic/Latino), 11 international. Average age 25. 125 applicants, 82% accepted, 39 enrolled. In 2010, 35 master's awarded. *Degree requirements:* For master's, thesis optional, internship, capstone seminar. *Entrance requirements:* For master's, GRE General Test, 3 letters of recommendation; minimum GPA of 3.2 (recommended). Additional exam requirements/recommendations for international students: Required—TOEFL (minimum score 550 paper-based; 213 computer-based; 80 iBT), TWE (minimum score 4); Recommended—IELTS (minimum score 7). *Application deadline:* For fall admission, 2/1 for domestic students, 1/5 for international students; for spring admission, 11/1 for domestic students, 8/1 for international students. Application fee: $50. Electronic applications accepted. *Expenses:* Tuition, state resident: full-time $17,304; part-time $701 per credit. Tuition, nonresident: full-time $29,554; part-time $1210 per credit. Required fees: $740; $214 per term. Tuition and fees vary according to program. *Financial support:* In 2010–11, 28 students received support. Scholarships/grants, tuition waivers (full and partial), unspecified assistantships, and student employment available. Financial award application deadline: 2/1. *Faculty research:* Nongovernmental organizations, religion and civil society, international development, development economics and policy, human rights and development, humanitarian intervention, ethnic conflict and civil war, post-conflict peace-building, corruption and transnational governance, civil society and public affairs, political constraints on rural development. Total annual research expenditures: $892,349. *Unit head:* Dr. Paul J. Nelson, Director, 412-648-7645, Fax: 412-648-2605, E-mail: pjnelson@pitt.edu. *Application contact:* Elizabeth Hruby, Graduate Enrollment Counselor, 412-648-7640, Fax: 412-648-7641, E-mail: eah44@pitt.edu.

University of Pittsburgh, Graduate School of Public and International Affairs, Public Policy and Management Program for Mid-Career Professionals, Pittsburgh, PA 15260. Offers development planning (MPPM); international development (MPPM); international political economy (MPPM); international security studies (MPPM); management of non profit organizations (MPPM); metropolitan management and regional development (MPPM); policy analysis and evaluation (MPPM). Part-time programs available. *Faculty:* 30 full-time (12 women), 67 part-time/adjunct (25 women). *Students:* 14 full-time (1 woman), 34 part-time (17 women), 8 international. Average age 38. 31 applicants, 74% accepted, 15 enrolled. In 2010, 14 master's awarded. *Degree requirements:* For master's, thesis optional, capstone seminar. *Entrance requirements:* For master's, 2 letters of recommendation, resume, 5 years of supervisory or budgetary experience. Additional exam requirements/recommendations for international students: Required—TOEFL (minimum score 600 paper-based; 250 computer-based; 100 iBT), TWE (minimum score 4); Recommended—IELTS (minimum score 7). *Application deadline:* For fall admission, 6/1 priority date for domestic students, 2/15 for international students; for spring admission, 1/1 priority date for domestic students, 8/1 for international students. Applications are processed on a rolling basis. Application fee: $50. Electronic applications accepted. *Expenses:* Tuition, state resident: full-time $17,304; part-time $701 per credit. Tuition, nonresident: full-time $29,554; part-time $1210 per credit. Required fees: $740; $214 per term. Tuition and fees vary according to program. *Financial support:* In 2010–11, 14 students received support. Scholarships/grants and tuition waivers (partial) available. Support available to part-time students. Financial award application deadline: 2/1. *Faculty research:* Nonprofit management, urban and regional affairs, policy analysis and evaluation, security and intelligence studies, global political economy, nongovernmental organizations, civil society, development planning and environmental sustainability, human security. Total annual research expenditures: $892,349. *Unit head:* Dr. George Dougherty, Director, Executive Education, 412-648-7603, Fax: 412-648-2605, E-mail: gwdjr@pitt.edu. *Application contact:* Michael T. Rizzi, Associate Director of Student Services, 412-648-7640, Fax: 412-648-7641, E-mail: rizzim@pitt.edu.

University of Pittsburgh, Katz Graduate School of Business, MBA/Master of International Development Joint Degree Program, Pittsburgh, PA 15260. Offers MID/MBA. *Accreditation:* AACSB. Part-time and evening/weekend programs available. *Faculty:* 60 full-time (18 women), 22 part-time/adjunct (5 women). *Students:* 2 full-time (both women). Average age 26. 2 applicants, 50% accepted, 0 enrolled. *Entrance requirements:* Additional exam requirements/recommendations for international students: Required—TOEFL (minimum 600 paper, 250 computer, 100 iBT) or IELTS. *Application deadline:* For fall admission, 4/1 priority date for domestic students, 2/1 priority date for international students. Application fee: $50. Electronic applications accepted. *Expenses:* Tuition, state resident: full-time $17,304; part-time $701 per credit. Tuition, nonresident: full-time $29,554; part-time $1210 per credit. Required fees: $740; $214 per term. Tuition and fees vary according to program. *Financial support:* Career-related internships or fieldwork and scholarships/grants available. Financial award application deadline: 3/1; financial award applicants required to submit FAFSA. *Faculty research:* Transitional economies, incentives and governance, corporate finance, mergers and acquisitions, global information systems and structures, consumer behavior and marketing models, entrepreneurship and globalization. *Unit head:* William T. Valenta, Assistant Dean, Director of MBA Program, 412-648-1610, Fax: 412-648-1659, E-mail: wtvalenta@katz.pitt.edu. *Application contact:* Cliff McCormick, Director of MBA Admissions, 412-648-1700, Fax: 412-648-1659, E-mail: mba@katz.pitt.edu.

University of San Francisco, College of Arts and Sciences, Department of Economics, Program in International and Development Economics, San Francisco, CA 94117-1080. Offers MA. *Faculty:* 8 full-time (2 women), 9 part-time/adjunct (3 women). *Students:* 39 full-time (21 women), 7 part-time (3 women); includes 8 minority (3 Asian, non-Hispanic/Latino; 2 Hispanic/Latino; 3 Two or more races, non-Hispanic/Latino), 17 international. Average age 28. 122 applicants, 51% accepted, 25 enrolled. In 2010, 13 master's awarded. *Expenses:* Tuition: Full-time $20,070; part-time $1115 per credit hour. Tuition and fees vary according to course load, degree level and program. *Financial support:* In 2010–11, 27 students received support.

International Development

University of San Francisco (continued)
Unit head: Dr. Elizabeth Katz, Co-Director, 415-422-2711, Fax: 415-422-6983. *Application contact:* Information Contact, 415-422-5135, Fax: 415-422-6983, E-mail: asgraduate@usfca.edu.

University of Southern Mississippi, Graduate School, College of Arts and Letters, Department of Political Science, International Development, and International Affairs, Hattiesburg, MS 39406-0001. Offers international development (PhD); political science (MA, MS). Part-time and evening/weekend programs available. Postbaccalaureate distance learning degree programs offered. *Faculty:* 14 full-time (2 women). *Students:* 33 full-time (14 women), 65 part-time (28 women); includes 19 Black or African American, non-Hispanic/Latino; 1 American Indian or Alaska Native, non-Hispanic/Latino; 2 Asian, non-Hispanic/Latino; 6 Hispanic/Latino, 7 international. Average age 36. 44 applicants, 64% accepted, 22 enrolled. In 2010, 10 master's, 2 doctorates awarded. *Degree requirements:* For master's, comprehensive exam, thesis (for some programs); for doctorate, comprehensive exam, thesis/dissertation. *Entrance requirements:* For master's, GRE General Test, minimum GPA of 2.75 in last 2 years, 3.0 in field of study; for doctorate, GRE General Test, minimum GPA of 3.5. Additional exam requirements/recommendations for international students: Required—TOEFL, IELTS. *Application deadline:* For fall admission, 3/1 priority date for domestic students, 3/1 for international students. Applications are processed on a rolling basis. Application fee: $50. *Financial support:* In 2010–11, 4 research assistantships with full and partial tuition reimbursements (averaging $9,000 per year), 8 teaching assistantships with full tuition reimbursements (averaging $7,000 per year) were awarded; career-related internships or fieldwork, Federal Work-Study, scholarships/grants, health care benefits, and unspecified assistantships also available. Financial award application deadline: 3/15; financial award applicants required to submit FAFSA. *Faculty research:* American politics, international politics, political theory, comparative politics, public law. *Unit head:* Dr. Allan McBride, Chair, 601-266-4310. *Application contact:* Dr. Mark Stedman, Director, Graduate Studies, 601-266-4310, Fax: 601-266-4172.

Walden University, Graduate Programs, School of Public Policy and Administration, Minneapolis, MN 55401. Offers criminal justice (MPA); emergency management (MPA); government management (Postbaccalaureate Certificate); health policy (MPA); homeland security policy (MPA); homeland security policy and coordination (MPA); interdisciplinary policy studies (MPA); international nongovernmental organizations (ngos) (MPA); law and public policy (MPA); local government management for sustainable communities (MPA); nonprofit management (Postbaccalaureate Certificate); nonprofit management and leadership (MPA, MS); policy analysis (MPA); public management and leadership (MPA); public policy and administration (MPA, PhD), including criminal justice (PhD), emergency management (PhD), health policy (PhD), health services (PhD), homeland security policy (PhD), homeland security policy and coordination (PhD), interdisciplinary policy studies (PhD), international nongovernmental organizations (PhD), law and public policy (PhD), local government management for sustainable communities (PhD), nonprofit management and leadership (PhD), policy analysis (PhD), public management and leadership (PhD), terrorism, mediation, and peace (PhD); terrorism, mediation, and peace (MPA). Part-time and evening/weekend programs available. Postbaccalaureate distance learning degree programs offered (minimal on-campus study). *Faculty:* 10 full-time (5 women), 117 part-time/adjunct (49 women). *Students:* 1,408 full-time (901 women), 599 part-time (392 women); includes 1,022 Black or African American, non-Hispanic/Latino; 11 American Indian or Alaska Native, non-Hispanic/Latino; 37 Asian, non-Hispanic/Latino; 64 Hispanic/Latino; 26 Two or more races, non-Hispanic/Latino, 47 international. Average age 40. In 2010, 311 master's, 23 doctorates awarded. *Degree requirements:* For doctorate, thesis/dissertation, residency. *Entrance requirements:* For master's, bachelor's degree or equivalent in related field, minimum GPA of 2.5; for doctorate, master's degree or equivalent in related field; minimum GPA of 3.0; official transcripts; three years of related professional/academic experience (preferred); access to computer and Internet. Additional exam requirements/recommendations for international students: Required—TOEFL (minimum score 550 paper-based; 213 computer-based), IELTS (minimum score 6.5), TOEFL (minimum score 550 paper-based; 213 computer-based), IELTS (minimum score 6.5), or Michigan English Language Assessment Battery (minimum score 82). *Application deadline:* Applications are processed on a rolling basis. Application fee: $50. Electronic applications accepted. *Expenses:* Tuition: Full-time $10,274; part-time $445 per credit. Tuition and fees vary according to course load, degree level and program. *Financial support:* Fellowships with tuition reimbursements, Federal Work-Study, scholarships/grants, unspecified assistantships, and family tuition reduction, active duty/veteran tuition reduction, group tuition reduction, interest-free payment plans available. Support available to part-time students. Financial award applicants required to submit FAFSA. *Unit head:* Dr. Mark Gordon, Associate Dean, 800-925-3368. *Application contact:* Jennifer Hall, Vice President of Enrollment Management, 866-4-WALDEN, E-mail: info@waldenu.edu.

International Trade Policy

The George Washington University, Elliott School of International Affairs, Program in International Trade and Investment Policy, Washington, DC 20052. Offers MA, JD/MA, MBA/MA. Part-time and evening/weekend programs available. *Students:* 41 full-time (19 women), 12 part-time (9 women); includes 2 Black or African American, non-Hispanic/Latino; 5 Asian, non-Hispanic/Latino; 1 Hispanic/Latino; 2 Two or more races, non-Hispanic/Latino, 11 international. Average age 26. 93 applicants, 70% accepted, 20 enrolled. In 2010, 20 master's awarded. *Degree requirements:* For master's, one foreign language, capstone project. *Entrance requirements:* For master's, GRE General Test, 2 years of a modern foreign language, 2 semesters of introductory economics. Additional exam requirements/recommendations for international students: Required—TOEFL. *Application deadline:* For fall admission, 2/1 for domestic students; for spring admission, 10/1 for domestic students. Application fee: $75. Electronic applications accepted. *Financial support:* In 2010–11, 11 students received support; fellowships with tuition reimbursements available, research assistantships with tuition reimbursements available, career-related internships or fieldwork, Federal Work-Study, institutionally sponsored loans, and tuition waivers available. Financial award application deadline: 1/15. *Unit head:* Steven Suranovic, Director, 202-994-7579, Fax: 202-994-5477, E-mail: smsuran@gwu.edu. *Application contact:* Jeff V. Miles, Director of Graduate Admissions, 202-994-7050, Fax: 202-994-9537, E-mail: esiagrad@gwu.edu.

Monterey Institute of International Studies, Graduate School of International Policy and Management, Program in International Trade Policy, Monterey, CA 93940-2691. Offers MA. *Degree requirements:* For master's, one foreign language. *Entrance requirements:* For master's, minimum GPA of 3.0, proficiency in a foreign language. Additional exam requirements/recommendations for international students: Required—TOEFL (minimum score 550 paper-based; 213 computer-based; 80 iBT). Electronic applications accepted. *Expenses:* Tuition: Full-time $32,000; part-time $1525 per credit hour. Required fees: $56.

Political Science

Acadia University, Faculty of Arts, Department of Political Science, Wolfville, NS B4P 2R6, Canada. Offers MA. *Faculty:* 7 full-time (2 women), 2 part-time/adjunct (0 women). *Students:* 3 full-time (2 women), 3 part-time (2 women). Average age 26. 12 applicants, 50% accepted, 3 enrolled. In 2010, 1 master's awarded. *Degree requirements:* For master's, thesis. *Entrance requirements:* For master's, honors degree or equivalent. Additional exam requirements/recommendations for international students: Required—TOEFL (minimum score 580 paper-based; 237 computer-based; 93 iBT), IELTS (minimum score 6.5). *Application deadline:* For fall admission, 2/1 priority date for domestic and international students. Applications are processed on a rolling basis. Application fee: $50. *Financial support:* Teaching assistantships available. Financial award application deadline: 2/1. *Faculty research:* Atlantic Canada, international relations and organization, human rights, Canadian politics, political thought, technology. *Unit head:* Dr. Malcolm Grieve, Head, 902-585-1507, Fax: 902-585-1070, E-mail: malcolm.grieve@acadiau.ca. *Application contact:* Danielle Fraser, Administrative Secretary, 902-585-1506, Fax: 902-585-1070, E-mail: polisci@acadiau.ca.

American Public University System, AMU/APU Graduate Programs, Charles Town, WV 25414. Offers accounting (MBA); administration and supervision (M Ed); air warfare (MA Military Studies); asymmetrical warfare (MA Military Studies); criminal justice (MA); emergency and disaster management (MA); entrepreneurship (MBA); environmental policy and management (MS); finance (MBA); general (MBA); global business management (MBA); guidance and counseling (M Ed); history (MA); homeland security (MA); homeland security resource allocation (MBA); humanities (MA); information technology (MS); information technology management (MBA); intelligence studies (MA); international relations and conflict resolution (MA); joint warfare (MA Military Studies); land warfare (MA Military Studies); legal studies (MA); management (MA), including defense mangement, general, human resource management, organizational leadership, public administration; marketing (MBA); military history (MA); national security studies (MA); naval warfare (MA Military Studies); nonprofit management (MBA); political science (MA); psychology (MA); public administration (MA); public health (MA); security management (MA); space studies (MS); sports management (MS); strategic leadership (MA Military Studies); teaching (M Ed), including elementary, secondary social sciences; transportation and logistics management (MA). Programs offered via distance learning only. Part-time and evening/weekend programs available. Postbaccalaureate distance learning degree programs offered (no on-campus study). *Faculty:* 253 full-time (134 women), 1,208 part-time/adjunct (570 women). *Students:* 956 full-time (422 women), 8,476 part-time (2,821 women); includes 2,511 minority (1,218 Black or African American, non-Hispanic/Latino; 68 American Indian or Alaska Native, non-Hispanic/Latino; 219 Asian, non-Hispanic/Latino; 705 Hispanic/Latino; 46 Native Hawaiian or other Pacific Islander, non-Hispanic/Latino; 255 Two or more races, non-Hispanic/Latino), 107 international. Average age 35. 9,550 applicants, 100% accepted. In 2010, 1,688 master's awarded. *Degree requirements:* For master's, comprehensive exam or practicum. *Entrance requirements:* For master's, official transcript showing earned bachelor's degree from institution accredited by recognized accrediting body. Additional exam requirements/recommendations for international students: Required—TOEFL (minimum score 550 paper-based; 213 computer-based), IELTS (minimum score 6.5). *Application deadline:*

Applications are processed on a rolling basis. Application fee: $0. Electronic applications accepted. *Financial support:* Applicants required to submit FAFSA. *Faculty research:* Military history, criminal justice, management performance, national security. *Unit head:* Dr. Frank McCluskey, Provost, 877-468-6268, Fax: 304-724-3780. *Application contact:* Terry Grant, Director of Enrollment Management, 877-468-6268, Fax: 304-724-3780, E-mail: info@apus.edu.

American University, School of Communication, Program in Political Communication, Washington, DC 20016-8001. Offers MA. Part-time and evening/weekend programs available. *Students:* 4 full-time (all women), 1 (woman) part-time. 13 applicants, 69% accepted, 5 enrolled. *Degree requirements:* For master's, comprehensive exam, thesis or alternative. *Entrance requirements:* For master's, GRE General Test. Additional exam requirements/recommendations for international students: Required—TOEFL (minimum score 600 paper-based; 250 computer-based; 100 iBT), IELTS (minimum score 7). *Application deadline:* For fall admission, 2/1 priority date for domestic students, 4/1 for international students; for spring admission, 11/15 for domestic students. Applications are processed on a rolling basis. Application fee: $50. Electronic applications accepted. *Financial support:* In 2010–11, 3 research assistantships with full tuition reimbursements (averaging $15,000 per year) were awarded; career-related internships or fieldwork, Federal Work-Study, institutionally sponsored loans, scholarships/grants, tuition waivers (partial), and unspecified assistantships also available. Financial award application deadline: 2/1; financial award applicants required to submit FAFSA. *Faculty research:* Polling and public opinion, political polling, advocacy communication, entertainment and politics, communication research and management, political communication theory, campaign ethics. *Unit head:* Prof. Dotty Lynch, Dean, 202-885-2968, E-mail: dlynch@american.edu. *Application contact:* Sharmeen Ahsan-Bracciale, Graduate Admissions Office, 202-885-2040, Fax: 202-885-2019, E-mail: gradcomm@american.edu.

American University, School of Public Affairs, Department of Government, Washington, DC 20016-8130. Offers political science (MA, PhD), including American politics (MA), comparative politics (MA); women, policy and political leadership (Certificate). Part-time and evening/weekend programs available. *Faculty:* 29 full-time (15 women), 24 part-time/adjunct (3 women). *Students:* 58 full-time (26 women), 33 part-time (16 women); includes 12 minority (2 Black or African American, non-Hispanic/Latino; 3 Asian, non-Hispanic/Latino; 7 Hispanic/Latino), 3 international. Average age 27. 162 applicants, 45% accepted, 28 enrolled. In 2010, 31 master's, 2 doctorates awarded. Terminal master's awarded for partial completion of doctoral program. *Degree requirements:* For master's, comprehensive exam; for doctorate, comprehensive exam, thesis/dissertation. *Entrance requirements:* For master's, GRE, 2 recommendations; for doctorate, GRE, statement of purpose; 3 recommendations; for Certificate, bachelor's degree. Additional exam requirements/recommendations for international students: Required—TOEFL. *Application deadline:* For fall admission, 2/1 for domestic students; for spring admission, 11/1 for domestic students. Application fee: $55. *Financial support:* Fellowships, research assistantships, teaching assistantships, career-related internships or fieldwork and institutionally sponsored loans available. Financial award application deadline: 2/1. *Faculty research:* Political leadership, interest groups, politics of regulation, public law, political behavior. *Unit head:* Dr.

Todd Eisenstadt, Chair, 202-885-6493, E-mail: eisensta@american.edu. *Application contact:* Dr. Todd Eisenstadt, Chair, 202-885-6493, E-mail: eisensta@american.edu.

The American University in Cairo, School of Humanities and Social Sciences, Department of Political Science, Cairo, Egypt. Offers MA. *Degree requirements:* For master's, thesis. *Entrance requirements:* Additional exam requirements/recommendations for international students: Required—English entrance exam and/or TOEFL. Electronic applications accepted. *Faculty research:* African and Middle East politics, international relations, development of human rights, international law.

The American University of Athens, School of Graduate Studies, Athens, Greece. Offers biomedical sciences (MS); business (MBA); business communication (MA); computer sciences (MS); engineering and applied sciences (MS); politics and policy making (MA); systems engineering (MS); telecommunications (MS). *Entrance requirements:* For master's, resume, 2 recommendation letters. Additional exam requirements/recommendations for international students: Required—TOEFL (minimum score 550 paper-based; 213 computer-based). *Faculty research:* Nanotechnology, environmental sciences, rock mechanics, human skin studies, Monte Carlo algorithms and software.

American University of Beirut, Graduate Programs, Faculty of Arts and Sciences, Beirut, Lebanon. Offers anthropology (MA); Arabic language and literature (MA); archaeology (MA); biology (MS); chemistry (MS); computational science (MS); computer science (MS); economics (MA); education (MA); English language (MA); English literature (MA); environmental policy planning (MSES); financial economics (MAFE); geology (MS); history (MA); mathematics (MA, MS); Middle Eastern studies (MA); philosophy (MA); physics (MS); political studies (MA); psychology (MA); public administration (MA); sociology (MA); statistics (MA, MS). Part-time programs available. *Faculty:* 229 full-time (98 women), 136 part-time/adjunct (79 women). *Students:* 158 full-time (104 women), 263 part-time (171 women). Average age 25. 356 applicants, 59% accepted, 127 enrolled. In 2010, 57 master's awarded. *Degree requirements:* For master's, one foreign language, comprehensive exam, thesis (for some programs). *Entrance requirements:* For master's, GRE, letter of recommendation. Additional exam requirements/recommendations for international students: Required—TOEFL (minimum score 600 paper-based; 250 computer-based; 97 iBT), IELTS (minimum score 7). *Application deadline:* For fall admission, 4/30 for domestic and international students; for spring admission, 11/1 for domestic and international students. Application fee: $50. *Expenses:* Tuition: Full-time $12,294; part-time $683 per credit. Required fees: $499; $499 per credit. Tuition and fees vary according to course load and program. *Financial support:* In 2010–11, 33 students received support. Career-related internships or fieldwork, institutionally sponsored loans, scholarships/grants, health care benefits, and unspecified assistantships available. Financial award application deadline: 2/4; financial award applicants required to submit FAFSA. *Faculty research:* Modern and contemporary world theatre; mineralogy, petrology, and geochemistry; cell differentiation and transformation; combinatorial technologies; philosophy of action; continental philosophy; Phoenician epigraphy; nascent complex societies and urbanism; the economies of the Arab world; environmental economics; tectonophysics; host-parasite interactions; innate immunity; insect-plant interactions; history of the Ottoman archives; decentralization; transparency and corruption. Total annual research expenditures: $622,243. *Unit head:* Dr. Patrick McGreevy, Dean, 961-137-4374 Ext. 3800, Fax: 961-174-4461, E-mail: pm07@aub.edu.lb. *Application contact:* Dr. Salim Kanaan, Director, Admissions Office, 961-135-0000 Ext. 2594, Fax: 961-175-0775, E-mail: sk00@aub.edu.lb.

Appalachian State University, Cratis D. Williams Graduate School, Department of Government and Justice Studies, Boone, NC 28608. Offers criminal justice (MS); political science (MA), including American government, environmental politics and policy analysis, international relations; public administration (MPA), including public management, town, city and county management. Part-time programs available. Postbaccalaureate distance learning degree programs offered (no on-campus study). *Faculty:* 24 full-time (5 women), 3 part-time/adjunct (2 women). *Students:* 72 full-time (29 women), 53 part-time (25 women); includes 6 Black or African American, non-Hispanic/Latino; 1 Asian, non-Hispanic/Latino; 3 Hispanic/Latino; 1 Two or more races, non-Hispanic/Latino. 86 applicants, 86% accepted, 58 enrolled. In 2010, 49 master's awarded. *Degree requirements:* For master's, variable foreign language requirement, comprehensive exam, thesis optional. *Entrance requirements:* For master's, GRE General Test, 3 letters of recommendation. Additional exam requirements/recommendations for international students: Required—TOEFL (minimum score 570 paper-based; 230 computer-based; 79 iBT), IELTS (minimum score 6.5). *Application deadline:* For fall admission, 7/1 for domestic students, 2/1 for international students; for spring admission, 11/1 for domestic students, 7/1 for international students. Applications are processed on a rolling basis. Application fee: $55. Electronic applications accepted. *Expenses:* Tuition, state resident: full-time $3428; part-time $428 per unit. Tuition, nonresident: full-time $14,518; part-time $1814 per unit. Required fees: $2320; $344 per unit. Tuition and fees vary according to campus/location. *Financial support:* In 2010–11, 20 research assistantships (averaging $8,000 per year) were awarded; fellowships, teaching assistantships, career-related internships or fieldwork, Federal Work-Study, scholarships/grants, and unspecified assistantships also available. Financial award application deadline: 4/1; financial award applicants required to submit FAFSA. *Faculty research:* Campaign finance, emerging democracies, bureaucratic politics, judicial behavior, administration of justice. Total annual research expenditures: $143,000. *Unit head:* Dr. Brian Ellison, Chairperson, 828-262-3085, E-mail: ellisonba@appstate.edu. *Application contact:* Sandy Krause, Director of Admissions and Recruiting, 828-262-2130, Fax: 828-262-2709, E-mail: krausesl@appstate.edu.

Arizona State University, College of Liberal Arts and Sciences, Department of Political Science, Tempe, AZ 85287-3902. Offers political science (MA, PhD). Part-time programs available. *Faculty:* 41 full-time (17 women), 1 (woman) part-time/adjunct. *Students:* 35 full-time (9 women), 11 part-time (3 women); includes 8 minority (1 Black or African American, non-Hispanic/Latino; 1 Asian, non-Hispanic/Latino; 4 Hispanic/Latino; 2 Two or more races, non-Hispanic/Latino), 7 international. Average age 30. 90 applicants, 20% accepted, 9 enrolled. In 2010, 9 master's, 5 doctorates awarded. Terminal master's awarded for partial completion of doctoral program. *Degree requirements:* For master's, thesis or alternative, interactive Program of Study (iPOS) submitted before completing 50 percent of required credit hours; for doctorate, comprehensive exam, thesis/dissertation, interactive Program of Study (iPOS) submitted before completing 50 percent of required credit hours. *Entrance requirements:* For master's and doctorate, GRE, minimum GPA of 3.0 or equivalent in last 2 years of work leading to bachelor's degree. Additional exam requirements/recommendations for international students: Required—TOEFL, IELTS, or Pearson Test of English. *Application deadline:* For fall admission, 2/1 for domestic and international students. Applications are processed on a rolling basis. Application fee: $70 ($90 for international students). Electronic applications accepted. *Expenses:* Tuition, state resident: full-time $8510; part-time $608 per credit. Tuition, nonresident: full-time $16,542; part-time $919 per credit. Required fees: $339; $110 per credit. Part-time tuition and fees vary according to course load. *Financial support:* In 2010–11, 31 teaching assistantships with full and partial tuition reimbursements (averaging $12,341 per year) were awarded; fellowships with full tuition reimbursements, research assistantships with full and partial tuition reimbursements, career-related internships or fieldwork, Federal Work-Study, institutionally sponsored loans, scholarships/grants, and tuition waivers (partial) also available. Financial award application deadline: 3/1; financial award applicants required to submit FAFSA. Total annual research expenditures: $1.1 million. *Unit head:* Dr. Patrick J. Kenney, Director, 480-965-4222, E-mail: pkenney@asu.edu. *Application contact:* Graduate Admissions, 480-965-6113.

Arkansas State University, Graduate School, College of Humanities and Social Sciences, Department of Political Science, Jonesboro, State University, AR 72467. Offers political science (MA); political science education (SCCT); public administration (MPA). *Accreditation:* NASPAA (one or more programs are accredited). Part-time programs available. *Faculty:* 8 full-time (3 women), 1 (woman) part-time/adjunct. *Students:* 26 full-time (13 women), 24 part-time (8 women); includes 14 minority (13 Black or African American, non-Hispanic/Latino; 1 American Indian or Alaska Native, non-Hispanic/Latino), 9 international. Average age 29. 36 applicants, 78% accepted, 21 enrolled. In 2010, 16 master's awarded. *Degree requirements:* For master's, comprehensive exam, thesis or alternative; for SCCT, comprehensive exam. *Entrance requirements:* For master's, GRE General Test or MAT, GMAT, appropriate bachelor's degree, letters of recommendation, official transcripts, immunization records, statement of purpose; for SCCT, GRE General Test or MAT, GMAT, interview, master's degree, official transcript, letters of recommendation, immunization records. Additional exam requirements/recommendations for international students: Required—TOEFL (minimum score 550 paper-based; 213 computer-based; 79 iBT), IELTS (minimum score 6), PTE: Pearson Test of English Academic (56). *Application deadline:* For fall admission, 7/1 for domestic and international students; for spring admission, 11/15 for domestic students, 11/14 for international students. Applications are processed on a rolling basis. Application fee: $30 ($40 for international students). Electronic applications accepted. *Expenses:* Tuition, state resident: full-time $3888; part-time $216 per credit hour. Tuition, nonresident: full-time $9918; part-time $551 per credit hour. International tuition: $8376 full-time. Required fees: $932; $49 per credit hour. $25 per term. One-time fee: $30. Tuition and fees vary according to course load and program. *Financial support:* In 2010–11, 15 students received support; teaching assistantships, career-related internships or fieldwork, scholarships/grants, and unspecified assistantships available. Financial award application deadline: 7/1; financial award applicants required to submit FAFSA. *Unit head:* Dr. Richard Wang, Chair, 870-972-3048, Fax: 870-972-2720, E-mail: rwang@astate.edu. *Application contact:* Dr. Andrew Sustich, Dean of the Graduate School, 870-972-3029, Fax: 870-972-3857, E-mail: sustich@astate.edu.

Ashland University, College of Arts and Sciences, Program in American History and Government, Ashland, OH 44805-3702. Offers MAHG. Part-time programs available. *Faculty:* 6 full-time (0 women), 36 part-time/adjunct (3 women). *Students:* 74 full-time (36 women), 65 part-time (31 women); includes 13 minority (1 Black or African American, non-Hispanic/Latino; 2 American Indian or Alaska Native, non-Hispanic/Latino; 4 Asian, non-Hispanic/Latino; 6 Hispanic/Latino). Average age 39. 91 applicants, 70% accepted, 44 enrolled. In 2010, 3 master's awarded. *Degree requirements:* For master's, capstone project or thesis. *Entrance requirements:* For master's, minimum undergraduate GPA of 2.75, 3.0 graduate. *Application deadline:* Applications are processed on a rolling basis. Application fee: $30. Electronic applications accepted. *Expenses:* Contact institution. *Financial support:* In 2010–11, 15 students received support. Application deadline: 4/15. *Faculty research:* American founding, United States Civil War, Progressive Era. *Unit head:* Dr. Peter W. Schramm, Chair, 419-289-5411, Fax: 419-289-5425, E-mail: pschramm@ashland.edu. *Application contact:* Christian A. Pascarella, Director, 419-289-5411, Fax: 419-289-5425, E-mail: cpascare@ashland.edu.

Auburn University, Graduate School, College of Liberal Arts, Department of Political Science, Auburn University, AL 36849. Offers public administration (MPA, PhD); MPA/MCP. Part-time programs available. *Faculty:* 22 full-time (8 women), 3 part-time/adjunct (1 woman). *Students:* 35 full-time (17 women), 34 part-time (18 women); includes 9 Black or African American, non-Hispanic/Latino; 2 Asian, non-Hispanic/Latino; 2 Hispanic/Latino, 9 international. Average age 33. 57 applicants, 54% accepted, 24 enrolled. In 2010, 13 master's, 6 doctorates awarded. *Degree requirements:* For doctorate, thesis/dissertation. *Entrance requirements:* For master's, GRE General Test, minimum GPA of 3.0 in political science, 2.5 overall; for doctorate, GRE General Test. *Application deadline:* For fall admission, 7/7 for domestic students; for spring admission, 11/24 for domestic students. Applications are processed on a rolling basis. Application fee: $50 ($60 for international students). Electronic applications accepted. *Expenses:* Tuition, state resident: full-time $7002. Tuition, nonresident: full-time $21,898. International tuition: $22,116 full-time. Required fees: $892. Tuition and fees vary according to course load and program. *Financial support:* Fellowships, research assistantships, teaching assistantships, career-related internships or fieldwork and Federal Work-Study available. Support available to part-time students. Financial award application deadline: 3/15; financial award applicants required to submit FAFSA. *Faculty research:* Policy evaluation, political economy, privatization, participation, election administration. Total annual research expenditures: $200,000. *Unit head:* Dr. Gerard Gryski, Chair, 334-844-9644. *Application contact:* Dr. George Flowers, Dean of the Graduate School, 334-844-2125.

Auburn University Montgomery, School of Sciences, Department of Public Administration and Political Science, Montgomery, AL 36124-4023. Offers MPA, MPS, PhD. PhD offered jointly with Auburn University. *Accreditation:* NASPAA (one or more programs are accredited). Part-time and evening/weekend programs available. *Degree requirements:* For master's, comprehensive exam; for doctorate, thesis/dissertation. *Entrance requirements:* For master's, GRE General Test or MAT; for doctorate, GRE General Test. Electronic applications accepted.

Augusta State University, Graduate Studies, College of Arts and Sciences, Department of Political Science, Augusta, GA 30904-2200. Offers MPA. Part-time and evening/weekend programs available. *Degree requirements:* For master's, comprehensive exam, thesis. *Entrance requirements:* For master's, GRE General Test. Electronic applications accepted. *Expenses:* Tuition, state resident: part-time $165 per hour. Tuition, nonresident: part-time $615 per hour. *Faculty research:* Political behavior, administrative law, political participation, human resources administration.

Ball State University, Graduate School, College of Sciences and Humanities, Department of Political Science, Program in Political Science, Muncie, IN 47306-1099. Offers MA. *Faculty:* 16. *Students:* 12 full-time (2 women), 14 part-time (5 women); includes 2 Black or African American, non-Hispanic/Latino, 3 international. Average age 25. 12 applicants, 83% accepted, 5 enrolled. In 2010, 4 master's awarded. Application fee: $50. *Expenses:* Tuition, state resident: full-time $6160; part-time $299 per credit hour. Tuition, nonresident: full-time $16,020; part-time $783 per credit hour. Required fees: $2278; $95 per credit hour. *Financial support:* In 2010–11, 5 teaching assistantships with full tuition reimbursements (averaging $8,441 per year) were awarded; career-related internships or fieldwork also available. Financial award application deadline: 3/1. *Faculty research:* Survey research, public policy. *Unit head:* Dr. Joseph Losco, Director, 765-285-8800, Fax: 765-285-5345. *Application contact:* Dr. Gary Crawley, Associate Provost for Research and Dean of the Graduate School, 765-285-8785, E-mail: gcrawley@bsu.edu.

Baylor University, Graduate School, College of Arts and Sciences, Department of Political Science, Waco, TX 76798. Offers international studies (MA); political science (MA, PhD); public policy and administration (MPPA); JD/MPPA. *Students:* 29 full-time (8 women), 1 part-time (0 women), 3 international. In 2010, 6 master's, 3 doctorates awarded. *Entrance requirements:* For master's, GRE General Test. *Application deadline:* Applications are processed on a rolling basis. Application fee: $25. *Financial support:* Research assistantships, career-related internships or fieldwork, Federal Work-Study, and institutionally sponsored loans available. Financial award application deadline: 3/1. *Unit head:* Dr. David Corey, Graduate Program Director, 254-710-3161, Fax: 254-710-3122, E-mail: david_d_corey@baylor.edu. *Application contact:* Jenice Langston, Administrative Assistant, 254-710-3161, Fax: 254-710-3870, E-mail: jenice_langston@baylor.edu.

Baylor University, Graduate School, College of Arts and Sciences, J. M. Dawson Institute of Church-State Studies, Waco, TX 76798. Offers MA, PhD. *Students:* 40 full-time (15 women), 3 part-time (2 women); includes 9 minority (2 Black or African American, non-Hispanic/Latino; 1 Asian, non-Hispanic/Latino; 4 Hispanic/Latino; 2 Two or more races, non-Hispanic/Latino), 7 international. In 2010, 3 master's, 2 doctorates awarded. *Degree requirements:* For master's, thesis, oral exam; for doctorate, one foreign language, thesis/dissertation, preliminary exams. *Entrance requirements:* For master's, GRE General Test; for doctorate, GRE General Test, MA or equivalent. *Application deadline:* For fall admission, 3/1 for domestic students. Applications are processed on a rolling basis. Application fee: $25. *Financial support:* Fellowships, research assistantships, teaching assistantships, Federal Work-Study and institutionally sponsored loans available. Financial award application deadline: 3/1. *Faculty research:* Religion and politics, religion and public education, religious freedom and international politics, First Amendment jurisprudence. *Unit head:* Dr. Christopher Marsh, Graduate Program Director, 254-710-4412, Fax: 254-710-1571, E-mail: chris_marsh@baylor.edu. *Application contact:*

Political Science

Baylor University (continued)
Suzanne Seller, Administrative Assistant, 254-710-1510, Fax: 254-710-1571, E-mail: suzanne_sellers@baylor.edu.

Boston College, Graduate School of Arts and Sciences, Department of Political Science, Chestnut Hill, MA 02467-3800. Offers MA, PhD. Terminal master's awarded for partial completion of doctoral program. *Degree requirements:* For master's, thesis or alternative; for doctorate, one foreign language, thesis/dissertation. *Entrance requirements:* For master's and doctorate, GRE General Test. Additional exam requirements/recommendations for international students: Required—TOEFL (minimum score 600 paper-based; 250 computer-based; 100 iBT). Electronic applications accepted. *Faculty research:* Political theory, American politics, international politics.

Boston University, Graduate School of Arts and Sciences, Department of Political Science, Boston, MA 02215. Offers MA, PhD. *Students:* 59 full-time (20 women), 4 part-time (2 women); includes 7 minority (2 Black or African American, non-Hispanic/Latino; 4 Asian, non-Hispanic/Latino; 1 Two or more races, non-Hispanic/Latino), 22 international. Average age 31. 156 applicants, 25% accepted, 14 enrolled. In 2010, 5 master's, 8 doctorates awarded. Terminal master's awarded for partial completion of doctoral program. *Degree requirements:* For master's, one foreign language; for doctorate, 2 foreign languages, comprehensive exam, thesis/dissertation. *Entrance requirements:* For master's and doctorate, GRE General Test, 3 letters of recommendation. Additional exam requirements/recommendations for international students: Required—TOEFL (minimum score 600 paper-based; 250 computer-based). *Application deadline:* For fall admission, 12/1 for domestic and international students. Application fee: $70. Electronic applications accepted. *Expenses:* Tuition: Full-time $39,314; part-time $1228 per credit. Required fees: $40 per semester. *Financial support:* In 2010–11, 16 students received support, including 1 fellowship with full tuition reimbursement available (averaging $19,300 per year), 11 teaching assistantships with full tuition reimbursements available (averaging $18,800 per year); career-related internships or fieldwork, Federal Work-Study, and stipends also available. Support available to part-time students. Financial award application deadline: 12/1; financial award applicants required to submit FAFSA. *Unit head:* Graham Wilson, Chairman, 617-353-2545, Fax: 617-353-5508, E-mail: gkwilson@bu.edu. *Application contact:* Linda Simons, Graduate Program Coordinator, 617-353-2541, Fax: 617-353-5508, E-mail: pograd@bu.edu.

Boston University, School of Education, Boston, MA 02215. Offers counseling (Ed M, CAGS), including community, school, sport psychology; counseling psychology (Ed D); curriculum and teaching (Ed M, Ed D, CAGS), including early childhood (Ed D), educational media and technology (Ed D), English and language arts (Ed D), mathematics (Ed D), physical education and coaching (Ed D), science (Ed D), social studies education (Ed D), special education (Ed D); developmental studies (Ed D), including literacy and language, reading education; developmental studies in literacy and language education (Ed M, CAGS); early childhood education (Ed M, CAGS); education of the deaf (Ed M, CAGS); educational leadership and development (Ed D), including educational administration (Ed M, Ed D, CAGS), higher education administration (Ed M, Ed D, CAGS); educational media and technology (Ed M, CAGS); elementary education (Ed M); English and language arts (Ed M, CAGS); English education (MAT); health education (Ed M, CAGS); Latin and classical studies (MAT); mathematics education (Ed M, MAT, CAGS); mathematics for teaching (MMT); modern foreign language education (MAT), including French, Spanish; physical education and coaching (Ed M, CAGS); policy, planning, and administration (Ed M, CAGS), including community education leadership, educational administration (Ed M, Ed D, CAGS), higher education administration (Ed M, Ed D, CAGS); reading education (Ed M, CAGS); science education (Ed M, MAT, CAGS), including biology (MAT), chemistry (MAT), earth science (MAT), general science (MAT), physics (MAT); social studies education (Ed M, MAT, CAGS), including history (MAT), political science (MAT); special education (Ed M, Ed D, CAGS), including disability studies (Ed M), moderate disabilities (Ed M), severe disabilities (Ed M), special education administration (Ed M); teaching English as a second language (Ed M, CAGS). Part-time programs available. *Faculty:* 57 full-time, 39 part-time/adjunct. *Students:* 245 full-time (191 women), 376 part-time (274 women); includes 83 minority (14 Black or African American, non-Hispanic/Latino; 2 American Indian or Alaska Native, non-Hispanic/Latino; 28 Asian, non-Hispanic/Latino; 31 Hispanic/Latino; 2 Native Hawaiian or other Pacific Islander, non-Hispanic/Latino; 6 Two or more races, non-Hispanic/Latino), 79 international. Average age 30. 1,270 applicants, 66% accepted, 292 enrolled. In 2010, 273 master's, 15 doctorates, 7 other advanced degrees awarded. Terminal master's awarded for partial completion of doctoral program. *Degree requirements:* For master's, thesis (for some programs); for doctorate, comprehensive exam, thesis/dissertation; for CAGS, comprehensive exam. *Entrance requirements:* For master's and CAGS, GRE General Test or Miller Analogies Test (MAT); for doctorate, GRE General Test. Additional exam requirements/recommendations for international students: Required—TOEFL, IELTS. *Application deadline:* For fall admission, 1/15 priority date for domestic and international students; for spring admission, 9/15 priority date for domestic and international students. Applications are processed on a rolling basis. Application fee: $70. Electronic applications accepted. *Expenses:* Tuition: Full-time $39,314; part-time $1228 per credit. Required fees: $40 per semester. *Financial support:* In 2010–11, 276 students received support, including 31 fellowships with full tuition reimbursements available, 16 research assistantships, 26 teaching assistantships with partial tuition reimbursements available; career-related internships or fieldwork, Federal Work-Study, and scholarships/grants also available. Support available to part-time students. Financial award applicants required to submit FAFSA. *Faculty research:* Deaf studies, social emotional learning, civic engagement and education, STEM education, pre-college educational pipelines. Total annual research expenditures: $2.6 million. *Unit head:* Dr. Hardin Coleman, Dean, 617-353-3213. *Application contact:* Dana Fernandez, Director of Enrollment, 617-353-4237, Fax: 617-353-8937, E-mail: sedgrad@bu.edu.

Bowling Green State University, Graduate College, College of Arts and Sciences, Department of Political Science, Program in Political Science, Bowling Green, OH 43403. Offers MA/MA. *Entrance requirements:* Additional exam requirements/recommendations for international students: Required—TOEFL. Electronic applications accepted.

Brandeis University, Graduate School of Arts and Sciences, Department of Politics, Waltham, MA 02454-9110. Offers MA, PhD. Part-time programs available. *Faculty:* 13 full-time (2 women). *Students:* 22 full-time (9 women), 5 international. 115 applicants, 17% accepted, 6 enrolled. In 2010, 4 master's, 4 doctorates awarded. Terminal master's awarded for partial completion of doctoral program. *Degree requirements:* For master's, thesis; for doctorate, one foreign language, comprehensive exam, thesis/dissertation. *Entrance requirements:* For master's and doctorate, GRE General Test, sample of written work, resume, 3 letters of recommendation. Additional exam requirements/recommendations for international students: Required—TOEFL (minimum score 600 paper-based; 250 computer-based; 100 iBT); Recommended—IELTS (minimum score 7). *Application deadline:* For fall admission, 1/15 priority date for domestic and international students. Applications are processed on a rolling basis. Application fee: $75. Electronic applications accepted. *Financial support:* In 2010–11, 13 students received support, including 11 fellowships with full tuition reimbursements available (averaging $20,000 per year), 2 teaching assistantships with partial tuition reimbursements available (averaging $3,200 per year); scholarships/grants, health care benefits, tuition waivers (full and partial), and unspecified assistantships also available. Financial award application deadline: 2/1; financial award applicants required to submit FAFSA. *Faculty research:* American institutions, international law and foreign policy, political theory, comparative politics, European politics. *Unit head:* Prof. Daniel Kryder, Director of Graduate Studies, 781-736-2778, Fax: 781-736-2777, E-mail: kryder@brandeis.edu. *Application contact:* Rosanne Colocouris, Department Administrator, 781-736-2755, Fax: 781-736-2777, E-mail: colocour@brandeis.edu.

Brigham Young University, Graduate Studies, Marriott School of Management, Master of Public Administration Program, Provo, UT 84602. Offers finance (MPA); human resources (MPA); local government (MPA); nonprofit management (MPA); JD/MPA. *Faculty:* 12 full-time (1 woman), 5 part-time/adjunct (0 women). *Students:* 121 full-time (58 women); includes 3 Black or African American, non-Hispanic/Latino; 1 American Indian or Alaska Native, non-Hispanic/Latino; 11 Asian, non-Hispanic/Latino; 8 Hispanic/Latino. Average age 27. 137 applicants, 64% accepted, 61 enrolled. In 2010, 47 master's awarded. *Entrance requirements:* For master's, GRE, GMAT, minimum GPA of 3.0. Additional exam requirements/recommendations for international students: Required—TOEFL (minimum score 580 paper-based; 85 iBT); IELTS (minimum score 7). *Application deadline:* For fall admission, 2/1 for domestic and international students. Application fee: $50. Electronic applications accepted. *Expenses:* Tuition: Full-time $5580; part-time $310 per credit hour. Tuition and fees vary according to program and student's religious affiliation. *Financial support:* In 2010–11, 73 students received support. Career-related internships or fieldwork and scholarships/grants available. Financial award application deadline: 4/15; financial award applicants required to submit FAFSA. *Faculty research:* Taxes, budgeting, nonprofit, ethics, decision modeling, work balance, organizational behavior. *Unit head:* Dr. David W. Hart, Director, 801-422-4221, Fax: 801-422-0311, E-mail: mpa@byu.edu. *Application contact:* Catherine Cooper, Director of Student Services, 801-422-4221, E-mail: mpa@byu.edu.

Brock University, Faculty of Graduate Studies, Faculty of Social Sciences, Program in Political Science, St. Catharines, ON L2S 3A1, Canada. Offers Canadian politics (MA); comparative politics (MA); international relations (MA); political theory or philosophy (MA); public policy (MA). Part-time programs available. *Degree requirements:* For master's, thesis optional. *Entrance requirements:* For master's, honors degree. Additional exam requirements/recommendations for international students: Required—TOEFL (minimum score 550 paper-based; 213 computer-based; 80 iBT), IELTS (minimum score 6.5), TWE (minimum score 4). Electronic applications accepted. *Faculty research:* Public administration reform, economic and social justice, politics of societies, Canadian politics, international relations.

Brooklyn College of the City University of New York, Division of Graduate Studies, Department of Political Science, Brooklyn, NY 11210-2889. Offers international affairs (MA); political science (MA, PhD); political science, urban policy and administration (MA). Part-time and evening/weekend programs available. *Students:* 23 full-time (13 women), 219 part-time (124 women); includes 119 minority (92 Black or African American, non-Hispanic/Latino; 12 Asian, non-Hispanic/Latino; 15 Hispanic/Latino), 28 international. Average age 30. 155 applicants, 80% accepted, 88 enrolled. In 2010, 49 master's awarded. *Degree requirements:* For master's, comprehensive exam (for some programs), thesis or alternative, foreign language exam (for international affairs program). *Entrance requirements:* For master's, 2 letters of recommendation, personal statement. Additional exam requirements/recommendations for international students: Required—TOEFL (minimum score 500 paper-based; 173 computer-based; 61 iBT). *Application deadline:* For fall admission, 5/1 for domestic and international students; for spring admission, 12/15 for domestic students, 11/1 for international students. *Expenses:* Tuition, state resident: full-time $7360; part-time $310 per credit hour. Tuition, nonresident: full-time $13,800; part-time $575 per credit hour. Required fees: $190 per semester. *Financial support:* Career-related internships or fieldwork and Federal Work-Study available. Support available to part-time students. Financial award application deadline: 5/1; financial award applicants required to submit FAFSA. *Faculty research:* Ethics and politics, politics of criminal justice, Western Europe, international law and politics, labor politics. *Unit head:* Dr. Paisley Currah, Acting Chairperson, 718-951-5306, E-mail: pcurrah@brooklyn.cuny.edu. *Application contact:* Hernan Sierra, Graduate Admissions Coordinator, 718-951-4536, Fax: 718-951-4506, E-mail: grads@brooklyn.cuny.edu.

Brown University, Graduate School, Department of Political Science, Providence, RI 02912. Offers PhD, MA/PhD. *Degree requirements:* For doctorate, thesis/dissertation. *Entrance requirements:* For doctorate, GRE General Test.

California Polytechnic State University, San Luis Obispo, College of Liberal Arts, Department of Political Science, San Luis Obispo, CA 93407. Offers MPP. Part-time programs available. *Faculty:* 2 full-time (1 woman). *Students:* 25 full-time (14 women), 8 part-time (4 women); includes 13 minority (2 Asian, non-Hispanic/Latino; 7 Hispanic/Latino; 4 Two or more races, non-Hispanic/Latino). Average age 28. 45 applicants, 69% accepted, 16 enrolled. In 2010, 13 master's awarded. *Degree requirements:* For master's, thesis or alternative. *Entrance requirements:* For master's, minimum GPA of 2.75 in last 90 quarter units of course work, three letters of recommendation. Additional exam requirements/recommendations for international students: Required—TOEFL (minimum score 550 paper-based; 213 computer-based) or IELTS (minimum score 6). *Application deadline:* For fall admission, 2/1 for domestic students, 11/30 for international students; for winter admission, 6/30 for international students. Application fee: $55. *Expenses:* Tuition, state resident: full-time $5386; part-time $3124 per year. Tuition, nonresident: full-time $11,160; part-time $248 per unit. Required fees: $2250; $614 per term. One-time fee: $2250 full-time; $1842 part-time. *Financial support:* Career-related internships or fieldwork, Federal Work-Study, and scholarships/grants available. Support available to part-time students. Financial award application deadline: 3/2; financial award applicants required to submit FAFSA. *Faculty research:* Public policy analysis, public finance, policy internship. *Unit head:* Dr. Elizabeth Lowham, Graduate Coordinator, 805-756-2919, Fax: 805-756-7168, E-mail: elowham@calpoly.edu. *Application contact:* Dr. Elizabeth Lowham, Graduate Coordinator, 805-756-2919, Fax: 805-756-7168, E-mail: elowham@calpoly.edu.

California State University, Chico, Graduate School, College of Behavioral and Social Sciences, Department of Political Science, Program in Political Science, Chico, CA 95929-0722. Offers MA. Part-time programs available. *Students:* 15 full-time (5 women), 15 part-time (8 women); includes 2 Black or African American, non-Hispanic/Latino; 1 Asian, non-Hispanic/Latino; 3 Hispanic/Latino, 2 international. Average age 29. 25 applicants, 88% accepted, 12 enrolled. In 2010, 4 master's awarded. *Entrance requirements:* For master's, 2 letters of recommendation. Additional exam requirements/recommendations for international students: Required—TOEFL (minimum score 550 paper-based; 213 computer-based; 80 iBT), IELTS (minimum score 6.5). *Application deadline:* For fall admission, 3/1 priority date for domestic students, 3/1 for international students; for spring admission, 9/15 priority date for domestic students, 9/15 for international students. Applications are processed on a rolling basis. Application fee: $55. Electronic applications accepted. *Financial support:* Career-related internships or fieldwork available. *Unit head:* Dr. Charles Turner, Graduate Coordinator, 530-898-5960. *Application contact:* Dr. Charles Turner, Graduate Coordinator, 530-898-5960.

California State University, Fullerton, Graduate Studies, College of Humanities and Social Sciences, Division of Politics, Administration, and Justice, Fullerton, CA 92834-9480. Offers political science (MA); public administration (MPA). *Accreditation:* NASPAA (one or more programs are accredited). Part-time programs available. *Students:* 27 full-time (16 women), 123 part-time (60 women); includes 5 Black or African American, non-Hispanic/Latino; 28 Asian, non-Hispanic/Latino; 38 Hispanic/Latino; 6 Two or more races, non-Hispanic/Latino, 4 international. Average age 31. 223 applicants, 31% accepted, 45 enrolled. In 2010, 57 master's awarded. *Degree requirements:* For master's, comprehensive exam, project or thesis. *Entrance requirements:* For master's, minimum GPA of 2.5 in last 60 units of course work, 12 units of course work in social sciences. Application fee: $55. *Financial support:* Career-related internships or fieldwork, Federal Work-Study, institutionally sponsored loans, and scholarships/grants available. Support available to part-time students. Financial award application deadline: 3/1; financial award applicants required to submit FAFSA. *Faculty research:* Emergency management plans. *Unit head:* Dr. Phil Gianos, Chair, 657-278-3521. *Application contact:* Admissions/Applications, 657-278-2371.

California State University, Long Beach, Graduate Studies, College of Liberal Arts, Department of Political Science, Long Beach, CA 90840. Offers MA. Part-time programs available. *Faculty:* 7 full-time (2 women). *Students:* 6 full-time (1 woman), 23 part-time (9 women); includes 1 Black or African American, non-Hispanic/Latino; 4 Asian, non-Hispanic/Latino; 9 Hispanic/Latino, 1 international. Average age 28. 61 applicants, 26% accepted, 8 enrolled. In 2010, 11 master's awarded. *Degree requirements:* For master's, one foreign language, comprehensive exam or thesis. *Entrance requirements:* For master's, GRE General Test, minimum GPA of 3.0 in field. *Application deadline:* For fall admission, 4/1 for domestic students. Applications are processed on a rolling basis. Application fee: $55. Electronic applications accepted. *Financial* *support:* In 2010–11, 6 students received support; teaching assistantships, Federal Work-Study, institutionally sponsored loans, and scholarships/grants available. Financial award application deadline: 3/2. *Faculty research:* Social welfare policy, international political economy, Marxism, voting behavior. *Unit head:* Dr. Teresa Wright, Chair, 562-985-4704, Fax: 562-985-4979, E-mail: twright@csulb.edu. *Application contact:* Dr. Liesl Haas, Graduate Advisor, 562-985-5860, Fax: 562-985-4979, E-mail: lhaas@csulb.edu.

California State University, Los Angeles, Graduate Studies, College of Natural and Social Sciences, Department of Political Science, Los Angeles, CA 90032-8530. Offers political science (MA); public administration (MS). Part-time and evening/weekend programs available. *Faculty:* 18 full-time (16 women), 4 part-time/adjunct (1 woman). *Students:* 21 full-time (12 women), 83 part-time (45 women); includes 68 minority (6 Black or African American, non-Hispanic/Latino; 8 Asian, non-Hispanic/Latino; 54 Hispanic/Latino), 6 international. Average age 30. 61 applicants, 95% accepted, 32 enrolled. In 2010, 39 master's awarded. *Degree requirements:* For master's, comprehensive exam or thesis. *Entrance requirements:* Additional exam requirements/recommendations for international students: Required—TOEFL (minimum score 500 paper-based; 173 computer-based). *Application deadline:* For fall admission, 5/1 for domestic and international students. Applications are processed on a rolling basis. Application fee: $55. Electronic applications accepted. *Financial support:* Career-related internships or fieldwork and Federal Work-Study available. Support available to part-time students. Financial award application deadline: 3/1. *Faculty research:* Government; public policy and law; international, political, and economic relations; comparative politics. *Unit head:* Dr. Scott Bowman, Chair, 323-343-2248, Fax: 323-343-6452, E-mail: sbowman@calstatela.edu. *Application contact:* Dr. Alan Muchlinski, Dean of Graduate Studies, 323-343-3820, Fax: 323-343-5653, E-mail: amuchli@exchange.calstatela.edu.

California State University, Northridge, Graduate Studies, College of Social and Behavioral Sciences, Department of Political Science, Northridge, CA 91330. Offers MA. *Degree requirements:* For master's, comprehensive exam. *Entrance requirements:* For master's, GRE (if cumulative undergraduate GPA less than 3.0), 2 letters of recommendation. Additional exam requirements/recommendations for international students: Required—TOEFL.

California State University, Sacramento, Graduate Studies, College of Social Sciences and Interdisciplinary Studies, Department of Government, Sacramento, CA 95819. Offers MA. Part-time programs available. *Degree requirements:* For master's, thesis or alternative, writing proficiency exam. *Entrance requirements:* For master's, GRE General Test, minimum GPA of 3.0 during previous 2 years. Additional exam requirements/recommendations for international students: Required—TOEFL. Electronic applications accepted.

Carleton University, Faculty of Graduate Studies, Faculty of Public Affairs and Management, Department of Political Science, Ottawa, ON K1S 5B6, Canada. Offers MA, PhD. *Degree requirements:* For master's, one foreign language, comprehensive exam, thesis optional; for doctorate, one foreign language, comprehensive exam, thesis/dissertation. *Entrance requirements:* For master's, honors degree in political science, minimum B average; for doctorate, master's degree in political science. Additional exam requirements/recommendations for international students: Required—TOEFL. *Faculty research:* Canadian politics, comparative politics, international relations, public administration and policy analysis, political theory.

Carleton University, Faculty of Graduate Studies, Faculty of Public Affairs and Management, Institute of Political Economy, Ottawa, ON K1S 5B6, Canada. Offers MA, PhD. *Degree requirements:* For master's, thesis optional. *Entrance requirements:* For master's, honors degree. Additional exam requirements/recommendations for international students: Required—TOEFL. *Faculty research:* Relationships between economy and politics as they affect the political, social and cultural life of societies; historical processes whereby social change is located in the interaction of the economic, political and cultural, and ideological moments of social life.

Case Western Reserve University, School of Graduate Studies, Department of Political Science, Cleveland, OH 44106. Offers MA, PhD. Part-time programs available. *Faculty:* 11 full-time (5 women), 2 part-time/adjunct (0 women). *Students:* 1 (woman) full-time. 8 applicants, 0% accepted, 0 enrolled. Terminal master's awarded for partial completion of doctoral program. *Degree requirements:* For master's, comprehensive exam; for doctorate, thesis/dissertation. *Entrance requirements:* For master's and doctorate, GRE General Test, undergraduate degree in political science. Additional exam requirements/recommendations for international students: Required—TOEFL (minimum score 550 paper-based; 215 computer-based; 79 iBT). *Application deadline:* For fall admission, 5/1 priority date for domestic students; for spring admission, 11/1 for domestic students. Applications are processed on a rolling basis. Application fee: $50. Electronic applications accepted. *Financial support:* Federal Work-Study available. Financial award application deadline: 2/1; financial award applicants required to submit FAFSA. *Faculty research:* American political institutions; elections and political parties both in the United States and abroad; legislative politics in particular; international relations with an emphasis on international political economy; the development and decline of nation-states; the politics of gender; public policy and public organizations; research methods; and comparative politics with regional concentrations including Western Europe, Africa, Central Asia and the Middle East. *Unit head:* Joseph White, Chairman, 216-368-2426, Fax: 216-368-4681, E-mail: joseph.white@case.edu. *Application contact:* Sharon Skowronski, Department Assistant, 216-368-2424, Fax: 216-368-4681, E-mail: sxs22@po.cwru.edu.

The Catholic University of America, School of Arts and Sciences, Department of Politics, Washington, DC 20064. Offers American government (MA, PhD); Congressional and presidential studies (MA); international affairs (MA); international political economics (MA); political theory (MA, PhD); world politics (MA, PhD); MA/JD. Part-time programs available. *Faculty:* 13 full-time (1 woman), 8 part-time/adjunct (0 women). *Students:* 28 full-time (8 women), 76 part-time (19 women); includes 4 Black or African American, non-Hispanic/Latino; 5 Asian, non-Hispanic/Latino; 5 Hispanic/Latino, 6 international. Average age 30. 111 applicants, 59% accepted, 25 enrolled. In 2010, 23 master's, 4 doctorates awarded. *Degree requirements:* For master's, one foreign language, comprehensive exam, thesis or alternative; for doctorate, variable foreign language requirement, comprehensive exam, thesis/dissertation. *Entrance requirements:* For master's, GRE General Test, statement of purpose, official copies of academic transcripts, three letters of recommendation, minimum GPA of 3.0; for doctorate, GRE General Test, statement of purpose, official copies of academic transcripts, three letters of recommendation. Additional exam requirements/recommendations for international students: Required—TOEFL (minimum score 580 paper-based; 237 computer-based). *Application deadline:* For fall admission, 8/1 priority date for domestic students, 7/15 for international students; for spring admission, 12/1 priority date for domestic students, 10/15 for international students. Applications are processed on a rolling basis. Application fee: $55. Electronic applications accepted. *Expenses:* Tuition: Full-time $33,580; part-time $1315 per credit hour. Required fees: $80; $40 per semester hour. One-time fee: $425. *Financial support:* Fellowships, research assistantships, teaching assistantships, Federal Work-Study, scholarships/grants, tuition waivers (full and partial), and unspecified assistantships available. Financial award application deadline: 2/1; financial award applicants required to submit FAFSA. *Faculty research:* Political philosophy, American political institutions and processes, political economy, international relations, U. S. political leadership since 1789. *Unit head:* Dr. Philip Henderson, Chair, 202-319-5128, Fax: 202-319-6289, E-mail: hendersp@cua.edu. *Application contact:* Andrew Woodall, Director of Graduate Admissions, 202-319-5057, Fax: 202-319-6533, E-mail: cua-admissions@cua.edu.

Central European University, Graduate Studies, School of Social Sciences and Humanities, Budapest, Hungary. Offers economics (MA, PhD); gender studies (MA, PhD); international relations and European studies (MA, PhD); mathematics and its applications (MS, PhD); medieval studies (MA, PhD); nationalism studies (MA, PhD); philosophy (MA, PhD); political science (MA, PhD); public policy (MA, PhD); sociology and social anthropology (MA, PhD). *Faculty:* 90 full-time (29 women), 13 part-time/adjunct (7 women). *Students:* 732 full-time (404 women). Average age 28. 3,639 applicants, 22% accepted, 416 enrolled. In 2010, 278 master's, 16 doctorates awarded. Terminal master's awarded for partial completion of doctoral program. *Degree requirements:* For master's, one foreign language, thesis; for doctorate, one foreign language, comprehensive exam, thesis/dissertation. *Entrance requirements:* For master's, interview; for doctorate, GRE, CEU subject test, interview. Additional exam requirements/recommendations for international students: Required—TOEFL (minimum score 570 paper-based; 230 computer-based); Recommended—IELTS (minimum score 6.5). *Application deadline:* For fall admission, 1/15 priority date for domestic and international students. Application fee: $0. Electronic applications accepted. Tuition and fees charges are reported in euros. *Expenses:* Tuition: Full-time 11,000 euros. Required fees: 250 euros. One-time fee: 200 euros full-time. Tuition and fees vary according to degree level, program, reciprocity agreements and student level. *Financial support:* In 2010–11, 402 students received support, including 416 fellowships with full and partial tuition reimbursements available (averaging $6,200 per year); career-related internships or fieldwork, institutionally sponsored loans, and scholarships/grants also available. Financial award application deadline: 1/5. *Faculty research:* Civil society, fiscal decentralization, party politics, political philosophy (especially liberalism, theory of democracy). Total annual research expenditures: $35,000. *Unit head:* Dr. Katalin Farkas, Provost/Academic Pro Rector, 361-327-3000 Ext. 2227, E-mail: farkask@ceu.hu. *Application contact:* Zsuzsanna Jaszberenyi, Admissions Officer, 361-327-3009, Fax: 361-327-3211, E-mail: admissions@ceu.hu.

Central Michigan University, Central Michigan University Off-Campus Programs, Program in Public Administration, Mount Pleasant, MI 48859. Offers public management (MPA); state and local government (MPA). *Accreditation:* NASPAA. Part-time and evening/weekend programs available. *Entrance requirements:* For master's, minimum GPA of 2.8. Additional exam requirements/recommendations for international students: Required—TOEFL. Electronic applications accepted. *Expenses:* Tuition, state resident: full-time $8208; part-time $456 per credit hour. Tuition, nonresident: full-time $13,788; part-time $766 per credit hour. One-time fee: $25. *Financial support:* Scholarships/grants available. Support available to part-time students. *Unit head:* Dr. Lawrence Sych, Program Director, 989-774-3316, E-mail: sych1l@cmich.edu. *Application contact:* 877-268-4636, E-mail: cmuoffcampus@cmich.edu.

Central Michigan University, College of Graduate Studies, College of Humanities and Social and Behavioral Sciences, Department of Political Science, Program in Political Science, Mount Pleasant, MI 48859. Offers political science (MA), including American politics, comparative/international politics. Part-time programs available. *Faculty:* 11 full-time (2 women), 1 part-time/adjunct (0 women). *Students:* 10 full-time (5 women), 7 part-time (0 women); includes 3 Black or African American, non-Hispanic/Latino; 1 American Indian or Alaska Native, non-Hispanic/Latino. Average age 25. *Degree requirements:* For master's, thesis or alternative. *Application deadline:* For fall admission, 6/1 for international students; for spring admission, 10/1 for international students. Applications are processed on a rolling basis. Application fee: $35 ($45 for international students). Electronic applications accepted. *Expenses:* Tuition, state resident: full-time $8208; part-time $456 per credit hour. Tuition, nonresident: full-time $13,788; part-time $766 per credit hour. One-time fee: $25. *Financial support:* Fellowships with tuition reimbursements, career-related internships or fieldwork, Federal Work-Study, unspecified assistantships, and out-of-state merit awards, non-resident graduate awards available. *Unit head:* Dr. Orlando J. Perez, Chairperson, 989-774-3442, Fax: 989-774-1136, E-mail: perez1oj@cmich.edu. *Application contact:* Laura Orta, Assistant Director of Graduate Programs, 989-774-2391, Fax: 989-774-1136, E-mail: orta1lj@cmich.edu.

Central Michigan University, College of Graduate Studies, College of Humanities and Social and Behavioral Sciences, Department of Political Science, Program in Public Administration, Mount Pleasant, MI 48859. Offers professional development in public administration (Graduate Certificate); public administration (MPA), including cognate courses option; public management (MPA); state and local government (MPA). Part-time programs available. *Faculty:* 11 full-time (2 women), 1 part-time/adjunct (0 women). *Students:* 10 full-time (2 women), 12 part-time (5 women); includes 1 American Indian or Alaska Native, non-Hispanic/Latino; 1 Asian, non-Hispanic/Latino, 4 international. Average age 32. *Degree requirements:* For master's, thesis or alternative. *Application deadline:* For fall admission, 6/1 for international students; for spring admission, 10/1 for international students. Applications are processed on a rolling basis. Application fee: $35 ($45 for international students). Electronic applications accepted. *Expenses:* Tuition, state resident: full-time $8208; part-time $456 per credit hour. Tuition, nonresident: full-time $13,788; part-time $766 per credit hour. One-time fee: $25. *Financial support:* Fellowships with tuition reimbursements, career-related internships or fieldwork, Federal Work-Study, unspecified assistantships, and out-of-state merit awards, non-resident graduate awards available. *Unit head:* Dr. Orlando J. Perez, Chairperson, 989-774-3442, Fax: 989-774-1136, E-mail: perez1oj@cmich.edu. *Application contact:* Laura Orta, Assistant Director of Graduate Programs, 989-774-2391, Fax: 989-774-1136, E-mail: orta1lj@cmich.edu.

Claremont Graduate University, Graduate Programs, School of Politics and Economics, Department of Politics and Policy, Claremont, CA 91711-6160. Offers American politics (MA, PhD); comparative politics (PhD); international political economy (MA); international studies (MA); political philosophy (PhD); political science (PhD); politics, economics and business (MA); public policy (MA, PhD); world politics (PhD); MBA/PhD. Part-time programs available. *Faculty:* 8 full-time (5 women), 3 part-time/adjunct (0 women). *Students:* 155 full-time (59 women), 15 part-time (6 women); includes 35 minority (5 Black or African American, non-Hispanic/Latino; 9 Asian, non-Hispanic/Latino; 17 Hispanic/Latino; 3 Native Hawaiian or other Pacific Islander, non-Hispanic/Latino; 1 Two or more races, non-Hispanic/Latino), 36 international. Average age 32. In 2010, 16 master's, 21 doctorates awarded. Terminal master's awarded for partial completion of doctoral program. *Entrance requirements:* For master's and doctorate, GRE General Test. Additional exam requirements/recommendations for international students: Required—TOEFL (minimum score 550 paper-based; 213 computer-based; 80 iBT). *Application deadline:* For fall admission, 2/1 priority date for domestic students. Applications are processed on a rolling basis. Application fee: $60. Electronic applications accepted. *Expenses:* Tuition: Full-time $35,748; part-time $1554 per unit. Required fees: $215 per semester. *Financial support:* Fellowships, research assistantships, teaching assistantships, Federal Work-Study, institutionally sponsored loans, and scholarships/grants available. Support available to part-time students. Financial award application deadline: 2/15; financial award applicants required to submit FAFSA. *Faculty research:* Environmental policy, international debt, global democratization, Third World development, public sector discrimination. *Unit head:* Jennifer Merolla, Chair, 909-621-8696, Fax: 909-621-8545, E-mail: jennifer.merolla@cgu.edu. *Application contact:* Lesa Hiben, Admissions Coordinator, 909-621-8699, Fax: 909-621-7545, E-mail: lesa.hiben@cga.edu.

Clark Atlanta University, School of Arts and Sciences, Department of Political Science, Atlanta, GA 30314. Offers MA, PhD. Part-time programs available. *Faculty:* 4 full-time (0 women), 1 part-time/adjunct (0 women). *Students:* 4 full-time (2 women), 42 part-time (23 women); includes 41 Black or African American, non-Hispanic/Latino, 2 international. Average age 39. 13 applicants, 85% accepted, 3 enrolled. In 2010, 2 doctorates awarded. Terminal master's awarded for partial completion of doctoral program. *Degree requirements:* For master's, one foreign language, comprehensive exam, thesis; for doctorate, 2 foreign languages, comprehensive exam, thesis/dissertation. *Entrance requirements:* For master's, GRE General Test, minimum GPA of 2.5; for doctorate, GRE General Test, minimum graduate GPA of 3.0. Additional exam requirements/recommendations for international students: Required—TOEFL (minimum score 500 paper-based; 173 computer-based; 61 iBT). *Application deadline:* For fall admission, 4/1 for domestic and international students; for spring admission, 11/1 for domestic and international students. Applications are processed on a rolling basis. Application fee: $40 ($55 for international students). *Expenses:* Tuition: Full-time $12,942; part-time $719 per credit hour. Required fees: $710; $355 per semester. *Financial support:* In 2010–11, 1 fellowship was awarded; scholarships/grants and unspecified assistantships also available. Financial award application deadline: 4/30; financial award applicants required to submit FAFSA. *Faculty research:* Public policy and education, rural politics, women and state economic programs, reconstruction after war in Africa, environmental policies. *Unit head:* Dr. Fragano Ledgister, Chairperson, 404-880-8737, Fax: 404-880-8717, E-mail: fledgister@cau.edu. *Application contact:* Michelle Clark-Davis, Graduate Program Admissions, 404-880-6605, E-mail: cauadmissions@cau.edu.

Political Science

The College of Saint Rose, Graduate Studies, School of Arts and Humanities, Program in History/Political Science, Albany, NY 12203-1419. Offers MA. Part-time and evening/weekend programs available. *Degree requirements:* For master's, final paper/project, thesis or comprehensive exam. *Entrance requirements:* For master's, minimum undergraduate GPA of 3.0, 12 undergraduate credits in US history and/or political science. Additional exam requirements/recommendations for international students: Required—TOEFL (minimum score 550 paper-based; 213 computer-based). Electronic applications accepted.

Colorado State University, Graduate School, College of Liberal Arts, Department of Political Science, Fort Collins, CO 80523-1782. Offers MA, PhD. Part-time programs available. *Faculty:* 15 full-time (7 women), 1 (woman) part-time/adjunct. *Students:* 30 full-time (13 women), 16 part-time (4 women); includes 3 minority (2 Hispanic/Latino; 1 Two or more races, non-Hispanic/Latino). Average age 29. 38 applicants, 61% accepted, 8 enrolled. In 2010, 15 master's, 2 doctorates awarded. *Degree requirements:* For master's, variable foreign language requirement, comprehensive exam (for some programs), thesis (for some programs); for doctorate, variable foreign language requirement, comprehensive exam (for some programs), thesis/dissertation (for some programs). *Entrance requirements:* For master's, GRE General Test (minimum score 1050 verbal and quantitative), minimum GPA of 3.0, BA/BS, letters of recommendation; for doctorate, GRE General Test (minimum combined score of 1200 on Verbal and Quantitative sections), minimum GPA of 3.5, 15-page writing sample, MA/MS or at least 24 credits in a master's program, letters of recommendation. Additional exam requirements/recommendations for international students: Required—TOEFL (minimum score 550 paper-based; 213 computer-based; 80 iBT). *Application deadline:* For fall admission, 2/15 priority date for domestic and international students; for spring admission, 10/15 priority date for domestic students, 8/1 priority date for international students. Applications are processed on a rolling basis. Application fee: $50. Electronic applications accepted. *Expenses:* Tuition, state resident: full-time $7434; part-time $413 per credit. Tuition, nonresident: full-time $19,022; part-time $1057 per credit. Required fees: $1729; $88 per credit. *Financial support:* In 2010–11, 27 students received support, including 2 research assistantships (averaging $14,427 per year), 25 teaching assistantships with full tuition reimbursements available (averaging $12,622 per year); fellowships, career-related internships or fieldwork, Federal Work-Study, institutionally sponsored loans, scholarships/grants, traineeships, and unspecified assistantships also available. Financial award application deadline: 3/1; financial award applicants required to submit FAFSA. *Faculty research:* Environmental politics and policy, international relations, politics of developing nations, state and local politics and administration, political behavior. Total annual research expenditures: $5,347. *Unit head:* Dr. Robert Duffy, Chair, 970-491-6225, Fax: 970-491-2490, E-mail: robert.duffy@colostate.edu. *Application contact:* Violet Marquart, Graduate Contact, 970-491-5157, Fax: 970-491-2490, E-mail: violet.marquart@colostate.edu.

Columbia University, Graduate School of Arts and Sciences, Division of Social Sciences, Department of Political Science, New York, NY 10027. Offers M Phil, MA, PhD, JD/MA, JD/PhD. *Degree requirements:* For master's, one foreign language; for doctorate, 2 foreign languages, thesis/dissertation. *Entrance requirements:* For master's and doctorate, GRE General Test. Additional exam requirements/recommendations for international students: Required—TOEFL. *Faculty research:* Comparative politics, American government, international relations.

Concordia University, School of Graduate Studies, Faculty of Arts and Science, Department of Political Science, Montréal, QC H3G 1M8, Canada. Offers political science (PhD); public policy and public administration (MA), including geography. *Degree requirements:* For master's, one foreign language, comprehensive exam, thesis optional, internship. *Entrance requirements:* For master's, honors degree or equivalent. Additional exam requirements/recommendations for international students: Required—TOEFL. *Faculty research:* International public policy and administration, Quebec public administration, public policy and social/political theory, geography and public policy, public administration and decision making.

Converse College, School of Education and Graduate Studies, Program in Liberal Arts, Spartanburg, SC 29302-0006. Offers English (MLA); history (MLA); political science (MLA). *Degree requirements:* For master's, capstone paper. *Entrance requirements:* For master's, minimum GPA of 3.0, 2 recommendations. *Expenses:* Tuition: Part-time $365 per credit hour.

Cornell University, Graduate School, Graduate Fields of Arts and Sciences, Field of Government, Ithaca, NY 14853-0001. Offers American politics (PhD); comparative politics (PhD); international relations (PhD); political methodology (PhD); political thought (PhD); public policy (PhD). *Faculty:* 45 full-time (14 women). *Students:* 74 full-time (40 women); includes 1 Black or African American, non-Hispanic/Latino; 5 Asian, non-Hispanic/Latino; 4 Hispanic/Latino, 22 international. Average age 28. 394 applicants, 9% accepted, 20 enrolled. In 2010, 12 doctorates awarded. *Degree requirements:* For doctorate, comprehensive exam, thesis/dissertation. *Entrance requirements:* For doctorate, GRE General Test, sample of written work, 3 letters of recommendation. Additional exam requirements/recommendations for international students: Required—TOEFL (minimum score 550 paper-based; 213 computer-based; 77 iBT). *Application deadline:* For fall admission, 1/15 for domestic students. Application fee: $80. Electronic applications accepted. *Expenses:* Tuition: Full-time $29,500. Required fees: $76. Tuition and fees vary according to degree level and program. *Financial support:* In 2010–11, 29 fellowships with full tuition reimbursements, 2 research assistantships with full tuition reimbursements, 29 teaching assistantships with full tuition reimbursements were awarded; institutionally sponsored loans, scholarships/grants, health care benefits, tuition waivers (full and partial), and unspecified assistantships also available. Financial award applicants required to submit FAFSA. *Faculty research:* Political theory, American politics, comparative politics, international relations, methodology. *Unit head:* Director of Graduate Studies, 607-255-3567, Fax: 607-255-4530. *Application contact:* Graduate Field Assistant, 607-255-3567, Fax: 607-255-4530, E-mail: cu_govt@cornell.edu.

Dalhousie University, Faculty of Arts and Social Science, Department of Political Science, Halifax, NS B3H 4R2, Canada. Offers MA, PhD. *Entrance requirements:* Additional exam requirements/recommendations for international students: Required—TOEFL, IELTS, CANTEST, CAEL, or Michigan English Language Assessment Battery. Electronic applications accepted. *Faculty research:* Canadian political behavior and institutions, international politics, foreign policy, African politics, liberalism and modern political theory.

Duke University, Graduate School, Department of Political Science, Durham, NC 27708. Offers AM, PhD, JD/AM, JD/PhD. *Faculty:* 40 full-time. *Students:* 98 full-time (32 women); includes 5 Black or African American, non-Hispanic/Latino; 2 American Indian or Alaska Native, non-Hispanic/Latino; 3 Asian, non-Hispanic/Latino; 6 Hispanic/Latino, 30 international. 359 applicants, 16% accepted, 24 enrolled. In 2010, 8 master's, 15 doctorates awarded. Terminal master's awarded for partial completion of doctoral program. *Degree requirements:* For doctorate, 2 foreign languages, thesis/dissertation. *Entrance requirements:* For master's and doctorate, GRE General Test. Additional exam requirements/recommendations for international students: Required—TOEFL (minimum score 550 paper-based; 213 computer-based; 83 iBT), IELTS (minimum score 7). *Application deadline:* For fall admission, 12/8 priority date for domestic and international students. Application fee: $75. Electronic applications accepted. *Financial support:* Fellowships, research assistantships, teaching assistantships, Federal Work-Study available. Financial award application deadline: 12/8. *Unit head:* Ward Michael, Director of Graduate Studies, 919-660-4327, Fax: 919-660-4330, E-mail: knigh021@duke.edu. *Application contact:* Elizabeth Hutton, Director of Admissions, 919-684-3913, Fax: 919-684-2277, E-mail: grad-admissions@duke.edu.

East Carolina University, Graduate School, Thomas Harriot College of Arts and Sciences, Department of Political Science, Greenville, NC 27858-4353. Offers public administration (MPA). *Accreditation:* NASPAA. Part-time and evening/weekend programs available. *Degree requirements:* For master's, one foreign language, comprehensive exam. *Entrance requirements:* For master's, GRE General Test. Additional exam requirements/recommendations for international students: Required—TOEFL. *Expenses:* Tuition, state resident: full-time $3130; part-time $391.25 per credit hour. Tuition, nonresident: full-time $13,817; part-time $1727.13 per credit hour. Required fees: $1916; $239.50 per credit hour. Tuition and fees vary according to campus/location and program.

Eastern Illinois University, Graduate School, College of Sciences, Department of Political Science, Charleston, IL 61920-3099. Offers MA.

Eastern Kentucky University, The Graduate School, College of Arts and Sciences, Department of Government, Program in Political Science, Richmond, KY 40475-3102. Offers MA. *Entrance requirements:* For master's, GRE General Test, minimum GPA of 2.5.

East Stroudsburg University of Pennsylvania, Graduate School, College of Arts and Sciences, Department of Political Science, East Stroudsburg, PA 18301-2999. Offers M Ed, MA. Part-time and evening/weekend programs available. *Degree requirements:* For master's, variable foreign language requirement, comprehensive exam, thesis or alternative. *Entrance requirements:* Additional exam requirements/recommendations for international students: Required—TOEFL (minimum score 560 paper-based; 220 computer-based; 83 iBT).

East Tennessee State University, School of Graduate Studies, College of Arts and Sciences, Department of Political Science, Johnson City, TN 37614. Offers MPA.

Emory University, Laney Graduate School, Department of Political Science, Atlanta, GA 30322-1100. Offers PhD. *Degree requirements:* For doctorate, comprehensive exam, thesis/dissertation. *Entrance requirements:* For doctorate, GRE General Test, minimum GPA of 3.0. Additional exam requirements/recommendations for international students: Required—TOEFL. Electronic applications accepted. *Expenses:* Tuition: Full-time $33,800. Required fees: $1300. *Faculty research:* Post-Soviet politics, comparative politics, international politics, judicial politics and methodology, American national political institutions.

Fairleigh Dickinson University, Metropolitan Campus, University College: Arts, Sciences, and Professional Studies, School of History, Political and International Studies, Program in Political Science, Teaneck, NJ 07666-1914. Offers MA. *Students:* 3 part-time (1 woman). Average age 35. 2 applicants, 0% accepted, 0 enrolled. *Application deadline:* Applications are processed on a rolling basis. Application fee: $40. *Application contact:* Susan Brooman, University Director of Graduate Admissions, 201-692-2554, Fax: 201-692-2560, E-mail: globaleducation@fdu.edu.

Fayetteville State University, Graduate School, Department of Geography, History and Political Science, Fayetteville, NC 28301-4298. Offers history (MA); political science (MA). Part-time and evening/weekend programs available. *Faculty:* 8 full-time (2 women). *Students:* 3 full-time (2 women), 6 part-time (3 women); includes 7 Black or African American, non-Hispanic/Latino. Average age 40. 4 applicants, 100% accepted, 4 enrolled. In 2010, 1 master's awarded. *Degree requirements:* For master's, comprehensive exam, internship. *Entrance requirements:* For master's, GRE General Test. *Application deadline:* For fall admission, 4/15 for domestic students; for spring admission, 10/15 for domestic students. Applications are processed on a rolling basis. Application fee: $35. Electronic applications accepted. *Unit head:* Dr. Adeguke Ademiluyi, Chairperson, 910-672-1137, E-mail: aademiluyi@uncfsu.edu. *Application contact:* Katrina Hoffman, Graduate Admissions Officer, 910-672-1374, Fax: 910-672-1470, E-mail: khoffma1@uncfsu.edu.

Florida Agricultural and Mechanical University, Division of Graduate Studies, Research, and Continuing Education, College of Arts and Sciences, Division of History and Political Sciences, Program in Applied Social Science, Tallahassee, FL 32307-3200. Offers African American history (MASS); criminal justice (MASS); economics (MASS); history (MASS); political science (MASS); public administration (MASS); public management (MASS); social work (MASS); sociology (MASS). Part-time programs available. *Degree requirements:* For master's, thesis optional. *Entrance requirements:* For master's, GRE General Test, minimum GPA of 3.0. *Faculty research:* Southern history, black history, election trends, presidential history.

Florida Atlantic University, Dorothy F. Schmidt College of Arts and Letters, Department of Political Science, Boca Raton, FL 33431-0991. Offers MA, MAT. Part-time programs available. *Faculty:* 16 full-time (4 women), 5 part-time/adjunct (1 woman). *Students:* 9 full-time (4 women), 22 part-time (10 women); includes 10 minority (2 Black or African American, non-Hispanic/Latino; 1 American Indian or Alaska Native, non-Hispanic/Latino; 2 Asian, non-Hispanic/Latino; 5 Hispanic/Latino), 1 international. Average age 31. 21 applicants, 57% accepted, 10 enrolled. In 2010, 10 master's awarded. *Degree requirements:* For master's, one foreign language, thesis or alternative. *Entrance requirements:* For master's, GRE General Test, minimum GPA of 3.0 during last 60 hours of course work. *Application deadline:* For fall admission, 7/1 for domestic students, 2/15 for international students; for spring admission, 11/1 for domestic students, 7/15 for international students. Applications are processed on a rolling basis. Application fee: $30. Electronic applications accepted. *Expenses:* Tuition, area resident: Part-time $319.96 per credit. Tuition, state resident: part-time $319.96 per credit. Tuition, nonresident: part-time $926.42 per credit. *Financial support:* Research assistantships, teaching assistantships with partial tuition reimbursements, career-related internships or fieldwork, Federal Work-Study, and institutionally sponsored loans available. Support available to part-time students. Financial award application deadline: 4/16. *Faculty research:* Public policy, comparative policy affecting women, Congress, international system, urban policy. *Unit head:* Dr. Timothy Lenz, Chair, 561-297-3212, Fax: 561-297-2997, E-mail: lenz@fau.edu. *Application contact:* Dr. Robert Rabil, Director of Graduate Studies, 561-297-3215, Fax: 561-297-2997, E-mail: rrabil@fau.edu.

Florida International University, College of Arts and Sciences, Department of Politics and International Relations, Program of Political Science, Miami, FL 33199. Offers MA, PhD. Part-time and evening/weekend programs available. *Students:* 23 full-time (6 women), 7 part-time (3 women); includes 4 Black or African American, non-Hispanic/Latino; 8 Hispanic/Latino, 11 international. Average age 27. 56 applicants, 16% accepted, 9 enrolled. In 2010, 3 doctorates awarded. *Degree requirements:* For master's, one foreign language, thesis or alternative, research project; for doctorate, one foreign language, comprehensive exam, thesis/dissertation. *Entrance requirements:* For master's, GRE General Test, minimum GPA of 3.2, 2 letters of recommendation; for doctorate, GRE General Test, minimum GPA of 3.2 (undergraduate), 3.25 (graduate); 2 letters of recommendation; master's thesis or other major paper. Additional exam requirements/recommendations for international students: Required—TOEFL (minimum score 550 paper-based; 80 iBT). *Application deadline:* For fall admission, 3/15 for domestic and international students. Application fee: $30. Electronic applications accepted. *Financial support:* Institutionally sponsored loans and scholarships/grants available. Financial award application deadline: 3/1; financial award applicants required to submit FAFSA. *Unit head:* Dr. Richard Olson, Chair, Politics and International Relations, 305-348-2556, Fax: 305-348-6138, E-mail: pir@fiu.edu. *Application contact:* Dr. Ronald Cox, Director of Graduate Studies, 305-348-2556, Fax: 305-348-6138, E-mail: pir@fiu.edu.

Florida State University, The Graduate School, College of Social Sciences and Public Policy, Department of Political Science, Tallahassee, FL 32306-2230. Offers MA, MS, PhD. Part-time programs available. *Faculty:* 23 full-time (3 women). *Students:* 57 full-time (16 women), 31 part-time (14 women); includes 16 minority (4 Black or African American, non-Hispanic/Latino; 3 Asian, non-Hispanic/Latino; 9 Hispanic/Latino), 3 international. Average age 27. 117 applicants, 56% accepted, 27 enrolled. In 2010, 55 master's, 7 doctorates awarded. Terminal master's awarded for partial completion of doctoral program. *Degree requirements:* For master's, thesis optional; for doctorate, comprehensive exam, thesis/dissertation. *Entrance requirements:* For master's, GRE General Test, minimum undergraduate GPA of 3.0; for doctorate, GRE General Test, minimum graduate GPA of 3.5, undergraduate 3.0. Additional exam requirements/recommendations for international students: Required—TOEFL (minimum score 600 paper-based; 250 computer-based; 100 iBT). *Application deadline:* For fall admission, 1/15 priority date for domestic and international students. Applications are processed on a rolling basis. Application fee: $30. Electronic applications accepted. *Expenses:* Tuition, state resident: full-time $8238.24. *Financial support:* In 2010–11, 37 students received support, including 3 fellowships with full tuition reimbursements available (averaging $18,000 per year), 28 research assistantships with full tuition reimbursements available (averaging $17,000 per year), 8 teaching assistantships with full tuition reimbursements available (averaging $17,000 per year); Federal Work-Study, institutionally sponsored loans, scholarships/grants, and unspecified assistantships also available. Financial award application deadline: 1/15; financial award applicants required to submit FAFSA. *Faculty research:* American government, international relations, comparative government, public policy. Total annual research expenditures: $230,000. *Unit head:* Dr. Charles Barrilleaux, Director of Graduate Studies, 850-644-7643, Fax: 850-644-1367, E-mail: cbarrile@fsu.edu. *Application contact:* Jerry Fisher, Academic Coordinator, 850-644-7305, Fax: 850-644-1367, E-mail: jfisher@admin.fsu.edu.

Fordham University, Graduate School of Arts and Sciences, Department of Political Science, New York, NY 10458. Offers elections and campaign management (MA). Part-time and evening/weekend programs available. *Faculty:* 18 full-time (2 women). *Students:* 5 full-time (0 women), 7 part-time (3 women); includes 1 Black or African American, non-Hispanic/Latino; 1 Hispanic/Latino, 4 international. Average age 30. 33 applicants, 76% accepted, 5 enrolled. In 2010, 8 master's awarded. *Degree requirements:* For master's, comprehensive exam. *Entrance requirements:* For master's, GRE General Test. Additional exam requirements/recommendations for international students: Required—TOEFL (minimum score 600 paper-based; 250 computer-based). *Application deadline:* For fall admission, 1/4 priority date for domestic students; for spring admission, 11/1 for domestic students. Application fee: $70. Electronic applications accepted. *Financial support:* In 2010–11, 5 students received support, including 5 research assistantships with tuition reimbursements available (averaging $14,720 per year); institutionally sponsored loans, tuition waivers (full and partial), and unspecified assistantships also available. Financial award application deadline: 1/4; financial award applicants required to submit FAFSA. *Faculty research:* Protest in emerging democracies, impact of religion on presidential elections, increasing partisan polarization in U. S. politics, comparative urban development, democracy vs. authoritarianism in the Middle East, election and campaign management. *Unit head:* Dr. Bruce Berg, Chair, 718-817-3950, Fax: 718-817-3972, E-mail: berg@fordham.edu. *Application contact:* Charlene Dundie, Director of Graduate Admissions, 718-817-4420, Fax: 718-817-3566, E-mail: dundie@fordham.edu.

Fordham University, Graduate School of Arts and Sciences, Program in International Political Economy and Development, Program in Elections and Campaign Management, New York, NY 10458. Offers MA. *Students:* 17 full-time (10 women), 20 part-time (4 women); includes 6 minority (3 Black or African American, non-Hispanic/Latino; 3 Hispanic/Latino), 5 international. 37 applicants, 86% accepted, 14 enrolled. In 2010, 13 master's awarded. Application fee: $70. *Unit head:* Dr. Costas Panagopoulos, Director, 718-817-3967. *Application contact:* Charlene Dundie, Director of Graduate Admissions, 718-817-4420, Fax: 718-817-3566, E-mail: dundie@fordham.edu.

George Mason University, College of Humanities and Social Sciences, Department of Public and International Affairs, Fairfax, VA 22030. Offers association management (Certificate); biodefense (MS, PhD); emergency management and homeland security (Certificate); nonprofit management (Certificate); political science (MA, PhD); public administration (MPA); public management (Certificate). *Accreditation:* NASPAA (one or more programs are accredited). *Faculty:* 38 full-time (14 women), 31 part-time/adjunct (8 women). *Students:* 134 full-time (76 women), 319 part-time (176 women); includes 63 minority (29 Black or African American, non-Hispanic/Latino; 9 Asian, non-Hispanic/Latino; 21 Hispanic/Latino; 1 Native Hawaiian or other Pacific Islander, non-Hispanic/Latino; 3 Two or more races, non-Hispanic/Latino), 16 international. Average age 31. 574 applicants, 58% accepted, 144 enrolled. In 2010, 140 master's, 3 doctorates, 11 other advanced degrees awarded. *Entrance requirements:* For master's, GRE General Test, minimum GPA of 3.0 in last 60 hours of course work. Additional exam requirements/recommendations for international students: Required—TOEFL (minimum score 570 paper-based; 230 computer-based; 88 iBT). *Application deadline:* For fall admission, 3/1 priority date for domestic students; for spring admission, 10/15 for domestic students. Application fee: $100. Electronic applications accepted. *Expenses:* Tuition, state resident: full-time $8192; part-time $440 per credit hour. Tuition, nonresident: full-time $22,952; part-time $1055 per credit hour. Required fees: $2364; $99 per credit hour. *Financial support:* In 2010–11, 30 students received support, including 3 fellowships with full tuition reimbursements available (averaging $18,000 per year), 10 research assistantships with full and partial tuition reimbursements available (averaging $12,271 per year), 18 teaching assistantships with full and partial tuition reimbursements available (averaging $10,428 per year); career-related internships or fieldwork, Federal Work-Study, scholarships/grants, unspecified assistantships, and health care benefits (full-time research or teaching assistantship recipients) also available. Financial award application deadline: 3/1; financial award applicants required to submit FAFSA. *Faculty research:* The Rehnquist Court and economic liberties; intersection of economic development with high-tech industry, telecommunications, and entrepreneurism; political economy of development; violence, terrorism and U. S. foreign policy; international security issues. Total annual research expenditures: $696,997. *Unit head:* Dr. Priscilla Regan, Chair, 703-993-1419, Fax: 703-993-1399, E-mail: pregan@gmu.edu. *Application contact:* Peg Koback, Information Contact, 703-993-9466, E-mail: mkoback@gmu.edu.

Georgetown University, Graduate School of Arts and Sciences, Department of Government, Program in Democracy and Governance, Washington, DC 20057. Offers MA.

Georgetown University, Graduate School of Arts and Sciences, School of Continuing Studies, Washington, DC 20057. Offers American studies (MALS); Catholic studies (MALS); classical civilizations (MALS); disability studies (MPS); ethics and the professions (MALS); human resources management (MPS); humanities (MALS); individualized study (MALS); international affairs (MALS); Islam and Muslim-Christian relations (MALS); journalism (MPS); liberal studies (DLS); literature and society (MALS); medieval and early modern European studies (MALS); public relations and corporate communications (MPS); real estate (MPS); religious studies (MALS); social and public policy (MALS); sports industry management (MPS); the theory and practice of American democracy (MALS); visual culture (MALS). *Entrance requirements:* Additional exam requirements/recommendations for international students: Required—TOEFL.

The George Washington University, College of Professional Studies, Graduate School of Political Management, Program in Legislative Affairs, Washington, DC 20052. Offers MA. Part-time and evening/weekend programs available. *Students:* 31 full-time (6 women), 61 part-time (26 women); includes 14 minority (3 Black or African American, non-Hispanic/Latino; 1 American Indian or Alaska Native, non-Hispanic/Latino; 2 Asian, non-Hispanic/Latino; 7 Hispanic/Latino; 1 Two or more races, non-Hispanic/Latino). Average age 32. 72 applicants, 94% accepted. In 2010, 54 master's awarded. *Degree requirements:* For master's, comprehensive exam. *Entrance requirements:* For master's, GRE General Test, minimum GPA of 3.0. Additional exam requirements/recommendations for international students: Required—TOEFL (minimum score 550 paper-based; 213 computer-based). *Application deadline:* For fall admission, 4/1 priority date for domestic and international students; for spring admission, 10/1 priority date for domestic and international students. Applications are processed on a rolling basis. Application fee: $75. Electronic applications accepted. *Financial support:* Application deadline: 2/1. *Unit head:* Dr. Steven E. Billet, Director, 202-994-6000, E-mail: sbillet@gwu.edu. *Application contact:* Information Contact, 202-994-6000, Fax: 202-994-6006, E-mail: gspmmail@gwu.edu.

The George Washington University, Columbian College of Arts and Sciences, Department of Political Science, Washington, DC 20052. Offers MA, PhD. Part-time and evening/weekend programs available. *Faculty:* 28 full-time (9 women). *Students:* 52 full-time (24 women), 44 part-time (13 women); includes 9 Asian, non-Hispanic/Latino; 2 Hispanic/Latino, 22 international. Average age 30. 367 applicants, 27% accepted, 20 enrolled. In 2010, 7 master's, 8 doctorates awarded. Terminal master's awarded for partial completion of doctoral program. *Degree requirements:* For master's, one foreign language, comprehensive exam, thesis or alternative; for doctorate, 2 foreign languages, thesis/dissertation, general exam. *Entrance requirements:* For master's and doctorate, GRE General Test, minimum GPA of 3.0. Additional exam requirements/recommendations for international students: Required—TOEFL (minimum score 550 paper-based; 213 computer-based; 80 iBT). *Application deadline:* For fall admission, 1/15 priority date for domestic students; for spring admission, 10/1 priority date for domestic students. Applications are processed on a rolling basis. Application fee: $75. Electronic applications accepted. *Financial support:* In 2010–11, 43 students received support; fellowships with tuition reimbursements available, teaching assistantships with tuition reimbursements available, Federal Work-Study and tuition waivers available. *Unit head:* Christopher J. Deering, Chair, 202-994-6564, E-mail: rocket@gwu.edu. *Application contact:* Christopher J. Deering, Chair, 202-994-6564, E-mail: rocket@gwu.edu.

The George Washington University, Elliott School of International Affairs, Program in Security Policy Studies, Washington, DC 20052. Offers MA, JD/MA. Part-time and evening/weekend programs available. *Students:* 51 full-time (15 women), 41 part-time (16 women); includes 1 Black or African American, non-Hispanic/Latino; 7 Asian, non-Hispanic/Latino; 1 Hispanic/Latino, 4 international. Average age 27. 284 applicants, 40% accepted, 25 enrolled. In 2010, 52 master's awarded. *Degree requirements:* For master's, one foreign language, capstone project. *Entrance requirements:* For master's, GRE General Test, 2 semesters of introductory economics, 2 years of a modern foreign language or 1 semester of statistics. Additional exam requirements/recommendations for international students: Required—TOEFL. *Application deadline:* For fall admission, 2/1 for domestic students; for spring admission, 10/1 for domestic students. Application fee: $75. Electronic applications accepted. *Financial support:* In 2010–11, 22 students received support; fellowships with tuition reimbursements available, research assistantships with tuition reimbursements available, career-related internships or fieldwork, Federal Work-Study, institutionally sponsored loans, and tuition waivers (full) available. Financial award application deadline: 1/15; financial award applicants required to submit FAFSA. *Faculty research:* U. S. arms transfer policies, military balance in the Third World, U. S. foreign policy, technology and security policy. *Unit head:* Joanna Spear, Director, 202-994-1088, E-mail: jspear@gwu.edu. *Application contact:* Jeff V. Miles, Director of Graduate Admissions, 202-994-7050, Fax: 202-994-9537, E-mail: esiagrad@gwu.edu.

Georgia State University, College of Arts and Sciences, Department of Political Science, Atlanta, GA 30302-3083. Offers MA, PhD. Part-time and evening/weekend programs available. Terminal master's awarded for partial completion of doctoral program. *Degree requirements:* For master's, thesis or alternative, exam; for doctorate, one foreign language, thesis/dissertation, exam. *Entrance requirements:* For master's, GRE General Test, 2 letters of recommendation; for doctorate, GRE General Test, 3 letters of recommendation, writing sample. Additional exam requirements/recommendations for international students: Required—TOEFL. Electronic applications accepted. *Faculty research:* International politics, American politics, comparative politics, public administration, international political economy.

Governors State University, College of Arts and Sciences, Program in Political and Justice Studies, University Park, IL 60466-0975. Offers MA. Part-time and evening/weekend programs available. *Degree requirements:* For master's, thesis or alternative. *Entrance requirements:* For master's, bachelor's degree in related field. *Expenses:* Tuition, state resident: full-time $5400; part-time $225 per credit hour. Tuition, nonresident: full-time $16,200; part-time $675 per credit hour. Required fees: $1358; $46 per credit hour. $126 per term. Tuition and fees vary according to degree level and program.

Graduate School and University Center of the City University of New York, Graduate Studies, Program in Political Science, New York, NY 10016-4039. Offers MA, PhD. Terminal master's awarded for partial completion of doctoral program. *Degree requirements:* For master's, one foreign language, thesis; for doctorate, one foreign language, thesis/dissertation. *Entrance requirements:* For master's and doctorate, GRE General Test. Additional exam requirements/recommendations for international students: Required—TOEFL. Electronic applications accepted.

Grambling State University, School of Graduate Studies and Research, College of Arts and Sciences, Program in Public Administration, Grambling, LA 71270. Offers health service administration (MPA); human resource management (MPA); public management (MPA); state and local government (MPA). *Accreditation:* NASPAA. Part-time programs available. *Degree requirements:* For master's, comprehensive exam (for some programs), thesis optional. *Entrance requirements:* For master's, GRE, minimum GPA of 2.75 on last degree. Additional exam requirements/recommendations for international students: Required—TOEFL (minimum score 500 paper-based; 173 computer-based; 61 iBT). Electronic applications accepted.

Harvard University, Graduate School of Arts and Sciences, Committee on Political Economy and Government, Cambridge, MA 02138. Offers PhD. *Entrance requirements:* For doctorate, GRE General Test or GMAT. Additional exam requirements/recommendations for international students: Required—TOEFL. *Expenses:* Tuition: Full-time $34,976. Required fees: $1166. Full-time tuition and fees vary according to program.

Harvard University, Graduate School of Arts and Sciences, Department of Government, Cambridge, MA 02138. Offers political science (PhD), including American politics, comparative politics, international relations, political thought, quantitative methods. *Degree requirements:* For doctorate, one foreign language, thesis/dissertation, general exams. *Entrance requirements:* For doctorate, GRE General Test. Additional exam requirements/recommendations for international students: Required—TOEFL. *Expenses:* Tuition: Full-time $34,976. Required fees: $1166. Full-time tuition and fees vary according to program.

Harvard University, John F. Kennedy School of Government, Cambridge, MA 02138. Offers MPA, MPAID, MPP, PhD, JD/MPP, MBA/MPP, MD/MPP. *Accreditation:* NASPAA. *Students:* 880 full-time (367 women), 32 part-time (12 women); includes 32 Black or African American, non-Hispanic/Latino; 7 American Indian or Alaska Native, non-Hispanic/Latino; 61 Asian, non-Hispanic/Latino; 53 Hispanic/Latino; 38 Two or more races, non-Hispanic/Latino, 344 international. Average age 31. 3,129 applicants, 28% accepted, 581 enrolled. In 2010, 513 master's awarded. *Degree requirements:* For doctorate, thesis/dissertation. *Entrance requirements:* For master's, GMAT or GRE General Test; for doctorate, GRE General Test. Additional exam requirements/recommendations for international students: Required—TOEFL (minimum score 600 paper-based; 250 computer-based; 100 iBT), TWE. Application fee: $100. Electronic applications accepted. *Expenses:* Tuition: Full-time $34,976. Required fees: $1166. Full-time tuition and fees vary according to program. *Financial support:* Fellowships, research assistantships, teaching assistantships, career-related internships or fieldwork, Federal Work-Study, institutionally sponsored loans, scholarships/grants, and unspecified assistantships available. Support available to part-time students. Financial award applicants required to submit CSS PROFILE or FAFSA. *Unit head:* Dr. David Ellwood, Dean, 617-495-1122. *Application contact:* 617-495-1155, Fax: 617-496-1165, E-mail: hks_admissions@harvard.edu.

Howard University, Graduate School, Department of Political Science, Program in Political Science, Washington, DC 20059-0002. Offers MA, PhD. *Degree requirements:* For master's, comprehensive exam. *Entrance requirements:* For master's, GRE General Test, minimum GPA of 3.0; for doctorate, GRE General Test, minimum GPA of 2.8.

Hult International Business School, Program in International Relations—Hult London Campus, London, MA WC 1B 4JP, United Kingdom. Offers conflict resolution (MA); diplomacy (MA); international public law (MA); international relations (MA); Middle East international security (MA); politics (MA); security studies (MA); terrorism (MA); U.S. foreign policy (MA). Part-time programs available. *Entrance requirements:* Additional exam requirements/recommendations for international students: Required—TOEFL (minimum score 580 paper-based; 237 computer-based), TWE (minimum score 5). Electronic applications accepted. *Faculty research:* American foreign politics, Middle East, security studies.

Idaho State University, Office of Graduate Studies, College of Arts and Sciences, Department of Political Science, Pocatello, ID 83209-8073. Offers political science (MA, DA); public administration (MPA). Part-time programs available. *Degree requirements:* For master's, comprehensive exam, thesis optional; for doctorate, comprehensive exam, thesis/dissertation, teaching internship. *Entrance requirements:* For master's, GRE General Test, minimum GPA of 3.0 in last 2 years of undergraduate study, 3 letters of recommendation; for doctorate, GRE General Test, major field of American politics, minimum GPA of 3.0 in last 2 years of

Political Science

Idaho State University *(continued)*
undergraduate study, 3 letters of recommendation. Additional exam requirements/recommendations for international students: Required—TOEFL (minimum score 550 paper-based; 213 computer-based; 80 iBT). Electronic applications accepted. *Faculty research:* International affairs, environmental policy, decision making, Constitution, executive/legislative relations.

Illinois State University, Graduate School, College of Arts and Sciences, Department of Politics and Government, Normal, IL 61790-2200. Offers MA, MS. *Degree requirements:* For master's, thesis or alternative. *Entrance requirements:* For master's, GRE General Test, minimum GPA of 3.0 in last 60 hours of course work, 15 hours of course work in political science. *Faculty research:* Political tolerance in a democracy under external threats: a survey of public opinion.

Indiana State University, College of Graduate and Professional Studies, College of Arts and Sciences, Department of Political Science, Terre Haute, IN 47809. Offers political science (MA, MS); public administration (MPA). *Degree requirements:* For master's, thesis (for some programs). *Entrance requirements:* For master's, GRE or minimum undergraduate GPA of 2.75, 18 semester hours of course work in political science. Additional exam requirements/recommendations for international students: Required—TOEFL (minimum score 550 paper-based). Electronic applications accepted.

Indiana University Bloomington, University Graduate School, College of Arts and Sciences, Department of Political Science, Bloomington, IN 47405-7000. Offers MA, PhD. *Faculty:* 26 full-time (9 women). *Students:* 83 full-time (27 women); includes 7 minority (2 Black or African American, non-Hispanic/Latino; 3 Asian, non-Hispanic/Latino; 1 Hispanic/Latino; 1 Two or more races, non-Hispanic/Latino), 15 international. Average age 31. 142 applicants, 14% accepted, 8 enrolled. In 2010, 4 master's, 5 doctorates awarded. Terminal master's awarded for partial completion of doctoral program. *Degree requirements:* For master's, thesis, 30 credit hours; for doctorate, comprehensive exam, thesis/dissertation. *Entrance requirements:* For master's, GRE, personal statement, transcripts, 3 letters of recommendation; for doctorate, GRE, sample of written work, 3 letters of recommendation. Additional exam requirements/recommendations for international students: Required—TOEFL (minimum score 640 paper-based; 273 computer-based; 112 iBT). *Application deadline:* For fall admission, 1/15 for domestic students, 12/1 for international students. Application fee: $55 ($65 for international students). Electronic applications accepted. *Financial support:* In 2010–11, 10 fellowships with full tuition reimbursements (averaging $16,000 per year), 9 research assistantships with full tuition reimbursements (averaging $15,450 per year), 19 teaching assistantships with full tuition reimbursements (averaging $15,175 per year) were awarded; Federal Work-Study, institutionally sponsored loans, scholarships/grants, health care benefits, and unspecified assistantships also available. Financial award application deadline: 2/25. *Faculty research:* American politics, international relations, public policy, political theory, comparative politics, theory and methodology. Total annual research expenditures: $291,773. *Unit head:* Russell Hanson, Chair, 812-855-1209, Fax: 812-855-2027, E-mail: hansonr@indiana.edu. *Application contact:* Sharon LaRoche, Graduate Secretary, 812-855-1208, Fax: 812-855-2027, E-mail: laroches@indiana.edu.

Indiana University–Purdue University Indianapolis, School of Liberal Arts, Department of Political Science, Indianapolis, IN 46202-2896. Offers MA, Certificate. *Students:* 1 full-time (0 women), 7 part-time (4 women); includes 3 minority (all Black or African American, non-Hispanic/Latino). Average age 27. 4 applicants, 75% accepted, 2 enrolled. *Unit head:* John McCormick, Chair, 317-274-7387. *Application contact:* Director of Research and Graduate Programs, 317-274-8305.

Institute for Christian Studies, Graduate Programs, Toronto, ON M5T 1R4, Canada. Offers education (M Phil F, PhD); history of philosophy (M Phil F, PhD); philosophical aesthetics (M Phil F, PhD); philosophy of religion (M Phil F, PhD); political theory (M Phil F, PhD); systematic philosophy (M Phil F, PhD); theology (M Phil F, PhD); worldview studies (MWS). Part-time programs available. Postbaccalaureate distance learning degree programs offered (minimal on-campus study). *Degree requirements:* For master's, one foreign language, thesis; for doctorate, 2 foreign languages, thesis/dissertation. *Entrance requirements:* For master's and doctorate, philosophy background. Additional exam requirements/recommendations for international students: Required—TOEFL (minimum score 600 paper-based; 250 computer-based). *Faculty research:* Human rights, anthropology of self, medieval discourse, gender and body, post-modern thought; biblical hermeneutics, creational aesthetics, ecumenism, epistemology, political theory and public policy, relational psychotherapy.

The Institute of World Politics, Graduate Programs in National Security, Intelligence, and International Affairs, Washington, DC 20036. Offers American foreign policy (Certificate); comparative political culture (Certificate); counterintelligence (Certificate); democracy building (Certificate); intelligence (Certificate); international politics (Certificate); national security affairs (Certificate); public diplomacy and political warfare (Certificate); statecraft and national security affairs (MA); statecraft and world politics (MA); strategic intelligence studies (MA). Part-time and evening/weekend programs available. *Degree requirements:* For master's, comprehensive exam, thesis optional. *Entrance requirements:* For master's, GRE General Test. Additional exam requirements/recommendations for international students: Required—TOEFL. Electronic applications accepted. *Faculty research:* Intelligence, national security, statecraft.

Iowa State University of Science and Technology, Graduate College, College of Liberal Arts and Sciences, Department of Political Science, Ames, IA 50011. Offers political science (MA); public administration (MPA); JD/MA. JD/MA offered jointly with Drake University. *Accreditation:* NASPAA. *Faculty:* 15 full-time (3 women), 6 part-time/adjunct (2 women). *Students:* 45 full-time (21 women), 62 part-time (20 women); includes 6 Black or African American, non-Hispanic/Latino; 5 Asian, non-Hispanic/Latino; 1 Hispanic/Latino, 14 international. 37 applicants, 78% accepted, 19 enrolled. In 2010, 16 master's awarded. *Degree requirements:* For master's, thesis (for some programs). *Entrance requirements:* For master's, GRE General Test, GMAT or LSAT. Additional exam requirements/recommendations for international students: Required—TOEFL (minimum score 570 paper-based; 80 iBT), IELTS (minimum score 6.5). *Application deadline:* For fall admission, 1/1 priority date for domestic and international students; for spring admission, 10/1 for domestic and international students. Applications are processed on a rolling basis. Application fee: $40 ($90 for international students). Electronic applications accepted. *Financial support:* In 2010–11, 18 research assistantships with full and partial tuition reimbursements (averaging $4,063 per year), 3 teaching assistantships with full and partial tuition reimbursements (averaging $6,713 per year) were awarded; fellowships, scholarships/grants, health care benefits, and unspecified assistantships also available. *Unit head:* Dr. James M. McCormick, Chair, 515-294-8682, Fax: 515-294-1003, E-mail: polsc@iastate.edu. *Application contact:* Dr. Mack Shelley, Director of Graduate Education, 515-294-1075, E-mail: polsci@iastate.edu.

Jackson State University, Graduate School, College of Liberal Arts, Department of Political Science, Jackson, MS 39217. Offers MA. Part-time and evening/weekend programs available. *Faculty:* 4 full-time (2 women). *Students:* 13 full-time (8 women), 9 part-time (6 women); includes 16 Black or African American, non-Hispanic/Latino; 1 Hispanic/Latino, 1 international. Average age 33. In 2010, 4 master's awarded. *Degree requirements:* For master's, comprehensive exam, thesis or alternative. *Entrance requirements:* For master's, GRE General Test. Additional exam requirements/recommendations for international students: Required—TOEFL (minimum score 520 paper-based; 195 computer-based; 67 iBT). *Application deadline:* For fall admission, 3/1 priority date for domestic students, 3/1 for international students; for spring admission, 10/1 for domestic and international students. Applications are processed on a rolling basis. Application fee: $25. *Expenses:* Tuition, state resident: full-time $5050; part-time $281 per credit hour. Tuition, nonresident: full-time $12,380; part-time $689 per credit hour. *Financial support:* Career-related internships or fieldwork, Federal Work-Study, scholarships/grants, and unspecified assistantships available. Support available to part-time students.

Financial award application deadline: 3/1; financial award applicants required to submit FAFSA. *Unit head:* Dr. D'Andra Orey, Chair, 601-979-2136, Fax: 601-979-2904, E-mail: emmanul.c.nwagboso@jsums.edu. *Application contact:* Sharlene Wilson, Director of Graduate Admissions, 601-979-2455, Fax: 601-979-4325, E-mail: sharlene.f.wilson@jsums.edu.

Jacksonville State University, College of Graduate Studies and Continuing Education, College of Arts and Sciences, Department of Political Science, Jacksonville, AL 36265-1602. Offers MPA. Part-time and evening/weekend programs available. *Degree requirements:* For master's, comprehensive exam, thesis (for some programs). *Entrance requirements:* For master's, GRE General Test or MAT. Electronic applications accepted.

James Madison University, The Graduate School, College of Arts and Letters, Department of Political Science, Program in Political Science, Harrisonburg, VA 22807. Offers MA. Part-time programs available. *Students:* 21 full-time (9 women); includes 1 minority (Hispanic/Latino). Average age 27. *Entrance requirements:* For master's, GRE General Test, GRE Writing Test, 2 letters of recommendation; resume; goals, language proficiency and policy interest statements. Additional exam requirements/recommendations for international students: Required—TOEFL. *Application deadline:* For fall admission, 5/1 priority date for domestic students; for spring admission, 9/1 priority date for domestic students. Applications are processed on a rolling basis. Application fee: $55. Electronic applications accepted. *Financial support:* Application deadline: 3/1. *Unit head:* Dr. Jessica Adolino, Academic Unit Head, 540-568-6149, E-mail: adolinjr@jmu.edu. *Application contact:* Lynette M. Bible, Director of Graduate Admissions, 540-568-6395, Fax: 540-568-7860, E-mail: biblem@jmu.edu.

The Johns Hopkins University, Zanvyl Krieger School of Arts and Sciences, Advanced Academic Programs, Program in Government, Baltimore, MD 21218-2699. Offers government (MA); national securities study (Certificate); MA/MBA. Part-time and evening/weekend programs available. *Faculty:* 4 full-time (2 women), 35 part-time/adjunct (5 women). *Students:* 249 full-time (110 women), 215 part-time (90 women); includes 103 minority (26 Black or African American, non-Hispanic/Latino; 3 American Indian or Alaska Native, non-Hispanic/Latino; 29 Asian, non-Hispanic/Latino; 36 Hispanic/Latino; 9 Two or more races, non-Hispanic/Latino), 9 international. Average age 28. 144 applicants, 73% accepted, 92 enrolled. In 2010, 89 master's awarded. *Degree requirements:* For master's, thesis. *Entrance requirements:* For master's, minimum GPA of 3.0. Additional exam requirements/recommendations for international students: Required—TOEFL (minimum score 250 computer-based; 100 iBT). *Application deadline:* For fall admission, 5/31 priority date for domestic students, 4/30 priority date for international students; for spring admission, 10/31 priority date for domestic and international students. Applications are processed on a rolling basis. Application fee: $75. Electronic applications accepted. *Financial support:* Applicants required to submit FAFSA. *Unit head:* Dr. Kathy Wagner, Associate Program Chair, 202-452-1953, E-mail: kwagner@jhu.edu. *Application contact:* Valana M. McMickens, Admissions Manager, 202-452-1941, Fax: 202-452-1970, E-mail: aapadmissions@jhu.edu.

The Johns Hopkins University, Zanvyl Krieger School of Arts and Sciences, Department of Political Science, Baltimore, MD 21218-2699. Offers MA, PhD. *Faculty:* 20 full-time (6 women), 3 part-time/adjunct (0 women). *Students:* 72 full-time (28 women); includes 2 Black or African American, non-Hispanic/Latino; 1 Hispanic/Latino, 30 international. Average age 29. 201 applicants, 11% accepted, 22 enrolled. In 2010, 3 master's, 3 doctorates awarded. *Degree requirements:* For doctorate, one foreign language, comprehensive exam, thesis/dissertation. *Entrance requirements:* For doctorate, GRE General Test. Additional exam requirements/recommendations for international students: Required—TOEFL (minimum score 600 paper-based; 250 computer-based; 100 iBT), IELTS. *Application deadline:* For fall admission, 1/15 for domestic and international students. Application fee: $75. Electronic applications accepted. *Financial support:* In 2010–11, 54 students received support, including 31 fellowships with full tuition reimbursements available (averaging $18,900 per year), 24 teaching assistantships with full tuition reimbursements available (averaging $18,900 per year); research assistantships with full tuition reimbursements available, Federal Work-Study and institutionally sponsored loans also available. Financial award application deadline: 4/15; financial award applicants required to submit FAFSA. *Faculty research:* American politics, comparative politics, international relations, political theory, urban politics. Total annual research expenditures: $104,641. *Unit head:* Dr. Richard Katz, Chair, 410-516-7534, Fax: 410-516-5515, E-mail: richard.katz@jhu.edu. *Application contact:* Barbara Hall, Academic Program Coordinator, 410-516-7540, Fax: 410-516-5515, E-mail: bhall@jhu.edu.

Kansas State University, Graduate School, College of Arts and Sciences, Department of Political Science, Manhattan, KS 66506. Offers political science (MA), including international service, political science; public administration (MPA). Part-time programs available. *Degree requirements:* For master's, thesis or alternative. *Entrance requirements:* For master's, GRE (recommended), minimum GPA of 3.0. Additional exam requirements/recommendations for international students: Required—TOEFL (minimum score 550 paper-based; 213 computer-based). Electronic applications accepted. *Faculty research:* Armed conflict, civil military relations, comparative public administration and policy, electoral competition, legislative studies.

Kaplan University, Davenport Campus, School of Legal Studies, Davenport, IA 52807-2095. Offers health care delivery (MS); pathway to paralegal (Postbaccalaureate Certificate); state and local government (MS). Part-time and evening/weekend programs available. Postbaccalaureate distance learning degree programs offered (no on-campus study). *Entrance requirements:* Additional exam requirements/recommendations for international students: Required—TOEFL (minimum score 550 paper-based; 218 computer-based; 80 iBT).

Kean University, College of Humanities and Social Sciences, Program in Political Science, Union, NJ 07083. Offers MA. Part-time and evening/weekend programs available. *Faculty:* 9 full-time (1 woman). *Students:* 6 full-time (5 women), 10 part-time (1 woman); includes 2 Black or African American, non-Hispanic/Latino; 1 Asian, non-Hispanic/Latino; 1 Hispanic/Latino. Average age 29. 10 applicants, 100% accepted, 7 enrolled. In 2010, 4 master's awarded. *Degree requirements:* For master's, comprehensive exam, thesis. *Entrance requirements:* For master's, GRE General Test, minimum GPA of 3.0, 3 letters of recommendation, transcripts. *Application deadline:* For fall admission, 6/1 for domestic students; for spring admission, 11/1 for domestic students. Application fee: $75 ($150 for international students). Electronic applications accepted. *Expenses:* Tuition, state resident: full-time $10,872; part-time $500 per credit. Tuition, nonresident: full-time $14,736; part-time $614 per credit. Required fees: $2740.80; $125 per credit. Part-time tuition and fees vary according to course load and degree level. *Financial support:* In 2010–11, 2 research assistantships with full tuition reimbursements (averaging $3,263 per year) were awarded; unspecified assistantships also available. Financial award applicants required to submit FAFSA. *Unit head:* Dr. Larry Chang, Program Coordinator, 908-737-3998, E-mail: lchang@kean.edu. *Application contact:* Steven Koch, Pre-Admissions Coordinator, 908-737-5924, Fax: 908-737-5925, E-mail: skoch@kean.edu.

Kent State University, College of Arts and Sciences, Department of Political Science, Kent, OH 44242-0001. Offers political science (MA); public administration (MPA); public policy (PhD). Part-time programs available. Postbaccalaureate distance learning degree programs offered. *Degree requirements:* For master's, thesis optional; for doctorate, 2 foreign languages, thesis/dissertation. *Entrance requirements:* For master's, GRE General Test, minimum GPA of 2.75; for doctorate, GRE General Test, minimum GPA of 3.0. Additional exam requirements/recommendations for international students: Required—TOEFL. Electronic applications accepted. *Expenses:* Tuition, state resident: full-time $7866; part-time $437 per credit hour. Tuition, nonresident: full-time $14,022; part-time $779 per credit hour.

Lamar University, College of Graduate Studies, College of Arts and Sciences, Department of Political Science, Beaumont, TX 77710. Offers public administration (MPA). Part-time programs available. *Faculty:* 4 full-time (0 women). *Students:* 4 full-time (2 women), 9 part-time (4 women); includes 4 Black or African American, non-Hispanic/Latino; 1 Hispanic/Latino, 2 international. Average age 29. 6 applicants, 50% accepted, 2 enrolled. In 2010, 4 master's awarded. *Entrance requirements:* For master's, GRE General Test. Additional exam requirements/recommendations for international students: Required—TOEFL. *Application deadline:* For fall admission, 8/1 for domestic students; for spring admission, 12/1 for domestic students. Applications are processed on a rolling basis. Application fee: $25 ($50 for international students). *Expenses:* Tuition, state resident: full-time $4160; part-time $208 per credit hour. Tuition, nonresident: full-time $10,360; part-time $518 per credit hour. *Financial support:* Fellowships, research assistantships, teaching assistantships, career-related internships or fieldwork, Federal Work-Study, and institutionally sponsored loans available. Financial award application deadline: 4/1. *Faculty research:* Political activities of administrators, administrative response to hurricane Rita, budgeting, environmental politics, urban planning. *Unit head:* Dr. Glenn Utter, Chair, 409-880-8526, Fax: 409-880-8710. *Application contact:* Dr. Terri Davis, Director, 409-880-8533, Fax: 409-880-1710, E-mail: davistb@hal.lamar.edu.

Lehigh University, College of Arts and Sciences, Department of Political Science, Bethlehem, PA 18015. Offers politics and policy (MA), including political theory. Part-time programs available. *Faculty:* 12 full-time (7 women). *Students:* 12 full-time (7 women), 3 part-time (2 women); includes 1 minority (Hispanic/Latino), 1 international. Average age 26. 22 applicants, 59% accepted, 11 enrolled. In 2010, 11 master's awarded. *Degree requirements:* For master's, thesis optional. *Entrance requirements:* For master's, GRE General Test. Additional exam requirements/recommendations for international students: Required—TOEFL (minimum score 560 paper-based; 223 computer-based). *Application deadline:* For fall admission, 7/15 for domestic and international students; for spring admission, 12/1 for domestic and international students. Applications are processed on a rolling basis. Application fee: $65. Electronic applications accepted. *Financial support:* In 2010–11, 10 students received support, including 8 fellowships, 2 teaching assistantships with full tuition reimbursements available; research assistantships, career-related internships or fieldwork and tuition waivers (partial) also available. Financial award application deadline: 1/15. *Faculty research:* American politics and institutions, comparative politics, public policy, political theory. *Unit head:* Dr. Richard K. Matthews, Chairman, 610-758-3343, Fax: 610-758-3348, E-mail: rm02@lehigh.edu. *Application contact:* Dr. Laura K. Olson, Director, Graduate Studies, 610-758-3346, Fax: 610-758-3348, E-mail: lko1@lehigh.edu.

Lincoln University, School of Graduate Studies and Continuing Education, Jefferson City, MO 65102. Offers business administration (MBA), including accounting, entrepreneurship, management, public administration and policy; educational leadership (Ed S), including elementary leadership, secondary leadership, superintendency; guidance and counseling (M Ed), including community/agency counseling, elementary school, secondary school; history (MA); school administration and supervision (M Ed), including elementary school administration, secondary school administration, special education administration; school teaching (M Ed), including elementary school teaching, secondary school teaching; social science (MA), including history, political science, sociology; sociology (MA); sociology/criminal justice (MA). Part-time and evening/weekend programs available. *Degree requirements:* For master's and Ed S, comprehensive exam, thesis optional. *Entrance requirements:* For master's and Ed S, GRE, MAT or GMAT, minimum GPA of 2.75 in major, 2.5 overall; 3 letters of recommendation; minimum C average in English composition; personal statement of purpose. Additional exam requirements/recommendations for international students: Required—TOEFL (minimum score 500 paper-based; 173 computer-based; 61 iBT). *Faculty research:* Suicide prevention.

Long Island University, Brooklyn Campus, Richard L. Conolly College of Liberal Arts and Sciences, Department of Political Science, Brooklyn, NY 11201-8423. Offers MA. Part-time and evening/weekend programs available. *Degree requirements:* For master's, thesis or alternative. *Entrance requirements:* For master's, 2 letters of recommendation. Additional exam requirements/recommendations for international students: Required—TOEFL (minimum score 550 paper-based; 173 computer-based). Electronic applications accepted.

Long Island University, C.W. Post Campus, College of Liberal Arts and Sciences, Department of Political Science/International Studies, Brookville, NY 11548-1300. Offers MA. Part-time and evening/weekend programs available. *Degree requirements:* For master's, comprehensive exam, thesis or alternative. *Entrance requirements:* For master's, GRE. Electronic applications accepted. *Faculty research:* International relations, Middle Eastern politics, political philosophy.

Louisiana State University and Agricultural and Mechanical College, Graduate School, College of Humanities and Social Sciences, Department of Political Science, Baton Rouge, LA 70803. Offers MA, PhD. *Faculty:* 25 full-time (6 women). *Students:* 40 full-time (16 women), 14 part-time (8 women); includes 2 Black or African American, non-Hispanic/Latino; 2 Asian, non-Hispanic/Latino; 2 Hispanic/Latino, 8 international. Average age 30. 58 applicants, 67% accepted, 3 enrolled. In 2010, 8 master's, 4 doctorates awarded. Terminal master's awarded for partial completion of doctoral program. *Degree requirements:* For master's, thesis or alternative; for doctorate, one foreign language, thesis/dissertation. *Entrance requirements:* For master's and doctorate, GRE General Test, minimum GPA of 3.0. Additional exam requirements/recommendations for international students: Required—TOEFL (minimum score 550 paper-based; 213 computer-based; 79 iBT) or IELTS (minimum score 6.5). *Application deadline:* For fall admission, 2/15 priority date for domestic students, 5/15 for international students; for spring admission, 10/15 for domestic and international students. Application fee: $50 ($70 for international students). Electronic applications accepted. *Financial support:* In 2010–11, 37 students received support, including 2 fellowships with full and partial tuition reimbursements available (averaging $17,716 per year), 5 research assistantships with full and partial tuition reimbursements available (averaging $15,000 per year), 21 teaching assistantships with full and partial tuition reimbursements available (averaging $11,904 per year); Federal Work-Study, institutionally sponsored loans, health care benefits, tuition waivers (full), and unspecified assistantships also available. Financial award application deadline: 3/1; financial award applicants required to submit FAFSA. *Faculty research:* American government and policy, political theory, international relations and comparative politics. Total annual research expenditures: $131,117. *Unit head:* Dr. Greg Stoner, Chair, 225-578-2141, Fax: 225-578-2540. *Application contact:* Dr. Kathleen Bratton, Director of Graduate Studies, 225-578-1912, Fax: 225-578-2540, E-mail: bratton@lsu.edu.

Loyola University Chicago, Graduate School, Department of Political Science, Chicago, IL 60660. Offers MA, PhD. Part-time and evening/weekend programs available. *Faculty:* 19 full-time (4 women). *Students:* 32 full-time (14 women), 20 part-time (13 women); includes 5 minority (4 Black or African American, non-Hispanic/Latino; 1 Hispanic/Latino), 4 international. Average age 27. 98 applicants, 39% accepted, 11 enrolled. In 2010, 10 master's, 2 doctorates awarded. Terminal master's awarded for partial completion of doctoral program. *Degree requirements:* For master's, comprehensive exam, thesis or alternative; for doctorate, comprehensive exam, thesis/dissertation. *Entrance requirements:* For master's and doctorate, GRE General Test. Additional exam requirements/recommendations for international students: Required—TOEFL (minimum score 550 paper-based; 213 computer-based; 79 iBT). *Application deadline:* For fall admission, 6/1 for domestic and international students; for spring admission, 10/1 for domestic and international students. Applications are processed on a rolling basis. Application fee: $0. Electronic applications accepted. *Expenses:* Tuition: Full-time $14,940; part-time $830 per credit hour. Required fees: $87 per semester. Part-time tuition and fees vary according to course load and program. *Financial support:* In 2010–11, 8 fellowships with full tuition reimbursements (averaging $14,000 per year), 8 research assistantships with full tuition reimbursements (averaging $14,000 per year) were awarded; Federal Work-Study, institutionally sponsored loans, scholarships/grants, tuition waivers (partial), and unspecified assistantships also available. Financial award application deadline: 2/15; financial award applicants required to submit FAFSA. *Faculty research:* American elections, parties and political institutions; comparative politics; foreign policy analysis; international relations theory; modern and contemporary political thought. *Unit head:* Prof. Peter J. Schraeder, Graduate Program Director, 773-508-3070, Fax: 773-508-3131, E-mail: pschrae@luc.edu. *Application contact:* Prof. Peter J. Schraeder, Graduate Program Director, 773-508-3070, Fax: 773-508-3131, E-mail: pschrae@luc.edu.

Marquette University, Graduate School, College of Arts and Sciences, Department of Political Science/International Affairs, Milwaukee, WI 53201-1881. Offers international affairs (MA);

political science (MA); political science/communication (MA); JD/MA; MA/MBA. Part-time programs available. *Faculty:* 16 full-time (4 women), 2 part-time/adjunct (both women). *Students:* 22 full-time (10 women), 4 part-time (all women); includes 1 minority (Asian, non-Hispanic/Latino), 4 international. Average age 27. 66 applicants, 65% accepted, 14 enrolled. In 2010, 11 master's awarded. *Degree requirements:* For master's, comprehensive exam, thesis optional. *Entrance requirements:* For master's, GRE General Test, official transcripts from all current and previous colleges/universities except Marquette, three letters of recommendation, statement of purpose. Additional exam requirements/recommendations for international students: Required—TOEFL (minimum score 530 paper-based; 78 computer-based). *Application deadline:* For fall admission, 2/15 for domestic and international students. Application fee: $50. Electronic applications accepted. *Expenses:* Tuition: Full-time $16,290; part-time $905 per credit hour. Tuition and fees vary according to program. *Financial support:* In 2010–11, 4 fellowships, 11 teaching assistantships were awarded; research assistantships, Federal Work-Study, institutionally sponsored loans, scholarships/grants, and tuition waivers (full and partial) also available. Support available to part-time students. Financial award application deadline: 2/15. *Faculty research:* Public opinion and electoral behavior, public policy analysis, Congress and the Presidency, judicial behavior, political system transitions. Total annual research expenditures: $187,654. *Unit head:* Dr. Barrett McCormick, Chair, 414-288-6842, Fax: 414-288-3360. *Application contact:* Dr. Lowell Barrington, Director of Graduate Studies, 414-288-5234, Fax: 414-288-3360.

Marshall University, Academic Affairs Division, College of Liberal Arts, Department of Political Science, Huntington, WV 25755. Offers MA. *Faculty:* 8 full-time (4 women). *Students:* 14 full-time (4 women), 4 part-time (2 women), 1 international. Average age 27. In 2010, 10 master's awarded. *Degree requirements:* For master's, thesis optional. *Entrance requirements:* For master's, GRE General Test. *Application fee:* $40. *Unit head:* Dr. MaryBeth Beller, Chairperson, 304-696-2763, Fax: 304-696-3245, E-mail: beller@marshall.edu. *Application contact:* Graduate Admissions, 304-746-1900, Fax: 304-746-1902, E-mail: services@marshall.edu.

Massachusetts Institute of Technology, School of Humanities, Arts, and Social Sciences, Department of Political Science, Cambridge, MA 02139. Offers SM, PhD. *Faculty:* 23 full-time (7 women). *Students:* 57 full-time (17 women); includes 5 minority (3 Asian, non-Hispanic/Latino; 2 Hispanic/Latino), 13 international. Average age 28. 436 applicants, 8% accepted, 17 enrolled. In 2010, 5 master's, 10 doctorates awarded. Terminal master's awarded for partial completion of doctoral program. *Degree requirements:* For master's, thesis; for doctorate, one foreign language, comprehensive exam, thesis/dissertation. *Entrance requirements:* For master's and doctorate, GRE General Test. Additional exam requirements/recommendations for international students: Required—TOEFL (minimum score 600 paper-based; 250 computer-based; 100 iBT), IELTS (minimum score 7). *Application deadline:* For fall admission, 12/15 for domestic and international students. Application fee: $75. Electronic applications accepted. *Expenses:* Tuition: Full-time $38,940; part-time $605 per unit. Required fees: $272. *Financial support:* In 2010–11, 55 students received support, including 14 fellowships with tuition reimbursements available (averaging $27,627 per year), 24 research assistantships with tuition reimbursements available (averaging $30,626 per year), 12 teaching assistantships with tuition reimbursements available (averaging $31,449 per year); Federal Work-Study, institutionally sponsored loans, scholarships/grants, health care benefits, and unspecified assistantships also available. *Faculty research:* International security, American politics, political economy, ethnic conflict and politics, models and methods. Total annual research expenditures: $2.1 million. *Unit head:* Prof. Richard Locke, Department Head, 617-253-5262, Fax: 617-258-6164. *Application contact:* Graduate Administrator, 617-253-4897, Fax: 617-258-6164, E-mail: twarog@mit.edu.

McGill University, Faculty of Graduate and Postdoctoral Studies, Faculty of Arts, Department of Political Science, Montréal, QC H3A 2T5, Canada. Offers MA, PhD.

McMaster University, School of Graduate Studies, Faculty of Social Sciences, Department of Political Science, Hamilton, ON L8S 4M2, Canada. Offers international relations (PhD); political science (MA); public and the global economy (MA); public policy (PhD); public policy and administration (MA). MA program in public policy and administration offered jointly with University of Guelph. Part-time programs available. *Degree requirements:* For master's, thesis or alternative. *Entrance requirements:* For master's, minimum B+ average. Additional exam requirements/recommendations for international students: Required—TOEFL (minimum score 580 paper-based; 237 computer-based). *Faculty research:* Organizational theory, internationalization of public policy, water resource policies, political interest intermediation, comparative politics.

Memorial University of Newfoundland, School of Graduate Studies, Department of Political Science, St. John's, NL A1C 5S7, Canada. Offers MA. Part-time and evening/weekend programs available. *Degree requirements:* For master's, thesis optional. *Entrance requirements:* For master's, minimum 2nd class bachelor's degree. Electronic applications accepted. *Faculty research:* Comparative politics, Canadian government and politics, Newfoundland politics, and the politics of multi-level systems.

Miami University, Graduate School, College of Arts and Science, Department of Political Science, Oxford, OH 45056. Offers MA. *Students:* 20 full-time (6 women), 2 part-time (both women); includes 3 minority (2 Black or African American, non-Hispanic/Latino; 1 Asian, non-Hispanic/Latino), 2 international. Average age 29. In 2010, 10 master's awarded. *Entrance requirements:* For master's, GRE General Test, minimum undergraduate GPA of 3.0 during previous 2 years or 2.75 overall. Additional exam requirements/recommendations for international students: Required—TOEFL. Application fee: $50. *Expenses:* Tuition, state resident: full-time $11,616; part-time $484 per credit hour. Tuition, nonresident: full-time $25,656; part-time $1069 per credit hour. Required fees: $528. *Financial support:* Fellowships with full tuition reimbursements, research assistantships with full tuition reimbursements, teaching assistantships with full tuition reimbursements, Federal Work-Study, institutionally sponsored loans, health care benefits, tuition waivers (full), and unspecified assistantships available. Financial award application deadline: 3/1; financial award applicants required to submit FAFSA. *Faculty research:* Constitutional rights and liberties, American foreign policy, world regional politics, public management, political philosophy, parties and interest groups, international law. *Unit head:* Dr. Steven DeLue, Interim Chair, 513-529-2000, E-mail: political@muohio.edu. *Application contact:* Dr. Steven DeLue, Interim Chair, 513-529-2000, E-mail: political@muohio.edu.

Michigan State University, The Graduate School, College of Social Science, Department of Political Science, East Lansing, MI 48824. Offers political science (MA, PhD); public policy (MPP). *Degree requirements:* For master's, practicum; for doctorate, comprehensive exam, presentation of dissertation. *Entrance requirements:* Additional exam requirements/recommendations for international students: Required—TOEFL. Electronic applications accepted.

Midwestern State University, Graduate Studies, College of Humanities and Social Sciences, Department of Political Science, Wichita Falls, TX 76308. Offers MA. *Faculty:* 4 full-time (0 women). *Students:* 6 full-time (3 women), 6 part-time (1 woman); includes 1 Black or African American, non-Hispanic/Latino; 1 Hispanic/Latino, 1 international. Average age 27. 4 applicants, 100% accepted, 3 enrolled. In 2010, 2 master's awarded. *Degree requirements:* For master's, one foreign language, comprehensive exam. *Entrance requirements:* For master's, GRE General Test. Additional exam requirements/recommendations for international students: Required—TOEFL (minimum score 550 paper-based; 213 computer-based). *Application deadline:* For fall admission, 7/1 priority date for domestic students, 4/1 for international students; for spring admission, 11/1 priority date for domestic students, 8/1 for international students. Applications are processed on a rolling basis. Application fee: $35 ($50 for international students). Electronic applications accepted. *Expenses:* Tuition, state resident: full-time $1620; part-time $90 per credit hour. Tuition, nonresident: full-time $2160; part-time $120 per credit hour. International tuition: $7200 full-time. *Financial support:* In 2010–11, 6 students received support, including 3 teaching assistantships with partial tuition reimbursements available (averaging $7,500 per year); career-related internships or fieldwork, Federal Work-Study, institutionally sponsored loans, scholarships/grants, and unspecified assistantships also available. Support available to part-time students. Financial award application deadline: 3/1; financial

Political Science

Midwestern State University *(continued)*
award applicants required to submit FAFSA. *Faculty research:* American politics, political behavior, political research methods, conflict processes, Latin American politics. *Unit head:* Dr. Steve Garrison, Chair, 940-397-6282, Fax: 940-397-4865, E-mail: steve.garrison@mwsu.edu. *Application contact:* 800-842-1922, Fax: 940-397-4672, E-mail: admissions@mwsu.edu.

Mississippi College, Graduate School, College of Arts and Sciences, School of Humanities and Social Sciences, Department of History, Political Science, Administration of Justice, and Paralegal Studies, Clinton, MS 39058. Offers administration of justice (MSS); history (M Ed, MA, MSS); paralegal studies (Certificate); political science (MSS); social sciences (M Ed, MSS). Part-time programs available. *Degree requirements:* For master's, one foreign language, comprehensive exam, thesis (for some programs). *Entrance requirements:* For master's, GRE or NTE, minimum GPA of 2.5. Additional exam requirements/recommendations for international students: Recommended—IELTS. Electronic applications accepted.

Mississippi State University, College of Arts and Sciences, Department of Political Science and Public Administration, Mississippi State, MS 39762. Offers political science (MA); public policy and administration (MPPA, PhD). *Accreditation:* NASPAA (one or more programs are accredited). Evening/weekend programs available. Postbaccalaureate distance learning degree programs offered (no on-campus study). *Faculty:* 13 full-time (4 women). *Students:* 61 full-time (31 women), 47 part-time (26 women); includes 37 minority (33 Black or African American, non-Hispanic/Latino; 1 American Indian or Alaska Native, non-Hispanic/Latino; 1 Asian, non-Hispanic/Latino; 1 Hispanic/Latino; 1 Two or more races, non-Hispanic/Latino), 4 international. Average age 30. 60 applicants, 62% accepted, 26 enrolled. In 2010, 32 master's, 2 doctorates awarded. *Degree requirements:* For master's, thesis optional, comprehensive oral or written exam; for doctorate, thesis/dissertation, comprehensive oral and written exam. *Entrance requirements:* For master's, GRE, minimum GPA of 3.0 on the last two years of undergraduate courses or graduate work; for doctorate, GRE General Test, minimum graduate GPA of 3.35. Additional exam requirements/recommendations for international students: Required—TOEFL (minimum score 600 paper-based; 250 computer-based; 100 iBT); Recommended—IELTS (minimum score 7.5). *Application deadline:* For fall admission, 8/1 priority date for domestic students, 5/1 for international students; for spring admission, 12/1 priority date for domestic students, 9/1 for international students. Applications are processed on a rolling basis. Application fee: $40. Electronic applications accepted. *Expenses:* Tuition, state resident: full-time $2730.50; part-time $304 per credit hour. Tuition, nonresident: full-time $6901; part-time $767 per credit hour. *Financial support:* In 2010–11, 3 research assistantships (averaging $10,144 per year), 8 teaching assistantships with full tuition reimbursements (averaging $10,138 per year) were awarded; Federal Work-Study, institutionally sponsored loans, scholarships/grants, and unspecified assistantships also available. Financial award application deadline: 4/1; financial award applicants required to submit FAFSA. *Faculty research:* American politics, international relations, state and local government, comparative government, public administration. Total annual research expenditures: $1.2 million. *Unit head:* Dr. K. C. Morrison, Department Head, 662-325-2711, Fax: 662-325-2716, E-mail: kcmorrison@ps.msstate.edu. *Application contact:* Dr. Edward French, Assistant Professor and Graduate Coordinator, 662-325-2711, Fax: 662-325-2716, E-mail: efrench@ps.msstate.edu.

Missouri State University, Graduate College, College of Humanities and Public Affairs, Department of Political Science, Springfield, MO 65897. Offers global studies (MGS); public administration (MPA). Part-time programs available. *Degree requirements:* For master's, variable foreign language requirement, comprehensive exam, thesis or alternative. *Entrance requirements:* For master's, GRE, minimum GPA of 3.0. Additional exam requirements/recommendations for international students: Required—TOEFL (minimum score 550 paper-based; 213 computer-based; 79 iBT). Electronic applications accepted. *Expenses:* Tuition, state resident: full-time $3348; part-time $186 per credit hour. Tuition, nonresident: full-time $6696; part-time $372 per credit hour. Required fees: $238 per semester. Tuition and fees vary according to course level, course load and program.

Montclair State University, The Graduate School, College of Humanities and Social Sciences, Department of Political Science and Law, Montclair, NJ 07043-1624. Offers law and governance (MA), including conflict management and peace studies, governance, compliance and regulation, intellectual property, law and governance, legal management. Part-time and evening/weekend programs available. *Faculty:* 13 full-time (6 women), 25 part-time/adjunct (8 women). *Students:* 9 full-time (5 women), 26 part-time (15 women); includes 10 Black or African American, non-Hispanic/Latino; 4 Asian, non-Hispanic/Latino; 2 Hispanic/Latino, 2 international. Average age 30. 19 applicants, 68% accepted, 10 enrolled. In 2010, 16 master's, 3 other advanced degrees awarded. *Degree requirements:* For master's, thesis or comprehensive exam. *Entrance requirements:* For master's, GRE, minimum cumulative GPA of 2.75 for undergraduate work. Additional exam requirements/recommendations for international students: Required—TOEFL (minimum iBT score of 83) or IELTS. *Expenses:* Tuition, state resident: part-time $501.34 per credit. Tuition, nonresident: part-time $773.88 per credit. Required fees: $71.15 per credit. *Financial support:* In 2010–11, 1 research assistantship with full tuition reimbursement (averaging $7,000 per year) was awarded; Federal Work-Study, scholarships/grants, and unspecified assistantships also available. Support available to part-time students. Financial award application deadline: 3/1. *Unit head:* Dr. William Berlin, Chair, 973-655-7576, E-mail: berlinw@mail.montclair.edu. *Application contact:* Amy Aiello, Director of Graduate Admissions and Operations, 973-655-5147, Fax: 973-655-7869, E-mail: graduate.school@montclair.edu.

Naval Postgraduate School, Graduate Programs, Department of National Security Affairs, Monterey, CA 93943. Offers intelligence (MA); international relations (MA); political science (MA); regional security education (MA); security building (MA); security studies (MA). Program only open to commissioned officers of the United States and friendly nations and select U.S. federal civilian employees. Part-time programs available. *Degree requirements:* For master's, thesis.

New Mexico State University, Graduate School, College of Arts and Sciences, Department of Government, Las Cruces, NM 88003-8001. Offers MA, MPA. *Accreditation:* NASPAA (one or more programs are accredited). Part-time and evening/weekend programs available. *Faculty:* 10 full-time (3 women), 1 part-time/adjunct (0 women). *Students:* 37 full-time (19 women), 22 part-time (8 women); includes 20 minority (3 Black or African American, non-Hispanic/Latino; 3 Asian, non-Hispanic/Latino; 14 Hispanic/Latino), 4 international. Average age 31. 53 applicants, 100% accepted, 38 enrolled. In 2010, 10 master's awarded. *Degree requirements:* For master's, comprehensive exam (for some programs), thesis optional. *Entrance requirements:* For master's, GRE (if GPA less than 3.0), writing sample, 3 letters of recommendation, resume. Additional exam requirements/recommendations for international students: Required—TOEFL (minimum score 530 paper-based; 197 computer-based). *Application deadline:* Applications are processed on a rolling basis. Application fee: $30 ($50 for international students). Electronic applications accepted. *Expenses:* Tuition, state resident: full-time $4536; part-time $242 per credit. Tuition, nonresident: full-time $15,816; part-time $712 per credit. Required fees: $636 per term. *Financial support:* In 2010–11, 4 research assistantships (averaging $15,012 per year), 14 teaching assistantships with tuition reimbursements (averaging $6,856 per year) were awarded; career-related internships or fieldwork, Federal Work-Study, scholarships/grants, health care benefits, and unspecified assistantships also available. Support available to part-time students. Financial award application deadline: 3/1. *Faculty research:* U. S.-Mexico border studies, public administration and policy, international relations, Latin America, American politics and theory. *Unit head:* Dr. Neil Harvey, Acting Head, 575-646-4935, Fax: 575-646-2052, E-mail: nharvey@nmsu.edu. *Application contact:* Rona M. Lujan, Department Secretary, 575-646-4734, Fax: 575-646-2052, E-mail: rona@nmsu.edu.

The New School: A University, The New School for Social Research, Department of Political Science, New York, NY 10003. Offers M Phil, MA, DS Sc, PhD. Part-time programs available. Terminal master's awarded for partial completion of doctoral program. *Degree requirements:* For master's, thesis; for doctorate, one foreign language, comprehensive exam, thesis/

dissertation, two methodology courses, PhD seminar, field seminars. *Entrance requirements:* For master's, GRE General Test; for doctorate, GRE General Test, MA. Additional exam requirements/recommendations for international students: Required—TOEFL (minimum score 600 paper-based; 250 computer-based; 100 iBT). Electronic applications accepted. *Faculty research:* Democratic transitions and institution; race, class and gender; immigration and incorporation.

New York University, Graduate School of Arts and Science, Department of Politics, New York, NY 10012-1019. Offers political campaign management (MA); politics (MA, PhD); JD/MA; MBA/MA. Part-time programs available. *Faculty:* 30 full-time (4 women). *Students:* 183 full-time (92 women), 54 part-time (29 women); includes 2 Black or African American, non-Hispanic/Latino; 14 Asian, non-Hispanic/Latino; 6 Hispanic/Latino, 111 international. Average age 28. 747 applicants, 34% accepted, 78 enrolled. In 2010, 78 master's, 9 doctorates awarded. Terminal master's awarded for partial completion of doctoral program. *Degree requirements:* For master's, one foreign language, thesis or alternative; for doctorate, 2 foreign languages, comprehensive exam, thesis/dissertation. *Entrance requirements:* For master's, GRE General Test; for doctorate, GRE General Test, master's degree in political science, minimum GPA of 2.5. Additional exam requirements/recommendations for international students: Required—TOEFL. *Application deadline:* For fall admission, 12/15 priority date for domestic students. Application fee: $90. *Financial support:* Fellowships with tuition reimbursements, teaching assistantships with tuition reimbursements, career-related internships or fieldwork, Federal Work-Study, and institutionally sponsored loans available. Financial award application deadline: 12/15; financial award applicants required to submit FAFSA. *Faculty research:* Comparative politics, democratic theory and practice, rational choice, political economy, international relations. *Unit head:* Michael Gilligan, Director of PhD Program, 212-998-8500, Fax: 212-995-4184, E-mail: politics.phd@nyu.edu. *Application contact:* Shinasi Rama, Director of Master's Program, 212-998-8500, Fax: 212-995-4184, E-mail: politics.masters@nyu.edu.

Northeastern Illinois University, Graduate College, College of Arts and Sciences, Department of Political Science, Program in Political Science, Chicago, IL 60625-4699. Offers MA. Part-time and evening/weekend programs available. *Faculty:* 9 full-time (2 women), 4 part-time/adjunct (3 women). *Students:* 14 full-time (6 women), 31 part-time (10 women); includes 8 minority (2 Black or African American, non-Hispanic/Latino; 2 Asian, non-Hispanic/Latino; 4 Hispanic/Latino), 4 international. Average age 36. 35 applicants, 77% accepted. In 2010, 10 master's awarded. *Degree requirements:* For master's, comprehensive exam, thesis optional. *Entrance requirements:* For master's, minimum GPA of 2.75. Additional exam requirements/recommendations for international students: Required—TOEFL (minimum score 550 paper-based; 213 computer-based; 79 iBT). *Application deadline:* For fall admission, 4/1 priority date for domestic students; for spring admission, 8/15 for domestic students. Applications are processed on a rolling basis. Application fee: $30. Electronic applications accepted. *Financial support:* In 2010–11, 13 students received support, including 2 research assistantships with full and partial tuition reimbursements available (averaging $6,600 per year); career-related internships or fieldwork, Federal Work-Study, institutionally sponsored loans, scholarships/grants, tuition waivers (full and partial), and unspecified assistantships also available. Support available to part-time students. Financial award applicants required to submit FAFSA. *Faculty research:* Chinese politics, Latin American democratization, Jewish feminism, administration and delegation. *Unit head:* Dr. David E. Leaman, Department Chair. *Application contact:* Dr. David E. Leaman, Department Chair.

Northeastern University, College of Social Sciences and Humanities, Department of Political Science, Boston, MA 02115-5096. Offers political science (MA); public administration (MPA, Certificate), including development administration (MPA), health administration and policy (MPA), state and local government (MPA), urban studies (Certificate); public and international affairs (PhD). Part-time and evening/weekend programs available. *Faculty:* 22 full-time (4 women), 10 part-time/adjunct (1 woman). *Students:* 64 full-time (30 women), 12 part-time (7 women). Average age 30. 132 applicants, 47% accepted, 23 enrolled. In 2010, 21 master's, 3 doctorates awarded. *Degree requirements:* For master's, thesis optional; for doctorate, thesis/dissertation. *Entrance requirements:* For master's, GRE General Test. Additional exam requirements/recommendations for international students: Required—TOEFL. *Application deadline:* Applications are processed on a rolling basis. Application fee: $50. *Financial support:* In 2010–11, 12 fellowships, 1 research assistantship with tuition reimbursement, 17 teaching assistantships with tuition reimbursements (averaging $14,035 per year) were awarded; career-related internships or fieldwork, Federal Work-Study, tuition waivers (full and partial), and unspecified assistantships also available. Support available to part-time students. Financial award application deadline: 2/1; financial award applicants required to submit FAFSA. *Faculty research:* Presidency, public opinion, Congress, democratization, national identity. *Unit head:* Dr. John Portz, Chair, 617-373-2796, Fax: 617-373-5311, E-mail: gradpolisci@neu.edu. *Application contact:* Brynn Thompson, Graduate Programs Assistant, 617-373-4404, Fax: 617-373-5311, E-mail: gradpolisci@neu.edu.

Northern Arizona University, Graduate College, College of Social and Behavioral Sciences, Department of Politics and International Affairs, Flagstaff, AZ 86011. Offers political science (MA, PhD); public administration (MPA); public management (Certificate). Part-time programs available. *Faculty:* 23 full-time (8 women). *Students:* 37 full-time (13 women), 39 part-time (26 women); includes 20 minority (3 Black or African American, non-Hispanic/Latino; 5 American Indian or Alaska Native, non-Hispanic/Latino; 4 Asian, non-Hispanic/Latino; 7 Hispanic/Latino; 1 Two or more races, non-Hispanic/Latino), 7 international. Average age 34. 47 applicants, 81% accepted, 27 enrolled. In 2010, 9 master's, 6 doctorates, 5 other advanced degrees awarded. *Degree requirements:* For master's, comprehensive exam (for some programs), thesis optional; for doctorate, one foreign language, comprehensive exam, thesis/dissertation. *Entrance requirements:* For master's, GRE (70th percentile ranking in each testing area preferred); for doctorate, GRE (minimum 70th percentile in each testing area preferred). Additional exam requirements/recommendations for international students: Required—TOEFL (minimum score 550 paper-based; 213 computer-based; 80 iBT), IELTS (minimum score 7). *Application deadline:* For fall admission, 2/1 priority date for domestic and international students. Applications are processed on a rolling basis. Application fee: $65. Electronic applications accepted. *Financial support:* In 2010–11, 1 fellowship, 13 teaching assistantships with partial tuition reimbursements (averaging $11,300 per year) were awarded; career-related internships or fieldwork, Federal Work-Study, scholarships/grants, health care benefits, tuition waivers (full and partial), and unspecified assistantships also available. Financial award applicants required to submit FAFSA. *Unit head:* Dr. Frederic Solop, Chair, 928-523-3135, Fax: 928-523-6777, E-mail: fred.solop@nau.edu. *Application contact:* Julie Hammond, Administrative Assistant, 928-523-6544, Fax: 928-523-6777, E-mail: political.science@nau.edu.

Northern Illinois University, Graduate School, College of Liberal Arts and Sciences, Department of Political Science, De Kalb, IL 60115-2854. Offers political science (MA, PhD); public administration (MPA). Part-time and evening/weekend programs available. *Faculty:* 24 full-time (5 women), 8 part-time/adjunct (2 women). *Students:* 88 full-time (33 women), 75 part-time (26 women); includes 8 Black or African American, non-Hispanic/Latino; 2 Asian, non-Hispanic/Latino; 6 Hispanic/Latino, 22 international. Average age 31. 91 applicants, 56% accepted, 30 enrolled. In 2010, 10 master's, 7 doctorates awarded. Terminal master's awarded for partial completion of doctoral program. *Degree requirements:* For master's, comprehensive exam, thesis optional; for doctorate, variable foreign language requirement, thesis/dissertation, candidacy exam, dissertation defense. *Entrance requirements:* For master's, GRE General Test, minimum GPA of 2.75, 9 hours of course work in political science; for doctorate, GRE General Test, minimum GPA of 2.75 (undergraduate), 3.2 (graduate); undergraduate major in related field. Additional exam requirements/recommendations for international students: Required—TOEFL (minimum score 550 paper-based; 213 computer-based). *Application deadline:* For fall admission, 3/1 priority date for domestic students, 5/1 for international students; for spring admission, 11/1 for domestic students, 10/1 for international students. Applications are processed on a rolling basis. Application fee: $30. Electronic applications accepted. *Expenses:* Tuition, state resident: full-time $7200; part-time $300 per credit hour. Tuition, nonresident: full-time $14,400; part-time $600 per credit hour. Required fees: $79 per credit hour. *Financial support:* In 2010–11, 1 research assistantship with full tuition reimbursement, 24 teaching assistantships with full tuition reimbursements were awarded; fellowships with full tuition reimbursements, career-related internships or fieldwork, Federal Work-Study, scholarships/grants, tuition waivers (full), and unspecified assistantships also available. Support available to part-time students. Financial award applicants required to submit FAFSA. *Faculty research:* Terrorism and dynamics of trade, U. S. foreign policy, political economy of development, biopolitical theory, women and politics. *Unit head:* Dr. Christopher Jones, Chair, 815-753-7040, Fax: 815-753-6302. *Application contact:* Dr. Dwight King, Director, Graduate Studies, 815-753-7054, E-mail: dking@niu.edu.

Northwestern University, The Graduate School, Judd A. and Marjorie Weinberg College of Arts and Sciences, Department of Political Science, Evanston, IL 60208. Offers MA, PhD, JD/PhD. Admissions and degrees offered through The Graduate School. Terminal master's awarded for partial completion of doctoral program. *Degree requirements:* For master's, thesis or alternative; for doctorate, thesis/dissertation, qualifying exams. *Entrance requirements:* For master's and doctorate, GRE General Test, sample of written work. Additional exam requirements/recommendations for international students: Required—TOEFL. *Faculty research:* Formal theory/formal political economy, political economy of development/state-business relations, labor market institutions and welfare policy, public opinion and political behavior, feminist political theory.

The Ohio State University, Graduate School, College of Arts and Sciences, Division of Social and Behavioral Sciences, Department of Political Science, Columbus, OH 43210. Offers MA, PhD. *Faculty:* 40. *Students:* 43 full-time (18 women), 45 part-time (13 women); includes 4 Black or African American, non-Hispanic/Latino; 3 Asian, non-Hispanic/Latino; 3 Hispanic/Latino, 23 international. Average age 29. In 2010, 20 master's, 15 doctorates awarded. *Degree requirements:* For master's, thesis optional; for doctorate, thesis/dissertation. *Entrance requirements:* For master's and doctorate, GRE General Test. Additional exam requirements/recommendations for international students: Recommended—TOEFL (minimum score 620 paper-based; 260 computer-based). *Application deadline:* For fall admission, 8/15 priority date for domestic students, 7/1 priority date for international students; for winter admission, 12/1 priority date for domestic students, 11/1 priority date for international students; for spring admission, 3/1 priority date for domestic students, 2/1 priority date for international students. Applications are processed on a rolling basis. Application fee: $40 ($50 for international students). Electronic applications accepted. *Expenses:* Tuition, state resident: full-time $10,605. Tuition, nonresident: full-time $26,535. Tuition and fees vary according to course load and program. *Financial support:* Fellowships, research assistantships, teaching assistantships, Federal Work-Study and institutionally sponsored loans available. Support available to part-time students. *Faculty research:* American, comparative, and international politics; political theory. *Unit head:* Dr. Herbert Weisberg, Chair, 614-292-6572, Fax: 614-292-1146, E-mail: weisberg.1@osu.edu. *Application contact:* 614-292-9444, Fax: 614-292-3895, E-mail: domestic.grad@osu.edu.

Ohio University, Graduate College, College of Arts and Sciences, Department of Political Science, Athens, OH 45701-2979. Offers political science (MA). Part-time and evening/weekend programs available. *Students:* 23 full-time (8 women), 6 part-time (3 women); includes 5 minority (1 Black or African American, non-Hispanic/Latino; 1 Asian, non-Hispanic/Latino; 1 Hispanic/Latino; 2 Two or more races, non-Hispanic/Latino), 1 international. 37 applicants, 68% accepted, 13 enrolled. In 2010, 38 master's awarded. *Degree requirements:* For master's, comprehensive exam, thesis or alternative. *Entrance requirements:* For master's, GRE General Test, minimum GPA of 3.0. Additional exam requirements/recommendations for international students: Required—TOEFL (minimum score 550 paper-based; 80 iBT) or IELTS (minimum score 6.5). *Application deadline:* For fall admission, 2/15 priority date for domestic and international students. Applications are processed on a rolling basis. Application fee: $50 ($55 for international students). Electronic applications accepted. *Financial support:* Research assistantships with full tuition reimbursements, teaching assistantships with full tuition reimbursements, career-related internships or fieldwork, Federal Work-Study, institutionally sponsored loans, and tuition waivers (partial) available. Financial award application deadline: 2/15. *Faculty research:* International relations, Latin American politics, public policy, economic development, political theory. *Unit head:* Dr. John Gilliom, Chair, 740-593-4368, Fax: 740-593-0394. *Application contact:* Dr. Delysa Burnier, Graduate Chair, 740-593-1337, Fax: 740-593-0394, E-mail: burnier@ohio.edu.

Oklahoma State University, College of Arts and Sciences, Department of Political Science, Stillwater, OK 74078. Offers fire and emergency management administration (MS, PhD); political science (MA). *Faculty:* 18 full-time (7 women), 7 part-time/adjunct (0 women). *Students:* 46 full-time (11 women), 86 part-time (20 women); includes 5 Black or African American, non-Hispanic/Latino; 5 American Indian or Alaska Native, non-Hispanic/Latino; 5 Hispanic/Latino, 24 international. Average age 35. 106 applicants, 45% accepted, 31 enrolled. In 2010, 23 master's awarded. *Degree requirements:* For master's, comprehensive exam, thesis or creative component; for doctorate, comprehensive exam, thesis/dissertation. *Entrance requirements:* For master's, GRE; for doctorate, GRE. Additional exam requirements/recommendations for international students: Required—TOEFL (minimum score 550 paper-based; 79 iBT). *Application deadline:* For fall admission, 3/1 priority date for international students; for spring admission, 8/1 priority date for international students. Applications are processed on a rolling basis. Application fee: $40 ($75 for international students). Electronic applications accepted. *Expenses:* Tuition, state resident: full-time $3716; part-time $154.85 per credit hour. Tuition, nonresident: full-time $14,892; part-time $621 per credit hour. Required fees: $2044; $85.20 per credit hour. One-time fee: $50. Tuition and fees vary according to course load and campus/location. *Financial support:* In 2010–11, 7 research assistantships (averaging $11,416 per year), 14 teaching assistantships (averaging $7,891 per year) were awarded; career-related internships or fieldwork, Federal Work-Study, scholarships/grants, health care benefits, tuition waivers (partial), and unspecified assistantships also available. Support available to part-time students. Financial award application deadline: 3/1; financial award applicants required to submit FAFSA. *Faculty research:* Fire and emergency management, environmental dispute resolution, voting and elections, women and politics, urban politics. *Unit head:* Dr. James Scott, Head, 405-744-5569, Fax: 405-744-6534. *Application contact:* Dr. Gordon Emslie, Dean, 405-744-6368, Fax: 405-744-0355, E-mail: grad-i@okstate.edu.

Penn State University Park, Graduate School, College of the Liberal Arts, Department of Political Science, State College, University Park, PA 16802-1503. Offers MA, PhD. *Unit head:* Dr. Donna Bahry, Head, 814-863-1449, E-mail: dlb46@psu.edu. *Application contact:* Dr. Donna Bahry, Head, 814-863-1449, E-mail: dlb46@psu.edu.

Pepperdine University, School of Public Policy, Malibu, CA 90263. Offers American politics (MPP); economics (MPP); international relations (MPP); public policy (MPP); state and local policy (MPP). *Faculty:* 7 full-time (2 women), 10 part-time/adjunct (0 women). *Students:* 123 full-time (72 women), 4 part-time (all women); includes 36 minority (11 Black or African American, non-Hispanic/Latino; 2 American Indian or Alaska Native, non-Hispanic/Latino; 11 Asian, non-Hispanic/Latino; 9 Hispanic/Latino; 3 Two or more races, non-Hispanic/Latino), 13 international. 168 applicants, 93% accepted, 66 enrolled. In 2010, 50 master's awarded. *Entrance requirements:* For master's, GRE or GMAT, 2 letters of recommendation, resume, two essays. Additional exam requirements/recommendations for international students: Required—TOEFL. *Application deadline:* For fall admission, 5/1 for domestic students. Applications are processed on a rolling basis. Application fee: $50. Electronic applications accepted. *Financial support:* Institutionally sponsored loans and scholarships/grants available. Financial award application deadline: 5/1; financial award applicants required to submit FAFSA. *Unit head:* Dr. James R. Wilburn, Dean, 310-506-7490, Fax: 310-506-7494, E-mail: james.wilburn@pepperdine.edu. *Application contact:* Melinda E. van Hemert, Director of Recruitment and Career Services, 310-506-7492, Fax: 310-506-7494, E-mail: melinda.vanhemert@pepperdine.edu.

Portland State University, Graduate Studies, College of Urban and Public Affairs, Hatfield School of Government, Division of Political Science, Portland, OR 97207-0751. Offers MA, MAT, MS, MST, PhD. Part-time programs available. *Faculty:* 10 full-time (2 women), 4 part-time/adjunct (1 woman). *Students:* 15 full-time (5 women), 13 part-time (4 women), 2 international. Average age 30. 11 applicants, 73% accepted, 7 enrolled. In 2010, 6 master's awarded. *Degree requirements:* For master's, one foreign language, comprehensive exam, thesis; for doctorate, comprehensive exam, thesis/dissertation, residency. *Entrance requirements:* For master's, GRE General Test or MAT, minimum GPA of 3.1, 2 letters of recommendation; for doctorate, GRE General Test. Additional exam requirements/recommendations for international students: Required—TOEFL (minimum score 550 paper-based; 213 computer-based). *Application deadline:* For fall admission, 4/1 priority date for domestic students, 3/1 priority date for international students. Applications are processed on a rolling basis. Application fee: $50. *Expenses:* Tuition, state resident: full-time $8505; part-time $315 per credit. Tuition, nonresident: full-time $13,284; part-time $492 per credit. Required fees: $1482; $21 per credit. $99 per term. One-time fee: $120. Part-time tuition and fees vary according to course load and program. *Financial support:* In 2010–11, 3 research assistantships with full tuition reimbursements (averaging $9,930 per year) were awarded; teaching assistantships, career-related internships or fieldwork, Federal Work-Study, and unspecified assistantships also available. Support available to part-time students. Financial award application deadline: 3/1; financial award applicants required to submit FAFSA. *Faculty research:* Congress, Presidency, political reform, international environment, hate speech. *Unit head:* David Kinsella, Chair, 503-725-3035, Fax: 503-725-8444, E-mail: kinsella@pdx.edu. *Application contact:* David Kinsella, Chair, 503-725-3035, Fax: 503-725-8444, E-mail: kinsella@pdx.edu.

Princeton University, Graduate School, Department of Politics, Princeton, NJ 08544-1019. Offers political philosophy (PhD); politics (PhD). *Degree requirements:* For doctorate, comprehensive exam, thesis/dissertation, teaching experience. *Entrance requirements:* For doctorate, GRE General Test, sample of written work, letters of recommendation. Additional exam requirements/recommendations for international students: Required—TOEFL (minimum score 600 paper-based; 250 computer-based). Electronic applications accepted. *Faculty research:* American politics, comparative politics, formal and quantitative methods, international relations, public law, political theory.

Purdue University, Graduate School, College of Liberal Arts, Department of Political Science, West Lafayette, IN 47907. Offers MA, PhD. Part-time and evening/weekend programs available. Terminal master's awarded for partial completion of doctoral program. *Degree requirements:* For doctorate, 2 foreign languages, thesis/dissertation. *Entrance requirements:* For master's and doctorate, GRE General Test, minimum GPA of 3.0. Additional exam requirements/recommendations for international students: Required—TOEFL. Electronic applications accepted. *Faculty research:* American politics, comparative politics, political theory, public policy/public administration, international relations.

Queen's University at Kingston, School of Graduate Studies and Research, Faculty of Arts and Sciences, Department of Political Studies, Kingston, ON K7L 3N6, Canada. Offers Canadian politics (PhD); comparative politics (PhD); gender and politics (PhD); international relations (PhD); political theory (PhD). *Degree requirements:* For master's, thesis or alternative; for doctorate, one foreign language, thesis/dissertation, qualifying exams. *Entrance requirements:* Additional exam requirements/recommendations for international students: Required—TOEFL (minimum score 600 paper-based; 250 computer-based). *Faculty research:* Canadian politics, comparative politics, political thought, international politics, women and politics.

Regent University, Graduate School, Robertson School of Government, Virginia Beach, VA 23464. Offers American government (MA); international politics (MA); political theory (MA); public administration (MA); JD/MA; M Div/MA; M Ed/MA; MBA/MA. Part-time and evening/weekend programs available. Postbaccalaureate distance learning degree programs offered (minimal on-campus study). *Faculty:* 6 full-time (1 woman), 11 part-time/adjunct (2 women). *Students:* 91 full-time (57 women), 62 part-time (37 women); includes 41 Black or African American, non-Hispanic/Latino; 3 Asian, non-Hispanic/Latino; 7 Hispanic/Latino, 1 international. Average age 30. 149 applicants, 61% accepted, 40 enrolled. In 2010, 59 master's awarded. *Degree requirements:* For master's, thesis optional, internship. *Entrance requirements:* For master's, GRE General Test or LSAT, minimum undergraduate GPA of 3.0, writing sample, resume, interview, references. Additional exam requirements/recommendations for international students: Required—TOEFL (minimum score 577 paper-based; 233 computer-based). *Application deadline:* For fall admission, 5/1 priority date for domestic students; for spring admission, 11/1 priority date for domestic students. Applications are processed on a rolling basis. Application fee: $50. Electronic applications accepted. *Expenses:* Contact institution. *Financial support:* Career-related internships or fieldwork, scholarships/grants, tuition waivers (full and partial), and unspecified assistantships available. Support available to part-time students. Financial award application deadline: 9/1; financial award applicants required to submit FAFSA. *Faculty research:* Education reform, political character issues, social capital concerns, administrative ethics, Biblical law and public policy. *Unit head:* Dr. Gary Roberts, Interim Dean, 757-352-4962, Fax: 757-352-4735, E-mail: garyrob@regent.edu. *Application contact:* Matthew Chadwick, Director of Enrollment Support Services, 800-373-5504, Fax: 757-352-4381, E-mail: admissions@regent.edu.

Rice University, Graduate Programs, School of Social Sciences, Department of Political Science, Houston, TX 77251-1892. Offers PhD. Terminal master's awarded for partial completion of doctoral program. *Degree requirements:* For doctorate, comprehensive exam, thesis/dissertation, 42 hours of coursework. *Entrance requirements:* For doctorate, GRE General Test. Additional exam requirements/recommendations for international students: Required—TOEFL (minimum score 600 paper-based; 250 computer-based; 90 iBT). Electronic applications accepted. *Faculty research:* Comparative government in Western Europe and the former Soviet Union, international relations, Congress and public policy in American government, minority politics.

Roosevelt University, Graduate Division, College of Arts and Sciences, Department of Political Science and Public Administration, Program in Political Science, Chicago, IL 60605. Offers MA. Part-time and evening/weekend programs available. *Degree requirements:* For master's, thesis or alternative. *Entrance requirements:* For master's, minimum GPA of 2.7. *Faculty research:* Metropolitan social movements, American politics, comparative politics, political theory.

Rutgers, The State University of New Jersey, Newark, Graduate School, Program in Political Science, Newark, NJ 07102. Offers American political system (MA); international relations (MA); JD/MA. Part-time and evening/weekend programs available. *Faculty:* 8 full-time (4 women), 2 part-time/adjunct (both women). *Students:* 7 full-time (3 women), 22 part-time (11 women); includes 6 Black or African American, non-Hispanic/Latino; 2 Asian, non-Hispanic/Latino; 2 Hispanic/Latino. 44 applicants, 61% accepted, 7 enrolled. In 2010, 10 master's awarded. *Degree requirements:* For master's, comprehensive exam, thesis optional. *Entrance requirements:* For master's, GRE, minimum undergraduate B average. *Application deadline:* For fall admission, 8/1 priority date for domestic students; for spring admission, 12/1 for domestic students. Applications are processed on a rolling basis. Application fee: $60. Electronic applications accepted. *Expenses:* Tuition, state resident: part-time $600 per credit. Tuition, nonresident: full-time $10,694. *Financial support:* Federal Work-Study and tuition waivers (full and partial) available. Support available to part-time students. Financial award application deadline: 3/1. *Faculty research:* Policymaking and policy evaluation in the United States; government and politics in Europe, Middle East, Asia, Africa, and Latin America. *Unit head:* Dr. Mara Sidney, Director, 973-353-5105, E-mail: msidney@andromeda.rutgers.edu. *Application contact:* Jason Hand, Director of Admissions, 973-353-5205, Fax: 973-353-1440.

Rutgers, The State University of New Jersey, New Brunswick, Graduate School-New Brunswick, Department of Political Science, Piscataway, NJ 08854-8097. Offers American politics (PhD); comparative politics (PhD); international relations (PhD); political theory (PhD); public law (PhD); women and politics (PhD). *Degree requirements:* For doctorate, one foreign language, comprehensive exam, thesis/dissertation. *Entrance requirements:* For doctorate, GRE General Test. Additional exam requirements/recommendations for international students:

Political Science

Rutgers, The State University of New Jersey, New Brunswick (continued)
Required—TOEFL. *Expenses:* Tuition, state resident: full-time $7200; part-time $600 per credit. Tuition, nonresident: full-time $11,124; part-time $927 per credit.

St. John's University, St. John's College of Liberal Arts and Sciences, Department of Government and Politics, Program in Government and Politics, Queens, NY 11439. Offers MA, JD/MA. Part-time and evening/weekend programs available. *Students:* 64 full-time (36 women), 43 part-time (24 women); includes 42 minority (12 Black or African American, non-Hispanic/Latino; 1 American Indian or Alaska Native, non-Hispanic/Latino; 9 Asian, non-Hispanic/Latino; 19 Hispanic/Latino; 1 Two or more races, non-Hispanic/Latino), 4 international. Average age 25. 124 applicants, 69% accepted, 45 enrolled. In 2010, 52 master's awarded. *Degree requirements:* For master's, comprehensive exam, thesis optional. *Entrance requirements:* For master's, minimum GPA of 3.0. Additional exam requirements/recommendations for international students: Required—TOEFL (minimum score 600 paper-based; 250 computer-based; 100 iBT), IELTS (minimum score 5.5). *Application deadline:* For fall admission, 5/1 priority date for domestic and international students; for spring admission, 11/1 priority date for domestic and international students. Applications are processed on a rolling basis. Application fee: $70. Electronic applications accepted. *Expenses:* Tuition: Full-time $17,100; part-time $950 per credit. Required fees: $340; $170 per semester. Tuition and fees vary according to program. *Financial support:* Research assistantships, scholarships/grants available. Support available to part-time students. Financial award application deadline: 3/1; financial award applicants required to submit FAFSA. *Unit head:* Dr. Luba Racanska, Chair, 718-990-6329, E-mail: racanskl@stjohns.edu. *Application contact:* Kathleen Davis, Director of Graduate Admissions, 718-990-1601, Fax: 718-990-5686, E-mail: gradhelp@stjohns.edu.

St. John's University, St. John's College of Liberal Arts and Sciences, Department of Government and Politics and Division of Library and Information Science, Program in Government Information Specialist, Queens, NY 11439. Offers MA/MLS. Part-time and evening/weekend programs available. *Students:* 1 (woman) full-time. Average age 24. 3 applicants, 33% accepted, 0 enrolled. *Entrance requirements:* Additional exam requirements/recommendations for international students: Required—TOEFL (minimum score 600 paper-based; 250 computer-based; 100 iBT), IELTS (minimum score 5.5). *Application deadline:* For fall admission, 5/1 priority date for domestic and international students; for spring admission, 11/1 priority date for domestic and international students. Applications are processed on a rolling basis. Application fee: $70. Electronic applications accepted. *Expenses:* Tuition: Full-time $17,100; part-time $950 per credit. Required fees: $340; $170 per semester. Tuition and fees vary according to program. *Financial support:* Research assistantships, career-related internships or fieldwork and scholarships/grants available. Support available to part-time students. Financial award application deadline: 3/1; financial award applicants required to submit FAFSA. *Unit head:* Dr. Luba Racanska, Chair, 718-990-6329, E-mail: racanskl@stjohns.edu. *Application contact:* Kathleen Davis, Director of Graduate Admission, 718-990-1601, Fax: 718-990-5686, E-mail: gradhelp@stjohns.edu.

Saint Louis University, Graduate Education, College of Arts and Sciences and Graduate Education, Department of Political Science, St. Louis, MO 63103-2097. Offers MA. Part-time programs available. *Entrance requirements:* For master's, GRE or LSAT, letters of recommendation, resume, writing sample. Additional exam requirements/recommendations for international students: Required—TOEFL (minimum score 525 paper-based; 194 computer-based). Electronic applications accepted. *Faculty research:* Part of Asia, Africa, Latin America, and Russia; international political economy; diplomacy and international organization; theories of democracy and justice; American political institutions.

St. Mary's University, Graduate School, Department of Political Science, San Antonio, TX 78228-8507. Offers international relations (MA); political communications and applied science (MA); political science (MA); public administration (MPA), including inter-American administration, public management; JD/MA; JD/MPA. Part-time programs available. *Degree requirements:* For master's, one foreign language, comprehensive exam. *Entrance requirements:* For master's, GRE General Test. Additional exam requirements/recommendations for international students: Required—TOEFL (minimum score 550 paper-based; 213 computer-based; 80 iBT). Electronic applications accepted. *Faculty research:* Voting rights, natural resources and urban policy, comparative politics and international relations.

Sam Houston State University, College of Humanities and Social Sciences, Department of Political Science, Huntsville, TX 77341. Offers political science (MA); public administration (MPA). Evening/weekend programs available. *Faculty:* 8 full-time (5 women). *Students:* 10 full-time (7 women), 25 part-time (20 women); includes 4 Black or African American, non-Hispanic/Latino; 2 Hispanic/Latino, 2 international. Average age 33. 18 applicants, 94% accepted, 13 enrolled. In 2010, 9 master's awarded. *Degree requirements:* For master's, thesis or alternative. *Entrance requirements:* For master's, GRE General Test. Additional exam requirements/recommendations for international students: Required—TOEFL (minimum score 550 paper-based; 213 computer-based; 79 iBT). *Application deadline:* For fall admission, 8/1 for domestic students; for spring admission, 12/1 for domestic students. Applications are processed on a rolling basis. Application fee: $20. *Expenses:* Tuition, state resident: full-time $1363; part-time $163 per credit hour. Tuition, nonresident: full-time $3856; part-time $473 per credit hour. *Financial support:* Research assistantships, teaching assistantships, career-related internships or fieldwork and institutionally sponsored loans available. Support available to part-time students. Financial award application deadline: 5/31; financial award applicants required to submit FAFSA. *Unit head:* Dr. Rhonda Callaway, Chair, 936-294-4108, Fax: 936-294-4172, E-mail: rlc005@shsu.edu. *Application contact:* Dr. Tamara Waggener, Advisor, 936-294-1466, E-mail: pol_taw@shsu.edu.

San Diego State University, Graduate and Research Affairs, College of Arts and Letters, Department of Political Science, San Diego, CA 92182. Offers MA. Part-time programs available. *Degree requirements:* For master's, thesis. *Entrance requirements:* For master's, GRE General Test, minimum GPA of 3.0, 2 letters of reference. Additional exam requirements/recommendations for international students: Required—TOEFL. Electronic applications accepted.

San Francisco State University, Division of Graduate Studies, College of Behavioral and Social Sciences, Department of Political Science, San Francisco, CA 94132-1722. Offers MA. *Financial support:* Research assistantships, teaching assistantships available. *Unit head:* Dr. James Martel, Chair, 415-338-1178, Fax: 415-338-2391. *Application contact:* Dr. Sujian Guo, Graduate Coordinator, 415-338-7523, E-mail: sguo@sfsu.edu.

Simon Fraser University, Graduate Studies, Faculty of Arts and Social Sciences, Department of Political Science, Burnaby, BC V5A 1S6, Canada. Offers MA, PhD. *Degree requirements:* For master's, thesis (for some programs); for doctorate, one foreign language, comprehensive exam, thesis/dissertation. *Entrance requirements:* For master's, minimum GPA of 3.0; for doctorate, minimum GPA of 3.67, master's in political science. Additional exam requirements/recommendations for international students: Required—TOEFL or IELTS. *Faculty research:* Theory, comparative government, public policy and administration, federalism, international relations, Canadian politics.

Sonoma State University, School of Social Sciences, Department of Political Science, Rohnert Park, CA 94928. Offers public administration (MPA). Part-time and evening/weekend programs available. *Faculty:* 3 full-time (1 woman), 3 part-time/adjunct (all women). *Students:* 1 (woman) full-time, 53 part-time (31 women); includes 18 minority (4 Black or African American, non-Hispanic/Latino; 4 Asian, non-Hispanic/Latino; 5 Hispanic/Latino; 1 Native Hawaiian or other Pacific Islander, non-Hispanic/Latino; 4 Two or more races, non-Hispanic/Latino). Average age 34. 22 applicants, 86% accepted, 10 enrolled. In 2010, 7 master's awarded. *Degree requirements:* For master's, thesis or alternative. *Entrance requirements:* For master's, GRE General Test, minimum GPA of 3.0. Additional exam requirements/recommendations for international students: Required—TOEFL (minimum score 500 paper-based; 173 computer-based). *Application deadline:* For fall admission, 11/30 for domestic students; for spring admission, 8/31 for domestic students. Application fee: $55. *Financial support:* Research assistantships, teaching assistantships, career-related internships or fieldwork and Federal Work-Study available. Support available to part-time students. Financial award application deadline: 3/2; financial award applicants required to submit FAFSA. *Unit head:* Dr. Robert McNamara, Chair, 707-664-2676. *Application contact:* Dr. David McCuan, Graduate Program Coordinator, 707-664-2179, Fax: 707-664-3920, E-mail: david.mccuan@sonoma.edu.

Southern Connecticut State University, School of Graduate Studies, School of Arts and Sciences, Department of Political Science, New Haven, CT 06515-1355. Offers MS. Part-time and evening/weekend programs available. *Faculty:* 7 full-time (2 women). *Students:* 8 full-time (2 women), 7 part-time (2 women); includes 2 Black or African American, non-Hispanic/Latino; 1 Hispanic/Latino, 1 international. 21 applicants, 14% accepted, 2 enrolled. In 2010, 4 master's awarded. *Degree requirements:* For master's, thesis or alternative. *Entrance requirements:* For master's, interview. *Application deadline:* For fall admission, 7/15 priority date for domestic students. Applications are processed on a rolling basis. Application fee: $50. Electronic applications accepted. *Expenses:* Tuition, state resident: full-time $5137; part-time $518 per credit. Tuition, nonresident: part-time $542 per credit. Required fees: $4008; $55 per semester. Tuition and fees vary according to program. *Financial support:* Application deadline: 4/15. *Unit head:* Dr. Arthur Paulson, Chairperson, 203-392-5657, Fax: 203-392-5670, E-mail: paulsona1@southernct.edu. *Application contact:* Dr. John Critzer, Graduate Coordinator, 203-392-5658, Fax: 203-392-5670, E-mail: critzerj1@southernct.edu.

Southern Illinois University Carbondale, Graduate School, College of Liberal Arts, Department of Political Science, Program in Political Science, Carbondale, IL 62901-4701. Offers MA, PhD, JD/PhD. Part-time programs available. *Degree requirements:* For doctorate, thesis/dissertation. *Entrance requirements:* For master's, GRE General Test, minimum GPA of 2.7; for doctorate, GRE General Test, minimum GPA of 3.5. Additional exam requirements/recommendations for international students: Required—TOEFL. *Faculty research:* Public law, international relations, comparative government, American government.

Southern University and Agricultural and Mechanical College, Graduate School, Nelson Mandela School of Public Policy and Urban Affairs, Department of Political Science and Geography, Baton Rouge, LA 70813. Offers social sciences (MA). *Degree requirements:* For master's, thesis. *Entrance requirements:* For master's, GMAT or GRE General Test, minimum GPA of 3.0. Additional exam requirements/recommendations for international students: Required—TOEFL. *Faculty research:* Redistricting, comparative studies, environmental politics, political geography, mayoral elections.

Stanford University, School of Humanities and Sciences, Department of Political Science, Stanford, CA 94305-9991. Offers MA, PhD. Terminal master's awarded for partial completion of doctoral program. *Degree requirements:* For doctorate, one foreign language, thesis/dissertation, oral exam. *Entrance requirements:* For master's and doctorate, GRE General Test. Additional exam requirements/recommendations for international students: Required—TOEFL. Electronic applications accepted. *Expenses:* Tuition: Full-time $38,700; part-time $860 per unit. One-time fee: $200 full-time.

State University of New York at Binghamton, Graduate School, School of Arts and Sciences, Department of Political Science, Binghamton, NY 13902-6000. Offers political science (MA, PhD); public policy (MA, PhD). *Faculty:* 17 full-time (4 women), 2 part-time/adjunct (1 woman). *Students:* 27 full-time (7 women), 21 part-time (8 women); includes 3 Black or African American, non-Hispanic/Latino, 16 international. Average age 29. 45 applicants, 44% accepted, 9 enrolled. In 2010, 9 master's, 5 doctorates awarded. Terminal master's awarded for partial completion of doctoral program. *Degree requirements:* For master's, thesis or alternative, written exam; for doctorate, 2 foreign languages, thesis/dissertation, written exam. *Entrance requirements:* For master's and doctorate, GRE General Test, GRE Subject Test. Additional exam requirements/recommendations for international students: Required—TOEFL (minimum score 550 paper-based; 213 computer-based; 80 iBT). *Application deadline:* For fall admission, 2/15 priority date for domestic and international students. Applications are processed on a rolling basis. Application fee: $60. Electronic applications accepted. *Financial support:* In 2010–11, 33 students received support, including 1 fellowship with full tuition reimbursement available (averaging $15,000 per year), 3 research assistantships with full tuition reimbursements available (averaging $15,000 per year), 24 teaching assistantships with full tuition reimbursements available (averaging $15,000 per year); career-related internships or fieldwork, Federal Work-Study, institutionally sponsored loans, scholarships/grants, health care benefits, tuition waivers (full), and unspecified assistantships also available. Financial award application deadline: 2/15; financial award applicants required to submit FAFSA. *Unit head:* Dr. David H. Clark, Chairperson, 607-777-6786, E-mail: dclark@binghamton.edu. *Application contact:* Catherine Smith, Recruiting and Admissions Coordinator, 607-777-2151, Fax: 607-777-2501, E-mail: cmsmith@binghamton.edu.

Stony Brook University, State University of New York, Graduate School, College of Arts and Sciences, Department of Political Science, Stony Brook, NY 11794. Offers political science (MA, PhD); public policy (MAPP); public policy and urban development (MA). Evening/weekend programs available. *Faculty:* 11 full-time (2 women), 5 part-time/adjunct (0 women). *Students:* 74 full-time (27 women), 20 part-time (12 women); includes 9 Black or African American, non-Hispanic/Latino; 9 Asian, non-Hispanic/Latino; 6 Hispanic/Latino; 2 Two or more races, non-Hispanic/Latino, 12 international. Average age 27. 136 applicants, 57% accepted, 46 enrolled. In 2010, 39 master's, 6 doctorates awarded. *Degree requirements:* For doctorate, thesis/dissertation. *Entrance requirements:* For master's and doctorate, GRE General Test. *Application deadline:* For fall admission, 1/15 for domestic students. Application fee: $100. *Expenses:* Tuition, state resident: full-time $8370; part-time $349 per credit. Tuition, nonresident: full-time $13,780; part-time $574 per credit. Required fees: $994. *Financial support:* In 2010–11, 30 teaching assistantships were awarded; fellowships, research assistantships also available. Total annual research expenditures: $17,036. *Unit head:* Dr. Jeffrey Segal, Chair, 631-632-7640. *Application contact:* Dr. Charles Taber, Director, 631-632-7667, Fax: 631-632-4116, E-mail: charles.taber@stonybrook.edu.

Suffolk University, College of Arts and Sciences, Department of Government, Boston, MA 02108-2770. Offers international relations (MSPS); political science (MSPS); professional politics (MSPS, CAGS); MPA/MSPS. Part-time and evening/weekend programs available. *Faculty:* 11 full-time (6 women), 15 part-time/adjunct (8 women). *Students:* 14 full-time (9 women), 24 part-time (16 women); includes 2 Black or African American, non-Hispanic/Latino; 1 Hispanic/Latino, 6 international. Average age 26. 73 applicants, 79% accepted, 31 enrolled. In 2010, 23 master's awarded. *Degree requirements:* For master's, thesis optional. *Entrance requirements:* For master's, GRE General Test or MAT, 2 letters of recommendation, resume. Additional exam requirements/recommendations for international students: Required—TOEFL (minimum score 550 paper-based; 213 computer-based; 80 iBT). *Application deadline:* For fall admission, 6/15 priority date for domestic students, 6/15 for international students; for spring admission, 11/1 priority date for domestic students, 11/1 for international students. Applications are processed on a rolling basis. Application fee: $50. Electronic applications accepted. *Expenses:* Contact institution. *Financial support:* In 2010–11, 32 students received support, including 27 fellowships with full and partial tuition reimbursements available (averaging $6,104 per year); career-related internships or fieldwork, Federal Work-Study, and institutionally sponsored loans also available. Support available to part-time students. Financial award application deadline: 4/1; financial award applicants required to submit FAFSA. *Faculty research:* Political parties, women in politics, Canadian politics, public policy, legislative policies. *Unit head:* Dr. Rachael Cobb, Chairperson, 617-305-6380, Fax: 617-367-4623, E-mail: rcobb@suffolk.edu. *Application contact:* Judith Reynolds, Director of Graduate Admissions, 617-573-8302, Fax: 617-305-1733, E-mail: grad.admission@suffolk.edu.

Sul Ross State University, School of Arts and Sciences, Department of Behavioral and Social Sciences, Program in Political Science, Alpine, TX 79832. Offers MA. Part-time and evening/weekend programs available. *Degree requirements:* For master's, thesis optional.

Entrance requirements: For master's, GRE General Test, minimum undergraduate GPA of 2.5 in last 60 hours. *Faculty research:* Local government, state government, borderland studies, British studies.

Syracuse University, Maxwell School of Citizenship and Public Affairs, Program in E-Government Management and Leadership, Syracuse, NY 13244. Offers CAS. Part-time programs available. *Entrance requirements:* For degree, Syracuse degree program matriculation. Additional exam requirements/recommendations for international students: Required—TOEFL (minimum score 100 iBT). Application fee: $75. Electronic applications accepted. *Expenses:* Tuition: Part-time $1162 per credit. *Application contact:* Margaret Lane, Director of Executive Education, 315-443-8708.

Syracuse University, Maxwell School of Citizenship and Public Affairs, Program in Political Science, Syracuse, NY 13244. Offers MA, PhD. *Students:* 63 full-time (32 women), 4 part-time (3 women); includes 4 minority (2 Black or African American, non-Hispanic/Latino; 1 Asian, non-Hispanic/Latino; 1 Two or more races, non-Hispanic/Latino), 29 international. Average age 30. 142 applicants, 23% accepted, 9 enrolled. In 2010, 13 master's, 2 doctorates awarded. *Degree requirements:* For doctorate, thesis/dissertation. *Entrance requirements:* For master's and doctorate, GRE General Test. Additional exam requirements/recommendations for international students: Required—TOEFL (minimum score 100 iBT). *Application deadline:* For fall admission, 2/1 priority date for domestic and international students. Application fee: $75. Electronic applications accepted. *Expenses:* Tuition: Part-time $1162 per credit. *Financial support:* Fellowships with full tuition reimbursements, research assistantships with full and partial tuition reimbursements, teaching assistantships with full and partial tuition reimbursements available. Financial award application deadline: 1/1. *Unit head:* Dr. Mark Rupert, Chair, 315-443-2416, Fax: 315-443-9082, E-mail: polisci@maxwell.syr.edu. *Application contact:* Candy Brooks, Recruiting Contact, 315-443-2416, E-mail: cbrooks01@syr.edu.

Tarleton State University, College of Graduate Studies, College of Liberal and Fine Arts, Department of Social Sciences, Stephenville, TX 76402. Offers history (MA); political science (MA). Part-time and evening/weekend programs available. Postbaccalaureate distance learning degree programs offered (minimal on-campus study). *Degree requirements:* For master's, variable foreign language requirement, comprehensive exam, thesis optional. *Entrance requirements:* For master's, GRE General Test, minimum GPA of 3.0. Additional exam requirements/recommendations for international students: Required—TOEFL (minimum score 550 paper-based; 213 computer-based; 80 iBT). Electronic applications accepted.

Teachers College, Columbia University, Graduate Faculty of Education, Department of Organization and Leadership, Program in Politics and Education, New York, NY 10027. Offers Ed M, MA, Ed D, PhD. *Faculty:* 8 full-time (1 woman), 1 (woman) part-time/adjunct. *Students:* 18 full-time (14 women), 18 part-time (11 women); includes 13 minority (4 Black or African American, non-Hispanic/Latino; 5 Asian, non-Hispanic/Latino; 3 Hispanic/Latino; 1 Two or more races, non-Hispanic/Latino), 1 international. Average age 32. 35 applicants, 71% accepted, 9 enrolled. In 2010, 13 master's, 1 doctorate awarded. *Degree requirements:* For master's, comprehensive exam, thesis or alternative; for doctorate, one foreign language, comprehensive exam, thesis/dissertation. *Entrance requirements:* For master's and doctorate, GRE. *Application deadline:* For fall admission, 1/15 priority date for domestic students; for spring admission, 11/1 priority date for domestic students. Application fee: $65. *Expenses:* Tuition: Full-time $28,272; part-time $1178 per credit. Required fees: $756; $378 per semester. *Financial support:* Career-related internships or fieldwork, Federal Work-Study, institutionally sponsored loans, and tuition waivers (full and partial) available. Support available to part-time students. Financial award application deadline: 2/1. *Faculty research:* Urban and social programs in education. *Unit head:* Prof. Jeffrey Henig, Program Coordinator, 212-678-3751, E-mail: henig@tc.edu. *Application contact:* Prof. Jeffrey Henig, Program Coordinator, 212-678-3751, E-mail: henig@tc.edu.

Temple University, College of Liberal Arts, Department of Political Science, Philadelphia, PA 19122-6096. Offers MA, PhD. Part-time programs available. *Faculty:* 23 full-time (7 women). *Students:* 46 full-time (15 women), 8 part-time (4 women); includes 4 Black or African American, non-Hispanic/Latino; 4 Asian, non-Hispanic/Latino; 1 Two or more races, non-Hispanic/Latino, 2 international. 67 applicants, 51% accepted, 11 enrolled. In 2010, 6 master's, 6 doctorates awarded. Terminal master's awarded for partial completion of doctoral program. *Degree requirements:* For master's, comprehensive exam; for doctorate, thesis/dissertation, preliminary and oral exams. *Entrance requirements:* For master's and doctorate, GRE General Test, minimum GPA of 3.0. Additional exam requirements/recommendations for international students: Required—TOEFL (minimum score 550 paper-based; 213 computer-based; 79 iBT). *Application deadline:* For fall admission, 1/15 for domestic students, 12/15 for international students; for spring admission, 10/15 for domestic students, 8/1 for international students. Applications are processed on a rolling basis. Application fee: $50. Electronic applications accepted. *Financial support:* Fellowships, research assistantships, teaching assistantships with tuition reimbursements, career-related internships or fieldwork, Federal Work-Study, institutionally sponsored loans, scholarships/grants, and tuition waivers (partial) available. Financial award application deadline: 1/15; financial award applicants required to submit FAFSA. *Faculty research:* American politics, international politics, comparative politics, political theory, urban politics, public policy. Total annual research expenditures: $20,000. *Unit head:* Dr. Richard Deeg, Chair, 215-204-7123, Fax: 215-204-3770, E-mail: rdeeg@temple.edu. *Application contact:* Dr. Richard Deeg, Chair, 215-204-7123, Fax: 215-204-3770, E-mail: rdeeg@temple.edu.

Texas A&M International University, Office of Graduate Studies and Research, College of Arts and Sciences, Department of Social Sciences, Laredo, TX 78041-1900. Offers history (MA); political science (MA); public administration (MPA). *Faculty:* 8 full-time (3 women). *Students:* 4 full-time (2 women), 52 part-time (27 women); includes 1 Asian, non-Hispanic/Latino; 52 Hispanic/Latino, 1 international. Average age 30. 35 applicants, 74% accepted, 19 enrolled. In 2010, 10 master's awarded. *Degree requirements:* For master's, thesis (for some programs). *Entrance requirements:* For master's, GRE General Test. Additional exam requirements/recommendations for international students: Required—TOEFL (minimum score 550 paper-based; 213 computer-based). *Application deadline:* For fall admission, 4/30 priority date for domestic students; for spring admission, 11/30 for domestic students, 10/1 for international students. Applications are processed on a rolling basis. Application fee: $25. *Financial support:* In 2010–11, 14 students received support, including 7 research assistantships. Financial award application deadline: 11/1. *Unit head:* Dr. Mohammed Ben-Ruwin, Chair, 956-328-2632, E-mail: mbenruwin@tamiu.edu. *Application contact:* Suzanne Hansen-Alford, Director of Admissions, 956-326-3023, Fax: 956-326-3021, E-mail: graduateschool@tamiu.edu.

Texas A&M University, College of Liberal Arts, Department of Political Science, College Station, TX 77843. Offers PhD. *Faculty:* 21. *Students:* 44 full-time (23 women), 6 part-time (2 women); includes 6 Black or African American, non-Hispanic/Latino; 2 Asian, non-Hispanic/Latino; 3 Hispanic/Latino, 10 international. Average age 30. In 2010, 12 doctorates awarded. *Degree requirements:* For doctorate, comprehensive exam, thesis/dissertation. *Entrance requirements:* For doctorate, GRE General Test, minimum GPA of 3.4. Additional exam requirements/recommendations for international students: Required—TOEFL. *Application deadline:* For fall admission, 12/20 for domestic and international students. Application fee: $50 ($75 for international students). Electronic applications accepted. *Financial support:* In 2010–11, fellowships (averaging $3,000 per year), research assistantships (averaging $15,600 per year) were awarded; institutionally sponsored loans and assistant lecturer positions also available. Financial award application deadline: 12/20; financial award applicants required to submit FAFSA. *Faculty research:* American politics, international relations, comparative politics, political theory, public policy. *Unit head:* Dr. James Rogers, Head, 979-845-8833, E-mail: rogers@politics.tamu.edu. *Application contact:* Dr. Cary J. Nederman, Graduate Advisor, 979-845-8594, Fax: 979-845-4845, E-mail: nederman@polisci.tamu.edu.

Texas A&M University–Kingsville, College of Graduate Studies, College of Arts and Sciences, Program in History and Political Science, Kingsville, TX 78363. Offers MA, MS. Part-time and evening/weekend programs available. *Degree requirements:* For master's, comprehensive

exam, thesis or alternative. *Entrance requirements:* For master's, GRE General Test. Additional exam requirements/recommendations for international students: Required—TOEFL.

Texas State University–San Marcos, Graduate School, College of Liberal Arts, Department of Political Science, Program in Political Science, San Marcos, TX 78666. Offers M Ed, MA. Part-time and evening/weekend programs available. *Faculty:* 12 full-time (3 women), 1 part-time/adjunct (0 women). *Students:* 42 full-time (18 women), 33 part-time (18 women); includes 3 Black or African American, non-Hispanic/Latino; 2 Asian, non-Hispanic/Latino; 16 Hispanic/Latino; 2 Two or more races, non-Hispanic/Latino. Average age 28. 26 applicants, 92% accepted, 19 enrolled. In 2010, 19 master's awarded. *Degree requirements:* For master's, comprehensive exam, thesis (for some programs). *Entrance requirements:* For master's, minimum GPA of 2.9 in last 60 hours of course work. Additional exam requirements/recommendations for international students: Required—TOEFL (minimum score 550 paper-based; 213 computer-based; 78 iBT). *Application deadline:* For fall admission, 6/15 priority date for domestic students, 6/1 priority date for international students; for spring admission, 10/15 priority date for domestic students, 10/1 priority date for international students. Applications are processed on a rolling basis. Application fee: $40 ($90 for international students). Electronic applications accepted. *Expenses:* Tuition, state resident: full-time $6024; part-time $251 per credit hour. Tuition, nonresident: full-time $13,536; part-time $564 per credit hour. Required fees: $1776; $50 per credit hour. $306 per semester. *Financial support:* In 2010–11, 34 students received support, including 2 research assistantships (averaging $4,991 per year), 8 teaching assistantships (averaging $5,076 per year); career-related internships or fieldwork, Federal Work-Study, institutionally sponsored loans, scholarships/grants, and unspecified assistantships also available. Support available to part-time students. Financial award application deadline: 4/1; financial award applicants required to submit FAFSA. *Faculty research:* Voting patterns, analyzing voting. Total annual research expenditures: $6,463. *Unit head:* Dr. Cecilia Castillio, Graduate Adviser, 512-245-7582, Fax: 512-345-7815, E-mail: cr09@txstate.edu. *Application contact:* Dr. J. Michael Willoughby, Dean of Graduate School, 512-245-2581, Fax: 512-245-8365, E-mail: gradcollege@txstate.edu.

Texas State University–San Marcos, Graduate School, Interdisciplinary Studies in Political Science, San Marcos, TX 78666. Offers MAIS. *Degree requirements:* For master's, comprehensive exam, thesis optional. *Entrance requirements:* For master's, minimum GPA of 2.9 or GRE (minimum combined score of 900 Verbal and Quantitative preferred). Additional exam requirements/recommendations for international students: Required—TOEFL (minimum score 550 paper-based; 213 computer-based; 78 iBT). *Application deadline:* For fall admission, 6/15 priority date for domestic students, 6/1 for international students; for spring admission, 10/15 priority date for domestic students, 10/1 for international students. Applications are processed on a rolling basis. Application fee: $40 ($90 for international students). *Expenses:* Tuition, state resident: full-time $6024; part-time $251 per credit hour. Tuition, nonresident: full-time $13,536; part-time $564 per credit hour. Required fees: $1776; $50 per credit hour. $306 per semester. *Financial support:* Application deadline: 4/1. *Unit head:* Dr. Cecilia Castillio, Graduate Advisor, 512-245-3255, Fax: 512-345-7815, E-mail: cr09@txstate.edu. *Application contact:* Dr. J. Michael Willoughby, Dean of Graduate School, 512-245-2581, Fax: 512-245-8365, E-mail: gradcollege@txstate.edu.

Texas Tech University, Graduate School, College of Arts and Sciences, Department of Political Science, Lubbock, TX 79409. Offers political science (MA, PhD); JD/MPA. *Accreditation:* NASPAA (one or more programs are accredited). Part-time programs available. *Faculty:* 12 full-time (2 women). *Students:* 57 full-time (21 women), 22 part-time (11 women); includes 1 Black or African American, non-Hispanic/Latino; 2 American Indian or Alaska Native, non-Hispanic/Latino; 1 Asian, non-Hispanic/Latino; 17 Hispanic/Latino; 1 Two or more races, non-Hispanic/Latino, 11 international. Average age 29. 73 applicants, 56% accepted, 20 enrolled. In 2010, 13 master's, 6 doctorates awarded. *Degree requirements:* For master's, thesis or alternative; for doctorate, thesis/dissertation. *Entrance requirements:* For master's and doctorate, GRE General Test, departmental application form, 3 letters of reference. Additional exam requirements/recommendations for international students: Required—TOEFL (minimum score 550 paper-based; 213 computer-based; 79 iBT). *Application deadline:* For fall admission, 6/1 priority date for domestic students, 1/15 priority date for international students; for spring admission, 9/1 priority date for domestic students, 6/15 priority date for international students. Applications are processed on a rolling basis. Application fee: $50 ($75 for international students). Electronic applications accepted. *Expenses:* Tuition, state resident: full-time $5495.76; part-time $228.99 per credit hour. Tuition, nonresident: full-time $12,936; part-time $538.99 per credit hour. Required fees: $2674; $36 per credit hour. $905 per semester. *Financial support:* In 2010–11, 31 students received support, including 14 teaching assistantships with partial tuition reimbursements available (averaging $5,100 per year). Financial award application deadline: 4/15; financial award applicants required to submit FAFSA. *Faculty research:* State politics, American institutions and behavior, Asian politics, international and comparative political relations and economics, public administration and organizations. Total annual research expenditures: $59,489. *Unit head:* Dr. Dennis Patterson, Chair, 806-742-3121, Fax: 806-742-0850, E-mail: dennis.patterson@ttu.edu. *Application contact:* Dr. Frank Thames, Associate Chair, 806-742-4049, Fax: 806-742-0850, E-mail: frank.thames@ttu.edu.

Texas Woman's University, Graduate School, College of Arts and Sciences, Department of History and Government, Denton, TX 76201. Offers government (MA); history (MA). Part-time and evening/weekend programs available. *Faculty:* 10 full-time (4 women), 1 (woman) part-time/adjunct. *Students:* 7 full-time (5 women), 31 part-time (28 women); includes 4 Black or African American, non-Hispanic/Latino; 2 American Indian or Alaska Native, non-Hispanic/Latino; 1 Asian, non-Hispanic/Latino; 2 Hispanic/Latino. Average age 39. 14 applicants, 100% accepted, 10 enrolled. In 2010, 7 master's awarded. *Degree requirements:* For master's, comprehensive exam, thesis. *Entrance requirements:* For master's, minimum GPA of 3.0, written statement of purpose; 2 letters of reference. Additional exam requirements/recommendations for international students: Required—TOEFL (minimum score 550 paper-based; 213 computer-based; 79 iBT). *Application deadline:* For fall admission, 7/1 priority date for domestic students, 3/1 for international students; for spring admission, 12/1 priority date for domestic students, 7/1 for international students. Applications are processed on a rolling basis. Application fee: $50 ($75 for international students). Electronic applications accepted. *Expenses:* Tuition, state resident: full-time $3834; part-time $213 per credit hour. Tuition, nonresident: full-time $9468; part-time $526 per credit hour. Required fees: $1247; $220 per credit hour. *Financial support:* In 2010–11, 16 students received support, including 14 research assistantships (averaging $11,520 per year), 2 teaching assistantships (averaging $11,520 per year); career-related internships or fieldwork, Federal Work-Study, institutionally sponsored loans, scholarships/grants, traineeships, health care benefits, and unspecified assistantships also available. Support available to part-time students. Financial award application deadline: 3/1; financial award applicants required to submit FAFSA. *Faculty research:* U. S. history, politics, and law; global history, politics, and law; Latin American and Caribbean history; legal studies; women in history, politics, and law. Total annual research expenditures: $505,193. *Unit head:* Dr. Mark Kessler, Chair, 940-898-2133, Fax: 940-898-2130, E-mail: historygov@twu.edu. *Application contact:* Dr. Samuel Wheeler, Assistant Director of Admissions, 940-898-3188, Fax: 940-898-3081, E-mail: wheelersr@twu.edu.

Troy University, Graduate School, College of Education, Program in Postsecondary Education, Troy, AL 36082. Offers adult education (M Ed); biology (M Ed); criminal justice (M Ed); English (M Ed); foundations of education (M Ed); general science (M Ed); higher education administration (M Ed); history (M Ed); instructional technology (M Ed); mathematics (M Ed); music industry (M Ed); physical fitness (M Ed); political science (M Ed); public administration (M Ed); social science (M Ed); teaching English (M Ed). *Accreditation:* NCATE. Part-time and evening/weekend programs available. *Students:* 314 full-time (247 women), 153 part-time (122 women); includes 255 minority (242 Black or African American, non-Hispanic/Latino; 3 American Indian or Alaska Native, non-Hispanic/Latino; 5 Asian, non-Hispanic/Latino; 5 Hispanic/Latino). Average age 34. 223 applicants, 89% accepted. In 2010, 364 master's awarded. *Degree requirements:* For master's, comprehensive exam, thesis. *Entrance requirements:* For master's, MAT (minimum score 385), minimum GPA of 2.5. Additional exam requirements/recommendations for inter-

Political Science

Troy University (continued)
national students: Required—TOEFL (minimum score 523 paper-based; 193 computer-based; 70 iBT), IELTS, or ACT compass ESL (minimum Listening, Reading, and Grammar score: 270). *Application deadline:* Applications are processed on a rolling basis. Application fee: $50. Electronic applications accepted. *Expenses:* Tuition, state resident: full-time $4428; part-time $246 per credit hour. Tuition, nonresident: full-time $8856; part-time $492 per credit hour. Required fees: $432; $24 per credit hour. $50 per term. Tuition and fees vary according to program. *Financial support:* Available to part-time students. Applicants required to submit FAFSA. *Unit head:* Dr. Andrew Creamer, Chair, 334-670-3350, Fax: 334-670-3296, E-mail: drcreamer@troy.edu. *Application contact:* Brenda K. Campbell, Director of Graduate Admissions, 334-670-3178, Fax: 334-670-3733, E-mail: bcamp@troy.edu.

Tulane University, School of Liberal Arts, Department of Political Science, New Orleans, LA 70118-5669. Offers MA, PhD, MA/JD. *Degree requirements:* For master's, one foreign language, thesis optional, seminar; for doctorate, 2 foreign languages, thesis/dissertation. *Entrance requirements:* For master's, GRE General Test, minimum B average in undergraduate course work; for doctorate, GRE General Test. Additional exam requirements/recommendations for international students: Required—TOEFL. Electronic applications accepted.

Universidad Nacional Pedro Henriquez Urena, Graduate School, Santo Domingo, Dominican Republic. Offers agricultural diversity (MS), including horticultural/fruit production, tropical animal production; conservation of monuments and cultural assets (M Arch); ecology and environment (MS); environmental engineering (MEE); international relations (MA); natural resource management (MS); political science (MA); project optimization (MPM); project feasibility (MPM); project management (MPM); sanitation engineering (ME); science for teachers (MS); tropical Caribbean architecture (M Arch).

Université de Montréal, Faculty of Arts and Sciences, Department of Political Science, Montréal, QC H3C 3J7, Canada. Offers M Sc, PhD. *Degree requirements:* For master's, thesis; for doctorate, thesis/dissertation, general exam. *Entrance requirements:* For master's, minimum GPA of 2.8; for doctorate, master's degree, minimum GPA of 3.0. Electronic applications accepted.

Université du Québec à Montréal, Graduate Programs, Program in Political Science, Montréal, QC H3C 3P8, Canada. Offers MA, PhD. Part-time programs available. *Degree requirements:* For master's, thesis; for doctorate, thesis/dissertation. *Entrance requirements:* For master's, appropriate bachelor's degree or equivalent, proficiency in French; for doctorate, appropriate master's degree or equivalent, proficiency in French.

Université Laval, Faculty of Social Sciences, Department of Political Science, Program in Policy Analysis, Québec, QC G1K 7P4, Canada. Offers MA. *Degree requirements:* For master's, thesis (for some programs). *Entrance requirements:* For master's, knowledge of French, comprehension of written English. Electronic applications accepted.

Université Laval, Faculty of Social Sciences, Department of Political Science, Programs in Political Science, Québec, QC G1K 7P4, Canada. Offers MA, PhD. Terminal master's awarded for partial completion of doctoral program. *Degree requirements:* For master's, thesis (for some programs); for doctorate, comprehensive exam, thesis/dissertation. *Entrance requirements:* For master's, knowledge of French; for doctorate, knowledge of French, comprehension of written English. Electronic applications accepted.

University at Albany, State University of New York, Nelson A. Rockefeller College of Public Affairs and Policy, Department of Political Science, Albany, NY 12222-0001. Offers MA, PhD. *Degree requirements:* For doctorate, one foreign language, thesis/dissertation. *Entrance requirements:* For doctorate, GRE General Test. Additional exam requirements/recommendations for international students: Required—TOEFL (minimum score 550 paper-based; 213 computer-based). Electronic applications accepted.

University at Buffalo, the State University of New York, Graduate School, College of Arts and Sciences, Department of Political Science, Buffalo, NY 14260. Offers MA, PhD. *Faculty:* 16 full-time (4 women), 3 part-time/adjunct (all women). *Students:* 25 full-time (9 women), 15 part-time (5 women); includes 3 Asian, non-Hispanic/Latino, 4 international. Average age 27. 48 applicants, 67% accepted, 14 enrolled. In 2010, 10 master's, 8 doctorates awarded. Terminal master's awarded for partial completion of doctoral program. *Degree requirements:* For master's, thesis or alternative, paper, project; for doctorate, comprehensive exam, thesis/dissertation. *Entrance requirements:* For master's, GRE General Test, minimum GPA of 3.0; for doctorate, GRE General Test, minimum GPA of 3.3. Additional exam requirements/recommendations for international students: Required—TOEFL (minimum score 550 paper-based; 213 computer-based; 79 iBT). *Application deadline:* For fall admission, 6/1 priority date for domestic students, 3/1 for international students; for spring admission, 11/1 priority date for domestic students, 10/1 for international students. Applications are processed on a rolling basis. Application fee: $75. Electronic applications accepted. *Financial support:* In 2010–11, 11 students received support, including 3 fellowships with full tuition reimbursements available (averaging $16,800 per year), 11 teaching assistantships with full tuition reimbursements available (averaging $10,400 per year); research assistantships, career-related internships or fieldwork, Federal Work-Study, health care benefits, tuition waivers (partial), and unspecified assistantships also available. Financial award application deadline: 2/1; financial award applicants required to submit FAFSA. *Faculty research:* American politics, public law, comparative politics, international politics. *Unit head:* Dr. James Campbell, Chairman, 716-645-8452, Fax: 716-645-2166, E-mail: jcampbel@buffalo.edu. *Application contact:* Mary E. OBrien, Graduate Coordinator, 716-645-3441, Fax: 716-645-2166, E-mail: meobrien@buffalo.edu.

The University of Akron, Graduate School, Buchtel College of Arts and Sciences, Department of Political Science, Akron, OH 44325. Offers applied politics (MA); political science (MA); JD/MAP. Part-time programs available. *Faculty:* 12 full-time (2 women), 11 part-time/adjunct (4 women). *Students:* 34 full-time (17 women), 17 part-time (9 women); includes 6 Black or African American, non-Hispanic/Latino; 1 Hispanic/Latino. Average age 29. 25 applicants, 64% accepted, 11 enrolled. In 2010, 14 master's awarded. *Degree requirements:* For master's, comprehensive exam, essay, seminars (political science), portfolio (applied politics). *Entrance requirements:* For master's, GRE, minimum GPA of 3.0, three letters of recommendation (two of which must be from faculty members), statement of purpose. Additional exam requirements/recommendations for international students: Required—TOEFL (minimum score 550 paper-based; 213 computer-based; 79 iBT). *Application deadline:* Applications are processed on a rolling basis. Application fee: $30 ($40 for international students). Electronic applications accepted. *Expenses:* Tuition, state resident: full-time $6800; part-time $378 per credit hour. Tuition, nonresident: full-time $11,644; part-time $647 per credit hour. Required fees: $1265. One-time fee: $30 full-time. *Financial support:* In 2010–11, 16 teaching assistantships with full tuition reimbursements were awarded. *Faculty research:* Public opinion and public policy, applied/electrical politics, international/comparative politics, the politics of criminal justice, conflict management. Total annual research expenditures: $9,809. *Unit head:* Dr. James McHugh, Chair, 330-972-6291, E-mail: mchugh@uakron.edu. *Application contact:* Dr. Steven Brooks, Graduate Director, 330-972-7944, E-mail: sbrooks@uakron.edu.

The University of Alabama, Graduate School, College of Arts and Sciences, Department of Political Science, Tuscaloosa, AL 35487. Offers political science (MA, PhD); public administration (MPA). Part-time programs available. *Faculty:* 12 full-time (4 women), 1 part-time/adjunct (0 women). *Students:* 52 full-time (20 women), 32 part-time (18 women); includes 14 minority (6 Black or African American, non-Hispanic/Latino; 1 American Indian or Alaska Native, non-Hispanic/Latino; 2 Asian, non-Hispanic/Latino; 3 Hispanic/Latino; 2 Two or more races, non-Hispanic/Latino), 4 international. Average age 28. 57 applicants, 51% accepted, 16 enrolled. In 2010, 11 master's, 4 doctorates awarded. Terminal master's awarded for partial completion of doctoral program. *Degree requirements:* For master's, thesis optional; for doctorate, comprehensive exam, thesis/dissertation. *Entrance requirements:* For master's and doctorate, GRE (minimum score: 1000), minimum undergraduate GPA of 3.0. Additional exam requirements/recommendations for international students: Required—TOEFL. *Application deadline:* For fall admission, 6/30 for domestic and international students; for spring admission, 10/15 for domestic and international students. Applications are processed on a rolling basis. Application fee: $50 ($60 for international students). Electronic applications accepted. *Expenses:* Tuition, state resident: full-time $7900. Tuition, nonresident: full-time $20,500. *Financial support:* In 2010–11, 15 students received support, including teaching assistantships with full tuition reimbursements available (averaging $10,908 per year); fellowships, career-related internships or fieldwork and Federal Work-Study also available. Financial award application deadline: 2/15. *Faculty research:* American politics, comparative politics, international relations, public administration, political theory. Total annual research expenditures: $167,549. *Unit head:* Dr. Carol A. Cassel, Chair and Professor, 205-348-5981, Fax: 205-348-5298, E-mail: ccassel@tenhoor.as.ua.edu. *Application contact:* Dr. Joseph Smith, Graduate Advisor, 205-348-3806, Fax: 205-348-5248, E-mail: josmith@bama.ua.edu.

University of Alberta, Faculty of Graduate Studies and Research, Department of Political Science, Edmonton, AB T6G 2E1, Canada. Offers MA, PhD. Part-time programs available. *Degree requirements:* For master's, thesis (for some programs); for doctorate, one foreign language, thesis/dissertation. *Entrance requirements:* Additional exam requirements/recommendations for international students: Required—TOEFL. *Faculty research:* Canadian politics, international relations, globalization, classical and contemporary political theory, gender and politics.

The University of Arizona, College of Social and Behavioral Sciences, Department of Political Science, Tucson, AZ 85721. Offers MA, PhD. *Faculty:* 16 full-time (7 women), 3 part-time/adjunct (1 woman). *Students:* 30 full-time (16 women), 1 (woman) part-time; includes 1 Black or African American, non-Hispanic/Latino; 2 Hispanic/Latino; 1 Two or more races, non-Hispanic/Latino, 3 international. Average age 30. 63 applicants, 6% accepted, 4 enrolled. In 2010, 4 master's, 1 doctorate awarded. Terminal master's awarded for partial completion of doctoral program. *Degree requirements:* For master's, thesis or alternative; for doctorate, variable foreign language requirement, comprehensive exam, thesis/dissertation. *Entrance requirements:* For master's, GRE General Test, minimum GPA of 3.2, 3 letters of recommendation, writing sample; for doctorate, GRE General Test, minimum GPA of 3.2, 3 letters of recommendation, statement of purpose, writing sample. Additional exam requirements/recommendations for international students: Required—TOEFL (minimum score 550 paper-based; 213 computer-based; 79 iBT). *Application deadline:* For fall admission, 1/15 for domestic and international students. Applications are processed on a rolling basis. Application fee: $65. Electronic applications accepted. *Expenses:* Tuition, state resident: full-time $7692. *Financial support:* In 2010–11, 1 research assistantship with full tuition reimbursement (averaging $17,906 per year), 27 teaching assistantships with full tuition reimbursements (averaging $18,850 per year) were awarded; institutionally sponsored loans, scholarships/grants, health care benefits, tuition waivers (full), and unspecified assistantships also available. Financial award application deadline: 3/6. *Faculty research:* Voting behavior, political participation, Soviet domestic and Sino-Soviet relations, presidential leadership and congressional behavior. Total annual research expenditures: $50,514. *Unit head:* Dr. William Dixon, Head, 520-621-5728, Fax: 520-621-5051, E-mail: dixonw@email.arizona.edu. *Application contact:* Victoria Healey, Coordinator, 520-621-7601, Fax: 520-621-5051, E-mail: vhealey@email.arizona.edu.

University of Arkansas, Graduate School, J. William Fulbright College of Arts and Sciences, Department of Political Science, Program in Political Science, Fayetteville, AR 72701-1201. Offers MA. *Students:* 18 full-time (9 women), 3 part-time (2 women); includes 1 minority (Asian, non-Hispanic/Latino), 3 international. 17 applicants, 82% accepted. In 2010, 7 master's awarded. *Degree requirements:* For master's, thesis or alternative. *Entrance requirements:* For master's, GRE General Test. *Application deadline:* For fall admission, 4/1 for international students; for spring admission, 10/1 for international students. Applications are processed on a rolling basis. Application fee: $40 ($50 for international students). Electronic applications accepted. *Financial support:* In 2010–11, 3 research assistantships, 4 teaching assistantships were awarded; fellowships, career-related internships or fieldwork and Federal Work-Study also available. Support available to part-time students. Financial award application deadline: 4/1; financial award applicants required to submit FAFSA. *Unit head:* Dr. Margaret Reid, Graduate Coordinator, 479-575-3356, E-mail: mreid@uark.edu. *Application contact:* Dr. Andrew Dowdle, Graduate Coordinator, 479-575-6445, E-mail: adowdle@uark.edu.

The University of British Columbia, Faculty of Arts and Faculty of Graduate Studies, Department of Political Science, Vancouver, BC V6T 1Z1, Canada. Offers MA, PhD. Part-time programs available. *Degree requirements:* For master's, thesis; for doctorate, comprehensive exam, thesis/dissertation. *Entrance requirements:* For master's, BA in political science; for doctorate, GRE, BA and MA in political science. Additional exam requirements/recommendations for international students: Required—TOEFL (minimum score 580 paper-based; 237 computer-based), TWE (minimum score 5). Electronic applications accepted. Tuition charges are reported in Canadian dollars. *Expenses:* Tuition, area resident: Full-time $4179 Canadian dollars. International tuition: $7344 Canadian dollars full-time. *Faculty research:* Canadian politics, international relations, political theory, comparative politics, public policy.

University of Calgary, Faculty of Graduate Studies, Faculty of Social Sciences, Department of Political Science, Calgary, AB T2N 1N4, Canada. Offers MA, PhD. *Degree requirements:* For master's, thesis; for doctorate, one foreign language, comprehensive exam, thesis/dissertation, prospectus, oral and written candidacy exams. *Entrance requirements:* For master's, minimum GPA of 3.4; for doctorate, minimum GPA of 3.7. Additional exam requirements/recommendations for international students: Required—TOEFL (minimum score 620 paper-based; 260 computer-based). Electronic applications accepted. *Faculty research:* Canadian politics, international relations, comparative politics, theory, public policy.

University of California, Berkeley, Graduate Division, College of Letters and Science, Charles and Louise Travers Department of Political Science, Berkeley, CA 94720-1500. Offers PhD. *Degree requirements:* For doctorate, thesis/dissertation, oral qualifying exams. *Entrance requirements:* For doctorate, GRE General Test, minimum GPA of 3.0, 3 letters of recommendation. Electronic applications accepted.

University of California, Davis, Graduate Studies, Program in Political Science, Davis, CA 95616. Offers MA, PhD. Terminal master's awarded for partial completion of doctoral program. *Degree requirements:* For master's, thesis; for doctorate, thesis/dissertation. *Entrance requirements:* For master's and doctorate, GRE General Test, minimum GPA of 3.0, writing sample. Additional exam requirements/recommendations for international students: Required—TOEFL (minimum score 550 paper-based; 213 computer-based). Electronic applications accepted. *Faculty research:* American government and politics, political theory, comparative politics, international relations, public law.

University of California, Irvine, School of Social Sciences, Department of Political Science, Irvine, CA 92697. Offers political psychology (PhD); political sciences (PhD); public choice (PhD). *Students:* 68 full-time (31 women), 2 part-time (0 women); includes 17 minority (1 Black or African American, non-Hispanic/Latino; 11 Asian, non-Hispanic/Latino; 4 Hispanic/Latino; 1 Two or more races, non-Hispanic/Latino), 2 international. Average age 28. 137 applicants, 18% accepted, 10 enrolled. In 2010, 7 doctorates awarded. *Degree requirements:* For doctorate, thesis/dissertation. *Entrance requirements:* For doctorate, GRE General Test, minimum GPA of 3.0. Additional exam requirements/recommendations for international students: Required—TOEFL (minimum score 550 paper-based; 213 computer-based). *Application deadline:* For fall admission, 1/15 priority date for domestic students, 1/15 for international students. Applications are processed on a rolling basis. Application fee: $80 ($100 for international students). Electronic applications accepted. *Financial support:* Fellowships, research assistantships with full tuition reimbursements, teaching assistantships, institutionally sponsored loans, traineeships, health care benefits, and unspecified assistantships available. Financial award application deadline: 3/1; financial award applicants required to submit FAFSA. *Faculty research:* Political behavior, political economy, international relations. *Unit head:* Prof. Mark Petracca, Chair,

949-824-4012, Fax: 949-824-8762, E-mail: mppetrac@uci.edu. *Application contact:* Wayne Sandholtz, Graduate Director, 949-824-5726, Fax: 949-824-8762, E-mail: wayne.sandholtz@uci.edu.

University of California, Los Angeles, Graduate Division, College of Letters and Science, Department of Political Science, Los Angeles, CA 90095. Offers MA, PhD. *Faculty:* 43 full-time (11 women). *Students:* 129 full-time (53 women); includes 32 minority (6 Black or African American, non-Hispanic/Latino; 12 Asian, non-Hispanic/Latino; 14 Hispanic/Latino), 27 international. Average age 30. 309 applicants, 5% accepted, 15 enrolled. In 2010, 12 master's, 20 doctorates awarded. *Degree requirements:* For master's, comprehensive exam; for doctorate, one foreign language, thesis/dissertation, oral and written qualifying exams. *Entrance requirements:* For master's, GRE General Test, minimum GPA of 3.0, sample of written work; for doctorate, GRE General Test, minimum undergraduate GPA of 3.0, sample of written work. *Application deadline:* For fall admission, 12/15 for domestic and international students. Application fee: $70 ($90 for international students). Electronic applications accepted. *Financial support:* In 2010–11, 85 fellowships with full tuition reimbursements, 33 research assistantships with full tuition reimbursements, 82 teaching assistantships with full tuition reimbursements were awarded; Federal Work-Study, institutionally sponsored loans, scholarships/grants, health care benefits, tuition waivers (full and partial), and unspecified assistantships also available. Financial award application deadline: 3/1; financial award applicants required to submit FAFSA. *Unit head:* Dr. Edmond Keller, Chair, 310-825-2566, E-mail: ekeller@ucla.edu. *Application contact:* Joseph Brown, Graduate Advisor, 310-825-3372, Fax: 310-825-0778, E-mail: joseph@polisci.ucla.edu.

University of California, Riverside, Graduate Division, Department of Political Science, Riverside, CA 92521-0102. Offers MA, PhD. Part-time programs available. Terminal master's awarded for partial completion of doctoral program. *Degree requirements:* For master's, comprehensive exams or thesis; for doctorate, thesis/dissertation, qualifying exams. *Entrance requirements:* For master's and doctorate, GRE General Test, minimum GPA of 3.2. Additional exam requirements/recommendations for international students: Required—TOEFL (minimum score 550 paper-based; 213 computer-based; 80 iBT). Electronic applications accepted. *Faculty research:* American politics, mass political behavior, comparative politics, international relations, political theory.

University of California, San Diego, Office of Graduate Studies, Department of Political Science, La Jolla, CA 92093. Offers Latin American studies (MA); political science (PhD); political science and international affairs (PhD). *Entrance requirements:* For master's and doctorate, GRE General Test. Electronic applications accepted.

University of California, San Diego, Office of Graduate Studies, Graduate School of International Relations and Pacific Studies, La Jolla, CA 92093. Offers economics and international affairs (PhD); Pacific international affairs (MPIA); political science and international affairs (PhD). *Degree requirements:* For master's, one foreign language; for doctorate, thesis/dissertation. *Entrance requirements:* For master's, GMAT or GRE General Test; for doctorate, GRE General Test. Additional exam requirements/recommendations for international students: Required—TOEFL (minimum score 550 paper-based; 213 computer-based). Electronic applications accepted. *Faculty research:* Pacific Rim as system and placement in global relations; studies in international economics, management and finance; analysis of patterns of policymaking in countries of the Pacific.

University of California, Santa Barbara, Graduate Division, College of Letters and Sciences, Division of Social Sciences, Department of Global and International Studies, Santa Barbara, CA 93106-7065. Offers global culture and religion (MA); global government and human rights (MA); political economy, sustainable development, and the environment (MA). *Faculty:* 14 full-time (5 women), 4 part-time/adjunct (1 woman). *Students:* 37 full-time (25 women); includes 6 Asian, non-Hispanic/Latino; 2 Hispanic/Latino; 1 Native Hawaiian or other Pacific Islander, non-Hispanic/Latino. Average age 28. 55 applicants, 42% accepted, 12 enrolled. In 2010, 14 master's awarded. *Degree requirements:* For master's, one foreign language, thesis or alternative, 2 years of a second language. *Entrance requirements:* For master's, GRE, 2 years of a second language with minimum B grade, 3 letters of recommendation, resume/curriculum vitae. Additional exam requirements/recommendations for international students: Required—TOEFL (minimum score 600 paper-based; 80 iBT), IELTS (minimum score 7). *Application deadline:* For fall admission, 12/15 for domestic and international students. Application fee: $70 ($90 for international students). Electronic applications accepted. *Financial support:* In 2010–11, 36 students received support, including 29 fellowships with partial tuition reimbursements available (averaging $6,805 per year), 31 teaching assistantships with partial tuition reimbursements available (averaging $8,175 per year); career-related internships or fieldwork also available. Financial award application deadline: 12/15; financial award applicants required to submit FAFSA. *Faculty research:* Global culture religion, global governance human rights, political economy, environment, sustainable development. Total annual research expenditures: $240,000. *Unit head:* Prof. Giles Gunn, Chair, 805-893-4299, Fax: 805-893-8003, E-mail: ggunn@global.ucsb.edu. *Application contact:* Jessea Gay Marie, Graduate Program Advisor/Internship Assistance Officer, 805-893-4668, Fax: 805-893-8003, E-mail: gd-global@global.ucsb.edu.

University of California, Santa Barbara, Graduate Division, College of Letters and Sciences, Division of Social Sciences, Department of Political Science, Santa Barbara, CA 93106-9420. Offers MA, PhD, MA/PhD. *Faculty:* 18 full-time (8 women), 1 part-time/adjunct (0 women). *Students:* 54 full-time (25 women); includes 1 Black or African American, non-Hispanic/Latino; 8 Asian, non-Hispanic/Latino; 7 Hispanic/Latino. Average age 31. 89 applicants, 28% accepted, 9 enrolled. In 2010, 4 master's, 3 doctorates awarded. Terminal master's awarded for partial completion of doctoral program. *Degree requirements:* For master's, thesis optional, comprehensive exam or field paper; for doctorate, one foreign language, thesis/dissertation, 2 comprehensive exams or 1 exam and field paper. *Entrance requirements:* For master's and doctorate, GRE General Test. Additional exam requirements/recommendations for international students: Required—TOEFL (minimum score 600 paper-based; 100 iBT), IELTS. *Application deadline:* For fall admission, 1/1 for domestic and international students. Application fee: $70 ($90 for international students). Electronic applications accepted. *Financial support:* In 2010–11, 47 students received support, including 31 fellowships with full and partial tuition reimbursements available (averaging $5,459 per year), 1 research assistantship with tuition reimbursement available (averaging $9,099 per year), 41 teaching assistantships with full and partial tuition reimbursements available (averaging $12,738 per year); tuition waivers (full and partial) also available. Financial award application deadline: 1/1; financial award applicants required to submit FAFSA. *Faculty research:* American politics, comparative politics, international relations, political theory. *Unit head:* Prof. Garrett Glasgow, Professor, 805-893-5304, Fax: 805-893-3309, E-mail: glasgow@polsci.ucsb.edu. *Application contact:* Linda James, Administrative Assistant, 805-893-3626, Fax: 805-893-3309, E-mail: james@polsci.ucsb.edu.

University of California, Santa Cruz, Division of Graduate Studies, Division of Social Sciences, Politics Department, Santa Cruz, CA 95064. Offers PhD. *Students:* 26 full-time (15 women), 2 part-time (1 woman); includes 5 minority (2 Black or African American, non-Hispanic/Latino; 3 Hispanic/Latino), 4 international. Average age 30. 40 applicants, 13% accepted, 3 enrolled. In 2010, 1 doctorate awarded. *Degree requirements:* For doctorate, qualifying exam. *Entrance requirements:* For doctorate, GRE. Additional exam requirements/recommendations for international students: Required—TOEFL (minimum score 550 paper-based; 220 computer-based; 83 iBT); Recommended—IELTS (minimum score 8). *Application deadline:* For fall admission, 1/4 for domestic and international students. Application fee: $70 ($90 for international students). Electronic applications accepted. *Financial support:* Fellowships, research assistantships, teaching assistantships, institutionally sponsored loans and tuition waivers available. Financial award applicants required to submit FAFSA. *Faculty research:* Political and social thought, political institutions, political economy, political and social forces. *Unit head:* Cindy Bale, Graduate Program Coordinator, 831-459-4450, E-mail: poliphd@ucsc.edu. *Application contact:* Cindy Bale, Graduate Program Coordinator, 831-459-4450, E-mail: poliphd@ucsc.edu.

University of Central Florida, College of Sciences, Department of Political Science, Orlando, FL 32816. Offers MA. Part-time and evening/weekend programs available. *Faculty:* 25 full-time (8 women), 8 part-time/adjunct (1 woman). *Students:* 35 full-time (13 women), 19 part-time (8 women); includes 3 Black or African American, non-Hispanic/Latino; 5 Hispanic/Latino, 2 international. Average age 27. 49 applicants, 47% accepted, 12 enrolled. In 2010, 16 master's awarded. *Degree requirements:* For master's, comprehensive exam, thesis. *Entrance requirements:* For master's, GRE General Test, minimum GPA of 3.0 in last 60 hours. Additional exam requirements/recommendations for international students: Required—TOEFL. *Application deadline:* For fall admission, 7/15 for domestic students; for spring admission, 12/1 for domestic students. Application fee: $30. Electronic applications accepted. *Expenses:* Tuition, state resident: part-time $256.56 per credit hour. Tuition, nonresident: part-time $1011.52 per credit hour. Part-time tuition and fees vary according to program. *Financial support:* In 2010–11, 9 students received support, including 2 fellowships with partial tuition reimbursements available (averaging $2,800 per year), 7 teaching assistantships with partial tuition reimbursements available (averaging $6,800 per year); career-related internships or fieldwork, Federal Work-Study, institutionally sponsored loans, tuition waivers (partial), and unspecified assistantships also available. Financial award application deadline: 3/1; financial award applicants required to submit FAFSA. *Faculty research:* Environment, presidential campaigning, term limits for elected officials. *Unit head:* Dr. Roger Handberg, Chair, 407-823-2608, Fax: 407-823-0051, E-mail: handberg@mail.ucf.edu. *Application contact:* Dr. Roger Handberg, Chair, 407-823-2608, Fax: 407-823-0051, E-mail: handberg@mail.ucf.edu.

University of Central Oklahoma, College of Graduate Studies and Research, College of Liberal Arts, Department of Political Science, Program in Political Science, Edmond, OK 73034-5209. Offers MA. Part-time programs available. *Entrance requirements:* Additional exam requirements/recommendations for international students: Required—TOEFL (minimum score 550 paper-based; 213 computer-based). Electronic applications accepted. *Faculty research:* U. S. Congress.

University of Chicago, Division of Social Sciences, Department of Political Science, Chicago, IL 60637-1513. Offers PhD. *Degree requirements:* For doctorate, one foreign language, thesis/dissertation, exam, qualifying paper. *Entrance requirements:* For doctorate, GRE General Test. Additional exam requirements/recommendations for international students: Required—TOEFL, IELTS (minimum score 7). Electronic applications accepted. *Faculty research:* Political philosophy, international political economy, strategic studies, public policy and race relations, comparative politics (China, Middle East, Soviet Union, Africa, India, Japan).

University of Cincinnati, Graduate School, McMicken College of Arts and Sciences, Department of Political Science, Cincinnati, OH 45221. Offers MA, PhD. Terminal master's awarded for partial completion of doctoral program. *Degree requirements:* For master's, thesis (for some programs); for doctorate, thesis/dissertation. *Entrance requirements:* For master's and doctorate, GRE General Test, GRE Subject Test. Additional exam requirements/recommendations for international students: Required—TOEFL. Electronic applications accepted. *Faculty research:* International security, methodology, American politics, comparative politics.

University of Colorado Boulder, Graduate School, College of Arts and Sciences, Department of Political Science, Boulder, CO 80309. Offers international affairs (MA); political science (MA, PhD); public policy (MA). *Faculty:* 27 full-time (9 women). *Students:* 65 full-time (31 women), 2 part-time (0 women); includes 7 minority (2 American Indian or Alaska Native, non-Hispanic/Latino; 2 Asian, non-Hispanic/Latino; 3 Hispanic/Latino), 7 international. Average age 30. 184 applicants, 15 enrolled. In 2010, 23 master's, 6 doctorates awarded. Terminal master's awarded for partial completion of doctoral program. *Degree requirements:* For master's, comprehensive exam, thesis; for doctorate, one foreign language, thesis/dissertation. *Entrance requirements:* For master's, GRE General Test, minimum undergraduate GPA of 3.0; for doctorate, GRE General Test, minimum GPA of 3.5 (undergraduate), 3.0 (graduate). *Application deadline:* For fall admission, 12/31 priority date for domestic students, 12/31 for international students. Application fee: $50 ($60 for international students). *Financial support:* In 2010–11, 10 fellowships (averaging $2,060 per year), 41 research assistantships (averaging $12,087 per year) were awarded; Federal Work-Study also available. Financial award application deadline: 12/31. *Faculty research:* American government and politics, comparative politics, international relations, public policy, law and politics, political philosophy, empirical theory and methodology. Total annual research expenditures: $92,305.

University of Colorado Denver, College of Liberal Arts and Sciences, Department of Political Science, Denver, CO 80217. Offers MA. Part-time and evening/weekend programs available. *Faculty:* 10 full-time (2 women), 3 part-time/adjunct (0 women). *Students:* 61 full-time (32 women), 36 part-time (20 women); includes 6 Black or African American, non-Hispanic/Latino; 6 American Indian or Alaska Native, non-Hispanic/Latino; 2 Asian, non-Hispanic/Latino; 10 Hispanic/Latino. Average age 32. 33 applicants, 82% accepted, 21 enrolled. In 2010, 23 master's awarded. *Degree requirements:* For master's, thesis or alternative, project or thesis, minimum of 33 credit hours. *Entrance requirements:* For master's, 18 hours of course work in political science; minimum GPA of 3.0 (3.2 preferred); statement of purpose; academic writing sample. Additional exam requirements/recommendations for international students: Required—TOEFL (minimum score 525 paper-based; 197 computer-based). *Application deadline:* For fall admission, 4/1 for domestic students; for spring admission, 10/1 for domestic students. Application fee: $50 ($75 for international students). Electronic applications accepted. *Expenses:* Tuition, state resident: full-time $7332; part-time $355 per credit hour. Tuition, nonresident: full-time $18,990; part-time $1055 per credit hour. Required fees: $998. Tuition and fees vary according to course level, course load, degree level, campus/location, program, reciprocity agreements and student level. *Financial support:* Research assistantships, teaching assistantships, Federal Work-Study, scholarships/grants, and unspecified assistantships available. Financial award application deadline: 4/1; financial award applicants required to submit FAFSA. *Faculty research:* Indigenous peoples in the international legal and political arena; political developments in Europe and the former Soviet Union; early Chinese industrialization, modern Chinese political and economic development, and human rights; congressional oversight and congressional-executive relations. *Unit head:* Jana Everett, Chair, 303-556-3515, Fax: 303-556-4861, E-mail: jana.everett@ucdenver.edu. *Application contact:* Political Science Department, 303-556-3556.

University of Colorado Denver, School of Public Affairs, Program in Public Affairs and Administration, Denver, CO 80127. Offers public administration (MPA), including domestic violence, emergency management and homeland security, environmental policy, management and law, homeland security and defense, local government, nonprofit management, public administration; public affairs (PhD). *Accreditation:* NASPAA. Part-time and evening/weekend programs available. Postbaccalaureate distance learning degree programs offered (no on-campus study). *Faculty:* 19 full-time (9 women), 14 part-time/adjunct (5 women). *Students:* 317 full-time (181 women), 167 part-time (100 women); includes 15 Black or African American, non-Hispanic/Latino; 2 American Indian or Alaska Native, non-Hispanic/Latino; 18 Asian, non-Hispanic/Latino; 29 Hispanic/Latino; 1 Two or more races, non-Hispanic/Latino, 36 international. Average age 30. 270 applicants, 66% accepted, 118 enrolled. In 2010, 119 master's, 4 doctorates awarded. *Degree requirements:* For master's, thesis or alternative, 36-39 credit hours; for doctorate, comprehensive exam, thesis/dissertation, minimum of 66 semester hours, including at least 30 hours of doctoral dissertation credits. *Entrance requirements:* For master's and doctorate, GRE, resume, essay, transcripts, recommendations. Additional exam requirements/recommendations for international students: Required—TOEFL (minimum score 550 paper-based; 223 computer-based). *Application deadline:* For fall admission, 2/1 for domestic students; for spring admission, 10/15 priority date for domestic students. Application fee: $50 ($75 for international students). Electronic applications accepted. *Expenses:* Contact institution. *Financial support:* Fellowships with partial tuition reimbursements, research assistantships with partial tuition reimbursements, teaching assistantships with partial tuition reimbursements, Federal Work-Study and scholarships/grants available. Support available to part-time students. Financial award application deadline: 4/1; financial award applicants required to submit FAFSA. *Faculty research:* Housing, education and the social and economic issues of

Political Science

University of Colorado Denver (continued)

vulnerable populations; nonprofit governance and management; education finance, effectiveness and reform; P-20 (preschool through graduate school) education initiatives; municipal government accountability. *Unit head:* Dr. Mary Guy, Program Director, 303-315-2007, Fax: 303-315-2229, E-mail: mary.guy@ucdenver.edu. *Application contact:* Annie Davies, Director of Marketing, Community Outreach and Alumni Affairs, 303-315-2896, Fax: 303-315-2229, E-mail: annie.davies@ucdenver.edu.

University of Connecticut, Graduate School, College of Liberal Arts and Sciences, Department of Political Science, Storrs, CT 06269. Offers MA, PhD. Terminal master's awarded for partial completion of doctoral program. *Degree requirements:* For master's, comprehensive exam; for doctorate, 2 foreign languages, thesis/dissertation. *Entrance requirements:* For master's and doctorate, GRE General Test. Additional exam requirements/recommendations for international students: Required—TOEFL (minimum score 550 paper-based; 213 computer-based). Electronic applications accepted.

University of Dallas, Braniff Graduate School of Liberal Arts, Institute of Philosophic Studies, Doctoral Program in Politics, Irving, TX 75062-4736. Offers PhD. *Degree requirements:* For doctorate, 2 foreign languages, comprehensive exam, thesis/dissertation. *Entrance requirements:* For doctorate, GRE General Test. Additional exam requirements/recommendations for international students: Required—TOEFL. *Expenses:* Tuition: Full-time $7500; part-time $720 per credit hour. Required fees: $500; $60 per credit hour. $300 per semester. One-time fee: $150. Tuition and fees vary according to program and student level. *Faculty research:* Classical, medieval, and modern political philosophy; American political thought and institutions; politics and literature.

University of Dallas, Braniff Graduate School of Liberal Arts, Master's Program in Politics, Irving, TX 75062-4736. Offers M Pol, MA. Part-time programs available. *Degree requirements:* For master's, one foreign language, comprehensive exam, thesis. *Entrance requirements:* For master's, GRE General Test. Additional exam requirements/recommendations for international students: Required—TOEFL. *Expenses:* Tuition: Full-time $7500; part-time $720 per credit hour. Required fees: $500; $60 per credit hour. $300 per semester. One-time fee: $150. Tuition and fees vary according to program and student level. *Faculty research:* Classical, medieval, and modern political philosophy; American political thought and institutions; politics and literature.

University of Delaware, College of Arts and Sciences, Department of Political Science and International Relations, Newark, DE 19716. Offers MA, PhD. Terminal master's awarded for partial completion of doctoral program. *Degree requirements:* For master's, research paper; for doctorate, one foreign language, comprehensive exam, thesis/dissertation. *Entrance requirements:* For master's and doctorate, GRE General Test, minimum GPA of 3.2 in major, 3.0 overall. Additional exam requirements/recommendations for international students: Required—TOEFL (minimum score 600 paper-based). Electronic applications accepted. *Faculty research:* Social constructivism. international migration, international security, democratization, human rights.

University of Florida, Graduate School, College of Liberal Arts and Sciences, Department of Political Science, Gainesville, FL 32611. Offers international development policy and administration (MA, Certificate); international relations (MA, MAT); political campaigning (MA, Certificate); political science (MA, MAT, PhD); public affairs (MA, Certificate); JD/MA. *Faculty:* 27 full-time (9 women), 3 part-time/adjunct (1 woman). *Students:* 115 full-time (43 women), 23 part-time (13 women); includes 6 Black or African American, non-Hispanic/Latino; 3 Asian, non-Hispanic/Latino; 10 Hispanic/Latino, 25 international. Average age 27. 185 applicants, 48% accepted, 35 enrolled. In 2010, 28 master's, 11 doctorates awarded. Terminal master's awarded for partial completion of doctoral program. *Degree requirements:* For master's, variable foreign language requirement, comprehensive exam (for some programs), thesis or alternative, internship (for some programs); for doctorate, variable foreign language requirement, comprehensive exam, thesis/dissertation. *Entrance requirements:* For master's and doctorate, GRE General Test, minimum GPA of 3.0. Additional exam requirements/recommendations for international students: Required—TOEFL (minimum score 550 paper-based; 213 computer-based; 80 iBT), IELTS (minimum score 6). *Application deadline:* For fall admission, 1/1 priority date for domestic students, 1/1 for international students. Applications are processed on a rolling basis. Application fee: $30. Electronic applications accepted. *Expenses:* Tuition, state resident: full-time $10,915.92. Tuition, nonresident: full-time $28,309. *Financial support:* In 2010–11, 104 students received support, including 50 fellowships, 13 research assistantships (averaging $15,878 per year), 41 teaching assistantships (averaging $16,099 per year); career-related internships or fieldwork, Federal Work-Study, institutionally sponsored loans, and unspecified assistantships also available. Financial award application deadline: 1/15; financial award applicants required to submit FAFSA. *Faculty research:* American political institutions, comparative democratization, political theory and judgment, religion and politics, theories of international relations. *Unit head:* Dr. Michael D. Martinez, Chair, 352-273-2363, Fax: 352-392-8127, E-mail: martinez@ufl.edu. *Application contact:* Dr. Dan O'Neill, Interim Graduate Coordinator, 352-273-2386, Fax: 352-392-8127, E-mail: doneill@ufl.edu.

University of Georgia, School of Public and International Affairs, Program in Political Science, Athens, GA 30602. Offers MA, PhD. *Faculty:* 17 full-time (3 women). *Students:* 80 full-time (29 women), 15 part-time (3 women); includes 2 Black or African American, non-Hispanic/Latino; 1 Asian, non-Hispanic/Latino; 1 Two or more races, non-Hispanic/Latino, 19 international. 177 applicants, 48% accepted, 44 enrolled. In 2010, 13 master's, 10 doctorates awarded. *Degree requirements:* For master's, one foreign language, thesis; for doctorate, one foreign language, thesis/dissertation. *Entrance requirements:* For master's and doctorate, GRE General Test. *Application deadline:* For fall admission, 7/1 priority date for domestic students; for spring admission, 11/15 for domestic students. Application fee: $50. Electronic applications accepted. *Expenses:* Tuition, state resident: full-time $7200; part-time $344 per credit hour. Tuition, nonresident: full-time $21,900; part-time $944 per credit hour. Tuition and fees vary according to course load and program. *Financial support:* Fellowships, research assistantships, teaching assistantships, unspecified assistantships available. *Unit head:* Dr. John A. Maltese, Head, 706-542-4147, E-mail: jmaltese@uga.edu. *Application contact:* Dr. Audrey A. Haynes, Graduate Coordinator, 706-542-2933, Fax: 706-542-4421, E-mail: polaah@uga.edu.

University of Guelph, Graduate Studies, College of Social and Applied Human Sciences, Department of Political Science, Guelph, ON N1G 2W1, Canada. Offers comparative politics (MA); international development (MA); political science (MA); public policy and public administration (MA); the Americas (Canada emphasis) (MA). MA in public policy and public administration offered in collaboration with Department of Political Science of McMaster University. *Degree requirements:* For master's, thesis or paper. *Entrance requirements:* For master's, minimum B average during previous 2 years of course work, 4 year Honours Degree in Political Science. Additional exam requirements/recommendations for international students: Required—TOEFL. Electronic applications accepted. *Faculty research:* Political ethics, constitutional power.

University of Hawaii at Manoa, Graduate Division, College of Social Sciences, Department of Political Science, Honolulu, HI 96822. Offers MA, PhD. Part-time programs available. *Faculty:* 30 full-time (12 women), 2 part-time/adjunct (1 woman). *Students:* 87 full-time (38 women), 31 part-time (17 women); includes 44 minority (10 Asian, non-Hispanic/Latino; 5 Hispanic/Latino; 16 Native Hawaiian or other Pacific Islander, non-Hispanic/Latino; 13 Two or more races, non-Hispanic/Latino), 36 international. Average age 34. 143 applicants, 35% accepted, 34 enrolled. In 2010, 16 master's, 13 doctorates awarded. Terminal master's awarded for partial completion of doctoral program. *Degree requirements:* For master's, thesis optional; for doctorate, comprehensive exam, thesis/dissertation. *Entrance requirements:* Additional exam requirements/recommendations for international students: Required—TOEFL (minimum score 540 paper-based; 207 computer-based; 76 iBT), IELTS (minimum score 5). *Application deadline:* For fall admission, 2/1 for domestic students, 1/15 for international students. Application fee: $60. *Financial support:* In 2010–11, 19 fellowships (averaging $5,008 per year), 9 research assistantships (averaging $16,175 per year), 13 teaching assistantships (averaging $15,466 per year) were awarded; career-related internships or fieldwork, Federal Work-Study, and institutionally sponsored loans also available. Support available to part-time students. Financial award application deadline: 3/1. *Faculty research:* Asia/Pacific, political economy, human rights, futures, postmodernism. Total annual research expenditures: $24,000. *Application contact:* Debora Halbert, Graduate Chair, 808-956-8357, Fax: 808-956-6877, E-mail: halbert@hawaii.edu.

University of Houston, College of Liberal Arts and Social Sciences, Department of Political Science, Houston, TX 77204. Offers political science (MA, PhD); public administration (MA). Part-time programs available. *Faculty:* 19 full-time (3 women), 7 part-time/adjunct (1 woman). *Students:* 61 full-time (29 women), 63 part-time (33 women); includes 12 Black or African American, non-Hispanic/Latino; 1 American Indian or Alaska Native, non-Hispanic/Latino; 3 Asian, non-Hispanic/Latino; 10 Hispanic/Latino; 2 Two or more races, non-Hispanic/Latino, 21 international. Average age 32. 128 applicants, 40% accepted, 32 enrolled. In 2010, 12 master's, 6 doctorates awarded. Terminal master's awarded for partial completion of doctoral program. *Degree requirements:* For master's, thesis optional; for doctorate, thesis/dissertation. *Entrance requirements:* For master's and doctorate, GRE. Additional exam requirements/recommendations for international students: Required—TOEFL (minimum score 550 paper-based; 213 computer-based; 79 iBT). *Application deadline:* For fall admission, 2/15 for domestic and international students; for spring admission, 10/1 for domestic and international students. Application fee: $0 ($75 for international students). *Expenses:* Tuition, state resident: full-time $8592; part-time $358 per credit hour. Tuition, nonresident: full-time $16,032; part-time $668 per credit hour. Required fees: $2889. Tuition and fees vary according to course load and program. *Financial support:* In 2010–11, 3 fellowships with full tuition reimbursements (averaging $2,500 per year), 1 research assistantship with full tuition reimbursement (averaging $10,400 per year), 26 teaching assistantships with full tuition reimbursements (averaging $11,168 per year) were awarded; career-related internships or fieldwork, Federal Work-Study, institutionally sponsored loans, scholarships/grants, health care benefits, and unspecified assistantships also available. Support available to part-time students. Financial award application deadline: 2/1. *Faculty research:* American politics, political theory, judicial process, public policy, comparative politics. *Unit head:* Dr. Gregory Weiher, Chairperson, 713-743-3890, Fax: 713-743-3927, E-mail: gweiher@uh.edu. *Application contact:* Edward Manouelian, Graduate Advisor, 713-743-3939, E-mail: eemanoue@central.uh.edu.

University of Idaho, College of Graduate Studies, College of Letters, Arts and Social Sciences, Department of Political Science and Public Affairs Research, Program in Political Science, Moscow, ID 83844-2282. Offers MA, PhD. *Students:* 8 full-time, 4 part-time. Average age 26. In 2010, 2 master's, 1 doctorate awarded. *Degree requirements:* For doctorate, thesis/dissertation. *Entrance requirements:* For master's, minimum GPA of 2.8; for doctorate, minimum undergraduate GPA of 2.8, 3.0 graduate. *Application deadline:* For fall admission, 8/1 for domestic students; for spring admission, 12/15 for domestic students. Applications are processed on a rolling basis. Application fee: $60. Electronic applications accepted. *Expenses:* Tuition, nonresident: part-time $580 per credit. Required fees: $306 per credit. *Financial support:* Applicants required to submit FAFSA. *Unit head:* Dr. Donald W. Crowley, Chair, 208-885-6328. *Application contact:* Dr. Donald W. Crowley, Chair, 208-885-6328.

University of Illinois at Chicago, Graduate College, College of Liberal Arts and Sciences, Department of Political Science, Chicago, IL 60607-7128. Offers MA, PhD. Part-time programs available. Terminal master's awarded for partial completion of doctoral program. *Degree requirements:* For master's, thesis or comprehensive exam. *Entrance requirements:* For master's, GRE General Test, minimum GPA of 3.0. Additional exam requirements/recommendations for international students: Required—TOEFL. Electronic applications accepted. *Faculty research:* Policy analysis/national urban politics and policy, electoral behavior.

University of Illinois at Springfield, Graduate Programs, College of Public Affairs and Administration, Department of Political Science, Springfield, IL 62703-5407. Offers MA. Part-time and evening/weekend programs available. *Degree requirements:* For master's, comprehensive exam, participant/observer case study, or thesis. *Entrance requirements:* Additional exam requirements/recommendations for international students: Required—TOEFL (minimum score 500 paper-based; 176 computer-based; 61 iBT). Electronic applications accepted. *Expenses:* Tuition, state resident: full-time $6774; part-time $282.25 per credit hour. Tuition, nonresident: full-time $15,078; part-time $628.25 per credit hour. Required fees: $15.25 per credit hour. $492 per term.

University of Illinois at Urbana–Champaign, Graduate College, College of Liberal Arts and Sciences, Department of Political Science, Champaign, IL 61820. Offers MA, PhD, PhD/JD. *Faculty:* 28 full-time (11 women), 1 part-time/adjunct (0 women). *Students:* 70 full-time (32 women), 2 part-time (1 woman); includes 9 minority (3 Black or African American, non-Hispanic/Latino; 5 Asian, non-Hispanic/Latino; 1 Hispanic/Latino), 9 international. 138 applicants, 8% accepted, 10 enrolled. In 2010, 9 master's, 4 doctorates awarded. *Entrance requirements:* For master's, GRE General Test, minimum GPA of 3.0; for doctorate, GRE General Test, writing sample, minimum GPA of 3.0. Additional exam requirements/recommendations for international students: Required—TOEFL (minimum score 79 iBT). *Application deadline:* Applications are processed on a rolling basis. Application fee: $75 ($90 for international students). Electronic applications accepted. *Financial support:* In 2010–11, 50 fellowships, 27 research assistantships, 43 teaching assistantships were awarded; tuition waivers (full and partial) also available. *Unit head:* William T. Bernhard, Head, 217-333-2602, Fax: 217-244-5712, E-mail: bernhard@illinois.edu. *Application contact:* Brenda R. Stamm, Office Administrator, 217-333-3880, Fax: 217-244-5712, E-mail: stamm@illinois.edu.

The University of Iowa, Graduate College, College of Liberal Arts and Sciences, Department of Political Science, Iowa City, IA 52242-1316. Offers MA, PhD. *Degree requirements:* For master's, thesis optional, exam; for doctorate, comprehensive exam, thesis/dissertation. *Entrance requirements:* For master's and doctorate, GRE General Test, minimum GPA of 3.0. Additional exam requirements/recommendations for international students: Required—TOEFL (minimum score 600 paper-based; 250 computer-based; 100 iBT). Electronic applications accepted.

The University of Kansas, Graduate Studies, College of Liberal Arts and Sciences, Department of Political Science, Lawrence, KS 66045. Offers MA, PhD. Part-time programs available. *Faculty:* 23 full-time (9 women). *Students:* 51 full-time (15 women), 8 part-time (4 women); includes 4 minority (1 Black or African American, non-Hispanic/Latino; 1 Asian, non-Hispanic/Latino; 2 Hispanic/Latino), 13 international. Average age 30. 62 applicants, 63% accepted, 11 enrolled. In 2010, 7 master's, 1 doctorate awarded. Terminal master's awarded for partial completion of doctoral program. *Degree requirements:* For master's, comprehensive exam, thesis or alternative; for doctorate, comprehensive exam, thesis/dissertation, research and responsible scholarship skills. *Entrance requirements:* For master's, GRE General Test, 3 letters of recommendation, curriculum vitae, transcripts, personal statement; for doctorate, GRE General Test, 3 letters of recommendation, transcripts, personal statement, curriculum vitae. Additional exam requirements/recommendations for international students: Required—TOEFL. *Application deadline:* For fall admission, 4/15 priority date for domestic and international students. Application fee: $55 ($65 for international students). Electronic applications accepted. *Expenses:* Tuition, state resident: full-time $7092; part-time $295.50 per credit hour. Tuition, nonresident: full-time $16,590; part-time $691.25 per credit hour. Required fees: $858; $71.49 per credit hour. Tuition and fees vary according to course load, campus/location and program. *Financial support:* Fellowships with full tuition reimbursements, research assistantships, teaching assistantships with full tuition reimbursements, scholarships/grants, health care benefits, and unspecified assistantships available. Financial award application deadline: 1/9. *Faculty research:* American politics, comparative politics, international relations, public policy, political theory. *Unit head:* Don Haider-Markel, Chair, 785-864-9034, Fax: 785-864-5700, E-mail: dhmarkel@ku.edu. *Application contact:* Prof. Mark Joslyn, Graduate Director, 785-864-9046, Fax: 785-864-5700, E-mail: mjoz@ku.edu.

University of Kentucky, Graduate School, College of Arts and Sciences, Program in Political Science, Lexington, KY 40506-0032. Offers MA, PhD. *Degree requirements:* For master's, comprehensive exam, thesis optional; for doctorate, comprehensive exam, thesis/dissertation. *Entrance requirements:* For master's, GRE General Test, minimum undergraduate GPA of 2.75; for doctorate, GRE General Test, minimum graduate GPA of 3.0. Additional exam requirements/recommendations for international students: Required—TOEFL (minimum score 550 paper-based; 213 computer-based). Electronic applications accepted. *Faculty research:* International political economy, critical policy studies, regional conflict and integration, race and American politics, media studies.

University of Lethbridge, School of Graduate Studies, Lethbridge, AB T1K 3M4, Canada. Offers accounting (MScM); addictions counseling (M Sc); agricultural biotechnology (M Sc); agricultural studies (M Sc, MA); anthropology (MA); archaeology (MA); art (MA, MFA); biochemistry (M Sc); biological sciences (M Sc); biomolecular science (PhD); biosystems and biodiversity (PhD); Canadian studies (MA); chemistry (M Sc); computer science (M Sc); computer science and geographical information science (M Sc); counseling psychology (M Ed); dramatic arts (MA); earth, space, and physical science (PhD); economics (MA); educational leadership (M Ed); English (MA); environmental science (M Sc); evolution and behavior (PhD); exercise science (M Sc); finance (MScM); French (MA); French/German (MA); French/Spanish (MA); general education (M Ed); general management (MScM); geography (M Sc, MA); German (MA); health science (M Sc); history (MA); human resource management and labour relations (MScM); individualized multidisciplinary (M Sc, MA); information systems (MScM); international management (MScM); kinesiology (M Sc, MA); management (M Sc, MA); marketing (MScM); mathematics (M Sc); music (M Mus, MA); Native American studies (MA); neuroscience (M Sc, PhD); new media (MA); nursing (M Sc); philosophy (MA); physics (M Sc); policy and strategy (MScM); political science (MA); psychology (M Sc, MA); religious studies (MA); social sciences (MA); sociology (MA); theatre and dramatic arts (MFA); theoretical and computational science (PhD); urban and regional studies (MA); women's studies (MA). Part-time and evening/weekend programs available. *Degree requirements:* For doctorate, comprehensive exam, thesis/dissertation. *Entrance requirements:* For master's, GMAT (M Sc in management), bachelor's degree in related field, minimum GPA of 3.0 during previous 20 graded semester courses, 2 years teaching or related experience (M Ed); for doctorate, master's degree, minimum graduate GPA of 3.5. Additional exam requirements/recommendations for international students: Required—TOEFL. *Faculty research:* Movement and brain plasticity, gibberellin physiology, photosynthesis, carbon cycling, molecular properties of main-group ring components.

University of Louisville, Graduate School, College of Arts and Sciences, Department of Political Science, Louisville, KY 40292-0001. Offers MA. Part-time and evening/weekend programs available. *Faculty:* 13 full-time (5 women), 3 part-time/adjunct (0 women). *Students:* 26 full-time (10 women), 11 part-time (5 women); includes 1 Black or African American, non-Hispanic/Latino; 1 Asian, non-Hispanic/Latino; 1 Hispanic/Latino, 3 international. Average age 27. 31 applicants, 55% accepted, 14 enrolled. In 2010, 9 master's awarded. *Degree requirements:* For master's, thesis or directed research paper. *Entrance requirements:* For master's, GRE General Test, 2 academic letters of recommendation. Additional exam requirements/recommendations for international students: Required—TOEFL. *Application deadline:* For fall admission, 8/1 for domestic and international students; for winter admission, 8/1 for domestic students; for spring admission, 12/1 for domestic and international students. Applications are processed on a rolling basis. Application fee: $30 ($40 for international students). *Expenses:* Tuition, state resident: full-time $9144; part-time $508 per credit hour. Tuition, nonresident: full-time $19,026; part-time $1057 per credit hour. Tuition and fees vary according to program and reciprocity agreements. *Financial support:* Research assistantships available. Financial award application deadline: 6/1. *Faculty research:* International law, politics of east Asia, comparative political systems, environmental policy, international relations. Total annual research expenditures: $45,000. *Unit head:* Dr. Ronald K. Vogel, Chair, 502-852-3312, Fax: 502-852-7923, E-mail: ron.vogel@louisvile.edu. *Application contact:* Libby Leggett, Director, Graduate Admissions, 502-852-3101, Fax: 502-852-6536, E-mail: gradadm@louisville.edu.

The University of Manchester, School of Social Sciences, Manchester, United Kingdom. Offers ethnographic documentary (M Phil); interdisciplinary study of culture (PhD); philosophy (PhD); politics (PhD); social anthropology (PhD); social anthropology with visual media (PhD); social change (PhD); social statistics (PhD); sociology (PhD); visual anthropology (M Phil).

University of Manitoba, Faculty of Graduate Studies, Faculty of Arts, Department of Political Studies, Winnipeg, MB R3T 2N2, Canada. Offers political studies (MA); public administration (MPA). *Degree requirements:* For master's, one foreign language, thesis or alternative.

University of Maryland, College Park, Academic Affairs, College of Behavioral and Social Sciences, Department of Government and Politics, College Park, MD 20742. Offers American politics (PhD); comparative politics (PhD); international relations (PhD); political economy (PhD); political theory (PhD). Part-time and evening/weekend programs available. *Faculty:* 46 full-time (14 women), 14 part-time/adjunct (4 women). *Students:* 131 full-time (58 women), 16 part-time (4 women); includes 5 Black or African American, non-Hispanic/Latino; 2 American Indian or Alaska Native, non-Hispanic/Latino; 8 Asian, non-Hispanic/Latino; 4 Hispanic/Latino, 23 international. 283 applicants, 14% accepted, 23 enrolled. In 2010, 12 doctorates awarded. *Degree requirements:* For doctorate, comprehensive exam, thesis/dissertation, written exams in 2 fields. *Entrance requirements:* For doctorate, GRE General Test, minimum GPA of 3.5, writing sample. Additional exam requirements/recommendations for international students: Required—TOEFL. *Application deadline:* For fall admission, 2/1 for domestic and international students. Applications are processed on a rolling basis. Application fee: $75. Electronic applications accepted. *Expenses:* Tuition, state resident: part-time $471 per credit hour. Tuition, nonresident: part-time $1016 per credit hour. Required fees: $337 per term. *Financial support:* In 2010–11, 6 fellowships with full and partial tuition reimbursements (averaging $19,085 per year), 73 teaching assistantships (averaging $15,935 per year) were awarded; research assistantships, career-related internships or fieldwork, Federal Work-Study, scholarships/grants, and unspecified assistantships also available. Support available to part-time students. Financial award applicants required to submit FAFSA. *Faculty research:* International development/conflict, international security, post-communist society, public service, dynamics of conflict and conflict resolution. Total annual research expenditures: $1.9 million. *Unit head:* Dr. Mark Lichbach, Chairman, 301-405-4156, Fax: 301-314-9690, E-mail: mlichbac@umd.edu. *Application contact:* Dean of Graduate School, 301-405-0358, Fax: 301-314-9305.

University of Massachusetts Amherst, Graduate School, College of Social and Behavioral Sciences, Department of Political Science, Amherst, MA 01003. Offers MA, PhD. Part-time programs available. *Faculty:* 36 full-time (15 women). *Students:* 30 full-time (15 women), 19 part-time (6 women); includes 2 minority (1 Black or African American, non-Hispanic/Latino; 1 Hispanic/Latino), 15 international. Average age 30. 107 applicants, 22% accepted, 6 enrolled. In 2010, 9 master's, 8 doctorates awarded. Terminal master's awarded for partial completion of doctoral program. *Degree requirements:* For master's, one foreign language, thesis or alternative; for doctorate, one foreign language, comprehensive exam, thesis/dissertation. *Entrance requirements:* For master's and doctorate, GRE General Test, writing sample, 3 letters of recommendation. Additional exam requirements/recommendations for international students: Required—TOEFL (minimum score 550 paper-based; 213 computer-based; 80 iBT), IELTS (minimum score 6.5). *Application deadline:* For fall admission, 1/15 for domestic and international students. Applications are processed on a rolling basis. Application fee: $50 ($65 for international students). Electronic applications accepted. *Expenses:* Tuition, state resident: full-time $2640. Required fees: $8282. One-time fee: $357 full-time. *Financial support:* In 2010–11, 12 research assistantships with full tuition reimbursements (averaging $7,348 per year), 32 teaching assistantships with full tuition reimbursements (averaging $12,976 per year) were awarded; fellowships, career-related internships or fieldwork, Federal Work-Study, scholarships/grants, traineeships, health care benefits, tuition waivers (full), and unspecified assistantships also available. Support available to part-time students. Financial award application deadline: 1/15; financial award applicants required to submit FAFSA. *Unit head:* Dr. Frederic C. Schaffer, Graduate Program Director, 413-545-0410, Fax: 413-545-3349. *Application contact:* Jean M. Ames, Supervisor of Admissions, 413-545-0722, Fax: 413-577-0010, E-mail: gradadm@grad.umass.edu.

University of Massachusetts Boston, Office of Graduate Studies, Division of Continuing Education and John W. McCormack Graduate School of Policy Studies, Program in Women in Politics and Government, Boston, MA 02125-3393. Offers Certificate. Part-time and evening/weekend programs available. *Degree requirements:* For Certificate, practicum, final project. *Entrance requirements:* For degree, interview, minimum GPA of 2.75.

University of Massachusetts Boston, Office of Graduate Studies, John W. McCormack Graduate School of Policy Studies, Boston, MA 02125-3393. Offers gerontology (MA, MS, PhD, Certificate), including gerontology (MS, PhD, Certificate), gerontology research (MA), management in aging services (MA); public affairs (MS); public policy (PhD); women in politics and government (Certificate). Certificate program in women in politics and government offered jointly with Division of Continuing Education. Part-time and evening/weekend programs available. *Degree requirements:* For doctorate, thesis/dissertation; for Certificate, practicum, final project. *Entrance requirements:* For doctorate, GRE General Test; for Certificate, interview, minimum GPA of 2.5.

University of Memphis, Graduate School, College of Arts and Sciences, Department of Political Science, Memphis, TN 38152. Offers MA. *Faculty:* 5 full-time (2 women). *Students:* 14 full-time (10 women), 2 part-time (1 woman); includes 1 Black or African American, non-Hispanic/Latino; 1 Asian, non-Hispanic/Latino. Average age 27. 10 applicants, 100% accepted, 3 enrolled. In 2010, 8 master's awarded. *Degree requirements:* For master's, comprehensive exam, thesis or alternative, internship. *Entrance requirements:* For master's, GRE General Test or GMAT, minimum GPA of 3.0. *Application deadline:* For fall admission, 8/1 for domestic students; for spring admission, 12/1 for domestic students. Applications are processed on a rolling basis. Application fee: $35 ($60 for international students). *Financial support:* In 2010–11, 10 students received support; research assistantships with full tuition reimbursements available, Federal Work-Study, scholarships/grants, and unspecified assistantships available. Financial award application deadline: 2/15; financial award applicants required to submit FAFSA. *Faculty research:* Political philosophy, comparative judicial studies, conflict studies, legislative studies, foreign policy. *Unit head:* Dr. Robert Blanton, Interim Chair, 901-678-2395, Fax: 901-678-2983, E-mail: rblanton@memphis.edu. *Application contact:* Dr. David Richards, Graduate Studies Coordinator, 901-678-3348, Fax: 901-678-2983, E-mail: drich1@memphis.edu.

University of Miami, Graduate School, College of Arts and Sciences, Department of Political Science, Coral Gables, FL 33124. Offers MPA, MPA/MPH. Part-time and evening/weekend programs available. *Degree requirements:* For master's, thesis optional. *Entrance requirements:* For master's, GRE General Test. Additional exam requirements/recommendations for international students: Required—TOEFL.

University of Michigan, Horace H. Rackham School of Graduate Studies, College of Literature, Science, and the Arts, Department of Political Science, Ann Arbor, MI 48109. Offers political science (AM, PhD); social work and political science (PhD); JD/AM. Terminal master's awarded for partial completion of doctoral program. *Degree requirements:* For master's, thesis; for doctorate, comprehensive exam, thesis/dissertation, oral defense of dissertation, preliminary exam. *Entrance requirements:* For master's and doctorate, GRE General Test. Additional exam requirements/recommendations for international students: Required—TOEFL. Electronic applications accepted. *Expenses:* Tuition, state resident: full-time $17,784; part-time $1116 per credit hour. Tuition, nonresident: full-time $35,944; part-time $2125 per credit hour. International tuition: $35,994 full-time. Required fees: $95 per semester. Tuition and fees vary according to course load, degree level and program. *Faculty research:* Political theory, American politics, world politics, comparative politics, methodology, public law.

University of Minnesota, Twin Cities Campus, Graduate School, College of Liberal Arts, Department of Political Science, Minneapolis, MN 55455-0213. Offers PhD. *Degree requirements:* For doctorate, thesis/dissertation, 1 foreign language or statistics. *Entrance requirements:* For doctorate, GRE. Additional exam requirements/recommendations for international students: Required—TOEFL; Recommended—IELTS. Electronic applications accepted. *Faculty research:* American politics, comparative politics, international relations, political theory, research methodology.

University of Mississippi, Graduate School, College of Liberal Arts, Department of Political Science, Oxford, University, MS 38677. Offers MA, PhD. *Students:* 23 full-time (7 women), 1 part-time (0 women); includes 4 minority (all Black or African American, non-Hispanic/Latino), 3 international. In 2010, 2 master's, 4 doctorates awarded. *Degree requirements:* For doctorate, thesis/dissertation. *Entrance requirements:* For master's, GRE General Test, minimum GPA of 3.0; for doctorate, GRE General Test. Additional exam requirements/recommendations for international students: Required—TOEFL. *Application deadline:* For fall admission, 2/15 for domestic students; for spring admission, 10/1 for domestic students. Applications are processed on a rolling basis. Application fee: $25. Electronic applications accepted. *Financial support:* Scholarships/grants available. Financial award application deadline: 3/1; financial award applicants required to submit FAFSA. *Unit head:* Dr. Richard G. Forgette, Chairman, 662-915-7401, Fax: 662-915-7808, E-mail: rforgett@olemiss.edu. *Application contact:* Dr. Christy M. Wyandt, Associate Dean, 662-915-7474, Fax: 662-915-7577, E-mail: cwyandt@olemiss.edu.

University of Missouri, Graduate School, College of Arts and Sciences, Department of Political Science, Columbia, MO 65211. Offers MA, PhD. Terminal master's awarded for partial completion of doctoral program. *Degree requirements:* For doctorate, one foreign language, comprehensive exam, thesis/dissertation. *Entrance requirements:* For master's, GRE General Test (minimum combined score 1000 Verbal and Quantitative), minimum GPA of 3.0 in last 60 hours and in political science courses; at least 12 hours of upper-level course work in political science; for doctorate, GRE General Test (minimum combined score 1200 Verbal and Quantitative), minimum GPA of 3.0 in last 60 hours and in political science courses; at least 12 hours of upper-level course work in political science. Additional exam requirements/recommendations for international students: Required—TOEFL (minimum score 570 paper-based; 240 computer-based; 88 iBT). Electronic applications accepted. *Faculty research:* American politics, comparative politics, international relations, public policy and administration.

University of Missouri–Kansas City, College of Arts and Sciences, Department of Political Science, Kansas City, MO 64110-2499. Offers MA, PhD. PhD (interdisciplinary) offered through the School of Graduate Studies. Part-time and evening/weekend programs available. *Faculty:* 6 full-time (2 women), 3 part-time/adjunct (0 women). *Students:* 2 full-time (1 woman), 14 part-time (3 women); includes 3 minority (2 Asian, non-Hispanic/Latino; 1 Hispanic/Latino). Average age 34. 12 applicants, 50% accepted, 5 enrolled. In 2010, 6 master's awarded. Terminal master's awarded for partial completion of doctoral program. *Degree requirements:* For master's, thesis optional; for doctorate, thesis/dissertation. *Entrance requirements:* For master's, GRE, minimum GPA of 3.0, course work in political science, 2 letters of recommendation; for doctorate, GRE, minimum GPA of 3.0, MA in political science or related area, writing sample. Additional exam requirements/recommendations for international students: Required—TOEFL (minimum score 550 paper-based; 213 computer-based; 80 iBT). *Application deadline:* For fall admission, 4/1 priority date for domestic and international students; for spring admission, 11/1 priority date for domestic and international students. Applications are processed on a rolling basis. Application fee: $45 ($50 for international students). Electronic applications accepted. *Expenses:* Tuition, state resident: full-time $5522.40; part-time $306.80 per credit hour. Tuition, nonresident: full-time $7128; part-time $792 per credit hour. Required fees: $261.15 per term. *Financial support:* In 2010–11, 3 research assistantships (averaging $9,678 per year), 1 teaching assistantship with partial tuition reimbursement (averaging $29,400 per year) were awarded; career-related internships or fieldwork and institutionally sponsored loans also available. Financial award application deadline: 3/1; financial award applicants required to submit FAFSA. *Faculty research:* Sex and gender, Chinese politics, voting behavior, politics of Presidency and social security, public law. *Unit head:* Dr. Harris Mirkin, Chair, 816-235-2792, Fax: 816-235-5594, E-mail: mirkinh@umkc.edu. *Application contact:* Dr. Harris Mirkin, Chair, 816-235-2792, Fax: 816-235-5594, E-mail: mirkinh@umkc.edu.

Political Science

University of Missouri–St. Louis, College of Arts and Sciences, Department of Political Science, St. Louis, MO 63121. Offers American politics (MA); comparative politics (MA); international politics (MA); political process and behavior (MA); political science (PhD); public administration and public policy (MA); urban and regional politics (MA). Part-time and evening/weekend programs available. *Faculty:* 18 full-time (7 women), 1 (woman) part-time/adjunct. *Students:* 15 full-time (7 women), 39 part-time (21 women); includes 13 minority (8 Black or African American, non-Hispanic/Latino; 2 American Indian or Alaska Native, non-Hispanic/Latino; 3 Asian, non-Hispanic/Latino), 3 international. Average age 35. 43 applicants, 47% accepted, 10 enrolled. In 2010, 4 master's, 5 doctorates awarded. Terminal master's awarded for partial completion of doctoral program. *Degree requirements:* For master's, thesis optional; for doctorate, thesis/dissertation. *Entrance requirements:* For master's, GRE General Test, 2 letters of recommendation; for doctorate, GRE General Test, 3 letters of recommendation. Additional exam requirements/recommendations for international students: Required—TOEFL (minimum score 550 paper-based; 213 computer-based). *Application deadline:* For fall admission, 2/15 priority date for domestic and international students; for spring admission, 10/15 priority date for domestic and international students. Applications are processed on a rolling basis. Application fee: $35 ($40 for international students). Electronic applications accepted. *Expenses:* Tuition, state resident: full-time $5522; part-time $306.80 per credit hour. Tuition, nonresident: full-time $14,253; part-time $792.10 per credit hour. Required fees: $658; $49 per credit hour. One-time fee: $12. Tuition and fees vary according to program. *Financial support:* In 2010–11, 8 research assistantships with full and partial tuition reimbursements (averaging $1,110 per year), 6 teaching assistantships with full and partial tuition reimbursements (averaging $10,800 per year) were awarded; fellowships, career-related internships or fieldwork also available. Support available to part-time students. Financial award application deadline: 3/15; financial award applicants required to submit FAFSA. *Faculty research:* Public policy, urban politics and administration, American government. *Unit head:* Dr. Kenneth Thomas, Director of Graduate Studies, 314-516-5521, Fax: 314-516-5268, E-mail: umslpolisci@umsl.edu. *Application contact:* 314-516-5458, Fax: 314-516-6996, E-mail: gradadm@umsl.edu.

University of Missouri–St. Louis, College of Business Administration, Program in Business Administration, St. Louis, MO 63121. Offers accounting (MBA); business administration (Certificate); finance (MBA); human resource management (Certificate); information systems (MBA); local government (Certificate); logistics and supply chain management (MBA, Certificate); marketing (MBA); marketing management (Certificate); operations management (MBA). *Accreditation:* AACSB. Part-time and evening/weekend programs available. *Faculty:* 30 full-time (5 women), 11 part-time/adjunct (2 women). *Students:* 132 full-time (57 women), 306 part-time (122 women); includes 55 minority (21 Black or African American, non-Hispanic/Latino; 20 Asian, non-Hispanic/Latino; 11 Hispanic/Latino; 1 Native Hawaiian or other Pacific Islander, non-Hispanic/Latino; 2 Two or more races, non-Hispanic/Latino), 6 international. Average age 30. 219 applicants, 60% accepted, 88 enrolled. In 2010, 114 master's, 9 other advanced degrees awarded. *Entrance requirements:* For master's, GMAT, 2 letters of recommendation. Additional exam requirements/recommendations for international students: Required—TOEFL (minimum score 550 paper-based; 213 computer-based). *Application deadline:* For fall admission, 7/1 for domestic students; for spring admission, 11/1 for domestic students. Applications are processed on a rolling basis. Application fee: $35 ($40 for international students). Electronic applications accepted. *Expenses:* Tuition, state resident: full-time $5522; part-time $306.80 per credit hour. Tuition, nonresident: full-time $14,253; part-time $792.10 per credit hour. Required fees: $658; $49 per credit hour. One-time fee: $12. Tuition and fees vary according to program. *Financial support:* In 2010–11, 22 research assistantships with full and partial tuition reimbursements (averaging $7,414 per year), 4 teaching assistantships with full and partial tuition reimbursements (averaging $13,950 per year) were awarded; career-related internships or fieldwork, Federal Work-Study, and institutionally sponsored loans also available. Support available to part-time students. Financial award application deadline: 4/1; financial award applicants required to submit FAFSA. *Faculty research:* Human resources, strategic management, marketing strategy, consumer behavior product development, advertising. *Unit head:* Karl Kottemann, Assistant Director, 314-516-5885, Fax: 314-516-6420, E-mail: mba@umsl.edu. *Application contact:* 314-516-5458, Fax: 314-516-6996, E-mail: gradadm@umsl.edu.

The University of Montana, Graduate School, College of Arts and Sciences, Department of Political Science, Program in Political Science, Missoula, MT 59812-0002. Offers MA. *Degree requirements:* For master's, thesis. *Entrance requirements:* For master's, GRE General Test.

University of Nebraska at Omaha, Graduate Studies, College of Arts and Sciences, Department of Political Science, Omaha, NE 68182. Offers MS. Part-time and evening/weekend programs available. *Faculty:* 9 full-time (3 women). *Students:* 5 full-time (2 women), 8 part-time (3 women); includes 2 minority (1 American Indian or Alaska Native, non-Hispanic/Latino; 1 Hispanic/Latino). Average age 31. 6 applicants, 33% accepted, 1 enrolled. In 2010, 8 master's awarded. *Degree requirements:* For master's, comprehensive exam, thesis (for some programs). *Entrance requirements:* For master's, 15 undergraduate political science hours, minimum undergraduate GPA of 3.0, 2 letters of recommendation. Additional exam requirements/recommendations for international students: Required—TOEFL (minimum score 500 paper-based; 173 computer-based; 61 iBT). *Application deadline:* For fall admission, 3/15 priority date for domestic students; for spring admission, 11/1 priority date for domestic students. Applications are processed on a rolling basis. Application fee: $45. Electronic applications accepted. *Financial support:* In 2010–11, 7 students received support; fellowships, research assistantships, teaching assistantships, Federal Work-Study, scholarships/grants, tuition waivers (partial), and unspecified assistantships available. Financial award application deadline: 3/1; financial award applicants required to submit FAFSA. *Unit head:* Dr. Randall Adkins, Chairperson, 402-554-2624. *Application contact:* Dr. Jody Neathery-Castro, Student Contact, 402-554-2624.

University of Nebraska–Lincoln, Graduate College, College of Arts and Sciences, Department of Political Science, Lincoln, NE 68588. Offers political science (MA, PhD); public policy analysis (Graduate Certificate). *Degree requirements:* For master's, thesis optional; for doctorate, variable foreign language requirement, comprehensive exam, thesis/dissertation. *Entrance requirements:* For master's and doctorate, GRE General Test, writing sample. Additional exam requirements/recommendations for international students: Required—TOEFL (minimum score 600 paper-based; 250 computer-based). Electronic applications accepted. *Faculty research:* Public policy; comparative politics; international relations; political theory, behavior, and methodology; American politics.

University of Nevada, Las Vegas, Graduate College, College of Liberal Arts, Department of Political Science, Las Vegas, NV 89154-5029. Offers ethics and policy studies (MA); political science (MA, PhD). Part-time programs available. *Faculty:* 13 full-time (3 women), 1 (woman) part-time/adjunct. *Students:* 12 full-time (6 women), 13 part-time (5 women); includes 15 minority (2 Black or African American, non-Hispanic/Latino; 2 Asian, non-Hispanic/Latino; 3 Hispanic/Latino; 1 Native Hawaiian or other Pacific Islander, non-Hispanic/Latino; 7 Two or more races, non-Hispanic/Latino), 3 international. Average age 33. 20 applicants, 55% accepted, 7 enrolled. In 2010, 7 master's awarded. *Degree requirements:* For master's, comprehensive exam (for some programs), thesis (for some programs); for doctorate, comprehensive exam, thesis/dissertation, oral examination. *Entrance requirements:* For master's and doctorate, GRE General Test. Additional exam requirements/recommendations for international students: Required—TOEFL (minimum score 550 paper-based; 213 computer-based; 80 iBT), IELTS (minimum score 7). *Application deadline:* For fall admission, 2/1 priority date for domestic and international students; for spring admission, 10/1 priority date for domestic and international students. Applications are processed on a rolling basis. Application fee: $60 ($95 for international students). Electronic applications accepted. *Expenses:* Tuition, area resident: Part-time $239.50 per credit. Tuition, state resident: part-time $239.50 per credit. Tuition, nonresident: part-time $503 per credit. Required fees: $108 per semester. Tuition and fees vary according to course load, program and reciprocity agreements. *Financial support:* In 2010–11, 10 students received support, including 10 research assistantships with partial tuition reimbursements available (averaging $10,725 per year); institutionally sponsored loans, scholarships/grants, health care benefits, and unspecified assistantships also available. Financial award application deadline: 3/1. *Faculty research:* Ancient political philosophy, international security, globalization, Islamic law, informal education in Senegal. Total annual research expenditures: $8,892. *Unit head:* Dr. John Tuman, Chair/Associate Professor, 702-895-5258, Fax: 702-895-1065, E-mail: john.tuman@unlv.edu. *Application contact:* Graduate College Admissions Evaluator, 702-895-3320, Fax: 702-895-4180, E-mail: gradcollege@unlv.edu.

University of Nevada, Reno, Graduate School, College of Liberal Arts, Department of Political Science, Program in Political Science, Reno, NV 89557. Offers MA, PhD. Terminal master's awarded for partial completion of doctoral program. *Degree requirements:* For master's, comprehensive exam, oral exam/thesis or professional paper; for doctorate, thesis/dissertation, 2 field exams, oral exam. *Entrance requirements:* For master's, GRE General Test, GMAT, LSAT, minimum GPA of 2.75; for doctorate, GRE General Test, GMAT, LSAT, minimum GPA of 3.0. Additional exam requirements/recommendations for international students: Required—TOEFL (minimum score 500 paper-based; 173 computer-based; 61 iBT), IELTS (minimum score 6). Electronic applications accepted. *Expenses:* Tuition, state resident: full-time $2219; part-time $246 per credit. Tuition, nonresident: part-time $510 per credit. International tuition: $9009 full-time. Required fees: $59 per term. One-time fee: $101. Tuition and fees vary according to course load. *Faculty research:* Analysis of political processes, institutions, and policies.

University of New Brunswick Fredericton, School of Graduate Studies, Faculty of Arts, Department of Political Science, Fredericton, NB E3B 5A3, Canada. Offers MA. Part-time programs available. *Faculty:* 7 full-time (2 women). *Students:* 10 full-time (4 women), 2 part-time (1 woman). In 2010, 3 master's awarded. *Degree requirements:* For master's, thesis (for some programs). *Entrance requirements:* For master's, minimum cumulative GPA of 3.3, 42 credit hours of course work in political science. *Application deadline:* For fall admission, 3/1 priority date for domestic students. Application fee: $50 Canadian dollars. Electronic applications accepted. *Expenses:* Tuition, area resident: Full-time $3708; part-time $927 per term. International tuition: $6300 full-time. Required fees: $50 per term. *Financial support:* In 2010–11, 2 fellowships, 3 research assistantships (averaging $12,540 per year), 3 teaching assistantships (averaging $3,145 per year) were awarded. *Faculty research:* Political theory, public policy, gender and politics, global political economy and Canadian politics. *Unit head:* Dr. Joanne Wright, Director of Graduate Studies, 506-458-7422, Fax: 506-453-4755, E-mail: jwright@unb.ca. *Application contact:* Deborah Sloan, Graduate Secretary, 506-453-4826, Fax: 506-453-4755, E-mail: dsloan@unb.ca.

University of New Hampshire, Graduate School, College of Liberal Arts, Department of Political Science, Program in Political Science, Durham, NH 03824. Offers MA. Part-time programs available. *Faculty:* 15 full-time. *Students:* 16 full-time (4 women), 10 part-time (4 women); includes 3 American Indian or Alaska Native, non-Hispanic/Latino. Average age 33. 24 applicants, 71% accepted, 12 enrolled. In 2010, 9 master's awarded. *Degree requirements:* For master's, thesis. *Entrance requirements:* For master's, GRE General Test. Additional exam requirements/recommendations for international students: Required—TOEFL (minimum score 550 paper-based; 213 computer-based; 80 iBT). *Application deadline:* For fall admission, 6/1 priority date for domestic students, 4/1 for international students; for spring admission, 12/1 for domestic students. Applications are processed on a rolling basis. Application fee: $65. Electronic applications accepted. *Financial support:* In 2010–11, 2 students received support, including 1 teaching assistantship; fellowships, research assistantships, career-related internships or fieldwork, Federal Work-Study, scholarships/grants, and tuition waivers (full and partial) also available. Support available to part-time students. Financial award application deadline: 2/15. *Unit head:* Dr. Dante Scala, Chairperson, 603-862-3225. *Application contact:* Janis Marshal, Administrative Assistant, 603-862-1750, E-mail: mpa.ma.political.science.grad@unh.edu.

University of New Mexico, Graduate School, College of Arts and Sciences, Department of Political Science, Albuquerque, NM 87131-2039. Offers MA, PhD. Part-time programs available. *Faculty:* 25 full-time (9 women), 15 part-time/adjunct (2 women). *Students:* 30 full-time (13 women), 7 part-time (3 women); includes 1 Black or African American, non-Hispanic/Latino; 1 Asian, non-Hispanic/Latino; 8 Hispanic/Latino, 5 international. Average age 32. 55 applicants, 22% accepted, 4 enrolled. In 2010, 3 master's, 1 doctorate awarded. Terminal master's awarded for partial completion of doctoral program. *Degree requirements:* For master's, comprehensive exam, thesis optional; for doctorate, comprehensive exam, thesis/dissertation, field research paper, minimum cumulative GPA of 3.5. *Entrance requirements:* For master's and doctorate, GRE General Test, 3 letters of recommendation, writing sample, letter of intent. Additional exam requirements/recommendations for international students: Required—TOEFL. *Application deadline:* For fall admission, 1/15 priority date for domestic and international students. Application fee: $50. Electronic applications accepted. *Expenses:* Tuition, state resident: full-time $5991; part-time $251 per credit hour. Tuition, nonresident: full-time $14,405; part-time $800.20 per credit hour. Tuition and fees vary according to course level, course load, program and reciprocity agreements. *Financial support:* In 2010–11, 31 students received support, including 4 fellowships (averaging $5,228 per year), 13 teaching assistantships with tuition reimbursements available (averaging $7,414 per year); scholarships/grants, health care benefits, and unspecified assistantships also available. Financial award application deadline: 1/15; financial award applicants required to submit FAFSA. *Faculty research:* Latin American politics, American politics, comparative politics, public policy, international relations, methodology. Total annual research expenditures: $250,000. *Unit head:* Dr. Mark Peceny, Chair, 505-277-5104, Fax: 505-277-2821, E-mail: markpec@unm.edu. *Application contact:* Sarah Marinelli, Graduate Program Assistant, 505-277-5104, Fax: 505-288-2821, E-mail: smarin12@unm.edu.

University of New Orleans, Graduate School, College of Liberal Arts, Department of Political Science, New Orleans, LA 70148. Offers political science (MA, PhD); public administration (MPA). Evening/weekend programs available. *Degree requirements:* For master's, one foreign language, thesis or alternative; for doctorate, one foreign language, thesis/dissertation. *Entrance requirements:* For master's, GRE General Test; for doctorate, GRE General Test, GRE Subject Test. Additional exam requirements/recommendations for international students: Required—TOEFL (minimum score 550 paper-based; 213 computer-based; 79 iBT). Electronic applications accepted. *Faculty research:* Judicial politics, public policy, voting rights, Southern politics, presidential-congressional relations.

The University of North Carolina at Chapel Hill, Graduate School, College of Arts and Sciences, Department of Political Science, Chapel Hill, NC 27599. Offers Latin American studies (Certificate); political science (MA, PhD); trans-Atlantic studies (MA). *Degree requirements:* For master's, comprehensive exam; for doctorate, one foreign language, comprehensive exam, thesis/dissertation. *Entrance requirements:* For master's and doctorate, GRE General Test, minimum GPA of 3.0 recommended. Electronic applications accepted.

The University of North Carolina at Charlotte, Graduate School, College of Arts and Sciences, Department of Sociology, Charlotte, NC 28223-0001. Offers health research (MA); mathematical sociology and quantitative methods (MA); organizations, occupations, and work (MA); political sociology (MA); race and gender (MA); social psychology (MA); social theory (MA); sociology of education (MA); stratification (MA). Part-time and evening/weekend programs available. *Faculty:* 18 full-time (10 women). *Students:* 11 full-time (7 women), 14 part-time (8 women); includes 6 minority (4 Black or African American, non-Hispanic/Latino; 2 Asian, non-Hispanic/Latino). Average age 29. 20 applicants, 60% accepted, 8 enrolled. In 2010, 2 master's awarded. *Degree requirements:* For master's, thesis or alternative, thesis or comprehensive exam. *Entrance requirements:* For master's, GRE or MAT, minimum GPA of 3.0 in last 2 years, 2.75 overall. Additional exam requirements/recommendations for international students: Required—TOEFL (minimum score 557 paper-based; 220 computer-based; 83 iBT). *Application deadline:* For fall admission, 7/1 for domestic students, 5/1 for international students; for spring admission, 11/1 for domestic students, 10/1 for international students. Applications are processed on a rolling basis. Application fee: $55. Electronic applications accepted. *Expenses:* Tuition, state resident: full-time $3464. Tuition, nonresident: full-time $14,297. Required fees: $2094. Tuition and fees vary according to course load. *Financial support:* In 2010–11, 6 students received support, including 1 fellowship (averaging $60,000 per year), 1 research assistantship (averaging $9,000 per year), 1 teaching assistantship (averaging $9,000 per year); career-related internships or fieldwork, institutionally sponsored loans, scholarships/grants, and unspecified assistantships also available. Support available to part-time students. Financial award application deadline: 4/1; financial award applicants required to submit FAFSA. *Faculty research:* Social psychology, sociology of education, social gerontology, quantitative methodology, medical sociology. Total annual research expenditures: $61,382. *Unit head:* Dr. Lisa Rachotte, Chair, 704-687-2288, Fax: 704-687-3091, E-mail: lrashott@uncc.edu. *Application contact:* Kathy B. Giddings, Director of Graduate Admissions, 704-687-5503, Fax: 704-687-3279, E-mail: gradadm@uncc.edu.

The University of North Carolina at Greensboro, Graduate School, College of Arts and Sciences, Department of Political Science, Greensboro, NC 27412-5001. Offers nonprofit management (Certificate); public affairs (MPA); urban and economic development (Certificate). *Accreditation:* NASPAA. *Degree requirements:* For master's, comprehensive exam. *Entrance requirements:* For master's, GRE General Test. Additional exam requirements/recommendations for international students: Required—TOEFL. Electronic applications accepted. *Faculty research:* U.S. Constitution, Canadian parliament, public management, ethical challenge of public service.

University of Northern British Columbia, Office of Graduate Studies, Prince George, BC V2N 4Z9, Canada. Offers business administration (Diploma); community health science (M Sc); disability management (MA); education (M Ed); first nations studies (MA); gender studies (MA); history (MA); interdisciplinary studies (MA); international studies (MA); mathematical, computer and physical sciences (M Sc); natural resources and environmental studies (M Sc, MA, MNRES, PhD); political science (MA); psychology (M Sc, PhD); social work (MSW). Part-time and evening/weekend programs available. Postbaccalaureate distance learning degree programs offered (no on-campus study). *Degree requirements:* For master's, thesis; for doctorate, thesis/dissertation. *Entrance requirements:* For master's, GRE, minimum B average in undergraduate course work; for doctorate, candidacy exam, minimum A average in graduate course work.

University of Northern Iowa, Graduate College, College of Social and Behavioral Sciences, Department of Political Science, Cedar Falls, IA 50614. Offers MA. *Entrance requirements:* For master's, minimum GPA of 3.0. Additional exam requirements/recommendations for international students: Required—TOEFL (minimum score 500 paper-based; 180 computer-based; 61 iBT). *Unit head:* Dr. Michael Licari, Head, 319-273-6048, Fax: 319-273-7103, E-mail: michael.licari@uni.edu. *Application contact:* Laurie S. Russell, Record Analyst, 319-273-2623, Fax: 319-273-6792, E-mail: laurie.russell@uni.edu.

University of North Texas, Toulouse Graduate School, College of Arts and Sciences, Department of Political Science, Denton, TX 76203. Offers MA, MS, PhD. Part-time and evening/weekend programs available. *Degree requirements:* For master's, variable foreign language requirement, thesis; for doctorate, variable foreign language requirement, comprehensive exam, thesis/dissertation. *Entrance requirements:* For master's, GRE General Test, minimum GPA of 3.0, 3 letters of recommendation; for doctorate, GRE General Test, minimum GPA of 3.0, 3 letters of recommendation, statement of interest. Additional exam requirements/recommendations for international students: Recommended—TOEFL (minimum score 550 paper-based; 213 computer-based; 79 iBT). *Expenses:* Tuition, state resident: full-time $4298; part-time $239 per credit hour. Tuition, nonresident: full-time $10,782; part-time $549 per credit hour. Required fees: $1292; $270 per credit hour. *Financial support:* Fellowships with full tuition reimbursements, research assistantships with partial tuition reimbursements, teaching assistantships with partial tuition reimbursements, career-related internships or fieldwork, Federal Work-Study, and institutionally sponsored loans available. Financial award applicants required to submit FAFSA. *Faculty research:* Political parties, international conflict, judicial politics, comparative politics. *Application contact:* Graduate Advisor, 940-565-2315, Fax: 940-565-4818, E-mail: paolino@unt.edu.

University of Notre Dame, Graduate School, College of Arts and Letters, Division of Social Science, Department of Political Science, Notre Dame, IN 46556. Offers PhD. *Degree requirements:* For doctorate, one foreign language, comprehensive exam, thesis/dissertation, candidacy exam. *Entrance requirements:* For doctorate, GRE General Test. Additional exam requirements/recommendations for international students: Required—TOEFL (minimum score 600 paper-based; 250 computer-based; 80 iBT). Electronic applications accepted. *Faculty research:* American government, comparative politics, international relations, political theory.

University of Oklahoma, College of Arts and Sciences, Department of Political Science, Program in Political Science, Norman, OK 73019-0390. Offers MA, PhD. *Students:* 31 full-time (12 women), 21 part-time (7 women); includes 3 minority (2 Asian, non-Hispanic/Latino; 1 Hispanic/Latino), 11 international. Average age 31. 40 applicants, 60% accepted, 11 enrolled. In 2010, 4 master's, 6 doctorates awarded. Terminal master's awarded for partial completion of doctoral program. *Degree requirements:* For master's, thesis or alternative; for doctorate, thesis/dissertation, language or quantitative techniques. *Entrance requirements:* For master's and doctorate, GRE General Test, 3 letters of recommendation. Additional exam requirements/recommendations for international students: Required—TOEFL (minimum score 600 paper-based; 250 computer-based; 79 iBT). *Application deadline:* For fall admission, 2/1 for domestic and international students; for spring admission, 10/15 for domestic students, 9/1 for international students. Applications are processed on a rolling basis. Application fee: $40 ($90 for international students). Electronic applications accepted. *Expenses:* Tuition, state resident: full-time $3893; part-time $162.20 per credit hour. Tuition, nonresident: full-time $14,167; part-time $590.30 per credit hour. Required fees: $2523; $94.60 per credit hour. Tuition and fees vary according to course load and degree level. *Financial support:* In 2010–11, 52 students received support. Unspecified assistantships and research assistantships with tuition waivers and health care benefits available. *Faculty research:* State formation and failing states, policy agenda setting in democratic institutions, civil rights and civil liberties in the U. S., humanitarian intervention, individual policy preferences under conditions of scientific uncertainty. *Unit head:* Greg Russell, Academic Chair, 405-325-5517, Fax: 405-325-0718, E-mail: grussell@ou.edu. *Application contact:* Mitchell P. Smith, Graduate Programs Director, 405-325-8893, Fax: 405-325-0718, E-mail: mps@ou.edu.

University of Oregon, Graduate School, College of Arts and Sciences, Department of Political Science, Eugene, OR 97403. Offers MA, MS, PhD. Terminal master's awarded for partial completion of doctoral program. *Degree requirements:* For master's, thesis or alternative; for doctorate, thesis/dissertation. *Entrance requirements:* For master's and doctorate, GRE General Test, minimum GPA of 3.0. Additional exam requirements/recommendations for international students: Required—TOEFL. *Faculty research:* Public policy, public choice, comparative politics, political economy, international relations.

University of Ottawa, Faculty of Graduate and Postdoctoral Studies, Faculty of Social Sciences, Department of Political Studies, Ottawa, ON K1N 6N5, Canada. Offers MA, PhD. *Degree requirements:* For master's, thesis or alternative, fluency in English and French; for doctorate, comprehensive exam, thesis/dissertation. *Entrance requirements:* For master's, honors bachelor's degree or equivalent, minimum B average; for doctorate, master's degree, minimum B+ average. Electronic applications accepted. *Faculty research:* Political thought and analysis of ideologies, Canadian and Québécois policies, international and comparative policies.

University of Pennsylvania, School of Arts and Sciences, Graduate Group in Political Science, Philadelphia, PA 19104. Offers AM, PhD, MGA/AM. *Faculty:* 34 full-time (11 women), 3 part-time/adjunct (1 woman). *Students:* 62 full-time (26 women), 8 part-time (4 women); includes 3 Black or African American, non-Hispanic/Latino; 1 Hispanic/Latino, 20 international. 342 applicants, 5% accepted, 9 enrolled. In 2010, 6 master's, 6 doctorates awarded. Terminal master's awarded for partial completion of doctoral program. *Degree requirements:* For doctorate, one foreign language, thesis/dissertation. *Entrance requirements:* For master's and doctorate, GRE General Test. Additional exam requirements/recommendations for international students: Required—TOEFL. *Application deadline:* For fall admission, 12/1 priority date for domestic

students. Application fee: $70. Electronic applications accepted. *Expenses:* Tuition: Full-time $25,660; part-time $4758 per course. Required fees: $2152; $270 per course. Tuition and fees vary according to course load, degree level and program. *Financial support:* Fellowships, research assistantships, teaching assistantships, institutionally sponsored loans, scholarships/grants, traineeships, health care benefits, and unspecified assistantships available. Financial award application deadline: 12/15. *Unit head:* Edward Mansfield, Department Chair, Political Science, 215-898-7657, E-mail: emansfie@sas.upenn.edu. *Application contact:* Pat Kozak, Administrative Coordinator, 215-898-5625, E-mail: pkozak@sas.upenn.edu.

University of Pittsburgh, Graduate School of Public and International Affairs, International Affairs Division, Pittsburgh, PA 15260. Offers global political economy (MPIA); human security (MPIA); security and intelligence studies (MPIA); JD/MPIA; MBA/MPIA; MID/MPIA; MPA/MPIA; MSIS/MPIA. Part-time and evening/weekend programs available. *Faculty:* 30 full-time (12 women), 67 part-time/adjunct (25 women). *Students:* 187 full-time (93 women), 26 part-time (7 women); includes 17 minority (9 Black or African American, non-Hispanic/Latino; 1 American Indian or Alaska Native, non-Hispanic/Latino; 4 Asian, non-Hispanic/Latino; 3 Hispanic/Latino), 17 international. Average age 25. 325 applicants, 73% accepted, 100 enrolled. In 2010, 92 master's awarded. *Degree requirements:* For master's, thesis optional, internship, capstone seminar. *Entrance requirements:* For master's, GRE General Test, 3 letters of recommendation, resume; minimum GPA of 3.2 (recommended). Additional exam requirements/recommendations for international students: Required—TOEFL (minimum score 550 paper-based; 213 computer-based), TWE (minimum score 4); Recommended—IELTS (minimum score 7). *Application deadline:* For fall admission, 3/1 for domestic students, 1/15 for international students; for spring admission, 11/1 for domestic students, 8/1 for international students. Application fee: $50. Electronic applications accepted. *Expenses:* Tuition, state resident: full-time $17,304; part-time $701 per credit. Tuition, nonresident: full-time $29,554; part-time $1210 per credit. Required fees: $740; $214 per term. Tuition and fees vary according to program. *Financial support:* In 2010–11, 44 students received support. Scholarships/grants, tuition waivers (full and partial), unspecified assistantships, and student employment available. Financial award application deadline: 2/1. *Faculty research:* International political economy, international security and intelligence, transnational organized crime, international trade, international finance, globalization, terrorism, multinational corporations and the global economy. Total annual research expenditures: $892,349. *Unit head:* Dr. Martin Staniland, Director, International Affairs and International Development Divisions, 412-648-7656, Fax: 412-648-2605, E-mail: mstan@pitt.edu. *Application contact:* Kelly C. McDevitt, Graduate Enrollment Counselor, 412-648-7640, Fax: 412-648-7641, E-mail: mcdevitt@pitt.edu.

University of Pittsburgh, Graduate School of Public and International Affairs, Public Policy and Management Program for Mid-Career Professionals, Pittsburgh, PA 15260. Offers development planning (MPPM); international development (MPPM); international political economy (MPPM); international security studies (MPPM); management of non profit organizations (MPPM); metropolitan management and regional development (MPPM); policy analysis and evaluation (MPPM). Part-time programs available. *Faculty:* 30 full-time (12 women), 67 part-time/adjunct (25 women). *Students:* 14 full-time (1 woman), 34 part-time (17 women), 8 international. Average age 38. 31 applicants, 74% accepted, 15 enrolled. In 2010, 14 master's awarded. *Degree requirements:* For master's, thesis optional, capstone seminar. *Entrance requirements:* For master's, 2 letters of recommendation, resume, 5 years of supervisory or budgetary experience. Additional exam requirements/recommendations for international students: Required—TOEFL (minimum score 600 paper-based; 250 computer-based; 100 iBT), TWE (minimum score 4); Recommended—IELTS (minimum score 7). *Application deadline:* For fall admission, 6/1 priority date for domestic students, 2/15 for international students; for spring admission, 1/1 priority date for domestic students, 8/1 for international students. Applications are processed on a rolling basis. Application fee: $50. Electronic applications accepted. *Expenses:* Tuition, state resident: full-time $17,304; part-time $701 per credit. Tuition, nonresident: full-time $29,554; part-time $1210 per credit. Required fees: $740; $214 per term. Tuition and fees vary according to program. *Financial support:* In 2010–11, 14 students received support. Scholarships/grants and tuition waivers (partial) available. Support available to part-time students. Financial award application deadline: 2/1. *Faculty research:* Nonprofit management, urban and regional affairs, policy analysis and evaluation, security and intelligence studies, global political economy, nongovernmental organizations, civil society, development planning and environmental sustainability, human security. Total annual research expenditures: $892,349. *Unit head:* Dr. George Dougherty, Director, Executive Education, 412-648-7603, Fax: 412-648-2605, E-mail: gwdjr@pitt.edu. *Application contact:* Michael T. Rizzi, Associate Director of Student Services, 412-648-7640, Fax: 412-648-7641, E-mail: rizzim@pitt.edu.

University of Pittsburgh, School of Arts and Sciences, Department of Political Science, Pittsburgh, PA 15260. Offers MA, PhD. Part-time programs available. *Faculty:* 25 full-time (8 women), 5 part-time/adjunct (0 women). *Students:* 44 full-time (17 women); includes 6 Asian, non-Hispanic/Latino; 8 Hispanic/Latino, 4 international. Average age 30. 125 applicants, 17% accepted, 9 enrolled. In 2010, 4 master's, 5 doctorates awarded. Terminal master's awarded for partial completion of doctoral program. *Degree requirements:* For master's, comprehensive exam; for doctorate, comprehensive exam, thesis/dissertation. *Entrance requirements:* For master's and doctorate, GRE General Test, minimum QPA of 3.0. Additional exam requirements/recommendations for international students: Required—TOEFL. *Application deadline:* For fall admission, 1/1 for domestic and international students. Applications are processed on a rolling basis. Application fee: $50. Electronic applications accepted. *Expenses:* Tuition, state resident: full-time $17,304; part-time $701 per credit. Tuition, nonresident: full-time $29,554; part-time $1210 per credit. Required fees: $740; $214 per term. Tuition and fees vary according to program. *Financial support:* In 2010–11, 28 students received support, including 16 fellowships with full tuition reimbursements available (averaging $18,546 per year), 1 research assistantship with full tuition reimbursement available (averaging $16,400 per year), 14 teaching assistantships with full tuition reimbursements available (averaging $16,140 per year); tuition waivers (partial) also available. Financial award application deadline: 1/1. *Unit head:* Prof. Barry Ames, Chairman, 412-648-7290, Fax: 412-648-7277, E-mail: barrya@pitt.edu. *Application contact:* Prof. David Barker, Director of Graduate Students, 412-648-7275, Fax: 412-648-7277, E-mail: dbarker@pitt.edu.

University of Regina, Faculty of Graduate Studies and Research, Faculty of Arts, Department of Political Science, Regina, SK S4S 0A2, Canada. Offers MA. Part-time programs available. *Faculty:* 10 full-time (5 women), 1 part-time/adjunct (0 women). *Students:* 8 full-time (3 women), 2 part-time (both women). 15 applicants, 40% accepted. In 2010, 3 master's awarded. *Degree requirements:* For master's, thesis. *Entrance requirements:* Additional exam requirements/recommendations for international students: Required—TOEFL (minimum score 580 paper-based; 80 iBT). *Application deadline:* For fall admission, 3/15 for domestic and international students; for winter admission, 9/15 for domestic and international students. Applications are processed on a rolling basis. Application fee: $100. Electronic applications accepted. Tuition and fees charges are reported in Canadian dollars. *Expenses:* Tuition, area resident: Full-time $3244.50 Canadian dollars; part-time $180.25 Canadian dollars per credit hour. International tuition: $4744.50 Canadian dollars full-time. Required fees: $494 Canadian dollars; $115.25 Canadian dollars per credit hour. $115.25 Canadian dollars per semester. Tuition and fees vary according to program. *Financial support:* In 2010–11, 2 teaching assistantships (averaging $6,924 per year) were awarded; fellowships, research assistantships, scholarships/grants also available. Financial award application deadline: 6/15. *Faculty research:* Canadian, comparative, and international politics; political theory. *Unit head:* Dr. Tom McIntosh, Head, 306-585-4400, Fax: 306-585-4815, E-mail: tom.mcintosh@uregina.ca. *Application contact:* Dr. Yuchao Zhu, Graduate Program Coordinator, 306-585-4060, Fax: 306-585-4815, E-mail: yuchao.zhu@uregina.ca.

University of Regina, Faculty of Graduate Studies and Research, Faculty of Arts, Program in Social and Political Thought, Regina, SK S4S 0A2, Canada. Offers MA. Part-time programs available. *Faculty:* 1 (woman) full-time. *Students:* 3 full-time (1 woman). 1 applicant, 100% accepted. In 2010, 3 master's awarded. *Degree requirements:* For master's, thesis. *Entrance*

Political Science

University of Regina (continued)
requirements: Additional exam requirements/recommendations for international students: Required—TOEFL (minimum score 580 paper-based; 80 iBT). *Application deadline:* For fall admission, 3/15 for domestic and international students. Application fee: $100. Electronic applications accepted. Tuition and fees charges are reported in Canadian dollars. *Expenses:* Tuition, area resident: Full-time $3244.50 Canadian dollars; part-time $180.25 Canadian dollars per credit hour. International tuition: $4744.50 Canadian dollars full-time. Required fees: $494 Canadian dollars; $115.25 Canadian dollars per credit hour. $115.25 Canadian dollars per semester. Tuition and fees vary according to program. *Financial support:* In 2010–11, 1 research assistantship (averaging $16,500 per year) was awarded; fellowships, teaching assistantships, scholarships/grants also available. Financial award application deadline: 5/15. *Faculty research:* Liberalism and freedom, neo-conservatism, Aristotle's ethics, Kant's ethical theory and political philosophy, Hegel's philosophy of right. *Unit head:* Dr. Shadia Drury, Program Coordinator, 306-585-4073, E-mail: shadia.drury@uregina.ca. *Application contact:* Dr. Shadia Drury, Graduate Program Coordinator, 306-585-4073, E-mail: shadia.drury@uregina.ca.

University of Rhode Island, Graduate School, College of Arts and Sciences, Department of Political Science, Kingston, RI 02881. Offers political science (MA), including American politics, comparative government, international relations, public policy; public policy and administration (MPA); MLIS/MPA. Part-time programs available. *Faculty:* 10 full-time (4 women). *Students:* 17 full-time (10 women), 31 part-time (19 women); includes 10 minority (4 Black or African American, non-Hispanic/Latino; 1 Asian, non-Hispanic/Latino; 5 Hispanic/Latino). In 2010, 22 master's awarded. *Degree requirements:* For master's, comprehensive exam (for some programs), thesis optional. *Entrance requirements:* For master's, GRE, GMAT or MAT, 2 letters of recommendation. Additional exam requirements/recommendations for international students: Required—TOEFL (minimum score 550 paper-based; 213 computer-based). *Application deadline:* For fall admission, 2/1 for international students; for spring admission, 7/15 for international students. Application fee: $65. Electronic applications accepted. *Expenses:* Tuition, state resident: full-time $9588; part-time $533 per credit hour. Tuition, nonresident: full-time $22,968; part-time $1276 per credit hour. Required fees: $1282; $68 per semester. Tuition and fees vary according to program. *Financial support:* In 2010–11, 4 teaching assistantships with full tuition reimbursements (averaging $9,263 per year) were awarded. Financial award applicants required to submit FAFSA. *Unit head:* Dr. Gerry Tyler, Department Chair, 401-874-4053, Fax: 401-874-4072, E-mail: gtyler@uri.edu. *Application contact:* Dr. Gerry Tyler, Department Chair, 401-874-4053, Fax: 401-874-4072, E-mail: gtyler@uri.edu.

University of Rochester, School of Arts and Sciences, Department of Political Science, Rochester, NY 14627. Offers MA, PhD, MPH/MS, MS/PhD. Terminal master's awarded for partial completion of doctoral program. *Degree requirements:* For doctorate, thesis/dissertation, qualifying exam. *Entrance requirements:* For master's and doctorate, GRE General Test. Additional exam requirements/recommendations for international students: Required—TOEFL.

University of Saskatchewan, College of Graduate Studies and Research, College of Arts and Sciences, Department of Political Studies, Saskatoon, SK S7N 5A2, Canada. Offers MA. *Degree requirements:* For master's, thesis. *Entrance requirements:* Additional exam requirements/recommendations for international students: Required—TOEFL (minimum score 80 iBT); Recommended—IELTS (minimum score 6.5). Electronic applications accepted.

University of South Africa, College of Human Sciences, Pretoria, South Africa. Offers adult education (M Ed); African languages (MA, PhD); African politics (MA, PhD); Afrikaans (MA, PhD); ancient history (MA, PhD); ancient Near Eastern studies (MA, PhD); anthropology (MA, PhD); applied linguistics (MA); Arabic (MA, PhD); archaeology (MA); art history (MA); Biblical archaeology (MA); Biblical studies (M Th, D Th, PhD); Christian spirituality (M Th, D Th); church history (M Th, D Th); classical studies (MA, PhD); clinical psychology (MA); communication (MA, PhD); comparative education (M Ed, Ed D); consulting psychology (D Admin, D Com, PhD); curriculum studies (M Ed, Ed D); development studies (M Admin, MA, D Admin, PhD); didactics (M Ed, Ed D); education (M Tech); education management (M Ed, Ed D); educational psychology (M Ed); English (MA); environmental education (M Ed); French (MA, PhD); German (MA, PhD); Greek (MA); guidance and counseling (M Ed); health studies (MA, PhD), including health sciences education (MA), health services management (MA), medical and surgical nursing science (critical care general) (MA), midwifery and neonatal nursing science (MA), trauma and emergency care (MA); history (MA, PhD); history of education (Ed D); inclusive education (M Ed, Ed D); information and communications technology policy and regulation (MA); information science (MA, MIS, PhD); international politics (MA, PhD); Islamic studies (MA, PhD); Italian (MA, PhD); Judaica (MA, PhD); linguistics (MA, PhD); mathematical education (M Ed); mathematics education (MA); missiology (M Th, D Th); modern Hebrew (MA, PhD); musicology (MA, MMus, D Mus, PhD); natural science education (M Ed); New Testament (M Th, D Th); Old Testament (D Th); pastoral therapy (M Th, D Th); philosophy (MA); philosophy of education (M Ed, Ed D); politics (MA, PhD); Portuguese (MA, PhD); practical theology (M Th, D Th); psychology (MA, MS, PhD); psychology of education (M Ed, Ed D); public health (MA); religious studies (MA, D Th, PhD); Romance languages (MA); Russian (MA, PhD); Semitic languages (MA, PhD); social behavior studies in HIV/AIDS (MA); social science (mental health) (MA); social science in development studies (MA); social science in psychology (MA); social science in social work (MA); social science in sociology (MA); social work (MSW, DSW, PhD); socio-education (M Ed, Ed D); sociolinguistics (MA); sociology (MA, PhD); Spanish (MA, PhD); systematic theology (M Th, D Th); TESOL (teaching English to speakers of other languages) (MA); theological ethics (M Th, D Th); theory of literature (MA, PhD); urban ministries (D Th); urban ministry (M Th).

University of South Carolina, The Graduate School, College of Arts and Sciences, Department of Political Science, Program in Political Science, Columbia, SC 29208. Offers MA, PhD. Part-time programs available. Terminal master's awarded for partial completion of doctoral program. *Degree requirements:* For master's, one foreign language, thesis; for doctorate, one foreign language, comprehensive exam, thesis/dissertation. *Entrance requirements:* For master's and doctorate, GRE General Test, minimum GPA of 3.5. Additional exam requirements/recommendations for international students: Required—TOEFL. Electronic applications accepted. *Faculty research:* American government and politics, comparative politics, political theory, international politics, public administration and policy.

The University of South Dakota, Graduate School, College of Arts and Sciences, Department of Political Science, Vermillion, SD 57069-2390. Offers American political institutions (PhD); political science (MA); public administration (MPA, PhD); public policy (PhD); JD/MA; JD/MPA. *Accreditation:* NASPAA (one or more programs are accredited). Part-time programs available. Postbaccalaureate distance learning degree programs offered. *Degree requirements:* For master's, comprehensive exam, thesis (for some programs). *Entrance requirements:* For master's, GRE or LSAT (MPA), GRE General Test (MA), minimum GPA of 2.7. Additional exam requirements/recommendations for international students: Required—TOEFL (minimum score 550 paper-based; 213 computer-based; 79 iBT). Electronic applications accepted.

University of Southern California, Graduate School, Annenberg School for Communication and Journalism, School of Communication, Program in Public Diplomacy, Los Angeles, CA 90089. Offers MPD. *Students:* 47 full-time, 2 part-time; includes 15 minority (2 Black or African American, non-Hispanic/Latino; 5 Hispanic/Latino; 7 Native Hawaiian or other Pacific Islander, non-Hispanic/Latino; 1 Two or more races, non-Hispanic/Latino), 11 international. Average age 26. 100 applicants, 51% accepted, 21 enrolled. In 2010, 23 master's awarded. *Degree requirements:* For master's, thesis. *Entrance requirements:* For master's, GRE, resume, writing samples, recommendation letters. Additional exam requirements/recommendations for international students: Required—TOEFL (minimum score 280 computer-based; 114 iBT). *Application deadline:* For fall admission, 12/15 priority date for domestic and international students. Application fee: $85. Electronic applications accepted. *Expenses:* Tuition: Full-time $31,240; part-time $1420 per unit. Required fees: $600. One-time fee: $35 full-time. Full-time tuition and fees vary according to degree level and program. *Financial support:* Career-related internships or fieldwork, Federal Work-Study, scholarships/grants, and tuition waivers available. Support available to part-time students. Financial award application deadline: 1/15; financial award applicants required to submit FAFSA. *Unit head:* Dr. Nicholas Cull, Director of Public Diplomacy Degree Program, 213-821-4080, E-mail: cull@usc.edu. *Application contact:* Allyson Hill, Assistant Dean, Admissions, 213-821-0770, Fax: 213-740-1933, E-mail: ascadm@usc.edu.

See Display on page 675 and Close-Up on page 727.

University of Southern California, Graduate School, Dana and David Dornsife College of Letters, Arts and Sciences, Political Science and International Relations (Joint PhD Program), Los Angeles, CA 90089. Offers PhD. *Faculty:* 29 full-time (12 women). *Students:* 53 full-time (25 women); includes 14 minority (3 Asian, non-Hispanic/Latino; 8 Hispanic/Latino; 3 Two or more races, non-Hispanic/Latino), 20 international. 117 applicants, 13% accepted, 8 enrolled. In 2010, 14 doctorates awarded. *Degree requirements:* For doctorate, variable foreign language requirement, comprehensive exam, thesis/dissertation. *Entrance requirements:* For doctorate, GRE (minimum score 1000). Additional exam requirements/recommendations for international students: Required—TOEFL (minimum score 600 paper-based; 250 computer-based; 100 iBT). *Application deadline:* For fall admission, 12/1 priority date for domestic and international students. Application fee: $85. Electronic applications accepted. *Expenses:* Tuition: Full-time $31,240; part-time $1420 per unit. Required fees: $600. One-time fee: $35 full-time. Full-time tuition and fees vary according to degree level and program. *Financial support:* In 2010–11, 37 students received support, including 14 fellowships with full tuition reimbursements available (averaging $23,000 per year), 1 research assistantship with full tuition reimbursement available (averaging $20,000 per year), 30 teaching assistantships with full tuition reimbursements available (averaging $20,000 per year); health care benefits also available. Financial award application deadline: 12/1. *Faculty research:* American politics, foreign policy analysis, international political economy, race/ethics politics, security studies. *Unit head:* Prof. Saori Katada, Director POIR Program, 213-740-8542, E-mail: skatada@usc.edu. *Application contact:* Veridiana Chavarin, Graduate Advisor, 213-740-1695, E-mail: vchavari@usc.edu.

University of Southern Mississippi, Graduate School, College of Arts and Letters, Department of Political Science, International Development, and International Affairs, Hattiesburg, MS 39406-0001. Offers international development (PhD); political science (MA, MS). Part-time and evening/weekend programs available. Postbaccalaureate distance learning degree programs offered. *Faculty:* 14 full-time (2 women). *Students:* 33 full-time (14 women), 65 part-time (28 women); includes 19 Black or African American, non-Hispanic/Latino; 1 American Indian or Alaska Native, non-Hispanic/Latino; 2 Asian, non-Hispanic/Latino; 6 Hispanic/Latino, 7 international. Average age 36. 44 applicants, 64% accepted, 22 enrolled. In 2010, 10 master's, 2 doctorates awarded. *Degree requirements:* For master's, comprehensive exam, thesis (for some programs); for doctorate, comprehensive exam, thesis/dissertation. *Entrance requirements:* For master's, GRE General Test, minimum GPA of 2.75 in last 2 years, 3.0 in field of study; for doctorate, GRE General Test, minimum GPA of 3.5. Additional exam requirements/recommendations for international students: Required—TOEFL, IELTS. *Application deadline:* For fall admission, 3/1 priority date for domestic students, 3/1 for international students. Applications are processed on a rolling basis. Application fee: $50. *Financial support:* In 2010–11, 4 research assistantships with full and partial tuition reimbursements (averaging $9,000 per year), 8 teaching assistantships with full tuition reimbursements (averaging $7,000 per year) were awarded; career-related internships or fieldwork, Federal Work-Study, scholarships/grants, health care benefits, and unspecified assistantships also available. Financial award application deadline: 3/15; financial award applicants required to submit FAFSA. *Faculty research:* American politics, international politics, political theory, comparative politics, public law. *Unit head:* Dr. Allan McBride, Chair, 601-266-4310. *Application contact:* Dr. Mark Stedman, Director, Graduate Studies, 601-266-4310, Fax: 601-266-4172.

University of South Florida, Graduate School, College of Arts and Sciences, Department of Government and International Affairs, Tampa, FL 33620-9951. Offers government (PhD); Latin American Caribbean and Latino Studies (MA); political science (MA); public administration (MPA). Part-time and evening/weekend programs available. *Faculty:* 5 full-time (1 woman), 1 part-time/adjunct (0 women). *Students:* 57 full-time (35 women), 84 part-time (42 women); includes 23 Black or African American, non-Hispanic/Latino; 1 American Indian or Alaska Native, non-Hispanic/Latino; 4 Asian, non-Hispanic/Latino; 18 Hispanic/Latino, 2 international. Average age 32. 151 applicants, 38% accepted, 41 enrolled. In 2010, 31 master's awarded. *Degree requirements:* For master's, comprehensive exam, thesis; for doctorate, comprehensive exam, thesis/dissertation. *Entrance requirements:* For master's, GRE (minimum score 470 verbal, 470 quantitative), minimum GPA of 3.0 in last 60 hours of course work. Additional exam requirements/recommendations for international students: Required—TOEFL (minimum score 550 paper-based; 213 computer-based). *Application deadline:* For fall admission, 2/15 for domestic students, 1/2 for international students; for spring admission, 10/15 for domestic students, 6/1 for international students. Applications are processed on a rolling basis. Application fee: $30. Electronic applications accepted. *Financial support:* In 2010–11, 12 teaching assistantships with tuition reimbursements (averaging $15,000 per year) were awarded; unspecified assistantships also available. Financial award application deadline: 4/1. *Unit head:* Dr. Mohsen Milani, Chairperson, 813-974-2384, Fax: 813-974-0832, E-mail: milani@chuma1.cas.usf.edu. *Application contact:* Dr. Stephen Tauber, Graduate Coordinator, 813-974-0781, Fax: 813-974-0832, E-mail: stauber@chuma1.cas.usf.edu.

The University of Tennessee, Graduate School, College of Arts and Sciences, Department of Political Science, Program in Political Science, Knoxville, TN 37996. Offers MA, PhD. Part-time programs available. *Degree requirements:* For master's, thesis or alternative; for doctorate, one foreign language, thesis/dissertation. *Entrance requirements:* For master's and doctorate, GRE General Test, minimum GPA of 2.7. Additional exam requirements/recommendations for international students: Required—TOEFL. Electronic applications accepted. *Expenses:* Tuition, state resident: full-time $7440; part-time $414 per credit hour. Tuition, nonresident: full-time $22,478; part-time $1250 per credit hour. Required fees: $922; $43 per credit hour. Tuition and fees vary according to program.

The University of Tennessee, Graduate School, College of Arts and Sciences, Department of Sociology, Knoxville, TN 37996. Offers criminology (MA, PhD); energy, environment, and resource policy (MA, PhD); political economy (MA, PhD). Part-time programs available. *Degree requirements:* For master's, thesis or alternative; for doctorate, thesis/dissertation. *Entrance requirements:* For master's, GRE General Test, minimum GPA of 3.0; for doctorate, GRE General Test, minimum GPA of 3.5. Additional exam requirements/recommendations for international students: Required—TOEFL. Electronic applications accepted. *Expenses:* Tuition, state resident: full-time $7440; part-time $414 per credit hour. Tuition, nonresident: full-time $22,478; part-time $1250 per credit hour. Required fees: $922; $43 per credit hour. Tuition and fees vary according to program.

The University of Texas at Arlington, Graduate School, College of Liberal Arts, Department of Political Science, Arlington, TX 76019. Offers MA. Part-time and evening/weekend programs available. *Faculty:* 14 full-time (4 women), 1 part-time/adjunct (0 women). *Students:* 14 full-time (11 women), 26 part-time (13 women); includes 18 minority (9 Black or African American, non-Hispanic/Latino; 2 Asian, non-Hispanic/Latino; 6 Hispanic/Latino; 1 Two or more races, non-Hispanic/Latino), 1 international. 23 applicants, 74% accepted, 11 enrolled. In 2010, 8 master's awarded. *Degree requirements:* For master's, comprehensive exam, thesis optional. *Entrance requirements:* For master's, GRE, minimum GPA of 3.0 in last 60 hours of course work. Additional exam requirements/recommendations for international students: Required—TOEFL (minimum score 550 paper-based; 213 computer-based). *Application deadline:* For fall admission, 6/15 for domestic students. Applications are processed on a rolling basis. Application fee: $35 ($50 for international students). Electronic applications accepted. *Expenses:* Tuition, state resident: full-time $7500. Tuition, nonresident: full-time $13,080. International tuition: $13,250 full-time. *Financial support:* In 2010–11, 2 students received support, including 2 fellowships with full tuition reimbursements available, 4 teaching assistantships (averaging $12,000 per year); career-related internships or fieldwork, institutionally sponsored loans, and scholarships/grants also available. Support available to part-time students. Financial award application deadline: 6/1; financial award applicants required to submit FAFSA. *Unit head:* Dr. Rebecca Deen, Chair, 817-272-2991, Fax: 817-272-2525, E-mail: deen@uta.edu. *Application contact:* Dr. Brent Boyea, Graduate Advisor, 817-272-2991, E-mail: boyea@uta.edu.

The University of Texas at Austin, Graduate School, College of Liberal Arts, Department of Government, Austin, TX 78712-1111. Offers PhD. *Degree requirements:* For doctorate, comprehensive exam, thesis/dissertation. *Entrance requirements:* For doctorate, GRE General Test. Electronic applications accepted.

The University of Texas at Brownsville, Graduate Studies, College of Liberal Arts, Department of Government, Brownsville, TX 78520-4991. Offers MAIS. Part-time and evening/weekend programs available. *Degree requirements:* For master's, comprehensive exam, thesis optional. *Entrance requirements:* For master's, GRE General Test. Additional exam requirements/recommendations for international students: Required—TOEFL.

The University of Texas at Dallas, School of Economic, Political and Policy Sciences, Program in Political Science, Richardson, TX 75080. Offers constitutional law (MA); legislative studies (MA); political science (MA, PhD). Part-time and evening/weekend programs available. *Faculty:* 14 full-time (3 women), 1 part-time/adjunct (0 women). *Students:* 34 full-time (16 women), 20 part-time (9 women); includes 22 minority (7 Black or African American, non-Hispanic/Latino; 1 American Indian or Alaska Native, non-Hispanic/Latino; 6 Asian, non-Hispanic/Latino; 7 Hispanic/Latino; 1 Two or more races, non-Hispanic/Latino), 4 international. Average age 31. 54 applicants, 56% accepted, 15 enrolled. In 2010, 17 master's, 8 doctorates awarded. Terminal master's awarded for partial completion of doctoral program. *Degree requirements:* For master's, thesis optional, independent study; for doctorate, thesis/dissertation, practicum research. *Entrance requirements:* For master's, GRE (minimum combined verbal and quantitative score of 1100), minimum undergraduate GPA of 3.0; for doctorate, GRE (minimum combined verbal and quantitative score of 1200, writing 4.5), minimum undergraduate GPA of 3.2. Additional exam requirements/recommendations for international students: Required—TOEFL (minimum score 550 paper-based; 215 computer-based). *Application deadline:* For fall admission, 7/15 for domestic students, 5/1 priority date for international students; for spring admission, 11/15 for domestic students, 9/1 priority date for international students. Applications are processed on a rolling basis. Application fee: $50 ($100 for international students). Electronic applications accepted. *Expenses:* Tuition, state resident: full-time $10,248; part-time $569 per credit hour. Tuition, nonresident: full-time $18,544; part-time $1030 per credit hour. Tuition and fees vary according to course load. *Financial support:* In 2010–11, 30 students received support, including 4 research assistantships with partial tuition reimbursements available (averaging $11,250 per year), 13 teaching assistantships with partial tuition reimbursements available (averaging $11,146 per year); career-related internships or fieldwork, Federal Work-Study, institutionally sponsored loans, and scholarships/grants also available. Support available to part-time students. Financial award application deadline: 4/30; financial award applicants required to submit FAFSA. *Faculty research:* Terrorism and democratic stability, redistricting and representation, trust and social exchange, how economic ideas impact political thought and public policy. *Unit head:* Dr. Robert C. Lowry, Program Head, 972-883-6720, Fax: 972-883-2735, E-mail: robert.lowry@utdallas.edu. *Application contact:* Dr. Linda Keith, Associate Program Head, 972-883-6481, Fax: 972-883-2735, E-mail: linda.keith@utdallas.edu.

The University of Texas at Dallas, School of Economic, Political and Policy Sciences, Program in Public Policy and Political Economy, Richardson, TX 75080. Offers international political economy (MS); public policy (MPP); public policy and political economy (PhD). Part-time and evening/weekend programs available. *Faculty:* 19 full-time (5 women), 1 (woman) part-time/adjunct. *Students:* 59 full-time (28 women), 41 part-time (17 women); includes 30 minority (14 Black or African American, non-Hispanic/Latino; 8 Asian, non-Hispanic/Latino; 8 Hispanic/Latino), 17 international. Average age 35. 84 applicants, 48% accepted, 24 enrolled. In 2010, 9 master's, 11 doctorates awarded. *Degree requirements:* For doctorate, thesis/dissertation. *Entrance requirements:* For master's and doctorate, GRE General Test, minimum GPA of 3.0 in upper-level course work in field. Additional exam requirements/recommendations for international students: Required—TOEFL (minimum score 550 paper-based; 215 computer-based). *Application deadline:* For fall admission, 7/15 for domestic students, 5/1 priority date for international students; for spring admission, 11/15 for domestic students, 9/1 priority date for international students. Applications are processed on a rolling basis. Application fee: $50 ($100 for international students). Electronic applications accepted. *Expenses:* Tuition, state resident: full-time $10,248; part-time $569 per credit hour. Tuition, nonresident: full-time $18,544; part-time $1030 per credit hour. Tuition and fees vary according to course load. *Financial support:* In 2010–11, 45 students received support, including 6 research assistantships with partial tuition reimbursements available (averaging $14,850 per year), 14 teaching assistantships with partial tuition reimbursements available (averaging $11,517 per year); career-related internships or fieldwork, Federal Work-Study, institutionally sponsored loans, scholarships/grants, and unspecified assistantships also available. Support available to part-time students. Financial award application deadline: 4/30; financial award applicants required to submit FAFSA. *Faculty research:* Ethnicity, community and local public good provision; community mental health policy; Texas Schools Project; biological and chemical arms control; cross-disciplinary applications of quantitative methodology. *Unit head:* Dr. Paul Jargowski, Program Head, 972-883-2992, Fax: 972-883-6297, E-mail: jargo@utdallas.edu. *Application contact:* Dr. Marie I. Chevrier, Associate Program Head, 972-883-2727, Fax: 972-883-6297, E-mail: chevrier@utdallas.edu.

See Close-Up on page 811.

The University of Texas at El Paso, Graduate School, College of Liberal Arts, Department of Political Science, El Paso, TX 79968-0001. Offers MA. Part-time and evening/weekend programs available. *Students:* 25 (10 women); includes 2 Black or African American, non-Hispanic/Latino; 12 Hispanic/Latino, 4 international. Average age 34. In 2010, 8 master's awarded. *Degree requirements:* For master's, thesis optional. *Entrance requirements:* For master's, GRE, minimum GPA of 3.0, letters of recommendation. Additional exam requirements/recommendations for international students: Required—TOEFL; Recommended—IELTS. *Application deadline:* For fall admission, 8/1 priority date for domestic students, 3/1 for international students; for spring admission, 11/1 priority date for domestic students, 9/1 for international students. Applications are processed on a rolling basis. Application fee: $45 ($80 for international students). Electronic applications accepted. *Financial support:* In 2010–11, research assistantships with partial tuition reimbursements (averaging $18,625 per year), 10 teaching assistantships with partial tuition reimbursements (averaging $14,900 per year) were awarded; fellowships with partial tuition reimbursements, institutionally sponsored loans, scholarships/grants, health care benefits, tuition waivers (partial), and unspecified assistantships also available. Support available to part-time students. Financial award application deadline: 3/15; financial award applicants required to submit FAFSA. *Unit head:* Dr. Gregory D. Schmidt, Chair, 915-747-5227, Fax: 915-747-6616, E-mail: gdschmidt@utep.edu. *Application contact:* Dr. Patricia D. Witherspoon, Dean of the Graduate School, 915-747-5491, Fax: 915-747-5788, E-mail: withersp@utep.edu.

The University of Texas at San Antonio, College of Liberal and Fine Arts, Department of Political Science and Geography, San Antonio, TX 78249-0617. Offers political science (MA). Part-time and evening/weekend programs available. *Faculty:* 11 full-time (2 women). *Students:* 21 full-time (11 women), 29 part-time (13 women); includes 25 minority (3 Black or African American, non-Hispanic/Latino; 22 Hispanic/Latino), 5 international. Average age 28. 28 applicants, 75% accepted, 14 enrolled. In 2010, 9 master's awarded. *Degree requirements:* For master's, comprehensive exam (for some programs), thesis (for some programs). *Entrance requirements:* For master's, GRE General Test. Additional exam requirements/recommendations for international students: Required—TOEFL (minimum score 500 paper-based; 173 computer-based; 61 iBT), IELTS (minimum score 5). *Application deadline:* For fall admission, 7/1 for domestic students, 4/1 for international students; for spring admission, 11/1 for domestic students, 9/1 for international students. Applications are processed on a rolling basis. Application

fee: $45 ($80 for international students). Electronic applications accepted. *Expenses:* Tuition, state resident: full-time $4172; part-time $231.75 per credit hour. Tuition, nonresident: full-time $15,332; part-time $851.75 per credit hour. *Financial support:* In 2010–11, 2 students received support, including 8 research assistantships (averaging $10,140 per year), 4 teaching assistantships (averaging $4,988 per year); scholarships/grants, tuition waivers, and unspecified assistantships also available. Support available to part-time students. Total annual research expenditures: $3,185. *Unit head:* Dr. Mansour El-Kikhia, Chair, 210-458-5600, Fax: 210-458-4629, E-mail: mansour.elkikhia@utsa.edu. *Application contact:* Veronica Ramirez, Assistant Dean of the Graduate School, 210-458-4330, Fax: 210-458-4332, E-mail: graduatestudies@utsa.edu.

The University of Texas at Tyler, College of Arts and Sciences, Department of Political Science, Tyler, TX 75799-0001. Offers MA. Part-time and evening/weekend programs available. *Degree requirements:* For master's, comprehensive exam, thesis optional. *Entrance requirements:* Additional exam requirements/recommendations for international students: Required—TOEFL (minimum score 79 computer-based). *Faculty research:* American politics, comparative politics, international relations, political theory and philosophy.

The University of Texas of the Permian Basin, Office of Graduate Studies, College of Arts and Sciences, Department of Social Sciences, Odessa, TX 79762-0001. Offers criminal justice administration (MS); political science (MPA). Part-time and evening/weekend programs available. *Degree requirements:* For master's, comprehensive exam (for some programs), thesis (for some programs). *Entrance requirements:* For master's, GRE General Test. Additional exam requirements/recommendations for international students: Required—TOEFL (minimum score 550 paper-based; 213 computer-based).

The University of Toledo, College of Graduate Studies, College of Language, Literature and Social Sciences, Department of Political Science and Public Administration, Toledo, OH 43606-3390. Offers health care administration (Certificate); management of non-profit organizations (Certificate); political science (MA); public administration (MPA), including health care policy, municipal administration, public administration. Part-time programs available. *Faculty:* 9. *Students:* 21 full-time (11 women), 13 part-time (8 women); includes 7 minority (5 Black or African American, non-Hispanic/Latino; 2 Hispanic/Latino), 2 international. Average age 30. 34 applicants, 59% accepted, 16 enrolled. In 2010, 14 master's, 7 other advanced degrees awarded. *Degree requirements:* For master's, thesis. *Entrance requirements:* For master's, GRE General Test, A minimum 2.7 cumulative point-hour ratio (on a 4.0 scale) for all previous academic work, a statement of purpose, 3 letters of recommendation and transcripts from all prior institutions attended; for Certificate, A minimum 2.7 cumulative point-hour ratio (on a 4.0 scale) for all previous academic work, a statement of purpose, 3 letters of recommendation and transcripts from all prior institutions attended. Additional exam requirements/recommendations for international students: Required—TOEFL (minimum score 550 paper-based; 213 computer-based; 80 iBT), IELTS (minimum score 6.5). *Application deadline:* For fall admission, 1/15 priority date for domestic and international students. Applications are processed on a rolling basis. Application fee: $45 ($75 for international students). Electronic applications accepted. *Expenses:* Tuition, state resident: full-time $11,426; part-time $476 per credit hour. Tuition, nonresident: full-time $21,660; part-time $903 per credit hour. One-time fee: $62. *Financial support:* Research assistantships with tuition reimbursements, teaching assistantships with tuition reimbursements, career-related internships or fieldwork, Federal Work-Study, institutionally sponsored loans, scholarships/grants, tuition waivers (full), and unspecified assistantships available. Support available to part-time students. *Faculty research:* Economic development, health care, Third World, criminal justice, Eastern Europe. *Unit head:* Dr. Mark E. Denham, Chair, 419-530-4151, E-mail: mark.denham@utoledo.edu. *Application contact:* Graduate School Office, 419-530-4723, Fax: 419-530-4724, E-mail: grdsch@utnet.utoledo.edu.

University of Toronto, School of Graduate Studies, Social Sciences Division, Department of Political Science, Toronto, ON M5S 1A1, Canada. Offers MA, PhD. Part-time programs available. *Degree requirements:* For master's, thesis optional; for doctorate, one foreign language, thesis/dissertation, reading competency in a language other than English. *Entrance requirements:* For master's, 3 letters of recommendation, writing sample; for doctorate, 4 letters of recommendation, writing sample.

University of Utah, Graduate School, College of Humanities, Program in Middle East Studies, Salt Lake City, UT 84112. Offers anthropology (MA); Arabic (MA, PhD); Arabic and linguistics (MA, PhD); Hebrew (MA); history (MA, PhD); Persian (MA, PhD); political science (MA, PhD); Turkish (MA). *Students:* 20 full-time (10 women), 15 part-time (5 women), 8 international. Average age 33. 28 applicants, 29% accepted, 3 enrolled. In 2010, 3 master's awarded. Terminal master's awarded for partial completion of doctoral program. *Degree requirements:* For master's, 2 foreign languages, comprehensive exam, thesis optional; for doctorate, 3 foreign languages, comprehensive exam, thesis/dissertation. *Entrance requirements:* For master's, GRE General Test, minimum GPA of 3.2; for doctorate, GRE General Test, MA in Middle East studies or equivalent, minimum GPA of 3.2. Additional exam requirements/recommendations for international students: Required—TOEFL (minimum score 580 paper-based; 237 computer-based; 92 iBT). *Application deadline:* For fall admission, 1/15 priority date for domestic and international students. Application fee: $55 ($65 for international students). Electronic applications accepted. *Expenses:* Tuition, area resident: Part-time $179.19 per credit hour. Tuition, state resident: full-time $4384. Tuition, nonresident: full-time $16,684; part-time $630.67 per credit hour. Required fees: $350 per semester. Tuition and fees vary according to course load, degree level and program. *Financial support:* In 2010–11, 17 students received support, including 11 fellowships with full tuition reimbursements available (averaging $14,000 per year), 6 teaching assistantships with full tuition reimbursements available (averaging $12,000 per year); unspecified assistantships also available. Financial award application deadline: 1/15. *Faculty research:* Arabic linguistics; Islamic studies; Middle Eastern history; political science; Judaic studies; anthropology; Arabic, Persian, Hebrew, and Turkish language and literature. *Application contact:* Peter von Sivers, Director of Graduate Studies, 801-581-8073, Fax: 801-581-6183, E-mail: peter.vonsivers@utah.edu.

University of Utah, Graduate School, College of Social and Behavioral Science, Department of Political Science, Program in Political Science, Salt Lake City, UT 84112-1107. Offers MA, MS, PhD. *Faculty:* 29 full-time (6 women), 2 part-time/adjunct (0 women). *Students:* 26 full-time (9 women), 38 part-time (11 women); includes 9 minority (1 Black or African American, non-Hispanic/Latino; 1 Asian, non-Hispanic/Latino; 5 Hispanic/Latino; 2 Two or more races, non-Hispanic/Latino), 10 international. Average age 34. 37 applicants, 59% accepted, 15 enrolled. In 2010, 8 master's, 3 doctorates awarded. Terminal master's awarded for partial completion of doctoral program. *Degree requirements:* For master's, variable foreign language requirement, thesis or research paper; for doctorate, variable foreign language requirement, comprehensive exam, thesis/dissertation. *Entrance requirements:* For master's and doctorate, GRE General Test, minimum GPA of 3.2. Additional exam requirements/recommendations for international students: Required—TOEFL (minimum score 580 paper-based; 237 computer-based; 92 iBT). *Application deadline:* For fall admission, 1/15 priority date for domestic and international students; for spring admission, 10/1 priority date for domestic and international students. Application fee: $55 ($65 for international students). *Expenses:* Tuition, area resident: Part-time $179.19 per credit hour. Tuition, state resident: full-time $4384. Tuition, nonresident: full-time $16,684; part-time $630.67 per credit hour. Required fees: $350 per semester. Tuition and fees vary according to course load, degree level and program. *Financial support:* In 2010–11, 15 students received support, including 2 fellowships with full tuition reimbursements available (averaging $15,000 per year), 9 teaching assistantships with full tuition reimbursements available (averaging $11,500 per year); research assistantships with full tuition reimbursements available, career-related internships or fieldwork also available. Financial award application deadline: 1/15; financial award applicants required to submit FAFSA. *Faculty research:* International relations, American government, comparative politics, political theory, Middle East politics, environmental politics, democratic theory, political participation, Latin-American politics, public administration. Total annual research expenditures: $1.3 million. *Unit head:* Dr. James J. Gosling, Chair, 801-585-0447, Fax: 801-585-6492, E-mail: pjg@poli-sci.utah.edu. *Application*

Political Science

University of Utah (continued)

contact: Mary Ann Underwood, Graduate Coordinator, 801-581-8608, Fax: 801-585-6492, E-mail: maryann.underwood@poli-sci.utah.edu.

University of Victoria, Faculty of Graduate Studies, Faculty of Social Sciences, Department of Political Science, Victoria, BC V8W 2Y2, Canada. Offers MA, PhD. Part-time programs available. *Degree requirements:* For master's, thesis; for doctorate, thesis/dissertation, candidacy exam. *Entrance requirements:* For master's, minimum B+ average in last 2 years of undergraduate course work. Additional exam requirements/recommendations for international students: Required—TOEFL (minimum score 600 paper-based; 250 computer-based). Electronic applications accepted. *Faculty research:* Political theory, political parties, international political economy, comparative public policy, British Columbian politics.

University of Virginia, College and Graduate School of Arts and Sciences, Department of Politics, Program in Government, Charlottesville, VA 22903. Offers MA, PhD, JD/MA, MBA/MA. *Students:* 33 full-time (12 women), 1 part-time (0 women); includes 1 Black or African American, non-Hispanic/Latino, 4 international. Average age 28. 91 applicants, 26% accepted, 10 enrolled. In 2010, 4 master's, 2 doctorates awarded. *Degree requirements:* For master's, 2 research/statistics courses or thesis; for doctorate, variable foreign language requirement, thesis/dissertation, 2 research/statistics courses. *Entrance requirements:* For master's and doctorate, GRE General Test, long writing sample; 2 letters of recommendation. Additional exam requirements/recommendations for international students: Required—TOEFL (minimum score 600 paper-based; 250 computer-based; 90 iBT), IELTS (minimum score 7). *Application deadline:* For fall admission, 12/4 for domestic and international students. Applications are processed on a rolling basis. Application fee: $60. Electronic applications accepted. *Financial support:* Fellowships, teaching assistantships available. Financial award application deadline: 12/4; financial award applicants required to submit FAFSA. *Unit head:* David Leblang, Chair, 434-924-3192, Fax: 434-924-3159. *Application contact:* David Leblang, Chair, 434-924-3192, Fax: 434-924-3159.

University of Washington, Graduate School, College of Arts and Sciences, Department of Political Science, Seattle, WA 98195. Offers MA, PhD. *Degree requirements:* For doctorate, thesis/dissertation. *Entrance requirements:* For master's and doctorate, GRE General Test, minimum GPA of 3.0. Additional exam requirements/recommendations for international students: Required—TOEFL. Electronic applications accepted. *Faculty research:* American politics, comparative politics, international relations, political theory, political economy.

University of Waterloo, Graduate Studies, Faculty of Arts, Department of Political Science, Global Governance Program, Waterloo, ON N2L 3G1, Canada. Offers MA, PhD. *Entrance requirements:* For doctorate, MA. Additional exam requirements/recommendations for international students: Required—TOEFL. Electronic applications accepted. *Faculty research:* Global political economy, global environment, peace and security, global justice and human rights, multilateral institutions and diplomacy.

The University of Western Ontario, Faculty of Graduate Studies, Social Sciences Division, Department of Political Science, London, ON N6A 5B8, Canada. Offers MA, MPA, PhD. Part-time programs available. *Degree requirements:* For master's, thesis; for doctorate, comprehensive exam, thesis/dissertation. *Entrance requirements:* For master's, minimum B average, honors BA in political science or equivalent, sample of written work; for doctorate, MA in political science or equivalent. *Faculty research:* Political theory, Canadian politics, local government, comparative politics, international relations.

University of West Florida, College of Arts and Sciences: Arts, Department of Government, Pensacola, FL 32514-5750. Offers political science (MA), including public administration, security and diplomacy. Part-time and evening/weekend programs available. *Faculty:* 3 full-time (1 woman), 1 part-time/adjunct (0 women). *Students:* 12 full-time (5 women), 10 part-time (7 women); includes 3 minority (1 Hispanic/Latino; 1 Native Hawaiian or other Pacific Islander, non-Hispanic/Latino; 1 Two or more races, non-Hispanic/Latino). Average age 28. 15 applicants, 87% accepted, 6 enrolled. In 2010, 5 master's awarded. *Degree requirements:* For master's, thesis or alternative. *Entrance requirements:* For master's, GRE General Test, minimum GPA of 3.0. Additional exam requirements/recommendations for international students: Required—TOEFL (minimum score 550 paper-based; 213 computer-based). *Application deadline:* For fall admission, 6/1 for domestic students, 5/15 for international students; for spring admission, 10/1 for domestic and international students. Applications are processed on a rolling basis. Application fee: $30. *Expenses:* Tuition, state resident: full-time $4982; part-time $208 per credit hour. Tuition, nonresident: full-time $20,059; part-time $836 per credit hour. Required fees: $1365; $57 per credit hour. *Financial support:* In 2010–11, 14 fellowships with partial tuition reimbursements (averaging $134 per year), 5 research assistantships (averaging $3,280 per year), 2 teaching assistantships with partial tuition reimbursements (averaging $5,000 per year) were awarded; unspecified assistantships also available. Financial award application deadline: 4/15; financial award applicants required to submit FAFSA. *Faculty research:* Political campaigns, elections, law enforcement, growth management. *Unit head:* Dr. Alfred Cuzan, Chairperson, 850-474-2337, E-mail: govt@uwf.edu. *Application contact:* Terry McCray, Assistant Director of Graduate Admissions, 850-473-7718, Fax: 850-473-7714, E-mail: gradadmissions@uwf.edu.

University of West Georgia, College of Arts and Sciences, Department of Political Science and Planning, Carrollton, GA 30118. Offers political science (Certificate); public administration (MPA); public management (Certificate); rural and small town planning (MS). *Accreditation:* NASPAA (one or more programs are accredited). Part-time programs available. *Faculty:* 5 full-time (0 women). *Students:* 19 full-time (5 women), 22 part-time (11 women); includes 11 Black or African American, non-Hispanic/Latino; 1 Native Hawaiian or other Pacific Islander, non-Hispanic/Latino. Average age 33. 26 applicants, 58% accepted, 6 enrolled. In 2010, 10 master's, 5 other advanced degrees awarded. *Degree requirements:* For master's, exit paper. *Entrance requirements:* For master's, GRE General Test. Additional exam requirements/recommendations for international students: Required—TOEFL. *Application deadline:* For fall admission, 7/17 priority date for domestic students; for spring admission, 11/20 for domestic students. Applications are processed on a rolling basis. Application fee: $30. Electronic applications accepted. *Expenses:* Tuition, state resident: full-time $4130; part-time $173 per semester hour. Tuition, nonresident: full-time $16,524; part-time $689 per semester hour. Required fees: $1586; $44.01 per semester hour. $397 per semester. Tuition and fees vary according to program. *Financial support:* In 2010–11, 4 students received support, including 4 research assistantships with partial tuition reimbursements available (averaging $3,000 per year); career-related internships or fieldwork and unspecified assistantships also available. Support available to part-time students. Financial award application deadline: 7/1; financial award applicants required to submit FAFSA. *Faculty research:* State and local government, environmental health, administrative studies. *Unit head:* Dr. Robert M. Schaefer, Chair, 678-839-6504, Fax: 678-839-5009, E-mail: rschaefe@westga.edu. *Application contact:* Dr. Charles W. Clark, Dean, 678-839-6419, E-mail: cclark@westga.edu.

University of Windsor, Faculty of Graduate Studies, Faculty of Arts and Social Sciences, Department of Political Science, Windsor, ON N9B 3P4, Canada. Offers MA. Part-time programs available. *Entrance requirements:* For master's, minimum B+ average. Additional exam requirements/recommendations for international students: Required—TOEFL (minimum score 600 paper-based; 250 computer-based). Electronic applications accepted. *Faculty research:* Canadian politics and government, local government, comparative political Canadian public administration, public policy.

University of Wisconsin–Madison, Graduate School, College of Letters and Science, Department of Political Science, Madison, WI 53706-1380. Offers PhD. *Degree requirements:* For doctorate, thesis/dissertation. *Entrance requirements:* For doctorate, GRE General Test. Electronic applications accepted. *Expenses:* Tuition, state resident: full-time $9887; part-time $617.96 per credit. Tuition, nonresident: full-time $24,054; part-time $1503.40 per credit. Required fees: $67.63 per credit. Tuition and fees vary according to reciprocity agreements. *Faculty research:* Comparative politics, American politics, international relations, political theory, political methodology.

University of Wisconsin–Milwaukee, Graduate School, College of Letters and Sciences, Department of Political Science, Milwaukee, WI 53201-0413. Offers MA, PhD. *Faculty:* 20 full-time (6 women). *Students:* 37 full-time (14 women), 17 part-time (8 women); includes 3 Asian, non-Hispanic/Latino; 1 Hispanic/Latino, 6 international. Average age 29. 57 applicants, 63% accepted, 11 enrolled. In 2010, 8 master's, 3 doctorates awarded. *Degree requirements:* For master's, thesis or alternative; for doctorate, one foreign language, thesis/dissertation. *Entrance requirements:* For master's and doctorate, GRE General Test, minimum GPA of 3.0. Additional exam requirements/recommendations for international students: Required—TOEFL (minimum score 550 paper-based; 79 iBT), IELTS (minimum score 6.5). *Application deadline:* For fall admission, 1/1 priority date for domestic students; for spring admission, 9/1 for domestic students. Applications are processed on a rolling basis. Application fee: $56 ($96 for international students). Electronic applications accepted. *Financial support:* In 2010–11, 1 fellowship, 2 research assistantships, 21 teaching assistantships were awarded; career-related internships or fieldwork, unspecified assistantships, and project assistantships also available. Support available to part-time students. Financial award application deadline: 4/15; financial award applicants required to submit FAFSA. Total annual research expenditures: $270,833. *Unit head:* Sara Benesh, Representative, 414-229-6720, Fax: 414-229-5021, E-mail: sbenesh@uwm.edu. *Application contact:* General Information Contact, 414-229-4982, Fax: 414-229-6967, E-mail: gradschool@uwm.edu.

University of Wyoming, College of Arts and Sciences, Department of Political Science, Program in Political Science, Laramie, WY 82070. Offers MA. Part-time programs available. *Degree requirements:* For master's, thesis or alternative. *Entrance requirements:* For master's, GRE General Test, bachelor's degree in political science, minimum GPA of 3.0. Additional exam requirements/recommendations for international students: Required—TOEFL (minimum score 525 paper-based; 195 computer-based). Electronic applications accepted. *Faculty research:* American government, public law, judicial politics, political theory, international relations.

Utah State University, School of Graduate Studies, College of Humanities, Arts and Social Sciences, Department of Political Science, Logan, UT 84322. Offers MA, MS. Part-time programs available. *Degree requirements:* For master's, one foreign language, thesis. *Entrance requirements:* For master's, GRE General Test, minimum GPA of 3.0. Additional exam requirements/recommendations for international students: Required—TOEFL. *Faculty research:* Political parties; social choice; international political economics; foreign policy; politics, markets, and public policy.

Vanderbilt University, Graduate School, Department of Political Science, Nashville, TN 37240-1001. Offers MA, MAT, PhD. *Faculty:* 23 full-time (10 women), 1 (woman) part-time/adjunct. *Students:* 37 full-time (15 women), 2 part-time (both women); includes 4 Black or African American, non-Hispanic/Latino; 2 Hispanic/Latino. Average age 29. 186 applicants, 12% accepted, 12 enrolled. In 2010, 4 master's, 5 doctorates awarded. Terminal master's awarded for partial completion of doctoral program. *Degree requirements:* For master's, thesis; for doctorate, thesis/dissertation, final and qualifying exams. *Entrance requirements:* For master's and doctorate, GRE General Test, writing sample. Additional exam requirements/recommendations for international students: Required—TOEFL (minimum score 570 paper-based; 230 computer-based; 88 iBT). *Application deadline:* For fall admission, 1/15 for domestic and international students. Application fee: $0. Electronic applications accepted. *Financial support:* Fellowships with full tuition reimbursements, research assistantships with full tuition reimbursements, teaching assistantships with full tuition reimbursements, Federal Work-Study, institutionally sponsored loans, scholarships/grants, and health care benefits available. Financial award application deadline: 1/15; financial award applicants required to submit CSS PROFILE or FAFSA. *Faculty research:* American politics, comparative politics, international politics, political theory, political culture and life. *Unit head:* John G. Geer, Chair, 615-343-5746, Fax: 615-343-6003, E-mail: j.geer@vanderbilt.edu. *Application contact:* Jonathan Hiskey, Director of Graduate Studies, 615-322-6236, Fax: 615-343-6003, E-mail: j.hiskey@vanderbilt.edu.

Villanova University, Graduate School of Liberal Arts and Sciences, Department of Political Science, Program in Political Science, Villanova, PA 19085-1699. Offers MA. Part-time programs available. *Faculty:* 7 full-time (2 women), 1 part-time/adjunct (0 women). *Students:* 35 full-time (8 women), 7 part-time (4 women); includes 7 minority (3 Black or African American, non-Hispanic/Latino; 2 Asian, non-Hispanic/Latino; 2 Hispanic/Latino), 2 international. Average age 29. 25 applicants, 92% accepted, 13 enrolled. In 2010, 22 master's awarded. *Degree requirements:* For master's, comprehensive exam, thesis or alternative. *Entrance requirements:* For master's, GRE, minimum GPA of 3.0. Additional exam requirements/recommendations for international students: Required—TOEFL. *Application deadline:* For fall admission, 2/1 priority date for domestic and international students; for spring admission, 11/15 priority date for domestic students, 10/15 priority date for international students. Applications are processed on a rolling basis. Application fee: $50. Electronic applications accepted. *Expenses:* Tuition: Part-time $700 per credit. Part-time tuition and fees vary according to degree level and program. *Financial support:* Scholarships/grants and unspecified assistantships available. Financial award application deadline: 3/15; financial award applicants required to submit FAFSA. *Unit head:* Dr. Markus Kreuzer, Director, 610-519-4710. *Application contact:* Dr. Adele Lindenmeyr, Information Contact, 610-519-7093, E-mail: matthew.kerbel@villanova.edu.

Virginia Commonwealth University, Graduate School, College of Humanities and Sciences, Wilder School of Government and Public Affairs, Richmond, VA 23284-9005. Offers MA, MPA, MS, MURP, PhD, CASR, CCJA, CPM, CURP, Certificate, Graduate Certificate, JD/MURP, MSW/Certificate. *Students:* 1,004 full-time (558 women), 1,058 part-time (655 women); includes 434 minority (259 Black or African American, non-Hispanic/Latino; 6 American Indian or Alaska Native, non-Hispanic/Latino; 88 Asian, non-Hispanic/Latino; 53 Hispanic/Latino; 3 Native Hawaiian or other Pacific Islander, non-Hispanic/Latino; 25 Two or more races, non-Hispanic/Latino), 117 international. *Expenses:* Tuition, state resident: full-time $4308; part-time $479 per credit hour. Tuition, nonresident: full-time $8942; part-time $994 per credit hour. Required fees: $2000; $85 per credit hour. Tuition and fees vary according to course level, course load, degree level, campus/location and program. *Unit head:* Dr. Niraj Verma, Director, L. Douglas Wilder School of Government and Public Affairs, 804-828-2292. *Application contact:* Dr. Niraj Verma, Director, L. Douglas Wilder School of Government and Public Affairs, 804-828-2292.

Virginia Polytechnic Institute and State University, Graduate School, College of Architecture and Urban Studies, School of Public and International Affairs, Blacksburg, VA 24061. Offers economic development (Certificate); government and international affairs (MPIA, PhD); homeland security policy (Certificate); local government management (Certificate); nonprofit and nongovernmental organization management (Certificate); planning, governance and globalization (PhD); public administration and public affairs (MPA, PhD); urban and regional planning (MURPL). *Accreditation:* ACSP. *Faculty:* 31 full-time (9 women). *Students:* 114 full-time (66 women), 105 part-time (54 women); includes 11 Black or African American, non-Hispanic/Latino; 1 American Indian or Alaska Native, non-Hispanic/Latino; 7 Asian, non-Hispanic/Latino; 8 Hispanic/Latino, 19 international. Average age 31. 166 applicants, 67% accepted, 53 enrolled. In 2010, 41 master's, 3 doctorates awarded. *Degree requirements:* For master's, comprehensive exam (for some programs), thesis (for some programs); for doctorate, comprehensive exam (for some programs), thesis/dissertation (for some programs). *Entrance requirements:* For master's and doctorate, GRE. Additional exam requirements/recommendations for international students: Required—TOEFL (minimum score 550 paper-based; 213 computer-based). *Application deadline:* For fall admission, 7/1 for domestic and international students; for spring admission, 12/1 for domestic and international students. Applications are processed on a rolling basis. Application fee: $65. Electronic applications accepted. *Expenses:* Tuition, state resident: full-time $9399; part-time $488 per credit hour. Tuition, nonresident: full-time $17,854; part-time $957.75 per credit hour. Required fees: $1534. Full-time tuition and fees vary according to program. *Financial support:* In 2010–11, 1 teaching assistantship with full tuition reimbursement (averaging $21,395 per year) was awarded; career-related internships or fieldwork, Federal Work-Study, scholarships/grants, health care benefits, and unspecified assistantships also available. Financial award application deadline: 1/15. *Faculty research:* Design theory, environmental planning, town planning, transportation planning. Total annual research expenditures: $610,749. *Unit head:* Dr. Karen M. Hult, UNIT HEAD, 540-231-5351, Fax: 540-231-9938, E-mail: khult@vt.edu. *Application contact:* Krystal D. Wright, Contact, 540-231-2291, Fax: 540-231-9938, E-mail: garch@vt.edu.

Virginia Polytechnic Institute and State University, Graduate School, College of Liberal Arts and Human Sciences, Department of Political Science, Blacksburg, VA 24061. Offers environmental politics and policy (Certificate); foundations of political analysis (Certificate); information policy and society (Certificate); political science (MA); security studies (Certificate). *Faculty:* 22 full-time (6 women), 1 (woman) part-time/adjunct. *Students:* 40 full-time (15 women), 49 part-time (19 women); includes 1 Black or African American, non-Hispanic/Latino; 1 American Indian or Alaska Native, non-Hispanic/Latino; 3 Asian, non-Hispanic/Latino; 4 Hispanic/Latino, 10 international. Average age 32. 49 applicants, 47% accepted, 13 enrolled. In 2010, 12 master's awarded. *Degree requirements:* For master's, comprehensive exam (for some programs), thesis (for some programs). *Entrance requirements:* For master's, GRE. Additional exam requirements/recommendations for international students: Required—TOEFL (minimum score 550 paper-based; 213 computer-based). *Application deadline:* For fall admission, 7/1 for domestic and international students; for spring admission, 12/1 for domestic and international students. Applications are processed on a rolling basis. Application fee: $65. Electronic applications accepted. *Expenses:* Tuition, state resident: full-time $9399; part-time $488 per credit hour. Tuition, nonresident: full-time $17,854; part-time $957.75 per credit hour. Required fees: $1534. Full-time tuition and fees vary according to program. *Financial support:* In 2010–11, 12 teaching assistantships with full tuition reimbursements (averaging $12,972 per year) were awarded; career-related internships or fieldwork, Federal Work-Study, scholarships/grants, health care benefits, and unspecified assistantships also available. Financial award application deadline: 1/15. *Faculty research:* Comparative politics, international relations, American government and politics, research methods. Total annual research expenditures: $24,854. *Unit head:* Dr. Ilja A. Luciak, UNIT HEAD, 540-231-6571, Fax: 540-231-6078, E-mail: iluciak@vt.edu. *Application contact:* Tim Luke, Contact, 540-231-6633, Fax: 540-231-6078, E-mail: twluke@vt.edu.

Virginia Polytechnic Institute and State University, VT Online, Blacksburg, VA 24061. Offers aerospace engineering (MS); business information systems (Graduate Certificate); career and technical education (MS); computer engineering (M Eng, MS); decision support systems (Graduate Certificate); eLearning leadership (MA); electrical engineering (M Eng, MS); engineering administration (MEA); environmental politics and policy (Graduate Certificate); foundations of political analysis (Graduate Certificate); health product risk management (Graduate Certificate); information policy and society (Graduate Certificate); information security (Graduate Certificate); instructional technology (MA); liberal arts (Graduate Certificate); life sciences: health product risk management (MS); natural resources (MNR, Graduate Certificate); networking (Graduate Certificate); nonprofit and nongovernmental organization management (Graduate Certificate); ocean engineering (MS); political science (MA); security studies (Graduate Certificate); software development (Graduate Certificate). *Expenses:* Tuition, state resident: full-time $9399; part-time $488 per credit hour. Tuition, nonresident: full-time $17,854; part-time $957.75 per credit hour. Required fees: $1534. Full-time tuition and fees vary according to program.

Washington State University, Graduate School, College of Liberal Arts, Department of Political Science, Program in Political Science, Pullman, WA 99164. Offers MA, PhD. *Faculty:* 22. *Students:* 30 full-time (7 women), 13 part-time (3 women); includes 1 Black or African American, non-Hispanic/Latino; 1 American Indian or Alaska Native, non-Hispanic/Latino; 5 Hispanic/Latino, 4 international. Average age 32. 45 applicants, 27% accepted, 4 enrolled. In 2010, 9 master's, 3 doctorates awarded. Terminal master's awarded for partial completion of doctoral program. *Degree requirements:* For master's, comprehensive exam (for some programs), thesis, oral exam; for doctorate, comprehensive exam, thesis/dissertation, oral exam, written exam. *Entrance requirements:* For master's, GRE General Test, minimum GPA of 3.0; for doctorate, GRE General Test, minimum GPA of 3.5. Additional exam requirements/recommendations for international students: Required—TOEFL. *Application deadline:* For fall admission, 2/1 for domestic and international students; for spring admission, 11/1 for domestic students, 7/1 for international students. Application fee: $50. Electronic applications accepted. *Expenses:* Tuition, state resident: full-time $8552; part-time $443 per credit. Tuition, nonresident: full-time $21,650; part-time $1083 per credit. Required fees: $846. *Financial support:* In 2010–11, 34 students received support, including 4 fellowships (averaging $2,656 per year), 6 research assistantships with full and partial tuition reimbursements available (averaging $13,917 per year), 12 teaching assistantships with full and partial tuition reimbursements available (averaging $13,056 per year). Financial award application deadline: 2/1; financial award applicants required to submit FAFSA. *Faculty research:* Political psychology and image theory, grass roots environmental policy, federal juvenile policy. *Unit head:* Dr. Andrew Mark Appleton, Director, 509-335-4025, Fax: 509-335-7990, E-mail: appleton@wsu.edu. *Application contact:* Graduate School Admissions, 800-GRADWSU, Fax: 509-335-1949, E-mail: gradsch@wsu.edu.

Washington University in St. Louis, Graduate School of Arts and Sciences, Department of Political Science, St. Louis, MO 63130-4899. Offers political economy and public policy (MA); political science (PhD). Terminal master's awarded for partial completion of doctoral program. *Degree requirements:* For master's, thesis or alternative; for doctorate, thesis/dissertation. *Entrance requirements:* For master's and doctorate, GRE General Test. Electronic applications accepted.

Wayne State University, College of Liberal Arts and Sciences, Department of Political Science, Detroit, MI 48202. Offers political science (MA, PhD); public administration (MPA), including criminal justice, public administration; JD/MA. *Accreditation:* NASPAA. Evening/weekend programs available. *Faculty:* 16 full-time (5 women), 2 part-time/adjunct (1 woman). *Students:* 44 full-time (19 women), 28 part-time (14 women); includes 7 minority (6 Black or African American, non-Hispanic/Latino; 1 Hispanic/Latino), 14 international. Average age 34. 29 applicants, 79% accepted, 15 enrolled. In 2010, 6 master's, 5 doctorates awarded. *Degree requirements:* For doctorate, thesis/dissertation. *Entrance requirements:* For master's, GRE General Test; for doctorate, GRE General Test, 3 letters of recommendation; autobiography; interview. Additional exam requirements/recommendations for international students: Required—TOEFL (minimum score 550 paper-based; 213 computer-based); Recommended—TWE (minimum score 6). *Application deadline:* For fall admission, 7/1 for domestic students, 6/1 for international students; for winter admission, 10/1 for international students; for spring admission, 2/1 for international students. Applications are processed on a rolling basis. Application fee: $30 ($50 for international students). Electronic applications accepted. *Expenses:* Tuition, state resident: full-time $7662; part-time $478.85 per credit hour. Tuition, nonresident: full-time $16,920; part-time $1057.55 per credit hour. Required fees: $571.20; $35.70 per credit hour. $188.05 per semester. Tuition and fees vary according to course load and program. *Financial support:* In 2010–11, 9 fellowships (averaging $10,889 per year), 13 teaching assistantships with tuition reimbursements (averaging $15,181 per year) were awarded; research assistantships with tuition reimbursements, career-related internships or fieldwork, Federal Work-Study, and institutionally sponsored loans also available. *Faculty research:* American politics and public policy, comparative politics and international relations, political theory, public administration, urban politics. *Unit head:* Daniel Geller, Chair, 313-577-6328, Fax: 313-993-3435, E-mail: av0844@wayne.edu. *Application contact:* Ewa Golebiowska, Associate Professor, 313-577-2630, Fax: 313-993-3435, E-mail: ewa_golebiowska@wayne.edu.

West Chester University of Pennsylvania, Office of Graduate Studies, College of Business and Public Affairs, Department of Political Science, West Chester, PA 19383. Offers general public administration (MPA); human resource management (MPA, Certificate); non profit administration (Certificate); nonprofit administration (MPA); public administration (Certificate). Part-time and evening/weekend programs available. *Students:* 22 full-time (12 women), 39 part-time (31 women); includes 16 minority (12 Black or African American, non-Hispanic/Latino; 4 Hispanic/Latino), 2 international. Average age 31. 41 applicants, 88% accepted, 17 enrolled. In 2010, 22 master's awarded. *Degree requirements:* For master's, capstone project. *Entrance requirements:* For master's and Certificate, statement of professional goals, resume, two letters of reference. Additional exam requirements/recommendations for international students: Required—TOEFL (minimum score 550 paper-based; 213 computer-based; 80 iBT). *Application deadline:* For fall admission, 4/15 priority date for domestic students, 3/15 for international students; for spring admission, 10/15 for domestic students, 9/1 for international students. Applications are processed on a rolling basis. Application fee: $35. Electronic applications accepted. *Expenses:* Tuition, state resident: full-time $6966; part-time $387 per credit. Tuition, nonresident: full-time $11,146; part-time $619 per credit. Required fees: $1614.40; $133.24 per credit. Part-time tuition and fees vary according to campus/location. *Financial support:* Unspecified assistantships available. Support available to part-time students. Financial award application deadline: 2/15; financial award applicants required to submit FAFSA. *Faculty research:* Public policy, economic development, public opinion, urban politics, public administration. *Unit head:* Dr. Christopher Fiorentino, Dean, College of Business and Public Affairs, 610-436-2930, E-mail: cfiorentino@wcupa.edu. *Application contact:* Dr. Lorraine Bernotsky, Graduate Coordinator, 610-738-0576, E-mail: lbernotsky@wcupa.edu.

Western Illinois University, School of Graduate Studies, College of Arts and Sciences, Department of Political Science, Macomb, IL 61455-1390. Offers MA. Part-time programs available. *Students:* 21 full-time (7 women), 5 part-time (2 women); includes 5 minority (2 Black or African American, non-Hispanic/Latino; 3 Hispanic/Latino), 3 international. Average age 27. 21 applicants, 62% accepted. In 2010, 13 master's awarded. *Degree requirements:* For master's, comprehensive exam, thesis or alternative. *Entrance requirements:* Additional exam requirements/recommendations for international students: Required—TOEFL (minimum score 550 paper-based; 213 computer-based; 80 iBT). *Application deadline:* Applications are processed on a rolling basis. Application fee: $30. Electronic applications accepted. *Expenses:* Tuition, state resident: full-time $6370; part-time $265.40 per credit hour. Tuition, nonresident: full-time $12,740; part-time $530.80 per credit hour. Required fees: $75.67 per credit hour. *Financial support:* In 2010–11, 13 students received support, including 13 research assistantships with full tuition reimbursements available (averaging $7,280 per year). Financial award applicants required to submit FAFSA. *Unit head:* Dr. Keith Boeckelman, Chairperson, 309-298-1055. *Application contact:* Evelyn Hoing, Assistant Director of Graduate Studies, 309-298-1806, Fax: 309-298-2345, E-mail: grad-office@wiu.edu.

Western Kentucky University, Graduate Studies, Potter College of Arts and Letters, Department of Political Science, Bowling Green, KY 42101. Offers MPA. *Accreditation:* NASPAA. Part-time and evening/weekend programs available. *Degree requirements:* For master's, comprehensive exam, final exam. *Entrance requirements:* For master's, GRE General Test, minimum GPA of 2.75. Additional exam requirements/recommendations for international students: Required—TOEFL (minimum score 555 paper-based; 213 computer-based; 79 iBT). *Faculty research:* Role of non-profits, comparative policy analysis, social welfare policy, rural administration, ethics and bureaucracy.

Western Michigan University, Graduate College, College of Arts and Sciences, Department of Political Science, Program in Political Science, Kalamazoo, MI 49008. Offers MA, PhD. *Degree requirements:* For master's, thesis optional, oral exams; for doctorate, thesis/dissertation, oral exam. *Entrance requirements:* For doctorate, GRE General Test.

Western Washington University, Graduate School, College of Humanities and Social Sciences, Department of Political Science, Bellingham, WA 98225-5996. Offers MA. Part-time programs available. *Degree requirements:* For master's, comprehensive exam, thesis (for some programs). *Entrance requirements:* For master's, GRE General Test, minimum GPA of 3.0 in last 60 semester hours or last 90 quarter hours. Additional exam requirements/recommendations for international students: Required—TOEFL (minimum score 567 paper-based; 227 computer-based). Electronic applications accepted. *Faculty research:* Elections, environment, identity, international relations.

West Texas A&M University, College of Education and Social Sciences, Department of History and Political Science, Program in Political Science, Canyon, TX 79016-0001. Offers MA. Part-time and evening/weekend programs available. *Degree requirements:* For master's, comprehensive exam, thesis optional. *Entrance requirements:* For master's, GRE General Test. Additional exam requirements/recommendations for international students: Required—TOEFL (minimum score 550 paper-based). Electronic applications accepted. *Faculty research:* American government, public administration, state and local government, international politics.

West Virginia University, Eberly College of Arts and Sciences, Department of Political Science, Morgantown, WV 26506. Offers American public policy and politics (MA); international and comparative public policy and politics (MA); political science (PhD); public policy analysis (PhD). Terminal master's awarded for partial completion of doctoral program. *Degree requirements:* For master's, thesis optional; for doctorate, comprehensive exam, thesis/dissertation. *Entrance requirements:* For master's, GRE General Test, minimum GPA of 2.75; for doctorate, GRE General Test, minimum GPA of 3.0. Additional exam requirements/recommendations for international students: Required—TOEFL. *Faculty research:* Public policy, research methods, foreign policy analysis, judicial politics, environmental and energy policy.

Wilfrid Laurier University, Faculty of Graduate and Postdoctoral Studies, Faculty of Arts, Department of Political Science, Waterloo, ON N2L 3C5, Canada. Offers Canadian political studies (MA); comparative politics/international relations (MA). Part-time programs available. *Faculty:* 20 full-time (6 women). *Students:* 18 full-time (7 women), 3 part-time (1 woman), 1 international. 68 applicants, 49% accepted, 13 enrolled. In 2010, 13 master's awarded. *Degree requirements:* For master's, thesis optional. *Entrance requirements:* For master's, honors bachelor's degree or the equivalent in political science, minimum B average in undergraduate course work. Additional exam requirements/recommendations for international students: Required—TOEFL (minimum score 89 iBT). *Application deadline:* For fall admission, 2/1 priority date for domestic and international students. Application fee: $100. Electronic applications accepted. Tuition and fee charges are reported in Canadian dollars. *Expenses:* Tuition, area resident: Full-time $15,300 Canadian dollars; part-time $1200 Canadian dollars per credit. International tuition: $21,300 Canadian dollars full-time. Required fees: $650 Canadian dollars; $100 Canadian dollars per credit. Tuition and fees vary according to course load, degree level, campus/location and program. *Financial support:* In 2010–11, 26 fellowships, 5 research assistantships, 26 teaching assistantships were awarded; career-related internships or fieldwork, scholarships/grants, health care benefits, and unspecified assistantships also available. *Faculty research:* Political behavior/political psychology, Canadian political studies, comparative, politics/relations, public opinion and electoral studies, international. *Unit head:* Dr. Andrea Perella, Graduate Coordinator, 519-884-0710 Ext. 2719, Fax: 519-746-3655, E-mail: aperrella@wlu.ca. *Application contact:* Jennifer Williams, Graduate Admission and Records Officer, 519-884-0710 Ext. 3536, Fax: 519-884-1020, E-mail: gradstudies@wlu.ca.

Wilfrid Laurier University, Faculty of Graduate and Postdoctoral Studies, Faculty of Arts and School of Business and Economics, Global Governance Program, Waterloo, ON N2L 3C5, Canada. Offers conflict and security (PhD); global environment (PhD); global justice and human rights (PhD); global political economy (PhD); global social governance (PhD); multilateral institutions and diplomacy (PhD). *Faculty:* 27 full-time (7 women). *Students:* 14 full-time (7 women), 4 international. 83 applicants, 5% accepted, 3 enrolled. *Degree requirements:* For doctorate, thesis/dissertation. *Entrance requirements:* For doctorate, MA in political science, history, economics, international development studies, international peace studies, globalization studies, environmental studies or related field with minimum A-. Additional exam requirements/recommendations for international students: Required—TOEFL (minimum score 89 iBT). *Application deadline:* For fall admission, 1/31 priority date for domestic and international students. Application fee: $100. Electronic applications accepted. Tuition and fees charges are reported in Canadian dollars. *Expenses:* Tuition, area resident: Full-time $15,300 Canadian

Political Science

Wilfrid Laurier University *(continued)*
dollars; part-time $1200 Canadian dollars per credit. International tuition: $21,300 Canadian dollars full-time. Required fees: $650 Canadian dollars; $100 Canadian dollars per credit. Tuition and fees vary according to course load, degree level, campus/location and program. *Financial support:* In 2010–11, 4 fellowships, 4 teaching assistantships were awarded; career-related internships or fieldwork, scholarships/grants, health care benefits, and unspecified assistantships also available. *Faculty research:* Global political economy, global environment, conflict and security, global justice and human rights, multilateral institutions and diplomacy. *Unit head:* Dr. Randall Wigle, Associate Director, 519-884-1970 Ext. 2438, Fax: 519-884-8454, E-mail: rwigle@wlu.ca. *Application contact:* Jennifer Willaims, Student Contact, 519-884-0710 Ext. 3536, Fax: 519-884-1020, E-mail: gradstudies@wlu.ca.

Wilfrid Laurier University, Faculty of Graduate and Postdoctoral Studies, Faculty of Arts and School of Business and Economics, International Public Policy Program, Waterloo, ON N2L 3C5, Canada. Offers global governance (MIPP); human security (MIPP); international economic relations (MIPP); international environmental policy (MIPP). *Faculty:* 17 full-time (8 women). *Students:* 16 full-time (9 women), 2 international. 90 applicants, 30% accepted, 14 enrolled. In 2010, 15 master's awarded. *Entrance requirements:* For master's, honours BA with minimum B average. Additional exam requirements/recommendations for international students: Required—TOEFL (minimum score 89 iBT). *Application deadline:* For fall admission, 2/1 priority date for domestic and international students. Application fee: $100. Electronic applications accepted. Tuition and fees charges are reported in Canadian dollars. *Expenses:* Tuition, area resident: Full-time $15,300 Canadian dollars; part-time $1200 Canadian dollars per credit. International tuition: $21,300 Canadian dollars full-time. Required fees: $650 Canadian dollars; $100 Canadian dollars per credit. Tuition and fees vary according to course load, degree level, campus/location and program. *Financial support:* In 2010–11, 5 fellowships, 5 teaching assistantships were awarded; career-related internships or fieldwork, scholarships/grants, health care benefits, and unspecified assistantships also available. *Faculty research:* International environmental policy, international economic relations, human security, global governance. *Unit head:* Dr. Terry Snodden, Graduate Coordinator, 519-884-0710 Ext. 2945, Fax: 519-884-8854, E-mail: tlevesque@wlu.ca. *Application contact:* Jennifer Williams, Graduate Admissions and Records Officer, 519-884-0710 Ext. 3536, Fax: 519-884-1020, E-mail: gradstudies@wlu.ca.

Yale University, Graduate School of Arts and Sciences, Department of Political Science, New Haven, CT 06520. Offers PhD. *Degree requirements:* For doctorate, one foreign language, thesis/dissertation. *Entrance requirements:* For doctorate, GRE General Test. *Faculty research:* U.N. and international security.

Yorktown University, School of Government, Denver, CO 80246. Offers American culture and the life of the citizen (MA); foundations of democracy in America and Western Europe (MA); political economy (MA); political theory (MA).

York University, Faculty of Graduate Studies, Faculty of Arts, Program in Political Science, Toronto, ON M3J 1P3, Canada. Offers MA, PhD. Part-time programs available. *Degree requirements:* For master's, thesis or alternative; for doctorate, one foreign language, comprehensive exam, thesis/dissertation. Electronic applications accepted.

York University, Faculty of Graduate Studies, Faculty of Arts, Program in Social and Political Thought, Toronto, ON M3J 1P3, Canada. Offers MA, PhD. Part-time programs available. *Degree requirements:* For master's, one foreign language, thesis or alternative, oral exams; for doctorate, one foreign language, comprehensive exam, thesis/dissertation. Electronic applications accepted.

Section 24
Psychology and Counseling

This section contains a directory of institutions offering graduate work in psychology and counseling, followed by in-depth entries submitted by institutions that chose to prepare detailed program descriptions. Additional information about programs listed in the directory but not augmented by an in-depth entry may be obtained by writing directly to the dean of a graduate school or chair of a department at the address given in the directory.

For programs offering related work, see also in this book *Criminology and Forensics, Family and Consumer Sciences,* and *Sociology, Anthropology, and Archaeology.* In the other guides in this series:

Graduate Programs in the Biological Sciences

See *Biological and Biomedical Sciences; Genetics, Developmental Biology, and Reproductive Biology; Neuroscience and Neurobiology;* and *Pharmacology and Toxicology*

Graduate Programs in Business, Education, Health, Information Studies, Law & Social Work

See *Education, Nursing (Psychiatric Nursing), Pharmacy and Pharmaceutical Sciences, Public Health,* and *Social Work*

CONTENTS

Program Directories

Psychology—General

Abilene Christian University, Graduate School, College of Arts and Sciences, Department of Psychology, Program in Psychology, Abilene, TX 79699-9100. Offers MS. *Students:* 5 full-time (4 women), 1 (woman) part-time; includes 1 Hispanic/Latino, 1 international. 7 applicants, 43% accepted, 1 enrolled. *Degree requirements:* For master's, comprehensive exam, thesis. *Entrance requirements:* For master's, GRE General Test. Additional exam requirements/recommendations for international students: Required—TOEFL (minimum score 550 paper-based; 213 computer-based). *Application deadline:* For fall admission, 4/1 priority date for domestic students; for spring admission, 11/1 for domestic students. Applications are processed on a rolling basis. Application fee: $40. Electronic applications accepted. *Expenses:* Tuition: Full-time $12,906; part-time $717 per hour. Required fees: $1250; $61.50 per unit. *Financial support:* In 2010–11, 4 students received support. Federal Work-Study available. Support available to part-time students. Financial award application deadline: 4/1; financial award applicants required to submit FAFSA. *Unit head:* Dr. Robert McKelvain, Graduate Advisor, 325-674-2286, Fax: 325-674-6968, E-mail: mckelvainr@acu.edu. *Application contact:* David Pittman, Graduate Admissions Counselor, 325-674-2656, Fax: 325-674-6717, E-mail: gradinfo@acu.edu.

Acadia University, Faculty of Pure and Applied Science, Department of Psychology, Wolfville, NS B4P 2R6, Canada. Offers clinical psychology (M Sc). *Faculty:* 11 full-time (6 women), 2 part-time/adjunct (both women). *Students:* 9 full-time (7 women), 1 (woman) part-time. Average age 26. 36 applicants, 22% accepted, 4 enrolled. In 2010, 3 master's awarded. *Degree requirements:* For master's, thesis. *Entrance requirements:* For master's, GRE General Test, GRE Subject Test, honors degree or equivalent. Additional exam requirements/recommendations for international students: Required—TOEFL (minimum score 580 paper-based; 237 computer-based; 93 iBT), IELTS (minimum score 6.5). *Application deadline:* For fall admission, 2/1 priority date for domestic and international students. Applications are processed on a rolling basis. Application fee: $50. *Financial support:* Teaching assistantships, career-related internships or fieldwork, scholarships/grants, and unspecified assistantships available. Financial award application deadline: 2/1. *Faculty research:* Social psychology, job stress, psychotherapy, cognition perception, development. *Unit head:* Dr. Peter McLeod, Head, 902-585-1301, Fax: 902-585-1078, E-mail: peter.mcleod@acadiau.ca. *Application contact:* Dr. Peter Horvath, Graduate Coordinator, 902-585-1200, Fax: 902-585-1078, E-mail: peter.horvath@acadiau.ca.

Adelphi University, Derner Institute of Advanced Psychological Studies, Garden City, NY 11530-0701. Offers clinical psychology (PhD); general psychology (MA); mental health counseling (MA); school psychology (MA). *Accreditation:* APA (one or more programs are accredited). Part-time programs available. *Students:* 186 full-time (154 women), 111 part-time (94 women); includes 63 minority (24 Black or African American, non-Hispanic/Latino; 2 American Indian or Alaska Native, non-Hispanic/Latino; 15 Asian, non-Hispanic/Latino; 17 Hispanic/Latino; 1 Native Hawaiian or other Pacific Islander, non-Hispanic/Latino; 4 Two or more races, non-Hispanic/Latino), 16 international. Average age 28. 566 applicants, 36% accepted, 100 enrolled. In 2010, 115 master's, 29 doctorates awarded. *Degree requirements:* For master's, comprehensive exam; for doctorate, thesis/dissertation, research (second year), 1 year internship. *Entrance requirements:* For master's, 3 letters of recommendation, minimum GPA of 3.0; for doctorate, GRE General Test, GRE Subject Test, interview; resume; undergraduate course work in psychology, experimental psychology, statistics, developmental psychology, and abnormal psychology. Additional exam requirements/recommendations for international students: Required—TOEFL (minimum score 550 paper-based; 213 computer-based; 80 iBT). *Application deadline:* For fall admission, 4/1 priority date for domestic students, 5/1 priority date for international students; for spring admission, 11/1 priority date for international students. Application fee: $50. Electronic applications accepted. *Expenses:* Contact institution. *Financial support:* In 2010–11, 107 research assistantships with full and partial tuition reimbursements (averaging $8,303 per year) were awarded; teaching assistantships, career-related internships or fieldwork, Federal Work-Study,

institutionally sponsored loans, and unspecified assistantships also available. Financial award application deadline: 2/15; financial award applicants required to submit FAFSA. *Faculty research:* Psychoanalytic processes, trauma and resilience, personality disorders, program evaluation, psychotherapy process. *Unit head:* Dr. Jacques P. Barber, Dean, 516-877-4803, E-mail: jcmuran@adelphi.edu. *Application contact:* Christine Murphy, Director of Admissions, 516-877-3050, Fax: 516-877-3039, E-mail: graduateadmissions@adelphi.edu.

See Close-Up on page 1117.

Adler School of Professional Psychology, Programs in Psychology, Chicago, IL 60602. Offers advanced Adlerian psychotherapy (Certificate); art therapy (MA); clinical neuropsychology (Certificate); clinical psychology (Psy D); community psychology (MA); counseling and organizational psychology (MA); counseling psychology (MA); forensic psychology (MA); gerontological counseling (MA); marriage and family counseling (MA); marriage and family therapy (Certificate); organizational psychology (MA); police psychology (MA); rehabilitation counseling (MA); sport and health psychology (MA); substance abuse counseling (Certificate); Psy D/Certificate; Psy D/MACAT; Psy D/MACP; Psy D/MAMFC; Psy D/MASAC. *Accreditation:* APA. Part-time and evening/weekend programs available. Postbaccalaureate distance learning degree programs offered (minimal on-campus study). *Faculty:* 40 full-time (18 women), 61 part-time/adjunct (31 women). *Students:* 688 full-time (532 women), 142 part-time (110 women). Average age 27.Terminal master's awarded for partial completion of doctoral program. *Degree requirements:* For master's, thesis or alternative, oral exam, practicum; for doctorate, thesis/dissertation, clinical exam, internship, oral exam, practicum, written qualifying exam. *Entrance requirements:* For master's, 12 semester hours in psychology, minimum GPA of 3.0; for doctorate, 18 semester hours in psychology, minimum GPA of 3.25; for Certificate, appropriate master's or doctoral degree. Additional exam requirements/recommendations for international students: Required—TOEFL (minimum score 550 paper-based; 213 computer-based; 79 iBT). *Application deadline:* For fall admission, 2/15 priority date for domestic students, 12/1 priority date for international students. Applications are processed on a rolling basis. Application fee: $50. Electronic applications accepted. *Financial support:* Career-related internships or fieldwork, Federal Work-Study, scholarships/grants, and tuition waivers (full and partial) available. Support available to part-time students. Financial award application deadline: 5/15; financial award applicants required to submit FAFSA. *Application contact:* Michelle Brice, Director of Admissions, 312-662-4113, Fax: 312-662-4199, E-mail: admissions@adler.edu.

See Display below and Close-Up on page 1119.

Alabama Agricultural and Mechanical University, School of Graduate Studies, School of Education, Department of Counseling and Special Education, Huntsville, AL 35811. Offers communicative disorders (M Ed, MS); psychology and counseling (MS, Ed S), including clinical psychology (MS), counseling and guidance, counseling psychology (MS), personnel management (MS), psychometry (MS), school psychology (MS); special education (M Ed, MS). *Accreditation:* CORE; NCATE. Part-time and evening/weekend programs available. *Degree requirements:* For master's, comprehensive exam. *Entrance requirements:* For master's, GRE General Test. Additional exam requirements/recommendations for international students: Required—TOEFL (minimum score 500 paper-based; 173 computer-based; 61 iBT). *Faculty research:* Increasing numbers of minorities in special education and speech-language pathology.

Alliant International University–Fresno, California School of Professional Psychology, Fresno, CA 93727. Offers PhD, Psy D. *Accreditation:* APA. *Degree requirements:* For doctorate, thesis/dissertation. *Entrance requirements:* For doctorate, interview, 3.0 GPA, letters of recommendation. *Faculty research:* Child and family, body image, psychoanalysis, neuropsychology, teaching of psychology.

Alliant International University–Los Angeles, California School of Professional Psychology, Alhambra, CA 91803-1360. Offers MA, PhD, Psy D. *Accreditation:* APA. *Degree requirements:*

For doctorate, comprehensive exam, thesis/dissertation. *Entrance requirements:* For doctorate, interview, minimum GPA of 3.0 in psychology and overall, letters of recommendation. Additional exam requirements/recommendations for international students: Required—TOEFL (minimum score 600 paper-based; 250 computer-based), TWE (minimum score 5). Electronic applications accepted. *Faculty research:* Family therapy, pregnancy-related issues, multi-cultural psychology, post-traumatic stress.

Alliant International University–Sacramento, California School of Professional Psychology, Sacramento, CA 95825. Offers MA, Psy D. Electronic applications accepted.

Alliant International University–San Diego, California School of Professional Psychology, San Diego, CA 92131-1799. Offers MA, PhD, Psy D. *Accreditation:* APA. Part-time programs available. *Degree requirements:* For doctorate, thesis/dissertation. *Entrance requirements:* For doctorate, interview, minimum GPA of 3.0 in both psychology and overall. *Faculty research:* Native American studies, cross-cultural family therapy, families.

Alliant International University–San Francisco, California School of Professional Psychology, San Francisco, CA 94133-1221. Offers Post-Doctoral MS, PhD, Psy D, Certificate. *Accreditation:* APA (one or more programs are accredited). *Degree requirements:* For doctorate, comprehensive exam, thesis/dissertation. *Entrance requirements:* For master's and doctorate, interview, minimum GPA of 3.0. Additional exam requirements/recommendations for international students: Required—TOEFL (minimum score 600 paper-based; 250 computer-based), TWE (minimum score 5). Electronic applications accepted. *Faculty research:* Multicultural issues, lesbian/gay/bisexual/transgender issues, health psychology, family systems, substance abuse.

American International College, School of Arts, Education and Sciences, Department of Psychology, Springfield, MA 01109-3189. Offers clinical psychology (MA); educational psychology (MA, Ed D); forensic psychology (MS). Part-time and evening/weekend programs available. *Degree requirements:* For master's, comprehensive exam (for some programs), thesis (for some programs), practicum. *Entrance requirements:* For master's, minimum GPA of 3.0; for doctorate, GRE General Test, interview. Additional exam requirements/recommendations for international students: Required—TOEFL. Electronic applications accepted.

American Public University System, AMU/APU Graduate Programs, Charles Town, WV 25414. Offers accounting (MBA); administration and supervision (M Ed); air warfare (MA Military Studies); asymmetrical warfare (MA Military Studies); criminal justice (MA); emergency and disaster management (MA); entrepreneurship (MBA); environmental policy and management (MS); finance (MBA); general (MBA); global business management (MBA); guidance and counseling (M Ed); history (MA); homeland security (MA); homeland security resource allocation (MBA); humanities (MA); information technology (MS); information technology management (MBA); intelligence studies (MA); international relations and conflict resolution (MA); joint warfare (MA Military Studies); land warfare (MA Military Studies); legal studies (MA); management (MA), including defense mangement, general, human resource management, organizational leadership, public administration; marketing (MBA); military history (MA); national security studies (MA); naval warfare (MA Military Studies); nonprofit management (MBA); political science (MA); psychology (MA); public administration (MA); public health (MA); security management (MA); space studies (MS); sports management (MS); strategic leadership (MA Military Studies); teaching (M Ed), including elementary, secondary social sciences; transportation and logistics management (MA). Programs offered via distance learning only. Part-time and evening/weekend programs available. Postbaccalaureate distance learning degree programs offered (no on-campus study). *Faculty:* 253 full-time (134 women), 1,208 part-time/adjunct (570 women). *Students:* 956 full-time (422 women), 8,476 part-time (2,821 women); includes 2,511 minority (1,218 Black or African American, non-Hispanic/Latino; 68 American Indian or Alaska Native, non-Hispanic/Latino; 219 Asian, non-Hispanic/Latino; 705 Hispanic/Latino; 46 Native Hawaiian or other Pacific Islander, non-Hispanic/Latino; 255 Two or more races, non-Hispanic/Latino), 107 international. Average age 35. 9,550 applicants, 100% accepted. In 2010, 1,688 master's awarded. *Degree requirements:* For master's, comprehensive exam or practicum. *Entrance requirements:* For master's, official transcript showing earned bachelor's degree from institution accredited by recognized accrediting body. Additional exam requirements/recommendations for international students: Required—TOEFL (minimum score 550 paper-based; 213 computer-based), IELTS (minimum score 6.5). *Application deadline:* Applications are processed on a rolling basis. Application fee: $0. Electronic applications accepted. *Financial support:* Applicants required to submit FAFSA. *Faculty research:* Military history, criminal justice, management performance, national security. *Unit head:* Dr. Frank McCluskey, Provost, 877-468-6268, Fax: 304-724-3780. *Application contact:* Terry Grant, Director of Enrollment Management, 877-468-6268, Fax: 304-724-3780, E-mail: info@apus.edu.

American University, College of Arts and Sciences, Department of Psychology, Washington, DC 22016-8062. Offers behavior, cognition, and neuroscience (PhD), including psychology; clinical psychology (PhD), including psychology; psychology (MA), including experimental/biological psychology, general psychology, personality/social psychology. *Accreditation:* APA. Part-time programs available. *Faculty:* 19 full-time (7 women), 6 part-time/adjunct (4 women). *Students:* 65 full-time (51 women), 47 part-time (41 women); includes 16 minority (4 Black or African American, non-Hispanic/Latino; 3 Asian, non-Hispanic/Latino; 9 Hispanic/Latino), 3 international. Average age 28. 445 applicants, 19% accepted, 36 enrolled. In 2010, 35 master's, 11 doctorates awarded. *Degree requirements:* For master's, comprehensive exam, thesis or alternative; for doctorate, comprehensive exam, thesis/dissertation, tools of research. *Entrance requirements:* For master's, GRE General Test, GRE Subject Test, recommendations; for doctorate, GRE General Test, GRE Subject Test. Additional exam requirements/recommendations for international students: Required—TOEFL. Application fee: $80. *Financial support:* Fellowships, research assistantships, teaching assistantships, career-related internships or fieldwork, Federal Work-Study, institutionally sponsored loans, tuition waivers (full and partial), and unspecified assistantships available. Support available to part-time students. Financial award application deadline: 2/1. *Faculty research:* Anxiety disorders, cognitive assessment, neuropsychology, conditioning and learning, psychopharmacology. *Unit head:* Dr. Anthony Riley, Chair, 202-885-1720, E-mail: alriley@american.edu. *Application contact:* Sara Holland, Senior Administrative Assistant, 202-885-1717, Fax: 202-885-1023, E-mail: holland@american.edu.

American University of Beirut, Graduate Programs, Faculty of Arts and Sciences, Beirut, Lebanon. Offers anthropology (MA); Arabic language and literature (MA); archaeology (MA); biology (MS); chemistry (MS); computational science (MS); computer science (MS); economics (MA); education (MA); English language (MA); English literature (MA); environmental policy planning (MSES); financial economics (MAFE); geology (MS); history (MA); mathematics (MA, MS); Middle Eastern studies (MA); philosophy (MA); physics (MS); political studies (MA); psychology (MA); public administration (MA); sociology (MA); statistics (MA, MS). Part-time programs available. *Faculty:* 229 full-time (98 women), 136 part-time/adjunct (79 women). *Students:* 158 full-time (104 women), 263 part-time (171 women). Average age 25. 356 applicants, 59% accepted, 127 enrolled. In 2010, 57 master's awarded. *Degree requirements:* For master's, one foreign language, comprehensive exam, thesis (for some programs). *Entrance requirements:* For master's, GRE, letter of recommendation. Additional exam requirements/recommendations for international students: Required—TOEFL (minimum score 600 paper-based; 250 computer-based; 97 iBT), IELTS (minimum score 7). *Application deadline:* For fall admission, 4/30 for domestic and international students; for spring admission, 11/1 for domestic and international students. Application fee: $50. *Expenses:* Tuition: Full-time $12,294; part-time $683 per credit. Required fees: $499; $499 per credit. Tuition and fees vary according to course load and program. *Financial support:* In 2010–11, 33 students received support. Career-related internships or fieldwork, institutionally sponsored loans, scholarships/grants, health care benefits, and unspecified assistantships available. Financial award application deadline: 2/4; financial award applicants required to submit FAFSA. *Faculty research:* Modern and contemporary world theatre; mineralogy, petrology, and geochemistry; cell differentiation and transformation; combinatorial technologies; philosophy of action; continental philosophy; Phoenician epigraphy; nascent complex societies and urbanism; the economies of the Arab world; environmental economics; tectonophysics; host-parasite interactions; innate immunity; insect-plant interactions; history of the Ottoman archives; decentralization; transparency and corruption. Total annual research expenditures: $622,243. *Unit head:* Dr. Patrick McGreevy, Dean, 961-137-4374 Ext. 3800, Fax: 961-174-4461, E-mail: pm07@aub.edu.lb. *Application contact:* Dr. Salim Kanaan, Director, Admissions Office, 961-135-0000 Ext. 2594, Fax: 961-175-0775, E-mail: sk00@aub.edu.lb.

Andrews University, School of Graduate Studies, School of Education, Department of Educational and Counseling Psychology, Berrien Springs, MI 49104. Offers community counseling (MA); counseling psychology (PhD); educational and developmental psychology (MA, Ed D, PhD), including educational and developmental psychology (MA), educational psychology (Ed D, PhD); school counseling (MA); school psychology (Ed S); special education (MS). *Accreditation:* ACA (one or more programs are accredited). Part-time programs available. Terminal master's awarded for partial completion of doctoral program. *Degree requirements:* For master's, thesis optional; for doctorate, thesis/dissertation. *Entrance requirements:* For master's, GRE Subject Test, minimum GPA of 2.6; for doctorate, GRE General Test, MA, minimum GPA of 3.5, sample of research. Additional exam requirements/recommendations for international students: Required—TOEFL (minimum score 550 paper-based). *Faculty research:* Testing methods, temperament, African-American studies, counseling process, multicultural issues.

Angelo State University, College of Graduate Studies, College of Liberal and Fine Arts, Department of Psychology, Sociology and Social Work, San Angelo, TX 76909. Offers psychology (MS), including applied psychology, counseling psychology, industrial and organizational psychology. Part-time and evening/weekend programs available. *Faculty:* 8 full-time (2 women). *Students:* 53 full-time (38 women), 10 part-time (7 women); includes 6 Black or African American, non-Hispanic/Latino; 12 Hispanic/Latino. Average age 29. 52 applicants, 69% accepted, 35 enrolled. In 2010, 13 master's awarded. *Degree requirements:* For master's, comprehensive exam, thesis optional. *Entrance requirements:* For master's, GRE General Test (for industrial and organizational psychology only), essay, letters of recommendation (for industrial and organizational psychology only). Additional exam requirements/recommendations for international students: Required—TOEFL or IELTS. *Application deadline:* For fall admission, 7/15 priority date for domestic students, 6/10 for international students; for spring admission, 12/1 priority date for domestic students, 11/1 for international students. Applications are processed on a rolling basis. Application fee: $40 ($50 for international students). Electronic applications accepted. *Expenses:* Tuition, state resident: full-time $4560; part-time $152 per credit hour. Tuition, nonresident: full-time $13,860; part-time $462 per credit hour. Required fees: $2132. Tuition and fees vary according to course load. *Financial support:* In 2010–11, 44 students received support, including 3 teaching assistantships (averaging $10,251 per year); career-related internships or fieldwork, Federal Work-Study, scholarships/grants, and unspecified assistantships also available. Support available to part-time students. Financial award application deadline: 3/1; financial award applicants required to submit FAFSA. Total annual research expenditures: $116,915. *Unit head:* Dr. William B. Davidson, Department Head, 325-942-2068 Ext. 248, Fax: 325-942-2290, E-mail: bill.davidson@angelo.edu. *Application contact:* Aly Hunter, Graduate Admissions Assistant, 325-942-2169, Fax: 325-942-2194, E-mail: aly.hunter@angelo.edu.

Antioch University Los Angeles, Graduate Programs, Program in Psychology, Culver City, CA 90230. Offers clinical psychology (MA); psychology (MA). Part-time programs available. *Degree requirements:* For master's, thesis (for some programs), internship. *Entrance requirements:* For master's, interview. Additional exam requirements/recommendations for international students: Required—TOEFL. *Faculty research:* Creativity and humor, ethnic humor, adult development, Jungian theory, psychoanalytic theory.

Antioch University Midwest, Graduate Programs, Individualized Liberal and Professional Studies Program, Yellow Springs, OH 45387-1609. Offers liberal and professional studies (MA), including counseling, creative writing, education, film studies, liberal studies, management, modern literature, psychology, theatre, visual arts. Part-time and evening/weekend programs available. Postbaccalaureate distance learning degree programs offered (minimal on-campus study). *Faculty:* 2 full-time (1 woman), 2 part-time/adjunct (both women). *Students:* 15 full-time (11 women), 34 part-time (22 women); includes 11 minority (8 Black or African American, non-Hispanic/Latino; 3 Hispanic/Latino). Average age 40. 13 applicants, 69% accepted, 5 enrolled. In 2010, 18 master's awarded. *Degree requirements:* For master's, thesis or alternative. *Entrance requirements:* For master's, resume, goal statement, interview. *Application deadline:* For fall admission, 8/1 for domestic students; for winter admission, 12/1 for domestic students; for spring admission, 3/10 for domestic students. Applications are processed on a rolling basis. Application fee: $50. Electronic applications accepted. *Expenses:* Contact institution. *Financial support:* Federal Work-Study available. Financial award applicants required to submit FAFSA. *Unit head:* Dr. Joseph Cronin, Chair, 937-769-1894, Fax: 937-769-1807, E-mail: jcronin@antioch.edu. *Application contact:* Seth Gordon, Assistant Director of Admissions, 937-769-1800 Ext. 1825, Fax: 937-769-1804, E-mail: sgordon@antioch.edu.

Antioch University Santa Barbara, Program in Psychology, Santa Barbara, CA 93101-1581. Offers MA. Part-time and evening/weekend programs available. *Degree requirements:* For master's, internship. *Entrance requirements:* Additional exam requirements/recommendations for international students: Required—TOEFL (minimum score 550 paper-based; 213 computer-based). Electronic applications accepted.

Antioch University Seattle, Graduate Programs, Program in Psychology, Seattle, WA 98121-1814. Offers MA, Psy D. Part-time and evening/weekend programs available. *Degree requirements:* For master's, internship. Electronic applications accepted. *Faculty research:* Trauma and post-traumatic stress disorders, workplace harassment and violence, multicultural issues and diversity.

Appalachian State University, Cratis D. Williams Graduate School, Department of Psychology, Boone, NC 28608. Offers clinical health psychology (MA); general experimental psychology (MA); industrial and organizational psychology (MA). Part-time programs available. *Faculty:* 31 full-time (10 women), 2 part-time/adjunct (1 woman). *Students:* 55 full-time (40 women), 11 part-time (9 women); includes 3 minority (2 Black or African American, non-Hispanic/Latino; 1 Two or more races, non-Hispanic/Latino). 158 applicants, 32% accepted, 28 enrolled. In 2010, 25 master's, 7 other advanced degrees awarded. *Degree requirements:* For master's, comprehensive exam, thesis optional, exit exam. *Entrance requirements:* For master's, GRE General Test, 3 letters of recommendation. Additional exam requirements/recommendations for international students: Required—TOEFL (minimum score 550 paper-based; 230 computer-based; 79 iBT) or IELTS (minimum score 6.5). *Application deadline:* For fall admission, 2/15 for domestic students, 2/1 for international students. Applications are processed on a rolling basis. Application fee: $55. Electronic applications accepted. *Expenses:* Tuition, state resident: full-time $3428; part-time $428 per unit. Tuition, nonresident: full-time $14,518; part-time $1814 per unit. Required fees: $2320; $344 per unit. Tuition and fees vary according to campus/location. *Financial support:* In 2010–11, 34 research assistantships (averaging $4,000 per year), 25 teaching assistantships (averaging $4,000 per year) were awarded; fellowships, career-related internships or fieldwork, Federal Work-Study, scholarships/grants, and unspecified assistantships also available. Financial award application deadline: 4/1; financial award applicants required to submit FAFSA. *Faculty research:* Eating disorders, school-based consultations, organizational behavior management, brain mechanisms of sound localization, parenting styles. Total annual research expenditures: $18,000. *Unit head:* Dr. James Denniston, Chair, 828-262-2272, Fax: 828-262-2272, E-mail: dennistonjc@appstate.edu. *Application contact:* Dr. Denise Martz, Graduate Coordinator, 828-262-2715, E-mail: martzdm@appstate.edu.

Arcadia University, Graduate Studies, Department of Education, Glenside, PA 19038-3295. Offers art education (M Ed, MA Ed); biology education (MA Ed); chemistry education (MA Ed); child development (CAS); computer education (M Ed, CAS); computer education 7-12 (MA Ed); early childhood education (M Ed, CAS), including individualized (M Ed), master teacher (M Ed),

Psychology—General

Arcadia University (continued)
research in child development (M Ed); educational leadership (M Ed, CAS); educational psychology (CAS); elementary education (M Ed, CAS); English education (MA Ed); environmental education (MA Ed, CAS); history education (MA Ed); language arts (M Ed, CAS); mathematics education (M Ed, MA Ed, CAS); music education (MA Ed); psychology (MA Ed); pupil personnel services (CAS); reading (M Ed, CAS); school library science (M Ed); science education (M Ed, CAS); secondary education (M Ed, CAS); special education (M Ed, Ed D, CAS); theater arts (MA Ed); written communication (MA Ed). *Accreditation:* NASAD. Part-time and evening/weekend programs available. Postbaccalaureate distance learning degree programs offered (minimal on-campus study). *Faculty:* 12 full-time (8 women), 38 part-time/adjunct (26 women). *Students:* 101 full-time (80 women), 667 part-time (508 women); includes 85 Black or African American, non-Hispanic/Latino; 10 Asian, non-Hispanic/Latino; 9 Hispanic/Latino; 5 Two or more races, non-Hispanic/Latino, 1 international. Average age 32. In 2010, 211 master's, 6 doctorates awarded. *Application deadline:* Applications are processed on a rolling basis. Application fee: $50. Electronic applications accepted. *Expenses:* Contact institution. *Financial support:* Career-related internships or fieldwork, tuition waivers (partial), and unspecified assistantships available. *Unit head:* Dr. Steven P. Gulkus. *Application contact:* 215-572-2925, Fax: 215-572-2126, E-mail: grad@arcadia.edu.

Arcadia University, Graduate Studies, Department of Psychology, Glenside, PA 19038-3295. Offers community counseling (MACP); school counseling (MACP). Part-time programs available. *Faculty:* 4 full-time (2 women), 6 part-time/adjunct (4 women). *Students:* 32 full-time (30 women), 37 part-time (32 women); includes 11 minority (6 Black or African American, non-Hispanic/Latino; 1 Asian, non-Hispanic/Latino; 3 Hispanic/Latino; 1 Two or more races, non-Hispanic/Latino). Average age 27. In 2010, 11 master's awarded. *Degree requirements:* For master's, practicum. *Entrance requirements:* For master's, GRE General Test or MAT. *Application deadline:* Applications are processed on a rolling basis. Application fee: $50. *Expenses:* Contact institution. *Financial support:* Research assistantships, career-related internships or fieldwork and unspecified assistantships available. Support available to part-time students. Financial award application deadline: 8/15. *Unit head:* Dr. Eleonora Bartoli, Director, 215-572-4693. *Application contact:* 215-572-2925, Fax: 215-572-2126, E-mail: grad@arcadia.edu.

Argosy University, Atlanta, College of Psychology and Behavioral Sciences, Atlanta, GA 30328. Offers clinical psychology (MA, Psy D, Postdoctoral Respecialization Certificate), including child and family psychology (Psy D), general adult clinical (Psy D), health psychology (Psy D), neuropsychology/geropsychology (Psy D); community counseling (MA), including marriage and family therapy; counselor education and supervision (Ed D); forensic psychology (MA); industrial organizational psychology (MA); marriage and family therapy (Certificate); sport-exercise psychology (MA). *Accreditation:* APA.

See Close-Up on page 1121.

Argosy University, Chicago, College of Psychology and Behavioral Sciences, Chicago, IL 60601. Offers clinical psychology (MA, Psy D), including child and adolescent psychology (Psy D), client-centered and experiential psychotherapies (Psy D), diversity and multicultural psychology (Psy D), family psychology (Psy D), forensic psychology (Psy D), health psychology (Psy D), neuropsychology (Psy D), organizational consulting (Psy D), psychoanalytic psychology (Psy D), psychology and spirituality (Psy D); community counseling (MA); counseling psychology (Ed D), including counselor education and supervision; counselor education and supervision (Ed D); industrial organizational psychology (MA). *Accreditation:* APA (one or more programs are accredited). Postbaccalaureate distance learning degree programs offered (minimal on-campus study).

See Close-Up on page 1123.

Argosy University, Dallas, College of Psychology and Behavioral Sciences, Farmers Branch, TX 75244. Offers MA, Ed D, Psy D.

See Close-Up on page 1125.

Argosy University, Denver, College of Psychology and Behavioral Sciences, Denver, CO 80231. Offers clinical mental health counseling (MA); clinical psychology (MA, Psy D); counseling psychology (Ed D); counselor education and supervision (Ed D); forensic psychology (MA); industrial organizational psychology (MA); marriage and family therapy (MA, DMFT).

See Close-Up on page 1127.

Argosy University, Hawai'i, College of Psychology and Behavioral Sciences, Honolulu, HI 96813. Offers MA, MS, Ed D, Psy D, Certificate, Postdoctoral Respecialization Certificate. *Accreditation:* APA.

See Close-Up on page 1129.

Argosy University, Inland Empire, College of Psychology and Behavioral Sciences, San Bernardino, CA 92408. Offers clinical psychology/marriage and family therapy (MA); counseling psychology (Ed D); counseling psychology/marriage and family therapy (MA); forensic psychology (MA); industrial organizational psychology (MA); sport-exercise psychology (MA).

See Close-Up on page 1131.

Argosy University, Los Angeles, College of Psychology and Behavioral Sciences, Santa Monica, CA 90045. Offers clinical psychology/marriage and family therapy (MA); counseling psychology (Ed D); counseling psychology/marriage and family therapy (MA); forensic psychology (MA).

See Close-Up on page 1133.

Argosy University, Nashville, College of Psychology and Behavioral Sciences, Nashville, TN 37214. Offers counselor education and supervision (Ed D); mental health counseling (MA).

See Close-Up on page 1135.

Argosy University, Orange County, College of Psychology and Behavioral Sciences, Orange, CA 92868. Offers MA, Ed D, Psy D. *Accreditation:* APA. Part-time and evening/weekend programs available. *Degree requirements:* For master's, comprehensive exam; for doctorate, comprehensive exam, thesis/dissertation. *Entrance requirements:* For master's and doctorate, 3 letters of recommendation, interview, resume. Additional exam requirements/recommendations for international students: Required—TOEFL. Electronic applications accepted. *Faculty research:* The psychological aspects of infertility medicine, depression, psychoanalytic therapy, experiential approaches to teaching.

See Close-Up on page 1137.

Argosy University, Phoenix, College of Psychology and Behavioral Sciences, Phoenix, AZ 85021. Offers MA, Psy D.

See Close-Up on page 1139.

Argosy University, Salt Lake City, College of Psychology and Behavioral Sciences, Draper, UT 84020. Offers counseling psychology (Ed D); counselor education and supervision (Ed D); forensic psychology (MA); marriage and family therapy (MA, DMFT); mental health counseling (MA).

See Close-Up on page 1141.

Argosy University, San Diego, College of Psychology and Behavioral Sciences, San Diego, CA 92108. Offers clinical psychology/marriage and family therapy (MA); counseling psychology (Ed D); counseling psychology/marriage and family therapy (MA); forensic psychology (MA).

See Close-Up on page 1143.

Argosy University, San Francisco Bay Area, College of Psychology and Behavioral Sciences, Alameda, CA 94501. Offers clinical psychology (MA, Psy D); counseling psychology (MA, Ed D); forensic psychology (MA); sport-exercise psychology (MA). *Accreditation:* APA (one or more programs are accredited).

See Close-Up on page 1145.

Argosy University, Sarasota, College of Psychology and Behavioral Sciences, Sarasota, FL 34235. Offers community counseling (MA); counseling psychology (Ed D); counselor education and supervision (Ed D); forensic psychology (MA); marriage and family therapy (MA); mental health counseling (MA); pastoral community counseling (Ed D).

See Close-Up on page 1147.

Argosy University, Schaumburg, College of Psychology and Behavioral Sciences, Schaumburg, IL 60173-5403. Offers clinical health psychology (Post-Graduate Certificate); clinical psychology (MA, Psy D), including child and family psychology (Psy D), clinical health psychology (Psy D), diversity and multicultural psychology (Psy D), forensic psychology (Psy D), neuropsychology (Psy D); community counseling (MA); counseling psychology (Ed D), including counselor education and supervision; counselor education and supervision (Ed D); forensic psychology (Post-Graduate Certificate); industrial organizational psychology (MA). *Accreditation:* ACA; APA.

See Close-Up on page 1149.

Argosy University, Seattle, College of Psychology and Behavioral Sciences, Seattle, WA 98121. Offers MA, Ed D, Psy D, Postdoctoral Respecialization Certificate.

See Close-Up on page 1151.

Argosy University, Tampa, College of Psychology and Behavioral Sciences, Tampa, FL 33607. Offers clinical psychology (MA, Psy D), including clinical psychology; counselor education and supervision (Ed D); industrial organizational psychology (MA); marriage and family therapy (MA); mental health counseling (MA).

See Close-Up on page 1153.

Argosy University, Twin Cities, College of Psychology and Behavioral Sciences, Eagan, MN 55121. Offers clinical psychology (MA, Psy D), including child and family psychology (Psy D), forensic psychology (Psy D), health and neuropsychology (Psy D), trauma (Psy D); forensic counseling (Post-Graduate Certificate); forensic psychology (MA); industrial organizational psychology (MA); marriage and family therapy (MA, DMFT), including forensic counseling (MA). *Accreditation:* AAMFT; AAMFT/COAMFTE; APA.

See Close-Up on page 1155.

Argosy University, Washington DC, College of Psychology and Behavioral Sciences, Arlington, VA 22209. Offers clinical psychology (MA, Psy D), including child and family psychology (Psy D), diversity and multicultural psychology (Psy D), forensic psychology (Psy D), health and neuropsychology (Psy D); community counseling (MA); counseling psychology (Ed D), including counselor education and supervision; counselor education and supervision (Ed D); forensic psychology (MA). *Accreditation:* APA.

See Close-Up on page 1157.

Arizona State University, College of Liberal Arts and Sciences, Department of Psychology, Tempe, AZ 85287-1104. Offers behavioral neuroscience (PhD); clinical psychology (PhD); cognition, action and perception (PhD); developmental psychology (PhD); quantitative psychology (PhD); social psychology (PhD). *Accreditation:* APA. *Faculty:* 72 full-time (36 women), 9 part-time/adjunct (6 women). *Students:* 113 full-time (79 women), 17 part-time (12 women); includes 24 minority (2 Black or African American, non-Hispanic/Latino; 10 Asian, non-Hispanic/Latino; 10 Hispanic/Latino; 2 Two or more races, non-Hispanic/Latino), 9 international. Average age 28. 519 applicants, 8% accepted, 30 enrolled. In 2010, 19 doctorates awarded. *Degree requirements:* For doctorate, comprehensive exam, thesis/dissertation, interactive Program of Study (iPOS) submitted before completing 50 percent of required credit hours. *Entrance requirements:* For doctorate, GRE General Test, GRE Subject Test, minimum GPA of 3.0 or equivalent in last 2 years of work leading to bachelor's degree. Additional exam requirements/recommendations for international students: Required—TOEFL, IELTS, or Pearson Test of English. *Application deadline:* For fall admission, 12/15 for domestic and international students. Application fee: $70 ($90 for international students). Electronic applications accepted. *Expenses:* Tuition, state resident: full-time $8510; part-time $608 per credit. Tuition, nonresident: full-time $16,542; part-time $919 per credit. Required fees: $339; $110 per credit. Part-time tuition and fees vary according to course load. *Financial support:* In 2010–11, 58 research assistantships with tuition reimbursements (averaging $15,281 per year), 48 teaching assistantships with tuition reimbursements (averaging $15,062 per year) were awarded; fellowships with full tuition reimbursements, career-related internships or fieldwork, Federal Work-Study, institutionally sponsored loans, scholarships/grants, and tuition waivers (full and partial) also available. Financial award application deadline: 3/1; financial award applicants required to submit FAFSA. Total annual research expenditures: $9.4 million. *Unit head:* Dr. Keith Crnic, Chair, 480-965-3061, E-mail: keith.crnic@asu.edu. *Application contact:* Graduate Admissions, 480-965-6113.

Arizona State University, New College of Interdisciplinary Arts and Sciences, Program in Psychology, Phoenix, AZ 85069-7100. Offers MS. Part-time and evening/weekend programs available. *Faculty:* 13 full-time (7 women). *Students:* 17 full-time (11 women), 2 part-time (both women); includes 3 minority (1 Black or African American, non-Hispanic/Latino; 1 Asian, non-Hispanic/Latino; 1 Hispanic/Latino), 1 international. Average age 25. 45 applicants, 62% accepted, 19 enrolled. *Degree requirements:* For master's, thesis or applied project, interactive Program of Study (iPOS) submitted before completing 50 percent of required credit hours. *Entrance requirements:* For master's, GRE, bachelor's degree in psychology or related field; minimum cumulative GPA of 3.0; successful completion of undergraduate statistics and research methods courses; three letters of recommendation from faculty; personal statement of research interests and goals. Additional exam requirements/recommendations for international students: Required—TOEFL, IELTS, or Pearson Test of English. *Application deadline:* Applications are processed on a rolling basis. Application fee: $70 ($90 for international students). Electronic applications accepted. *Expenses:* Tuition, state resident: full-time $8510; part-time $608 per credit. Tuition, nonresident: full-time $16,542; part-time $919 per credit. Required fees: $339; $110 per credit. Part-time tuition and fees vary according to course load. *Financial support:* In 2010–11, 1 research assistantship with full and partial tuition reimbursement (averaging $12,400 per year) was awarded; teaching assistantships with full and partial tuition reimbursements, institutionally sponsored loans, scholarships/grants, and tuition waivers (full and partial) also available. Financial award application deadline: 3/1; financial award applicants required to submit FAFSA. *Faculty research:* Emotion; stress; social identity, intergroup relations and prejudice; psychology and the legal system; discursive psychology; cognitive neuroscience, bilingualism and cognition; social psychology and bullying; health related decision-making; psychophysiology; attention, eye-tracking and natural behavior. *Unit head:* Dr. Paul Miller, Director, 602-543-6014, E-mail: paul.miller@asu.edu. *Application contact:* Graduate Admissions, 480-965-6113.

Arkansas Tech University, Graduate College, College of Arts and Humanities, Russellville, AR 72801. Offers communication (MLA); English (M Ed, MA); fine arts (MLA); history (MA); multi-media journalism (MA); psychology (MS); social science (MLA); Spanish (MA, MLA); teaching English as a second language (MA, MLA). Part-time programs available. *Students:* 39 full-time (23 women), 87 part-time (69 women); includes 13 minority (3 Black or African American, non-Hispanic/Latino; 1 American Indian or Alaska Native, non-Hispanic/Latino; 1 Asian, non-Hispanic/Latino; 8 Hispanic/Latino), 14 international. Average age 32. In 2010, 54 master's awarded. *Degree requirements:* For master's, comprehensive exam (for some programs), thesis (for some programs), project. *Entrance requirements:* For master's, GRE

General Test or MAT. Additional exam requirements/recommendations for international students: Required—TOEFL (minimum score 550 paper-based; 213 computer-based; 79 iBT), IELTS (minimum score 6). *Application deadline:* For fall admission, 3/1 priority date for domestic students, 5/1 priority date for international students; for spring admission, 10/1 priority date for domestic and international students. Applications are processed on a rolling basis. Application fee: $0 ($50 for international students). Electronic applications accepted. *Expenses:* Tuition, state resident: full-time $4680; part-time $195 per credit hour. Tuition, nonresident: full-time $9360; part-time $390 per credit hour. Required fees: $714; $14 per credit hour. One-time fee: $326 part-time. Tuition and fees vary according to course load. *Financial support:* In 2010–11, teaching assistantships with full tuition reimbursements (averaging $4,000 per year); research assistantships, career-related internships or fieldwork, Federal Work-Study, scholarships/grants, health care benefits, and unspecified assistantships also available. Support available to part-time students. Financial award application deadline: 4/15; financial award applicants required to submit FAFSA. *Unit head:* Dr. Micheal Tarver, Dean, 479-968-0274, Fax: 479-964-0812, E-mail: mtarver@atu.edu. *Application contact:* Dr. Mary B. Gunter, Dean of Graduate College, 479-968-0398, Fax: 479-964-0542, E-mail: graduate.school@atu.edu.

Assumption College, Graduate School, Counseling Psychology Program, Worcester, MA 01609-1296. Offers child and family interventions (MA); cognitive-behavioral therapies (MA); counseling psychology (CAGS); general psychology (MA). Part-time and evening/weekend programs available. *Faculty:* 4 full-time (1 woman), 8 part-time/adjunct (2 women). *Students:* 74 full-time (66 women), 35 part-time (33 women); includes 18 minority (5 Black or African American, non-Hispanic/Latino; 2 Asian, non-Hispanic/Latino; 8 Hispanic/Latino; 3 Two or more races, non-Hispanic/Latino). Average age 24. 100 applicants, 78% accepted. In 2010, 20 master's, 2 other advanced degrees awarded. *Degree requirements:* For master's, comprehensive exam, internship, practicum, oral exam; for CAGS, comprehensive exam, oral exam. *Entrance requirements:* For master's, 3 letters of recommendation, resume, essay; for CAGS, 3 letters of recommendation, resume, interview, essay. Additional exam requirements/recommendations for international students: Required—TOEFL (minimum score 540 paper-based; 200 computer-based; 76 iBT), IELTS (minimum score 6). *Application deadline:* For fall admission, 6/1 priority date for domestic students, 5/1 priority date for international students; for spring admission, 11/1 priority date for domestic students, 9/1 priority date for international students. Applications are processed on a rolling basis. Application fee: $30. Electronic applications accepted. *Expenses:* Tuition: Part-time $503 per credit. Required fees: $20 per semester. One-time fee: $100. Part-time tuition and fees vary according to campus/location. *Financial support:* In 2010–11, 21 students received support, including 19 fellowships with partial tuition reimbursements available (averaging $8,206 per year), 2 teaching assistantships with full tuition reimbursements available (averaging $7,575 per year). Financial award application deadline: 3/1; financial award applicants required to submit FAFSA. *Faculty research:* Mood disorders, adjustment to life-threatening illness, perception of movement, socioemotional development of young children, discovery versus disclosure. *Unit head:* Dr. Leonard A. Doerfler, Director, 508-767-7549, Fax: 508-767-7263, E-mail: doerfler@assumption.edu. *Application contact:* Daniel Provost, Director of Graduate Enrollment Management and Services, 508-767-7426, Fax: 508-767-7030, E-mail: dprovost@assumption.edu.

Auburn University, Graduate School, College of Liberal Arts, Department of Psychology, Auburn University, AL 36849. Offers applied behavior analysis in developmental disabilities (MS); clinical psychology (PhD); experimental psychology (PhD); industrial/organizational psychology (PhD). *Accreditation:* APA (one or more programs are accredited). Part-time programs available. *Faculty:* 24 full-time (7 women), 4 part-time/adjunct (3 women). *Students:* 36 full-time (28 women), 57 part-time (33 women); includes 6 Black or African American, non-Hispanic/Latino; 4 Asian, non-Hispanic/Latino; 5 Hispanic/Latino. Average age 26. 293 applicants, 9% accepted, 19 enrolled. In 2010, 20 master's, 11 doctorates awarded. *Degree requirements:* For doctorate, thesis/dissertation. *Entrance requirements:* For master's, GRE General Test, GRE Subject Test, minimum GPA of 3.25 in psychology, 3.0 overall; for doctorate, GRE General Test, GRE Subject Test. *Application deadline:* For fall admission, 7/7 for domestic students; for spring admission, 11/24 for domestic students. Applications are processed on a rolling basis. Application fee: $50 ($60 for international students). Electronic applications accepted. *Expenses:* Tuition, state resident: full-time $7002. Tuition, nonresident: full-time $21,898. International tuition: $22,116 full-time. Required fees: $892. Tuition and fees vary according to course load and program. *Financial support:* Research assistantships, teaching assistantships, Federal Work-Study available. Support available to part-time students. Financial award application deadline: 3/15; financial award applicants required to submit FAFSA. *Faculty research:* Clinical psychology, learning, industrial psychology, organizational psychology. Total annual research expenditures: $200,000. *Unit head:* Dr. Barry Burkhart, Chair, 334-844-6476. *Application contact:* Dr. George Flowers, Dean of the Graduate School, 334-844-2125.

Auburn University Montgomery, School of Sciences, Department of Psychology, Montgomery, AL 36124-4023. Offers MSPG. Part-time and evening/weekend programs available. *Degree requirements:* For master's, comprehensive exam, thesis optional. *Entrance requirements:* For master's, GRE General Test or MAT. Electronic applications accepted. *Faculty research:* Community service, diagnosis, behavior modification.

Augusta State University, Graduate Studies, College of Arts and Sciences, Department of Psychology, Augusta, GA 30904-2200. Offers MS. Part-time programs available. *Degree requirements:* For master's, thesis optional, written/oral exam. *Entrance requirements:* For master's, GRE General Test, minimum GPA of 2.5, bachelor's degree in psychology or equivalent course work. *Expenses:* Tuition, state resident: part-time $165 per hour. Tuition, nonresident: part-time $615 per hour. *Faculty research:* Developmental, cognitive, gender and aging issues, consumer behavior, conditioned taste aversions, circadian rhythms, use of slang and offensive language.

Austin Peay State University, College of Graduate Studies, College of Behavioral and Health Sciences, Department of Psychology, Clarksville, TN 37044. Offers counseling (MS); counseling and guidance (Ed S); psychology (MA). Part-time programs available. Postbaccalaureate distance learning degree programs offered (no on-campus study). *Faculty:* 11 full-time (6 women), 1 (woman) part-time/adjunct. *Students:* 61 full-time (54 women), 24 part-time (19 women); includes 16 minority (10 Black or African American, non-Hispanic/Latino; 2 Asian, non-Hispanic/Latino; 2 Hispanic/Latino; 2 Two or more races, non-Hispanic/Latino), 1 international. Average age 29. 52 applicants, 100% accepted, 31 enrolled. In 2010, 23 master's awarded. *Degree requirements:* For master's, comprehensive exam, thesis (for some programs). *Entrance requirements:* For master's, GRE General Test, minimum undergraduate GPA of 2.5, 3 letters of recommendation, bachelor's degree. Additional exam requirements/recommendations for international students: Required—TOEFL (minimum score 500 paper-based; 173 computer-based). *Application deadline:* For fall admission, 3/27 priority date for domestic students; for spring admission, 11/1 priority date for domestic students. Applications are processed on a rolling basis. Application fee: $25. Electronic applications accepted. *Expenses:* Tuition, state resident: full-time $6480; part-time $324 per credit hour. Tuition, nonresident: full-time $17,960; part-time $898 per credit hour. Required fees: $1244; $61.20 per credit hour. *Financial support:* In 2010–11, research assistantships with full tuition reimbursements (averaging $5,174 per year); career-related internships or fieldwork, Federal Work-Study, institutionally sponsored loans, scholarships/grants, and unspecified assistantships also available. Support available to part-time students. Financial award application deadline: 3/1; financial award applicants required to submit FAFSA. *Unit head:* Dr. Samuel Fung, Chair, 931-221-7233, Fax: 931-221-6267, E-mail: fungs@apsu.edu. *Application contact:* Dr. Dixie Dennis, Dean, College of Graduate Studies, 931-221-7662, Fax: 931-221-7641, E-mail: dennisdi@apsu.edu.

Avila University, Department of Psychology, Kansas City, MO 64145-1698. Offers counseling psychology (MS); general psychology (MS). Part-time and evening/weekend programs available. *Faculty:* 6 full-time (5 women), 20 part-time/adjunct (9 women). *Students:* 122 full-time (96 women), 21 part-time (16 women); includes 35 minority (26 Black or African American, non-Hispanic/Latino; 2 Asian, non-Hispanic/Latino; 6 Hispanic/Latino; 1 Two or more races, non-Hispanic/Latino), 6 international. Average age 32. 76 applicants, 53% accepted, 28 enrolled. In 2010, 3,631 master's awarded. *Degree requirements:* For master's, capstone project. *Entrance requirements:* For master's, minimum GPA of 3.0 in last 60 hours, 2 letters of recommendation, letter of intent, resume. Additional exam requirements/recommendations for international students: Required—TOEFL (minimum score 500 paper-based). *Application deadline:* Applications are processed on a rolling basis. Application fee: $0. Electronic applications accepted. *Expenses:* Tuition: Full-time $5580; part-time $465 per credit hour. Required fees: $348; $29 per credit hour. *Financial support:* In 2010–11, 132 students received support, including 1 research assistantship with partial tuition reimbursement available, 1 teaching assistantship (averaging $2,400 per year); career-related internships or fieldwork, scholarships/grants, and unspecified assistantships also available. Support available to part-time students. Financial award applicants required to submit FAFSA. *Faculty research:* Neuro/biofeedback, emotional regulation, perception, mindful wellness, trauma and restorative justice. *Unit head:* Robin M. Schluter, Director of Graduate Psychology, 816-501-2969, Fax: 816-501-2455, E-mail: robin.schluter@avila.edu. *Application contact:* Jennifer A. Manczuk, Graduate Program Liaison, 816-501-3698, Fax: 816-501-2455, E-mail: gradpsych@avila.edu.

Azusa Pacific University, School of Behavioral and Applied Sciences, Department of Graduate Psychology, Azusa, CA 91702-7000. Offers clinical psychology (MA, Psy D), including family therapy (MA). *Accreditation:* APA (one or more programs are accredited). Part-time and evening/weekend programs available. *Faculty:* 14 full-time (8 women), 2 part-time/adjunct (1 woman). *Students:* 186 full-time (134 women), 45 part-time (35 women); includes 68 minority (14 Black or African American, non-Hispanic/Latino; 26 Asian, non-Hispanic/Latino; 27 Hispanic/Latino; 1 Native Hawaiian or other Pacific Islander, non-Hispanic/Latino), 11 international. Average age 30. In 2010, 73 master's, 16 doctorates awarded. *Degree requirements:* For master's, comprehensive exam, 250 hours of clinical experience, individual and group therapy. *Entrance requirements:* For master's, interview, minimum GPA of 3.0, Minnesota Multiphasic Personality Inventory. Additional exam requirements/recommendations for international students: Required—TOEFL (minimum score 600 paper-based). *Application deadline:* For fall admission, 6/30 priority date for domestic students. Applications are processed on a rolling basis. Application fee: $45 ($65 for international students). *Unit head:* Dr. Robert Welsh, Chair, 626-815-5008. *Application contact:* Linda Witte, Graduate Admissions Office, 626-969-3434.

Ball State University, Graduate School, College of Sciences and Humanities, Department of Psychological Science, Muncie, IN 47306-1099. Offers clinical psychology (MA); cognitive and social processes (MA). *Faculty:* 20. *Students:* 35 full-time (23 women), 3 part-time (all women); includes 1 Black or African American, non-Hispanic/Latino; 1 American Indian or Alaska Native, non-Hispanic/Latino; 2 Asian, non-Hispanic/Latino; 1 Hispanic/Latino, 1 international. Average age 24. 75 applicants, 33% accepted, 17 enrolled. In 2010, 22 master's awarded. Application fee: $50. *Expenses:* Tuition, state resident: full-time $6160; part-time $299 per credit hour. Tuition, nonresident: full-time $16,020; part-time $783 per credit hour. Required fees: $2278; $95 per credit hour. *Financial support:* In 2010–11, 19 teaching assistantships (averaging $7,959 per year) were awarded; research assistantships with full tuition reimbursements. Financial award application deadline: 3/1. *Unit head:* Dr. Bernard Whitley, Chairman, 765-285-1690, Fax: 765-285-8980. *Application contact:* Dr. Kerri Pickel, Graduate Program Director, 765-285-1690, Fax: 765-285-8980, E-mail: kpickel@bsu.edu.

Barry University, School of Arts and Sciences, Department of Psychology, Miami Shores, FL 33161-6695. Offers clinical psychology (MS); school psychology (MS, SSP). Part-time and evening/weekend programs available. *Degree requirements:* For master's, thesis, practicum. *Entrance requirements:* For master's, GRE General Test, minimum GPA of 3.0, course work in psychology. Electronic applications accepted. *Faculty research:* Closed head injury, memory and aging, infant/mother interaction, evolutionary aspects of behavior, gender roles.

See Display on next page and Close-Up on page 1159.

Baylor University, Graduate School, College of Arts and Sciences, Department of Psychology and Neuroscience, Program in Psychology, Waco, TX 76798. Offers MA, PhD. *Students:* 19 full-time (13 women); includes 1 Hispanic/Latino, 1 international. In 2010, 1 doctorate awarded. *Degree requirements:* For doctorate, comprehensive exam. *Entrance requirements:* For master's and doctorate, GRE General Test. *Application deadline:* Applications are processed on a rolling basis. Application fee: $25. *Unit head:* Dr. Matthew Stanford, Graduate Program Director, 254-710-2236, Fax: 254-710-3033, E-mail: matthew_stanford@baylor.edu. *Application contact:* Barbara Prisco, Graduate Coordinator, 254-757-0535, Fax: 254-710-3033, E-mail: barbara_prisco@baylor.edu.

See Close-Up on page 1161.

Biola University, Rosemead School of Psychology, La Mirada, CA 90639-0001. Offers PhD, Psy D. *Accreditation:* APA. *Faculty:* 17 full-time (5 women), 6 part-time/adjunct (3 women). *Students:* 86 full-time (57 women), 10 part-time (7 women); includes 5 Black or African American, non-Hispanic/Latino; 21 Asian, non-Hispanic/Latino; 4 Hispanic/Latino, 6 international. 135 applicants, 33% accepted, 24 enrolled. In 2010, 17 doctorates awarded. *Degree requirements:* For doctorate, comprehensive exam, thesis/dissertation, internship. *Entrance requirements:* For doctorate, GRE General Test, GRE Subject Test, Minnesota Multiphasic Personality Inventory, interview, 30 undergraduate credits in psychology, minimum GPA of 3.0. Additional exam requirements/recommendations for international students: Required—TOEFL. *Application deadline:* For fall admission, 1/15 for domestic and international students. Application fee: $45. Electronic applications accepted. *Expenses:* Contact institution. *Financial support:* Research assistantships, teaching assistantships, career-related internships or fieldwork, institutionally sponsored loans, scholarships/grants, and unspecified assistantships available. Support available to part-time students. Financial award application deadline: 3/2; financial award applicants required to submit FAFSA. *Faculty research:* Integration of psychology and theology, practice of psychotherapy, therapy process and outcomes. *Unit head:* Dr. Clark Campbell, Administrative Dean, 562-903-4867, Fax: 562-903-4864. *Application contact:* Roy M. Allinson, Director of Graduate Admissions, 562-903-4752, Fax: 562-903-4709, E-mail: admissions@biola.edu.

Boston College, Graduate School of Arts and Sciences, Department of Psychology, Chestnut Hill, MA 02467-3800. Offers MA, PhD. *Degree requirements:* For doctorate, thesis/dissertation, fieldwork. *Entrance requirements:* For master's, GRE General Test; for doctorate, GRE General Test, GRE Subject Test. Additional exam requirements/recommendations for international students: Required—TOEFL (minimum score 600 paper-based; 250 computer-based; 100 iBT). Electronic applications accepted. *Faculty research:* Social, cognitive, and biological processes.

Boston Graduate School of Psychoanalysis, Master's Program—New York, New York, NY 10011. Offers MA. Part-time programs available. *Faculty:* 12 full-time (10 women), 11 part-time/adjunct (7 women). *Students:* 8 full-time (4 women), 24 part-time (16 women). 16 applicants, 100% accepted, 13 enrolled. In 2010, 4 master's awarded. *Degree requirements:* For master's, thesis. *Entrance requirements:* For master's, interview, BA, writing sample. *Application deadline:* Applications are processed on a rolling basis. Application fee: $100. *Expenses:* Tuition: Full-time $13,500; part-time $500 per credit. Required fees: $50; $860 per semester. *Financial support:* Career-related internships or fieldwork available. Financial award applicants required to submit FAFSA. *Unit head:* Dr. Mimi Crowell, Dean, 212-260-7050, Fax: 212-228-6410, E-mail: bgsp-ny.registrar@bgsp.edu. *Application contact:* Stephen Guttman, Registrar, 212-260-7050, Fax: 212-228-6410, E-mail: bgsp-ny.registrar@bgsp.edu.

Boston University, Graduate School of Arts and Sciences, Department of Psychology, Boston, MA 02215. Offers MA, PhD. *Accreditation:* APA (one or more programs are accredited). *Students:* 132 full-time (103 women), 10 part-time (8 women); includes 30 minority (7 Black or African American, non-Hispanic/Latino; 15 Asian, non-Hispanic/Latino; 6 Hispanic/Latino; 2 Two or more races, non-Hispanic/Latino), 14 international. Average age 27. 936 applicants, 17% accepted, 55 enrolled. In 2010, 83 master's, 19 doctorates awarded. Terminal master's awarded for partial completion of doctoral program. *Degree requirements:* For master's, one foreign language, comprehensive exam; for doctorate, one foreign language, comprehensive

Psychology—General

Boston University (continued)

exam, thesis/dissertation. *Entrance requirements:* For master's and doctorate, GRE General Test. Additional exam requirements/recommendations for international students: Required—TOEFL. *Application deadline:* For fall admission, 12/1 for domestic and international students. Application fee: $70. Electronic applications accepted. *Expenses:* Tuition: Full-time $39,314; part-time $1228 per credit. Required fees: $40 per semester. *Financial support:* In 2010–11, 85 students received support, including 4 fellowships (averaging $19,300 per year), 56 research assistantships with full tuition reimbursements available (averaging $18,800 per year), 23 teaching assistantships with full tuition reimbursements available (averaging $18,800 per year); career-related internships or fieldwork, Federal Work-Study, and unspecified assistantships also available. Support available to part-time students. Financial award application deadline: 12/1; financial award applicants required to submit FAFSA. *Unit head:* Michael Lyons, Chairman, 617-353-3820, Fax: 617-353-6933, E-mail: mlyons@bu.edu. *Application contact:* Michael Lyons, Chairman, 617-353-3820, Fax: 617-353-6933, E-mail: mlyons@bu.edu.

Bowling Green State University, Graduate College, College of Arts and Sciences, Department of Psychology, Bowling Green, OH 43403. Offers clinical psychology (MA, PhD); developmental psychology (MA, PhD); experimental psychology (MA, PhD); industrial/organizational psychology (MA, PhD); quantitative psychology (MA, PhD). *Accreditation:* APA (one or more programs are accredited). *Degree requirements:* For doctorate, thesis/dissertation. *Entrance requirements:* For doctorate, GRE General Test, GRE Subject Test. Additional exam requirements/recommendations for international students: Required—TOEFL. Electronic applications accepted. *Faculty research:* Personnel psychology, developmental-mathematical models, behavioral medication, brain process, child/adolescent social cognition.

Brandeis University, Graduate School of Arts and Sciences, Department of Psychology, Waltham, MA 02454-9110. Offers brain, body and behavior (PhD); cognitive neuroscience (PhD); general psychology (MA); social/developmental psychology (PhD). Part-time programs available. *Faculty:* 17 full-time (4 women), 2 part-time/adjunct (1 woman). *Students:* 47 full-time (32 women); includes 2 Asian, non-Hispanic/Latino, 12 international. 164 applicants, 27% accepted, 24 enrolled. In 2010, 8 master's, 4 doctorates awarded. Terminal master's awarded for partial completion of doctoral program. *Degree requirements:* For master's, thesis; for doctorate, comprehensive exam, thesis/dissertation. *Entrance requirements:* For master's and doctorate, GRE General Test, GRE Subject Test (recommended), 3 letters of recommendation, statement of purpose. Additional exam requirements/recommendations for international students: Required—TOEFL (minimum score 600 paper-based; 250 computer-based; 100 iBT); Recommended—IELTS (minimum score 7). *Application deadline:* For fall admission, 1/15 priority date for domestic and international students. Applications are processed on a rolling basis. Application fee: $75. Electronic applications accepted. *Financial support:* In 2010–11, 16 fellowships with full tuition reimbursements (averaging $20,000 per year), 3 research assistantships with full tuition reimbursements (averaging $20,000 per year), 9 teaching assistantships with partial tuition reimbursements (averaging $3,200 per year) were awarded; institutionally sponsored loans, scholarships/grants, health care benefits, tuition waivers (full and partial), and unspecified assistantships also available. Support available to part-time students. Financial award application deadline: 4/15; financial award applicants required to submit FAFSA. *Faculty research:* Cognitive neuroscience, social developmental psychology, brain body and behavior. *Unit head:* Prof. Paul DiZio, Director of Graduate Studies, 781-736-3300, Fax: 781-736-3291, E-mail: dizio@brandeis.edu. *Application contact:* Phil Gnatowski, Department Administrator, 781-736-3303, Fax: 781-736-3291, E-mail: gnat@brandeis.edu.

Brenau University, Sydney O. Smith Graduate School, College of Health and Science, Gainesville, GA 30501. Offers family nurse practitioner (MSN); nurse educator (MSN); nursing management (MSN); occupational therapy (MS); psychology (MS). *Accreditation:* AOTA; NLN. Part-time and evening/weekend programs available. *Faculty:* 14 full-time (12 women), 9 part-time/adjunct (all women). *Students:* 136 full-time (129 women), 106 part-time (96 women); includes 82 minority (61 Black or African American, non-Hispanic/Latino; 1 American Indian or Alaska Native, non-Hispanic/Latino; 4 Asian, non-Hispanic/Latino; 12 Hispanic/Latino; 4 Two or more races, non-Hispanic/Latino), 1 international. Average age 33. In 2010, 35 master's awarded. *Degree requirements:* For master's, comprehensive exam (for some programs), thesis (for some programs), clinical practicum hours. *Entrance requirements:* For master's, GRE General Test or MAT (for some programs), interview, writing sample, references (for some programs). Additional exam requirements/recommendations for international students: Required—TOEFL (minimum score 500 paper-based; 173 computer-based; 61 iBT); Recommended—IELTS (minimum score 5). *Application deadline:* Applications are processed on a rolling basis. Application fee: $35. Electronic applications accepted. *Expenses:* Contact institution. *Financial support:* In 2010–11, 32 students received support. Scholarships/grants and traineeships available. Support available to part-time students. Financial award application deadline: 7/15; financial award applicants required to submit FAFSA. *Unit head:* Dr. Gale Starich, Dean, 777-718-5305, Fax: 770-297-5929, E-mail: gstarich@brenau.edu. *Application contact:* Christina White, Admissions Coordinator, 770-718-5320, Fax: 770-770-5338, E-mail: cwhite@brenau.edu.

Bridgewater State University, School of Graduate Studies, School of Arts and Sciences, Department of Psychology, Bridgewater, MA 02325-0001. Offers MA. Part-time and evening/weekend programs available. *Entrance requirements:* For master's, GRE General Test.

Brigham Young University, Graduate Studies, College of Family, Home, and Social Sciences, Department of Psychology, Provo, UT 84602. Offers clinical psychology (PhD); general psychology (MS); psychology (PhD), including applied social psychology, behavioral neuroscience. *Accreditation:* APA (one or more programs are accredited). *Faculty:* 32 full-time (6 women), 2 part-time/adjunct (2 women). *Students:* 82 full-time (27 women); includes 3 Black or African American, non-Hispanic/Latino; 1 American Indian or Alaska Native, non-Hispanic/Latino; 6 Asian, non-Hispanic/Latino; 5 Hispanic/Latino; 68 Native Hawaiian or other Pacific Islander, non-Hispanic/Latino, 8 international. Average age 26. 91 applicants, 25% accepted, 18 enrolled. In 2010, 12 master's, 18 doctorates awarded. *Degree requirements:* For master's, thesis; for doctorate, comprehensive exam, thesis/dissertation, publishable paper. *Entrance requirements:* For master's and doctorate, GRE General Test, minimum GPA of 3.0 in last 60 hours of upper division course work. Additional exam requirements/recommendations for international students: Required—TOEFL. *Application deadline:* For fall admission, 1/5 for domestic students. Application fee: $50. Electronic applications accepted. *Expenses:* Tuition: Full-time $5580; part-time $310 per credit hour. Tuition and fees vary according to program and student's religious affiliation. *Financial support:* In 2010–11, 82 students received support, including 20 research assistantships with partial tuition reimbursements available (averaging $10,000 per year), 30 teaching assistantships with partial tuition reimbursements available (averaging $10,000 per year); fellowships, career-related internships or fieldwork, scholarships/grants, tuition waivers (partial), and unspecified assistantships also available. Financial award application deadline: 5/31. *Faculty research:* Psychotherapy process, Alzheimer's disease/dementia, psychology and law, health, psychology, developmental. Total annual research expenditures: $1 million. *Unit head:* Dr. Ramona Hopkins, Chair, 801-422-1170, Fax: 801-422-0602, E-mail: ramona_hopkins@byu.edu. *Application contact:* Karen A. Christensen, Coordinator of Student Programs, 801-422-4560, Fax: 801-422-0602, E-mail: karen@byu.edu.

Brock University, Faculty of Graduate Studies, Faculty of Social Sciences, Program in Psychology, St. Catharines, ON L2S 3A1, Canada. Offers behavioral neuroscience (MA, PhD); life span development (MA, PhD); social personality (MA, PhD). Part-time programs available. *Degree requirements:* For master's, thesis; for doctorate, thesis/dissertation. *Entrance requirements:* For master's, GRE, honors degree; for doctorate, GRE, master's degree. Additional exam requirements/recommendations for international students: Required—TOEFL (minimum score 550 paper-based; 213 computer-based; 80 iBT), IELTS (minimum score 6.5), TWE (minimum score 4). Electronic applications accepted. *Faculty research:* Social personality, behavioral neuroscience, life-span development.

Brooklyn College of the City University of New York, Division of Graduate Studies, Department of Psychology, Brooklyn, NY 11210-2889. Offers experimental psychology (MA);

industrial and organizational psychology (MA), including human relations, organizational behavior; mental health counseling (MA); psychology (PhD). Part-time programs available. *Students:* 83 full-time (68 women), 142 part-time (108 women); includes 102 minority (64 Black or African American, non-Hispanic/Latino; 18 Asian, non-Hispanic/Latino; 20 Hispanic/Latino), 16 international. Average age 30. 331 applicants, 44% accepted, 88 enrolled. In 2010, 75 master's awarded. *Degree requirements:* For master's, comprehensive exam, thesis (for some programs). *Entrance requirements:* For master's, minimum GPA of 3.0, 2 letters of recommendation, essay; for doctorate, GRE. Additional exam requirements/recommendations for international students: Required—TOEFL (minimum score 520 paper-based; 190 computer-based; 69 iBT). *Application deadline:* For fall admission, 3/1 for domestic students, 2/1 for international students; for spring admission, 11/1 for domestic students, 10/1 for international students. Applications are processed on a rolling basis. Application fee: $125. Electronic applications accepted. *Expenses:* Tuition, state resident: full-time $7360; part-time $310 per credit hour. Tuition, nonresident: full-time $13,800; part-time $575 per credit hour. Required fees: $190 per semester. *Financial support:* Career-related internships or fieldwork, Federal Work-Study, institutionally sponsored loans, scholarships/grants, and tuition waivers (partial) available. Support available to part-time students. Financial award application deadline: 5/1; financial award applicants required to submit FAFSA. *Unit head:* Dr. Margaret-Ellen Pipe, Chairperson, 718-951-5601, Fax: 718-951-4814, E-mail: mepipe@brooklyn.cuny.edu. *Application contact:* Hernan Sierra, Graduate Admissions Coordinator, 718-951-4536, Fax: 718-951-4506, E-mail: grads@brooklyn.cuny.edu.

Brown University, Graduate School, Department of Psychology, Providence, RI 02912. Offers behavioral neuroscience (PhD); cognitive processes (PhD); sensation and perception (PhD); social/developmental (PhD); MS/PhD. *Degree requirements:* For doctorate, thesis/dissertation. *Entrance requirements:* For doctorate, GRE General Test, GRE Subject Test.

Bucknell University, Graduate Studies, College of Arts and Sciences, Department of Psychology, Lewisburg, PA 17837. Offers MA, MS. Part-time programs available. *Degree requirements:* For master's, thesis. *Entrance requirements:* For master's, GRE General Test, GRE Subject Test, minimum GPA of 2.8. Additional exam requirements/recommendations for international students: Required—TOEFL. *Expenses:* Tuition: Full-time $36,992; part-time $4624 per course.

California Coast University, School of Behavioral Science, Santa Ana, CA 92701. Offers psychology (MS). Postbaccalaureate distance learning degree programs offered (no on-campus study).

California Institute of Integral Studies, School of Consciousness and Transformation, San Francisco, CA 94103. Offers creative inquiry/interdisciplinary arts (MFA); cultural anthropology and social transformation (MA); East-West psychology (MA, PhD); integrative health studies (MA); philosophy and religion (MA, PhD), including Asian and comparative studies, philosophy, cosmology, and consciousness, women's spirituality; social and cultural anthropology (PhD); transformative leadership (MA); transformative studies (PhD); writing and consciousness (MFA). Part-time and evening/weekend programs available. Postbaccalaureate distance learning degree programs offered (minimal on-campus study). *Students:* 455 full-time (315 women), 133 part-time (90 women); includes 47 Black or African American, non-Hispanic/Latino; 3 American Indian or Alaska Native, non-Hispanic/Latino; 21 Asian, non-Hispanic/Latino; 41 Hispanic/Latino, 40 international. Average age 37. 265 applicants, 91% accepted, 163 enrolled. In 2010, 64 master's, 22 doctorates awarded. Terminal master's awarded for partial completion of doctoral program. *Degree requirements:* For master's, thesis optional; for doctorate, comprehensive exam, thesis/dissertation, 1 foreign language (Asian comparative studies). *Entrance requirements:* For master's, minimum GPA of 3.0, letters of recommendation, writing sample; for doctorate, master's degree, minimum GPA of 3.0, letters of recommendation, writing sample. Additional exam requirements/recommendations for international students: Required—TOEFL. *Application deadline:* For fall admission, 2/1 priority date for domestic and international students; for spring admission, 10/15 priority date for domestic and international students. Applications are processed on a rolling basis. Application fee: $65. Electronic applications accepted. *Expenses:* Tuition: Full-time $15,660; part-time $870 per semester hour. Required fees: $95 per semester. *Financial support:* In 2010–11, 255 students received support; research assistantships, teaching assistantships, career-related internships or fieldwork, Federal Work-Study, scholarships/grants, and tuition waivers (partial) available. Support available to part-time students. Financial award application deadline: 4/15; financial award applicants required to submit FAFSA. *Faculty research:* Ecology and sustainability, philosophy and religion, East-West psychology, integrative health, social and cultural anthropology, transformative leadership. *Application contact:* Allyson Werner, Associate Director of Admissions, 415-575-6155, Fax: 415-575-1268.

California Institute of Integral Studies, School of Professional Psychology, San Francisco, CA 94103. Offers clinical psychology (Psy D); community mental health (MA); drama therapy (MA); expressive arts therapy (MA); integral counseling psychology (MA); integral counseling psychology-weekend (MA); somatic psychology (MA). *Accreditation:* APA. Part-time and evening/weekend programs available. *Students:* 651 full-time (476 women), 74 part-time (62 women); includes 146 minority (32 Black or African American, non-Hispanic/Latino; 1 American Indian or Alaska Native, non-Hispanic/Latino; 53 Asian, non-Hispanic/Latino; 43 Hispanic/Latino; 17 Two or more races, non-Hispanic/Latino), 52 international. Average age 37. 556 applicants, 72% accepted, 247 enrolled. In 2010, 148 master's, 27 doctorates awarded. *Degree requirements:* For doctorate, comprehensive exam, thesis/dissertation. *Entrance requirements:* For master's, minimum GPA of 3.0, letters of recommendation, writing sample; for doctorate, GRE, MA in psychology or social work with appropriate practical experience for advanced standing, or BA with a minimum GPA of 3.1; letters of recommendation; writing sample. Additional exam requirements/recommendations for international students: Required—TOEFL. *Application deadline:* For fall admission, 2/1 priority date for domestic and international students; for spring admission, 10/15 priority date for domestic and international students. Applications are processed on a rolling basis. Application fee: $65. Electronic applications accepted. *Expenses:* Tuition: Full-time $15,660; part-time $870 per semester hour. Required fees: $95 per semester. *Financial support:* Research assistantships with tuition reimbursements, teaching assistantships with tuition reimbursements, career-related internships or fieldwork, Federal Work-Study, scholarships/grants, and tuition waivers (partial) available. Support available to part-time students. Financial award application deadline: 4/15; financial award applicants required to submit FAFSA. *Faculty research:* Transpersonal psychology, somatic psychology, expressive arts therapy, drama therapy, community mental health, ecopsychology. *Application contact:* David Townes, Senior Admissions Counselor, 415-575-6152, Fax: 415-575-1268, E-mail: dtownes@ciis.edu.

California Lutheran University, Graduate Studies, Department of Psychology, Thousand Oaks, CA 91360-2787. Offers clinical psychology (MS, Psy D); marital and family therapy (MS). Part-time programs available. *Faculty:* 3 full-time (2 women), 12 part-time/adjunct (10 women). *Students:* 178 full-time (152 women), 11 part-time (9 women); includes 67 minority (5 Black or African American, non-Hispanic/Latino; 1 American Indian or Alaska Native, non-Hispanic/Latino; 7 Asian, non-Hispanic/Latino; 46 Hispanic/Latino; 1 Native Hawaiian or other Pacific Islander, non-Hispanic/Latino; 7 Two or more races, non-Hispanic/Latino), 5 international. Average age 31. 224 applicants, 67% accepted, 103 enrolled. In 2010, 68 master's awarded. *Degree requirements:* For master's, thesis or comprehensive exams; for doctorate, internship. *Entrance requirements:* For master's, GRE General Test, interview, minimum GPA of 3.0. *Application deadline:* For fall admission, 2/15 priority date for domestic students. Applications are processed on a rolling basis. Application fee: $50. *Unit head:* Dr. Mindy Puopolo, Director, 805-493-3528. *Application contact:* 805-493-3127, Fax: 805-493-3542, E-mail: clugrad@clunet.edu.

California Polytechnic State University, San Luis Obispo, College of Liberal Arts, Department of Psychology and Child Development, San Luis Obispo, CA 93407. Offers psychology (MS). Part-time programs available. *Faculty:* 2 full-time (1 woman). *Students:* 37 full-time (30 women), 9 part-time (8 women); includes 9 minority (1 Black or African American, non-Hispanic/Latino; 6 Hispanic/Latino; 2 Two or more races, non-Hispanic/Latino). Average age 29. 58 applicants, 31% accepted, 14 enrolled. In 2010, 7 master's awarded. *Degree requirements:* For master's, comprehensive exam, thesis (for some programs). *Entrance requirements:* For master's, GRE General Test, minimum GPA of 3.0 in last 90 quarter units of course work, 4 letters of recommendation, interview. Additional exam requirements/recommendations for international students: Required—TOEFL (minimum score 550 paper-based; 213 computer-based) or IELTS (minimum score 6). *Application deadline:* For fall admission, 12/1 for domestic students, 11/30 for international students. Application fee: $55. Electronic applications accepted. *Expenses:* Tuition, state resident: full-time $5386; part-time $3124 per year. Tuition, nonresident: full-time $11,160; part-time $248 per unit. Required fees: $2250; $614 per term. One-time fee: $2250 full-time; $1842 part-time. *Financial support:* Career-related internships or fieldwork, Federal Work-Study, and institutionally sponsored loans available. Support available to part-time students. Financial award application deadline: 3/2; financial award applicants required to submit FAFSA. *Faculty research:* Eating disorders, mood disorders, neuropsychology, forensic psychology, group therapy. *Unit head:* Dr. Kelly Moreno, Graduate Coordinator, 805-756-2805, Fax: 805-756-1134, E-mail: kmoreno@calpoly.edu. *Application contact:* Margaret Booker, Administrative Analyst, 805-756-2456, Fax: 805-756-1134, E-mail: mbooker@calpoly.edu.

California State Polytechnic University, Pomona, Academic Affairs, College of Letters, Arts, and Social Sciences, Program in Psychology, Pomona, CA 91768-2557. Offers MS. Part-time programs available. *Students:* 26 full-time (19 women), 4 part-time (all women); includes 12 minority (5 Asian, non-Hispanic/Latino; 6 Hispanic/Latino; 1 Two or more races, non-Hispanic/Latino), 3 international. Average age 28. 114 applicants, 15% accepted, 14 enrolled. In 2010, 10 master's awarded. *Degree requirements:* For master's, thesis or alternative. *Application deadline:* For fall admission, 4/15 for domestic students. Applications are processed on a rolling basis. Application fee: $55. Electronic applications accepted. *Expenses:* Tuition, state resident: full-time $5386; part-time $2850 per year. Tuition, nonresident: full-time $12,082; part-time $248 per credit. Required fees: $577; $248 per credit. $577 per year. Tuition and fees vary according to course load and program. *Financial support:* Application deadline: 3/2. *Unit head:* Dr. Jeffery Mio, Director of Graduate Studies, 909-869-3899, E-mail: jsmio@csupomona.edu. *Application contact:* Scott J. Duncan, Director, Admissions, 909-869-3258, Fax: 909-869-4529, E-mail: sjduncan@csupomona.edu.

California State University, Bakersfield, Division of Graduate Studies, School of Humanities and Social Sciences, Program in Psychology, Bakersfield, CA 93311. Offers MA. Part-time programs available. *Degree requirements:* For master's, comprehensive exam, thesis. *Entrance requirements:* For master's, GRE General Test, 3 letters of recommendation.

California State University, Chico, Graduate School, College of Behavioral and Social Sciences, Department of Psychology, Program in Psychological Science, Chico, CA 95929-0722. Offers MA. *Students:* 9 full-time (7 women), 10 part-time (4 women); includes 1 American Indian or Alaska Native, non-Hispanic/Latino; 1 Asian, non-Hispanic/Latino, 1 international. Average age 29. 23 applicants, 52% accepted, 7 enrolled. In 2010, 8 master's awarded. *Degree requirements:* For master's, thesis or alternative. *Entrance requirements:* For master's, GRE General Test or MAT, 3 letters of recommendation on departmental form. Additional exam requirements/recommendations for international students: Required—TOEFL (minimum score 550 paper-based; 213 computer-based; 80 iBT), IELTS (minimum score 6.5). *Application deadline:* For fall admission, 3/1 for domestic and international students. Application fee: $55. *Unit head:* Dr. Linda Kline, Graduate Coordinator, 530-898-6263. *Application contact:* Dr. Linda Kline, Graduate Coordinator, 530-898-6263.

California State University, Dominguez Hills, College of Natural and Behavioral Sciences, Program in Psychology, Carson, CA 90747-0001. Offers clinical psychology (MA). Part-time and evening/weekend programs available. *Faculty:* 7 full-time (4 women). *Students:* 31 full-time (22 women), 28 part-time (26 women); includes 10 Black or African American, non-Hispanic/Latino; 2 Asian, non-Hispanic/Latino; 27 Hispanic/Latino; 1 Two or more races, non-Hispanic/Latino, 2 international. Average age 30. 59 applicants, 44% accepted, 15 enrolled. In 2010, 4 master's awarded. Terminal master's awarded for partial completion of doctoral program. *Degree requirements:* For master's, comprehensive exam, thesis optional. *Entrance requirements:* For master's, GRE General Test or MAT, interview, minimum GPA of 3.0, prerequisite psychology courses. Additional exam requirements/recommendations for international students: Required—TOEFL (minimum score 550 paper-based). *Application deadline:* For fall admission, 3/1 for domestic and international students. Application fee: $55. Electronic applications accepted. *Faculty research:* Culture and health, neuropsychology and HIV, psychohistory of the Holocaust, community and adolescents, malingering. *Unit head:* Dr. L. Mark Carrier, Chair, 310-243-3499, E-mail: lcarrier@csudh.edu. *Application contact:* Dr. Karen I. Mason, Coordinator, 310-243-3642, Fax: 310-516-3642, E-mail: kmason@csudh.edu.

California State University, Fresno, Division of Graduate Studies, College of Science and Mathematics, Department of Psychology, Fresno, CA 93740-8027. Offers MA, MS. *Degree requirements:* For master's, thesis. *Entrance requirements:* For master's, GRE General Test, GRE Subject Test, minimum GPA of 3.0. Additional exam requirements/recommendations for international students: Required—TOEFL. Electronic applications accepted. *Faculty research:* Oncology prediction, parenting stress, wellness, aging and memory, retrieval inhibition, anger, minority mental health.

California State University, Fullerton, Graduate Studies, College of Humanities and Social Sciences, Department of Psychology, Fullerton, CA 92834-9480. Offers clinical/community psychology (MS); psychology (MA). Part-time programs available. *Students:* 67 full-time (49 women), 9 part-time (5 women); includes 2 Black or African American, non-Hispanic/Latino; 5 Asian, non-Hispanic/Latino; 8 Hispanic/Latino; 3 Two or more races, non-Hispanic/Latino, 2 international. Average age 25. 169 applicants, 22% accepted, 37 enrolled. In 2010, 33 master's awarded. *Degree requirements:* For master's, thesis. *Entrance requirements:* For master's, GRE General Test, GRE Subject Test, undergraduate major in psychology or related field. Application fee: $55. *Financial support:* Career-related internships or fieldwork, Federal Work-Study, institutionally sponsored loans, and scholarships/grants available. Support available to part-time students. Financial award application deadline: 3/1; financial award applicants required to submit FAFSA. *Unit head:* Dr. Daniel Kee, Chair, 657-278-3514. *Application contact:* Admissions/Applications, 657-278-2371.

California State University, Long Beach, Graduate Studies, College of Liberal Arts, Department of Psychology, Long Beach, CA 90840. Offers human factors (MS); industrial/organizational psychology (MS); psychology (MA). Part-time and evening/weekend programs available. *Faculty:* 18 full-time (5 women), 1 part-time/adjunct (0 women). *Students:* 43 full-time (31 women), 27 part-time (17 women); includes 4 Black or African American, non-Hispanic/Latino; 10 Asian, non-Hispanic/Latino; 11 Hispanic/Latino, 2 international. Average age 27. 203 applicants, 16% accepted, 30 enrolled. In 2010, 19 master's awarded. *Degree requirements:* For master's, comprehensive exam, thesis. *Entrance requirements:* For master's, GRE General Test, GRE Subject Test. *Application deadline:* For fall admission, 3/1 for domestic students. Applications are processed on a rolling basis. Application fee: $55. Electronic applications accepted. *Financial support:* Federal Work-Study, institutionally sponsored loans, and scholarships/grants available. Financial award application deadline: 3/2. *Faculty research:* Physiological psychology, social and personality psychology, community-clinical psychology, industrial-organizational psychology, developmental psychology. *Unit head:* Dr. Kenneth Green, Chair, 562-985-5049, Fax: 562-985-8004, E-mail: kgreen@csulb.edu. *Application contact:* Dr. Kenneth Green, Chair, 562-985-5049, Fax: 562-985-8004, E-mail: kgreen@csulb.edu.

California State University, Los Angeles, Graduate Studies, College of Natural and Social Sciences, Department of Psychology, Los Angeles, CA 90032-8530. Offers MA, MS. Part-time and evening/weekend programs available. *Faculty:* 6 full-time (2 women), 8 part-time/adjunct (6 women). *Students:* 24 full-time (19 women), 54 part-time (44 women); includes 41 minority (9 Black or African American, non-Hispanic/Latino; 10 Asian, non-Hispanic/Latino; 20 Hispanic/Latino; 1 Native Hawaiian or other Pacific Islander, non-Hispanic/Latino; 1 Two or more races,

Psychology—General

California State University, Los Angeles (continued)
non-Hispanic/Latino), 7 international. Average age 29. 41 applicants, 100% accepted, 27 enrolled. In 2010, 51 master's awarded. *Degree requirements:* For master's, comprehensive exam or thesis. *Entrance requirements:* Additional exam requirements/recommendations for international students: Required—TOEFL (minimum score 500 paper-based; 173 computer-based). *Application deadline:* For fall admission, 5/1 for domestic and international students. Applications are processed on a rolling basis. Application fee: $55. Electronic applications accepted. *Financial support:* Career-related internships or fieldwork and Federal Work-Study available. Support available to part-time students. Financial award application deadline: 3/1. *Faculty research:* Binaural resolution of the size of an acoustic array, response and generalization of matching to sample in children. *Unit head:* Dr. Kaveri Subrahmanyam, Chair, 323-343-2250, Fax: 323-343-2281, E-mail: ksubrah@exchange.calstatela.edu. *Application contact:* Dr. Alan Muchlinski, Dean of Graduate Studies, 323-343-3820, Fax: 323-343-5653, E-mail: amuchli@exchange.calstatela.edu.

California State University, Northridge, Graduate Studies, College of Social and Behavioral Sciences, Department of Psychology, Northridge, CA 91330. Offers clinical psychology (MA); general-experimental psychology (MA); human factors and applied experimental psychology (MA). *Degree requirements:* For master's, thesis. *Entrance requirements:* For master's, GRE General Test, GRE Subject Test, minimum GPA of 3.0, letters of recommendation. Additional exam requirements/recommendations for international students: Required—TOEFL.

California State University, Sacramento, Graduate Studies, College of Social Sciences and Interdisciplinary Studies, Department of Psychology, Sacramento, CA 95819. Offers counseling psychology (MA). Part-time programs available. *Degree requirements:* For master's, thesis, writing proficiency exam. *Entrance requirements:* For master's, GRE Subject Test, minimum GPA of 3.0 during previous 2 years. Additional exam requirements/recommendations for international students: Required—TOEFL. Electronic applications accepted.

California State University, San Bernardino, Graduate Studies, College of Social and Behavioral Sciences, Department of Psychology, San Bernardino, CA 92407-2397. Offers child development (MA), including psychology-life span; clinical/counseling psychology (MS), including clinical psychology; general/experimental psychology (MA), including psychology; industrial/organizational psychology (MS), including organizational psychology. *Degree requirements:* For master's, comprehensive exam, thesis (for some programs), advancement to candidacy. *Entrance requirements:* For master's, writing exam, minimum GPA of 3.0 in major. *Faculty research:* Perceptual development, human memory, psychopharmacology, psychology of women, language acquisition.

California State University, San Marcos, College of Arts and Sciences, Program in Psychology, San Marcos, CA 92096-0001. Offers MA. *Degree requirements:* For master's, thesis. *Entrance requirements:* For master's, GRE General Test, GRE Subject Test (recommended), 3 letters of recommendation. Additional exam requirements/recommendations for international students: Required—TOEFL (minimum score 550 paper-based). *Faculty research:* Psychopharmacology, recovery from major surgery, computer literacy in children, neuropsychology of hemispheric differences, conservation psychology.

California State University, Stanislaus, College of Human and Health Sciences, Program in Psychology (MA/MS), Turlock, CA 95382. Offers behavior analysis (MS); counseling psychology (MS); psychology (MA). Part-time programs available. *Students:* 26 full-time (20 women), 39 part-time (36 women); includes 24 minority (1 Black or African American, non-Hispanic/Latino; 1 American Indian or Alaska Native, non-Hispanic/Latino; 4 Asian, non-Hispanic/Latino; 15 Hispanic/Latino; 3 Two or more races, non-Hispanic/Latino). Average age 30. 62 applicants, 48% accepted, 24 enrolled. In 2010, 13 master's awarded. *Degree requirements:* For master's, thesis. *Entrance requirements:* For master's, GRE, minimum GPA of 3.0, 3 letters of reference, 16 PSYC prerequisites, department approval, personal statement. Additional exam requirements/recommendations for international students: Required—TOEFL (minimum score 550 paper-based; 213 computer-based). *Application deadline:* For fall admission, 5/1 for domestic students; for spring admission, 1/7 for domestic students. Application fee: $55. Electronic applications accepted. Tuition and fees vary according to program. *Financial support:* Fellowships, career-related internships or fieldwork and Federal Work-Study available. Financial award application deadline: 3/1; financial award applicants required to submit FAFSA. *Faculty research:* Hedonic tone judgment, syntax and autism, early literacy assessment and native and non-native languages. *Unit head:* Dr. Bruce Hesse, Psychology Professor, Graduate Academic Director, 209-667-3555, E-mail: bhesse@csustan.edu. *Application contact:* Graduate School, 209-667-3129, Fax: 209-664-7025, E-mail: graduate_school@csustan.edu.

Cambridge College, School of Psychology and Counseling, Cambridge, MA 02138-5304. Offers addiction counseling (M Ed); alcohol and drug counseling (Certificate); counseling psychology (M Ed, CAGS); counseling psychology: forensic counseling (M Ed); marriage and family therapy (M Ed); mental health and addiction counseling (M Ed); mental health counseling (M Ed); mental health counseling for school guidance counselors (Post Master's Certificate); psychological studies (M Ed); school adjustment and mental health counseling (M Ed); school adjustment, mental health and addiction counseling (M Ed); school guidance counselor (M Ed); trauma studies (Certificate). Part-time and evening/weekend programs available. *Faculty:* 4 full-time (2 women), 83 part-time/adjunct (48 women). *Students:* 436 full-time (351 women), 351 part-time (274 women); includes 321 Black or African American, non-Hispanic/Latino; 3 American Indian or Alaska Native, non-Hispanic/Latino; 4 Asian, non-Hispanic/Latino; 87 Hispanic/Latino; 4 Two or more races, non-Hispanic/Latino, 6 international. Average age 37. In 2010, 284 master's, 16 other advanced degrees awarded. *Degree requirements:* For master's and other advanced degree, thesis, practicum/internship. *Entrance requirements:* For master's, resume, 2 professional references; for other advanced degree, official transcripts, documents for transfer credit evaluation, resume, written personal statement/essay, 2 professional references, health insurance, immunizations form. Additional exam requirements/recommendations for international students: Required—TOEFL (minimum score 550 paper-based; 213 computer-based; 79 iBT); Recommended—IELTS (minimum score 6). *Application deadline:* Applications are processed on a rolling basis. Application fee: $30. Electronic applications accepted. *Expenses:* Contact institution. *Financial support:* Career-related internships or fieldwork, Federal Work-Study, and scholarships/grants available. Financial award applicants required to submit FAFSA. *Faculty research:* Trauma, drug and alcohol counseling, cross-cultural issues, school counseling, trauma in schools. *Unit head:* Dr. Niti Seth, Dean, 617-873-0208, Fax: 617-349-3561, E-mail: nseth@cambridgecollege.edu. *Application contact:* Elaine M. Lapomardo, Dean of Enrollment Management, 617-873-0274, Fax: 617-349-3561, E-mail: elaine.lapomardo@cambridgecollege.edu.

Cameron University, Office of Graduate Studies, Program in Behavioral Sciences, Lawton, OK 73505-6377. Offers MS. Part-time and evening/weekend programs available. *Degree requirements:* For master's, comprehensive exam, thesis optional. *Entrance requirements:* Additional exam requirements/recommendations for international students: Required—TOEFL (minimum score 550 paper-based; 213 computer-based). Electronic applications accepted. *Faculty research:* Student burnout, attention deficit hyperactivity disorder, group decision making, counseling outcomes, smoking cessation.

Capella University, Harold Abel School of Psychology, Minneapolis, MN 55402. Offers child and adolescent development (MS); clinical psychology (MS, Psy D); counseling psychology (MS); educational psychology (MS, PhD); evaluation, research, and measurement (MS); general psychology (MS, PhD); industrial/organizational psychology (MS, PhD); leadership coaching psychology (MS); organizational leader development (MS); school psychology (MS); sport psychology (MS). Part-time and evening/weekend programs available. Postbaccalaureate distance learning degree programs offered (minimal on-campus study). Terminal master's awarded for partial completion of doctoral program. *Degree requirements:* For master's, thesis optional, project; for doctorate, thesis/dissertation. *Entrance requirements:* For degree, master's degree in school psychology. Additional exam requirements/recommendations for international students: Required—TOEFL (minimum score 550 paper-based; 213 computer-based), TWE (minimum score 4); Recommended—IELTS. Electronic applications accepted. *Expenses:* Tuition: Full-time $11,880; part-time $440 per credit hour.

Cardinal Stritch University, College of Arts and Sciences, Department of Psychology, Milwaukee, WI 53217-3985. Offers clinical psychology (MA). Part-time and evening/weekend programs available. *Degree requirements:* For master's, thesis, portfolio, clinical practicum. *Entrance requirements:* For master's, GRE General Test, GRE Subject Test (psychology), interview, minimum GPA of 3.0, 3 letters of recommendation.

Carleton University, Faculty of Graduate Studies, Faculty of Arts and Social Sciences, Department of Psychology, Ottawa, ON K1S 5B6, Canada. Offers neuroscience (M Sc); psychology (MA, PhD). Part-time programs available. *Degree requirements:* For master's, thesis; for doctorate, comprehensive exam, thesis/dissertation. *Entrance requirements:* For master's, honors degree; for doctorate, GRE, master's degree. Additional exam requirements/recommendations for international students: Required—TOEFL. *Faculty research:* Behavioral neuroscience, social and personality psychology, cognitive/perception, developmental psychology, computer user research and evaluation, forensic psychology, health psychology.

Carlos Albizu University, Graduate Programs, San Juan, PR 00901. Offers clinical psychology (MS, PhD, Psy D); general psychology (PhD); industrial/organizational psychology (MS, PhD); speech and language pathology (MS). *Accreditation:* APA (one or more programs are accredited). Part-time and evening/weekend programs available. Terminal master's awarded for partial completion of doctoral program. *Degree requirements:* For master's, one foreign language, comprehensive exam, thesis; for doctorate, one foreign language, comprehensive exam, thesis/dissertation, written qualifying exams. *Entrance requirements:* For master's, GRE General Test or EXADEP, interview; minimum GPA of 3.0 (industrial/organizational psychology), 3.25 (speech and language pathology); for doctorate, GRE General Test or EXADEP, interview; minimum GPA of 3.0 (industrial/organizational psychology), 3.25 (PhD and Psy D in clinical psychology). *Faculty research:* Psychotherapeutic techniques for Hispanics, psychology of the aged, school dropouts, stress, violence.

Carlos Albizu University, Miami Campus, Graduate Programs, Miami, FL 33172-2209. Offers clinical psychology (Psy D); entrepreneurship (MBA); exceptional student education (MS); industrial/organizational psychology (MS); marriage and family therapy (MS); mental health counseling (MS); nonprofit management (MBA); organizational management (MBA); psychology (MS); school counseling (MS); teaching English as a second language (MS). *Accreditation:* APA. Part-time and evening/weekend programs available. *Faculty:* 21 full-time (12 women), 37 part-time/adjunct (18 women). *Students:* 496 full-time (400 women), 242 part-time (192 women); includes 590 minority (58 Black or African American, non-Hispanic/Latino; 2 American Indian or Alaska Native, non-Hispanic/Latino; 5 Asian, non-Hispanic/Latino; 523 Hispanic/Latino; 2 Two or more races, non-Hispanic/Latino), 15 international. Average age 36. 141 applicants, 84% accepted, 118 enrolled. In 2010, 159 master's, 20 doctorates awarded. Terminal master's awarded for partial completion of doctoral program. *Degree requirements:* For master's, one foreign language, comprehensive exam, integrative project (MBA), research project (exceptional student education, teaching English as a second language); for doctorate, one foreign language, comprehensive exam, internship, project. *Entrance requirements:* For master's, 3 letters of recommendation, interview, minimum GPA of 3.0, resume, statement of purpose, official transcripts; for doctorate, 3 letters of recommendation, minimum GPA of 3.0, resume, interview. *Application deadline:* For fall admission, 8/1 priority date for domestic students; for spring admission, 11/30 priority date for domestic students. Applications are processed on a rolling basis. Application fee: $50. Electronic applications accepted. *Expenses:* Tuition: Full-time $9360; part-time $520 per credit. Required fees: $298 per term. Tuition and fees vary according to course load, degree level and program. *Financial support:* In 2010–11, 106 students received support. Federal Work-Study, scholarships/grants, and tuition discounts available. Financial award application deadline: 6/1; financial award applicants required to submit FAFSA. *Faculty research:* Psychotherapy, forensic psychology, neuropsychology, marketing strategy, entrepreneurship, special education. *Unit head:* Dr. Carmen S. Roca, Chancellor, 305-593-1223 Ext. 120, Fax: 305-629-8052, E-mail: croca@albizu.edu. *Application contact:* Vanessa Almendarez, Secretary, 305-593-1223 Ext. 137, Fax: 305-593-1854, E-mail: valmendarez@albizu.edu.

Carnegie Mellon University, College of Humanities and Social Sciences, Department of Psychology, Pittsburgh, PA 15213-3891. Offers cognitive neuroscience (PhD); cognitive psychology (PhD); developmental psychology (PhD); social/personality/health psychology (PhD). *Degree requirements:* For doctorate, comprehensive exam, thesis/dissertation. *Entrance requirements:* For doctorate, GRE General Test. Additional exam requirements/recommendations for international students: Required—TOEFL. *Faculty research:* Artificial intelligence, stress and the immune system, children's learning strategies, neural basis of cognition.

Case Western Reserve University, School of Graduate Studies, Department of Psychology, Cleveland, OH 44106. Offers clinical psychology (PhD); experimental psychology (PhD). *Accreditation:* APA. Part-time programs available. *Faculty:* 14 full-time (7 women), 15 part-time/adjunct (6 women). *Students:* 40 full-time (32 women); includes 1 Asian, non-Hispanic/Latino; 2 Hispanic/Latino, 1 international. Average age 27. 211 applicants, 3% accepted, 7 enrolled. In 2010, 5 doctorates awarded. *Degree requirements:* For doctorate, thesis/dissertation, internship. *Entrance requirements:* For doctorate, GRE General Test, GRE Subject Test. Additional exam requirements/recommendations for international students: Required—TOEFL (minimum score 550 paper-based; 213 computer-based; 79 iBT). *Application deadline:* For fall admission, 1/5 priority date for domestic students. Application fee: $50. Electronic applications accepted. *Financial support:* Fellowships, research assistantships, teaching assistantships, tuition waivers (full and partial) available. Financial award application deadline: 2/1. *Faculty research:* Adolescent suicide, cognitive processing, repressive responses, visual perception, impact of HIV infection, neuropsychology. *Unit head:* Dr. Lee Thompson, Chair, 216-368-2685, Fax: 216-368-4891, E-mail: cwrupsych@gmail.com. *Application contact:* Dr. James C. Overholser, Director of Clinical Training, 216-368-2686, Fax: 216-368-4891, E-mail: cwrupsych@gmail.com.

Castleton State College, Division of Graduate Studies, Department of Psychology, Castleton, VT 05735. Offers forensic psychology (MA). *Degree requirements:* For master's, thesis. *Entrance requirements:* For master's, GRE General Test, minimum undergraduate GPA of 3.5, previous course work in research methodology and statistics. Additional exam requirements/recommendations for international students: Required—TOEFL. *Faculty research:* Psychology and law, juvenile delinquency, criminal psychology, correctional psychology, police psychology.

The Catholic University of America, School of Arts and Sciences, Department of Psychology, Washington, DC 20064. Offers applied experimental psychology (PhD); clinical psychology (PhD); general psychology (MA); human factors (MA); MA/JD. *Accreditation:* APA (one or more programs are accredited). Part-time programs available. *Faculty:* 12 full-time (6 women), 7 part-time/adjunct (2 women). *Students:* 39 full-time (25 women), 31 part-time (28 women); includes 6 Black or African American, non-Hispanic/Latino; 4 Asian, non-Hispanic/Latino; 4 Hispanic/Latino, 1 international. Average age 29. 229 applicants, 22% accepted, 17 enrolled. In 2010, 22 master's, 8 doctorates awarded. *Degree requirements:* For master's, comprehensive exam, thesis (for some programs); for doctorate, comprehensive exam, thesis/dissertation. *Entrance requirements:* For master's, GRE General Test, statement of purpose, official copies of academic transcripts, three letters of recommendation; for doctorate, GRE General Test, GRE Subject Test, statement of purpose, official copies of academic transcripts, three letters of recommendation. Additional exam requirements/recommendations for international students: Required—TOEFL (minimum score 580 paper-based; 237 computer-based). *Application deadline:* For fall admission, 8/1 priority date for domestic students, 7/15 for international students; for spring admission, 12/1 priority date for domestic students, 10/15 for international students. Applications are processed on a rolling basis. Application fee: $55. Electronic applications accepted. *Expenses:* Tuition: Full-time $33,580; part-time $1315 per credit hour. Required fees: $80; $40 per semester hour. One-time fee: $425. *Financial support:* Fellowships, research assistantships, teaching assistantships, Federal Work-Study, scholarships/grants, tuition waivers (full and partial), and unspecified assistantships available. Financial award application deadline: 2/1; financial award applicants required to submit FAFSA. *Faculty research:* Clinical psychology, applied cognitive science, psychopathology, cognitive neuroscience, psychotherapy. Total annual research expenditures: $409,988. *Unit head:* Dr. Marc M. Sebrechts, Chair, 202-319-5750, Fax: 202-319-6263, E-mail: sebrechts@cua.edu. *Application contact:* Andrew Woodall, Director of Graduate Admissions, 202-319-5057, Fax: 202-319-6533, E-mail: cua-admissions@cua.edu.

Central Connecticut State University, School of Graduate Studies, School of Arts and Sciences, Department of Psychology, New Britain, CT 06050-4010. Offers community psychology (MA); general psychology (MA); health psychology (MA). Part-time and evening/weekend programs available. *Faculty:* 20 full-time (12 women), 22 part-time/adjunct (6 women). *Students:* 26 full-time (20 women), 25 part-time (20 women); includes 6 minority (1 Black or African American, non-Hispanic/Latino; 4 Hispanic/Latino; 1 Two or more races, non-Hispanic/Latino). Average age 26. 65 applicants, 57% accepted, 19 enrolled. In 2010, 7 master's awarded. *Degree requirements:* For master's, comprehensive exam, thesis or alternative. *Entrance requirements:* For master's, minimum undergraduate GPA of 2.7, essay. Additional exam requirements/recommendations for international students: Required—TOEFL. *Application deadline:* For fall admission, 4/25 for domestic students; for spring admission, 12/1 for domestic students. Applications are processed on a rolling basis. Application fee: $50. Electronic applications accepted. *Expenses:* Tuition, area resident: Full-time $5012; part-time $470 per credit. Tuition, state resident: full-time $7518; part-time $482 per credit. Tuition, nonresident: full-time $13,962; part-time $482 per credit. Required fees: $3772. One-time fee: $62 part-time. *Financial support:* In 2010–11, 8 students received support, including 4 research assistantships; career-related internships or fieldwork, Federal Work-Study, scholarships/grants, and unspecified assistantships also available. Support available to part-time students. Financial award application deadline: 2/15; financial award applicants required to submit FAFSA. *Faculty research:* Clinical psychology, general psychology, child development, cognitive development, drugs/behavior. *Unit head:* Dr. Laura Bowman, Chair, 860-832-3100. *Application contact:* Dr. Laura Bowman, Chair, 860-832-3100.

Central Michigan University, College of Graduate Studies, College of Humanities and Social and Behavioral Sciences, Department of Psychology, Mount Pleasant, MI 48859. Offers clinical psychology (MA, PhD); experimental psychology (MS, PhD), including applied experimental psychology (PhD), experimental psychology (MS); industrial and organizational psychology (MA, PhD), including industrial and organizational psychology, occupational health psychology (PhD); neuroscience (MS, PhD); school psychology (PhD, S Psy S), including psychological services (S Psy S), school psychology (PhD). *Accreditation:* APA (one or more programs are accredited). *Faculty:* 28 full-time (9 women), 1 part-time/adjunct (0 women). *Students:* 65 full-time (39 women), 82 part-time (56 women); includes 2 Black or African American, non-Hispanic/Latino; 1 American Indian or Alaska Native, non-Hispanic/Latino; 1 Asian, non-Hispanic/Latino; 2 Hispanic/Latino, 12 international. Average age 27. In 2010, 5 other advanced degrees awarded. Terminal master's awarded for partial completion of doctoral program. *Degree requirements:* For master's, thesis or alternative; for doctorate, thesis/dissertation; for S Psy S, thesis. *Entrance requirements:* For doctorate, GRE. Application fee: $35 ($45 for international students). Electronic applications accepted. *Expenses:* Tuition, state resident: full-time $8208; part-time $456 per credit hour. Tuition, nonresident: full-time $13,788; part-time $766 per credit hour. One-time fee: $25. *Financial support:* Fellowships with tuition reimbursements, research assistantships with tuition reimbursements, teaching assistantships with tuition reimbursements, career-related internships or fieldwork, Federal Work-Study, unspecified assistantships, and out-of-state merit awards; non-resident graduate awards available. *Faculty research:* Experimental psychology, clinical psychology, industrial/organizational psychology, school psychology, neuroscience. *Unit head:* Dr. Hajime Otani, Chairperson, 989-774-6461, Fax: 989-774-2553, E-mail: otani1h@cmich.edu. *Application contact:* Barbara Houghton, Office Supervisor, 989-774-6461, Fax: 989-774-2553, E-mail: hough1ba@cmich.edu.

Central Washington University, Graduate Studies and Research, College of the Sciences, Department of Psychology, Ellensburg, WA 98926. Offers experimental psychology (MS); mental health counseling (MS); school counseling (M Ed); school psychology (M Ed). Evening/weekend programs available. *Degree requirements:* For master's, thesis. *Entrance requirements:* For master's, GRE General Test, minimum GPA of 3.0. Additional exam requirements/recommendations for international students: Required—TOEFL (minimum score 550 paper-based; 213 computer-based; 79 iBT).

Chestnut Hill College, School of Graduate Studies, Division of Psychology, Philadelphia, PA 19118-2693. Offers clinical and counseling psychology (MA, MS, CAS); clinical psychology (Psy D). Part-time and evening/weekend programs available. *Faculty:* 10 full-time (5 women), 31 part-time/adjunct (18 women). *Students:* 150 full-time (128 women), 223 part-time (180 women); includes 59 minority (35 Black or African American, non-Hispanic/Latino; 12 Asian, non-Hispanic/Latino; 11 Hispanic/Latino; 1 Two or more races, non-Hispanic/Latino), 8 international. Average age 32. 266 applicants, 53% accepted, 89 enrolled. In 2010, 74 master's, 7 doctorates awarded. *Degree requirements:* For master's, thesis optional, practica; for doctorate, comprehensive exam, thesis/dissertation, internship, practica, clinical competency exam. *Entrance requirements:* For master's, GRE General Test, writing sample, letters of recommendation; for doctorate, GRE General Test, master's degree in clinical counseling or closely related field, transcripts, letters of recommendation, statement of professional goals, writing sample; for CAS, GRE General Test, official transcripts, letters of recommendation, statement of professional goals, writing sample. Additional exam requirements/recommendations for international students: Required—TOEFL (minimum score 500 paper-based; 213 computer-based). *Application deadline:* For fall admission, 7/17 priority date for domestic students, 7/15 priority date for international students; for spring admission, 12/15 priority date for domestic and international students. Applications are processed on a rolling basis. Application fee: $55. *Expenses:* Tuition: Part-time $560 per credit hour. One-time fee: $55. Tuition and fees vary according to degree level and program. *Faculty research:* Adolescent development, trauma and sexual abuse, cultural diversity, family psychology and family therapy, psychodynamic therapy. *Unit head:* Dr. Joseph Micucci, Division Chair, 215-248-7162, Fax: 215-248-7155. *Application contact:* Amy Boorse, Administrative Assistant, School of Graduate Studies Office, 215-248-7170, Fax: 215-248-7161, E-mail: gradadmissions@chc.edu.

The Chicago School of Professional Psychology, Program in Business Psychology, Chicago, IL 60610. Offers Psy D. *Degree requirements:* For doctorate, thesis/dissertation optional. *Entrance requirements:* For doctorate, GRE. Additional exam requirements/recommendations for international students: Required—TOEFL.

The Chicago School of Professional Psychology at Irvine, Program in Psychology, Irvine, CA 92612. Offers generalist (Psy D); psychodynamic psychotherapy (Psy D).

The Chicago School of Professional Psychology at Westwood, Program in Psychology, Los Angeles, CA 90024. Offers generalist (Psy D); psychodynamic psychotherapy (Psy D).

The Chicago School of Professional Psychology: Online, Program in International Psychology, Chicago, IL 60654. Offers PhD.

The Chicago School of Professional Psychology: Online, Program in Psychology, Chicago, IL 60654. Offers child and adolescent psychology (MA); generalist (MA); gerontology (MA); international psychology (MA); organizational leadership (MA); sport and exercise psychology (MA).

The Citadel, The Military College of South Carolina, Citadel Graduate College, Department of Psychology, Charleston, SC 29409. Offers psychology (MA), including clinical counseling; school psychology (Ed S), including school psychology. Part-time and evening/weekend programs available. *Faculty:* 10 full-time (3 women), 2 part-time/adjunct (1 woman). *Students:*

69 full-time (58 women), 62 part-time (56 women); includes 4 Black or African American, non-Hispanic/Latino; 1 Asian, non-Hispanic/Latino; 2 Hispanic/Latino, 1 international. Average age 27. In 2010, 16 master's, 14 other advanced degrees awarded. *Degree requirements:* For master's, comprehensive exam, thesis optional; for Ed S, comprehensive exam, thesis, internship. *Entrance requirements:* For master's, GRE (minimum score 1000) or MAT (minimum score 410), minimum undergraduate GPA of 3.0; 2 letters of reference; for Ed S, GRE (minimum 1000) or MAT with prior permission (minimum 410), minimum undergraduate or graduate GPA of 3.0; 2 letters of reference. Additional exam requirements/recommendations for international students: Required—TOEFL (minimum score 550 paper-based; 213 computer-based). *Application deadline:* For fall admission, 3/15 for domestic students. Application fee: $30. Electronic applications accepted. *Expenses:* Tuition, state resident: part-time $460 per credit hour. Tuition, nonresident: part-time $756 per credit hour. Required fees: $40 per term. *Financial support:* Research assistantships, career-related internships or fieldwork, health care benefits, and unspecified assistantships available. Support available to part-time students. Financial award application deadline: 7/1; financial award applicants required to submit FAFSA. *Faculty research:* Ostracism and social exclusion, bullying, social concerns of special-needs children, childhood obesity, phantom limb pain, validation of psychological tests, perfectionism, school-based interventions with at-risk children. *Unit head:* Dr. P. Michael Politano, Department Head, 843-953-5230, Fax: 843-953-6797, E-mail: politanom@citadel.edu. *Application contact:* Dr. William G. Johnson, Program Director, 843-953-6827, Fax: 843-953-6769, E-mail: will.johnson@citadel.edu.

City College of the City University of New York, Graduate School, College of Liberal Arts and Science, Division of Social Science, Department of Psychology, New York, NY 10031-9198. Offers clinical psychology (PhD); experimental cognition (PhD); general psychology (MA); mental health counseling (MA). PhD program offered jointly with Graduate School and University Center of the City University of New York. *Accreditation:* APA (one or more programs are accredited). Part-time programs available. *Degree requirements:* For master's, one foreign language, comprehensive exam, thesis. *Entrance requirements:* For master's, GRE. Additional exam requirements/recommendations for international students: Required—TOEFL (minimum score 550 paper-based; 79 iBT). Electronic applications accepted. *Faculty research:* Social/personality psychology, physiological psychology, cognition and development.

Claremont Graduate University, Graduate Programs, School of Behavioral and Organizational Sciences, Department of Psychology, Claremont, CA 91711-6160. Offers advanced study in evaluation (Certificate); cognitive psychology (MA, PhD); developmental psychology (MA, PhD); evaluation and applied research methods (MA, PhD); health behavior research and evaluation (MA, PhD); human resource development and evaluation (MA); industrial/organizational psychology (MA, PhD); organizational behavior (MA, PhD); organizational psychology (MA, PhD); social psychology (MA, PhD); MBA/PhD. Part-time programs available. *Faculty:* 15 full-time (6 women), 5 part-time/adjunct (2 women). *Students:* 248 full-time (169 women), 15 part-time (9 women); includes 68 minority (14 Black or African American, non-Hispanic/Latino; 1 American Indian or Alaska Native, non-Hispanic/Latino; 27 Asian, non-Hispanic/Latino; 19 Hispanic/Latino; 2 Native Hawaiian or other Pacific Islander, non-Hispanic/Latino; 5 Two or more races, non-Hispanic/Latino), 29 international. Average age 30. In 2010, 45 master's, 21 doctorates, 4 other advanced degrees awarded. Terminal master's awarded for partial completion of doctoral program. *Entrance requirements:* For master's and doctorate, GRE General Test. Additional exam requirements/recommendations for international students: Required—TOEFL (minimum score 550 paper-based; 213 computer-based; 80 iBT). *Application deadline:* For fall admission, 1/15 priority date for domestic students. Applications are processed on a rolling basis. Application fee: $60. Electronic applications accepted. *Expenses:* Tuition: Full-time $35,748; part-time $1554 per unit. Required fees: $215 per semester. *Financial support:* Fellowships, research assistantships, teaching assistantships, Federal Work-Study, institutionally sponsored loans, scholarships/grants, and tuition waivers (full and partial) available. Support available to part-time students. Financial award application deadline: 2/15; financial award applicants required to submit FAFSA. *Faculty research:* Social intervention, diversity in organizations, eyewitness memory, aging and cognition, drug policy. *Unit head:* Stewart Donaldson, Dean, 909-607-9001, Fax: 909-621-8905, E-mail: stewart.donaldson@cgu.edu. *Application contact:* Paul Thomas, Director, External Affairs, 909-607-9016, Fax: 909-621-8905, E-mail: paul.thomas@cgu.edu.

Clemson University, Graduate School, College of Business and Behavioral Science, Department of Psychology, Program in Human Factors Psychology, Clemson, SC 29634. Offers PhD. *Students:* 14 full-time (8 women), 1 part-time (0 women); includes 1 Two or more races, non-Hispanic/Latino. Average age 28. 17 applicants, 35% accepted, 4 enrolled. In 2010, 6 doctorates awarded. *Degree requirements:* For doctorate, thesis/dissertation. *Entrance requirements:* For doctorate, GRE General Test. Additional exam requirements/recommendations for international students: Required—TOEFL. *Application deadline:* For fall admission, 1/15 for domestic students. Applications are processed on a rolling basis. Application fee: $70 ($80 for international students). Electronic applications accepted. *Expenses:* Contact institution. *Financial support:* In 2010–11, 14 students received support, including 3 fellowships with full and partial tuition reimbursements available (averaging $7,167 per year), 5 research assistantships with partial tuition reimbursements available (averaging $13,400 per year), 9 teaching assistantships with partial tuition reimbursements available (averaging $12,000 per year); career-related internships or fieldwork, institutionally sponsored loans, scholarships/grants, health care benefits, and unspecified assistantships also available. Support available to part-time students. *Faculty research:* Transportation safety, human factors in health care, human-computer interaction, ergonomics, vision and visual performance. *Unit head:* Dr. Patrick Raymark, Chair, 864-656-4715, Fax: 864-656-0358, E-mail: praymar@clemson.edu. *Application contact:* Dr. Lee Gugerty, 864-656-4467, Fax: 864-656-0358, E-mail: gugerty@clemson.edu.

Cleveland State University, College of Graduate Studies, College of Sciences and Health Professions, Department of Psychology, Cleveland, OH 44115. Offers adult development and aging (PhD); clinical psychology (MA); consumer/industrial research (MA); diversity management (MA); experimental research psychology (MA); school psychology (Psy S). *Accreditation:* APA. *Faculty:* 20 full-time (7 women), 16 part-time/adjunct (8 women). *Students:* 63 full-time (45 women), 43 part-time (27 women); includes 15 Black or African American, non-Hispanic/Latino; 1 American Indian or Alaska Native, non-Hispanic/Latino; 3 Asian, non-Hispanic/Latino; 3 Hispanic/Latino, 1 international. Average age 30. 164 applicants, 44% accepted, 62 enrolled. In 2010, 39 master's, 8 other advanced degrees awarded. Terminal master's awarded for partial completion of doctoral program. *Degree requirements:* For master's, comprehensive exam (for some programs), thesis (for some programs); for doctorate, comprehensive exam, thesis/dissertation; for Psy S, internship. *Entrance requirements:* For master's and doctorate, GRE General Test. Additional exam requirements/recommendations for international students: Required—TOEFL (minimum score 525 paper-based; 197 computer-based). *Application deadline:* For fall admission, 2/1 priority date for domestic and international students. Application fee: $30. Electronic applications accepted. *Expenses:* Tuition, state resident: full-time $8447; part-time $469 per credit hour. Tuition, nonresident: full-time $16,020; part-time $890 per credit hour. Required fees: $50. *Financial support:* In 2010–11, 45 students received support. Career-related internships or fieldwork, Federal Work-Study, scholarships/grants, tuition waivers (partial), and unspecified assistantships available. Financial award applicants required to submit FAFSA. *Faculty research:* Cognitive and social psychology, consumer psychology, clinical psychology, school psychology, aging. Total annual research expenditures: $112,607. *Unit head:* Dr. Kathleen M. McNamara, Chairperson, 216-687-2545, Fax: 216-687-9294, E-mail: k.mcnamara@csuohio.edu. *Application contact:* Karen R. Colston, Administrative Coordinator, 216-687-2552, Fax: 216-687-9294, E-mail: k.colston@csuohio.edu.

The College at Brockport, State University of New York, School of Science and Mathematics, Department of Psychology, Brockport, NY 14420-2997. Offers MA. Part-time programs available. *Students:* 14 full-time (12 women), 5 part-time (all women); includes 1 Hispanic/Latino. 27 applicants, 37% accepted, 8 enrolled. In 2010, 8 master's awarded. *Degree requirements:* For master's, thesis optional. *Entrance requirements:* For master's, GRE General Test, letters of recommendation, interview, minimum GPA of 3.0. Additional exam requirements/

Psychology—General

The College at Brockport, State University of New York (continued)

recommendations for international students: Required—TOEFL (minimum score 550 paper-based; 213 computer-based; 79 iBT). *Application deadline:* For fall admission, 4/1 priority date for domestic and international students. Application fee: $50. Electronic applications accepted. *Financial support:* In 2010–11, 2 teaching assistantships with full tuition reimbursements (averaging $6,000 per year) were awarded; Federal Work-Study, scholarships/grants, and unspecified assistantships also available. Support available to part-time students. Financial award application deadline: 3/15; financial award applicants required to submit FAFSA. *Faculty research:* Positive psychology, decision-making and applied behavior analysis, family processes and close relationships, cognition and neuropsychology, social/personality and industrial/organizational psychology. *Unit head:* Dr. Melissa M. Brown, Chairperson, 585-395-2488, Fax: 585-395-2116, E-mail: mmbrown@brockport.edu. *Application contact:* Dr. Janet Gillespie, Graduate Director, 585-395-2433, Fax: 585-395-2116, E-mail: jgillesp@brockport.edu.

College of Saint Elizabeth, Department of Psychology, Morristown, NJ 07960-6989. Offers counseling psychology (MA); forensic psychology (MA); student affairs in higher education (Certificate). Part-time and evening/weekend programs available. *Faculty:* 4 full-time (3 women), 9 part-time/adjunct (all women). *Students:* 33 full-time (31 women), 67 part-time (57 women); includes 13 Black or African American, non-Hispanic/Latino; 4 Asian, non-Hispanic/Latino; 12 Hispanic/Latino, 2 international. Average age 30. 86 applicants, 41% accepted, 27 enrolled. In 2010, 22 master's awarded. *Degree requirements:* For master's, thesis or alternative, portfolio. *Entrance requirements:* For master's, minimum GPA of 3.0, BA in psychology (preferred), 12 credits of course work in psychology. Additional exam requirements/recommendations for international students: Required—TOEFL (minimum score 550 paper-based). *Application deadline:* For fall admission, 4/1 priority date for domestic students; for spring admission, 11/15 for domestic students. Applications are processed on a rolling basis. Application fee: $35. Electronic applications accepted. *Expenses:* Tuition: Part-time $857 per credit. Required fees: $70 per credit. *Financial support:* Career-related internships or fieldwork, tuition waivers (partial), and unspecified assistantships available. Support available to part-time students. Financial award application deadline: 3/15; financial award applicants required to submit FAFSA. *Faculty research:* Family systems, dissociative identity disorder, multicultural counseling, outcomes assessment. *Unit head:* Dr. Valerie Scott, Director of the Graduate Program in Counseling Psychology, 973-290-4102, Fax: 973-290-4676, E-mail: vscott@cse.edu. *Application contact:* Dean Donna Tatarka, Dean of Admission, 973-290-4705, Fax: 973-290-4710, E-mail: dtatarka@cse.edu.

College of St. Joseph, Graduate Programs, Division of Psychology and Human Services, Rutland, VT 05701-3899. Offers alcohol and substance abuse counseling (MS); clinical mental health counseling (MS); clinical psychology (MS); community counseling (MS); school guidance counseling (MS). Part-time and evening/weekend programs available. *Faculty:* 4 full-time (1 woman), 8 part-time/adjunct (4 women). *Students:* 30 full-time (25 women), 32 part-time (26 women); includes 1 Asian, non-Hispanic/Latino. Average age 35. 22 applicants, 91% accepted, 17 enrolled. In 2010, 12 master's awarded. *Degree requirements:* For master's, comprehensive exam, thesis. *Entrance requirements:* For master's, 2 letters of reference, interview. *Application deadline:* Applications are processed on a rolling basis. Application fee: $35. Electronic applications accepted. *Expenses:* Tuition: Full-time $14,200; part-time $400 per credit hour. Required fees: $45 per semester. *Financial support:* In 2010–11, 3 students received support, including teaching assistantships with tuition reimbursements available (averaging $3,000 per year); career-related internships or fieldwork, Federal Work-Study, and unspecified assistantships also available. Support available to part-time students. Financial award application deadline: 3/1. *Unit head:* Dr. Craig Knapp, Chair, 802-773-5900 Ext. 3219, Fax: 802-776-5258, E-mail: cknapp@csj.edu. *Application contact:* Alan Young, Dean of Admissions, 802-773-5900 Ext. 3227, Fax: 802-776-5310, E-mail: alanyoung@csj.edu.

Colorado State University, Graduate School, College of Natural Sciences, Department of Psychology, Fort Collins, CO 80523-1876. Offers psychology (MS, PhD). *Accreditation:* APA. Postbaccalaureate distance learning degree programs offered (no on-campus study). *Faculty:* 25 full-time (12 women), 2 part-time/adjunct (0 women). *Students:* 64 full-time (42 women), 50 part-time (30 women); includes 26 minority (2 Black or African American, non-Hispanic/Latino; 1 American Indian or Alaska Native, non-Hispanic/Latino; 5 Asian, non-Hispanic/Latino; 11 Hispanic/Latino; 7 Two or more races, non-Hispanic/Latino), 3 international. Average age 28. 449 applicants, 6% accepted, 25 enrolled. In 2010, 16 master's, 15 doctorates awarded. Terminal master's awarded for partial completion of doctoral program. *Degree requirements:* For master's, comprehensive exam (for some programs), thesis (for some programs); for doctorate, comprehensive exam, thesis/dissertation. *Entrance requirements:* For master's, GRE General Test, GRE Subject Test, minimum GPA of 3.0; transcripts; 3 letters of recommendation; resume or curriculum vitae; statement of interest; sample of scientific writing (for some areas of study); for doctorate, GRE General Test, GRE Subject Test, minimum GPA of 3.0; 3 letters of recommendation; resume or curriculum vitae; sample of scientific writing (for some areas of study). Additional exam requirements/recommendations for international students: Required—TOEFL (minimum score 550 paper-based; 213 computer-based; 80 iBT). *Application deadline:* For fall admission, 12/15 priority date for domestic and international students. Application fee: $50. Electronic applications accepted. *Expenses:* Tuition, state resident: full-time $7434; part-time $413 per credit. Tuition, nonresident: full-time $19,022; part-time $1057 per credit. Required fees: $1729; $88 per credit. *Financial support:* In 2010–11, 76 students received support, including 3 fellowships (averaging $28,970 per year), 22 research assistantships with full tuition reimbursements available (averaging $10,268 per year), 51 teaching assistantships with full tuition reimbursements available (averaging $11,161 per year); health care benefits also available. Financial award application deadline: 1/15; financial award applicants required to submit FAFSA. *Faculty research:* Environmental psychology, cognitive learning, health psychology, counseling and clinical issues, industrial and organizational psychology. Total annual research expenditures: $4.4 million. *Unit head:* Dr. Ernest L. Chavez, Chair and Professor, 970-491-6364, Fax: 970-491-1032, E-mail: ernest.chavez@colostate.edu. *Application contact:* Linda Thornton, Graduate Contact, 970-491-5212, Fax: 970-491-1032, E-mail: linda.thornton@colostate.edu.

Columbia University, Graduate School of Arts and Sciences, Division of Natural Sciences, Department of Psychology, New York, NY 10027. Offers experimental psychology (M Phil, MA, PhD); psychobiology (M Phil, MA, PhD); social psychology (M Phil, MA, PhD); JD/MA; JD/PhD; MD/PhD. *Degree requirements:* For master's, thesis; for doctorate, thesis/dissertation. *Entrance requirements:* For master's and doctorate, GRE General Test. Additional exam requirements/recommendations for international students: Required—TOEFL.

Concordia University, School of Graduate Studies, Faculty of Arts and Science, Department of Psychology, Program in Psychology (General), Montréal, QC H3G 1M8, Canada. Offers MA, PhD. *Degree requirements:* For master's, comprehensive exam, thesis; for doctorate, comprehensive exam, thesis/dissertation. *Entrance requirements:* For master's, GRE General Test, GRE Subject Test, honors degree in psychology or equivalent; for doctorate, master's degree in psychology. *Faculty research:* Appetitive motivation and drug dependence, human information processing, psychology of physical activity.

Concordia University Chicago, College of Graduate and Innovative Programs, Program in Psychology, River Forest, IL 60305-1499. Offers MA. Part-time and evening/weekend programs available. *Degree requirements:* For master's, comprehensive exam, thesis optional. *Entrance requirements:* For master's, minimum GPA of 2.9. Additional exam requirements/recommendations for international students: Required—TOEFL (minimum score 550 paper-based; 195 computer-based). Electronic applications accepted. *Faculty research:* Lutheran high school counseling research.

Concordia University Wisconsin, Graduate Programs, Department of Psychology, Mequon, WI 53097-2402. Offers professional counseling (MPC).

Connecticut College, Department of Psychology, New London, CT 06320-4196. Offers MA. Part-time programs available. *Degree requirements:* For master's, comprehensive exam (for some programs), thesis. *Entrance requirements:* For master's, GRE General Test. Additional exam requirements/recommendations for international students: Required—TOEFL (minimum score 600 paper-based). *Expenses:* Tuition: Part-time $44.13 per credit hour. *Faculty research:* Behavioral medicine, personality-social psychology, clinical, neuroscience/psychobiology.

Cornell University, Graduate School, Graduate Fields of Arts and Sciences, Field of Psychology, Ithaca, NY 14853-0001. Offers biopsychology (PhD); human experimental psychology (PhD); personality and social psychology (PhD). *Faculty:* 40 full-time (15 women). *Students:* 39 full-time (25 women); includes 1 Black or African American, non-Hispanic/Latino; 4 Asian, non-Hispanic/Latino; 2 Hispanic/Latino, 13 international. Average age 27. 273 applicants, 5% accepted, 10 enrolled. In 2010, 4 doctorates awarded. *Degree requirements:* For doctorate, comprehensive exam, thesis/dissertation, 2 semesters of teaching experience. *Entrance requirements:* For doctorate, GRE General Test, 3 letters of recommendation. Additional exam requirements/recommendations for international students: Required—TOEFL (minimum score 550 paper-based; 213 computer-based; 77 iBT). *Application deadline:* For fall admission, 12/15 for domestic students. Application fee: $80. Electronic applications accepted. *Expenses:* Tuition: Full-time $29,500. Required fees: $76. Tuition and fees vary according to degree level and program. *Financial support:* In 2010–11, 12 fellowships with full tuition reimbursements, 2 research assistantships with full tuition reimbursements, 23 teaching assistantships with full tuition reimbursements were awarded; institutionally sponsored loans, scholarships/grants, health care benefits, tuition waivers (full and partial), and unspecified assistantships also available. Financial award applicants required to submit FAFSA. *Faculty research:* Sensory and perceptual systems, social cognition, cognitive development, quantitative and computational modeling, behavioral neuroscience. *Unit head:* Director of Graduate Studies, 607-255-6364, Fax: 607-255-8433. *Application contact:* Graduate Field Assistant, 607-255-3834, Fax: 607-255-8433, E-mail: psychapp@cornell.edu.

Dalhousie University, Faculty of Science, Department of Psychology, Halifax, NS B3H 4R2, Canada. Offers clinical psychology (PhD); psychology (M Sc, PhD); psychology/neuroscience (M Sc, PhD). *Accreditation:* APA (one or more programs are accredited). *Degree requirements:* For master's, thesis; for doctorate, thesis/dissertation. *Entrance requirements:* For doctorate, GRE General Test. Additional exam requirements/recommendations for international students: Required—TOEFL, IELTS, CANTEST, CAEL, or Michigan English Language Assessment Battery. Electronic applications accepted. *Faculty research:* Physiological psychology, psychology of learning, learning and behavior, forensic clinical health psychology, development perception and cognition.

Dartmouth College, Arts and Sciences Graduate Programs, Department of Psychological and Brain Sciences, Hanover, NH 03755. Offers cognitive neuroscience (PhD); psychology (PhD). *Degree requirements:* For doctorate, thesis/dissertation. *Entrance requirements:* For doctorate, GRE General Test, GRE Subject Test. Additional exam requirements/recommendations for international students: Required—TOEFL. *Faculty research:* Behavioral neuroscience, cognitive neuroscience, cognitive science, social/personality psychology.

DePaul University, College of Liberal Arts and Sciences, Department of Psychology, Chicago, IL 60604-2287. Offers clinical psychology (MA, PhD), including child clinical psychology, community clinical psychology; experimental psychology (MA, PhD); general psychology (MS); industrial/organizational psychology (MA, PhD); MA/PhD. *Accreditation:* APA (one or more programs are accredited). *Faculty:* 31 full-time (19 women), 6 part-time/adjunct (4 women). *Students:* 43 full-time (26 women), 57 part-time (39 women); includes 11 Black or African American, non-Hispanic/Latino; 5 Asian, non-Hispanic/Latino; 10 Hispanic/Latino; 4 Two or more races, non-Hispanic/Latino, 2 international. Average age 28. 332 applicants, 14% accepted, 23 enrolled. In 2010, 14 master's, 17 doctorates awarded. *Degree requirements:* For master's, thesis, oral exam; for doctorate, comprehensive exam, thesis/dissertation, oral and written exams. *Entrance requirements:* For master's and doctorate, GRE General Test, GRE Subject Test, 32 quarter hours of course work in psychology, 3 letters of recommendation. Additional exam requirements/recommendations for international students: Required—TOEFL. Application fee: $40. Electronic applications accepted. *Financial support:* In 2010–11, 48 students received support, including 35 research assistantships with full tuition reimbursements available (averaging $11,800 per year), 13 teaching assistantships with full tuition reimbursements available (averaging $11,800 per year); career-related internships or fieldwork, scholarships/grants, traineeships, tuition waivers (full and partial), and unspecified assistantships also available. Financial award application deadline: 1/10. *Faculty research:* Adolescent stress and depression, minority adolescents sexuality, public policy, community influences in child adjustment. *Unit head:* Dr. Christopher B. Keys, Chairman, 773-325-7887, Fax: 773-325-7888. *Application contact:* Alison Pereida Knapp, Graduate Admissions Assistant, 773-325-7887, Fax: 773-325-7888.

Drexel University, College of Arts and Sciences, Department of Psychology, Philadelphia, PA 19104-2875. Offers clinical psychology (PhD), including clinical psychology, forensic psychology, health psychology, neuropsychology; law-psychology (PhD); psychology (MS); JD/PhD. *Accreditation:* APA (one or more programs are accredited). *Degree requirements:* For doctorate, thesis/dissertation, internship. *Entrance requirements:* For doctorate, GRE General Test. Additional exam requirements/recommendations for international students: Required—TOEFL. Electronic applications accepted. *Expenses:* Contact institution. *Faculty research:* Neurosciences, rehabilitation psychology, cognitive science, neurological assessment.

Duke University, Graduate School, Department of Psychology and Neuroscience, Durham, NC 27708. Offers biological psychology (PhD); clinical psychology (PhD); cognitive psychology (PhD); developmental psychology (PhD); experimental psychology (PhD); health psychology (PhD); human social development (PhD); JD/MA. *Accreditation:* APA (one or more programs are accredited). *Faculty:* 40 full-time. *Students:* 92 full-time (67 women); includes 6 Black or African American, non-Hispanic/Latino; 2 Asian, non-Hispanic/Latino; 7 Hispanic/Latino, 13 international. 483 applicants, 8% accepted, 23 enrolled. In 2010, 24 doctorates awarded. *Degree requirements:* For doctorate, thesis/dissertation. *Entrance requirements:* For doctorate, GRE General Test. Additional exam requirements/recommendations for international students: Required—TOEFL (minimum score 550 paper-based; 213 computer-based; 83 iBT), IELTS (minimum score 7). *Application deadline:* For fall admission, 12/8 priority date for domestic and international students. Application fee: $75. Electronic applications accepted. *Financial support:* Fellowships, research assistantships, teaching assistantships, career-related internships or fieldwork and Federal Work-Study available. Financial award application deadline: 12/8. *Unit head:* Melanie Bonner, Director of Graduate Studies, 919-660-5715, Fax: 919-660-5726, E-mail: morrell@duke.edu. *Application contact:* Elizabeth Hutton, Director of Admissions, 919-684-3913, Fax: 919-684-2277, E-mail: grad-admissions@duke.edu.

Duquesne University, Graduate School of Liberal Arts, Department of Psychology, Pittsburgh, PA 15282-0001. Offers clinical psychology (PhD). *Accreditation:* APA. *Faculty:* 14 full-time (5 women). *Students:* 46 full-time (24 women); includes 1 Hispanic/Latino, 4 international. Average age 25. 133 applicants, 6% accepted, 8 enrolled. In 2010, 11 doctorates awarded. *Degree requirements:* For doctorate, comprehensive exam, thesis/dissertation. *Entrance requirements:* For doctorate, GRE General Test, MA in psychology. Additional exam requirements/recommendations for international students: Required—TOEFL. *Application deadline:* For fall admission, 12/15 for domestic and international students. Electronic applications accepted. *Expenses:* Tuition: Part-time $884 per credit. Required fees: $84 per credit. Tuition and fees vary according to course load. *Financial support:* In 2010–11, 9 research assistantships with full tuition reimbursements (averaging $15,000 per year), 14 teaching assistantships with full tuition reimbursements (averaging $15,000 per year) were awarded; fellowships with full tuition reimbursements, career-related internships or fieldwork, scholarships/grants, tuition waivers (partial), and unspecified assistantships also available. Financial award application deadline: 5/1. *Faculty research:* Emotion, language motivation, imagination, development. *Unit head:* Dr. Daniel Burston, Chair, 412-396-5067.

East Carolina University, Graduate School, Thomas Harriot College of Arts and Sciences, Department of Psychology, Program in General Psychology, Greenville, NC 27858-4353. Offers MA. *Degree requirements:* For master's, one foreign language, comprehensive exam, thesis. *Entrance requirements:* For master's, GRE General Test, GRE Subject Test. Additional exam requirements/recommendations for international students: Required—TOEFL. *Expenses:* Tuition, state resident: full-time $3130; part-time $391.25 per credit hour. Tuition, nonresident: full-time $13,817; part-time $1727.13 per credit hour. Required fees: $1916; $239.50 per credit hour. Tuition and fees vary according to campus/location and program.

East Central University, School of Graduate Studies, Department of Psychology, Ada, OK 74820-6899. Offers MSPS. Part-time and evening/weekend programs available. *Entrance requirements:* For master's, GRE General Test, MAT. Electronic applications accepted.

Eastern Illinois University, Graduate School, College of Sciences, Department of Psychology, Charleston, IL 61920-3099. Offers clinical psychology (MA); school psychology (SSP). *Degree requirements:* For master's, comprehensive exam; for SSP, thesis. *Entrance requirements:* For master's and SSP, GRE General Test.

Eastern Kentucky University, The Graduate School, College of Arts and Sciences, Department of Psychology, Richmond, KY 40475-3102. Offers clinical psychology (MS); industrial/organizational psychology (MS); school psychology (Psy S). Part-time programs available. *Entrance requirements:* For master's and Psy S, GRE General Test, minimum GPA of 2.5. *Faculty research:* Autism, social psychology, parenting, assessment of depression/anxiety, reading.

Eastern Michigan University, Graduate School, College of Arts and Sciences, Department of Psychology, Ypsilanti, MI 48197. Offers clinical behavioral psychology (MS); clinical psychology (MS, PhD); experimental psychology (MS). *Accreditation:* APA. *Faculty:* 24 full-time (14 women). *Students:* 55 full-time (39 women), 35 part-time (28 women); includes 8 minority (1 Black or African American, non-Hispanic/Latino; 5 Asian, non-Hispanic/Latino; 2 Hispanic/Latino), 3 international. Average age 27. 234 applicants, 13% accepted, 26 enrolled. In 2010, 21 master's, 9 doctorates awarded. *Degree requirements:* For master's, 600-hour practicum; for doctorate, 1500-hour practicum; 2000-hour internship. *Entrance requirements:* For master's and doctorate, GRE. *Application deadline:* For fall admission, 2/15 for domestic students. Application fee: $35. *Financial support:* Fellowships available. *Unit head:* Dr. Carol Freedman-Doan, Department Head, 734-487-1155, Fax: 734-487-6553, E-mail: cfreedman@emich.edu. *Application contact:* Dawn Stentzel, Graduate Secretary, 734-487-1155, Fax: 734-487-6553, E-mail: dstentzel@emich.edu.

Eastern Washington University, Graduate Studies, College of Social and Behavioral Sciences, Department of Psychology, Cheney, WA 99004-2431. Offers clinical psychology (MS); experimental psychology (MS); psychology (MS); school psychology (MS). *Degree requirements:* For master's, comprehensive exam, thesis or alternative. *Entrance requirements:* For master's, GRE General Test, minimum GPA of 3.0.

East Tennessee State University, School of Graduate Studies, College of Arts and Sciences, Department of Psychology, Johnson City, TN 37614. Offers clinical psychology (PhD); experiential psychology (PhD); general psychology (MA). *Faculty:* 10 full-time (1 woman). *Students:* 35 full-time (19 women), 8 part-time (6 women); includes 2 minority (1 Hispanic/Latino; 1 Two or more races, non-Hispanic/Latino), 1 international. Average age 27. 82 applicants, 27% accepted, 13 enrolled. In 2010, 5 master's awarded. *Degree requirements:* For master's, thesis; for doctorate, thesis/dissertation. *Entrance requirements:* For master's, GRE General Test, GRE Subject Test, minimum GPA of 3.0. Additional exam requirements/recommendations for international students: Required—TOEFL (minimum score 550 paper-based; 213 computer-based; 79 iBT). *Application deadline:* For fall admission, 2/1 for domestic and international students. Application fee: $25 ($35 for international students). Electronic applications accepted. *Financial support:* In 2010–11, 2 research assistantships with full tuition reimbursements (averaging $5,500 per year), 5 teaching assistantships with full tuition reimbursements (averaging $5,500 per year) were awarded; career-related internships or fieldwork, institutionally sponsored loans, scholarships/grants, and unspecified assistantships also available. Financial award application deadline: 7/1; financial award applicants required to submit FAFSA. *Faculty research:* Language acquisition, recovery of brain function after injury or damage, violence in domestic relationships and road rage, reasons for living, unhealthy tanning behaviors. Total annual research expenditures: $83,798. *Unit head:* Dr. Wallace Dixon, Chair, 423-439-6656, Fax: 423-439-5695, E-mail: dixonw@etsu.edu. *Application contact:* Admissions and Records Clerk, 423-439-4221, Fax: 423-439-5624, E-mail: gradsch@etsu.edu.

Emory University, Laney Graduate School, Department of Psychology, Atlanta, GA 30322-1100. Offers clinical psychology (PhD); cognition and development (PhD); neuroscience and animal behavior (PhD). *Accreditation:* APA. *Degree requirements:* For doctorate, comprehensive exam, thesis/dissertation. *Entrance requirements:* For doctorate, GRE General Test, minimum GPA of 3.25. Additional exam requirements/recommendations for international students: Required—TOEFL. Electronic applications accepted. *Expenses:* Tuition: Full-time $33,800. Required fees: $1300. *Faculty research:* Neuroscience and animal behavior; adult and child psychopathology, cognition development assessment.

Emporia State University, Graduate School, Teachers College, Department of Psychology, Art Therapy, Rehabilitation and Mental Health Counseling, Program in Psychology, Emporia, KS 66801-5087. Offers general psychology (MS); industrial/organizational psychology (MS). Part-time programs available. *Students:* 15 full-time (9 women), 10 part-time (8 women); includes 2 minority (1 Black or African American, non-Hispanic/Latino; 1 Two or more races, non-Hispanic/Latino), 6 international. 10 applicants, 60% accepted, 5 enrolled. In 2010, 6 master's awarded. *Degree requirements:* For master's, comprehensive exam or thesis, internship. *Entrance requirements:* For master's, GRE General Test or MAT, graduate essay exam, appropriate bachelor's degree, letters of recommendation. Additional exam requirements/recommendations for international students: Required—TOEFL (minimum score 520 paper-based; 133 computer-based; 68 iBT). *Application deadline:* For fall admission, 6/1 priority date for domestic students; for spring admission, 10/1 for domestic students. Applications are processed on a rolling basis. Application fee: $30 ($75 for international students). Electronic applications accepted. *Expenses:* Tuition, state resident: full-time $4382; part-time $183 per credit hour. Tuition, nonresident: full-time $13,572; part-time $566 per credit hour. Required fees: $1022; $62 per credit hour. Tuition and fees vary according to course level, course load and campus/location. *Financial support:* Career-related internships or fieldwork, Federal Work-Study, institutionally sponsored loans, health care benefits, and unspecified assistantships available. Financial award application deadline: 3/15; financial award applicants required to submit FAFSA. *Faculty research:* Driving under the influence (DUI) personality, lifestyles and imposter phenomenon. *Unit head:* Dr. Brian W. Schrader, Chair, 620-341-5317, E-mail: bschrade@emporia.edu. *Application contact:* Mary Sewell, Admissions Coordinator, 800-950-GRAD, Fax: 620-341-5909, E-mail: msewell@emporia.edu.

Evangel University, Department of Psychology, Springfield, MO 65802. Offers clinical psychology (MS); counseling psychology (MS). Part-time programs available. *Faculty:* 3 full-time (2 women), 9 part-time/adjunct (4 women). *Students:* 23 full-time (15 women), 18 part-time (14 women). Average age 27. 17 applicants, 100% accepted, 15 enrolled. In 2010, 8 master's awarded. *Degree requirements:* For master's, comprehensive exam, thesis optional. *Entrance requirements:* For master's, GRE General Test or MAT, minimum undergraduate GPA of 3.0, undergraduate major or minor in psychology. Additional exam requirements/recommendations for international students: Required—TOEFL (minimum score 550 paper-based; 213 computer-based). *Application deadline:* For fall admission, 2/1 priority date for domestic students; for spring admission, 10/15 priority date for domestic students. Applications are processed on a rolling basis. Application fee: $25. Electronic applications accepted. *Financial support:* In 2010–11, 6 students received support. Career-related internships or fieldwork, scholarships/grants, and unspecified assistantships available. Support available to part-time students. Financial award application deadline: 3/1; financial award applicants required to submit FAFSA. *Unit head:* Dr. Grant Jones, Chair, 417-865-2815 Ext. 8619, E-mail: jonesg@evangel.edu. *Application contact:* Charity H. Fahlstrom, Admissions Representative, Graduate and Professional Studies Admissions, 417-865-2815 Ext. 7227, Fax: 417-575-5484, E-mail: fahlstromc@evangel.edu.

Fairleigh Dickinson University, College at Florham, Maxwell Becton College of Arts and Sciences, Department of Psychology, Madison, NJ 07940-1099. Offers clinical mental health counseling (MA); counseling (MA); industrial/organizational psychology (MA); organizational behavior (MA, Certificate), including organizational behavior (MA), organizational leadership (Certificate); MA/MBA. *Students:* 73 full-time (52 women), 43 part-time (29 women), 2 international. Average age 31. 50 applicants, 68% accepted, 15 enrolled. In 2010, 34 master's awarded. *Application deadline:* Applications are processed on a rolling basis. Application fee: $40. *Application contact:* Susan Brooman, University Director, Graduate Admissions, 973-443-8905, Fax: 973-443-8088, E-mail: grad@fdu.edu.

Fairleigh Dickinson University, Metropolitan Campus, University College: Arts, Sciences, and Professional Studies, School of Psychology, Teaneck, NJ 07666-1914. Offers clinical psychology (MA, PhD); clinical psychopharmacology (MA); forensic psychology (MA); general-theoretical psychology (MA, Certificate); school psychology (MA, Psy D). *Accreditation:* APA (one or more programs are accredited). *Students:* 205 full-time (141 women), 47 part-time (30 women), 8 international. Average age 32. 183 applicants, 73% accepted, 66 enrolled. In 2010, 47 master's, 15 doctorates awarded. *Application deadline:* Applications are processed on a rolling basis. Application fee: $40. *Application contact:* Susan Brooman, University Director of Graduate Admissions, 201-692-2554, Fax: 201-692-2560, E-mail: globaleducation@fdu.edu.

Fayetteville State University, Graduate School, Program in Psychology, Fayetteville, NC 28301-4298. Offers MA. Part-time and evening/weekend programs available. *Faculty:* 14 full-time (6 women). *Students:* 19 full-time (16 women), 20 part-time (16 women); includes 22 Black or African American, non-Hispanic/Latino; 1 American Indian or Alaska Native, non-Hispanic/Latino. Average age 32. 16 applicants, 100% accepted, 16 enrolled. In 2010, 8 master's awarded. *Degree requirements:* For master's, comprehensive exam, internship. *Application deadline:* For fall admission, 4/15 for domestic students. Applications are processed on a rolling basis. Application fee: $35. Electronic applications accepted. *Faculty research:* Coping strategies, reasons for living, hypnosis, cultural differences in expression of emotions, ethics, morals, stress, adult development. *Unit head:* Dr. Thomas Van Cantfort, Head, 910-672-1413, Fax: 910-672-1043, E-mail: tvancantfort@uncfsu.edu. *Application contact:* Katrina Hoffman, Graduate Admissions Officer, 910-672-1374, Fax: 910-672-1470, E-mail: khoffma1@uncfsu.edu.

Fielding Graduate University, Graduate Programs, School of Psychology, Santa Barbara, CA 93105-3538. Offers clinical psychology (PhD); clinical psychology respecialization (Post-Doctoral Certificate); media psychology (PhD); media psychology and social change (MA); neuropsychology (Post-Doctoral Certificate). *Accreditation:* APA. Postbaccalaureate distance learning degree programs offered (minimal on-campus study). *Faculty:* 27 full-time (15 women), 8 part-time/adjunct (2 women). *Students:* 534 full-time (396 women), 69 part-time (48 women); includes 147 minority (41 Black or African American, non-Hispanic/Latino; 7 American Indian or Alaska Native, non-Hispanic/Latino; 25 Asian, non-Hispanic/Latino; 57 Hispanic/Latino; 17 Two or more races, non-Hispanic/Latino), 20 international. Average age 42. 333 applicants, 35% accepted, 76 enrolled. In 2010, 9 master's, 39 doctorates, 16 other advanced degrees awarded. Terminal master's awarded for partial completion of doctoral program. *Degree requirements:* For master's, thesis or alternative, capstone project; for doctorate, comprehensive exam, thesis/dissertation. *Entrance requirements:* For doctorate, writing sample, minimum GPA of 3.0, 3 letters of recommendation, resume. *Application deadline:* For fall admission, 2/25 for domestic and international students; for spring admission, 8/25 for domestic and international students. Application fee: $75. Electronic applications accepted. *Expenses:* Contact institution. *Financial support:* In 2010–11, 79 students received support. Scholarships/grants and health care benefits available. Support available to part-time students. *Unit head:* Dr. Gerardo Rodriguez-.Menendez, Interim Dean, 805-898-2909, E-mail: grodriguez@fielding.edu. *Application contact:* Admission Counselor, 800-340-1099, Fax: 805-687-9793, E-mail: psyadmissions@fielding.edu.

Fisk University, Division of Graduate Studies, Department of Psychology, Nashville, TN 37208-3051. Offers clinical psychology (MA); psychology (MA). *Degree requirements:* For master's, thesis. *Entrance requirements:* For master's, GRE General Test, GRE Subject Test, minimum GPA of 3.0. Electronic applications accepted. *Faculty research:* Ethnic and gender identity, development, female adolescent development, juvenile delinquency prevention.

Florida Agricultural and Mechanical University, Division of Graduate Studies, Research, and Continuing Education, College of Arts and Sciences, Department of Psychology, Tallahassee, FL 32307-3200. Offers community psychology (MS); school psychology (MS). *Degree requirements:* For master's, thesis. *Entrance requirements:* For master's, GRE General Test, minimum GPA of 3.0. Additional exam requirements/recommendations for international students: Required—TOEFL.

Florida Atlantic University, Charles E. Schmidt College of Science, Department of Psychology, Boca Raton, FL 33431-0991. Offers MA, PhD. *Faculty:* 26 full-time (7 women), 7 part-time/adjunct (3 women). *Students:* 39 full-time (20 women), 14 part-time (8 women); includes 11 minority (1 Black or African American, non-Hispanic/Latino; 3 Asian, non-Hispanic/Latino; 6 Hispanic/Latino; 1 Two or more races, non-Hispanic/Latino), 4 international. Average age 30. 137 applicants, 51% accepted, 32 enrolled. In 2010, 15 master's, 4 doctorates awarded. Terminal master's awarded for partial completion of doctoral program. *Degree requirements:* For master's, one foreign language, thesis or alternative; for doctorate, one foreign language, comprehensive exam, thesis/dissertation. *Entrance requirements:* For master's and doctorate, GRE General Test, minimum GPA of 3.0 during previous 2 years. *Application deadline:* For fall admission, 5/1 for domestic students, 5/15 for international students. Application fee: $30. Electronic applications accepted. *Expenses:* Tuition, area resident: Part-time $319.96 per credit. Tuition, state resident: part-time $319.96 per credit. Tuition, nonresident: part-time $926.42 per credit. *Financial support:* Research assistantships with partial tuition reimbursements, teaching assistantships with partial tuition reimbursements, Federal Work-Study, institutionally sponsored loans, scholarships/grants, and unspecified assistantships available. Financial award application deadline: 3/1; financial award applicants required to submit FAFSA. *Faculty research:* Cognition, psychobiology, developmental psychology, social psychology, neuroscience. *Unit head:* Dr. David L. Wolgin, Chair, 561-297-3366, Fax: 561-297-2160, E-mail: wolgindl@fau.edu. *Application contact:* Dr. David F. Bjorklund, Graduate Program Coordinator, 561-297-3368, Fax: 561-297-2160, E-mail: dbjorklu@fau.edu.

Florida Institute of Technology, Graduate Programs, College of Psychology and Liberal Arts, School of Psychology, Melbourne, FL 32901-6975. Offers applied behavior analysis (MS); applied behavior analysis and organizational behavior management (MS); behavior analysis (PhD); clinical psychology (Psy D); industrial/organizational psychology (MS, PhD); organizational behavior management (MS). *Accreditation:* APA (one or more programs are accredited). Part-time programs available. *Faculty:* 21 full-time (10 women), 6 part-time/adjunct (2 women). *Students:* 220 full-time (167 women), 11 part-time (10 women); includes 25 minority (5 Black or African American, non-Hispanic/Latino; 4 Asian, non-Hispanic/Latino; 16 Hispanic/Latino), 22 international. Average age 27. 378 applicants, 42% accepted, 77 enrolled. In 2010, 57 master's, 13 doctorates awarded. Terminal master's awarded for partial completion of doctoral program. *Degree requirements:* For master's, comprehensive exam (for some programs), thesis (for some programs), BCBA certification, final exam; for doctorate, comprehensive exam, thesis/dissertation, internship, full time resident of school for 4 years (8 semesters, 3 summers). *Entrance requirements:* For master's, GRE General Test, 3 letters of recommendation, minimum GPA of 3.0, resume, statement of objectives; for doctorate, GRE General Test, GRE Subject Test (psychology), 3 letters of recommendation, minimum GPA of 3.2, resume, statement of objectives. Additional exam requirements/recommendations for international students: Required—TOEFL (minimum score 550 paper-based; 213 computer-

Psychology—General

Florida Institute of Technology (continued)

based; 79 iBT). *Application deadline:* For fall admission, 4/1 for international students; for spring admission, 9/30 for international students. Applications are processed on a rolling basis. Application fee: $50. Electronic applications accepted. *Expenses:* Tuition: Part-time $1040 per credit hour. Tuition and fees vary according to campus/location. *Financial support:* In 2010–11, 4 fellowships with full and partial tuition reimbursements (averaging $3,775 per year), 32 research assistantships with full and partial tuition reimbursements (averaging $5,602 per year), 8 teaching assistantships with full and partial tuition reimbursements (averaging $4,570 per year) were awarded; career-related internships or fieldwork, institutionally sponsored loans, tuition waivers (partial), unspecified assistantships, and tuition remissions also available. Support available to part-time students. Financial award application deadline: 3/1; financial award applicants required to submit FAFSA. *Faculty research:* Addictions, neuropsychology, child abuse, assessment, psychological trauma. Total annual research expenditures: $1.8 million. *Unit head:* Dr. Mary Beth Kenkel, Dean, 321-674-8142, Fax: 321-674-7105, E-mail: mkenkel@fit.edu. *Application contact:* Cheryl A. Brown, Associate Director of Graduate Admissions, 321-674-7581, Fax: 321-723-9468, E-mail: cbrown@fit.edu.

Florida International University, College of Arts and Sciences, Department of Psychology, Miami, FL 33199. Offers MS, PhD. Program is fall admission only. Part-time and evening/weekend programs available. *Faculty:* 31 full-time (17 women), 21 part-time/adjunct (6 women). *Students:* 111 full-time (77 women), 31 part-time (24 women); includes 9 Black or African American, non-Hispanic/Latino; 1 American Indian or Alaska Native, non-Hispanic/Latino; 5 Asian, non-Hispanic/Latino; 64 Hispanic/Latino, 13 international. Average age 29. 260 applicants, 21% accepted, 52 enrolled. In 2010, 20 master's, 9 doctorates awarded. Terminal master's awarded for partial completion of doctoral program. *Degree requirements:* For master's, thesis; for doctorate, comprehensive exam, thesis/dissertation. *Entrance requirements:* For master's, GRE General Test, minimum GPA of 3.0, resume, 3 letters of recommendation; for doctorate, GRE General Test, 3 letters of recommendation, resume, letter of intent, two writing samples, minimum GPA of 3.0. Additional exam requirements/recommendations for international students: Required—TOEFL (minimum score 550 paper-based; 80 iBT). *Application deadline:* For fall admission, 12/15 for domestic and international students. Application fee: $30. Electronic applications accepted. *Financial support:* Institutionally sponsored loans and scholarships/grants available. Financial award application deadline: 3/1. *Faculty research:* Legal psychology, organizational and industrial psychology, child behavior psychology. *Unit head:* Dr. Mary Levitt, Chair, 305-348-2880, Fax: 305-348-3879, E-mail: mary.levitt@fiu.edu. *Application contact:* Lara Wilson, Senior Secretary, 305-348-2881, Fax: 305-348-3879, E-mail: lara.wilson@fiu.edu.

Florida State University, The Graduate School, College of Arts and Sciences, Department of Psychology, Tallahassee, FL 32306. Offers applied behavior analysis (MS); clinical psychology (PhD); cognitive psychology (PhD); developmental psychology (PhD); neuroscience (PhD); social psychology (PhD). *Accreditation:* APA (one or more programs are accredited). *Faculty:* 42 full-time (18 women). *Students:* 158 full-time (102 women), 8 part-time (5 women); includes 9 Black or African American, non-Hispanic/Latino; 4 Asian, non-Hispanic/Latino; 11 Hispanic/Latino, 3 international. Average age 26. 550 applicants, 11% accepted, 38 enrolled. In 2010, 40 master's, 22 doctorates awarded. Terminal master's awarded for partial completion of doctoral program. *Degree requirements:* For master's, comprehensive exam; for doctorate, thesis/dissertation, preliminary exam. *Entrance requirements:* For master's and doctorate, GRE General Test, minimum GPA of 3.0. Additional exam requirements/recommendations for international students: Required—TOEFL (minimum score 550 paper-based; 213 computer-based; 80 iBT). Application fee: $30. Electronic applications accepted. *Expenses:* Tuition, state resident: full-time $8238.24. *Financial support:* In 2010–11, 157 students received support, including 35 fellowships with full tuition reimbursements available (averaging $20,000 per year), 38 research assistantships with full tuition reimbursements available (averaging $20,000 per year), 84 teaching assistantships with full tuition reimbursements available (averaging $16,500 per year); career-related internships or fieldwork, Federal Work-Study, institutionally sponsored loans, scholarships/grants, traineeships, health care benefits, and unspecified assistantships also available. Financial award applicants required to submit FAFSA. Total annual research expenditures: $8.1 million. *Unit head:* Dr. Janet Kistner, Chairman, 850-644-2040, Fax: 850-644-7739, E-mail: kistner@psy.fsu.edu. *Application contact:* Cherie P. Miller, Graduate Program Assistant, 850-644-2499, Fax: 850-644-7739, E-mail: grad-info@psy.fsu.edu.

Fordham University, Graduate School of Arts and Sciences, Department of Psychology, New York, NY 10458. Offers applied developmental psychology (PhD); clinical psychology (PhD); psychometrics (PhD). *Faculty:* 25 full-time (8 women), 3 part-time/adjunct (2 women). *Students:* 94 full-time (68 women), 29 part-time (22 women); includes 6 Black or African American, non-Hispanic/Latino; 1 American Indian or Alaska Native, non-Hispanic/Latino; 11 Asian, non-Hispanic/Latino; 6 Hispanic/Latino, 12 international. Average age 29. 478 applicants, 8% accepted, 27 enrolled. In 2010, 20 doctorates awarded. Terminal master's awarded for partial completion of doctoral program. *Degree requirements:* For doctorate, comprehensive exam, thesis/dissertation. *Entrance requirements:* For doctorate, GRE General Test, GRE Subject Test. Additional exam requirements/recommendations for international students: Required—TOEFL (minimum score 600 paper-based; 250 computer-based). *Application deadline:* For fall admission, 12/14 for domestic students. Application fee: $65. Electronic applications accepted. *Financial support:* In 2010–11, 73 students received support, including 4 fellowships with tuition reimbursements available (averaging $18,500 per year), 40 research assistantships with tuition reimbursements available (averaging $15,125 per year), 16 teaching assistantships with tuition reimbursements available (averaging $10,209 per year); career-related internships or fieldwork, institutionally sponsored loans, tuition waivers (full and partial), and unspecified assistantships also available. Financial award application deadline: 12/14; financial award applicants required to submit FAFSA. Total annual research expenditures: $848,459. *Unit head:* Dr. Frederick Wertz, Chair, 718-817-3777, Fax: 718-817-3785, E-mail: wertz@fordham.edu. *Application contact:* Charlene Dundie, Director of Graduate Admissions, 718-817-4420, Fax: 718-817-3566, E-mail: dundie@fordham.edu.

Fort Hays State University, Graduate School, College of Arts and Sciences, Department of Psychology, Hays, KS 67601-4099. Offers psychology (MS); school psychology (Ed S). *Degree requirements:* For master's and Ed S, comprehensive exam, thesis. *Entrance requirements:* For master's, GRE General Test. Additional exam requirements/recommendations for international students: Required—TOEFL (minimum score 550 paper-based; 213 computer-based). Electronic applications accepted. *Faculty research:* Memory, learning, motivation, clinical and experimental psychology, history and systems of psychological stressors in rural environments.

Framingham State University, Division of Graduate and Continuing Education, Program in Counseling Psychology, Framingham, MA 01701-9101. Offers MA. Part-time and evening/weekend programs available.

Francis Marion University, Graduate Programs, Department of Psychology, Florence, SC 29502-0547. Offers applied psychology (MS), including clinical/counseling, school psychology; school psychology (SSP). Part-time and evening/weekend programs available. *Faculty:* 10 full-time (4 women), 5 part-time/adjunct (4 women). *Students:* 17 full-time (16 women), 26 part-time (25 women); includes 6 Black or African American, non-Hispanic/Latino. Average age 25. 44 applicants, 61% accepted, 14 enrolled. In 2010, 9 master's awarded. *Degree requirements:* For master's, internship. *Entrance requirements:* For master's, GRE General Test. *Application deadline:* For fall admission, 3/15 for domestic students; for spring admission, 10/15 for domestic students. Applications are processed on a rolling basis. Application fee: $30. *Expenses:* Tuition, state resident: full-time $8667; part-time $433.35 per credit hour. Tuition, nonresident: full-time $17,334; part-time $866.70 per credit hour. Required fees: $335; $12.25 per credit hour. $30 per semester. *Financial support:* In 2010–11, 13 students received support, including 2 research assistantships (averaging $7,000 per year), 3 teaching assistantships (averaging $8,000 per year); career-related internships or fieldwork, unspecified assistantships, and scholarships with out-of-state waivers also available. Support available to part-time students. Financial award application deadline: 3/1; financial award applicants required to submit FAFSA. *Faculty research:* Parenting and family relationships, child development, applied behavioral analysis, posttraumatic stress disorder, clinical psychology in adults. *Unit head:* Dr. John R. Hester, Chair, 843-661-1635, Fax: 843-661-1628. *Application contact:* Jennifer Taylor, Administrative Assistant, 843-661-1378, Fax: 843-661-1628.

Frostburg State University, Graduate School, College of Liberal Arts and Sciences, Department of Psychology, Frostburg, MD 21532-1099. Offers counseling psychology (MS). Part-time and evening/weekend programs available. *Degree requirements:* For master's, internship. *Entrance requirements:* For master's, GRE General Test or MAT, interview, minimum GPA of 3.0, resume. Additional exam requirements/recommendations for international students: Required—TOEFL. Electronic applications accepted.

Fuller Theological Seminary, Graduate School of Psychology, Pasadena, CA 91182. Offers MA, MS, PhD, Psy D, Certificate. *Accreditation:* APA (one or more programs are accredited). Terminal master's awarded for partial completion of doctoral program. *Degree requirements:* For master's, practicum; for doctorate, thesis/dissertation, internships. *Entrance requirements:* For master's, GRE General Test; for doctorate, GRE General Test, GRE Subject Test, interview. Additional exam requirements/recommendations for international students: Required—TOEFL. *Faculty research:* Psychology of religion, depression, shame, psychoneuroimmunology, marital intimacy, sex roles, psychoanalytic theory, men's issues, family relations.

Gardner-Webb University, Graduate School, School of Psychology, Boiling Springs, NC 28017. Offers mental health counseling (MA); school counseling (MA). Part-time and evening/weekend programs available. *Faculty:* 6 full-time (3 women). *Students:* 3 full-time (all women), 88 part-time (75 women); includes 17 Black or African American, non-Hispanic/Latino; 1 Asian, non-Hispanic/Latino; 2 Hispanic/Latino. Average age 36. In 2010, 22 master's awarded. *Degree requirements:* For master's, comprehensive exam. *Entrance requirements:* For master's, GRE General Test, MAT, minimum GPA of 2.7. *Application deadline:* For fall admission, 7/1 priority date for domestic students. Applications are processed on a rolling basis. Application fee: $40. Electronic applications accepted. *Expenses:* Tuition: Part-time $325 per credit hour. *Financial support:* Unspecified assistantships available. *Unit head:* Dr. David Carscaddon, Chair, 704-406-4437, Fax: 704-406-4329, E-mail: dcarscaddon@gardner-webb.edu. *Application contact:* Office of Graduate Admisisons, 877-498-4723, Fax: 704-406-3895, E-mail: gradinfo@gardner-webb.edu.

Geneva College, Program in Counseling, Beaver Falls, PA 15010-3599. Offers marriage and family (MA); mental health (MA); school counseling (MA). *Accreditation:* ACA. Part-time and evening/weekend programs available. *Degree requirements:* For master's, comprehensive exam, internship. *Entrance requirements:* For master's, GRE General Test or MAT, minimum GPA of 3.0 (preferred), letters of recommendation, faith statement. Additional exam requirements/recommendations for international students: Required—TOEFL. Electronic applications accepted.

George Mason University, College of Humanities and Social Sciences, Department of Psychology, Fairfax, VA 22030. Offers aviation psychology (Certificate); cognitive neuroscience (Certificate); psychology (MA, PhD); school psychology (Certificate); usability (Certificate). *Accreditation:* APA. *Faculty:* 46 full-time (20 women), 15 part-time/adjunct (7 women). *Students:* 113 full-time (75 women), 119 part-time (78 women); includes 5 Black or African American, non-Hispanic/Latino; 10 Asian, non-Hispanic/Latino; 11 Hispanic/Latino; 3 Two or more races, non-Hispanic/Latino, 9 international. Average age 27. 693 applicants, 23% accepted, 76 enrolled. In 2010, 57 master's, 15 doctorates, 8 other advanced degrees awarded. Terminal master's awarded for partial completion of doctoral program. *Degree requirements:* For master's, comprehensive exam, thesis (for biopsychology); for doctorate, comprehensive exam, thesis/dissertation, 2nd year project. *Entrance requirements:* For master's, GRE General Test, minimum GPA of 3.25 in last 60 hours of course work, undergraduate course work in psychology, 3 letters of recommendation, resume; for doctorate, GRE General Test, minimum undergraduate GPA of 3.5, 3 letters of recommendation, resume, expanded goals statement. Additional exam requirements/recommendations for international students: Required—TOEFL (minimum score 570 paper-based; 230 computer-based; 88 iBT). *Application deadline:* For fall admission, 3/1 priority date for domestic students; for spring admission, 10/15 for domestic students. Application fee: $100. Electronic applications accepted. *Expenses:* Tuition, state resident: full-time $8192; part-time $440 per credit hour. Tuition, nonresident: full-time $22,952; part-time $1055 per credit hour. Required fees: $2364; $99 per credit hour. *Financial support:* In 2010–11, 110 students received support, including 3 fellowships with full tuition reimbursements available (averaging $18,000 per year), 76 research assistantships with full and partial tuition reimbursements available (averaging $11,036 per year), 52 teaching assistantships with full and partial tuition reimbursements available (averaging $8,237 per year); career-related internships or fieldwork, Federal Work-Study, scholarships/grants, traineeships, tuition waivers (partial), unspecified assistantships, and health care benefits (full-time research or teaching assistantship recipients) also available. Support available to part-time students. Financial award application deadline: 3/1; financial award applicants required to submit FAFSA. *Faculty research:* Applied developmental psychology, biopsychology, clinical psychology, human factors/applied cognition psychology, industrial/organizational psychology, school psychology. Total annual research expenditures: $4.5 million. *Unit head:* Dr. Deborah Boehm-Davis, Chairperson, 703-993-1398, Fax: 703-993-1359, E-mail: dbdavis@gmu.edu. *Application contact:* Darby Wiggins, Graduate Program Assistant, 703-993-1548, E-mail: dwiggin3@gmu.edu.

Georgetown University, Graduate School of Arts and Sciences, Department of Psychology, Washington, DC 20057. Offers PhD, JD/MPP. *Degree requirements:* For doctorate, thesis/dissertation. *Entrance requirements:* For doctorate, GRE General Test, GRE Subject Test. Additional exam requirements/recommendations for international students: Required—TOEFL.

The George Washington University, Columbian College of Arts and Sciences, Department of Psychology, Washington, DC 20052. Offers applied social psychology (PhD); clinical psychology (PhD); cognitive neuroscience (PhD). *Accreditation:* APA. Part-time and evening/weekend programs available. *Faculty:* 26 full-time (14 women), 14 part-time/adjunct (9 women). *Students:* 131 full-time (103 women), 75 part-time (55 women); includes 14 Black or African American, non-Hispanic/Latino; 2 American Indian or Alaska Native, non-Hispanic/Latino; 18 Asian, non-Hispanic/Latino; 16 Hispanic/Latino, 4 international. Average age 29. 797 applicants, 6% accepted, 9 enrolled. In 2010, 41 doctorates awarded. *Degree requirements:* For doctorate, thesis/dissertation or alternative, general exam. *Entrance requirements:* For doctorate, GRE General Test, minimum GPA of 3.0. Additional exam requirements/recommendations for international students: Required—TOEFL (minimum score 550 paper-based; 213 computer-based; 80 iBT). *Application deadline:* For fall admission, 1/15 for domestic and international students. Application fee: $75. *Financial support:* In 2010–11, 62 students received support; fellowships with tuition reimbursements available, teaching assistantships with tuition reimbursements available, career-related internships or fieldwork, Federal Work-Study, and tuition waivers available. *Unit head:* Dr. Paul Poppen, Chair, 202-994-6324, E-mail: pjp@gwu.edu. *Application contact:* Information Contact, 202-994-6320, Fax: 202-994-1602, E-mail: psydept@gwu.edu.

The George Washington University, Columbian College of Arts and Sciences, Program in Professional Psychology, Washington, DC 20052. Offers Psy D. *Accreditation:* APA. *Faculty:* 1 (woman) full-time, 2 part-time/adjunct (1 woman). *Students:* 95 full-time (75 women), 51 part-time (37 women); includes 9 Black or African American, non-Hispanic/Latino; 2 American Indian or Alaska Native, non-Hispanic/Latino; 11 Asian, non-Hispanic/Latino; 8 Hispanic/Latino. Average age 29. 342 applicants, 11% accepted, 36 enrolled. In 2010, 33 doctorates awarded. *Entrance requirements:* For doctorate, GRE General Test, interview, minimum GPA of 3.0. Additional exam requirements/recommendations for international students: Required—TOEFL (minimum score 550 paper-based; 213 computer-based; 80 iBT). *Application deadline:* For fall admission, 12/1 priority date for domestic students. Applications are processed on a rolling basis. Application fee: $75. Electronic applications accepted. *Financial support:* Fellowships with partial tuition reimbursements available. *Unit head:* Dr. Dorothy Holmes, Director,

202-496-6282, Fax: 202-496-6263, E-mail: crescent@gwu.edu. *Application contact:* Dr. Dorothy Holmes, Director, 202-496-6282, Fax: 202-496-6263, E-mail: crescent@gwu.edu.

Georgia Institute of Technology, Graduate Studies and Research, College of Sciences, School of Psychology, Atlanta, GA 30332-0001. Offers human computer interaction (MSHCI); psychology (MS, MS Psy, PhD), including engineering psychology (PhD), experimental psychology (PhD), industrial/organizational psychology (PhD). Terminal master's awarded for partial completion of doctoral program. *Degree requirements:* For master's, thesis; for doctorate, thesis/dissertation. *Entrance requirements:* For master's and doctorate, GRE General Test, GRE Subject Test, minimum GPA of 3.0. Additional exam requirements/recommendations for international students: Required—TOEFL. Electronic applications accepted. *Faculty research:* Experimental, industrial-organizational, and engineering psychology; cognitive aging and processes; leadership; human factors.

Georgia Southern University, Jack N. Averitt College of Graduate Studies, College of Liberal Arts and Social Sciences, Department of Psychology, Statesboro, GA 30460. Offers MS, Psy D. *Students:* 39 full-time (24 women), 4 part-time (2 women); includes 5 Black or African American, non-Hispanic/Latino; 1 Asian, non-Hispanic/Latino; 1 Hispanic/Latino. Average age 26. 64 applicants, 45% accepted, 18 enrolled. In 2010, 5 master's awarded. Terminal master's awarded for partial completion of doctoral program. *Degree requirements:* For master's, comprehensive exam, thesis (for some programs), terminal exam; for doctorate, comprehensive exam, thesis/dissertation, clinical qualifying exam, practicum, internship. *Entrance requirements:* For master's, GRE General Test, minimum GPA of 3.0, introductory courses in psychology and statistics, letters of recommendation; for doctorate, GRE General Test; GRE Subject Test (if no undergraduate degree in psychology), minimum undergraduate GPA of 3.25; 3 letters of reference; statement of purpose. Additional exam requirements/recommendations for international students: Required—TOEFL (minimum score 550 paper-based; 213 computer-based; 80 iBT). *Application deadline:* For fall admission, 1/15 priority date for domestic students, 1/15 for international students. Applications are processed on a rolling basis. Application fee: $50. Electronic applications accepted. *Expenses:* Tuition, state resident: full-time $6000; part-time $250 per semester hour. Tuition, nonresident: full-time $23,976; part-time $999 per semester hour. Required fees: $1644. *Financial support:* In 2010–11, 38 students received support, including fellowships with partial tuition reimbursements available (averaging $12,000 per year), research assistantships with partial tuition reimbursements available (averaging $7,200 per year), teaching assistantships with partial tuition reimbursements available (averaging $7,200 per year); career-related internships or fieldwork, Federal Work-Study, scholarships/grants, tuition waivers (partial), and unspecified assistantships also available. Support available to part-time students. Financial award application deadline: 4/15; financial award applicants required to submit FAFSA. *Faculty research:* Psychology of religion, health and psychological response to illness, cognition and perception, adult and child attachment, psychology of teaching. Total annual research expenditures: $50,396. *Unit head:* Dr. Michael E. Nielsen, Chair, 912-478-5539, Fax: 912-478-0751, E-mail: mnielsen@georgiasouthern.edu. *Application contact:* Dr. Charles Ziglar, Coordinator for Graduate Student Recruitment, 912-478-5635, Fax: 912-478-0740, E-mail: gradadmissions@georgiasouthern.edu.

Georgia State University, College of Arts and Sciences, Department of Psychology, Atlanta, GA 30302-3083. Offers MA, PhD. *Accreditation:* APA (one or more programs are accredited). *Degree requirements:* For master's, thesis; for doctorate, comprehensive exam, thesis/dissertation. *Entrance requirements:* For doctorate, GRE General Test, departmental supplemental form. Additional exam requirements/recommendations for international students: Required—TOEFL. Electronic applications accepted. *Faculty research:* Social psychology, developmental and comparative psychology, neuropsychology, clinical psychology, neuropsychology.

Golden Gate University, Ageno School of Business, San Francisco, CA 94105-2968. Offers accounting (MBA); business administration (EMBA, MBA, PMBA, DBA); finance (MBA, MS, Certificate); financial planning (MS, Certificate); healthcare information systems (Certificate); human resource management (MBA, MS); human resources management (Certificate); information systems (MS); information technology (MBA); information technology management (Certificate); integrated marketing and communications (MS, Certificate); international business (MBA); management (MBA); marketing (MBA, MS, Certificate); operations supply chain management (Certificate); psychology (MA, Certificate); public administration (EMPA); public relations (MS, Certificate); technical market analysis (Certificate); JD/MBA. Part-time and evening/weekend programs available. *Faculty:* 16 full-time (4 women), 241 part-time/adjunct (72 women). *Students:* 421 full-time (235 women), 744 part-time (425 women); includes 526 minority (114 Black or African American, non-Hispanic/Latino; 2 American Indian or Alaska Native, non-Hispanic/Latino; 296 Asian, non-Hispanic/Latino; 73 Hispanic/Latino; 29 Native Hawaiian or other Pacific Islander, non-Hispanic/Latino; 12 Two or more races, non-Hispanic/Latino), 100 international. Average age 32. 681 applicants, 78% accepted, 270 enrolled. In 2010, 550 master's, 13 doctorates awarded. *Degree requirements:* For doctorate, thesis/dissertation. *Entrance requirements:* For master's, GMAT (MBA), minimum GPA of 2.5 (MS). Additional exam requirements/recommendations for international students: Required—TOEFL. *Application deadline:* For fall admission, 5/15 for domestic and international students; for winter admission, 1/15 for domestic and international students; for spring admission, 9/15 for domestic and international students. Applications are processed on a rolling basis. Application fee: $70 ($110 for international students). Electronic applications accepted. *Expenses:* Contact institution. *Financial support:* Career-related internships or fieldwork, Federal Work-Study, institutionally sponsored loans, and scholarships/grants available. Support available to part-time students. Financial award applicants required to submit FAFSA. *Unit head:* Dr. Paul Fouts, Dean, 415-442-7026, Fax: 415-442-6579. *Application contact:* Angela Melero, Enrollment Services, 415-442-7800, Fax: 415-442-7807, E-mail: info@ggu.edu.

Governors State University, College of Education, Program in Psychology, University Park, IL 60466-0975. Offers MA. Part-time and evening/weekend programs available. *Degree requirements:* For master's, thesis or alternative, practicum. *Entrance requirements:* For master's, GRE or MAT. *Expenses:* Tuition, state resident: full-time $5400; part-time $225 per credit hour. Tuition, nonresident: full-time $16,200; part-time $675 per credit hour. Required fees: $1358; $46 per credit hour. $126 per term. Tuition and fees vary according to degree level and program.

Graduate School and University Center of the City University of New York, Graduate Studies, Program in Psychology, New York, NY 10016-4039. Offers basic applied neurocognition (PhD); biopsychology (PhD); clinical psychology (PhD); developmental psychology (PhD); environmental psychology (PhD); experimental psychology (PhD); industrial psychology (PhD); learning processes (PhD); neuropsychology (PhD); psychology (PhD); social personality (PhD). *Degree requirements:* For doctorate, one foreign language, thesis/dissertation. *Entrance requirements:* For doctorate, GRE General Test. Additional exam requirements/recommendations for international students: Required—TOEFL. Electronic applications accepted.

Grand Canyon University, College of Doctoral Studies, Phoenix, AZ 85017-1097. Offers business administration (DBA); general psychology (PhD), including cognition and instruction, industrial and organizational psychology; organizational leadership (Ed D, PhD), including behavioral health (PhD), education and effective schools (PhD), higher education (PhD), instructional leadership (PhD), organizational development (Ed D). *Faculty:* 2 full-time (1 woman), 12 part-time/adjunct (5 women). *Students:* 968 part-time (711 women); includes 316 minority (283 Black or African American, non-Hispanic/Latino; 12 American Indian or Alaska Native, non-Hispanic/Latino; 3 Asian, non-Hispanic/Latino; 11 Hispanic/Latino; 1 Native Hawaiian or other Pacific Islander, non-Hispanic/Latino; 6 Two or more races, non-Hispanic/Latino). *Degree requirements:* For doctorate, comprehensive exam, thesis/dissertation. *Entrance requirements:* For doctorate, minimum GPA of 3.4 on earned advanced degree from regionally-accredited institution; transcripts; goals statement. Application fee: $0. *Unit head:* Dr. Hank Radda, Dean, 602-639-7255, E-mail: hank.radda@gcu.edu. *Application contact:* Hector Leal, Associate Vice President of Internet Enrollment, 800-639-7144, E-mail: hector.leal@.gcu.edu.

Hardin-Simmons University, Graduate School, Cynthia Ann Parker College of Liberal Arts, Department of Psychology, Abilene, TX 79698-0001. Offers family psychology (MA). Part-time programs available. *Faculty:* 6 full-time (2 women). *Students:* 14 full-time (11 women), 3 part-time (all women); includes 1 Black or African American, non-Hispanic/Latino; 1 Hispanic/Latino. Average age 27. 14 applicants, 57% accepted, 8 enrolled. In 2010, 9 master's awarded. *Degree requirements:* For master's, comprehensive exam, clinical experience, project. *Entrance requirements:* For master's, 21 semester hours of course work in psychology (18 in upper division classes); minimum undergraduate GPA of 3.0 in major, 2.7 overall; writing sample; letters of recommendation. Additional exam requirements/recommendations for international students: Required—TOEFL (minimum score 550 paper-based; 213 computer-based; 75 iBT). *Application deadline:* For fall admission, 8/15 priority date for domestic students, 4/1 for international students; for spring admission, 1/5 priority date for domestic students, 9/1 for international students. Applications are processed on a rolling basis. Application fee: $50. *Expenses:* Tuition: Full-time $12,150; part-time $675 per credit hour. Required fees: $650; $110 per semester. Tuition and fees vary according to degree level. *Financial support:* In 2010–11, 17 students received support, including 16 fellowships (averaging $600 per year); career-related internships or fieldwork and scholarships/grants also available. Support available to part-time students. Financial award application deadline: 6/30; financial award applicants required to submit FAFSA. *Faculty research:* Spirituality in marriage, intimacy and sexuality in marriage, sex education in the church, role of faith in marital satisfaction, family stress management. *Unit head:* Dr. Doug Thomas, Head, 325-670-1534, Fax: 325-670-1458, E-mail: dthomas@hsutx.edu. *Application contact:* Dr. Nancy Kucinski, Dean of Graduate Studies, 325-670-1298, Fax: 325-670-1564, E-mail: gradoff@hsutx.edu.

Harvard University, Graduate School of Arts and Sciences, Department of Psychology, Cambridge, MA 02138. Offers psychology (PhD), including behavior and decision analysis, cognition, developmental psychology, experimental psychology, personality, psychobiology, psychopathology; social psychology (PhD). *Accreditation:* APA. *Degree requirements:* For doctorate, thesis/dissertation, general exams. *Entrance requirements:* For doctorate, GRE General Test. Additional exam requirements/recommendations for international students: Required—TOEFL. *Expenses:* Tuition: Full-time $34,976. Required fees: $1166. Full-time tuition and fees vary according to program.

Hodges University, Graduate Programs, Naples, FL 34119. Offers business administration (MBA); computer information technology (MS); criminal justice (MCJ); education (MPS); information systems management (MIS); interdisciplinary (MPS); legal studies (MS); management (MSM); mental health counseling (MS); psychology (MPS); public administration (MPA). Part-time and evening/weekend programs available. Postbaccalaureate distance learning degree programs offered (no on-campus study). *Faculty:* 25 full-time (9 women), 5 part-time/adjunct (4 women). *Students:* 27 full-time (15 women), 228 part-time (146 women); includes 76 minority (35 Black or African American, non-Hispanic/Latino; 5 Asian, non-Hispanic/Latino; 36 Hispanic/Latino). Average age 36. 92 applicants, 91% accepted, 81 enrolled. In 2010, 92 master's awarded. *Degree requirements:* For master's, comprehensive exam (for some programs), thesis (for some programs). *Entrance requirements:* For master's, in-house entrance exam. *Application deadline:* Applications are processed on a rolling basis. Application fee: $50. Electronic applications accepted. *Expenses:* Tuition: Full-time $16,605; part-time $615 per credit hour. Required fees: $190 per trimester. *Financial support:* In 2010–11, 200 students received support. Federal Work-Study and scholarships/grants available. Financial award application deadline: 7/9; financial award applicants required to submit FAFSA. *Unit head:* Terry McMahan, President, 239-513-1122, Fax: 239-598-6253, E-mail: tmcmahan@hodges.edu. *Application contact:* Rita Lampus, Vice President of Student Enrollment Management, 239-513-1122, Fax: 239-598-6253, E-mail: rlampus@hodges.edu.

Hood College, Graduate School, Programs in Human Sciences, Frederick, MD 21701-8575. Offers human sciences (MA), including psychology; thanatology (MA, Certificate). Part-time and evening/weekend programs available. *Faculty:* 5 full-time (3 women), 7 part-time/adjunct (4 women). *Students:* 19 full-time (13 women), 66 part-time (60 women); includes 13 Black or African American, non-Hispanic/Latino; 2 American Indian or Alaska Native, non-Hispanic/Latino; 1 Asian, non-Hispanic/Latino; 2 Hispanic/Latino; 1 Two or more races, non-Hispanic/Latino, 2 international. Average age 34. 40 applicants, 85% accepted, 19 enrolled. In 2010, 40 master's, 27 other advanced degrees awarded. *Degree requirements:* For master's, comprehensive exam, capstone/research project. *Entrance requirements:* For master's, minimum GPA of 2.75. Additional exam requirements/recommendations for international students: Required—TOEFL (minimum score 575 paper-based; 231 computer-based; 89 iBT). *Application deadline:* For fall admission, 7/15 for domestic and international students; for spring admission, 12/15 for domestic and international students. Applications are processed on a rolling basis. Application fee: $35. Electronic applications accepted. *Expenses:* Tuition: Full-time $6480; part-time $360 per credit. Required fees: $100; $50 per term. *Financial support:* Applicants required to submit FAFSA. *Faculty research:* Mind-body medicine and multicultural healing, the New Orleans jazz funeral, death practices in African-American culture, bereavement theories and gender differences, Piaget's theory of cognitive development as a formal mathematical model. *Unit head:* Dr. Terry Martin, Director, 301-696-3759, Fax: 301-696-3597, E-mail: tmartin@hood.edu. *Application contact:* Dr. Allen P. Flora, Dean of Graduate School, 301-696-3811, Fax: 301-696-3597, E-mail: gofurther@hood.edu.

Houston Baptist University, College of Education and Behavioral Sciences, Program in Psychology, Houston, TX 77074-3298. Offers MAP. Part-time and evening/weekend programs available. *Degree requirements:* For master's, comprehensive exam. *Entrance requirements:* For master's, GRE General Test, minimum GPA of 3.0. Additional exam requirements/recommendations for international students: Required—TOEFL (minimum score 550 paper-based; 213 computer-based).

Howard University, Graduate School, Department of Psychology, Washington, DC 20059-0002. Offers clinical psychology (PhD); developmental psychology (PhD); experimental psychology (PhD); neuropsychology (PhD); personality psychology (PhD); psychology (MS); social psychology (PhD). *Accreditation:* APA (one or more programs are accredited). Part-time programs available. *Degree requirements:* For master's, thesis; for doctorate, comprehensive exam, thesis/dissertation, qualifying exam. *Entrance requirements:* For master's, GRE General Test, minimum GPA of 2.5, bachelor's degree in psychology or related field; for doctorate, GRE General Test, minimum GPA of 3.0. *Faculty research:* Personality and psychophysiology, educational and social development of African-American children, child and adult psychopathology.

Humboldt State University, Academic Programs, College of Professional Studies, Department of Psychology, Arcata, CA 95521-8299. Offers psychology (MA), including academic research, counseling, school psychology. *Students:* 45 full-time (31 women), 12 part-time (8 women); includes 12 minority (2 Asian, non-Hispanic/Latino; 7 Hispanic/Latino; 3 Two or more races, non-Hispanic/Latino). Average age 28. 35 applicants, 86% accepted, 9 enrolled. In 2010, 24 master's awarded. *Degree requirements:* For master's, thesis. *Entrance requirements:* For master's, appropriate bachelor's degree, minimum GPA of 2.5. Additional exam requirements/recommendations for international students: Required—TOEFL (minimum score 500 paper-based; 173 computer-based). *Application deadline:* For fall admission, 2/1 for domestic students, 2/15 for international students. Applications are processed on a rolling basis. Application fee: $55. Tuition and fees vary according to program. *Financial support:* Career-related internships or fieldwork available. Financial award application deadline: 3/1; financial award applicants required to submit FAFSA. *Faculty research:* School psychology, counseling, eating disorders, mood induction, depression. *Unit head:* Dr. Gregg Gold, Chair, 707-826-3740, Fax: 707-826-4993, E-mail: gjg14@humboldt.edu. *Application contact:* Dr. Chris Aberson, Coordinator, 707-826-3670, Fax: 707-826-4993, E-mail: cla18@humboldt.edu.

Hunter College of the City University of New York, Graduate School, School of Arts and Sciences, Department of Psychology, New York, NY 10021-5085. Offers animal behavior and conservation (MA); applied and evaluative psychology (MA); biopsychology and behavioral neuroscience (PhD); biopsychology and comparative psychology (MA); social, cognitive, and

Psychology—General

Hunter College of the City University of New York (continued)
developmental psychology (MA). Part-time and evening/weekend programs available. *Faculty:* 9 full-time (1 woman), 1 part-time/adjunct (0 women). *Students:* 10 full-time (7 women), 79 part-time (61 women); includes 3 Black or African American, non-Hispanic/Latino; 7 Asian, non-Hispanic/Latino; 9 Hispanic/Latino, 2 international. Average age 27. 151 applicants, 34% accepted, 21 enrolled. In 2010, 13 master's awarded. *Degree requirements:* For master's, comprehensive exam, thesis. *Entrance requirements:* For master's, GRE General Test, minimum 12 credits of course work in psychology, including statistics and experimental psychology; 2 letters of recommendation. Additional exam requirements/recommendations for international students: Required—TOEFL. *Application deadline:* For fall admission, 4/1 for domestic students, 2/1 for international students; for spring admission, 11/1 for domestic students, 9/1 for international students. Applications are processed on a rolling basis. Application fee: $125. *Financial support:* Federal Work-Study, scholarships/grants, and tuition waivers (partial) available. Support available to part-time students. *Faculty research:* Personality, cognitive and linguistic development, hormonal and neural control of behavior, gender and culture, social cognition of health and attitudes. *Unit head:* Dr. Jeffrey Parsons, Chairperson, 212-772-5550, Fax: 212-772-5620, E-mail: jeffrey.parsons@hunter.cuny.edu. *Application contact:* Martin Braun, Acting Program Director, 212-772-4482, Fax: 212-650-3336, E-mail: cbraun@hunter.cuny.edu.

Idaho State University, Office of Graduate Studies, College of Arts and Sciences, Department of Psychology, Pocatello, ID 83209-8112. Offers clinical psychology (PhD); psychology (MS). *Accreditation:* APA (one or more programs are accredited). Part-time programs available. *Degree requirements:* For master's, comprehensive exam, thesis, active participation in the research process; for doctorate, comprehensive exam, thesis/dissertation, 1 year full-time clinical internship. *Entrance requirements:* For master's, GRE General Test, GRE Subject Test, BS in psychology, minimum GPA of 3.0 in last 2 years of undergraduate courses; for doctorate, GRE General Test, GRE Subject Test, MS in psychology, recommendation from Clinical Admissions Committee. Additional exam requirements/recommendations for international students: Required—TOEFL (minimum score 550 paper-based; 213 computer-based; 80 iBT). Electronic applications accepted. *Faculty research:* Substance abuse, sexual decision making, trauma, behavioral pharmacology, developmental psychopathology, working memory and strategies, goal setting, person perception, developmental psychobiology, parent-child interactions.

Illinois Institute of Technology, Graduate College, College of Psychology, Chicago, IL 60616. Offers clinical psychology (PhD); industrial/organizational psychology (PhD); personnel/human resource development (MS); rehabilitation (PhD); rehabilitation counseling (MS). *Accreditation:* APA (one or more programs are accredited); CORE. Part-time and evening/weekend programs available. *Faculty:* 21 full-time (7 women), 6 part-time/adjunct (4 women). *Students:* 160 full-time (111 women), 39 part-time (33 women); includes 36 minority (8 Black or African American, non-Hispanic/Latino; 1 American Indian or Alaska Native, non-Hispanic/Latino; 15 Asian, non-Hispanic/Latino; 12 Hispanic/Latino), 16 international. Average age 29. 253 applicants, 40% accepted, 43 enrolled. In 2010, 31 master's, 14 doctorates awarded. Terminal master's awarded for partial completion of doctoral program. *Degree requirements:* For master's, thesis (for some programs); for doctorate, comprehensive exam, thesis/dissertation, 96-108 credit hours, internship (for clinical and industrial/organizational specializations). *Entrance requirements:* For master's, GRE General Test (minimum score 900 Quantitative and Verbal, 2.5 Analytical Writing), minimum high school GPA of 3.0; at least 18 credit hours of undergraduate study in psychology with at least one course each in experimental psychology and statistics; official transcripts; 3 letters of recommendation; personal statement; for doctorate, GRE General Test (minimum score 1000 Quantitative and Verbal, 3.0 Analytical Writing), minimum high school GPA of 3.0; at least 18 credit hours of undergraduate study in psychology with at least one course each in experimental psychology and statistics; official transcripts; 3 letters of recommendation; personal statement. Additional exam requirements/recommendations for international students: Required—TOEFL (minimum score 550 paper-based; 213 computer-based; 80 iBT); Recommended—IELTS (minimum score 5.5). *Application deadline:* For fall admission, 1/15 for domestic and international students. Application fee: $50. Electronic applications accepted. *Expenses:* Tuition: Full-time $18,576; part-time $1032 per credit hour. Required fees: $583 per semester. One-time fee: $150. Tuition and fees vary according to program and student level. *Financial support:* In 2010–11, 23 research assistantships with full and partial tuition reimbursements (averaging $223 per year) were awarded; fellowships with full and partial tuition reimbursements, career-related internships or fieldwork, Federal Work-Study, institutionally sponsored loans, scholarships/grants, traineeships, health care benefits, tuition waivers (partial), and unspecified assistantships also available. Support available to part-time students. Financial award application deadline: 1/15; financial award applicants required to submit FAFSA. *Faculty research:* Health psychology, behavioral medicine, attachment, child social and emotional development, educational assessment. Total annual research expenditures: $1.6 million. *Unit head:* Dr. M. Ellen Mitchell, Dean, 312-567-3362, Fax: 312-567-3493, E-mail: mitchelle@iit.edu. *Application contact:* Institute of Psychology Graduate Admissions, 312-567-3500, Fax: 312-567-3493, E-mail: psychology@iit.edu.

Illinois State University, Graduate School, College of Arts and Sciences, Department of Psychology, Normal, IL 61790-2200. Offers psychology (MA, MS), including clinical psychology, counseling psychology, developmental psychology, educational psychology, experimental psychology, measurement-evaluation, organizational-industrial psychology; school psychology (PhD, SSP). *Accreditation:* APA. *Degree requirements:* For master's, thesis or alternative; for doctorate, variable foreign language requirement, thesis/dissertation, 2 terms of residency, internship, practicum. *Entrance requirements:* For master's, GRE General Test, GRE Subject Test, minimum GPA of 3.0 in last 60 hours of course work; for doctorate, GRE General Test. *Faculty research:* Comprehensive evaluation system for the central region professional development grant, Illinois school psychology internship consortium, for children's sake.

Immaculata University, College of Graduate Studies, Department of Psychology, Immaculata, PA 19345. Offers clinical psychology (Psy D); counseling psychology (MA, Certificate), including school guidance counselor (Certificate), school psychologist (Certificate). *Accreditation:* APA. Part-time and evening/weekend programs available. *Students:* 123 full-time (100 women), 201 part-time (159 women). Average age 34. 83 applicants, 76% accepted, 55 enrolled. In 2010, 37 master's, 13 doctorates awarded. Terminal master's awarded for partial completion of doctoral program. *Degree requirements:* For master's, comprehensive exam, thesis optional; for doctorate, comprehensive exam, thesis/dissertation. *Entrance requirements:* For master's, GRE General Test or MAT, minimum GPA of 3.0; for doctorate, GRE General Test or MAT, minimum GPA of 3.5. Additional exam requirements/recommendations for international students: Required—TOEFL, IELTS. *Application deadline:* Applications are processed on a rolling basis. Application fee: $50. Electronic applications accepted. *Financial support:* Application deadline: 5/1. *Faculty research:* Supervision ethics, psychology of teaching, gender. *Unit head:* Dr. Jed A. Yalof, Chair, 610-647-4400 Ext. 3503, Fax: 610-993-8550, E-mail: jyalof@immaculata.edu. *Application contact:* Office of Graduate Admission, 610-647-4400 Ext. 3211, Fax: 610-993-8550, E-mail: graduate@immaculata.edu.

Indiana State University, College of Graduate and Professional Studies, College of Arts and Sciences, Department of Psychology, Terre Haute, IN 47809. Offers clinical psychology (Psy D); general psychology (MA, MS). *Accreditation:* APA (one or more programs are accredited). Terminal master's awarded for partial completion of doctoral program. *Degree requirements:* For master's, thesis (for some programs); for doctorate, comprehensive exam, thesis/dissertation, internship, professional research project. *Entrance requirements:* For master's, GRE General Test, 12 semester hours of course work in psychology, minimum GPA of 2.75; for doctorate, GRE General Test, minimum GPA of 3.0. Additional exam requirements/recommendations for international students: Required—TOEFL (minimum score 550 paper-based). Electronic applications accepted.

Indiana University Bloomington, University Graduate School, College of Arts and Sciences, Department of Criminal Justice, Bloomington, IN 47405. Offers criminal justice (MA, PhD); criminology (MA, PhD); cross-cultural perspectives of crime and justice (MA, PhD); law and society (MA, PhD); psychology and the law (MA). Part-time programs available. *Faculty:* 15 full-time (5 women). *Students:* 39 full-time (23 women); includes 6 minority (4 Black or African American, non-Hispanic/Latino; 2 American Indian or Alaska Native, non-Hispanic/Latino), 3 international. Average age 31. 30 applicants, 30% accepted, 4 enrolled. In 2010, 3 master's, 2 doctorates awarded. Terminal master's awarded for partial completion of doctoral program. *Degree requirements:* For master's, thesis optional; for doctorate, thesis/dissertation, foreign language or research practicum. *Entrance requirements:* For master's and doctorate, GRE General Test. Additional exam requirements/recommendations for international students: Required—TOEFL (minimum score 600 paper-based; 250 computer-based; 100 iBT). *Application deadline:* For fall admission, 1/15 for domestic students, 12/1 for international students. Application fee: $55 ($65 for international students). Electronic applications accepted. *Expenses:* Contact institution. *Financial support:* In 2010–11, 4 fellowships with full tuition reimbursements (averaging $25,000 per year), 3 research assistantships with full tuition reimbursements (averaging $11,721 per year), 21 teaching assistantships with full tuition reimbursements (averaging $11,721 per year) were awarded; Federal Work-Study, health care benefits, tuition waivers (full), and unspecified assistantships also available. Financial award application deadline: 1/15. *Faculty research:* Violence, crime, juveniles, psychology and law, cross-cultural studies. *Unit head:* Dr. Roger J. R. Levesque, Chair, 812-856-1210, E-mail: rlevesqu@indiana.edu. *Application contact:* Ruth Cord, Graduate Secretary, 812-856-4675, Fax: 812-855-5522, E-mail: rkapusti@indiana.edu.

Indiana University Bloomington, University Graduate School, College of Arts and Sciences, Department of Psychological and Brain Sciences, Bloomington, IN 47405-7000. Offers biology and behavior (PhD); clinical science (PhD); cognitive psychology (PhD); developmental psychology (PhD); psychological and brain sciences (MA); social psychology (PhD). *Accreditation:* APA (one or more programs are accredited). *Faculty:* 53 full-time (16 women). *Students:* 85 full-time (45 women), 1 (woman) part-time; includes 13 minority (3 Black or African American, non-Hispanic/Latino; 3 Asian, non-Hispanic/Latino; 6 Hispanic/Latino; 1 Two or more races, non-Hispanic/Latino), 19 international. Average age 28. 363 applicants, 10% accepted, 20 enrolled. In 2010, 3 master's, 17 doctorates awarded. *Degree requirements:* For doctorate, comprehensive exam, thesis/dissertation, 1st and 2nd year projects, 1 year as associate instructor, qualifying exam, student teaching. *Entrance requirements:* For doctorate, GRE. Additional exam requirements/recommendations for international students: Required—TOEFL (minimum score 550 paper-based; 213 computer-based). *Application deadline:* For fall admission, 12/15 for domestic students, 12/1 for international students. Application fee: $55 ($65 for international students). Electronic applications accepted. *Financial support:* In 2010–11, 32 fellowships with full tuition reimbursements (averaging $23,580 per year), 7 research assistantships with full tuition reimbursements (averaging $17,850 per year), 7 teaching assistantships with full tuition reimbursements (averaging $17,850 per year) were awarded; scholarships/grants, health care benefits, and unspecified assistantships also available. *Unit head:* Dr. Linda B. Smith, Chair, 812-855-3991, Fax: 812-855-4691, E-mail: smith4@indiana.edu. *Application contact:* Patricia G. Crouch, Academic Services Coordinator, 812-855-4528, Fax: 812-855-4691, E-mail: pcrouch@indiana.edu.

Indiana University of Pennsylvania, School of Graduate Studies and Research, College of Natural Sciences and Mathematics, Department of Psychology, Indiana, PA 15705-1087. Offers clinical psychology (Psy D); psychology (MA). *Accreditation:* APA (one or more programs are accredited). Part-time programs available. *Faculty:* 13 full-time (9 women). *Students:* 43 full-time (35 women), 22 part-time (20 women); includes 5 minority (3 Asian, non-Hispanic/Latino; 2 Hispanic/Latino), 1 international. Average age 27. 136 applicants, 13% accepted, 17 enrolled. In 2010, 12 master's, 13 doctorates awarded. Terminal master's awarded for partial completion of doctoral program. *Degree requirements:* For doctorate, comprehensive exam, thesis/dissertation, internship, practicum. *Entrance requirements:* For master's, GRE General Test; for doctorate, GRE General Test, minimum GPA of 3.0, interview, letters of recommendation. Additional exam requirements/recommendations for international students: Required—TOEFL. *Application deadline:* For fall admission, 1/10 for domestic students. Applications are processed on a rolling basis. Application fee: $40. *Financial support:* In 2010–11, 4 fellowships (averaging $2,000 per year), 35 research assistantships with full and partial tuition reimbursements (averaging $4,213 per year), 2 teaching assistantships (averaging $21,967 per year) were awarded; Federal Work-Study and scholarships/grants also available. Financial award application deadline: 3/15; financial award applicants required to submit FAFSA. *Unit head:* Dr. Mary Lou Zanich, Chairperson, 724-357-2426, E-mail: mtzanich@iup.edu. *Application contact:* Dr. Donald Robertson, Graduate Coordinator, 724-357-4522, E-mail: durobert@iup.edu.

Indiana University–Purdue University Indianapolis, School of Science, Department of Psychology, Indianapolis, IN 46202-3275. Offers clinical rehabilitation psychology (MS); industrial/organizational psychology (MS); psychobiology of addictions (MS, PhD). *Accreditation:* APA (one or more programs are accredited). *Faculty:* 10 full-time (2 women). *Students:* 51 full-time (43 women), 11 part-time (10 women); includes 4 minority (2 Black or African American, non-Hispanic/Latino; 2 Asian, non-Hispanic/Latino), 3 international. Average age 28. 116 applicants, 25% accepted, 18 enrolled. In 2010, 11 master's, 4 doctorates awarded. Terminal master's awarded for partial completion of doctoral program. *Degree requirements:* For master's, thesis; for doctorate, thesis/dissertation. *Entrance requirements:* For master's, GRE General Test, minimum undergraduate GPA of 3.0; for doctorate, GRE General Test, GRE Subject Test (clinical rehabilitation psychology), minimum undergraduate GPA of 3.2. *Application deadline:* For fall admission, 1/1 priority date for domestic students. Application fee: $55 ($65 for international students). *Financial support:* In 2010–11, 5 fellowships with partial tuition reimbursements (averaging $12,218 per year), 23 teaching assistantships with partial tuition reimbursements (averaging $7,553 per year) were awarded; research assistantships with partial tuition reimbursements, career-related internships or fieldwork, Federal Work-Study, and institutionally sponsored loans also available. Financial award application deadline: 3/1; financial award applicants required to submit FAFSA. *Faculty research:* Psychiatric rehabilitation, chronic stress, neurological research, language and cognitive development in infants, alcoholism and psychopathology. *Unit head:* Dr. J. Gregor Fetterman, Chairman, 317-274-6945, Fax: 317-274-6756, E-mail: gfetter@iupui.edu. *Application contact:* Dr. J. Gregor Fetterman, Chairman, 317-274-6945, Fax: 317-274-6756, E-mail: gfetter@iupui.edu.

Institute of Transpersonal Psychology, Global Online Programs, Palo Alto, CA 94303. Offers psychology (PhD); transpersonal psychology (MTP); transpersonal studies (Certificate). Postbaccalaureate distance learning degree programs offered (minimal on-campus study). Terminal master's awarded for partial completion of doctoral program. *Degree requirements:* For master's, thesis (for some programs); for doctorate, thesis/dissertation. *Entrance requirements:* For master's and doctorate, bachelor's degree. Additional exam requirements/recommendations for international students: Required—TOEFL. *Expenses:* Contact institution.

Institute of Transpersonal Psychology, Low-Residency Programs, Palo Alto, CA 94303. Offers counseling psychology (online) (MA); spiritual guidance (MA); women's spirituality (MA). Postbaccalaureate distance learning degree programs offered (minimal on-campus study).

Institute of Transpersonal Psychology, Residential Programs, Palo Alto, CA 94303. Offers counseling psychology (MA); spiritually oriented clinical psychology (Psy D); transpersonal psychology (MA, PhD). Part-time and evening/weekend programs available. Terminal master's awarded for partial completion of doctoral program. *Degree requirements:* For doctorate, thesis/dissertation. *Entrance requirements:* For master's and doctorate, bachelor's degree.

Inter American University of Puerto Rico, Metropolitan Campus, Graduate Programs, Program in Psychology, San Juan, PR 00919-1293. Offers counseling psychology (MA, PhD); industrial/organizational psychology (MA, PhD); labor relations (MA); school psychology (MA, PhD). *Degree requirements:* For master's, comprehensive exam. *Entrance requirements:* For master's, GRE or EXADEP, interview. Electronic applications accepted.

Inter American University of Puerto Rico, San Germán Campus, Graduate Studies Center, Program in Psychology, San Germán, PR 00683-5008. Offers counseling psychology (MA, PhD); school psychology (MA, PhD). Part-time and evening/weekend programs available. *Degree requirements:* For master's, comprehensive exam, thesis; for doctorate, comprehensive exam, thesis/dissertation. *Entrance requirements:* For master's, GRE General Test or EXADEP, minimum GPA of 3.0; for doctorate, GRE, EXADEP or MAT, minimum GPA of 3.0. *Expenses:* Tuition: Part-time $202 per credit. Required fees: $258 per semester.

Iona College, School of Arts and Science, Department of Psychology, New Rochelle, NY 10801-1890. Offers experimental psychology (MA); industrial-organizational psychology (MA); mental health counseling (MA); psychology (MA); school psychology (MA). Part-time and evening/weekend programs available. *Faculty:* 10 full-time (7 women), 12 part-time/adjunct (7 women). *Students:* 86 full-time (70 women), 36 part-time (30 women); includes 21 minority (6 Black or African American, non-Hispanic/Latino; 1 American Indian or Alaska Native, non-Hispanic/Latino; 2 Asian, non-Hispanic/Latino; 12 Hispanic/Latino), 2 international. Average age 25. 153 applicants, 78% accepted, 50 enrolled. In 2010, 36 master's awarded. *Degree requirements:* For master's, thesis. *Entrance requirements:* For master's, GRE or minimum GPA of 3.0. Additional exam requirements/recommendations for international students: Required—TOEFL (minimum score 550 paper-based; 213 computer-based). *Application deadline:* Applications are processed on a rolling basis. Application fee: $50. Electronic applications accepted. *Expenses:* Tuition: Part-time $830 per credit. Required fees: $225 per credit. *Financial support:* Career-related internships or fieldwork, tuition waivers (partial), and unspecified assistantships available. Support available to part-time students. Financial award application deadline: 4/15; financial award applicants required to submit FAFSA. *Unit head:* Dr. Paul Greene, Chair, 914-633-2048, E-mail: pgreene@iona.edu. *Application contact:* Veronica Jarek-Prinz, Director of Graduate Admissions, 914-633-2420, Fax: 914-633-2277, E-mail: vjarekprinz@iona.edu.

Iowa State University of Science and Technology, Graduate College, College of Liberal Arts and Sciences, Department of Psychology, Ames, IA 50011. Offers cognitive psychology (PhD); counseling psychology (PhD); social psychology (PhD). *Accreditation:* APA. *Faculty:* 34 full-time (14 women), 1 part-time/adjunct (0 women). *Students:* 73 full-time (42 women), 27 part-time (18 women); includes 8 Black or African American, non-Hispanic/Latino; 4 Asian, non-Hispanic/Latino; 4 Hispanic/Latino, 17 international. 88 applicants, 13% accepted, 9 enrolled. In 2010, 4 doctorates awarded. *Degree requirements:* For doctorate, comprehensive exam, thesis/dissertation. *Entrance requirements:* For doctorate, GRE General Test, GRE Subject Test (psychology), 3 letters of recommendation. Additional exam requirements/recommendations for international students: Required—TOEFL (minimum score 560 paper-based; 79 iBT), IELTS (minimum score 6.5). *Application deadline:* For fall admission, 1/2 priority date for domestic and international students. Application fee: $30 ($70 for international students). Electronic applications accepted. *Financial support:* In 2010–11, fellowships with full tuition reimbursements (averaging $14,055 per year), 7 research assistantships with full tuition reimbursements (averaging $13,169 per year), 57 teaching assistantships with full tuition reimbursements (averaging $9,432 per year) were awarded; scholarships/grants, health care benefits, and unspecified assistantships also available. *Faculty research:* Counseling psychology, cognitive psychology, social psychology, health psychology, psychology and public policy. *Unit head:* Carolyn Cutrona, Chair, 515-294-0283, Fax: 515-294-6424, E-mail: ccutrona@iastate.edu. *Application contact:* Ann Schmidt, Graduate Admissions Secretary, 515-294-1743, Fax: 515-294-6424, E-mail: psychadm@iastate.edu.

Jackson State University, Graduate School, College of Liberal Arts, Department of Psychology, Jackson, MS 39217. Offers clinical psychology (PhD). *Accreditation:* APA. *Faculty:* 8 full-time (5 women), 1 part-time/adjunct (0 women). *Students:* 28 full-time (22 women), 11 part-time (10 women); includes 24 Black or African American, non-Hispanic/Latino; 2 Asian, non-Hispanic/Latino. Average age 32. In 2010, 10 doctorates awarded. *Degree requirements:* For doctorate, comprehensive exam, thesis/dissertation. *Entrance requirements:* For doctorate, MAT, GRE. Additional exam requirements/recommendations for international students: Required—TOEFL (minimum score 520 paper-based; 195 computer-based; 67 iBT). *Application deadline:* For fall admission, 1/15 for domestic and international students. Application fee: $25. *Expenses:* Tuition, state resident: full-time $5050; part-time $281 per credit hour. Tuition, nonresident: full-time $12,380; part-time $689 per credit hour. *Financial support:* Fellowships, research assistantships, teaching assistantships, career-related internships or fieldwork, Federal Work-Study, scholarships/grants, tuition waivers (full), and unspecified assistantships available. Support available to part-time students. Financial award application deadline: 3/1; financial award applicants required to submit FAFSA. *Unit head:* Dr. Keith Hudson, Director, 601-979-5590, Fax: 601-979-3947, E-mail: keith.l.hudson@jsums.edu. *Application contact:* Sharlene Wilson, Director of Graduate Admissions, 601-979-2455, Fax: 601-977-4325, E-mail: sharlene.f.wilson@jsums.edu.

Jacksonville State University, College of Graduate Studies and Continuing Education, College of Arts and Sciences, Department of Psychology, Jacksonville, AL 36265-1602. Offers MS. Part-time and evening/weekend programs available. *Degree requirements:* For master's, comprehensive exam, thesis (for some programs). *Entrance requirements:* For master's, GRE General Test or MAT. Electronic applications accepted.

James Madison University, The Graduate School, College of Integrated Science and Technology, Department of Graduate Psychology, Harrisonburg, VA 22807. Offers assessment and measurement (PhD); clinical mental health counseling (M Ed, MA, Ed S); college student personnel administration (M Ed); combined-integrated clinical and school psychology (Psy D); psychological sciences (MA); school counseling (Ed S); school psychology (M Ed, MA, Ed S), including school counseling (M Ed, Ed S), school psychology (MA, Ed S). *Accreditation:* ACA (one or more programs are accredited); APA (one or more programs are accredited). Part-time and evening/weekend programs available. *Faculty:* 34 full-time (20 women), 20 part-time/adjunct (9 women). *Students:* 131 full-time (91 women), 37 part-time (31 women); includes 21 minority (11 Black or African American, non-Hispanic/Latino; 3 Asian, non-Hispanic/Latino; 5 Hispanic/Latino; 2 Two or more races, non-Hispanic/Latino), 5 international. Average age 27. In 2010, 49 master's, 13 doctorates, 26 other advanced degrees awarded. *Degree requirements:* For doctorate, thesis/dissertation; for Ed S, thesis. *Entrance requirements:* For master's, GRE General Test, GRE Subject Test; for doctorate, GRE General Test. Additional exam requirements/recommendations for international students: Required—TOEFL. *Application deadline:* For fall admission, 2/1 priority date for domestic students; for spring admission, 9/1 for domestic students. Applications are processed on a rolling basis. Application fee: $55. Electronic applications accepted. *Financial support:* In 2010–11, 106 students received support, including 3 teaching assistantships with full tuition reimbursements available (averaging $8,664 per year); career-related internships or fieldwork, Federal Work-Study, and 79 graduate assistantships ($7382), 24 doctoral assistantships ($14,50) also available. Financial award application deadline: 3/1; financial award applicants required to submit FAFSA. *Unit head:* Harriet C. Cobb, Academic Unit Head, 540-568-6834, Fax: 540-568-3322, E-mail: cobbhc@jmu.edu. *Application contact:* Harriet C. Cobb, Academic Unit Head, 540-568-6834, Fax: 540-568-3322, E-mail: cobbhc@jmu.edu.

John F. Kennedy University, Graduate School of Holistic Studies, Department of Integral Studies, Program in Integral Psychology, Pleasant Hill, CA 94523-4817. Offers dream studies (Certificate); integral psychology (MA); life coaching (Certificate). Part-time and evening/weekend programs available.

John F. Kennedy University, Graduate School of Professional Psychology, Pleasant Hill, CA 94523-4817. Offers MA, Psy D, Certificate. *Accreditation:* APA. Part-time and evening/weekend programs available. *Degree requirements:* For master's, thesis or alternative. *Entrance requirements:* For master's, interview. Additional exam requirements/recommendations for international students: Required—TOEFL.

The Johns Hopkins University, Zanvyl Krieger School of Arts and Sciences, Department of Psychological and Brain Sciences, Baltimore, MD 21218. Offers PhD. *Faculty:* 16 full-time (8 women), 8 part-time/adjunct (1 woman). *Students:* 30 full-time (15 women); includes 8 minority (2 Black or African American, non-Hispanic/Latino; 4 Asian, non-Hispanic/Latino; 2 Hispanic/Latino), 9 international. Average age 26. 91 applicants, 14% accepted, 7 enrolled. In 2010, 1 doctorate awarded. *Degree requirements:* For doctorate, thesis/dissertation, research project, teaching experience. *Entrance requirements:* For doctorate, GRE General Test, GRE Subject Test. Additional exam requirements/recommendations for international students: Required—TOEFL (minimum score 600 paper-based; 250 computer-based; 100 iBT), IELTS. *Application deadline:* For fall admission, 12/15 priority date for domestic students, 12/15 for international students. Application fee: $75. Electronic applications accepted. *Financial support:* In 2010–11, 8 fellowships with partial tuition reimbursements (averaging $25,333 per year), 18 teaching assistantships with full tuition reimbursements (averaging $25,333 per year) were awarded; Federal Work-Study, tuition waivers (full), and unspecified assistantships also available. Financial award application deadline: 4/15; financial award applicants required to submit FAFSA. *Faculty research:* Biopsychology, cognitive psychology, cognitive neuroscience, developmental psychology, neurobiology. Total annual research expenditures: $2.5 million. *Unit head:* Dr. Steven Yantis, Chair, 410-516-5328, Fax: 410-516-4478, E-mail: psychair@jhu.edu. *Application contact:* Hope Stein, Admissions Coordinator, 410-516-6175, Fax: 410-516-4478, E-mail: hope.stein@jhu.edu.

Kansas State University, Graduate School, College of Arts and Sciences, Department of Psychology, Manhattan, KS 66506. Offers MS, PhD. Part-time programs available. *Degree requirements:* For master's, thesis or alternative; for doctorate, thesis/dissertation, preliminary exam. *Entrance requirements:* For master's, GRE General Test, minimum undergraduate GPA of 3.0; for doctorate, GRE General Test, minimum GPA of 3.0. Additional exam requirements/recommendations for international students: Required—TOEFL (minimum score 600 paper-based; 250 computer-based). Electronic applications accepted. *Faculty research:* Personal and occupational health, neurological bases of drug use and abuse, measurement and reduction of prejudice, judgment and decision making, visual perception.

Kean University, College of Humanities and Social Sciences, Program in Psychology, Union, NJ 07083. Offers human behavior and organizational psychology (MA); psychological services (MA). Part-time and evening/weekend programs available. *Faculty:* 17 full-time (13 women). *Students:* 24 full-time (20 women), 20 part-time (13 women); includes 12 Black or African American, non-Hispanic/Latino; 5 Asian, non-Hispanic/Latino; 5 Hispanic/Latino; 1 Two or more races, non-Hispanic/Latino, 2 international. Average age 27. 41 applicants, 83% accepted, 26 enrolled. In 2010, 18 master's awarded. *Degree requirements:* For master's, comprehensive exam, thesis, research, two semesters advanced seminar. *Entrance requirements:* For master's, GRE General Test, minimum GPA of 3.0, 2 letters of recommendation, interview, 12 credits in behavioral sciences, transcripts. *Application deadline:* For fall admission, 6/1 for domestic students; for spring admission, 11/1 for domestic students. Application fee: $75 ($150 for international students). Electronic applications accepted. *Expenses:* Tuition, state resident: full-time $10,872; part-time $500 per credit. Tuition, nonresident: full-time $14,736; part-time $614 per credit. Required fees: $2740.80; $125 per credit. Part-time tuition and fees vary according to course load and degree level. *Financial support:* In 2010–11, 2 research assistantships with full tuition reimbursements (averaging $3,263 per year) were awarded; unspecified assistantships also available. Financial award applicants required to submit FAFSA. *Unit head:* Dr. Joanne Walsh, Program Coordinator, 908-737-5888, E-mail: jwalsh@kean.edu. *Application contact:* Reenat Hasan, Pre-Admissions Coordinator, 908-737-5923, Fax: 908-737-5925, E-mail: rhasan@exchange.kean.edu.

Kent State University, College of Arts and Sciences, Department of Psychology, Kent, OH 44242-0001. Offers clinical psychology (MA, PhD); experimental psychology (MA, PhD). *Accreditation:* APA (one or more programs are accredited). *Degree requirements:* For master's, thesis; for doctorate, thesis/dissertation. *Entrance requirements:* For master's, GRE, minimum GPA of 3.0, minimum 18 semester hours in psychology with one course in statistics and one experimental course with a lab component; for doctorate, GRE, minimum GPA of 3.0. Additional exam requirements/recommendations for international students: Required—TOEFL (minimum score 525 paper-based), Michigan English Language Assessment Battery (minimum score: 77). *Expenses:* Tuition, state resident: full-time $7866; part-time $437 per credit hour. Tuition, nonresident: full-time $14,022; part-time $779 per credit hour.

Lakehead University, Graduate Studies, Department of Psychology, Thunder Bay, ON P7B 5E1, Canada. Offers clinical psychology (PhD); experimental psychology (MA). Part-time and evening/weekend programs available. *Degree requirements:* For master's, thesis optional; for doctorate, thesis/dissertation, 2 comprehensive exams, internship. *Entrance requirements:* For master's, GRE, honors degree in psychology, advanced course work in statistics, minimum B average; for doctorate, GRE, minimum B average. Additional exam requirements/recommendations for international students: Required—TOEFL. *Faculty research:* Chaos theory, health psychology, counseling psychology, gerontology, women's studies.

Lamar University, College of Graduate Studies, College of Arts and Sciences, Department of Psychology, Beaumont, TX 77710. Offers community/clinical psychology (MS); industrial/organizational psychology (MS). Part-time programs available. *Faculty:* 7 full-time (4 women). *Students:* 17 full-time (12 women), 10 part-time (4 women); includes 2 Black or African American, non-Hispanic/Latino; 2 Hispanic/Latino, 1 international. Average age 29. 25 applicants, 60% accepted, 9 enrolled. In 2010, 26 master's awarded. *Degree requirements:* For master's, thesis, practicum. *Entrance requirements:* For master's, GRE General Test, minimum GPA of 2.75 in last 60 hours of undergraduate course work. Additional exam requirements/recommendations for international students: Required—TOEFL. *Application deadline:* For fall admission, 8/1 for domestic students; for spring admission, 12/1 for domestic students. Application fee: $25 ($50 for international students). *Expenses:* Tuition, state resident: full-time $4160; part-time $208 per credit hour. Tuition, nonresident: full-time $10,360; part-time $518 per credit hour. *Financial support:* In 2010–11, 12 students received support, including 3 teaching assistantships (averaging $4,500 per year); fellowships, research assistantships, career-related internships or fieldwork, Federal Work-Study, scholarships/grants, and tuition waivers (partial) also available. Support available to part-time students. Financial award application deadline: 4/1. *Faculty research:* Groupthink, health psychology, school psychology, behavioral neuroscience. *Application contact:* Assistant Dean, 409-880-7978, E-mail: westgate@hal.lamar.edu.

La Salle University, School of Arts and Sciences, Program in Psychology, Philadelphia, PA 19141-1199. Offers clinical psychology (Psy D); family psychology (Psy D); rehabilitation psychology (Psy D). *Accreditation:* AAMFT/COAMFTE. Part-time and evening/weekend programs available. *Entrance requirements:* For doctorate, GRE, minimum GPA of 3.0. *Expenses:* Contact institution. *Faculty research:* Cognitive therapy, attribution theory, treatment of addiction.

Laurentian University, School of Graduate Studies and Research, Programme in Psychology, Sudbury, ON P3E 2C6, Canada. Offers applied psychology (MA); experimental psychology (MA).

Lehigh University, College of Arts and Sciences, Department of Psychology, Bethlehem, PA 18015. Offers human cognition and development (MS, PhD). *Faculty:* 14 full-time (8 women). *Students:* 17 full-time (13 women), 3 part-time (2 women), 4 international. Average age 27. 90 applicants, 9% accepted, 7 enrolled. In 2010, 1 master's, 2 doctorates awarded. *Degree requirements:* For master's, thesis; for doctorate, comprehensive exam, thesis/dissertation. *Entrance requirements:* For master's and doctorate, GRE General Test. Additional exam requirements/recommendations for international students: Required—TOEFL. *Application deadline:* For fall admission, 1/15 for domestic and international students. Application fee: $75. Electronic applications accepted. *Expenses:* Contact institution. *Financial support:* In 2010–11, 15 students received support, including 1 fellowship with full tuition reimbursement available (averaging $25,000 per year), 3 research assistantships with full tuition reimbursements available (averaging $18,400 per year), 11 teaching assistantships with full tuition reimbursements available (averaging $18,400 per year); scholarships/grants, tuition waivers (full and

Psychology—General

Lehigh University (continued)
partial), and unspecified assistantships also available. Financial award application deadline: 1/15. *Faculty research:* Cognition, memory, language, and their development; prosocial cognition, emotion, and action; conflict and cooperation between and within groups; self-control of cognition and emotion; optimizing developmental and relational outcomes. Total annual research expenditures: $281,626. *Unit head:* Ageliki Nicolopoulou, Chairperson, 610-758-4702, Fax: 610-758-6277, E-mail: agn3@lehigh.edu. *Application contact:* Dr. Michael Gill, Program Director, 610-758-3630, Fax: 610-758-6277, E-mail: inpsy@lehigh.edu.

Lesley University, Graduate School of Arts and Social Sciences, Cambridge, MA 02138-2790. Offers clinical mental health counseling (MA), including expressive therapies counseling, holistic counseling, school and community counseling; counseling psychology (MA, CAGS), including professional counseling (MA), school counseling (MA); creative arts in learning (CAGS); creative writing (MFA); ecological teaching and learning (MS); environmental education (MS); expressive therapies (MA, PhD, CAGS), including art (MA), dance (MA), expressive therapies, music (MA); independent studies (CAGS); independent study (MA); intercultural relations (MA, CAGS); interdisciplinary studies (MA), including individualized studies, integrative holistic health, women's studies; urban environmental leadership (MA); visual arts (MFA). Part-time and evening/weekend programs available. Postbaccalaureate distance learning degree programs offered (minimal on-campus study). *Degree requirements:* For master's, internship, practicum, thesis (expressive therapies); for doctorate, thesis/dissertation, arts apprenticeship, field placement; for CAGS, thesis, internship (counseling psychology, expressive therapies). *Entrance requirements:* For master's, MAT (counseling psychology), interview, writing samples, art portfolio; for doctorate, GRE or MAT; for CAGS, interview, master's degree. Additional exam requirements/recommendations for international students: Required—TOEFL (minimum score 550 paper-based; 213 computer-based; 80 iBT). Electronic applications accepted. *Faculty research:* Psychotherapy and culture; psychotherapy and psychological trauma; women's issues in art, teaching and psychotherapy; community based art, psycho-spiritual inquiry.

LeTourneau University, School of Graduate and Professional Studies, Longview, TX 75607-7001. Offers business administration (MBA); counseling (MA); curriculum and instruction (M Ed); educational administration (M Ed); engineering (M Sc); psychology (MA); strategic leadership (MSL); teaching and learning (M Ed). Part-time and evening/weekend programs available. Postbaccalaureate distance learning degree programs offered (no on-campus study). *Faculty:* 9 full-time (1 woman), 62 part-time/adjunct (26 women). *Students:* 329 full-time (233 women); includes 152 Black or African American, non-Hispanic/Latino; 1 American Indian or Alaska Native, non-Hispanic/Latino; 5 Asian, non-Hispanic/Latino; 23 Hispanic/Latino. Average age 36. 138 applicants, 90% accepted, 120 enrolled. In 2010, 129 master's awarded. *Entrance requirements:* For master's, GRE (for MA in counseling and M Sc in engineering), minimum GPA of 2.8. Additional exam requirements/recommendations for international students: Required—TOEFL. *Application deadline:* Applications are processed on a rolling basis. Application fee: $0. Electronic applications accepted. *Expenses:* Tuition: Full-time $13,020; part-time $620 per credit hour. *Financial support:* Applicants required to submit FAFSA. *Unit head:* Dr. Carol Green, Vice President, 903-233-4010, Fax: 903-233-3227, E-mail: carolgreen@letu.edu. *Application contact:* Chris Fontaine, Assistant Vice President for Enrollment Management and Marketing, 903-233-4071, Fax: 903-233-3227, E-mail: chrisfontaine@letu.edu.

Lewis & Clark College, Graduate School of Education and Counseling, Department of Counseling Psychology, Portland, OR 97219-7899. Offers addictions treatment (MA, MS); community counseling (MA, MS), including professional mental health counseling; marriage, couple and family therapy (MA, MS); psychological and cultural studies (MA, MS); school psychology (Ed S). *Accreditation:* AAMFT/COAMFTE; ACA. Part-time and evening/weekend programs available. *Faculty:* 10 full-time (6 women), 29 part-time/adjunct (19 women). *Students:* 182 full-time (148 women), 65 part-time (55 women); includes 2 Black or African American, non-Hispanic/Latino; 6 Asian, non-Hispanic/Latino; 10 Hispanic/Latino; 13 Two or more races, non-Hispanic/Latino, 4 international. Average age 31. 231 applicants, 62% accepted, 69 enrolled. In 2010, 60 master's awarded. *Degree requirements:* For master's, thesis proposal (MS). *Entrance requirements:* For master's, GRE General Test, minimum undergraduate GPA of 2.75. Additional exam requirements/recommendations for international students: Required—TOEFL (minimum score 575 paper-based; 233 computer-based). *Application deadline:* For fall admission, 2/1 priority date for domestic and international students; for spring admission, 10/1 priority date for domestic and international students. Application fee: $50. Electronic applications accepted. *Expenses:* Tuition: Part-time $713 per semester hour. Tuition and fees vary according to course level and campus/location. *Financial support:* In 2010–11, 33 students received support. Career-related internships or fieldwork, Federal Work-Study, institutionally sponsored loans, scholarships/grants, health care benefits, and tuition waivers (partial) available. Support available to part-time students. Financial award application deadline: 3/1; financial award applicants required to submit FAFSA. *Unit head:* Dr. Teresa McDowell, Chair, 503-768-6060, Fax: 503-768-6065, E-mail: cpsy@lclark.edu. *Application contact:* Becky Haas, Director of Admissions, 503-768-6200, Fax: 503-768-6205, E-mail: gseadmit@lclark.edu.

Lipscomb University, Programs in Counseling, Nashville, TN 37204-3951. Offers counseling psychology (Certificate); professional counseling (MS); psychology (MS). Part-time and evening/weekend programs available. Postbaccalaureate distance learning degree programs offered (minimal on-campus study). *Faculty:* 5 full-time (1 woman), 12 part-time/adjunct (7 women). *Students:* 88 full-time (70 women), 46 part-time (28 women); includes 16 Black or African American, non-Hispanic/Latino; 1 American Indian or Alaska Native, non-Hispanic/Latino; 2 Asian, non-Hispanic/Latino; 3 Hispanic/Latino, 1 international. Average age 30. 101 applicants, 60% accepted, 46 enrolled. In 2010, 35 master's awarded. *Entrance requirements:* For master's, GRE, resume, 3 reference letters, minimum GPA of 3.0. Application fee: $50. Electronic applications accepted. *Expenses:* Tuition: Full-time $18,149; part-time $943 per hour. Tuition and fees vary according to program. *Faculty research:* Cognitive psychology, neuroscience, health psychology, grief issues. *Unit head:* Dr. Jake Morris, Graduate Program Director and Professor of Psychology, 615-966-5906, E-mail: jake.morris@lipscomb.edu. *Application contact:* Elena Zemmel, Administrative Assistant, 615-966-5906, E-mail: elena.zemmel@lipscomb.edu.

Loma Linda University, School of Science and Technology, Department of Psychology, Loma Linda, CA 92350. Offers PhD, Psy D. *Accreditation:* APA. *Degree requirements:* For doctorate, comprehensive exam, thesis/dissertation. *Entrance requirements:* For doctorate, GRE General Test. Additional exam requirements/recommendations for international students: Required—TOEFL (minimum score 550 paper-based; 213 computer-based), MTELP. Electronic applications accepted.

Long Island University, Brooklyn Campus, Richard L. Conolly College of Liberal Arts and Sciences, Department of Psychology, Brooklyn, NY 11201-8423. Offers clinical psychology (PhD); psychology (MA). *Accreditation:* APA (one or more programs are accredited). Part-time and evening/weekend programs available. Terminal master's awarded for partial completion of doctoral program. *Degree requirements:* For master's, thesis or alternative; for doctorate, thesis/dissertation. *Entrance requirements:* For master's, GRE Subject Test, GRE General Test, 2 letters of recommendation; for doctorate, GRE Subject Test, GRE General Test. Additional exam requirements/recommendations for international students: Required—TOEFL (minimum score 500 paper-based; 173 computer-based). Electronic applications accepted.

Long Island University, C.W. Post Campus, College of Liberal Arts and Sciences, Department of Psychology, Brookville, NY 11548-1300. Offers clinical psychology (Psy D); psychology (MA). *Accreditation:* APA. Part-time programs available. *Degree requirements:* For master's, thesis; for doctorate, thesis/dissertation, internship. *Entrance requirements:* For master's, GRE General Test, GRE Subject Test, minimum GPA of 3.0 in psychology, 2.8 overall; for doctorate, GRE General Test, GRE Subject Test, bachelor's degree in psychology, minimum GPA of 3.25. Electronic applications accepted. *Faculty research:* Visual perception, animal learning, attachment, neuropsychology, developmental disabilities, severe mental illness.

Louisiana State University and Agricultural and Mechanical College, Graduate School, College of Humanities and Social Sciences, Department of Psychology, Baton Rouge, LA 70803. Offers biological psychology (MA, PhD); clinical psychology (MA, PhD); cognitive psychology (MA, PhD); developmental psychology (MA, PhD); industrial/organizational psychology (MA, PhD); school psychology (MA, PhD). PhD programs offered jointly with Southeastern Louisiana University. *Accreditation:* APA (one or more programs are accredited). *Faculty:* 26 full-time (10 women). *Students:* 96 full-time (68 women), 24 part-time (19 women); includes 7 Black or African American, non-Hispanic/Latino; 2 American Indian or Alaska Native, non-Hispanic/Latino; 1 Asian, non-Hispanic/Latino; 5 Hispanic/Latino, 2 international. Average age 27. 289 applicants, 11% accepted, 17 enrolled. In 2010, 16 master's, 11 doctorates awarded. Terminal master's awarded for partial completion of doctoral program. *Degree requirements:* For master's, thesis; for doctorate, thesis/dissertation, 1 year internship. *Entrance requirements:* For master's and doctorate, GRE General Test, minimum GPA of 3.0. Additional exam requirements/recommendations for international students: Required—TOEFL (minimum score 550 paper-based; 213 computer-based; 79 iBT) or IELTS (minimum score 6.5). *Application deadline:* For fall admission, 1/15 for domestic and international students. Applications are processed on a rolling basis. Application fee: $50 ($70 for international students). Electronic applications accepted. *Financial support:* In 2010–11, 115 students received support, including 5 fellowships (averaging $25,207 per year), 25 research assistantships with partial tuition reimbursements available (averaging $18,083 per year), 48 teaching assistantships with partial tuition reimbursements available (averaging $13,043 per year); career-related internships or fieldwork, Federal Work-Study, institutionally sponsored loans, scholarships/grants, health care benefits, and tuition waivers (full and partial) also available. Financial award applicants required to submit FAFSA. *Faculty research:* Clinical psychology, autism, anxiety, addition, neuropsychology, school psychology, cognitive psychology, experimental psychology. Total annual research expenditures: $1.3 million. *Unit head:* Dr. Robert Matthews, Chair, 225-578-8745, Fax: 225-578-4125, E-mail: psmath@lsu.edu. *Application contact:* Dr. Jason Hicks, Coordinator of Graduate Studies, 225-578-4109, Fax: 225-578-4125, E-mail: jhicks@lsu.edu.

Louisiana Tech University, Graduate School, College of Education, Department of Behavioral Sciences and Psychology, Ruston, LA 71272. Offers counseling (MA); counseling psychology (PhD); industrial/organizational psychology (MA); special education (MA). *Accreditation:* APA (one or more programs are accredited). Part-time programs available. *Degree requirements:* For master's, thesis or alternative; for doctorate, thesis/dissertation. *Entrance requirements:* For master's and doctorate, GRE General Test.

Loyola University Chicago, Graduate School, Department of Psychology, Chicago, IL 60660. Offers applied social psychology (MA, PhD); clinical psychology (MA, PhD); developmental psychology (MA, PhD). *Accreditation:* APA (one or more programs are accredited). *Faculty:* 27 full-time (12 women), 1 part-time/adjunct (0 women). *Students:* 99 full-time (84 women), 3 part-time (all women); includes 23 minority (7 Black or African American, non-Hispanic/Latino; 1 American Indian or Alaska Native, non-Hispanic/Latino; 3 Asian, non-Hispanic/Latino; 9 Hispanic/Latino; 3 Two or more races, non-Hispanic/Latino), 6 international. Average age 29. 384 applicants, 6% accepted, 14 enrolled. In 2010, 14 master's, 8 doctorates awarded. Terminal master's awarded for partial completion of doctoral program. *Degree requirements:* For master's, comprehensive exam, thesis; for doctorate, comprehensive exam, thesis/dissertation. *Entrance requirements:* For master's and doctorate, GRE General Test, GRE Subject Test. Application fee: $50. Electronic applications accepted. *Expenses:* Tuition: Full-time $14,940; part-time $830 per credit hour. Required fees: $87 per semester. Part-time tuition and fees vary according to course load and program. *Financial support:* In 2010–11, 7 fellowships with full tuition reimbursements (averaging $12,000 per year), 24 research assistantships with full tuition reimbursements (averaging $12,000 per year), 10 teaching assistantships with full tuition reimbursements (averaging $12,000 per year) were awarded; career-related internships or fieldwork, Federal Work-Study, scholarships/grants, and traineeships also available. Financial award applicants required to submit FAFSA. *Faculty research:* Cognitive development, hearing and vision, attitude and prejudice, child and family, AIDS and health promotion. Total annual research expenditures: $2.5 million. *Unit head:* Dr. R. Scott Tindale, Chair, 773-508-3014, E-mail: rtindal@luc.edu. *Application contact:* Ron Martin, Assistant Director of Enrollment Management, 312-915-8950, Fax: 312-915-8905, E-mail: gradapp@luc.edu.

Loyola University Maryland, Graduate Programs, Loyola College of Arts and Sciences, Department of Psychology, Baltimore, MD 21210-2699. Offers clinical psychology (MS, Psy D, CAS); counseling psychology (MS, CAS). *Accreditation:* APA. Part-time and evening/weekend programs available. *Entrance requirements:* For master's, doctorate, and CAS, GRE General Test, GRE Subject Test (recommended). Additional exam requirements/recommendations for international students: Required—TOEFL (minimum score 550 paper-based; 213 computer-based).

Madonna University, Department of Psychology, Livonia, MI 48150-1173. Offers clinical psychology (MSCP). Part-time and evening/weekend programs available. *Degree requirements:* For master's, thesis or alternative. *Entrance requirements:* Additional exam requirements/recommendations for international students: Required—TOEFL. Electronic applications accepted.

Mansfield University of Pennsylvania, Graduate Studies, Program in Organizational Leadership, Mansfield, PA 16933. Offers MA. Postbaccalaureate distance learning degree programs offered. *Expenses:* Tuition, state resident: full-time $6966; part-time $387 per credit hour. Tuition, nonresident: full-time $11,146; part-time $619 per credit hour. Required fees: $1456; $68 per credit hour.

Marietta College, Program in Psychology, Marietta, OH 45750-4000. Offers MAP.

Marist College, Graduate Programs, School of Social and Behavioral Sciences, Poughkeepsie, NY 12601-1387. Offers education (M Ed, MA); mental health counseling (MA); school psychology (MA, Adv C). Part-time and evening/weekend programs available. *Degree requirements:* For master's, thesis optional. *Entrance requirements:* For master's, GRE General Test, letters of recommendation, minimum undergraduate GPA of 3.0, interview. Additional exam requirements/recommendations for international students: Required—TOEFL (minimum score 550 paper-based; 213 computer-based; 80 iBT); Recommended—IELTS (minimum score 6.5). Electronic applications accepted. *Faculty research:* AIDS prevention, educational intervention, humanistic counseling research, aging and development, neuroimaging.

Marquette University, Graduate School, College of Arts and Sciences, Department of Psychology, Milwaukee, WI 53201-1881. Offers PhD. *Accreditation:* APA. *Faculty:* 18 full-time (8 women), 5 part-time/adjunct (3 women). *Students:* 43 full-time (29 women), 4 part-time (all women); includes 4 minority (1 Black or African American, non-Hispanic/Latino; 2 Hispanic/Latino; 1 Two or more races, non-Hispanic/Latino), 2 international. Average age 27. 119 applicants, 12% accepted, 6 enrolled. In 2010, 3 doctorates awarded. *Degree requirements:* For doctorate, thesis/dissertation, internship, qualifying exam. *Entrance requirements:* For doctorate, GRE General Test, sample of scholarly writing, official transcripts from all current and previous colleges/universities except Marquette, personal statement, three letters of reference. Additional exam requirements/recommendations for international students: Required—TOEFL (minimum score 530 paper-based; 78 computer-based). *Application deadline:* For fall admission, 12/1 for domestic and international students. Application fee: $50. Electronic applications accepted. *Expenses:* Tuition: Full-time $16,290; part-time $905 per credit hour. Tuition and fees vary according to program. *Financial support:* In 2010–11, 1 fellowship, 1 research assistantship, 17 teaching assistantships were awarded; career-related internships or fieldwork, Federal Work-Study, institutionally sponsored loans, scholarships/grants, and tuition waivers (full and partial) also available. Support available to part-time students. Financial award application deadline: 2/15. *Faculty research:* Mental imagery, moral development, organizational behavior, depression, psychotherapy outcomes. Total annual research expenditures: $138,300. *Unit head:* Dr. Alan Burkard, Chair, 414-288-7218, Fax: 414-288-5333. *Application contact:* Dr. Steve Saunders, Information Contact, 414-288-7459.

Marshall University, Academic Affairs Division, College of Liberal Arts, Department of Psychology, Huntington, WV 25755. Offers clinical psychology (MA); general psychology (MA); industrial and organizational psychology (MA); psychology (Psy D). *Accreditation:* APA. *Faculty:* 17 full-time (5 women), 1 (woman) part-time/adjunct. *Students:* 98 full-time (67 women), 32 part-time (26 women); includes 7 Black or African American, non-Hispanic/Latino; 1 Asian, non-Hispanic/Latino; 1 Hispanic/Latino; 1 Native Hawaiian or other Pacific Islander, non-Hispanic/Latino, 4 international. Average age 28. In 2010, 33 master's, 4 doctorates awarded. *Degree requirements:* For master's, thesis optional. *Entrance requirements:* For master's, GRE General Test or MAT. *Application deadline:* For fall admission, 3/1 for domestic students; for spring admission, 11/1 for domestic students. Application fee: $40. *Financial support:* Teaching assistantships with tuition reimbursements available. *Unit head:* Dr. Steven Mewaldt, Chairperson, 304-696-2777, E-mail: mewaldt@marshall.edu. *Application contact:* Graduate Admissions, 304-746-1900, Fax: 304-746-1902, E-mail: services@marshall.edu.

Martin University, Division of Psychology, Indianapolis, IN 46218-3867. Offers community psychology (MS). Part-time and evening/weekend programs available. *Degree requirements:* For master's, thesis. *Entrance requirements:* For master's, GRE General Test, GRE Subject Test.

Marywood University, Academic Affairs, Reap College of Education and Human Development, Department of Psychology and Counseling, Program in Psychology, Scranton, PA 18509-1598. Offers clinical services (MA); general theoretical (MA). *Entrance requirements:* Additional exam requirements/recommendations for international students: Required—TOEFL (minimum score 550 paper-based; 213 computer-based; 79 iBT). Electronic applications accepted. *Expenses:* Tuition: Part-time $735 per credit. Required fees: $470 per semester. Tuition and fees vary according to degree level and campus/location. *Faculty research:* Personality disorders, counselor training, preschool development, self-esteem measurement, family dynamics.

Massachusetts School of Professional Psychology, Graduate Programs, Boston, MA 02132. Offers applied psychology in higher education student personnel administration (MA); clinical psychology (Psy D); counseling psychology (MA); counseling psychology and community mental health (MA); counseling psychology and global mental health (MA); executive coaching (Graduate Certificate); forensic and counseling psychology (MA); leadership psychology (Psy D); organizational psychology (MA); primary care psychology (MA); respecialization in clinical psychology (Certificate); school psychology (Psy D); MA/CAGS. *Accreditation:* APA. *Faculty:* 24 full-time (11 women), 13 part-time/adjunct (9 women). *Students:* 515. Average age 28. *Degree requirements:* For master's, comprehensive exam (for some programs); for doctorate, thesis/dissertation (for some programs). Application fee: $50. Electronic applications accepted. *Expenses:* Tuition: Full-time $32,352; part-time $1011 per credit. Full-time tuition and fees vary according to degree level. *Financial support:* Teaching assistantships, career-related internships or fieldwork available. Financial award applicants required to submit FAFSA. *Unit head:* Dr. Nicholas A. Covino, President, 617-327-6777, Fax: 617-327-4447. *Application contact:* Admissions and Marketing, 617-327-6777 Ext. 210, Fax: 617-327-4447, E-mail: admissions@mspp.edu.

McGill University, Faculty of Graduate and Postdoctoral Studies, Faculty of Medicine, Department of Psychiatry, Montréal, QC H3A 2T5, Canada. Offers M Sc.

McGill University, Faculty of Graduate and Postdoctoral Studies, Faculty of Science, Department of Psychology, Montréal, QC H3A 2T5, Canada. Offers clinical psychology (PhD); experimental psychology (M Sc, MA, PhD). *Accreditation:* APA (one or more programs are accredited).

McMaster University, School of Graduate Studies, Faculty of Science, Department of Psychology, Hamilton, ON L8S 4M2, Canada. Offers M Sc, PhD. *Degree requirements:* For doctorate, comprehensive exam, thesis/dissertation. *Entrance requirements:* For doctorate, GRE General Test, honors degree, minimum B+ average. Additional exam requirements/recommendations for international students: Required—TOEFL (minimum score 550 paper-based; 213 computer-based).

McNeese State University, Doré School of Graduate Studies, Burton College of Education, Department of Psychology, Lake Charles, LA 70609. Offers addiction treatment (MA); applied behavior analysis (MA); counseling psychology (MA); general/experimental psychology (MA). Evening/weekend programs available. *Faculty:* 6 full-time (3 women). *Students:* 46 full-time (31 women), 29 part-time (21 women); includes 11 minority (6 Black or African American, non-Hispanic/Latino; 1 Asian, non-Hispanic/Latino; 2 Hispanic/Latino; 2 Two or more races, non-Hispanic/Latino), 4 international. In 2010, 14 master's awarded. *Entrance requirements:* For master's, GRE. *Application deadline:* For fall admission, 5/15 priority date for domestic and international students; for spring admission, 10/15 priority date for domestic and international students. Applications are processed on a rolling basis. Application fee: $20 ($30 for international students). Tuition and fees vary according to course load. *Financial support:* Application deadline: 5/1. *Unit head:* Dr. Dena L. Matzenbacher, Head, 337-475-5457, Fax: 337-562-4115, E-mail: dena@mcneese.edu. *Application contact:* Dr. George F. Mead, Interim Dean of Dore' School of Graduate Studies, 337-475-5396, Fax: 337-475-5397, E-mail: admissions@mcneese.edu.

Medaille College, Programs in Psychology, Buffalo, NY 14214-2695. Offers mental health counseling (MA); psychology (MA). Part-time and evening/weekend programs available. *Faculty:* 9 full-time (6 women), 9 part-time/adjunct (6 women). *Students:* 186 full-time (165 women); includes 22 Black or African American, non-Hispanic/Latino; 3 Asian, non-Hispanic/Latino; 2 Hispanic/Latino; 2 Two or more races, non-Hispanic/Latino. Average age 31. In 2010, 69 master's awarded. *Degree requirements:* For master's, comprehensive exam (for some programs), thesis (for some programs). *Entrance requirements:* For master's, GRE General Test (psychology), minimum GPA of 2.75 (psychology). Additional exam requirements/recommendations for international students: Required—TOEFL (minimum score 550 paper-based; 213 computer-based). *Application deadline:* Applications are processed on a rolling basis. Application fee: $35. Electronic applications accepted. *Financial support:* In 2010–11, 90 students received support. Federal Work-Study available. Financial award applicants required to submit FAFSA. *Faculty research:* Schizophrenia, Parkinson's Disease, eyewitness testimony, methodology. *Unit head:* Dr. Judith Horowitz, Dean of Adult and Graduate Studies, 716-880-2229, Fax: 716-884-0291, E-mail: jhorowitz@medaille.edu. *Application contact:* Jacqueline Matheny, Executive Director of Marketing and Enrollment, 716-932-2541, Fax: 716-632-1811, E-mail: jmatheny@medaille.edu.

Memorial University of Newfoundland, School of Graduate Studies, Department of Psychology, St. John's, NL A1C 5S7, Canada. Offers applied social psychology (MASP); experimental psychology (M Sc, PhD). Part-time programs available. *Degree requirements:* For master's, workterms (MASP), thesis (M Sc); for doctorate, comprehensive exam, thesis/dissertation, oral thesis defense. *Entrance requirements:* For master's, GRE, honors bachelor's degree of high second class standing or equivalent; for doctorate, GRE, master's or honors degree. Electronic applications accepted. *Faculty research:* Behavioral neuroscience, cognition, theory and research on abnormal behavior.

Mercy College, School of Social and Behavioral Sciences, Program in Psychology, Dobbs Ferry, NY 10522-1189. Offers MS. Part-time and evening/weekend programs available. Postbaccalaureate distance learning degree programs offered (no on-campus study). *Students:* 21 full-time (17 women), 34 part-time (27 women); includes 16 Black or African American, non-Hispanic/Latino; 1 American Indian or Alaska Native, non-Hispanic/Latino; 1 Asian, non-Hispanic/Latino; 11 Hispanic/Latino; 2 Two or more races, non-Hispanic/Latino, 2 international. Average age 32. 69 applicants, 43% accepted, 25 enrolled. In 2010, 6 master's awarded. *Degree requirements:* For master's, written comprehensive exam or 6 credit thesis. *Entrance requirements:* For master's, BA in psychology, sociology, behavioral science or education; interview; letters of recommendation; minimum GPA of 3.0; resume; 3- to 5-page essay stating reason for pursuing master's degree in psychology. Additional exam requirements/recommendations for international students: Required—TOEFL (minimum score 600 paper-based; 250 computer-based; 100 iBT), IELTS (minimum score 8). *Application deadline:* For fall admission, 8/1 for international students. Applications are processed on a rolling basis. Application fee: $40. Electronic applications accepted. *Expenses:* Tuition: Full-time $13,572; part-time $754 per credit hour. Required fees: $130 per term. *Financial support:* Career-related internships or fieldwork, Federal Work-Study, scholarships/grants, and unspecified assistantships available. Support available to part-time students. Financial award applicants required to submit FAFSA. *Unit head:* Dr. Mary Knopp Kelly, Chair/Associate Professor, 914-674-7809, E-mail: mkkelly@mercy.edu. *Application contact:* Allison Gurdineer, Senior Associate Director of Recruitment, 914-674-6701, E-mail: agurdineer@mercy.edu.

Metropolitan State University, College of Professional Studies, St. Paul, MN 55106-5000. Offers psychology (MA); urban secondary education (Certificate). Part-time and evening/weekend programs available. *Students:* 40 full-time (29 women), 37 part-time (28 women); includes 11 Black or African American, non-Hispanic/Latino; 4 Asian, non-Hispanic/Latino; 2 Hispanic/Latino; 5 Two or more races, non-Hispanic/Latino. Average age 36. In 2010, 2 master's awarded. *Degree requirements:* For master's, thesis. *Entrance requirements:* For master's, resume, letters of reference, minimum GPA of 3.0. Additional exam requirements/recommendations for international students: Required—TOEFL (minimum score 550 paper-based; 213 computer-based). *Application deadline:* For fall admission, 8/1 priority date for domestic students; for spring admission, 12/1 priority date for domestic students. Electronic applications accepted. *Expenses:* Tuition, state resident: full-time $5827; part-time $291 per credit hour. Tuition, nonresident: full-time $11,654; part-time $583 per credit hour. Required fees: $10 per credit hour. Tuition and fees vary according to degree level. *Financial support:* Applicants required to submit FAFSA. *Unit head:* Dr. Daniel Abebe, Interim Dean, 651-793-1333, Fax: 651-793-1355, E-mail: daniel.abebe@metrostate.edu. *Application contact:* Lucille Maghrak, Graduate Studies Coordinator, 651-793-1932, E-mail: lucille.maghrak@metrostate.edu.

Miami University, Graduate School, College of Arts and Science, Department of Psychology, Oxford, OH 45056. Offers PhD. *Accreditation:* APA. *Students:* 69 full-time (42 women), 1 (woman) part-time; includes 8 minority (3 Black or African American, non-Hispanic/Latino; 5 Asian, non-Hispanic/Latino), 6 international. Average age 28. In 2010, 15 doctorates awarded. *Degree requirements:* For doctorate, comprehensive exam, thesis/dissertation. *Entrance requirements:* For doctorate, GRE General Test, minimum GPA of 2.75 (undergraduate), 3.0 (graduate). Additional exam requirements/recommendations for international students: Required—TOEFL. Application fee: $50. *Expenses:* Tuition, state resident: full-time $11,616; part-time $484 per credit hour. Tuition, nonresident: full-time $25,656; part-time $1069 per credit hour. Required fees: $528. *Financial support:* Fellowships with full tuition reimbursements, research assistantships with full tuition reimbursements, teaching assistantships with full tuition reimbursements, career-related internships or fieldwork, Federal Work-Study, health care benefits, tuition waivers (full), and unspecified assistantships available. Financial award application deadline: 3/1. *Unit head:* Dr. Leonard Mark, Professor and Interim Chair, 513-529-2400, Fax: 513-529-2420, E-mail: marksl@muohio.edu. *Application contact:* Pam Turner, Senior Graduate Program Assistant, 513-529-7224, Fax: 513-529-2420, E-mail: turnerpr@muohio.edu.

Michigan School of Professional Psychology, MA and PsyD Programs in Clinical Psychology, Farmington Hills, MI 48334. Offers MA, Psy D. Part-time programs available. *Faculty:* 7 full-time (3 women), 20 part-time/adjunct (11 women). *Students:* 120 full-time (92 women), 18 part-time (16 women); includes 29 minority (22 Black or African American, non-Hispanic/Latino; 4 Asian, non-Hispanic/Latino; 3 Hispanic/Latino). 126 applicants, 75% accepted, 77 enrolled. In 2010, 41 master's, 20 doctorates awarded. *Degree requirements:* For master's, thesis, practicum; for doctorate, comprehensive exam, thesis/dissertation, internship, practicum. *Entrance requirements:* For master's, undergraduate degree from accredited institution with minimum GPA of 2.5; major in psychology, social work, counseling or equivalent; for doctorate, undergraduate degree from accredited institution with minimum GPA of 2.5; graduate degree from accredited institution with minimum GPA of 3.25; undergraduate or graduate degree in psychology, social work, counseling or equivalent; 500 practicum hours or equivalent field experience. Additional exam requirements/recommendations for international students: Required—TOEFL (minimum score 550 paper-based; 213 computer-based; 79 iBT). *Application deadline:* Applications are processed on a rolling basis. Application fee: $75. Tuition and fees vary according to course load and degree level. *Financial support:* In 2010–11, 6 students received support, including 3 research assistantships (averaging $12,000 per year), 1 teaching assistantship (averaging $12,000 per year); career-related internships or fieldwork, institutionally sponsored loans, and scholarships/grants also available. Financial award application deadline: 6/30; financial award applicants required to submit FAFSA. *Faculty research:* Qualitative research, existential, phenomenological psychology, clinical practice, humanistic. *Unit head:* Dr. Kerry Moustakas, President, 248-476-1122, Fax: 248-476-1125. *Application contact:* Amanda Ming, Admissions and Recruitment Coordinator, 248-476-1122 Ext. 117, Fax: 248-476-1125, E-mail: aming@mispp.edu.

Michigan State University, The Graduate School, College of Social Science, Department of Psychology, East Lansing, MI 48824. Offers MA, PhD. *Accreditation:* APA (one or more programs are accredited). *Entrance requirements:* Additional exam requirements/recommendations for international students: Required—TOEFL (minimum score 550 paper-based; 213 computer-based), Michigan State University ELT (minimum score 85), Michigan English Language Assessment Battery (minimum score 83). Electronic applications accepted.

Middle Tennessee State University, College of Graduate Studies, College of Behavioral and Health Sciences, Department of Psychology, Program in Psychology, Murfreesboro, TN 37132. Offers MA. Part-time and evening/weekend programs available. Postbaccalaureate distance learning degree programs offered. *Students:* 32 full-time (27 women), 77 part-time (52 women); includes 11 Black or African American, non-Hispanic/Latino; 6 Asian, non-Hispanic/Latino; 2 Hispanic/Latino. 141 applicants, 64% accepted, 90 enrolled. In 2010, 37 master's awarded. *Degree requirements:* For master's, one foreign language, comprehensive exam, thesis. *Entrance requirements:* For master's, GRE. Additional exam requirements/recommendations for international students: Required—TOEFL (minimum score 525 paper-based; 195 computer-based; 71 iBT) or IELTS (minimum score 6). *Application deadline:* For fall admission, 6/1 for domestic and international students. Applications are processed on a rolling basis. Application fee: $25 ($30 for international students). Electronic applications accepted. *Expenses:* Tuition, state resident: full-time $4632. Tuition, nonresident: full-time $11,520. *Financial support:* Application deadline: 5/1. *Unit head:* Dr. Dennis Papini, Chair, 615-898-2706, Fax: 615-898-5027. *Application contact:* Dr. Michael Allen, Dean and Vice Provost for Research, 615-898-2840, Fax: 615-904-8020, E-mail: mallen@mtsu.edu.

Midwestern State University, Graduate Studies, College of Humanities and Social Sciences, Department of Psychology, Wichita Falls, TX 76308. Offers MA. Part-time and evening/weekend programs available. *Faculty:* 4 full-time (0 women). *Students:* 13 full-time (12 women), 4 part-time (2 women); includes 1 Black or African American, non-Hispanic/Latino; 1 Asian, non-Hispanic/Latino; 2 Hispanic/Latino. Average age 27. 15 applicants, 47% accepted, 6 enrolled. In 2010, 7 master's awarded. *Degree requirements:* For master's, one foreign language, comprehensive exam, thesis optional. *Entrance requirements:* For master's, GRE General Test, 3 recommendation forms. Additional exam requirements/recommendations for international students: Required—TOEFL (minimum score 550 paper-based; 213 computer-based). *Application deadline:* For fall admission, 7/1 priority date for domestic students, 4/1 for international students; for spring admission, 11/1 priority date for domestic students, 8/1 for international students. Applications are processed on a rolling basis. Application fee: $35 ($50 for international students). Electronic applications accepted. *Expenses:* Tuition, state resident: full-time $1620; part-time $90 per credit hour. Tuition, nonresident: full-time $2160; part-time $120 per credit hour. International tuition: $7200 full-time. *Financial support:* In 2010–11, 16 students received support, including 4 teaching assistantships with partial tuition reimbursements available (averaging $1,875 per year); career-related internships or fieldwork, Federal Work-Study, institutionally sponsored loans, scholarships/grants, tuition waivers (partial), and

Psychology—General

Midwestern State University (continued)

unspecified assistantships also available. Support available to part-time students. Financial award application deadline: 3/1; financial award applicants required to submit FAFSA. *Faculty research:* Child assessment and treatment outcomes, Christianity as it relates to psychology, treatment of behavioral/emotional problems in childhood, -people struggling with HIV/AIDS, educational psychology. *Unit head:* Dr. David Carlston, Graduate Coordinator, 940-397-4718, Fax: 940-397-4929, E-mail: david.carlston@mwsu.edu. *Application contact:* Dr. David Carlston, Graduate Coordinator, 940-397-4718, Fax: 940-397-4929, E-mail: david.carlston@mwsu.edu.

Millersville University of Pennsylvania, College of Graduate and Professional Studies, School of Education, Department of Psychology, Millersville, PA 17551-0302. Offers school counseling (M Ed); school psychology (MS), including clinical psychology, school psychology. Part-time programs available. *Faculty:* 19 full-time (13 women), 8 part-time/adjunct (5 women). *Students:* 64 full-time (54 women), 68 part-time (53 women); includes 2 Black or African American, non-Hispanic/Latino; 1 Asian, non-Hispanic/Latino; 1 Hispanic/Latino, 3 international. Average age 28. 89 applicants, 70% accepted, 37 enrolled. In 2010, 37 master's awarded. *Degree requirements:* For master's, comprehensive exam, thesis optional. *Entrance requirements:* For master's, GRE, 3 letters of recommendation, interview (in-person). Additional exam requirements/recommendations for international students: Required—TOEFL (minimum score 500 paper-based; 183 computer-based; 65 iBT) or IELTS (minimum score 6). *Application deadline:* For fall admission, 1/15 for domestic and international students; for winter admission, 10/1 for domestic and international students; for spring admission, 10/1 for domestic and international students. Application fee: $40 ($50 for international students). Electronic applications accepted. *Expenses:* Tuition, state resident: full-time $6966; part-time $387 per credit. Tuition, nonresident: full-time $11,146; part-time $619 per credit. Required fees: $1829.50; $88 per credit. One-time fee: $60 part-time. Tuition and fees vary according to course load. *Financial support:* In 2010–11, 44 students received support, including 44 research assistantships with full and partial tuition reimbursements available (averaging $5,033 per year); institutionally sponsored loans and unspecified assistantships also available. Support available to part-time students. Financial award application deadline: 3/15; financial award applicants required to submit FAFSA. *Unit head:* Dr. Helena Tuleya-Payne, Chair, 717-872-3925, Fax: 717-871-2480, E-mail: helena.tuleya-payne@millersville.edu. *Application contact:* Dr. Victor S. DeSantis, Dean of Graduate and Professional Studies, 717-872-3099, Fax: 717-872-3453, E-mail: victor.desantis@millersville.edu.

Minnesota State University Mankato, College of Graduate Studies, College of Social and Behavioral Sciences, Department of Psychology, Mankato, MN 56001. Offers clinical psychology (MA); industrial/organizational psychology (MA); school psychology (Psy D). Part-time programs available. *Students:* 57 full-time (38 women), 1 part-time (0 women). *Degree requirements:* For master's, one foreign language, comprehensive exam, thesis (for some programs). *Entrance requirements:* For master's, GRE General Test, GRE Subject Test (clinical psychology), minimum GPA of 3.0 during previous 2 years, 3 letters of reference. Additional exam requirements/recommendations for international students: Required—TOEFL. *Application deadline:* For fall admission, 1/1 priority date for domestic students. Applications are processed on a rolling basis. Application fee: $40. Electronic applications accepted. *Financial support:* Research assistantships, teaching assistantships with full tuition reimbursements, career-related internships or fieldwork, Federal Work-Study, institutionally sponsored loans, and unspecified assistantships available. Support available to part-time students. Financial award application deadline: 3/15; financial award applicants required to submit FAFSA. *Faculty research:* Professional competency in hospitals, mood disturbance, 360-degree feedback, employee selection, planning fallacy. *Unit head:* Dr. Barry Ries, Chairperson, 507-389-2724. *Application contact:* 507-389-2321, E-mail: grad@mnsu.edu.

Mississippi State University, College of Arts and Sciences, Department of Psychology, Mississippi State, MS 39762. Offers cognitive science (PhD); psychology (MS), including clinical psychology, experimental psychology. *Faculty:* 12 full-time (4 women). *Students:* 40 full-time (27 women), 7 part-time (5 women); includes 4 minority (3 Black or African American, non-Hispanic/Latino; 1 Two or more races, non-Hispanic/Latino), 3 international. Average age 26. 77 applicants, 36% accepted, 19 enrolled. In 2010, 10 master's, 1 doctorate awarded. Terminal master's awarded for partial completion of doctoral program. *Degree requirements:* For master's, comprehensive exam, thesis; for doctorate, thesis/dissertation, qualifying exam, comprehensive written and oral exam. *Entrance requirements:* For master's, GRE General Test, minimum GPA of 2.75 on last two years of undergraduate courses; for doctorate, GRE General Test, proficiency in at least 1 computer language. Additional exam requirements/recommendations for international students: Required—TOEFL (minimum score 475 paper-based; 153 computer-based; 53 iBT); Recommended—IELTS (minimum score 4.5). *Application deadline:* For fall admission, 1/15 priority date for domestic students, 5/1 for international students; for spring admission, 11/1 priority date for domestic students, 9/1 for international students. Applications are processed on a rolling basis. Application fee: $40. Electronic applications accepted. *Expenses:* Tuition, state resident: full-time $2730.50; part-time $304 per credit hour. Tuition, nonresident: full-time $6901; part-time $767 per credit hour. *Financial support:* In 2010–11, 6 research assistantships with full tuition reimbursements (averaging $11,925 per year), 13 teaching assistantships with full tuition reimbursements (averaging $9,755 per year) were awarded; career-related internships or fieldwork, Federal Work-Study, institutionally sponsored loans, scholarships/grants, and unspecified assistantships also available. Financial award application deadline: 4/1; financial award applicants required to submit FAFSA. *Faculty research:* Personality type, alcoholism, blindness and low vision, mental retardation, language comprehension. Total annual research expenditures: $2.4 million. *Unit head:* Dr. Stephen B. Klein, Department Head, 662-325-3202, Fax: 662-325-7212, E-mail: sbkl@ra.msstate.edu. *Application contact:* Dr. Kevin J. Armstrong, Graduate Coordinator, 662-325-3202, Fax: 662-325-7212, E-mail: grad@psychology.msstate.edu.

Missouri State University, Graduate College, College of Health and Human Services, Department of Psychology, Springfield, MO 65897. Offers psychology (MS), including clinical psychology, experimental psychology, industrial/organizational psychology. *Degree requirements:* For master's, comprehensive exam, thesis. *Entrance requirements:* For master's, GRE General Test, GRE Subject Test, minimum GPA of 3.25 in major, 3.0 overall; 20 hours of course work in psychology (experimental and statistics). Additional exam requirements/recommendations for international students: Required—TOEFL (minimum score 550 paper-based; 213 computer-based; 79 iBT). Electronic applications accepted. *Expenses:* Tuition, state resident: full-time $3348; part-time $186 per credit hour. Tuition, nonresident: full-time $6696; part-time $372 per credit hour. Required fees: $238 per semester. Tuition and fees vary according to course level, course load and program. *Faculty research:* Work-family conflict, child forensic psychology, sports psychology, body image assessment, visual learning.

Monmouth University, The Graduate School, Department of Psychology, West Long Branch, NJ 07764-1898. Offers mental health counseling (MS); psychological counseling (MA, PMC). *Accreditation:* ACA. Part-time and evening/weekend programs available. *Faculty:* 8 full-time (4 women), 8 part-time/adjunct (6 women). *Students:* 168 full-time (142 women), 122 part-time (108 women); includes 21 Black or African American, non-Hispanic/Latino; 32 American Indian or Alaska Native, non-Hispanic/Latino; 8 Asian, non-Hispanic/Latino; 18 Hispanic/Latino; 5 Two or more races, non-Hispanic/Latino, 1 international. Average age 30. 173 applicants, 74% accepted, 94 enrolled. In 2010, 54 master's awarded. *Degree requirements:* For master's, thesis optional, fieldwork. *Entrance requirements:* For master's, GRE General Test, minimum GPA of 3.0 in major, 24 credits in psychology. Additional exam requirements/recommendations for international students: Required—TOEFL (minimum score 550 paper-based; 213 computer-based; 79 iBT), IELTS (minimum score 5) or Michigan English Language Assessment Battery (minimum score 77), Cambridge A, B, C. *Application deadline:* For fall admission, 7/15 priority date for domestic students, 6/1 for international students; for spring admission, 11/15 priority date for domestic students, 11/1 for international students. Applications are processed on a rolling basis. Application fee: $50. Electronic applications accepted. *Expenses:* Tuition: Full-time $19,572; part-time $816 per credit. Required fees: $628; $157 per semester. *Financial support:* In 2010–11, 224 students received support, including 222 fellowships (averaging $2,288 per year), 18 research assistantships (averaging $7,400 per year); career-related internships or fieldwork, scholarships/grants, and unspecified assistantships also available. Support available to part-time students. Financial award applicants required to submit FAFSA. *Faculty research:* Violent crime, single parenting, the African-American male, counseling older women, successful behavior for under-achieving youth. *Unit head:* Dr. George Kapalka, Director, 732-263-5583, Fax: 732-263-5159, E-mail: gkapalka@monmouth.edu. *Application contact:* Kevin Roane, Director, Office of Graduate Admission, 732-571-3452, Fax: 732-263-5123, E-mail: gradadm@monmouth.edu.

Montana State University, College of Graduate Studies, College of Letters and Science, Department of Psychology, Bozeman, MT 59717. Offers MS. Part-time programs available. *Faculty:* 8 full-time (2 women), 5 part-time/adjunct (4 women). *Students:* 4 full-time (3 women), 6 part-time (5 women). Average age 25. 22 applicants, 36% accepted, 6 enrolled. In 2010, 4 master's awarded. *Degree requirements:* For master's, comprehensive exam, thesis (for some programs). *Entrance requirements:* For master's, GRE General Test. Additional exam requirements/recommendations for international students: Required—TOEFL (minimum score 550 paper-based; 213 computer-based). *Application deadline:* For fall admission, 7/15 priority date for domestic students, 5/15 priority date for international students; for spring admission, 12/1 priority date for domestic students, 10/1 priority date for international students. Applications are processed on a rolling basis. Application fee: $30. Electronic applications accepted. *Expenses:* Tuition, state resident: full-time $5553.90. Tuition, nonresident: full-time $14,646. Required fees: $1233. *Financial support:* In 2010–11, 9 students received support, including 10 teaching assistantships with full tuition reimbursements available (averaging $10,244 per year); unspecified assistantships also available. Financial award application deadline: 3/1; financial award applicants required to submit FAFSA. *Faculty research:* Psychological study of social cognitive, neuro and eating behaviors. Total annual research expenditures: $135,020. *Unit head:* Dr. Keith Hutchison, Interim Department Head, 406-994-5528, Fax: 406-994-3804, E-mail: khutch@montana.edu. *Application contact:* Dr. Carl A. Fox, Vice Provost for Graduate Education, 406-994-4145, Fax: 406-994-7433, E-mail: gradstudy@montana.edu.

Montana State University Billings, College of Arts and Sciences, Department of Psychology, Billings, MT 59101-0298. Offers MS. Part-time programs available. *Degree requirements:* For master's, thesis optional. *Entrance requirements:* For master's, GRE General Test, 3 letters of recommendation, resume.

Montclair State University, The Graduate School, College of Humanities and Social Sciences, Department of Psychology, Montclair, NJ 07043-1624. Offers educational psychology (MA), including child/adolescent clinical psychology, clinical psychology for Spanish/English bilinguals, educational psychology; psychology (MA), including industrial and organizational psychology; school psychology (Certificate). Part-time and evening/weekend programs available. *Faculty:* 25 full-time (11 women), 37 part-time/adjunct (21 women). *Students:* 43 full-time (31 women), 33 part-time (22 women); includes 8 Black or African American, non-Hispanic/Latino; 3 Asian, non-Hispanic/Latino; 10 Hispanic/Latino, 2 international. Average age 26. 117 applicants, 33% accepted, 24 enrolled. In 2010, 23 master's, 1 other advanced degree awarded. *Degree requirements:* For master's, comprehensive exam, thesis or alternative. *Entrance requirements:* For master's, GRE General Test, 2 letters of recommendation. Additional exam requirements/recommendations for international students: Required—TOEFL (minimum iBT score of 83) or IELTS. *Application deadline:* For fall admission, 6/1 for international students; for spring admission, 11/1 for international students. Applications are processed on a rolling basis. Application fee: $60. Electronic applications accepted. *Expenses:* Tuition, state resident: part-time $501.34 per credit. Tuition, nonresident: part-time $773.88 per credit. Required fees: $71.15 per credit. *Financial support:* In 2010–11, 13 research assistantships with full tuition reimbursements (averaging $7,000 per year) were awarded; Federal Work-Study, scholarships/grants, and unspecified assistantships also available. Support available to part-time students. Financial award application deadline: 3/1; financial award applicants required to submit FAFSA. *Faculty research:* Legal decision-making, leadership development, bias and stereotype threat in the selection process, nature of pre-linguistic thought in infants, lateralized cortical contributions to memory, pediatric neuro-imaging, the production and perception of speech, school-based assessment and intervention for bullying, cognitive processes in reading, identification of autism in toddlers. Total annual research expenditures: $300,000. *Unit head:* Dr. Peter Vietze, Chairperson, 973-655-5201. *Application contact:* Amy Aiello, Director of Admissions and Operations, 973-655-5147, Fax: 973-655-7869, E-mail: graduate.school@montclair.edu.

Morehead State University, Graduate Programs, College of Science and Technology, Department of Psychology, Morehead, KY 40351. Offers clinical/counseling psychology (MS); general/experimental psychology (MS). Part-time and evening/weekend programs available. *Degree requirements:* For master's, comprehensive exam, thesis optional. *Entrance requirements:* For master's, GRE General Test, 18 undergraduate hours in psychology, minimum GPA of 3.0, 3 letters of recommendation. Additional exam requirements/recommendations for international students: Required—TOEFL (minimum score 500 paper-based; 173 computer-based). Electronic applications accepted. *Faculty research:* Mood induction effects, serotonin receptor activity, stress, perceptual processes.

Morgan State University, School of Graduate Studies, College of Liberal Arts, Department of Psychology, Baltimore, MD 21251. Offers psychometrics (MS, PhD). *Entrance requirements:* For master's and doctorate, GRE.

Mountain State University, School of Graduate Studies, Program in Psychology, Beckley, WV 25802-9003. Offers MA. *Faculty:* 3 full-time (2 women), 1 part-time/adjunct (0 women). *Students:* 2 full-time (both women), 2 part-time (1 woman). Average age 30. 43 applicants, 51% accepted, 4 enrolled. *Entrance requirements:* For master's, transcripts, 2 references. *Expenses:* Tuition: Full-time $4800; part-time $400 per credit hour. Required fees: $2250; $2250 per credit hour. Tuition and fees vary according to degree level and program. *Unit head:* Dr. William White, Interim Dean, School of Graduate Studies, 304-929-1658, E-mail: wwhite@mountainstate.edu. *Application contact:* Anita Diaz, Enrollment Coordinator of Graduate Studies, 304-929-1731, Fax: 304-929-1710, E-mail: adiaz@mountainstate.edu.

Mount Aloysius College, Program in Psychology, Cresson, PA 16630-1999. Offers MS. *Entrance requirements:* For master's, GRE General Test.

Mount Holyoke College, Department of Psychology and Education, South Hadley, MA 01075. Offers MA.

Mount St. Mary's College, Graduate Division, Program in Counseling Psychology, Los Angeles, CA 90049-1599. Offers counseling psychology (MS); marriage and family therapy (MS); psychology (MS). Part-time and evening/weekend programs available. *Degree requirements:* For master's, research project. *Entrance requirements:* For master's, minimum GPA of 3.0.

Murray State University, College of Humanities and Fine Arts, Program in Psychology, Murray, KY 42071. Offers clinical psychology (MA, MS); psychology (MA, MS). Part-time programs available. *Degree requirements:* For master's, one foreign language, comprehensive exam (for some programs), thesis. *Entrance requirements:* For master's, GRE General Test. Additional exam requirements/recommendations for international students: Required—TOEFL.

National-Louis University, College of Arts and Sciences, Chicago, IL 60603. Offers counseling and human services (MS); language and academic development (M Ed, Certificate); psychology (MA, PhD, Certificate); public policy (MA); written communication (MS, Certificate). Part-time and evening/weekend programs available. Postbaccalaureate distance learning degree programs offered (minimal on-campus study). *Students:* 29 full-time (22 women), 489 part-time (405 women); includes 186 minority (137 Black or African American, non-Hispanic/Latino; 8 Asian, non-Hispanic/Latino; 32 Hispanic/Latino; 9 Two or more races, non-Hispanic/Latino), 2 international. Average age 38. In 2010, 245 master's, 9 doctorates, 24 other advanced degrees awarded. *Degree requirements:* For master's and Certificate, comprehensive exam (for some programs), thesis (for some programs); for doctorate, thesis/dissertation. *Entrance* *requirements:* For master's, MAT or GRE, 3 professional or academic references, interview, minimum GPA of 3.0; for doctorate, GRE General Test, MAT, or Watson-Glaser Critical Thinking Appraisal, three professional or academic references, statement of academic and professional goals, 3 years of experience in field, interview, master's degree, resume, writing sample; for Certificate, GRE, MAT, or Watson-Glaser Critical Thinking Appraisal, three professional or academic references, statement of academic and professional goals, interview, minimum GPA of 3.0. Additional exam requirements/recommendations for international students: Required—Department of Language Studies Assessment or TOEFL (minimum score 550 paper-based; 213 computer-based; 79 iBT). *Application deadline:* Applications are processed on a rolling basis. Application fee: $40. Electronic applications accepted. *Financial support:* Career-related internships or fieldwork, Federal Work-Study, institutionally sponsored loans, scholarships/grants, and tuition waivers available. Support available to part-time students. Financial award applicants required to submit FAFSA. *Unit head:* Dr. Stephen Thompson, Interim Dean, 224-233-2539, Fax: 224-233-2539, E-mail: sthompson@nl.edu. *Application contact:* Dr. George Valcourt, Vice President of Enrollment and Student Services, 888-658-8632, Fax: 312-261-3550, E-mail: george.valcourt@nl.edu.

National University, Academic Affairs, College of Letters and Sciences, Department of Psychology, La Jolla, CA 92037-1011. Offers counseling psychology (MA); human behavior (MA). Part-time and evening/weekend programs available. Postbaccalaureate distance learning degree programs offered (no on-campus study). *Faculty:* 17 full-time (8 women), 209 part-time/adjunct (121 women). *Students:* 429 full-time (355 women), 466 part-time (356 women); includes 664 minority (113 Black or African American, non-Hispanic/Latino; 8 American Indian or Alaska Native, non-Hispanic/Latino; 41 Asian, non-Hispanic/Latino; 188 Hispanic/Latino; 303 Native Hawaiian or other Pacific Islander, non-Hispanic/Latino; 11 Two or more races, non-Hispanic/Latino), 2 international. Average age 36. 623 applicants, 100% accepted, 353 enrolled. In 2010, 266 master's awarded. *Degree requirements:* For master's, thesis (for some programs). *Entrance requirements:* For master's, interview, minimum GPA of 2.5. Additional exam requirements/recommendations for international students: Required—TOEFL (minimum score 550 paper-based; 213 computer-based; 79 iBT), IELTS (minimum score 6). *Application deadline:* Applications are processed on a rolling basis. Application fee: $60 ($65 for international students). Electronic applications accepted. *Expenses:* Tuition: Full-time $9450; part-time $350 per unit. Required fees: $350 per unit. One-time fee: $60. *Financial support:* Career-related internships or fieldwork, institutionally sponsored loans, scholarships/grants, and tuition waivers (partial) available. Support available to part-time students. Financial award application deadline: 6/30; financial award applicants required to submit FAFSA. *Unit head:* Dr. Roland Fleck, Chair and Professor, 858-642-8577, Fax: 858-642-8715, E-mail: rfleck@nu.edu. *Application contact:* Dominick Giovanniello, Associate Regional Dean—San Diego, 800-NAT-UNIV, Fax: 858-541-7792, E-mail: dgiovann@nu.edu.

New Mexico Highlands University, Graduate Studies, College of Arts and Sciences, Department of Behavioral Sciences, Las Vegas, NM 87701. Offers psychology (MS), including clinical psychology, general psychology. Part-time programs available. *Faculty:* 11 full-time (6 women). *Students:* 22 full-time (16 women), 13 part-time (8 women); includes 2 Black or African American, non-Hispanic/Latino; 1 American Indian or Alaska Native, non-Hispanic/Latino; 19 Hispanic/Latino. Average age 28. 8 applicants, 100% accepted, 7 enrolled. In 2010, 3 master's awarded. *Degree requirements:* For master's, comprehensive exam, thesis or alternative. *Entrance requirements:* For master's, minimum undergraduate GPA of 3.0. Additional exam requirements/recommendations for international students: Required—TOEFL (minimum score 540 paper-based; 207 computer-based). *Application deadline:* For fall admission, 8/1 priority date for domestic students. Applications are processed on a rolling basis. Application fee: $15. *Expenses:* Tuition, state resident: full-time $2544. Required fees: $624; $132 per credit hour. *Financial support:* In 2010–11, 28 students received support; teaching assistantships, career-related internships or fieldwork, Federal Work-Study, institutionally sponsored loans, scholarships/grants, tuition waivers (full and partial), and unspecified assistantships available. Support available to part-time students. Financial award application deadline: 3/1; financial award applicants required to submit FAFSA. *Faculty research:* Southwest Native American resettlement development, community-level interventions, neurochemistry of personality, comparative criminal justice, social theory and activism. *Unit head:* Dr. Ian Williamson, Chair, 505-454-3342, E-mail: iwilliamson@nmhu.edu. *Application contact:* Diane Trujillo, Administrative Assistant for Graduate Studies, 505-454-3266, Fax: 505-426-2117, E-mail: dtrujillo@nmhu.edu.

New Mexico State University, Graduate School, College of Arts and Sciences, Department of Psychology, Las Cruces, NM 88003-8001. Offers MA, PhD. Part-time programs available. *Faculty:* 12 full-time (3 women). *Students:* 36 full-time (20 women), 11 part-time (3 women); includes 8 minority (1 Asian, non-Hispanic/Latino; 6 Hispanic/Latino; 1 Two or more races, non-Hispanic/Latino). Average age 30. 60 applicants, 52% accepted, 30 enrolled. In 2010, 6 master's, 4 doctorates awarded. *Degree requirements:* For master's, thesis; for doctorate, comprehensive exam, thesis/dissertation. *Entrance requirements:* For master's, GRE General Test, letters of recommendation, curriculum vitae; for doctorate, GRE General Test, letters of recommendation, master's thesis or proposal, curriculum vitae. *Application deadline:* For fall admission, 2/1 priority date for domestic students, 2/1 for international students. Applications are processed on a rolling basis. Application fee: $30 ($50 for international students). Electronic applications accepted. *Expenses:* Tuition, state resident: full-time $4536; part-time $242 per credit. Tuition, nonresident: full-time $15,816; part-time $712 per credit. Required fees: $636 per term. *Financial support:* In 2010–11, 7 research assistantships with partial tuition reimbursements (averaging $7,499 per year), 29 teaching assistantships with partial tuition reimbursements (averaging $5,793 per year) were awarded; fellowships, career-related internships or fieldwork, Federal Work-Study, and health care benefits also available. Support available to part-time students. Financial award application deadline: 2/15. *Faculty research:* Engineering, cognitive, and social psychology; human/computer interaction; cognitive science. *Unit head:* Dr. James E. McDonald, Head, 575-646-5130, Fax: 575-646-6212, E-mail: jemcdon@nmsu.edu. *Application contact:* Dr. Laura J. Madson, Associate Professor/Chair of Graduate Committee, 575-646-6207, Fax: 575-646-6212, E-mail: lmadson@nmsu.edu.

The New School: A University, The New School for Social Research, Department of Psychology, New York, NY 10011. Offers clinical psychology (PhD); cognitive, social and developmental psychology (PhD); general psychology (MA). *Accreditation:* APA (one or more programs are accredited). Part-time programs available. Terminal master's awarded for partial completion of doctoral program. *Degree requirements:* For master's, comprehensive exam (for some programs), thesis (for some programs); for doctorate, thesis/dissertation, qualifying exam. *Entrance requirements:* For master's, GRE General Test; for doctorate, GRE General Test, MA. Additional exam requirements/recommendations for international students: Required—TOEFL (minimum score 600 paper-based; 250 computer-based; 100 iBT). Electronic applications accepted. *Faculty research:* Consciousness, memory, language, perceptions, psychopathology.

New York University, Graduate School of Arts and Science, Department of Psychology, New York, NY 10012-1019. Offers cognition and perception (PhD); community psychology (PhD); general psychology (MA); industrial/organizational psychology (MA); psychotherapy and psychoanalysis (Advanced Certificate); social/personality psychology (PhD). Part-time programs available. *Students:* 157 full-time (113 women), 257 part-time (175 women); includes 18 Black or African American, non-Hispanic/Latino; 1 American Indian or Alaska Native, non-Hispanic/Latino; 29 Asian, non-Hispanic/Latino; 24 Hispanic/Latino, 64 international. Average age 32. 834 applicants, 39% accepted, 82 enrolled. In 2010, 73 master's, 14 doctorates, 13 other advanced degrees awarded. Terminal master's awarded for partial completion of doctoral program. *Degree requirements:* For master's, comprehensive exam, thesis or alternative; for doctorate, thesis/dissertation. *Entrance requirements:* For master's, GRE General Test, minimum GPA of 3.0; for doctorate, GRE General Test, GRE Subject Test; for Advanced Certificate, doctoral degree, minimum GPA of 3.0. Additional exam requirements/recommendations for international students: Required—TOEFL. *Application deadline:* For fall admission, 12/15 for domestic students. Application fee: $90. *Financial support:* Fellowships with tuition reimbursements, research assistantships with tuition reimbursements, teaching assistantships with tuition

reimbursements, career-related internships or fieldwork, Federal Work-Study, institutionally sponsored loans, scholarships/grants, traineeships, health care benefits, and unspecified assistantships available. Financial award application deadline: 12/15; financial award applicants required to submit FAFSA. *Faculty research:* Vision, memory, social cognition, social and cognitive development, relationships. *Unit head:* Madeline Heilman, Director of PhD Program, 212-998-7900, Fax: 212-995-4018, E-mail: psychq@psych.nyu.edu. *Application contact:* Barry Cohen, Director of MA Program, 212-998-7900, Fax: 212-995-4018, E-mail: psychq@psych.nyu.edu.

New York University, Steinhardt School of Culture, Education, and Human Development, Department of Applied Psychology, Programs in Educational and Developmental Psychology, New York, NY 10012-1019. Offers educational psychology (MA); human development and social intervention (MA); psychological development (PhD); psychology and social intervention (PhD). *Accreditation:* APA (one or more programs are accredited). Part-time programs available. *Faculty:* 24 full-time (16 women). *Students:* 52 full-time (48 women), 33 part-time (29 women); includes 9 Black or African American, non-Hispanic/Latino; 8 Asian, non-Hispanic/Latino; 7 Hispanic/Latino, 14 international. Average age 29. 230 applicants, 35% accepted, 33 enrolled. In 2010, 26 master's, 4 doctorates awarded. *Degree requirements:* For master's, thesis (for some programs); for doctorate, thesis/dissertation. *Entrance requirements:* For doctorate, GRE General Test, interview. Additional exam requirements/recommendations for international students: Required—TOEFL. *Application deadline:* For fall admission, 12/1 priority date for domestic and international students. Applications are processed on a rolling basis. Application fee: $75. Electronic applications accepted. *Financial support:* Teaching assistantships with partial tuition reimbursements, career-related internships or fieldwork, Federal Work-Study, institutionally sponsored loans, and tuition waivers (partial) available. Support available to part-time students. Financial award application deadline: 2/1; financial award applicants required to submit FAFSA. *Faculty research:* High risk children and youth; child and adolescent developments; families and schooling; infant cognition; exploration, language, and symbolic play in toddlerhood. *Unit head:* Dr. LaRue Allen, Director, 212-998-5555, Fax: 212-995-4358. *Application contact:* 212-998-5030, Fax: 212-995-4328, E-mail: steinhardt.gradadmissions@nyu.edu.

Norfolk State University, School of Graduate Studies, School of Liberal Arts, Department of Psychology, Norfolk, VA 23504. Offers community/clinical psychology (MA); psychology (Psy D). Psy D offered through the Virginia Consortium for Professional Psychology; for information call 757-431-4950. Part-time programs available. *Degree requirements:* For master's, comprehensive exam, thesis or alternative; for doctorate, comprehensive exam, thesis/dissertation. *Entrance requirements:* For master's, minimum GPA of 2.7.

North Carolina Central University, Division of Academic Affairs, College of Behavioral and Social Sciences, Department of Psychology, Durham, NC 27707-3129. Offers MA. Part-time and evening/weekend programs available. *Degree requirements:* For master's, one foreign language, comprehensive exam, thesis. *Entrance requirements:* For master's, GRE, minimum GPA of 3.0 in major, 2.5 overall. Additional exam requirements/recommendations for international students: Required—TOEFL. *Faculty research:* Aggression, hypertension, faces, anger, teaching.

North Carolina State University, Graduate School, College of Humanities and Social Sciences, Department of Psychology, Raleigh, NC 27695. Offers developmental psychology (PhD); ergonomics and experimental psychology (PhD); industrial/organizational psychology (PhD); psychology in the public interest (PhD); school psychology (PhD). *Accreditation:* APA. *Degree requirements:* For doctorate, comprehensive exam, thesis/dissertation. *Entrance requirements:* For doctorate, GRE General Test, GRE Subject Test (industrial/organizational psychology), MAT (recommended), minimum GPA of 3.0 in major. Electronic applications accepted. *Faculty research:* Cognitive and social development (human factors, families, the workplace, community issues and health, aging).

Northcentral University, Graduate Studies, Prescott Valley, AZ 86314. Offers business (MBA, DBA, PhD, CAGS); education (M Ed, Ed D, PhD, CAGS); marriage and family therapy (MA, PhD); psychology (MA, PhD, CAGS). Evening/weekend programs available. Postbaccalaureate distance learning degree programs offered (no on-campus study). *Faculty:* 18 full-time (7 women), 449 part-time/adjunct (199 women). *Students:* 8,363 full-time (4,501 women); includes 896 minority (606 Black or African American, non-Hispanic/Latino; 35 American Indian or Alaska Native, non-Hispanic/Latino; 92 Asian, non-Hispanic/Latino; 142 Hispanic/Latino; 13 Native Hawaiian or other Pacific Islander, non-Hispanic/Latino; 8 Two or more races, non-Hispanic/Latino). Average age 43. In 2010, 367 master's, 150 doctorates, 33 other advanced degrees awarded. *Entrance requirements:* For master's, bachelor's degree from regionally-accredited institution, current resume; for doctorate and CAGS, master's degree from regionally-accredited university. Additional exam requirements/recommendations for international students: Required—TOEFL (minimum score 95 computer-based), IELTS (minimum score 7), Pearson Test of English (minimum score: 65). *Application deadline:* Applications are processed on a rolling basis. Application fee: $75. *Financial support:* Scholarships/grants available. *Unit head:* Dr. Clinton D. Gardner, President and Provost, 888-327-2877, Fax: 928-759-6381, E-mail: president@ncu.edu. *Application contact:* Kevin Lustig, Vice President, Enrollment Services, 480-478-7490, Fax: 928-759-6285, E-mail: klustig@ncu.edu.

North Dakota State University, College of Graduate and Interdisciplinary Studies, College of Science and Mathematics, Department of Psychology, Fargo, ND 58108. Offers clinical psychology (MS); cognitive and visual neuroscience (PhD); health and social psychology (PhD); psychology (MS). *Faculty:* 18 full-time (4 women), 2 part-time/adjunct (1 woman). *Students:* 20 full-time (11 women), 3 part-time (0 women); includes 1 Two or more races, non-Hispanic/Latino, 2 international. Average age 24. 41 applicants, 27% accepted, 6 enrolled. In 2010, 7 master's, 2 doctorates awarded. *Degree requirements:* For master's, thesis; for doctorate, thesis/dissertation. *Entrance requirements:* For master's and doctorate, GRE General Test, GRE Subject Test. Additional exam requirements/recommendations for international students: Required—TOEFL (minimum score 525 paper-based; 197 computer-based; 71 iBT). *Application deadline:* For fall admission, 3/1 for domestic and international students. Application fee: $45 ($60 for international students). Electronic applications accepted. *Financial support:* In 2010–11, 2 fellowships with full tuition reimbursements (averaging $16,000 per year), 23 research assistantships with full tuition reimbursements (averaging $16,000 per year), 11 teaching assistantships with full tuition reimbursements (averaging $6,000 per year) were awarded; career-related internships or fieldwork, Federal Work-Study, institutionally sponsored loans, tuition waivers (full and partial), and unspecified assistantships also available. Support available to part-time students. Financial award application deadline: 3/1. *Faculty research:* Cognition science, neuropsychology, group behavior, applied behavior analysis, behavior therapy. Total annual research expenditures: $2 million. *Unit head:* Dr. Paul D. Rokke, Chair, 701-231-8622, Fax: 701-231-8426, E-mail: paul.rokke@ndsu.edu. *Application contact:* Dr. Paul D. Rokke, Chair, 701-231-8622, Fax: 701-231-8426, E-mail: paul.rokke@ndsu.edu.

Northeastern State University, Graduate College, College of Education, Department of Psychology and Counseling, Tahlequah, OK 74464-2399. Offers counseling psychology (MS); school counseling (M Ed); substance abuse counseling (MS). Part-time and evening/weekend programs available. *Students:* 89 full-time (72 women), 100 part-time (80 women); includes 52 minority (5 Black or African American, non-Hispanic/Latino; 41 American Indian or Alaska Native, non-Hispanic/Latino; 2 Asian, non-Hispanic/Latino; 4 Hispanic/Latino), 4 international. In 2010, 40 master's awarded. *Degree requirements:* For master's, thesis (for some programs), written and oral examinations. *Entrance requirements:* For master's, GRE, minimum GPA of 2.5. *Application deadline:* Applications are processed on a rolling basis. Application fee: $0. *Expenses:* Tuition, state resident: part-time $144 per credit hour. Tuition, nonresident: part-time $384.05 per credit hour. Required fees: $34.90 per credit hour. Tuition and fees vary according to program. *Financial support:* Teaching assistantships, career-related internships or fieldwork and Federal Work-Study available. Financial award application deadline: 3/1. *Unit head:* Dr. Kathryn Sanders, Chair, 918-456-5511 Ext. 3016, Fax: 918-458-2397, E-mail: sanderka@

Psychology—General

Northeastern State University (continued)
nsuok.edu. *Application contact:* Margie Railey, Administrative Assistant, 918-456-5511 Ext. 2093, Fax: 918-458-2061, E-mail: railey@nsouk.edu.

Northern Arizona University, Graduate College, College of Social and Behavioral Sciences, Department of Psychology, Flagstaff, AZ 86011. Offers clinical health psychology (MA); general psychology (MA); teaching psychology (MA). Part-time programs available. *Faculty:* 20 full-time (10 women). *Students:* 33 full-time (16 women), 5 part-time (2 women); includes 7 minority (1 American Indian or Alaska Native, non-Hispanic/Latino; 3 Asian, non-Hispanic/Latino; 3 Hispanic/Latino), 2 international. Average age 30. 74 applicants, 24% accepted, 18 enrolled. In 2010, 10 master's awarded. *Degree requirements:* For master's, comprehensive exam (for some programs), thesis (for some programs), oral defense. *Entrance requirements:* For master's, GRE General Test. Additional exam requirements/recommendations for international students: Required—TOEFL (minimum score 550 paper-based; 213 computer-based; 80 iBT), IELTS (minimum score 7). *Application deadline:* For fall admission, 2/1 priority date for domestic and international students. Applications are processed on a rolling basis. Application fee: $65. Electronic applications accepted. *Financial support:* In 2010–11, 11 teaching assistantships with partial tuition reimbursements (averaging $9,709 per year) were awarded; career-related internships or fieldwork, Federal Work-Study, institutionally sponsored loans, scholarships/grants, health care benefits, tuition waivers (full and partial), and unspecified assistantships also available. Support available to part-time students. Financial award applicants required to submit FAFSA. *Unit head:* Dr. Laurie Dickson, Chair, 928-523-1829, Fax: 928-523-6777, E-mail: laurie.dickson@nau.edu. *Application contact:* Janina Burton, Graduate Coordinator, 928-523-3063, Fax: 928-523-6777, E-mail: janina.burton@nau.edu.

Northern Illinois University, Graduate School, College of Liberal Arts and Sciences, Department of Psychology, De Kalb, IL 60115-2854. Offers MA, PhD. *Accreditation:* APA (one or more programs are accredited). *Faculty:* 26 full-time (11 women), 5 part-time/adjunct (1 woman). *Students:* 119 full-time (81 women), 18 part-time (11 women); includes 3 Black or African American, non-Hispanic/Latino; 2 American Indian or Alaska Native, non-Hispanic/Latino; 2 Asian, non-Hispanic/Latino; 6 Hispanic/Latino; 4 Two or more races, non-Hispanic/Latino, 6 international. Average age 28. 376 applicants, 14% accepted, 36 enrolled. In 2010, 19 master's, 10 doctorates awarded. *Degree requirements:* For master's, comprehensive exam, thesis optional; for doctorate, thesis/dissertation, candidacy exam, dissertation defense. *Entrance requirements:* For master's, GRE General Test, minimum GPA of 3.0 for last 2 years of undergraduate work; for doctorate, GRE General Test, minimum undergraduate GPA of 2.75, graduate 3.2; master's degree with research thesis. Additional exam requirements/recommendations for international students: Required—TOEFL (minimum score 550 paper-based; 213 computer-based). *Application deadline:* For fall admission, 3/1 for domestic students, 5/1 for international students; for spring admission, 11/1 for domestic students, 10/1 for international students. Applications are processed on a rolling basis. Application fee: $30. Electronic applications accepted. *Expenses:* Tuition, state resident: full-time $7200; part-time $300 per credit hour. Tuition, nonresident: full-time $14,400; part-time $600 per credit hour. Required fees: $79 per credit hour. *Financial support:* In 2010–11, 22 research assistantships with full tuition reimbursements, 85 teaching assistantships with full tuition reimbursements were awarded; fellowships with full tuition reimbursements, career-related internships or fieldwork, Federal Work-Study, scholarships/grants, tuition waivers (full), and staff assistantships also available. Support available to part-time students. Financial award applicants required to submit FAFSA. *Faculty research:* Neglect syndrome, ADHD, workplace discrimination, adolescent suicide, social dilemmas. *Unit head:* Dr. Gregory A. Waas, Chair, 815-753-7065, E-mail: gwaas@niu.edu. *Application contact:* Dr. Gregory A. Waas, Chair, 815-753-7065, E-mail: gwaas@niu.edu.

Northern Michigan University, College of Graduate Studies, College of Arts and Sciences, Department of Psychology, Marquette, MI 49855-5301. Offers MS. Part-time and evening/weekend programs available. *Degree requirements:* For master's, thesis (for some programs). *Entrance requirements:* For master's, GRE, minimum GPA of 3.0.

Northwestern State University of Louisiana, Graduate Studies and Research, Department of Psychology, Natchitoches, LA 71497. Offers clinical psychology (MS). *Degree requirements:* For master's, comprehensive exam, thesis or alternative. *Entrance requirements:* For master's, GRE General Test, GRE Subject Test, minimum undergraduate GPA of 2.5.

Northwestern University, The Graduate School, Judd A. and Marjorie Weinberg College of Arts and Sciences, Department of Psychology, Evanston, IL 60208. Offers brain, behavior and cognition (PhD); clinical psychology (PhD); cognitive psychology (PhD); personality (PhD); social psychology (PhD); JD/PhD. Admissions and degrees offered through The Graduate School. *Accreditation:* APA (one or more programs are accredited). Part-time programs available. *Degree requirements:* For doctorate, thesis/dissertation. *Entrance requirements:* For doctorate, GRE General Test, GRE Subject Test. Additional exam requirements/recommendations for international students: Required—TOEFL. Electronic applications accepted. *Faculty research:* Memory and higher order cognition, anxiety and depression, effectiveness of psychotherapy, social cognition, molecular basis of memory.

Northwest Missouri State University, Graduate School, College of Education and Human Services, Department of Psychology and Sociology, Maryville, MO 64468-6001. Offers guidance and counseling (MS Ed). Part-time programs available. *Faculty:* 11 full-time (9 women). *Students:* 15 full-time (all women), 31 part-time (28 women); includes 1 Black or African American, non-Hispanic/Latino. 1 applicant, 0% accepted, 0 enrolled. In 2010, 15 master's awarded. *Degree requirements:* For master's, comprehensive exam, thesis. *Entrance requirements:* For master's, GRE General Test, minimum undergraduate GPA of 2.5, 3.0 in major; writing sample. Additional exam requirements/recommendations for international students: Required—TOEFL (minimum score 550 paper-based; 213 computer-based). *Application deadline:* For fall admission, 3/1 for domestic and international students. Applications are processed on a rolling basis. Application fee: $0 ($50 for international students). Electronic applications accepted. *Financial support:* In 2010–11, 4 research assistantships with full tuition reimbursements (averaging $6,000 per year) were awarded; unspecified assistantships also available. Financial award application deadline: 4/1; financial award applicants required to submit FAFSA. *Unit head:* Dr. Carla Edwards, Chairperson, 660-562-1263. *Application contact:* Dr. Gregory Haddock, Dean of Graduate School, 660-562-1145, Fax: 660-562-1096, E-mail: gradsch@nwmissouri.edu.

Northwest University, College of Social and Behavioral Sciences, Kirkland, WA 98033. Offers counseling psychology (MA, Psy D); international care and community development (MA). Evening/weekend programs available. *Faculty:* 5 full-time (2 women), 11 part-time/adjunct (5 women). *Students:* 82 full-time (64 women), 10 part-time (8 women); includes 18 minority (3 Black or African American, non-Hispanic/Latino; 8 Asian, non-Hispanic/Latino; 7 Hispanic/Latino), 1 international. 114 applicants, 68% accepted, 58 enrolled. In 2010, 39 master's awarded. *Entrance requirements:* For master's, 3 character references. Additional exam requirements/recommendations for international students: Required—TOEFL (minimum score 580 paper-based; 237 computer-based). *Application deadline:* For fall admission, 12/1 priority date for domestic and international students; for spring admission, 4/1 priority date for domestic and international students. Applications are processed on a rolling basis. Application fee: $75. *Expenses:* Contact institution. *Financial support:* Career-related internships or fieldwork, health care benefits, and international student scholarships available. Financial award application deadline: 6/30. *Unit head:* Dr. Matt Nelson, Dean, 425-889-5328, Fax: 425-739-4602, E-mail: matt.nelson@northwestu.edu. *Application contact:* Shoshana Weed, Director of Student Services, 425-889-5249, Fax: 425-739-4602, E-mail: shoshana.weed@northwestu.edu.

Notre Dame de Namur University, Division of Academic Affairs, College of Arts and Sciences, Department of Clinical Psychology and Gerontology, Belmont, CA 94002-1908. Offers clinical psychology (MS); clinical psychology: marital and family therapy (MS). Part-time and evening/weekend programs available. *Faculty:* 3 full-time (all women), 6 part-time/adjunct (5 women). *Students:* 26 full-time (24 women), 68 part-time (58 women); includes 34 minority (4

Black or African American, non-Hispanic/Latino; 2 American Indian or Alaska Native, non-Hispanic/Latino; 8 Asian, non-Hispanic/Latino; 17 Hispanic/Latino; 2 Native Hawaiian or other Pacific Islander, non-Hispanic/Latino; 1 Two or more races, non-Hispanic/Latino), 3 international. Average age 35. 66 applicants, 47% accepted, 26 enrolled. In 2010, 15 master's awarded. *Entrance requirements:* For master's, interview, minimum GPA of 2.5. Additional exam requirements/recommendations for international students: Required—TOEFL (minimum score 550 paper-based; 213 computer-based; 79 iBT). *Application deadline:* For fall admission, 8/1 priority date for domestic students; for spring admission, 12/1 priority date for domestic students. Applications are processed on a rolling basis. Application fee: $60. Electronic applications accepted. *Expenses:* Tuition: Full-time $14,220; part-time $790 per credit. Required fees: $35 per semester. Tuition and fees vary according to program. *Financial support:* Career-related internships or fieldwork available. Support available to part-time students. Financial award applicants required to submit FAFSA. *Unit head:* Dr. Nusha Askari, Chair, 650-508-3728, E-mail: naskari@ndnu.edu. *Application contact:* Candace Hallmark, Associate Director of Admissions, 650-508-3600, Fax: 650-508-3426, E-mail: grad.admit@ndnu.edu.

Nova Southeastern University, Center for Psychological Studies, Fort Lauderdale, FL 33314-7796. Offers MS, PhD, Psy D, Psy S, SPS. *Accreditation:* APA (one or more programs are accredited). Postbaccalaureate distance learning degree programs offered. *Faculty:* 34 full-time (11 women), 68 part-time/adjunct (32 women). *Students:* 915 full-time (771 women), 771 part-time (694 women); includes 723 minority (278 Black or African American, non-Hispanic/Latino; 2 American Indian or Alaska Native, non-Hispanic/Latino; 42 Asian, non-Hispanic/Latino; 382 Hispanic/Latino; 2 Native Hawaiian or other Pacific Islander, non-Hispanic/Latino; 17 Two or more races, non-Hispanic/Latino), 39 international. Average age 30. 1,433 applicants, 49% accepted, 520 enrolled. In 2010, 382 master's, 83 doctorates, 34 other advanced degrees awarded. Terminal master's awarded for partial completion of doctoral program. *Degree requirements:* For master's, comprehensive exam, 3 practica; for doctorate, thesis/dissertation, clinical internship, competency exam; for other advanced degree, comprehensive exam, internship. *Entrance requirements:* For doctorate, GRE General Test, GRE Subject Test (recommended), minimum undergraduate GPA of 3.0; for other advanced degree, GRE General Test. Additional exam requirements/recommendations for international students: Required—TOEFL (minimum score 550 paper-based; 213 computer-based). *Application deadline:* Applications are processed on a rolling basis. Application fee: $50. Electronic applications accepted. *Expenses:* Contact institution. *Financial support:* In 2010–11, 5 research assistantships, 34 teaching assistantships (averaging $1,000 per year) were awarded; career-related internships or fieldwork, Federal Work-Study, institutionally sponsored loans, scholarships/grants, and unspecified assistantships also available. Support available to part-time students. Financial award application deadline: 4/1. *Faculty research:* Clinical and child clinical psychology, geriatrics, interpersonal violence. *Unit head:* Karen Grosby, Dean, 954-262-5701, Fax: 954-262-3859, E-mail: grosby@nova.edu. *Application contact:* Carlos Perez, Enrollment Management, 954-262-5790, Fax: 954-262-3893, E-mail: cpsinfo@cps.nova.edu.

The Ohio State University, Graduate School, College of Arts and Sciences, Division of Social and Behavioral Sciences, Department of Psychology, Columbus, OH 43210. Offers behavioral neuroscience (PhD); clinical psychology (PhD); cognitive psychology (PhD); developmental psychology (PhD); mental retardation and developmental disabilities (PhD); psychology (MA); quantitative psychology (PhD); social psychology (PhD). *Accreditation:* APA (one or more programs are accredited). *Faculty:* 60. *Students:* 106 full-time (65 women), 42 part-time (31 women); includes 5 Black or African American, non-Hispanic/Latino; 1 American Indian or Alaska Native, non-Hispanic/Latino; 5 Asian, non-Hispanic/Latino; 10 Hispanic/Latino; 3 Two or more races, non-Hispanic/Latino, 23 international. Average age 27. In 2010, 21 master's, 22 doctorates awarded. *Degree requirements:* For doctorate, thesis/dissertation. *Entrance requirements:* For master's and doctorate, GRE General Test. Additional exam requirements/recommendations for international students: Required—TOEFL (minimum score 600 paper-based; 250 computer-based). *Application deadline:* For fall admission, 12/31 for domestic students, 11/30 for international students. Applications are processed on a rolling basis. Application fee: $40 ($50 for international students). Electronic applications accepted. *Expenses:* Tuition, state resident: full-time $10,605. Tuition, nonresident: full-time $26,535. Tuition and fees vary according to course load and program. *Financial support:* Fellowships, research assistantships, teaching assistantships available. *Unit head:* Dr. Richard Petty, Chair, 614-292-1640, E-mail: petty.1@osu.edu. *Application contact:* 614-292-9444, Fax: 614-292-3895, E-mail: domestic.grad@osu.edu.

Ohio University, Graduate College, College of Arts and Sciences, Department of Psychology, Athens, OH 45701-2979. Offers clinical psychology (PhD); experimental psychology (PhD); organizational psychology (PhD). *Accreditation:* APA. *Students:* 70 full-time (43 women), 23 part-time (14 women); includes 11 minority (3 Black or African American, non-Hispanic/Latino; 2 Asian, non-Hispanic/Latino; 3 Hispanic/Latino; 3 Two or more races, non-Hispanic/Latino), 12 international. 167 applicants, 13% accepted, 13 enrolled. In 2010, 20 doctorates awarded. *Degree requirements:* For doctorate, one foreign language, comprehensive exam, thesis/dissertation. *Entrance requirements:* For doctorate, GRE General Test, GRE Subject Test. Additional exam requirements/recommendations for international students: Required—TOEFL (minimum score 550 paper-based; 80 iBT) or IELTS (minimum score 6.5). *Application deadline:* For fall admission, 1/1 for domestic and international students. Application fee: $50 ($55 for international students). Electronic applications accepted. *Financial support:* Fellowships with full tuition reimbursements, research assistantships with full tuition reimbursements, teaching assistantships with full tuition reimbursements, career-related internships or fieldwork, Federal Work-Study, institutionally sponsored loans, traineeships, tuition waivers (partial), and unspecified assistantships available. Financial award application deadline: 1/15. *Faculty research:* Health, cognitive, child clinical, and social psychology. Total annual research expenditures: $11.2 million. *Unit head:* Dr. Bruce Carlson, Chair, 740-593-1077, Fax: 740-593-0053, E-mail: carlsonb@ohio.edu. *Application contact:* Karyl Jones, Administrative Secretary, 740-593-1090, Fax: 740-593-0579, E-mail: psychology@ohio.edu.

Oklahoma State University, College of Arts and Sciences, Department of Psychology, Stillwater, OK 74078. Offers clinical psychology (PhD); general psychology (MS); lifespan development psychology (PhD). *Accreditation:* APA (one or more programs are accredited). *Faculty:* 26 full-time (13 women), 1 (woman) part-time/adjunct. *Students:* 40 full-time (29 women), 12 part-time (6 women); includes 2 Black or African American, non-Hispanic/Latino; 2 American Indian or Alaska Native, non-Hispanic/Latino; 4 Hispanic/Latino, 1 international. Average age 28. 169 applicants, 10% accepted, 13 enrolled. In 2010, 7 master's, 10 doctorates awarded. *Degree requirements:* For master's, thesis or alternative; for doctorate, comprehensive exam, thesis/dissertation. *Entrance requirements:* For master's and doctorate, GRE General Test. Additional exam requirements/recommendations for international students: Required—TOEFL (minimum score 550 paper-based; 79 iBT). *Application deadline:* For fall admission, 3/1 priority date for international students; for spring admission, 8/1 priority date for international students. Applications are processed on a rolling basis. Application fee: $40 ($75 for international students). Electronic applications accepted. *Expenses:* Tuition, state resident: full-time $3716; part-time $154.85 per credit hour. Tuition, nonresident: full-time $14,892; part-time $621 per credit hour. Required fees: $2044; $85.20 per credit hour. One-time fee: $50. Tuition and fees vary according to course load and campus/location. *Financial support:* In 2010–11, 12 research assistantships (averaging $14,763 per year), 38 teaching assistantships (averaging $13,475 per year) were awarded; career-related internships or fieldwork, Federal Work-Study, scholarships/grants, health care benefits, tuition waivers (partial), and unspecified assistantships also available. Support available to part-time students. Financial award application deadline: 3/1; financial award applicants required to submit FAFSA. *Unit head:* Dr. Larry Mullins, Head, 405-744-6028, Fax: 405-744-8067. *Application contact:* Dr. Gordon Emslie, Dean, 405-744-6368, Fax: 405-744-0355, E-mail: grad-i@okstate.edu.

Old Dominion University, College of Sciences, Doctoral Program in Psychology, Norfolk, VA 23529. Offers applied experimental psychology (PhD); human factors psychology (PhD); industrial/organizational psychology (PhD). *Faculty:* 21 full-time (9 women). *Students:* 32 full-time (21 women), 12 part-time (8 women); includes 2 minority (1 Black or African American, non-Hispanic/Latino; 1 Hispanic/Latino), 4 international. Average age 29. 59 applicants, 24% accepted, 12 enrolled. In 2010, 1 doctorate awarded. *Degree requirements:* For doctorate, thesis/dissertation, candidacy exam. *Entrance requirements:* For doctorate, GRE General Test, GRE Subject Test, 3 recommendation letters. Additional exam requirements/recommendations for international students: Required—TOEFL (minimum score 550 paper-based). *Application deadline:* For winter admission, 1/5 for domestic and international students. Application fee: $50. Electronic applications accepted. *Expenses:* Tuition, state resident: full-time $8592; part-time $358 per credit. Tuition, nonresident: full-time $21,672; part-time $903 per credit. Required fees: $119 per semester. One-time fee: $50. *Financial support:* In 2010–11, 33 students received support, including 4 fellowships with full tuition reimbursements available (averaging $18,000 per year), 4 research assistantships with full tuition reimbursements available (averaging $12,000 per year), 25 teaching assistantships with full tuition reimbursements available (averaging $12,000 per year). Financial award application deadline: 1/15. *Faculty research:* Human factors, industrial psychology, organizational psychology, applied experimental (health, developmental, quantitative). Total annual research expenditures: $978,563. *Unit head:* Dr. Bryan E. Porter, Graduate Program Director, 757-683-4458, Fax: 757-683-5087, E-mail: bporter@odu.edu. *Application contact:* Dr. Bryan E. Porter, Graduate Program Director, 757-683-4458, Fax: 757-683-5087, E-mail: bporter@odu.edu.

Old Dominion University, College of Sciences, Program in Psychology, Norfolk, VA 23529. Offers MS. Part-time programs available. *Faculty:* 20 full-time (9 women). *Students:* 16 full-time (12 women), 4 part-time (3 women); includes 3 minority (2 Black or African American, non-Hispanic/Latino; 1 Asian, non-Hispanic/Latino), 1 international. Average age 26. 28 applicants, 61% accepted, 7 enrolled. In 2010, 11 master's awarded. *Degree requirements:* For master's, comprehensive exam, thesis optional. *Entrance requirements:* For master's, GRE General Test, minimum GPA of 3.0 in major, previous course work in psychology. Additional exam requirements/recommendations for international students: Required—TOEFL. *Application deadline:* For fall admission, 5/15 for domestic and international students. Applications are processed on a rolling basis. Application fee: $40. Electronic applications accepted. *Expenses:* Tuition, state resident: full-time $8592; part-time $358 per credit. Tuition, nonresident: full-time $21,672; part-time $903 per credit. Required fees: $119 per semester. One-time fee: $50. *Financial support:* In 2010–11, 7 students received support, including research assistantships with partial tuition reimbursements available (averaging $9,000 per year), 7 teaching assistantships with partial tuition reimbursements available (averaging $9,000 per year); career-related internships or fieldwork, scholarships/grants, and tuition waivers (partial) also available. Financial award application deadline: 2/15; financial award applicants required to submit FAFSA. *Faculty research:* Social psychology, developmental psychology, physiopsychology, clinical psychology, industrial/organizational psychology. *Unit head:* Dr. Louis H. Janda, Graduate Program Director, 757-683-4211, Fax: 757-683-5087, E-mail: ljanda@odu.edu. *Application contact:* Dr. Louis H. Janda, Graduate Program Director, 757-683-4211, Fax: 757-683-5087, E-mail: ljanda@odu.edu.

Our Lady of the Lake University of San Antonio, School of Professional Studies, Program in Psychology, San Antonio, TX 78207-4689. Offers counseling psychology (MS, Psy D); marriage and family therapy (MS); school psychology (MS). *Accreditation:* APA (one or more programs are accredited). Part-time and evening/weekend programs available. *Students:* 118 full-time (97 women), 94 part-time (85 women); includes 119 minority (20 Black or African American, non-Hispanic/Latino; 2 Asian, non-Hispanic/Latino; 90 Hispanic/Latino; 2 Native Hawaiian or other Pacific Islander, non-Hispanic/Latino; 5 Two or more races, non-Hispanic/Latino), 5 international. Average age 30. In 2010, 842 master's, 4 doctorates awarded. *Degree requirements:* For master's, comprehensive exam, thesis optional, practicum; for doctorate, thesis/dissertation, internship, qualifying exam. *Entrance requirements:* For master's and doctorate, GRE General Test or MAT, interview. Additional exam requirements/recommendations for international students: Required—TOEFL. *Application deadline:* For fall admission, 3/1 priority date for domestic and international students. Applications are processed on a rolling basis. Application fee: $25 ($50 for international students). Electronic applications accepted. *Expenses:* Tuition: Full-time $13,500; part-time $750 per contact hour. Required fees: $330. Tuition and fees vary according to course level, degree level and campus/location. *Financial support:* Research assistantships, teaching assistantships, career-related internships or fieldwork available. Support available to part-time students. Financial award application deadline: 4/15. *Faculty research:* Marriage and family therapy, supervision, cross-cultural counseling, violence. *Unit head:* Dr. Joan Biever, Chair, 210-434-6711, E-mail: jbiever@lake.ollusa.edu. *Application contact:* 210-434-6711, Fax: 210-431-4036, E-mail: gradadm@lake.ollusa.edu.

Pace University, Dyson College of Arts and Sciences, Department of Psychology, Program in Psychology, New York, NY 10038. Offers MA. *Entrance requirements:* Additional exam requirements/recommendations for international students: Required—TOEFL. Electronic applications accepted.

Pacifica Graduate Institute, Graduate Programs, Carpinteria, CA 93013. Offers clinical psychology (PhD); counseling psychology (MA); depth psychology (MA, PhD); mythological studies (MA, PhD). Terminal master's awarded for partial completion of doctoral program. *Degree requirements:* For master's, thesis (for some programs), practicum; for doctorate, comprehensive exam, thesis/dissertation, internship. *Entrance requirements:* For master's, resume, 3 letters of recommendation, writing sample, interview; for doctorate, resumé, 4 letters of recommendation, writing sample, interview. Additional exam requirements/recommendations for international students: Required—TOEFL. *Faculty research:* Imaginal and archetypal theory; post-Colonial psychoanalytic and Jungian theory; myth literature as it applies to the theory and practice of psychology.

Pacific University, School of Professional Psychology, Forest Grove, OR 97116-1797. Offers clinical psychology (MS, Psy D); counseling psychology (MA). *Accreditation:* APA (one or more programs are accredited). Part-time programs available. *Degree requirements:* For master's, comprehensive exam (for some programs), thesis (for some programs); for doctorate, comprehensive exam, thesis/dissertation. *Entrance requirements:* For master's, course work in introductory psychology, statistics, and abnormal psychology; minimum GPA of 3.0; for doctorate, GRE General Test, minimum GPA of 3.0, undergraduate course work in psychology, minimum GPA of 3.1 in last 2 years. Additional exam requirements/recommendations for international students: Required—TOEFL (minimum score 600 paper-based; 105 computer-based). Electronic applications accepted. *Expenses:* Contact institution. *Faculty research:* Neuropsychological assessment, assessment and treatment of anxiety, forensic psychology, cross-cultural psychology, child and adolescent psychopathology.

Palo Alto University, Distance Learning Program in Psychology, Palo Alto, CA 94303-4232. Offers MS. Postbaccalaureate distance learning degree programs offered (no on-campus study). *Entrance requirements:* For master's, GRE General Test. Additional exam requirements/recommendations for international students: Required—TOEFL (minimum score 550 paper-based; 220 computer-based). Electronic applications accepted.

Palo Alto University, Program in Clinical Psychology, Palo Alto, CA 94303-4232. Offers PhD, JD/PhD, MBA/PhD. JD/PhD offered jointly with Golden Gate University; MBA/PhD with Masagung Graduate School of Management. *Accreditation:* APA. *Degree requirements:* For doctorate, comprehensive exam, thesis/dissertation, 2000 hour clinical internship, oral clinical competency exam. *Entrance requirements:* For doctorate, GRE General Test, BA or MA in psychology or related area, minimum undergraduate GPA of 3.0, 3.3 graduate. Additional exam requirements/recommendations for international students: Required—TOEFL. Electronic applications accepted. *Faculty research:* Child/family studies, health psychology, neuropsychology, personality development, assessment.

Penn State Harrisburg, Graduate School, School of Behavioral Sciences and Education, Middletown, PA 17057-4898. Offers M Ed, MA, D Ed. Part-time and evening/weekend programs available. *Financial support:* Career-related internships or fieldwork available. *Unit head:* Dr. William D. Milheim, Director, 717-948-6205, Fax: 717-948-6209, E-mail: wdm2@psu.edu. *Application contact:* Robert Coffman, Director of Admissions, 717-948-6214, E-mail: rwc11@psu.edu.

Penn State University Park, Graduate School, College of the Liberal Arts, Department of Psychology, State College, University Park, PA 16802-1503. Offers MS, PhD. *Accreditation:* APA (one or more programs are accredited). *Unit head:* Dr. Melvin M. Mark, Interim Head, 814-865-9515, Fax: 814-863-7002, E-mail: m5m@psu.edu. *Application contact:* Dr. Melvin M. Mark, Interim Head, 814-865-9515, Fax: 814-863-7002, E-mail: m5m@psu.edu.

Pepperdine University, Graduate School of Education and Psychology, Division of Psychology, Doctor of Psychology Program, Malibu, CA 90263. Offers Psy D. *Faculty:* 50 full-time (29 women), 114 part-time/adjunct (68 women). *Students:* 76 full-time (62 women), 69 part-time (60 women); includes 41 minority (12 Black or African American, non-Hispanic/Latino; 1 American Indian or Alaska Native, non-Hispanic/Latino; 10 Asian, non-Hispanic/Latino; 18 Hispanic/Latino), 2 international. 164 applicants, 25% accepted, 28 enrolled. In 2010, 28 doctorates awarded. *Entrance requirements:* For doctorate, GRE General Test, GRE Subject Test (psychology), autobiographical statement of three to ten typed pages, brief resume of professional experience, two recommendations. Additional exam requirements/recommendations for international students: Required—TOEFL. *Application deadline:* For fall admission, 11/15 priority date for domestic students. Application fee: $55. *Unit head:* Dr. Edward Shafranske, Director, 310-568-5747, E-mail: edward.shafranske@pepperdine.edu. *Application contact:* Deanna Schwartz, Psychology Admissions Manager, 310-568-5777, E-mail: deanna.lazaro@pepperdine.edu.

Philadelphia College of Osteopathic Medicine, Graduate and Professional Programs, Department of Psychology, Philadelphia, PA 19131-1694. Offers clinical psychology (Psy D); counseling and clinical health psychology (MS); organizational leadership and development (MS); psychology (Certificate, Post-Doctoral Certificate); school psychology (MS, Psy D, Ed S). *Accreditation:* APA. *Degree requirements:* For master's, thesis; for doctorate, comprehensive exam, thesis/dissertation, final project, fieldwork. *Entrance requirements:* For master's, GRE or MAT, minimum GPA of 3.0; course work in biology, chemistry, English, physics; for other advanced degree, PRAXIS. *Faculty research:* Depression in primary care, integrated primary care, geriatric mental health.

See Display on next page and Close-Up on page 1167.

Pittsburg State University, Graduate School, College of Education, Department of Psychology and Counseling, Program in Psychology, Pittsburg, KS 66762. Offers MS. *Degree requirements:* For master's, thesis or alternative. *Entrance requirements:* For master's, GRE General Test, minimum GPA of 2.8.

Polytechnic Institute of NYU, Department of Humanities and Social Sciences, Major in Environment-Behavior Studies, Brooklyn, NY 11201-2990. Offers MS, Graduate Certificate. Part-time and evening/weekend programs available. *Students:* 1 applicant, 100% accepted, 0 enrolled. *Degree requirements:* For master's, comprehensive exam (for some programs), thesis (for some programs). *Entrance requirements:* Additional exam requirements/recommendations for international students: Required—TOEFL (minimum score 550 paper-based; 213 computer-based; 80 iBT); Recommended—IELTS (minimum score 6.5). *Application deadline:* For fall admission, 7/31 priority date for domestic students, 4/30 priority date for international students; for spring admission, 12/31 priority date for domestic students, 11/30 priority date for international students. Applications are processed on a rolling basis. Application fee: $55. Electronic applications accepted. *Expenses:* Tuition: Full-time $21,492; part-time $1194 per credit. Required fees: $385 per semester. Tuition and fees vary according to course load. *Financial support:* Institutionally sponsored loans, scholarships/grants, and unspecified assistantships available. Support available to part-time students. *Unit head:* Prof. Kristen Day, Head, 718-260-3999, E-mail: kday@poly.edu. *Application contact:* JeanCarlo Bonilla, Director of Graduate Enrollment Management, 718-260-3182, Fax: 718-260-3624, E-mail: gradinfo@poly.edu.

Pontifical Catholic University of Puerto Rico, College of Graduate Studies in Behavioral Science and Community Affairs, Ponce, PR 00717-0777. Offers clinical psychology (PhD, Psy D); clinical social work (MSW); criminology (MA); industrial psychology (PhD); psychology (PhD); public administration (MSS); rehabilitation counseling (MA). Part-time and evening/weekend programs available. *Degree requirements:* For master's, thesis; for doctorate, comprehensive exam, thesis/dissertation. *Entrance requirements:* For master's, EXADEP, GRE General Test, 3 letters of recommendation, interview, minimum GPA of 2.75.

Pontificia Universidad Catolica Madre y Maestra, Graduate School, Faculty of Social and Administrative Sciences, Santiago, Dominican Republic. Offers business administration (MBA), including business development, finance, international business, management skills (M Mgmt, MBA), marketing, operations, strategic cost management, strategy, tourist destination planning and management; law (LL M), including civil law, corporate business law, criminal law, international relations, real estate law; management (M Mgmt), including higher financial management, insurance program administration, management skills (M Mgmt, MBA); psychology (MA), including clinical child and adolescent psychology, forensic psychology; strategic human resources (EMBA).

Portland State University, Graduate Studies, College of Liberal Arts and Sciences, Department of Psychology, Portland, OR 97207-0751. Offers MA, MS, PhD. *Faculty:* 17 full-time (9 women), 20 part-time/adjunct (6 women). *Students:* 48 full-time (33 women), 11 part-time (9 women); includes 12 minority (1 Black or African American, non-Hispanic/Latino; 2 American Indian or Alaska Native, non-Hispanic/Latino; 3 Asian, non-Hispanic/Latino; 4 Hispanic/Latino; 1 Native Hawaiian or other Pacific Islander, non-Hispanic/Latino; 1 Two or more races, non-Hispanic/Latino), 2 international. Average age 30. 16 applicants, 88% accepted, 11 enrolled. In 2010, 11 master's awarded. *Degree requirements:* For master's, variable foreign language requirement, thesis; for doctorate, variable foreign language requirement, comprehensive exam, thesis/dissertation. *Entrance requirements:* For master's, GRE General Test, minimum GPA of 3.0 in upper-division course work or 2.75 overall, 3 letters of recommendation. Additional exam requirements/recommendations for international students: Required—TOEFL (minimum score 550 paper-based; 213 computer-based). *Application deadline:* For fall admission, 12/15 for domestic and international students. Application fee: $50. *Expenses:* Tuition, state resident: full-time $8505; part-time $315 per credit. Tuition, nonresident: full-time $13,284; part-time $492 per credit. Required fees: $1482; $21 per credit, $99 per term. One-time fee: $120. Part-time tuition and fees vary according to course load and program. *Financial support:* In 2010–11, 1 research assistantship with full tuition reimbursement (averaging $10,657 per year), 37 teaching assistantships with full tuition reimbursements (averaging $10,094 per year) were awarded; career-related internships or fieldwork, Federal Work-Study, scholarships/grants, tuition waivers (partial), and unspecified assistantships also available. Support available to part-time students. Financial award application deadline: 3/1; financial award applicants required to submit FAFSA. *Faculty research:* Organizational psychology, work and the family, quantitative psychology, decision-making, psychosocial factors affecting health. Total annual research expenditures: $1.2 million. *Unit head:* Dr. Sherwin Davidson, Chair, 503-725-4854, Fax: 503-725-3904, E-mail: davidsons@pdx.edu. *Application contact:* Dr. Sherwin Davidson, Chair, 503-725-4854, Fax: 503-725-3904, E-mail: davidsons@pdx.edu.

Portland State University, Graduate Studies, Systems Science Program, Portland, OR 97207-0751. Offers computational intelligence (Certificate); computer modeling and simulation (Certificate); systems science (MS); systems science/anthropology (PhD); systems science/business administration (PhD); systems science/civil engineering (PhD); systems science/economics (PhD); systems science/engineering management (PhD); systems science/general (PhD); systems science/mathematical sciences (PhD); systems science/mechanical engineering (PhD); systems science/psychology (PhD); systems science/sociology (PhD). *Faculty:* 4 full-time (0 women), 1 part-time/adjunct (0 women). *Students:* 15 full-time (4 women), 35 part-time (11

Psychology—General

Portland State University (continued)
women); includes 1 American Indian or Alaska Native, non-Hispanic/Latino; 1 Asian, non-Hispanic/Latino; 1 Two or more races, non-Hispanic/Latino; 4 international. Average age 39. 8 applicants, 88% accepted, 5 enrolled. In 2010, 2 master's, 4 doctorates awarded. *Degree requirements:* For doctorate, variable foreign language requirement, thesis/dissertation. *Entrance requirements:* For master's, 2 letters of recommendation; for doctorate, GMAT, GRE General Test, minimum undergraduate GPA of 3.0. Additional exam requirements/recommendations for international students: Required—TOEFL. *Application deadline:* For fall admission, 2/1 for domestic students; for spring admission, 11/1 for domestic students. Application fee: $50. *Expenses:* Tuition, state resident: full-time $8505; part-time $315 per credit. Tuition, nonresident: full-time $13,284; part-time $492 per credit. Required fees: $1482; $21 per credit. $99 per term. One-time fee: $120. Part-time tuition and fees vary according to course load and program. *Financial support:* In 2010–11, 1 research assistantship with full tuition reimbursement (averaging $7,704 per year) was awarded; teaching assistantships with full tuition reimbursements, career-related internships or fieldwork, Federal Work-Study, scholarships/grants, and unspecified assistantships also available. Support available to part-time students. Financial award application deadline: 3/1; financial award applicants required to submit FAFSA. *Faculty research:* Systems theory and methodology, artificial intelligence neural networks, information theory, nonlinear dynamics/chaos, modeling and simulation. *Unit head:* George Lendaris, Acting Director, 503-725-4960. *Application contact:* Dawn Sharafi, Administrative Assistant, 503-725-4960, E-mail: dawn@sysc.pdx.edu.

Princeton University, Graduate School, Department of Psychology, Princeton, NJ 08544-1019. Offers neuroscience (PhD); psychology (PhD). *Degree requirements:* For doctorate, thesis/dissertation. *Entrance requirements:* For doctorate, GRE General Test, GRE Subject Test. Additional exam requirements/recommendations for international students: Required—TOEFL (minimum score 550 paper-based). Electronic applications accepted.

Purdue University, Graduate School, College of Liberal Arts, Department of Psychological Sciences, West Lafayette, IN 47907. Offers PhD. *Accreditation:* APA. *Entrance requirements:* For doctorate, GRE General Test. Additional exam requirements/recommendations for international students: Required—TOEFL. Electronic applications accepted. *Faculty research:* Career development of women in science, development of friendships during childhood and adolescence, social competence, human information processing.

Queens College of the City University of New York, Division of Graduate Studies, Mathematics and Natural Sciences Division, Department of Psychology, Flushing, NY 11367-1597. Offers clinical behavioral applications in mental health settings (MA); psychology (MA). Part-time programs available. *Faculty:* 27 full-time (13 women). *Students:* 13 full-time (10 women), 92 part-time (78 women); includes 7 Black or African American, non-Hispanic/Latino; 1 American Indian or Alaska Native, non-Hispanic/Latino; 7 Asian, non-Hispanic/Latino; 14 Hispanic/Latino, 6 international. 134 applicants, 47% accepted, 48 enrolled. In 2010, 28 master's awarded. *Degree requirements:* For master's, comprehensive exam, thesis or alternative. *Entrance requirements:* For master's, GRE, minimum GPA of 3.0. Additional exam requirements/recommendations for international students: Required—TOEFL. *Application deadline:* For fall admission, 4/1 for domestic students; for spring admission, 11/1 for domestic students. Applications are processed on a rolling basis. Application fee: $125. *Financial support:* Career-related internships or fieldwork, Federal Work-Study, institutionally sponsored loans, and tuition waivers (partial) available. Support available to part-time students. Financial award application deadline: 4/1; financial award applicants required to submit FAFSA. *Unit head:* Dr. Richard Bodnar, Chairperson, 718-997-3200. *Application contact:* Dr. Philip Ramsey, Graduate Adviser, 718-997-3200, E-mail: philip_ramsey@qc.edu.

Queen's University at Kingston, School of Graduate Studies and Research, Faculty of Arts and Sciences, Department of Psychology, Kingston, ON K7L 3N6, Canada. Offers brain behavior and cognitive science (MA, PhD); clinical psychology (MA, PhD); developmental psychology (MA, PhD); social personality psychology (MA, PhD). *Accreditation:* APA (one or more programs are accredited). *Degree requirements:* For master's, thesis; for doctorate, comprehensive exam, thesis/dissertation. *Entrance requirements:* For master's and doctorate, GRE General Test. Additional exam requirements/recommendations for international students: Required—TOEFL. *Faculty research:* Human development, social, personality, behavioral neuroscience, forensic.

Radford University, College of Graduate and Professional Studies, College of Humanities and Behavioral Sciences, Program in Psychology, Radford, VA 24142. Offers clinical psychology (MA, MS); experimental psychology (MA, MS); general psychology (MS); industrial/organizational psychology (MA, MS). Part-time programs available. *Faculty:* 18 full-time (7 women), 4 part-time/adjunct (2 women). *Students:* 41 full-time (29 women); includes 6 minority (4 Black or African American, non-Hispanic/Latino; 1 Asian, non-Hispanic/Latino; 1 Hispanic/Latino). Average age 23. 107 applicants, 71% accepted, 23 enrolled. In 2010, 21 master's awarded. *Degree requirements:* For master's, comprehensive exam, thesis (for some programs). *Entrance requirements:* For master's, GRE, minimum GPA of 3.0; 3 letters of reference; essay. Additional exam requirements/recommendations for international students: Required—TOEFL (minimum score 550 paper-based; 213 computer-based; 79 iBT). *Application deadline:* For fall admission, 2/15 priority date for domestic students, 12/1 for international students; for spring admission, 7/1 for international students. Applications are processed on a rolling basis. Application fee: $50. Electronic applications accepted. *Expenses:* Tuition, state resident: full-time $5746; part-time $239 per credit hour. Tuition, nonresident: full-time $14,174; part-time $591 per credit hour. Required fees: $2634; $111 per credit hour. *Financial support:* In 2010–11, 33 students received support, including 18 research assistantships with partial tuition reimbursements available (averaging $8,000 per year), 14 teaching assistantships with partial tuition reimbursements available (averaging $8,700 per year); career-related internships or fieldwork, institutionally sponsored loans, scholarships/grants, and unspecified assistantships also available. Financial award application deadline: 3/1; financial award applicants required to submit FAFSA. *Unit head:* Dr. Hilary M. Lips, Chair, 540-831-5387, Fax: 540-831-6113, E-mail: hlips@radford.edu. *Application contact:* Rebecca Conner, Graduate Admissions Office, 540-831-5431, Fax: 540-831-6061, E-mail: gradcollege@radford.edu.

Regis University, College for Professional Studies, School of Humanities and Social Sciences, MA Program, Denver, CO 80221-1099. Offers communication (MA); fine arts (Certificate); interdisciplinary studies (MA); mediation and conflict resolution (Certificate); psychology (MA); social justice, peace, and reconciliation (Certificate); technical communication (Certificate). Program also offered in Henderson and Las Vegas (Summerlin), NV. Part-time and evening/weekend programs available. Postbaccalaureate distance learning degree programs offered (minimal on-campus study). *Degree requirements:* For master's, thesis, research project. *Entrance requirements:* For master's, resume, recommendations. Additional exam requirements/recommendations for international students: Required—TOEFL (minimum score 213 computer-based), TWE (minimum score 5). Electronic applications accepted. *Expenses:* Contact institution. *Faculty research:* Independent/nonresidential graduate study: new methods and models, adult learning and the capstone experience, Goal Setting, behavior of Adult students, Innovative Studies for Community Colleges.

Rhode Island College, School of Graduate Studies, Faculty of Arts and Sciences, Department of Psychology, Providence, RI 02908-1991. Offers health psychology (CGS); psychology (MA). Part-time and evening/weekend programs available. *Faculty:* 3 full-time (1 woman). *Students:* 4 full-time (all women), 11 part-time (7 women); includes 2 minority (1 American Indian or Alaska Native, non-Hispanic/Latino; 1 Hispanic/Latino). Average age 32. In 2010, 4 master's awarded. *Degree requirements:* For master's, comprehensive exam. *Entrance requirements:* For master's, GRE, 3 letters of recommendation. Additional exam requirements/recommendations for international students: Recommended—TOEFL (minimum score 550 paper-based; 213 computer-based; 79 iBT). *Application deadline:* For fall admission, 3/1 for domestic students; for spring admission, 11/1 for domestic students. Applications are processed on a rolling basis. Application fee: $50. *Expenses:* Tuition, state resident: full-time $8208; part-time $342 per credit hour. Tuition, nonresident: full-time $16,080; part-time $670 per credit

hour. Required fees: $554; $20 per credit. $72 per term. *Financial support:* In 2010–11, 3 teaching assistantships with full tuition reimbursements (averaging $4,550 per year) were awarded; Federal Work-Study, scholarships/grants, health care benefits, and unspecified assistantships also available. Support available to part-time students. Financial award application deadline: 5/15; financial award applicants required to submit FAFSA. *Unit head:* Dr. Thomas Malloy, Chair, 401-456-8015. *Application contact:* Graduate Studies, 401-456-8700.

Rice University, Graduate Programs, School of Humanities, Department of Religious Studies, Houston, TX 77251-1892. Offers African religions (PhD); African-American religions (PhD); contemplative studies (PhD); gnosticism, esotericism, mysticism (PhD); Islam (PhD); Jewish thought and philosophy (PhD); modern Christianity in thought and popular culture (PhD); psychology of religion (PhD); the Bible and beyond (PhD). *Degree requirements:* For doctorate, 2 foreign languages, comprehensive exam, thesis/dissertation. *Entrance requirements:* For doctorate, GRE, letters of recommendation, writing sample. Additional exam requirements/recommendations for international students: Required—TOEFL (minimum score 600 paper-based; 90 iBT). Electronic applications accepted. *Faculty research:* Origins and historical development of Islam, history of Christianity, the study of comparative religion, African-American religion, religion and culture.

Rice University, Graduate Programs, School of Social Sciences, Department of Psychology, Houston, TX 77251-1892. Offers cognitive sciences (MA, PhD); industrial-organizational/social psychology (MA, PhD); psychology (MA, PhD). Terminal master's awarded for partial completion of doctoral program. *Degree requirements:* For master's, thesis; for doctorate, thesis/dissertation. *Entrance requirements:* For doctorate, GRE General Test, minimum GPA of 3.0. Additional exam requirements/recommendations for international students: Required—TOEFL. Electronic applications accepted. *Faculty research:* Cognitive, cognitive neuropsychology, human factors, human-computer interaction, industrial-organizational psychology.

Richmont Graduate University, Graduate Programs, Atlanta, GA 30327. Offers Christian psychological studies (MS); marriage and family therapy (MA); professional counseling (MA).

Rivier College, School of Graduate Studies, Department of Psychology, Nashua, NH 03060. Offers clinical psychology (MS); experimental psychology (MS). *Faculty:* 5 full-time (2 women). *Students:* 10 full-time (7 women). Average age 28. 9 applicants, 11% accepted, 1 enrolled. In 2010, 4 master's awarded. Application fee: $25. *Expenses:* Tuition: Part-time $456 per credit. *Unit head:* Dr. Howard Goodman, Department Coordinator, 603-897-8602, E-mail: hgoodman@rivier.edu. *Application contact:* Mathew Kittredge, Director of Graduate Admissions, 603-897-8229, Fax: 603-897-8810, E-mail: mkittredge@rivier.edu.

Rochester Institute of Technology, Graduate Enrollment Services, College of Liberal Arts, Department of Psychology, Rochester, NY 14623-5603. Offers MS. Part-time programs available. *Students:* 47 full-time (37 women), 4 part-time (all women); includes 1 Black or African American, non-Hispanic/Latino; 1 Asian, non-Hispanic/Latino; 1 Two or more races, non-Hispanic/Latino, 3 international. Average age 27. 64 applicants, 58% accepted, 16 enrolled. In 2010, 18 master's awarded. *Degree requirements:* For master's, thesis. *Entrance requirements:* For master's, GRE, minimum GPA of 3.0. Additional exam requirements/recommendations for international students: Required—TOEFL (minimum score 580 paper-based; 237 computer-based; 92 iBT) or IELTS (minimum score 7). *Application deadline:* For fall admission, 2/1 priority date for domestic and international students; for winter admission, 11/1 for domestic and international students; for spring admission, 2/1 for domestic and international students. Applications are processed on a rolling basis. Electronic applications accepted. *Expenses:* Tuition: Full-time $33,234; part-time $924 per credit hour. Required fees: $219. *Financial support:* Research assistantships with partial tuition reimbursements, teaching assistantships with partial tuition reimbursements, career-related internships or fieldwork, scholarships/grants, and unspecified assistantships available. Support available to part-time students. Financial award applicants required to submit FAFSA. *Faculty research:* Perception, cognitive neuroscience, human factors in complex systems, developmental psychopathology, hemispheric specialization. *Unit head:* Dr. Andrew Herbert, Chair, 585-475-4554, Fax: 585-475-7120, E-mail: psychdept@rit.edu. *Application contact:* Diane Ellison, Assistant Vice President, Graduate Enrollment Services, 585-475-2229, Fax: 585-475-7164, E-mail: gradinfo@rit.edu.

Roosevelt University, Graduate Division, College of Arts and Sciences, Department of Psychology, Program in Clinical Psychology, Chicago, IL 60605. Offers MA, Psy D.

Rosalind Franklin University of Medicine and Science, College of Health Professions, Department of Psychology, North Chicago, IL 60064-3095. Offers clinical counseling (MS); psychology (MS, PhD). *Accreditation:* APA. Terminal master's awarded for partial completion of doctoral program. *Degree requirements:* For master's, capstone experience. *Entrance requirements:* For master's, minimum GPA of 3.0, bachelor's degree (preferably in related subject); for doctorate, GRE, minimum GPA of 3.0, bachelor's or master's degree. Additional exam requirements/recommendations for international students: Required—TOEFL. *Faculty research:* Anxiety, pain, psychopathy, epilepsy, neuropsychology.

Rowan University, Graduate School, College of Liberal Arts and Sciences, Department of Psychology, Glassboro, NJ 08028-1701. Offers applied behavioral analysis (MA); clinical mental health counseling (MA); mental health counseling (MA). Part-time and evening/weekend programs available. *Faculty:* 7 full-time (4 women), 6 part-time/adjunct (1 woman). *Students:* 7 part-time (all women). Average age 30. 66 applicants, 48% accepted. In 2010, 10 master's awarded. *Degree requirements:* For master's, thesis. *Entrance requirements:* For master's, GRE General Test. Additional exam requirements/recommendations for international students: Required—TOEFL. *Application deadline:* Applications are processed on a rolling basis. Application fee: $65 ($200 for international students). Electronic applications accepted. *Expenses:* Tuition, area resident: Part-time $602 per semester hour. Tuition, nonresident: part-time $602 per semester hour. Required fees: $100 per semester hour. One-time fee: $10 part-time. *Financial support:* Career-related internships or fieldwork, scholarships/grants, health care benefits, and unspecified assistantships available. *Unit head:* Dr. Horacio Sosa, Dean, College of Graduate and Continuing Education, 856-256-4747, Fax: 856-256-5638, E-mail: sosa@rowan.edu. *Application contact:* Karen Haynes, Graduate Coordinator, 856-256-4052, Fax: 856-256-4436, E-mail: haynes@rowan.edu.

Rutgers, The State University of New Jersey, Camden, Graduate School of Arts and Sciences, Program in Psychology, Camden, NJ 08102. Offers MA. Part-time and evening/weekend programs available. *Faculty:* 11 full-time (6 women), 2 part-time/adjunct (0 women). *Students:* 13 full-time (7 women), 16 part-time (10 women); includes 2 Black or African American, non-Hispanic/Latino; 2 Hispanic/Latino, 4 international. Average age 27. 71 applicants, 32% accepted, 7 enrolled. In 2010, 1 master's awarded. *Degree requirements:* For master's, thesis, 30 credits. *Entrance requirements:* For master's, GRE, 3 letters of recommendation; statement of personal, professional, and academic goals; prerequisite course work in introductory psychology, statistics and experimental psychology. Additional exam requirements/recommendations for international students: Required—TOEFL, IELTS. *Application deadline:* For fall admission, 3/1 priority date for domestic students; for spring admission, 12/1 priority date for domestic students. Applications are processed on a rolling basis. Application fee: $65. Electronic applications accepted. *Expenses:* Tuition, state resident: full-time $4963; part-time $319 per credit. Tuition, nonresident: full-time $10,493; part-time $680 per credit. *Financial support:* In 2010–11, 21 students received support, including 9 fellowships with partial tuition reimbursements available (averaging $622 per year); Federal Work-Study, scholarships/grants, and tuition waivers (partial) also available. Financial award application deadline: 3/15; financial award applicants required to submit FAFSA. *Faculty research:* Cognitive psychology, sexuality, health psychology, personality psychology, clinical psychology. Total annual research expenditures: $232,175. *Unit head:* Dr. Mary Bravo, Director, 856-225-6431, E-mail: gradpsych@camden.rutgers.edu. *Application contact:* Dr. Mary Bravo, Director, 856-225-6431, E-mail: gradpsych@camden.rutgers.edu.

Rutgers, The State University of New Jersey, Newark, Graduate School, Program in Psychology, Newark, NJ 07102. Offers cognitive neuroscience (PhD); cognitive science (PhD); perception (PhD); psychobiology (PhD); social cognition (PhD). *Faculty:* 15 full-time (5 women), 6 part-time/adjunct (all women). *Students:* 23 full-time (19 women), 2 part-time (1 woman); includes 3 Black or African American, non-Hispanic/Latino; 1 Asian, non-Hispanic/Latino; 2 Hispanic/Latino. 48 applicants, 17% accepted, 6 enrolled. In 2010, 4 doctorates awarded. *Degree requirements:* For doctorate, comprehensive exam, thesis/dissertation. *Entrance requirements:* For doctorate, GRE General Test, GRE Subject Test, minimum undergraduate B average. *Application deadline:* For fall admission, 2/1 for domestic students; for spring admission, 11/1 for domestic students. Application fee: $60. Electronic applications accepted. *Expenses:* Tuition, state resident: part-time $600 per credit. Tuition, nonresident: full-time $10,694. *Financial support:* In 2010–11, 16 students received support, including 9 fellowships with full and partial tuition reimbursements available (averaging $18,000 per year), 8 teaching assistantships with full and partial tuition reimbursements available (averaging $23,112 per year); career-related internships or fieldwork, health care benefits, and minority scholarships also available. Financial award application deadline: 2/1. *Faculty research:* Visual perception (luminance, motion), neuroendocrine mechanisms in behavior (reproduction, pain), attachment theory, connectionist modeling of cognition. *Unit head:* Dr. Kenneth Kressel, Director, 973-353-5440 Ext. 232, Fax: 973-353-1171, E-mail: kkressel@andromeda.rutgers.edu. *Application contact:* Jason Hand, Director of Admissions, 973-353-5205, Fax: 973-353-1440.

See Display on page 991 and Close-Up on page 1169.

Rutgers, The State University of New Jersey, New Brunswick, Graduate School-New Brunswick, Program in Psychology, Piscataway, NJ 08854-8097. Offers behavioral neuroscience (PhD); clinical psychology (PhD); cognitive psychology (PhD); interdisciplinary health psychology (PhD); social psychology (PhD). *Accreditation:* APA. *Degree requirements:* For doctorate, comprehensive exam, thesis/dissertation. *Entrance requirements:* For doctorate, GRE General Test, 3 letters of recommendation. Additional exam requirements/recommendations for international students: Required—TOEFL (minimum score 577 paper-based; 233 computer-based). Electronic applications accepted. *Expenses:* Tuition, state resident: full-time $7200; part-time $600 per credit. Tuition, nonresident: full-time $11,124; part-time $927 per credit. *Faculty research:* Learning and memory, behavioral ecology, hormones and behavior, psychopharmacology, anxiety disorders.

Sage Graduate School, Graduate School, School of Health Sciences, Department of Psychology, Troy, NY 12180-4115. Offers community psychology (MA), including child care and children's services, community counseling, community health education, community psychology, general psychology; counseling and community psychology (MA). Part-time and evening/weekend programs available. *Faculty:* 3 full-time (all women), 8 part-time/adjunct (7 women). *Students:* 39 full-time (38 women), 49 part-time (43 women); includes 12 minority (8 Black or African American, non-Hispanic/Latino; 1 Asian, non-Hispanic/Latino; 3 Hispanic/Latino). Average age 29. 72 applicants, 46% accepted, 20 enrolled. In 2010, 27 master's awarded. *Degree requirements:* For master's, thesis or alternative. *Entrance requirements:* For master's, GRE General Test. Additional exam requirements/recommendations for international students: Required—TOEFL (minimum score 550 paper-based; 213 computer-based). *Application deadline:* Applications are processed on a rolling basis. Application fee: $40. *Expenses:* Tuition: Full-time $10,980; part-time $610 per credit hour. Tuition and fees vary according to course load, degree level and program. *Financial support:* Fellowships, research assistantships, Federal Work-Study, scholarships/grants, and unspecified assistantships available. Support available to part-time students. Financial award application deadline: 3/1; financial award applicants required to submit FAFSA. *Faculty research:* Effectiveness of arts integration programs in elementary/secondary schools, literacy-based substance abuse program, outcome evaluation of program to increase college entry among urban youth. *Unit head:* Dr. Esther Haskevitz, Interim Dean, School of Health Sciences, 518-244-2296, Fax: 518-244-4571, E-mail: haskve@sage.edu. *Application contact:* Dr. Jean Poppei, Chair, 518-244-2076, Fax: 518-244-4545, E-mail: poppej@sage.edu.

St. Cloud State University, School of Graduate Studies, College of Education, Department of Counselor Education, Higher Education, and Educational Psychology, St. Cloud, MN 56301-4498. Offers college counseling and student development (MS); higher education administration (MS, Ed D); rehabilitation counseling (MS); school counseling (MS). *Degree requirements:* For master's, thesis or alternative. *Entrance requirements:* For master's, GRE General Test, minimum GPA of 2.75. Additional exam requirements/recommendations for international students: Required—Michigan English Language Assessment Battery; Recommended—TOEFL (minimum score 550 paper-based; 213 computer-based), IELTS (minimum score 6.5). Electronic applications accepted.

St. John's University, St. John's College of Liberal Arts and Sciences, Department of Psychology, Queens, NY 11439. Offers clinical psychology (MA, PhD), including clinical psychology (MA), clinical psychology-child (PhD), clinical psychology-general (PhD); general experimental psychology (MA); school psychology (MS, Psy D). *Accreditation:* APA (one or more programs are accredited). Part-time and evening/weekend programs available. *Students:* 149 full-time (125 women), 103 part-time (88 women); includes 53 minority (14 Black or African American, non-Hispanic/Latino; 15 Asian, non-Hispanic/Latino; 20 Hispanic/Latino; 4 Two or more races, non-Hispanic/Latino), 12 international. Average age 26. 526 applicants, 23% accepted, 55 enrolled. In 2010, 57 master's, 37 doctorates awarded. *Degree requirements:* For master's, comprehensive exam, thesis optional; for doctorate, comprehensive exam, thesis/dissertation, internship. *Entrance requirements:* For master's, GRE, GRE subject (varies), minimum GPA of 3.0, 2 writing samples, transcripts, 3 letters of recommendation, personal essay; for doctorate, GRE General Test, GRE Subject Test, interview. Additional exam requirements/recommendations for international students: Required—TOEFL (minimum score 600 paper-based; 250 computer-based; 100 iBT), IELTS (minimum score 5.5). *Application deadline:* For fall admission, 1/15 priority date for domestic and international students; for spring admission, 11/1 priority date for domestic and international students. Applications are processed on a rolling basis. Application fee: $70. Electronic applications accepted. *Expenses:* Contact institution. *Financial support:* Fellowships, research assistantships, career-related internships or fieldwork, scholarships/grants, and unspecified assistantships available. Support available to part-time students. Financial award application deadline: 3/1; financial award applicants required to submit FAFSA. *Faculty research:* Clinical psychology, school psychology, developmental psychopathology, risky behaviors and health, cognitive behavior treatments for trauma, assessment and treatment of anger problems, development of mathematical reasoning, personality disorders and depression. Total annual research expenditures: $1.1 million. *Unit head:* Dr. Raymond DiGiuseppe, Chair, 718-990-1955, E-mail: digiuser@stjohns.edu. *Application contact:* Kathleen Davis, Director of Graduate Admissions, 718-990-1601, Fax: 718-990-5686, E-mail: gradhelp@stjohns.edu.

Saint Joseph's University, College of Arts and Sciences, Department of Criminal Justice, Philadelphia, PA 19131-1395. Offers administration/police executive (MS); behavior analysis (MS, Post-Master's Certificate); criminal justice (MS, Post-Master's Certificate); criminology (MS); federal law (MS); intelligence and crime (MS); probation, parole, and corrections (MS). Part-time and evening/weekend programs available. Postbaccalaureate distance learning degree programs offered (no on-campus study). *Faculty:* 6 full-time (all women), 37 part-time/adjunct (26 women). *Students:* 50 full-time (35 women), 406 part-time (267 women). Average age 34. 193 applicants, 85% accepted, 140 enrolled. In 2010, 124 master's awarded. *Degree requirements:* For master's, thesis. *Entrance requirements:* For master's, GRE General Test or minimum GPA of 3.0, 2 letters of recommendation. Additional exam requirements/recommendations for international students: Required—TOEFL (minimum score 550 paper-based; 213 computer-based; 79 iBT). *Application deadline:* For fall admission, 7/15 priority date for domestic students, 4/15 for international students; for winter admission, 1/15 for international students; for spring admission, 11/15 priority date for domestic students, 10/15 for international students. Applications are processed on a rolling basis. Application fee: $35. Electronic applications accepted. *Expenses:* Tuition: Part-time $729 per credit. Tuition and

Psychology—General

Saint Joseph's University (continued)

fees vary according to course load, degree level and program. *Financial support:* Career-related internships or fieldwork and unspecified assistantships available. Financial award applicants required to submit FAFSA. *Unit head:* Patricia Griffin, Director, 610-660-1294, E-mail: pgriffin@sju.edu. *Application contact:* Kate McConnell, Director, Graduate College of Arts and Sciences Admissions and Retention, 610-660-3184, Fax: 610-660-3230, E-mail: kate.mconnell@sju.edu.

Saint Joseph's University, College of Arts and Sciences, Department of Psychology, Philadelphia, PA 19131-1395. Offers MS. Evening/weekend programs available. *Faculty:* 12 full-time (6 women), 1 (woman) part-time/adjunct. *Students:* 27 full-time (23 women); includes 3 Black or African American, non-Hispanic/Latino; 1 Asian, non-Hispanic/Latino; 1 Two or more races, non-Hispanic/Latino. Average age 24. 59 applicants, 36% accepted, 19 enrolled. In 2010, 12 master's awarded. *Entrance requirements:* For master's, GRE General Test, 2 letters of recommendation, official transcripts, personal statement, psychology insert. Additional exam requirements/recommendations for international students: Required—TOEFL (minimum score 550 paper-based; 213 computer-based; 79 iBT). *Application deadline:* For fall admission, 3/1 priority date for domestic and international students; for winter admission, 1/15 for international students; for spring admission, 11/15 for domestic students, 10/15 for international students. Application fee: $35. Electronic applications accepted. *Expenses:* Tuition: Part-time $729 per credit. Tuition and fees vary according to course load, degree level and program. *Financial support:* Teaching assistantships, unspecified assistantships available. Financial award applicants required to submit FAFSA. *Faculty research:* Early child care and development, preschool quality. Total annual research expenditures: $374,500. *Unit head:* Dr. Jodi Mindell, Director, 610-660-1806, E-mail: jmindell@sju.edu. *Application contact:* Kate McConnell, Director, Graduate College of Arts and Sciences Admissions and Retention, 610-660-3184, Fax: 610-660-3230, E-mail: kate.mcconnell@sju.edu.

Saint Louis University, Graduate Education, College of Arts and Sciences and Graduate Education, Department of Psychology, St. Louis, MO 63103-2097. Offers clinical psychology (MS-R, PhD); experimental psychology (MS-R, PhD); industrial-organizational psychology (PhD); psychology (PhD). *Accreditation:* APA (one or more programs are accredited). Part-time programs available. *Degree requirements:* For master's, comprehensive exam, thesis; for doctorate, thesis/dissertation, clinical internship (for clinical psychology PhD). *Entrance requirements:* For master's, GRE General Test, interview, letters of recommendation, resume; for doctorate, GRE General Test, interview, letters of recommendation, resumé, transcripts, goal statement. Additional exam requirements/recommendations for international students: Required—TOEFL (minimum score 550 paper-based; 213 computer-based). Electronic applications accepted. *Faculty research:* Violence and trauma; neural basis of learning and memory function; eating disorders; body image and health behavior; prejudice, stereotyping, and victimization; memory, cognitive aging and language processing.

Saint Mary's University, Faculty of Science, Department of Psychology, Halifax, NS B3H 3C3, Canada. Offers applied psychology (M Sc, PhD), including industrial/organizational psychology (M Sc). Part-time programs available. *Degree requirements:* For master's, thesis, 500-hour internship; for doctorate, comprehensive exam, thesis/dissertation, research project. *Entrance requirements:* For master's and doctorate, GRE General Test. *Faculty research:* Assessment, health psychology, social psychology, cognition.

St. Mary's University, Graduate School, Department of Psychology, San Antonio, TX 78228-8507. Offers clinical psychology (MA, MS); industrial/organizational psychology (MA, MS). Part-time programs available. *Degree requirements:* For master's, comprehensive exam. *Entrance requirements:* For master's, GRE General Test, letters of recommendation, work experience. Additional exam requirements/recommendations for international students: Required—TOEFL (minimum score 550 paper-based; 213 computer-based; 80 iBT). Electronic applications accepted.

Saint Xavier University, Graduate Studies, School of Arts and Sciences, Department of Psychology, Chicago, IL 60655-3105. Offers adult counseling (Certificate); child/adolescent counseling (Certificate); core counseling (Certificate); counseling psychology (MA). Part-time and evening/weekend programs available. *Entrance requirements:* For master's, GRE General Test, minimum GPA of 3.0, interview.

Salem State University, School of Graduate Studies, Program in Counseling and Psychological Services, Salem, MA 01970-5353. Offers MS, Graduate Certificate. Part-time and evening/weekend programs available. *Students:* 48 full-time (36 women), 54 part-time (40 women); includes 3 Black or African American, non-Hispanic/Latino; 3 Asian, non-Hispanic/Latino; 6 Hispanic/Latino, 6 international. 33 applicants, 88% accepted, 29 enrolled. In 2010, 24 master's, 4 other advanced degrees awarded. *Entrance requirements:* For master's, GRE or MAT. Additional exam requirements/recommendations for international students: Required—TOEFL (minimum score 550 paper-based; 80 iBT) or IELTS (minimum score 5.5). *Application deadline:* For fall admission, 5/1 for domestic students; for spring admission, 10/1 for domestic students. Applications are processed on a rolling basis. Application fee: $50. *Expenses:* Tuition, state resident: full-time $2520; part-time $290 per credit hour. Tuition, nonresident: full-time $4140; part-time $380 per credit hour. Required fees: $2700. *Financial support:* Career-related internships or fieldwork, Federal Work-Study, scholarships/grants, and unspecified assistantships available. Support available to part-time students. Financial award application deadline: 5/1; financial award applicants required to submit FAFSA. *Unit head:* Dr. Patrice Miller, Coordinator, 978-542-6075, Fax: 978-542-6596, E-mail: pmiller@salemstate.edu. *Application contact:* Dr. Lee A. Brossoit, Assistant Dean of Graduate Admissions, 978-542-6673, Fax: 978-542-7215, E-mail: lbrossoit@salemstate.edu.

Sam Houston State University, College of Humanities and Social Sciences, Department of Psychology and Philosophy, Huntsville, TX 77341. Offers clinical psychology (PhD); psychology (MA). *Accreditation:* APA. Part-time programs available. *Faculty:* 13 full-time (5 women), 1 part-time/adjunct (0 women). *Students:* 62 full-time (52 women), 31 part-time (24 women); includes 5 Black or African American, non-Hispanic/Latino; 3 Asian, non-Hispanic/Latino; 6 Hispanic/Latino, 5 international. Average age 26. 113 applicants, 29% accepted, 24 enrolled. In 2010, 20 master's, 4 doctorates awarded. *Degree requirements:* For master's, thesis. *Entrance requirements:* For master's, GRE General Test or MAT, minimum GPA of 3.0. Additional exam requirements/recommendations for international students: Required—TOEFL (minimum score 550 paper-based; 213 computer-based; 79 iBT). *Application deadline:* For fall admission, 8/1 for domestic students; for spring admission, 12/1 for domestic students. Applications are processed on a rolling basis. Application fee: $20. *Expenses:* Tuition, state resident: full-time $1363; part-time $163 per credit hour. Tuition, nonresident: full-time $3856; part-time $473 per credit hour. *Financial support:* Research assistantships, teaching assistantships, career-related internships or fieldwork and institutionally sponsored loans available. Support available to part-time students. Financial award application deadline: 5/31; financial award applicants required to submit FAFSA. *Unit head:* Dr. Christopher Wilson, Chair, 936-294-3052, Fax: 936-294-3798, E-mail: psy_dcw@shsu.edu. *Application contact:* Dr. Jeffrey Anastasi, Coordinator, 936-294-3049, Fax: 936-294-3798, E-mail: jsa001@shsu.edu.

San Diego State University, Graduate and Research Affairs, College of Sciences, Department of Psychology, San Diego, CA 92182. Offers clinical psychology (MS, PhD); industrial and organizational psychology (MS); program evaluation (MS); psychology (MA). PhD offered jointly with University of California, San Diego. *Accreditation:* APA (one or more programs are accredited). Terminal master's awarded for partial completion of doctoral program. *Degree requirements:* For master's, thesis, oral exam; for doctorate, thesis/dissertation. *Entrance requirements:* For master's, GRE General Test, GRE Subject Test, 3 letters of recommendation; for doctorate, GRE General Test, GRE Subject Test, minimum GPA of 3.0, 3 letters of recommendation. Additional exam requirements/recommendations for international students: Required—TOEFL. Electronic applications accepted.

San Francisco State University, Division of Graduate Studies, College of Behavioral and Social Sciences, Department of Psychology, San Francisco, CA 94132-1722. Offers clinical psychology (MS); developmental psychology (MA); industrial/organizational psychology (MS); psychological research (MA); school psychology (MS); social psychology (MA). *Financial support:* Teaching assistantships available. Financial award application deadline: 3/1. *Unit head:* Dr. Julia Lewis, Chair, 415-338-7555, E-mail: jmlewis@sfsu.edu. *Application contact:* Leslye M. Tinson, Assistant to the Chair, 415-338-7555, E-mail: ltinson@sfsu.edu.

San Jose State University, Graduate Studies and Research, College of Social Sciences, Department of Psychology, San Jose, CA 95192-0001. Offers clinical psychology (MS); experimental psychology (MA); industrial/organizational psychology (MS); psychology (MA). *Degree requirements:* For master's, comprehensive exam, thesis (for some programs). *Entrance requirements:* For master's, GRE General Test, minimum GPA of 3.0. Electronic applications accepted. *Faculty research:* Drug and alcohol abuse, neurohormonal mechanisms in motion sickness, behavior modification, sleep research, genetics.

Saybrook University, Graduate College of Psychology and Humanistic Studies, San Francisco, CA 94111-1920. Offers clinical psychology (Psy D); human science (MA, PhD), including consciousness and spirituality, humanistic and transpersonal psychology, integrative health studies, organizational systems, social transformation, transformative social change (MA); organizational systems (MA, PhD), including consciousness and spirituality, humanistic and transpersonal psychology, integrative health studies, leadership of sustainable systems (MA), organizational systems, social transformation; psychology (MA, PhD), including clinical psychology (PhD), consciousness and spirituality, creativity studies (MA), humanistic and transpersonal psychology, integrative health studies, Jungian studies, marriage and family therapy (MA), organizational systems, social transformation. Postbaccalaureate distance learning degree programs offered (minimal on-campus study). *Faculty:* 15 full-time (5 women), 83 part-time/adjunct (34 women). *Students:* 479 full-time (333 women); includes 30 Black or African American, non-Hispanic/Latino; 1 American Indian or Alaska Native, non-Hispanic/Latino; 13 Asian, non-Hispanic/Latino; 18 Hispanic/Latino, 18 international. Average age 43. 280 applicants, 52% accepted, 105 enrolled. In 2010, 28 master's, 43 doctorates awarded. Terminal master's awarded for partial completion of doctoral program. *Degree requirements:* For master's, thesis or alternative; for doctorate, thesis/dissertation. *Entrance requirements:* Additional exam requirements/recommendations for international students: Required—TOEFL (minimum score 580 paper-based; 237 computer-based; 93 iBT). *Application deadline:* For fall admission, 6/1 priority date for domestic students; for spring admission, 12/16 priority date for domestic students. Application fee: $50. Electronic applications accepted. *Financial support:* In 2010–11, 335 students received support. Scholarships/grants available. Financial award applicants required to submit FAFSA. *Faculty research:* Humanistic theory, health studies, organizational systems, consciousness and spirituality, social transformation. Total annual research expenditures: $90,000. *Unit head:* Mark Schulman, President, 800-825-4480, Fax: 415-433-9271. *Application contact:* Director of Admissions, 800-825-4480, Fax: 415-433-9271, E-mail: admissions@saybrook.edu.

Saybrook University, LIOS Graduate College, Kirkland, WA 98033. Offers leadership and organization development (MA); systems counseling (MA). *Faculty:* 10 full-time (5 women), 5 part-time/adjunct (2 women). *Students:* 108 full-time (87 women); includes 16 minority (4 Black or African American, non-Hispanic/Latino; 1 American Indian or Alaska Native, non-Hispanic/Latino; 3 Asian, non-Hispanic/Latino; 3 Hispanic/Latino; 1 Native Hawaiian or other Pacific Islander, non-Hispanic/Latino; 4 Two or more races, non-Hispanic/Latino), 3 international. Average age 35. 55 applicants, 69% accepted, 34 enrolled. In 2010, 45 master's awarded. *Degree requirements:* For master's, thesis (for some programs), oral exams. *Entrance requirements:* For master's, bachelor's degree from an accredited university or college. Additional exam requirements/recommendations for international students: Recommended—IELTS, TWE. *Application deadline:* For fall admission, 6/1 priority date for domestic and international students; for winter admission, 12/2 priority date for domestic and international students. Applications are processed on a rolling basis. Application fee: $50. *Financial support:* In 2010–11, 101 students received support. Federal Work-Study and scholarships/grants available. Financial award application deadline: 6/1; financial award applicants required to submit FAFSA. *Unit head:* Dr. Judy Heinrich, Dean, 425-968-3400, Fax: 425-968-3406, E-mail: jheinrich@lios.saybrook.edu. *Application contact:* Jennifer Herron, Director, Academic Admissions, 425-968-3400, Fax: 425-968-4306, E-mail: jherron@lios.saybrook.edu.

The School of Professional Psychology at Forest Institute, Graduate Programs, Springfield, MO 65807. Offers applied behavior analysis (MS); clinical psychology (MA, Psy D); counseling psychology (MA); marriage and family therapy (MA, PGC). *Accreditation:* AAMFT/COAMFTE; APA (one or more programs are accredited). *Faculty:* 17 full-time (8 women), 18 part-time/adjunct (10 women). *Students:* 214 full-time (144 women), 46 part-time (35 women); includes 35 minority (11 Black or African American, non-Hispanic/Latino; 9 American Indian or Alaska Native, non-Hispanic/Latino; 5 Asian, non-Hispanic/Latino; 10 Hispanic/Latino), 3 international. Average age 28. 176 applicants, 69% accepted, 45 enrolled. In 2010, 35 master's, 31 doctorates awarded. Terminal master's awarded for partial completion of doctoral program. *Degree requirements:* For master's, thesis, practicum; for doctorate, comprehensive exam, thesis/dissertation, internship, practicum. *Entrance requirements:* For master's, GRE General Test, interview, minimum GPA of 3.0, 12 hours in psychology; for doctorate, GRE General Test, interview, minimum GPA of 3.0, 18 hours in psychology. Additional exam requirements/recommendations for international students: Required—TOEFL (minimum score 550 paper-based; 213 computer-based). *Application deadline:* For fall admission, 1/15 priority date for domestic and international students; for spring admission, 8/1 priority date for domestic and international students. Applications are processed on a rolling basis. Application fee: $50. Electronic applications accepted. *Financial support:* In 2010–11, 59 students received support; fellowships with partial tuition reimbursements available, teaching assistantships, career-related internships or fieldwork, Federal Work-Study, scholarships/grants, tuition waivers (partial), and unspecified assistantships available. Financial award applicants required to submit FAFSA. *Faculty research:* Forensics/corrections, marriage and family therapy, child and adolescent, integrated health care, neuropsychology. *Unit head:* Dr. Mark E. Skrade, President, 417-823-3477, Fax: 417-823-3442, E-mail: mskrade@forest.edu. *Application contact:* Bethany Ritter, Admissions Counselor, 417-823-3477, Fax: 417-823-3442, E-mail: britter@forest.edu.

Seattle University, College of Arts and Sciences, Department of Psychology, Seattle, WA 98122-1090. Offers existential and phenomenological therapeutic psychology (MA Psych). *Degree requirements:* For master's, thesis. *Entrance requirements:* For master's, interview, minimum GPA of 3.0, previous undergraduate course work in psychology. *Faculty research:* Healing, transformations in relationships, therapy, dialogical research.

Seton Hall University, College of Arts and Sciences, Department of Psychology, South Orange, NJ 07079-2697. Offers experimental psychology (MS), including behavioral neuroscience. Part-time and evening/weekend programs available. *Entrance requirements:* For master's, GRE. Additional exam requirements/recommendations for international students: Required—TOEFL. Electronic applications accepted. *Faculty research:* Behavioral neuroscience, cognitive psychology, social psychology, perception/motor skills, memory, depression, anxiety.

Seton Hall University, College of Education and Human Services, Department of Professional Psychology and Family Therapy, South Orange, NJ 07079-2697. Offers counseling psychology (MA, PhD); marriage and family therapy (MS, PhD, Ed S); psychological studies (MA); school psychology (Ed S). *Accreditation:* APA. Part-time and evening/weekend programs available. Postbaccalaureate distance learning degree programs offered (minimal on-campus study). Terminal master's awarded for partial completion of doctoral program. *Degree requirements:* For master's, comprehensive exam, case study; for doctorate, comprehensive exam, thesis/dissertation, internship; for Ed S, comprehensive exam, internship. *Entrance requirements:* For master's, GRE or MAT; for doctorate, GRE, interview; for Ed S, GRE or MAT, interview. *Faculty research:* Counseling process, ethics, family systems, child pathology.

Shippensburg University of Pennsylvania, School of Graduate Studies, College of Arts and Sciences, Department of Psychology, Shippensburg, PA 17257-2299. Offers applied track (MS); general/reading track (MS); research track (MS). Part-time and evening/weekend programs available. *Faculty:* 9 full-time (3 women). *Students:* 22 full-time (13 women), 7 part-time (5 women); includes 5 minority (2 Black or African American, non-Hispanic/Latino; 1 Asian, non-Hispanic/Latino; 2 Hispanic/Latino), 2 international. Average age 24. 54 applicants, 46% accepted, 15 enrolled. In 2010, 14 master's awarded. *Degree requirements:* For master's, comprehensive exam (for some programs), thesis (for some programs). *Entrance requirements:* For master's, minimum GPA of 2.75, 1 course in statistics, 6 undergraduate credit hours in psychology, supplemental form with personal goals statement. Additional exam requirements/recommendations for international students: Required—TOEFL (minimum score 580 paper-based; 237 computer-based); Recommended—IELTS (minimum score 6). *Application deadline:* For fall admission, 4/1 priority date for domestic students, 3/1 for international students; for spring admission, 11/1 priority date for domestic students, 7/1 for international students. Applications are processed on a rolling basis. Application fee: $30. Electronic applications accepted. *Expenses:* Tuition, state resident: full-time $6966. Tuition, nonresident: full-time $11,146. Required fees: $1802. *Financial support:* In 2010–11, 8 research assistantships with full tuition reimbursements (averaging $5,000 per year) were awarded; career-related internships or fieldwork, scholarships/grants, unspecified assistantships, and resident hall director and student payroll positions also available. Support available to part-time students. Financial award application deadline: 3/1; financial award applicants required to submit FAFSA. *Unit head:* Dr. Suzanne Morin, Chairperson, 717-477-1657, Fax: 717-477-4057, E-mail: smmori@ship.edu. *Application contact:* Jeremy R. Goshorn, Associate Dean of Graduate Admissions, 717-477-1231, Fax: 717-477-4016, E-mail: jrgoshorn@ship.edu.

Simmons College, College of Arts and Sciences Graduate Studies, Program in Behavior Analysis, Boston, MA 02115. Offers MS, PhD. Part-time programs available. *Degree requirements:* For doctorate, thesis/dissertation. Electronic applications accepted. *Expenses:* Contact institution. *Faculty research:* Verbal behavior for children with autism spectrum disorder, stimulus equivalence for teaching academic skills, analysis and treatment of obesity and health related issues, innovative pedagogy in higher education, organizational behavior management.

Simon Fraser University, Graduate Studies, Faculty of Arts and Social Sciences, Department of Psychology, Burnaby, BC V5A 1S6, Canada. Offers MA, PhD. *Accreditation:* APA (one or more programs are accredited). *Degree requirements:* For master's, thesis; for doctorate, thesis/dissertation. *Entrance requirements:* For master's and doctorate, GRE, minimum GPA of 3.5. Additional exam requirements/recommendations for international students: Required—TOEFL or IELTS. *Expenses:* Contact institution. *Faculty research:* Social cognition/biological neuropsychology, theory and methods.

Southeastern Baptist Theological Seminary, Graduate and Professional Programs, Wake Forest, NC 27588-1889. Offers advanced biblical studies (M Div); Christian education (M Div, MACE); Christian ethics (PhD); Christian ministry (M Div); Christian planting (M Div); church music (MACM); counseling (MACO); evangelism (PhD); language (M Div); ministry (D Min); New Testament (PhD); Old Testament (PhD); philosophy (PhD); theology (Th M, PhD); women's studies (M Div). *Accreditation:* ACIPE; ATS (one or more programs are accredited). *Degree requirements:* For master's, thesis (for some programs), oral exam; for doctorate, thesis/dissertation, fieldwork; for M Div, supervised ministry. *Entrance requirements:* For master's, Cooperative English Test, minimum GPA of 2.0, M Div or equivalent (Th M); for doctorate, GRE General Test or MAT, Cooperative English Test, M Div or equivalent, 3 years of professional experience.

Southeastern Louisiana University, College of Arts, Humanities and Social Sciences, Department of Psychology, Hammond, LA 70402. Offers MA. Part-time programs available. *Faculty:* 6 full-time (4 women). *Students:* 19 full-time (15 women), 10 part-time (9 women); includes 2 minority (1 Black or African American, non-Hispanic/Latino; 1 Asian, non-Hispanic/Latino), 1 international. Average age 24. 42 applicants, 57% accepted, 14 enrolled. In 2010, 7 master's awarded. *Degree requirements:* For master's, comprehensive exam, thesis. *Entrance requirements:* For master's, GRE (minimum combined score 950), minimum GPA of 3.0, 18 undergraduate hours in psychology/educational psychology, 3 letters of reference. Additional exam requirements/recommendations for international students: Required—TOEFL (minimum score 500 paper-based; 173 computer-based; 61 iBT). *Application deadline:* For fall admission, 7/15 priority date for domestic students, 6/1 priority date for international students; for spring admission, 12/1 priority date for domestic students, 10/1 priority date for international students. Applications are processed on a rolling basis. Application fee: $20 ($30 for international students). Electronic applications accepted. *Expenses:* Tuition, state resident: full-time $3533. Tuition, nonresident: full-time $12,002. Required fees: $907. Tuition and fees vary according to degree level. *Financial support:* In 2010–11, 10 students received support, including 10 research assistantships (averaging $9,220 per year); career-related internships or fieldwork, Federal Work-Study, and institutionally sponsored loans also available. Support available to part-time students. Financial award application deadline: 5/1; financial award applicants required to submit FAFSA. *Faculty research:* Evolution and religion, eating disorders, body image and adult psychopathology (clinical psychology), performance system management (industrial/organizational psychology), social cognition, the impact of trauma on children. *Unit head:* Dr. Matt Rossano, Department Head, 985-549-2154, Fax: 985-549-6892, E-mail: mrossano@selu.edu. *Application contact:* Sandra Meyers, Graduate Admissions Analyst, 985-549-5620, Fax: 985-549-5632, E-mail: admissions@selu.edu.

Southern Adventist University, School of Education and Psychology, Collegedale, TN 37315-0370. Offers clinical mental health counseling (MS); inclusive education (MS Ed); instructional leadership (MS Ed); literacy education (MS Ed); outdoor teacher education (MS Ed); school counseling (MS). *Accreditation:* NCATE. Part-time and evening/weekend programs available. *Degree requirements:* For master's, comprehensive exam (for some programs), thesis optional, position paper (MS), portfolio (MS Ed in outdoor teacher education). *Entrance requirements:* For master's, interview (MS); 9 semester hours of upper division course work in psychology or related field, including 1 course in psychology research or statistics; 9 semester hours of education (MS Ed). Additional exam requirements/recommendations for international students: Required—TOEFL (minimum score 600 paper-based; 250 computer-based; 100 iBT). Electronic applications accepted.

Southern California Seminary, Graduate and Professional Programs, El Cajon, CA 92019. Offers Biblical studies (MABS); counseling psychology (MACP); marriage and family therapy (MAMFT); psychology (Psy D); religious studies (MRS); theology (M Div). Part-time and evening/weekend programs available. Postbaccalaureate distance learning degree programs offered (minimal on-campus study). *Students:* 37 full-time (8 women), 80 part-time (37 women); includes 55 minority (20 Black or African American, non-Hispanic/Latino; 14 Asian, non-Hispanic/Latino; 16 Hispanic/Latino; 1 Native Hawaiian or other Pacific Islander, non-Hispanic/Latino; 4 Two or more races, non-Hispanic/Latino), 5 international. Average age 41. In 2010, 7 first professional degrees, 50 master's, 4 doctorates awarded. *Degree requirements:* For master's, thesis (for some programs); for doctorate, thesis/dissertation; for M Div, 2 foreign languages. *Entrance requirements:* For doctorate, master's degree in psychology. Additional exam requirements/recommendations for international students: Required—TOEFL (minimum score 550 paper-based). *Application deadline:* For fall admission, 8/13 for domestic and international students; for spring admission, 12/11 for domestic students, 12/15 for international students. Applications are processed on a rolling basis. Application fee: $31 ($126 for international students). Electronic applications accepted. *Expenses:* Tuition: Part-time $339 per unit. Part-time tuition and fees vary according to degree level, campus/location and program. *Financial support:* In 2010–11, 14 students received support. Federal Work-Study, scholarships/grants, and tuition waivers (partial) available. Financial award application deadline: 3/1; financial award applicants required to submit FAFSA. *Unit head:* Dr. Chuck Emert, Vice-President of Academics, 619-201-8995, Fax: 619-201-8975. *Application contact:* Thomas Pittman, Admissions Officer and Director of Student Services, 888-389-7244, Fax: 619-201-8975, E-mail: thpittman@socalsem.edu.

Southern Connecticut State University, School of Graduate Studies, School of Arts and Sciences, Department of Psychology, New Haven, CT 06515-1355. Offers MA. Part-time and evening/weekend programs available. *Faculty:* 20 full-time (13 women). *Students:* 19 full-time (15 women), 14 part-time (12 women); includes 2 Black or African American, non-Hispanic/Latino; 3 Asian, non-Hispanic/Latino; 1 Hispanic/Latino. 61 applicants, 23% accepted, 11 enrolled. In 2010, 18 master's awarded. *Degree requirements:* For master's, thesis or alternative. *Entrance requirements:* For master's, interview, previous course work in psychology. *Application deadline:* For fall admission, 5/15 priority date for domestic students. Applications are processed on a rolling basis. Application fee: $50. Electronic applications accepted. *Expenses:* Tuition, state resident: full-time $5137; part-time $518 per credit. Tuition, nonresident: part-time $542 per credit. Required fees: $4008; $55 per semester. Tuition and fees vary according to program. *Financial support:* Teaching assistantships available. Financial award application deadline: 4/15; financial award applicants required to submit FAFSA. *Unit head:* Dr. Claire Novosad, Chairperson, 203-392-6863, Fax: 203-392-6805, E-mail: novosadc1@southernct.edu. *Application contact:* Dr. William Hauselt, Coordinator, 203-392-6874, Fax: 203-392-6805, E-mail: hauseltw1@southernct.edu.

Southern Illinois University Carbondale, Graduate School, College of Education, Department of Behavior Analysis and Therapy, Carbondale, IL 62901-4701. Offers MS.

Southern Illinois University Carbondale, Graduate School, College of Liberal Arts, Department of Psychology, Carbondale, IL 62901-4701. Offers clinical psychology (MA, MS, PhD); counseling psychology (MA, MS, PhD); experimental psychology (MA, MS, PhD). *Accreditation:* APA (one or more programs are accredited). *Degree requirements:* For master's, thesis; for doctorate, thesis/dissertation. *Entrance requirements:* For master's, GRE General Test, GRE Subject Test, minimum GPA of 2.7; for doctorate, GRE General Test, GRE Subject Test, minimum GPA of 3.25. Additional exam requirements/recommendations for international students: Required—TOEFL. *Faculty research:* Developmental neuropsychology; smoking, affect, and cognition; personality measurement; vocational psychology; program evaluation.

Southern Illinois University Edwardsville, Graduate School, School of Education, Department of Psychology, Edwardsville, IL 62026. Offers clinical child and school psychology (MS); clinical-adult psychology (MA); industrial-organizational psychology (MA); school psychology (SD). Part-time programs available. *Faculty:* 20 full-time (9 women). *Students:* 48 full-time (36 women), 41 part-time (35 women); includes 10 minority (3 Black or African American, non-Hispanic/Latino; 1 Asian, non-Hispanic/Latino; 4 Hispanic/Latino; 2 Two or more races, non-Hispanic/Latino), 3 international. Average age 26. 171 applicants, 16% accepted. In 2010, 36 master's, 10 other advanced degrees awarded. *Degree requirements:* For master's, thesis (for some programs), research paper; for SD, thesis. *Entrance requirements:* For master's, GRE. Additional exam requirements/recommendations for international students: Required—TOEFL (minimum score 550 paper-based; 213 computer-based; 79 iBT), IELTS (minimum score 6.5). *Application deadline:* For fall and spring admission, 2/1 for domestic and international students. Application fee: $30. Electronic applications accepted. *Expenses:* Tuition, state resident: full-time $6012; part-time $1503 per semester. Tuition, nonresident: full-time $15,030; part-time $3758 per semester. Required fees: $1711; $675 per semester. *Financial support:* In 2010–11, fellowships with full tuition reimbursements (averaging $8,370 per year), 4 research assistantships with full tuition reimbursements (averaging $8,064 per year), 33 teaching assistantships with full tuition reimbursements (averaging $8,064 per year) were awarded; career-related internships or fieldwork, Federal Work-Study, institutionally sponsored loans, scholarships/grants, traineeships, and unspecified assistantships also available. Support available to part-time students. Financial award application deadline: 3/1; financial award applicants required to submit FAFSA. *Unit head:* Dr. Lynn Bartels, Co-Chair, 618-650-2202, E-mail: lbartel@siue.edu. *Application contact:* Dr. Lynn Bartels, Co-Chair, 618-650-2202, E-mail: lbartel@siue.edu.

Southern Methodist University, Dedman College, Department of Psychology, Dallas, TX 75275. Offers clinical psychology (PhD). *Accreditation:* APA. *Faculty:* 18 full-time (7 women), 8 part-time/adjunct (7 women). *Students:* 7 full-time (all women), 19 part-time (16 women); includes 1 American Indian or Alaska Native, non-Hispanic/Latino; 1 Hispanic/Latino, 1 international. Average age 30. 80 applicants, 10% accepted, 5 enrolled. In 2010, 1 doctorate awarded. Terminal master's awarded for partial completion of doctoral program. *Degree requirements:* For doctorate, comprehensive exam, thesis/dissertation, oral exam, practicum, research presentation and publication. *Entrance requirements:* For doctorate, GRE General Test, minimum GPA of 3.4. Additional exam requirements/recommendations for international students: Required—TOEFL (minimum score 550 paper-based). *Application deadline:* For fall admission, 12/1 priority date for domestic and international students. Application fee: $75. Electronic applications accepted. *Financial support:* In 2010–11, 23 students received support, including 23 research assistantships with full tuition reimbursements available (averaging $14,000 per year); career-related internships or fieldwork, institutionally sponsored loans, health care benefits, and unspecified assistantships also available. Financial award application deadline: 12/1; financial award applicants required to submit FAFSA. *Faculty research:* Experimental, social, developmental, and cognitive psychology; anger/violence; mood disorders; depression and anxiety; family assessment and development; chronic pain and mental health. *Unit head:* Dr. Ernest Jouriles, Chair, 214-768-2360, Fax: 214-768-3910, E-mail: ejourile@mail.smu.edu. *Application contact:* Dr. Robert B. Hampson, Director of Graduate Studies, 214-768-2734, Fax: 214-768-3910, E-mail: rhampson@smu.edu.

Southern Nazarene University, Graduate College, School of Psychology, Bethany, OK 73008. Offers counseling psychology (MSCP); marriage and family therapy (MA). *Degree requirements:* For master's, thesis optional. *Entrance requirements:* For master's, English proficiency exam, minimum GPA of 3.0 in last 60 hours/major, 2.7 overall. *Expenses:* Tuition: Part-time $575 per credit hour.

Southern New Hampshire University, School of Liberal Arts, Manchester, NH 03106-1045. Offers clinical services for adults psychiatric disabilities (Certificate); clinical services for children and adolescents with psychiatric disabilities (Certificate); clinical services for persons with co-occurring substance abuse and psychiatric disabilities (Certificate); community mental health (MS); fiction writing (MFA); non-fiction writing (MFA); teaching English as a foreign language (MS). Part-time and evening/weekend programs available. *Degree requirements:* For master's, one foreign language, thesis. *Entrance requirements:* For master's, minimum GPA of 2.75: MS-TEFL, 3.0: MFA. Additional exam requirements/recommendations for international students: Required—TOEFL (minimum score 550 paper-based; 213 computer-based; 79 iBT), IELTS (minimum score 6.5), TWE (minimum score 5). Electronic applications accepted. *Expenses:* Contact institution. *Faculty research:* Action research, state of the art practice in behavioral health services, wraparound approaches to working with youth, learning styles.

Southern Oregon University, Graduate Studies, College of Arts and Sciences, Department of Psychology, Ashland, OR 97520. Offers mental health counseling (MAP). Part-time programs available. *Faculty:* 13 full-time (7 women). *Students:* 40 full-time (31 women), 4 part-time (1 woman); includes 5 minority (1 Black or African American, non-Hispanic/Latino; 2 Asian, non-Hispanic/Latino; 2 Hispanic/Latino), 1 international. Average age 37. 58 applicants, 43% accepted, 21 enrolled. In 2010, 20 master's awarded. *Degree requirements:* For master's, thesis, portfolio, oral defense. *Entrance requirements:* For master's, GRE General Test, minimum GPA of 3.0. *Application deadline:* Applications are processed on a rolling basis. Application fee: $50. *Expenses:* Tuition, state resident: full-time $9450; part-time $350 per credit. Tuition, nonresident: full-time $15,000; part-time $350 per credit. Required fees: $60 per quarter. *Financial support:* Scholarships/grants and unspecified assistantships available. Financial award applicants required to submit FAFSA. *Unit head:* Dr. Dan Deneui, Chair, 541-552-6913, E-mail: deneuid@sou.edu. *Application contact:* Wri Courtney, Graduate Coordinator, 541-552-6947, E-mail: map@sou.edu.

Psychology—General

Southern University and Agricultural and Mechanical College, Graduate School, College of Sciences, Department of Psychology, Baton Rouge, LA 70813. Offers rehabilitation counseling (MS). *Degree requirements:* For master's, comprehensive exam, thesis optional. *Entrance requirements:* For master's, GMAT or GRE General Test. Additional exam requirements/recommendations for international students: Required—TOEFL (minimum score 525 paper-based; 193 computer-based). *Faculty research:* Cultural diversity, professional preparation and participation of minorities, needs and satisfaction of students with disabilities, prediction model for rehabilitation outcome, diabetes.

Southwestern College, Program in Psychodrama and Action Methods, Santa Fe, NM 87502-4788. Offers Certificate. *Entrance requirements:* For degree, 3 letters of reference.

Spalding University, Graduate Studies, College of Social Sciences and Humanities, School of Professional Psychology, Louisville, KY 40203-2188. Offers clinical psychology (MA, Psy D). *Accreditation:* APA (one or more programs are accredited). Part-time programs available. *Faculty:* 8 full-time (4 women), 15 part-time/adjunct (4 women). *Students:* 100 full-time (77 women), 53 part-time (38 women); includes 20 minority (5 Black or African American, non-Hispanic/Latino; 4 Asian, non-Hispanic/Latino; 5 Hispanic/Latino; 6 Two or more races, non-Hispanic/Latino), 3 international. Average age 29. 78 applicants, 41% accepted, 32 enrolled. In 2010, 13 master's, 15 doctorates awarded. Terminal master's awarded for partial completion of doctoral program. *Degree requirements:* For master's, comprehensive exam; for doctorate, thesis/dissertation. *Entrance requirements:* For master's and doctorate, GRE General Test, 18 hours of undergraduate course work in psychology, interview, letters of recommendation, writing sample, autobiographical statement, transcripts. Additional exam requirements/recommendations for international students: Required—TOEFL (minimum score 535 paper-based; 203 computer-based). *Application deadline:* For fall admission, 1/15 priority date for domestic students, 1/15 for international students. Application fee: $30. *Financial support:* In 2010–11, 66 students received support, including 51 research assistantships with partial tuition reimbursements available (averaging $4,944 per year); career-related internships or fieldwork, Federal Work-Study, scholarships/grants, and unspecified assistantships also available. Financial award application deadline: 3/15; financial award applicants required to submit FAFSA. *Faculty research:* Substance abuse, prayer research, end-of-life issues, complementary and alternative medicine, research methodology and statistical inference. *Unit head:* Dr. Steven Katsikas, Chair, 502-585-9911 Ext. 2700, E-mail: skatsikas@spalding.edu. *Application contact:* Elizabeth A. Simpson, Administrative Assistant, 502-585-7127, Fax: 502-585-7159, E-mail: esimpson@spalding.edu.

Stanford University, School of Humanities and Sciences, Department of Psychology, Stanford, CA 94305-9991. Offers PhD. *Degree requirements:* For doctorate, thesis/dissertation, oral exam. *Entrance requirements:* For doctorate, GRE General Test, GRE Subject Test. Additional exam requirements/recommendations for international students: Required—TOEFL. Electronic applications accepted. *Expenses:* Tuition: Full-time $38,700; part-time $860 per unit. One-time fee: $200 full-time.

State University of New York at Binghamton, Graduate School, School of Arts and Sciences, Department of Psychology, Binghamton, NY 13902-6000. Offers behavioral neuroscience (MA, PhD); clinical psychology (MA, PhD); cognitive and behavioral science (MA, PhD). *Accreditation:* APA (one or more programs are accredited). *Faculty:* 30 full-time (13 women), 4 part-time/adjunct (1 woman). *Students:* 54 full-time (34 women), 32 part-time (24 women); includes 1 Black or African American, non-Hispanic/Latino; 1 Asian, non-Hispanic/Latino; 6 Hispanic/Latino, 4 international. Average age 27. 294 applicants, 10% accepted, 20 enrolled. In 2010, 12 doctorates awarded. Terminal master's awarded for partial completion of doctoral program. *Degree requirements:* For master's, thesis; for doctorate, thesis/dissertation, departmental qualifying exam. *Entrance requirements:* For master's and doctorate, GRE General Test, GRE Subject Test. Additional exam requirements/recommendations for international students: Required—TOEFL (minimum score 550 paper-based; 213 computer-based; 80 iBT). *Application deadline:* Applications are processed on a rolling basis. Application fee: $60. Electronic applications accepted. *Financial support:* In 2010–11, 67 students received support, including 6 fellowships with full tuition reimbursements available (averaging $17,500 per year), 21 research assistantships with full tuition reimbursements available (averaging $17,500 per year), 36 teaching assistantships with full tuition reimbursements available (averaging $17,500 per year); career-related internships or fieldwork, Federal Work-Study, institutionally sponsored loans, scholarships/grants, health care benefits, tuition waivers (full and partial), and unspecified assistantships also available. Financial award application deadline: 2/15; financial award applicants required to submit FAFSA. *Unit head:* Dr. Celia Klin, Chair, 607-777-4991, E-mail: cklin@binghamton.edu. *Application contact:* Catherine Smith, Recruiting and Admissions Coordinator, 607-777-2151, Fax: 607-777-2501, E-mail: cmsmith@binghamton.edu.

State University of New York at New Paltz, Graduate School, School of Liberal Arts and Sciences, Department of Psychology, New Paltz, NY 12561. Offers mental health counseling (MS); psychology (MA); school counseling (MS). Part-time and evening/weekend programs available. *Faculty:* 11 full-time (7 women), 2 part-time/adjunct (both women). *Students:* 52 full-time (41 women), 18 part-time (14 women); includes 2 Black or African American, non-Hispanic/Latino; 1 Asian, non-Hispanic/Latino; 1 Hispanic/Latino; 3 Two or more races, non-Hispanic/Latino, 3 international. Average age 27. 103 applicants, 42% accepted, 33 enrolled. In 2010, 9 master's awarded. *Degree requirements:* For master's, comprehensive exam, thesis. *Entrance requirements:* For master's, GRE General Test, minimum GPA of 3.0. Additional exam requirements/recommendations for international students: Required—TOEFL (minimum score 550 paper-based; 213 computer-based; 80 iBT), IELTS (minimum score 6.5). *Application deadline:* For fall admission, 1/20 priority date for domestic and international students; for spring admission, 11/15 for domestic and international students. Application fee: $50. Electronic applications accepted. *Expenses:* Tuition, state resident: full-time $8370; part-time $349 per credit hour. Tuition, nonresident: full-time $13,780; part-time $574 per credit hour. Required fees: $1165; $33.80 per credit hour. $175 per term. Tuition and fees vary according to program. *Financial support:* In 2010–11, 8 students received support, including 1 research assistantship (averaging $5,000 per year), 6 teaching assistantships with partial tuition reimbursements available (averaging $5,000 per year); career-related internships or fieldwork, Federal Work-Study, institutionally sponsored loans, traineeships, tuition waivers (full), and unspecified assistantships also available. Financial award application deadline: 8/1; financial award applicants required to submit FAFSA. *Faculty research:* Disaster mental health, women's objectification, mate selection, cultural psychology, achievement motivation. *Unit head:* Dr. Glenn Geher, Chair, 845-257-3091, E-mail: geherg@newpaltz.edu. *Application contact:* Dr. Jonathan Raskin, Coordinator, 845-257-3471, E-mail: raskinj@newpaltz.edu.

State University of New York at Plattsburgh, Faculty of Arts and Science, Department of Psychology, Plattsburgh, NY 12901-2681. Offers school psychology (MA, CAS). Part-time programs available. *Degree requirements:* For master's, thesis, internship. *Entrance requirements:* For master's, GRE General Test, minimum GPA of 3.0. Additional exam requirements/recommendations for international students: Required—TOEFL (minimum score 550 paper-based; 213 computer-based; 79 iBT). *Faculty research:* Alzheimer's disease, adolescent behavior, intellectual assessment, learning disabilities, reading skill acquisition.

Stephen F. Austin State University, Graduate School, College of Liberal Arts, Department of Psychology, Nacogdoches, TX 75962. Offers MA. *Degree requirements:* For master's, comprehensive exam, thesis. *Entrance requirements:* For master's, GRE General Test. Additional exam requirements/recommendations for international students: Required—TOEFL.

Stony Brook University, State University of New York, Graduate School, College of Arts and Sciences, Department of Psychology, Stony Brook, NY 11794. Offers biopsychology (PhD); clinical psychology (PhD); cognitive/experimental psychology (PhD); social and health psychology (PhD). *Accreditation:* APA. *Faculty:* 27 full-time (12 women), 2 part-time/adjunct (1 woman). *Students:* 99 full-time (70 women), 1 part-time (0 women); includes 3 Black or African American, non-Hispanic/Latino; 8 Asian, non-Hispanic/Latino; 11 Hispanic/Latino; 1 Two or more races, non-Hispanic/Latino, 10 international. Average age 27. 477 applicants, 6% accepted. In 2010, 22 doctorates awarded. *Degree requirements:* For doctorate, thesis/dissertation. *Entrance requirements:* For doctorate, GRE General Test, GRE Subject Test. Additional exam requirements/recommendations for international students: Required—TOEFL. *Application deadline:* For fall admission, 1/15 for domestic students. Application fee: $60. *Expenses:* Tuition, state resident: full-time $8370; part-time $349 per credit. Tuition, nonresident: full-time $13,780; part-time $574 per credit. Required fees: $994. *Financial support:* In 2010–11, 15 research assistantships, 62 teaching assistantships were awarded; fellowships, career-related internships or fieldwork also available. *Faculty research:* Behavior therapy, memory and cognition, child and family studies, quantitative methods, health psychology. Total annual research expenditures: $4.9 million. *Unit head:* Dr. Nancy Squires, Chair, 631-632-7855, Fax: 631-632-7876, E-mail: nancy.squires@stonybrook.edu. *Application contact:* Graduate Director, 631-632-7855, Fax: 631-632-7876.

Suffolk University, College of Arts and Sciences, Department of Psychology, Boston, MA 02108-2770. Offers clinical psychology (PhD). *Accreditation:* APA. *Faculty:* 17 full-time (9 women), 2 part-time/adjunct (0 women). *Students:* 32 full-time (30 women), 36 part-time (30 women); includes 4 Asian, non-Hispanic/Latino; 6 Hispanic/Latino, 3 international. Average age 29. 278 applicants, 9% accepted, 13 enrolled. In 2010, 7 doctorates awarded. *Degree requirements:* For doctorate, thesis/dissertation, practicum. *Entrance requirements:* For doctorate, GRE General Test or MAT, 2 letters of recommendation, resume. Additional exam requirements/recommendations for international students: Required—TOEFL (minimum score 550 paper-based; 213 computer-based; 80 iBT). *Application deadline:* For fall admission, 12/15 for domestic and international students. Applications are processed on a rolling basis. Application fee: $50. Electronic applications accepted. *Expenses:* Contact institution. *Financial support:* In 2010–11, 51 students received support, including 37 fellowships with full and partial tuition reimbursements available (averaging $20,063 per year); career-related internships or fieldwork, Federal Work-Study, and institutionally sponsored loans also available. Support available to part-time students. Financial award application deadline: 4/1; financial award applicants required to submit FAFSA. *Faculty research:* Olfaction decision-making in substance-dependent individuals, ego development, experiential avoidance in generalized anxiety disorder. *Unit head:* Dr. Gary Fireman, Chairperson, 617-305-6368, Fax: 617-367-2924, E-mail: gfireman@suffolk.edu. *Application contact:* Judith Reynolds, Director of Graduate Admissions, 617-573-8302, Fax: 617-305-1733, E-mail: grad.admission@suffolk.edu.

Sul Ross State University, School of Arts and Sciences, Department of Behavioral and Social Sciences, Program in Psychology, Alpine, TX 79832. Offers MA. *Entrance requirements:* For master's, GRE General Test, minimum GPA of 2.5 in last 60 hours of undergraduate work.

Temple University, College of Liberal Arts, Department of Psychology, Philadelphia, PA 19122-6096. Offers brain and cognitive sciences (PhD); clinical psychology (PhD); developmental psychology (PhD); psychology (MA); social psychology (PhD). *Accreditation:* APA. *Faculty:* 29 full-time (11 women). *Students:* 88 full-time (69 women), 14 part-time (12 women); includes 1 Black or African American, non-Hispanic/Latino; 1 American Indian or Alaska Native, non-Hispanic/Latino; 4 Asian, non-Hispanic/Latino; 2 Hispanic/Latino, 6 international. 538 applicants, 6% accepted, 16 enrolled. In 2010, 10 master's, 15 doctorates awarded. *Degree requirements:* For doctorate, thesis/dissertation. *Entrance requirements:* For doctorate, GRE General Test, minimum GPA of 3.0. Additional exam requirements/recommendations for international students: Required—TOEFL (minimum score 550 paper-based; 213 computer-based; 79 iBT). *Application deadline:* For fall admission, 12/15 for domestic and international students. Application fee: $50. Electronic applications accepted. *Financial support:* Fellowships, research assistantships, teaching assistantships, career-related internships or fieldwork, Federal Work-Study, institutionally sponsored loans, and unspecified assistantships available. Financial award application deadline: 12/15; financial award applicants required to submit FAFSA. Total annual research expenditures: $4 million. *Unit head:* Dr. Marsha Weinraub, Chair, 215-204-7321, Fax: 215-204-5539, E-mail: mweinrau@temple.edu. *Application contact:* Dr. Marsha Weinraub, Chair, 215-204-7321, Fax: 215-204-5539, E-mail: mweinrau@temple.edu.

Tennessee State University, The School of Graduate Studies and Research, College of Education, Department of Psychology, Nashville, TN 37209-1561. Offers counseling and guidance (MS), including counseling, elementary school counseling, organizational counseling, secondary school counseling; counseling psychology (PhD); psychology (MS, PhD); school psychology (MS, PhD). *Accreditation:* APA. *Degree requirements:* For doctorate, thesis/dissertation (for some programs). *Entrance requirements:* For master's, GRE General Test or MAT; for doctorate, GRE General Test or MAT, minimum GPA of 3.25, work experience. Electronic applications accepted.

Texas A&M International University, Office of Graduate Studies and Research, College of Arts and Sciences, Department of Behavioral Sciences, Laredo, TX 78041-1900. Offers counseling psychology (MACP); criminal justice (MS); psychology (MS); sociology (MA). *Faculty:* 9 full-time (5 women), 2 part-time/adjunct (1 woman). *Students:* 12 full-time (8 women), 116 part-time (80 women); includes 1 Black or African American, non-Hispanic/Latino; 1 Asian, non-Hispanic/Latino; 120 Hispanic/Latino, 1 international. Average age 29. 20 applicants, 90% accepted, 10 enrolled. In 2010, 16 master's awarded. *Degree requirements:* For master's, thesis (for some programs). *Entrance requirements:* For master's, GRE General Test. Additional exam requirements/recommendations for international students: Required—TOEFL (minimum score 550 paper-based; 213 computer-based; 79 iBT). *Application deadline:* For fall admission, 4/30 priority date for domestic students; for spring admission, 11/30 for domestic students. Applications are processed on a rolling basis. Application fee: $25. *Financial support:* In 2010–11, 17 students received support, including 2 fellowships, 6 research assistantships; teaching assistantships. Financial award application deadline: 11/1. *Unit head:* Dr. Frances P. Bernat, Chair, 956-326-2475, Fax: 956-326-2474, E-mail: gvillagran@tamiu.edu. *Application contact:* Suzanne Hansen-Alford, Director of Graduate Recruiting, 956-326-3023, Fax: 956-326-3021, E-mail: graduateschool@tamiu.edu.

Texas A&M University, College of Liberal Arts, Department of Psychology, College Station, TX 77843. Offers behavioral and cellular neuroscience (PhD); clinical psychology (PhD); cognitive psychology (PhD); developmental psychology (PhD); industrial/organizational psychology (PhD); social psychology (PhD). *Accreditation:* APA. *Faculty:* 39. *Students:* 91 full-time (57 women), 14 part-time (11 women); includes 7 Black or African American, non-Hispanic/Latino; 8 Asian, non-Hispanic/Latino; 17 Hispanic/Latino, 7 international. In 2010, 12 doctorates awarded. *Degree requirements:* For doctorate, comprehensive exam (for some programs), thesis/dissertation. *Entrance requirements:* For doctorate, GRE General Test. Additional exam requirements/recommendations for international students: Required—TOEFL. *Application deadline:* For fall admission, 1/5 for domestic and international students. Application fee: $50 ($75 for international students). Electronic applications accepted. *Financial support:* Fellowships with partial tuition reimbursements, research assistantships with partial tuition reimbursements, teaching assistantships with partial tuition reimbursements, career-related internships or fieldwork, institutionally sponsored loans, health care benefits, and unspecified assistantships available. Financial award application deadline: 1/5; financial award applicants required to submit FAFSA. *Unit head:* Ludy T. Benjamin, Head, 979-845-2540, Fax: 979-845-4727, E-mail: lbenjamin@tamu.edu. *Application contact:* Julie Austin, Graduate Admissions Supervisor, 979-458-1710, Fax: 979-845-4727, E-mail: gradadv@psyc.tamu.edu.

Texas A&M University–Commerce, Graduate School, College of Education and Human Services, Department of Psychology and Special Education, Commerce, TX 75429-3011. Offers cognition and instruction (PhD); psychology (MA, MS); special education (M Ed, MA, MS). Part-time programs available. Terminal master's awarded for partial completion of doctoral program. *Degree requirements:* For master's, comprehensive exam, thesis (for some programs); for doctorate, thesis/dissertation, departmental qualifying exam. *Entrance requirements:* For master's, GRE General Test; for doctorate, GRE General Test, 3 letters of recommendation. Electronic applications accepted. *Faculty research:* Human learning, study skills, multicultural bilingual, diversity and special education, educationally handicapped.

Texas A&M University–Corpus Christi, Graduate Studies and Research, College of Liberal Arts, Program in Psychology, Corpus Christi, TX 78412-5503. Offers MA. Part-time and evening/weekend programs available. *Degree requirements:* For master's, comprehensive exam, thesis (for some programs). *Entrance requirements:* For master's, GRE General Test. Additional exam requirements/recommendations for international students: Required—TOEFL. Electronic applications accepted.

Texas A&M University–Kingsville, College of Graduate Studies, College of Arts and Sciences, Department of Psychology and Sociology, Kingsville, TX 78363. Offers gerontology (MS); psychology (MA, MS); sociology (MA, MS). Part-time and evening/weekend programs available. *Degree requirements:* For master's, comprehensive exam, thesis or alternative. *Entrance requirements:* For master's, GRE General Test, minimum GPA of 2.5. Additional exam requirements/recommendations for international students: Required—TOEFL. *Faculty research:* Hispanic female voting behavior, attitudes toward criminal justice, immigration of aged into south Texas, folk medicine.

Texas A&M University–Texarkana, Graduate Studies and Research, College of Health and Behavioral Sciences, Texarkana, TX 75505-5518. Offers counseling psychology (MS). Part-time and evening/weekend programs available. *Degree requirements:* For master's, comprehensive exam (for some programs), thesis or alternative. *Entrance requirements:* For master's, minimum GPA of 3.0 in last 60 hours of bachelor's degree. Additional exam requirements/recommendations for international students: Required—TOEFL. Electronic applications accepted.

Texas Christian University, College of Science and Engineering, Department of Psychology, Fort Worth, TX 76129-0002. Offers experimental psychology (PhD), including cognitive psychology, learning, neuropsychology, social psychology; psychology (MA, MS). In 2010, 7 master's, 3 doctorates awarded. Terminal master's awarded for partial completion of doctoral program. *Degree requirements:* For master's, thesis; for doctorate, thesis/dissertation. *Entrance requirements:* For master's and doctorate, GRE General Test. Additional exam requirements/recommendations for international students: Required—TOEFL. *Application deadline:* For fall admission, 3/1 for domestic and international students; for spring admission, 12/1 for domestic students. Applications are processed on a rolling basis. Application fee: $50. Electronic applications accepted. *Expenses:* Tuition: Full-time $18,720; part-time $1040 per credit hour. Tuition and fees vary according to course load and program. *Financial support:* In 2010–11, 20 students received support; teaching assistantships with full tuition reimbursements available, unspecified assistantships available. Financial award application deadline: 3/1. *Unit head:* Dr. Charles Lord, Coordinator of Graduate Studies, 817-257-7410, Fax: 817-257-7681, E-mail: c.lord@tcu.edu. *Application contact:* Tami Joyce, Department Manager, 817-257-7410, Fax: 817-257-7681, E-mail: t.joyce@tcu.edu.

Texas Southern University, College of Liberal Arts and Behavioral Sciences, Department of Psychology, Houston, TX 77004-4584. Offers MA. *Faculty:* 4 full-time (2 women), 1 part-time/adjunct (0 women). *Students:* 28 full-time (19 women), 36 part-time (30 women); includes 57 Black or African American, non-Hispanic/Latino; 1 Asian, non-Hispanic/Latino; 2 Hispanic/Latino. Average age 33. 15 applicants, 87% accepted, 10 enrolled. In 2010, 8 master's awarded. *Application deadline:* For fall admission, 7/1 for domestic and international students; for spring admission, 11/1 for domestic and international students. Applications are processed on a rolling basis. Application fee: $50. Electronic applications accepted. *Expenses:* Tuition, state resident: full-time $1875; part-time $100 per credit hour. Tuition, nonresident: full-time $6641; part-time $343 per credit hour. Tuition and fees vary according to course level, course load and degree level. *Financial support:* In 2010–11, 1 teaching assistantship (averaging $6,720 per year) was awarded; scholarships/grants and unspecified assistantships also available. *Unit head:* Dr. Leon H. Belcher, Chair, 713-313-7062, E-mail: belcher_lh@tsu.edu. *Application contact:* Dr. Gregory Maddox, Dean of the Graduate School, 713-313-7011 Ext. 4410, Fax: 713-639-1876, E-mail: maddox_gh@tsu.edu.

Texas State University–San Marcos, Graduate School, College of Liberal Arts, Department of Psychology, San Marcos, TX 78666. Offers health psychology (MA). *Faculty:* 13 full-time (6 women), 1 part-time/adjunct (0 women). *Students:* 44 full-time (32 women), 11 part-time (7 women); includes 1 Black or African American, non-Hispanic/Latino; 1 Asian, non-Hispanic/Latino; 13 Hispanic/Latino; 1 Two or more races, non-Hispanic/Latino. Average age 27. 49 applicants, 69% accepted, 28 enrolled. In 2010, 16 master's awarded. *Degree requirements:* For master's, comprehensive exam, thesis (for some programs). *Entrance requirements:* For master's, GRE General Test, minimum GPA of 3.0 in last 60 hours, in psychology, and in psychology core courses; 3 letters of recommendation; statement of purpose. Additional exam requirements/recommendations for international students: Required—TOEFL (minimum score 550 paper-based; 213 computer-based; 78 iBT). *Application deadline:* For fall admission, 3/15 for domestic and international students. Applications are processed on a rolling basis. Application fee: $40 ($90 for international students). Electronic applications accepted. *Expenses:* Tuition, state resident: full-time $6024; part-time $251 per credit hour. Tuition, nonresident: full-time $13,536; part-time $564 per credit hour. Required fees: $1776; $50 per credit hour. $306 per semester. *Financial support:* In 2010–11, 26 students received support, including 6 research assistantships (averaging $3,887 per year), 25 teaching assistantships (averaging $2,652 per year); Federal Work-Study, institutionally sponsored loans, scholarships/grants, health care benefits, and unspecified assistantships also available. Support available to part-time students. Financial award application deadline: 4/1. *Faculty research:* Stress and alcohol. Total annual research expenditures: $17,023. *Unit head:* Dr. Shirley Ogletree, Graduate Advisor, 512-245-2526, Fax: 512-245-3153, E-mail: so01@txstate.edu. *Application contact:* Dr. J. Michael Willoughby, Dean of Graduate College, 512-245-2581, Fax: 512-245-8365, E-mail: gradcollege@txstate.edu.

Texas State University–San Marcos, Graduate School, Interdisciplinary Studies Program in Educational Administration and Psychological Services, San Marcos, TX 78666. Offers MAIS. *Degree requirements:* For master's, comprehensive exam. *Entrance requirements:* Additional exam requirements/recommendations for international students: Required—TOEFL (minimum score 550 paper-based; 213 computer-based; 78 iBT). *Application deadline:* For fall admission, 6/15 priority date for domestic students; for spring admission, 10/15 priority date for domestic students. Applications are processed on a rolling basis. Application fee: $40 ($90 for international students). *Expenses:* Tuition, state resident: full-time $6024; part-time $251 per credit hour. Tuition, nonresident: full-time $13,536; part-time $564 per credit hour. Required fees: $1776; $50 per credit hour. $306 per semester. *Financial support:* Application deadline: 4/1. *Unit head:* Dr. Stan Carpenter, Dean, 512-245-2575, Fax: 512-245-8345, E-mail: sc33@txstate.edu. *Application contact:* Dr. J. Michael Willoughby, Dean of Graduate School, 512-245-2581, Fax: 512-245-8365, E-mail: gradcollege@txstate.edu.

Texas State University–San Marcos, Graduate School, Interdisciplinary Studies Program in Psychology, San Marcos, TX 78666. Offers MAIS, MSIS. *Degree requirements:* For master's, comprehensive exam. *Entrance requirements:* Additional exam requirements/recommendations for international students: Required—TOEFL (minimum score 550 paper-based; 213 computer-based; 78 iBT). *Application deadline:* For fall admission, 6/15 priority date for domestic students, 6/1 for international students; for spring admission, 10/15 priority date for domestic students, 10/1 for international students. Applications are processed on a rolling basis. Application fee: $40 ($90 for international students). *Expenses:* Tuition, state resident: full-time $6024; part-time $251 per credit hour. Tuition, nonresident: full-time $13,536; part-time $564 per credit hour. Required fees: $1776; $50 per credit hour. $306 per semester. *Financial support:* Application deadline: 4/1. *Unit head:* Dr. Paula Williams, Advisor, 512-245-3159, E-mail: pw04@txstate.edu. *Application contact:* Dr. J. Michael Willoughby, Dean of Graduate School, 512-245-2581, Fax: 512-245-8365, E-mail: gradcollege@txstate.edu.

Texas Tech University, Graduate School, College of Arts and Sciences, Department of Psychology, Lubbock, TX 79409-2051. Offers clinical psychology (PhD); counseling psychology (MA, PhD); experimental psychology (MA, PhD); psychology (MA, PhD). *Accreditation:* APA (one or more programs are accredited). Part-time programs available. *Faculty:* 25 full-time (11 women). *Students:* 91 full-time (57 women), 18 part-time (17 women); includes 2 Black or African American, non-Hispanic/Latino; 1 American Indian or Alaska Native, non-Hispanic/Latino; 1 Asian, non-Hispanic/Latino; 9 Hispanic/Latino; 1 Two or more races, non-Hispanic/Latino, 7 international. Average age 27. 276 applicants, 11% accepted, 19 enrolled. In 2010, 18 master's, 13 doctorates awarded. *Degree requirements:* For doctorate, comprehensive exam, thesis/dissertation, 100 credit hours of organized courses, research credits, and practica. *Entrance requirements:* For master's and doctorate, GRE General Test, GRE Subject Test, departmental application form, essays. Additional exam requirements/recommendations for international students: Required—TOEFL (minimum score 550 paper-based; 213 computer-based; 79 iBT). *Application deadline:* For fall admission, 6/1 priority date for domestic students, 1/15 priority date for international students; for spring admission, 9/1 priority date for domestic students, 6/15 priority date for international students. Applications are processed on a rolling basis. Application fee: $50 ($75 for international students). Electronic applications accepted. *Expenses:* Tuition, state resident: full-time $5495.76; part-time $228.99 per credit hour. Tuition, nonresident: full-time $12,936; part-time $538.99 per credit hour. Required fees: $2674; $36 per credit hour. $905 per semester. *Financial support:* In 2010–11, 85 students received support, including 13 research assistantships with partial tuition reimbursements available (averaging $5,707 per year), 32 teaching assistantships with partial tuition reimbursements available (averaging $5,672 per year). Financial award application deadline: 4/15; financial award applicants required to submit FAFSA. *Faculty research:* Failure/success in relationships, peer rejection in school, stress and coping, group processes, clinical and health psychology. Total annual research expenditures: $202,278. *Unit head:* Dr. Lee M. Cohen, Chair, 806-742-3711 Ext. 222, Fax: 806-742-0818, E-mail: lee.cohen@ttu.edu. *Application contact:* Kay Hill, Admissions Coordinator, 806-742-3711 Ext. 222, Fax: 806-742-0818, E-mail: kay.hill@ttu.edu.

Texas Woman's University, Graduate School, College of Arts and Sciences, Department of Psychology and Philosophy, Denton, TX 76201. Offers counseling psychology (MA, PhD); school psychology (PhD, SSP). *Accreditation:* APA (one or more programs are accredited). *Faculty:* 16 full-time (9 women). *Students:* 81 full-time (72 women), 52 part-time (46 women); includes 11 Black or African American, non-Hispanic/Latino; 1 American Indian or Alaska Native, non-Hispanic/Latino; 6 Asian, non-Hispanic/Latino; 13 Hispanic/Latino, 1 international. Average age 30. 169 applicants, 27% accepted, 33 enrolled. In 2010, 15 master's, 9 doctorates awarded. Terminal master's awarded for partial completion of doctoral program. *Degree requirements:* For master's, thesis; for doctorate, comprehensive exam, thesis/dissertation, internship, residency. *Entrance requirements:* For master's, GRE (preferred minimum score 500 Verbal, 500 Quantitative, 4 Analytical), BA/BS or 18 hours in psychology; minimum GPA of 3.0, 3.5 in undergraduate psychology classes; 3 letters of reference; curriculum vitae; essays; for doctorate, GRE (preferred minimum score 500 Verbal, 500 Quantitative, 4 Analytical), 3 letters of reference, minimum GPA of 3.5 overall and in psychology undergraduate classes, BS/BA in psychology or 18 hours of required psychology classes, curriculum vitae, essays. Additional exam requirements/recommendations for international students: Required—TOEFL (minimum score 550 paper-based; 213 computer-based; 79 iBT). *Application deadline:* For fall admission, 12/15 priority date for domestic and international students. Applications are processed on a rolling basis. Application fee: $50 ($75 for international students). Electronic applications accepted. *Expenses:* Tuition, state resident: full-time $3834; part-time $213 per credit hour. Tuition, nonresident: full-time $9468; part-time $526 per credit hour. Required fees: $1247; $220 per credit hour. *Financial support:* In 2010–11, 49 students received support, including 29 research assistantships (averaging $10,746 per year), 9 teaching assistantships (averaging $10,746 per year); career-related internships or fieldwork, Federal Work-Study, institutionally sponsored loans, scholarships/grants, traineeships, health care benefits, and unspecified assistantships also available. Support available to part-time students. Financial award application deadline: 3/1; financial award applicants required to submit FAFSA. *Faculty research:* Women's anger, school neuropsychological theory and assessment, body image dysfunction, traumatic stress, classical ethics, mental health and behavioral needs of adolescents in alternative education. *Unit head:* Dr. Dan Miller, Chair, 940-898-2303, Fax: 940-898-2301, E-mail: dmiller@twu.edu. *Application contact:* Dr. Samuel Wheeler, Assistant Director of Admissions, 940-898-3188, Fax: 940-898-3081, E-mail: wheelersr@twu.edu.

Trevecca Nazarene University, Graduate Division, Graduate Psychology Programs, Nashville, TN 37210-2877. Offers clinical counseling (PhD); counseling (MA); counseling psychology (MA); marriage and family therapy (MMFT). Part-time and evening/weekend programs available. *Faculty:* 5 full-time (1 woman), 17 part-time/adjunct (10 women). *Students:* 245 full-time (175 women), 48 part-time (36 women); includes 62 minority (50 Black or African American, non-Hispanic/Latino; 1 American Indian or Alaska Native, non-Hispanic/Latino; 5 Hispanic/Latino; 6 Two or more races, non-Hispanic/Latino). Average age 34. In 2010, 72 master's awarded. *Degree requirements:* For master's, comprehensive exam; for doctorate, comprehensive exam, thesis/dissertation. *Entrance requirements:* For master's, GRE General Test or MAT, minimum GPA of 2.7, 2 reference assessment forms; for doctorate, GRE, minimum GPA of 3.25, 3 recommendation forms, 400-word letter of intent, interview. Additional exam requirements/recommendations for international students: Required—TOEFL (minimum score 550 paper-based; 213 computer-based). *Application deadline:* Applications are processed on a rolling basis. *Expenses:* Contact institution. *Financial support:* Applicants required to submit FAFSA. *Unit head:* Dr. Peter Wilson, Director, 615-248-1384, Fax: 615-248-1662, E-mail: pwilson@trevecca.edu. *Application contact:* Heather Ambrefe, Administrative Assistant, 615-248-1384, Fax: 615-248-1662, E-mail: admissions_psy@trevecca.edu.

Tufts University, Graduate School of Arts and Sciences, Department of Psychology, Medford, MA 02155. Offers MS, PhD. Terminal master's awarded for partial completion of doctoral program. *Degree requirements:* For master's, thesis; for doctorate, one foreign language, thesis/dissertation. *Entrance requirements:* For master's and doctorate, GRE General Test, GRE Subject Test. Additional exam requirements/recommendations for international students: Required—TOEFL (minimum score 550 paper-based; 213 computer-based; 80 iBT). Electronic applications accepted. *Expenses:* Tuition: Full-time $39,624; part-time $3962 per course. Required fees: $40 per year. Full-time tuition and fees vary according to degree level, program and student level. Part-time tuition and fees vary according to course load.

Tulane University, School of Science and Engineering, Department of Psychology, New Orleans, LA 70118-5669. Offers MS, PhD. *Accreditation:* APA (one or more programs are accredited). Terminal master's awarded for partial completion of doctoral program. *Degree requirements:* For master's, variable foreign language requirement, thesis; for doctorate, thesis/dissertation. *Entrance requirements:* For master's, GRE General Test, minimum B average in undergraduate course work; for doctorate, GRE General Test. Additional exam requirements/recommendations for international students: Required—TOEFL. Electronic applications accepted. *Faculty research:* Hormones and behavior, aggression, personnel selection, cognitive development, stereotyping, diabetes.

Uniformed Services University of the Health Sciences, School of Medicine, Graduate Programs in the Biomedical Sciences and Public Health, Department of Medical and Clinical Psychology, Bethesda, MD 20814. Offers clinical psychology (PhD); medical and clinical psychology (clinical/dual track) (PhD); medical and clinical psychology (research track) (PhD). Clinical psychology available to active duty military only. *Accreditation:* APA. Terminal master's awarded for partial completion of doctoral program. *Degree requirements:* For doctorate, comprehensive exam, thesis/dissertation, qualifying exam. *Entrance requirements:* For doctorate, GRE General Test, minimum GPA of 3.0, U.S. citizenship. Additional exam requirements/recommendations for international students: Required—TOEFL. Electronic applications accepted. *Faculty research:* Addictive and appetitive behavior, psychopharmacology, stress and eating, obesity, health.

Union College, Graduate Programs, Department of Psychology, Barbourville, KY 40906-1499. Offers clinical psychology (MA); counseling psychology (MA); school psychology (MA).

Union Institute & University, Master of Arts Program–Online, Montpelier, VT 05602. Offers creativity studies (MA); education (MA); health and wellness (MA); history and culture (MA);

Psychology—General

Union Institute & University (continued)
leadership, public policy, and social issues (MA); literature and writing (MA); psychology (MA). Part-time programs available. Postbaccalaureate distance learning degree programs offered (no on-campus study). *Faculty:* 2 full-time (1 woman), 18 part-time/adjunct (11 women). *Students:* 27 full-time (26 women), 119 part-time (98 women); includes 34 minority (25 Black or African American, non-Hispanic/Latino; 3 American Indian or Alaska Native, non-Hispanic/Latino; 6 Hispanic/Latino). Average age 40. In 2010, 26 master's awarded. *Degree requirements:* For master's, thesis. *Application deadline:* Applications are processed on a rolling basis. Application fee: $50. Electronic applications accepted. *Expenses:* Tuition: Full-time $16,430; part-time $685 per credit hour. Required fees: $174; $44 per term. Tuition and fees vary according to course load, degree level and program. *Financial support:* Career-related internships or fieldwork and tuition waivers available. Financial award applicants required to submit FAFSA. *Unit head:* Dr. Brian Webb, Program Director, 802-828-8777, E-mail: brian.webb@tui.edu. *Application contact:* Diane Robinson, Director of Admissions, 888-828-8575, E-mail: diane.robinson@myunion.edu.

Union Institute & University, Programs in Psychology and Counseling, Brattleboro, VT 05301. Offers clinical mental health counseling (MA); clinical psychology (Psy D); counseling psychology (MA); counselor education and supervision (CAGS); developmental psychology (MA); educational psychology (MA); human development and wellness (CAGS); organizational psychology (MA); psychology education (CAGS). Psy D offered in Ohio and Vermont. Postbaccalaureate distance learning degree programs offered (minimal on-campus study). *Faculty:* 6 full-time (4 women), 17 part-time/adjunct (6 women). *Students:* 93 full-time (66 women), 11 part-time (10 women); includes 14 minority (6 Black or African American, non-Hispanic/Latino; 1 Asian, non-Hispanic/Latino; 7 Hispanic/Latino). Average age 44. In 2010, 21 master's awarded. *Degree requirements:* For master's, thesis, internship (depending on concentration); for doctorate, thesis/dissertation, internship, practicum. *Application deadline:* Applications are processed on a rolling basis. Application fee: $50. Electronic applications accepted. *Expenses:* Tuition: Full-time $16,430; part-time $685 per credit hour. Required fees: $174; $44 per term. Tuition and fees vary according to course load, degree level and program. *Financial support:* Federal Work-Study available. Financial award applicants required to submit FAFSA. *Unit head:* Dr. Bill Lax, Dean, 802-254-0152, E-mail: bill.lax@myunion.edu. *Application contact:* Diane Robinson, Director of Admissions, 888-828-8575, E-mail: diane.robinson@myunion.edu.

Universidad de las Americas, A.C., Program in Psychology, Mexico City, Mexico. Offers family therapy (MA).

Universidad de las Américas–Puebla, Division of Graduate Studies, School of Social Sciences, Program in Psychology, Puebla, Mexico. Offers MA. Part-time and evening/weekend programs available. *Degree requirements:* For master's, one foreign language, thesis. *Entrance requirements:* For master's, minimum B+ average. *Faculty research:* Testing, social hemispheric specialization, clinical psychology.

Université de Montréal, Faculty of Arts and Sciences, Department of Psychology, Montréal, QC H3C 3J7, Canada. Offers M Sc, PhD. Terminal master's awarded for partial completion of doctoral program. *Degree requirements:* For master's, one foreign language, thesis; for doctorate, one foreign language, thesis/dissertation, general exam. Electronic applications accepted. *Faculty research:* Vision, marital counseling, memory.

Université de Sherbrooke, Faculty of Letters and Human Sciences, Department of Psychology, Sherbrooke, QC J1K 2R1, Canada. Offers gerontology (MA). *Degree requirements:* For master's, thesis. *Faculty research:* Human relations.

Université du Québec à Montréal, Graduate Programs, Program in Psychology, Montréal, QC H3C 3P8, Canada. Offers D Ps, PhD. Programs offered jointly with Université du Québec à Trois-Rivières. Part-time programs available. *Degree requirements:* For doctorate, thesis/dissertation. *Entrance requirements:* For doctorate, appropriate master's degree or equivalent, proficiency in French.

Université du Québec à Trois-Rivières, Graduate Programs, Program in Psychology, Trois-Rivières, QC G9A 5H7, Canada. Offers PhD, Certificate. Part-time programs available. *Degree requirements:* For doctorate, thesis/dissertation. *Entrance requirements:* For doctorate, appropriate master's degree, proficiency in French. *Faculty research:* Child and family development, gerontology, mental health.

Université Laval, Faculty of Social Sciences, School of Psychology, Programs in Psychology, Québec, QC G1K 7P4, Canada. Offers clinical psychology (PhD); community psychology (PhD); psychology (PhD, Psy D). *Degree requirements:* For doctorate, comprehensive exam, thesis/dissertation. *Entrance requirements:* For doctorate, comprehension of written English, knowledge of French, interview. Electronic applications accepted.

University at Albany, State University of New York, College of Arts and Sciences, Department of Psychology, Albany, NY 12222-0001. Offers autism (Certificate); biopsychology (PhD); clinical psychology (PhD); general/experimental psychology (PhD); industrial/organizational psychology (PhD); psychology (MA); social/personality psychology (PhD). *Accreditation:* APA (one or more programs are accredited). *Degree requirements:* For doctorate, thesis/dissertation. *Entrance requirements:* For doctorate, GRE General Test, GRE Subject Test. Additional exam requirements/recommendations for international students: Required—TOEFL (minimum score 550 paper-based; 213 computer-based). Electronic applications accepted.

University at Buffalo, the State University of New York, Graduate School, College of Arts and Sciences, Department of Psychology, Buffalo, NY 14260. Offers behavioral neuroscience (PhD); clinical psychology (PhD); cognitive psychology (PhD); general psychology (MA); social-personality psychology (PhD). *Accreditation:* APA (one or more programs are accredited). *Faculty:* 26 full-time (8 women), 10 part-time/adjunct (5 women). *Students:* 88 full-time (60 women), 6 part-time (4 women); includes 21 minority (2 Black or African American, non-Hispanic/Latino; 2 American Indian or Alaska Native, non-Hispanic/Latino; 7 Asian, non-Hispanic/Latino; 9 Hispanic/Latino; 1 Two or more races, non-Hispanic/Latino), 11 international. Average age 27. 367 applicants, 12% accepted, 21 enrolled. In 2010, 14 master's, 6 doctorates awarded. Terminal master's awarded for partial completion of doctoral program. *Degree requirements:* For master's, project; for doctorate, thesis/dissertation. *Entrance requirements:* For master's and doctorate, GRE General Test. Additional exam requirements/recommendations for international students: Required—TOEFL (minimum score 550 paper-based; 213 computer-based; 79 iBT). *Application deadline:* For fall admission, 12/1 for domestic and international students. Application fee: $75. Electronic applications accepted. *Financial support:* In 2010–11, 65 students received support, including 8 fellowships with full tuition reimbursements available (averaging $13,700 per year), 16 research assistantships with full tuition reimbursements available (averaging $13,700 per year), 38 teaching assistantships with full tuition reimbursements available (averaging $13,700 per year); career-related internships or fieldwork, Federal Work-Study, institutionally sponsored loans, scholarships/grants, and tuition waivers (partial) also available. Financial award application deadline: 12/1; financial award applicants required to submit FAFSA. *Faculty research:* Neural, endocrine, and molecular bases of behavior; adult mood and anxiety disorders; relationship dysfunction; attention deficit/hyperactivity disorder; psycho-linguistics. Total annual research expenditures: $7.9 million. *Unit head:* Dr. Paul A. Luce, Chair, 716-645-3650 Ext. 203, Fax: 716-645-3801, E-mail: psychair@acsu.buffalo.edu. *Application contact:* Mary Claire Schnepf, Coordinator of Admissions, 716-645-3660, Fax: 716-645-3801, E-mail: psych@abuffalo.edu.

The University of Akron, Graduate School, Buchtel College of Arts and Sciences, Department of Psychology, Akron, OH 44325. Offers counseling psychology (MA, PhD); industrial/organizational psychology (MA, PhD); psychology (MA). *Accreditation:* APA (one or more programs are accredited). *Faculty:* 20 full-time (10 women), 2 part-time/adjunct (1 woman). *Students:* 60 full-time (44 women), 19 part-time (17 women); includes 5 Black or African American, non-Hispanic/Latino; 3 Asian, non-Hispanic/Latino; 2 Hispanic/Latino; 1 Two or more races, non-Hispanic/Latino, 3 international. Average age 27. 124 applicants, 5% accepted, 6 enrolled. In 2010, 15 master's, 14 doctorates awarded. Terminal master's awarded for partial completion of doctoral program. *Degree requirements:* For master's, thesis optional, thesis or specialty exam; for doctorate, one foreign language, comprehensive exam, thesis/dissertation. *Entrance requirements:* For master's, GRE General Test, minimum GPA of 2.75, 3.0 in psychology courses; three letters of recommendation; personal statement; curriculum vitae; for doctorate, GRE General Test, minimum graduate GPA of 3.25, three letters of recommendation, personal statement, statement of purpose, curriculum vitae. Additional exam requirements/recommendations for international students: Required—TOEFL (minimum score 550 paper-based; 213 computer-based; 79 iBT). *Application deadline:* For fall admission, 1/15 for domestic and international students. Application fee: $30 ($40 for international students). Electronic applications accepted. *Expenses:* Tuition, state resident: full-time $6800; part-time $378 per credit hour. Tuition, nonresident: full-time $11,644; part-time $647 per credit hour. Required fees: $1265. One-time fee: $30 full-time. *Financial support:* In 2010–11, 7 research assistantships with full tuition reimbursements, 54 teaching assistantships with full tuition reimbursements were awarded; career-related internships or fieldwork, Federal Work-Study, and institutionally sponsored loans also available. *Faculty research:* Social cognitive determinants of behavior, the application of psychological principles to the workplace and career planning/development, the psychological processes of aging. Total annual research expenditures: $314,132. *Unit head:* Dr. Paul Levy, Chair, 330-972-8367, E-mail: plevy@uakron.edu. *Application contact:* Dr. Paul Levy, Chair, 330-972-8367, E-mail: plevy@uakron.edu.

The University of Alabama, Graduate School, College of Arts and Sciences, Department of Psychology, Tuscaloosa, AL 35487. Offers clinical psychology (PhD); experimental psychology (PhD). *Accreditation:* APA. *Faculty:* 22 full-time (10 women), 2 part-time/adjunct (both women). *Students:* 75 full-time (57 women), 23 part-time (16 women); includes 17 minority (8 Black or African American, non-Hispanic/Latino; 5 Asian, non-Hispanic/Latino; 4 Hispanic/Latino), 6 international. Average age 28. 261 applicants, 15% accepted, 23 enrolled. In 2010, 15 doctorates awarded. *Degree requirements:* For doctorate, thesis/dissertation, internship (for clinical psychology). *Entrance requirements:* For doctorate, GRE. Additional exam requirements/recommendations for international students: Required—TOEFL (minimum score 550 paper-based). *Application deadline:* For fall admission, 12/1 for domestic and international students. Application fee: $50 ($60 for international students). Electronic applications accepted. *Expenses:* Tuition, state resident: full-time $7900. Tuition, nonresident: full-time $20,500. *Financial support:* In 2010–11, 73 students received support, including 12 fellowships with full tuition reimbursements available (averaging $15,000 per year), 34 research assistantships with full and partial tuition reimbursements available (averaging $11,142 per year), 26 teaching assistantships with tuition reimbursements available (averaging $11,142 per year); career-related internships or fieldwork, institutionally sponsored loans, scholarships/grants, health care benefits, and unspecified assistantships also available. Financial award application deadline: 12/1. *Faculty research:* Cognitive development/disability, child clinical, psychology and law, health/aging, social psychology. Total annual research expenditures: $2 million. *Unit head:* Dr. Beverly E. Thorn, Chair, 205-348-1919, Fax: 205-348-8648, E-mail: bthorn@bama.ua.edu. *Application contact:* Colett Thomas, Information Contact, 205-348-1913, Fax: 205-348-8648, E-mail: cthomas@as.ua.edu.

The University of Alabama at Birmingham, College of Arts and Sciences, Program in Psychology, Birmingham, AL 35294. Offers MA, PhD. *Accreditation:* APA (one or more programs are accredited). *Students:* 67 full-time (56 women), 4 part-time (3 women); includes 14 minority (7 Black or African American, non-Hispanic/Latino; 2 Asian, non-Hispanic/Latino; 3 Hispanic/Latino; 2 Two or more races, non-Hispanic/Latino), 2 international. Average age 28. 163 applicants, 15% accepted, 10 enrolled. In 2010, 11 master's, 11 doctorates awarded. *Application deadline:* Applications are processed on a rolling basis. Electronic applications accepted. *Expenses:* Tuition, state resident: full-time $5482. Tuition, nonresident: full-time $12,430. Tuition and fees vary according to program. *Financial support:* Career-related internships or fieldwork available. *Faculty research:* Biological basis of behavior structure, function of the nervous system. *Unit head:* Dr. Karlene Ball, Chair, 205-934-2610, Fax: 205-975-2295. *Application contact:* Julie Bryant, Director of Graduate Admissions, 205-934-8227, Fax: 205-934-8413, E-mail: jbryant@uab.edu.

The University of Alabama in Huntsville, School of Graduate Studies, College of Liberal Arts, Department of Psychology, Huntsville, AL 35899. Offers experimental psychology (MA); industrial and organizational psychology (MA). Part-time and evening/weekend programs available. *Faculty:* 7 full-time (4 women). *Students:* 6 full-time (3 women), 4 part-time (3 women). Average age 24. 9 applicants, 56% accepted, 3 enrolled. In 2010, 6 master's awarded. *Degree requirements:* For master's, comprehensive exam, thesis or alternative, oral and written exams. *Entrance requirements:* For master's, GRE General Test, 15 hours of course work in psychology, minimum GPA of 3.25, sample of written work. Additional exam requirements/recommendations for international students: Required—TOEFL (minimum score 500 paper-based; 173 computer-based; 62 iBT). *Application deadline:* For fall admission, 7/15 for domestic students, 4/1 for international students; for spring admission, 11/30 for domestic students, 9/1 for international students. Applications are processed on a rolling basis. Application fee: $40 ($50 for international students). Electronic applications accepted. *Expenses:* Tuition, state resident: full-time $7250; part-time $407.75 per credit hour. Tuition, nonresident: full-time $17,358; part-time $970.05 per credit hour. Required fees: $246.80 per semester. Tuition and fees vary according to course load and program. *Financial support:* In 2010–11, 8 students received support, including 2 teaching assistantships with full tuition reimbursements available (averaging $8,460 per year); career-related internships or fieldwork, Federal Work-Study, institutionally sponsored loans, scholarships/grants, health care benefits, tuition waivers (full), and unspecified assistantships also available. Support available to part-time students. Financial award application deadline: 4/1; financial award applicants required to submit FAFSA. *Faculty research:* Personal and social cognition, development and aging, human factors, perception, biological psychology: hormones and behavior. Total annual research expenditures: $228,509. *Unit head:* Dr. Jeffrey Neuschatz, Assistant Chair, 256-824-2321, Fax: 256-824-2387, E-mail: neuschaj@uah.edu. *Application contact:* Kathy Biggs, Graduate Studies Admissions Manager, 256-824-6199, Fax: 256-824-6405, E-mail: deangrad@uah.edu.

University of Alaska Anchorage, College of Arts and Sciences, Department of Psychology, Anchorage, AK 99508. Offers clinical psychology (MS); clinical-community psychology with rural-indigenous emphasis (PhD). Part-time programs available. *Degree requirements:* For master's, thesis. *Entrance requirements:* For master's, GRE General Test, GRE Subject Test, interview, references; for doctorate, interview, bachelor's or master's degree in psychology. Additional exam requirements/recommendations for international students: Required—TOEFL (minimum score 550 paper-based; 213 computer-based). *Faculty research:* Substance abuse, childhood autism, biofeedback, psychological assessment, mental health in Native Alaskans.

University of Alaska Fairbanks, College of Liberal Arts, Department of Psychology, Fairbanks, AK 99775-6480. Offers clinical-community psychology (PhD), including rural cross-cultural emphasis. Program offered jointly with University of Alaska Anchorage. *Faculty:* 8 full-time (5 women). *Students:* 2 full-time (both women), 28 part-time (25 women); includes 9 minority (2 American Indian or Alaska Native, non-Hispanic/Latino; 2 Hispanic/Latino; 5 Two or more races, non-Hispanic/Latino), 1 international. Average age 31. 36 applicants, 39% accepted, 12 enrolled. *Degree requirements:* For doctorate, comprehensive exam, thesis/dissertation, oral exam, oral defense. *Entrance requirements:* For doctorate, disclosure statement. Additional exam requirements/recommendations for international students: Required—TOEFL (minimum score 550 paper-based; 213 computer-based; 80 iBT). *Application deadline:* For fall admission, 12/15 for domestic and international students. Application fee: $60. *Expenses:* Tuition, state resident: full-time $5688; part-time $316 per credit. Tuition, nonresident: full-time $11,628; part-time $646 per credit. Required fees: $289 per semester. Tuition and fees vary according to course load and reciprocity agreements. *Financial support:* In 2010–11, 7 research assistantships with tuition reimbursements (averaging $16,679 per year), 6 teaching assistantships with tuition reimbursements (averaging $17,997 per year) were awarded; fellowships with tuition reimbursements, career-related internships or fieldwork, Federal Work-Study, scholarships/grants, health care benefits, and unspecified assistantships also available. Support available to part-time students. Financial award application deadline: 7/1; financial award applicants required to submit FAFSA. *Faculty research:* Clinical and community psychology; rural, indigenous, and cultural psychology. Total annual research expenditures: $42,389. *Unit head:* Dr. Dani Sheppard, Department Chair, 907-474-7007, Fax: 907-474-5781, E-mail: fypsych@uaf.edu. *Application contact:* Dr. Dani Sheppard, Department Chair, 907-474-7007, Fax: 907-474-5781, E-mail: fypsych@uaf.edu.

University of Alberta, Faculty of Graduate Studies and Research, Department of Psychology, Edmonton, AB T6G 2E1, Canada. Offers M Sc, MA, PhD. Terminal master's awarded for partial completion of doctoral program. *Degree requirements:* For master's, thesis (for some programs); for doctorate, thesis/dissertation. *Entrance requirements:* For master's and doctorate, GRE. Additional exam requirements/recommendations for international students: Required—TOEFL (minimum score 550 paper-based; 213 computer-based). Electronic applications accepted. *Faculty research:* Animal behavior processes; cognitive, social and perceptual processes; development and aging; neuroscience.

The University of Arizona, College of Science, Department of Psychology, Tucson, AZ 85721. Offers MA, PhD. *Accreditation:* APA (one or more programs are accredited). *Faculty:* 20 full-time (7 women), 3 part-time/adjunct (1 woman). *Students:* 63 full-time (41 women), 18 part-time (12 women); includes 1 Asian, non-Hispanic/Latino; 12 Hispanic/Latino; 5 Two or more races, non-Hispanic/Latino, 10 international. Average age 31. 364 applicants, 4% accepted, 11 enrolled. In 2010, 11 master's, 8 doctorates awarded. *Degree requirements:* For doctorate, comprehensive exam, thesis/dissertation. *Entrance requirements:* For master's, GRE General Test, 3 letters of recommendation, statement of purpose; for doctorate, GRE General Test, 3 letters of recommendation. Additional exam requirements/recommendations for international students: Required—TOEFL (minimum score 550 paper-based; 213 computer-based; 79 iBT). *Application deadline:* For fall admission, 12/15 for domestic and international students. Applications are processed on a rolling basis. Application fee: $65. Electronic applications accepted. *Expenses:* Tuition, state resident: full-time $7692. *Financial support:* In 2010–11, 19 research assistantships with full tuition reimbursements (averaging $17,892 per year), 44 teaching assistantships with full tuition reimbursements (averaging $17,892 per year) were awarded; scholarships/grants, health care benefits, and unspecified assistantships also available. Financial award application deadline: 1/1; financial award applicants required to submit FAFSA. *Faculty research:* Cognitive neuroscience, aging, law and psychology, psycholinguistics, family psychology. Total annual research expenditures: $5 million. *Unit head:* Dr. Alfred W. Kaszniak, Head, 520-621-5149, Fax: 520-621-9306, E-mail: kaszniak@u.arizona.edu. *Application contact:* Beth Owens, Information Contact, 520-621-7456, Fax: 520-621-9306, E-mail: psycgrad@u.arizona.edu.

University of Arkansas, Graduate School, J. William Fulbright College of Arts and Sciences, Department of Psychology, Fayetteville, AR 72701-1201. Offers MA, PhD. *Accreditation:* APA (one or more programs are accredited). *Students:* 28 full-time (19 women), 15 part-time (8 women); includes 2 minority (both Hispanic/Latino), 1 international. 18 applicants, 100% accepted. In 2010, 8 master's, 8 doctorates awarded. *Degree requirements:* For master's, thesis; for doctorate, variable foreign language requirement, thesis/dissertation. *Entrance requirements:* For doctorate, GRE General Test, GRE Subject Test. *Application deadline:* For fall admission, 4/1 for international students; for spring admission, 10/1 for international students. Applications are processed on a rolling basis. Application fee: $40 ($50 for international students). Electronic applications accepted. *Financial support:* In 2010–11, 28 fellowships with tuition reimbursements, 30 research assistantships, 4 teaching assistantships were awarded; career-related internships or fieldwork, Federal Work-Study, and traineeships also available. Support available to part-time students. Financial award application deadline: 4/1; financial award applicants required to submit FAFSA. *Unit head:* Dr. Doug Behrend, Departmental Chairperson, 479-575-4256, Fax: 479-575-3219, E-mail: psycapp@uark.edu. *Application contact:* Dr. Doug Behrend, Departmental Chairperson, 479-575-4256, Fax: 479-575-3219, E-mail: psycapp@uark.edu.

University of Arkansas at Little Rock, Graduate School, College of Arts, Humanities, and Social Science, Department of Psychology, Little Rock, AR 72204-1099. Offers applied psychology (MAP). Part-time and evening/weekend programs available. *Entrance requirements:* For master's, GRE General Test, minimum GPA of 2.7. *Faculty research:* Psychological methods and theories in business industry, government, and organizations; personnel program evaluation; training; affirmative action; organizational analysis and development.

The University of British Columbia, Faculty of Arts and Faculty of Graduate Studies, Department of Psychology, Vancouver, BC V6T 1Z4, Canada. Offers behavioral neuroscience (MA, PhD); clinical psychology (MA, PhD); cognitive science (MA, PhD); developmental psychology (MA, PhD); health psychology (MA, PhD); quantitative methods (MA, PhD); social/personality psychology (MA, PhD). *Accreditation:* APA (one or more programs are accredited). Terminal master's awarded for partial completion of doctoral program. *Degree requirements:* For master's, thesis; for doctorate, comprehensive exam, thesis/dissertation. *Entrance requirements:* For master's and doctorate, GRE General Test. Additional exam requirements/recommendations for international students: Required—TOEFL (minimum score 550 paper-based; 230 computer-based; 80 iBT). Electronic applications accepted. Tuition charges are reported in Canadian dollars. *Expenses:* Tuition, area resident: Full-time $4179 Canadian dollars. International tuition: $7344 Canadian dollars full-time. *Faculty research:* Clinical, developmental, social/personality, cognition, behavioral neuroscience.

University of Calgary, Faculty of Graduate Studies, Faculty of Social Sciences, Department of Psychology, Calgary, AB T2N 1N4, Canada. Offers clinical psychology (M Sc, PhD); psychology (M Sc, PhD). *Degree requirements:* For master's, thesis; for doctorate, thesis/dissertation. *Entrance requirements:* For master's, GRE General Test, bachelor's degree in psychology, minimum GPA of 3.4. Additional exam requirements/recommendations for international students: Required—TOEFL (minimum score 550 paper-based; 213 computer-based). Electronic applications accepted. *Faculty research:* Cognition and cognitive development, social psychology, theoretical psychology, perception, aging.

University of California, Berkeley, Graduate Division, College of Letters and Science, Department of Psychology, Berkeley, CA 94720-1500. Offers PhD. *Accreditation:* APA. *Degree requirements:* For doctorate, thesis/dissertation, qualifying exam. *Entrance requirements:* For doctorate, GRE General Test, GRE Subject Test, minimum GPA of 3.0, 3 letters of recommendation. Electronic applications accepted.

University of California, Davis, Graduate Studies, Program in Psychology, Davis, CA 95616. Offers PhD. *Degree requirements:* For doctorate, thesis/dissertation. *Entrance requirements:* For doctorate, GRE General Test, GRE Subject Test, minimum GPA of 3.0. Additional exam requirements/recommendations for international students: Required—TOEFL (minimum score 550 paper-based; 213 computer-based). Electronic applications accepted. *Faculty research:* Social personality, perception, cognition, psychobiology.

University of California, Irvine, School of Social Ecology, Department of Psychology and Social Behavior, Irvine, CA 92697. Offers PhD. *Students:* 61 full-time (40 women); includes 14 minority (1 Black or African American, non-Hispanic/Latino; 9 Asian, non-Hispanic/Latino; 3 Hispanic/Latino; 1 Two or more races, non-Hispanic/Latino), 1 international. Average age 28. 209 applicants, 4% accepted, 9 enrolled. In 2010, 5 doctorates awarded. *Degree requirements:* For doctorate, thesis/dissertation, research project. *Entrance requirements:* For doctorate, GRE General Test, minimum GPA of 3.0. Additional exam requirements/recommendations for international students: Required—TOEFL (minimum score 550 paper-based; 213 computer-based). *Application deadline:* For fall admission, 12/15 priority date for domestic and international students. Applications are processed on a rolling basis. Application fee: $80 ($100 for international students). Electronic applications accepted. *Financial support:* Fellowships, research assistantships with full tuition reimbursements, teaching assistantships, institutionally sponsored loans, traineeships, health care benefits, and unspecified assistantships available. Financial award application deadline: 3/1; financial award applicants required to submit FAFSA. *Faculty research:* Psychosocial development in children, adolescents, and adults; gerontology, childhood behavior disorders, and developmental psychopathology; sex differences; attitude change; social psychology. *Unit head:* Prof. Peter H. Ditto, Chair, 949-824-8168, Fax: 949-824-3002, E-mail: phditto@uci.edu. *Application contact:* Susan A. Morrison, PSB Research & Graduate Program Coordinator, 949-824-9526, Fax: 949-824-3002, E-mail: samorris@uci.edu.

University of California, Irvine, School of Social Sciences, Department of Cognitive Science, Irvine, CA 92697. Offers psychology (PhD). *Students:* 56 full-time (22 women), 2 part-time (1 woman); includes 15 minority (8 Asian, non-Hispanic/Latino; 7 Hispanic/Latino), 5 international. Average age 28. 94 applicants, 23% accepted, 10 enrolled. In 2010, 9 doctorates awarded. *Degree requirements:* For doctorate, thesis/dissertation. *Entrance requirements:* For doctorate, GRE General Test, minimum GPA of 3.0. Additional exam requirements/recommendations for international students: Required—TOEFL (minimum score 550 paper-based; 213 computer-based). *Application deadline:* For fall admission, 1/15 priority date for domestic and international students. Applications are processed on a rolling basis. Application fee: $80 ($100 for international students). Electronic applications accepted. *Financial support:* Fellowships, research assistantships with full tuition reimbursements, teaching assistantships, institutionally sponsored loans, traineeships, health care benefits, and unspecified assistantships available. Financial award application deadline: 3/1; financial award applicants required to submit FAFSA. *Faculty research:* Mathematical psychology, visual and auditory perception, cognitive development, problem solving, experimental psychology. *Unit head:* Prof. Michael David Lee, Chair, 949-824-2969, Fax: 949-824-2307, E-mail: mdlee@uci.edu. *Application contact:* Prof. Geoff Iverson, Professor and Graduate Director, 949-824-4023, Fax: 949-824-2357, E-mail: giverson@uci.edu.

University of California, Los Angeles, Graduate Division, College of Letters and Science, Department of Psychology, Los Angeles, CA 90034. Offers MA, PhD. *Accreditation:* APA (one or more programs are accredited). *Faculty:* 67 full-time (28 women). *Students:* 196 full-time (138 women); includes 54 minority (7 Black or African American, non-Hispanic/Latino; 25 Asian, non-Hispanic/Latino; 18 Hispanic/Latino; 4 Two or more races, non-Hispanic/Latino), 6 international. Average age 27. 781 applicants, 6% accepted, 42 enrolled. In 2010, 30 master's, 38 doctorates awarded. Terminal master's awarded for partial completion of doctoral program. *Degree requirements:* For master's, comprehensive exam; for doctorate, thesis/dissertation, oral and written qualifying exams, teaching experience. *Entrance requirements:* For master's, GRE General Test, GRE Subject Test, minimum GPA of 3.0; for doctorate, GRE General Test, GRE Subject Test, MAT, minimum undergraduate GPA of 3.0. Additional exam requirements/recommendations for international students: Required—TOEFL. Application fee: $70 ($90 for international students). Electronic applications accepted. *Financial support:* In 2010–11, 148 fellowships with full and partial tuition reimbursements, 69 research assistantships with full and partial tuition reimbursements, 116 teaching assistantships with full and partial tuition reimbursements were awarded; Federal Work-Study, institutionally sponsored loans, scholarships/grants, health care benefits, tuition waivers (full and partial), and unspecified assistantships also available. Financial award application deadline: 3/1; financial award applicants required to submit FAFSA. *Unit head:* Dr. Bruce Baker, Chair, 310-825-2288, E-mail: baker@psych.ucla.edu. *Application contact:* Department Office, 310-825-2617, E-mail: gradadm@psych.ucla.edu.

University of California, Riverside, Graduate Division, Department of Psychology, Riverside, CA 92521-0102. Offers MA, PhD. *Accreditation:* APA. *Degree requirements:* For doctorate, comprehensive exam, thesis/dissertation, 3 quarters of teaching experience, qualifying exams. *Entrance requirements:* For doctorate, GRE General Test, minimum GPA of 3.2. Additional exam requirements/recommendations for international students: Required—TOEFL (minimum score 550 paper-based; 213 computer-based; 80 iBT). Electronic applications accepted. *Faculty research:* Neuroscience, personality and social psychology, developmental psychology, cognition, health psychology, quantitative psychology.

University of California, San Diego, Office of Graduate Studies, Department of Psychology, La Jolla, CA 92093. Offers PhD. *Degree requirements:* For doctorate, thesis/dissertation. *Entrance requirements:* For doctorate, GRE General Test. Electronic applications accepted.

University of California, San Diego, Office of Graduate Studies, Interdisciplinary Program in Cognitive Science, La Jolla, CA 92093. Offers cognitive science/anthropology (PhD); cognitive science/communication (PhD); cognitive science/computer science and engineering (PhD); cognitive science/linguistics (PhD); cognitive science/neuroscience (PhD); cognitive science/philosophy (PhD); cognitive science/psychology (PhD); cognitive science/sociology (PhD). Admissions offered through affiliated departments. *Degree requirements:* For doctorate, thesis/dissertation. *Entrance requirements:* For doctorate, GRE General Test, acceptance into one of the eight participating departments. *Faculty research:* Language and cognition, philosophy of mind, visual perception, biological anthropology, sociolinguistics.

University of California, Santa Barbara, Graduate Division, College of Letters and Sciences, Division of Mathematics, Life, and Physical Sciences, Department of Psychology, Santa Barbara, CA 93106-9660. Offers cognitive science (PhD); psychology (PhD); quantitative methods in the social sciences (PhD). *Faculty:* 33 full-time (10 women). *Students:* 59 full-time (36 women); includes 2 Black or African American, non-Hispanic/Latino; 8 Asian, non-Hispanic/Latino. Average age 27. 240 applicants, 6% accepted, 5 enrolled. In 2010, 8 doctorates awarded. Terminal master's awarded for partial completion of doctoral program. *Degree requirements:* For doctorate, comprehensive exam, thesis/dissertation, teaching assistant training, progress report, papers, mini-convention presentation, 1 quarter of student teaching or teaching assistant class with section lab. *Entrance requirements:* For doctorate, GRE General Test. Additional exam requirements/recommendations for international students: Required—TOEFL (minimum score 550 paper-based; 80 iBT), IELTS (minimum score 7). *Application deadline:* For fall admission, 12/1 for domestic and international students. Application fee: $70 ($90 for international students). Electronic applications accepted. *Financial support:* In 2010–11, 59 students received support, including 60 fellowships with full and partial tuition reimbursements available (averaging $6,819 per year), 29 research assistantships with full and partial tuition reimbursements available (averaging $10,114 per year), 48 teaching assistantships with full and partial tuition reimbursements available (averaging $11,597 per year); tuition waivers (full and partial) also available. Financial award application deadline: 12/15; financial award applicants required to submit FAFSA. *Faculty research:* Social psychology; developmental and evolutionary psychology; neuroscience and behavior; cognition, perception and cognitive neuroscience. Total annual research expenditures: $6 million. *Unit head:* Greg Ashby, Chair, 805-893-2130, Fax: 805-893-4303. *Application contact:* Greg Ashby, Chair, 805-893-2130, Fax: 805-893-4303.

University of California, Santa Cruz, Division of Graduate Studies, Division of Social Sciences, Department of Psychology, Santa Cruz, CA 95064. Offers PhD. *Students:* 58 full-time (41 women), 5 part-time (all women); includes 24 minority (2 Black or African American, non-Hispanic/Latino; 1 American Indian or Alaska Native, non-Hispanic/Latino; 5 Asian, non-Hispanic/Latino; 15 Hispanic/Latino; 1 Two or more races, non-Hispanic/Latino), 2 international. Average age 31. 162 applicants, 9% accepted, 9 enrolled. In 2010, 8 doctorates awarded. *Degree requirements:* For doctorate, thesis/dissertation, qualifying exam, seminars. *Entrance requirements:* For doctorate, GRE General Test. Additional exam requirements/recommendations for international students: Required—TOEFL (minimum score 550 paper-based; 220 computer-based; 83 iBT); Recommended—IELTS (minimum score 8). *Application deadline:* For fall admission, 1/15 for domestic and international students. Application fee: $70 ($90 for international students). Electronic applications accepted. *Financial support:* Fellowships, research assistantships, teaching assistantships, institutionally sponsored loans and tuition waivers available. Financial award applicants required to submit FAFSA. *Faculty research:* Cognitive psychology, developmental psychology, social psychology. *Unit head:* Allison Land, Graduate

Psychology—General

University of California, Santa Cruz (continued)
Program Coordinator, 831-459-4932, E-mail: allison@ucsc.edu. *Application contact:* Allison Land, Graduate Program Coordinator, 831-459-4932, E-mail: allison@ucsc.edu.

University of Central Arkansas, Graduate School, College of Health and Behavioral Sciences, Department of Counseling and Psychology, Conway, AR 72035-0001. Offers community counseling (MS); counseling psychology (MS); school psychology (MS, PhD). *Accreditation:* APA. *Faculty:* 17 full-time (4 women). *Students:* 64 full-time (50 women), 41 part-time (36 women); includes 12 Black or African American, non-Hispanic/Latino; 2 Asian, non-Hispanic/Latino; 1 Hispanic/Latino, 2 international. Average age 27. 41 applicants, 80% accepted, 32 enrolled. In 2010, 45 master's, 3 doctorates awarded. Terminal master's awarded for partial completion of doctoral program. *Degree requirements:* For master's, comprehensive exam, thesis optional, internship; for doctorate, comprehensive exam, thesis/dissertation, internship. *Entrance requirements:* For master's, GRE General Test, minimum GPA of 2.75; for doctorate, GRE General Test, minimum GPA of 3.25. Additional exam requirements/recommendations for international students: Required—TOEFL (minimum score 550 paper-based; 213 computer-based). *Application deadline:* For fall admission, 3/1 priority date for domestic students; for spring admission, 10/1 priority date for domestic students. Applications are processed on a rolling basis. Application fee: $25 ($50 for international students). *Financial support:* In 2010–11, 17 research assistantships with partial tuition reimbursements (averaging $6,000 per year) were awarded; career-related internships or fieldwork, Federal Work-Study, scholarships/grants, tuition waivers (partial), and unspecified assistantships also available. Support available to part-time students. Financial award application deadline: 6/30; financial award applicants required to submit FAFSA. *Unit head:* Dr. David Skotko, Chair, 501-450-3175, Fax: 501-450-5424, E-mail: davids@uca.edu. *Application contact:* Susan Wood, Administrative Assistant, 501-450-3124, Fax: 501-450-5678, E-mail: swood@uca.edu.

University of Central Florida, College of Sciences, Department of Psychology, Orlando, FL 32816. Offers applied experimental and human factors psychology (MA, PhD); clinical psychology (MA, MS, PhD); industrial/organizational psychology (MS, PhD). *Accreditation:* APA. Part-time and evening/weekend programs available. *Faculty:* 48 full-time (18 women), 9 part-time/adjunct (4 women). *Students:* 174 full-time (105 women), 17 part-time (12 women); includes 10 Black or African American, non-Hispanic/Latino; 9 Asian, non-Hispanic/Latino; 20 Hispanic/Latino; 1 Two or more races, non-Hispanic/Latino, 10 international. Average age 27. 468 applicants, 17% accepted, 44 enrolled. In 2010, 36 master's, 7 doctorates awarded. *Degree requirements:* For doctorate, thesis/dissertation, candidacy exam. *Entrance requirements:* For master's, GRE General Test, minimum GPA of 3.0 in last 60 hours. Additional exam requirements/recommendations for international students: Required—TOEFL. *Application deadline:* For fall admission, 2/15 for domestic students. Application fee: $30. Electronic applications accepted. *Expenses:* Tuition, state resident: part-time $256.56 per credit hour. Tuition, nonresident: part-time $1011.52 per credit hour. Part-time tuition and fees vary according to program. *Financial support:* In 2010–11, 128 students received support, including 20 fellowships with partial tuition reimbursements available (averaging $7,400 per year), 59 research assistantships with partial tuition reimbursements available (averaging $10,300 per year), 99 teaching assistantships with partial tuition reimbursements available (averaging $8,000 per year); career-related internships or fieldwork, Federal Work-Study, institutionally sponsored loans, tuition waivers (partial), and unspecified assistantships also available. Financial award application deadline: 3/1; financial award applicants required to submit FAFSA. *Faculty research:* Professional ethical decision making, electronic selection systems, psychometrics. *Unit head:* Dr. Robert Dipboye, Chair, 407-823-2216, E-mail: rdipboye@mail.ucf.edu. *Application contact:* Dr. Robert Dipboye, Chair, 407-823-2216, E-mail: rdipboye@mail.ucf.edu.

University of Central Missouri, The Graduate School, College of Arts, Humanities and Social Sciences, Warrensburg, MO 64093. Offers English (MA); history (MA); mass communication (MA); music (MA); psychology (MS); speech communication (MA); teaching English as a second language (MA); theatre (MA). Part-time programs available. *Entrance requirements:* Additional exam requirements/recommendations for international students: Required—TOEFL (minimum score 550 paper-based; 79 computer-based). Electronic applications accepted.

University of Central Oklahoma, College of Graduate Studies and Research, College of Education, Department of Psychology, Program in General Psychology, Edmond, OK 73034-5209. Offers MA. *Degree requirements:* For master's, thesis. *Entrance requirements:* For master's, GRE General Test. Additional exam requirements/recommendations for international students: Required—TOEFL (minimum score 550 paper-based; 213 computer-based). Electronic applications accepted.

University of Chicago, Division of Social Sciences, Department of Psychology, Chicago, IL 60637-1513. Offers PhD. *Degree requirements:* For doctorate, one foreign language, thesis/dissertation, exams. *Entrance requirements:* For doctorate, GRE General Test, GRE Subject Test. Additional exam requirements/recommendations for international students: Required—TOEFL, IELTS (minimum score 7). Electronic applications accepted.

University of Cincinnati, Graduate School, McMicken College of Arts and Sciences, Department of Psychology, Cincinnati, OH 45221. Offers clinical psychology (PhD); experimental psychology (PhD). *Accreditation:* APA. *Degree requirements:* For doctorate, comprehensive exam, thesis/dissertation. *Entrance requirements:* For doctorate, GRE General Test. Additional exam requirements/recommendations for international students: Required—TOEFL. *Faculty research:* Neuropsychology, human factors, health.

University of Colorado at Colorado Springs, College of Letters, Arts and Sciences, Department of Psychology, Colorado Springs, CO 80933-7150. Offers MA, PhD. *Accreditation:* APA. Part-time programs available. *Faculty:* 14 full-time (7 women), 1 part-time/adjunct (0 women). *Students:* 51 full-time (30 women), 3 part-time (0 women); includes 1 Black or African American, non-Hispanic/Latino; 1 Asian, non-Hispanic/Latino; 3 Hispanic/Latino; 1 Two or more races, non-Hispanic/Latino, 1 international. Average age 27. 69 applicants, 65% accepted, 19 enrolled. In 2010, 12 master's, 3 doctorates awarded. *Degree requirements:* For master's, thesis; for doctorate, comprehensive exam, thesis/dissertation. *Entrance requirements:* For master's, GRE, BA in psychology or equivalent background; minimum GPA of 3.0. *Application deadline:* For fall admission, 1/1 for domestic students. Applications are processed on a rolling basis. Application fee: $60 ($75 for international students). *Expenses:* Tuition, state resident: full-time $7916. Tuition, nonresident: full-time $16,610. Tuition and fees vary according to course load, degree level, program, reciprocity agreements and student level. *Financial support:* Research assistantships, teaching assistantships, career-related internships or fieldwork, Federal Work-Study, and scholarships/grants available. Support available to part-time students. Financial award application deadline: 3/1; financial award applicants required to submit FAFSA. *Faculty research:* Aging, social psychology, learning and memory, personality disorders, psychology and law. Total annual research expenditures: $240,375. *Unit head:* Dr. Michael Kisley, Director, Graduate Training, 719-255-4177, Fax: 719-255-4166, E-mail: mkisley@uccs.edu. *Application contact:* Dr. David Dubois, Graduate Student Advisor, 719-255-4500, Fax: 719-255-4166, E-mail: ddubois@uccs.edu.

University of Colorado Boulder, Graduate School, College of Arts and Sciences, Department of Psychology and Neuroscience, Boulder, CO 80309. Offers MA, PhD. *Accreditation:* APA (one or more programs are accredited). *Faculty:* 39 full-time (12 women). *Students:* 123 full-time (60 women), 7 part-time (6 women); includes 4 minority (1 Asian, non-Hispanic/Latino; 3 Hispanic/Latino), 8 international. Average age 30. 412 applicants, 7 enrolled. In 2010, 17 master's, 25 doctorates awarded. *Degree requirements:* For master's, comprehensive exam; for doctorate, thesis/dissertation. *Entrance requirements:* For master's, GRE General Test, minimum undergraduate GPA of 2.75; for doctorate, GRE General Test. *Application deadline:* For fall admission, 1/1 for domestic students, 12/1 for international students. Application fee: $50 ($60 for international students). *Financial support:* In 2010–11, 33 fellowships (averaging $13,156 per year), 41 research assistantships (averaging $13,718 per year) were awarded; tuition waivers (full) also available. Financial award application deadline: 1/1. *Faculty research:* Clinical psychology, behavioral genetics, behavioral neuroscience, cognitive psychology, social psychology. Total annual research expenditures: $17.5 million.

University of Connecticut, Graduate School, College of Liberal Arts and Sciences, Department of Psychology, Storrs, CT 06269. Offers behavioral neuroscience (PhD); biopsychology (PhD); clinical psychology (MA, PhD); cognition and instruction (PhD); developmental psychology (MA, PhD); ecological psychology (PhD); experimental psychology (PhD); general psychology (MA, PhD); health psychology (Graduate Certificate); industrial/organizational psychology (PhD); language and cognition (PhD); neuroscience (PhD); occupational health psychology (Graduate Certificate); social psychology (MA, PhD). *Accreditation:* APA. Terminal master's awarded for partial completion of doctoral program. *Degree requirements:* For master's, comprehensive exam; for doctorate, thesis/dissertation. *Entrance requirements:* For master's and doctorate, GRE General Test, GRE Subject Test. Additional exam requirements/recommendations for international students: Required—TOEFL (minimum score 550 paper-based; 213 computer-based). Electronic applications accepted.

University of Dallas, Braniff Graduate School of Liberal Arts, Program in Psychology, Irving, TX 75062-4736. Offers M Psych, MA. Part-time programs available. *Degree requirements:* For master's, one foreign language, comprehensive exam (for some programs), thesis (for some programs). *Entrance requirements:* Additional exam requirements/recommendations for international students: Required—TOEFL. *Expenses:* Tuition: Full-time $7500; part-time $720 per credit hour. Required fees: $500; $60 per credit hour. $300 per semester. One-time fee: $150. Tuition and fees vary according to program and student level.

University of Dayton, Graduate School, College of Arts and Sciences, Department of Psychology, Dayton, OH 45469-1300. Offers clinical psychology (MA); general psychology (MA). *Faculty:* 18 full-time (5 women), 2 part-time/adjunct (1 woman). *Students:* 21 full-time (17 women), 3 part-time (2 women); includes 5 minority (2 Black or African American, non-Hispanic/Latino; 1 American Indian or Alaska Native, non-Hispanic/Latino; 1 Asian, non-Hispanic/Latino; 1 Hispanic/Latino), 1 international. Average age 25. 72 applicants, 18% accepted, 8 enrolled. In 2010, 15 master's awarded. *Degree requirements:* For master's, thesis. *Entrance requirements:* For master's, GRE General Test, GRE Subject Test (recommended). Additional exam requirements/recommendations for international students: Required—TOEFL (minimum score 550 paper-based; 213 computer-based; 80 iBT). *Application deadline:* For fall admission, 3/1 priority date for domestic students, 2/1 priority date for international students. Application fee: $0 ($50 for international students). Electronic applications accepted. *Expenses:* Tuition: Full-time $7800; part-time $650 per credit hour. *Financial support:* In 2010–11, 21 students received support, including 3 fellowships, 10 research assistantships with full tuition reimbursements available (averaging $10,298 per year); institutionally sponsored loans, traineeships, health care benefits, and tuition waivers (partial) also available. Financial award application deadline: 3/1; financial award applicants required to submit FAFSA. *Faculty research:* Cognitive processes, interpersonal processes, television and children, perception, personality psychology, family relationship issues, conduct disorders, trauma/revictimization, community problems. *Unit head:* Dr. Carolyn Roecker-Phelps, Chair, 937-229-2713, Fax: 937-229-3900, E-mail: biers@udayton.edu. *Application contact:* Alexander Popovski, Associate Director of International and Graduate Admissions, 937-229-2357, Fax: 937-229-4729, E-mail: alex.popovski@notes.udayton.edu.

University of Delaware, College of Arts and Sciences, Department of Psychology, Newark, DE 19716. Offers behavioral neuroscience (PhD); clinical psychology (PhD); cognitive psychology (PhD); social psychology (PhD). *Accreditation:* APA. *Degree requirements:* For doctorate, thesis/dissertation. *Entrance requirements:* For doctorate, GRE General Test. Additional exam requirements/recommendations for international students: Required—TOEFL (minimum score 600 paper-based; 250 computer-based). Electronic applications accepted. *Faculty research:* Emotion development, neural and cognitive aspects of memory, neural control of feeding, intergroup relations, social cognition and communication.

University of Denver, Division of Arts, Humanities and Social Sciences, Department of Psychology, Denver, CO 80208. Offers affective science (PhD); affective/social psychology (PhD); clinical child psychology (PhD); developmental cognitive neuroscience (PhD); developmental psychology (PhD). Incidental Master's program available. *Accreditation:* APA. *Faculty:* 18 full-time (8 women), 5 part-time/adjunct (4 women). *Students:* 32 full-time (31 women), 2 part-time (1 woman); includes 6 minority (3 Asian, non-Hispanic/Latino; 2 Hispanic/Latino; 1 Two or more races, non-Hispanic/Latino), 2 international. Average age 26. 320 applicants, 5% accepted, 13 enrolled. In 2010, 6 doctorates awarded. Terminal master's awarded for partial completion of doctoral program. *Degree requirements:* For doctorate, one foreign language, comprehensive exam (for some programs), thesis/dissertation. *Entrance requirements:* For doctorate, GRE General Test. Additional exam requirements/recommendations for international students: Required—TOEFL (minimum score 550 paper-based; 80 iBT). *Application deadline:* For fall admission, 12/1 for domestic students. Applications are processed on a rolling basis. Application fee: $60. Electronic applications accepted. *Expenses:* Tuition: Full-time $35,604; part-time $29,670 per year. Required fees: $687 per year. Tuition and fees vary according to program. *Financial support:* In 2010–11, 12 research assistantships with full and partial tuition reimbursements (averaging $15,500 per year), 22 teaching assistantships with full and partial tuition reimbursements (averaging $16,773 per year) were awarded; career-related internships or fieldwork, Federal Work-Study, institutionally sponsored loans, scholarships/grants, and unspecified assistantships also available. Support available to part-time students. Financial award application deadline: 1/1; financial award applicants required to submit FAFSA. *Faculty research:* Developmental neuropsychology, self-esteem and peer relationships, child abuse and neglect, marital and family interactions, adolescent peer and romantic relationships. *Unit head:* Dr. Rob Roberts, Chair, 303-871-3792, Fax: 303-871-4747. *Application contact:* Paula Plank-Houghtaling, Graduate Secretary, 303-871-3803, Fax: 303-871-4747, E-mail: info@psy.du.edu.

University of Denver, Graduate School of Professional Psychology, Denver, CO 80208. Offers clinical psychology (Psy D); forensic psychology (MA); international disaster psychology (MA); psychology (MA); sport and performance psychology (MA). *Accreditation:* APA. *Faculty:* 15 full-time (8 women), 24 part-time/adjunct (11 women). *Students:* 209 full-time (170 women), 36 part-time (25 women); includes 26 minority (7 Black or African American, non-Hispanic/Latino; 2 American Indian or Alaska Native, non-Hispanic/Latino; 5 Asian, non-Hispanic/Latino; 9 Hispanic/Latino; 3 Two or more races, non-Hispanic/Latino), 4 international. Average age 26. 612 applicants, 30% accepted, 124 enrolled. In 2010, 74 master's, 38 doctorates awarded. *Degree requirements:* For master's, comprehensive exam (for some programs); for doctorate, comprehensive exam (for some programs), paper, clinical internship. *Entrance requirements:* For master's and doctorate, GRE General Test. Additional exam requirements/recommendations for international students: Required—TOEFL (minimum score 550 paper-based; 80 iBT). Application fee: $60. Electronic applications accepted. *Expenses:* Tuition: Full-time $35,604; part-time $29,670 per year. Required fees: $687 per year. Tuition and fees vary according to program. *Financial support:* In 2010–11, 38 teaching assistantships with full and partial tuition reimbursements (averaging $2,952 per year) were awarded; career-related internships or fieldwork, Federal Work-Study, institutionally sponsored loans, scholarships/grants, unspecified assistantships, and clinical assistantships also available. Support available to part-time students. Financial award application deadline: 3/1; financial award applicants required to submit FAFSA. *Unit head:* Dr. Peter Buirski, Dean, 303-871-2382, E-mail: pbuirski@du.edu. *Application contact:* Admissions Counselor, 303-871-3736, Fax: 303-871-7656, E-mail: gsppinfo@du.edu.

University of Detroit Mercy, College of Liberal Arts and Education, Department of Psychology, Detroit, MI 48221. Offers clinical psychology (MA, PhD); industrial/organizational psychology (MA); school psychology (Spec). *Accreditation:* APA. Evening/weekend programs available. *Degree requirements:* For doctorate, departmental qualifying exam. *Faculty research:* Gerontology.

University of Florida, Graduate School, College of Liberal Arts and Sciences, Department of Psychology, Gainesville, FL 32611. Offers behavior analysis (PhD); behavioral neuroscience

(MS, PhD); cognitive and sensory processes (PhD); counseling psychology (PhD); developmental psychology (PhD); social psychology (MS, PhD); JD/PhD. *Faculty:* 29 full-time (10 women). *Students:* 106 full-time (82 women), 14 part-time (7 women); includes 3 Black or African American, non-Hispanic/Latino; 2 American Indian or Alaska Native, non-Hispanic/Latino; 7 Asian, non-Hispanic/Latino; 12 Hispanic/Latino, 11 international. Average age 27. 614 applicants, 7% accepted, 36 enrolled. In 2010, 25 master's, 13 doctorates awarded. *Degree requirements:* For master's, comprehensive exam, thesis or alternative; for doctorate, comprehensive exam, thesis/dissertation. *Entrance requirements:* For master's and doctorate, GRE General Test, minimum GPA of 3.0. Additional exam requirements/recommendations for international students: Required—TOEFL (minimum score 550 paper-based; 213 computer-based; 80 iBT), IELTS (minimum score 6). *Application deadline:* For fall admission, 12/9 priority date for domestic students, 12/9 for international students. Applications are processed on a rolling basis. Application fee: $30. Electronic applications accepted. *Expenses:* Tuition, state resident: full-time $10,915.92. Tuition, nonresident: full-time $28,309. *Financial support:* In 2010–11, 105 students received support, including 19 fellowships, 24 research assistantships (averaging $18,742 per year), 62 teaching assistantships (averaging $19,797 per year); career-related internships or fieldwork and unspecified assistantships also available. Financial award application deadline: 12/9; financial award applicants required to submit FAFSA. *Faculty research:* Behavior analysis, behavioral and cognitive neuroscience, counseling, developmental psychology, social psychology. Total annual research expenditures: $2.7 million. *Unit head:* Dr. Neil E. Rowland, Chair, 352-273-2128, Fax: 352-392-7985, E-mail: nrowland@ufl.edu. *Application contact:* Dr. Clive D. Wynne, Graduate Coordinator, 352-392-0601, Fax: 352-392-7985, E-mail: wynne@ufl.edu.

University of Georgia, College of Arts and Sciences, Department of Psychology, Athens, GA 30602. Offers MS, PhD. *Accreditation:* APA (one or more programs are accredited). *Faculty:* 31 full-time (11 women), 2 part-time/adjunct (1 woman). *Students:* 100 full-time (70 women), 11 part-time (9 women); includes 6 Black or African American, non-Hispanic/Latino; 3 Asian, non-Hispanic/Latino; 2 Hispanic/Latino, 10 international. 473 applicants, 7% accepted, 21 enrolled. In 2010, 19 master's, 17 doctorates awarded. *Degree requirements:* For master's, thesis; for doctorate, one foreign language, thesis/dissertation. *Entrance requirements:* For master's and doctorate, GRE General Test. Additional exam requirements/recommendations for international students: Required—TOEFL. *Application deadline:* For fall admission, 12/1 for domestic students; for spring admission, 11/15 for domestic students. Application fee: $50. Electronic applications accepted. *Expenses:* Tuition, state resident: full-time $7200; part-time $344 per credit hour. Tuition, nonresident: full-time $21,900; part-time $944 per credit hour. Tuition and fees vary according to course load and program. *Financial support:* Fellowships, research assistantships, teaching assistantships, unspecified assistantships available. *Unit head:* Dr. W. Keith Campbell, Head, 706-542-2174, Fax: 706-542-3275, E-mail: wkc@uga.edu. *Application contact:* Dr. Billy R. Hammond, Graduate Coordinator, 706-542-4812, Fax: 706-542-3275, E-mail: bhammond@uga.edu.

University of Guelph, Graduate Studies, College of Social and Applied Human Sciences, Department of Psychology, Guelph, ON N1G 2W1, Canada. Offers applied social psychology (MA, PhD); clinical psychology applied development emphasis (PhD); clinical psychology applied developmental emphasis (MA); industrial/organizational psychology (MA, PhD); neuroscience and applied cognitive science (MA, PhD). *Degree requirements:* For master's, thesis; for doctorate, comprehensive exam, thesis/dissertation. *Entrance requirements:* For master's, GRE General Test, GRE Subject Test, minimum B+ average during previous 2 years of course work; for doctorate, GRE General Test, GRE Subject Test, minimum A- average. Additional exam requirements/recommendations for international students: Required—TOEFL (minimum score 89 iBT). Electronic applications accepted. *Faculty research:* Organizational psychology, reading comprehension and mathematical ability, drug addiction and relapse, gender issues and culture, memory, clinical psychology.

University of Hartford, College of Arts and Sciences, Department of Psychology, West Hartford, CT 06117-1599. Offers clinical practices (MA, Psy D), including clinical practices (Psy D), psychology (MA); general experimental psychology (MA); organizational behavior (MS); school psychology (MS). *Accreditation:* APA. Part-time programs available. *Degree requirements:* For master's, comprehensive exam, thesis (for some programs). *Entrance requirements:* For master's, GRE General Test, GRE Subject Test, minimum GPA of 3.0; for doctorate, GRE General Test, GRE Subject Test. Additional exam requirements/recommendations for international students: Required—TOEFL (minimum score 550 paper-based; 213 computer-based). Electronic applications accepted. *Expenses:* Contact institution.

University of Hawaii at Manoa, Graduate Division, College of Social Sciences, Department of Psychology, Honolulu, HI 96822. Offers clinical psychology (PhD); community and cultural psychology (PhD); community and culture (MA); psychology (MA, PhD, Graduate Certificate). *Accreditation:* APA (one or more programs are accredited). Part-time programs available. *Faculty:* 35 full-time (12 women), 2 part-time/adjunct (1 woman). *Students:* 75 full-time (56 women), 17 part-time (12 women); includes 34 minority (1 Black or African American, non-Hispanic/Latino; 1 American Indian or Alaska Native, non-Hispanic/Latino; 12 Asian, non-Hispanic/Latino; 3 Hispanic/Latino; 6 Native Hawaiian or other Pacific Islander, non-Hispanic/Latino; 11 Two or more races, non-Hispanic/Latino), 13 international. Average age 31. 203 applicants, 10% accepted, 17 enrolled. In 2010, 9 master's, 4 doctorates awarded. Terminal master's awarded for partial completion of doctoral program. *Degree requirements:* For master's, comprehensive exam, thesis; for doctorate, comprehensive exam, thesis/dissertation. *Entrance requirements:* For master's and doctorate, GRE General Test, GRE Subject Test. Additional exam requirements/recommendations for international students: Required—TOEFL (minimum score 600 paper-based; 250 computer-based; 100 iBT), IELTS (minimum score 7). *Application deadline:* For fall admission, 1/1 for domestic and international students. Application fee: $60. *Financial support:* In 2010–11, 13 fellowships (averaging $6,425 per year), 42 research assistantships (averaging $14,690 per year), 14 teaching assistantships (averaging $14,802 per year) were awarded; career-related internships or fieldwork, institutionally sponsored loans, and tuition waivers (full and partial) also available. Financial award application deadline: 1/1. *Faculty research:* Cross-cultural psychology, health psychology, marine mammals, child/adult psychopathology. Total annual research expenditures: $1.3 million. *Application contact:* Charlene Baker, Graduate Chair, 808-956-8414, Fax: 808-956-4700, E-mail: bakercha@hawaii.edu.

University of Houston, College of Liberal Arts and Social Sciences, Department of Psychology, Houston, TX 77204. Offers clinical psychology (PhD); developmental psychology (PhD); industrial/organizational psychology (PhD); psychology (MA); social psychology (PhD). *Accreditation:* APA (one or more programs are accredited). *Faculty:* 28 full-time (12 women), 7 part-time/adjunct (4 women). *Students:* 117 full-time (86 women), 22 part-time (16 women); includes 7 Black or African American, non-Hispanic/Latino; 10 Asian, non-Hispanic/Latino; 16 Hispanic/Latino; 4 Two or more races, non-Hispanic/Latino, 17 international. Average age 27. 460 applicants, 6% accepted, 28 enrolled. In 2010, 19 master's, 20 doctorates awarded. *Degree requirements:* For master's, comprehensive exam, thesis; for doctorate, comprehensive exam, thesis/dissertation. *Entrance requirements:* For master's, GRE General Test, career statement, 3 letters of recommendation; for doctorate, GRE General Test, 3 letters of recommendation. Additional exam requirements/recommendations for international students: Required—TOEFL (minimum score 550 paper-based; 79 iBT). *Application deadline:* For fall admission, 12/15 for domestic and international students. Application fee: $40 ($75 for international students). Electronic applications accepted. *Expenses:* Tuition, state resident: full-time $8592; part-time $358 per credit hour. Tuition, nonresident: full-time $16,032; part-time $668 per credit hour. Required fees: $2889. Tuition and fees vary according to course load and program. *Financial support:* In 2010–11, 23 fellowships with full tuition reimbursements (averaging $2,828 per year), 39 research assistantships with full tuition reimbursements (averaging $7,864 per year), 62 teaching assistantships with full tuition reimbursements (averaging $9,312 per year) were awarded; career-related internships or fieldwork, Federal Work-Study, institutionally sponsored loans, scholarships/grants, health care benefits, and unspecified assistantships also available. Support available to part-time students. Financial award application deadline: 2/1; financial award applicants required to submit FAFSA. *Faculty research:* Health psychology, depression, child/family process, organizational effectiveness, close relationships. *Unit head:* Dr. David Francis, Chairperson, 713-743-7036, Fax: 713-743-8588, E-mail: dfrancis@uh.edu. *Application contact:* Patti Tolar, Academic Affairs Coordinator, 713-743-5544, Fax: 713-743-8588, E-mail: ptolar@uh.edu.

University of Houston–Clear Lake, School of Human Sciences and Humanities, Programs in Human Sciences, Houston, TX 77058-1098. Offers behavioral sciences (MA), including criminology, cross cultural studies, general psychology, sociology; clinical psychology (MA); criminology (MA); cross cultural studies (MA); family therapy (MA); fitness and human performance (MA); school psychology (MA). *Accreditation:* AAMFT/COAMFTE. Part-time and evening/weekend programs available. Postbaccalaureate distance learning degree programs offered (minimal on-campus study). *Degree requirements:* For master's, thesis or alternative. *Entrance requirements:* For master's, GRE General Test. Additional exam requirements/recommendations for international students: Required—TOEFL (minimum score 550 paper-based; 213 computer-based). Electronic applications accepted. *Faculty research:* Smoking cessation, adolescent sexuality, white collar crime, serial murder, human factors/human computer interaction.

University of Houston–Victoria, School of Arts and Sciences, Program in Psychology, Victoria, TX 77901-4450. Offers counseling psychology (MA); school psychology (MA). Part-time and evening/weekend programs available. Postbaccalaureate distance learning degree programs offered (minimal on-campus study). *Faculty:* 6 full-time (4 women). *Students:* 43 full-time (33 women), 64 part-time (56 women); includes 34 Black or African American, non-Hispanic/Latino; 2 Asian, non-Hispanic/Latino; 23 Hispanic/Latino; 2 Two or more races, non-Hispanic/Latino. Average age 33. 61 applicants, 77% accepted, 35 enrolled. In 2010, 9 master's awarded. *Degree requirements:* For master's, project or thesis. *Entrance requirements:* For master's, GRE General Test. Additional exam requirements/recommendations for international students: Required—TOEFL (minimum score 550 paper-based; 213 computer-based). *Application deadline:* For fall admission, 6/1 for international students; for spring admission, 10/1 for international students. Applications are processed on a rolling basis. Application fee: $0. Electronic applications accepted. *Expenses:* Tuition, state resident: full-time $4050; part-time $225 per credit hour. Tuition, nonresident: full-time $8730; part-time $485 per credit hour. Required fees: $810; $54 per credit hour. Tuition and fees vary according to course load. *Financial support:* In 2010–11, research assistantships with partial tuition reimbursements (averaging $2,000 per year), teaching assistantships with partial tuition reimbursements (averaging $2,000 per year) were awarded; Federal Work-Study, scholarships/grants, and unspecified assistantships also available. Support available to part-time students. Financial award application deadline: 4/15; financial award applicants required to submit FAFSA. *Unit head:* Dr. Rick Harrington, Chair, 361-570-4205, Fax: 361-570-4229, E-mail: harringtonr@unh.edu. *Application contact:* Tracey Fox, Director of Services, 361-570-4233, Fax: 361-580-5507, E-mail: admissions@uhv.edu.

University of Idaho, College of Graduate Studies, College of Letters, Arts and Social Sciences, Department of Psychology and Communication Studies, Moscow, ID 83844-2282. Offers psychology (MS). *Faculty:* 7 full-time, 8 part-time/adjunct. *Students:* 15 full-time, 15 part-time. Average age 31. In 2010, 4 master's awarded. *Entrance requirements:* For master's, GRE, minimum GPA of 2.8. *Application deadline:* For fall admission, 8/1 for domestic students; for spring admission, 12/15 for domestic students. Applications are processed on a rolling basis. Application fee: $60. Electronic applications accepted. *Expenses:* Tuition, nonresident: part-time $580 per credit. Required fees: $306 per credit. *Financial support:* Fellowships, research assistantships, teaching assistantships available. Financial award applicants required to submit FAFSA. *Faculty research:* Clinical, experimental, and cognitive psychology. *Unit head:* Dr. Richard D. Locke, Chair, 208-885-6324, E-mail: cberreth@uidaho.edu. *Application contact:* Dr. Richard D. Locke, Chair, 208-885-6324, E-mail: cberreth@uidaho.edu.

University of Illinois at Chicago, Graduate College, College of Liberal Arts and Sciences, Department of Psychology, Chicago, IL 60607-7128. Offers PhD. *Accreditation:* APA. *Degree requirements:* For doctorate, thesis/dissertation, departmental qualifying exam. *Entrance requirements:* For doctorate, GRE General Test, minimum GPA of 2.75. Additional exam requirements/recommendations for international students: Required—TOEFL. Electronic applications accepted.

University of Illinois at Urbana–Champaign, Graduate College, College of Liberal Arts and Sciences, Department of Psychology, Champaign, IL 61820. Offers MA, MS, PhD. *Accreditation:* APA (one or more programs are accredited). *Faculty:* 54 full-time (19 women), 3 part-time/adjunct (all women). *Students:* 142 full-time (94 women), 5 part-time (3 women); includes 26 minority (5 Black or African American, non-Hispanic/Latino; 11 Asian, non-Hispanic/Latino; 7 Hispanic/Latino; 1 Native Hawaiian or other Pacific Islander, non-Hispanic/Latino; 2 Two or more races, non-Hispanic/Latino), 41 international. 628 applicants, 7% accepted, 14 enrolled. In 2010, 27 master's, 27 doctorates awarded. *Entrance requirements:* For master's and doctorate, GRE General Test, minimum GPA of 3.0. Additional exam requirements/recommendations for international students: Required—TOEFL (minimum score: 79 iBT) or IELTS (minimum score 6.5). *Application deadline:* Applications are processed on a rolling basis. Application fee: $75 ($90 for international students). Electronic applications accepted. *Financial support:* In 2010–11, 33 fellowships with full tuition reimbursements, 79 research assistantships with full tuition reimbursements, 73 teaching assistantships with full tuition reimbursements were awarded; tuition waivers (full) also available. *Unit head:* Dr. David E. Irwin, Head, 217-333-0632, Fax: 217-244-5876, E-mail: irwin@illinois.edu. *Application contact:* Lori Hendricks, Administrative Aide, 217-333-2169, Fax: 217-244-5876, E-mail: lahendri@illinois.edu.

University of Indianapolis, Graduate Programs, School of Psychological Sciences, Indianapolis, IN 46227-3697. Offers clinical psychology (Psy D); clinical psychology/mental health counseling (MA). *Accreditation:* APA. *Faculty:* 6 full-time (1 woman), 1 (woman) part-time/adjunct. *Students:* 118 full-time (105 women), 44 part-time (37 women); includes 2 minority (1 Black or African American, non-Hispanic/Latino; 1 Hispanic/Latino), 11 international. Average age 26. *Degree requirements:* For master's, practicum; for doctorate, comprehensive exam, thesis/dissertation, 1200 hours of clinical practicum, 2000 hour internship. *Entrance requirements:* For master's, GRE, 3 letters of recommendation; for doctorate, GRE, minimum GPA of 3.0, 18 hours of course work in psychology, 3 letters of recommendation. Additional exam requirements/recommendations for international students: Required—TOEFL (minimum score 550 paper-based; 213 computer-based). *Application deadline:* For fall admission, 2/25 for domestic students. Application fee: $50. Tuition and fees vary according to course load, degree level and program. *Financial support:* Federal Work-Study available. *Unit head:* Dr. Rick Holigrocki, Acting Dean, 317-788-6126, Fax: 317-788-3480, E-mail: rholigrocki@uindy.edu. *Application contact:* Dr. Rick Holigrocki, Acting Dean, 317-788-6126, E-mail: rholigrocki@uindy.edu.

The University of Iowa, Graduate College, College of Education, Department of Psychological and Quantitative Foundations, Iowa City, IA 52242-1316. Offers counseling psychology (PhD); educational measurement and statistics (MA, PhD); educational psychology (MA, PhD); school psychology (PhD, Ed S); JD/PhD. *Accreditation:* APA. *Degree requirements:* For master's, thesis optional, exam; for doctorate, comprehensive exam, thesis/dissertation; for Ed S, exam. *Entrance requirements:* For master's, doctorate, and Ed S, GRE General Test, minimum GPA of 3.0. Additional exam requirements/recommendations for international students: Required—TOEFL (minimum score 550 paper-based; 213 computer-based; 81 iBT). Electronic applications accepted.

The University of Iowa, Graduate College, College of Liberal Arts and Sciences, Department of Psychology, Iowa City, IA 52242-1316. Offers neural and behavioral sciences (PhD); psychology (MA, PhD). *Degree requirements:* For master's, thesis optional, exam; for doctorate, comprehensive exam, thesis/dissertation. *Entrance requirements:* For master's and doctorate, GRE General Test, minimum GPA of 3.0. Additional exam requirements/recommendations for

Psychology—General

The University of Iowa (continued)
international students: Required—TOEFL (minimum score 550 paper-based; 213 computer-based; 81 iBT). Electronic applications accepted.

The University of Kansas, Graduate Studies, College of Liberal Arts and Sciences, Department of Applied Behavioral Science, Lawrence, KS 66045. Offers applied behavioral science (MA); behavioral psychology (PhD). *Faculty:* 16 full-time (6 women). *Students:* 48 full-time (33 women), 1 (woman) part-time; includes 6 minority (3 Black or African American, non-Hispanic/Latino; 1 Asian, non-Hispanic/Latino; 1 Hispanic/Latino; 1 Two or more races, non-Hispanic/Latino), 5 international. Average age 31. 46 applicants, 24% accepted, 9 enrolled. In 2010, 8 master's, 5 doctorates awarded. Terminal master's awarded for partial completion of doctoral program. *Degree requirements:* For master's, thesis; for doctorate, thesis/dissertation, comprehensive oral and written exams, journal reviews. *Entrance requirements:* For master's and doctorate, curriculum vitae, 3 letters of recommendation. Additional exam requirements/recommendations for international students: Required—TOEFL. *Application deadline:* For fall admission, 12/15 priority date for domestic and international students. Applications are processed on a rolling basis. Application fee: $55 ($65 for international students). Electronic applications accepted. *Expenses:* Tuition, state resident: full-time $7092; part-time $295.50 per credit hour. Tuition, nonresident: full-time $16,590; part-time $691.25 per credit hour. Required fees: $858; $71.49 per credit hour. Tuition and fees vary according to course load, campus/location and program. *Financial support:* Fellowships, research assistantships with full and partial tuition reimbursements, teaching assistantships with full and partial tuition reimbursements, career-related internships or fieldwork, traineeships, tuition waivers (full), and unspecified assistantships available. Financial award application deadline: 12/15; financial award applicants required to submit CSS PROFILE or FAFSA. *Faculty research:* Early childhood, developmental disabilities, community health and development, adults with disabilities, applied behavior analysis. *Unit head:* Dr. Edward K. Morris, Chair, 785-864-4840, Fax: 785-864-5202, E-mail: ekm@ku.edu. *Application contact:* Dr. Florence DiGennaro Reed, Graduate Director, 785-864-4840, Fax: 785-864-5202, E-mail: fdreed@ku.edu.

The University of Kansas, Graduate Studies, College of Liberal Arts and Sciences, Department of Psychology, Lawrence, KS 66045. Offers clinical child psychology (MA, PhD); clinical health and rehabilitation (PhD); cognitive psychology (PhD); developmental psychology (PhD); quantitative psychology (PhD); social psychology (MA). *Accreditation:* APA (one or more programs are accredited). *Faculty:* 27 full-time (8 women), 9 part-time/adjunct (4 women). *Students:* 122 full-time (87 women), 1 (woman) part-time; includes 17 minority (4 Black or African American, non-Hispanic/Latino; 8 Asian, non-Hispanic/Latino; 4 Hispanic/Latino; 1 Native Hawaiian or other Pacific Islander, non-Hispanic/Latino), 9 international. Average age 28. 348 applicants, 11% accepted, 25 enrolled. In 2010, 16 master's, 16 doctorates awarded. *Degree requirements:* For master's, thesis; for doctorate, variable foreign language requirement, comprehensive exam, thesis/dissertation. *Entrance requirements:* For doctorate, GRE General Test, minimum GPA of 3.0; undergraduate degree with 15 hours of course work in psychology, curriculum vitae, writing sample (clinical program only). Additional exam requirements/recommendations for international students: Required—TOEFL. *Application deadline:* For fall admission, 12/1 for domestic and international students. Application fee: $55 ($65 for international students). Electronic applications accepted. *Expenses:* Tuition, state resident: full-time $7092; part-time $295.50 per credit hour. Tuition, nonresident: full-time $16,590; part-time $691.25 per credit hour. Required fees: $858; $71.49 per credit hour. Tuition and fees vary according to course load, campus/location and program. *Financial support:* Fellowships with full tuition reimbursements, research assistantships with partial tuition reimbursements, teaching assistantships with full and partial tuition reimbursements, career-related internships or fieldwork and unspecified assistantships available. Financial award application deadline: 12/1; financial award applicants required to submit FAFSA. *Faculty research:* Information processing in depression, rape and other forms of sexual coercion, motions on physical function, processes of memory and understanding text, social stigmas and hostile group environments. *Unit head:* Dr. Ruth Ann Atchley, Chair, 785-864-9821, Fax: 785-864-5696, E-mail: ratchley@ku.edu. *Application contact:* Cathy L. O'Keefe, Graduate Admissions Officer, 785-864-4195, Fax: 785-864-5696, E-mail: psycgrad@ku.edu.

University of Kentucky, Graduate School, College of Arts and Sciences, Program in Psychology, Lexington, KY 40506-0032. Offers clinical psychology (MA); experimental psychology (MA). *Accreditation:* APA (one or more programs are accredited). *Degree requirements:* For master's, comprehensive exam, thesis; for doctorate, comprehensive exam, thesis/dissertation. *Entrance requirements:* For master's, GRE General Test, minimum undergraduate GPA of 2.75; for doctorate, GRE General Test, minimum graduate GPA of 3.0. Additional exam requirements/recommendations for international students: Required—TOEFL (minimum score 550 paper-based; 213 computer-based). Electronic applications accepted. *Faculty research:* Psychopharmacology and teratology, behavioral neuroscience, social psychology, cognitive psychology, development and developmental psychobiology.

University of La Verne, College of Arts and Sciences, Department of Psychology, La Verne, CA 91750-4443. Offers clinical-community psychology (Psy D); counseling (MS), including counseling, marriage and family therapy. *Accreditation:* APA (one or more programs are accredited). Part-time programs available. *Faculty:* 13 full-time (6 women), 25 part-time/adjunct (17 women). *Students:* 101 full-time (89 women), 78 part-time (63 women); includes 102 minority (27 Black or African American, non-Hispanic/Latino; 14 Asian, non-Hispanic/Latino; 61 Hispanic/Latino). Average age 29. In 2010, 53 master's, 8 doctorates awarded. *Degree requirements:* For master's, thesis, competency exam, personal psychotherapy; for doctorate, thesis/dissertation, clinical internship, competency exams, practicum, personal psychotherapy. *Entrance requirements:* For master's, minimum undergraduate GPA of 3.0, 3 letters of recommendation, interview; for doctorate, minimum GPA of 3.25 undergraduate, 3.65 graduate; 3 recommendations; interview; curriculum vitae. Additional exam requirements/recommendations for international students: Required—TOEFL (minimum score 600 paper-based; 250 computer-based). *Application deadline:* Applications are processed on a rolling basis. *Expenses:* Contact institution. *Financial support:* Career-related internships or fieldwork, institutionally sponsored loans, and scholarships/grants available. Financial award application deadline: 3/2; financial award applicants required to submit FAFSA. *Faculty research:* Developmental therapy and counseling. *Unit head:* Dr. Glenn Gamst, Department Chair, 909-593-3511 Ext. 4176, E-mail: ggamst@laverne.edu. *Application contact:* Barbara Cox, Admissions Information Specialist, 909-593-3511 Ext. 4004, Fax: 909-392-2761, E-mail: gradadmission@laverne.edu.

University of Lethbridge, School of Graduate Studies, Lethbridge, AB T1K 3M4, Canada. Offers accounting (MScM); addictions counseling (M Sc); agricultural biotechnology (M Sc); agricultural studies (M Sc, MA); anthropology (MA); archaeology (MA); art (MA, MFA); biochemistry (M Sc); biological sciences (M Sc); biomolecular science (PhD); biosystems and biodiversity (PhD); Canadian studies (MA); chemistry (M Sc); computer science (M Sc); computer science and geographical information science (M Sc); counseling psychology (M Ed); dramatic arts (MA); earth, space, and physical science (PhD); economics (MA); educational leadership (M Ed); English (MA); environmental science (M Sc); evolution and behavior (PhD); exercise science (M Sc); finance (MScM); French (MA); French/German (MA); French/Spanish (MA); general education (M Ed); general management (MScM); geography (M Sc, MA); German (MA); health science (M Sc); history (MA); human resource management and labour relations (MScM); individualized multidisciplinary (M Sc, MA); information systems (MScM); international management (MScM); kinesiology (M Sc, MA); management (M Sc, MA); marketing (MScM); mathematics (M Sc); music (M Mus, MA); Native American studies (MA); neuroscience (M Sc, PhD); new media (MA); nursing (M Sc); philosophy (MA); physics (M Sc); policy and strategy (MScM); political science (MA); psychology (M Sc, MA); religious studies (MA); social sciences (MA); sociology (MA); theatre and dramatic arts (MFA); theoretical and computational science (PhD); urban and regional studies (MA); women's studies (MA). Part-time and evening/weekend programs available. *Degree requirements:* For doctorate, comprehensive exam, thesis/dissertation. *Entrance requirements:* For master's, GMAT (M Sc in management), bachelor's degree in related field, minimum GPA of 3.0 during previous 20 graded semester courses, 2 years teaching or related experience (M Ed); for doctorate, master's degree, minimum graduate GPA of 3.5. Additional exam requirements/recommendations for international students: Required—TOEFL. *Faculty research:* Movement and brain plasticity, gibberellin physiology, photosynthesis, carbon cycling, molecular properties of main-group ring components.

University of Louisiana at Lafayette, College of Liberal Arts, Department of Psychology, Program in Psychology, Lafayette, LA 70504. Offers MS. *Degree requirements:* For master's, comprehensive exam, thesis (for some programs). *Entrance requirements:* For master's, GRE General Test. Additional exam requirements/recommendations for international students: Required—TOEFL (minimum score 550 paper-based; 213 computer-based).

University of Louisiana at Monroe, Graduate School, College of Education and Human Development, Department of Psychology, Monroe, LA 71209-0001. Offers general psychology (MS); school psychology (MS, SSP). Part-time and evening/weekend programs available. *Faculty:* 9 full-time (3 women), 2 part-time/adjunct (1 woman). *Students:* 22 full-time (16 women), 11 part-time (6 women); includes 7 Black or African American, non-Hispanic/Latino; 1 Asian, non-Hispanic/Latino; 1 Hispanic/Latino. Average age 29. In 2010, 4 master's, 3 other advanced degrees awarded. *Degree requirements:* For master's, thesis; for SSP, comprehensive exam, thesis, field and practicum experiences (400 hours), internship (1250 hours). *Entrance requirements:* For master's, minimum GPA of 2.75 or GRE General Test; for SSP, GRE General Test, minimum GPA of 3.25. Additional exam requirements/recommendations for international students: Required—TOEFL (minimum score 500 paper-based; 173 computer-based; 61 iBT). *Application deadline:* For fall admission, 8/22 priority date for domestic students, 7/1 for international students; for winter admission, 12/14 priority date for domestic students; for spring admission, 1/19 for domestic students, 11/1 for international students. Applications are processed on a rolling basis. Application fee: $20 ($30 for international students). Electronic applications accepted. *Expenses:* Tuition, state resident: full-time $2991; part-time $197 per credit hour. Tuition, nonresident: full-time $2991; part-time $197 per credit hour. International tuition: $10,288 full-time. *Financial support:* In 2010–11, 12 research assistantships with full tuition reimbursements (averaging $2,500 per year) were awarded; career-related internships or fieldwork, Federal Work-Study, and unspecified assistantships also available. Financial award application deadline: 4/1; financial award applicants required to submit FAFSA. *Faculty research:* Identity development comparison, alcohol and drug problems. *Unit head:* Dr. David Williamson, Head, 318-342-1331, Fax: 318-342-1352, E-mail: williamson@ulm.edu. *Application contact:* Dr. David Williamson, Head, 318-342-1331, Fax: 318-342-1352, E-mail: williamson@ulm.edu.

University of Louisville, Graduate School, College of Arts and Sciences, Department of Psychological and Brain Sciences, Louisville, KY 40292-0001. Offers clinical psychology (PhD); experimental psychology (PhD). *Accreditation:* APA. *Faculty:* 22 full-time (9 women), 4 part-time/adjunct (1 woman). *Students:* 66 full-time (43 women), 1 part-time (0 women); includes 2 Black or African American, non-Hispanic/Latino; 3 Asian, non-Hispanic/Latino; 1 Hispanic/Latino, 9 international. Average age 30. 142 applicants, 3% accepted, 4 enrolled. In 2010, 4 doctorates awarded. *Degree requirements:* For doctorate, thesis/dissertation, preliminary exam, research, internship. *Entrance requirements:* For doctorate, GRE General Test. Additional exam requirements/recommendations for international students: Required—TOEFL. *Application deadline:* For fall admission, 12/1 for domestic and international students. Application fee: $50. Electronic applications accepted. *Expenses:* Tuition, state resident: full-time $9144; part-time $508 per credit hour. Tuition, nonresident: full-time $19,026; part-time $1057 per credit hour. Tuition and fees vary according to program and reciprocity agreements. *Financial support:* In 2010–11, 39 students received support, including 12 fellowships (averaging $22,000 per year), 27 teaching assistantships (averaging $22,000 per year); career-related internships or fieldwork also available. *Faculty research:* Health psychology, geropsychology, psychopathology, cognitive and development sciences, vision and hearing sciences. *Unit head:* Dr. Suzanne Meeks, Chair, 502-852-6068, Fax: 502-852-8904, E-mail: smeeks@louisville.edu. *Application contact:* Mary E. Leggett, Director, Graduate Admissions, 502-852-3101, Fax: 502-852-6536, E-mail: gradadm@louisville.edu.

University of Maine, Graduate School, College of Liberal Arts and Sciences, Department of Psychology, Orono, ME 04469. Offers clinical (PhD); developmental (MA, PhD); experimental (MA); psychological sciences (MA, PhD). *Accreditation:* APA (one or more programs are accredited). *Faculty:* 14 full-time (6 women), 3 part-time/adjunct (2 women). *Students:* 27 full-time (17 women), 10 part-time (6 women); includes 2 minority (1 Asian, non-Hispanic/Latino; 1 Hispanic/Latino), 2 international. Average age 28. 147 applicants, 5% accepted, 7 enrolled. In 2010, 5 master's, 4 doctorates awarded. *Degree requirements:* For master's, thesis; for doctorate, thesis/dissertation. *Entrance requirements:* For master's and doctorate, GRE General Test, GRE Subject Test. Additional exam requirements/recommendations for international students: Required—TOEFL. *Application deadline:* For fall admission, 2/1 priority date for domestic students. Applications are processed on a rolling basis. Application fee: $65. Electronic applications accepted. *Expenses:* Tuition, state resident: full-time $400. Tuition, nonresident: full-time $1050. *Financial support:* In 2010–11, 3 research assistantships with tuition reimbursements (averaging $14,063 per year), 21 teaching assistantships with tuition reimbursements (averaging $12,790 per year) were awarded; Federal Work-Study, institutionally sponsored loans, and tuition waivers (full and partial) also available. Financial award application deadline: 3/1. *Faculty research:* Social development, hypertension and aging, attitude change, self-confidence in achievement situations, health psychology. *Unit head:* Dr. Michael Robbins, Chair, 207-581-2051, Fax: 207-581-6128. *Application contact:* Scott G. Delcourt, Associate Dean of the Graduate School, 207-581-3291, Fax: 207-581-3232, E-mail: graduate@maine.edu.

The University of Manchester, School of Psychological Sciences, Manchester, United Kingdom. Offers audiology (M Phil, PhD); clinical psychology (M Phil, PhD, Psy D); psychology (M Phil, PhD).

University of Manitoba, Faculty of Graduate Studies, Faculty of Arts, Department of Psychology, Winnipeg, MB R3T 2N2, Canada. Offers clinical psychology (PhD); psychology (MA, PhD); school psychology (MA). *Accreditation:* APA (one or more programs are accredited). *Degree requirements:* For master's, thesis; for doctorate, one foreign language, thesis/dissertation. *Entrance requirements:* For master's and doctorate, GRE General Test.

University of Mary Hardin-Baylor, Graduate Studies in Counseling and Psychology, Belton, TX 76513. Offers clinical mental health counseling (MA); marriage and family Christian counseling (MA); psychology and counseling (MA); school counseling and psychology (MA). Part-time and evening/weekend programs available. *Faculty:* 7 full-time (4 women). *Students:* 33 full-time (23 women), 18 part-time (10 women); includes 11 minority (6 Black or African American, non-Hispanic/Latino; 4 Hispanic/Latino; 1 Two or more races, non-Hispanic/Latino), 1 international. Average age 29. 46 applicants, 50% accepted, 19 enrolled. In 2010, 44 master's awarded. *Degree requirements:* For master's, comprehensive exam. *Entrance requirements:* For master's, GRE General Test, minimum GPA of 3.0 in last 60 hours or 2.75 overall. *Application deadline:* For fall admission, 6/1 priority date for domestic students; for spring admission, 11/1 for domestic students. Applications are processed on a rolling basis. Application fee: $35 ($135 for international students). Electronic applications accepted. *Financial support:* Research assistantships with full tuition reimbursements, Federal Work-Study and scholarships (for some active duty military personnel only) available. Support available to part-time students. Financial award applicants required to submit FAFSA. *Unit head:* Dr. Isaac Gusukuma, Interim Graduate Program Director, 254-295-5017, E-mail: isaac.gusukuma@umhb.edu. *Application contact:* Dr. Isaac Gusukuma, Interim Graduate Program Director, 254-295-5017, E-mail: isaac.gusukuma@umhb.edu.

University of Maryland, Baltimore County, Graduate School, College of Arts, Humanities and Social Sciences, Department of Psychology, Baltimore, MD 21250. Offers applied developmental psychology (PhD); human services psychology (MA, PhD), including applied behavioral analysis (MA), human services psychology/clinical (PhD); industrial organizational psychology (MPS); psychology (MPS). *Accreditation:* APA (one or more programs are accredited). *Faculty:* 24 full-time (9 women), 11 part-time/adjunct (4 women). *Students:* 105 full-time (88 women), 17 part-time (15 women); includes 6 Black or African American, non-Hispanic/Latino; 10 Asian, non-Hispanic/Latino; 3 Hispanic/Latino, 7 international. Average age 28. 206 applicants, 22% accepted, 21 enrolled. In 2010, 25 master's, 11 doctorates awarded. Terminal master's awarded for partial completion of doctoral program. *Degree requirements:* For master's, thesis or alternative; for doctorate, comprehensive exam, thesis/dissertation. *Entrance requirements:* For master's, GRE General Test; for doctorate, GRE General Test, GRE Subject Test. Additional exam requirements/recommendations for international students: Required—TOEFL. *Application deadline:* For fall admission, 12/1 for domestic and international students. Application fee: $70. Electronic applications accepted. *Financial support:* In 2010–11, fellowships with full and partial tuition reimbursements (averaging $22,000 per year), 29 research assistantships with full and partial tuition reimbursements (averaging $14,857 per year), 28 teaching assistantships with full and partial tuition reimbursements (averaging $14,857 per year) were awarded; career-related internships or fieldwork, Federal Work-Study, health care benefits, tuition waivers (full and partial), and unspecified assistantships also available. Financial award application deadline: 3/1; financial award applicants required to submit FAFSA. *Faculty research:* Prevention and treatment of behavior problems, early intervention, cultural contexts, applications to education, behavioral medicine. Total annual research expenditures: $2.3 million. *Unit head:* Dr. Linda Baker, Chair, 410-455-2415, Fax: 410-455-1055, E-mail: baker@umbc.edu. *Application contact:* Nicole Mooney, Program Management Specialist, 410-455-2567, Fax: 410-455-1055, E-mail: psycdept@umbc.edu.

University of Maryland, College Park, Academic Affairs, College of Behavioral and Social Sciences, Department of Psychology, College Park, MD 20742. Offers clinical psychology (PhD); developmental psychology (PhD); experimental psychology (PhD); industrial psychology (MA, MS, PhD); social psychology (PhD). *Accreditation:* APA (one or more programs are accredited). *Faculty:* 70 full-time (34 women), 16 part-time/adjunct (10 women). *Students:* 83 full-time (63 women), 6 part-time (4 women); includes 4 Black or African American, non-Hispanic/Latino; 6 Asian, non-Hispanic/Latino; 6 Hispanic/Latino, 13 international. 653 applicants, 4% accepted, 13 enrolled. In 2010, 8 master's, 18 doctorates awarded. *Degree requirements:* For master's, thesis; for doctorate, variable foreign language requirement, comprehensive exam, thesis/dissertation. *Entrance requirements:* For master's and doctorate, GRE General Test, GRE Subject Test, minimum GPA of 3.5, research and/or work experience, 3 letters of recommendation. *Application deadline:* For fall admission, 12/1 for domestic and international students. Applications are processed on a rolling basis. Application fee: $75. Electronic applications accepted. *Expenses:* Tuition, state resident: part-time $471 per credit hour. Tuition, nonresident: part-time $1016 per credit hour. Required fees: $337 per term. *Financial support:* In 2010–11, 14 fellowships with full and partial tuition reimbursements (averaging $20,179 per year), 5 research assistantships (averaging $18,414 per year), 54 teaching assistantships (averaging $17,209 per year) were awarded; career-related internships or fieldwork, Federal Work-Study, and scholarships/grants also available. Support available to part-time students. Financial award applicants required to submit FAFSA. *Faculty research:* Social stereotyping and prejudice, anxiety disorders, auditory neuroethology, counseling and social psychology. Total annual research expenditures: $4 million. *Unit head:* Thomas S. Wallsten, Chair, 301-405-3562, Fax: 301-314-9566, E-mail: twallst@umd.edu. *Application contact:* Dean of Graduate School, 301-405-0358, Fax: 301-314-9305.

University of Massachusetts Amherst, Graduate School, College of Natural Sciences, Department of Psychology, Amherst, MA 01003. Offers clinical psychology (MS, PhD); cognitive psychology (MS, PhD); developmental science (MS, PhD); psychology of peace and violence (MS, PhD); social psychology (MS, PhD). *Accreditation:* APA (one or more programs are accredited). *Faculty:* 47 full-time (23 women). *Students:* 54 full-time (42 women), 6 part-time (4 women); includes 16 minority (3 Black or African American, non-Hispanic/Latino; 6 Asian, non-Hispanic/Latino; 4 Hispanic/Latino; 3 Two or more races, non-Hispanic/Latino), 3 international. Average age 29. 435 applicants, 4% accepted, 8 enrolled. In 2010, 12 master's, 16 doctorates awarded. Terminal master's awarded for partial completion of doctoral program. *Degree requirements:* For master's, thesis; for doctorate, comprehensive exam, thesis/dissertation. *Entrance requirements:* For master's and doctorate, GRE General Test, 3 letters of recommendation. Additional exam requirements/recommendations for international students: Required—TOEFL (minimum score 550 paper-based; 213 computer-based; 80 iBT), IELTS (minimum score 6.5). *Application deadline:* For fall admission, 12/1 for domestic and international students. Applications are processed on a rolling basis. Application fee: $50 ($65 for international students). Electronic applications accepted. *Expenses:* Tuition, state resident: full-time $2640. Required fees: $8282. One-time fee: $357 full-time. *Financial support:* In 2010–11, 8 fellowships with full tuition reimbursements (averaging $12,569 per year), 41 research assistantships with full tuition reimbursements (averaging $10,714 per year), 55 teaching assistantships with full tuition reimbursements (averaging $10,951 per year) were awarded; career-related internships or fieldwork, Federal Work-Study, scholarships/grants, traineeships, health care benefits, tuition waivers (full), and unspecified assistantships also available. Support available to part-time students. Financial award application deadline: 12/1; financial award applicants required to submit FAFSA. *Unit head:* Dr. Linda M. Isbell, Graduate Program Director, 413-545-2503, Fax: 413-545-0996. *Application contact:* Jean M. Ames, Supervisor of Admissions, 413-545-0722, Fax: 413-577-0010, E-mail: gradadm@grad.umass.edu.

University of Massachusetts Dartmouth, Graduate School, College of Arts and Sciences, Department of Psychology, North Dartmouth, MA 02747-2300. Offers behavior analyst (Post-baccalaureate Certificate); clinical psychology (MA); general psychology (MA). Part-time programs available. *Faculty:* 18 full-time (9 women), 8 part-time/adjunct (4 women). *Students:* 22 full-time (19 women), 62 part-time (52 women); includes 7 Black or African American, non-Hispanic/Latino; 2 Hispanic/Latino; 1 Two or more races, non-Hispanic/Latino, 1 international. Average age 30. 110 applicants, 43% accepted, 36 enrolled. In 2010, 14 master's awarded. *Degree requirements:* For master's, thesis (for some programs). *Entrance requirements:* For master's, GRE General Test, minimum GPA of 2.75, 3 letters of recommendation. Additional exam requirements/recommendations for international students: Required—TOEFL (minimum score 500 paper-based). *Application deadline:* For fall admission, 3/31 for domestic students, 1/31 for international students. Application fee: $40 ($60 for international students). Electronic applications accepted. *Expenses:* Tuition, state resident: full-time $2071; part-time $86 per credit. Tuition, nonresident: full-time $8099; part-time $337 per credit. Required fees: $9446; $394 per credit. One-time fee: $75. Part-time tuition and fees vary according to class time, course load, degree level and reciprocity agreements. *Financial support:* In 2010–11, 1 research assistantship with full tuition reimbursement (averaging $10,000 per year), 9 teaching assistantships with full tuition reimbursements (averaging $3,500 per year) were awarded; career-related internships or fieldwork, Federal Work-Study, and unspecified assistantships also available. Support available to part-time students. Financial award application deadline: 3/1; financial award applicants required to submit FAFSA. *Faculty research:* Nonverbal communication, behavioral medicine, anxiety disorder, intimate relationships, learning. Total annual research expenditures: $129,359. *Unit head:* Dr. Paul Donnelly, Director, Clinical Psychology, 508-999-8334, E-mail: pdonnelly@umassd.edu. *Application contact:* Elan Turcotte-Shamski, Graduate Admissions Officer, 508-999-8604, Fax: 508-999-8183, E-mail: graduate@umassd.edu.

University of Massachusetts Lowell, College of Arts and Sciences, Department of Psychology, Lowell, MA 01854-2881. Offers community social psychology (MA). Part-time programs available. *Degree requirements:* For master's, thesis optional. *Entrance requirements:* For master's, GRE General Test or MAT. Electronic applications accepted. *Faculty research:* Domestic violence, youth sports, teen pregnancy, substance abuse, family and work roles.

University of Memphis, Graduate School, College of Arts and Sciences, Department of Psychology, Memphis, TN 38152-3230. Offers psychology (MS, PhD), including clinical (PhD), experimental (PhD), general psychology (MS), school (PhD); school psychology (MA, Ed S); MS/PhD. *Faculty:* 28 full-time (9 women), 4 part-time/adjunct (0 women). *Students:* 114 full-time (81 women), 21 part-time (15 women); includes 14 Black or African American, non-Hispanic/Latino; 1 American Indian or Alaska Native, non-Hispanic/Latino; 4 Asian, non-Hispanic/Latino; 3 Hispanic/Latino; 4 Two or more races, non-Hispanic/Latino, 7 international. Average age 27. 220 applicants, 15% accepted, 29 enrolled. In 2010, 31 master's, 9 doctorates awarded. *Degree requirements:* For master's, comprehensive exam (for some programs), thesis (for some programs), 37 credit hours (MA); 33 credit hours with thesis or 36 with exam (MS); for doctorate, comprehensive exam (for some programs), thesis/dissertation, 80 semester hours, major area paper; clinical: 1 year placement and 1 year internship; internship (school psychology). *Entrance requirements:* For master's, GRE; for doctorate, GRE (minimum combined score of 1100), minimum GPA of 2.75, 18 hours of undergraduate psychology courses, transcripts, personal statement, letters of recommendation; for Ed S, GRE (minimum combined score of 1100), minimum GPA of 2.75, 18 hours of undergraduate psychology courses, letters of recommendation. Additional exam requirements/recommendations for international students: Required—TOEFL (minimum score 550 paper-based; 210 computer-based; 79 iBT). *Application deadline:* For fall admission, 12/5 for domestic students. Applications are processed on a rolling basis. Application fee: $35 ($60 for international students). Electronic applications accepted. *Financial support:* In 2010–11, 66 students received support; fellowships with full tuition reimbursements available, research assistantships with full tuition reimbursements available, teaching assistantships with full tuition reimbursements available, Federal Work-Study, scholarships/grants, tuition waivers (partial), and unspecified assistantships available. Financial award application deadline: 2/15; financial award applicants required to submit FAFSA. *Faculty research:* Clinical health; school, child and family psychology; psychotherapy; cognitive and behavioral neuroscience; industrial-organizational psychology. *Unit head:* Dr. Robert Cohen, Coordinator of Graduate Programs, 901-678-4679, Fax: 901-678-2579, E-mail: rcohen@memphis.edu. *Application contact:* Lynell Connable, Graduate Secretary, 901-678-4340, Fax: 901-678-2579, E-mail: dconnabl@memphis.edu.

University of Miami, Graduate School, College of Arts and Sciences, Department of Psychology, Coral Gables, FL 33124. Offers adult clinical (PhD); behavioral neuroscience (PhD); child clinical (PhD); developmental psychology (PhD); health clinical (PhD); psychology (MS). *Accreditation:* APA (one or more programs are accredited). *Degree requirements:* For doctorate, comprehensive exam, thesis/dissertation. *Entrance requirements:* For doctorate, GRE General Test, minimum GPA of 3.5. Additional exam requirements/recommendations for international students: Required—TOEFL. Electronic applications accepted. *Faculty research:* Behavioral factors in cardiovascular disease and cancer adult psychopathology, developmental disabilities, social and emotional development, mechanisms of coping.

University of Michigan, Horace H. Rackham School of Graduate Studies, College of Literature, Science, and the Arts, Department of Psychology, Ann Arbor, MI 48109. Offers biopsychology (PhD); clinical psychology (PhD); cognition and perception (PhD); developmental psychology (PhD); personality and social contexts (PhD); social psychology (PhD). *Accreditation:* APA. *Faculty:* 83 full-time (39 women), 30 part-time/adjunct (14 women). *Students:* 132 full-time (92 women); includes 13 Black or African American, non-Hispanic/Latino; 2 American Indian or Alaska Native, non-Hispanic/Latino; 18 Asian, non-Hispanic/Latino; 7 Hispanic/Latino; 2 Two or more races, non-Hispanic/Latino, 20 international. Average age 27. 608 applicants, 6% accepted, 24 enrolled. In 2010, 28 doctorates awarded. *Degree requirements:* For doctorate, comprehensive exam, thesis/dissertation, oral defense of dissertation, preliminary exam. *Entrance requirements:* For doctorate, GRE General Test. Additional exam requirements/recommendations for international students: Required—TOEFL. *Application deadline:* For fall admission, 12/1 for domestic and international students. Application fee: $65 ($75 for international students). Electronic applications accepted. *Expenses:* Tuition, state resident: full-time $17,784; part-time $1116 per credit hour. Tuition, nonresident: full-time $35,944; part-time $2125 per credit hour. International tuition: $35,994 full-time. Required fees: $95 per semester. Tuition and fees vary according to course load, degree level and program. *Financial support:* In 2010–11, 118 students received support, including 55 fellowships with full tuition reimbursements available (averaging $20,900 per year), 15 research assistantships with full tuition reimbursements available (averaging $25,950 per year), 52 teaching assistantships with full tuition reimbursements available (averaging $22,670 per year); career-related internships or fieldwork also available. Financial award application deadline: 4/15. Total annual research expenditures: $7.4 million. *Unit head:* Prof. Theresa Lee, Chair, 734-764-7429. *Application contact:* Laurie Brannan, Psychology Student Academic Affairs, 731-764-2580, Fax: 734-615-7584, E-mail: psych.saa@umich.edu.

University of Michigan, Horace H. Rackham School of Graduate Studies, College of Literature, Science, and the Arts, Department of Women's Studies, Ann Arbor, MI 48109. Offers English and women's studies (PhD); history and women's studies (PhD); lesbian, gay, bisexual, transgender, queer (LGBTQ) studies (Certificate); psychology and women's studies (PhD); sociology and women's studies (PhD); women's studies (Certificate). *Faculty:* 77 full-time (71 women). *Students:* 71 full-time (63 women); includes 6 Black or African American, non-Hispanic/Latino; 11 Asian, non-Hispanic/Latino; 7 Hispanic/Latino; 4 Two or more races, non-Hispanic/Latino. Average age 30. 101 applicants, 10% accepted, 9 enrolled. In 2010, 5 doctorates, 8 other advanced degrees awarded. *Degree requirements:* For doctorate, variable foreign language requirement, comprehensive exam (for some programs), thesis/dissertation. *Entrance requirements:* For doctorate, GRE General Test, previous undergraduate course work in women's studies; for Certificate, GRE General Test, previous course work in women's studies. Additional exam requirements/recommendations for international students: Required—TOEFL. *Application deadline:* For fall admission, 12/1 for domestic and international students. Application fee: $65 ($75 for international students). Electronic applications accepted. *Expenses:* Tuition, state resident: full-time $17,784; part-time $1116 per credit hour. Tuition, nonresident: full-time $35,944; part-time $2125 per credit hour. International tuition: $35,994 full-time. Required fees: $95 per semester. Tuition and fees vary according to course load, degree level and program. *Financial support:* In 2010–11, 39 students received support, including 21 fellowships with full tuition reimbursements available (averaging $16,800 per year), 18 teaching assistantships with full tuition reimbursements available (averaging $17,270 per year); career-related internships or fieldwork, institutionally sponsored loans, scholarships/grants, traineeships, health care benefits, and unspecified assistantships also available. *Faculty research:* Gender issues, LGBTQ studies, sexuality, women and science, global feminism. *Unit head:* Elizabeth R. Cole, Chair, Department of Women's Studies, Professor of Women's Studies, Professor of Afroamerican and African Studies, Professor of Psychology, 734-763-2047, Fax: 734-647-4943, E-mail: wsdgradInquiry@umich.edu. *Application contact:* Aimee Germain, Graduate Program Coordinator, 734-763-2047, Fax: 734-647-4943, E-mail: wsdgradinquiry@umich.edu.

University of Michigan, Horace H. Rackham School of Graduate Studies, Combined Program in Education and Psychology, Ann Arbor, MI 48109. Offers PhD. *Accreditation:* Teacher Education Accreditation Council. *Faculty:* 17 part-time/adjunct (8 women). *Students:* 31 full-time (24 women); includes 8 Black or African American, non-Hispanic/Latino; 2 Asian, non-Hispanic/Latino; 6 Hispanic/Latino, 4 international. Average age 27. 75 applicants, 13% accepted, 7 enrolled. In 2010, 5 doctorates awarded. *Degree requirements:* For doctorate, thesis/dissertation, independent research project, preliminary exam, oral defense of dissertation. *Entrance requirements:* For doctorate, GRE General Test with Analytical Writing Test. Additional exam requirements/recommendations for international students: Required—TOEFL (minimum score 600 paper-based; 250 computer-based; 100 iBT). *Application deadline:* For fall admission, 12/1 for domestic and international students. Application fee: $65 ($75 for international students). Electronic applications accepted. *Expenses:* Tuition, state resident: full-time $17,784; part-time $1116 per credit hour. Tuition, nonresident: full-time $35,944; part-time $2125 per credit hour. International tuition: $35,994 full-time. Required fees: $95 per semester. Tuition and fees vary according to course load, degree level and program. *Financial support:* In 2010–11, 31 students received support, including 13 fellowships with full tuition reimbursements available (averaging $24,776 per year), 7 research assistantships with full tuition reimbursements available (averaging $28,459 per year), 8 teaching assistantships with full tuition reimbursements available (averaging $28,621 per year); institutionally sponsored loans, scholarships/grants, traineeships, tuition waivers (full and partial), and unspecified assistantships also available. Financial award application deadline: 12/1. *Faculty research:* Human development

Psychology—General

University of Michigan (continued)
in context of schools, families, communities; cognitive and learning sciences; motivation and self-regulated learning; culture, ethnicity, social and class influences on learning and motivation. *Unit head:* Dr. Tabbye M. Chavous, Director, 734-647-0626, Fax: 734-615-2164, E-mail: tchavous@umich.edu. *Application contact:* Janie Knieper, Administrative Specialist, 734-647-0626, Fax: 734-763-0680, E-mail: cpep@umich.edu.

University of Minnesota, Twin Cities Campus, Graduate School, College of Liberal Arts, Department of Psychology, Minneapolis, MN 55455-0213. Offers biological psychopathology (PhD); clinical psychology (PhD); cognitive and biological psychology (PhD); counseling psychology (PhD); industrial/organizational psychology (PhD); personality, individual differences, and behavior genetics (PhD); quantitative/psychometric methods (PhD); school psychology (PhD); social psychology (PhD). *Accreditation:* APA. *Degree requirements:* For doctorate, comprehensive exam, thesis/dissertation. *Entrance requirements:* For doctorate, GRE General Test, GRE Subject Test (recommended), 12 credits of upper-level psychology courses, including a course in statistics or psychological measurement. Additional exam requirements/recommendations for international students: Required—TOEFL (minimum score 79 iBT).

University of Mississippi, Graduate School, College of Liberal Arts, Department of Psychology, Oxford, University, MS 38677. Offers clinical psychology (PhD); experimental psychology (PhD); psychology (MA). *Accreditation:* APA (one or more programs are accredited). *Students:* 55 full-time (42 women), 6 part-time (4 women); includes 10 minority (8 Black or African American, non-Hispanic/Latino; 1 Asian, non-Hispanic/Latino; 1 Hispanic/Latino), 1 international. In 2010, 4 master's, 4 doctorates awarded. *Degree requirements:* For master's, thesis; for doctorate, thesis/dissertation. *Entrance requirements:* For master's, GRE General Test, minimum GPA of 3.0; for doctorate, GRE General Test. Additional exam requirements/recommendations for international students: Required—TOEFL. *Application deadline:* For fall admission, 1/15 for domestic students; for spring admission, 10/1 for domestic students. Applications are processed on a rolling basis. Application fee: $25. Electronic applications accepted. *Financial support:* Scholarships/grants available. Financial award application deadline: 3/1; financial award applicants required to submit FAFSA. *Unit head:* Dr. Michael T. Allen, Chairman, 662-915-5190, Fax: 662-915-5398, E-mail: psych@olemiss.edu. *Application contact:* Dr. Christy M. Wyandt, Associate Dean, 662-915-7474, Fax: 662-915-7577, E-mail: cwyandt@olemiss.edu.

University of Missouri, Graduate School, College of Arts and Sciences, Department of Psychological Sciences, Columbia, MO 65211. Offers MA, MS, PhD. *Accreditation:* APA (one or more programs are accredited). Terminal master's awarded for partial completion of doctoral program. *Degree requirements:* For doctorate, comprehensive exam, thesis/dissertation. *Entrance requirements:* For master's, GRE General Test, minimum GPA of 3.0; for doctorate, GRE General Test; GRE Subject Test (strongly recommended), minimum GPA of 3.0. Additional exam requirements/recommendations for international students: Required—TOEFL (minimum score 500 paper-based; 173 computer-based; 61 iBT). Electronic applications accepted. *Faculty research:* Clinical psychology, cognition and neuroscience, developmental psychology, quantitative psychology and social/personality psychology, as well as a dual program in child clinical & developmental psychology.

University of Missouri–Kansas City, College of Arts and Sciences, Department of Psychology, Kansas City, MO 64110-2499. Offers clinical psychology (PhD); community psychology (PhD); health psychology (PhD); psychology (MA). PhD (interdisciplinary) offered through the School of Graduate Studies. *Accreditation:* APA. *Faculty:* 14 full-time (10 women), 4 part-time/adjunct (3 women). *Students:* 17 full-time (11 women), 7 part-time (all women); includes 1 Black or African American, non-Hispanic/Latino; 1 Asian, non-Hispanic/Latino; 3 Hispanic/Latino. Average age 30. 89 applicants, 9% accepted, 6 enrolled. In 2010, 6 master's, 4 doctorates awarded. Terminal master's awarded for partial completion of doctoral program. *Degree requirements:* For master's, thesis; for doctorate, comprehensive exam, thesis/dissertation, residency. *Entrance requirements:* For master's, GRE, minimum GPA of 3.5, letter of recommendation; for doctorate, GRE, minimum GPA of 3.25. Additional exam requirements/recommendations for international students: Required—TOEFL (minimum score 550 paper-based; 213 computer-based; 80 iBT). *Application deadline:* For fall admission, 1/15 for domestic and international students. Applications are processed on a rolling basis. Application fee: $45 ($50 for international students). Electronic applications accepted. *Expenses:* Tuition, state resident: full-time $5522.40; part-time $306.80 per credit hour. Tuition, nonresident: full-time $7128; part-time $792 per credit hour. Required fees: $261.15 per term. *Financial support:* In 2010–11, 18 research assistantships (averaging $11,778 per year), 6 teaching assistantships (averaging $11,500 per year) were awarded; career-related internships or fieldwork, Federal Work-Study, and institutionally sponsored loans also available. Support available to part-time students. Financial award application deadline: 3/1; financial award applicants required to submit FAFSA. *Faculty research:* HIV/AIDS research group, psycho-oncology, sensory and cognitive neuroscience, cognitive psychophysiology, obesity and related metabolic disorders. Total annual research expenditures: $933,609. *Unit head:* Dr. Tamera Murdock, Chairperson/Professor, 816-235-1318, Fax: 816-235-1062, E-mail: murdockt@umkc.edu. *Application contact:* Dr. Lisa Terre, Director, Graduate Programs, 816-235-1318, Fax: 816-235-1062, E-mail: terrel@umkc.edu.

University of Missouri–St. Louis, College of Arts and Sciences, Department of Psychology, St. Louis, MO 63121. Offers behavioral neuroscience (PhD); clinical community psychology (PhD); clinical psychology respecialization (Certificate); general psychology (MA); industrial/organizational psychology (PhD); trauma studies (Certificate). *Accreditation:* APA (one or more programs are accredited). Evening/weekend programs available. *Faculty:* 19 full-time (9 women), 5 part-time/adjunct (3 women). *Students:* 44 full-time (34 women), 35 part-time (25 women); includes 7 minority (1 Black or African American, non-Hispanic/Latino; 1 American Indian or Alaska Native, non-Hispanic/Latino; 3 Asian, non-Hispanic/Latino; 2 Hispanic/Latino). Average age 27. 220 applicants, 10% accepted, 18 enrolled. In 2010, 10 master's, 6 doctorates awarded. Terminal master's awarded for partial completion of doctoral program. *Degree requirements:* For master's, thesis; for doctorate, thesis/dissertation. *Entrance requirements:* For master's, GRE General Test, 3 letters of recommendation; for doctorate, GRE General Test, GRE Subject Test, 3 letters of recommendation. Additional exam requirements/recommendations for international students: Required—TOEFL (minimum score 550 paper-based; 213 computer-based). *Application deadline:* For fall admission, 1/15 for domestic and international students. Application fee: $35 ($40 for international students). Electronic applications accepted. *Expenses:* Tuition, state resident: full-time $5522; part-time $306.80 per credit hour. Tuition, nonresident: full-time $14,253; part-time $792.10 per credit hour. Required fees: $658; $49 per credit hour. One-time fee: $12. Tuition and fees vary according to program. *Financial support:* In 2010–11, 5 research assistantships with full and partial tuition reimbursements (averaging $13,352 per year), 26 teaching assistantships with full and partial tuition reimbursements (averaging $11,000 per year) were awarded; fellowships with full tuition reimbursements also available. Financial award applicants required to submit FAFSA. *Faculty research:* Bereavement and loss, neuroscience, post-traumatic stress disorder, conflict and negotiation, social psychology. *Unit head:* Dr. George Taylor, Chair, 314-516-5391, Fax: 314-516-5392, E-mail: umslpsychology@msx.umsl.edu. *Application contact:* 314-516-5458, Fax: 314-516-6996, E-mail: gradadm@umsl.edu.

The University of Montana, Graduate School, College of Arts and Sciences, Department of Psychology, Missoula, MT 59812-0002. Offers clinical psychology (PhD); experimental psychology (PhD), including animal behavior psychology, developmental psychology; school psychology (MA, PhD, Ed S). *Accreditation:* APA (one or more programs are accredited). Terminal master's awarded for partial completion of doctoral program. *Degree requirements:* For master's, thesis; for doctorate, thesis/dissertation. *Entrance requirements:* For master's, doctorate, and Ed S, GRE General Test. Additional exam requirements/recommendations for international students: Required—TOEFL.

University of Nebraska at Omaha, Graduate Studies, College of Arts and Sciences, Department of Psychology, Omaha, NE 68182. Offers developmental psychology (PhD); industrial/organizational psychology (MS, PhD); psychobiology (PhD); psychology (MA); school psychology (MS, Ed S). Part-time programs available. *Faculty:* 18 full-time (8 women). *Students:* 50 full-time (38 women), 41 part-time (32 women); includes 9 minority (2 Black or African American, non-Hispanic/Latino; 1 American Indian or Alaska Native, non-Hispanic/Latino; 1 Asian, non-Hispanic/Latino; 5 Hispanic/Latino), 2 international. Average age 26. 92 applicants, 39% accepted, 34 enrolled. In 2010, 17 master's, 2 doctorates, 6 other advanced degrees awarded. *Degree requirements:* For master's, comprehensive exam, thesis (for some programs). *Entrance requirements:* For master's, GRE General Test, GRE Subject Test, previous course work in psychology, including statistics and a laboratory course; minimum GPA of 3.0, 3 letters of recommendation; for doctorate, GRE General Test. Additional exam requirements/recommendations for international students: Required—TOEFL (minimum score 500 paper-based; 173 computer-based; 61 iBT). *Application deadline:* For fall admission, 1/5 for domestic students. Application fee: $45. Electronic applications accepted. *Financial support:* In 2010–11, 66 students received support; fellowships, research assistantships with tuition reimbursements available, teaching assistantships with tuition reimbursements available, career-related internships or fieldwork, Federal Work-Study, institutionally sponsored loans, scholarships/grants, tuition waivers (partial), and unspecified assistantships available. Support available to part-time students. Financial award application deadline: 3/1; financial award applicants required to submit FAFSA. *Unit head:* Dr. Brigette Ryalls, Chairperson, 402-554-2592. *Application contact:* Dr. Joseph Brown, Student Contact, 402-554-2592.

University of Nebraska–Lincoln, Graduate College, College of Arts and Sciences, Department of Psychology, Lincoln, NE 68588. Offers biopsychology (PhD); clinical psychology (PhD); cognitive psychology (PhD); developmental psychology (PhD); psychology (MA); social/personality psychology (PhD); JD/MA; JD/PhD. *Accreditation:* APA (one or more programs are accredited). *Degree requirements:* For master's, thesis optional; for doctorate, comprehensive exam, thesis/dissertation. *Entrance requirements:* For master's and doctorate, GRE General Test. Additional exam requirements/recommendations for international students: Required—TOEFL (minimum score 550 paper-based; 213 computer-based). Electronic applications accepted. *Faculty research:* Law and psychology, rural mental health, chronic mental illness, neuropsychology, child clinical psychology.

University of Nevada, Las Vegas, Graduate College, College of Liberal Arts, Department of Psychology, Las Vegas, NV 89154-5030. Offers MA, PhD. *Accreditation:* APA. Part-time programs available. *Faculty:* 22 full-time (9 women), 4 part-time/adjunct (2 women). *Students:* 60 full-time (44 women), 18 part-time (12 women); includes 3 Black or African American, non-Hispanic/Latino; 2 American Indian or Alaska Native, non-Hispanic/Latino; 2 Asian, non-Hispanic/Latino; 2 Hispanic/Latino, 3 international. Average age 32. 149 applicants, 11% accepted, 12 enrolled. In 2010, 10 master's, 9 doctorates awarded. *Degree requirements:* For master's, comprehensive exam, thesis, oral defense of dissertation; for doctorate, comprehensive exam, thesis/dissertation, oral defense of dissertation. *Entrance requirements:* For master's and doctorate, GRE General and Subject Tests. Additional exam requirements/recommendations for international students: Required—TOEFL (minimum score 550 paper-based; 213 computer-based; 80 iBT), IELTS (minimum score 7). *Application deadline:* For fall admission, 12/1 priority date for domestic and international students. Applications are processed on a rolling basis. Application fee: $60 ($95 for international students). Electronic applications accepted. *Expenses:* Tuition, area resident: Part-time $239.50 per credit. Tuition, state resident: part-time $239.50 per credit. Tuition, nonresident: part-time $503 per credit. Required fees: $108 per semester. Tuition and fees vary according to course load, program and reciprocity agreements. *Financial support:* In 2010–11, 55 students received support, including 10 research assistantships with partial tuition reimbursements available (averaging $12,000 per year), 45 teaching assistantships with partial tuition reimbursements available (averaging $12,000 per year); institutionally sponsored loans, scholarships/grants, health care benefits, and unspecified assistantships also available. Financial award application deadline: 3/1. *Faculty research:* Schizophrenia and bipolar disorders, childhood anxiety and school refusal, development of stereotypes in infants, cognitive processes in text comprehension, drug abuse and child neglect. Total annual research expenditures: $597,979. *Unit head:* Dr. Mark Ashcraft, Chair/Professor, 702-895-3305, Fax: 702-895-0195, E-mail: mark.ashcraft@unlv.edu. *Application contact:* Graduate College Admissions Evaluator, 702-895-3320, Fax: 702-895-4180, E-mail: gradcollege@unlv.edu.

University of Nevada, Reno, Graduate School, College of Liberal Arts, Department of Psychology, Reno, NV 89557. Offers behavior analysis (MA, PhD); clinical psychology (MA, PhD); cognitive brain science (MA, PhD). *Accreditation:* APA (one or more programs are accredited). Terminal master's awarded for partial completion of doctoral program. *Degree requirements:* For master's, thesis optional; for doctorate, thesis/dissertation. *Entrance requirements:* For master's, GRE General Test, GRE Subject Test, minimum GPA of 2.75; for doctorate, GRE General Test, GRE Subject Test, minimum GPA of 3.0. Additional exam requirements/recommendations for international students: Required—TOEFL (minimum score 500 paper-based; 173 computer-based; 61 iBT), IELTS (minimum score 6). Electronic applications accepted. *Expenses:* Tuition, state resident: full-time $2219; part-time $246 per credit. Tuition, nonresident: part-time $510 per credit. International tuition: $9009 full-time. Required fees: $59 per term. One-time fee: $101. Tuition and fees vary according to course load. *Faculty research:* Cognitive psychology, social psychological theory, animal and human intelligence, psychotherapy outcome, perception.

University of New Brunswick Saint John, Department of Psychology, Saint John, NB E2L 4L5, Canada. Offers applied and experimental psychology (PhD); clinical psychology (PhD); experimental psychology (MA). Part-time programs available. *Faculty:* 9 full-time (4 women), 1 part-time/adjunct (0 women). *Students:* 4 full-time (1 woman). In 2010, 1 doctorate awarded. *Degree requirements:* For master's, thesis. *Entrance requirements:* For master's, GRE General and Subject Tests, honours thesis. Additional exam requirements/recommendations for international students: Required—TOEFL (minimum score 550 paper-based), TWE. *Application deadline:* For fall admission, 2/1 for domestic students. Application fee: $50. *Financial support:* In 2010–11, 2 research assistantships (averaging $9,000 per year), 7 teaching assistantships (averaging $4,500 per year) were awarded; fellowships, unspecified assistantships also available. Support available to part-time students. Financial award application deadline: 2/1. *Faculty research:* Psychopharmacology and addictions, forensic psychology and criminal justice, interpersonal relations, perception and graphical perception, lie detection, children's play and peer relationships, classical and operant conditioning. *Unit head:* Dr. Lily Both, Director of Graduate Studies, 506-648-5769, Fax: 506-648-5780, E-mail: lboth@unbsj.ca. *Application contact:* Frances Stevens, Secretary, 506-648-5640, Fax: 506-648-5780, E-mail: fstevens@unb.ca.

University of New Hampshire, Graduate School, College of Liberal Arts, Department of Psychology, Durham, NH 03824. Offers PhD. *Faculty:* 23 full-time (7 women). *Students:* 27 full-time (19 women), 5 part-time (4 women); includes 1 minority (Two or more races, non-Hispanic/Latino), 1 international. Average age 34. 86 applicants, 9% accepted, 6 enrolled. In 2010, 6 doctorates awarded. *Degree requirements:* For doctorate, thesis/dissertation. *Entrance requirements:* For doctorate, GRE General Test, GRE Subject Test. Additional exam requirements/recommendations for international students: Required—TOEFL (minimum score 550 paper-based; 213 computer-based; 80 iBT). *Application deadline:* For fall admission, 6/15 priority date for domestic students, 4/15 for international students; for spring admission, 12/1 for domestic students. Applications are processed on a rolling basis. Application fee: $65. Electronic applications accepted. *Financial support:* In 2010–11, 29 students received support, including 2 fellowships, 27 teaching assistantships; research assistantships, career-related internships or fieldwork, Federal Work-Study, scholarships/grants, and tuition waivers (full and partial) also available. Support available to part-time students. Financial award application deadline: 2/15. *Faculty research:* History of psychology; cognition and perception; learning, developmental, physiological, and social psychology. *Unit head:* Dr. Robert Mair, Chairperson, 603-862-3198. *Application contact:* Donna Hardy, Administrative Assistant, 603-862-3167, E-mail: psychology.ph.d@unh.edu.

University of New Mexico, Graduate School, College of Arts and Sciences, Department of Psychology, Albuquerque, NM 87131-2039. Offers clinical psychology (MS, PhD); psychology (PhD). *Accreditation:* APA (one or more programs are accredited). *Faculty:* 53 full-time (21 women), 22 part-time/adjunct (15 women). *Students:* 73 full-time (55 women), 8 part-time (6 women); includes 1 American Indian or Alaska Native, non-Hispanic/Latino; 2 Asian, non-Hispanic/Latino; 14 Hispanic/Latino, 5 international. Average age 31. 189 applicants, 8% accepted, 12 enrolled. In 2010, 12 master's, 10 doctorates awarded. Terminal master's awarded for partial completion of doctoral program. *Degree requirements:* For master's, thesis; for doctorate, comprehensive exam, thesis/dissertation, pre-doctoral internship. *Entrance requirements:* For doctorate, GRE General Test, GRE Subject Test (psychology), minimum GPA of 3.0. Additional exam requirements/recommendations for international students: Required—TOEFL. *Application deadline:* For fall admission, 1/15 priority date for domestic and international students. Applications are processed on a rolling basis. Application fee: $50. Electronic applications accepted. *Expenses:* Tuition, state resident: full-time $5991; part-time $251 per credit hour. Tuition, nonresident: full-time $14,405; part-time $800.20 per credit hour. Tuition and fees vary according to course level, course load, program and reciprocity agreements. *Financial support:* In 2010–11, 78 students received support, including 2 fellowships (averaging $13,124 per year), 40 research assistantships with full and partial tuition reimbursements available (averaging $11,759 per year), 14 teaching assistantships with full and partial tuition reimbursements available (averaging $9,711 per year); career-related internships or fieldwork, Federal Work-Study, institutionally sponsored loans, scholarships/grants, health care benefits, tuition waivers (full and partial), and unspecified assistantships also available. Financial award application deadline: 3/1; financial award applicants required to submit FAFSA. *Faculty research:* Addictions, clinical, cognition, brain and behavior, developmental, evolutionary, functional neuroimaging, health psychology, learning and memory, neuropsychology. Total annual research expenditures: $953,743. *Unit head:* Dr. Jane Ellen Smith, Chair, 505-277-4121, Fax: 505-277-1394, E-mail: janellen@unm.edu. *Application contact:* Program Advisement Coordinator, 505-277-5009, Fax: 505-277-1394.

University of New Orleans, Graduate School, College of Sciences, Department of Psychology, New Orleans, LA 70148. Offers MS, PhD. *Degree requirements:* For doctorate, thesis/dissertation. *Entrance requirements:* For doctorate, GRE General Test, minimum GPA of 3.0, 21 hours of course work in psychology. Additional exam requirements/recommendations for international students: Required—TOEFL (minimum score 550 paper-based; 213 computer-based; 79 iBT). Electronic applications accepted. *Faculty research:* Biofeedback, visual and auditory perception, psychopharmacology, neuropeptides.

The University of North Carolina at Chapel Hill, Graduate School, College of Arts and Sciences, Department of Psychology, Chapel Hill, NC 27599. Offers biological psychology (PhD); clinical psychology (PhD); cognitive psychology (PhD); developmental psychology (PhD); quantitative psychology (PhD); social psychology (PhD). *Accreditation:* APA. *Degree requirements:* For doctorate, comprehensive exam, thesis/dissertation. *Entrance requirements:* For doctorate, GRE General Test, minimum GPA of 3.0. Electronic applications accepted. *Faculty research:* Expressed emotion, cognitive development, social cognitive neuroscience, human memory personality.

The University of North Carolina at Charlotte, Graduate School, College of Arts and Sciences, Department of Psychology, Charlotte, NC 28223-0001. Offers community/clinical psychology (MA); health psychology (PhD); industrial/organizational psychology (MA); organizational science (PhD). Part-time programs available. *Faculty:* 27 full-time (11 women), 1 part-time/adjunct (0 women). *Students:* 67 full-time (50 women), 18 part-time (14 women); includes 19 minority (8 Black or African American, non-Hispanic/Latino; 3 Asian, non-Hispanic/Latino; 4 Hispanic/Latino; 1 Native Hawaiian or other Pacific Islander, non-Hispanic/Latino; 3 Two or more races, non-Hispanic/Latino), 3 international. Average age 29. 317 applicants, 9% accepted, 21 enrolled. In 2010, 14 master's, 1 doctorate awarded. *Degree requirements:* For master's, thesis; for doctorate, thesis/dissertation. *Entrance requirements:* For master's, GRE General Test, GRE Subject Test, minimum GPA of 3.0 in undergraduate major, 2.8 overall. Additional exam requirements/recommendations for international students: Required—TOEFL (minimum score 557 paper-based; 220 computer-based; 83 iBT). *Application deadline:* Applications are processed on a rolling basis. Application fee: $55. Electronic applications accepted. *Expenses:* Tuition, state resident: full-time $3464. Tuition, nonresident: full-time $14,297. Required fees: $2094. Tuition and fees vary according to course load. *Financial support:* In 2010–11, 44 students received support, including 12 research assistantships (averaging $14,191 per year), 31 teaching assistantships (averaging $10,710 per year); career-related internships or fieldwork, Federal Work-Study, institutionally sponsored loans, scholarships/grants, and administrative assistantships also available. Support available to part-time students. Financial award application deadline: 4/1; financial award applicants required to submit FAFSA. *Faculty research:* Health psychology, industrial-organizational psychology, cognitive science. Total annual research expenditures: $435,127. *Unit head:* Dr. Brian L. Cutler, Chair, 704-687-4731, Fax: 704-687-3096, E-mail: blcutler@uncc.edu. *Application contact:* Kathy B. Giddings, Director of Graduate Admissions, 704-687-5503, Fax: 704-687-3279, E-mail: gradadm@uncc.edu.

The University of North Carolina at Greensboro, Graduate School, College of Arts and Sciences, Department of Psychology, Greensboro, NC 27412-5001. Offers clinical psychology (MA, PhD); cognitive psychology (MA, PhD); developmental psychology (MA, PhD); social psychology (MA, PhD). *Accreditation:* APA (one or more programs are accredited). Terminal master's awarded for partial completion of doctoral program. *Degree requirements:* For master's, comprehensive exam, thesis; for doctorate, one foreign language, thesis/dissertation, preliminary exam. *Entrance requirements:* For master's and doctorate, GRE General Test. Additional exam requirements/recommendations for international students: Required—TOEFL. Electronic applications accepted. *Faculty research:* Sensory and perceptual determinants; evoked potential: disorders, deafness, and development.

The University of North Carolina Wilmington, College of Arts and Sciences, Department of Psychology, Wilmington, NC 28403-3297. Offers MA. Part-time programs available. *Faculty:* 24 full-time (12 women). *Students:* 31 full-time (23 women), 33 part-time (20 women); includes 2 Black or African American, non-Hispanic/Latino; 1 Asian, non-Hispanic/Latino; 4 Hispanic/Latino; 2 Two or more races, non-Hispanic/Latino, 1 international. Average age 26. 121 applicants, 21% accepted, 23 enrolled. In 2010, 18 master's awarded. *Degree requirements:* For master's, comprehensive exam, thesis. *Entrance requirements:* For master's, GRE General Test, GRE Subject Test, minimum B average in undergraduate major. Additional exam requirements/recommendations for international students: Required—TOEFL (minimum score 550 paper-based; 217 computer-based; 79 iBT), IELTS (minimum score 6.5). *Application deadline:* For fall admission, 1/15 for domestic students. Applications are processed on a rolling basis. Application fee: $60. *Financial support:* In 2010–11, 16 teaching assistantships with partial tuition reimbursements (averaging $10,000 per year) were awarded; career-related internships or fieldwork and Federal Work-Study also available. Financial award application deadline: 3/15. *Unit head:* Dr. Mark Galizio, Department Chair, 910-962-3370, Fax: 910-962-7010, E-mail: galiziom@uncw.edu. *Application contact:* Dr. Richard Ogle, Graduate Coordinator, 910-962-7753, E-mail: ogler@uncw.edu.

University of North Dakota, Graduate School, College of Arts and Sciences, Department of Psychology, Grand Forks, ND 58202. Offers clinical psychology (PhD); counseling psychology (PhD); experimental psychology (PhD); forensic psychology (MA, MS); psychology (MA). *Accreditation:* APA (one or more programs are accredited). *Faculty:* 22 full-time (7 women), 2 part-time/adjunct (1 woman). *Students:* 55 full-time (46 women), 81 part-time (69 women); includes 24 minority (4 Black or African American, non-Hispanic/Latino; 12 American Indian or Alaska Native, non-Hispanic/Latino; 2 Asian, non-Hispanic/Latino; 4 Hispanic/Latino; 2 Two or more races, non-Hispanic/Latino), 2 international. Average age 29. 126 applicants, 25% accepted, 27 enrolled. In 2010, 25 master's, 9 doctorates awarded. *Degree requirements:* For master's, thesis, final exam; for doctorate, comprehensive exam, thesis/dissertation, internship, final exam. *Entrance requirements:* For master's, GRE General Test, GRE Subject Test, minimum GPA of 3.0; for doctorate, GRE General Test, GRE Subject Test, minimum GPA of 3.5. Additional exam requirements/recommendations for international students: Required—TOEFL (minimum score 550 paper-based; 213 computer-based; 79 iBT), IELTS (minimum score 6.5). *Application deadline:* For fall admission, 1/15 for domestic and international students. Application fee: $35. Electronic applications accepted. *Expenses:* Tuition, state resident: full-time $5857; part-time $306.74 per credit. Tuition, nonresident: full-time $15,666; part-time $729.77 per credit. Required fees: $53.42 per credit. Tuition and fees vary according to course load, program and reciprocity agreements. *Financial support:* In 2010–11, 28 students received support, including 21 teaching assistantships with full and partial tuition reimbursements available (averaging $8,993 per year); fellowships with full and partial tuition reimbursements available, research assistantships with full and partial tuition reimbursements available, career-related internships or fieldwork, Federal Work-Study, institutionally sponsored loans, scholarships/grants, health care benefits, tuition waivers (full and partial), and unspecified assistantships also available. Support available to part-time students. Financial award application deadline: 3/15; financial award applicants required to submit FAFSA. *Faculty research:* Developmental psychology, clinical social psychology, educational psychology, personality disorders. Total annual research expenditures: $323,990. *Unit head:* Dr. Mark Grabe, Chairperson, 701-777-3451, E-mail: mark.grabe@und.nodak.edu. *Application contact:* Matt Anderson, Admissions Specialist, 701-777-2947, Fax: 701-777-3619, E-mail: matthew.anderson@gradschool.und.edu.

University of Northern British Columbia, Office of Graduate Studies, Prince George, BC V2N 4Z9, Canada. Offers business administration (Diploma); community health science (M Sc); disability management (MA); education (M Ed); first nations studies (MA); gender studies (MA); history (MA); interdisciplinary studies (MA); international studies (MA); mathematical, computer and physical sciences (M Sc); natural resources and environmental studies (M Sc, MA, MNRES, PhD); political science (MA); psychology (M Sc, PhD); social work (MSW). Part-time and evening/weekend programs available. Postbaccalaureate distance learning degree programs offered (no on-campus study). *Degree requirements:* For master's, thesis; for doctorate, thesis/dissertation. *Entrance requirements:* For master's, GRE, minimum B average in undergraduate course work; for doctorate, candidacy exam, minimum A average in graduate course work.

University of Northern Colorado, Graduate School, College of Education and Behavioral Sciences, School of Psychological Sciences, Greeley, CO 80639. Offers MA, PhD. Part-time programs available. *Faculty:* 28 full-time (15 women). *Students:* 24 full-time (12 women), 12 part-time (10 women); includes 1 Black or African American, non-Hispanic/Latino; 1 American Indian or Alaska Native, non-Hispanic/Latino; 3 Hispanic/Latino. Average age 34. 17 applicants, 88% accepted, 9 enrolled. In 2010, 8 master's, 6 doctorates awarded. *Degree requirements:* For master's, comprehensive exam, thesis or alternative; for doctorate, comprehensive exam, thesis/dissertation. *Entrance requirements:* For master's and doctorate, GRE General Test, letters of recommendation. *Application deadline:* Applications are processed on a rolling basis. Application fee: $50 ($60 for international students). Electronic applications accepted. *Expenses:* Tuition, state resident: full-time $6199; part-time $344 per credit hour. Tuition, nonresident: full-time $14,834; part-time $824 per credit hour. Required fees: $1091; $60.60 per credit hour. Tuition and fees vary according to course load, degree level and program. *Financial support:* In 2010–11, 5 research assistantships (averaging $3,418 per year), 8 teaching assistantships (averaging $4,898 per year) were awarded; fellowships, unspecified assistantships also available. Financial award application deadline: 3/1; financial award applicants required to submit FAFSA. *Unit head:* Dr. Mark Alcorn, Director, 970-351-2957, Fax: 970-351-1103. *Application contact:* Linda Sisson, Graduate Student Admission Coordinator, 970-351-1807, Fax: 970-351-2371, E-mail: linda.sisson@unco.edu.

University of Northern Iowa, Graduate College, College of Social and Behavioral Sciences, Department of Psychology, Cedar Falls, IA 50614. Offers MA. Part-time programs available. *Students:* 26 full-time (17 women), 1 part-time (0 women); includes 2 minority (1 Hispanic/Latino; 1 Two or more races, non-Hispanic/Latino), 2 international. 73 applicants, 22% accepted, 11 enrolled. In 2010, 14 master's awarded. *Degree requirements:* For master's, comprehensive exam, thesis. *Entrance requirements:* For master's, GRE, minimum GPA of 3.0, 3 letters of recommendation. Additional exam requirements/recommendations for international students: Required—TOEFL (minimum score 500 paper-based; 180 computer-based; 61 iBT). *Application deadline:* For fall admission, 4/30 for domestic students. Applications are processed on a rolling basis. Application fee: $50 ($70 for international students). Electronic applications accepted. *Financial support:* Career-related internships or fieldwork, Federal Work-Study, and tuition waivers (full and partial) available. Support available to part-time students. Financial award application deadline: 2/1. *Unit head:* Dr. Carolyn Hildebrandt, Interim Department Head, 319-273-7179, Fax: 319-273-6188, E-mail: carolyn.hildebrandt@uni.edu. *Application contact:* Laurie S. Russell, Record Analyst, 319-273-2623, Fax: 319-273-2885, E-mail: laurie.russell@uni.edu.

University of North Florida, College of Arts and Sciences, Department of Psychology, Jacksonville, FL 32224. Offers counseling psychology (MAC); general psychology (MA). Part-time and evening/weekend programs available. *Faculty:* 13 full-time (5 women), 3 part-time/adjunct (1 woman). *Students:* 35 full-time (21 women), 16 part-time (11 women); includes 1 Black or African American, non-Hispanic/Latino; 1 Asian, non-Hispanic/Latino; 5 Hispanic/Latino; 2 Two or more races, non-Hispanic/Latino, 1 international. Average age 28. 61 applicants, 38% accepted, 12 enrolled. In 2010, 14 master's awarded. *Degree requirements:* For master's, comprehensive exam, thesis optional, practicum. *Entrance requirements:* For master's, GRE General Test, 2 letters of recommendation, minimum GPA of 3.0 in last 60 hours of course work. Additional exam requirements/recommendations for international students: Required—TOEFL (minimum score 500 paper-based; 173 computer-based; 61 iBT). *Application deadline:* For fall admission, 6/1 priority date for domestic students, 4/1 for international students. Applications are processed on a rolling basis. Application fee: $30. Electronic applications accepted. *Expenses:* Tuition, state resident: full-time $7646.40; part-time $318.60 per credit hour. Tuition, nonresident: full-time $23,502; part-time $979.24 per credit hour. Required fees: $1208.88; $50.37 per credit hour. Tuition and fees vary according to course load and program. *Financial support:* In 2010–11, 25 students received support, including 1 research assistantship (averaging $1,684 per year), 4 teaching assistantships (averaging $5,186 per year); Federal Work-Study, scholarships/grants, and tuition waivers (partial) also available. Financial award application deadline: 4/1; financial award applicants required to submit FAFSA. *Faculty research:* Sensory perception, social cognition, sexual behavior, evolutionary psychology, psychology and law. Total annual research expenditures: $68,727. *Unit head:* Dr. Michael Toglia, Chair, 904-620-1624, E-mail: m.toglia@unf.edu. *Application contact:* Lillith Richardson, Assistant Director, The Graduate School, 904-620-1360, Fax: 904-620-1362, E-mail: graduateschool@unf.edu.

University of North Texas, Toulouse Graduate School, College of Arts and Sciences, Department of Psychology, Denton, TX 76203. Offers clinical psychology (PhD); counseling psychology (MA, MS, PhD); experimental psychology (MA, MS, PhD); health psychology and behavioral medicine (PhD). *Accreditation:* APA (one or more programs are accredited). Terminal master's awarded for partial completion of doctoral program. *Degree requirements:* For master's, comprehensive exam, thesis or alternative; for doctorate, one foreign language, comprehensive exam, thesis/dissertation. *Entrance requirements:* For master's and doctorate, GRE General Test, interview. Additional exam requirements/recommendations for international students: Recommended—TOEFL (minimum score 550 paper-based; 213 computer-based; 79 iBT). *Application deadline:* Applications are processed on a rolling basis. Electronic applications accepted. *Expenses:* Tuition, state resident: full-time $4298; part-time $239 per credit hour. Tuition, nonresident: full-time $10,782; part-time $549 per credit hour. Required fees: $1292; $270 per credit hour. *Financial support:* Fellowships, research assistantships, teaching assistantships, career-related internships or fieldwork, Federal Work-Study, and institutionally sponsored loans available. Financial award applicants required to submit FAFSA. *Application contact:* Graduate Coordinator, 940-565-2671, Fax: 940-565-4682, E-mail: amym@unt.edu.

University of North Texas, Toulouse Graduate School, College of Public Affairs and Community Service, Department of Behavior Analysis, Denton, TX 76203. Offers MS. *Accreditation:*

Psychology—General

University of North Texas (continued)
APA. *Degree requirements:* For master's, thesis. *Entrance requirements:* For master's, GRE General Test. Additional exam requirements/recommendations for international students: Recommended—TOEFL (minimum score 550 paper-based; 213 computer-based; 79 iBT). *Application deadline:* Applications are processed on a rolling basis. Electronic applications accepted. *Expenses:* Tuition, state resident: full-time $4298; part-time $239 per credit hour. Tuition, nonresident: full-time $10,782; part-time $549 per credit hour. Required fees: $1292; $270 per credit hour. *Financial support:* Fellowships, teaching assistantships, career-related internships or fieldwork, Federal Work-Study, scholarships/grants, and tuition waivers (partial) available. Support available to part-time students. Financial award applicants required to submit FAFSA. *Faculty research:* Human operant research, applied behavior analysis, animal training, autism. *Application contact:* Graduate Advisor, 940-369-7961, Fax: 940-565-2467, E-mail: manish.vaidya@unt.edu.

University of Notre Dame, Graduate School, College of Arts and Letters, Division of Social Science, Department of Psychology, Notre Dame, IN 46556. Offers cognitive psychology (PhD); counseling psychology (PhD); developmental psychology (PhD); quantitative psychology (PhD). *Accreditation:* APA. *Degree requirements:* For doctorate, comprehensive exam, thesis/dissertation, candidacy exam. *Entrance requirements:* For doctorate, GRE General Test, GRE Subject Test (strongly recommended). Additional exam requirements/recommendations for international students: Required—TOEFL (minimum score 600 paper-based; 250 computer-based; 80 iBT). Electronic applications accepted. *Faculty research:* Cognitive and socio-emotional development, statistical methods and quantitative models applicable to psychology, interpersonal relations, life span development and developmental delay, childhood depression, structural equation and dynamical systems.

University of Oklahoma, College of Arts and Sciences, Department of Psychology, Norman, OK 73019. Offers organizational dynamics (MA), including organizational dynamics; psychology (MS, PhD), including industrial and organizational psychology, psychology. *Faculty:* 25 full-time (12 women), 1 part-time/adjunct (0 women). *Students:* 75 full-time (31 women), 33 part-time (18 women); includes 12 minority (3 Black or African American, non-Hispanic/Latino; 3 American Indian or Alaska Native, non-Hispanic/Latino; 4 Asian, non-Hispanic/Latino; 1 Native Hawaiian or other Pacific Islander, non-Hispanic/Latino; 1 Two or more races, non-Hispanic/Latino), 5 international. Average age 30. 81 applicants, 26% accepted, 20 enrolled. In 2010, 17 master's, 11 doctorates awarded. Terminal master's awarded for partial completion of doctoral program. *Degree requirements:* For master's, thesis or alternative; for doctorate, thesis/dissertation, general exam. *Entrance requirements:* For master's, GRE General Test, GRE Subject Test, minimum GPA of 3.0, 3 letters of recommendation; for doctorate, GRE General Test, GRE Subject Test, 3 letters of recommendation. Additional exam requirements/recommendations for international students: Required—TOEFL (minimum score 550 paper-based; 213 computer-based; 79 iBT). *Application deadline:* For fall admission, 4/1 priority date for domestic students, 4/1 for international students; for spring admission, 11/1 for domestic students, 9/1 for international students. Applications are processed on a rolling basis. Application fee: $40 ($90 for international students). Electronic applications accepted. *Expenses:* Tuition, state resident: full-time $3893; part-time $162.20 per credit hour. Tuition, nonresident: full-time $14,167; part-time $590.30 per credit hour. Required fees: $2523; $94.60 per credit hour. Tuition and fees vary according to course load and degree level. *Financial support:* In 2010–11, 104 students received support, including 13 fellowships with full tuition reimbursements available (averaging $5,846 per year), 7 research assistantships with partial tuition reimbursements available (averaging $12,177 per year), 35 teaching assistantships with partial tuition reimbursements available (averaging $13,421 per year); institutionally sponsored loans, scholarships/grants, health care benefits, and unspecified assistantships also available. Financial award application deadline: 3/1; financial award applicants required to submit FAFSA. *Faculty research:* Industrial organizational psychology including leadership and creativity; cognitive psychology with an emphasis in modeling, memory, and decision science; quantitative methods (measurement, modeling, and statistics); social psychology (self and stereotype thinking); personality and animal behavior. Total annual research expenditures: $2 million. *Unit head:* Dr. Jorge Mendoza, Chair, 405-325-4511, Fax: 405-325-4737, E-mail: jmendoza@ou.edu. *Application contact:* Kathryn Paine, Graduate Admissions Coordinator, 405-325-4512, Fax: 405-325-4737, E-mail: kpaine@ou.edu.

University of Oregon, Graduate School, College of Arts and Sciences, Department of Psychology, Eugene, OR 97403. Offers clinical psychology (PhD); cognitive psychology (MA, MS, PhD); developmental psychology (MA, MS, PhD); physiological psychology (MA, MS, PhD); psychology (MA, MS, PhD); social/personality psychology (MA, MS, PhD). *Accreditation:* APA (one or more programs are accredited). Terminal master's awarded for partial completion of doctoral program. *Degree requirements:* For doctorate, thesis/dissertation. *Entrance requirements:* For master's, GRE General Test, minimum GPA of 3.0; for doctorate, GRE General Test. Additional exam requirements/recommendations for international students: Required—TOEFL.

University of Ottawa, Faculty of Graduate and Postdoctoral Studies, Faculty of Social Sciences, School of Psychology, Ottawa, ON K1N 6N5, Canada. Offers PhD. *Accreditation:* APA. *Degree requirements:* For doctorate, thesis/dissertation. *Entrance requirements:* For doctorate, minimum B+ average. Electronic applications accepted. *Faculty research:* Behavioral neuroscience, social psychology, developmental psychology, cognition.

University of Pennsylvania, School of Arts and Sciences, Graduate Group in Psychology, Philadelphia, PA 19104. Offers PhD. *Accreditation:* APA. *Faculty:* 59 full-time (17 women), 12 part-time/adjunct (4 women). *Students:* 52 full-time (33 women); includes 5 Asian, non-Hispanic/Latino; 1 Hispanic/Latino, 12 international. 602 applicants, 4% accepted, 12 enrolled. In 2010, 7 doctorates awarded. *Degree requirements:* For doctorate, thesis/dissertation. *Entrance requirements:* For doctorate, GRE General Test, GRE Subject Test. Additional exam requirements/recommendations for international students: Required—TOEFL. *Application deadline:* For fall admission, 12/1 priority date for domestic students. Application fee: $70. Electronic applications accepted. *Expenses:* Tuition: Full-time $25,660; part-time $4758 per course. Required fees: $2152; $270 per course. Tuition and fees vary according to course load, degree level and program. *Financial support:* In 2010–11, 10 fellowships, 2 research assistantships, 20 teaching assistantships were awarded; institutionally sponsored loans, scholarships/grants, traineeships, health care benefits, and unspecified assistantships also available. Financial award application deadline: 12/15. *Faculty research:* Cognitive psychology, sensation and perception, biological psychology, clinical psychology, social psychology. *Unit head:* Robert DeRubeis, Department Chair, Psychology, 215-898-6230, E-mail: derubeis@psych.upenn.edu. *Application contact:* Michael Kahana, Director of Graduate Studies, 215-898-0911, E-mail: dgs@psych.upenn.edu.

University of Philosophical Research, Program in Transformational Psychology, Los Angeles, CA 90027. Offers MA. *Degree requirements:* For master's, thesis.

University of Phoenix, College of Social Science, Phoenix, AZ 85034-7209. Offers clinical mental health counseling (MSC); community counseling (MSC); psychology (MS). Programs are offered at the online campus. Evening/weekend programs available. Postbaccalaureate distance learning degree programs offered. *Students:* 4,215 full-time (3,585 women); includes 1,544 minority (1,161 Black or African American, non-Hispanic/Latino; 34 American Indian or Alaska Native, non-Hispanic/Latino; 32 Asian, non-Hispanic/Latino; 280 Hispanic/Latino; 22 Native Hawaiian or other Pacific Islander, non-Hispanic/Latino; 15 Two or more races, non-Hispanic/Latino), 85 international. Average age 38. *Entrance requirements:* For master's, minimum undergraduate GPA of 2.5 from accredited university, 3 years of work experience, citizen of the United States or have valid visa. Additional exam requirements/recommendations for international students: Required—TOEFL (minimum paper score 550, computer score 213, iBT 79), Test of English for International Communication, or IELTS. *Application deadline:* Applications are processed on a rolling basis. Application fee: $45. Electronic applications accepted. *Expenses:* Tuition: Full-time $16,440. One-time fee: $45 full-time. Full-time tuition and fees vary according to course load, degree level, campus/location and program. *Financial support:* Scholarships/grants available. Financial award applicants required to submit FAFSA. *Unit head:* Rob Olding, Associate Dean, Human Service/Psychology, 602-551-3073, E-mail: rob.olding@phoenix.edu. *Application contact:* Rob Olding, Associate Dean, Human Service/Psychology, 602-551-3073, E-mail: rob.olding@phoenix.edu.

University of Phoenix–Birmingham Campus, College of Social and Behavioral Science, Birmingham, AL 35244. Offers administration of justice and security (MS); psychology (MS).

University of Phoenix–Chattanooga Campus, College of Social Services, Chattanooga, TN 37421-3707. Offers industrial/organizational psychology (PhD); psychology (MSP). Postbaccalaureate distance learning degree programs offered.

University of Phoenix–Cincinnati Campus, College of Social Services, West Chester, OH 45069-4875. Offers psychology (MS). Evening/weekend programs available. Postbaccalaureate distance learning degree programs offered. *Degree requirements:* For master's, thesis (for some programs). *Entrance requirements:* For master's, minimum undergraduate GPA of 2.5, 3 years of work experience. Additional exam requirements/recommendations for international students: Required—TOEFL (minimum score 550 paper-based; 79 iBT). Electronic applications accepted.

University of Phoenix–Jersey City Campus, College of Social Services, Jersey City, NJ 07310. Offers psychology (MS). Postbaccalaureate distance learning degree programs offered.

University of Phoenix–Milwaukee Campus, College of Social Sciences, Milwaukee, WI 53045. Offers industrial/organizational psychology (PhD); psychology (MS).

University of Phoenix–Philadelphia Campus, College of Social Services, Wayne, PA 19087-2121. Offers psychology (MS). Evening/weekend programs available. *Degree requirements:* For master's, thesis (for some programs). *Entrance requirements:* For master's, minimum undergraduate GPA of 2.5, 3 years work experience. Additional exam requirements/recommendations for international students: Required—TOEFL (minimum score 550 paper-based; 213 computer-based; 79 iBT). Electronic applications accepted.

University of Phoenix–Phoenix Campus, College of Social Sciences, Phoenix, AZ 85040-1958. Offers community counseling (MC); counseling (MSC); psychology (MSP). Evening/weekend programs available. Postbaccalaureate distance learning degree programs offered. *Students:* 181 full-time (140 women); includes 23 minority (7 Black or African American, non-Hispanic/Latino; 2 Asian, non-Hispanic/Latino; 14 Hispanic/Latino), 7 international. Average age 34. *Entrance requirements:* For master's, minimum undergraduate GPA of 2.5 from accredited university, 3 years of work experience, citizen of the United States or have valid visa. Additional exam requirements/recommendations for international students: Required—TOEFL (minimum paper score 500, computer score 213, iBT 79), Test of English for International Communication, or IELTS. *Application deadline:* Applications are processed on a rolling basis. Application fee: $45. Electronic applications accepted. *Expenses:* Tuition: Full-time $13,560. One-time fee: $45 full-time. Full-time tuition and fees vary according to course load, degree level, campus/location and program. *Financial support:* Scholarships/grants available. Financial award applicants required to submit FAFSA. *Unit head:* Dr. Lynn Hall, Dean/Executive Director, 520-247-4364, E-mail: lynn.hall@phoenix.edu. *Application contact:* Campus Information Center, 866-766-0766.

University of Phoenix–Southern Arizona Campus, College of Social Sciences, Tucson, AZ 85711. Offers psychology (MS). Evening/weekend programs available. *Degree requirements:* For master's, thesis (for some programs). *Entrance requirements:* For master's, minimum undergraduate GPA of 2.5, 3 years of work experience, RN license. Additional exam requirements/recommendations for international students: Required—TOEFL (minimum score 550 paper-based; 213 computer-based; 79 iBT). Electronic applications accepted.

University of Phoenix–Southern California Campus, College of Social Sciences, Costa Mesa, CA 92626. Offers administration of justice and security (MS); community counseling (MSC); marriage, family and child therapy (MSC); mental health counseling (MSC); psychology (MS); school counseling (MSC). Evening/weekend programs available. *Degree requirements:* For master's, thesis (for some programs). *Entrance requirements:* For master's, minimum undergraduate GPA of 3.0, 3 years work experience. Additional exam requirements/recommendations for international students: Required—TOEFL (minimum score 550 paper-based; 213 computer-based; 79 iBT). Electronic applications accepted.

University of Phoenix–Washington D.C. Campus, College of Social Sciences, Washington, DC 20001. Offers industrial/organizational psychology (PhD); psychology (MS).

University of Pittsburgh, School of Arts and Sciences, Department of Psychology, Pittsburgh, PA 15260. Offers MS, PhD. *Accreditation:* APA (one or more programs are accredited). *Faculty:* 39 full-time (16 women), 8 part-time/adjunct (4 women). *Students:* 96 full-time (82 women); includes 2 Black or African American, non-Hispanic/Latino; 4 Asian, non-Hispanic/Latino; 5 Hispanic/Latino, 11 international. 429 applicants, 7% accepted, 14 enrolled. In 2010, 8 master's, 17 doctorates awarded. Terminal master's awarded for partial completion of doctoral program. *Degree requirements:* For master's, comprehensive exam, thesis; for doctorate, comprehensive exam, thesis/dissertation. *Entrance requirements:* For doctorate, GRE General Test, minimum GPA of 3.0. Additional exam requirements/recommendations for international students: Required—TOEFL, TOEFL (minimum score 550 paper-based; 80 internet-based) or IELTS (minimum score 7). *Application deadline:* For fall admission, 12/1 for domestic and international students. Application fee: $50. Electronic applications accepted. *Expenses:* Tuition, state resident: full-time $17,304; part-time $701 per credit. Tuition, nonresident: full-time $29,554; part-time $1210 per credit. Required fees: $740; $214 per term. Tuition and fees vary according to program. *Financial support:* In 2010–11, 100 students received support, including 18 fellowships with full tuition reimbursements available (averaging $18,546 per year), 42 research assistantships with full tuition reimbursements available (averaging $14,400 per year), 34 teaching assistantships with full tuition reimbursements available (averaging $16,140 per year); career-related internships or fieldwork, scholarships/grants, traineeships, health care benefits, and unspecified assistantships also available. Financial award application deadline: 12/1. *Faculty research:* Behavioral medicine and psychoneuroimmunology; learning, reasoning and memory; psychopathology and behavioral problems; social cognition; social influence and group processes; social and cognitive development. Total annual research expenditures: $16.5 million. *Unit head:* Dr. Daniel S. Shaw, Chairman, 412-624-4501, Fax: 412-624-4428, E-mail: casey@pitt.edu. *Application contact:* Graduate Program Coordinator, 412-624-4502, Fax: 412-624-4428, E-mail: psygrad@pitt.edu.

University of Puerto Rico, Río Piedras, College of Social Sciences, Department of Psychology, San Juan, PR 00931-3300. Offers clinical psychology (MA); industrial organizational psychology (MA); investigative academic psychology (MA); psychology (PhD); social-community psychology (MA). Part-time programs available. *Degree requirements:* For master's, comprehensive exam, thesis; for doctorate, comprehensive exam, thesis/dissertation, internship. *Entrance requirements:* For master's, GRE or PAEG, interview, minimum GPA of 3.0; for doctorate, GRE or PAEG, interview, master's degree, minimum GPA of 3.0. *Faculty research:* Intervention on Depressed Latino Youth, biosychosocial training.

University of Regina, Faculty of Graduate Studies and Research, Faculty of Arts, Department of Psychology, Regina, SK S4S 0A2, Canada. Offers clinical psychology (MA, PhD); experimental and applied psychology (MA, PhD). *Faculty:* 19 full-time (9 women). *Students:* 51 full-time (39 women), 3 part-time (2 women). 44 applicants, 41% accepted. In 2010, 12 master's, 4 doctorates awarded. *Degree requirements:* For master's, thesis; for doctorate, comprehensive exam, thesis/dissertation. *Entrance requirements:* For master's, GRE General Test, GRE Subject Test; for doctorate, GRE General Test, GRE Subject Test (optional for those with a master's degree from a Canadian university). Additional exam requirements/recommendations for international students: Required—TOEFL (minimum score 580 paper-based; 80 iBT).

Application deadline: For fall admission, 2/15 for domestic and international students. Application fee: $100. Electronic applications accepted. Tuition and fees charges are reported in Canadian dollars. *Expenses:* Tuition, area resident: Full-time $3244.50 Canadian dollars; part-time $180.25 Canadian dollars per credit hour. International tuition: $4744.50 Canadian dollars full-time. Required fees: $494 Canadian dollars; $115.25 Canadian dollars per credit hour. $115.25 Canadian dollars per semester. Tuition and fees vary according to program. *Financial support:* In 2010–11, 9 fellowships (averaging $20,333 per year), 3 research assistantships (averaging $16,500 per year), 21 teaching assistantships (averaging $6,884 per year) were awarded; career-related internships or fieldwork and scholarships/grants also available. Financial award application deadline: 6/15. *Faculty research:* Clinical, experimental, cognitive, and applied psychology; post-traumatic stress disorder, anxiety, and panic disorder; traumatic brain injury; chronic pain; perception and memory. *Unit head:* Dr. Richard MacLennan, Head, 306-585-4458, Fax: 306-585-5429, E-mail: richard.maclennan@uregina.ca. *Application contact:* Dr. Richard MacLennan, Graduate Program Coordinator, 306-585-4458, Fax: 306-585-5429, E-mail: richard.maclennan@uregina.ca.

University of Rhode Island, Graduate School, College of Arts and Sciences, Department of Psychology, Kingston, RI 02881. Offers behavioral science (PhD); clinical psychology (MA, PhD); school psychology (MS, PhD). *Accreditation:* APA (one or more programs are accredited). Part-time programs available. *Faculty:* 20 full-time (10 women). *Students:* 75 full-time (56 women), 32 part-time (28 women); includes 24 minority (12 Black or African American, non-Hispanic/Latino; 4 Asian, non-Hispanic/Latino; 7 Hispanic/Latino; 1 Two or more races, non-Hispanic/Latino), 6 international. In 2010, 16 master's, 14 doctorates awarded. *Degree requirements:* For master's, comprehensive exam, thesis optional; for doctorate, thesis/dissertation. *Entrance requirements:* For master's and doctorate, GRE, 3 letters of recommendation. Additional exam requirements/recommendations for international students: Required—TOEFL (minimum score 550 paper-based; 213 computer-based). Application fee: $65. Electronic applications accepted. *Expenses:* Tuition, state resident: full-time $9588; part-time $533 per credit hour. Tuition, nonresident: full-time $22,968; part-time $1276 per credit hour. Required fees: $1282; $68 per semester. Tuition and fees vary according to program. *Financial support:* In 2010–11, 5 research assistantships with full and partial tuition reimbursements (averaging $2,927 per year), 20 teaching assistantships with full and partial tuition reimbursements (averaging $12,479 per year) were awarded. Financial award applicants required to submit FAFSA. Total annual research expenditures: $193,164. *Unit head:* Dr. Patricia Morokoff, Chairperson, 401-874-4239, Fax: 401-874-2157, E-mail: morokoff@uri.edu. *Application contact:* Dr. Patricia Morokoff, Chairperson, 401-874-4239, Fax: 401-874-2157, E-mail: morokoff@uri.edu.

University of Rochester, School of Arts and Sciences, Department of Clinical and Social Sciences in Psychology, Program in Social-Personality Psychology, Rochester, NY 14627.

University of Saint Francis, Graduate School, Department of Psychology and Counseling, Fort Wayne, IN 46808-3994. Offers general psychology (MS); mental health counseling (MS); pastoral counseling (MS); school counseling (MS Ed). Part-time and evening/weekend programs available. *Entrance requirements:* For master's, interview, minimum undergraduate GPA of 3.0. *Expenses:* Tuition: Part-time $770 per semester hour. Part-time tuition and fees vary according to program.

University of Saint Mary, Graduate Programs, Program in Psychology, Leavenworth, KS 66048-5082. Offers MA. Part-time and evening/weekend programs available. *Degree requirements:* For master's, thesis. *Entrance requirements:* For master's, minimum undergraduate GPA of 2.75.

University of St. Thomas, Graduate Studies, Graduate School of Professional Psychology, St. Paul, MN 55105-1096. Offers counseling psychology (MA, Psy D); marriage and family psychology (MA, Certificate). *Accreditation:* APA. Part-time and evening/weekend programs available. *Faculty:* 11 full-time (5 women), 13 part-time/adjunct (6 women). *Students:* 68 full-time (54 women), 141 part-time (113 women); includes 5 Black or African American, non-Hispanic/Latino; 13 Asian, non-Hispanic/Latino; 3 Hispanic/Latino, 4 international. Average age 29. 578 applicants, 42% accepted. In 2010, 22 master's, 11 doctorates awarded. *Degree requirements:* For master's, comprehensive exam, practicum; for doctorate, comprehensive exam, thesis/dissertation, qualifying exam, practicum, internship. *Entrance requirements:* For master's, GRE, minimum GPA of 2.75, letters of recommendation, personal statement; for doctorate, GRE, minimum GPA of 3.2, letters of recommendation, personal statement. Additional exam requirements/recommendations for international students: Required—TOEFL (minimum score 550 paper-based; 213 computer-based; 80 iBT). *Application deadline:* For fall admission, 3/1 priority date for domestic students; for winter admission, 2/1 priority date for domestic students; for spring admission, 9/15 priority date for domestic students, 3/1 for international students. Application fee: $50. *Expenses:* Contact institution. *Financial support:* In 2010–11, 2 fellowships (averaging $5,000 per year) were awarded; research assistantships, institutionally sponsored loans and scholarships/grants also available. Support available to part-time students. Financial award application deadline: 8/1; financial award applicants required to submit FAFSA. *Faculty research:* Elderly, eating disorders, anxiety, family. *Unit head:* Dr. Christopher S. Vye, Associate Dean, 651-962-4666, Fax: 651-962-4666, E-mail: bnolan@stthomas.edu. *Application contact:* Laurie Dupont, Administrative Assistant, 651-962-4669, Fax: 651-962-4651, E-mail: ldupont@stthomas.edu.

University of Saskatchewan, College of Graduate Studies and Research, College of Arts and Sciences, Department of Psychology, Saskatoon, SK S7N 5A2, Canada. Offers MA, PhD. *Accreditation:* APA (one or more programs are accredited). *Degree requirements:* For master's, thesis; for doctorate, comprehensive exam (for some programs), thesis/dissertation. *Entrance requirements:* Additional exam requirements/recommendations for international students: Required—TOEFL (minimum score 80 iBT); Recommended—IELTS (minimum score 6.5). Electronic applications accepted.

University of South Africa, College of Human Sciences, Pretoria, South Africa. Offers adult education (M Ed); African languages (MA, PhD); African politics (MA, PhD); Afrikaans (MA, PhD); ancient history (MA, PhD); ancient Near Eastern studies (MA, PhD); anthropology (MA, PhD); applied linguistics (MA); Arabic (MA, PhD); archaeology (MA); art history (MA); Biblical archaeology (MA); Biblical studies (M Th, D Th, PhD); Christian spirituality (M Th, D Th); church history (M Th, D Th); classical studies (MA, PhD); clinical psychology (MA); communication (MA, PhD); comparative education (M Ed, Ed D); consulting psychology (D Admin, D Com, PhD); curriculum studies (M Ed, Ed D); development studies (M Admin, MA, D Admin, PhD); didactics (M Ed, Ed D); education (M Tech); education management (M Ed, Ed D); educational psychology (M Ed); English (MA); environmental education (M Ed); French (MA, PhD); German (MA, PhD); Greek (MA); guidance and counseling (M Ed); health studies (MA, PhD), including health sciences education (MA), health services management (MA), medical and surgical nursing science (critical care general) (MA), midwifery and neonatal nursing science (MA), trauma and emergency care (MA); history (MA, PhD); history of education (Ed D); inclusive education (M Ed, Ed D); information and communications technology policy and regulation (MA); information science (MA, MIS, PhD); international politics (MA, PhD); Islamic studies (MA, PhD); Italian (MA, PhD); Judaica (MA, PhD); linguistics (MA, PhD); mathematical education (M Ed); mathematics education (MA); missiology (M Th, D Th); modern Hebrew (MA, PhD); musicology (MA, MMus, D Mus, PhD); natural science education (M Ed); New Testament (M Th, D Th); Old Testament (D Th); pastoral therapy (M Th, D Th); philosophy (MA); philosophy of education (M Ed, Ed D); politics (MA, PhD); Portuguese (MA, PhD); practical theology (M Th, D Th); psychology (MA, MS, PhD); psychology of education (M Ed, Ed D); public health (MA); religious studies (MA, D Th, PhD); Romance languages (MA); Russian (MA, PhD); Semitic languages (MA, PhD); social behavior studies in HIV/AIDS (MA); social science (mental health) (MA); social science in development studies (MA); social science in psychology (MA); social science in social work (MA); social science in sociology (MA); social work (MSW, DSW, PhD); socio-education (M Ed, Ed D); sociolinguistics (MA); sociology (MA, PhD); Spanish (MA, PhD); systematic theology (M Th, D Th); TESOL (teaching English to speakers of other languages) (MA); theological ethics (M Th, D Th); theory of literature (MA, PhD); urban ministries (D Th); urban ministry (M Th).

University of South Alabama, Graduate School, College of Arts and Sciences, Department of Psychology, Mobile, AL 36688. Offers clinical and counseling psychology (PhD); psychology (MS). Part-time and evening/weekend programs available. *Faculty:* 10 full-time (4 women). *Students:* 14 full-time (11 women), 9 part-time (5 women); includes 3 minority (2 Black or African American, non-Hispanic/Latino; 1 Hispanic/Latino). 47 applicants, 26% accepted, 9 enrolled. In 2010, 10 master's awarded. *Degree requirements:* For master's, comprehensive exam, thesis optional. *Entrance requirements:* For master's, GRE General Test, GRE Subject Test (recommended), minimum GPA of 3.0, major in psychology or equivalent. Additional exam requirements/recommendations for international students: Required—TOEFL. *Application deadline:* For fall admission, 3/1 priority date for domestic students, 3/1 for international students. Applications are processed on a rolling basis. Application fee: $35. *Expenses:* Tuition, state resident: part-time $300 per credit hour. Tuition, nonresident: part-time $600 per credit hour. Required fees: $150 per semester. *Financial support:* Fellowships, research assistantships available. Support available to part-time students. Financial award application deadline: 4/1. *Faculty research:* Language acquisition and development. *Unit head:* Dr. Larry Christensen, Chair, 251-460-6371. *Application contact:* Dr. Lisa Turner, Graduate Coordinator, 251-460-6371.

University of South Carolina, The Graduate School, College of Arts and Sciences, Department of Psychology, Columbia, SC 29208. Offers clinical/community psychology (MA, PhD), including clinical/community psychology (PhD), general psychology (MA); experimental psychology (MA, PhD); school psychology (PhD). *Accreditation:* APA (one or more programs are accredited). Terminal master's awarded for partial completion of doctoral program. *Degree requirements:* For master's, thesis; for doctorate, comprehensive exam, thesis/dissertation. *Entrance requirements:* For master's and doctorate, GRE General Test. Additional exam requirements/recommendations for international students: Required—TOEFL. Electronic applications accepted. *Faculty research:* Developmental cognitive neuroscience, alcohol and drug addictions, reading and language processing, child and family, prevention.

The University of South Dakota, Graduate School, College of Arts and Sciences, Department of Psychology, Vermillion, SD 57069-2390. Offers clinical psychology (MA, PhD); human factors (MA, PhD). *Accreditation:* APA (one or more programs are accredited). *Degree requirements:* For master's, comprehensive exam, thesis; for doctorate, comprehensive exam, thesis/dissertation. *Entrance requirements:* For master's, GRE, minimum GPA of 2.7; for doctorate, GRE General Test, GRE Subject Test, minimum GPA of 2.7. Additional exam requirements/recommendations for international students: Required—TOEFL (minimum score 550 paper-based; 213 computer-based; 79 iBT). Electronic applications accepted. *Faculty research:* Human-computer interactions, perceptual-cognitive processing, medical psychology, depression, moral psychology.

University of Southern California, Graduate School, Dana and David Dornsife College of Letters, Arts and Sciences, Department of Psychology, Los Angeles, CA 90089. Offers brain and cognitive science (PhD); clinical science (PhD); developmental psychology (PhD); human behavior (MHB); quantitative methods (PhD); social psychology (PhD). *Accreditation:* APA. *Faculty:* 34 full-time (10 women), 15 part-time/adjunct (9 women). *Students:* 105 full-time (65 women), 3 part-time (all women); includes 32 minority (4 Black or African American, non-Hispanic/Latino; 17 Asian, non-Hispanic/Latino; 9 Hispanic/Latino; 2 Two or more races, non-Hispanic/Latino), 22 international. 543 applicants, 5% accepted, 14 enrolled. In 2010, 17 master's, 12 doctorates awarded. *Degree requirements:* For doctorate, comprehensive exam, thesis/dissertation, one-year internship (for clinical science students). *Entrance requirements:* For doctorate, GRE. Additional exam requirements/recommendations for international students: Recommended—TOEFL (minimum score 600 paper-based; 250 computer-based; 100 iBT). *Application deadline:* For fall admission, 12/1 for domestic and international students. Application fee: $85. Electronic applications accepted. *Expenses:* Tuition: Full-time $31,240; part-time $1420 per unit. Required fees: $600. One-time fee: $35 full-time. Full-time tuition and fees vary according to degree level and program. *Financial support:* In 2010–11, 85 students received support, including 30 fellowships with full tuition reimbursements available (averaging $24,000 per year), 12 research assistantships with full tuition reimbursements available (averaging $19,250 per year), 40 teaching assistantships with full tuition reimbursements available (averaging $19,250 per year); scholarships/grants, traineeships, health care benefits, and unspecified assistantships also available. Financial award application deadline: 12/1. *Faculty research:* Affective neuroscience; children and families; vision, culture and ethnicity; intergroup relations; aggression and violence; language and reading development; substance abuse. *Unit head:* Dr. Margaret Gatz, Chair and Professor, 213-740-2212, Fax: 213-746-9028, E-mail: gatz@usc.edu. *Application contact:* Irene Takaragawa, Graduate Advisor, 213-740-2205, Fax: 213-746-9082, E-mail: itakarag@usc.edu.

University of Southern Mississippi, Graduate School, College of Education and Psychology, Department of Psychology, Hattiesburg, MS 39406-0001. Offers clinical psychology (MA, PhD); counseling psychology (MA, PhD); experimental psychology (MA, PhD); school psychology (MA, PhD). *Accreditation:* APA (one or more programs are accredited). *Faculty:* 32 full-time (9 women). *Students:* 98 full-time (75 women), 42 part-time (33 women); includes 8 Black or African American, non-Hispanic/Latino; 3 Asian, non-Hispanic/Latino; 5 Hispanic/Latino, 7 international. Average age 29. 219 applicants, 16% accepted, 31 enrolled. In 2010, 27 master's, 13 doctorates awarded. Terminal master's awarded for partial completion of doctoral program. *Degree requirements:* For master's, comprehensive exam, thesis; for doctorate, comprehensive exam, thesis/dissertation. *Entrance requirements:* For master's, GRE General Test, minimum GPA of 3.0; for doctorate, GRE General Test, interview, minimum GPA of 3.5. Additional exam requirements/recommendations for international students: Required—TOEFL, IELTS. *Application deadline:* For fall admission, 3/1 priority date for domestic students, 3/1 for international students. Applications are processed on a rolling basis. Application fee: $50. *Financial support:* In 2010–11, 48 research assistantships with full tuition reimbursements (averaging $8,802 per year), 48 teaching assistantships with full tuition reimbursements (averaging $6,500 per year) were awarded; career-related internships or fieldwork, Federal Work-Study, institutionally sponsored loans, scholarships/grants, health care benefits, and unspecified assistantships also available. Financial award application deadline: 3/15; financial award applicants required to submit FAFSA. *Faculty research:* Dolphin cognition, sleep, neuropsychology, health-related behaviors, psychopathology. Total annual research expenditures: $101,200. *Unit head:* Dr. Joesph Olmi, Chair, 601-266-4177, Fax: 601-266-5580. *Application contact:* Susan King, Graduate Secretary, 601-266-4177, Fax: 601-266-5580.

University of South Florida, Graduate School, College of Arts and Sciences, Department of Psychology, Tampa, FL 33620-9951. Offers clinical psychology (PhD); cognitive and neural sciences (PhD); industrial-organizational psychology (PhD). *Accreditation:* APA. *Faculty:* 17 full-time (4 women). *Students:* 101 full-time (55 women), 24 part-time (16 women); includes 3 Black or African American, non-Hispanic/Latino; 9 Asian, non-Hispanic/Latino; 8 Hispanic/Latino; 1 Two or more races, non-Hispanic/Latino, 12 international. Average age 28. 452 applicants, 8% accepted, 22 enrolled. In 2010, 11 doctorates awarded. *Degree requirements:* For doctorate, comprehensive exam, thesis/dissertation, internship. *Entrance requirements:* For doctorate, GRE General Test, minimum GPA of 3.0 in last 60 hours of course work. Additional exam requirements/recommendations for international students: Required—TOEFL (minimum score 550 paper-based; 213 computer-based). *Application deadline:* For fall admission, 12/1 for domestic and international students. Application fee: $30. Electronic applications accepted. *Expenses:* Contact institution. *Financial support:* In 2010–11, 18 research assistantships (averaging $13,719 per year), 63 teaching assistantships with tuition reimbursements (averaging $13,724 per year) were awarded; tuition waivers (partial) and unspecified assistantships also available. Financial award applicants required to submit FAFSA. *Faculty research:* Clinical, cognitive, neuroscience, social, industrial/organizational. Total annual research expenditures: $3.5 million. *Unit head:* Michael Brannick, Chairperson, 813-974-0478, Fax:

Psychology—General

University of South Florida (continued)
813-974-4617, E-mail: mbrannick@usf.edu. *Application contact:* William Sacco, Program Director, 813-974-0375, Fax: 813-974-4617, E-mail: sacco@cas.usf.edu.

The University of Tennessee, Graduate School, College of Arts and Sciences, Department of Psychology, Knoxville, TN 37996. Offers clinical psychology (PhD); experimental psychology (MA, PhD); psychology (MA). *Accreditation:* APA (one or more programs are accredited). Terminal master's awarded for partial completion of doctoral program. *Degree requirements:* For master's, thesis; for doctorate, thesis/dissertation. *Entrance requirements:* For master's and doctorate, GRE General Test, GRE Subject Test, minimum GPA of 2.7. Additional exam requirements/recommendations for international students: Required—TOEFL. Electronic applications accepted. *Expenses:* Tuition, state resident: full-time $7440; part-time $414 per credit hour. Tuition, nonresident: full-time $22,478; part-time $1250 per credit hour. Required fees: $922; $43 per credit hour. Tuition and fees vary according to program.

The University of Tennessee at Chattanooga, Graduate School, College of Arts and Sciences, Department of Psychology, Chattanooga, TN 37403. Offers industrial/organizational psychology (MS); research psychology (MS). Part-time and evening/weekend programs available. *Faculty:* 6 full-time (1 woman). *Students:* 46 full-time (27 women), 6 part-time (3 women); includes 6 minority (3 Black or African American, non-Hispanic/Latino; 1 Asian, non-Hispanic/Latino; 1 Hispanic/Latino; 1 Two or more races, non-Hispanic/Latino), 1 international. Average age 25. 60 applicants, 70% accepted, 32 enrolled. In 2010, 24 master's awarded. *Degree requirements:* For master's, thesis (for some programs), practicum (industrial/organizational psychology). *Entrance requirements:* For master's, GRE General Test, minimum GPA of 2.5 on all undergraduate coursework or 3.0 in senior year. Additional exam requirements/recommendations for international students: Required—TOEFL (minimum score 550 paper-based; 213 computer-based; 79 iBT), IELTS (minimum score 6). *Application deadline:* For fall admission, 8/1 priority date for domestic students, 6/1 for international students; for spring admission, 12/1 priority date for domestic students, 10/1 for international students. Applications are processed on a rolling basis. Application fee: $35. Electronic applications accepted. *Financial support:* In 2010–11, 20 research assistantships with full and partial tuition reimbursements (averaging $5,500 per year) were awarded; career-related internships or fieldwork, scholarships/grants, and unspecified assistantships also available. Support available to part-time students. *Faculty research:* Decision processes, philosophical psychology, memory, social cognition, employee selection. Total annual research expenditures: $35,031. *Unit head:* Dr. Paul J. Watson, Department Head, 423-425-4262, Fax: 423-425-4284, E-mail: paul-watson@utc.edu. *Application contact:* Dr. Jerald Ainsworth, Dean of Graduate Studies, 423-425-4478, Fax: 423-425-5223, E-mail: jerald-ainsworth@utc.edu.

The University of Texas at Arlington, Graduate School, College of Science, Department of Psychology, Arlington, TX 76019. Offers experimental psychology (PhD); health psychology (PhD); industrial organizational psychology (MS); psychology (MS). Part-time programs available. *Faculty:* 21 full-time (8 women), 1 part-time/adjunct (0 women). *Students:* 62 full-time (41 women), 10 part-time (7 women); includes 5 Black or African American, non-Hispanic/Latino; 2 Asian, non-Hispanic/Latino; 6 Hispanic/Latino, 7 international. 72 applicants, 90% accepted, 22 enrolled. In 2010, 16 master's, 6 doctorates awarded. Terminal master's awarded for partial completion of doctoral program. *Degree requirements:* For master's, comprehensive exam or thesis; for doctorate, thesis/dissertation (for some programs). *Entrance requirements:* For master's and doctorate, GRE General Test, minimum GPA of 3.0 in last 60 hours of course work. Additional exam requirements/recommendations for international students: Required—TOEFL (minimum score 550 paper-based; 213 computer-based). *Application deadline:* For fall admission, 6/15 for domestic students. Applications are processed on a rolling basis. Application fee: $35 ($50 for international students). *Expenses:* Tuition, state resident: full-time $7500. Tuition, nonresident: full-time $13,080. International tuition: $13,250 full-time. *Financial support:* In 2010–11, 4 fellowships (averaging $1,000 per year), 2 research assistantships with tuition reimbursements (averaging $15,000 per year), 28 teaching assistantships with tuition reimbursements (averaging $15,000 per year) were awarded; career-related internships or fieldwork, Federal Work-Study, institutionally sponsored loans, scholarships/grants, traineeships, tuition waivers (partial), and unspecified assistantships also available. Financial award application deadline: 6/1; financial award applicants required to submit FAFSA. *Unit head:* Dr. Robert Gatchel, Chair, 817-272-2281, Fax: 817-272-2364, E-mail: gatchel@uta.edu. *Application contact:* Dr. Jared Kenworthy, Graduate Advisor, Psychological Sciences, 817-272-2281, Fax: 817-272-2364, E-mail: kenworthy@uta.edu.

The University of Texas at Austin, Graduate School, College of Liberal Arts, Department of Psychology, Austin, TX 78712-1111. Offers PhD. *Accreditation:* APA. *Degree requirements:* For doctorate, thesis/dissertation. *Entrance requirements:* For doctorate, GRE General Test. Electronic applications accepted. *Faculty research:* Behavioral neuroscience, sensory neuroscience, evolutionary psychology, cognitive processes in psychopathology, cognitive processes and their development.

The University of Texas at Brownsville, Graduate Studies, College of Liberal Arts, Department of Behavioral Sciences, Brownsville, TX 78520-4991. Offers MAIS. Part-time and evening/weekend programs available. *Degree requirements:* For master's, thesis or comprehensive exam. *Entrance requirements:* For master's, GRE General Test. Additional exam requirements/recommendations for international students: Required—TOEFL. *Faculty research:* Memory, socio-political structure of South America, cartography of Mexico and Central America, family economic structure of Spain.

The University of Texas at Dallas, School of Behavioral and Brain Sciences, Program in Psychological Sciences, Richardson, TX 75080. Offers early childhood disorders (MS); psychological sciences (MS, PhD). Part-time and evening/weekend programs available. *Faculty:* 12 full-time (7 women). *Students:* 52 full-time (42 women), 18 part-time (16 women); includes 23 minority (7 Black or African American, non-Hispanic/Latino; 5 Asian, non-Hispanic/Latino; 10 Hispanic/Latino; 1 Two or more races, non-Hispanic/Latino), 8 international. Average age 29. 97 applicants, 34% accepted, 22 enrolled. In 2010, 21 master's, 4 doctorates awarded. *Degree requirements:* For master's, directed project or internship; for doctorate, thesis/dissertation. *Entrance requirements:* For master's and doctorate, GRE General Test, minimum GPA of 3.0 in upper-level course work. Additional exam requirements/recommendations for international students: Required—TOEFL (minimum score 550 paper-based; 215 computer-based). *Application deadline:* For fall admission, 7/15 for domestic students, 5/1 priority date for international students; for spring admission, 11/15 for domestic students, 9/1 priority date for international students. Applications are processed on a rolling basis. Application fee: $50 ($100 for international students). Electronic applications accepted. *Expenses:* Tuition, state resident: full-time $10,248; part-time $569 per credit hour. Tuition, nonresident: full-time $18,544; part-time $1030 per credit hour. Tuition and fees vary according to course load. *Financial support:* In 2010–11, 35 students received support, including 4 research assistantships with partial tuition reimbursements available (averaging $10,242 per year), 14 teaching assistantships with partial tuition reimbursements available (averaging $12,025 per year); career-related internships or fieldwork, Federal Work-Study, scholarships/grants, and unspecified assistantships also available. Support available to part-time students. Financial award application deadline: 4/30; financial award applicants required to submit FAFSA. *Faculty research:* Neurocognitive development in young adulthood, infant learning, infant and toddler eye tracking, social aggression. *Unit head:* Dr. Marion K. Underwood, Program Head, 972-883-2470, Fax: 972-883-2491, E-mail: undrwd@utdallas.edu. *Application contact:* Dr. Robert D. Stillman, Associate Dean of Graduate Programs, 972-883-3630, Fax: 972-883-2491, E-mail: stillman@utdallas.edu.

The University of Texas at El Paso, Graduate School, College of Liberal Arts, Department of Psychology, El Paso, TX 79968-0001. Offers clinical psychology (MA); experimental psychology (MA); psychology (PhD). Part-time and evening/weekend programs available. *Students:* 47 (28 women); includes 1 Asian, non-Hispanic/Latino; 19 Hispanic/Latino, 6 international. Average age 34. In 2010, 11 master's, 5 doctorates awarded. *Degree requirements:* For master's,

thesis; for doctorate, thesis/dissertation. *Entrance requirements:* For master's, GRE, letters of recommendation; for doctorate, GRE, statement of purpose, letters of recommendation. Additional exam requirements/recommendations for international students: Required—TOEFL; Recommended—IELTS. *Application deadline:* For fall admission, 8/1 for domestic students, 3/1 for international students; for spring admission, 11/1 for domestic students, 9/1 for international students. Applications are processed on a rolling basis. Application fee: $45 ($80 for international students). Electronic applications accepted. *Financial support:* In 2010–11, research assistantships with partial tuition reimbursements (averaging $18,625 per year), teaching assistantships with partial tuition reimbursements (averaging $14,900 per year) were awarded; fellowships with partial tuition reimbursements, institutionally sponsored loans, scholarships/grants, health care benefits, tuition waivers (partial), and unspecified assistantships also available. Support available to part-time students. Financial award application deadline: 3/15; financial award applicants required to submit FAFSA. *Unit head:* Dr. Edward Casta?eda, Chair, 915-747-5551, Fax: 915-747-6553, E-mail: ecastaneda9@utep.edu. *Application contact:* Dr. Patricia D. Witherspoon, Dean of the Graduate School, 915-747-5491, Fax: 915-747-5788, E-mail: withersp@utep.edu.

The University of Texas at San Antonio, College of Liberal and Fine Arts, Department of Psychology, San Antonio, TX 78249-0617. Offers MS. Part-time and evening/weekend programs available. *Faculty:* 14 full-time (8 women), 1 (woman) part-time/adjunct. *Students:* 31 full-time (22 women), 14 part-time (8 women); includes 21 minority (2 Black or African American, non-Hispanic/Latino; 2 Asian, non-Hispanic/Latino; 17 Hispanic/Latino), 4 international. Average age 25. 42 applicants, 57% accepted, 24 enrolled. In 2010, 10 master's awarded. *Degree requirements:* For master's, comprehensive exam (for some programs), thesis (for some programs). *Entrance requirements:* For master's, GRE General Test, minimum GPA of 3.0 in last 60 hours and in all psychology courses. Additional exam requirements/recommendations for international students: Required—TOEFL (minimum score 500 paper-based; 173 computer-based; 61 iBT), IELTS (minimum score 5). *Application deadline:* For fall admission, 7/1 for domestic students, 4/1 for international students; for spring admission, 11/1 for domestic students, 9/1 for international students. Applications are processed on a rolling basis. Application fee: $45 ($80 for international students). Electronic applications accepted. *Expenses:* Tuition, state resident: full-time $4172; part-time $231.75 per credit hour. Tuition, nonresident: full-time $15,332; part-time $851.75 per credit hour. *Financial support:* In 2010–11, 6 students received support, including 9 research assistantships (averaging $11,691 per year), 6 teaching assistantships (averaging $6,133 per year); career-related internships or fieldwork, scholarships/grants, tuition waivers, and unspecified assistantships also available. Support available to part-time students. Total annual research expenditures: $201,776. *Unit head:* Dr. Robert W. Fuhrman, Department Chair, 210-458-4372, Fax: 210-458-5728, E-mail: robert.fuhrman@utsa.edu. *Application contact:* Veronica Ramirez, Assistant Dean of the Graduate School, 210-458-4330, Fax: 210-458-4332, E-mail: graduatestudies@utsa.edu.

The University of Texas at Tyler, College of Education and Psychology, Department of Psychology and Counseling, Tyler, TX 75799-0001. Offers clinical psychology (MS), including neuropsychology, school psychology; counseling psychology (MA), including general, marriage and family; interdisciplinary studies (MSIS); school counseling (MA). Part-time and evening/weekend programs available. *Degree requirements:* For master's, comprehensive exam, thesis optional. *Entrance requirements:* For master's, GRE General Test, minimum GPA of 3.0. Additional exam requirements/recommendations for international students: Required—TOEFL (minimum score 79 computer-based). Electronic applications accepted. *Faculty research:* Neuropsychology, child abuse, psychometric properties of psychological instruments, maternal behavior, clinical practice issues, victimization of women, post-traumatic stress disorder.

The University of Texas of the Permian Basin, Office of Graduate Studies, College of Arts and Sciences, Department of Psychology, Odessa, TX 79762-0001. Offers applied research psychology (MA); clinical psychology (MA). Part-time and evening/weekend programs available. *Degree requirements:* For master's, comprehensive exam, thesis, practicum. *Entrance requirements:* For master's, GRE General Test, 3 letters of recommendation. Additional exam requirements/recommendations for international students: Required—TOEFL (minimum score 550 paper-based; 213 computer-based).

The University of Texas–Pan American, College of Social and Behavioral Sciences, Department of Psychology and Anthropology, Edinburg, TX 78539. Offers psychology (MA), including clinical psychology, experimental psychology. Part-time and evening/weekend programs available. *Degree requirements:* For master's, comprehensive exam, thesis optional, internship. *Entrance requirements:* For master's, GRE, letters of recommendation. Additional exam requirements/recommendations for international students: Required—TOEFL. Electronic applications accepted. *Faculty research:* Biofeedback, acculturation, health, stress/trauma, neuropsychological assessment, false memories, children's theory of mind.

University of the Pacific, College of the Pacific, Department of Psychology, Stockton, CA 95211-0197. Offers MA. *Faculty:* 6 full-time (3 women), 1 part-time/adjunct (0 women). *Students:* 15 part-time (10 women); includes 2 Asian, non-Hispanic/Latino; 1 Hispanic/Latino, 2 international. Average age 25. 31 applicants, 26% accepted, 7 enrolled. In 2010, 1 master's awarded. *Degree requirements:* For master's, thesis. *Entrance requirements:* For master's, GRE General Test. Additional exam requirements/recommendations for international students: Required—TOEFL (minimum score 475 paper-based; 150 computer-based). *Application deadline:* For fall admission, 3/1 priority date for domestic students. Applications are processed on a rolling basis. Application fee: $75. *Financial support:* In 2010–11, 7 teaching assistantships were awarded; institutionally sponsored loans also available. Support available to part-time students. Financial award application deadline: 3/1; financial award applicants required to submit FAFSA. *Unit head:* Dr. Carolynn Kohn, Chairperson, 209-946-2133, E-mail: rhannon@pacific.edu. *Application contact:* Information Contact, 209-946-2261.

University of the Rockies, Graduate Programs, Colorado Springs, CO 80903. Offers MA, Psy D.

University of the West, Department of Psychology, Rosemead, CA 91770. Offers MA. *Degree requirements:* For master's, comprehensive exam.

The University of Toledo, College of Graduate Studies, College of Language, Literature and Social Sciences, Department of Psychology, Toledo, OH 43606-3390. Offers clinical psychology (MA, PhD); experimental psychology (MA, PhD). *Accreditation:* APA. *Faculty:* 22. *Students:* 34 full-time (26 women), 3 part-time (1 woman), 7 international. Average age 26. 192 applicants, 7% accepted, 9 enrolled. In 2010, 2 master's, 8 doctorates awarded. *Degree requirements:* For master's, comprehensive exam, thesis; for doctorate, comprehensive exam, thesis/dissertation. *Entrance requirements:* For master's and doctorate, GRE General Test, GRE Subject Test, A minimum 2.7 cumulative point-hour ratio (on a 4.0 scale) for all previous academic work. Three Letters of Recommendation, a statement of purpose, and transcripts from all prior institutions attended. Additional exam requirements/recommendations for international students: Required—TOEFL (minimum score 550 paper-based; 213 computer-based; 80 iBT), IELTS (minimum score 6.5). *Application deadline:* For fall admission, 1/15 priority date for domestic and international students. Applications are processed on a rolling basis. Application fee: $45 ($75 for international students). Electronic applications accepted. *Expenses:* Tuition, state resident: full-time $11,426; part-time $476 per credit hour. Tuition, nonresident: full-time $21,660; part-time $903 per credit hour. One-time fee: $62. *Financial support:* Research assistantships with tuition reimbursements, teaching assistantships with tuition reimbursements, career-related internships or fieldwork, Federal Work-Study, institutionally sponsored loans, scholarships/grants, tuition waivers (full and partial), and unspecified assistantships available. Support available to part-time students. *Faculty research:* Neural taste response. *Unit head:* Dr. J. D. Jasper, Chair, 419-530-4130, E-mail: jjasper@utnet.utoledo.edu. *Application contact:* Graduate School Office, 419-530-4723, Fax: 419-530-4724, E-mail: grdsch@utnet.utoledo.edu.

University of Toronto, School of Graduate Studies, Life Sciences Division, Department of Psychology, Toronto, ON M5S 1A1, Canada. Offers MA, PhD. *Accreditation:* APA (one or more programs are accredited). *Degree requirements:* For master's, thesis; for doctorate, thesis/dissertation, oral exam. *Entrance requirements:* For master's, minimum A– average in last two years, 6 full courses in psychology, laboratory experience; for doctorate, minimum A– average, research experience.

University of Tulsa, Graduate School, College of Arts and Sciences, Department of Psychology, Tulsa, OK 74104-3189. Offers clinical psychology (MA, PhD); industrial/organizational psychology (MA, PhD); JD/MA. *Accreditation:* APA (one or more programs are accredited). Part-time programs available. *Faculty:* 13 full-time (5 women), 1 (woman) part-time/adjunct. *Students:* 42 full-time (31 women), 21 part-time (18 women); includes 3 Black or African American, non-Hispanic/Latino; 1 American Indian or Alaska Native, non-Hispanic/Latino; 1 Asian, non-Hispanic/Latino; 2 Hispanic/Latino, 4 international. Average age 27. 121 applicants, 30% accepted, 15 enrolled. In 2010, 5 master's, 15 doctorates awarded. Terminal master's awarded for partial completion of doctoral program. *Degree requirements:* For doctorate, comprehensive exam, thesis/dissertation. *Entrance requirements:* For master's and doctorate, GRE General Test. Additional exam requirements/recommendations for international students: Required—TOEFL (minimum score 575 paper-based; 231 computer-based; 91 iBT), IELTS (minimum score 6.5). Application fee: $40. Electronic applications accepted. *Expenses:* Tuition: Full-time $16,902; part-time $939 per credit hour. Required fees: $1020; $4 per credit hour. Tuition and fees vary according to course load. *Financial support:* In 2010–11, 47 students received support, including 10 fellowships with full and partial tuition reimbursements available (averaging $7,051 per year), 13 research assistantships with full and partial tuition reimbursements available (averaging $12,391 per year), 31 teaching assistantships with full and partial tuition reimbursements available (averaging $11,675 per year); career-related internships or fieldwork, Federal Work-Study, scholarships/grants, health care benefits, tuition waivers (full and partial), and unspecified assistantships also available. Support available to part-time students. Financial award application deadline: 2/1; financial award applicants required to submit FAFSA. *Faculty research:* Traumatic stress studies, randomized control trials of exposure treatments, pain modulation, neuropsychological assessment of health/mental health, psychological assessment, psychometrics, ethics, longitudinal assessment of child development, trauma and journalism, MMPI studies, personnel testing and selection, training, performance appraisal, organizational development, job attitudes and motivation, leadership. Total annual research expenditures: $414,625. *Unit head:* Dr. Judy Berry, Chairperson, 918-631-2834, Fax: 918-631-2833, E-mail: judy-berry@utulsa.edu. *Application contact:* Graduate School, 918-631-2336, Fax: 918-631-2156, E-mail: grad@utulsa.edu.

University of Utah, Graduate School, College of Social and Behavioral Science, Department of Psychology, Salt Lake City, UT 84112. Offers clinical psychology (PhD); psychology (PhD). *Accreditation:* APA. *Faculty:* 33 full-time (16 women), 2 part-time/adjunct (0 women). *Students:* 50 full-time (38 women), 7 part-time (4 women); includes 5 minority (4 Asian, non-Hispanic/Latino; 1 Hispanic/Latino), 3 international. Average age 29. 216 applicants, 6% accepted, 13 enrolled. In 2010, 10 doctorates awarded. *Degree requirements:* For doctorate, thesis/dissertation. *Entrance requirements:* For doctorate, GRE General Test. Additional exam requirements/recommendations for international students: Required—TOEFL (minimum score 500 paper-based; 173 computer-based). *Application deadline:* For fall admission, 12/15 for domestic and international students. Applications are processed on a rolling basis. Application fee: $55 ($65 for international students). Electronic applications accepted. *Expenses:* Tuition, area resident: Part-time $179.19 per credit hour. Tuition, state resident: full-time $4384. Tuition, nonresident: full-time $16,684; part-time $630.67 per credit hour. Required fees: $350 per semester. Tuition and fees vary according to course load, degree level and program. *Financial support:* In 2010–11, 43 students received support, including 2 fellowships with full tuition reimbursements available (averaging $14,000 per year), 2 research assistantships with full tuition reimbursements available (averaging $14,000 per year), 33 teaching assistantships with full tuition reimbursements available (averaging $14,000 per year); career-related internships or fieldwork also available. Financial award applicants required to submit FAFSA. *Faculty research:* Cognitive neuroscience, health, social cognition, psychopathology, cognitive and social development. Total annual research expenditures: $813,660. *Unit head:* Dr. Cynthia A. Berg, Chair, 801-581-8925, Fax: 801-581-5841, E-mail: cynthia.berg@psych.utah.edu. *Application contact:* Nancy Seegmiller, Administrative Assistant, 801-581-8925, Fax: 801-581-5841, E-mail: nancy.seegmiller@psych.utah.edu.

University of Vermont, Graduate College, College of Arts and Sciences, Department of Psychology, Burlington, VT 05405. Offers clinical psychology (PhD); psychology (PhD). *Accreditation:* APA. *Students:* 59 (42 women); includes 2 Black or African American, non-Hispanic/Latino; 1 Asian, non-Hispanic/Latino; 4 Hispanic/Latino, 2 international. 322 applicants, 7% accepted, 16 enrolled. In 2010, 18 doctorates awarded. *Degree requirements:* For doctorate, thesis/dissertation. *Entrance requirements:* For doctorate, GRE General Test. Additional exam requirements/recommendations for international students: Required—TOEFL (minimum score 550 paper-based; 213 computer-based; 80 iBT). *Application deadline:* For fall admission, 12/1 for domestic students. Application fee: $40. Electronic applications accepted. *Expenses:* Tuition, state resident: part-time $537 per credit hour. Tuition, nonresident: part-time $1355 per credit hour. *Financial support:* Fellowships, research assistantships, teaching assistantships available. Financial award application deadline: 2/1. *Unit head:* Dr. William Falls, Chairperson, 802-656-2670. *Application contact:* Dr. Rex Forehand, Coordinator, 802-656-2670.

University of Victoria, Faculty of Graduate Studies, Faculty of Social Sciences, Department of Psychology, Victoria, BC V8W 2Y2, Canada. Offers clinical psychology (PhD); clinical psychology (neuropsychology) (M Sc); cognition and brain science (M Sc, PhD); experimental neuropsychology (M Sc, PhD); individualized study (M Sc, PhD); life span development psychology (PhD); life span developmental psychology (M Sc); social psychology (M Sc, PhD). *Accreditation:* APA (one or more programs are accredited). *Degree requirements:* For master's, thesis; for doctorate, thesis/dissertation, candidacy exam. *Entrance requirements:* For master's and doctorate, GRE General Test. Additional exam requirements/recommendations for international students: Required—TOEFL (minimum score 600 paper-based; 250 computer-based). Electronic applications accepted. *Faculty research:* Life span development psychology and aging, behavioral neuroscience, cognitive psychology, behavioral psychology, environmental psychology.

University of Virginia, College and Graduate School of Arts and Sciences, Department of Psychology, Charlottesville, VA 22903. Offers MA, PhD. *Accreditation:* APA (one or more programs are accredited). *Faculty:* 31 full-time (8 women), 2 part-time/adjunct (0 women). *Students:* 81 full-time (58 women), 2 part-time (both women); includes 6 Black or African American, non-Hispanic/Latino; 2 Asian, non-Hispanic/Latino, 11 international. Average age 27. 541 applicants, 4% accepted, 15 enrolled. In 2010, 10 master's, 9 doctorates awarded. *Degree requirements:* For master's, pre-dissertation research project; for doctorate, comprehensive exam, thesis/dissertation. *Entrance requirements:* For master's and doctorate, GRE General Test, 3 or more letters of recommendation. Additional exam requirements/recommendations for international students: Required—TOEFL (minimum score 600 paper-based; 250 computer-based; 90 iBT), IELTS (minimum score 7). *Application deadline:* For fall admission, 12/1 for domestic and international students. Applications are processed on a rolling basis. Application fee: $60. Electronic applications accepted. *Financial support:* Fellowships, research assistantships, teaching assistantships available. Financial award applicants required to submit FAFSA. *Unit head:* Dennis R. Proffitt, Chair, 434-982-4750, Fax: 434-982-4766, E-mail: psy-dept@virginia.edu. *Application contact:* Debbie Snow, Psychology Department Admission Secretary, 434-982-4750, Fax: 434-982-4766, E-mail: dsnow@virginia.edu.

University of Washington, Graduate School, College of Arts and Sciences, Department of Psychology, Seattle, WA 98195. Offers animal behavior (PhD); child psychology (PhD); clinical psychology (PhD); cognition and perception (PhD); developmental psychology (PhD); quantitative psychology (PhD); social psychology and personality (PhD). *Accreditation:* APA. *Degree requirements:* For doctorate, thesis/dissertation. *Entrance requirements:* For doctorate, GRE

General Test, minimum GPA of 3.0. Electronic applications accepted. *Faculty research:* Addictive behaviors, artificial intelligence, child psychopathology, mechanisms and development of vision, physiology of ingestive behaviors.

University of Waterloo, Graduate Studies, Faculty of Arts, Department of Psychology, Waterloo, ON N2L 3G1, Canada. Offers MA, MA Sc, PhD. *Accreditation:* APA (one or more programs are accredited). Terminal master's awarded for partial completion of doctoral program. *Degree requirements:* For master's, thesis (for some programs); for doctorate, thesis/dissertation. *Entrance requirements:* For master's, GRE, honors degree in psychology, minimum B average; for doctorate, GRE, master's degree in psychology, minimum B average. Additional exam requirements/recommendations for international students: Required—TOEFL, TWE. Electronic applications accepted. *Faculty research:* Memory and attention, attitudes and behavior in the workplace, object recognition, judgment and decision making, communication and knowledge in toddlers.

The University of Western Ontario, Faculty of Graduate Studies, Biosciences Division, Department of Psychology, London, ON N6A 5B8, Canada. Offers MA, PhD. *Degree requirements:* For master's, thesis; for doctorate, thesis/dissertation. *Entrance requirements:* For master's, minimum B average during last 2 years; for doctorate, MA in psychology. Additional exam requirements/recommendations for international students: Required—TOEFL. *Faculty research:* Clinical, applied and social/personality psychology; psychobiology; cognitive processes.

University of West Florida, College of Arts and Sciences: Arts, Department of Psychology, Pensacola, FL 32514-5750. Offers counseling (MA); counseling-licensed mental health counselor (MA); general (MA); industrial-organizational (MA). Part-time programs available. *Faculty:* 10 full-time (4 women), 1 part-time/adjunct (0 women). *Students:* 67 full-time (45 women), 39 part-time (30 women); includes 16 minority (5 Black or African American, non-Hispanic/Latino; 2 Asian, non-Hispanic/Latino; 5 Hispanic/Latino; 1 Native Hawaiian or other Pacific Islander, non-Hispanic/Latino; 3 Two or more races, non-Hispanic/Latino), 4 international. Average age 26. 143 applicants, 53% accepted, 32 enrolled. In 2010, 34 master's awarded. *Degree requirements:* For master's, thesis (for some programs). *Entrance requirements:* For master's, GRE General Test, GRE Subject Test, minimum GPA of 3.0. Additional exam requirements/recommendations for international students: Required—TOEFL (minimum score 550 paper-based; 213 computer-based). *Application deadline:* For fall admission, 6/1 for domestic students, 5/15 for international students; for spring admission, 10/1 for domestic and international students. Applications are processed on a rolling basis. Application fee: $30. *Expenses:* Tuition, state resident: full-time $4982; part-time $208 per credit hour. Tuition, nonresident: full-time $20,059; part-time $836 per credit hour. Required fees: $1365; $57 per credit hour. *Financial support:* In 2010–11, 19 fellowships with partial tuition reimbursements (averaging $1,090 per year), 30 research assistantships with partial tuition reimbursements (averaging $3,500 per year), 5 teaching assistantships with partial tuition reimbursements (averaging $4,552 per year) were awarded; career-related internships or fieldwork and unspecified assistantships also available. Financial award application deadline: 4/15; financial award applicants required to submit FAFSA. *Faculty research:* Prose recall, brain imaging, peak performance, biofeedback and pain control, comparable worth. Total annual research expenditures: $15,000. *Unit head:* Dr. Laura L. K. Bryan, Chairperson, 850-474-3493. *Application contact:* Terry McCray, Assistant Director of Graduate Admissions, 850-473-7718, Fax: 850-473-7714, E-mail: gradadmissions@uwf.edu.

University of West Georgia, College of Arts and Sciences, Department of Psychology, Carrollton, GA 30118. Offers individual, organizational, and community transformation: consciousness and society (Psy D); psychology (MA). Part-time programs available. *Faculty:* 14 full-time (2 women). *Students:* 53 full-time (33 women), 27 part-time (12 women); includes 9 Black or African American, non-Hispanic/Latino; 1 American Indian or Alaska Native, non-Hispanic/Latino; 3 Hispanic/Latino, 3 international. Average age 31. 67 applicants, 31% accepted, 15 enrolled. In 2010, 11 master's awarded. Terminal master's awarded for partial completion of doctoral program. *Degree requirements:* For master's, one foreign language, comprehensive exam, thesis optional; for doctorate, comprehensive exam, thesis/dissertation. *Entrance requirements:* For master's, GRE General Test, interview, minimum GPA of 2.5, written statement; for doctorate, GRE or MAT, interview, written statement. *Application deadline:* For fall admission, 7/17 for domestic students; for spring admission, 11/20 for domestic students. Applications are processed on a rolling basis. Application fee: $30. Electronic applications accepted. *Expenses:* Tuition, state resident: full-time $4130; part-time $173 per semester hour. Tuition, nonresident: full-time $16,524; part-time $689 per semester hour. Required fees: $1586; $44.01 per semester hour. $397 per semester. Tuition and fees vary according to program. *Financial support:* In 2010–11, 12 students received support, including 12 research assistantships with full tuition reimbursements available (averaging $3,000 per year); career-related internships or fieldwork, tuition waivers (full), and unspecified assistantships also available. Support available to part-time students. Financial award application deadline: 7/1; financial award applicants required to submit FAFSA. *Faculty research:* Creativity, inspiration and consciousness; symbolism and metaphor in psychotherapy; spirituality of children; feminism and culture; mind/body connection. Total annual research expenditures: $30,000. *Unit head:* Dr. Donadrian Lawrence Rice, Chair, 678-839-6510, Fax: 678-839-0611, E-mail: drice@westga.edu. *Application contact:* Dr. Charles W. Clark, Dean, 678-839-6508, E-mail: cclark@westga.edu.

University of Windsor, Faculty of Graduate Studies, Faculty of Arts and Social Sciences, Department of Psychology, Windsor, ON N9B 3P4, Canada. Offers adult clinical (MA, PhD); applied social psychology (MA, PhD); child clinical (MA, PhD); clinical neuropsychology (MA, PhD). *Accreditation:* APA (one or more programs are accredited). *Degree requirements:* For master's, thesis; for doctorate, comprehensive exam, thesis/dissertation. *Entrance requirements:* For master's, GRE General Test, GRE Subject Test in psychology, minimum B average; for doctorate, GRE General Test, GRE Subject Test in psychology, master's degree. Additional exam requirements/recommendations for international students: Required—TOEFL (minimum score 600 paper-based; 250 computer-based). Electronic applications accepted. *Faculty research:* Gambling, suicidology, emotional competence, psychotherapy and trauma.

University of Wisconsin–Eau Claire, College of Arts and Sciences, Department of Psychology, Eau Claire, WI 54702-4004. Offers school psychology (MSE, Ed S). Part-time programs available. *Faculty:* 18 full-time (9 women). *Students:* 14 full-time (13 women), 10 part-time (6 women), 1 international. Average age 28. 25 applicants, 28% accepted, 5 enrolled. In 2010, 8 master's, 6 other advanced degrees awarded. *Degree requirements:* For master's, comprehensive exam, thesis, National Certified School Psychologist Professional Exam, written exam, externship. *Entrance requirements:* For master's, GRE, minimum undergraduate GPA of 3.0; courses in exceptional children and youth, statistics, psychopathology, and theories of counseling. Additional exam requirements/recommendations for international students: Required—TOEFL (minimum score 550 paper-based; 213 computer-based; 79 iBT); Recommended—IELTS (minimum score 7). *Application deadline:* For fall admission, 3/1 priority date for domestic and international students. Applications are processed on a rolling basis. Application fee: $56. *Expenses:* Tuition, state resident: full-time $7001; part-time $389 per credit. Tuition, nonresident: full-time $16,771; part-time $932 per credit. Required fees: $1057; $58.49 per credit. *Financial support:* In 2010–11, 15 students received support, including 6 fellowships (averaging $993 per year); Federal Work-Study and unspecified assistantships also available. Financial award application deadline: 3/1; financial award applicants required to submit FAFSA. *Unit head:* Dr. Lori Bica, Chair, 715-836-5733, Fax: 715-836-2214, E-mail: bicala@uwec.edu. *Application contact:* Dr. Barbara Lozar, Professor, 715-836-5733, E-mail: lozarb@uwec.edu.

University of Wisconsin–La Crosse, Office of University Graduate Studies, College of Liberal Studies, Department of Psychology, La Crosse, WI 54601-3742. Offers school psychology (MS Ed, Ed S); student affairs administration (MS Ed). Part-time programs available. Post-baccalaureate distance learning degree programs offered (no on-campus study). *Students:* 112 full-time (85 women), 36 part-time (31 women); includes 16 minority (5 Black or African American, non-Hispanic/Latino; 2 American Indian or Alaska Native, non-Hispanic/Latino; 2

Psychology—General

University of Wisconsin–La Crosse (continued)
Asian, non-Hispanic/Latino; 3 Hispanic/Latino; 1 Native Hawaiian or other Pacific Islander, non-Hispanic/Latino; 3 Two or more races, non-Hispanic/Latino). 190 applicants, 45% accepted, 66 enrolled. In 2010, 58 master's awarded. *Degree requirements:* For master's, thesis, seminar, or comprehensive exams. *Entrance requirements:* Additional exam requirements/ recommendations for international students: Required—TOEFL (minimum score 550 paper-based; 213 computer-based; 79 iBT). Application fee: $56. Electronic applications accepted. *Expenses:* Tuition, state resident: full-time $7121; part-time $395.61 per credit. Tuition, nonresident: full-time $16,891; part-time $938.41 per credit. Part-time tuition and fees vary according to course load, program and reciprocity agreements. *Financial support:* Research assistantships with partial tuition reimbursements, Federal Work-Study, scholarships/grants, and health care benefits available. Support available to part-time students. *Unit head:* Dr. Betsy Morgan, Chair, 608-785-6888, Fax: 608-785-8443, E-mail: morgan.bets@uwlax.edu. *Application contact:* Kathryn Kiefer, Director of Admissions, 608-785-8939, E-mail: admissions@uwlax.edu.

University of Wisconsin–Madison, Graduate School, College of Letters and Science, Department of Psychology, Madison, WI 53706-1380. Offers biology of brain and behavior (PhD); clinical psychology (PhD); cognitive neurosciences (PhD); developmental psychology (PhD); perception (PhD); psychology (PhD); social and personality psychology (PhD). *Accreditation:* APA. *Degree requirements:* For doctorate, comprehensive exam, thesis/ dissertation. *Entrance requirements:* For doctorate, GRE General Test, minimum undergraduate GPA of 3.0. Additional exam requirements/recommendations for international students: Required—TOEFL. Electronic applications accepted. *Expenses:* Tuition, state resident: full-time $9887; part-time $617.96 per credit. Tuition, nonresident: full-time $24,054; part-time $1503.40 per credit. Required fees: $67.63 per credit. Tuition and fees vary according to reciprocity agreements.

University of Wisconsin–Milwaukee, Graduate School, College of Letters and Sciences, Department of Psychology, Milwaukee, WI 53201-0413. Offers clinical psychology (MS, PhD); psychology (MS, PhD). *Accreditation:* APA (one or more programs are accredited). *Faculty:* 24 full-time (8 women). *Students:* 58 full-time (35 women), 15 part-time (11 women); includes 1 Black or African American, non-Hispanic/Latino; 1 American Indian or Alaska Native, non-Hispanic/Latino; 2 Asian, non-Hispanic/Latino; 4 Hispanic/Latino, 6 international. Average age 29. 257 applicants, 10% accepted, 14 enrolled. In 2010, 15 master's, 5 doctorates awarded. *Degree requirements:* For master's, thesis; for doctorate, variable foreign language requirement, thesis/dissertation. *Entrance requirements:* For master's and doctorate, GRE General Test, GRE Subject Test. Additional exam requirements/recommendations for international students: Required—TOEFL (minimum score 550 paper-based; 79 iBT), IELTS (minimum score 6.5). *Application deadline:* For fall admission, 1/1 priority date for domestic students; for spring admission, 9/1 for domestic students. Applications are processed on a rolling basis. Application fee: $56 ($96 for international students). Electronic applications accepted. *Financial support:* In 2010–11, 8 fellowships, 6 research assistantships, 46 teaching assistantships were awarded; career-related internships or fieldwork, unspecified assistantships, and project assistantships also available. Support available to part-time students. Financial award application deadline: 4/15; financial award applicants required to submit FAFSA. Total annual research expenditures: $1.4 million. *Unit head:* Hobart Davies, Representative, 414-229-6594, Fax: 414-229-5219, E-mail: hobart@uwm.edu. *Application contact:* General Information Contact, 414-229-4982, Fax: 414-229-6967, E-mail: gradschool@uwm.edu.

University of Wisconsin–Oshkosh, The Office of Graduate Studies, College of Letters and Science, Department of Psychology, Oshkosh, WI 54901. Offers experimental psychology (MS); industrial/organizational psychology (MS). *Degree requirements:* For master's, thesis. *Entrance requirements:* For master's, GRE, 10 semester hours of undergraduate course work in psychology. Additional exam requirements/recommendations for international students: Required—TOEFL (minimum score 550 paper-based; 213 computer-based; 79 iBT). Electronic applications accepted. *Faculty research:* Performance evaluation, training, biological bases of behavior, tactile perception, aging.

University of Wisconsin–Whitewater, School of Graduate Studies, College of Letters and Sciences, Department of Psychology, Whitewater, WI 53190-1790. Offers school psychology (MS Ed, Ed S). Part-time and evening/weekend programs available. Postbaccalaureate distance learning degree programs offered (no on-campus study). *Degree requirements:* For master's, comprehensive exam or thesis. *Entrance requirements:* For master's, MAT or GRE, interview, minimum GPA of 3.0, 3 letters of recommendation. Additional exam requirements/ recommendations for international students: Required—TOEFL (minimum score 550 paper-based; 213 computer-based). Electronic applications accepted. *Faculty research:* School violence/youth violence; anger/aggression interventions; women's mental health; pedagogy of empathy, social psychology, and personality.

University of Wyoming, College of Arts and Sciences, Department of Psychology, Laramie, WY 82070. Offers MA, MS, PhD. *Accreditation:* APA (one or more programs are accredited). Terminal master's awarded for partial completion of doctoral program. *Degree requirements:* For master's, thesis; for doctorate, comprehensive exam, thesis/dissertation. *Entrance requirements:* For master's and doctorate, GRE General Test, GRE Subject Test, minimum GPA of 3.0. Additional exam requirements/recommendations for international students: Required—TOEFL. *Faculty research:* Child development, health psychology, psychology and law, social psychology, mood/anxiety disorders.

Utah State University, School of Graduate Studies, College of Education and Human Services, Department of Psychology, Logan, UT 84322. Offers clinical/counseling/school psychology (PhD); research and evaluation methodology (PhD); school counseling (MS); school psychology (MS). *Accreditation:* APA (one or more programs are accredited). Part-time and evening/ weekend programs available. Postbaccalaureate distance learning degree programs offered (no on-campus study). Terminal master's awarded for partial completion of doctoral program. *Degree requirements:* For master's, thesis (for some programs); for doctorate, thesis/ dissertation. *Entrance requirements:* For master's, GRE General Test (school psychology), MAT (school counseling), minimum GPA of 3.5; for doctorate, GRE General Test, minimum GPA of 3.5. Additional exam requirements/recommendations for international students: Required—TOEFL. *Faculty research:* Hearing loss detection in infancy, ADHD, eating disorders, domestic violence, neuropsychology, bilingual/Spanish speaking students/parents.

Valdosta State University, Department of Psychology and Counseling, Valdosta, GA 31698. Offers clinical/counseling psychology (MS); industrial/organizational psychology (MS); school counseling (M Ed, Ed S); school psychology (Ed S). Part-time and evening/weekend programs available. *Faculty:* 19 full-time (6 women). *Students:* 65 full-time (47 women), 41 part-time (35 women); includes 38 minority (29 Black or African American, non-Hispanic/Latino; 3 Asian, non-Hispanic/Latino; 4 Hispanic/Latino; 2 Two or more races, non-Hispanic/Latino). Average age 27. 61 applicants, 51% accepted, 27 enrolled. In 2010, 43 master's awarded. *Degree requirements:* For master's, thesis or alternative, comprehensive written and/or oral exams; for Ed S, thesis. *Entrance requirements:* For master's and Ed S, GRE General Test or MAT. Additional exam requirements/recommendations for international students: Required—TOEFL (minimum score 523 paper-based; 193 computer-based). *Application deadline:* For fall admission, 7/1 for domestic and international students; for spring admission, 11/15 for domestic and international students. Applications are processed on a rolling basis. Application fee: $35. Electronic applications accepted. *Expenses:* Tuition, state resident: full-time $5256; part-time $197 per credit hour. Tuition, nonresident: full-time $14,490; part-time $710 per credit hour. Required fees: $855 per semester. Tuition and fees vary according to course load and campus/location. *Financial support:* In 2010–11, 6 students received support, including 2 research assistantships with full tuition reimbursements available (averaging $3,652 per year); institutionally sponsored loans and unspecified assistantships also available. Support available to part-time students. Financial award application deadline: 7/1; financial award applicants required to submit FAFSA. *Faculty research:* Using Bender-Gestalt to predict graphomotor dimensions of the draw-a-person test, neurobehavioral hemispheric dominance. *Unit head:* Dr. Robert Bauer, Chair, 229-333-5930, Fax: 229-259-5576, E-mail: bbauer@valdosta.edu. *Application contact:* Rebecca Waters, Coordinator of Graduate Admissions, 229-333-5694, Fax: 229-245-3853, E-mail: rlwaters@valdosta.edu.

Valparaiso University, Graduate School, Department of Psychology, Valparaiso, IN 46383. Offers business management (for counseling students) (Certificate); clinical mental health counseling (MA); community counseling (MA); JD/MA. Part-time and evening/weekend programs available. *Faculty:* 9 part-time/adjunct (5 women). *Students:* 40 full-time (34 women), 12 part-time (8 women); includes 3 Black or African American, non-Hispanic/Latino; 2 Hispanic/ Latino, 2 international. Average age 28. In 2010, 22 master's awarded. *Degree requirements:* For master's, thesis or alternative, internship. *Entrance requirements:* For master's, minimum GPA of 3.0; 15 credits in the social/behavioral sciences (psychology, sociology, human development, etc.) with a minimum GPA of 3.0; course in introductory psychology; recent statistics course with minimum B average. Additional exam requirements/recommendations for international students: Required—TOEFL (minimum score 550 paper-based; 213 computer-based; 80 iBT). *Application deadline:* For fall admission, 3/1 priority date for domestic students. Applications are processed on a rolling basis. Application fee: $30 ($50 for international students). Electronic applications accepted. *Expenses:* Tuition: Full-time $9540; part-time $530 per credit hour. Required fees: $292; $95 per semester. Tuition and fees vary according to program. *Financial support:* Career-related internships or fieldwork, traineeships, and unspecified assistantships available. Support available to part-time students. Financial award applicants required to submit FAFSA. *Faculty research:* Environmental psychology, human sexuality, developmental psychopathology, social psychology. *Unit head:* Dr. David Simpson, Director of Graduate Programs, 219-464-6941, Fax: 219-464-6878, E-mail: david.simpson@valpo.edu. *Application contact:* Laura Groth, Coordinator of Student Services and Support, 219-464-5313, Fax: 219-464-5381, E-mail: laura.groth@valpo.edu.

Vanderbilt University, Graduate School, Program in Psychological Sciences, Nashville, TN 37240-1001. Offers MA, MS, PhD. *Accreditation:* APA (one or more programs are accredited). *Faculty:* 25 full-time (5 women), 2 part-time/adjunct (both women). *Students:* 100 full-time (67 women), 2 part-time (both women); includes 5 Black or African American, non-Hispanic/Latino; 5 Asian, non-Hispanic/Latino; 5 Hispanic/Latino; 1 Two or more races, non-Hispanic/Latino. Average age 28. 492 applicants, 7% accepted, 19 enrolled. In 2010, 2 master's, 5 doctorates awarded. *Degree requirements:* For doctorate, comprehensive exam, thesis/dissertation, final and qualifying exams. *Entrance requirements:* For doctorate, GRE General Test, GRE Subject Test. Additional exam requirements/recommendations for international students: Required—TOEFL (minimum score 570 paper-based; 230 computer-based; 88 iBT). *Application deadline:* For fall admission, 12/15 for domestic and international students. Application fee: $0. Electronic applications accepted. *Financial support:* Fellowships with full and partial tuition reimbursements, research assistantships with full and partial tuition reimbursements, teaching assistantships with full and partial tuition reimbursements, career-related internships or fieldwork, Federal Work-Study, institutionally sponsored loans, scholarships/grants, traineeships, and health care benefits available. Financial award application deadline: 1/15; financial award applicants required to submit CSS PROFILE or FAFSA. *Faculty research:* Clinical, cognitive, developmental, and social psychology; neuroscience; vision; behavior. *Unit head:* Andrew J. Tomarken, Co-Chair, 615-322-4177, Fax: 615-343-8449, E-mail: andrew.j.tomarken@vanderbilt.edu. *Application contact:* Thomas J. Palmeri, Co-Director of Graduate Studies, 615-343-7900, Fax: 615-343-8449, E-mail: thomas.j.palmeri@vanderbilt.edu.

Vanderbilt University, Peabody College, Department of Psychology and Human Development, Nashville, TN 37240-1001. Offers child studies (M Ed). *Accreditation:* APA. Part-time programs available. *Faculty:* 36 full-time (18 women), 2 part-time/adjunct (0 women). *Students:* 17 full-time (all women), 2 part-time (both women); includes 5 minority (3 Black or African American, non-Hispanic/Latino; 1 Asian, non-Hispanic/Latino; 1 Hispanic/Latino). Average age 25. 46 applicants, 37% accepted, 10 enrolled. In 2010, 8 master's awarded. *Degree requirements:* For master's, comprehensive exam, thesis optional. *Entrance requirements:* For master's, GRE General Test. Additional exam requirements/recommendations for international students: Required—TOEFL (minimum score 550 paper-based; 213 computer-based). *Application deadline:* For fall admission, 12/31 for domestic and international students; for spring admission, 11/1 for domestic and international students. Applications are processed on a rolling basis. Application fee: $0. Electronic applications accepted. *Financial support:* In 2010–11, 17 students received support, including 6 research assistantships with full and partial tuition reimbursements, 7 teaching assistantships with full and partial tuition reimbursements available; fellowships with full and partial tuition reimbursements available, Federal Work-Study, institutionally sponsored loans, scholarships/grants, tuition waivers (partial), and unspecified assistantships also available. Financial award application deadline: 2/1; financial award applicants required to submit FAFSA. *Faculty research:* Child clinical psychology and developmental psychopathology; cognitive psychology, language and social development; educational and developmental neuroscience; quantitative methods and evaluation. *Unit head:* Dr. David Cole, Acting Chair, 615-322-8141, Fax: 615-343-9494, E-mail: david.cole@vanderbilt.edu. *Application contact:* Sharone Hall, Educational Coordinator, 615-343-4963, Fax: 615-343-9494, E-mail: sharone.k.hall@vanderbilt.edu.

Villanova University, Graduate School of Liberal Arts and Sciences, Department of Psychology, Villanova, PA 19085-1699. Offers MS. Part-time and evening/weekend programs available. *Faculty:* 10 full-time (1 woman), 3 part-time/adjunct (2 women). *Students:* 47 full-time (28 women); includes 3 minority (2 Hispanic/Latino; 1 Two or more races, non-Hispanic/Latino). Average age 24. 115 applicants, 43% accepted, 20 enrolled. In 2010, 26 master's awarded. *Degree requirements:* For master's, thesis. *Entrance requirements:* For master's, GRE General Test, minimum GPA of 3.0. Additional exam requirements/recommendations for international students: Required—TOEFL. *Application deadline:* For fall admission, 3/1 priority date for domestic and international students; for spring admission, 11/15 priority date for domestic and international students. Applications are processed on a rolling basis. Application fee: $50. Electronic applications accepted. *Expenses:* Tuition: Part-time $700 per credit. Part-time tuition and fees vary according to degree level and program. *Financial support:* Research assistantships, Federal Work-Study, scholarships/grants, and unspecified assistantships available. Financial award applicants required to submit FAFSA. *Unit head:* Dr. Thomas Toppino, Chair, 610-519-4720. *Application contact:* Dr. Adele Lindenmeyr, Dean, Graduate School of Liberal Arts and Sciences, 610-519-7093, Fax: 610-519-7096.

Virginia Commonwealth University, Graduate School, College of Humanities and Sciences, Department of Psychology, Program in General Psychology, Richmond, VA 23284-9005. Offers biopsychology (PhD); developmental psychology (PhD); social psychology (PhD). *Students:* 22 full-time (16 women), 9 part-time (4 women); includes 6 minority (4 Black or African American, non-Hispanic/Latino; 1 Asian, non-Hispanic/Latino; 1 Hispanic/Latino), 1 international. 68 applicants, 6% accepted, 1 enrolled. In 2010, 3 doctorates awarded. *Degree requirements:* For doctorate, thesis/dissertation. *Entrance requirements:* For doctorate, GRE General Test. Additional exam requirements/recommendations for international students: Required—TOEFL (minimum score 600 paper-based; 250 computer-based; 100 iBT); Recommended—IELTS (minimum score 6.5). *Application deadline:* For fall admission, 12/15 for domestic students. Application fee: $50. Electronic applications accepted. *Expenses:* Tuition, state resident: full-time $4308; part-time $479 per credit hour. Tuition, nonresident: full-time $8942; part-time $994 per credit hour. Required fees: $2000; $85 per credit hour. Tuition and fees vary according to course level, course load, degree level, campus/location and program. *Financial support:* Fellowships, research assistantships, teaching assistantships, Federal Work-Study, institutionally sponsored loans, and scholarships/grants available. Support available to part-time students. *Faculty research:* Biopsychology, developmental and social psychology. *Unit head:* Dr. Michael Southam-Gerow, Director, Graduate Programs in Psychology, 804-828-1193, Fax: 804-828-2237, E-mail: masouthamger@vcu.edu. *Application contact:* Dr. Joseph Porter, Director, Biopsychology Division, 804-828-0096, Fax: 804-828-2237, E-mail: jporter@vcu.edu.

Virginia Polytechnic Institute and State University, Graduate School, College of Science, Department of Psychology, Blacksburg, VA 24061. Offers MS, PhD. *Accreditation:* APA (one or more programs are accredited). *Faculty:* 23 full-time (7 women). *Students:* 73 full-time (49 women), 2 part-time (1 woman); includes 7 Black or African American, non-Hispanic/Latino; 2 Asian, non-Hispanic/Latino; 4 Hispanic/Latino, 7 international. Average age 27. 199 applicants, 12% accepted, 15 enrolled. In 2010, 11 master's, 12 doctorates awarded. *Degree requirements:* For master's, comprehensive exam (for some programs), thesis (for some programs); for doctorate, comprehensive exam (for some programs), thesis/dissertation (for some programs). *Entrance requirements:* For master's and doctorate, GRE. Additional exam requirements/recommendations for international students: Required—TOEFL (minimum score 550 paper-based; 213 computer-based). *Application deadline:* For fall admission, 7/1 for domestic and international students; for spring admission, 12/1 for domestic and international students. Applications are processed on a rolling basis. Application fee: $65. Electronic applications accepted. *Expenses:* Tuition, state resident: full-time $9399; part-time $488 per credit hour. Tuition, nonresident: full-time $17,854; part-time $957.75 per credit hour. Required fees: $1534. Full-time tuition and fees vary according to program. *Financial support:* In 2010–11, 12 research assistantships with full tuition reimbursements (averaging $20,573 per year), 40 teaching assistantships with full tuition reimbursements (averaging $18,272 per year) were awarded; career-related internships or fieldwork, Federal Work-Study, scholarships/grants, health care benefits, and unspecified assistantships also available. Financial award application deadline: 1/15. *Faculty research:* Infant development from electrophysical point of view, work motivation and personnel selection, EEG, ERP and hypnosis with reference to chronic pain, intimate violence. Total annual research expenditures: $2.4 million. *Unit head:* Dr. Robert S. Stephens, UNIT HEAD, 540-231-6304, Fax: 540-231-3652, E-mail: stephens@vt.edu. *Application contact:* Kirby Deater-Deckard, Contact, 540-231-6581, Fax: 540-231-3652, E-mail: kirbydd@vt.edu.

Virginia State University, School of Graduate Studies, Research, and Outreach, School of Engineering, Science and Technology, Department of Psychology, Petersburg, VA 23806-0001. Offers behavioral and community health sciences (PhD); clinical health psychology (PhD); clinical psychology (MS); general psychology (MS). *Degree requirements:* For master's, one foreign language, thesis. *Entrance requirements:* For master's, GRE General Test. *Expenses:* Tuition, state resident: full-time $5576; part-time $335 per credit hour. Tuition, nonresident: full-time $13,402; part-time $670 per credit hour.

Wake Forest University, Graduate School of Arts and Sciences, Department of Psychology, Winston-Salem, NC 27109. Offers MA. *Degree requirements:* For master's, one foreign language, comprehensive exam, thesis. *Entrance requirements:* For master's, GRE General Test. Additional exam requirements/recommendations for international students: Required—TOEFL (minimum score 213 computer-based; 79 iBT). Electronic applications accepted. *Faculty research:* Developmental, social, personality, experimental, and physiological psychology.

Walden University, Graduate Programs, School of Psychology, Minneapolis, MN 55401. Offers clinical child psychology (Post-Doctoral Certificate); clinical psychology (MS, Post-Doctoral Certificate), including counseling (MS); counseling psychology (Post-Doctoral Certificate); forensic psychology (MS), including forensic psychology in the community, general program, mental health applications, program planning and evaluation in forensic settings, psychology and legal systems; general psychology (Post-Doctoral Certificate); health psychology (Post-Doctoral Certificate); organizational psychology (Post-Doctoral Certificate); organizational psychology and development (Postbaccalaureate Certificate); psychology (MS, PhD), including clinical psychology (PhD), counseling psychology (PhD), crisis management and response (MS), general program (MS), general psychology (PhD), health psychology, leadership development and coaching (MS), media psychology (MS), organizational psychology (PhD), organizational psychology and development (MS), organizational psychology and nonprofit management (MS), program evaluation and research (MS), psychology of culture (MS), psychology, public administration, and social change (MS), social psychology (MS), terrorism and security (MS); teaching online (Post-Master's Certificate). Part-time and evening/weekend programs available. Postbaccalaureate distance learning degree programs offered (minimal on-campus study). *Faculty:* 41 full-time (25 women), 254 part-time/adjunct (131 women). *Students:* 3,463 full-time (2,737 women), 1,400 part-time (1,130 women); includes 1,491 Black or African American, non-Hispanic/Latino; 59 American Indian or Alaska Native, non-Hispanic/Latino; 89 Asian, non-Hispanic/Latino; 283 Hispanic/Latino; 76 Two or more races, non-Hispanic/Latino, 126 international. Average age 40. In 2010, 559 master's, 100 doctorates awarded. Terminal master's awarded for partial completion of doctoral program. *Degree requirements:* For master's, thesis optional; for doctorate, thesis/dissertation, residency. *Entrance requirements:* For master's, bachelor's degree or equivalent in related field; minimum GPA of 2.5; official transcripts; goal statement; access to computer and Internet; for doctorate, master's degree or equivalent in related field; minimum GPA of 3.0; 3 years of related professional/academic experience (preferred). Additional exam requirements/recommendations for international students: Required—TOEFL (minimum score 550 paper-based; 213 computer-based), IELTS (minimum score 6.5), TOEFL (minimum score 550 paper-based; 213 computer-based), IELTS (minimum score 6.5), or Michigan English Language Assessment Battery (minimum score 82). *Application deadline:* Applications are processed on a rolling basis. Application fee: $50. Electronic applications accepted. *Expenses:* Tuition: Full-time $10,274; part-time $445 per credit. Tuition and fees vary according to course load, degree level and program. *Financial support:* In 2010–11, 1 fellowship was awarded; Federal Work-Study, scholarships/grants, unspecified assistantships, and family tuition reduction, active duty/veteran tuition reduction, group tuition reduction, interest-free payment plans also available. Support available to part-time students. Financial award applicants required to submit FAFSA. *Unit head:* Dr. Melanie Storms, Associate Dean, 800-925-3368. *Application contact:* Jennifer Hall, Vice President of Enrollment Management, 866-4-WALDEN, E-mail: info@waldenu.edu.

Washburn University, College of Arts and Sciences, Department of Psychology, Topeka, KS 66621. Offers clinical psychology (MA). Part-time programs available. *Faculty:* 8 full-time (4 women). *Students:* 22 full-time (16 women), 5 part-time (4 women). Average age 28. In 2010, 4 master's awarded. *Degree requirements:* For master's, thesis. *Entrance requirements:* For master's, GRE General Test, 15 hours of course work in psychology. Additional exam requirements/recommendations for international students: Recommended—TOEFL (minimum score 550 paper-based; 80 iBT). *Application deadline:* For fall admission, 3/15 for domestic students; for spring admission, 12/1 for domestic students. Electronic applications accepted. *Expenses:* Tuition, state resident: full-time $5130; part-time $285 per credit hour. Tuition, nonresident: full-time $10,476; part-time $582 per credit hour. Required fees: $86; $43 per semester. Tuition and fees vary according to program. *Financial support:* Applicants required to submit FAFSA. *Faculty research:* Metacognition, anxiety disorders, gender roles in relationships, rural psychology, sports performance psychology. *Unit head:* Dr. David Provorse, Chair, 785-670-1565, Fax: 785-670-1004, E-mail: dave.provorse@washburn.edu. *Application contact:* Dr. David Provorse, Chair, 785-670-1565, Fax: 785-670-1004, E-mail: dave.provorse@washburn.edu.

Washington College, Graduate Programs, Department of Psychology, Chestertown, MD 21620-1197. Offers MA. Part-time and evening/weekend programs available. *Entrance requirements:* For master's, GRE General Test. *Expenses:* Tuition: Part-time $1125 per course. Required fees: $100 per course.

Washington State University, Graduate School, College of Liberal Arts, Department of Psychology, Pullman, WA 99164. Offers clinical psychology (PhD); experimental psychology (PhD); psychology (MS). *Accreditation:* APA (one or more programs are accredited). *Faculty:* 22. *Students:* 49 full-time (34 women), 4 part-time (2 women); includes 2 Asian, non-Hispanic/Latino; 5 Hispanic/Latino, 7 international. Average age 29. 262 applicants, 6% accepted, 12 enrolled. In 2010, 7 master's, 8 doctorates awarded. *Degree requirements:* For master's, comprehensive exam (for some programs), thesis (for some programs), oral exam; for doctorate, comprehensive exam, thesis/dissertation, oral exam, written exam. *Entrance requirements:* For master's, GRE General Test, minimum undergraduate GPA of 3.0; research experiences; clinical experiences; at least 18 hours of psychology, including a class in statistics; three letters of recommendation, official transcripts; for doctorate, GRE General Test, three letters of reference; summary data form; at least 18 credits of study in psychology; at least one course in statistics and research methodology; official transcripts; minimum cumulative undergraduate GPA of 3.0 or master's degree in psychology. Additional exam requirements/recommendations for international students: Required—TOEFL, IELTS. *Application deadline:* For fall admission, 12/15 priority date for domestic and international students. Applications are processed on a rolling basis. Application fee: $50. *Expenses:* Tuition, state resident: full-time $8552; part-time $443 per credit. Tuition, nonresident: full-time $21,650; part-time $1083 per credit. Required fees: $846. *Financial support:* In 2010–11, 5 research assistantships with full and partial tuition reimbursements (averaging $13,917 per year), 39 teaching assistantships with full and partial tuition reimbursements (averaging $13,056 per year) were awarded; fellowships, career-related internships or fieldwork, Federal Work-Study, institutionally sponsored loans, and unspecified assistantships also available. Financial award application deadline: 2/15; financial award applicants required to submit FAFSA. *Faculty research:* Childhood conduct disorders, etiology of depression, treatment of reading disorders, applied behavior analysis, selective attention. *Unit head:* Dr. John Hinson, Chair, 509-335-1089, Fax: 509-335-5043, E-mail: hinson@mail.wsu.edu. *Application contact:* Graduate School Admissions, 800-GRADWSU, Fax: 509-335-1949, E-mail: gradsch@wsu.edu.

Washington University in St. Louis, Graduate School of Arts and Sciences, Department of Philosophy, Program in Philosophy/Neuroscience/Psychology, St. Louis, MO 63130-4899. Offers PhD. *Degree requirements:* For doctorate, thesis/dissertation. *Entrance requirements:* For doctorate, GRE General Test, sample of written work. Electronic applications accepted.

Washington University in St. Louis, Graduate School of Arts and Sciences, Department of Psychology, St. Louis, MO 63130-4899. Offers clinical psychology (PhD); general experimental psychology (PhD); social psychology (PhD). *Accreditation:* APA. Terminal master's awarded for partial completion of doctoral program. *Degree requirements:* For doctorate, thesis/dissertation. *Entrance requirements:* For doctorate, GRE General Test. Electronic applications accepted.

Wayne State University, College of Liberal Arts and Sciences, Department of Psychology, Detroit, MI 48202. Offers industrial and organizational psychology (PhD). *Accreditation:* APA (one or more programs are accredited). *Faculty:* 20 full-time (7 women), 4 part-time/adjunct (2 women). *Students:* 95 full-time (74 women), 23 part-time (17 women); includes 17 minority (7 Black or African American, non-Hispanic/Latino; 2 American Indian or Alaska Native, non-Hispanic/Latino; 5 Asian, non-Hispanic/Latino; 2 Hispanic/Latino; 1 Two or more races, non-Hispanic/Latino), 8 international. Average age 28. 230 applicants, 9% accepted, 13 enrolled. In 2010, 20 master's, 12 doctorates awarded. *Degree requirements:* For doctorate, thesis/dissertation. *Entrance requirements:* For doctorate, GRE General Test, GRE Subject Test, letters of recommendation. Additional exam requirements/recommendations for international students: Required—TOEFL (minimum score 550 paper-based; 213 computer-based); Recommended—TWE (minimum score 6). *Application deadline:* For fall admission, 6/1 for international students; for winter admission, 10/1 for international students; for spring admission, 2/1 for international students. Applications are processed on a rolling basis. Application fee: $30 ($50 for international students). Electronic applications accepted. *Expenses:* Tuition, state resident: full-time $7662; part-time $478.85 per credit hour. Tuition, nonresident: full-time $16,920; part-time $1057.55 per credit hour. Required fees: $571.20; $35.70 per credit hour. $188.05 per semester. Tuition and fees vary according to course load and program. *Financial support:* In 2010–11, 12 fellowships with tuition reimbursements (averaging $19,631 per year), 25 research assistantships with tuition reimbursements (averaging $17,161 per year), 49 teaching assistantships with tuition reimbursements (averaging $15,579 per year) were awarded; career-related internships or fieldwork also available. Financial award application deadline: 2/1. *Faculty research:* Clinical neuropsychology, high risk factors in development, human aging and neuroscience, industrial/organizational psychology, health psychology. Total annual research expenditures: $172,430. *Unit head:* Douglas Whitman, Chair, 313-577-2803, Fax: 313-577-7636, E-mail: dwhitman@wayne.edu. *Application contact:* Dr. Melissa Kaplan-Estrin, Graduate Director, 313-577-2824, Fax: 313-577-7636, E-mail: mkestrin@sun.science.wayne.edu.

West Chester University of Pennsylvania, Office of Graduate Studies, College of Arts and Sciences, Department of Psychology, West Chester, PA 19383. Offers clinical mental health (Certificate); clinical psychology (MA); general psychology (MA); industrial psychology (MA). Part-time and evening/weekend programs available. *Students:* 79 full-time (56 women), 33 part-time (22 women); includes 16 minority (4 Black or African American, non-Hispanic/Latino; 1 American Indian or Alaska Native, non-Hispanic/Latino; 5 Asian, non-Hispanic/Latino; 6 Hispanic/Latino), 4 international. Average age 27. 192 applicants, 53% accepted, 40 enrolled. In 2010, 43 master's, 4 other advanced degrees awarded. *Degree requirements:* For master's, comprehensive exam, thesis (for some programs). *Entrance requirements:* For master's, GRE General Test or MAT, minimum GPA of 3.0, 3.25 in psychology; three letters of reference. Additional exam requirements/recommendations for international students: Required—TOEFL (minimum score 550 paper-based; 213 computer-based; 80 iBT). *Application deadline:* For fall admission, 4/15 priority date for domestic students, 3/15 for international students; for spring admission, 10/15 for domestic students, 9/1 for international students. Applications are processed on a rolling basis. Application fee: $35. Electronic applications accepted. *Expenses:* Tuition, state resident: full-time $6966; part-time $387 per credit. Tuition, nonresident: full-time $11,146; part-time $619 per credit. Required fees: $1614.40; $133.24 per credit. Part-time tuition and fees vary according to campus/location. *Financial support:* Unspecified assistantships available. Support available to part-time students. Financial award application deadline: 2/15; financial award applicants required to submit FAFSA. *Faculty research:* Animal learning and cognition. *Unit head:* Dr. Loretta Rieser-Danner, Acting Chairperson, 610-436-3106, E-mail: lrieser-danner@wcupa.edu. *Application contact:* Dr. Julian Azorlosa, Graduate Coordinator, 610-738-0430, E-mail: jazorlosa@wcupa.edu.

Western Carolina University, Graduate School, College of Education and Allied Professions, Department of Psychology, Cullowhee, NC 28723. Offers general psychology (MA); school psychology (MA). Part-time programs available. *Degree requirements:* For master's, comprehensive exam, thesis. *Entrance requirements:* For master's, GRE General Test, appropriate undergraduate degree, interview, 3 letters of recommendation. Additional exam requirements/recommendations for international students: Required—TOEFL (minimum score 550 paper-based; 270 computer-based; 79 iBT). *Faculty research:* Five-factor model of personality, evolutionary psychology, stress and worry, body image and physical attractiveness, moral decision-making, memory, learning styles.

Western Illinois University, School of Graduate Studies, College of Arts and Sciences, Department of Psychology, Macomb, IL 61455-1390. Offers clinical/community mental health (MS); general psychology (MS); psychology (MS, SSP); school psychology (SSP). Part-time programs available. *Students:* 44 full-time (31 women), 15 part-time (7 women); includes 4 minority (1 American Indian or Alaska Native, non-Hispanic/Latino; 3 Asian, non-Hispanic/Latino), 2 international. Average age 26. 94 applicants, 34% accepted. In 2010, 11 master's, 8 other advanced degrees awarded. *Degree requirements:* For master's, comprehensive exam (for some programs), thesis or alternative. *Entrance requirements:* For master's and SSP, GRE General Test. Additional exam requirements/recommendations for international students: Required—TOEFL (minimum score 550 paper-based; 213 computer-based; 80 iBT). *Application deadline:* Applications are processed on a rolling basis. Application fee: $30. Electronic applications accepted. *Expenses:* Tuition, state resident: full-time $6370; part-time $265.40 per credit hour. Tuition, nonresident: full-time $12,740; part-time $530.80 per credit hour. Required fees: $75.67 per credit hour. *Financial support:* In 2010–11, 37 students received support, including 37 research assistantships with full tuition reimbursements available (averaging $7,280 per year). Financial award applicants required to submit FAFSA. *Unit head:* Dr. Steven Dworkin, Chairperson, 309-298-1593. *Application contact:* Evelyn Hoing, Assistant Director of Graduate Studies, 309-298-1806, Fax: 309-298-2345, E-mail: grad-office@wiu.edu.

Psychology—General

Western Kentucky University, Graduate Studies, College of Education and Behavioral Sciences, Department of Psychology, Bowling Green, KY 42101. Offers clinical psychology (MA); experimental psychology (MA); general psychology (MA); industrial/organizational psychology (MA); school psychology (Ed S). *Degree requirements:* For master's, comprehensive exam, thesis (for some programs); for Ed S, thesis, oral exam. *Entrance requirements:* For master's, GRE General Test; for Ed S, GRE General Test, minimum GPA of 3.5. Additional exam requirements/recommendations for international students: Required—TOEFL (minimum score 555 paper-based; 213 computer-based; 79 iBT). *Faculty research:* Neural regeneration, enhancing mobility in the elderly, improvement in visual processing in older adults, lifespan development.

Western Michigan University, Graduate College, College of Arts and Sciences, Department of Psychology, Kalamazoo, MI 49008. Offers behavior analysis (MA, PhD); clinical psychology (PhD); industrial/organizational psychology (MA). *Accreditation:* APA (one or more programs are accredited). *Degree requirements:* For master's, variable foreign language requirement, thesis, oral exams; for doctorate, 2 foreign languages, comprehensive exam, thesis/dissertation, oral exams. *Entrance requirements:* For master's and doctorate, GRE General Test.

Western Washington University, Graduate School, College of Humanities and Social Sciences, Department of Psychology, Bellingham, WA 98225-5996. Offers experimental psychology (MS); mental health counseling (MS); school counseling (M Ed). *Accreditation:* ACA (one or more programs are accredited). *Degree requirements:* For master's, comprehensive exam, thesis (for some programs). *Entrance requirements:* For master's, GRE General Test, minimum GPA of 3.0 in last 60 semester hours or last 90 quarter hours. Additional exam requirements/recommendations for international students: Required—TOEFL (minimum score 567 paper-based; 227 computer-based). *Faculty research:* Social, cognitive, behavioral neuroscience, counseling/clinical, developmental.

Westfield State University, Division of Graduate and Continuing Education, Department of Psychology, Westfield, MA 01086. Offers applied behavior analysis (MA); mental health counseling (MA); school guidance (MA). Part-time and evening/weekend programs available. *Degree requirements:* For master's, comprehensive exam. *Entrance requirements:* For master's, GRE General Test, MAT, minimum undergraduate GPA of 2.7.

West Texas A&M University, College of Education and Social Sciences, Department of Behavioral Sciences, Canyon, TX 79016-0001. Offers psychology (MA). Part-time and evening/weekend programs available. *Degree requirements:* For master's, comprehensive exam, thesis optional. *Entrance requirements:* For master's, GRE General Test, 3 letters of recommendation; interview; minimum GPA of 3.25 in psychology, 3.0 overall. Additional exam requirements/recommendations for international students: Required—TOEFL (minimum score 550 paper-based). Electronic applications accepted. *Faculty research:* Application of sociological principles to historical and contemporary analyses of social systems.

West Virginia University, Eberly College of Arts and Sciences, Department of Psychology, Morgantown, WV 26506. Offers behavior analysis (PhD); clinical psychology (MA, PhD); development psychology (PhD); psychology (MS). *Accreditation:* APA (one or more programs are accredited). Part-time programs available. Terminal master's awarded for partial completion of doctoral program. *Degree requirements:* For master's, thesis optional; for doctorate, comprehensive exam, thesis/dissertation. *Entrance requirements:* For master's and doctorate, GRE General Test, minimum GPA of 3.0. Additional exam requirements/recommendations for international students: Required—TOEFL. *Faculty research:* Adult and child clinical psychology, behavioral assessment and therapy, child and adolescent behavior, life span development, experimental and applied behavior analysis.

Wheaton College, Graduate School, Department of Psychology, Wheaton, IL 60187-5593. Offers clinical psychology (MA, Psy D); counseling ministries (MA). *Accreditation:* APA (one or more programs are accredited). Terminal master's awarded for partial completion of doctoral program. *Degree requirements:* For master's, thesis or alternative; for doctorate, thesis/dissertation, internship. *Entrance requirements:* For master's, GRE General Test, 18 hours of course work in psychology; for doctorate, GRE General Test.

Wichita State University, Graduate School, Fairmount College of Liberal Arts and Sciences, Department of Psychology, Wichita, KS 67260. Offers clinical (PhD); community (PhD); human factors (PhD). *Accreditation:* APA. Part-time programs available. *Unit head:* Dr. Alex Chaparro, Chair, 316-978-3170, Fax: 316-978-3006, E-mail: alex.chaparro@wichita.edu. *Application contact:* Dr. Robert Zettle, Graduate Coordinator, 316-978-3170, E-mail: robert.zettle@wichita.edu.

Widener University, School of Human Service Professions, Institute for Graduate Clinical Psychology, Law-Psychology Program, Chester, PA 19013-5792. Offers JD/Psy D. *Faculty:* 15 full-time (6 women), 18 part-time/adjunct (10 women). *Students:* 11 full-time (7 women), 1 (woman) part-time; includes 1 minority (Two or more races, non-Hispanic/Latino). Average age 23. 21 applicants, 19% accepted. *Application deadline:* For fall admission, 2/1 for domestic students. Applications are processed on a rolling basis. Application fee: $60. Electronic applications accepted. *Financial support:* In 2010–11, 12 students received support; research assistantships, career-related internships or fieldwork, Federal Work-Study, institutionally sponsored loans, and scholarships/grants available. Financial award application deadline: 5/31. *Unit head:* Dr. Amiram Elwork, Director, 610-499-1206, Fax: 610-499-4625, E-mail: amiram.elwork@widener.edu. *Application contact:* Maureen A. Brennan, Admissions Coordinator, 610-499-1206, Fax: 610-499-4625, E-mail: maureen.a.brennan@widener.edu.

Wilfrid Laurier University, Faculty of Graduate and Postdoctoral Studies, Faculty of Science, Department of Psychology, Waterloo, ON N2L 3C5, Canada. Offers behavioral neuroscience (M Sc, PhD); cognitive neuroscience (M Sc, PhD); community psychology (MA, PhD); social and developmental psychology (MA, PhD). Part-time programs available. *Faculty:* 32 full-time (12 women), 8 part-time/adjunct (1 woman). *Students:* 68 full-time (49 women), 4 part-time (3 women), 2 international. 94 applicants, 51% accepted, 27 enrolled. In 2010, 27 master's, 5 doctorates awarded. *Degree requirements:* For master's, thesis; for doctorate, thesis/dissertation. *Entrance requirements:* For master's, GRE General Test, honors BA or the equivalent in psychology, minimum B average in undergraduate course work; for doctorate, GRE General Test, master's degree, minimum A- average. Additional exam requirements/recommendations for international students: Required— TOEFL (minimum score 89 iBT). *Application deadline:* For fall admission, 1/15 priority date for domestic and international students. Application fee: $100. Electronic applications accepted. Tuition and fees charges are reported in Canadian dollars. *Expenses:* Tuition, area resident: Full-time $15,300 Canadian dollars; part-time $1200 Canadian dollars per credit. International tuition: $21,300 Canadian dollars full-time. Required fees: $650 Canadian dollars; $100 Canadian dollars per credit. Tuition and fees vary according to course load, degree level, campus/location and program. *Financial support:* In 2010–11, 116 fellowships, 116 teaching assistantships were awarded; career-related internships or fieldwork, scholarships/grants, health care benefits, and unspecified assistantships also available. *Faculty research:* Brain and cognition, community psychology, social and developmental psychology. *Unit head:* Dr. Alexandra Gottardo, Graduate Coordinator, 519-884-0710 Ext. 2169, Fax: 519-746-7605, E-mail: agottard@wlu.ca. *Application contact:* Rosemary Springett, Graduate

Admissions and Records Officer, 519-884-0710 Ext. 3078, Fax: 519-884-1020, E-mail: gradstudies@wlu.ca.

William Carey University, School of Psychology and Counseling, Hattiesburg, MS 39401-5499. Offers counseling psychology (MS). Part-time programs available. *Entrance requirements:* For master's, GRE, PRAXIS, MAT, minimum GPA of 2.5. Additional exam requirements/recommendations for international students: Required—TOEFL (minimum score 550 paper-based; 213 computer-based). *Expenses:* Contact institution. *Faculty research:* Addiction prevention, psychometric measurement, crisis counseling, gerontology.

Winthrop University, College of Arts and Sciences, Department of Psychology, Rock Hill, SC 29733. Offers MS, SSP. *Degree requirements:* For master's and SSP, comprehensive exam. *Entrance requirements:* For master's, GRE General Test, interview, minimum GPA of 3.0, 3 letters of recommendation, 15 hours of psychology courses in specified subject areas. Electronic applications accepted.

Wisconsin School of Professional Psychology, Program in Clinical Psychology, Milwaukee, WI 53225-4960. Offers MA, Psy D. *Accreditation:* APA. Part-time and evening/weekend programs available. Terminal master's awarded for partial completion of doctoral program. *Degree requirements:* For master's, candidacy exam, 500 hours of supervised clinical practica; for doctorate, thesis/dissertation, 1 year clinical intern and practicum experience (2000 hrs), candidacy and clinical exams. *Entrance requirements:* For master's, GRE General Test, GRE Subject Test, bachelor's degree in psychology, writing sample; for doctorate, GRE General Test, GRE Subject Test, master's degree in clinical psychology or equivalent, writing sample. *Faculty research:* Violence prevention, psychology of women, forensic psychology, custody evaluation, aging, harm reduction in AODA.

Wright Institute, Doctoral Program in Clinical Psychology, Berkeley, CA 94704-1796. Offers Psy D. *Accreditation:* APA. *Faculty:* 28 full-time (19 women), 93 part-time/adjunct (53 women). *Students:* 355 full-time (254 women); includes 95 minority (14 Black or African American, non-Hispanic/Latino; 2 American Indian or Alaska Native, non-Hispanic/Latino; 33 Asian, non-Hispanic/Latino; 29 Hispanic/Latino; 17 Two or more races, non-Hispanic/Latino). Average age 34. 323 applicants, 40% accepted, 59 enrolled. In 2010, 45 degrees awarded. *Median time to degree:* Of those who began their doctoral program in fall 2002, 100% received their degree in 8 years or less. *Degree requirements:* For doctorate, comprehensive exam, thesis/dissertation. *Entrance requirements:* For doctorate, GRE General Test, statistics, human development, theories of personality or abnormal psychology. Additional exam requirements/recommendations for international students: Required—TOEFL (minimum score 600 paper-based). *Application deadline:* For fall admission, 1/15 priority date for domestic students, 1/15 for international students. Application fee: $50. Electronic applications accepted. *Expenses:* Tuition: Full-time $26,600. *Financial support:* In 2010–11, 150 students received support, including 4 research assistantships (averaging $1,600 per year), 25 teaching assistantships (averaging $1,600 per year); career-related internships or fieldwork, Federal Work-Study, and scholarships/grants also available. Financial award application deadline: 11/30; financial award applicants required to submit FAFSA. *Faculty research:* Time-limited dynamic psychotherapy; mindfulness/ACT; psychotherapy integration; empathy, altruism and survivor guilt; culturally-informed practice. *Unit head:* Dr. Charles Alexander, Dean, 510-841-9230 Ext. 101, E-mail: calexander@wi.edu. *Application contact:* Melissa Delaney, Director of Admissions, 510-841-9230 Ext. 170, Fax: 510-841-0167, E-mail: mdelaney@wi.edu.

Wright State University, School of Graduate Studies, College of Science and Mathematics, Department of Psychology, Dayton, OH 45435. Offers human factors and industrial/organizational psychology (MS, PhD). *Degree requirements:* For master's, thesis; for doctorate, thesis/dissertation. *Entrance requirements:* For master's, GRE General Test. Additional exam requirements/recommendations for international students: Required—TOEFL.

Wright State University, School of Professional Psychology, Dayton, OH 45435. Offers clinical psychology (Psy D). *Accreditation:* APA. *Degree requirements:* For doctorate, thesis/dissertation. *Entrance requirements:* For doctorate, GRE General Test, GRE Subject Test. Additional exam requirements/recommendations for international students: Required—TOEFL. *Expenses:* Contact institution.

Xavier University, College of Social Sciences, Health and Education, Department of Psychology, Cincinnati, OH 45207. Offers clinical psychology (Psy D); psychology (MA), including general experimental psychology, industrial-organizational psychology. *Accreditation:* APA (one or more programs are accredited). *Faculty:* 16 full-time (8 women), 5 part-time/adjunct (2 women). *Students:* 87 full-time (65 women), 26 part-time (21 women); includes 11 minority (4 Black or African American, non-Hispanic/Latino; 1 American Indian or Alaska Native, non-Hispanic/Latino; 3 Asian, non-Hispanic/Latino; 3 Hispanic/Latino), 2 international. Average age 27. 292 applicants, 22% accepted, 25 enrolled. In 2010, 26 master's, 16 doctorates awarded. *Degree requirements:* For master's, one foreign language, comprehensive exam, thesis, internship; for doctorate, one foreign language, comprehensive exam, thesis/dissertation, internship. *Entrance requirements:* For master's and doctorate, GRE. Additional exam requirements/recommendations for international students: Required—TOEFL, IELTS. *Application deadline:* For fall admission, 12/15 for domestic and international students. Application fee: $35. Electronic applications accepted. *Expenses:* Contact institution. *Financial support:* In 2010–11, 54 students received support, including 41 research assistantships with partial tuition reimbursements available, 13 teaching assistantships with partial tuition reimbursements available; scholarships/grants and unspecified assistantships also available. Financial award application deadline: 3/1; financial award applicants required to submit FAFSA. *Faculty research:* Older adults, clinical child and adolescent issues, personnel selection and employee behavior, at-risk youth, sexual abuse. *Unit head:* Dr. Karl Stukenberg, Chair, 513-745-1041, Fax: 513-745-3327, E-mail: stukenb@xavier.edu. *Application contact:* Margaret Maybury, Assistant Director, Enrollment and Student Services, 513-745-1053, Fax: 513-745-3347, E-mail: maybury@xavier.edu.

Yale University, Graduate School of Arts and Sciences, Department of Psychology, New Haven, CT 06520. Offers behavioral neuroscience (PhD); clinical psychology (PhD); cognitive psychology (PhD); developmental psychology (PhD); social/personality psychology (PhD). *Accreditation:* APA. *Degree requirements:* For doctorate, thesis/dissertation. *Entrance requirements:* For doctorate, GRE General Test.

Yeshiva University, Ferkauf Graduate School of Psychology, New York, NY 10033-3201. Offers MA, PhD, Psy D. *Accreditation:* APA (one or more programs are accredited). Part-time programs available. *Degree requirements:* For doctorate, comprehensive exam, thesis/dissertation. *Entrance requirements:* For master's and doctorate, GRE General Test.

York University, Faculty of Graduate Studies, Faculty of Health, Program in Psychology, Toronto, ON M3J 1P3, Canada. Offers MA, PhD. *Accreditation:* APA (one or more programs are accredited). Part-time programs available. *Degree requirements:* For master's, thesis, practicum; for doctorate, thesis/dissertation, practicum. *Entrance requirements:* For master's, GRE. Electronic applications accepted.

Youngstown State University, Graduate School, College of Liberal Arts and Social Sciences, Department of Psychology, Youngstown, OH 44555-0001. Offers applied behavior analysis (MS).

Addictions/Substance Abuse Counseling

Adler School of Professional Psychology, Programs in Psychology, Chicago, IL 60602. Offers advanced Adlerian psychotherapy (Certificate); art therapy (MA); clinical neuropsychology (Certificate); clinical psychology (Psy D); community psychology (MA); counseling and organizational psychology (MA); counseling psychology (MA); forensic psychology (MA); gerontological counseling (MA); marriage and family counseling (MA); marriage and family therapy (Certificate); organizational psychology (MA); police psychology (MA); rehabilitation counseling (MA); sport and health psychology (MA); substance abuse counseling (Certificate); Psy D/Certificate; Psy D/MACAT; Psy D/MACP; Psy D/MAMFC; Psy D/MASAC. *Accreditation:* APA. Part-time and evening/weekend programs available. Postbaccalaureate distance learning degree programs offered (minimal on-campus study). *Faculty:* 40 full-time (18 women), 61 part-time/adjunct (31 women). *Students:* 688 full-time (532 women), 142 part-time (110 women). Average age 27.Terminal master's awarded for partial completion of doctoral program. *Degree requirements:* For master's, thesis or alternative, oral exam, practicum; for doctorate, thesis/dissertation, clinical exam, internship, oral exam, practicum, written qualifying exam. *Entrance requirements:* For master's, 12 semester hours in psychology, minimum GPA of 3.0; for doctorate, 18 semester hours in psychology, minimum GPA of 3.25; for Certificate, appropriate master's or doctoral degree. Additional exam requirements/recommendations for international students: Required—TOEFL (minimum score 550 paper-based; 213 computer-based; 79 iBT). *Application deadline:* For fall admission, 2/15 priority date for domestic students, 12/1 priority date for international students. Applications are processed on a rolling basis. Application fee: $50. Electronic applications accepted. *Financial support:* Career-related internships or fieldwork, Federal Work-Study, scholarships/grants, and tuition waivers (full and partial) available. Support available to part-time students. Financial award application deadline: 5/15; financial award applicants required to submit FAFSA. *Application contact:* Michelle Brice, Director of Admissions, 312-662-4113, Fax: 312-662-4199, E-mail: admissions@adler.edu.

See Display on page 912 and Close-Up on page 1119.

Alliant International University–Los Angeles, California School of Professional Psychology, Program in Marital and Family Therapy, Alhambra, CA 91803-1360. Offers biofeedback (MA); chemical dependency (MA); gerontology (MA); Latin American family therapy (MA). *Accreditation:* AAMFT/COAMFTE.

Argosy University, Hawai'i, College of Psychology and Behavioral Sciences, Program in Substance Abuse Counseling, Honolulu, HI 96813. Offers Certificate.

See Close-Up on page 1129.

Cambridge College, School of Psychology and Counseling, Cambridge, MA 02138-5304. Offers addiction counseling (M Ed); alcohol and drug counseling (Certificate); counseling psychology (M Ed, CAGS); counseling psychology: forensic counseling (M Ed); marriage and family therapy (M Ed); mental health and addiction counseling (M Ed); mental health counseling (M Ed); mental health counseling for school guidance counselors (Post Master's Certificate); psychological studies (M Ed); school adjustment and mental health counseling (M Ed); school adjustment, mental health and addiction counseling (M Ed); school guidance counselor (M Ed); trauma studies (Certificate). Part-time and evening/weekend programs available. *Faculty:* 4 full-time (2 women), 83 part-time/adjunct (48 women). *Students:* 436 full-time (351 women), 351 part-time (274 women); includes 321 Black or African American, non-Hispanic/Latino; 3 American Indian or Alaska Native, non-Hispanic/Latino; 4 Asian, non-Hispanic/Latino; 87 Hispanic/Latino; 4 Two or more races, non-Hispanic/Latino, 6 international. Average age 37. In 2010, 284 master's, 16 other advanced degrees awarded. *Degree requirements:* For master's and other advanced degree, thesis, practicum/internship. *Entrance requirements:* For master's, resume, 2 professional references; for other advanced degree, official transcripts, documents for transfer credit evaluation, resume, written personal statement/essay, 2 professional references, health insurance, immunizations form. Additional exam requirements/recommendations for international students: Required—TOEFL (minimum score 550 paper-based; 213 computer-based; 79 iBT); Recommended—IELTS (minimum score 6). *Application deadline:* Applications are processed on a rolling basis. Application fee: $30. Electronic applications accepted. *Expenses:* Contact institution. *Financial support:* Career-related internships or fieldwork, Federal Work-Study, and scholarships/grants available. Financial award applicants required to submit FAFSA. *Faculty research:* Trauma, drug and alcohol counseling, cross-cultural issues, school counseling, trauma in schools. *Unit head:* Dr. Niti Seth, Dean, 617-873-0208, Fax: 617-349-3561, E-mail: nseth@cambridgecollege.edu. *Application contact:* Elaine M. Lapomardo, Dean of Enrollment Management, 617-873-0274, Fax: 617-349-3561, E-mail: elaine.lapomardo@cambridgecollege.edu.

Capella University, School of Human Services, Minneapolis, MN 55402. Offers addictions counseling (Certificate); counseling studies (MS, PhD); criminal justice (MS, PhD, Certificate); diversity studies (Certificate); general human services (MS, PhD); health care administration (MS, PhD, Certificate); management of nonprofit agencies (MS, PhD, Certificate); marital, couple and family counseling/therapy (MS); marriage and family services (Certificate); mental health counseling (MS); professional counseling (Certificate); social and community services (MS, PhD, Certificate). Part-time and evening/weekend programs available. Postbaccalaureate distance learning degree programs offered (minimal on-campus study). Terminal master's awarded for partial completion of doctoral program. *Degree requirements:* For master's, thesis optional, integrative project; for doctorate, comprehensive exam, thesis/dissertation. *Entrance requirements:* Additional exam requirements/recommendations for international students: Required—TOEFL (minimum score 550 paper-based; 213 computer-based), TWE (minimum score 4). Electronic applications accepted. *Expenses:* Tuition: Full-time $11,880; part-time $440 per credit hour. *Faculty research:* Compulsive and addictive behaviors, substance abuse, assessment of psychopathology and neuropsychology.

Cleveland State University, College of Graduate Studies, College of Education and Human Services, Department of Counseling, Administration, Supervision and Adult Learning (CASAL), Cleveland, OH 44115. Offers accelerated degree in adult learning and development (M Ed); adult learning and development (M Ed); chemical dependency counseling (Certificate); community agency counseling (M Ed); counseling and pupil personnel administration (Ed S); early childhood mental health counseling (Certificate); educational administration and supervision (M Ed); school administration (Ed S); school counseling (M Ed). *Accreditation:* ACA (one or more programs are accredited). Part-time and evening/weekend programs available. *Faculty:* 14 full-time (8 women), 16 part-time/adjunct (6 women). *Students:* 64 full-time (53 women), 285 part-time (223 women); includes 108 Black or African American, non-Hispanic/Latino; 3 Asian, non-Hispanic/Latino; 8 Hispanic/Latino; 1 Two or more races, non-Hispanic/Latino, 4 international. Average age 35. 235 applicants, 56% accepted, 104 enrolled. In 2010, 128 master's, 10 other advanced degrees awarded. *Degree requirements:* For master's, comprehensive exam (for some programs), thesis optional; for other advanced degree, comprehensive exam, thesis optional, internship. *Entrance requirements:* For master's, GRE General Test or MAT, letter of recommendation, minimum GPA of 2.75. Additional exam requirements/recommendations for international students: Required—TOEFL (minimum score 525 paper-based; 197 computer-based), IELTS (minimum score 6). *Application deadline:* For fall admission, 6/21 for domestic students, 5/15 for international students; for spring admission, 8/31 for domestic students, 11/1 for international students. Application fee: $30. Electronic applications accepted. *Expenses:* Tuition: state resident: full-time $8447; part-time $469 per credit hour. Tuition, nonresident: full-time $16,020; part-time $890 per credit hour. Required fees: $50. *Financial support:* In 2010–11, 17 students received support, including 7 research assistantships with full and partial tuition reimbursements available (averaging $9,882 per year), 6 teaching assistantships with full and partial tuition reimbursements available (averaging $9,882 per year); scholarships/grants, tuition waivers (full), and unspecified assistantships also available. Support available to part-time students. *Faculty research:* Education law, career development, women in school administration, psychopharmacology, counseling and spirituality. Total annual research expenditures: $433,211. *Unit head:* Dr. Ann L. Bauer, Chairperson,

216-687-4582, Fax: 216-687-5378, E-mail: a.l.bauer@csuohio.edu. *Application contact:* Deborah L. Brown, Interim Assistant Director, Graduate Admissions, 216-523-7572, Fax: 216-687-5400, E-mail: d.l.brown@csuohio.edu.

The College of New Jersey, Graduate Division, School of Education, Department of Counselor Education, Program in Community Counseling: Substance Abuse and Addiction Specialization, Ewing, NJ 08628. Offers MA, Certificate. Part-time programs available. *Students:* 3 full-time (all women), 4 part-time (all women); includes 1 Hispanic/Latino. 14 applicants, 29% accepted, 2 enrolled. In 2010, 1 other advanced degree awarded. *Degree requirements:* For master's, comprehensive exam. *Entrance requirements:* For master's, GRE, minimum GPA of 3.0 in field or 2.75 overall; for Certificate, previous master's degree or higher. Additional exam requirements/recommendations for international students: Required—TOEFL. *Application deadline:* For fall admission, 2/1 for domestic students; for spring admission, 10/1 for domestic students. Application fee: $70. Electronic applications accepted. *Financial support:* Tuition waivers (partial) and unspecified assistantships available. Financial award application deadline: 5/1; financial award applicants required to submit FAFSA. *Unit head:* Dr. Mark Woodford, Coordinator, 609-771-3018, Fax: 609-637-5166, E-mail: woodford@tcnj.edu. *Application contact:* Susan L. Hydro, Assistant Dean, Office of Graduate Studies, 609-771-2300, Fax: 609-637-5105, E-mail: graduate@tcnj.edu.

College of St. Joseph, Graduate Programs, Division of Psychology and Human Services, Program in Alcohol and Substance Abuse Counseling, Rutland, VT 05701-3899. Offers MS. Part-time programs available. *Faculty:* 4 full-time (1 woman), 7 part-time/adjunct (4 women). *Students:* 4 full-time (2 women), 2 part-time (1 woman). Average age 46. 2 applicants, 100% accepted, 1 enrolled. *Degree requirements:* For master's, comprehensive exam. *Entrance requirements:* For master's, 2 letters of reference, interview. *Application deadline:* Applications are processed on a rolling basis. Application fee: $35. Electronic applications accepted. *Expenses:* Tuition: Full-time $14,200; part-time $400 per credit hour. Required fees: $45 per semester. *Financial support:* Application deadline: 3/1. *Unit head:* Dr. Craig Knapp, Chair, 802-773-5900 Ext. 3219, Fax: 802-776-5258, E-mail: cknapp@csj.edu. *Application contact:* Alan Young, Dean of Admissions, 802-773-5900 Ext. 3227, Fax: 802-776-5310, E-mail: alanyoung@csj.edu.

The College of William and Mary, School of Education, Program in Counselor Education, Williamsburg, VA 23187-8795. Offers community and addictions counseling (M Ed); community counseling (M Ed); counselor education (PhD); family counseling (M Ed); school counseling (M Ed). *Accreditation:* ACA; NCATE. Part-time and evening/weekend programs available. *Faculty:* 6 full-time (3 women), 7 part-time/adjunct (6 women). *Students:* 68 full-time (59 women), 8 part-time (4 women); includes 16 minority (9 Black or African American, non-Hispanic/Latino; 2 Asian, non-Hispanic/Latino; 3 Hispanic/Latino; 2 Two or more races, non-Hispanic/Latino), 2 international. Average age 29. 148 applicants, 41% accepted, 31 enrolled. In 2010, 27 master's, 1 doctorate awarded. *Degree requirements:* For doctorate, comprehensive exam, thesis/dissertation. *Entrance requirements:* For master's, GRE, minimum GPA of 3.0; for doctorate, GRE, minimum GPA of 3.5. Additional exam requirements/recommendations for international students: Required—TOEFL. *Application deadline:* For fall admission, 1/15 for domestic and international students. Application fee: $50. Electronic applications accepted. *Expenses:* Tuition, state resident: full-time $6400; part-time $345 per credit hour. Tuition, nonresident: full-time $19,720; part-time $920 per credit hour. Required fees: $4368. *Financial support:* In 2010–11, 54 students received support, including 1 fellowship with full tuition reimbursement available (averaging $20,000 per year), 48 research assistantships with full tuition reimbursements available (averaging $13,000 per year); career-related internships or fieldwork, Federal Work-Study, institutionally sponsored loans, scholarships/grants, and unspecified assistantships also available. Financial award application deadline: 1/15; financial award applicants required to submit FAFSA. *Faculty research:* Sexuality, multicultural education, substance abuse, transpersonal psychology. *Unit head:* Dr. Charles McAdams, Area Coordinator, 757-221-2338, E-mail: crmcad@wm.edu. *Application contact:* Dorothy Smith Osborne, Assistant Dean for Admission, 757-221-2317, Fax: 757-221-2293, E-mail: dsosbo@wm.edu.

Coppin State University, Division of Graduate Studies, Division of Arts and Sciences, Department of Applied Psychology and Rehabilitation Counseling, Program in Alcohol and Substance Abuse Counseling, Baltimore, MD 21216-3698. Offers MS. Part-time programs available. *Degree requirements:* For master's, comprehensive exam (for some programs), thesis optional, internship, clinical requirement. *Entrance requirements:* For master's, GRE General Test, interview, minimum GPA of 3.0.

East Carolina University, Graduate School, School of Allied Health Sciences, Program in Rehabilitation Studies, Greenville, NC 27858-4353. Offers rehabilitation counseling (MS); substance abuse and clinical counseling (MS); vocational evaluation (MS). *Accreditation:* CORE. Part-time and evening/weekend programs available. *Degree requirements:* For master's, comprehensive exam, thesis or alternative, internship. *Entrance requirements:* For master's, GRE General Test or MAT. Additional exam requirements/recommendations for international students: Required—TOEFL. *Expenses:* Tuition, state resident: full-time $3130; part-time $391.25 per credit hour. Tuition, nonresident: full-time $13,817; part-time $1727.13 per credit hour. Required fees: $1916; $239.50 per credit hour. Tuition and fees vary according to campus/location and program.

Eastern Michigan University, Graduate School, College of Health and Human Services, School of Social Work, Ypsilanti, MI 48197. Offers family and children's services (MSW); mental health and chemical dependency (MSW); services to the aging (MSW). *Accreditation:* CSWE. Part-time and evening/weekend programs available. *Faculty:* 19 full-time (15 women). *Students:* 20 full-time (18 women), 201 part-time (181 women); includes 89 minority (81 Black or African American, non-Hispanic/Latino; 1 American Indian or Alaska Native, non-Hispanic/Latino; 1 Asian, non-Hispanic/Latino; 4 Hispanic/Latino; 2 Two or more races, non-Hispanic/Latino), 1 international. Average age 36. 300 applicants, 33% accepted, 89 enrolled. In 2010, 76 master's awarded. *Entrance requirements:* Additional exam requirements/recommendations for international students: Required—TOEFL. *Application deadline:* For fall admission, 1/15 priority date for domestic students. Applications are processed on a rolling basis. Application fee: $35. *Financial support:* Fellowships, research assistantships with full tuition reimbursements, teaching assistantships with full tuition reimbursements, career-related internships or fieldwork, Federal Work-Study, institutionally sponsored loans, scholarships/grants, tuition waivers (partial), and unspecified assistantships available. Support available to part-time students. Financial award applicants required to submit FAFSA. *Unit head:* Dr. Ann Alvarez, Director, 734-487-0393, Fax: 734-487-6832, E-mail: aalvare4@emich.edu. *Application contact:* Julie Harkema, Admissions Director, 734-487-4206, Fax: 734-487-6832, E-mail: jharkema@emich.edu.

Governors State University, College of Health Professions, Program in Addictions Studies, University Park, IL 60466-0975. Offers MHS. Part-time and evening/weekend programs available. *Degree requirements:* For master's, comprehensive exam, thesis or alternative, internship. *Entrance requirements:* For master's, minimum undergraduate GPA of 2.5; 9 hours of course work in behavioral sciences; 6 hours of course work in biological sciences or chemistry, statistics or research methods. *Expenses:* Tuition, state resident: full-time $5400; part-time $225 per credit hour. Tuition, nonresident: full-time $16,200; part-time $675 per credit hour. Required fees: $1358; $46 per credit hour. $126 per term. Tuition and fees vary according to degree level and program.

Grand Canyon University, College of Nursing and Health Sciences, Phoenix, AZ 85017-1097. Offers addiction counseling (MS); health care administration (MS); health care informatics (MS); marriage and family therapy (MS); professional counseling (MS); public health (MS). Part-time and evening/weekend programs available. Postbaccalaureate distance learning degree

Addictions/Substance Abuse Counseling

Grand Canyon University (continued)
programs offered (no on-campus study). *Faculty:* 2 full-time (1 woman), 54 part-time/adjunct (36 women). *Students:* 2 full-time (both women), 1,818 part-time (1,476 women); includes 414 minority (346 Black or African American, non-Hispanic/Latino; 14 American Indian or Alaska Native, non-Hispanic/Latino; 4 Asian, non-Hispanic/Latino; 29 Hispanic/Latino; 3 Native Hawaiian or other Pacific Islander, non-Hispanic/Latino; 18 Two or more races, non-Hispanic/Latino), 1 international. Average age 44. In 2010, 103 master's awarded. *Entrance requirements:* For master's, undergraduate degree with minimum GPA of 2.8. Additional exam requirements/recommendations for international students: Required—TOEFL (minimum score 575 paper-based; 233 computer-based; 90 iBT), IELTS (minimum score 7). *Application deadline:* For fall admission, 8/21 for domestic students, 7/2 for international students; for spring admission, 12/24 for domestic students, 11/1 for international students. Application fee: $0. *Financial support:* Federal Work-Study available. Support available to part-time students. Financial award applicants required to submit FAFSA. *Unit head:* Dr. Mark Wooden, Dean, 602-639-6815, E-mail: mark.wooden@gcu.edu. *Application contact:* Andrea Wolochuk, Information Contact, 602-639-6429, E-mail: awolochuk@gcu.edu.

Hazelden Graduate School of Addiction Studies, Graduate Programs, Center City, MN 55012. Offers addiction counseling (MA, Certificate). Part-time programs available. *Entrance requirements:* Additional exam requirements/recommendations for international students: Required—TOEFL.

Indiana University–Purdue University Indianapolis, School of Science, Department of Psychology, Psychobiology of Addictions Program, Indianapolis, IN 46202-2896. Offers MS, PhD. *Faculty:* 7 full-time (3 women). *Students:* 13 full-time (9 women), 5 part-time (4 women); includes 1 minority (Black or African American, non-Hispanic/Latino). Average age 29. 14 applicants, 36% accepted, 4 enrolled. *Entrance requirements:* For master's, GRE General Test, minimum undergraduate GPA of 3.2. *Application deadline:* For fall admission, 1/1 for domestic students. Application fee: $55 ($65 for international students). *Financial support:* Fellowships with partial tuition reimbursements, research assistantships with partial tuition reimbursements, teaching assistantships with partial tuition reimbursements, career-related internships or fieldwork and Federal Work-Study available. Financial award application deadline: 3/1; financial award applicants required to submit FAFSA. *Faculty research:* Behavioral genetics, behavior pharmacology, animal models, developmental psychology, neurobehavioral toxicology, neuropsychology of learning and memory, animal models of fetal alcohol syndrome. *Unit head:* Dr. J. Gregor Fetterman, Chairman, 317-274-6945, Fax: 317-274-6756, E-mail: gfetter@iupui.edu. *Application contact:* Dr. J. Gregor Fetterman, Chairman, 317-274-6945, Fax: 317-274-6756, E-mail: gfetter@iupui.edu.

Indiana Wesleyan University, Graduate School, College of Arts and Sciences, Marion, IN 46953. Offers addictions counseling (MS); clinical mental health counseling (MS); community counseling (MS); marriage and family therapy (MS); school counseling (MS); student development counseling and administration (MS). *Accreditation:* ACA. Part-time programs available. *Degree requirements:* For master's, thesis or alternative. *Entrance requirements:* For master's, GRE General Test. Additional exam requirements/recommendations for international students: Required—TOEFL. Electronic applications accepted. *Expenses:* Contact institution. *Faculty research:* Community counseling, multicultural counseling, addictions.

The Johns Hopkins University, Bloomberg School of Public Health, Department of Mental Health, Baltimore, MD 21218-2699. Offers children's mental health services (PhD); drug dependence epidemiology (PhD); mental health (MHS, Dr PH); psychiatric epidemiology (PhD). *Faculty:* 26 full-time (14 women), 46 part-time/adjunct (18 women). *Students:* 49 full-time (37 women), 5 part-time (4 women); includes 1 Native Hawaiian or other Pacific Islander, non-Hispanic/Latino; 6 Two or more races, non-Hispanic/Latino. Average age 33. 73 applicants, 67% accepted, 27 enrolled. In 2010, 21 master's, 8 doctorates awarded. *Degree requirements:* For master's, thesis (for some programs); for doctorate, thesis/dissertation, 1 year full-time residency, oral and written exams. *Entrance requirements:* For master's, GRE General Test, MCAT, 3 letters of recommendation, curriculum vitae; for doctorate, GRE General Test, MCAT or GMAT, 3 letters of recommendation, curriculum vitae. Additional exam requirements/recommendations for international students: Required—TOEFL (minimum score 600 paper-based; 250 computer-based; 100 iBT). *Application deadline:* For fall admission, 12/1 priority date for domestic and international students. Applications are processed on a rolling basis. Application fee: $45. Electronic applications accepted. *Financial support:* In 2010–11, 1 fellowship (averaging $32,000 per year) was awarded; Federal Work-Study, institutionally sponsored loans, scholarships/grants, traineeships, and stipends also available. Support available to part-time students. Financial award application deadline: 3/15; financial award applicants required to submit FAFSA. *Faculty research:* Etiology, development and prevention of aggressive and antisocial behavior; epidemiology of mental disorders; genetic epidemiology of mental disorders; brain and behavior. Total annual research expenditures: $12 million. *Unit head:* Dr. William W. Eaton, Chair, 410-955-3910, Fax: 410-614-7469, E-mail: weaton@jhsph.edu. *Application contact:* Patricia E. Scott, Senior Academic Program Coordinator, 410-955-1906, Fax: 410-955-9088, E-mail: mhdept@jhsph.edu.

Kean University, College of Education, Program in Counselor Education, Union, NJ 07083. Offers alcohol and drug abuse counseling (MA); clinical mental heath counseling (MA); school counseling (MA). *Accreditation:* ACA; NCATE. Part-time programs available. *Faculty:* 5 full-time (3 women). *Students:* 66 full-time (59 women), 216 part-time (192 women); includes 44 Black or African American, non-Hispanic/Latino; 4 Asian, non-Hispanic/Latino; 44 Hispanic/Latino; 1 Two or more races, non-Hispanic/Latino, 1 international. Average age 32. 152 applicants, 72% accepted, 61 enrolled. In 2010, 48 master's awarded. *Degree requirements:* For master's, comprehensive exam, practicum, internship. *Entrance requirements:* For master's, GRE General Test or MAT, minimum GPA of 3.0, 2 letters of recommendation, interview. *Application deadline:* For fall admission, 6/1 for domestic students; for spring admission, 11/1 for domestic students. Application fee: $75 ($150 for international students). Electronic applications accepted. *Expenses:* Tuition, state resident: full-time $10,872; part-time $500 per credit. Tuition, nonresident: full-time $14,736; part-time $614 per credit. Required fees: $2740.80; $125 per credit. Part-time tuition and fees vary according to course load and degree level. *Financial support:* In 2010–11, 2 research assistantships with full tuition reimbursements (averaging $3,263 per year) were awarded; unspecified assistantships also available. Financial award applicants required to submit FAFSA. *Unit head:* Dr. J. Barry Mascari, Program Coordinator, 908-737-3863, E-mail: jmascari@kean.edu. *Application contact:* Steven Koch, Pre-Admissions Coordinator, 908-737-5924, Fax: 908-737-5925, E-mail: skoch@kean.edu.

Lewis & Clark College, Graduate School of Education and Counseling, Department of Counseling Psychology, Program in Addictions Treatment, Portland, OR 97219-7899. Offers MA, MS. Part-time and evening/weekend programs available. *Faculty:* 1 full-time (0 women), 4 part-time/adjunct (3 women). *Students:* 26 full-time (19 women), 8 part-time (all women); includes 2 Hispanic/Latino; 1 Two or more races, non-Hispanic/Latino, 1 international. Average age 33. 23 applicants, 87% accepted, 12 enrolled. In 2010, 8 master's awarded. *Degree requirements:* For master's, thesis (MS). *Entrance requirements:* For master's, GRE General Test, minimum undergraduate GPA of 2.75. Additional exam requirements/recommendations for international students: Required—TOEFL (minimum score 575 paper-based; 233 computer-based). *Application deadline:* For fall admission, 2/1 priority date for domestic and international students; for spring admission, 10/1 priority date for domestic and international students. Application fee: $50. Electronic applications accepted. *Expenses:* Tuition: Part-time $713 per semester hour. Tuition and fees vary according to course level and campus/location. *Financial support:* In 2010–11, 1 student received support. Career-related internships or fieldwork, Federal Work-Study, institutionally sponsored loans, scholarships/grants, health care benefits, and tuition waivers (partial) available. Support available to part-time students. Financial award applicants required to submit FAFSA. *Unit head:* Dr. Boyd Pidcock, Program Coordinator, 503-768-6060, Fax: 503-768-6065, E-mail: cpsy@lclark.edu. *Application contact:* Becky Haas, Director of Admissions, 503-768-6200, Fax: 503-768-6205, E-mail: gseadmit@lclark.edu.

Long Island University, C.W. Post Campus, School of Health Professions and Nursing, Master of Social Work Program, Brookville, NY 11548-1300. Offers alcohol and substance abuse (MSW); child and family welfare (MSW); forensic social work (MSW); gerontology (MSW); nonprofit management (MSW). *Accreditation:* CSWE.

Maryville University of Saint Louis, School of Health Professions, Program in Rehabilitation Counseling, St. Louis, MO 63141-7299. Offers marriage and family therapy (MARC); music therapy (MARC); rehabilitation counseling (CAGS); substance abuse (MARC). *Accreditation:* CORE. Part-time and evening/weekend programs available. *Students:* 21 full-time (16 women), 29 part-time (21 women); includes 11 minority (all Black or African American, non-Hispanic/Latino). Average age 33. In 2010, 19 master's awarded. *Degree requirements:* For master's, internship, seminar. *Entrance requirements:* For master's, minimum cumulative GPA of 3.0, 2 letters of recommendation, interview. Additional exam requirements/recommendations for international students: Required—TOEFL (minimum score 550 paper-based). *Application deadline:* For fall admission, 1/15 for domestic students; for spring admission, 10/1 for domestic students. Application fee: $40 ($60 for international students). Electronic applications accepted. *Expenses:* Tuition: Full-time $21,100; part-time $633.50 per credit hour. Required fees: $150 per semester. *Financial support:* Career-related internships or fieldwork, Federal Work-Study, and campus employment available. Financial award application deadline: 3/1; financial award applicants required to submit FAFSA. *Unit head:* Dr. Michael Kiener, Interim Director, 314-529-9443, Fax: 314-529-9495, E-mail: mkiener@maryville.edu. *Application contact:* Dr. Michael Kiener, Interim Director, 314-529-9443, Fax: 314-529-9495, E-mail: mkiener@maryville.edu.

McNeese State University, Doré School of Graduate Studies, Burton College of Education, Department of Psychology, Lake Charles, LA 70609. Offers addiction treatment (MA); applied behavior analysis (MA); counseling psychology (MA); general/experimental psychology (MA). Evening/weekend programs available. *Faculty:* 6 full-time (3 women). *Students:* 46 full-time (31 women), 29 part-time (21 women); includes 11 minority (6 Black or African American, non-Hispanic/Latino; 1 Asian, non-Hispanic/Latino; 2 Hispanic/Latino; 2 Two or more races, non-Hispanic/Latino), 4 international. In 2010, 14 master's awarded. *Entrance requirements:* For master's, GRE. *Application deadline:* For fall admission, 5/15 priority date for domestic and international students; for spring admission, 10/15 priority date for domestic and international students. Applications are processed on a rolling basis. Application fee: $20 ($30 for international students). Tuition and fees vary according to course load. *Financial support:* Application deadline: 5/1. *Unit head:* Dr. Dena L. Matzenbacher, Head, 337-475-5457, Fax: 337-562-4115, E-mail: dena@mcneese.edu. *Application contact:* Dr. George F. Mead, Interim Dean of Dore' School of Graduate Studies, 337-475-5396, Fax: 337-475-5397, E-mail: admissions@mcneese.edu.

Mercy College, School of Social and Behavioral Sciences, Program in Counseling, Dobbs Ferry, NY 10522-1189. Offers alcohol and substance abuse counseling (Certificate); counseling (MS); family counseling (Certificate). Part-time and evening/weekend programs available. Postbaccalaureate distance learning degree programs offered (no on-campus study). *Students:* 118 full-time (101 women), 207 part-time (183 women); includes 90 Black or African American, non-Hispanic/Latino; 1 American Indian or Alaska Native, non-Hispanic/Latino; 3 Asian, non-Hispanic/Latino; 127 Hispanic/Latino; 5 Two or more races, non-Hispanic/Latino. Average age 34. 194 applicants, 50% accepted, 74 enrolled. In 2010, 77 master's, 17 other advanced degrees awarded. *Degree requirements:* For master's, comprehensive exam. *Entrance requirements:* For master's, interview, two professional letters of recommendation, minimum undergraduate GPA of 3.0, resume. Additional exam requirements/recommendations for international students: Required—TOEFL (minimum score 600 paper-based; 250 computer-based; 100 iBT), IELTS (minimum score 8). *Application deadline:* For fall admission, 8/1 for international students. Applications are processed on a rolling basis. Application fee: $40. Electronic applications accepted. *Expenses:* Tuition: Full-time $13,572; part-time $754 per credit hour. Required fees: $130 per term. *Financial support:* Career-related internships or fieldwork, Federal Work-Study, scholarships/grants, and unspecified assistantships available. Support available to part-time students. Financial award applicants required to submit FAFSA. *Faculty research:* Ethics, drug abuse problems, human development, domestic violence. *Unit head:* Dr. Arthur McCann, Assistant Professor, Psychology and Behavioral Science, 914-674-7670, E-mail: amccann@mercy.edu. *Application contact:* Allison Gurdineer, Senior Associate Director of Recruitment, 914-674-7601, E-mail: agurdineer@mercy.edu.

Montclair State University, The Graduate School, College of Education and Human Services, Department of Counseling, Human Development, and Educational Leadership, Montclair, NJ 07043-1624. Offers advanced counseling (Certificate); certified alcohol and drug counselor (Certificate); counseling (MA), including addictions counseling, community counseling, school counseling, student affairs; counselor education (PhD); director of school counseling services (Certificate); educational leadership (MA), including adult and organizational learning, educational leadership; principal (Certificate); school business administrator (Certificate); school counselor (Certificate); substance awareness coordinator (Certificate); supervisor (Certificate). *Accreditation:* NCATE. Part-time and evening/weekend programs available. *Faculty:* 18 full-time (12 women), 37 part-time/adjunct (26 women). *Students:* 169 full-time (125 women), 385 part-time (281 women); includes 51 Black or African American, non-Hispanic/Latino; 13 Asian, non-Hispanic/Latino; 49 Hispanic/Latino; 1 Native Hawaiian or other Pacific Islander, non-Hispanic/Latino; 1 Two or more races, non-Hispanic/Latino, 4 international. Average age 31. 270 applicants, 57% accepted, 124 enrolled. In 2010, 172 master's, 13 other advanced degrees awarded. *Degree requirements:* For master's, comprehensive exam, thesis or alternative; for doctorate, comprehensive exam, thesis/dissertation. *Entrance requirements:* For master's, GRE General Test, interview, 2 letters of recommendation; for doctorate, GRE General Test, interview, 3 letters of recommendation. Additional exam requirements/recommendations for international students: Required—TOEFL (minimum iBT score of 83) or IELTS. *Application deadline:* For fall admission, 6/1 for international students; for spring admission, 10/1 for international students. Applications are processed on a rolling basis. Application fee: $60. Electronic applications accepted. *Expenses:* Tuition, state resident: part-time $501.34 per credit. Tuition, nonresident: part-time $773.88 per credit. Required fees: $71.15 per credit. *Financial support:* In 2010–11, 10 research assistantships with full tuition reimbursements (averaging $7,000 per year), 4 teaching assistantships (averaging $15,000 per year) were awarded; Federal Work-Study, scholarships/grants, and unspecified assistantships also available. Support available to part-time students. Financial award application deadline: 3/1; financial award applicants required to submit FAFSA. *Faculty research:* Multicultural counseling competence and training; adoption triad adjustment, issues and counseling; substance abuse treatment with underserved populations; role of data in school change; adult development: pedagogical issues for adult students and special populations. *Unit head:* Dr. Larry Burlew, Chairperson, 973-655-7611. *Application contact:* Amy Aiello, Director of Graduate Admissions and Operations, 973-655-5147, Fax: 973-655-7869, E-mail: graduate.school@montclair.edu.

Northeastern State University, Graduate College, College of Education, Department of Psychology and Counseling, Program in Substance Abuse Counseling, Tahlequah, OK 74464-2399. Offers MS. *Students:* 10 full-time (7 women), 15 part-time (9 women); includes 1 Black or African American, non-Hispanic/Latino; 6 American Indian or Alaska Native, non-Hispanic/Latino; 1 Asian, non-Hispanic/Latino. *Expenses:* Tuition, state resident: part-time $144 per credit hour. Tuition, nonresident: part-time $384.05 per credit hour. Required fees: $34.90 per credit hour. Tuition and fees vary according to program. *Unit head:* Dr. Kathryn Sanders, Chair, 918-456-5511 Ext. 3016, Fax: 918-458-2397, E-mail: sanderka@nsuok.edu. *Application contact:* Margie Railey, Administrative Assistant, 918-456-5511 Ext. 2093, Fax: 918-458-2061, E-mail: railey@nsouk.edu.

Pace University, Dyson College of Arts and Sciences, Department of Psychology, Program in Counseling-Substance Abuse, New York, NY 10038. Offers loss and grief (MS); mental health (MS); substance abuse (MS). Offered at Pleasantville, NY location only. Part-time and evening/weekend programs available. *Degree requirements:* For master's, comprehensive exam, qualifying exams, internship. *Entrance requirements:* For master's, GRE, interview. Additional exam requirements/recommendations for international students: Required—TOEFL. Electronic applications accepted.

Palm Beach Atlantic University, School of Education and Behavioral Studies, West Palm Beach, FL 33416-4708. Offers counseling psychology (MSCP), including addictions/mental health, marriage and family therapy, mental health counseling, school guidance counseling. Part-time and evening/weekend programs available. *Faculty:* 13 full-time (3 women), 10 part-time/adjunct (5 women). *Students:* 250 full-time (209 women), 61 part-time (47 women); includes 63 Black or African American, non-Hispanic/Latino; 2 Asian, non-Hispanic/Latino; 37 Hispanic/Latino; 1 Native Hawaiian or other Pacific Islander, non-Hispanic/Latino, 7 international. Average age 35. 108 applicants, 92% accepted, 83 enrolled. In 2010, 96 master's awarded. *Entrance requirements:* For master's, GRE, minimum GPA of 3.0. Additional exam requirements/recommendations for international students: Required—TOEFL (minimum score 550 paper-based; 213 computer-based). *Application deadline:* For fall admission, 7/15 priority date for domestic students; for spring admission, 11/15 priority date for domestic students. Applications are processed on a rolling basis. Application fee: $45. Electronic applications accepted. *Expenses:* Tuition: Full-time $8280; part-time $460 per credit hour. Required fees: $99 per semester. Tuition and fees vary according to course load, degree level and campus/location. *Financial support:* Applicants required to submit FAFSA. *Unit head:* Dr. Lisa Stubbs, Program Director, 561-803-2286. *Application contact:* Graduate Admissions, 888-468-6722, E-mail: grad@pba.edu.

St. Mary's University, Graduate School, Department of Counseling and Human Services, San Antonio, TX 78228-8507. Offers community counseling (MA); counseling (Sp C); counseling education and supervision (PhD); marriage and family relations (Certificate); marriage and family therapy (MA, PhD); mental health (MA); mental health and substance abuse counseling (Certificate); substance abuse (MA). *Accreditation:* AAMFT/COAMFTE (one or more programs are accredited); ACA (one or more programs are accredited). Postbaccalaureate distance learning degree programs offered (minimal on-campus study). *Degree requirements:* For master's, comprehensive exam, internship; for doctorate, comprehensive exam, thesis/dissertation, internship. *Entrance requirements:* For master's, GRE General Test, MAT; for doctorate, GRE General Test, recommendation from employers, admissions committee and department faculty. Additional exam requirements/recommendations for international students: Required—TOEFL (minimum score 550 paper-based; 213 computer-based; 80 iBT). Electronic applications accepted. *Expenses:* Contact institution.

Shippensburg University of Pennsylvania, School of Graduate Studies, College of Education and Human Services, Department of Counseling, Shippensburg, PA 17257-2299. Offers Adlerian studies (Certificate); advanced study in counseling (Certificate); alcohol and drug counseling (Certificate); counseling (M Ed, MS), including clinical mental health counseling (MS), college counseling (MS), college student personnel services (MS), elementary school counseling (M Ed), secondary school counseling (MS); couple and family counseling (Certificate). *Accreditation:* ACA (one or more programs are accredited); NCATE. Part-time and evening/weekend programs available. *Faculty:* 8 full-time (4 women), 5 part-time/adjunct (3 women). *Students:* 79 full-time (66 women), 105 part-time (92 women); includes 28 minority (20 Black or African American, non-Hispanic/Latino; 3 Asian, non-Hispanic/Latino; 4 Hispanic/Latino; 1 Two or more races, non-Hispanic/Latino), 2 international. Average age 29. 129 applicants, 45% accepted, 43 enrolled. In 2010, 45 master's awarded. *Degree requirements:* For master's, fieldwork, research project, internship, candidacy. *Entrance requirements:* For master's, GRE or MAT (mental health, student personnel, and college counseling applicants if GPA is less than 2.75), minimum GPA of 2.75 (3.0 for M Ed), resume, 3 letters of recommendation, supplemental data forms, one year of relevant work experience, on-campus interview, autobiographical statement. Additional exam requirements/recommendations for international students: Required—TOEFL (minimum score 580 paper-based; 237 computer-based); Recommended—IELTS (minimum score 6). *Application deadline:* For fall admission, 3/1 for international students; for spring admission, 7/1 for international students. Applications are processed on a rolling basis. Application fee: $30. Electronic applications accepted. *Expenses:* Tuition, state resident: full-time $6966. Tuition, nonresident: full-time $11,146. Required fees: $1802. *Financial support:* In 2010–11, 49 research assistantships with full tuition reimbursements (averaging $5,000 per year) were awarded; career-related internships or fieldwork, scholarships/grants, unspecified assistantships, and resident hall director and student payroll positions also available. Support available to part-time students. Financial award application deadline: 3/1; financial award applicants required to submit FAFSA. *Unit head:* Dr. Jan Arminio, Chairperson, 717-477-1668, Fax: 717-477-4016, E-mail: jlarmi@ship.edu. *Application contact:* Jeremy R. Goshorn, Associate Dean of Graduate Admissions, 717-477-1231, Fax: 717-477-4016, E-mail: jrgoshorn@ship.edu.

Southeastern Louisiana University, College of Education and Human Development, Department of Counseling and Human Development, Hammond, LA 70402. Offers counselor education (M Ed), including community counseling, marriage and family therapy, school counseling, substance abuse counseling. *Accreditation:* ACA; NCATE. Part-time programs available. *Faculty:* 7 full-time (5 women). *Students:* 62 full-time (58 women), 47 part-time (44 women); includes 26 minority (21 Black or African American, non-Hispanic/Latino; 1 American Indian or Alaska Native, non-Hispanic/Latino; 1 Asian, non-Hispanic/Latino; 2 Hispanic/Latino; 1 Two or more races, non-Hispanic/Latino). Average age 29. 50 applicants, 52% accepted, 16 enrolled. In 2010, 22 master's awarded. *Degree requirements:* For master's, comprehensive exam, 100-hour practicum, 600-hour internship. *Entrance requirements:* For master's, GRE (verbal and quantitative). Additional exam requirements/recommendations for international students: Required—TOEFL (minimum score 500 paper-based; 173 computer-based; 61 iBT). *Application deadline:* For fall admission, 7/15 priority date for domestic students, 6/1 priority date for international students; for spring admission, 12/1 priority date for domestic students, 10/1 priority date for international students. Applications are processed on a rolling basis. Application fee: $20 ($30 for international students). Electronic applications accepted. *Expenses:* Tuition, state resident: full-time $3533. Tuition, nonresident: full-time $12,002. Required fees: $907. Tuition and fees vary according to degree level. *Financial support:* In 2010–11, 5 students received support. Career-related internships or fieldwork, Federal Work-Study, institutionally sponsored loans, unspecified assistantships, and administrative assistantships available. Support available to part-time students. Financial award application deadline: 5/1; financial award applicants required to submit FAFSA. *Faculty research:* Play therapy, grief and loss, addictions, gratitude, couples relationships enrichment/spirituality. *Unit head:* Dr. June Williams, Interim Department Head, 985-549-2309, Fax: 985-549-3758, E-mail: jwilliams@selu.edu. *Application contact:* Sandra Meyers, Graduate Admissions Analyst, 985-549-2066, Fax: 985-549-5632, E-mail: admissions@selu.edu.

Southern New Hampshire University, School of Liberal Arts, Manchester, NH 03106-1045. Offers clinical services for adults psychiatric disabilities (Certificate); clinical services for children and adolescents with psychiatric disabilities (Certificate); clinical services for persons with co-occurring substance abuse and psychiatric disabilities (Certificate); community mental health (MS); fiction writing (MFA); non-fiction writing (MFA); teaching English as a foreign language (MS). Part-time and evening/weekend programs available. *Degree requirements:* For master's, one foreign language, thesis. *Entrance requirements:* For master's, minimum GPA of 2.75: MS-TEFL, 3.0: MFA. Additional exam requirements/recommendations for international students: Required—TOEFL (minimum score 550 paper-based; 213 computer-based; 79 iBT), IELTS (minimum score 6.5), TWE (minimum score 5). Electronic applications accepted. *Expenses:* Contact institution. *Faculty research:* Action research, state of the art practice in behavioral health services, wraparound approaches to working with youth, learning styles.

Springfield College, Graduate Programs, Programs in Rehabilitation Counseling and Services, Springfield, MA 01109-3797. Offers alcohol rehabilitation/substance abuse counseling (M Ed, MS); deaf counseling (M Ed, MS); developmental disabilities (M Ed, MS); general counseling and casework (M Ed, MS); psychiatric rehabilitation/mental health counseling (M Ed, MS); special services (M Ed, MS). *Accreditation:* CORE (one or more programs are accredited). Part-time programs available. *Degree requirements:* For master's, comprehensive exam.

Entrance requirements: Additional exam requirements/recommendations for international students: Required—TOEFL (minimum score 550 paper-based; 213 computer-based). Electronic applications accepted.

Stony Brook University, State University of New York, Stony Brook University Medical Center, School of Medicine, Program in Public Health, Stony Brook, NY 11794. Offers community health (MPH); evaluation sciences (MPH); family violence (MPH); health economics (MPH); population health (MPH); substance abuse (MPH). *Accreditation:* CEPH. *Faculty:* 7 full-time (5 women), 1 part-time/adjunct (0 women). *Students:* 21 full-time (15 women), 19 part-time (17 women); includes 2 Black or African American, non-Hispanic/Latino; 8 Asian, non-Hispanic/Latino; 2 Hispanic/Latino, 4 international. Average age 39. 90 applicants, 62% accepted. In 2010, 17 master's awarded. *Entrance requirements:* For master's, GRE, 3 references. Additional exam requirements/recommendations for international students: Required—TOEFL. *Application deadline:* For fall admission, 1/15 for domestic and international students. Application fee: $100. Electronic applications accepted. *Expenses:* Tuition, state resident: full-time $8370; part-time $349 per credit. Tuition, nonresident: full-time $13,780; part-time $574 per credit. Required fees: $994. *Faculty research:* Population health, health service research, health economics. *Unit head:* Dr. Raymond L. Goldsteen, Director, 631-444-2074, Fax: 631-444-3480, E-mail: raymond.goldsteen@stonybrook.edu. *Application contact:* Dr. Raymond L. Goldsteen, Director, 631-444-2074, Fax: 631-444-3480, E-mail: raymond.goldsteen@stonybrook.edu.

Syracuse University, College of Human Ecology, Program in Addiction Studies, Syracuse, NY 13244. Offers CAS. Part-time programs available. *Students:* 2 full-time (both women), 1 (woman) part-time; includes 1 minority (Hispanic/Latino). Average age 39. 3 applicants, 100% accepted, 3 enrolled. *Entrance requirements:* Additional exam requirements/recommendations for international students: Required—TOEFL (minimum score 100 iBT). *Application deadline:* For fall admission, 3/15 priority date for domestic and international students. Application fee: $75. Electronic applications accepted. *Expenses:* Tuition: Part-time $1162 per credit. *Financial support:* Application deadline: 1/1. *Unit head:* Dr. Maureen Thompson, Program Contact, 315-443-9815, Fax: 315-443-2562, E-mail: mlthomps@syr.edu. *Application contact:* Felecia Otero, Director of College Admissions, 315-443-5555, Fax: 315-443-2562, E-mail: inquire@hshp.syr.edu.

Troy University, Graduate School, College of Education, Program in Counseling and Psychology, Troy, AL 36082. Offers agency counseling (Ed S); clinical mental health (MS); community counseling (MS, Ed S); corrections counseling (MS); rehabilitation counseling (MS); school psychology (MS, Ed S); school psychometry (MS); social service counseling (MS); student affairs counseling (MS); substance abuse counseling (MS). *Accreditation:* ACA; CORE; NCATE. Part-time and evening/weekend programs available. *Students:* 419 full-time (338 women), 720 part-time (603 women); includes 696 minority (592 Black or African American, non-Hispanic/Latino; 8 American Indian or Alaska Native, non-Hispanic/Latino; 4 Asian, non-Hispanic/Latino; 46 Hispanic/Latino; 46 Two or more races, non-Hispanic/Latino). Average age 33. 326 applicants, 90% accepted. In 2010, 198 master's, 1 other advanced degree awarded. *Degree requirements:* For master's, comprehensive exam, thesis. *Entrance requirements:* For master's, MAT, minimum GPA of 2.5. Additional exam requirements/recommendations for international students: Required—TOEFL (minimum score 523 paper-based; 193 computer-based; 70 iBT), IELTS (minimum score 6). *Application deadline:* Applications are processed on a rolling basis. Application fee: $50. Electronic applications accepted. *Expenses:* Tuition, state resident: full-time $4428; part-time $246 per credit hour. Tuition, nonresident: full-time $8856; part-time $492 per credit hour. Required fees: $432; $24 per credit hour. $50 per term. Tuition and fees vary according to program. *Unit head:* Dr. Andrew Creamer, Chair, 334-670-3350, Fax: 334-670-32961, E-mail: drcreamer@troy.edu. *Application contact:* Brenda K. Campbell, Director of Graduate Admissions, 334-670-3178, Fax: 334-670-3733, E-mail: bcamp@troy.edu.

United States International University, School of Arts and Sciences, Nairobi, Kenya. Offers counseling psychology (MA), including chemical dependency, health psychology; international relations (MA), including development studies, diplomacy and foreign policy, peace and conflict studies. Part-time and evening/weekend programs available. *Faculty:* 43 full-time (14 women), 69 part-time/adjunct (28 women). *Students:* 94 full-time (60 women), 22 part-time (all women). Average age 30. 93 applicants, 80% accepted, 64 enrolled. In 2010, 33 master's awarded. *Degree requirements:* For master's, thesis, practicum. *Entrance requirements:* For master's, GRE General Test, 2 letters of recommendation, resume. Additional exam requirements/recommendations for international students: Required—TOEFL. *Application deadline:* For fall admission, 6/30 priority date for domestic and international students. Application fee: $50. *Financial support:* In 2010–11, 56 students received support, including 3 research assistantships (averaging $1,400 per year), 7 teaching assistantships (averaging $1,400 per year); career-related internships or fieldwork, scholarships/grants, and unspecified assistantships also available. Support available to part-time students. Financial award application deadline: 6/30; financial award applicants required to submit FAFSA. *Faculty research:* Trauma in children, African intellectualism, psychological assessment tools. *Unit head:* Prof. Mulinge Munyae, Dean, 254-02-3606-434, E-mail: mmulinge@usiu.ac.ke. *Application contact:* George Lumbasi, Director of Admissions, 254-02-3606563, Fax: 254-02-3606100, E-mail: glumbasi@usiu.ac.ke.

Universidad Central del Caribe, Program in Substance Abuse Counseling, Bayamón, PR 00960-6032. Offers MHS.

University of Arkansas at Pine Bluff, School of Arts and Sciences, Pine Bluff, AR 71601-2799. Offers addiction studies (MS).

University of California, Berkeley, UC Berkeley Extension, Certificate Programs in Behavioral and Health Sciences, Berkeley, CA 94720-1500. Offers alcohol and drug abuse studies (Certificate).

University of Central Oklahoma, College of Graduate Studies and Research, College of Liberal Arts, Department of Sociology, Criminal Justice and Substance Abuse Studies, Edmond, OK 73034-5209. Offers criminal justice management and administration (MA). Part-time programs available. *Entrance requirements:* Additional exam requirements/recommendations for international students: Required—TOEFL (minimum score 550 paper-based; 213 computer-based). Electronic applications accepted. *Faculty research:* Gender issues, violent offenders.

University of Detroit Mercy, College of Liberal Arts and Education, Department of Counseling and Addiction Studies, Program in Addiction Studies, Detroit, MI 48221. Offers Certificate. Part-time programs available.

University of Detroit Mercy, College of Liberal Arts and Education, Department of Counseling and Addiction Studies, Program in Counseling, Detroit, MI 48221. Offers addiction counseling (MA); community counseling (MA); school counseling (MA). *Accreditation:* ACA. Part-time and evening/weekend programs available. *Degree requirements:* For master's, thesis or alternative. *Entrance requirements:* For master's, minimum GPA of 2.75.

University of Illinois at Springfield, Graduate Programs, College of Education and Human Services, Program in Human Services, Springfield, IL 62703-5407. Offers alcoholism and substance abuse (MA); child and family services (MA); gerontology (MA); social services administration (MA). Part-time and evening/weekend programs available. Postbaccalaureate distance learning degree programs offered (no on-campus study). *Degree requirements:* For master's, internship; project or thesis. *Entrance requirements:* For master's, minimum undergraduate GPA of 3.0, 2 letters of recommendation. Additional exam requirements/recommendations for international students: Required—TOEFL (minimum score 500 paper-based; 176 computer-based; 61 iBT). Electronic applications accepted. *Expenses:* Tuition, state resident: full-time $6774; part-time $282.25 per credit hour. Tuition, nonresident: full-time $15,078; part-time $628.25 per credit hour. Required fees: $15.25 per credit hour. $492 per term.

Addictions/Substance Abuse Counseling

University of Lethbridge, School of Graduate Studies, Lethbridge, AB T1K 3M4, Canada. Offers accounting (MScM); addictions counseling (M Sc); agricultural biotechnology (M Sc); agricultural studies (M Sc, MA); anthropology (MA); archaeology (MA); art (MA, MFA); biochemistry (M Sc); biological sciences (M Sc); biomolecular science (PhD); biosystems and biodiversity (PhD); Canadian studies (MA); chemistry (M Sc); computer science (M Sc); computer science and geographical information science (M Sc); counseling psychology (M Ed); dramatic arts (MA); earth, space, and physical science (PhD); economics (MA); educational leadership (M Ed); English (MA); environmental science (M Sc); evolution and behavior (PhD); exercise science (M Sc); finance (MScM); French (MA); French/German (MA); French/Spanish (MA); general education (M Ed); general management (MScM); geography (M Sc, MA); German (MA); health science (M Sc); history (MA); human resource management and labour relations (MScM); individualized multidisciplinary (M Sc, MA); information systems (MScM); international management (MScM); kinesiology (M Sc, MA); management (M Sc, MA); marketing (MScM); mathematics (M Sc); music (M Mus, MA); Native American studies (MA); neuroscience (M Sc, PhD); new media (MA); nursing (M Sc); philosophy (MA); physics (M Sc); policy and strategy (MScM); political science (MA); psychology (M Sc, MA); religious studies (MA); social sciences (MA); sociology (MA); theatre and dramatic arts (MFA); theoretical and computational science (PhD); urban and regional studies (MA); women's studies (MA). Part-time and evening/weekend programs available. *Degree requirements:* For doctorate, comprehensive exam, thesis/dissertation. *Entrance requirements:* For master's, GMAT (M Sc in management), bachelor's degree in related field, minimum GPA of 3.0 during previous 20 graded semester courses, 2 years teaching or related experience (M Ed); for doctorate, master's degree, minimum graduate GPA of 3.5. Additional exam requirements/recommendations for international students: Required—TOEFL. *Faculty research:* Movement and brain plasticity, gibberellin physiology, photosynthesis, carbon cycling, molecular properties of main-group ring components.

University of Louisiana at Monroe, Graduate School, College of Education and Human Development, Department of Educational Leadership and Counseling, Program in Substance Abuse Counseling, Monroe, LA 71209-0001. Offers MA. Part-time and evening/weekend programs available. *Students:* 1 full-time (0 women), 5 part-time (3 women); includes 1 Black or African American, non-Hispanic/Latino; 1 Asian, non-Hispanic/Latino. Average age 37. In 2010, 6 master's awarded. *Degree requirements:* For master's, thesis optional, 600 hours clinical internship. *Entrance requirements:* For master's, GRE General Test, minimum GPA of 2.8 in last 60 hours. Additional exam requirements/recommendations for international students: Required—TOEFL (minimum score 500 paper-based; 173 computer-based; 61 iBT). *Application deadline:* For fall admission, 8/24 priority date for domestic students, 7/1 for international students; for winter admission, 12/14 for domestic students; for spring admission, 1/19 for domestic students, 11/1 for international students. Applications are processed on a rolling basis. Application fee: $20 ($30 for international students). Electronic applications accepted. *Expenses:* Tuition, state resident: full-time $2991; part-time $197 per credit hour. Tuition, nonresident: full-time $2991; part-time $197 per credit hour. International tuition: $10,288 full-time. *Financial support:* Career-related internships or fieldwork, Federal Work-Study, and unspecified assistantships available. Financial award application deadline: 4/1; financial award applicants required to submit FAFSA. *Faculty research:* Addictionology. *Unit head:* Dr. Mitchell Young, Coordinator, 318-342-1255, Fax: 318-342-3131, E-mail: myoung@ulm.edu. *Application contact:* Dr. Mitchell Young, Coordinator, 318-342-1255, Fax: 318-342-3131, E-mail: myoung@ulm.edu.

University of Louisville, Graduate School, Raymond A. Kent School of Social Work, Louisville, KY 40292-0001. Offers marriage and family therapy (PMC), including mental health; social work (MSSW, PhD), including alcohol and drug counseling (MSSW), gerontology (MSSW), marriage and family (PhD), school social work (MSSW). *Accreditation:* AAMFT/COAMFTE; CSWE (one or more programs are accredited). Part-time and evening/weekend programs available. *Faculty:* 23 full-time (15 women), 38 part-time/adjunct (21 women). *Students:* 259 full-time (209 women), 71 part-time (60 women); includes 84 minority (66 Black or African American, non-Hispanic/Latino; 1 American Indian or Alaska Native, non-Hispanic/Latino; 3 Asian, non-Hispanic/Latino; 6 Hispanic/Latino; 8 Two or more races, non-Hispanic/Latino), 7 international. Average age 32. 249 applicants, 78% accepted, 141 enrolled. In 2010, 141 master's, 7 doctorates awarded. *Degree requirements:* For doctorate, comprehensive exam, thesis/dissertation. *Entrance requirements:* For master's, GRE or minimum GPA of 2.75; for doctorate, GRE General Test, interview, writing sample. Additional exam requirements/recommendations for international students: Required—TOEFL (minimum score 550 paper-based; 213 computer-based; 79 iBT). *Application deadline:* For fall admission, 7/31 for domestic and international students. Applications are processed on a rolling basis. Application fee: $50. Electronic applications accepted. *Expenses:* Tuition, state resident: full-time $9144; part-time $508 per credit hour. Tuition, nonresident: full-time $19,026; part-time $1057 per credit hour. Tuition and fees vary according to program and reciprocity agreements. *Financial support:* In 2010–11, 70 students received support, including 9 research assistantships with full tuition reimbursements available (averaging $19,000 per year), 1 teaching assistantship (averaging $19,000 per year); Federal Work-Study, institutionally sponsored loans, scholarships/grants, health care benefits, and unspecified assistantships also available. Support available to part-time students. Financial award application deadline: 5/15; financial award applicants required to submit FAFSA. *Faculty research:* Child welfare, substance abuse, gerontology, family functioning, health behavior. Total annual research expenditures: $2.8 million. *Unit head:* Dr. Terry Singer, Dean, 502-852-6402, Fax: 502-852-0422, E-mail: terry.singer@louisville.edu. *Application contact:* Libby Leggett, Director, Graduate Admissions, 502-852-3101, Fax: 502-852-6536, E-mail: gradadm@louisville.edu.

University of Mary, School of Education and Behavioral Sciences, Department of Behavioral Sciences, Bismarck, ND 58504-9652. Offers addiction counseling (MSC); community counseling (MSC); school counseling (MSC); student affairs counseling (MSC). Part-time programs available. Postbaccalaureate distance learning degree programs offered (minimal on-campus study). *Faculty:* 11 part-time/adjunct (8 women). *Students:* 32 full-time (21 women), 25 part-time (21 women); includes 4 Black or African American, non-Hispanic/Latino; 1 American Indian or Alaska Native, non-Hispanic/Latino. Average age 32. 27 applicants, 100% accepted, 27 enrolled. In 2010, 14 master's awarded. *Degree requirements:* For master's, thesis, internship. *Entrance requirements:* For master's, coursework/experience in psychology, statistics, minimum GPA of 3.0. Additional exam requirements/recommendations for international students: Required—TOEFL (minimum score 500 paper-based; 197 computer-based; 71 iBT). *Application deadline:* For fall admission, 8/1 priority date for domestic students. Application fee: $40. *Expenses:* Tuition: Full-time $10,800; part-time $450 per credit. Tuition and fees vary according to course load, degree level, program and student level. *Financial support:* Application deadline: 8/1. *Unit head:* James Renner, Program Director for Counseling Graduate Studies, 701-355-8177, Fax: 701-255-7687, E-mail: jrenner@umary.edu. *Application contact:* Jeanette Shaeffer, Accelerated and Distance Education Administrative Assistant, 701-355-8128, Fax: 701-255-7687, E-mail: jgschae@umary.edu.

University of New England, Westbrook College of Health Professions, School of Social Work, Biddeford, ME 04005-9526. Offers addictions counseling (Certificate); gerontology (Certificate); social work (MSW). *Accreditation:* CSWE. Part-time programs available. *Students:* 361 full-time (323 women), 61 part-time (57 women); includes 83 minority (48 Black or African American, non-Hispanic/Latino; 3 American Indian or Alaska Native, non-Hispanic/Latino; 5 Asian, non-Hispanic/Latino; 16 Hispanic/Latino; 2 Native Hawaiian or other Pacific Islander, non-Hispanic/Latino; 9 Two or more races, non-Hispanic/Latino). 276 applicants, 75% accepted, 181 enrolled. In 2010, 44 master's awarded. *Degree requirements:* For master's, field internships. *Entrance requirements:* Additional exam requirements/recommendations for international students: Required—TOEFL (minimum score 550 paper-based; 213 computer-based). *Application deadline:* For fall admission, 1/15 priority date for domestic students; for spring admission, 3/31 priority date for domestic students, 3/31 for international students. Applications are processed on a rolling basis. Application fee: $40. Electronic applications accepted. *Financial support:* In 2010–11, 40 students received support. Scholarships/grants and tuition waivers (partial) available. Financial award application deadline: 5/1; financial award applicants required to submit FAFSA. *Faculty research:* Domestic violence, solution-focused practice, empowerment models, adverse childhood experiences. *Unit head:* Martha Wilson, Director, 207-221-4513, E-mail: mwilson@une.edu. *Application contact:* Stacy Gato, Assistant Director of Graduate Admissions, 207-221-4225, Fax: 207-221-4898, E-mail: gradadmissions@une.edu.

University of Oklahoma, College of Arts and Sciences, Department of Human Relations, Norman, OK 73019-0390. Offers human relations (MHR), including affirmative action, chemical addictions counseling, family relations, general, human resources, juvenile justice; human relations licensure (Graduate Certificate). Part-time and evening/weekend programs available. Postbaccalaureate distance learning degree programs offered (minimal on-campus study). *Faculty:* 25 full-time (16 women), 27 part-time/adjunct (13 women). *Students:* 315 full-time (216 women), 499 part-time (312 women); includes 258 minority (159 Black or African American, non-Hispanic/Latino; 39 American Indian or Alaska Native, non-Hispanic/Latino; 14 Asian, non-Hispanic/Latino; 24 Hispanic/Latino; 2 Native Hawaiian or other Pacific Islander, non-Hispanic/Latino; 20 Two or more races, non-Hispanic/Latino), 24 international. Average age 34. 262 applicants, 89% accepted, 151 enrolled. In 2010, 384 master's awarded. *Degree requirements:* For master's, thesis optional. *Entrance requirements:* For master's, minimum GPA of 3.0 in last 60 hours of undergraduate course work, resume, 3 letters of reference. Additional exam requirements/recommendations for international students: Required—TOEFL (minimum score 550 paper-based; 213 computer-based; 79 iBT). *Application deadline:* For fall admission, 4/1 priority date for domestic students, 4/1 for international students; for spring admission, 11/1 for domestic students, 9/1 for international students. Applications are processed on a rolling basis. Application fee: $40 ($90 for international students). Electronic applications accepted. *Expenses:* Tuition, state resident: full-time $3893; part-time $162.20 per credit hour. Tuition, nonresident: full-time $14,167; part-time $590.30 per credit hour. Required fees: $2523; $94.60 per credit hour. Tuition and fees vary according to course load and degree level. *Financial support:* In 2010–11, 201 students received support, including 12 research assistantships with partial tuition reimbursements available (averaging $10,699 per year), 1 teaching assistantship (averaging $10,800 per year); career-related internships or fieldwork, scholarships/grants, and unspecified assistantships also available. Financial award applicants required to submit FAFSA. *Faculty research:* Non-profit organizations, high risk youth, trauma, women's studies, impact of war on women and children. Total annual research expenditures: $30,549. *Unit head:* Dr. Susan Marcus-Mendoza, Dept Chair, 405-325-1756, Fax: 405-325-4402, E-mail: smmendoza@ou.edu. *Application contact:* Lawana Miller, Admissions Coordinator, 405-325-1756, Fax: 405-325-4402, E-mail: lmiller@ou.edu.

Waynesburg University, Graduate and Professional Studies, Waynesburg, PA 15370-1222. Offers business (MBA), including finance, health systems, human resources, leadership, market development; counseling (MA), including addictions counseling, clinical mental health; education (MAT); nursing (MSN), including administration, education, informatics, palliative care; nursing practice (DNP); special education (M Ed); technology (M Ed); MSN/MBA. *Accreditation:* AACN. Part-time and evening/weekend programs available. *Degree requirements:* For doctorate, thesis/dissertation. *Entrance requirements:* Additional exam requirements/recommendations for international students: Required—TOEFL. Electronic applications accepted.

Applied Behavior Analysis

Auburn University, Graduate School, College of Liberal Arts, Department of Psychology, Auburn University, AL 36849. Offers applied behavior analysis in developmental disabilities (MS); clinical psychology (PhD); experimental psychology (PhD); industrial/organizational psychology (PhD). *Accreditation:* APA (one or more programs are accredited). Part-time programs available. *Faculty:* 24 full-time (7 women), 4 part-time/adjunct (3 women). *Students:* 36 full-time (28 women), 57 part-time (33 women); includes 6 Black or African American, non-Hispanic/Latino; 4 Asian, non-Hispanic/Latino; 5 Hispanic/Latino. Average age 26. 293 applicants, 9% accepted, 19 enrolled. In 2010, 20 master's, 11 doctorates awarded. *Degree requirements:* For doctorate, thesis/dissertation. *Entrance requirements:* For master's, GRE General Test, GRE Subject Test, minimum GPA of 3.25 in psychology, 3.0 overall; for doctorate, GRE General Test, GRE Subject Test. *Application deadline:* For fall admission, 7/7 for domestic students; for spring admission, 11/24 for domestic students. Applications are processed on a rolling basis. Application fee: $50 ($60 for international students). Electronic applications accepted. *Expenses:* Tuition, state resident: full-time $7002. Tuition, nonresident: full-time $21,898. International tuition: $22,116 full-time. Required fees: $892. Tuition and fees vary according to course load and program. *Financial support:* Research assistantships, teaching assistantships, Federal Work-Study available. Support available to part-time students. Financial award application deadline: 3/15; financial award applicants required to submit FAFSA. *Faculty research:* Clinical psychology, learning, industrial psychology, organizational psychology. Total annual research expenditures: $200,000. *Unit head:* Dr. Barry Burkhart, Chair, 334-844-6476. *Application contact:* Dr. George Flowers, Dean of the Graduate School, 334-844-2125.

Ball State University, Graduate School, Teachers College, Department of Special Education, Muncie, IN 47306-1099. Offers applied behavior analysis (MA); special education (MA, MAE, Ed D, Ed S). *Accreditation:* NCATE. *Faculty:* 12. *Students:* 65 full-time (54 women), 253 part-time (222 women); includes 11 Black or African American, non-Hispanic/Latino; 2 Asian, non-Hispanic/Latino; 9 Hispanic/Latino, 17 international. Average age 33. 211 applicants, 87% accepted, 90 enrolled. In 2010, 62 master's, 3 doctorates awarded. *Degree requirements:* For doctorate, thesis/dissertation; for Ed S, thesis. *Entrance requirements:* For doctorate, GRE General Test, interview, minimum graduate GPA of 3.2; for Ed S, GRE General Test. Application fee: $50. *Expenses:* Tuition, state resident: full-time $6160; part-time $299 per credit hour. Tuition, nonresident: full-time $16,020; part-time $783 per credit hour. Required fees: $2278; $95 per credit hour. *Financial support:* In 2010–11, 4 research assistantships with full tuition reimbursements (averaging $10,394 per year), 14 teaching assistantships (averaging $8,374 per year) were awarded; career-related internships or fieldwork also available. Financial award application deadline: 3/1. *Faculty research:* Language development and utilization in the handicapped (preschool through adult). *Unit head:* John Merbler, Chairperson, 765-285-5700, Fax: 765-285-4280, E-mail: jmerbler@bsu.edu. *Application contact:* Dr. Robert Morris, Associate Provost for Research and Dean of the Graduate School, 765-285-1300, E-mail: rmorris@bsu.edu.

Caldwell College, Graduate Studies, Program in Applied Behavior Analysis, Caldwell, NJ 07006-6195. Offers MA, PhD. *Entrance requirements:* For master's, GRE, minimum GPA of 3.0, writing sample. Additional exam requirements/recommendations for international students: Required—TOEFL (minimum score 580 paper-based; 237 computer-based).

California State University, Stanislaus, College of Human and Health Sciences, Program in Psychology (MA/MS), Turlock, CA 95382. Offers behavior analysis (MS); counseling psychology (MS); psychology (MA). Part-time programs available. *Students:* 26 full-time (20 women), 39 part-time (36 women); includes 24 minority (1 Black or African American, non-Hispanic/Latino; 1 American Indian or Alaska Native, non-Hispanic/Latino; 4 Asian, non-Hispanic/Latino; 15 Hispanic/Latino; 3 Two or more races, non-Hispanic/Latino). Average age 30. 62 applicants, 48% accepted, 24 enrolled. In 2010, 13 master's awarded. *Degree requirements:* For master's, thesis. *Entrance requirements:* For master's, GRE, minimum GPA of 3.0, 3 letters of reference, 16 PSYC prerequisites, department approval, personal statement. Additional exam requirements/recommendations for international students: Required—TOEFL (minimum score 550 paper-based; 213 computer-based). *Application deadline:* For fall admission, 5/1 for domestic students; for spring admission, 1/7 for domestic students. Application fee: $55. Electronic applications accepted. Tuition and fees vary according to program. *Financial support:* Fellowships, career-related internships or fieldwork and Federal Work-Study available. Financial award application deadline: 3/1; financial award applicants required to submit FAFSA. *Faculty research:* Hedonic tone judgment, syntax and autism, early literacy assessment and native and non-native languages. *Unit head:* Dr. Bruce Hesse, Psychology Professor, Graduate Academic Director, 209-667-3555, E-mail: bhesse@csustan.edu. *Application contact:* Graduate School, 209-667-3129, Fax: 209-664-7025, E-mail: graduate_school@csustan.edu.

The Chicago School of Professional Psychology, Program in Applied Behavior Analysis, Chicago, IL 60610. Offers applied behavior analysis (Psy D); clinical psychology (applied behavior analysis specialization) (MA). *Degree requirements:* For master's, thesis, practicum; for doctorate, thesis/dissertation, practicum. *Entrance requirements:* For doctorate, GRE. Additional exam requirements/recommendations for international students: Required—TOEFL.

The Chicago School of Professional Psychology, Program in Clinical Psychology, Chicago, IL 60610. Offers applied behavior analysis (MA); clinical psychology (Psy D); counseling (MA). *Accreditation:* APA. *Degree requirements:* For master's, thesis (for some programs); for doctorate, comprehensive exam, thesis/dissertation. *Entrance requirements:* For master's, minimum undergraduate GPA of 3.0, 1 course in psychology, 1 course in either statistics or research methods; for doctorate, GRE, 18 hours of psychology credit (including courses in statistics, normal psychology and human development); minimum GPA of 3.2. Additional exam requirements/recommendations for international students: Required—TOEFL. Electronic applications accepted.

The Chicago School of Professional Psychology at Downtown Los Angeles, Program in Applied Behavior Analysis, Los Angeles, CA 90017. Offers Psy D.

The Chicago School of Professional Psychology at Downtown Los Angeles, Program in Clinical Psychology, Los Angeles, CA 90017. Offers applied behavior analysis (MA); clinical psychology (Psy D); marital and family therapy (MA).

Florida Institute of Technology, Graduate Programs, College of Psychology and Liberal Arts, School of Psychology, Melbourne, FL 32901-6975. Offers applied behavior analysis (MS); applied behavior analysis and organizational behavior management (MS); behavior analysis (PhD); clinical psychology (Psy D); industrial/organizational psychology (MS, PhD); organizational behavior management (MS). *Accreditation:* APA (one or more programs are accredited). Part-time programs available. *Faculty:* 21 full-time (10 women), 6 part-time/adjunct (2 women). *Students:* 220 full-time (167 women), 11 part-time (10 women); includes 25 minority (5 Black or African American, non-Hispanic/Latino; 4 Asian, non-Hispanic/Latino; 16 Hispanic/Latino), 22 international. Average age 27. 378 applicants, 42% accepted, 77 enrolled. In 2010, 57 master's, 13 doctorates awarded. Terminal master's awarded for partial completion of doctoral program. *Degree requirements:* For master's, comprehensive exam (for some programs), thesis (for some programs), BCBA certification, final exam; for doctorate, comprehensive exam, thesis/dissertation, internship, full time resident of school for 4 years (8 semesters, 3 summers). *Entrance requirements:* For master's, GRE General Test, 3 letters of recommendation, minimum GPA of 3.0, resume, statement of objectives; for doctorate, GRE General Test, GRE Subject Test (psychology), 3 letters of recommendation, minimum GPA of 3.2, resume, statement of objectives. Additional exam requirements/recommendations for international students: Required—TOEFL (minimum score 550 paper-based; 213 computer-based; 79 iBT). *Application deadline:* For fall admission, 4/1 for international students; for spring admission, 9/30 for international students. Applications are processed on a rolling basis. Application fee: $50. Electronic applications accepted. *Expenses:* Tuition: Part-time $1040 per credit hour. Tuition and fees vary according to campus/location. *Financial support:* In 2010–11, 4 fellowships with full and partial tuition reimbursements (averaging $3,775 per year), 32 research assistantships with full and partial tuition reimbursements (averaging $5,602 per year), 8 teaching assistantships with full and partial tuition reimbursements (averaging $4,570 per year) were awarded; career-related internships or fieldwork, institutionally sponsored loans, tuition waivers (partial), unspecified assistantships, and tuition remissions also available. Support available to part-time students. Financial award application deadline: 3/1; financial award applicants required to submit FAFSA. *Faculty research:* Addictions, neuropsychology, child abuse, assessment, psychological trauma. Total annual research expenditures: $1.8 million. *Unit head:* Dr. Mary Beth Kenkel, Dean, 321-674-8142, Fax: 321-674-7105, E-mail: mkenkel@fit.edu. *Application contact:* Cheryl A. Brown, Associate Director of Graduate Admissions, 321-674-7581, Fax: 321-723-9468, E-mail: cbrown@fit.edu.

Florida State University, The Graduate School, College of Arts and Sciences, Department of Psychology, Program in Applied Behavior Analysis, Tallahassee, FL 32306. Offers MS. *Faculty:* 4 full-time (2 women). *Students:* 26 full-time (24 women); includes 3 Black or African American, non-Hispanic/Latino; 4 Hispanic/Latino. Average age 25. 62 applicants, 44% accepted, 16 enrolled. In 2010, 17 master's awarded. *Degree requirements:* For master's, comprehensive exam. *Entrance requirements:* For master's, GRE General Test (suggested minimum total score of 1000), minimum GPA of 3.0. Additional exam requirements/recommendations for international students: Required—TOEFL (minimum score 550 paper-based; 213 computer-based; 80 iBT). *Application deadline:* For fall admission, 2/1 for domestic and international students. Application fee: $30. Electronic applications accepted. *Expenses:* Contact institution. *Financial support:* In 2010–11, 26 students received support, including research assistantships with full tuition reimbursements available (averaging $20,000 per year), 26 teaching assistantships with full tuition reimbursements available (averaging $16,500 per year); career-related internships or fieldwork, Federal Work-Study, institutionally sponsored loans, and unspecified assistantships also available. Financial award applicants required to submit FAFSA. *Unit head:* Dr. Jon Bailey, Head, 850-644-1877, Fax: 850-645-7518, E-mail: bailey@psy.fsu.edu. *Application contact:* Cherie P. Miller, Graduate Program Assistant, 850-644-2499, Fax: 850-644-7739, E-mail: grad-info@psy.fsu.edu.

Johnson State College, Graduate Program in Education, Program in Applied Behavior Analysis, Johnson, VT 05656. Offers children's mental health (MA Ed). *Entrance requirements:* Additional exam requirements/recommendations for international students: Required—TOEFL. *Expenses:* Tuition, state resident: part-time $437 per credit. Tuition, nonresident: part-time $943 per credit.

Long Island University at Riverhead, Education Division, Riverhead, NY 11901. Offers applied behavior analysis (Advanced Certificate); childhood education (MS Ed), including childhood education, elementary education; literacy education (MS Ed); teaching students with disabilities (MS Ed). *Accreditation:* Teacher Education Accreditation Council. Part-time and evening/weekend programs available. *Faculty:* 1 full-time (0 women), 11 part-time/adjunct (7 women). *Students:* 29 full-time (25 women), 90 part-time (82 women). Average age 30. 48 applicants, 69% accepted, 33 enrolled. In 2010, 38 master's awarded. *Degree requirements:* For master's, thesis (for some programs); for Advanced Certificate, comprehensive exam (for some programs). *Entrance requirements:* For master's, minimum GPA of 2.75, writing sample, letter of reference, interview, official college transcripts. Additional exam requirements/recommendations for international students: Required—TOEFL (minimum score 550 paper-based; 250 computer-based). *Application deadline:* Applications are processed on a rolling basis. Electronic applications accepted. *Expenses:* Tuition: Part-time $982 per credit. *Financial support:* In 2010–11, 105 students received support. Scholarships/grants and tuition waivers (partial) available. Support available to part-time students. Financial award applicants required to submit FAFSA. *Unit head:* Dr. R. Lawrence McCann, Director, 631-287-8211, E-mail: admissions@southampton.liu.edu. *Application contact:* Andrea Borra, Director of Graduate Admissions and Program Administration, 631-287-8010 Ext. 8326, Fax: 631-287-8253, E-mail: andrea.borra@liu.edu.

McNeese State University, Doré School of Graduate Studies, Burton College of Education, Department of Psychology, Lake Charles, LA 70609. Offers addiction treatment (MA); applied behavior analysis (MA); counseling psychology (MA); general/experimental psychology (MA). Evening/weekend programs available. *Faculty:* 6 full-time (3 women). *Students:* 46 full-time (31 women), 29 part-time (21 women); includes 11 minority (6 Black or African American, non-Hispanic/Latino; 1 Asian, non-Hispanic/Latino; 2 Hispanic/Latino; 2 Two or more races, non-Hispanic/Latino), 4 international. In 2010, 14 master's awarded. *Entrance requirements:* For master's, GRE. *Application deadline:* For fall admission, 5/15 priority date for domestic and international students; for spring admission, 10/15 priority date for domestic and international students. Applications are processed on a rolling basis. Application fee: $20 ($30 for international students). Tuition and fees vary according to course load. *Financial support:* Application deadline: 5/1. *Unit head:* Dr. Dena L. Matzenbacher, Head, 337-475-5457, Fax: 337-562-4115, E-mail: dena@mcneese.edu. *Application contact:* Dr. George F. Mead, Interim Dean of Doré School of Graduate Studies, 337-475-5396, Fax: 337-475-5397, E-mail: admissions@mcneese.edu.

Mercy College, School of Education, Program in Applied Behavior Analysis, Dobbs Ferry, NY 10522-1189. Offers Post Master's Certificate. *Students:* 4 part-time (2 women); includes 1 Black or African American, non-Hispanic/Latino; 1 Asian, non-Hispanic/Latino. Average age 40. 11 applicants, 64% accepted, 3 enrolled. *Entrance requirements:* For degree, master's degree. Additional exam requirements/recommendations for international students: Required—TOEFL (minimum score 600 paper-based; 250 computer-based; 100 iBT), IELTS (minimum score 8). *Application deadline:* For fall admission, 8/1 for international students. Applications are processed on a rolling basis. Application fee: $40. Electronic applications accepted. *Expenses:* Tuition: Full-time $13,572; part-time $754 per credit hour. Required fees: $130 per term. *Unit head:* Dr. Andrew Peiser, Chairperson, 914-674-7489, Fax: 914-674-7352, E-mail: apeiser@mercy.edu. *Application contact:* Mary Ellen Hoffman, Director, Graduate Education Programs, 914-674-7334, E-mail: mhoffman@mercy.edu.

Northeastern University, Bouvé College of Health Sciences Graduate School, Department of Counseling and Applied Educational Psychology, Program in Applied Behavior Analysis, Boston, MA 02115-5096. Offers MS. Part-time programs available. *Faculty:* 10 part-time/adjunct (5 women). *Students:* 38 full-time (32 women), 21 part-time (19 women). Average age 29. 35 applicants, 97% accepted, 10 enrolled. In 2010, 30 master's awarded. *Degree requirements:* For master's, thesis. *Entrance requirements:* For master's, GRE General Test or MAT. Additional exam requirements/recommendations for international students: Required—TOEFL (minimum score 100 iBT). *Application deadline:* For fall admission, 8/1 for domestic students; for spring admission, 12/1 for domestic students. Applications are processed on a rolling basis. Application fee: $50. Electronic applications accepted. *Financial support:* Career-related internships or fieldwork available. Support available to part-time students. Financial award application deadline: 3/1; financial award applicants required to submit FAFSA. *Faculty research:* Stimulus control, failure-to-thrive children, severe behavior disorders, autism. *Unit head:* Karen Gould, Director, 781-440-0400 Ext. 215, E-mail: kgould@mayinstitute.org. *Application contact:* Margaret Schnabel, Director of Graduate Admissions, 617-373-2708, E-mail: bouvegrad@neu.edu.

Oklahoma City University, Petree College of Arts and Sciences, Division of Education and Kinesiology Exercise Studies, Programs in Education, Oklahoma City, OK 73106-1402. Offers applied behavioral studies (M Ed); early childhood education (M Ed); elementary education (M Ed). Part-time and evening/weekend programs available. *Degree requirements:* For master's, thesis optional. *Entrance requirements:* For master's, minimum GPA of 3.0. Additional exam requirements/recommendations for international students: Required—TOEFL (minimum score 550 paper-based). *Faculty research:* Adult literacy, cognition, reading strategies.

Oklahoma State University, College of Education, School of Applied Health and Educational Psychology, Stillwater, OK 74078. Offers applied behavioral studies (Ed D); applied health and educational psychology (MS, PhD, Ed S). *Accreditation:* APA (one or more programs are accredited). Part-time programs available. *Faculty:* 38 full-time (17 women), 19 part-time/adjunct (11 women). *Students:* 199 full-time (144 women), 146 part-time (104 women); includes 25 Black or African American, non-Hispanic/Latino; 27 American Indian or Alaska Native, non-Hispanic/Latino; 12 Asian, non-Hispanic/Latino; 12 Hispanic/Latino, 13 international. Average age 31. 247 applicants, 35% accepted, 65 enrolled. In 2010, 72 master's, 16 doctorates awarded. *Degree requirements:* For master's, thesis (for some programs); for doctorate, comprehensive exam, thesis/dissertation. *Entrance requirements:* For master's and doctorate, GRE or GMAT. Additional exam requirements/recommendations for international students: Required—TOEFL (minimum score 550 paper-based; 79 iBT). *Application deadline:* For fall admission, 3/1 priority date for international students; for spring admission, 8/1 priority date for international students. Applications are processed on a rolling basis. Application fee: $40 ($75 for international students). Electronic applications accepted. *Expenses:* Tuition, state resident: full-time $3716; part-time $154.85 per credit hour. Tuition, nonresident: full-time $14,892; part-time $621 per credit hour. Required fees: $2044; $85.20 per credit hour. One-time fee: $50. Tuition and fees vary according to course load and campus/location. *Financial support:* In 2010–11, 30 research assistantships (averaging $6,839 per year), 64 teaching assistantships (averaging $8,416 per year) were awarded; career-related internships or fieldwork, Federal Work-Study, scholarships/grants, health care benefits, tuition waivers (partial), and unspecified assistantships also available. Support available to part-time students. Financial award application deadline: 3/1; financial award applicants required to submit FAFSA. *Unit head:* Dr. John Romans, Head, 405-744-6040, Fax: 405-744-6779. *Application contact:* Dr. Gordon Emslie, Dean, 405-744-6368, Fax: 405-744-0355, E-mail: grad-i@okstate.edu.

Rowan University, Graduate School, College of Liberal Arts and Sciences, Department of Psychology, Program in Applied Behavioral Analysis, Glassboro, NJ 08028-1701. Offers MA. *Students:* 3 part-time (all women). Average age 45. 32 applicants, 72% accepted, 3 enrolled. *Entrance requirements:* For master's, GRE General Test. Additional exam requirements/recommendations for international students: Required—TOEFL. *Application deadline:* Applications are processed on a rolling basis. Application fee: $65 ($200 for international students). Electronic applications accepted. *Expenses:* Tuition, area resident: Part-time $602 per semester hour. Tuition, nonresident: part-time $602 per semester hour. Required fees: $100 per semester hour. One-time fee: $10 part-time. *Unit head:* Dr. Horacio Sosa, Dean, College of Graduate and Continuing Education, 856-256-4747, Fax: 856-256-5638, E-mail: lalovic-hand@rowan.edu. *Application contact:* Karen Haynes, Graduate Coordinator, 856-256-4052, Fax: 856-256-4436, E-mail: haynes@rowan.edu.

Sage Graduate School, Graduate School, School of Education, Program in Applied Behavior Analysis and Autism, Troy, NY 12180-4115. Offers MS, Post Master's Certificate. Part-time and evening/weekend programs available. *Faculty:* 12 full-time (8 women), 27 part-time/adjunct (23 women). *Students:* 2 full-time (1 woman), 97 part-time (92 women); includes 10 minority (1 Black or African American, non-Hispanic/Latino; 2 Asian, non-Hispanic/Latino; 6 Hispanic/Latino; 1 Two or more races, non-Hispanic/Latino). Average age 29. 230 applicants, 39% accepted, 56 enrolled. In 2010, 8 master's awarded. *Entrance requirements:* Additional exam requirements/recommendations for international students: Required—TOEFL (minimum score 550 paper-based; 213 computer-based). *Application deadline:* Applications are processed on a rolling basis. Application fee: $40. *Expenses:* Tuition: Full-time $10,980; part-time $610 per credit hour. Tuition and fees vary according to course load, degree level and program. *Financial support:* Federal Work-Study, scholarships/grants, tuition waivers (partial), and unspecified assistantships available. Support available to part-time students. Financial award

Applied Behavior Analysis

Sage Graduate School (continued)
applicants required to submit FAFSA. *Unit head:* Dr. Lori Quigley, Dean, School of Education, 518-244-2326, Fax: 518-244-4571, E-mail: l.quigley@sage.edu. *Application contact:* Dr. Dana Reineke, Director, Center for Applied Behavior Analysis, 518-244-2227, Fax: 518-244-6880, E-mail: caba@sage.edu.

St. Cloud State University, School of Graduate Studies, College of Education, Department of Educational Leadership and Community Psychology, Program in Applied Behavior Analysis, St. Cloud, MN 56301-4498. Offers MS. Part-time programs available. Postbaccalaureate distance learning degree programs offered (no on-campus study). *Degree requirements:* For master's, comprehensive exam (for some programs), thesis or alternative. *Entrance requirements:* For master's, GRE General Test, minimum GPA of 2.75. Additional exam requirements/recommendations for international students: Required—Michigan English Language Assessment Battery; Recommended—TOEFL (minimum score 550 paper-based; 213 computer-based), IELTS (minimum score 6.5).

Saint Peter's College, Graduate Programs in Education, Jersey City, NJ 07306-5997. Offers director of school counseling services (Certificate); educational leadership (MA Ed, Ed D); middle school mathematics (Certificate); professional/associate counselor (Certificate); reading (MA Ed); school business administrator (Certificate); school counseling (MA, Certificate); special education (MA Ed, Certificate), including applied behavioral analysis (MA Ed), literacy (MA Ed), teacher of students with disabilities (Certificate); teaching (MA Ed, Certificate), including 6-8 middle school education, K-12 secondary education, K-5 elementary education. *Accreditation:* Teacher Education Accreditation Council. Part-time and evening/weekend programs available. *Students:* 132 applicants, 70% accepted, 63 enrolled. *Degree requirements:* For master's, comprehensive exam; for doctorate, comprehensive exam, thesis/dissertation. *Entrance requirements:* For master's and doctorate, GRE or MAT. Additional exam requirements/recommendations for international students: Required—TOEFL (minimum score 79 computer-based). *Application deadline:* Applications are processed on a rolling basis. Electronic applications accepted. *Financial support:* Applicants required to submit FAFSA. *Unit head:* Dr. Anthony Sciarrillo, Chairperson. *Application contact:* Stephanie Autenrieth, Director, Graduate and Professional Studies Admission, 201-761-6474, Fax: 201-435-5270, E-mail: sautenrieth@spc.edu.

The School of Professional Psychology at Forest Institute, Graduate Programs, Springfield, MO 65807. Offers applied behavior analysis (MS); clinical psychology (MA, Psy D); counseling psychology (MA); marriage and family therapy (MA, PGC). *Accreditation:* AAMFT/COAMFTE; APA (one or more programs are accredited). *Faculty:* 17 full-time (8 women), 18 part-time/adjunct (10 women). *Students:* 214 full-time (144 women), 46 part-time (35 women); includes 35 minority (11 Black or African American, non-Hispanic/Latino; 9 American Indian or Alaska Native, non-Hispanic/Latino; 5 Asian, non-Hispanic/Latino; 10 Hispanic/Latino), 3 international. Average age 28. 176 applicants, 69% accepted, 45 enrolled. In 2010, 35 master's, 31 doctorates awarded. Terminal master's awarded for partial completion of doctoral program. *Degree requirements:* For master's, thesis, practicum; for doctorate, comprehensive exam, thesis/dissertation, internship, practicum. *Entrance requirements:* For master's, GRE General Test, interview, minimum GPA of 3.0, 12 hours in psychology; for doctorate, GRE General Test, interview, minimum GPA of 3.0, 18 hours in psychology. Additional exam requirements/recommendations for international students: Required—TOEFL (minimum score 550 paper-based; 213 computer-based). *Application deadline:* For fall admission, 1/15 priority date for domestic and international students; for spring admission, 8/1 priority date for domestic and international students. Applications are processed on a rolling basis. Application fee: $50. Electronic applications accepted. *Financial support:* In 2010–11, 59 students received support; fellowships with partial tuition reimbursements available, teaching assistantships, career-related internships or fieldwork, Federal Work-Study, scholarships/grants, tuition waivers (partial), and unspecified assistantships available. Financial award applicants required to submit FAFSA. *Faculty research:* Forensics/corrections, marriage and family therapy, child and adolescent, integrated health care, neuropsychology. *Unit head:* Dr. Mark E. Skrade, President, 417-823-3477, Fax: 417-823-3442, E-mail: mskrade@forest.edu. *Application contact:* Bethany Ritter, Admissions Counselor, 417-823-3477, Fax: 417-823-3442, E-mail: britter@forest.edu.

Simmons College, College of Arts and Sciences Graduate Studies, Department of Education, Program in Special Education, Boston, MA 02115. Offers applied behavior analysis (PhD); assistive technology (MS Ed, Ed S); behavioral education (MS Ed, Ed S); health professions education (PhD); language and literacy (MS Ed, Ed S); moderate disabilities (Ed S); moderate special needs (MS Ed); severe disabilities (Ed S); severe special needs (MS Ed); special education administration (MS Ed, PhD, Ed S). Part-time and evening/weekend programs available. *Degree requirements:* For master's, student teaching. *Entrance requirements:* For doctorate, GRE, research proposal, interview, BCBA credential. Additional exam requirements/recommendations for international students: Required—TOEFL (minimum score 600 paper-based; 250 computer-based; 100 iBT). Electronic applications accepted. *Expenses:* Contact institution. *Faculty research:* Development and application of the IEP for teachers, assistive technology, language-based disabilities, applied behavior analysis, communication challenges between general and special education teachers.

Spalding University, Graduate Studies, College of Social Sciences and Humanities, Program in Applied Behavior Analysis, Louisville, KY 40203-2188. Offers MA. *Faculty:* 2 full-time (0 women), 2 part-time/adjunct (0 women). *Students:* 41 full-time (34 women), 8 part-time (6 women); includes 6 minority (4 Black or African American, non-Hispanic/Latino; 2 Hispanic/Latino). Average age 32. 39 applicants, 62% accepted, 24 enrolled. *Entrance requirements:* For master's, GRE, 12 hours in psychology (developmental, research methods, learning, behavioral modifications, applied behavioral analysis), letters of recommendation, writing sample. Additional exam requirements/recommendations for international students: Required—TOEFL (minimum score 535 paper-based; 203 computer-based). *Application deadline:* For fall admission, 2/15 priority date for domestic students. Application fee: $30. *Financial support:* In 2010–11, 4 students received support, including 1 research assistantship (averaging $4,500 per year); unspecified assistantships also available. Financial award application deadline: 3/15; financial award applicants required to submit FAFSA. *Unit head:* Dr. Nicholas Weatherly, Program Director, 502-585-9111 Ext. 2750, E-mail: nweatherly@spalding.edu. *Application contact:* Debbie Pierce, Admissions Office, 502-585-7111 Ext. 2698, E-mail: dpierce@spalding.edu.

Teachers College, Columbia University, Graduate Faculty of Education, Department of Health and Behavior Studies, Program in Applied Behavior Analysis, New York, NY 10027. Offers MA, Ed D, PhD. *Faculty:* 7 full-time (4 women), 11 part-time/adjunct (10 women). *Students:* 1 (woman) full-time, 52 part-time (46 women); includes 14 minority (5 Black or African American, non-Hispanic/Latino; 4 Asian, non-Hispanic/Latino; 3 Hispanic/Latino; 2 Two or more races, non-Hispanic/Latino), 11 international. Average age 28. 40 applicants, 75% accepted, 17 enrolled. In 2010, 17 master's, 5 doctorates awarded. *Degree requirements:* For doctorate, comprehensive exam, thesis/dissertation. *Entrance requirements:* For doctorate, writing sample. *Application deadline:* For fall admission, 1/2 priority date for domestic students; for spring admission, 11/15 for domestic students. Applications are processed on a rolling basis. Electronic applications accepted. *Expenses:* Tuition: Full-time $28,272; part-time $1178 per credit. Required fees: $756; $378 per semester. *Financial support:* Applicants required to submit FAFSA. *Faculty research:* Communication skills, academic skills (reading and math), behavior problems, and cultural differences in individuals with autism as well as transition support services and teacher preparation for these individuals. *Unit head:* Prof. R. Douglas Greer, Program Coordinator, 212-678-3880, E-mail: rdg13@columbia.edu. *Application contact:* Elizabeth Puleio, Admissions Contact, 212-678-3710.

Temple University, College of Education, Department of Curriculum, Instruction, and Technology in Education, Philadelphia, PA 19122-6096. Offers applied behavioral analysis (MS Ed); career and technical education (MS Ed); early childhood education and elementary education (MS Ed); English education (MS Ed); language arts education (Ed D); math/science education (Ed D); mathematics education (MS Ed); science education (MS Ed); second and foreign language education (MS Ed); special education (MS Ed); teaching English as a second language (MS Ed). Part-time and evening/weekend programs available. *Faculty:* 26 full-time (15 women). *Students:* 87 full-time (58 women), 195 part-time (130 women); includes 14 Black or African American, non-Hispanic/Latino; 8 Asian, non-Hispanic/Latino; 7 Hispanic/Latino; 1 Two or more races, non-Hispanic/Latino, 12 international. 181 applicants, 71% accepted, 85 enrolled. In 2010, 117 master's, 3 doctorates awarded. Terminal master's awarded for partial completion of doctoral program. *Degree requirements:* For master's, thesis or alternative; for doctorate, thesis/dissertation. *Entrance requirements:* For master's and doctorate, GRE General Test or MAT, minimum GPA of 3.0. Additional exam requirements/recommendations for international students: Required—TOEFL (minimum score 550 paper-based; 213 computer-based; 79 iBT). *Application deadline:* For fall admission, 4/1 for domestic students, 12/15 for international students; for spring admission, 10/1 for domestic students, 8/1 for international students. Application fee: $50. Electronic applications accepted. *Financial support:* Fellowships, research assistantships with full tuition reimbursements, teaching assistantships with full tuition reimbursements available. Financial award application deadline: 1/15; financial award applicants required to submit FAFSA. *Faculty research:* School improvement, problem-solving, literacy, language development. *Unit head:* Dr. Michael W. Smith, Chair, 215-204-6387, Fax: 215-204-1414, E-mail: mwsmith@temple.edu. *Application contact:* Dr. Margo Greicar, Director for Graduate Academic & Student Affairs, 215-204-8011, Fax: 215-204-4383, E-mail: margo.greicar@temple.edu.

Tennessee Technological University, Graduate School, College of Education, Department of Curriculum and Instruction, Program in Exceptional Learning, Cookeville, TN 38505. Offers applied behavior and learning (PhD); literacy (PhD); program planning and evaluation (PhD). *Students:* 11 full-time (8 women), 10 part-time (8 women); includes 3 Black or African American, non-Hispanic/Latino; 1 Asian, non-Hispanic/Latino. 18 applicants, 17% accepted, 2 enrolled. In 2010, 5 doctorates awarded. *Degree requirements:* For doctorate, comprehensive exam, thesis/dissertation. *Entrance requirements:* For doctorate, GRE, minimum GPA of 3.0. Additional exam requirements/recommendations for international students: Required—TOEFL (minimum score 550 paper-based; 79 iBT), IELTS (minimum score 5.5). *Application deadline:* For fall admission, 8/1 for domestic students, 5/1 for international students; for spring admission, 12/1 for domestic students, 10/1 for international students. Application fee: $25 ($30 for international students). Electronic applications accepted. *Expenses:* Tuition, state resident: full-time $7934; part-time $388 per credit hour. Tuition, nonresident: full-time $19,758; part-time $962 per credit hour. *Financial support:* In 2010–11, 4 fellowships (averaging $8,000 per year), 10 research assistantships (averaging $12,000 per year), 1 teaching assistantship (averaging $12,000 per year) were awarded. Financial award application deadline: 4/1. *Unit head:* Dr. Lisa Zagumny, Interim Director, 931-372-3078, Fax: 931-372-3517. *Application contact:* Shelia K. Kendrick, Coordinator of Graduate Admissions, 931-372-3808, Fax: 931-372-3497, E-mail: skendrick@tntech.edu.

The University of Kansas, Graduate Studies, College of Liberal Arts and Sciences, Department of Applied Behavioral Science, Lawrence, KS 66045. Offers applied behavioral science (MA); behavioral psychology (PhD). *Faculty:* 16 full-time (6 women). *Students:* 48 full-time (33 women), 1 (woman) part-time; includes 6 minority (3 Black or African American, non-Hispanic/Latino; 1 Asian, non-Hispanic/Latino; 1 Hispanic/Latino; 1 Two or more races, non-Hispanic/Latino), 5 international. Average age 31. 46 applicants, 24% accepted, 9 enrolled. In 2010, 8 master's, 5 doctorates awarded. Terminal master's awarded for partial completion of doctoral program. *Degree requirements:* For master's, thesis; for doctorate, thesis/dissertation, comprehensive oral and written exams, journal reviews. *Entrance requirements:* For master's and doctorate, curriculum vitae, 3 letters of recommendation. Additional exam requirements/recommendations for international students: Required—TOEFL. *Application deadline:* For fall admission, 12/15 priority date for domestic and international students. Applications are processed on a rolling basis. Application fee: $55 ($65 for international students). Electronic applications accepted. *Expenses:* Tuition, state resident: full-time $7092; part-time $295.50 per credit hour. Tuition, nonresident: full-time $16,590; part-time $691.25 per credit hour. Required fees: $858; $71.49 per credit hour. Tuition and fees vary according to course load, campus/location and program. *Financial support:* Fellowships, research assistantships with full and partial tuition reimbursements, teaching assistantships with full and partial tuition reimbursements, career-related internships or fieldwork, traineeships, tuition waivers (full), and unspecified assistantships available. Financial award application deadline: 12/15; financial award applicants required to submit CSS PROFILE or FAFSA. *Faculty research:* Early childhood, developmental disabilities, community health and development, adults with disabilities, applied behavior analysis. *Unit head:* Dr. Edward K. Morris, Chair, 785-864-4840, Fax: 785-864-5202, E-mail: ekm@ku.edu. *Application contact:* Dr. Florence DiGennaro Reed, Graduate Director, 785-864-4840, Fax: 785-864-5202, E-mail: fdreed@ku.edu.

University of Maryland, Baltimore County, Graduate School, College of Arts, Humanities and Social Sciences, Department of Psychology, Program in Human Services Psychology, Baltimore, MD 21250. Offers applied behavioral analysis (MA); human services psychology/clinical (PhD). *Faculty:* 17 full-time (5 women), 11 part-time/adjunct (4 women). *Students:* 81 full-time (67 women), 14 part-time (12 women); includes 12 Black or African American, non-Hispanic/Latino; 5 Asian, non-Hispanic/Latino; 7 Hispanic/Latino. Average age 29. 142 applicants, 32% accepted, 12 enrolled. In 2010, 24 master's, 9 doctorates awarded. Terminal master's awarded for partial completion of doctoral program. *Degree requirements:* For master's, thesis; for doctorate, comprehensive exam, thesis/dissertation. *Entrance requirements:* For master's, GRE General Test, minimum GPA of 3.0; for doctorate, GRE General Test, GRE Subject Test, minimum GPA of 3.0. Additional exam requirements/recommendations for international students: Required—TOEFL. *Application deadline:* For fall admission, 12/1 for domestic and international students. Application fee: $70. Electronic applications accepted. *Financial support:* In 2010–11, 1 student received support, including fellowships with full and partial tuition reimbursements available (averaging $2,200 per year), 23 research assistantships with full and partial tuition reimbursements available (averaging $14,857 per year), 13 teaching assistantships with full and partial tuition reimbursements available (averaging $14,857 per year); career-related internships or fieldwork, Federal Work-Study, scholarships/grants, health care benefits, tuition waivers, and unspecified assistantships also available. Financial award application deadline: 3/1; financial award applicants required to submit FAFSA. *Faculty research:* Addictive behaviors, cardiovascular and cerebrovascular disease, family violence, pediatric psychology, community prevention. Total annual research expenditures: $1.8 million. *Unit head:* Dr. Carlo C. DiClememte, Director, 410-455-2567, Fax: 410-455-1055, E-mail: diclemen@umbc.edu. *Application contact:* Nicole Mooney, Program Management Specialist, 410-455-2567, Fax: 410-455-1055, E-mail: psycdept@umbc.edu.

University of North Florida, College of Education and Human Services, Department of Exceptional Student and Deaf Education, Jacksonville, FL 32224. Offers American sign language/English interpreting (M Ed); applied behavior analysis (M Ed); autism (M Ed); deaf education (M Ed); disability services (M Ed); exceptional student education (M Ed). *Accreditation:* NCATE. Part-time and evening/weekend programs available. *Faculty:* 11 full-time (9 women), 2 part-time/adjunct (both women). *Students:* 30 full-time (28 women), 51 part-time (49 women); includes 4 Black or African American, non-Hispanic/Latino; 3 Asian, non-Hispanic/Latino; 7 Hispanic/Latino, 1 international. Average age 30. 54 applicants, 74% accepted, 32 enrolled. In 2010, 22 master's awarded. *Entrance requirements:* For master's, GRE General Test, minimum GPA of 3.0 in last 60 hours, interview, 3 letters of recommendation. Additional exam requirements/recommendations for international students: Required—TOEFL (minimum score 500 paper-based; 173 computer-based). *Application deadline:* For fall admission, 7/1 priority date for domestic students, 5/1 for international students; for spring admission, 11/1 priority date for domestic students, 10/1 for international students. Applications are processed on a rolling basis. Application fee: $30. Electronic applications accepted. *Expenses:* Tuition, state resident: full-time $7646.40; part-time $318.60 per credit hour. Tuition, nonresident: full-time $23,502; part-time $979.24 per credit hour. Required fees: $1208.88; $50.37 per credit hour. Tuition and fees vary according to course load and program. *Financial support:* In 2010–11, 38 students received support, including 1 research assistantship (averaging $6,150 per year); teaching assistantships, career-related internships or fieldwork, Federal Work-Study, scholarships/

grants, tuition waivers (partial), and unspecified assistantships also available. Support available to part-time students. Financial award application deadline: 4/1; financial award applicants required to submit FAFSA. *Faculty research:* Transition, integrating technology into teacher education, written language development, professional school development, learning strategies. Total annual research expenditures: $892,583. *Unit head:* Dr. Karen Patterson, Chair, 904-620-2930, Fax: 904-620-3895, E-mail: karen.patterson@unf.edu. *Application contact:* Lillith Richardson, Assistant Director, The Graduate School, 904-620-1360, Fax: 904-620-1362, E-mail: graduateschool@unf.edu.

University of Southern Maine, School of Education and Human Development, Program in Educational Psychology, Portland, ME 04104-9300. Offers applied behavior analysis (MS, Certificate). Part-time and evening/weekend programs available. *Students:* 4 full-time (3 women), 5 part-time (3 women). 15 applicants, 60% accepted, 6 enrolled. In 2010, 4 master's awarded. *Entrance requirements:* For master's, GRE or MAT. Additional exam requirements/recommendations for international students: Required—TOEFL (minimum score 550 paper-based; 213 computer-based; 79 iBT). *Application deadline:* For fall admission, 5/1 priority date for domestic students; for spring admission, 10/15 priority date for domestic students. Applications are processed on a rolling basis. Application fee: $65. Electronic applications accepted. *Financial support:* Federal Work-Study, institutionally sponsored loans, scholarships/grants, and unspecified assistantships available. Support available to part-time students. Financial award application deadline: 3/1. *Unit head:* Dr. E. Michael Brady, Chair, Human Resource Development Department, 207-780-5316, Fax: 207-780-5043, E-mail: mbrady@usm.maine.edu. *Application contact:* Mary Sloan, Director of Graduate Admissions, 207-780-4386, Fax: 207-780-4969, E-mail: msloan@usm.maine.edu.

University of South Florida, Graduate School, College of Behavioral and Community Sciences, Program in Applied Behavior Analysis, Tampa, FL 33620-9951. Offers MA. *Accreditation:* ACA. *Faculty:* 14 full-time (9 women). *Students:* 26 full-time (20 women), 28 part-time (25 women); includes 2 Black or African American, non-Hispanic/Latino; 2 Asian, non-Hispanic/Latino; 10 Hispanic/Latino; 1 Two or more races, non-Hispanic/Latino. Average age 25. 89 applicants, 42% accepted, 20 enrolled. In 2010, 17 master's awarded. *Degree requirements:* For master's, comprehensive exam, thesis. *Entrance requirements:* For master's, GRE General Test, minimum GPA of 3.0 in last 60 hours of coursework. Additional exam requirements/recommendations for international students: Required—TOEFL (minimum score 550 paper-based; 213 computer-based). *Application deadline:* For fall admission, 2/15 for domestic students, 1/2 for international students. Application fee: $30. *Financial support:* Unspecified assistantships available. Financial award application deadline: 4/1. *Unit head:* Dr. Raymond G. Miltenberger, Director, 813-974-5079, Fax: 813-974-6115, E-mail: rmiltenberger@fmhi.usf.edu. *Application contact:* Dr. Raymond G. Miltenberger, Director, 813-974-5079, Fax: 813-974-6115, E-mail: rmiltenberger@fmhi.usf.edu.

Western New England University, School of Arts and Sciences, Program in Behavior Analysis, Springfield, MA 01119. Offers applied behavior analysis (Postbaccalaureate Certificate); behavior analysis (PhD). Part-time programs available. *Students:* 22 part-time (18 women); includes 1 Asian, non-Hispanic/Latino; 3 Hispanic/Latino. *Entrance requirements:* For doctorate, GRE, master's degree in behavior analysis with minimum GPA of 3.6. *Application deadline:* For fall admission, 1/15 for domestic and international students. Application fee: $30. *Expenses:* Tuition: Full-time $35,582. *Financial support:* Available to part-time students. Applicants required to submit FAFSA. *Unit head:* Gregory Hanley, Director, 413-796-2367, E-mail: ghanley@wnec.edu. *Application contact:* Assistant Vice President, Graduate Studies and Continuing Education, 413-782-1517, Fax: 413-782-1777, E-mail: study@wnec.edu.

Westfield State University, Division of Graduate and Continuing Education, Department of Psychology, Westfield, MA 01086. Offers applied behavior analysis (MA); mental health counseling (MA); school guidance (MA). Part-time and evening/weekend programs available. *Degree requirements:* For master's, comprehensive exam. *Entrance requirements:* For master's, GRE General Test, MAT, minimum undergraduate GPA of 2.7.

Wright State University, School of Graduate Studies, College of Liberal Arts, Program in Applied Behavioral Science, Dayton, OH 45435. Offers criminal justice and social problems (MA); international and comparative politics (MA). *Degree requirements:* For master's, thesis optional. *Entrance requirements:* Additional exam requirements/recommendations for international students: Required—TOEFL. *Faculty research:* Training and development, criminal justice and social problems, community systems, human factors, industrial/organizational psychology.

Youngstown State University, Graduate School, College of Liberal Arts and Social Sciences, Department of Psychology, Youngstown, OH 44555-0001. Offers applied behavior analysis (MS).

Applied Psychology

Angelo State University, College of Graduate Studies, College of Liberal and Fine Arts, Department of Psychology, Sociology and Social Work, San Angelo, TX 76909. Offers psychology (MS), including applied psychology, counseling psychology, industrial and organizational psychology. Part-time and evening/weekend programs available. *Faculty:* 8 full-time (2 women). *Students:* 53 full-time (38 women), 10 part-time (7 women); includes 6 Black or African American, non-Hispanic/Latino; 12 Hispanic/Latino. Average age 29. 52 applicants, 69% accepted, 35 enrolled. In 2010, 13 master's awarded. *Degree requirements:* For master's, comprehensive exam, thesis optional. *Entrance requirements:* For master's, GRE General Test (for industrial and organizational psychology only), essay, letters of recommendation (for industrial and organizational psychology only). Additional exam requirements/recommendations for international students: Required—TOEFL or IELTS. *Application deadline:* For fall admission, 7/15 priority date for domestic students, 6/10 for international students; for spring admission, 12/1 priority date for domestic students, 11/1 for international students. Applications are processed on a rolling basis. Application fee: $40 ($50 for international students). Electronic applications accepted. *Expenses:* Tuition, state resident: full-time $4560; part-time $152 per credit hour. Tuition, nonresident: full-time $13,860; part-time $462 per credit hour. Required fees: $2132. Tuition and fees vary according to course load. *Financial support:* In 2010–11, 44 students received support, including 3 teaching assistantships (averaging $10,251 per year); career-related internships or fieldwork, Federal Work-Study, scholarships/grants, and unspecified assistantships also available. Support available to part-time students. Financial award application deadline: 3/1; financial award applicants required to submit FAFSA. Total annual research expenditures: $116,915. *Unit head:* Dr. William B. Davidson, Department Head, 325-942-2068 Ext. 248, Fax: 325-942-2290, E-mail: bill.davidson@angelo.edu. *Application contact:* Aly Hunter, Graduate Admissions Assistant, 325-942-2169, Fax: 325-942-2194, E-mail: aly.hunter@angelo.edu.

Antioch University New England, Graduate School, Department of Applied Psychology, Keene, NH 03431-3552. Offers autism spectrum disorders (Certificate); clinical mental health counseling (MA); dance/movement therapy and counseling (M Ed, MA); marriage and family therapy (MA, PhD). *Degree requirements:* For master's, internship, practicum. *Entrance requirements:* For master's, previous course work and work experience in psychology. Additional exam requirements/recommendations for international students: Required—TOEFL (minimum score 600 paper-based; 250 computer-based). Electronic applications accepted. *Expenses:* Contact institution. *Faculty research:* Diversity, descendents of survivors of the Holocaust and American slavery.

Arizona State University, College of Technology and Innovation, Applied Psychology Program, Mesa, AZ 85212. Offers MS. Part-time programs available. *Faculty:* 5 full-time (1 woman). *Students:* 9 full-time (4 women), 4 part-time (2 women); includes 3 minority (2 Asian, non-Hispanic/Latino; 1 Hispanic/Latino). Average age 30. 18 applicants, 39% accepted, 4 enrolled. In 2010, 3 degrees awarded. Terminal master's awarded for partial completion of doctoral program. *Degree requirements:* For master's, thesis or applied project with oral defense and exam; interactive Program of Study (iPOS) submitted before completing 50 percent of required credit hours. *Entrance requirements:* For master's, GRE, minimum GPA of 3.0 or equivalent in last 2 years of work leading to bachelor's degree. Additional exam requirements/recommendations for international students: Required—TOEFL, IELTS, or Pearson Test of English. *Application deadline:* For fall admission, 1/31 for domestic and international students; for spring admission, 9/30 for domestic and international students. Application fee: $70 ($90 for international students). Electronic applications accepted. *Expenses:* Tuition, state resident: full-time $8510; part-time $608 per credit. Tuition, nonresident: full-time $16,542; part-time $919 per credit. Required fees: $339; $110 per credit. Part-time tuition and fees vary according to course load. *Financial support:* In 2010–11, 4 research assistantships with full and partial tuition reimbursements (averaging $19,060 per year) were awarded; fellowships with full tuition reimbursements, teaching assistantships with full and partial tuition reimbursements, career-related internships or fieldwork, Federal Work-Study, institutionally sponsored loans, scholarships/grants, health care benefits, and tuition waivers (full and partial) also available. Support available to part-time students. Financial award application deadline: 3/1; financial award applicants required to submit FAFSA. Total annual research expenditures: $602,827. *Unit head:* Dr. Mitzi Montoya, Vice Provost and Dean, 480-727-1955, Fax: 480-727-1538, E-mail: mitzi.montoya@asu.edu. *Application contact:* Graduate Admissions, 480-965-6113.

Athabasca University, Graduate Centre for Applied Psychology, Athabasca, AB T9S 3A3, Canada. Offers art therapy (MC); career counseling (MC); counseling (Advanced Certificate); counseling psychology (MC); school counseling (MC).

Boston College, Lynch Graduate School of Education, Program in Applied Developmental and Educational Psychology, Chestnut Hill, MA 02467-3800. Offers MA, PhD. Part-time and evening/weekend programs available. *Students:* 48 full-time (42 women), 9 part-time (6 women); includes 5 Black or African American, non-Hispanic/Latino; 2 Asian, non-Hispanic/Latino; 4 Hispanic/Latino, 11 international. 173 applicants, 47% accepted, 30 enrolled. In 2010, 16 master's, 1 doctorate awarded. Terminal master's awarded for partial completion of doctoral program. *Degree requirements:* For master's, comprehensive exam; for doctorate, comprehensive exam, thesis/dissertation. *Entrance requirements:* For master's and doctorate, GRE General Test. Additional exam requirements/recommendations for international students: Required—TOEFL (minimum score 550 paper-based; 213 computer-based; 81 iBT). Application fee: $70. Electronic applications accepted. *Financial support:* Fellowships with full and partial tuition reimbursements, research assistantships with full and partial tuition reimbursements, teaching assistantships with full and partial tuition reimbursements, career-related internships or fieldwork, Federal Work-Study, scholarships/grants, traineeships, health care benefits, tuition waivers (full and partial), and unspecified assistantships available. Support available to part-time students. Financial award applicants required to submit FAFSA. *Faculty research:* Cognitive learning and culture, effects of social policy reform on children and families, psychosocial trauma, human rights and international justice, positive youth development, children and adolescents living in poverty. *Unit head:* Dr. M. Brinton Lykes, Chairperson, 617-552-4214, Fax: 617-552-0812. *Application contact:* Adam Poluzzi, Director, Graduate Admission and Financial Aid, 617-552-4214, Fax: 617-552-0398, E-mail: poluzzi@bc.edu.

California State University, Chico, Graduate School, College of Behavioral and Social Sciences, Department of Psychology, Program in Applied Psychology, Chico, CA 95929-0722. Offers MA. *Students:* 24 full-time (22 women), 1 (woman) part-time; includes 1 Black or African American, non-Hispanic/Latino; 1 Asian, non-Hispanic/Latino; 6 Hispanic/Latino, 1 international. Average age 27. 27 applicants, 44% accepted, 10 enrolled. In 2010, 10 master's awarded. *Degree requirements:* For master's, thesis or alternative. *Entrance requirements:* For master's, GRE General Test or MAT, 3 letters of recommendation on departmental form. Additional exam requirements/recommendations for international students: Required—TOEFL (minimum score 550 paper-based; 213 computer-based; 80 iBT), IELTS (minimum score 6.5). *Application deadline:* For fall admission, 3/1 for domestic and international students. Application fee: $55. *Unit head:* Dr. Linda Kline, Graduate Coordinator, 530-898-6263. *Application contact:* Dr. Linda Kline, Graduate Coordinator, 530-898-6263.

California State University, Northridge, Graduate Studies, College of Social and Behavioral Sciences, Department of Psychology, Northridge, CA 91330. Offers clinical psychology (MA); general-experimental psychology (MA); human factors and applied experimental psychology (MA). *Degree requirements:* For master's, thesis. *Entrance requirements:* For master's, GRE General Test, GRE Subject Test, minimum GPA of 3.0, letters of recommendation. Additional exam requirements/recommendations for international students: Required—TOEFL.

The Catholic University of America, School of Arts and Sciences, Department of Psychology, Washington, DC 20064. Offers applied experimental psychology (PhD); clinical psychology (PhD); general psychology (MA); human factors (MA); MA/JD. *Accreditation:* APA (one or more programs are accredited). Part-time programs available. *Faculty:* 12 full-time (6 women), 7 part-time/adjunct (2 women). *Students:* 39 full-time (25 women), 31 part-time (28 women); includes 6 Black or African American, non-Hispanic/Latino; 4 Asian, non-Hispanic/Latino; 4 Hispanic/Latino, 1 international. Average age 29. 229 applicants, 22% accepted, 17 enrolled. In 2010, 22 master's, 8 doctorates awarded. *Degree requirements:* For master's, comprehensive exam, thesis (for some programs); for doctorate, comprehensive exam, thesis/dissertation. *Entrance requirements:* For master's, GRE General Test, statement of purpose, official copies of academic transcripts, three letters of recommendation; for doctorate, GRE General Test, GRE Subject Test, statement of purpose, official copies of academic transcripts, three letters of recommendation. Additional exam requirements/recommendations for international students: Required—TOEFL (minimum score 580 paper-based; 237 computer-based). *Application deadline:* For fall admission, 8/1 priority date for domestic students, 7/15 for international students; for spring admission, 12/1 priority date for domestic students, 10/15 for international students. Applications are processed on a rolling basis. Application fee: $55. Electronic applications accepted. *Expenses:* Tuition: Full-time $33,580; part-time $1315 per credit hour. Required fees: $80; $40 per semester hour. One-time fee: $425. *Financial support:* Fellowships, research assistantships, teaching assistantships, Federal Work-Study, scholarships/grants, tuition waivers (full and partial), and unspecified assistantships available. Financial award application deadline: 2/1; financial award applicants required to submit FAFSA. *Faculty research:* Clinical psychology, applied cognitive science, psychopathology, cognitive neuroscience, psychotherapy. Total annual research expenditures: $409,988. *Unit head:* Dr. Marc M. Sebrechts, Chair, 202-319-5750, Fax: 202-319-6263, E-mail: sebrechts@cua.edu. *Application contact:* Andrew Woodall, Director of Graduate Admissions, 202-319-5057, Fax: 202-319-6533, E-mail: cua-admissions@cua.edu.

Central Michigan University, College of Graduate Studies, College of Humanities and Social and Behavioral Sciences, Department of Psychology, Program in Experimental Psychology,

Applied Psychology

Central Michigan University (continued)

Mount Pleasant, MI 48859. Offers applied experimental psychology (PhD); experimental psychology (MS). Part-time programs available. *Students:* 13 full-time (3 women), 17 part-time (9 women); includes 1 Black or African American, non-Hispanic/Latino, 1 international. Average age 27. *Degree requirements:* For master's, thesis or alternative; for doctorate, thesis/dissertation. *Application deadline:* For fall admission, 2/1 for domestic and international students. Application fee: $35 ($45 for international students). Electronic applications accepted. *Expenses:* Tuition, state resident: full-time $8208; part-time $456 per credit hour. Tuition, nonresident: full-time $13,788; part-time $766 per credit hour. One-time fee: $25. *Financial support:* In 2010–11, 3 fellowships with tuition reimbursements were awarded; research assistantships with tuition reimbursements, career-related internships or fieldwork, Federal Work-Study, unspecified assistantships, and out-of-state merit awards, non-resident graduate awards also available. *Faculty research:* Behavioral neuroscience, human development, perception and cognition, social/personal problem solving, psychophysiology. *Unit head:* Dr. Hajime Otani, Chairperson, 989-774-6494, Fax: 989-774-2553, E-mail: otani1h@cmich.edu. *Application contact:* Dr. Mark Reilly, Graduate Coordinator, 989-774-2343, Fax: 989-774-2553, E-mail: reill1mp@cmich.edu.

The Chicago School of Professional Psychology, Program in Applied Behavior Analysis, Chicago, IL 60610. Offers applied behavior analysis (Psy D); clinical psychology (applied behavior analysis specialization) (MA). *Degree requirements:* For master's, thesis, practicum; for doctorate, thesis/dissertation, practicum. *Entrance requirements:* For doctorate, GRE. Additional exam requirements/recommendations for international students: Required—TOEFL.

The Chicago School of Professional Psychology: Online, Program in Applied Forensic Psychology Services, Chicago, IL 60654. Offers MA, Certificate.

The Chicago School of Professional Psychology: Online, Program in Applied Industrial and Organizational Psychology, Chicago, IL 60654. Offers MA, Certificate.

Clemson University, Graduate School, College of Business and Behavioral Science, Department of Psychology, Program in Applied Psychology, Clemson, SC 29634. Offers MS. *Students:* 4 full-time (2 women). Average age 31. 37 applicants, 11% accepted, 2 enrolled. In 2010, 11 master's awarded. *Degree requirements:* For master's, thesis, internship. *Entrance requirements:* For master's, GRE General Test. Additional exam requirements/recommendations for international students: Required—TOEFL. *Application deadline:* For fall admission, 1/15 for domestic students. Application fee: $70 ($80 for international students). Electronic applications accepted. *Expenses:* Contact institution. *Financial support:* In 2010–11, 1 student received support, including 1 research assistantship with partial tuition reimbursement available (averaging $12,000 per year); fellowships with full and partial tuition reimbursements available, teaching assistantships with partial tuition reimbursements available, career-related internships or fieldwork, institutionally sponsored loans, scholarships/grants, health care benefits, and unspecified assistantships also available. Support available to part-time students. Financial award application deadline: 3/15; financial award applicants required to submit FAFSA. *Faculty research:* Personnel selection and evaluation, occupational health, motivation and decision-making, human factors, transportation safety. *Unit head:* Dr. Patrick Raymark, Chair, 864-656-4715, Fax: 864-656-0358, E-mail: praymar@clemson.edu. *Application contact:* Dr. Robert Sinclair, Graduate Program Coordinator, 864-656-3931, Fax: 864-656-0358, E-mail: rsincla@clemson.edu.

Coppin State University, Division of Graduate Studies, Division of Arts and Sciences, Department of Applied Psychology and Rehabilitation Counseling, Baltimore, MD 21216-3698. Offers alcohol and substance abuse counseling (MS); rehabilitation counseling (M Ed). *Accreditation:* CORE (one or more programs are accredited). Part-time and evening/weekend programs available. *Degree requirements:* For master's, comprehensive exam, thesis optional, fieldwork/internship. *Entrance requirements:* For master's, GRE, minimum GPA of 3.0, interview.

Eastern Washington University, Graduate Studies, College of Education and Human Development, Program in Mental Health Counseling, Cheney, WA 99004-2431. Offers applied psychology (MS); mental health counseling (MS).

Eastern Washington University, Graduate Studies, College of Education and Human Development, Program in School Counseling, Cheney, WA 99004-2431. Offers applied psychology (MS); school counseling (MS). *Accreditation:* ACA. *Degree requirements:* For master's, comprehensive exam, thesis or alternative. *Entrance requirements:* For master's, GRE General Test, minimum GPA of 3.0.

Fairfield University, Graduate School of Education and Allied Professions, Department of Psychological and Educational Consultation, Fairfield, CT 06824-5195. Offers applied psychology (MA), including foundations of advanced psychology, human services, industrial/organizational; educational technology (MA); school library media specialist (MA); school psychology (MA, CAS); special education (MA, CAS). Part-time and evening/weekend programs available. *Faculty:* 6 full-time (2 women), 7 part-time/adjunct (4 women). *Students:* 52 full-time (46 women), 144 part-time (120 women); includes 2 Black or African American, non-Hispanic/Latino; 1 American Indian or Alaska Native, non-Hispanic/Latino; 2 Asian, non-Hispanic/Latino; 14 Hispanic/Latino, 2 international. 136 applicants, 63% accepted, 59 enrolled. In 2010, 44 master's, 14 other advanced degrees awarded. *Degree requirements:* For master's, comprehensive exam, thesis optional. *Entrance requirements:* For master's, PRAXIS I (PPST), minimum QPA of 3.0, 2 recommendations, resume. Additional exam requirements/recommendations for international students: Required—TOEFL (minimum score 550 paper-based; 213 computer-based; 84 iBT). Application fee: $60. Electronic applications accepted. *Expenses:* Tuition: Part-time $600 per hour. Part-time tuition and fees vary according to degree level and program. *Financial support:* Unspecified assistantships available. Financial award applicants required to submit FAFSA. *Faculty research:* Child neuropsychology, disabilities, effect of pre-treatment orientation on treatment, autism, technology in business and classroom, collaboration with schools, communities and industry. *Unit head:* Dr. David Zera, Chair, 203-254-4250, Fax: 203-254-4047, E-mail: dzera@fairfield.edu. *Application contact:* Marianne Gumpper, Director of Graduate and Continuing Studies Admissions, 203-254-4184, Fax: 203-254-4073, E-mail: gradadmis@fairfield.edu.

Fordham University, Graduate School of Arts and Sciences, Department of Psychology, Program in Applied Developmental Psychology, New York, NY 10458. Offers PhD. *Students:* 20 full-time (18 women), 11 part-time (8 women); includes 5 Black or African American, non-Hispanic/Latino; 2 Asian, non-Hispanic/Latino; 1 Hispanic/Latino, 3 international. Average age 29. 23 applicants, 52% accepted, 6 enrolled. In 2010, 4 doctorates awarded. *Degree requirements:* For doctorate, comprehensive exam, thesis/dissertation. *Entrance requirements:* For doctorate, GRE General Test, GRE Subject Test. Additional exam requirements/recommendations for international students: Required—TOEFL (minimum score 600 paper-based; 250 computer-based). *Application deadline:* For fall admission, 12/14 for domestic students. Application fee: $70. Electronic applications accepted. *Financial support:* In 2010–11, 15 students received support, including 4 fellowships with tuition reimbursements available (averaging $21,300 per year), 11 research assistantships with tuition reimbursements available (averaging $18,836 per year), 1 teaching assistantship with tuition reimbursement available (averaging $20,600 per year); career-related internships or fieldwork, institutionally sponsored loans, tuition waivers (full and partial), and unspecified assistantships also available. Financial award application deadline: 12/14. *Faculty research:* Development of citizenship, impact of participation in community service, impact of poverty on children, development of moral reasoning and behavior. Total annual research expenditures: $1.4 million. *Unit head:* Dr. Ann D'Allesandro, Director, 718-817-3789, Fax: 718-817-3785, E-mail: sherrod@fordham.edu. *Application contact:* Charlene Dundie, Director of Graduate Admissions, 718-817-4420, Fax: 718-817-3566, E-mail: dundie@fordham.edu.

Francis Marion University, Graduate Programs, Department of Psychology, Florence, SC 29502-0547. Offers applied psychology (MS), including clinical/counseling, school psychology; school psychology (SSP). Part-time and evening/weekend programs available. *Faculty:* 10 full-time (4 women), 5 part-time/adjunct (4 women). *Students:* 17 full-time (16 women), 26 part-time (25 women); includes 6 Black or African American, non-Hispanic/Latino. Average age 25. 44 applicants, 61% accepted, 14 enrolled. In 2010, 9 master's awarded. *Degree requirements:* For master's, internship. *Entrance requirements:* For master's, GRE General Test. *Application deadline:* For fall admission, 3/15 for domestic students; for spring admission, 10/15 for domestic students. Applications are processed on a rolling basis. Application fee: $30. *Expenses:* Tuition, state resident: full-time $8667; part-time $433.35 per credit hour. Tuition, nonresident: full-time $17,334; part-time $866.70 per credit hour. Required fees: $335; $12.25 per credit hour. $30 per semester. *Financial support:* In 2010–11, 13 students received support, including 2 research assistantships (averaging $7,000 per year), 3 teaching assistantships (averaging $8,000 per year); career-related internships or fieldwork, unspecified assistantships, and scholarships with out-of-state waivers also available. Support available to part-time students. Financial award application deadline: 3/1; financial award applicants required to submit FAFSA. *Faculty research:* Parenting and family relationships, child development, applied behavioral analysis, posttraumatic stress disorder, clinical psychology in adults. *Unit head:* Dr. John R. Hester, Chair, 843-661-1635, Fax: 843-661-1628. *Application contact:* Jennifer Taylor, Administrative Assistant, 843-661-1378, Fax: 843-661-1628.

The George Washington University, Columbian College of Arts and Sciences, Department of Psychology, Washington, DC 20052. Offers applied social psychology (PhD); clinical psychology (PhD); cognitive neuroscience (PhD). *Accreditation:* APA. Part-time and evening/weekend programs available. *Faculty:* 26 full-time (14 women), 14 part-time/adjunct (9 women). *Students:* 131 full-time (103 women), 75 part-time (55 women); includes 14 Black or African American, non-Hispanic/Latino; 2 American Indian or Alaska Native, non-Hispanic/Latino; 18 Asian, non-Hispanic/Latino; 16 Hispanic/Latino, 4 international. Average age 29. 797 applicants, 6% accepted, 9 enrolled. In 2010, 41 doctorates awarded. *Degree requirements:* For doctorate, thesis/dissertation or alternative, general exam. *Entrance requirements:* For doctorate, GRE General Test, minimum GPA of 3.0. Additional exam requirements/recommendations for international students: Required—TOEFL (minimum score 550 paper-based; 213 computer-based; 80 iBT). *Application deadline:* For fall admission, 1/15 for domestic and international students. Application fee: $75. *Financial support:* In 2010–11, 62 students received support; fellowships with tuition reimbursements available, teaching assistantships with tuition reimbursements available, career-related internships or fieldwork, Federal Work-Study, and tuition waivers available. *Unit head:* Dr. Paul Poppen, Chair, 202-994-6324, E-mail: pjp@gwu.edu. *Application contact:* Information Contact, 202-994-6320, Fax: 202-994-1602, E-mail: psydept@gwu.edu.

Hofstra University, College of Liberal Arts and Sciences, Program in Applied Organizational Psychology, Hempstead, NY 11549. Offers PhD. *Students:* 19 full-time (11 women), 11 part-time (7 women); includes 10 minority (6 Black or African American, non-Hispanic/Latino; 4 Asian, non-Hispanic/Latino), 2 international. Average age 30. 20 applicants, 50% accepted, 10 enrolled. In 2010, 8 doctorates awarded. *Degree requirements:* For doctorate, comprehensive exam, thesis/dissertation. *Entrance requirements:* For doctorate, GRE, 2 letters of recommendation; Essay; Interview. Additional exam requirements/recommendations for international students: Required—TOEFL (minimum score 550 paper-based; 213 computer-based; 80 iBT). *Application deadline:* For fall admission, 2/1 for domestic and international students. Application fee: $70 ($75 for international students). Electronic applications accepted. *Expenses:* Tuition: Full-time $18,000; part-time $1000 per credit hour. Required fees: $970; $145 per term. Tuition and fees vary according to program. *Financial support:* In 2010–11, 21 students received support, including 21 fellowships with full and partial tuition reimbursements available (averaging $6,979 per year); research assistantships with full and partial tuition reimbursements available, career-related internships or fieldwork, Federal Work-Study, institutionally sponsored loans, scholarships/grants, tuition waivers (full and partial), and unspecified assistantships also available. Support available to part-time students. Financial award applicants required to submit FAFSA. *Faculty research:* Customer satisfaction, personnel selection and decision-making, team effectiveness, occupational health, positive organizational behavior. *Unit head:* Dr. Terri Shapiro, Associate Director, 516-463-6345, Fax: 516-463-7306, E-mail: psytzs@hofstra.edu. *Application contact:* Carol Drummer, Dean of Graduate Admissions, 516-463-4876, Fax: 516-463-4664, E-mail: gradstudent@hofstra.edu.

Hunter College of the City University of New York, Graduate School, School of Arts and Sciences, Department of Psychology, New York, NY 10021-5085. Offers animal behavior and conservation (MA); applied and evaluative psychology (MA); biopsychology and behavioral neuroscience (PhD); biopsychology and comparative psychology (MA); social, cognitive, and developmental psychology (MA). Part-time and evening/weekend programs available. *Faculty:* 9 full-time (1 woman), 1 part-time/adjunct (0 women). *Students:* 10 full-time (7 women), 79 part-time (61 women); includes 3 Black or African American, non-Hispanic/Latino; 7 Asian, non-Hispanic/Latino; 9 Hispanic/Latino, 2 international. Average age 27. 151 applicants, 34% accepted, 21 enrolled. In 2010, 13 master's awarded. *Degree requirements:* For master's, comprehensive exam, thesis. *Entrance requirements:* For master's, GRE General Test, minimum 12 credits of course work in psychology, including statistics and experimental psychology; 2 letters of recommendation. Additional exam requirements/recommendations for international students: Required—TOEFL. *Application deadline:* For fall admission, 4/1 for domestic students, 2/1 for international students; for spring admission, 11/1 for domestic students, 9/1 for international students. Applications are processed on a rolling basis. Application fee: $125. *Financial support:* Federal Work-Study, scholarships/grants, and tuition waivers (partial) available. Support available to part-time students. *Faculty research:* Personality, cognitive and linguistic development, hormonal and neural control of behavior, gender and culture, social cognition of health and attitudes. *Unit head:* Dr. Jeffrey Parsons, Chairperson, 212-772-5550, Fax: 212-772-5620, E-mail: jeffrey.parsons@hunter.cuny.edu. *Application contact:* Martin Braun, Acting Program Director, 212-772-4482, Fax: 212-650-3336, E-mail: cbraun@hunter.cuny.edu.

Indiana University South Bend, College of Liberal Arts and Sciences, South Bend, IN 46634-7111. Offers applied mathematics and computer science (MS); applied psychology (MA); English (MA); liberal studies (MLS). Part-time and evening/weekend programs available. *Faculty:* 79 full-time (33 women). *Students:* 34 full-time (18 women), 100 part-time (69 women); includes 23 minority (15 Black or African American, non-Hispanic/Latino; 2 American Indian or Alaska Native, non-Hispanic/Latino; 3 Asian, non-Hispanic/Latino; 2 Hispanic/Latino; 1 Two or more races, non-Hispanic/Latino), 16 international. Average age 37. 44 applicants, 84% accepted, 27 enrolled. In 2010, 21 master's awarded. *Degree requirements:* For master's, thesis (for some programs). *Entrance requirements:* For master's, minimum GPA of 3.0. Additional exam requirements/recommendations for international students: Required—TOEFL. *Application deadline:* For fall admission, 7/31 priority date for domestic students, 7/1 priority date for international students; for spring admission, 3/31 priority date for domestic students, 11/1 priority date for international students. Applications are processed on a rolling basis. Application fee: $50 ($60 for international students). *Financial support:* In 2010–11, 5 students received support, including 5 teaching assistantships; Federal Work-Study also available. Support available to part-time students. *Faculty research:* Artificial intelligence, bioinformatics, English language and literature, creative writing, computer networks. Total annual research expenditures: $127,000. *Unit head:* Dr. Lynn R. Williams, Dean, 574-520-4322, Fax: 574-520-4528, E-mail: lwilliam@iusb.edu. *Application contact:* Dr. Lynn R. Williams, Dean, 574-520-4322, Fax: 574-520-4528, E-mail: lwilliam@iusb.edu.

Laurentian University, School of Graduate Studies and Research, Programme in Psychology, Sudbury, ON P3E 2C6, Canada. Offers applied psychology (MA); experimental psychology (MA).

Loras College, Graduate Division, Program in Applied Psychology, Dubuque, IA 52004-0178. Offers MA. Part-time and evening/weekend programs available. *Degree requirements:* For master's, comprehensive exam, thesis (for some programs). *Entrance requirements:* For master's, Ohio State University Psychological Test or GRE General Test, minimum undergraduate GPA of 2.75.

Applied Psychology

Loyola University Chicago, Graduate School, Department of Psychology, Program in Applied Social Psychology, Chicago, IL 60660. Offers MA, PhD. *Faculty:* 7 full-time (3 women), 2 part-time/adjunct (1 woman). *Students:* 36 full-time (28 women), 2 part-time (both women); includes 8 minority (2 Black or African American, non-Hispanic/Latino; 1 Asian, non-Hispanic/Latino; 3 Hispanic/Latino; 2 Two or more races, non-Hispanic/Latino), 3 international. Average age 30. 70 applicants, 19% accepted, 6 enrolled. In 2010, 8 master's, 5 doctorates awarded. Terminal master's awarded for partial completion of doctoral program. *Degree requirements:* For master's, thesis; for doctorate, comprehensive exam, thesis/dissertation, internship. *Entrance requirements:* For master's and doctorate, GRE General Test, GRE Subject Test, sample of written work. *Application deadline:* For fall admission, 1/15 for domestic and international students. Applications are processed on a rolling basis. Application fee: $50. *Expenses:* Tuition: Full-time $14,940; part-time $830 per credit hour. Required fees: $87 per semester. Part-time tuition and fees vary according to course load and program. *Financial support:* In 2010–11, 1 fellowship with tuition reimbursement (averaging $14,000 per year), 5 research assistantships with tuition reimbursements (averaging $14,000 per year), 1 teaching assistantship (averaging $14,000 per year) were awarded; career-related internships or fieldwork, Federal Work-Study, and scholarships/grants also available. Financial award application deadline: 1/15; financial award applicants required to submit FAFSA. *Faculty research:* Program evaluation, attitudes and prejudice, psychological well-being, mass media, groups and organizations and communities. Total annual research expenditures: $200,000. *Unit head:* Dr. Scott Tindale, 773-508-3014. *Application contact:* Dr. Scott Tindale, 773-508-3014.

Lynn University, College of Liberal Education, Boca Raton, FL 33431-5598. Offers applied psychology (MS); criminal justice administration (MS); emergency planning and administration (MS, Certificate). Part-time and evening/weekend programs available. Postbaccalaureate distance learning degree programs offered. *Entrance requirements:* For master's, GRE, resume, 2 letters of recommendation, minimum undergraduate GPA of 3.0. Additional exam requirements/recommendations for international students: Required—TOEFL (minimum score 550 paper-based; 213 computer-based). *Faculty research:* Terrorism, criminological theory, corrections, emergency planning.

Massachusetts School of Professional Psychology, Graduate Programs, Boston, MA 02132. Offers applied psychology in higher education student personnel administration (MA); clinical psychology (Psy D); counseling psychology (MA); counseling psychology and community mental health (MA); counseling psychology and global mental health (MA); executive coaching (Graduate Certificate); forensic and counseling psychology (MA); leadership psychology (Psy D); organizational psychology (MA); primary care psychology (MA); respecialization in clinical psychology (Certificate); school psychology (Psy D); MA/CAGS. *Accreditation:* APA. *Faculty:* 24 full-time (11 women), 13 part-time/adjunct (9 women). *Students:* 515. Average age 28. *Degree requirements:* For master's, comprehensive exam (for some programs); for doctorate, thesis/dissertation (for some programs). Application fee: $50. Electronic applications accepted. *Expenses:* Tuition: Full-time $32,352; part-time $1011 per credit. Full-time tuition and fees vary according to degree level. *Financial support:* Teaching assistantships, career-related internships or fieldwork available. Financial award applicants required to submit FAFSA. *Unit head:* Dr. Nicholas A. Covino, President, 617-327-6777, Fax: 617-327-4447. *Application contact:* Admissions and Marketing, 617-327-6777 Ext. 210, Fax: 617-327-4447, E-mail: admissions@mspp.edu.

Memorial University of Newfoundland, School of Graduate Studies, Department of Psychology, St. John's, NL A1C 5S7, Canada. Offers applied social psychology (MASP); experimental psychology (M Sc, PhD). Part-time programs available. *Degree requirements:* For master's, workterms (MASP), thesis (M Sc); for doctorate, comprehensive exam, thesis/dissertation, oral thesis defense. *Entrance requirements:* For master's, GRE, honors bachelor's degree of high second class standing or equivalent; for doctorate, GRE, master's or honors degree. Electronic applications accepted. *Faculty research:* Behavioral neuroscience, cognition, theory and research on abnormal behavior.

New York University, Steinhardt School of Culture, Education, and Human Development, Department of Applied Psychology, New York, NY 10012-1019. Offers counselor education (MA, PhD, Advanced Certificate), including counseling and guidance (MA, Advanced Certificate), counseling for mental health and wellness (MA), counseling psychology (PhD); educational and developmental psychology (MA, PhD), including educational psychology (MA), human development and social intervention (MA), psychological development (PhD), psychology and social intervention (PhD). *Accreditation:* APA (one or more programs are accredited). Part-time programs available. *Faculty:* 34 full-time (22 women), 54 part-time/adjunct (33 women). *Students:* 200 full-time (156 women), 92 part-time (75 women); includes 36 Black or African American, non-Hispanic/Latino; 1 American Indian or Alaska Native, non-Hispanic/Latino; 24 Asian, non-Hispanic/Latino; 29 Hispanic/Latino, 37 international. Average age 29. 1,104 applicants, 26% accepted, 89 enrolled. In 2010, 94 master's, 12 doctorates awarded. Terminal master's awarded for partial completion of doctoral program. *Degree requirements:* For master's, thesis (for some programs); for doctorate, thesis/dissertation. *Entrance requirements:* For doctorate, GRE General Test, interview. Additional exam requirements/recommendations for international students: Required—TOEFL. *Application deadline:* For fall admission, 12/1 priority date for domestic and international students; for spring admission, 11/1 for domestic and international students. Applications are processed on a rolling basis. Application fee: $75. Electronic applications accepted. *Financial support:* Fellowships with full and partial tuition reimbursements, research assistantships with full and partial tuition reimbursements, teaching assistantships with full and partial tuition reimbursements, career-related internships or fieldwork, Federal Work-Study, institutionally sponsored loans, scholarships/grants, tuition waivers (partial), and unspecified assistantships available. Support available to part-time students. Financial award application deadline: 2/1; financial award applicants required to submit FAFSA. *Faculty research:* Urban children; adolescents and families; culture, race and ethnicity; risk-taking behaviors and health; early childhood. *Unit head:* Dr. Jacqueline Mattis, Chairperson, 212-998-9404, Fax: 212-995-4358, E-mail: jacqueline.mattis@nyu.edu. *Application contact:* 212-998-5030, Fax: 212-995-4328, E-mail: steinhardt.gradadmissions@nyu.edu.

Northeastern University, Bouvé College of Health Sciences Graduate School, Department of Counseling and Applied Educational Psychology, Boston, MA 02115-5096. Offers applied behavior analysis (MS); college student development and counseling (MS, CAGS); counseling psychology (MS, PhD, CAGS); school psychology (MS, PhD, CAGS). *Accreditation:* APA (one or more programs are accredited). Part-time and evening/weekend programs available. *Faculty:* 19 full-time (12 women), 25 part-time/adjunct (14 women). *Students:* 254 full-time (208 women), 49 part-time (43 women). 469 applicants, 42% accepted, 75 enrolled. In 2010, 174 master's, 1 doctorate, 25 other advanced degrees awarded. *Degree requirements:* For doctorate, comprehensive exam, thesis/dissertation, qualifying exams; for CAGS, comprehensive exam. *Entrance requirements:* For master's and CAGS, GRE General Test or MAT; for doctorate, GRE General Test. Additional exam requirements/recommendations for international students: Required—TOEFL (minimum score 100 iBT). *Application deadline:* Applications are processed on a rolling basis. Application fee: $50. Electronic applications accepted. *Financial support:* Research assistantships, teaching assistantships with full tuition reimbursements, career-related internships or fieldwork, Federal Work-Study, scholarships/grants, tuition waivers (partial), and unspecified assistantships available. Support available to part-time students. Financial award application deadline: 3/1; financial award applicants required to submit FAFSA. *Faculty research:* Early intervention, career development and choice, crisis intervention, family systems, bilingual education in special education, eating disorders. *Unit head:* Dr. Y. Barry Chung, Chairman, 617-373-8120, Fax: 617-373-8892, E-mail: y.chunk@neu.edu. *Application contact:* Margaret Schnabel, Director of Graduate Admissions, 617-373-2708, E-mail: bouvegrad@neu.edu.

Oklahoma State University, College of Education, School of Applied Health and Educational Psychology, Stillwater, OK 74078. Offers applied behavioral studies (Ed D); applied health and educational psychology (MS, PhD, Ed S). *Accreditation:* APA (one or more programs are accredited). Part-time programs available. *Faculty:* 38 full-time (17 women), 19 part-time/adjunct (11 women). *Students:* 199 full-time (144 women), 146 part-time (104 women); includes 25 Black or African American, non-Hispanic/Latino; 27 American Indian or Alaska Native, non-Hispanic/Latino; 12 Asian, non-Hispanic/Latino; 12 Hispanic/Latino, 13 international. Average age 31. 247 applicants, 35% accepted, 65 enrolled. In 2010, 72 master's, 16 doctorates awarded. *Degree requirements:* For master's, thesis (for some programs); for doctorate, comprehensive exam, thesis/dissertation. *Entrance requirements:* For master's and doctorate, GRE or GMAT. Additional exam requirements/recommendations for international students: Required—TOEFL (minimum score 550 paper-based; 79 iBT). *Application deadline:* For fall admission, 3/1 priority date for international students; for spring admission, 8/1 priority date for international students. Applications are processed on a rolling basis. Application fee: $40 ($75 for international students). Electronic applications accepted. *Expenses:* Tuition, state resident: full-time $3716; part-time $154.85 per credit hour. Tuition, nonresident: full-time $14,892; part-time $621 per credit hour. Required fees: $2044; $85.20 per credit hour. One-time fee: $50. Tuition and fees vary according to course load and campus/location. *Financial support:* In 2010–11, 30 research assistantships (averaging $6,839 per year), 64 teaching assistantships (averaging $8,416 per year) were awarded; career-related internships or fieldwork, Federal Work-Study, scholarships/grants, health care benefits, tuition waivers (partial), and unspecified assistantships also available. Support available to part-time students. Financial award application deadline: 3/1; financial award applicants required to submit FAFSA. *Unit head:* Dr. John Romans, Head, 405-744-6040, Fax: 405-744-6779. *Application contact:* Dr. Gordon Emslie, Dean, 405-744-6368, Fax: 405-744-0355, E-mail: grad-i@okstate.edu.

Old Dominion University, College of Sciences, Doctoral Program in Psychology, Norfolk, VA 23529. Offers applied experimental psychology (PhD); human factors psychology (PhD); industrial/organizational psychology (PhD). *Faculty:* 21 full-time (9 women). *Students:* 32 full-time (21 women), 12 part-time (8 women); includes 2 minority (1 Black or African American, non-Hispanic/Latino; 1 Hispanic/Latino), 4 international. Average age 29. 59 applicants, 24% accepted, 12 enrolled. In 2010, 1 doctorate awarded. *Degree requirements:* For doctorate, thesis/dissertation, candidacy exam. *Entrance requirements:* For doctorate, GRE General Test, GRE Subject Test, 3 recommendation letters. Additional exam requirements/recommendations for international students: Required—TOEFL (minimum score 550 paper-based). *Application deadline:* For winter admission, 1/5 for domestic and international students. Application fee: $50. Electronic applications accepted. *Expenses:* Tuition, state resident: full-time $8592; part-time $358 per credit. Tuition, nonresident: full-time $21,672; part-time $903 per credit. Required fees: $119 per semester. One-time fee: $50. *Financial support:* In 2010–11, 33 students received support, including 4 fellowships with full tuition reimbursements available (averaging $18,000 per year), 4 research assistantships with full tuition reimbursements available (averaging $12,000 per year), 25 teaching assistantships with full tuition reimbursements available (averaging $12,000 per year). Financial award application deadline: 1/15. *Faculty research:* Human factors, industrial psychology, organizational psychology, applied experimental (health, developmental, quantitative). Total annual research expenditures: $978,563. *Unit head:* Dr. Bryan E. Porter, Graduate Program Director, 757-683-4458, Fax: 757-683-5087, E-mail: bporter@odu.edu. *Application contact:* Dr. Bryan E. Porter, Graduate Program Director, 757-683-4458, Fax: 757-683-5087, E-mail: bporter@odu.edu.

Rowan University, Graduate School, College of Liberal Arts and Sciences, Program in Mental Health Counseling and Applied Psychology, Glassboro, NJ 08028-1701. Offers MA. *Accreditation:* ACA. Part-time and evening/weekend programs available. In 2010, 31 master's awarded. *Degree requirements:* For master's, thesis. *Entrance requirements:* For master's, GRE General Test. Additional exam requirements/recommendations for international students: Required—TOEFL. *Application deadline:* Applications are processed on a rolling basis. Application fee: $65 ($200 for international students). Electronic applications accepted. *Expenses:* Tuition, area resident: Part-time $602 per semester hour. Tuition, nonresident: part-time $602 per semester hour. Required fees: $100 per semester hour. One-time fee: $10 part-time. *Financial support:* Career-related internships or fieldwork, scholarships/grants, health care benefits, and unspecified assistantships available. *Unit head:* Dr. Horacio Sosa, Dean, College of Graduate and Continuing Education, 856-256-4747, Fax: 856-256-5638, E-mail: sosa@rowan.edu. *Application contact:* Karen Haynes, Graduate Coordinator, 856-256-4052, Fax: 856-256-4436, E-mail: haynes@rowan.edu.

Rutgers, The State University of New Jersey, New Brunswick, Graduate School of Applied and Professional Psychology, Piscataway, NJ 08854. Offers Psy M, Psy D. *Accreditation:* APA (one or more programs are accredited). *Faculty:* 20 full-time (11 women), 14 part-time/adjunct (11 women). *Students:* 187 full-time (141 women), 8 part-time (all women); includes 17 Black or African American, non-Hispanic/Latino; 13 Asian, non-Hispanic/Latino; 14 Hispanic/Latino, 1 international. Average age 31. 505 applicants, 10% accepted, 35 enrolled. In 2010, 37 master's, 27 doctorates awarded. *Degree requirements:* For doctorate, comprehensive exam, thesis/dissertation, 1 year internship. *Entrance requirements:* For doctorate, GRE General Test, GRE Subject Test, bachelor's degree in psychology or equivalent. Additional exam requirements/recommendations for international students: Required—TOEFL. *Application deadline:* For fall admission, 1/5 for domestic and international students. Application fee: $65. Electronic applications accepted. *Expenses:* Contact institution. *Financial support:* In 2010–11, 32 students received support, including 43 fellowships with partial tuition reimbursements available (averaging $10,000 per year), 1 research assistantship with full tuition reimbursement available (averaging $16,988 per year), 8 teaching assistantships with full tuition reimbursements available (averaging $16,988 per year); career-related internships or fieldwork, Federal Work-Study, institutionally sponsored loans, scholarships/grants, traineeships, and unspecified assistantships also available. Support available to part-time students. Financial award application deadline: 3/15; financial award applicants required to submit FAFSA. *Faculty research:* Organizational psychology, behavior modification, long- and short-term dynamic therapy, school psychology, addictive behaviors. *Unit head:* Dr. Stanley B. Messer, Dean, 732-445-2000 Ext. 110, Fax: 732-445-4888, E-mail: smesser@rci.rutgers.edu. *Application contact:* Jennifer Leon, Associate Dean, 732-445-2000 Ext. 113, Fax: 732-445-4888, E-mail: j.leon@rutgers.edu.

Saint Mary's University, Faculty of Science, Department of Psychology, Halifax, NS B3H 3C3, Canada. Offers applied psychology (M Sc, PhD), including industrial/organizational psychology (M Sc). Part-time programs available. *Degree requirements:* For master's, thesis, 500-hour internship; for doctorate, comprehensive exam, thesis/dissertation, research project. *Entrance requirements:* For master's and doctorate, GRE General Test. *Faculty research:* Assessment, health psychology, social psychology, cognition.

Shippensburg University of Pennsylvania, School of Graduate Studies, College of Arts and Sciences, Department of Psychology, Shippensburg, PA 17257-2299. Offers applied track (MS); general/reading track (MS); research track (MS). Part-time and evening/weekend programs available. *Faculty:* 9 full-time (3 women). *Students:* 22 full-time (13 women), 7 part-time (5 women); includes 5 minority (2 Black or African American, non-Hispanic/Latino; 1 Asian, non-Hispanic/Latino; 2 Hispanic/Latino), 2 international. Average age 24. 54 applicants, 46% accepted, 15 enrolled. In 2010, 14 master's awarded. *Degree requirements:* For master's, comprehensive exam (for some programs), thesis (for some programs). *Entrance requirements:* For master's, minimum GPA of 2.75, 1 course in statistics, 6 undergraduate credit hours in psychology, supplemental form with personal goals statement. Additional exam requirements/recommendations for international students: Required—TOEFL (minimum score 580 paper-based; 237 computer-based); Recommended—IELTS (minimum score 6). *Application deadline:* For fall admission, 4/1 priority date for domestic students, 3/1 for international students; for spring admission, 11/1 priority date for domestic students, 7/1 for international students. Applications are processed on a rolling basis. Application fee: $30. Electronic applications accepted. *Expenses:* Tuition, state resident: full-time $6966. Tuition, nonresident: full-time $11,146. Required fees: $1802. *Financial support:* In 2010–11, 8 research assistantships with full tuition reimbursements (averaging $5,000 per year) were awarded; career-related internships or fieldwork, scholarships/grants, unspecified assistantships, and resident hall director and student payroll positions also available. Support available to part-time students. Financial award application deadline: 3/1; financial award applicants required to submit FAFSA. *Unit head:* Dr. Suzanne Morin, Chairperson, 717-477-1657, Fax: 717-477-4057, E-mail: smmori@

Applied Psychology

Shippensburg University of Pennsylvania (continued)
ship.edu. *Application contact:* Jeremy R. Goshorn, Associate Dean of Graduate Admissions, 717-477-1231, Fax: 717-477-4016, E-mail: jrgoshorn@ship.edu.

Teachers College, Columbia University, Graduate Faculty of Education, Department of Health and Behavior Studies, Program in Applied Educational Psychology–School Psychology, New York, NY 10027. Offers Ed M, MA, Ed D, PhD. *Accreditation:* APA (one or more programs are accredited). *Faculty:* 4 full-time (2 women), 12 part-time/adjunct (10 women). *Students:* 47 full-time (43 women), 49 part-time (42 women); includes 19 minority (4 Black or African American, non-Hispanic/Latino; 6 Asian, non-Hispanic/Latino; 4 Hispanic/Latino; 3 Native Hawaiian or other Pacific Islander, non-Hispanic/Latino; 2 Two or more races, non-Hispanic/Latino), 5 international. Average age 26. 143 applicants, 29% accepted, 22 enrolled. In 2010, 123 master's, 3 doctorates awarded. *Degree requirements:* For master's, project; for doctorate, comprehensive exam, thesis/dissertation. *Entrance requirements:* For master's, GRE General Test (for Ed M); for doctorate, GRE General Test. *Application deadline:* For fall admission, 12/15 for domestic students. Application fee: $65. *Expenses:* Tuition: Full-time $28,272; part-time $1178 per credit. Required fees: $756; $378 per semester. *Financial support:* Fellowships, research assistantships, career-related internships or fieldwork, Federal Work-Study, institutionally sponsored loans, and tuition waivers (full and partial) available. Support available to part-time students. Financial award application deadline: 2/1; financial award applicants required to submit FAFSA. *Faculty research:* Psychoeducational assessment, observation and concept acquisition in young children, reading, mathematical thinking, memory. *Unit head:* Prof. Marla Brassard, Chair, 212-678-3942, E-mail: brassard@tc.edu. *Application contact:* Prof. Marla Brassard, Chair, 212-678-3942, E-mail: brassard@tc.edu.

University of Arkansas at Little Rock, Graduate School, College of Arts, Humanities, and Social Science, Department of Psychology, Little Rock, AR 72204-1099. Offers applied psychology (MAP). Part-time and evening/weekend programs available. *Entrance requirements:* For master's, GRE General Test, minimum GPA of 2.7. *Faculty research:* Psychological methods and theories in business industry, government, and organizations; personnel program evaluation; training; affirmative action; organizational analysis and development.

University of Baltimore, Graduate School, The Yale Gordon College of Liberal Arts, Program in Applied Psychology, Baltimore, MD 21201-5779. Offers applied psychology (MS), including counseling, industrial and organizational psychology, psychological applications. Part-time and evening/weekend programs available. *Degree requirements:* For master's, thesis optional. *Entrance requirements:* For master's, GRE, minimum GPA of 3.0. Additional exam requirements/recommendations for international students: Required—TOEFL (minimum score 550 paper-based; 213 computer-based). Electronic applications accepted. *Expenses:* Contact institution. *Faculty research:* Participatory decision making, counter productive workplace behavior, organizational consulting, substance abuse treatment, cognitive functioning in head injured.

University of Calgary, Faculty of Graduate Studies, Faculty of Education, Division of Applied Psychology, Calgary, AB T2N 1N4, Canada. Offers counseling psychology (M Ed, M Sc, PhD); human development and learning (M Ed, M Sc, PhD); school psychology (M Ed, M Sc, PhD); special education (M Ed, M Sc, PhD). Part-time programs available. *Degree requirements:* For master's, thesis (for some programs), final oral exam; for doctorate, thesis/dissertation, candidacy exam, final oral exam. *Entrance requirements:* For master's, minimum GPA of 3.0, 3 letters of reference; for doctorate, minimum GPA of 3.5, 3 letters of reference. *Faculty research:* Counselor education, family life studies, learning and cognition.

University of Central Florida, College of Sciences, Department of Psychology, Program in Applied Experimental and Human Factors Psychology, Orlando, FL 32816. Offers MA, PhD. *Students:* 41 full-time (18 women), 6 part-time (4 women); includes 1 Black or African American, non-Hispanic/Latino; 3 Asian, non-Hispanic/Latino; 3 Hispanic/Latino, 2 international. Average age 30. 45 applicants, 31% accepted, 9 enrolled. In 2010, 2 master's, 6 doctorates awarded. *Degree requirements:* For doctorate, thesis/dissertation, departmental candidacy exam. *Entrance requirements:* For doctorate, GRE General Test, minimum GPA of 3.2 in last 60 hours or master's qualifying exam. Additional exam requirements/recommendations for international students: Required—TOEFL. *Application deadline:* For fall admission, 2/1 for domestic students. Application fee: $30. Electronic applications accepted. *Expenses:* Tuition, state resident: part-time $256.56 per credit hour. Tuition, nonresident: part-time $1011.52 per credit hour. Part-time tuition and fees vary according to program. *Financial support:* In 2010–11, 36 students received support, including 6 fellowships (averaging $3,300 per year), 31 research assistantships with partial tuition reimbursements available (averaging $9,400 per year), 23 teaching assistantships with partial tuition reimbursements available (averaging $8,200 per year); career-related internships or fieldwork, Federal Work-Study, institutionally sponsored loans, tuition waivers (partial), and unspecified assistantships also available. Financial award application deadline: 3/1; financial award applicants required to submit FAFSA. *Faculty research:* Visual performance, team training, controls/displays, synthetic speech, alarms/warning. *Unit head:* Dr. Eduardo Salas, Program Director, 407-882-1325, Fax: 407-882-1550, E-mail: esalas@ist.ucf.edu. *Application contact:* Dr. Eduardo Salas, Program Director, 407-882-1325, Fax: 407-882-1550, E-mail: esalas@ist.ucf.edu.

University of Guelph, Graduate Studies, College of Social and Applied Human Sciences, Department of Psychology, Guelph, ON N1G 2W1, Canada. Offers applied social psychology (MA, PhD); clinical psychology applied development emphasis (PhD); clinical psychology applied developmental emphasis (MA); industrial/organizational psychology (MA, PhD); neuroscience and applied cognitive science (MA, PhD). *Degree requirements:* For master's, thesis; for doctorate, comprehensive exam, thesis/dissertation. *Entrance requirements:* For master's, GRE General Test, GRE Subject Test, minimum B+ average during previous 2 years of course work; for doctorate, GRE General Test, GRE Subject Test, minimum A- average. Additional exam requirements/recommendations for international students: Required—TOEFL (minimum score 89 iBT). Electronic applications accepted. *Faculty research:* Organizational psychology, reading comprehension and mathematical ability, drug addiction and relapse, gender issues and culture, memory, clinical psychology.

University of Maryland, Baltimore County, Graduate School, College of Arts, Humanities and Social Sciences, Department of Psychology, Program in Applied Developmental Psychology, Baltimore, MD 21250. Offers PhD. *Faculty:* 7 full-time (4 women), 11 part-time/adjunct (4 women). *Students:* 26 full-time (23 women), 3 part-time (all women); includes 6 minority (1 Black or African American, non-Hispanic/Latino; 4 Asian, non-Hispanic/Latino; 1 Hispanic/Latino). Average age 29. 20 applicants, 30% accepted, 2 enrolled. In 2010, 2 doctorates awarded. *Degree requirements:* For doctorate, comprehensive exam, thesis/dissertation. *Entrance requirements:* For doctorate, GRE General Test, GRE Subject Test, minimum GPA of 3.0. Additional exam requirements/recommendations for international students: Required—TOEFL. *Application deadline:* For fall admission, 1/9 for domestic and international students. Application fee: $70. Electronic applications accepted. *Financial support:* In 2010–11, fellowships with partial tuition reimbursements (averaging $2,200 per year), 3 research assistantships with full and partial tuition reimbursements (averaging $14,857 per year), 10 teaching assistantships with full and partial tuition reimbursements (averaging $14,857 per year) were awarded; career-related internships or fieldwork, Federal Work-Study, health care benefits, and unspecified assistantships also available. Financial award application deadline: 3/1; financial award applicants required to submit FAFSA. *Faculty research:* Early intervention and development, schooling and development, cultural aspects of development, development in high risk children, social-emotional development. Total annual research expenditures: $1.8 million. *Unit head:* Dr. Susan Sonnenschein, Director, 410-455-2361, Fax: 410-455-1055, E-mail: sonnenschein@umbc.edu. *Application contact:* Nicole Mooney, Program Management Specialist, 410-455-2567, Fax: 410-455-1055, E-mail: psycdept@umbc.edu.

University of New Brunswick Saint John, Department of Psychology, Saint John, NB E2L 4L5, Canada. Offers applied and experimental psychology (PhD); clinical psychology (PhD); experimental psychology (MA). Part-time programs available. *Faculty:* 9 full-time (4 women), 1 part-time/adjunct (0 women). *Students:* 4 full-time (1 woman). In 2010, 1 doctorate awarded. *Degree requirements:* For master's, thesis. *Entrance requirements:* For master's, GRE General and Subject Tests, honours thesis. Additional exam requirements/recommendations for international students: Required—TOEFL (minimum score 550 paper-based), TWE. *Application deadline:* For fall admission, 2/1 for domestic students. Application fee: $50. *Financial support:* In 2010–11, 2 research assistantships (averaging $9,000 per year), 7 teaching assistantships (averaging $4,500 per year) were awarded; fellowships, unspecified assistantships also available. Support available to part-time students. Financial award application deadline: 2/1. *Faculty research:* Psychopharmacology and addictions, forensic psychology and criminal justice, interpersonal relations, perception and graphical perception, lie detection, children's play and peer relationships, classical and operant conditioning. *Unit head:* Dr. Lily Both, Director of Graduate Studies, 506-648-5769, Fax: 506-648-5780, E-mail: lboth@unbsj.ca. *Application contact:* Frances Stevens, Secretary, 506-648-5640, Fax: 506-648-5780, E-mail: fstevens@unb.ca.

University of Pennsylvania, Graduate School of Education, Division of Applied Psychology and Human Development, Philadelphia, PA 19104. Offers M Phil, MS Ed, PhD. Part-time programs available. *Students:* 139 full-time (114 women), 25 part-time (20 women); includes 24 Black or African American, non-Hispanic/Latino; 4 Asian, non-Hispanic/Latino; 8 Hispanic/Latino, 13 international. 215 applicants, 60% accepted, 88 enrolled. In 2010, 80 master's, 6 doctorates awarded. Terminal master's awarded for partial completion of doctoral program. *Degree requirements:* For master's, exam; for doctorate, thesis/dissertation, exam. *Entrance requirements:* For master's, GRE General Test; for doctorate, GRE General Test, GRE Subject Test. *Application deadline:* For fall admission, 12/15 priority date for domestic students. Applications are processed on a rolling basis. Application fee: $70. Electronic applications accepted. *Expenses:* Contact institution. *Financial support:* Fellowships, research assistantships, institutionally sponsored loans, scholarships/grants, traineeships, health care benefits, and unspecified assistantships available. *Faculty research:* Multivariate analysis, therapeutic intervention at a preschool level, actuarial systems for assessment of children.

University of Pittsburgh, School of Education, Department of Psychology in Education, Program in Applied Developmental Psychology, Pittsburgh, PA 15260. Offers M Ed, MS, PhD. Part-time and evening/weekend programs available. *Students:* 47 full-time (38 women), 48 part-time (38 women); includes 18 minority (12 Black or African American, non-Hispanic/Latino; 3 Asian, non-Hispanic/Latino; 1 Hispanic/Latino; 2 Two or more races, non-Hispanic/Latino), 8 international. Average age 30. 129 applicants, 58% accepted, 50 enrolled. In 2010, 32 master's, 2 doctorates awarded. *Degree requirements:* For master's, thesis. *Entrance requirements:* For doctorate, GRE. Additional exam requirements/recommendations for international students: Required—TOEFL. *Application deadline:* For fall admission, 2/1 for domestic students, 2/1 priority date for international students; for spring admission, 7/1 priority date for international students. Applications are processed on a rolling basis. Application fee: $50. Electronic applications accepted. *Expenses:* Tuition, state resident: full-time $17,304; part-time $701 per credit. Tuition, nonresident: full-time $29,554; part-time $1210 per credit. Required fees: $740; $214 per term. Tuition and fees vary according to program. *Financial support:* Tuition waivers (partial) available. Support available to part-time students. Financial award applicants required to submit FAFSA. *Unit head:* Dr. Carl N. Johnson, Chairman, 412-624-6942, Fax: 412-624-7231, E-mail: johnson@pitt.edu. *Application contact:* Maggie Sikora, Graduate Enrollment Manager, 412-648-2230, Fax: 412-648-1899, E-mail: soeinfo@pitt.edu.

University of Regina, Faculty of Graduate Studies and Research, Faculty of Arts, Department of Psychology, Regina, SK S4S 0A2, Canada. Offers clinical psychology (MA, PhD); experimental and applied psychology (MA, PhD). *Faculty:* 19 full-time (9 women). *Students:* 51 full-time (39 women), 3 part-time (2 women). 44 applicants, 41% accepted. In 2010, 12 master's, 4 doctorates awarded. *Degree requirements:* For master's, thesis; for doctorate, comprehensive exam, thesis/dissertation. *Entrance requirements:* For master's, GRE General Test, GRE Subject Test; for doctorate, GRE General Test, GRE Subject Test (optional for those with a master's degree from a Canadian university). Additional exam requirements/recommendations for international students: Required—TOEFL (minimum score 580 paper-based; 80 iBT). *Application deadline:* For fall admission, 2/15 for domestic and international students. Application fee: $100. Electronic applications accepted. Tuition and fees charges are reported in Canadian dollars. *Expenses:* Tuition, area resident: Full-time $3244.50 Canadian dollars; part-time $180.25 Canadian dollars per credit hour. International tuition: $4744.50 Canadian dollars full-time. Required fees: $494 Canadian dollars; $115.25 Canadian dollars per credit hour. $115.25 Canadian dollars per semester. Tuition and fees vary according to program. *Financial support:* In 2010–11, 9 fellowships (averaging $20,333 per year), 3 research assistantships (averaging $16,500 per year), 21 teaching assistantships (averaging $6,884 per year) were awarded; career-related internships or fieldwork and scholarships/grants also available. Financial award application deadline: 6/15. *Faculty research:* Clinical, experimental, cognitive, and applied psychology; post-traumatic stress disorder, anxiety, and panic disorder; traumatic brain injury; chronic pain; perception and memory. *Unit head:* Dr. Richard MacLennan, Head, 306-585-4458, Fax: 306-585-5429, E-mail: richard.maclennan@uregina.ca. *Application contact:* Dr. Richard MacLennan, Graduate Program Coordinator, 306-585-4458, Fax: 306-585-5429, E-mail: richard.maclennan@uregina.ca.

University of South Carolina Aiken, Program in Applied Clinical Psychology, Aiken, SC 29801-6309. Offers MS. Part-time programs available. *Faculty:* 7 full-time (5 women). *Students:* 23 full-time (19 women), 7 part-time (all women); includes 7 minority (2 Black or African American, non-Hispanic/Latino; 1 Asian, non-Hispanic/Latino; 2 Hispanic/Latino; 2 Two or more races, non-Hispanic/Latino). Average age 26. 50 applicants, 54% accepted, 15 enrolled. In 2010, 8 master's awarded. *Degree requirements:* For master's, thesis. *Entrance requirements:* For master's, GRE General Test, GRE Subject Test (psychology). Additional exam requirements/recommendations for international students: Required—TOEFL (minimum score 550 paper-based; 213 computer-based). *Application deadline:* For fall admission, 5/1 priority date for domestic and international students. Applications are processed on a rolling basis. Application fee: $45. Electronic applications accepted. *Expenses:* Tuition, state resident: full-time $10,490; part-time $440 per credit hour. Tuition, nonresident: full-time $22,550; part-time $945 per credit hour. Required fees: $290; $9 per credit hour. $25 per semester. *Financial support:* In 2010–11, 21 students received support, including 21 research assistantships with partial tuition reimbursements available (averaging $3,805 per year); career-related internships or fieldwork, Federal Work-Study, scholarships/grants, tuition waivers (partial), and unspecified assistantships also available. Financial award application deadline: 3/15; financial award applicants required to submit FAFSA. *Faculty research:* Clinical, addictive behaviors, anxiety disorders, child clinical, social and personality psychology. Total annual research expenditures: $59,500. *Unit head:* Dr. Jane Stafford, Director, 803-641-3358, Fax: 803-641-3720, E-mail: jstafford@usca.edu. *Application contact:* Karen Morris, Graduate Studies Coordinator, 803-641-3489, Fax: 803-641-3720, E-mail: karenm@usca.edu.

The University of Tennessee, Graduate School, College of Education, Health and Human Sciences, Department of Educational Psychology and Counseling, Knoxville, TN 37996. Offers adult education (MS); applied educational psychology (MS); collaborative learning (Ed D); college student personnel (MS); mental health counseling (MS); rehabilitation counseling (MS); school counseling (MS). *Accreditation:* ACA (one or more programs are accredited); CORE (one or more programs are accredited); NCATE. Part-time and evening/weekend programs available. *Degree requirements:* For master's, thesis optional. *Entrance requirements:* For master's, GRE General Test, minimum GPA of 2.7. Additional exam requirements/recommendations for international students: Required—TOEFL. Electronic applications accepted. *Expenses:* Tuition, state resident: full-time $7440; part-time $414 per credit hour. Tuition, nonresident: full-time $22,478; part-time $1250 per credit hour. Required fees: $922; $43 per credit hour. Tuition and fees vary according to program.

The University of Texas of the Permian Basin, Office of Graduate Studies, College of Arts and Sciences, Department of Psychology, Odessa, TX 79762-0001. Offers applied research psychology (MA); clinical psychology (MA). Part-time and evening/weekend programs available.

Degree requirements: For master's, comprehensive exam, thesis, practicum. *Entrance requirements:* For master's, GRE General Test, 3 letters of recommendation. Additional exam requirements/recommendations for international students: Required—TOEFL (minimum score 550 paper-based; 213 computer-based).

University of Windsor, Faculty of Graduate Studies, Faculty of Arts and Social Sciences, Department of Psychology, Windsor, ON N9B 3P4, Canada. Offers adult clinical (MA, PhD); applied social psychology (MA, PhD); child clinical (MA, PhD); clinical neuropsychology (MA, PhD). *Accreditation:* APA (one or more programs are accredited). *Degree requirements:* For master's, thesis; for doctorate, comprehensive exam, thesis/dissertation. *Entrance requirements:* For master's, GRE General Test, GRE Subject Test in psychology, minimum B average; for doctorate, GRE General Test, GRE Subject Test in psychology, master's degree. Additional exam requirements/recommendations for international students: Required—TOEFL (minimum score 600 paper-based; 250 computer-based). Electronic applications accepted. *Faculty research:* Gambling, suicidology, emotional competence, psychotherapy and trauma.

University of Wisconsin–Stout, Graduate School, College of Human Development, Program in Applied Psychology, Menomonie, WI 54751. Offers MS. Part-time programs available. *Degree requirements:* For master's, thesis. *Entrance requirements:* For master's, GRE General Test, GRE Subject Test, minimum GPA of 3.0, 15 semester credits of undergraduate course work in psychology, 8 semester credits in research methods and statistics. Additional exam requirements/recommendations for international students: Required—TOEFL (minimum score 500 paper-based; 173 computer-based; 61 iBT). Electronic applications accepted. *Faculty research:* Health complementary therapies, motivation, group dynamics, social reasoning, stress.

Clinical Psychology

Abilene Christian University, Graduate School, College of Arts and Sciences, Department of Psychology, Program in Clinical Psychology, Abilene, TX 79699-9100. Offers MS. Part-time programs available. *Students:* 11 full-time (10 women), 2 part-time (1 woman); includes 2 Hispanic/Latino, 1 international. 17 applicants, 47% accepted, 5 enrolled. In 2010, 4 master's awarded. *Degree requirements:* For master's, thesis, practicum. *Entrance requirements:* For master's, GRE General Test. Additional exam requirements/recommendations for international students: Required—TOEFL (minimum score 550 paper-based; 213 computer-based). *Application deadline:* For fall admission, 4/1 priority date for domestic students; for spring admission, 11/1 for domestic students. Applications are processed on a rolling basis. Application fee: $40. Electronic applications accepted. *Expenses:* Tuition: Full-time $12,906; part-time $717 per hour. Required fees: $1250; $61.50 per unit. *Financial support:* In 2010–11, 11 students received support. Career-related internships or fieldwork and Federal Work-Study available. Support available to part-time students. Financial award application deadline: 4/1; financial award applicants required to submit FAFSA. *Unit head:* Dr. Robert McKelvain, Graduate Advisor, 325-674-2286, Fax: 325-674-6968, E-mail: mckelvainr@acu.edu. *Application contact:* David Pittman, Graduate Admissions Counselor, 325-674-2656, Fax: 325-674-6717, E-mail: gradinfo@acu.edu.

Acadia University, Faculty of Pure and Applied Science, Department of Psychology, Wolfville, NS B4P 2R6, Canada. Offers clinical psychology (M Sc). *Faculty:* 11 full-time (6 women), 2 part-time/adjunct (both women). *Students:* 9 full-time (7 women), 1 (woman) part-time. Average age 26. 36 applicants, 22% accepted, 4 enrolled. In 2010, 3 master's awarded. *Degree requirements:* For master's, thesis. *Entrance requirements:* For master's, GRE General Test, GRE Subject Test, honors degree or equivalent. Additional exam requirements/recommendations for international students: Required—TOEFL (minimum score 580 paper-based; 237 computer-based; 93 iBT), IELTS (minimum score 6.5). *Application deadline:* For fall admission, 2/1 priority date for domestic and international students. Applications are processed on a rolling basis. Application fee: $50. *Financial support:* Teaching assistantships, career-related internships or fieldwork, scholarships/grants, and unspecified assistantships available. Financial award application deadline: 2/1. *Faculty research:* Social psychology, job stress, psychotherapy, cognition perception, development. *Unit head:* Dr. Peter McLeod, Head, 902-585-1301, Fax: 902-585-1078, E-mail: peter.mcleod@acadiau.ca. *Application contact:* Dr. Peter Horvath, Graduate Coordinator, 902-585-1200, Fax: 902-585-1078, E-mail: peter.horvath@acadiau.ca.

Adelphi University, Derner Institute of Advanced Psychological Studies, Program in Clinical Psychology, Garden City, NY 11530-0701. Offers PhD. *Students:* 79 full-time (59 women), 35 part-time (29 women); includes 6 Black or African American, non-Hispanic/Latino; 8 Asian, non-Hispanic/Latino; 5 Hispanic/Latino; 1 Two or more races, non-Hispanic/Latino, 13 international. Average age 31. In 2010, 12 doctorates awarded. *Degree requirements:* For doctorate, thesis/dissertation, research (second year), 1 year internship. *Entrance requirements:* For doctorate, GRE General Test, GRE Subject Test, interview; resume, undergraduate courses in psychology, experimental psychology, statistics, developmental psychology, and abnormal psychology. Additional exam requirements/recommendations for international students: Required—TOEFL (minimum score 550 paper-based; 213 computer-based; 80 iBT). *Application deadline:* For fall admission, 1/15 priority date for domestic and international students. Application fee: $50. Electronic applications accepted. *Financial support:* Research assistantships with full and partial tuition reimbursements, teaching assistantships, career-related internships or fieldwork, Federal Work-Study, institutionally sponsored loans, and unspecified assistantships available. Financial award application deadline: 2/15; financial award applicants required to submit FAFSA. *Unit head:* Dr. J. Christopher Muran, Associate Dean, 516-877-4803, E-mail: jcmuran@adelphi.edu. *Application contact:* Christine Murphy, Director of Admissions, 516-877-3050, Fax: 516-877-3039, E-mail: graduateadmissions@adelphi.edu.

Adler Graduate School, Program in Adlerian Counseling and Psychotherapy, Richfield, MN 55423. Offers art therapy (MA); clinical mental health counseling (MA); marriage and family therapy (MA); non-clinical Adlerian studies (MA); online Adlerian studies (MA); organizational wellness and transformation (MA); parent coaching (Certificate); personal and professional life coaching (Certificate); school counseling (MA). Part-time and evening/weekend programs available. *Faculty:* 11 full-time (4 women), 48 part-time/adjunct (28 women). *Students:* 442 part-time (361 women). Average age 37. *Degree requirements:* For master's, thesis or alternative, 500-700 hour internship (depending on license choice). *Entrance requirements:* For master's, minimum undergraduate GPA of 3.0, 12 credits of course work in psychology or related field. *Application deadline:* Applications are processed on a rolling basis. Application fee: $50. *Expenses:* Tuition: Part-time $455 per credit. *Financial support:* Career-related internships or fieldwork and tuition waivers available. Support available to part-time students. Financial award applicants required to submit FAFSA. *Unit head:* Dr. Dan Haugen, President, 612-861-7554 Ext. 107, Fax: 612-861-7559, E-mail: haugen@alfredadler.edu. *Application contact:* Evelyn B. Haas, Director of Student Services and Admissions, 612-861-7554 Ext. 103, Fax: 612-861-7559, E-mail: ev@alfredadler.edu.

Adler School of Professional Psychology, Programs in Psychology, Chicago, IL 60602. Offers advanced Adlerian psychotherapy (Certificate); art therapy (MA); clinical neuropsychology (Certificate); clinical psychology (Psy D); community psychology (MA); counseling and organizational psychology (MA); counseling psychology (MA); forensic psychology (MA); gerontological counseling (MA); marriage and family counseling (MA); marriage and family therapy (Certificate); organizational psychology (MA); police psychology (MA); rehabilitation counseling (MA); sport and health psychology (MA); substance abuse counseling (Certificate); Psy D/Certificate; Psy D/MACAT; Psy D/MACP; Psy D/MAMFC; Psy D/MASAC. *Accreditation:* APA. Part-time and evening/weekend programs available. Postbaccalaureate distance learning degree programs offered (minimal on-campus study). *Faculty:* 40 full-time (18 women), 61 part-time/adjunct (31 women). *Students:* 688 full-time (532 women), 142 part-time (110 women). Average age 27. Terminal master's awarded for partial completion of doctoral program. *Degree requirements:* For master's, thesis or alternative, oral exam, practicum; for doctorate, thesis/dissertation, clinical exam, internship, oral exam, practicum, written qualifying exam. *Entrance requirements:* For master's, 12 semester hours in psychology, minimum GPA of 3.0; for doctorate, 18 semester hours in psychology, minimum GPA of 3.25; for Certificate, appropriate master's or doctoral degree. Additional exam requirements/recommendations for international students: Required—TOEFL (minimum score 550 paper-based; 213 computer-based; 79 iBT). *Application deadline:* For fall admission, 2/15 priority date for domestic students, 12/1 priority date for international students. Applications are processed on a rolling basis. Application fee: $50. Electronic applications accepted. *Financial support:* Career-related internships or fieldwork, Federal Work-Study, scholarships/grants, and tuition waivers (full and partial) available. Support available to part-time students. Financial award application deadline: 5/15; financial award applicants required to submit FAFSA. *Application contact:* Michelle Brice, Director of Admissions, 312-662-4113, Fax: 312-662-4199, E-mail: admissions@adler.edu.

See Display on page 912 and Close-Up on page 1119.

Alabama Agricultural and Mechanical University, School of Graduate Studies, School of Education, Department of Counseling and Special Education, Huntsville, AL 35811. Offers communicative disorders (M Ed, MS); psychology and counseling (MS, Ed S), including clinical psychology (MS), counseling and guidance, counseling psychology (MS), personnel management (MS), psychometry (MS), school psychology (MS); special education (M Ed, MS). *Accreditation:* CORE; NCATE. Part-time and evening/weekend programs available. *Degree requirements:* For master's, comprehensive exam. *Entrance requirements:* For master's, GRE General Test. Additional exam requirements/recommendations for international students: Required—TOEFL (minimum score 500 paper-based; 173 computer-based; 61 iBT). *Faculty research:* Increasing numbers of minorities in special education and speech-language pathology.

Alliant International University–Fresno, California School of Professional Psychology, PhD Program in Clinical Psychology, Fresno, CA 93727. Offers PhD. *Degree requirements:* For doctorate, thesis/dissertation. *Entrance requirements:* For doctorate, interview, minimum GPA of 3.0 in both psychology and overall, letters of recommendation. Additional exam requirements/recommendations for international students: Required—TOEFL (minimum score 600 paper-based; 250 computer-based), TWE (minimum score 5). *Faculty research:* Teaching, ecosystemic child psychology, health psychology, clinical forensic psychology.

Alliant International University–Fresno, California School of Professional Psychology, Psy D Program in Clinical Psychology, Fresno, CA 93727. Offers Psy D. *Accreditation:* APA. *Degree requirements:* For doctorate, comprehensive exam, thesis/dissertation. *Entrance requirements:* For doctorate, interview, minimum GPA of 3.0 in both psychology and overall, letters of recommendation. Additional exam requirements/recommendations for international students: Required—TOEFL (minimum score 600 paper-based; 250 computer-based), TWE (minimum score 5). Electronic applications accepted. *Faculty research:* Ecosystemic child clinical health psychology, eating disorders.

Alliant International University–Los Angeles, California School of Professional Psychology, PhD Program in Clinical Psychology, Alhambra, CA 91803-1360. Offers PhD. *Accreditation:* APA. *Degree requirements:* For doctorate, comprehensive exam, thesis/dissertation. *Entrance requirements:* For doctorate, interview, minimum GPA of 3.0 in both psychology and overall. Additional exam requirements/recommendations for international students: Required—TOEFL (minimum score 600 paper-based; 250 computer-based), TWE (minimum score 5). Electronic applications accepted. *Faculty research:* Multicultural and community clinical psychology, health psychology, individual and family psychology.

Alliant International University–Los Angeles, California School of Professional Psychology, Psy D Program in Clinical Psychology, Alhambra, CA 91803-1360. Offers Psy D. *Accreditation:* APA. *Degree requirements:* For doctorate, thesis/dissertation. *Entrance requirements:* For doctorate, interview, minimum GPA of 3.0 in both psychology and overall. Additional exam requirements/recommendations for international students: Required—TOEFL (minimum score 600 paper-based; 250 computer-based), TWE. Electronic applications accepted. *Faculty research:* Child and family psychology, multicultural and community psychology, acculturation, lesbian and gay issues, women's health.

Alliant International University–Sacramento, California School of Professional Psychology, Program in Clinical Psychology, Sacramento, CA 95825. Offers Psy D. *Entrance requirements:* For doctorate, minimum GPA of 3.0, letters of recommendation, interview. Electronic applications accepted. *Faculty research:* Health psychology, infant-preschool mental health, community mental, health trauma, aging.

Alliant International University–San Diego, California School of Professional Psychology, PhD Program in Clinical Psychology, San Diego, CA 92131-1799. Offers PhD. *Accreditation:* APA. *Degree requirements:* For doctorate, thesis/dissertation. *Entrance requirements:* For doctorate, interview, minimum GPA of 3.0 in both psychology and overall. Additional exam requirements/recommendations for international students: Required—TOEFL (minimum score 600 paper-based; 250 computer-based), TWE (minimum score 5). Electronic applications accepted. *Faculty research:* Family conflict in adolescence, anxiety disorders, PTSD, childhood psychopathology, regressed memory.

Alliant International University–San Diego, California School of Professional Psychology, Psy D Program in Clinical Psychology, San Diego, CA 92131-1799. Offers Psy D. *Accreditation:* APA. *Degree requirements:* For doctorate, thesis/dissertation. *Entrance requirements:* For doctorate, interview, minimum GPA of 3.0 in both psychology and overall. Additional exam requirements/recommendations for international students: Required—TOEFL (minimum score 600 paper-based; 250 computer-based), TWE (minimum score 5). Electronic applications accepted. *Faculty research:* Forensic psychology, health psychology, integrative psychology, family and child psychology.

Alliant International University–San Diego, Marshall Goldsmith School of Management, Organizational Psychology Division, San Diego, CA 92131-1799. Offers clinical/industrial organizational psychology (PhD); consulting psychology (PhD); industrial/organizational psychology (MA, MS, PhD); organizational behavior (MA). Part-time and evening/weekend programs available. Terminal master's awarded for partial completion of doctoral program. *Degree requirements:* For doctorate, thesis/dissertation. *Entrance requirements:* For master's and doctorate, interview, minimum GPA of 3.0 in both psychology and overall. Additional exam requirements/recommendations for international students: Required—TOEFL (minimum score 600 paper-based; 250 computer-based), TWE (minimum score 5). Electronic applications accepted. *Faculty research:* Cultural diversity in the workplace, work motivation, personnel, performance management.

Clinical Psychology

Alliant International University–San Francisco, California School of Professional Psychology, PhD Program in Clinical Psychology, San Francisco, CA 94133-1221. Offers PhD. *Degree requirements:* For doctorate, thesis/dissertation. *Entrance requirements:* For doctorate, interview, minimum GPA of 3.0 in both psychology and overall. Additional exam requirements/ recommendations for international students: Required—TOEFL (minimum score 600 paper-based; 250 computer-based), TWE (minimum score 5). Electronic applications accepted. *Faculty research:* Social model of disability, feminist models of clinical training, post-traumatic stress disorder, HIV, psychology of women.

Alliant International University–San Francisco, California School of Professional Psychology, Psy D Program in Clinical Psychology, San Francisco, CA 94133-1221. Offers Psy D, Certificate. *Accreditation:* APA (one or more programs are accredited). *Degree requirements:* For doctorate, thesis/dissertation. *Entrance requirements:* For doctorate, interview, minimum GPA of 3.0 in both psychology and overall. Additional exam requirements/recommendations for international students: Required—TOEFL (minimum score 600 paper-based; 250 computer-based), TWE (minimum score 5). Electronic applications accepted. *Faculty research:* Health psychology, family and child psychology, psychodynamic psychology, multicultural and community psychology, gender issues.

American International College, School of Arts, Education and Sciences, Department of Psychology, Program in Clinical Psychology, Springfield, MA 01109-3189. Offers MA. *Degree requirements:* For master's, practicum. *Entrance requirements:* For master's, minimum B average in undergraduate course work. Additional exam requirements/recommendations for international students: Required—TOEFL. Electronic applications accepted.

American University, College of Arts and Sciences, Department of Psychology, Washington, DC 22016-8062. Offers behavior, cognition, and neuroscience (PhD), including psychology; clinical psychology (PhD), including psychology; psychology (MA), including experimental/ biological psychology, general psychology, personality/social psychology. *Accreditation:* APA. Part-time programs available. *Faculty:* 19 full-time (7 women), 6 part-time/adjunct (4 women). *Students:* 65 full-time (51 women), 47 part-time (41 women); includes 16 minority (4 Black or African American, non-Hispanic/Latino; 3 Asian, non-Hispanic/Latino; 9 Hispanic/Latino), 3 international. Average age 28. 445 applicants, 19% accepted, 36 enrolled. In 2010, 35 master's, 11 doctorates awarded. *Degree requirements:* For master's, comprehensive exam, thesis or alternative; for doctorate, comprehensive exam, thesis/dissertation, tools of research. *Entrance requirements:* For master's, GRE General Test, GRE Subject Test, recommendations; for doctorate, GRE General Test, GRE Subject Test. Additional exam requirements/ recommendations for international students: Required—TOEFL. Application fee: $80. *Financial support:* Fellowships, research assistantships, teaching assistantships, career-related internships or fieldwork, Federal Work-Study, institutionally sponsored loans, tuition waivers (full and partial), and unspecified assistantships available. Support available to part-time students. Financial award application deadline: 2/1. *Faculty research:* Anxiety disorders, cognitive assessment, neuropsychology, conditioning and learning, psychopharmacology. *Unit head:* Dr. Anthony Riley, Chair, 202-885-1720, E-mail: alriley@american.edu. *Application contact:* Sara Holland, Senior Administrative Assistant, 202-885-1717, Fax: 202-885-1023, E-mail: holland@ american.edu.

Antioch University Los Angeles, Graduate Programs, Program in Psychology, Culver City, CA 90230. Offers clinical psychology (MA); psychology (MA). Part-time programs available. *Degree requirements:* For master's, thesis (for some programs), internship. *Entrance requirements:* For master's, interview. Additional exam requirements/recommendations for international students: Required—TOEFL. *Faculty research:* Creativity and humor, ethnic humor, adult development, Jungian theory, psychoanalytic theory.

Antioch University New England, Graduate School, Department of Applied Psychology, Program in Clinical Mental Health Counseling, Keene, NH 03431-3552. Offers MA. *Accreditation:* ACA. *Degree requirements:* For master's, internship, practicum. *Entrance requirements:* For master's, previous course work and work experience in psychology. Additional exam requirements/recommendations for international students: Required—TOEFL (minimum score 600 paper-based; 250 computer-based). Electronic applications accepted. *Expenses:* Contact institution. *Faculty research:* Multicultural issues in field supervision.

Antioch University New England, Graduate School, Department of Clinical Psychology, Keene, NH 03431-3552. Offers Psy D. *Accreditation:* APA. *Degree requirements:* For doctorate, thesis/dissertation, internship, practicum. *Entrance requirements:* For doctorate, GRE General Test, GRE Subject Test, previous course work in psychology. Additional exam requirements/ recommendations for international students: Required—TOEFL (minimum score 600 paper-based; 250 computer-based). *Expenses:* Contact institution. *Faculty research:* Psychotherapy outcome and process in private practice, neuropsychiatric evaluations, effects of trauma on adults, supervision, clinical training evaluation.

Antioch University Santa Barbara, Program in Clinical Psychology, Santa Barbara, CA 93101-1581. Offers Psy D. *Entrance requirements:* Additional exam requirements/ recommendations for international students: Required—TOEFL (minimum score 550 paper-based; 213 computer-based). Electronic applications accepted.

Appalachian State University, Cratis D. Williams Graduate School, Department of Human Development and Psychological Counseling, Boone, NC 28608. Offers clinical mental health counseling (MA); college student development (MA); marriage and family therapy (MA); school counseling (MA). *Accreditation:* AAMFT/COAMFTE; ACA; NCATE. Part-time programs available. *Faculty:* 14 full-time (9 women), 7 part-time/adjunct (all women). *Students:* 140 full-time (101 women), 25 part-time (20 women); includes 8 Black or African American, non-Hispanic/Latino; 1 Asian, non-Hispanic/Latino; 1 Hispanic/Latino; 1 Two or more races, non-Hispanic/Latino. 233 applicants, 53% accepted, 74 enrolled. In 2010, 53 master's awarded. *Degree requirements:* For master's, comprehensive exam (for some programs), thesis optional, internships. *Entrance requirements:* For master's, GRE General Test, 3 letters of recommendation. Additional exam requirements/recommendations for international students: Required—TOEFL (minimum score 570 paper-based; 230 computer-based; 79 iBT), IELTS (minimum score 6.5). *Application deadline:* For fall admission, 2/1 priority date for domestic students, 2/1 for international students; for spring admission, 2/1 for international students. Applications are processed on a rolling basis. Application fee: $55. Electronic applications accepted. *Expenses:* Tuition, state resident: full-time $3428; part-time $428 per unit. Tuition, nonresident: full-time $14,518; part-time $1814 per unit. Required fees: $2320; $344 per unit. Tuition and fees vary according to campus/location. *Financial support:* In 2010–11, 20 research assistantships (averaging $8,000 per year), 7 teaching assistantships (averaging $8,000 per year) were awarded; fellowships, career-related internships or fieldwork, Federal Work-Study, scholarships/grants, and unspecified assistantships also available. Financial award application deadline: 4/1; financial award applicants required to submit FAFSA. *Faculty research:* Multicultural counseling, addictions counseling, play therapy, expressive arts, child and adolescent therapy, sexual abuse counseling. *Unit head:* Dr. Lee Baruth, Chairman, 828-262-2055, E-mail: baruthlg@appstate.edu. *Application contact:* Sandy Krause, Director of Admissions and Recruiting, 828-262-2130, Fax: 828-262-2709, E-mail: krausesl@appstate.edu.

Appalachian State University, Cratis D. Williams Graduate School, Department of Psychology, Boone, NC 28608. Offers clinical health psychology (MA); general experimental psychology (MA); industrial and organizational psychology (MA). Part-time programs available. *Faculty:* 31 full-time (10 women), 2 part-time/adjunct (1 woman). *Students:* 55 full-time (40 women), 11 part-time (9 women); includes 3 minority (2 Black or African American, non-Hispanic/Latino; 1 Two or more races, non-Hispanic/Latino). 158 applicants, 32% accepted, 28 enrolled. In 2010, 25 master's, 7 other advanced degrees awarded. *Degree requirements:* For master's, comprehensive exam, thesis optional, exit exam. *Entrance requirements:* For master's, GRE General Test, 3 letters of recommendation. Additional exam requirements/recommendations for international students: Required—TOEFL (minimum score 550 paper-based; 230 computer-based; 79 iBT) or IELTS (minimum score 6.5). *Application deadline:* For fall admission, 2/15 for domestic students, 2/1 for international students. Applications are processed on a rolling basis. Application fee: $55. Electronic applications accepted. *Expenses:* Tuition, state resident: full-time $3428; part-time $428 per unit. Tuition, nonresident: full-time $14,518; part-time $1814 per unit. Required fees: $2320; $344 per unit. Tuition and fees vary according to campus/location. *Financial support:* In 2010–11, 34 research assistantships (averaging $4,000 per year), 25 teaching assistantships (averaging $4,000 per year) were awarded; fellowships, career-related internships or fieldwork, Federal Work-Study, scholarships/grants, and unspecified assistantships also available. Financial award application deadline: 4/1; financial award applicants required to submit FAFSA. *Faculty research:* Eating disorders, school-based consultations, organizational behavior management, brain mechanisms of sound localization, parenting styles. Total annual research expenditures: $18,000. *Unit head:* Dr. James Denniston, Chair, 828-262-2272, Fax: 828-262-2272, E-mail: dennistonjc@appstate.edu. *Application contact:* Dr. Denise Martz, Graduate Coordinator, 828-262-2715, E-mail: martzdm@appstate.edu.

Argosy University, Atlanta, College of Psychology and Behavioral Sciences, Atlanta, GA 30328. Offers clinical psychology (MA, Psy D, Postdoctoral Respecialization Certificate), including child and family psychology (Psy D), general adult clinical (Psy D), health psychology (Psy D), neuropsychology/geropsychology (Psy D); community counseling (MA), including marriage and family therapy; counselor education and supervision (Ed D); forensic psychology (MA); industrial organizational psychology (MA); marriage and family therapy (Certificate); sport-exercise psychology (MA). *Accreditation:* APA.

See Close-Up on page 1121.

Argosy University, Chicago, College of Psychology and Behavioral Sciences, Doctoral Program in Clinical Psychology, Chicago, IL 60601. Offers child and adolescent psychology (Psy D); client-centered and experiential psychotherapies (Psy D); diversity and multicultural psychology (Psy D); family psychology (Psy D); forensic psychology (Psy D); health psychology (Psy D); neuropsychology (Psy D); organizational consulting (Psy D); psychoanalytic psychology (Psy D); psychology and spirituality (Psy D). *Accreditation:* APA.

See Close-Up on page 1123.

Argosy University, Chicago, College of Psychology and Behavioral Sciences, Master's Program in Clinical Psychology, Chicago, IL 60601. Offers MA.

See Close-Up on page 1123.

Argosy University, Dallas, College of Psychology and Behavioral Sciences, Program in Clinical Psychology, Farmers Branch, TX 75244. Offers MA, Psy D.

See Close-Up on page 1125.

Argosy University, Denver, College of Psychology and Behavioral Sciences, Denver, CO 80231. Offers clinical mental health counseling (MA); clinical psychology (MA, Psy D); counseling psychology (Ed D); counselor education and supervision (Ed D); forensic psychology (MA); industrial organizational psychology (MA); marriage and family therapy (MA, DMFT).

See Close-Up on page 1127.

Argosy University, Hawai'i, College of Psychology and Behavioral Sciences, Program in Clinical Psychology, Honolulu, HI 96813. Offers clinical psychology (MA, Psy D, Postdoctoral Respecialization Certificate), including child and family clinical practice (Psy D), diversity in clinical practice (Psy D). *Accreditation:* APA.

See Close-Up on page 1129.

Argosy University, Inland Empire, College of Psychology and Behavioral Sciences, San Bernardino, CA 92408. Offers clinical psychology/marriage and family therapy (MA); counseling psychology (Ed D); counseling psychology/marriage and family therapy (MA); forensic psychology (MA); industrial organizational psychology (MA); sport-exercise psychology (MA).

See Close-Up on page 1131.

Argosy University, Los Angeles, College of Psychology and Behavioral Sciences, Santa Monica, CA 90045. Offers clinical psychology/marriage and family therapy (MA); counseling psychology (Ed D); counseling psychology/marriage and family therapy (MA); forensic psychology (MA).

See Close-Up on page 1133.

Argosy University, Orange County, College of Psychology and Behavioral Sciences, Program in Clinical Psychology, Orange, CA 92868. Offers child and adolescent psychology (Psy D); forensic psychology (Psy D); marriage and family therapy (MA). *Accreditation:* APA.

See Close-Up on page 1137.

Argosy University, Phoenix, College of Psychology and Behavioral Sciences, Program in Clinical Psychology, Phoenix, AZ 85021. Offers clinical psychology (MA); neuropsychology (Psy D); sports-exercise psychology (Psy D). *Accreditation:* APA (one or more programs are accredited).

See Close-Up on page 1139.

Argosy University, San Diego, College of Psychology and Behavioral Sciences, San Diego, CA 92108. Offers clinical psychology/marriage and family therapy (MA); counseling psychology (Ed D); counseling psychology/marriage and family therapy (MA); forensic psychology (MA).

See Close-Up on page 1143.

Argosy University, San Francisco Bay Area, College of Psychology and Behavioral Sciences, Alameda, CA 94501. Offers clinical psychology (MA, Psy D); counseling psychology (MA, Ed D); forensic psychology (MA); sport-exercise psychology (MA). *Accreditation:* APA (one or more programs are accredited).

See Close-Up on page 1145.

Argosy University, Schaumburg, College of Psychology and Behavioral Sciences, Schaumburg, IL 60173-5403. Offers clinical health psychology (Post-Graduate Certificate); clinical psychology (MA, Psy D), including child and family psychology (Psy D), clinical health psychology (Psy D), diversity and multicultural psychology (Psy D), forensic psychology (Psy D), neuropsychology (Psy D); community counseling (MA); counseling psychology (Ed D), including counselor education and supervision; counselor education and supervision (Ed D); forensic psychology (Post-Graduate Certificate); industrial organizational psychology (MA). *Accreditation:* ACA; APA.

See Close-Up on page 1149.

Argosy University, Seattle, College of Psychology and Behavioral Sciences, Program in Clinical Psychology, Seattle, WA 98121. Offers MA, Psy D, Postdoctoral Respecialization Certificate.

See Close-Up on page 1151.

Argosy University, Tampa, College of Psychology and Behavioral Sciences, Program in Clinical Psychology, Tampa, FL 33607. Offers clinical psychology (MA, Psy D), including child and adolescent psychology (Psy D), geropsychology (Psy D), marriage/couples and family therapy (Psy D), neuropsychology (Psy D). *Accreditation:* APA.

See Close-Up on page 1153.

Argosy University, Twin Cities, College of Psychology and Behavioral Sciences, Eagan, MN 55121. Offers clinical psychology (MA, Psy D), including child and family psychology (Psy D), forensic psychology (Psy D), health and neuropsychology (Psy D), trauma (Psy D); forensic counseling (Post-Graduate Certificate); forensic psychology (MA); industrial organizational psychology (MA); marriage and family therapy (MA, DMFT), including forensic counseling (MA). *Accreditation:* AAMFT; AAMFT/COAMFTE; APA.

See Close-Up on page 1155.

Argosy University, Washington DC, College of Psychology and Behavioral Sciences, Arlington, VA 22209. Offers clinical psychology (MA, Psy D), including child and family psychology (Psy D), diversity and multicultural psychology (Psy D), forensic psychology (Psy D), health and neuropsychology (Psy D); community counseling (MA); counseling psychology (Ed D), including counselor education and supervision; counselor education and supervision (Ed D); forensic psychology (MA). *Accreditation:* APA.

See Close-Up on page 1157.

Arizona State University, College of Liberal Arts and Sciences, Department of Psychology, Tempe, AZ 85287-1104. Offers behavioral neuroscience (PhD); clinical psychology (PhD); cognition, action and perception (PhD); developmental psychology (PhD); quantitative psychology (PhD); social psychology (PhD). *Accreditation:* APA. *Faculty:* 72 full-time (36 women), 9 part-time/adjunct (6 women). *Students:* 113 full-time (79 women), 17 part-time (12 women); includes 24 minority (2 Black or African American, non-Hispanic/Latino; 10 Asian, non-Hispanic/Latino; 10 Hispanic/Latino; 2 Two or more races, non-Hispanic/Latino), 9 international. Average age 28. 519 applicants, 8% accepted, 30 enrolled. In 2010, 19 doctorates awarded. *Degree requirements:* For doctorate, comprehensive exam, thesis/dissertation, interactive Program of Study (iPOS) submitted before completing 50 percent of required credit hours. *Entrance requirements:* For doctorate, GRE General Test, GRE Subject Test, minimum GPA of 3.0 or equivalent in last 2 years of work leading to bachelor's degree. Additional exam requirements/recommendations for international students: Required—TOEFL, IELTS, or Pearson Test of English. *Application deadline:* For fall admission, 12/15 for domestic and international students. Application fee: $70 ($90 for international students). Electronic applications accepted. *Expenses:* Tuition, state resident: full-time $8510; part-time $608 per credit. Tuition, nonresident: full-time $16,542; part-time $919 per credit. Required fees: $339; $110 per credit. Part-time tuition and fees vary according to course load. *Financial support:* In 2010–11, 58 research assistantships with tuition reimbursements (averaging $15,281 per year), 48 teaching assistantships with tuition reimbursements (averaging $15,062 per year) were awarded; fellowships with full tuition reimbursements, career-related internships or fieldwork, Federal Work-Study, institutionally sponsored loans, scholarships/grants, and tuition waivers (full and partial) also available. Financial award application deadline: 3/1; financial award applicants required to submit FAFSA. Total annual research expenditures: $9.4 million. *Unit head:* Dr. Keith Crnic, Chair, 480-965-3061, E-mail: keith.crnic@asu.edu. *Application contact:* Graduate Admissions, 480-965-6113.

Azusa Pacific University, School of Behavioral and Applied Sciences, Department of Graduate Psychology, Azusa, CA 91702-7000. Offers clinical psychology (MA, Psy D), including family therapy (MA). *Accreditation:* APA (one or more programs are accredited). Part-time and evening/weekend programs available. *Faculty:* 14 full-time (8 women), 2 part-time/adjunct (1 woman). *Students:* 186 full-time (134 women), 45 part-time (35 women); includes 68 minority (14 Black or African American, non-Hispanic/Latino; 26 Asian, non-Hispanic/Latino; 27 Hispanic/Latino; 1 Native Hawaiian or other Pacific Islander, non-Hispanic/Latino), 11 international. Average age 30. In 2010, 73 master's, 16 doctorates awarded. *Degree requirements:* For master's, comprehensive exam, 250 hours of clinical experience, individual and group therapy. *Entrance requirements:* For master's, interview, minimum GPA of 3.0, Minnesota Multiphasic Personality Inventory. Additional exam requirements/recommendations for international students: Required—TOEFL (minimum score 600 paper-based). *Application deadline:* For fall admission, 6/30 priority date for domestic students. Applications are processed on a rolling basis. Application fee: $45 ($65 for international students). *Unit head:* Dr. Robert Welsh, Chair, 626-815-5008. *Application contact:* Linda Witte, Graduate Admissions Office, 626-969-3434.

Ball State University, Graduate School, College of Sciences and Humanities, Department of Psychological Science, Program in Clinical Psychology, Muncie, IN 47306-1099. Offers MA. *Faculty:* 20. *Students:* 20 full-time (18 women), 3 part-time (all women); includes 2 Black or African American, non-Hispanic/Latino, 1 international. Average age 23. 59 applicants, 27% accepted, 10 enrolled. In 2010, 15 master's awarded. *Entrance requirements:* For master's, GRE General Test, interview. Application fee: $50. *Expenses:* Tuition, state resident: full-time $6160; part-time $299 per credit hour. Tuition, nonresident: full-time $16,020; part-time $783 per credit hour. Required fees: $2278; $95 per credit hour. *Financial support:* In 2010–11, 9 teaching assistantships (averaging $8,676 per year) were awarded. Financial award application deadline: 3/1. *Unit head:* Dr. Kerri Pickel, Graduate Program Director, 765-285-1690, Fax: 765-285-8980, E-mail: kpickel@bsu.edu. *Application contact:* Dr. Kerri Pickel, Graduate Program Director, 765-285-1690, Fax: 765-285-8980, E-mail: kpickel@bsu.edu.

Barry University, School of Arts and Sciences, Department of Psychology, Miami Shores, FL 33161-6695. Offers clinical psychology (MS); school psychology (MS, SSP). Part-time and evening/weekend programs available. *Degree requirements:* For master's, thesis, practicum. *Entrance requirements:* For master's, GRE General Test, minimum GPA of 3.0, course work in psychology. Electronic applications accepted. *Faculty research:* Closed head injury, memory and aging, infant/mother interaction, evolutionary aspects of behavior, gender roles.

See Display on page 916 and Close-Up on page 1159.

Baylor University, Graduate School, College of Arts and Sciences, Department of Psychology and Neuroscience, Program in Clinical Psychology, Waco, TX 76798. Offers MSCP, Psy D. *Accreditation:* APA. *Students:* 32 full-time (24 women); includes 8 minority (6 Asian, non-Hispanic/Latino; 2 Hispanic/Latino), 1 international. In 2010, 6 master's, 5 doctorates awarded. *Degree requirements:* For doctorate, comprehensive exam. *Entrance requirements:* For master's, GRE General Test; for doctorate, GRE General Test, interview. *Application deadline:* For fall admission, 2/1 for domestic students. Applications are processed on a rolling basis. Application fee: $25. *Financial support:* Research assistantships, teaching assistantships, career-related internships or fieldwork, institutionally sponsored loans, tuition waivers (partial), and practicum stipends available. Financial award applicants required to submit FAFSA. *Faculty research:* Professional training in clinical psychology, human systems and dynamics, social skills validation, child therapy and assessment. *Unit head:* Dr. Gary Elkins, Graduate Program Director, 254-710-2961, Fax: 254-710-3033, E-mail: gary_elkins@baylor.edu. *Application contact:* Barbara Prisco, Graduate Coordinator, 254-757-0535, Fax: 254-710-2470, E-mail: barbara_prisco@baylor.edu.

Benedictine University, Graduate Programs, Program in Clinical Psychology, Lisle, IL 60532-0900. Offers MS. Part-time programs available. *Faculty:* 1 full-time (0 women), 7 part-time/adjunct (4 women). *Students:* 44 full-time (38 women), 34 part-time (30 women); includes 12 minority (5 Black or African American, non-Hispanic/Latino; 3 Asian, non-Hispanic/Latino; 4 Hispanic/Latino). Average age 33. 44 applicants, 59% accepted, 20 enrolled. In 2010, 18 master's awarded. *Degree requirements:* For master's, comprehensive exam, internship. *Entrance requirements:* For master's, MAT. Additional exam requirements/recommendations for international students: Required—TOEFL (minimum score 550 paper-based; 213 computer-based). *Application deadline:* For fall admission, 9/1 for domestic students; for winter admission, 12/1 for domestic students; for spring admission, 2/15 for domestic students. Applications are processed on a rolling basis. Application fee: $40. Electronic applications accepted. *Financial support:* Career-related internships or fieldwork and health care benefits available. Support available to part-time students. *Unit head:* Dr. James Crissmon, Director, 630-829-6490, E-mail: jcrissmon@ben.edu. *Application contact:* Kari Gibbons, Director, Admissions, 630-829-6200, Fax: 630-829-6584, E-mail: kgibbons@ben.edu.

Bethany University, Program in Clinical Psychology, Scotts Valley, CA 95066-2820. Offers MS. Part-time and evening/weekend programs available.

Bowling Green State University, Graduate College, College of Arts and Sciences, Department of Psychology, Bowling Green, OH 43403. Offers clinical psychology (MA, PhD); developmental psychology (MA, PhD); experimental psychology (MA, PhD); industrial/organizational psychology (MA, PhD); quantitative psychology (MA, PhD). *Accreditation:* APA (one or more programs are accredited). *Degree requirements:* For doctorate, thesis/dissertation. *Entrance requirements:* For doctorate, GRE General Test, GRE Subject Test. Additional exam requirements/recommendations for international students: Required—TOEFL. Electronic applications accepted. *Faculty research:* Personnel psychology, developmental-mathematical models, behavioral medication, brain process, child/adolescent social cognition.

Brigham Young University, Graduate Studies, College of Family, Home, and Social Sciences, Department of Psychology, Provo, UT 84602. Offers clinical psychology (PhD); general psychology (MS); psychology (PhD), including applied social psychology, behavioral neuroscience. *Accreditation:* APA (one or more programs are accredited). *Faculty:* 32 full-time (6 women), 4 part-time/adjunct (2 women). *Students:* 82 full-time (27 women); includes 3 Black or African American, non-Hispanic/Latino; 1 American Indian or Alaska Native, non-Hispanic/Latino; 6 Asian, non-Hispanic/Latino; 5 Hispanic/Latino; 68 Native Hawaiian or other Pacific Islander, non-Hispanic/Latino, 8 international. Average age 26. 91 applicants, 25% accepted, 18 enrolled. In 2010, 12 master's, 18 doctorates awarded. *Degree requirements:* For master's, thesis; for doctorate, comprehensive exam, thesis/dissertation, publishable paper. *Entrance requirements:* For master's and doctorate, GRE General Test, minimum GPA of 3.0 in last 60 hours of upper division course work. Additional exam requirements/recommendations for international students: Required—TOEFL. *Application deadline:* For fall admission, 1/5 for domestic students. Application fee: $50. Electronic applications accepted. *Expenses:* Tuition: Full-time $5580; part-time $310 per credit hour. Tuition and fees vary according to program and student's religious affiliation. *Financial support:* In 2010–11, 82 students received support, including 20 research assistantships with partial tuition reimbursements available (averaging $10,000 per year), 30 teaching assistantships with partial tuition reimbursements available (averaging $10,000 per year); fellowships, career-related internships or fieldwork, scholarships/grants, tuition waivers (partial), and unspecified assistantships also available. Financial award application deadline: 5/31. *Faculty research:* Psychotherapy process, Alzheimer's disease/dementia, psychology and law, health, psychology, developmental. Total annual research expenditures: $1 million. *Unit head:* Dr. Ramona Hopkins, Chair, 801-422-1170, Fax: 801-422-0602, E-mail: ramona_hopkins@byu.edu. *Application contact:* Karen A. Christensen, Coordinator of Student Programs, 801-422-4560, Fax: 801-422-0602, E-mail: karen@byu.edu.

California Institute of Integral Studies, School of Professional Psychology, San Francisco, CA 94103. Offers clinical psychology (Psy D); community mental health (MA); drama therapy (MA); expressive arts therapy (MA); integral counseling psychology (MA); integral counseling psychology-weekend (MA); somatic psychology (MA). *Accreditation:* APA. Part-time and evening/weekend programs available. *Students:* 651 full-time (476 women), 74 part-time (62 women); includes 146 minority (32 Black or African American, non-Hispanic/Latino; 1 American Indian or Alaska Native, non-Hispanic/Latino; 53 Asian, non-Hispanic/Latino; 43 Hispanic/Latino; 17 Two or more races, non-Hispanic/Latino), 52 international. Average age 37. 556 applicants, 72% accepted, 247 enrolled. In 2010, 148 master's, 27 doctorates awarded. *Degree requirements:* For doctorate, comprehensive exam, thesis/dissertation. *Entrance requirements:* For master's, minimum GPA of 3.0, letters of recommendation, writing sample; for doctorate, GRE, MA in psychology or social work with appropriate practical experience for advanced standing, or BA with a minimum GPA of 3.1; letters of recommendation; writing sample. Additional exam requirements/recommendations for international students: Required—TOEFL. *Application deadline:* For fall admission, 2/1 priority date for domestic and international students; for spring admission, 10/15 priority date for domestic and international students. Applications are processed on a rolling basis. Application fee: $65. Electronic applications accepted. *Expenses:* Tuition: Full-time $15,660; part-time $870 per semester hour. Required fees: $95 per semester. *Financial support:* Research assistantships with tuition reimbursements, teaching assistantships with tuition reimbursements, career-related internships or fieldwork, Federal Work-Study, scholarships/grants, and tuition waivers (partial) available. Support available to part-time students. Financial award application deadline: 4/15; financial award applicants required to submit FAFSA. *Faculty research:* Transpersonal psychology, somatic psychology, expressive arts therapy, drama therapy, community mental health, ecopsychology. *Application contact:* David Townes, Senior Admissions Counselor, 415-575-6152, Fax: 415-575-1268, E-mail: dtownes@ciis.edu.

California Lutheran University, Graduate Studies, Department of Psychology, Thousand Oaks, CA 91360-2787. Offers clinical psychology (MS, Psy D); marital and family therapy (MS). Part-time programs available. *Faculty:* 3 full-time (2 women), 12 part-time/adjunct (10 women). *Students:* 178 full-time (152 women), 11 part-time (9 women); includes 67 minority (5 Black or African American, non-Hispanic/Latino; 1 American Indian or Alaska Native, non-Hispanic/Latino; 7 Asian, non-Hispanic/Latino; 46 Hispanic/Latino; 1 Native Hawaiian or other Pacific Islander, non-Hispanic/Latino; 7 Two or more races, non-Hispanic/Latino), 5 international. Average age 31. 224 applicants, 67% accepted, 103 enrolled. In 2010, 68 master's awarded. *Degree requirements:* For master's, thesis or comprehensive exams; for doctorate, internship. *Entrance requirements:* For master's, GRE General Test, interview, minimum GPA of 3.0. *Application deadline:* For fall admission, 2/15 priority date for domestic students. Applications are processed on a rolling basis. Application fee: $50. *Unit head:* Dr. Mindy Puopolo, Director, 805-493-3528. *Application contact:* 805-493-3127, Fax: 805-493-3542, E-mail: clugrad@clunet.edu.

California State University, Dominguez Hills, College of Natural and Behavioral Sciences, Program in Psychology, Carson, CA 90747-0001. Offers clinical psychology (MA). Part-time and evening/weekend programs available. *Faculty:* 7 full-time (4 women). *Students:* 31 full-time (22 women), 28 part-time (26 women); includes 10 Black or African American, non-Hispanic/Latino; 2 Asian, non-Hispanic/Latino; 27 Hispanic/Latino; 1 Two or more races, non-Hispanic/Latino, 2 international. Average age 30. 59 applicants, 44% accepted, 15 enrolled. In 2010, 4 master's awarded. Terminal master's awarded for partial completion of doctoral program. *Degree requirements:* For master's, comprehensive exam, thesis optional. *Entrance requirements:* For master's, GRE General Test or MAT, interview, minimum GPA of 3.0, prerequisite psychology courses. Additional exam requirements/recommendations for international students: Required—TOEFL (minimum score 550 paper-based). *Application deadline:* For fall admission, 3/1 for domestic and international students. Application fee: $55. Electronic applications accepted. *Faculty research:* Culture and health, neuropsychology and HIV, psychohistory of the Holocaust, community and adolescents, malingering. *Unit head:* Dr. L. Mark Carrier, Chair, 310-243-3499, E-mail: lcarrier@csudh.edu. *Application contact:* Dr. Karen I. Mason, Coordinator, 310-243-3642, Fax: 310-516-3642, E-mail: kmason@csudh.edu.

California State University, Fullerton, Graduate Studies, College of Humanities and Social Sciences, Department of Psychology, Fullerton, CA 92834-9480. Offers clinical/community psychology (MS); psychology (MA). Part-time programs available. *Students:* 67 full-time (49 women), 9 part-time (5 women); includes 2 Black or African American, non-Hispanic/Latino; 5 Asian, non-Hispanic/Latino; 8 Hispanic/Latino; 3 Two or more races, non-Hispanic/Latino, 2 international. Average age 25. 169 applicants, 22% accepted, 37 enrolled. In 2010, 33 master's awarded. *Degree requirements:* For master's, thesis. *Entrance requirements:* For master's, GRE General Test, GRE Subject Test, undergraduate major in psychology or related field. Application fee: $55. *Financial support:* Career-related internships or fieldwork, Federal Work-Study, institutionally sponsored loans, and scholarships/grants available. Support available to part-time students. Financial award application deadline: 3/1; financial award applicants required to submit FAFSA. *Unit head:* Dr. Daniel Kee, Chair, 657-278-3514. *Application contact:* Admissions/Applications, 657-278-2371.

California State University, Northridge, Graduate Studies, College of Social and Behavioral Sciences, Department of Psychology, Northridge, CA 91330. Offers clinical psychology (MA); general-experimental psychology (MA); human factors and applied experimental psychology (MA). *Degree requirements:* For master's, thesis. *Entrance requirements:* For master's, GRE

Clinical Psychology

California State University, Northridge (continued)
General Test, GRE Subject Test, minimum GPA of 3.0, letters of recommendation. Additional exam requirements/recommendations for international students: Required—TOEFL.

California State University, San Bernardino, Graduate Studies, College of Social and Behavioral Sciences, Department of Psychology, Program in Clinical/Counseling Psychology, San Bernardino, CA 92407-2397. Offers clinical psychology (MS). *Degree requirements:* For master's, comprehensive exam or thesis. *Entrance requirements:* For master's, minimum GPA of 3.0 in major. *Faculty research:* Psychology of women, fathering, depression, families, cross-cultural counseling.

Capella University, Harold Abel School of Psychology, Minneapolis, MN 55402. Offers child and adolescent development (MS); clinical psychology (MS, Psy D); counseling psychology (MS); educational psychology (MS, PhD); evaluation, research, and measurement (MS); general psychology (MS, PhD); industrial/organizational psychology (MS, PhD); leadership coaching psychology (MS); organizational leader development (MS); school psychology (MS); sport psychology (MS). Part-time and evening/weekend programs available. Postbaccalaureate distance learning degree programs offered (minimal on-campus study). Terminal master's awarded for partial completion of doctoral program. *Degree requirements:* For master's, thesis optional, project; for doctorate, thesis/dissertation. *Entrance requirements:* For degree, master's degree in school psychology. Additional exam requirements/recommendations for international students: Required—TOEFL (minimum score 550 paper-based; 213 computer-based), TWE (minimum score 4); Recommended—IELTS. Electronic applications accepted. *Expenses:* Tuition: Full-time $11,880; part-time $440 per credit hour.

Cardinal Stritch University, College of Arts and Sciences, Department of Psychology, Milwaukee, WI 53217-3985. Offers clinical psychology (MA). Part-time and evening/weekend programs available. *Degree requirements:* For master's, thesis, portfolio, clinical practicum. *Entrance requirements:* For master's, GRE General Test, GRE Subject Test (psychology), interview, minimum GPA of 3.0, 3 letters of recommendation.

Carlos Albizu University, Graduate Programs, San Juan, PR 00901. Offers clinical psychology (MS, PhD, Psy D); general psychology (PhD); industrial/organizational psychology (MS, PhD); speech and language pathology (MS). *Accreditation:* APA (one or more programs are accredited). Part-time and evening/weekend programs available. Terminal master's awarded for partial completion of doctoral program. *Degree requirements:* For master's, one foreign language, comprehensive exam, thesis; for doctorate, one foreign language, comprehensive exam, thesis/dissertation, written qualifying exams. *Entrance requirements:* For master's, GRE General Test or EXADEP, interview; minimum GPA of 3.0 (industrial/organizational psychology), 3.25 (speech and language pathology); for doctorate, GRE General Test or EXADEP, interview; minimum GPA of 3.0 (industrial/organizational psychology), 3.25 (PhD and Psy D in clinical psychology). *Faculty research:* Psychotherapeutic techniques for Hispanics, psychology of the aged, school dropouts, stress, violence.

Carlos Albizu University, Miami Campus, Graduate Programs, Miami, FL 33172-2209. Offers clinical psychology (Psy D); entrepreneurship (MBA); exceptional student education (MS); industrial/organizational psychology (MS); marriage and family therapy (MS); mental health counseling (MS); nonprofit management (MBA); organizational management (MBA); psychology (MS); school counseling (MS); teaching English as a second language (MS). *Accreditation:* APA. Part-time and evening/weekend programs available. *Faculty:* 21 full-time (12 women), 37 part-time/adjunct (18 women). *Students:* 496 full-time (400 women), 242 part-time (192 women); includes 590 minority (58 Black or African American, non-Hispanic/Latino; 2 American Indian or Alaska Native, non-Hispanic/Latino; 5 Asian, non-Hispanic/Latino; 523 Hispanic/Latino; 2 Two or more races, non-Hispanic/Latino), 15 international. Average age 36. 141 applicants, 84% accepted, 118 enrolled. In 2010, 159 master's, 20 doctorates awarded. Terminal master's awarded for partial completion of doctoral program. *Degree requirements:* For master's, one foreign language, comprehensive exam, integrative project (MBA), research project (exceptional student education, teaching English as a second language); for doctorate, one foreign language, comprehensive exam, internship, project. *Entrance requirements:* For master's, 3 letters of recommendation, interview, minimum GPA of 3.0, resume, statement of purpose, official transcripts; for doctorate, 3 letters of recommendation, minimum GPA of 3.0, resume, interview. *Application deadline:* For fall admission, 8/1 priority date for domestic students; for spring admission, 11/30 priority date for domestic students. Applications are processed on a rolling basis. Application fee: $50. Electronic applications accepted. *Expenses:* Tuition: Full-time $9360; part-time $520 per credit. Required fees: $298 per term. Tuition and fees vary according to course load, degree level and program. *Financial support:* In 2010–11, 106 students received support. Federal Work-Study, scholarships/grants, and tuition discounts available. Financial award application deadline: 6/1; financial award applicants required to submit FAFSA. *Faculty research:* Psychotherapy, forensic psychology, neuropsychology, marketing strategy, entrepreneurship, special education. *Unit head:* Dr. Carmen S. Roca, Chancellor, 305-593-1223 Ext. 120, Fax: 305-629-8052, E-mail: croca@albizu.edu. *Application contact:* Vanessa Almendarez, Secretary, 305-593-1223 Ext. 137, Fax: 305-593-1854, E-mail: valmendarez@albizu.edu.

Case Western Reserve University, School of Graduate Studies, Department of Psychology, Program in Clinical Psychology, Cleveland, OH 44106. Offers PhD. *Accreditation:* APA. Part-time programs available. *Faculty:* 7 full-time (5 women), 12 part-time/adjunct (6 women). *Students:* 32 full-time (30 women); includes 2 Two or more races, non-Hispanic/Latino. Average age 27. 211 applicants, 3% accepted, 6 enrolled. In 2010, 4 doctorates awarded. *Degree requirements:* For doctorate, thesis/dissertation, internship. *Entrance requirements:* For doctorate, GRE General Test, GRE Subject Test. Additional exam requirements/recommendations for international students: Required—TOEFL (minimum score 550 paper-based; 213 computer-based; 79 iBT). *Application deadline:* For fall admission, 1/5 for domestic students. Application fee: $50. Electronic applications accepted. *Financial support:* Fellowships, research assistantships, teaching assistantships available. Financial award application deadline: 2/15; financial award applicants required to submit FAFSA. *Faculty research:* Pediatric psychology, family functioning, depression, geriatric psychopathology, creativity and play. *Unit head:* Director of Clinical Training. *Application contact:* Dr. James C. Overholser, Director of Clinical Training, 216-368-2686, Fax: 216-368-4891, E-mail: cwrupsych@gmail.com.

The Catholic University of America, School of Arts and Sciences, Department of Psychology, Washington, DC 20064. Offers applied experimental psychology (PhD); clinical psychology (PhD); general psychology (MA); human factors (MA); MA/JD. *Accreditation:* APA (one or more programs are accredited). Part-time programs available. *Faculty:* 12 full-time (6 women), 7 part-time/adjunct (2 women). *Students:* 39 full-time (25 women), 31 part-time (28 women); includes 6 Black or African American, non-Hispanic/Latino; 4 Asian, non-Hispanic/Latino; 4 Hispanic/Latino, 1 international. Average age 29. 229 applicants, 22% accepted, 17 enrolled. In 2010, 22 master's, 8 doctorates awarded. *Degree requirements:* For master's, comprehensive exam, thesis (for some programs); for doctorate, comprehensive exam, thesis/dissertation. *Entrance requirements:* For master's, GRE General Test, statement of purpose, official copies of academic transcripts, three letters of recommendation; for doctorate, GRE General Test, GRE Subject Test, statement of purpose, official copies of academic transcripts, three letters of recommendation. Additional exam requirements/recommendations for international students: Required—TOEFL (minimum score 580 paper-based; 237 computer-based). *Application deadline:* For fall admission, 8/1 priority date for domestic students, 7/15 for international students; for spring admission, 12/1 priority date for domestic students, 10/15 for international students. Applications are processed on a rolling basis. Application fee: $55. Electronic applications accepted. *Expenses:* Tuition: Full-time $33,580; part-time $1315 per credit hour. Required fees: $80; $40 per semester hour. One-time fee: $425. *Financial support:* Fellowships, research assistantships, teaching assistantships, Federal Work-Study, scholarships/grants, tuition waivers (full and partial), and unspecified assistantships available. Financial award application deadline: 2/1; financial award applicants required to submit FAFSA. *Faculty research:* Clinical psychology, applied cognitive science, psychopathology, cognitive neuroscience, psychotherapy. Total annual research expenditures: $409,988. *Unit head:* Dr. Marc M. Sebrechts, Chair, 202-319-5750, Fax: 202-319-6263, E-mail: sebrechts@cua.edu. *Application contact:* Andrew Woodall, Director of Graduate Admissions, 202-319-5057, Fax: 202-319-6533, E-mail: cua-admissions@cua.edu.

Central Michigan University, College of Graduate Studies, College of Humanities and Social and Behavioral Sciences, Department of Psychology, Program in Clinical Psychology, Mount Pleasant, MI 48859. Offers MS, PhD. *Accreditation:* APA. *Students:* 15 full-time (12 women), 20 part-time (15 women); includes 1 Black or African American, non-Hispanic/Latino, 4 international. Average age 26.Terminal master's awarded for partial completion of doctoral program. *Degree requirements:* For master's, thesis, completion of first 2 years of the PhD program in clinical psychology; for doctorate, thesis/dissertation. *Entrance requirements:* For master's and doctorate, GRE. *Application deadline:* For fall admission, 1/15 for domestic and international students. Application fee: $35 ($45 for international students). Electronic applications accepted. *Expenses:* Tuition, state resident: full-time $8208; part-time $456 per credit hour. Tuition, nonresident: full-time $13,788; part-time $766 per credit hour. One-time fee: $25. *Financial support:* In 2010–11, 3 fellowships with tuition reimbursements were awarded; research assistantships with tuition reimbursements, career-related internships or fieldwork, Federal Work-Study, unspecified assistantships, and out-of-state merit awards, non-resident graduate awards also available. *Faculty research:* Applied youth development; emotional processes, personality disorders, and assessment; influence of affective variables on cognitive performance; post-traumatic stress disorder and panic disorder; validation of clinical inferences from psychological tests. *Unit head:* Dr. Hajime Otani, Chair, 989-774-6461, Fax: 989-774-2553, E-mail: otani1h@cmich.edu. *Application contact:* Dr. Reid Skeel, Director, Clinical Psychology, 989-774-6463, Fax: 989-774-2553, E-mail: skeel1rl@cmich.edu.

Chestnut Hill College, School of Graduate Studies, Division of Psychology, Program in Clinical and Counseling Psychology, Philadelphia, PA 19118-2693. Offers MA, MS, CAS. Part-time and evening/weekend programs available. *Faculty:* 10 full-time (5 women), 31 part-time/adjunct (18 women). *Students:* 95 full-time (83 women), 165 part-time (131 women); includes 43 minority (30 Black or African American, non-Hispanic/Latino; 6 Asian, non-Hispanic/Latino; 7 Hispanic/Latino), 5 international. Average age 32. 107 applicants, 92% accepted, 70 enrolled. In 2010, 74 master's awarded. *Degree requirements:* For master's, thesis optional, practica. *Entrance requirements:* For master's, GRE, writing sample, letters of recommendation. Additional exam requirements/recommendations for international students: Required—TOEFL (minimum score 550 paper-based; 213 computer-based). *Application deadline:* For fall admission, 7/17 priority date for domestic students, 7/15 priority date for international students; for spring admission, 12/15 priority date for domestic and international students. Applications are processed on a rolling basis. Application fee: $55. *Expenses:* Tuition: Part-time $560 per credit hour. One-time fee: $55. Tuition and fees vary according to degree level and program. *Faculty research:* Play therapy, eating disorders, addictions, group psychology and group therapy, health psychology. *Unit head:* Dr. Joseph Micucci, Chair, Psychology Division, 215-348-7162, Fax: 215-753-3619, E-mail: micucci@chc.edu. *Application contact:* Amy Boorse, Administrative Assistant, School of Graduate Studies Office, 215-248-7170, Fax: 215-248-7161, E-mail: gradadmissions@chc.edu.

Chestnut Hill College, School of Graduate Studies, Division of Psychology, Program in Clinical Psychology, Philadelphia, PA 19118-2693. Offers Psy D. *Accreditation:* APA. Part-time and evening/weekend programs available. *Faculty:* 10 full-time (5 women), 31 part-time/adjunct (18 women). *Students:* 55 full-time (45 women), 58 part-time (49 women); includes 16 minority (5 Black or African American, non-Hispanic/Latino; 6 Asian, non-Hispanic/Latino; 4 Hispanic/Latino; 1 Two or more races, non-Hispanic/Latino), 3 international. Average age 31. 159 applicants, 27% accepted, 19 enrolled. In 2010, 7 doctorates awarded. *Degree requirements:* For doctorate, comprehensive exam, thesis/dissertation, internships, practica. *Entrance requirements:* For doctorate, GRE, letters of recommendation, writing sample, master's degree in clinical/counseling psychology or closely related field. Additional exam requirements/recommendations for international students: Required—TOEFL (minimum score 500 paper-based; 213 computer-based). *Application deadline:* For fall admission, 7/17 priority date for domestic students, 7/15 priority date for international students; for spring admission, 12/15 priority date for domestic and international students. Applications are processed on a rolling basis. Application fee: $80. *Expenses:* Tuition: Part-time $560 per credit hour. One-time fee: $55. Tuition and fees vary according to degree level and program. *Faculty research:* Psychological testing and assessment, GLBT issues, autism and developmental disorders, stepfamilies, gender issues. *Unit head:* Dr. Joseph Micucci, Chair, Division of Psychology, 215-248-7162, Fax: 215-753-3619, E-mail: micucci@chc.edu. *Application contact:* Eileem Webb, Director of Psy D Admissions, 215-248-7077, Fax: 215-753-3619, E-mail: profpsyc@chc.edu.

The Chicago School of Professional Psychology, Program in Applied Behavior Analysis, Chicago, IL 60610. Offers applied behavior analysis (Psy D); clinical psychology (applied behavior analysis specialization) (MA). *Degree requirements:* For master's, thesis, practicum; for doctorate, thesis/dissertation, practicum. *Entrance requirements:* For doctorate, GRE. Additional exam requirements/recommendations for international students: Required—TOEFL.

The Chicago School of Professional Psychology, Program in Clinical Forensic Psychology, Chicago, IL 60610. Offers Psy D. *Degree requirements:* For doctorate, thesis/dissertation. *Entrance requirements:* For doctorate, GRE. Additional exam requirements/recommendations for international students: Required—TOEFL, IELTS.

The Chicago School of Professional Psychology, Program in Clinical Psychology, Chicago, IL 60610. Offers applied behavior analysis (MA); clinical psychology (Psy D); counseling (MA). *Accreditation:* APA. *Degree requirements:* For master's, thesis (for some programs); for doctorate, comprehensive exam, thesis/dissertation. *Entrance requirements:* For master's, minimum undergraduate GPA of 3.0, 1 course in psychology, 1 course in either statistics or research methods; for doctorate, GRE, 18 hours of psychology credit (including courses in statistics, normal psychology and human development); minimum GPA of 3.2. Additional exam requirements/recommendations for international students: Required—TOEFL. Electronic applications accepted.

The Chicago School of Professional Psychology at Downtown Los Angeles, Program in Clinical Forensic Psychology, Los Angeles, CA 90017. Offers Psy D.

The Chicago School of Professional Psychology at Downtown Los Angeles, Program in Clinical Psychology, Los Angeles, CA 90017. Offers applied behavior analysis (MA); clinical psychology (Psy D); marital and family therapy (MA).

The Chicago School of Professional Psychology at Grayslake, Program in Clinical Counseling Psychology, Chicago, IL 60610. Offers counseling (MA), including child and adolescent treatment, generalist, health psychology, Latino mental health, supervision and leadership in mental health, treatment of addiction disorders.

The Chicago School of Professional Psychology at Irvine, Program in Clinical Forensic Psychology, Irvine, CA 92612. Offers Psy D.

The Chicago School of Professional Psychology at Westwood, Program in Clinical Psychology, Los Angeles, CA 90024. Offers marital and family therapy (MA).

City College of the City University of New York, Graduate School, College of Liberal Arts and Science, Division of Social Science, Department of Psychology, New York, NY 10031-9198. Offers clinical psychology (PhD); experimental cognition (PhD); general psychology (MA); mental health counseling (MA). PhD program offered jointly with Graduate School and University Center of the City University of New York. *Accreditation:* APA (one or more programs are accredited). Part-time programs available. *Degree requirements:* For master's, one foreign language, comprehensive exam, thesis. *Entrance requirements:* For master's, GRE. Additional exam requirements/recommendations for international students: Required—TOEFL (minimum score 550 paper-based; 79 iBT). Electronic applications accepted. *Faculty research:* Social/personality psychology, physiological psychology, cognition and development.

Clark University, Graduate School, Department of Psychology, Program in Clinical Psychology, Worcester, MA 01610-1477. Offers PhD. *Accreditation:* APA. *Students:* 24 full-time (19 women); includes 4 minority (1 American Indian or Alaska Native, non-Hispanic/Latino; 3 Hispanic/Latino), 1 international. Average age 28. In 2010, 4 doctorates awarded. *Degree requirements:* For doctorate, thesis/dissertation. *Entrance requirements:* For doctorate, GRE General Test. Additional exam requirements/recommendations for international students: Required—TOEFL. *Application deadline:* For fall admission, 12/28 priority date for domestic students. Applications are processed on a rolling basis. Application fee: $50. *Expenses:* Tuition: Full-time $37,000; part-time $1156 per credit hour. Required fees: $30; $1156 per credit hour. *Financial support:* In 2010–11, fellowships with full tuition reimbursements (averaging $15,700 per year), research assistantships with full tuition reimbursements (averaging $15,700 per year), teaching assistantships with full tuition reimbursements (averaging $15,700 per year) were awarded; tuition waivers (full) also available. *Faculty research:* Development of psychological processes in sociocultural context, conceptualizing and reasoning, symbolization, psychotherapy, metaphor, emotions and personalities. *Unit head:* Dr. James Cordova, Chair, 508-793-7268. *Application contact:* Peggy Moskowitz, Graduate School Secretary, 508-793-7274, Fax: 508-793-7265, E-mail: psychology@clarku.edu.

Cleveland State University, College of Graduate Studies, College of Sciences and Health Professions, Department of Psychology, Cleveland, OH 44115. Offers adult development and aging (PhD); clinical psychology (MA); consumer/industrial research (MA); diversity management (MA); experimental research psychology (MA); school psychology (Psy S). *Accreditation:* APA. *Faculty:* 20 full-time (7 women), 16 part-time/adjunct (8 women). *Students:* 63 full-time (45 women), 43 part-time (27 women); includes 15 Black or African American, non-Hispanic/Latino; 1 American Indian or Alaska Native, non-Hispanic/Latino; 3 Asian, non-Hispanic/Latino; 3 Hispanic/Latino, 1 international. Average age 30. 164 applicants, 44% accepted, 62 enrolled. In 2010, 39 master's, 8 other advanced degrees awarded. Terminal master's awarded for partial completion of doctoral program. *Degree requirements:* For master's, comprehensive exam (for some programs), thesis (for some programs); for doctorate, comprehensive exam, thesis/dissertation; for Psy S, internship. *Entrance requirements:* For master's and doctorate, GRE General Test. Additional exam requirements/recommendations for international students: Required—TOEFL (minimum score 525 paper-based; 197 computer-based). *Application deadline:* For fall admission, 2/1 priority date for domestic and international students. Application fee: $30. Electronic applications accepted. *Expenses:* Tuition, state resident: full-time $8447; part-time $469 per credit hour. Tuition, nonresident: full-time $16,020; part-time $890 per credit hour. Required fees: $50. *Financial support:* In 2010–11, 45 students received support. Career-related internships or fieldwork, Federal Work-Study, scholarships/grants, tuition waivers (partial), and unspecified assistantships available. Financial award applicants required to submit FAFSA. *Faculty research:* Cognitive and social psychology, consumer psychology, clinical psychology, school psychology, aging. Total annual research expenditures: $112,607. *Unit head:* Dr. Kathleen M. McNamara, Chairperson, 216-687-2545, Fax: 216-687-9294, E-mail: k.mcnamara@csuohio.edu. *Application contact:* Karen R. Colston, Administrative Coordinator, 216-687-2552, Fax: 216-687-9294, E-mail: k.colston@csuohio.edu.

College of St. Joseph, Graduate Programs, Division of Psychology and Human Services, Program in Clinical Mental Health Counseling, Rutland, VT 05701-3899. Offers MS. Part-time programs available. *Faculty:* 4 full-time (1 woman), 7 part-time/adjunct (4 women). *Students:* 10 full-time (8 women), 11 part-time (9 women). Average age 36. 5 applicants, 80% accepted, 4 enrolled. In 2010, 3 master's awarded. *Degree requirements:* For master's, comprehensive exam. *Entrance requirements:* For master's, 2 letters of reference, interview. *Application deadline:* Applications are processed on a rolling basis. Application fee: $35. Electronic applications accepted. *Expenses:* Tuition: Full-time $14,200; part-time $400 per credit hour. Required fees: $45 per semester. *Financial support:* In 2010–11, 1 student received support. Career-related internships or fieldwork, Federal Work-Study, and unspecified assistantships available. Support available to part-time students. Financial award application deadline: 3/1. *Unit head:* Dr. Craig Knapp, Chair, 802-773-5900 Ext. 3219, Fax: 802-776-5258, E-mail: cknapp@csj.edu. *Application contact:* Alan Young, Dean of Admissions, 802-773-5900 Ext. 3227, Fax: 802-776-5310, E-mail: alanyoung@csj.edu.

College of St. Joseph, Graduate Programs, Division of Psychology and Human Services, Program in Clinical Psychology, Rutland, VT 05701-3899. Offers MS. Part-time and evening/weekend programs available. *Faculty:* 4 full-time (1 woman), 6 part-time/adjunct (3 women). *Students:* 7 full-time (all women), 8 part-time (5 women); includes 1 Asian, non-Hispanic/Latino. Average age 33. 6 applicants, 100% accepted, 5 enrolled. In 2010, 5 master's awarded. *Degree requirements:* For master's, comprehensive exam, thesis optional. *Entrance requirements:* For master's, 2 letters of reference, interview. *Application deadline:* Applications are processed on a rolling basis. Application fee: $35. Electronic applications accepted. *Expenses:* Tuition: Full-time $14,200; part-time $400 per credit hour. Required fees: $45 per semester. *Financial support:* In 2010–11, 2 students received support, including teaching assistantships with tuition reimbursements available (averaging $3,000 per year); unspecified assistantships also available. Financial award application deadline: 3/1. *Unit head:* Dr. Craig Knapp, Chair, 802-773-5900 Ext. 3219, Fax: 802-776-5258, E-mail: cknapp@csj.edu. *Application contact:* Alan Young, Dean of Admissions, 802-773-5900 Ext. 3227, Fax: 802-776-5310, E-mail: alanyoung@csj.edu.

Concordia University, School of Graduate Studies, Faculty of Arts and Science, Department of Psychology, Program in Psychology (Clinical), Montréal, QC H3G 1M8, Canada. Offers MA, PhD, Certificate. *Accreditation:* APA (one or more programs are accredited). *Degree requirements:* For master's, comprehensive exam, thesis; for doctorate, comprehensive exam, thesis/dissertation. *Entrance requirements:* For master's, GRE General Test, GRE Subject Test, honors degree in psychology or equivalent; for doctorate, master's degree in psychology. *Faculty research:* Developmental-clinical psychology, sensory deficits, sexual dysfunction.

Dalhousie University, Faculty of Science, Department of Psychology, Halifax, NS B3H 4R2, Canada. Offers clinical psychology (PhD); psychology (M Sc, PhD); psychology/neuroscience (M Sc, PhD). *Accreditation:* APA (one or more programs are accredited). *Degree requirements:* For master's, thesis; for doctorate, thesis/dissertation. *Entrance requirements:* For doctorate, GRE General Test. Additional exam requirements/recommendations for international students: Required—TOEFL, IELTS, CANTEST, CAEL, or Michigan English Language Assessment Battery. Electronic applications accepted. *Faculty research:* Physiological psychology, psychology of learning, learning and behavior, forensic clinical health psychology, development perception and cognition.

DePaul University, College of Liberal Arts and Sciences, Department of Psychology, Chicago, IL 60604-2287. Offers clinical psychology (MA, PhD), including child clinical psychology, community clinical psychology; experimental psychology (MA, PhD); general psychology (MS); industrial/organizational psychology (MA, PhD); MA/PhD. *Accreditation:* APA (one or more programs are accredited). *Faculty:* 31 full-time (19 women), 6 part-time/adjunct (4 women). *Students:* 43 full-time (26 women), 57 part-time (39 women); includes 11 Black or African American, non-Hispanic/Latino; 5 Asian, non-Hispanic/Latino; 10 Hispanic/Latino; 4 Two or more races, non-Hispanic/Latino, 2 international. Average age 28. 332 applicants, 14% accepted, 23 enrolled. In 2010, 14 master's, 17 doctorates awarded. *Degree requirements:* For master's, thesis, oral exam; for doctorate, comprehensive exam, thesis/dissertation, oral and written exams. *Entrance requirements:* For master's and doctorate, GRE General Test, GRE Subject Test, 32 quarter hours of course work in psychology, 3 letters of recommendation. Additional exam requirements/recommendations for international students: Required—TOEFL. Application fee: $40. Electronic applications accepted. *Financial support:* In 2010–11, 48 students received support, including 35 research assistantships with full tuition reimbursements available (averaging $11,800 per year), 13 teaching assistantships with full tuition reimbursements available (averaging $11,800 per year); career-related internships or fieldwork, scholarships/grants,

traineeships, tuition waivers (full and partial), and unspecified assistantships also available. Financial award application deadline: 1/10. *Faculty research:* Adolescent stress and depression, minority adolescents sexuality, public policy, community influences in child adjustment. *Unit head:* Dr. Christopher B. Keys, Chairman, 773-325-7887, Fax: 773-325-7888. *Application contact:* Alison Pereida Knapp, Graduate Admissions Assistant, 773-325-7887, Fax: 773-325-7888.

Drexel University, College of Arts and Sciences, Department of Psychology, Clinical Psychology Program, Philadelphia, PA 19104-2875. Offers clinical psychology (PhD); forensic psychology (PhD); health psychology (PhD); neuropsychology (PhD). *Accreditation:* APA. Terminal master's awarded for partial completion of doctoral program. *Degree requirements:* For doctorate, thesis/dissertation, qualifying exam. *Entrance requirements:* For doctorate, GRE General Test, GRE Subject Test, minimum GPA of 3.0. Electronic applications accepted. *Expenses:* Contact institution. *Faculty research:* Cognitive behavioral therapy, stress and coping, eating disorders, substance abuse, developmental disabilities.

Drexel University, College of Arts and Sciences, Department of Psychology, Program in Law-Psychology, Philadelphia, PA 19104-2875. Offers JD/PhD. Electronic applications accepted. *Expenses:* Contact institution. *Faculty research:* Mental health law issues, professional ethics, social science applications to law.

Duke University, Graduate School, Department of Psychology and Neuroscience, Durham, NC 27708. Offers biological psychology (PhD); clinical psychology (PhD); cognitive psychology (PhD); developmental psychology (PhD); experimental psychology (PhD); health psychology (PhD); human social development (PhD); JD/MA. *Accreditation:* APA (one or more programs are accredited). *Faculty:* 40 full-time. *Students:* 92 full-time (67 women); includes 6 Black or African American, non-Hispanic/Latino; 2 Asian, non-Hispanic/Latino; 7 Hispanic/Latino, 13 international. 483 applicants, 8% accepted, 23 enrolled. In 2010, 24 doctorates awarded. *Degree requirements:* For doctorate, thesis/dissertation. *Entrance requirements:* For doctorate, GRE General Test. Additional exam requirements/recommendations for international students: Required—TOEFL (minimum score 550 paper-based; 213 computer-based; 83 iBT), IELTS (minimum score 7). *Application deadline:* For fall admission, 12/8 priority date for domestic and international students. Application fee: $75. Electronic applications accepted. *Financial support:* Fellowships, research assistantships, teaching assistantships, career-related internships or fieldwork and Federal Work-Study available. Financial award application deadline: 12/8. *Unit head:* Melanie Bonner, Director of Graduate Studies, 919-660-5715, Fax: 919-660-5726, E-mail: morrell@duke.edu. *Application contact:* Elizabeth Hutton, Director of Admissions, 919-684-3913, Fax: 919-684-2277, E-mail: grad-admissions@duke.edu.

Duquesne University, Graduate School of Liberal Arts, Department of Psychology, Pittsburgh, PA 15282-0001. Offers clinical psychology (PhD). *Accreditation:* APA. *Faculty:* 14 full-time (5 women). *Students:* 46 full-time (24 women); includes 1 Hispanic/Latino, 4 international. Average age 25. 133 applicants, 6% accepted, 8 enrolled. In 2010, 11 doctorates awarded. *Degree requirements:* For doctorate, comprehensive exam, thesis/dissertation. *Entrance requirements:* For doctorate, GRE General Test, MA in psychology. Additional exam requirements/recommendations for international students: Required—TOEFL. *Application deadline:* For fall admission, 12/15 for domestic and international students. Electronic applications accepted. *Expenses:* Tuition: Part-time $884 per credit. Required fees: $84 per credit. Tuition and fees vary according to course load. *Financial support:* In 2010–11, 9 research assistantships with full tuition reimbursements (averaging $15,000 per year), 14 teaching assistantships with full tuition reimbursements (averaging $15,000 per year) were awarded; fellowships with full tuition reimbursements, career-related internships or fieldwork, scholarships/grants, tuition waivers (partial), and unspecified assistantships also available. Financial award application deadline: 5/1. *Faculty research:* Emotion, language motivation, imagination, development. *Unit head:* Dr. Daniel Burston, Chair, 412-396-5067. *Application contact:* Dr. Daniel Buston, Chair, 412-396-5067.

East Carolina University, Graduate School, Thomas Harriot College of Arts and Sciences, Department of Psychology, Program in Clinical Psychology, Greenville, NC 27858-4353. Offers MA. *Degree requirements:* For master's, one foreign language, comprehensive exam, thesis. *Entrance requirements:* For master's, GRE General Test, GRE Subject Test. Additional exam requirements/recommendations for international students: Required—TOEFL. *Expenses:* Tuition, state resident: full-time $3130; part-time $391.25 per credit hour. Tuition, nonresident: full-time $13,817; part-time $1727.13 per credit hour. Required fees: $1916; $239.50 per credit hour. Tuition and fees vary according to campus/location and program.

Eastern Illinois University, Graduate School, College of Sciences, Charleston, IL 61920-3099. Offers biological sciences (MS); chemistry (MS); communication disorders and sciences (MS); economics (MA); mathematics and computer science (MA), including mathematics, mathematics education; natural sciences (MS); political science (MA); psychology (MA, SSP), including clinical psychology (MA), school psychology (SSP). Part-time programs available. *Degree requirements:* For SSP, thesis. *Entrance requirements:* For degree, GRE General Test.

Eastern Illinois University, Graduate School, College of Sciences, Department of Psychology, Program in Clinical Psychology, Charleston, IL 61920-3099. Offers MA. *Degree requirements:* For master's, comprehensive exam. *Entrance requirements:* For master's, GRE General Test.

Eastern Kentucky University, The Graduate School, College of Arts and Sciences, Department of Psychology, Richmond, KY 40475-3102. Offers clinical psychology (MS); industrial/organizational psychology (MS); school psychology (Psy S). Part-time programs available. *Entrance requirements:* For master's and Psy S, GRE General Test, minimum GPA of 2.5. *Faculty research:* Autism, social psychology, parenting, assessment of depression/anxiety, reading.

Eastern Michigan University, Graduate School, College of Arts and Sciences, Department of Psychology, Ypsilanti, MI 48197. Offers clinical behavioral psychology (MS); clinical psychology (MS, PhD); experimental psychology (MS). *Accreditation:* APA. *Faculty:* 24 full-time (14 women). *Students:* 55 full-time (39 women), 35 part-time (28 women); includes 8 minority (1 Black or African American, non-Hispanic/Latino; 5 Asian, non-Hispanic/Latino; 2 Hispanic/Latino), 3 international. Average age 27. 234 applicants, 13% accepted, 26 enrolled. In 2010, 21 master's, 9 doctorates awarded. *Degree requirements:* For master's, 600-hour practicum; for doctorate, 1500-hour practicum; 2000-hour internship. *Entrance requirements:* For master's and doctorate, GRE. *Application deadline:* For fall admission, 2/15 for domestic students. Application fee: $35. *Financial support:* Fellowships available. *Unit head:* Dr. Carol Freedman-Doan, Department Head, 734-487-1155, Fax: 734-487-6553, E-mail: cfreedman@emich.edu. *Application contact:* Dawn Stentzel, Graduate Secretary, 734-487-1155, Fax: 734-487-6553, E-mail: dstentzel@emich.edu.

Eastern Virginia Medical School, The Virginia Consortium Program in Clinical Psychology, Norfolk, VA 23501-1980. Offers Psy D. Program offered jointly with The College of William and Mary, Norfolk State University, and Old Dominion University. *Faculty:* 33. *Students:* 44 full-time (33 women); includes 4 Black or African American, non-Hispanic/Latino; 5 Asian, non-Hispanic/Latino; 4 Hispanic/Latino. 169 applicants, 4% accepted, 6 enrolled. In 2010, 14 doctorates awarded. *Entrance requirements:* For doctorate, GRE, BS in behavioral sciences or equivalent. Additional exam requirements/recommendations for international students: Required—TOEFL. *Application deadline:* For fall admission, 1/15 for domestic students. Application fee: $40. *Expenses:* Contact institution. *Unit head:* Dr. Michael L. Stutts, Director, 757-446-8400, Fax: 757-446-8401, E-mail: stuttsml@evms.edu. *Application contact:* Eileen O'Neill, Administrative Coordinator, 757-368-1820, Fax: 757-446-8401, E-mail: exoneill@odu.edu.

Eastern Washington University, Graduate Studies, College of Social and Behavioral Sciences, Department of Psychology, Cheney, WA 99004-2431. Offers clinical psychology (MS); experimental psychology (MS); psychology (MS); school psychology (MS). *Degree requirements:* For master's, comprehensive exam, thesis or alternative. *Entrance requirements:* For master's, GRE General Test, minimum GPA of 3.0.

Clinical Psychology

East Tennessee State University, School of Graduate Studies, College of Arts and Sciences, Department of Psychology, Johnson City, TN 37614. Offers clinical psychology (PhD); experiential psychology (PhD); general psychology (MA). *Faculty:* 10 full-time (1 woman). *Students:* 35 full-time (19 women), 8 part-time (6 women); includes 2 minority (1 Hispanic/Latino; 1 Two or more races, non-Hispanic/Latino), 1 international. Average age 27. 82 applicants, 27% accepted, 13 enrolled. In 2010, 5 master's awarded. *Degree requirements:* For master's, thesis; for doctorate, thesis/dissertation. *Entrance requirements:* For master's, GRE General Test, GRE Subject Test, minimum GPA of 3.0. Additional exam requirements/recommendations for international students: Required—TOEFL (minimum score 550 paper-based; 213 computer-based; 79 iBT). *Application deadline:* For fall admission, 2/1 for domestic and international students. Application fee: $25 ($35 for international students). Electronic applications accepted. *Financial support:* In 2010–11, 2 research assistantships with full tuition reimbursements (averaging $5,500 per year), 5 teaching assistantships with full tuition reimbursements (averaging $5,500 per year) were awarded; career-related internships or fieldwork, institutionally sponsored loans, scholarships/grants, and unspecified assistantships also available. Financial award application deadline: 7/1; financial award applicants required to submit FAFSA. *Faculty research:* Language acquisition, recovery of brain function after injury or damage, violence in domestic relationships and road rage, reasons for living, unhealthy tanning behaviors. Total annual research expenditures: $83,798. *Unit head:* Dr. Wallace Dixon, Chair, 423-439-6656, Fax: 423-439-5695, E-mail: dixonw@etsu.edu. *Application contact:* Admissions and Records Clerk, 423-439-4221, Fax: 423-439-5624, E-mail: gradsch@etsu.edu.

Emory University, Laney Graduate School, Department of Psychology, Atlanta, GA 30322-1100. Offers clinical psychology (PhD); cognition and development (PhD); neuroscience and animal behavior (PhD). *Accreditation:* APA. *Degree requirements:* For doctorate, comprehensive exam, thesis/dissertation. *Entrance requirements:* For doctorate, GRE General Test, minimum GPA of 3.25. Additional exam requirements/recommendations for international students: Required—TOEFL. Electronic applications accepted. *Expenses:* Tuition: Full-time $33,800. Required fees: $1300. *Faculty research:* Neuroscience and animal behavior; adult and child psychopathology, cognition development assessment.

Emporia State University, Graduate School, Teachers College, Department of Psychology, Art Therapy, Rehabilitation and Mental Health Counseling, Program in Clinical Psychology, Emporia, KS 66801-5087. Offers MS. Part-time programs available. *Students:* 26 full-time (17 women), 5 part-time (all women); includes 2 minority (1 Asian, non-Hispanic/Latino; 1 Two or more races, non-Hispanic/Latino), 1 international. 13 applicants, 69% accepted, 9 enrolled. In 2010, 11 master's awarded. *Degree requirements:* For master's, comprehensive exam, clinical internship. *Entrance requirements:* For master's, GRE or MAT, 24 hours of course work in undergraduate psychology, 3 letters of recommendation. Additional exam requirements/recommendations for international students: Required—TOEFL (minimum score 520 paper-based; 133 computer-based; 68 iBT). *Application deadline:* For fall admission, 8/15 for domestic students. Applications are processed on a rolling basis. Application fee: $30 ($75 for international students). Electronic applications accepted. *Expenses:* Tuition, state resident: full-time $4382; part-time $183 per credit hour. Tuition, nonresident: full-time $13,572; part-time $566 per credit hour. Required fees: $1022; $62 per credit hour. Tuition and fees vary according to course level, course load and campus/location. *Financial support:* Career-related internships or fieldwork, Federal Work-Study, institutionally sponsored loans, health care benefits, and unspecified assistantships available. Support available to part-time students. Financial award application deadline: 3/15; financial award applicants required to submit FAFSA. *Unit head:* Dr. Brian W. Schrader, Chair, 620-341-5317, E-mail: schrade@emporia.edu. *Application contact:* Mary Sewell, Admissions Coordinator, 800-950-GRAD, Fax: 620-341-5909, E-mail: msewell@emporia.edu.

Evangel University, Department of Psychology, Springfield, MO 65802. Offers clinical psychology (MS); counseling psychology (MS). Part-time programs available. *Faculty:* 3 full-time (2 women), 9 part-time/adjunct (4 women). *Students:* 23 full-time (15 women), 18 part-time (14 women). Average age 27. 17 applicants, 100% accepted, 15 enrolled. In 2010, 8 master's awarded. *Degree requirements:* For master's, comprehensive exam, thesis optional. *Entrance requirements:* For master's, GRE General Test or MAT, minimum undergraduate GPA of 3.0, undergraduate major or minor in psychology. Additional exam requirements/recommendations for international students: Required—TOEFL (minimum score 550 paper-based; 213 computer-based). *Application deadline:* For fall admission, 2/1 priority date for domestic students; for spring admission, 10/15 priority date for domestic students. Applications are processed on a rolling basis. Application fee: $25. Electronic applications accepted. *Financial support:* In 2010–11, 6 students received support. Career-related internships or fieldwork, scholarships/grants, and unspecified assistantships available. Support available to part-time students. Financial award application deadline: 3/1; financial award applicants required to submit FAFSA. *Unit head:* Dr. Grant Jones, Chair, 417-865-2815 Ext. 8619, E-mail: jonesg@evangel.edu. *Application contact:* Charity H. Fahlstrom, Admissions Representative, Graduate and Professional Studies Admissions, 417-865-2815 Ext. 7227, Fax: 417-575-5484, E-mail: fahlstromc@evangel.edu.

Fairfield University, Graduate School of Education and Allied Professions, Department of Counselor Education, Fairfield, CT 06824-5195. Offers clinical mental health counseling (MA, CAS); school counseling (MA, CAS). *Accreditation:* ACA (one or more programs are accredited). Part-time and evening/weekend programs available. *Faculty:* 4 full-time (all women), 4 part-time/adjunct (3 women). *Students:* 25 full-time (21 women), 78 part-time (52 women); includes 3 Black or African American, non-Hispanic/Latino; 1 Asian, non-Hispanic/Latino; 7 Hispanic/Latino. 52 applicants, 29% accepted, 8 enrolled. In 2010, 28 master's, 2 other advanced degrees awarded. *Degree requirements:* For master's, comprehensive exam, thesis or alternative. *Entrance requirements:* For master's, PRAXIS I (PPST), minimum QPA of 3.0, 2 recommendations, resume. Additional exam requirements/recommendations for international students: Required—TOEFL (minimum score 550 paper-based; 213 computer-based; 84 iBT). *Application deadline:* For fall admission, 2/15 for domestic and international students; for spring admission, 10/1 for domestic and international students. Application fee: $60. Electronic applications accepted. *Expenses:* Tuition: Part-time $600 per hour. Part-time tuition and fees vary according to degree level and program. *Financial support:* Career-related internships or fieldwork and unspecified assistantships available. Financial award applicants required to submit FAFSA. *Faculty research:* Corrective feedback in group setting, applying group concepts to teaching counselor education curriculum, assessment and program evaluation, spirituality and counseling, clinical supervision, developmental school counseling, wellness and multicultural counseling. *Unit head:* Dr. Diana Hulse, Chair, 203-254-4000 Ext. 2245, Fax: 203-254-4047, E-mail: dhulse@fairfield.edu. *Application contact:* Marianne Gumpper, Director of Graduate and Continuing Studies Admissions, 203-254-4184, Fax: 203-254-4073, E-mail: gradadmis@fairfield.edu.

Fairleigh Dickinson University, College at Florham, Maxwell Becton College of Arts and Sciences, Department of Psychology, Program in Clinical Mental Health Counseling, Madison, NJ 07940-1099. Offers MA. *Students:* 20 full-time (13 women), 2 part-time (1 woman). Average age 26. 1 applicant, 100% accepted, 0 enrolled. *Unit head:* Dr. Ketrin Maxwell, Director. *Application contact:* Susan Brooman, University Director, Graduate Admissions, 973-443-8905, Fax: 973-443-8088, E-mail: grad@fdu.edu.

Fairleigh Dickinson University, Metropolitan Campus, University College: Arts, Sciences, and Professional Studies, School of Psychology, Program in Clinical Psychology, Teaneck, NJ 07666-1914. Offers MA, PhD. *Accreditation:* APA. *Students:* 81 full-time (53 women), 4 international. Average age 30. 20 applicants, 80% accepted, 14 enrolled. In 2010, 4 doctorates awarded. *Application deadline:* Applications are processed on a rolling basis. Application fee: $40. *Application contact:* Susan Brooman, University Director of Graduate Admissions, 201-692-2554, Fax: 201-692-2560, E-mail: globaleducation@fdu.edu.

Fairleigh Dickinson University, Metropolitan Campus, University College: Arts, Sciences, and Professional Studies, School of Psychology, Program in Clinical Psychopharmacology, Teaneck, NJ 07666-1914. Offers MA. *Students:* 1 full-time (0 women), 37 part-time (23 women), 1 international. Average age 48. 23 applicants, 100% accepted, 16 enrolled. In 2010, 18 master's awarded. *Application contact:* Susan Brooman, University Director of Graduate Admissions, 201-692-2554, Fax: 201-692-2560, E-mail: globaleducation@fdu.edu.

Fielding Graduate University, Graduate Programs, School of Psychology, Santa Barbara, CA 93105-3538. Offers clinical psychology (PhD); clinical psychology respecialization (Post-Doctoral Certificate); media psychology (PhD); media psychology and social change (MA); neuropsychology (Post-Doctoral Certificate). *Accreditation:* APA. Postbaccalaureate distance learning degree programs offered (minimal on-campus study). *Faculty:* 27 full-time (15 women), 8 part-time/adjunct (2 women). *Students:* 534 full-time (396 women), 69 part-time (48 women); includes 147 minority (41 Black or African American, non-Hispanic/Latino; 7 American Indian or Alaska Native, non-Hispanic/Latino; 25 Asian, non-Hispanic/Latino; 57 Hispanic/Latino; 17 Two or more races, non-Hispanic/Latino), 20 international. Average age 42. 333 applicants, 35% accepted, 76 enrolled. In 2010, 9 master's, 39 doctorates, 16 other advanced degrees awarded. Terminal master's awarded for partial completion of doctoral program. *Degree requirements:* For master's, thesis or alternative, capstone project; for doctorate, comprehensive exam, thesis/dissertation. *Entrance requirements:* For doctorate, writing sample, minimum GPA of 3.0, 3 letters of recommendation, resume. *Application deadline:* For fall admission, 2/25 for domestic and international students; for spring admission, 8/25 for domestic and international students. Application fee: $75. Electronic applications accepted. *Expenses:* Contact institution. *Financial support:* In 2010–11, 79 students received support. Scholarships/grants and health care benefits available. Support available to part-time students. *Unit head:* Dr. Gerardo Rodriguez-Menendez, Interim Dean, 805-898-2909, E-mail: grodriguez@fielding.edu. *Application contact:* Admission Counselor, 800-340-1099, Fax: 805-687-9793, E-mail: psyadmissions@fielding.edu.

Fisk University, Division of Graduate Studies, Department of Psychology, Nashville, TN 37208-3051. Offers clinical psychology (MA); psychology (MA). *Degree requirements:* For master's, thesis. *Entrance requirements:* For master's, GRE General Test, GRE Subject Test, minimum GPA of 3.0. Electronic applications accepted. *Faculty research:* Ethnic and gender identity, development, female adolescent development, juvenile delinquency prevention.

Florida Institute of Technology, Graduate Programs, College of Psychology and Liberal Arts, School of Psychology, Melbourne, FL 32901-6975. Offers applied behavior analysis (MS); applied behavior analysis and organizational behavior management (MS); behavior analysis (PhD); clinical psychology (Psy D); industrial/organizational psychology (MS, PhD); organizational behavior management (MS). *Accreditation:* APA (one or more programs are accredited). Part-time programs available. *Faculty:* 21 full-time (10 women), 6 part-time/adjunct (2 women). *Students:* 220 full-time (167 women), 11 part-time (10 women); includes 25 minority (5 Black or African American, non-Hispanic/Latino; 4 Asian, non-Hispanic/Latino; 16 Hispanic/Latino), 22 international. Average age 27. 378 applicants, 42% accepted, 77 enrolled. In 2010, 57 master's, 13 doctorates awarded. Terminal master's awarded for partial completion of doctoral program. *Degree requirements:* For master's, comprehensive exam (for some programs), thesis (for some programs), BCBA certification, final exam; for doctorate, comprehensive exam, thesis/dissertation, internship, full time resident of school for 4 years (8 semesters, 3 summers). *Entrance requirements:* For master's, GRE General Test, 3 letters of recommendation, minimum GPA of 3.0, resume, statement of objectives; for doctorate, GRE General Test, GRE Subject Test (psychology), 3 letters of recommendation, minimum GPA of 3.2, resume, statement of objectives. Additional exam requirements/recommendations for international students: Required—TOEFL (minimum score 550 paper-based; 213 computer-based; 79 iBT). *Application deadline:* For fall admission, 4/1 for international students; for spring admission, 9/30 for international students. Applications are processed on a rolling basis. Application fee: $50. Electronic applications accepted. *Expenses:* Tuition: Part-time $1040 per credit hour. Tuition and fees vary according to campus/location. *Financial support:* In 2010–11, 4 fellowships with full and partial tuition reimbursements (averaging $3,775 per year), 32 research assistantships with full and partial tuition reimbursements (averaging $5,602 per year), 8 teaching assistantships with full and partial tuition reimbursements (averaging $4,570 per year) were awarded; career-related internships or fieldwork, institutionally sponsored loans, tuition waivers (partial), unspecified assistantships, and tuition remissions also available. Support available to part-time students. Financial award application deadline: 3/1; financial award applicants required to submit FAFSA. *Faculty research:* Addictions, neuropsychology, child abuse, assessment, psychological trauma. Total annual research expenditures: $1.8 million. *Unit head:* Dr. Mary Beth Kenkel, Dean, 321-674-8142, Fax: 321-674-7105, E-mail: mkenkel@fit.edu. *Application contact:* Cheryl A. Brown, Associate Director of Graduate Admissions, 321-674-7581, Fax: 321-723-9468, E-mail: cbrown@fit.edu.

Florida International University, College of Education, Department of Educational Leadership and Policy Studies, Miami, FL 33199. Offers adult education (MS); adult education in human resource development (Ed D); clinical mental health counseling (MS); conflict resolution and consensus building (Certificate); counselor education (MS); educational administration and supervision (Ed D); educational leadership (MS, Certificate, Ed S); higher education (Ed D); higher education administration (MS); human resource development (MS); instruction in urban settings (MS); international/intercultural education (MS); learning technologies (MS); multicultural-bilingual (MS); multicultural-TESOL (MS); recreation and sport management (MS); recreation therapy (MS); rehabilitation counseling (MS); school counseling (MS); school psychology (Ed S); urban education (MS). Part-time and evening/weekend programs available. *Students:* 164 full-time (124 women), 308 part-time (234 women); includes 107 Black or African American, non-Hispanic/Latino; 3 American Indian or Alaska Native, non-Hispanic/Latino; 8 Asian, non-Hispanic/Latino; 223 Hispanic/Latino, 12 international. Average age 31. 544 applicants, 41% accepted, 197 enrolled. In 2010, 123 master's, 5 doctorates, 16 other advanced degrees awarded. *Degree requirements:* For doctorate, thesis/dissertation. *Entrance requirements:* For master's, minimum GPA of 3.0; for doctorate and other advanced degree, GRE General Test. Additional exam requirements/recommendations for international students: Required—TOEFL (minimum score 550 paper-based; 213 computer-based; 80 iBT), IELTS (minimum score 6.3). *Application deadline:* For fall admission, 6/1 priority date for domestic students, 4/1 for international students; for winter admission, 10/1 priority date for domestic students, 9/1 for international students; for spring admission, 3/1 priority date for domestic students, 2/1 for international students. Applications are processed on a rolling basis. Application fee: $30. Electronic applications accepted. *Financial support:* Fellowships, research assistantships with full and partial tuition reimbursements, teaching assistantships with full and partial tuition reimbursements, Federal Work-Study and tuition waivers (full and partial) available. Support available to part-time students. Financial award applicants required to submit FAFSA. *Unit head:* Dr. Patricia Barbetta, Dean of Graduate Studies, 305-348-2835, Fax: 305-348-2081, E-mail: barbetta@fiu.edu. *Application contact:* Nanett Rojas, Graduate Admission, 305-348-7442, Fax: 305-348-7441, E-mail: nanett.rojas@fiu.edu.

Florida State University, The Graduate School, College of Arts and Sciences, Department of Psychology, Program in Clinical Psychology, Tallahassee, FL 32306. Offers PhD. *Accreditation:* APA. *Faculty:* 14 full-time (7 women). *Students:* 50 full-time (40 women), 6 part-time (4 women); includes 2 Black or African American, non-Hispanic/Latino; 1 American Indian or Alaska Native, non-Hispanic/Latino; 4 Hispanic/Latino. Average age 25. 230 applicants, 5% accepted, 5 enrolled. In 2010, 9 doctorates awarded. Terminal master's awarded for partial completion of doctoral program. *Degree requirements:* For doctorate, thesis/dissertation, preliminary exam, independent project. *Entrance requirements:* For doctorate, GRE General Test (suggested minimum total score of 1200), minimum GPA of 3.3, research experience, letters of recommendation. Additional exam requirements/recommendations for international students: Required—TOEFL (minimum score 550 paper-based; 213 computer-based; 80 iBT). *Application deadline:* For fall admission, 12/1 for domestic and international students. Application fee: $30. Electronic applications accepted. *Expenses:* Tuition, state resident: full-time $8238.24. *Financial support:* In 2010–11, 49 students received support, including 14 fellowships with full tuition reimbursements available (averaging $20,000 per year), 10 research assistantships with full tuition reimbursements available (averaging $20,000 per year), 25 teaching assistantships with full tuition reimbursements available (averaging $16,500 per year); career-related internships or fieldwork, Federal Work-Study, institutionally sponsored loans, scholarships/grants, traineeships, health care benefits, and unspecified assistantships also available. Financial award applicants required to submit FAFSA. *Faculty research:* Antisocial behavior, depression, addictive behavior, developmental psychopathology, anxiety. Total annual research expenditures: $3.2 million. *Unit head:* Dr. Jeanette Taylor, Director, 850-644-7243, Fax: 850-644-7739, E-mail: taylor@psy.fsu.edu. *Application contact:* Cherie P. Miller, Graduate Program Assistant, 850-644-2499, Fax: 850-644-7739, E-mail: grad-info@psy.fsu.edu.

Fordham University, Graduate School of Arts and Sciences, Department of Psychology, Program in Clinical Psychology, New York, NY 10458. Offers PhD. *Students:* 53 full-time (37 women), 27 part-time (16 women); includes 24 minority (9 Black or African American, non-Hispanic/Latino; 1 American Indian or Alaska Native, non-Hispanic/Latino; 8 Asian, non-Hispanic/Latino; 6 Hispanic/Latino), 4 international. Average age 28. 496 applicants, 4% accepted, 11 enrolled. In 2010, 13 doctorates awarded. Terminal master's awarded for partial completion of doctoral program. *Degree requirements:* For doctorate, comprehensive exam, thesis/dissertation, clinical internship. *Entrance requirements:* For doctorate, GRE General Test, GRE Subject Test. Additional exam requirements/recommendations for international students: Required—TOEFL (minimum score 600 paper-based; 250 computer-based). *Application deadline:* For fall admission, 12/14 for domestic students. Application fee: $70. Electronic applications accepted. *Financial support:* In 2010–11, 32 students received support, including 3 fellowships with tuition reimbursements available (averaging $21,133 per year), 22 research assistantships with tuition reimbursements available (averaging $18,688 per year), 7 teaching assistantships with tuition reimbursements available (averaging $17,216 per year); career-related internships or fieldwork, institutionally sponsored loans, tuition waivers (full and partial), and unspecified assistantships also available. Financial award application deadline: 12/14. Total annual research expenditures: $2 million. *Unit head:* Dr. Barry Rosenfeld, Director, 718-817-3782, Fax: 718-817-3785. *Application contact:* Charlene Dundie, Director of Graduate Admissions, 718-817-4420, Fax: 718-817-3566, E-mail: dundie@fordham.edu.

Francis Marion University, Graduate Programs, Department of Psychology, Florence, SC 29502-0547. Offers applied psychology (MS), including clinical/counseling, school psychology; school psychology (SSP). Part-time and evening/weekend programs available. *Faculty:* 10 full-time (4 women), 5 part-time/adjunct (4 women). *Students:* 17 full-time (16 women), 26 part-time (25 women); includes 6 Black or African American, non-Hispanic/Latino. Average age 25. 44 applicants, 61% accepted, 14 enrolled. In 2010, 9 master's awarded. *Degree requirements:* For master's, internship. *Entrance requirements:* For master's, GRE General Test. *Application deadline:* For fall admission, 3/15 for domestic students; for spring admission, 10/15 for domestic students. Applications are processed on a rolling basis. Application fee: $30. *Expenses:* Tuition, state resident: full-time $8667; part-time $433.35 per credit hour. Tuition, nonresident: full-time $17,334; part-time $866.70 per credit hour. Required fees: $335; $12.25 per credit hour. $30 per semester. *Financial support:* In 2010–11, 13 students received support, including 2 research assistantships (averaging $7,000 per year), 3 teaching assistantships (averaging $8,000 per year); career-related internships or fieldwork, unspecified assistantships, and scholarships with out-of-state waivers also available. Support available to part-time students. Financial award application deadline: 3/1; financial award applicants required to submit FAFSA. *Faculty research:* Parenting and family relationships, child development, applied behavioral analysis, posttraumatic stress disorder, clinical psychology in adults. *Unit head:* Dr. John R. Hester, Chair, 843-661-1635, Fax: 843-661-1628. *Application contact:* Jennifer Taylor, Administrative Assistant, 843-661-1378, Fax: 843-661-1628.

Fuller Theological Seminary, Graduate School of Psychology, Department of Clinical Psychology, Pasadena, CA 91182. Offers PhD, Psy D. *Accreditation:* APA (one or more programs are accredited). *Degree requirements:* For doctorate, thesis/dissertation, internships. *Entrance requirements:* For doctorate, GRE General Test, GRE Subject Test, interview. Additional exam requirements/recommendations for international students: Required—TOEFL. *Expenses:* Contact institution. *Faculty research:* Psychoneuroimmunology, psychology of religion, coping, shame, depression.

Gallaudet University, The Graduate School, Washington, DC 20002-3625. Offers administration (MS); audiology (Au D, PhD); change leadership in education (Ed S); clinical psychology (PhD); deaf education (Ed D, PhD); deaf education: advanced studies (MA); deaf education: special programs in deaf education (MA); deaf history (Certificate); deaf studies (MA); education: teacher preparation (MA, MA Missions), including deaf education (MA), early childhood education and deaf education (MA), elementary education and deaf education (MA Missions), secondary education and deaf education (MA); hearing, speech and language sciences (MS); international development (MA); interpretation (MA, PhD); leadership (Certificate); leisure services administration (MS); linguistics (MA, PhD); management (Certificate); mental health counseling (MA); school counseling (MA); school counseling (summer session) (MA); school psychology (Psy S); sign language teaching (MA); social work (MSW); special education administration (PhD); speech-language pathology (PhD). Part-time programs available. *Faculty:* 116 full-time (86 women). *Students:* 291 full-time (224 women), 122 part-time (97 women); includes 142 minority (36 Black or African American, non-Hispanic/Latino; 3 American Indian or Alaska Native, non-Hispanic/Latino; 13 Asian, non-Hispanic/Latino; 29 Hispanic/Latino; 61 Two or more races, non-Hispanic/Latino), 28 international. Average age 30. 442 applicants, 52% accepted, 145 enrolled. In 2010, 116 master's, 17 doctorates, 16 other advanced degrees awarded. Terminal master's awarded for partial completion of doctoral program. *Degree requirements:* For master's, comprehensive exam (for some programs), thesis optional; for doctorate, comprehensive exam, thesis/dissertation. *Entrance requirements:* For master's and doctorate, GRE General Test or MAT, letters of recommendation, interviews, goals statement, ASL proficiency interview, written English competency. Additional exam requirements/recommendations for international students: Required—TOEFL. *Application deadline:* For fall admission, 2/15 for domestic students. Applications are processed on a rolling basis. Application fee: $50. Electronic applications accepted. *Expenses:* Tuition: Full-time $11,930; part-time $663 per credit. Required fees: $188 per semester. *Financial support:* In 2010–11, 219 students received support; fellowships, research assistantships, teaching assistantships, career-related internships or fieldwork, Federal Work-Study, scholarships/grants, tuition waivers (partial), and unspecified assistantships available. Support available to part-time students. Financial award applicants required to submit FAFSA. *Faculty research:* Bimodal bilingualism development, audiology, telecommunications access, early childhood education, linguistics, visual language and visual learning, rehabilitation and hearing enhancement. *Unit head:* Dr. Carol J. Erting, Dean, 202-651-5520, Fax: 202-651-5027, E-mail: carol.erting@gallaudet.edu. *Application contact:* Wednesday Luria, Coordinator of Prospective Graduate Student Services, 202-651-5400, Fax: 202-651-5295, E-mail: graduate.school@gallaudet.edu.

George Fox University, Program in Clinical Psychology, Newberg, OR 97132-2697. Offers MA, Psy D. *Accreditation:* APA. *Faculty:* 9 full-time (4 women), 3 part-time/adjunct (1 woman). *Students:* 92 full-time (62 women), 12 part-time (7 women); includes 1 Black or African American, non-Hispanic/Latino; 1 American Indian or Alaska Native, non-Hispanic/Latino; 4 Asian, non-Hispanic/Latino; 5 Hispanic/Latino; 1 Native Hawaiian or other Pacific Islander, non-Hispanic/Latino, 2 international. Average age 29. 81 applicants, 56% accepted, 20 enrolled. In 2010, 21 master's, 18 doctorates awarded. *Degree requirements:* For master's, comprehensive exam, 60 semester hours of required and elective courses; for doctorate, thesis/dissertation, internship. *Entrance requirements:* For master's and doctorate, GRE General Test, bachelor's degree from regionally-accredited university or college, minimum undergraduate GPA of 3.0 during previous 2 years, interview. Additional exam requirements/recommendations for international students: Required—TOEFL (minimum score 577 paper-based; 233 computer-based; 90 iBT), IELTS (minimum score 7). *Application deadline:* For fall admission, 1/15 priority date for domestic and international students. Application fee: $40. Electronic applications accepted. *Expenses:* Contact institution. *Financial support:* Scholarships/grants available. Financial award application deadline: 5/15; financial award applicants required to submit FAFSA. *Faculty research:* Psychological assessment, impact of psychological services on medical outcome, spirituality and wellness, effectiveness of clinical training and supervision, shame. *Unit head:*

Dr. Wayne Adams, Professor and Director, Graduate Department of Clinical Psychology, 800-765-4369 Ext. 2372, E-mail: wadams@georgefox.edu. *Application contact:* Adina McConaughey, Admission Counselor, 800-631-0921 Ext. 2263, Fax: 503-554-2263, E-mail: psyd@georgefox.edu.

George Fox University, School of Education, Graduate Department of Counseling, Newberg, OR 97132-2697. Offers clinical mental health counseling (MA); marriage, couple and family counseling (MA, Certificate); mental health trauma (Certificate); school counseling (MA, Certificate); school psychology (Certificate, Ed S). Part-time programs available. *Faculty:* 9 full-time (3 women), 7 part-time/adjunct (4 women). *Students:* 119 full-time (95 women), 115 part-time (93 women); includes 34 minority (9 Black or African American, non-Hispanic/Latino; 5 American Indian or Alaska Native, non-Hispanic/Latino; 8 Asian, non-Hispanic/Latino; 10 Hispanic/Latino; 1 Native Hawaiian or other Pacific Islander, non-Hispanic/Latino; 1 Two or more races, non-Hispanic/Latino). Average age 34. 114 applicants, 55% accepted, 45 enrolled. In 2010, 66 master's, 3 other advanced degrees awarded. *Degree requirements:* For master's, clinical project. *Entrance requirements:* For master's, MAT or GRE, bachelor's degree from regionally-accredited college or university, minimum cumulative GPA of 3.0, 1 professional and 1 academic reference, resume, on-campus interview. Additional exam requirements/recommendations for international students: Required—TOEFL (minimum score 577 paper-based; 233 computer-based; 90 iBT), IELTS (minimum score 7). *Application deadline:* For fall admission, 5/30 for domestic and international students; for winter admission, 11/1 for domestic and international students; for spring admission, 2/28 for domestic and international students. Applications are processed on a rolling basis. Application fee: $40. Electronic applications accepted. *Expenses:* Contact institution. *Financial support:* Career-related internships or fieldwork available. *Unit head:* Dr. Richard Shaw, Associate Professor of Marriage and Family Therapy/Chair, 503-554-6142, E-mail: rshaw@georgefox.edu. *Application contact:* Kathy Grant, Admissions Counselor, 800-493-4937, Fax: 503-554-6111, E-mail: counseling@georgefox.edu.

The George Washington University, Columbian College of Arts and Sciences, Department of Psychology, Washington, DC 20052. Offers applied social psychology (PhD); clinical psychology (PhD); cognitive neuroscience (PhD). *Accreditation:* APA. Part-time and evening/weekend programs available. *Faculty:* 26 full-time (14 women), 14 part-time/adjunct (9 women). *Students:* 131 full-time (103 women), 75 part-time (55 women); includes 14 Black or African American, non-Hispanic/Latino; 2 American Indian or Alaska Native, non-Hispanic/Latino; 18 Asian, non-Hispanic/Latino; 16 Hispanic/Latino, 4 international. Average age 29. 797 applicants, 6% accepted, 9 enrolled. In 2010, 41 doctorates awarded. *Degree requirements:* For doctorate, thesis/dissertation or alternative, general exam. *Entrance requirements:* For doctorate, GRE General Test, minimum GPA of 3.0. Additional exam requirements/recommendations for international students: Required—TOEFL (minimum score 550 paper-based; 213 computer-based; 80 iBT). *Application deadline:* For fall admission, 1/15 for domestic and international students. Application fee: $75. *Financial support:* In 2010–11, 62 students received support; fellowships with tuition reimbursements available, teaching assistantships with tuition reimbursements available, career-related internships or fieldwork, Federal Work-Study, and tuition waivers available. *Unit head:* Dr. Paul Poppen, Chair, 202-994-6324, E-mail: pjp@gwu.edu. *Application contact:* Information Contact, 202-994-6320, Fax: 202-994-1602, E-mail: psydept@gwu.edu.

Georgian Court University, School of Arts and Sciences, Lakewood, NJ 08701-2697. Offers biology (MA); Catholic school leadership (Certificate); clinical mental health counseling (MA); holistic health studies (MA); mathematics (MA); pastoral ministry (Certificate); religious education (Certificate); school psychology (Certificate); theology (MA, Certificate). Part-time and evening/weekend programs available. *Faculty:* 19 full-time (11 women), 7 part-time/adjunct (5 women). *Students:* 61 full-time (59 women), 143 part-time (113 women); includes 20 minority (5 Black or African American, non-Hispanic/Latino; 3 Asian, non-Hispanic/Latino; 11 Hispanic/Latino; 1 Two or more races, non-Hispanic/Latino), 1 international. Average age 39. 139 applicants, 59% accepted, 50 enrolled. In 2010, 5 master's awarded. *Degree requirements:* For master's, comprehensive exam (for some programs), thesis (for some programs). *Entrance requirements:* For master's, GRE, MAT, or NTE/PRAXIS, 3 letters of recommendation. Additional exam requirements/recommendations for international students: Required—TOEFL (minimum score 550 paper-based; 213 computer-based). *Application deadline:* For fall admission, 8/1 priority date for domestic students, 4/1 for international students; for spring admission, 1/1 priority date for domestic students, 7/1 for international students. Applications are processed on a rolling basis. Application fee: $40. Electronic applications accepted. *Expenses:* Tuition: Full-time $12,510; part-time $695 per credit. Required fees: $416 per year. Tuition and fees vary according to campus/location and program. *Financial support:* Scholarships/grants, health care benefits, and unspecified assistantships available. Financial award application deadline: 4/15; financial award applicants required to submit FAFSA. *Unit head:* Dr. Linda James, Dean, 732-987-2617, Fax: 732-987-2007. *Application contact:* Patrick Givens, Assistant Director of Admissions, 732-987-2736, Fax: 732-987-2084, E-mail: graduateadmissions@georgian.edu.

Graduate School and University Center of the City University of New York, Graduate Studies, Program in Psychology, New York, NY 10016-4039. Offers basic applied neurocognition (PhD); biopsychology (PhD); clinical psychology (PhD); developmental psychology (PhD); environmental psychology (PhD); experimental psychology (PhD); industrial psychology (PhD); learning processes (PhD); neuropsychology (PhD); psychology (PhD); social personality (PhD). *Degree requirements:* For doctorate, one foreign language, thesis/dissertation. *Entrance requirements:* For doctorate, GRE General Test. Additional exam requirements/recommendations for international students: Required—TOEFL. Electronic applications accepted.

Hawai'i Pacific University, College of Humanities and Social Sciences, Program in Clinical Mental Health Counseling, Honolulu, HI 96813. Offers MA.

Hofstra University, College of Liberal Arts and Sciences, Program in Clinical Psychology, Hempstead, NY 11549. Offers PhD. *Accreditation:* APA; NCATE. *Students:* 80 full-time (54 women); includes 9 minority (3 Black or African American, non-Hispanic/Latino; 5 Asian, non-Hispanic/Latino; 1 Hispanic/Latino), 1 international. Average age 27. 168 applicants, 10% accepted, 14 enrolled. In 2010, 13 doctorates awarded. *Degree requirements:* For doctorate, comprehensive exam, thesis/dissertation, 1st year qualifying examination, 2nd year research project, successful practicum/externship placements, written presentation and successful oral defense of dissertation, completion of full-time internship. *Entrance requirements:* For doctorate, GRE General Test, GRE Subject Test (Psychology), 3 letters of recommendation; Interview; Essay; Curriculum vitae. Additional exam requirements/recommendations for international students: Required—TOEFL (minimum score 550 paper-based; 213 computer-based; 80 iBT). *Application deadline:* For fall admission, 12/15 for domestic and international students. Application fee: $70 ($75 for international students). Electronic applications accepted. *Expenses:* Tuition: Full-time $18,000; part-time $1000 per credit hour. Required fees: $970; $145 per term. Tuition and fees vary according to program. *Financial support:* In 2010–11, 62 students received support, including 46 fellowships with full and partial tuition reimbursements available (averaging $7,939 per year), 6 research assistantships with full and partial tuition reimbursements available (averaging $1,601 per year); career-related internships or fieldwork, Federal Work-Study, institutionally sponsored loans, scholarships/grants, tuition waivers (full and partial), unspecified assistantships, and scholarships also available. Support available to part-time students. Financial award applicants required to submit FAFSA. *Faculty research:* Parent-child interaction training, treatment of anger, cognitions of cocaine-addicted schizophrenics, applications of mindfulness in treatment of psychopathology, virtual reality exposure therapy for phobia and trauma treatment. *Unit head:* Dr. Mitchell L. Schare, Program Director, 516-463-5662, Fax: 516-463-6052, E-mail: psymls@hofstra.edu. *Application contact:* Carol Drummer, Dean of Graduate Admissions, 516-463-4876, Fax: 516-463-4664, E-mail: gradstudent@hofstra.edu.

Howard University, Graduate School, Department of Psychology, Washington, DC 20059-0002. Offers clinical psychology (PhD); developmental psychology (PhD); experimental psychology (PhD); neuropsychology (PhD); personality psychology (PhD); psychology (MS); social psychology (PhD). *Accreditation:* APA (one or more programs are accredited). Part-time programs available. *Degree requirements:* For master's, thesis; for doctorate, comprehensive

Clinical Psychology

Howard University (continued)
exam, thesis/dissertation, qualifying exam. *Entrance requirements:* For master's, GRE General Test, minimum GPA of 2.5, bachelor's degree in psychology or related field; for doctorate, GRE General Test, minimum GPA of 3.0. *Faculty research:* Personality and psychophysiology, educational and social development of African-American children, child and adult psychopathology.

Idaho State University, Office of Graduate Studies, College of Arts and Sciences, Department of Psychology, Program in Clinical Psychology, Pocatello, ID 83209-8112. Offers PhD. *Degree requirements:* For doctorate, comprehensive exam, thesis/dissertation, 1 year full-time clinical internship. *Entrance requirements:* For doctorate, GRE General Test, GRE Subject Test, MS in psychology. Additional exam requirements/recommendations for international students: Required—TOEFL (minimum score 550 paper-based; 213 computer-based; 80 iBT). Electronic applications accepted. *Faculty research:* Pre-adolescent behavior, substance abuse training, trauma related problems.

Illinois Institute of Technology, Graduate College, College of Psychology, Chicago, IL 60616. Offers clinical psychology (PhD); industrial/organizational psychology (PhD); personnel/human resource development (MS); rehabilitation (PhD); rehabilitation counseling (MS). *Accreditation:* APA (one or more programs are accredited); CORE. Part-time and evening/weekend programs available. *Faculty:* 21 full-time (7 women), 6 part-time/adjunct (4 women). *Students:* 160 full-time (111 women), 39 part-time (33 women); includes 36 minority (8 Black or African American, non-Hispanic/Latino; 1 American Indian or Alaska Native, non-Hispanic/Latino; 15 Asian, non-Hispanic/Latino; 12 Hispanic/Latino), 16 international. Average age 29. 253 applicants, 40% accepted, 43 enrolled. In 2010, 31 master's, 14 doctorates awarded. Terminal master's awarded for partial completion of doctoral program. *Degree requirements:* For master's, thesis (for some programs); for doctorate, comprehensive exam, thesis/dissertation, 96-108 credit hours, internship (for clinical and industrial/organizational specializations). *Entrance requirements:* For master's, GRE General Test (minimum score 900 Quantitative and Verbal, 2.5 Analytical Writing), minimum high school GPA of 3.0; at least 18 credit hours of undergraduate study in psychology with at least one course each in experimental psychology and statistics; official transcripts; 3 letters of recommendation; personal statement; for doctorate, GRE General Test (minimum score 1000 Quantitative and Verbal, 3.0 Analytical Writing), minimum high school GPA of 3.0; at least 18 credit hours of undergraduate study in psychology with at least one course each in experimental psychology and statistics; official transcripts; 3 letters of recommendation; personal statement. Additional exam requirements/recommendations for international students: Required—TOEFL (minimum score 550 paper-based; 213 computer-based; 80 iBT); Recommended—IELTS (minimum score 5.5). *Application deadline:* For fall admission, 1/15 for domestic and international students. Application fee: $50. Electronic applications accepted. *Expenses:* Tuition: Full-time $18,576; part-time $1032 per credit hour. Required fees: $583 per semester. One-time fee: $150. Tuition and fees vary according to program and student level. *Financial support:* In 2010–11, 23 research assistantships with full and partial tuition reimbursements (averaging $223 per year) were awarded; fellowships with full and partial tuition reimbursements, career-related internships or fieldwork, Federal Work-Study, institutionally sponsored loans, scholarships/grants, traineeships, health care benefits, tuition waivers (partial), and unspecified assistantships also available. Support available to part-time students. Financial award application deadline: 1/15; financial award applicants required to submit FAFSA. *Faculty research:* Health psychology, behavioral medicine, attachment, child social and emotional development, educational assessment. Total annual research expenditures: $1.6 million. *Unit head:* Dr. M. Ellen Mitchell, Dean, 312-567-3362, Fax: 312-567-3493, E-mail: mitchelle@iit.edu. *Application contact:* Institute of Psychology Graduate Admissions, 312-567-3500, Fax: 312-567-3493, E-mail: psychology@iit.edu.

Illinois State University, Graduate School, College of Arts and Sciences, Department of Psychology, Normal, IL 61790-2200. Offers psychology (MA, MS), including clinical psychology, counseling psychology, developmental psychology, educational psychology, experimental psychology, measurement-evaluation, organizational-industrial psychology; school psychology (PhD, SSP). *Accreditation:* APA. *Degree requirements:* For master's, thesis or alternative; for doctorate, variable foreign language requirement, thesis/dissertation, 2 terms of residency, internship, practicum. *Entrance requirements:* For master's, GRE General Test, GRE Subject Test, minimum GPA of 3.0 in last 60 hours of course work; for doctorate, GRE General Test. *Faculty research:* Comprehensive evaluation system for the central region professional development grant, Illinois school psychology internship consortium, for children's sake.

Immaculata University, College of Graduate Studies, Department of Psychology, Immaculata, PA 19345. Offers clinical psychology (Psy D); counseling psychology (MA, Certificate), including school guidance counselor (Certificate), school psychologist (Certificate). *Accreditation:* APA. Part-time and evening/weekend programs available. *Students:* 123 full-time (100 women), 201 part-time (159 women). Average age 34. 83 applicants, 76% accepted, 55 enrolled. In 2010, 37 master's, 13 doctorates awarded. Terminal master's awarded for partial completion of doctoral program. *Degree requirements:* For master's, comprehensive exam, thesis optional; for doctorate, comprehensive exam, thesis/dissertation. *Entrance requirements:* For master's, GRE General Test or MAT, minimum GPA of 3.0; for doctorate, GRE General Test or MAT, minimum GPA of 3.5. Additional exam requirements/recommendations for international students: Required—TOEFL, IELTS. *Application deadline:* Applications are processed on a rolling basis. Application fee: $50. Electronic applications accepted. *Financial support:* Application deadline: 5/1. *Faculty research:* Supervision ethics, psychology of teaching, gender. *Unit head:* Dr. Jed A. Yalof, Chair, 610-647-4400 Ext. 3503, Fax: 610-993-8550, E-mail: jyalof@immaculata.edu. *Application contact:* Office of Graduate Admission, 610-647-4400 Ext. 3211, Fax: 610-993-8550, E-mail: graduate@immaculata.edu.

Indiana State University, College of Graduate and Professional Studies, College of Arts and Sciences, Department of Psychology, Terre Haute, IN 47809. Offers clinical psychology (Psy D); general psychology (MA, MS). *Accreditation:* APA (one or more programs are accredited). Terminal master's awarded for partial completion of doctoral program. *Degree requirements:* For master's, thesis (for some programs); for doctorate, comprehensive exam, thesis/dissertation, internship, professional research project. *Entrance requirements:* For master's, GRE General Test, 12 semester hours of course work in psychology, minimum GPA of 2.75; for doctorate, GRE General Test, minimum GPA of 3.0. Additional exam requirements/recommendations for international students: Required—TOEFL (minimum score 550 paper-based). Electronic applications accepted.

Indiana University of Pennsylvania, School of Graduate Studies and Research, College of Natural Sciences and Mathematics, Department of Psychology, Program in Clinical Psychology, Indiana, PA 15705-1087. Offers Psy D. *Accreditation:* APA. Part-time programs available. *Faculty:* 13 full-time (9 women). *Students:* 43 full-time (35 women), 22 part-time (20 women); includes 5 minority (3 Asian, non-Hispanic/Latino; 2 Hispanic/Latino), 1 international. Average age 27. 136 applicants, 13% accepted, 17 enrolled. In 2010, 13 doctorates awarded. *Degree requirements:* For doctorate, comprehensive exam, thesis/dissertation, internship, practicum. *Entrance requirements:* For doctorate, GRE General Test, minimum GPA of 3.0, 3 letters of recommendation, interview. Additional exam requirements/recommendations for international students: Required—TOEFL. *Application deadline:* For fall admission, 1/10 for domestic students. Application fee: $40. *Financial support:* In 2010–11, 4 fellowships (averaging $2,000 per year), 35 research assistantships with full and partial tuition reimbursements (averaging $4,213 per year), 2 teaching assistantships (averaging $21,967 per year) were awarded; Federal Work-Study and scholarships/grants also available. Financial award application deadline: 3/15; financial award applicants required to submit FAFSA. *Unit head:* Dr. Beverly Goodwin, Graduate Coordinator, 724-357-4522, E-mail: beverly.goodwin@iup.edu. *Application contact:* Dr. Donald Robertson, Graduate Coordinator, 724-357-4522, E-mail: durobert@iup.edu.

Indiana University–Purdue University Indianapolis, School of Science, Department of Psychology, Indianapolis, IN 46202-3275. Offers clinical rehabilitation psychology (MS); industrial/organizational psychology (MS); psychobiology of addictions (MS, PhD). *Accreditation:* APA (one or more programs are accredited). *Faculty:* 10 full-time (2 women). *Students:* 51 full-time (43 women), 11 part-time (10 women); includes 4 minority (2 Black or African American, non-Hispanic/Latino; 2 Asian, non-Hispanic/Latino), 3 international. Average age 28. 116 applicants, 25% accepted, 18 enrolled. In 2010, 11 master's, 4 doctorates awarded. Terminal master's awarded for partial completion of doctoral program. *Degree requirements:* For master's, thesis; for doctorate, thesis/dissertation. *Entrance requirements:* For master's, GRE General Test, minimum undergraduate GPA of 3.0; for doctorate, GRE General Test, GRE Subject Test (clinical rehabilitation psychology), minimum undergraduate GPA of 3.2. *Application deadline:* For fall admission, 1/1 priority date for domestic students. Application fee: $55 ($65 for international students). *Financial support:* In 2010–11, 5 fellowships with partial tuition reimbursements (averaging $12,218 per year), 23 teaching assistantships with partial tuition reimbursements (averaging $7,553 per year) were awarded; research assistantships with partial tuition reimbursements, career-related internships or fieldwork, Federal Work-Study, and institutionally sponsored loans also available. Financial award application deadline: 3/1; financial award applicants required to submit FAFSA. *Faculty research:* Psychiatric rehabilitation, chronic stress, neurological research, language and cognitive development in infants, alcoholism and psychopathology. *Unit head:* Dr. J. Gregor Fetterman, Chairman, 317-274-6945, Fax: 317-274-6756, E-mail: gfetter@iupui.edu. *Application contact:* Dr. J. Gregor Fetterman, Chairman, 317-274-6945, Fax: 317-274-6756, E-mail: gfetter@iupui.edu.

The Institute for the Psychological Sciences, Program in Clinical Psychology, Arlington, VA 30327. Offers MS, Psy D. Part-time programs available. *Faculty:* 9 full-time (2 women), 3 part-time/adjunct (0 women). *Students:* 68 full-time (49 women), 5 part-time (3 women); includes 15 minority (11 Hispanic/Latino; 4 Two or more races, non-Hispanic/Latino), 12 international. 46 applicants, 76% accepted, 24 enrolled. In 2010, 19 master's, 2 doctorates awarded. *Degree requirements:* For master's, comprehensive exam; for doctorate, comprehensive exam, thesis/dissertation. *Entrance requirements:* For master's and doctorate, GRE. Additional exam requirements/recommendations for international students: Required—TOEFL. *Application deadline:* For fall admission, 5/4 for domestic and international students. Applications are processed on a rolling basis. Application fee: $50. *Expenses:* Tuition: Full-time $19,600; part-time $800 per credit hour. Required fees: $445. *Financial support:* Scholarships/grants and unspecified assistantships available. Financial award application deadline: 3/15; financial award applicants required to submit FAFSA. *Unit head:* Fr. Charles Sikorsky, President, 703-416-1441 Ext. 102, Fax: 703-416-8588, E-mail: csikorsky@ipsciences.edu. *Application contact:* Anne-Marie Dardis, Director of Admissions, 703-416-1441 Ext. 117, Fax: 703-416-8588, E-mail: amdardis@ipsciences.edu.

Institute of Transpersonal Psychology, Residential Programs, Palo Alto, CA 94303. Offers counseling psychology (MA); spiritually oriented clinical psychology (Psy D); transpersonal psychology (MA, PhD). Part-time and evening/weekend programs available. Terminal master's awarded for partial completion of doctoral program. *Degree requirements:* For doctorate, thesis/dissertation. *Entrance requirements:* For master's and doctorate, bachelor's degree.

Jackson State University, Graduate School, College of Liberal Arts, Department of Psychology, Jackson, MS 39217. Offers clinical psychology (PhD). *Accreditation:* APA. *Faculty:* 8 full-time (5 women), 1 part-time/adjunct (0 women). *Students:* 28 full-time (22 women), 11 part-time (10 women); includes 24 Black or African American, non-Hispanic/Latino; 2 Asian, non-Hispanic/Latino. Average age 32. In 2010, 10 doctorates awarded. *Degree requirements:* For doctorate, comprehensive exam, thesis/dissertation. *Entrance requirements:* For doctorate, MAT, GRE. Additional exam requirements/recommendations for international students: Required—TOEFL (minimum score 520 paper-based; 195 computer-based; 67 iBT). *Application deadline:* For fall admission, 1/15 for domestic and international students. Application fee: $25. *Expenses:* Tuition, state resident: full-time $5050; part-time $281 per credit hour. Tuition, nonresident: full-time $12,380; part-time $689 per credit hour. *Financial support:* Fellowships, research assistantships, teaching assistantships, career-related internships or fieldwork, Federal Work-Study, scholarships/grants, tuition waivers (full), and unspecified assistantships available. Support available to part-time students. Financial award application deadline: 3/1; financial award applicants required to submit FAFSA. *Unit head:* Dr. Keith Hudson, Director, 601-979-5590, Fax: 601-979-3947, E-mail: keith.l.hudson@jsums.edu. *Application contact:* Sharlene Wilson, Director of Graduate Admissions, 601-979-2455, Fax: 601-977-4325, E-mail: sharlene.f.wilson@jsums.edu.

James Madison University, The Graduate School, College of Integrated Science and Technology, Department of Graduate Psychology, Clinical Mental Health Counseling Program, Harrisonburg, VA 22807. Offers M Ed, MA, Ed S. *Accreditation:* ACA (one or more programs are accredited); APA (one or more programs are accredited). Part-time and evening/weekend programs available. *Students:* 65 full-time (48 women), 24 part-time (21 women); includes 9 minority (6 Black or African American, non-Hispanic/Latino; 1 Asian, non-Hispanic/Latino; 2 Hispanic/Latino), 1 international. Average age 27. In 2010, 31 master's, 15 other advanced degrees awarded. *Degree requirements:* For Ed S, comprehensive exam, thesis, internship. *Entrance requirements:* For master's, GRE General Test, 3 reference forms, interview, criminal history check. Additional exam requirements/recommendations for international students: Required—TOEFL. *Application deadline:* For fall admission, 2/1 priority date for domestic students. Applications are processed on a rolling basis. Application fee: $55. Electronic applications accepted. *Financial support:* In 2010–11, 53 students received support, including 1 teaching assistantship with full tuition reimbursement available (averaging $8,664 per year); career-related internships or fieldwork, Federal Work-Study, and 52 graduate assistantships ($7382) also available. Financial award application deadline: 3/1; financial award applicants required to submit FAFSA. *Unit head:* Dr. A. Renee Staton, Program Director, 540-568-7867. *Application contact:* Dr. A. Renee Staton, Program Director, 540-568-7867.

James Madison University, The Graduate School, College of Integrated Science and Technology, Department of Graduate Psychology, Program in Combined-Integrated Clinical and School Psychology, Harrisonburg, VA 22807. Offers Psy D. Part-time and evening/weekend programs available. *Students:* 20 full-time (16 women); includes 2 minority (1 Black or African American, non-Hispanic/Latino; 1 Asian, non-Hispanic/Latino), 3 international. Average age 27. In 2010, 4 doctorates awarded. *Degree requirements:* For doctorate, thesis/dissertation, 12-month internship. *Entrance requirements:* For doctorate, GRE General Test, GRE Subject Test (advanced psychology), 3 letters of recommendation. Additional exam requirements/recommendations for international students: Required—TOEFL. *Application deadline:* For fall admission, 2/1 for domestic students. Applications are processed on a rolling basis. Application fee: $55. Electronic applications accepted. *Financial support:* In 2010–11, 17 students received support. 17 doctoral assistantships ($14,500) available. Financial award application deadline: 3/1; financial award applicants required to submit FAFSA. *Unit head:* Dr. Gregg R. Henriques, Program Director, 540-568-7857, E-mail: henrigg@jmu.edu. *Application contact:* Dr. Gregg R. Henriques, Program Director, 540-568-7857, E-mail: henrigg@jmu.edu.

The Johns Hopkins University, Bloomberg School of Public Health, Department of Mental Health, Baltimore, MD 21218-2699. Offers children's mental health services (PhD); drug dependence epidemiology (PhD); mental health (MHS, Dr PH); psychiatric epidemiology (PhD). *Faculty:* 26 full-time (14 women), 46 part-time/adjunct (18 women). *Students:* 49 full-time (37 women), 5 part-time (4 women); includes 1 Native Hawaiian or other Pacific Islander, non-Hispanic/Latino; 6 Two or more races, non-Hispanic/Latino. Average age 33. 73 applicants, 67% accepted, 27 enrolled. In 2010, 21 master's, 8 doctorates awarded. *Degree requirements:* For master's, thesis (for some programs); for doctorate, thesis/dissertation, 1 year full-time residency, oral and written exams. *Entrance requirements:* For master's, GRE General Test, MCAT, 3 letters of recommendation, curriculum vitae; for doctorate, GRE General Test, MCAT or GMAT, 3 letters of recommendation, curriculum vitae. Additional exam requirements/recommendations for international students: Required—TOEFL (minimum score 600 paper-based; 250 computer-based; 100 iBT). *Application deadline:* For fall admission, 12/1 priority date for domestic and international students. Applications are processed on a rolling basis. Application fee: $45. Electronic applications accepted. *Financial support:* In 2010–11, 1 fellowship (averaging $32,000 per year) was awarded; Federal Work-Study, institutionally sponsored loans, scholarships/grants, traineeships, and stipends also available. Support available to part-time students. Financial award application deadline: 3/15; financial award applicants required to submit FAFSA. *Faculty research:* Etiology, development and prevention of aggressive and antisocial behavior; epidemiology of mental disorders; genetic epidemiology of mental disorders; brain and behavior. Total annual research expenditures: $12 million. *Unit head:* Dr. William W. Eaton, Chair, 410-955-3910, Fax: 410-614-7469, E-mail: weaton@jhsph.edu. *Application contact:* Patricia E. Scott, Senior Academic Program Coordinator, 410-955-1906, Fax: 410-955-9088, E-mail: mhdept@jhsph.edu.

Kean University, College of Education, Program in Counselor Education, Union, NJ 07083. Offers alcohol and drug abuse counseling (MA); clinical mental heath counseling (MA); school counseling (MA). *Accreditation:* ACA; NCATE. Part-time programs available. *Faculty:* 5 full-time (3 women). *Students:* 66 full-time (59 women), 216 part-time (192 women); includes 44 Black or African American, non-Hispanic/Latino; 4 Asian, non-Hispanic/Latino; 44 Hispanic/Latino; 1 Two or more races, non-Hispanic/Latino, 1 international. Average age 32. 152 applicants, 72% accepted, 61 enrolled. In 2010, 48 master's awarded. *Degree requirements:* For master's, comprehensive exam, practicum, internship. *Entrance requirements:* For master's, GRE General Test or MAT, minimum GPA of 3.0, 2 letters of recommendation, interview. *Application deadline:* For fall admission, 6/1 for domestic students; for spring admission, 11/1 for domestic students. Application fee: $75 ($150 for international students). Electronic applications accepted. *Expenses:* Tuition, state resident: full-time $10,872; part-time $500 per credit. Tuition, nonresident: full-time $14,736; part-time $614 per credit. Required fees: $2740.80; $125 per credit. Part-time tuition and fees vary according to course load and degree level. *Financial support:* In 2010–11, 2 research assistantships with full tuition reimbursements (averaging $3,263 per year) were awarded; unspecified assistantships also available. Financial award applicants required to submit FAFSA. *Unit head:* Dr. J. Barry Mascari, Program Coordinator, 908-737-3863, E-mail: jmascari@kean.edu. *Application contact:* Steven Koch, Pre-Admissions Coordinator, 908-737-5924, Fax: 908-737-5925, E-mail: skoch@kean.edu.

Kean University, Nathan Weiss Graduate College, Program in School and Clinical Psychology, Union, NJ 07083. Offers Psy D. Evening/weekend programs available. *Faculty:* 3 full-time (1 woman). *Students:* 17 full-time (16 women); includes 1 Black or African American, non-Hispanic/Latino, 1 international. Average age 26. 20 applicants, 55% accepted, 8 enrolled. *Degree requirements:* For doctorate, comprehensive exam, thesis/dissertation, externship. *Entrance requirements:* For doctorate, GRE General Test (minimum score 500 verbal, 500 quantitative, 4.0 writing), GRE Subject Test in psychology taken within the last 5 years (minimum score 550), minimum undergraduate GPA of 3.3, graduate 3.5; 3 letters of recommendation (at least one from a professor); personal interview; prerequisite coursework in theories of personality, abnormal psychology, tests and measurements, statistics, and experimental psychology; personal statement; 3 letters of recommendation. *Application deadline:* For fall admission, 1/30 for domestic students. Application fee: $75 ($150 for international students). Electronic applications accepted. *Expenses:* Contact institution. *Financial support:* In 2010–11, 13 research assistantships with full tuition reimbursements (averaging $3,263 per year) were awarded; unspecified assistantships also available. Financial award applicants required to submit FAFSA. *Unit head:* Dr. Frank Gardner, Program Coordinator, 908-737-5862, E-mail: fgardner@kean.edu. *Application contact:* Reenat Hasan, Pre-Admissions Coordinator, 908-737-5923, Fax: 908-737-5925, E-mail: hasanr@kean.edu.

Kent State University, College of Arts and Sciences, Department of Psychology, Kent, OH 44242-0001. Offers clinical psychology (MA, PhD); experimental psychology (MA, PhD). *Accreditation:* APA (one or more programs are accredited). *Degree requirements:* For master's, thesis; for doctorate, thesis/dissertation. *Entrance requirements:* For master's, GRE, minimum GPA of 3.0, minimum 18 semester hours in psychology with one course in statistics and one experimental course with a lab component; for doctorate, GRE, minimum GPA of 3.0. Additional exam requirements/recommendations for international students: Required—TOEFL (minimum score 525 paper-based), Michigan English Language Assessment Battery (minimum score: 77). *Expenses:* Tuition, state resident: full-time $7866; part-time $437 per credit hour. Tuition, nonresident: full-time $14,022; part-time $779 per credit hour.

Lakehead University, Graduate Studies, Department of Psychology, Thunder Bay, ON P7B 5E1, Canada. Offers clinical psychology (PhD); experimental psychology (MA). Part-time and evening/weekend programs available. *Degree requirements:* For master's, thesis optional; for doctorate, thesis/dissertation, 2 comprehensive exams, internship. *Entrance requirements:* For master's, GRE, honors degree in psychology, advanced course work in statistics, minimum B average; for doctorate, GRE, minimum B average. Additional exam requirements/recommendations for international students: Required—TOEFL. *Faculty research:* Chaos theory, health psychology, counseling psychology, gerontology, women's studies.

Lamar University, College of Graduate Studies, College of Arts and Sciences, Department of Psychology, Beaumont, TX 77710. Offers community/clinical psychology (MS); industrial/organizational psychology (MS). Part-time programs available. *Faculty:* 7 full-time (4 women). *Students:* 17 full-time (12 women), 10 part-time (4 women); includes 2 Black or African American, non-Hispanic/Latino; 2 Hispanic/Latino, 1 international. Average age 29. 25 applicants, 60% accepted, 9 enrolled. In 2010, 26 master's awarded. *Degree requirements:* For master's, thesis, practicum. *Entrance requirements:* For master's, GRE General Test, minimum GPA of 2.75 in last 60 hours of undergraduate course work. Additional exam requirements/recommendations for international students: Required—TOEFL. *Application deadline:* For fall admission, 8/1 for domestic students; for spring admission, 12/1 for domestic students. Application fee: $25 ($50 for international students). *Expenses:* Tuition, state resident: full-time $4160; part-time $208 per credit hour. Tuition, nonresident: full-time $10,360; part-time $518 per credit hour. *Financial support:* In 2010–11, 12 students received support, including 3 teaching assistantships (averaging $4,500 per year); fellowships, research assistantships, career-related internships or fieldwork, Federal Work-Study, scholarships/grants, and tuition waivers (partial) also available. Support available to part-time students. Financial award application deadline: 4/1. *Faculty research:* Groupthink, health psychology, school psychology, behavioral neuroscience. *Application contact:* Assistant Dean, 409-880-7978, E-mail: westgate@hal.lamar.edu.

La Salle University, School of Arts and Sciences, Program in Clinical-Counseling Psychology, Philadelphia, PA 19141-1199. Offers MA. *Accreditation:* APA. Part-time and evening/weekend programs available. *Degree requirements:* For master's, comprehensive exam. *Entrance requirements:* For master's, GRE or MAT, 15 undergraduate credits in psychology. *Expenses:* Contact institution. *Faculty research:* Cognitive therapy, attribution theory, work habits, single parent families, treatment of addictions.

La Salle University, School of Arts and Sciences, Program in Psychology, Philadelphia, PA 19141-1199. Offers clinical psychology (Psy D); family psychology (Psy D); rehabilitation psychology (Psy D). *Accreditation:* AAMFT/COAMFTE. Part-time and evening/weekend programs available. *Entrance requirements:* For doctorate, GRE, minimum GPA of 3.0. *Expenses:* Contact institution. *Faculty research:* Cognitive therapy, attribution theory, treatment of addiction.

Lesley University, Graduate School of Arts and Social Sciences, Cambridge, MA 02138-2790. Offers clinical mental health counseling (MA), including expressive therapies counseling, holistic counseling, school and community counseling; counseling psychology (MA, CAGS), including professional counseling (MA), school counseling (MA); creative arts in learning (CAGS); creative writing (MFA); ecological teaching and learning (MS); environmental education (MS); expressive therapies (MA, PhD, CAGS), including art (MA), dance (MA), expressive therapies, music (MA); independent studies (CAGS); independent study (MA); intercultural relations (MA, CAGS); interdisciplinary studies (MA), including individualized studies, integrative holistic health, women's studies; urban environmental leadership (MA); visual arts (MFA). Part-time and evening/weekend programs available. Postbaccalaureate distance learning degree programs offered (minimal on-campus study). *Degree requirements:* For master's, internship, practicum, thesis (expressive therapies); for doctorate, thesis/dissertation, arts apprenticeship, field placement; for CAGS, thesis, internship (counseling psychology, expressive therapies). *Entrance requirements:* For master's, MAT (counseling psychology), interview, writing samples, art portfolio; for doctorate, GRE or MAT; for CAGS, interview, master's degree. Additional exam requirements/recommendations for international students: Required—TOEFL (minimum score 550 paper-based; 213 computer-based; 80 iBT). Electronic applications accepted. *Faculty research:* Psychotherapy and culture; psychotherapy and psychological trauma; women's issues in art, teaching and psychotherapy; community based art, psycho-spiritual inquiry.

Long Island University, Brooklyn Campus, Richard L. Conolly College of Liberal Arts and Sciences, Department of Psychology, Program in Clinical Psychology, Brooklyn, NY 11201-8423. Offers PhD. *Accreditation:* APA. *Degree requirements:* For doctorate, thesis/dissertation. *Entrance requirements:* For doctorate, GRE Subject Test, GRE General Test. Additional exam requirements/recommendations for international students: Required—TOEFL (minimum score 500 paper-based; 173 computer-based). Electronic applications accepted. *Faculty research:* Ethnicity and human development.

Long Island University, C.W. Post Campus, College of Liberal Arts and Sciences, Department of Psychology, Program in Clinical Psychology, Brookville, NY 11548-1300. Offers Psy D. *Accreditation:* APA. *Degree requirements:* For doctorate, thesis/dissertation, internship. *Entrance requirements:* For doctorate, GRE General Test, GRE Subject Test, GRE Analytical Writing, bachelor's degree in psychology, minimum GPA of 3.25, 18 credit hours of undergraduate psychology, 3 letters of recommendation. *Expenses:* Contact institution. *Faculty research:* Family violence, schizophrenia, developmental disabilities, psychotherapy, terror and trauma.

Louisiana State University and Agricultural and Mechanical College, Graduate School, College of Humanities and Social Sciences, Department of Psychology, Baton Rouge, LA 70803. Offers biological psychology (MA, PhD); clinical psychology (MA, PhD); cognitive psychology (MA, PhD); developmental psychology (MA, PhD); industrial/organizational psychology (MA, PhD); school psychology (MA, PhD). PhD programs offered jointly with Southeastern Louisiana University. *Accreditation:* APA (one or more programs are accredited). *Faculty:* 26 full-time (10 women). *Students:* 96 full-time (68 women), 24 part-time (19 women); includes 7 Black or African American, non-Hispanic/Latino; 2 American Indian or Alaska Native, non-Hispanic/Latino; 1 Asian, non-Hispanic/Latino; 5 Hispanic/Latino, 2 international. Average age 27. 289 applicants, 11% accepted, 17 enrolled. In 2010, 16 master's, 11 doctorates awarded. Terminal master's awarded for partial completion of doctoral program. *Degree requirements:* For master's, thesis; for doctorate, thesis/dissertation, 1 year internship. *Entrance requirements:* For master's and doctorate, GRE General Test, minimum GPA of 3.0. Additional exam requirements/recommendations for international students: Required—TOEFL (minimum score 550 paper-based; 213 computer-based; 79 iBT) or IELTS (minimum score 6.5). *Application deadline:* For fall admission, 1/15 for domestic and international students. Applications are processed on a rolling basis. Application fee: $50 ($70 for international students). Electronic applications accepted. *Financial support:* In 2010–11, 115 students received support, including 5 fellowships (averaging $25,207 per year), 25 research assistantships with partial tuition reimbursements available (averaging $18,083 per year), 48 teaching assistantships with partial tuition reimbursements available (averaging $13,043 per year); career-related internships or fieldwork, Federal Work-Study, institutionally sponsored loans, scholarships/grants, health care benefits, and tuition waivers (full and partial) also available. Financial award applicants required to submit FAFSA. *Faculty research:* Clinical psychology, autism, anxiety, addition, neuropsychology, school psychology, cognitive psychology, experimental psychology. Total annual research expenditures: $1.3 million. *Unit head:* Dr. Robert Matthews, Chair, 225-578-8745, Fax: 225-578-4125, E-mail: psmath@lsu.edu. *Application contact:* Dr. Jason Hicks, Coordinator of Graduate Studies, 225-578-4109, Fax: 225-578-4125, E-mail: jhicks@lsu.edu.

Loyola University Chicago, Graduate School, Department of Psychology, Program in Clinical Psychology, Chicago, IL 60660. Offers MA, PhD. *Accreditation:* APA. *Faculty:* 8 full-time (6 women). *Students:* 36 full-time (31 women); includes 7 minority (3 Black or African American, non-Hispanic/Latino; 2 Asian, non-Hispanic/Latino; 2 Hispanic/Latino). Average age 27. 293 applicants, 2% accepted, 5 enrolled. In 2010, 3 master's, 2 doctorates awarded. Terminal master's awarded for partial completion of doctoral program. *Degree requirements:* For master's, thesis; for doctorate, comprehensive exam, thesis/dissertation. *Entrance requirements:* For doctorate, GRE General Test, GRE Subject Test, letters of recommendation, personal statement, curriculum vitae, transcript. *Application deadline:* For fall admission, 12/1 for domestic students. Electronic applications accepted. *Expenses:* Tuition: Full-time $14,940; part-time $830 per credit hour. Required fees: $87 per semester. Part-time tuition and fees vary according to course load and program. *Financial support:* In 2010–11, 5 students received support, including 7 fellowships with full tuition reimbursements available (averaging $16,500 per year), 11 research assistantships with full tuition reimbursements available (averaging $16,500 per year), 5 teaching assistantships with full tuition reimbursements available (averaging $16,500 per year); career-related internships or fieldwork, scholarships/grants, and unspecified assistantships also available. Financial award application deadline: 12/1. *Faculty research:* Child and family, AIDS, ethics and professional practice, psychotherapy, stress and coping, positive youth development, pediatric psychology, adolescence, inner city youth, emerging adulthood, mental health services, exposure to violence, obesity, spina bifida, asthma. *Unit head:* Dr. Grayson Holmbeck, Director, 773-508-2967, Fax: 773-508-8713, E-mail: gholmbe@luc.edu. *Application contact:* Jacquie Hamilton, Senior Secretary, 773-508-2974, Fax: 773-508-8713, E-mail: jhamilt@luc.edu.

Loyola University Maryland, Graduate Programs, Loyola College of Arts and Sciences, Department of Psychology, Program in Clinical Psychology, Baltimore, MD 21210-2699. Offers MS, Psy D, CAS. *Accreditation:* APA. Part-time and evening/weekend programs available. *Entrance requirements:* For master's, doctorate, and CAS, GRE General Test, GRE Subject Test (recommended). Additional exam requirements/recommendations for international students: Required—TOEFL (minimum score 550 paper-based; 213 computer-based).

Lynchburg College, Graduate Studies, School of Education and Human Development, M Ed Program in Clinical Mental Health Counseling, Lynchburg, VA 24501-3199. Offers M Ed. Part-time and evening/weekend programs available. *Faculty:* 6 full-time (4 women). *Students:* 15 full-time (10 women), 17 part-time (12 women); includes 6 minority (5 Black or African American, non-Hispanic/Latino; 1 American Indian or Alaska Native, non-Hispanic/Latino), 1 international. Average age 32. 34 applicants, 44% accepted. In 2010, 6 master's awarded. *Degree requirements:* For master's, comprehensive exam, completion of counseling internship. *Entrance requirements:* For master's, GRE, official transcripts, personal essay, 3 letters of recommendation. Additional exam requirements/recommendations for international students: Required—TOEFL (minimum score 530 paper-based; 197 computer-based; 71 iBT), IELTS (minimum score 6.5). *Application deadline:* For fall admission, 7/31 for domestic students, 6/1 for international students; for spring admission, 11/30 for domestic students, 10/15 for international students. Applications are processed on a rolling basis. Application fee: $30. Electronic applications accepted. *Expenses:* Tuition: Full-time $7200; part-time $400 per credit hour. Required fees: $20; $5.10 per credit hour. $15 per term. Tuition and fees vary according to degree level and program. *Financial support:* Fellowships, research assistantships, Federal Work-Study, scholarships/grants, health care benefits, and unspecified assistantships available. Support available to part-time students. Financial award application deadline: 7/31; financial award applicants required to submit FAFSA. *Unit head:* Dr. Mandy Perryman, Assistant Professor and Program Director, Counselor Education, 434-544-8067, E-mail: perryman@lynchburg.edu. *Application contact:* Dr. Mandy Perryman, Assistant Professor and Program Director, Counselor Education, 434-544-8067, E-mail: perryman@lynchburg.edu.

Madonna University, Department of Psychology, Livonia, MI 48150-1173. Offers clinical psychology (MSCP). Part-time and evening/weekend programs available. *Degree requirements:* For master's, thesis or alternative. *Entrance requirements:* Additional exam requirements/recommendations for international students: Required—TOEFL. Electronic applications accepted.

Marquette University, Graduate School, College of Education, Milwaukee, WI 53201-1881. Offers clinical mental health counseling (MS); college student personnel administration (M Ed); counseling (MA); counseling psychology (PhD); curriculum and instruction (MA); education

Clinical Psychology

Marquette University (continued)
(PhD); educational administration (M Ed); educational policy and foundations (MA); educational psychology (MA); elementary education (Certificate); literacy (MA); principal (Certificate); reading specialist (Certificate); reading teacher (Certificate); secondary education (Certificate); superintendent (Certificate). *Accreditation:* NCATE. Part-time programs available. *Faculty:* 24 full-time (15 women), 35 part-time/adjunct (27 women). *Students:* 91 full-time (66 women), 208 part-time (133 women); includes 47 minority (21 Black or African American, non-Hispanic/Latino; 2 American Indian or Alaska Native, non-Hispanic/Latino; 7 Asian, non-Hispanic/Latino; 14 Hispanic/Latino; 3 Two or more races, non-Hispanic/Latino), 3 international. Average age 31. 326 applicants, 58% accepted, 99 enrolled. In 2010, 62 master's, 9 doctorates, 4 other advanced degrees awarded. Terminal master's awarded for partial completion of doctoral program. *Degree requirements:* For master's, comprehensive exam, thesis (for some programs); for doctorate, thesis/dissertation, qualifying exam, supporting minor. *Entrance requirements:* For master's, GRE General Test or MAT, official transcripts from all current and previous colleges/universities except Marquette, three letters of recommendation, statement of purpose; for doctorate, GRE General Test, MAT, sample of written work, official transcripts from all current and previous colleges/universities except Marquette, three letters of recommendation, statement of purpose, resume/vita; for Certificate, GRE General Test or MAT, master's degree. Additional exam requirements/recommendations for international students: Required—TOEFL (minimum score 530 paper-based; 78 computer-based). *Application deadline:* For fall admission, 1/15 for domestic and international students. Application fee: $50. *Expenses:* Contact institution. *Financial support:* In 2010–11, 3 fellowships, 17 research assistantships, 17 teaching assistantships were awarded; Federal Work-Study, institutionally sponsored loans, scholarships/grants, and tuition waivers (full and partial) also available. Support available to part-time students. Financial award application deadline: 2/15. *Faculty research:* Parenting, psychology of motivation, reading assessment, socialization of educational administrators, education philosophy of Cardinal Newman. Total annual research expenditures: $239,042. *Unit head:* Dr. Bill Henk, Dean, 414-288-7376. *Application contact:* Erin Fox, Director of Graduate Admissions, 414-288-7182, Fax: 414-288-1902.

Marshall University, Academic Affairs Division, College of Liberal Arts, Department of Psychology, Huntington, WV 25755. Offers clinical psychology (MA); general psychology (MA); industrial and organizational psychology (MA); psychology (Psy D). *Accreditation:* APA. *Faculty:* 17 full-time (5 women), 1 (woman) part-time/adjunct. *Students:* 98 full-time (67 women), 32 part-time (26 women); includes 7 Black or African American, non-Hispanic/Latino; 1 Asian, non-Hispanic/Latino; 1 Hispanic/Latino; 1 Native Hawaiian or other Pacific Islander, non-Hispanic/Latino, 4 international. Average age 28. In 2010, 33 master's, 4 doctorates awarded. *Degree requirements:* For master's, thesis optional. *Entrance requirements:* For master's, GRE General Test or MAT. *Application deadline:* For fall admission, 3/1 for domestic students; for spring admission, 11/1 for domestic students. Application fee: $40. *Financial support:* Teaching assistantships with tuition reimbursements available. *Unit head:* Dr. Steven Mewaldt, Chairperson, 304-696-2777, E-mail: mewaldt@marshall.edu. *Application contact:* Graduate Admissions, 304-746-1900, Fax: 304-746-1902, E-mail: services@marshall.edu.

Marywood University, Academic Affairs, Reap College of Education and Human Development, Department of Psychology and Counseling, Program in Clinical Psychology, Scranton, PA 18509-1598. Offers Psy D. *Accreditation:* APA. *Entrance requirements:* Additional exam requirements/recommendations for international students: Required—TOEFL (minimum score 550 paper-based; 213 computer-based; 79 iBT). Electronic applications accepted. *Expenses:* Contact institution.

Marywood University, Academic Affairs, Reap College of Education and Human Development, Department of Psychology and Counseling, Program in Psychology, Scranton, PA 18509-1598. Offers clinical services (MA); general theoretical (MA). *Entrance requirements:* Additional exam requirements/recommendations for international students: Required—TOEFL (minimum score 550 paper-based; 213 computer-based; 79 iBT). Electronic applications accepted. *Expenses:* Tuition: Part-time $735 per credit. Required fees: $470 per semester. Tuition and fees vary according to degree level and campus/location. *Faculty research:* Personality disorders, counselor training, preschool development, self-esteem measurement, family dynamics.

Massachusetts School of Professional Psychology, Graduate Programs, Boston, MA 02132. Offers applied psychology in higher education student personnel administration (MA); clinical psychology (Psy D); counseling psychology (MA); counseling psychology and community mental health (MA); counseling psychology and global mental health (MA); executive coaching (Graduate Certificate); forensic and counseling psychology (MA); leadership psychology (Psy D); organizational psychology (MA); primary care psychology (MA); respecialization in clinical psychology (Certificate); school psychology (Psy D); MA/CAGS. *Accreditation:* APA. *Faculty:* 24 full-time (11 women), 13 part-time/adjunct (9 women). *Students:* 515. Average age 28. *Degree requirements:* For master's, comprehensive exam (for some programs); for doctorate, thesis/dissertation (for some programs). Application fee: $50. Electronic applications accepted. *Expenses:* Tuition: Full-time $32,352; part-time $1011 per credit. Full-time tuition and fees vary according to degree level. *Financial support:* Teaching assistantships, career-related internships or fieldwork available. Financial award applicants required to submit FAFSA. *Unit head:* Dr. Nicholas A. Covino, President, 617-327-6777, Fax: 617-327-4447. *Application contact:* Admissions and Marketing, 617-327-6777 Ext. 210, Fax: 617-327-4447, E-mail: admissions@mspp.edu.

McGill University, Faculty of Graduate and Postdoctoral Studies, Faculty of Science, Department of Psychology, Montréal, QC H3A 2T5, Canada. Offers clinical psychology (PhD); experimental psychology (M Sc, MA, PhD). *Accreditation:* APA (one or more programs are accredited).

Messiah College, Program in Counseling, Grantham, PA 17027. Offers clinical mental health counseling (MAC); counseling (CAGS); marriage, couple, and family counseling (MAC); school counseling (MAC). Part-time programs available. *Entrance requirements:* For master's, minimum undergraduate cumulative GPA of 3.0, 2 recommendations, resume or curriculum vitae, interview; for CAGS, bachelor's degree, minimum undergraduate cumulative GPA of 3.0, essay, two recommendations, resume or curriculum vitae, interview. *Application deadline:* Applications are processed on a rolling basis. Application fee: $30. Electronic applications accepted. *Financial support:* Applicants required to submit FAFSA. *Unit head:* Dr. John Addleman, Director, 717-796-1800 Ext. 2980, Fax: 717-691-2386, E-mail: jaddlemn@messiah.edu. *Application contact:* Dr. John Addleman, Director, 717-796-1800 Ext. 2980, Fax: 717-691-2386, E-mail: jaddlemn@messiah.edu.

Michigan School of Professional Psychology, MA and PsyD Programs in Clinical Psychology, Farmington Hills, MI 48334. Offers MA, Psy D. Part-time programs available. *Faculty:* 7 full-time (3 women), 20 part-time/adjunct (11 women). *Students:* 120 full-time (92 women), 18 part-time (16 women); includes 29 minority (22 Black or African American, non-Hispanic/Latino; 4 Asian, non-Hispanic/Latino; 3 Hispanic/Latino). 126 applicants, 75% accepted, 77 enrolled. In 2010, 41 master's, 20 doctorates awarded. *Degree requirements:* For master's, thesis, practicum; for doctorate, comprehensive exam, thesis/dissertation, internship, practicum. *Entrance requirements:* For master's, undergraduate degree from accredited institution with minimum GPA of 2.5; major in psychology, social work, counseling or equivalent; for doctorate, undergraduate degree from accredited institution with minimum GPA of 2.5; graduate degree from accredited institution with minimum GPA of 3.25; undergraduate or graduate degree in psychology, social work, counseling or equivalent; 500 practicum hours or equivalent field experience. Additional exam requirements/recommendations for international students: Required—TOEFL (minimum score 550 paper-based; 213 computer-based; 79 iBT). *Application deadline:* Applications are processed on a rolling basis. Application fee: $75. Tuition and fees vary according to course load and degree level. *Financial support:* In 2010–11, 6 students received support, including 3 research assistantships (averaging $12,000 per year), 1 teaching assistantship (averaging $12,000 per year); career-related internships or fieldwork, institutionally sponsored loans, and scholarships/grants also available. Financial award application deadline:

6/30; financial award applicants required to submit FAFSA. *Faculty research:* Qualitative research, existential, phenomenological psychology, clinical practice, humanistic. *Unit head:* Dr. Kerry Moustakas, President, 248-476-1122, Fax: 248-476-1125. *Application contact:* Amanda Ming, Admissions and Recruitment Coordinator, 248-476-1122 Ext. 117, Fax: 248-476-1125, E-mail: aming@mispp.edu.

Middle Tennessee State University, College of Graduate Studies, College of Behavioral and Health Sciences, Department of Psychology, Murfreesboro, TN 37132. Offers clinical psychology (MA); experimental psychology (MA); industrial/organizational psychology (MA); psychology (MA); quantitative psychology (MA); school psychology (MA, Ed S). Part-time and evening/weekend programs available. Postbaccalaureate distance learning degree programs offered. *Faculty:* 36 full-time (16 women), 2 part-time/adjunct (0 women). *Students:* 32 full-time (27 women), 84 part-time (58 women); includes 11 Black or African American, non-Hispanic/Latino; 6 Asian, non-Hispanic/Latino; 2 Hispanic/Latino. Average age 26. 251 applicants, 55% accepted. In 2010, 52 master's, 10 other advanced degrees awarded. *Degree requirements:* For master's, variable foreign language requirement, comprehensive exam, thesis (for some programs). *Entrance requirements:* Additional exam requirements/recommendations for international students: Required—TOEFL (minimum score 525 paper-based; 195 computer-based; 71 iBT) or IELTS (minimum score 6). *Application deadline:* For fall admission, 6/1 for domestic and international students. Applications are processed on a rolling basis. Application fee: $25 ($30 for international students). Electronic applications accepted. *Expenses:* Tuition, state resident: full-time $4632. Tuition, nonresident: full-time $11,520. *Financial support:* In 2010–11, 16 students received support. Career-related internships or fieldwork and institutionally sponsored loans available. Support available to part-time students. Financial award application deadline: 5/1; financial award applicants required to submit FAFSA. *Faculty research:* Industrial/organizational, social/personality/sports, counseling/clinical/school, cognitive/language/learning/perception, developmental/aging. *Unit head:* Dr. Dennis Papini, Chair, 615-898-2706, Fax: 615-898-5027, E-mail: dpapini@mtsu.edu. *Application contact:* Dr. Michael Allen, Dean and Vice Provost for Research, 615-898-2840, Fax: 615-904-8020, E-mail: mallen@mtsu.edu.

Midwestern University, Downers Grove Campus, College of Health Sciences, Illinois Campus, Program in Clinical Psychology, Downers Grove, IL 60515-1235. Offers MA, Psy D. *Faculty:* 10 full-time (7 women). *Students:* 63 full-time (49 women), 18 part-time (14 women); includes 6 Black or African American, non-Hispanic/Latino; 2 Asian, non-Hispanic/Latino; 3 Hispanic/Latino, 2 international. Average age 28. 77 applicants, 61% accepted, 26 enrolled. In 2010, 16 master's awarded. *Degree requirements:* For doctorate, thesis/dissertation, qualifying examination. *Entrance requirements:* For master's and doctorate, GRE, minimum overall GPA of 2.75, 3 letters of recommendation. Additional exam requirements/recommendations for international students: Required—TOEFL. *Application deadline:* Applications are processed on a rolling basis. Application fee: $50. *Unit head:* Dr. Frank J. Prerost, Director, 630-515-7405, Fax: 630-971-6402, E-mail: fprero@midwestern.edu. *Application contact:* Michael Laken, Director of Admissions, 630-515-6171, Fax: 630-971-6086, E-mail: admissil@midwestern.edu.

Midwestern University, Glendale Campus, College of Health Sciences, Arizona Campus, Program in Clinical Psychology, Glendale, AZ 85308. Offers Psy D. *Faculty:* 5 full-time (3 women). *Students:* 36 full-time (27 women), 1 (woman) part-time; includes 1 Black or African American, non-Hispanic/Latino; 1 Hispanic/Latino, 1 international. Average age 27. 31 applicants, 55% accepted, 11 enrolled. *Unit head:* Dr. Philinda Hutchings, Program Director and Professor, 623-572-3861, Fax: 623-572-3449. *Application contact:* James Walter, Director of Admissions, 888-247-9277, Fax: 623-572-3229, E-mail: admissaz@midwestern.edu.

Millersville University of Pennsylvania, College of Graduate and Professional Studies, School of Education, Department of Psychology, Program in Psychology, Millersville, PA 17551-0302. Offers clinical psychology (MS); school psychology (MS). Part-time programs available. *Faculty:* 19 full-time (13 women), 8 part-time/adjunct (5 women). *Students:* 53 full-time (45 women), 41 part-time (34 women); includes 3 Black or African American, non-Hispanic/Latino; 1 Hispanic/Latino, 3 international. Average age 28. 65 applicants, 78% accepted, 30 enrolled. In 2010, 23 master's awarded. *Degree requirements:* For master's, comprehensive exam, thesis optional. *Entrance requirements:* For master's, GRE, 3 letters of recommendation; interview (in-person). Additional exam requirements/recommendations for international students: Required—TOEFL (minimum score 500 paper-based; 183 computer-based; 65 iBT) or IELTS (minimum score 6). *Application deadline:* For fall admission, 1/15 for domestic and international students; for winter admission, 10/1 for domestic and international students; for spring admission, 10/1 for domestic and international students. Application fee: $40 ($50 for international students). Electronic applications accepted. *Expenses:* Tuition, state resident: full-time $6966; part-time $387 per credit. Tuition, nonresident: full-time $11,146; part-time $619 per credit. Required fees: $1829.50; $88 per credit. One-time fee: $60 part-time. Tuition and fees vary according to course load. *Financial support:* In 2010–11, 35 students received support, including 35 research assistantships with full and partial tuition reimbursements available (averaging $4,997 per year); institutionally sponsored loans and unspecified assistantships also available. Support available to part-time students. Financial award application deadline: 3/15; financial award applicants required to submit FAFSA. *Faculty research:* Parenting and alcohol risk, time perceptions, time management, stress and coping, autism and behavioral disorders. *Unit head:* Dr. Claudia Haferkamp, Director of Clinical Psychology Program, 717-872-3826, Fax: 717-871-2480, E-mail: claudia.haferkamp@millersville.edu. *Application contact:* Dr. Victor S. DeSantis, Dean of Graduate and Professional Studies, 717-872-3099, Fax: 717-872-3453, E-mail: victor.desantis@millersville.edu.

Minnesota State University Mankato, College of Graduate Studies, College of Social and Behavioral Sciences, Department of Psychology, Mankato, MN 56001. Offers clinical psychology (MA); industrial/organizational psychology (MA); school psychology (Psy D). Part-time programs available. *Students:* 57 full-time (38 women), 1 part-time (0 women). *Degree requirements:* For master's, one foreign language, comprehensive exam, thesis (for some programs). *Entrance requirements:* For master's, GRE General Test, GRE Subject Test (clinical psychology), minimum GPA of 3.0 during previous 2 years, 3 letters of reference. Additional exam requirements/recommendations for international students: Required—TOEFL. *Application deadline:* For fall admission, 1/1 priority date for domestic students. Applications are processed on a rolling basis. Application fee: $40. Electronic applications accepted. *Financial support:* Research assistantships, teaching assistantships with full tuition reimbursements, career-related internships or fieldwork, Federal Work-Study, institutionally sponsored loans, and unspecified assistantships available. Support available to part-time students. Financial award application deadline: 3/15; financial award applicants required to submit FAFSA. *Faculty research:* Professional competency in hospitals, mood disturbance, 360-degree feedback, employee selection, planning fallacy. *Unit head:* Dr. Barry Ries, Chairperson, 507-389-2724. *Application contact:* 507-389-2321, E-mail: grad@mnsu.edu.

Mississippi State University, College of Arts and Sciences, Department of Psychology, Mississippi State, MS 39762. Offers cognitive science (PhD); psychology (MS), including clinical psychology, experimental psychology. *Faculty:* 12 full-time (4 women). *Students:* 40 full-time (27 women), 7 part-time (5 women); includes 4 minority (3 Black or African American, non-Hispanic/Latino; 1 Two or more races, non-Hispanic/Latino), 3 international. Average age 26. 77 applicants, 36% accepted, 19 enrolled. In 2010, 10 master's, 1 doctorate awarded. Terminal master's awarded for partial completion of doctoral program. *Degree requirements:* For master's, comprehensive exam, thesis; for doctorate, thesis/dissertation, qualifying exam, comprehensive written and oral exam. *Entrance requirements:* For master's, GRE General Test, minimum GPA of 2.75 on last two years of undergraduate courses; for doctorate, GRE General Test, proficiency in at least 1 computer language. Additional exam requirements/recommendations for international students: Required—TOEFL (minimum score 475 paper-based; 153 computer-based; 53 iBT); Recommended—IELTS (minimum score 4.5). *Application deadline:* For fall admission, 1/15 priority date for domestic students, 5/1 for international students; for spring admission, 11/1 priority date for domestic students, 9/1 for international students. Applications are processed on a rolling basis. Application fee: $40. Electronic applications accepted. *Expenses:* Tuition, state resident: full-time $2730.50; part-time $304 per credit hour. Tuition, nonresident: full-time $6901; part-time $767 per credit hour. *Financial support:* In 2010–11, 6 research assistantships with full tuition reimbursements (averaging $11,925 per year), 13 teaching assistantships with full tuition reimbursements (averaging $9,755 per year) were awarded; career-related internships or fieldwork, Federal Work-Study, institutionally sponsored loans, scholarships/grants, and unspecified assistantships also available. Financial award application deadline: 4/1; financial award applicants required to submit FAFSA. *Faculty research:* Personality type, alcoholism, blindness and low vision, mental retardation, language comprehension. Total annual research expenditures: $2.4 million. *Unit head:* Dr. Stephen B. Klein, Department Head, 662-325-3202, Fax: 662-325-7212, E-mail: sbkl@ra.msstate.edu. *Application contact:* Dr. Kevin J. Armstrong, Graduate Coordinator, 662-325-3202, Fax: 662-325-7212, E-mail: grad@psychology.msstate.edu.

Missouri State University, Graduate College, College of Health and Human Services, Department of Psychology, Springfield, MO 65897. Offers psychology (MS), including clinical psychology, experimental psychology, industrial/organizational psychology. *Degree requirements:* For master's, comprehensive exam, thesis. *Entrance requirements:* For master's, GRE General Test, GRE Subject Test, minimum GPA of 3.25 in major, 3.0 overall; 20 hours of course work in psychology (experimental and statistics). Additional exam requirements/recommendations for international students: Required—TOEFL (minimum score 550 paper-based; 213 computer-based; 79 iBT). Electronic applications accepted. *Expenses:* Tuition, state resident: full-time $3348; part-time $186 per credit hour. Tuition, nonresident: full-time $6696; part-time $372 per credit hour. Required fees: $238 per semester. Tuition and fees vary according to course level, course load and program. *Faculty research:* Work-family conflict, child forensic psychology, sports psychology, body image assessment, visual learning.

Montclair State University, The Graduate School, College of Humanities and Social Sciences, Department of Psychology, Montclair, NJ 07043-1624. Offers educational psychology (MA), including child/adolescent clinical psychology, clinical psychology for Spanish/English bilinguals, educational psychology; psychology (MA), including industrial and organizational psychology; school psychology (Certificate). Part-time and evening/weekend programs available. *Faculty:* 25 full-time (11 women), 37 part-time/adjunct (21 women). *Students:* 43 full-time (31 women), 33 part-time (22 women); includes 8 Black or African American, non-Hispanic/Latino; 3 Asian, non-Hispanic/Latino; 10 Hispanic/Latino, 2 international. Average age 26. 117 applicants, 33% accepted, 24 enrolled. In 2010, 23 master's, 1 other advanced degree awarded. *Degree requirements:* For master's, comprehensive exam, thesis or alternative. *Entrance requirements:* For master's, GRE General Test, 2 letters of recommendation. Additional exam requirements/recommendations for international students: Required—TOEFL (minimum iBT score of 83) or IELTS. *Application deadline:* For fall admission, 6/1 for international students; for spring admission, 11/1 for international students. Applications are processed on a rolling basis. Application fee: $60. Electronic applications accepted. *Expenses:* Tuition, state resident: part-time $501.34 per credit. Tuition, nonresident: part-time $773.88 per credit. Required fees: $71.15 per credit. *Financial support:* In 2010–11, 13 research assistantships with full tuition reimbursements (averaging $7,000 per year) were awarded; Federal Work-Study, scholarships/grants, and unspecified assistantships also available. Support available to part-time students. Financial award application deadline: 3/1; financial award applicants required to submit FAFSA. *Faculty research:* Legal decision-making, leadership development, bias and stereotype threat in the selection process, nature of pre-linguistic thought in infants, lateralized cortical contributions to memory, pediatric neuro-imaging, the production and perception of speech, school-based assessment and intervention for bullying, cognitive processes in reading, identification of autism in toddlers. Total annual research expenditures: $300,000. *Unit head:* Dr. Peter Vietze, Chairperson, 973-655-5201. *Application contact:* Amy Aiello, Director of Admissions and Operations, 973-655-5147, Fax: 973-655-7869, E-mail: graduate.school@montclair.edu.

Morehead State University, Graduate Programs, College of Science and Technology, Department of Psychology, Morehead, KY 40351. Offers clinical/counseling psychology (MS); general/experimental psychology (MS). Part-time and evening/weekend programs available. *Degree requirements:* For master's, comprehensive exam, thesis optional. *Entrance requirements:* For master's, GRE General Test, 18 undergraduate hours in psychology, minimum GPA of 3.0, 3 letters of recommendation. Additional exam requirements/recommendations for international students: Required—TOEFL (minimum score 500 paper-based; 173 computer-based). Electronic applications accepted. *Faculty research:* Mood induction effects, serotonin receptor activity, stress, perceptual processes.

Murray State University, College of Humanities and Fine Arts, Program in Psychology, Murray, KY 42071. Offers clinical psychology (MA, MS); psychology (MA, MS). Part-time programs available. *Degree requirements:* For master's, one foreign language, comprehensive exam (for some programs), thesis. *Entrance requirements:* For master's, GRE General Test. Additional exam requirements/recommendations for international students: Required—TOEFL.

Naropa University, Graduate Programs, Program in Transpersonal Psychology, Boulder, CO 80302-6697. Offers ecopsychology (MA); transpersonal psychology (MA). Part-time and evening/weekend programs available. Postbaccalaureate distance learning degree programs offered (minimal on-campus study). *Faculty:* 1 full-time (0 women), 13 part-time/adjunct (7 women). *Students:* 1 full-time (0 women), 12 part-time (11 women); includes 2 minority (1 Hispanic/Latino; 1 Two or more races, non-Hispanic/Latino). Average age 45. 17 applicants, 59% accepted, 4 enrolled. In 2010, 5 master's awarded. *Degree requirements:* For master's, thesis, service learning. *Entrance requirements:* For master's, interview (by phone or in-person), technology form, resume, letter of interest, 3 letters of recommendation. Additional exam requirements/recommendations for international students: Required—TOEFL (minimum score 600 paper-based; 250 computer-based). *Application deadline:* For fall admission, 1/15 for domestic and international students. Applications are processed on a rolling basis. Application fee: $60. Electronic applications accepted. *Expenses:* Tuition: Full-time $17,820; part-time $810 per credit. Required fees: $305 per semester. Tuition and fees vary according to course load, program and reciprocity agreements. *Financial support:* In 2010–11, 3 students received support. Career-related internships or fieldwork, Federal Work-Study, scholarships/grants, health care benefits, and tuition waivers (partial) available. Support available to part-time students. Financial award application deadline: 3/1; financial award applicants required to submit FAFSA. *Unit head:* Dr. MacAndrew Jack, Director, Graduate School of Psychology, 303-245-4752, E-mail: mjack@naropa.edu. *Application contact:* Office of Admissions, 303-546-3572, Fax: 303-546-3583, E-mail: admissions@naropa.edu.

New Mexico Highlands University, Graduate Studies, College of Arts and Sciences, Department of Behavioral Sciences, Las Vegas, NM 87701. Offers psychology (MS), including clinical psychology, general psychology. Part-time programs available. *Faculty:* 11 full-time (6 women). *Students:* 22 full-time (16 women), 13 part-time (8 women); includes 2 Black or African American, non-Hispanic/Latino; 1 American Indian or Alaska Native, non-Hispanic/Latino; 19 Hispanic/Latino. Average age 28. 8 applicants, 100% accepted, 7 enrolled. In 2010, 3 master's awarded. *Degree requirements:* For master's, comprehensive exam, thesis or alternative. *Entrance requirements:* For master's, minimum undergraduate GPA of 3.0. Additional exam requirements/recommendations for international students: Required—TOEFL (minimum score 540 paper-based; 207 computer-based). *Application deadline:* For fall admission, 8/1 priority date for domestic students. Applications are processed on a rolling basis. Application fee: $15. *Expenses:* Tuition, state resident: full-time $2544. Required fees: $624; $132 per credit hour. *Financial support:* In 2010–11, 28 students received support; teaching assistantships, career-related internships or fieldwork, Federal Work-Study, institutionally sponsored loans, scholarships/grants, tuition waivers (full and partial), and unspecified assistantships available. Support available to part-time students. Financial award application deadline: 3/1; financial award applicants required to submit FAFSA. *Faculty research:* Southwest Native American resettlement development, community-level interventions, neurochemistry of personality, comparative criminal justice, social theory and activism. *Unit head:* Dr. Ian Williamson, Chair, 505-454-3342, E-mail: iwilliamson@nmhu.edu. *Application contact:* Diane Trujillo, Administrative Assistant for Graduate Studies, 505-454-3266, Fax: 505-426-2117, E-mail: dtrujillo@nmhu.edu.

The New School: A University, The New School for Social Research, Department of Psychology, New York, NY 10011. Offers clinical psychology (PhD); cognitive, social and developmental psychology (PhD); general psychology (MA). *Accreditation:* APA (one or more programs are accredited). Part-time programs available. Terminal master's awarded for partial completion of doctoral program. *Degree requirements:* For master's, comprehensive exam (for some programs), thesis (for some programs); for doctorate, thesis/dissertation, qualifying exam. *Entrance requirements:* For master's, GRE General Test; for doctorate, GRE General Test, MA. Additional exam requirements/recommendations for international students: Required—TOEFL (minimum score 600 paper-based; 250 computer-based; 100 iBT). Electronic applications accepted. *Faculty research:* Consciousness, memory, language, perceptions, psychopathology.

Norfolk State University, School of Graduate Studies, School of Liberal Arts, Department of Psychology, Program in Community/Clinical Psychology, Norfolk, VA 23504. Offers MA. *Degree requirements:* For master's, comprehensive exam, thesis or alternative. *Entrance requirements:* For master's, minimum GPA of 2.7.

North Dakota State University, College of Graduate and Interdisciplinary Studies, College of Science and Mathematics, Department of Psychology, Fargo, ND 58108. Offers clinical psychology (MS); cognitive and visual neuroscience (PhD); health and social psychology (PhD); psychology (MS). *Faculty:* 18 full-time (4 women), 2 part-time/adjunct (1 woman). *Students:* 20 full-time (11 women), 3 part-time (0 women); includes 1 Two or more races, non-Hispanic/Latino, 2 international. Average age 24. 41 applicants, 27% accepted, 6 enrolled. In 2010, 7 master's, 2 doctorates awarded. *Degree requirements:* For master's, thesis; for doctorate, thesis/dissertation. *Entrance requirements:* For master's and doctorate, GRE General Test, GRE Subject Test. Additional exam requirements/recommendations for international students: Required—TOEFL (minimum score 525 paper-based; 197 computer-based; 71 iBT). *Application deadline:* For fall admission, 3/1 for domestic and international students. Application fee: $45 ($60 for international students). Electronic applications accepted. *Financial support:* In 2010–11, 2 fellowships with full tuition reimbursements (averaging $16,000 per year), 23 research assistantships with full tuition reimbursements (averaging $16,000 per year), 11 teaching assistantships with full tuition reimbursements (averaging $6,000 per year) were awarded; career-related internships or fieldwork, Federal Work-Study, institutionally sponsored loans, tuition waivers (full and partial), and unspecified assistantships also available. Support available to part-time students. Financial award application deadline: 3/1. *Faculty research:* Cognition science, neuropsychology, group behavior, applied behavior analysis, behavior therapy. Total annual research expenditures: $2 million. *Unit head:* Dr. Paul D. Rokke, Chair, 701-231-8622, Fax: 701-231-8426, E-mail: paul.rokke@ndsu.edu. *Application contact:* Dr. Paul D. Rokke, Chair, 701-231-8622, Fax: 701-231-8426, E-mail: paul.rokke@ndsu.edu.

Northern Arizona University, Graduate College, College of Social and Behavioral Sciences, Department of Psychology, Flagstaff, AZ 86011. Offers clinical health psychology (MA); general psychology (MA); teaching psychology (MA). Part-time programs available. *Faculty:* 20 full-time (10 women). *Students:* 33 full-time (16 women), 5 part-time (2 women); includes 7 minority (1 American Indian or Alaska Native, non-Hispanic/Latino; 3 Asian, non-Hispanic/Latino; 3 Hispanic/Latino), 2 international. Average age 30. 74 applicants, 24% accepted, 18 enrolled. In 2010, 10 master's awarded. *Degree requirements:* For master's, comprehensive exam (for some programs), thesis (for some programs), oral defense. *Entrance requirements:* For master's, GRE General Test. Additional exam requirements/recommendations for international students: Required—TOEFL (minimum score 550 paper-based; 213 computer-based; 80 iBT), IELTS (minimum score 7). *Application deadline:* For fall admission, 2/1 priority date for domestic and international students. Applications are processed on a rolling basis. Application fee: $65. Electronic applications accepted. *Financial support:* In 2010–11, 11 teaching assistantships with partial tuition reimbursements (averaging $9,709 per year) were awarded; career-related internships or fieldwork, Federal Work-Study, institutionally sponsored loans, scholarships/grants, health care benefits, tuition waivers (full and partial), and unspecified assistantships also available. Support available to part-time students. Financial award applicants required to submit FAFSA. *Unit head:* Dr. Laurie Dickson, Chair, 928-523-1829, Fax: 928-523-6777, E-mail: laurie.dickson@nau.edu. *Application contact:* Janina Burton, Graduate Coordinator, 928-523-3063, Fax: 928-523-6777, E-mail: janina.burton@nau.edu.

Northern Kentucky University, Office of Graduate Programs, College of Education and Human Services, Program in Community Counseling, Highland Heights, KY 41099. Offers clinical mental health counseling (MA); college student development administration (Certificate); community counseling (Certificate). Part-time and evening/weekend programs available. *Faculty:* 12 full-time (7 women), 1 part-time/adjunct (0 women). *Students:* 17 full-time (16 women), 24 part-time (19 women). Average age 32. 36 applicants, 61% accepted, 19 enrolled. In 2010, 12 master's, 6 other advanced degrees awarded. *Degree requirements:* For master's, comprehensive exam, internship. *Entrance requirements:* For master's, GRE, minimum GPA of 2.75, 3 letters of reference, criminal background check (state and federal), resume. Additional exam requirements/recommendations for international students: Required—TOEFL (minimum score 550 paper-based; 213 computer-based; 79 iBT); Recommended—IELTS (minimum score 6.5). *Application deadline:* For fall admission, 7/1 for domestic students, 6/1 priority date for international students; for spring admission, 11/1 for domestic students, 10/1 priority date for international students. Applications are processed on a rolling basis. Application fee: $40. Electronic applications accepted. *Expenses:* Tuition, state resident: full-time $7254; part-time $403 per credit hour. Tuition, nonresident: full-time $12,492; part-time $694 per credit hour. Tuition and fees vary according to degree level and program. *Financial support:* Applicants required to submit FAFSA. *Faculty research:* Ethical decision-making in counseling, clinical supervision in counseling, expectations about counseling inventory development. *Unit head:* Dr. Jacqueline Smith, Director, 859-572-6149, E-mail: smithjac@nku.edu. *Application contact:* Dr. Peg Griffin, Director, Graduate Programs, 859-572-6934, Fax: 859-572-6670, E-mail: griffinp@nku.edu.

Northwestern State University of Louisiana, Graduate Studies and Research, Department of Psychology, Natchitoches, LA 71497. Offers clinical psychology (MS). *Degree requirements:* For master's, comprehensive exam, thesis or alternative. *Entrance requirements:* For master's, GRE General Test, GRE Subject Test, minimum undergraduate GPA of 2.5.

Northwestern University, The Graduate School, Judd A. and Marjorie Weinberg College of Arts and Sciences, Department of Psychology, Evanston, IL 60208. Offers brain, behavior and cognition (PhD); clinical psychology (PhD); cognitive psychology (PhD); personality (PhD); social psychology (PhD); JD/PhD. Admissions and degrees offered through The Graduate School. *Accreditation:* APA (one or more programs are accredited). Part-time programs available. *Degree requirements:* For doctorate, thesis/dissertation. *Entrance requirements:* For doctorate, GRE General Test, GRE Subject Test. Additional exam requirements/recommendations for international students: Required—TOEFL. Electronic applications accepted. *Faculty research:* Memory and higher order cognition, anxiety and depression, effectiveness of psychotherapy, social cognition, molecular basis of memory.

Northwestern University, The Graduate School and Northwestern University Feinberg School of Medicine, Program in Clinical Psychology, Evanston, IL 60208. Offers clinical psychology (PhD), including clinical neuropsychology, general clinical. PhD admissions and degree offered through The Graduate School. *Accreditation:* APA. *Degree requirements:* For doctorate, thesis/dissertation, clinical internship. *Entrance requirements:* For doctorate, GRE General Test, GRE Subject Test, minimum GPA of 3.2, course work in psychology. Additional exam requirements/recommendations for international students: Required—TOEFL. *Faculty research:* Cancer and cardiovascular risk reduction, evaluation of mental health services and policy, neuropsychological assessment, outcome of psychotherapy, cognitive therapy, pediatric and clinical child psychology.

Notre Dame de Namur University, Division of Academic Affairs, College of Arts and Sciences, Department of Clinical Psychology and Gerontology, Program in Clinical Psychology, Belmont, CA 94002-1908. Offers MS. Part-time programs available. *Students:* 25 full-time (21 women), 45 part-time (38 women); includes 3 Black or African American, non-Hispanic/Latino;

Clinical Psychology

Notre Dame de Namur University *(continued)*
9 Asian, non-Hispanic/Latino; 12 Hispanic/Latino, 2 international. Average age 34. In 2010, 24 master's awarded. *Entrance requirements:* Additional exam requirements/recommendations for international students: Required—TOEFL (minimum score 550 paper-based; 213 computer-based; 79 iBT). Application fee: $60. *Expenses:* Tuition: Full-time $14,220; part-time $790 per credit. Required fees: $35 per semester. Tuition and fees vary according to program. *Financial support:* Available to part-time students. Applicants required to submit FAFSA. *Unit head:* Dr. Nusha Askari, 650-508-3728, E-mail: naskari@ndnu.edu. *Application contact:* Candace Hallmark, Associate Director of Admissions, 650-508-3592, Fax: 650-508-3426, E-mail: grad.admit@ndnu.edu.

Nova Southeastern University, Center for Psychological Studies, Program in Clinical Psychology, Fort Lauderdale, FL 33314-7796. Offers PhD, Psy D, SPS. *Accreditation:* APA. *Faculty:* 31 full-time (9 women), 12 part-time/adjunct (6 women). *Students:* 524 full-time (421 women); includes 30 Black or African American, non-Hispanic/Latino; 2 American Indian or Alaska Native, non-Hispanic/Latino; 18 Asian, non-Hispanic/Latino; 95 Hispanic/Latino; 1 Two or more races, non-Hispanic/Latino, 13 international. 474 applicants, 30% accepted, 95 enrolled. In 2010, 83 doctorates awarded. *Degree requirements:* For doctorate, thesis/dissertation, clinical internship, competency exam; for SPS, comprehensive exam, internship. *Entrance requirements:* For doctorate, GRE General Test, GRE Subject Test (recommended), 18 credits of course work in psychology including 1 hour of experimental psychology and 3 hours of statistics, minimum undergraduate GPA of 3.0; for SPS, GRE General Test. Additional exam requirements/recommendations for international students: Required—TOEFL (minimum score 550 paper-based; 213 computer-based). *Application deadline:* For fall admission, 1/8 for domestic students. Application fee: $50. Electronic applications accepted. *Expenses:* Contact institution. *Financial support:* In 2010–11, 5 research assistantships, 33 teaching assistantships (averaging $1,000 per year) were awarded; career-related internships or fieldwork, Federal Work-Study, scholarships/grants, and unspecified assistantships also available. Financial award application deadline: 4/1. *Faculty research:* Eating disorders, neuropsychology, family violence, sports psychology, child-pediatric psychology. *Unit head:* Karen Grosby, Dean, 954-262-5701, Fax: 954-262-3859, E-mail: grosby@nova.edu. *Application contact:* Carlos Perez, Enrollment Management, 954-262-5790, Fax: 954-262-3893, E-mail: cpsinfo@cps.nova.edu.

The Ohio State University, Graduate School, College of Arts and Sciences, Division of Social and Behavioral Sciences, Department of Psychology, Columbus, OH 43210. Offers behavioral neuroscience (PhD); clinical psychology (PhD); cognitive psychology (PhD); developmental psychology (PhD); mental retardation and developmental disabilities (PhD); psychology (MA); quantitative psychology (PhD); social psychology (PhD). *Accreditation:* APA (one or more programs are accredited). *Faculty:* 60. *Students:* 106 full-time (65 women), 42 part-time (31 women); includes 5 Black or African American, non-Hispanic/Latino; 1 American Indian or Alaska Native, non-Hispanic/Latino; 5 Asian, non-Hispanic/Latino; 10 Hispanic/Latino; 3 Two or more races, non-Hispanic/Latino, 23 international. Average age 27. In 2010, 21 master's, 22 doctorates awarded. *Degree requirements:* For doctorate, thesis/dissertation. *Entrance requirements:* For master's and doctorate, GRE General Test. Additional exam requirements/recommendations for international students: Required—TOEFL (minimum score 600 paper-based; 250 computer-based). *Application deadline:* For fall admission, 12/31 for domestic students, 11/30 for international students. Applications are processed on a rolling basis. Application fee: $40 ($50 for international students). Electronic applications accepted. *Expenses:* Tuition, state resident: full-time $10,605. Tuition, nonresident: full-time $26,535. Tuition and fees vary according to course load and program. *Financial support:* Fellowships, research assistantships, teaching assistantships available. *Unit head:* Dr. Richard Petty, Chair, 614-292-1640, E-mail: petty.1@osu.edu. *Application contact:* 614-292-9444, Fax: 614-292-3895, E-mail: domestic.grad@osu.edu.

Ohio University, Graduate College, College of Arts and Sciences, Department of Psychology, Program in Clinical Psychology, Athens, OH 45701-2979. Offers PhD. *Accreditation:* APA. *Students:* 41 full-time (32 women), 15 part-time (9 women); includes 9 minority (3 Black or African American, non-Hispanic/Latino; 2 Asian, non-Hispanic/Latino; 1 Hispanic/Latino; 3 Two or more races, non-Hispanic/Latino), 6 international. Average age 28. 122 applicants, 8% accepted, 7 enrolled. In 2010, 12 doctorates awarded. *Degree requirements:* For doctorate, one foreign language, comprehensive exam, thesis/dissertation. *Entrance requirements:* For doctorate, GRE General Test, GRE Subject Test, minimum graduate GPA of 3.4. Additional exam requirements/recommendations for international students: Required—TOEFL. *Application deadline:* For fall admission, 1/1 for domestic students. Application fee: $50 ($55 for international students). *Financial support:* In 2010–11, 41 students received support, including 6 fellowships with full tuition reimbursements available (averaging $16,400 per year), 1 research assistantship with full tuition reimbursement available (averaging $13,200 per year), 9 teaching assistantships with full tuition reimbursements available (averaging $13,200 per year); career-related internships or fieldwork, Federal Work-Study, institutionally sponsored loans, traineeships, tuition waivers (full), and unspecified assistantships also available. Financial award application deadline: 1/15. *Faculty research:* Health psychology, child clinical psychology, psychotherapy outcomes. Total annual research expenditures: $7.3 million. *Unit head:* Christine Gidycz, Director of Clinical Studies, 740-593-1092, Fax: 740-593-0579, E-mail: gidycz@ohio.edu. *Application contact:* Karyl Jones, Administrative Secretary, 740-593-1090, Fax: 740-593-0579, E-mail: psychology@ohio.edu.

Oklahoma State University, College of Arts and Sciences, Department of Psychology, Stillwater, OK 74078. Offers clinical psychology (PhD); general psychology (MS); lifespan development psychology (PhD). *Accreditation:* APA (one or more programs are accredited). *Faculty:* 26 full-time (13 women), 1 (woman) part-time/adjunct. *Students:* 40 full-time (29 women), 12 part-time (6 women); includes 2 Black or African American, non-Hispanic/Latino; 2 American Indian or Alaska Native, non-Hispanic/Latino; 4 Hispanic/Latino, 1 international. Average age 28. 169 applicants, 10% accepted, 13 enrolled. In 2010, 7 master's, 10 doctorates awarded. *Degree requirements:* For master's, thesis or alternative; for doctorate, comprehensive exam, thesis/dissertation. *Entrance requirements:* For master's and doctorate, GRE General Test. Additional exam requirements/recommendations for international students: Required—TOEFL (minimum score 550 paper-based; 79 iBT). *Application deadline:* For fall admission, 3/1 priority date for international students; for spring admission, 8/1 priority date for international students. Applications are processed on a rolling basis. Application fee: $40 ($75 for international students). Electronic applications accepted. *Expenses:* Tuition, state resident: full-time $3716; part-time $154.85 per credit hour. Tuition, nonresident: full-time $14,892; part-time $621 per credit hour. Required fees: $2044; $85.20 per credit hour. One-time fee: $50. Tuition and fees vary according to course load and campus/location. *Financial support:* In 2010–11, 12 research assistantships (averaging $14,763 per year), 38 teaching assistantships (averaging $13,475 per year) were awarded; career-related internships or fieldwork, Federal Work-Study, scholarships/grants, health care benefits, tuition waivers (partial), and unspecified assistantships also available. Support available to part-time students. Financial award application deadline: 3/1; financial award applicants required to submit FAFSA. *Unit head:* Dr. Larry Mullins, Head, 405-744-6028, Fax: 405-744-8067. *Application contact:* Dr. Gordon Emslie, Dean, 405-744-6368, Fax: 405-744-0355, E-mail: grad-i@okstate.edu.

Old Dominion University, College of Sciences, Virginia Consortium Program in Clinical Psychology, Norfolk, VA 23529. Offers Psy D. Program offered jointly with The College of William and Mary, Eastern Virginia Medical School, Norfolk State University. *Faculty:* 10 full-time (5 women). *Students:* 20 part-time (15 women); includes 4 minority (1 Black or African American, non-Hispanic/Latino; 2 Asian, non-Hispanic/Latino; 1 Hispanic/Latino), 1 international. Average age 28. 207 applicants, 8% accepted, 6 enrolled. In 2010, 4 doctorates awarded. *Degree requirements:* For doctorate, comprehensive exam, thesis/dissertation, internship. *Entrance requirements:* For doctorate, GRE General Test. Additional exam requirements/recommendations for international students: Required—TOEFL. *Application deadline:* For fall admission, 1/2 for domestic and international students. Application fee: $40. *Expenses:* Contact institution. *Financial support:* In 2010–11, 26 research assistantships with partial tuition reimbursements (averaging $7,550 per year), 3 teaching assistantships with partial tuition reimbursements (averaging $8,000 per year) were awarded; career-related internships or fieldwork, scholarships/grants, and unspecified assistantships also available. Financial award application deadline: 1/2; financial award applicants required to submit FAFSA. *Faculty research:* Depression, coping with stress, minority and women's issues, family therapy, neuropsychology, assessment, alcohol abuse. *Unit head:* Dr. Louis Janda, Graduate Program Director, 757-683-4211, Fax: 757-368-1823, E-mail: ljanda@odu.edu. *Application contact:* Eileen O'Neill, Coordinator, 757-368-1820, Fax: 757-368-1823, E-mail: exoneill@odu.edu.

Pace University, Dyson College of Arts and Sciences, Department of Psychology, Program in School-Clinical Child Psychology, New York, NY 10038. Offers school psychology (MS Ed); school-clinical psychology (Psy D). *Accreditation:* APA (one or more programs are accredited). Terminal master's awarded for partial completion of doctoral program. *Degree requirements:* For master's, comprehensive exam, qualifying exams, internship; for doctorate, comprehensive exam, qualifying exams, externship, internship, project. *Entrance requirements:* For master's, GRE General Test, GRE Subject Test, interview; for doctorate, GRE General Test, GRE Subject Test (psychology), interview, transcripts, 3 letters of reference. Additional exam requirements/recommendations for international students: Required—TOEFL. Electronic applications accepted.

Pacifica Graduate Institute, Graduate Programs, Carpinteria, CA 93013. Offers clinical psychology (PhD); counseling psychology (MA); depth psychology (MA, PhD); mythological studies (MA, PhD). Terminal master's awarded for partial completion of doctoral program. *Degree requirements:* For master's, thesis (for some programs), practicum; for doctorate, comprehensive exam, thesis/dissertation, internship. *Entrance requirements:* For master's, resume, 3 letters of recommendation, writing sample, interview; for doctorate, resumé, 4 letters of recommendation, writing sample, interview. Additional exam requirements/recommendations for international students: Required—TOEFL. *Faculty research:* Imaginal and archetypal theory; post-Colonial psychoanalytic and Jungian theory; myth literature as it applies to the theory and practice of psychology.

Palo Alto University, PGSP-Stanford Psy D Consortium Program, Palo Alto, CA 94303-4232. Offers Psy D. Program offered jointly with Stanford University. *Accreditation:* APA. *Degree requirements:* For doctorate, thesis/dissertation. *Entrance requirements:* For doctorate, GRE, BA or MA in psychology or related area, minimum undergraduate GPA of 3.0, minimum graduate GPA of 3.3. Additional exam requirements/recommendations for international students: Required—TOEFL. Electronic applications accepted. *Faculty research:* Biopsychosocial research, neurobiology, psychopharmacology.

Palo Alto University, Program in Clinical Psychology, Palo Alto, CA 94303-4232. Offers PhD, JD/PhD, MBA/PhD. JD/PhD offered jointly with Golden Gate University; MBA/PhD with Masagung Graduate School of Management. *Accreditation:* APA. *Degree requirements:* For doctorate, comprehensive exam, thesis/dissertation, 2000 hour clinical internship, oral clinical competency exam. *Entrance requirements:* For doctorate, GRE General Test, BA or MA in psychology or related area, minimum undergraduate GPA of 3.0, 3.3 graduate. Additional exam requirements/recommendations for international students: Required—TOEFL. Electronic applications accepted. *Faculty research:* Child/family studies, health psychology, neuropsychology, personality development, assessment.

Pepperdine University, Graduate School of Education and Psychology, Division of Psychology, MA Program in Clinical Psychology (Day Format), Malibu, CA 90263. Offers marriage and family therapy (MA). *Faculty:* 50 full-time (29 women), 114 part-time/adjunct (68 women). *Students:* 91 full-time (79 women); includes 22 minority (7 Black or African American, non-Hispanic/Latino; 1 American Indian or Alaska Native, non-Hispanic/Latino; 7 Asian, non-Hispanic/Latino; 7 Native Hawaiian or other Pacific Islander, non-Hispanic/Latino). 204 applicants, 36% accepted, 44 enrolled. *Entrance requirements:* For master's, GRE (taken within last five years) or MAT (taken within last two years), two professional recommendations, two- to five-page typed personal statement. Additional exam requirements/recommendations for international students: Required—TOEFL. *Application deadline:* For fall admission, 2/1 for domestic students. Application fee: $55. *Unit head:* Duncan Wigg, Director, 949-223-2522, E-mail: duncan.wigg@pepperdine.edu. *Application contact:* Deanna Schwartz, Psychology Admissions Manager, 310-568-5777, E-mail: deanna.lazaro@pepperdine.edu.

Pepperdine University, Graduate School of Education and Psychology, Division of Psychology, MA Program in Clinical Psychology (Evening Format), Malibu, CA 90263. Offers marriage and family therapy (MA). *Accreditation:* APA. Part-time and evening/weekend programs available. *Faculty:* 50 full-time (29 women), 114 part-time/adjunct (68 women). *Students:* 197 full-time (171 women), 355 part-time (309 women); includes 150 minority (48 Black or African American, non-Hispanic/Latino; 3 American Indian or Alaska Native, non-Hispanic/Latino; 38 Asian, non-Hispanic/Latino; 58 Hispanic/Latino; 2 Native Hawaiian or other Pacific Islander, non-Hispanic/Latino; 1 Two or more races, non-Hispanic/Latino), 4 international. 246 applicants, 75% accepted, 147 enrolled. *Entrance requirements:* For master's, GRE (taken within last five years) or MAT (taken within last two years), two professional recommendations, two- to five-page typed personal statement. Additional exam requirements/recommendations for international students: Required—TOEFL. *Application deadline:* For fall admission, 6/1 priority date for domestic students; for spring admission, 10/1 priority date for domestic students. Applications are processed on a rolling basis. Application fee: $55. *Financial support:* Research assistantships, teaching assistantships available. Financial award application deadline: 7/1; financial award applicants required to submit FAFSA. *Unit head:* Duncan Wigg, Director, 949-223-2522, E-mail: duncan.wigg@pepperdine.edu. *Application contact:* Deanna Schwartz, Psychology Admissions Manager, 310-568-5777, E-mail: deanna.lazaro@pepperdine.edu.

Philadelphia College of Osteopathic Medicine, Graduate and Professional Programs, Department of Psychology, Philadelphia, PA 19131-1694. Offers clinical psychology (Psy D); counseling and clinical health psychology (MS); organizational leadership and development (MS); psychology (Certificate, Post-Doctoral Certificate); school psychology (MS, Psy D, Ed S). *Accreditation:* APA. *Degree requirements:* For master's, thesis; for doctorate, comprehensive exam, thesis/dissertation, final project, fieldwork. *Entrance requirements:* For master's, GRE or MAT, minimum GPA of 3.0; course work in biology, chemistry, English, physics; for other advanced degree, PRAXIS. *Faculty research:* Depression in primary care, integrated primary care, geriatric mental health.

See Display on page 932 and Close-Up on page 1167.

Ponce School of Medicine, Program in Clinical Psychology, Ponce, PR 00732-7004. Offers PhD, Psy D. *Accreditation:* APA. *Faculty:* 13 full-time (5 women), 5 part-time/adjunct (4 women). *Students:* 215 full-time (189 women); includes 192 Hispanic/Latino. Average age 27. 133 applicants, 45% accepted, 48 enrolled. In 2010, 27 doctorates awarded. *Degree requirements:* For doctorate, one foreign language, comprehensive exam, thesis/dissertation, internship. *Entrance requirements:* For doctorate, GRE General Test or EXADEP, proficiency in Spanish and English; 2 letters of recommendation; minimum undergraduate GPA of 2.7, graduate 3.0; criminal background check. *Application deadline:* For fall admission, 3/15 for domestic and international students. Application fee: $100. *Expenses:* Tuition: Full-time $22,983.70; part-time $200 per credit. Required fees: $2728.60. Full-time tuition and fees vary according to course level. *Financial support:* In 2010–11, 14 students received support; fellowships, scholarships/grants available. Financial award application deadline: 4/30; financial award applicants required to submit FAFSA. *Unit head:* Dr. Jose Pons, Head, 787-840-2575, E-mail: jpons@psm.edu. *Application contact:* Maria Colon, Admissions Officer, 787-840-2575 Ext. 2143, E-mail: mcolon@psm.edu.

Pontifical Catholic University of Puerto Rico, College of Graduate Studies in Behavioral Science and Community Affairs, Program in Clinical Psychology (Doctorate), Ponce, PR 00717-0777. Offers PhD, Psy D. Part-time and evening/weekend programs available. *Degree* *requirements:* For doctorate, comprehensive exam, thesis/dissertation. *Entrance requirements:* For doctorate, EXADEP, minimum GPA of 2.75.

Pontificia Universidad Catolica Madre y Maestra, Graduate School, Faculty of Social and Administrative Sciences, Santiago, Dominican Republic. Offers business administration (MBA), including business development, finance, international business, management skills (M Mgmt, MBA), marketing, operations, strategic cost management, strategy, tourist destination planning and management; law (LL M), including civil law, corporate business law, criminal law, international relations, real estate law; management (M Mgmt), including higher financial management, insurance program administration, management skills (M Mgmt, MBA); psychology (MA), including clinical child and adolescent psychology, forensic psychology; strategic human resources (EMBA).

Prairie View A&M University, College of Arts and Sciences, Department of Biology, Prairie View, TX 77446-0519. Offers bio- environmental toxicology (MS); biology (MS). Part-time and evening/weekend programs available. *Faculty:* 5 full-time (2 women). *Students:* 6 full-time (4 women), 3 part-time (2 women); includes all Black or African American, non-Hispanic/Latino. Average age 25. 14 applicants, 86% accepted. In 2010, 1 master's awarded. *Degree requirements:* For master's, comprehensive exam, thesis optional. *Entrance requirements:* For master's, GRE General Test. Additional exam requirements/recommendations for international students: Required—TOEFL. *Application deadline:* For fall admission, 7/1 for domestic and international students; for spring admission, 11/1 for domestic and international students. Applications are processed on a rolling basis. *Expenses:* Tuition, state resident: full-time $3586.14; part-time $119.06 per credit hour. Tuition, nonresident: part-time $511.23 per credit hour. *Financial support:* In 2010–11, 3 students received support, including 3 teaching assistantships (averaging $13,440 per year); Federal Work-Study and unspecified assistantships also available. Financial award application deadline: 4/1; financial award applicants required to submit FAFSA. *Faculty research:* Geonomics, hypertension, control of gene express, proteins, kigands that interact with hormone receptors, prostate cancer, renin-angiotensin yeast metabolism. *Unit head:* Dr. Harriette Howard-Lee-Block, Head, 936-261-3160, Fax: 936-261-3179, E-mail: hlblock@pvamu.edu. *Application contact:* Dr. Seab A. Smith, Associate Professor, 936-261-3169, Fax: 936-261-3179, E-mail: sasmith@pvamu.edu.

Prairie View A&M University, College of Juvenile Justice and Psychology, Prairie View, TX 77446-0519. Offers clinical adolescent psychology (PhD); juvenile forensic psychology (MSJFP); juvenile justice (MSJJ, PhD). Part-time and evening/weekend programs available. *Faculty:* 12 full-time (7 women). *Students:* 48 full-time (35 women), 30 part-time (22 women); includes 64 Black or African American, non-Hispanic/Latino; 3 Hispanic/Latino, 4 international. Average age 26. 55 applicants, 60% accepted, 33 enrolled. In 2010, 20 master's, 1 doctorate awarded. *Degree requirements:* For master's, comprehensive exam (for some programs), thesis (for some programs); for doctorate, comprehensive exam, thesis/dissertation. *Entrance requirements:* For master's, GRE, minimum GPA of 2.75; for doctorate, GRE, previous course work in clinical adolescent psychology, minimum GPA of 3.5. Additional exam requirements/recommendations for international students: Required—TOEFL. *Application deadline:* For fall admission, 3/1 for domestic and international students; for spring admission, 10/1 for domestic and international students. Applications are processed on a rolling basis. Application fee: $50. *Expenses:* Tuition, state resident: full-time $3586.14; part-time $119.06 per credit hour. Tuition, nonresident: part-time $511.23 per credit hour. *Financial support:* In 2010–11, 23 students received support, including 12 research assistantships (averaging $15,000 per year), 11 teaching assistantships (averaging $20,000 per year); career-related internships or fieldwork, Federal Work-Study, institutionally sponsored loans, tuition waivers (full and partial), and unspecified assistantships also available. Support available to part-time students. Financial award application deadline: 3/1; financial award applicants required to submit FAFSA. *Faculty research:* Juvenile justice, juvenile forensic psychology, teen court, graduate education, capital punishment. Total annual research expenditures: $2,888. *Unit head:* Dr. Dennis E. Daniels, Interim Dean, 936-261-5205, Fax: 936-261-5252, E-mail: dedaniels@pvamu.edu. *Application contact:* Sandy Siegmund, Executive Secretary, Graduate Program, 936-261-5234, Fax: 936-261-5249, E-mail: sisiegmund@pvamu.edu.

Queens College of the City University of New York, Division of Graduate Studies, Mathematics and Natural Sciences Division, Department of Psychology, Flushing, NY 11367-1597. Offers clinical behavioral applications in mental health settings (MA); psychology (MA). Part-time programs available. *Faculty:* 27 full-time (13 women). *Students:* 13 full-time (10 women), 92 part-time (78 women); includes 7 Black or African American, non-Hispanic/Latino; 1 American Indian or Alaska Native, non-Hispanic/Latino; 7 Asian, non-Hispanic/Latino; 14 Hispanic/Latino, 6 international. 134 applicants, 47% accepted, 48 enrolled. In 2010, 28 master's awarded. *Degree requirements:* For master's, comprehensive exam, thesis or alternative. *Entrance requirements:* For master's, GRE, minimum GPA of 3.0. Additional exam requirements/recommendations for international students: Required—TOEFL. *Application deadline:* For fall admission, 4/1 for domestic students; for spring admission, 11/1 for domestic students. Applications are processed on a rolling basis. Application fee: $125. *Financial support:* Career-related internships or fieldwork, Federal Work-Study, institutionally sponsored loans, and tuition waivers (partial) available. Support available to part-time students. Financial award application deadline: 4/1; financial award applicants required to submit FAFSA. *Unit head:* Dr. Richard Bodnar, Chairperson, 718-997-3200. *Application contact:* Dr. Philip Ramsey, Graduate Adviser, 718-997-3200, E-mail: philip_ramsey@qc.edu.

Queen's University at Kingston, School of Graduate Studies and Research, Faculty of Arts and Sciences, Department of Psychology, Kingston, ON K7L 3N6, Canada. Offers brain behavior and cognitive science (MA, PhD); clinical psychology (MA, PhD); developmental psychology (MA, PhD); social personality psychology (MA, PhD). *Accreditation:* APA (one or more programs are accredited). *Degree requirements:* For master's, thesis; for doctorate, comprehensive exam, thesis/dissertation. *Entrance requirements:* For master's and doctorate, GRE General Test. Additional exam requirements/recommendations for international students: Required—TOEFL. *Faculty research:* Human development, social, personality, behavioral neuroscience, forensic.

Quincy University, Program in Counseling, Quincy, IL 62301-2699. Offers education (MS Ed), including clinical mental health counseling, school counseling. Part-time and evening/weekend programs available. *Faculty:* 2 full-time (1 woman). *Students:* 2 full-time (both women), 17 part-time (15 women); includes 1 Black or African American, non-Hispanic/Latino; 1 Two or more races, non-Hispanic/Latino. In 2010, 17 master's awarded. *Degree requirements:* For master's, comprehensive exam, practicum, internship. *Entrance requirements:* For master's, MAT or GRE. Additional exam requirements/recommendations for international students: Required—TOEFL (minimum score 550 paper-based). *Application deadline:* Applications are processed on a rolling basis. Application fee: $25. Electronic applications accepted. *Expenses:* Tuition: Full-time $8880; part-time $370 per semester hour. Required fees: $360; $15 per semester hour. Tuition and fees vary according to course load, campus/location and program. *Financial support:* Available to part-time students. Applicants required to submit FAFSA. *Unit head:* Dr. Kenneth Oliver, Director, 217-228-5432 Ext. 3113, E-mail: oliveke@quincy.edu. *Application contact:* Jennifer Bang, Coordinator of Adult Studies, 217-228-5404, Fax: 217-228-5479, E-mail: admissions@quincy.edu.

Radford University, College of Graduate and Professional Studies, College of Humanities and Behavioral Sciences, Program in Psychology, Radford, VA 24142. Offers clinical psychology (MA, MS); experimental psychology (MA, MS); general psychology (MS); industrial/organizational psychology (MA, MS). Part-time programs available. *Faculty:* 18 full-time (7 women), 4 part-time/adjunct (2 women). *Students:* 41 full-time (29 women); includes 6 minority (4 Black or African American, non-Hispanic/Latino; 1 Asian, non-Hispanic/Latino; 1 Hispanic/Latino). Average age 23. 107 applicants, 71% accepted, 23 enrolled. In 2010, 21 master's awarded. *Degree requirements:* For master's, comprehensive exam, thesis (for some programs). *Entrance requirements:* For master's, GRE, minimum GPA of 3.0; 3 letters of reference; essay. Additional exam requirements/recommendations for international students: Required—TOEFL (minimum

score 550 paper-based; 213 computer-based; 79 iBT). *Application deadline:* For fall admission, 2/15 priority date for domestic students, 12/1 for international students; for spring admission, 7/1 for international students. Applications are processed on a rolling basis. Application fee: $50. Electronic applications accepted. *Expenses:* Tuition, state resident: full-time $5746; part-time $239 per credit hour. Tuition, nonresident: full-time $14,174; part-time $591 per credit hour. Required fees: $2634; $111 per credit hour. *Financial support:* In 2010–11, 33 students received support, including 18 research assistantships with partial tuition reimbursements available (averaging $8,000 per year), 14 teaching assistantships with partial tuition reimbursements available (averaging $8,700 per year); career-related internships or fieldwork, institutionally sponsored loans, scholarships/grants, and unspecified assistantships also available. Financial award application deadline: 3/1; financial award applicants required to submit FAFSA. *Unit head:* Dr. Hilary M. Lips, Chair, 540-831-5387, Fax: 540-831-6113, E-mail: hlips@radford.edu. *Application contact:* Rebecca Conner, Graduate Admissions Office, 540-831-5431, Fax: 540-831-6061, E-mail: gradcollege@radford.edu.

Regent University, Graduate School, School of Psychology and Counseling, Virginia Beach, VA 23464-9800. Offers clinical psychology (MA, Psy D); counseling studies (CAGS); counselor education and supervision (PhD); human services counseling (MA), including community counseling, school counseling; M Div/MA; M Ed/MA; MBA/MA. PhD program offered online only. *Accreditation:* ACA; APA (one or more programs are accredited). Part-time and evening/weekend programs available. Postbaccalaureate distance learning degree programs offered (minimal on-campus study). *Faculty:* 31 full-time (16 women), 23 part-time/adjunct (14 women). *Students:* 235 full-time (190 women), 203 part-time (158 women); includes 104 Black or African American, non-Hispanic/Latino; 7 Asian, non-Hispanic/Latino; 11 Hispanic/Latino, 13 international. Average age 35. 436 applicants, 49% accepted, 111 enrolled. In 2010, 82 master's, 57 doctorates awarded. *Degree requirements:* For master's, thesis or alternative, internship, practicum, written competency exam; for doctorate, thesis/dissertation or alternative. *Entrance requirements:* For master's, GRE General Test including writing exam, minimum undergraduate GPA of 2.75, 3 recommendations, resume, transcripts, writing sample; for doctorate, GRE General Test including writing exam, GRE Subject Test, minimum undergraduate GPA of 3.0, 3.5 (PhD), 10-15 minute VHS tape demonstrating counseling skills, writing sample, 3 recommendations, resume. Additional exam requirements/recommendations for international students: Required—TOEFL (minimum score 577 paper-based; 233 computer-based). *Application deadline:* For fall admission, 4/1 priority date for domestic students; for spring admission, 11/1 priority date for domestic students. Applications are processed on a rolling basis. Application fee: $50. Electronic applications accepted. *Expenses:* Contact institution. *Financial support:* Research assistantships with full and partial tuition reimbursements, teaching assistantships with full and partial tuition reimbursements, career-related internships or fieldwork, scholarships/grants, and tuition waivers (full and partial) available. Support available to part-time students. Financial award application deadline: 9/1; financial award applicants required to submit FAFSA. *Faculty research:* Marriage enrichment, AIDS counseling, troubled youth, faith and learning, trauma. *Unit head:* Dr. William Hathaway, Acting Dean, 757-352-4294, Fax: 757-352-4282, E-mail: willhat@regent.edu. *Application contact:* Matthew Chadwick, Director of Enrollment Support Services, 800-373-5504, Fax: 757-352-4381, E-mail: admissions@regent.edu.

Rivier College, School of Graduate Studies, Department of Psychology, Nashua, NH 03060. Offers clinical psychology (MS); experimental psychology (MS). *Faculty:* 5 full-time (2 women). *Students:* 10 full-time (7 women). Average age 28. 9 applicants, 11% accepted, 1 enrolled. In 2010, 4 master's awarded. Application fee: $25. *Expenses:* Tuition: Part-time $456 per credit. *Unit head:* Dr. Howard Goodman, Department Coordinator, 603-897-8602, E-mail: hgoodman@rivier.edu. *Application contact:* Mathew Kittredge, Director of Graduate Admissions, 603-897-8229, Fax: 603-897-8810, E-mail: mkittredge@rivier.edu.

Roosevelt University, Graduate Division, College of Arts and Sciences, Department of Psychology, Program in Clinical Professional Psychology, Chicago, IL 60605. Offers MA. *Accreditation:* APA.

Rowan University, Graduate School, College of Liberal Arts and Sciences, Department of Psychology, Program in Clinical Mental Health Counseling, Glassboro, NJ 08028-1701. Offers MA. Part-time and evening/weekend programs available. *Students:* 34 applicants, 26% accepted, 9 enrolled. *Entrance requirements:* For master's, GRE General Test. Additional exam requirements/recommendations for international students: Required—TOEFL. *Application deadline:* Applications are processed on a rolling basis. Application fee: $65 ($200 for international students). Electronic applications accepted. *Expenses:* Tuition, area resident: Part-time $602 per semester hour. Tuition, nonresident: part-time $602 per semester hour. Required fees: $100 per semester hour. One-time fee: $10 part-time. *Financial support:* Career-related internships or fieldwork, Federal Work-Study, and unspecified assistantships available. Support available to part-time students. *Unit head:* Dr. Horacio Sosa, Dean, College of Graduate and Continuing Education, 856-256-4747, Fax: 856-256-5638, E-mail: lalovic-hand@rowan.edu. *Application contact:* Karen Haynes, Graduate Coordinator, 856-256-4052, Fax: 856-256-4436, E-mail: haynes@rowan.edu.

Rutgers, The State University of New Jersey, New Brunswick, Graduate School-New Brunswick, Program in Psychology, Piscataway, NJ 08854-8097. Offers behavioral neuroscience (PhD); clinical psychology (PhD); cognitive psychology (PhD); interdisciplinary health psychology (PhD); social psychology (PhD). *Accreditation:* APA. *Degree requirements:* For doctorate, comprehensive exam, thesis/dissertation. *Entrance requirements:* For doctorate, GRE General Test, 3 letters of recommendation. Additional exam requirements/recommendations for international students: Required—TOEFL (minimum score 577 paper-based; 233 computer-based). Electronic applications accepted. *Expenses:* Tuition, state resident: full-time $7200; part-time $600 per credit. Tuition, nonresident: full-time $11,124; part-time $927 per credit. *Faculty research:* Learning and memory, behavioral ecology, hormones and behavior, psychopharmacology, anxiety disorders.

Rutgers, The State University of New Jersey, New Brunswick, Graduate School of Applied and Professional Psychology, Department of Clinical Psychology, Piscataway, NJ 08854-8097. Offers Psy M, Psy D. *Accreditation:* APA (one or more programs are accredited). *Faculty:* 14 full-time (6 women), 10 part-time/adjunct (7 women). *Students:* 103 full-time (71 women); includes 9 Asian, non-Hispanic/Latino; 13 Hispanic/Latino, 6 international. Average age 32. 414 applicants, 7% accepted, 17 enrolled. In 2010, 10 master's, 9 doctorates awarded. *Degree requirements:* For doctorate, comprehensive exam, thesis/dissertation, 1 year internship. *Entrance requirements:* For doctorate, GRE General Test, GRE Subject Test, bachelor's degree in psychology or equivalent. Additional exam requirements/recommendations for international students: Required—TOEFL. *Application deadline:* For fall admission, 1/5 for domestic and international students. Application fee: $65. Electronic applications accepted. *Expenses:* Contact institution. *Financial support:* In 2010–11, 19 fellowships with partial tuition reimbursements (averaging $12,679 per year), 3 teaching assistantships with full tuition reimbursements (averaging $16,988 per year) were awarded; research assistantships with full tuition reimbursements, career-related internships or fieldwork, Federal Work-Study, institutionally sponsored loans, scholarships/grants, traineeships, and unspecified assistantships also available. Support available to part-time students. Financial award application deadline: 3/15; financial award applicants required to submit FAFSA. *Faculty research:* Long- and short-term dynamic therapy, community psychology, cognitive-behavioral therapy: anxiety and depressive disorders, addictive behaviors: eating disorders and alcoholism. *Unit head:* Dr. Brenna H. Bry, Chair, 732-445-2000 Ext. 114, Fax: 732-445-4888, E-mail: bbry@rci.rutgers.edu. *Application contact:* Alicia M. Picone, Administrative Assistant, 732-445-2000 Ext. 117, Fax: 732-445-4888, E-mail: clinpsyd@rci.rutgers.edu.

St. John's University, St. John's College of Liberal Arts and Sciences, Department of Psychology, Program in Clinical Psychology, Queens, NY 11439. Offers clinical psychology (MA); clinical psychology-child (PhD); clinical psychology-general (PhD). *Accreditation:* APA. *Students:* 35 full-time (29 women), 31 part-time (23 women); includes 17 minority (6 Black or

Clinical Psychology

St. John's University (continued)
African American, non-Hispanic/Latino; 6 Asian, non-Hispanic/Latino; 3 Hispanic/Latino; 2 Two or more races, non-Hispanic/Latino), 5 international. Average age 27. 308 applicants, 7% accepted, 10 enrolled. In 2010, 12 master's, 11 doctorates awarded. *Degree requirements:* For doctorate, comprehensive exam, thesis/dissertation, internship, externship. *Entrance requirements:* For doctorate, GRE General Test, GRE Subject Test, 24 credits of undergraduate course work in psychology, 2 writing samples. Additional exam requirements/recommendations for international students: Required—TOEFL (minimum score 600 paper-based; 250 computer-based; 100 iBT), IELTS (minimum score 5.5). *Application deadline:* For fall admission, 1/15 priority date for domestic and international students. Applications are processed on a rolling basis. Application fee: $70. Electronic applications accepted. *Expenses:* Contact institution. *Financial support:* Fellowships, research assistantships, career-related internships or fieldwork and scholarships/grants available. Support available to part-time students. Financial award application deadline: 3/1; financial award applicants required to submit FAFSA. *Faculty research:* Cognitive-behavioral therapy, sucking cessation pedagogical research and implicit attitudes. *Unit head:* Dr. Jeffrey S. Nevid, Director, 718-990-1548, E-mail: nevidj@stjohns.edu. *Application contact:* Kathleen Davis, Director of Graduate Admission, 718-990-1601, Fax: 718-990-5686, E-mail: gradhelp@stjohns.edu.

Saint Louis University, Graduate Education, College of Arts and Sciences and Graduate Education, Department of Psychology, St. Louis, MO 63103-2097. Offers clinical psychology (MS-R, PhD); experimental psychology (MS-R, PhD); industrial-organizational psychology (PhD); psychology (PhD). *Accreditation:* APA (one or more programs are accredited). Part-time programs available. *Degree requirements:* For master's, comprehensive exam, thesis; for doctorate, thesis/dissertation, clinical internship (for clinical psychology PhD). *Entrance requirements:* For master's, GRE General Test, interview, letters of recommendation, resume; for doctorate, GRE General Test, interview, letters of recommendation, resumé, transcripts, goal statement. Additional exam requirements/recommendations for international students: Required—TOEFL (minimum score 550 paper-based; 213 computer-based). Electronic applications accepted. *Faculty research:* Violence and trauma; neural basis of learning and memory function; eating disorders; body image and health behavior; prejudice, stereotyping, and victimization; memory, cognitive aging and language processing.

St. Mary's University, Graduate School, Department of Psychology, Program in Clinical Psychology, San Antonio, TX 78228-8507. Offers MA, MS. Part-time programs available. *Degree requirements:* For master's, comprehensive exam, practica. *Entrance requirements:* For master's, GRE General Test. Additional exam requirements/recommendations for international students: Required—TOEFL (minimum score 550 paper-based; 213 computer-based; 80 iBT). Electronic applications accepted.

Saint Michael's College, Graduate Programs, Program in Clinical Psychology, Colchester, VT 05439. Offers MA. Part-time and evening/weekend programs available. *Degree requirements:* For master's, thesis or alternative, internship, practicum, research seminar. *Entrance requirements:* For master's, GRE General Test, GRE Subject Test, undergraduate major in psychology or related area, minimum 12 credits in psychology, minimum GPA of 3.0. Electronic applications accepted. *Faculty research:* Psychodynamic psychotherapy, family therapy, philosophical foundations of clinical psychology.

Sam Houston State University, College of Humanities and Social Sciences, Department of Psychology and Philosophy, Huntsville, TX 77341. Offers clinical psychology (PhD); psychology (MA). *Accreditation:* APA. Part-time programs available. *Faculty:* 13 full-time (5 women), 1 part-time/adjunct (0 women). *Students:* 62 full-time (52 women), 31 part-time (24 women); includes 5 Black or African American, non-Hispanic/Latino; 3 Asian, non-Hispanic/Latino; 6 Hispanic/Latino, 5 international. Average age 26. 113 applicants, 29% accepted, 24 enrolled. In 2010, 20 master's, 4 doctorates awarded. *Degree requirements:* For master's, thesis. *Entrance requirements:* For master's, GRE General Test or MAT, minimum GPA of 3.0. Additional exam requirements/recommendations for international students: Required—TOEFL (minimum score 550 paper-based; 213 computer-based; 79 iBT). *Application deadline:* For fall admission, 8/1 for domestic students; for spring admission, 12/1 for domestic students. Applications are processed on a rolling basis. Application fee: $20. *Expenses:* Tuition, state resident: full-time $1363; part-time $163 per credit hour. Tuition, nonresident: full-time $3856; part-time $473 per credit hour. *Financial support:* Research assistantships, teaching assistantships, career-related internships or fieldwork and institutionally sponsored loans available. Support available to part-time students. Financial award application deadline: 5/31; financial award applicants required to submit FAFSA. *Unit head:* Dr. Christopher Wilson, Chair, 936-294-3052, Fax: 936-294-3798, E-mail: psy_dcw@shsu.edu. *Application contact:* Dr. Jeffrey Anastasi, Coordinator, 936-294-3049, Fax: 936-294-3798, E-mail: jsa001@shsu.edu.

San Diego State University, Graduate and Research Affairs, College of Sciences, Department of Psychology, San Diego, CA 92182. Offers clinical psychology (MS, PhD); industrial and organizational psychology (MS); program evaluation (MS); psychology (MA). PhD offered jointly with University of California, San Diego. *Accreditation:* APA (one or more programs are accredited). Terminal master's awarded for partial completion of doctoral program. *Degree requirements:* For master's, thesis, oral exam; for doctorate, thesis/dissertation. *Entrance requirements:* For master's, GRE General Test, GRE Subject Test, 3 letters of recommendation; for doctorate, GRE General Test, GRE Subject Test, minimum GPA of 3.0, 3 letters of recommendation. Additional exam requirements/recommendations for international students: Required—TOEFL. Electronic applications accepted.

San Francisco State University, Division of Graduate Studies, College of Behavioral and Social Sciences, Department of Psychology, San Francisco, CA 94132-1722. Offers clinical psychology (MS); developmental psychology (MA); industrial/organizational psychology (MS); psychological research (MA); school psychology (MS); social psychology (MA). *Financial support:* Teaching assistantships available. Financial award application deadline: 3/1. *Unit head:* Dr. Julia Lewis, Chair, 415-338-7555, E-mail: jmlewis@sfsu.edu. *Application contact:* Leslye M. Tinson, Assistant to the Chair, 415-338-7555, E-mail: ltinson@sfsu.edu.

San Jose State University, Graduate Studies and Research, College of Social Sciences, Department of Psychology, San Jose, CA 95192-0001. Offers clinical psychology (MS); experimental psychology (MA); industrial/organizational psychology (MS); psychology (MA). *Degree requirements:* For master's, comprehensive exam, thesis (for some programs). *Entrance requirements:* For master's, GRE General Test, minimum GPA of 3.0. Electronic applications accepted. *Faculty research:* Drug and alcohol abuse, neurohormonal mechanisms in motion sickness, behavior modification, sleep research, genetics.

Saybrook University, Graduate College of Psychology and Humanistic Studies, San Francisco, CA 94111-1920. Offers clinical psychology (Psy D); human science (MA, PhD), including consciousness and spirituality, humanistic and transpersonal psychology, integrative health studies, organizational systems, social transformation, transformative social change (MA); organizational systems (MA, PhD), including consciousness and spirituality, humanistic and transpersonal psychology, integrative health studies, leadership of sustainable systems (MA), organizational systems, social transformation; psychology (MA, PhD), including clinical psychology (PhD), consciousness and spirituality, creativity studies (MA), humanistic and transpersonal psychology, integrative health studies, Jungian studies, marriage and family therapy (MA), organizational systems, social transformation. Postbaccalaureate distance learning degree programs offered (minimal on-campus study). *Faculty:* 15 full-time (5 women), 83 part-time/adjunct (34 women). *Students:* 479 full-time (333 women); includes 30 Black or African American, non-Hispanic/Latino; 1 American Indian or Alaska Native, non-Hispanic/Latino; 13 Asian, non-Hispanic/Latino; 18 Hispanic/Latino, 18 international. Average age 43. 280 applicants, 52% accepted, 105 enrolled. In 2010, 28 master's, 43 doctorates awarded. Terminal master's awarded for partial completion of doctoral program. *Degree requirements:* For master's, thesis or alternative; for doctorate, thesis/dissertation. *Entrance requirements:* Additional exam requirements/recommendations for international students: Required—TOEFL (minimum score 580 paper-based; 237 computer-based; 93 iBT). *Application deadline:* For fall admission, 6/1 priority date for domestic students; for spring admission, 12/16 priority date for domestic students. Application fee: $50. Electronic applications accepted. *Financial support:* In 2010–11, 335 students received support. Scholarships/grants available. Financial award applicants required to submit FAFSA. *Faculty research:* Humanistic theory, health studies, organizational systems, consciousness and spirituality, social transformation. Total annual research expenditures: $90,000. *Unit head:* Mark Schulman, President, 800-825-4480, Fax: 415-433-9271. *Application contact:* Director of Admissions, 800-825-4480, Fax: 415-433-9271, E-mail: admissions@saybrook.edu.

The School of Professional Psychology at Forest Institute, Graduate Programs, Springfield, MO 65807. Offers applied behavior analysis (MS); clinical psychology (MA, Psy D); counseling psychology (MA); marriage and family therapy (MA, PGC). *Accreditation:* AAMFT/COAMFTE; APA (one or more programs are accredited). *Faculty:* 17 full-time (8 women), 18 part-time/adjunct (10 women). *Students:* 214 full-time (144 women), 46 part-time (35 women); includes 35 minority (11 Black or African American, non-Hispanic/Latino; 9 American Indian or Alaska Native, non-Hispanic/Latino; 5 Asian, non-Hispanic/Latino; 10 Hispanic/Latino), 3 international. Average age 28. 176 applicants, 69% accepted, 45 enrolled. In 2010, 35 master's, 31 doctorates awarded. Terminal master's awarded for partial completion of doctoral program. *Degree requirements:* For master's, thesis, practicum; for doctorate, comprehensive exam, thesis/dissertation, internship, practicum. *Entrance requirements:* For master's, GRE General Test, interview, minimum GPA of 3.0, 12 hours in psychology; for doctorate, GRE General Test, interview, minimum GPA of 3.0, 18 hours in psychology. Additional exam requirements/recommendations for international students: Required—TOEFL (minimum score 550 paper-based; 213 computer-based). *Application deadline:* For fall admission, 1/15 priority date for domestic and international students; for spring admission, 8/1 priority date for domestic and international students. Applications are processed on a rolling basis. Application fee: $50. Electronic applications accepted. *Financial support:* In 2010–11, 59 students received support; fellowships with partial tuition reimbursements available, teaching assistantships, career-related internships or fieldwork, Federal Work-Study, scholarships/grants, tuition waivers (partial), and unspecified assistantships available. Financial award applicants required to submit FAFSA. *Faculty research:* Forensics/corrections, marriage and family therapy, child and adolescent, integrated health care, neuropsychology. *Unit head:* Dr. Mark E. Skrade, President, 417-823-3477, Fax: 417-823-3442, E-mail: mskrade@forest.edu. *Application contact:* Bethany Ritter, Admissions Counselor, 417-823-3477, Fax: 417-823-3442, E-mail: britter@forest.edu.

Seattle Pacific University, PhD in Clinical Psychology Program, Seattle, WA 98119-1997. Offers PhD. *Accreditation:* APA. *Faculty:* 8 full-time (5 women), 3 part-time/adjunct (0 women). *Students:* 44 full-time (36 women), 29 part-time (23 women); includes 12 minority (5 Asian, non-Hispanic/Latino; 3 Hispanic/Latino; 4 Two or more races, non-Hispanic/Latino). Average age 29. 127 applicants, 8% accepted, 10 enrolled. In 2010, 13 doctorates awarded. *Degree requirements:* For doctorate, thesis/dissertation, clinical internship, practicum. *Entrance requirements:* For doctorate, GRE (preferred minimum score 1100 verbal and quantitative, taken within the last five years). Additional exam requirements/recommendations for international students: Required—TOEFL (minimum score 600 paper-based; 250 computer-based). *Application deadline:* For fall admission, 12/15 for domestic and international students. Electronic applications accepted. *Expenses:* Contact institution. *Financial support:* In 2010–11, 65 students received support; fellowships, scholarships/grants available. Financial award applicants required to submit FAFSA. *Faculty research:* Social network support, attachment, integration of faith and family psychology, developmental psychology. *Unit head:* Dr. Jay Skidmore, Chair, 206-281-2916. *Application contact:* Dr. Jay Skidmore, Chair, 206-281-2916.

Shippensburg University of Pennsylvania, School of Graduate Studies, College of Education and Human Services, Department of Counseling, Shippensburg, PA 17257-2299. Offers Adlerian studies (Certificate); advanced study in counseling (Certificate); alcohol and drug counseling (Certificate); counseling (M Ed, MS), including clinical mental health counseling (MS), college counseling (MS), college student personnel services (MS), elementary school counseling (M Ed), secondary school counseling (MS); couple and family counseling (Certificate). *Accreditation:* ACA (one or more programs are accredited); NCATE. Part-time and evening/weekend programs available. *Faculty:* 8 full-time (4 women), 5 part-time/adjunct (3 women). *Students:* 79 full-time (66 women), 105 part-time (92 women); includes 28 minority (20 Black or African American, non-Hispanic/Latino; 3 Asian, non-Hispanic/Latino; 4 Hispanic/Latino; 1 Two or more races, non-Hispanic/Latino), 2 international. Average age 29. 129 applicants, 45% accepted, 43 enrolled. In 2010, 45 master's awarded. *Degree requirements:* For master's, fieldwork, research project, internship, candidacy. *Entrance requirements:* For master's, GRE or MAT (mental health, student personnel, and college counseling applicants if GPA is less than 2.75), minimum GPA of 2.75 (3.0 for M Ed), resume, 3 letters of recommendation, supplemental data forms, one year of relevant work experience, on-campus interview, autobiographical statement. Additional exam requirements/recommendations for international students: Required—TOEFL (minimum score 580 paper-based; 237 computer-based); Recommended—IELTS (minimum score 6). *Application deadline:* For fall admission, 3/1 for international students; for spring admission, 7/1 for international students. Applications are processed on a rolling basis. Application fee: $30. Electronic applications accepted. *Expenses:* Tuition, state resident: full-time $6966. Tuition, nonresident: full-time $11,146. Required fees: $1802. *Financial support:* In 2010–11, 49 research assistantships with full tuition reimbursements (averaging $5,000 per year) were awarded; career-related internships or fieldwork, scholarships/grants, unspecified assistantships, and resident hall director and student payroll positions also available. Support available to part-time students. Financial award application deadline: 3/1; financial award applicants required to submit FAFSA. *Unit head:* Dr. Jan Arminio, Chairperson, 717-477-1668, Fax: 717-477-4016, E-mail: jlarmi@ship.edu. *Application contact:* Jeremy R. Goshorn, Associate Dean of Graduate Admissions, 717-477-1231, Fax: 717-477-4016, E-mail: jrgoshorn@ship.edu.

Southeastern Oklahoma State University, School of Behavioral Sciences, Durant, OK 74701-0609. Offers clinical mental health counseling (MS). Part-time and evening/weekend programs available. *Faculty:* 10 full-time (3 women). *Students:* 29 full-time (23 women), 14 part-time (12 women); includes 2 Black or African American, non-Hispanic/Latino; 12 American Indian or Alaska Native, non-Hispanic/Latino; 1 Asian, non-Hispanic/Latino; 1 Hispanic/Latino, 2 international. Average age 35. 12 applicants, 100% accepted, 12 enrolled. *Degree requirements:* For master's, thesis optional. *Entrance requirements:* For master's, GRE General Test, minimum GPA of 3.0 in last 60 hours or 2.75 overall. Additional exam requirements/recommendations for international students: Required—TOEFL (minimum score 550 paper-based; 213 computer-based). *Application deadline:* For fall admission, 8/1 for domestic students, 6/1 for international students; for spring admission, 1/5 for domestic students, 11/1 for international students. Application fee: $20 ($55 for international students). Electronic applications accepted. *Financial support:* Fellowships, research assistantships, teaching assistantships, Federal Work-Study available. Support available to part-time students. Financial award application deadline: 6/15. *Unit head:* Dr. Kimberly Donovan, Program Coordinator, 580-745-2312, E-mail: kdonovan@se.edu. *Application contact:* Carrie Williamson, Graduate Secretary, 580-745-2200, Fax: 580-745-7474, E-mail: cwilliamson@se.edu.

Southern Illinois University Carbondale, Graduate School, College of Liberal Arts, Department of Psychology, Carbondale, IL 62901-4701. Offers clinical psychology (MA, MS, PhD); counseling psychology (MA, MS, PhD); experimental psychology (MA, MS, PhD). *Accreditation:* APA (one or more programs are accredited). *Degree requirements:* For master's, thesis; for doctorate, thesis/dissertation. *Entrance requirements:* For master's, GRE General Test, GRE Subject Test, minimum GPA of 2.7; for doctorate, GRE General Test, GRE Subject Test, minimum GPA of 3.25. Additional exam requirements/recommendations for international students: Required—TOEFL. *Faculty research:* Developmental neuropsychology; smoking, affect, and cognition; personality measurement; vocational psychology; program evaluation.

Southern Illinois University Edwardsville, Graduate School, School of Education, Department of Psychology, Program in Clinical-Adult Psychology, Edwardsville, IL 62026-0001. Offers MA.

Part-time programs available. *Students:* 18 full-time (14 women), 11 part-time (8 women); includes 4 minority (2 Black or African American, non-Hispanic/Latino; 1 Hispanic/Latino; 1 Two or more races, non-Hispanic/Latino), 1 international. Average age 26. In 2010, 15 master's awarded. *Degree requirements:* For master's, comprehensive exam, thesis. *Entrance requirements:* For master's, GRE. Additional exam requirements/recommendations for international students: Required—TOEFL (minimum score 550 paper-based; 213 computer-based; 79 iBT), IELTS (minimum score 6.5). *Application deadline:* For fall admission, 2/1 for domestic and international students. Application fee: $30. Electronic applications accepted. *Expenses:* Tuition, state resident: full-time $6012; part-time $1503 per semester. Tuition, nonresident: full-time $15,030; part-time $3758 per semester. Required fees: $1711; $675 per semester. *Financial support:* Career-related internships or fieldwork, Federal Work-Study, institutionally sponsored loans, scholarships/grants, traineeships, and unspecified assistantships available. Support available to part-time students. Financial award application deadline: 3/1; financial award applicants required to submit FAFSA. *Unit head:* Dr. Andrew Pomerantz, Director, 618-650-2202, E-mail: apomera@siue.edu. *Application contact:* Dr. Andrew Pomerantz, Director, 618-650-2202, E-mail: apomera@siue.edu.

Southern Illinois University Edwardsville, Graduate School, School of Education, Department of Psychology, Program in Clinical Child and School Psychology, Edwardsville, IL 62026-0001. Offers MS. Part-time programs available. *Students:* 15 full-time (13 women), 9 part-time (8 women); includes 2 minority (1 Asian, non-Hispanic/Latino; 1 Two or more races, non-Hispanic/Latino), 1 international. Average age 26. In 2010, 10 master's awarded. *Degree requirements:* For master's, thesis (for some programs), research project. *Entrance requirements:* For master's, GRE. Additional exam requirements/recommendations for international students: Required—TOEFL (minimum score 550 paper-based; 213 computer-based; 79 iBT), IELTS (minimum score 6.5). *Application deadline:* For fall admission, 2/1 for domestic and international students. Application fee: $30. Electronic applications accepted. *Expenses:* Tuition, state resident: full-time $6012; part-time $1503 per semester. Tuition, nonresident: full-time $15,030; part-time $3758 per semester. Required fees: $1711; $675 per semester. *Financial support:* Career-related internships or fieldwork, Federal Work-Study, institutionally sponsored loans, scholarships/grants, traineeships, and unspecified assistantships available. Support available to part-time students. Financial award application deadline: 3/1; financial award applicants required to submit FAFSA. *Unit head:* Dr. Emily Krohn, Director, 618-650-2202, E-mail: ekrohn@siue.edu. *Application contact:* Dr. Emily Krohn, Director, 618-650-2202, E-mail: ekrohn@siue.edu.

Southern Methodist University, Dedman College, Department of Psychology, Program in Clinical Psychology, Dallas, TX 75275. Offers PhD. *Accreditation:* APA. *Faculty:* 16 full-time (6 women), 7 part-time/adjunct (all women). *Students:* 84 applicants, 8% accepted, 4 enrolled. In 2010, 1 doctorate awarded. *Degree requirements:* For doctorate, comprehensive exam, thesis/dissertation, research presentation and publication. *Entrance requirements:* For doctorate, GRE General Test, minimum GPA of 3.0, 3 letters of recommendation. Additional exam requirements/recommendations for international students: Required—TOEFL (minimum score 550 paper-based). *Application deadline:* For fall admission, 1/1 priority date for domestic and international students. Application fee: $60. Electronic applications accepted. *Financial support:* In 2010–11, 9 students received support, including 8 research assistantships with full tuition reimbursements available (averaging $14,000 per year); career-related internships or fieldwork also available. Financial award application deadline: 1/1; financial award applicants required to submit FAFSA. *Faculty research:* Family violence, family assessment, anxiety disorders, personality disorders. Total annual research expenditures: $500,000. *Unit head:* Dr. Robert B. Hampson, Director, 214-768-2734, Fax: 214-768-3910, E-mail: rhampson@smu.edu. *Application contact:* Ann Conner, Assistant to Director of Graduate Studies, 214-768-4924, Fax: 214-768-3910, E-mail: aconner@smu.edu.

Southern New Hampshire University, School of Liberal Arts, Manchester, NH 03106-1045. Offers clinical services for adults psychiatric disabilities (Certificate); clinical services for children and adolescents with psychiatric disabilities (Certificate); clinical services for persons with co-occurring substance abuse and psychiatric disabilities (Certificate); community mental health (MS); fiction writing (MFA); non-fiction writing (MFA); teaching English as a foreign language (MS). Part-time and evening/weekend programs available. *Degree requirements:* For master's, one foreign language, thesis. *Entrance requirements:* For master's, minimum GPA of 2.75: MS-TEFL, 3.0: MFA. Additional exam requirements/recommendations for international students: Required—TOEFL (minimum score 550 paper-based; 213 computer-based; 79 iBT), IELTS (minimum score 6.5), TWE (minimum score 5). Electronic applications accepted. *Expenses:* Contact institution. *Faculty research:* Action research, state of the art practice in behavioral health services, wraparound approaches to working with youth, learning styles.

Spalding University, Graduate Studies, College of Social Sciences and Humanities, School of Professional Psychology, Louisville, KY 40203-2188. Offers clinical psychology (MA, Psy D). *Accreditation:* APA (one or more programs are accredited). Part-time programs available. *Faculty:* 8 full-time (4 women), 15 part-time/adjunct (4 women). *Students:* 100 full-time (77 women), 53 part-time (38 women); includes 20 minority (5 Black or African American, non-Hispanic/Latino; 4 Asian, non-Hispanic/Latino; 5 Hispanic/Latino; 6 Two or more races, non-Hispanic/Latino), 3 international. Average age 29. 78 applicants, 41% accepted, 32 enrolled. In 2010, 13 master's, 15 doctorates awarded. Terminal master's awarded for partial completion of doctoral program. *Degree requirements:* For master's, comprehensive exam; for doctorate, thesis/dissertation. *Entrance requirements:* For master's and doctorate, GRE General Test, 18 hours of undergraduate course work in psychology, interview, letters of recommendation, writing sample, autobiographical statement, transcripts. Additional exam requirements/recommendations for international students: Required—TOEFL (minimum score 535 paper-based; 203 computer-based). *Application deadline:* For fall admission, 1/15 priority date for domestic students, 1/15 for international students. Application fee: $30. *Financial support:* In 2010–11, 66 students received support, including 51 research assistantships with partial tuition reimbursements available (averaging $4,944 per year); career-related internships or fieldwork, Federal Work-Study, scholarships/grants, and unspecified assistantships also available. Financial award application deadline: 3/15; financial award applicants required to submit FAFSA. *Faculty research:* Substance abuse, prayer research, end-of-life issues, complementary and alternative medicine, research methodology and statistical inference. *Unit head:* Dr. Steven Katsikas, Chair, 502-585-9911 Ext. 2700, E-mail: skatsikas@spalding.edu. *Application contact:* Elizabeth A. Simpson, Administrative Assistant, 502-585-7127, Fax: 502-585-7159, E-mail: esimpson@spalding.edu.

State University of New York at Binghamton, Graduate School, School of Arts and Sciences, Department of Psychology, Specialization in Clinical Psychology, Binghamton, NY 13902-6000. Offers MA, PhD. *Accreditation:* APA (one or more programs are accredited). *Students:* 20 full-time (16 women), 18 part-time (14 women); includes 1 Black or African American, non-Hispanic/Latino; 2 Hispanic/Latino, 1 international. Average age 28. 242 applicants, 6% accepted, 7 enrolled. In 2010, 8 doctorates awarded. *Degree requirements:* For master's, thesis; for doctorate, thesis/dissertation, departmental qualifying exam. *Entrance requirements:* For master's and doctorate, GRE General Test, GRE Subject Test. Additional exam requirements/recommendations for international students: Required—TOEFL (minimum score 550 paper-based; 213 computer-based; 80 iBT). *Application deadline:* For fall admission, 12/15 priority date for domestic and international students. Applications are processed on a rolling basis. Application fee: $60. Electronic applications accepted. *Financial support:* In 2010–11, 29 students received support, including 2 fellowships with full tuition reimbursements available (averaging $17,500 per year), 17 research assistantships with full tuition reimbursements available (averaging $17,500 per year), 8 teaching assistantships with full tuition reimbursements available (averaging $17,500 per year); career-related internships or fieldwork, Federal Work-Study, institutionally sponsored loans, scholarships/grants, traineeships, health care benefits, tuition waivers (full and partial), and unspecified assistantships also available. Financial award application deadline: 2/15; financial award applicants required to submit FAFSA. *Unit head:* Dr. Stephen Lisman, Graduate Coordinator, 607-777-4929, E-mail: slisman@binghamton.edu. *Application contact:* Catherine Smith, Recruiting and Admissions Coordinator, 607-777-2151, Fax: 607-777-2501, E-mail: cmsmith@binghamton.edu.

Stony Brook University, State University of New York, Graduate School, College of Arts and Sciences, Department of Psychology, Program in Clinical Psychology, Stony Brook, NY 11794. Offers PhD. *Accreditation:* APA. *Students:* 30 full-time (26 women); includes 2 Asian, non-Hispanic/Latino; 2 Hispanic/Latino; 1 Two or more races, non-Hispanic/Latino. Average age 27. 336 applicants, 3% accepted, 7 enrolled. In 2010, 8 doctorates awarded. *Degree requirements:* For doctorate, thesis/dissertation. *Entrance requirements:* For doctorate, GRE General Test, GRE Subject Test. Additional exam requirements/recommendations for international students: Required—TOEFL. *Application deadline:* For fall admission, 1/15 for domestic students. Application fee: $100. *Expenses:* Tuition, state resident: full-time $8370; part-time $349 per credit. Tuition, nonresident: full-time $13,780; part-time $574 per credit. Required fees: $994. *Unit head:* Dr. Joanne Davila, Area Head, 631-632-7855, E-mail: joanne.davila@stonybrook.edu. *Application contact:* Graduate Director, 631-632-7855, Fax: 631-632-7876.

Suffolk University, College of Arts and Sciences, Department of Psychology, Boston, MA 02108-2770. Offers clinical psychology (PhD). *Accreditation:* APA. *Faculty:* 17 full-time (9 women), 2 part-time/adjunct (0 women). *Students:* 32 full-time (30 women), 36 part-time (30 women); includes 4 Asian, non-Hispanic/Latino; 6 Hispanic/Latino, 3 international. Average age 29. 278 applicants, 9% accepted, 13 enrolled. In 2010, 7 doctorates awarded. *Degree requirements:* For doctorate, thesis/dissertation, practicum. *Entrance requirements:* For doctorate, GRE General Test or MAT, 2 letters of recommendation, resume. Additional exam requirements/recommendations for international students: Required—TOEFL (minimum score 550 paper-based; 213 computer-based; 80 iBT). *Application deadline:* For fall admission, 12/15 for domestic and international students. Applications are processed on a rolling basis. Application fee: $50. Electronic applications accepted. *Expenses:* Contact institution. *Financial support:* In 2010–11, 51 students received support, including 37 fellowships with full and partial tuition reimbursements available (averaging $20,063 per year); career-related internships or fieldwork, Federal Work-Study, and institutionally sponsored loans also available. Support available to part-time students. Financial award application deadline: 4/1; financial award applicants required to submit FAFSA. *Faculty research:* Olfaction decision-making in substance-dependent individuals, ego development, experiential avoidance in generalized anxiety disorder. *Unit head:* Dr. Gary Fireman, Chairperson, 617-305-6368, Fax: 617-367-2924, E-mail: gfireman@suffolk.edu. *Application contact:* Judith Reynolds, Director of Graduate Admissions, 617-573-8302, Fax: 617-305-1733, E-mail: grad.admission@suffolk.edu.

Syracuse University, College of Arts and Sciences, Program in Clinical Psychology, Syracuse, NY 13244. Offers PhD. *Accreditation:* APA. *Students:* 25 full-time (19 women); includes 3 minority (2 Asian, non-Hispanic/Latino; 1 Hispanic/Latino), 1 international. Average age 27. 135 applicants, 6% accepted, 3 enrolled. In 2010, 2 doctorates awarded. *Degree requirements:* For doctorate, thesis/dissertation. *Entrance requirements:* For doctorate, GRE General Test, GRE Subject Test. Additional exam requirements/recommendations for international students: Required—TOEFL (minimum score 100 iBT). *Application deadline:* For fall admission, 1/1 priority date for domestic and international students. Application fee: $75. Electronic applications accepted. *Expenses:* Tuition: Part-time $1162 per credit. *Financial support:* Fellowships with full tuition reimbursements, research assistantships with full and partial tuition reimbursements, teaching assistantships with full and partial tuition reimbursements available. Financial award application deadline: 1/1; financial award applicants required to submit FAFSA. *Unit head:* Dr. Kevin S. Masters, Graduate Director, 315-443-3666, Fax: 315-443-4085, E-mail: kemaster@syr.edu. *Application contact:* Sue Bova, Information Contact, 315-443-1050, E-mail: skbova@syr.edu.

Syracuse University, School of Education, Program in Clinical Mental Health Counseling, Syracuse, NY 13244. Offers MS. *Students:* 14 full-time (11 women), 3 part-time (1 woman), 2 international. Average age 27. 37 applicants, 65% accepted, 7 enrolled. *Entrance requirements:* For master's, GRE General Test or MAT, interview. Additional exam requirements/recommendations for international students: Required—TOEFL (minimum score 100 iBT). *Application deadline:* For fall admission, 2/1 priority date for domestic students; for spring admission, 10/15 priority date for domestic and international students. Electronic applications accepted. *Expenses:* Tuition: Part-time $1162 per credit. *Financial support:* Fellowships with full tuition reimbursements available. Financial award application deadline: 1/1. *Unit head:* Dr. Dennis Gilbride, Department Chair, 315-443-2266, E-mail: ddgilbri@syr.edu. *Application contact:* Liza Rochelson, Graduate Recruiter, School of Education, 315-443-2505, E-mail: e-gradrcrt@syr.edu.

Teachers College, Columbia University, Graduate Faculty of Education, Department of Counseling and Clinical Psychology, Program in Clinical Psychology, New York, NY 10027-6696. Offers PhD. *Accreditation:* APA. *Faculty:* 6 full-time (4 women), 25 part-time/adjunct (15 women). *Students:* 25 full-time (16 women), 20 part-time (14 women); includes 9 minority (2 Black or African American, non-Hispanic/Latino; 5 Asian, non-Hispanic/Latino; 1 Hispanic/Latino; 1 Two or more races, non-Hispanic/Latino), 7 international. Average age 30. 419 applicants, 68% accepted. In 2010, 7 doctorates awarded. *Degree requirements:* For doctorate, comprehensive exam, thesis/dissertation, twelve-month clinical internship, original piece of empirical research. *Entrance requirements:* For doctorate, GRE. *Application deadline:* For fall admission, 12/15 for domestic students. Application fee: $65. *Expenses:* Tuition: Full-time $28,272; part-time $1178 per credit. Required fees: $756; $378 per semester. *Financial support:* Career-related internships or fieldwork, Federal Work-Study, institutionally sponsored loans, and tuition waivers (partial) available. Support available to part-time students. Financial award application deadline: 2/1. *Faculty research:* Psychotherapy education, trauma, stress, psychopathology, life span and aging issues. *Unit head:* Prof. Barry Farber, Program Coordinator, 212-678-3267, E-mail: farber@tc.edu. *Application contact:* David Estrella, Senior Associate Director of Admission, 212-678-3305, E-mail: dpe2103@columbia.edu.

Temple University, College of Liberal Arts, Department of Psychology, Philadelphia, PA 19122-6096. Offers brain and cognitive sciences (PhD); clinical psychology (PhD); developmental psychology (PhD); psychology (MA); social psychology (PhD). *Accreditation:* APA. *Faculty:* 29 full-time (11 women). *Students:* 88 full-time (69 women), 14 part-time (12 women); includes 1 Black or African American, non-Hispanic/Latino; 1 American Indian or Alaska Native, non-Hispanic/Latino; 4 Asian, non-Hispanic/Latino; 2 Hispanic/Latino, 6 international. 538 applicants, 6% accepted, 16 enrolled. In 2010, 10 master's, 15 doctorates awarded. *Degree requirements:* For doctorate, thesis/dissertation. *Entrance requirements:* For doctorate, GRE General Test, minimum GPA of 3.0. Additional exam requirements/recommendations for international students: Required—TOEFL (minimum score 550 paper-based; 213 computer-based; 79 iBT). *Application deadline:* For fall admission, 12/15 for domestic and international students. Application fee: $50. Electronic applications accepted. *Financial support:* Fellowships, research assistantships, teaching assistantships, career-related internships or fieldwork, Federal Work-Study, institutionally sponsored loans, and unspecified assistantships available. Financial award application deadline: 12/15; financial award applicants required to submit FAFSA. Total annual research expenditures: $4 million. *Unit head:* Dr. Marsha Weinraub, Chair, 215-204-7321, Fax: 215-204-5539, E-mail: mweinrau@temple.edu. *Application contact:* Dr. Marsha Weinraub, Chair, 215-204-7321, Fax: 215-204-5539, E-mail: mweinrau@temple.edu.

Texas A&M University, College of Liberal Arts, Department of Psychology, College Station, TX 77843. Offers behavioral and cellular neuroscience (PhD); clinical psychology (PhD); cognitive psychology (PhD); developmental psychology (PhD); industrial/organizational psychology (PhD); social psychology (PhD). *Accreditation:* APA. *Faculty:* 39. *Students:* 91 full-time (57 women), 14 part-time (11 women); includes 7 Black or African American, non-Hispanic/Latino; 8 Asian, non-Hispanic/Latino; 17 Hispanic/Latino, 7 international. In 2010, 12 doctorates awarded. *Degree requirements:* For doctorate, comprehensive exam (for some programs), thesis/dissertation. *Entrance requirements:* For doctorate, GRE General Test. Additional exam requirements/recommendations for international students: Required—TOEFL. *Application deadline:* For fall admission, 1/5 for domestic and international students. Application fee: $50 ($75 for international students). Electronic applications accepted. *Financial support:* Fellowships with partial tuition reimbursements, research assistantships with partial tuition reimbursements, teaching assistantships with partial tuition reimbursements, career-related

Clinical Psychology

Texas A&M University (continued)
internships or fieldwork, institutionally sponsored loans, health care benefits, and unspecified assistantships available. Financial award application deadline: 1/5; financial award applicants required to submit FAFSA. *Unit head:* Ludy T. Benjamin, Head, 979-845-2540, Fax: 979-845-4727, E-mail: lbenjamin@tamu.edu. *Application contact:* Julie Austin, Graduate Admissions Supervisor, 979-458-1710, Fax: 979-845-4727, E-mail: gradadv@psyc.tamu.edu.

Texas Tech University, Graduate School, College of Arts and Sciences, Department of Psychology, Lubbock, TX 79409-2051. Offers clinical psychology (PhD); counseling psychology (MA, PhD); experimental psychology (MA, PhD); psychology (MA, PhD). *Accreditation:* APA (one or more programs are accredited). Part-time programs available. *Faculty:* 25 full-time (11 women). *Students:* 91 full-time (57 women), 18 part-time (17 women); includes 2 Black or African American, non-Hispanic/Latino; 1 American Indian or Alaska Native, non-Hispanic/Latino; 1 Asian, non-Hispanic/Latino; 9 Hispanic/Latino; 1 Two or more races, non-Hispanic/Latino, 7 international. Average age 27. 276 applicants, 11% accepted, 19 enrolled. In 2010, 18 master's, 13 doctorates awarded. *Degree requirements:* For doctorate, comprehensive exam, thesis/dissertation, 100 credit hours of organized courses, research credits, and practica. *Entrance requirements:* For master's and doctorate, GRE General Test, GRE Subject Test, departmental application form, essays. Additional exam requirements/recommendations for international students: Required—TOEFL (minimum score 550 paper-based; 213 computer-based; 79 iBT). *Application deadline:* For fall admission, 6/1 priority date for domestic students, 1/15 priority date for international students; for spring admission, 9/1 priority date for domestic students, 6/15 priority date for international students. Applications are processed on a rolling basis. Application fee: $50 ($75 for international students). Electronic applications accepted. *Expenses:* Tuition, state resident: full-time $5495.76; part-time $228.99 per credit hour. Tuition, nonresident: full-time $12,936; part-time $538.99 per credit hour. Required fees: $2674; $36 per credit hour. $905 per semester. *Financial support:* In 2010–11, 85 students received support, including 13 research assistantships with partial tuition reimbursements available (averaging $5,707 per year), 32 teaching assistantships with partial tuition reimbursements available (averaging $5,672 per year). Financial award application deadline: 4/15; financial award applicants required to submit FAFSA. *Faculty research:* Failure/success in relationships, peer rejection in school, stress and coping, group processes, clinical and health psychology. Total annual research expenditures: $202,278. *Unit head:* Dr. Lee M. Cohen, Chair, 806-742-3711 Ext. 222, Fax: 806-742-0818, E-mail: lee.cohen@ttu.edu. *Application contact:* Kay Hill, Admissions Coordinator, 806-742-3711 Ext. 222, Fax: 806-742-0818, E-mail: kay.hill@ttu.edu.

Towson University, Program in Clinical Psychology, Towson, MD 21252-0001. Offers MA. Part-time and evening/weekend programs available. *Students:* 101 full-time (83 women), 29 part-time (18 women); includes 22 minority (13 Black or African American, non-Hispanic/Latino; 5 Asian, non-Hispanic/Latino; 3 Hispanic/Latino; 1 Two or more races, non-Hispanic/Latino), 1 international. Average age 26. In 2010, 45 master's awarded. *Degree requirements:* For master's, thesis (for some programs), exams. *Entrance requirements:* For master's, GRE, minimum GPA of 3.0, 15 credits in related course work. Additional exam requirements/recommendations for international students: Required—TOEFL. *Application deadline:* For fall admission, 2/1 for domestic and international students. Application fee: $50. Electronic applications accepted. *Expenses:* Tuition, state resident: part-time $324 per credit. Tuition, nonresident: part-time $681 per credit. Required fees: $95 per term. *Financial support:* Federal Work-Study and unspecified assistantships available. Financial award application deadline: 4/1; financial award applicants required to submit FAFSA. *Faculty research:* Cognitive behavior, issues affecting the aging, relaxation hypnosis and imagery, medicalization of male sexuality. *Unit head:* Dr. Elizabeth Katz, Graduate Program Director, 410-704-3201, Fax: 410-704-3800, E-mail: ekatz@towson.edu. *Application contact:* The Graduate School, 410-704-2501, Fax: 410-704-4675, E-mail: grads@towson.edu.

Troy University, Graduate School, College of Education, Program in Counseling and Psychology, Troy, AL 36082. Offers agency counseling (Ed S); clinical mental health (MS); community counseling (MS, Ed S); corrections counseling (MS); rehabilitation counseling (MS); school psychology (MS, Ed S); school psychometry (MS); social service counseling (MS); student affairs counseling (MS); substance abuse counseling (MS). *Accreditation:* ACA; CORE; NCATE. Part-time and evening/weekend programs available. *Students:* 419 full-time (338 women), 720 part-time (603 women); includes 696 minority (592 Black or African American, non-Hispanic/Latino; 8 American Indian or Alaska Native, non-Hispanic/Latino; 4 Asian, non-Hispanic/Latino; 46 Hispanic/Latino; 46 Two or more races, non-Hispanic/Latino). Average age 33. 326 applicants, 90% accepted. In 2010, 198 master's, 1 other advanced degree awarded. *Degree requirements:* For master's, comprehensive exam, thesis. *Entrance requirements:* For master's, MAT, minimum GPA of 2.5. Additional exam requirements/recommendations for international students: Required—TOEFL (minimum score 523 paper-based; 193 computer-based; 70 iBT), IELTS (minimum score 6). *Application deadline:* Applications are processed on a rolling basis. Application fee: $50. Electronic applications accepted. *Expenses:* Tuition, state resident: full-time $4428; part-time $246 per credit hour. Tuition, nonresident: full-time $8856; part-time $492 per credit hour. Required fees: $432; $24 per credit hour. $50 per term. Tuition and fees vary according to program. *Unit head:* Dr. Andrew Creamer, Chair, 334-670-3350, Fax: 334-670-32961, E-mail: drcreamer@troy.edu. *Application contact:* Brenda K. Campbell, Director of Graduate Admissions, 334-670-3178, Fax: 334-670-3733, E-mail: bcamp@troy.edu.

Uniformed Services University of the Health Sciences, School of Medicine, Graduate Programs in the Biomedical Sciences and Public Health, Department of Medical and Clinical Psychology, Bethesda, MD 20814. Offers clinical psychology (PhD); medical and clinical psychology (clinical/dual track) (PhD); medical and clinical psychology (research track) (PhD). Clinical psychology available to active duty military only. *Accreditation:* APA. Terminal master's awarded for partial completion of doctoral program. *Degree requirements:* For doctorate, comprehensive exam, thesis/dissertation, qualifying exam. *Entrance requirements:* For doctorate, GRE General Test, minimum GPA of 3.0, U.S. citizenship. Additional exam requirements/recommendations for international students: Required—TOEFL. Electronic applications accepted. *Faculty research:* Addictive and appetitive behavior, psychopharmacology, stress and eating, obesity, health.

Union College, Graduate Programs, Department of Psychology, Barbourville, KY 40906-1499. Offers clinical psychology (MA); counseling psychology (MA); school psychology (MA).

Union Institute & University, Programs in Psychology and Counseling, Brattleboro, VT 05301. Offers clinical mental health counseling (MA); clinical psychology (Psy D); counseling psychology (MA); counselor education and supervision (CAGS); developmental psychology (MA); educational psychology (MA); human development and wellness (CAGS); organizational psychology (MA); psychology education (CAGS). Psy D offered in Ohio and Vermont. Postbaccalaureate distance learning degree programs offered (minimal on-campus study). *Faculty:* 6 full-time (4 women), 17 part-time/adjunct (6 women). *Students:* 93 full-time (66 women), 11 part-time (10 women); includes 14 minority (6 Black or African American, non-Hispanic/Latino; 1 Asian, non-Hispanic/Latino; 7 Hispanic/Latino). Average age 44. In 2010, 21 master's awarded. *Degree requirements:* For master's, thesis, internship (depending on concentration); for doctorate, thesis/dissertation, internship, practicum. *Application deadline:* Applications are processed on a rolling basis. Application fee: $50. Electronic applications accepted. *Expenses:* Tuition: Full-time $16,430; part-time $685 per credit hour. Required fees: $174; $44 per term. Tuition and fees vary according to course load, degree level and program. *Financial support:* Federal Work-Study available. Financial award applicants required to submit FAFSA. *Unit head:* Dr. Bill Lax, Dean, 802-254-0152, E-mail: bill.lax@myunion.edu. *Application contact:* Diane Robinson, Director of Admissions, 888-828-8575, E-mail: diane.robinson@myunion.edu.

Universidad de Iberoamerica, Graduate School, San Jose, Costa Rica. Offers clinical neuropsychology (PhD); clinical psychology (M Psych); educational psychology (M Psych); forensic psychology (M Psych); hospital management (MHA); intensive care nursing (MN); medicine (MD). *Entrance requirements:* For master's, 2 letters of recommendation, interview.

Université Laval, Faculty of Social Sciences, School of Psychology, Programs in Psychology, Québec, QC G1K 7P4, Canada. Offers clinical psychology (PhD); community psychology (PhD); psychology (PhD, Psy D). *Degree requirements:* For doctorate, comprehensive exam, thesis/dissertation. *Entrance requirements:* For doctorate, comprehension of written English, knowledge of French, interview. Electronic applications accepted.

University at Albany, State University of New York, College of Arts and Sciences, Department of Psychology, Albany, NY 12222-0001. Offers autism (Certificate); biopsychology (PhD); clinical psychology (PhD); general/experimental psychology (PhD); industrial/organizational psychology (PhD); psychology (MA); social/personality psychology (PhD). *Accreditation:* APA (one or more programs are accredited). *Degree requirements:* For doctorate, thesis/dissertation. *Entrance requirements:* For doctorate, GRE General Test, GRE Subject Test. Additional exam requirements/recommendations for international students: Required—TOEFL (minimum score 550 paper-based; 213 computer-based). Electronic applications accepted.

University at Buffalo, the State University of New York, Graduate School, College of Arts and Sciences, Department of Psychology, Buffalo, NY 14260. Offers behavioral neuroscience (PhD); clinical psychology (PhD); cognitive psychology (PhD); general psychology (MA); social-personality psychology (PhD). *Accreditation:* APA (one or more programs are accredited). *Faculty:* 26 full-time (8 women), 10 part-time/adjunct (5 women). *Students:* 88 full-time (60 women), 6 part-time (4 women); includes 21 minority (2 Black or African American, non-Hispanic/Latino; 2 American Indian or Alaska Native, non-Hispanic/Latino; 7 Asian, non-Hispanic/Latino; 9 Hispanic/Latino; 1 Two or more races, non-Hispanic/Latino), 11 international. Average age 27. 367 applicants, 12% accepted, 21 enrolled. In 2010, 14 master's, 6 doctorates awarded. Terminal master's awarded for partial completion of doctoral program. *Degree requirements:* For master's, project; for doctorate, thesis/dissertation. *Entrance requirements:* For master's and doctorate, GRE General Test. Additional exam requirements/recommendations for international students: Required—TOEFL (minimum score 550 paper-based; 213 computer-based; 79 iBT). *Application deadline:* For fall admission, 12/1 for domestic and international students. Application fee: $75. Electronic applications accepted. *Financial support:* In 2010–11, 65 students received support, including 8 fellowships with full tuition reimbursements available (averaging $13,700 per year), 16 research assistantships with full tuition reimbursements available (averaging $13,700 per year), 38 teaching assistantships with full tuition reimbursements available (averaging $13,700 per year); career-related internships or fieldwork, Federal Work-Study, institutionally sponsored loans, scholarships/grants, and tuition waivers (partial) also available. Financial award application deadline: 12/1; financial award applicants required to submit FAFSA. *Faculty research:* Neural, endocrine, and molecular bases of behavior; adult mood and anxiety disorders; relationship dysfunction; attention deficit/hyperactivity disorder; psycho-linguistics. Total annual research expenditures: $7.9 million. *Unit head:* Dr. Paul A. Luce, Chair, 716-645-3650 Ext. 203, Fax: 716-645-3801, E-mail: psychair@acsu.buffalo.edu. *Application contact:* Mary Claire Schnepf, Coordinator of Admissions, 716-645-3660, Fax: 716-645-3801, E-mail: psych@abuffalo.edu.

The University of Alabama, Graduate School, College of Arts and Sciences, Department of Psychology, Tuscaloosa, AL 35487. Offers clinical psychology (PhD); experimental psychology (PhD). *Accreditation:* APA. *Faculty:* 22 full-time (10 women), 2 part-time/adjunct (both women). *Students:* 75 full-time (57 women), 23 part-time (16 women); includes 17 minority (8 Black or African American, non-Hispanic/Latino; 5 Asian, non-Hispanic/Latino; 4 Hispanic/Latino), 6 international. Average age 28. 261 applicants, 15% accepted, 23 enrolled. In 2010, 15 doctorates awarded. *Degree requirements:* For doctorate, thesis/dissertation, internship (for clinical psychology). *Entrance requirements:* For doctorate, GRE. Additional exam requirements/recommendations for international students: Required—TOEFL (minimum score 550 paper-based). *Application deadline:* For fall admission, 12/1 for domestic and international students. Application fee: $50 ($60 for international students). Electronic applications accepted. *Expenses:* Tuition, state resident: full-time $7900. Tuition, nonresident: full-time $20,500. *Financial support:* In 2010–11, 73 students received support, including 12 fellowships with full tuition reimbursements available (averaging $15,000 per year), 34 research assistantships with full and partial tuition reimbursements available (averaging $11,142 per year), 26 teaching assistantships with tuition reimbursements available (averaging $11,142 per year); career-related internships or fieldwork, institutionally sponsored loans, scholarships/grants, health care benefits, and unspecified assistantships also available. Financial award application deadline: 12/1. *Faculty research:* Cognitive development/disability, child clinical, psychology and law, health/aging, social psychology. Total annual research expenditures: $2 million. *Unit head:* Dr. Beverly E. Thorn, Chair, 205-348-1919, Fax: 205-348-8648, E-mail: bthorn@bama.ua.edu. *Application contact:* Colett Thomas, Information Contact, 205-348-1913, Fax: 205-348-8648, E-mail: cthomas@as.ua.edu.

University of Alaska Anchorage, College of Arts and Sciences, Department of Psychology, Anchorage, AK 99508. Offers clinical psychology (MS); clinical-community psychology with rural-indigenous emphasis (PhD). Part-time programs available. *Degree requirements:* For master's, thesis. *Entrance requirements:* For master's, GRE General Test, GRE Subject Test, interview, references; for doctorate, interview, bachelor's or master's degree in psychology. Additional exam requirements/recommendations for international students: Required—TOEFL (minimum score 550 paper-based; 213 computer-based). *Faculty research:* Substance abuse, childhood autism, biofeedback, psychological assessment, mental health in Native Alaskans.

University of Alaska Fairbanks, College of Liberal Arts, Department of Psychology, Fairbanks, AK 99775-6480. Offers clinical-community psychology (PhD), including rural cross-cultural emphasis. Program offered jointly with University of Alaska Anchorage. *Faculty:* 8 full-time (5 women). *Students:* 2 full-time (both women), 28 part-time (25 women); includes 9 minority (2 American Indian or Alaska Native, non-Hispanic/Latino; 2 Hispanic/Latino; 5 Two or more races, non-Hispanic/Latino), 1 international. Average age 31. 36 applicants, 39% accepted, 12 enrolled. *Degree requirements:* For doctorate, comprehensive exam, thesis/dissertation, oral exam, oral defense. *Entrance requirements:* For doctorate, disclosure statement. Additional exam requirements/recommendations for international students: Required—TOEFL (minimum score 550 paper-based; 213 computer-based; 80 iBT). *Application deadline:* For fall admission, 12/15 for domestic and international students. Application fee: $60. *Expenses:* Tuition, state resident: full-time $5688; part-time $316 per credit. Tuition, nonresident: full-time $11,628; part-time $646 per credit. Required fees: $289 per semester. Tuition and fees vary according to course load and reciprocity agreements. *Financial support:* In 2010–11, 7 research assistantships with tuition reimbursements (averaging $16,679 per year), 6 teaching assistantships with tuition reimbursements (averaging $17,997 per year) were awarded; fellowships with tuition reimbursements, career-related internships or fieldwork, Federal Work-Study, scholarships/grants, health care benefits, and unspecified assistantships also available. Support available to part-time students. Financial award application deadline: 7/1; financial award applicants required to submit FAFSA. *Faculty research:* Clinical and community psychology; rural, indigenous, and cultural psychology. Total annual research expenditures: $42,389. *Unit head:* Dr. Dani Sheppard, Department Chair, 907-474-7007, Fax: 907-474-5781, E-mail: fypsych@uaf.edu. *Application contact:* Dr. Dani Sheppard, Department Chair, 907-474-7007, Fax: 907-474-5781, E-mail: fypsych@uaf.edu.

The University of British Columbia, Faculty of Arts and Faculty of Graduate Studies, Department of Psychology, Vancouver, BC V6T 1Z4, Canada. Offers behavioral neuroscience (MA, PhD); clinical psychology (MA, PhD); cognitive science (MA, PhD); developmental psychology (MA, PhD); health psychology (MA, PhD); quantitative methods (MA, PhD); social/personality psychology (MA, PhD). *Accreditation:* APA (one or more programs are accredited). Terminal master's awarded for partial completion of doctoral program. *Degree requirements:* For master's, thesis; for doctorate, comprehensive exam, thesis/dissertation. *Entrance requirements:* For master's and doctorate, GRE General Test. Additional exam requirements/recommendations for international students: Required—TOEFL (minimum score 550 paper-based; 230 computer-based; 80 iBT). Electronic applications accepted. Tuition charges are reported in Canadian dollars. *Expenses:* Tuition, area resident: Full-time $4179 Canadian dollars. International tuition: $7344 Canadian dollars full-time. *Faculty research:* Clinical, developmental, social/personality, cognition, behavioral neuroscience.

University of Calgary, Faculty of Graduate Studies, Faculty of Social Sciences, Department of Psychology, Program in Clinical Psychology, Calgary, AB T2N 1N4, Canada. Offers M Sc, PhD. *Degree requirements:* For master's, thesis, practical training; for doctorate, thesis/dissertation, practical training. *Entrance requirements:* For master's, GRE General Test, bachelor's degree in psychology or equivalent, minimum GPA of 3.6; for doctorate, GRE General Test, bachelor's degree in psychology, master's degree. Additional exam requirements/recommendations for international students: Required—TOEFL (minimum score 600 paper-based; 250 computer-based). Electronic applications accepted. *Faculty research:* Depression, schizophrenia, aging, neuropsychology, cognitive and linguistic development in infancy.

University of California, San Diego, Office of Graduate Studies, Group in Clinical Psychology, La Jolla, CA 92093. Offers PhD. Program offered jointly with San Diego State University. *Accreditation:* APA. Electronic applications accepted.

University of California, Santa Barbara, Graduate Division, Gevirtz Graduate School of Education, Santa Barbara, CA 93106-9490. Offers counseling, clinical and school psychology (PhD), including clinical psychology, counseling psychology, school psychology; education (M Ed, MA, PhD), including child and adolescent development (MA, PhD), cultural perspectives and comparative education (MA, PhD), educational leadership and organizations (MA, PhD), research methodology (MA, PhD), special education disabilities and risk studies (MA), special education, disabilities and risk studies (PhD), teaching (M Ed), teaching and learning (MA, PhD); educational leadership (Ed D); school psychology (M Ed); MA/PhD. *Accreditation:* APA (one or more programs are accredited). Postbaccalaureate distance learning degree programs offered (minimal on-campus study). *Faculty:* 40 full-time (22 women), 5 part-time/adjunct (1 woman). *Students:* 411 full-time (325 women); includes 19 Black or African American, non-Hispanic/Latino; 3 American Indian or Alaska Native, non-Hispanic/Latino; 59 Asian, non-Hispanic/Latino; 67 Hispanic/Latino. Average age 29. 683 applicants, 38% accepted, 154 enrolled. In 2010, 128 master's, 58 doctorates awarded. Terminal master's awarded for partial completion of doctoral program. *Degree requirements:* For master's, comprehensive exam (for some programs), thesis (for some programs); for doctorate, comprehensive exam (for some programs), thesis/dissertation. *Entrance requirements:* For master's and doctorate, GRE. Additional exam requirements/recommendations for international students: Required—TOEFL (minimum score 550 paper-based; 80 iBT), IELTS (minimum score 7). Application fee: $70 ($90 for international students). Electronic applications accepted. *Financial support:* In 2010–11, 269 students received support, including 222 fellowships with partial tuition reimbursements available (averaging $5,615 per year), 75 research assistantships with full tuition reimbursements available (averaging $6,470 per year), 65 teaching assistantships with partial tuition reimbursements available (averaging $7,059 per year); career-related internships or fieldwork also available. Financial award applicants required to submit FAFSA. *Faculty research:* Needs of diverse students, school accountability and leadership, school violence, language learning and literacy, science/math education. Total annual research expenditures: $3.1 million. *Unit head:* Carol North Dixon, Graduate Advisor, 805-893-2185, E-mail: dixon@education.ucsb.edu. *Application contact:* Kathryn Marie Tucciarone, Student Affairs Officer, 805-893-2137, Fax: 805-893-2588, E-mail: katiet@education.ucsb.edu.

University of Central Florida, College of Sciences, Department of Psychology, Program in Clinical Psychology, Orlando, FL 32816. Offers MA, MS, PhD. *Accreditation:* APA. Part-time and evening/weekend programs available. *Students:* 63 full-time (45 women), 2 part-time (both women); includes 2 Black or African American, non-Hispanic/Latino; 1 Asian, non-Hispanic/Latino; 8 Hispanic/Latino, 4 international. Average age 25. 339 applicants, 12% accepted, 21 enrolled. In 2010, 16 master's, 1 doctorate awarded. *Degree requirements:* For master's, thesis or alternative, clinical internship; for doctorate, thesis/dissertation, candidacy exam, internship. *Entrance requirements:* For master's and doctorate, GRE General Test, minimum GPA of 3.0 in last 60 hours, resume. Additional exam requirements/recommendations for international students: Required—TOEFL. *Application deadline:* For fall admission, 2/15 for domestic students. Application fee: $30. Electronic applications accepted. *Expenses:* Tuition, state resident: part-time $256.56 per credit hour. Tuition, nonresident: part-time $1011.52 per credit hour. Part-time tuition and fees vary according to program. *Financial support:* In 2010–11, 39 students received support, including 8 fellowships with partial tuition reimbursements available (averaging $9,100 per year), 1 research assistantship with partial tuition reimbursement available (averaging $7,400 per year), 39 teaching assistantships with partial tuition reimbursements available (averaging $8,500 per year); career-related internships or fieldwork, Federal Work-Study, institutionally sponsored loans, tuition waivers (partial), and unspecified assistantships also available. Financial award application deadline: 3/1; financial award applicants required to submit FAFSA. *Faculty research:* Professional ethical decision making, computer experience and anxiety, effects of expert testimony on decision-making in a rape trial, religiosity, relationship beliefs and marital adjustment. *Unit head:* Dr. Deborah Beidel, Director, 407-254-3908, E-mail: dbeidel@mail.ucf.edu. *Application contact:* Dr. Deborah Beidel, Director, 407-254-3908, E-mail: dbeidel@mail.ucf.edu.

University of Cincinnati, Graduate School, McMicken College of Arts and Sciences, Department of Psychology, Cincinnati, OH 45221. Offers clinical psychology (PhD); experimental psychology (PhD). *Accreditation:* APA. *Degree requirements:* For doctorate, comprehensive exam, thesis/dissertation. *Entrance requirements:* For doctorate, GRE General Test. Additional exam requirements/recommendations for international students: Required—TOEFL. *Faculty research:* Neuropsychology, human factors, health.

University of Colorado Denver, College of Liberal Arts and Sciences, Department of Psychology, Denver, CO 80217-3364. Offers clinical psychology (MA). Part-time and evening/weekend programs available. *Faculty:* 20 full-time (11 women), 1 (woman) part-time/adjunct. *Students:* 24 full-time (18 women), 6 part-time (4 women); includes 3 Asian, non-Hispanic/Latino; 1 Hispanic/Latino, 1 international. Average age 28. 120 applicants, 10% accepted, 12 enrolled. In 2010, 16 master's awarded. *Degree requirements:* For master's, thesis or alternative, 31-33 semester hours, thesis or internship, minimum GPA of 3.0; for doctorate, comprehensive exam, thesis/dissertation, 69 credits of coursework, minimum of 12 clinical practicum hours, 30 dissertation hours, three credits of pre-doctoral internship. *Entrance requirements:* For master's, GRE General Test; GRE Subject Test (recommended), undergraduate courses in psychological statistics, abnormal psychology and introductory psychology; minimum GPA of 3.0; letters of recommendation; personal statement; resume; for doctorate, GRE General Test, minimum GPA of 3.5; undergraduate courses in introductory psychology, psychological statistics, research methods and abnormal psychology; letters of recommendation; personal statement; resume. Additional exam requirements/recommendations for international students: Required—TOEFL (minimum score 525 paper-based; 197 computer-based). *Application deadline:* For fall admission, 2/1 for domestic students, 1/15 for international students. Application fee: $50 ($75 for international students). Electronic applications accepted. *Expenses:* Tuition, state resident: full-time $7332; part-time $355 per credit hour. Tuition, nonresident: full-time $18,990; part-time $1055 per credit hour. Required fees: $998. Tuition and fees vary according to course level, course load, degree level, campus/location, program, reciprocity agreements and student level. *Financial support:* Fellowships, research assistantships, teaching assistantships, career-related internships or fieldwork, Federal Work-Study, scholarships/grants, and unspecified assistantships available. Financial award application deadline: 4/1; financial award applicants required to submit FAFSA. *Faculty research:* Organizational behavior, body image perception, professional ethics, infant perception and cognition, charismatic leadership. *Unit head:* Dr. Peter Kaplan, Program Director, 303-556-2601, Fax: 303-556-3520, E-mail: peter.kaplan@ucdenver.edu. *Application contact:* Gay Freebern, Program Assistant, 303-556-8565, Fax: 303-556-3520, E-mail: gay.freebern@ucdenver.edu.

University of Connecticut, Graduate School, College of Liberal Arts and Sciences, Department of Psychology, Storrs, CT 06269. Offers behavioral neuroscience (PhD); biopsychology (PhD); clinical psychology (MA, PhD); cognition and instruction (PhD); developmental psychology (MA, PhD); ecological psychology (PhD); experimental psychology (PhD); general psychology (MA, PhD); health psychology (Graduate Certificate); industrial/organizational psychology (PhD); language and cognition (PhD); neuroscience (PhD); occupational health psychology (Graduate Certificate); social psychology (MA, PhD). *Accreditation:* APA. Terminal master's awarded for partial completion of doctoral program. *Degree requirements:* For master's, comprehensive exam; for doctorate, thesis/dissertation. *Entrance requirements:* For master's and doctorate, GRE General Test, GRE Subject Test. Additional exam requirements/recommendations for international students: Required—TOEFL (minimum score 550 paper-based; 213 computer-based). Electronic applications accepted.

University of Dayton, Graduate School, College of Arts and Sciences, Department of Psychology, Program in Clinical Psychology, Dayton, OH 45469-1300. Offers MA. *Faculty:* 10 full-time (4 women), 1 (woman) part-time/adjunct. *Students:* 16 full-time (12 women), 3 part-time (2 women); includes 3 minority (1 Black or African American, non-Hispanic/Latino; 1 Asian, non-Hispanic/Latino; 1 Hispanic/Latino), 1 international. Average age 25. 55 applicants, 15% accepted, 8 enrolled. In 2010, 11 master's awarded. *Degree requirements:* For master's, thesis, clinical practicum. *Entrance requirements:* For master's, GRE General Test, GRE Subject Test (recommended), minimum undergraduate GPA of 3.0, 3.3 during final 2 years of course work. Additional exam requirements/recommendations for international students: Required—TOEFL (minimum score 550 paper-based; 213 computer-based; 80 iBT). *Application deadline:* For fall admission, 3/1 priority date for domestic and international students; for winter admission, 7/1 priority date for international students; for spring admission, 1/1 priority date for international students. Application fee: $0 ($50 for international students). Electronic applications accepted. *Expenses:* Tuition: Full-time $7800; part-time $650 per credit hour. *Financial support:* In 2010–11, 16 students received support, including 3 fellowships with full tuition reimbursements available (averaging $10,298 per year), 5 research assistantships with full tuition reimbursements available (averaging $10,298 per year); institutionally sponsored loans, traineeships, and tuition waivers (partial) also available. Financial award application deadline: 3/1. *Faculty research:* Family relationship issues, conduct disorders, trauma/revictimization, community problems. *Unit head:* Dr. Roger N. Reeb, Director, 937-229-2395, Fax: 937-229-3900, E-mail: roger.reeb@notes.udayton.edu. *Application contact:* Alex Popovski, Associate Director of Graduate and International Admissions, 937-229-2357, Fax: 937-229-4729, E-mail: alex.popovski@notes.udayton.edu.

University of Delaware, College of Arts and Sciences, Department of Psychology, Newark, DE 19716. Offers behavioral neuroscience (PhD); clinical psychology (PhD); cognitive psychology (PhD); social psychology (PhD). *Accreditation:* APA. *Degree requirements:* For doctorate, thesis/dissertation. *Entrance requirements:* For doctorate, GRE General Test. Additional exam requirements/recommendations for international students: Required—TOEFL (minimum score 600 paper-based; 250 computer-based). Electronic applications accepted. *Faculty research:* Emotion development, neural and cognitive aspects of memory, neural control of feeding, intergroup relations, social cognition and communication.

University of Denver, Division of Arts, Humanities and Social Sciences, Department of Psychology, Denver, CO 80208. Offers affective science (PhD); affective/social psychology (PhD); clinical child psychology (PhD); developmental cognitive neuroscience (PhD); developmental psychology (PhD). Incidental Master's program available. *Accreditation:* APA. *Faculty:* 18 full-time (8 women), 5 part-time/adjunct (4 women). *Students:* 32 full-time (31 women), 2 part-time (1 woman); includes 6 minority (3 Asian, non-Hispanic/Latino; 2 Hispanic/Latino; 1 Two or more races, non-Hispanic/Latino), 2 international. Average age 26. 320 applicants, 5% accepted, 13 enrolled. In 2010, 6 doctorates awarded. Terminal master's awarded for partial completion of doctoral program. *Degree requirements:* For doctorate, one foreign language, comprehensive exam (for some programs), thesis/dissertation. *Entrance requirements:* For doctorate, GRE General Test. Additional exam requirements/recommendations for international students: Required—TOEFL (minimum score 550 paper-based; 80 iBT). *Application deadline:* For fall admission, 12/1 for domestic students. Applications are processed on a rolling basis. Application fee: $60. Electronic applications accepted. *Expenses:* Tuition: Full-time $35,604; part-time $29,670 per year. Required fees: $687 per year. Tuition and fees vary according to program. *Financial support:* In 2010–11, 12 research assistantships with full and partial tuition reimbursements (averaging $15,500 per year), 22 teaching assistantships with full and partial tuition reimbursements (averaging $16,773 per year) were awarded; career-related internships or fieldwork, Federal Work-Study, institutionally sponsored loans, scholarships/grants, and unspecified assistantships also available. Support available to part-time students. Financial award application deadline: 1/1; financial award applicants required to submit FAFSA. *Faculty research:* Developmental neuropsychology, self-esteem and peer relationships, child abuse and neglect, marital and family interactions, adolescent peer and romantic relationships. *Unit head:* Dr. Rob Roberts, Chair, 303-871-3792, Fax: 303-871-4747. *Application contact:* Paula Plank-Houghtaling, Graduate Secretary, 303-871-3803, Fax: 303-871-4747, E-mail: info@psy.du.edu.

University of Denver, Graduate School of Professional Psychology, Denver, CO 80208. Offers clinical psychology (Psy D); forensic psychology (MA); international disaster psychology (MA); psychology (MA); sport and performance psychology (MA). *Accreditation:* APA. *Faculty:* 15 full-time (8 women), 24 part-time/adjunct (11 women). *Students:* 209 full-time (170 women), 36 part-time (25 women); includes 26 minority (7 Black or African American, non-Hispanic/Latino; 2 American Indian or Alaska Native, non-Hispanic/Latino; 5 Asian, non-Hispanic/Latino; 9 Hispanic/Latino; 3 Two or more races, non-Hispanic/Latino), 4 international. Average age 26. 612 applicants, 30% accepted, 124 enrolled. In 2010, 74 master's, 38 doctorates awarded. *Degree requirements:* For master's, comprehensive exam (for some programs); for doctorate, comprehensive exam (for some programs), paper, clinical internship. *Entrance requirements:* For master's and doctorate, GRE General Test. Additional exam requirements/recommendations for international students: Required—TOEFL (minimum score 550 paper-based; 80 iBT). Application fee: $60. Electronic applications accepted. *Expenses:* Tuition: Full-time $35,604; part-time $29,670 per year. Required fees: $687 per year. Tuition and fees vary according to program. *Financial support:* In 2010–11, 38 teaching assistantships with full and partial tuition reimbursements (averaging $2,952 per year) were awarded; career-related internships or fieldwork, Federal Work-Study, institutionally sponsored loans, scholarships/grants, unspecified assistantships, and clinical assistantships also available. Support available to part-time students. Financial award application deadline: 3/1; financial award applicants required to submit FAFSA. *Unit head:* Dr. Peter Buirski, Dean, 303-871-2382, E-mail: pbuirski@du.edu. *Application contact:* Admissions Counselor, 303-871-3736, Fax: 303-871-7656, E-mail: gsppinfo@du.edu.

University of Detroit Mercy, College of Liberal Arts and Education, Department of Psychology, Program in Clinical Psychology, Detroit, MI 48221. Offers MA, PhD. *Accreditation:* APA. *Degree requirements:* For doctorate, departmental qualifying exam.

University of Florida, Graduate School, College of Public Health and Health Professions, Department of Clinical and Health Psychology, Gainesville, FL 32611. Offers PhD. *Accreditation:* APA. *Faculty:* 21 full-time (8 women), 2 part-time/adjunct (1 woman). *Students:* 58 full-time (42 women), 14 part-time (11 women); includes 5 Black or African American, non-Hispanic/Latino; 1 American Indian or Alaska Native, non-Hispanic/Latino; 4 Asian, non-Hispanic/Latino; 4 Hispanic/Latino. Average age 29. 614 applicants, 7% accepted, 36 enrolled. In 2010, 18 doctorates awarded. *Degree requirements:* For doctorate, comprehensive exam, thesis/dissertation, pre-doctoral internship. *Entrance requirements:* For doctorate, GRE General Test minimum score 1000, minimum GPA of 3.0. Additional exam requirements/recommendations for international students: Required—TOEFL (minimum score 550 paper-based; 213 computer-based; 80 iBT), IELTS (minimum score 6). *Application deadline:* For fall admission, 12/1 for domestic and international students. Application fee: $30. Electronic applications accepted. *Expenses:* Tuition, state resident: full-time $10,915.92. Tuition, nonresident: full-time $28,309. *Financial support:* In 2010–11, 59 students received support, including 8 fellowships with partial tuition reimbursements available, 51 research assistantships with partial tuition reimbursements available (averaging $16,870 per year); career-related internships or fieldwork, Federal

Clinical Psychology

University of Florida (continued)

Work-Study, institutionally sponsored loans, scholarships/grants, and unspecified assistantships also available. Financial award application deadline: 12/1; financial award applicants required to submit FAFSA. *Faculty research:* Clinical child and pediatric psychology, medical psychology, neuropsychology, health promotion and aging. Total annual research expenditures: $3.6 million. *Unit head:* Dr. Russell M. Bauer, Chair, 352-273-6140, Fax: 352-273-6156, E-mail: rbauer@phhp.ufl.edu. *Application contact:* Dr. Stephen R. Boggs, Director, Clinical Psychology Doctoral Program, 352-273-6146, Fax: 352-273-6156, E-mail: sboggs@phhp.ufl.edu.

University of Guelph, Graduate Studies, College of Social and Applied Human Sciences, Department of Psychology, Guelph, ON N1G 2W1, Canada. Offers applied social psychology (MA, PhD); clinical psychology applied development emphasis (PhD); clinical psychology applied developmental emphasis (MA); industrial/organizational psychology (MA, PhD); neuroscience and applied cognitive science (MA, PhD). *Degree requirements:* For master's, thesis; for doctorate, comprehensive exam, thesis/dissertation. *Entrance requirements:* For master's, GRE General Test, GRE Subject Test, minimum B+ average during previous 2 years of course work; for doctorate, GRE General Test, GRE Subject Test, minimum A- average. Additional exam requirements/recommendations for international students: Required—TOEFL (minimum score 89 iBT). Electronic applications accepted. *Faculty research:* Organizational psychology, reading comprehension and mathematical ability, drug addiction and relapse, gender issues and culture, memory, clinical psychology.

University of Hartford, College of Arts and Sciences, Department of Psychology, Program in Clinical Practices, West Hartford, CT 06117-1599. Offers clinical practices (Psy D); psychology (MA). *Accreditation:* APA. *Degree requirements:* For master's, comprehensive exam, thesis optional. *Entrance requirements:* For master's, GRE General Test, GRE Subject Test, minimum GPA of 3.0, 3 letters of recommendation. Additional exam requirements/recommendations for international students: Required—TOEFL (minimum score 550 paper-based; 213 computer-based). Electronic applications accepted. *Faculty research:* Attachment issues, child abuse prevention, master's psychologist issues, neuropsychology.

University of Hawaii at Manoa, Graduate Division, College of Social Sciences, Department of Psychology, Honolulu, HI 96822. Offers clinical psychology (PhD); community and cultural psychology (PhD); community and culture (MA); psychology (MA, PhD, Graduate Certificate). *Accreditation:* APA (one or more programs are accredited). Part-time programs available. *Faculty:* 35 full-time (12 women), 2 part-time/adjunct (1 woman). *Students:* 75 full-time (56 women), 17 part-time (12 women); includes 34 minority (1 Black or African American, non-Hispanic/Latino; 1 American Indian or Alaska Native, non-Hispanic/Latino; 12 Asian, non-Hispanic/Latino; 3 Hispanic/Latino; 6 Native Hawaiian or other Pacific Islander, non-Hispanic/Latino; 11 Two or more races, non-Hispanic/Latino), 13 international. Average age 31. 203 applicants, 10% accepted, 17 enrolled. In 2010, 9 master's, 4 doctorates awarded. Terminal master's awarded for partial completion of doctoral program. *Degree requirements:* For master's, comprehensive exam, thesis; for doctorate, comprehensive exam, thesis/dissertation. *Entrance requirements:* For master's and doctorate, GRE General Test, GRE Subject Test. Additional exam requirements/recommendations for international students: Required—TOEFL (minimum score 600 paper-based; 250 computer-based; 100 iBT), IELTS (minimum score 7). *Application deadline:* For fall admission, 1/1 for domestic and international students. Application fee: $60. *Financial support:* In 2010–11, 13 fellowships (averaging $6,425 per year), 42 research assistantships (averaging $14,690 per year), 14 teaching assistantships (averaging $14,802 per year) were awarded; career-related internships or fieldwork, institutionally sponsored loans, and tuition waivers (full and partial) also available. Financial award application deadline: 1/1. *Faculty research:* Cross-cultural psychology, health psychology, marine mammals, child/adult psychopathology. Total annual research expenditures: $1.3 million. *Application contact:* Charlene Baker, Graduate Chair, 808-956-8414, Fax: 808-956-4700, E-mail: bakercha@hawaii.edu.

University of Houston, College of Liberal Arts and Social Sciences, Department of Psychology, Houston, TX 77204. Offers clinical psychology (PhD); developmental psychology (PhD); industrial/organizational psychology (PhD); psychology (MA); social psychology (PhD). *Accreditation:* APA (one or more programs are accredited). *Faculty:* 28 full-time (12 women), 7 part-time/adjunct (4 women). *Students:* 117 full-time (86 women), 22 part-time (16 women); includes 7 Black or African American, non-Hispanic/Latino; 10 Asian, non-Hispanic/Latino; 16 Hispanic/Latino; 4 Two or more races, non-Hispanic/Latino, 17 international. Average age 27. 460 applicants, 6% accepted, 28 enrolled. In 2010, 19 master's, 20 doctorates awarded. *Degree requirements:* For master's, comprehensive exam, thesis; for doctorate, comprehensive exam, thesis/dissertation. *Entrance requirements:* For master's, GRE General Test, career statement, 3 letters of recommendation; for doctorate, GRE General Test, 3 letters of recommendation. Additional exam requirements/recommendations for international students: Required—TOEFL (minimum score 550 paper-based; 79 iBT). *Application deadline:* For fall admission, 12/15 for domestic and international students. Application fee: $40 ($75 for international students). Electronic applications accepted. *Expenses:* Tuition, state resident: full-time $8592; part-time $358 per credit hour. Tuition, nonresident: full-time $16,032; part-time $668 per credit hour. Required fees: $2889. Tuition and fees vary according to course load and program. *Financial support:* In 2010–11, 23 fellowships with full tuition reimbursements (averaging $2,828 per year), 39 research assistantships with full tuition reimbursements (averaging $7,864 per year), 62 teaching assistantships with full tuition reimbursements (averaging $9,312 per year) were awarded; career-related internships or fieldwork, Federal Work-Study, institutionally sponsored loans, scholarships/grants, health care benefits, and unspecified assistantships also available. Support available to part-time students. Financial award application deadline: 2/1; financial award applicants required to submit FAFSA. *Faculty research:* Health psychology, depression, child/family process, organizational effectiveness, close relationships. *Unit head:* Dr. David Francis, Chairperson, 713-743-7036, Fax: 713-743-8588, E-mail: dfrancis@uh.edu. *Application contact:* Patti Tolar, Academic Affairs Coordinator, 713-743-5544, Fax: 713-743-8588, E-mail: ptolar@uh.edu.

University of Houston–Clear Lake, School of Human Sciences and Humanities, Programs in Human Sciences, Houston, TX 77058-1098. Offers behavioral sciences (MA), including criminology, cross cultural studies, general psychology, sociology; clinical psychology (MA); criminology (MA); cross cultural studies (MA); family therapy (MA); fitness and human performance (MA); school psychology (MA). *Accreditation:* AAMFT/COAMFTE. Part-time and evening/weekend programs available. Postbaccalaureate distance learning degree programs offered (minimal on-campus study). *Degree requirements:* For master's, thesis or alternative. *Entrance requirements:* For master's, GRE General Test. Additional exam requirements/recommendations for international students: Required—TOEFL (minimum score 550 paper-based; 213 computer-based). Electronic applications accepted. *Faculty research:* Smoking cessation, adolescent sexuality, white collar crime, serial murder, human factors/human computer interaction.

University of Indianapolis, Graduate Programs, School of Psychological Sciences, Indianapolis, IN 46227-3697. Offers clinical psychology (Psy D); clinical psychology/mental health counseling (MA). *Accreditation:* APA. *Faculty:* 6 full-time (1 woman), 1 (woman) part-time/adjunct. *Students:* 118 full-time (105 women), 44 part-time (37 women); includes 2 minority (1 Black or African American, non-Hispanic/Latino; 1 Hispanic/Latino), 11 international. Average age 26. *Degree requirements:* For master's, practicum; for doctorate, comprehensive exam, thesis/dissertation, 1200 hours of clinical practicum, 2000 hour internship. *Entrance requirements:* For master's, GRE, 3 letters of recommendation; for doctorate, GRE, minimum GPA of 3.0, 18 hours of course work in psychology, 3 letters of recommendation. Additional exam requirements/recommendations for international students: Required—TOEFL (minimum score 550 paper-based; 213 computer-based). *Application deadline:* For fall admission, 2/25 for domestic students. Application fee: $50. Tuition and fees vary according to course load, degree level and program. *Financial support:* Federal Work-Study available. *Unit head:* Dr. Rick Holigrocki, Acting Dean, 317-788-6126, Fax: 317-788-3480, E-mail: rholigrocki@uindy.edu. *Application contact:* Dr. Rick Holigrocki, Acting Dean, 317-788-6126, E-mail: rholigrocki@uindy.edu.

The University of Kansas, Graduate Studies, College of Liberal Arts and Sciences, Department of Psychology and Department of Psychology, Program in Clinical Child Psychology, Lawrence, KS 66045. Offers MA, PhD. *Accreditation:* APA. *Faculty:* 4 full-time (1 woman). *Students:* 25 full-time (18 women); includes 5 minority (1 Black or African American, non-Hispanic/Latino; 2 Asian, non-Hispanic/Latino; 1 Hispanic/Latino; 1 Native Hawaiian or other Pacific Islander, non-Hispanic/Latino). Average age 28. 124 applicants, 6% accepted, 5 enrolled. In 2010, 3 master's, 5 doctorates awarded. *Degree requirements:* For master's, thesis; for doctorate, comprehensive exam, thesis/dissertation, clinical internship. *Entrance requirements:* For master's, GRE General Test, GRE Subject Test; for doctorate, GRE General Test, GRE Subject Test, minimum GPA of 3.5. Additional exam requirements/recommendations for international students: Required—TOEFL. *Application deadline:* For fall admission, 12/1 for domestic and international students. Application fee: $55 ($65 for international students). Electronic applications accepted. *Expenses:* Tuition, state resident: full-time $7092; part-time $295.50 per credit hour. Tuition, nonresident: full-time $16,590; part-time $691.25 per credit hour. Required fees: $858; $71.49 per credit hour. Tuition and fees vary according to course load, campus/location and program. *Financial support:* Fellowships with tuition reimbursements, research assistantships with full tuition reimbursements, teaching assistantships with full tuition reimbursements, career-related internships or fieldwork, scholarships/grants, traineeships, health care benefits, and unspecified assistantships available. Financial award application deadline: 12/1. *Faculty research:* Pediatric psychology; serious emotional disorders; responses to disasters and terrorism; anxiety, stress, and coping; psychotherapy with children; childhood obesity; child maltreatment; classification issues. *Unit head:* Dr. Michael Roberts, Director, 785-864-4226, Fax: 785-864-5024, E-mail: mroberts@ku.edu. *Application contact:* Tammie Zordel, Graduate Admissions, 785-864-4226, Fax: 785-864-5024, E-mail: ccpp@ku.edu.

University of Kentucky, Graduate School, College of Arts and Sciences, Program in Psychology, Lexington, KY 40506-0032. Offers clinical psychology (MA); experimental psychology (MA). *Accreditation:* APA (one or more programs are accredited). *Degree requirements:* For master's, comprehensive exam, thesis; for doctorate, comprehensive exam, thesis/dissertation. *Entrance requirements:* For master's, GRE General Test, minimum undergraduate GPA of 2.75; for doctorate, GRE General Test, minimum graduate GPA of 3.0. Additional exam requirements/recommendations for international students: Required—TOEFL (minimum score 550 paper-based; 213 computer-based). Electronic applications accepted. *Faculty research:* Psychopharmacology and teratology, behavioral neuroscience, social psychology, cognitive psychology, development and developmental psychobiology.

University of La Verne, College of Arts and Sciences, Department of Psychology, Program in Clinical-Community Psychology, La Verne, CA 91750-4443. Offers Psy D. Part-time programs available. *Faculty:* 13 full-time (6 women), 25 part-time/adjunct (17 women). *Students:* 65 full-time (56 women), 26 part-time (17 women); includes 48 minority (11 Black or African American, non-Hispanic/Latino; 11 Asian, non-Hispanic/Latino; 26 Hispanic/Latino). Average age 28. In 2010, 8 doctorates awarded. *Degree requirements:* For doctorate, thesis/dissertation, clinical internship, competency exams, practicum, personal psychotherapy. *Entrance requirements:* For doctorate, minimum GPA of 3.0 undergraduate, 3.5 graduate; 3 letters of recommendation; curriculum vitae. Additional exam requirements/recommendations for international students: Required—TOEFL (minimum score 600 paper-based; 250 computer-based). *Application deadline:* For fall admission, 1/15 for domestic and international students. Application fee: $75. *Expenses:* Contact institution. *Financial support:* Career-related internships or fieldwork, institutionally sponsored loans, scholarships/grants, and unspecified assistantships available. Financial award application deadline: 3/2; financial award applicants required to submit FAFSA. *Unit head:* Dr. Jerry Kernes, Chairperson, 909-593-3511 Ext. 4414, E-mail: jkernes@laverne.edu. *Application contact:* Barbara Cox, Admissions Information Specialist, 909-593-3511 Ext. 4004, Fax: 909-392-2761, E-mail: gradadmission@laverne.edu.

University of Louisville, Graduate School, College of Arts and Sciences, Department of Psychological and Brain Sciences, Louisville, KY 40292-0001. Offers clinical psychology (PhD); experimental psychology (PhD). *Accreditation:* APA. *Faculty:* 22 full-time (9 women), 4 part-time/adjunct (1 woman). *Students:* 66 full-time (43 women), 1 part-time (0 women); includes 2 Black or African American, non-Hispanic/Latino; 3 Asian, non-Hispanic/Latino; 1 Hispanic/Latino, 9 international. Average age 30. 142 applicants, 3% accepted, 4 enrolled. In 2010, 4 doctorates awarded. *Degree requirements:* For doctorate, thesis/dissertation, preliminary exam, research, internship. *Entrance requirements:* For doctorate, GRE General Test. Additional exam requirements/recommendations for international students: Required—TOEFL. *Application deadline:* For fall admission, 12/1 for domestic and international students. Application fee: $50. Electronic applications accepted. *Expenses:* Tuition, state resident: full-time $9144; part-time $508 per credit hour. Tuition, nonresident: full-time $19,026; part-time $1057 per credit hour. Tuition and fees vary according to program and reciprocity agreements. *Financial support:* In 2010–11, 39 students received support, including 12 fellowships (averaging $22,000 per year), 27 teaching assistantships (averaging $22,000 per year); career-related internships or fieldwork also available. *Faculty research:* Health psychology, geropsychology, psychopathology, cognitive and development sciences, vision and hearing sciences. *Unit head:* Dr. Suzanne Meeks, Chair, 502-852-6068, Fax: 502-852-8904, E-mail: smeeks@louisville.edu. *Application contact:* Mary E. Leggett, Director, Graduate Admissions, 502-852-3101, Fax: 502-852-6536, E-mail: gradadm@louisville.edu.

University of Maine, Graduate School, College of Liberal Arts and Sciences, Department of Psychology, Orono, ME 04469. Offers clinical (PhD); developmental (MA, PhD); experimental (MA); psychological sciences (MA, PhD). *Accreditation:* APA (one or more programs are accredited). *Faculty:* 14 full-time (6 women), 3 part-time/adjunct (2 women). *Students:* 27 full-time (17 women), 10 part-time (6 women); includes 2 minority (1 Asian, non-Hispanic/Latino; 1 Hispanic/Latino), 2 international. Average age 28. 147 applicants, 5% accepted, 7 enrolled. In 2010, 5 master's, 4 doctorates awarded. *Degree requirements:* For master's, thesis; for doctorate, thesis/dissertation. *Entrance requirements:* For master's and doctorate, GRE General Test, GRE Subject Test. Additional exam requirements/recommendations for international students: Required—TOEFL. *Application deadline:* For fall admission, 2/1 priority date for domestic students. Applications are processed on a rolling basis. Application fee: $65. Electronic applications accepted. *Expenses:* Tuition, state resident: full-time $400. Tuition, nonresident: full-time $1050. *Financial support:* In 2010–11, 3 research assistantships with tuition reimbursements (averaging $14,063 per year), 21 teaching assistantships with tuition reimbursements (averaging $12,790 per year) were awarded; Federal Work-Study, institutionally sponsored loans, and tuition waivers (full and partial) also available. Financial award application deadline: 3/1. *Faculty research:* Social development, hypertension and aging, attitude change, self-confidence in achievement situations, health psychology. *Unit head:* Dr. Michael Robbins, Chair, 207-581-2051, Fax: 207-581-6128. *Application contact:* Scott G. Delcourt, Associate Dean of the Graduate School, 207-581-3291, Fax: 207-581-3232, E-mail: graduate@maine.edu.

The University of Manchester, School of Psychological Sciences, Manchester, United Kingdom. Offers audiology (M Phil, PhD); clinical psychology (M Phil, PhD, Psy D); psychology (M Phil, PhD).

University of Manitoba, Faculty of Graduate Studies, Faculty of Arts, Department of Psychology, Winnipeg, MB R3T 2N2, Canada. Offers clinical psychology (PhD); psychology (MA, PhD); school psychology (MA). *Accreditation:* APA (one or more programs are accredited). *Degree requirements:* For master's, thesis; for doctorate, one foreign language, thesis/dissertation. *Entrance requirements:* For master's and doctorate, GRE General Test.

University of Mary Hardin-Baylor, Graduate Studies in Counseling and Psychology, Belton, TX 76513. Offers clinical mental health counseling (MA); marriage and family Christian counseling (MA); psychology and counseling (MA); school counseling and psychology (MA). Part-time and evening/weekend programs available. *Faculty:* 7 full-time (4 women). *Students:* 33 full-time (23 women), 18 part-time (10 women); includes 11 minority (6 Black or African

American, non-Hispanic/Latino; 4 Hispanic/Latino; 1 Two or more races, non-Hispanic/Latino), 1 international. Average age 29. 46 applicants, 50% accepted, 19 enrolled. In 2010, 44 master's awarded. *Degree requirements:* For master's, comprehensive exam. *Entrance requirements:* For master's, GRE General Test, minimum GPA of 3.0 in last 60 hours or 2.75 overall. *Application deadline:* For fall admission, 6/1 priority date for domestic students; for spring admission, 11/1 for domestic students. Applications are processed on a rolling basis. Application fee: $35 ($135 for international students). Electronic applications accepted. *Financial support:* Research assistantships with full tuition reimbursements, Federal Work-Study and scholarships (for some active duty military personnel only) available. Support available to part-time students. Financial award applicants required to submit FAFSA. *Unit head:* Dr. Isaac Gusukuma, Interim Graduate Program Director, 254-295-5017, E-mail: isaac.gusukuma@umhb.edu. *Application contact:* Dr. Isaac Gusukuma, Interim Graduate Program Director, 254-295-5017, E-mail: isaac.gusukuma@umhb.edu.

University of Maryland, College Park, Academic Affairs, College of Behavioral and Social Sciences, Department of Psychology, College Park, MD 20742. Offers clinical psychology (PhD); developmental psychology (PhD); experimental psychology (PhD); industrial psychology (MA, MS, PhD); social psychology (PhD). *Accreditation:* APA (one or more programs are accredited). *Faculty:* 70 full-time (34 women), 16 part-time/adjunct (10 women). *Students:* 83 full-time (63 women), 6 part-time (4 women); includes 4 Black or African American, non-Hispanic/Latino; 6 Asian, non-Hispanic/Latino; 6 Hispanic/Latino, 13 international. 653 applicants, 4% accepted, 13 enrolled. In 2010, 8 master's, 18 doctorates awarded. *Degree requirements:* For master's, thesis; for doctorate, variable foreign language requirement, comprehensive exam, thesis/dissertation. *Entrance requirements:* For master's and doctorate, GRE General Test, GRE Subject Test, minimum GPA of 3.5, research and/or work experience, 3 letters of recommendation. *Application deadline:* For fall admission, 12/1 for domestic and international students. Applications are processed on a rolling basis. Application fee: $75. Electronic applications accepted. *Expenses:* Tuition, state resident: part-time $471 per credit hour. Tuition, nonresident: part-time $1016 per credit hour. Required fees: $337 per term. *Financial support:* In 2010–11, 14 fellowships with full and partial tuition reimbursements (averaging $20,179 per year), 5 research assistantships (averaging $18,414 per year), 54 teaching assistantships (averaging $17,209 per year) were awarded; career-related internships or fieldwork, Federal Work-Study, and scholarships/grants also available. Support available to part-time students. Financial award applicants required to submit FAFSA. *Faculty research:* Social stereotyping and prejudice, anxiety disorders, auditory neuroethology, counseling and social psychology. Total annual research expenditures: $4 million. *Unit head:* Thomas S. Wallsten, Chair, 301-405-3562, Fax: 301-314-9566, E-mail: twallst@umd.edu. *Application contact:* Dean of Graduate School, 301-405-0358, Fax: 301-314-9305.

University of Massachusetts Amherst, Graduate School, College of Natural Sciences, Department of Psychology, Amherst, MA 01003. Offers clinical psychology (MS, PhD); cognitive psychology (MS, PhD); developmental science (MS, PhD); psychology of peace and violence (MS, PhD); social psychology (MS, PhD). *Accreditation:* APA (one or more programs are accredited). *Faculty:* 47 full-time (23 women). *Students:* 54 full-time (42 women), 6 part-time (4 women); includes 16 minority (3 Black or African American, non-Hispanic/Latino; 6 Asian, non-Hispanic/Latino; 4 Hispanic/Latino; 3 Two or more races, non-Hispanic/Latino), 3 international. Average age 29. 435 applicants, 4% accepted, 8 enrolled. In 2010, 12 master's, 16 doctorates awarded. Terminal master's awarded for partial completion of doctoral program. *Degree requirements:* For master's, thesis; for doctorate, comprehensive exam, thesis/dissertation. *Entrance requirements:* For master's and doctorate, GRE General Test, 3 letters of recommendation. Additional exam requirements/recommendations for international students: Required—TOEFL (minimum score 550 paper-based; 213 computer-based; 80 iBT), IELTS (minimum score 6.5). *Application deadline:* For fall admission, 12/1 for domestic and international students. Applications are processed on a rolling basis. Application fee: $50 ($65 for international students). Electronic applications accepted. *Expenses:* Tuition, state resident: full-time $2640. Required fees: $8282. One-time fee: $357 full-time. *Financial support:* In 2010–11, 8 fellowships with full tuition reimbursements (averaging $12,569 per year), 41 research assistantships with full tuition reimbursements (averaging $10,714 per year), 55 teaching assistantships with full tuition reimbursements (averaging $10,951 per year) were awarded; career-related internships or fieldwork, Federal Work-Study, scholarships/grants, traineeships, health care benefits, tuition waivers (full), and unspecified assistantships also available. Support available to part-time students. Financial award application deadline: 12/1; financial award applicants required to submit FAFSA. *Unit head:* Dr. Linda M. Isbell, Graduate Program Director, 413-545-2503, Fax: 413-545-0996. *Application contact:* Jean M. Ames, Supervisor of Admissions, 413-545-0722, Fax: 413-577-0010, E-mail: gradadm@grad.umass.edu.

University of Massachusetts Boston, Office of Graduate Studies, College of Liberal Arts, Program in Clinical Psychology, Boston, MA 02125-3393. Offers PhD. *Accreditation:* APA. *Degree requirements:* For doctorate, thesis/dissertation, practicum, qualifying exam, internship, dissertation. *Entrance requirements:* For doctorate, GRE General Test, GRE Subject Test, minimum GPA of 2.75. *Faculty research:* Community psychology, psychology, racism and mental health, gender and culture, posttraumatic stress disorder.

University of Massachusetts Dartmouth, Graduate School, College of Arts and Sciences, Department of Psychology, North Dartmouth, MA 02747-2300. Offers behavior analyst (Post-baccalaureate Certificate); clinical psychology (MA); general psychology (MA). Part-time programs available. *Faculty:* 18 full-time (9 women), 8 part-time/adjunct (4 women). *Students:* 22 full-time (19 women), 62 part-time (52 women); includes 7 Black or African American, non-Hispanic/Latino; 2 Hispanic/Latino; 1 Two or more races, non-Hispanic/Latino, 1 international. Average age 30. 110 applicants, 43% accepted, 36 enrolled. In 2010, 14 master's awarded. *Degree requirements:* For master's, thesis (for some programs). *Entrance requirements:* For master's, GRE General Test, minimum GPA of 2.75, 3 letters of recommendation. Additional exam requirements/recommendations for international students: Required—TOEFL (minimum score 500 paper-based). *Application deadline:* For fall admission, 3/31 for domestic students, 1/31 for international students. Application fee: $40 ($60 for international students). Electronic applications accepted. *Expenses:* Tuition, state resident: full-time $2071; part-time $86 per credit. Tuition, nonresident: full-time $8099; part-time $337 per credit. Required fees: $9446; $394 per credit. One-time fee: $75. Part-time tuition and fees vary according to class time, course load, degree level and reciprocity agreements. *Financial support:* In 2010–11, 1 research assistantship with full tuition reimbursement (averaging $10,000 per year), 9 teaching assistantships with full tuition reimbursements (averaging $3,500 per year) were awarded; career-related internships or fieldwork, Federal Work-Study, and unspecified assistantships also available. Support available to part-time students. Financial award application deadline: 3/1; financial award applicants required to submit FAFSA. *Faculty research:* Nonverbal communication, behavioral medicine, anxiety disorder, intimate relationships, learning. Total annual research expenditures: $129,359. *Unit head:* Dr. Paul Donnelly, Director, Clinical Psychology, 508-999-8334, E-mail: pdonnelly@umassd.edu. *Application contact:* Elan Turcotte-Shamski, Graduate Admissions Officer, 508-999-8604, Fax: 508-999-8183, E-mail: graduate@umassd.edu.

University of Memphis, Graduate School, College of Arts and Sciences, Department of Psychology, Memphis, TN 38152-3230. Offers psychology (MS, PhD), including clinical (PhD), experimental (PhD), general psychology (MS), school (PhD); school psychology (MA, Ed S); MS/PhD. *Faculty:* 28 full-time (9 women), 4 part-time/adjunct (0 women). *Students:* 114 full-time (81 women), 21 part-time (15 women); includes 14 Black or African American, non-Hispanic/Latino; 1 American Indian or Alaska Native, non-Hispanic/Latino; 4 Asian, non-Hispanic/Latino; 3 Hispanic/Latino; 4 Two or more races, non-Hispanic/Latino, 7 international. Average age 27. 220 applicants, 15% accepted, 29 enrolled. In 2010, 31 master's, 9 doctorates awarded. *Degree requirements:* For master's, comprehensive exam (for some programs), thesis (for some programs), 37 credit hours (MA); 33 credit hours with thesis or 36 with exam (MS); for doctorate, comprehensive exam (for some programs), thesis/dissertation, 80 semester hours, major area paper; clinical: 1 year placement and 1 year internship; internship (school psychology). *Entrance requirements:* For master's, GRE; for doctorate, GRE (minimum combined score of 1100), minimum GPA of 2.75, 18 hours of undergraduate psychology courses, transcripts, personal statement, letters of recommendation; for Ed S, GRE (minimum combined score of 1100), minimum GPA of 2.75, 18 hours of undergraduate psychology courses, letters of recommendation. Additional exam requirements/recommendations for international students: Required—TOEFL (minimum score 550 paper-based; 210 computer-based; 79 iBT). *Application deadline:* For fall admission, 12/5 for domestic students. Applications are processed on a rolling basis. Application fee: $35 ($60 for international students). Electronic applications accepted. *Financial support:* In 2010–11, 66 students received support; fellowships with full tuition reimbursements available, research assistantships with full tuition reimbursements available, teaching assistantships with full tuition reimbursements available, Federal Work-Study, scholarships/grants, tuition waivers (partial), and unspecified assistantships available. Financial award application deadline: 2/15; financial award applicants required to submit FAFSA. *Faculty research:* Clinical health; school, child and family psychology; psychotherapy; cognitive and behavioral neuroscience; industrial-organizational psychology. *Unit head:* Dr. Robert Cohen, Coordinator of Graduate Programs, 901-678-4679, Fax: 901-678-2579, E-mail: rcohen@memphis.edu. *Application contact:* Lynell Connable, Graduate Secretary, 901-678-4340, Fax: 901-678-2579, E-mail: dconnabl@memphis.edu.

University of Miami, Graduate School, College of Arts and Sciences, Department of Psychology, Coral Gables, FL 33124. Offers adult clinical (PhD); behavioral neuroscience (PhD); child clinical (PhD); developmental psychology (PhD); health clinical (PhD); psychology (MS). *Accreditation:* APA (one or more programs are accredited). *Degree requirements:* For doctorate, comprehensive exam, thesis/dissertation. *Entrance requirements:* For doctorate, GRE General Test, minimum GPA of 3.5. Additional exam requirements/recommendations for international students: Required—TOEFL. Electronic applications accepted. *Faculty research:* Behavioral factors in cardiovascular disease and cancer adult psychopathology, developmental disabilities, social and emotional development, mechanisms of coping.

University of Michigan, Horace H. Rackham School of Graduate Studies, College of Literature, Science, and the Arts, Department of Psychology, Ann Arbor, MI 48109. Offers biopsychology (PhD); clinical psychology (PhD); cognition and perception (PhD); developmental psychology (PhD); personality and social contexts (PhD); social psychology (PhD). *Accreditation:* APA. *Faculty:* 83 full-time (39 women), 30 part-time/adjunct (14 women). *Students:* 132 full-time (92 women); includes 13 Black or African American, non-Hispanic/Latino; 2 American Indian or Alaska Native, non-Hispanic/Latino; 18 Asian, non-Hispanic/Latino; 7 Hispanic/Latino; 2 Two or more races, non-Hispanic/Latino, 20 international. Average age 27. 608 applicants, 6% accepted, 24 enrolled. In 2010, 28 doctorates awarded. *Degree requirements:* For doctorate, comprehensive exam, thesis/dissertation, oral defense of dissertation, preliminary exam. *Entrance requirements:* For doctorate, GRE General Test. Additional exam requirements/recommendations for international students: Required—TOEFL. *Application deadline:* For fall admission, 12/1 for domestic and international students. Application fee: $65 ($75 for international students). Electronic applications accepted. *Expenses:* Tuition, state resident: full-time $17,784; part-time $1116 per credit hour. Tuition, nonresident: full-time $35,944; part-time $2125 per credit hour. International tuition: $35,994 full-time. Required fees: $95 per semester. Tuition and fees vary according to course load, degree level and program. *Financial support:* In 2010–11, 118 students received support, including 55 fellowships with full tuition reimbursements available (averaging $20,900 per year), 15 research assistantships with full tuition reimbursements available (averaging $25,950 per year), 52 teaching assistantships with full tuition reimbursements available (averaging $22,670 per year); career-related internships or fieldwork also available. Financial award application deadline: 4/15. Total annual research expenditures: $7.4 million. *Unit head:* Prof. Theresa Lee, Chair, 734-764-7429. *Application contact:* Laurie Brannan, Psychology Student Academic Affairs, 731-764-2580, Fax: 734-615-7584, E-mail: psych.saa@umich.edu.

University of Michigan–Dearborn, College of Arts, Sciences, and Letters, Master of Science in Psychology Program, Dearborn, MI 48128. Offers clinical health psychology (MS); health psychology (MS). Part-time programs available. *Faculty:* 11 full-time (5 women). *Students:* 24 full-time (21 women), 10 part-time (9 women); includes 2 Black or African American, non-Hispanic/Latino; 2 Asian, non-Hispanic/Latino; 1 Hispanic/Latino; 1 Native Hawaiian or other Pacific Islander, non-Hispanic/Latino. Average age 31. 49 applicants, 71% accepted, 23 enrolled. In 2010, 9 master's awarded. *Degree requirements:* For master's, oral defense of thesis. *Entrance requirements:* For master's, GRE, 3 letters of recommendation. Additional exam requirements/recommendations for international students: Required—TOEFL (minimum score 560 paper-based; 220 computer-based). *Application deadline:* For fall admission, 3/15 for domestic and international students. Application fee: $60 ($75 for international students). *Financial support:* In 2010–11, 4 students received support. Scholarships/grants available. *Faculty research:* Cardiovascular reactivity, coping, addiction, psychoneuroimmunology. *Unit head:* Dr. Pam McAuslan, Program Director, 313-593-5376, E-mail: pmcausla@umd.umich.edu. *Application contact:* Carol Ligienza, Coordinator, CASL Graduate Programs, 313-593-1183, Fax: 313-583-6700, E-mail: caslgrad@umd.umich.edu.

University of Minnesota, Twin Cities Campus, Graduate School, College of Liberal Arts, Department of Psychology, Program in Clinical Psychology, Minneapolis, MN 55455-0213. Offers PhD. *Accreditation:* APA. *Degree requirements:* For doctorate, comprehensive exam, thesis/dissertation, internship. *Entrance requirements:* For doctorate, GRE General Test, minimum GPA of 3.5; 12 credits of upper-level psychology courses, including statistics or psychological measurement; previous course work in abnormal psychology. Additional exam requirements/recommendations for international students: Required—TOEFL (minimum score 550 paper-based; 213 computer-based; 79 iBT).

University of Mississippi, Graduate School, College of Liberal Arts, Department of Psychology, Oxford, University, MS 38677. Offers clinical psychology (PhD); experimental psychology (PhD); psychology (MA). *Accreditation:* APA (one or more programs are accredited). *Students:* 55 full-time (42 women), 6 part-time (4 women); includes 10 minority (8 Black or African American, non-Hispanic/Latino; 1 Asian, non-Hispanic/Latino; 1 Hispanic/Latino), 1 international. In 2010, 4 master's, 4 doctorates awarded. *Degree requirements:* For master's, thesis; for doctorate, thesis/dissertation. *Entrance requirements:* For master's, GRE General Test, minimum GPA of 3.0; for doctorate, GRE General Test. Additional exam requirements/recommendations for international students: Required—TOEFL. *Application deadline:* For fall admission, 1/15 for domestic students; for spring admission, 10/1 for domestic students. Applications are processed on a rolling basis. Application fee: $25. Electronic applications accepted. *Financial support:* Scholarships/grants available. Financial award application deadline: 3/1; financial award applicants required to submit FAFSA. *Unit head:* Dr. Michael T. Allen, Chairman, 662-915-5190, Fax: 662-915-5398, E-mail: psych@olemiss.edu. *Application contact:* Dr. Christy M. Wyandt, Associate Dean, 662-915-7474, Fax: 662-915-7577, E-mail: cwyandt@olemiss.edu.

University of Missouri–Kansas City, College of Arts and Sciences, Department of Psychology, Kansas City, MO 64110-2499. Offers clinical psychology (PhD); community psychology (PhD); health psychology (PhD); psychology (MA). PhD (interdisciplinary) offered through the School of Graduate Studies. *Accreditation:* APA. *Faculty:* 14 full-time (10 women), 4 part-time/adjunct (3 women). *Students:* 17 full-time (11 women), 7 part-time (all women); includes 1 Black or African American, non-Hispanic/Latino; 1 Asian, non-Hispanic/Latino; 3 Hispanic/Latino. Average age 30. 89 applicants, 9% accepted, 6 enrolled. In 2010, 6 master's, 4 doctorates awarded. Terminal master's awarded for partial completion of doctoral program. *Degree requirements:* For master's, thesis; for doctorate, comprehensive exam, thesis/dissertation, residency. *Entrance requirements:* For master's, GRE, minimum GPA of 3.5, letter of recommendation; for doctorate, GRE, minimum GPA of 3.25. Additional exam requirements/recommendations for international students: Required—TOEFL (minimum score 550 paper-based; 213 computer-based; 80 iBT). *Application deadline:* For fall admission, 1/15 for domestic and international students. Applications are processed on a rolling basis. Application fee: $45 ($50 for international students). Electronic applications accepted. *Expenses:* Tuition, state resident: full-time $5522.40; part-time $306.80 per credit hour. Tuition, nonresident: full-time $7128; part-time $792 per credit hour. Required fees: $261.15 per term. *Financial support:* In 2010–11, 18 research assistantships

Clinical Psychology

University of Missouri–Kansas City (continued)
(averaging $11,778 per year), 6 teaching assistantships (averaging $11,500 per year) were awarded; career-related internships or fieldwork, Federal Work-Study, and institutionally sponsored loans also available. Support available to part-time students. Financial award application deadline: 3/1; financial award applicants required to submit FAFSA. *Faculty research:* HIV/AIDS research group, psycho-oncology, sensory and cognitive neuroscience, cognitive psychophysiology, obesity and related metabolic disorders. Total annual research expenditures: $933,609. *Unit head:* Dr. Tamera Murdock, Chairperson/Professor, 816-235-1318, Fax: 816-235-1062, E-mail: murdockt@umkc.edu. *Application contact:* Dr. Lisa Terre, Director, Graduate Programs, 816-235-1318, Fax: 816-235-1062, E-mail: terrel@umkc.edu.

University of Missouri–St. Louis, College of Arts and Sciences, Department of Psychology, St. Louis, MO 63121. Offers behavioral neuroscience (PhD); clinical community psychology (PhD); clinical psychology respecialization (Certificate); general psychology (MA); industrial/organizational psychology (PhD); trauma studies (Certificate). *Accreditation:* APA (one or more programs are accredited). Evening/weekend programs available. *Faculty:* 19 full-time (9 women), 5 part-time/adjunct (3 women). *Students:* 44 full-time (34 women), 35 part-time (25 women); includes 7 minority (1 Black or African American, non-Hispanic/Latino; 1 American Indian or Alaska Native, non-Hispanic/Latino; 3 Asian, non-Hispanic/Latino; 2 Hispanic/Latino). Average age 27. 220 applicants, 10% accepted, 18 enrolled. In 2010, 10 master's, 6 doctorates awarded. Terminal master's awarded for partial completion of doctoral program. *Degree requirements:* For master's, thesis; for doctorate, thesis/dissertation. *Entrance requirements:* For master's, GRE General Test, 3 letters of recommendation; for doctorate, GRE General Test, GRE Subject Test, 3 letters of recommendation. Additional exam requirements/recommendations for international students: Required—TOEFL (minimum score 550 paper-based; 213 computer-based). *Application deadline:* For fall admission, 1/15 for domestic and international students. Application fee: $35 ($40 for international students). Electronic applications accepted. *Expenses:* Tuition, state resident: full-time $5522; part-time $306.80 per credit hour. Tuition, nonresident: full-time $14,253; part-time $792.10 per credit hour. Required fees: $658; $49 per credit hour. One-time fee: $12. Tuition and fees vary according to program. *Financial support:* In 2010–11, 5 research assistantships with full and partial tuition reimbursements (averaging $13,352 per year), 26 teaching assistantships with full and partial tuition reimbursements (averaging $11,000 per year) were awarded; fellowships with full tuition reimbursements also available. Financial award applicants required to submit FAFSA. *Faculty research:* Bereavement and loss, neuroscience, post-traumatic stress disorder, conflict and negotiation, social psychology. *Unit head:* Dr. George Taylor, Chair, 314-516-5391, Fax: 314-516-5392, E-mail: umslpsychology@msx.umsl.edu. *Application contact:* 314-516-5458, Fax: 314-516-6996, E-mail: gradadm@umsl.edu.

The University of Montana, Graduate School, College of Arts and Sciences, Department of Psychology, Missoula, MT 59812-0002. Offers clinical psychology (PhD); experimental psychology (PhD), including animal behavior psychology, developmental psychology; school psychology (MA, PhD, Ed S). *Accreditation:* APA (one or more programs are accredited). Terminal master's awarded for partial completion of doctoral program. *Degree requirements:* For master's, thesis; for doctorate, thesis/dissertation. *Entrance requirements:* For master's, doctorate, and Ed S, GRE General Test. Additional exam requirements/recommendations for international students: Required—TOEFL.

University of Nebraska–Lincoln, Graduate College, College of Arts and Sciences, Department of Psychology, Lincoln, NE 68588. Offers biopsychology (PhD); clinical psychology (PhD); cognitive psychology (PhD); developmental psychology (PhD); psychology (MA); social/personality psychology (PhD); JD/MA; JD/PhD. *Accreditation:* APA (one or more programs are accredited). *Degree requirements:* For master's, thesis optional; for doctorate, comprehensive exam, thesis/dissertation. *Entrance requirements:* For master's and doctorate, GRE General Test. Additional exam requirements/recommendations for international students: Required—TOEFL (minimum score 550 paper-based; 213 computer-based). Electronic applications accepted. *Faculty research:* Law and psychology, rural mental health, chronic mental illness, neuropsychology, child clinical psychology.

University of Nevada, Las Vegas, Graduate College, College of Education, Department of Counselor Education, Las Vegas, NV 89154-3066. Offers clinical mental health counseling (MS); community mental health counseling (Advanced Certificate); rehabilitation counseling (Advanced Certificate); school counseling (M Ed). *Faculty:* 7 full-time (2 women), 10 part-time/adjunct (7 women). *Students:* 62 full-time (54 women), 60 part-time (53 women); includes 50 minority (8 Black or African American, non-Hispanic/Latino; 1 American Indian or Alaska Native, non-Hispanic/Latino; 2 Asian, non-Hispanic/Latino; 17 Hispanic/Latino; 1 Native Hawaiian or other Pacific Islander, non-Hispanic/Latino; 21 Two or more races, non-Hispanic/Latino), 1 international. Average age 33. 102 applicants, 82% accepted, 58 enrolled. In 2010, 24 master's, 4 other advanced degrees awarded. *Degree requirements:* For master's, comprehensive exam (for some programs), thesis (for some programs); for Advanced Certificate, thesis (for some programs). *Entrance requirements:* Additional exam requirements/recommendations for international students: Required—TOEFL (minimum score 550 paper-based; 213 computer-based; 80 iBT), IELTS (minimum score 7). *Application deadline:* For fall admission, 2/1 priority date for domestic and international students. Applications are processed on a rolling basis. Application fee: $60 ($95 for international students). Electronic applications accepted. *Expenses:* Tuition, area resident: Part-time $239.50 per credit. Tuition, state resident: part-time $239.50 per credit. Tuition, nonresident: part-time $503 per credit. Required fees: $108 per semester. Tuition and fees vary according to course load, program and reciprocity agreements. *Financial support:* In 2010–11, 10 students received support, including 6 research assistantships with partial tuition reimbursements available (averaging $10,000 per year), 4 teaching assistantships with partial tuition reimbursements available (averaging $10,000 per year); institutionally sponsored loans, scholarships/grants, health care benefits, and unspecified assistantships also available. Financial award application deadline: 3/1. *Faculty research:* Multicultural issues in counseling, counseling with returning veterans, counseling depression and suicide, effective play therapy, ethics and counseling. Total annual research expenditures: $4,627. *Unit head:* Dr. Jesse Brinson, Interim Chair/ Associate Professor, 702-895-1390, Fax: 702-895-5550, E-mail: brinson@unlv.nevada.edu. *Application contact:* Graduate College Admissions Evaluator, 702-895-3320, Fax: 702-895-4180, E-mail: gradcollege@unlv.edu.

University of Nevada, Reno, Graduate School, College of Liberal Arts, Department of Psychology, Program in Clinical Psychology, Reno, NV 89557. Offers PhD. Terminal master's awarded for partial completion of doctoral program. *Degree requirements:* For doctorate, comprehensive exam, thesis/dissertation. *Entrance requirements:* For doctorate, GRE Subject Test (psychology), minimum GPA of 3.0. Additional exam requirements/recommendations for international students: Required—TOEFL (minimum score 500 paper-based; 173 computer-based; 61 iBT), IELTS (minimum score 6). Electronic applications accepted. *Expenses:* Tuition, state resident: full-time $2219; part-time $246 per credit. Tuition, nonresident: part-time $510 per credit. International tuition: $9009 full-time. Required fees: $59 per term. One-time fee: $101. Tuition and fees vary according to course load. *Faculty research:* Health behavior, domestic violence, verbal relations, anxiety.

University of New Brunswick Saint John, Department of Psychology, Saint John, NB E2L 4L5, Canada. Offers applied and experimental psychology (PhD); clinical psychology (PhD); experimental psychology (MA). Part-time programs available. *Faculty:* 9 full-time (4 women), 1 part-time/adjunct (0 women). *Students:* 4 full-time (1 woman). In 2010, 1 doctorate awarded. *Degree requirements:* For master's, thesis. *Entrance requirements:* For master's, GRE General and Subject Tests, honours thesis. Additional exam requirements/recommendations for international students: Required—TOEFL (minimum score 550 paper-based), TWE. *Application deadline:* For fall admission, 2/1 for domestic students. Application fee: $50. *Financial support:* In 2010–11, 2 research assistantships (averaging $9,000 per year), 7 teaching assistantships (averaging $4,500 per year) were awarded; fellowships, unspecified assistantships also available. Support available to part-time students. Financial award application deadline: 2/1. *Faculty*

research: Psychopharmacology and addictions, forensic psychology and criminal justice, interpersonal relations, perception and graphical perception, lie detection, children's play and peer relationships, classical and operant conditioning. *Unit head:* Dr. Lily Both, Director of Graduate Studies, 506-648-5769, Fax: 506-648-5780, E-mail: lboth@unbsj.ca. *Application contact:* Frances Stevens, Secretary, 506-648-5640, Fax: 506-648-5780, E-mail: fstevens@unb.ca.

University of New Mexico, Graduate School, College of Arts and Sciences, Department of Psychology, Program in Clinical Psychology, Albuquerque, NM 87131-2039. Offers MS, PhD. *Accreditation:* APA (one or more programs are accredited). *Students:* 6 full-time (5 women); includes 2 Hispanic/Latino. Average age 34. *Degree requirements:* For master's, thesis; for doctorate, comprehensive exam, thesis/dissertation, pre-doctoral internship. *Entrance requirements:* For doctorate, GRE General Test, GRE Subject Test (psychology), minimum GPA of 3.0. Additional exam requirements/recommendations for international students: Required—TOEFL. *Application deadline:* For fall admission, 1/15 priority date for domestic and international students. Applications are processed on a rolling basis. Application fee: $50. Electronic applications accepted. *Expenses:* Tuition, state resident: full-time $5991; part-time $251 per credit hour. Tuition, nonresident: full-time $14,405; part-time $800.20 per credit hour. Tuition and fees vary according to course level, course load, program and reciprocity agreements. *Financial support:* In 2010–11, 6 students received support, including 3 research assistantships with full and partial tuition reimbursements available (averaging $13,050 per year), 3 teaching assistantships with full and partial tuition reimbursements available (averaging $10,996 per year); fellowships, career-related internships or fieldwork, Federal Work-Study, scholarships/grants, health care benefits, tuition waivers (full and partial), and unspecified assistantships also available. Financial award application deadline: 3/1; financial award applicants required to submit FAFSA. *Faculty research:* Addictive behaviors; cognitive, behavioral, community psychology; cross-cultural issues; eating disorders; empirically-supported treatment; health psychology; neurobiological, psychological trauma and sexual victimization. *Unit head:* Dr. Sarah Erickson, Director of Clinical Training, 505-277-4121, Fax: 505-277-1394, E-mail: erickson@unm.edu. *Application contact:* Tonya Bryant, Coordinator, Program Advisement, 505-277-5009, Fax: 505-277-1394, E-mail: advising@unm.edu.

The University of North Carolina at Chapel Hill, Graduate School, College of Arts and Sciences, Department of Psychology, Chapel Hill, NC 27599. Offers biological psychology (PhD); clinical psychology (PhD); cognitive psychology (PhD); developmental psychology (PhD); quantitative psychology (PhD); social psychology (PhD). *Accreditation:* APA. *Degree requirements:* For doctorate, comprehensive exam, thesis/dissertation. *Entrance requirements:* For doctorate, GRE General Test, minimum GPA of 3.0. Electronic applications accepted. *Faculty research:* Expressed emotion, cognitive development, social cognitive neuroscience, human memory personality.

The University of North Carolina at Charlotte, Graduate School, College of Arts and Sciences, Department of Psychology, Charlotte, NC 28223-0001. Offers community/clinical psychology (MA); health psychology (PhD); industrial/organizational psychology (MA); organizational science (PhD). Part-time programs available. *Faculty:* 27 full-time (11 women), 1 part-time/adjunct (0 women). *Students:* 67 full-time (50 women), 18 part-time (14 women); includes 19 minority (8 Black or African American, non-Hispanic/Latino; 3 Asian, non-Hispanic/Latino; 4 Hispanic/Latino; 1 Native Hawaiian or other Pacific Islander, non-Hispanic/Latino; 3 Two or more races, non-Hispanic/Latino), 3 international. Average age 29. 317 applicants, 9% accepted, 21 enrolled. In 2010, 14 master's, 1 doctorate awarded. *Degree requirements:* For master's, thesis; for doctorate, thesis/dissertation. *Entrance requirements:* For master's, GRE General Test, GRE Subject Test, minimum GPA of 3.0 in undergraduate major, 2.8 overall. Additional exam requirements/recommendations for international students: Required—TOEFL (minimum score 557 paper-based; 220 computer-based; 83 iBT). *Application deadline:* Applications are processed on a rolling basis. Application fee: $55. Electronic applications accepted. *Expenses:* Tuition, state resident: full-time $3464. Tuition, nonresident: full-time $14,297. Required fees: $2094. Tuition and fees vary according to course load. *Financial support:* In 2010–11, 44 students received support, including 12 research assistantships (averaging $14,191 per year), 31 teaching assistantships (averaging $10,710 per year); career-related internships or fieldwork, Federal Work-Study, institutionally sponsored loans, scholarships/grants, and administrative assistantships also available. Support available to part-time students. Financial award application deadline: 4/1; financial award applicants required to submit FAFSA. *Faculty research:* Health psychology, industrial-organizational psychology, cognitive science. Total annual research expenditures: $435,127. *Unit head:* Dr. Brian L. Cutler, Chair, 704-687-4731, Fax: 704-687-3096, E-mail: blcutler@uncc.edu. *Application contact:* Kathy B. Giddings, Director of Graduate Admissions, 704-687-5503, Fax: 704-687-3279, E-mail: gradadm@uncc.edu.

The University of North Carolina at Greensboro, Graduate School, College of Arts and Sciences, Department of Psychology, Greensboro, NC 27412-5001. Offers clinical psychology (MA, PhD); cognitive psychology (MA, PhD); developmental psychology (MA, PhD); social psychology (MA, PhD). *Accreditation:* APA (one or more programs are accredited). Terminal master's awarded for partial completion of doctoral program. *Degree requirements:* For master's, comprehensive exam, thesis; for doctorate, one foreign language, thesis/dissertation, preliminary exam. *Entrance requirements:* For master's and doctorate, GRE General Test. Additional exam requirements/recommendations for international students: Required—TOEFL. Electronic applications accepted. *Faculty research:* Sensory and perceptual determinants; evoked potential: disorders, deafness, and development.

University of North Dakota, Graduate School, College of Arts and Sciences, Department of Psychology, Grand Forks, ND 58202. Offers clinical psychology (PhD); counseling psychology (PhD); experimental psychology (PhD); forensic psychology (MA, MS); psychology (MA). *Accreditation:* APA (one or more programs are accredited). *Faculty:* 22 full-time (7 women), 2 part-time/adjunct (1 woman). *Students:* 55 full-time (46 women), 81 part-time (69 women); includes 24 minority (4 Black or African American, non-Hispanic/Latino; 12 American Indian or Alaska Native, non-Hispanic/Latino; 2 Asian, non-Hispanic/Latino; 4 Hispanic/Latino; 2 Two or more races, non-Hispanic/Latino), 2 international. Average age 29. 126 applicants, 25% accepted, 27 enrolled. In 2010, 25 master's, 9 doctorates awarded. *Degree requirements:* For master's, thesis, final exam; for doctorate, comprehensive exam, thesis/dissertation, internship, final exam. *Entrance requirements:* For master's, GRE General Test, GRE Subject Test, minimum GPA of 3.0; for doctorate, GRE General Test, GRE Subject Test, minimum GPA of 3.5. Additional exam requirements/recommendations for international students: Required—TOEFL (minimum score 550 paper-based; 213 computer-based; 79 iBT), IELTS (minimum score 6.5). *Application deadline:* For fall admission, 1/15 for domestic and international students. Application fee: $35. Electronic applications accepted. *Expenses:* Tuition, state resident: full-time $5857; part-time $306.74 per credit. Tuition, nonresident: full-time $15,666; part-time $729.77 per credit. Required fees: $53.42 per credit. Tuition and fees vary according to course load, program and reciprocity agreements. *Financial support:* In 2010–11, 28 students received support, including 21 teaching assistantships with full and partial tuition reimbursements available (averaging $8,993 per year); fellowships with full and partial tuition reimbursements available, research assistantships with full and partial tuition reimbursements available, career-related internships or fieldwork, Federal Work-Study, institutionally sponsored loans, scholarships/grants, health care benefits, tuition waivers (full and partial), and unspecified assistantships also available. Support available to part-time students. Financial award application deadline: 3/15; financial award applicants required to submit FAFSA. *Faculty research:* Developmental psychology, clinical social psychology, educational psychology, personality disorders. Total annual research expenditures: $323,990. *Unit head:* Dr. Mark Grabe, Chairperson, 701-777-3451, E-mail: mark.grabe@und.nodak.edu. *Application contact:* Matt Anderson, Admissions Specialist, 701-777-2947, Fax: 701-777-3619, E-mail: matthew.anderson@gradschool.und.edu.

University of North Texas, Toulouse Graduate School, College of Arts and Sciences, Department of Psychology, Denton, TX 76203. Offers clinical psychology (PhD); counseling psychology (MA, MS, PhD); experimental psychology (MA, MS, PhD); health psychology and behavioral medicine (PhD). *Accreditation:* APA (one or more programs are accredited). Terminal master's awarded for partial completion of doctoral program. *Degree requirements:* For master's, comprehensive exam, thesis or alternative; for doctorate, one foreign language, comprehensive exam, thesis/dissertation. *Entrance requirements:* For master's and doctorate, GRE General Test, interview. Additional exam requirements/recommendations for international students: Recommended—TOEFL (minimum score 550 paper-based; 213 computer-based; 79 iBT). *Application deadline:* Applications are processed on a rolling basis. Electronic applications accepted. *Expenses:* Tuition, state resident: full-time $4298; part-time $239 per credit hour. Tuition, nonresident: full-time $10,782; part-time $549 per credit hour. Required fees: $1292; $270 per credit hour. *Financial support:* Fellowships, research assistantships, teaching assistantships, career-related internships or fieldwork, Federal Work-Study, and institutionally sponsored loans available. Financial award applicants required to submit FAFSA. *Application contact:* Graduate Coordinator, 940-565-2671, Fax: 940-565-4682, E-mail: amym@unt.edu.

University of Oregon, Graduate School, College of Arts and Sciences, Department of Psychology, Program in Clinical Psychology, Eugene, OR 97403. Offers PhD. *Accreditation:* APA. *Degree requirements:* For doctorate, thesis/dissertation. *Entrance requirements:* For doctorate, GRE General Test. Additional exam requirements/recommendations for international students: Required—TOEFL.

University of Phoenix, College of Social Science, Phoenix, AZ 85034-7209. Offers clinical mental health counseling (MSC); community counseling (MSC); psychology (MS). Programs are offered at the online campus. Evening/weekend programs available. Postbaccalaureate distance learning degree programs offered. *Students:* 4,215 full-time (3,585 women); includes 1,544 minority (1,161 Black or African American, non-Hispanic/Latino; 34 American Indian or Alaska Native, non-Hispanic/Latino; 32 Asian, non-Hispanic/Latino; 280 Hispanic/Latino; 22 Native Hawaiian or other Pacific Islander, non-Hispanic/Latino; 15 Two or more races, non-Hispanic/Latino), 85 international. Average age 38. *Entrance requirements:* For master's, minimum undergraduate GPA of 2.5 from accredited university, 3 years of work experience, citizen of the United States or have valid visa. Additional exam requirements/recommendations for international students: Required—TOEFL (minimum paper score 550, computer score 213, iBT 79), Test of English for International Communication, or IELTS. *Application deadline:* Applications are processed on a rolling basis. Application fee: $45. Electronic applications accepted. *Expenses:* Tuition: Full-time $16,440. One-time fee: $45 full-time. Full-time tuition and fees vary according to course load, degree level, campus/location and program. *Financial support:* Scholarships/grants available. Financial award applicants required to submit FAFSA. *Unit head:* Rob Olding, Associate Dean, Human Service/Psychology, 602-551-3073, E-mail: rob.olding@phoenix.edu. *Application contact:* Rob Olding, Associate Dean, Human Service/Psychology, 602-551-3073, E-mail: rob.olding@phoenix.edu.

University of Puerto Rico, Río Piedras, College of Social Sciences, Department of Psychology, San Juan, PR 00931-3300. Offers clinical psychology (MA); industrial organizational psychology (MA); investigative academic psychology (MA); psychology (PhD); social-community psychology (MA). Part-time programs available. *Degree requirements:* For master's, comprehensive exam, thesis; for doctorate, comprehensive exam, thesis/dissertation, internship. *Entrance requirements:* For master's, GRE or PAEG, interview, minimum GPA of 3.0; for doctorate, GRE or PAEG, interview, master's degree, minimum GPA of 3.0. *Faculty research:* Intervention on Depressed Latino Youth, biosychosocial training.

University of Regina, Faculty of Graduate Studies and Research, Faculty of Arts, Department of Psychology, Regina, SK S4S 0A2, Canada. Offers clinical psychology (MA, PhD); experimental and applied psychology (MA, PhD). *Faculty:* 19 full-time (9 women). *Students:* 51 full-time (39 women), 3 part-time (2 women). 44 applicants, 41% accepted. In 2010, 12 master's, 4 doctorates awarded. *Degree requirements:* For master's, thesis; for doctorate, comprehensive exam, thesis/dissertation. *Entrance requirements:* For master's, GRE General Test, GRE Subject Test; for doctorate, GRE General Test, GRE Subject Test (optional for those with a master's degree from a Canadian university). Additional exam requirements/recommendations for international students: Required—TOEFL (minimum score 580 paper-based; 80 iBT). *Application deadline:* For fall admission, 2/15 for domestic and international students. Application fee: $100. Electronic applications accepted. Tuition and fees charges are reported in Canadian dollars. *Expenses:* Tuition, area resident: Full-time $3244.50 Canadian dollars; part-time $180.25 Canadian dollars per credit hour. International tuition: $4744.50 Canadian dollars full-time. Required fees: $494 Canadian dollars; $115.25 Canadian dollars per credit hour. $115.25 Canadian dollars per semester. Tuition and fees vary according to program. *Financial support:* In 2010–11, 9 fellowships (averaging $20,333 per year), 3 research assistantships (averaging $16,500 per year), 21 teaching assistantships (averaging $6,884 per year) were awarded; career-related internships or fieldwork and scholarships/grants also available. Financial award application deadline: 6/15. *Faculty research:* Clinical, experimental, cognitive, and applied psychology; post-traumatic stress disorder, anxiety, and panic disorder; traumatic brain injury; chronic pain; perception and memory. *Unit head:* Dr. Richard MacLennan, Head, 306-585-4458, Fax: 306-585-5429, E-mail: richard.maclennan@uregina.ca. *Application contact:* Dr. Richard MacLennan, Graduate Program Coordinator, 306-585-4458, Fax: 306-585-5429, E-mail: richard.maclennan@uregina.ca.

University of Rhode Island, Graduate School, College of Arts and Sciences, Department of Psychology, Kingston, RI 02881. Offers behavioral science (PhD); clinical psychology (MA, PhD); school psychology (MS, PhD). *Accreditation:* APA (one or more programs are accredited). Part-time programs available. *Faculty:* 20 full-time (10 women). *Students:* 75 full-time (56 women), 32 part-time (28 women); includes 24 minority (12 Black or African American, non-Hispanic/Latino; 4 Asian, non-Hispanic/Latino; 7 Hispanic/Latino; 1 Two or more races, non-Hispanic/Latino), 6 international. In 2010, 16 master's, 14 doctorates awarded. *Degree requirements:* For master's, comprehensive exam, thesis optional; for doctorate, thesis/dissertation. *Entrance requirements:* For master's and doctorate, GRE, 3 letters of recommendation. Additional exam requirements/recommendations for international students: Required—TOEFL (minimum score 550 paper-based; 213 computer-based). Application fee: $65. Electronic applications accepted. *Expenses:* Tuition, state resident: full-time $9588; part-time $533 per credit hour. Tuition, nonresident: full-time $22,968; part-time $1276 per credit hour. Required fees: $1282; $68 per semester. Tuition and fees vary according to program. *Financial support:* In 2010–11, 5 research assistantships with full and partial tuition reimbursements (averaging $2,927 per year), 20 teaching assistantships with full and partial tuition reimbursements (averaging $12,479 per year) were awarded. Financial award applicants required to submit FAFSA. Total annual research expenditures: $193,164. *Unit head:* Dr. Patricia Morokoff, Chairperson, 401-874-4239, Fax: 401-874-2157, E-mail: morokoff@uri.edu. *Application contact:* Dr. Patricia Morokoff, Chairperson, 401-874-4239, Fax: 401-874-2157, E-mail: morokoff@uri.edu.

University of Rochester, School of Arts and Sciences, Department of Clinical and Social Sciences in Psychology, Program in Clinical Psychology, Rochester, NY 14627.

University of South Africa, College of Human Sciences, Pretoria, South Africa. Offers adult education (M Ed); African languages (MA, PhD); African politics (MA, PhD); Afrikaans (MA, PhD); ancient history (MA, PhD); ancient Near Eastern studies (MA, PhD); anthropology (MA, PhD); applied linguistics (MA); Arabic (MA, PhD); archaeology (MA); art history (MA); Biblical archaeology (MA); Biblical studies (M Th, D Th, PhD); Christian spirituality (M Th, D Th); church history (M Th, D Th); classical studies (MA, PhD); clinical psychology (MA); communication (MA, PhD); comparative education (M Ed, Ed D); consulting psychology (D Admin, D Com, PhD); curriculum studies (M Ed, Ed D); development studies (M Admin, MA, D Admin, PhD); didactics (M Ed, Ed D); education (M Tech); education management (M Ed, Ed D); educational psychology (M Ed); English (MA); environmental education (M Ed); French (MA, PhD); German (MA, PhD); Greek (MA); guidance and counseling (M Ed); health studies (MA, PhD), including health sciences education (MA), health services management (MA), medical and surgical nursing science (critical care general) (MA), midwifery and neonatal nursing science (MA), trauma and emergency care (MA); history (MA, PhD); history of education (Ed D); inclusive education (M Ed, Ed D); information and communications technology policy and regulation (MA); information science (MA, MIS, PhD); international politics (MA, PhD); Islamic studies (MA, PhD); Italian (MA, PhD); Judaica (MA, PhD); linguistics (MA, PhD); mathematical education (M Ed); mathematics education (MA); missiology (M Th, D Th); modern Hebrew (MA, PhD); musicology (MA, MMus, D Mus, PhD); natural science education (M Ed); New Testament (M Th, D Th); Old Testament (D Th); pastoral therapy (M Th, D Th); philosophy (MA); philosophy of education (M Ed, Ed D); politics (MA, PhD); Portuguese (MA, PhD); practical theology (M Th, D Th); psychology (MA, MS, PhD); psychology of education (M Ed, Ed D); public health (MA); religious studies (MA, D Th, PhD); Romance languages (MA); Russian (MA, PhD); Semitic languages (MA, PhD); social behavior studies in HIV/AIDS (MA); social science (mental health) (MA); social science in development studies (MA); social science in psychology (MA); social science in social work (MA); social science in sociology (MA); social work (MSW, DSW, PhD); socio-education (M Ed, Ed D); sociolinguistics (MA); sociology (MA, PhD); Spanish (MA, PhD); systematic theology (M Th, D Th); TESOL (teaching English to speakers of other languages) (MA); theological ethics (M Th, D Th); theory of literature (MA, PhD); urban ministries (D Th); urban ministry (M Th).

University of South Alabama, Graduate School, College of Arts and Sciences, Department of Psychology, Mobile, AL 36688. Offers clinical and counseling psychology (PhD); psychology (MS). Part-time and evening/weekend programs available. *Faculty:* 10 full-time (4 women). *Students:* 14 full-time (11 women), 9 part-time (5 women); includes 3 minority (2 Black or African American, non-Hispanic/Latino; 1 Hispanic/Latino). 47 applicants, 26% accepted, 9 enrolled. In 2010, 10 master's awarded. *Degree requirements:* For master's, comprehensive exam, thesis optional. *Entrance requirements:* For master's, GRE General Test, GRE Subject Test (recommended), minimum GPA of 3.0, major in psychology or equivalent. Additional exam requirements/recommendations for international students: Required—TOEFL. *Application deadline:* For fall admission, 3/1 priority date for domestic students, 3/1 for international students. Applications are processed on a rolling basis. Application fee: $35. *Expenses:* Tuition, state resident: part-time $300 per credit hour. Tuition, nonresident: part-time $600 per credit hour. Required fees: $150 per semester. *Financial support:* Fellowships, research assistantships. Support available to part-time students. Financial award application deadline: 4/1. *Faculty research:* Language acquisition and development. *Unit head:* Dr. Larry Christensen, Chair, 251-460-6371. *Application contact:* Dr. Lisa Turner, Graduate Coordinator, 251-460-6371.

University of South Alabama, Graduate School, Program in Clinical and Counseling Psychology, Mobile, AL 36688-0002. Offers PhD. *Students:* 12 full-time (11 women); includes 2 minority (both Asian, non-Hispanic/Latino). 21 applicants, 29% accepted, 6 enrolled. *Entrance requirements:* For doctorate, GRE. Additional exam requirements/recommendations for international students: Required—TOEFL. *Application deadline:* For fall admission, 2/15 for domestic students; for spring admission, 5/1 for domestic students. Applications are processed on a rolling basis. Application fee: $35. Electronic applications accepted. *Expenses:* Tuition, state resident: part-time $300 per credit hour. Tuition, nonresident: part-time $600 per credit hour. Required fees: $150 per semester. *Unit head:* Dr. Martin Rohling, Director of Clinical Training, 251-460-6371, E-mail: mrohling@usouthal.edu. *Application contact:* Dr. B. Keith Harrison, Dean of the Graduate School, 251-460-6310.

University of South Carolina, The Graduate School, College of Arts and Sciences, Department of Psychology, Program in Clinical/Community Psychology, Columbia, SC 29208. Offers clinical/community psychology (PhD); general psychology (MA). *Accreditation:* APA. *Degree requirements:* For master's, comprehensive exam, thesis; for doctorate, comprehensive exam, thesis/dissertation. *Entrance requirements:* For doctorate, GRE General Test, minimum GPA of 3.2. Additional exam requirements/recommendations for international students: Required—TOEFL. Electronic applications accepted. *Faculty research:* Developmental psychopathology, health disparities, community-level interventions for psychological well being.

University of South Carolina Aiken, Program in Applied Clinical Psychology, Aiken, SC 29801-6309. Offers MS. Part-time programs available. *Faculty:* 7 full-time (5 women). *Students:* 23 full-time (19 women), 7 part-time (all women); includes 7 minority (2 Black or African American, non-Hispanic/Latino; 1 Asian, non-Hispanic/Latino; 2 Hispanic/Latino; 2 Two or more races, non-Hispanic/Latino). Average age 26. 50 applicants, 54% accepted, 15 enrolled. In 2010, 8 master's awarded. *Degree requirements:* For master's, thesis. *Entrance requirements:* For master's, GRE General Test, GRE Subject Test (psychology). Additional exam requirements/recommendations for international students: Required—TOEFL (minimum score 550 paper-based; 213 computer-based). *Application deadline:* For fall admission, 5/1 priority date for domestic and international students. Applications are processed on a rolling basis. Application fee: $45. Electronic applications accepted. *Expenses:* Tuition, state resident: full-time $10,490; part-time $440 per credit hour. Tuition, nonresident: full-time $22,550; part-time $945 per credit hour. Required fees: $290; $9 per credit hour. $25 per semester. *Financial support:* In 2010–11, 21 students received support, including 21 research assistantships with partial tuition reimbursements available (averaging $3,805 per year); career-related internships or fieldwork, Federal Work-Study, scholarships/grants, tuition waivers (partial), and unspecified assistantships also available. Financial award application deadline: 3/15; financial award applicants required to submit FAFSA. *Faculty research:* Clinical, addictive behaviors, anxiety disorders, child clinical, social and personality psychology. Total annual research expenditures: $59,500. *Unit head:* Dr. Jane Stafford, Director, 803-641-3358, Fax: 803-641-3720, E-mail: jstafford@usca.edu. *Application contact:* Karen Morris, Graduate Studies Coordinator, 803-641-3489, Fax: 803-641-3720, E-mail: karenm@usca.edu.

The University of South Dakota, Graduate School, College of Arts and Sciences, Department of Psychology, Vermillion, SD 57069-2390. Offers clinical psychology (MA, PhD); human factors (MA, PhD). *Accreditation:* APA (one or more programs are accredited). *Degree requirements:* For master's, comprehensive exam, thesis; for doctorate, comprehensive exam, thesis/dissertation. *Entrance requirements:* For master's, GRE, minimum GPA of 2.7; for doctorate, GRE General Test, GRE Subject Test, minimum GPA of 2.7. Additional exam requirements/recommendations for international students: Required—TOEFL (minimum score 550 paper-based; 213 computer-based; 79 iBT). Electronic applications accepted. *Faculty research:* Human-computer interactions, perceptual-cognitive processing, medical psychology, depression, moral psychology.

University of Southern California, Graduate School, Dana and David Dornsife College of Letters, Arts and Sciences, Department of Psychology, Los Angeles, CA 90089. Offers brain and cognitive science (PhD); clinical science (PhD); developmental psychology (PhD); human behavior (MHB); quantitative methods (PhD); social psychology (PhD). *Accreditation:* APA. *Faculty:* 34 full-time (10 women), 15 part-time/adjunct (9 women). *Students:* 105 full-time (65 women), 3 part-time (all women); includes 32 minority (4 Black or African American, non-Hispanic/Latino; 17 Asian, non-Hispanic/Latino; 9 Hispanic/Latino; 2 Two or more races, non-Hispanic/Latino), 22 international. 543 applicants, 5% accepted, 14 enrolled. In 2010, 17 master's, 12 doctorates awarded. *Degree requirements:* For doctorate, comprehensive exam, thesis/dissertation, one-year internship (for clinical science students). *Entrance requirements:* For doctorate, GRE. Additional exam requirements/recommendations for international students: Recommended—TOEFL (minimum score 600 paper-based; 250 computer-based; 100 iBT). *Application deadline:* For fall admission, 12/1 for domestic and international students. Application fee: $85. Electronic applications accepted. *Expenses:* Tuition: Full-time $31,240; part-time $1420 per unit. Required fees: $600. One-time fee: $35 full-time. Full-time tuition and fees vary according to degree level and program. *Financial support:* In 2010–11, 85 students received support, including 30 fellowships with full tuition reimbursements available (averaging $24,000 per year), 12 research assistantships with full tuition reimbursements available (averaging $19,250 per year), 40 teaching assistantships with full tuition reimbursements available (averaging $19,250 per year); scholarships/grants, traineeships, health care benefits, and unspecified assistantships also available. Financial award application deadline: 12/1. *Faculty research:* Affective neuroscience; children and families; vision, culture and ethnicity; intergroup relations; aggression and violence; language and reading development; substance abuse. *Unit head:* Dr. Margaret Gatz, Chair and Professor, 213-740-2212, Fax: 213-746-9028, E-mail:

Clinical Psychology

University of Southern California (continued)

gatz@usc.edu. *Application contact:* Irene Takaragawa, Graduate Advisor, 213-740-2205, Fax: 213-746-9082, E-mail: itakarag@usc.edu.

University of Southern Mississippi, Graduate School, College of Education and Psychology, Department of Psychology, Hattiesburg, MS 39406-0001. Offers clinical psychology (MA, PhD); counseling psychology (MA, PhD); experimental psychology (MA, PhD); school psychology (MA, PhD). *Accreditation:* APA (one or more programs are accredited). *Faculty:* 32 full-time (9 women). *Students:* 98 full-time (75 women), 42 part-time (33 women); includes 8 Black or African American, non-Hispanic/Latino; 3 Asian, non-Hispanic/Latino; 5 Hispanic/Latino, 7 international. Average age 29. 219 applicants, 16% accepted, 31 enrolled. In 2010, 27 master's, 13 doctorates awarded. Terminal master's awarded for partial completion of doctoral program. *Degree requirements:* For master's, comprehensive exam, thesis; for doctorate, comprehensive exam, thesis/dissertation. *Entrance requirements:* For master's, GRE General Test, minimum GPA of 3.0; for doctorate, GRE General Test, interview, minimum GPA of 3.5. Additional exam requirements/recommendations for international students: Required—TOEFL, IELTS. *Application deadline:* For fall admission, 3/1 priority date for domestic students, 3/1 for international students. Applications are processed on a rolling basis. Application fee: $50. *Financial support:* In 2010–11, 48 research assistantships with full tuition reimbursements (averaging $8,802 per year), 48 teaching assistantships with full tuition reimbursements (averaging $6,500 per year) were awarded; career-related internships or fieldwork, Federal Work-Study, institutionally sponsored loans, scholarships/grants, health care benefits, and unspecified assistantships also available. Financial award application deadline: 3/15; financial award applicants required to submit FAFSA. *Faculty research:* Dolphin cognition, sleep, neuropsychology, health-related behaviors, psychopathology. Total annual research expenditures: $101,200. *Unit head:* Dr. Joesph Olmi, Chair, 601-266-4177, Fax: 601-266-5580. *Application contact:* Susan King, Graduate Secretary, 601-266-4177, Fax: 601-266-5580.

University of South Florida, Graduate School, College of Arts and Sciences, Department of Psychology, Tampa, FL 33620-9951. Offers clinical psychology (PhD); cognitive and neural sciences (PhD); industrial-organizational psychology (PhD). *Accreditation:* APA. *Faculty:* 17 full-time (4 women). *Students:* 101 full-time (55 women), 24 part-time (16 women); includes 3 Black or African American, non-Hispanic/Latino; 9 Asian, non-Hispanic/Latino; 8 Hispanic/Latino; 1 Two or more races, non-Hispanic/Latino, 12 international. Average age 28. 452 applicants, 8% accepted, 22 enrolled. In 2010, 11 doctorates awarded. *Degree requirements:* For doctorate, comprehensive exam, thesis/dissertation, internship. *Entrance requirements:* For doctorate, GRE General Test, minimum GPA of 3.0 in last 60 hours of course work. Additional exam requirements/recommendations for international students: Required—TOEFL (minimum score 550 paper-based; 213 computer-based). *Application deadline:* For fall admission, 12/1 for domestic and international students. Application fee: $30. Electronic applications accepted. *Expenses:* Contact institution. *Financial support:* In 2010–11, 18 research assistantships (averaging $13,719 per year), 63 teaching assistantships with tuition reimbursements (averaging $13,724 per year) were awarded; tuition waivers (partial) and unspecified assistantships also available. Financial award applicants required to submit FAFSA. *Faculty research:* Clinical, cognitive, neuroscience, social, industrial/organizational. Total annual research expenditures: $3.5 million. *Unit head:* Michael Brannick, Chairperson, 813-974-0478, Fax: 813-974-4617, E-mail: mbrannick@usf.edu. *Application contact:* William Sacco, Program Director, 813-974-0375, Fax: 813-974-4617, E-mail: sacco@cas.usf.edu.

The University of Tennessee, Graduate School, College of Arts and Sciences, Department of Psychology, Knoxville, TN 37996. Offers clinical psychology (PhD); experimental psychology (MA, PhD); psychology (MA). *Accreditation:* APA (one or more programs are accredited). Terminal master's awarded for partial completion of doctoral program. *Degree requirements:* For master's, thesis; for doctorate, thesis/dissertation. *Entrance requirements:* For master's and doctorate, GRE General Test, GRE Subject Test, minimum GPA of 2.7. Additional exam requirements/recommendations for international students: Required—TOEFL. Electronic applications accepted. *Expenses:* Tuition, state resident: full-time $7440; part-time $414 per credit hour. Tuition, nonresident: full-time $22,478; part-time $1250 per credit hour. Required fees: $922; $43 per credit hour. Tuition and fees vary according to program.

The University of Texas at El Paso, Graduate School, College of Liberal Arts, Department of Psychology, El Paso, TX 79968-0001. Offers clinical psychology (MA); experimental psychology (MA); psychology (PhD). Part-time and evening/weekend programs available. *Students:* 47 (28 women); includes 1 Asian, non-Hispanic/Latino; 19 Hispanic/Latino, 6 international. Average age 34. In 2010, 11 master's, 5 doctorates awarded. *Degree requirements:* For master's, thesis; for doctorate, thesis/dissertation. *Entrance requirements:* For master's, GRE, letters of recommendation; for doctorate, GRE, statement of purpose, letters of recommendation. Additional exam requirements/recommendations for international students: Required—TOEFL; Recommended—IELTS. *Application deadline:* For fall admission, 8/1 for domestic students, 3/1 for international students; for spring admission, 11/1 for domestic students, 9/1 for international students. Applications are processed on a rolling basis. Application fee: $45 ($80 for international students). Electronic applications accepted. *Financial support:* In 2010–11, research assistantships with partial tuition reimbursements (averaging $18,625 per year), teaching assistantships with partial tuition reimbursements (averaging $14,900 per year) were awarded; fellowships with partial tuition reimbursements, institutionally sponsored loans, scholarships/grants, health care benefits, tuition waivers (partial), and unspecified assistantships also available. Support available to part-time students. Financial award application deadline: 3/15; financial award applicants required to submit FAFSA. *Unit head:* Dr. Edward Casta?eda, Chair, 915-747-5551, Fax: 915-747-6553, E-mail: ecastaneda9@utep.edu. *Application contact:* Dr. Patricia D. Witherspoon, Dean of the Graduate School, 915-747-5491, Fax: 915-747-5788, E-mail: withersp@utep.edu.

The University of Texas at Tyler, College of Education and Psychology, Department of Psychology and Counseling, Tyler, TX 75799-0001. Offers clinical psychology (MS), including neuropsychology, school psychology; counseling psychology (MA), including general, marriage and family; interdisciplinary studies (MSIS); school counseling (MA). Part-time and evening/weekend programs available. *Degree requirements:* For master's, comprehensive exam, thesis optional. *Entrance requirements:* For master's, GRE General Test, minimum GPA of 3.0. Additional exam requirements/recommendations for international students: Required—TOEFL (minimum score 79 computer-based). Electronic applications accepted. *Faculty research:* Neuropsychology, child abuse, psychometric properties of psychological instruments, maternal behavior, clinical practice issues, victimization of women, post-traumatic stress disorder.

The University of Texas of the Permian Basin, Office of Graduate Studies, College of Arts and Sciences, Department of Psychology, Odessa, TX 79762-0001. Offers applied research psychology (MA); clinical psychology (MA). Part-time and evening/weekend programs available. *Degree requirements:* For master's, comprehensive exam, thesis, practicum. *Entrance requirements:* For master's, GRE General Test, 3 letters of recommendation. Additional exam requirements/recommendations for international students: Required—TOEFL (minimum score 550 paper-based; 213 computer-based).

The University of Texas–Pan American, College of Social and Behavioral Sciences, Department of Psychology and Anthropology, Edinburg, TX 78539. Offers psychology (MA), including clinical psychology, experimental psychology. Part-time and evening/weekend programs available. *Degree requirements:* For master's, comprehensive exam, thesis optional, internship. *Entrance requirements:* For master's, GRE, letters of recommendation. Additional exam requirements/recommendations for international students: Required—TOEFL. Electronic applications accepted. *Faculty research:* Biofeedback, acculturation, health, stress/trauma, neuropsychological assessment, false memories, children's theory of mind.

The University of Texas Southwestern Medical Center at Dallas, Southwestern Graduate School of Biomedical Sciences, Division of Clinical Science, Clinical Psychology Program, Dallas, TX 75390. Offers PhD. *Accreditation:* APA. *Faculty:* 41 full-time (20 women), 30 part-time/adjunct (11 women). *Students:* 40 full-time (31 women); includes 10 minority (3 Black or African American, non-Hispanic/Latino; 3 Asian, non-Hispanic/Latino; 4 Hispanic/Latino), 1 international. Average age 26. 214 applicants, 10% accepted, 9 enrolled. In 2010, 12 doctorates awarded. *Degree requirements:* For doctorate, thesis/dissertation, clinical and qualifying exams. *Entrance requirements:* For doctorate, GRE General Test, minimum undergraduate GPA of 3.0. *Application deadline:* For fall admission, 1/1 for domestic students. Application fee: $0. Electronic applications accepted. *Financial support:* Research assistantships, career-related internships or fieldwork and institutionally sponsored loans available. Financial award application deadline: 3/1; financial award applicants required to submit FAFSA. *Faculty research:* Health psychology, depression, cross-cultural research, neuropsychology, sequelae children's illness. *Unit head:* Dr. C. Munro Cullum, Chair, 214-648-4640, Fax: 214-648-5250, E-mail: munro.cullum@utsouthwestern.edu. *Application contact:* Kimberly Jones, Education Coordinator, 214-648-5267, Fax: 214-648-5297, E-mail: kelsey.stutzman@utsouthwestern.edu.

University of the Cumberlands, Program in Clinical Psychology, Williamsburg, KY 40769-1372. Offers PhD. Part-time and evening/weekend programs available. Postbaccalaureate distance learning degree programs offered (minimal on-campus study). *Expenses:* Tuition: Full-time $6984; part-time $291 per credit hour. Required fees: $50 per term. Tuition and fees vary according to course level, course load and program. *Unit head:* Dr. Peter Geissler, Professor, 800-323-4574, E-mail: peter.geissler@ucumberlands.edu. *Application contact:* Donna Stanfill, Director, Graduate Admissions, 606-549-2200 Ext. 4496, Fax: 606-539-4534, E-mail: donna.stanfill@cumberlandcollege.edu.

University of the District of Columbia, College of Arts and Sciences, Department of Psychology and Counseling, Program in Clinical Psychology, Washington, DC 20008-1175. Offers MS. *Expenses:* Tuition, state resident: full-time $7580; part-time $421 per credit. Tuition, nonresident: full-time $14,580; part-time $810 per credit. Required fees: $620; $30 per credit. One-time fee: $100 part-time.

The University of Toledo, College of Graduate Studies, College of Language, Literature and Social Sciences, Department of Psychology, Toledo, OH 43606-3390. Offers clinical psychology (MA, PhD); experimental psychology (MA, PhD). *Accreditation:* APA. *Faculty:* 22. *Students:* 34 full-time (26 women), 3 part-time (1 woman), 7 international. Average age 26. 192 applicants, 7% accepted, 9 enrolled. In 2010, 2 master's, 8 doctorates awarded. *Degree requirements:* For master's, comprehensive exam, thesis; for doctorate, comprehensive exam, thesis/dissertation. *Entrance requirements:* For master's and doctorate, GRE General Test, GRE Subject Test, A minimum 2.7 cumulative point-hour ratio (on a 4.0 scale) for all previous academic work. Three Letters of Recommendation, a statement of purpose, and transcripts from all prior institutions attended. Additional exam requirements/recommendations for international students: Required—TOEFL (minimum score 550 paper-based; 213 computer-based; 80 iBT), IELTS (minimum score 6.5). *Application deadline:* For fall admission, 1/15 priority date for domestic and international students. Applications are processed on a rolling basis. Application fee: $45 ($75 for international students). Electronic applications accepted. *Expenses:* Tuition, state resident: full-time $11,426; part-time $476 per credit hour. Tuition, nonresident: full-time $21,660; part-time $903 per credit hour. One-time fee: $62. *Financial support:* Research assistantships with tuition reimbursements, teaching assistantships with tuition reimbursements, career-related internships or fieldwork, Federal Work-Study, institutionally sponsored loans, scholarships/grants, tuition waivers (full and partial), and unspecified assistantships available. Support available to part-time students. *Faculty research:* Neural taste response. *Unit head:* Dr. J. D. Jasper, Chair, 419-530-4130, E-mail: jjasper@utnet.utoledo.edu. *Application contact:* Graduate School Office, 419-530-4723, Fax: 419-530-4724, E-mail: grdsch@utnet.utoledo.edu.

University of Tulsa, Graduate School, College of Arts and Sciences, Department of Psychology, Program in Clinical Psychology, Tulsa, OK 74104-3189. Offers MA, PhD, JD/MA. *Accreditation:* APA (one or more programs are accredited). Part-time programs available. *Faculty:* 9 full-time (4 women), 1 (woman) part-time/adjunct. *Students:* 23 full-time (18 women), 16 part-time (14 women); includes 3 minority (2 Black or African American, non-Hispanic/Latino; 1 Hispanic/Latino), 2 international. Average age 29. 74 applicants, 18% accepted, 8 enrolled. In 2010, 1 master's, 13 doctorates awarded. Terminal master's awarded for partial completion of doctoral program. *Degree requirements:* For master's, thesis (for some programs), 6 credit hours of practicum training; for doctorate, comprehensive exam, thesis/dissertation, 1 year pre-doctoral internship. *Entrance requirements:* For master's and doctorate, GRE General Test, interview, resume. Additional exam requirements/recommendations for international students: Required—TOEFL (minimum score 575 paper-based; 231 computer-based; 91 iBT), IELTS (minimum score 6.5). *Application deadline:* For fall admission, 12/1 for domestic and international students. Application fee: $40. Electronic applications accepted. *Expenses:* Tuition: Full-time $16,902; part-time $939 per credit hour. Required fees: $1020; $4 per credit hour. Tuition and fees vary according to course load. *Financial support:* In 2010–11, 28 students received support, including 6 fellowships with full and partial tuition reimbursements available (averaging $9,916 per year), 12 research assistantships with full and partial tuition reimbursements available (averaging $10,382 per year), 14 teaching assistantships with full and partial tuition reimbursements available (averaging $11,640 per year); career-related internships or fieldwork, Federal Work-Study, health care benefits, tuition waivers (full and partial), and unspecified assistantships also available. Support available to part-time students. Financial award application deadline: 2/1; financial award applicants required to submit FAFSA. *Faculty research:* Traumatic stress studies, randomized control trials of exposure treatments, pain modulation, neuropsychological assessment of health/mental health, psychological assessment, psychometrics, ethics, longitudinal assessment of child development, trauma and journalism, MMPI studies. Total annual research expenditures: $414,625. *Unit head:* Dr. Michael Basso, Director, 918-631-3151, Fax: 918-631-2836, E-mail: michael-basso@utulsa.edu. *Application contact:* Information Contact, 800-882-4723, E-mail: grad@utulsa.edu.

University of Utah, Graduate School, College of Social and Behavioral Science, Department of Psychology, Salt Lake City, UT 84112. Offers clinical psychology (PhD); psychology (PhD). *Accreditation:* APA. *Faculty:* 33 full-time (16 women), 2 part-time/adjunct (0 women). *Students:* 50 full-time (38 women), 7 part-time (4 women); includes 5 minority (4 Asian, non-Hispanic/Latino; 1 Hispanic/Latino), 3 international. Average age 29. 216 applicants, 6% accepted, 13 enrolled. In 2010, 10 doctorates awarded. *Degree requirements:* For doctorate, thesis/dissertation. *Entrance requirements:* For doctorate, GRE General Test. Additional exam requirements/recommendations for international students: Required—TOEFL (minimum score 500 paper-based; 173 computer-based). *Application deadline:* For fall admission, 12/15 for domestic and international students. Applications are processed on a rolling basis. Application fee: $55 ($65 for international students). Electronic applications accepted. *Expenses:* Tuition, area resident: Part-time $179.19 per credit hour. Tuition, state resident: full-time $4384. Tuition, nonresident: full-time $16,684; part-time $630.67 per credit hour. Required fees: $350 per semester. Tuition and fees vary according to course load, degree level and program. *Financial support:* In 2010–11, 43 students received support, including 2 fellowships with full tuition reimbursements available (averaging $14,000 per year), 2 research assistantships with full tuition reimbursements available (averaging $14,000 per year), 33 teaching assistantships with full tuition reimbursements available (averaging $14,000 per year); career-related internships or fieldwork also available. Financial award applicants required to submit FAFSA. *Faculty research:* Cognitive neuroscience, health, social cognition, psychopathology, cognitive and social development. Total annual research expenditures: $813,660. *Unit head:* Dr. Cynthia A. Berg, Chair, 801-581-8925, Fax: 801-581-5841, E-mail: cynthia.berg@psych.utah.edu. *Application contact:* Nancy Seegmiller, Administrative Assistant, 801-581-8925, Fax: 801-581-5841, E-mail: nancy.seegmiller@psych.utah.edu.

University of Vermont, Graduate College, College of Arts and Sciences, Department of Psychology, Burlington, VT 05405. Offers clinical psychology (PhD); psychology (PhD). *Accreditation:* APA. *Students:* 59 (42 women); includes 2 Black or African American, non-Hispanic/Latino; 1 Asian, non-Hispanic/Latino; 4 Hispanic/Latino, 2 international. 322 applicants, 7% accepted, 16 enrolled. In 2010, 18 doctorates awarded. *Degree requirements:* For doctorate, thesis/dissertation. *Entrance requirements:* For doctorate, GRE General Test. Additional exam requirements/recommendations for international students: Required—TOEFL (minimum score 550 paper-based; 213 computer-based; 80 iBT). *Application deadline:* For fall admission, 12/1 for domestic students. Application fee: $40. Electronic applications accepted. *Expenses:* Tuition, state resident: part-time $537 per credit hour. Tuition, nonresident: part-time $1355 per credit hour. *Financial support:* Fellowships, research assistantships, teaching assistantships available. Financial award application deadline: 2/1. *Unit head:* Dr. William Falls, Chairperson, 802-656-2670. *Application contact:* Dr. Rex Forehand, Coordinator, 802-656-2670.

University of Victoria, Faculty of Graduate Studies, Faculty of Social Sciences, Department of Psychology, Victoria, BC V8W 2Y2, Canada. Offers clinical psychology (PhD); clinical psychology (neuropsychology) (M Sc); cognition and brain science (M Sc, PhD); experimental neuropsychology (M Sc, PhD); individualized study (M Sc, PhD); life span development psychology (PhD); life span developmental psychology (M Sc); social psychology (M Sc, PhD). *Accreditation:* APA (one or more programs are accredited). *Degree requirements:* For master's, thesis; for doctorate, thesis/dissertation, candidacy exam. *Entrance requirements:* For master's and doctorate, GRE General Test. Additional exam requirements/recommendations for international students: Required—TOEFL (minimum score 600 paper-based; 250 computer-based). Electronic applications accepted. *Faculty research:* Life span development psychology and aging, behavioral neuroscience, cognitive psychology, behavioral psychology, environmental psychology.

University of Virginia, Curry School of Education, Department of Human Services, Program in Clinical and School Psychology, Charlottesville, VA 22903. Offers PhD. *Students:* 29 full-time (25 women); includes 4 Black or African American, non-Hispanic/Latino; 1 Asian, non-Hispanic/Latino; 1 Hispanic/Latino; 1 Two or more races, non-Hispanic/Latino. Average age 27. 130 applicants, 8% accepted, 7 enrolled. In 2010, 9 doctorates awarded. *Unit head:* Dr. Peter L. Sheras, Director of Clinical Training, 434-924-0795, E-mail: pls@virginia.edu. *Application contact:* Lynn Renfroe, Information Contact, 434-924-6254, E-mail: ldr9t@virginia.edu.

University of Washington, Graduate School, College of Arts and Sciences, Department of Psychology, Seattle, WA 98195. Offers animal behavior (PhD); child psychology (PhD); clinical psychology (PhD); cognition and perception (PhD); developmental psychology (PhD); quantitative psychology (PhD); social psychology and personality (PhD). *Accreditation:* APA. *Degree requirements:* For doctorate, thesis/dissertation. *Entrance requirements:* For doctorate, GRE General Test, minimum GPA of 3.0. Electronic applications accepted. *Faculty research:* Addictive behaviors, artificial intelligence, child psychopathology, mechanisms and development of vision, physiology of ingestive behaviors.

University of Windsor, Faculty of Graduate Studies, Faculty of Arts and Social Sciences, Department of Psychology, Windsor, ON N9B 3P4, Canada. Offers adult clinical (MA, PhD); applied social psychology (MA, PhD); child clinical (MA, PhD); clinical neuropsychology (MA, PhD). *Accreditation:* APA (one or more programs are accredited). *Degree requirements:* For master's, thesis; for doctorate, comprehensive exam, thesis/dissertation. *Entrance requirements:* For master's, GRE General Test, GRE Subject Test in psychology, minimum B average; for doctorate, GRE General Test, GRE Subject Test in psychology, master's degree. Additional exam requirements/recommendations for international students: Required—TOEFL (minimum score 600 paper-based; 250 computer-based). Electronic applications accepted. *Faculty research:* Gambling, suicidology, emotional competence, psychotherapy and trauma.

University of Wisconsin–Madison, Graduate School, College of Letters and Science, Department of Psychology, Program in Clinical Psychology, Madison, WI 53706-1380. Offers PhD. *Accreditation:* APA. *Degree requirements:* For doctorate, comprehensive exam, thesis/dissertation. *Entrance requirements:* For doctorate, GRE General Test, minimum undergraduate GPA of 3.0. Additional exam requirements/recommendations for international students: Required—TOEFL. Electronic applications accepted. *Expenses:* Tuition, state resident: full-time $9887; part-time $617.96 per credit. Tuition, nonresident: full-time $24,054; part-time $1503.40 per credit. Required fees: $67.63 per credit. Tuition and fees vary according to reciprocity agreements.

University of Wisconsin–Milwaukee, Graduate School, College of Letters and Sciences, Department of Psychology, Milwaukee, WI 53201-0413. Offers clinical psychology (MS, PhD); psychology (MS, PhD). *Accreditation:* APA (one or more programs are accredited). *Faculty:* 24 full-time (8 women). *Students:* 58 full-time (35 women), 15 part-time (11 women); includes 1 Black or African American, non-Hispanic/Latino; 1 American Indian or Alaska Native, non-Hispanic/Latino; 2 Asian, non-Hispanic/Latino; 4 Hispanic/Latino, 6 international. Average age 29. 257 applicants, 10% accepted, 14 enrolled. In 2010, 15 master's, 5 doctorates awarded. *Degree requirements:* For master's, thesis; for doctorate, variable foreign language requirement, thesis/dissertation. *Entrance requirements:* For master's and doctorate, GRE General Test, GRE Subject Test. Additional exam requirements/recommendations for international students: Required—TOEFL (minimum score 550 paper-based; 79 iBT), IELTS (minimum score 6.5). *Application deadline:* For fall admission, 1/1 priority date for domestic students; for spring admission, 9/1 for domestic students. Applications are processed on a rolling basis. Application fee: $56 ($96 for international students). Electronic applications accepted. *Financial support:* In 2010–11, 8 fellowships, 6 research assistantships, 46 teaching assistantships were awarded; career-related internships or fieldwork, unspecified assistantships, and project assistantships also available. Support available to part-time students. Financial award application deadline: 4/15; financial award applicants required to submit FAFSA. Total annual research expenditures: $1.4 million. *Unit head:* Hobart Davies, Representative, 414-229-6594, Fax: 414-229-5219, E-mail: hobart@uwm.edu. *Application contact:* General Information Contact, 414-229-4982, Fax: 414-229-6967, E-mail: gradschool@uwm.edu.

Utah State University, School of Graduate Studies, College of Education and Human Services, Department of Psychology, Logan, UT 84322. Offers clinical/counseling/school psychology (PhD); research and evaluation methodology (PhD); school counseling (MS); school psychology (MS). *Accreditation:* APA (one or more programs are accredited). Part-time and evening/weekend programs available. Postbaccalaureate distance learning degree programs offered (no on-campus study). Terminal master's awarded for partial completion of doctoral program. *Degree requirements:* For master's, thesis (for some programs); for doctorate, thesis/dissertation. *Entrance requirements:* For master's, GRE General Test (school psychology), MAT (school counseling), minimum GPA of 3.5; for doctorate, GRE General Test, minimum GPA of 3.5. Additional exam requirements/recommendations for international students: Required—TOEFL. *Faculty research:* Hearing loss detection in infancy, ADHD, eating disorders, domestic violence, neuropsychology, bilingual/Spanish speaking students/parents.

Valdosta State University, Department of Psychology and Counseling, Valdosta, GA 31698. Offers clinical/counseling psychology (MS); industrial/organizational psychology (MS); school counseling (M Ed, Ed S); school psychology (Ed S). Part-time and evening/weekend programs available. *Faculty:* 19 full-time (6 women). *Students:* 65 full-time (47 women), 41 part-time (35 women); includes 38 minority (29 Black or African American, non-Hispanic/Latino; 3 Asian, non-Hispanic/Latino; 4 Hispanic/Latino; 2 Two or more races, non-Hispanic/Latino). Average age 27. 61 applicants, 51% accepted, 27 enrolled. In 2010, 43 master's awarded. *Degree requirements:* For master's, thesis or alternative, comprehensive written and/or oral exams; for Ed S, thesis. *Entrance requirements:* For master's and Ed S, GRE General Test or MAT. Additional exam requirements/recommendations for international students: Required—TOEFL (minimum score 523 paper-based; 193 computer-based). *Application deadline:* For fall admission, 7/1 for domestic and international students; for spring admission, 11/15 for domestic and international students. Applications are processed on a rolling basis. Application fee: $35. Electronic applications accepted. *Expenses:* Tuition, state resident: full-time $5256; part-time $197 per credit hour. Tuition, nonresident: full-time $14,490; part-time $710 per credit hour. Required fees: $855 per semester. Tuition and fees vary according to course load and campus/location. *Financial support:* In 2010–11, 6 students received support, including 2 research assistantships with full tuition reimbursements available (averaging $3,652 per year); institutionally sponsored loans and unspecified assistantships also available. Support available

to part-time students. Financial award application deadline: 7/1; financial award applicants required to submit FAFSA. *Faculty research:* Using Bender-Gestalt to predict graphomotor dimensions of the draw-a-person test, neurobehavioral hemispheric dominance. *Unit head:* Dr. Robert Bauer, Chair, 229-333-5930, Fax: 229-259-5576, E-mail: bbauer@valdosta.edu. *Application contact:* Rebecca Waters, Coordinator of Graduate Admissions, 229-333-5694, Fax: 229-245-3853, E-mail: rlwaters@valdosta.edu.

Valparaiso University, Graduate School, Department of Psychology, Valparaiso, IN 46383. Offers business management (for counseling students) (Certificate); clinical mental health counseling (MA); community counseling (MA); JD/MA. Part-time and evening/weekend programs available. *Faculty:* 9 part-time/adjunct (5 women). *Students:* 40 full-time (34 women), 12 part-time (8 women); includes 3 Black or African American, non-Hispanic/Latino; 2 Hispanic/Latino, 2 international. Average age 28. In 2010, 22 master's awarded. *Degree requirements:* For master's, thesis or alternative, internship. *Entrance requirements:* For master's, minimum GPA of 3.0; 15 credits in the social/behavioral sciences (psychology, sociology, human development, etc.) with a minimum GPA of 3.0; course in introductory psychology; recent statistics course with minimum B average. Additional exam requirements/recommendations for international students: Required—TOEFL (minimum score 550 paper-based; 213 computer-based; 80 iBT). *Application deadline:* For fall admission, 3/1 priority date for domestic students. Applications are processed on a rolling basis. Application fee: $30 ($50 for international students). Electronic applications accepted. *Expenses:* Tuition: Full-time $9540; part-time $530 per credit hour. Required fees: $292; $95 per semester. Tuition and fees vary according to program. *Financial support:* Career-related internships or fieldwork, traineeships, and unspecified assistantships available. Support available to part-time students. Financial award applicants required to submit FAFSA. *Faculty research:* Environmental psychology, human sexuality, developmental psychopathology, social psychology. *Unit head:* Dr. David Simpson, Director of Graduate Programs, 219-464-6941, Fax: 219-464-6878, E-mail: david.simpson@valpo.edu. *Application contact:* Laura Groth, Coordinator of Student Services and Support, 219-464-5313, Fax: 219-464-5381, E-mail: laura.groth@valpo.edu.

Vanguard University of Southern California, Graduate Program in Clinical Psychology, Costa Mesa, CA 92626-9601. Offers clinical psychology (MS). Part-time and evening/weekend programs available. *Degree requirements:* For master's, thesis or alternative, completion of personal therapy. *Entrance requirements:* For master's, minimum GPA of 3.0. Additional exam requirements/recommendations for international students: Required—TOEFL (minimum score 550 paper-based; 213 computer-based; 79 iBT). Electronic applications accepted. *Expenses:* Contact institution. *Faculty research:* Children, play therapy, death and dying, trauma, marital and family counseling.

Virginia Commonwealth University, Graduate School, College of Humanities and Sciences, Department of Psychology, Program in Clinical Psychology, Richmond, VA 23284-9005. Offers behavioral medicine (PhD); clinical child psychology (PhD). *Accreditation:* APA. *Students:* 34 full-time (29 women), 19 part-time (17 women); includes 15 minority (2 Black or African American, non-Hispanic/Latino; 3 Asian, non-Hispanic/Latino; 8 Hispanic/Latino; 2 Two or more races, non-Hispanic/Latino), 1 international. 198 applicants, 5% accepted, 6 enrolled. In 2010, 8 doctorates awarded. *Degree requirements:* For doctorate, thesis/dissertation. *Entrance requirements:* For doctorate, GRE General Test. Additional exam requirements/recommendations for international students: Required—TOEFL (minimum score 600 paper-based; 250 computer-based; 100 iBT); Recommended—IELTS (minimum score 6.5). *Application deadline:* For fall admission, 12/1 for domestic students. Application fee: $50. Electronic applications accepted. *Expenses:* Tuition, state resident: full-time $4308; part-time $479 per credit hour. Tuition, nonresident: full-time $8942; part-time $994 per credit hour. Required fees: $2000; $85 per credit hour. Tuition and fees vary according to course level, course load, degree level, campus/location and program. *Financial support:* Fellowships, research assistantships, teaching assistantships, Federal Work-Study, institutionally sponsored loans, and scholarships/grants available. Support available to part-time students. *Faculty research:* Clinical child/adolescent and behavioral medicine. *Unit head:* Dr. Michael Southam-Gerow, Director of Graduate Programs in Psychology, 804-828-1193, Fax: 804-828-2237, E-mail: masouthamger@vcu.edu. *Application contact:* Dr. Bruce D. Rybarczyk, Director, Clinical Psychology Program, 804-828-1675, Fax: 804-828-2237, E-mail: bdrybarczyk@vcu.edu.

Virginia State University, School of Graduate Studies, Research, and Outreach, School of Engineering, Science and Technology, Department of Psychology, Petersburg, VA 23806-0001. Offers behavioral and community health sciences (PhD); clinical health psychology (PhD); clinical psychology (MS); general psychology (MS). *Degree requirements:* For master's, one foreign language, thesis. *Entrance requirements:* For master's, GRE General Test. *Expenses:* Tuition, state resident: full-time $5576; part-time $335 per credit hour. Tuition, nonresident: full-time $13,402; part-time $670 per credit hour.

Walden University, Graduate Programs, School of Psychology, Minneapolis, MN 55401. Offers clinical child psychology (Post-Doctoral Certificate); clinical psychology (MS, Post-Doctoral Certificate), including counseling (MS); counseling psychology (Post-Doctoral Certificate); forensic psychology (MS), including forensic psychology in the community, general program, mental health applications, program planning and evaluation in forensic settings, psychology and legal systems; general psychology (Post-Doctoral Certificate); health psychology (Post-Doctoral Certificate); organizational psychology (Post-Doctoral Certificate); organizational psychology and development (Postbaccalaureate Certificate); psychology (MS, PhD), including clinical psychology (PhD), counseling psychology (PhD), crisis management and response (MS), general program (MS), general psychology (PhD), health psychology, leadership development and coaching (MS), media psychology (MS), organizational psychology (PhD), organizational psychology and development (MS), organizational psychology and nonprofit management (MS), program evaluation and research (MS), psychology of culture (MS), psychology, public administration, and social change (MS), social psychology (MS), terrorism and security (MS); teaching online (Post-Master's Certificate). Part-time and evening/weekend programs available. Postbaccalaureate distance learning degree programs offered (minimal on-campus study). *Faculty:* 41 full-time (25 women), 254 part-time/adjunct (131 women). *Students:* 3,463 full-time (2,737 women), 1,400 part-time (1,130 women); includes 1,491 Black or African American, non-Hispanic/Latino; 59 American Indian or Alaska Native, non-Hispanic/Latino; 89 Asian, non-Hispanic/Latino; 283 Hispanic/Latino; 76 Two or more races, non-Hispanic/Latino, 126 international. Average age 40. In 2010, 559 master's, 100 doctorates awarded. Terminal master's awarded for partial completion of doctoral program. *Degree requirements:* For master's, thesis optional; for doctorate, thesis/dissertation, residency. *Entrance requirements:* For master's, bachelor's degree or equivalent in related field; minimum GPA of 2.5; official transcripts; goal statement; access to computer and Internet; for doctorate, master's degree or equivalent in related field, minimum GPA of 3.0; 3 years of related professional/academic experience (preferred). Additional exam requirements/recommendations for international students: Required—TOEFL (minimum score 550 paper-based; 213 computer-based), IELTS (minimum score 6.5), TOEFL (minimum score 550 paper-based; 213 computer-based), IELTS (minimum score 6.5), or Michigan English Language Assessment Battery (minimum score 82). *Application deadline:* Applications are processed on a rolling basis. Application fee: $50. Electronic applications accepted. *Expenses:* Tuition: Full-time $10,274; part-time $445 per credit. Tuition and fees vary according to course load, degree level and program. *Financial support:* In 2010–11, 1 fellowship was awarded; Federal Work-Study, scholarships/grants, unspecified assistantships, and family tuition reduction, active duty/veteran tuition reduction, group tuition reduction, interest-free payment plans also available. Support available to part-time students. Financial award applicants required to submit FAFSA. *Unit head:* Dr. Melanie Storms, Associate Dean, 800-925-3368. *Application contact:* Jennifer Hall, Vice President of Enrollment Management, 866-4-WALDEN, E-mail: info@waldenu.edu.

Washburn University, College of Arts and Sciences, Department of Psychology, Topeka, KS 66621. Offers clinical psychology (MA). Part-time programs available. *Faculty:* 8 full-time (4 women). *Students:* 22 full-time (16 women), 5 part-time (4 women). Average age 28. In 2010, 4 master's awarded. *Degree requirements:* For master's, thesis. *Entrance requirements:* For

Clinical Psychology

Washburn University (continued)

master's, GRE General Test, 15 hours of course work in psychology. Additional exam requirements/recommendations for international students: Recommended—TOEFL (minimum score 550 paper-based; 80 iBT). *Application deadline:* For fall admission, 3/15 for domestic students; for spring admission, 12/1 for domestic students. Electronic applications accepted. *Expenses:* Tuition, state resident: full-time $5130; part-time $285 per credit hour. Tuition, nonresident: full-time $10,476; part-time $582 per credit hour. Required fees: $86; $43 per semester. Tuition and fees vary according to program. *Financial support:* Applicants required to submit FAFSA. *Faculty research:* Metacognition, anxiety disorders, gender roles in relationships, rural psychology, sports performance psychology. *Unit head:* Dr. David Provorse, Chair, 785-670-1565, Fax: 785-670-1004, E-mail: dave.provorse@washburn.edu. *Application contact:* Dr. David Provorse, Chair, 785-670-1565, Fax: 785-670-1004, E-mail: dave.provorse@washburn.edu.

Washington State University, Graduate School, College of Liberal Arts, Department of Psychology, Pullman, WA 99164. Offers clinical psychology (PhD); experimental psychology (PhD); psychology (MS). *Accreditation:* APA (one or more programs are accredited). *Faculty:* 22. *Students:* 49 full-time (34 women), 4 part-time (2 women); includes 2 Asian, non-Hispanic/Latino; 5 Hispanic/Latino, 7 international. Average age 29. 262 applicants, 6% accepted, 12 enrolled. In 2010, 7 master's, 8 doctorates awarded. *Degree requirements:* For master's, comprehensive exam (for some programs), thesis (for some programs), oral exam; for doctorate, comprehensive exam, thesis/dissertation, oral exam, written exam. *Entrance requirements:* For master's, GRE General Test, minimum undergraduate GPA of 3.0; research experiences; clinical experiences; at least 18 hours of psychology, including a class in statistics; three letters of recommendation, official transcripts; for doctorate, GRE General Test, three letters of reference; summary data form; at least 18 credits of study in psychology; at least one course in statistics and research methodology; official transcripts; minimum cumulative undergraduate GPA of 3.0 or master's degree in psychology. Additional exam requirements/recommendations for international students: Required—TOEFL, IELTS. *Application deadline:* For fall admission, 12/15 priority date for domestic and international students. Applications are processed on a rolling basis. Application fee: $50. *Expenses:* Tuition, state resident: full-time $8552; part-time $443 per credit. Tuition, nonresident: full-time $21,650; part-time $1083 per credit. Required fees: $846. *Financial support:* In 2010–11, 5 research assistantships with full and partial tuition reimbursements (averaging $13,917 per year), 39 teaching assistantships with full and partial tuition reimbursements (averaging $13,056 per year) were awarded; fellowships, career-related internships or fieldwork, Federal Work-Study, institutionally sponsored loans, and unspecified assistantships also available. Financial award application deadline: 2/15; financial award applicants required to submit FAFSA. *Faculty research:* Childhood conduct disorders, etiology of depression, treatment of reading disorders, applied behavior analysis, selective attention. *Unit head:* Dr. John Hinson, Chair, 509-335-1089, Fax: 509-335-5043, E-mail: hinson@mail.wsu.edu. *Application contact:* Graduate School Admissions, 800-GRADWSU, Fax: 509-335-1949, E-mail: gradsch@wsu.edu.

Washington University in St. Louis, Graduate School of Arts and Sciences, Department of Psychology, St. Louis, MO 63130-4899. Offers clinical psychology (PhD); general experimental psychology (PhD); social psychology (PhD). *Accreditation:* APA. Terminal master's awarded for partial completion of doctoral program. *Degree requirements:* For doctorate, thesis/dissertation. *Entrance requirements:* For doctorate, GRE General Test. Electronic applications accepted.

Waynesburg University, Graduate and Professional Studies, Waynesburg, PA 15370-1222. Offers business (MBA), including finance, health systems, human resources, leadership, market development; counseling (MA), including addictions counseling, clinical mental health; education (MAT); nursing (MSN), including administration, education, informatics, palliative care; nursing practice (DNP); special education (M Ed); technology (M Ed); MSN/MBA. *Accreditation:* AACN. Part-time and evening/weekend programs available. *Degree requirements:* For doctorate, thesis/dissertation. *Entrance requirements:* Additional exam requirements/recommendations for international students: Required—TOEFL. Electronic applications accepted.

Wayne State University, College of Education, Division of Theoretical and Behavioral Foundations, Detroit, MI 48202. Offers counseling (M Ed, MA, Ed D, PhD, Ed S); education evaluation and research (M Ed, Ed D, PhD); educational psychology (M Ed, Ed D, PhD, Ed S); educational sociology (M Ed, Ed D, PhD, Ed S); history and philosophy of education (M Ed, Ed D, PhD); rehabilitation counseling and community inclusion (MA, Ed S); school and community psychology (MA, Ed S); school clinical psychology (Ed S). *Accreditation:* ACA (one or more programs are accredited); CORE (one or more programs are accredited). Evening/weekend programs available. *Faculty:* 100 full-time (50 women), 60 part-time/adjunct (35 women). *Students:* 193 full-time (156 women), 202 part-time (164 women); includes 168 minority (150 Black or African American, non-Hispanic/Latino; 3 American Indian or Alaska Native, non-Hispanic/Latino; 8 Asian, non-Hispanic/Latino; 5 Hispanic/Latino; 2 Two or more races, non-Hispanic/Latino), 17 international. Average age 36. 97 applicants, 55% accepted, 35 enrolled. In 2010, 42 master's, 9 doctorates, 2 other advanced degrees awarded. *Degree requirements:* For doctorate, thesis/dissertation. *Entrance requirements:* For master's, GRE; for doctorate, GRE, interview, minimum GPA of 3.0, curriculum vitae, references. Additional exam requirements/recommendations for international students: Required—TOEFL (minimum score 550 paper-based; 213 computer-based), TWE (minimum score 6). *Application deadline:* For fall admission, 7/1 for domestic students, 6/1 for international students; for winter admission, 10/1 for international students; for spring admission, 2/1 for international students. Application fee: $20 ($30 for international students). Electronic applications accepted. *Expenses:* Tuition, state resident: full-time $7662; part-time $478.85 per credit hour. Tuition, nonresident: full-time $16,920; part-time $1057.55 per credit hour. Required fees: $571.20; $35.70 per credit hour. $188.05 per semester. Tuition and fees vary according to course load and program. *Financial support:* In 2010–11, 2 fellowships with tuition reimbursements (averaging $16,875 per year), 3 research assistantships with tuition reimbursements (averaging $17,785 per year), 1 teaching assistantship (averaging $15,181 per year) were awarded; career-related internships or fieldwork, Federal Work-Study, and institutionally sponsored loans also available. *Faculty research:* Adolescents at risk, supervision of counseling. *Unit head:* Dr. JoAnne Holbert, Assistant Dean, 313-577-1721, E-mail: jholbert@wayne.edu. *Application contact:* Janice Green, Assistant Dean, 313-577-1605, E-mail: jwgreen@wayne.edu.

West Chester University of Pennsylvania, Office of Graduate Studies, College of Arts and Sciences, Department of Psychology, West Chester, PA 19383. Offers clinical mental health (Certificate); clinical psychology (MA); general psychology (MA); industrial psychology (MA). Part-time and evening/weekend programs available. *Students:* 79 full-time (56 women), 33 part-time (22 women); includes 16 minority (4 Black or African American, non-Hispanic/Latino; 1 American Indian or Alaska Native, non-Hispanic/Latino; 5 Asian, non-Hispanic/Latino; 6 Hispanic/Latino), 4 international. Average age 27. 192 applicants, 53% accepted, 40 enrolled. In 2010, 43 master's, 4 other advanced degrees awarded. *Degree requirements:* For master's, comprehensive exam, thesis (for some programs). *Entrance requirements:* For master's, GRE General Test or MAT, minimum GPA of 3.0, 3.25 in psychology; three letters of reference. Additional exam requirements/recommendations for international students: Required—TOEFL (minimum score 550 paper-based; 213 computer-based; 80 iBT). *Application deadline:* For fall admission, 4/15 priority date for domestic students, 3/15 for international students; for spring admission, 10/15 for domestic students, 9/1 for international students. Applications are processed on a rolling basis. Application fee: $35. Electronic applications accepted. *Expenses:* Tuition, state resident: full-time $6966; part-time $387 per credit. Tuition, nonresident: full-time $11,146; part-time $619 per credit. Required fees: $1614.40; $133.24 per credit. Part-time tuition and fees vary according to campus/location. *Financial support:* Unspecified assistantships available. Support available to part-time students. Financial award application deadline: 2/15; financial award applicants required to submit FAFSA. *Faculty research:* Animal learning and cognition. *Unit head:* Dr. Loretta Rieser-Danner, Acting Chairperson, 610-436-3106, E-mail: lrieser-danner@wcupa.edu. *Application contact:* Dr. Julian Azorlosa, Graduate Coordinator, 610-738-0430, E-mail: jazorlosa@wcupa.edu.

Western Illinois University, School of Graduate Studies, College of Arts and Sciences, Department of Psychology, Macomb, IL 61455-1390. Offers clinical/community mental health (MS); general psychology (MS); psychology (MS, SSP); school psychology (SSP). Part-time programs available. *Students:* 44 full-time (31 women), 15 part-time (7 women); includes 4 minority (1 American Indian or Alaska Native, non-Hispanic/Latino; 3 Asian, non-Hispanic/Latino), 2 international. Average age 26. 94 applicants, 34% accepted. In 2010, 11 master's, 8 other advanced degrees awarded. *Degree requirements:* For master's, comprehensive exam (for some programs), thesis or alternative. *Entrance requirements:* For master's and SSP, GRE General Test. Additional exam requirements/recommendations for international students: Required—TOEFL (minimum score 550 paper-based; 213 computer-based; 80 iBT). *Application deadline:* Applications are processed on a rolling basis. Application fee: $30. Electronic applications accepted. *Expenses:* Tuition, state resident: full-time $6370; part-time $265.40 per credit hour. Tuition, nonresident: full-time $12,740; part-time $530.80 per credit hour. Required fees: $75.67 per credit hour. *Financial support:* In 2010–11, 37 students received support, including 37 research assistantships with full tuition reimbursements available (averaging $7,280 per year). Financial award applicants required to submit FAFSA. *Unit head:* Dr. Steven Dworkin, Chairperson, 309-298-1593. *Application contact:* Evelyn Hoing, Assistant Director of Graduate Studies, 309-298-1806, Fax: 309-298-2345, E-mail: grad-office@wiu.edu.

Western Kentucky University, Graduate Studies, College of Education and Behavioral Sciences, Department of Psychology, Bowling Green, KY 42101. Offers clinical psychology (MA); experimental psychology (MA); general psychology (MA); industrial/organizational psychology (MA); school psychology (Ed S). *Degree requirements:* For master's, comprehensive exam, thesis (for some programs); for Ed S, thesis, oral exam. *Entrance requirements:* For master's, GRE General Test; for Ed S, GRE General Test, minimum GPA of 3.5. Additional exam requirements/recommendations for international students: Required—TOEFL (minimum score 555 paper-based; 213 computer-based; 79 iBT). *Faculty research:* Neural regeneration, enhancing mobility in the elderly, improvement in visual processing in older adults, lifespan development.

Western Michigan University, Graduate College, College of Arts and Sciences, Department of Psychology, Kalamazoo, MI 49008. Offers behavior analysis (MA, PhD); clinical psychology (PhD); industrial/organizational psychology (MA). *Accreditation:* APA (one or more programs are accredited). *Degree requirements:* For master's, variable foreign language requirement, thesis, oral exams; for doctorate, 2 foreign languages, comprehensive exam, thesis/dissertation, oral exams. *Entrance requirements:* For master's and doctorate, GRE General Test.

West Virginia University, Eberly College of Arts and Sciences, Department of Psychology, Morgantown, WV 26506. Offers behavior analysis (PhD); clinical psychology (MA, PhD); development psychology (PhD); psychology (MS). *Accreditation:* APA (one or more programs are accredited). Part-time programs available. Terminal master's awarded for partial completion of doctoral program. *Degree requirements:* For master's, thesis optional; for doctorate, comprehensive exam, thesis/dissertation. *Entrance requirements:* For master's and doctorate, GRE General Test, minimum GPA of 3.0. Additional exam requirements/recommendations for international students: Required—TOEFL. *Faculty research:* Adult and child clinical psychology, behavioral assessment and therapy, child and adolescent behavior, life span development, experimental and applied behavior analysis.

Wheaton College, Graduate School, Department of Psychology, Wheaton, IL 60187-5593. Offers clinical psychology (MA, Psy D); counseling ministries (MA). *Accreditation:* APA (one or more programs are accredited). Terminal master's awarded for partial completion of doctoral program. *Degree requirements:* For master's, thesis or alternative; for doctorate, thesis/dissertation, internship. *Entrance requirements:* For master's, GRE General Test, 18 hours of course work in psychology; for doctorate, GRE General Test.

Wichita State University, Graduate School, Fairmount College of Liberal Arts and Sciences, Department of Psychology, Wichita, KS 67260. Offers clinical (PhD); community (PhD); human factors (PhD). *Accreditation:* APA. Part-time programs available. *Unit head:* Dr. Alex Chaparro, Chair, 316-978-3170, Fax: 316-978-3006, E-mail: alex.chaparro@wichita.edu. *Application contact:* Dr. Robert Zettle, Graduate Coordinator, 316-978-3170, E-mail: robert.zettle@wichita.edu.

Widener University, School of Human Service Professions, Institute for Graduate Clinical Psychology, Program in Clinical Psychology, Chester, PA 19013-5792. Offers Psy D, Psy D/M Ed, Psy D/MA, Psy D/MBA, Psy D/MHA, Psy D/MPA, Psy D/MSHR. *Accreditation:* APA. *Students:* 163 full-time (120 women), 3 part-time (2 women); includes 7 Black or African American, non-Hispanic/Latino; 10 Asian, non-Hispanic/Latino; 11 Hispanic/Latino; 3 Two or more races, non-Hispanic/Latino, 3 international. Average age 24. In 2010, 26 doctorates awarded. *Degree requirements:* For doctorate, thesis/dissertation, final oral and written qualifying exams. *Entrance requirements:* For doctorate, GRE General Test or MAT. *Application deadline:* For fall admission, 12/31 for domestic students. Application fee: $75. Electronic applications accepted. *Expenses:* Contact institution. *Financial support:* Career-related internships or fieldwork, Federal Work-Study, institutionally sponsored loans, scholarships/grants, and stipends available. Financial award application deadline: 4/15. *Faculty research:* Cognitive and personality diagnostic testing, depression, child and adolescent competencies, learning disabilities, family therapy. *Unit head:* Dr. Virginia Brabender, Associate Dean/Director, 610-499-1208, Fax: 610-499-4625, E-mail: graduate.psychology@widener.edu. *Application contact:* Ellen Madison, Admissions Coordinator, 611-499-1206, Fax: 610-499-4625, E-mail: ellen.t.madison@widener.edu.

Widener University, School of Human Service Professions, Institute for Graduate Clinical Psychology, Program in Clinical Psychology and Health and Medical Services Administration, Chester, PA 19013-5792. Offers Psy D/MBA, Psy D/MHA. *Accreditation:* APA (one or more programs are accredited); CAHME. *Faculty:* 15 full-time (6 women), 18 part-time/adjunct (10 women). *Students:* 2 full-time (both women). Average age 28. *Application deadline:* For fall admission, 12/31 for domestic students. Application fee: $75. Electronic applications accepted. *Financial support:* Career-related internships or fieldwork, Federal Work-Study, and institutionally sponsored loans available. Financial award application deadline: 5/31. *Faculty research:* Psychosocial competence, family systems, medical care systems and financing. *Unit head:* Dr. Hal Shorey, Director, 610-499-4598, Fax: 610-499-4625. *Application contact:* Admissions Coordinator.

William Paterson University of New Jersey, College of Humanities and Social Sciences, Wayne, NJ 07470-8420. Offers clinical and counseling psychology (MA); English (MA); history (MA); public policy and international affairs (MA); sociology (MA). Part-time and evening/weekend programs available. Electronic applications accepted.

Wisconsin School of Professional Psychology, Program in Clinical Psychology, Milwaukee, WI 53225-4960. Offers MA, Psy D. *Accreditation:* APA. Part-time and evening/weekend programs available. Terminal master's awarded for partial completion of doctoral program. *Degree requirements:* For master's, candidacy exam, 500 hours of supervised clinical practica; for doctorate, thesis/dissertation, 1 year clinical intern and practicum experience (2000 hrs), candidacy and clinical exams. *Entrance requirements:* For master's, GRE General Test, GRE Subject Test, bachelor's degree in psychology, writing sample; for doctorate, GRE General Test, GRE Subject Test, master's degree in clinical psychology or equivalent, writing sample. *Faculty research:* Violence prevention, psychology of women, forensic psychology, custody evaluation, aging, harm reduction in AODA.

Wright Institute, Doctoral Program in Clinical Psychology, Berkeley, CA 94704-1796. Offers Psy D. *Accreditation:* APA. *Faculty:* 28 full-time (19 women), 93 part-time/adjunct (53 women). *Students:* 355 full-time (254 women); includes 95 minority (14 Black or African American, non-Hispanic/Latino; 2 American Indian or Alaska Native, non-Hispanic/Latino; 33 Asian, non-Hispanic/Latino; 29 Hispanic/Latino; 17 Two or more races, non-Hispanic/Latino). Average

age 34. 323 applicants, 40% accepted, 59 enrolled. In 2010, 45 degrees awarded. *Median time to degree:* Of those who began their doctoral program in fall 2002, 100% received their degree in 8 years or less. *Degree requirements:* For doctorate, comprehensive exam, thesis/dissertation. *Entrance requirements:* For doctorate, GRE General Test, statistics, human development, theories of personality or abnormal psychology. Additional exam requirements/recommendations for international students: Required—TOEFL (minimum score 600 paper-based). *Application deadline:* For fall admission, 1/15 priority date for domestic students, 1/15 for international students. Application fee: $50. Electronic applications accepted. *Expenses:* Tuition: Full-time $26,600. *Financial support:* In 2010–11, 150 students received support, including 4 research assistantships (averaging $1,600 per year), 25 teaching assistantships (averaging $1,600 per year); career-related internships or fieldwork, Federal Work-Study, and scholarships/grants also available. Financial award application deadline: 11/30; financial award applicants required to submit FAFSA. *Faculty research:* Time-limited dynamic psychotherapy; mindfulness/ACT; psychotherapy integration; empathy, altruism and survivor guilt; culturally-informed practice. *Unit head:* Dr. Charles Alexander, Dean, 510-841-9230 Ext. 101, E-mail: calexander@wi.edu. *Application contact:* Melissa Delaney, Director of Admissions, 510-841-9230 Ext. 170, Fax: 510-841-0167, E-mail: mdelaney@wi.edu.

Wright State University, School of Professional Psychology, Dayton, OH 45435. Offers clinical psychology (Psy D). *Accreditation:* APA. *Degree requirements:* For doctorate, thesis/dissertation. *Entrance requirements:* For doctorate, GRE General Test, GRE Subject Test. Additional exam requirements/recommendations for international students: Required—TOEFL. *Expenses:* Contact institution.

Xavier University, College of Social Sciences, Health and Education, Department of Psychology, Cincinnati, OH 45207. Offers clinical psychology (Psy D); psychology (MA), including general experimental psychology, industrial-organizational psychology. *Accreditation:* APA (one or more programs are accredited). *Faculty:* 16 full-time (8 women), 5 part-time/adjunct (2 women). *Students:* 87 full-time (65 women), 26 part-time (21 women); includes 11 minority (4 Black or African American, non-Hispanic/Latino; 1 American Indian or Alaska Native, non-Hispanic/Latino; 3 Asian, non-Hispanic/Latino; 3 Hispanic/Latino), 2 international. Average age 27. 292 applicants, 22% accepted, 25 enrolled. In 2010, 26 master's, 16 doctorates awarded. *Degree*

requirements: For master's, one foreign language, comprehensive exam, thesis, internship; for doctorate, one foreign language, comprehensive exam, thesis/dissertation, internship. *Entrance requirements:* For master's and doctorate, GRE. Additional exam requirements/recommendations for international students: Required—TOEFL, IELTS. *Application deadline:* For fall admission, 12/15 for domestic and international students. Application fee: $35. Electronic applications accepted. *Expenses:* Contact institution. *Financial support:* In 2010–11, 54 students received support, including 41 research assistantships with partial tuition reimbursements available, 13 teaching assistantships with partial tuition reimbursements available; scholarships/grants and unspecified assistantships also available. Financial award application deadline: 3/1; financial award applicants required to submit FAFSA. *Faculty research:* Older adults, clinical child and adolescent issues, personnel selection and employee behavior, at-risk youth, sexual abuse. *Unit head:* Dr. Karl Stukenberg, Chair, 513-745-1041, Fax: 513-745-3327, E-mail: stukenb@xavier.edu. *Application contact:* Margaret Maybury, Assistant Director, Enrollment and Student Services, 513-745-1053, Fax: 513-745-3347, E-mail: maybury@xavier.edu.

Yale University, Graduate School of Arts and Sciences, Department of Psychology, New Haven, CT 06520. Offers behavioral neuroscience (PhD); clinical psychology (PhD); cognitive psychology (PhD); developmental psychology (PhD); social/personality psychology (PhD). *Accreditation:* APA. *Degree requirements:* For doctorate, thesis/dissertation. *Entrance requirements:* For doctorate, GRE General Test.

Yeshiva University, Ferkauf Graduate School of Psychology, Program in Clinical Psychology, New York, NY 10033-3201. Offers Psy D. *Accreditation:* APA. Part-time programs available. *Degree requirements:* For doctorate, comprehensive exam, thesis/dissertation. *Entrance requirements:* For doctorate, GRE General Test. *Faculty research:* Psychotherapy, family therapy, psychoanalysis, cognitive behavior therapy.

Yeshiva University, Ferkauf Graduate School of Psychology, Program in School/Clinical-Child Psychology, New York, NY 10033-3201. Offers Psy D. *Accreditation:* APA. Part-time programs available. *Degree requirements:* For doctorate, comprehensive exam, thesis/dissertation. *Entrance requirements:* For doctorate, GRE General Test. *Faculty research:* Testing, early childhood intervention, child and adolescent psychotherapy, clinical child psychology.

Cognitive Sciences

Arizona State University, College of Liberal Arts and Sciences, Department of Psychology, Tempe, AZ 85287-1104. Offers behavioral neuroscience (PhD); clinical psychology (PhD); cognition, action and perception (PhD); developmental psychology (PhD); quantitative psychology (PhD); social psychology (PhD). *Accreditation:* APA. *Faculty:* 72 full-time (36 women), 9 part-time/adjunct (6 women). *Students:* 113 full-time (79 women), 17 part-time (12 women); includes 24 minority (2 Black or African American, non-Hispanic/Latino; 10 Asian, non-Hispanic/Latino; 10 Hispanic/Latino; 2 Two or more races, non-Hispanic/Latino), 9 international. Average age 28. 519 applicants, 8% accepted, 30 enrolled. In 2010, 19 doctorates awarded. *Degree requirements:* For doctorate, comprehensive exam, thesis/dissertation, interactive Program of Study (iPOS) submitted before completing 50 percent of required credit hours. *Entrance requirements:* For doctorate, GRE General Test, GRE Subject Test, minimum GPA of 3.0 or equivalent in last 2 years of work leading to bachelor's degree. Additional exam requirements/recommendations for international students: Required—TOEFL, IELTS, or Pearson Test of English. *Application deadline:* For fall admission, 12/15 for domestic and international students. Application fee: $70 ($90 for international students). Electronic applications accepted. *Expenses:* Tuition, state resident: full-time $8510; part-time $608 per credit. Tuition, nonresident: full-time $16,542; part-time $919 per credit. Required fees: $339; $110 per credit. Part-time tuition and fees vary according to course load. *Financial support:* In 2010–11, 58 research assistantships with tuition reimbursements (averaging $15,281 per year), 48 teaching assistantships with tuition reimbursements (averaging $15,062 per year) were awarded; fellowships with full tuition reimbursements, career-related internships or fieldwork, Federal Work-Study, institutionally sponsored loans, scholarships/grants, and tuition waivers (full and partial) also available. Financial award application deadline: 3/1; financial award applicants required to submit FAFSA. Total annual research expenditures: $9.4 million. *Unit head:* Dr. Keith Crnic, Chair, 480-965-3061, E-mail: keith.crnic@asu.edu. *Application contact:* Graduate Admissions, 480-965-6113.

Arizona State University, College of Technology and Innovation, Department of Engineering, Mesa, AZ 85212. Offers computing studies (MCST); simulation, modeling, and applied cognitive science (PhD). Part-time programs available. *Faculty:* 30 full-time (8 women). *Students:* 33 full-time (9 women), 12 part-time (10 women); includes 7 minority (1 Black or African American, non-Hispanic/Latino; 4 Asian, non-Hispanic/Latino; 2 Hispanic/Latino), 29 international. Average age 26. 208 applicants, 97% accepted, 15 enrolled. In 2010, 8 master's awarded. *Degree requirements:* For master's, thesis or applied project with oral defense; interactive Program of Study (iPOS) submitted before completing 50 percent of required credit hours; for doctorate, comprehensive exam, thesis/dissertation, interactive Program of Study (iPOS) submitted before completing 50 percent of required credit hours. *Entrance requirements:* For master's, GRE, minimum GPA of 3.0 or equivalent in last 2 years of work leading to bachelor's degree; for doctorate, GRE, master's degree in psychology, engineering, cognitive science, or computer science; 3 letters of recommendation; statement of research interests. Additional exam requirements/recommendations for international students: Required—TOEFL, IELTS, or Pearson Test of English. *Application deadline:* For fall admission, 1/31 for domestic and international students; for spring admission, 9/30 for domestic students, 8/30 for international students. Application fee: $70 ($90 for international students). Electronic applications accepted. *Expenses:* Tuition, state resident: full-time $8510; part-time $608 per credit. Tuition, nonresident: full-time $16,542; part-time $919 per credit. Required fees: $339; $110 per credit. Part-time tuition and fees vary according to course load. *Financial support:* In 2010–11, 3 research assistantships with full and partial tuition reimbursements (averaging $14,832 per year), 1 teaching assistantship with full and partial tuition reimbursement (averaging $10,400 per year) were awarded; fellowships with full and partial tuition reimbursements, career-related internships or fieldwork, Federal Work-Study, scholarships/grants, health care benefits, tuition waivers (full and partial), and unspecified assistantships also available. Support available to part-time students. Financial award application deadline: 3/1; financial award applicants required to submit FAFSA. *Faculty research:* Software process and automated workflow, software architecture, dotal technologies, relational database systems, embedded systems. Total annual research expenditures: $595,649. *Unit head:* Dr. Chell Roberts, Executive Dean/Chair, 480-727-1353, Fax: 480-727-1089, E-mail: chell.roberts@asu.edu. *Application contact:* Graduate Admissions, 480-965-6113.

Ball State University, Graduate School, College of Sciences and Humanities, Department of Psychological Science, Program in Cognitive and Social Processes, Muncie, IN 47306-1099. Offers MA. *Faculty:* 20. *Students:* 15 full-time (5 women); includes 1 Black or African American, non-Hispanic/Latino; 1 Hispanic/Latino, 1 international. Average age 27. 7 applicants, 0% accepted, 0 enrolled. In 2010, 7 master's awarded. Application fee: $50. *Expenses:* Tuition, state resident: full-time $6160; part-time $299 per credit hour. Tuition, nonresident: full-time $16,020; part-time $783 per credit hour. Required fees: $2278; $95 per credit hour. *Financial support:* Research assistantships with full tuition reimbursements, teaching assistantships available. *Unit head:* Dr. Kerri Pickel, Graduate Program Director, 765-285-1690, Fax: 765-285-8980, E-mail: kpickel@bsu.edu. *Application contact:* Dr. Kerri Pickel, Graduate Program Director, 765-285-1690, Fax: 765-285-8980, E-mail: kpickel@bsu.edu.

Boston University, Graduate School of Arts and Sciences, Department of Cognitive and Neural Systems, Boston, MA 02215. Offers MA, PhD. *Students:* 46 full-time (9 women), 7 part-time (2 women); includes 6 minority (4 Asian, non-Hispanic/Latino; 1 Hispanic/Latino; 1 Two or more races, non-Hispanic/Latino), 15 international. Average age 30. 61 applicants, 31% accepted, 8 enrolled.Terminal master's awarded for partial completion of doctoral program. *Degree requirements:* For master's, one foreign language, comprehensive exam; for doctorate, one foreign language, comprehensive exam, thesis/dissertation. *Entrance requirements:* For master's and doctorate, GRE General Test, GRE Subject Test (recommended), 3 letters of recommendation. Additional exam requirements/recommendations for international students: Required—TOEFL (minimum score 550 paper-based; 213 computer-based). *Application deadline:* For fall admission, 1/15 for domestic and international students; for spring admission, 10/15 for domestic and international students. Application fee: $70. Electronic applications accepted. *Expenses:* Tuition: Full-time $39,314; part-time $1228 per credit. Required fees: $40 per semester. *Financial support:* In 2010–11, 2 fellowships with full tuition reimbursements (averaging $19,300 per year), 35 research assistantships with full tuition reimbursements (averaging $18,800 per year), 2 teaching assistantships with full tuition reimbursements were awarded; Federal Work-Study and unspecified assistantships also available. Support available to part-time students. Financial award application deadline: 1/15; financial award applicants required to submit FAFSA. *Unit head:* Ennio Mingolla, Chairman, 617-353-9485, Fax: 617-353-7755, E-mail: ennio@bu.edu. *Application contact:* Carol Y. Jefferson, Administrative Assistant, 617-353-7676, Fax: 617-353-7755, E-mail: caroly@bu.edu.

Brandeis University, Graduate School of Arts and Sciences, Department of Psychology, Waltham, MA 02454-9110. Offers brain, body and behavior (PhD); cognitive neuroscience (PhD); general psychology (MA); social/developmental psychology (PhD). Part-time programs available. *Faculty:* 17 full-time (4 women), 2 part-time/adjunct (1 woman). *Students:* 47 full-time (32 women); includes 2 Asian, non-Hispanic/Latino, 12 international. 164 applicants, 27% accepted, 24 enrolled. In 2010, 8 master's, 4 doctorates awarded. Terminal master's awarded for partial completion of doctoral program. *Degree requirements:* For master's, thesis; for doctorate, comprehensive exam, thesis/dissertation. *Entrance requirements:* For master's and doctorate, GRE General Test, GRE Subject Test (recommended), 3 letters of recommendation, statement of purpose. Additional exam requirements/recommendations for international students: Required—TOEFL (minimum score 600 paper-based; 250 computer-based; 100 iBT); Recommended—IELTS (minimum score 7). *Application deadline:* For fall admission, 1/15 priority date for domestic and international students. Applications are processed on a rolling basis. Application fee: $75. Electronic applications accepted. *Financial support:* In 2010–11, 16 fellowships with full tuition reimbursements (averaging $20,000 per year), 3 research assistantships with full tuition reimbursements (averaging $20,000 per year), 9 teaching assistantships with partial tuition reimbursements (averaging $3,200 per year) were awarded; institutionally sponsored loans, scholarships/grants, health care benefits, tuition waivers (full and partial), and unspecified assistantships also available. Support available to part-time students. Financial award application deadline: 4/15; financial award applicants required to submit FAFSA. *Faculty research:* Cognitive neuroscience, social developmental psychology, brain body and behavior. *Unit head:* Prof. Paul DiZio, Director of Graduate Studies, 781-736-3300, Fax: 781-736-3291, E-mail: dizio@brandeis.edu. *Application contact:* Phil Gnatowski, Department Administrator, 781-736-3303, Fax: 781-736-3291, E-mail: gnat@brandeis.edu.

Brown University, Graduate School, Department of Cognitive and Linguistic Sciences, Providence, RI 02912. Offers cognitive science (Sc M, PhD); linguistics (AM, PhD). *Degree requirements:* For master's, one foreign language, thesis or alternative; for doctorate, 2 foreign languages, thesis/dissertation.

Brown University, Graduate School, Department of Psychology, Providence, RI 02912. Offers behavioral neuroscience (PhD); cognitive processes (PhD); sensation and perception (PhD); social/developmental (PhD); MS/PhD. *Degree requirements:* For doctorate, thesis/dissertation. *Entrance requirements:* For doctorate, GRE General Test, GRE Subject Test.

Carleton University, Faculty of Graduate Studies, Faculty of Arts and Social Sciences, Program in Cognitive Science, Ottawa, ON K1S 5B6, Canada. Offers PhD. *Degree requirements:* For doctorate, thesis/dissertation. *Entrance requirements:* For doctorate, master's degree. *Faculty research:* Language, attention, artificial intelligence, symbol recognition, consciousness.

Carnegie Mellon University, College of Humanities and Social Sciences, Department of Psychology, Area of Cognitive Neuroscience, Pittsburgh, PA 15213-3891. Offers PhD. *Degree requirements:* For doctorate, comprehensive exam, thesis/dissertation. *Entrance requirements:* For doctorate, GRE General Test. Additional exam requirements/recommendations for international students: Required—TOEFL.

Carnegie Mellon University, College of Humanities and Social Sciences, Department of Psychology, Area of Cognitive Psychology, Pittsburgh, PA 15213-3891. Offers PhD. *Degree*

Cognitive Sciences

Carnegie Mellon University (continued)
requirements: For doctorate, comprehensive exam, thesis/dissertation. *Entrance requirements:* For doctorate, GRE General Test. Additional exam requirements/recommendations for international students: Required—TOEFL.

Case Western Reserve University, School of Graduate Studies, Department of Cognitive Science, Cleveland, OH 44106. Offers cognitive linguistics (MA). Part-time programs available. *Faculty:* 6 full-time (2 women), 2 part-time/adjunct (1 woman). *Students:* 2 full-time (0 women), 4 part-time (0 women). Average age 30. 7 applicants, 57% accepted, 2 enrolled. In 2010, 3 master's awarded. *Degree requirements:* For master's, thesis. *Entrance requirements:* For master's, GRE, recommendations, writing sample. Additional exam requirements/recommendations for international students: Required—TOEFL (minimum score 550 paper-based; 213 computer-based; 79 iBT). *Application deadline:* For fall admission, 5/1 priority date for domestic students. Application fee: $50. Electronic applications accepted. *Faculty research:* Integrated, trans-disciplinary research into human higher-order cognition with emphases including the workings of the human mind in design, art, and technology, the interaction of brain and culture in development and evolution, the origins of human higher-order cognition. *Unit head:* Dr. Todd Oakley, Chair, 216-368-4753, E-mail: cogsci@case.edu. *Application contact:* Dr. Todd Oakley, Co-Director of Admission, 216-368-4753, E-mail: coglingadmission@case.edu.

Claremont Graduate University, Graduate Programs, School of Behavioral and Organizational Sciences, Department of Psychology, Claremont, CA 91711-6160. Offers advanced study in evaluation (Certificate); cognitive psychology (MA, PhD); developmental psychology (MA, PhD); evaluation and applied research methods (MA, PhD); health behavior research and evaluation (MA, PhD); human resource development and evaluation (MA); industrial/organizational psychology (MA, PhD); organizational behavior (MA, PhD); organizational psychology (MA, PhD); social psychology (MA, PhD); MBA/PhD. Part-time programs available. *Faculty:* 15 full-time (6 women), 5 part-time/adjunct (2 women). *Students:* 248 full-time (169 women), 15 part-time (9 women); includes 68 minority (14 Black or African American, non-Hispanic/Latino; 1 American Indian or Alaska Native, non-Hispanic/Latino; 27 Asian, non-Hispanic/Latino; 19 Hispanic/Latino; 2 Native Hawaiian or other Pacific Islander, non-Hispanic/Latino; 5 Two or more races, non-Hispanic/Latino), 29 international. Average age 30. In 2010, 45 master's, 21 doctorates, 4 other advanced degrees awarded. Terminal master's awarded for partial completion of doctoral program. *Entrance requirements:* For master's and doctorate, GRE General Test. Additional exam requirements/recommendations for international students: Required—TOEFL (minimum score 550 paper-based; 213 computer-based; 80 iBT). *Application deadline:* For fall admission, 1/15 priority date for domestic students. Applications are processed on a rolling basis. Application fee: $60. Electronic applications accepted. *Expenses:* Tuition: Full-time $35,748; part-time $1554 per unit. Required fees: $215 per semester. *Financial support:* Fellowships, research assistantships, teaching assistantships, Federal Work-Study, institutionally sponsored loans, scholarships/grants, and tuition waivers (full and partial) available. Support available to part-time students. Financial award application deadline: 2/15; financial award applicants required to submit FAFSA. *Faculty research:* Social intervention, diversity in organizations, eyewitness memory, aging and cognition, drug policy. *Unit head:* Stewart Donaldson, Dean, 909-607-9001, Fax: 909-621-8905, E-mail: stewart.donaldson@cgu.edu. *Application contact:* Paul Thomas, Director, External Affairs, 909-607-9016, Fax: 909-621-8905, E-mail: paul.thomas@cgu.edu.

Cornell University, Graduate School, Graduate Fields of Arts and Sciences, Field of Information Science, Ithaca, NY 14853-0001. Offers cognition (PhD); human computer interaction (PhD); information systems (PhD); social aspects of information (PhD). *Faculty:* 33 full-time (10 women). *Students:* 23 full-time (9 women); includes 1 Black or African American, non-Hispanic/Latino; 2 Asian, non-Hispanic/Latino, 10 international. Average age 28. 98 applicants, 15% accepted, 8 enrolled. In 2010, 2 degrees awarded. *Degree requirements:* For doctorate, comprehensive exam, thesis/dissertation. *Entrance requirements:* For doctorate, GRE General Test, 3 letters of recommendation. Additional exam requirements/recommendations for international students: Required—TOEFL (minimum score 550 paper-based; 213 computer-based; 77 iBT). *Application deadline:* For fall admission, 1/1 for domestic students. Application fee: $80. Electronic applications accepted. *Expenses:* Tuition: Full-time $29,500. Required fees: $76. Tuition and fees vary according to degree level and program. *Financial support:* In 2010–11, 5 fellowships with full tuition reimbursements, 10 research assistantships with full tuition reimbursements, 5 teaching assistantships with full tuition reimbursements were awarded; institutionally sponsored loans, scholarships/grants, tuition waivers (full and partial), and unspecified assistantships also available. Financial award applicants required to submit FAFSA. *Faculty research:* Digital libraries, game theory, data mining, human-computer interaction, computational linguistics. *Unit head:* Director of Graduate Studies, 607-255-5925. *Application contact:* Graduate Field Assistant, 607-255-5925, E-mail: info@infosci.cornell.edu.

Dartmouth College, Arts and Sciences Graduate Programs, Department of Psychological and Brain Sciences, Program in Cognitive Neuroscience, Hanover, NH 03755. Offers PhD. *Entrance requirements:* Additional exam requirements/recommendations for international students: Required—TOEFL.

Duke University, Graduate School, Department of Psychology and Neuroscience, Durham, NC 27708. Offers biological psychology (PhD); clinical psychology (PhD); cognitive psychology (PhD); developmental psychology (PhD); experimental psychology (PhD); health psychology (PhD); human social development (PhD); JD/MA. *Accreditation:* APA (one or more programs are accredited). *Faculty:* 92 full-time. *Students:* 92 full-time (67 women); includes 6 Black or African American, non-Hispanic/Latino; 2 Asian, non-Hispanic/Latino; 7 Hispanic/Latino, 13 international. 483 applicants, 8% accepted, 23 enrolled. In 2010, 24 doctorates awarded. *Degree requirements:* For doctorate, thesis/dissertation. *Entrance requirements:* For doctorate, GRE General Test. Additional exam requirements/recommendations for international students: Required—TOEFL (minimum score 550 paper-based; 213 computer-based; 83 iBT), IELTS (minimum score 7). *Application deadline:* For fall admission, 12/8 priority date for domestic and international students. Application fee: $75. Electronic applications accepted. *Financial support:* Fellowships, research assistantships, teaching assistantships, career-related internships or fieldwork and Federal Work-Study available. Financial award application deadline: 12/8. *Unit head:* Melanie Bonner, Director of Graduate Studies, 919-660-5715, Fax: 919-660-5726, E-mail: morrell@duke.edu. *Application contact:* Elizabeth Hutton, Director of Admissions, 919-684-3913, Fax: 919-684-2277, E-mail: grad-admissions@duke.edu.

Emory University, Laney Graduate School, Department of Psychology, Atlanta, GA 30322-1100. Offers clinical psychology (PhD); cognition and development (PhD); neuroscience and animal behavior (PhD). *Accreditation:* APA. *Degree requirements:* For doctorate, comprehensive exam, thesis/dissertation. *Entrance requirements:* For doctorate, GRE General Test, minimum GPA of 3.25. Additional exam requirements/recommendations for international students: Required—TOEFL. Electronic applications accepted. *Expenses:* Tuition: Full-time $33,800. Required fees: $1300. *Faculty research:* Neuroscience and animal behavior; adult and child psychopathology, cognition development assessment.

Florida State University, The Graduate School, College of Arts and Sciences, Department of Psychology, Program in Cognitive Psychology, Tallahassee, FL 32306. Offers PhD. *Faculty:* 7 full-time (1 woman). *Students:* 24 full-time (6 women), 1 international. Average age 28. 49 applicants, 14% accepted, 5 enrolled. In 2010, 1 doctorate awarded. Terminal master's awarded for partial completion of doctoral program. *Degree requirements:* For doctorate, thesis/dissertation, preliminary exam. *Entrance requirements:* For doctorate, GRE General Test (suggested minimum total score of 1000), minimum GPA of 3.0, research experience, letters of recommendation. Additional exam requirements/recommendations for international students: Required—TOEFL (minimum score 550 paper-based; 213 computer-based; 80 iBT). *Application deadline:* For fall admission, 12/15 for domestic and international students. Application fee: $30. Electronic applications accepted. *Expenses:* Tuition, state resident: full-time $8238.24. *Financial support:* In 2010–11, 24 students received support, including 4 fellowships with full tuition reimbursements available (averaging $20,000 per year), 7 research assistantships with full tuition reimbursements available (averaging $20,000 per year), 13 teaching assistantships with full tuition reimbursements available (averaging $16,500 per year); Federal Work-Study, institutionally sponsored loans, scholarships/grants, traineeships, health care benefits, and unspecified assistantships also available. *Faculty research:* Memory, learning and reading disabilities; expert performance; aging. Total annual research expenditures: $639,161. *Unit head:* Dr. Michael Kaschak, Director, 850-644-9363, Fax: 850-644-7739, E-mail: kaschak@psy.fsu.edu. *Application contact:* Cherie P. Miller, Graduate Program Assistant, 850-644-2499, Fax: 850-644-7739, E-mail: grad-info@psy.fsu.edu.

George Mason University, College of Humanities and Social Sciences, Department of Psychology, Fairfax, VA 22030. Offers aviation psychology (Certificate); cognitive neuroscience (Certificate); psychology (MA, PhD); school psychology (Certificate); usability (Certificate). *Accreditation:* APA. *Faculty:* 46 full-time (20 women), 15 part-time/adjunct (7 women). *Students:* 113 full-time (75 women), 119 part-time (78 women); includes 5 Black or African American, non-Hispanic/Latino; 10 Asian, non-Hispanic/Latino; 11 Hispanic/Latino; 3 Two or more races, non-Hispanic/Latino, 9 international. Average age 27. 693 applicants, 23% accepted, 76 enrolled. In 2010, 57 master's, 15 doctorates, 8 other advanced degrees awarded. Terminal master's awarded for partial completion of doctoral program. *Degree requirements:* For master's, comprehensive exam, thesis (for biopsychology); for doctorate, comprehensive exam, thesis/dissertation, 2nd year project. *Entrance requirements:* For master's, GRE General Test, minimum GPA of 3.25 in last 60 hours of course work, undergraduate course work in psychology, 3 letters of recommendation, resume; for doctorate, GRE General Test, minimum undergraduate GPA of 3.5, 3 letters of recommendation, resume, expanded goals statement. Additional exam requirements/recommendations for international students: Required—TOEFL (minimum score 570 paper-based; 230 computer-based; 88 iBT). *Application deadline:* For fall admission, 3/1 priority date for domestic students; for spring admission, 10/15 for domestic students. Application fee: $100. Electronic applications accepted. *Expenses:* Tuition, state resident: full-time $8192; part-time $440 per credit hour. Tuition, nonresident: full-time $22,952; part-time $1055 per credit hour. Required fees: $2364; $99 per credit hour. *Financial support:* In 2010–11, 110 students received support, including 3 fellowships with full tuition reimbursements available (averaging $18,000 per year), 76 research assistantships with full and partial tuition reimbursements available (averaging $11,036 per year), 52 teaching assistantships with full and partial tuition reimbursements available (averaging $8,237 per year); career-related internships or fieldwork, Federal Work-Study, scholarships/grants, traineeships, tuition waivers (partial), unspecified assistantships, and health care benefits (full-time research or teaching assistantship recipients) also available. Support available to part-time students. Financial award application deadline: 3/1; financial award applicants required to submit FAFSA. *Faculty research:* Applied developmental psychology, biopsychology, clinical psychology, human factors/applied cognition psychology, industrial/organizational psychology, school psychology. Total annual research expenditures: $4.5 million. *Unit head:* Dr. Deborah Boehm-Davis, Chairperson, 703-993-1398, Fax: 703-993-1359, E-mail: dbdavis@gmu.edu. *Application contact:* Darby Wiggins, Graduate Program Assistant, 703-993-1548, E-mail: dwiggin3@gmu.edu.

The George Washington University, Columbian College of Arts and Sciences, Department of Psychology, Washington, DC 20052. Offers applied social psychology (PhD); clinical psychology (PhD); cognitive neuroscience (PhD). *Accreditation:* APA. Part-time and evening/weekend programs available. *Faculty:* 26 full-time (14 women), 14 part-time/adjunct (9 women). *Students:* 131 full-time (103 women), 75 part-time (55 women); includes 14 Black or African American, non-Hispanic/Latino; 2 American Indian or Alaska Native, non-Hispanic/Latino; 18 Asian, non-Hispanic/Latino; 16 Hispanic/Latino, 4 international. Average age 29. 797 applicants, 6% accepted, 9 enrolled. In 2010, 41 doctorates awarded. *Degree requirements:* For doctorate, thesis/dissertation or alternative, general exam. *Entrance requirements:* For doctorate, GRE General Test, minimum GPA of 3.0. Additional exam requirements/recommendations for international students: Required—TOEFL (minimum score 550 paper-based; 213 computer-based; 80 iBT). *Application deadline:* For fall admission, 1/15 for domestic and international students. Application fee: $75. *Financial support:* In 2010–11, 62 students received support; fellowships with tuition reimbursements available, teaching assistantships with tuition reimbursements available, career-related internships or fieldwork, Federal Work-Study, and tuition waivers available. *Unit head:* Dr. Paul Poppen, Chair, 202-994-6324, E-mail: pjp@gwu.edu. *Application contact:* Information Contact, 202-994-6320, Fax: 202-994-1602, E-mail: psydept@gwu.edu.

Graduate School and University Center of the City University of New York, Graduate Studies, Program in Psychology, New York, NY 10016-4039. Offers basic applied neurocognition (PhD); biopsychology (PhD); clinical psychology (PhD); developmental psychology (PhD); environmental psychology (PhD); experimental psychology (PhD); industrial psychology (PhD); learning processes (PhD); neuropsychology (PhD); psychology (PhD); social personality (PhD). *Degree requirements:* For doctorate, one foreign language, thesis/dissertation. *Entrance requirements:* For doctorate, GRE General Test. Additional exam requirements/recommendations for international students: Required—TOEFL. Electronic applications accepted.

Grand Canyon University, College of Doctoral Studies, Phoenix, AZ 85017-1097. Offers business administration (DBA); general psychology (PhD), including cognition and instruction, industrial and organizational psychology; organizational leadership (Ed D, PhD), including behavioral health (PhD), education and effective schools (PhD), higher education (PhD), instructional leadership (PhD), organizational development (Ed D). *Faculty:* 2 full-time (1 woman), 12 part-time/adjunct (5 women). *Students:* 968 part-time (711 women); includes 316 minority (283 Black or African American, non-Hispanic/Latino; 12 American Indian or Alaska Native, non-Hispanic/Latino; 3 Asian, non-Hispanic/Latino; 11 Hispanic/Latino; 1 Native Hawaiian or other Pacific Islander, non-Hispanic/Latino; 6 Two or more races, non-Hispanic/Latino). *Degree requirements:* For doctorate, comprehensive exam, thesis/dissertation. *Entrance requirements:* For doctorate, minimum GPA of 3.4 on earned advanced degree from regionally-accredited institution; transcripts; goals statement. Application fee: $0. *Unit head:* Dr. Hank Radda, Dean, 602-639-7255, E-mail: hank.radda@gcu.edu. *Application contact:* Hector Leal, Associate Vice President of Internet Enrollment, 800-639-7144, E-mail: hector.leal@.gcu.edu.

Harvard University, Graduate School of Arts and Sciences, Department of Psychology, Cambridge, MA 02138. Offers psychology (PhD), including behavior and decision analysis, cognition, developmental psychology, experimental psychology, personality, psychobiology, psychopathology; social psychology (PhD). *Accreditation:* APA. *Degree requirements:* For doctorate, thesis/dissertation, general exams. *Entrance requirements:* For doctorate, GRE General Test. Additional exam requirements/recommendations for international students: Required—TOEFL. *Expenses:* Tuition: Full-time $34,976. Required fees: $1166. Full-time tuition and fees vary according to program.

Harvard University, Harvard Graduate School of Education, Master's Programs in Education, Cambridge, MA 02138. Offers arts in education (Ed M); education policy and management (Ed M); higher education (Ed M); human development and psychology (Ed M); international education policy (Ed M); language and literacy (Ed M); learning and teaching (Ed M); mid-career mathematics and science (teaching certificate) (Ed M); mind brain and education (Ed M); prevention science and practice (Ed M); school leadership (Ed M); special studies (Ed M); teaching and curriculum (teaching certificate) (Ed M); technology innovation and education (Ed M). Part-time programs available. *Faculty:* 79 full-time (42 women), 58 part-time/adjunct (24 women). *Students:* 601 full-time (453 women), 77 part-time (53 women); includes 198 minority (59 Black or African American, non-Hispanic/Latino; 3 American Indian or Alaska Native, non-Hispanic/Latino; 59 Asian, non-Hispanic/Latino; 48 Hispanic/Latino; 2 Native Hawaiian or other Pacific Islander, non-Hispanic/Latino; 27 Two or more races, non-Hispanic/Latino), 75 international. Average age 28. 1,667 applicants, 53% accepted, 633 enrolled. In 2010, 634 master's awarded. *Entrance requirements:* For master's, GRE General Test, statement of purpose, 3 letters of recommendation, resume, official transcripts. Additional exam requirements/recommendations for international students: Required—TOEFL (minimum score 600 paper-based; 250 computer-based; 100 iBT), TWE (minimum score 5). *Application deadline:* For fall admission, 1/3 for domestic and international students. Application fee: $85. Electronic applications accepted. *Expenses:* Contact institution. *Financial support:* In 2010–11, 422 students received support, including 24 fellowships with full and partial tuition reimbursements available (averaging $11,886 per year); career-related internships or fieldwork, Federal Work-Study, institutionally sponsored loans, scholarships/grants, health care benefits, tuition waivers (full and partial), and unspecified assistantships also available. Support available to part-time students. Financial award application deadline: 2/1; financial award applicants required to submit FAFSA. *Faculty research:* Learning and development, educational leadership and organizations, educational policy analysis. Total annual research expenditures: $23 million. *Unit head:* Jennifer L. Petrallia, Assistant Dean, 617-495-8445. *Application contact:* Information Contact, 617-495-3414, Fax: 617-496-3577, E-mail: gseadmissions@harvard.edu.

Hunter College of the City University of New York, Graduate School, School of Arts and Sciences, Department of Psychology, New York, NY 10021-5085. Offers animal behavior and conservation (MA); applied and evaluative psychology (MA); biopsychology and behavioral neuroscience (PhD); biopsychology and comparative psychology (MA); social, cognitive, and developmental psychology (MA). Part-time and evening/weekend programs available. *Faculty:* 9 full-time (1 woman), 1 part-time/adjunct (0 women). *Students:* 10 full-time (7 women), 79 part-time (61 women); includes 3 Black or African American, non-Hispanic/Latino; 7 Asian, non-Hispanic/Latino; 9 Hispanic/Latino, 2 international. Average age 27. 151 applicants, 34% accepted, 21 enrolled. In 2010, 13 master's awarded. *Degree requirements:* For master's, comprehensive exam, thesis. *Entrance requirements:* For master's, GRE General Test, minimum 12 credits of course work in psychology, including statistics and experimental psychology; 2 letters of recommendation. Additional exam requirements/recommendations for international students: Required—TOEFL. *Application deadline:* For fall admission, 4/1 for domestic students, 2/1 for international students; for spring admission, 11/1 for domestic students, 9/1 for international students. Applications are processed on a rolling basis. Application fee: $125. *Financial support:* Federal Work-Study, scholarships/grants, and tuition waivers (partial) available. Support available to part-time students. *Faculty research:* Personality, cognitive and linguistic development, hormonal and neural control of behavior, gender and culture, social cognition of health and attitudes. *Unit head:* Dr. Jeffrey Parsons, Chairperson, 212-772-5550, Fax: 212-772-5620, E-mail: jeffrey.parsons@hunter.cuny.edu. *Application contact:* Martin Braun, Acting Program Director, 212-772-4482, Fax: 212-650-3336, E-mail: cbraun@hunter.cuny.edu.

Indiana University Bloomington, University Graduate School, College of Arts and Sciences, Cognitive Science Program, Bloomington, IN 47406-7512. Offers PhD. *Faculty:* 78 full-time (17 women). *Students:* 21 full-time (5 women); includes 3 minority (1 Asian, non-Hispanic/Latino; 1 Hispanic/Latino; 1 Two or more races, non-Hispanic/Latino), 5 international. Average age 30. 86 applicants, 8% accepted, 5 enrolled. In 2010, 6 doctorates awarded. *Degree requirements:* For doctorate, comprehensive exam, thesis/dissertation, research project. *Entrance requirements:* For doctorate, GRE, 3 letters of reference, departmental questions form. Additional exam requirements/recommendations for international students: Required—TOEFL (minimum score 600 paper-based; 94 iBT). *Application deadline:* For fall admission, 1/15 for domestic students, 12/1 for international students. Application fee: $55 ($65 for international students). Electronic applications accepted. *Financial support:* In 2010–11, 18 students received support, including 8 fellowships with full tuition reimbursements available (averaging $24,000 per year), 5 research assistantships with full tuition reimbursements available (averaging $17,140 per year), 5 teaching assistantships with full and partial tuition reimbursements available (averaging $16,347 per year). *Faculty research:* Learning concepts, neural network models, language, animal cognition, dynamic and robotics systems approaches to behavior and cognition. *Unit head:* Robert Goldstone, Director, 812-856-3889, E-mail: rgoldsto@indiana.edu. *Application contact:* Susan Towle, Information Contact, 812-855-0031, E-mail: stowle@indiana.edu.

Indiana University Bloomington, University Graduate School, College of Arts and Sciences, Department of Psychological and Brain Sciences, Bloomington, IN 47405-7000. Offers biology and behavior (PhD); clinical science (PhD); cognitive psychology (PhD); developmental psychology (PhD); psychological and brain sciences (MA); social psychology (PhD). *Accreditation:* APA (one or more programs are accredited). *Faculty:* 53 full-time (16 women). *Students:* 85 full-time (45 women), 1 (woman) part-time; includes 13 minority (3 Black or African American, non-Hispanic/Latino; 3 Asian, non-Hispanic/Latino; 6 Hispanic/Latino; 1 Two or more races, non-Hispanic/Latino), 19 international. Average age 28. 363 applicants, 10% accepted, 20 enrolled. In 2010, 3 master's, 17 doctorates awarded. *Degree requirements:* For doctorate, comprehensive exam, thesis/dissertation, 1st and 2nd year projects, 1 year as associate instructor, qualifying exam, student teaching. *Entrance requirements:* For doctorate, GRE. Additional exam requirements/recommendations for international students: Required—TOEFL (minimum score 550 paper-based; 213 computer-based). *Application deadline:* For fall admission, 12/15 for domestic students, 12/1 for international students. Application fee: $55 ($65 for international students). Electronic applications accepted. *Financial support:* In 2010–11, 32 fellowships with full tuition reimbursements (averaging $23,580 per year), 7 research assistantships with full tuition reimbursements (averaging $17,850 per year), 7 teaching assistantships with full tuition reimbursements (averaging $17,850 per year) were awarded; scholarships/grants, health care benefits, and unspecified assistantships also available. *Unit head:* Dr. Linda B. Smith, Chair, 812-855-3991, Fax: 812-855-4691, E-mail: smith4@indiana.edu. *Application contact:* Patricia G. Crouch, Academic Services Coordinator, 812-855-4528, Fax: 812-855-4691, E-mail: pcrouch@indiana.edu.

Iowa State University of Science and Technology, Graduate College, College of Liberal Arts and Sciences, Department of Psychology, Ames, IA 50011. Offers cognitive psychology (PhD); counseling psychology (PhD); social psychology (PhD). *Accreditation:* APA. *Faculty:* 34 full-time (14 women), 1 part-time/adjunct (0 women). *Students:* 73 full-time (42 women), 27 part-time (18 women); includes 8 Black or African American, non-Hispanic/Latino; 4 Asian, non-Hispanic/Latino; 4 Hispanic/Latino, 17 international. 88 applicants, 13% accepted, 9 enrolled. In 2010, 4 doctorates awarded. *Degree requirements:* For doctorate, comprehensive exam, thesis/dissertation. *Entrance requirements:* For doctorate, GRE General Test, GRE Subject Test (psychology), 3 letters of recommendation. Additional exam requirements/recommendations for international students: Required—TOEFL (minimum score 560 paper-based; 79 iBT), IELTS (minimum score 6.5). *Application deadline:* For fall admission, 1/2 priority date for domestic and international students. Application fee: $30 ($70 for international students). Electronic applications accepted. *Financial support:* In 2010–11, fellowships with full tuition reimbursements (averaging $14,055 per year), 7 research assistantships with full tuition reimbursements (averaging $13,169 per year), 57 teaching assistantships with full tuition reimbursements (averaging $9,432 per year) were awarded; scholarships/grants, health care benefits, and unspecified assistantships also available. *Faculty research:* Counseling psychology, cognitive psychology, social psychology, health psychology, psychology and public policy. *Unit head:* Carolyn Cutrona, Chair, 515-294-0283, Fax: 515-294-6424, E-mail: ccutrona@iastate.edu. *Application contact:* Ann Schmidt, Graduate Admissions Secretary, 515-294-1743, Fax: 515-294-6424, E-mail: psychadm@iastate.edu.

The Johns Hopkins University, Zanvyl Krieger School of Arts and Sciences, Department of Cognitive Science, Baltimore, MD 21218-2699. Offers PhD. *Faculty:* 7 full-time (3 women). *Students:* 15 full-time (10 women); includes 2 minority (1 Black or African American, non-Hispanic/Latino; 1 Hispanic/Latino), 3 international. Average age 25. 56 applicants, 11% accepted, 6 enrolled. In 2010, 3 doctorates awarded. Terminal master's awarded for partial completion of doctoral program. *Degree requirements:* For doctorate, thesis/dissertation, 2 research papers. *Entrance requirements:* For doctorate, GRE General Test, letters of recommendation, sample of work. Additional exam requirements/recommendations for international students: Required—TOEFL (minimum score 600 paper-based; 250 computer-based; 100 iBT), IELTS. *Application deadline:* For fall admission, 1/15 for domestic and international students. Application fee: $75. Electronic applications accepted. *Financial support:* In 2010–11, 1 fellowship with full tuition reimbursement (averaging $30,000 per year), research assistantships with full tuition reimbursements (averaging $20,000 per year), 19 teaching assistantships with full tuition reimbursements (averaging $30,000 per year) were awarded; scholarships/grants, health care benefits, and fellowship award, 19 teaching assistantships ($30,000 average) also available. Financial award application deadline: 1/15; financial award applicants required

to submit FAFSA. *Faculty research:* Acquisition and development, cognitive neuropsychology and neuroscience, computational studies, psycholinguistics and cognitive psychology, theoretical linguistics. Total annual research expenditures: $1.8 million. *Unit head:* Dr. Barbara Landau, Dick & Lydia Todd Professor, Department Chair, 410-516-5255, Fax: 410-516-8020, E-mail: landau@cogsci.jhu.edu. *Application contact:* Barbara Ann Fisher, Academic Program Coordinator, 410-516-5250, Fax: 410-516-8020, E-mail: fisher@cogsci.jhu.edu.

Louisiana State University and Agricultural and Mechanical College, Graduate School, College of Humanities and Social Sciences, Department of Psychology, Baton Rouge, LA 70803. Offers biological psychology (MA, PhD); clinical psychology (MA, PhD); cognitive psychology (MA, PhD); developmental psychology (MA, PhD); industrial/organizational psychology (MA, PhD); school psychology (MA, PhD). PhD programs offered jointly with Southeastern Louisiana University. *Accreditation:* APA (one or more programs are accredited). *Faculty:* 26 full-time (10 women). *Students:* 96 full-time (68 women), 24 part-time (19 women); includes 7 Black or African American, non-Hispanic/Latino; 2 American Indian or Alaska Native, non-Hispanic/Latino; 1 Asian, non-Hispanic/Latino; 5 Hispanic/Latino, 2 international. Average age 27. 289 applicants, 11% accepted, 17 enrolled. In 2010, 16 master's, 11 doctorates awarded. Terminal master's awarded for partial completion of doctoral program. *Degree requirements:* For master's, thesis; for doctorate, thesis/dissertation, 1 year internship. *Entrance requirements:* For master's and doctorate, GRE General Test, minimum GPA of 3.0. Additional exam requirements/recommendations for international students: Required—TOEFL (minimum score 550 paper-based; 213 computer-based; 79 iBT) or IELTS (minimum score 6.5). *Application deadline:* For fall admission, 1/15 for domestic and international students. Applications are processed on a rolling basis. Application fee: $50 ($70 for international students). Electronic applications accepted. *Financial support:* In 2010–11, 115 students received support, including 5 fellowships (averaging $25,207 per year), 25 research assistantships with partial tuition reimbursements available (averaging $18,083 per year), 48 teaching assistantships with partial tuition reimbursements available (averaging $13,043 per year); career-related internships or fieldwork, Federal Work-Study, institutionally sponsored loans, scholarships/grants, health care benefits, and tuition waivers (full and partial) also available. Financial award applicants required to submit FAFSA. *Faculty research:* Clinical psychology, autism, anxiety, addition, neuropsychology, school psychology, cognitive psychology, experimental psychology. Total annual research expenditures: $1.3 million. *Unit head:* Dr. Robert Matthews, Chair, 225-578-8745, Fax: 225-578-4125, E-mail: psmath@lsu.edu. *Application contact:* Dr. Jason Hicks, Coordinator of Graduate Studies, 225-578-4109, Fax: 225-578-4125, E-mail: jhicks@lsu.edu.

Massachusetts Institute of Technology, School of Science, Department of Brain and Cognitive Sciences, Cambridge, MA 02139-4307. Offers cognitive science (PhD); neuroscience (PhD). *Faculty:* 37 full-time (14 women). *Students:* 96 full-time (33 women); includes 24 minority (2 Black or African American, non-Hispanic/Latino; 1 American Indian or Alaska Native, non-Hispanic/Latino; 9 Asian, non-Hispanic/Latino; 10 Hispanic/Latino; 2 Two or more races, non-Hispanic/Latino), 16 international. Average age 27. 415 applicants, 8% accepted, 16 enrolled. In 2010, 13 doctorates awarded. *Degree requirements:* For doctorate, comprehensive exam, thesis/dissertation. *Entrance requirements:* For doctorate, GRE General Test. Additional exam requirements/recommendations for international students: Required—TOEFL (minimum score 577 paper-based; 233 computer-based; 90 iBT), IELTS (minimum score 7). *Application deadline:* For fall admission, 12/1 for domestic and international students. Application fee: $75. Electronic applications accepted. *Expenses:* Tuition: Full-time $38,940; part-time $605 per unit. Required fees: $272. *Financial support:* In 2010–11, 83 students received support, including 72 fellowships with tuition reimbursements available (averaging $28,951 per year), 18 research assistantships with tuition reimbursements available (averaging $30,165 per year), 6 teaching assistantships with tuition reimbursements available (averaging $31,586 per year); Federal Work-Study, institutionally sponsored loans, scholarships/grants, traineeships, health care benefits, and unspecified assistantships also available. *Faculty research:* Vision–perception and physiology; learning, memory, and executive control—molecular and systems approaches; sensorimotor systems—physiology and computation; neural and cognitive development and plasticity; language and high-level cognition—learning, acquisition, and computation. Total annual research expenditures: $28.3 million. *Unit head:* Prof. Mriganka Sur, Department Head, 617-253-5748, E-mail: bcs-info@mit.edu. *Application contact:* Academic Office, 617-253-7403, Fax: 617-253-9216, E-mail: bcs-admissions@mit.edu.

Mississippi State University, College of Arts and Sciences, Department of Psychology, Mississippi State, MS 39762. Offers cognitive science (PhD); psychology (MS), including clinical psychology, experimental psychology. *Faculty:* 12 full-time (4 women). *Students:* 40 full-time (27 women), 7 part-time (5 women); includes 4 minority (3 Black or African American, non-Hispanic/Latino; 1 Two or more races, non-Hispanic/Latino), 3 international. Average age 26. 77 applicants, 36% accepted, 19 enrolled. In 2010, 10 master's, 1 doctorate awarded. Terminal master's awarded for partial completion of doctoral program. *Degree requirements:* For master's, comprehensive exam, thesis; for doctorate, thesis/dissertation, qualifying exam, comprehensive written and oral exam. *Entrance requirements:* For master's, GRE General Test, minimum GPA of 2.75 on last two years of undergraduate courses; for doctorate, GRE General Test, proficiency in at least 1 computer language. Additional exam requirements/recommendations for international students: Required—TOEFL (minimum score 475 paper-based; 153 computer-based; 53 iBT); Recommended—IELTS (minimum score 4.5). *Application deadline:* For fall admission, 1/15 priority date for domestic students, 5/1 for international students; for spring admission, 11/1 priority date for domestic students, 9/1 for international students. Applications are processed on a rolling basis. Application fee: $40. Electronic applications accepted. *Expenses:* Tuition, state resident: full-time $2730.50; part-time $304 per credit hour. Tuition, nonresident: full-time $6901; part-time $767 per credit hour. *Financial support:* In 2010–11, 6 research assistantships with full tuition reimbursements (averaging $11,925 per year), 13 teaching assistantships with full tuition reimbursements (averaging $9,755 per year) were awarded; career-related internships or fieldwork, Federal Work-Study, institutionally sponsored loans, scholarships/grants, and unspecified assistantships also available. Financial award application deadline: 4/1; financial award applicants required to submit FAFSA. *Faculty research:* Personality type, alcoholism, blindness and low vision, mental retardation, language comprehension. Total annual research expenditures: $2.4 million. *Unit head:* Dr. Stephen B. Klein, Department Head, 662-325-3202, Fax: 662-325-7212, E-mail: sbkl@ra.msstate.edu. *Application contact:* Dr. Kevin J. Armstrong, Graduate Coordinator, 662-325-3202, Fax: 662-325-7212, E-mail: grad@psychology.msstate.edu.

The New School: A University, The New School for Social Research, Department of Psychology, New York, NY 10011. Offers clinical psychology (PhD); cognitive, social and developmental psychology (PhD); general psychology (MA). *Accreditation:* APA (one or more programs are accredited). Part-time programs available. Terminal master's awarded for partial completion of doctoral program. *Degree requirements:* For master's, comprehensive exam (for some programs), thesis (for some programs); for doctorate, thesis/dissertation, qualifying exam. *Entrance requirements:* For master's, GRE General Test; for doctorate, GRE General Test, MA. Additional exam requirements/recommendations for international students: Required—TOEFL (minimum score 600 paper-based; 250 computer-based; 100 iBT). Electronic applications accepted. *Faculty research:* Consciousness, memory, language, perceptions, psychopathology.

New York University, Graduate School of Arts and Science, Department of Psychology, New York, NY 10012-1019. Offers cognition and perception (PhD); community psychology (PhD); general psychology (MA); industrial/organizational psychology (MA); psychotherapy and psychoanalysis (Advanced Certificate); social/personality psychology (PhD). Part-time programs available. *Students:* 157 full-time (113 women), 257 part-time (175 women); includes 18 Black or African American, non-Hispanic/Latino; 1 American Indian or Alaska Native, non-Hispanic/Latino; 29 Asian, non-Hispanic/Latino; 24 Hispanic/Latino, 64 international. Average age 32. 834 applicants, 39% accepted, 82 enrolled. In 2010, 73 master's, 14 doctorates, 13 other advanced degrees awarded. Terminal master's awarded for partial completion of doctoral program. *Degree requirements:* For master's, comprehensive exam, thesis or alternative; for doctorate, thesis/dissertation. *Entrance requirements:* For master's, GRE General Test, minimum GPA of 3.0; for doctorate, GRE General Test, GRE Subject Test; for Advanced Certificate,

Cognitive Sciences

New York University (continued)
doctoral degree, minimum GPA of 3.0. Additional exam requirements/recommendations for international students: Required—TOEFL. *Application deadline:* For fall admission, 12/15 for domestic students. Application fee: $90. *Financial support:* Fellowships with tuition reimbursements, research assistantships with tuition reimbursements, teaching assistantships with tuition reimbursements, career-related internships or fieldwork, Federal Work-Study, institutionally sponsored loans, scholarships/grants, traineeships, health care benefits, and unspecified assistantships available. Financial award application deadline: 12/15; financial award applicants required to submit FAFSA. *Faculty research:* Vision, memory, social cognition, social and cognitive development, relationships. *Unit head:* Madeline Heilman, Director of PhD Program, 212-998-7900, Fax: 212-995-4018, E-mail: psychq@psych.nyu.edu. *Application contact:* Barry Cohen, Director of MA Program, 212-998-7900, Fax: 212-995-4018, E-mail: psychq@psych.nyu.edu.

North Dakota State University, College of Graduate and Interdisciplinary Studies, College of Science and Mathematics, Department of Psychology, Fargo, ND 58108. Offers clinical psychology (MS); cognitive and visual neuroscience (PhD); health and social psychology (PhD); psychology (MS). *Faculty:* 18 full-time (4 women), 2 part-time/adjunct (1 woman). *Students:* 20 full-time (11 women), 3 part-time (0 women); includes 1 Two or more races, non-Hispanic/Latino, 2 international. Average age 24. 41 applicants, 27% accepted, 6 enrolled. In 2010, 7 master's, 2 doctorates awarded. *Degree requirements:* For master's, thesis; for doctorate, thesis/dissertation. *Entrance requirements:* For master's and doctorate, GRE General Test, GRE Subject Test. Additional exam requirements/recommendations for international students: Required—TOEFL (minimum score 525 paper-based; 197 computer-based; 71 iBT). *Application deadline:* For fall admission, 3/1 for domestic and international students. Application fee: $45 ($60 for international students). Electronic applications accepted. *Financial support:* In 2010–11, 2 fellowships with full tuition reimbursements (averaging $16,000 per year), 23 research assistantships with full tuition reimbursements (averaging $16,000 per year), 11 teaching assistantships with full tuition reimbursements (averaging $6,000 per year) were awarded; career-related internships or fieldwork, Federal Work-Study, institutionally sponsored loans, tuition waivers (full and partial), and unspecified assistantships also available. Support available to part-time students. Financial award application deadline: 3/1. *Faculty research:* Cognition science, neuropsychology, group behavior, applied behavior analysis, behavior therapy. Total annual research expenditures: $2 million. *Unit head:* Dr. Paul D. Rokke, Chair, 701-231-8622, Fax: 701-231-8426, E-mail: paul.rokke@ndsu.edu. *Application contact:* Dr. Paul D. Rokke, Chair, 701-231-8622, Fax: 701-231-8426, E-mail: paul.rokke@ndsu.edu.

Northwestern University, The Graduate School, Judd A. and Marjorie Weinberg College of Arts and Sciences, Department of Psychology, Evanston, IL 60208. Offers brain, behavior and cognition (PhD); clinical psychology (PhD); cognitive psychology (PhD); personality (PhD); social psychology (PhD); JD/PhD. Admissions and degrees offered through The Graduate School. *Accreditation:* APA (one or more programs are accredited). Part-time programs available. *Degree requirements:* For doctorate, thesis/dissertation. *Entrance requirements:* For doctorate, GRE General Test, GRE Subject Test. Additional exam requirements/recommendations for international students: Required—TOEFL. Electronic applications accepted. *Faculty research:* Memory and higher order cognition, anxiety and depression, effectiveness of psychotherapy, social cognition, molecular basis of memory.

The Ohio State University, Graduate School, College of Arts and Sciences, Division of Social and Behavioral Sciences, Department of Psychology, Columbus, OH 43210. Offers behavioral neuroscience (PhD); clinical psychology (PhD); cognitive psychology (PhD); developmental psychology (PhD); mental retardation and developmental disabilities (PhD); psychology (MA); quantitative psychology (PhD); social psychology (PhD). *Accreditation:* APA (one or more programs are accredited). *Faculty:* 60. *Students:* 106 full-time (65 women), 42 part-time (31 women); includes 5 Black or African American, non-Hispanic/Latino; 1 American Indian or Alaska Native, non-Hispanic/Latino; 5 Asian, non-Hispanic/Latino; 10 Hispanic/Latino; 3 Two or more races, non-Hispanic/Latino, 23 international. Average age 27. In 2010, 21 master's, 22 doctorates awarded. *Degree requirements:* For doctorate, thesis/dissertation. *Entrance requirements:* For master's and doctorate, GRE General Test. Additional exam requirements/recommendations for international students: Required—TOEFL (minimum score 600 paper-based; 250 computer-based). *Application deadline:* For fall admission, 12/31 for domestic students, 11/30 for international students. Applications are processed on a rolling basis. Application fee: $40 ($50 for international students). Electronic applications accepted. *Expenses:* Tuition, state resident: full-time $10,605. Tuition, nonresident: full-time $26,535. Tuition and fees vary according to course load and program. *Financial support:* Fellowships, research assistantships, teaching assistantships available. *Unit head:* Dr. Richard Petty, Chair, 614-292-1640, E-mail: petty.1@osu.edu. *Application contact:* 614-292-9444, Fax: 614-292-3895, E-mail: domestic.grad@osu.edu.

Queen's University at Kingston, School of Graduate Studies and Research, Faculty of Arts and Sciences, Department of Psychology, Kingston, ON K7L 3N6, Canada. Offers brain behavior and cognitive science (MA, PhD); clinical psychology (MA, PhD); developmental psychology (MA, PhD); social personality psychology (MA, PhD). *Accreditation:* APA (one or more programs are accredited). *Degree requirements:* For master's, thesis; for doctorate, comprehensive exam, thesis/dissertation. *Entrance requirements:* For master's and doctorate, GRE General Test. Additional exam requirements/recommendations for international students: Required—TOEFL. *Faculty research:* Human development, social, personality, behavioral neuroscience, forensic.

Rensselaer Polytechnic Institute, Graduate School, School of Humanities, Arts, and Social Sciences, Program in Cognitive Science, Troy, NY 12180-3590. Offers MS, PhD. *Faculty:* 16 full-time (1 woman). *Students:* 21 full-time (4 women), 2 part-time (both women), 4 international. Average age 23. 39 applicants, 13% accepted, 4 enrolled. In 2010, 1 master's, 1 doctorate awarded. *Degree requirements:* For doctorate, thesis/dissertation. *Entrance requirements:* For doctorate, GRE General Test. Additional exam requirements/recommendations for international students: Required—TOEFL (minimum score 600 paper-based; 250 computer-based; 88 iBT), IELTS (minimum score 7.5). *Application deadline:* For fall admission, 1/15 priority date for domestic and international students. Applications are processed on a rolling basis. Application fee: $75. Electronic applications accepted. *Expenses:* Tuition: Full-time $39,600; part-time $1650 per credit. Required fees: $1896. *Financial support:* In 2010–11, 5 students received support, including 1 fellowship with full tuition reimbursement available (averaging $23,500 per year), 13 research assistantships with full tuition reimbursements available (averaging $17,500 per year), 2 teaching assistantships with full tuition reimbursements available (averaging $17,500 per year); institutionally sponsored loans, scholarships/grants, and unspecified assistantships also available. Financial award application deadline: 1/15. *Faculty research:* Perception and action, logic, artificial intelligence, cognitive engineering, computational cognitive modeling. Total annual research expenditures: $2.8 million. *Unit head:* Dr. Selmer Bringsjord, Professor and Chair, 518-276-8105, Fax: 518-276-8268, E-mail: brings@rpi.edu. *Application contact:* Betty Osganian, Student Services Administrator, 518-276-6473, Fax: 518-276-8268, E-mail: osgane@rpi.edu.

Rice University, Graduate Programs, School of Social Sciences, Department of Psychology, Houston, TX 77251-1892. Offers cognitive sciences (MA, PhD); industrial-organizational/social psychology (MA, PhD); psychology (MA, PhD). Terminal master's awarded for partial completion of doctoral program. *Degree requirements:* For master's, thesis; for doctorate, thesis/dissertation. *Entrance requirements:* For doctorate, GRE General Test, minimum GPA of 3.0. Additional exam requirements/recommendations for international students: Required—TOEFL. Electronic applications accepted. *Faculty research:* Cognitive, cognitive neuropsychology, human factors, human-computer interaction, industrial-organizational psychology.

Rutgers, The State University of New Jersey, Newark, Graduate School, Program in Psychology, Newark, NJ 07102. Offers cognitive neuroscience (PhD); cognitive science (PhD); perception (PhD); psychobiology (PhD); social cognition (PhD). *Faculty:* 15 full-time (5 women), 6 part-time/adjunct (all women). *Students:* 23 full-time (19 women), 2 part-time (1 woman); includes 3 Black or African American, non-Hispanic/Latino; 1 Asian, non-Hispanic/Latino; 2 Hispanic/Latino. 48 applicants, 17% accepted, 6 enrolled. In 2010, 4 doctorates awarded. *Degree requirements:* For doctorate, comprehensive exam, thesis/dissertation. *Entrance requirements:* For doctorate, GRE General Test, GRE Subject Test, minimum undergraduate B average. *Application deadline:* For fall admission, 2/1 for domestic students; for spring admission, 11/1 for domestic students. Application fee: $60. Electronic applications accepted. *Expenses:* Tuition, state resident: part-time $600 per credit. Tuition, nonresident: full-time $10,694. *Financial support:* In 2010–11, 16 students received support, including 9 fellowships with full and partial tuition reimbursements available (averaging $18,000 per year), 8 teaching assistantships with full and partial tuition reimbursements available (averaging $23,112 per year); career-related internships or fieldwork, health care benefits, and minority scholarships also available. Financial award application deadline: 2/1. *Faculty research:* Visual perception (luminance, motion), neuroendocrine mechanisms in behavior (reproduction, pain), attachment theory, connectionist modeling of cognition. *Unit head:* Dr. Kenneth Kressel, Director, 973-353-5440 Ext. 232, Fax: 973-353-1171, E-mail: kkressel@andromeda.rutgers.edu. *Application contact:* Jason Hand, Director of Admissions, 973-353-5205, Fax: 973-353-1440.

See Display on next page and Close-Up on page 1169.

Rutgers, The State University of New Jersey, New Brunswick, Graduate School-New Brunswick, Program in Psychology, Piscataway, NJ 08854-8097. Offers behavioral neuroscience (PhD); clinical psychology (PhD); cognitive psychology (PhD); interdisciplinary health psychology (PhD); social psychology (PhD). *Accreditation:* APA. *Degree requirements:* For doctorate, comprehensive exam, thesis/dissertation. *Entrance requirements:* For doctorate, GRE General Test, 3 letters of recommendation. Additional exam requirements/recommendations for international students: Required—TOEFL (minimum score 577 paper-based; 233 computer-based). Electronic applications accepted. *Expenses:* Tuition, state resident: full-time $7200; part-time $600 per credit. Tuition, nonresident: full-time $11,124; part-time $927 per credit. *Faculty research:* Learning and memory, behavioral ecology, hormones and behavior, psychopharmacology, anxiety disorders.

State University of New York at Binghamton, Graduate School, School of Arts and Sciences, Department of Psychology, Specialization in Cognitive and Behavioral Science, Binghamton, NY 13902-6000. Offers MA, PhD. *Students:* 16 full-time (6 women), 3 part-time (2 women); includes 1 Asian, non-Hispanic/Latino; 1 Hispanic/Latino, 3 international. Average age 27. 25 applicants, 24% accepted, 5 enrolled. In 2010, 2 doctorates awarded. *Degree requirements:* For master's, thesis; for doctorate, thesis/dissertation, departmental qualifying exam. *Entrance requirements:* For master's and doctorate, GRE General Test, GRE Subject Test. Additional exam requirements/recommendations for international students: Required—TOEFL (minimum score 550 paper-based; 213 computer-based; 80 iBT). *Application deadline:* For fall admission, 1/15 priority date for domestic and international students. Applications are processed on a rolling basis. Application fee: $60. Electronic applications accepted. *Financial support:* In 2010–11, 17 students received support, including 1 fellowship with full tuition reimbursement available (averaging $17,500 per year), 16 teaching assistantships with full tuition reimbursements available (averaging $17,500 per year); career-related internships or fieldwork, Federal Work-Study, institutionally sponsored loans, scholarships/grants, traineeships, health care benefits, tuition waivers (full and partial), and unspecified assistantships also available. Financial award application deadline: 2/15; financial award applicants required to submit FAFSA. *Unit head:* Dr. Albrecht Inhoff, Graduate Coordinator, 607-777-3958, E-mail: inhoff@binghamton.edu. *Application contact:* Catherine Smith, Recruiting and Admissions Coordinator, 607-777-2151, Fax: 607-777-2501, E-mail: cmsmith@binghamton.edu.

Temple University, College of Liberal Arts, Department of Psychology, Philadelphia, PA 19122-6096. Offers brain and cognitive sciences (PhD); clinical psychology (PhD); developmental psychology (PhD); psychology (MA); social psychology (PhD). *Accreditation:* APA. *Faculty:* 29 full-time (11 women). *Students:* 88 full-time (69 women), 14 part-time (12 women); includes 1 Black or African American, non-Hispanic/Latino; 1 American Indian or Alaska Native, non-Hispanic/Latino; 4 Asian, non-Hispanic/Latino; 2 Hispanic/Latino, 6 international. 538 applicants, 6% accepted, 16 enrolled. In 2010, 10 master's, 15 doctorates awarded. *Degree requirements:* For doctorate, thesis/dissertation. *Entrance requirements:* For doctorate, GRE General Test, minimum GPA of 3.0. Additional exam requirements/recommendations for international students: Required—TOEFL (minimum score 550 paper-based; 213 computer-based; 79 iBT). *Application deadline:* For fall admission, 12/15 for domestic and international students. Application fee: $50. Electronic applications accepted. *Financial support:* Fellowships, research assistantships, teaching assistantships, career-related internships or fieldwork, Federal Work-Study, institutionally sponsored loans, and unspecified assistantships available. Financial award application deadline: 12/15; financial award applicants required to submit FAFSA. Total annual research expenditures: $4 million. *Unit head:* Dr. Marsha Weinraub, Chair, 215-204-7321, Fax: 215-204-5539, E-mail: mweinrau@temple.edu. *Application contact:* Dr. Marsha Weinraub, Chair, 215-204-7321, Fax: 215-204-5539, E-mail: mweinrau@temple.edu.

Texas A&M University, College of Liberal Arts, Department of Psychology, College Station, TX 77843. Offers behavioral and cellular neuroscience (PhD); clinical psychology (PhD); cognitive psychology (PhD); developmental psychology (PhD); industrial/organizational psychology (PhD); social psychology (PhD). *Accreditation:* APA. *Faculty:* 39. *Students:* 91 full-time (57 women), 14 part-time (11 women); includes 7 Black or African American, non-Hispanic/Latino; 8 Asian, non-Hispanic/Latino; 17 Hispanic/Latino, 7 international. In 2010, 12 doctorates awarded. *Degree requirements:* For doctorate, comprehensive exam (for some programs), thesis/dissertation. *Entrance requirements:* For doctorate, GRE General Test. Additional exam requirements/recommendations for international students: Required—TOEFL. *Application deadline:* For fall admission, 1/5 for domestic and international students. Application fee: $50 ($75 for international students). Electronic applications accepted. *Financial support:* Fellowships with partial tuition reimbursements, research assistantships with partial tuition reimbursements, teaching assistantships with partial tuition reimbursements, career-related internships or fieldwork, institutionally sponsored loans, health care benefits, and unspecified assistantships available. Financial award application deadline: 1/5; financial award applicants required to submit FAFSA. *Unit head:* Ludy T. Benjamin, Head, 979-845-2540, Fax: 979-845-4727, E-mail: lbenjamin@tamu.edu. *Application contact:* Julie Austin, Graduate Admissions Supervisor, 979-458-1710, Fax: 979-845-4727, E-mail: gradadv@psyc.tamu.edu.

Texas A&M University–Commerce, Graduate School, College of Education and Human Services, Department of Psychology and Special Education, Commerce, TX 75429-3011. Offers cognition and instruction (PhD); psychology (MA, MS); special education (M Ed, MA, MS). Part-time programs available. Terminal master's awarded for partial completion of doctoral program. *Degree requirements:* For master's, comprehensive exam, thesis (for some programs); for doctorate, thesis/dissertation, departmental qualifying exam. *Entrance requirements:* For master's, GRE General Test; for doctorate, GRE General Test, 3 letters of recommendation. Electronic applications accepted. *Faculty research:* Human learning, study skills, multicultural bilingual, diversity and special education, educationally handicapped.

Texas Christian University, College of Science and Engineering, Department of Psychology, Fort Worth, TX 76129-0002. Offers experimental psychology (PhD), including cognitive psychology, learning, neuropsychology, social psychology; psychology (MA, MS). In 2010, 7 master's, 3 doctorates awarded. Terminal master's awarded for partial completion of doctoral program. *Degree requirements:* For master's, thesis; for doctorate, thesis/dissertation. *Entrance requirements:* For master's and doctorate, GRE General Test. Additional exam requirements/recommendations for international students: Required—TOEFL. *Application deadline:* For fall admission, 3/1 for domestic and international students; for spring admission, 12/1 for domestic students. Applications are processed on a rolling basis. Application fee: $50. Electronic applications accepted. *Expenses:* Tuition: Full-time $18,720; part-time $1040 per credit hour. Tuition and fees vary according to course load and program. *Financial support:* In 2010–11, 20 students received support; teaching assistantships with full tuition reimbursements available, unspecified assistantships available. Financial award application deadline: 3/1. *Unit head:* Dr. Charles Lord, Coordinator of Graduate Studies, 817-257-7410, Fax: 817-257-7681, E-mail: c.lord@tcu.edu. *Application contact:* Tami Joyce, Department Manager, 817-257-7410, Fax: 817-257-7681, E-mail: t.joyce@tcu.edu.

University at Buffalo, the State University of New York, Graduate School, College of Arts and Sciences, Department of Psychology, Buffalo, NY 14260. Offers behavioral neuroscience (PhD); clinical psychology (PhD); cognitive psychology (PhD); general psychology (MA); social-personality psychology (PhD). *Accreditation:* APA (one or more programs are accredited). *Faculty:* 26 full-time (8 women), 10 part-time/adjunct (5 women). *Students:* 88 full-time (60 women), 6 part-time (4 women); includes 21 minority (2 Black or African American, non-Hispanic/Latino; 2 American Indian or Alaska Native, non-Hispanic/Latino; 7 Asian, non-Hispanic/Latino; 9 Hispanic/Latino; 1 Two or more races, non-Hispanic/Latino), 11 international. Average age 27. 367 applicants, 12% accepted, 21 enrolled. In 2010, 14 master's, 6 doctorates awarded. Terminal master's awarded for partial completion of doctoral program. *Degree requirements:* For master's, project; for doctorate, thesis/dissertation. *Entrance requirements:* For master's and doctorate, GRE General Test. Additional exam requirements/recommendations for international students: Required—TOEFL (minimum score 550 paper-based; 213 computer-based; 79 iBT). *Application deadline:* For fall admission, 12/1 for domestic and international students. Application fee: $75. Electronic applications accepted. *Financial support:* In 2010–11, 65 students received support, including 8 fellowships with full tuition reimbursements available (averaging $13,700 per year), 16 research assistantships with full tuition reimbursements available (averaging $13,700 per year), 38 teaching assistantships with full tuition reimbursements available (averaging $13,700 per year); career-related internships or fieldwork, Federal Work-Study, institutionally sponsored loans, scholarships/grants, and tuition waivers (partial) also available. Financial award application deadline: 12/1; financial award applicants required to submit FAFSA. *Faculty research:* Neural, endocrine, and molecular bases of behavior; adult mood and anxiety disorders; relationship dysfunction; attention deficit/hyperactivity disorder; psycho-linguistics. Total annual research expenditures: $7.9 million. *Unit head:* Dr. Paul A. Luce, Chair, 716-645-3650 Ext. 203, Fax: 716-645-3801, E-mail: psychair@acsu.buffalo.edu. *Application contact:* Mary Claire Schnepf, Coordinator of Admissions, 716-645-3660, Fax: 716-645-3801, E-mail: psych@abuffalo.edu.

The University of British Columbia, Faculty of Arts and Faculty of Graduate Studies, Department of Psychology, Vancouver, BC V6T 1Z4, Canada. Offers behavioral neuroscience (MA, PhD); clinical psychology (MA, PhD); cognitive science (MA, PhD); developmental psychology (MA, PhD); health psychology (MA, PhD); quantitative methods (MA, PhD); social/personality psychology (MA, PhD). *Accreditation:* APA (one or more programs are accredited). Terminal master's awarded for partial completion of doctoral program. *Degree requirements:* For master's, thesis; for doctorate, comprehensive exam, thesis/dissertation. *Entrance requirements:* For master's and doctorate, GRE General Test. Additional exam requirements/recommendations for international students: Required—TOEFL (minimum score 550 paper-based; 230 computer-based; 80 iBT). Electronic applications accepted. Tuition charges are reported in Canadian dollars. *Expenses:* Tuition, area resident: Full-time $4179 Canadian dollars. International tuition: $7344 Canadian dollars full-time. *Faculty research:* Clinical, developmental, social/personality, cognition, behavioral neuroscience.

University of California, Merced, Division of Graduate Studies, School of Social Sciences, Humanities and Arts, Merced, CA 95343. Offers social and cognitive sciences (MA, PhD); world cultures (MA, PhD).

University of California, San Diego, Office of Graduate Studies, Department of Cognitive Science, La Jolla, CA 92093. Offers PhD. *Degree requirements:* For doctorate, one foreign language, thesis/dissertation. *Entrance requirements:* For doctorate, GRE General Test. Additional exam requirements/recommendations for international students: Required—TOEFL (minimum score 550 paper-based; 213 computer-based; 79 iBT). Electronic applications accepted. *Faculty research:* Neural networks, neurobiology of cognition, cognitive modeling, distributed cognition, psycholinguistics.

University of California, San Diego, Office of Graduate Studies, Interdisciplinary Program in Cognitive Science, La Jolla, CA 92093. Offers cognitive science/anthropology (PhD); cognitive science/communication (PhD); cognitive science/computer science and engineering (PhD); cognitive science/linguistics (PhD); cognitive science/neuroscience (PhD); cognitive science/philosophy (PhD); cognitive science/psychology (PhD); cognitive science/sociology (PhD). Admissions offered through affiliated departments. *Degree requirements:* For doctorate, thesis/dissertation. *Entrance requirements:* For doctorate, GRE General Test, acceptance into one of the eight participating departments. *Faculty research:* Language and cognition, philosophy of mind, visual perception, biological anthropology, sociolinguistics.

University of California, Santa Barbara, Graduate Division, College of Engineering, Department of Computer Science, Santa Barbara, CA 93106-5110. Offers cognitive science (PhD); computational science and engineering (PhD); computer science (MS, PhD); technology and society (PhD). *Faculty:* 33 full-time (5 women), 5 part-time/adjunct (0 women). *Students:* 135 full-time (31 women); includes 51 Asian, non-Hispanic/Latino; 4 Hispanic/Latino. Average age 27. 481 applicants, 20% accepted, 30 enrolled. In 2010, 33 master's, 12 doctorates awarded. Terminal master's awarded for partial completion of doctoral program. *Degree requirements:* For master's, comprehensive exam (for some programs), thesis (for some programs), project (for some programs); for doctorate, thesis/dissertation. *Entrance requirements:* For master's and doctorate, GRE. Additional exam requirements/recommendations for international students: Required—TOEFL (minimum score 600 paper-based; 100 iBT), IELTS (minimum score 7). *Application deadline:* For fall admission, 12/15 for domestic and international students. Application fee: $70 ($90 for international students). Electronic applications accepted. *Financial support:* In 2010–11, 117 students received support, including 36 fellowships with full and partial tuition reimbursements available (averaging $10,486 per year), 77 research assistantships with full and partial tuition reimbursements available (averaging $12,464 per year), 47 teaching assistantships with partial tuition reimbursements available (averaging $10,383 per year); career-related internships or fieldwork, Federal Work-Study, institutionally sponsored loans, scholarships/grants, health care benefits, tuition waivers (full and partial), and unspecified assistantships also available. Financial award application deadline: 12/15; financial award applicants required to submit FAFSA. *Faculty research:* Networking and security, database systems, computational science and engineering, programming languages and software engineering, human computer interaction. Total annual research expenditures: $8 million. *Unit head:* Subhash Suri, Chair, 805-893-5334, Fax: 805-893-8553, E-mail: suri@cs.ucsb.edu. *Application contact:* Morgan Marcos, Graduate Program Assistant, 805-893-4322, Fax: 805-893-8553, E-mail: mmarcos@cs.ucsb.edu.

University of California, Santa Barbara, Graduate Division, College of Letters and Sciences, Division of Humanities and Fine Arts, Department of Linguistics, Santa Barbara, CA 93106-9580. Offers applied linguistics (PhD); cognitive science (PhD); language, interaction, and social organizations (PhD); linguistics (PhD); translation studies (PhD); MA/PhD. *Faculty:* 9 full-time (5 women), 1 part-time/adjunct (0 women). *Students:* 28 full-time (14 women); includes 1 Asian, non-Hispanic/Latino. Average age 31. 62 applicants, 23% accepted, 8 enrolled. In 2010, 2 doctorates awarded. Terminal master's awarded for partial completion of doctoral program. *Degree requirements:* For doctorate, one foreign language, comprehensive exam, thesis/dissertation. *Entrance requirements:* For doctorate, GRE. Additional exam requirements/

GRADUATE PROGRAM IN PSYCHOLOGY
Rutgers, The State University of New Jersey

The graduate program in psychology offers training in the behavioral sciences including concentrations in perception, cognitive science, cognitive neuroscience, social, developmental, and biopsychology. There is a strong emphasis on research, empirical methods, teaching, and presentation skills throughout the duration of graduate studies.

For more information, please contact:
Alan Gilchrist, Ph.D., Professor
Department of Psychology
Rutgers, The State University of New Jersey
Smith Hall, Room 342
101 Warren Street
Newark, NJ 07102
newarkadmissions@ugadm.rutgers.edu

http://psychology.rutgers.edu/

Cognitive Sciences

University of California, Santa Barbara *(continued)*
recommendations for international students: Required—TOEFL (minimum score 550 paper-based; 80 iBT), IELTS (minimum score 7). *Application deadline:* For fall admission, 12/1 for domestic and international students. Application fee: $70 ($90 for international students). Electronic applications accepted. *Financial support:* In 2010–11, 22 students received support, including 20 fellowships with full and partial tuition reimbursements available (averaging $16,513 per year), 2 research assistantships with full and partial tuition reimbursements available (averaging $12,185 per year), 10 teaching assistantships with full and partial tuition reimbursements available (averaging $6,586 per year). Financial award application deadline: 12/1; financial award applicants required to submit FAFSA. *Faculty research:* Sociolinguistics, linguistic theory, discourse, psycho-linguistics, anthropological linguistics. *Unit head:* Joni Schwartz, Director, 805-893-3237, Fax: 805-893-7492, E-mail: joni@hfa.ucsb.edu. *Application contact:* Cami Helmuth, Graduate Program Advisor, 805-893-7490, Fax: 805-893-7492, E-mail: helmuth@hfa.uscb.edu.

University of California, Santa Barbara, Graduate Division, College of Letters and Sciences, Division of Mathematics, Life, and Physical Sciences, Department of Geography, Santa Barbara, CA 93106-4060. Offers cognitive science (PhD); geography (MA, PhD); quantitative methods in the social sciences (PhD); transportation (PhD); MA/PhD. *Faculty:* 23 full-time (4 women), 11 part-time/adjunct (4 women). *Students:* 71 full-time (32 women); includes 2 Black or African American, non-Hispanic/Latino; 14 Asian, non-Hispanic/Latino; 6 Hispanic/Latino. Average age 31. 82 applicants, 33% accepted, 18 enrolled. In 2010, 3 master's, 13 doctorates awarded. Terminal master's awarded for partial completion of doctoral program. *Degree requirements:* For master's, comprehensive exam (for some programs), thesis or alternative; for doctorate, comprehensive exam, thesis/dissertation. *Entrance requirements:* For master's and doctorate, GRE (minimum verbal/quantitative score 1100). Additional exam requirements/recommendations for international students: Required—TOEFL (minimum score 550 paper-based; 80 iBT), IELTS (minimum score 7). *Application deadline:* For fall admission, 2/1 for domestic and international students. Application fee: $70 ($90 for international students). Electronic applications accepted. *Financial support:* In 2010–11, 61 students received support, including 49 fellowships with full and partial tuition reimbursements available (averaging $8,958 per year), 32 research assistantships with full and partial tuition reimbursements available (averaging $10,335 per year), 29 teaching assistantships with partial tuition reimbursements available (averaging $9,384 per year). Financial award applicants required to submit FAFSA. *Faculty research:* Earth system science, human environment relations, modeling, measurement and computation. *Unit head:* Dr. Dar Alexander Roberts, Professor/Chair, 805-880-2531, Fax: 805-893-2578, E-mail: dar@geog.ucsb.edu. *Application contact:* Jose Luis Saleta, Student Programs Manager, 805-456-2829, Fax: 805-893-2578, E-mail: saleta@geog.ucsb.edu.

University of California, Santa Barbara, Graduate Division, College of Letters and Sciences, Division of Mathematics, Life, and Physical Sciences, Department of Psychology, Santa Barbara, CA 93106-9660. Offers cognitive science (PhD); psychology (PhD); quantitative methods in the social sciences (PhD). *Faculty:* 33 full-time (10 women). *Students:* 59 full-time (36 women); includes 2 Black or African American, non-Hispanic/Latino; 8 Asian, non-Hispanic/Latino. Average age 27. 240 applicants, 6% accepted, 5 enrolled. In 2010, 8 doctorates awarded. Terminal master's awarded for partial completion of doctoral program. *Degree requirements:* For doctorate, comprehensive exam, thesis/dissertation, teaching assistant training, progress report, papers, mini-convention presentation, 1 quarter of student teaching or teaching assistant class with section lab. *Entrance requirements:* For doctorate, GRE General Test. Additional exam requirements/recommendations for international students: Required—TOEFL (minimum score 550 paper-based; 80 iBT), IELTS (minimum score 7). *Application deadline:* For fall admission, 12/1 for domestic and international students. Application fee: $70 ($90 for international students). Electronic applications accepted. *Financial support:* In 2010–11, 59 students received support, including 60 fellowships with full and partial tuition reimbursements available (averaging $6,819 per year), 29 research assistantships with full and partial tuition reimbursements available (averaging $10,114 per year), 48 teaching assistantships with full and partial tuition reimbursements available (averaging $11,597 per year); tuition waivers (full and partial) also available. Financial award application deadline: 12/15; financial award applicants required to submit FAFSA. *Faculty research:* Social psychology; developmental and evolutionary psychology; neuroscience and behavior; cognition, perception and cognitive neuroscience. Total annual research expenditures: $6 million. *Unit head:* Greg Ashby, Chair, 805-893-2130, Fax: 805-893-4303. *Application contact:* Greg Ashby, Chair, 805-893-2130, Fax: 805-893-4303.

University of California, Santa Barbara, Graduate Division, College of Letters and Sciences, Division of Social Sciences, Department of Communication, Santa Barbara, CA 93106-4020. Offers cognitive science (PhD); feminist studies (PhD); quantitative methods in the social science (PhD); society and technology (PhD); MA/PhD. *Faculty:* 20 full-time (9 women). *Students:* 39 full-time (26 women); includes 3 Black or African American, non-Hispanic/Latino; 5 Asian, non-Hispanic/Latino; 6 Hispanic/Latino. Average age 30. 169 applicants, 6% accepted, 5 enrolled. In 2010, 3 doctorates awarded. Terminal master's awarded for partial completion of doctoral program. *Degree requirements:* For doctorate, comprehensive exam, thesis/dissertation. *Entrance requirements:* For doctorate, GRE. Additional exam requirements/recommendations for international students: Required—TOEFL (minimum score 550 paper-based; 80 iBT), IELTS (minimum score 7). *Application deadline:* For fall admission, 12/1 for domestic and international students. Application fee: $70 ($90 for international students). Electronic applications accepted. *Financial support:* In 2010–11, 39 students received support, including 39 fellowships with full and partial tuition reimbursements available (averaging $6,045 per year), 5 research assistantships with full and partial tuition reimbursements available (averaging $9,646 per year), 29 teaching assistantships with partial tuition reimbursements available (averaging $14,294 per year); career-related internships or fieldwork, health care benefits, and tuition waivers (full and partial) also available. Support available to part-time students. Financial award application deadline: 12/1. *Faculty research:* Interpersonal, intercultural, organizational, health, media. *Unit head:* Prof. Linda L. Putnam, Professor, 805-893-7935, Fax: 805-893-7102, E-mail: lputnam@comm.ucsb.edu. *Application contact:* Nancy Siris-Rawls, Graduate Program Assistant, 805-893-3046, Fax: 805-893-7102, E-mail: nsiris@comm.ucsb.edu.

University of Connecticut, Graduate School, College of Liberal Arts and Sciences, Department of Psychology, Storrs, CT 06269. Offers behavioral neuroscience (PhD); biopsychology (PhD); clinical psychology (MA, PhD); cognition and instruction (PhD); developmental psychology (MA, PhD); ecological psychology (PhD); experimental psychology (PhD); general psychology (MA, PhD); health psychology (Graduate Certificate); industrial/organizational psychology (PhD); language and cognition (PhD); neuroscience (PhD); occupational health psychology (Graduate Certificate); social psychology (MA, PhD). *Accreditation:* APA. Terminal master's awarded for partial completion of doctoral program. *Degree requirements:* For master's, comprehensive exam; for doctorate, thesis/dissertation. *Entrance requirements:* For master's and doctorate, GRE General Test, GRE Subject Test. Additional exam requirements/recommendations for international students: Required—TOEFL (minimum score 550 paper-based; 213 computer-based). Electronic applications accepted.

University of Connecticut, Graduate School, Neag School of Education, Department of Educational Psychology, Program in Cognition and Instruction, Storrs, CT 06269. Offers MA, PhD, Post-Master's Certificate. *Degree requirements:* For master's, comprehensive exam; for doctorate, thesis/dissertation. *Entrance requirements:* For doctorate, GRE General Test. Additional exam requirements/recommendations for international students: Required—TOEFL (minimum score 550 paper-based; 213 computer-based). Electronic applications accepted.

University of Delaware, College of Arts and Sciences, Department of Psychology, Newark, DE 19716. Offers behavioral neuroscience (PhD); clinical psychology (PhD); cognitive psychology (PhD); social psychology (PhD). *Accreditation:* APA. *Degree requirements:* For doctorate, thesis/dissertation. *Entrance requirements:* For doctorate, GRE General Test. Additional exam requirements/recommendations for international students: Required—TOEFL

(minimum score 600 paper-based; 250 computer-based). Electronic applications accepted. *Faculty research:* Emotion development, neural and cognitive aspects of memory, neural control of feeding, intergroup relations, social cognition and communication.

University of Florida, Graduate School, College of Liberal Arts and Sciences, Department of Psychology, Gainesville, FL 32611. Offers behavior analysis (PhD); behavioral neuroscience (MS, PhD); cognitive and sensory processes (PhD); counseling psychology (PhD); developmental psychology (PhD); social psychology (MS, PhD); JD/PhD. *Faculty:* 29 full-time (10 women). *Students:* 106 full-time (82 women), 14 part-time (7 women); includes 3 Black or African American, non-Hispanic/Latino; 2 American Indian or Alaska Native, non-Hispanic/Latino; 7 Asian, non-Hispanic/Latino; 12 Hispanic/Latino, 11 international. Average age 27. 614 applicants, 7% accepted, 36 enrolled. In 2010, 25 master's, 13 doctorates awarded. *Degree requirements:* For master's, comprehensive exam, thesis or alternative; for doctorate, comprehensive exam, thesis/dissertation. *Entrance requirements:* For master's and doctorate, GRE General Test, minimum GPA of 3.0. Additional exam requirements/recommendations for international students: Required—TOEFL (minimum score 550 paper-based; 213 computer-based; 80 iBT), IELTS (minimum score 6). *Application deadline:* For fall admission, 12/9 priority date for domestic students, 12/9 for international students. Applications are processed on a rolling basis. Application fee: $30. Electronic applications accepted. *Expenses:* Tuition, state resident: full-time $10,915.92. Tuition, nonresident: full-time $28,309. *Financial support:* In 2010–11, 105 students received support, including 19 fellowships, 24 research assistantships (averaging $18,742 per year), 62 teaching assistantships (averaging $19,797 per year); career-related internships or fieldwork and unspecified assistantships also available. Financial award application deadline: 12/9; financial award applicants required to submit FAFSA. *Faculty research:* Behavior analysis, behavioral and cognitive neuroscience, counseling, developmental psychology, social psychology. Total annual research expenditures: $2.7 million. *Unit head:* Dr. Neil E. Rowland, Chair, 352-273-2128, Fax: 352-392-7985, E-mail: nrowland@ufl.edu. *Application contact:* Dr. Clive D. Wynne, Graduate Coordinator, 352-392-0601, Fax: 352-392-7985, E-mail: wynne@ufl.edu.

University of Guelph, Graduate Studies, College of Social and Applied Human Sciences, Department of Psychology, Guelph, ON N1G 2W1, Canada. Offers applied social psychology (MA, PhD); clinical psychology applied development emphasis (PhD); clinical psychology applied developmental emphasis (MA); industrial/organizational psychology (MA, PhD); neuroscience and applied cognitive science (MA, PhD). *Degree requirements:* For master's, thesis; for doctorate, comprehensive exam, thesis/dissertation. *Entrance requirements:* For master's, GRE General Test, GRE Subject Test, minimum B+ average during previous 2 years of course work; for doctorate, GRE General Test, GRE Subject Test, minimum A- average. Additional exam requirements/recommendations for international students: Required—TOEFL (minimum score 89 iBT). Electronic applications accepted. *Faculty research:* Organizational psychology, reading comprehension and mathematical ability, drug addiction and relapse, gender issues and culture, memory, clinical psychology.

The University of Kansas, Graduate Studies, College of Liberal Arts and Sciences, Department of Psychology, Lawrence, KS 66045. Offers clinical child psychology (MA, PhD); clinical health and rehabilitation (PhD); cognitive psychology (PhD); developmental psychology (PhD); quantitative psychology (PhD); social psychology (MA). *Accreditation:* APA (one or more programs are accredited). *Faculty:* 27 full-time (8 women), 9 part-time/adjunct (4 women). *Students:* 122 full-time (87 women), 1 (woman) part-time; includes 17 minority (4 Black or African American, non-Hispanic/Latino; 8 Asian, non-Hispanic/Latino; 4 Hispanic/Latino; 1 Native Hawaiian or other Pacific Islander, non-Hispanic/Latino), 9 international. Average age 28. 348 applicants, 11% accepted, 25 enrolled. In 2010, 16 master's, 16 doctorates awarded. *Degree requirements:* For master's, thesis; for doctorate, variable foreign language requirement, comprehensive exam, thesis/dissertation. *Entrance requirements:* For doctorate, GRE General Test, minimum GPA of 3.0; undergraduate degree with 15 hours of course work in psychology, curriculum vitae, writing sample (clinical program only). Additional exam requirements/recommendations for international students: Required—TOEFL. *Application deadline:* For fall admission, 12/1 for domestic and international students. Application fee: $55 ($65 for international students). Electronic applications accepted. *Expenses:* Tuition, state resident: full-time $7092; part-time $295.50 per credit hour. Tuition, nonresident: full-time $16,590; part-time $691.25 per credit hour. Required fees: $858; $71.49 per credit hour. Tuition and fees vary according to course load, campus/location and program. *Financial support:* Fellowships with full tuition reimbursements, research assistantships with partial tuition reimbursements, teaching assistantships with full and partial tuition reimbursements, career-related internships or fieldwork and unspecified assistantships available. Financial award application deadline: 12/1; financial award applicants required to submit FAFSA. *Faculty research:* Information processing in depression, rape and other forms of sexual coercion, motions on physical function, processes of memory and understanding text, social stigmas and hostile group environments. *Unit head:* Dr. Ruth Ann Atchley, Chair, 785-864-9821, Fax: 785-864-5696, E-mail: ratchley@ku.edu. *Application contact:* Cathy L. O'Keefe, Graduate Admissions Officer, 785-864-4195, Fax: 785-864-5696, E-mail: psycgrad@ku.edu.

University of Louisiana at Lafayette, College of Sciences, Institute of Cognitive Science, Lafayette, LA 70504. Offers PhD. *Degree requirements:* For doctorate, comprehensive exam, thesis/dissertation. *Entrance requirements:* For doctorate, GRE General Test, minimum GPA of 3.25. Additional exam requirements/recommendations for international students: Required—TOEFL (minimum score 550 paper-based; 213 computer-based). Electronic applications accepted. *Faculty research:* Computational models of cognition, comparative cognition, cognitive development, computational cognitive neuroscience, memory.

University of Maryland, Baltimore County, Graduate School, College of Natural and Mathematical Sciences, Department of Biological Sciences and Department of Psychology, Program in Neurosciences and Cognitive Sciences, Baltimore, MD 21250. Offers PhD. *Faculty:* 4 full-time (3 women). *Students:* 2 full-time (0 women); includes 1 Asian, non-Hispanic/Latino; 1 Hispanic/Latino. Average age 30. 7 applicants, 0% accepted, 0 enrolled. *Degree requirements:* For doctorate, comprehensive exam (for some programs), thesis/dissertation. *Entrance requirements:* For doctorate, GRE General Test, minimum GPA of 3.0. Additional exam requirements/recommendations for international students: Required—TOEFL. *Application deadline:* For fall admission, 1/15 for domestic students, 12/15 for international students. Applications are processed on a rolling basis. Application fee: $50. Electronic applications accepted. *Financial support:* In 2010–11, 5 students received support, including 3 research assistantships with full tuition reimbursements available (averaging $22,300 per year), 2 teaching assistantships with full tuition reimbursements available (averaging $21,300 per year). *Unit head:* Dr. Jeff Leips, Director, 410-455-3669, Fax: 410-455-3875, E-mail: biograd@umbc.edu. *Application contact:* Dr. Jeff Leips, Director, 410-455-3669, Fax: 410-455-3875, E-mail: biograd@umbc.edu.

University of Maryland, College Park, Academic Affairs, College of Behavioral and Social Sciences, Program in Neurosciences and Cognitive Sciences, College Park, MD 20742. Offers PhD. *Students:* 49 full-time (28 women), 3 part-time (2 women); includes 3 Black or African American, non-Hispanic/Latino; 1 Asian, non-Hispanic/Latino, 13 international. 105 applicants, 17% accepted, 7 enrolled. In 2010, 7 doctorates awarded. *Degree requirements:* For doctorate, comprehensive exam, thesis/dissertation. *Entrance requirements:* For doctorate, GRE General Test, 3 letters of recommendation. Additional exam requirements/recommendations for international students: Required—TOEFL. *Application deadline:* For fall admission, 12/15 for domestic and international students. Applications are processed on a rolling basis. Application fee: $75. Electronic applications accepted. *Expenses:* Tuition, state resident: part-time $471 per credit hour. Tuition, nonresident: part-time $1016 per credit hour. Required fees: $337 per term. *Financial support:* In 2010–11, 11 fellowships with full and partial tuition reimbursements (averaging $17,924 per year), 12 research assistantships (averaging $18,643 per year), 26 teaching assistantships (averaging $17,870 per year) were awarded; Federal Work-Study and scholarships/grants also available. Support available to part-time students. Financial award applicants required to submit FAFSA. *Faculty research:* Molecular neurobiology, cognition, neural and behavioral systems language, memory, human development. *Unit head:* Dr. Cynthia F. Moss, Director, 301-405-0353, Fax: 301-405-7104, E-mail: moss@umd.edu. *Application contact:* Dean of Graduate School, 301-405-0358, Fax: 301-314-9305.

University of Massachusetts Amherst, Graduate School, College of Natural Sciences, Department of Psychology, Amherst, MA 01003. Offers clinical psychology (MS, PhD); cognitive psychology (MS, PhD); developmental science (MS, PhD); psychology of peace and violence (MS, PhD); social psychology (MS, PhD). *Accreditation:* APA (one or more programs are accredited). *Faculty:* 47 full-time (23 women). *Students:* 54 full-time (42 women), 6 part-time (4 women); includes 16 minority (3 Black or African American, non-Hispanic/Latino; 6 Asian, non-Hispanic/Latino; 4 Hispanic/Latino; 3 Two or more races, non-Hispanic/Latino), 3 international. Average age 29. 435 applicants, 4% accepted, 8 enrolled. In 2010, 12 master's, 16 doctorates awarded. Terminal master's awarded for partial completion of doctoral program. *Degree requirements:* For master's, thesis; for doctorate, comprehensive exam, thesis/dissertation. *Entrance requirements:* For master's and doctorate, GRE General Test, 3 letters of recommendation. Additional exam requirements/recommendations for international students: Required—TOEFL (minimum score 550 paper-based; 213 computer-based; 80 iBT), IELTS (minimum score 6.5). *Application deadline:* For fall admission, 12/1 for domestic and international students. Applications are processed on a rolling basis. Application fee: $50 ($65 for international students). Electronic applications accepted. *Expenses:* Tuition, state resident: full-time $2640. Required fees: $8282. One-time fee: $357 full-time. *Financial support:* In 2010–11, 8 fellowships with full tuition reimbursements (averaging $12,569 per year), 41 research assistantships with full tuition reimbursements (averaging $10,714 per year), 55 teaching assistantships with full tuition reimbursements (averaging $10,951 per year) were awarded; career-related internships or fieldwork, Federal Work-Study, scholarships/grants, traineeships, health care benefits, tuition waivers (full), and unspecified assistantships also available. Support available to part-time students. Financial award application deadline: 12/1; financial award applicants required to submit FAFSA. *Unit head:* Dr. Linda M. Isbell, Graduate Program Director, 413-545-2503, Fax: 413-545-0996. *Application contact:* Jean M. Ames, Supervisor of Admissions, 413-545-0722, Fax: 413-577-0010, E-mail: gradadm@grad.umass.edu.

University of Massachusetts Amherst, Graduate School, Interdisciplinary Programs, Program in Neuroscience and Behavior, Amherst, MA 01003. Offers animal behavior and learning (PhD); molecular and cellular neuroscience (PhD); neural and behavioral development (PhD); neuroendocrinology (PhD); neuroscience and behavior (MS); sensorimotor, cognitive, and computational neuroscience (PhD). *Students:* 31 full-time (19 women); includes 5 minority (2 Asian, non-Hispanic/Latino; 3 Hispanic/Latino), 2 international. Average age 26. 77 applicants, 30% accepted, 10 enrolled. In 2010, 2 master's, 4 doctorates awarded. Terminal master's awarded for partial completion of doctoral program. *Degree requirements:* For master's, thesis or alternative; for doctorate, comprehensive exam, thesis/dissertation. *Entrance requirements:* For master's and doctorate, GRE General Test. Additional exam requirements/recommendations for international students: Required—TOEFL (minimum score 550 paper-based; 213 computer-based; 80 iBT), IELTS (minimum score 6.5). *Application deadline:* For fall admission, 1/2 for domestic and international students. Applications are processed on a rolling basis. Application fee: $50 ($65 for international students). Electronic applications accepted. *Expenses:* Tuition, state resident: full-time $2640. Required fees: $8282. One-time fee: $357 full-time. *Financial support:* In 2010–11, 8 fellowships with full tuition reimbursements (averaging $11,100 per year), 3 research assistantships with full tuition reimbursements (averaging $1,529 per year) were awarded; teaching assistantships, career-related internships or fieldwork, Federal Work-Study, scholarships/grants, traineeships, health care benefits, tuition waivers (full), and unspecified assistantships also available. Support available to part-time students. Financial award application deadline: 1/2; financial award applicants required to submit FAFSA. *Unit head:* Dr. Neil Berthier, Graduate Program Director, 413-545-2046, Fax: 413-545-3243. *Application contact:* Jean M. Ames, Supervisor of Admissions, 413-545-0722, Fax: 413-577-0010, E-mail: gradadm@grad.umass.edu.

University of Minnesota, Twin Cities Campus, Graduate School, College of Liberal Arts, Department of Psychology, Program in Cognitive and Biological Psychology, Minneapolis, MN 55455-0213. Offers PhD. *Degree requirements:* For doctorate, comprehensive exam, thesis/dissertation. *Entrance requirements:* For doctorate, GRE General Test, GRE Subject Test (recommended), 12 credits of upper-level psychology courses, including a course in statistics or psychological measurement. Additional exam requirements/recommendations for international students: Required—TOEFL (minimum score 550 paper-based; 213 computer-based; 79 iBT).

University of Nebraska–Lincoln, Graduate College, College of Arts and Sciences, Department of Psychology, Lincoln, NE 68588. Offers biopsychology (PhD); clinical psychology (PhD); cognitive psychology (PhD); developmental psychology (PhD); psychology (MA); social/personality psychology (PhD); JD/MA; JD/PhD. *Accreditation:* APA (one or more programs are accredited). *Degree requirements:* For master's, thesis optional; for doctorate, comprehensive exam, thesis/dissertation. *Entrance requirements:* For master's and doctorate, GRE General Test. Additional exam requirements/recommendations for international students: Required—TOEFL (minimum score 550 paper-based; 213 computer-based). Electronic applications accepted. *Faculty research:* Law and psychology, rural mental health, chronic mental illness, neuropsychology, child clinical psychology.

University of Nebraska–Lincoln, Graduate College, College of Education and Human Sciences, Department of Educational Psychology, Lincoln, NE 68588. Offers cognition, learning and development (MA); counseling psychology (MA); educational psychology (MA, Ed S); psychological studies in education (PhD), including cognition, learning and development, counseling psychology, quantitative, qualitative, and psychometric methods, school psychology; quantitative, qualitative, and psychometric methods (MA); school psychology (MA, Ed S). *Accreditation:* APA (one or more programs are accredited); NCATE. *Degree requirements:* For master's, thesis optional. *Entrance requirements:* For master's, GRE General Test. Additional exam requirements/recommendations for international students: Required—TOEFL (minimum score 500 paper-based; 173 computer-based). Electronic applications accepted. *Faculty research:* Measurement and assessment, metacognition, academic skills, child development, multicultural education and counseling.

University of Nevada, Reno, Graduate School, College of Liberal Arts, Department of Psychology, Program in Cognitive Brain Science, Reno, NV 89557. Offers MA, PhD. Terminal master's awarded for partial completion of doctoral program. *Degree requirements:* For master's, thesis optional; for doctorate, comprehensive exam, thesis/dissertation. *Entrance requirements:* For master's, GRE General Test, minimum GPA of 2.75; for doctorate, GRE General Test, minimum GPA of 3.0. Additional exam requirements/recommendations for international students: Required—TOEFL (minimum score 500 paper-based; 173 computer-based; 61 iBT), IELTS (minimum score 6). Electronic applications accepted. *Expenses:* Tuition, state resident: full-time $2219; part-time $246 per credit. Tuition, nonresident: part-time $510 per credit. International tuition: $9009 full-time. Required fees: $59 per term. One-time fee: $101. Tuition and fees vary according to course load. *Faculty research:* Comparative psychology, cognition, perception.

The University of North Carolina at Chapel Hill, Graduate School, College of Arts and Sciences, Department of Psychology, Chapel Hill, NC 27599. Offers biological psychology (PhD); clinical psychology (PhD); cognitive psychology (PhD); developmental psychology (PhD); quantitative psychology (PhD); social psychology (PhD). *Accreditation:* APA. *Degree requirements:* For doctorate, comprehensive exam, thesis/dissertation. *Entrance requirements:* For doctorate, GRE General Test, minimum GPA of 3.0. Electronic applications accepted. *Faculty research:* Expressed emotion, cognitive development, social cognitive neuroscience, human memory personality.

The University of North Carolina at Greensboro, Graduate School, College of Arts and Sciences, Department of Psychology, Greensboro, NC 27412-5001. Offers clinical psychology (MA, PhD); cognitive psychology (MA, PhD); developmental psychology (MA, PhD); social psychology (MA, PhD). *Accreditation:* APA (one or more programs are accredited). Terminal master's awarded for partial completion of doctoral program. *Degree requirements:* For master's, comprehensive exam, thesis; for doctorate, one foreign language, thesis/dissertation, preliminary exam. *Entrance requirements:* For master's and doctorate, GRE General Test. Additional exam requirements/recommendations for international students: Required—TOEFL. Electronic applications accepted. *Faculty research:* Sensory and perceptual determinants; evoked potential: disorders, deafness, and development.

University of Notre Dame, Graduate School, College of Arts and Letters, Division of Social Science, Department of Psychology, Notre Dame, IN 46556. Offers cognitive psychology (PhD); counseling psychology (PhD); developmental psychology (PhD); quantitative psychology (PhD). *Accreditation:* APA. *Degree requirements:* For doctorate, comprehensive exam, thesis/dissertation, candidacy exam. *Entrance requirements:* For doctorate, GRE General Test, GRE Subject Test (strongly recommended). Additional exam requirements/recommendations for international students: Required—TOEFL (minimum score 600 paper-based; 250 computer-based; 80 iBT). Electronic applications accepted. *Faculty research:* Cognitive and socio-emotional development, statistical methods and quantitative models applicable to psychology, interpersonal relations, life span development and developmental delay, childhood depression, structural equation and dynamical systems.

University of Oregon, Graduate School, College of Arts and Sciences, Department of Psychology, Eugene, OR 97403. Offers clinical psychology (PhD); cognitive psychology (MA, MS, PhD); developmental psychology (MA, MS, PhD); physiological psychology (MA, MS, PhD); psychology (MA, MS, PhD); social/personality psychology (MA, MS, PhD). *Accreditation:* APA (one or more programs are accredited). Terminal master's awarded for partial completion of doctoral program. *Degree requirements:* For doctorate, thesis/dissertation. *Entrance requirements:* For master's, GRE General Test, minimum GPA of 3.0; for doctorate, GRE General Test. Additional exam requirements/recommendations for international students: Required—TOEFL.

University of Pittsburgh, School of Education, Department of Instruction and Learning, Program in Cognitive Studies, Pittsburgh, PA 15260. Offers PhD. *Students:* 1 full-time (0 women), 1 (woman) part-time. Average age 31. *Degree requirements:* For doctorate, thesis/dissertation. *Entrance requirements:* For doctorate, GRE General Test. Additional exam requirements/recommendations for international students: Required—TOEFL. *Application deadline:* For fall admission, 2/1 for domestic and international students. Application fee: $50. Electronic applications accepted. *Expenses:* Tuition, state resident: full-time $17,304; part-time $701 per credit. Tuition, nonresident: full-time $29,554; part-time $1210 per credit. Required fees: $740; $214 per term. Tuition and fees vary according to program. *Financial support:* Research assistantships available. Financial award application deadline: 3/15; financial award applicants required to submit FAFSA. *Unit head:* Dr. Richard Donato, Chairman, 412-624-7248, Fax: 412-648-7081, E-mail: donato@pitt.edu. *Application contact:* Information Contact, 412-648-2230, Fax: 412-648-1899, E-mail: soeinfo@pitt.edu.

University of Rochester, School of Arts and Sciences, Department of Brain and Cognitive Sciences, Rochester, NY 14627. Offers MS, PhD. Terminal master's awarded for partial completion of doctoral program. *Degree requirements:* For doctorate, thesis/dissertation, qualifying exam. *Entrance requirements:* For master's and doctorate, GRE General Test. Additional exam requirements/recommendations for international students: Required—TOEFL. Electronic applications accepted.

University of Southern California, Graduate School, Dana and David Dornsife College of Letters, Arts and Sciences, Department of Psychology, Los Angeles, CA 90089. Offers brain and cognitive science (PhD); clinical science (PhD); developmental psychology (PhD); human behavior (MHB); quantitative methods (PhD); social psychology (PhD). *Accreditation:* APA. *Faculty:* 34 full-time (10 women), 15 part-time/adjunct (9 women). *Students:* 105 full-time (65 women), 3 part-time (all women); includes 32 minority (4 Black or African American, non-Hispanic/Latino; 17 Asian, non-Hispanic/Latino; 9 Hispanic/Latino; 2 Two or more races, non-Hispanic/Latino), 22 international. 543 applicants, 5% accepted, 14 enrolled. In 2010, 17 master's, 12 doctorates awarded. *Degree requirements:* For doctorate, comprehensive exam, thesis/dissertation, one-year internship (for clinical science students). *Entrance requirements:* For doctorate, GRE. Additional exam requirements/recommendations for international students: Recommended—TOEFL (minimum score 600 paper-based; 250 computer-based; 100 iBT). *Application deadline:* For fall admission, 12/1 for domestic and international students. Application fee: $85. Electronic applications accepted. *Expenses:* Tuition: Full-time $31,240; part-time $1420 per unit. Required fees: $600. One-time fee: $35 full-time. Full-time tuition and fees vary according to degree level and program. *Financial support:* In 2010–11, 85 students received support, including 30 fellowships with full tuition reimbursements available (averaging $24,000 per year), 12 research assistantships with full tuition reimbursements available (averaging $19,250 per year), 40 teaching assistantships with full tuition reimbursements available (averaging $19,250 per year); scholarships/grants, traineeships, health care benefits, and unspecified assistantships also available. Financial award application deadline: 12/1. *Faculty research:* Affective neuroscience; children and families; vision, culture and ethnicity; intergroup relations; aggression and violence; language and reading development; substance abuse. *Unit head:* Dr. Margaret Gatz, Chair and Professor, 213-740-2212, Fax: 213-746-9028, E-mail: gatz@usc.edu. *Application contact:* Irene Takaragawa, Graduate Advisor, 213-740-2205, Fax: 213-746-9082, E-mail: itakarag@usc.edu.

University of South Florida, Graduate School, College of Arts and Sciences, Department of Psychology, Tampa, FL 33620-9951. Offers clinical psychology (PhD); cognitive and neural sciences (PhD); industrial-organizational psychology (PhD). *Accreditation:* APA. *Faculty:* 17 full-time (4 women). *Students:* 101 full-time (55 women), 24 part-time (16 women); includes 3 Black or African American, non-Hispanic/Latino; 9 Asian, non-Hispanic/Latino; 8 Hispanic/Latino; 1 Two or more races, non-Hispanic/Latino, 12 international. Average age 28. 452 applicants, 8% accepted, 22 enrolled. In 2010, 11 doctorates awarded. *Degree requirements:* For doctorate, comprehensive exam, thesis/dissertation, internship. *Entrance requirements:* For doctorate, GRE General Test, minimum GPA of 3.0 in last 60 hours of course work. Additional exam requirements/recommendations for international students: Required—TOEFL (minimum score 550 paper-based; 213 computer-based). *Application deadline:* For fall admission, 12/1 for domestic and international students. Application fee: $30. Electronic applications accepted. *Expenses:* Contact institution. *Financial support:* In 2010–11, 18 research assistantships (averaging $13,719 per year), 63 teaching assistantships with tuition reimbursements (averaging $13,724 per year) were awarded; tuition waivers (partial) and unspecified assistantships also available. Financial award applicants required to submit FAFSA. *Faculty research:* Clinical, cognitive, neuroscience, social, industrial/organizational. Total annual research expenditures: $3.5 million. *Unit head:* Michael Brannick, Chairperson, 813-974-0478, Fax: 813-974-4617, E-mail: mbrannick@usf.edu. *Application contact:* William Sacco, Program Director, 813-974-0375, Fax: 813-974-4617, E-mail: sacco@cas.usf.edu.

The University of Texas at Austin, Graduate School, College of Education, Department of Educational Psychology, Austin, TX 78712-1111. Offers academic educational psychology (M Ed, MA); counseling psychology (PhD); counselor education (M Ed); human development and culture (PhD); learning, cognition and instruction (PhD); quantitative methods (PhD); school psychology (PhD). *Accreditation:* APA (one or more programs are accredited). *Degree requirements:* For master's, thesis optional; for doctorate, thesis/dissertation. *Entrance requirements:* For master's and doctorate, GRE General Test, 3 letters of recommendation. Additional exam requirements/recommendations for international students: Required—TOEFL.

The University of Texas at Dallas, School of Behavioral and Brain Sciences, Program in Cognition and Neuroscience, Richardson, TX 75080. Offers applied cognition and neuroscience (MS); cognition and neuroscience (PhD). Part-time and evening/weekend programs available. *Faculty:* 25 full-time (8 women). *Students:* 85 full-time (48 women), 35 part-time (20 women); includes 25 minority (3 Black or African American, non-Hispanic/Latino; 14 Asian, non-Hispanic/Latino; 8 Hispanic/Latino), 16 international. Average age 30. 88 applicants, 51%

Cognitive Sciences

The University of Texas at Dallas (continued)
accepted, 17 enrolled. In 2010, 33 master's, 2 doctorates awarded. *Degree requirements:* For master's, internship; for doctorate, thesis/dissertation. *Entrance requirements:* For master's and doctorate, GRE General Test, minimum GPA of 3.0 in upper-level coursework in field. Additional exam requirements/recommendations for international students: Required—TOEFL (minimum score 550 paper-based; 215 computer-based). *Application deadline:* For fall admission, 7/15 for domestic students, 5/1 priority date for international students; for spring admission, 11/15 for domestic students, 9/1 priority date for international students. Applications are processed on a rolling basis. Application fee: $50 ($100 for international students). Electronic applications accepted. *Expenses:* Tuition, state resident: full-time $10,248; part-time $569 per credit hour. Tuition, nonresident: full-time $18,544; part-time $1030 per credit hour. Tuition and fees vary according to course load. *Financial support:* In 2010–11, 75 students received support, including 17 research assistantships with partial tuition reimbursements available (averaging $14,189 per year), 26 teaching assistantships with partial tuition reimbursements available (averaging $13,259 per year); career-related internships or fieldwork, Federal Work-Study, institutionally sponsored loans, scholarships/grants, and unspecified assistantships also available. Support available to part-time students. Financial award application deadline: 4/30; financial award applicants required to submit FAFSA. *Faculty research:* Neural plasticity, neuroimaging, face recognition, cognitive and neurobiological mechanisms of human memory, treatment interventions for semantic memory retrieval problems. *Unit head:* Dr. James C. Bartlett, Program Head, 972-883-2079, Fax: 972-883-2491, E-mail: jbartlet@utdallas.edu. *Application contact:* Mary Felipe, Program Assistant, 972-883-2358, Fax: 972-883-2491, E-mail: mary.felipe@utdallas.edu.

University of Washington, Graduate School, College of Arts and Sciences, Department of Psychology, Seattle, WA 98195. Offers animal behavior (PhD); child psychology (PhD); clinical psychology (PhD); cognition and perception (PhD); developmental psychology (PhD); quantitative psychology (PhD); social psychology and personality (PhD). *Accreditation:* APA. *Degree requirements:* For doctorate, thesis/dissertation. *Entrance requirements:* For doctorate, GRE General Test, minimum GPA of 3.0. Electronic applications accepted. *Faculty research:* Addictive behaviors, artificial intelligence, child psychopathology, mechanisms and development of vision, physiology of ingestive behaviors.

University of Wisconsin–Madison, Graduate School, College of Letters and Science, Department of Psychology, Program in Cognitive Neurosciences, Madison, WI 53706-1380. Offers PhD. *Degree requirements:* For doctorate, comprehensive exam, thesis/dissertation. *Entrance requirements:* For doctorate, GRE General Test, minimum undergraduate GPA of 3.0. Additional exam requirements/recommendations for international students: Required—TOEFL. Electronic applications accepted. *Expenses:* Tuition, state resident: full-time $9887; part-time $617.96 per credit. Tuition, nonresident: full-time $24,054; part-time $1503.40 per credit. Required fees: $67.63 per credit. Tuition and fees vary according to reciprocity agreements.

University of Wisconsin–Madison, Graduate School, College of Letters and Science, Department of Psychology, Program in Perception, Madison, WI 53706-1380. Offers PhD. *Degree requirements:* For doctorate, comprehensive exam, thesis/dissertation. *Entrance requirements:* For doctorate, GRE General Test, minimum GPA of 3.0. Electronic applications accepted. *Expenses:* Tuition, state resident: full-time $9887; part-time $617.96 per credit. Tuition, nonresident: full-time $24,054; part-time $1503.40 per credit. Required fees: $67.63 per credit. Tuition and fees vary according to reciprocity agreements.

Virginia Polytechnic Institute and State University, Graduate School, College of Liberal Arts and Human Sciences, School of Education, Department of Teaching and Learning, Blacksburg, VA 24061. Offers career and technical education (MS Ed, Ed D, PhD, Ed S); cognition and education (Certificate); counselor education (MA, PhD); curriculum and instruction (MA Ed, Ed D, PhD, Ed S); educational research, evaluation (PhD); higher education administration (Certificate); integrative STEM education (Certificate). *Accreditation:* NCATE. Postbaccalaureate distance learning degree programs offered (no on-campus study). *Students:* 265 full-time (186 women), 301 part-time (217 women); includes 38 Black or African American, non-Hispanic/Latino; 1 American Indian or Alaska Native, non-Hispanic/Latino; 6 Asian, non-Hispanic/Latino; 8 Hispanic/Latino, 41 international. Average age 34. 248 applicants, 78% accepted, 154 enrolled. In 2010, 257 master's, 23 doctorates, 2 other advanced degrees awarded. Terminal master's awarded for partial completion of doctoral program. *Degree requirements:* For master's, comprehensive exam (for some programs), thesis (for some programs); for doctorate, comprehensive exam (for some programs), thesis/dissertation (for some programs). *Entrance requirements:* For master's and doctorate, GRE. Additional exam requirements/recommendations for international students: Required—TOEFL (minimum score 550 paper-based; 213 computer-based). *Application deadline:* For fall admission, 7/1 for domestic and international students; for spring admission, 12/1 for domestic and international students. Applications are processed on a rolling basis. Application fee: $65. Electronic applications accepted. *Expenses:* Tuition, state resident: full-time $9399; part-time $488 per credit hour. Tuition, nonresident: full-time $17,854; part-time $957.75 per credit hour. Required fees: $1534. Full-time tuition and fees vary according to program. *Financial support:* Career-related internships or fieldwork, Federal Work-Study, scholarships/grants, health care benefits, and unspecified assistantships available. Financial award application deadline: 1/15. *Faculty research:* Instructional technology, teacher evaluation, school change, literacy, teaching strategies. *Unit head:* Dr. Daisy L. Stewart, UNIT HEAD, 540-231-8180, Fax: 540-231-3717, E-mail: daisys@vt.edu. *Application contact:* Dr. Daisy L. Stewart, UNIT HEAD, 540-231-8180, Fax: 540-231-3717, E-mail: daisys@vt.edu.

Wilfrid Laurier University, Faculty of Graduate and Postdoctoral Studies, Faculty of Science, Department of Psychology, Waterloo, ON N2L 3C5, Canada. Offers behavioral neuroscience (M Sc, PhD); cognitive neuroscience (M Sc, PhD); community psychology (MA, PhD); social and developmental psychology (MA, PhD). Part-time programs available. *Faculty:* 32 full-time (12 women), 8 part-time/adjunct (1 woman). *Students:* 68 full-time (49 women), 4 part-time (3 women), 2 international. 94 applicants, 51% accepted, 27 enrolled. In 2010, 27 master's, 5 doctorates awarded. *Degree requirements:* For master's, thesis; for doctorate, thesis/dissertation. *Entrance requirements:* For master's, GRE General Test, honors BA or the equivalent in psychology, minimum B average in undergraduate course work; for doctorate, GRE General Test, master's degree, minimum A- average. Additional exam requirements/recommendations for international students: Required—TOEFL (minimum score 89 iBT). *Application deadline:* For fall admission, 1/15 priority date for domestic and international students. Application fee: $100. Electronic applications accepted. Tuition and fees charges are reported in Canadian dollars. *Expenses:* Tuition, area resident: Full-time $15,300 Canadian dollars; part-time $1200 Canadian dollars per credit. International tuition: $21,300 Canadian dollars full-time. Required fees: $650 Canadian dollars; $100 Canadian dollars per credit. Tuition and fees vary according to course load, degree level, campus/location and program. *Financial support:* In 2010–11, 116 fellowships, 116 teaching assistantships were awarded; career-related internships or fieldwork, scholarships/grants, health care benefits, and unspecified assistantships also available. *Faculty research:* Brain and cognition, community psychology, social and developmental psychology. *Unit head:* Dr. Alexandra Gottardo, Graduate Coordinator, 519-884-0710 Ext. 2169, Fax: 519-746-7605, E-mail: agottard@wlu.ca. *Application contact:* Rosemary Springett, Graduate Admissions and Records Officer, 519-884-0710 Ext. 3078, Fax: 519-884-1020, E-mail: gradstudies@wlu.ca.

Yale University, Graduate School of Arts and Sciences, Department of Psychology, New Haven, CT 06520. Offers behavioral neuroscience (PhD); clinical psychology (PhD); cognitive psychology (PhD); developmental psychology (PhD); social/personality psychology (PhD). *Accreditation:* APA. *Degree requirements:* For doctorate, thesis/dissertation. *Entrance requirements:* For doctorate, GRE General Test.

Counseling Psychology

Abilene Christian University, Graduate School, College of Arts and Sciences, Department of Psychology, Program in Counseling Psychology, Abilene, TX 79699-9100. Offers MS. Part-time programs available. *Students:* 6 full-time (3 women), 5 part-time (2 women), 1 international. 16 applicants, 50% accepted, 4 enrolled. In 2010, 11 master's awarded. *Degree requirements:* For master's, comprehensive exam, thesis, practicum. *Entrance requirements:* For master's, GRE General Test. Additional exam requirements/recommendations for international students: Required—TOEFL (minimum score 550 paper-based; 213 computer-based). *Application deadline:* For fall admission, 4/1 priority date for domestic students; for spring admission, 11/1 for domestic students. Applications are processed on a rolling basis. Application fee: $40. Electronic applications accepted. *Expenses:* Tuition: Full-time $12,906; part-time $717 per hour. Required fees: $1250; $61.50 per unit. *Financial support:* In 2010–11, 6 students received support. Applicants required to submit FAFSA. *Unit head:* Dr. Robert McKelvain, Graduate Advisor, 325-674-2286, Fax: 325-674-6968, E-mail: mckevainr@acu.edu. *Application contact:* David Pittman, Graduate Admissions Counselor, 325-674-2656, Fax: 325-674-6717, E-mail: gradinfo@acu.edu.

Adelphi University, Derner Institute of Advanced Psychological Studies, Program in Mental Health Counseling, Garden City, NY 11530-0701. Offers MA. *Students:* 29 full-time (28 women), 4 part-time (3 women); includes 8 minority (1 Black or African American, non-Hispanic/Latino; 3 Asian, non-Hispanic/Latino; 2 Hispanic/Latino; 2 Two or more races, non-Hispanic/Latino). Average age 25. In 2010, 18 master's awarded. *Degree requirements:* For master's, comprehensive exam. *Entrance requirements:* For master's, GRE General Test, GRE Subject Test, minimum cumulative GPA of 3.1; interview; course work in developmental psychology, research methods, and psycho-pathology; 2 letters of recommendation. Additional exam requirements/recommendations for international students: Required—TOEFL (minimum score 550 paper-based; 213 computer-based; 80 iBT). *Application deadline:* For fall admission, 4/1 priority date for domestic students, 5/1 priority date for international students. Application fee: $50. Electronic applications accepted. *Financial support:* Research assistantships with full and partial tuition reimbursements, career-related internships or fieldwork, Federal Work-Study, institutionally sponsored loans, and unspecified assistantships available. *Unit head:* Dr. Errol Rodriguez, Assistant Dean, 516-237-8572, E-mail: erodriguez@adelphi.edu. *Application contact:* Christine Murphy, Director of Admissions, 516-877-3050, Fax: 516-877-3039, E-mail: graduateadmissions@adelphi.edu.

Adler Graduate School, Program in Adlerian Counseling and Psychotherapy, Richfield, MN 55423. Offers art therapy (MA); clinical mental health counseling (MA); marriage and family therapy (MA); non-clinical Adlerian studies (MA); online Adlerian studies (MA); organizational wellness and transformation (MA); parent coaching (Certificate); personal and professional life coaching (Certificate); school counseling (MA). Part-time and evening/weekend programs available. *Faculty:* 11 full-time (4 women), 48 part-time/adjunct (28 women). *Students:* 442 part-time (361 women). Average age 37. *Degree requirements:* For master's, thesis or alternative, 500-700 hour internship (depending on license choice). *Entrance requirements:* For master's, minimum undergraduate GPA of 3.0, 12 credits of course work in psychology or related field. *Application deadline:* Applications are processed on a rolling basis. Application fee: $50. *Expenses:* Tuition: Part-time $455 per credit. *Financial support:* Career-related internships or fieldwork and tuition waivers available. Support available to part-time students. Financial award applicants required to submit FAFSA. *Unit head:* Dr. Dan Haugen, President, 612-861-7554 Ext. 107, Fax: 612-861-7559, E-mail: haugen@alfredadler.edu. *Application contact:* Evelyn B. Haas, Director of Student Services and Admissions, 612-861-7554 Ext. 103, Fax: 612-861-7559, E-mail: ev@alfredadler.edu.

Adler School of Professional Psychology, Programs in Psychology, Chicago, IL 60602. Offers advanced Adlerian psychotherapy (Certificate); art therapy (MA); clinical neuropsychology (Certificate); clinical psychology (Psy D); community psychology (MA); counseling and organizational psychology (MA); counseling psychology (MA); forensic psychology (MA); gerontological counseling (MA); marriage and family counseling (MA); marriage and family therapy (Certificate); organizational psychology (MA); police psychology (MA); rehabilitation counseling (MA); sport and health psychology (MA); substance abuse counseling (Certificate); Psy D/Certificate; Psy D/MACAT; Psy D/MACP; Psy D/MAMFC; Psy D/MASAC. *Accreditation:* APA. Part-time and evening/weekend programs available. Postbaccalaureate distance learning degree programs offered (minimal on-campus study). *Faculty:* 40 full-time (18 women), 61 part-time/adjunct (31 women). *Students:* 688 full-time (532 women), 142 part-time (110 women). Average age 27. Terminal master's awarded for partial completion of doctoral program. *Degree requirements:* For master's, thesis or alternative, oral exam, practicum; for doctorate, thesis/dissertation, clinical exam, internship, oral exam, practicum, written qualifying exam. *Entrance requirements:* For master's, 12 semester hours in psychology, minimum GPA of 3.0; for doctorate, 18 semester hours in psychology, minimum GPA of 3.25; for Certificate, appropriate master's or doctoral degree. Additional exam requirements/recommendations for international students: Required—TOEFL (minimum score 550 paper-based; 213 computer-based; 79 iBT). *Application deadline:* For fall admission, 2/15 priority date for domestic students, 12/1 priority date for international students. Applications are processed on a rolling basis. Application fee: $50. Electronic applications accepted. *Financial support:* Career-related internships or fieldwork, Federal Work-Study, scholarships/grants, and tuition waivers (full and partial) available. Support available to part-time students. Financial award application deadline: 5/15; financial award applicants required to submit FAFSA. *Application contact:* Michelle Brice, Director of Admissions, 312-662-4113, Fax: 312-662-4199, E-mail: admissions@adler.edu.

See Display on page 912 and Close-Up on page 1119.

Alabama Agricultural and Mechanical University, School of Graduate Studies, School of Education, Department of Counseling and Special Education, Huntsville, AL 35811. Offers communicative disorders (M Ed, MS); psychology and counseling (MS, Ed S), including clinical psychology (MS), counseling and guidance, counseling psychology (MS), personnel management (MS), psychometry (MS), school psychology (MS); special education (M Ed, MS). *Accreditation:* CORE; NCATE. Part-time and evening/weekend programs available. *Degree requirements:* For master's, comprehensive exam. *Entrance requirements:* For master's, GRE General Test. Additional exam requirements/recommendations for international students: Required—TOEFL (minimum score 500 paper-based; 173 computer-based; 61 iBT). *Faculty research:* Increasing numbers of minorities in special education and speech-language pathology.

Alaska Pacific University, Graduate Programs, Department of Counseling, Psychological Studies, and Human Services, Program in Counseling Psychology, Anchorage, AK 99508-4672. Offers MSCP.

Alliant International University–México City, Programs in Arts and Science, Mexico City, Mexico. Offers counseling psychology (MA); international relations (MA). Part-time programs available. *Degree requirements:* For master's, thesis optional. *Entrance requirements:* For master's, GRE General Test, letters of recommendation. Additional exam requirements/recommendations for international students: Required—TOEFL. Electronic applications accepted.

Amberton University, Graduate School, Program in Counseling, Garland, TX 75041-5595. Offers MA. *Entrance requirements:* For master's, minimum GPA of 3.0.

Amridge University, Graduate and Professional Programs, Montgomery, AL 36117. Offers behavioral leadership and management (MA); Biblical exposition (MA); biblical studies (MA, PhD); family therapy (D Min); historical and theological studies (MA); leadership and management (MS); marriage and family therapy (M Div, MA, PhD); ministerial leadership (M Div, MS); pastoral counseling (M Div, MS); pastoral ministry (MA); professional counseling (M Div, MA, PhD); theology (D Min). Part-time and evening/weekend programs available. Postbaccalaureate distance learning degree programs offered (no on-campus study). *Faculty:* 39 full-time (6 women), 39 part-time/adjunct (5 women). *Students:* 119 full-time (54 women), 260 part-time (149 women); includes 160 minority (153 Black or African American, non-Hispanic/Latino; 1 Asian, non-Hispanic/Latino; 6 Hispanic/Latino). Average age 35. *Degree requirements:* For master's, one foreign language, comprehensive exam (for some programs), thesis (for some programs); for doctorate, comprehensive exam (for some programs), thesis/dissertation; for M Div, comprehensive exam (for some programs). *Entrance requirements:* For M Div, master's, and doctorate, GRE General Test or MAT. Additional exam requirements/recommendations for international students: Required—TOEFL. *Application deadline:* For fall admission, 9/1 priority date for domestic students; for spring admission, 1/1 priority date for domestic students. Applications are processed on a rolling basis. Application fee: $75. Electronic applications accepted. *Financial support:* Federal Work-Study and scholarships/grants available. Support available to part-time students. Financial award applicants required to submit FAFSA. *Faculty research:* Homiletics, hermeneutics, ancient Near Eastern history. *Unit head:* Director of Enrollment Management, 800-351-4040 Ext. 7513, Fax: 334-387-3878. *Application contact:* Ora Davis, Admissions Officer, 334-387-3877 Ext. 7524, Fax: 334-387-3878, E-mail: admissions@amridgeuniversity.edu.

Andrews University, School of Graduate Studies, School of Education, Department of Educational and Counseling Psychology, Program in Counseling Psychology, Berrien Springs, MI 49104. Offers PhD. *Degree requirements:* For doctorate, thesis/dissertation. *Entrance requirements:* Additional exam requirements/recommendations for international students: Required—TOEFL (minimum score 550 paper-based).

Angelo State University, College of Graduate Studies, College of Liberal and Fine Arts, Department of Psychology, Sociology and Social Work, San Angelo, TX 76909. Offers psychology (MS), including applied psychology, counseling psychology, industrial and organizational psychology. Part-time and evening/weekend programs available. *Faculty:* 8 full-time (2 women). *Students:* 53 full-time (38 women), 10 part-time (7 women); includes 6 Black or African American, non-Hispanic/Latino; 12 Hispanic/Latino. Average age 29. 52 applicants, 69% accepted, 35 enrolled. In 2010, 13 master's awarded. *Degree requirements:* For master's, comprehensive exam, thesis optional. *Entrance requirements:* For master's, GRE General Test (for industrial and organizational psychology only), essay, letters of recommendation (for industrial and organizational psychology only). Additional exam requirements/recommendations for international students: Required—TOEFL or IELTS. *Application deadline:* For fall admission, 7/15 priority date for domestic students, 6/10 for international students; for spring admission, 12/1 priority date for domestic students, 11/1 for international students. Applications are processed on a rolling basis. Application fee: $40 ($50 for international students). Electronic applications accepted. *Expenses:* Tuition, state resident: full-time $4560; part-time $152 per credit hour. Tuition, nonresident: full-time $13,860; part-time $462 per credit hour. Required fees: $2132. Tuition and fees vary according to course load. *Financial support:* In 2010–11, 44 students received support, including 3 teaching assistantships (averaging $10,251 per year); career-related internships or fieldwork, Federal Work-Study, scholarships/grants, and unspecified assistantships also available. Support available to part-time students. Financial award application deadline: 3/1; financial award applicants required to submit FAFSA. Total annual research expenditures: $116,915. *Unit head:* Dr. William B. Davidson, Department Head, 325-942-2068 Ext. 248, Fax: 325-942-2290, E-mail: bill.davidson@angelo.edu. *Application contact:* Aly Hunter, Graduate Admissions Assistant, 325-942-2169, Fax: 325-942-2194, E-mail: aly.hunter@angelo.edu.

Anna Maria College, Graduate Division, Program in Counseling Psychology, Paxton, MA 01612. Offers counseling psychology (MA). Part-time and evening/weekend programs available. *Degree requirements:* For master's, comprehensive exam, practicum. *Entrance requirements:* Additional exam requirements/recommendations for international students: Required—TOEFL (minimum score 500 paper-based). Electronic applications accepted.

Antioch University Midwest, Graduate Programs, Individualized Liberal and Professional Studies Program, Yellow Springs, OH 45387-1609. Offers liberal and professional studies (MA), including counseling, creative writing, education, film studies, liberal studies, management, modern literature, psychology, theatre, visual arts. Part-time and evening/weekend programs available. Postbaccalaureate distance learning degree programs offered (minimal on-campus study). *Faculty:* 2 full-time (1 woman), 2 part-time/adjunct (both women). *Students:* 15 full-time (11 women), 34 part-time (22 women); includes 11 minority (8 Black or African American, non-Hispanic/Latino; 3 Hispanic/Latino). Average age 40. 13 applicants, 69% accepted, 5 enrolled. In 2010, 18 master's awarded. *Degree requirements:* For master's, thesis or alternative. *Entrance requirements:* For master's, resume, goal statement, interview. *Application deadline:* For fall admission, 8/1 for domestic students; for winter admission, 12/1 for domestic students; for spring admission, 3/10 for domestic students. Applications are processed on a rolling basis. Application fee: $50. Electronic applications accepted. *Expenses:* Contact institution. *Financial support:* Federal Work-Study available. Financial award applicants required to submit FAFSA. *Unit head:* Dr. Joseph Cronin, Chair, 937-769-1894, Fax: 937-769-1807, E-mail: jcronin@antioch.edu. *Application contact:* Seth Gordon, Assistant Director of Admissions, 937-769-1800 Ext. 1825, Fax: 937-769-1804, E-mail: sgordon@antioch.edu.

Antioch University New England, Graduate School, Department of Applied Psychology, Program in Clinical Mental Health Counseling, Keene, NH 03431-3552. Offers MA. *Accreditation:* ACA. *Degree requirements:* For master's, internship, practicum. *Entrance requirements:* For master's, previous course work and work experience in psychology. Additional exam requirements/recommendations for international students: Required—TOEFL (minimum score 600 paper-based; 250 computer-based). Electronic applications accepted. *Expenses:* Contact institution. *Faculty research:* Multicultural issues in field supervision.

Appalachian State University, Cratis D. Williams Graduate School, Department of Human Development and Psychological Counseling, Boone, NC 28608. Offers clinical mental health counseling (MA); college student development (MA); marriage and family therapy (MA); school counseling (MA). *Accreditation:* AAMFT/COAMFTE; ACA; NCATE. Part-time programs available. *Faculty:* 14 full-time (9 women), 7 part-time/adjunct (all women). *Students:* 140 full-time (101 women), 25 part-time (20 women); includes 8 Black or African American, non-Hispanic/Latino; 1 Asian, non-Hispanic/Latino; 1 Hispanic/Latino; 1 Two or more races, non-Hispanic/Latino. 233 applicants, 53% accepted, 74 enrolled. In 2010, 53 master's awarded. *Degree requirements:* For master's, comprehensive exam (for some programs), thesis optional, internships. *Entrance requirements:* For master's, GRE General Test, 3 letters of recommendation. Additional exam requirements/recommendations for international students: Required—TOEFL (minimum score 570 paper-based; 230 computer-based; 79 iBT), IELTS (minimum score 6.5). *Application deadline:* For fall admission, 2/1 priority date for domestic students, 2/1 for international students; for spring admission, 2/1 for international students. Applications are processed on a rolling basis. Application fee: $55. Electronic applications accepted. *Expenses:* Tuition, state resident: full-time $3428; part-time $428 per unit. Tuition, nonresident: full-time $14,518; part-time $1814 per unit. Required fees: $2320; $344 per unit. Tuition and fees vary according to campus/location. *Financial support:* In 2010–11, 20 research assistantships (averaging $8,000 per year), 7 teaching assistantships (averaging $8,000 per year) were awarded; fellowships, career-related internships or fieldwork, Federal Work-Study, scholarships/grants, and unspecified assistantships also available. Financial award application deadline: 4/1; financial award applicants required to submit FAFSA. *Faculty research:* Multicultural counseling, addictions counseling, play therapy, expressive arts, child and adolescent therapy, sexual abuse counseling. *Unit head:* Dr. Lee Baruth, Chairman, 828-262-2055, E-mail: baruthlg@appstate.edu. *Application contact:* Sandy Krause, Director of Admissions and Recruiting, 828-262-2130, Fax: 828-262-2709, E-mail: krausesl@appstate.edu.

Argosy University, Chicago, College of Psychology and Behavioral Sciences, Doctoral Program in Clinical Psychology, Chicago, IL 60601. Offers child and adolescent psychology (Psy D); client-centered and experiential psychotherapies (Psy D); diversity and multicultural psychology (Psy D); family psychology (Psy D); forensic psychology (Psy D); health psychology (Psy D); neuropsychology (Psy D); organizational consulting (Psy D); psychoanalytic psychology (Psy D); psychology and spirituality (Psy D). *Accreditation:* APA.

See Close-Up on page 1123.

Argosy University, Chicago, College of Psychology and Behavioral Sciences, Program in Counseling Psychology, Chicago, IL 60601. Offers counselor education and supervision (Ed D). Postbaccalaureate distance learning degree programs offered (minimal on-campus study).

See Close-Up on page 1123.

Argosy University, Denver, College of Psychology and Behavioral Sciences, Denver, CO 80231. Offers clinical mental health counseling (MA); clinical psychology (MA, Psy D); counseling psychology (Ed D); counselor education and supervision (Ed D); forensic psychology (MA); industrial organizational psychology (MA); marriage and family therapy (MA, DMFT).

See Close-Up on page 1127.

Argosy University, Hawai'i, College of Psychology and Behavioral Sciences, Program in Counseling Psychology, Honolulu, HI 96813. Offers Ed D.

See Close-Up on page 1129.

Argosy University, Inland Empire, College of Psychology and Behavioral Sciences, San Bernardino, CA 92408. Offers clinical psychology/marriage and family therapy (MA); counseling psychology (Ed D); counseling psychology/marriage and family therapy (MA); forensic psychology (MA); industrial organizational psychology (MA); sport-exercise psychology (MA).

See Close-Up on page 1131.

Argosy University, Los Angeles, College of Psychology and Behavioral Sciences, Santa Monica, CA 90045. Offers clinical psychology/marriage and family therapy (MA); counseling psychology (Ed D); counseling psychology/marriage and family therapy (MA); forensic psychology (MA).

See Close-Up on page 1133.

Argosy University, Nashville, College of Psychology and Behavioral Sciences, Nashville, TN 37214. Offers counselor education and supervision (Ed D); mental health counseling (MA).

See Close-Up on page 1135.

Argosy University, Orange County, College of Psychology and Behavioral Sciences, Program in Counseling Psychology, Orange, CA 92868. Offers counseling psychology (Ed D); marriage and family therapy (MA).

See Close-Up on page 1137.

Argosy University, Phoenix, College of Psychology and Behavioral Sciences, Program in Mental Health Counseling, Phoenix, AZ 85021. Offers MA.

See Close-Up on page 1139.

Argosy University, Salt Lake City, College of Psychology and Behavioral Sciences, Draper, UT 84020. Offers counseling psychology (Ed D); counselor education and supervision (Ed D); forensic psychology (MA); marriage and family therapy (MA, DMFT); mental health counseling (MA).

See Close-Up on page 1141.

Argosy University, San Diego, College of Psychology and Behavioral Sciences, San Diego, CA 92108. Offers clinical psychology/marriage and family therapy (MA); counseling psychology (Ed D); counseling psychology/marriage and family therapy (MA); forensic psychology (MA).

See Close-Up on page 1143.

Argosy University, San Francisco Bay Area, College of Psychology and Behavioral Sciences, Program in Counseling Psychology, Alameda, CA 94501. Offers MA, Ed D.

See Close-Up on page 1145.

Argosy University, Sarasota, College of Psychology and Behavioral Sciences, Sarasota, FL 34235. Offers community counseling (MA); counseling psychology (Ed D); counselor education and supervision (Ed D); forensic psychology (MA); marriage and family therapy (MA); mental health counseling (MA); pastoral community counseling (Ed D).

See Close-Up on page 1147.

Argosy University, Schaumburg, College of Psychology and Behavioral Sciences, Schaumburg, IL 60173-5403. Offers clinical health psychology (Post-Graduate Certificate); clinical psychology (MA, Psy D), including child and family psychology (Psy D), clinical health psychology (Psy D), diversity and multicultural psychology (Psy D), forensic psychology (Psy D), neuropsychology (Psy D); community counseling (MA); counseling psychology (Ed D), including counselor education and supervision; counselor education and supervision (Ed D); forensic psychology (Post-Graduate Certificate); industrial organizational psychology (MA). *Accreditation:* ACA; APA.

See Close-Up on page 1149.

Argosy University, Seattle, College of Psychology and Behavioral Sciences, Program in Counseling Psychology, Seattle, WA 98121. Offers MA, Ed D.

See Close-Up on page 1151.

Argosy University, Tampa, College of Psychology and Behavioral Sciences, Tampa, FL 33607. Offers clinical psychology (MA, Psy D), including clinical psychology; counselor education and supervision (Ed D); industrial organizational psychology (MA); marriage and family therapy (MA); mental health counseling (MA).

See Close-Up on page 1153.

Argosy University, Washington DC, College of Psychology and Behavioral Sciences, Arlington, VA 22209. Offers clinical psychology (MA, Psy D), including child and family psychology (Psy D), diversity and multicultural psychology (Psy D), forensic psychology (Psy D), health and neuropsychology (Psy D); community counseling (MA); counseling psychology (Ed D), including counselor education and supervision; counselor education and supervision (Ed D); forensic psychology (MA). *Accreditation:* APA.

See Close-Up on page 1157.

Counseling Psychology

Arizona State University, School of Letters and Sciences, Program in Counseling Psychology, Tempe, AZ 85287-0811. Offers PhD. *Accreditation:* APA. *Faculty:* 10 full-time (4 women). *Students:* 28 full-time (17 women), 16 part-time (10 women); includes 21 minority (2 Black or African American, non-Hispanic/Latino; 2 American Indian or Alaska Native, non-Hispanic/Latino; 6 Asian, non-Hispanic/Latino; 11 Hispanic/Latino), 3 international. Average age 30. 138 applicants, 7% accepted, 7 enrolled. In 2010, 4 doctorates awarded. *Degree requirements:* For doctorate, comprehensive exam, thesis/dissertation, internship/practica, interactive Program of Study (iPOS) submitted before completing 50 percent of required credit hours. *Entrance requirements:* For doctorate, GRE, minimum GPA of 3.0 or equivalent in last 2 years of work leading to bachelor's degree, 3 letters of recommendation, personal statement describing history and academic/professional goals, completed Biographical Information form, 7-page sample of expository writing. Additional exam requirements/recommendations for international students: Required—TOEFL, IELTS, or Pearson Test of English. *Application deadline:* For fall admission, 12/1 for domestic and international students. Application fee: $70 ($90 for international students). Electronic applications accepted. *Expenses:* Tuition, state resident: full-time $8510; part-time $608 per credit. Tuition, nonresident: full-time $16,542; part-time $919 per credit. Required fees: $339; $110 per credit. Part-time tuition and fees vary according to course load. *Financial support:* In 2010–11, 8 research assistantships with full and partial tuition reimbursements (averaging $9,164 per year), 15 teaching assistantships with full and partial tuition reimbursements (averaging $10,313 per year) were awarded; fellowships with full and partial tuition reimbursements, career-related internships or fieldwork, institutionally sponsored loans, scholarships/grants, traineeships, health care benefits, and tuition waivers (full and partial) also available. Financial award application deadline: 3/1; financial award applicants required to submit FAFSA. *Unit head:* Dr. Terence Tracey, Program Leader, 480-965-6159, E-mail: terence.tracey@asu.edu. *Application contact:* Graduate Admissions, 480-965-6113.

Arkansas State University, Graduate School, College of Education, Department of Psychology and Counseling, Jonesboro, State University, AR 72467. Offers college student personnel services (MS); mental health counseling (Certificate); psychology and counseling (Ed S); rehabilitation counseling (MRC); school counseling (MSE); student affairs (Certificate). *Accreditation:* ACA (one or more programs are accredited); CORE (one or more programs are accredited); NCATE. Part-time programs available. *Faculty:* 11 full-time (6 women), 6 part-time/adjunct (2 women). *Students:* 40 full-time (27 women), 87 part-time (69 women); includes 38 minority (37 Black or African American, non-Hispanic/Latino; 1 Two or more races, non-Hispanic/Latino), 1 international. Average age 34. 55 applicants, 56% accepted, 28 enrolled. In 2010, 24 master's, 19 other advanced degrees awarded. *Degree requirements:* For master's and other advanced degree, comprehensive exam, thesis or alternative. *Entrance requirements:* For master's, GRE General Test or MAT (MSE), appropriate bachelor's degree, interview, letters of reference, official transcripts, immunization records, written statement, 2-3 page autobiography; for other advanced degree, GRE General Test, interview, master's degree, letters of reference, official transcript, personal statement, immunization records. Additional exam requirements/recommendations for international students: Required—TOEFL (minimum score 550 paper-based; 213 computer-based; 79 iBT), IELTS (minimum score 6), PTE: Pearson Test of English Academic (56). *Application deadline:* Applications are processed on a rolling basis. Application fee: $30 ($40 for international students). Electronic applications accepted. *Expenses:* Tuition, state resident: full-time $3888; part-time $216 per credit hour. Tuition, nonresident: full-time $9918; part-time $551 per credit hour. International tuition: $8376 full-time. Required fees: $932; $49 per credit hour. $25 per term. One-time fee: $30. Tuition and fees vary according to course load and program. *Financial support:* In 2010–11, 25 students received support; teaching assistantships, career-related internships or fieldwork, scholarships/grants, and unspecified assistantships available. Financial award application deadline: 7/1; financial award applicants required to submit FAFSA. *Unit head:* Dr. Loretta McGregor, Chair, 870-972-3064, Fax: 870-972-3962, E-mail: lmcgregor@astate.edu. *Application contact:* Dr. Andrew Sustich, Dean of the Graduate School, 870-972-3029, Fax: 870-972-3857, E-mail: sustich@astate.edu.

Assumption College, Graduate School, Counseling Psychology Program, Worcester, MA 01609-1296. Offers child and family interventions (MA); cognitive-behavioral therapies (MA); counseling psychology (CAGS); general psychology (MA). Part-time and evening/weekend programs available. *Faculty:* 4 full-time (1 woman), 8 part-time/adjunct (2 women). *Students:* 74 full-time (66 women), 35 part-time (33 women); includes 18 minority (5 Black or African American, non-Hispanic/Latino; 2 Asian, non-Hispanic/Latino; 8 Hispanic/Latino; 3 Two or more races, non-Hispanic/Latino). Average age 24. 100 applicants, 78% accepted. In 2010, 20 master's, 2 other advanced degrees awarded. *Degree requirements:* For master's, comprehensive exam, internship, practicum, oral exam; for CAGS, comprehensive exam, oral exam. *Entrance requirements:* For master's, 3 letters of recommendation, resume, essay; for CAGS, 3 letters of recommendation, resume, interview, essay. Additional exam requirements/recommendations for international students: Required—TOEFL (minimum score 540 paper-based; 200 computer-based; 76 iBT), IELTS (minimum score 6). *Application deadline:* For fall admission, 6/1 priority date for domestic students, 5/1 priority date for international students; for spring admission, 11/1 priority date for domestic students, 9/1 priority date for international students. Applications are processed on a rolling basis. Application fee: $30. Electronic applications accepted. *Expenses:* Tuition: Part-time $503 per credit. Required fees: $20 per semester. One-time fee: $100. Part-time tuition and fees vary according to campus/location. *Financial support:* In 2010–11, 21 students received support, including 19 fellowships with partial tuition reimbursements available (averaging $8,206 per year), 2 teaching assistantships with full tuition reimbursements available (averaging $7,575 per year). Financial award application deadline: 3/1; financial award applicants required to submit FAFSA. *Faculty research:* Mood disorders, adjustment to life-threatening illness, perception of movement, socioemotional development of young children, discovery versus disclosure. *Unit head:* Dr. Leonard A. Doerfler, Director, 508-767-7549, Fax: 508-767-7263, E-mail: doerfler@assumption.edu. *Application contact:* Daniel Provost, Director of Graduate Enrollment Management and Services, 508-767-7426, Fax: 508-767-7030, E-mail: dprovost@assumption.edu.

Athabasca University, Graduate Centre for Applied Psychology, Athabasca, AB T9S 3A3, Canada. Offers art therapy (MC); career counseling (MC); counseling (Advanced Certificate); counseling psychology (MC); school counseling (MC).

Avila University, Department of Psychology, Kansas City, MO 64145-1698. Offers counseling psychology (MS); general psychology (MS). Part-time and evening/weekend programs available. *Faculty:* 6 full-time (5 women), 20 part-time/adjunct (9 women). *Students:* 122 full-time (96 women), 21 part-time (16 women); includes 35 minority (26 Black or African American, non-Hispanic/Latino; 2 Asian, non-Hispanic/Latino; 6 Hispanic/Latino; 1 Two or more races, non-Hispanic/Latino), 6 international. Average age 32. 76 applicants, 53% accepted, 28 enrolled. In 2010, 3,631 master's awarded. *Degree requirements:* For master's, capstone project. *Entrance requirements:* For master's, minimum GPA of 3.0 in last 60 hours, 2 letters of recommendation, letter of intent, resume. Additional exam requirements/recommendations for international students: Required—TOEFL (minimum score 500 paper-based). *Application deadline:* Applications are processed on a rolling basis. Application fee: $0. Electronic applications accepted. *Expenses:* Tuition: Full-time $5580; part-time $465 per credit hour. Required fees: $348; $29 per credit hour. *Financial support:* In 2010–11, 132 students received support, including 1 research assistantship with partial tuition reimbursement available, 1 teaching assistantship (averaging $2,400 per year); career-related internships or fieldwork, scholarships/grants, and unspecified assistantships also available. Support available to part-time students. Financial award applicants required to submit FAFSA. *Faculty research:* Neuro/biofeedback, emotional regulation, perception, mindful wellness, trauma and restorative justice. *Unit head:* Robin M. Schluter, Director of Graduate Psychology, 816-501-2969, Fax: 816-501-2455, E-mail: robin.schluter@avila.edu. *Application contact:* Jennifer A. Manczuk, Graduate Program Liaison, 816-501-3698, Fax: 816-501-2455, E-mail: gradpsych@avila.edu.

Ball State University, Graduate School, Teachers College, Department of Counseling Psychology and Guidance Services, Program in Counseling Psychology, Muncie, IN 47306-1099. Offers MA, PhD. *Accreditation:* ACA; APA. *Faculty:* 12. *Students:* 87 full-time (60 women), 71 part-time (56 women); includes 4 Black or African American, non-Hispanic/Latino; 1 Hispanic/Latino; 1 Two or more races, non-Hispanic/Latino, 19 international. Average age 24. 232 applicants, 28% accepted, 52 enrolled. In 2010, 37 master's, 5 doctorates awarded. *Degree requirements:* For doctorate, thesis/dissertation. *Entrance requirements:* For doctorate, GRE General Test, interview, minimum graduate GPA of 3.2, resume. Application fee: $50. *Expenses:* Tuition, state resident: full-time $6160; part-time $299 per credit hour. Tuition, nonresident: full-time $16,020; part-time $783 per credit hour. Required fees: $2278; $95 per credit hour. *Financial support:* In 2010–11, 1 research assistantship with full tuition reimbursement (averaging $12,360 per year), 31 teaching assistantships with tuition reimbursements (averaging $10,244 per year) were awarded. Financial award application deadline: 3/1. *Unit head:* Dr. Sharon Bowman, Head, 765-285-8040, E-mail: sbowman@bsu.edu. *Application contact:* Associate Provost for Research and Dean of the Graduate School.

Bemidji State University, School of Graduate Studies, Bemidji, MN 56601-2699. Offers biology (MS); counseling psychology (MS); education (M Ed, MS); English (MA, MS); environmental studies (MS); mathematics (MS); mathematics (elementary and middle level education) (MS); special education (M Sp Ed, MS). Part-time programs available. Postbaccalaureate distance learning degree programs offered (no on-campus study). *Faculty:* 142 full-time (61 women), 37 part-time/adjunct (22 women). *Students:* 82 full-time (51 women), 350 part-time (210 women); includes 21 minority (6 Black or African American, non-Hispanic/Latino; 3 American Indian or Alaska Native, non-Hispanic/Latino; 6 Asian, non-Hispanic/Latino; 6 Hispanic/Latino), 8 international. Average age 35. 491 applicants, 93% accepted, 307 enrolled. In 2010, 97 master's awarded. *Degree requirements:* For master's, comprehensive exam, thesis (for some programs). *Entrance requirements:* For master's, GRE, letters of recommendation, letters of interest. Additional exam requirements/recommendations for international students: Required—TOEFL (minimum score 550 paper-based; 213 computer-based; 80 iBT). *Application deadline:* Applications are processed on a rolling basis. Application fee: $20. Electronic applications accepted. *Expenses:* Tuition, state resident: full-time $6605; part-time $330 per credit. Tuition, nonresident: full-time $6605; part-time $330 per credit. Required fees: $107.97 per credit. *Financial support:* In 2010–11, 110 students received support, including 40 research assistantships with partial tuition reimbursements available (averaging $7,196 per year), 40 teaching assistantships with partial tuition reimbursements available (averaging $7,196 per year); career-related internships or fieldwork, Federal Work-Study, scholarships/grants, health care benefits, and unspecified assistantships also available. Support available to part-time students. Financial award application deadline: 4/15; financial award applicants required to submit FAFSA. *Unit head:* Dr. Patricia Rogers, Dean, 218-755-2027, Fax: 218-755-2258, E-mail: progers@bemidjistate.edu. *Application contact:* Joan Miller, Senior Office and Administrative Specialist, 218-755-2027, Fax: 218-755-2258, E-mail: jmiller@bemidjistate.edu.

Bethel University, Graduate School, Program in Counseling Psychology, St. Paul, MN 55112-6999. Offers child and adolescent and community counseling (MA). Part-time and evening/weekend programs available. *Faculty:* 5 full-time (2 women), 11 part-time/adjunct (4 women). *Students:* 84 full-time (72 women), 3 part-time (all women); includes 1 Black or African American, non-Hispanic/Latino; 1 Asian, non-Hispanic/Latino; 1 Hispanic/Latino; 4 Two or more races, non-Hispanic/Latino. Average age 32. 42 applicants, 100% accepted, 41 enrolled. In 2010, 32 master's awarded. *Degree requirements:* For master's, comprehensive exam, thesis optional, practicum. *Entrance requirements:* For master's, MAT, minimum GPA of 3.0, course work in psychology and statistics, letters of reference. Additional exam requirements/recommendations for international students: Required—TOEFL (minimum score 550 paper-based; 213 computer-based; 80 iBT). *Application deadline:* For fall admission, 5/1 priority date for domestic students. Applications are processed on a rolling basis. Electronic applications accepted. *Expenses:* Tuition: Full-time $5400; part-time $450 per credit. Tuition and fees vary according to course level, course load, degree level and program. *Financial support:* Applicants required to submit FAFSA. *Unit head:* Dr. Diane Dahl, Assistant Dean, 651-635-8000, Fax: 651-635-8004, E-mail: diane-dahl@bethel.edu. *Application contact:* Paul Ives, Director of Admissions, 651-635-8000, Fax: 651-635-8004, E-mail: gs@bethel.edu.

Boston College, Lynch Graduate School of Education, Program in Counseling Psychology, Chestnut Hill, MA 02467-3800. Offers MA, PhD, MA/MA. *Accreditation:* APA (one or more programs are accredited). *Students:* 205 full-time (175 women), 7 part-time (6 women); includes 12 Black or African American, non-Hispanic/Latino; 15 Asian, non-Hispanic/Latino; 12 Hispanic/Latino, 17 international. 661 applicants, 42% accepted, 99 enrolled. In 2010, 73 master's, 6 doctorates awarded. Terminal master's awarded for partial completion of doctoral program. *Degree requirements:* For master's, comprehensive exam; for doctorate, comprehensive exam, thesis/dissertation. *Entrance requirements:* For master's and doctorate, GRE General Test. Additional exam requirements/recommendations for international students: Required—TOEFL (minimum score 550 paper-based; 213 computer-based; 81 iBT). Application fee: $70. Electronic applications accepted. *Financial support:* Fellowships with full and partial tuition reimbursements, research assistantships with full and partial tuition reimbursements, teaching assistantships with full and partial tuition reimbursements, career-related internships or fieldwork, Federal Work-Study, scholarships/grants, traineeships, health care benefits, tuition waivers (full and partial), and unspecified assistantships available. Support available to part-time students. Financial award applicants required to submit FAFSA. *Faculty research:* Reducing non-academic barriers to learning; race, gender, culture and social class issues in mental health; domestic violence; career development; community intervention and prevention. *Unit head:* Dr. M. Brinton Lykes, Chairperson, 617-552-4214, Fax: 617-552-0812. *Application contact:* Adam Poluzzi, Director, Graduate Admission and Financial Aid, 617-552-4214, Fax: 617-552-0398, E-mail: poluzzi@bc.edu.

Boston Graduate School of Psychoanalysis, Program in Psychoanalytic Counseling, Brookline, MA 02446-4602. Offers MA. *Faculty:* 11 full-time (7 women), 16 part-time/adjunct (8 women). *Students:* 18 full-time (12 women), 1 (woman) part-time; includes 2 Black or African American, non-Hispanic/Latino; 2 Asian, non-Hispanic/Latino; 1 Hispanic/Latino, 4 international. 36 applicants, 86% accepted. In 2010, 9 master's awarded. *Degree requirements:* For master's, thesis, 100-hour practicum, 600-hour internship. *Entrance requirements:* For master's, interview, BA, personal statement, writing sample, 3 letters of recommendation. Additional exam requirements/recommendations for international students: Required—TOEFL (minimum score 550 paper-based; 213 computer-based; 79 iBT). *Application deadline:* For fall admission, 4/15 priority date for domestic and international students; for spring admission, 11/15 priority date for domestic and international students. Applications are processed on a rolling basis. Application fee: $100. *Expenses:* Tuition: Full-time $13,500; part-time $500 per credit. Required fees: $50; $860 per semester. *Financial support:* Career-related internships or fieldwork and unspecified assistantships available. Financial award applicants required to submit FAFSA. *Faculty research:* Emotional learning in the classroom, addictions, the effect of extra-analytic contact with analysis, the geriatric setting, siblings. *Unit head:* Dr. Jane Snyder, President, 617-277-3915. *Application contact:* Stephanie Woolbert, Admissions Coordinator, 617-277-3915, Fax: 617-277-0312, E-mail: admissions@bgsp.edu.

Boston University, School of Education, Boston, MA 02215. Offers counseling (Ed M, CAGS), including community, school, sport psychology; counseling psychology (Ed D); curriculum and teaching (Ed M, Ed D, CAGS), including early childhood (Ed D), educational media and technology (Ed D), English and language arts (Ed D), mathematics (Ed D), physical education and coaching (Ed D), science (Ed D), social studies education (Ed D), special education (Ed D); developmental studies (Ed D), including literacy and language, reading education; developmental studies in literacy and language education (Ed M, CAGS); early childhood education (Ed M, CAGS); education of the deaf (Ed M, CAGS); educational leadership and development (Ed D), including educational administration (Ed M, Ed D, CAGS), higher education administration (Ed M, Ed D, CAGS); educational media and technology (Ed M, CAGS); elementary education (Ed M); English and language arts (Ed M, CAGS); English education (MAT); health education (Ed M, CAGS); Latin and classical studies (MAT); mathematics education (Ed M, MAT, CAGS); mathematics for teaching (MMT); modern foreign language education (MAT), including French, Spanish; physical education and coaching (Ed M, CAGS); policy, planning, and administration (Ed M, CAGS), including community education leadership, educational administration (Ed M, Ed D, CAGS), higher education administration (Ed M, Ed D, CAGS); reading education (Ed M, CAGS); science education (Ed M, MAT, CAGS), including biology (MAT), chemistry (MAT), earth science (MAT), general science (MAT), physics (MAT); social studies education (Ed M, MAT, CAGS), including history (MAT), political science (MAT); special education (Ed M, Ed D, CAGS), including disability studies (Ed M), moderate disabilities (Ed M), severe disabilities (Ed M), special education administration (Ed M); teaching English as a second language (Ed M, CAGS). Part-time programs available. *Faculty:* 57 full-time, 39 part-time/adjunct. *Students:* 245 full-time (191 women), 376 part-time (274 women); includes 83 minority (14 Black or African American, non-Hispanic/Latino; 2 American Indian or Alaska Native, non-Hispanic/Latino; 28 Asian, non-Hispanic/Latino; 31 Hispanic/Latino; 2 Native Hawaiian or other Pacific Islander, non-Hispanic/Latino; 6 Two or more races, non-Hispanic/Latino), 79 international. Average age 30. 1,270 applicants, 66% accepted, 292 enrolled. In 2010, 273 master's, 15 doctorates, 7 other advanced degrees awarded. Terminal master's awarded for partial completion of doctoral program. *Degree requirements:* For master's, thesis (for some programs); for doctorate, comprehensive exam, thesis/dissertation; for CAGS, comprehensive exam. *Entrance requirements:* For master's and CAGS, GRE General Test or Miller Analogies Test (MAT); for doctorate, GRE General Test. Additional exam requirements/recommendations for international students: Required—TOEFL, IELTS. *Application deadline:* For fall admission, 1/15 priority date for domestic and international students; for spring admission, 9/15 priority date for domestic and international students. Applications are processed on a rolling basis. Application fee: $70. Electronic applications accepted. *Expenses:* Tuition: Full-time $39,314; part-time $1228 per credit. Required fees: $40 per semester. *Financial support:* In 2010–11, 276 students received support, including 31 fellowships with full tuition reimbursements available, 16 research assistantships, 26 teaching assistantships with partial tuition reimbursements available; career-related internships or fieldwork, Federal Work-Study, and scholarships/grants also available. Support available to part-time students. Financial award applicants required to submit FAFSA. *Faculty research:* Deaf studies, social emotional learning, civic engagement and education, STEM education, pre-college educational pipelines. Total annual research expenditures: $2.6 million. *Unit head:* Dr. Hardin Coleman, Dean, 617-353-3213. *Application contact:* Dana Fernandez, Director of Enrollment, 617-353-4237, Fax: 617-353-8937, E-mail: sedgrad@bu.edu.

Bowie State University, Graduate Programs, Program in Counseling Psychology, Bowie, MD 20715-9465. Offers MA. Part-time and evening/weekend programs available. *Degree requirements:* For master's, comprehensive exam, thesis optional, research paper, practicum. *Entrance requirements:* For master's, minimum GPA of 2.5, 3 recommendations. Electronic applications accepted. *Expenses:* Tuition, state resident: full-time $4080; part-time $340 per credit. Tuition, nonresident: full-time $7752; part-time $646 per credit. Required fees: $2128; $340 per credit.

Bowie State University, Graduate Programs, Program in Mental Health Counseling, Bowie, MD 20715-9465. Offers MA. Part-time and evening/weekend programs available. *Degree requirements:* For master's, comprehensive exam. *Entrance requirements:* For master's, 3 letters of recommendation, minimum GPA of 3.0, 12 undergraduate credit hours in counseling or psychology. Electronic applications accepted. *Expenses:* Tuition, state resident: full-time $4080; part-time $340 per credit. Tuition, nonresident: full-time $7752; part-time $646 per credit. Required fees: $2128; $340 per credit.

Bowling Green State University, Graduate College, College of Education and Human Development, School of Education and Intervention Services, Intervention Services Division, Program in Counseling, Bowling Green, OH 43403. Offers mental health counseling (MA); school counseling (M Ed). *Accreditation:* ACA; NCATE. Part-time programs available. *Degree requirements:* For master's, thesis or alternative. *Entrance requirements:* For master's, GRE General Test. Additional exam requirements/recommendations for international students: Required—TOEFL. Electronic applications accepted. *Faculty research:* Perfectionism, multicultural counseling, suicide, ethics and legal issues related to counseling, play therapy.

Brigham Young University, Graduate Studies, David O. McKay School of Education, Department of Counseling Psychology and Special Education, Provo, UT 84602-1001. Offers counseling psychology (PhD); school psychology (Ed S); special education (MS). Part-time programs available. *Faculty:* 12 full-time (7 women), 7 part-time/adjunct (2 women). *Students:* 61 full-time (41 women), 19 part-time (17 women); includes 1 Black or African American, non-Hispanic/Latino; 2 American Indian or Alaska Native, non-Hispanic/Latino; 3 Asian, non-Hispanic/Latino; 1 Hispanic/Latino; 2 Native Hawaiian or other Pacific Islander, non-Hispanic/Latino, 6 international. Average age 30. 91 applicants, 19% accepted, 17 enrolled. In 2010, 14 master's, 6 doctorates, 10 other advanced degrees awarded. *Degree requirements:* For master's, comprehensive exam, thesis; for doctorate, comprehensive exam, thesis/dissertation. *Entrance requirements:* For master's and doctorate, GRE General Test, minimum GPA of 3.0 in last 60 hours of undergraduate coursework. Additional exam requirements/recommendations for international students: Required—TOEFL (minimum score 580 paper-based; 237 computer-based), IELTS (minimum score 7). *Application deadline:* For fall admission, 1/15 for domestic and international students. Application fee: $50. Electronic applications accepted. *Expenses:* Tuition: Full-time $5580; part-time $310 per credit hour. Tuition and fees vary according to program and student's religious affiliation. *Financial support:* In 2010–11, 53 students received support, including 42 research assistantships with partial tuition reimbursements available (averaging $6,715 per year), 4 teaching assistantships with partial tuition reimbursements available (averaging $6,778 per year); institutionally sponsored loans and tuition waivers (partial) also available. Financial award application deadline: 3/15. *Faculty research:* Group psychotherapy, career development of Native Americans, multicultural psychology, gender issues in education, crisis management in schools. *Unit head:* Dr. Timothy B. Smith, Professor and Development Chair, 801-422-3857, Fax: 801-422-0198. *Application contact:* Diane E. Hancock, Department Secretary, 801-422-3859, Fax: 801-422-0198, E-mail: diane_hancock@byu.edu.

Brooklyn College of the City University of New York, Division of Graduate Studies, Department of Health and Nutrition Science, Brooklyn, NY 11210-2889. Offers community health (MA, MPH, MS), including community health education (MA), computer science and health science (MS), health care management (MPH), health care policy and administration (MPH), thanatology (MA); grief counseling (CAS); nutrition (MS); public health (MPH), including community-public health. Part-time and evening/weekend programs available. *Students:* 16 full-time (13 women), 179 part-time (158 women); includes 94 minority (67 Black or African American, non-Hispanic/Latino; 17 Asian, non-Hispanic/Latino; 10 Hispanic/Latino), 15 international. Average age 34. 123 applicants, 75% accepted, 38 enrolled. In 2010, 43 master's, 1 other advanced degree awarded. *Degree requirements:* For master's, thesis or alternative. *Entrance requirements:* For master's, GRE, essay, 2 letters of recommendation. Additional exam requirements/recommendations for international students: Required—TOEFL. *Application deadline:* For fall admission, 3/1 priority date for domestic students, 2/1 priority date for international students; for spring admission, 11/1 priority date for domestic students, 10/1 priority date for international students. Applications are processed on a rolling basis. Application fee: $125. Electronic applications accepted. *Expenses:* Tuition, state resident: full-time $7360; part-time $310 per credit hour. Tuition, nonresident: full-time $13,800; part-time $575 per credit hour. Required fees: $190 per semester. *Financial support:* Career-related internships or fieldwork, Federal Work-Study, institutionally sponsored loans, and scholarships/grants available. Support available to part-time students. Financial award application deadline: 5/1; financial award applicants required to submit FAFSA. *Faculty research:* Medical ethics, relocation stress, risk reduction, disease prevention, history of public health, computer applications. *Unit head:* Dr. Janet Kolmer Grommet, Chairperson, 718-951-5026, Fax: 718-951-4670, E-mail: jgrommet@brooklyn.cuny.edu. *Application contact:* Hernan Sierra, Graduate Admissions Coordinator, 718-951-4536, Fax: 718-951-4506, E-mail: grads@brooklyn.cuny.edu.

Brooklyn College of the City University of New York, Division of Graduate Studies, Department of Psychology, Brooklyn, NY 11210-2889. Offers experimental psychology (MA); industrial and organizational psychology (MA), including human relations, organizational behavior; mental health counseling (MA); psychology (PhD). Part-time programs available. *Students:* 83 full-time (68 women), 142 part-time (108 women); includes 102 minority (64 Black or African American, non-Hispanic/Latino; 18 Asian, non-Hispanic/Latino; 20 Hispanic/Latino), 16 international. Average age 30. 331 applicants, 44% accepted, 88 enrolled. In 2010, 75 master's awarded. *Degree requirements:* For master's, comprehensive exam, thesis (for some programs). *Entrance requirements:* For master's, minimum GPA of 3.0, 2 letters of recommendation, essay; for doctorate, GRE. Additional exam requirements/recommendations for international students: Required—TOEFL (minimum score 520 paper-based; 190 computer-based; 69 iBT). *Application deadline:* For fall admission, 3/1 for domestic students, 2/1 for international students; for spring admission, 11/1 for domestic students, 10/1 for international students. Applications are processed on a rolling basis. Application fee: $125. Electronic applications accepted. *Expenses:* Tuition, state resident: full-time $7360; part-time $310 per credit hour. Tuition, nonresident: full-time $13,800; part-time $575 per credit hour. Required fees: $190 per semester. *Financial support:* Career-related internships or fieldwork, Federal Work-Study, institutionally sponsored loans, scholarships/grants, and tuition waivers (partial) available. Support available to part-time students. Financial award application deadline: 5/1; financial award applicants required to submit FAFSA. *Unit head:* Dr. Margaret-Ellen Pipe, Chairperson, 718-951-5601, Fax: 718-951-4814, E-mail: mepipe@brooklyn.cuny.edu. *Application contact:* Hernan Sierra, Graduate Admissions Coordinator, 718-951-4536, Fax: 718-951-4506, E-mail: grads@brooklyn.cuny.edu.

Caldwell College, Graduate Studies, Program in Counseling Psychology, Caldwell, NJ 07006-6195. Offers art therapy (MA); counseling psychology (MA); school counseling (MA). Part-time and evening/weekend programs available. *Degree requirements:* For master's, comprehensive exam, practicum. *Entrance requirements:* For master's, GRE General Test, minimum GPA of 3.0. Additional exam requirements/recommendations for international students: Required—TOEFL (minimum score 580 paper-based; 237 computer-based). Electronic applications accepted.

California Baptist University, Program in Counseling Psychology, Riverside, CA 92504-3206. Offers professional counseling (MS); professional ministry (MS). Part-time programs available. *Faculty:* 13 full-time (8 women), 15 part-time/adjunct (8 women). *Students:* 151 full-time (126 women), 50 part-time (42 women); includes 107 minority (34 Black or African American, non-Hispanic/Latino; 2 American Indian or Alaska Native, non-Hispanic/Latino; 7 Asian, non-Hispanic/Latino; 61 Hispanic/Latino; 3 Two or more races, non-Hispanic/Latino), 1 international. 97 applicants, 91% accepted, 76 enrolled. In 2010, 51 master's awarded. *Degree requirements:* For master's, comprehensive exam, 24 hours (individual) or 50 hours (group) psychotherapy, 300 hours of field work. *Entrance requirements:* For master's, Minnesota Multiphasic Personality Inventory, Myers-Briggs Type Indicator, course work in developmental psychology, theories of personality, and statistics; minimum undergraduate GPA of 2.75. Additional exam requirements/recommendations for international students: Required—TOEFL (minimum score 575 paper-based; 230 computer-based; 89 iBT). *Application deadline:* For fall admission, 9/1 for domestic students, 7/1 for international students; for spring admission, 1/3 for domestic students, 10/15 for international students. Applications are processed on a rolling basis. Application fee: $45. Electronic applications accepted. *Expenses:* Contact institution. *Financial support:* Career-related internships or fieldwork, Federal Work-Study, scholarships/grants, traineeships, and unspecified assistantships available. Support available to part-time students. Financial award applicants required to submit FAFSA. *Unit head:* Dr. Mischa Routon, Director, 951-343-4206, Fax: 951-343-4569, E-mail: mrouton@calbaptist.edu. *Application contact:* Gail Ronveaux, Dean of Graduate Enrollment, 951-343-5045, Fax: 951-343-5095, E-mail: graduateadmissions@calbaptist.edu.

California Institute of Integral Studies, School of Professional Psychology, San Francisco, CA 94103. Offers clinical psychology (Psy D); community mental health (MA); drama therapy (MA); expressive arts therapy (MA); integral counseling psychology (MA); integral counseling psychology-weekend (MA); somatic psychology (MA). *Accreditation:* APA. Part-time and evening/weekend programs available. *Students:* 651 full-time (476 women), 74 part-time (62 women); includes 146 minority (32 Black or African American, non-Hispanic/Latino; 1 American Indian or Alaska Native, non-Hispanic/Latino; 53 Asian, non-Hispanic/Latino; 43 Hispanic/Latino; 17 Two or more races, non-Hispanic/Latino), 52 international. Average age 37. 556 applicants, 72% accepted, 247 enrolled. In 2010, 148 master's, 27 doctorates awarded. *Degree requirements:* For doctorate, comprehensive exam, thesis/dissertation. *Entrance requirements:* For master's, minimum GPA of 3.0, letters of recommendation, writing sample; for doctorate, GRE, MA in psychology or social work with appropriate practical experience for advanced standing, or BA with a minimum GPA of 3.1; letters of recommendation; writing sample. Additional exam requirements/recommendations for international students: Required—TOEFL. *Application deadline:* For fall admission, 2/1 priority date for domestic and international students; for spring admission, 10/15 priority date for domestic and international students. Applications are processed on a rolling basis. Application fee: $65. Electronic applications accepted. *Expenses:* Tuition: Full-time $15,660; part-time $870 per semester hour. Required fees: $95 per semester. *Financial support:* Research assistantships with tuition reimbursements, teaching assistantships with tuition reimbursements, career-related internships or fieldwork, Federal Work-Study, scholarships/grants, and tuition waivers (partial) available. Support available to part-time students. Financial award application deadline: 4/15; financial award applicants required to submit FAFSA. *Faculty research:* Transpersonal psychology, somatic psychology, expressive arts therapy, drama therapy, community mental health, ecopsychology. *Application contact:* David Townes, Senior Admissions Counselor, 415-575-6152, Fax: 415-575-1268, E-mail: dtownes@ciis.edu.

California State University, Bakersfield, Division of Graduate Studies, School of Humanities and Social Sciences, Program in Counseling Psychology, Bakersfield, CA 93311. Offers MS.

California State University, Sacramento, Graduate Studies, College of Social Sciences and Interdisciplinary Studies, Department of Psychology, Sacramento, CA 95819. Offers counseling psychology (MA). Part-time programs available. *Degree requirements:* For master's, thesis, writing proficiency exam. *Entrance requirements:* For master's, GRE Subject Test, minimum GPA of 3.0 during previous 2 years. Additional exam requirements/recommendations for international students: Required—TOEFL. Electronic applications accepted.

California State University, San Bernardino, Graduate Studies, College of Social and Behavioral Sciences, Department of Psychology, Program in Clinical/Counseling Psychology, San Bernardino, CA 92407-2397. Offers clinical psychology (MS). *Degree requirements:* For master's, comprehensive exam or thesis. *Entrance requirements:* For master's, minimum GPA of 3.0 in major. *Faculty research:* Psychology of women, fathering, depression, families, cross-cultural counseling.

California State University, Stanislaus, College of Human and Health Sciences, Program in Psychology (MA/MS), Turlock, CA 95382. Offers behavior analysis (MS); counseling psychology (MS); psychology (MA). Part-time programs available. *Students:* 26 full-time (20 women), 39 part-time (36 women); includes 24 minority (1 Black or African American, non-Hispanic/Latino; 1 American Indian or Alaska Native, non-Hispanic/Latino; 4 Asian, non-Hispanic/Latino; 15 Hispanic/Latino; 3 Two or more races, non-Hispanic/Latino). Average age 30. 62 applicants, 48% accepted, 24 enrolled. In 2010, 13 master's awarded. *Degree requirements:* For master's, thesis. *Entrance requirements:* For master's, GRE, minimum GPA of 3.0, 3 letters of reference, 16 PSYC prerequisites, department approval, personal statement. Additional exam requirements/recommendations for international students: Required—TOEFL (minimum score 550 paper-based; 213 computer-based). *Application deadline:* For fall admission, 5/1 for domestic students; for spring admission, 1/7 for domestic students. Application fee: $55. Electronic applications accepted. Tuition and fees vary according to program. *Financial support:* Fellowships, career-related internships or fieldwork and Federal Work-Study available. Financial award application deadline: 3/1; financial award applicants required to submit FAFSA. *Faculty research:* Hedonic tone judgment, syntax and autism, early literacy assessment and native and non-native languages. *Unit head:* Dr. Bruce Hesse, Psychology Professor, Graduate Academic Director,

Counseling Psychology

California State University, Stanislaus *(continued)*
209-667-3555, E-mail: bhesse@csustan.edu. *Application contact:* Graduate School, 209-667-3129, Fax: 209-664-7025, E-mail: graduate_school@csustan.edu.

Cambridge College, School of Psychology and Counseling, Cambridge, MA 02138-5304. Offers addiction counseling (M Ed); alcohol and drug counseling (Certificate); counseling psychology (M Ed, CAGS); counseling psychology: forensic counseling (M Ed); marriage and family therapy (M Ed); mental health and addiction counseling (M Ed); mental health counseling (M Ed); mental health counseling for school guidance counselors (Post Master's Certificate); psychological studies (M Ed); school adjustment and mental health counseling (M Ed); school adjustment, mental health and addiction counseling (M Ed); school guidance counselor (M Ed); trauma studies (Certificate). Part-time and evening/weekend programs available. *Faculty:* 4 full-time (2 women), 83 part-time/adjunct (48 women). *Students:* 436 full-time (351 women), 351 part-time (274 women); includes 321 Black or African American, non-Hispanic/Latino; 3 American Indian or Alaska Native, non-Hispanic/Latino; 4 Asian, non-Hispanic/Latino; 87 Hispanic/Latino; 4 Two or more races, non-Hispanic/Latino, 6 international. Average age 37. In 2010, 284 master's, 16 other advanced degrees awarded. *Degree requirements:* For master's and other advanced degree, thesis, practicum/internship. *Entrance requirements:* For master's, resume, 2 professional references; for other advanced degree, official transcripts, documents for transfer credit evaluation, resume, written personal statement/essay, 2 professional references, health insurance, immunizations form. Additional exam requirements/recommendations for international students: Required—TOEFL (minimum score 550 paper-based; 213 computer-based; 79 iBT); Recommended—IELTS (minimum score 6). *Application deadline:* Applications are processed on a rolling basis. Application fee: $30. Electronic applications accepted. *Expenses:* Contact institution. *Financial support:* Career-related internships or fieldwork, Federal Work-Study, and scholarships/grants available. Financial award applicants required to submit FAFSA. *Faculty research:* Trauma, drug and alcohol counseling, cross-cultural issues, school counseling, trauma in schools. *Unit head:* Dr. Niti Seth, Dean, 617-873-0208, Fax: 617-349-3561, E-mail: nseth@cambridgecollege.edu. *Application contact:* Elaine M. Lapomardo, Dean of Enrollment Management, 617-873-0274, Fax: 617-349-3561, E-mail: elaine.lapomardo@cambridgecollege.edu.

Capella University, Harold Abel School of Psychology, Minneapolis, MN 55402. Offers child and adolescent development (MS); clinical psychology (MS, Psy D); counseling psychology (MS); educational psychology (MS, PhD); evaluation, research, and measurement (MS); general psychology (MS, PhD); industrial/organizational psychology (MS, PhD); leadership coaching psychology (MS); organizational leader development (MS); school psychology (MS); sport psychology (MS). Part-time and evening/weekend programs available. Postbaccalaureate distance learning degree programs offered (minimal on-campus study). Terminal master's awarded for partial completion of doctoral program. *Degree requirements:* For master's, thesis optional, project; for doctorate, thesis/dissertation. *Entrance requirements:* For degree, master's degree in school psychology. Additional exam requirements/recommendations for international students: Required—TOEFL (minimum score 550 paper-based; 213 computer-based), TWE (minimum score 4); Recommended—IELTS. Electronic applications accepted. *Expenses:* Tuition: Full-time $11,880; part-time $440 per credit hour.

Capella University, School of Human Services, Minneapolis, MN 55402. Offers addictions counseling (Certificate); counseling studies (MS, PhD); criminal justice (MS, PhD, Certificate); diversity studies (Certificate); general human services (MS, PhD); health care administration (MS, PhD, Certificate); management of nonprofit agencies (MS, PhD, Certificate); marital, couple and family counseling/therapy (MS); marriage and family services (Certificate); mental health counseling (MS); professional counseling (Certificate); social and community services (MS, PhD, Certificate). Part-time and evening/weekend programs available. Postbaccalaureate distance learning degree programs offered (minimal on-campus study). Terminal master's awarded for partial completion of doctoral program. *Degree requirements:* For master's, thesis optional, integrative project; for doctorate, comprehensive exam, thesis/dissertation. *Entrance requirements:* Additional exam requirements/recommendations for international students: Required—TOEFL (minimum score 550 paper-based; 213 computer-based), TWE (minimum score 4). Electronic applications accepted. *Expenses:* Tuition: Full-time $11,880; part-time $440 per credit hour. *Faculty research:* Compulsive and addictive behaviors, substance abuse, assessment of psychopathology and neuropsychology.

Carlos Albizu University, Miami Campus, Graduate Programs, Miami, FL 33172-2209. Offers clinical psychology (Psy D); entrepreneurship (MBA); exceptional student education (MS); industrial/organizational psychology (MS); marriage and family therapy (MS); mental health counseling (MS); nonprofit management (MBA); organizational management (MBA); psychology (MS); school counseling (MS); teaching English as a second language (MS). *Accreditation:* APA. Part-time and evening/weekend programs available. *Faculty:* 21 full-time (12 women), 37 part-time/adjunct (18 women). *Students:* 496 full-time (400 women), 242 part-time (192 women); includes 590 minority (58 Black or African American, non-Hispanic/Latino; 2 American Indian or Alaska Native, non-Hispanic/Latino; 5 Asian, non-Hispanic/Latino; 523 Hispanic/Latino; 2 Two or more races, non-Hispanic/Latino), 15 international. Average age 36. 141 applicants, 84% accepted, 118 enrolled. In 2010, 159 master's, 20 doctorates awarded. Terminal master's awarded for partial completion of doctoral program. *Degree requirements:* For master's, one foreign language, comprehensive exam, integrative project (MBA), research project (exceptional student education, teaching English as a second language); for doctorate, one foreign language, comprehensive exam, internship, project. *Entrance requirements:* For master's, 3 letters of recommendation, interview, minimum GPA of 3.0, resume, statement of purpose, official transcripts; for doctorate, 3 letters of recommendation, minimum GPA of 3.0, resume, interview. *Application deadline:* For fall admission, 8/1 priority date for domestic students; for spring admission, 11/30 priority date for domestic students. Applications are processed on a rolling basis. Application fee: $50. Electronic applications accepted. *Expenses:* Tuition: Full-time $9360; part-time $520 per credit. Required fees: $298 per term. Tuition and fees vary according to course load, degree level and program. *Financial support:* In 2010–11, 106 students received support. Federal Work-Study, scholarships/grants, and tuition discounts available. Financial award application deadline: 6/1; financial award applicants required to submit FAFSA. *Faculty research:* Psychotherapy, forensic psychology, neuropsychology, marketing strategy, entrepreneurship, special education. *Unit head:* Dr. Carmen S. Roca, Chancellor, 305-593-1223 Ext. 120, Fax: 305-629-8052, E-mail: croca@albizu.edu. *Application contact:* Vanessa Almendarez, Secretary, 305-593-1223 Ext. 137, Fax: 305-593-1854, E-mail: valmendarez@albizu.edu.

Carlow University, School for Social Change, Pittsburgh, PA 15213-3165. Offers counseling psychology (Psy D); professional counseling (MS); professional counseling: school counseling (MS). *Accreditation:* APA. Part-time and evening/weekend programs available. *Students:* 206 full-time (184 women), 21 part-time (18 women); includes 41 Black or African American, non-Hispanic/Latino; 1 American Indian or Alaska Native, non-Hispanic/Latino; 2 Asian, non-Hispanic/Latino; 3 Hispanic/Latino. Average age 31. 298 applicants, 36% accepted, 71 enrolled. In 2010, 50 master's awarded. *Entrance requirements:* Additional exam requirements/recommendations for international students: Required—TOEFL (minimum score 550 paper-based; 213 computer-based). *Application deadline:* For fall admission, 6/15 priority date for domestic and international students; for spring admission, 11/15 priority date for domestic and international students. Applications are processed on a rolling basis. Application fee: $20. Electronic applications accepted. *Expenses:* Tuition: Full-time $9900; part-time $660 per credit. Tuition and fees vary according to course load, degree level and program. *Financial support:* Federal Work-Study available. Financial award application deadline: 4/1; financial award applicants required to submit FAFSA. *Unit head:* Dr. Robert A. Reed, Chair, Department of Psychology and Counseling, 412-575-6349, E-mail: reedra@carlow.edu. *Application contact:* Jo Danhires, Administrative Assistant of Admissions, 412-578-6059, Fax: 412-578-6321, E-mail: gradstudies@carlow.edu.

Centenary College, Program in Counseling Psychology, Hackettstown, NJ 07840-2100. Offers counseling (MA); counseling psychology (MA). Part-time and evening/weekend programs available. Postbaccalaureate distance learning degree programs offered (minimal on-campus study). *Degree requirements:* For master's, thesis, fieldwork.

Central Michigan University, Central Michigan University Off-Campus Programs, Program in Counseling, Mount Pleasant, MI 48859. Offers professional counseling (MA); school counseling (MA). *Accreditation:* Teacher Education Accreditation Council. Part-time and evening/weekend programs available. *Entrance requirements:* For master's, MAT, minimum GPA of 2.7. Additional exam requirements/recommendations for international students: Required—TOEFL. Electronic applications accepted. *Expenses:* Tuition, state resident: full-time $8208; part-time $456 per credit hour. Tuition, nonresident: full-time $13,788; part-time $766 per credit hour. One-time fee: $25. *Financial support:* Scholarships/grants available. Support available to part-time students. *Unit head:* Dr. Suzanne Shellady, Chair, 989-774-3507, E-mail: shell1sm@cmich.edu. *Application contact:* 877-268-4636, E-mail: cmuoffcampus@cmich.edu.

Central Michigan University, College of Graduate Studies, College of Humanities and Social and Behavioral Sciences, Department of Psychology, Mount Pleasant, MI 48859. Offers clinical psychology (MA, PhD); experimental psychology (MS, PhD), including applied experimental psychology (PhD), experimental psychology (MS); industrial and organizational psychology (MA, PhD), including industrial and organizational psychology, occupational health psychology (PhD); neuroscience (MS, PhD); school psychology (PhD, S Psy S), including psychological services (S Psy S), school psychology (PhD). *Accreditation:* APA (one or more programs are accredited). *Faculty:* 28 full-time (9 women), 1 part-time/adjunct (0 women). *Students:* 65 full-time (39 women), 82 part-time (56 women); includes 2 Black or African American, non-Hispanic/Latino; 1 American Indian or Alaska Native, non-Hispanic/Latino; 1 Asian, non-Hispanic/Latino; 2 Hispanic/Latino, 12 international. Average age 27. In 2010, 5 other advanced degrees awarded. Terminal master's awarded for partial completion of doctoral program. *Degree requirements:* For master's, thesis or alternative; for doctorate, thesis/dissertation; for S Psy S, thesis. *Entrance requirements:* For doctorate, GRE. *Application fee:* $35 ($45 for international students). Electronic applications accepted. *Expenses:* Tuition, state resident: full-time $8208; part-time $456 per credit hour. Tuition, nonresident: full-time $13,788; part-time $766 per credit hour. One-time fee: $25. *Financial support:* Fellowships with tuition reimbursements, research assistantships with tuition reimbursements, teaching assistantships with tuition reimbursements, career-related internships or fieldwork, Federal Work-Study, unspecified assistantships, and out-of-state merit awards, non-resident graduate awards available. *Faculty research:* Experimental psychology, clinical psychology, industrial/organizational psychology, school psychology, neuroscience. *Unit head:* Dr. Hajime Otani, Chairperson, 989-774-6461, Fax: 989-774-2553, E-mail: otani1h@cmich.edu. *Application contact:* Barbara Houghton, Office Supervisor, 989-774-6461, Fax: 989-774-2553, E-mail: hough1ba@cmich.edu.

Central Washington University, Graduate Studies and Research, College of the Sciences, Department of Psychology, Program in Mental Health Counseling, Ellensburg, WA 98926. Offers MS. *Accreditation:* ACA. *Degree requirements:* For master's, thesis, internship. *Entrance requirements:* For master's, GRE General Test, minimum GPA of 3.0. Additional exam requirements/recommendations for international students: Required—TOEFL (minimum score 550 paper-based; 213 computer-based; 79 iBT).

Chaminade University of Honolulu, Graduate Services, Program in Counseling Psychology, Honolulu, HI 96816-1578. Offers MSCP. Part-time and evening/weekend programs available. *Degree requirements:* For master's, comprehensive exam. *Entrance requirements:* For master's, minimum undergraduate GPA of 3.0, 3 letters of recommendation. Additional exam requirements/recommendations for international students: Required—TOEFL (minimum score 550 paper-based). *Faculty research:* Taoist/Buddhist psychology, psychology of T'ai Chi Ch'uan, sleep disorders, drug/alcohol prevention with adolescent girls, anger/aggression with kids.

Chatham University, Program in Counseling Psychology, Pittsburgh, PA 15232-2826. Offers child, adolescent and family (MSCP); counseling psychology (Psy D); health and holistic (MSCP); infant mental health (MSCP); organization and supervision (MSCP); sport and exercise (MSCP). Part-time and evening/weekend programs available. *Degree requirements:* For master's, thesis optional, supervised internship; for doctorate, thesis/dissertation, internship. *Entrance requirements:* For master's, minimum GPA of 3.0; 2 letters of recommendation; resume; prerequisite coursework in statistics, biology, and psychology; for doctorate, GRE. Additional exam requirements/recommendations for international students: Required—TOEFL (minimum score 600 paper-based; 250 computer-based; 100 iBT), IELTS (minimum score 6.5), TWE. Electronic applications accepted. *Faculty research:* Trauma and recovery, hypnosis, psychospiritual dimensions of healing, psychotherapy of schizophrenia.

Chestnut Hill College, School of Graduate Studies, Division of Psychology, Program in Clinical and Counseling Psychology, Philadelphia, PA 19118-2693. Offers MA, MS, CAS. Part-time and evening/weekend programs available. *Faculty:* 10 full-time (5 women), 31 part-time/adjunct (18 women). *Students:* 95 full-time (83 women), 165 part-time (131 women); includes 43 minority (30 Black or African American, non-Hispanic/Latino; 6 Asian, non-Hispanic/Latino; 7 Hispanic/Latino), 5 international. Average age 32. 107 applicants, 92% accepted, 70 enrolled. In 2010, 74 master's awarded. *Degree requirements:* For master's, thesis optional, practica. *Entrance requirements:* For master's, GRE, writing sample, letters of recommendation. Additional exam requirements/recommendations for international students: Required—TOEFL (minimum score 550 paper-based; 213 computer-based). *Application deadline:* For fall admission, 7/17 priority date for domestic students, 7/15 priority date for international students; for spring admission, 12/15 priority date for domestic and international students. Applications are processed on a rolling basis. Application fee: $55. *Expenses:* Tuition: Part-time $560 per credit hour. One-time fee: $55. Tuition and fees vary according to degree level and program. *Faculty research:* Play therapy, eating disorders, addictions, group psychology and group therapy, health psychology. *Unit head:* Dr. Joseph Micucci, Chair, Psychology Division, 215-348-7162, Fax: 215-753-3619, E-mail: micucci@chc.edu. *Application contact:* Amy Boorse, Administrative Assistant, School of Graduate Studies Office, 215-248-7170, Fax: 215-248-7161, E-mail: gradadmissions@chc.edu.

The Chicago School of Professional Psychology at Grayslake, Program in Clinical Counseling Psychology, Chicago, IL 60610. Offers counseling (MA), including child and adolescent treatment, generalist, health psychology, Latino mental health, supervision and leadership in mental health, treatment of addiction disorders.

City College of the City University of New York, Graduate School, College of Liberal Arts and Science, Program in Mental Health Counseling, New York, NY 10031-9198. Offers MA.

City University of Seattle, Graduate Division, Division of Arts and Sciences, Bellevue, WA 98005. Offers counseling psychology (MA). Part-time and evening/weekend programs available. *Degree requirements:* For master's, comprehensive exam (for some programs), thesis (for some programs). *Entrance requirements:* Additional exam requirements/recommendations for international students: Recommended—TOEFL (minimum score 567 paper-based; 227 computer-based; 87 iBT), IELTS, TWE. Electronic applications accepted. *Expenses:* Contact institution.

Clemson University, Graduate School, College of Health, Education, and Human Development, Eugene T. Moore School of Education, Program in Counselor Education, Clemson, SC 29634. Offers clinical mental health counseling (M Ed); community mental health (M Ed); school counseling (K-12) (M Ed); student affairs (higher education) (M Ed). *Accreditation:* ACA; NCATE. Part-time and evening/weekend programs available. *Students:* 122 full-time (98 women), 41 part-time (29 women); includes 12 Black or African American, non-Hispanic/Latino; 4 Asian, non-Hispanic/Latino; 2 Hispanic/Latino; 2 international. Average age 28. 197 applicants, 62% accepted, 57 enrolled. In 2010, 76 master's awarded. *Degree requirements:* For master's, comprehensive exam. *Entrance requirements:* For master's, GRE General Test. Additional exam requirements/recommendations for international students: Required—TOEFL; Recommended—IELTS. *Application deadline:* For fall admission, 2/1 priority date for domestic students; for spring admission, 10/1 for domestic students. Applications are processed on a rolling basis. Application fee: $70 ($80 for international students). Electronic applications accepted. *Expenses:* Contact institution. *Financial support:* In 2010–11, 78 students received support, including 9 research assistantships with partial tuition reimbursements available (averaging $8,074 per year), 9 teaching assistantships with partial tuition reimbursements available (averaging $11,092 per year); institutionally sponsored loans, health care benefits, and unspecified assistantships also available. Financial award application deadline: 6/1; financial award applicants required to submit FAFSA. *Faculty research:* At-risk youth, ethnic identity development across the life span, postsecondary transitions and college readiness, distance and distributed learning environments, the student veteran experience in college, student development theory. *Unit head:* Dr. Michael J. Padilla, Director/ Associate Dean, 864-656-4444, Fax: 864-656-0311, E-mail: padilla@clemson.edu. *Application contact:* Dr. David Fleming, Graduate Coordinator, 864-656-1881, Fax: 864-656-0311, E-mail: dflemin@clemson.edu.

Cleveland State University, College of Graduate Studies, College of Education and Human Services, Department of Counseling, Administration, Supervision and Adult Learning (CASAL), Cleveland, OH 44115. Offers accelerated degree in adult learning and development (M Ed); adult learning and development (M Ed); chemical dependency counseling (Certificate); community agency counseling (M Ed); counseling and pupil personnel administration (Ed S); early childhood mental health counseling (Certificate); educational administration and supervision (M Ed); school administration (Ed S); school counseling (M Ed). *Accreditation:* ACA (one or more programs are accredited). Part-time and evening/weekend programs available. *Faculty:* 14 full-time (8 women), 16 part-time/adjunct (6 women). *Students:* 64 full-time (53 women), 285 part-time (223 women); includes 108 Black or African American, non-Hispanic/Latino; 3 Asian, non-Hispanic/Latino; 8 Hispanic/Latino; 1 Two or more races, non-Hispanic/Latino, 4 international. Average age 35. 235 applicants, 56% accepted, 104 enrolled. In 2010, 128 master's, 10 other advanced degrees awarded. *Degree requirements:* For master's, comprehensive exam (for some programs), thesis optional; for other advanced degree, comprehensive exam, thesis optional, internship. *Entrance requirements:* For master's, GRE General Test or MAT, letter of recommendation, minimum GPA of 2.75. Additional exam requirements/recommendations for international students: Required—TOEFL (minimum score 525 paper-based; 197 computer-based), IELTS (minimum score 6). *Application deadline:* For fall admission, 6/21 for domestic students, 5/15 for international students; for spring admission, 8/31 for domestic students, 11/1 for international students. Application fee: $30. Electronic applications accepted. *Expenses:* Tuition, state resident: full-time $8447; part-time $469 per credit hour. Tuition, nonresident: full-time $16,020; part-time $890 per credit hour. Required fees: $50. *Financial support:* In 2010–11, 17 students received support, including 7 research assistantships with full and partial tuition reimbursements available (averaging $9,882 per year), 6 teaching assistantships with full and partial tuition reimbursements available (averaging $9,882 per year); scholarships/grants, tuition waivers (full), and unspecified assistantships also available. Support available to part-time students. *Faculty research:* Education law, career development, women in school administration, psychopharmacology, counseling and spirituality. Total annual research expenditures: $433,211. *Unit head:* Dr. Ann L. Bauer, Chairperson, 216-687-4582, Fax: 216-687-5378, E-mail: a.l.bauer@csuohio.edu. *Application contact:* Deborah L. Brown, Interim Assistant Director, Graduate Admissions, 216-523-7572, Fax: 216-687-5400, E-mail: d.l.brown@csuohio.edu.

Cleveland State University, College of Graduate Studies, College of Education and Human Services, Program in Urban Education, Cleveland, OH 44115. Offers counseling (PhD); counseling psychology (PhD); leadership and lifelong learning (PhD); learning and development (PhD); policy studies (PhD); school administration (PhD). Part-time programs available. *Faculty:* 16 full-time (8 women), 15 part-time/adjunct (12 women). *Students:* 30 full-time (21 women), 84 part-time (59 women); includes 27 Black or African American, non-Hispanic/Latino; 3 Asian, non-Hispanic/Latino; 3 Hispanic/Latino, 9 international. Average age 42. 53 applicants, 36% accepted, 13 enrolled. In 2010, 17 doctorates awarded. *Degree requirements:* For doctorate, one foreign language, comprehensive exam, thesis/dissertation. *Entrance requirements:* For doctorate, GRE General Test, minimum graduate GPA of 3.25. Additional exam requirements/recommendations for international students: Required—TOEFL (minimum score 525 paper-based; 197 computer-based), IELTS (minimum score 6). *Application deadline:* For fall admission, 2/5 for domestic students. Application fee: $30. *Expenses:* Tuition, state resident: full-time $8447; part-time $469 per credit hour. Tuition, nonresident: full-time $16,020; part-time $890 per credit hour. Required fees: $50. *Financial support:* In 2010–11, 7 students received support, including 4 research assistantships with full and partial tuition reimbursements available (averaging $7,800 per year), 3 teaching assistantships with full and partial tuition reimbursements available (averaging $7,800 per year); tuition waivers (full) and unspecified assistantships also available. Financial award applicants required to submit FAFSA. *Faculty research:* Equity issues (race, ethnicity, and gender), education development consequences for special needs of urban populations, urban education programming, counseling the violent or aggressive adolescent. Total annual research expenditures: $5,662. *Unit head:* Dr. Joshua Bagakas, Director, 216-687-4591, Fax: 216-875-9697, E-mail: j.bagakas@csuohio.edu. *Application contact:* Wanda Butler, Administrative Assistant, 216-687-4697, Fax: 216-875-9697, E-mail: w.pruett-butler@csuohio.edu.

The College at Brockport, State University of New York, School of Education and Human Services, Department of Counselor Education, Brockport, NY 14420-2997. Offers college counseling (MS Ed); mental health counseling (MS); school counseling (MS Ed, CAS). *Accreditation:* ACA (one or more programs are accredited). Part-time programs available. *Students:* 27 full-time (17 women), 56 part-time (39 women); includes 18 minority (14 Black or African American, non-Hispanic/Latino; 2 Asian, non-Hispanic/Latino; 2 Hispanic/Latino). 87 applicants, 26% accepted, 17 enrolled. In 2010, 19 master's, 2 other advanced degrees awarded. *Degree requirements:* For master's, thesis, internship. *Entrance requirements:* For master's, group interview, letters of recommendation, written objectives; for CAS, master's degree, New York state school counselor certificate. Additional exam requirements/recommendations for international students: Required—TOEFL (minimum score 550 paper-based; 213 computer-based; 79 iBT). *Application deadline:* For fall admission, 2/1 priority date for domestic and international students; for spring admission, 9/1 priority date for domestic and international students. Application fee: $80. Electronic applications accepted. *Financial support:* In 2010–11, 1 teaching assistantship with full tuition reimbursement (averaging $6,000 per year) was awarded; Federal Work-Study, scholarships/grants, and unspecified assistantships also available. Support available to part-time students. Financial award application deadline: 3/15; financial award applicants required to submit FAFSA. *Faculty research:* Gender and diversity issues; counseling outcomes; spirituality; school, college and mental health counseling; obesity. *Unit head:* Dr. Thomas J. Hernandez, Chairperson, 585-395-2258, Fax: 585-395-2366, E-mail: thernandez@brockport.edu. *Application contact:* Dr. Thomas J. Hernandez, Chairperson, 585-395-2258, Fax: 585-395-2366, E-mail: thernandez@brockport.edu.

The College of New Rochelle, Graduate School, Division of Human Services, Program in Guidance and Counseling, New Rochelle, NY 10805-2308. Offers MS. Part-time programs available. *Degree requirements:* For master's, internship. *Entrance requirements:* For master's, interview, minimum GPA of 3.0.

The College of New Rochelle, Graduate School, Division of Human Services, Program in Mental Health Counseling, New Rochelle, NY 10805-2308. Offers Certificate. *Degree requirements:* For Certificate, internship.

College of Saint Elizabeth, Department of Psychology, Morristown, NJ 07960-6989. Offers counseling psychology (MA); forensic psychology (MA); student affairs in higher education (Certificate). Part-time and evening/weekend programs available. *Faculty:* 4 full-time (3 women), 9 part-time/adjunct (all women). *Students:* 33 full-time (31 women), 67 part-time (57 women); includes 13 Black or African American, non-Hispanic/Latino; 4 Asian, non-Hispanic/Latino; 12 Hispanic/Latino, 2 international. Average age 30. 86 applicants, 41% accepted, 27 enrolled. In 2010, 22 master's awarded. *Degree requirements:* For master's, thesis or alternative, portfolio. *Entrance requirements:* For master's, minimum GPA of 3.0, BA in psychology (preferred), 12 credits of course work in psychology. Additional exam requirements/recommendations for international students: Required—TOEFL (minimum score 550 paper-based). *Application deadline:* For fall admission, 4/1 priority date for domestic students; for spring admission, 11/15 for domestic students. Applications are processed on a rolling basis. Application fee: $35. Electronic applications accepted. *Expenses:* Tuition: Part-time $857 per credit. Required fees: $70 per credit. *Financial support:* Career-related internships or fieldwork, tuition waivers (partial), and unspecified assistantships available. Support available to part-time students. Financial award application deadline: 3/15; financial award applicants required to submit FAFSA. *Faculty research:* Family systems, dissociative identity disorder, multicultural counseling, outcomes assessment. *Unit head:* Dr. Valerie Scott, Director of the Graduate Program in Counseling Psychology, 973-290-4102, Fax: 973-290-4676, E-mail: vscott@cse.edu. *Application contact:* Dean Donna Tatarka, Dean of Admission, 973-290-4705, Fax: 973-290-4710, E-mail: dtatarka@cse.edu.

College of St. Joseph, Graduate Programs, Division of Psychology and Human Services, Program in Clinical Mental Health Counseling, Rutland, VT 05701-3899. Offers MS. Part-time programs available. *Faculty:* 4 full-time (1 woman), 7 part-time/adjunct (4 women). *Students:* 10 full-time (8 women), 11 part-time (9 women). Average age 36. 5 applicants, 80% accepted, 4 enrolled. In 2010, 3 master's awarded. *Degree requirements:* For master's, comprehensive exam. *Entrance requirements:* For master's, 2 letters of reference, interview. *Application deadline:* Applications are processed on a rolling basis. Application fee: $35. Electronic applications accepted. *Expenses:* Tuition: Full-time $14,200; part-time $400 per credit hour. Required fees: $45 per semester. *Financial support:* In 2010–11, 1 student received support. Career-related internships or fieldwork, Federal Work-Study, and unspecified assistantships available. Support available to part-time students. Financial award application deadline: 3/1. *Unit head:* Dr. Craig Knapp, Chair, 802-773-5900 Ext. 3219, Fax: 802-776-5258, E-mail: cknapp@csj.edu. *Application contact:* Alan Young, Dean of Admissions, 802-773-5900 Ext. 3227, Fax: 802-776-5310, E-mail: alanyoung@csj.edu.

College of Staten Island of the City University of New York, Graduate Programs, Program in Mental Health Counseling, Staten Island, NY 10314-6600. Offers MA. *Faculty:* 5 full-time (all women), 2 part-time/adjunct (both women). *Students:* 32 full-time (25 women); includes 1 Black or African American, non-Hispanic/Latino; 4 Hispanic/Latino. Average age 27. 89 applicants, 28% accepted, 21 enrolled. *Degree requirements:* For master's, comprehensive exam, 700 hours total for practicum internships. *Entrance requirements:* For master's, BA/BS with five undergraduate courses in psychology; minimum GPA of 3.0; 2 letters of recommendation, one from former professor. Additional exam requirements/recommendations for international students: Required—TOEFL (minimum score 600 paper-based; 250 computer-based; 100 iBT), IELTS (minimum score 7). *Application deadline:* For fall admission, 3/10 priority date for domestic and international students. Application fee: $125. Electronic applications accepted. *Expenses:* Tuition, state resident: full-time $7730; part-time $325 per credit. Tuition, nonresident: full-time $14,520; part-time $605 per credit. Required fees: $378. *Financial support:* In 2010–11, 2 students received support. Federal Work-Study available. *Unit head:* Dr. Judith Kuppersmith, Director, 718-982-4185, E-mail: judith.kuppersmith@csi.cuny.edu. *Application contact:* Sasha Spence, Assistant Director of Graduate Recruitment and Admissions, 718-982-2699, Fax: 718-982-2500, E-mail: sasha.spence@csi.cuny.edu.

Colorado Christian University, Program in Counseling, Lakewood, CO 80226. Offers MAC. Part-time and evening/weekend programs available. *Faculty:* 12 full-time (5 women), 56 part-time/adjunct (39 women). *Students:* 35 full-time (28 women), 71 part-time (57 women); includes 5 Black or African American, non-Hispanic/Latino; 3 Asian, non-Hispanic/Latino; 11 Hispanic/Latino. 33 applicants, 21% accepted. *Degree requirements:* For master's, thesis optional. *Entrance requirements:* For master's, GRE General Test, 3 letters of recommendation. Additional exam requirements/recommendations for international students: Required—TOEFL. *Application deadline:* For fall admission, 8/25 priority date for domestic and international students; for spring admission, 1/12 priority date for domestic and international students. Applications are processed on a rolling basis. Application fee: $40. Electronic applications accepted. *Expenses:* Contact institution. *Financial support:* In 2010–11, 27 students received support. Scholarships/grants and tuition waivers (full and partial) available. Support available to part-time students. Financial award application deadline: 3/1; financial award applicants required to submit FAFSA. *Unit head:* Dr. Laverne Jordan, Dean of Social Sciences and Humanities, 303-963-3300, Fax: 303-963-3301, E-mail: agsadmission@ccu.edu. *Application contact:* College of Adult and Graduate Studies, 303-963-3300, Fax: 303-963-3301, E-mail: agsadmission@ccu.edu.

Columbus State University, Graduate Studies, College of Education and Health Professions, Department of Counseling, Foundations, and Leadership, Columbus, GA 31907-5645. Offers community counseling (MS); curriculum and leadership (Ed D); educational leadership (M Ed, Ed S); school counseling (M Ed). *Accreditation:* ACA; NCATE. Part-time and evening/weekend programs available. Postbaccalaureate distance learning degree programs offered (minimal on-campus study). *Faculty:* 12 full-time (5 women), 12 part-time/adjunct (6 women). *Students:* 120 full-time (101 women), 99 part-time (72 women); includes 84 minority (78 Black or African American, non-Hispanic/Latino; 1 Asian, non-Hispanic/Latino; 3 Hispanic/Latino; 2 Two or more races, non-Hispanic/Latino), 1 international. Average age 35. 134 applicants, 75% accepted, 74 enrolled. In 2010, 57 master's, 33 other advanced degrees awarded. *Degree requirements:* For master's, thesis, exit exam; for Ed S, thesis or alternative. *Entrance requirements:* For master's, GRE General Test, minimum GPA of 2.75; for doctorate, minimum graduate GPA of 3.5, four years of professional service; for Ed S, GRE General Test. Additional exam requirements/recommendations for international students: Required—TOEFL (minimum score 550 paper-based; 213 computer-based; 79 iBT). *Application deadline:* For fall admission, 6/30 for domestic students, 6/31 for international students; for spring admission, 11/1 for domestic and international students. Applications are processed on a rolling basis. Application fee: $30. Electronic applications accepted. *Expenses:* Tuition, state resident: full-time $5573; part-time $232 per semester hour. Tuition, nonresident: full-time $13,968; part-time $582 per semester hour. Required fees: $1300; $650 per semester. Tuition and fees vary according to degree level and program. *Financial support:* In 2010–11, 126 students received support, including 10 research assistantships with partial tuition reimbursements available (averaging $3,000 per year); career-related internships or fieldwork, Federal Work-Study, institutionally sponsored loans, scholarships/grants, tuition waivers (partial), and unspecified assistantships also available. Support available to part-time students. Financial award application deadline: 5/1; financial award applicants required to submit FAFSA. *Unit head:* Dr. Michael L. Baltimore, Chair, 706-568-5088, Fax: 706-569-3134, E-mail: baltimore_michael@colstate.edu. *Application contact:* Katie Thornton, Graduate Admissions Specialist, 706-568-2035, Fax: 706-568-2462, E-mail: thornton_katie@colstate.edu.

Concordia University Chicago, College of Graduate and Innovative Programs, Program in Community Counseling, River Forest, IL 60305-1499. Offers MA. *Accreditation:* ACA. *Degree requirements:* For master's, final project. *Entrance requirements:* For master's, minimum GPA of 2.9. Additional exam requirements/recommendations for international students: Required—TOEFL (minimum score 550 paper-based; 195 computer-based). Electronic applications accepted.

Concordia University Wisconsin, Graduate Programs, Department of Psychology, Program in Professional Counseling, Mequon, WI 53097-2402. Offers MPC. Postbaccalaureate distance learning degree programs offered (minimal on-campus study). *Degree requirements:* For master's, comprehensive exam, thesis or alternative. *Entrance requirements:* For master's, minimum GPA of 3.0. Additional exam requirements/recommendations for international students: Required—TOEFL.

Dallas Baptist University, College of Humanities and Social Sciences, Counseling Program (Main Campus), Dallas, TX 75211-9299. Offers MA. Part-time and evening/weekend programs available. *Entrance requirements:* For master's, GRE General Test, minimum GPA of 3.0. Additional exam requirements/recommendations for international students: Required—TOEFL.

Counseling Psychology

Dallas Baptist University (continued)
Electronic applications accepted. *Expenses:* Tuition: Full-time $11,394; part-time $633 per credit hour. *Faculty research:* Therapy effectiveness.

Dallas Baptist University, College of Humanities and Social Sciences, Counseling Program (North Campus), Dallas, TX 75211-9299. Offers). Part-time and evening/weekend programs available. *Expenses:* Tuition: Full-time $11,394; part-time $633 per credit hour.

Dominican University of California, Graduate Programs, School of Education and Counseling Psychology, Department of Counseling Psychology, San Rafael, CA 94901-2298. Offers MFT, MS. Part-time programs available. *Faculty:* 3 full-time (2 women), 9 part-time/adjunct (7 women). *Students:* 55 full-time (52 women), 39 part-time (33 women); includes 15 minority (3 Black or African American, non-Hispanic/Latino; 1 American Indian or Alaska Native, non-Hispanic/Latino; 9 Hispanic/Latino; 2 Two or more races, non-Hispanic/Latino), 4 international. Average age 38. 59 applicants, 54% accepted, 23 enrolled. In 2010, 20 master's awarded. *Degree requirements:* For master's, comprehensive exam (for some programs), thesis (for some programs). *Entrance requirements:* For master's, minimum GPA of 3.0 for last 60 units. Additional exam requirements/recommendations for international students: Required—TOEFL (minimum score 550 paper-based; 213 computer-based; 80 iBT), IELTS. *Application deadline:* For fall admission, 6/15 priority date for domestic and international students; for spring admission, 11/15 priority date for domestic and international students. Applications are processed on a rolling basis. Application fee: $40. Electronic applications accepted. *Expenses:* Contact institution. *Financial support:* In 2010–11, 39 students received support, including 38 fellowships (averaging $2,704 per year); career-related internships or fieldwork, scholarships/grants, traineeships, health care benefits, tuition waivers (partial), and tuition discounts also available. Support available to part-time students. Financial award application deadline: 3/2; financial award applicants required to submit FAFSA. *Unit head:* Dr. Charles R. Billings, Chair, 415-485-3263. *Application contact:* Moriah Dunning, Associate Director of Graduate Admissions, 415-485-3246, Fax: 415-485-3214, E-mail: moriah.dunning@dominican.edu.

Eastern Nazarene College, Adult and Graduate Studies, Program in Marriage and Family Therapy, Quincy, MA 02170. Offers MS. Part-time and evening/weekend programs available. *Entrance requirements:* For master's, 3 letters of recommendation, resume. Additional exam requirements/recommendations for international students: Required—TOEFL (minimum score 550 paper-based).

Eastern University, Department of Counseling Psychology, St. Davids, PA 19087-3696. Offers community/clinical counseling (MA); school counseling (MA, Certificate); school psychology (MS, Certificate). *Degree requirements:* For master's, internship. *Entrance requirements:* For master's, minimum GPA of 2.5. Additional exam requirements/recommendations for international students: Required—TOEFL.

Eastern Washington University, Graduate Studies, College of Education and Human Development, Program in Mental Health Counseling, Cheney, WA 99004-2431. Offers applied psychology (MS); mental health counseling (MS).

Emporia State University, Graduate School, Teachers College, Department of Psychology, Art Therapy, Rehabilitation and Mental Health Counseling, Program in Mental Health Counseling, Emporia, KS 66801-5087. Offers MS. *Accreditation:* ACA. Part-time programs available. *Students:* 19 full-time (15 women), 9 part-time (6 women), 1 international. 7 applicants, 100% accepted, 4 enrolled. In 2010, 14 master's awarded. *Degree requirements:* For master's, comprehensive exam, internship. *Entrance requirements:* For master's, GRE or MAT. Additional exam requirements/recommendations for international students: Required—TOEFL (minimum score 520 paper-based; 133 computer-based; 68 iBT). *Application deadline:* For fall admission, 8/15 for domestic students. Applications are processed on a rolling basis. Application fee: $30 ($75 for international students). Electronic applications accepted. *Expenses:* Tuition, state resident: full-time $4382; part-time $183 per credit hour. Tuition, nonresident: full-time $13,572; part-time $566 per credit hour. Required fees: $1022; $62 per credit hour. Tuition and fees vary according to course level, course load and campus/location. *Financial support:* Federal Work-Study, institutionally sponsored loans, health care benefits, and unspecified assistantships available. Financial award application deadline: 3/15; financial award applicants required to submit FAFSA. *Unit head:* Dr. Brian A. Schrader, Chair, 620-341-5317, E-mail: bschrade@emporia.edu. *Application contact:* Mary Sewell, Admissions Coordinator, 800-950-GRAD, Fax: 620-341-5909, E-mail: msewell@emporia.edu.

Evangel University, Department of Psychology, Springfield, MO 65802. Offers clinical psychology (MS); counseling psychology (MS). Part-time programs available. *Faculty:* 3 full-time (2 women), 9 part-time/adjunct (4 women). *Students:* 23 full-time (15 women), 18 part-time (14 women). Average age 27. 17 applicants, 100% accepted, 15 enrolled. In 2010, 8 master's awarded. *Degree requirements:* For master's, comprehensive exam, thesis optional. *Entrance requirements:* For master's, GRE General Test or MAT, minimum undergraduate GPA of 3.0, undergraduate major or minor in psychology. Additional exam requirements/recommendations for international students: Required—TOEFL (minimum score 550 paper-based; 213 computer-based). *Application deadline:* For fall admission, 2/1 priority date for domestic students; for spring admission, 10/15 priority date for domestic students. Applications are processed on a rolling basis. Application fee: $25. Electronic applications accepted. *Financial support:* In 2010–11, 6 students received support. Career-related internships or fieldwork, scholarships/grants, and unspecified assistantships available. Support available to part-time students. Financial award application deadline: 3/1; financial award applicants required to submit FAFSA. *Unit head:* Dr. Grant Jones, Chair, 417-865-2815 Ext. 8619, E-mail: jonesg@evangel.edu. *Application contact:* Charity H. Fahlstrom, Admissions Representative, Graduate and Professional Studies Admissions, 417-865-2815 Ext. 7227, Fax: 417-575-5484, E-mail: fahlstromc@evangel.edu.

Fairfield University, Graduate School of Education and Allied Professions, Department of Counselor Education, Fairfield, CT 06824-5195. Offers clinical mental health counseling (MA, CAS); school counseling (MA, CAS). *Accreditation:* ACA (one or more programs are accredited). Part-time and evening/weekend programs available. *Faculty:* 4 full-time (all women), 4 part-time/adjunct (3 women). *Students:* 25 full-time (21 women), 78 part-time (52 women); includes 3 Black or African American, non-Hispanic/Latino; 1 Asian, non-Hispanic/Latino; 7 Hispanic/Latino. 52 applicants, 29% accepted, 8 enrolled. In 2010, 28 master's, 2 other advanced degrees awarded. *Degree requirements:* For master's, comprehensive exam, thesis or alternative. *Entrance requirements:* For master's, PRAXIS I (PPST), minimum QPA of 3.0, 2 recommendations, resume. Additional exam requirements/recommendations for international students: Required—TOEFL (minimum score 550 paper-based; 213 computer-based; 84 iBT). *Application deadline:* For fall admission, 2/15 for domestic and international students; for spring admission, 10/1 for domestic and international students. Application fee: $60. Electronic applications accepted. *Expenses:* Tuition: Part-time $600 per hour. Part-time tuition and fees vary according to degree level and program. *Financial support:* Career-related internships or fieldwork and unspecified assistantships available. Financial award applicants required to submit FAFSA. *Faculty research:* Corrective feedback in group setting, applying group concepts to teaching counselor education curriculum, assessment and program evaluation, spirituality and counseling, clinical supervision, developmental school counseling, wellness and multicultural counseling. *Unit head:* Dr. Diana Hulse, Chair, 203-254-4000 Ext. 2245, Fax: 203-254-4047, E-mail: dhulse@fairfield.edu. *Application contact:* Marianne Gumpper, Director of Graduate and Continuing Studies Admissions, 203-254-4184, Fax: 203-254-4073, E-mail: gradadmis@fairfield.edu.

Fairleigh Dickinson University, College at Florham, Maxwell Becton College of Arts and Sciences, Department of Psychology, Program in Clinical Mental Health Counseling, Madison, NJ 07940-1099. Offers MA. *Students:* 20 full-time (13 women), 2 part-time (1 woman). Average age 26. 1 applicant, 100% accepted, 0 enrolled. *Unit head:* Dr. Ketrin Maxwell, Director.

Application contact: Susan Brooman, University Director, Graduate Admissions, 973-443-8905, Fax: 973-443-8088, E-mail: grad@fdu.edu.

Fairleigh Dickinson University, College at Florham, Maxwell Becton College of Arts and Sciences, Department of Psychology, Program in Counseling, Madison, NJ 07940-1099. Offers MA. *Students:* 44 full-time (32 women), 22 part-time (19 women), 1 international. Average age 31. 22 applicants, 55% accepted, 4 enrolled. In 2010, 20 master's awarded. *Application contact:* Susan Brooman, University Director, Graduate Admissions, 973-443-8905, Fax: 973-443-8088, E-mail: grad@fdu.edu.

Felician College, Program in Counseling Psychology, Lodi, NJ 07644-2117. Offers MA.

See Display on next page and Close-Up on page 1163.

Fitchburg State University, Division of Graduate and Continuing Education, Programs in Counseling, Fitchburg, MA 01420-2697. Offers elementary school guidance counseling (MS); mental health counseling (MS); secondary school guidance counseling (MS). *Accreditation:* NCATE. Part-time and evening/weekend programs available. *Students:* 17 full-time (15 women), 52 part-time (47 women); includes 2 Black or African American, non-Hispanic/Latino; 3 Hispanic/Latino, 1 international. Average age 32. 24 applicants, 79% accepted, 12 enrolled. In 2010, 23 master's awarded. *Entrance requirements:* For master's, GRE General Test or MAT, letters of recommendation, resume. Additional exam requirements/recommendations for international students: Required—TOEFL (minimum score 550 paper-based; 213 computer-based; 79 iBT). *Application deadline:* Applications are processed on a rolling basis. Application fee: $25 ($50 for international students). *Expenses:* Tuition, area resident: Part-time $150 per credit. Tuition, state resident: part-time $150 per credit. Tuition, nonresident: part-time $150 per credit. Required fees: $127 per credit. *Financial support:* In 2010–11, research assistantships with partial tuition reimbursements (averaging $5,500 per year); Federal Work-Study, scholarships/grants, and unspecified assistantships also available. Support available to part-time students. Financial award application deadline: 3/1; financial award applicants required to submit FAFSA. *Unit head:* Dr. John Hancock, Chair, 978-665-3604, Fax: 978-665-3658, E-mail: gce@fitchburgstate.edu. *Application contact:* Director of Admissions, 978-665-3144, Fax: 978-665-4540, E-mail: admissions@fitchburgstate.edu.

Florida Atlantic University, College of Education, Department of Counselor Education, Boca Raton, FL 33431-0991. Offers counselor education (M Ed, PhD, Ed S); marriage and family therapy (Ed S); mental health counseling (M Ed, Ed S); rehabilitation counseling (M Ed); school counseling (M Ed, Ed S). *Accreditation:* ACA; NCATE. Part-time and evening/weekend programs available. *Faculty:* 10 full-time (5 women), 1 (woman) part-time/adjunct. *Students:* 75 full-time (60 women), 82 part-time (68 women); includes 46 minority (22 Black or African American, non-Hispanic/Latino; 4 Asian, non-Hispanic/Latino; 20 Hispanic/Latino), 1 international. Average age 32. 118 applicants, 35% accepted, 37 enrolled. In 2010, 51 master's, 1 doctorate awarded. *Degree requirements:* For Ed S, departmental qualifying exam. *Entrance requirements:* For master's, GRE General Test, minimum GPA of 3.0 during previous 2 years; for Ed S, GRE General Test, minimum graduate GPA of 3.25. Additional exam requirements/recommendations for international students: Required—TOEFL. *Application deadline:* For fall admission, 3/1 for domestic students, 2/1 for international students; for spring admission, 9/15 for domestic students, 7/1 for international students. Applications are processed on a rolling basis. Application fee: $30. *Expenses:* Tuition, area resident: Part-time $319.96 per credit. Tuition, state resident: part-time $319.96 per credit. Tuition, nonresident: part-time $926.42 per credit. *Financial support:* Research assistantships with partial tuition reimbursements, teaching assistantships, career-related internships or fieldwork, scholarships/grants, and unspecified assistantships available. *Faculty research:* Brief therapy, psychological type, marriage and family counseling, international programs, integrated services. *Unit head:* Dr. Irene Johnson, Chair, 561-297-2136, Fax: 561-297-2309. *Application contact:* Darlene Epperson, Office Assistant, 561-297-3601, Fax: 561-297-2309, E-mail: frederic@fau.edu.

Florida International University, College of Education, Department of Educational Leadership and Policy Studies, Miami, FL 33199. Offers adult education (MS); adult education in human resource development (Ed D); clinical mental health counseling (MS); conflict resolution and consensus building (Certificate); counselor education (MS); educational administration and supervision (Ed D); educational leadership (MS, Certificate, Ed S); higher education (Ed D); higher education administration (MS); human resource development (MS); instruction in urban settings (MS); international/intercultural education (MS); learning technologies (MS); multicultural-bilingual (MS); multicultural-TESOL (MS); recreation and sport management (MS); recreation therapy (MS); rehabilitation counseling (MS); school counseling (MS); school psychology (Ed S); urban education (MS). Part-time and evening/weekend programs available. *Students:* 164 full-time (124 women), 308 part-time (234 women); includes 107 Black or African American, non-Hispanic/Latino; 3 American Indian or Alaska Native, non-Hispanic/Latino; 8 Asian, non-Hispanic/Latino; 223 Hispanic/Latino, 12 international. Average age 31. 544 applicants, 41% accepted, 197 enrolled. In 2010, 123 master's, 5 doctorates, 16 other advanced degrees awarded. *Degree requirements:* For doctorate, thesis/dissertation. *Entrance requirements:* For master's, minimum GPA of 3.0; for doctorate and other advanced degree, GRE General Test. Additional exam requirements/recommendations for international students: Required—TOEFL (minimum score 550 paper-based; 213 computer-based; 80 iBT), IELTS (minimum score 6.3). *Application deadline:* For fall admission, 6/1 priority date for domestic students, 4/1 for international students; for winter admission, 10/1 priority date for domestic students, 9/1 for international students; for spring admission, 3/1 priority date for domestic students, 2/1 for international students. Applications are processed on a rolling basis. Application fee: $30. Electronic applications accepted. *Financial support:* Fellowships, research assistantships with full and partial tuition reimbursements, teaching assistantships with full and partial tuition reimbursements, Federal Work-Study and tuition waivers (full and partial) available. Support available to part-time students. Financial award applicants required to submit FAFSA. *Unit head:* Dr. Patricia Barbetta, Dean of Graduate Studies, 305-348-2835, Fax: 305-348-2081, E-mail: barbetta@fiu.edu. *Application contact:* Nanett Rojas, Graduate Admission, 305-348-7442, Fax: 305-348-7441, E-mail: nanett.rojas@fiu.edu.

Florida State University, The Graduate School, College of Education, Department of Educational Psychology and Learning Systems, Program in Psychological Services, Tallahassee, FL 32306. Offers MS, PhD, Ed S. *Accreditation:* ACA (one or more programs are accredited). *Faculty:* 9 full-time (6 women), 1 part-time/adjunct (0 women). *Students:* 49 full-time (39 women), 5 part-time (4 women); includes 15 minority (8 Black or African American, non-Hispanic/Latino; 1 Asian, non-Hispanic/Latino; 6 Hispanic/Latino), 1 international. Average age 28. 79 applicants, 47% accepted, 25 enrolled. In 2010, 20 master's, 16 other advanced degrees awarded. *Degree requirements:* For master's and Ed S, comprehensive exam, thesis optional. *Entrance requirements:* For master's and Ed S, GRE General Test, minimum GPA of 3.0. Additional exam requirements/recommendations for international students: Required—TOEFL (minimum score 550 paper-based; 213 computer-based; 80 iBT). *Application deadline:* For fall admission, 1/15 for domestic and international students. Applications are processed on a rolling basis. Application fee: $30. Electronic applications accepted. *Expenses:* Tuition, state resident: full-time $8238.24. *Financial support:* Fellowships with full and partial tuition reimbursements, research assistantships with full and partial tuition reimbursements, teaching assistantships with full and partial tuition reimbursements, career-related internships or fieldwork available. Financial award applicants required to submit FAFSA. *Faculty research:* Social, emotional, and vocational capabilities of learners; rehabilitation counseling; technology and learners; talent identification. *Unit head:* Dr. Frances Prevatt, Program Leader, 850-644-9445, Fax: 850-644-8776, E-mail: fprevatt@fsu.edu. *Application contact:* Terri Wehnert, Program Assistant, 850-644-8046, Fax: 850-644-8776, E-mail: tmpowell@fsu.edu.

Fordham University, Graduate School of Education, Division of Psychological and Educational Services, New York, NY 10023. Offers counseling and personnel services (MSE, Adv C); counseling psychology (PhD); educational psychology (MSE, PhD); school psychology (PhD); urban and urban bilingual school psychology (Adv C). *Accreditation:* APA (one or more programs are accredited); NCATE. *Degree requirements:* For doctorate, thesis/dissertation. *Entrance requirements:* For doctorate, GRE General Test.

Fort Valley State University, College of Graduate Studies and Extended Education, Department of Counseling Psychology, Program in Mental Health Counseling, Fort Valley, GA 31030. Offers MS. Part-time programs available. *Degree requirements:* For master's, comprehensive exam (for some programs), thesis optional. *Entrance requirements:* For master's, GRE General Test or MAT.

Franciscan University of Steubenville, Graduate Programs, Department of Counseling, Steubenville, OH 43952-1763. Offers MA. Part-time programs available. *Degree requirements:* For master's, case presentation, integrative paper. *Entrance requirements:* For master's, GRE General Test or MAT, minimum undergraduate GPA of 3.0.

Francis Marion University, Graduate Programs, Department of Psychology, Florence, SC 29502-0547. Offers applied psychology (MS), including clinical/counseling, school psychology; school psychology (SSP). Part-time and evening/weekend programs available. *Faculty:* 10 full-time (4 women), 5 part-time/adjunct (4 women). *Students:* 17 full-time (16 women), 26 part-time (25 women); includes 6 Black or African American, non-Hispanic/Latino. Average age 25. 44 applicants, 61% accepted, 14 enrolled. In 2010, 9 master's awarded. *Degree requirements:* For master's, internship. *Entrance requirements:* For master's, GRE General Test. *Application deadline:* For fall admission, 3/15 for domestic students; for spring admission, 10/15 for domestic students. Applications are processed on a rolling basis. Application fee: $30. *Expenses:* Tuition, state resident: full-time $8667; part-time $433.35 per credit hour. Tuition, nonresident: full-time $17,334; part-time $866.70 per credit hour. Required fees: $335; $12.25 per credit hour. $30 per semester. *Financial support:* In 2010–11, 13 students received support, including 2 research assistantships (averaging $7,000 per year), 3 teaching assistantships (averaging $8,000 per year); career-related internships or fieldwork, unspecified assistantships, and scholarships with out-of-state waivers also available. Support available to part-time students. Financial award application deadline: 3/1; financial award applicants required to submit FAFSA. *Faculty research:* Parenting and family relationships, child development, applied behavioral analysis, posttraumatic stress disorder, clinical psychology in adults. *Unit head:* Dr. John R. Hester, Chair, 843-661-1635, Fax: 843-661-1628. *Application contact:* Jennifer Taylor, Administrative Assistant, 843-661-1378, Fax: 843-661-1628.

Frostburg State University, Graduate School, College of Liberal Arts and Sciences, Department of Psychology, Program in Counseling Psychology, Frostburg, MD 21532-1099. Offers MS. Part-time and evening/weekend programs available. *Degree requirements:* For master's, internship. *Entrance requirements:* For master's, GRE General Test or MAT, interview, minimum GPA of 3.0, resume. Additional exam requirements/recommendations for international students: Required—TOEFL. Electronic applications accepted.

Gallaudet University, The Graduate School, Washington, DC 20002-3625. Offers administration (MS); audiology (Au D, PhD); change leadership in education (Ed S); clinical psychology (PhD); deaf education (Ed D, PhD); deaf education: advanced studies (MA); deaf education: special programs in deaf education (MA); deaf history (Certificate); deaf studies (MA); education: teacher preparation (MA, MA Missions), including deaf education (MA), early childhood education and deaf education (MA), elementary education and deaf education (MA Missions), secondary education and deaf education (MA); hearing, speech and language sciences (MS); international development (MA); interpretation (MA, PhD); leadership (Certificate); leisure services administration (MS); linguistics (MA, PhD); management (Certificate); mental health counseling (MA); school counseling (MA); school counseling (summer session) (MA); school psychology (Psy S); sign language teaching (MA); social work (MSW); special education administration (PhD); speech-language pathology (PhD). Part-time programs available. *Faculty:* 116 full-time (86 women). *Students:* 291 full-time (224 women), 122 part-time (97 women); includes 142 minority (36 Black or African American, non-Hispanic/Latino; 3 American Indian or Alaska Native, non-Hispanic/Latino; 13 Asian, non-Hispanic/Latino; 29 Hispanic/Latino; 61 Two or more races, non-Hispanic/Latino), 28 international. Average age 30. 442 applicants, 52%

accepted, 145 enrolled. In 2010, 116 master's, 17 doctorates, 16 other advanced degrees awarded. Terminal master's awarded for partial completion of doctoral program. *Degree requirements:* For master's, comprehensive exam (for some programs), thesis optional; for doctorate, comprehensive exam, thesis/dissertation. *Entrance requirements:* For master's and doctorate, GRE General Test or MAT, letters of recommendation, interviews, goals statement, ASL proficiency interview, written English competency. Additional exam requirements/recommendations for international students: Required—TOEFL. *Application deadline:* For fall admission, 2/15 for domestic students. Applications are processed on a rolling basis. Application fee: $50. Electronic applications accepted. *Expenses:* Tuition: Full-time $11,930; part-time $663 per credit. Required fees: $188 per semester. *Financial support:* In 2010–11, 219 students received support; fellowships, research assistantships, teaching assistantships, career-related internships or fieldwork, Federal Work-Study, scholarships/grants, tuition waivers (partial), and unspecified assistantships available. Support available to part-time students. Financial award applicants required to submit FAFSA. *Faculty research:* Bimodal bilingualism development, audiology, telecommunications access, early childhood education, linguistics, visual language and visual learning, rehabilitation and hearing enhancement. *Unit head:* Dr. Carol J. Erting, Dean, 202-651-5520, Fax: 202-651-5027, E-mail: carol.erting@gallaudet.edu. *Application contact:* Wednesday Luria, Coordinator of Prospective Graduate Student Services, 202-651-5400, Fax: 202-651-5295, E-mail: graduate.school@gallaudet.edu.

Gannon University, School of Graduate Studies, College of Humanities, Education, and Social Sciences, School of Humanities, Program in Counseling Psychology, Erie, PA 16541-0001. Offers PhD. *Accreditation:* ACA. Part-time and evening/weekend programs available. *Students:* 10 part-time (8 women), 1 international. Average age 42. In 2010, 1 doctorate awarded. *Degree requirements:* For doctorate, thesis/dissertation, internship. *Entrance requirements:* For doctorate, GRE General Test, master's degree, minimum QPA of 3.5. Additional exam requirements/recommendations for international students: Required—TOEFL (minimum score 79 iBT). *Application deadline:* Applications are processed on a rolling basis. Application fee: $50. Electronic applications accepted. *Expenses:* Contact institution. *Financial support:* Career-related internships or fieldwork, Federal Work-Study, scholarships/grants, and unspecified assistantships available. Financial award application deadline: 7/1; financial award applicants required to submit FAFSA. *Unit head:* Dr. Linda Fleming, Director, 814-871-7262, Fax: 814-871-5511, E-mail: fleming006@gannon.edu. *Application contact:* Kara Morgan, Assistant Director of Graduate Admissions, 814-871-5831, Fax: 814-871-5827, E-mail: graduate@gannon.edu.

Gardner-Webb University, Graduate School, School of Psychology, Program in Mental Health Counseling, Boiling Springs, NC 28017. Offers MA. *Accreditation:* ACA. Part-time and evening/weekend programs available. *Faculty:* 6 full-time (3 women). *Students:* 3 full-time (all women), 51 part-time (44 women); includes 8 Black or African American, non-Hispanic/Latino; 2 Hispanic/Latino. Average age 32. In 2010, 8 master's awarded. *Degree requirements:* For master's, comprehensive exam. *Entrance requirements:* For master's, GRE General Test, MAT, minimum GPA of 2.7. *Application deadline:* For fall admission, 7/1 priority date for domestic students. Applications are processed on a rolling basis. Application fee: $40. Electronic applications accepted. *Expenses:* Tuition: Part-time $325 per credit hour. *Financial support:* Unspecified assistantships available. *Unit head:* Dr. Frieda Brown, Coordinator, 704-406-4436, Fax: 704-406-4329, E-mail: fbrown@gardner-webb.edu. *Application contact:* Office of Graduate Admisisons, 877-498-4723, Fax: 704-406-3895, E-mail: gradinfo@gardner-webb.edu.

Geneva College, Program in Counseling, Beaver Falls, PA 15010-3599. Offers marriage and family (MA); mental health (MA); school counseling (MA). *Accreditation:* ACA. Part-time and evening/weekend programs available. *Degree requirements:* For master's, comprehensive exam, internship. *Entrance requirements:* For master's, GRE General Test or MAT, minimum GPA of 3.0 (preferred), letters of recommendation, faith statement. Additional exam requirements/recommendations for international students: Required—TOEFL. Electronic applications accepted.

George Fox University, School of Education, Graduate Department of Counseling, Newberg, OR 97132-2697. Offers clinical mental health counseling (MA); marriage, couple and family

Counseling Psychology

George Fox University (continued)
counseling (MA, Certificate); mental health trauma (Certificate); school counseling (MA, Certificate); school psychology (Certificate, Ed S). Part-time programs available. *Faculty:* 9 full-time (3 women), 7 part-time/adjunct (4 women). *Students:* 119 full-time (95 women), 115 part-time (93 women); includes 34 minority (9 Black or African American, non-Hispanic/Latino; 5 American Indian or Alaska Native, non-Hispanic/Latino; 8 Asian, non-Hispanic/Latino; 10 Hispanic/Latino; 1 Native Hawaiian or other Pacific Islander, non-Hispanic/Latino; 1 Two or more races, non-Hispanic/Latino). Average age 34. 114 applicants, 55% accepted, 45 enrolled. In 2010, 66 master's, 3 other advanced degrees awarded. *Degree requirements:* For master's, clinical project. *Entrance requirements:* For master's, MAT or GRE, bachelor's degree from regionally-accredited college or university, minimum cumulative GPA of 3.0, 1 professional and 1 academic reference, resume, on-campus interview. Additional exam requirements/recommendations for international students: Required—TOEFL (minimum score 577 paper-based; 233 computer-based; 90 iBT), IELTS (minimum score 7). *Application deadline:* For fall admission, 5/30 for domestic and international students; for winter admission, 11/1 for domestic and international students; for spring admission, 2/28 for domestic and international students. Applications are processed on a rolling basis. Application fee: $40. Electronic applications accepted. *Expenses:* Contact institution. *Financial support:* Career-related internships or fieldwork available. *Unit head:* Dr. Richard Shaw, Associate Professor of Marriage and Family Therapy/Chair, 503-554-6142, E-mail: rshaw@georgefox.edu. *Application contact:* Kathy Grant, Admissions Counselor, 800-493-4937, Fax: 503-554-6111, E-mail: counseling@georgefox.edu.

Georgian Court University, School of Arts and Sciences, Lakewood, NJ 08701-2697. Offers biology (MA); Catholic school leadership (Certificate); clinical mental health counseling (MA); holistic health studies (MA); mathematics (MA); pastoral ministry (Certificate); religious education (Certificate); school psychology (Certificate); theology (MA, Certificate). Part-time and evening/weekend programs available. *Faculty:* 19 full-time (11 women), 7 part-time/adjunct (5 women). *Students:* 61 full-time (59 women), 143 part-time (113 women); includes 20 minority (5 Black or African American, non-Hispanic/Latino; 3 Asian, non-Hispanic/Latino; 11 Hispanic/Latino; 1 Two or more races, non-Hispanic/Latino), 1 international. Average age 39. 139 applicants, 59% accepted, 50 enrolled. In 2010, 5 master's awarded. *Degree requirements:* For master's, comprehensive exam (for some programs), thesis (for some programs). *Entrance requirements:* For master's, GRE, MAT, or NTE/PRAXIS, 3 letters of recommendation. Additional exam requirements/recommendations for international students: Required—TOEFL (minimum score 550 paper-based; 213 computer-based). *Application deadline:* For fall admission, 8/1 priority date for domestic students, 4/1 for international students; for spring admission, 1/1 priority date for domestic students, 7/1 for international students. Applications are processed on a rolling basis. Application fee: $40. Electronic applications accepted. *Expenses:* Tuition: Full-time $12,510; part-time $695 per credit. Required fees: $416 per year. Tuition and fees vary according to campus/location and program. *Financial support:* Scholarships/grants, health care benefits, and unspecified assistantships available. Financial award application deadline: 4/15; financial award applicants required to submit FAFSA. *Unit head:* Dr. Linda James, Dean, 732-987-2617, Fax: 732-987-2007. *Application contact:* Patrick Givens, Assistant Director of Admissions, 732-987-2736, Fax: 732-987-2084, E-mail: graduateadmissions@georgian.edu.

Georgia State University, College of Education, Department of Counseling and Psychological Services, Program in Professional Counseling, Atlanta, GA 30302-3083. Offers counseling psychology (PhD); counselor education and practice (PhD); professional counseling (MS, Ed S). *Accreditation:* ACA (one or more programs are accredited); APA (one or more programs are accredited). *Degree requirements:* For master's, comprehensive exam; for doctorate, comprehensive exam, thesis/dissertation. *Entrance requirements:* For master's, GRE General Test, minimum GPA of 2.5; for doctorate, GRE General Test, minimum GPA of 3.3; for Ed S, GRE General Test, minimum graduate GPA of 3.25. *Faculty research:* Dropout prevention, school reform, school violence, lifestyle correlates, stress management.

Goddard College, Graduate Division, Master of Arts in Psychology and Counseling Program, Plainfield, VT 05667-9432. Offers organizational development (MA); psychology and counseling (MA); sexual orientation (MA). Part-time programs available. Postbaccalaureate distance learning degree programs offered (minimal on-campus study). *Degree requirements:* For master's, thesis. *Entrance requirements:* For master's, recent undergraduate degree in psychology or closely related field (preparatory semester at Goddard can substitute), 3 letters of recommendation, interview. Electronic applications accepted.

Gonzaga University, School of Education, Program in Counseling Psychology, Spokane, WA 99258. Offers MAC, MAP. *Accreditation:* ACA. *Degree requirements:* For master's, comprehensive exam. *Entrance requirements:* For master's, GRE General Test or MAT, minimum B average in undergraduate course work. Additional exam requirements/recommendations for international students: Required—TOEFL.

Governors State University, College of Education, Program in Counseling, University Park, IL 60466-0975. Offers MA. *Accreditation:* ACA. Part-time and evening/weekend programs available. *Degree requirements:* For master's, practicum. *Entrance requirements:* For master's, minimum GPA of 2.5 in last 60 hours of course work or minimum GPA of 2.25 and GRE General Test. *Expenses:* Tuition, state resident: full-time $5400; part-time $225 per credit hour. Tuition, nonresident: full-time $16,200; part-time $675 per credit hour. Required fees: $1358; $46 per credit hour. $126 per term. Tuition and fees vary according to degree level and program.

Grace College, Graduate School in Counseling and Interpersonal Relations, Program in Counseling, Winona Lake, IN 46590-1294. Offers counseling (MA); interpersonal relations (MA). *Accreditation:* ACA. Part-time and evening/weekend programs available. *Degree requirements:* For master's, comprehensive exam, portfolio. *Entrance requirements:* For master's, GRE (counseling). Additional exam requirements/recommendations for international students: Required—TOEFL. Electronic applications accepted.

Grace University, College of Graduate Studies, Counseling Program, Omaha, NE 68108. Offers MA. *Entrance requirements:* For master's, minimum undergraduate GPA of 3.0.

Grand Canyon University, College of Nursing and Health Sciences, Phoenix, AZ 85017-1097. Offers addiction counseling (MS); health care administration (MS); health care informatics (MS); marriage and family therapy (MS); professional counseling (MS); public health (MS). Part-time and evening/weekend programs available. Postbaccalaureate distance learning degree programs offered (no on-campus study). *Faculty:* 2 full-time (1 woman), 54 part-time/adjunct (36 women). *Students:* 2 full-time (both women), 1,818 part-time (1,476 women); includes 414 minority (346 Black or African American, non-Hispanic/Latino; 14 American Indian or Alaska Native, non-Hispanic/Latino; 4 Asian, non-Hispanic/Latino; 29 Hispanic/Latino; 3 Native Hawaiian or other Pacific Islander, non-Hispanic/Latino; 18 Two or more races, non-Hispanic/Latino), 1 international. Average age 44. In 2010, 103 master's awarded. *Entrance requirements:* For master's, undergraduate degree with minimum GPA of 2.8. Additional exam requirements/recommendations for international students: Required—TOEFL (minimum score 575 paper-based; 233 computer-based; 90 iBT), IELTS (minimum score 7). *Application deadline:* For fall admission, 8/21 for domestic students, 7/2 for international students; for spring admission, 12/24 for domestic students, 11/1 for international students. Application fee: $0. *Financial support:* Federal Work-Study available. Support available to part-time students. Financial award applicants required to submit FAFSA. *Unit head:* Dr. Mark Wooden, Dean, 602-639-6815, E-mail: mark.wooden@gcu.edu. *Application contact:* Andrea Wolochuk, Information Contact, 602-639-6429, E-mail: awolochuk@gcu.edu.

Harding University, College of Bible and Religion, Program in Marriage and Family Therapy, Searcy, AR 72149-0001. Offers marriage and family therapy (MS); mental health counseling (MS). Part-time programs available. *Faculty:* 4 full-time (0 women), 4 part-time/adjunct (1 woman). *Students:* 29 full-time (19 women), 3 part-time (all women); includes 2 Black or African American, non-Hispanic/Latino; 1 Hispanic/Latino. Average age 27. 27 applicants, 70% accepted, 19 enrolled. In 2010, 13 master's awarded. *Degree requirements:* For master's, comprehensive exam, 15-month practicum. *Entrance requirements:* For master's, GRE General Test, minimum undergraduate GPA of 2.75, graduate 3.0. *Application deadline:* For fall admission, 4/1 priority date for domestic students. Applications are processed on a rolling basis. Application fee: $40. *Expenses:* Tuition: Full-time $10,098; part-time $561 per credit hour. Required fees: $22.50 per credit hour. *Financial support:* In 2010–11, 6 students received support. Scholarships/grants available. *Faculty research:* Forgiveness, substance abuse, post traumatic stress disorder. *Unit head:* Dr. Lewis L. Moore, Chairman, 501-279-4347, Fax: 501-279-4417, E-mail: lmoore@harding.edu. *Application contact:* Ruth Ann Dawson, Office Manager, 501-279-4347, Fax: 501-279-4417, E-mail: radawson@harding.edu.

Heidelberg University, Program in Counseling, Tiffin, OH 44883-2462. Offers MA. *Accreditation:* ACA. Part-time and evening/weekend programs available. *Degree requirements:* For master's, thesis or alternative, counseling practicum, internship. *Entrance requirements:* For master's, GRE General Test, 12 hours course work in behavioral sciences, minimum GPA of 2.9, 3 letters of reference. Additional exam requirements/recommendations for international students: Required—TOEFL. *Expenses:* Tuition: Full-time $8910; part-time $495 per credit hour.

Henderson State University, Graduate Studies, School of Education, Department of Counselor Education, Arkadelphia, AR 71999-0001. Offers clinical mental health counseling (MSE); elementary school counseling (MSE); secondary school counseling (MSE). *Accreditation:* ACA; NCATE. Part-time programs available. *Entrance requirements:* For master's, GRE General Test or MAT, letters of recommendation, minimum GPA of 2.7, teacher certification. Additional exam requirements/recommendations for international students: Required—TOEFL (minimum score 550 paper-based; 213 computer-based); Recommended—IELTS (minimum score 6). Electronic applications accepted. *Expenses:* Tuition, state resident: full-time $3978; part-time $221 per credit hour. Tuition, nonresident: full-time $7956; part-time $442 per credit hour. Tuition and fees vary according to course load.

Hodges University, Graduate Programs, Naples, FL 34119. Offers business administration (MBA); computer information technology (MS); criminal justice (MCJ); education (MPS); information systems management (MIS); interdisciplinary (MPS); legal studies (MS); management (MSM); mental health counseling (MS); psychology (MPS); public administration (MPA). Part-time and evening/weekend programs available. Postbaccalaureate distance learning degree programs offered (no on-campus study). *Faculty:* 25 full-time (9 women), 5 part-time/adjunct (4 women). *Students:* 27 full-time (15 women), 228 part-time (146 women); includes 76 minority (35 Black or African American, non-Hispanic/Latino; 5 Asian, non-Hispanic/Latino; 36 Hispanic/Latino). Average age 36. 92 applicants, 91% accepted, 81 enrolled. In 2010, 92 master's awarded. *Degree requirements:* For master's, comprehensive exam (for some programs), thesis (for some programs). *Entrance requirements:* For master's, in-house entrance exam. *Application deadline:* Applications are processed on a rolling basis. Application fee: $50. Electronic applications accepted. *Expenses:* Tuition: Full-time $16,605; part-time $615 per credit hour. Required fees: $190 per trimester. *Financial support:* In 2010–11, 200 students received support. Federal Work-Study and scholarships/grants available. Financial award application deadline: 7/9; financial award applicants required to submit FAFSA. *Unit head:* Terry McMahan, President, 239-513-1122, Fax: 239-598-6253, E-mail: tmcmahan@hodges.edu. *Application contact:* Rita Lampus, Vice President of Student Enrollment Management, 239-513-1122, Fax: 239-598-6253, E-mail: rlampus@hodges.edu.

Hofstra University, School of Education, Health, and Human Services, Programs in Counseling, Hempstead, NY 11549. Offers counseling (MS Ed, PD); creative arts therapy (MA); gerontology (MS, Advanced Certificate); marriage and family therapy (MA); mental health counseling (MA); rehabilitation counseling (MS Ed, CAS, PD); rehabilitation counseling in mental health (MS Ed, CAS); school counselor-bilingual extension (Advanced Certificate). Part-time and evening/weekend programs available. *Students:* 145 full-time (132 women), 80 part-time (74 women); includes 41 minority (23 Black or African American, non-Hispanic/Latino; 5 Asian, non-Hispanic/Latino; 11 Hispanic/Latino; 1 Native Hawaiian or other Pacific Islander, non-Hispanic/Latino; 1 Two or more races, non-Hispanic/Latino), 8 international. Average age 30. 187 applicants, 63% accepted, 67 enrolled. In 2010, 79 master's, 1 other advanced degree awarded. *Degree requirements:* For master's, comprehensive exam (for some programs), thesis (for some programs), internship, practicum, student teaching, seminars. *Entrance requirements:* For master's, GRE, interview, letters of recommendation, portfolio, essay, professional experience, certification; for other advanced degree, GRE, interview, letters of recommendation, essay, professional experience, resume, master's degree. Additional exam requirements/recommendations for international students: Required—TOEFL (minimum score 550 paper-based; 213 computer-based; 80 iBT). *Application deadline:* Applications are processed on a rolling basis. Application fee: $70 ($75 for international students). Electronic applications accepted. *Expenses:* Tuition: Full-time $18,000; part-time $1000 per credit hour. Required fees: $970; $145 per term. Tuition and fees vary according to program. *Financial support:* In 2010–11, 102 students received support, including 27 fellowships with full and partial tuition reimbursements available (averaging $2,466 per year), 4 research assistantships with full and partial tuition reimbursements available (averaging $14,567 per year); career-related internships or fieldwork, Federal Work-Study, institutionally sponsored loans, scholarships/grants, tuition waivers (full and partial), unspecified assistantships, and scholarships also available. Support available to part-time students. Financial award applicants required to submit FAFSA. *Faculty research:* Bereavement, loss, and trauma counseling, creativity for non-artists. *Unit head:* Dr. Darra Pace, Chairperson, 516-463-6476, Fax: 516-463-6415, E-mail: cprdzp@hofstra.edu. *Application contact:* Carol Drummer, Dean of Graduate Admissions, 516-463-4876, Fax: 516-463-4664, E-mail: gradstudent@hofstra.edu.

Holy Family University, Graduate School, School of Arts and Sciences, Program in Counseling Psychology, Philadelphia, PA 19114. Offers MS. Part-time and evening/weekend programs available. *Students:* 5 full-time (3 women), 152 part-time (64 women); includes 6 Black or African American, non-Hispanic/Latino; 1 Asian, non-Hispanic/Latino; 2 Hispanic/Latino. Average age 28. 71 applicants, 83% accepted, 30 enrolled. In 2010, 18 master's awarded. *Entrance requirements:* For master's, baccalaureate degree from accredited college or university; minimum undergraduate cumulative GPA of 3.0; 2 letters of recommendation; personal statement; official transcripts; interview. *Application deadline:* For fall admission, 8/1 for domestic students; for winter admission, 1/1 for domestic students. Applications are processed on a rolling basis. Application fee: $25. Electronic applications accepted. *Expenses:* Tuition: Full-time $14,400; part-time $600 per credit hour. Required fees: $85 per term. *Financial support:* Application deadline: 5/1. *Unit head:* Dr. George Colton, Director, 267-341-4035. *Application contact:* Gidget Marie Montelibans, Graduate Admissions Counselor, 267-341-3558, Fax: 215-637-1478, E-mail: gmontelibano@holyfamily.edu.

See Display on next page and Close-Up on page 1165.

Holy Names University, Graduate Division, Department of Counseling Psychology, Oakland, CA 94619-1699. Offers counseling psychology (MA); forensic psychology (MA, Certificate); pastoral counseling (MA, Certificate). Part-time and evening/weekend programs available. *Faculty:* 1 (woman) full-time, 9 part-time/adjunct (5 women). *Students:* 49 full-time (39 women), 25 part-time (24 women); includes 30 Black or African American, non-Hispanic/Latino; 4 Asian, non-Hispanic/Latino; 13 Hispanic/Latino, 1 international. Average age 32. 22 applicants, 68% accepted, 11 enrolled. In 2010, 13 master's awarded. *Degree requirements:* For master's, comprehensive paper, seminars. *Entrance requirements:* For master's, minimum undergraduate GPA of 2.6 overall, 3.0 in major. Additional exam requirements/recommendations for international students: Required—TOEFL (minimum score 550 paper-based; 213 computer-based; 80 iBT). *Application deadline:* For fall admission, 8/1 priority date for domestic students, 8/1 for international students; for spring admission, 12/1 priority date for domestic students, 12/1 for international students. Applications are processed on a rolling basis. Application fee: $0. *Expenses:* Tuition: Full-time $13,788; part-time $766 per credit. Required fees: $340; $170 per semester. *Financial support:* In 2010–11, 38 students received support. Available to part-time students. Application deadline: 3/2. *Faculty research:* Cognitive psychology, anger management, grief and grief counseling, post-modernism and psychotherapy, spirituality and psychology. *Unit head:* Dr. Helen Shoemaker, Program Director, 510-436-1543, E-mail: shoemaker@hnu.edu. *Application contact:* 800-430-1321, Fax: 510-436-1325, E-mail: adulted@hnu.edu.

Houston Baptist University, College of Education and Behavioral Sciences, Program in Christian Counseling, Houston, TX 77074-3298. Offers MACC. *Degree requirements:* For master's, comprehensive exam. *Entrance requirements:* For master's, GRE General Test, minimum GPA of 3.0. Additional exam requirements/recommendations for international students: Required—TOEFL (minimum score 550 paper-based; 213 computer-based).

Howard University, School of Education, Department of Human Development and Psychoeducational Studies, Program in Counseling Psychology, Washington, DC 20059-0002. Offers M Ed, PhD. *Accreditation:* APA. Part-time programs available. *Faculty:* 4 full-time (2 women), 1 (woman) part-time/adjunct. *Students:* 33 full-time (26 women), 10 part-time (8 women); includes 39 Black or African American, non-Hispanic/Latino; 1 Asian, non-Hispanic/Latino, 3 international. Average age 28. 44 applicants, 34% accepted, 9 enrolled. In 2010, 6 master's awarded. *Degree requirements:* For master's, comprehensive exam, thesis (for some programs), expository writing exam; for doctorate, one foreign language, comprehensive exam, thesis/dissertation, expository writing exam, internship. *Entrance requirements:* For master's, minimum GPA of 2.7; for doctorate, GRE General Test, minimum GPA of 3.4. Additional exam requirements/recommendations for international students: Required—TOEFL (minimum score 550 paper-based). *Application deadline:* For fall admission, 12/15 priority date for domestic students; for spring admission, 11/1 for domestic students. Application fee: $45. Electronic applications accepted. *Financial support:* In 2010–11, 9 students received support, including 1 fellowship with full and partial tuition reimbursement available (averaging $10,000 per year), 8 research assistantships with full and partial tuition reimbursements available (averaging $7,762 per year); career-related internships or fieldwork, institutionally sponsored loans, scholarships/grants, and unspecified assistantships also available. Financial award application deadline: 12/15; financial award applicants required to submit FAFSA. *Faculty research:* Cultural issues in counseling and psychotherapy, counseling theory construction, self-actualization black psychology. *Unit head:* Dr. Kamilah Woodson, Assistant Professor/Coordinator, Doctoral Program, 202-805-0611, Fax: 202-806-5205, E-mail: kwoodson@howard.edu. *Application contact:* Frazier Tate-Jackson, Administrative Assistant, Department of Human Development and Psychoeducational Studies, 202-806-7350, Fax: 202-806-5205, E-mail: fjackson@howard.edu.

Humboldt State University, Academic Programs, College of Professional Studies, Department of Psychology, Arcata, CA 95521-8299. Offers psychology (MA), including academic research, counseling, school psychology. *Students:* 45 full-time (31 women), 12 part-time (8 women); includes 12 minority (2 Asian, non-Hispanic/Latino; 7 Hispanic/Latino; 3 Two or more races, non-Hispanic/Latino). Average age 28. 35 applicants, 86% accepted, 9 enrolled. In 2010, 24 master's awarded. *Degree requirements:* For master's, thesis. *Entrance requirements:* For master's, appropriate bachelor's degree, minimum GPA of 2.5. Additional exam requirements/recommendations for international students: Required—TOEFL (minimum score 500 paper-based; 173 computer-based). *Application deadline:* For fall admission, 2/1 for domestic students, 2/15 for international students. Applications are processed on a rolling basis. Application fee: $55. Tuition and fees vary according to program. *Financial support:* Career-related internships or fieldwork available. Financial award application deadline: 3/1; financial award applicants required to submit FAFSA. *Faculty research:* School psychology, counseling, eating disorders, mood induction, depression. *Unit head:* Dr. Gregg Gold, Chair, 707-826-3740, Fax: 707-826-4993, E-mail: gjg14@humboldt.edu. *Application contact:* Dr. Chris Aberson, Coordinator, 707-826-3670, Fax: 707-826-4993, E-mail: cla18@humboldt.edu.

Husson University, School of Graduate and Professional Studies, Program in Counseling Psychology, Bangor, ME 04401-2999. Offers MS.

Idaho State University, Office of Graduate Studies, Kasiska College of Health Professions, Department of Counseling, Pocatello, ID 83209-8120. Offers counseling (M Coun, Ed S),

including marriage and family counseling (M Coun), mental health counseling (M Coun), school counseling (M Coun), student affairs and college counseling (M Coun); counselor education and counseling (PhD). *Accreditation:* ACA (one or more programs are accredited). Part-time programs available. *Degree requirements:* For master's, comprehensive exam, thesis, 4 semesters resident graduate study, practicum/internship; for doctorate, comprehensive exam, thesis/dissertation, 3 semesters internship, 4 consecutive semesters doctoral-level study on campus; for Ed S, comprehensive exam, thesis, case studies, oral exam. *Entrance requirements:* For master's, GRE General Test, MAT, minimum GPA of 3.0, bachelors degree, interview, 3 letters of recommendation; for doctorate, GRE General Test, MAT, minimum graduate GPA of 3.0, resume, interview, counseling license, master's degree; for Ed S, GRE General Test, minimum graduate GPA of 3.0, master's degree in counseling, 3 letters of recommendation, 2 years work experience. Additional exam requirements/recommendations for international students: Required—TOEFL (minimum score 600 paper-based; 213 computer-based; 80 iBT). Electronic applications accepted. *Faculty research:* Group counseling, multicultural counseling, family counseling, child therapy, supervision.

Illinois State University, Graduate School, College of Arts and Sciences, Department of Psychology, Normal, IL 61790-2200. Offers psychology (MA, MS), including clinical psychology, counseling psychology, developmental psychology, educational psychology, experimental psychology, measurement-evaluation, organizational-industrial psychology; school psychology (PhD, SSP). *Accreditation:* APA. *Degree requirements:* For master's, thesis or alternative; for doctorate, variable foreign language requirement, thesis/dissertation, 2 terms of residency, internship, practicum. *Entrance requirements:* For master's, GRE General Test, GRE Subject Test, minimum GPA of 3.0 in last 60 hours of course work; for doctorate, GRE General Test. *Faculty research:* Comprehensive evaluation system for the central region professional development grant, Illinois school psychology internship consortium, for children's sake.

Immaculata University, College of Graduate Studies, Department of Psychology, Immaculata, PA 19345. Offers clinical psychology (Psy D); counseling psychology (MA, Certificate), including school guidance counselor (Certificate), school psychologist (Certificate). *Accreditation:* APA. Part-time and evening/weekend programs available. *Students:* 123 full-time (100 women), 201 part-time (159 women). Average age 34. 83 applicants, 76% accepted, 55 enrolled. In 2010, 37 master's, 13 doctorates awarded. Terminal master's awarded for partial completion of doctoral program. *Degree requirements:* For master's, comprehensive exam, thesis optional; for doctorate, comprehensive exam, thesis/dissertation. *Entrance requirements:* For master's, GRE General Test or MAT, minimum GPA of 3.0; for doctorate, GRE General Test or MAT, minimum GPA of 3.5. Additional exam requirements/recommendations for international students: Required—TOEFL, IELTS. *Application deadline:* Applications are processed on a rolling basis. Application fee: $50. Electronic applications accepted. *Financial support:* Application deadline: 5/1. *Faculty research:* Supervision ethics, psychology of teaching, gender. *Unit head:* Dr. Jed A. Yalof, Chair, 610-647-4400 Ext. 3503, Fax: 610-993-8550, E-mail: jyalof@immaculata.edu. *Application contact:* Office of Graduate Admission, 610-647-4400 Ext. 3211, Fax: 610-993-8550, E-mail: graduate@immaculata.edu.

Indiana State University, College of Graduate and Professional Studies, College of Education, Department of Communication Disorders, Counseling and School and Educational Psychology, Terre Haute, IN 47809. Offers counseling psychology (MS, PhD); counselor education (PhD); mental health counseling (MS); school counseling (M Ed); school psychology (PhD, Ed S); MA/MS. *Accreditation:* ACA; NCATE. Part-time and evening/weekend programs available. *Degree requirements:* For master's, thesis optional; for doctorate, thesis/dissertation, research tools proficiency tests. *Entrance requirements:* For master's, GRE General Test or MAT, minimum undergraduate GPA of 2.75; for doctorate, GRE General Test, master's degree, minimum undergraduate GPA of 3.5. Electronic applications accepted. *Faculty research:* Vocational development supervision.

Indiana Wesleyan University, Graduate School, College of Arts and Sciences, Marion, IN 46953. Offers addictions counseling (MS); clinical mental health counseling (MS); community counseling (MS); marriage and family therapy (MS); school counseling (MS); student

Counseling Psychology

Indiana Wesleyan University (continued)
development counseling and administration (MS). *Accreditation:* ACA. Part-time programs available. *Degree requirements:* For master's, thesis or alternative. *Entrance requirements:* For master's, GRE General Test. Additional exam requirements/recommendations for international students: Required—TOEFL. Electronic applications accepted. *Expenses:* Contact institution. *Faculty research:* Community counseling, multicultural counseling, addictions.

Institute of Transpersonal Psychology, Low-Residency Programs, Palo Alto, CA 94303. Offers counseling psychology (online) (MA); spiritual guidance (MA); women's spirituality (MA). Postbaccalaureate distance learning degree programs offered (minimal on-campus study).

Institute of Transpersonal Psychology, Residential Programs, Palo Alto, CA 94303. Offers counseling psychology (MA); spiritually oriented clinical psychology (Psy D); transpersonal psychology (MA, PhD). Part-time and evening/weekend programs available. Terminal master's awarded for partial completion of doctoral program. *Degree requirements:* For doctorate, thesis/dissertation. *Entrance requirements:* For master's and doctorate, bachelor's degree.

Instituto Tecnologico de Santo Domingo, Graduate School, Area of Humanities and Social Sciences, Santo Domingo, Dominican Republic. Offers accounting (Certificate); adult education (Certificate); applied linguistics (MA); economics (MA); education (M Ed); educational psychology (MA, Certificate); gender and development (MA, Certificate); humanistic studies (MA); international marketing management (Certificate); international relations in the Caribbean basin (Certificate); intervention systems in family therapy (MA); linguistic and literary communication (Certificate); pedagogical support (MA); social science education (M Ed); sustainable human development (MA); terminal illness and death psychology (Certificate); youth and adult education (M Ed).

Inter American University of Puerto Rico, Aguadilla Campus, Graduate School, Aguadilla, PR 00605. Offers accounting (MBA); counseling psychology specializing in family (MS); criminal justice (MA); educative management and leadership (MA); elementary education (M Ed); finance (MBA); human resources (MBA); industrial management (MBA); management information systems (MBA); marketing (MBA). Part-time and evening/weekend programs available. *Degree requirements:* For master's, comprehensive exam. *Entrance requirements:* For master's, EXADEP, 2 letters of recommendation, minimum GPA of 2.5. Electronic applications accepted.

Inter American University of Puerto Rico, Metropolitan Campus, Graduate Programs, Program in Psychology, San Juan, PR 00919-1293. Offers counseling psychology (MA, PhD); industrial/organizational psychology (MA, PhD); labor relations (MA); school psychology (MA, PhD). *Degree requirements:* For master's, comprehensive exam. *Entrance requirements:* For master's, GRE or EXADEP, interview. Electronic applications accepted.

Inter American University of Puerto Rico, San Germán Campus, Graduate Studies Center, Program in Psychology, San Germán, PR 00683-5008. Offers counseling psychology (MA, PhD); school psychology (MA, PhD). Part-time and evening/weekend programs available. *Degree requirements:* For master's, comprehensive exam, thesis; for doctorate, comprehensive exam, thesis/dissertation. *Entrance requirements:* For master's, GRE General Test or EXADEP, minimum GPA of 3.0; for doctorate, GRE, EXADEP or MAT, minimum GPA of 3.0. *Expenses:* Tuition: Part-time $202 per credit. Required fees: $258 per semester.

Iona College, School of Arts and Science, Department of Psychology, New Rochelle, NY 10801-1890. Offers experimental psychology (MA); industrial-organizational psychology (MA); mental health counseling (MA); psychology (MA); school psychology (MA). Part-time and evening/weekend programs available. *Faculty:* 10 full-time (7 women), 12 part-time/adjunct (7 women). *Students:* 86 full-time (70 women), 36 part-time (30 women); includes 21 minority (6 Black or African American, non-Hispanic/Latino; 1 American Indian or Alaska Native, non-Hispanic/Latino; 2 Asian, non-Hispanic/Latino; 12 Hispanic/Latino), 2 international. Average age 25. 153 applicants, 78% accepted, 50 enrolled. In 2010, 36 master's awarded. *Degree requirements:* For master's, thesis. *Entrance requirements:* For master's, GRE or minimum GPA of 3.0. Additional exam requirements/recommendations for international students: Required—TOEFL (minimum score 550 paper-based; 213 computer-based). *Application deadline:* Applications are processed on a rolling basis. Application fee: $50. Electronic applications accepted. *Expenses:* Tuition: Part-time $830 per credit. Required fees: $225 per credit. *Financial support:* Career-related internships or fieldwork, tuition waivers (partial), and unspecified assistantships available. Support available to part-time students. Financial award application deadline: 4/15; financial award applicants required to submit FAFSA. *Unit head:* Dr. Paul Greene, Chair, 914-633-2048, E-mail: pgreene@iona.edu. *Application contact:* Veronica Jarek-Prinz, Director of Graduate Admissions, 914-633-2420, Fax: 914-633-2277, E-mail: vjarekprinz@iona.edu.

Iowa State University of Science and Technology, Graduate College, College of Liberal Arts and Sciences, Department of Psychology, Ames, IA 50011. Offers cognitive psychology (PhD); counseling psychology (PhD); social psychology (PhD). *Accreditation:* APA. *Faculty:* 34 full-time (14 women), 1 part-time/adjunct (0 women). *Students:* 73 full-time (42 women), 27 part-time (18 women); includes 8 Black or African American, non-Hispanic/Latino; 4 Asian, non-Hispanic/Latino; 4 Hispanic/Latino, 17 international. 88 applicants, 13% accepted, 9 enrolled. In 2010, 4 doctorates awarded. *Degree requirements:* For doctorate, comprehensive exam, thesis/dissertation. *Entrance requirements:* For doctorate, GRE General Test, GRE Subject Test (psychology), 3 letters of recommendation. Additional exam requirements/recommendations for international students: Required—TOEFL (minimum score 560 paper-based; 79 iBT), IELTS (minimum score 6.5). *Application deadline:* For fall admission, 1/2 priority date for domestic and international students. Application fee: $30 ($70 for international students). Electronic applications accepted. *Financial support:* In 2010–11, fellowships with full tuition reimbursements (averaging $14,055 per year), 7 research assistantships with full tuition reimbursements (averaging $13,169 per year), 57 teaching assistantships with full tuition reimbursements (averaging $9,432 per year) were awarded; scholarships/grants, health care benefits, and unspecified assistantships also available. *Faculty research:* Counseling psychology, cognitive psychology, social psychology, health psychology, psychology and public policy. *Unit head:* Carolyn Cutrona, Chair, 515-294-0283, Fax: 515-294-6424, E-mail: ccutrona@iastate.edu. *Application contact:* Ann Schmidt, Graduate Admissions Secretary, 515-294-1743, Fax: 515-294-6424, E-mail: psychadm@iastate.edu.

James Madison University, The Graduate School, College of Integrated Science and Technology, Department of Graduate Psychology, Clinical Mental Health Counseling Program, Harrisonburg, VA 22807. Offers M Ed, MA, Ed S. *Accreditation:* ACA (one or more programs are accredited); APA (one or more programs are accredited). Part-time and evening/weekend programs available. *Students:* 65 full-time (48 women), 24 part-time (21 women); includes 9 minority (6 Black or African American, non-Hispanic/Latino; 1 Asian, non-Hispanic/Latino; 2 Hispanic/Latino), 1 international. Average age 27. In 2010, 31 master's, 15 other advanced degrees awarded. *Degree requirements:* For Ed S, comprehensive exam, thesis, internship. *Entrance requirements:* For master's, GRE General Test, 3 reference forms, interview, criminal history check. Additional exam requirements/recommendations for international students: Required—TOEFL. *Application deadline:* For fall admission, 2/1 priority date for domestic students. Applications are processed on a rolling basis. Application fee: $55. Electronic applications accepted. *Financial support:* In 2010–11, 53 students received support, including 1 teaching assistantship with full tuition reimbursement available (averaging $8,664 per year); career-related internships or fieldwork, Federal Work-Study, and 52 graduate assistantships ($7382) also available. Financial award application deadline: 3/1; financial award applicants required to submit FAFSA. *Unit head:* Dr. A. Renee Staton, Program Director, 540-568-7867. *Application contact:* Dr. A. Renee Staton, Program Director, 540-568-7867.

John Carroll University, Graduate School, Program in Community Counseling, University Heights, OH 44118-4581. Offers clinical counseling (Certificate); community counseling (MA). *Accreditation:* ACA. Part-time and evening/weekend programs available. *Degree requirements:* For master's, comprehensive exam, internship, practicum. *Entrance requirements:* For master's, MAT or GRE, minimum GPA of 2.75, statement of volunteer experience, interview, 12-18 hours social science course work, survey. Additional exam requirements/recommendations for international students: Required—TOEFL. Electronic applications accepted. *Faculty research:* Child and adolescent development, HIV, hypnosis, wellness, women's issues.

John F. Kennedy University, Graduate School of Holistic Studies, Department of Counseling Psychology, Program in Counseling Psychology, Pleasant Hill, CA 94523-4817. Offers holistic studies (MA); somatic psychology (MA); transpersonal psychology (MA). Part-time and evening/weekend programs available. *Degree requirements:* For master's, thesis or alternative. *Entrance requirements:* For master's, interview. Additional exam requirements/recommendations for international students: Required—TOEFL.

John F. Kennedy University, Graduate School of Professional Psychology, Program in Counseling Psychology, Pleasant Hill, CA 94523-4817. Offers MA. Part-time and evening/weekend programs available. *Degree requirements:* For master's, thesis or alternative. *Entrance requirements:* For master's, interview. Additional exam requirements/recommendations for international students: Required—TOEFL.

Kean University, College of Education, Program in Counselor Education, Union, NJ 07083. Offers alcohol and drug abuse counseling (MA); clinical mental heath counseling (MA); school counseling (MA). *Accreditation:* ACA; NCATE. Part-time programs available. *Faculty:* 5 full-time (3 women). *Students:* 66 full-time (59 women), 216 part-time (192 women); includes 44 Black or African American, non-Hispanic/Latino; 4 Asian, non-Hispanic/Latino; 44 Hispanic/Latino; 1 Two or more races, non-Hispanic/Latino, 1 international. Average age 32. 152 applicants, 72% accepted, 61 enrolled. In 2010, 48 master's awarded. *Degree requirements:* For master's, comprehensive exam, practicum, internship. *Entrance requirements:* For master's, GRE General Test or MAT, minimum GPA of 3.0, 2 letters of recommendation, interview. *Application deadline:* For fall admission, 6/1 for domestic students; for spring admission, 11/1 for domestic students. Application fee: $75 ($150 for international students). Electronic applications accepted. *Expenses:* Tuition, state resident: full-time $10,872; part-time $500 per credit. Tuition, nonresident: full-time $14,736; part-time $614 per credit. Required fees: $2740.80; $125 per credit. Part-time tuition and fees vary according to course load and degree level. *Financial support:* In 2010–11, 2 research assistantships with full tuition reimbursements (averaging $3,263 per year) were awarded; unspecified assistantships also available. Financial award applicants required to submit FAFSA. *Unit head:* Dr. J. Barry Mascari, Program Coordinator, 908-737-3863, E-mail: jmascari@kean.edu. *Application contact:* Steven Koch, Pre-Admissions Coordinator, 908-737-5924, Fax: 908-737-5925, E-mail: skoch@kean.edu.

Kean University, College of Humanities and Social Sciences, Program in Psychology, Union, NJ 07083. Offers human behavior and organizational psychology (MA); psychological services (MA). Part-time and evening/weekend programs available. *Faculty:* 17 full-time (13 women). *Students:* 24 full-time (20 women), 20 part-time (13 women); includes 12 Black or African American, non-Hispanic/Latino; 5 Asian, non-Hispanic/Latino; 5 Hispanic/Latino; 1 Two or more races, non-Hispanic/Latino, 2 international. Average age 27. 41 applicants, 83% accepted, 26 enrolled. In 2010, 18 master's awarded. *Degree requirements:* For master's, comprehensive exam, thesis, research, two semesters advanced seminar. *Entrance requirements:* For master's, GRE General Test, minimum GPA of 3.0, 2 letters of recommendation, interview, 12 credits in behavioral sciences, transcripts. *Application deadline:* For fall admission, 6/1 for domestic students; for spring admission, 11/1 for domestic students. Application fee: $75 ($150 for international students). Electronic applications accepted. *Expenses:* Tuition, state resident: full-time $10,872; part-time $500 per credit. Tuition, nonresident: full-time $14,736; part-time $614 per credit. Required fees: $2740.80; $125 per credit. Part-time tuition and fees vary according to course load and degree level. *Financial support:* In 2010–11, 2 research assistantships with full tuition reimbursements (averaging $3,263 per year) were awarded; unspecified assistantships also available. Financial award applicants required to submit FAFSA. *Unit head:* Dr. Joanne Walsh, Program Coordinator, 908-737-5888, E-mail: jwalsh@kean.edu. *Application contact:* Reenat Hasan, Pre-Admissions Coordinator, 908-737-5923, Fax: 908-737-5925, E-mail: rhasan@exchange.kean.edu.

Kent State University, Graduate School of Education, Health, and Human Services, School of Lifespan Development and Educational Sciences, Program in Clinical Mental Health Counseling, Kent, OH 44242-0001. Offers M Ed. *Accreditation:* ACA; NCATE. *Faculty:* 9 full-time (4 women), 18 part-time/adjunct (12 women). *Students:* 69 full-time (60 women), 61 part-time (49 women); includes 18 Black or African American, non-Hispanic/Latino; 1 Hispanic/Latino. 72 applicants, 56% accepted. In 2010, 33 master's awarded. *Degree requirements:* For master's, thesis (for some programs). *Entrance requirements:* Additional exam requirements/recommendations for international students: Required—TOEFL. *Application deadline:* For fall admission, 6/1 for domestic students; for spring admission, 10/1 for domestic students. Application fee: $30 ($60 for international students). Electronic applications accepted. *Expenses:* Tuition, state resident: full-time $7866; part-time $437 per credit hour. Tuition, nonresident: full-time $14,022; part-time $779 per credit hour. *Financial support:* In 2010–11, research assistantships with full tuition reimbursements (averaging $8,313 per year); career-related internships or fieldwork, Federal Work-Study, institutionally sponsored loans, scholarships/grants, health care benefits, unspecified assistantships, and 1 administrative assistantship (averaging $8,313 per year) also available. Support available to part-time students. Financial award application deadline: 4/1; financial award applicants required to submit FAFSA. *Faculty research:* Group work, personality assessment, family/child therapy, substance abuse counseling, clinical supervision. *Unit head:* Dr. Jason McGlothlin, Coordinator, 330-672-0716, E-mail: jmcgloth@kent.edu. *Application contact:* Nancy Miller, Academic Program Coordinator, Office of Graduate Student Services, 330-672-2576, Fax: 330-672-9162, E-mail: ogs@kent.edu.

Kutztown University of Pennsylvania, College of Education, Program in Counseling Psychology, Kutztown, PA 19530-0730. Offers agency counseling (MA); marital and family therapy (MA). Part-time and evening/weekend programs available. *Faculty:* 8 full-time (3 women). *Students:* 28 full-time (25 women), 26 part-time (23 women); includes 5 minority (3 Black or African American, non-Hispanic/Latino; 2 American Indian or Alaska Native, non-Hispanic/Latino). Average age 27. 36 applicants, 47% accepted, 11 enrolled. In 2010, 10 master's awarded. *Degree requirements:* For master's, comprehensive exam, thesis optional. *Entrance requirements:* For master's, GRE General Test, interview. Additional exam requirements/recommendations for international students: Required—TOEFL (minimum score 550 paper-based; 79 iBT). *Application deadline:* For fall admission, 2/1 for domestic and international students; for spring admission, 8/1 for domestic and international students. Application fee: $35. Electronic applications accepted. *Expenses:* Tuition, state resident: full-time $6966; part-time $387 per credit. Tuition, nonresident: full-time $11,146; part-time $619 per credit hour. Required fees: $1499; $54 per credit. $68 per year. *Financial support:* Career-related internships or fieldwork, Federal Work-Study, scholarships/grants, and unspecified assistantships available. Financial award application deadline: 3/1; financial award applicants required to submit FAFSA. *Faculty research:* Family addictions. *Unit head:* Dr. Deborah Barlieb, Chairperson, 610-683-4204, Fax: 610-683-1585, E-mail: barlieb@kutztown.edu. *Application contact:* Kelly D. Burr, Associate Director, Graduate Admissions, 610-683-4200, Fax: 610-683-1393, E-mail: graduate@kutztown.edu.

Lancaster Bible College, Graduate School, Lancaster, PA 17601-5036. Offers adult ministries (MA); Bible (MA); children and family ministry (MA); consulting resource teacher (M Ed); elementary school counseling (M Ed); leadership (PhD); leadership studies (MA); marriage and family counseling (MA); mental health counseling (MA); pastoral studies (MA); secondary school counseling (M Ed); student ministry (MA). Part-time and evening/weekend programs available. *Faculty:* 8 full-time (1 woman), 5 part-time/adjunct (1 woman). *Students:* 94 full-time (47 women), 89 part-time (45 women); includes 21 minority (15 Black or African American, non-Hispanic/Latino; 5 Asian, non-Hispanic/Latino; 1 Hispanic/Latino). Average age 36. *Degree requirements:* For master's, comprehensive exam (for some programs), thesis (for some programs). *Entrance requirements:* For master's, bachelor's degree with a minimum of 30 credits of course work in Bible, minimum undergraduate GPA of 3.0, interview. Additional exam requirements/recommendations for international students: Required—TOEFL. *Application deadline:* Applications are processed on a rolling basis. Application fee: $25. *Expenses:* Tuition: Part-time $1491 per course. Required fees: $35 per semester. *Financial support:* In 2010–11, 31 students received support; teaching assistantships, scholarships/grants and unspecified assistantships available. Support available to part-time students. Financial award application deadline: 6/1; financial award applicants required to submit FAFSA. *Unit head:* Dr. Gary Bredfeldt, Associate Vice President/Dean of iLead Center, 717-560-8297, Fax: 717-560-8236. *Application contact:* Mark Wilson, Admissions Counselor, 717-560-8229, E-mail: mwilson@lbc.edu.

La Salle University, School of Arts and Sciences, Program in Clinical-Counseling Psychology, Philadelphia, PA 19141-1199. Offers MA. *Accreditation:* APA. Part-time and evening/weekend programs available. *Degree requirements:* For master's, comprehensive exam. *Entrance requirements:* For master's, GRE or MAT, 15 undergraduate credits in psychology. *Expenses:* Contact institution. *Faculty research:* Cognitive therapy, attribution theory, work habits, single parent families, treatment of addictions.

Lee University, Graduate Studies in Counseling, Cleveland, TN 37320-3450. Offers college student development (MS); holistic child development (MS); marriage and family therapy (MS); school counseling (MS). Part-time programs available. *Faculty:* 7 full-time (3 women), 6 part-time/adjunct (2 women). *Students:* 74 full-time (64 women), 36 part-time (30 women); includes 2 Black or African American, non-Hispanic/Latino; 2 American Indian or Alaska Native, non-Hispanic/Latino; 1 Asian, non-Hispanic/Latino; 2 Hispanic/Latino; 1 Native Hawaiian or other Pacific Islander, non-Hispanic/Latino, 4 international. Average age 27. 53 applicants, 91% accepted, 34 enrolled. In 2010, 19 master's awarded. *Degree requirements:* For master's, variable foreign language requirement, comprehensive exam, thesis, internship. *Entrance requirements:* For master's, GRE General Test or MAT, minimum undergraduate GPA of 3.0, 3 letters of recommendation, interview. Additional exam requirements/recommendations for international students: Required—TOEFL (minimum score 450 paper-based; 45 computer-based). *Application deadline:* For fall admission, 4/1 priority date for domestic and international students; for spring admission, 10/1 priority date for domestic and international students. Applications are processed on a rolling basis. Application fee: $25. *Expenses:* Tuition: Full-time $12,120; part-time $506 per credit hour. Required fees: $560; $305 per semester. Part-time tuition and fees vary according to course load and campus/location. *Financial support:* Teaching assistantships, career-related internships or fieldwork, Federal Work-Study, institutionally sponsored loans, scholarships/grants, and unspecified assistantships available. Financial award application deadline: 3/1; financial award applicants required to submit FAFSA. *Unit head:* Dr. Trevor Milliron, Director, 423-614-8126, Fax: 423-614-8129, E-mail: tmilliron@leeuniversity.edu. *Application contact:* Vicki Glasscock, Graduate Admissions Director, 423-614-8059, E-mail: vglasscock@leeuniversity.edu.

Lehigh University, College of Education, Program in Counseling Psychology, Bethlehem, PA 18015. Offers counseling and human services (M Ed); counseling psychology (PhD); elementary counseling with certification (M Ed); international counseling (Certificate); international counseling with certification (M Ed); secondary school counseling (M Ed). *Accreditation:* APA (one or more programs are accredited). Part-time and evening/weekend programs available. Postbaccalaureate distance learning degree programs offered (minimal on-campus study). *Faculty:* 5 full-time (4 women), 6 part-time/adjunct (4 women). *Students:* 51 full-time (44 women), 34 part-time (29 women); includes 9 minority (7 Black or African American, non-Hispanic/Latino; 2 Hispanic/Latino), 4 international. Average age 29. 204 applicants, 29% accepted, 25 enrolled. In 2010, 24 master's, 3 doctorates awarded. *Degree requirements:* For doctorate, comprehensive exam, thesis/dissertation. *Entrance requirements:* For master's, minimum GPA of 3.0, 2 letters of recommendation, essay, transcript; for doctorate, GRE General Test (Verbal and Quantitative), 2 letters of recommendation, transcript, essay; for Certificate, minimum GPA of 3.0. Additional exam requirements/recommendations for international students: Required—TOEFL (minimum score 600 paper-based; 250 computer-based; 93 iBT). *Application deadline:* For fall admission, 3/1 for domestic students, 11/15 for international students; for winter admission, 2/1 for international students. Application fee: $65. Electronic applications accepted. *Financial support:* In 2010–11, 21 students received support, including 1 research assistantship with full and partial tuition reimbursement available (averaging $16,000 per year); fellowships with full and partial tuition reimbursements available, career-related internships or fieldwork, Federal Work-Study, institutionally sponsored loans, scholarships/grants, and tuition waivers (full and partial) also available. Financial award application deadline: 2/15; financial award applicants required to submit FAFSA. *Faculty research:* Supervision, violence prevention, multicultural training and counseling, career development and health interventions, intersection of identities. *Unit head:* Dr. Arpana Inman, Coordinator, 610-758-4443, Fax: 610-758-3227, E-mail: agi2@lehigh.edu. *Application contact:* Donna M. Johnson, Coordinator, 610-758-3231, Fax: 610-758-6223, E-mail: dmj4@lehigh.edu.

Lesley University, Graduate School of Arts and Social Sciences, Program in Counseling Psychology, Cambridge, MA 02138-2790. Offers professional counseling (MA); school counseling (MA). Part-time and evening/weekend programs available. Postbaccalaureate distance learning degree programs offered (no on-campus study). Terminal master's awarded for partial completion of doctoral program. *Degree requirements:* For master's, internship, practicum. *Entrance requirements:* For master's, MAT. Additional exam requirements/recommendations for international students: Required—TOEFL (minimum score 550 paper-based; 213 computer-based; 80 iBT).

Lewis & Clark College, Graduate School of Education and Counseling, Department of Counseling Psychology, Portland, OR 97219-7899. Offers addictions treatment (MA, MS); community counseling (MA, MS), including professional mental health counseling; marriage, couple and family therapy (MA, MS); psychological and cultural studies (MA, MS); school psychology (Ed S). *Accreditation:* AAMFT/COAMFTE; ACA. Part-time and evening/weekend programs available. *Faculty:* 10 full-time (6 women), 29 part-time/adjunct (19 women). *Students:* 182 full-time (148 women), 65 part-time (55 women); includes 2 Black or African American, non-Hispanic/Latino; 6 Asian, non-Hispanic/Latino; 10 Hispanic/Latino; 13 Two or more races, non-Hispanic/Latino, 4 international. Average age 31. 231 applicants, 62% accepted, 69 enrolled. In 2010, 60 master's awarded. *Degree requirements:* For master's, thesis proposal (MS). *Entrance requirements:* For master's, GRE General Test, minimum undergraduate GPA of 2.75. Additional exam requirements/recommendations for international students: Required—TOEFL (minimum score 575 paper-based; 233 computer-based). *Application deadline:* For fall admission, 2/1 priority date for domestic and international students; for spring admission, 10/1 priority date for domestic and international students. Application fee: $50. Electronic applications accepted. *Expenses:* Tuition: Part-time $713 per semester hour. Tuition and fees vary according to course level and campus/location. *Financial support:* In 2010–11, 33 students received support. Career-related internships or fieldwork, Federal Work-Study, institutionally sponsored loans, scholarships/grants, health care benefits, and tuition waivers (partial) available. Support available to part-time students. Financial award application deadline: 3/1; financial award applicants required to submit FAFSA. *Unit head:* Dr. Teresa McDowell, Chair, 503-768-6060, Fax: 503-768-6065, E-mail: cpsy@lclark.edu. *Application contact:* Becky Haas, Director of Admissions, 503-768-6200, Fax: 503-768-6205, E-mail: gseadmit@lclark.edu.

Lewis University, College of Arts and Sciences, Program in Counseling Psychology, Romeoville, IL 60446. Offers child and adolescent counseling (MA); mental health counseling (MA). Part-time and evening/weekend programs available. *Faculty:* 9 full-time (6 women), 5 part-time/adjunct (2 women). *Students:* 38 full-time (34 women), 78 part-time (69 women); includes 13 Black or African American, non-Hispanic/Latino; 3 Asian, non-Hispanic/Latino; 9 Hispanic/Latino. Average age 29. In 2010, 27 master's awarded. *Degree requirements:* For master's, comprehensive exam (for some programs), thesis optional, practicum, internship. *Entrance requirements:* For master's, writing assessment, 15 hours of psychology, including statistics or research; 2 letters of recommendation; minimum GPA of 3.0 in last 60 hours; interview. Additional exam requirements/recommendations for international students: Required—TOEFL (minimum score 550 paper-based; 213 computer-based). *Application deadline:* For fall admission, 5/1 priority date for international students; for spring admission, 11/15 priority date for international students. Applications are processed on a rolling basis. Application fee: $40. Electronic applications accepted. *Expenses:* Tuition: Full-time $13,320; part-time $740 per credit hour. Tuition and fees vary according to program. *Financial support:* Federal Work-Study, scholarships/grants, tuition waivers, and unspecified assistantships available. Financial award application deadline: 5/1; financial award applicants required to submit FAFSA. *Faculty research:* Cognitive development, attitude formation, juvenile delinquency, gender issues, work-family conflict. *Unit head:* Dr. Katherine Helm, Director, 815-838-0500 Ext. 5604, Fax: 815-836-5032, E-mail: helmka@lewisu.edu. *Application contact:* Nancy Hanley, Information Contact, 815-838-0500 Ext. 5604, E-mail: hanleyna@lewisu.edu.

Liberty University, College of Arts and Sciences, Lynchburg, VA 24502. Offers counseling (MA); human services (MA); nursing (MSN); pastoral care and counseling (PhD); professional counseling (PhD). *Accreditation:* AACN. Part-time programs available. Postbaccalaureate distance learning degree programs offered (minimal on-campus study). *Students:* 2,021 full-time (1,587 women), 4,301 part-time (3,346 women); includes 1,698 minority (1,424 Black or African American, non-Hispanic/Latino; 20 American Indian or Alaska Native, non-Hispanic/Latino; 59 Asian, non-Hispanic/Latino; 181 Hispanic/Latino; 10 Native Hawaiian or other Pacific Islander, non-Hispanic/Latino; 4 Two or more races, non-Hispanic/Latino), 93 international. Average age 36. In 2010, 865 master's, 12 doctorates awarded. *Degree requirements:* For master's, comprehensive exam (for some programs); for doctorate, comprehensive exam, thesis/dissertation. *Entrance requirements:* For master's, GRE General Test (MSN), minimum undergraduate GPA of 3.0; for doctorate, GRE General Test, minimum master's GPA of 3.25. Additional exam requirements/recommendations for international students: Required—TOEFL (minimum score 600 paper-based; 250 computer-based; 100 iBT). *Application deadline:* For fall admission, 6/1 priority date for domestic students; for spring admission, 11/1 priority date for domestic students. Applications are processed on a rolling basis. Application fee: $50. Electronic applications accepted. *Financial support:* Teaching assistantships with tuition reimbursements, Federal Work-Study available. *Faculty research:* God concept and adult attachment, building marital strength, image of God and gender, breastfeeding behavior among adolescent mothers, osteoporosis. *Unit head:* Dr. Ronald E. Hawkins, Dean, 434-592-4030, Fax: 434-522-0416, E-mail: rehawkin@liberty.edu. *Application contact:* Jay Bridge, Director of Graduate Admissions, 800-424-9595, Fax: 800-628-7977, E-mail: gradadmissions@liberty.edu.

Lindenwood University, Graduate Programs, School of Education, St. Charles, MO 63301-1695. Offers education (MA); educational administration (MA, Ed D, Ed S); instructional leadership (Ed D, Ed S); library media (MA); professional and school counseling (MA); professional counseling (MA); school administration (Ed S); school counseling (MA); teaching (MA). Part-time and evening/weekend programs available. *Faculty:* 33 full-time (13 women), 176 part-time/adjunct (83 women). *Students:* 543 full-time (389 women), 1,827 part-time (1,426 women); includes 510 minority (478 Black or African American, non-Hispanic/Latino; 3 American Indian or Alaska Native, non-Hispanic/Latino; 14 Asian, non-Hispanic/Latino; 14 Hispanic/Latino; 1 Two or more races, non-Hispanic/Latino), 20 international. Average age 35. 248 applicants, 120 enrolled. In 2010, 730 master's, 62 doctorates, 67 other advanced degrees awarded. *Degree requirements:* For master's, thesis (for some programs); for doctorate, thesis/dissertation, minimum GPA of 3.0; for Ed S, comprehensive exam, project, minimum GPA of 3.0. *Entrance requirements:* For master's, interview, minimum GPA of 3.0, writing sample, letter of recommendation; for doctorate, GRE, minimum graduate GPA of 3.4, resume, interview, writing sample, 4 letters of recommendation; for Ed S, master's degree in education, relevant work experience. Additional exam requirements/recommendations for international students: Required—TOEFL (minimum score 550 paper-based; 213 computer-based; 80 iBT). *Application deadline:* For fall admission, 8/27 priority date for domestic and international students; for spring admission, 1/28 priority date for domestic and international students. Applications are processed on a rolling basis. Application fee: $30 ($100 for international students). Electronic applications accepted. *Expenses:* Tuition: Full-time $13,260; part-time $380 per credit hour. Required fees: $340. One-time fee: $30. Tuition and fees vary according to course level and course load. *Financial support:* In 2010–11, 177 students received support. Career-related internships or fieldwork, institutionally sponsored loans, tuition waivers (partial), and unspecified assistantships available. Financial award application deadline: 6/30; financial award applicants required to submit FAFSA. *Unit head:* Dr. Cynthia Bice, Dean, 636-949-4618, Fax: 636-949-4197, E-mail: cbice@lindenwood.edu. *Application contact:* Brett Barger, Dean of Evening Admissions and Extension Campuses, 636-949-4934, Fax: 636-949-4109, E-mail: adultadmissions@lindenwood.edu.

Lindsey Wilson College, School of Professional Counseling, Columbia, KY 42728. Offers counseling and human development (M Ed). *Accreditation:* ACA. Part-time and evening/weekend programs available.

Lipscomb University, Programs in Counseling, Nashville, TN 37204-3951. Offers counseling psychology (Certificate); professional counseling (MS); psychology (MS). Part-time and evening/weekend programs available. Postbaccalaureate distance learning degree programs offered (minimal on-campus study). *Faculty:* 5 full-time (1 woman), 12 part-time/adjunct (7 women). *Students:* 88 full-time (70 women), 46 part-time (28 women); includes 16 Black or African American, non-Hispanic/Latino; 1 American Indian or Alaska Native, non-Hispanic/Latino; 2 Asian, non-Hispanic/Latino; 3 Hispanic/Latino, 1 international. Average age 30. 101 applicants, 60% accepted, 46 enrolled. In 2010, 35 master's awarded. *Entrance requirements:* For master's, GRE, resume, 3 reference letters, minimum GPA of 3.0. Application fee: $50. Electronic applications accepted. *Expenses:* Tuition: Full-time $18,149; part-time $943 per hour. Tuition and fees vary according to program. *Faculty research:* Cognitive psychology, neuroscience, health psychology, grief issues. *Unit head:* Dr. Jake Morris, Graduate Program Director and Professor of Psychology, 615-966-5906, E-mail: jake.morris@lipscomb.edu. *Application contact:* Elena Zemmel, Administrative Assistant, 615-966-5906, E-mail: elena.zemmel@lipscomb.edu.

Long Island University, Brentwood Campus, School of Education, Brentwood, NY 11717. Offers childhood education (MS); early childhood education (MS); literacy (MS); mental health counseling (MS); school counseling (MS); special education (MS). Part-time and evening/weekend programs available.

Long Island University, Rockland Graduate Campus, Graduate School, Program in Counseling and Development, Orangeburg, NY 10962. Offers mental health counseling (MS); school counselor (MS Ed). Part-time and evening/weekend programs available. *Faculty:* 1 (woman) full-time, 8 part-time/adjunct (7 women). *Students:* 44 full-time (28 women), 28 part-time (21 women). In 2010, 32 master's awarded. *Entrance requirements:* For master's, transcripts, letters of recommendation, personal statement, interview. Additional exam requirements/recommendations for international students: Required—TOEFL (minimum score 79 iBT). *Application deadline:* Applications are processed on a rolling basis. Application fee: $30. *Expenses:* Tuition: Part-time $1028 per credit. Required fees: $340 per semester. *Financial support:* Applicants required to submit FAFSA. *Unit head:* Dr. Thomas Nardi, Program Director, 845-359-7200 Ext. 5429, Fax: 845-359-7248, E-mail: thomas.nardi@liu.edu. *Application contact:* Carolyn Reiter, Director of Admissions and Marketing, 845-359-7200 Ext. 5417, Fax: 845-359-7200, E-mail: carolyn.reiter@liu.edu.

Long Island University, Westchester Graduate Campus, Program in Mental Health Counseling, Purchase, NY 10577. Offers MS.

Louisiana State University in Shreveport, College of Education and Human Development, Program in Counseling Psychology, Shreveport, LA 71115-2399. Offers MS. *Students:* 29 full-time (24 women), 11 part-time (10 women); includes 10 minority (7 Black or African American, non-Hispanic/Latino; 3 Hispanic/Latino). Average age 29. 28 applicants, 93% accepted, 10 enrolled. In 2010, 14 master's awarded. *Degree requirements:* For master's, comprehensive exam, internship (600 clock hours). *Entrance requirements:* For master's,

Counseling Psychology

Louisiana State University in Shreveport (continued)
GRE, references. Additional exam requirements/recommendations for international students: Required—TOEFL (minimum score 500 paper-based; 173 computer-based; 61 iBT). *Application deadline:* For fall admission, 6/30 for domestic and international students; for spring admission, 11/30 for domestic and international students. Applications are processed on a rolling basis. Application fee: $10 ($20 for international students). *Expenses:* Tuition, state resident: full-time $3272; part-time $181.80 per credit hour. Tuition, nonresident: full-time $7902; part-time $471.19 per credit hour. Required fees: $850; $47 per credit hour. *Financial support:* In 2010–11, 3 research assistantships with partial tuition reimbursements (averaging $30,000 per year) were awarded. *Unit head:* Dr. Meredith G. Nelson, Program Director, 318-797-5199, Fax: 318-798-4171, E-mail: mnelson@pilot.lsus.edu. *Application contact:* Yvonne Yarbrough, Secretary, Graduate Studies, 318-797-5247, Fax: 318-798-4120, E-mail: yyarbrou@lsus.edu.

Louisiana Tech University, Graduate School, College of Education, Department of Behavioral Sciences and Psychology, Ruston, LA 71272. Offers counseling (MA); counseling psychology (PhD); industrial/organizational psychology (MA); special education (MA). *Accreditation:* APA (one or more programs are accredited). Part-time programs available. *Degree requirements:* For master's, thesis or alternative; for doctorate, thesis/dissertation. *Entrance requirements:* For master's and doctorate, GRE General Test.

Loyola University Chicago, School of Education, Program in Counseling Psychology, Chicago, IL 60660. Offers PhD. Offered through the Graduate School. *Accreditation:* APA. *Faculty:* 5 full-time (4 women), 4 part-time/adjunct (2 women). *Students:* 21. Average age 26. 55 applicants, 7% accepted, 4 enrolled. In 2010, 6 doctorates awarded. *Degree requirements:* For doctorate, comprehensive exam, thesis/dissertation. *Entrance requirements:* For doctorate, GRE General Test, GRE Subject Test, interview; minimum graduate GPA of 3.5, undergraduate 3.0; letters of recommendation. Additional exam requirements/recommendations for international students: Required—TOEFL (minimum score 550 paper-based; 213 computer-based; 79 iBT). *Application deadline:* For fall admission, 12/1 for domestic and international students. Application fee: $50. Electronic applications accepted. *Expenses:* Tuition: Full-time $14,940; part-time $830 per credit hour. Required fees: $87 per semester. Part-time tuition and fees vary according to course load and program. *Financial support:* In 2010–11, 4 fellowships with full tuition reimbursements (averaging $14,000 per year), 10 research assistantships with full tuition reimbursements (averaging $12,500 per year) were awarded; teaching assistantships with full tuition reimbursements, career-related internships or fieldwork, Federal Work-Study, traineeships, and unspecified assistantships also available. Financial award application deadline: 2/1; financial award applicants required to submit FAFSA. *Faculty research:* Career choice and development, multicultural counseling, psychological measurement, prevention and intervention, family therapy. *Unit head:* Dr. Anita Thomas, Director, 312-915-7403, E-mail: athoma9@luc.edu. *Application contact:* Marie Rosin-Dittmar, Information Contact, 312-915-6800, E-mail: schleduc@luc.edu.

Loyola University Maryland, Graduate Programs, Loyola College of Arts and Sciences, Department of Psychology, Program in Counseling Psychology, Baltimore, MD 21210-2699. Offers MS, CAS. Part-time and evening/weekend programs available. *Entrance requirements:* For master's and CAS, GRE General Test, GRE Subject Test (recommended). Additional exam requirements/recommendations for international students: Required—TOEFL (minimum score 550 paper-based; 213 computer-based).

Lynchburg College, Graduate Studies, School of Education and Human Development, M Ed Program in Clinical Mental Health Counseling, Lynchburg, VA 24501-3199. Offers M Ed. Part-time and evening/weekend programs available. *Faculty:* 6 full-time (4 women). *Students:* 15 full-time (10 women), 17 part-time (12 women); includes 6 minority (5 Black or African American, non-Hispanic/Latino; 1 American Indian or Alaska Native, non-Hispanic/Latino), 1 international. Average age 32. 34 applicants, 44% accepted. In 2010, 6 master's awarded. *Degree requirements:* For master's, comprehensive exam, completion of counseling internship. *Entrance requirements:* For master's, GRE, official transcripts, personal essay, 3 letters of recommendation. Additional exam requirements/recommendations for international students: Required—TOEFL (minimum score 530 paper-based; 197 computer-based; 71 iBT), IELTS (minimum score 6.5). *Application deadline:* For fall admission, 7/31 for domestic students, 6/1 for international students; for spring admission, 11/30 for domestic students, 10/15 for international students. Applications are processed on a rolling basis. Application fee: $30. Electronic applications accepted. *Expenses:* Tuition: Full-time $7200; part-time $400 per credit hour. Required fees: $20; $5.10 per credit hour. $15 per term. Tuition and fees vary according to degree level and program. *Financial support:* Fellowships, research assistantships, Federal Work-Study, scholarships/grants, health care benefits, and unspecified assistantships available. Support available to part-time students. Financial award application deadline: 7/31; financial award applicants required to submit FAFSA. *Unit head:* Dr. Mandy Perryman, Assistant Professor and Program Director, Counselor Education, 434-544-8067, E-mail: perryman@lynchburg.edu. *Application contact:* Dr. Mandy Perryman, Assistant Professor and Program Director, Counselor Education, 434-544-8067, E-mail: perryman@lynchburg.edu.

Marist College, Graduate Programs, School of Social and Behavioral Sciences, Poughkeepsie, NY 12601-1387. Offers education (M Ed, MA); mental health counseling (MA); school psychology (MA, Adv C). Part-time and evening/weekend programs available. *Degree requirements:* For master's, thesis optional. *Entrance requirements:* For master's, GRE General Test, letters of recommendation, minimum undergraduate GPA of 3.0, interview. Additional exam requirements/recommendations for international students: Required—TOEFL (minimum score 550 paper-based; 213 computer-based; 80 iBT); Recommended—IELTS (minimum score 6.5). Electronic applications accepted. *Faculty research:* AIDS prevention, educational intervention, humanistic counseling research, aging and development, neuroimaging.

Marquette University, Graduate School, College of Education, Milwaukee, WI 53201-1881. Offers clinical mental health counseling (MS); college student personnel administration (M Ed); counseling (MA); counseling psychology (PhD); curriculum and instruction (MA); education (PhD); educational administration (M Ed); educational policy and foundations (MA); educational psychology (MA); elementary education (Certificate); literacy (MA); principal (Certificate); reading specialist (Certificate); reading teacher (Certificate); secondary education (Certificate); superintendent (Certificate). *Accreditation:* NCATE. Part-time programs available. *Faculty:* 24 full-time (15 women), 35 part-time/adjunct (27 women). *Students:* 91 full-time (66 women), 208 part-time (133 women); includes 47 minority (21 Black or African American, non-Hispanic/Latino; 2 American Indian or Alaska Native, non-Hispanic/Latino; 7 Asian, non-Hispanic/Latino; 14 Hispanic/Latino; 3 Two or more races, non-Hispanic/Latino), 3 international. Average age 31. 326 applicants, 58% accepted, 99 enrolled. In 2010, 62 master's, 9 doctorates, 4 other advanced degrees awarded. Terminal master's awarded for partial completion of doctoral program. *Degree requirements:* For master's, comprehensive exam, thesis (for some programs); for doctorate, thesis/dissertation, qualifying exam, supporting minor. *Entrance requirements:* For master's, GRE General Test or MAT, official transcripts from all current and previous colleges/universities except Marquette, three letters of recommendation, statement of purpose; for doctorate, GRE General Test, MAT, sample of written work, official transcripts from all current and previous colleges/universities except Marquette, three letters of recommendation, statement of purpose, resume/vita; for Certificate, GRE General Test or MAT, master's degree. Additional exam requirements/recommendations for international students: Required—TOEFL (minimum score 530 paper-based; 78 computer-based). *Application deadline:* For fall admission, 1/15 for domestic and international students. Application fee: $50. *Expenses:* Contact institution. *Financial support:* In 2010–11, 3 fellowships, 17 research assistantships, 17 teaching assistantships were awarded; Federal Work-Study, institutionally sponsored loans, scholarships/grants, and tuition waivers (full and partial) also available. Support available to part-time students. Financial award application deadline: 2/15. *Faculty research:* Parenting, psychology of motivation, reading assessment, socialization of educational administrators, education philosophy of Cardinal Newman. Total annual research expenditures: $239,042. *Unit head:* Dr. Bill Henk, Dean, 414-288-7376. *Application contact:* Erin Fox, Director of Graduate Admissions, 414-288-7182, Fax: 414-288-1902.

Mars Hill Graduate School, Graduate Programs, Seattle, WA 98121. Offers Christian studies (MA); counseling psychology (MA); divinity (MS). Part-time programs available. *Entrance requirements:* For master's, MAT.

Marylhurst University, Department of Art Therapy Counseling, Marylhurst, OR 97036-0261. Offers art therapy (PGC); art therapy counseling (MA); counseling (PGC). Part-time programs available. *Faculty:* 3 full-time (all women), 4 part-time/adjunct (all women). *Students:* 5 full-time (3 women), 25 part-time (20 women); includes 1 American Indian or Alaska Native, non-Hispanic/Latino; 1 Asian, non-Hispanic/Latino; 4 Hispanic/Latino; 1 Two or more races, non-Hispanic/Latino. Average age 34. 30 applicants, 83% accepted, 18 enrolled. In 2010, 18 master's awarded. *Degree requirements:* For master's, comprehensive exam, practica. *Entrance requirements:* For master's, MAT, minimum GPA of 3.0, course work in psychology and art, slide portfolio, letters of reference, resume, autobiography, portfolio. Additional exam requirements/recommendations for international students: Required—TOEFL (minimum score 550 paper-based; 213 computer-based; 80 iBT). *Application deadline:* For fall admission, 1/31 priority date for domestic and international students. Applications are processed on a rolling basis. Application fee: $50. Electronic applications accepted. *Expenses:* Contact institution. *Financial support:* Scholarships/grants available. Support available to part-time students. Financial award applicants required to submit FAFSA. *Faculty research:* Scientific approaches to art therapy research, child and adolescent psychotherapy, multicultural counseling. *Unit head:* Christine Turner, Chair, 503-636-8141, Fax: 503-636-9526, E-mail: cturner@marylhurst.edu. *Application contact:* Maruska Lynch, Graduate Admissions Specialist, 800-634-9982 Ext. 6322, Fax: 503-699-6320, E-mail: admissions@marylhurst.edu.

Marymount University, School of Education and Human Services, Program in Community Counseling, Arlington, VA 22207-4299. Offers MA, Certificate. *Accreditation:* ACA (one or more programs are accredited). Part-time and evening/weekend programs available. *Entrance requirements:* For master's, GRE, 2 letters of recommendation, interview, resume, personal statement; for Certificate, master's degree in counseling. Additional exam requirements/recommendations for international students: Required—TOEFL (minimum score 600 paper-based; 250 computer-based; 96 iBT), IELTS (minimum score 6.5). Electronic applications accepted.

Marywood University, Academic Affairs, Reap College of Education and Human Development, Department of Psychology and Counseling, Program in Mental Health Counseling, Scranton, PA 18509-1598. Offers MA. *Accreditation:* ACA. *Entrance requirements:* Additional exam requirements/recommendations for international students: Required—TOEFL (minimum score 550 paper-based; 213 computer-based; 79 iBT). Electronic applications accepted. *Expenses:* Tuition: Part-time $735 per credit. Required fees: $470 per semester. Tuition and fees vary according to degree level and campus/location.

Massachusetts School of Professional Psychology, Graduate Programs, Boston, MA 02132. Offers applied psychology in higher education student personnel administration (MA); clinical psychology (Psy D); counseling psychology (MA); counseling psychology and community mental health (MA); counseling psychology and global mental health (MA); executive coaching (Graduate Certificate); forensic and counseling psychology (MA); leadership psychology (Psy D); organizational psychology (MA); primary care psychology (MA); respecialization in clinical psychology (Certificate); school psychology (Psy D); MA/CAGS. *Accreditation:* APA. *Faculty:* 24 full-time (11 women), 13 part-time/adjunct (9 women). *Students:* 515. Average age 28. *Degree requirements:* For master's, comprehensive exam (for some programs); for doctorate, thesis/dissertation (for some programs). Application fee: $50. Electronic applications accepted. *Expenses:* Tuition: Full-time $32,352; part-time $1011 per credit. Full-time tuition and fees vary according to degree level. *Financial support:* Teaching assistantships, career-related internships or fieldwork available. Financial award applicants required to submit FAFSA. *Unit head:* Dr. Nicholas A. Covino, President, 617-327-6777, Fax: 617-327-4447. *Application contact:* Admissions and Marketing, 617-327-6777 Ext. 210, Fax: 617-327-4447, E-mail: admissions@mspp.edu.

McGill University, Faculty of Graduate and Postdoctoral Studies, Faculty of Education, Department of Educational and Counseling Psychology, Montréal, QC H3A 2T5, Canada. Offers counseling psychology (MA, PhD); educational psychology (M Ed, MA, PhD); school/applied child psychology and applied developmental psychology (M Ed, MA, PhD, Diploma), including school psychology. *Accreditation:* APA.

McKendree University, Graduate Programs, Master of Arts in Professional Counseling Program, Lebanon, IL 62254-1299. Offers MAPC. Part-time and evening/weekend programs available. *Faculty:* 2 full-time (1 woman), 8 part-time/adjunct (3 women). *Students:* 20 full-time (13 women), 49 part-time (40 women). Average age 32. 43 applicants, 37% accepted, 8 enrolled. In 2010, 16 master's awarded. *Degree requirements:* For master's, comprehensive exam, internship. *Entrance requirements:* For master's, official transcripts from institutions attended, minimum GPA of 3.0, three letters of recommendation, personal statement, interview, completion of six hours in behavior science. *Application deadline:* For fall admission, 8/1 for domestic and international students; for spring admission, 11/1 for domestic and international students. Applications are processed on a rolling basis. Application fee: $0. Electronic applications accepted. *Expenses:* Tuition: Full-time $6750; part-time $375 per credit hour. One-time fee: $100. Tuition and fees vary according to program. *Financial support:* Application deadline: 6/30. *Unit head:* Dr. Jim Cook, Director, 618-537-6875, E-mail: jhcook@mckendree.edu. *Application contact:* Brie L. Knaus, Graduate Admission Counselor, 618-537-6574, Fax: 618-537-6410, E-mail: blknaus@mckendree.edu.

McNeese State University, Doré School of Graduate Studies, Burton College of Education, Department of Psychology, Lake Charles, LA 70609. Offers addiction treatment (MA); applied behavior analysis (MA); counseling psychology (MA); general/experimental psychology (MA). Evening/weekend programs available. *Faculty:* 6 full-time (3 women). *Students:* 46 full-time (31 women), 29 part-time (21 women); includes 11 minority (6 Black or African American, non-Hispanic/Latino; 1 Asian, non-Hispanic/Latino; 2 Hispanic/Latino; 2 Two or more races, non-Hispanic/Latino), 4 international. In 2010, 14 master's awarded. *Entrance requirements:* For master's, GRE. *Application deadline:* For fall admission, 5/15 priority date for domestic and international students; for spring admission, 10/15 priority date for domestic and international students. Applications are processed on a rolling basis. Application fee: $20 ($30 for international students). Tuition and fees vary according to course load. *Financial support:* Application deadline: 5/1. *Unit head:* Dr. Dena L. Matzenbacher, Head, 337-475-5457, Fax: 337-562-4115, E-mail: dena@mcneese.edu. *Application contact:* Dr. George F. Mead, Interim Dean of Dore' School of Graduate Studies, 337-475-5396, Fax: 337-475-5397, E-mail: admissions@mcneese.edu.

Medaille College, Programs in Psychology, Buffalo, NY 14214-2695. Offers mental health counseling (MA); psychology (MA). Part-time and evening/weekend programs available. *Faculty:* 9 full-time (6 women), 9 part-time/adjunct (6 women). *Students:* 186 full-time (165 women); includes 22 Black or African American, non-Hispanic/Latino; 3 Asian, non-Hispanic/Latino; 2 Hispanic/Latino; 2 Two or more races, non-Hispanic/Latino. Average age 31. In 2010, 69 master's awarded. *Degree requirements:* For master's, comprehensive exam (for some programs), thesis (for some programs). *Entrance requirements:* For master's, GRE General Test (psychology), minimum GPA of 2.75 (psychology). Additional exam requirements/recommendations for international students: Required—TOEFL (minimum score 550 paper-based; 213 computer-based). *Application deadline:* Applications are processed on a rolling basis. Application fee: $35. Electronic applications accepted. *Financial support:* In 2010–11, 90 students received support. Federal Work-Study available. Financial award applicants required to submit FAFSA. *Faculty research:* Schizophrenia, Parkinson's Disease, eyewitness testimony, methodology. *Unit head:* Dr. Judith Horowitz, Dean of Adult and Graduate Studies, 716-880-2229, Fax: 716-884-0291, E-mail: jhorowitz@medaille.edu. *Application contact:* Jacqueline Matheny, Executive Director of Marketing and Enrollment, 716-932-2541, Fax: 716-632-1811, E-mail: jmatheny@medaille.edu.

Mercy College, School of Social and Behavioral Sciences, Program in Counseling, Dobbs Ferry, NY 10522-1189. Offers alcohol and substance abuse counseling (Certificate); counseling (MS); family counseling (Certificate). Part-time and evening/weekend programs available. Postbaccalaureate distance learning degree programs offered (no on-campus study). *Students:* 118 full-time (101 women), 207 part-time (183 women); includes 90 Black or African American, non-Hispanic/Latino; 1 American Indian or Alaska Native, non-Hispanic/Latino; 3 Asian, non-Hispanic/Latino; 127 Hispanic/Latino; 5 Two or more races, non-Hispanic/Latino. Average age 34. 194 applicants, 50% accepted, 74 enrolled. In 2010, 77 master's, 17 other advanced degrees awarded. *Degree requirements:* For master's, comprehensive exam. *Entrance requirements:* For master's, interview, two professional letters of recommendation, minimum undergraduate GPA of 3.0, resume. Additional exam requirements/recommendations for international students: Required—TOEFL (minimum score 600 paper-based; 250 computer-based; 100 iBT), IELTS (minimum score 8). *Application deadline:* For fall admission, 8/1 for international students. Applications are processed on a rolling basis. Application fee: $40. Electronic applications accepted. *Expenses:* Tuition: Full-time $13,572; part-time $754 per credit hour. Required fees: $130 per term. *Financial support:* Career-related internships or fieldwork, Federal Work-Study, scholarships/grants, and unspecified assistantships available. Support available to part-time students. Financial award applicants required to submit FAFSA. *Faculty research:* Ethics, drug abuse problems, human development, domestic violence. *Unit head:* Dr. Arthur McCann, Assistant Professor, Psychology and Behavioral Science, 914-674-7670, E-mail: amccann@mercy.edu. *Application contact:* Allison Gurdineer, Senior Associate Director of Recruitment, 914-674-7601, E-mail: agurdineer@mercy.edu.

Mercy College, School of Social and Behavioral Sciences, Program in Mental Health Counseling, Dobbs Ferry, NY 10522-1189. Offers MS. Part-time and evening/weekend programs available. *Students:* 39 full-time (34 women), 53 part-time (46 women); includes 35 Black or African American, non-Hispanic/Latino; 2 Asian, non-Hispanic/Latino; 26 Hispanic/Latino, 1 international. Average age 36. 91 applicants, 44% accepted, 31 enrolled. In 2010, 15 master's awarded. *Degree requirements:* For master's, comprehensive exam. *Entrance requirements:* For master's, resume, interview, two professional letters of recommendation, 2- to 3-page essay on reason(s) for pursuing counseling degree. Additional exam requirements/recommendations for international students: Required—TOEFL (minimum score 600 paper-based; 250 computer-based; 100 iBT), IELTS (minimum score 8). *Application deadline:* For fall admission, 8/1 for international students. Applications are processed on a rolling basis. Application fee: $40. Electronic applications accepted. *Expenses:* Tuition: Full-time $13,572; part-time $754 per credit hour. Required fees: $130 per term. *Financial support:* Career-related internships or fieldwork, Federal Work-Study, scholarships/grants, and unspecified assistantships available. Support available to part-time students. Financial award applicants required to submit FAFSA. *Unit head:* Dr. Arthur McCann, Chair, Department of Counseling, 914-674-7401, E-mail: dtrevouledes@mercy.edu. *Application contact:* Allison Gurdineer, Senior Associate Director of Recruitment, 914-674-7601, E-mail: agurdineer@mercy.edu.

Messiah College, Program in Counseling, Grantham, PA 17027. Offers clinical mental health counseling (MAC); counseling (CAGS); marriage, couple, and family counseling (MAC); school counseling (MAC). Part-time programs available. *Entrance requirements:* For master's, minimum undergraduate cumulative GPA of 3.0, 2 recommendations, resume or curriculum vitae, interview; for CAGS, bachelor's degree, minimum undergraduate cumulative GPA of 3.0, essay, two recommendations, resume or curriculum vitae, interview. *Application deadline:* Applications are processed on a rolling basis. Application fee: $30. Electronic applications accepted. *Financial support:* Applicants required to submit FAFSA. *Unit head:* Dr. John Addleman, Director, 717-796-1800 Ext. 2980, Fax: 717-691-2386, E-mail: jaddlemn@messiah.edu. *Application contact:* Dr. John Addleman, Director, 717-796-1800 Ext. 2980, Fax: 717-691-2386, E-mail: jaddlemn@messiah.edu.

Michigan Theological Seminary, Graduate Programs, Plymouth, MI 48170. Offers Bible (Graduate Certificate); Christian education (MA); counseling psychology (MA); divinity (M Div); theological studies (MA). Part-time and evening/weekend programs available. *Degree requirements:* For master's, one foreign language, thesis; for M Div, 2 foreign languages. *Faculty research:* Judaism, cults, world religions.

Mid-America Christian University, Program in Counseling, Oklahoma City, OK 73170-4504. Offers marital and family therapy (MS); pastoral/spiritual direction (MS); professional counselor (MS). *Entrance requirements:* For master's, MAT, bachelor's degree from a regionally accredited college or university, minimum overall cumulative GPA of 2.75 of bachelor course work. Additional exam requirements/recommendations for international students: Required—TOEFL (minimum score 550 paper-based; 213 computer-based).

MidAmerica Nazarene University, Graduate Studies in Counseling, Olathe, KS 66062-1899. Offers counseling (MAC); play therapy (PMC). *Accreditation:* ACA. Evening/weekend programs available. *Entrance requirements:* For master's, Minnesota Multiphasic Personality Inventory, minimum GPA of 3.0. *Expenses:* Contact institution.

Middle Tennessee State University, College of Graduate Studies, College of Education, Department of Educational Leadership, Program in Professional Counseling, Murfreesboro, TN 37132. Offers curriculum and instruction (Ed S), including school psychology; mental health counseling (M Ed); school counseling (M Ed). *Accreditation:* ACA; NCATE. Part-time and evening/weekend programs available. Postbaccalaureate distance learning degree programs offered. *Students:* 7 part-time (6 women). 35 applicants, 69% accepted. In 2010, 15 master's awarded. *Degree requirements:* For master's, comprehensive exam. *Entrance requirements:* For master's, GRE or MAT. Additional exam requirements/recommendations for international students: Required—TOEFL (minimum score 525 paper-based; 195 computer-based; 71 iBT) or IELTS (minimum score 6). *Application deadline:* For fall admission, 6/1 for domestic and international students. Applications are processed on a rolling basis. Application fee: $25 ($30 for international students). Electronic applications accepted. *Expenses:* Tuition, state resident: full-time $4632. Tuition, nonresident: full-time $11,520. *Financial support:* Application deadline: 5/1. *Application contact:* Dr. Michael Allen, Dean and Vice Provost for Research, 615-898-2840, Fax: 615-904-8020, E-mail: mallen@mtsu.edu.

Minnesota State University Mankato, College of Graduate Studies, College of Education, Department of Counseling and Student Personnel, Mankato, MN 56001. Offers college student affairs (MS); counselor education and supervision (Ed D); marriage and family counseling (Certificate); mental health counseling (MS); professional school counseling (MS). *Accreditation:* ACA (one or more programs are accredited); NCATE. *Students:* 78 full-time (64 women), 35 part-time (25 women). *Degree requirements:* For master's, comprehensive exam, thesis or alternative. *Entrance requirements:* For master's, GRE General Test or MAT (if GPA less than 3.0 for last 2 years), minimum GPA of 3.0 during previous 2 years, 3 letters of reference. Additional exam requirements/recommendations for international students: Required—TOEFL. *Application deadline:* For fall admission, 1/15 priority date for domestic students. Applications are processed on a rolling basis. Application fee: $40. Electronic applications accepted. *Financial support:* Research assistantships with full tuition reimbursements, teaching assistantships with full tuition reimbursements, career-related internships or fieldwork, Federal Work-Study, institutionally sponsored loans, and unspecified assistantships available. Support available to part-time students. Financial award application deadline: 3/15; financial award applicants required to submit FAFSA. *Unit head:* Dr. Jacqueline Lewis, Chairperson, 507-389-5658. *Application contact:* 507-389-2321, E-mail: grad@mnsu.edu.

Mississippi College, Graduate School, School of Education, Department of Psychology and Counseling, Clinton, MS 39058. Offers counseling (Ed S); marriage and family counseling (MS); mental health counseling (MS); school counseling (M Ed). Part-time programs available. *Degree requirements:* For master's and Ed S, comprehensive exam, thesis optional. *Entrance requirements:* For master's, GRE or NTE. Additional exam requirements/recommendations for international students: Recommended—IELTS. Electronic applications accepted.

Monmouth University, The Graduate School, Department of Psychology, West Long Branch, NJ 07764-1898. Offers mental health counseling (MS); psychological counseling (MA, PMC). *Accreditation:* ACA. Part-time and evening/weekend programs available. *Faculty:* 8 full-time (4 women), 8 part-time/adjunct (6 women). *Students:* 168 full-time (142 women), 122 part-time (108 women); includes 21 Black or African American, non-Hispanic/Latino; 32 American Indian or Alaska Native, non-Hispanic/Latino; 8 Asian, non-Hispanic/Latino; 18 Hispanic/Latino; 5 Two or more races, non-Hispanic/Latino, 1 international. Average age 30. 173 applicants, 74% accepted, 94 enrolled. In 2010, 54 master's awarded. *Degree requirements:* For master's, thesis optional, fieldwork. *Entrance requirements:* For master's, GRE General Test, minimum GPA of 3.0 in major, 24 credits in psychology. Additional exam requirements/recommendations for international students: Required—TOEFL (minimum score 550 paper-based; 213 computer-based; 79 iBT), IELTS (minimum score 5) or Michigan English Language Assessment Battery (minimum score 77), Cambridge A, B, C. *Application deadline:* For fall admission, 7/15 priority date for domestic students, 6/1 for international students; for spring admission, 11/15 priority date for domestic students, 11/1 for international students. Applications are processed on a rolling basis. Application fee: $50. Electronic applications accepted. *Expenses:* Tuition: Full-time $19,572; part-time $816 per credit. Required fees: $628; $157 per semester. *Financial support:* In 2010–11, 224 students received support, including 222 fellowships (averaging $2,288 per year), 18 research assistantships (averaging $7,400 per year); career-related internships or fieldwork, scholarships/grants, and unspecified assistantships also available. Support available to part-time students. Financial award applicants required to submit FAFSA. *Faculty research:* Violent crime, single parenting, the African-American male, counseling older women, successful behavior for under-achieving youth. *Unit head:* Dr. George Kapalka, Director, 732-263-5583, Fax: 732-263-5159, E-mail: gkapalka@monmouth.edu. *Application contact:* Kevin Roane, Director, Office of Graduate Admission, 732-571-3452, Fax: 732-263-5123, E-mail: gradadm@monmouth.edu.

Montclair State University, The Graduate School, College of Education and Human Services, Department of Counseling, Human Development, and Educational Leadership, Montclair, NJ 07043-1624. Offers advanced counseling (Certificate); certified alcohol and drug counselor (Certificate); counseling (MA), including addictions counseling, community counseling, school counseling, student affairs; counselor education (PhD); director of school counseling services (Certificate); educational leadership (MA), including adult and organizational learning, educational leadership; principal (Certificate); school business administrator (Certificate); school counselor (Certificate); substance awareness coordinator (Certificate); supervisor (Certificate). *Accreditation:* NCATE. Part-time and evening/weekend programs available. *Faculty:* 18 full-time (12 women), 37 part-time/adjunct (26 women). *Students:* 169 full-time (125 women), 385 part-time (281 women); includes 51 Black or African American, non-Hispanic/Latino; 13 Asian, non-Hispanic/Latino; 49 Hispanic/Latino; 1 Native Hawaiian or other Pacific Islander, non-Hispanic/Latino; 1 Two or more races, non-Hispanic/Latino, 4 international. Average age 31. 270 applicants, 57% accepted, 124 enrolled. In 2010, 172 master's, 13 other advanced degrees awarded. *Degree requirements:* For master's, comprehensive exam, thesis or alternative; for doctorate, comprehensive exam, thesis/dissertation. *Entrance requirements:* For master's, GRE General Test, interview, 2 letters of recommendation; for doctorate, GRE General Test, interview, 3 letters of recommendation. Additional exam requirements/recommendations for international students: Required—TOEFL (minimum iBT score of 83) or IELTS. *Application deadline:* For fall admission, 6/1 for international students; for spring admission, 10/1 for international students. Applications are processed on a rolling basis. Application fee: $60. Electronic applications accepted. *Expenses:* Tuition, state resident: part-time $501.34 per credit. Tuition, nonresident: part-time $773.88 per credit. Required fees: $71.15 per credit. *Financial support:* In 2010–11, 10 research assistantships with full tuition reimbursements (averaging $7,000 per year), 4 teaching assistantships (averaging $15,000 per year) were awarded; Federal Work-Study, scholarships/grants, and unspecified assistantships also available. Support available to part-time students. Financial award application deadline: 3/1; financial award applicants required to submit FAFSA. *Faculty research:* Multicultural counseling competence and training; adoption triad adjustment, issues and counseling; substance abuse treatment with underserved populations; role of data in school change; adult development: pedagogical issues for adult students and special populations. *Unit head:* Dr. Larry Burlew, Chairperson, 973-655-7611. *Application contact:* Amy Aiello, Director of Graduate Admissions and Operations, 973-655-5147, Fax: 973-655-7869, E-mail: graduate.school@montclair.edu.

Morehead State University, Graduate Programs, College of Science and Technology, Department of Psychology, Morehead, KY 40351. Offers clinical/counseling psychology (MS); general/experimental psychology (MS). Part-time and evening/weekend programs available. *Degree requirements:* For master's, comprehensive exam, thesis optional. *Entrance requirements:* For master's, GRE General Test, 18 undergraduate hours in psychology, minimum GPA of 3.0, 3 letters of recommendation. Additional exam requirements/recommendations for international students: Required—TOEFL (minimum score 500 paper-based; 173 computer-based). Electronic applications accepted. *Faculty research:* Mood induction effects, serotonin receptor activity, stress, perceptual processes.

Mount St. Mary's College, Graduate Division, Program in Counseling Psychology, Los Angeles, CA 90049-1599. Offers counseling psychology (MS); marriage and family therapy (MS); psychology (MS). Part-time and evening/weekend programs available. *Degree requirements:* For master's, research project. *Entrance requirements:* For master's, minimum GPA of 3.0.

Naropa University, Graduate Programs, Program in Transpersonal Counseling Psychology, Boulder, CO 80302-6697. Offers art therapy (MA); counseling psychology (MA); wilderness therapy (MA). *Faculty:* 8 full-time (5 women), 27 part-time/adjunct (20 women). *Students:* 159 full-time (121 women), 70 part-time (54 women); includes 25 minority (2 Black or African American, non-Hispanic/Latino; 3 American Indian or Alaska Native, non-Hispanic/Latino; 2 Asian, non-Hispanic/Latino; 10 Hispanic/Latino; 8 Two or more races, non-Hispanic/Latino), 6 international. Average age 30. 237 applicants, 53% accepted, 84 enrolled. In 2010, 53 master's awarded. *Degree requirements:* For master's, internships. *Entrance requirements:* For master's, in-person interview, course work in psychology, 3 letters of recommendation, resume. Additional exam requirements/recommendations for international students: Required—TOEFL (minimum score 600 paper-based; 250 computer-based). *Application deadline:* For fall admission, 1/15 priority date for domestic and international students. Applications are processed on a rolling basis. Application fee: $60. Electronic applications accepted. *Expenses:* Tuition: Full-time $17,820; part-time $810 per credit. Required fees: $305 per semester. Tuition and fees vary according to course load, program and reciprocity agreements. *Financial support:* In 2010–11, 67 students received support, including 21 research assistantships with partial tuition reimbursements available (averaging $2,692 per year), 4 teaching assistantships with partial tuition reimbursements available (averaging $2,866 per year); career-related internships or fieldwork, Federal Work-Study, scholarships/grants, health care benefits, tuition waivers (partial), and unspecified assistantships also available. Support available to part-time students. Financial award application deadline: 3/1; financial award applicants required to submit FAFSA. *Unit head:* Dr. MacAndrew Jack, Director, Graduate School of Psychology. *Application contact:* Office of Admissions, 303-546-3572, Fax: 303-546-3583, E-mail: admissions@naropa.edu.

National University, Academic Affairs, College of Letters and Sciences, Department of Psychology, La Jolla, CA 92037-1011. Offers counseling psychology (MA); human behavior (MA). Part-time and evening/weekend programs available. Postbaccalaureate distance learning degree programs offered (no on-campus study). *Faculty:* 17 full-time (8 women), 209 part-time/adjunct (121 women). *Students:* 429 full-time (355 women), 466 part-time (356 women); includes 664 minority (113 Black or African American, non-Hispanic/Latino; 8 American Indian or Alaska Native, non-Hispanic/Latino; 41 Asian, non-Hispanic/Latino; 188 Hispanic/Latino; 303 Native Hawaiian or other Pacific Islander, non-Hispanic/Latino; 11 Two or more races, non-Hispanic/Latino), 2 international. Average age 36. 623 applicants, 100% accepted, 353 enrolled. In 2010, 266 master's awarded. *Degree requirements:* For master's, thesis (for some programs). *Entrance requirements:* For master's, interview, minimum GPA of 2.5. Additional exam requirements/recommendations for international students: Required—TOEFL (minimum

Counseling Psychology

National University (continued)
score 550 paper-based; 213 computer-based; 79 iBT), IELTS (minimum score 6). *Application deadline:* Applications are processed on a rolling basis. Application fee: $60 ($65 for international students). Electronic applications accepted. *Expenses:* Tuition: Full-time $9450; part-time $350 per unit. Required fees: $350 per unit. One-time fee: $60. *Financial support:* Career-related internships or fieldwork, institutionally sponsored loans, scholarships/grants, and tuition waivers (partial) available. Support available to part-time students. Financial award application deadline: 6/30; financial award applicants required to submit FAFSA. *Unit head:* Dr. Roland Fleck, Chair and Professor, 858-642-8577, Fax: 858-642-8715, E-mail: rfleck@nu.edu. *Application contact:* Dominick Giovanniello, Associate Regional Dean—San Diego, 800-NAT-UNIV, Fax: 858-541-7792, E-mail: dgiovann@nu.edu.

New England College, Program in Community Mental Health Counseling, Henniker, NH 03242-3293. Offers human services (MS); mental health counseling (MS). Part-time and evening/weekend programs available. *Degree requirements:* For master's, internship.

New Jersey City University, Graduate Studies and Continuing Education, Debra Cannon Partridge Wolfe College of Education, Program in Counseling, Jersey City, NJ 07305-1597. Offers MA. Part-time and evening/weekend programs available.

New Mexico State University, Graduate School, College of Education, Department of Counseling and Educational Psychology, Las Cruces, NM 88003-8001. Offers counseling and guidance (MA); counseling psychology (PhD); school psychology (Ed S). *Accreditation:* ACA; APA (one or more programs are accredited); NCATE. Part-time programs available. *Faculty:* 11 full-time (7 women), 2 part-time/adjunct (1 woman). *Students:* 69 full-time (54 women), 35 part-time (28 women); includes 52 minority (3 Black or African American, non-Hispanic/Latino; 2 American Indian or Alaska Native, non-Hispanic/Latino; 2 Asian, non-Hispanic/Latino; 44 Hispanic/Latino; 1 Two or more races, non-Hispanic/Latino), 2 international. Average age 30. 135 applicants, 89% accepted, 40 enrolled. In 2010, 11 master's, 4 doctorates, 7 other advanced degrees awarded. *Degree requirements:* For master's, comprehensive exam, thesis optional, internship; for doctorate, comprehensive exam, thesis/dissertation, internship; for Ed S, thesis or alternative, internship. *Entrance requirements:* For master's, doctorate, and Ed S, GRE General Test, minimum GPA of 3.0. *Application deadline:* For fall admission, 12/15 for domestic students; for spring admission, 4/1 priority date for domestic students. Application fee: $30 ($50 for international students). Electronic applications accepted. *Expenses:* Tuition, state resident: full-time $4536; part-time $242 per credit. Tuition, nonresident: full-time $15,816; part-time $712 per credit. Required fees: $636 per term. *Financial support:* In 2010–11, 15 research assistantships with partial tuition reimbursements (averaging $10,567 per year), 30 teaching assistantships with partial tuition reimbursements (averaging $6,880 per year) were awarded; fellowships with partial tuition reimbursements, career-related internships or fieldwork, Federal Work-Study, institutionally sponsored loans, scholarships/grants, traineeships, health care benefits, and unspecified assistantships also available. Support available to part-time students. Financial award application deadline: 4/1. *Faculty research:* Multicultural counseling, integrative health psychology group, career development school counseling. *Unit head:* Dr. Michael Waldo, Head, 575-646-2121, Fax: 575-646-8035, E-mail: miwaldo@nmsu.edu. *Application contact:* Elena Luna, Coordinator, 575-646-3498, Fax: 575-646-7721, E-mail: rosluna@nmsu.edu.

New York Institute of Technology, Graduate Division, School of Health Professions, Program in Mental Health Counseling, Old Westbury, NY 11568-8000. Offers MS. *Students:* 9 full-time (all women), 8 part-time (5 women); includes 4 minority (3 Black or African American, non-Hispanic/Latino; 1 Hispanic/Latino). Average age 32. In 2010, 4 master's awarded. *Degree requirements:* For master's, thesis, internship. *Entrance requirements:* For master's, minimum GPA of 3.0, interview, 3 letters of reference. Additional exam requirements/recommendations for international students: Required—TOEFL (minimum score 550 paper-based; 213 computer-based). *Application deadline:* For fall admission, 7/1 priority date for domestic students; for spring admission, 12/1 priority date for domestic students. Application fee: $50. *Expenses:* Tuition: Part-time $835 per credit. *Financial support:* Research assistantships with partial tuition reimbursements, career-related internships or fieldwork, institutionally sponsored loans, and unspecified assistantships available. Support available to part-time students. Financial award applicants required to submit FAFSA. *Unit head:* Dr. Oren Shtayermman, Coordinator, 516-686-1084, E-mail: oshtayer@nyit.edu. *Application contact:* Dr. Jacquelyn Nealon, Dean of Admissions and Financial Aid, 516-686-7925, Fax: 516-686-7613, E-mail: jnealon@nyit.edu.

New York University, Steinhardt School of Culture, Education, and Human Development, Department of Applied Psychology, Program in Counselor Education, New York, NY 10012-1019. Offers counseling and guidance (MA, Advanced Certificate), including bilingual school counseling (MA), school counseling (MA); counseling for mental health and wellness (MA); counseling psychology (PhD). *Accreditation:* APA (one or more programs are accredited). Part-time programs available. *Faculty:* 10 full-time (6 women). *Students:* 148 full-time (108 women), 59 part-time (46 women); includes 27 Black or African American, non-Hispanic/Latino; 1 American Indian or Alaska Native, non-Hispanic/Latino; 16 Asian, non-Hispanic/Latino; 22 Hispanic/Latino, 23 international. Average age 30. 874 applicants, 24% accepted, 84 enrolled. In 2010, 68 master's, 8 doctorates awarded. *Degree requirements:* For master's, thesis (for some programs); for doctorate, thesis/dissertation. *Entrance requirements:* For doctorate, GRE General Test, interview. Additional exam requirements/recommendations for international students: Required—TOEFL. *Application deadline:* For fall admission, 12/1 priority date for domestic and international students. Applications are processed on a rolling basis. Application fee: $75. Electronic applications accepted. *Financial support:* Fellowships with full and partial tuition reimbursements, research assistantships, teaching assistantships with partial tuition reimbursements, career-related internships or fieldwork, Federal Work-Study, institutionally sponsored loans, scholarships/grants, tuition waivers (partial), and unspecified assistantships available. Support available to part-time students. Financial award application deadline: 2/1; financial award applicants required to submit FAFSA. *Faculty research:* Cross-cultural counseling; group dynamics; culture, race and ethnicity; religiosity and psychological development; well-being and mental health. *Application contact:* 212-998-5030, Fax: 212-995-4328, E-mail: steinhardt.gradadmissions@nyu.edu.

Nicholls State University, Graduate Studies, College of Education, Department of Psychology and Counselor Education, Thibodaux, LA 70310. Offers psychological counseling (MA); school psychology (SSP). *Accreditation:* NCATE. Part-time and evening/weekend programs available. *Degree requirements:* For master's, comprehensive exam; for SSP, comprehensive exam, internship. *Entrance requirements:* For master's, GRE General Test. Electronic applications accepted.

Northeastern State University, Graduate College, College of Education, Department of Psychology and Counseling, Program in Counseling Psychology, Tahlequah, OK 74464-2399. Offers MS. Part-time and evening/weekend programs available. *Students:* 48 full-time (37 women), 56 part-time (43 women); includes 32 minority (2 Black or African American, non-Hispanic/Latino; 26 American Indian or Alaska Native, non-Hispanic/Latino; 4 Hispanic/Latino), 3 international. In 2010, 22 master's awarded. *Degree requirements:* For master's, thesis, internship, practicum. *Entrance requirements:* For master's, GRE, minimum GPA of 2.5. Additional exam requirements/recommendations for international students: Required—TOEFL (minimum score 213 computer-based). *Application deadline:* For fall admission, 3/1 priority date for domestic students; for spring admission, 10/1 for domestic students. Applications are processed on a rolling basis. Application fee: $0 ($25 for international students). Electronic applications accepted. *Expenses:* Tuition, state resident: part-time $144 per credit hour. Tuition, nonresident: part-time $384.05 per credit hour. Required fees: $34.90 per credit hour. Tuition and fees vary according to program. *Financial support:* Teaching assistantships, career-related internships or fieldwork and Federal Work-Study available. Financial award application deadline: 3/1. *Application contact:* Margie Railey, Administrative Assistant, 918-456-5511 Ext. 2093, Fax: 918-458-2061, E-mail: railey@nsouk.edu.

Northeastern University, Bouvé College of Health Sciences Graduate School, Department of Counseling and Applied Educational Psychology, Program in Counseling Psychology, Boston, MA 02115-5096. Offers MS, PhD, CAGS. *Accreditation:* APA (one or more programs are accredited). Part-time programs available. *Students:* 64 full-time (54 women), 11 part-time (10 women). 228 applicants, 27% accepted, 21 enrolled. In 2010, 13 master's, 6 doctorates awarded. *Degree requirements:* For doctorate, comprehensive exam, thesis/dissertation, qualifying exams; for CAGS, comprehensive exam. *Entrance requirements:* For master's and CAGS, GRE General Test or MAT; for doctorate, GRE General Test. Additional exam requirements/recommendations for international students: Required—TOEFL (minimum score 100 iBT). *Application deadline:* For fall admission, 6/1 for domestic and international students; for winter admission, 1/5 for domestic and international students. Applications are processed on a rolling basis. Application fee: $50. Electronic applications accepted. *Financial support:* In 2010–11, 2 teaching assistantships with full tuition reimbursements (averaging $13,832 per year) were awarded; career-related internships or fieldwork, Federal Work-Study, tuition waivers (partial), and unspecified assistantships also available. Support available to part-time students. Financial award application deadline: 3/1; financial award applicants required to submit FAFSA. *Faculty research:* Culture, gender and political psychology; child and adolescent counseling; health psychology forensic counseling; early intervention. *Unit head:* Dr. Mary B. Ballou, Director, 617-373-5937, Fax: 617-373-8892, E-mail: m.ballou@neu.edu. *Application contact:* Margaret Schnabel, Director of Graduate Admissions, 617-373-2708, E-mail: bouvegrad@neu.edu.

Northern Arizona University, Graduate College, College of Education, Department of Educational Psychology, Flagstaff, AZ 86011. Offers counseling (MA); educational psychology (PhD), including counseling psychology, learning and instruction, school psychology; human relations (M Ed); school counseling (M Ed); school psychology (MA, Certificate); student affairs (M Ed). Part-time programs available. Postbaccalaureate distance learning degree programs offered. *Faculty:* 19 full-time (9 women). *Students:* 230 full-time (176 women), 217 part-time (167 women); includes 168 minority (27 Black or African American, non-Hispanic/Latino; 19 American Indian or Alaska Native, non-Hispanic/Latino; 8 Asian, non-Hispanic/Latino; 105 Hispanic/Latino; 2 Native Hawaiian or other Pacific Islander, non-Hispanic/Latino; 7 Two or more races, non-Hispanic/Latino), 2 international. 736 applicants, 84% accepted. In 2010, 194 master's, 6 doctorates awarded. Terminal master's awarded for partial completion of doctoral program. *Degree requirements:* For master's, internship (for some programs); for doctorate, comprehensive exam, thesis/dissertation, internship. *Entrance requirements:* Additional exam requirements/recommendations for international students: Required—TOEFL (minimum score 550 paper-based; 213 computer-based; 80 iBT), IELTS (minimum score 7). *Application deadline:* For fall admission, 9/15 for domestic students; for spring admission, 1/15 for domestic students. Applications are processed on a rolling basis. Application fee: $65. Electronic applications accepted. *Financial support:* In 2010–11, 20 students received support, including 1 research assistantship with partial tuition reimbursement available (averaging $10,222 per year), 14 teaching assistantships with partial tuition reimbursements available (averaging $9,660 per year); career-related internships or fieldwork, Federal Work-Study, scholarships/grants, health care benefits, tuition waivers (full and partial), and unspecified assistantships also available. Financial award applicants required to submit FAFSA. *Unit head:* Dr. Kathy Bohan, Chair, 928-523-0362, Fax: 928-523-9284, E-mail: kathy.bohan@nau.edu. *Application contact:* Hope DeMello, Administrative Assistant, 928-523-7103, Fax: 928-523-9284, E-mail: eps@nau.edu.

Northern Kentucky University, Office of Graduate Programs, College of Education and Human Services, Program in Community Counseling, Highland Heights, KY 41099. Offers clinical mental health counseling (MA); college student development administration (Certificate); community counseling (Certificate). Part-time and evening/weekend programs available. *Faculty:* 12 full-time (7 women), 1 part-time/adjunct (0 women). *Students:* 17 full-time (16 women), 24 part-time (19 women). Average age 32. 36 applicants, 61% accepted, 19 enrolled. In 2010, 12 master's, 6 other advanced degrees awarded. *Degree requirements:* For master's, comprehensive exam, internship. *Entrance requirements:* For master's, GRE, minimum GPA of 2.75, 3 letters of reference, criminal background check (state and federal), resume. Additional exam requirements/recommendations for international students: Required—TOEFL (minimum score 550 paper-based; 213 computer-based; 79 iBT); Recommended—IELTS (minimum score 6.5). *Application deadline:* For fall admission, 7/1 for domestic students, 6/1 priority date for international students; for spring admission, 11/1 for domestic students, 10/1 priority date for international students. Applications are processed on a rolling basis. Application fee: $40. Electronic applications accepted. *Expenses:* Tuition, state resident: full-time $7254; part-time $403 per credit hour. Tuition, nonresident: full-time $12,492; part-time $694 per credit hour. Tuition and fees vary according to degree level and program. *Financial support:* Applicants required to submit FAFSA. *Faculty research:* Ethical decision-making in counseling, clinical supervision in counseling, expectations about counseling inventory development. *Unit head:* Dr. Jacqueline Smith, Director, 859-572-6149, E-mail: smithjac@nku.edu. *Application contact:* Dr. Peg Griffin, Director, Graduate Programs, 859-572-6934, Fax: 859-572-6670, E-mail: griffinp@nku.edu.

Northwestern Oklahoma State University, School of Professional Studies, Program in Counseling Psychology, Alva, OK 73717-2799. Offers MCP. Part-time programs available. *Faculty:* 5 full-time (2 women), 2 part-time/adjunct (1 woman). *Students:* 33 full-time (25 women), 22 part-time (16 women); includes 2 American Indian or Alaska Native, non-Hispanic/Latino; 1 Hispanic/Latino. Average age 31. 10 applicants, 90% accepted, 9 enrolled. In 2010, 15 master's awarded. *Degree requirements:* For master's, comprehensive exam. *Entrance requirements:* For master's, GRE General Test or MAT, minimum GPA of 2.75. *Application deadline:* Applications are processed on a rolling basis. Application fee: $15. *Financial support:* Fellowships, Federal Work-Study available. Support available to part-time students. Financial award application deadline: 5/1; financial award applicants required to submit FAFSA. *Unit head:* Dr. Nancy Knous, Coordinator, 580-327-8443. *Application contact:* Sabrina Watson, Coordinator of Graduate Studies, 580-327-8410, E-mail: sdwatson@nwosu.edu.

Northwestern University, The Graduate School, Interdepartmental Programs, Program in Counseling Psychology, Evanston, IL 60201. Offers MA. Admissions and degrees offered through The Graduate School. Part-time programs available. *Degree requirements:* For master's, comprehensive exam. *Entrance requirements:* For master's, GRE General Test. Electronic applications accepted. *Faculty research:* Family psychology, adult development and pathology, minority counseling, groups and systems, clinical training, stress and coping, health psychology.

Northwest University, College of Social and Behavioral Sciences, Kirkland, WA 98033. Offers counseling psychology (MA, Psy D); international care and community development (MA). Evening/weekend programs available. *Faculty:* 5 full-time (2 women), 11 part-time/adjunct (5 women). *Students:* 82 full-time (64 women), 10 part-time (8 women); includes 18 minority (3 Black or African American, non-Hispanic/Latino; 8 Asian, non-Hispanic/Latino; 7 Hispanic/Latino), 1 international. 114 applicants, 68% accepted, 58 enrolled. In 2010, 39 master's awarded. *Entrance requirements:* For master's, 3 character references. Additional exam requirements/recommendations for international students: Required—TOEFL (minimum score 580 paper-based; 237 computer-based). *Application deadline:* For fall admission, 12/1 priority date for domestic and international students; for spring admission, 4/1 priority date for domestic and international students. Applications are processed on a rolling basis. Application fee: $75. *Expenses:* Contact institution. *Financial support:* Career-related internships or fieldwork, health care benefits, and international student scholarships available. Financial award application deadline: 6/30. *Unit head:* Dr. Matt Nelson, Dean, 425-889-5328, Fax: 425-739-4602, E-mail: matt.nelson@northwestu.edu. *Application contact:* Shoshana Weed, Director of Student Services, 425-889-5249, Fax: 425-739-4602, E-mail: shoshana.weed@northwestu.edu.

Nova Southeastern University, Center for Psychological Studies, Master's Programs in Counseling, Mental Health, School Guidance, and Clinical Pharmacology, Fort Lauderdale, FL 33314-7796. Offers clinical pharmacology (MS); mental health counseling (MS); school guidance and counseling (MS). Part-time and evening/weekend programs available. *Faculty:* 7 full-time (2 women), 27 part-time/adjunct (8 women). *Students:* 331 full-time (299 women), 706 part-time

(637 women); includes 520 minority (219 Black or African American, non-Hispanic/Latino; 20 Asian, non-Hispanic/Latino; 264 Hispanic/Latino; 1 Native Hawaiian or other Pacific Islander, non-Hispanic/Latino; 16 Two or more races, non-Hispanic/Latino), 22 international. Average age 32. 562 applicants, 65% accepted, 262 enrolled. In 2010, 382 master's awarded. *Degree requirements:* For master's, comprehensive exam, 3 practica. *Entrance requirements:* Additional exam requirements/recommendations for international students: Required—TOEFL (minimum score 550 paper-based; 213 computer-based). *Application deadline:* For fall admission, 7/29 for domestic students; for winter admission, 11/29 for domestic students; for spring admission, 3/29 for domestic students. Applications are processed on a rolling basis. Application fee: $50. Electronic applications accepted. *Financial support:* Career-related internships or fieldwork, Federal Work-Study, and institutionally sponsored loans available. Financial award application deadline: 4/1. *Faculty research:* Clinical and child clinical psychology, geriatrics, interpersonal violence. *Unit head:* Karen S. Grosby, Dean, 954-262-5701, Fax: 954-262-3859. *Application contact:* Carlos Perez, Enrollment Management, 954-262-5790, Fax: 954-262-3893, E-mail: cpsinfo@cps.nova.edu.

Nyack College, Alliance Graduate School of Counseling, Nyack, NY 10960-3698. Offers marriage and family therapy (MA); mental health counseling (MA). Part-time programs available. *Students:* 66 full-time (59 women), 190 part-time (154 women); includes 182 minority (103 Black or African American, non-Hispanic/Latino; 30 Asian, non-Hispanic/Latino; 40 Hispanic/Latino; 9 Two or more races, non-Hispanic/Latino), 7 international. Average age 40. In 2010, 50 master's awarded. *Degree requirements:* For master's, comprehensive exam, counselor-in-training therapy, internship, CPCE exam. *Entrance requirements:* Additional exam requirements/recommendations for international students: Required—TOEFL (minimum score 220 computer-based; 83 iBT). *Application deadline:* Applications are processed on a rolling basis. Application fee: $35. Electronic applications accepted. *Expenses:* Contact institution. *Unit head:* Dr. Carol Robles, Director, 845-770-5730, Fax: 845-348-3923. *Application contact:* Traci Piescki, Director of Admissions, 800-541-6891, Fax: 845-348-3912, E-mail: admissions. grad@nyack.edu.

Oakland University, Graduate Study and Lifelong Learning, School of Education and Human Services, Department of Counseling, Rochester, MI 48309-4401. Offers MA, PhD, Certificate. *Accreditation:* ACA (one or more programs are accredited). Part-time and evening/weekend programs available. *Degree requirements:* For doctorate, thesis/dissertation. *Entrance requirements:* Additional exam requirements/recommendations for international students: Required—TOEFL (minimum score 550 paper-based; 213 computer-based). Electronic applications accepted.

Ottawa University, Graduate Studies-Arizona, Program in Professional Counseling, Ottawa, KS 66067-3399. Offers Christian counseling (MA); expressive arts therapy (MA); marriage and family therapy (MA); treatment of trauma, abuse and deprivation (MA). Programs offered in Mesa, Phoenix, Tempe and West Valley, AZ. Part-time and evening/weekend programs available. Postbaccalaureate distance learning degree programs offered. *Degree requirements:* For master's, comprehensive exam, thesis or alternative, field experience, practicum. *Entrance requirements:* For master's, minimum undergraduate GPA of 3.0; course work in theories of personality, abnormal psychology, and human growth and development. Additional exam requirements/recommendations for international students: Required—TOEFL (minimum score 550 paper-based; 213 computer-based).

Our Lady of the Lake University of San Antonio, School of Professional Studies, Program in Psychology, San Antonio, TX 78207-4689. Offers counseling psychology (MS, Psy D); marriage and family therapy (MS); school psychology (MS). *Accreditation:* APA (one or more programs are accredited). Part-time and evening/weekend programs available. *Students:* 118 full-time (97 women), 94 part-time (85 women); includes 119 minority (20 Black or African American, non-Hispanic/Latino; 2 Asian, non-Hispanic/Latino; 90 Hispanic/Latino; 2 Native Hawaiian or other Pacific Islander, non-Hispanic/Latino; 5 Two or more races, non-Hispanic/Latino), 5 international. Average age 30. In 2010, 842 master's, 4 doctorates awarded. *Degree requirements:* For master's, comprehensive exam, thesis optional, practicum; for doctorate, thesis/dissertation, internship, qualifying exam. *Entrance requirements:* For master's and doctorate, GRE General Test or MAT, interview. Additional exam requirements/recommendations for international students: Required—TOEFL. *Application deadline:* For fall admission, 3/1 priority date for domestic and international students. Applications are processed on a rolling basis. Application fee: $25 ($50 for international students). Electronic applications accepted. *Expenses:* Tuition: Full-time $13,500; part-time $750 per contact hour. Required fees: $330. Tuition and fees vary according to course level, degree level and campus/location. *Financial support:* Research assistantships, teaching assistantships, career-related internships or fieldwork available. Support available to part-time students. Financial award application deadline: 4/15. *Faculty research:* Marriage and family therapy, supervision, cross-cultural counseling, violence. *Unit head:* Dr. Joan Biever, Chair, 210-434-6711, E-mail: jbiever@lake.ollusa.edu. *Application contact:* 210-434-6711, Fax: 210-431-4036, E-mail: gradadm@lake.ollusa.edu.

Pace University, Dyson College of Arts and Sciences, Department of Psychology, Program in Counseling-Substance Abuse, New York, NY 10038. Offers loss and grief (MS); mental health (MS); substance abuse (MS). Offered at Pleasantville, NY location only. Part-time and evening/weekend programs available. *Degree requirements:* For master's, comprehensive exam, qualifying exams, internship. *Entrance requirements:* For master's, GRE, interview. Additional exam requirements/recommendations for international students: Required—TOEFL. Electronic applications accepted.

Pacifica Graduate Institute, Graduate Programs, Carpinteria, CA 93013. Offers clinical psychology (PhD); counseling psychology (MA); depth psychology (MA, PhD); mythological studies (MA, PhD). Terminal master's awarded for partial completion of doctoral program. *Degree requirements:* For master's, thesis (for some programs), practicum; for doctorate, comprehensive exam, thesis/dissertation, internship. *Entrance requirements:* For master's, resume, 3 letters of recommendation, writing sample, interview; for doctorate, resumé, 4 letters of recommendation, writing sample, interview. Additional exam requirements/recommendations for international students: Required—TOEFL. *Faculty research:* Imaginal and archetypal theory; post-Colonial psychoanalytic and Jungian theory; myth literature as it applies to the theory and practice of psychology.

Palm Beach Atlantic University, School of Education and Behavioral Studies, West Palm Beach, FL 33416-4708. Offers counseling psychology (MSCP), including addictions/mental health, marriage and family therapy, mental health counseling, school guidance counseling. Part-time and evening/weekend programs available. *Faculty:* 13 full-time (3 women), 10 part-time/adjunct (5 women). *Students:* 250 full-time (209 women), 61 part-time (47 women); includes 63 Black or African American, non-Hispanic/Latino; 2 Asian, non-Hispanic/Latino; 37 Hispanic/Latino; 1 Native Hawaiian or other Pacific Islander, non-Hispanic/Latino, 7 international. Average age 35. 108 applicants, 92% accepted, 83 enrolled. In 2010, 96 master's awarded. *Entrance requirements:* For master's, GRE, minimum GPA of 3.0. Additional exam requirements/recommendations for international students: Required—TOEFL (minimum score 550 paper-based; 213 computer-based). *Application deadline:* For fall admission, 7/15 priority date for domestic students; for spring admission, 11/15 priority date for domestic students. Applications are processed on a rolling basis. Application fee: $45. Electronic applications accepted. *Expenses:* Tuition: Full-time $8280; part-time $460 per credit hour. Required fees: $99 per semester. Tuition and fees vary according to course load, degree level and campus/location. *Financial support:* Applicants required to submit FAFSA. *Unit head:* Dr. Lisa Stubbs, Program Director, 561-803-2286. *Application contact:* Graduate Admissions, 888-468-6722, E-mail: grad@pba.edu.

Penn State University Park, Graduate School, College of Education, Department of Counselor Education, Counseling Psychology and Rehabilitation Services, State College, University Park, PA 16802-1503. Offers M Ed, MS, PhD. *Accreditation:* ACA (one or more programs are accredited); APA (one or more programs are accredited); NCATE.

Perelandra College, Program in Counseling, La Mesa, CA 91941. Offers MA. *Degree requirements:* For master's, practicum.

Philadelphia College of Osteopathic Medicine, Graduate and Professional Programs, Department of Psychology, Philadelphia, PA 19131-1694. Offers clinical psychology (Psy D); counseling and clinical health psychology (MS); organizational leadership and development (MS); psychology (Certificate, Post-Doctoral Certificate); school psychology (MS, Psy D, Ed S). *Accreditation:* APA. *Degree requirements:* For master's, thesis; for doctorate, comprehensive exam, thesis/dissertation, final project, fieldwork. *Entrance requirements:* For master's, GRE or MAT, minimum GPA of 3.0; course work in biology, chemistry, English, physics; for other advanced degree, PRAXIS. *Faculty research:* Depression in primary care, integrated primary care, geriatric mental health.

See Display on page 932 and Close-Up on page 1167.

Phoenix Seminary, Graduate Programs, Phoenix, AZ 85018. Offers Biblical and theological studies (Graduate Diploma); Biblical communication (M Div); Biblical leadership (MA); Christian counseling (Graduate Diploma); counseling and family (M Div); leadership development (M Div); ministry (D Min); professional counseling (MA). *Accreditation:* ATS (one or more programs are accredited). Part-time and evening/weekend programs available. *Faculty:* 6 full-time (0 women), 7 part-time/adjunct (0 women). *Students:* 30 full-time (4 women), 160 part-time (50 women); includes 40 minority (18 Black or African American, non-Hispanic/Latino; 8 Asian, non-Hispanic/Latino; 12 Hispanic/Latino; 2 Two or more races, non-Hispanic/Latino). Average age 37. 49 applicants, 96% accepted, 37 enrolled. In 2010, 21 master's, 5 doctorates, 8 other advanced degrees awarded. *Degree requirements:* For master's, 2 foreign languages, comprehensive exam; for doctorate, 2 foreign languages, thesis/dissertation. *Entrance requirements:* For master's, undergraduate degree with minimum GPA of 2.5; for doctorate, M Div (94 hours) with minimum GPA of 3.0. Additional exam requirements/recommendations for international students: Required—TOEFL (minimum score 587 paper-based; 240 computer-based; 92 iBT), TWE (minimum score 4.5). *Application deadline:* For fall admission, 6/1 for domestic students; for spring admission, 11/1 for domestic students. Applications are processed on a rolling basis. Application fee: $90. *Expenses:* Tuition: Full-time $10,105; part-time $430 per semester hour. Required fees: $430 per semester hour. $60 per semester. One-time fee: $160. *Financial support:* In 2010–11, 123 students received support. Institutionally sponsored loans and scholarships/grants available. Support available to part-time students. Financial award application deadline: 6/1; financial award applicants required to submit FAFSA. *Application contact:* Roma Royer, Director of Admissions and Academic Services, 602-850-8000 Ext. 111, Fax: 602-850-8080, E-mail: rroyer@ps.edu.

Prescott College, Graduate Programs, Program in Counseling and Psychology, Prescott, AZ 86301. Offers adventure-based psychotherapy (MA); counseling psychology (MA); ecopsychology (MA); ecotherapy (MA); equine-assisted mental health (MA); expressive arts therapy (MA); somatic psychology (MA); student-directed independent study (MA). Part-time programs available. Postbaccalaureate distance learning degree programs offered (minimal on-campus study). *Faculty:* 3 full-time (all women), 25 part-time/adjunct (18 women). *Students:* 71 full-time (55 women), 59 part-time (50 women); includes 16 minority (4 Black or African American, non-Hispanic/Latino; 2 American Indian or Alaska Native, non-Hispanic/Latino; 1 Asian, non-Hispanic/Latino; 3 Hispanic/Latino; 1 Native Hawaiian or other Pacific Islander, non-Hispanic/Latino; 5 Two or more races, non-Hispanic/Latino), 5 international. Average age 38. 107 applicants, 79% accepted, 54 enrolled. In 2010, 23 master's awarded. *Degree requirements:* For master's, thesis, fieldwork or internship, practicum. *Entrance requirements:* For master's, 2 letters of recommendation, resume. Additional exam requirements/recommendations for international students: Required—TOEFL (minimum score 500 paper-based; 173 computer-based). *Application deadline:* For fall admission, 4/15 priority date for domestic and international students; for spring admission, 9/15 priority date for domestic and international students. Applications are processed on a rolling basis. Application fee: $40. Electronic applications accepted. *Expenses:* Tuition: Full-time $15,600; part-time $650 per credit. Required fees: $50 per term. One-time fee: $190. Tuition and fees vary according to course load and degree level. *Financial support:* Career-related internships or fieldwork, Federal Work-Study, and scholarships/grants available. Financial award applicants required to submit FAFSA. *Unit head:* Camille Smith, Chair, 602-373-3881, Fax: 928-776-5151, E-mail: csmith@prescott.edu. *Application contact:* Kerstin Alicki, Admissions Counselor, 877-412-8705, Fax: 928-277-4695, E-mail: admissions@prescott.edu.

Providence College and Theological Seminary, Theological Seminary, Otterburne, MB R0A 1G0, Canada. Offers children's ministry (Certificate); Christian studies (MA, Certificate); counseling (MA); cross-cultural discipleship (Certificate); divinity (M Div); educational studies (MA), including counseling psychology, educational ministries, student development, teaching English to speakers of other languages, training teachers of English to speakers of other languages; global studies (MA); lay counseling (Diploma); ministry (D Min); teaching English to speakers of other languages (Certificate); theological studies (MA); training teacher of English to speakers of other languages (Certificate); youth ministry (Certificate). *Accreditation:* ATS. Part-time programs available. *Degree requirements:* For master's, variable foreign language requirement, thesis (for some programs); for doctorate, thesis/dissertation; for M Div, 2 foreign languages, comprehensive exam, thesis/dissertation (for some programs). *Entrance requirements:* Additional exam requirements/recommendations for international students: Recommended—TOEFL (minimum score 550 paper-based; 213 computer-based). *Faculty research:* Studies in Isaiah, theology of sin.

Purdue University Calumet, Graduate Studies Office, School of Education, Program in Counseling, Hammond, IN 46323-2094. Offers human services (MS Ed); mental health counseling (MS Ed); school counseling (MS Ed). *Entrance requirements:* Additional exam requirements/recommendations for international students: Required—TOEFL. Application fee: $30. *Expenses:* Tuition, state resident: full-time $6867. Tuition, nonresident: full-time $14,157. *Financial support:* Application deadline: 3/1. *Unit head:* Dr. Robert Colon, Director, Graduate Studies in Education, 219-989-2867, E-mail: colon2@purduecal.edu. *Application contact:* Dr. Lisa Hollingsworth, Program Chair, 219-989-2789, E-mail: hollings@purduecal.edu.

Quincy University, Program in Counseling, Quincy, IL 62301-2699. Offers education (MS Ed), including clinical mental health counseling, school counseling. Part-time and evening/weekend programs available. *Faculty:* 2 full-time (1 woman). *Students:* 2 full-time (both women), 17 part-time (15 women); includes 1 Black or African American, non-Hispanic/Latino; 1 Two or more races, non-Hispanic/Latino. In 2010, 17 master's awarded. *Degree requirements:* For master's, comprehensive exam, practicum, internship. *Entrance requirements:* For master's, MAT or GRE. Additional exam requirements/recommendations for international students: Required—TOEFL (minimum score 550 paper-based). *Application deadline:* Applications are processed on a rolling basis. Application fee: $25. Electronic applications accepted. *Expenses:* Tuition: Full-time $8880; part-time $370 per semester hour. Required fees: $360; $15 per semester hour. Tuition and fees vary according to course load, campus/location and program. *Financial support:* Available to part-time students. Applicants required to submit FAFSA. *Unit head:* Dr. Kenneth Oliver, Director, 217-228-5432 Ext. 3113, E-mail: oliveke@quincy.edu. *Application contact:* Jennifer Bang, Coordinator of Adult Studies, 217-228-5404, Fax: 217-228-5479, E-mail: admissions@quincy.edu.

Radford University, College of Graduate and Professional Studies, College of Education and Human Development, Department of Counselor Education, Radford, VA 24142. Offers community counseling (MS); school counseling (MS); student affairs—administration (MS); student affairs—counseling (MS). *Accreditation:* ACA; NCATE. Part-time and evening/weekend programs available. *Faculty:* 8 full-time (5 women), 19 part-time/adjunct (12 women). *Students:* 60 full-time (44 women), 43 part-time (35 women); includes 6 minority (3 Black or African American, non-Hispanic/Latino; 1 American Indian or Alaska Native, non-Hispanic/Latino; 1 Asian, non-Hispanic/Latino; 1 Hispanic/Latino). Average age 29. 56 applicants, 82% accepted, 23 enrolled. In 2010, 32 master's awarded. *Degree requirements:* For master's, comprehensive exam, thesis optional. *Entrance requirements:* For master's, GRE or MAT, minimum GPA of 2.75, 3

Counseling Psychology

Radford University (continued)
letters of reference. Additional exam requirements/recommendations for international students: Required—TOEFL (minimum score 550 paper-based; 213 computer-based; 79 iBT). *Application deadline:* For fall admission, 2/15 priority date for domestic students, 12/1 for international students; for spring admission, 7/1 for international students. Applications are processed on a rolling basis. Application fee: $50. Electronic applications accepted. *Expenses:* Tuition, state resident: full-time $5746; part-time $239 per credit hour. Tuition, nonresident: full-time $14,174; part-time $591 per credit hour. Required fees: $2634; $111 per credit hour. *Financial support:* In 2010–11, 26 students received support, including 12 research assistantships with partial tuition reimbursements available (averaging $8,000 per year), 8 teaching assistantships with partial tuition reimbursements available (averaging $8,700 per year); career-related internships or fieldwork, Federal Work-Study, institutionally sponsored loans, scholarships/grants, and unspecified assistantships also available. Financial award application deadline: 3/1; financial award applicants required to submit FAFSA. *Unit head:* Dr. Alan Forrest, Chair, 540-831-5487, Fax: 540-831-6755, E-mail: aforrest@radford.edu. *Application contact:* Rebecca Conner, Graduate Admissions, 540-831-5431, Fax: 540-831-6061, E-mail: gradcollege@radford.edu.

Radford University, College of Graduate and Professional Studies, College of Humanities and Behavioral Sciences, Program in Counseling Psychology, Radford, VA 24142. Offers Psy D. *Faculty:* 4 full-time (3 women). *Students:* 10 full-time (8 women); includes 2 minority (1 Black or African American, non-Hispanic/Latino; 1 Asian, non-Hispanic/Latino). Average age 28. 10 applicants, 70% accepted, 4 enrolled. *Degree requirements:* For doctorate, thesis/dissertation. *Entrance requirements:* For doctorate, GRE General Test, master's degree; minimum GPA of 3.5; letter of interest; curriculum vitae; writing sample; 3 letters of recommendation. Additional exam requirements/recommendations for international students: Required—TOEFL (minimum score 550 paper-based; 213 computer-based; 79 iBT). *Application deadline:* For fall admission, 1/15 for domestic students, 12/1 for international students. Applications are processed on a rolling basis. Application fee: $50. Electronic applications accepted. *Expenses:* Tuition, state resident: full-time $5746; part-time $239 per credit hour. Tuition, nonresident: full-time $14,174; part-time $591 per credit hour. Required fees: $2634; $111 per credit hour. *Financial support:* In 2010–11, 10 students received support, including 10 research assistantships with full tuition reimbursements available (averaging $13,800 per year); career-related internships or fieldwork, Federal Work-Study, institutionally sponsored loans, and scholarships/grants also available. Financial award application deadline: 3/1; financial award applicants required to submit FAFSA. *Unit head:* Dr. James L. Werth, Program Director, 540-831-6817, Fax: 540-831-6113, E-mail: jwerth@radford.edu. *Application contact:* Rebecca Conner, Graduate Admissions, 540-831-5431, Fax: 540-831-6061, E-mail: gradcollege@radford.edu.

Regent University, Graduate School, School of Psychology and Counseling, Virginia Beach, VA 23464-9800. Offers clinical psychology (MA, Psy D); counseling studies (CAGS); counselor education and supervision (PhD); human services counseling (MA), including community counseling, school counseling; M Div/MA; M Ed/MA; MBA/MA. PhD program offered online only. *Accreditation:* ACA; APA (one or more programs are accredited). Part-time and evening/weekend programs available. Postbaccalaureate distance learning degree programs offered (minimal on-campus study). *Faculty:* 31 full-time (16 women), 23 part-time/adjunct (14 women). *Students:* 235 full-time (190 women), 203 part-time (158 women); includes 104 Black or African American, non-Hispanic/Latino; 7 Asian, non-Hispanic/Latino; 11 Hispanic/Latino, 13 international. Average age 35. 436 applicants, 49% accepted, 111 enrolled. In 2010, 82 master's, 57 doctorates awarded. *Degree requirements:* For master's, thesis or alternative, internship, practicum, written competency exam; for doctorate, thesis/dissertation or alternative. *Entrance requirements:* For master's, GRE General Test including writing exam, minimum undergraduate GPA of 2.75, 3 recommendations, resume, transcripts, writing sample; for doctorate, GRE General Test including writing exam, GRE Subject Test, minimum undergraduate GPA of 3.0, 3.5 (PhD), 10-15 minute VHS tape demonstrating counseling skills, writing sample, 3 recommendations, resume. Additional exam requirements/recommendations for international students: Required—TOEFL (minimum score 577 paper-based; 233 computer-based). *Application deadline:* For fall admission, 4/1 priority date for domestic students; for spring admission, 11/1 priority date for domestic students. Applications are processed on a rolling basis. Application fee: $50. Electronic applications accepted. *Expenses:* Contact institution. *Financial support:* Research assistantships with full and partial tuition reimbursements, teaching assistantships with full and partial tuition reimbursements, career-related internships or fieldwork, scholarships/grants, and tuition waivers (full and partial) available. Support available to part-time students. Financial award application deadline: 9/1; financial award applicants required to submit FAFSA. *Faculty research:* Marriage enrichment, AIDS counseling, troubled youth, faith and learning, trauma. *Unit head:* Dr. William Hathaway, Acting Dean, 757-352-4294, Fax: 757-352-4282, E-mail: willhat@regent.edu. *Application contact:* Matthew Chadwick, Director of Enrollment Support Services, 800-373-5504, Fax: 757-352-4381, E-mail: admissions@regent.edu.

Regis University, College for Professional Studies, School of Education and Counseling, Department of Counseling, Denver, CO 80221-1099. Offers community counseling (MAC); counseling children and adolescents (Post-Graduate Certificate); marriage and family therapy (MA, Post-Graduate Certificate); transformative counseling (Post-Graduate Certificate). Program offered in Henderson and Las Vegas (Summerlin), NV. *Accreditation:* ACA. Part-time and evening/weekend programs available. *Degree requirements:* For master's, internships, practicum. *Entrance requirements:* For master's, interview, 2 recommendations, resume, criminal background check. Additional exam requirements/recommendations for international students: Required—TOEFL (minimum score 213 computer-based), TWE (minimum score 5). *Expenses:* Contact institution. *Faculty research:* Group development, counselor education, counsel and therapy, influence of technology on psychology, dream finding groups, adult development, depression.

Rhode Island College, School of Graduate Studies, Feinstein School of Education and Human Development, Department of Counseling, Educational Leadership, and School Psychology, Providence, RI 02908-1991. Offers agency counseling (MA); co-occurring disorders (MA, CGS); educational leadership (M Ed); educational psychology (MA); mental health counseling (CAGS); school counseling (MA, CAGS); school psychology (CAGS). *Accreditation:* NCATE. Part-time and evening/weekend programs available. *Faculty:* 10 full-time (5 women), 12 part-time/adjunct (7 women). *Students:* 31 full-time (26 women), 137 part-time (101 women); includes 13 minority (9 Black or African American, non-Hispanic/Latino; 2 Asian, non-Hispanic/Latino; 2 Hispanic/Latino). Average age 34. In 2010, 43 master's, 21 other advanced degrees awarded. *Degree requirements:* For master's and other advanced degree, comprehensive exam (for some programs), thesis (for some programs). *Entrance requirements:* For master's, GRE General Test or MAT, undergraduate transcripts; minimum undergraduate GPA of 3.0; for other advanced degree, GRE or MAT (for most programs), undergraduate transcripts; minimum undergraduate GPA of 3.0; copy of teaching certificate (when applicable); 3 letters of recommendation; current resume. Additional exam requirements/recommendations for international students: Recommended—TOEFL (minimum score 550 paper-based; 213 computer-based; 79 iBT). *Application deadline:* For fall admission, 3/1 for domestic students; for spring admission, 11/1 for domestic students. Applications are processed on a rolling basis. Application fee: $50. *Expenses:* Tuition, state resident: full-time $8208; part-time $342 per credit hour. Tuition, nonresident: full-time $16,080; part-time $670 per credit hour. Required fees: $554; $20 per credit. $72 per term. *Financial support:* Teaching assistantships with full tuition reimbursements, career-related internships or fieldwork, Federal Work-Study, scholarships/grants, health care benefits, and unspecified assistantships available. Support available to part-time students. Financial award application deadline: 5/15; financial award applicants required to submit FAFSA. *Unit head:* Dr. Monica Darcy, Chair, 401-456-8023. *Application contact:* Graduate Studies, 401-456-8700.

Richmont Graduate University, Graduate Programs, Atlanta, GA 30327. Offers Christian psychological studies (MS); marriage and family therapy (MA); professional counseling (MA).

Rivier College, School of Graduate Studies, Department of Education, Nashua, NH 03060. Offers curriculum and instruction (M Ed); early childhood education (M Ed); educational administration (M Ed); educational studies (M Ed); elementary education (M Ed); elementary education and general special education (M Ed); emotional and behavioral disorders (M Ed); general social education (M Ed); leadership and learning (Ed D, CAGS); learning disabilities (M Ed); learning disabilities and reading (M Ed); mental health counseling (MA); reading (M Ed); school counseling (M Ed). Part-time and evening/weekend programs available. *Faculty:* 15 full-time (10 women), 19 part-time/adjunct (14 women). *Students:* 103 full-time (92 women), 368 part-time (310 women); includes 7 Black or African American, non-Hispanic/Latino; 5 Asian, non-Hispanic/Latino; 6 Hispanic/Latino. Average age 35. 212 applicants, 28% accepted, 38 enrolled. In 2010, 95 master's, 18 other advanced degrees awarded. *Degree requirements:* For master's, comprehensive exam (for some programs), internships. *Entrance requirements:* For master's, GRE General Test or MAT. *Application deadline:* Applications are processed on a rolling basis. Application fee: $25. *Expenses:* Tuition: Part-time $456 per credit. *Financial support:* Available to part-time students. Application deadline: 2/1. *Unit head:* Dr. Mary McNeil, Chairman, 603-897-8582, E-mail: mmcneil@rivier.edu. *Application contact:* Mathew Kittredge, Director of Graduate Admissions, 603-897-8229, Fax: 603-897-8810, E-mail: mkittredge@rivier.edu.

Rosemont College, Schools of Graduate and Professional Studies, Program in Counseling Psychology, Rosemont, PA 19010-1699. Offers human services (MA); school counseling (MA). Part-time and evening/weekend programs available. *Degree requirements:* For master's, thesis or alternative, practicum. *Entrance requirements:* For master's, minimum undergraduate GPA of 3.0, 3 letters of recommendation. Additional exam requirements/recommendations for international students: Required—TOEFL. Electronic applications accepted. *Expenses:* Contact institution. *Faculty research:* Addictions counseling.

Rowan University, Graduate School, College of Liberal Arts and Sciences, Department of Psychology, Program in Mental Health Counseling, Glassboro, NJ 08028-1701. Offers MA. *Accreditation:* ACA. Part-time and evening/weekend programs available. *Students:* 1 (woman) part-time. Average age 31. 1 applicant, 100% accepted, 1 enrolled. In 2010, 8 master's awarded. *Degree requirements:* For master's, thesis. *Entrance requirements:* For master's, GRE General Test. Additional exam requirements/recommendations for international students: Required—TOEFL. *Application deadline:* For spring admission, 2/15 for domestic students. Applications are processed on a rolling basis. Application fee: $65 ($200 for international students). Electronic applications accepted. *Expenses:* Tuition, area resident: Part-time $602 per semester hour. Tuition, nonresident: part-time $602 per semester hour. Required fees: $100 per semester hour. One-time fee: $10 part-time. *Financial support:* Career-related internships or fieldwork, scholarships/grants, health care benefits, and unspecified assistantships available. *Unit head:* Dr. Horacio Sosa, Dean, College of Graduate and Continuing Education, 856-256-4747, Fax: 856-256-5638, E-mail: lalovic-hand@rowan.edu. *Application contact:* Karen Haynes, Graduate Coordinator, 856-256-4052, Fax: 856-256-4436, E-mail: haynes@rowan.edu.

Rowan University, Graduate School, College of Liberal Arts and Sciences, Program in Mental Health Counseling and Applied Psychology, Glassboro, NJ 08028-1701. Offers MA. *Accreditation:* ACA. Part-time and evening/weekend programs available. In 2010, 31 master's awarded. *Degree requirements:* For master's, thesis. *Entrance requirements:* For master's, GRE General Test. Additional exam requirements/recommendations for international students: Required—TOEFL. *Application deadline:* Applications are processed on a rolling basis. Application fee: $65 ($200 for international students). Electronic applications accepted. *Expenses:* Tuition, area resident: Part-time $602 per semester hour. Tuition, nonresident: part-time $602 per semester hour. Required fees: $100 per semester hour. One-time fee: $10 part-time. *Financial support:* Career-related internships or fieldwork, scholarships/grants, health care benefits, and unspecified assistantships available. *Unit head:* Dr. Horacio Sosa, Dean, College of Graduate and Continuing Education, 856-256-4747, Fax: 856-256-5638, E-mail: sosa@rowan.edu. *Application contact:* Karen Haynes, Graduate Coordinator, 856-256-4052, Fax: 856-256-4436, E-mail: haynes@rowan.edu.

Rutgers, The State University of New Jersey, New Brunswick, Graduate School of Education, Department of Educational Psychology, Programs in School Counseling and Counseling Psychology, Piscataway, NJ 08854-8097. Offers Ed M. Part-time and evening/weekend programs available. *Faculty:* 3 full-time (2 women). *Students:* 31 full-time (21 women), 25 part-time (20 women). 94 applicants, 52% accepted, 24 enrolled. In 2010, 29 master's awarded. *Entrance requirements:* For master's, GRE General Test, 3 letters of recommendation. Additional exam requirements/recommendations for international students: Required—TOEFL (minimum score 550 paper-based; 233 computer-based; 83 iBT). *Application deadline:* For fall admission, 2/1 for domestic and international students; for spring admission, 11/1 for domestic and international students. Application fee: $65. Electronic applications accepted. *Expenses:* Tuition, state resident: full-time $7200; part-time $600 per credit. Tuition, nonresident: full-time $11,124; part-time $927 per credit. *Financial support:* Application deadline: 3/15. *Faculty research:* Children and family in cross-cultural context, attachment theory, multicultural counseling, therapy relationship. *Unit head:* Dr. Lorraine D. McCune, Chairperson, 732-932-7496 Ext. 8310, Fax: 732-932-6829, E-mail: mccune@rutgers.edu. *Application contact:* Dr. William Firestone, Associate Dean for Academic Affairs, 732-932-7496 Ext. 8102, Fax: 732-932-8206, E-mail: william.firestone@gse.rutgers.edu.

Sage Graduate School, Graduate School, School of Health Sciences, Department of Psychology, Program in Counseling and Community Psychology, Troy, NY 12180-4115. Offers MA. *Faculty:* 3 full-time (all women), 8 part-time/adjunct (7 women). *Students:* 31 full-time (30 women), 37 part-time (32 women); includes 8 minority (5 Black or African American, non-Hispanic/Latino; 1 Asian, non-Hispanic/Latino; 2 Hispanic/Latino). Average age 29. 62 applicants, 44% accepted, 13 enrolled. In 2010, 22 master's awarded. *Degree requirements:* For master's, externship, internship, thesis or research seminar. *Entrance requirements:* For master's, minimum undergraduate GPA of 3.0, interview. *Application deadline:* Applications are processed on a rolling basis. Application fee: $40. *Expenses:* Tuition: Full-time $10,980; part-time $610 per credit hour. Tuition and fees vary according to course load, degree level and program. *Unit head:* Dr. Esther Haskevitz, Interim Dean, School of Health Sciences, 518-244-2296, Fax: 518-244-4571, E-mail: haskve@sage.edu. *Application contact:* Dr. Jean Poppei, Director, 518-244-2076, Fax: 518-244-4545, E-mail: poppej@sage.edu.

St. Bonaventure University, School of Graduate Studies, School of Education, Program in Counselor Education, St. Bonaventure, NY 14778-2284. Offers community mental health counseling (MS Ed); school counseling (MS Ed); school counselor (Adv C). *Accreditation:* ACA. Part-time and evening/weekend programs available. *Faculty:* 4 full-time (1 woman), 8 part-time/adjunct (3 women). *Students:* 115 full-time (94 women), 24 part-time (17 women); includes 8 minority (4 Black or African American, non-Hispanic/Latino; 4 Hispanic/Latino), 2 international. Average age 29. 110 applicants, 65% accepted, 50 enrolled. In 2010, 23 master's, 8 Adv Cs awarded. *Degree requirements:* For master's, comprehensive exam, thesis optional, completion of internship, submission of porfolio. *Entrance requirements:* For master's, interview, writing sample, minimum undergraduate GPA of 3.0, references. Additional exam requirements/recommendations for international students: Required—TOEFL (minimum score 550 paper-based; 213 computer-based). *Application deadline:* For fall admission, 8/15 priority date for domestic students, 2/1 priority date for international students; for spring admission, 10/15 priority date for domestic students, 7/1 priority date for international students. Applications are processed on a rolling basis. Application fee: $30. Electronic applications accepted. *Expenses:* Tuition: Part-time $670 per credit hour. *Financial support:* In 2010–11, 5 research assistantships with full and partial tuition reimbursements were awarded; career-related internships or fieldwork, Federal Work-Study, scholarships/grants, health care benefits, tuition waivers (partial), and unspecified assistantships also available. Support available to part-time students. Financial award application deadline: 4/15; financial award applicants required to submit FAFSA. *Unit head:* Dr. Craig Zuckerman, Director, 716-375-2374, Fax: 716-375-2360, E-mail: czuck@sbu.edu. *Application contact:* Bruce Campbell, Director of Graduate Admissions, 716-375-2429, E-mail: gradsch@sbu.edu.

St. Edward's University, New College, Program in Counseling, Austin, TX 78704. Offers MA. Part-time and evening/weekend programs available. *Students:* 97 full-time (80 women), 157 part-time (128 women); includes 57 minority (11 Black or African American, non-Hispanic/Latino; 1 American Indian or Alaska Native, non-Hispanic/Latino; 1 Asian, non-Hispanic/Latino; 38 Hispanic/Latino; 1 Native Hawaiian or other Pacific Islander, non-Hispanic/Latino; 5 Two or more races, non-Hispanic/Latino). Average age 33. 111 applicants, 70% accepted, 59 enrolled. In 2010, 65 master's awarded. *Degree requirements:* For master's, minimum of 24 resident hours. *Entrance requirements:* For master's, GRE General Test, minimum GPA of 3.0 in last 60 hours or 2.75 overall. Additional exam requirements/recommendations for international students: Required—TOEFL (minimum score 550 paper-based; 213 computer-based; 79 iBT) or IELTS (minimum score 6). *Application deadline:* For fall admission, 7/1 for domestic and international students; for spring admission, 11/1 for domestic and international students. Applications are processed on a rolling basis. Application fee: $45 ($50 for international students). Electronic applications accepted. *Expenses:* Tuition: Full-time $16,200; part-time $900 per credit hour. Required fees: $50 per trimester. Full-time tuition and fees vary according to course load and program. *Financial support:* In 2010–11, 4 students received support. Scholarships/grants available. *Unit head:* Dr. Elizabeth Katz, Director, 512-464-8833, Fax: 512-448-8492, E-mail: elizk@stedwards.edu. *Application contact:* Anna Alkin, Graduate Admissions Coordinator, 512-448-8745, Fax: 512-428-1032, E-mail: annaa@stedwards.edu.

St. John Fisher College, Wegmans School of Nursing, Program in Mental Health Counseling, Rochester, NY 14618-3597. Offers MS. *Accreditation:* ACA. Part-time programs available. *Faculty:* 5 full-time (2 women), 1 part-time/adjunct (0 women). *Students:* 39 full-time (33 women), 25 part-time (23 women); includes 13 minority (5 Black or African American, non-Hispanic/Latino; 7 Hispanic/Latino; 1 Two or more races, non-Hispanic/Latino). Average age 31. 79 applicants, 68% accepted, 33 enrolled. In 2010, 20 master's awarded. *Degree requirements:* For master's, practicum experience, internship. *Entrance requirements:* For master's, GRE (if GPA below 3.0), 2 letters of recommendation, personal statement, current resume, interview. Additional exam requirements/recommendations for international students: Required—TOEFL (minimum score 575 paper-based; 233 computer-based; 80 iBT). *Application deadline:* Applications are processed on a rolling basis. Application fee: $30. Electronic applications accepted. *Expenses:* Tuition: Part-time $705 per credit hour. Required fees: $25 per semester. *Financial support:* In 2010–11, 52 students received support. Scholarships/grants available. Financial award applicants required to submit FAFSA. *Faculty research:* Social class issues, clinical supervision, counselor education, play therapy. *Unit head:* Dr. Rachel Jordan, Director, 585-899-3858, E-mail: rjordan@sjfc.edu. *Application contact:* Jose Perales, Director of Graduate Admissions, 585-385-8067, E-mail: jperales@sjfc.edu.

Saint Joseph College, Department of Counselor Education, West Hartford, CT 06117-2700. Offers community counseling (MA); school counseling (MA). Part-time and evening/weekend programs available. *Students:* 57 full-time (54 women), 80 part-time (70 women); includes 1 Black or African American, non-Hispanic/Latino; 4 Hispanic/Latino; 1 Two or more races, non-Hispanic/Latino. *Degree requirements:* For master's, comprehensive exam, thesis optional. *Entrance requirements:* For master's, 2 letters of recommendation. *Application deadline:* Applications are processed on a rolling basis. Application fee: $50. Electronic applications accepted. *Expenses:* Tuition: Full-time $11,340; part-time $630 per credit. Required fees: $540; $30 per credit. Tuition and fees vary according to course load, campus/location and program. *Financial support:* Career-related internships or fieldwork and unspecified assistantships available. Support available to part-time students. Financial award applicants required to submit FAFSA. *Application contact:* Graduate Admissions Office, 860-231-5261, E-mail: graduate@sjc.edu.

Saint Martin's University, Graduate Programs, Program in Counseling Psychology, Lacey, WA 98503. Offers MAC. Part-time and evening/weekend programs available. *Faculty:* 3 full-time (2 women), 3 part-time/adjunct (all women). *Students:* 40 full-time (29 women), 58 part-time (52 women); includes 4 Black or African American, non-Hispanic/Latino; 4 American Indian or Alaska Native, non-Hispanic/Latino; 5 Asian, non-Hispanic/Latino; 5 Hispanic/Latino; 1 Two or more races, non-Hispanic/Latino, 5 international. Average age 36. 24 applicants, 79% accepted, 18 enrolled. In 2010, 17 master's awarded. *Degree requirements:* For master's, clinical experience, interview. *Entrance requirements:* For master's, BA in psychology or related field, clinical experience. Additional exam requirements/recommendations for international students: Required—TOEFL. *Application deadline:* For fall admission, 7/1 for domestic students, 2/15 for international students; for spring admission, 11/1 priority date for domestic students, 7/1 for international students. Applications are processed on a rolling basis. Application fee: $35. *Financial support:* In 2010–11, 97 students received support. Career-related internships or fieldwork, Federal Work-Study, and institutionally sponsored loans available. Support available to part-time students. Financial award application deadline: 3/1; financial award applicants required to submit FAFSA. *Faculty research:* Alcohol studies, clinical effectiveness, social justice, parent adolescent interaction. *Unit head:* Dr. Godfrey J. Ellis, Director, 360-438-4560, E-mail: gellis@stmartin.edu. *Application contact:* Sandy Brandt, Administrative Assistant, 360-438-4560, E-mail: sbrandt@stmartin.edu.

St. Mary's University, Graduate School, Department of Counseling and Human Services, Program in Mental Health, San Antonio, TX 78228-8507. Offers MA. Part-time programs available. *Degree requirements:* For master's, comprehensive exam, internship. *Entrance requirements:* For master's, GRE, MAT. Additional exam requirements/recommendations for international students: Required—TOEFL (minimum score 550 paper-based; 213 computer-based; 80 iBT). Electronic applications accepted.

Saint Mary's University of Minnesota, Schools of Graduate and Professional Programs, Graduate School of Health and Human Services, Counseling and Psychological Services Program, Winona, MN 55987-1399. Offers counseling and psychological services (MA). *Unit head:* Dr. Christina Huck, Director, 612-728-5113, Fax: 612-728-5121, E-mail: chuck@smumn.edu. *Application contact:* Yasin Alsaidi, Director of Admissions for Graduate and Professional Programs, 612-728-5207, Fax: 612-728-5121, E-mail: yalsaidi@smumn.edu.

Saint Mary's University of Minnesota, Schools of Graduate and Professional Programs, Graduate School of Health and Human Services, Counseling Psychology Program, Winona, MN 55987-1399. Offers Psy D. *Unit head:* Dr. Kenneth Solberg, Director, 612-238-4548, E-mail: ksolberg@smumn.edu. *Application contact:* Yasin Alsaidi, Director of Admissions for Graduate and Professional Programs, 612-728-5207, Fax: 612-728-5121, E-mail: yalsaidi@smumn.edu.

Saint Paul University, Faculty of Human Sciences, Program in Counseling and Spirituality, Ottawa, ON K1S 1C4, Canada. Offers individual or marital/couple counseling (MA); spiritual care (MA). Part-time programs available. *Degree requirements:* For master's, research project or thesis. *Entrance requirements:* For master's, honors BA in human sciences, minimum B average, 12 theology credits.

St. Thomas University, Biscayne College, Department of Social Sciences and Counseling, Program in Mental Health Counseling, Miami Gardens, FL 33054-6459. Offers MS. Part-time and evening/weekend programs available. *Degree requirements:* For master's, comprehensive exam. *Entrance requirements:* For master's, interview, minimum GPA of 3.0 or GRE. Additional exam requirements/recommendations for international students: Required—TOEFL (minimum score 550 paper-based; 213 computer-based; 79 iBT). Electronic applications accepted.

Saint Xavier University, Graduate Studies, School of Arts and Sciences, Department of Psychology, Chicago, IL 60655-3105. Offers adult counseling (Certificate); child/adolescent counseling (Certificate); core counseling (Certificate); counseling psychology (MA). Part-time and evening/weekend programs available. *Entrance requirements:* For master's, GRE General Test, minimum GPA of 3.0, interview.

Salem State University, School of Graduate Studies, Program in Counseling and Psychological Services, Salem, MA 01970-5353. Offers MS, Graduate Certificate. Part-time and evening/weekend programs available. *Students:* 48 full-time (36 women), 54 part-time (40 women); includes 3 Black or African American, non-Hispanic/Latino; 3 Asian, non-Hispanic/Latino; 6 Hispanic/Latino, 6 international. 33 applicants, 88% accepted, 29 enrolled. In 2010, 24 master's, 4 other advanced degrees awarded. *Entrance requirements:* For master's, GRE or MAT. Additional exam requirements/recommendations for international students: Required—TOEFL (minimum score 550 paper-based; 80 iBT) or IELTS (minimum score 5.5). *Application deadline:* For fall admission, 5/1 for domestic students; for spring admission, 10/1 for domestic students. Applications are processed on a rolling basis. Application fee: $50. *Expenses:* Tuition, state resident: full-time $2520; part-time $290 per credit hour. Tuition, nonresident: full-time $4140; part-time $380 per credit hour. Required fees: $2700. *Financial support:* Career-related internships or fieldwork, Federal Work-Study, scholarships/grants, and unspecified assistantships available. Support available to part-time students. Financial award application deadline: 5/1; financial award applicants required to submit FAFSA. *Unit head:* Dr. Patrice Miller, Coordinator, 978-542-6075, Fax: 978-542-6596, E-mail: pmiller@salemstate.edu. *Application contact:* Dr. Lee A. Brossoit, Assistant Dean of Graduate Admissions, 978-542-6673, Fax: 978-542-7215, E-mail: lbrossoit@salemstate.edu.

Salem State University, School of Graduate Studies, Program of Advanced Professional Studies in Counseling, Salem, MA 01970-5353. Offers Graduate Certificate. Part-time and evening/weekend programs available. *Students:* 7 part-time (5 women), 1 international. Average age 32. 4 applicants, 50% accepted, 2 enrolled. *Entrance requirements:* Additional exam requirements/recommendations for international students: Required—TOEFL (minimum score 550 paper-based; 80 iBT) or IELTS (minimum score 5.5). *Application deadline:* For fall admission, 5/1 for domestic students; for spring admission, 10/1 for domestic students. Applications are processed on a rolling basis. Application fee: $50. *Expenses:* Tuition, state resident: full-time $2520; part-time $290 per credit hour. Tuition, nonresident: full-time $4140; part-time $380 per credit hour. Required fees: $2700. *Financial support:* Career-related internships or fieldwork, Federal Work-Study, scholarships/grants, and unspecified assistantships available. Support available to part-time students. Financial award application deadline: 5/1; financial award applicants required to submit FAFSA. *Unit head:* Dr. Patrice Miller, Program Coordinator, 978-542-6075, Fax: 978-542-7215, E-mail: pmiller@salemstate.edu. *Application contact:* Dr. Lee A. Brossoit, Assistant Dean of Graduate Admissions, 978-542-6675, Fax: 978-542-7215, E-mail: lbrossoit@salemstate.edu.

Salve Regina University, Graduate Studies, Holistic Graduate Programs, Newport, RI 02840-4192. Offers expressive and creative arts (CAGS); holistic counseling (MA); holistic leadership (MA, CAGS); mental health (CAGS). Part-time and evening/weekend programs available. *Degree requirements:* For master's, internship, project. *Entrance requirements:* For master's, GMAT, GRE General Test, or MAT. Additional exam requirements/recommendations for international students: Required—TOEFL (minimum score 600 paper-based; 250 computer-based; 100 iBT) or IELTS. Electronic applications accepted. *Expenses:* Tuition: Full-time $7740; part-time $430 per credit. Required fees: $40 per semester. Tuition and fees vary according to course level and degree level.

Salve Regina University, Graduate Studies, Program in Rehabilitation Counseling, Newport, RI 02840-4192. Offers mental health counseling (CAGS); rehabilitation counseling (MA). *Accreditation:* CORE. Part-time and evening/weekend programs available. *Entrance requirements:* For master's, GMAT, GRE General Test or MAT. Additional exam requirements/recommendations for international students: Required—TOEFL (minimum score 600 paper-based; 250 computer-based; 100 iBT) or IELTS. Electronic applications accepted. *Expenses:* Tuition: Full-time $7740; part-time $430 per credit. Required fees: $40 per semester. Tuition and fees vary according to course level and degree level.

San Francisco State University, Division of Graduate Studies, College of Health and Human Services, Department of Counseling, San Francisco, CA 94132-1722. Offers counseling (MS); marriage, family, and child counseling (MSC); rehabilitation counseling (MS). *Accreditation:* ACA (one or more programs are accredited). Part-time programs available. *Application deadline:* Applications are processed on a rolling basis. *Unit head:* Dr. Robert Williams, Chair, 415-338-2005. *Application contact:* Couryll Pineda, Academic Office Coordinator, 415-338-2005, E-mail: counsel@sfsu.edu.

Santa Clara University, School of Education and Counseling Psychology, Department of Counseling Psychology, Santa Clara, CA 95053. Offers counseling (MA); counseling psychology (MA). Part-time and evening/weekend programs available. *Students:* 83 full-time (68 women), 147 part-time (123 women); includes 71 minority (4 Black or African American, non-Hispanic/Latino; 1 American Indian or Alaska Native, non-Hispanic/Latino; 29 Asian, non-Hispanic/Latino; 34 Hispanic/Latino; 1 Native Hawaiian or other Pacific Islander, non-Hispanic/Latino; 2 Two or more races, non-Hispanic/Latino), 11 international. Average age 33. 137 applicants, 68% accepted, 43 enrolled. In 2010, 68 master's awarded. *Degree requirements:* For master's, comprehensive exam. *Entrance requirements:* For master's, GRE or MAT, statement of purpose, letters of recommendation, transcripts. Additional exam requirements/recommendations for international students: Required—TOEFL (minimum score 600 paper-based; 100 computer-based; 100 iBT). *Application deadline:* For fall admission, 6/15 for domestic and international students; for winter admission, 10/15 for domestic and international students; for spring admission, 1/31 for domestic and international students. Applications are processed on a rolling basis. Application fee: $50. Electronic applications accepted. *Expenses:* Contact institution. *Financial support:* In 2010–11, 35 students received support; fellowships, Federal Work-Study, institutionally sponsored loans, and scholarships/grants available. Support available to part-time students. Financial award application deadline: 5/15; financial award applicants required to submit FAFSA. *Unit head:* Dr. Atom Yee, Interim Dean, 408-554-4455, Fax: 408-554-5038, E-mail: ayee@scu.edu. *Application contact:* Paul Somoff, Admissions and Financial Aid Coordinator, 408-554-7884, Fax: 408-554-4367, E-mail: psomoff@scu.edu.

Saybrook University, LIOS Graduate College, Systems Counseling Track, San Francisco, CA 94111-1920. Offers MA. Program offered jointly with Bastyr University. *Faculty:* 10 full-time (6 women), 5 part-time/adjunct (2 women). *Students:* 90 full-time. Average age 40. 55 applicants, 96% accepted, 50 enrolled. In 2010, 51 master's awarded. *Degree requirements:* For master's, thesis (for some programs), oral exams. *Entrance requirements:* For master's, bachelor's degree from an accredited university or college. *Application deadline:* Applications are processed on a rolling basis. Application fee: $65. *Financial support:* In 2010–11, 41 students received support. Career-related internships or fieldwork, Federal Work-Study, and scholarships/grants available. Financial award applicants required to submit FAFSA. *Faculty research:* Family systems theory, marriage and family therapy, systems consultation, family and culture of origin, personal authority. *Unit head:* Dr. Timothy Weber, Head, 425-939-8170, Fax: 425-939-8110, E-mail: tweber@lios.org. *Application contact:* Jennifer Herron, Director, Academic Admissions, 425-939-8124, Fax: 425-939-8110, E-mail: jherron@lios.org.

The School of Professional Psychology at Forest Institute, Graduate Programs, Springfield, MO 65807. Offers applied behavior analysis (MS); clinical psychology (MA, Psy D); counseling psychology (MA); marriage and family therapy (MA, PGC). *Accreditation:* AAMFT/COAMFTE; APA (one or more programs are accredited). *Faculty:* 17 full-time (8 women), 18 part-time/adjunct (10 women). *Students:* 214 full-time (144 women), 46 part-time (35 women); includes 35 minority (11 Black or African American, non-Hispanic/Latino; 9 American Indian or Alaska Native, non-Hispanic/Latino; 5 Asian, non-Hispanic/Latino; 10 Hispanic/Latino), 3 international. Average age 28. 176 applicants, 69% accepted, 45 enrolled. In 2010, 35 master's, 31 doctorates awarded. Terminal master's awarded for partial completion of doctoral program. *Degree requirements:* For master's, thesis, practicum; for doctorate, comprehensive exam, thesis/dissertation, internship, practicum. *Entrance requirements:* For master's, GRE General Test, interview, minimum GPA of 3.0, 12 hours in psychology; for doctorate, GRE General Test, interview, minimum GPA of 3.0, 18 hours in psychology. Additional exam requirements/recommendations for international students: Required—TOEFL (minimum score 550 paper-based; 213 computer-based). *Application deadline:* For fall admission, 1/15 priority date for domestic and international students; for spring admission, 8/1 priority date for domestic and

Counseling Psychology

The School of Professional Psychology at Forest Institute (continued)
international students. Applications are processed on a rolling basis. Application fee: $50. Electronic applications accepted. *Financial support:* In 2010–11, 59 students received support; fellowships with partial tuition reimbursements available, teaching assistantships, career-related internships or fieldwork, Federal Work-Study, scholarships/grants, tuition waivers (partial), and unspecified assistantships available. Financial award applicants required to submit FAFSA. *Faculty research:* Forensics/corrections, marriage and family therapy, child and adolescent, integrated health care, neuropsychology. *Unit head:* Dr. Mark E. Skrade, President, 417-823-3477, Fax: 417-823-3442, E-mail: mskrade@forest.edu. *Application contact:* Bethany Ritter, Admissions Counselor, 417-823-3477, Fax: 417-823-3442, E-mail: britter@forest.edu.

Seton Hall University, College of Education and Human Services, Department of Professional Psychology and Family Therapy, Program in Counseling Psychology, South Orange, NJ 07079-2697. Offers MA, PhD. *Accreditation:* APA. *Degree requirements:* For doctorate, comprehensive exam, thesis/dissertation, internship. *Entrance requirements:* For doctorate, GRE, interview. *Faculty research:* Vocational indecision, coping skills, cognitive behavioral interventions, vocational development.

Shippensburg University of Pennsylvania, School of Graduate Studies, College of Education and Human Services, Department of Counseling, Shippensburg, PA 17257-2299. Offers Adlerian studies (Certificate); advanced study in counseling (Certificate); alcohol and drug counseling (Certificate); counseling (M Ed, MS), including clinical mental health counseling (MS), college counseling (MS), college student personnel services (MS), elementary school counseling (M Ed), secondary school counseling (MS); couple and family counseling (Certificate). *Accreditation:* ACA (one or more programs are accredited); NCATE. Part-time and evening/weekend programs available. *Faculty:* 8 full-time (4 women), 5 part-time/adjunct (3 women). *Students:* 79 full-time (66 women), 105 part-time (92 women); includes 28 minority (20 Black or African American, non-Hispanic/Latino; 3 Asian, non-Hispanic/Latino; 4 Hispanic/Latino; 1 Two or more races, non-Hispanic/Latino), 2 international. Average age 29. 129 applicants, 45% accepted, 43 enrolled. In 2010, 45 master's awarded. *Degree requirements:* For master's, fieldwork, research project, internship, candidacy. *Entrance requirements:* For master's, GRE or MAT (mental health, student personnel, and college counseling applicants if GPA is less than 2.75), minimum GPA of 2.75 (3.0 for M Ed), resume, 3 letters of recommendation, supplemental data forms, one year of relevant work experience, on-campus interview, autobiographical statement. Additional exam requirements/recommendations for international students: Required—TOEFL (minimum score 580 paper-based; 237 computer-based); Recommended—IELTS (minimum score 6). *Application deadline:* For fall admission, 3/1 for international students; for spring admission, 7/1 for international students. Applications are processed on a rolling basis. Application fee: $30. Electronic applications accepted. *Expenses:* Tuition, state resident: full-time $6966. Tuition, nonresident: full-time $11,146. Required fees: $1802. *Financial support:* In 2010–11, 49 research assistantships with full tuition reimbursements (averaging $5,000 per year) were awarded; career-related internships or fieldwork, scholarships/grants, unspecified assistantships, and resident hall director and student payroll positions also available. Support available to part-time students. Financial award application deadline: 3/1; financial award applicants required to submit FAFSA. *Unit head:* Dr. Jan Arminio, Chairperson, 717-477-1668, Fax: 717-477-4016, E-mail: jlarmi@ship.edu. *Application contact:* Jeremy R. Goshorn, Associate Dean of Graduate Admissions, 717-477-1231, Fax: 717-477-4016, E-mail: jrgoshorn@ship.edu.

Simpson University, MA in Counseling Psychology Program, Redding, CA 96003-8606. Offers MA. Evening/weekend programs available. *Degree requirements:* For master's, completed portfolio, clinical evaluation project. *Entrance requirements:* For master's, BA, minimum GPA of 3.0, resume, 3 letters of recommendation, personal statement, official transcripts. Additional exam requirements/recommendations for international students: Required—TOEFL (minimum score 550 paper-based; 213 computer-based; 79 iBT). Electronic applications accepted. *Faculty research:* Development of executive functioning in young children, cognitive neuropsychology, historical issues in the neurosciences, neurotheology.

Sonoma State University, School of Social Sciences, Department of Counseling, Rohnert Park, CA 94928. Offers counseling (MA); marriage, family, and child counseling (MA); pupil personnel services (MA). *Accreditation:* ACA. Part-time programs available. *Faculty:* 6 full-time (4 women), 5 part-time/adjunct (3 women). *Students:* 57 full-time (45 women), 40 part-time (33 women); includes 1 Black or African American, non-Hispanic/Latino; 1 American Indian or Alaska Native, non-Hispanic/Latino; 4 Asian, non-Hispanic/Latino; 12 Hispanic/Latino; 4 Two or more races, non-Hispanic/Latino, 1 international. Average age 32. 158 applicants, 26% accepted, 15 enrolled. In 2010, 21 master's awarded. *Degree requirements:* For master's, internship. *Entrance requirements:* For master's, minimum GPA of 3.0. Additional exam requirements/recommendations for international students: Required—TOEFL (minimum score 500 paper-based; 173 computer-based). *Application deadline:* For fall admission, 11/30 for domestic students. Application fee: $55. *Financial support:* Career-related internships or fieldwork available. Financial award application deadline: 3/2; financial award applicants required to submit FAFSA. *Unit head:* Dr. Adam Hill, Program Coordinator, 707-664-2340, E-mail: adam.hill@sonoma.edu. *Application contact:* Jaymala Madathil, Administrative Analyst, 707-664-4067, Fax: 707-664-2038, E-mail: jaymala.madathil@sonoma.edu.

Southeastern Oklahoma State University, School of Behavioral Sciences, Durant, OK 74701-0609. Offers clinical mental health counseling (MS). Part-time and evening/weekend programs available. *Faculty:* 10 full-time (3 women). *Students:* 29 full-time (23 women), 14 part-time (12 women); includes 2 Black or African American, non-Hispanic/Latino; 12 American Indian or Alaska Native, non-Hispanic/Latino; 1 Asian, non-Hispanic/Latino; 1 Hispanic/Latino, 2 international. Average age 35. 12 applicants, 100% accepted, 12 enrolled. *Degree requirements:* For master's, thesis optional. *Entrance requirements:* For master's, GRE General Test, minimum GPA of 3.0 in last 60 hours or 2.75 overall. Additional exam requirements/recommendations for international students: Required—TOEFL (minimum score 550 paper-based; 213 computer-based). *Application deadline:* For fall admission, 8/1 for domestic students, 6/1 for international students; for spring admission, 1/5 for domestic students, 11/1 for international students. Application fee: $20 ($55 for international students). Electronic applications accepted. *Financial support:* Fellowships, research assistantships, teaching assistantships, Federal Work-Study available. Support available to part-time students. Financial award application deadline: 6/15. *Unit head:* Dr. Kimberly Donovan, Program Coordinator, 580-745-2312, E-mail: kdonovan@se.edu. *Application contact:* Carrie Williamson, Graduate Secretary, 580-745-2200, Fax: 580-745-7474, E-mail: cwilliamson@se.edu.

Southeastern University, Department of Behavioral and Social Sciences, Lakeland, FL 33801-6099. Offers human services (MA); professional counseling (MS); school counseling (MS). Evening/weekend programs available.

Southeast Missouri State University, School of Graduate Studies, Department of Educational Leadership and Counseling, Counseling Program, Cape Girardeau, MO 63701-4799. Offers career counseling (MA); community counseling (MA); counseling education (Ed S); mental health counseling (MA); school counseling (MA), including elementary counseling, secondary counseling. *Accreditation:* ACA; NCATE. Part-time and evening/weekend programs available. Postbaccalaureate distance learning degree programs offered. *Faculty:* 12 full-time (6 women). *Students:* 29 full-time (26 women), 53 part-time (48 women); includes 5 minority (3 Black or African American, non-Hispanic/Latino; 1 American Indian or Alaska Native, non-Hispanic/Latino; 1 Hispanic/Latino), 1 international. Average age 33. 31 applicants, 94% accepted, 20 enrolled. In 2010, 16 master's, 7 other advanced degrees awarded. *Degree requirements:* For master's, comprehensive exam, portfolio, oral exam, minimum GPA of 3.25; for Ed S, oral exam, minimum GPA of 3.25. *Entrance requirements:* For master's, GRE General Test or MAT, minimum undergraduate GPA of 3.0; 18 undergraduate hours in social science including statistics; teaching certification for school counselor or evidence of competency; for Ed S, GRE General Test or MAT, master's degree; teacher certification; recommendations. Additional exam requirements/recommendations for international students: Required—TOEFL (minimum score 550 paper-based; 213 computer-based; 79 iBT); Recommended—IELTS (minimum score 6). *Application deadline:* For fall admission, 8/1 for domestic students, 6/1 for international students; for spring admission, 11/21 for domestic students, 10/1 for international students. Applications are processed on a rolling basis. Application fee: $25 ($35 for international students). Electronic applications accepted. *Expenses:* Tuition, state resident: full-time $4698; part-time $261 per credit hour. Tuition, nonresident: full-time $8379; part-time $465.50 per credit hour. *Financial support:* In 2010–11, 8 students received support. Career-related internships or fieldwork, Federal Work-Study, institutionally sponsored loans, scholarships/grants, tuition waivers (full), and unspecified assistantships available. Financial award application deadline: 6/30; financial award applicants required to submit FAFSA. *Faculty research:* Counselor development, marriage and family counseling, multicultural counseling. *Unit head:* Dr. David Stader, 573-651-2417, E-mail: dstader@semo.edu. *Application contact:* Gail Amick, Administrative Secretary, 573-651-2049, Fax: 573-651-2001, E-mail: gamick@semo.edu.

Southern Adventist University, School of Education and Psychology, Collegedale, TN 37315-0370. Offers clinical mental health counseling (MS); inclusive education (MS Ed); instructional leadership (MS Ed); literacy education (MS Ed); outdoor teacher education (MS Ed); school counseling (MS). *Accreditation:* NCATE. Part-time and evening/weekend programs available. *Degree requirements:* For master's, comprehensive exam (for some programs), thesis optional, position paper (MS), portfolio (MS Ed in outdoor teacher education). *Entrance requirements:* For master's, interview (MS); 9 semester hours of upper division course work in psychology or related field, including 1 course in psychology research or statistics; 9 semester hours of education (MS Ed). Additional exam requirements/recommendations for international students: Required—TOEFL (minimum score 600 paper-based; 250 computer-based; 100 iBT). Electronic applications accepted.

Southern California Seminary, Graduate and Professional Programs, El Cajon, CA 92019. Offers Biblical studies (MABS); counseling psychology (MACP); marriage and family therapy (MAMFT); psychology (Psy D); religious studies (MRS); theology (M Div). Part-time and evening/weekend programs available. Postbaccalaureate distance learning degree programs offered (minimal on-campus study). *Students:* 37 full-time (8 women), 80 part-time (37 women); includes 55 minority (20 Black or African American, non-Hispanic/Latino; 14 Asian, non-Hispanic/Latino; 16 Hispanic/Latino; 1 Native Hawaiian or other Pacific Islander, non-Hispanic/Latino; 4 Two or more races, non-Hispanic/Latino), 5 international. Average age 41. In 2010, 7 first professional degrees, 50 master's, 4 doctorates awarded. *Degree requirements:* For master's, thesis (for some programs); for doctorate, thesis/dissertation; for M Div, 2 foreign languages. *Entrance requirements:* For doctorate, master's degree in psychology. Additional exam requirements/recommendations for international students: Required—TOEFL (minimum score 550 paper-based). *Application deadline:* For fall admission, 8/13 for domestic and international students; for spring admission, 12/11 for domestic students, 12/15 for international students. Applications are processed on a rolling basis. Application fee: $31 ($126 for international students). Electronic applications accepted. *Expenses:* Tuition: Part-time $339 per unit. Part-time tuition and fees vary according to degree level, campus/location and program. *Financial support:* In 2010–11, 14 students received support. Federal Work-Study, scholarships/grants, and tuition waivers (partial) available. Financial award application deadline: 3/1; financial award applicants required to submit FAFSA. *Unit head:* Dr. Chuck Emert, Vice-President of Academics, 619-201-8995, Fax: 619-201-8975. *Application contact:* Thomas Pittman, Admissions Officer and Director of Student Services, 888-389-7244, Fax: 619-201-8975, E-mail: thpittman@socalsem.edu.

Southern Illinois University Carbondale, Graduate School, College of Liberal Arts, Department of Psychology, Carbondale, IL 62901-4701. Offers clinical psychology (MA, MS, PhD); counseling psychology (MA, MS, PhD); experimental psychology (MA, MS, PhD). *Accreditation:* APA (one or more programs are accredited). *Degree requirements:* For master's, thesis; for doctorate, thesis/dissertation. *Entrance requirements:* For master's, GRE General Test, GRE Subject Test, minimum GPA of 2.7; for doctorate, GRE General Test, GRE Subject Test, minimum GPA of 3.25. Additional exam requirements/recommendations for international students: Required—TOEFL. *Faculty research:* Developmental neuropsychology; smoking, affect, and cognition; personality measurement; vocational psychology; program evaluation.

Southern Nazarene University, Graduate College, School of Psychology, Bethany, OK 73008. Offers counseling psychology (MSCP); marriage and family therapy (MA). *Degree requirements:* For master's, thesis optional. *Entrance requirements:* For master's, English proficiency exam, minimum GPA of 3.0 in last 60 hours/major, 2.7 overall. *Expenses:* Tuition: Part-time $575 per credit hour.

Southern Oregon University, Graduate Studies, College of Arts and Sciences, Department of Psychology, Ashland, OR 97520. Offers mental health counseling (MAP). Part-time programs available. *Faculty:* 13 full-time (7 women). *Students:* 40 full-time (31 women), 4 part-time (1 woman); includes 5 minority (1 Black or African American, non-Hispanic/Latino; 2 Asian, non-Hispanic/Latino; 2 Hispanic/Latino), 1 international. Average age 37. 58 applicants, 43% accepted, 21 enrolled. In 2010, 20 master's awarded. *Degree requirements:* For master's, thesis, portfolio, oral defense. *Entrance requirements:* For master's, GRE General Test, minimum GPA of 3.0. *Application deadline:* Applications are processed on a rolling basis. Application fee: $50. *Expenses:* Tuition, state resident: full-time $9450; part-time $350 per credit. Tuition, nonresident: full-time $15,000; part-time $350 per credit. Required fees: $400 per quarter. *Financial support:* Scholarships/grants and unspecified assistantships available. Financial award applicants required to submit FAFSA. *Unit head:* Dr. Dan Deneui, Chair, 541-552-6913, E-mail: deneuid@sou.edu. *Application contact:* Wri Courtney, Graduate Coordinator, 541-552-6947, E-mail: map@sou.edu.

South University, Graduate Programs, College of Arts and Sciences, Program in Professional Counseling, Savannah, GA 31406. Offers MA.

See Close-Up on page 1179.

South University, Program in Professional Counseling, Montgomery, AL 36116-1120. Offers MA.

See Close-Up on page 1173.

South University, Program in Professional Counseling, Columbia, SC 29203. Offers MA.

See Close-Up on page 1171.

South University, Program in Professional Counseling, Royal Palm Beach, FL 33411. Offers MA.

See Close-Up on page 1183.

South University, Program in Professional Counseling, Glen Allen, VA 23060. Offers MA.

See Close-Up on page 1177.

South University, Program in Professional Counseling, Virginia Beach, VA 23452. Offers MA.

See Close-Up on page 1181.

South University, Program in Professional Counseling, Novi, MI 48377. Offers MA.

See Close-Up on page 1175.

Southwestern Assemblies of God University, Thomas F. Harrison School of Graduate Studies, Program in Counseling Psychology, Waxahachie, TX 75165-5735. Offers counseling psychology (clinical) (MCP); human services counseling (MS). Part-time programs available. *Degree requirements:* For master's, comprehensive written and oral exams. *Entrance requirements:* For master's, GRE General Test, minimum GPA of 2.5. Electronic applications accepted.

Southwestern College, Program in Art Therapy/Counseling, Santa Fe, NM 87502-4788. Offers MA. Part-time and evening/weekend programs available. *Degree requirements:* For master's, internship. *Entrance requirements:* For master's, resume, slide portfolio, interview, 3 letters of reference. Additional exam requirements/recommendations for international students: Required—TOEFL.

Southwestern College, Program in Counseling, Santa Fe, NM 87502-4788. Offers MA. Part-time and evening/weekend programs available. *Degree requirements:* For master's, internship. *Entrance requirements:* For master's, resume, 3 letters of reference, interview. Additional exam requirements/recommendations for international students: Required—TOEFL.

Southwestern College, Program in Grief, Loss and Trauma Counseling, Santa Fe, NM 87502-4788. Offers MA, Certificate. Part-time and evening/weekend programs available. Postbaccalaureate distance learning degree programs offered (minimal on-campus study). *Entrance requirements:* For master's, interview, references, resume; for Certificate, 3 letters of reference, interview.

Spring Arbor University, School of Graduate and Professional Studies, Spring Arbor, MI 49283-9799. Offers counseling (MAC); family studies (MAFS); nursing (MSN); organizational management (MAOM). Part-time and evening/weekend programs available. Postbaccalaureate distance learning degree programs offered (no on-campus study). *Faculty:* 16 full-time (7 women), 100 part-time/adjunct (56 women). *Students:* 407 full-time (324 women), 357 part-time (293 women); includes 171 Black or African American, non-Hispanic/Latino; 3 American Indian or Alaska Native, non-Hispanic/Latino; 9 Asian, non-Hispanic/Latino; 19 Hispanic/Latino, 2 international. Average age 39. In 2010, 279 master's awarded. *Entrance requirements:* For master's, bachelor's degree from regionally-accredited college or university, minimum GPA of 3.0 for at least the last two years of the bachelor's degree, at least two recommendations from professional/academic individuals. Additional exam requirements/recommendations for international students: Required—TOEFL (minimum score 600 paper-based; 220 computer-based). *Application deadline:* Applications are processed on a rolling basis. Application fee: $40. Electronic applications accepted. *Expenses:* Tuition: Full-time $6300; part-time $525 per credit hour. Required fees: $240; $120 per semester. Tuition and fees vary according to course load and program. *Financial support:* Scholarships/grants available. Support available to part-time students. Financial award applicants required to submit FAFSA. *Unit head:* Natalie Gianetti, Dean, 517-750-1200 Ext. 1343, Fax: 517-750-6602, E-mail: gianetti@arbor.edu. *Application contact:* Greg Bentle, Coordinator of Graduate Recruitment, 517-750-6763, Fax: 517-750-6624, E-mail: gbentle@arbor.edu.

Springfield College, Graduate Programs, Program in Human Services, Springfield, MA 01109-3797. Offers human services (MS), including community counseling psychology, mental health counseling, organizational management and leadership. Part-time programs available. *Degree requirements:* For master's, comprehensive exam, thesis (for some programs), research project. *Entrance requirements:* For master's, GRE. Additional exam requirements/recommendations for international students: Required—TOEFL (minimum score 550 paper-based; 213 computer-based). Electronic applications accepted. *Expenses:* Contact institution.

Springfield College, Graduate Programs, Programs in Psychology and Counseling, Springfield, MA 01109-3797. Offers athletic counseling (M Ed, MS, CAGS); industrial/organizational psychology (M Ed, MS, CAGS); marriage and family therapy (M Ed, MS, CAGS); mental health counseling (M Ed, MS, CAGS); school guidance and counseling (M Ed, MS, CAGS); student personnel in higher education (M Ed, MS, CAGS). Part-time programs available. *Degree requirements:* For master's, research project, portfolio. *Entrance requirements:* Additional exam requirements/recommendations for international students: Required—TOEFL (minimum score 550 paper-based; 213 computer-based). Electronic applications accepted.

Stanford University, School of Education, Program in Psychological Studies in Education, Stanford, CA 94305-9991. Offers child and adolescent development (PhD); counseling psychology (PhD); educational psychology (PhD). *Degree requirements:* For doctorate, thesis/dissertation. *Entrance requirements:* For doctorate, GRE General Test. Electronic applications accepted. *Expenses:* Tuition: Full-time $38,700; part-time $860 per unit. One-time fee: $200 full-time.

State University of New York at New Paltz, Graduate School, School of Liberal Arts and Sciences, Department of Psychology, New Paltz, NY 12561. Offers mental health counseling (MS); psychology (MA); school counseling (MS). Part-time and evening/weekend programs available. *Faculty:* 11 full-time (7 women), 2 part-time/adjunct (both women). *Students:* 52 full-time (41 women), 18 part-time (14 women); includes 2 Black or African American, non-Hispanic/Latino; 1 Asian, non-Hispanic/Latino; 1 Hispanic/Latino; 3 Two or more races, non-Hispanic/Latino, 3 international. Average age 27. 103 applicants, 42% accepted, 33 enrolled. In 2010, 9 master's awarded. *Degree requirements:* For master's, comprehensive exam, thesis. *Entrance requirements:* For master's, GRE General Test, minimum GPA of 3.0. Additional exam requirements/recommendations for international students: Required—TOEFL (minimum score 550 paper-based; 213 computer-based; 80 iBT), IELTS (minimum score 6.5). *Application deadline:* For fall admission, 1/20 priority date for domestic and international students; for spring admission, 11/15 for domestic and international students. Application fee: $50. Electronic applications accepted. *Expenses:* Tuition, state resident: full-time $8370; part-time $349 per credit hour. Tuition, nonresident: full-time $13,780; part-time $574 per credit hour. Required fees: $1165; $33.80 per credit hour. $175 per term. Tuition and fees vary according to program. *Financial support:* In 2010–11, 8 students received support, including 1 research assistantship (averaging $5,000 per year), 6 teaching assistantships with partial tuition reimbursements available (averaging $5,000 per year); career-related internships or fieldwork, Federal Work-Study, institutionally sponsored loans, traineeships, tuition waivers (full), and unspecified assistantships also available. Financial award application deadline: 8/1; financial award applicants required to submit FAFSA. *Faculty research:* Disaster mental health, women's objectification, mate selection, cultural psychology, achievement motivation. *Unit head:* Dr. Glenn Geher, Chair, 845-257-3091, E-mail: geherg@newpaltz.edu. *Application contact:* Dr. Jonathan Raskin, Coordinator, 845-257-3471, E-mail: raskinj@newpaltz.edu.

State University of New York at Oswego, Graduate Studies, School of Education, Department of Counseling and Psychological Services, Program in Counseling Services, Oswego, NY 13126. Offers MS, CAS, MS/CAS. *Faculty:* 8 full-time (5 women), 6 part-time/adjunct (3 women). *Students:* 22 full-time (18 women), 7 part-time (5 women); includes 1 minority (Asian, non-Hispanic/Latino). Average age 27. 45 applicants, 62% accepted. In 2010, 27 master's, 3 other advanced degrees awarded. *Degree requirements:* For master's, comprehensive exam, thesis optional, fieldwork; for CAS, thesis, fieldwork. *Entrance requirements:* For master's, GRE General Test, interview, minimum GPA of 3.0; for CAS, GRE General Test, GRE Subject Test, 18 hours of course work in behavioral science or education, interview, minimum GPA of 3.0. Additional exam requirements/recommendations for international students: Required—TOEFL (minimum score 560 paper-based; 220 computer-based). *Application deadline:* For fall admission, 2/1 for domestic and international students. Application fee: $50. *Expenses:* Tuition, state resident: full-time $8370; part-time $349 per credit hour. Tuition, nonresident: full-time $13,780; part-time $574 per credit hour. Required fees: $853; $22.59 per credit hour. *Financial support:* In 2010–11, 10 students received support, including 2 fellowships with full tuition reimbursements available (averaging $5,100 per year), 8 teaching assistantships with partial tuition reimbursements available (averaging $3,800 per year); career-related internships or fieldwork, Federal Work-Study, institutionally sponsored loans, and scholarships/grants also available. Support available to part-time students. Financial award application deadline: 4/1; financial award applicants required to submit FAFSA. *Faculty research:* Psychological applications in education and human services, evaluation of standard tests for admissions criteria. *Unit head:* Dr. Michael LeBlanc, Coordinator, 315-312-4051, E-mail: michael.leblanc@oswego.edu. *Application contact:* Dr. David W. King, Dean of Graduate Studies, 315-312-3152, Fax: 315-312-3228, E-mail: david.king@oswego.edu.

State University of New York at Oswego, Graduate Studies, School of Education, Department of Counseling and Psychological Services, Program in Mental Health Counseling, Oswego, NY 13126. Offers MS. Part-time programs available. *Faculty:* 8 full-time (5 women), 6 part-time/adjunct (3 women). *Students:* 35 full-time (26 women), 9 part-time (all women); includes 4 minority (2 Black or African American, non-Hispanic/Latino; 1 Hispanic/Latino; 1 Two or more races, non-Hispanic/Latino). Average age 28. 30 applicants, 87% accepted. In 2010, 15 master's awarded. *Degree requirements:* For master's, comprehensive exam, thesis optional. *Entrance requirements:* For master's, GRE General Test, interview, minimum GPA of 3.0. Additional exam requirements/recommendations for international students: Required—TOEFL (minimum score 560 paper-based; 220 computer-based). *Application deadline:* For fall admission, 2/1 for domestic and international students. Application fee: $50. *Expenses:* Tuition, state resident: full-time $8370; part-time $349 per credit hour. Tuition, nonresident: full-time $13,780; part-time $574 per credit hour. Required fees: $853; $22.59 per credit hour. *Financial support:* In 2010–11, 18 students received support, including 1 fellowship with full tuition reimbursement available (averaging $5,100 per year), 17 teaching assistantships with partial tuition reimbursements available (averaging $3,800 per year); career-related internships or fieldwork, Federal Work-Study, institutionally sponsored loans, and scholarships/grants also available. Support available to part-time students. Financial award application deadline: 4/1; financial award applicants required to submit FAFSA. *Unit head:* Dr. Jodi Mullen, Coordinator, 315-312-3234, E-mail: jodi.mullen@oswego.edu. *Application contact:* Dr. David W. King, Dean of Graduate Studies, 315-312-3152, Fax: 315-312-3228, E-mail: david.king@oswego.edu.

Stephens College, Division of Graduate and Continuing Studies, Programs in Counseling, Columbia, MO 65215-0002. Offers counseling (M Ed), including marriage and family therapy, professional counseling, school counseling. Part-time and evening/weekend programs available. *Faculty:* 1 (woman) full-time, 13 part-time/adjunct (10 women). *Students:* 130 full-time (114 women), 22 part-time (all women); includes 12 Black or African American, non-Hispanic/Latino; 1 American Indian or Alaska Native, non-Hispanic/Latino; 3 Asian, non-Hispanic/Latino; 3 Hispanic/Latino; 1 Two or more races, non-Hispanic/Latino. Average age 34. 52 applicants, 44% accepted, 23 enrolled. In 2010, 31 master's awarded. *Degree requirements:* For master's, thesis. *Entrance requirements:* For master's, minimum GPA of 3.0 in last 60 hours. Additional exam requirements/recommendations for international students: Required—TOEFL (minimum score 213 computer-based). *Application deadline:* For fall admission, 7/25 priority date for domestic and international students; for winter admission, 12/1 priority date for domestic and international students; for spring admission, 4/25 priority date for domestic and international students. Applications are processed on a rolling basis. Application fee: $40. Electronic applications accepted. *Financial support:* In 2010–11, 62 students received support. Scholarships/grants and unspecified assistantships available. Financial award application deadline: 12/5; financial award applicants required to submit FAFSA. *Unit head:* Dr. Linda Thompson, Program Chair, 800-388-7579. *Application contact:* Jennifer Deaver, Assistant Director of Marketing and Recruitment, 800-388-7579, E-mail: online@stephens.edu.

Suffolk University, College of Arts and Sciences, Department of Education and Human Services, Boston, MA 02108-2770. Offers administration of higher education (M Ed, CAGS), including administration of higher education (M Ed), leadership (CAGS); human resource, learning and performance (MS, CAGS, Graduate Certificate), including global human resources (Graduate Certificate), human resources (MS, Graduate Certificate), organizational development (CAGS, Graduate Certificate), organizational learning and development (MS, Graduate Certificate); mental health counseling (MS, CAGS); school counseling (M Ed, CAGS); school teaching (M Ed, CAGS), including foundations of education (M Ed), middle school teaching (M Ed), secondary school teaching (M Ed); MPA/MSMHC; MS/Certificate. Part-time and evening/weekend programs available. *Faculty:* 8 full-time (4 women), 9 part-time/adjunct (3 women). *Students:* 62 full-time (49 women), 126 part-time (94 women); includes 6 Black or African American, non-Hispanic/Latino; 1 American Indian or Alaska Native, non-Hispanic/Latino; 3 Asian, non-Hispanic/Latino; 5 Hispanic/Latino, 7 international. Average age 28. 170 applicants, 78% accepted, 61 enrolled. In 2010, 80 master's, 2 other advanced degrees awarded. *Entrance requirements:* For master's, GRE General Test or MAT, 2 letters of recommendation, resume. Additional exam requirements/recommendations for international students: Required—TOEFL (minimum score 550 paper-based; 213 computer-based; 80 iBT). *Application deadline:* For fall admission, 6/15 priority date for domestic students, 6/15 for international students; for spring admission, 11/1 priority date for domestic students, 11/1 for international students. Applications are processed on a rolling basis. Application fee: $50. Electronic applications accepted. *Expenses:* Contact institution. *Financial support:* In 2010–11, 110 students received support, including 34 fellowships with full and partial tuition reimbursements available (averaging $10,596 per year); career-related internships or fieldwork, Federal Work-Study, and institutionally sponsored loans also available. Support available to part-time students. Financial award application deadline: 4/1; financial award applicants required to submit FAFSA. *Faculty research:* Predicting competent Head Start preschools, cultural differences. *Unit head:* Dr. Donna Qualters, Interim Chair & Director, 617-573-8264 Ext. 8261, Fax: 617-305-1743, E-mail: dqualters@suffolk.edu. *Application contact:* Judith Reynolds, Director of Graduate Admissions, 617-573-8302, Fax: 617-305-1733, E-mail: grad.admission@suffolk.edu.

Tarleton State University, College of Graduate Studies, College of Education, Department of Psychology and Counseling, Stephenville, TX 76402. Offers counseling and psychology (M Ed), including counseling, counseling psychology, educational psychology; educational administration (M Ed); secondary education (Certificate); special education (Certificate). Part-time and evening/weekend programs available. Postbaccalaureate distance learning degree programs offered (minimal on-campus study). *Degree requirements:* For master's, comprehensive exam, thesis optional. *Entrance requirements:* For master's, GRE General Test, minimum GPA of 3.0. Additional exam requirements/recommendations for international students: Required—TOEFL (minimum score 550 paper-based; 213 computer-based; 80 iBT). Electronic applications accepted.

Teachers College, Columbia University, Graduate Faculty of Education, Department of Counseling and Clinical Psychology, Program in Counseling Psychology, New York, NY 10027. Offers Ed M, Ed D, PhD. *Accreditation:* APA (one or more programs are accredited). Part-time programs available. *Faculty:* 7 full-time (3 women), 9 part-time/adjunct (4 women). *Students:* 174 full-time (153 women), 84 part-time (78 women); includes 107 minority (36 Black or African American, non-Hispanic/Latino; 29 Asian, non-Hispanic/Latino; 30 Hispanic/Latino; 1 Native Hawaiian or other Pacific Islander, non-Hispanic/Latino; 11 Two or more races, non-Hispanic/Latino), 33 international. Average age 27. 493 applicants, 35% accepted, 87 enrolled. In 2010, 184 master's, 9 doctorates awarded. *Degree requirements:* For master's, comprehensive exam, special project; for doctorate, comprehensive exam, thesis/dissertation, research competence project. *Entrance requirements:* For doctorate, GRE General Test. *Application deadline:* For fall admission, 1/15 for domestic students. Application fee: $65. Electronic applications accepted. *Expenses:* Tuition: Full-time $28,272; part-time $1178 per credit. Required fees: $756; $378 per semester. *Financial support:* Fellowships, research assistantships, teaching assistantships, career-related internships or fieldwork, Federal Work-Study, institutionally sponsored loans, and tuition waivers (full and partial) available. Support available to part-time students. Financial award application deadline: 2/1. *Faculty research:* Career development, mentoring racial identity, adult development, gender issues. *Unit head:* Prof. George V. Gushue, Director of Training, 212-678-3397. *Application contact:* Prof. George V. Gushue, Director of Training, 212-678-3397.

Temple University, College of Education, Department of Psychological Studies in Education, Counseling Psychology Program, Philadelphia, PA 19122-6096. Offers Ed M, PhD. *Accreditation:* APA (one or more programs are accredited). Part-time programs available. Terminal master's awarded for partial completion of doctoral program. *Degree requirements:* For master's, thesis or alternative; for doctorate, thesis/dissertation. *Entrance requirements:* For master's, GRE General Test or MAT, minimum GPA of 2.8; for doctorate, GRE General Test, GRE Subject Test in psychology. *Faculty research:* Multi-cultural and diversity training, health psychology/supervision/addictions.

Counseling Psychology

Tennessee State University, The School of Graduate Studies and Research, College of Education, Department of Psychology, Nashville, TN 37209-1561. Offers counseling and guidance (MS), including counseling, elementary school counseling, organizational counseling, secondary school counseling; counseling psychology (PhD); psychology (MS, PhD); school psychology (MS, PhD). *Accreditation:* APA. *Degree requirements:* For doctorate, thesis/dissertation (for some programs). *Entrance requirements:* For master's, GRE General Test or MAT; for doctorate, GRE General Test or MAT, minimum GPA of 3.25, work experience. Electronic applications accepted.

Texas A&M International University, Office of Graduate Studies and Research, College of Arts and Sciences, Department of Behavioral Sciences, Laredo, TX 78041-1900. Offers counseling psychology (MACP); criminal justice (MS); psychology (MS); sociology (MA). *Faculty:* 9 full-time (5 women), 2 part-time/adjunct (1 woman). *Students:* 12 full-time (8 women), 116 part-time (80 women); includes 1 Black or African American, non-Hispanic/Latino; 1 Asian, non-Hispanic/Latino; 120 Hispanic/Latino, 1 international. Average age 29. 20 applicants, 90% accepted, 10 enrolled. In 2010, 16 master's awarded. *Degree requirements:* For master's, thesis (for some programs). *Entrance requirements:* For master's, GRE General Test. Additional exam requirements/recommendations for international students: Required—TOEFL (minimum score 550 paper-based; 213 computer-based; 79 iBT). *Application deadline:* For fall admission, 4/30 priority date for domestic students; for spring admission, 11/30 for domestic students. Applications are processed on a rolling basis. Application fee: $25. *Financial support:* In 2010–11, 17 students received support, including 2 fellowships, 6 research assistantships; teaching assistantships. Financial award application deadline: 11/1. *Unit head:* Dr. Frances P. Bernat, Chair, 956-326-2475, Fax: 956-326-2474, E-mail: gvillagran@tamiu.edu. *Application contact:* Suzanne Hansen-Alford, Director of Graduate Recruiting, 956-326-3023, Fax: 956-326-3021, E-mail: graduateschool@tamiu.edu.

Texas A&M University, College of Education and Human Development, Department of Educational Psychology, College Station, TX 77843. Offers bilingual education (M Ed, PhD); cognition, creativity, instruction and development (MS, PhD); counseling psychology (PhD); educational psychology (PhD); educational technology (PhD); research, measurement and statistics (MS); research, measurement, and statistics (PhD); school psychology (PhD); special education (M Ed, PhD). *Accreditation:* APA (one or more programs are accredited). Part-time and evening/weekend programs available. Postbaccalaureate distance learning degree programs offered (no on-campus study). *Faculty:* 49. *Students:* 160 full-time (123 women), 147 part-time (120 women); includes 106 minority (24 Black or African American, non-Hispanic/Latino; 16 Asian, non-Hispanic/Latino; 66 Hispanic/Latino), 45 international. In 2010, 36 master's, 31 doctorates awarded. *Degree requirements:* For master's, thesis optional; for doctorate, thesis/dissertation. *Entrance requirements:* For master's and doctorate, GRE General Test. Additional exam requirements/recommendations for international students: Required—TOEFL. Application fee: $50 ($75 for international students). Electronic applications accepted. *Financial support:* In 2010–11, fellowships (averaging $12,000 per year), research assistantships (averaging $9,000 per year), teaching assistantships (averaging $9,000 per year) were awarded; career-related internships or fieldwork, institutionally sponsored loans, scholarships/grants, and unspecified assistantships also available. Financial award applicants required to submit FAFSA. *Unit head:* Dr. Victor Willson, Head, 979-845-1800. *Application contact:* Carol A. Wagner, Director of Advising, 979-845-1833, Fax: 979-862-1256, E-mail: epsyadvisor@tamu.edu.

Texas A&M University–Commerce, Graduate School, College of Education and Human Services, Department of Counseling, Commerce, TX 75429-3011. Offers M Ed, MS, PhD. *Accreditation:* ACA (one or more programs are accredited). Part-time programs available. Terminal master's awarded for partial completion of doctoral program. *Degree requirements:* For master's, comprehensive exam, thesis (for some programs); for doctorate, thesis/dissertation, departmental qualifying exam. *Entrance requirements:* For master's and doctorate, GRE General Test. *Faculty research:* Emergency responders, efficacy and effect of web-based instruction, family violence, play therapy.

Texas A&M University–Texarkana, Graduate Studies and Research, College of Health and Behavioral Sciences, Texarkana, TX 75505-5518. Offers counseling psychology (MS). Part-time and evening/weekend programs available. *Degree requirements:* For master's, comprehensive exam (for some programs), thesis or alternative. *Entrance requirements:* For master's, minimum GPA of 3.0 in last 60 hours of bachelor's degree. Additional exam requirements/recommendations for international students: Required—TOEFL. Electronic applications accepted.

Texas Tech University, Graduate School, College of Arts and Sciences, Department of Psychology, Lubbock, TX 79409-2051. Offers clinical psychology (PhD); counseling psychology (MA, PhD); experimental psychology (MA, PhD); psychology (MA, PhD). *Accreditation:* APA (one or more programs are accredited). Part-time programs available. *Faculty:* 25 full-time (11 women). *Students:* 91 full-time (57 women), 18 part-time (17 women); includes 2 Black or African American, non-Hispanic/Latino; 1 American Indian or Alaska Native, non-Hispanic/Latino; 1 Asian, non-Hispanic/Latino; 9 Hispanic/Latino; 1 Two or more races, non-Hispanic/Latino, 7 international. Average age 27. 276 applicants, 11% accepted, 19 enrolled. In 2010, 18 master's, 13 doctorates awarded. *Degree requirements:* For doctorate, comprehensive exam, thesis/dissertation, 100 credit hours of organized courses, research credits, and practica. *Entrance requirements:* For master's and doctorate, GRE General Test, GRE Subject Test, departmental application form, essays. Additional exam requirements/recommendations for international students: Required—TOEFL (minimum score 550 paper-based; 213 computer-based; 79 iBT). *Application deadline:* For fall admission, 6/1 priority date for domestic students, 1/15 priority date for international students; for spring admission, 9/1 priority date for domestic students, 6/15 priority date for international students. Applications are processed on a rolling basis. Application fee: $50 ($75 for international students). Electronic applications accepted. *Expenses:* Tuition, state resident: full-time $5495.76; part-time $228.99 per credit hour. Tuition, nonresident: full-time $12,936; part-time $538.99 per credit hour. Required fees: $2674; $36 per credit hour. $905 per semester. *Financial support:* In 2010–11, 85 students received support, including 13 research assistantships with partial tuition reimbursements available (averaging $5,707 per year), 32 teaching assistantships with partial tuition reimbursements available (averaging $5,672 per year). Financial award application deadline: 4/15; financial award applicants required to submit FAFSA. *Faculty research:* Failure/success in relationships, peer rejection in school, stress and coping, group processes, clinical and health psychology. Total annual research expenditures: $202,278. *Unit head:* Dr. Lee M. Cohen, Chair, 806-742-3711 Ext. 222, Fax: 806-742-0818, E-mail: lee.cohen@ttu.edu. *Application contact:* Kay Hill, Admissions Coordinator, 806-742-3711 Ext. 222, Fax: 806-742-0818, E-mail: kay.hill@ttu.edu.

Texas Wesleyan University, Graduate Programs, Programs in Education, Fort Worth, TX 76105-1536. Offers education (M Ed, Ed D); marriage and family therapy (MSMFT); professional counseling (MA); school counseling (MS). Part-time and evening/weekend programs available. Postbaccalaureate distance learning degree programs offered (no on-campus study). *Entrance requirements:* For master's, GRE General Test, minimum GPA of 3.0 in final 60 hours of undergraduate course work, interview. Tuition and fees vary according to course level, degree level and program. *Faculty research:* Teacher effectiveness, bilingual education, analytic teaching.

Texas Woman's University, Graduate School, College of Arts and Sciences, Department of Psychology and Philosophy, Denton, TX 76201. Offers counseling psychology (MA, PhD); school psychology (PhD, SSP). *Accreditation:* APA (one or more programs are accredited). *Faculty:* 16 full-time (9 women). *Students:* 81 full-time (72 women), 52 part-time (46 women); includes 11 Black or African American, non-Hispanic/Latino; 1 American Indian or Alaska Native, non-Hispanic/Latino; 6 Asian, non-Hispanic/Latino; 13 Hispanic/Latino, 1 international. Average age 30. 169 applicants, 27% accepted, 33 enrolled. In 2010, 15 master's, 9 doctorates awarded. Terminal master's awarded for partial completion of doctoral program. *Degree requirements:* For master's, thesis; for doctorate, comprehensive exam, thesis/dissertation, internship, residency. *Entrance requirements:* For master's, GRE (preferred minimum score 500 Verbal, 500 Quantitative, 4 Analytical), BA/BS or 18 hours in psychology; minimum GPA of 3.0, 3.5 in undergraduate psychology classes; 3 letters of reference; curriculum vitae; essays; for doctorate, GRE (preferred minimum score 500 Verbal, 500 Quantitative, 4 Analytical), 3 letters of reference, minimum GPA of 3.5 overall and in psychology undergraduate classes, BS/BA in psychology or 18 hours of required psychology classes, curriculum vitae, essays. Additional exam requirements/recommendations for international students: Required—TOEFL (minimum score 550 paper-based; 213 computer-based; 79 iBT). *Application deadline:* For fall admission, 12/15 priority date for domestic and international students. Applications are processed on a rolling basis. Application fee: $50 ($75 for international students). Electronic applications accepted. *Expenses:* Tuition, state resident: full-time $3834; part-time $213 per credit hour. Tuition, nonresident: full-time $9468; part-time $526 per credit hour. Required fees: $1247; $220 per credit hour. *Financial support:* In 2010–11, 49 students received support, including 29 research assistantships (averaging $10,746 per year), 9 teaching assistantships (averaging $10,746 per year); career-related internships or fieldwork, Federal Work-Study, institutionally sponsored loans, scholarships/grants, traineeships, health care benefits, and unspecified assistantships also available. Support available to part-time students. Financial award application deadline: 3/1; financial award applicants required to submit FAFSA. *Faculty research:* Women's anger, school neuropsychological theory and assessment, body image dysfunction, traumatic stress, classical ethics, mental health and behavioral needs of adolescents in alternative education. *Unit head:* Dr. Dan Miller, Chair, 940-898-2303, Fax: 940-898-2301, E-mail: dmiller@twu.edu. *Application contact:* Dr. Samuel Wheeler, Assistant Director of Admissions, 940-898-3188, Fax: 940-898-3081, E-mail: wheelersr@twu.edu.

Towson University, Program in Counseling Psychology, Towson, MD 21252-0001. Offers CAS. Part-time and evening/weekend programs available. *Students:* 1 (woman) full-time, 7 part-time (all women); includes 1 minority (Black or African American, non-Hispanic/Latino). Average age 43. In 2010, 1 CAS awarded. Application fee: $50. *Expenses:* Tuition, state resident: part-time $324 per credit. Tuition, nonresident: part-time $681 per credit. Required fees: $95 per term. *Financial support:* Application deadline: 4/1. *Unit head:* Christa Schmidt, Graduate Program Director, 410-704-3063, E-mail: ckschmidt@towson.edu. *Application contact:* The Graduate School, 410-704-2501, Fax: 410-704-4675, E-mail: grads@towson.edu.

Trevecca Nazarene University, Graduate Division, Graduate Psychology Programs, Major in Counseling Psychology, Nashville, TN 37210-2877. Offers MA. Part-time and evening/weekend programs available. *Students:* 41 full-time (28 women), 12 part-time (9 women); includes 13 minority (11 Black or African American, non-Hispanic/Latino; 2 Two or more races, non-Hispanic/Latino). *Degree requirements:* For master's, comprehensive exam, practicum. *Entrance requirements:* For master's, GRE General Test or MAT, minimum GPA of 2.7, 2 reference assessment forms. Additional exam requirements/recommendations for international students: Required—TOEFL (minimum score 550 paper-based; 213 computer-based). *Application deadline:* Applications are processed on a rolling basis. Application fee: $25. *Expenses:* Contact institution. *Financial support:* Applicants required to submit FAFSA. *Unit head:* Dr. Peter Wilson, Director of Graduate Psychology Program, 615-248-1384, Fax: 615-248-1662, E-mail: admissions_psy@trevecca.edu. *Application contact:* Heather Ambrefe, Administrative Assistant, 615-248-1384, Fax: 615-248-1662, E-mail: admissions_psy@trevecca.edu.

Trinity International University, Trinity Evangelical Divinity School, Deerfield, IL 60015-1284. Offers Biblical and Near Eastern archaeology and languages (MA); Christian studies (MA, Certificate); Christian thought (MA); church history (MA, Th M); congregational ministry: pastor-teacher (M Div); congregational ministry: team ministry (M Div); counseling ministries (MA); counseling psychology (MA); cross-cultural ministry (M Div); educational studies (PhD); evangelism (MA); history of Christianity in America (MA); intercultural studies (MA, PhD); leadership and ministry management (D Min); military chaplaincy (D Min); ministry (MA); mission and evangelism (Th M); missions and evangelism (D Min); New Testament (MA, Th M); Old Testament (Th M); Old Testament and Semitic languages (MA); pastoral care (M Div); pastoral care and counseling (D Min); pastoral counseling and psychology (Th M); pastoral theology (Th M); philosophy of religion (MA); preaching (D Min); religion (MA); research ministry (M Div); systematic theology (Th M); theological studies (PhD); urban ministry (MA). *Accreditation:* ATS (one or more programs are accredited). Part-time programs available. Postbaccalaureate distance learning degree programs offered (minimal on-campus study). *Degree requirements:* For master's, comprehensive exam, thesis, fieldwork; for doctorate, comprehensive exam (for some programs), thesis/dissertation; for M Div, 2 foreign languages, fieldwork; for Certificate, comprehensive exam, integrative papers. *Entrance requirements:* For M Div, GRE, MAT; for master's, GRE, MAT, minimum cumulative undergraduate GPA of 3.0; for doctorate, GRE, minimum cumulative graduate GPA of 3.2; for Certificate, GRE, MAT, minimum undergraduate GPA of 2.5. Additional exam requirements/recommendations for international students: Required—TOEFL (minimum score 580 paper-based; 237 computer-based), TWE (minimum score 4). Electronic applications accepted.

Trinity International University, Trinity Graduate School, Deerfield, IL 60015-1284. Offers bioethics (MA); communication and culture (MA); counseling psychology (MA); instructional leadership (M Ed); teaching (MA). Part-time and evening/weekend programs available. Postbaccalaureate distance learning degree programs offered (minimal on-campus study). *Degree requirements:* For master's, comprehensive exam. *Entrance requirements:* For master's, GRE General Test or MAT, minimum undergraduate GPA of 3.0. Additional exam requirements/recommendations for international students: Required—TOEFL (minimum score 580 paper-based; 237 computer-based), TWE (minimum score 4). Electronic applications accepted.

Trinity International University, South Florida Campus, Graduate School, Miami, FL 33132-1996. Offers MA.

Trinity Western University, School of Graduate Studies, Program in Counseling Psychology, Langley, BC V2Y 1Y1, Canada. Offers MA. *Accreditation:* ACA. Part-time programs available. *Degree requirements:* For master's, comprehensive exam, thesis. *Entrance requirements:* For master's, GRE (if out of school for 5 years prior to applying), BA in honors psychology, minimum GPA of 3.0 for 3rd and 4th year of BA. Additional exam requirements/recommendations for international students: Required—TOEFL (minimum score 600 paper-based; 250 computer-based). *Faculty research:* Meaning, group counseling, trauma, counseling supervision.

Union College, Graduate Programs, Department of Psychology, Barbourville, KY 40906-1499. Offers clinical psychology (MA); counseling psychology (MA); school psychology (MA).

Union Institute & University, Programs in Psychology and Counseling, Brattleboro, VT 05301. Offers clinical mental health counseling (MA); clinical psychology (Psy D); counseling psychology (MA); counselor education and supervision (CAGS); developmental psychology (MA); educational psychology (MA); human development and wellness (CAGS); organizational psychology (MA); psychology education (CAGS). Psy D offered in Ohio and Vermont. Postbaccalaureate distance learning degree programs offered (minimal on-campus study). *Faculty:* 6 full-time (4 women), 17 part-time/adjunct (6 women). *Students:* 93 full-time (66 women), 11 part-time (10 women); includes 14 minority (6 Black or African American, non-Hispanic/Latino; 1 Asian, non-Hispanic/Latino; 7 Hispanic/Latino). Average age 44. In 2010, 21 master's awarded. *Degree requirements:* For master's, thesis, internship (depending on concentration); for doctorate, thesis/dissertation, internship, practicum. *Application deadline:* Applications are processed on a rolling basis. Application fee: $50. Electronic applications accepted. *Expenses:* Tuition: Full-time $16,430; part-time $685 per credit hour. Required fees: $174; $44 per term. Tuition and fees vary according to course load, degree level and program. *Financial support:* Federal Work-Study available. Financial award applicants required to submit FAFSA. *Unit head:* Dr. Bill Lax, Dean, 802-254-0152, E-mail: bill.lax@myunion.edu. *Application contact:* Diane Robinson, Director of Admissions, 888-828-8575, E-mail: diane.robinson@myunion.edu.

United States International University, School of Arts and Sciences, Nairobi, Kenya. Offers counseling psychology (MA), including chemical dependency, health psychology; international relations (MA), including development studies, diplomacy and foreign policy, peace and conflict studies. Part-time and evening/weekend programs available. *Faculty:* 43 full-time (14 women), 69 part-time/adjunct (28 women). *Students:* 94 full-time (60 women), 22 part-time (all women). Average age 30. 93 applicants, 80% accepted, 64 enrolled. In 2010, 33 master's awarded. *Degree requirements:* For master's, thesis, practicum. *Entrance requirements:* For master's, GRE General Test, 2 letters of recommendation, resume. Additional exam requirements/recommendations for international students: Required—TOEFL. *Application deadline:* For fall admission, 6/30 priority date for domestic and international students. Application fee: $50. *Financial support:* In 2010–11, 56 students received support, including 3 research assistantships (averaging $1,400 per year), 7 teaching assistantships (averaging $1,400 per year); career-related internships or fieldwork, scholarships/grants, and unspecified assistantships also available. Support available to part-time students. Financial award application deadline: 6/30; financial award applicants required to submit FAFSA. *Faculty research:* Trauma in children, African intellectualism, psychological assessment tools. *Unit head:* Prof. Mulinge Munyae, Dean, 254-02-3606-434, E-mail: mmulinge@usiu.ac.ke. *Application contact:* George Lumbasi, Director of Admissions, 254-02-3606563, Fax: 254-02-3606100, E-mail: glumbasi@usiu.ac.ke.

Universidad del Turabo, Graduate Programs, School of Social Sciences and Humanities, Programs in Psychology, Program in Counseling Psychology, Gurabo, PR 00778-3030. Offers M Psych, Psy D, Certificate.

Universidad Metropolitana, School of Social Sciences, Humanities and Communications, Program in Counseling Psychology, San Juan, PR 00928-1150. Offers MA.

University at Albany, State University of New York, School of Education, Department of Educational and Counseling Psychology, Albany, NY 12222-0001. Offers counseling psychology (MS, PhD, CAS); educational psychology (Ed D); educational psychology and statistics (MS); measurements and evaluation (Ed D); rehabilitation counseling (MS), including counseling psychology; school counselor (CAS); school psychology (Psy D, CAS); special education (MS); statistics and research design (Ed D). *Accreditation:* APA (one or more programs are accredited). Evening/weekend programs available. *Degree requirements:* For doctorate, thesis/dissertation. *Entrance requirements:* For doctorate, GRE General Test. Additional exam requirements/recommendations for international students: Required—TOEFL (minimum score 550 paper-based; 213 computer-based). Electronic applications accepted.

University at Buffalo, the State University of New York, Graduate School, Graduate School of Education, Department of Counseling, School, and Educational Psychology, Buffalo, NY 14260. Offers counseling/school psychology (PhD); counselor education (PhD); educational psychology (MA, PhD); general education (Ed M); mental health counseling (MS); rehabilitation counseling (MS); school counseling (Ed M, Certificate); Singapore school counseling (Ed M). *Accreditation:* CORE (one or more programs are accredited). Part-time programs available. Postbaccalaureate distance learning degree programs offered (no on-campus study). *Faculty:* 21 full-time (12 women), 30 part-time/adjunct (26 women). *Students:* 156 full-time (125 women), 112 part-time (87 women); includes 25 Black or African American, non-Hispanic/Latino; 3 American Indian or Alaska Native, non-Hispanic/Latino; 2 Asian, non-Hispanic/Latino; 8 Hispanic/Latino, 24 international. Average age 30. 403 applicants, 40% accepted, 108 enrolled. In 2010, 35 master's, 12 doctorates, 19 other advanced degrees awarded. *Degree requirements:* For master's, comprehensive exam (for some programs), thesis (for some programs); for doctorate, comprehensive exam, thesis/dissertation. *Entrance requirements:* For master's and doctorate, GRE General Test, interview, letters of reference. Additional exam requirements/recommendations for international students: Required—TOEFL (minimum score 79 iBT). *Application deadline:* For fall admission, 2/1 priority date for domestic and international students. Application fee: $50. Electronic applications accepted. *Financial support:* In 2010–11, 10 fellowships with full tuition reimbursements (averaging $9,474 per year), 24 research assistantships with full tuition reimbursements (averaging $9,301 per year) were awarded; teaching assistantships with tuition reimbursements, career-related internships or fieldwork, Federal Work-Study, institutionally sponsored loans, and unspecified assistantships also available. Financial award application deadline: 2/1; financial award applicants required to submit FAFSA. *Faculty research:* Multicultural counseling, class size effects, good work in counseling, eating disorders, outcome assessment, change agents and therapeutic factors in group counseling. *Unit head:* Dr. Timothy Janikowski, Chair, 716-645-2484, Fax: 716-645-6616, E-mail: tjanikow@buffalo.edu. *Application contact:* Rochelle Cohen, Admissions Assistant, 716-645-2110, Fax: 716-645-7937, E-mail: recohen@buffalo.edu.

The University of Akron, Graduate School, Buchtel College of Arts and Sciences, Department of Psychology, Collaborative Program in Counseling Psychology, Akron, OH 44325. Offers MA, PhD. *Accreditation:* APA (one or more programs are accredited). *Students:* 17 full-time (14 women), 10 part-time (9 women); includes 3 minority (1 Black or African American, non-Hispanic/Latino; 2 Hispanic/Latino), 1 international. Average age 28. 6 applicants, 17% accepted, 1 enrolled. In 2010, 7 doctorates awarded. *Degree requirements:* For master's, thesis or specialty exam; for doctorate, comprehensive exam, thesis/dissertation. *Entrance requirements:* For master's, GRE General Test, bachelor's degree in psychology or its equivalent, three letters of recommendation, current vita, declaration of intent outlining goals and interests; for doctorate, GRE General Test, bachelor's degree in psychology or equivalent; current vita; declaration of intent outlining goals and interests; three letters of recommendation. Additional exam requirements/recommendations for international students: Required—TOEFL (minimum score 550 paper-based; 213 computer-based; 79 iBT). *Application deadline:* For fall admission, 12/1 for domestic and international students. Application fee: $30 ($40 for international students). Electronic applications accepted. *Expenses:* Tuition, state resident: full-time $6800; part-time $378 per credit hour. Tuition, nonresident: full-time $11,644; part-time $647 per credit hour. Required fees: $1265. One-time fee: $30 full-time. *Financial support:* Fellowships with full tuition reimbursements, research assistantships with full tuition reimbursements, teaching assistantships with full tuition reimbursements, career-related internships or fieldwork, Federal Work-Study, and institutionally sponsored loans available. *Faculty research:* Counseling process and outcome, suicide, diversity issues and counseling psychology (e.g., gender, race, ethnicity, sexual orientation) vocational psychology, assessment. *Unit head:* Dr. Linda Subich, Coordinator, 330-972-8379, E-mail: lsubich@uakron.edu. *Application contact:* Dr. Linda Subich, Coordinator, 330-972-8379, E-mail: lsubich@uakron.edu.

The University of Akron, Graduate School, College of Education, Department of Counseling, Program in Counseling Psychology, Akron, OH 44325. Offers PhD. *Accreditation:* APA. *Students:* 14 full-time (9 women), 17 part-time (14 women). Average age 32. 31 applicants, 0% accepted, 0 enrolled. In 2010, 2 doctorates awarded. *Degree requirements:* For doctorate, one foreign language, comprehensive exam, thesis/dissertation, written and oral exams. *Entrance requirements:* For doctorate, GRE, interview; minimum GPA of 3.25; three letters of recommendation; declaration of intent outlining occupational goals, interests, and commitment to program; current vita. Additional exam requirements/recommendations for international students: Required—TOEFL (minimum score 550 paper-based; 213 computer-based). *Application deadline:* For fall admission, 12/15 for domestic and international students. Application fee: $30 ($40 for international students). Electronic applications accepted. *Expenses:* Tuition, state resident: full-time $6800; part-time $378 per credit hour. Tuition, nonresident: full-time $11,644; part-time $647 per credit hour. Required fees: $1265. One-time fee: $30 full-time. *Unit head:* Dr. James Rogers, Coordinator, 330-972-8635, E-mail: jrrogers@uakron.edu. *Application contact:* Dr. James Rogers, Coordinator, 330-972-8635, E-mail: jrrogers@uakron.edu.

University of Alberta, Faculty of Graduate Studies and Research, Department of Educational Psychology, Edmonton, AB T6G 2E1, Canada. Offers counseling psychology (M Ed, PhD); educational psychology (M Ed, PhD); instructional technology (M Ed); school counseling (M Ed); school psychology (M Ed, PhD); special education (M Ed, PhD); special education-deafness studies (M Ed); teaching English as a second language (M Ed). Part-time programs available. *Degree requirements:* For master's, thesis optional; for doctorate, comprehensive exam, thesis/dissertation. *Entrance requirements:* For master's and doctorate, minimum GPA of 3.0.

Additional exam requirements/recommendations for international students: Required—TOEFL. *Faculty research:* Human learning, development and assessment.

University of Baltimore, Graduate School, The Yale Gordon College of Liberal Arts, Program in Applied Psychology, Baltimore, MD 21201-5779. Offers applied psychology (MS), including counseling, industrial and organizational psychology, psychological applications. Part-time and evening/weekend programs available. *Degree requirements:* For master's, thesis optional. *Entrance requirements:* For master's, GRE, minimum GPA of 3.0. Additional exam requirements/recommendations for international students: Required—TOEFL (minimum score 550 paper-based; 213 computer-based). Electronic applications accepted. *Expenses:* Contact institution. *Faculty research:* Participatory decision making, counter productive workplace behavior, organizational consulting, substance abuse treatment, cognitive functioning in head injured.

The University of British Columbia, Faculty of Education, Department of Educational and Counseling Psychology, and Special Education, Vancouver, BC V6T 1Z1, Canada. Offers counseling psychology (M Ed, MA, PhD); development, learning and culture (PhD); guidance studies (Diploma); human development, learning and culture (M Ed, MA); measurement and evaluation and research methodology (M Ed); measurement, evaluation and research methodology (MA); measurement, evaluation, and research methodology (PhD); school psychology (M Ed, MA, PhD); special education (M Ed, MA, PhD, Diploma). Part-time programs available. *Degree requirements:* For master's, thesis (for some programs); for doctorate, comprehensive exam, thesis/dissertation. *Entrance requirements:* For master's, GRE General Test (counseling psychology MA); for doctorate, GRE General Test. Additional exam requirements/recommendations for international students: Required—TOEFL. Electronic applications accepted. Tuition charges are reported in Canadian dollars. *Expenses:* Tuition, area resident: Full-time $4179 Canadian dollars. International tuition: $7344 Canadian dollars full-time. *Faculty research:* Women, family, social problems, career transition, stress and coping problems.

University of Calgary, Faculty of Graduate Studies, Faculty of Education, Division of Applied Psychology, Calgary, AB T2N 1N4, Canada. Offers counseling psychology (M Ed, M Sc, PhD); human development and learning (M Ed, M Sc, PhD); school psychology (M Ed, M Sc, PhD); special education (M Ed, M Sc, PhD). Part-time programs available. *Degree requirements:* For master's, thesis (for some programs), final oral exam; for doctorate, thesis/dissertation, candidacy exam, final oral exam. *Entrance requirements:* For master's, minimum GPA of 3.0, 3 letters of reference; for doctorate, minimum GPA of 3.5, 3 letters of reference. *Faculty research:* Counselor education, family life studies, learning and cognition.

University of California, Berkeley, UC Berkeley Extension, Certificate Programs in Behavioral and Health Sciences, Berkeley, CA 94720-1500. Offers alcohol and drug abuse studies (Certificate).

University of California, Santa Barbara, Graduate Division, Gevirtz Graduate School of Education, Santa Barbara, CA 93106-9490. Offers counseling, clinical and school psychology (PhD), including clinical psychology, counseling psychology, school psychology; education (M Ed, MA, PhD), including child and adolescent development (MA, PhD), cultural perspectives and comparative education (MA, PhD), educational leadership and organizations (MA, PhD), research methodology (MA, PhD), special education disabilities and risk studies (MA), special education, disabilities and risk studies (PhD), teaching (M Ed), teaching and learning (MA, PhD); educational leadership (Ed D); school psychology (M Ed); MA/PhD. *Accreditation:* APA (one or more programs are accredited). Postbaccalaureate distance learning degree programs offered (minimal on-campus study). *Faculty:* 40 full-time (22 women), 5 part-time/adjunct (1 woman). *Students:* 411 full-time (325 women); includes 19 Black or African American, non-Hispanic/Latino; 3 American Indian or Alaska Native, non-Hispanic/Latino; 59 Asian, non-Hispanic/Latino; 67 Hispanic/Latino. Average age 29. 683 applicants, 38% accepted, 154 enrolled. In 2010, 128 master's, 58 doctorates awarded. Terminal master's awarded for partial completion of doctoral program. *Degree requirements:* For master's, comprehensive exam (for some programs), thesis (for some programs); for doctorate, comprehensive exam (for some programs), thesis/dissertation. *Entrance requirements:* For master's and doctorate, GRE. Additional exam requirements/recommendations for international students: Required—TOEFL (minimum score 550 paper-based; 80 iBT), IELTS (minimum score 7). Application fee: $70 ($90 for international students). Electronic applications accepted. *Financial support:* In 2010–11, 269 students received support, including 222 fellowships with partial tuition reimbursements available (averaging $5,615 per year), 75 research assistantships with full tuition reimbursements available (averaging $6,470 per year), 65 teaching assistantships with partial tuition reimbursements available (averaging $7,059 per year); career-related internships or fieldwork also available. Financial award applicants required to submit FAFSA. *Faculty research:* Needs of diverse students, school accountability and leadership, school violence, language learning and literacy, science/math education. Total annual research expenditures: $3.1 million. *Unit head:* Carol North Dixon, Graduate Advisor, 805-893-2185, E-mail: dixon@education.ucsb.edu. *Application contact:* Kathryn Marie Tucciarone, Student Affairs Officer, 805-893-2137, Fax: 805-893-2588, E-mail: katiet@education.ucsb.edu.

University of Central Arkansas, Graduate School, College of Health and Behavioral Sciences, Department of Counseling and Psychology, Program in Counseling Psychology, Conway, AR 72035-0001. Offers MS. *Students:* 18 full-time (15 women), 11 part-time (10 women); includes 5 minority (3 Black or African American, non-Hispanic/Latino; 1 Asian, non-Hispanic/Latino; 1 Hispanic/Latino). Average age 27. 16 applicants, 56% accepted, 5 enrolled. In 2010, 11 master's awarded. *Degree requirements:* For master's, comprehensive exam, thesis optional. *Entrance requirements:* For master's, GRE General Test, minimum GPA of 2.7. Additional exam requirements/recommendations for international students: Required—TOEFL (minimum score 550 paper-based; 213 computer-based). *Application deadline:* For fall admission, 3/1 priority date for domestic and international students; for spring admission, 10/1 priority date for domestic and international students. Applications are processed on a rolling basis. Application fee: $25 ($40 for international students). *Financial support:* Federal Work-Study, scholarships/grants, and unspecified assistantships available. Financial award applicants required to submit FAFSA. *Unit head:* Dr. Elson Bihm, Head, 501-450-3193, Fax: 501-450-5424, E-mail: elsonb@uca.edu. *Application contact:* Susan Wood, Administrative Assistant, 501-450-3124, Fax: 501-450-5678, E-mail: swood@uca.edu.

University of Central Missouri, The Graduate School, College of Education, Warrensburg, MO 64093. Offers career and technical education administration (MS); career and technical education industry training (MS); career and technical education leadership/teaching (MS); college student personnel administration (MS); counseling (MS); curriculum and instruction (Ed S); educational leadership (Ed D); educational technology (MS); elementary education/educational foundations and literacy (MSE); elementary school administration (MSE); elementary school principalship (Ed S); human services/learning resources (Ed S); human services/professional counseling (Ed S); human services/special education (Ed S); human services/technology and occupational education (Ed S); K-12 education/educational foundations and literacy (MSE); K-12 special education (MSE); library science and information services (MS); literacy education (MSE); secondary education/educational foundations & literacy (MSE); secondary school administration (MSE); secondary school principalship (Ed S); superintendency (Ed S); teaching (MAT). Ed D offered jointly with University of Missouri. Part-time programs available. Postbaccalaureate distance learning degree programs offered. *Entrance requirements:* Additional exam requirements/recommendations for international students: Required—TOEFL (minimum score 550 paper-based; 79 computer-based). Electronic applications accepted.

University of Central Oklahoma, College of Graduate Studies and Research, College of Education, Department of Psychology, Program in Counseling Psychology, Edmond, OK 73034-5209. Offers MS. *Entrance requirements:* For master's, GRE General Test. Additional exam requirements/recommendations for international students: Required—TOEFL (minimum score 550 paper-based; 213 computer-based). Electronic applications accepted.

Counseling Psychology

University of Colorado Denver, School of Education and Human Development, Program in Counseling Psychology and Counselor Education, Denver, CO 80217-3364. Offers school counseling (MA). *Accreditation:* ACA; NCATE. Part-time and evening/weekend programs available. *Students:* 183 full-time (159 women), 40 part-time (38 women); includes 5 Black or African American, non-Hispanic/Latino; 1 American Indian or Alaska Native, non-Hispanic/Latino; 6 Asian, non-Hispanic/Latino; 10 Hispanic/Latino, 4 international. Average age 30. 90 applicants, 54% accepted, 31 enrolled. In 2010, 43 master's awarded. *Degree requirements:* For master's, thesis or alternative, 63-66 hours. *Entrance requirements:* For master's, GRE, letters of recommendation, interview, resume. Additional exam requirements/recommendations for international students: Required—TOEFL (minimum score 525 paper-based; 197 computer-based). *Application deadline:* For fall admission, 1/15 for domestic students; for spring admission, 9/15 for domestic students. Application fee: $50 ($75 for international students). Electronic applications accepted. *Expenses:* Contact institution. *Financial support:* Research assistantships, Federal Work-Study and scholarships/grants available. Financial award application deadline: 4/1; financial award applicants required to submit FAFSA. *Faculty research:* Spiritual issues in counseling, multicultural and diversity issues in counseling, adolescent suicide, career development. *Unit head:* Dr. Marsha Wiggins, Division Coordinator, 303-315-6332, E-mail: marsha.wiggins@ucdenver.edu. *Application contact:* Student Services Coordinator, 303-315-6300, Fax: 303-315-6311, E-mail: education@ucdenver.edu.

University of Connecticut, Graduate School, Neag School of Education, Department of Educational Psychology, Program in Counseling Psychology, Storrs, CT 06269. Offers counseling psychology (PhD); school counseling (MA, Post-Master's Certificate). *Accreditation:* ACA. Terminal master's awarded for partial completion of doctoral program. *Degree requirements:* For master's, comprehensive exam, thesis or alternative; for doctorate, thesis/dissertation. *Entrance requirements:* For doctorate, GRE General Test. Additional exam requirements/recommendations for international students: Required—TOEFL (minimum score 550 paper-based; 213 computer-based). Electronic applications accepted.

University of Denver, Morgridge College of Education, Denver, CO 80208. Offers counseling psychology (MA, PhD); curriculum and instruction (MA, PhD, Certificate), including curriculum leadership (MA, PhD); educational administration and policy studies (Certificate); educational psychology (MA, PhD, Ed S), including child and family studies (MA, PhD), quantitative research methods (MA, PhD), school psychology (PhD, Ed S); higher education and adult studies (MA, PhD); library and information science (MLIS); library and information sciences (Certificate); school administration (PhD). *Accreditation:* ALA; APA (one or more programs are accredited). Part-time and evening/weekend programs available. Postbaccalaureate distance learning degree programs offered (no on-campus study). *Faculty:* 48 full-time (33 women), 68 part-time/adjunct (52 women). *Students:* 405 full-time (311 women), 423 part-time (326 women); includes 171 minority (53 Black or African American, non-Hispanic/Latino; 5 American Indian or Alaska Native, non-Hispanic/Latino; 17 Asian, non-Hispanic/Latino; 88 Hispanic/Latino; 8 Two or more races, non-Hispanic/Latino), 19 international. Average age 33. 934 applicants, 66% accepted, 381 enrolled. In 2010, 203 master's, 59 doctorates, 108 other advanced degrees awarded. Terminal master's awarded for partial completion of doctoral program. *Degree requirements:* For master's, comprehensive exam; for doctorate, 2 foreign languages, comprehensive exam, thesis/dissertation. *Entrance requirements:* For master's and doctorate, GRE General Test or GMAT. Additional exam requirements/recommendations for international students: Required—TOEFL (minimum score 550 paper-based; 80 iBT). *Application deadline:* Applications are processed on a rolling basis. Application fee: $60. Electronic applications accepted. *Expenses:* Tuition: Full-time $35,604; part-time $29,670 per year. Required fees: $687 per year. Tuition and fees vary according to program. *Financial support:* In 2010–11, 1 research assistantship with full and partial tuition reimbursement (averaging $18,297 per year), 26 teaching assistantships with full and partial tuition reimbursements (averaging $12,341 per year) were awarded; career-related internships or fieldwork, Federal Work-Study, institutionally sponsored loans, scholarships/grants, and unspecified assistantships also available. Support available to part-time students. Financial award application deadline: 3/1; financial award applicants required to submit FAFSA. *Faculty research:* Parkinson's disease, personnel training, development and assessments, gifted education, service-learning, transportation, public schools. *Unit head:* Dr. Gregory M. Anderson, Dean, 303-871-3665, E-mail: gregory.m.anderson@du.edu. *Application contact:* Janet Erickson, Director of Graduate Admission, 303-871-2485, E-mail: edinfo@du.edu.

University of Florida, Graduate School, College of Liberal Arts and Sciences, Department of Psychology, Gainesville, FL 32611. Offers behavior analysis (PhD); behavioral neuroscience (MS, PhD); cognitive and sensory processes (PhD); counseling psychology (PhD); developmental psychology (PhD); social psychology (MS, PhD); JD/PhD. *Faculty:* 29 full-time (10 women). *Students:* 106 full-time (82 women), 14 part-time (7 women); includes 3 Black or African American, non-Hispanic/Latino; 2 American Indian or Alaska Native, non-Hispanic/Latino; 7 Asian, non-Hispanic/Latino; 12 Hispanic/Latino, 11 international. Average age 27. 614 applicants, 7% accepted, 36 enrolled. In 2010, 25 master's, 13 doctorates awarded. *Degree requirements:* For master's, comprehensive exam, thesis or alternative; for doctorate, comprehensive exam, thesis/dissertation. *Entrance requirements:* For master's and doctorate, GRE General Test, minimum GPA of 3.0. Additional exam requirements/recommendations for international students: Required—TOEFL (minimum score 550 paper-based; 213 computer-based; 80 iBT), IELTS (minimum score 6). *Application deadline:* For fall admission, 12/9 priority date for domestic students, 12/9 for international students. Applications are processed on a rolling basis. Application fee: $30. Electronic applications accepted. *Expenses:* Tuition, state resident: full-time $10,915.92. Tuition, nonresident: full-time $28,309. *Financial support:* In 2010–11, 105 students received support, including 19 fellowships, 24 research assistantships (averaging $18,742 per year), 62 teaching assistantships (averaging $19,797 per year); career-related internships or fieldwork and unspecified assistantships also available. Financial award application deadline: 12/9; financial award applicants required to submit FAFSA. *Faculty research:* Behavior analysis, behavioral and cognitive neuroscience, counseling, developmental psychology, social psychology. Total annual research expenditures: $2.7 million. *Unit head:* Dr. Neil E. Rowland, Chair, 352-273-2128, Fax: 352-392-7985, E-mail: nrowland@ufl.edu. *Application contact:* Dr. Clive D. Wynne, Graduate Coordinator, 352-392-0601, Fax: 352-392-7985, E-mail: wynne@ufl.edu.

University of Great Falls, Graduate Studies, Program in Counseling, Great Falls, MT 59405. Offers MSC. Part-time and evening/weekend programs available. *Degree requirements:* For master's, thesis optional, internship. *Entrance requirements:* For master's, GRE General Test, 3 letters of recommendation. Additional exam requirements/recommendations for international students: Required—TOEFL (minimum score 500 paper-based; 205 computer-based). Electronic applications accepted. *Faculty research:* Self concept and adolescent offenders, juvenile delinquency, community mental health counseling.

University of Hawaii at Hilo, Program in Counseling Psychology, Hilo, HI 96720-4091. Offers MA. *Degree requirements:* For master's, project or thesis.

University of Houston, College of Education, Department of Educational Psychology, Houston, TX 77204. Offers administration and supervision—higher education (M Ed); counseling (M Ed); counseling psychology (PhD); educational psychology (M Ed); school psychology (PhD); school psychology and individual differences (PhD); special education (M Ed). *Accreditation:* NCATE. Part-time and evening/weekend programs available. *Faculty:* 21 full-time (10 women), 14 part-time/adjunct (9 women). *Students:* 149 full-time (126 women), 125 part-time (111 women); includes 99 minority (30 Black or African American, non-Hispanic/Latino; 3 American Indian or Alaska Native, non-Hispanic/Latino; 22 Asian, non-Hispanic/Latino; 38 Hispanic/Latino; 1 Native Hawaiian or other Pacific Islander, non-Hispanic/Latino; 5 Two or more races, non-Hispanic/Latino), 15 international. Average age 29. 99 applicants, 54% accepted, 42 enrolled. In 2010, 52 master's, 18 doctorates awarded. *Degree requirements:* For master's, comprehensive exam or thesis; for doctorate, comprehensive exam, thesis/dissertation. *Entrance requirements:* For master's, GRE, transcripts, 3 letters of recommendation, curriculum vita, goal statement; for doctorate, GRE, transcripts, 3 letters of recommendation, curriculum vita, goal statement, writing sample, interview. Additional exam requirements/recommendations for international students: Required—TOEFL (minimum score 550 paper-based; 79 iBT), IELTS (minimum score 6.5). *Application deadline:* For fall admission, 1/15 for domestic and international students; for spring admission, 9/15 for domestic and international students. Application fee: $45 ($75 for international students). Electronic applications accepted. *Expenses:* Tuition, state resident: full-time $8592; part-time $358 per credit hour. Tuition, nonresident: full-time $16,032; part-time $668 per credit hour. Required fees: $2889. Tuition and fees vary according to course load and program. *Financial support:* In 2010–11, 5 fellowships with full tuition reimbursements (averaging $2,000 per year), 8 research assistantships with full tuition reimbursements (averaging $8,664 per year), 56 teaching assistantships with full tuition reimbursements (averaging $8,760 per year) were awarded; career-related internships or fieldwork, Federal Work-Study, institutionally sponsored loans, scholarships/grants, health care benefits, and unspecified assistantships also available. Support available to part-time students. Financial award application deadline: 2/1. *Faculty research:* Evidence-based assessment and intervention, multicultural issues in psychology, social and cultural context of learning, systemic barriers to college, motivational aspects of self-regulated learning. *Unit head:* Dr. Tom Kubiszyn, Chairperson, 713-743-9865, Fax: 713-743-4996, E-mail: tkubiszyn@uh.edu. *Application contact:* Jeylan Yassin, Coordinator of Institutional Effectiveness, 713-743-5019, E-mail: jyassin@uh.edu.

University of Houston–Victoria, School of Arts and Sciences, Program in Psychology, Victoria, TX 77901-4450. Offers counseling psychology (MA); school psychology (MA). Part-time and evening/weekend programs available. Postbaccalaureate distance learning degree programs offered (minimal on-campus study). *Faculty:* 6 full-time (4 women). *Students:* 43 full-time (33 women), 64 part-time (56 women); includes 34 Black or African American, non-Hispanic/Latino; 2 Asian, non-Hispanic/Latino; 23 Hispanic/Latino; 2 Two or more races, non-Hispanic/Latino. Average age 33. 61 applicants, 77% accepted, 35 enrolled. In 2010, 9 master's awarded. *Degree requirements:* For master's, project or thesis. *Entrance requirements:* For master's, GRE General Test. Additional exam requirements/recommendations for international students: Required—TOEFL (minimum score 550 paper-based; 213 computer-based). *Application deadline:* For fall admission, 6/1 for international students; for spring admission, 10/1 for international students. Applications are processed on a rolling basis. Application fee: $0. Electronic applications accepted. *Expenses:* Tuition, state resident: full-time $4050; part-time $225 per credit hour. Tuition, nonresident: full-time $8730; part-time $485 per credit hour. Required fees: $810; $54 per credit hour. Tuition and fees vary according to course load. *Financial support:* In 2010–11, research assistantships with partial tuition reimbursements (averaging $2,000 per year), teaching assistantships with partial tuition reimbursements (averaging $2,000 per year) were awarded; Federal Work-Study, scholarships/grants, and unspecified assistantships also available. Support available to part-time students. Financial award application deadline: 4/15; financial award applicants required to submit FAFSA. *Unit head:* Dr. Rick Harrington, Chair, 361-570-4205, Fax: 361-570-4229, E-mail: harringtonr@uhv.edu. *Application contact:* Tracey Fox, Director of Services, 361-570-4233, Fax: 361-580-5507, E-mail: admissions@uhv.edu.

University of Indianapolis, Graduate Programs, School of Psychological Sciences, Indianapolis, IN 46227-3697. Offers clinical psychology (Psy D); clinical psychology/mental health counseling (MA). *Accreditation:* APA. *Faculty:* 6 full-time (1 woman), 1 (woman) part-time/adjunct. *Students:* 118 full-time (105 women), 44 part-time (37 women); includes 2 minority (1 Black or African American, non-Hispanic/Latino; 1 Hispanic/Latino), 11 international. Average age 26. *Degree requirements:* For master's, practicum; for doctorate, comprehensive exam, thesis/dissertation, 1200 hours of clinical practicum, 2000 hour internship. *Entrance requirements:* For master's, GRE, 3 letters of recommendation; for doctorate, GRE, minimum GPA of 3.0, 18 hours of course work in psychology, 3 letters of recommendation. Additional exam requirements/recommendations for international students: Required—TOEFL (minimum score 550 paper-based; 213 computer-based). *Application deadline:* For fall admission, 2/25 for domestic students. Application fee: $50. Tuition and fees vary according to course load, degree level and program. *Financial support:* Federal Work-Study available. *Unit head:* Dr. Rick Holigrocki, Acting Dean, 317-788-6126, Fax: 317-788-3480, E-mail: rholigrocki@uindy.edu. *Application contact:* Dr. Rick Holigrocki, Acting Dean, 317-788-6126, E-mail: rholigrocki@uindy.edu.

The University of Iowa, Graduate College, College of Education, Department of Psychological and Quantitative Foundations, Iowa City, IA 52242-1316. Offers counseling psychology (PhD); educational measurement and statistics (MA, PhD); educational psychology (MA, PhD); school psychology (PhD, Ed S); JD/PhD. *Accreditation:* APA. *Degree requirements:* For master's, thesis optional, exam; for doctorate, comprehensive exam, thesis/dissertation; for Ed S, exam. *Entrance requirements:* For master's, doctorate, and Ed S, GRE General Test, minimum GPA of 3.0. Additional exam requirements/recommendations for international students: Required—TOEFL (minimum score 550 paper-based; 213 computer-based; 81 iBT). Electronic applications accepted.

The University of Kansas, Graduate Studies, School of Education, Department of Psychology and Research in Education, Program in Counseling Psychology, Lawrence, KS 66045. Offers MS, PhD. *Accreditation:* APA (one or more programs are accredited). Part-time programs available. *Students:* 65 full-time (44 women), 4 part-time (2 women); includes 8 minority (4 Black or African American, non-Hispanic/Latino; 1 Asian, non-Hispanic/Latino; 1 Hispanic/Latino; 2 Two or more races, non-Hispanic/Latino), 2 international. Average age 29. 91 applicants, 40% accepted, 22 enrolled. In 2010, 20 master's, 9 doctorates awarded. Terminal master's awarded for partial completion of doctoral program. *Degree requirements:* For master's, thesis or alternative; for doctorate, comprehensive exam, thesis/dissertation. *Entrance requirements:* For master's and doctorate, GRE General Test, minimum GPA of 3.0. Additional exam requirements/recommendations for international students: Required—TOEFL. *Application deadline:* For fall admission, 12/15 for domestic and international students. Application fee: $55 ($65 for international students). Electronic applications accepted. *Expenses:* Tuition, state resident: full-time $7092; part-time $295.50 per credit hour. Tuition, nonresident: full-time $16,590; part-time $691.25 per credit hour. Required fees: $858; $71.49 per credit hour. Tuition and fees vary according to course load, campus/location and program. *Financial support:* Fellowships, research assistantships with full and partial tuition reimbursements, teaching assistantships with full and partial tuition reimbursements, career-related internships or fieldwork, scholarships/grants, and unspecified assistantships available. Financial award application deadline: 1/15. *Faculty research:* Career development, assessment and intervention, multi-cultural counseling, counselor training, positive psychology. *Unit head:* James Litchenberg, Professor and Director of Training, 785-864-3931, Fax: 785-864-3820, E-mail: jlicht@ku.edu. *Application contact:* Admissions Coordinator, 785-864-3931, Fax: 785-864-3820, E-mail: preadmit@ku.edu.

University of Kentucky, Graduate School, College of Education, Program in Educational and Counseling Psychology, Lexington, KY 40506-0032. Offers counseling psychology (MS Ed, PhD, Ed S); educational and counseling psychology (MS Ed); educational psychology (Ed D, PhD, Ed S); school psychometrist and school psychology (MA Ed). *Accreditation:* APA (one or more programs are accredited); NCATE. *Degree requirements:* For master's, comprehensive exam, thesis optional; for doctorate, comprehensive exam, thesis/dissertation; for Ed S, comprehensive exam. *Entrance requirements:* For master's, GRE General Test, minimum undergraduate GPA of 2.75; for doctorate, GRE General Test, minimum graduate GPA of 3.0; for Ed S, GRE General Test. Additional exam requirements/recommendations for international students: Required—TOEFL (minimum score 550 paper-based; 213 computer-based). Electronic applications accepted.

University of La Verne, College of Arts and Sciences, Department of Psychology, Programs in Counseling, La Verne, CA 91750-4443. Offers counseling (MS), including student services; marriage and family therapy (MS). Part-time programs available. *Faculty:* 13 full-time (6 women), 25 part-time/adjunct (17 women). *Students:* 36 full-time (33 women), 52 part-time (46 women); includes 54 minority (16 Black or African American, non-Hispanic/Latino; 3 Asian, non-Hispanic/Latino; 35 Hispanic/Latino). Average age 29. In 2010, 36 master's awarded. *Degree requirements:* For master's, thesis, competency exam, personal psychotherapy. *Entrance* *requirements:* For master's, minimum undergraduate GPA of 3.0; 3 letters of recommendations; interview. Additional exam requirements/recommendations for international students: Required—TOEFL (minimum score 600 paper-based; 250 computer-based). *Application deadline:* Applications are processed on a rolling basis. Application fee: $50. *Expenses:* Contact institution. *Financial support:* Career-related internships or fieldwork, institutionally sponsored loans, and scholarships/grants available. Financial award application deadline: 3/2; financial award applicants required to submit FAFSA. *Unit head:* Patricia Long, 909-593-3511 Ext. 4091, E-mail: plong@laverne.edu. *Application contact:* Barbara Cox, Program and Admission Specialist, 909-593-3511 Ext. 4004, Fax: 909-392-2761, E-mail: gradadmission@laverne.edu.

University of Lethbridge, School of Graduate Studies, Lethbridge, AB T1K 3M4, Canada. Offers accounting (MScM); addictions counseling (M Sc); agricultural biotechnology (M Sc); agricultural studies (M Sc, MA); anthropology (MA); archaeology (MA); art (MA, MFA); biochemistry (M Sc); biological sciences (M Sc); biomolecular science (PhD); biosystems and biodiversity (PhD); Canadian studies (MA); chemistry (M Sc); computer science (M Sc); computer science and geographical information science (M Sc); counseling psychology (M Ed); dramatic arts (MA); earth, space, and physical science (PhD); economics (MA); educational leadership (M Ed); English (MA); environmental science (M Sc); evolution and behavior (PhD); exercise science (M Sc); finance (MScM); French (MA); French/German (MA); French/Spanish (MA); general education (M Ed); general management (MScM); geography (M Sc, MA); German (MA); health science (M Sc); history (MA); human resource management and labour relations (MScM); individualized multidisciplinary (M Sc, MA); information systems (MScM); international management (MScM); kinesiology (M Sc, MA); management (M Sc, MA); marketing (MScM); mathematics (M Sc); music (M Mus, MA); Native American studies (MA); neuroscience (M Sc, PhD); new media (MA); nursing (M Sc); philosophy (MA); physics (M Sc); policy and strategy (MScM); political science (MA); psychology (M Sc, MA); religious studies (MA); social sciences (MA); sociology (MA); theatre and dramatic arts (MFA); theoretical and computational science (PhD); urban and regional studies (MA); women's studies (MA). Part-time and evening/weekend programs available. *Degree requirements:* For doctorate, comprehensive exam, thesis/dissertation. *Entrance requirements:* For master's, GMAT (M Sc in management), bachelor's degree in related field, minimum GPA of 3.0 during previous 20 graded semester courses, 2 years teaching or related experience (M Ed); for doctorate, master's degree, minimum graduate GPA of 3.5. Additional exam requirements/recommendations for international students: Required—TOEFL. *Faculty research:* Movement and brain plasticity, gibberellin physiology, photosynthesis, carbon cycling, molecular properties of main-group ring components.

The University of Manchester, School of Education, Manchester, United Kingdom. Offers counseling (D Couns); counseling psychology (D Couns); education (M Phil, Ed D, PhD); educational and child psychology (Ed D); educational psychology (Ed D).

University of Mary Hardin-Baylor, Graduate Studies in Counseling and Psychology, Belton, TX 76513. Offers clinical mental health counseling (MA); marriage and family Christian counseling (MA); psychology and counseling (MA); school counseling and psychology (MA). Part-time and evening/weekend programs available. *Faculty:* 7 full-time (4 women). *Students:* 33 full-time (23 women), 18 part-time (10 women); includes 11 minority (6 Black or African American, non-Hispanic/Latino; 4 Hispanic/Latino; 1 Two or more races, non-Hispanic/Latino), 1 international. Average age 29. 46 applicants, 50% accepted, 19 enrolled. In 2010, 44 master's awarded. *Degree requirements:* For master's, comprehensive exam. *Entrance requirements:* For master's, GRE General Test, minimum GPA of 3.0 in last 60 hours or 2.75 overall. *Application deadline:* For fall admission, 6/1 priority date for domestic students; for spring admission, 11/1 for domestic students. Applications are processed on a rolling basis. Application fee: $35 ($135 for international students). Electronic applications accepted. *Financial support:* Research assistantships with full tuition reimbursements, Federal Work-Study and scholarships (for some active duty military personnel only) available. Support available to part-time students. Financial award applicants required to submit FAFSA. *Unit head:* Dr. Isaac Gusukuma, Interim Graduate Program Director, 254-295-5017, E-mail: isaac.gusukuma@umhb.edu. *Application contact:* Dr. Isaac Gusukuma, Interim Graduate Program Director, 254-295-5017, E-mail: isaac.gusukuma@umhb.edu.

University of Maryland, College Park, Academic Affairs, College of Education, Department of Counseling and Personnel Services, College Park, MD 20742. Offers college student personnel (M Ed, MA); college student personnel administration (PhD); community counseling (CAGS); community/career counseling (M Ed, MA); counseling and personnel services (M Ed, MA, PhD), including art therapy (M Ed), college student personnel (M Ed), counseling and personnel services (PhD), counseling psychology (M Ed), mental health counseling (M Ed), school counseling (M Ed); counseling psychology (PhD); counselor education (PhD); rehabilitation counseling (M Ed, MA, AGSC); school counseling (M Ed, MA); school psychology (M Ed, MA, PhD). *Accreditation:* ACA (one or more programs are accredited); APA (one or more programs are accredited); CORE (one or more programs are accredited); NCATE. Part-time and evening/weekend programs available. Postbaccalaureate distance learning degree programs offered (no on-campus study). *Faculty:* 33 full-time (18 women), 1 (woman) part-time/adjunct. *Students:* 136 full-time (105 women), 16 part-time (11 women); includes 23 Black or African American, non-Hispanic/Latino; 19 Asian, non-Hispanic/Latino; 12 Hispanic/Latino; 5 Two or more races, non-Hispanic/Latino, 11 international. 407 applicants, 11% accepted, 25 enrolled. In 2010, 38 master's, 15 doctorates, 4 other advanced degrees awarded. *Degree requirements:* For master's, thesis (for some programs); for doctorate, thesis/dissertation. *Entrance requirements:* For master's, GRE General Test or MAT, minimum GPA of 3.0, 3 letters of recommendation; for doctorate, GRE General Test or MAT, minimum GPA of 3.5, 3 letters of recommendation. Additional exam requirements/recommendations for international students: Required—TOEFL. *Application deadline:* For fall admission, 12/15 for domestic and international students; for spring admission, 6/1 for international students. Applications are processed on a rolling basis. Application fee: $75. Electronic applications accepted. *Expenses:* Tuition, state resident: part-time $471 per credit hour. Tuition, nonresident: part-time $1016 per credit hour. Required fees: $337 per term. *Financial support:* In 2010–11, 15 fellowships with partial tuition reimbursements (averaging $11,738 per year), 3 research assistantships (averaging $17,258 per year), 83 teaching assistantships with tuition reimbursements (averaging $16,131 per year) were awarded; career-related internships or fieldwork, Federal Work-Study, and scholarships/grants also available. Support available to part-time students. Financial award applicants required to submit FAFSA. *Faculty research:* Educational psychology, counseling, health. Total annual research expenditures: $838,213. *Unit head:* Dr. Dennis Kivlighan, Chair, 301-405-2858, E-mail: dennisk@umd.edu. *Application contact:* Dean of Graduate School, 301-405-0358.

University of Massachusetts Boston, Office of Graduate Studies, Graduate College of Education, Counseling and School Psychology Department, Boston, MA 02125-3393. Offers family therapy (M Ed, CAGS); forensic counseling (M Ed, CAGS); mental health counseling (M Ed, CAGS); rehabilitation counseling (M Ed, CAGS); school guidance counseling (M Ed, CAGS); school psychology (M Ed, CAGS). *Degree requirements:* For master's and CAGS, comprehensive exam. *Entrance requirements:* For master's, GRE General Test or MAT; for CAGS, minimum GPA of 2.75.

University of Medicine and Dentistry of New Jersey, School of Health Related Professions, Department of Psychiatric Rehabilitation and Counseling Professions, Newark, NJ 07107-1709. Offers professional counseling (Certificate); psychiatric rehabilitation (MS, PhD); rehabilitation counseling (MS), including psychiatric rehabilitation, vocational rehabilitation. *Accreditation:* CORE. *Students:* 8 full-time (all women), 58 part-time (41 women); includes 15 Black or African American, non-Hispanic/Latino; 4 Asian, non-Hispanic/Latino; 10 Hispanic/Latino, 2 international. Average age 34. 42 applicants, 69% accepted, 23 enrolled. In 2010, 25 master's awarded. *Degree requirements:* For master's, internship, practicum. *Entrance requirements:* For master's, minimum 2 years of psychiatric rehabilitation or related professional experience or GRE General Test, interview; for doctorate, GRE General Test. Additional exam requirements/recommendations for international students: Required—TOEFL. *Application deadline:* Applications are processed on a rolling basis. Application fee: $50. Electronic applications accepted. *Financial support:* Traineeships available. *Unit head:* Dr. Kenneth J. Gill, Chairperson/Director, 908-889-2438, Fax: 908-889-2432, E-mail: kgill@umdnj.edu. *Application contact:* Douglas Lomonaco, Assistant Dean, 973-972-5454, Fax: 973-972-7463, E-mail: shrpadm@umdnj.edu.

University of Memphis, Graduate School, College of Education, Department of Counseling, Educational Psychology and Research, Memphis, TN 38152. Offers counseling (MS, Ed D), including community counseling (MS), rehabilitation counseling (MS), school counseling (MS); counseling psychology (PhD); educational psychology and research (MS, PhD), including educational psychology, educational research. *Accreditation:* ACA (one or more programs are accredited); APA (one or more programs are accredited); CORE (one or more programs are accredited); NCATE. *Faculty:* 26 full-time (13 women), 9 part-time/adjunct (5 women). *Students:* 95 full-time (73 women), 104 part-time (81 women); includes 56 Black or African American, non-Hispanic/Latino; 3 American Indian or Alaska Native, non-Hispanic/Latino; 1 Asian, non-Hispanic/Latino; 2 Hispanic/Latino, 5 international. Average age 33. 118 applicants, 63% accepted, 36 enrolled. In 2010, 46 master's, 14 doctorates awarded. *Degree requirements:* For master's, comprehensive exam, thesis or alternative; for doctorate, comprehensive exam, thesis/dissertation. *Entrance requirements:* For master's, GRE General Test or MAT, minimum GPA of 2.5; for doctorate, GRE General Test. *Application deadline:* For fall admission, 10/1 for domestic students; for spring admission, 4/1 for domestic students. Application fee: $35 ($60 for international students). *Financial support:* In 2010–11, 130 students received support; fellowships with full tuition reimbursements available, research assistantships with full tuition reimbursements available, teaching assistantships with full tuition reimbursements available, career-related internships or fieldwork, Federal Work-Study, scholarships/grants, and unspecified assistantships available. Financial award application deadline: 2/15; financial award applicants required to submit FAFSA. *Faculty research:* Anger management, aging and disability, supervision, multicultural counseling. *Unit head:* Dr. Douglas C. Strohmer, Chair, 901-678-2841, Fax: 901-678-5114. *Application contact:* Dr. Ernest A. Rakow, Associate Dean of Administration and Graduate Programs, 901-678-2399, Fax: 901-678-4778.

University of Miami, Graduate School, School of Education, Department of Educational and Psychological Studies, Program in Counseling Psychology, Coral Gables, FL 33124. Offers PhD. *Accreditation:* APA. *Faculty:* 8 full-time (3 women). *Students:* 34 full-time (25 women); includes 11 minority (2 Black or African American, non-Hispanic/Latino; 7 Hispanic/Latino; 2 Two or more races, non-Hispanic/Latino), 2 international. Average age 29. 150 applicants, 5% accepted, 6 enrolled. In 2010, 6 doctorates awarded. *Degree requirements:* For doctorate, thesis/dissertation, qualifying exam. *Entrance requirements:* For doctorate, GRE General Test. Additional exam requirements/recommendations for international students: Required—TOEFL (minimum score 550 paper-based; 80 iBT); Recommended—IELTS (minimum score 6.5). *Application deadline:* For fall admission, 12/1 for domestic students, 10/15 for international students. Application fee: $65. Electronic applications accepted. *Financial support:* In 2010–11, 22 students received support. Career-related internships or fieldwork, institutionally sponsored loans, health care benefits, and unspecified assistantships available. Financial award application deadline: 3/1; financial award applicants required to submit FAFSA. *Faculty research:* Cocaine recidivism, family systems, behavior and health, nontraditional families, stress and coping. *Unit head:* Dr. Brian Lewis, Clinical Assistant Professor and Director of Training, 305-284-2260, Fax: 305-284-3003, E-mail: blewis@miami.edu. *Application contact:* Lois Heffernan, Graduate Admissions Coordinator, 305-284-2167, Fax: 305-284-3003, E-mail: lheffernan@miami.edu.

University of Minnesota, Twin Cities Campus, Graduate School, College of Liberal Arts, Department of Psychology, Program in Counseling Psychology, Minneapolis, MN 55455-0213. Offers PhD. *Accreditation:* APA. *Degree requirements:* For doctorate, comprehensive exam, thesis/dissertation, internship. *Entrance requirements:* For doctorate, GRE General Test, GRE Subject Test (recommended), 12 credits of upper-level psychology courses, including a course in statistics or psychological measurement. Additional exam requirements/recommendations for international students: Required—TOEFL (minimum score 550 paper-based; 213 computer-based; 79 iBT).

University of Missouri, Graduate School, College of Education, Department of Educational, School, and Counseling Psychology, Columbia, MO 65211. Offers counseling psychology (M Ed, MA, PhD, Ed S); educational psychology (M Ed, MA, PhD, Ed S); learning and instruction (M Ed); school psychology (M Ed, MA, PhD, Ed S). *Accreditation:* APA (one or more programs are accredited). Part-time programs available. *Degree requirements:* For doctorate, thesis/dissertation. *Entrance requirements:* For master's, doctorate, and Ed S, GRE General Test, minimum GPA of 3.0. Additional exam requirements/recommendations for international students: Required—TOEFL (minimum score 580 paper-based; 237 computer-based; 92 iBT).

University of Missouri–Kansas City, School of Education, Kansas City, MO 64110-2499. Offers administration (Ed D); counseling and guidance (MA, Ed S); counseling psychology (PhD); curriculum and instruction (MA, Ed S); education (PhD); educational administration (Ed S); reading education (MA, Ed S); special education (MA). PhD (education) offered through the School of Graduate Studies. *Accreditation:* NCATE. Part-time and evening/weekend programs available. *Faculty:* 61 full-time (51 women), 38 part-time/adjunct (28 women). *Students:* 213 full-time (154 women), 410 part-time (300 women); includes 127 minority (91 Black or African American, non-Hispanic/Latino; 1 American Indian or Alaska Native, non-Hispanic/Latino; 14 Asian, non-Hispanic/Latino; 20 Hispanic/Latino; 1 Two or more races, non-Hispanic/Latino), 19 international. Average age 33. 422 applicants, 243 enrolled. In 2010, 152 master's, 5 doctorates, 33 other advanced degrees awarded. *Degree requirements:* For doctorate, thesis/dissertation, internship, practicum. *Entrance requirements:* For master's, GRE, minimum GPA of 2.75, 2 letters of reference, written statement of purpose; for doctorate, GRE, minimum GPA of 3.0; for Ed S, minimum GPA of 3.0. Additional exam requirements/recommendations for international students: Required—TOEFL (minimum score 550 paper-based; 213 computer-based; 80 iBT). *Application deadline:* For fall admission, 4/1 priority date for domestic and international students; for spring admission, 11/1 priority date for domestic and international students. Applications are processed on a rolling basis. Application fee: $45 ($50 for international students). *Expenses:* Tuition, state resident: full-time $5522.40; part-time $306.80 per credit hour. Tuition, nonresident: full-time $7128; part-time $792 per credit hour. Required fees: $261.15 per term. *Financial support:* In 2010–11, 19 research assistantships with partial tuition reimbursements (averaging $10,920 per year) were awarded; career-related internships or fieldwork, Federal Work-Study, institutionally sponsored loans, and tuition waivers (full and partial) also available. Support available to part-time students. Financial award application deadline: 3/1; financial award applicants required to submit FAFSA. *Faculty research:* Urban education, inquiry-based field study, theories of counseling and psychotherapy, school literacy, educational technology. Total annual research expenditures: $340,644. *Unit head:* Dr. Wanda Blanchett, Dean, 816-235-2234, Fax: 816-235-5270, E-mail: education@umkc.edu. *Application contact:* Erica Hernandez-Scott, Student Recruiter, 816-235-1295, Fax: 816-235-5270, E-mail: hernandeze@umkc.edu.

The University of Montana, Graduate School, School of Education, Department of Educational Leadership and Counseling, Program in Counselor Education, Missoula, MT 59812-0002. Offers counselor education (Ed S); counselor education and supervision (Ed D); mental health counseling (MA); school counseling (MA). *Accreditation:* ACA. *Degree requirements:* For doctorate, thesis/dissertation. *Entrance requirements:* For master's, doctorate, and Ed S, GRE General Test. Additional exam requirements/recommendations for international students: Required—TOEFL.

University of Nebraska–Lincoln, Graduate College, College of Education and Human Sciences, Department of Educational Psychology, Lincoln, NE 68588. Offers cognition, learning and development (MA); counseling psychology (MA); educational psychology (MA, Ed S); psychological studies in education (PhD), including cognition, learning and development, counseling psychology, quantitative, qualitative, and psychometric methods, school psychology; quantitative, qualitative, and psychometric methods (MA); school psychology (MA, Ed S).

Counseling Psychology

University of Nebraska–Lincoln (continued)
Accreditation: APA (one or more programs are accredited); NCATE. Degree requirements: For master's, thesis optional. Entrance requirements: For master's, GRE General Test. Additional exam requirements/recommendations for international students: Required—TOEFL (minimum score 500 paper-based; 173 computer-based). Electronic applications accepted. Faculty research: Measurement and assessment, metacognition, academic skills, child development, multicultural education and counseling.

The University of North Carolina at Greensboro, Graduate School, School of Education, Department of Counseling and Educational Development, Greensboro, NC 27412-5001. Offers advanced school counseling (PMC); counseling and counselor education (PhD); counseling and educational development (MS); couple and family counseling (PMC); school counseling (PMC); MS/Ed S. Accreditation: ACA (one or more programs are accredited); NCATE. Degree requirements: For master's, comprehensive exam, practicum, internship; for doctorate, comprehensive exam, thesis/dissertation. Entrance requirements: For master's, doctorate, and PMC, GRE General Test. Additional exam requirements/recommendations for international students: Required—TOEFL. Electronic applications accepted. Faculty research: Gerontology, invitational theory, career development, marriage and family therapy, drug and alcohol abuse prevention.

University of North Dakota, Graduate School, College of Education and Human Development, Department of Counseling, Grand Forks, ND 58202. Offers MA. Faculty: 12 full-time (7 women), 1 (woman) part-time/adjunct. Students: 50 full-time (37 women), 35 part-time (26 women); includes 7 minority (1 Black or African American, non-Hispanic/Latino; 4 American Indian or Alaska Native, non-Hispanic/Latino; 1 Asian, non-Hispanic/Latino; 1 Hispanic/Latino), 3 international. Average age 30. 61 applicants, 34% accepted, 14 enrolled. In 2010, 17 master's awarded. Degree requirements: For master's, comprehensive exam, thesis or alternative. Entrance requirements: For master's, GRE General Test or MAT, minimum GPA of 3.0. Additional exam requirements/recommendations for international students: Required—TOEFL (minimum score 550 paper-based; 213 computer-based; 79 iBT), IELTS (minimum score 6.5). Application deadline: For fall admission, 3/21 for domestic and international students. Application fee: $35. Electronic applications accepted. Expenses: Tuition, state resident: full-time $5857; part-time $306.74 per credit. Tuition, nonresident: full-time $15,666; part-time $729.77 per credit. Required fees: $53.42 per credit. Tuition and fees vary according to course load, program and reciprocity agreements. Financial support: In 2010–11, 22 students received support, including 3 research assistantships with full tuition reimbursements available (averaging $7,768 per year), 13 teaching assistantships with full tuition reimbursements available (averaging $6,351 per year); fellowships with full and partial tuition reimbursements available, career-related internships or fieldwork, Federal Work-Study, institutionally sponsored loans, scholarships/grants, tuition waivers (full and partial), and unspecified assistantships also available. Support available to part-time students. Financial award application deadline: 3/15; financial award applicants required to submit FAFSA. Faculty research: Group dynamics, addictive behavior, item response theory, geopsychology, women's health. Total annual research expenditures: $5,217. Unit head: Dr. Dorlene Walker, Graduate Director, 701-777-3737, Fax: 701-777-3184, E-mail: dorlene.walker@und.edu. Application contact: Staci Wells, Admissions Associate, 701-777-2945, Fax: 701-777-3619, E-mail: staci.wells@gradschool.und.edu.

University of Northern Iowa, Graduate College, College of Social and Behavioral Sciences, School of Applied Human Sciences, Program in Counseling, Cedar Falls, IA 50614. Offers mental health counseling (MA); school counseling (MAE). Accreditation: ACA (one or more programs are accredited). Part-time and evening/weekend programs available. Students: 52 full-time (40 women), 43 part-time (37 women); includes 7 minority (4 Black or African American, non-Hispanic/Latino; 1 Asian, non-Hispanic/Latino; 2 Hispanic/Latino), 4 international. 75 applicants, 35% accepted, 17 enrolled. In 2010, 22 master's awarded. Degree requirements: For master's, comprehensive exam, thesis or alternative. Entrance requirements: For master's, minimum GPA of 3.0. Additional exam requirements/recommendations for international students: Required—TOEFL (minimum score 500 paper-based; 180 computer-based; 61 iBT). Application deadline: For fall admission, 8/1 priority date for domestic students. Applications are processed on a rolling basis. Application fee: $50 ($70 for international students). Electronic applications accepted. Financial support: Career-related internships or fieldwork, Federal Work-Study, and tuition waivers (full and partial) available. Support available to part-time students. Financial award application deadline: 2/1. Unit head: Dr. Jan Bartlett, Coordinator, 319-273-7979, Fax: 319-273-5175, E-mail: jan.bartlett@uni.edu. Application contact: Laurie S. Russell, Record Analyst, 319-273-2623, Fax: 319-273-2885, E-mail: laurie.russell@uni.edu.

University of North Florida, College of Arts and Sciences, Department of Psychology, Jacksonville, FL 32224. Offers counseling psychology (MAC); general psychology (MA). Part-time and evening/weekend programs available. Faculty: 13 full-time (5 women), 3 part-time/adjunct (1 woman). Students: 35 full-time (21 women), 16 part-time (11 women); includes 1 Black or African American, non-Hispanic/Latino; 1 Asian, non-Hispanic/Latino; 5 Hispanic/Latino; 2 Two or more races, non-Hispanic/Latino, 1 international. Average age 28. 61 applicants, 38% accepted, 12 enrolled. In 2010, 14 master's awarded. Degree requirements: For master's, comprehensive exam, thesis optional, practicum. Entrance requirements: For master's, GRE General Test, 2 letters of recommendation, minimum GPA of 3.0 in last 60 hours of course work. Additional exam requirements/recommendations for international students: Required—TOEFL (minimum score 500 paper-based; 173 computer-based; 61 iBT). Application deadline: For fall admission, 6/1 priority date for domestic students, 4/1 for international students. Applications are processed on a rolling basis. Application fee: $30. Electronic applications accepted. Expenses: Tuition, state resident: full-time $7646.40; part-time $318.60 per credit hour. Tuition, nonresident: full-time $23,502; part-time $979.24 per credit hour. Required fees: $1208.88; $50.37 per credit hour. Tuition and fees vary according to course load and program. Financial support: In 2010–11, 25 students received support, including 1 research assistantship (averaging $1,684 per year), 4 teaching assistantships (averaging $5,186 per year); Federal Work-Study, scholarships/grants, and tuition waivers (partial) also available. Financial award application deadline: 4/1; financial award applicants required to submit FAFSA. Faculty research: Sensory perception, social cognition, sexual behavior, evolutionary psychology, psychology and law. Total annual research expenditures: $68,727. Unit head: Dr. Michael Toglia, Chair, 904-620-1624, E-mail: m.toglia@unf.edu. Application contact: Lillith Richardson, Assistant Director, The Graduate School, 904-620-1360, Fax: 904-620-1362, E-mail: graduateschool@unf.edu.

University of North Texas, Toulouse Graduate School, College of Arts and Sciences, Department of Psychology, Denton, TX 76203. Offers clinical psychology (PhD); counseling psychology (MA, MS, PhD); experimental psychology (MA, MS, PhD); health psychology and behavioral medicine (PhD). Accreditation: APA (one or more programs are accredited). Terminal master's awarded for partial completion of doctoral program. Degree requirements: For master's, comprehensive exam, thesis or alternative; for doctorate, one foreign language, comprehensive exam, thesis/dissertation. Entrance requirements: For master's and doctorate, GRE General Test, interview. Additional exam requirements/recommendations for international students: Recommended—TOEFL (minimum score 550 paper-based; 213 computer-based; 79 iBT). Application deadline: Applications are processed on a rolling basis. Electronic applications accepted. Expenses: Tuition, state resident: full-time $4298; part-time $239 per credit hour. Tuition, nonresident: full-time $10,782; part-time $549 per credit hour. Required fees: $1292; $270 per credit hour. Financial support: Fellowships, research assistantships, teaching assistantships, career-related internships or fieldwork, Federal Work-Study, and institutionally sponsored loans available. Financial award applicants required to submit FAFSA. Application contact: Graduate Coordinator, 940-565-2671, Fax: 940-565-4682, E-mail: amym@unt.edu.

University of Notre Dame, Graduate School, College of Arts and Letters, Division of Social Science, Department of Psychology, Notre Dame, IN 46556. Offers cognitive psychology (PhD); counseling psychology (PhD); developmental psychology (PhD); quantitative psychology (PhD). Accreditation: APA. Degree requirements: For doctorate, comprehensive exam, thesis/

dissertation, candidacy exam. Entrance requirements: For doctorate, GRE General Test, GRE Subject Test (strongly recommended). Additional exam requirements/recommendations for international students: Required—TOEFL (minimum score 600 paper-based; 250 computer-based; 80 iBT). Electronic applications accepted. Faculty research: Cognitive and socio-emotional development, statistical methods and quantitative models applicable to psychology, interpersonal relations, life span development and developmental delay, childhood depression, structural equation and dynamical systems.

University of Oklahoma, Jeannine Rainbolt College of Education, Department of Educational Psychology, Program in Counseling Psychology, Norman, OK 73019. Offers PhD. Accreditation: APA. Students: 25 full-time (15 women), 16 part-time (11 women); includes 10 minority (2 Black or African American, non-Hispanic/Latino; 4 American Indian or Alaska Native, non-Hispanic/Latino; 1 Asian, non-Hispanic/Latino; 1 Hispanic/Latino; 2 Two or more races, non-Hispanic/Latino), 2 international. Average age 32. 34 applicants, 15% accepted, 5 enrolled. In 2010, 9 doctorates awarded. Degree requirements: For doctorate, thesis/dissertation, general exam. Entrance requirements: For doctorate, GRE General Test, master's degree, 3 letters of recommendation, interview, curriculum vitae. Additional exam requirements/recommendations for international students: Required—TOEFL (minimum score 550 paper-based; 213 computer-based; 79 iBT). Application deadline: For fall admission, 1/10 for domestic and international students; for spring admission, 11/1 for domestic students, 9/1 for international students. Applications are processed on a rolling basis. Application fee: $40 ($90 for international students). Electronic applications accepted. Expenses: Tuition, state resident: full-time $3893; part-time $162.20 per credit hour. Tuition, nonresident: full-time $14,167; part-time $590.30 per credit hour. Required fees: $2523; $94.60 per credit hour. Tuition and fees vary according to course load and degree level. Financial support: In 2010–11, 40 students received support. Career-related internships or fieldwork, Federal Work-Study, institutionally sponsored loans, scholarships/grants, health care benefits, and unspecified assistantships available. Support available to part-time students. Financial award application deadline: 3/1; financial award applicants required to submit FAFSA. Faculty research: Domestic violence, marriage and family, multicultural, training and supervision, trauma. Unit head: Dr. Terri K. Debacker, Chair, 405-325-1068, Fax: 405-325-6655, E-mail: debacker@ou.edu. Application contact: Rashida Y. Douglas, Graduate Programs Officer, 405-325-4525, Fax: 405-325-6655, E-mail: ryd618@ou.edu.

University of Pennsylvania, Graduate School of Education, Division of Applied Psychology and Human Development, Program in Counseling and Psychological Services, Philadelphia, PA 19104. Offers PhD. Students: 33 full-time (27 women), 5 part-time (4 women); includes 5 Black or African American, non-Hispanic/Latino; 1 Asian, non-Hispanic/Latino; 1 Hispanic/Latino, 11 international. 48 applicants, 83% accepted, 24 enrolled. Degree requirements: For doctorate, thesis/dissertation, exams. Entrance requirements: For doctorate, GRE General Test, GRE Subject Test. Application deadline: For fall admission, 12/15 priority date for domestic students. Applications are processed on a rolling basis. Application fee: $70. Electronic applications accepted. Expenses: Contact institution. Financial support: Fellowships, institutionally sponsored loans, scholarships/grants, traineeships, health care benefits, and unspecified assistantships available. Faculty research: Therapeutic interventions at a preschool level, childhood stress, college psychology, school and community psychology. Application contact: Michele King-Griffin, 215-898-4610, E-mail: griffinm@gse.upenn.edu.

University of Pennsylvania, Graduate School of Education, Division of Applied Psychology and Human Development, Program in Professional Counseling and Mental Health Services, Philadelphia, PA 19104. Offers counseling and mental health services (MS Ed); professional counseling (M Phil); school counseling (MS Ed). Students: 71 full-time (62 women), 15 part-time (12 women); includes 14 Black or African American, non-Hispanic/Latino; 4 Asian, non-Hispanic/Latino; 7 Hispanic/Latino. 71 applicants, 77% accepted, 43 enrolled. In 2010, 12 master's awarded. Degree requirements: For master's, exam. Entrance requirements: For master's, GRE General Test. Application deadline: For fall admission, 12/15 priority date for domestic students. Applications are processed on a rolling basis. Application fee: $70. Electronic applications accepted. Expenses: Contact institution. Financial support: Applicants required to submit FAFSA. Faculty research: Counseling in school, college, or agency.

University of Phoenix, College of Social Science, Phoenix, AZ 85034-7209. Offers clinical mental health counseling (MSC); community counseling (MSC); psychology (MS). Programs are offered at the online campus. Evening/weekend programs available. Postbaccalaureate distance learning degree programs offered. Students: 4,215 full-time (3,585 women); includes 1,544 minority (1,161 Black or African American, non-Hispanic/Latino; 34 American Indian or Alaska Native, non-Hispanic/Latino; 32 Asian, non-Hispanic/Latino; 280 Hispanic/Latino; 22 Native Hawaiian or other Pacific Islander, non-Hispanic/Latino; 15 Two or more races, non-Hispanic/Latino), 85 international. Average age 38. Entrance requirements: For master's, minimum undergraduate GPA of 2.5 from accredited university, 3 years of work experience, citizen of the United States or have valid visa. Additional exam requirements/recommendations for international students: Required—TOEFL (minimum paper score 550, computer score 213, iBT 79), Test of English for International Communication, or IELTS. Application deadline: Applications are processed on a rolling basis. Application fee: $45. Electronic applications accepted. Expenses: Tuition: Full-time $16,440. One-time fee: $45 full-time. Full-time tuition and fees vary according to course load, degree level, campus/location and program. Financial support: Scholarships/grants available. Financial award applicants required to submit FAFSA. Unit head: Rob Olding, Associate Dean, Human Service/Psychology, 602-551-3073, E-mail: rob.olding@phoenix.edu. Application contact: Rob Olding, Associate Dean, Human Service/Psychology, 602-551-3073, E-mail: rob.olding@phoenix.edu.

University of Phoenix–Las Vegas Campus, College of Human Services, Las Vegas, NV 89128. Offers marriage, family, and child therapy (MSC); mental health counseling (MSC); school counseling (MSC). Postbaccalaureate distance learning degree programs offered. Entrance requirements: For master's, minimum undergraduate GPA of 2.5, 3 years of work experience. Additional exam requirements/recommendations for international students: Required—TOEFL (minimum score 550 paper-based; 213 computer-based; 79 iBT). Electronic applications accepted.

University of Phoenix–Phoenix Campus, College of Social Sciences, Phoenix, AZ 85040-1958. Offers community counseling (MC); counseling (MSC); psychology (MSP). Evening/weekend programs available. Postbaccalaureate distance learning degree programs offered. Students: 181 full-time (140 women); includes 23 minority (7 Black or African American, non-Hispanic/Latino; 2 Asian, non-Hispanic/Latino; 14 Hispanic/Latino), 7 international. Average age 34. Entrance requirements: For master's, minimum undergraduate GPA of 2.5 from accredited university, 3 years of work experience, citizen of the United States or have valid visa. Additional exam requirements/recommendations for international students: Required—TOEFL (minimum paper score 500, computer score 213, iBT 79), Test of English for International Communication, or IELTS. Application deadline: Applications are processed on a rolling basis. Application fee: $45. Electronic applications accepted. Expenses: Tuition: Full-time $13,560. One-time fee: $45 full-time. Full-time tuition and fees vary according to course load, degree level, campus/location and program. Financial support: Scholarships/grants available. Financial award applicants required to submit FAFSA. Unit head: Dr. Lynn Hall, Dean/Executive Director, 520-247-4364, E-mail: lynn.hall@phoenix.edu. Application contact: Campus Information Center, 866-766-0766.

University of Phoenix–Puerto Rico Campus, College of Human Services, Guaynabo, PR 00968. Offers marriage and family counseling (MSC); mental health counseling (MSC). Evening/weekend programs available. Degree requirements: For master's, thesis (for some programs). Entrance requirements: For master's, Counselor Preparation Comprehensive Examination, minimum undergraduate GPA of 2.5, 3 years work experience. Additional exam requirements/recommendations for international students: Required—TOEFL (minimum score 550 paper-based; 213 computer-based; 79 iBT). Electronic applications accepted.

University of Phoenix–Southern California Campus, College of Social Sciences, Costa Mesa, CA 92626. Offers administration of justice and security (MS); community counseling (MSC); marriage, family and child therapy (MSC); mental health counseling (MSC); psychology (MS); school counseling (MSC). Evening/weekend programs available. *Degree requirements:* For master's, thesis (for some programs). *Entrance requirements:* For master's, minimum undergraduate GPA of 3.0, 3 years work experience. Additional exam requirements/recommendations for international students: Required—TOEFL (minimum score 550 paper-based; 213 computer-based; 79 iBT). Electronic applications accepted.

University of Puget Sound, Graduate Studies, School of Education, Program in Counseling, Tacoma, WA 98416. Offers mental health counseling (M Ed); pastoral counseling (M Ed); school counseling (M Ed). *Accreditation:* NCATE. Part-time programs available. *Entrance requirements:* For master's, GRE General Test, minimum GPA of 3.0. Additional exam requirements/recommendations for international students: Required—TOEFL (minimum score 550 paper-based; 213 computer-based; 80 iBT). Electronic applications accepted. *Expenses:* Contact institution. *Faculty research:* Cross-role professional preparation, suicide prevention.

University of Rhode Island, Graduate School, College of Human Science and Services, Department of Human Development and Family Studies, Kingston, RI 02881. Offers college student personnel (MS); human development and family studies (MS); marriage and family therapy (MS). *Accreditation:* AAMFT/COAMFTE. Part-time programs available. *Faculty:* 12 full-time (9 women), 3 part-time/adjunct (all women). *Students:* 38 full-time (30 women), 16 part-time (11 women); includes 6 minority (2 Black or African American, non-Hispanic/Latino; 4 Hispanic/Latino). In 2010, 23 master's awarded. *Degree requirements:* For master's, comprehensive exam (for some programs), thesis optional. *Entrance requirements:* For master's, GRE or MAT, 2 letters of recommendation. Additional exam requirements/recommendations for international students: Required—TOEFL (minimum score 550 paper-based; 213 computer-based). Application fee: $65. Electronic applications accepted. *Expenses:* Tuition, state resident: full-time $9588; part-time $533 per credit hour. Tuition, nonresident: full-time $22,968; part-time $1276 per credit hour. Required fees: $1282; $68 per semester. Tuition and fees vary according to program. *Financial support:* In 2010–11, 3 research assistantships with full and partial tuition reimbursements (averaging $11,578 per year), 4 teaching assistantships with full and partial tuition reimbursements (averaging $8,105 per year) were awarded. Financial award applicants required to submit FAFSA. Total annual research expenditures: $1.2 million. *Unit head:* Dr. Jerome Adams, Chair, 401-874-5962, Fax: 401-874-4020, E-mail: jadams@uri.edu. *Application contact:* Dr. Jerome Adams, Chair, 401-874-5962, Fax: 401-874-4020, E-mail: jadams@uri.edu.

University of Saint Francis, Graduate School, Department of Psychology and Counseling, Fort Wayne, IN 46808-3994. Offers general psychology (MS); mental health counseling (MS); pastoral counseling (MS); school counseling (MS Ed). Part-time and evening/weekend programs available. *Entrance requirements:* For master's, interview, minimum undergraduate GPA of 3.0. *Expenses:* Tuition: Part-time $770 per semester hour. Part-time tuition and fees vary according to program.

University of St. Thomas, Graduate Studies, Graduate School of Professional Psychology, St. Paul, MN 55105-1096. Offers counseling psychology (MA, Psy D); marriage and family psychology (MA, Certificate). *Accreditation:* APA. Part-time and evening/weekend programs available. *Faculty:* 11 full-time (5 women), 13 part-time/adjunct (6 women). *Students:* 68 full-time (54 women), 141 part-time (113 women); includes 5 Black or African American, non-Hispanic/Latino; 13 Asian, non-Hispanic/Latino; 3 Hispanic/Latino, 4 international. Average age 29. 578 applicants, 42% accepted. In 2010, 22 master's, 11 doctorates awarded. *Degree requirements:* For master's, comprehensive exam, practicum; for doctorate, comprehensive exam, thesis/dissertation, qualifying exam, practicum, internship. *Entrance requirements:* For master's, GRE, minimum GPA of 2.75, letters of recommendation, personal statement; for doctorate, GRE, minimum GPA of 3.2, letters of recommendation, personal statement. Additional exam requirements/recommendations for international students: Required—TOEFL (minimum score 550 paper-based; 213 computer-based; 80 iBT). *Application deadline:* For fall admission, 3/1 priority date for domestic students; for winter admission, 2/1 priority date for domestic students; for spring admission, 9/15 priority date for domestic students, 3/1 for international students. Application fee: $50. *Expenses:* Contact institution. *Financial support:* In 2010–11, 2 fellowships (averaging $5,000 per year) were awarded; research assistantships, institutionally sponsored loans and scholarships/grants also available. Support available to part-time students. Financial award application deadline: 8/1; financial award applicants required to submit FAFSA. *Faculty research:* Elderly, eating disorders, anxiety, family. *Unit head:* Dr. Christopher S. Vye, Associate Dean, 651-962-4666, Fax: 651-962-4666, E-mail: bnolan@stthomas.edu. *Application contact:* Laurie Dupont, Administrative Assistant, 651-962-4669, Fax: 651-962-4651, E-mail: ldupont@stthomas.edu.

University of San Diego, School of Leadership and Education Sciences, Program in Counseling, San Diego, CA 92110-2492. Offers clinical mental health counseling (MA); school counseling (MA). *Accreditation:* ACA. Part-time and evening/weekend programs available. *Faculty:* 6 full-time (2 women), 16 part-time/adjunct (10 women). *Students:* 68 full-time (58 women), 28 part-time (25 women); includes 43 minority (5 Black or African American, non-Hispanic/Latino; 8 Asian, non-Hispanic/Latino; 22 Hispanic/Latino; 1 Native Hawaiian or other Pacific Islander, non-Hispanic/Latino; 7 Two or more races, non-Hispanic/Latino), 3 international. Average age 27. 132 applicants, 70% accepted, 54 enrolled. In 2010, 34 master's awarded. *Degree requirements:* For master's, comprehensive exam. *Entrance requirements:* For master's, minimum GPA of 3.0, interview with faculty member. Additional exam requirements/recommendations for international students: Required—TOEFL (minimum score 580 paper-based; 237 computer-based; 83 iBT), TWE. *Application deadline:* For fall admission, 3/1 priority date for domestic students, 3/1 for international students. Application fee: $45. Electronic applications accepted. *Expenses:* Tuition: Full-time $21,744; part-time $1208 per unit. Required fees: $224. Full-time tuition and fees vary according to course load and degree level. *Financial support:* Career-related internships or fieldwork, Federal Work-Study, institutionally sponsored loans, unspecified assistantships, and stipends available. Support available to part-time students. Financial award application deadline: 4/1; financial award applicants required to submit FAFSA. *Faculty research:* Action research, forensic psychology, lifespan and career development, multicultural counseling, school counseling. *Unit head:* Dr. Lonnie Rowell, Graduate Program Co-Director, 619-260-4212, Fax: 619-260-8095. *Application contact:* Stephen Pultz, Director of Admissions and Enrollment, 619-260-4506, Fax: 619-260-6836, E-mail: admissions@sandiego.edu.

University of San Francisco, School of Education, Department of Counseling Psychology, San Francisco, CA 94117-1080. Offers counseling (MA), including educational counseling, life transitions counseling, marital and family therapy; counseling psychology (Ed D). *Faculty:* 7 full-time (3 women), 37 part-time/adjunct (26 women). *Students:* 300 full-time (240 women), 14 part-time (10 women); includes 119 minority (14 Black or African American, non-Hispanic/Latino; 43 Asian, non-Hispanic/Latino; 46 Hispanic/Latino; 16 Two or more races, non-Hispanic/Latino), 7 international. Average age 31. 439 applicants, 58% accepted, 142 enrolled. In 2010, 138 master's awarded. *Degree requirements:* For doctorate, thesis/dissertation. *Entrance requirements:* For doctorate, GRE General Test. Application fee: $55 ($65 for international students). *Expenses:* Tuition: Full-time $20,070; part-time $1115 per credit hour. Tuition and fees vary according to course load, degree level and program. *Financial support:* In 2010–11, 245 students received support; fellowships, research assistantships, teaching assistantships available. Financial award application deadline: 3/2; financial award applicants required to submit FAFSA. *Unit head:* Dr. Brian Gerrard, Chair, 415-422-6868. *Application contact:* Beth Teague, Associate Director of Graduate Outreach, 415-422-5467, E-mail: schoolofeducation@usfca.edu.

The University of Scranton, College of Graduate and Continuing Education, Department of Counseling and Human Services, Scranton, PA 18510. Offers community counseling (MS); professional counseling (CAGS); rehabilitation counseling (MS); school counseling (MS). *Accreditation:* ACA (one or more programs are accredited). Part-time and evening/weekend programs available. *Faculty:* 9 full-time (6 women), 10 part-time/adjunct (5 women). *Students:* 128 full-time (99 women), 18 part-time (12 women); includes 5 Black or African American, non-Hispanic/Latino; 3 Asian, non-Hispanic/Latino; 3 Hispanic/Latino, 2 international. Average age 28. 110 applicants, 50% accepted. In 2010, 57 master's awarded. *Degree requirements:* For master's, comprehensive exam, capstone experience. *Entrance requirements:* For master's, minimum GPA of 2.75. Additional exam requirements/recommendations for international students: Required—TOEFL (minimum score 500 paper-based; 173 computer-based), IELTS (minimum score 5.5). *Application deadline:* For fall admission, 3/1 for domestic students. Application fee: $0. *Financial support:* In 2010–11, 20 students received support, including 20 teaching assistantships with full and partial tuition reimbursements available (averaging $4,400 per year); fellowships, career-related internships or fieldwork, Federal Work-Study, and unspecified assistantships also available. Support available to part-time students. Financial award application deadline: 3/1. *Unit head:* Dr. Lee Ann Eschbach, Chair, 570-941-6299, Fax: 570-941-4201, E-mail: eschbach@scranton.edu. *Application contact:* Joseph M. Robach, Director of Admissions, 570-941-4385, Fax: 570-941-5928, E-mail: robachj2@scranton.edu.

University of South Africa, College of Human Sciences, Pretoria, South Africa. Offers adult education (M Ed); African languages (MA, PhD); African politics (MA, PhD); Afrikaans (MA, PhD); ancient history (MA, PhD); ancient Near Eastern studies (MA, PhD); anthropology (MA, PhD); applied linguistics (MA); Arabic (MA, PhD); archaeology (MA); art history (MA); Biblical archaeology (MA); Biblical studies (M Th, D Th, PhD); Christian spirituality (M Th, D Th); church history (M Th, D Th); classical studies (MA, PhD); clinical psychology (MA); communication (MA, PhD); comparative education (M Ed, Ed D); consulting psychology (D Admin, D Com, PhD); curriculum studies (M Ed, Ed D); development studies (M Admin, MA, D Admin, PhD); didactics (M Ed, Ed D); education (M Tech); education management (M Ed, Ed D); educational psychology (M Ed); English (MA); environmental education (M Ed); French (MA, PhD); German (MA, PhD); Greek (MA); guidance and counseling (M Ed); health studies (MA, PhD), including health sciences education (MA), health services management (MA), medical and surgical nursing science (critical care general) (MA), midwifery and neonatal nursing science (MA), trauma and emergency care (MA); history (MA, PhD); history of education (Ed D); inclusive education (M Ed, Ed D); information and communications technology policy and regulation (MA); information science (MA, MIS, PhD); international politics (MA, PhD); Islamic studies (MA, PhD); Italian (MA, PhD); Judaica (MA, PhD); linguistics (MA, PhD); mathematical education (M Ed); mathematics education (MA); missiology (M Th, D Th); modern Hebrew (MA, PhD); musicology (MA, MMus, D Mus, PhD); natural science education (M Ed); New Testament (M Th, D Th); Old Testament (D Th); pastoral therapy (M Th, D Th); philosophy (MA); philosophy of education (M Ed, Ed D); politics (MA, PhD); Portuguese (MA, PhD); practical theology (M Th, D Th); psychology (MA, MS, PhD); psychology of education (M Ed, Ed D); public health (MA); religious studies (MA, D Th, PhD); Romance languages (MA); Russian (MA, PhD); Semitic languages (MA, PhD); social behavior studies in HIV/AIDS (MA); social science (mental health) (MA); social science in development studies (MA); social science in psychology (MA); social science in social work (MA); social science in sociology (MA); social work (MSW, DSW, PhD); socio-education (M Ed, Ed D); sociolinguistics (MA); sociology (MA, PhD); Spanish (MA, PhD); systematic theology (M Th, D Th); TESOL (teaching English to speakers of other languages) (MA); theological ethics (M Th, D Th); theory of literature (MA, PhD); urban ministries (D Th); urban ministry (M Th).

University of South Alabama, Graduate School, College of Arts and Sciences, Department of Psychology, Mobile, AL 36688. Offers clinical and counseling psychology (PhD); psychology (MS). Part-time and evening/weekend programs available. *Faculty:* 10 full-time (4 women). *Students:* 14 full-time (11 women), 9 part-time (5 women); includes 3 minority (2 Black or African American, non-Hispanic/Latino; 1 Hispanic/Latino). 47 applicants, 26% accepted, 9 enrolled. In 2010, 10 master's awarded. *Degree requirements:* For master's, comprehensive exam, thesis optional. *Entrance requirements:* For master's, GRE General Test, GRE Subject Test (recommended), minimum GPA of 3.0, major in psychology or equivalent. Additional exam requirements/recommendations for international students: Required—TOEFL. *Application deadline:* For fall admission, 3/1 priority date for domestic students, 3/1 for international students. Applications are processed on a rolling basis. Application fee: $35. *Expenses:* Tuition, state resident: part-time $300 per credit hour. Tuition, nonresident: part-time $600 per credit hour. Required fees: $150 per semester. *Financial support:* Fellowships, research assistantships available. Support available to part-time students. Financial award application deadline: 4/1. *Faculty research:* Language acquisition and development. *Unit head:* Dr. Larry Christensen, Chair, 251-460-6371. *Application contact:* Dr. Lisa Turner, Graduate Coordinator, 251-460-6371.

University of South Alabama, Graduate School, Program in Clinical and Counseling Psychology, Mobile, AL 36688-0002. Offers PhD. *Students:* 12 full-time (11 women); includes 2 minority (both Asian, non-Hispanic/Latino). 21 applicants, 29% accepted, 6 enrolled. *Entrance requirements:* For doctorate, GRE. Additional exam requirements/recommendations for international students: Required—TOEFL. *Application deadline:* For fall admission, 2/15 for domestic students; for spring admission, 5/1 for domestic students. Applications are processed on a rolling basis. Application fee: $35. Electronic applications accepted. *Expenses:* Tuition, state resident: part-time $300 per credit hour. Tuition, nonresident: part-time $600 per credit hour. Required fees: $150 per semester. *Unit head:* Dr. Martin Rohling, Director of Clinical Training, 251-460-6371, E-mail: mrohling@usouthal.edu. *Application contact:* Dr. B. Keith Harrison, Dean of the Graduate School, 251-460-6310.

University of Southern Maine, School of Education and Human Development, Program in Counselor Education, Portland, ME 04104-9300. Offers clinical mental health (MS); counseling (CAS); mental health rehabilitation technician/community (Certificate); rehabilitation counseling (MS); school counseling (MS). *Accreditation:* ACA (one or more programs are accredited); CORE; Teacher Education Accreditation Council. Part-time and evening/weekend programs available. *Faculty:* 9 full-time (5 women), 3 part-time/adjunct (1 woman). *Students:* 52 full-time (45 women), 88 part-time (63 women); includes 8 minority (1 Black or African American, non-Hispanic/Latino; 2 American Indian or Alaska Native, non-Hispanic/Latino; 2 Asian, non-Hispanic/Latino; 3 Hispanic/Latino). 103 applicants, 58% accepted, 47 enrolled. In 2010, 39 master's, 1 other advanced degree awarded. *Degree requirements:* For master's, comprehensive exam, thesis or alternative; for other advanced degree, thesis or alternative. *Entrance requirements:* For master's, GRE General Test or MAT, interview; for other advanced degree, master's degree. Additional exam requirements/recommendations for international students: Required—TOEFL (minimum score 550 paper-based; 213 computer-based; 79 iBT). *Application deadline:* For fall admission, 11/15 for domestic students. Application fee: $65. Electronic applications accepted. *Financial support:* In 2010–11, 15 students received support, including 5 research assistantships with partial tuition reimbursements available (averaging $4,500 per year); career-related internships or fieldwork, Federal Work-Study, institutionally sponsored loans, scholarships/grants, and unspecified assistantships also available. Support available to part-time students. Financial award application deadline: 3/1; financial award applicants required to submit FAFSA. *Faculty research:* Counselor licensure. *Unit head:* Dr. E. Michael Brady, Chair, Human Resource Development Department, 207-780-5316, Fax: 207-780-5043, E-mail: mbrady@usm.maine.edu. *Application contact:* Mary Sloan, Director of Graduate Admissions, 207-780-4386, Fax: 207-780-4969, E-mail: msloan@usm.maine.edu.

University of Southern Mississippi, Graduate School, College of Education and Psychology, Department of Psychology, Hattiesburg, MS 39406-0001. Offers clinical psychology (MA, PhD); counseling psychology (MA, PhD); experimental psychology (MA, PhD); school psychology (MA, PhD). *Accreditation:* APA (one or more programs are accredited). *Faculty:* 32 full-time (9 women). *Students:* 98 full-time (75 women), 42 part-time (33 women); includes 8 Black or African American, non-Hispanic/Latino; 3 Asian, non-Hispanic/Latino; 5 Hispanic/Latino, 7 international. Average age 29. 219 applicants, 16% accepted, 31 enrolled. In 2010, 27 master's, 13 doctorates awarded. Terminal master's awarded for partial completion of doctoral program. *Degree requirements:* For master's, comprehensive exam, thesis; for doctorate, comprehensive exam, thesis/dissertation. *Entrance requirements:* For master's, GRE General Test, minimum

Counseling Psychology

University of Southern Mississippi (continued)

GPA of 3.0; for doctorate, GRE General Test, interview, minimum GPA of 3.5. Additional exam requirements/recommendations for international students: Required—TOEFL, IELTS. *Application deadline:* For fall admission, 3/1 priority date for domestic students, 3/1 for international students. Applications are processed on a rolling basis. Application fee: $50. *Financial support:* In 2010–11, 48 research assistantships with full tuition reimbursements (averaging $8,802 per year), 48 teaching assistantships with full tuition reimbursements (averaging $6,500 per year) were awarded; career-related internships or fieldwork, Federal Work-Study, institutionally sponsored loans, scholarships/grants, health care benefits, and unspecified assistantships also available. Financial award application deadline: 3/15; financial award applicants required to submit FAFSA. *Faculty research:* Dolphin cognition, sleep, neuropsychology, health-related behaviors, psychopathology. Total annual research expenditures: $101,200. *Unit head:* Dr. Joesph Olmi, Chair, 601-266-4177, Fax: 601-266-5580. *Application contact:* Susan King, Graduate Secretary, 601-266-4177, Fax: 601-266-5580.

The University of Tennessee, Graduate School, College of Education, Health and Human Sciences, Department of Educational Psychology and Counseling, Knoxville, TN 37996. Offers adult education (MS); applied educational psychology (MS); collaborative learning (Ed D); college student personnel (MS); mental health counseling (MS); rehabilitation counseling (MS); school counseling (MS). *Accreditation:* ACA (one or more programs are accredited); CORE (one or more programs are accredited); NCATE. Part-time and evening/weekend programs available. *Degree requirements:* For master's, thesis optional. *Entrance requirements:* For master's, GRE General Test, minimum GPA of 2.7. Additional exam requirements/recommendations for international students: Required—TOEFL. Electronic applications accepted. *Expenses:* Tuition, state resident: full-time $7440; part-time $414 per credit hour. Tuition, nonresident: full-time $22,478; part-time $1250 per credit hour. Required fees: $922; $43 per credit hour. Tuition and fees vary according to program.

The University of Texas at Austin, Graduate School, College of Education, Department of Educational Psychology, Austin, TX 78712-1111. Offers academic educational psychology (M Ed, MA); counseling psychology (PhD); counselor education (M Ed); human development and culture (PhD); learning, cognition and instruction (PhD); quantitative methods (PhD); school psychology (PhD). *Accreditation:* APA (one or more programs are accredited). *Degree requirements:* For master's, thesis optional; for doctorate, thesis/dissertation. *Entrance requirements:* For master's and doctorate, GRE General Test, 3 letters of recommendation. Additional exam requirements/recommendations for international students: Required—TOEFL.

The University of Texas at Tyler, College of Education and Psychology, Department of Psychology and Counseling, Tyler, TX 75799-0001. Offers clinical psychology (MS), including neuropsychology, school psychology; counseling psychology (MA), including general, marriage and family; interdisciplinary studies (MSIS); school counseling (MA). Part-time and evening/weekend programs available. *Degree requirements:* For master's, comprehensive exam, thesis optional. *Entrance requirements:* For master's, GRE General Test, minimum GPA of 3.0. Additional exam requirements/recommendations for international students: Required—TOEFL (minimum score 79 computer-based). Electronic applications accepted. *Faculty research:* Neuropsychology, child abuse, psychometric properties of psychological instruments, maternal behavior, clinical practice issues, victimization of women, post-traumatic stress disorder.

University of the Cumberlands, Program in Professional Counseling, Williamsburg, KY 40769-1372. Offers MA. Program also offered in San Francisco. Part-time and evening/weekend programs available. Postbaccalaureate distance learning degree programs offered (minimal on-campus study). *Faculty:* 2 full-time (1 woman), 2 part-time/adjunct (1 woman). *Students:* 12 full-time (10 women), 3 part-time (2 women); includes 1 Black or African American, non-Hispanic/Latino. Average age 33. *Application deadline:* Applications are processed on a rolling basis. Application fee: $30. Electronic applications accepted. *Expenses:* Tuition: Full-time $6984; part-time $291 per credit hour. Required fees: $50 per term. Tuition and fees vary according to course level, course load and program. *Unit head:* Dr. Dennis Trickett, Department Chair, 606-539-4153, E-mail: dennis.trickett@ucumberlands.edu. *Application contact:* Donna Stanfill, Director, Graduate Admissions, 606-549-2200 Ext. 4496, Fax: 606-539-4534, E-mail: donna.stanfill@cumberlandcollege.edu.

University of the District of Columbia, College of Arts and Sciences, Department of Psychology and Counseling, Program in Counseling, Washington, DC 20008-1175. Offers MS. *Expenses:* Tuition, state resident: full-time $7580; part-time $421 per credit. Tuition, nonresident: full-time $14,580; part-time $810 per credit. Required fees: $620; $30 per credit. One-time fee: $100 part-time.

University of the Southwest, Graduate Programs, Hobbs, NM 88240-9129. Offers business administration (MBA); curriculum and instruction (MSE); curriculum and instruction: reading (MSE); early childhood education (MSE); educational administration (MSE); educational diagnostician (MSE); mental health counseling (MSE); school counseling (MSE); special education (MSE); sports management (MBA). Part-time and evening/weekend programs available. Postbaccalaureate distance learning degree programs offered (no on-campus study). *Faculty:* 13 full-time (6 women), 28 part-time/adjunct (17 women). *Students:* 169 full-time (125 women), 59 part-time (42 women); includes 87 minority (16 Black or African American, non-Hispanic/Latino; 68 Hispanic/Latino; 3 Two or more races, non-Hispanic/Latino), 1 international. Average age 36. 94 applicants, 65% accepted, 36 enrolled. In 2010, 41 master's awarded. *Degree requirements:* For master's, comprehensive exam. *Application deadline:* For fall admission, 3/1 priority date for domestic students; for spring admission, 10/1 for domestic students. Applications are processed on a rolling basis. Application fee: $50. Electronic applications accepted. *Expenses:* Tuition: Part-time $512 per credit hour. *Financial support:* In 2010–11, 188 students received support; research assistantships with partial tuition reimbursements available, Federal Work-Study, scholarships/grants, and tuition waivers (partial) available. Support available to part-time students. Financial award application deadline: 4/1; financial award applicants required to submit FAFSA. *Unit head:* Dr. Mary Harris, Dean of Education, 575-492-2162 Ext. 2162, Fax: 575-392-6006, E-mail: mharris@usw.edu. *Application contact:* Melissa Mitchell, Graduate Program Advisor, 575-492-2142 Ext. 2142, Fax: 575-392-6006, E-mail: mmitchell@usw.edu.

University of Utah, Graduate School, College of Education, Department of Educational Psychology, Salt Lake City, UT 84112. Offers counseling psychology (PhD); educational psychology (MA); instructional design and educational technology (M Ed); learning and cognition (MS, PhD); professional counseling (MS); professional psychology (M Ed); reading and literacy (M Ed, PhD); school counseling (M Ed, MS); school psychology (MS, PhD); statistics (M Stat). *Accreditation:* APA (one or more programs are accredited). Evening/weekend programs available. Postbaccalaureate distance learning degree programs offered (minimal on-campus study). *Faculty:* 20 full-time (10 women), 6 part-time/adjunct (4 women). *Students:* 119 full-time (96 women), 105 part-time (72 women); includes 25 minority (1 American Indian or Alaska Native, non-Hispanic/Latino; 6 Asian, non-Hispanic/Latino; 13 Hispanic/Latino; 1 Native Hawaiian or other Pacific Islander, non-Hispanic/Latino; 4 Two or more races, non-Hispanic/Latino), 3 international. Average age 33. 238 applicants, 34% accepted, 60 enrolled. In 2010, 40 master's, 18 doctorates awarded. *Degree requirements:* For master's, variable foreign language requirement, comprehensive exam, thesis (for some programs); for doctorate, variable foreign language requirement, thesis/dissertation, oral exam. *Entrance requirements:* For master's and doctorate, GRE General Test, minimum GPA of 3.0. Additional exam requirements/recommendations for international students: Required—TOEFL (minimum score 500 paper-based; 173 computer-based). *Application deadline:* For fall admission, 4/1 for domestic and international students; for spring admission, 11/1 for domestic and international students. Application fee: $55 ($65 for international students). *Expenses:* Contact institution. *Financial support:* In 2010–11, 90 students received support, including 45 fellowships with full and partial tuition reimbursements available (averaging $11,500 per year), 13 research assistantships with full and partial tuition reimbursements available (averaging $11,500 per year), 32 teaching assistantships with full and partial tuition reimbursements available (averaging $11,500 per year); career-related internships or fieldwork, Federal Work-Study, institutionally sponsored loans, scholarships/grants, and unspecified assistantships also available. Financial award application deadline: 2/1; financial award applicants required to submit FAFSA. *Faculty research:* Autism, computer technology and instruction, cognitive behavior, aging, group counseling. Total annual research expenditures: $902,082. *Unit head:* Dr. Elaine Clark, Chair, 801-581-7148, Fax: 801-581-5566, E-mail: clark@ed.utah.edu. *Application contact:* Kendra Lee Wiebke, Academic Program Specialist, 801-581-7148, Fax: 801-581-5566, E-mail: kendra.wiebke@utah.edu.

University of Vermont, Graduate College, College of Education and Social Services, Department of Integrated Professional Studies, Counseling Program, Burlington, VT 05405. Offers MS. *Accreditation:* ACA; NCATE. *Faculty:* 3 full-time (2 women), 6 part-time/adjunct (2 women). *Students:* 36 (32 women); includes 1 Asian, non-Hispanic/Latino, 2 international. 60 applicants, 80% accepted, 17 enrolled. In 2010, 17 master's awarded. *Entrance requirements:* For master's, GRE General Test, resume. Additional exam requirements/recommendations for international students: Required—TOEFL (minimum score 550 paper-based; 213 computer-based; 80 iBT). *Application deadline:* For fall admission, 2/1 priority date for domestic students. Applications are processed on a rolling basis. Application fee: $40. Electronic applications accepted. *Expenses:* Tuition, state resident: part-time $537 per credit hour. Tuition, nonresident: part-time $1355 per credit hour. *Financial support:* Fellowships, research assistantships, teaching assistantships available. Financial award application deadline: 2/1. *Faculty research:* Women and tenure, counseling children and adolescents. *Unit head:* Anne Geroski, Coordinator, 802-656-3888, Fax: 802-656-3173. *Application contact:* Anne Geroski, Coordinator, 802-656-3888, Fax: 802-656-3173.

University of Victoria, Faculty of Graduate Studies, Faculty of Education, Department of Educational Psychology and Leadership Studies, Victoria, BC V8W 2Y2, Canada. Offers aboriginal communities counseling (M Ed); counseling (M Ed, MA); educational psychology (M Ed, MA, PhD), including counseling psychology (M Ed, MA), leadership studies (PhD), learning and development (MA, PhD), measurement and evaluation, special education (M Ed, MA); leadership studies (M Ed, MA). Part-time programs available. *Degree requirements:* For master's, thesis (for some programs), comprehensive exam (M Ed); for doctorate, comprehensive exam, thesis/dissertation, candidacy exam. *Entrance requirements:* For master's, 2 years of work experience in a relevant field; for doctorate, GRE, 2 years of work experience in a relevant field, minimum B average. Additional exam requirements/recommendations for international students: Required—TOEFL (minimum score 575 paper-based; 233 computer-based), IELTS (minimum score 7). *Faculty research:* Learning and development (child, adolescent and adult), special education and exceptional children.

The University of Western Ontario, Faculty of Graduate Studies, Social Sciences Division, Faculty of Education, Program in Counseling Psychology, London, ON N6A 5B8, Canada. Offers M Ed. Part-time programs available. *Entrance requirements:* For master's, minimum B average, 3 yr experience in helping profession. *Faculty research:* Women's issues in counseling, causes for sexual harassment in the workplace, counselor memory and confidence in clinical judgements.

University of West Florida, College of Arts and Sciences: Arts, Department of Psychology, Pensacola, FL 32514-5750. Offers counseling (MA); counseling-licensed mental health counselor (MA); general (MA); industrial-organizational (MA). Part-time programs available. *Faculty:* 10 full-time (4 women), 1 part-time/adjunct (0 women). *Students:* 67 full-time (45 women), 39 part-time (30 women); includes 16 minority (5 Black or African American, non-Hispanic/Latino; 2 Asian, non-Hispanic/Latino; 5 Hispanic/Latino; 1 Native Hawaiian or other Pacific Islander, non-Hispanic/Latino; 3 Two or more races, non-Hispanic/Latino), 4 international. Average age 26. 143 applicants, 53% accepted, 32 enrolled. In 2010, 34 master's awarded. *Degree requirements:* For master's, thesis (for some programs). *Entrance requirements:* For master's, GRE General Test, GRE Subject Test, minimum GPA of 3.0. Additional exam requirements/recommendations for international students: Required—TOEFL (minimum score 550 paper-based; 213 computer-based). *Application deadline:* For fall admission, 6/1 for domestic students, 5/15 for international students; for spring admission, 10/1 for domestic and international students. Applications are processed on a rolling basis. Application fee: $30. *Expenses:* Tuition, state resident: full-time $4982; part-time $208 per credit hour. Tuition, nonresident: full-time $20,059; part-time $836 per credit hour. Required fees: $1365; $57 per credit hour. *Financial support:* In 2010–11, 19 fellowships with partial tuition reimbursements (averaging $1,090 per year), 30 research assistantships with partial tuition reimbursements (averaging $3,500 per year), 5 teaching assistantships with partial tuition reimbursements (averaging $4,552 per year) were awarded; career-related internships or fieldwork and unspecified assistantships also available. Financial award application deadline: 4/15; financial award applicants required to submit FAFSA. *Faculty research:* Prose recall, brain imaging, peak performance, biofeedback and pain control, comparable worth. Total annual research expenditures: $15,000. *Unit head:* Dr. Laura L. K. Bryan, Chairperson, 850-474-3493. *Application contact:* Terry McCray, Assistant Director of Graduate Admissions, 850-473-7718, Fax: 850-473-7714, E-mail: gradadmissions@uwf.edu.

University of Wisconsin–Madison, Graduate School, School of Education, Department of Counseling Psychology, Program in Counseling Psychology, Madison, WI 53706-1380. Offers PhD. *Accreditation:* APA. *Degree requirements:* For doctorate, thesis/dissertation. Application fee: $56. *Expenses:* Tuition, state resident: full-time $9887; part-time $617.96 per credit. Tuition, nonresident: full-time $24,054; part-time $1503.40 per credit. Required fees: $67.63 per credit. Tuition and fees vary according to reciprocity agreements. *Unit head:* Dr. Bruce Wampold, Chair, 608-263-9503, E-mail: wampold@education.wisc.edu. *Application contact:* Dr. Bruce Wampold, Chair, 608-263-9503, E-mail: wampold@education.wisc.edu.

University of Wisconsin–Milwaukee, Graduate School, School of Education, Department of Educational Psychology, Milwaukee, WI 53201-0413. Offers counseling (school, community) (MS); counseling psychology (PhD); learning and development (MS); research methodology (MS, PhD); school psychology (PhD). *Accreditation:* APA. Part-time programs available. *Faculty:* 22 full-time (14 women). *Students:* 158 full-time (130 women), 62 part-time (48 women); includes 14 Black or African American, non-Hispanic/Latino; 8 Asian, non-Hispanic/Latino; 5 Hispanic/Latino, 10 international. Average age 30. 278 applicants, 41% accepted. In 2010, 69 master's, 8 doctorates awarded. *Degree requirements:* For master's, comprehensive exam, thesis; for doctorate, thesis/dissertation. *Entrance requirements:* For master's, minimum GPA of 3.0; for doctorate, GRE General Test, minimum GPA of 3.0. Additional exam requirements/recommendations for international students: Required—TOEFL (minimum score 550 paper-based; 79 iBT), IELTS (minimum score 6.5). *Application deadline:* For fall admission, 1/1 priority date for domestic students; for spring admission, 9/1 for domestic students. Applications are processed on a rolling basis. Application fee: $56 ($96 for international students). Electronic applications accepted. *Financial support:* In 2010–11, 14 fellowships, 1 research assistantship, 8 teaching assistantships were awarded; career-related internships or fieldwork, health care benefits, unspecified assistantships, and project assistantships also available. Support available to part-time students. Financial award application deadline: 4/15; financial award applicants required to submit FAFSA. *Unit head:* Nadya Fouad, Graduate Program Representative, 414-229-4599, Fax: 414-229-4939, E-mail: nadya@uwm.edu. *Application contact:* General Information Contact, 414-229-4982, Fax: 414-229-6967, E-mail: gradschool@uwm.edu.

University of Wisconsin–Stout, Graduate School, College of Human Development, Program in Mental Health Counseling, Menomonie, WI 54751. Offers MS. Part-time programs available. *Degree requirements:* For master's, comprehensive exam or thesis. *Entrance requirements:* For master's, minimum GPA of 2.75. Additional exam requirements/recommendations for international students: Required—TOEFL (minimum score 500 paper-based; 173 computer-based; 61 iBT). Electronic applications accepted. *Faculty research:* Body image, gender issues, eating disorders, cognitive behavioral therapy.

University of Wisconsin–Stout, Graduate School, School of Education, Program in School Counseling, Menomonie, WI 54751. Offers MS. Part-time programs available. *Degree requirements:* For master's, thesis. *Entrance requirements:* For master's, minimum GPA of 2.75. Additional exam requirements/recommendations for international students: Required—TOEFL (minimum score 500 paper-based; 173 computer-based; 61 iBT). Electronic applications accepted. *Faculty research:* Adventure-based learning, body image, domestic violence, resilience, school climate.

Utah State University, School of Graduate Studies, College of Education and Human Services, Department of Psychology, Logan, UT 84322. Offers clinical/counseling/school psychology (PhD); research and evaluation methodology (PhD); school counseling (MS); school psychology (MS). *Accreditation:* APA (one or more programs are accredited). Part-time and evening/weekend programs available. Postbaccalaureate distance learning degree programs offered (no on-campus study). Terminal master's awarded for partial completion of doctoral program. *Degree requirements:* For master's, thesis (for some programs); for doctorate, thesis/dissertation. *Entrance requirements:* For master's, GRE General Test (school psychology), MAT (school counseling), minimum GPA of 3.5; for doctorate, GRE General Test, minimum GPA of 3.5. Additional exam requirements/recommendations for international students: Required—TOEFL. *Faculty research:* Hearing loss detection in infancy, ADHD, eating disorders, domestic violence, neuropsychology, bilingual/Spanish speaking students/parents.

Valdosta State University, Department of Psychology and Counseling, Valdosta, GA 31698. Offers clinical/counseling psychology (MS); industrial/organizational psychology (MS); school counseling (M Ed, Ed S); school psychology (Ed S). Part-time and evening/weekend programs available. *Faculty:* 19 full-time (6 women). *Students:* 65 full-time (47 women), 41 part-time (35 women); includes 38 minority (29 Black or African American, non-Hispanic/Latino; 3 Asian, non-Hispanic/Latino; 4 Hispanic/Latino; 2 Two or more races, non-Hispanic/Latino). Average age 27. 61 applicants, 51% accepted, 27 enrolled. In 2010, 43 master's awarded. *Degree requirements:* For master's, thesis or alternative, comprehensive written and/or oral exams; for Ed S, thesis. *Entrance requirements:* For master's and Ed S, GRE General Test or MAT. Additional exam requirements/recommendations for international students: Required—TOEFL (minimum score 523 paper-based; 193 computer-based). *Application deadline:* For fall admission, 7/1 for domestic and international students; for spring admission, 11/15 for domestic and international students. Applications are processed on a rolling basis. Application fee: $35. Electronic applications accepted. *Expenses:* Tuition, state resident: full-time $5256; part-time $197 per credit hour. Tuition, nonresident: full-time $14,490; part-time $710 per credit hour. Required fees: $855 per semester. Tuition and fees vary according to course load and campus/location. *Financial support:* In 2010–11, 6 students received support, including 2 research assistantships with full tuition reimbursements available (averaging $3,652 per year); institutionally sponsored loans and unspecified assistantships also available. Support available to part-time students. Financial award application deadline: 7/1; financial award applicants required to submit FAFSA. *Faculty research:* Using Bender-Gestalt to predict graphomotor dimensions of the draw-a-person test, neurobehavioral hemispheric dominance. *Unit head:* Dr. Robert Bauer, Chair, 229-333-5930, Fax: 229-259-5576, E-mail: bbauer@valdosta.edu. *Application contact:* Rebecca Waters, Coordinator of Graduate Admissions, 229-333-5694, Fax: 229-245-3853, E-mail: rlwaters@valdosta.edu.

Valparaiso University, Graduate School, Department of Psychology, Valparaiso, IN 46383. Offers business management (for counseling students) (Certificate); clinical mental health counseling (MA); community counseling (MA); JD/MA. Part-time and evening/weekend programs available. *Faculty:* 9 part-time/adjunct (5 women). *Students:* 40 full-time (34 women), 12 part-time (8 women); includes 3 Black or African American, non-Hispanic/Latino; 2 Hispanic/Latino, 2 international. Average age 28. In 2010, 22 master's awarded. *Degree requirements:* For master's, thesis or alternative, internship. *Entrance requirements:* For master's, minimum GPA of 3.0; 15 credits in the social/behavioral sciences (psychology, sociology, human development, etc.) with a minimum GPA of 3.0; course in introductory psychology; recent statistics course with minimum B average. Additional exam requirements/recommendations for international students: Required—TOEFL (minimum score 550 paper-based; 213 computer-based; 80 iBT). *Application deadline:* For fall admission, 3/1 priority date for domestic students. Applications are processed on a rolling basis. Application fee: $30 ($50 for international students). Electronic applications accepted. *Expenses:* Tuition: Full-time $9540; part-time $530 per credit hour. Required fees: $292; $95 per semester. Tuition and fees vary according to program. *Financial support:* Career-related internships or fieldwork, traineeships, and unspecified assistantships available. Support available to part-time students. Financial award applicants required to submit FAFSA. *Faculty research:* Environmental psychology, human sexuality, developmental psychopathology, social psychology. *Unit head:* Dr. David Simpson, Director of Graduate Programs, 219-464-6941, Fax: 219-464-6878, E-mail: david.simpson@valpo.edu. *Application contact:* Laura Groth, Coordinator of Student Services and Support, 219-464-5313, Fax: 219-464-5381, E-mail: laura.groth@valpo.edu.

Virginia Commonwealth University, Graduate School, College of Humanities and Sciences, Department of Psychology, Program in Counseling Psychology, Richmond, VA 23284-9005. Offers PhD. *Accreditation:* ACA; APA. *Students:* 28 full-time (23 women), 11 part-time (9 women); includes 10 minority (7 Black or African American, non-Hispanic/Latino; 2 Asian, non-Hispanic/Latino; 1 Hispanic/Latino), 2 international. 144 applicants, 7% accepted, 6 enrolled. In 2010, 11 doctorates awarded. *Degree requirements:* For doctorate, thesis/dissertation. *Entrance requirements:* For doctorate, GRE General Test, GRE Subject Test. Additional exam requirements/recommendations for international students: Required—TOEFL (minimum score 600 paper-based; 250 computer-based; 100 iBT); Recommended—IELTS (minimum score 6.5). *Application deadline:* For fall admission, 12/1 for domestic students. Application fee: $50. Electronic applications accepted. *Expenses:* Tuition, state resident: full-time $4308; part-time $479 per credit hour. Tuition, nonresident: full-time $8942; part-time $994 per credit hour. Required fees: $2000; $85 per credit hour. Tuition and fees vary according to course level, course load, degree level, campus/location and program. *Financial support:* Fellowships, research assistantships, teaching assistantships, Federal Work-Study, institutionally sponsored loans, and scholarships/grants available. Support available to part-time students. *Unit head:* Dr. Michael Southam-Gerow, Director, Graduate Programs in Psychology, 804-828-1193, Fax: 804-828-2237, E-mail: masouthamger@vcu.edu. *Application contact:* Dr. Marilyn Stern, Co-director, Counseling Psychology Training Program, 804-827-0400, Fax: 804-828-2237, E-mail: mstern@vcu.edu.

Virginia Commonwealth University, Graduate School, School of Allied Health Professions, Program in Patient Counseling, Richmond, VA 23284-9005. Offers MS, CPC. *Accreditation:* ACA. *Students:* 19 full-time (10 women), 1 (woman) part-time; includes 7 minority (all Black or African American, non-Hispanic/Latino). 20 applicants, 30% accepted, 6 enrolled. In 2010, 7 master's awarded. *Entrance requirements:* For master's, GRE General Test. Additional exam requirements/recommendations for international students: Required—TOEFL (minimum score 600 paper-based; 250 computer-based; 100 iBT). *Application deadline:* For fall admission, 2/1 for domestic students. Applications are processed on a rolling basis. Application fee: $50. Electronic applications accepted. *Expenses:* Tuition, state resident: full-time $4308; part-time $479 per credit hour. Tuition, nonresident: full-time $8942; part-time $994 per credit hour. Required fees: $2000; $85 per credit hour. Tuition and fees vary according to course level, course load, degree level, campus/location and program. *Financial support:* Application deadline: 3/1. *Unit head:* Dr. D. Mark Cooper, Chair, Department of Patient Counseling, 804-828-0540, Fax: 804-828-0542, E-mail: dmcooper@vcu.edu. *Application contact:* Christine Stevens, Admissions Contact, 804-828-0540, Fax: 804-828-0542, E-mail: cstevens3@vcu.edu.

Walden University, Graduate Programs, School of Counseling and Social Service, Minneapolis, MN 55401. Offers career counseling (MS); counselor education and supervision (PhD), including consultation, counseling and social change, forensic mental health counseling, general program, nonprofit management and leadership, trauma and crisis; human services (PhD), including clinical social work, counseling, criminal justice, disaster, crisis and intervention, family studies and intervention strategies, general program, human services administration, public health, self-designed, social policy analysis and planning; marriage, couple, and family counseling (MS), including forensic counseling, trauma and crisis counseling; mental health counseling (MS), including forensic counseling. Part-time and evening/weekend programs available. Postbaccalaureate distance learning degree programs offered (minimal on-campus study). *Faculty:* 25 full-time (17 women), 241 part-time/adjunct (162 women). *Students:* 2,687 full-time (2,269 women), 536 part-time (473 women); includes 1,582 minority (1,319 Black or African American, non-Hispanic/Latino; 34 American Indian or Alaska Native, non-Hispanic/Latino; 29 Asian, non-Hispanic/Latino; 142 Hispanic/Latino; 58 Two or more races, non-Hispanic/Latino), 47 international. Average age 38. In 2010, 182 master's, 8 doctorates awarded. *Degree requirements:* For master's, residency (for some programs); for doctorate, thesis/dissertation, residency. *Entrance requirements:* For master's, bachelor's degree or equivalent in related field, minimum GPA of 2.5; for doctorate, master's degree or equivalent in related field; minimum GPA of 3.0; official transcripts; three years' related professional/academic experience (preferred); access to computer and Internet. Additional exam requirements/recommendations for international students: Required—TOEFL (minimum score 550 paper-based; 213 computer-based), IELTS (minimum score 6.5), TOEFL (minimum score 550 paper-based; 213 computer-based), IELTS (minimum score 6.5), or Michigan English Language Assessment Battery (minimum score 82). *Application deadline:* Applications are processed on a rolling basis. Application fee: $50. Electronic applications accepted. *Expenses:* Tuition: Full-time $10,274; part-time $445 per credit. Tuition and fees vary according to course load, degree level and program. *Financial support:* Fellowships, Federal Work-Study, scholarships/grants, unspecified assistantships, and family tuition reduction, active duty/veteran tuition reduction, group tuition reduction, interest-free payment plans available. Support available to part-time students. Financial award applicants required to submit FAFSA. *Unit head:* Dr. Savitri Dixon-Saxon, Associate Dean, 800-925-3368. *Application contact:* Jennifer Hall, Vice President of Enrollment Management, 866-4-WALDEN, E-mail: info@waldenu.edu.

Walden University, Graduate Programs, School of Psychology, Minneapolis, MN 55401. Offers clinical child psychology (Post-Doctoral Certificate); clinical psychology (MS, Post-Doctoral Certificate), including counseling (MS); counseling psychology (Post-Doctoral Certificate); forensic psychology (MS), including forensic psychology in the community, general program, mental health applications, program planning and evaluation in forensic settings, psychology and legal systems; general psychology (Post-Doctoral Certificate); health psychology (Post-Doctoral Certificate); organizational psychology (Post-Doctoral Certificate); organizational psychology and development (Postbaccalaureate Certificate); psychology (MS, PhD), including clinical psychology (PhD), counseling psychology (PhD), crisis management and response (MS), general program (MS), general psychology (PhD), health psychology, leadership development and coaching (MS), media psychology (MS), organizational psychology (PhD), organizational psychology and development (MS), organizational psychology and nonprofit management (MS), program evaluation and research (MS), psychology of culture (MS), psychology, public administration, and social change (MS), social psychology (MS), terrorism and security (MS); teaching online (Post-Master's Certificate). Part-time and evening/weekend programs available. Postbaccalaureate distance learning degree programs offered (minimal on-campus study). *Faculty:* 41 full-time (25 women), 254 part-time/adjunct (131 women). *Students:* 3,463 full-time (2,737 women), 1,400 part-time (1,130 women); includes 1,491 Black or African American, non-Hispanic/Latino; 59 American Indian or Alaska Native, non-Hispanic/Latino; 89 Asian, non-Hispanic/Latino; 283 Hispanic/Latino; 76 Two or more races, non-Hispanic/Latino, 126 international. Average age 40. In 2010, 559 master's, 100 doctorates awarded. Terminal master's awarded for partial completion of doctoral program. *Degree requirements:* For master's, thesis optional; for doctorate, thesis/dissertation, residency. *Entrance requirements:* For master's, bachelor's degree or equivalent in related field; minimum GPA of 2.5; official transcripts; goal statement; access to computer and Internet; for doctorate, master's degree or equivalent in related field; minimum GPA of 3.0; 3 years of related professional/academic experience (preferred). Additional exam requirements/recommendations for international students: Required—TOEFL (minimum score 550 paper-based; 213 computer-based), IELTS (minimum score 6.5), TOEFL (minimum score 550 paper-based; 213 computer-based), IELTS (minimum score 6.5), or Michigan English Language Assessment Battery (minimum score 82). *Application deadline:* Applications are processed on a rolling basis. Application fee: $50. Electronic applications accepted. *Expenses:* Tuition: Full-time $10,274; part-time $445 per credit. Tuition and fees vary according to course load, degree level and program. *Financial support:* In 2010–11, 1 fellowship was awarded; Federal Work-Study, scholarships/grants, unspecified assistantships, and family tuition reduction, active duty/veteran tuition reduction, group tuition reduction, interest-free payment plans also available. Support available to part-time students. Financial award applicants required to submit FAFSA. *Unit head:* Dr. Melanie Storms, Associate Dean, 800-925-3368. *Application contact:* Jennifer Hall, Vice President of Enrollment Management, 866-4-WALDEN, E-mail: info@waldenu.edu.

Walla Walla University, Graduate School, School of Education and Psychology, Specialization in Counseling Psychology, College Place, WA 99324-1198. Offers MA. Part-time programs available. *Faculty:* 6 full-time (2 women). *Students:* 16 full-time (8 women), 8 part-time (4 women); includes 1 American Indian or Alaska Native, non-Hispanic/Latino; 1 Hispanic/Latino. Average age 34. 17 applicants, 65% accepted, 10 enrolled. *Degree requirements:* For master's, thesis (for some programs). *Entrance requirements:* For master's, GRE General Test, minimum GPA of 2.75, course work in education and psychology. Additional exam requirements/recommendations for international students: Required—TOEFL (minimum score 550 paper-based; 213 computer-based; 79 iBT). *Application deadline:* For fall admission, 4/1 priority date for domestic students. Applications are processed on a rolling basis. Application fee: $50. Electronic applications accepted. *Financial support:* Teaching assistantships with partial tuition reimbursements available. Financial award application deadline: 4/1; financial award applicants required to submit FAFSA. *Faculty research:* Instructional psychology, moral development. *Unit head:* Dr. Lee Stough, Program Director, 509-527-2943, Fax: 509-527-2248, E-mail: lee.stough@wallawalla.edu. *Application contact:* Dr. Joe G. Galusha, Dean of Graduate Studies, 509-527-2421, Fax: 509-527-2237, E-mail: joe.galusha@wallawalla.edu.

Walsh University, Graduate Studies, Program in Counseling and Human Development, North Canton, OH 44720-3396. Offers mental health counseling (MA); school counseling (MA). *Accreditation:* ACA. Part-time and evening/weekend programs available. *Faculty:* 5 full-time (4 women), 3 part-time/adjunct (all women). *Students:* 32 full-time (23 women), 54 part-time (46 women); includes 3 Black or African American, non-Hispanic/Latino; 1 American Indian or Alaska Native, non-Hispanic/Latino; 1 Hispanic/Latino, 3 international. Average age 31. 36 applicants, 61% accepted, 19 enrolled. In 2010, 22 master's awarded. *Degree requirements:* For master's, comprehensive exam, internship, practicum. *Entrance requirements:* For master's, GRE General Test, MAT, interview, minimum GPA of 3.0, writing sample, reference forms, moral affidavit. Additional exam requirements/recommendations for international students: Required—TOEFL (minimum score 500 paper-based; 173 computer-based; 61 iBT). *Application deadline:* For fall admission, 7/15 priority date for domestic students. Applications are processed on a rolling basis. Application fee: $25. Electronic applications accepted. *Expenses:* Tuition: Full-time $13,080; part-time $545 per credit hour. *Financial support:* In 2010–11, 79 students received support, including 12 research assistantships with tuition reimbursements available (averaging $6,020 per year); tuition waivers (partial) and tuition discounts also available. Financial award application deadline: 12/31. *Faculty research:* Mind-body connections in trauma and trauma counseling, grief/loss issues regarding counselor training, supervision, family counseling and counselor education, refugee mental health, grief counseling and grief counseling training. *Unit head:* Dr. Linda Barclay, Program Director, 330-490-7264, Fax: 330-490-7323, E-mail: lbarclay@walsh.edu. *Application contact:* Christine Haver, Assistant Director for Graduate and Transfer Admissions, 330-490-7177, Fax: 330-244-4925, E-mail: chaver@walsh.edu.

Washington Adventist University, Program in Counseling Psychology, Takoma Park, MD 20912. Offers MA. Part-time programs available.

Washington Adventist University, Program in Professional Counseling Psychology, Takoma Park, MD 20912. Offers MA. Part-time programs available.

Counseling Psychology

Washington State University, Graduate School, College of Education, Department of Educational Leadership and Counseling Psychology, Program in Counseling Psychology, Pullman, WA 99164. Offers counseling psychology (Ed M, MA, PhD); school psychologist (Certificate). *Accreditation:* APA (one or more programs are accredited). *Faculty:* 18. *Students:* 54 full-time (41 women), 6 part-time (2 women); includes 7 minority (3 Asian, non-Hispanic/Latino; 4 Hispanic/Latino), 7 international. Average age 29. 319 applicants, 5% accepted, 15 enrolled. In 2010, 7 master's, 8 doctorates awarded. Terminal master's awarded for partial completion of doctoral program. *Degree requirements:* For master's, comprehensive exam (for some programs), thesis (for some programs), oral or written exam; for doctorate, comprehensive exam, thesis/dissertation, oral and written exam. *Entrance requirements:* For master's and doctorate, GRE General Test, minimum GPA of 3.0, 3 letters of recommendation. Additional exam requirements/recommendations for international students: Required—TOEFL (minimum score 550 paper-based; 213 computer-based). *Application deadline:* For fall admission, 2/1 for domestic and international students. Application fee: $50. Electronic applications accepted. *Expenses:* Tuition, state resident: full-time $8552; part-time $443 per credit. Tuition, nonresident: full-time $21,650; part-time $1083 per credit. Required fees: $846. *Financial support:* In 2010–11, 4 research assistantships with partial tuition reimbursements (averaging $18,204 per year), 31 teaching assistantships with partial tuition reimbursements (averaging $18,204 per year) were awarded; career-related internships or fieldwork, Federal Work-Study, institutionally sponsored loans, scholarships/grants, tuition waivers (partial), and unspecified assistantships also available. Financial award application deadline: 4/1; financial award applicants required to submit FAFSA. *Faculty research:* Hypnosis supervision, multicultural counseling, American Indian mental health, eating disorders. Total annual research expenditures: $934,000. *Unit head:* Dr. Kelly Ward, Chair, 509-335-9117, Fax: 509-335-7977, E-mail: kaward@wsu.edu. *Application contact:* Graduate School Admissions, 800-GRADWSU, Fax: 509-335-1949, E-mail: gradsch@wsu.edu.

Wayland Baptist University, Graduate Programs, Program in Counseling, Plainview, TX 79072-6998. Offers counseling (MA); government administration (MPA); homeland security (MPA); justice administration (MPA). Part-time and evening/weekend programs available. Postbaccalaureate distance learning degree programs offered. *Degree requirements:* For master's, comprehensive exam. *Entrance requirements:* For master's, GRE, MAT. Additional exam requirements/recommendations for international students: Required—TOEFL (minimum score 500 paper-based; 173 computer-based; 61 iBT). Electronic applications accepted.

Waynesburg University, Graduate and Professional Studies, Waynesburg, PA 15370-1222. Offers business (MBA), including finance, health systems, human resources, leadership, market development; counseling (MA), including addictions counseling, clinical mental health; education (MAT); nursing (MSN), including administration, education, informatics, palliative care; nursing practice (DNP); special education (M Ed); technology (M Ed); MSN/MBA. *Accreditation:* AACN. Part-time and evening/weekend programs available. *Degree requirements:* For doctorate, thesis/dissertation. *Entrance requirements:* Additional exam requirements/recommendations for international students: Required—TOEFL. Electronic applications accepted.

Webster University, College of Arts and Sciences, Department of Behavioral and Social Sciences, Program in Counseling, St. Louis, MO 63119-3194. Offers MA. Part-time programs available. *Entrance requirements:* Additional exam requirements/recommendations for international students: Required—TOEFL. *Expenses:* Tuition: Part-time $585 per credit hour. Tuition and fees vary according to degree level, campus/location and program.

Western Kentucky University, Graduate Studies, College of Education and Behavioral Sciences, Department of Counseling and Student Affairs, Bowling Green, KY 42101. Offers counseling (MA Ed), including marriage and family therapy, mental health counseling; school counseling (P-12) (MA Ed); student affairs in higher education (MA Ed). *Accreditation:* ACA; NCATE. Part-time and evening/weekend programs available. *Degree requirements:* For master's, comprehensive exam, thesis optional. *Entrance requirements:* For master's, GRE General Test. Additional exam requirements/recommendations for international students: Required—TOEFL (minimum score 555 paper-based; 213 computer-based; 79 iBT). *Faculty research:* Counselor education, research for residential workers.

Western Michigan University, Graduate College, College of Education and Human Development, Department of Counselor Education and Counseling Psychology, Kalamazoo, MI 49008. Offers counseling psychology (MA, PhD); counselor education (MA, PhD); human resources development (MA). *Accreditation:* ACA (one or more programs are accredited); APA (one or more programs are accredited); CORE; NCATE. *Degree requirements:* For doctorate, thesis/dissertation, oral exams. *Entrance requirements:* For doctorate, GRE General Test.

Western Washington University, Graduate School, College of Humanities and Social Sciences, Department of Psychology, Program in Mental Health Counseling, Bellingham, WA 98225-5996. Offers MS. *Accreditation:* ACA. *Degree requirements:* For master's, thesis optional. *Entrance requirements:* For master's, GRE General Test, minimum GPA of 3.0 in last 60 semester hours or last 90 quarter hours. Additional exam requirements/recommendations for international students: Required—TOEFL (minimum score 567 paper-based; 227 computer-based). Electronic applications accepted.

Westfield State University, Division of Graduate and Continuing Education, Department of Psychology, Westfield, MA 01086. Offers applied behavior analysis (MA); mental health counseling (MA); school guidance (MA). Part-time and evening/weekend programs available. *Degree requirements:* For master's, comprehensive exam. *Entrance requirements:* For master's, GRE General Test, MAT, minimum undergraduate GPA of 2.7.

Westminster College, Program in Counseling Psychology, Salt Lake City, UT 84105-3697. Offers MSPC. Part-time and evening/weekend programs available. *Faculty:* 8 full-time (all women), 3 part-time/adjunct (all women). *Students:* 27 full-time (18 women), 9 part-time (8 women); includes 1 Asian, non-Hispanic/Latino; 2 Hispanic/Latino; 1 Two or more races, non-Hispanic/Latino. Average age 28. 41 applicants, 46% accepted, 13 enrolled. In 2010, 10 master's awarded. *Degree requirements:* For master's, comprehensive exam, thesis, internship. *Entrance requirements:* For master's, GRE, 3 professional or academic letters of recommendation, background check, baccalaureate degree, official transcripts, personal statement. Additional exam requirements/recommendations for international students: Required—TOEFL (minimum score 600 paper-based). *Application deadline:* For fall admission, 4/15 for domestic students, 4/16 for international students. Applications are processed on a rolling basis. Application fee: $50. Electronic applications accepted. *Expenses:* Contact institution. *Financial support:* In 2010–11, 26 students received support. Career-related internships or fieldwork and tuition reimbursement, tuition remission available. Support available to part-time students. Financial award applicants required to submit FAFSA. *Faculty research:* Trauma, substance abuse treatment, object relations, refugee populations, attachment theory. *Unit head:* Janine Wanlass, Director, 801-832-2428, E-mail: jwanlass@westminstercollege.edu. *Application contact:* Joel Bauman, Vice President of Enrollment Services, 801-832-2200, Fax: 801-832-3101, E-mail: admission@westminstercollege.edu.

West Virginia University, College of Human Resources and Education, Department of Counseling, Rehabilitation Counseling, and Counseling Psychology, Program in Counseling Psychology, Morgantown, WV 26506. Offers PhD. *Accreditation:* ACA; APA. *Degree requirements:* For doctorate, comprehensive exam, thesis/dissertation, APA-approved 1 year internship. *Entrance requirements:* For doctorate, GRE General Test, interview. Additional exam requirements/recommendations for international students: Required—TOEFL (minimum score 550 paper-based; 213 computer-based; 65 iBT). Electronic applications accepted.

William Carey University, School of Psychology and Counseling, Hattiesburg, MS 39401-5499. Offers counseling psychology (MS). Part-time programs available. *Entrance requirements:* For master's, GRE, PRAXIS, MAT, minimum GPA of 2.5. Additional exam requirements/recommendations for international students: Required—TOEFL (minimum score 550 paper-based; 213 computer-based). *Expenses:* Contact institution. *Faculty research:* Addiction prevention, psychometric measurement, crisis counseling, gerontology.

William Paterson University of New Jersey, College of Humanities and Social Sciences, Wayne, NJ 07470-8420. Offers clinical and counseling psychology (MA); English (MA); history (MA); public policy and international affairs (MA); sociology (MA). Part-time and evening/weekend programs available. Electronic applications accepted.

Wright Institute, Program in Counseling Psychology, Berkeley, CA 94704-1796. Offers MA. Part-time and evening/weekend programs available. *Faculty:* 5 full-time (3 women), 17 part-time/adjunct (13 women). *Students:* 85 full-time (69 women); includes 4 Black or African American, non-Hispanic/Latino; 3 Asian, non-Hispanic/Latino; 7 Hispanic/Latino; 7 Two or more races, non-Hispanic/Latino. Average age 38. 90 applicants, 54% accepted, 40 enrolled. In 2010, 30 degrees awarded. *Degree requirements:* For master's, comprehensive exam. *Entrance requirements:* Additional exam requirements/recommendations for international students: Required—TOEFL. *Application deadline:* Applications are processed on a rolling basis. Application fee: $50. Electronic applications accepted. *Expenses:* Tuition: Full-time $26,600. *Financial support:* In 2010–11, 22 students received support. Career-related internships or fieldwork, Federal Work-Study, and scholarships/grants available. Financial award application deadline: 11/30; financial award applicants required to submit FAFSA. *Faculty research:* Neuroscience, attachment, PTSD, psychotherapy process and outcome. *Unit head:* Dr. Milena Esherick, Program Director, 510-841-9230. *Application contact:* Melissa Delaney, Director of Admissions, 510-841-9230 Ext. 170, Fax: 510-841-0167, E-mail: mdelaney@wi.edu.

Yeshiva University, Ferkauf Graduate School of Psychology, Program in Mental Health Counseling Psychology, New York, NY 10033-3201. Offers MA. Part-time programs available. *Entrance requirements:* For master's, GRE General Test. *Faculty research:* Substance abuse treatment, group therapy.

Youngstown State University, Graduate School, Beeghly College of Education, Department of Counseling, Youngstown, OH 44555-0001. Offers community counseling (MS Ed); school counseling (MS Ed). *Accreditation:* ACA; NCATE. Part-time and evening/weekend programs available. *Degree requirements:* For master's, comprehensive exam. *Entrance requirements:* For master's, MAT, interview, minimum GPA of 2.7. Additional exam requirements/recommendations for international students: Required—TOEFL. *Faculty research:* Suicide, euthanasia, ethical issues, marriage and family.

Developmental Psychology

Andrews University, School of Graduate Studies, School of Education, Department of Educational and Counseling Psychology, Program in Educational and Developmental Psychology, Berrien Springs, MI 49104. Offers educational and developmental psychology (MA); educational psychology (Ed D, PhD). *Degree requirements:* For master's, thesis optional. *Entrance requirements:* For master's, GRE. Additional exam requirements/recommendations for international students: Required—TOEFL (minimum score 550 paper-based).

Arizona State University, College of Liberal Arts and Sciences, Department of Psychology, Tempe, AZ 85287-1104. Offers behavioral neuroscience (PhD); clinical psychology (PhD); cognition, action and perception (PhD); developmental psychology (PhD); quantitative psychology (PhD); social psychology (PhD). *Accreditation:* APA. *Faculty:* 72 full-time (36 women), 9 part-time/adjunct (6 women). *Students:* 113 full-time (79 women), 17 part-time (12 women); includes 24 minority (2 Black or African American, non-Hispanic/Latino; 10 Asian, non-Hispanic/Latino; 10 Hispanic/Latino; 2 Two or more races, non-Hispanic/Latino), 9 international. Average age 28. 519 applicants, 8% accepted, 30 enrolled. In 2010, 19 doctorates awarded. *Degree requirements:* For doctorate, comprehensive exam, thesis/dissertation, interactive Program of Study (iPOS) submitted before completing 50 percent of required credit hours. *Entrance requirements:* For doctorate, GRE General Test, GRE Subject Test, minimum GPA of 3.0 or equivalent in last 2 years of work leading to bachelor's degree. Additional exam requirements/recommendations for international students: Required—TOEFL, IELTS, or Pearson Test of English. *Application deadline:* For fall admission, 12/15 for domestic and international students. Application fee: $70 ($90 for international students). Electronic applications accepted. *Expenses:* Tuition, state resident: full-time $8510; part-time $608 per credit. Tuition, nonresident: full-time $16,542; part-time $919 per credit. Required fees: $339; $110 per credit. Part-time tuition and fees vary according to course load. *Financial support:* In 2010–11, 58 research assistantships with tuition reimbursements (averaging $15,281 per year), 48 teaching assistantships with tuition reimbursements (averaging $15,062 per year) were awarded; fellowships with full tuition reimbursements, career-related internships or fieldwork, Federal Work-Study, institutionally sponsored loans, scholarships/grants, and tuition waivers (full and partial) also available. Financial award application deadline: 3/1; financial award applicants required to submit FAFSA. Total annual research expenditures: $9.4 million. *Unit head:* Dr. Keith Crnic, Chair, 480-965-3061, E-mail: keith.crnic@asu.edu. *Application contact:* Graduate Admissions, 480-965-6113.

Bethel University, Graduate School, Program in Counseling Psychology, St. Paul, MN 55112-6999. Offers child and adolescent and community counseling (MA). Part-time and evening/weekend programs available. *Faculty:* 5 full-time (2 women), 11 part-time/adjunct (4 women). *Students:* 84 full-time (72 women), 3 part-time (all women); includes 1 Black or African American, non-Hispanic/Latino; 1 Asian, non-Hispanic/Latino; 1 Hispanic/Latino; 4 Two or more races, non-Hispanic/Latino. Average age 32. 42 applicants, 100% accepted, 41 enrolled. In 2010, 32 master's awarded. *Degree requirements:* For master's, comprehensive exam, thesis optional, practicum. *Entrance requirements:* For master's, MAT, minimum GPA of 3.0, course work in psychology and statistics, letters of reference. Additional exam requirements/recommendations for international students: Required—TOEFL (minimum score 550 paper-based; 213 computer-based; 80 iBT). *Application deadline:* For fall admission, 5/1 priority date for domestic students. Applications are processed on a rolling basis. Electronic applications accepted. *Expenses:* Tuition: Full-time $5400; part-time $450 per credit. Tuition and fees vary according to course level, course load, degree level and program. *Financial support:* Applicants required to submit FAFSA. *Unit head:* Dr. Diane Dahl, Assistant Dean, 651-635-8000, Fax: 651-635-8004, E-mail: diane-dahl@bethel.edu. *Application contact:* Paul Ives, Director of Admissions, 651-635-8000, Fax: 651-635-8004, E-mail: gs@bethel.edu.

Boston College, Lynch Graduate School of Education, Program in Applied Developmental and Educational Psychology, Chestnut Hill, MA 02467-3800. Offers MA, PhD. Part-time and evening/weekend programs available. *Students:* 48 full-time (42 women), 9 part-time (6 women); includes 5 Black or African American, non-Hispanic/Latino; 2 Asian, non-Hispanic/Latino; 4 Hispanic/Latino, 11 international. 173 applicants, 47% accepted, 30 enrolled. In 2010, 16 master's, 1 doctorate awarded. Terminal master's awarded for partial completion of doctoral program. *Degree requirements:* For master's, comprehensive exam; for doctorate, comprehensive exam, thesis/dissertation. *Entrance requirements:* For master's and doctorate, GRE General Test. Additional exam requirements/recommendations for international students: Required—TOEFL (minimum score 550 paper-based; 213 computer-based; 81 iBT). Application fee: $70. Electronic applications accepted. *Financial support:* Fellowships with full and partial tuition reimbursements, research assistantships with full and partial tuition reimbursements, teaching assistantships with full and partial tuition reimbursements, career-related internships or fieldwork, Federal Work-Study, scholarships/grants, traineeships, health care benefits, tuition waivers (full and partial), and unspecified assistantships available. Support available to part-time students. Financial award applicants required to submit FAFSA. *Faculty research:* Cognitive learning and culture, effects of social policy reform on children and families, psychosocial trauma, human rights and international justice, positive youth development, children and adolescents living in poverty. *Unit head:* Dr. M. Brinton Lykes, Chairperson, 617-552-4214, Fax: 617-552-0812. *Application contact:* Adam Poluzzi, Director, Graduate Admission and Financial Aid, 617-552-4214, Fax: 617-552-0398, E-mail: poluzzi@bc.edu.

Bowling Green State University, Graduate College, College of Arts and Sciences, Department of Psychology, Bowling Green, OH 43403. Offers clinical psychology (MA, PhD); developmental psychology (MA, PhD); experimental psychology (MA, PhD); industrial/organizational psychology (MA, PhD); quantitative psychology (MA, PhD). *Accreditation:* APA (one or more programs are accredited). *Degree requirements:* For doctorate, thesis/dissertation. *Entrance requirements:* For doctorate, GRE General Test, GRE Subject Test. Additional exam requirements/recommendations for international students: Required—TOEFL. Electronic applications accepted. *Faculty research:* Personnel psychology, developmental-mathematical models, behavioral medication, brain process, child/adolescent social cognition.

Brandeis University, Graduate School of Arts and Sciences, Department of Psychology, Waltham, MA 02454-9110. Offers brain, body and behavior (PhD); cognitive neuroscience (PhD); general psychology (MA); social/developmental psychology (PhD). Part-time programs available. *Faculty:* 17 full-time (4 women), 2 part-time/adjunct (1 woman). *Students:* 47 full-time (32 women); includes 2 Asian, non-Hispanic/Latino, 12 international. 164 applicants, 27% accepted, 24 enrolled. In 2010, 8 master's, 4 doctorates awarded. Terminal master's awarded for partial completion of doctoral program. *Degree requirements:* For master's, thesis; for doctorate, comprehensive exam, thesis/dissertation. *Entrance requirements:* For master's and doctorate, GRE General Test, GRE Subject Test (recommended), 3 letters of recommendation, statement of purpose. Additional exam requirements/recommendations for international students: Required—TOEFL (minimum score 600 paper-based; 250 computer-based; 100 iBT); Recommended—IELTS (minimum score 7). *Application deadline:* For fall admission, 1/15 priority date for domestic and international students. Applications are processed on a rolling basis. Application fee: $75. Electronic applications accepted. *Financial support:* In 2010–11, 16 fellowships with full tuition reimbursements (averaging $20,000 per year), 3 research assistantships with full tuition reimbursements (averaging $20,000 per year), 9 teaching assistantships with partial tuition reimbursements (averaging $3,200 per year) were awarded; institutionally sponsored loans, scholarships/grants, health care benefits, tuition waivers (full and partial), and unspecified assistantships also available. Support available to part-time students. Financial award application deadline: 4/15; financial award applicants required to submit FAFSA. *Faculty research:* Cognitive neuroscience, social developmental psychology, brain body and behavior. *Unit head:* Prof. Paul DiZio, Director of Graduate Studies, 781-736-3300, Fax: 781-736-3291, E-mail: dizio@brandeis.edu. *Application contact:* Phil Gnatowski, Department Administrator, 781-736-3303, Fax: 781-736-3291, E-mail: gnat@brandeis.edu.

Brown University, Graduate School, Department of Psychology, Providence, RI 02912. Offers behavioral neuroscience (PhD); cognitive processes (PhD); sensation and perception (PhD); social/developmental (PhD); MS/PhD. *Degree requirements:* For doctorate, thesis/dissertation. *Entrance requirements:* For doctorate, GRE General Test, GRE Subject Test.

Capella University, Harold Abel School of Psychology, Minneapolis, MN 55402. Offers child and adolescent development (MS); clinical psychology (MS, Psy D); counseling psychology (MS); educational psychology (MS, PhD); evaluation, research, and measurement (MS); general psychology (MS, PhD); industrial/organizational psychology (MS, PhD); leadership coaching psychology (MS); organizational leader development (MS); school psychology (MS); sport psychology (MS). Part-time and evening/weekend programs available. Postbaccalaureate distance learning degree programs offered (minimal on-campus study). Terminal master's awarded for partial completion of doctoral program. *Degree requirements:* For master's, thesis optional, project; for doctorate, thesis/dissertation. *Entrance requirements:* For degree, master's degree in school psychology. Additional exam requirements/recommendations for international students: Required—TOEFL (minimum score 550 paper-based; 213 computer-based), TWE (minimum score 4); Recommended—IELTS. Electronic applications accepted. *Expenses:* Tuition: Full-time $11,880; part-time $440 per credit hour.

Carnegie Mellon University, College of Humanities and Social Sciences, Department of Psychology, Area of Developmental Psychology, Pittsburgh, PA 15213-3891. Offers PhD. *Degree requirements:* For doctorate, comprehensive exam, thesis/dissertation. *Entrance requirements:* For doctorate, GRE General Test. Additional exam requirements/recommendations for international students: Required—TOEFL. *Faculty research:* Cognitive development, language acquisition.

Chatham University, Program in Counseling Psychology, Pittsburgh, PA 15232-2826. Offers child, adolescent and family (MSCP); counseling psychology (Psy D); health and holistic (MSCP); infant mental health (MSCP); organization and supervision (MSCP); sport and exercise (MSCP). Part-time and evening/weekend programs available. *Degree requirements:* For master's, thesis optional, supervised internship; for doctorate, thesis/dissertation, internship. *Entrance requirements:* For master's, minimum GPA of 3.0; 2 letters of recommendation; resume; prerequisite coursework in statistics, biology, and psychology; for doctorate, GRE. Additional exam requirements/recommendations for international students: Required—TOEFL (minimum score 600 paper-based; 250 computer-based; 100 iBT), IELTS (minimum score 6.5), TWE. Electronic applications accepted. *Faculty research:* Trauma and recovery, hypnosis, psychospiritual dimensions of healing, psychotherapy of schizophrenia.

Claremont Graduate University, Graduate Programs, School of Behavioral and Organizational Sciences, Department of Psychology, Claremont, CA 91711-6160. Offers advanced study in evaluation (Certificate); cognitive psychology (MA, PhD); developmental psychology (MA, PhD); evaluation and applied research methods (MA, PhD); health behavior research and evaluation (MA, PhD); human resource development and evaluation (MA); industrial/organizational psychology (MA, PhD); organizational behavior (MA, PhD); organizational psychology (MA, PhD); social psychology (MA, PhD); MBA/PhD. Part-time programs available. *Faculty:* 15 full-time (6 women), 5 part-time/adjunct (2 women). *Students:* 248 full-time (169 women), 15 part-time (9 women); includes 68 minority (14 Black or African American, non-Hispanic/Latino; 1 American Indian or Alaska Native, non-Hispanic/Latino; 27 Asian, non-Hispanic/Latino; 19 Hispanic/Latino; 2 Native Hawaiian or other Pacific Islander, non-Hispanic/Latino; 5 Two or more races, non-Hispanic/Latino), 29 international. Average age 30. In 2010, 45 master's, 21 doctorates, 4 other advanced degrees awarded. Terminal master's awarded for partial completion of doctoral program. *Entrance requirements:* For master's and doctorate, GRE General Test. Additional exam requirements/recommendations for international students: Required—TOEFL (minimum score 550 paper-based; 213 computer-based; 80 iBT). *Application deadline:* For fall admission, 1/15 priority date for domestic students. Applications are processed on a rolling basis. Application fee: $60. Electronic applications accepted. *Expenses:* Tuition: Full-time $35,748; part-time $1554 per unit. Required fees: $215 per semester. *Financial support:* Fellowships, research assistantships, teaching assistantships, Federal Work-Study, institutionally sponsored loans, scholarships/grants, and tuition waivers (full and partial) available. Support available to part-time students. Financial award application deadline: 2/15; financial award applicants required to submit FAFSA. *Faculty research:* Social intervention, diversity in

organizations, eyewitness memory, aging and cognition, drug policy. *Unit head:* Stewart Donaldson, Dean, 909-607-9001, Fax: 909-621-8905, E-mail: stewart.donaldson@cgu.edu. *Application contact:* Paul Thomas, Director, External Affairs, 909-607-9016, Fax: 909-621-8905, E-mail: paul.thomas@cgu.edu.

Clark University, Graduate School, Department of Psychology, Program in Developmental Psychology, Worcester, MA 01610-1477. Offers PhD. *Students:* 11 full-time (10 women); includes 1 minority (Asian, non-Hispanic/Latino), 5 international. Average age 28. In 2010, 3 doctorates awarded. *Degree requirements:* For doctorate, thesis/dissertation. *Entrance requirements:* For doctorate, GRE General Test. Additional exam requirements/recommendations for international students: Required—TOEFL. *Application deadline:* For fall admission, 12/28 priority date for domestic students. Applications are processed on a rolling basis. Application fee: $50. *Expenses:* Tuition: Full-time $37,000; part-time $1156 per credit hour. Required fees: $30; $1156 per credit hour. *Financial support:* In 2010–11, fellowships with full tuition reimbursements (averaging $15,700 per year), research assistantships with full tuition reimbursements (averaging $15,700 per year), teaching assistantships with full tuition reimbursements (averaging $15,700 per year) were awarded; tuition waivers (full) also available. *Faculty research:* Development of psychological processes in sociocultural context, conceptualizing and reasoning, symbolization, psychotherapy, metaphor, emotions and personalities. *Unit head:* Dr. Michael Bamberg, Chair, 508-793-7274. *Application contact:* Peggy Moskowitz, Graduate School Secretary, 508-793-7274, Fax: 508-793-7265, E-mail: psychology@clarku.edu.

Cornell University, Graduate School, Graduate Fields of Human Ecology, Field of Human Development, Ithaca, NY 14853-0001. Offers developmental psychology (PhD), including cognitive development, developmental psychopathology, ecology of human development, social and personality development; human development and family studies (PhD), including ecology of human development, family studies and the life course. *Faculty:* 32 full-time (16 women). *Students:* 44 full-time (29 women); includes 1 Asian, non-Hispanic/Latino, 1 Hispanic/Latino, 12 international. Average age 27. 110 applicants, 26% accepted, 19 enrolled. In 2010, 2 doctorates awarded. *Degree requirements:* For doctorate, comprehensive exam, thesis/dissertation, pre-doctoral research project, teaching experience. *Entrance requirements:* For doctorate, GRE General Test, 2 letters of recommendation. Additional exam requirements/recommendations for international students: Required—TOEFL (minimum score 550 paper-based; 213 computer-based; 77 iBT). *Application deadline:* For fall admission, 1/15 for domestic students. Application fee: $70. Electronic applications accepted. *Expenses:* Tuition: Full-time $29,500. Required fees: $76. Tuition and fees vary according to degree level and program. *Financial support:* In 2010–11, 26 students received support, including 4 fellowships with full tuition reimbursements available, 9 research assistantships with full tuition reimbursements available, 18 teaching assistantships with full tuition reimbursements available; institutionally sponsored loans, scholarships/grants, health care benefits, tuition waivers (full and partial), and unspecified assistantships also available. Financial award applicants required to submit FAFSA. *Faculty research:* Cognitive development, developmental psychopathology, ecology of human development, family studies and the life course, social and personality development. *Unit head:* Director of Graduate Studies, 607-255-3181, Fax: 607-255-9856. *Application contact:* Graduate Field Assistant, 607-255-3181, Fax: 607-255-9856, E-mail: hdfs@cornell.edu.

Duke University, Graduate School, Department of Psychology and Neuroscience, Durham, NC 27708. Offers biological psychology (PhD); clinical psychology (PhD); cognitive psychology (PhD); developmental psychology (PhD); experimental psychology (PhD); health psychology (PhD); human social development (PhD); JD/MA. *Accreditation:* APA (one or more programs are accredited). *Faculty:* 40 full-time. *Students:* 92 full-time (67 women); includes 6 Black or African American, non-Hispanic/Latino; 2 Asian, non-Hispanic/Latino; 7 Hispanic/Latino, 13 international. 483 applicants, 8% accepted, 23 enrolled. In 2010, 24 doctorates awarded. *Degree requirements:* For doctorate, thesis/dissertation. *Entrance requirements:* For doctorate, GRE General Test. Additional exam requirements/recommendations for international students: Required—TOEFL (minimum score 550 paper-based; 213 computer-based; 83 iBT), IELTS (minimum score 7). *Application deadline:* For fall admission, 12/8 priority date for domestic and international students. Application fee: $75. Electronic applications accepted. *Financial support:* Fellowships, research assistantships, teaching assistantships, career-related internships or fieldwork and Federal Work-Study available. Financial award application deadline: 12/8. *Unit head:* Melanie Bonner, Director of Graduate Studies, 919-660-5715, Fax: 919-660-5726, E-mail: morrell@duke.edu. *Application contact:* Elizabeth Hutton, Director of Admissions, 919-684-3913, Fax: 919-684-2277, E-mail: grad-admissions@duke.edu.

Emory University, Laney Graduate School, Department of Psychology, Atlanta, GA 30322-1100. Offers clinical psychology (PhD); cognition and development (PhD); neuroscience and animal behavior (PhD). *Accreditation:* APA. *Degree requirements:* For doctorate, comprehensive exam, thesis/dissertation. *Entrance requirements:* For doctorate, GRE General Test, minimum GPA of 3.25. Additional exam requirements/recommendations for international students: Required—TOEFL. Electronic applications accepted. *Expenses:* Tuition: Full-time $33,800. Required fees: $1300. *Faculty research:* Neuroscience and animal behavior; adult and child psychopathology, cognition development assessment.

Erikson Institute, Academic Programs, Chicago, IL 60654. Offers administration (Certificate); bilingual/ESL (Certificate); child development (MS); early childhood education (MS); infant mental health (Certificate); infant studies (Certificate); MS/MSW. MS/MSW offered jointly with Loyola University Chicago. Part-time and evening/weekend programs available. *Degree requirements:* For master's, comprehensive exam, internship; for Certificate, internship. *Entrance requirements:* For master's and Certificate, minimum GPA of 2.75. Additional exam requirements/recommendations for international students: Required—TOEFL. *Expenses:* Tuition: Part-time $810 per credit. Required fees: $420 per year. *Faculty research:* Assessment strategies from early childhood through elementary years; language, literacy, and the arts in children's development; inclusive special education; parent-child relationships; cognitive development.

Florida State University, The Graduate School, College of Arts and Sciences, Department of Psychology, Program in Developmental Psychology, Tallahassee, FL 32306. Offers PhD. *Faculty:* 10 full-time (3 women). *Students:* 12 full-time (7 women); includes 2 Black or African American, non-Hispanic/Latino, 1 international. Average age 26. 26 applicants, 19% accepted, 5 enrolled. In 2010, 1 doctorate awarded. Terminal master's awarded for partial completion of doctoral program. *Degree requirements:* For doctorate, thesis/dissertation, preliminary exam. *Entrance requirements:* For doctorate, GRE General Test (suggested minimum total score of 1000), minimum GPA of 3.0, research experience, letters of recommendation. Additional exam requirements/recommendations for international students: Required—TOEFL (minimum score 550 paper-based; 213 computer-based; 80 iBT). *Application deadline:* For fall admission, 1/10 for domestic students, 1/13 for international students. Application fee: $30. Electronic applications accepted. *Expenses:* Tuition, state resident: full-time $8238.24. *Financial support:* In 2010–11, 12 students received support, including 9 fellowships with full tuition reimbursements available (averaging $20,000 per year), 3 research assistantships with full tuition reimbursements available (averaging $20,000 per year), teaching assistantships with full tuition reimbursements available (averaging $16,500 per year); Federal Work-Study, institutionally sponsored loans, scholarships/grants, health care benefits, and unspecified assistantships also available. *Faculty research:* Learning disabilities, phonological processing, psychology of reading, emergent literacy, aging. *Unit head:* Dr. Christopher Schatschneider, Director, 850-644-4323, Fax: 850-644-7739, E-mail: schatschneider@psy.fsu.edu. *Application contact:* Cherie P. Miller, Graduate Program Assistant, 850-644-2499, Fax: 850-644-7739, E-mail: grad-info@psy.fsu.edu.

Fordham University, Graduate School of Arts and Sciences, Department of Psychology, Program in Applied Developmental Psychology, New York, NY 10458. Offers PhD. *Students:* 20 full-time (18 women), 11 part-time (8 women); includes 5 Black or African American, non-Hispanic/Latino; 2 Asian, non-Hispanic/Latino; 1 Hispanic/Latino, 3 international. Average age 29. 23 applicants, 52% accepted, 6 enrolled. In 2010, 4 doctorates awarded. *Degree requirements:* For doctorate, comprehensive exam, thesis/dissertation. *Entrance requirements:* For doctorate, GRE General Test, GRE Subject Test. Additional exam requirements/

Developmental Psychology

Fordham University (continued)

recommendations for international students: Required—TOEFL (minimum score 600 paper-based; 250 computer-based). *Application deadline:* For fall admission, 12/14 for domestic students. Application fee: $70. Electronic applications accepted. *Financial support:* In 2010–11, 15 students received support, including 4 fellowships with tuition reimbursements available (averaging $21,300 per year), 11 research assistantships with tuition reimbursements available (averaging $18,836 per year), 1 teaching assistantship with tuition reimbursement available (averaging $20,600 per year); career-related internships or fieldwork, institutionally sponsored loans, tuition waivers (full and partial), and unspecified assistantships also available. Financial award application deadline: 12/14. *Faculty research:* Development of citizenship, impact of participation in community service, impact of poverty on children, development of moral reasoning and behavior. Total annual research expenditures: $1.4 million. *Unit head:* Dr. Ann D'Allesandro, Director, 718-817-3789, Fax: 718-817-3785, E-mail: sherrod@fordham.edu. *Application contact:* Charlene Dundie, Director of Graduate Admissions, 718-817-4420, Fax: 718-817-3566, E-mail: dundie@fordham.edu.

Graduate School and University Center of the City University of New York, Graduate Studies, Program in Psychology, New York, NY 10016-4039. Offers basic applied neurocognition (PhD); biopsychology (PhD); clinical psychology (PhD); developmental psychology (PhD); environmental psychology (PhD); experimental psychology (PhD); industrial psychology (PhD); learning processes (PhD); neuropsychology (PhD); psychology (PhD); social personality (PhD). *Degree requirements:* For doctorate, one foreign language, thesis/dissertation. *Entrance requirements:* For doctorate, GRE General Test. Additional exam requirements/recommendations for international students: Required—TOEFL. Electronic applications accepted.

Harvard University, Graduate School of Arts and Sciences, Department of Psychology, Cambridge, MA 02138. Offers psychology (PhD), including behavior and decision analysis, cognition, developmental psychology, experimental psychology, personality, psychobiology, psychopathology; social psychology (PhD). *Accreditation:* APA. *Degree requirements:* For doctorate, thesis/dissertation, general exams. *Entrance requirements:* For doctorate, GRE General Test. Additional exam requirements/recommendations for international students: Required—TOEFL. *Expenses:* Tuition: Full-time $34,976. Required fees: $1166. Full-time tuition and fees vary according to program.

Howard University, Graduate School, Department of Psychology, Washington, DC 20059-0002. Offers clinical psychology (PhD); developmental psychology (PhD); experimental psychology (PhD); neuropsychology (PhD); personality psychology (PhD); psychology (MS); social psychology (PhD). *Accreditation:* APA (one or more programs are accredited). Part-time programs available. *Degree requirements:* For master's, thesis; for doctorate, comprehensive exam, thesis/dissertation, qualifying exam. *Entrance requirements:* For master's, GRE General Test, minimum GPA of 2.5, bachelor's degree in psychology or related field; for doctorate, GRE General Test, minimum GPA of 3.0. *Faculty research:* Personality and psychophysiology, educational and social development of African-American children, child and adult psychopathology.

Illinois State University, Graduate School, College of Arts and Sciences, Department of Psychology, Normal, IL 61790-2200. Offers psychology (MA, MS), including clinical psychology, counseling psychology, developmental psychology, educational psychology, experimental psychology, measurement-evaluation, organizational-industrial psychology; school psychology (PhD, SSP). *Accreditation:* APA. *Degree requirements:* For master's, thesis or alternative; for doctorate, variable foreign language requirement, thesis/dissertation, 2 terms of residency, internship, practicum. *Entrance requirements:* For master's, GRE General Test, GRE Subject Test, minimum GPA of 3.0 in last 60 hours of course work; for doctorate, GRE General Test. *Faculty research:* Comprehensive evaluation system for the central region professional development grant, Illinois school psychology internship consortium, for children's sake.

Indiana University Bloomington, University Graduate School, College of Arts and Sciences, Department of Psychological and Brain Sciences, Bloomington, IN 47405-7000. Offers biology and behavior (PhD); clinical science (PhD); cognitive psychology (PhD); developmental psychology (PhD); psychological and brain sciences (MA); social psychology (PhD). *Accreditation:* APA (one or more programs are accredited). *Faculty:* 53 full-time (16 women). *Students:* 85 full-time (45 women), 1 (woman) part-time; includes 13 minority (3 Black or African American, non-Hispanic/Latino; 3 Asian, non-Hispanic/Latino; 6 Hispanic/Latino; 1 Two or more races, non-Hispanic/Latino), 19 international. Average age 28. 363 applicants, 10% accepted, 20 enrolled. In 2010, 3 master's, 17 doctorates awarded. *Degree requirements:* For doctorate, comprehensive exam, thesis/dissertation, 1st and 2nd year projects, 1 year as associate instructor, qualifying exam, student teaching. *Entrance requirements:* For doctorate, GRE. Additional exam requirements/recommendations for international students: Required—TOEFL (minimum score 550 paper-based; 213 computer-based). *Application deadline:* For fall admission, 12/15 for domestic students, 12/1 for international students. Application fee: $55 ($65 for international students). Electronic applications accepted. *Financial support:* In 2010–11, 32 fellowships with full tuition reimbursements (averaging $23,580 per year), 7 research assistantships with full tuition reimbursements (averaging $17,850 per year), 7 teaching assistantships with full tuition reimbursements (averaging $17,850 per year) were awarded; scholarships/grants, health care benefits, and unspecified assistantships also available. *Unit head:* Dr. Linda B. Smith, Chair, 812-855-3991, Fax: 812-855-4691, E-mail: smith4@indiana.edu. *Application contact:* Patricia G. Crouch, Academic Services Coordinator, 812-855-4528, Fax: 812-855-4691, E-mail: pcrouch@indiana.edu.

Louisiana State University and Agricultural and Mechanical College, Graduate School, College of Humanities and Social Sciences, Department of Psychology, Baton Rouge, LA 70803. Offers biological psychology (MA, PhD); clinical psychology (MA, PhD); cognitive psychology (MA, PhD); developmental psychology (MA, PhD); industrial/organizational psychology (MA, PhD); school psychology (MA, PhD). PhD programs offered jointly with Southeastern Louisiana University. *Accreditation:* APA (one or more programs are accredited). *Faculty:* 26 full-time (10 women). *Students:* 96 full-time (68 women), 24 part-time (19 women); includes 7 Black or African American, non-Hispanic/Latino; 2 American Indian or Alaska Native, non-Hispanic/Latino; 1 Asian, non-Hispanic/Latino; 5 Hispanic/Latino, 2 international. Average age 27. 289 applicants, 11% accepted, 17 enrolled. In 2010, 16 master's, 11 doctorates awarded. Terminal master's awarded for partial completion of doctoral program. *Degree requirements:* For master's, thesis; for doctorate, thesis/dissertation, 1 year internship. *Entrance requirements:* For master's and doctorate, GRE General Test, minimum GPA of 3.0. Additional exam requirements/recommendations for international students: Required—TOEFL (minimum score 550 paper-based; 213 computer-based; 79 iBT) or IELTS (minimum score 6.5). *Application deadline:* For fall admission, 1/15 for domestic and international students. Applications are processed on a rolling basis. Application fee: $50 ($70 for international students). Electronic applications accepted. *Financial support:* In 2010–11, 115 students received support, including 5 fellowships (averaging $25,207 per year), 25 research assistantships with partial tuition reimbursements available (averaging $18,083 per year), 48 teaching assistantships with partial tuition reimbursements available (averaging $13,043 per year); career-related internships or fieldwork, Federal Work-Study, institutionally sponsored loans, scholarships/grants, health care benefits, and tuition waivers (full and partial) also available. Financial award applicants required to submit FAFSA. *Faculty research:* Clinical psychology, autism, anxiety, addition, neuropsychology, school psychology, cognitive psychology, experimental psychology. Total annual research expenditures: $1.3 million. *Unit head:* Dr. Robert Matthews, Chair, 225-578-8745, Fax: 225-578-4125, E-mail: psmath@lsu.edu. *Application contact:* Dr. Jason Hicks, Coordinator of Graduate Studies, 225-578-4109, Fax: 225-578-4125, E-mail: jhicks@lsu.edu.

Loyola University Chicago, Graduate School, Department of Psychology, Program in Developmental Psychology, Chicago, IL 60660. Offers MA, PhD. *Faculty:* 6 full-time (4 women), 1 (woman) part-time/adjunct. *Students:* 13 full-time (11 women); includes 6 minority (1 American Indian or Alaska Native, non-Hispanic/Latino; 1 Asian, non-Hispanic/Latino; 3 Hispanic/Latino; 1 Two or more races, non-Hispanic/Latino). Average age 26. 21 applicants, 14% accepted, 3 enrolled. In 2010, 3 master's, 1 doctorate awarded. *Degree requirements:* For doctorate, comprehensive exam, thesis/dissertation, internship or student teaching. *Entrance requirements:* For doctorate, GRE General Test, GRE Subject Test. Additional exam requirements/recommendations for international students: Required—TOEFL (minimum score 500 paper-based). *Application deadline:* For fall admission, 1/15 for domestic students. Application fee: $50. Electronic applications accepted. *Expenses:* Tuition: Full-time $14,940; part-time $830 per credit hour. Required fees: $87 per semester. Part-time tuition and fees vary according to course load and program. *Financial support:* In 2010–11, 5 students received support, including fellowships with full tuition reimbursements available (averaging $14,000 per year), research assistantships with full tuition reimbursements available (averaging $14,000 per year), teaching assistantships with full tuition reimbursements available (averaging $14,000 per year); career-related internships or fieldwork, scholarships/grants, and unspecified assistantships also available. Financial award application deadline: 2/1; financial award applicants required to submit FAFSA. *Faculty research:* Cognitive development, parenting, bilingualism, memory development, emotion development, aggression and violence, racism stereotyping. Total annual research expenditures: $10,000. *Unit head:* Dr. Denise Davidson, Director, 773-508-3008, Fax: 773-508-2813, E-mail: ddavids@luc.edu. *Application contact:* Ron Martin, Assistant Director of Enrollment Management, 312-915-8950, Fax: 312-915-8905, E-mail: gradapp@luc.edu.

McGill University, Faculty of Graduate and Postdoctoral Studies, Faculty of Education, Department of Educational and Counseling Psychology, Montréal, QC H3A 2T5, Canada. Offers counseling psychology (MA, PhD); educational psychology (M Ed, MA, PhD); school/applied child psychology and applied developmental psychology (M Ed, MA, PhD, Diploma), including school psychology. *Accreditation:* APA.

The New School: A University, The New School for Social Research, Department of Psychology, New York, NY 10011. Offers clinical psychology (PhD); cognitive, social and developmental psychology (PhD); general psychology (MA). *Accreditation:* APA (one or more programs are accredited). Part-time programs available. Terminal master's awarded for partial completion of doctoral program. *Degree requirements:* For master's, comprehensive exam (for some programs), thesis (for some programs); for doctorate, thesis/dissertation, qualifying exam. *Entrance requirements:* For master's, GRE General Test; for doctorate, GRE General Test, MA. Additional exam requirements/recommendations for international students: Required—TOEFL (minimum score 600 paper-based; 250 computer-based; 100 iBT). Electronic applications accepted. *Faculty research:* Consciousness, memory, language, perceptions, psychopathology.

New York University, Steinhardt School of Culture, Education, and Human Development, Department of Applied Psychology, Programs in Educational and Developmental Psychology, New York, NY 10012-1019. Offers educational psychology (MA); human development and social intervention (MA); psychological development (PhD); psychology and social intervention (PhD). *Accreditation:* APA (one or more programs are accredited). Part-time programs available. *Faculty:* 24 full-time (16 women). *Students:* 52 full-time (48 women), 33 part-time (29 women); includes 9 Black or African American, non-Hispanic/Latino; 8 Asian, non-Hispanic/Latino; 7 Hispanic/Latino, 14 international. Average age 29. 230 applicants, 35% accepted, 33 enrolled. In 2010, 26 master's, 4 doctorates awarded. *Degree requirements:* For master's, thesis (for some programs); for doctorate, thesis/dissertation. *Entrance requirements:* For doctorate, GRE General Test, interview. Additional exam requirements/recommendations for international students: Required—TOEFL. *Application deadline:* For fall admission, 12/1 priority date for domestic and international students. Applications are processed on a rolling basis. Application fee: $75. Electronic applications accepted. *Financial support:* Teaching assistantships with partial tuition reimbursements, career-related internships or fieldwork, Federal Work-Study, institutionally sponsored loans, and tuition waivers (partial) available. Support available to part-time students. Financial award application deadline: 2/1; financial award applicants required to submit FAFSA. *Faculty research:* High risk children and youth; child and adolescent developments; families and schooling; infant cognition; exploration, language, and symbolic play in toddlerhood. *Unit head:* Dr. LaRue Allen, Director, 212-998-5555, Fax: 212-995-4358. *Application contact:* 212-998-5030, Fax: 212-995-4328, E-mail: steinhardt.gradadmissions@nyu.edu.

North Carolina State University, Graduate School, College of Humanities and Social Sciences, Department of Psychology, Raleigh, NC 27695. Offers developmental psychology (PhD); ergonomics and experimental psychology (PhD); industrial/organizational psychology (PhD); psychology in the public interest (PhD); school psychology (PhD). *Accreditation:* APA. *Degree requirements:* For doctorate, comprehensive exam, thesis/dissertation. *Entrance requirements:* For doctorate, GRE General Test, GRE Subject Test (industrial/organizational psychology), MAT (recommended), minimum GPA of 3.0 in major. Electronic applications accepted. *Faculty research:* Cognitive and social development (human factors, families, the workplace, community issues and health, aging).

The Ohio State University, Graduate School, College of Arts and Sciences, Division of Social and Behavioral Sciences, Department of Psychology, Columbus, OH 43210. Offers behavioral neuroscience (PhD); clinical psychology (PhD); cognitive psychology (PhD); developmental psychology (PhD); mental retardation and developmental disabilities (PhD); psychology (MA); quantitative psychology (PhD); social psychology (PhD). *Accreditation:* APA (one or more programs are accredited). *Faculty:* 60. *Students:* 106 full-time (65 women), 42 part-time (31 women); includes 5 Black or African American, non-Hispanic/Latino; 1 American Indian or Alaska Native, non-Hispanic/Latino; 5 Asian, non-Hispanic/Latino; 10 Hispanic/Latino; 3 Two or more races, non-Hispanic/Latino, 23 international. Average age 27. In 2010, 21 master's, 22 doctorates awarded. *Degree requirements:* For doctorate, thesis/dissertation. *Entrance requirements:* For master's and doctorate, GRE General Test. Additional exam requirements/recommendations for international students: Required—TOEFL (minimum score 600 paper-based; 250 computer-based). *Application deadline:* For fall admission, 12/31 for domestic students, 11/30 for international students. Applications are processed on a rolling basis. Application fee: $40 ($50 for international students). Electronic applications accepted. *Expenses:* Tuition, state resident: full-time $10,605. Tuition, nonresident: full-time $26,535. Tuition and fees vary according to course load and program. *Financial support:* Fellowships, research assistantships, teaching assistantships available. *Unit head:* Dr. Richard Petty, Chair, 614-292-1640, E-mail: petty.1@osu.edu. *Application contact:* 614-292-9444, Fax: 614-292-3895, E-mail: domestic.grad@osu.edu.

Pontificia Universidad Catolica Madre y Maestra, Graduate School, Faculty of Social and Administrative Sciences, Santiago, Dominican Republic. Offers business administration (MBA), including business development, finance, international business, management skills (M Mgmt, MBA), marketing, operations, strategic cost management, strategy, tourist destination planning and management; law (LL M), including civil law, corporate business law, criminal law, international relations, real estate law; management (M Mgmt), including higher financial management, insurance program administration, management skills (M Mgmt, MBA); psychology (MA), including clinical child and adolescent psychology, forensic psychology; strategic human resources (EMBA).

Queen's University at Kingston, School of Graduate Studies and Research, Faculty of Arts and Sciences, Department of Psychology, Kingston, ON K7L 3N6, Canada. Offers brain behavior and cognitive science (MA, PhD); clinical psychology (MA, PhD); developmental psychology (MA, PhD); social personality psychology (MA, PhD). *Accreditation:* APA (one or more programs are accredited). *Degree requirements:* For master's, thesis; for doctorate, comprehensive exam, thesis/dissertation. *Entrance requirements:* For master's and doctorate, GRE General Test. Additional exam requirements/recommendations for international students: Required—TOEFL. *Faculty research:* Human development, social, personality, behavioral neuroscience, forensic.

San Francisco State University, Division of Graduate Studies, College of Behavioral and Social Sciences, Department of Psychology, San Francisco, CA 94132-1722. Offers clinical psychology (MS); developmental psychology (MA); industrial/organizational psychology (MS); psychological research (MA); school psychology (MS); social psychology (MA). *Financial support:* Teaching assistantships available. Financial award application deadline: 3/1. *Unit* head: Dr. Julia Lewis, Chair, 415-338-7555, E-mail: jmlewis@sfsu.edu. *Application contact:* Leslye M. Tinson, Assistant to the Chair, 415-338-7555, E-mail: ltinson@sfsu.edu.

Stanford University, School of Education, Program in Psychological Studies in Education, Stanford, CA 94305-9991. Offers child and adolescent development (PhD); counseling psychology (PhD); educational psychology (PhD). *Degree requirements:* For doctorate, thesis/ dissertation. *Entrance requirements:* For doctorate, GRE General Test. Electronic applications accepted. *Expenses:* Tuition: Full-time $38,700; part-time $860 per unit. One-time fee: $200 full-time.

Teachers College, Columbia University, Graduate Faculty of Education, Department of Human Development, Program in Developmental Psychology, New York, NY 10027-6696. Offers MA, Ed D, PhD. *Faculty:* 5 full-time (3 women), 4 part-time/adjunct (2 women). *Students:* 45 full-time (40 women), 52 part-time (44 women); includes 43 minority (12 Black or African American, non-Hispanic/Latino; 12 Asian, non-Hispanic/Latino; 14 Hispanic/Latino; 1 Native Hawaiian or other Pacific Islander, non-Hispanic/Latino; 4 Two or more races, non-Hispanic/ Latino), 15 international. Average age 27. 102 applicants, 79% accepted, 35 enrolled. In 2010, 45 master's, 1 doctorate awarded. *Degree requirements:* For master's, special research project; for doctorate, thesis/dissertation, integrative project. *Entrance requirements:* For doctorate, GRE General Test. *Application deadline:* For fall admission, 12/15 for domestic students. Application fee: $65. *Expenses:* Tuition: Full-time $28,272; part-time $1178 per credit. Required fees: $756; $378 per semester. *Financial support:* Research assistantships, teaching assistantships, career-related internships or fieldwork, Federal Work-Study, institutionally sponsored loans, and tuition waivers (full and partial) available. Support available to part-time students. Financial award application deadline: 2/1; financial award applicants required to submit FAFSA. *Faculty research:* Language development in infants, psychology of mathematics education, intellectual development, testing and assessment, cognitive development. *Unit head:* Prof. Jeanne Brooks-Gunn, Program Coordinator, 212-678-4190, Fax: 212-678-4171, E-mail: brooks-gunn@columbia.edu. *Application contact:* David Estrella, Associate Director of Admission, 212-678-3710, Fax: 212-678-4171, E-mail: tcinfo@tc.edu.

Temple University, College of Liberal Arts, Department of Psychology, Philadelphia, PA 19122-6096. Offers brain and cognitive sciences (PhD); clinical psychology (PhD); developmental psychology (PhD); psychology (MA); social psychology (PhD). *Accreditation:* APA. *Faculty:* 29 full-time (11 women). *Students:* 88 full-time (69 women), 14 part-time (12 women); includes 1 Black or African American, non-Hispanic/Latino; 1 American Indian or Alaska Native, non-Hispanic/Latino; 4 Asian, non-Hispanic/Latino; 2 Hispanic/Latino, 6 international. 538 applicants, 6% accepted, 16 enrolled. In 2010, 10 master's, 15 doctorates awarded. *Degree requirements:* For doctorate, thesis/dissertation. *Entrance requirements:* For doctorate, GRE General Test, minimum GPA of 3.0. Additional exam requirements/recommendations for international students: Required—TOEFL (minimum score 550 paper-based; 213 computer-based; 79 iBT). *Application deadline:* For fall admission, 12/15 for domestic and international students. Application fee: $50. Electronic applications accepted. *Financial support:* Fellowships, research assistantships, teaching assistantships, career-related internships or fieldwork, Federal Work-Study, institutionally sponsored loans, and unspecified assistantships available. Financial award application deadline: 12/15; financial award applicants required to submit FAFSA. Total annual research expenditures: $4 million. *Unit head:* Dr. Marsha Weinraub, Chair, 215-204-7321, Fax: 215-204-5539, E-mail: mweinrau@temple.edu. *Application contact:* Dr. Marsha Weinraub, Chair, 215-204-7321, Fax: 215-204-5539, E-mail: mweinrau@temple.edu.

Texas A&M University, College of Liberal Arts, Department of Psychology, College Station, TX 77843. Offers behavioral and cellular neuroscience (PhD); clinical psychology (PhD); cognitive psychology (PhD); developmental psychology (PhD); industrial/organizational psychology (PhD); social psychology (PhD). *Accreditation:* APA. *Faculty:* 39. *Students:* 91 full-time (57 women), 14 part-time (11 women); includes 7 Black or African American, non-Hispanic/Latino; 8 Asian, non-Hispanic/Latino; 17 Hispanic/Latino, 7 international. In 2010, 12 doctorates awarded. *Degree requirements:* For doctorate, comprehensive exam (for some programs), thesis/dissertation. *Entrance requirements:* For doctorate, GRE General Test. Additional exam requirements/recommendations for international students: Required—TOEFL. *Application deadline:* For fall admission, 1/5 for domestic and international students. Application fee: $50 ($75 for international students). Electronic applications accepted. *Financial support:* Fellowships with partial tuition reimbursements, research assistantships with partial tuition reimbursements, teaching assistantships with partial tuition reimbursements, career-related internships or fieldwork, institutionally sponsored loans, health care benefits, and unspecified assistantships available. Financial award application deadline: 1/5; financial award applicants required to submit FAFSA. *Unit head:* Ludy T. Benjamin, Head, 979-845-2540, Fax: 979-845-4727, E-mail: lbenjamin@tamu.edu. *Application contact:* Julie Austin, Graduate Admissions Supervisor, 979-458-1710, Fax: 979-845-4727, E-mail: gradadv@psyc.tamu.edu.

Union Institute & University, Programs in Psychology and Counseling, Brattleboro, VT 05301. Offers clinical mental health counseling (MA); clinical psychology (Psy D); counseling psychology (MA); counselor education and supervision (CAGS); developmental psychology (MA); educational psychology (MA); human development and wellness (CAGS); organizational psychology (MA); psychology education (CAGS). Psy D offered in Ohio and Vermont. Postbaccalaureate distance learning degree programs offered (minimal on-campus study). *Faculty:* 6 full-time (4 women), 17 part-time/adjunct (6 women). *Students:* 93 full-time (66 women), 11 part-time (10 women); includes 14 minority (6 Black or African American, non-Hispanic/Latino; 1 Asian, non-Hispanic/Latino; 7 Hispanic/Latino). Average age 44. In 2010, 21 master's awarded. *Degree requirements:* For master's, thesis, internship (depending on concentration); for doctorate, thesis/dissertation, internship, practicum. *Application deadline:* Applications are processed on a rolling basis. Application fee: $50. Electronic applications accepted. *Expenses:* Tuition: Full-time $16,430; part-time $685 per credit hour. Required fees: $174; $44 per term. Tuition and fees vary according to course load, degree level and program. *Financial support:* Federal Work-Study available. Financial award applicants required to submit FAFSA. *Unit head:* Dr. Bill Lax, Dean, 802-254-0152, E-mail: bill.lax@myunion.edu. *Application contact:* Diane Robinson, Director of Admissions, 888-828-8575, E-mail: diane.robinson@myunion.edu.

Université de Montréal, Faculty of Arts and Sciences, School of Psychoeducation, Montréal, QC H3C 3J7, Canada. Offers M Sc, PhD. Part-time programs available. *Degree requirements:* For master's, one foreign language, thesis. Electronic applications accepted. *Faculty research:* Child maladjustment, family, prevention, treatment, antisocial behavior.

The University of British Columbia, Faculty of Arts and Faculty of Graduate Studies, Department of Psychology, Vancouver, BC V6T 1Z4, Canada. Offers behavioral neuroscience (MA, PhD); clinical psychology (MA, PhD); cognitive science (MA, PhD); developmental psychology (MA, PhD); health psychology (MA, PhD); quantitative methods (MA, PhD); social/ personality psychology (MA, PhD). *Accreditation:* APA (one or more programs are accredited). Terminal master's awarded for partial completion of doctoral program. *Degree requirements:* For master's, thesis; for doctorate, comprehensive exam, thesis/dissertation. *Entrance requirements:* For master's and doctorate, GRE General Test. Additional exam requirements/ recommendations for international students: Required—TOEFL (minimum score 550 paper-based; 230 computer-based; 80 iBT). Electronic applications accepted. Tuition charges are reported in Canadian dollars. *Expenses:* Tuition: area resident: Full-time $4179 Canadian dollars. International tuition: $7344 Canadian dollars full-time. *Faculty research:* Clinical, developmental, social/personality, cognition, behavioral neuroscience.

University of California, Santa Barbara, Graduate Division, Gevirtz Graduate School of Education, Santa Barbara, CA 93106-9490. Offers counseling, clinical and school psychology (PhD), including clinical psychology, counseling psychology, school psychology; education (M Ed, MA, PhD), including child and adolescent development (MA, PhD), cultural perspectives and comparative education (MA, PhD), educational leadership and organizations (MA, PhD), research methodology (MA, PhD), special education disabilities and risk studies (MA), special education, disabilities and risk studies (PhD), teaching (M Ed), teaching and learning (MA, PhD); educational leadership (Ed D); school psychology (M Ed); MA/PhD. *Accreditation:* APA (one or more programs are accredited). Postbaccalaureate distance learning degree programs offered (minimal on-campus study). *Faculty:* 40 full-time (22 women), 5 part-time/ adjunct (1 woman). *Students:* 411 full-time (325 women); includes 19 Black or African American, non-Hispanic/Latino; 3 American Indian or Alaska Native, non-Hispanic/Latino; 59 Asian, non-Hispanic/Latino; 67 Hispanic/Latino. Average age 29. 683 applicants, 38% accepted, 154 enrolled. In 2010, 128 master's, 58 doctorates awarded. Terminal master's awarded for partial completion of doctoral program. *Degree requirements:* For master's, comprehensive exam (for some programs), thesis (for some programs); for doctorate, comprehensive exam (for some programs), thesis/dissertation. *Entrance requirements:* For master's and doctorate, GRE. Additional exam requirements/recommendations for international students: Required—TOEFL (minimum score 550 paper-based; 80 iBT), IELTS (minimum score 7). Application fee: $70 ($90 for international students). Electronic applications accepted. *Financial support:* In 2010–11, 269 students received support, including 222 fellowships with partial tuition reimbursements available (averaging $5,615 per year), 75 research assistantships with full tuition reimbursements available (averaging $6,470 per year), 65 teaching assistantships with partial tuition reimbursements available (averaging $7,059 per year); career-related internships or fieldwork also available. Financial award applicants required to submit FAFSA. *Faculty research:* Needs of diverse students, school accountability and leadership, school violence, language learning and literacy, science/math education. Total annual research expenditures: $3.1 million. *Unit head:* Carol North Dixon, Graduate Advisor, 805-893-2185, E-mail: dixon@education.ucsb.edu. *Application contact:* Kathryn Marie Tucciarone, Student Affairs Officer, 805-893-2137, Fax: 805-893-2588, E-mail: katiet@education.ucsb.edu.

University of Connecticut, Graduate School, College of Liberal Arts and Sciences, Department of Psychology, Storrs, CT 06269. Offers behavioral neuroscience (PhD); biopsychology (PhD); clinical psychology (MA, PhD); cognition and instruction (PhD); developmental psychology (MA, PhD); ecological psychology (PhD); experimental psychology (PhD); general psychology (MA, PhD); health psychology (Graduate Certificate); industrial/organizational psychology (PhD); language and cognition (PhD); neuroscience (PhD); occupational health psychology (Graduate Certificate); social psychology (MA, PhD). *Accreditation:* APA. Terminal master's awarded for partial completion of doctoral program. *Degree requirements:* For master's, comprehensive exam; for doctorate, thesis/dissertation. *Entrance requirements:* For master's and doctorate, GRE General Test, GRE Subject Test. Additional exam requirements/recommendations for international students: Required—TOEFL (minimum score 550 paper-based; 213 computer-based). Electronic applications accepted.

University of Denver, Division of Arts, Humanities and Social Sciences, Department of Psychology, Denver, CO 80208. Offers affective science (PhD); affective/social psychology (PhD); clinical child psychology (PhD); developmental cognitive neuroscience (PhD); developmental psychology (PhD). Incidental Master's program available. *Accreditation:* APA. *Faculty:* 18 full-time (8 women), 5 part-time/adjunct (4 women). *Students:* 32 full-time (31 women), 2 part-time (1 woman); includes 6 minority (3 Asian, non-Hispanic/Latino; 2 Hispanic/ Latino; 1 Two or more races, non-Hispanic/Latino), 2 international. Average age 26. 320 applicants, 5% accepted, 13 enrolled. In 2010, 6 doctorates awarded. Terminal master's awarded for partial completion of doctoral program. *Degree requirements:* For doctorate, one foreign language, comprehensive exam (for some programs), thesis/dissertation. *Entrance requirements:* For doctorate, GRE General Test. Additional exam requirements/recommendations for international students: Required—TOEFL (minimum score 550 paper-based; 80 iBT). *Application deadline:* For fall admission, 12/1 for domestic students. Applications are processed on a rolling basis. Application fee: $60. Electronic applications accepted. *Expenses:* Tuition: Full-time $35,604; part-time $29,670 per year. Required fees: $687 per year. Tuition and fees vary according to program. *Financial support:* In 2010–11, 12 research assistantships with full and partial tuition reimbursements (averaging $15,500 per year), 22 teaching assistantships with full and partial tuition reimbursements (averaging $16,773 per year) were awarded; career-related internships or fieldwork, Federal Work-Study, institutionally sponsored loans, scholarships/grants, and unspecified assistantships also available. Support available to part-time students. Financial award application deadline: 1/1; financial award applicants required to submit FAFSA. *Faculty research:* Developmental neuropsychology, self-esteem and peer relationships, child abuse and neglect, marital and family interactions, adolescent peer and romantic relationships. *Unit head:* Dr. Rob Roberts, Chair, 303-871-3792, Fax: 303-871-4747. *Application contact:* Paula Plank-Houghtaling, Graduate Secretary, 303-871-3803, Fax: 303-871-4747, E-mail: info@psy.du.edu.

University of Florida, Graduate School, College of Liberal Arts and Sciences, Department of Psychology, Gainesville, FL 32611. Offers behavior analysis (PhD); behavioral neuroscience (MS, PhD); cognitive and sensory processes (PhD); counseling psychology (PhD); developmental psychology (PhD); social psychology (MS, PhD); JD/PhD. *Faculty:* 29 full-time (10 women). *Students:* 106 full-time (82 women), 14 part-time (7 women); includes 3 Black or African American, non-Hispanic/Latino; 2 American Indian or Alaska Native, non-Hispanic/Latino; 7 Asian, non-Hispanic/Latino; 12 Hispanic/Latino, 11 international. Average age 27. 614 applicants, 7% accepted, 36 enrolled. In 2010, 25 master's, 13 doctorates awarded. *Degree requirements:* For master's, comprehensive exam, thesis or alternative; for doctorate, comprehensive exam, thesis/dissertation. *Entrance requirements:* For master's and doctorate, GRE General Test, minimum GPA of 3.0. Additional exam requirements/recommendations for international students: Required—TOEFL (minimum score 550 paper-based; 213 computer-based; 80 iBT), IELTS (minimum score 6). *Application deadline:* For fall admission, 12/9 priority date for domestic students, 12/9 for international students. Applications are processed on a rolling basis. Application fee: $30. Electronic applications accepted. *Expenses:* Tuition, state resident: full-time $10,915.92. Tuition, nonresident: full-time $28,309. *Financial support:* In 2010–11, 105 students received support, including 19 fellowships, 24 research assistantships (averaging $18,742 per year), 62 teaching assistantships (averaging $19,797 per year); career-related internships or fieldwork and unspecified assistantships also available. Financial award application deadline: 12/9; financial award applicants required to submit FAFSA. *Faculty research:* Behavior analysis, behavioral and cognitive neuroscience, counseling, developmental psychology, social psychology. Total annual research expenditures: $2.7 million. *Unit head:* Dr. Neil E. Rowland, Chair, 352-273-2128, Fax: 352-392-7985, E-mail: nrowland@ufl.edu. *Application contact:* Dr. Clive D. Wynne, Graduate Coordinator, 352-392-0601, Fax: 352-392-7985, E-mail: wynne@ufl.edu.

University of Houston, College of Liberal Arts and Social Sciences, Department of Psychology, Houston, TX 77204. Offers clinical psychology (PhD); developmental psychology (PhD); industrial/organizational psychology (PhD); psychology (MA); social psychology (PhD). *Accreditation:* APA (one or more programs are accredited). *Faculty:* 28 full-time (12 women), 7 part-time/adjunct (4 women). *Students:* 117 full-time (86 women), 22 part-time (16 women); includes 7 Black or African American, non-Hispanic/Latino; 10 Asian, non-Hispanic/Latino; 16 Hispanic/Latino; 4 Two or more races, non-Hispanic/Latino, 17 international. Average age 27. 460 applicants, 6% accepted, 28 enrolled. In 2010, 19 master's, 20 doctorates awarded. *Degree requirements:* For master's, comprehensive exam, thesis; for doctorate, comprehensive exam, thesis/dissertation. *Entrance requirements:* For master's, GRE General Test, career statement, 3 letters of recommendation; for doctorate, GRE General Test, 3 letters of recommendation. Additional exam requirements/recommendations for international students: Required—TOEFL (minimum score 550 paper-based; 79 iBT). *Application deadline:* For fall admission, 12/15 for domestic and international students. Application fee: $40 ($75 for international students). Electronic applications accepted. *Expenses:* Tuition, state resident: full-time $8592; part-time $358 per credit hour. Tuition, nonresident: full-time $16,032; part-time $668 per credit hour. Required fees: $2889. Tuition and fees vary according to course load and program. *Financial support:* In 2010–11, 23 fellowships with full tuition reimbursements (averaging $2,828 per year), 39 research assistantships with full tuition reimbursements (averaging $7,864 per year), 62 teaching assistantships with full tuition reimbursements (averaging $9,312 per year) were awarded; career-related internships or fieldwork, Federal Work-Study, institutionally sponsored loans, scholarships/grants, health care benefits, and unspecified

Developmental Psychology

University of Houston (continued)

assistantships also available. Support available to part-time students. Financial award application deadline: 2/1; financial award applicants required to submit FAFSA. *Faculty research:* Health psychology, depression, child/family process, organizational effectiveness, close relationships. *Unit head:* Dr. David Francis, Chairperson, 713-743-7036, Fax: 713-743-8588, E-mail: dfrancis@uh.edu. *Application contact:* Patti Tolar, Academic Affairs Coordinator, 713-743-5544, Fax: 713-743-8588, E-mail: ptolar@uh.edu.

The University of Kansas, Graduate Studies, College of Liberal Arts and Sciences, Department of Psychology, Lawrence, KS 66045. Offers clinical child psychology (MA, PhD); clinical health and rehabilitation (PhD); cognitive psychology (PhD); developmental psychology (PhD); quantitative psychology (PhD); social psychology (MA). *Accreditation:* APA (one or more programs are accredited). *Faculty:* 27 full-time (8 women), 9 part-time/adjunct (4 women). *Students:* 122 full-time (87 women), 1 (woman) part-time; includes 17 minority (4 Black or African American, non-Hispanic/Latino; 8 Asian, non-Hispanic/Latino; 4 Hispanic/Latino; 1 Native Hawaiian or other Pacific Islander, non-Hispanic/Latino), 9 international. Average age 28. 348 applicants, 11% accepted, 25 enrolled. In 2010, 16 master's, 16 doctorates awarded. *Degree requirements:* For master's, thesis; for doctorate, variable foreign language requirement, comprehensive exam, thesis/dissertation. *Entrance requirements:* For doctorate, GRE General Test, minimum GPA of 3.0; undergraduate degree with 15 hours of course work in psychology, curriculum vitae, writing sample (clinical program only). Additional exam requirements/recommendations for international students: Required—TOEFL. *Application deadline:* For fall admission, 12/1 for domestic and international students. Application fee: $55 ($65 for international students). Electronic applications accepted. *Expenses:* Tuition, state resident: full-time $7092; part-time $295.50 per credit hour. Tuition, nonresident: full-time $16,590; part-time $691.25 per credit hour. Required fees: $858; $71.49 per credit hour. Tuition and fees vary according to course load, campus/location and program. *Financial support:* Fellowships with full tuition reimbursements, research assistantships with partial tuition reimbursements, teaching assistantships with full and partial tuition reimbursements, career-related internships or fieldwork and unspecified assistantships available. Financial award application deadline: 12/1; financial award applicants required to submit FAFSA. *Faculty research:* Information processing in depression, rape and other forms of sexual coercion, motions on physical function, processes of memory and understanding text, social stigmas and hostile group environments. *Unit head:* Dr. Ruth Ann Atchley, Chair, 785-864-9821, Fax: 785-864-5696, E-mail: ratchley@ku.edu. *Application contact:* Cathy L. O'Keefe, Graduate Admissions Officer, 785-864-4195, Fax: 785-864-5696, E-mail: psycgrad@ku.edu.

The University of Kansas, Graduate Studies, College of Liberal Arts and Sciences, Program in Child Language, Lawrence, KS 66045. Offers MA, PhD. *Faculty:* 23 full-time (12 women). *Students:* 5 full-time (4 women), 1 international. Average age 27. 3 applicants, 33% accepted, 0 enrolled. In 2010, 2 master's, 2 doctorates awarded. *Degree requirements:* For master's, thesis; for doctorate, comprehensive exam, thesis/dissertation, written preliminary exam; training in responsible research and research skills. *Entrance requirements:* For master's and doctorate, GRE, minimum GPA of 3.5, 3 letters of reference. Additional exam requirements/recommendations for international students: Required—TOEFL. *Application deadline:* For fall admission, 1/15 priority date for domestic and international students; for spring admission, 11/1 for domestic and international students. Applications are processed on a rolling basis. Application fee: $55 ($65 for international students). Electronic applications accepted. *Expenses:* Tuition, state resident: full-time $7092; part-time $295.50 per credit hour. Tuition, nonresident: full-time $16,590; part-time $691.25 per credit hour. Required fees: $858; $71.49 per credit hour. Tuition and fees vary according to course load, campus/location and program. *Financial support:* Fellowships with full tuition reimbursements, research assistantships with full tuition reimbursements, teaching assistantships with full tuition reimbursements, career-related internships or fieldwork, traineeships, and unspecified assistantships available. Financial award application deadline: 2/1. *Faculty research:* Etiology of language impairments, word recognition processes, cultural context and linguistic patterns, language acquisition. *Unit head:* Mabel Rice, Director, 785-864-4570, E-mail: mabel@ku.edu. *Application contact:* Susan Kemper, Graduate Adviser, 785-864-0748, E-mail: skemper@ku.edu.

University of Maine, Graduate School, College of Liberal Arts and Sciences, Department of Psychology, Orono, ME 04469. Offers clinical (PhD); developmental (MA, PhD); experimental (MA); psychological sciences (MA, PhD). *Accreditation:* APA (one or more programs are accredited). *Faculty:* 14 full-time (6 women), 3 part-time/adjunct (2 women). *Students:* 27 full-time (17 women), 10 part-time (6 women); includes 2 minority (1 Asian, non-Hispanic/Latino; 1 Hispanic/Latino), 2 international. Average age 28. 147 applicants, 5% accepted, 7 enrolled. In 2010, 5 master's, 4 doctorates awarded. *Degree requirements:* For master's, thesis; for doctorate, thesis/dissertation. *Entrance requirements:* For master's and doctorate, GRE General Test, GRE Subject Test. Additional exam requirements/recommendations for international students: Required—TOEFL. *Application deadline:* For fall admission, 2/1 priority date for domestic students. Applications are processed on a rolling basis. Application fee: $65. Electronic applications accepted. *Expenses:* Tuition, state resident: full-time $400. Tuition, nonresident: full-time $1050. *Financial support:* In 2010–11, 3 research assistantships with tuition reimbursements (averaging $14,063 per year), 21 teaching assistantships with tuition reimbursements (averaging $12,790 per year) were awarded; Federal Work-Study, institutionally sponsored loans, and tuition waivers (full and partial) also available. Financial award application deadline: 3/1. *Faculty research:* Social development, hypertension and aging, attitude change, self-confidence in achievement situations, health psychology. *Unit head:* Dr. Michael Robbins, Chair, 207-581-2051, Fax: 207-581-6128. *Application contact:* Scott G. Delcourt, Associate Dean of the Graduate School, 207-581-3291, Fax: 207-581-3232, E-mail: graduate@maine.edu.

The University of Manchester, School of Education, Manchester, United Kingdom. Offers counseling (D Couns); counseling psychology (D Couns); education (M Phil, Ed D, PhD); educational and child psychology (Ed D); educational psychology (Ed D).

University of Maryland, Baltimore County, Graduate School, College of Arts, Humanities and Social Sciences, Department of Psychology, Program in Applied Developmental Psychology, Baltimore, MD 21250. Offers PhD. *Faculty:* 7 full-time (4 women), 11 part-time/adjunct (4 women). *Students:* 26 full-time (23 women), 3 part-time (all women); includes 6 minority (1 Black or African American, non-Hispanic/Latino; 4 Asian, non-Hispanic/Latino; 1 Hispanic/Latino). Average age 29. 20 applicants, 30% accepted, 2 enrolled. In 2010, 2 doctorates awarded. *Degree requirements:* For doctorate, comprehensive exam, thesis/dissertation. *Entrance requirements:* For doctorate, GRE General Test, GRE Subject Test, minimum GPA of 3.0. Additional exam requirements/recommendations for international students: Required—TOEFL. *Application deadline:* For fall admission, 1/9 for domestic and international students. Application fee: $70. Electronic applications accepted. *Financial support:* In 2010–11, fellowships with partial tuition reimbursements (averaging $2,200 per year), 3 research assistantships with full and partial tuition reimbursements (averaging $14,857 per year), 10 teaching assistantships with full and partial tuition reimbursements (averaging $14,857 per year) were awarded; career-related internships or fieldwork, Federal Work-Study, health care benefits, and unspecified assistantships also available. Financial award application deadline: 3/1; financial award applicants required to submit FAFSA. *Faculty research:* Early intervention and development, schooling and development, cultural aspects of development, development in high risk children, social-emotional development. Total annual research expenditures: $1.8 million. *Unit head:* Dr. Susan Sonnenschein, Director, 410-455-2361, Fax: 410-455-1055, E-mail: sonnenschein@umbc.edu. *Application contact:* Nicole Mooney, Program Management Specialist, 410-455-2567, Fax: 410-455-1055, E-mail: psycdept@umbc.edu.

University of Maryland, College Park, Academic Affairs, College of Behavioral and Social Sciences, Department of Psychology, College Park, MD 20742. Offers clinical psychology (PhD); developmental psychology (PhD); experimental psychology (PhD); industrial psychology (MA, MS, PhD); social psychology (PhD). *Accreditation:* APA (one or more programs are accredited). *Faculty:* 70 full-time (34 women), 16 part-time/adjunct (10 women). *Students:* 83 full-time (63 women), 6 part-time (4 women); includes 4 Black or African American, non-Hispanic/Latino; 6 Asian, non-Hispanic/Latino; 6 Hispanic/Latino, 13 international. 653 applicants, 4% accepted, 13 enrolled. In 2010, 8 master's, 18 doctorates awarded. *Degree requirements:* For master's, thesis; for doctorate, variable foreign language requirement, comprehensive exam, thesis/dissertation. *Entrance requirements:* For master's and doctorate, GRE General Test, GRE Subject Test, minimum GPA of 3.5, research and/or work experience, 3 letters of recommendation. *Application deadline:* For fall admission, 12/1 for domestic and international students. Applications are processed on a rolling basis. Application fee: $75. Electronic applications accepted. *Expenses:* Tuition, state resident: part-time $471 per credit hour. Tuition, nonresident: part-time $1016 per credit hour. Required fees: $337 per term. *Financial support:* In 2010–11, 14 fellowships with full and partial tuition reimbursements (averaging $20,179 per year), 5 research assistantships (averaging $18,414 per year), 54 teaching assistantships (averaging $17,209 per year) were awarded; career-related internships or fieldwork, Federal Work-Study, and scholarships/grants also available. Support available to part-time students. Financial award applicants required to submit FAFSA. *Faculty research:* Social stereotyping and prejudice, anxiety disorders, auditory neuroethology, counseling and social psychology. Total annual research expenditures: $4 million. *Unit head:* Thomas S. Wallsten, Chair, 301-405-3562, Fax: 301-314-9566, E-mail: twallst@umd.edu. *Application contact:* Dean of Graduate School, 301-405-0358, Fax: 301-314-9305.

University of Massachusetts Amherst, Graduate School, College of Natural Sciences, Department of Psychology, Amherst, MA 01003. Offers clinical psychology (MS, PhD); cognitive psychology (MS, PhD); developmental science (MS, PhD); psychology of peace and violence (MS, PhD); social psychology (MS, PhD). *Accreditation:* APA (one or more programs are accredited). *Faculty:* 47 full-time (23 women). *Students:* 54 full-time (42 women), 6 part-time (4 women); includes 16 minority (3 Black or African American, non-Hispanic/Latino; 6 Asian, non-Hispanic/Latino; 4 Hispanic/Latino; 3 Two or more races, non-Hispanic/Latino), 3 international. Average age 29. 435 applicants, 4% accepted, 8 enrolled. In 2010, 12 master's, 16 doctorates awarded. Terminal master's awarded for partial completion of doctoral program. *Degree requirements:* For master's, thesis; for doctorate, comprehensive exam, thesis/dissertation. *Entrance requirements:* For master's and doctorate, GRE General Test, 3 letters of recommendation. Additional exam requirements/recommendations for international students: Required—TOEFL (minimum score 550 paper-based; 213 computer-based; 80 iBT), IELTS (minimum score 6.5). *Application deadline:* For fall admission, 12/1 for domestic and international students. Applications are processed on a rolling basis. Application fee: $50 ($65 for international students). Electronic applications accepted. *Expenses:* Tuition, state resident: full-time $2640. Required fees: $8282. One-time fee: $357 full-time. *Financial support:* In 2010–11, 8 fellowships with full tuition reimbursements (averaging $12,569 per year), 41 research assistantships with full tuition reimbursements (averaging $10,714 per year), 55 teaching assistantships with full tuition reimbursements (averaging $10,951 per year) were awarded; career-related internships or fieldwork, Federal Work-Study, scholarships/grants, traineeships, health care benefits, tuition waivers (full), and unspecified assistantships also available. Support available to part-time students. Financial award application deadline: 12/1; financial award applicants required to submit FAFSA. *Unit head:* Dr. Linda M. Isbell, Graduate Program Director, 413-545-2503, Fax: 413-545-0996. *Application contact:* Jean M. Ames, Supervisor of Admissions, 413-545-0722, Fax: 413-577-0010, E-mail: gradadm@grad.umass.edu.

University of Miami, Graduate School, College of Arts and Sciences, Department of Psychology, Coral Gables, FL 33124. Offers adult clinical (PhD); behavioral neuroscience (PhD); child clinical (PhD); developmental psychology (PhD); health clinical (PhD); psychology (MS). *Accreditation:* APA (one or more programs are accredited). *Degree requirements:* For doctorate, comprehensive exam, thesis/dissertation. *Entrance requirements:* For doctorate, GRE General Test, minimum GPA of 3.5. Additional exam requirements/recommendations for international students: Required—TOEFL. Electronic applications accepted. *Faculty research:* Behavioral factors in cardiovascular disease and cancer adult psychopathology, developmental disabilities, social and emotional development, mechanisms of coping.

University of Michigan, Horace H. Rackham School of Graduate Studies, College of Literature, Science, and the Arts, Department of Psychology, Ann Arbor, MI 48109. Offers biopsychology (PhD); clinical psychology (PhD); cognition and perception (PhD); developmental psychology (PhD); personality and social contexts (PhD); social psychology (PhD). *Accreditation:* APA. *Faculty:* 83 full-time (39 women), 30 part-time/adjunct (14 women). *Students:* 132 full-time (92 women); includes 13 Black or African American, non-Hispanic/Latino; 2 American Indian or Alaska Native, non-Hispanic/Latino; 18 Asian, non-Hispanic/Latino; 7 Hispanic/Latino; 2 Two or more races, non-Hispanic/Latino, 20 international. Average age 27. 608 applicants, 6% accepted, 24 enrolled. In 2010, 28 doctorates awarded. *Degree requirements:* For doctorate, comprehensive exam, thesis/dissertation, oral defense of dissertation, preliminary exam. *Entrance requirements:* For doctorate, GRE General Test. Additional exam requirements/recommendations for international students: Required—TOEFL. *Application deadline:* For fall admission, 12/1 for domestic and international students. Application fee: $65 ($75 for international students). Electronic applications accepted. *Expenses:* Tuition, state resident: full-time $17,784; part-time $1116 per credit hour. Tuition, nonresident: full-time $35,944; part-time $2125 per credit hour. International tuition: $35,994 full-time. Required fees: $95 per semester. Tuition and fees vary according to course load, degree level and program. *Financial support:* In 2010–11, 118 students received support, including 55 fellowships with full tuition reimbursements available (averaging $20,900 per year), 15 research assistantships with full tuition reimbursements available (averaging $25,950 per year), 52 teaching assistantships with full tuition reimbursements available (averaging $22,670 per year); career-related internships or fieldwork also available. Financial award application deadline: 4/15. Total annual research expenditures: $7.4 million. *Unit head:* Prof. Theresa Lee, Chair, 734-764-7429. *Application contact:* Laurie Brannan, Psychology Student Academic Affairs, 731-764-2580, Fax: 734-615-7584, E-mail: psych.saa@umich.edu.

The University of Montana, Graduate School, College of Arts and Sciences, Department of Psychology, Missoula, MT 59812-0002. Offers clinical psychology (PhD); experimental psychology (PhD), including animal behavior psychology, developmental psychology; school psychology (MA, PhD, Ed S). *Accreditation:* APA (one or more programs are accredited). Terminal master's awarded for partial completion of doctoral program. *Degree requirements:* For master's, thesis; for doctorate, thesis/dissertation. *Entrance requirements:* For master's, doctorate, and Ed S, GRE General Test. Additional exam requirements/recommendations for international students: Required—TOEFL.

University of Nebraska at Omaha, Graduate Studies, College of Arts and Sciences, Department of Psychology, Omaha, NE 68182. Offers developmental psychology (PhD); industrial/organizational psychology (MS, PhD); psychobiology (PhD); psychology (MA); school psychology (MS, Ed S). Part-time programs available. *Faculty:* 18 full-time (8 women). *Students:* 50 full-time (38 women), 41 part-time (32 women); includes 9 minority (2 Black or African American, non-Hispanic/Latino; 1 American Indian or Alaska Native, non-Hispanic/Latino; 1 Asian, non-Hispanic/Latino; 5 Hispanic/Latino), 2 international. Average age 26. 92 applicants, 39% accepted, 34 enrolled. In 2010, 17 master's, 2 doctorates, 6 other advanced degrees awarded. *Degree requirements:* For master's, comprehensive exam, thesis (for some programs). *Entrance requirements:* For master's, GRE General Test, GRE Subject Test, previous course work in psychology, including statistics and a laboratory course; minimum GPA of 3.0, 3 letters of recommendation; for doctorate, GRE General Test. Additional exam requirements/recommendations for international students: Required—TOEFL (minimum score 500 paper-based; 173 computer-based; 61 iBT). *Application deadline:* For fall admission, 1/5 for domestic students. Application fee: $45. Electronic applications accepted. *Financial support:* In 2010–11, 66 students received support; fellowships, research assistantships with tuition reimbursements available, teaching assistantships with tuition reimbursements available, career-related internships or fieldwork, Federal Work-Study, institutionally sponsored loans, scholarships/grants, tuition waivers (partial), and unspecified assistantships available. Support available to part-time students. Financial award application deadline: 3/1; financial award applicants required to submit FAFSA. *Unit head:* Dr. Brigette Ryalls, Chairperson, 402-554-2592. *Application contact:* Dr. Joseph Brown, Student Contact, 402-554-2592.

University of Nebraska–Lincoln, Graduate College, College of Arts and Sciences, Department of Psychology, Lincoln, NE 68588. Offers biopsychology (PhD); clinical psychology (PhD); cognitive psychology (PhD); developmental psychology (PhD); psychology (MA); social/personality psychology (PhD); JD/MA; JD/PhD. *Accreditation:* APA (one or more programs are accredited). *Degree requirements:* For master's, thesis optional; for doctorate, comprehensive exam, thesis/dissertation. *Entrance requirements:* For master's and doctorate, GRE General Test. Additional exam requirements/recommendations for international students: Required—TOEFL (minimum score 550 paper-based; 213 computer-based). Electronic applications accepted. *Faculty research:* Law and psychology, rural mental health, chronic mental illness, neuropsychology, child clinical psychology.

University of Nebraska–Lincoln, Graduate College, College of Education and Human Sciences, Department of Educational Psychology, Lincoln, NE 68588. Offers cognition, learning and development (MA); counseling psychology (MA); educational psychology (MA, Ed S); psychological studies in education (PhD), including cognition, learning and development, counseling psychology, quantitative, qualitative, and psychometric methods, school psychology; quantitative, qualitative, and psychometric methods (MA); school psychology (MA, Ed S). *Accreditation:* APA (one or more programs are accredited); NCATE. *Degree requirements:* For master's, thesis optional. *Entrance requirements:* For master's, GRE General Test. Additional exam requirements/recommendations for international students: Required—TOEFL (minimum score 500 paper-based; 173 computer-based). Electronic applications accepted. *Faculty research:* Measurement and assessment, metacognition, academic skills, child development, multicultural education and counseling.

The University of North Carolina at Chapel Hill, Graduate School, College of Arts and Sciences, Department of Psychology, Chapel Hill, NC 27599. Offers biological psychology (PhD); clinical psychology (PhD); cognitive psychology (PhD); developmental psychology (PhD); quantitative psychology (PhD); social psychology (PhD). *Accreditation:* APA. *Degree requirements:* For doctorate, comprehensive exam, thesis/dissertation. *Entrance requirements:* For doctorate, GRE General Test, minimum GPA of 3.0. Electronic applications accepted. *Faculty research:* Expressed emotion, cognitive development, social cognitive neuroscience, human memory personality.

The University of North Carolina at Greensboro, Graduate School, College of Arts and Sciences, Department of Psychology, Greensboro, NC 27412-5001. Offers clinical psychology (MA, PhD); cognitive psychology (MA, PhD); developmental psychology (MA, PhD); social psychology (MA, PhD). *Accreditation:* APA (one or more programs are accredited). Terminal master's awarded for partial completion of doctoral program. *Degree requirements:* For master's, comprehensive exam, thesis; for doctorate, one foreign language, thesis/dissertation, preliminary exam. *Entrance requirements:* For master's and doctorate, GRE General Test. Additional exam requirements/recommendations for international students: Required—TOEFL. Electronic applications accepted. *Faculty research:* Sensory and perceptual determinants; evoked potential: disorders, deafness, and development.

University of Notre Dame, Graduate School, College of Arts and Letters, Division of Social Science, Department of Psychology, Notre Dame, IN 46556. Offers cognitive psychology (PhD); counseling psychology (PhD); developmental psychology (PhD); quantitative psychology (PhD). *Accreditation:* APA. *Degree requirements:* For doctorate, comprehensive exam, thesis/dissertation, candidacy exam. *Entrance requirements:* For doctorate, GRE General Test, GRE Subject Test (strongly recommended). Additional exam requirements/recommendations for international students: Required—TOEFL (minimum score 600 paper-based; 250 computer-based; 80 iBT). Electronic applications accepted. *Faculty research:* Cognitive and socio-emotional development, statistical methods and quantitative models applicable to psychology, interpersonal relations, life span development and developmental delay, childhood depression, structural equation and dynamical systems.

University of Oregon, Graduate School, College of Arts and Sciences, Department of Psychology, Eugene, OR 97403. Offers clinical psychology (PhD); cognitive psychology (MA, MS, PhD); developmental psychology (MA, MS, PhD); physiological psychology (MA, MS, PhD); psychology (MA, MS, PhD); social/personality psychology (MA, MS, PhD). *Accreditation:* APA (one or more programs are accredited). Terminal master's awarded for partial completion of doctoral program. *Degree requirements:* For doctorate, thesis/dissertation. *Entrance requirements:* For master's, GRE General Test, minimum GPA of 3.0; for doctorate, GRE General Test. Additional exam requirements/recommendations for international students: Required—TOEFL.

University of Pittsburgh, School of Education, Department of Psychology in Education, Program in Applied Developmental Psychology, Pittsburgh, PA 15260. Offers M Ed, MS, PhD. Part-time and evening/weekend programs available. *Students:* 47 full-time (38 women), 48 part-time (38 women); includes 18 minority (12 Black or African American, non-Hispanic/Latino; 3 Asian, non-Hispanic/Latino; 1 Hispanic/Latino; 2 Two or more races, non-Hispanic/Latino), 8 international. Average age 30. 129 applicants, 58% accepted, 50 enrolled. In 2010, 32 master's, 2 doctorates awarded. *Degree requirements:* For master's, thesis. *Entrance requirements:* For doctorate, GRE. Additional exam requirements/recommendations for international students: Required—TOEFL. *Application deadline:* For fall admission, 2/1 for domestic students, 2/1 priority date for international students; for spring admission, 7/1 priority date for international students. Applications are processed on a rolling basis. Application fee: $50. Electronic applications accepted. *Expenses:* Tuition, state resident: full-time $17,304; part-time $701 per credit. Tuition, nonresident: full-time $29,554; part-time $1210 per credit. Required fees: $740; $214 per term. Tuition and fees vary according to program. *Financial support:* Tuition waivers (partial) available. Support available to part-time students. Financial award applicants required to submit FAFSA. *Unit head:* Dr. Carl N. Johnson, Chairman, 412-624-6942, Fax: 412-624-7231, E-mail: johnson@pitt.edu. *Application contact:* Maggie Sikora, Graduate Enrollment Manager, 412-648-2230, Fax: 412-648-1899, E-mail: soeinfo@pitt.edu.

University of Rochester, School of Arts and Sciences, Department of Clinical and Social Sciences in Psychology, Program in Developmental Psychology, Rochester, NY 14627.

University of Southern California, Graduate School, Dana and David Dornsife College of Letters, Arts and Sciences, Department of Psychology, Los Angeles, CA 90089. Offers brain and cognitive science (PhD); clinical science (PhD); developmental psychology (PhD); human behavior (MHB); quantitative methods (PhD); social psychology (PhD). *Accreditation:* APA. *Faculty:* 34 full-time (10 women), 15 part-time/adjunct (9 women). *Students:* 105 full-time (65 women), 3 part-time (all women); includes 32 minority (4 Black or African American, non-Hispanic/Latino; 17 Asian, non-Hispanic/Latino; 9 Hispanic/Latino; 2 Two or more races, non-Hispanic/Latino), 22 international. 543 applicants, 5% accepted, 14 enrolled. In 2010, 17 master's, 12 doctorates awarded. *Degree requirements:* For doctorate, comprehensive exam, thesis/dissertation, one-year internship (for clinical science students). *Entrance requirements:* For doctorate, GRE. Additional exam requirements/recommendations for international students: Recommended—TOEFL (minimum score 600 paper-based; 250 computer-based; 100 iBT). *Application deadline:* For fall admission, 12/1 for domestic and international students. Application fee: $85. Electronic applications accepted. *Expenses:* Tuition: Full-time $31,240; part-time $1420 per unit. Required fees: $600. One-time fee: $35 full-time. Full-time tuition and fees vary according to degree level and program. *Financial support:* In 2010–11, 85 students received support, including 30 fellowships with full tuition reimbursements available (averaging $24,000 per year), 12 research assistantships with full tuition reimbursements available (averaging $19,250 per year), 40 teaching assistantships with full tuition reimbursements available (averaging $19,250 per year); scholarships/grants, traineeships, health care benefits, and unspecified assistantships also available. Financial award application deadline: 12/1. *Faculty research:* Affective neuroscience; children and families; vision, culture and ethnicity; intergroup relations; aggression and violence; language and reading development; substance abuse. *Unit head:* Dr. Margaret Gatz, Chair and Professor, 213-740-2212, Fax: 213-746-9028, E-mail: gatz@usc.edu. *Application contact:* Irene Takaragawa, Graduate Advisor, 213-740-2205, Fax: 213-746-9082, E-mail: itakarag@usc.edu.

University of Victoria, Faculty of Graduate Studies, Faculty of Social Sciences, Department of Psychology, Victoria, BC V8W 2Y2, Canada. Offers clinical psychology (PhD); clinical psychology (neuropsychology) (M Sc); cognition and brain science (M Sc, PhD); experimental neuropsychology (M Sc, PhD); individualized study (M Sc, PhD); life span development psychology (PhD); life span developmental psychology (M Sc); social psychology (M Sc, PhD). *Accreditation:* APA (one or more programs are accredited). *Degree requirements:* For master's, thesis; for doctorate, thesis/dissertation, candidacy exam. *Entrance requirements:* For master's and doctorate, GRE General Test. Additional exam requirements/recommendations for international students: Required—TOEFL (minimum score 600 paper-based; 250 computer-based). Electronic applications accepted. *Faculty research:* Life span development psychology and aging, behavioral neuroscience, cognitive psychology, behavioral psychology, environmental psychology.

University of Washington, Graduate School, College of Arts and Sciences, Department of Psychology, Seattle, WA 98195. Offers animal behavior (PhD); child psychology (PhD); clinical psychology (PhD); cognition and perception (PhD); developmental psychology (PhD); quantitative psychology (PhD); social psychology and personality (PhD). *Accreditation:* APA. *Degree requirements:* For doctorate, thesis/dissertation. *Entrance requirements:* For doctorate, GRE General Test, minimum GPA of 3.0. Electronic applications accepted. *Faculty research:* Addictive behaviors, artificial intelligence, child psychopathology, mechanisms and development of vision, physiology of ingestive behaviors.

University of Wisconsin–Madison, Graduate School, College of Letters and Science, Department of Psychology, Program in Developmental Psychology, Madison, WI 53706-1380. Offers PhD. *Degree requirements:* For doctorate, comprehensive exam, thesis/dissertation. *Entrance requirements:* For doctorate, GRE General Test, minimum undergraduate GPA of 3.0. Additional exam requirements/recommendations for international students: Required—TOEFL. Electronic applications accepted. *Expenses:* Tuition, state resident: full-time $9887; part-time $617.96 per credit. Tuition, nonresident: full-time $24,054; part-time $1503.40 per credit. Required fees: $67.63 per credit. Tuition and fees vary according to reciprocity agreements.

University of Wisconsin–Milwaukee, Graduate School, School of Education, Department of Educational Psychology, Milwaukee, WI 53201-0413. Offers counseling (school, community) (MS); counseling psychology (PhD); learning and development (MS); research methodology (MS, PhD); school psychology (PhD). *Accreditation:* APA. Part-time programs available. *Faculty:* 22 full-time (14 women). *Students:* 158 full-time (130 women), 62 part-time (48 women); includes 14 Black or African American, non-Hispanic/Latino; 8 Asian, non-Hispanic/Latino; 5 Hispanic/Latino, 10 international. Average age 30. 278 applicants, 41% accepted. In 2010, 69 master's, 8 doctorates awarded. *Degree requirements:* For master's, comprehensive exam, thesis; for doctorate, thesis/dissertation. *Entrance requirements:* For master's, minimum GPA of 3.0; for doctorate, GRE General Test, minimum GPA of 3.0. Additional exam requirements/recommendations for international students: Required—TOEFL (minimum score 550 paper-based; 79 iBT), IELTS (minimum score 6.5). *Application deadline:* For fall admission, 1/1 priority date for domestic students; for spring admission, 9/1 for domestic students. Applications are processed on a rolling basis. Application fee: $56 ($96 for international students). Electronic applications accepted. *Financial support:* In 2010–11, 14 fellowships, 1 research assistantship, 8 teaching assistantships were awarded; career-related internships or fieldwork, health care benefits, unspecified assistantships, and project assistantships also available. Support available to part-time students. Financial award application deadline: 4/15; financial award applicants required to submit FAFSA. *Unit head:* Nadya Fouad, Graduate Program Representative, 414-229-4599, Fax: 414-229-4939, E-mail: nadya@uwm.edu. *Application contact:* General Information Contact, 414-229-4982, Fax: 414-229-6967, E-mail: gradschool@uwm.edu.

Virginia Commonwealth University, Graduate School, College of Humanities and Sciences, Department of Psychology, Program in General Psychology, Richmond, VA 23284-9005. Offers biopsychology (PhD); developmental psychology (PhD); social psychology (PhD). *Students:* 22 full-time (16 women), 9 part-time (4 women); includes 6 minority (4 Black or African American, non-Hispanic/Latino; 1 Asian, non-Hispanic/Latino; 1 Hispanic/Latino), 1 international. 68 applicants, 6% accepted, 1 enrolled. In 2010, 3 doctorates awarded. *Degree requirements:* For doctorate, thesis/dissertation. *Entrance requirements:* For doctorate, GRE General Test. Additional exam requirements/recommendations for international students: Required—TOEFL (minimum score 600 paper-based; 250 computer-based; 100 iBT); Recommended—IELTS (minimum score 6.5). *Application deadline:* For fall admission, 12/15 for domestic students. Application fee: $50. Electronic applications accepted. *Expenses:* Tuition, state resident: full-time $4308; part-time $479 per credit hour. Tuition, nonresident: full-time $8942; part-time $994 per credit hour. Required fees: $2000; $85 per credit hour. Tuition and fees vary according to course level, course load, degree level, campus/location and program. *Financial support:* Fellowships, research assistantships, teaching assistantships, Federal Work-Study, institutionally sponsored loans, and scholarships/grants available. Support available to part-time students. *Faculty research:* Biopsychology, developmental and social psychology. *Unit head:* Dr. Michael Southam-Gerow, Director, Graduate Programs in Psychology, 804-828-1193, Fax: 804-828-2237, E-mail: masouthamger@vcu.edu. *Application contact:* Dr. Joseph Porter, Director, Biopsychology Division, 804-828-0096, Fax: 804-828-2237, E-mail: jporter@vcu.edu.

Walden University, Graduate Programs, School of Psychology, Minneapolis, MN 55401. Offers clinical child psychology (Post-Doctoral Certificate); clinical psychology (MS, Post-Doctoral Certificate), including counseling (MS); counseling psychology (Post-Doctoral Certificate); forensic psychology (MS), including forensic psychology in the community, general program, mental health applications, program planning and evaluation in forensic settings, psychology and legal systems; general psychology (Post-Doctoral Certificate); health psychology (Post-Doctoral Certificate); organizational psychology (Post-Doctoral Certificate); organizational psychology and development (Postbaccalaureate Certificate); psychology (MS, PhD), including clinical psychology (PhD), counseling psychology (PhD), crisis management and response (MS), general program (MS), general psychology (PhD), health psychology, leadership development and coaching (MS), media psychology (MS), organizational psychology (PhD), organizational psychology and development (MS), organizational psychology and nonprofit management (MS), program evaluation and research (MS), psychology of culture (MS), psychology, public administration, and social change (MS), social psychology (MS), terrorism and security (MS); teaching online (Post-Master's Certificate). Part-time and evening/weekend programs available. Postbaccalaureate distance learning degree programs offered (minimal on-campus study). *Faculty:* 41 full-time (25 women), 254 part-time/adjunct (131 women). *Students:* 3,463 full-time (2,737 women), 1,400 part-time (1,130 women); includes 1,491 Black or African American, non-Hispanic/Latino; 59 American Indian or Alaska Native, non-Hispanic/Latino; 89 Asian, non-Hispanic/Latino; 283 Hispanic/Latino; 76 Two or more races, non-Hispanic/Latino, 126 international. Average age 40. In 2010, 559 master's, 100 doctorates awarded. Terminal master's awarded for partial completion of doctoral program. *Degree requirements:* For master's, thesis optional; for doctorate, thesis/dissertation, residency. *Entrance requirements:* For master's, bachelor's degree or equivalent in related field; minimum GPA of 2.5; official transcripts; goal statement; access to computer and Internet; for doctorate, master's degree or equivalent in related field; minimum GPA of 3.0; 3 years of related professional/academic experience (preferred). Additional exam requirements/recommendations for international students: Required—TOEFL (minimum score 550 paper-based; 213 computer-based), IELTS (minimum score 6.5), TOEFL (minimum score 550 paper-based; 213 computer-based), IELTS (minimum score 6.5), or Michigan English Language Assessment Battery (minimum score 82). *Application deadline:* Applications are processed on a rolling basis. Application fee: $50. Electronic applications accepted. *Expenses:* Tuition: Full-time $10,274; part-time $445 per

Walden University (continued)
credit. Tuition and fees vary according to course load, degree level and program. *Financial support:* In 2010–11, 1 fellowship was awarded; Federal Work-Study, scholarships/grants, unspecified assistantships, and family tuition reduction, active duty/veteran tuition reduction, group tuition reduction, interest-free payment plans also available. Support available to part-time students. Financial award applicants required to submit FAFSA. *Unit head:* Dr. Melanie Storms, Associate Dean, 800-925-3368. *Application contact:* Jennifer Hall, Vice President of Enrollment Management, 866-4-WALDEN, E-mail: info@waldenu.edu.

West Virginia University, Eberly College of Arts and Sciences, Department of Psychology, Morgantown, WV 26506. Offers behavior analysis (PhD); clinical psychology (MA, PhD); development psychology (PhD); psychology (MS). *Accreditation:* APA (one or more programs are accredited). Part-time programs available. Terminal master's awarded for partial completion of doctoral program. *Degree requirements:* For master's, thesis optional; for doctorate, comprehensive exam, thesis/dissertation. *Entrance requirements:* For master's and doctorate, GRE General Test, minimum GPA of 3.0. Additional exam requirements/recommendations for international students: Required—TOEFL. *Faculty research:* Adult and child clinical psychology, behavioral assessment and therapy, child and adolescent behavior, life span development, experimental and applied behavior analysis.

Wilfrid Laurier University, Faculty of Graduate and Postdoctoral Studies, Faculty of Science, Department of Psychology, Waterloo, ON N2L 3C5, Canada. Offers behavioral neuroscience (M Sc, PhD); cognitive neuroscience (M Sc, PhD); community psychology (MA, PhD); social and developmental psychology (MA, PhD). Part-time programs available. *Faculty:* 32 full-time (12 women), 8 part-time/adjunct (1 woman). *Students:* 68 full-time (49 women), 4 part-time (3 women), 2 international. 94 applicants, 51% accepted, 27 enrolled. In 2010, 27 master's, 5 doctorates awarded. *Degree requirements:* For master's, thesis; for doctorate, thesis/dissertation. *Entrance requirements:* For master's, GRE General Test, honors BA or the equivalent in psychology, minimum B average in undergraduate course work; for doctorate, GRE General Test, master's degree, minimum A- average. Additional exam requirements/recommendations for international students: Required—TOEFL (minimum score 89 iBT). *Application deadline:* For fall admission, 1/15 priority date for domestic and international students. Application fee: $100. Electronic applications accepted. Tuition and fees charges are reported in Canadian dollars. *Expenses:* Tuition, area resident: Full-time $15,300 Canadian dollars; part-time $1200 Canadian dollars per credit. International tuition: $21,300 Canadian dollars full-time. Required fees: $650 Canadian dollars; $100 Canadian dollars per credit. Tuition and fees vary according to course load, degree level, campus/location and program. *Financial support:* In 2010–11, 116 fellowships, 116 teaching assistantships were awarded; career-related internships or fieldwork, scholarships/grants, health care benefits, and unspecified assistantships also available. *Faculty research:* Brain and cognition, community psychology, social and developmental psychology. *Unit head:* Dr. Alexandra Gottardo, Graduate Coordinator, 519-884-0710 Ext. 2169, Fax: 519-746-7605, E-mail: agottard@wlu.ca. *Application contact:* Rosemary Springett, Graduate Admissions and Records Officer, 519-884-0710 Ext. 3078, Fax: 519-884-1020, E-mail: gradstudies@wlu.ca.

Yale University, Graduate School of Arts and Sciences, Department of Psychology, New Haven, CT 06520. Offers behavioral neuroscience (PhD); clinical psychology (PhD); cognitive psychology (PhD); developmental psychology (PhD); social/personality psychology (PhD). *Accreditation:* APA. *Degree requirements:* For doctorate, thesis/dissertation. *Entrance requirements:* For doctorate, GRE General Test.

Experimental Psychology

American University, College of Arts and Sciences, Department of Psychology, Washington, DC 22016-8062. Offers behavior, cognition, and neuroscience (PhD), including psychology; clinical psychology (PhD), including psychology; psychology (MA), including experimental/biological psychology, general psychology, personality/social psychology. *Accreditation:* APA. Part-time programs available. *Faculty:* 19 full-time (7 women), 6 part-time/adjunct (4 women). *Students:* 65 full-time (51 women), 47 part-time (41 women); includes 16 minority (4 Black or African American, non-Hispanic/Latino; 3 Asian, non-Hispanic/Latino; 9 Hispanic/Latino), 3 international. Average age 28. 445 applicants, 19% accepted, 36 enrolled. In 2010, 35 master's, 11 doctorates awarded. *Degree requirements:* For master's, comprehensive exam, thesis or alternative; for doctorate, comprehensive exam, thesis/dissertation, tools of research. *Entrance requirements:* For master's, GRE General Test, GRE Subject Test, recommendations; for doctorate, GRE General Test, GRE Subject Test. Additional exam requirements/recommendations for international students: Required—TOEFL. Application fee: $80. *Financial support:* Fellowships, research assistantships, teaching assistantships, career-related internships or fieldwork, Federal Work-Study, institutionally sponsored loans, tuition waivers (full and partial), and unspecified assistantships available. Support available to part-time students. Financial award application deadline: 2/1. *Faculty research:* Anxiety disorders, cognitive assessment, neuropsychology, conditioning and learning, psychopharmacology. *Unit head:* Dr. Anthony Riley, Chair, 202-885-1720, E-mail: alriley@american.edu. *Application contact:* Sara Holland, Senior Administrative Assistant, 202-885-1717, Fax: 202-885-1023, E-mail: holland@american.edu.

Appalachian State University, Cratis D. Williams Graduate School, Department of Psychology, Boone, NC 28608. Offers clinical health psychology (MA); general experimental psychology (MA); industrial and organizational psychology (MA). Part-time programs available. *Faculty:* 31 full-time (10 women), 2 part-time/adjunct (1 woman). *Students:* 55 full-time (40 women), 11 part-time (9 women); includes 3 minority (2 Black or African American, non-Hispanic/Latino; 1 Two or more races, non-Hispanic/Latino). 158 applicants, 32% accepted, 28 enrolled. In 2010, 25 master's, 7 other advanced degrees awarded. *Degree requirements:* For master's, comprehensive exam, thesis optional, exit exam. *Entrance requirements:* For master's, GRE General Test, 3 letters of recommendation. Additional exam requirements/recommendations for international students: Required—TOEFL (minimum score 550 paper-based; 230 computer-based; 79 iBT) or IELTS (minimum score 6.5). *Application deadline:* For fall admission, 2/15 for domestic students, 2/1 for international students. Applications are processed on a rolling basis. Application fee: $55. Electronic applications accepted. *Expenses:* Tuition, state resident: full-time $3428; part-time $428 per unit. Tuition, nonresident: full-time $14,518; part-time $1814 per unit. Required fees: $2320; $344 per unit. Tuition and fees vary according to campus/location. *Financial support:* In 2010–11, 34 research assistantships (averaging $4,000 per year), 25 teaching assistantships (averaging $4,000 per year) were awarded; fellowships, career-related internships or fieldwork, Federal Work-Study, scholarships/grants, and unspecified assistantships also available. Financial award application deadline: 4/1; financial award applicants required to submit FAFSA. *Faculty research:* Eating disorders, school-based consultations, organizational behavior management, brain mechanisms of sound localization, parenting styles. Total annual research expenditures: $18,000. *Unit head:* Dr. James Denniston, Chair, 828-262-2272, Fax: 828-262-2272, E-mail: dennistonjc@appstate.edu. *Application contact:* Dr. Denise Martz, Graduate Coordinator, 828-262-2715, E-mail: martzdm@appstate.edu.

Auburn University, Graduate School, College of Liberal Arts, Department of Psychology, Auburn University, AL 36849. Offers applied behavior analysis in developmental disabilities (MS); clinical psychology (PhD); experimental psychology (PhD); industrial/organizational psychology (PhD). *Accreditation:* APA (one or more programs are accredited). Part-time programs available. *Faculty:* 24 full-time (7 women), 4 part-time/adjunct (3 women). *Students:* 36 full-time (28 women), 57 part-time (33 women); includes 6 Black or African American, non-Hispanic/Latino; 4 Asian, non-Hispanic/Latino; 5 Hispanic/Latino. Average age 26. 293 applicants, 9% accepted, 19 enrolled. In 2010, 20 master's, 11 doctorates awarded. *Degree requirements:* For doctorate, thesis/dissertation. *Entrance requirements:* For master's, GRE General Test, GRE Subject Test, minimum GPA of 3.25 in psychology, 3.0 overall; for doctorate, GRE General Test, GRE Subject Test. *Application deadline:* For fall admission, 7/7 for domestic students; for spring admission, 11/24 for domestic students. Applications are processed on a rolling basis. Application fee: $50 ($60 for international students). Electronic applications accepted. *Expenses:* Tuition, state resident: full-time $7002. Tuition, nonresident: full-time $21,898. International tuition: $22,116 full-time. Required fees: $892. Tuition and fees vary according to course load and program. *Financial support:* Research assistantships, teaching assistantships, Federal Work-Study available. Support available to part-time students. Financial award application deadline: 3/15; financial award applicants required to submit FAFSA. *Faculty research:* Clinical psychology, learning, industrial psychology, organizational psychology. Total annual research expenditures: $200,000. *Unit head:* Dr. Barry Burkhart, Chair, 334-844-6476. *Application contact:* Dr. George Flowers, Dean of the Graduate School, 334-844-2125.

Bowling Green State University, Graduate College, College of Arts and Sciences, Department of Psychology, Bowling Green, OH 43403. Offers clinical psychology (MA, PhD); developmental psychology (MA, PhD); experimental psychology (MA, PhD); industrial/organizational psychology (MA, PhD); quantitative psychology (MA, PhD). *Accreditation:* APA (one or more programs are accredited). *Degree requirements:* For doctorate, thesis/dissertation. *Entrance requirements:* For doctorate, GRE General Test, GRE Subject Test. Additional exam requirements/recommendations for international students: Required—TOEFL. Electronic applications accepted. *Faculty research:* Personnel psychology, developmental-mathematical models, behavioral medication, brain process, child/adolescent social cognition.

Brooklyn College of the City University of New York, Division of Graduate Studies, Department of Psychology, Brooklyn, NY 11210-2889. Offers experimental psychology (MA); industrial and organizational psychology (MA), including human relations, organizational behavior; mental health counseling (MA); psychology (PhD). Part-time programs available. *Students:* 83 full-time (68 women), 142 part-time (108 women); includes 102 minority (64 Black or African American, non-Hispanic/Latino; 18 Asian, non-Hispanic/Latino; 20 Hispanic/Latino), 16 international. Average age 30. 331 applicants, 44% accepted, 88 enrolled. In 2010, 75 master's awarded. *Degree requirements:* For master's, comprehensive exam, thesis (for some programs). *Entrance requirements:* For master's, minimum GPA of 3.0, 2 letters of recommendation, essay; for doctorate, GRE. Additional exam requirements/recommendations for international students: Required—TOEFL (minimum score 520 paper-based; 190 computer-based; 69 iBT). *Application deadline:* For fall admission, 3/1 for domestic students, 2/1 for international students; for spring admission, 11/1 for domestic students, 10/1 for international students. Applications are processed on a rolling basis. Application fee: $125. Electronic applications accepted. *Expenses:* Tuition, state resident: full-time $7360; part-time $310 per credit hour. Tuition, nonresident: full-time $13,800; part-time $575 per credit hour. Required fees: $190 per semester. *Financial support:* Career-related internships or fieldwork, Federal Work-Study, institutionally sponsored loans, scholarships/grants, and tuition waivers (partial) available. Support available to part-time students. Financial award application deadline: 5/1; financial award applicants required to submit FAFSA. *Unit head:* Dr. Margaret-Ellen Pipe, Chairperson, 718-951-5601, Fax: 718-951-4814, E-mail: mepipe@brooklyn.cuny.edu. *Application contact:* Hernan Sierra, Graduate Admissions Coordinator, 718-951-4536, Fax: 718-951-4506, E-mail: grads@brooklyn.cuny.edu.

California State University, Northridge, Graduate Studies, College of Social and Behavioral Sciences, Department of Psychology, Northridge, CA 91330. Offers clinical psychology (MA); general-experimental psychology (MA); human factors and applied experimental psychology (MA). *Degree requirements:* For master's, thesis. *Entrance requirements:* For master's, GRE General Test, GRE Subject Test, minimum GPA of 3.0, letters of recommendation. Additional exam requirements/recommendations for international students: Required—TOEFL.

California State University, San Bernardino, Graduate Studies, College of Social and Behavioral Sciences, Department of Psychology, Program in General/Experimental Psychology, San Bernardino, CA 92407-2397. Offers psychology (MA). *Degree requirements:* For master's, thesis. *Entrance requirements:* For master's, minimum GPA of 3.0 in major.

Case Western Reserve University, School of Graduate Studies, Department of Psychology, Program in Experimental Psychology, Cleveland, OH 44106. Offers PhD. *Faculty:* 7 full-time (3 women), 3 part-time/adjunct (0 women). *Students:* 8 full-time (2 women); includes 1 Asian, non-Hispanic/Latino, 1 international. Average age 27. 211 applicants, 3% accepted, 1 enrolled. In 2010, 1 doctorate awarded. *Degree requirements:* For doctorate, thesis/dissertation, internship. *Entrance requirements:* For doctorate, GRE General Test, GRE Subject Test. Additional exam requirements/recommendations for international students: Required—TOEFL (minimum score 550 paper-based; 213 computer-based; 79 iBT). *Application deadline:* For fall admission, 2/15 priority date for domestic students. Application fee: $50. Electronic applications accepted. *Financial support:* Research assistantships, teaching assistantships available. *Faculty research:* Development and evaluation of cognitive behavioral treatments for anxiety and mood disorders, evaluating treatments for PTSD, depression and bipolar disorder in youth, family relations and emotional expressions. *Application contact:* Dr. James C. Overholser, Director of Clinical Training, 216-368-2686, Fax: 216-368-4891, E-mail: cwrupsych@gmail.com.

The Catholic University of America, School of Arts and Sciences, Department of Psychology, Washington, DC 20064. Offers applied experimental psychology (PhD); clinical psychology (PhD); general psychology (MA); human factors (MA); MA/JD. *Accreditation:* APA (one or more programs are accredited). Part-time programs available. *Faculty:* 12 full-time (6 women), 7 part-time/adjunct (2 women). *Students:* 39 full-time (25 women), 31 part-time (28 women); includes 6 Black or African American, non-Hispanic/Latino; 4 Asian, non-Hispanic/Latino; 4 Hispanic/Latino, 1 international. Average age 29. 229 applicants, 22% accepted, 17 enrolled. In 2010, 22 master's, 8 doctorates awarded. *Degree requirements:* For master's, comprehensive exam, thesis (for some programs); for doctorate, comprehensive exam, thesis/dissertation. *Entrance requirements:* For master's, GRE General Test, statement of purpose, official copies of academic transcripts, three letters of recommendation; for doctorate, GRE General Test, GRE Subject Test, statement of purpose, official copies of academic transcripts, three letters of recommendation. Additional exam requirements/recommendations for international students: Required—TOEFL (minimum score 580 paper-based; 237 computer-based). *Application deadline:* For fall admission, 8/1 priority date for domestic students, 7/15 for international students; for spring admission, 12/1 priority date for domestic students, 10/15 for international students. Applications are processed on a rolling basis. Application fee: $55. Electronic applications accepted. *Expenses:* Tuition: Full-time $33,580; part-time $1315 per credit hour. Required fees: $80; $40 per semester hour. One-time fee: $425. *Financial support:* Fellowships, research assistantships, teaching assistantships, Federal Work-Study, scholarships/grants, tuition waivers (full and partial), and unspecified assistantships available. Financial award application deadline: 2/1; financial award applicants required to submit FAFSA. *Faculty research:* Clinical psychology, applied cognitive science, psychopathology, cognitive neuroscience, psychotherapy. Total annual research expenditures: $409,988. *Unit head:* Dr. Marc M. Sebrechts, Chair, 202-319-5750, Fax: 202-319-6263, E-mail: sebrechts@cua.edu. *Application contact:* Andrew Woodall, Director of Graduate Admissions, 202-319-5057, Fax: 202-319-6533, E-mail: cua-admissions@cua.edu.

Central Michigan University, College of Graduate Studies, College of Humanities and Social and Behavioral Sciences, Department of Psychology, Program in Experimental Psychology, Mount Pleasant, MI 48859. Offers applied experimental psychology (PhD); experimental psychology (MS). Part-time programs available. *Students:* 13 full-time (3 women), 17 part-time (9 women); includes 1 Black or African American, non-Hispanic/Latino, 1 international. Average age 27. *Degree requirements:* For master's, thesis or alternative; for doctorate, thesis/dissertation. *Application deadline:* For fall admission, 2/1 for domestic and international students. Application fee: $35 ($45 for international students). Electronic applications accepted. *Expenses:* Tuition, state resident: full-time $8208; part-time $456 per credit hour. Tuition, nonresident: full-time $13,788; part-time $766 per credit hour. One-time fee: $25. *Financial support:* In 2010–11, 3 fellowships with tuition reimbursements were awarded; research assistantships with tuition reimbursements, career-related internships or fieldwork, Federal Work-Study, unspecified assistantships, and out-of-state merit awards, non-resident graduate awards also available. *Faculty research:* Behavioral neuroscience, human development, perception and cognition, social/personal problem solving, psychophysiology. *Unit head:* Dr. Hajime Otani, Chairperson, 989-774-6494, Fax: 989-774-2553, E-mail: otani1h@cmich.edu. *Application contact:* Dr. Mark Reilly, Graduate Coordinator, 989-774-2343, Fax: 989-774-2553, E-mail: reill1mp@cmich.edu.

Central Washington University, Graduate Studies and Research, College of the Sciences, Department of Psychology, Program in Experimental Psychology, Ellensburg, WA 98926. Offers MS. *Degree requirements:* For master's, thesis. *Entrance requirements:* For master's, GRE General Test, minimum GPA of 3.0. Additional exam requirements/recommendations for international students: Required—TOEFL (minimum score 550 paper-based; 213 computer-based; 79 iBT).

City College of the City University of New York, Graduate School, College of Liberal Arts and Science, Division of Social Science, Department of Psychology, New York, NY 10031-9198. Offers clinical psychology (PhD); experimental cognition (PhD); general psychology (MA); mental health counseling (MA). PhD program offered jointly with Graduate School and University Center of the City University of New York. *Accreditation:* APA (one or more programs are accredited). Part-time programs available. *Degree requirements:* For master's, one foreign language, comprehensive exam, thesis. *Entrance requirements:* For master's, GRE. Additional exam requirements/recommendations for international students: Required—TOEFL (minimum score 550 paper-based; 79 iBT). Electronic applications accepted. *Faculty research:* Social/personality psychology, physiological psychology, cognition and development.

Cleveland State University, College of Graduate Studies, College of Sciences and Health Professions, Department of Psychology, Cleveland, OH 44115. Offers adult development and aging (PhD); clinical psychology (MA); consumer/industrial research (MA); diversity management (MA); experimental research psychology (MA); school psychology (Psy S). *Accreditation:* APA. *Faculty:* 20 full-time (7 women), 16 part-time/adjunct (8 women). *Students:* 63 full-time (45 women), 43 part-time (27 women); includes 15 Black or African American, non-Hispanic/Latino; 1 American Indian or Alaska Native, non-Hispanic/Latino; 3 Asian, non-Hispanic/Latino; 3 Hispanic/Latino, 1 international. Average age 30. 164 applicants, 44% accepted, 62 enrolled. In 2010, 39 master's, 8 other advanced degrees awarded. Terminal master's awarded for partial completion of doctoral program. *Degree requirements:* For master's, comprehensive exam (for some programs), thesis (for some programs); for doctorate, comprehensive exam, thesis/dissertation; for Psy S, internship. *Entrance requirements:* For master's and doctorate, GRE General Test. Additional exam requirements/recommendations for international students: Required—TOEFL (minimum score 525 paper-based; 197 computer-based). *Application deadline:* For fall admission, 2/1 priority date for domestic and international students. Application fee: $30. Electronic applications accepted. *Expenses:* Tuition, state resident: full-time $8447; part-time $469 per credit hour. Tuition, nonresident: full-time $16,020; part-time $890 per credit hour. Required fees: $50. *Financial support:* In 2010–11, 45 students received support. Career-related internships or fieldwork, Federal Work-Study, scholarships/grants, tuition waivers (partial), and unspecified assistantships available. Financial award applicants required to submit FAFSA. *Faculty research:* Cognitive and social psychology, consumer psychology, clinical psychology, school psychology, aging. Total annual research expenditures: $112,607. *Unit head:* Dr. Kathleen M. McNamara, Chairperson, 216-687-2545, Fax: 216-687-9294, E-mail: k.mcnamara@csuohio.edu. *Application contact:* Karen R. Colston, Administrative Coordinator, 216-687-2552, Fax: 216-687-9294, E-mail: k.colston@csuohio.edu.

The College of William and Mary, Faculty of Arts and Sciences, Department of Psychology, Williamsburg, VA 23187-8795. Offers MA. *Faculty:* 20 full-time (8 women). *Students:* 14 full-time (6 women); includes 1 minority (Asian, non-Hispanic/Latino), 1 international. Average age 24. 79 applicants, 13% accepted, 6 enrolled. In 2010, 5 master's awarded. *Degree requirements:* For master's, thesis. *Entrance requirements:* For master's, GRE. Additional exam requirements/recommendations for international students: Required—TOEFL. *Application deadline:* For fall admission, 2/15 for domestic and international students. Application fee: $45. *Expenses:* Tuition, state resident: full-time $6400; part-time $345 per credit hour. Tuition, nonresident: full-time $19,720; part-time $920 per credit hour. Required fees: $4368. *Faculty research:* Personality, developmental, clinical and neuroscience, social psychology. Total annual research expenditures: $460,047. *Unit head:* Dr. Constance Pilkington, Chair, 757-221-3875, E-mail: cjpilk@wm.edu. *Application contact:* Tracy Coates, Administrator of Graduate Student Services, 757-221-3870, Fax: 757-221-3896, E-mail: tlcoates@wm.edu.

Columbia University, Graduate School of Arts and Sciences, Division of Natural Sciences, Department of Psychology, New York, NY 10027. Offers experimental psychology (M Phil, MA, PhD); psychobiology (M Phil, MA, PhD); social psychology (M Phil, MA, PhD); JD/MA; JD/PhD; MD/PhD. *Degree requirements:* For master's, thesis; for doctorate, thesis/dissertation. *Entrance requirements:* For master's and doctorate, GRE General Test. Additional exam requirements/recommendations for international students: Required—TOEFL.

Cornell University, Graduate School, Graduate Fields of Arts and Sciences, Field of Psychology, Ithaca, NY 14853-0001. Offers biopsychology (PhD); human experimental psychology (PhD); personality and social psychology (PhD). *Faculty:* 40 full-time (15 women). *Students:* 39 full-time (25 women); includes 1 Black or African American, non-Hispanic/Latino; 4 Asian, non-Hispanic/Latino; 2 Hispanic/Latino, 13 international. Average age 27. 273 applicants, 5% accepted, 10 enrolled. In 2010, 4 doctorates awarded. *Degree requirements:* For doctorate, comprehensive exam, thesis/dissertation, 2 semesters of teaching experience. *Entrance requirements:* For doctorate, GRE General Test, 3 letters of recommendation. Additional exam requirements/recommendations for international students: Required—TOEFL (minimum score 550 paper-based; 213 computer-based; 77 iBT). *Application deadline:* For fall admission, 12/15 for domestic students. Application fee: $80. Electronic applications accepted. *Expenses:* Tuition: Full-time $29,500. Required fees: $76. Tuition and fees vary according to degree level and program. *Financial support:* In 2010–11, 12 fellowships with full tuition reimbursements, 2 research assistantships with full tuition reimbursements, 23 teaching assistantships with full tuition reimbursements were awarded; institutionally sponsored loans, scholarships/grants, health care benefits, tuition waivers (full and partial), and unspecified assistantships also available. Financial award applicants required to submit FAFSA. *Faculty research:* Sensory and perceptual systems, social cognition, cognitive development, quantitative and computational modeling, behavioral neuroscience. *Unit head:* Director of Graduate Studies, 607-255-6364, Fax: 607-255-8433. *Application contact:* Graduate Field Assistant, 607-255-3834, Fax: 607-255-8433, E-mail: psychapp@cornell.edu.

Dallas Baptist University, Gary Cook School of Leadership, Program in Christian Education, Dallas, TX 75211-9299. Offers adult ministry (MA); business ministry (MA); childhood ministry (MA); collegiate ministry (MA); communication ministry (MA); counseling ministry (MA); education ministry (MA); general ministry (MA); missions ministry (MA); student ministry (MA); worship ministry (MA). Part-time and evening/weekend programs available. *Entrance requirements:* For master's, minimum GPA of 3.0. Additional exam requirements/recommendations for international students: Required—TOEFL. Electronic applications accepted. *Expenses:* Tuition: Full-time $11,394; part-time $633 per credit hour.

DePaul University, College of Liberal Arts and Sciences, Department of Psychology, Chicago, IL 60604-2287. Offers clinical psychology (MA, PhD), including child clinical psychology, community clinical psychology; experimental psychology (MA, PhD); general psychology (MS); industrial/organizational psychology (MA, PhD); MA/PhD. *Accreditation:* APA (one or more programs are accredited). *Faculty:* 31 full-time (19 women), 6 part-time/adjunct (4 women). *Students:* 43 full-time (26 women), 57 part-time (39 women); includes 11 Black or African American, non-Hispanic/Latino; 5 Asian, non-Hispanic/Latino; 10 Hispanic/Latino; 4 Two or more races, non-Hispanic/Latino, 2 international. Average age 28. 332 applicants, 14% accepted, 23 enrolled. In 2010, 14 master's, 17 doctorates awarded. *Degree requirements:* For master's, thesis, oral exam; for doctorate, comprehensive exam, thesis/dissertation, oral and written exams. *Entrance requirements:* For master's and doctorate, GRE General Test, GRE Subject Test, 32 quarter hours of course work in psychology, 3 letters of recommendation. Additional exam requirements/recommendations for international students: Required—TOEFL. Application fee: $40. Electronic applications accepted. *Financial support:* In 2010–11, 48 students received support, including 35 research assistantships with full tuition reimbursements available (averaging $11,800 per year), 13 teaching assistantships with full tuition reimbursements available (averaging $11,800 per year); career-related internships or fieldwork, scholarships/grants, traineeships, tuition waivers (full and partial), and unspecified assistantships also available. Financial award application deadline: 1/10. *Faculty research:* Adolescent stress and depression, minority adolescents sexuality, public policy, community influences in child adjustment. *Unit head:* Dr. Christopher B. Keys, Chairman, 773-325-7887, Fax: 773-325-7888. *Application contact:* Alison Pereida Knapp, Graduate Admissions Assistant, 773-325-7887, Fax: 773-325-7888.

Duke University, Graduate School, Department of Psychology and Neuroscience, Durham, NC 27708. Offers biological psychology (PhD); clinical psychology (PhD); cognitive psychology (PhD); developmental psychology (PhD); experimental psychology (PhD); health psychology (PhD); human social development (PhD); JD/MA. *Accreditation:* APA (one or more programs are accredited). *Faculty:* 40 full-time. *Students:* 92 full-time (67 women); includes 6 Black or African American, non-Hispanic/Latino; 2 Asian, non-Hispanic/Latino; 7 Hispanic/Latino, 13 international. 483 applicants, 8% accepted, 23 enrolled. In 2010, 24 doctorates awarded. *Degree requirements:* For doctorate, thesis/dissertation. *Entrance requirements:* For doctorate, GRE General Test. Additional exam requirements/recommendations for international students: Required—TOEFL (minimum score 550 paper-based; 213 computer-based; 83 iBT), IELTS (minimum score 7). *Application deadline:* For fall admission, 12/8 priority date for domestic and international students. Application fee: $75. Electronic applications accepted. *Financial support:* Fellowships, research assistantships, teaching assistantships, career-related internships or fieldwork and Federal Work-Study available. Financial award application deadline: 12/8. *Unit head:* Melanie Bonner, Director of Graduate Studies, 919-660-5715, Fax: 919-660-5726, E-mail: morrell@duke.edu. *Application contact:* Elizabeth Hutton, Director of Admissions, 919-684-3913, Fax: 919-684-2277, E-mail: grad-admissions@duke.edu.

Eastern Washington University, Graduate Studies, College of Social and Behavioral Sciences, Department of Psychology, Cheney, WA 99004-2431. Offers clinical psychology (MS); experimental psychology (MS); psychology (MS); school psychology (MS). *Degree requirements:* For master's, comprehensive exam, thesis or alternative. *Entrance requirements:* For master's, GRE General Test, minimum GPA of 3.0.

Fairleigh Dickinson University, Metropolitan Campus, University College: Arts, Sciences, and Professional Studies, School of Psychology, Program in General-Theoretical Psychology, Teaneck, NJ 07666-1914. Offers MA, Certificate. *Students:* 9 full-time (5 women), 7 part-time (5 women), 1 international. Average age 27. 24 applicants, 79% accepted, 5 enrolled. In 2010, 18 master's awarded. *Application deadline:* Applications are processed on a rolling basis. Application fee: $40. *Application contact:* Susan Brooman, University Director of Graduate Admissions, 201-692-2554, Fax: 201-692-2560, E-mail: globaleducation@fdu.edu.

Georgia Institute of Technology, Graduate Studies and Research, College of Sciences, School of Psychology, Atlanta, GA 30332-0001. Offers human computer interaction (MSHCI); psychology (MS, MS Psy, PhD), including engineering psychology (PhD), experimental psychology (PhD), industrial/organizational psychology (PhD). Terminal master's awarded for partial completion of doctoral program. *Degree requirements:* For master's, thesis; for doctorate, thesis/dissertation. *Entrance requirements:* For master's and doctorate, GRE General Test, GRE Subject Test, minimum GPA of 3.0. Additional exam requirements/recommendations for international students: Required—TOEFL. Electronic applications accepted. *Faculty research:* Experimental, industrial-organizational, and engineering psychology; cognitive aging and processes; leadership; human factors.

Graduate School and University Center of the City University of New York, Graduate Studies, Program in Psychology, New York, NY 10016-4039. Offers basic applied neurocognition (PhD); biopsychology (PhD); clinical psychology (PhD); developmental psychology (PhD); environmental psychology (PhD); experimental psychology (PhD); industrial psychology (PhD); learning processes (PhD); neuropsychology (PhD); psychology (PhD); social personality (PhD). *Degree requirements:* For doctorate, one foreign language, thesis/dissertation. *Entrance requirements:* For doctorate, GRE General Test. Additional exam requirements/recommendations for international students: Required—TOEFL. Electronic applications accepted.

Harvard University, Graduate School of Arts and Sciences, Department of Psychology, Cambridge, MA 02138. Offers psychology (PhD), including behavior and decision analysis, cognition, developmental psychology, experimental psychology, personality, psychobiology, psychopathology; social psychology (PhD). *Accreditation:* APA. *Degree requirements:* For doctorate, thesis/dissertation, general exams. *Entrance requirements:* For doctorate, GRE General Test. Additional exam requirements/recommendations for international students: Required—TOEFL. *Expenses:* Tuition: Full-time $34,976. Required fees: $1166. Full-time tuition and fees vary according to program.

Howard University, Graduate School, Department of Psychology, Washington, DC 20059-0002. Offers clinical psychology (PhD); developmental psychology (PhD); experimental psychology (PhD); neuropsychology (PhD); personality psychology (PhD); psychology (MS); social psychology (PhD). *Accreditation:* APA (one or more programs are accredited). Part-time programs available. *Degree requirements:* For master's, thesis; for doctorate, comprehensive exam, thesis/dissertation, qualifying exam. *Entrance requirements:* For master's, GRE General Test, minimum GPA of 2.5, bachelor's degree in psychology or related field; for doctorate, GRE General Test, minimum GPA of 3.0. *Faculty research:* Personality and psychophysiology, educational and social development of African-American children, child and adult psychopathology.

Illinois State University, Graduate School, College of Arts and Sciences, Department of Psychology, Normal, IL 61790-2200. Offers psychology (MA, MS), including clinical psychology, counseling psychology, developmental psychology, educational psychology, experimental psychology, measurement-evaluation, organizational-industrial psychology; school psychology (PhD, SSP). *Accreditation:* APA. *Degree requirements:* For master's, thesis or alternative; for doctorate, variable foreign language requirement, thesis/dissertation, 2 terms of residency, internship, practicum. *Entrance requirements:* For master's, GRE General Test, GRE Subject Test, minimum GPA of 3.0 in last 60 hours of course work; for doctorate, GRE General Test. *Faculty research:* Comprehensive evaluation system for the central region professional development grant, Illinois school psychology internship consortium, for children's sake.

Iona College, School of Arts and Science, Department of Psychology, New Rochelle, NY 10801-1890. Offers experimental psychology (MA); industrial-organizational psychology (MA);

Experimental Psychology

Iona College (continued)
mental health counseling (MA); psychology (MA); school psychology (MA). Part-time and evening/weekend programs available. *Faculty:* 10 full-time (7 women), 12 part-time/adjunct (7 women). *Students:* 86 full-time (70 women), 36 part-time (30 women); includes 21 minority (6 Black or African American, non-Hispanic/Latino; 1 American Indian or Alaska Native, non-Hispanic/Latino; 2 Asian, non-Hispanic/Latino; 12 Hispanic/Latino), 2 international. Average age 25. 153 applicants, 78% accepted, 50 enrolled. In 2010, 36 master's awarded. *Degree requirements:* For master's, thesis. *Entrance requirements:* For master's, GRE or minimum GPA of 3.0. Additional exam requirements/recommendations for international students: Required—TOEFL (minimum score 550 paper-based; 213 computer-based). *Application deadline:* Applications are processed on a rolling basis. Application fee: $50. Electronic applications accepted. *Expenses:* Tuition: Part-time $830 per credit. Required fees: $225 per credit. *Financial support:* Career-related internships or fieldwork, tuition waivers (partial), and unspecified assistantships available. Support available to part-time students. Financial award application deadline: 4/15; financial award applicants required to submit FAFSA. *Unit head:* Dr. Paul Greene, Chair, 914-633-2048, E-mail: pgreene@iona.edu. *Application contact:* Veronica Jarek-Prinz, Director of Graduate Admissions, 914-633-2420, Fax: 914-633-2277, E-mail: vjarekprinz@iona.edu.

Kent State University, College of Arts and Sciences, Department of Psychology, Kent, OH 44242-0001. Offers clinical psychology (MA, PhD); experimental psychology (MA, PhD). *Accreditation:* APA (one or more programs are accredited). *Degree requirements:* For master's, thesis; for doctorate, thesis/dissertation. *Entrance requirements:* For master's, GRE, minimum GPA of 3.0, minimum 18 semester hours in psychology with one course in statistics and one experimental course with a lab component; for doctorate, GRE, minimum GPA of 3.0. Additional exam requirements/recommendations for international students: Required—TOEFL (minimum score 525 paper-based), Michigan English Language Assessment Battery (minimum score: 77). *Expenses:* Tuition, state resident: full-time $7866; part-time $437 per credit hour. Tuition, nonresident: full-time $14,022; part-time $779 per credit hour.

Lakehead University, Graduate Studies, Department of Psychology, Thunder Bay, ON P7B 5E1, Canada. Offers clinical psychology (PhD); experimental psychology (MA). Part-time and evening/weekend programs available. *Degree requirements:* For master's, thesis optional; for doctorate, thesis/dissertation, 2 comprehensive exams, internship. *Entrance requirements:* For master's, GRE, honors degree in psychology, advanced course work in statistics, minimum B average; for doctorate, GRE, minimum B average. Additional exam requirements/recommendations for international students: Required—TOEFL. *Faculty research:* Chaos theory, health psychology, counseling psychology, gerontology, women's studies.

Laurentian University, School of Graduate Studies and Research, Programme in Psychology, Sudbury, ON P3E 2C6, Canada. Offers applied psychology (MA); experimental psychology (MA).

McGill University, Faculty of Graduate and Postdoctoral Studies, Faculty of Science, Department of Psychology, Montréal, QC H3A 2T5, Canada. Offers clinical psychology (PhD); experimental psychology (M Sc, MA, PhD). *Accreditation:* APA (one or more programs are accredited).

McNeese State University, Doré School of Graduate Studies, Burton College of Education, Department of Psychology, Lake Charles, LA 70609. Offers addiction treatment (MA); applied behavior analysis (MA); counseling psychology (MA); general/experimental psychology (MA). Evening/weekend programs available. *Faculty:* 6 full-time (3 women). *Students:* 46 full-time (31 women), 29 part-time (21 women); includes 11 minority (6 Black or African American, non-Hispanic/Latino; 1 Asian, non-Hispanic/Latino; 2 Hispanic/Latino; 2 Two or more races, non-Hispanic/Latino), 4 international. In 2010, 14 master's awarded. *Entrance requirements:* For master's, GRE. *Application deadline:* For fall admission, 5/15 priority date for domestic and international students; for spring admission, 10/15 priority date for domestic and international students. Applications are processed on a rolling basis. Application fee: $20 ($30 for international students). Tuition and fees vary according to course load. *Financial support:* Application deadline: 5/1. *Unit head:* Dr. Dena L. Matzenbacher, Head, 337-475-5457, Fax: 337-562-4115, E-mail: dena@mcneese.edu. *Application contact:* Dr. George F. Mead, Interim Dean of Dore' School of Graduate Studies, 337-475-5396, Fax: 337-475-5397, E-mail: admissions@mcneese.edu.

Memorial University of Newfoundland, School of Graduate Studies, Department of Psychology, St. John's, NL A1C 5S7, Canada. Offers applied social psychology (MASP); experimental psychology (M Sc, PhD). Part-time programs available. *Degree requirements:* For master's, workterms (MASP), thesis (M Sc); for doctorate, comprehensive exam, thesis/dissertation, oral thesis defense. *Entrance requirements:* For master's, GRE, honors bachelor's degree of high second class standing or equivalent; for doctorate, GRE, master's or honors degree. Electronic applications accepted. *Faculty research:* Behavioral neuroscience, cognition, theory and research on abnormal behavior.

Middle Tennessee State University, College of Graduate Studies, College of Behavioral and Health Sciences, Department of Psychology, Murfreesboro, TN 37132. Offers clinical psychology (MA); experimental psychology (MA); industrial/organizational psychology (MA); psychology (MA); quantitative psychology (MA); school psychology (MA, Ed S). Part-time and evening/weekend programs available. Postbaccalaureate distance learning degree programs offered. *Faculty:* 36 full-time (16 women), 2 part-time/adjunct (0 women). *Students:* 32 full-time (27 women), 84 part-time (58 women); includes 11 Black or African American, non-Hispanic/Latino; 6 Asian, non-Hispanic/Latino; 2 Hispanic/Latino. Average age 26. 251 applicants, 55% accepted. In 2010, 52 master's, 10 other advanced degrees awarded. *Degree requirements:* For master's, variable foreign language requirement, comprehensive exam, thesis (for some programs). *Entrance requirements:* Additional exam requirements/recommendations for international students: Required—TOEFL (minimum score 525 paper-based; 195 computer-based; 71 iBT) or IELTS (minimum score 6). *Application deadline:* For fall admission, 6/1 for domestic and international students. Applications are processed on a rolling basis. Application fee: $25 ($30 for international students). Electronic applications accepted. *Expenses:* Tuition, state resident: full-time $4632. Tuition, nonresident: full-time $11,520. *Financial support:* In 2010–11, 16 students received support. Career-related internships or fieldwork and institutionally sponsored loans available. Support available to part-time students. Financial award application deadline: 5/1; financial award applicants required to submit FAFSA. *Faculty research:* Industrial/organizational, social/personality/sports, counseling/clinical/school, cognitive/language/learning/perception, developmental/aging. *Unit head:* Dr. Dennis Papini, Chair, 615-898-2706, Fax: 615-898-5027, E-mail: dpapini@mtsu.edu. *Application contact:* Dr. Michael Allen, Dean and Vice Provost for Research, 615-898-2840, Fax: 615-904-8020, E-mail: mallen@mtsu.edu.

Mississippi State University, College of Arts and Sciences, Department of Psychology, Mississippi State, MS 39762. Offers cognitive science (PhD); psychology (MS), including clinical psychology, experimental psychology. *Faculty:* 12 full-time (4 women). *Students:* 40 full-time (27 women), 7 part-time (5 women); includes 4 minority (3 Black or African American, non-Hispanic/Latino; 1 Two or more races, non-Hispanic/Latino), 3 international. Average age 26. 77 applicants, 36% accepted, 19 enrolled. In 2010, 10 master's, 1 doctorate awarded. Terminal master's awarded for partial completion of doctoral program. *Degree requirements:* For master's, comprehensive exam, thesis; for doctorate, thesis/dissertation, qualifying exam, comprehensive written and oral exam. *Entrance requirements:* For master's, GRE General Test, minimum GPA of 2.75 on last two years of undergraduate courses; for doctorate, GRE General Test, proficiency in at least 1 computer language. Additional exam requirements/recommendations for international students: Required—TOEFL (minimum score 475 paper-based; 153 computer-based; 53 iBT); Recommended—IELTS (minimum score 4.5). *Application deadline:* For fall admission, 1/15 priority date for domestic students, 5/1 for international students; for spring admission, 11/1 priority date for domestic students, 9/1 for international students. Applications are processed on a rolling basis. Application fee: $40. Electronic applications accepted. *Expenses:* Tuition, state resident: full-time $2730.50; part-time $304 per credit hour. Tuition, nonresident: full-time $6901; part-time $767 per credit hour. *Financial support:* In 2010–11, 6 research assistantships with full tuition reimbursements (averaging $11,925 per year), 13 teaching assistantships with full tuition reimbursements (averaging $9,755 per year) were awarded; career-related internships or fieldwork, Federal Work-Study, institutionally sponsored loans, scholarships/grants, and unspecified assistantships also available. Financial award application deadline: 4/1; financial award applicants required to submit FAFSA. *Faculty research:* Personality type, alcoholism, blindness and low vision, mental retardation, language comprehension. Total annual research expenditures: $2.4 million. *Unit head:* Dr. Stephen B. Klein, Department Head, 662-325-3202, Fax: 662-325-7212, E-mail: sbkl@ra.msstate.edu. *Application contact:* Dr. Kevin J. Armstrong, Graduate Coordinator, 662-325-3202, Fax: 662-325-7212, E-mail: grad@psychology.msstate.edu.

Missouri State University, Graduate College, College of Health and Human Services, Department of Psychology, Springfield, MO 65897. Offers psychology (MS), including clinical psychology, experimental psychology, industrial/organizational psychology. *Degree requirements:* For master's, comprehensive exam, thesis. *Entrance requirements:* For master's, GRE General Test, GRE Subject Test, minimum GPA of 3.25 in major, 3.0 overall; 20 hours of course work in psychology (experimental and statistics). Additional exam requirements/recommendations for international students: Required—TOEFL (minimum score 550 paper-based; 213 computer-based; 79 iBT). Electronic applications accepted. *Expenses:* Tuition, state resident: full-time $3348; part-time $186 per credit hour. Tuition, nonresident: full-time $6696; part-time $372 per credit hour. Required fees: $238 per semester. Tuition and fees vary according to course level, course load and program. *Faculty research:* Work-family conflict, child forensic psychology, sports psychology, body image assessment, visual learning.

Morehead State University, Graduate Programs, College of Science and Technology, Department of Psychology, Morehead, KY 40351. Offers clinical/counseling psychology (MS); general/experimental psychology (MS). Part-time and evening/weekend programs available. *Degree requirements:* For master's, comprehensive exam, thesis optional. *Entrance requirements:* For master's, GRE General Test, 18 undergraduate hours in psychology, minimum GPA of 3.0, 3 letters of recommendation. Additional exam requirements/recommendations for international students: Required—TOEFL (minimum score 500 paper-based; 173 computer-based). Electronic applications accepted. *Faculty research:* Mood induction effects, serotonin receptor activity, stress, perceptual processes.

North Carolina State University, Graduate School, College of Humanities and Social Sciences, Department of Psychology, Raleigh, NC 27695. Offers developmental psychology (PhD); ergonomics and experimental psychology (PhD); industrial/organizational psychology (PhD); psychology in the public interest (PhD); school psychology (PhD). *Accreditation:* APA. *Degree requirements:* For doctorate, comprehensive exam, thesis/dissertation. *Entrance requirements:* For doctorate, GRE General Test, GRE Subject Test (industrial/organizational psychology), MAT (recommended), minimum GPA of 3.0 in major. Electronic applications accepted. *Faculty research:* Cognitive and social development (human factors, families, the workplace, community issues and health, aging).

Northeastern University, College of Science, Department of Psychology, Boston, MA 02115-5096. Offers experimental psychology (MA, PhD). *Faculty:* 24 full-time (8 women), 8 part-time/adjunct (6 women). *Students:* 28 full-time (19 women). 107 applicants, 11% accepted, 8 enrolled. In 2010, 5 master's, 3 doctorates awarded. *Degree requirements:* For doctorate, thesis/dissertation. *Entrance requirements:* For master's and doctorate, GRE General Test. Additional exam requirements/recommendations for international students: Required—TOEFL. *Application deadline:* For fall admission, 1/1 for domestic and international students. Applications are processed on a rolling basis. Application fee: $50. Electronic applications accepted. *Financial support:* In 2010–11, 1 fellowship with full tuition reimbursement, 22 teaching assistantships with full tuition reimbursements (averaging $16,760 per year) were awarded; research assistantships with full tuition reimbursements, career-related internships or fieldwork and traineeships also available. Financial award application deadline: 1/15; financial award applicants required to submit FAFSA. *Faculty research:* Behavioral, neuroscience language and cognition, perception, personality and social. *Unit head:* Dr. Rhea Eskew, Chair, 617-373-3076, Fax: 617-373-8714, E-mail: psychology@neu.edu. *Application contact:* Rhonda Johnson, Graduate Coordinator, 617-373-3076, Fax: 617-373-8714, E-mail: psychology@neu.edu.

Ohio University, Graduate College, College of Arts and Sciences, Department of Psychology, Program in Experimental Psychology, Athens, OH 45701-2979. Offers PhD. *Students:* 17 full-time (7 women), 6 part-time (4 women); includes 2 minority (both Hispanic/Latino), 5 international. Average age 28. 29 applicants, 24% accepted, 3 enrolled. In 2010, 4 doctorates awarded. *Degree requirements:* For doctorate, one foreign language, comprehensive exam, thesis/dissertation. *Entrance requirements:* For doctorate, GRE General Test, GRE Subject Test, minimum graduate GPA of 3.4. Additional exam requirements/recommendations for international students: Required—TOEFL. *Application deadline:* For fall admission, 1/1 for domestic students. Application fee: $50 ($55 for international students). *Financial support:* In 2010–11, 14 students received support, including 5 fellowships with full tuition reimbursements available (averaging $16,400 per year), research assistantships with full tuition reimbursements available (averaging $13,200 per year), 8 teaching assistantships with full tuition reimbursements available (averaging $13,200 per year); Federal Work-Study, institutionally sponsored loans, tuition waivers (full), and unspecified assistantships also available. Financial award application deadline: 1/15. *Faculty research:* Cognitive psychology, quantitative psychology, social psychology, judgment and decision-making, health psychology. Total annual research expenditures: $3.8 million. *Unit head:* Dr. Jeffrey Vancouver, Director of Experimental Studies, 740-593-1071, Fax: 740-593-0579, E-mail: vancouve@ohio.edu. *Application contact:* Karyl Jones, Administrative Secretary, 740-593-1090, Fax: 740-593-0579, E-mail: psychology@ohio.edu.

Old Dominion University, College of Sciences, Doctoral Program in Psychology, Norfolk, VA 23529. Offers applied experimental psychology (PhD); human factors psychology (PhD); industrial/organizational psychology (PhD). *Faculty:* 21 full-time (9 women). *Students:* 32 full-time (21 women), 12 part-time (8 women); includes 2 minority (1 Black or African American, non-Hispanic/Latino; 1 Hispanic/Latino), 4 international. Average age 29. 59 applicants, 24% accepted, 12 enrolled. In 2010, 1 doctorate awarded. *Degree requirements:* For doctorate, thesis/dissertation, candidacy exam. *Entrance requirements:* For doctorate, GRE General Test, GRE Subject Test, 3 recommendation letters. Additional exam requirements/recommendations for international students: Required—TOEFL (minimum score 550 paper-based). *Application deadline:* For winter admission, 1/5 for domestic and international students. Application fee: $50. Electronic applications accepted. *Expenses:* Tuition, state resident: full-time $8592; part-time $358 per credit. Tuition, nonresident: full-time $21,672; part-time $903 per credit. Required fees: $119 per semester. One-time fee: $50. *Financial support:* In 2010–11, 33 students received support, including 4 fellowships with full tuition reimbursements available (averaging $18,000 per year), 4 research assistantships with full tuition reimbursements available (averaging $12,000 per year), 25 teaching assistantships with full tuition reimbursements available (averaging $12,000 per year). Financial award application deadline: 1/15. *Faculty research:* Human factors, industrial psychology, organizational psychology, applied experimental (health, developmental, quantitative). Total annual research expenditures: $978,563. *Unit head:* Dr. Bryan E. Porter, Graduate Program Director, 757-683-4458, Fax: 757-683-5087, E-mail: bporter@odu.edu. *Application contact:* Dr. Bryan E. Porter, Graduate Program Director, 757-683-4458, Fax: 757-683-5087, E-mail: bporter@odu.edu.

Radford University, College of Graduate and Professional Studies, College of Humanities and Behavioral Sciences, Program in Psychology, Radford, VA 24142. Offers clinical psychology (MA, MS); experimental psychology (MA, MS); general psychology (MS); industrial/organizational psychology (MA, MS). Part-time programs available. *Faculty:* 18 full-time (7 women), 4 part-time/adjunct (2 women). *Students:* 41 full-time (29 women); includes 6 minority (4 Black or African American, non-Hispanic/Latino; 1 Asian, non-Hispanic/Latino; 1 Hispanic/Latino). Average

age 23. 107 applicants, 71% accepted, 23 enrolled. In 2010, 21 master's awarded. *Degree requirements:* For master's, comprehensive exam, thesis (for some programs). *Entrance requirements:* For master's, GRE, minimum GPA of 3.0; 3 letters of reference; essay. Additional exam requirements/recommendations for international students: Required—TOEFL (minimum score 550 paper-based; 213 computer-based; 79 iBT). *Application deadline:* For fall admission, 2/15 priority date for domestic students, 12/1 for international students; for spring admission, 7/1 for international students. Applications are processed on a rolling basis. Application fee: $50. Electronic applications accepted. *Expenses:* Tuition, state resident: full-time $5746; part-time $239 per credit hour. Tuition, nonresident: full-time $14,174; part-time $591 per credit hour. Required fees: $2634; $111 per credit hour. *Financial support:* In 2010–11, 33 students received support, including 18 research assistantships with partial tuition reimbursements available (averaging $8,000 per year), 14 teaching assistantships with partial tuition reimbursements available (averaging $8,700 per year); career-related internships or fieldwork, institutionally sponsored loans, scholarships/grants, and unspecified assistantships also available. Financial award application deadline: 3/1; financial award applicants required to submit FAFSA. *Unit head:* Dr. Hilary M. Lips, Chair, 540-831-5387, Fax: 540-831-6113, E-mail: hlips@radford.edu. *Application contact:* Rebecca Conner, Graduate Admissions Office, 540-831-5431, Fax: 540-831-6061, E-mail: gradcollege@radford.edu.

Rivier College, School of Graduate Studies, Department of Psychology, Nashua, NH 03060. Offers clinical psychology (MS); experimental psychology (MS). *Faculty:* 5 full-time (2 women). *Students:* 10 full-time (7 women). Average age 28. 9 applicants, 11% accepted, 1 enrolled. In 2010, 4 master's awarded. Application fee: $25. *Expenses:* Tuition: Part-time $456 per credit. *Unit head:* Dr. Howard Goodman, Department Coordinator, 603-897-8602, E-mail: hgoodman@rivier.edu. *Application contact:* Mathew Kittredge, Director of Graduate Admissions, 603-897-8229, Fax: 603-897-8810, E-mail: mkittredge@rivier.edu.

St. John's University, St. John's College of Liberal Arts and Sciences, Department of Psychology, Program in General Experimental Psychology, Queens, NY 11439. Offers MA. Part-time and evening/weekend programs available. *Students:* 17 full-time (13 women), 6 part-time (5 women); includes 8 minority (3 Black or African American, non-Hispanic/Latino; 2 Asian, non-Hispanic/Latino; 2 Hispanic/Latino; 1 Two or more races, non-Hispanic/Latino), 2 international. Average age 26. 41 applicants, 54% accepted, 8 enrolled. In 2010, 12 master's awarded. *Degree requirements:* For master's, comprehensive exam, thesis optional. *Entrance requirements:* For master's, minimum GPA of 3.0, 2 writing samples. Additional exam requirements/recommendations for international students: Required—TOEFL (minimum score 600 paper-based; 250 computer-based; 100 iBT), IELTS (minimum score 5.5). *Application deadline:* For fall admission, 5/1 priority date for domestic and international students; for spring admission, 11/1 priority date for domestic and international students. Applications are processed on a rolling basis. Application fee: $70. Electronic applications accepted. *Expenses:* Tuition: Full-time $17,100; part-time $950 per credit. Required fees: $340; $170 per semester. Tuition and fees vary according to program. *Financial support:* Research assistantships, career-related internships or fieldwork, scholarships/grants, and unspecified assistantships available. Support available to part-time students. Financial award application deadline: 3/1; financial award applicants required to submit FAFSA. *Faculty research:* Learning and memory neuropsychology, perception, social psychology, developmental psychology. *Unit head:* Dr. Leonard Brosgole, Coordinator, 718-990-1552, E-mail: brosgoll@stjohns.edu. *Application contact:* Kathleen Davis, Director of Graduate Admission, 718-990-1601, Fax: 718-990-5686, E-mail: gradhelp@stjohns.edu.

Saint Louis University, Graduate Education, College of Arts and Sciences and Graduate Education, Department of Psychology, St. Louis, MO 63103-2097. Offers clinical psychology (MS-R, PhD); experimental psychology (MS-R, PhD); industrial-organizational psychology (PhD); psychology (PhD). *Accreditation:* APA (one or more programs are accredited). Part-time programs available. *Degree requirements:* For master's, comprehensive exam, thesis; for doctorate, thesis/dissertation, clinical internship (for clinical psychology PhD). *Entrance requirements:* For master's, GRE General Test, interview, letters of recommendation, resume; for doctorate, GRE General Test, interview, letters of recommendation, resumé, transcripts, goal statement. Additional exam requirements/recommendations for international students: Required—TOEFL (minimum score 550 paper-based; 213 computer-based). Electronic applications accepted. *Faculty research:* Violence and trauma; neural basis of learning and memory function; eating disorders; body image and health behavior; prejudice, stereotyping, and victimization; memory, cognitive aging and language processing.

San Jose State University, Graduate Studies and Research, College of Social Sciences, Department of Psychology, San Jose, CA 95192-0001. Offers clinical psychology (MS); experimental psychology (MA); industrial/organizational psychology (MS); psychology (MA). *Degree requirements:* For master's, comprehensive exam, thesis (for some programs). *Entrance requirements:* For master's, GRE General Test, minimum GPA of 3.0. Electronic applications accepted. *Faculty research:* Drug and alcohol abuse, neurohormonal mechanisms in motion sickness, behavior modification, sleep research, genetics.

Seton Hall University, College of Arts and Sciences, Department of Psychology, South Orange, NJ 07079-2697. Offers experimental psychology (MS), including behavioral neuroscience. Part-time and evening/weekend programs available. *Entrance requirements:* For master's, GRE. Additional exam requirements/recommendations for international students: Required—TOEFL. Electronic applications accepted. *Faculty research:* Behavioral neuroscience, cognitive psychology, social psychology, perception/motor skills, memory, depression, anxiety.

Southern Illinois University Carbondale, Graduate School, College of Liberal Arts, Department of Psychology, Carbondale, IL 62901-4701. Offers clinical psychology (MA, MS, PhD); counseling psychology (MA, MS, PhD); experimental psychology (MA, MS, PhD). *Accreditation:* APA (one or more programs are accredited). *Degree requirements:* For master's, thesis; for doctorate, thesis/dissertation. *Entrance requirements:* For master's, GRE General Test, GRE Subject Test, minimum GPA of 2.7; for doctorate, GRE General Test, GRE Subject Test, minimum GPA of 3.25. Additional exam requirements/recommendations for international students: Required—TOEFL. *Faculty research:* Developmental neuropsychology; smoking, affect, and cognition; personality measurement; vocational psychology; program evaluation.

Stony Brook University, State University of New York, Graduate School, College of Arts and Sciences, Department of Psychology, Program in Cognitive/Experimental Psychology, Stony Brook, NY 11794. Offers PhD. *Students:* 20 full-time (7 women); includes 1 Hispanic/Latino, 3 international. Average age 28. 53 applicants, 23% accepted, 5 enrolled. In 2010, 3 doctorates awarded. *Degree requirements:* For doctorate, thesis/dissertation. *Entrance requirements:* For doctorate, GRE General Test, GRE Subject Test. Additional exam requirements/recommendations for international students: Required—TOEFL. *Application deadline:* For fall admission, 1/15 for domestic students. Application fee: $100. *Expenses:* Tuition, state resident: full-time $8370; part-time $349 per credit. Tuition, nonresident: full-time $13,780; part-time $574 per credit. Required fees: $994. *Unit head:* Dr. Gregory Zelinsky, Area Head, 631-632-7855, E-mail: gregory.zelinsky@stonybrook.edu. *Application contact:* Graduate Director, 631-632-7855, Fax: 631-632-7876.

Syracuse University, College of Arts and Sciences, Program in Experimental Psychology, Syracuse, NY 13244. Offers PhD. Part-time programs available. *Students:* 9 full-time (7 women); includes 1 minority (Asian, non-Hispanic/Latino), 2 international. Average age 29. 20 applicants, 0% accepted, 0 enrolled. In 2010, 1 doctorate awarded. *Degree requirements:* For doctorate, thesis/dissertation. *Entrance requirements:* For doctorate, GRE General Test. Additional exam requirements/recommendations for international students: Required—TOEFL (minimum score 100 iBT). *Application deadline:* For fall admission, 1/10 priority date for domestic and international students. Application fee: $75. Electronic applications accepted. *Expenses:* Tuition: Part-time $1162 per credit. *Financial support:* Fellowships with full tuition reimbursements, research assistantships with full tuition reimbursements, teaching assistantships with full tuition reimbursements available. Financial award application deadline: 1/1. *Unit*

head: Dr. William Hoyer, Graduate Director, 315-443-3663, E-mail: wjhoyer@syr.edu. *Application contact:* Sue Bova, Information Contact, 315-443-1050, E-mail: skbova@syr.edu.

Texas Christian University, College of Science and Engineering, Department of Psychology, Fort Worth, TX 76129-0002. Offers experimental psychology (PhD), including cognitive psychology, learning, neuropsychology, social psychology; psychology (MA, MS). In 2010, 7 master's, 3 doctorates awarded. Terminal master's awarded for partial completion of doctoral program. *Degree requirements:* For master's, thesis; for doctorate, thesis/dissertation. *Entrance requirements:* For master's and doctorate, GRE General Test. Additional exam requirements/recommendations for international students: Required—TOEFL. *Application deadline:* For fall admission, 3/1 for domestic and international students; for spring admission, 12/1 for domestic students. Applications are processed on a rolling basis. Application fee: $50. Electronic applications accepted. *Expenses:* Tuition: full-time $18,720; part-time $1040 per credit hour. Tuition and fees vary according to course load and program. *Financial support:* In 2010–11, 20 students received support; teaching assistantships with full tuition reimbursements available, unspecified assistantships available. Financial award application deadline: 3/1. *Unit head:* Dr. Charles Lord, Coordinator of Graduate Studies, 817-257-7410, Fax: 817-257-7681, E-mail: c.lord@tcu.edu. *Application contact:* Tami Joyce, Department Manager, 817-257-7410, Fax: 817-257-7681, E-mail: t.joyce@tcu.edu.

Texas Tech University, Graduate School, College of Arts and Sciences, Department of Psychology, Lubbock, TX 79409-2051. Offers clinical psychology (PhD); counseling psychology (MA, PhD); experimental psychology (MA, PhD); psychology (MA, PhD). *Accreditation:* APA (one or more programs are accredited). Part-time programs available. *Faculty:* 25 full-time (11 women). *Students:* 91 full-time (57 women), 18 part-time (17 women); includes 2 Black or African American, non-Hispanic/Latino; 1 American Indian or Alaska Native, non-Hispanic/Latino; 1 Asian, non-Hispanic/Latino; 9 Hispanic/Latino; 1 Two or more races, non-Hispanic/Latino, 7 international. Average age 27. 276 applicants, 11% accepted, 19 enrolled. In 2010, 18 master's, 13 doctorates awarded. *Degree requirements:* For doctorate, comprehensive exam, thesis/dissertation, 100 credit hours of organized courses, research credits, and practica. *Entrance requirements:* For master's and doctorate, GRE General Test, GRE Subject Test, departmental application form, essays. Additional exam requirements/recommendations for international students: Required—TOEFL (minimum score 550 paper-based; 213 computer-based; 79 iBT). *Application deadline:* For fall admission, 6/1 priority date for domestic students, 1/15 priority date for international students; for spring admission, 9/1 priority date for domestic students, 6/15 priority date for international students. Applications are processed on a rolling basis. Application fee: $50 ($75 for international students). Electronic applications accepted. *Expenses:* Tuition, state resident: full-time $5495.76; part-time $228.99 per credit hour. Tuition, nonresident: full-time $12,936; part-time $538.99 per credit hour. Required fees: $2674; $36 per credit hour. $905 per semester. *Financial support:* In 2010–11, 85 students received support, including 13 research assistantships with partial tuition reimbursements available (averaging $5,707 per year), 32 teaching assistantships with partial tuition reimbursements available (averaging $5,672 per year). Financial award application deadline: 4/15; financial award applicants required to submit FAFSA. *Faculty research:* Failure/success in relationships, peer rejection in school, stress and coping, group processes, clinical and health psychology. Total annual research expenditures: $202,278. *Unit head:* Dr. Lee M. Cohen, Chair, 806-742-3711 Ext. 222, Fax: 806-742-0818, E-mail: lee.cohen@ttu.edu. *Application contact:* Kay Hill, Admissions Coordinator, 806-742-3711 Ext. 222, Fax: 806-742-0818, E-mail: kay.hill@ttu.edu.

University at Albany, State University of New York, College of Arts and Sciences, Department of Psychology, Albany, NY 12222-0001. Offers autism (Certificate); biopsychology (PhD); clinical psychology (PhD); general/experimental psychology (PhD); industrial/organizational psychology (PhD); psychology (MA); social/personality psychology (PhD). *Accreditation:* APA (one or more programs are accredited). *Degree requirements:* For doctorate, thesis/dissertation. *Entrance requirements:* For doctorate, GRE General Test, GRE Subject Test. Additional exam requirements/recommendations for international students: Required—TOEFL (minimum score 550 paper-based; 213 computer-based). Electronic applications accepted.

The University of Alabama, Graduate School, College of Arts and Sciences, Department of Psychology, Tuscaloosa, AL 35487. Offers clinical psychology (PhD); experimental psychology (PhD). *Accreditation:* APA. *Faculty:* 22 full-time (10 women), 2 part-time/adjunct (both women). *Students:* 75 full-time (57 women), 23 part-time (16 women); includes 17 minority (8 Black or African American, non-Hispanic/Latino; 5 Asian, non-Hispanic/Latino; 4 Hispanic/Latino), 6 international. Average age 28. 261 applicants, 15% accepted, 23 enrolled. In 2010, 15 doctorates awarded. *Degree requirements:* For doctorate, thesis/dissertation, internship (for clinical psychology). *Entrance requirements:* For doctorate, GRE. Additional exam requirements/recommendations for international students: Required—TOEFL (minimum score 550 paper-based). *Application deadline:* For fall admission, 12/1 for domestic and international students. Application fee: $50 ($60 for international students). Electronic applications accepted. *Expenses:* Tuition, state resident: full-time $7900. Tuition, nonresident: full-time $20,500. *Financial support:* In 2010–11, 73 students received support, including 12 fellowships with full tuition reimbursements available (averaging $15,000 per year), 34 research assistantships with full and partial tuition reimbursements available (averaging $11,142 per year), 26 teaching assistantships with tuition reimbursements available (averaging $11,142 per year); career-related internships or fieldwork, institutionally sponsored loans, scholarships/grants, health care benefits, and unspecified assistantships also available. Financial award application deadline: 12/1. *Faculty research:* Cognitive development/disability, child clinical, psychology and law, health/aging, social psychology. Total annual research expenditures: $2 million. *Unit head:* Dr. Beverly E. Thorn, Chair, 205-348-1919, Fax: 205-348-8648, E-mail: bthorn@bama.ua.edu. *Application contact:* Colett Thomas, Information Contact, 205-348-1913, Fax: 205-348-8648, E-mail: cthomas@as.ua.edu.

The University of Alabama in Huntsville, School of Graduate Studies, College of Liberal Arts, Department of Psychology, Huntsville, AL 35899. Offers experimental psychology (MA); industrial and organizational psychology (MA). Part-time and evening/weekend programs available. *Faculty:* 7 full-time (4 women). *Students:* 6 full-time (3 women), 4 part-time (3 women). Average age 24. 9 applicants, 56% accepted, 3 enrolled. In 2010, 6 master's awarded. *Degree requirements:* For master's, comprehensive exam, thesis or alternative, oral and written exams. *Entrance requirements:* For master's, GRE General Test, 15 hours of course work in psychology, minimum GPA of 3.25, sample of written work. Additional exam requirements/recommendations for international students: Required—TOEFL (minimum score 500 paper-based; 173 computer-based; 62 iBT). *Application deadline:* For fall admission, 7/15 for domestic students, 4/1 for international students; for spring admission, 11/30 for domestic students, 9/1 for international students. Applications are processed on a rolling basis. Application fee: $40 ($50 for international students). Electronic applications accepted. *Expenses:* Tuition, state resident: full-time $7250; part-time $407.75 per credit hour. Tuition, nonresident: full-time $17,358; part-time $970.05 per credit hour. Required fees: $246.80 per semester. Tuition and fees vary according to course load and program. *Financial support:* In 2010–11, 8 students received support, including 2 teaching assistantships with full tuition reimbursements available (averaging $8,460 per year); career-related internships or fieldwork, Federal Work-Study, institutionally sponsored loans, scholarships/grants, health care benefits, tuition waivers (full), and unspecified assistantships also available. Support available to part-time students. Financial award application deadline: 4/1; financial award applicants required to submit FAFSA. *Faculty research:* Personal and social cognition, development and aging, human factors, perception, biological psychology: hormones and behavior. Total annual research expenditures: $228,509. *Unit head:* Dr. Jeffrey Neuschatz, Assistant Chair, 256-824-2321, Fax: 256-824-2387, E-mail: neuschaj@uah.edu. *Application contact:* Kathy Biggs, Graduate Studies Admissions Manager, 256-824-6199, Fax: 256-824-6405, E-mail: deangrad@uah.edu.

University of Central Florida, College of Sciences, Department of Psychology, Program in Applied Experimental and Human Factors Psychology, Orlando, FL 32816. Offers MA, PhD. *Students:* 41 full-time (18 women), 6 part-time (4 women); includes 1 Black or African American,

Experimental Psychology

University of Central Florida (continued)
non-Hispanic/Latino; 3 Asian, non-Hispanic/Latino; 3 Hispanic/Latino, 2 international. Average age 30. 45 applicants, 31% accepted, 9 enrolled. In 2010, 2 master's, 6 doctorates awarded. *Degree requirements:* For doctorate, thesis/dissertation, departmental candidacy exam. *Entrance requirements:* For doctorate, GRE General Test, minimum GPA of 3.2 in last 60 hours or master's qualifying exam. Additional exam requirements/recommendations for international students: Required—TOEFL. *Application deadline:* For fall admission, 2/1 for domestic students. Application fee: $30. Electronic applications accepted. *Expenses:* Tuition, state resident: part-time $256.56 per credit hour. Tuition, nonresident: part-time $1011.52 per credit hour. Part-time tuition and fees vary according to program. *Financial support:* In 2010–11, 36 students received support, including 6 fellowships (averaging $3,300 per year), 31 research assistantships with partial tuition reimbursements available (averaging $9,400 per year), 23 teaching assistantships with partial tuition reimbursements available (averaging $8,200 per year); career-related internships or fieldwork, Federal Work-Study, institutionally sponsored loans, tuition waivers (partial), and unspecified assistantships also available. Financial award application deadline: 3/1; financial award applicants required to submit FAFSA. *Faculty research:* Visual performance, team training, controls/displays, synthetic speech, alarms/warning. *Unit head:* Dr. Eduardo Salas, Program Director, 407-882-1325, Fax: 407-882-1550, E-mail: esalas@ist.ucf.edu. *Application contact:* Dr. Eduardo Salas, Program Director, 407-882-1325, Fax: 407-882-1550, E-mail: esalas@ist.ucf.edu.

University of Cincinnati, Graduate School, McMicken College of Arts and Sciences, Department of Psychology, Cincinnati, OH 45221. Offers clinical psychology (PhD); experimental psychology (PhD). *Accreditation:* APA. *Degree requirements:* For doctorate, comprehensive exam, thesis/dissertation. *Entrance requirements:* For doctorate, GRE General Test. Additional exam requirements/recommendations for international students: Required—TOEFL. *Faculty research:* Neuropsychology, human factors, health.

University of Connecticut, Graduate School, College of Liberal Arts and Sciences, Department of Psychology, Storrs, CT 06269. Offers behavioral neuroscience (PhD); biopsychology (PhD); clinical psychology (MA, PhD); cognition and instruction (PhD); developmental psychology (MA, PhD); ecological psychology (PhD); experimental psychology (PhD); general psychology (MA, PhD); health psychology (Graduate Certificate); industrial/organizational psychology (PhD); language and cognition (PhD); neuroscience (PhD); occupational health psychology (Graduate Certificate); social psychology (MA, PhD). *Accreditation:* APA. Terminal master's awarded for partial completion of doctoral program. *Degree requirements:* For master's, comprehensive exam; for doctorate, thesis/dissertation. *Entrance requirements:* For master's and doctorate, GRE General Test, GRE Subject Test. Additional exam requirements/recommendations for international students: Required—TOEFL (minimum score 550 paper-based; 213 computer-based). Electronic applications accepted.

University of Hartford, College of Arts and Sciences, Department of Psychology, Program in General Experimental Psychology, West Hartford, CT 06117-1599. Offers MA. Part-time programs available. *Degree requirements:* For master's, comprehensive exam, thesis or alternative. *Entrance requirements:* For master's, GRE General Test, GRE Subject Test, minimum GPA of 3.0, 3 letters of recommendation. Additional exam requirements/recommendations for international students: Required—TOEFL (minimum score 550 paper-based; 213 computer-based). Electronic applications accepted. *Faculty research:* Decision making, social judgment and stereotyping, stress and health.

University of Kentucky, Graduate School, College of Arts and Sciences, Program in Psychology, Lexington, KY 40506-0032. Offers clinical psychology (MA); experimental psychology (MA). *Accreditation:* APA (one or more programs are accredited). *Degree requirements:* For master's, comprehensive exam, thesis; for doctorate, comprehensive exam, thesis/dissertation. *Entrance requirements:* For master's, GRE General Test, minimum undergraduate GPA of 2.75; for doctorate, GRE General Test, minimum graduate GPA of 3.0. Additional exam requirements/recommendations for international students: Required—TOEFL (minimum score 550 paper-based; 213 computer-based). Electronic applications accepted. *Faculty research:* Psychopharmacology and teratology, behavioral neuroscience, social psychology, cognitive psychology, development and developmental psychobiology.

University of Louisiana at Monroe, Graduate School, College of Education and Human Development, Department of Psychology, Program in General Psychology, Monroe, LA 71209-0001. Offers MS. Part-time and evening/weekend programs available. *Faculty:* 7 full-time (1 woman). *Students:* 15 full-time (9 women), 9 part-time (6 women); includes 5 Black or African American, non-Hispanic/Latino; 1 Asian, non-Hispanic/Latino; 1 Hispanic/Latino. Average age 29. In 2010, 4 master's awarded. *Degree requirements:* For master's, comprehensive exam, thesis. *Entrance requirements:* For master's, minimum GPA of 2.5 or GRE General Test. Additional exam requirements/recommendations for international students: Required—TOEFL (minimum score 500 paper-based; 173 computer-based; 61 iBT). *Application deadline:* For fall admission, 8/24 priority date for domestic students, 7/1 for international students; for winter admission, 12/14 priority date for domestic students; for spring admission, 1/19 for domestic students, 11/1 for international students. Applications are processed on a rolling basis. Application fee: $20 ($30 for international students). Electronic applications accepted. *Expenses:* Tuition, state resident: full-time $2991; part-time $197 per credit hour. Tuition, nonresident: full-time $2991; part-time $197 per credit hour. International tuition: $10,288 full-time. *Financial support:* In 2010–11, 12 research assistantships (averaging $2,500 per year) were awarded; career-related internships or fieldwork, Federal Work-Study, and unspecified assistantships also available. Financial award application deadline: 4/1; financial award applicants required to submit FAFSA. *Unit head:* Dr. Joe McGahan, Coordinator, 818-342-1338, Fax: 318-342-1352, E-mail: mcgahan@ulm.edu. *Application contact:* Dr. Joe McGahan, Coordinator, 818-342-1338, Fax: 318-342-1352, E-mail: mcgahan@ulm.edu.

University of Louisville, Graduate School, College of Arts and Sciences, Department of Psychological and Brain Sciences, Louisville, KY 40292-0001. Offers clinical psychology (PhD); experimental psychology (PhD). *Accreditation:* APA. *Faculty:* 22 full-time (9 women), 4 part-time/adjunct (1 woman). *Students:* 66 full-time (43 women), 1 part-time (0 women); includes 2 Black or African American, non-Hispanic/Latino; 3 Asian, non-Hispanic/Latino; 1 Hispanic/Latino, 9 international. Average age 30. 142 applicants, 3% accepted, 4 enrolled. In 2010, 4 doctorates awarded. *Degree requirements:* For doctorate, thesis/dissertation, preliminary exam, research, internship. *Entrance requirements:* For doctorate, GRE General Test. Additional exam requirements/recommendations for international students: Required—TOEFL. *Application deadline:* For fall admission, 12/1 for domestic and international students. Application fee: $50. Electronic applications accepted. *Expenses:* Tuition, state resident: full-time $9144; part-time $508 per credit hour. Tuition, nonresident: full-time $19,026; part-time $1057 per credit hour. Tuition and fees vary according to program and reciprocity agreements. *Financial support:* In 2010–11, 39 students received support, including 12 fellowships (averaging $22,000 per year), 27 teaching assistantships (averaging $22,000 per year); career-related internships or fieldwork also available. *Faculty research:* Health psychology, geropsychology, psychopathology, cognitive and development sciences, vision and hearing sciences. *Unit head:* Dr. Suzanne Meeks, Chair, 502-852-6068, Fax: 502-852-8904, E-mail: smeeks@louisville.edu. *Application contact:* Mary E. Leggett, Director, Graduate Admissions, 502-852-3101, Fax: 502-852-6536, E-mail: gradadm@louisville.edu.

University of Maine, Graduate School, College of Liberal Arts and Sciences, Department of Psychology, Orono, ME 04469. Offers clinical (PhD); developmental (MA, PhD); experimental (MA); psychological sciences (MA, PhD). *Accreditation:* APA (one or more programs are accredited). *Faculty:* 14 full-time (6 women), 3 part-time/adjunct (2 women). *Students:* 27 full-time (17 women), 10 part-time (6 women); includes 2 minority (1 Asian, non-Hispanic/Latino; 1 Hispanic/Latino), 2 international. Average age 28. 147 applicants, 5% accepted, 7 enrolled. In 2010, 5 master's, 4 doctorates awarded. *Degree requirements:* For master's, thesis; for doctorate, thesis/dissertation. *Entrance requirements:* For master's and doctorate, GRE General Test, GRE Subject Test. Additional exam requirements/recommendations for international students: Required—TOEFL. *Application deadline:* For fall admission, 2/1 priority date for domestic students. Applications are processed on a rolling basis. Application fee: $65. Electronic applications accepted. *Expenses:* Tuition, state resident: full-time $400. Tuition, nonresident: full-time $1050. *Financial support:* In 2010–11, 3 research assistantships with tuition reimbursements (averaging $14,063 per year), 21 teaching assistantships with tuition reimbursements (averaging $12,790 per year) were awarded; Federal Work-Study, institutionally sponsored loans, and tuition waivers (full and partial) also available. Financial award application deadline: 3/1. *Faculty research:* Social development, hypertension and aging, attitude change, self-confidence in achievement situations, health psychology. *Unit head:* Dr. Michael Robbins, Chair, 207-581-2051, Fax: 207-581-6128. *Application contact:* Scott G. Delcourt, Associate Dean of the Graduate School, 207-581-3291, Fax: 207-581-3232, E-mail: graduate@maine.edu.

University of Maryland, College Park, Academic Affairs, College of Behavioral and Social Sciences, Department of Psychology, College Park, MD 20742. Offers clinical psychology (PhD); developmental psychology (PhD); experimental psychology (PhD); industrial psychology (MA, MS, PhD); social psychology (PhD). *Accreditation:* APA (one or more programs are accredited). *Faculty:* 70 full-time (34 women), 16 part-time/adjunct (10 women). *Students:* 83 full-time (63 women), 6 part-time (4 women); includes 4 Black or African American, non-Hispanic/Latino; 6 Asian, non-Hispanic/Latino; 6 Hispanic/Latino, 13 international. 653 applicants, 4% accepted, 13 enrolled. In 2010, 8 master's, 18 doctorates awarded. *Degree requirements:* For master's, thesis; for doctorate, variable foreign language requirement, comprehensive exam, thesis/dissertation. *Entrance requirements:* For master's and doctorate, GRE General Test, GRE Subject Test, minimum GPA of 3.5, research and/or work experience, 3 letters of recommendation. *Application deadline:* For fall admission, 12/1 for domestic and international students. Applications are processed on a rolling basis. Application fee: $75. Electronic applications accepted. *Expenses:* Tuition, state resident: part-time $471 per credit hour. Tuition, nonresident: part-time $1016 per credit hour. Required fees: $337 per term. *Financial support:* In 2010–11, 14 fellowships with full and partial tuition reimbursements (averaging $20,179 per year), 5 research assistantships (averaging $18,414 per year), 54 teaching assistantships (averaging $17,209 per year) were awarded; career-related internships or fieldwork, Federal Work-Study, and scholarships/grants also available. Support available to part-time students. Financial award applicants required to submit FAFSA. *Faculty research:* Social stereotyping and prejudice, anxiety disorders, auditory neuroethology, counseling and social psychology. Total annual research expenditures: $4 million. *Unit head:* Thomas S. Wallsten, Chair, 301-405-3562, Fax: 301-314-9566, E-mail: twallst@umd.edu. *Application contact:* Dean of Graduate School, 301-405-0358, Fax: 301-314-9305.

University of Memphis, Graduate School, College of Arts and Sciences, Department of Psychology, Memphis, TN 38152-3230. Offers psychology (MS, PhD), including clinical (PhD), experimental (PhD), general psychology (MS), school (PhD); school psychology (MA, Ed S); MS/PhD. *Faculty:* 28 full-time (9 women), 4 part-time/adjunct (0 women). *Students:* 114 full-time (81 women), 21 part-time (15 women); includes 14 Black or African American, non-Hispanic/Latino; 1 American Indian or Alaska Native, non-Hispanic/Latino; 4 Asian, non-Hispanic/Latino; 3 Hispanic/Latino; 4 Two or more races, non-Hispanic/Latino, 7 international. Average age 27. 220 applicants, 15% accepted, 29 enrolled. In 2010, 31 master's, 9 doctorates awarded. *Degree requirements:* For master's, comprehensive exam (for some programs), thesis (for some programs), 37 credit hours (MA); 33 credit hours with thesis or 36 with exam (MS); for doctorate, comprehensive exam (for some programs), thesis/dissertation, 80 semester hours, major area paper; clinical: 1 year placement and 1 year internship; internship (school psychology). *Entrance requirements:* For master's, GRE; for doctorate, GRE (minimum combined score of 1100), minimum GPA of 2.75, 18 hours of undergraduate psychology courses, transcripts, personal statement, letters of recommendation; for Ed S, GRE (minimum combined score of 1100), minimum GPA of 2.75, 18 hours of undergraduate psychology courses, letters of recommendation. Additional exam requirements/recommendations for international students: Required—TOEFL (minimum score 550 paper-based; 210 computer-based; 79 iBT). *Application deadline:* For fall admission, 12/5 for domestic students. Applications are processed on a rolling basis. Application fee: $35 ($60 for international students). Electronic applications accepted. *Financial support:* In 2010–11, 66 students received support; fellowships with full tuition reimbursements available, research assistantships with full tuition reimbursements available, teaching assistantships with full tuition reimbursements available, Federal Work-Study, scholarships/grants, tuition waivers (partial), and unspecified assistantships available. Financial award application deadline: 2/15; financial award applicants required to submit FAFSA. *Faculty research:* Clinical health; school, child and family psychology; psychotherapy; cognitive and behavioral neuroscience; industrial-organizational psychology. *Unit head:* Dr. Robert Cohen, Coordinator of Graduate Programs, 901-678-4679, Fax: 901-678-2579, E-mail: rcohen@memphis.edu. *Application contact:* Lynell Connable, Graduate Secretary, 901-678-4340, Fax: 901-678-2579, E-mail: dconnabl@memphis.edu.

University of Michigan, Horace H. Rackham School of Graduate Studies, College of Literature, Science, and the Arts, Department of Psychology, Ann Arbor, MI 48109. Offers biopsychology (PhD); clinical psychology (PhD); cognition and perception (PhD); developmental psychology (PhD); personality and social contexts (PhD); social psychology (PhD). *Accreditation:* APA. *Faculty:* 83 full-time (39 women), 30 part-time/adjunct (14 women). *Students:* 132 full-time (92 women); includes 13 Black or African American, non-Hispanic/Latino; 2 American Indian or Alaska Native, non-Hispanic/Latino; 18 Asian, non-Hispanic/Latino; 7 Hispanic/Latino; 2 Two or more races, non-Hispanic/Latino, 20 international. Average age 27. 608 applicants, 6% accepted, 24 enrolled. In 2010, 28 doctorates awarded. *Degree requirements:* For doctorate, comprehensive exam, thesis/dissertation, oral defense of dissertation, preliminary exam. *Entrance requirements:* For doctorate, GRE General Test. Additional exam requirements/recommendations for international students: Required—TOEFL. *Application deadline:* For fall admission, 12/1 for domestic and international students. Application fee: $65 ($75 for international students). Electronic applications accepted. *Expenses:* Tuition, state resident: full-time $17,784; part-time $1116 per credit hour. Tuition, nonresident: full-time $35,944; part-time $2125 per credit hour. International tuition: $35,994 full-time. Required fees: $95 per semester. Tuition and fees vary according to course load, degree level and program. *Financial support:* In 2010–11, 118 students received support, including 55 fellowships with full tuition reimbursements available (averaging $20,900 per year), 15 research assistantships with full tuition reimbursements available (averaging $25,950 per year), 52 teaching assistantships with full tuition reimbursements available (averaging $22,670 per year); career-related internships or fieldwork also available. Financial award application deadline: 4/15. Total annual research expenditures: $7.4 million. *Unit head:* Prof. Theresa Lee, Chair, 734-764-7429. *Application contact:* Laurie Brannan, Psychology Student Academic Affairs, 731-764-2580, Fax: 734-615-7584, E-mail: psych.saa@umich.edu.

University of Mississippi, Graduate School, College of Liberal Arts, Department of Psychology, Oxford, University, MS 38677. Offers clinical psychology (PhD); experimental psychology (PhD); psychology (MA). *Accreditation:* APA (one or more programs are accredited). *Students:* 55 full-time (42 women), 6 part-time (4 women); includes 10 minority (8 Black or African American, non-Hispanic/Latino; 1 Asian, non-Hispanic/Latino; 1 Hispanic/Latino), 1 international. In 2010, 4 master's, 4 doctorates awarded. *Degree requirements:* For master's, thesis; for doctorate, thesis/dissertation. *Entrance requirements:* For master's, GRE General Test, minimum GPA of 3.0; for doctorate, GRE General Test. Additional exam requirements/recommendations for international students: Required—TOEFL. *Application deadline:* For fall admission, 1/15 for domestic students; for spring admission, 10/1 for domestic students. Applications are processed on a rolling basis. Application fee: $25. Electronic applications accepted. *Financial support:* Scholarships/grants available. Financial award application deadline: 3/1; financial award applicants required to submit FAFSA. *Unit head:* Dr. Michael T. Allen, Chairman, 662-915-5190, Fax: 662-915-5398, E-mail: psych@olemiss.edu. *Application contact:* Dr. Christy M. Wyandt, Associate Dean, 662-915-7474, Fax: 662-915-7577, E-mail: cwyandt@olemiss.edu.

The University of Montana, Graduate School, College of Arts and Sciences, Department of Psychology, Missoula, MT 59812-0002. Offers clinical psychology (PhD); experimental psychology (PhD), including animal behavior psychology, developmental psychology; school psychology (MA, PhD, Ed S). *Accreditation:* APA (one or more programs are accredited). Terminal master's awarded for partial completion of doctoral program. *Degree requirements:* For master's, thesis; for doctorate, thesis/dissertation. *Entrance requirements:* For master's, doctorate, and Ed S, GRE General Test. Additional exam requirements/recommendations for international students: Required—TOEFL.

University of New Brunswick Saint John, Department of Psychology, Saint John, NB E2L 4L5, Canada. Offers applied and experimental psychology (PhD); clinical psychology (PhD); experimental psychology (MA). Part-time programs available. *Faculty:* 9 full-time (4 women), 1 part-time/adjunct (0 women). *Students:* 4 full-time (1 woman). In 2010, 1 doctorate awarded. *Degree requirements:* For master's, thesis. *Entrance requirements:* For master's, GRE General and Subject Tests, honours thesis. Additional exam requirements/recommendations for international students: Required—TOEFL (minimum score 550 paper-based), TWE. *Application deadline:* For fall admission, 2/1 for domestic students. Application fee: $50. *Financial support:* In 2010–11, 2 research assistantships (averaging $9,000 per year), 7 teaching assistantships (averaging $4,500 per year) were awarded; fellowships, unspecified assistantships also available. Support available to part-time students. Financial award application deadline: 2/1. *Faculty research:* Psychopharmacology and addictions, forensic psychology and criminal justice, interpersonal relations, perception and graphical perception, lie detection, children's play and peer relationships, classical and operant conditioning. *Unit head:* Dr. Lily Both, Director of Graduate Studies, 506-648-5769, Fax: 506-648-5780, E-mail: lboth@unbsj.ca. *Application contact:* Frances Stevens, Secretary, 506-648-5640, Fax: 506-648-5780, E-mail: fstevens@unb.ca.

The University of North Carolina at Chapel Hill, Graduate School, College of Arts and Sciences, Department of Psychology, Chapel Hill, NC 27599. Offers biological psychology (PhD); clinical psychology (PhD); cognitive psychology (PhD); developmental psychology (PhD); quantitative psychology (PhD); social psychology (PhD). *Accreditation:* APA. *Degree requirements:* For doctorate, comprehensive exam, thesis/dissertation. *Entrance requirements:* For doctorate, GRE General Test, minimum GPA of 3.0. Electronic applications accepted. *Faculty research:* Expressed emotion, cognitive development, social cognitive neuroscience, human memory personality.

University of North Dakota, Graduate School, College of Arts and Sciences, Department of Psychology, Grand Forks, ND 58202. Offers clinical psychology (PhD); counseling psychology (PhD); experimental psychology (PhD); forensic psychology (MA, MS); psychology (MA). *Accreditation:* APA (one or more programs are accredited). *Faculty:* 22 full-time (7 women), 2 part-time/adjunct (1 woman). *Students:* 55 full-time (46 women), 81 part-time (69 women); includes 24 minority (4 Black or African American, non-Hispanic/Latino; 12 American Indian or Alaska Native, non-Hispanic/Latino; 2 Asian, non-Hispanic/Latino; 4 Hispanic/Latino; 2 Two or more races, non-Hispanic/Latino), 2 international. Average age 29. 126 applicants, 25% accepted, 27 enrolled. In 2010, 25 master's, 9 doctorates awarded. *Degree requirements:* For master's, thesis, final exam; for doctorate, comprehensive exam, thesis/dissertation, internship, final exam. *Entrance requirements:* For master's, GRE General Test, GRE Subject Test, minimum GPA of 3.0; for doctorate, GRE General Test, GRE Subject Test, minimum GPA of 3.5. Additional exam requirements/recommendations for international students: Required—TOEFL (minimum score 550 paper-based; 213 computer-based; 79 iBT), IELTS (minimum score 6.5). *Application deadline:* For fall admission, 1/15 for domestic and international students. Application fee: $35. Electronic applications accepted. *Expenses:* Tuition, state resident: full-time $5857; part-time $306.74 per credit. Tuition, nonresident: full-time $15,666; part-time $729.77 per credit. Required fees: $53.42 per credit. Tuition and fees vary according to course load, program and reciprocity agreements. *Financial support:* In 2010–11, 28 students received support, including 21 teaching assistantships with full and partial tuition reimbursements available (averaging $8,993 per year); fellowships with full and partial tuition reimbursements available, research assistantships with full and partial tuition reimbursements available, career-related internships or fieldwork, Federal Work-Study, institutionally sponsored loans, scholarships/grants, health care benefits, tuition waivers (full and partial), and unspecified assistantships also available. Support available to part-time students. Financial award application deadline: 3/15; financial award applicants required to submit FAFSA. *Faculty research:* Developmental psychology, clinical social psychology, educational psychology, personality disorders. Total annual research expenditures: $323,990. *Unit head:* Dr. Mark Grabe, Chairperson, 701-777-3451, E-mail: mark.grabe@und.nodak.edu. *Application contact:* Matt Anderson, Admissions Specialist, 701-777-2947, Fax: 701-777-3619, E-mail: matthew.anderson@gradschool.und.edu.

University of North Texas, Toulouse Graduate School, College of Arts and Sciences, Department of Psychology, Denton, TX 76203. Offers clinical psychology (PhD); counseling psychology (MA, MS, PhD); experimental psychology (MA, MS, PhD); health psychology and behavioral medicine (PhD). *Accreditation:* APA (one or more programs are accredited). Terminal master's awarded for partial completion of doctoral program. *Degree requirements:* For master's, comprehensive exam, thesis or alternative; for doctorate, one foreign language, comprehensive exam, thesis/dissertation. *Entrance requirements:* For master's and doctorate, GRE General Test, interview. Additional exam requirements/recommendations for international students: Recommended—TOEFL (minimum score 550 paper-based; 213 computer-based; 79 iBT). *Application deadline:* Applications are processed on a rolling basis. Electronic applications accepted. *Expenses:* Tuition, state resident: full-time $4298; part-time $239 per credit hour. Tuition, nonresident: full-time $10,782; part-time $549 per credit hour. Required fees: $1292; $270 per credit hour. *Financial support:* Fellowships, research assistantships, teaching assistantships, career-related internships or fieldwork, Federal Work-Study, and institutionally sponsored loans available. Financial award applicants required to submit FAFSA. *Application contact:* Graduate Coordinator, 940-565-2671, Fax: 940-565-4682, E-mail: amym@unt.edu.

University of Regina, Faculty of Graduate Studies and Research, Faculty of Arts, Department of Psychology, Regina, SK S4S 0A2, Canada. Offers clinical psychology (MA, PhD); experimental and applied psychology (MA, PhD). *Faculty:* 19 full-time (9 women). *Students:* 51 full-time (39 women), 3 part-time (2 women). 44 applicants, 41% accepted. In 2010, 12 master's, 4 doctorates awarded. *Degree requirements:* For master's, thesis; for doctorate, comprehensive exam, thesis/dissertation. *Entrance requirements:* For master's, GRE General Test, GRE Subject Test; for doctorate, GRE General Test, GRE Subject Test (optional for those with a master's degree from a Canadian university). Additional exam requirements/recommendations for international students: Required—TOEFL (minimum score 580 paper-based; 80 iBT). *Application deadline:* For fall admission, 2/15 for domestic and international students. Application fee: $100. Electronic applications accepted. Tuition and fees charges are reported in Canadian dollars. *Expenses:* Tuition, area resident: full-time $3244.50 Canadian dollars; part-time $180.25 Canadian dollars per credit hour. International tuition: $4744.50 Canadian dollars full-time. Required fees: $494 Canadian dollars; $115.25 Canadian dollars per credit hour. $115.25 Canadian dollars per semester. Tuition and fees vary according to program. *Financial support:* In 2010–11, 9 fellowships (averaging $20,333 per year), 3 research assistantships (averaging $16,500 per year), 21 teaching assistantships (averaging $6,884 per year) were awarded; career-related internships or fieldwork and scholarships/grants also available. Financial award application deadline: 6/15. *Faculty research:* Clinical, experimental, cognitive, and applied psychology; post-traumatic stress disorder, anxiety, and panic disorder; traumatic brain injury; chronic pain; perception and memory. *Unit head:* Dr. Richard MacLennan, Head, 306-585-4458, Fax: 306-585-5429, E-mail: richard.maclennan@uregina.ca. *Application contact:* Dr. Richard MacLennan, Graduate Program Coordinator, 306-585-4458, Fax: 306-585-5429, E-mail: richard.maclennan@uregina.ca.

University of South Carolina, The Graduate School, College of Arts and Sciences, Department of Psychology, Program in Experimental Psychology, Columbia, SC 29208. Offers MA, PhD. Terminal master's awarded for partial completion of doctoral program. *Degree requirements:* For master's, comprehensive exam, thesis; for doctorate, comprehensive exam, thesis/dissertation. *Entrance requirements:* For master's and doctorate, GRE General Test. Additional exam requirements/recommendations for international students: Required—TOEFL. Electronic applications accepted. *Faculty research:* Cognition, development, neuroscience.

University of Southern Mississippi, Graduate School, College of Education and Psychology, Department of Psychology, Hattiesburg, MS 39406-0001. Offers clinical psychology (MA, PhD); counseling psychology (MA, PhD); experimental psychology (MA, PhD); school psychology (MA, PhD). *Accreditation:* APA (one or more programs are accredited). *Faculty:* 32 full-time (9 women). *Students:* 98 full-time (75 women), 42 part-time (33 women); includes 8 Black or African American, non-Hispanic/Latino; 3 Asian, non-Hispanic/Latino; 5 Hispanic/Latino, 7 international. Average age 29. 219 applicants, 16% accepted, 31 enrolled. In 2010, 27 master's, 13 doctorates awarded. Terminal master's awarded for partial completion of doctoral program. *Degree requirements:* For master's, comprehensive exam, thesis; for doctorate, comprehensive exam, thesis, dissertation. *Entrance requirements:* For master's, GRE General Test, minimum GPA of 3.0; for doctorate, GRE General Test, interview, minimum GPA of 3.5. Additional exam requirements/recommendations for international students: Required—TOEFL, IELTS. *Application deadline:* For fall admission, 3/1 priority date for domestic students, 3/1 for international students. Applications are processed on a rolling basis. Application fee: $50. *Financial support:* In 2010–11, 48 research assistantships with full tuition reimbursements (averaging $8,802 per year), 48 teaching assistantships with full tuition reimbursements (averaging $6,500 per year) were awarded; career-related internships or fieldwork, Federal Work-Study, institutionally sponsored loans, scholarships/grants, health care benefits, and unspecified assistantships also available. Financial award application deadline: 3/15; financial award applicants required to submit FAFSA. *Faculty research:* Dolphin cognition, sleep, neuropsychology, health-related behaviors, psychopathology. Total annual research expenditures: $101,200. *Unit head:* Dr. Joesph Olmi, Chair, 601-266-4177, Fax: 601-266-5580. *Application contact:* Susan King, Graduate Secretary, 601-266-4177, Fax: 601-266-5580.

The University of Tennessee, Graduate School, College of Arts and Sciences, Department of Psychology, Knoxville, TN 37996. Offers clinical psychology (PhD); experimental psychology (MA, PhD); psychology (MA). *Accreditation:* APA (one or more programs are accredited). Terminal master's awarded for partial completion of doctoral program. *Degree requirements:* For master's, thesis; for doctorate, thesis/dissertation. *Entrance requirements:* For master's and doctorate, GRE General Test, GRE Subject Test, minimum GPA of 2.7. Additional exam requirements/recommendations for international students: Required—TOEFL. Electronic applications accepted. *Expenses:* Tuition, state resident: full-time $7440; part-time $414 per credit hour. Tuition, nonresident: full-time $22,478; part-time $1250 per credit hour. Required fees: $922; $43 per credit hour. Tuition and fees vary according to program.

The University of Tennessee at Chattanooga, Graduate School, College of Arts and Sciences, Department of Psychology, Chattanooga, TN 37403. Offers industrial/organizational psychology (MS); research psychology (MS). Part-time and evening/weekend programs available. *Faculty:* 6 full-time (1 woman). *Students:* 46 full-time (27 women), 6 part-time (3 women); includes 6 minority (3 Black or African American, non-Hispanic/Latino; 1 Asian, non-Hispanic/Latino; 1 Hispanic/Latino; 1 Two or more races, non-Hispanic/Latino), 1 international. Average age 25. 60 applicants, 70% accepted, 32 enrolled. In 2010, 24 master's awarded. *Degree requirements:* For master's, thesis (for some programs), practicum (industrial/organizational psychology). *Entrance requirements:* For master's, GRE General Test, minimum GPA of 2.5 on all undergraduate coursework or 3.0 in senior year. Additional exam requirements/recommendations for international students: Required—TOEFL (minimum score 550 paper-based; 213 computer-based; 79 iBT), IELTS (minimum score 6). *Application deadline:* For fall admission, 8/1 priority date for domestic students, 6/1 for international students; for spring admission, 12/1 priority date for domestic students, 10/1 for international students. Applications are processed on a rolling basis. Application fee: $35. Electronic applications accepted. *Financial support:* In 2010–11, 20 research assistantships with full and partial tuition reimbursements (averaging $5,500 per year) were awarded; career-related internships or fieldwork, scholarships/grants, and unspecified assistantships also available. Support available to part-time students. *Faculty research:* Decision processes, philosophical psychology, memory, social cognition, employee selection. Total annual research expenditures: $35,031. *Unit head:* Dr. Paul J. Watson, Department Head, 423-425-4262, Fax: 423-425-4284, E-mail: paul-watson@utc.edu. *Application contact:* Dr. Jerald Ainsworth, Dean of Graduate Studies, 423-425-4478, Fax: 423-425-5223, E-mail: jerald-ainsworth@utc.edu.

The University of Texas at Arlington, Graduate School, College of Science, Department of Psychology, Arlington, TX 76019. Offers experimental psychology (PhD); health psychology (PhD); industrial organizational psychology (MS); psychology (MS). Part-time programs available. *Faculty:* 21 full-time (8 women), 1 part-time/adjunct (0 women). *Students:* 62 full-time (41 women), 10 part-time (7 women); includes 5 Black or African American, non-Hispanic/Latino; 2 Asian, non-Hispanic/Latino; 6 Hispanic/Latino, 7 international. 72 applicants, 90% accepted, 22 enrolled. In 2010, 16 master's, 6 doctorates awarded. Terminal master's awarded for partial completion of doctoral program. *Degree requirements:* For master's, comprehensive exam or thesis; for doctorate, thesis/dissertation (for some programs). *Entrance requirements:* For master's and doctorate, GRE General Test, minimum GPA of 3.0 in last 60 hours of course work. Additional exam requirements/recommendations for international students: Required—TOEFL (minimum score 550 paper-based; 213 computer-based). *Application deadline:* For fall admission, 6/15 for domestic students. Applications are processed on a rolling basis. Application fee: $35 ($50 for international students). *Expenses:* Tuition, state resident: full-time $7500. Tuition, nonresident: full-time $13,080. International tuition: $13,250 full-time. *Financial support:* In 2010–11, 4 fellowships (averaging $1,000 per year), 2 research assistantships with tuition reimbursements (averaging $15,000 per year), 28 teaching assistantships with tuition reimbursements (averaging $15,000 per year) were awarded; career-related internships or fieldwork, Federal Work-Study, institutionally sponsored loans, scholarships/grants, traineeships, tuition waivers (partial), and unspecified assistantships also available. Financial award application deadline: 6/1; financial award applicants required to submit FAFSA. *Unit head:* Dr. Robert Gatchel, Chair, 817-272-2281, Fax: 817-272-2364, E-mail: gatchel@uta.edu. *Application contact:* Dr. Jared Kenworthy, Graduate Advisor, Psychological Sciences, 817-272-2281, Fax: 817-272-2364, E-mail: kenworthy@uta.edu.

The University of Texas at El Paso, Graduate School, College of Liberal Arts, Department of Psychology, El Paso, TX 79968-0001. Offers clinical psychology (MA); experimental psychology (MA); psychology (PhD). Part-time and evening/weekend programs available. *Students:* 47 (28 women); includes 1 Asian, non-Hispanic/Latino; 19 Hispanic/Latino, 6 international. Average age 34. In 2010, 11 master's, 5 doctorates awarded. *Degree requirements:* For master's, thesis; for doctorate, thesis/dissertation. *Entrance requirements:* For master's, GRE, letters of recommendation; for doctorate, GRE, statement of purpose, letters of recommendation. Additional exam requirements/recommendations for international students: Required—TOEFL; Recommended—IELTS. *Application deadline:* For fall admission, 8/1 for domestic students, 3/1 for international students; for spring admission, 11/1 for domestic students, 9/1 for international students. Applications are processed on a rolling basis. Application fee: $45 ($80 for international students). Electronic applications accepted. *Financial support:* In 2010–11, research assistantships with partial tuition reimbursements (averaging $18,625 per year), teaching assistantships with partial tuition reimbursements (averaging $14,900 per year) were awarded; fellowships with partial tuition reimbursements, institutionally sponsored loans, scholarships/grants, health care benefits, tuition waivers (partial), and unspecified assistantships also available. Support available to part-time students. Financial award application deadline: 3/15; financial award applicants required to submit FAFSA. *Unit head:* Dr. Edward Casta?eda, Chair, 915-747-5551, Fax: 915-747-6553, E-mail: ecastaneda9@utep.edu. *Application contact:* Dr. Patricia D. Witherspoon, Dean of the Graduate School, 915-747-5491, Fax: 915-747-5788, E-mail: withersp@utep.edu.

The University of Texas of the Permian Basin, Office of Graduate Studies, College of Arts and Sciences, Department of Psychology, Odessa, TX 79762-0001. Offers applied research psychology (MA); clinical psychology (MA). Part-time and evening/weekend programs available. *Degree requirements:* For master's, comprehensive exam, thesis, practicum. *Entrance requirements:* For master's, GRE General Test, 3 letters of recommendation. Additional exam requirements/recommendations for international students: Required—TOEFL (minimum score 550 paper-based; 213 computer-based).

Experimental Psychology

The University of Texas–Pan American, College of Social and Behavioral Sciences, Department of Psychology and Anthropology, Edinburg, TX 78539. Offers psychology (MA), including clinical psychology, experimental psychology. Part-time and evening/weekend programs available. *Degree requirements:* For master's, comprehensive exam, thesis optional, internship. *Entrance requirements:* For master's, GRE, letters of recommendation. Additional exam requirements/recommendations for international students: Required—TOEFL. Electronic applications accepted. *Faculty research:* Biofeedback, acculturation, health, stress/trauma, neuropsychological assessment, false memories, children's theory of mind.

The University of Toledo, College of Graduate Studies, College of Language, Literature and Social Sciences, Department of Psychology, Toledo, OH 43606-3390. Offers clinical psychology (MA, PhD); experimental psychology (MA, PhD). *Accreditation:* APA. *Faculty:* 22. *Students:* 34 full-time (26 women), 3 part-time (1 woman), 7 international. Average age 26. 192 applicants, 7% accepted, 9 enrolled. In 2010, 2 master's, 8 doctorates awarded. *Degree requirements:* For master's, comprehensive exam, thesis; for doctorate, comprehensive exam, thesis/dissertation. *Entrance requirements:* For master's and doctorate, GRE General Test, GRE Subject Test, A minimum 2.7 cumulative point-hour ratio (on a 4.0 scale) for all previous academic work. Three Letters of Recommendation, a statement of purpose, and transcripts from all prior institutions attended. Additional exam requirements/recommendations for international students: Required—TOEFL (minimum score 550 paper-based; 213 computer-based; 80 iBT), IELTS (minimum score 6.5). *Application deadline:* For fall admission, 1/15 priority date for domestic and international students. Applications are processed on a rolling basis. Application fee: $45 ($75 for international students). Electronic applications accepted. *Expenses:* Tuition, state resident: full-time $11,426; part-time $476 per credit hour. Tuition, nonresident: full-time $21,660; part-time $903 per credit hour. One-time fee: $62. *Financial support:* Research assistantships with tuition reimbursements, teaching assistantships with tuition reimbursements, career-related internships or fieldwork, Federal Work-Study, institutionally sponsored loans, scholarships/grants, tuition waivers (full and partial), and unspecified assistantships available. Support available to part-time students. *Faculty research:* Neural taste response. *Unit head:* Dr. J. D. Jasper, Chair, 419-530-4130, E-mail: jjasper@utnet.utoledo.edu. *Application contact:* Graduate School Office, 419-530-4723, Fax: 419-530-4724, E-mail: grdsch@utnet.utoledo.edu.

University of Victoria, Faculty of Graduate Studies, Faculty of Social Sciences, Department of Psychology, Victoria, BC V8W 2Y2, Canada. Offers clinical psychology (PhD); clinical psychology (neuropsychology) (M Sc); cognition and brain science (M Sc, PhD); experimental neuropsychology (M Sc, PhD); individualized study (M Sc, PhD); life span development psychology (PhD); life span developmental psychology (M Sc); social psychology (M Sc, PhD). *Accreditation:* APA (one or more programs are accredited). *Degree requirements:* For master's, thesis; for doctorate, thesis/dissertation, candidacy exam. *Entrance requirements:* For master's and doctorate, GRE General Test. Additional exam requirements/recommendations for international students: Required—TOEFL (minimum score 600 paper-based; 250 computer-based). Electronic applications accepted. *Faculty research:* Life span development psychology and aging, behavioral neuroscience, cognitive psychology, behavioral psychology, environmental psychology.

University of Wisconsin–Oshkosh, The Office of Graduate Studies, College of Letters and Science, Department of Psychology, Oshkosh, WI 54901. Offers experimental psychology (MS); industrial/organizational psychology (MS). *Degree requirements:* For master's, thesis. *Entrance requirements:* For master's, GRE, 10 semester hours of undergraduate course work in psychology. Additional exam requirements/recommendations for international students: Required—TOEFL (minimum score 550 paper-based; 213 computer-based; 79 iBT). Electronic applications accepted. *Faculty research:* Performance evaluation, training, biological bases of behavior, tactile perception, aging.

Washington State University, Graduate School, College of Liberal Arts, Department of Psychology, Pullman, WA 99164. Offers clinical psychology (PhD); experimental psychology (PhD); psychology (MS). *Accreditation:* APA (one or more programs are accredited). *Faculty:* 22. *Students:* 49 full-time (34 women), 4 part-time (2 women); includes 2 Asian, non-Hispanic/Latino; 5 Hispanic/Latino, 7 international. Average age 29. 262 applicants, 6% accepted, 12 enrolled. In 2010, 7 master's, 8 doctorates awarded. *Degree requirements:* For master's, comprehensive exam (for some programs), thesis (for some programs), oral exam; for doctorate, comprehensive exam, thesis/dissertation, oral exam, written exam. *Entrance requirements:* For master's, GRE General Test, minimum undergraduate GPA of 3.0; research experiences; clinical experiences; at least 18 hours of psychology, including a class in statistics; three letters of recommendation, official transcripts; for doctorate, GRE General Test, three letters of reference; summary data form; at least 18 credits of study in psychology; at least one course in statistics and research methodology; official transcripts; minimum cumulative undergraduate GPA of 3.0 or master's degree in psychology. Additional exam requirements/recommendations for international students: Required—TOEFL, IELTS. *Application deadline:* For fall admission, 12/15 priority date for domestic and international students. Applications are processed on a rolling basis. Application fee: $50. *Expenses:* Tuition, state resident: full-time $8552; part-time $443 per credit. Tuition, nonresident: full-time $21,650; part-time $1083 per credit. Required fees: $846. *Financial support:* In 2010–11, 5 research assistantships with full and partial tuition reimbursements (averaging $13,917 per year), 39 teaching assistantships with full and partial tuition reimbursements (averaging $13,056 per year) were awarded; fellowships, career-related internships or fieldwork, Federal Work-Study, institutionally sponsored loans, and unspecified assistantships also available. Financial award application deadline: 2/15; financial award applicants required to submit FAFSA. *Faculty research:* Childhood conduct disorders, etiology of depression, treatment of reading disorders, applied behavior analysis, selective attention. *Unit head:* Dr. John Hinson, Chair, 509-335-1089, Fax: 509-335-5043, E-mail: hinson@mail.wsu.edu. *Application contact:* Graduate School Admissions, 800-GRADWSU, Fax: 509-335-1949, E-mail: gradsch@wsu.edu.

Washington University in St. Louis, Graduate School of Arts and Sciences, Department of Psychology, St. Louis, MO 63130-4899. Offers clinical psychology (PhD); general experimental psychology (PhD); social psychology (PhD). *Accreditation:* APA. Terminal master's awarded for partial completion of doctoral program. *Degree requirements:* For doctorate, thesis/dissertation. *Entrance requirements:* For doctorate, GRE General Test. Electronic applications accepted.

Western Kentucky University, Graduate Studies, College of Education and Behavioral Sciences, Department of Psychology, Bowling Green, KY 42101. Offers clinical psychology (MA); experimental psychology (MA); general psychology (MA); industrial/organizational psychology (MA); school psychology (Ed S). *Degree requirements:* For master's, comprehensive exam, thesis (for some programs); for Ed S, thesis, oral exam. *Entrance requirements:* For master's, GRE General Test; for Ed S, GRE General Test, minimum GPA of 3.5. Additional exam requirements/recommendations for international students: Required—TOEFL (minimum score 555 paper-based; 213 computer-based; 79 iBT). *Faculty research:* Neural regeneration, enhancing mobility in the elderly, improvement in visual processing in older adults, lifespan development.

Western Washington University, Graduate School, College of Humanities and Social Sciences, Department of Psychology, Program in Experimental Psychology, Bellingham, WA 98225-5996. Offers MS. *Degree requirements:* For master's, thesis. *Entrance requirements:* For master's, GRE General Test, minimum GPA of 3.0 in last 60 semester hours or last 90 quarter hours. Additional exam requirements/recommendations for international students: Required—TOEFL (minimum score 567 paper-based; 227 computer-based). Electronic applications accepted.

Xavier University, College of Social Sciences, Health and Education, Department of Psychology, Cincinnati, OH 45207. Offers clinical psychology (Psy D); psychology (MA), including general experimental psychology, industrial-organizational psychology. *Accreditation:* APA (one or more programs are accredited). *Faculty:* 16 full-time (8 women), 5 part-time/adjunct (2 women). *Students:* 87 full-time (65 women), 26 part-time (21 women); includes 11 minority (4 Black or African American, non-Hispanic/Latino; 1 American Indian or Alaska Native, non-Hispanic/Latino; 3 Asian, non-Hispanic/Latino; 3 Hispanic/Latino), 2 international. Average age 27. 292 applicants, 22% accepted, 25 enrolled. In 2010, 26 master's, 16 doctorates awarded. *Degree requirements:* For master's, one foreign language, comprehensive exam, thesis, internship; for doctorate, one foreign language, comprehensive exam, thesis/dissertation, internship. *Entrance requirements:* For master's and doctorate, GRE. Additional exam requirements/recommendations for international students: Required—TOEFL, IELTS. *Application deadline:* For fall admission, 12/15 for domestic and international students. Application fee: $35. Electronic applications accepted. *Expenses:* Contact institution. *Financial support:* In 2010–11, 54 students received support, including 41 research assistantships with partial tuition reimbursements available, 13 teaching assistantships with partial tuition reimbursements available; scholarships/grants and unspecified assistantships also available. Financial award application deadline: 3/1; financial award applicants required to submit FAFSA. *Faculty research:* Older adults, clinical child and adolescent issues, personnel selection and employee behavior, at-risk youth, sexual abuse. *Unit head:* Dr. Karl Stukenberg, Chair, 513-745-1041, Fax: 513-745-3327, E-mail: stukenb@xavier.edu. *Application contact:* Margaret Maybury, Assistant Director, Enrollment and Student Services, 513-745-1053, Fax: 513-745-3347, E-mail: maybury@xavier.edu.

Forensic Psychology

Adler School of Professional Psychology, Programs in Psychology, Chicago, IL 60602. Offers advanced Adlerian psychotherapy (Certificate); art therapy (MA); clinical neuropsychology (Certificate); clinical psychology (Psy D); community psychology (MA); counseling and organizational psychology (MA); counseling psychology (MA); forensic psychology (MA); gerontological counseling (MA); marriage and family counseling (MA); marriage and family therapy (Certificate); organizational psychology (MA); police psychology (MA); rehabilitation counseling (MA); sport and health psychology (MA); substance abuse counseling (Certificate); Psy D/Certificate; Psy D/MACAT; Psy D/MACP; Psy D/MAMFC; Psy D/MASAC. *Accreditation:* APA. Part-time and evening/weekend programs available. Postbaccalaureate distance learning degree programs offered (minimal on-campus study). *Faculty:* 40 full-time (18 women), 61 part-time/adjunct (31 women). *Students:* 688 full-time (532 women), 142 part-time (110 women). Average age 27.Terminal master's awarded for partial completion of doctoral program. *Degree requirements:* For master's, thesis or alternative, oral exam, practicum; for doctorate, thesis/dissertation, clinical exam, internship, oral exam, practicum, written qualifying exam. *Entrance requirements:* For master's, 12 semester hours in psychology, minimum GPA of 3.0; for doctorate, 18 semester hours in psychology, minimum GPA of 3.25; for Certificate, appropriate master's or doctoral degree. Additional exam requirements/recommendations for international students: Required—TOEFL (minimum score 550 paper-based; 213 computer-based; 79 iBT). *Application deadline:* For fall admission, 2/15 priority date for domestic students, 12/1 priority date for international students. Applications are processed on a rolling basis. Application fee: $50. Electronic applications accepted. *Financial support:* Career-related internships or fieldwork, Federal Work-Study, scholarships/grants, and tuition waivers (full and partial) available. Support available to part-time students. Financial award application deadline: 5/15; financial award applicants required to submit FAFSA. *Application contact:* Michelle Brice, Director of Admissions, 312-662-4113, Fax: 312-662-4199, E-mail: admissions@adler.edu.

See Display on page 912 and Close-Up on page 1119.

Alliant International University–Fresno, Center for Forensic Studies, Fresno, CA 93727. Offers forensic psychology (PhD, Psy D). *Degree requirements:* For doctorate, thesis/dissertation. *Entrance requirements:* For doctorate, interview; master's degree in psychology, forensic psychology, criminology, criminal justice, social work or law; minimum GPA of 3.0 in psychology and overall. Additional exam requirements/recommendations for international students: Required—TOEFL (minimum score 600 paper-based; 250 computer-based), TWE (minimum score 5). Electronic applications accepted. *Faculty research:* Domestic violence, serial killers, court evaluations, drug and alcohol abuse.

Alliant International University–Irvine, Center for Forensic Studies, Irvine, CA 92612. Offers Psy D.

Alliant International University–Los Angeles, Center for Forensic Studies, Alhambra, CA 91803-1360. Offers forensic psychology (Psy D). *Degree requirements:* For doctorate, thesis/dissertation. *Entrance requirements:* For doctorate, interview; master's degree in psychology, forensic psychology, criminology, criminal justice, social work or law; minimum GPA of 3.0 in psychology and overall. Additional exam requirements/recommendations for international students: Required—TOEFL (minimum score 600 paper-based; 250 computer-based), TWE (minimum score 5). *Faculty research:* Court testimony.

American International College, School of Arts, Education and Sciences, Department of Psychology, Program in Forensic Psychology, Springfield, MA 01109-3189. Offers MS. Part-time and evening/weekend programs available. *Degree requirements:* For master's, comprehensive exam (for some programs), thesis optional. *Entrance requirements:* For master's, minimum B-average in undergraduate course work, BS or BA. Additional exam requirements/recommendations for international students: Required—TOEFL. Electronic applications accepted.

Argosy University, Atlanta, College of Psychology and Behavioral Sciences, Atlanta, GA 30328. Offers clinical psychology (MA, Psy D, Postdoctoral Respecialization Certificate), including child and family psychology (Psy D), general adult clinical (Psy D), health psychology (Psy D), neuropsychology/geropsychology (Psy D); community counseling (MA), including marriage and family therapy; counselor education and supervision (Ed D); forensic psychology (MA); industrial organizational psychology (MA); marriage and family therapy (Certificate); sport-exercise psychology (MA). *Accreditation:* APA.

See Close-Up on page 1121.

Argosy University, Chicago, College of Psychology and Behavioral Sciences, Doctoral Program in Clinical Psychology, Chicago, IL 60601. Offers child and adolescent psychology (Psy D); client-centered and experiential psychotherapies (Psy D); diversity and multicultural psychology (Psy D); family psychology (Psy D); forensic psychology (Psy D); health psychology (Psy D); neuropsychology (Psy D); organizational consulting (Psy D); psychoanalytic psychology (Psy D); psychology and spirituality (Psy D). *Accreditation:* APA.

See Close-Up on page 1123.

Argosy University, Dallas, College of Psychology and Behavioral Sciences, Program in Forensic Psychology, Farmers Branch, TX 75244. Offers MA.

See Close-Up on page 1125.

Argosy University, Denver, College of Psychology and Behavioral Sciences, Denver, CO 80231. Offers clinical mental health counseling (MA); clinical psychology (MA, Psy D); counseling psychology (Ed D); counselor education and supervision (Ed D); forensic psychology (MA); industrial organizational psychology (MA); marriage and family therapy (MA, DMFT).

See Close-Up on page 1127.

Argosy University, Hawai'i, College of Psychology and Behavioral Sciences, Program in Forensic Psychology, Honolulu, HI 96813. Offers MA.

See Close-Up on page 1129.

Argosy University, Inland Empire, College of Psychology and Behavioral Sciences, San Bernardino, CA 92408. Offers clinical psychology/marriage and family therapy (MA); counseling psychology (Ed D); counseling psychology/marriage and family therapy (MA); forensic psychology (MA); industrial organizational psychology (MA); sport-exercise psychology (MA).

See Close-Up on page 1131.

Argosy University, Los Angeles, College of Psychology and Behavioral Sciences, Santa Monica, CA 90045. Offers clinical psychology/marriage and family therapy (MA); counseling psychology (Ed D); counseling psychology/marriage and family therapy (MA); forensic psychology (MA).

See Close-Up on page 1133.

Argosy University, Orange County, College of Psychology and Behavioral Sciences, Program in Forensic Psychology, Orange, CA 92868. Offers MA.

See Close-Up on page 1137.

Argosy University, Phoenix, College of Psychology and Behavioral Sciences, Program in Forensic Psychology, Phoenix, AZ 85021. Offers MA.

See Close-Up on page 1139.

Argosy University, Salt Lake City, College of Psychology and Behavioral Sciences, Draper, UT 84020. Offers counseling psychology (Ed D); counselor education and supervision (Ed D); forensic psychology (MA); marriage and family therapy (MA, DMFT); mental health counseling (MA).

See Close-Up on page 1141.

Argosy University, San Diego, College of Psychology and Behavioral Sciences, San Diego, CA 92108. Offers clinical psychology/marriage and family therapy (MA); counseling psychology (Ed D); counseling psychology/marriage and family therapy (MA); forensic psychology (MA).

See Close-Up on page 1143.

Argosy University, San Francisco Bay Area, College of Psychology and Behavioral Sciences, Program in Forensic Psychology, Alameda, CA 94501. Offers MA.

See Close-Up on page 1145.

Argosy University, Sarasota, College of Psychology and Behavioral Sciences, Sarasota, FL 34235. Offers community counseling (MA); counseling psychology (Ed D); counselor education and supervision (Ed D); forensic psychology (MA); marriage and family therapy (MA); mental health counseling (MA); pastoral community counseling (Ed D).

See Close-Up on page 1147.

Argosy University, Schaumburg, College of Psychology and Behavioral Sciences, Schaumburg, IL 60173-5403. Offers clinical health psychology (Post-Graduate Certificate); clinical psychology (MA, Psy D), including child and family psychology (Psy D), clinical health psychology (Psy D), diversity and multicultural psychology (Psy D), forensic psychology (Psy D), neuropsychology (Psy D); community counseling (MA); counseling psychology (Ed D), including counselor education and supervision; counselor education and supervision (Ed D); forensic psychology (Post-Graduate Certificate); industrial organizational psychology (MA). *Accreditation:* ACA; APA.

See Close-Up on page 1149.

Argosy University, Twin Cities, College of Psychology and Behavioral Sciences, Eagan, MN 55121. Offers clinical psychology (MA, Psy D), including child and family psychology (Psy D), forensic psychology (Psy D), health and neuropsychology (Psy D), trauma (Psy D); forensic counseling (Post-Graduate Certificate); forensic psychology (MA); industrial organizational psychology (MA); marriage and family therapy (MA, DMFT), including forensic counseling (MA). *Accreditation:* AAMFT; AAMFT/COAMFTE; APA.

See Close-Up on page 1155.

Argosy University, Washington DC, College of Psychology and Behavioral Sciences, Arlington, VA 22209. Offers clinical psychology (MA, Psy D), including child and family psychology (Psy D), diversity and multicultural psychology (Psy D), forensic psychology (Psy D), health and neuropsychology (Psy D); community counseling (MA); counseling psychology (Ed D), including counselor education and supervision; counselor education and supervision (Ed D); forensic psychology (MA). *Accreditation:* APA.

See Close-Up on page 1157.

California Baptist University, Program in Forensic Psychology, Riverside, CA 92504-3206. Offers MA. Part-time programs available. *Faculty:* 3 full-time (2 women), 2 part-time/adjunct (1 woman). *Students:* 13 full-time (11 women), 7 part-time (5 women); includes 1 Black or African American, non-Hispanic/Latino; 3 Asian, non-Hispanic/Latino; 7 Hispanic/Latino. 10 applicants, 100% accepted, 9 enrolled. In 2010, 9 master's awarded. *Entrance requirements:* For master's, Minnesota Multiphasic Personality Inventory-2, minimum GPA of 2.75; 15 units of pre-requisite coursework. Additional exam requirements/recommendations for international students: Required—TOEFL (minimum score 575 paper-based; 230 computer-based; 89 iBT). *Application deadline:* For fall admission, 8/1 priority date for domestic students, 7/1 for international students; for spring admission, 12/1 priority date for domestic students, 10/15 for international students. Applications are processed on a rolling basis. Application fee: $45. Electronic applications accepted. *Expenses:* Tuition: Full-time $8532; part-time $474 per unit. Required fees: $355 per semester. One-time fee: $45 full-time. Tuition and fees vary according to course load and program. *Financial support:* Federal Work-Study and scholarships/grants available. Support available to part-time students. Financial award applicants required to submit FAFSA. *Unit head:* Dr. Anne-Marie Larsen, Director, 951-343-4761, E-mail: alarsen@calbaptist.edu. *Application contact:* Gail Ronveaux, Dean of Graduate Enrollment, 951-343-5045, Fax: 951-343-5095, E-mail: graduateadmissions@calbaptist.edu.

Cambridge College, School of Psychology and Counseling, Cambridge, MA 02138-5304. Offers addiction counseling (M Ed); alcohol and drug counseling (Certificate); counseling psychology (M Ed, CAGS); counseling psychology: forensic counseling (M Ed); marriage and family therapy (M Ed); mental health and addiction counseling (M Ed); mental health counseling (M Ed); mental health counseling for school guidance counselors (Post Master's Certificate); psychological studies (M Ed); school adjustment and mental health counseling (M Ed); school adjustment, mental health and addiction counseling (M Ed); school guidance counselor (M Ed); trauma studies (Certificate). Part-time and evening/weekend programs available. *Faculty:* 4 full-time (2 women), 83 part-time/adjunct (48 women). *Students:* 436 full-time (351 women), 351 part-time (274 women); includes 321 Black or African American, non-Hispanic/Latino; 3 American Indian or Alaska Native, non-Hispanic/Latino; 4 Asian, non-Hispanic/Latino; 87 Hispanic/Latino; 4 Two or more races, non-Hispanic/Latino, 6 international. Average age 37. In 2010, 284 master's, 16 other advanced degrees awarded. *Degree requirements:* For master's

and other advanced degree, thesis, practicum/internship. *Entrance requirements:* For master's, resume, 2 professional references; for other advanced degree, official transcripts, documents for transfer credit evaluation, resume, written personal statement/essay, 2 professional references, health insurance, immunizations form. Additional exam requirements/recommendations for international students: Required—TOEFL (minimum score 550 paper-based; 213 computer-based; 79 iBT); Recommended—IELTS (minimum score 6). *Application deadline:* Applications are processed on a rolling basis. Application fee: $30. Electronic applications accepted. *Expenses:* Contact institution. *Financial support:* Career-related internships or fieldwork, Federal Work-Study, and scholarships/grants available. Financial award applicants required to submit FAFSA. *Faculty research:* Trauma, drug and alcohol counseling, cross-cultural issues, school counseling, trauma in schools. *Unit head:* Dr. Niti Seth, Dean, 617-873-0208, Fax: 617-349-3561, E-mail: nseth@cambridgecollege.edu. *Application contact:* Elaine M. Lapomardo, Dean of Enrollment Management, 617-873-0274, Fax: 617-349-3561, E-mail: elaine.lapomardo@cambridgecollege.edu.

Castleton State College, Division of Graduate Studies, Department of Psychology, Castleton, VT 05735. Offers forensic psychology (MA). *Degree requirements:* For master's, thesis. *Entrance requirements:* For master's, GRE General Test, minimum undergraduate GPA of 3.5, previous course work in research methodology and statistics. Additional exam requirements/recommendations for international students: Required—TOEFL. *Faculty research:* Psychology and law, juvenile delinquency, criminal psychology, correctional psychology, police psychology.

The Chicago School of Professional Psychology, Program in Clinical Forensic Psychology, Chicago, IL 60610. Offers Psy D. *Degree requirements:* For doctorate, thesis/dissertation. *Entrance requirements:* For doctorate, GRE. Additional exam requirements/recommendations for international students: Required—TOEFL, IELTS.

The Chicago School of Professional Psychology, Program in Forensic Psychology, Chicago, IL 60610. Offers MA. *Degree requirements:* For master's, thesis optional. *Entrance requirements:* For master's, GRE (highly recommended), 1 course each in research methods, statistics, and psychology. Additional exam requirements/recommendations for international students: Required—TOEFL (minimum score 550 paper-based; 213 computer-based; 79 iBT).

The Chicago School of Professional Psychology at Downtown Los Angeles, Program in Clinical Forensic Psychology, Los Angeles, CA 90017. Offers Psy D.

The Chicago School of Professional Psychology at Irvine, Program in Clinical Forensic Psychology, Irvine, CA 92612. Offers Psy D.

The Chicago School of Professional Psychology: Online, Program in Applied Forensic Psychology Services, Chicago, IL 60654. Offers MA, Certificate.

College of Saint Elizabeth, Department of Psychology, Morristown, NJ 07960-6989. Offers counseling psychology (MA); forensic psychology (MA); student affairs in higher education (Certificate). Part-time and evening/weekend programs available. *Faculty:* 4 full-time (3 women), 9 part-time/adjunct (all women). *Students:* 33 full-time (31 women), 67 part-time (57 women); includes 13 Black or African American, non-Hispanic/Latino; 4 Asian, non-Hispanic/Latino; 12 Hispanic/Latino, 2 international. Average age 30. 86 applicants, 41% accepted, 27 enrolled. In 2010, 22 master's awarded. *Degree requirements:* For master's, thesis or alternative, portfolio. *Entrance requirements:* For master's, minimum GPA of 3.0, BA in psychology (preferred), 12 credits of course work in psychology. Additional exam requirements/recommendations for international students: Required—TOEFL (minimum score 550 paper-based). *Application deadline:* For fall admission, 4/1 priority date for domestic students; for spring admission, 11/15 for domestic students. Applications are processed on a rolling basis. Application fee: $35. Electronic applications accepted. *Expenses:* Tuition: Part-time $857 per credit. Required fees: $70 per credit. *Financial support:* Career-related internships or fieldwork, tuition waivers (partial), and unspecified assistantships available. Support available to part-time students. Financial award application deadline: 3/15; financial award applicants required to submit FAFSA. *Faculty research:* Family systems, dissociative identity disorder, multicultural counseling, outcomes assessment. *Unit head:* Dr. Valerie Scott, Director of the Graduate Program in Counseling Psychology, 973-290-4102, Fax: 973-290-4676, E-mail: vscott@cse.edu. *Application contact:* Dean Donna Tatarka, Dean of Admission, 973-290-4705, Fax: 973-290-4710, E-mail: dtatarka@cse.edu.

Drexel University, College of Arts and Sciences, Department of Psychology, Clinical Psychology Program, Philadelphia, PA 19104-2875. Offers clinical psychology (PhD); forensic psychology (PhD); health psychology (PhD); neuropsychology (PhD). *Accreditation:* APA. Terminal master's awarded for partial completion of doctoral program. *Degree requirements:* For doctorate, thesis/dissertation, qualifying exam. *Entrance requirements:* For doctorate, GRE General Test, GRE Subject Test, minimum GPA of 3.0. Electronic applications accepted. *Expenses:* Contact institution. *Faculty research:* Cognitive behavioral therapy, stress and coping, eating disorders, substance abuse, developmental disabilities.

Fairleigh Dickinson University, Metropolitan Campus, University College: Arts, Sciences, and Professional Studies, School of Psychology, Program in Forensic Psychology, Teaneck, NJ 07666-1914. Offers MA. *Students:* 19 full-time (17 women), 2 international. Average age 26. 61 applicants, 64% accepted, 10 enrolled. In 2010, 7 master's awarded. *Application contact:* Susan Brooman, University Director of Graduate Admissions, 201-692-2554, Fax: 201-692-2560, E-mail: globaleducation@fdu.edu.

Holy Names University, Graduate Division, Department of Counseling Psychology, Oakland, CA 94619-1699. Offers counseling psychology (MA); forensic psychology (MA, Certificate); pastoral counseling (MA, Certificate). Part-time and evening/weekend programs available. *Faculty:* 1 (woman) full-time, 9 part-time/adjunct (5 women). *Students:* 49 full-time (39 women), 25 part-time (24 women); includes 30 Black or African American, non-Hispanic/Latino; 4 Asian, non-Hispanic/Latino; 13 Hispanic/Latino, 1 international. Average age 32. 22 applicants, 68% accepted, 11 enrolled. In 2010, 13 master's awarded. *Degree requirements:* For master's, comprehensive paper, seminars. *Entrance requirements:* For master's, minimum undergraduate GPA of 2.6 overall, 3.0 in major. Additional exam requirements/recommendations for international students: Required—TOEFL (minimum score 550 paper-based; 213 computer-based; 80 iBT). *Application deadline:* For fall admission, 8/1 priority date for domestic students, 8/1 for international students; for spring admission, 12/1 priority date for domestic students, 12/1 for international students. Applications are processed on a rolling basis. Application fee: $0. *Expenses:* Tuition: Full-time $13,788; part-time $766 per credit. Required fees: $340; $170 per semester. *Financial support:* In 2010–11, 38 students received support. Available to part-time students. Application deadline: 3/2. *Faculty research:* Cognitive psychology, anger management, grief and grief counseling, post-modernism and psychotherapy, spirituality and psychology. *Unit head:* Dr. Helen Shoemaker, Program Director, 510-436-1543, E-mail: shoemaker@hnu.edu. *Application contact:* 800-430-1321, Fax: 510-436-1325, E-mail: adulted@hnu.edu.

John Jay College of Criminal Justice of the City University of New York, Graduate Studies, Program in Forensic Psychology, New York, NY 10019-1093. Offers MA, PhD. Part-time and evening/weekend programs available. *Degree requirements:* For master's, thesis or alternative, externship. *Entrance requirements:* For master's, GRE General Test, minimum B average in major. Additional exam requirements/recommendations for international students: Required—TOEFL (minimum score 500 paper-based; 173 computer-based).

John Jay College of Criminal Justice of the City University of New York, Graduate Studies, Programs in Criminal Justice, New York, NY 10019-1093. Offers criminal justice (MA, PhD); criminology and deviance (PhD); forensic psychology (PhD); forensic science (PhD); law and philosophy (PhD); organizational behavior (PhD); public policy (PhD). Part-time and evening/weekend programs available. Terminal master's awarded for partial completion of doctoral program. *Degree requirements:* For master's, thesis or alternative; for doctorate, one foreign language, thesis/dissertation. *Entrance requirements:* For master's, GRE General Test, minimum B average; for doctorate, GRE General Test. Additional exam requirements/

Forensic Psychology

John Jay College of Criminal Justice of the City University of New York (continued)
recommendations for international students: Required—TOEFL (minimum score 500 paper-based; 173 computer-based).

Marymount University, School of Education and Human Services, Program in Forensic Psychology, Arlington, VA 22207-4299. Offers MA. Part-time and evening/weekend programs available. *Entrance requirements:* For master's, GRE, 2 letters of recommendation, resume. Additional exam requirements/recommendations for international students: Required—TOEFL (minimum score 600 paper-based; 250 computer-based; 96 iBT), IELTS (minimum score 6.5). Electronic applications accepted.

Massachusetts School of Professional Psychology, Graduate Programs, Boston, MA 02132. Offers applied psychology in higher education student personnel administration (MA); clinical psychology (Psy D); counseling psychology (MA); counseling psychology and community mental health (MA); counseling psychology and global mental health (MA); executive coaching (Graduate Certificate); forensic and counseling psychology (MA); leadership psychology (Psy D); organizational psychology (MA); primary care psychology (MA); respecialization in clinical psychology (Certificate); school psychology (Psy D); MA/CAGS. *Accreditation:* APA. *Faculty:* 24 full-time (11 women), 13 part-time/adjunct (9 women). *Students:* 515. Average age 28. *Degree requirements:* For master's, comprehensive exam (for some programs); for doctorate, thesis/dissertation (for some programs). Application fee: $50. Electronic applications accepted. *Expenses:* Tuition: Full-time $32,352; part-time $1011 per credit. Full-time tuition and fees vary according to degree level. *Financial support:* Teaching assistantships, career-related internships or fieldwork available. Financial award applicants required to submit FAFSA. *Unit head:* Dr. Nicholas A. Covino, President, 617-327-6777, Fax: 617-327-4447. *Application contact:* Admissions and Marketing, 617-327-6777 Ext. 210, Fax: 617-327-4447, E-mail: admissions@mspp.edu.

Oklahoma State University Center for Health Sciences, Graduate Program in Forensic Sciences, Tulsa, OK 74107-1898. Offers forensic DNA/molecular biology (MS); forensic examination of questioned documents (Certificate); forensic pathology (MS); forensic psychology (MS); forensic toxicology (MS). Part-time and evening/weekend programs available. Postbaccalaureate distance learning degree programs offered (no on-campus study). *Faculty:* 2 full-time (0 women), 14 part-time/adjunct (5 women). *Students:* 7 full-time (6 women), 21 part-time (12 women); includes 5 minority (2 Black or African American, non-Hispanic/Latino; 2 Asian, non-Hispanic/Latino; 1 Hispanic/Latino). Average age 34. 21 applicants, 57% accepted, 7 enrolled. In 2010, 6 master's awarded. *Degree requirements:* For master's, comprehensive exam (for some programs), thesis (for some programs). *Entrance requirements:* For master's, MAT (MFSA) or GRE General Test, professional experience (MFSA). Additional exam requirements/recommendations for international students: Required—TOEFL (minimum score 600 paper-based; 250 computer-based), TWE (minimum score 5). *Application deadline:* For fall admission, 3/1 for domestic and international students; for spring admission, 10/1 for domestic and international students. Application fee: $40 ($75 for international students). *Financial support:* In 2010–11, 10 students received support, including 10 research assistantships (averaging $29,000 per year); career-related internships or fieldwork, Federal Work-Study, and tuition waivers (partial) also available. Support available to part-time students. Financial award application deadline: 4/1; financial award applicants required to submit FAFSA. *Faculty research:* DNA typing, DNA polymorphism, identification through DNA, disease transmission, forensic dentistry, neurotoxicity of HIV, forensic toxicology method development, toxin detection and characterization. Total annual research expenditures: $58,000. *Unit head:* Dr. Robert T. Allen, Director, 918-561-1108, Fax: 918-561-8414. *Application contact:* Cathy Newsome, Coordinator, 918-561-1108, Fax: 918-561-8414, E-mail: cathy.newsome@okstate.edu.

Pontificia Universidad Catolica Madre y Maestra, Graduate School, Faculty of Social and Administrative Sciences, Santiago, Dominican Republic. Offers business administration (MBA), including business development, finance, international business, management skills (M Mgmt, MBA), marketing, operations, strategic cost management, strategy, tourist destination planning and management; law (LL M), including civil law, corporate business law, criminal law, international relations, real estate law; management (M Mgmt), including higher financial management, insurance program administration, management skills (M Mgmt, MBA); psychology (MA), including clinical child and adolescent psychology, forensic psychology; strategic human resources (EMBA).

Prairie View A&M University, College of Juvenile Justice and Psychology, Prairie View, TX 77446-0519. Offers clinical adolescent psychology (PhD); juvenile forensic psychology (MSJFP); juvenile justice (MSJJ, PhD). Part-time and evening/weekend programs available. *Faculty:* 12 full-time (7 women). *Students:* 48 full-time (35 women), 30 part-time (22 women); includes 64 Black or African American, non-Hispanic/Latino; 3 Hispanic/Latino, 4 international. Average age 26. 55 applicants, 60% accepted, 33 enrolled. In 2010, 20 master's, 1 doctorate awarded. *Degree requirements:* For master's, comprehensive exam (for some programs), thesis (for some programs); for doctorate, comprehensive exam, thesis/dissertation. *Entrance requirements:* For master's, GRE, minimum GPA of 2.75; for doctorate, GRE, previous course work in clinical adolescent psychology, minimum GPA of 3.5. Additional exam requirements/recommendations for international students: Required—TOEFL. *Application deadline:* For fall admission, 3/1 for domestic and international students; for spring admission, 10/1 for domestic and international students. Applications are processed on a rolling basis. Application fee: $50. *Expenses:* Tuition, state resident: full-time $3586.14; part-time $119.06 per credit hour. Tuition, nonresident: part-time $511.23 per credit hour. *Financial support:* In 2010–11, 23 students received support, including 12 research assistantships (averaging $15,000 per year), 11 teaching assistantships (averaging $20,000 per year); career-related internships or fieldwork, Federal Work-Study, institutionally sponsored loans, tuition waivers (full and partial), and unspecified assistantships also available. Support available to part-time students. Financial award application deadline: 3/1; financial award applicants required to submit FAFSA. *Faculty research:* Juvenile justice, juvenile forensic psychology, teen court, graduate education, capital punishment. Total annual research expenditures: $2,888. *Unit head:* Dr. Dennis E. Daniels, Interim Dean, 936-261-5205, Fax: 936-261-5252, E-mail: dedaniels@pvamu.edu. *Application contact:* Sandy Siegmund, Executive Secretary, Graduate Program, 936-261-5234, Fax: 936-261-5249, E-mail: sisiegmund@pvamu.edu.

Roger Williams University, Feinstein College of Arts and Sciences, Program in Forensic Psychology, Bristol, RI 02809. Offers MA. Part-time programs available. *Degree requirements:* For master's, thesis optional. *Entrance requirements:* For master's, GRE, 3 letters of recommendation. Additional exam requirements/recommendations for international students: Recommended—IELTS. Electronic applications accepted. *Expenses:* Contact institution.

Sage Graduate School, Graduate School, School of Health Sciences, Program in Forensic Mental Health, Troy, NY 12180-4115. Offers MS, Certificate. Part-time and evening/weekend programs available. *Faculty:* 1 (woman) full-time, 1 (woman) part-time/adjunct. *Students:* 23 full-time (20 women), 25 part-time (22 women); includes 8 minority (5 Black or African American, non-Hispanic/Latino; 1 Hispanic/Latino; 2 Two or more races, non-Hispanic/Latino). Average age 27. 50 applicants, 52% accepted, 12 enrolled. In 2010, 4 master's, 2 other advanced degrees awarded. *Entrance requirements:* Additional exam requirements/recommendations for international students: Required—TOEFL (minimum score 550 paper-based; 213 computer-based). *Application deadline:* Applications are processed on a rolling basis. Application fee: $40. *Expenses:* Tuition: Full-time $10,980; part-time $610 per credit hour. Tuition and fees vary according to course load, degree level and program. *Financial support:* Fellowships, research assistantships, Federal Work-Study, scholarships/grants, and unspecified assistantships available. Support available to part-time students. *Unit head:* Dr. Maureen McLeod, Chair, 518-244-2245, E-mail: mcleom@sage.edu. *Application contact:* Wendy D. Diefendorf, Director of Graduate and Adult Admission, 518-244-2443, Fax: 518-244-6880, E-mail: diefew@sage.edu.

Tiffin University, Program in Criminal Justice, Tiffin, OH 44883-2161. Offers crime analysis (MSCJ); criminal behavior (MSCJ); forensic psychology (MSCJ); homeland security administration (MSCJ); justice administration (MSCJ). Part-time and evening/weekend programs available. Postbaccalaureate distance learning degree programs offered (no on-campus study). *Faculty:* 13 full-time (3 women), 20 part-time/adjunct (9 women). *Students:* 120 full-time (84 women), 312 part-time (205 women). Average age 31. 185 applicants, 58% accepted, 104 enrolled. In 2010, 340 master's awarded. *Degree requirements:* For master's, thesis optional. *Entrance requirements:* For master's, minimum undergraduate GPA of 2.5, work experience. Additional exam requirements/recommendations for international students: Required—TOEFL (minimum score 550 paper-based; 213 computer-based). *Application deadline:* For fall admission, 9/3 for domestic students, 8/1 for international students; for spring admission, 1/9 priority date for domestic students, 12/1 for international students. Applications are processed on a rolling basis. Application fee: $0. Electronic applications accepted. *Financial support:* In 2010–11, 64 students received support. Available to part-time students. Application deadline: 7/31. *Faculty research:* Terrorism, intelligence, homeland security, guns and crime. *Unit head:* Dr. Tim Shaw, Dean of Criminal Justice and Social Sciences, 419-448-3305, Fax: 419-443-5002, E-mail: shawta@tiffin.edu. *Application contact:* Kristi Krintzline, Director of Graduate Admissions, 800-968-6446 Ext. 3445, Fax: 419-443-5002, E-mail: krintzlineka@tiffin.edu.

Universidad de Iberoamerica, Graduate School, San Jose, Costa Rica. Offers clinical neuropsychology (PhD); clinical psychology (M Psych); educational psychology (M Psych); forensic psychology (M Psych); hospital management (MHA); intensive care nursing (MN); medicine (MD). *Entrance requirements:* For master's, 2 letters of recommendation, interview.

University of Denver, Graduate School of Professional Psychology, Denver, CO 80208. Offers clinical psychology (Psy D); forensic psychology (MA); international disaster psychology (MA); psychology (MA); sport and performance psychology (MA). *Accreditation:* APA. *Faculty:* 15 full-time (8 women), 24 part-time/adjunct (11 women). *Students:* 209 full-time (170 women), 36 part-time (25 women); includes 26 minority (7 Black or African American, non-Hispanic/Latino; 2 American Indian or Alaska Native, non-Hispanic/Latino; 5 Asian, non-Hispanic/Latino; 9 Hispanic/Latino; 3 Two or more races, non-Hispanic/Latino), 4 international. Average age 26. 612 applicants, 30% accepted, 124 enrolled. In 2010, 74 master's, 38 doctorates awarded. *Degree requirements:* For master's, comprehensive exam (for some programs); for doctorate, comprehensive exam (for some programs), paper, clinical internship. *Entrance requirements:* For master's and doctorate, GRE General Test. Additional exam requirements/recommendations for international students: Required—TOEFL (minimum score 550 paper-based; 80 iBT). Application fee: $60. Electronic applications accepted. *Expenses:* Tuition: Full-time $35,604; part-time $29,670 per year. Required fees: $687 per year. Tuition and fees vary according to program. *Financial support:* In 2010–11, 38 teaching assistantships with full and partial tuition reimbursements (averaging $2,952 per year) were awarded; career-related internships or fieldwork, Federal Work-Study, institutionally sponsored loans, scholarships/grants, unspecified assistantships, and clinical assistantships also available. Support available to part-time students. Financial award application deadline: 3/1; financial award applicants required to submit FAFSA. *Unit head:* Dr. Peter Buirski, Dean, 303-871-2382, E-mail: pbuirski@du.edu. *Application contact:* Admissions Counselor, 303-871-3736, Fax: 303-871-7656, E-mail: gsppinfo@du.edu.

University of Massachusetts Boston, Office of Graduate Studies, Graduate College of Education, Counseling and School Psychology Department, Program in Mental Health Counseling, Boston, MA 02125-3393. Offers forensic counseling (M Ed, CAGS).

University of New Haven, Graduate School, College of Arts and Sciences, Program in Community Psychology, West Haven, CT 06516-1916. Offers applications of psychology (Certificate); community clinical services (MA); forensic psychology (Certificate). Part-time and evening/weekend programs available. *Students:* 22 full-time (19 women), 11 part-time (7 women); includes 6 Black or African American, non-Hispanic/Latino; 2 Hispanic/Latino, 2 international. Average age 29. 29 applicants, 100% accepted, 12 enrolled. In 2010, 24 master's awarded. *Degree requirements:* For master's, thesis or alternative. *Entrance requirements:* Additional exam requirements/recommendations for international students: Required—TOEFL (minimum score 520 paper-based; 190 computer-based; 70 iBT); Recommended—IELTS (minimum score 5.5). *Application deadline:* For fall admission, 5/31 for international students; for winter admission, 10/15 for international students; for spring admission, 1/15 for international students. Applications are processed on a rolling basis. Application fee: $50. Electronic applications accepted. *Financial support:* Research assistantships with partial tuition reimbursements, teaching assistantships with partial tuition reimbursements, career-related internships or fieldwork, Federal Work-Study, scholarships/grants, tuition waivers, and unspecified assistantships available. Support available to part-time students. Financial award application deadline: 5/1; financial award applicants required to submit FAFSA. *Unit head:* Dr. Michael A. Morris, Coordinator, 203-932-7281. *Application contact:* Eloise Gormley, Director of Graduate Admissions, 203-932-7449, Fax: 203-932-7137, E-mail: gradinfo@newhaven.edu.

University of New Haven, Graduate School, Henry C. Lee College of Criminal Justice and Forensic Sciences, Program in Criminal Justice, West Haven, CT 06516-1916. Offers crime analysis (MS); criminal justice (PhD); criminal justice management (MS); forensic computer investigation (MS, Certificate); forensic psychology (MS); victim advocacy and services management (Certificate); victimology (MS). Part-time and evening/weekend programs available. *Students:* 47 full-time (29 women), 42 part-time (25 women); includes 17 Black or African American, non-Hispanic/Latino; 5 Hispanic/Latino, 6 international. Average age 29. 95 applicants, 96% accepted, 54 enrolled. In 2010, 12 master's, 12 other advanced degrees awarded. *Degree requirements:* For master's, thesis or alternative. *Entrance requirements:* Additional exam requirements/recommendations for international students: Required—TOEFL (minimum score 520 paper-based; 190 computer-based; 70 iBT), IELTS (minimum score 5.5). *Application deadline:* For fall admission, 5/31 for international students; for winter admission, 10/15 for international students; for spring admission, 1/15 for international students. Applications are processed on a rolling basis. Application fee: $50. Electronic applications accepted. *Financial support:* Research assistantships with partial tuition reimbursements, teaching assistantships with partial tuition reimbursements, career-related internships or fieldwork, Federal Work-Study, scholarships/grants, tuition waivers, and unspecified assistantships available. Support available to part-time students. Financial award applicants required to submit FAFSA. *Unit head:* Dr. James J. Cassidy, Coordinator, 203-932-7374. *Application contact:* Eloise Gormley, Director of Graduate Admissions, 203-932-7449, Fax: 203-932-7137, E-mail: gradinfo@newhaven.edu.

University of North Dakota, Graduate School, College of Arts and Sciences, Department of Psychology, Grand Forks, ND 58202. Offers clinical psychology (PhD); counseling psychology (PhD); experimental psychology (PhD); forensic psychology (MA, MS); psychology (MA). *Accreditation:* APA (one or more programs are accredited). *Faculty:* 22 full-time (7 women), 2 part-time/adjunct (1 woman). *Students:* 55 full-time (46 women), 81 part-time (69 women); includes 24 minority (4 Black or African American, non-Hispanic/Latino; 12 American Indian or Alaska Native, non-Hispanic/Latino; 2 Asian, non-Hispanic/Latino; 4 Hispanic/Latino; 2 Two or more races, non-Hispanic/Latino), 2 international. Average age 29. 126 applicants, 25% accepted, 27 enrolled. In 2010, 25 master's, 9 doctorates awarded. *Degree requirements:* For master's, thesis, final exam; for doctorate, comprehensive exam, thesis/dissertation, internship, final exam. *Entrance requirements:* For master's, GRE General Test, GRE Subject Test, minimum GPA of 3.0; for doctorate, GRE General Test, GRE Subject Test, minimum GPA of 3.5. Additional exam requirements/recommendations for international students: Required—TOEFL (minimum score 550 paper-based; 213 computer-based; 79 iBT), IELTS (minimum score 6.5). *Application deadline:* For fall admission, 1/15 for domestic and international students. Application fee: $35. Electronic applications accepted. *Expenses:* Tuition, state resident: full-time $5857; part-time $306.74 per credit. Tuition, nonresident: full-time $15,666; part-time $729.77 per credit. Required fees: $53.42 per credit. Tuition and fees vary according to course load, program and reciprocity agreements. *Financial support:* In 2010–11, 28 students received support, including 21 teaching assistantships with full and partial tuition reimbursements available (averaging $8,993 per year); fellowships with full and partial tuition reimbursements available, research assistantships with full and partial tuition reimbursements available, career-related internships or fieldwork, Federal Work-Study, institutionally sponsored loans, scholarships/grants, health care benefits, tuition waivers (full and partial), and unspecified assistantships also available. Support available to part-time students. Financial award application deadline: 3/15; financial award applicants required to submit FAFSA. *Faculty research:* Developmental psychology, clinical social psychology, educational psychology, personality disorders. Total annual research expenditures: $323,990. *Unit head:* Dr. Mark Grabe, Chairperson, 701-777-3451, E-mail: mark.grabe@und.nodak.edu. *Application contact:* Matt Anderson, Admissions Specialist, 701-777-2947, Fax: 701-777-3619, E-mail: matthew.anderson@gradschool.und.edu.

Walden University, Graduate Programs, School of Counseling and Social Service, Minneapolis, MN 55401. Offers career counseling (MS); counselor education and supervision (PhD), including consultation, counseling and social change, forensic mental health counseling, general program, nonprofit management and leadership, trauma and crisis; human services (PhD), including clinical social work, counseling, criminal justice, disaster, crisis and intervention, family studies and intervention strategies, general program, human services administration, public health, self-designed, social policy analysis and planning; marriage, couple, and family counseling (MS), including forensic counseling, trauma and crisis counseling; mental health counseling (MS), including forensic counseling. Part-time and evening/weekend programs available. Postbaccalaureate distance learning degree programs offered (minimal on-campus study). *Faculty:* 25 full-time (17 women), 241 part-time/adjunct (162 women). *Students:* 2,687 full-time (2,269 women), 536 part-time (473 women); includes 1,582 minority (1,319 Black or African American, non-Hispanic/Latino; 34 American Indian or Alaska Native, non-Hispanic/Latino; 29 Asian, non-Hispanic/Latino; 142 Hispanic/Latino; 58 Two or more races, non-Hispanic/Latino), 47 international. Average age 38. In 2010, 182 master's, 8 doctorates awarded. *Degree requirements:* For master's, residency (for some programs); for doctorate, thesis/dissertation, residency. *Entrance requirements:* For master's, bachelor's degree or equivalent in related field, minimum GPA of 2.5; for doctorate, master's degree or equivalent in related field; minimum GPA of 3.0; official transcripts; three years' related professional/academic experience (preferred); access to computer and Internet. Additional exam requirements/recommendations for international students: Required—TOEFL (minimum score 550 paper-based; 213 computer-based), IELTS (minimum score 6.5), TOEFL (minimum score 550 paper-based; 213 computer-based), IELTS (minimum score 6.5), or Michigan English Language Assessment Battery (minimum score 82). *Application deadline:* Applications are processed on a rolling basis. Application fee: $50. Electronic applications accepted. *Expenses:* Tuition: Full-time $10,274; part-time $445 per credit. Tuition and fees vary according to course load, degree level and program. *Financial support:* Fellowships, Federal Work-Study, scholarships/grants, unspecified assistantships, and family tuition reduction, active duty/veteran tuition reduction, group tuition reduction, interest-free payment plans available. Support available to part-time students. Financial award applicants required to submit FAFSA. *Unit head:* Dr. Savitri Dixon-Saxon, Associate Dean, 800-925-3368. *Application contact:* Jennifer Hall, Vice President of Enrollment Management, 866-4-WALDEN, E-mail: info@waldenu.edu.

Walden University, Graduate Programs, School of Psychology, Minneapolis, MN 55401. Offers clinical child psychology (Post-Doctoral Certificate); clinical psychology (MS, Post-Doctoral Certificate), including counseling (MS); counseling psychology (Post-Doctoral Certificate); forensic psychology (MS), including forensic psychology in the community, general program, mental health applications, program planning and evaluation in forensic settings, psychology and legal systems; general psychology (Post-Doctoral Certificate); health psychology (Post-Doctoral Certificate); organizational psychology (Post-Doctoral Certificate); organizational psychology and development (Postbaccalaureate Certificate); psychology (MS, PhD), including clinical psychology (PhD), counseling psychology (PhD), crisis management and response (MS), general program (MS), general psychology (PhD), health psychology, leadership development and coaching (MS), media psychology (MS), organizational psychology (PhD), organizational psychology and development (MS), organizational psychology and nonprofit management (MS), program evaluation and research (MS), psychology of culture (MS), psychology, public administration, and social change (MS), social psychology (MS), terrorism and security (MS); teaching online (Post-Master's Certificate). Part-time and evening/weekend programs available. Postbaccalaureate distance learning degree programs offered (minimal on-campus study). *Faculty:* 41 full-time (25 women), 254 part-time/adjunct (131 women). *Students:* 3,463 full-time (2,737 women), 1,400 part-time (1,130 women); includes 1,491 Black or African American, non-Hispanic/Latino; 59 American Indian or Alaska Native, non-Hispanic/Latino; 89 Asian, non-Hispanic/Latino; 283 Hispanic/Latino; 76 Two or more races, non-Hispanic/Latino, 126 international. Average age 40. In 2010, 559 master's, 100 doctorates awarded. Terminal master's awarded for partial completion of doctoral program. *Degree requirements:* For master's, thesis optional; for doctorate, thesis/dissertation, residency. *Entrance requirements:* For master's, bachelor's degree or equivalent in related field; minimum GPA of 2.5; official transcripts; goal statement; access to computer and Internet; for doctorate, master's degree or equivalent in related field; minimum GPA of 3.0; 3 years of related professional/academic experience (preferred). Additional exam requirements/recommendations for international students: Required—TOEFL (minimum score 550 paper-based; 213 computer-based), IELTS (minimum score 6.5), TOEFL (minimum score 550 paper-based; 213 computer-based), IELTS (minimum score 6.5), or Michigan English Language Assessment Battery (minimum score 82). *Application deadline:* Applications are processed on a rolling basis. Application fee: $50. Electronic applications accepted. *Expenses:* Tuition: Full-time $10,274; part-time $445 per credit. Tuition and fees vary according to course load, degree level and program. *Financial support:* In 2010–11, 1 fellowship was awarded; Federal Work-Study, scholarships/grants, unspecified assistantships, and family tuition reduction, active duty/veteran tuition reduction, group tuition reduction, interest-free payment plans also available. Support available to part-time students. Financial award applicants required to submit FAFSA. *Unit head:* Dr. Melanie Storms, Associate Dean, 800-925-3368. *Application contact:* Jennifer Hall, Vice President of Enrollment Management, 866-4-WALDEN, E-mail: info@waldenu.edu.

Genetic Counseling

Arcadia University, Graduate Studies, Program in Genetic Counseling, Glenside, PA 19038-3295. Offers MSGC. *Faculty:* 3 full-time (all women), 18 part-time/adjunct (14 women). *Students:* 27 full-time (all women); includes 1 minority (Asian, non-Hispanic/Latino). Average age 25. In 2010, 14 master's awarded. *Degree requirements:* For master's, thesis. *Entrance requirements:* For master's, GRE. Additional exam requirements/recommendations for international students: Required—TOEFL. *Application deadline:* For fall admission, 3/1 for domestic students. Application fee: $50. *Expenses:* Contact institution. *Financial support:* In 2010–11, 9 students received support. Tuition waivers (partial) and unspecified assistantships available. *Unit head:* Kathleen Valverde, Director, 215-572-4058. *Application contact:* 215-572-2910, Fax: 215-572-4049, E-mail: admiss@arcadia.edu.

Brandeis University, Graduate School of Arts and Sciences, Program in Genetic Counseling, Waltham, MA 02454-9110. Offers MS. *Faculty:* 6 part-time/adjunct (5 women). *Students:* 21 full-time (all women), 3 international. 122 applicants, 9% accepted, 10 enrolled. In 2010, 11 master's awarded. *Degree requirements:* For master's, thesis. *Entrance requirements:* For master's, GRE General Test, resume, 3 letters of recommendation, statement of purpose. Additional exam requirements/recommendations for international students: Required—TOEFL (minimum score 600 paper-based; 250 computer-based; 100 iBT); Recommended—IELTS (minimum score 7). *Application deadline:* For fall admission, 2/1 for domestic and international students. Application fee: $75. Electronic applications accepted. *Expenses:* Contact institution. *Financial support:* In 2010–11, 20 students received support. Career-related internships or fieldwork, scholarships/grants, and tuition waivers (partial) available. Financial award application deadline: 4/15; financial award applicants required to submit FAFSA. *Faculty research:* Genetics, clinical genetics, human reproductive biology, counseling, genetic counseling. *Unit head:* Dr. Judith Tsipis, Director, 781-736-3179, Fax: 781-736-3107, E-mail: tsipis@brandeis.edu. *Application contact:* Missy Goldberg, Department Administrator, 781-736-3179, Fax: 781-736-3107, E-mail: goldberg@brandeis.edu.

California State University, Stanislaus, College of Natural Sciences, Program in Genetic Counseling (MS), Turlock, CA 95382. Offers MS. *Students:* 18 full-time (17 women); includes 3 minority (all Asian, non-Hispanic/Latino), 3 international. Average age 29. 65 applicants, 14% accepted, 9 enrolled. *Degree requirements:* For master's, thesis. *Entrance requirements:* For master's, GRE, minimum GPA of 3.0, 3 letters of reference, personal statement. Additional exam requirements/recommendations for international students: Required—TOEFL (minimum score 550 paper-based; 213 computer-based). *Application deadline:* For fall admission, 5/1 for domestic students; for spring admission, 1/7 for domestic students. Application fee: $55. Electronic applications accepted. *Expenses:* Contact institution. *Unit head:* Dr. Janey Youngblom, Program Director, 209-667-3153, E-mail: jyoungblom1@csustan.edu. *Application contact:* Extended Education, 209-667-3111, E-mail: extendeded@csustan.edu.

Case Western Reserve University, School of Medicine and School of Graduate Studies, Graduate Programs in Medicine, Department of Genetics, Program in Genetic Counseling, Cleveland, OH 44106. Offers MS. *Degree requirements:* For master's, thesis. *Entrance requirements:* For master's, GRE General Test. Additional exam requirements/recommendations for international students: Required—TOEFL. *Faculty research:* Genetic testing, ethical issues in genetics, cancer genetics, reproductive genetics, prenatal diagnosis.

The Johns Hopkins University, Bloomberg School of Public Health, Department of Health, Behavior and Society, Baltimore, MD 21218-2699. Offers genetic counseling (Sc M); health education and health communication (MHS); social and behavioral sciences (Dr PH, PhD, Sc D); social factors in health (MHS). *Faculty:* 43 full-time (30 women), 59 part-time/adjunct (40 women). *Students:* 114 full-time (105 women), 5 part-time (all women); includes 43 minority (14 Black or African American, non-Hispanic/Latino; 15 Asian, non-Hispanic/Latino; 6 Hispanic/Latino; 8 Two or more races, non-Hispanic/Latino), 11 international. Average age 28. 227 applicants, 31% accepted, 26 enrolled. In 2010, 21 master's, 10 doctorates awarded. *Degree requirements:* For master's, comprehensive exam (for some programs), thesis (for some programs); for doctorate, comprehensive exam, thesis/dissertation. *Entrance requirements:* For master's, GRE, curriculum vitae, 3 letters of recommendation; for doctorate, GRE, transcripts, curriculum vitae, 3 recommendation letters. Additional exam requirements/recommendations for international students: Required—TOEFL (minimum score 600 paper-based; 250 computer-based; 100 iBT). *Application deadline:* For fall admission, 12/1 for domestic and international students. Applications are processed on a rolling basis. Application fee: $45. Electronic applications accepted. *Financial support:* In 2010–11, 96 students received support, including 17 fellowships with tuition reimbursements available (averaging $23,634 per year), 30 research assistantships (averaging $7,800 per year), 25 teaching assistantships (averaging $2,759 per year); career-related internships or fieldwork, Federal Work-Study, scholarships/grants, traineeships, health care benefits, unspecified assistantships, and stipends also available. Financial award application deadline: 3/15. *Faculty research:* Social determinants of health and structural and community-level inventions to improve health, communication and health education, behavioral and social aspects of genetic counseling. Total annual research expenditures: $6.3 million. *Unit head:* Georgean Smith, Administrator, 410-502-3715, Fax: 410-502-4333, E-mail: gcsmith@jhsph.edu. *Application contact:* Barbara W. Diehl, Senior Academic Program Coordinator, 410-502-4415, Fax: 410-502-4333, E-mail: bdiehl@jhsph.edu.

Long Island University, C.W. Post Campus, College of Liberal Arts and Sciences, Department of Biology, Brookville, NY 11548-1300. Offers biology (MS); biology education (MS); genetic counseling (MS). Part-time and evening/weekend programs available. *Degree requirements:* For master's, thesis optional. *Entrance requirements:* For master's, GRE General Test, minimum GPA of 2.75 in major. Electronic applications accepted. *Faculty research:* Immunology, molecular biology, systematics, behavioral ecology, microbiology.

McGill University, Faculty of Graduate and Postdoctoral Studies, Faculty of Medicine, Department of Human Genetics, Montréal, QC H3A 2T5, Canada. Offers genetic counseling (M Sc); human genetics (M Sc, PhD).

Mount Sinai School of Medicine, Graduate School of Biological Sciences, New York, NY 10029-6504. Offers biomedical sciences (MS, PhD); clinical research education (MS, PhD); community medicine (MPH); genetic counseling (MS); neurosciences (PhD); MD/PhD. *Faculty:* 126 full-time (40 women). *Students:* 438 full-time (260 women); includes 29 Black or African American, non-Hispanic/Latino; 3 American Indian or Alaska Native, non-Hispanic/Latino; 86 Asian, non-Hispanic/Latino; 18 Hispanic/Latino, 99 international. 924 applicants, 29% accepted, 104 enrolled. In 2010, 58 master's, 36 doctorates awarded. Terminal master's awarded for partial completion of doctoral program. *Degree requirements:* For master's, thesis; for doctorate, comprehensive exam, thesis/dissertation. *Entrance requirements:* For master's, GRE General Test; for doctorate, GRE General Test, GRE Subject Test, 3 years of college pre-med course work. Additional exam requirements/recommendations for international students: Required—TOEFL. *Application deadline:* For fall admission, 12/15 for domestic and international students. Applications are processed on a rolling basis. Application fee: $80. Electronic applications accepted. *Expenses:* Tuition: Full-time $25,600; part-time $800 per credit hour. Required fees: $1600. Full-time tuition and fees vary according to program. *Financial support:* In 2010–11, fellowships with full tuition reimbursements (averaging $32,000 per year), research assistantships with full tuition reimbursements (averaging $32,000 per year) were awarded; Federal Work-Study, institutionally sponsored loans, scholarships/grants, health care benefits, and unspecified assistantships also available. Financial award application deadline: 4/30; financial award applicants required to submit FAFSA. *Faculty research:* Cancer, genetics and genomics, immunology, neuroscience, developmental and stem cell biology, translational research. Total annual research expenditures: $264.9 million. *Unit head:* Dr. John Morrison, Dean, 212-241-6546, Fax: 212-241-0651, E-mail: john.morrison@mssm.edu. *Application contact:* Lily Recanati, Manager, 212-241-2793, Fax: 212-241-0651, E-mail: lily.recantati@mssm.edu.

Northwestern University, The Graduate School, Program in Genetic Counseling, Evanston, IL 60208. Offers MS. *Degree requirements:* For master's, thesis. *Entrance requirements:* For master's, GRE General Test, interview. Additional exam requirements/recommendations for international students: Required—TOEFL. *Faculty research:* Preimplantation genetic diagnosis, gene expression in preimplantation embryos, fetal cells in maternal blood: first trimester prenatal screening for Down's Syndrome, genetic counseling efficacy and counseling issues in prenatal diagnosis.

Sarah Lawrence College, Graduate Studies, Joan H. Marks Graduate Program in Human Genetics, Bronxville, NY 10708-5999. Offers MS. Part-time programs available. *Degree*

Genetic Counseling

Sarah Lawrence College (continued)
requirements: For master's, thesis, fieldwork. *Entrance requirements:* For master's, previous course work in biology, chemistry, developmental biology, genetics, probability and statistics. *Expenses:* Contact institution.

Université de Montréal, Faculty of Medicine, Program in Genetic Counseling, Montréal, QC H3C 3J7, Canada. Offers DESS.

The University of Alabama at Birmingham, School of Health Professions, Program in Genetic Counseling, Birmingham, AL 35294. Offers MS. *Students:* 6 full-time (4 women). Average age 24. 25 applicants, 40% accepted, 6 enrolled. *Expenses:* Tuition, state resident: full-time $5482. Tuition, nonresident: full-time $12,430. Tuition and fees vary according to program. *Unit head:* Janelle Chiasera, 205-934-5994. *Application contact:* Julie Bryant, Director of Graduate Admissions, 205-934-8227, Fax: 205-934-8413, E-mail: jbryant@uab.edu.

University of Arkansas for Medical Sciences, Graduate School, Program in Genetic Counseling, Little Rock, AR 72205-7199. Offers MS. *Degree requirements:* For master's, thesis. *Entrance requirements:* For master's, GRE. Additional exam requirements/recommendations for international students: Required—TOEFL.

The University of British Columbia, Faculty of Medicine, Department of Medical Genetics, M Sc Program in Genetic Counselling, Vancouver, BC V6H 3N1, Canada. Offers M Sc. Electronic applications accepted. Tuition charges are reported in Canadian dollars. *Expenses:* Tuition, area resident: Full-time $4179 Canadian dollars. International tuition: $7344 Canadian dollars full-time.

University of California, Irvine, School of Medicine, Department of Pediatrics, Program in Genetic Counseling, Irvine, CA 92697. Offers MS. *Students:* 11 full-time (10 women), 1 (woman) part-time; includes 3 minority (2 Asian, non-Hispanic/Latino; 1 Two or more races, non-Hispanic/Latino). Average age 28. 77 applicants, 6% accepted, 5 enrolled. In 2010, 6 master's awarded. *Degree requirements:* For master's, thesis. *Entrance requirements:* For master's, GRE General Test, minimum GPA of 3.0. Additional exam requirements/recommendations for international students: Required—TOEFL (minimum score 550 paper-based; 213 computer-based). *Application deadline:* For fall admission, 1/15 priority date for domestic students, 1/15 for international students. Applications are processed on a rolling basis. Application fee: $80 ($100 for international students). Electronic applications accepted. *Financial support:* In 2010–11, 3 students received support; research assistantships with full tuition reimbursements available, teaching assistantships, career-related internships or fieldwork, institutionally sponsored loans, traineeships, health care benefits, and unspecified assistantships available. Financial award application deadline: 3/1; financial award applicants required to submit FAFSA. *Faculty research:* Gene mapping and linkage analysis, delineation of new malformation and chromosomal syndromes, ethical and counseling issues in genetics. *Application contact:* Nancy Oropeza, Supervising Admin Specialist, 714-456-7570, Fax: 714-456-5330, E-mail: noropeza@uci.edu.

University of Cincinnati, Graduate School, College of Allied Health Sciences, Program in Genetic Counseling, Cincinnati, OH 45221. Offers medical genetics (MS). Part-time programs available. *Degree requirements:* For master's, thesis. *Entrance requirements:* For master's, GRE General Test. Additional exam requirements/recommendations for international students: Required—TOEFL. Electronic applications accepted. *Faculty research:* Lysosomal disease, Tourette's syndrome, epidemiology of Down syndrome, genetic counseling, genetic disease treatment.

University of Colorado Denver, School of Medicine, Graduate Program in Genetic Counseling, Aurora, CO 80045. Offers MS. *Students:* 12 full-time (all women). Average age 25. 68 applicants, 9% accepted, 6 enrolled. In 2010, 6 master's awarded. *Degree requirements:* For master's, thesis or alternative, 43 core semester hours. *Entrance requirements:* For master's, GRE, minimum undergraduate GPA of 3.0; 4 letters of recommendations; prerequisite coursework in biology, general chemistry, general biochemistry, general genetics, general psychology; experience in counseling and laboratory settings and strong understanding of genetic counseling field (highly recommended). Additional exam requirements/recommendations for international students: Required—TOEFL. *Application deadline:* For fall admission, 1/1 for domestic students. Application fee: $65. Electronic applications accepted. *Expenses:* Contact institution. *Financial support:* Career-related internships or fieldwork and Federal Work-Study available. Financial award application deadline: 4/1. *Faculty research:* Psychosocial aspects of genetic counseling, clinical cytogenetics and molecular genetics, human inborn errors of metabolism, congenital malformations and disorders of the newborn, cancer genetics and genetic counseling. *Unit head:* Carol Walton, Director, 303-724-2370, E-mail: walton.carol@tchden.org. *Application contact:* Dr. Norma Wagoner, Associate Dean for Admissions, 303-724-8025, E-mail: somadmin@ucdenver.edu.

University of Maryland, Baltimore, School of Medicine, Genetic Counseling Training Program, Baltimore, MD 21201. Offers MGC. Part-time tuition and fees vary according to course load, degree level and program. *Unit head:* Dr. E. Albert Reece, Dean and Vice President for Medical Affairs, 410-706-7410, Fax: 410-706-0235, E-mail: deanmed@som.umaryland.edu. *Application contact:* Dr. E. Albert Reece, Dean and Vice President for Medical Affairs, 410-706-7410, Fax: 410-706-0235, E-mail: deanmed@som.umaryland.edu.

University of Michigan, Horace H. Rackham School of Graduate Studies, Program in Biomedical Sciences (PIBS), Department of Human Genetics, Ann Arbor, MI 48109. Offers genetic counseling (MS); human genetics (MS, PhD). *Faculty:* 33 full-time (14 women). *Students:* 38 full-time (29 women); includes 8 minority (1 Black or African American, non-Hispanic/Latino; 5 Asian, non-Hispanic/Latino; 1 Hispanic/Latino; 1 Two or more races, non-Hispanic/Latino). Average age 28. 187 applicants, 16 enrolled. In 2010, 8 master's, 3 doctorates awarded. Terminal master's awarded for partial completion of doctoral program. *Degree requirements:* For master's, research project; for doctorate, thesis/dissertation, oral preliminary exam, oral defense of dissertation. *Entrance requirements:* For master's, GRE General Test, 3 letters of recommendation, advocacy experience; for doctorate, GRE General Test, 3 letters of recommendation. Additional exam requirements/recommendations for international students: Required—TOEFL (minimum score 84 iBT). *Application deadline:* For fall admission, 12/1 for domestic students, 12/1 priority date for international students. Application fee: $65 ($75 for international students). Electronic applications accepted. *Expenses:* Tuition, state resident: full-time $17,784; part-time $1116 per credit hour. Tuition, nonresident: full-time $35,944; part-time $2125 per credit hour. International tuition: $35,994 full-time. Required fees: $95 per semester. Tuition and fees vary according to course load, degree level and program. *Financial support:* In 2010–11, 32 students received support, including 24 fellowships with full tuition reimbursements available (averaging $26,500 per year), 3 teaching assistantships with full tuition reimbursements available (averaging $17,270 per year); scholarships/grants, traineeships, health care benefits, and unspecified assistantships also available. Financial award application deadline: 12/1; financial award applicants required to submit FAFSA. *Faculty research:* Molecular, developmental, statistical, and population genetics. Total annual research expenditures: $8.4 million. *Unit head:* Dr. Sally A. Camper, Chair, 734-763-0682, Fax: 734-763-3784, E-mail: scamper@umich.edu. *Application contact:* Michelle S. Melis, Director of Student Life, 734-615-6538, Fax: 734-647-7022, E-mail: msmtegan@umich.edu.

University of Minnesota, Twin Cities Campus, Graduate School, Program in Molecular, Cellular, Developmental Biology and Genetics, Minneapolis, MN 55455-0213. Offers genetic counseling (MS); molecular, cellular, developmental biology and genetics (PhD). Terminal master's awarded for partial completion of doctoral program. *Degree requirements:* For master's, thesis optional; for doctorate, thesis/dissertation. *Entrance requirements:* For master's and doctorate, GRE General Test. Additional exam requirements/recommendations for international students: Required—TOEFL (minimum score 625 paper-based; 263 computer-based; 80 iBT). Electronic applications accepted. *Faculty research:* Membrane receptors and membrane transport, cell interactions, cytoskeleton and cell mobility, regulation of gene expression, plant cell and molecular biology.

The University of North Carolina at Greensboro, Graduate School, Program in Genetic Counseling, Greensboro, NC 27412-5001. Offers MS. Electronic applications accepted.

University of Oklahoma Health Sciences Center, College of Medicine and Graduate College, Department of Genetic Counseling, Oklahoma City, OK 73190. Offers MS. *Entrance requirements:* For master's, GRE General Test, 3 letters of recommendation.

University of Pittsburgh, Graduate School of Public Health, Department of Human Genetics, Pittsburgh, PA 15260. Offers genetic counseling (MS); human genetics (MS, PhD); public health genetics (MPH, Certificate). *Faculty:* 9 full-time (5 women), 5 part-time/adjunct (2 women). *Students:* 40 full-time (31 women), 27 part-time (23 women); includes 5 Asian, non-Hispanic/Latino; 1 Hispanic/Latino, 22 international. Average age 28. 111 applicants, 53% accepted, 21 enrolled. In 2010, 14 master's, 7 doctorates awarded. Terminal master's awarded for partial completion of doctoral program. *Degree requirements:* For master's, thesis (for some programs); for doctorate, thesis/dissertation. *Entrance requirements:* For master's, GRE General Test, previous course work in biochemistry, calculus, and genetics; for doctorate, GRE General Test. Additional exam requirements/recommendations for international students: Required—TOEFL (minimum score 550 paper-based; 213 computer-based; 80 iBT). *Application deadline:* For fall admission, 4/1 for international students; for winter admission, 9/1 for international students; for spring admission, 2/1 for international students. Applications are processed on a rolling basis. Application fee: $115. Electronic applications accepted. *Expenses:* Tuition, state resident: full-time $17,304; part-time $701 per credit. Tuition, nonresident: full-time $29,554; part-time $1210 per credit. Required fees: $740; $214 per term. Tuition and fees vary according to program. *Financial support:* In 2010–11, 20 students received support, including 20 research assistantships with full tuition reimbursements available (averaging $21,834 per year). *Faculty research:* Genetic mechanisms related to the transition from normal to disease states, how genes and the environment interact to affect the distribution of health and disease in human populations. Total annual research expenditures: $5.8 million. *Unit head:* Dr. Mohammad Kamboh, Chairman, 412-624-3066, Fax: 412-624-3020, E-mail: kamboh@pitt.edu. *Application contact:* Jeanette Norbut, Administrative Secretary, 412-624-3018, Fax: 412-624-3020, E-mail: jeanette.norbut@hgen.pitt.edu.

University of South Carolina, School of Medicine and The Graduate School, Graduate Programs in Medicine, Program in Genetic Counseling, Columbia, SC 29203. Offers MS. *Degree requirements:* For master's, comprehensive exam, internship, practicum. *Entrance requirements:* For master's, GRE General Test. Electronic applications accepted. *Expenses:* Contact institution. *Faculty research:* Genetic counseling, international, transition, prenatal diagnosis.

The University of Texas Health Science Center at Houston, Graduate School of Biomedical Sciences, Program in Genetic Counseling, Houston, TX 77225-0036. Offers MS. *Degree requirements:* For master's, thesis. *Entrance requirements:* For master's, GRE General Test. Additional exam requirements/recommendations for international students: Required—TOEFL. Electronic applications accepted. *Faculty research:* Psychosocial aspects of genetic counseling, risk assessment, cancer genetic counseling, multicultural genetic counseling, prenatal counseling.

University of Toronto, School of Graduate Studies, Life Sciences Division, Department of Molecular and Medical Genetics, Toronto, ON M5S 1A1, Canada. Offers genetic counseling (M Sc); molecular and medical genetics (M Sc, PhD). *Degree requirements:* For master's, thesis; for doctorate, thesis/dissertation. *Entrance requirements:* For master's, B Sc or equivalent; for doctorate, M Sc or equivalent, minimum B+ average. Additional exam requirements/recommendations for international students: Required—TOEFL, IELTS (minimum score: 7), Michigan English Language Assessment Battery (minimum score: 85) or COPE (minimum score: 4). *Faculty research:* Structural biology, developmental genetics, molecular medicine, genetic counseling.

University of Wisconsin–Madison, Graduate School, College of Agricultural and Life Sciences and Graduate Programs in Medicine, Department of Genetics, Program in Genetic Counseling, Madison, WI 53706-1380. Offers MS. *Expenses:* Tuition, state resident: full-time $9887; part-time $617.96 per credit. Tuition, nonresident: full-time $24,054; part-time $1503.40 per credit. Required fees: $67.63 per credit. Tuition and fees vary according to reciprocity agreements.

Wayne State University, School of Medicine, Graduate Programs in Medicine, Genetic Counseling Graduate Program, Detroit, MI 48202. Offers MS. *Faculty:* 6 full-time (1 woman). *Students:* 13 full-time (11 women); includes 1 minority (Asian, non-Hispanic/Latino), 2 international. Average age 27. 34 applicants, 21% accepted, 7 enrolled. In 2010, 6 master's awarded. *Degree requirements:* For master's, research project, internship. *Entrance requirements:* For master's, GRE, interview, recommendations, personal statement. *Expenses:* Tuition, state resident: full-time $7662; part-time $478.85 per credit hour. Tuition, nonresident: full-time $16,920; part-time $1057.55 per credit hour. Required fees: $571.20; $35.70 per credit hour. $188.05 per semester. Tuition and fees vary according to course load and program. *Unit head:* Dr. Kenneth C. Palmer, Assistant Dean, 313-577-1455, E-mail: kpalmer@med.wayne.edu. *Application contact:* Dr. Kenneth C. Palmer, Assistant Dean, 313-577-1455, E-mail: kpalmer@med.wayne.edu.

Health Psychology

Adler School of Professional Psychology, Programs in Psychology, Chicago, IL 60602. Offers advanced Adlerian psychotherapy (Certificate); art therapy (MA); clinical neuropsychology (Certificate); clinical psychology (Psy D); community psychology (MA); counseling and organizational psychology (MA); counseling psychology (MA); forensic psychology (MA); gerontological counseling (MA); marriage and family counseling (MA); marriage and family therapy (Certificate); organizational psychology (MA); police psychology (MA); rehabilitation counseling (MA); sport and health psychology (MA); substance abuse counseling (Certificate); Psy D/Certificate; Psy D/MACAT; Psy D/MACP; Psy D/MAMFC; Psy D/MASAC. *Accreditation:* APA. Part-time and evening/weekend programs available. Postbaccalaureate distance learning degree programs offered (minimal on-campus study). *Faculty:* 40 full-time (18 women), 61 part-time/adjunct (31 women). *Students:* 688 full-time (532 women), 142 part-time (110 women). Average age 27. Terminal master's awarded for partial completion of doctoral program. *Degree requirements:* For master's, thesis or alternative, oral exam, practicum; for doctorate, thesis/dissertation, clinical exam, internship, oral exam, practicum, written qualifying exam. *Entrance requirements:*

For master's, 12 semester hours in psychology, minimum GPA of 3.0; for doctorate, 18 semester hours in psychology, minimum GPA of 3.25; for Certificate, appropriate master's or doctoral degree. Additional exam requirements/recommendations for international students: Required—TOEFL (minimum score 550 paper-based; 213 computer-based; 79 iBT). *Application deadline:* For fall admission, 2/15 priority date for domestic students, 12/1 priority date for international students. Applications are processed on a rolling basis. Application fee: $50. Electronic applications accepted. *Financial support:* Career-related internships or fieldwork, Federal Work-Study, scholarships/grants, and tuition waivers (full and partial) available. Support available to part-time students. Financial award application deadline: 5/15; financial award applicants required to submit FAFSA. *Application contact:* Michelle Brice, Director of Admissions, 312-662-4113, Fax: 312-662-4199, E-mail: admissions@adler.edu.

See Display on page 912 and Close-Up on page 1119.

Appalachian State University, Cratis D. Williams Graduate School, Department of Psychology, Boone, NC 28608. Offers clinical health psychology (MA); general experimental psychology (MA); industrial and organizational psychology (MA). Part-time programs available. *Faculty:* 31 full-time (10 women), 2 part-time/adjunct (1 woman). *Students:* 55 full-time (40 women), 11 part-time (9 women); includes 3 minority (2 Black or African American, non-Hispanic/Latino; 1 Two or more races, non-Hispanic/Latino). 158 applicants, 32% accepted, 28 enrolled. In 2010, 25 master's, 7 other advanced degrees awarded. *Degree requirements:* For master's, comprehensive exam, thesis optional, exit exam. *Entrance requirements:* For master's, GRE General Test, 3 letters of recommendation. Additional exam requirements/recommendations for international students: Required—TOEFL (minimum score 550 paper-based; 230 computer-based; 79 iBT) or IELTS (minimum score 6.5). *Application deadline:* For fall admission, 2/15 for domestic students, 2/1 for international students. Applications are processed on a rolling basis. Application fee: $55. Electronic applications accepted. *Expenses:* Tuition, state resident: full-time $3428; part-time $428 per unit. Tuition, nonresident: full-time $14,518; part-time $1814 per unit. Required fees: $2320; $344 per unit. Tuition and fees vary according to campus/location. *Financial support:* In 2010–11, 34 research assistantships (averaging $4,000 per year), 25 teaching assistantships (averaging $4,000 per year) were awarded; fellowships, career-related internships or fieldwork, Federal Work-Study, scholarships/grants, and unspecified assistantships also available. Financial award application deadline: 4/1; financial award applicants required to submit FAFSA. *Faculty research:* Eating disorders, school-based consultations, organizational behavior management, brain mechanisms of sound localization, parenting styles. Total annual research expenditures: $18,000. *Unit head:* Dr. James Denniston, Chair, 828-262-2272, Fax: 828-262-2272, E-mail: dennistonjc@appstate.edu. *Application contact:* Dr. Denise Martz, Graduate Coordinator, 828-262-2715, E-mail: martzdm@appstate.edu.

Argosy University, Atlanta, College of Psychology and Behavioral Sciences, Atlanta, GA 30328. Offers clinical psychology (MA, Psy D, Postdoctoral Respecialization Certificate), including child and family psychology (Psy D), general adult clinical (Psy D), health psychology (Psy D), neuropsychology/geropsychology (Psy D); community counseling (MA), including marriage and family therapy; counselor education and supervision (Ed D); forensic psychology (MA); industrial organizational psychology (MA); marriage and family therapy (Certificate); sport-exercise psychology (MA). *Accreditation:* APA.

See Close-Up on page 1121.

Argosy University, Chicago, College of Psychology and Behavioral Sciences, Doctoral Program in Clinical Psychology, Chicago, IL 60601. Offers child and adolescent psychology (Psy D); client-centered and experiential psychotherapies (Psy D); diversity and multicultural psychology (Psy D); family psychology (Psy D); forensic psychology (Psy D); health psychology (Psy D); neuropsychology (Psy D); organizational consulting (Psy D); psychoanalytic psychology (Psy D); psychology and spirituality (Psy D). *Accreditation:* APA.

See Close-Up on page 1123.

Argosy University, Schaumburg, College of Psychology and Behavioral Sciences, Schaumburg, IL 60173-5403. Offers clinical health psychology (Post-Graduate Certificate); clinical psychology (MA, Psy D), including child and family psychology (Psy D), clinical health psychology (Psy D), diversity and multicultural psychology (Psy D), forensic psychology (Psy D), neuropsychology (Psy D); community counseling (MA); counseling psychology (Ed D), including counselor education and supervision; counselor education and supervision (Ed D); forensic psychology (Post-Graduate Certificate); industrial organizational psychology (MA). *Accreditation:* ACA; APA.

See Close-Up on page 1149.

Argosy University, Twin Cities, College of Psychology and Behavioral Sciences, Eagan, MN 55121. Offers clinical psychology (MA, Psy D), including child and family psychology (Psy D), forensic psychology (Psy D), health and neuropsychology (Psy D), trauma (Psy D); forensic counseling (Post-Graduate Certificate); forensic psychology (MA); industrial organizational psychology (MA); marriage and family therapy (MA, DMFT), including forensic counseling (MA). *Accreditation:* AAMFT; AAMFT/COAMFTE; APA.

See Close-Up on page 1155.

Argosy University, Washington DC, College of Psychology and Behavioral Sciences, Arlington, VA 22209. Offers clinical psychology (MA, Psy D), including child and family psychology (Psy D), diversity and multicultural psychology (Psy D), forensic psychology (Psy D), health and neuropsychology (Psy D); community counseling (MA); counseling psychology (Ed D), including counselor education and supervision; counselor education and supervision (Ed D); forensic psychology (MA). *Accreditation:* APA.

See Close-Up on page 1157.

Bastyr University, School of Nutrition and Exercise Science, Kenmore, WA 98028-4966. Offers nutrition (MS); nutrition and clinical health psychology (MS). *Accreditation:* ADtA. Part-time programs available. *Students:* 91 full-time (88 women), 26 part-time (25 women). Average age 31. In 2010, 36 master's awarded. *Degree requirements:* For master's, thesis optional. *Entrance requirements:* For master's, 1 year of course work in chemistry, biochemistry, physiology and nutrition. Additional exam requirements/recommendations for international students: Required—TOEFL (minimum score 550 paper-based; 213 computer-based; 79 iBT). *Application deadline:* For fall admission, 3/15 priority date for domestic and international students. Applications are processed on a rolling basis. Application fee: $75. *Expenses:* Tuition: Full-time $19,995; part-time $528 per credit hour. *Financial support:* Career-related internships or fieldwork, Federal Work-Study, and scholarships/grants available. Support available to part-time students. Financial award application deadline: 4/15; financial award applicants required to submit FAFSA. *Unit head:* Debra Boutin, Chair, 425-823-1300, Fax: 425-823-6222. *Application contact:* Admissions Office, 425-602-3330, Fax: 425-602-3090, E-mail: admissions@bastyr.edu.

California Institute of Integral Studies, School of Consciousness and Transformation, San Francisco, CA 94103. Offers creative inquiry/interdisciplinary arts (MFA); cultural anthropology and social transformation (MA); East-West psychology (MA, PhD); integrative health studies (MA); philosophy and religion (MA, PhD), including Asian and comparative studies, philosophy, cosmology, and consciousness, women's spirituality; social and cultural anthropology (PhD); transformative leadership (MA); transformative studies (PhD); writing and consciousness (MFA). Part-time and evening/weekend programs available. Postbaccalaureate distance learning degree programs offered (minimal on-campus study). *Students:* 455 full-time (315 women), 133 part-time (90 women); includes 47 Black or African American, non-Hispanic/Latino; 3 American Indian or Alaska Native, non-Hispanic/Latino; 21 Asian, non-Hispanic/Latino; 41 Hispanic/Latino, 40 international. Average age 37. 265 applicants, 91% accepted, 163 enrolled. In 2010, 64 master's, 22 doctorates awarded. Terminal master's awarded for partial completion of doctoral program. *Degree requirements:* For master's, thesis optional; for doctorate, comprehensive exam, thesis/dissertation, 1 foreign language (Asian comparative studies). *Entrance requirements:* For master's, minimum GPA of 3.0, letters of recommendation, writing sample; for doctorate, master's degree, minimum GPA of 3.0, letters of recommendation, writing sample. Additional exam requirements/recommendations for international students: Required—TOEFL. *Application deadline:* For fall admission, 2/1 priority date for domestic and international students; for spring admission, 10/15 priority date for domestic and international students. Applications are processed on a rolling basis. Application fee: $65. Electronic applications accepted. *Expenses:* Tuition: Full-time $15,660; part-time $870 per semester hour. Required fees: $95 per semester. *Financial support:* In 2010–11, 255 students received support; research assistantships, teaching assistantships, career-related internships or fieldwork, Federal Work-Study, scholarships/grants, and tuition waivers (partial) available. Support available to part-time students. Financial award application deadline: 4/15; financial award applicants required to submit FAFSA. *Faculty research:* Ecology and sustainability, philosophy and religion, East-West psychology, integrative health, social and cultural anthropology, transformative leadership. *Application contact:* Allyson Werner, Associate Director of Admissions, 415-575-6155, Fax: 415-575-1268.

California Institute of Integral Studies, School of Professional Psychology, San Francisco, CA 94103. Offers clinical psychology (Psy D); community mental health (MA); drama therapy (MA); expressive arts therapy (MA); integral counseling psychology (MA); integral counseling psychology-weekend (MA); somatic psychology (MA). *Accreditation:* APA. Part-time and evening/weekend programs available. *Students:* 651 full-time (476 women), 74 part-time (62 women); includes 146 minority (32 Black or African American, non-Hispanic/Latino; 1 American Indian or Alaska Native, non-Hispanic/Latino; 53 Asian, non-Hispanic/Latino; 43 Hispanic/Latino; 17 Two or more races, non-Hispanic/Latino), 52 international. Average age 37. 556 applicants, 72% accepted, 247 enrolled. In 2010, 148 master's, 27 doctorates awarded. *Degree requirements:* For doctorate, comprehensive exam, thesis/dissertation. *Entrance requirements:* For master's, minimum GPA of 3.0, letters of recommendation, writing sample; for doctorate, GRE, MA in psychology or social work with appropriate practical experience for advanced standing, or BA with a minimum GPA of 3.1; letters of recommendation; writing sample. Additional exam requirements/recommendations for international students: Required—TOEFL. *Application deadline:* For fall admission, 2/1 priority date for domestic and international students; for spring admission, 10/15 priority date for domestic and international students. Applications are processed on a rolling basis. Application fee: $65. Electronic applications accepted. *Expenses:* Tuition: Full-time $15,660; part-time $870 per semester hour. Required fees: $95 per semester. *Financial support:* Research assistantships with tuition reimbursements, teaching assistantships with tuition reimbursements, career-related internships or fieldwork, Federal Work-Study, scholarships/grants, and tuition waivers (partial) available. Support available to part-time students. Financial award application deadline: 4/15; financial award applicants required to submit FAFSA. *Faculty research:* Transpersonal psychology, somatic psychology, expressive arts therapy, drama therapy, community mental health, ecopsychology. *Application contact:* David Townes, Senior Admissions Counselor, 415-575-6152, Fax: 415-575-1268, E-mail: dtownes@ciis.edu.

Central Connecticut State University, School of Graduate Studies, School of Arts and Sciences, Department of Psychology, New Britain, CT 06050-4010. Offers community psychology (MA); general psychology (MA); health psychology (MA). Part-time and evening/weekend programs available. *Faculty:* 20 full-time (12 women), 22 part-time/adjunct (6 women). *Students:* 26 full-time (20 women), 25 part-time (20 women); includes 6 minority (1 Black or African American, non-Hispanic/Latino; 4 Hispanic/Latino; 1 Two or more races, non-Hispanic/Latino). Average age 26. 65 applicants, 57% accepted, 19 enrolled. In 2010, 7 master's awarded. *Degree requirements:* For master's, comprehensive exam, thesis or alternative. *Entrance requirements:* For master's, minimum undergraduate GPA of 2.7, essay. Additional exam requirements/recommendations for international students: Required—TOEFL. *Application deadline:* For fall admission, 4/25 for domestic students; for spring admission, 12/1 for domestic students. Applications are processed on a rolling basis. Application fee: $50. Electronic applications accepted. *Expenses:* Tuition, area resident: Full-time $5012; part-time $470 per credit. Tuition, state resident: full-time $7518; part-time $482 per credit. Tuition, nonresident: full-time $13,962; part-time $482 per credit. Required fees: $3772. One-time fee: $62 part-time. *Financial support:* In 2010–11, 8 students received support, including 4 research assistantships; career-related internships or fieldwork, Federal Work-Study, scholarships/grants, and unspecified assistantships also available. Support available to part-time students. Financial award application deadline: 2/15; financial award applicants required to submit FAFSA. *Faculty research:* Clinical psychology, general psychology, child development, cognitive development, drugs/behavior. *Unit head:* Dr. Laura Bowman, Chair, 860-832-3100. *Application contact:* Dr. Laura Bowman, Chair, 860-832-3100.

Central Michigan University, College of Graduate Studies, College of Humanities and Social and Behavioral Sciences, Department of Psychology, Program in Industrial and Organizational Psychology, Mount Pleasant, MI 48859. Offers industrial and organizational psychology (MA, PhD); occupational health psychology (PhD). *Students:* 18 full-time (7 women), 19 part-time (8 women); includes 1 American Indian or Alaska Native, non-Hispanic/Latino; 1 Asian, non-Hispanic/Latino; 1 Hispanic/Latino, 4 international. Average age 26. *Degree requirements:* For master's, thesis; for doctorate, comprehensive exam, thesis/dissertation. *Entrance requirements:* For master's and doctorate, GRE. *Application deadline:* For fall admission, 1/1 for domestic and international students. Application fee: $35 ($45 for international students). Electronic applications accepted. *Expenses:* Tuition, state resident: full-time $8208; part-time $456 per credit hour. Tuition, nonresident: full-time $13,788; part-time $766 per credit hour. One-time fee: $25. *Financial support:* Fellowships with tuition reimbursements, research assistantships with tuition reimbursements, career-related internships or fieldwork, Federal Work-Study, unspecified assistantships, and out-of-state merit awards, non-resident graduate awards available. *Faculty research:* Job stress, retirement, leadership, and careers; personality in the workplace, personnel selection, and structural equation modeling in I/O psychology; personnel psychology, evolutionary psychology, and influences on HRM utilization; occupational health psychology and job stress; work attitudes, psychological ownership in work, and performance appraisal. *Unit head:* Dr. Hajime Otani, Chairperson, 989-774-6461, Fax: 989-774-2553, E-mail: otani1h@cmich.edu. *Application contact:* Dr. Terry Beehr, Graduate Coordinator, 989-774-6466, Fax: 989-774-2553, E-mail: beehr1ta@cmich.edu.

Chatham University, Program in Counseling Psychology, Pittsburgh, PA 15232-2826. Offers child, adolescent and family (MSCP); counseling psychology (Psy D); health and holistic (MSCP); infant mental health (MSCP); organization and supervision (MSCP); sport and exercise (MSCP). Part-time and evening/weekend programs available. *Degree requirements:* For master's, thesis optional, supervised internship; for doctorate, thesis/dissertation, internship. *Entrance requirements:* For master's, minimum GPA of 3.0; 2 letters of recommendation; resume; prerequisite coursework in statistics, biology, and psychology; for doctorate, GRE. Additional exam requirements/recommendations for international students: Required—TOEFL (minimum score 600 paper-based; 250 computer-based; 100 iBT), IELTS (minimum score 6.5), TWE. Electronic applications accepted. *Faculty research:* Trauma and recovery, hypnosis, psychospiritual dimensions of healing, psychotherapy of schizophrenia.

Claremont Graduate University, Graduate Programs, School of Behavioral and Organizational Sciences, Department of Psychology, Claremont, CA 91711-6160. Offers advanced study in evaluation (Certificate); cognitive psychology (MA, PhD); developmental psychology (MA, PhD); evaluation and applied research methods (MA, PhD); health behavior research and evaluation (MA, PhD); human resource development and evaluation (MA); industrial/organizational psychology (MA, PhD); organizational behavior (MA, PhD); organizational psychology (MA, PhD); social psychology (MA, PhD); MBA/PhD. Part-time programs available. *Faculty:* 15 full-time (6 women), 5 part-time/adjunct (2 women). *Students:* 248 full-time (169 women), 15 part-time (9 women); includes 68 minority (14 Black or African American, non-Hispanic/Latino; 1 American Indian or Alaska Native, non-Hispanic/Latino; 27 Asian, non-Hispanic/Latino; 19 Hispanic/Latino; 2 Native Hawaiian or other Pacific Islander, non-Hispanic/Latino; 5 Two or more races, non-Hispanic/Latino), 29 international. Average age 30. In 2010, 45 master's, 21 doctorates, 4 other advanced degrees awarded. Terminal master's awarded for partial completion of doctoral program. *Entrance requirements:* For master's and doctorate,

Health Psychology

Claremont Graduate University (continued)
GRE General Test. Additional exam requirements/recommendations for international students: Required—TOEFL (minimum score 550 paper-based; 213 computer-based; 80 iBT). *Application deadline:* For fall admission, 1/15 priority date for domestic students. Applications are processed on a rolling basis. Application fee: $60. Electronic applications accepted. *Expenses:* Tuition: Full-time $35,748; part-time $1554 per unit. Required fees: $215 per semester. *Financial support:* Fellowships, research assistantships, teaching assistantships, Federal Work-Study, institutionally sponsored loans, scholarships/grants, and tuition waivers (full and partial) available. Support available to part-time students. Financial award application deadline: 2/15; financial award applicants required to submit FAFSA. *Faculty research:* Social intervention, diversity in organizations, eyewitness memory, aging and cognition, drug policy. *Unit head:* Stewart Donaldson, Dean, 909-607-9001, Fax: 909-621-8905, E-mail: stewart.donaldson@cgu.edu. *Application contact:* Paul Thomas, Director, External Affairs, 909-607-9016, Fax: 909-621-8905, E-mail: paul.thomas@cgu.edu.

Drexel University, College of Arts and Sciences, Department of Psychology, Clinical Psychology Program, Philadelphia, PA 19104-2875. Offers clinical psychology (PhD); forensic psychology (PhD); health psychology (PhD); neuropsychology (PhD). *Accreditation:* APA. Terminal master's awarded for partial completion of doctoral program. *Degree requirements:* For doctorate, thesis/dissertation, qualifying exam. *Entrance requirements:* For doctorate, GRE General Test, GRE Subject Test, minimum GPA of 3.0. Electronic applications accepted. *Expenses:* Contact institution. *Faculty research:* Cognitive behavioral therapy, stress and coping, eating disorders, substance abuse, developmental disabilities.

Drexel University, College of Arts and Sciences, Department of Psychology, Program in Law-Psychology, Philadelphia, PA 19104-2875. Offers JD/PhD. Electronic applications accepted. *Expenses:* Contact institution. *Faculty research:* Mental health law issues, professional ethics, social science applications to law.

Duke University, Graduate School, Department of Psychology and Neuroscience, Durham, NC 27708. Offers biological psychology (PhD); clinical psychology (PhD); cognitive psychology (PhD); developmental psychology (PhD); experimental psychology (PhD); health psychology (PhD); human social development (PhD); JD/MA. *Accreditation:* APA (one or more programs are accredited). *Faculty:* 40 full-time. *Students:* 92 full-time (67 women); includes 6 Black or African American, non-Hispanic/Latino; 2 Asian, non-Hispanic/Latino; 7 Hispanic/Latino, 13 international. 483 applicants, 8% accepted, 23 enrolled. In 2010, 24 doctorates awarded. *Degree requirements:* For doctorate, thesis/dissertation. *Entrance requirements:* For doctorate, GRE General Test. Additional exam requirements/recommendations for international students: Required—TOEFL (minimum score 550 paper-based; 213 computer-based; 83 iBT), IELTS (minimum score 7). *Application deadline:* For fall admission, 12/8 priority date for domestic and international students. Application fee: $75. Electronic applications accepted. *Financial support:* Fellowships, research assistantships, teaching assistantships, career-related internships or fieldwork and Federal Work-Study available. Financial award application deadline: 12/8. *Unit head:* Melanie Bonner, Director of Graduate Studies, 919-660-5715, Fax: 919-660-5726, E-mail: morrell@duke.edu. *Application contact:* Elizabeth Hutton, Director of Admissions, 919-684-3913, Fax: 919-684-2277, E-mail: grad-admissions@duke.edu.

East Carolina University, Graduate School, Thomas Harriot College of Arts and Sciences, Department of Psychology, Program in Health Psychology, Greenville, NC 27858-4353. Offers PhD. *Entrance requirements:* For doctorate, GRE. *Expenses:* Tuition, state resident: full-time $3130; part-time $391.25 per credit hour. Tuition, nonresident: full-time $13,817; part-time $1727.13 per credit hour. Required fees: $1916; $239.50 per credit hour. Tuition and fees vary according to campus/location and program.

Georgian Court University, School of Arts and Sciences, Lakewood, NJ 08701-2697. Offers biology (MA); Catholic school leadership (Certificate); clinical mental health counseling (MA); holistic health studies (MA); mathematics (MA); pastoral ministry (Certificate); religious education (Certificate); school psychology (Certificate); theology (MA, Certificate). Part-time and evening/weekend programs available. *Faculty:* 19 full-time (11 women), 7 part-time/adjunct (5 women). *Students:* 61 full-time (59 women), 143 part-time (113 women); includes 20 minority (5 Black or African American, non-Hispanic/Latino; 3 Asian, non-Hispanic/Latino; 11 Hispanic/Latino; 1 Two or more races, non-Hispanic/Latino), 1 international. Average age 39. 139 applicants, 59% accepted, 50 enrolled. In 2010, 5 master's awarded. *Degree requirements:* For master's, comprehensive exam (for some programs), thesis (for some programs). *Entrance requirements:* For master's, GRE, MAT, or NTE/PRAXIS, 3 letters of recommendation. Additional exam requirements/recommendations for international students: Required—TOEFL (minimum score 550 paper-based; 213 computer-based). *Application deadline:* For fall admission, 8/1 priority date for domestic students, 4/1 for international students; for spring admission, 1/1 priority date for domestic students, 7/1 for international students. Applications are processed on a rolling basis. Application fee: $40. Electronic applications accepted. *Expenses:* Tuition: Full-time $12,510; part-time $695 per credit. Required fees: $416 per year. Tuition and fees vary according to campus/location and program. *Financial support:* Scholarships/grants, health care benefits, and unspecified assistantships available. Financial award application deadline: 4/15; financial award applicants required to submit FAFSA. *Unit head:* Dr. Linda James, Dean, 732-987-2617, Fax: 732-987-2007. *Application contact:* Patrick Givens, Assistant Director of Admissions, 732-987-2736, Fax: 732-987-2084, E-mail: graduateadmissions@georgian.edu.

John F. Kennedy University, Graduate School of Holistic Studies, Department of Counseling Psychology, Program in Counseling Psychology, Pleasant Hill, CA 94523-4817. Offers holistic studies (MA); somatic psychology (MA); transpersonal psychology (MA). Part-time and evening/weekend programs available. *Degree requirements:* For master's, thesis or alternative. *Entrance requirements:* For master's, interview. Additional exam requirements/recommendations for international students: Required—TOEFL.

Lesley University, Graduate School of Arts and Social Sciences, Self-Designed Master's Program in Interdisciplinary Studies, Cambridge, MA 02138-2790. Offers individualized studies (MA); integrative holistic health (MA); women's studies (MA). Part-time and evening/weekend programs available. Postbaccalaureate distance learning degree programs offered (no on-campus study). *Entrance requirements:* For master's, 3 letters of recommendation. Additional exam requirements/recommendations for international students: Required—TOEFL (minimum score 550 paper-based; 213 computer-based; 80 iBT).

North Dakota State University, College of Graduate and Interdisciplinary Studies, College of Science and Mathematics, Department of Psychology, Fargo, ND 58108. Offers clinical psychology (MS); cognitive and visual neuroscience (PhD); health and social psychology (PhD); psychology (MS). *Faculty:* 18 full-time (4 women), 2 part-time/adjunct (1 woman). *Students:* 20 full-time (11 women), 3 part-time (0 women); includes 1 Two or more races, non-Hispanic/Latino, 2 international. Average age 24. 41 applicants, 27% accepted, 6 enrolled. In 2010, 7 master's, 2 doctorates awarded. *Degree requirements:* For master's, thesis; for doctorate, thesis/dissertation. *Entrance requirements:* For master's and doctorate, GRE General Test, GRE Subject Test. Additional exam requirements/recommendations for international students: Required—TOEFL (minimum score 525 paper-based; 197 computer-based; 71 iBT). *Application deadline:* For fall admission, 3/1 for domestic and international students. Application fee: $45 ($60 for international students). Electronic applications accepted. *Financial support:* In 2010–11, 2 fellowships with full tuition reimbursements (averaging $16,000 per year), 23 research assistantships with full tuition reimbursements (averaging $16,000 per year), 11 teaching assistantships with full tuition reimbursements (averaging $6,000 per year) were awarded; career-related internships or fieldwork, Federal Work-Study, institutionally sponsored loans, tuition waivers (full and partial), and unspecified assistantships also available. Support available to part-time students. Financial award application deadline: 3/1. *Faculty research:* Cognition science, neuropsychology, group behavior, applied behavior analysis, behavior therapy. Total annual research expenditures: $2 million. *Unit head:* Dr. Paul D. Rokke, Chair, 701-231-8622, Fax: 701-231-8426, E-mail: paul.rokke@ndsu.edu. *Application contact:* Dr. Paul D. Rokke, Chair, 701-231-8622, Fax: 701-231-8426, E-mail: paul.rokke@ndsu.edu.

Northern Kentucky University, Office of Graduate Programs, College of Arts and Sciences, Program in Industrial-Organizational Psychology, Highland Heights, KY 41099. Offers industrial psychology (Certificate); industrial-organizational psychology (MS); occupational health psychology (Certificate); organizational psychology (Certificate). Part-time and evening/weekend programs available. *Faculty:* 4 full-time (2 women), 1 part-time/adjunct (0 women). *Students:* 10 full-time (6 women), 26 part-time (19 women); includes 5 minority (2 Black or African American, non-Hispanic/Latino; 2 Asian, non-Hispanic/Latino; 1 Two or more races, non-Hispanic/Latino), 2 international. Average age 29. 43 applicants, 49% accepted, 14 enrolled. In 2010, 4 master's, 2 other advanced degrees awarded. *Degree requirements:* For master's, thesis optional, capstone. *Entrance requirements:* For master's, GRE (minimum score 450 verbal, 450 quantitative, 3.5 writing), minimum GPA of 3.0, at least 9 semester hours of undergraduate psychology, 1 course in statistics, 3 letters of recommendation, letter of intent. Additional exam requirements/recommendations for international students: Required—TOEFL (minimum score 550 paper-based; 213 computer-based; 79 iBT); Recommended—IELTS (minimum score 6.5). *Application deadline:* For fall admission, 8/1 for domestic students, 6/1 for international students; for spring admission, 12/1 for domestic students, 10/1 for international students. Applications are processed on a rolling basis. Application fee: $40. Electronic applications accepted. *Expenses:* Tuition, state resident: full-time $7254; part-time $403 per credit hour. Tuition, nonresident: full-time $12,492; part-time $694 per credit hour. Tuition and fees vary according to degree level and program. *Financial support:* Unspecified assistantships available. Financial award applicants required to submit FAFSA. *Faculty research:* Attitude development, employee surveys, factor analysis, the effect of gender and racial stereotypes on employment decisions, social conflict and human factors in the workplace, workplace abuse and bullying, psychological testing/measurement, leader social-cognitive skills. *Unit head:* Dr. Philip Moberg, Director, Master's Program, 859-572-1913, Fax: 859-572-6085, E-mail: mobergp1@nku.edu. *Application contact:* Dr. Peg Griffin, Director of Graduate Programs, 859-572-6934, Fax: 859-572-6670, E-mail: griffinp@nku.edu.

Philadelphia College of Osteopathic Medicine, Graduate and Professional Programs, Department of Psychology, Philadelphia, PA 19131-1694. Offers clinical psychology (Psy D); counseling and clinical health psychology (MS); organizational leadership and development (MS); psychology (Certificate, Post-Doctoral Certificate); school psychology (MS, Psy D, Ed S). *Accreditation:* APA. *Degree requirements:* For master's, thesis; for doctorate, comprehensive exam, thesis/dissertation, final project, fieldwork. *Entrance requirements:* For master's, GRE or MAT, minimum GPA of 3.0; course work in biology, chemistry, English, physics; for other advanced degree, PRAXIS. *Faculty research:* Depression in primary care, integrated primary care, geriatric mental health.

See Display on page 932 and Close-Up on page 1167.

Prescott College, Graduate Programs, Program in Counseling and Psychology, Prescott, AZ 86301. Offers adventure-based psychotherapy (MA); counseling psychology (MA); ecopsychology (MA); ecotherapy (MA); equine-assisted mental health (MA); expressive arts therapy (MA); somatic psychology (MA); student-directed independent study (MA). Part-time programs available. Postbaccalaureate distance learning degree programs offered (minimal on-campus study). *Faculty:* 3 full-time (all women), 25 part-time/adjunct (18 women). *Students:* 71 full-time (55 women), 59 part-time (50 women); includes 16 minority (4 Black or African American, non-Hispanic/Latino; 2 American Indian or Alaska Native, non-Hispanic/Latino; 1 Asian, non-Hispanic/Latino; 3 Hispanic/Latino; 1 Native Hawaiian or other Pacific Islander, non-Hispanic/Latino; 5 Two or more races, non-Hispanic/Latino), 5 international. Average age 38. 107 applicants, 79% accepted, 54 enrolled. In 2010, 23 master's awarded. *Degree requirements:* For master's, thesis, fieldwork or internship, practicum. *Entrance requirements:* For master's, 2 letters of recommendation, resume. Additional exam requirements/recommendations for international students: Required—TOEFL (minimum score 500 paper-based; 173 computer-based). *Application deadline:* For fall admission, 4/15 priority date for domestic and international students; for spring admission, 9/15 priority date for domestic and international students. Applications are processed on a rolling basis. Application fee: $40. Electronic applications accepted. *Expenses:* Tuition: Full-time $15,600; part-time $650 per credit. Required fees: $50 per term. One-time fee: $190. Tuition and fees vary according to course load and degree level. *Financial support:* Career-related internships or fieldwork, Federal Work-Study, and scholarships/grants available. Financial award applicants required to submit FAFSA. *Unit head:* Camille Smith, Chair, 602-373-3881, Fax: 928-776-5151, E-mail: csmith@prescott.edu. *Application contact:* Kerstin Alicki, Admissions Counselor, 877-412-8705, Fax: 928-277-4695, E-mail: admissions@prescott.edu.

Rhode Island College, School of Graduate Studies, Faculty of Arts and Sciences, Department of Psychology, Providence, RI 02908-1991. Offers health psychology (CGS); psychology (MA). Part-time and evening/weekend programs available. *Faculty:* 3 full-time (1 woman). *Students:* 4 full-time (all women), 11 part-time (7 women); includes 2 minority (1 American Indian or Alaska Native, non-Hispanic/Latino; 1 Hispanic/Latino). Average age 32. In 2010, 4 master's awarded. *Degree requirements:* For master's, comprehensive exam. *Entrance requirements:* For master's, GRE, 3 letters of recommendation. Additional exam requirements/recommendations for international students: Recommended—TOEFL (minimum score 550 paper-based; 213 computer-based; 79 iBT). *Application deadline:* For fall admission, 3/1 for domestic students; for spring admission, 11/1 for domestic students. Applications are processed on a rolling basis. Application fee: $50. *Expenses:* Tuition, state resident: full-time $8208; part-time $342 per credit hour. Tuition, nonresident: full-time $16,080; part-time $670 per credit hour. Required fees: $554; $20 per credit. $72 per term. *Financial support:* In 2010–11, 3 teaching assistantships with full tuition reimbursements (averaging $4,550 per year) were awarded; Federal Work-Study, scholarships/grants, health care benefits, and unspecified assistantships also available. Support available to part-time students. Financial award application deadline: 5/15; financial award applicants required to submit FAFSA. *Unit head:* Dr. Thomas Malloy, Chair, 401-456-8015. *Application contact:* Graduate Studies, 401-456-8700.

Rutgers, The State University of New Jersey, New Brunswick, Graduate School-New Brunswick, Program in Psychology, Piscataway, NJ 08854-8097. Offers behavioral neuroscience (PhD); clinical psychology (PhD); cognitive psychology (PhD); interdisciplinary health psychology (PhD); social psychology (PhD). *Accreditation:* APA. *Degree requirements:* For doctorate, comprehensive exam, thesis/dissertation. *Entrance requirements:* For doctorate, GRE General Test, 3 letters of recommendation. Additional exam requirements/recommendations for international students: Required—TOEFL (minimum score 577 paper-based; 233 computer-based). Electronic applications accepted. *Expenses:* Tuition, state resident: full-time $7200; part-time $600 per credit. Tuition, nonresident: full-time $11,124; part-time $927 per credit. *Faculty research:* Learning and memory, behavioral ecology, hormones and behavior, psychopharmacology, anxiety disorders.

San Diego State University, Graduate and Research Affairs, College of Health and Human Services, Graduate School of Public Health, San Diego, CA 92182. Offers environmental health (MPH); epidemiology (MPH, PhD), including biostatistics (MPH); global emergency preparedness and response (MS); global health (PhD); health behavior (PhD); health promotion (MPH); health services administration (MPH); toxicology (MS); MPH/MA; MSW/MPH. *Accreditation:* ABET (one or more programs are accredited); CAHME (one or more programs are accredited); CEPH (one or more programs are accredited). Part-time programs available. *Degree requirements:* For master's, comprehensive exam (for some programs), thesis (for some programs); for doctorate, thesis/dissertation. *Entrance requirements:* For master's, GMAT (MPH in health services administration), GRE General Test; for doctorate, GRE General Test. Additional exam requirements/recommendations for international students: Required—TOEFL. *Faculty research:* Evaluation of tobacco, AIDS prevalence and prevention, mammography, infant death project, Alzheimer's in elderly Chinese.

Saybrook University, Graduate College of Psychology and Humanistic Studies, San Francisco, CA 94111-1920. Offers clinical psychology (Psy D); human science (MA, PhD), including consciousness and spirituality, humanistic and transpersonal psychology, integrative health studies, organizational systems, social transformation, transformative social change (MA); organizational systems (MA, PhD), including consciousness and spirituality, humanistic and transpersonal psychology, integrative health studies, leadership of sustainable systems (MA), organizational systems, social transformation; psychology (MA, PhD), including clinical psychology (PhD), consciousness and spirituality, creativity studies (MA), humanistic and transpersonal psychology, integrative health studies, Jungian studies, marriage and family therapy (MA), organizational systems, social transformation. Postbaccalaureate distance learning degree programs offered (minimal on-campus study). *Faculty:* 15 full-time (5 women), 83 part-time/adjunct (34 women). *Students:* 479 full-time (333 women); includes 30 Black or African American, non-Hispanic/Latino; 1 American Indian or Alaska Native, non-Hispanic/Latino; 13 Asian, non-Hispanic/Latino; 18 Hispanic/Latino, 18 international. Average age 43. 280 applicants, 52% accepted, 105 enrolled. In 2010, 28 master's, 43 doctorates awarded. Terminal master's awarded for partial completion of doctoral program. *Degree requirements:* For master's, thesis or alternative; for doctorate, thesis/dissertation. *Entrance requirements:* Additional exam requirements/recommendations for international students: Required—TOEFL (minimum score 580 paper-based; 237 computer-based; 93 iBT). *Application deadline:* For fall admission, 6/1 priority date for domestic students; for spring admission, 12/16 priority date for domestic students. Application fee: $50. Electronic applications accepted. *Financial support:* In 2010–11, 335 students received support. Scholarships/grants available. Financial award applicants required to submit FAFSA. *Faculty research:* Humanistic theory, health studies, organizational systems, consciousness and spirituality, social transformation. Total annual research expenditures: $90,000. *Unit head:* Mark Schulman, President, 800-825-4480, Fax: 415-433-9271. *Application contact:* Director of Admissions, 800-825-4480, Fax: 415-433-9271, E-mail: admissions@saybrook.edu.

Southwestern College, Program in Integral Somatic Psychology, Santa Fe, NM 87502-4788. Offers Certificate.

Stony Brook University, State University of New York, Graduate School, College of Arts and Sciences, Department of Psychology, Program in Social and Health Psychology, Stony Brook, NY 11794. Offers PhD. *Students:* 17 full-time (12 women); includes 1 Asian, non-Hispanic/Latino; 4 Hispanic/Latino, 2 international. Average age 28. 85 applicants, 6% accepted, 1 enrolled. In 2010, 6 doctorates awarded. *Degree requirements:* For doctorate, thesis/dissertation. *Entrance requirements:* For doctorate, GRE General Test, GRE Subject Test. Additional exam requirements/recommendations for international students: Required—TOEFL. *Application deadline:* For fall admission, 1/15 for domestic students. Application fee: $100. *Expenses:* Tuition, state resident: full-time $8370; part-time $349 per credit. Tuition, nonresident: full-time $13,780; part-time $574 per credit. Required fees: $994. *Unit head:* Dr. Marci Lobel, Head, 631-632-7651, E-mail: marci.lobel@stonybrook.edu. *Application contact:* Dr. Marci Lobel, Head, 631-632-7651, E-mail: marci.lobel@stonybrook.edu.

Texas State University–San Marcos, Graduate School, College of Liberal Arts, Department of Psychology, San Marcos, TX 78666. Offers health psychology (MA). *Faculty:* 13 full-time (6 women), 1 part-time/adjunct (0 women). *Students:* 44 full-time (32 women), 11 part-time (7 women); includes 1 Black or African American, non-Hispanic/Latino; 1 Asian, non-Hispanic/Latino; 13 Hispanic/Latino; 1 Two or more races, non-Hispanic/Latino. Average age 27. 49 applicants, 69% accepted, 28 enrolled. In 2010, 16 master's awarded. *Degree requirements:* For master's, comprehensive exam, thesis (for some programs). *Entrance requirements:* For master's, GRE General Test, minimum GPA of 3.0 in last 60 hours, in psychology, and in psychology core courses; 3 letters of recommendation; statement of purpose. Additional exam requirements/recommendations for international students: Required—TOEFL (minimum score 550 paper-based; 213 computer-based; 78 iBT). *Application deadline:* For fall admission, 3/15 for domestic and international students. Applications are processed on a rolling basis. Application fee: $40 ($90 for international students). Electronic applications accepted. *Expenses:* Tuition, state resident: full-time $6024; part-time $251 per credit hour. Tuition, nonresident: full-time $13,536; part-time $564 per credit hour. Required fees: $1776; $50 per credit hour. $306 per semester. *Financial support:* In 2010–11, 26 students received support, including 6 research assistantships (averaging $3,887 per year), 25 teaching assistantships (averaging $2,652 per year); Federal Work-Study, institutionally sponsored loans, scholarships/grants, health care benefits, and unspecified assistantships also available. Support available to part-time students. Financial award application deadline: 4/1. *Faculty research:* Stress and alcohol. Total annual research expenditures: $17,023. *Unit head:* Dr. Shirley Ogletree, Graduate Advisor, 512-245-2526, Fax: 512-245-3153, E-mail: so01@txstate.edu. *Application contact:* Dr. J. Michael Willoughby, Dean of Graduate College, 512-245-2581, Fax: 512-245-8365, E-mail: gradcollege@txstate.edu.

United States International University, School of Arts and Sciences, Nairobi, Kenya. Offers counseling psychology (MA), including chemical dependency, health psychology; international relations (MA), including development studies, diplomacy and foreign policy, peace and conflict studies. Part-time and evening/weekend programs available. *Faculty:* 43 full-time (14 women), 69 part-time/adjunct (28 women). *Students:* 94 full-time (60 women), 22 part-time (all women). Average age 30. 93 applicants, 80% accepted, 64 enrolled. In 2010, 33 master's awarded. *Degree requirements:* For master's, thesis, practicum. *Entrance requirements:* For master's, GRE General Test, 2 letters of recommendation, resume. Additional exam requirements/recommendations for international students: Required—TOEFL. *Application deadline:* For fall admission, 6/30 priority date for domestic and international students. Application fee: $50. *Financial support:* In 2010–11, 56 students received support, including 3 research assistantships (averaging $1,400 per year), 7 teaching assistantships (averaging $1,400 per year); career-related internships or fieldwork, scholarships/grants, and unspecified assistantships also available. Support available to part-time students. Financial award application deadline: 6/30; financial award applicants required to submit FAFSA. *Faculty research:* Trauma in children, African intellectualism, psychological assessment tools. *Unit head:* Prof. Mulinge Munyae, Dean, 254-02-3606-434, E-mail: mmulinge@usiu.ac.ke. *Application contact:* George Lumbasi, Director of Admissions, 254-02-3606563, Fax: 254-02-3606100, E-mail: glumbasi@usiu.ac.ke.

The University of British Columbia, Faculty of Arts and Faculty of Graduate Studies, Department of Psychology, Vancouver, BC V6T 1Z4, Canada. Offers behavioral neuroscience (MA, PhD); clinical psychology (MA, PhD); cognitive science (MA, PhD); developmental psychology (MA, PhD); health psychology (MA, PhD); quantitative methods (MA, PhD); social/personality psychology (MA, PhD). *Accreditation:* APA (one or more programs are accredited). Terminal master's awarded for partial completion of doctoral program. *Degree requirements:* For master's, thesis; for doctorate, comprehensive exam, thesis/dissertation. *Entrance requirements:* For master's and doctorate, GRE General Test. Additional exam requirements/recommendations for international students: Required—TOEFL (minimum score 550 paper-based; 230 computer-based; 80 iBT). Electronic applications accepted. Tuition charges are reported in Canadian dollars. *Expenses:* Tuition, area resident: Full-time $4179 Canadian dollars. International tuition: $7344 Canadian dollars full-time. *Faculty research:* Clinical, developmental, social/personality, cognition, behavioral neuroscience.

University of Connecticut, Graduate School, College of Liberal Arts and Sciences, Department of Psychology, Storrs, CT 06269. Offers behavioral neuroscience (PhD); biopsychology (PhD); clinical psychology (MA, PhD); cognition and instruction (PhD); developmental psychology (MA, PhD); ecological psychology (PhD); experimental psychology (PhD); general psychology (MA, PhD); health psychology (Graduate Certificate); industrial/organizational psychology (PhD); language and cognition (PhD); neuroscience (PhD); occupational health psychology (Graduate Certificate); social psychology (MA, PhD). *Accreditation:* APA. Terminal master's awarded for partial completion of doctoral program. *Degree requirements:* For master's, comprehensive exam; for doctorate, thesis/dissertation. *Entrance requirements:* For master's and doctorate, GRE General Test, GRE Subject Test. Additional exam requirements/recommendations for international students: Required—TOEFL (minimum score 550 paper-based; 213 computer-based). Electronic applications accepted.

University of Florida, Graduate School, College of Public Health and Health Professions, Department of Clinical and Health Psychology, Gainesville, FL 32611. Offers PhD. *Accreditation:* APA. *Faculty:* 21 full-time (8 women), 2 part-time/adjunct (1 woman). *Students:* 58 full-time (42 women), 14 part-time (11 women); includes 5 Black or African American, non-Hispanic/Latino; 1 American Indian or Alaska Native, non-Hispanic/Latino; 4 Asian, non-Hispanic/Latino; 4 Hispanic/Latino. Average age 29. 614 applicants, 7% accepted, 36 enrolled. In 2010, 18 doctorates awarded. *Degree requirements:* For doctorate, comprehensive exam, thesis/dissertation, pre-doctoral internship. *Entrance requirements:* For doctorate, GRE General Test minimum score 1000, minimum GPA of 3.0. Additional exam requirements/recommendations for international students: Required—TOEFL (minimum score 550 paper-based; 213 computer-based; 80 iBT), IELTS (minimum score 6). *Application deadline:* For fall admission, 12/1 for domestic and international students. Application fee: $30. Electronic applications accepted. *Expenses:* Tuition, state resident: full-time $10,915.92. Tuition, nonresident: full-time $28,309. *Financial support:* In 2010–11, 59 students received support, including 8 fellowships with partial tuition reimbursements available, 51 research assistantships with partial tuition reimbursements available (averaging $16,870 per year); career-related internships or fieldwork, Federal Work-Study, institutionally sponsored loans, scholarships/grants, and unspecified assistantships also available. Financial award application deadline: 12/1; financial award applicants required to submit FAFSA. *Faculty research:* Clinical child and pediatric psychology, medical psychology, neuropsychology, health promotion and aging. Total annual research expenditures: $3.6 million. *Unit head:* Dr. Russell M. Bauer, Chair, 352-273-6140, Fax: 352-273-6156, E-mail: rbauer@phhp.ufl.edu. *Application contact:* Dr. Stephen R. Boggs, Director, Clinical Psychology Doctoral Program, 352-273-6146, Fax: 352-273-6156, E-mail: sboggs@phhp.ufl.edu.

University of Michigan–Dearborn, College of Arts, Sciences, and Letters, Master of Science in Psychology Program, Dearborn, MI 48128. Offers clinical health psychology (MS); health psychology (MS). Part-time programs available. *Faculty:* 11 full-time (5 women). *Students:* 24 full-time (21 women), 10 part-time (9 women); includes 2 Black or African American, non-Hispanic/Latino; 2 Asian, non-Hispanic/Latino; 1 Hispanic/Latino; 1 Native Hawaiian or other Pacific Islander, non-Hispanic/Latino. Average age 31. 49 applicants, 71% accepted, 23 enrolled. In 2010, 9 master's awarded. *Degree requirements:* For master's, oral defense of thesis. *Entrance requirements:* For master's, GRE, 3 letters of recommendation. Additional exam requirements/recommendations for international students: Required—TOEFL (minimum score 560 paper-based; 220 computer-based). *Application deadline:* For fall admission, 3/15 for domestic and international students. Application fee: $60 ($75 for international students). *Financial support:* In 2010–11, 4 students received support. Scholarships/grants available. *Faculty research:* Cardiovascular reactivity, coping, addiction, psychoneuroimmunology. *Unit head:* Dr. Pam McAuslan, Program Director, 313-593-5376, E-mail: pmcausla@umd.umich.edu. *Application contact:* Carol Ligienza, Coordinator, CASL Graduate Programs, 313-593-1183, Fax: 313-583-6700, E-mail: caslgrad@umd.umich.edu.

University of Missouri–Kansas City, College of Arts and Sciences, Department of Psychology, Kansas City, MO 64110-2499. Offers clinical psychology (PhD); community psychology (PhD); health psychology (PhD); psychology (MA). PhD (interdisciplinary) offered through the School of Graduate Studies. *Accreditation:* APA. *Faculty:* 14 full-time (10 women), 4 part-time/adjunct (3 women). *Students:* 17 full-time (11 women), 7 part-time (all women); includes 1 Black or African American, non-Hispanic/Latino; 1 Asian, non-Hispanic/Latino; 3 Hispanic/Latino. Average age 30. 89 applicants, 9% accepted, 6 enrolled. In 2010, 6 master's, 4 doctorates awarded. Terminal master's awarded for partial completion of doctoral program. *Degree requirements:* For master's, thesis; for doctorate, comprehensive exam, thesis/dissertation, residency. *Entrance requirements:* For master's, GRE, minimum GPA of 3.5, letter of recommendation; for doctorate, GRE, minimum GPA of 3.25. Additional exam requirements/recommendations for international students: Required—TOEFL (minimum score 550 paper-based; 213 computer-based; 80 iBT). *Application deadline:* For fall admission, 1/15 for domestic and international students. Applications are processed on a rolling basis. Application fee: $45 ($50 for international students). Electronic applications accepted. *Expenses:* Tuition, state resident: full-time $5522.40; part-time $306.80 per credit hour. Tuition, nonresident: full-time $7128; part-time $792 per credit hour. Required fees: $261.15 per term. *Financial support:* In 2010–11, 18 research assistantships (averaging $11,778 per year), 6 teaching assistantships (averaging $11,500 per year) were awarded; career-related internships or fieldwork, Federal Work-Study, and institutionally sponsored loans also available. Support available to part-time students. Financial award application deadline: 3/1; financial award applicants required to submit FAFSA. *Faculty research:* HIV/AIDS research group, psycho-oncology, sensory and cognitive neuroscience, cognitive psychophysiology, obesity and related metabolic disorders. Total annual research expenditures: $933,609. *Unit head:* Dr. Tamera Murdock, Chairperson/Professor, 816-235-1318, Fax: 816-235-1062, E-mail: murdockt@umkc.edu. *Application contact:* Dr. Lisa Terre, Director, Graduate Programs, 816-235-1318, Fax: 816-235-1062, E-mail: terrel@umkc.edu.

The University of North Carolina at Charlotte, Graduate School, College of Arts and Sciences, Department of Psychology, Charlotte, NC 28223-0001. Offers community/clinical psychology (MA); health psychology (PhD); industrial/organizational psychology (MA); organizational science (PhD). Part-time programs available. *Faculty:* 27 full-time (11 women), 1 part-time/adjunct (0 women). *Students:* 67 full-time (50 women), 18 part-time (14 women); includes 19 minority (8 Black or African American, non-Hispanic/Latino; 3 Asian, non-Hispanic/Latino; 4 Hispanic/Latino; 1 Native Hawaiian or other Pacific Islander, non-Hispanic/Latino; 3 Two or more races, non-Hispanic/Latino), 3 international. Average age 29. 317 applicants, 9% accepted, 21 enrolled. In 2010, 14 master's, 1 doctorate awarded. *Degree requirements:* For master's, thesis; for doctorate, thesis/dissertation. *Entrance requirements:* For master's, GRE General Test, GRE Subject Test, minimum GPA of 3.0 in undergraduate major, 2.8 overall. Additional exam requirements/recommendations for international students: Required—TOEFL (minimum score 557 paper-based; 220 computer-based; 83 iBT). *Application deadline:* Applications are processed on a rolling basis. Application fee: $55. Electronic applications accepted. *Expenses:* Tuition, state resident: full-time $3464. Tuition, nonresident: full-time $14,297. Required fees: $2094. Tuition and fees vary according to course load. *Financial support:* In 2010–11, 44 students received support, including 12 research assistantships (averaging $14,191 per year), 31 teaching assistantships (averaging $10,710 per year); career-related internships or fieldwork, Federal Work-Study, institutionally sponsored loans, scholarships/grants, and administrative assistantships also available. Support available to part-time students. Financial award application deadline: 4/1; financial award applicants required to submit FAFSA. *Faculty research:* Health psychology, industrial-organizational psychology, cognitive science. Total annual research expenditures: $435,127. *Unit head:* Dr. Brian L. Cutler, Chair, 704-687-4731, Fax: 704-687-3096, E-mail: blcutler@uncc.edu. *Application contact:* Kathy B. Giddings, Director of Graduate Admissions, 704-687-5503, Fax: 704-687-3279, E-mail: gradadm@uncc.edu.

University of North Texas, Toulouse Graduate School, College of Arts and Sciences, Department of Psychology, Denton, TX 76203. Offers clinical psychology (PhD); counseling psychology (MA, MS, PhD); experimental psychology (MA, MS, PhD); health psychology and behavioral medicine (PhD). *Accreditation:* APA (one or more programs are accredited). Terminal master's awarded for partial completion of doctoral program. *Degree requirements:* For master's, comprehensive exam, thesis or alternative; for doctorate, one foreign language, comprehensive exam, thesis/dissertation. *Entrance requirements:* For master's and doctorate, GRE General Test, interview. Additional exam requirements/recommendations for international students: Recommended—TOEFL (minimum score 550 paper-based; 213 computer-based; 79 iBT). *Application deadline:* Applications are processed on a rolling basis. Electronic applications accepted. *Expenses:* Tuition, state resident: full-time $4298; part-time $239 per credit hour. Tuition, nonresident: full-time $10,782; part-time $549 per credit hour. Required fees: $1292; $270 per credit hour. *Financial support:* Fellowships, research assistantships, teaching assistantships, career-related internships or fieldwork, Federal Work-Study, and institutionally sponsored

Health Psychology

University of North Texas *(continued)*
loans available. Financial award applicants required to submit FAFSA. *Application contact:* Graduate Coordinator, 940-565-2671, Fax: 940-565-4682, E-mail: amym@unt.edu.

The University of Texas at Arlington, Graduate School, College of Science, Department of Psychology, Arlington, TX 76019. Offers experimental psychology (PhD); health psychology (PhD); industrial organizational psychology (MS); psychology (MS). Part-time programs available. *Faculty:* 21 full-time (8 women), 1 part-time/adjunct (0 women). *Students:* 62 full-time (41 women), 10 part-time (7 women); includes 5 Black or African American, non-Hispanic/Latino; 2 Asian, non-Hispanic/Latino; 6 Hispanic/Latino, 7 international. 72 applicants, 90% accepted, 22 enrolled. In 2010, 16 master's, 6 doctorates awarded. Terminal master's awarded for partial completion of doctoral program. *Degree requirements:* For master's, comprehensive exam or thesis; for doctorate, thesis/dissertation (for some programs). *Entrance requirements:* For master's and doctorate, GRE General Test, minimum GPA of 3.0 in last 60 hours of course work. Additional exam requirements/recommendations for international students: Required—TOEFL (minimum score 550 paper-based; 213 computer-based). *Application deadline:* For fall admission, 6/15 for domestic students. Applications are processed on a rolling basis. Application fee: $35 ($50 for international students). *Expenses:* Tuition, state resident: full-time $7500. Tuition, nonresident: full-time $13,080. International tuition: $13,250 full-time. *Financial support:* In 2010–11, 4 fellowships (averaging $1,000 per year), 2 research assistantships with tuition reimbursements (averaging $15,000 per year), 28 teaching assistantships with tuition reimbursements (averaging $15,000 per year) were awarded; career-related internships or fieldwork, Federal Work-Study, institutionally sponsored loans, scholarships/grants, traineeships, tuition waivers (partial), and unspecified assistantships also available. Financial award application deadline: 6/1; financial award applicants required to submit FAFSA. *Unit head:* Dr. Robert Gatchel, Chair, 817-272-2281, Fax: 817-272-2364, E-mail: gatchel@uta.edu. *Application contact:* Dr. Jared Kenworthy, Graduate Advisor, Psychological Sciences, 817-272-2281, Fax: 817-272-2364, E-mail: kenworthy@uta.edu.

University of the Sciences in Philadelphia, College of Graduate Studies, Program in Health Psychology, Philadelphia, PA 19104-4495. Offers MS. *Entrance requirements:* For master's, bachelor's degree in related field, minimum GPA of 3.0 in major. Additional exam requirements/recommendations for international students: Required—TOEFL, TWE. *Expenses:* Contact institution. *Faculty research:* Stress and immune system, women's health and breast cancer, memory, health care policy.

Virginia Commonwealth University, Graduate School, College of Humanities and Sciences, Department of Psychology, Richmond, VA 23284-9005. Offers clinical psychology (PhD), including behavioral medicine, clinical child psychology; counseling psychology (PhD); general psychology (PhD), including biopsychology, developmental psychology, social psychology; health psychology (PhD). *Accreditation:* APA. *Students:* 87 full-time (71 women), 39 part-time (30 women); includes 33 minority (15 Black or African American, non-Hispanic/Latino; 6 Asian, non-Hispanic/Latino; 10 Hispanic/Latino; 2 Two or more races, non-Hispanic/Latino), 4 international. 433 applicants, 7% accepted, 16 enrolled. In 2010, 22 doctorates awarded. *Degree requirements:* For doctorate, thesis/dissertation. *Entrance requirements:* For doctorate, GRE General Test. Additional exam requirements/recommendations for international students: Required—TOEFL (minimum score 600 paper-based; 250 computer-based; 100 iBT); Recommended—IELTS (minimum score 6.5). *Application deadline:* For fall admission, 12/1 for domestic students. Application fee: $50. Electronic applications accepted. *Expenses:* Tuition, state resident: full-time $4308; part-time $479 per credit hour. Tuition, nonresident: full-time $8942; part-time $994 per credit hour. Required fees: $2000; $85 per credit hour. Tuition and fees vary according to course level, course load, degree level, campus/location and program. *Financial support:* Fellowships, research assistantships, teaching assistantships, Federal Work-Study, institutionally sponsored loans, and scholarships/grants available. Support available to part-time students. *Faculty research:* Biopsychology, clinical psychology, counseling psychology, developmental psychology, health psychology, social psychology. *Unit head:* Dr. Michael Southam-Gerow, Director, Graduate Programs in Psychology, 804-828-1193, Fax: 804-828-2237, E-mail: masouthamger@vcu.edu. *Application contact:* Dr. Michael Southam-Gerow, Director, Graduate Programs in Psychology, 804-828-1193, Fax: 804-828-2237, E-mail: masouthamger@vcu.edu.

Virginia State University, School of Graduate Studies, Research, and Outreach, School of Engineering, Science and Technology, Department of Psychology, Petersburg, VA 23806-0001. Offers behavioral and community health sciences (PhD); clinical health psychology (PhD); clinical psychology (MS); general psychology (MS). *Degree requirements:* For master's, one foreign language, thesis. *Entrance requirements:* For master's, GRE General Test. *Expenses:* Tuition, state resident: full-time $5576; part-time $335 per credit hour. Tuition, nonresident: full-time $13,402; part-time $670 per credit hour.

Walden University, Graduate Programs, School of Psychology, Minneapolis, MN 55401. Offers clinical child psychology (Post-Doctoral Certificate); clinical psychology (MS, Post-Doctoral Certificate), including counseling (MS); counseling psychology (Post-Doctoral Certificate); forensic psychology (MS), including forensic psychology in the community, general program, mental health applications, program planning and evaluation in forensic settings, psychology and legal systems; general psychology (Post-Doctoral Certificate); health psychology (Post-Doctoral Certificate); organizational psychology (Post-Doctoral Certificate); organizational psychology and development (Postbaccalaureate Certificate); psychology (MS, PhD), including clinical psychology (PhD), counseling psychology (PhD), crisis management and response (MS), general program (MS), general psychology (PhD), health psychology, leadership development and coaching (MS), media psychology (MS), organizational psychology (PhD), organizational psychology and development (MS), organizational psychology and nonprofit management (MS), program evaluation and research (MS), psychology of culture (MS), psychology, public administration, and social change (MS), social psychology (MS), terrorism and security (MS); teaching online (Post-Master's Certificate). Part-time and evening/weekend programs available. Postbaccalaureate distance learning degree programs offered (minimal on-campus study). *Faculty:* 41 full-time (25 women), 254 part-time/adjunct (131 women). *Students:* 3,463 full-time (2,737 women), 1,400 part-time (1,130 women); includes 1,491 Black or African American, non-Hispanic/Latino; 59 American Indian or Alaska Native, non-Hispanic/Latino; 89 Asian, non-Hispanic/Latino; 283 Hispanic/Latino; 76 Two or more races, non-Hispanic/Latino, 126 international. Average age 40. In 2010, 559 master's, 100 doctorates awarded. Terminal master's awarded for partial completion of doctoral program. *Degree requirements:* For master's, thesis optional; for doctorate, thesis/dissertation, residency. *Entrance requirements:* For master's, bachelor's degree or equivalent in related field; minimum GPA of 2.5; official transcripts; goal statement; access to computer and Internet; for doctorate, master's degree or equivalent in related field; minimum GPA of 3.0; 3 years of related professional/academic experience (preferred). Additional exam requirements/recommendations for international students: Required—TOEFL (minimum score 550 paper-based; 213 computer-based), IELTS (minimum score 6.5), TOEFL (minimum score 550 paper-based; 213 computer-based), IELTS (minimum score 6.5), or Michigan English Language Assessment Battery (minimum score 82). *Application deadline:* Applications are processed on a rolling basis. Application fee: $50. Electronic applications accepted. *Expenses:* Tuition: Full-time $10,274; part-time $445 per credit. Tuition and fees vary according to course load, degree level and program. *Financial support:* In 2010–11, 1 fellowship was awarded; Federal Work-Study, scholarships/grants, unspecified assistantships, and family tuition reduction, active duty/veteran tuition reduction, group tuition reduction, interest-free payment plans also available. Support available to part-time students. Financial award applicants required to submit FAFSA. *Unit head:* Dr. Melanie Storms, Associate Dean, 800-925-3368. *Application contact:* Jennifer Hall, Vice President of Enrollment Management, 866-4-WALDEN, E-mail: info@waldenu.edu.

West Chester University of Pennsylvania, Office of Graduate Studies, College of Health Sciences, Department of Health, West Chester, PA 19383. Offers emergency preparedness (Certificate); health care management (MPH, Certificate), including administration (MPH), community (MPH), environment (MPH), health care management (Certificate), integrative (MPH), nutrition (MPH); integrative health (Certificate); school health (M Ed). *Accreditation:* CEPH. Part-time and evening/weekend programs available. *Students:* 84 full-time (61 women), 97 part-time (75 women); includes 66 minority (53 Black or African American, non-Hispanic/Latino; 2 American Indian or Alaska Native, non-Hispanic/Latino; 9 Asian, non-Hispanic/Latino; 2 Hispanic/Latino), 20 international. Average age 30. 114 applicants, 81% accepted, 48 enrolled. In 2010, 57 master's, 9 other advanced degrees awarded. *Degree requirements:* For master's, thesis (for some programs), minimum GPA of 3.0. *Entrance requirements:* For master's, one-page statement of career objectives, two letters of reference. Additional exam requirements/recommendations for international students: Required—TOEFL (minimum score 550 paper-based; 213 computer-based; 80 iBT). *Application deadline:* For fall admission, 4/15 priority date for domestic students, 3/15 for international students; for spring admission, 10/15 for domestic students, 9/1 for international students. Applications are processed on a rolling basis. Application fee: $35. Electronic applications accepted. *Expenses:* Tuition, state resident: full-time $6966; part-time $387 per credit. Tuition, nonresident: full-time $11,146; part-time $619 per credit. Required fees: $1614.40; $133.24 per credit. Part-time tuition and fees vary according to campus/location. *Financial support:* Unspecified assistantships available. Support available to part-time students. Financial award application deadline: 2/15; financial award applicants required to submit FAFSA. *Faculty research:* Health school communities, community health issues and evidence-based programs, environment and health, nutrition and health, integrative health. *Unit head:* Dr. Bethann Cinelli, Chair, 610-436-2267, E-mail: bcinelli@wcupa.edu. *Application contact:* Dr. Lynn Carson, Graduate Coordinator, 610-436-2138, E-mail: lcarson@wcupa.edu.

Yeshiva University, Ferkauf Graduate School of Psychology, Program in Clinical Health Psychology, New York, NY 10033-3201. Offers PhD. *Accreditation:* APA. Part-time programs available. *Degree requirements:* For doctorate, comprehensive exam, thesis/dissertation. *Entrance requirements:* For doctorate, GRE General Test. *Faculty research:* Dieting, substance abuse, adolescent depression and suicide, cancer research, MS research.

Human Development

Argosy University, Chicago, College of Psychology and Behavioral Sciences, Doctoral Program in Clinical Psychology, Chicago, IL 60601. Offers child and adolescent psychology (Psy D); client-centered and experiential psychotherapies (Psy D); diversity and multicultural psychology (Psy D); family psychology (Psy D); forensic psychology (Psy D); health psychology (Psy D); neuropsychology (Psy D); organizational consulting (Psy D); psychoanalytic psychology (Psy D); psychology and spirituality (Psy D). *Accreditation:* APA.

See Close-Up on page 1123.

Arizona State University, College of Liberal Arts and Sciences, School of Social and Family Dynamics, Tempe, AZ 85287-3701. Offers family and human development (MS, PhD); infant-family practice (MAS); marriage and family therapy (MAS); sociology (MA, PhD). *Faculty:* 60 full-time (39 women), 2 part-time/adjunct (both women). *Students:* 91 full-time (82 women), 32 part-time (27 women); includes 28 minority (3 Black or African American, non-Hispanic/Latino; 2 American Indian or Alaska Native, non-Hispanic/Latino; 4 Asian, non-Hispanic/Latino; 17 Hispanic/Latino; 1 Native Hawaiian or other Pacific Islander, non-Hispanic/Latino; 1 Two or more races, non-Hispanic/Latino), 10 international. Average age 27. 186 applicants, 38% accepted, 44 enrolled. In 2010, 32 master's, 7 doctorates awarded. Terminal master's awarded for partial completion of doctoral program. *Degree requirements:* For master's, thesis or alternative, interactive Program of Study (iPOS) submitted before completing 50 percent of required credit hours; for doctorate, thesis/dissertation, interactive Program of Study (iPOS) submitted before completing 50 percent of required credit hours. *Entrance requirements:* For master's and doctorate, GRE, minimum GPA of 3.0 or equivalent in last 2 years of work leading to bachelor's degree. Additional exam requirements/recommendations for international students: Required—TOEFL, IELTS, or Pearson Test of English. *Application deadline:* For fall admission, 1/15 for domestic and international students. Application fee: $70 ($90 for international students). Electronic applications accepted. *Expenses:* Contact institution. *Financial support:* In 2010–11, 22 research assistantships with full and partial tuition reimbursements (averaging $14,111 per year), 27 teaching assistantships with full and partial tuition reimbursements (averaging $12,750 per year) were awarded; fellowships with full tuition reimbursements, career-related internships or fieldwork, Federal Work-Study, institutionally sponsored loans, scholarships/grants, and tuition waivers (full and partial) also available. Financial award application deadline: 3/1; financial award applicants required to submit FAFSA. Total annual research expenditures: $4.2 million. *Unit head:* Dr. Richard Fabes, Director, 480-965-4892, E-mail: rf@asu.edu. *Application contact:* Graduate Admissions, 480-965-6113.

Auburn University, Graduate School, College of Human Sciences, Department of Human Development and Family Studies, Auburn University, AL 36849. Offers MS, PhD. *Accreditation:* AAMFT/COAMFTE (one or more programs are accredited). Part-time programs available. *Faculty:* 20 full-time (12 women), 1 (woman) part-time/adjunct. *Students:* 28 full-time (24 women), 26 part-time (22 women); includes 10 Black or African American, non-Hispanic/Latino; 6 Asian, non-Hispanic/Latino; 2 Hispanic/Latino, 6 international. Average age 28. 56 applicants, 55% accepted, 18 enrolled. In 2010, 15 master's, 2 doctorates awarded. *Degree requirements:* For master's, thesis, oral exam; for doctorate, thesis/dissertation. *Entrance requirements:* For master's, GRE General Test; for doctorate, GRE General Test, master's degree. *Application deadline:* For fall admission, 7/7 for domestic students; for spring admission, 11/24 for domestic students. Applications are processed on a rolling basis. Application fee: $50 ($60 for international students). *Expenses:* Tuition, state resident: full-time $7002. Tuition, nonresident: full-time $21,898. International tuition: $22,116 full-time. Required fees: $892. Tuition and fees vary according to course load and program. *Financial support:* Research assistantships, teaching assistantships, Federal Work-Study available. Support available to part-time students. Financial award application deadline: 3/15; financial award applicants required to submit FAFSA. *Faculty research:* Family influences on personality and social development, parent-child relations, infancy, day care, parent education. *Unit head:* Dr. Leanne K. Lamke, Head, 334-844-3231, E-mail: mbradbar@humsci.auburn.edu. *Application contact:* Dr. George Flowers, Dean of the Graduate School, 334-844-2125.

Boston University, School of Education, Boston, MA 02215. Offers counseling (Ed M, CAGS), including community, school, sport psychology; counseling psychology (Ed D); curriculum and teaching (Ed M, Ed D, CAGS), including early childhood (Ed D), educational media and technology (Ed D), English and language arts (Ed D), mathematics (Ed D), physical education and coaching (Ed D), science (Ed D), social studies education (Ed D), special education

(Ed D); developmental studies (Ed D), including literacy and language, reading education; developmental studies in literacy and language education (Ed M, CAGS); early childhood education (Ed M, CAGS); education of the deaf (Ed M, CAGS); educational leadership and development (Ed D), including educational administration (Ed M, Ed D, CAGS), higher education administration (Ed M, Ed D, CAGS); educational media and technology (Ed M, CAGS); elementary education (Ed M); English and language arts (Ed M, CAGS); English education (MAT); health education (Ed M, CAGS); Latin and classical studies (MAT); mathematics education (Ed M, MAT, CAGS); mathematics for teaching (MMT); modern foreign language education (MAT), including French, Spanish; physical education and coaching (Ed M, CAGS); policy, planning, and administration (Ed M, CAGS), including community education leadership, educational administration (Ed M, Ed D, CAGS), higher education administration (Ed M, Ed D, CAGS); reading education (Ed M, CAGS); science education (Ed M, MAT, CAGS), including biology (MAT), chemistry (MAT), earth science (MAT), general science (MAT), physics (MAT); social studies education (Ed M, MAT, CAGS), including history (MAT), political science (MAT); special education (Ed M, Ed D, CAGS), including disability studies (Ed M), moderate disabilities (Ed M), severe disabilities (Ed M), special education administration (Ed M); teaching English as a second language (Ed M, CAGS). Part-time programs available. *Faculty:* 57 full-time, 39 part-time/adjunct. *Students:* 245 full-time (191 women), 376 part-time (274 women); includes 83 minority (14 Black or African American, non-Hispanic/Latino; 2 American Indian or Alaska Native, non-Hispanic/Latino; 28 Asian, non-Hispanic/Latino; 31 Hispanic/Latino; 2 Native Hawaiian or other Pacific Islander, non-Hispanic/Latino; 6 Two or more races, non-Hispanic/Latino), 79 international. Average age 30. 1,270 applicants, 66% accepted, 292 enrolled. In 2010, 273 master's, 15 doctorates, 7 other advanced degrees awarded. Terminal master's awarded for partial completion of doctoral program. *Degree requirements:* For master's, thesis (for some programs); for doctorate, comprehensive exam, thesis/dissertation; for CAGS, comprehensive exam. *Entrance requirements:* For master's and CAGS, GRE General Test or Miller Analogies Test (MAT); for doctorate, GRE General Test. Additional exam requirements/recommendations for international students: Required—TOEFL, IELTS. *Application deadline:* For fall admission, 1/15 priority date for domestic and international students; for spring admission, 9/15 priority date for domestic and international students. Applications are processed on a rolling basis. Application fee: $70. Electronic applications accepted. *Expenses:* Tuition: Full-time $39,314; part-time $1228 per credit. Required fees: $40 per semester. *Financial support:* In 2010–11, 276 students received support, including 31 fellowships with full tuition reimbursements available, 16 research assistantships, 26 teaching assistantships with partial tuition reimbursements available; career-related internships or fieldwork, Federal Work-Study, and scholarships/grants also available. Support available to part-time students. Financial award applicants required to submit FAFSA. *Faculty research:* Deaf studies, social emotional learning, civic engagement and education, STEM education, pre-college educational pipelines. Total annual research expenditures: $2.6 million. *Unit head:* Dr. Hardin Coleman, Dean, 617-353-3213. *Application contact:* Dana Fernandez, Director of Enrollment, 617-353-4237, Fax: 617-353-8937, E-mail: sedgrad@bu.edu.

Bowling Green State University, Graduate College, College of Education and Human Development, School of Family and Consumer Sciences, Bowling Green, OH 43403. Offers food and nutrition (MFCS); human development and family studies (MFCS). Part-time programs available. *Degree requirements:* For master's, thesis. *Entrance requirements:* For master's, GRE General Test, minimum GPA of 3.0. Additional exam requirements/recommendations for international students: Required—TOEFL. Electronic applications accepted. *Faculty research:* Public health, wellness, social issues and policies, ethnic foods, nutrition and aging.

Bradley University, Graduate School, College of Education and Health Sciences, Department of Educational Leadership and Human Development, Peoria, IL 61625-0002. Offers human development counseling (MA), including community and agency counseling, school counseling; leadership in educational administration (MA); leadership in human service administration (MA). *Accreditation:* ACA; NCATE. Part-time and evening/weekend programs available. *Degree requirements:* For master's, comprehensive exam, thesis optional. *Entrance requirements:* For master's, GRE General Test or MAT, interview, 3 letters of recommendation. Additional exam requirements/recommendations for international students: Required—TOEFL (minimum score 550 paper-based; 213 computer-based; 79 iBT).

Brigham Young University, Graduate Studies, College of Family, Home, and Social Sciences, Program in Marriage, Family and Human Development, Provo, UT 84602. Offers MS, PhD. *Accreditation:* AAMFT/COAMFTE. *Faculty:* 23 full-time (4 women). *Students:* 22 full-time (18 women), 4 international. Average age 33. 18 applicants, 61% accepted, 9 enrolled. In 2010, 8 master's, 2 doctorates awarded. *Degree requirements:* For master's, thesis; for doctorate, comprehensive exam, thesis/dissertation, 2 publishable papers. *Entrance requirements:* For master's and doctorate, GRE General Test, minimum GPA of 3.0 in last 60 semester hours, letters of recommendation. Additional exam requirements/recommendations for international students: Required—TOEFL (minimum score 580 paper-based; 237 computer-based; 85 iBT), IELTS (minimum score 7). *Application deadline:* For fall admission, 1/10 for domestic and international students. Application fee: $50. Electronic applications accepted. *Expenses:* Tuition: Full-time $5580; part-time $310 per credit hour. Tuition and fees vary according to program and student's religious affiliation. *Financial support:* In 2010–11, 18 students received support, including 18 research assistantships with full and partial tuition reimbursements available (averaging $5,800 per year), 3 teaching assistantships with full and partial tuition reimbursements available (averaging $5,800 per year); scholarships/grants and unspecified assistantships also available. Financial award application deadline: 3/27. *Faculty research:* Family studies and family process, marriage, adolescence and emerging adulthood, adult development and aging, child development. *Unit head:* Dr. Richard Miller, Director, School of Life, 801-422-2069, Fax: 801-422-0230, E-mail: rick_miller@byu.edu. *Application contact:* Graduate Secretary, 801-422-2060, E-mail: mfhdgrad@byu.edu.

Brock University, Faculty of Graduate Studies, Faculty of Social Sciences, Program in Psychology, St. Catharines, ON L2S 3A1, Canada. Offers behavioral neuroscience (MA, PhD); life span development (MA, PhD); social personality (MA, PhD). Part-time programs available. *Degree requirements:* For master's, thesis; for doctorate, thesis/dissertation. *Entrance requirements:* For master's, GRE, honors degree; for doctorate, GRE, master's degree. Additional exam requirements/recommendations for international students: Required—TOEFL (minimum score 550 paper-based; 213 computer-based; 80 iBT), IELTS (minimum score 6.5), TWE (minimum score 4). Electronic applications accepted. *Faculty research:* Social personality, behavioral neuroscience, life-span development.

California State University, San Bernardino, Graduate Studies, College of Social and Behavioral Sciences, Department of Psychology, Program in Child Development, San Bernardino, CA 92407-2397. Offers psychology-life span (MA). *Degree requirements:* For master's, comprehensive exam. *Entrance requirements:* For master's, minimum GPA of 3.0 in major.

Central Michigan University, College of Graduate Studies, College of Education and Human Services, Department of Human Environmental Studies, Mount Pleasant, MI 48859. Offers apparel product development and merchandising technology (MS); gerontology (Graduate Certificate); human development and family studies (MA); nutrition and dietetics (MS). Part-time and evening/weekend programs available. *Faculty:* 15 full-time (11 women), 1 (woman) part-time/adjunct. *Students:* 6 full-time (4 women), 24 part-time (22 women); includes 2 Black or African American, non-Hispanic/Latino, 4 international. *Degree requirements:* For master's, thesis or alternative. *Application deadline:* Applications are processed on a rolling basis. Application fee: $35 ($45 for international students). Electronic applications accepted. *Expenses:* Tuition, state resident: full-time $8208; part-time $456 per credit hour. Tuition, nonresident: full-time $13,788; part-time $766 per credit hour. One-time fee: $25. *Financial support:* Fellowships with tuition reimbursements, research assistantships, career-related internships or fieldwork, Federal Work-Study, unspecified assistantships, and out-of-state merit awards, non-resident graduate awards available. *Faculty research:* Human growth and development, family studies and human sexuality, human nutrition and dietetics, apparel and textile retailing, computer-aided design for apparel. *Unit head:* Dr. Megan P. Goodwin, Chairperson, 989-774-3218, Fax: 989-774-2435, E-mail: goodw1mp@cmich.edu. *Application contact:* Dr. Candace Maylee, Assistant Coordinator of Graduate Programs, 989-774-2613, Fax: 989-774-2435, E-mail: mayle1ce@cmich.edu.

Claremont Graduate University, Graduate Programs, School of Educational Studies, Claremont, CA 91711-6160. Offers Africana education (Certificate); education and policy (MA, PhD); higher education/student affairs (MA, PhD); human development (MA, PhD); public school administration (MA, PhD); quantitative evaluation (MA, PhD); special education (MA, PhD); teacher education (MA); teaching and learning (MA, PhD); urban leadership (PhD); MBA/PhD. PhD program offered jointly with San Diego State University. Part-time programs available. *Faculty:* 16 full-time (8 women), 2 part-time/adjunct (1 woman). *Students:* 296 full-time (200 women), 154 part-time (112 women); includes 228 minority (55 Black or African American, non-Hispanic/Latino; 4 American Indian or Alaska Native, non-Hispanic/Latino; 48 Asian, non-Hispanic/Latino; 99 Hispanic/Latino; 3 Native Hawaiian or other Pacific Islander, non-Hispanic/Latino; 19 Two or more races, non-Hispanic/Latino), 11 international. Average age 38. In 2010, 83 master's, 26 doctorates, 9 other advanced degrees awarded. Terminal master's awarded for partial completion of doctoral program. *Entrance requirements:* For master's and doctorate, GRE General Test. Additional exam requirements/recommendations for international students: Required—TOEFL (minimum score 550 paper-based; 213 computer-based; 80 iBT). *Application deadline:* For fall admission, 2/1 priority date for domestic students. Applications are processed on a rolling basis. Application fee: $60. Electronic applications accepted. *Expenses:* Tuition: Full-time $35,748; part-time $1554 per unit. Required fees: $215 per semester. *Financial support:* Fellowships, research assistantships, Federal Work-Study, institutionally sponsored loans, and scholarships/grants available. Support available to part-time students. Financial award application deadline: 2/15; financial award applicants required to submit FAFSA. *Faculty research:* Education administration, K-12 and higher education, multicultural education, education policy, diversity in higher education, faculty issues. *Unit head:* Margaret Grogan, Dean, 909-621-8075, Fax: 909-621-8734, E-mail: margaret.grogan@cgu.edu. *Application contact:* Margaret Grogan, Dean, 909-621-8075, Fax: 909-621-8734, E-mail: margaret.grogan@cgu.edu.

Clemson University, Graduate School, College of Health, Education, and Human Development, Program in Youth Development, Clemson, SC 29634. Offers MS. *Faculty:* 4 full-time (2 women). *Students:* 18 full-time (13 women), 27 part-time (15 women); includes 11 Black or African American, non-Hispanic/Latino; 1 Hispanic/Latino. Average age 30. 11 applicants, 73% accepted, 5 enrolled. In 2010, 6 master's awarded. *Entrance requirements:* For master's, GRE General Test. Additional exam requirements/recommendations for international students: Required—TOEFL. *Application deadline:* Applications are processed on a rolling basis. Application fee: $70 ($80 for international students). Electronic applications accepted. *Expenses:* Contact institution. *Financial support:* In 2010–11, 2 students received support. Total annual research expenditures: $61,948. *Unit head:* Dr. Kathy Headley, Associate Dean for Research and Graduate Programs, 864-656-2181, Fax: 864-656-5488, E-mail: ksn1177@clemson.edu. *Application contact:* Dr. William Quinn, Graduate Program Coordinator, 864-656-1501, Fax: 864-656-5488, E-mail: wquinn@clemson.edu.

Colorado State University, Graduate School, College of Applied Human Sciences, Department of Human Development and Family Studies, Fort Collins, CO 80523-1570. Offers MS, PhD. *Accreditation:* AAMFT/COAMFTE. Part-time programs available. *Faculty:* 14 full-time (10 women). *Students:* 30 full-time (28 women), 6 part-time (5 women); includes 1 minority (Black or African American, non-Hispanic/Latino), 4 international. Average age 28. 108 applicants, 29% accepted, 16 enrolled. In 2010, 10 master's awarded. Terminal master's awarded for partial completion of doctoral program. *Degree requirements:* For master's, thesis or alternative; for doctorate, comprehensive exam (for some programs), thesis/dissertation, competency exams. *Entrance requirements:* For master's, GRE General Test, minimum GPA of 3.0; course work in human development, family studies, and statistics; letters of recommendation; interview; BS/BA in human development and family studies or related field; for doctorate, GRE General Test (50th percentile on Verbal and Quantitative sections and 4.5 on Analytical Writing section), minimum GPA of 3.0; coursework in human development, family studies, and statistics; letters of recommendation; departmental application; interview; BS/BA or master's degree in related field. Additional exam requirements/recommendations for international students: Required—TOEFL (minimum score 550 paper-based; 213 computer-based; 80 iBT). *Application deadline:* For fall admission, 1/2 for domestic and international students. Application fee: $50. Electronic applications accepted. *Expenses:* Tuition, state resident: full-time $7434; part-time $413 per credit. Tuition, nonresident: full-time $19,022; part-time $1057 per credit. Required fees: $1729; $88 per credit. *Financial support:* In 2010–11, 32 students received support, including 1 fellowship (averaging $37,368 per year), 11 research assistantships with full and partial tuition reimbursements available (averaging $7,481 per year), 20 teaching assistantships with full and partial tuition reimbursements available (averaging $8,405 per year); career-related internships or fieldwork, Federal Work-Study, institutionally sponsored loans, scholarships/grants, health care benefits, and unspecified assistantships also available. Financial award application deadline: 2/15; financial award applicants required to submit FAFSA. *Faculty research:* Promoting resiliency and optimal development; gender, culture and diversity; gerontology/aging; child and adolescent health; disabilities. Total annual research expenditures: $824,524. *Unit head:* Dr. Lise Youngblade, Department Head, 970-491-5558, Fax: 970-491-7975, E-mail: lise.youngblade@colostate.edu. *Application contact:* Dr. Karen C. Barrett, Graduate Chair, 970-491-7382, Fax: 970-491-7975, E-mail: karen.barrett@colostate.edu.

Cornell University, Graduate School, Graduate Fields of Human Ecology, Field of Human Development, Ithaca, NY 14853-0001. Offers developmental psychology (PhD), including cognitive development, developmental psychopathology, ecology of human development, social and personality development; human development and family studies (PhD), including ecology of human development, family studies and the life course. *Faculty:* 32 full-time (16 women). *Students:* 44 full-time (29 women); includes 1 Asian, non-Hispanic/Latino; 1 Hispanic/Latino, 12 international. Average age 27. 110 applicants, 26% accepted, 19 enrolled. In 2010, 2 doctorates awarded. *Degree requirements:* For doctorate, comprehensive exam, thesis/dissertation, pre-doctoral research project, teaching experience. *Entrance requirements:* For doctorate, GRE General Test, 2 letters of recommendation. Additional exam requirements/recommendations for international students: Required—TOEFL (minimum score 550 paper-based; 213 computer-based; 77 iBT). *Application deadline:* For fall admission, 1/15 for domestic students. Application fee: $70. Electronic applications accepted. *Expenses:* Tuition: Full-time $29,500. Required fees: $76. Tuition and fees vary according to degree level and program. *Financial support:* In 2010–11, 26 students received support, including 4 fellowships with full tuition reimbursements available, 9 research assistantships with full tuition reimbursements available, 18 teaching assistantships with full tuition reimbursements available; institutionally sponsored loans, scholarships/grants, health care benefits, tuition waivers (full and partial), and unspecified assistantships also available. Financial award applicants required to submit FAFSA. *Faculty research:* Cognitive development, developmental psychopathology, ecology of human development, family studies and the life course, social and personality development. *Unit head:* Director of Graduate Studies, 607-255-3181, Fax: 607-255-9856. *Application contact:* Graduate Field Assistant, 607-255-3181, Fax: 607-255-9856, E-mail: hdfs@cornell.edu.

DePaul University, School of Education, Chicago, IL 60106. Offers bilingual and bicultural education (M Ed, MA); curriculum studies (M Ed, MA, Ed D); educational leadership (M Ed, MA, Ed D), including administration and supervision (M Ed, MA), Catholic school leadership (M Ed, MA), physical education (M Ed, MA); human development and learning (MA); human services and counseling (M Ed, MA), including agencies, family concerns, and higher education, elementary schools, human services management, secondary schools; reading and learning disabilities (M Ed, MA); social culture studies in education and development (M Ed, MA), including curriculum studies/development; teaching and learning (early childhood, elementary and secondary) (M Ed), including elementary education (M Ed, MA), secondary education (M Ed, MA); teaching and learning (early childhood, elementary, and secondary) (MA), including elementary education (M Ed, MA), secondary education (M Ed, MA). Part-time and evening/

Human Development

DePaul University (continued)

weekend programs available. *Faculty:* 61 full-time (40 women), 66 part-time/adjunct (41 women). *Students:* 944 full-time (753 women), 534 part-time (415 women); includes 355 minority (166 Black or African American, non-Hispanic/Latino; 1 American Indian or Alaska Native, non-Hispanic/Latino; 41 Asian, non-Hispanic/Latino; 124 Hispanic/Latino; 3 Native Hawaiian or other Pacific Islander, non-Hispanic/Latino; 20 Two or more races, non-Hispanic/Latino), 21 international. Average age 30. 635 applicants, 74% accepted, 318 enrolled. In 2010, 604 master's, 5 doctorates awarded. *Degree requirements:* For doctorate, thesis/dissertation. *Entrance requirements:* For master's, interview, minimum GPA of 2.75, 2 letters of recommendation; for doctorate, interview, master's degree, writing sample, 3 letters of recommendation. Additional exam requirements/recommendations for international students: Required—TOEFL (minimum score 550 paper-based; 213 computer-based; 80 iBT). *Application deadline:* Applications are processed on a rolling basis. Application fee: $40. Electronic applications accepted. *Financial support:* In 2010–11, 14 research assistantships with tuition reimbursements (averaging $5,800 per year) were awarded; career-related internships or fieldwork also available. *Faculty research:* Reflective teaching, children at risk, loss, ethnicity, urban education. Total annual research expenditures: $1.6 million. *Unit head:* Dr. Marie Donovan, Dean, 773-325-7581, Fax: 773-325-7713, E-mail: mdonovan@depaul.edu. *Application contact:* Brandon Washington, Data Project Manager, 773-325-1152, Fax: 773-325-2270, E-mail: bwashin3@depaul.edu.

Duke University, Graduate School, Department of Psychology and Neuroscience, Durham, NC 27708. Offers biological psychology (PhD); clinical psychology (PhD); cognitive psychology (PhD); developmental psychology (PhD); experimental psychology (PhD); health psychology (PhD); human social development (PhD); JD/MA. *Accreditation:* APA (one or more programs are accredited). *Faculty:* 40 full-time. *Students:* 92 full-time (67 women); includes 6 Black or African American, non-Hispanic/Latino; 2 Asian, non-Hispanic/Latino; 7 Hispanic/Latino, 13 international. 483 applicants, 8% accepted, 23 enrolled. In 2010, 24 doctorates awarded. *Degree requirements:* For doctorate, thesis/dissertation. *Entrance requirements:* For doctorate, GRE General Test. Additional exam requirements/recommendations for international students: Required—TOEFL (minimum score 550 paper-based; 213 computer-based; 83 iBT), IELTS (minimum score 7). *Application deadline:* For fall admission, 12/8 priority date for domestic and international students. Application fee: $75. Electronic applications accepted. *Financial support:* Fellowships, research assistantships, teaching assistantships, career-related internships or fieldwork and Federal Work-Study available. Financial award application deadline: 12/8. *Unit head:* Melanie Bonner, Director of Graduate Studies, 919-660-5715, Fax: 919-660-5726, E-mail: morrell@duke.edu. *Application contact:* Elizabeth Hutton, Director of Admissions, 919-684-3913, Fax: 919-684-2277, E-mail: grad-admissions@duke.edu.

East Tennessee State University, School of Graduate Studies, College of Education, Department of Human Development and Learning, Johnson City, TN 37614. Offers advanced practitioner (M Ed); community agency counseling (M Ed, MA); comprehensive concentration (M Ed); counseling (M Ed, MA); early childhood (PhD); early childhood education (M Ed, MA); early childhood general (M Ed); early childhood special education (M Ed); early childhood teaching (M Ed); elementary and secondary (school counseling) (M Ed, MA); marriage and family therapy (M Ed, MA); modified concentration (M Ed). *Accreditation:* ACA; NCATE. Part-time programs available. *Faculty:* 21 full-time (13 women). *Students:* 102 full-time (84 women), 45 part-time (44 women); includes 11 minority (7 Black or African American, non-Hispanic/Latino; 4 Two or more races, non-Hispanic/Latino), 5 international. Average age 33. 143 applicants, 46% accepted, 45 enrolled. In 2010, 48 master's awarded. Terminal master's awarded for partial completion of doctoral program. *Degree requirements:* For master's, comprehensive exam, thesis optional, internship, student teaching, culminating experience; for doctorate, comprehensive exam, thesis/dissertation, research apprenticeship. *Entrance requirements:* For master's, GRE General Test, minimum GPA of 3.0; for doctorate, GRE General Test, professional resume, master's degree in early childhood or related field, interview. Additional exam requirements/recommendations for international students: Required—TOEFL (minimum score 550 paper-based; 213 computer-based; 79 iBT). *Application deadline:* For fall admission, 2/1 priority date for domestic and international students. Application fee: $25 ($35 for international students). Electronic applications accepted. *Financial support:* In 2010–11, 12 research assistantships with full tuition reimbursements (averaging $5,500 per year) were awarded; teaching assistantships with full tuition reimbursements, career-related internships or fieldwork, institutionally sponsored loans, scholarships/grants, traineeships, and unspecified assistantships also available. Financial award application deadline: 7/1; financial award applicants required to submit FAFSA. *Faculty research:* Drug and alcohol abuse, marriage and family counseling, severe mental retardation, parenting of children with disabilities. Total annual research expenditures: $405,136. *Unit head:* Dr. Patricia Robertson, Chair, 423-439-7693, Fax: 423-439-7790, E-mail: robertpe@etsu.edu. *Application contact:* Admissions and Records Clerk, 423-439-4221, Fax: 423-439-5624, E-mail: gradsch@etsu.edu.

Erikson Institute, Academic Programs, Chicago, IL 60654. Offers administration (Certificate); bilingual/ESL (Certificate); child development (MS); early childhood education (MS); infant mental health (Certificate); infant studies (Certificate); MS/MSW. MS/MSW offered jointly with Loyola University Chicago. Part-time and evening/weekend programs available. *Degree requirements:* For master's, comprehensive exam, internship; for Certificate, internship. *Entrance requirements:* For master's and Certificate, minimum GPA of 2.75. Additional exam requirements/recommendations for international students: Required—TOEFL. *Expenses:* Tuition: Part-time $810 per credit. Required fees: $420 per year. *Faculty research:* Assessment strategies from early childhood through elementary years; language, literacy, and the arts in children's development; inclusive special education; parent-child relationships; cognitive development.

Fielding Graduate University, Graduate Programs, School of Human and Organization Development, Santa Barbara, CA 93105-3538. Offers evidence-based coaching (Certificate); human and organizational systems (PhD); human development (PhD); integral studies (Certificate); organization management and development (MA, Certificate). Postbaccalaureate distance learning degree programs offered (minimal on-campus study). *Faculty:* 25 full-time (11 women), 11 part-time/adjunct (3 women). *Students:* 455 full-time (325 women), 148 part-time (112 women); includes 124 minority (69 Black or African American, non-Hispanic/Latino; 6 American Indian or Alaska Native, non-Hispanic/Latino; 19 Asian, non-Hispanic/Latino; 20 Hispanic/Latino; 10 Two or more races, non-Hispanic/Latino), 65 international. Average age 48. 179 applicants, 94% accepted, 109 enrolled. In 2010, 49 master's, 32 doctorates, 55 other advanced degrees awarded. Terminal master's awarded for partial completion of doctoral program. *Degree requirements:* For master's, thesis or alternative; for doctorate, comprehensive exam, thesis/dissertation. *Entrance requirements:* For master's, minimum GPA of 2.5, letter of recommendation; for doctorate, 2 letters of recommendation, writing sample, resume, self-assessment statement. *Application deadline:* For fall admission, 3/1 for domestic and international students; for spring admission, 9/1 for domestic and international students. Application fee: $75. Electronic applications accepted. *Expenses:* Contact institution. *Financial support:* In 2010–11, 27 students received support. Scholarships/grants and health care benefits available. Support available to part-time students. *Unit head:* Dr. Charles McClintock, Dean, 805-898-2930, Fax: 805-687-4590, E-mail: cmcclintock@fielding.edu. *Application contact:* Carmen Kuchera, Admission Counselor, 800-340-1099, Fax: 805-687-9793, E-mail: hodadmissions@fielding.edu.

The George Washington University, Graduate School of Education and Human Development, Individualized Master's Program, Washington, DC 20052. Offers MA Ed. *Students:* 1 (woman) full-time, 3 part-time (all women); includes 1 Asian, non-Hispanic/Latino, 1 international. Average age 44. 6 applicants, 100% accepted, 2 enrolled. In 2010, 3 master's awarded. *Degree requirements:* For master's, comprehensive exam. *Entrance requirements:* For master's, GRE General Test or MAT, minimum GPA of 2.75. *Application deadline:* For fall admission, 3/1 priority date for domestic students; for spring admission, 10/1 for domestic students. Applications are processed on a rolling basis. Application fee: $75. *Financial support:* Application deadline: 1/15. *Application contact:* Sarah Lang, Director of Graduate Admissions, 202-994-1447, Fax: 202-994-7207, E-mail: slang@gwu.edu.

Harvard University, Harvard Graduate School of Education, Doctoral Program in Education, Cambridge, MA 02138. Offers culture, communities and education (Ed D); education policy, leadership and instructional practice (Ed D); higher education (Ed D); human development and education (Ed D); quantitative policy analysis in education (Ed D). *Faculty:* 79 full-time (42 women), 58 part-time/adjunct (24 women). *Students:* 276 full-time (188 women), 18 part-time (10 women); includes 98 minority (33 Black or African American, non-Hispanic/Latino; 1 American Indian or Alaska Native, non-Hispanic/Latino; 31 Asian, non-Hispanic/Latino; 25 Hispanic/Latino; 1 Native Hawaiian or other Pacific Islander, non-Hispanic/Latino; 7 Two or more races, non-Hispanic/Latino), 34 international. Average age 34. 485 applicants, 9% accepted, 29 enrolled. In 2010, 54 doctorates awarded. Terminal master's awarded for partial completion of doctoral program. *Degree requirements:* For doctorate, thesis/dissertation. *Entrance requirements:* For doctorate, GRE General Test, statement of purpose, 3 letters of recommendation, resume, official transcripts. Additional exam requirements/recommendations for international students: Required—TOEFL (minimum score 600 paper-based; 250 computer-based; 100 iBT), TWE (minimum score 5). *Application deadline:* For fall admission, 12/15 for domestic and international students. Application fee: $85. Electronic applications accepted. *Expenses:* Contact institution. *Financial support:* In 2010–11, 241 students received support, including 74 fellowships with full and partial tuition reimbursements available (averaging $13,993 per year), 40 research assistantships (averaging $10,322 per year), 133 teaching assistantships (averaging $10,500 per year); career-related internships or fieldwork, Federal Work-Study, institutionally sponsored loans, scholarships/grants, health care benefits, tuition waivers (full and partial), and unspecified assistantships also available. Support available to part-time students. Financial award application deadline: 2/1; financial award applicants required to submit FAFSA. *Faculty research:* Learning and development, educational leadership and organizations, education policy analysis. Total annual research expenditures: $23 million. *Unit head:* Dr. Shu-Ling Chen, Assistant Dean for Doctoral Studies, 617-496-4406. *Application contact:* Information Contact, 617-495-3414, Fax: 617-496-3577, E-mail: gseadmissions@harvard.edu.

Harvard University, Harvard Graduate School of Education, Master's Programs in Education, Cambridge, MA 02138. Offers arts in education (Ed M); education policy and management (Ed M); higher education (Ed M); human development and psychology (Ed M); international education policy (Ed M); language and literacy (Ed M); learning and teaching (Ed M); mid-career mathematics and science (teaching certificate) (Ed M); mind brain and education (Ed M); prevention science and practice (Ed M); school leadership (Ed M); special studies (Ed M); teaching and curriculum (teaching certificate) (Ed M); technology innovation and education (Ed M). Part-time programs available. *Faculty:* 79 full-time (42 women), 58 part-time/adjunct (24 women). *Students:* 601 full-time (453 women), 77 part-time (53 women); includes 198 minority (59 Black or African American, non-Hispanic/Latino; 3 American Indian or Alaska Native, non-Hispanic/Latino; 59 Asian, non-Hispanic/Latino; 48 Hispanic/Latino; 2 Native Hawaiian or other Pacific Islander, non-Hispanic/Latino; 27 Two or more races, non-Hispanic/Latino), 75 international. Average age 28. 1,667 applicants, 53% accepted, 633 enrolled. In 2010, 634 master's awarded. *Entrance requirements:* For master's, GRE General Test, statement of purpose, 3 letters of recommendation, resume, official transcripts. Additional exam requirements/recommendations for international students: Required—TOEFL (minimum score 600 paper-based; 250 computer-based; 100 iBT), TWE (minimum score 5). *Application deadline:* For fall admission, 1/3 for domestic and international students. Application fee: $85. Electronic applications accepted. *Expenses:* Contact institution. *Financial support:* In 2010–11, 422 students received support, including 24 fellowships with full and partial tuition reimbursements available (averaging $11,886 per year); career-related internships or fieldwork, Federal Work-Study, institutionally sponsored loans, scholarships/grants, health care benefits, tuition waivers (full and partial), and unspecified assistantships also available. Support available to part-time students. Financial award application deadline: 2/1; financial award applicants required to submit FAFSA. *Faculty research:* Learning and development, educational leadership and organizations, educational policy analysis. Total annual research expenditures: $23 million. *Unit head:* Jennifer L. Petrallia, Assistant Dean, 617-495-8445. *Application contact:* Information Contact, 617-495-3414, Fax: 617-496-3577, E-mail: gseadmissions@harvard.edu.

Hofstra University, School of Education, Health, and Human Services, Programs in Learning and Teaching, Hempstead, NY 11549. Offers learning and teaching (Ed D), including applied linguistics, art education, arts and humanities, early childhood education, English education, human development, math education, math, science, and technology, multicultural education, physical education, science education, social studies education, special education. Part-time and evening/weekend programs available. *Students:* 2 full-time (both women), 26 part-time (21 women); includes 2 Black or African American, non-Hispanic/Latino, 1 international. Average age 36. 26 applicants, 38% accepted, 9 enrolled. *Degree requirements:* For doctorate, comprehensive exam, thesis/dissertation. *Entrance requirements:* For doctorate, GRE, 3 letters of recommendation, essay, interview, 2 years full-time teaching. Additional exam requirements/recommendations for international students: Required—TOEFL (minimum score 550 paper-based; 213 computer-based; 80 iBT). *Application deadline:* Applications are processed on a rolling basis. Application fee: $70 ($75 for international students). Electronic applications accepted. *Expenses:* Tuition: Full-time $18,000; part-time $1000 per credit hour. Required fees: $970; $145 per term. Tuition and fees vary according to program. *Financial support:* In 2010–11, 27 students received support, including 22 fellowships with full and partial tuition reimbursements available (averaging $5,468 per year); research assistantships with full and partial tuition reimbursements available, Federal Work-Study, institutionally sponsored loans, scholarships/grants, tuition waivers (full and partial), and scholarships also available. Support available to part-time students. Financial award applicants required to submit FAFSA. *Faculty research:* Critical thinking, professional development, teacher quality, quantitative research. *Unit head:* Dr. Esther Fusco, Chairperson, 516-463-7704, Fax: 516-463-6196, E-mail: catajs@hofstra.edu. *Application contact:* Carol Drummer, Dean of Graduate Admissions, 516-463-4876, Fax: 516-463-4664, E-mail: gradstudent@hofstra.edu.

Hood College, Graduate School, Programs in Human Sciences, Frederick, MD 21701-8575. Offers human sciences (MA), including psychology; thanatology (MA, Certificate). Part-time and evening/weekend programs available. *Faculty:* 5 full-time (3 women), 7 part-time/adjunct (4 women). *Students:* 19 full-time (13 women), 66 part-time (60 women); includes 13 Black or African American, non-Hispanic/Latino; 2 American Indian or Alaska Native, non-Hispanic/Latino; 1 Asian, non-Hispanic/Latino; 2 Hispanic/Latino; 1 Two or more races, non-Hispanic/Latino, 2 international. Average age 34. 40 applicants, 85% accepted, 19 enrolled. In 2010, 40 master's, 27 other advanced degrees awarded. *Degree requirements:* For master's, comprehensive exam, capstone/research project. *Entrance requirements:* For master's, minimum GPA of 2.75. Additional exam requirements/recommendations for international students: Required—TOEFL (minimum score 575 paper-based; 231 computer-based; 89 iBT). *Application deadline:* For fall admission, 7/15 for domestic and international students; for spring admission, 12/15 for domestic and international students. Applications are processed on a rolling basis. Application fee: $35. Electronic applications accepted. *Expenses:* Tuition: Full-time $6480; part-time $360 per credit. Required fees: $100; $50 per term. *Financial support:* Applicants required to submit FAFSA. *Faculty research:* Mind-body medicine and multicultural healing, the New Orleans jazz funeral, death practices in African-American culture, bereavement theories and gender differences, Piaget's theory of cognitive development as a formal mathematical model. *Unit head:* Dr. Terry Martin, Director, 301-696-3759, Fax: 301-696-3597, E-mail: tmartin@hood.edu. *Application contact:* Dr. Allen P. Flora, Dean of Graduate School, 301-696-3811, Fax: 301-696-3597, E-mail: gofurther@hood.edu.

Indiana University Bloomington, School of Health, Physical Education and Recreation, Department of Applied Health Science, Bloomington, IN 47405-7000. Offers health behavior (PhD); health promotion (MS); human development/family studies (MS); nutrition science (MS); public health (MPH); safety management (MS); school and college health programs (MS). *Accreditation:* CEPH (one or more programs are accredited). *Faculty:* 24 full-time (12 women). *Students:* 143 full-time (105 women), 32 part-time (20 women); includes 36 Black or African American, non-Hispanic/Latino; 2 American Indian or Alaska Native, non-Hispanic/

Latino; 2 Asian, non-Hispanic/Latino; 7 Hispanic/Latino; 1 Two or more races, non-Hispanic/Latino, 28 international. Average age 30. 135 applicants, 80% accepted, 73 enrolled. In 2010, 49 master's, 7 doctorates awarded. *Degree requirements:* For master's, thesis optional; for doctorate, thesis/dissertation. *Entrance requirements:* For master's, GRE (MS in nutrition science), 3 recommendations; for doctorate, GRE, 3 recommendations. Additional exam requirements/recommendations for international students: Required—TOEFL (minimum score 550 paper-based; 213 computer-based; 79 iBT). *Application deadline:* For fall admission, 4/30 priority date for domestic students, 12/1 priority date for international students; for spring admission, 11/15 priority date for domestic students, 9/1 priority date for international students. Application fee: $55 ($65 for international students). *Financial support:* Fellowships, research assistantships with full and partial tuition reimbursements, teaching assistantships with full and partial tuition reimbursements, career-related internships or fieldwork, Federal Work-Study, institutionally sponsored loans, scholarships/grants, tuition waivers (partial), and fee remissions available. Financial award application deadline: 3/1. *Faculty research:* Cancer education, HIV/AIDS and drug education, public health, parent-child interactions, safety education. Total annual research expenditures: $2.8 million. *Unit head:* Dr. Mohammad R. Torabi, Chair, 812-855-4808, Fax: 812-855-3936, E-mail: torabi@indiana.edu. *Application contact:* Dr. Mohammad R. Torabi, Chair, 812-855-4808, Fax: 812-855-3936, E-mail: torabi@indiana.edu.

Iowa State University of Science and Technology, Graduate College, College of Human Sciences, Department of Human Development and Family Studies, Ames, IA 50011. Offers human development and family studies (MFCS, MS, PhD). *Accreditation:* AAMFT/COAMFTE. *Faculty:* 19 full-time (15 women), 6 part-time/adjunct (5 women). *Students:* 62 full-time (55 women), 21 part-time (17 women); includes 2 Black or African American, non-Hispanic/Latino; 1 Asian, non-Hispanic/Latino; 4 Hispanic/Latino, 10 international. 34 applicants, 74% accepted, 11 enrolled. In 2010, 11 master's, 9 doctorates awarded. *Degree requirements:* For master's, thesis; for doctorate, thesis/dissertation. *Entrance requirements:* For master's and doctorate, GRE General Test. Additional exam requirements/recommendations for international students: Required—TOEFL (minimum score 550 paper-based; 79 iBT), IELTS (minimum score 6.5). *Application deadline:* For fall admission, 1/15 priority date for domestic and international students. Application fee: $40 ($90 for international students). Electronic applications accepted. *Financial support:* In 2010–11, 36 research assistantships with full and partial tuition reimbursements (averaging $12,375 per year), 11 teaching assistantships with full and partial tuition reimbursements (averaging $11,066 per year) were awarded; fellowships, scholarships/grants also available. *Faculty research:* Child development, early childhood education, family resource management and housing, life span studies. *Unit head:* Dr. Dianne Draper, Interim Chair, 515-294-6316, Fax: 515-294-2502, E-mail: hdfs-grad-adm@iastate.edu. *Application contact:* Dr. Dianne Draper, Interim Chair, 515-294-6316, Fax: 515-294-2502, E-mail: hdfs-grad-adm@iastate.edu.

Kansas State University, Graduate School, College of Human Ecology, Program in Human Ecology, Manhattan, KS 66506. Offers apparel and textiles (PhD); family life education and consultation (PhD); food service and hospitality management (PhD); lifespan and human development (PhD); marriage and family therapy (PhD); personal financial planning (PhD). *Degree requirements:* For doctorate, thesis/dissertation. Electronic applications accepted.

Kansas State University, Graduate School, College of Human Ecology, School of Family Studies and Human Services, Manhattan, KS 66506. Offers communication sciences and disorders (MS); early childhood education (MS); family studies (MS); life span human development (MS); marriage and family therapy (MS). *Accreditation:* AAMFT/COAMFTE; ASHA. Part-time programs available. *Degree requirements:* For master's, thesis or alternative, oral exam, residency. *Entrance requirements:* For master's, GRE, minimum GPA of 3.0 in last 2 years of undergraduate study. Additional exam requirements/recommendations for international students: Required—TOEFL (minimum score 600 paper-based; 250 computer-based). Electronic applications accepted. *Faculty research:* Health and security of military families, personal and family risk assessment and evaluation, disorders of communication and swallowing, families and health.

Kent State University, Graduate School of Education, Health, and Human Services, School of Lifespan Development and Educational Sciences, Program in Counseling and Human Development Services, Kent, OH 44242-0001. Offers PhD. *Accreditation:* ACA; NCATE. *Faculty:* 9 full-time (4 women), 18 part-time/adjunct (12 women). *Students:* 58 full-time (47 women), 10 part-time (7 women); includes 11 Black or African American, non-Hispanic/Latino; 3 Asian, non-Hispanic/Latino. 28 applicants, 54% accepted. In 2010, 5 doctorates awarded. *Degree requirements:* For doctorate, comprehensive exam, thesis/dissertation. *Entrance requirements:* For doctorate, GRE General Test. Additional exam requirements/recommendations for international students: Required—TOEFL. *Application deadline:* For fall admission, 2/15 for domestic students. Application fee: $30 ($60 for international students). Electronic applications accepted. *Expenses:* Tuition, state resident: full-time $7866; part-time $437 per credit hour. Tuition, nonresident: full-time $14,022; part-time $779 per credit hour. *Financial support:* In 2010–11, 13 fellowships with full tuition reimbursements (averaging $11,000 per year), research assistantships with full tuition reimbursements (averaging $11,000 per year), teaching assistantships with full tuition reimbursements (averaging $11,000 per year) were awarded; career-related internships or fieldwork, Federal Work-Study, institutionally sponsored loans, scholarships/grants, health care benefits, unspecified assistantships, and 1 administrative assistantship (averaging $11,000 per year) also available. Support available to part-time students. Financial award application deadline: 4/1; financial award applicants required to submit FAFSA. *Faculty research:* Family/child therapy, clinical supervision, group work, experiential training methods. *Unit head:* Dr. John L. West, Coordinator, 330-672-0713, Fax: 330-672-5396, E-mail: jwest@kent.edu. *Application contact:* Nancy Miller, Academic Program Coordinator, Office of Graduate Student Services, 330-672-2576, Fax: 330-672-9162, E-mail: ogs@kent.edu.

Kent State University, Graduate School of Education, Health, and Human Services, School of Lifespan Development and Educational Sciences, Program in Family Studies, Kent, OH 44242-0001. Offers gerontology (MA); human development and family studies (MA). *Faculty:* 8 full-time (6 women), 12 part-time/adjunct (11 women). *Students:* 3 full-time (all women), 12 part-time (11 women); includes 2 Black or African American, non-Hispanic/Latino. 10 applicants, 70% accepted. In 2010, 4 master's awarded. Application fee: $30 ($60 for international students). *Expenses:* Tuition, state resident: full-time $7866; part-time $437 per credit hour. Tuition, nonresident: full-time $14,022; part-time $779 per credit hour. *Financial support:* In 2010–11, research assistantships (averaging $8,313 per year); 2 administrative assistantships (averaging $8,313 per year) also available. *Unit head:* Dr. Rhonda Richardson, Coordinator, 330-672-2026, E-mail: rrichard@kent.edu. *Application contact:* Nancy Miller, Academic Program Coordinator, 330-672-2576, Fax: 330-672-9162, E-mail: ogs@kent.edu.

Laurentian University, School of Graduate Studies and Research, Programme in Human Development, Sudbury, ON P3E 2C6, Canada. Offers M Sc, MA. Interdisciplinary program consisting of the Departments of Psychology, Sociology, and Human Movement. Part-time programs available. *Degree requirements:* For master's, thesis or alternative. *Entrance requirements:* For master's, honors degree with second class or better. *Faculty research:* Aging and well-being, physical, social and cognitive development of children, social cognition and social relationships including peers and family, education and schooling.

Lehigh University, College of Arts and Sciences, Department of Psychology, Bethlehem, PA 18015. Offers human cognition and development (MS, PhD). *Faculty:* 14 full-time (8 women). *Students:* 17 full-time (13 women), 3 part-time (2 women), 4 international. Average age 27. 90 applicants, 9% accepted, 7 enrolled. In 2010, 1 master's, 2 doctorates awarded. *Degree requirements:* For master's, thesis; for doctorate, comprehensive exam, thesis/dissertation. *Entrance requirements:* For master's and doctorate, GRE General Test. Additional exam requirements/recommendations for international students: Required—TOEFL. *Application deadline:* For fall admission, 1/15 for domestic and international students. Application fee: $75. Electronic applications accepted. *Expenses:* Contact institution. *Financial support:* In 2010–11, 15 students received support, including 1 fellowship with full tuition reimbursement available

(averaging $25,000 per year), 3 research assistantships with full tuition reimbursements available (averaging $18,400 per year), 11 teaching assistantships with full tuition reimbursements available (averaging $18,400 per year); scholarships/grants, tuition waivers (full and partial), and unspecified assistantships also available. Financial award application deadline: 1/15. *Faculty research:* Cognition, memory, language, and their development; prosocial cognition, emotion, and action; conflict and cooperation between and within groups; self-control of cognition and emotion; optimizing developmental and relational outcomes. Total annual research expenditures: $281,626. *Unit head:* Ageliki Nicolopoulou, Chairperson, 610-758-4702, Fax: 610-758-6277, E-mail: agn3@lehigh.edu. *Application contact:* Dr. Michael Gill, Program Director, 610-758-3630, Fax: 610-758-6277, E-mail: inpsy@lehigh.edu.

Lindsey Wilson College, School of Professional Counseling, Columbia, KY 42728. Offers counseling and human development (M Ed). *Accreditation:* ACA. Part-time and evening/weekend programs available.

Marywood University, Academic Affairs, Reap College of Education and Human Development, Department of Human Development, Doctoral Program in Human Development, Scranton, PA 18509-1598. Offers PhD. *Entrance requirements:* Additional exam requirements/recommendations for international students: Required—TOEFL (minimum score 550 paper-based; 213 computer-based; 79 iBT). Electronic applications accepted. *Expenses:* Contact institution.

Montana State University, College of Graduate Studies, College of Education, Health, and Human Development, Department of Health and Human Development, Bozeman, MT 59717. Offers family and consumer sciences (MS). *Accreditation:* ACA. Part-time programs available. Postbaccalaureate distance learning degree programs offered (no on-campus study). *Faculty:* 27 full-time (20 women), 7 part-time/adjunct (6 women). *Students:* 62 full-time (53 women), 27 part-time (22 women); includes 8 minority (2 American Indian or Alaska Native, non-Hispanic/Latino; 2 Asian, non-Hispanic/Latino; 3 Hispanic/Latino; 1 Two or more races, non-Hispanic/Latino), 1 international. Average age 29. 45 applicants, 56% accepted, 24 enrolled. In 2010, 26 master's awarded. *Degree requirements:* For master's, comprehensive exam. *Entrance requirements:* For master's, GRE (minimum scores: verbal 480; quantitative 480). Additional exam requirements/recommendations for international students: Required—TOEFL (minimum score 550 paper-based; 213 computer-based). *Application deadline:* For fall admission, 7/15 priority date for domestic students, 5/15 priority date for international students; for spring admission, 12/1 priority date for domestic students, 10/1 priority date for international students. Applications are processed on a rolling basis. Application fee: $30. Electronic applications accepted. *Expenses:* Tuition, state resident: full-time $5553.90. Tuition, nonresident: full-time $14,646. Required fees: $1233. *Financial support:* In 2010–11, 35 students received support, including 31 teaching assistantships with partial tuition reimbursements available (averaging $9,000 per year); career-related internships or fieldwork, scholarships/grants, and unspecified assistantships also available. Financial award application deadline: 3/1; financial award applicants required to submit FAFSA. *Faculty research:* Community food systems, ethic of care for teachers and coaches, influence of public policy on families and communities, cost effectiveness of early childhood education, exercise metabolism, winter sport performance enhancement, assessment of physical activity. Total annual research expenditures: $4 million. *Unit head:* Dr. Mark Nelson, Department Head, 404-994-3810, Fax: 404-994-2013, E-mail: markn@montana.edu. *Application contact:* Dr. Carl A. Fox.

National-Louis University, National College of Education, Chicago, IL 60603. Offers administration and supervision (M Ed, Ed D, CAS, Ed S); curriculum and instruction (M Ed, MS Ed, CAS); early childhood administration (M Ed, CAS); early childhood education (M Ed, MAT, MS Ed, CAS); education (Ed D); educational psychology/human learning and development (M Ed, MS Ed, CAS, Ed S); elementary education (MAT); interdisciplinary curriculum and instruction (M Ed); mathematics education (M Ed, MS Ed, CAS); reading and language (M Ed, MS Ed, CAS); school psychology (M Ed, Ed S); science education (M Ed, MS Ed, CAS); secondary education (MAT); special education (M Ed, MAT, CAS); technology in education (M Ed, CAS). *Accreditation:* NCATE. Part-time and evening/weekend programs available. *Students:* 501 full-time (370 women), 2,650 part-time (2,011 women); includes 572 minority (258 Black or African American, non-Hispanic/Latino; 2 American Indian or Alaska Native, non-Hispanic/Latino; 60 Asian, non-Hispanic/Latino; 210 Hispanic/Latino; 6 Native Hawaiian or other Pacific Islander, non-Hispanic/Latino; 36 Two or more races, non-Hispanic/Latino), 4 international. Average age 34. In 2010, 1,711 master's, 76 doctorates, 86 other advanced degrees awarded. *Degree requirements:* For doctorate, comprehensive exam, thesis/dissertation. *Entrance requirements:* For master's, MAT or GRE, minimum GPA of 3.0; for doctorate, GRE General Test, minimum GPA of 3.25, interview, resume, writing sample, 4 recommendations. Additional exam requirements/recommendations for international students: Required—TOEFL (minimum score 550 paper-based; 213 computer-based; 79 iBT). *Application deadline:* Applications are processed on a rolling basis. Application fee: $40. *Financial support:* Fellowships, research assistantships, teaching assistantships, career-related internships or fieldwork, Federal Work-Study, institutionally sponsored loans, and scholarships/grants available. Support available to part-time students. Financial award applicants required to submit FAFSA. *Unit head:* Dr. Alison Hilsabeck, Dean, 312-361-3580, Fax: 312-261-2580, E-mail: ahilsabeck@nl.edu. *Application contact:* Dr. George Valcourt, Vice President of Enrollment and Student Services, 312-261-3550, Fax: 312-261-3550, E-mail: george.valcourt@nl.edu.

New York University, Steinhardt School of Culture, Education, and Human Development, New York, NY 10003. Offers MA, MFA, MM, MS, DPS, DPT, Ed D, PhD, Advanced Certificate, MA/MA, MM/Advanced Certificate. *Accreditation:* Teacher Education Accreditation Council. Part-time programs available. *Faculty:* 262 full-time (154 women), 644 part-time/adjunct (524 women). *Students:* 2,305 full-time (1,758 women), 1,385 part-time (1,059 women); includes 253 Black or African American, non-Hispanic/Latino; 4 American Indian or Alaska Native, non-Hispanic/Latino; 312 Asian, non-Hispanic/Latino; 187 Hispanic/Latino, 536 international. Average age 30. 5,812 applicants, 49% accepted, 1293 enrolled. In 2010, 1,225 master's, 101 doctorates, 21 other advanced degrees awarded. *Degree requirements:* For master's, thesis (for some programs); for doctorate, comprehensive exam (for some programs), thesis/dissertation. *Entrance requirements:* For doctorate, GRE General Test, interview. Additional exam requirements/recommendations for international students: Required—TOEFL. *Application deadline:* For fall admission, 12/1 priority date for domestic students, 12/1 for international students; for spring admission, 1/1 for domestic and international students. Applications are processed on a rolling basis. Application fee: $75. Electronic applications accepted. *Expenses:* Contact institution. *Financial support:* Fellowships with full and partial tuition reimbursements, research assistantships with full and partial tuition reimbursements, teaching assistantships with full and partial tuition reimbursements, career-related internships or fieldwork, Federal Work-Study, institutionally sponsored loans, scholarships/grants, traineeships, tuition waivers (partial), and unspecified assistantships available. Support available to part-time students. Financial award application deadline: 2/1; financial award applicants required to submit FAFSA. *Faculty research:* Equity, urban adolescents, arts in education, globalization, community and public health. Total annual research expenditures: $22.8 million. *Unit head:* Dr. Mary Brabeck, Dean, 212-998-5000. *Application contact:* John Myers, Director of Enrollment Management, 212-998-5030, Fax: 212-995-4328, E-mail: steinhardt.gradadmissions@nyu.edu.

New York University, Steinhardt School of Culture, Education, and Human Development, Department of Applied Psychology, Programs in Educational and Developmental Psychology, New York, NY 10012-1019. Offers educational psychology (MA); human development and social intervention (MA); psychological development (PhD); psychology and social intervention (PhD). *Accreditation:* APA (one or more programs are accredited). Part-time programs available. *Faculty:* 24 full-time (16 women). *Students:* 52 full-time (48 women), 33 part-time (29 women); includes 9 Black or African American, non-Hispanic/Latino; 8 Asian, non-Hispanic/Latino; 7 Hispanic/Latino, 14 international. Average age 29. 230 applicants, 35% accepted, 33 enrolled. In 2010, 26 master's, 4 doctorates awarded. *Degree requirements:* For master's, thesis (for some programs); for doctorate, thesis/dissertation. *Entrance requirements:* For doctorate, GRE General Test, interview. Additional exam requirements/recommendations for international

Human Development

New York University (continued)
students: Required—TOEFL. *Application deadline:* For fall admission, 12/1 priority date for domestic and international students. Applications are processed on a rolling basis. Application fee: $75. Electronic applications accepted. *Financial support:* Teaching assistantships with partial tuition reimbursements, career-related internships or fieldwork, Federal Work-Study, institutionally sponsored loans, and tuition waivers (partial) available. Support available to part-time students. Financial award application deadline: 2/1; financial award applicants required to submit FAFSA. *Faculty research:* High risk children and youth; child and adolescent developments; families and schooling; infant cognition; exploration, language, and symbolic play in toddlerhood. *Unit head:* Dr. LaRue Allen, Director, 212-998-5555, Fax: 212-995-4358. *Application contact:* 212-998-5030, Fax: 212-995-4328, E-mail: steinhardt.gradadmissions@nyu.edu.

New York University, Steinhardt School of Culture, Education, and Human Development, Department of Humanities and Social Sciences in the Professions, Program in International Education, New York, NY 10012-1019. Offers human development and social intervention (MA); international education (MA, PhD, Advanced Certificate), including cross cultural exchange and training (PhD), global education (PhD), international development education (PhD). Part-time programs available. *Faculty:* 3 full-time (2 women). *Students:* 73 full-time (62 women), 61 part-time (51 women); includes 8 Black or African American, non-Hispanic/Latino; 22 Asian, non-Hispanic/Latino; 7 Hispanic/Latino, 29 international. Average age 27. 264 applicants, 72% accepted, 52 enrolled. In 2010, 58 master's, 1 doctorate, 1 other advanced degree awarded. *Degree requirements:* For master's, thesis (for some programs); for doctorate, thesis/dissertation. *Entrance requirements:* For doctorate, GRE General Test, interview; for Advanced Certificate, master's degree. Additional exam requirements/recommendations for international students: Required—TOEFL. *Application deadline:* For fall admission, 12/1 priority date for domestic and international students; for spring admission, 11/1 for domestic and international students. Applications are processed on a rolling basis. Application fee: $75. Electronic applications accepted. *Financial support:* Fellowships with full and partial tuition reimbursements, career-related internships or fieldwork, Federal Work-Study, institutionally sponsored loans, and scholarships/grants available. Support available to part-time students. Financial award application deadline: 2/1; financial award applicants required to submit FAFSA. *Faculty research:* Civic education, ethnic identity among students and teachers, comparative education, education during emergencies, cross-cultural exchange. *Unit head:* Dr. Philip Hosay, Director, 212-998-5496, Fax: 212-995-4832, E-mail: pmh2@nyu.edu. *Application contact:* 212-998-5030, Fax: 212-995-4328, E-mail: steinhardt.gradadmissions@nyu.edu.

North Dakota State University, College of Graduate and Interdisciplinary Studies, College of Human Development and Education, Program in Human Development, Fargo, ND 58108. Offers PhD. *Students:* 11 full-time (8 women), 17 part-time (13 women); includes 1 Black or African American, non-Hispanic/Latino, 1 international. 7 applicants, 71% accepted, 1 enrolled. In 2010, 8 doctorates awarded. *Degree requirements:* For doctorate, comprehensive exam, thesis/dissertation. *Entrance requirements:* Additional exam requirements/recommendations for international students: Required—TOEFL (minimum score 525 paper-based; 197 computer-based; 71 iBT). *Application deadline:* For fall admission, 2/1 priority date for domestic and international students. Applications are processed on a rolling basis. Application fee: $45 ($60 for international students). *Financial support:* In 2010–11, 12 students received support; research assistantships with full tuition reimbursements available, teaching assistantships with full tuition reimbursements available, scholarships/grants, tuition waivers (partial), and unspecified assistantships available. *Faculty research:* Gerontology, wellness, counselor education. Total annual research expenditures: $1.3 million. *Unit head:* Dr. Greg Sanders, Coordinator, 701-231-8211, E-mail: greg.sanders@ndsu.edu. *Application contact:* Dr. Greg Sanders, Coordinator, 701-231-8211, E-mail: greg.sanders@ndsu.edu.

Northern Arizona University, Graduate College, College of Social and Behavioral Sciences, Institute for Human Development, Flagstaff , AZ 86011. Offers assistive technology (Certificate); disability policy and practice (Certificate); positive behavior support (Certificate). Part-time programs available. *Faculty:* 1 (woman) full-time. *Students:* 2 full-time (both women), 49 part-time (43 women); includes 7 minority (1 Black or African American, non-Hispanic/Latino; 1 American Indian or Alaska Native, non-Hispanic/Latino; 4 Hispanic/Latino; 1 Two or more races, non-Hispanic/Latino), 1 international. Average age 25. 53 applicants, 68% accepted, 32 enrolled. In 2010, 21 Certificates awarded. *Entrance requirements:* Additional exam requirements/recommendations for international students: Required—TOEFL (minimum score 550 paper-based; 213 computer-based; 80 iBT), IELTS (minimum score 7). *Application deadline:* For fall admission, 3/1 priority date for international students; for spring admission, 9/15 priority date for international students. Applications are processed on a rolling basis. Application fee: $65. Electronic applications accepted. *Unit head:* Richard Carroll, Executive Director, 928-523-4791, Fax: 928-523-9127, E-mail: richard.carroll@nau.edu. *Application contact:* Karen Applequist, Graduate Coordinator, 928-523-9276, E-mail: karen.applequist@nau.edu.

Northwestern University, The Graduate School, School of Education and Social Policy, Program in Human Development and Social Policy, Evanston, IL 60208. Offers PhD. Admissions and degrees offered through The Graduate School. *Degree requirements:* For doctorate, comprehensive exam, thesis/dissertation. *Entrance requirements:* For doctorate, GRE General Test. Additional exam requirements/recommendations for international students: Required—TOEFL (minimum score 600 paper-based; 250 computer-based; 100 iBT). Electronic applications accepted. *Faculty research:* Individual development and the personal narrative; the life course and culture; development, intervention and culture; the life course and policy; analysis of policy effects on lives.

The Ohio State University, Graduate School, College of Education and Human Ecology, Department of Human Development and Family Science, Columbus, OH 43210. Offers M Ed, MS, PhD. *Faculty:* 24. *Students:* 23 full-time (20 women), 17 part-time (13 women); includes 2 Black or African American, non-Hispanic/Latino; 1 American Indian or Alaska Native, non-Hispanic/Latino; 1 Asian, non-Hispanic/Latino, 9 international. Average age 28. In 2010, 9 master's, 3 doctorates awarded. *Degree requirements:* For master's, thesis optional; for doctorate, thesis/dissertation. *Entrance requirements:* For master's and doctorate, GRE General Test. Additional exam requirements/recommendations for international students: Required—TOEFL (minimum score 577 paper-based; 233 computer-based). *Application deadline:* For fall admission, 8/15 priority date for domestic students, 7/1 priority date for international students; for winter admission, 12/1 priority date for domestic students, 11/1 priority date for international students; for spring admission, 3/1 priority date for domestic students, 2/1 priority date for international students. Applications are processed on a rolling basis. Application fee: $40 ($50 for international students). Electronic applications accepted. *Expenses:* Tuition, state resident: full-time $10,605. Tuition, nonresident: full-time $26,535. Tuition and fees vary according to course load and program. *Financial support:* Fellowships, research assistantships, teaching assistantships, Federal Work-Study and institutionally sponsored loans available. Support available to part-time students. *Unit head:* Julianne Serovich, Chair, 614-292-5685, Fax: 614-292-4365, E-mail: jserovich@ehe.osu.edu. *Application contact:* 614-292-9444, Fax: 614-292-3895, E-mail: domestic.grad@osu.edu.

Oklahoma State University, College of Arts and Sciences, Department of Psychology, Stillwater, OK 74078. Offers clinical psychology (PhD); general psychology (MS); lifespan development psychology (PhD). *Accreditation:* APA (one or more programs are accredited). *Faculty:* 26 full-time (13 women), 1 (woman) part-time/adjunct. *Students:* 40 full-time (29 women), 12 part-time (6 women); includes 2 Black or African American, non-Hispanic/Latino; 2 American Indian or Alaska Native, non-Hispanic/Latino; 4 Hispanic/Latino, 1 international. Average age 28. 169 applicants, 10% accepted, 13 enrolled. In 2010, 7 master's, 10 doctorates awarded. *Degree requirements:* For master's, thesis or alternative; for doctorate, comprehensive exam, thesis/dissertation. *Entrance requirements:* For master's and doctorate, GRE General Test. Additional exam requirements/recommendations for international students: Required—TOEFL (minimum score 550 paper-based; 79 iBT). *Application deadline:* For fall admission, 3/1 priority date for international students; for spring admission, 8/1 priority date for international students. Applications are processed on a rolling basis. Application fee: $40 ($75 for international students). Electronic applications accepted. *Expenses:* Tuition, state resident: full-time $3716; part-time $154.85 per credit hour. Tuition, nonresident: full-time $14,892; part-time $621 per credit hour. Required fees: $2044; $85.20 per credit hour. One-time fee: $50. Tuition and fees vary according to course load and campus/location. *Financial support:* In 2010–11, 12 research assistantships (averaging $14,763 per year), 38 teaching assistantships (averaging $13,475 per year) were awarded; career-related internships or fieldwork, Federal Work-Study, scholarships/grants, health care benefits, tuition waivers (partial), and unspecified assistantships also available. Support available to part-time students. Financial award application deadline: 3/1; financial award applicants required to submit FAFSA. *Unit head:* Dr. Larry Mullins, Head, 405-744-6028, Fax: 405-744-8067. *Application contact:* Dr. Gordon Emslie, Dean, 405-744-6368, Fax: 405-744-0355, E-mail: grad-i@okstate.edu.

Oregon State University, Graduate School, College of Health and Human Sciences, Department of Human Development and Family Sciences, Corvallis, OR 97331. Offers gerontology (MAIS); human development and family studies (MS, PhD). *Degree requirements:* For doctorate, thesis/dissertation. *Entrance requirements:* For master's and doctorate, GRE, minimum GPA of 3.0 in last 90 hours. Additional exam requirements/recommendations for international students: Required—TOEFL.

Our Lady of the Lake University of San Antonio, School of Professional Studies, Program in Human Sciences, San Antonio, TX 78207-4689. Offers MA. Part-time and evening/weekend programs available. *Students:* 7 full-time (4 women), 30 part-time (26 women); includes 22 minority (8 Black or African American, non-Hispanic/Latino; 13 Hispanic/Latino; 1 Two or more races, non-Hispanic/Latino). Average age 37. In 2010, 19 master's awarded. *Entrance requirements:* For master's, GRE General Test or MAT, interview. Additional exam requirements/recommendations for international students: Required—TOEFL. *Application deadline:* Applications are processed on a rolling basis. Application fee: $25 ($50 for international students). Electronic applications accepted. *Expenses:* Tuition: Full-time $13,500; part-time $750 per contact hour. Required fees: $330. Tuition and fees vary according to course level, degree level and campus/location. *Financial support:* Application deadline: 4/15. *Unit head:* Dr. Steve Blanchard, Chair, 210-434-6711 Ext. 2273, E-mail: blank@lake.ollusa.com. *Application contact:* 210-434-6711 Ext. 2314, Fax: 210-431-4036, E-mail: gradadm@lake.ollusa.edu.

Pacific Oaks College, Graduate School, Program in Human Development, Pasadena, CA 91103. Offers MA. Part-time and evening/weekend programs available. Postbaccalaureate distance learning degree programs offered (minimal on-campus study). *Degree requirements:* For master's, thesis. *Entrance requirements:* Additional exam requirements/recommendations for international students: Required—TOEFL (minimum score 550 paper-based; 213 computer-based). *Faculty research:* Bicultural development, teaching adults, art education, literacy development, adolescent development.

Penn State University Park, Graduate School, College of Health and Human Development, Department of Human Development and Family Studies, State College, University Park, PA 16802-1503. Offers MS, PhD. *Unit head:* Dr. Steven H. Zarit, Head, 814-865-5260, Fax: 814-863-7963, E-mail: z67@psu.edu. *Application contact:* Dr. Douglas M. Teti, Professor/Graduate Program Director, 814-865-2644, E-mail: dmt16@psu.edu.

Purdue University, Graduate School, College of Consumer and Family Sciences, Department of Child Development and Family Studies, West Lafayette, IN 47907. Offers developmental studies (MS, PhD); family studies (MS, PhD); marriage and family therapy (MS, PhD). *Accreditation:* AAMFT/COAMFTE (one or more programs are accredited). Part-time programs available. Terminal master's awarded for partial completion of doctoral program. *Degree requirements:* For master's, thesis; for doctorate, thesis/dissertation. *Entrance requirements:* For master's and doctorate, GRE General Test. Additional exam requirements/recommendations for international students: Required—TWE. Electronic applications accepted. *Faculty research:* Inclusion of children with special needs, families as learning environments, relationships in child care, work-family relations, AIDS prevention.

Saint Joseph College, Department of Gerontology, West Hartford, CT 06117-2700. Offers human development/gerontology (MA, Certificate). Part-time and evening/weekend programs available. *Students:* 17 part-time (all women). *Entrance requirements:* For master's, 2 letters of recommendation. *Application deadline:* Applications are processed on a rolling basis. Application fee: $50. Electronic applications accepted. *Expenses:* Tuition: Full-time $11,340; part-time $630 per credit. Required fees: $540; $30 per credit. Tuition and fees vary according to course load, campus/location and program. *Financial support:* Career-related internships or fieldwork and unspecified assistantships available. Support available to part-time students. Financial award applicants required to submit FAFSA. *Application contact:* Graduate Admissions Office, 860-231-5261, E-mail: graduate@sjc.edu.

St. Lawrence University, Department of Education, Program in Counseling and Human Development, Canton, NY 13617-1455. Offers mental health counseling (MS); school counseling (M Ed, CAS). Part-time and evening/weekend programs available. *Entrance requirements:* For master's, GRE General Test. *Faculty research:* Defense mechanisms and mediation.

Saint Louis University, Graduate Education, College of Education and Public Service and Graduate Education, Department of Counseling and Family Therapy, St. Louis, MO 63103-2097. Offers counseling and family therapy (PhD); human development counseling (MA); marriage and family therapy (Certificate); school counseling (MA, MA-R). *Accreditation:* AAMFT/COAMFTE; NCATE. Part-time programs available. *Degree requirements:* For master's, comprehensive exam, thesis (for some programs); for doctorate, comprehensive exam, thesis/dissertation, preliminary oral and written exams. *Entrance requirements:* For master's, GRE General Test, letters of recommendation, resume; for doctorate, GRE General Test, letters of recommendation, resumé, transcripts, goal statement. Additional exam requirements/recommendations for international students: Required—TOEFL (minimum score 550 paper-based; 213 computer-based). Electronic applications accepted. *Faculty research:* Medical family therapy/collaborative health care multicultural counseling, mental health needs of diverse, minority, or Immigrant/refugee populations, divorce, aging families.

Saint Mary's University of Minnesota, Schools of Graduate and Professional Programs, Graduate School of Business and Technology, Human Development Program, Winona, MN 55987-1399. Offers MA. *Unit head:* Dr. Larry Gorrell, Director, 612-728-5103, Fax: 612-728-5121, E-mail: lgorrell@smumn.edu. *Application contact:* Yasin Alsaidi, Director of Admissions for Graduate and Professional Programs, 612-728-5207, Fax: 612-728-5121, E-mail: yalsaidi@smumn.edu.

South Dakota State University, Graduate School, College of Education and Human Sciences, Department of Human Development, Consumer and Family Sciences, Brookings, SD 57007. Offers MFCS. *Entrance requirements:* For master's, resume. Additional exam requirements/recommendations for international students: Required—TOEFL (minimum score 525 paper-based).

Southern Illinois University Carbondale, Graduate School, College of Education, Department of Educational Psychology and Special Education, Program in Educational Psychology, Carbondale, IL 62901-4701. Offers counselor education (MS Ed, PhD); educational psychology (PhD); human learning and development (MS Ed); measurement and statistics (PhD). *Accreditation:* NCATE. *Degree requirements:* For master's, thesis; for doctorate, thesis/dissertation. *Entrance requirements:* For master's, GRE General Test, minimum GPA of 2.7; for doctorate, minimum GPA of 3.25. Additional exam requirements/recommendations for international students: Required—TOEFL. *Faculty research:* Career development, problem solving, learning and instruction, cognitive development, family assessment.

Texas A&M University, College of Education and Human Development, Department of Educational Psychology, College Station, TX 77843. Offers bilingual education (M Ed, PhD); cognition, creativity, instruction and development (MS, PhD); counseling psychology (PhD);

educational psychology (PhD); educational technology (PhD); research, measurement and statistics (MS); research, measurement, and statistics (PhD); school psychology (PhD); special education (M Ed, PhD). *Accreditation:* APA (one or more programs are accredited). Part-time and evening/weekend programs available. Postbaccalaureate distance learning degree programs offered (no on-campus study). *Faculty:* 49. *Students:* 160 full-time (123 women), 147 part-time (120 women); includes 106 minority (24 Black or African American, non-Hispanic/Latino; 16 Asian, non-Hispanic/Latino; 66 Hispanic/Latino), 45 international. In 2010, 36 master's, 31 doctorates awarded. *Degree requirements:* For master's, thesis optional; for doctorate, thesis/dissertation. *Entrance requirements:* For master's and doctorate, GRE General Test. Additional exam requirements/recommendations for international students: Required—TOEFL. Application fee: $50 ($75 for international students). Electronic applications accepted. *Financial support:* In 2010–11, fellowships (averaging $12,000 per year), research assistantships (averaging $9,000 per year), teaching assistantships (averaging $9,000 per year) were awarded; career-related internships or fieldwork, institutionally sponsored loans, scholarships/grants, and unspecified assistantships also available. Financial award applicants required to submit FAFSA. *Unit head:* Dr. Victor Willson, Head, 979-845-1800. *Application contact:* Carol A. Wagner, Director of Advising, 979-845-1833, Fax: 979-862-1256, E-mail: epsyadvisor@tamu.edu.

Texas Tech University, Graduate School, College of Human Sciences, Department of Human Development and Family Studies, Lubbock, TX 79409. Offers gerontology (MS); human development and family studies (MS, PhD). *Accreditation:* AAMFT/COAMFTE (one or more programs are accredited). Part-time programs available. *Faculty:* 17 full-time (13 women), 2 part-time/adjunct (both women). *Students:* 42 full-time (38 women), 14 part-time (6 women); includes 1 American Indian or Alaska Native, non-Hispanic/Latino; 1 Asian, non-Hispanic/Latino; 3 Hispanic/Latino, 14 international. Average age 32. 46 applicants, 43% accepted, 10 enrolled. In 2010, 6 master's, 3 doctorates awarded. *Degree requirements:* For master's, thesis; for doctorate, comprehensive exam, thesis/dissertation. *Entrance requirements:* For master's and doctorate, GRE General Test. Additional exam requirements/recommendations for international students: Required—TOEFL (minimum score 550 paper-based; 213 computer-based; 79 iBT). *Application deadline:* For fall admission, 6/1 priority date for domestic students, 1/15 priority date for international students; for spring admission, 9/1 priority date for domestic students, 6/15 priority date for international students. Applications are processed on a rolling basis. Application fee: $50 ($75 for international students). Electronic applications accepted. *Expenses:* Tuition, state resident: full-time $5495.76; part-time $228.99 per credit hour. Tuition, nonresident: full-time $12,936; part-time $538.99 per credit hour. Required fees: $2674; $36 per credit hour. $905 per semester. *Financial support:* In 2010–11, 40 students received support, including 8 research assistantships with partial tuition reimbursements available (averaging $3,281 per year), 14 teaching assistantships with partial tuition reimbursements available (averaging $3,551 per year). Financial award application deadline: 4/15; financial award applicants required to submit FAFSA. *Faculty research:* Parenting, marital and premarital relationships, adolescent risky behaviors, life span; child development. Total annual research expenditures: $509,694. *Unit head:* Dr. Jean Pearson Scott, Chairperson, 806-742-3000 Ext. 271, Fax: 806-742-0285, E-mail: jean.scott@ttu.edu. *Application contact:* Monya Castle, Graduate Secretary, 806-742-3000 Ext. 250, Fax: 806-742-0285, E-mail: monya.castle@ttu.edu.

Union Institute & University, Programs in Psychology and Counseling, Brattleboro, VT 05301. Offers clinical mental health counseling (MA); clinical psychology (Psy D); counseling psychology (MA); counselor education and supervision (CAGS); developmental psychology (MA); educational psychology (MA); human development and wellness (CAGS); organizational psychology (MA); psychology education (CAGS). Psy D offered in Ohio and Vermont. Postbaccalaureate distance learning degree programs offered (minimal on-campus study). *Faculty:* 6 full-time (4 women), 17 part-time/adjunct (6 women). *Students:* 93 full-time (66 women), 11 part-time (10 women); includes 14 minority (6 Black or African American, non-Hispanic/Latino; 1 Asian, non-Hispanic/Latino; 7 Hispanic/Latino). Average age 44. In 2010, 21 master's awarded. *Degree requirements:* For master's, thesis, internship (depending on concentration); for doctorate, thesis/dissertation, internship, practicum. *Application deadline:* Applications are processed on a rolling basis. Application fee: $50. Electronic applications accepted. *Expenses:* Tuition: Full-time $16,430; part-time $685 per credit hour. Required fees: $174; $44 per term. Tuition and fees vary according to course load, degree level and program. *Financial support:* Federal Work-Study available. Financial award applicants required to submit FAFSA. *Unit head:* Dr. Bill Lax, Dean, 802-254-0152, E-mail: bill.lax@myunion.edu. *Application contact:* Diane Robinson, Director of Admissions, 888-828-8575, E-mail: diane.robinson@myunion.edu.

The University of Alabama, Graduate School, College of Human Environmental Sciences, Department of Human Development and Family Studies, Tuscaloosa, AL 35487. Offers MSHES. *Faculty:* 8 full-time (5 women). *Students:* 25 full-time (24 women), 15 part-time (14 women); includes 12 minority (9 Black or African American, non-Hispanic/Latino; 1 Asian, non-Hispanic/Latino; 2 Two or more races, non-Hispanic/Latino). Average age 27. 27 applicants, 70% accepted, 13 enrolled. In 2010, 14 master's awarded. *Degree requirements:* For master's, thesis (for some programs). *Entrance requirements:* For master's, GRE General Test or MAT, minimum GPA of 3.0. Additional exam requirements/recommendations for international students: Required—TOEFL. *Application deadline:* For fall admission, 2/1 priority date for domestic and international students. Applications are processed on a rolling basis. Application fee: $50 ($60 for international students). Electronic applications accepted. *Expenses:* Tuition, state resident: full-time $7900. Tuition, nonresident: full-time $20,500. *Financial support:* In 2010–11, 10 students received support, including 1 fellowship with full tuition reimbursement available (averaging $15,000 per year), 4 research assistantships with full tuition reimbursements available (averaging $10,908 per year), 5 teaching assistantships (averaging $10,000 per year); career-related internships or fieldwork, Federal Work-Study, scholarships/grants, health care benefits, and unspecified assistantships also available. Financial award application deadline: 2/15. *Faculty research:* Parent/child relationships, preschool curricula and quality measures for child care programs, family strengths and adolescent behaviors, depression in mothers and infants, word association and word learning in young children. *Unit head:* Dr. Carroll M. Tingle, Chair, 205-348-6158, Fax: 205-348-8153, E-mail: ctingle@ches.ua.edu. *Application contact:* Dr. Maria Hernandez-Reif, Associate Professor, 205-348-5894, Fax: 205-348-8153, E-mail: mhernandez-reif@ches.ua.edu.

The University of Arizona, College of Education, Department of Disability and Psychoeducational Studies, Division of Family Studies and Human Development, Tucson, AZ 85721. Offers M Ed. *Faculty:* 17 full-time (9 women). *Students:* 62 full-time (48 women), 39 part-time (34 women); includes 3 Black or African American, non-Hispanic/Latino; 1 Asian, non-Hispanic/Latino; 9 Hispanic/Latino; 11 Two or more races, non-Hispanic/Latino, 9 international. Average age 36. 30 applicants, 70% accepted, 14 enrolled. In 2010, 25 master's awarded. Terminal master's awarded for partial completion of doctoral program. *Entrance requirements:* Additional exam requirements/recommendations for international students: Required—TOEFL (minimum score 600 paper-based). *Application deadline:* For fall admission, 2/1 for domestic students. Applications are processed on a rolling basis. Application fee: $65. *Expenses:* Tuition, state resident: full-time $7692. *Financial support:* In 2010–11, 4 research assistantships with full tuition reimbursements (averaging $12,828 per year), 4 teaching assistantships with full tuition reimbursements (averaging $12,378 per year) were awarded. *Unit head:* Dr. Ron Marx, Dean, 520-621-1081, E-mail: ronmarx@email.arizona.edu. *Application contact:* Cecilia Carlon, Administrative Assistant, 520-626-1248, E-mail: ccarlon@email.arizona.edu.

The University of British Columbia, Faculty of Education, Department of Educational and Counseling Psychology, and Special Education, Vancouver, BC V6T 1Z1, Canada. Offers counseling psychology (M Ed, MA, PhD); development, learning and culture (PhD); guidance studies (Diploma); human development, learning and culture (M Ed, MA); measurement and evaluation and research methodology (M Ed); measurement, evaluation and research methodology (MA); measurement, evaluation, and research methodology (PhD); school psychology (M Ed, MA, PhD); special education (M Ed, MA, PhD, Diploma). Part-time programs available. *Degree requirements:* For master's, thesis (for some programs); for doctorate,

comprehensive exam, thesis/dissertation. *Entrance requirements:* For master's, GRE General Test (counseling psychology MA); for doctorate, GRE General Test. Additional exam requirements/recommendations for international students: Required—TOEFL. Electronic applications accepted. Tuition charges are reported in Canadian dollars. *Expenses:* Tuition, area resident: Full-time $4179 Canadian dollars. International tuition: $7344 Canadian dollars full-time. *Faculty research:* Women, family, social problems, career transition, stress and coping problems.

University of Calgary, Faculty of Graduate Studies, Faculty of Education, Division of Applied Psychology, Calgary, AB T2N 1N4, Canada. Offers counseling psychology (M Ed, M Sc, PhD); human development and learning (M Ed, M Sc, PhD); school psychology (M Ed, M Sc, PhD); special education (M Ed, M Sc, PhD). Part-time programs available. *Degree requirements:* For master's, thesis (for some programs), final oral exam; for doctorate, thesis/dissertation, candidacy exam, final oral exam. *Entrance requirements:* For master's, minimum GPA of 3.0, 3 letters of reference; for doctorate, minimum GPA of 3.5, 3 letters of reference. *Faculty research:* Counselor education, family life studies, learning and cognition.

University of California, Berkeley, Graduate Division, School of Education, Programs in Education, Berkeley, CA 94720-1500. Offers development in mathematics and science (MA); education in mathematics, science, and technology (MA, PhD); human development and education (MA, PhD); special education (PhD); MA/Credential; PhD/Credential; PhD/MA. Terminal master's awarded for partial completion of doctoral program. *Degree requirements:* For master's, exam or thesis; for doctorate, thesis/dissertation, oral qualifying exam. *Entrance requirements:* For master's and doctorate, GRE General Test, minimum GPA of 3.0 during last 2 years of undergraduate course work. Electronic applications accepted. *Faculty research:* Human development, social and moral educational psychology, developmental teacher preparation.

University of California, Davis, Graduate Studies, Graduate Group in Human Development, Davis, CA 95616. Offers PhD. *Degree requirements:* For doctorate, thesis/dissertation. *Entrance requirements:* For doctorate, GRE General Test, GRE Subject Test, minimum GPA of 3.0. Additional exam requirements/recommendations for international students: Required—TOEFL (minimum score 550 paper-based; 213 computer-based). Electronic applications accepted. *Faculty research:* Life span socioemotional and cognitive development, individual differences, relationship between biological and behavioral development, cross-cultural and cross-generational development.

University of Central Oklahoma, College of Graduate Studies and Research, College of Education, Department of Human Environmental Sciences, Edmond, OK 73034-5209. Offers family and child studies (MS); family and consumer science education (MS); interior design (MS); nutrition-food management (MS). Part-time programs available. *Entrance requirements:* Additional exam requirements/recommendations for international students: Required—TOEFL (minimum score 550 paper-based; 213 computer-based). Electronic applications accepted. *Faculty research:* Dietetics and food science.

University of Chicago, Division of Social Sciences, Department of Comparative Human Development, Chicago, IL 60637-1513. Offers PhD. *Degree requirements:* For doctorate, one foreign language, thesis/dissertation, pre-doctoral written exams. *Entrance requirements:* For doctorate, GRE General Test, GRE Subject Test. Additional exam requirements/recommendations for international students: Required—TOEFL, IELTS (minimum score 7). Electronic applications accepted.

University of Colorado Denver, School of Education and Human Development, Programs in Educational and School Psychology, Denver, CO 80217. Offers educational psychology (MA), including educational assessment, human development, human learning, individually structured, partner schools, research and evaluation; school psychology (Ed S). Part-time and evening/weekend programs available. *Students:* 123 full-time (111 women), 57 part-time (51 women); includes 4 Black or African American, non-Hispanic/Latino; 1 American Indian or Alaska Native, non-Hispanic/Latino; 5 Asian, non-Hispanic/Latino; 8 Hispanic/Latino, 5 international. Average age 30. 97 applicants, 79% accepted, 54 enrolled. In 2010, 62 master's, 14 other advanced degrees awarded. *Degree requirements:* For master's, recommended plan of study includes 9 hours of core courses, embedded within a minimum of 36 to 38 hours of relevant coursework; for Ed S, comprehensive exam, minimum of 75 semester hours (61 hours of coursework, 6 of 500-hour practicum in field, and 8 of 1200-hour internship); Praxis II. *Entrance requirements:* For master's, GRE if undergraduate GPA below 2.75, resume, written statement, letters of recommendation, transcripts; for Ed S, GRE, resume, written statement, letters of recommendation, transcripts. Additional exam requirements/recommendations for international students: Required—TOEFL. *Application deadline:* For fall admission, 4/15 for domestic students; for spring admission, 9/15 for domestic students. Application fee: $50 ($75 for international students). Electronic applications accepted. *Expenses:* Contact institution. *Financial support:* Application deadline: 4/1. *Faculty research:* Crisis response and Intervention, school violence prevention; immigrant experience, educational environments for English language learners, culturally competent assessment and intervention, child and youth suicide. *Application contact:* Student Services Center, 303-315-6300, Fax: 303-315-6311, E-mail: education@ucdenver.edu.

University of Connecticut, Graduate School, College of Liberal Arts and Sciences, Department of Human Development and Family Studies, Storrs, CT 06269. Offers culture, health and human development (Graduate Certificate); human development and family studies (MA, PhD). *Accreditation:* AAMFT/COAMFTE (one or more programs are accredited). Terminal master's awarded for partial completion of doctoral program. *Degree requirements:* For master's, comprehensive exam; for doctorate, thesis/dissertation. *Entrance requirements:* For doctorate, GRE General Test. Additional exam requirements/recommendations for international students: Required—TOEFL (minimum score 550 paper-based; 213 computer-based). Electronic applications accepted.

University of Dayton, Graduate School, School of Education and Allied Professions, Department of Counselor Education and Human Services, Dayton, OH 45469-1300. Offers college student personnel (MS Ed); community counseling (MS Ed); higher education administration (MS Ed); human services (MS Ed); school counseling (MS Ed); school psychology (MS Ed, Ed S). *Accreditation:* ACA; NCATE. Part-time and evening/weekend programs available. *Faculty:* 12 full-time (9 women), 32 part-time/adjunct (18 women). *Students:* 269 full-time (219 women), 180 part-time (150 women); includes 84 minority (69 Black or African American, non-Hispanic/Latino; 2 American Indian or Alaska Native, non-Hispanic/Latino; 8 Asian, non-Hispanic/Latino; 3 Hispanic/Latino; 2 Two or more races, non-Hispanic/Latino), 2 international. Average age 32. 246 applicants, 48% accepted, 89 enrolled. In 2010, 157 master's, 10 Ed Ss awarded. *Degree requirements:* For master's, comprehensive exam (for some programs), thesis (for some programs), exit exam. *Entrance requirements:* For master's, MAT or GRE (if GPA less than 2.75), interview, writing sample. Additional exam requirements/recommendations for international students: Required—TOEFL (minimum score 550 paper-based; 213 computer-based; 80 iBT). *Application deadline:* For fall admission, 4/10 for domestic students, 3/1 priority date for international students; for winter admission, 9/10 for domestic students, 7/1 priority date for international students; for spring admission, 1/10 for domestic students, 1/1 priority date for international students. Application fee: $0 ($50 for international students). Electronic applications accepted. *Expenses:* Tuition: Full-time $7800; part-time $650 per credit hour. *Financial support:* In 2010–11, 7 research assistantships with full tuition reimbursements (averaging $8,400 per year) were awarded; career-related internships or fieldwork, institutionally sponsored loans, health care benefits, and unspecified assistantships also available. Financial award applicants required to submit FAFSA. *Faculty research:* Anger as part of the grief process, inclusion of children with severe disabilities, comparisons of school counselors in Bosnia and the U. S., graduate and professional student socialization, use of cohort groups in doctoral programs, bullying in schools, impact of space on learning, sophomore experience. *Unit head:* Dr. Alan Demmitt, Chairperson, 937-229-3644, Fax: 937-229-1055. *Application contact:*

Human Development

University of Dayton (continued)

Alexander Popovski, Associate Director of Graduate and International Admissions, 937-229-2357, Fax: 937-229-4729, E-mail: alex.popovski@notes.udayton.edu.

University of Delaware, College of Human Services, Education and Public Policy, Department of Individual and Family Studies, Newark, DE 19716. Offers human development and family studies (MS, PhD). Part-time programs available. Terminal master's awarded for partial completion of doctoral program. *Degree requirements:* For master's, thesis or alternative; for doctorate, comprehensive exam, thesis/dissertation. *Entrance requirements:* For master's and doctorate, GRE General Test, 3 letters of recommendation. Additional exam requirements/recommendations for international students: Required—TOEFL. Electronic applications accepted. *Faculty research:* Early childhood inclusive education, relationships, family risk and resilience, disability issues, program development and evaluation.

University of Guelph, Graduate Studies, College of Social and Applied Human Sciences, Department of Family Relations and Applied Nutrition, Guelph, ON N1G 2W1, Canada. Offers applied nutrition (MAN); family relations and human development (M Sc, PhD), including applied human nutrition, couple and family therapy (M Sc), family relations and human development. *Accreditation:* AAMFT/COAMFTE (one or more programs are accredited). Part-time programs available. *Degree requirements:* For master's, thesis (for some programs); for doctorate, comprehensive exam, thesis/dissertation. *Entrance requirements:* For master's, minimum B+ average; for doctorate, master's degree in family relations and human development or related field with a minimum B+ average or master's degree in applied human nutrition. Additional exam requirements/recommendations for international students: Required—TOEFL (minimum score 600 paper-based; 250 computer-based). Electronic applications accepted. *Faculty research:* Child and adolescent development, social gerontology, family roles and relations, couple and family therapy, applied human nutrition.

University of Illinois at Chicago, Graduate College, College of Applied Health Sciences, Department of Disability and Human Development, Chicago, IL 60607-7128. Offers disability and human development (MS); disability studies (PhD). *Accreditation:* AOTA. Part-time programs available. *Degree requirements:* For master's, thesis optional; for doctorate, thesis/dissertation. *Entrance requirements:* For master's and doctorate, GRE General Test. Additional exam requirements/recommendations for international students: Required—TOEFL. Electronic applications accepted. *Faculty research:* Emerging trends in disability, demography and financial structure of disability services, aging and disability, empowerment of people with disabilities, health promotion in disabilities.

University of Illinois at Springfield, Graduate Programs, College of Education and Human Services, Program in Human Development Counseling, Springfield, IL 62703-5407. Offers MA. *Accreditation:* ACA. Part-time and evening/weekend programs available. *Degree requirements:* For master's, project, thesis, or comprehensive exam. *Entrance requirements:* For master's, minimum undergraduate GPA of 3.0 in last 60 hours of coursework, personal references, interview. Additional exam requirements/recommendations for international students: Required—TOEFL (minimum score 500 paper-based; 176 computer-based; 61 iBT). Electronic applications accepted. *Expenses:* Tuition, state resident: full-time $6774; part-time $282.25 per credit hour. Tuition, nonresident: full-time $15,078; part-time $628.25 per credit hour. Required fees: $15.25 per credit hour. $492 per term.

University of Illinois at Urbana–Champaign, Graduate College, College of Agricultural, Consumer and Environmental Sciences, Department of Human and Community Development, Champaign, IL 61820. Offers agricultural education (MS); human and community development (MS, PhD); MS/MSW. *Faculty:* 16 full-time (10 women), 1 part-time/adjunct (0 women). *Students:* 40 full-time (31 women), 5 part-time (1 woman); includes 11 minority (4 Black or African American, non-Hispanic/Latino; 3 Asian, non-Hispanic/Latino; 2 Hispanic/Latino; 2 Two or more races, non-Hispanic/Latino), 4 international. 44 applicants, 41% accepted, 17 enrolled. In 2010, 3 master's, 4 doctorates awarded. *Entrance requirements:* For master's and doctorate, GRE, minimum GPA of 3.0. Additional exam requirements/recommendations for international students: Required—TOEFL (minimum score 550 paper-based; 213 computer-based; 79 iBT). *Application deadline:* Applications are processed on a rolling basis. Application fee: $75 ($90 for international students). Electronic applications accepted. *Financial support:* In 2010–11, 10 fellowships, 19 research assistantships, 20 teaching assistantships were awarded; tuition waivers (full and partial) also available. *Unit head:* Robert Hughes, Head, 217-333-3790, Fax: 217-244-7877, E-mail: hughesro@illinois.edu. *Application contact:* Andrea L. Ray, Office Manager, 217-333-3165, Fax: 217-244-7877, E-mail: aray@illinois.edu.

University of Maine, Graduate School, College of Education and Human Development, Department of Human Development and Family Relations, Orono, ME 04469. Offers human development (MS). Part-time programs available. *Students:* 16 full-time (14 women), 2 part-time (1 woman); includes 2 minority (both American Indian or Alaska Native, non-Hispanic/Latino), 1 international. Average age 27. 12 applicants, 75% accepted, 9 enrolled. In 2010, 4 master's awarded. *Degree requirements:* For master's, thesis. *Entrance requirements:* For master's, GRE General Test. Additional exam requirements/recommendations for international students: Required—TOEFL. *Application deadline:* For fall admission, 2/1 priority date for domestic students. Applications are processed on a rolling basis. Application fee: $65. Electronic applications accepted. *Expenses:* Tuition, state resident: full-time $400. Tuition, nonresident: full-time $1050. *Financial support:* Career-related internships or fieldwork, Federal Work-Study, institutionally sponsored loans, tuition waivers (full and partial), and unspecified assistantships available. Financial award application deadline: 3/1. *Faculty research:* Methods to assess nutrient intake and risk, carnitine-supplemented diets for protein-calorie malnutrition, nutrition education, grandfathers' perceptions of relations to grandchildren, social participation of spouses in distressed and nondistressed marriages. *Unit head:* Dr. Janet Spector, Coordinator, 207-581-3162, Fax: 207-581-3120. *Application contact:* Scott G. Delcourt, Associate Dean of the Graduate School, 207-581-3291, Fax: 207-581-3232, E-mail: graduate@maine.edu.

University of Maryland, College Park, Academic Affairs, College of Education, Department of Human Development, College Park, MD 20742. Offers early childhood/elementary education (M Ed, MA, Ed D, PhD); human development (M Ed, MA, Ed D, PhD). *Accreditation:* NCATE. Part-time and evening/weekend programs available. Postbaccalaureate distance learning degree programs offered. *Faculty:* 55 full-time (50 women), 16 part-time/adjunct (12 women). *Students:* 58 full-time (51 women), 27 part-time (23 women); includes 7 Black or African American, non-Hispanic/Latino; 8 Asian, non-Hispanic/Latino; 7 Hispanic/Latino; 1 Two or more races, non-Hispanic/Latino, 9 international. 110 applicants, 25% accepted, 22 enrolled. In 2010, 16 master's, 9 doctorates awarded. *Degree requirements:* For master's, comprehensive exam, thesis optional; for doctorate, comprehensive exam, thesis/dissertation, essay, exam, research paper. *Entrance requirements:* For master's, GRE General Test, minimum GPA of 3.0, 3 letters of recommendation; for doctorate, GRE General Test or MAT, minimum undergraduate GPA of 3.0, graduate 3.5; 3 letters of recommendation. Additional exam requirements/recommendations for international students: Required—TOEFL. *Application deadline:* For fall admission, 3/15 for domestic students, 12/15 for international students; for spring admission, 10/1 priority date for domestic students, 6/1 for international students. Applications are processed on a rolling basis. Application fee: $75. Electronic applications accepted. *Expenses:* Tuition, state resident: part-time $471 per credit hour. Tuition, nonresident: part-time $1016 per credit hour. Required fees: $337 per term. *Financial support:* In 2010–11, 11 fellowships with full and partial tuition reimbursements (averaging $15,838 per year), 1 research assistantship (averaging $16,049 per year), 37 teaching assistantships (averaging $17,132 per year) were awarded; Federal Work-Study and scholarships/grants also available. Support available to part-time students. Financial award applicants required to submit FAFSA. *Faculty research:* Developmental science, educational psychology, cognitive development, language development. Total annual research expenditures: $2.6 million. *Unit head:* Dr. Allan L. Wigfield, Chair, 301-405-1659, Fax: 301-405-2891, E-mail: awigfiel@umd.edu. *Application contact:* Dr. Charles A. Caramello, Dean of Graduate School, 301-405-0358, Fax: 301-314-9305, E-mail: ccaramel@umd.edu.

University of Missouri, Graduate School, College of Human Environmental Science, Department of Human Development and Family Studies, Columbia, MO 65211. Offers MA, MS, PhD. *Entrance requirements:* For master's, GRE General Test, minimum GPA of 3.0. Additional exam requirements/recommendations for international students: Required—TOEFL (minimum score 550 paper-based; 213 computer-based; 80 iBT).

University of Nebraska–Lincoln, Graduate College, College of Education and Human Sciences, Department of Child, Youth and Family Studies, Lincoln, NE 68588. Offers child development/early childhood education (MS, PhD); child, youth and family studies (MS); family and consumer sciences education (MS, PhD); family financial planning (MS); family science (MS, PhD); gerontology (PhD); human sciences (PhD), including child, youth and family studies, gerontology, medical family therapy; marriage and family therapy (MS); medical family therapy (PhD); youth development (MS). *Accreditation:* AAMFT/COAMFTE (one or more programs are accredited). Postbaccalaureate distance learning degree programs offered. *Degree requirements:* For master's, thesis optional. *Entrance requirements:* For master's, GRE. Additional exam requirements/recommendations for international students: Required—TOEFL (minimum score 550 paper-based; 213 computer-based). Electronic applications accepted. *Faculty research:* Marriage and family therapy, child development/early childhood education, family financial management.

University of Nebraska–Lincoln, Graduate College, College of Education and Human Sciences, Department of Special Education and Communication Disorders, Lincoln, NE 68588. Offers audiology research (PhD); clinical audiology (Au D); educational studies (PhD); human sciences (PhD), including communication disorders; special education (M Ed, MA, Ed S), including special education (M Ed, MA), special education and communication disorders (Ed S); speech-language pathology and audiology (MS, Au D), including audiology and hearing science (Au D), speech-language pathology (Au D), speech-language pathology and audiology (MS). *Accreditation:* ASHA (one or more programs are accredited); NCATE. *Degree requirements:* For master's, thesis optional. *Entrance requirements:* For master's, GRE General Test. Additional exam requirements/recommendations for international students: Required—TOEFL. Electronic applications accepted. *Faculty research:* Curriculum-based assessment, paraprofessional and parent training, behavior management for special needs individuals, augmentative communication, speech/language disorders.

University of Nebraska–Lincoln, Graduate College, College of Education and Human Sciences, Department of Textiles, Clothing and Design, Lincoln, NE 68588. Offers human sciences (PhD), including textiles, clothing and design (MS, PhD); merchandising (MS); textile history/quilt studies (MA); textile science (MS); textile-apparel (MA); textiles, clothing and design (MA, MS), including textiles, clothing and design (MS, PhD). Part-time programs available. Postbaccalaureate distance learning degree programs offered (minimal on-campus study). *Degree requirements:* For master's, thesis optional. *Entrance requirements:* For master's, GRE General Test. Additional exam requirements/recommendations for international students: Required—TOEFL (minimum score 550 paper-based; 213 computer-based). Electronic applications accepted. *Faculty research:* Merchandising, textile science, fiber arts, textile history, quilt studies.

University of Nevada, Reno, Graduate School, College of Education, Department of Human Development and Family Studies, Reno, NV 89557. Offers MS. *Degree requirements:* For master's, thesis optional. *Entrance requirements:* For master's, GRE General Test, minimum GPA of 2.75. Additional exam requirements/recommendations for international students: Required—TOEFL (minimum score 500 paper-based; 173 computer-based; 61 iBT), IELTS (minimum score 6). Electronic applications accepted. *Expenses:* Tuition, state resident: full-time $2219; part-time $246 per credit. Tuition, nonresident: part-time $510 per credit. International tuition: $9009 full-time. Required fees: $59 per term. One-time fee: $101. Tuition and fees vary according to course load. *Faculty research:* Early childhood/adolescent development, family studies.

The University of North Carolina at Greensboro, Graduate School, School of Human Environmental Sciences, Department of Human Development and Family Studies, Greensboro, NC 27412-5001. Offers M Ed, MS, PhD. *Degree requirements:* For master's, one foreign language; for doctorate, one foreign language, thesis/dissertation. *Entrance requirements:* For master's and doctorate, GRE General Test. Additional exam requirements/recommendations for international students: Required—TOEFL. Electronic applications accepted. *Expenses:* Contact institution. *Faculty research:* Adolescent mothers, multi-handicapped, older adults.

University of North Texas, Toulouse Graduate School, College of Education, Department of Educational Psychology, Program in Development and Family Studies, Denton, TX 76203. Offers MS, Certificate. Evening/weekend programs available. *Degree requirements:* For master's, comprehensive exam, thesis optional. *Entrance requirements:* For master's, GRE General Test, resume, references. Additional exam requirements/recommendations for international students: Recommended—TOEFL (minimum score 550 paper-based; 213 computer-based). *Application deadline:* Applications are processed on a rolling basis. Electronic applications accepted. *Expenses:* Tuition, state resident: full-time $4298; part-time $239 per credit hour. Tuition, nonresident: full-time $10,782; part-time $549 per credit hour. Required fees: $1292; $270 per credit hour. *Financial support:* Teaching assistantships, career-related internships or fieldwork, Federal Work-Study, and institutionally sponsored loans available. Financial award applicants required to submit FAFSA. *Faculty research:* Parent-child issues, cognitive development, social development. *Application contact:* Becky Glover, Graduate Advisor, 940-565-4876, E-mail: becky.glover@unt.edu.

University of Pennsylvania, Graduate School of Education, Division of Applied Psychology and Human Development, Interdisciplinary Studies in Human Development, Philadelphia, PA 19104. Offers MS Ed, PhD. Part-time programs available. *Students:* 35 full-time (25 women), 5 part-time (4 women); includes 11 Black or African American, non-Hispanic/Latino; 1 Hispanic/Latino, 13 international. 96 applicants, 36% accepted, 21 enrolled. In 2010, 17 master's, 5 doctorates awarded. Terminal master's awarded for partial completion of doctoral program. *Degree requirements:* For master's, exam; for doctorate, thesis/dissertation, exam. *Entrance requirements:* For master's, GRE General Test; for doctorate, GRE General Test, GRE Subject Test. *Application deadline:* For fall admission, 12/15 priority date for domestic students. Applications are processed on a rolling basis. Application fee: $70. Electronic applications accepted. *Expenses:* Contact institution. *Financial support:* Fellowships, research assistantships, institutionally sponsored loans, scholarships/grants, traineeships, health care benefits, and unspecified assistantships available. *Faculty research:* Child development, risk and resilience among vulnerable youth in high-risk environments.

University of Rochester, Margaret Warner Graduate School of Education and Human Development, Master's Program in Human Development, Rochester, NY 14627.

University of St. Thomas, Graduate Studies, School of Education, Program in Organization Learning and Development, St. Paul, MN 55105-1096. Offers career development (Certificate); e-learning (Certificate); human resource development (Certificate); human resource management (Certificate); human resources and change leadership (MA); learning technology (Certificate); learning technology for learning development and change (MA); organization development (Ed D, Certificate). Part-time and evening/weekend programs available. Postbaccalaureate distance learning degree programs offered (minimal on-campus study). *Faculty:* 6 full-time (4 women), 15 part-time/adjunct (8 women). *Students:* 8 full-time (7 women), 156 part-time (118 women); includes 30 minority (12 Black or African American, non-Hispanic/Latino; 7 Asian, non-Hispanic/Latino; 7 Hispanic/Latino; 1 Native Hawaiian or other Pacific Islander, non-Hispanic/Latino; 3 Two or more races, non-Hispanic/Latino), 6 international. Average age 37. 165 applicants, 71% accepted, 102 enrolled. In 2010, 38 master's, 9 doctorates, 15 other advanced degrees awarded. *Degree requirements:* For doctorate, comprehensive exam, thesis/dissertation. *Entrance requirements:* For master's, minimum GPA of 3.0, 2 letters of reference, personal statement; for doctorate, minimum GPA of 3.5, interview; for Certificate, minimum graduate GPA of 3.25. Additional exam requirements/recommendations for international students:

Required—TOEFL (minimum score 550 paper-based; 213 computer-based). *Application deadline:* For fall admission, 8/1 priority date for domestic and international students; for winter admission, 12/1 priority date for domestic students, 12/1 for international students; for spring admission, 12/1 priority date for domestic and international students. Applications are processed on a rolling basis. Application fee: $50. *Expenses:* Contact institution. *Financial support:* Fellowships, research assistantships, institutionally sponsored loans and scholarships/grants available. Support available to part-time students. Financial award applicants required to submit FAFSA. *Faculty research:* Workplace conflict, physician leaders, entrepreneurship education, mentoring. *Unit head:* Dr. David W. Jamieson, Department Chair, 651-962-4387, Fax: 651-962-4169, E-mail: jami9859@stthomas.edu. *Application contact:* Liz G. Knight, Department Coordinator, 651-962-4459, Fax: 651-962-4169, E-mail: egknight@stthomas.edu.

University of South Africa, College of Human Sciences, Pretoria, South Africa. Offers adult education (M Ed); African languages (MA, PhD); African politics (MA, PhD); Afrikaans (MA, PhD); ancient history (MA, PhD); ancient Near Eastern studies (MA, PhD); anthropology (MA, PhD); applied linguistics (MA); Arabic (MA, PhD); archaeology (MA); art history (MA); Biblical archaeology (MA); Biblical studies (M Th, D Th, PhD); Christian spirituality (M Th, D Th); church history (M Th, D Th); classical studies (MA, PhD); clinical psychology (MA); communication (MA, PhD); comparative education (M Ed, Ed D); consulting psychology (D Admin, D Com, PhD); curriculum studies (M Ed, Ed D); development studies (M Admin, MA, D Admin, PhD); didactics (M Ed, Ed D); education (M Tech); education management (M Ed, Ed D); educational psychology (M Ed); English (MA); environmental education (M Ed); French (MA, PhD); German (MA, PhD); Greek (MA); guidance and counseling (M Ed); health studies (MA, PhD), including health sciences education (MA), health services management (MA), medical and surgical nursing science (critical care general) (MA), midwifery and neonatal nursing science (MA), trauma and emergency care (MA); history (MA, PhD); history of education (Ed D); inclusive education (M Ed, Ed D); information and communications technology policy and regulation (MA); information science (MA, MIS, PhD); international politics (MA, PhD); Islamic studies (MA, PhD); Italian (MA, PhD); Judaica (MA, PhD); linguistics (MA, PhD); mathematical education (M Ed); mathematics education (MA); missiology (M Th, D Th); modern Hebrew (MA, PhD); musicology (MA, MMus, D Mus, PhD); natural science education (M Ed); New Testament (M Th, D Th); Old Testament (D Th); pastoral therapy (M Th, D Th); philosophy (MA); philosophy of education (M Ed, Ed D); politics (MA, PhD); Portuguese (MA, PhD); practical theology (M Th, D Th); psychology (MA, MS, PhD); psychology of education (M Ed, Ed D); public health (MA); religious studies (MA, D Th, PhD); Romance languages (MA); Russian (MA, PhD); Semitic languages (MA, PhD); social behavior studies in HIV/AIDS (MA); social science (mental health) (MA); social science in development studies (MA); social science in psychology (MA); social science in social work (MA); social science in sociology (MA); social work (MSW, DSW, PhD); socio-education (M Ed, Ed D); sociolinguistics (MA); sociology (MA, PhD); Spanish (MA, PhD); systematic theology (M Th, D Th); TESOL (teaching English to speakers of other languages) (MA); theological ethics (M Th, D Th); theory of literature (MA, PhD); urban ministries (D Th); urban ministry (M Th).

The University of Texas at Austin, Graduate School, College of Education, Department of Educational Psychology, Austin, TX 78712-1111. Offers academic educational psychology (M Ed, MA); counseling psychology (PhD); counselor education (M Ed); human development and culture (PhD); learning, cognition and instruction (PhD); quantitative methods (PhD); school psychology (PhD). *Accreditation:* APA (one or more programs are accredited). *Degree requirements:* For master's, thesis optional; for doctorate, thesis/dissertation. *Entrance requirements:* For master's and doctorate, GRE General Test, 3 letters of recommendation. Additional exam requirements/recommendations for international students: Required—TOEFL.

University of Utah, Graduate School, College of Social and Behavioral Science, Department of Family and Consumer Studies, Salt Lake City, UT 84112-0080. Offers early childhood education (M Ed); human development and social policy (MS). Part-time and evening/weekend programs available. *Faculty:* 17 full-time (8 women). *Students:* 18 full-time (17 women), 9 part-time (6 women); includes 1 minority (Native Hawaiian or other Pacific Islander, non-Hispanic/Latino), 1 international. Average age 31. 25 applicants, 80% accepted, 17 enrolled. In 2010, 9 master's awarded. *Degree requirements:* For master's, comprehensive exam (for some programs), thesis or alternative. *Entrance requirements:* For master's, GRE General Test, minimum undergraduate GPA of 3.0, courses in research methods and statistics. Additional exam requirements/recommendations for international students: Required—TOEFL (minimum score 500 paper-based; 173 computer-based). *Application deadline:* For fall admission, 3/1 priority date for domestic and international students. Application fee: $55 ($65 for international students). Electronic applications accepted. *Expenses:* Tuition, area resident: Part-time $179.19 per credit hour. Tuition, state resident: full-time $4384. Tuition, nonresident: full-time $16,684; part-time $630.67 per credit hour. Required fees: $350 per semester. Tuition and fees vary according to course load, degree level and program. *Financial support:* In 2010–11, 10 students received support, including 9 teaching assistantships with partial tuition reimbursements available (averaging $5,500 per year). Financial award application deadline: 2/1. *Faculty research:* Social, physical, educational and economic contexts of families and communities. Total annual research expenditures: $20,724. *Unit head:* Dr. Russell A. Isabella, Chair, 801-581-7712, Fax: 801-581-5156, E-mail: russ@fcs.utah.edu. *Application contact:* Dr. Marissa Diener, Graduate Director, 801-581-6521, E-mail: marissa.diener@fcs.utah.edu.

University of Victoria, Faculty of Graduate Studies, Faculty of Education, Department of Educational Psychology and Leadership Studies, Victoria, BC V8W 2Y2, Canada. Offers aboriginal communities counseling (M Ed); counseling (M Ed, MA); educational psychology (M Ed, MA, PhD), including counseling psychology (M Ed, MA), leadership studies (PhD), learning and development (MA, PhD), measurement and evaluation, special education (M Ed, MA); leadership studies (M Ed, MA). Part-time programs available. *Degree requirements:* For master's, thesis (for some programs), comprehensive exam (M Ed); for doctorate, comprehensive exam, thesis/dissertation, candidacy exam. *Entrance requirements:* For master's, 2 years of work experience in a relevant field; for doctorate, GRE, 2 years of work experience in a relevant field, minimum B average. Additional exam requirements/recommendations for international students: Required—TOEFL (minimum score 575 paper-based; 233 computer-based), IELTS (minimum score 7). *Faculty research:* Learning and development (child, adolescent and adult), special education and exceptional children.

University of Victoria, Faculty of Graduate Studies, Faculty of Human and Social Development, Studies in Policy and Practice Program, Victoria, BC V8W 2Y2, Canada. Offers MA. Part-time programs available. *Degree requirements:* For master's, thesis. *Entrance requirements:* For master's, resume. Additional exam requirements/recommendations for international students: Required—TOEFL (minimum score 575 paper-based; 233 computer-based), IELTS (minimum score 7). Electronic applications accepted. *Faculty research:* Women's issues, public policy formation and implementation, health promotion and education, children, youth and families.

University of Washington, Graduate School, College of Education, Program in Educational Psychology, Seattle, WA 98195. Offers educational psychology (PhD); human development and cognition (M Ed); learning sciences (M Ed, PhD); measurement, statistics and research design (M Ed); school psychology (M Ed). *Accreditation:* APA. *Degree requirements:* For master's, thesis optional; for doctorate, thesis/dissertation. *Entrance requirements:* For master's and doctorate, GRE General Test, minimum GPA of 3.0. Additional exam requirements/recommendations for international students: Required—TOEFL.

University of Wisconsin–Madison, Graduate School, School of Human Ecology, Program in Human Development and Family Studies, Madison, WI 53706-1380. Offers MS, PhD. Part-time programs available. *Faculty:* 12 full-time (9 women). *Students:* 19 full-time (18 women), 4 part-time (all women); includes 1 Black or African American, non-Hispanic/Latino; 2 Asian, non-Hispanic/Latino; 3 Hispanic/Latino. Average age 31. 64 applicants, 8% accepted, 5 enrolled. In 2010, 3 master's, 6 doctorates awarded. Terminal master's awarded for partial completion of doctoral program. *Degree requirements:* For master's, thesis; for doctorate, comprehensive exam, thesis/dissertation. *Entrance requirements:* For master's, GRE General Test, 3 letters of recommendation; for doctorate, GRE General Test, MS or MA, 3 letters of recommendation. Additional exam requirements/recommendations for international students: Required—TOEFL (minimum score 580 paper-based; 237 computer-based; 92 iBT). *Application deadline:* For fall admission, 1/3 for domestic and international students. Application fee: $56. Electronic applications accepted. *Expenses:* Tuition, state resident: full-time $9887; part-time $617.96 per credit. Tuition, nonresident: full-time $24,054; part-time $1503.40 per credit. Required fees: $67.63 per credit. Tuition and fees vary according to reciprocity agreements. *Financial support:* Fellowships with full tuition reimbursements, research assistantships with full tuition reimbursements, teaching assistantships with full tuition reimbursements, institutionally sponsored loans, scholarships/grants, health care benefits, and unspecified assistantships available. *Faculty research:* Human development, adolescence, adulthood, prevention, intervention. *Unit head:* Linda J. Roberts, Chair, 608-263-2290, E-mail: ljroberts@wisc.edu. *Application contact:* Jane A. Weier, Program Assistant, 608-263-2381, Fax: 608-265-1172, E-mail: jaweier@wisc.edu.

University of Wisconsin–Stevens Point, College of Professional Studies, School of Health Promotion and Human Development, Stevens Point, WI 54481-3897. Offers human and community resources (MS); nutritional sciences (MS). Part-time programs available. *Degree requirements:* For master's, thesis or alternative. *Entrance requirements:* For master's, minimum GPA of 2.75.

University of Wisconsin–Stout, Graduate School, College of Human Development, Program in Family Studies and Human Development, Menomonie, WI 54751. Offers MS. Part-time programs available. *Degree requirements:* For master's, thesis. *Entrance requirements:* For master's, minimum GPA of 2.75. Additional exam requirements/recommendations for international students: Required—TOEFL (minimum score 500 paper-based; 173 computer-based; 61 iBT). Electronic applications accepted. *Faculty research:* Diversity, work and family medical ethics, family policy, dementia and families.

Utah State University, School of Graduate Studies, College of Education and Human Services, Department of Family, Consumer, and Human Development, Logan, UT 84322. Offers family and human development (MFHD); family, consumer, and human development (MS, PhD), including adolescence/youth (MS), adult development/aging (MS), consumer science (MS), infancy/childhood (MS), marriage and family relations (MS), marriage and family therapy (MS). *Accreditation:* AAMFT/COAMFTE (one or more programs are accredited). Part-time and evening/weekend programs available. Postbaccalaureate distance learning degree programs offered (minimal on-campus study). *Degree requirements:* For master's, thesis; for doctorate, comprehensive exam, thesis/dissertation, competencies. *Entrance requirements:* For master's, GRE General Test or MAT, minimum GPA of 3.0, 3 letters of recommendation; for doctorate, GRE, minimum GPA of 3.0, 3 letters of recommendation. Additional exam requirements/recommendations for international students: Required—TOEFL. Electronic applications accepted. *Faculty research:* Marriage and family relations, adolescent problem behavior, family financial management, early literacy, mental health in the elderly, parent child attachment.

Vanderbilt University, Peabody College, Department of Human and Organizational Development, Nashville, TN 37240-1001. Offers community development and action (M Ed); human development counseling (M Ed). *Accreditation:* ACA; NCATE. Part-time programs available. *Faculty:* 32 full-time (14 women), 20 part-time/adjunct (11 women). *Students:* 82 full-time (67 women), 9 part-time (7 women); includes 18 minority (8 Black or African American, non-Hispanic/Latino; 1 American Indian or Alaska Native, non-Hispanic/Latino; 4 Asian, non-Hispanic/Latino; 4 Hispanic/Latino; 1 Two or more races, non-Hispanic/Latino), 1 international. Average age 27. 161 applicants, 60% accepted, 48 enrolled. In 2010, 45 master's awarded. *Degree requirements:* For master's, comprehensive exam, thesis optional. *Entrance requirements:* For master's, GRE General Test, MAT. Additional exam requirements/recommendations for international students: Required—TOEFL (minimum score 550 paper-based; 213 computer-based). *Application deadline:* For fall admission, 12/31 priority date for domestic and international students; for spring admission, 11/1 priority date for domestic and international students. Applications are processed on a rolling basis. Application fee: $0. Electronic applications accepted. *Financial support:* In 2010–11, 85 students received support, including 20 research assistantships with full and partial tuition reimbursements available, 20 teaching assistantships with full and partial tuition reimbursements available; fellowships with full and partial tuition reimbursements available, Federal Work-Study, institutionally sponsored loans, scholarships/grants, tuition waivers (partial), and unspecified assistantships also available. Support available to part-time students. Financial award application deadline: 2/1; financial award applicants required to submit FAFSA. *Faculty research:* Community psychology, community development and urban policy, counseling and mental health services, organizational development and institutional change; youth physical and behavioral health in schools and communities. *Unit head:* Dr. Marybeth Shinn, Chair, 615-322-6881, Fax: 615-322-1141, E-mail: marybeth.shinn@vanderbilt.edu. *Application contact:* Sherrie Lane, Office Assistant, 615-322-8484, Fax: 615-322-1141, E-mail: sherrie.a.lane@vanderbilt.edu.

Washington State University, Graduate School, College of Agricultural, Human, and Natural Resource Sciences, Department of Human Development, Pullman, WA 99164. Offers MA. Part-time programs available. *Faculty:* 10. *Students:* 17 full-time (16 women); includes 1 minority (Black or African American, non-Hispanic/Latino), 6 international. Average age 27. 23 applicants, 39% accepted, 8 enrolled. In 2010, 6 master's awarded. *Degree requirements:* For master's, comprehensive exam (for some programs), thesis (for some programs), oral exam. *Entrance requirements:* For master's, GRE General Test, bachelor's degree in human development or related field; written statement specifying qualifications, educational goals, and career objectives; official copies of all college transcripts; three letters of reference. Additional exam requirements/recommendations for international students: Required—TOEFL or IELTS. *Application deadline:* For fall admission, 1/10 priority date for domestic students, 1/10 for international students. Application fee: $50. Electronic applications accepted. *Expenses:* Tuition, state resident: full-time $8552; part-time $443 per credit. Tuition, nonresident: full-time $21,650; part-time $1083 per credit. Required fees: $846. *Financial support:* In 2010–11, 12 students received support, including 2 research assistantships with partial tuition reimbursements available (averaging $18,204 per year), 5 teaching assistantships with partial tuition reimbursements available (averaging $18,204 per year); Federal Work-Study, institutionally sponsored loans, tuition waivers (partial), and teaching associateships also available. Financial award application deadline: 2/15; financial award applicants required to submit FAFSA. *Faculty research:* Family processes, social development of children, quality child care, community collaborations, parent-child relationships. Total annual research expenditures: $438,000. *Unit head:* Dr. Thomas G. Power, Chair, 509-355-9540, Fax: 509-335-2456, E-mail: tompower@wsu.edu. *Application contact:* Graduate School Admissions, 800-GRADWSU, Fax: 509-335-1949, E-mail: gradsch@wsu.edu.

West Virginia University, Davis College of Agriculture, Forestry and Consumer Sciences, Division of Resource Management and Sustainable Development, Morgantown, WV 26506. Offers agricultural and extension education (MS, PhD), including agricultural and extension education, teaching vocational-agriculture (MS); agricultural and resource economics (MS); human and community development (PhD); natural resource economics (PhD); resource management (PhD); resource management and sustainable development (PhD). Part-time programs available. *Degree requirements:* For master's, thesis; for doctorate, comprehensive exam, thesis/dissertation. *Entrance requirements:* For master's, GRE General Test. Additional exam requirements/recommendations for international students: Required—TOEFL. *Faculty research:* Environmental economics, energy economics, agriculture.

Wheelock College, Graduate Programs, Division of Arts and Sciences, Boston, MA 02215-4176. Offers human development (MS). *Entrance requirements:* Additional exam requirements/recommendations for international students: Required—TOEFL. Electronic applications accepted.

Industrial and Organizational Psychology

Adler School of Professional Psychology, Programs in Psychology, Chicago, IL 60602. Offers advanced Adlerian psychotherapy (Certificate); art therapy (MA); clinical neuropsychology (Certificate); clinical psychology (Psy D); community psychology (MA); counseling and organizational psychology (MA); counseling psychology (MA); forensic psychology (MA); gerontological counseling (MA); marriage and family counseling (MA); marriage and family therapy (Certificate); organizational psychology (MA); police psychology (MA); rehabilitation counseling (MA); sport and health psychology (MA); substance abuse counseling (Certificate); Psy D/Certificate; Psy D/MACAT; Psy D/MACP; Psy D/MAMFC; Psy D/MASAC. *Accreditation:* APA. Part-time and evening/weekend programs available. Postbaccalaureate distance learning degree programs offered (minimal on-campus study). *Faculty:* 40 full-time (18 women), 61 part-time/adjunct (31 women). *Students:* 688 full-time (532 women), 142 part-time (110 women). Average age 27.Terminal master's awarded for partial completion of doctoral program. *Degree requirements:* For master's, thesis or alternative, oral exam, practicum; for doctorate, thesis/dissertation, clinical exam, internship, oral exam, practicum, written qualifying exam. *Entrance requirements:* For master's, 12 semester hours in psychology, minimum GPA of 3.0; for doctorate, 18 semester hours in psychology, minimum GPA of 3.25; for Certificate, appropriate master's or doctoral degree. Additional exam requirements/recommendations for international students: Required—TOEFL (minimum score 550 paper-based; 213 computer-based; 79 iBT). *Application deadline:* For fall admission, 2/15 priority date for domestic students, 12/1 priority date for international students. Applications are processed on a rolling basis. Application fee: $50. Electronic applications accepted. *Financial support:* Career-related internships or fieldwork, Federal Work-Study, scholarships/grants, and tuition waivers (full and partial) available. Support available to part-time students. Financial award application deadline: 5/15; financial award applicants required to submit FAFSA. *Application contact:* Michelle Brice, Director of Admissions, 312-662-4113, Fax: 312-662-4199, E-mail: admissions@adler.edu.

See Display on page 912 and Close-Up on page 1119.

Alliant International University–Fresno, Marshall Goldsmith School of Management, Organizational Psychology Division, Fresno, CA 93727. Offers organizational behavior (MA); organizational development (Psy D); MA/PhD; Psy D/MA. Part-time and evening/weekend programs available. *Degree requirements:* For doctorate, thesis/dissertation. *Entrance requirements:* For doctorate, interview, minimum GPA of 3.0. Additional exam requirements/recommendations for international students: Required—TOEFL (minimum score 600 paper-based; 250 computer-based), TWE (minimum score 5). Electronic applications accepted. *Faculty research:* Leadership, ethics and management, career development, human resources management.

Alliant International University–Los Angeles, Marshall Goldsmith School of Management, Organizational Psychology Division, Alhambra, CA 91803-1360. Offers industrial/organizational psychology (MA, PhD). Part-time programs available. Terminal master's awarded for partial completion of doctoral program. *Degree requirements:* For doctorate, thesis/dissertation. *Entrance requirements:* For master's and doctorate, interview, minimum GPA of 3.0 in both psychology and overall. Additional exam requirements/recommendations for international students: Required—TOEFL (minimum score 600 paper-based; 250 computer-based), TWE (minimum score 5). Electronic applications accepted. *Faculty research:* Organizational transitions, productivity, work force demographics, management technology, comparative and international research.

Alliant International University–Sacramento, Marshall Goldsmith School of Management, Program in Organizational Development, Sacramento, CA 95825. Offers Psy D. *Entrance requirements:* For doctorate, minimum GPA of 3.0, interview, letters of recommendation.

Alliant International University–San Diego, Marshall Goldsmith School of Management, Organizational Psychology Division, San Diego, CA 92131-1799. Offers clinical/industrial organizational psychology (PhD); consulting psychology (PhD); industrial/organizational psychology (MA, MS, PhD); organizational behavior (MA). Part-time and evening/weekend programs available. Terminal master's awarded for partial completion of doctoral program. *Degree requirements:* For doctorate, thesis/dissertation. *Entrance requirements:* For master's and doctorate, interview, minimum GPA of 3.0 in both psychology and overall. Additional exam requirements/recommendations for international students: Required—TOEFL (minimum score 600 paper-based; 250 computer-based), TWE (minimum score 5). Electronic applications accepted. *Faculty research:* Cultural diversity in the workplace, work motivation, personnel, performance management.

Alliant International University–San Francisco, Marshall Goldsmith School of Management, Organizational Psychology Division, San Francisco, CA 94133-1221. Offers organization development (MA); organizational psychology (MA, PhD). Part-time and evening/weekend programs available. Terminal master's awarded for partial completion of doctoral program. *Degree requirements:* For doctorate, thesis/dissertation. *Entrance requirements:* For master's and doctorate, interview, minimum GPA of 3.0. Additional exam requirements/recommendations for international students: Required—TOEFL (minimum score 650 paper-based; 250 computer-based), TWE (minimum score 5). Electronic applications accepted. *Faculty research:* Leadership, ethics and management, career development, organizational behavior, strategic change.

American InterContinental University Online, Program in Business Administration, Hoffman Estates, IL 60192. Offers accounting and finance (MBA); finance (MBA); healthcare management (MBA); human resource management (MBA); international business (MBA); management (MBA); marketing (MBA); operations management (MBA); organizational psychology and development (MBA); project management (MBA). Evening/weekend programs available. Postbaccalaureate distance learning degree programs offered (no on-campus study). *Entrance requirements:* Additional exam requirements/recommendations for international students: Required—TOEFL (minimum score 550 paper-based; 213 computer-based). Electronic applications accepted.

Angelo State University, College of Graduate Studies, College of Liberal and Fine Arts, Department of Psychology, Sociology and Social Work, San Angelo, TX 76909. Offers psychology (MS), including applied psychology, counseling psychology, industrial and organizational psychology. Part-time and evening/weekend programs available. *Faculty:* 8 full-time (2 women). *Students:* 53 full-time (38 women), 10 part-time (7 women); includes 6 Black or African American, non-Hispanic/Latino; 12 Hispanic/Latino. Average age 29. 52 applicants, 69% accepted, 35 enrolled. In 2010, 13 master's awarded. *Degree requirements:* For master's, comprehensive exam, thesis optional. *Entrance requirements:* For master's, GRE General Test (for industrial and organizational psychology only), essay, letters of recommendation (for industrial and organizational psychology only). Additional exam requirements/recommendations for international students: Required—TOEFL or IELTS. *Application deadline:* For fall admission, 7/15 priority date for domestic students, 6/10 for international students; for spring admission, 12/1 priority date for domestic students, 11/1 for international students. Applications are processed on a rolling basis. Application fee: $40 ($50 for international students). Electronic applications accepted. *Expenses:* Tuition, state resident: full-time $4560; part-time $152 per credit hour. Tuition, nonresident: full-time $13,860; part-time $462 per credit hour. Required fees: $2132. Tuition and fees vary according to course load. *Financial support:* In 2010–11, 44 students received support, including 3 teaching assistantships (averaging $10,251 per year); career-related internships or fieldwork, Federal Work-Study, scholarships/grants, and unspecified assistantships also available. Support available to part-time students. Financial award application deadline: 3/1; financial award applicants required to submit FAFSA. Total annual research expenditures: $116,915. *Unit head:* Dr. William B. Davidson, Department Head, 325-942-2068 Ext. 248, Fax: 325-942-2290, E-mail: bill.davidson@angelo.edu. *Application contact:* Aly Hunter, Graduate Admissions Assistant, 325-942-2169, Fax: 325-942-2194, E-mail: aly.hunter@angelo.edu.

Antioch University Seattle, Graduate Programs, Center for Creative Change, Seattle, WA 98121-1814. Offers environment and community (MA); management (MS); organizational psychology (MA); strategic communications (MA); whole system design (MA). Evening/weekend programs available. Electronic applications accepted. *Expenses:* Contact institution.

Appalachian State University, Cratis D. Williams Graduate School, Department of Psychology, Boone, NC 28608. Offers clinical health psychology (MA); general experimental psychology (MA); industrial and organizational psychology (MA). Part-time programs available. *Faculty:* 31 full-time (10 women), 2 part-time/adjunct (1 woman). *Students:* 55 full-time (40 women), 11 part-time (9 women); includes 3 minority (2 Black or African American, non-Hispanic/Latino; 1 Two or more races, non-Hispanic/Latino). 158 applicants, 32% accepted, 28 enrolled. In 2010, 25 master's, 7 other advanced degrees awarded. *Degree requirements:* For master's, comprehensive exam, thesis optional, exit exam. *Entrance requirements:* For master's, GRE General Test, 3 letters of recommendation. Additional exam requirements/recommendations for international students: Required—TOEFL (minimum score 550 paper-based; 230 computer-based; 79 iBT) or IELTS (minimum score 6.5). *Application deadline:* For fall admission, 2/15 for domestic students, 2/1 for international students. Applications are processed on a rolling basis. Application fee: $55. Electronic applications accepted. *Expenses:* Tuition, state resident: full-time $3428; part-time $428 per unit. Tuition, nonresident: full-time $14,518; part-time $1814 per unit. Required fees: $2320; $344 per unit. Tuition and fees vary according to campus/location. *Financial support:* In 2010–11, 34 research assistantships (averaging $4,000 per year), 25 teaching assistantships (averaging $4,000 per year) were awarded; fellowships, career-related internships or fieldwork, Federal Work-Study, scholarships/grants, and unspecified assistantships also available. Financial award application deadline: 4/1; financial award applicants required to submit FAFSA. *Faculty research:* Eating disorders, school-based consultations, organizational behavior management, brain mechanisms of sound localization, parenting styles. Total annual research expenditures: $18,000. *Unit head:* Dr. James Denniston, Chair, 828-262-2272, Fax: 828-262-2272, E-mail: dennistonjc@appstate.edu. *Application contact:* Dr. Denise Martz, Graduate Coordinator, 828-262-2715, E-mail: martzdm@appstate.edu.

Argosy University, Atlanta, College of Psychology and Behavioral Sciences, Atlanta, GA 30328. Offers clinical psychology (MA, Psy D, Postdoctoral Respecialization Certificate), including child and family psychology (Psy D), general adult clinical (Psy D), health psychology (Psy D), neuropsychology/geropsychology (Psy D); community counseling (MA), including marriage and family therapy; counselor education and supervision (Ed D); forensic psychology (MA); industrial organizational psychology (MA); marriage and family therapy (Certificate); sport-exercise psychology (MA). *Accreditation:* APA.

See Close-Up on page 1121.

Argosy University, Chicago, College of Psychology and Behavioral Sciences, Chicago, IL 60601. Offers clinical psychology (MA, Psy D), including child and adolescent psychology (Psy D), client-centered and experiential psychotherapies (Psy D), diversity and multicultural psychology (Psy D), family psychology (Psy D), forensic psychology (Psy D), health psychology (Psy D), neuropsychology (Psy D), organizational consulting (Psy D), psychoanalytic psychology (Psy D), psychology and spirituality (Psy D); community counseling (MA); counseling psychology (Ed D), including counselor education and supervision; counselor education and supervision (Ed D); industrial organizational psychology (MA). *Accreditation:* APA (one or more programs are accredited). Postbaccalaureate distance learning degree programs offered (minimal on-campus study).

See Close-Up on page 1123.

Argosy University, Dallas, College of Psychology and Behavioral Sciences, Program in Industrial Organizational Psychology, Farmers Branch, TX 75244. Offers MA.

See Close-Up on page 1125.

Argosy University, Denver, College of Psychology and Behavioral Sciences, Denver, CO 80231. Offers clinical mental health counseling (MA); clinical psychology (MA, Psy D); counseling psychology (Ed D); counselor education and supervision (Ed D); forensic psychology (MA); industrial organizational psychology (MA); marriage and family therapy (MA, DMFT).

See Close-Up on page 1127.

Argosy University, Inland Empire, College of Psychology and Behavioral Sciences, San Bernardino, CA 92408. Offers clinical psychology/marriage and family therapy (MA); counseling psychology (Ed D); counseling psychology/marriage and family therapy (MA); forensic psychology (MA); industrial organizational psychology (MA); sport-exercise psychology (MA).

See Close-Up on page 1131.

Argosy University, Phoenix, College of Psychology and Behavioral Sciences, Program in Industrial Organizational Psychology, Phoenix, AZ 85021. Offers MA.

See Close-Up on page 1139.

Argosy University, Schaumburg, College of Psychology and Behavioral Sciences, Schaumburg, IL 60173-5403. Offers clinical health psychology (Post-Graduate Certificate); clinical psychology (MA, Psy D), including child and family psychology (Psy D), clinical health psychology (Psy D), diversity and multicultural psychology (Psy D), forensic psychology (Psy D), neuropsychology (Psy D); community counseling (MA); counseling psychology (Ed D), including counselor education and supervision; counselor education and supervision (Ed D); forensic psychology (Post-Graduate Certificate); industrial organizational psychology (MA). *Accreditation:* ACA; APA.

See Close-Up on page 1149.

Argosy University, Tampa, College of Psychology and Behavioral Sciences, Tampa, FL 33607. Offers clinical psychology (MA, Psy D), including clinical psychology; counselor education and supervision (Ed D); industrial organizational psychology (MA); marriage and family therapy (MA); mental health counseling (MA).

See Close-Up on page 1153.

Argosy University, Twin Cities, College of Psychology and Behavioral Sciences, Eagan, MN 55121. Offers clinical psychology (MA, Psy D), including child and family psychology (Psy D), forensic psychology (Psy D), health and neuropsychology (Psy D), trauma (Psy D); forensic counseling (Post-Graduate Certificate); forensic psychology (MA); industrial organizational psychology (MA); marriage and family therapy (MA, DMFT), including forensic counseling (MA). *Accreditation:* AAMFT; AAMFT/COAMFTE; APA.

See Close-Up on page 1155.

Auburn University, Graduate School, College of Liberal Arts, Department of Psychology, Auburn University, AL 36849. Offers applied behavior analysis in developmental disabilities (MS); clinical psychology (PhD); experimental psychology (PhD); industrial/organizational psychology (PhD). *Accreditation:* APA (one or more programs are accredited). Part-time programs available. *Faculty:* 24 full-time (7 women), 4 part-time/adjunct (3 women). *Students:* 36 full-time (28 women), 57 part-time (33 women); includes 6 Black or African American, non-Hispanic/Latino; 4 Asian, non-Hispanic/Latino; 5 Hispanic/Latino. Average age 26. 293 applicants, 9% accepted, 19 enrolled. In 2010, 20 master's, 11 doctorates awarded. *Degree requirements:* For doctorate, thesis/dissertation. *Entrance requirements:* For master's, GRE General Test, GRE Subject Test, minimum GPA of 3.25 in psychology, 3.0 overall; for doctorate, GRE General Test, GRE Subject Test. *Application deadline:* For fall admission, 7/7 for domestic students; for spring admission, 11/24 for domestic students. Applications are processed on a rolling basis. Application fee: $50 ($60 for international students). Electronic applications accepted. *Expenses:* Tuition, state resident: full-time $7002. Tuition, nonresident: full-time $21,898. International tuition: $22,116 full-time. Required fees: $892. Tuition and fees vary according to course load and program. *Financial support:* Research assistantships, teaching assistantships, Federal Work-Study available. Support available to part-time students. Financial award application deadline: 3/15; financial award applicants required to submit FAFSA. *Faculty research:* Clinical psychology, learning, industrial psychology, organizational psychology. Total annual research expenditures: $200,000. *Unit head:* Dr. Barry Burkhart, Chair, 334-844-6476. *Application contact:* Dr. George Flowers, Dean of the Graduate School, 334-844-2125.

Bayamón Central University, Graduate Programs, Program in Organizational Psychology, Bayamón, PR 00960-1725. Offers MA. Part-time and evening/weekend programs available. *Degree requirements:* For master's, comprehensive exam. *Entrance requirements:* For master's, EXADEP, bachelor's degree in psychology or related field.

Bernard M. Baruch College of the City University of New York, Weissman School of Arts and Sciences, Program in Industrial Organizational Psychology, New York, NY 10010-5585. Offers MS.

Bernard M. Baruch College of the City University of New York, Zicklin School of Business, Program in Industrial and Organizational Psychology, New York, NY 10010-5585. Offers MBA, MS, PhD, Certificate. PhD offered jointly with Graduate School and University Center of the City University of New York. Part-time and evening/weekend programs available. *Degree requirements:* For master's, thesis or alternative; for doctorate, comprehensive exam, thesis/dissertation. *Entrance requirements:* For master's, GMAT or GRE General Test, 2 letters of recommendation, resumé, 2 years of work experience; for doctorate, GMAT or GRE General Test. Additional exam requirements/recommendations for international students: Required—TOEFL (minimum score 590 paper-based; 243 computer-based), TWE. *Faculty research:* Job attitudes, power and leadership in organizations, measurement issues in organizational behavior, work motivation, fair employment practices.

Bowling Green State University, Graduate College, College of Arts and Sciences, Department of Psychology, Bowling Green, OH 43403. Offers clinical psychology (MA, PhD); developmental psychology (MA, PhD); experimental psychology (MA, PhD); industrial/organizational psychology (MA, PhD); quantitative psychology (MA, PhD). *Accreditation:* APA (one or more programs are accredited). *Degree requirements:* For doctorate, thesis/dissertation. *Entrance requirements:* For doctorate, GRE General Test, GRE Subject Test. Additional exam requirements/recommendations for international students: Required—TOEFL. Electronic applications accepted. *Faculty research:* Personnel psychology, developmental-mathematical models, behavioral medication, brain process, child/adolescent social cognition.

Brooklyn College of the City University of New York, Division of Graduate Studies, Department of Psychology, Program in Industrial and Organizational Psychology, Brooklyn, NY 11210-2889. Offers human relations (MA); organizational behavior (MA). *Students:* 6 full-time (5 women), 100 part-time (78 women); includes 63 minority (42 Black or African American, non-Hispanic/Latino; 8 Asian, non-Hispanic/Latino; 13 Hispanic/Latino), 10 international. Average age 30. 93 applicants, 69% accepted, 41 enrolled. In 2010, 39 master's awarded. *Degree requirements:* For master's, comprehensive exam, thesis. *Entrance requirements:* For master's, 2 letters of recommendation. Additional exam requirements/recommendations for international students: Required—TOEFL (minimum score 520 paper-based; 190 computer-based; 69 iBT). *Application deadline:* For fall admission, 3/1 priority date for domestic students, 2/1 for international students. Applications are processed on a rolling basis. Electronic applications accepted. *Expenses:* Tuition, state resident: full-time $7360; part-time $310 per credit hour. Tuition, nonresident: full-time $13,800; part-time $575 per credit hour. Required fees: $190 per semester. *Unit head:* Benzion Chanowitz, Graduate Advisor, 718-951-5601, E-mail: bchanowitz@brooklyn.cuny.edu. *Application contact:* Hernan Sierra, Graduate Admissions Coordinator, 718-951-4536, Fax: 718-951-4506, E-mail: grads@brooklyn.cuny.edu.

California State University, Long Beach, Graduate Studies, College of Liberal Arts, Department of Psychology, Long Beach, CA 90840. Offers human factors (MS); industrial/organizational psychology (MS); psychology (MA). Part-time and evening/weekend programs available. *Faculty:* 18 full-time (5 women), 1 part-time/adjunct (0 women). *Students:* 43 full-time (31 women), 27 part-time (17 women); includes 4 Black or African American, non-Hispanic/Latino; 10 Asian, non-Hispanic/Latino; 11 Hispanic/Latino, 2 international. Average age 27. 203 applicants, 16% accepted, 30 enrolled. In 2010, 19 master's awarded. *Degree requirements:* For master's, comprehensive exam, thesis. *Entrance requirements:* For master's, GRE General Test, GRE Subject Test. *Application deadline:* For fall admission, 3/1 for domestic students. Applications are processed on a rolling basis. Application fee: $55. Electronic applications accepted. *Financial support:* Federal Work-Study, institutionally sponsored loans, and scholarships/grants available. Financial award application deadline: 3/2. *Faculty research:* Physiological psychology, social and personality psychology, community-clinical psychology, industrial-organizational psychology, developmental psychology. *Unit head:* Dr. Kenneth Green, Chair, 562-985-5049, Fax: 562-985-8004, E-mail: kgreen@csulb.edu. *Application contact:* Dr. Kenneth Green, Chair, 562-985-5049, Fax: 562-985-8004, E-mail: kgreen@csulb.edu.

California State University, San Bernardino, Graduate Studies, College of Social and Behavioral Sciences, Department of Psychology, Program in Industrial/Organizational Psychology, San Bernardino, CA 92407-2397. Offers organizational psychology (MS). *Degree requirements:* For master's, thesis. *Entrance requirements:* For master's, minimum GPA of 3.0 in major.

Capella University, Harold Abel School of Psychology, Minneapolis, MN 55402. Offers child and adolescent development (MS); clinical psychology (MS, Psy D); counseling psychology (MS); educational psychology (MS, PhD); evaluation, research, and measurement (MS); general psychology (MS, PhD); industrial/organizational psychology (MS, PhD); leadership coaching psychology (MS); organizational leader development (MS); school psychology (MS); sport psychology (MS). Part-time and evening/weekend programs available. Postbaccalaureate distance learning degree programs offered (minimal on-campus study). Terminal master's awarded for partial completion of doctoral program. *Degree requirements:* For master's, thesis optional, project; for doctorate, thesis/dissertation. *Entrance requirements:* For degree, master's degree in school psychology. Additional exam requirements/recommendations for international students: Required—TOEFL (minimum score 550 paper-based; 213 computer-based), TWE (minimum score 4); Recommended—IELTS. Electronic applications accepted. *Expenses:* Tuition: Full-time $11,880; part-time $440 per credit hour.

Carlos Albizu University, Graduate Programs, San Juan, PR 00901. Offers clinical psychology (MS, PhD, Psy D); general psychology (PhD); industrial/organizational psychology (MS, PhD); speech and language pathology (MS). *Accreditation:* APA (one or more programs are accredited). Part-time and evening/weekend programs available. Terminal master's awarded for partial completion of doctoral program. *Degree requirements:* For master's, one foreign language, comprehensive exam, thesis; for doctorate, one foreign language, comprehensive exam, thesis/dissertation, written qualifying exams. *Entrance requirements:* For master's, GRE General Test or EXADEP, interview; minimum GPA of 3.0 (industrial/organizational psychology), 3.25 (speech and language pathology); for doctorate, GRE General Test or EXADEP, interview; minimum GPA of 3.0 (industrial/organizational psychology), 3.25 (PhD and Psy D in clinical psychology). *Faculty research:* Psychotherapeutic techniques for Hispanics, psychology of the aged, school dropouts, stress, violence.

Carlos Albizu University, Miami Campus, Graduate Programs, Miami, FL 33172-2209. Offers clinical psychology (Psy D); entrepreneurship (MBA); exceptional student education (MS); industrial/organizational psychology (MS); marriage and family therapy (MS); mental health counseling (MS); nonprofit management (MBA); organizational management (MBA); psychology (MS); school counseling (MS); teaching English as a second language (MS). *Accreditation:* APA. Part-time and evening/weekend programs available. *Faculty:* 21 full-time (12 women), 37 part-time/adjunct (18 women). *Students:* 496 full-time (400 women), 242 part-time (192 women); includes 590 minority (58 Black or African American, non-Hispanic/Latino; 2 American Indian or Alaska Native, non-Hispanic/Latino; 5 Asian, non-Hispanic/Latino; 523 Hispanic/Latino; 2 Two or more races, non-Hispanic/Latino), 15 international. Average age 36. 141 applicants, 84% accepted, 118 enrolled. In 2010, 159 master's, 20 doctorates awarded. Terminal master's awarded for partial completion of doctoral program. *Degree requirements:* For master's, one foreign language, comprehensive exam, integrative project (MBA), research project (exceptional student education, teaching English as a second language); for doctorate, one foreign language, comprehensive exam, internship, project. *Entrance requirements:* For master's, 3 letters of recommendation, interview, minimum GPA of 3.0, resume, statement of purpose, official transcripts; for doctorate, 3 letters of recommendation, minimum GPA of 3.0, resume, interview. *Application deadline:* For fall admission, 8/1 priority date for domestic students; for spring admission, 11/30 priority date for domestic students. Applications are processed on a rolling basis. Application fee: $50. Electronic applications accepted. *Expenses:* Tuition: Full-time $9360; part-time $520 per credit. Required fees: $298 per term. Tuition and fees vary according to course load, degree level and program. *Financial support:* In 2010–11, 106 students received support. Federal Work-Study, scholarships/grants, and tuition discounts available. Financial award application deadline: 6/1; financial award applicants required to submit FAFSA. *Faculty research:* Psychotherapy, forensic psychology, neuropsychology, marketing strategy, entrepreneurship, special education. *Unit head:* Dr. Carmen S. Roca, Chancellor, 305-593-1223 Ext. 120, Fax: 305-629-8052, E-mail: croca@albizu.edu. *Application contact:* Vanessa Almendarez, Secretary, 305-593-1223 Ext. 137, Fax: 305-593-1854, E-mail: valmendarez@albizu.edu.

Central Michigan University, College of Graduate Studies, College of Humanities and Social and Behavioral Sciences, Department of Psychology, Program in Industrial and Organizational Psychology, Mount Pleasant, MI 48859. Offers industrial and organizational psychology (MA, PhD); occupational health psychology (PhD). *Students:* 18 full-time (7 women), 19 part-time (8 women); includes 1 American Indian or Alaska Native, non-Hispanic/Latino; 1 Asian, non-Hispanic/Latino; 1 Hispanic/Latino, 4 international. Average age 26. *Degree requirements:* For master's, thesis; for doctorate, comprehensive exam, thesis/dissertation. *Entrance requirements:* For master's and doctorate, GRE. *Application deadline:* For fall admission, 1/1 for domestic and international students. Application fee: $35 ($45 for international students). Electronic applications accepted. *Expenses:* Tuition, state resident: full-time $8208; part-time $456 per credit hour. Tuition, nonresident: full-time $13,788; part-time $766 per credit hour. One-time fee: $25. *Financial support:* Fellowships with tuition reimbursements, research assistantships with tuition reimbursements, career-related internships or fieldwork, Federal Work-Study, unspecified assistantships, and out-of-state merit awards, non-resident graduate awards available. *Faculty research:* Job stress, retirement, leadership, and careers; personality in the workplace, personnel selection, and structural equation modeling in I/O psychology; personnel psychology, evolutionary psychology, and influences on HRM utilization; occupational health psychology and job stress; work attitudes, psychological ownership in work, and performance appraisal. *Unit head:* Dr. Hajime Otani, Chairperson, 989-774-6461, Fax: 989-774-2553, E-mail: otani1h@cmich.edu. *Application contact:* Dr. Terry Beehr, Graduate Coordinator, 989-774-6466, Fax: 989-774-2553, E-mail: beehr1ta@cmich.edu.

Chatham University, Program in Counseling Psychology, Pittsburgh, PA 15232-2826. Offers child, adolescent and family (MSCP); counseling psychology (Psy D); health and holistic (MSCP); infant mental health (MSCP); organization and supervision (MSCP); sport and exercise (MSCP). Part-time and evening/weekend programs available. *Degree requirements:* For master's, thesis optional, supervised internship; for doctorate, thesis/dissertation, internship. *Entrance requirements:* For master's, minimum GPA of 3.0; 2 letters of recommendation; resume; prerequisite coursework in statistics, biology, and psychology; for doctorate, GRE. Additional exam requirements/recommendations for international students: Required—TOEFL (minimum score 600 paper-based; 250 computer-based; 100 iBT), IELTS (minimum score 6.5), TWE. Electronic applications accepted. *Faculty research:* Trauma and recovery, hypnosis, psychospiritual dimensions of healing, psychotherapy of schizophrenia.

The Chicago School of Professional Psychology, Program in Industrial and Organizational Psychology, Chicago, IL 60610. Offers business psychology (Psy D); industrial and organizational psychology (MA). Part-time and evening/weekend programs available. *Degree requirements:* For master's, internship; for doctorate, thesis/dissertation, internship. *Entrance requirements:* For master's, 1 course each in psychology, statistics, and research methods; for doctorate, GRE, writing test, 12 hours of psychology credit including a course in statistics and research methods. Additional exam requirements/recommendations for international students: Required—TOEFL (minimum score 550 paper-based; 213 computer-based; 79 iBT).

The Chicago School of Professional Psychology at Downtown Los Angeles, Program in Industrial and Organizational Psychology, Los Angeles, CA 90017. Offers MA.

The Chicago School of Professional Psychology: Online, PhD Program in Organizational Leadership, Chicago, IL 60654. Offers PhD.

The Chicago School of Professional Psychology: Online, Program in Applied Industrial and Organizational Psychology, Chicago, IL 60654. Offers MA, Certificate.

Claremont Graduate University, Graduate Programs, School of Behavioral and Organizational Sciences, Department of Psychology, Claremont, CA 91711-6160. Offers advanced study in evaluation (Certificate); cognitive psychology (MA, PhD); developmental psychology (MA, PhD); evaluation and applied research methods (MA, PhD); health behavior research and evaluation (MA, PhD); human resource development and evaluation (MA); industrial/organizational psychology (MA, PhD); organizational behavior (MA, PhD); organizational psychology (MA, PhD); social psychology (MA, PhD); MBA/PhD. Part-time programs available. *Faculty:* 15 full-time (6 women), 5 part-time/adjunct (2 women). *Students:* 248 full-time (169 women), 15 part-time (9 women); includes 68 minority (14 Black or African American, non-Hispanic/Latino; 1 American Indian or Alaska Native, non-Hispanic/Latino; 27 Asian, non-Hispanic/Latino; 19 Hispanic/Latino; 2 Native Hawaiian or other Pacific Islander, non-Hispanic/Latino; 5 Two or more races, non-Hispanic/Latino), 29 international. Average age 30. In 2010, 45 master's, 21 doctorates, 4 other advanced degrees awarded. Terminal master's awarded for partial completion of doctoral program. *Entrance requirements:* For master's and doctorate, GRE General Test. Additional exam requirements/recommendations for international students: Required—TOEFL (minimum score 550 paper-based; 213 computer-based; 80 iBT). *Application deadline:* For fall admission, 1/15 priority date for domestic students. Applications are processed on a rolling basis. Application fee: $60. Electronic applications accepted. *Expenses:* Tuition: Full-time $35,748; part-time $1554 per unit. Required fees: $215 per semester. *Financial support:* Fellowships, research assistantships, teaching assistantships, Federal Work-Study, institutionally sponsored loans, scholarships/grants, and tuition waivers (full and partial) available. Support available to part-time students. Financial award application deadline: 2/15; financial award applicants required to submit FAFSA. *Faculty research:* Social intervention, diversity in organizations, eyewitness memory, aging and cognition, drug policy. *Unit head:* Stewart Donaldson, Dean, 909-607-9001, Fax: 909-621-8905, E-mail: stewart.donaldson@cgu.edu. *Application contact:* Paul Thomas, Director, External Affairs, 909-607-9016, Fax: 909-621-8905, E-mail: paul.thomas@cgu.edu.

Clemson University, Graduate School, College of Business and Behavioral Science, Department of Psychology, Program in Industrial/Organizational Psychology, Clemson, SC 29634. Offers PhD. *Students:* 21 full-time (18 women), 5 part-time (3 women); includes 1 Black or African American, non-Hispanic/Latino, 2 international. Average age 28. 85 applicants, 7% accepted, 6 enrolled. In 2010, 3 doctorates awarded. *Degree requirements:* For doctorate, thesis/dissertation. *Entrance requirements:* For doctorate, GRE General Test. Additional exam requirements/recommendations for international students: Required—TOEFL. *Application deadline:* For fall admission, 1/15 for domestic students. Application fee: $70 ($80 for international students). Electronic applications accepted. *Expenses:* Contact institution. *Financial*

Industrial and Organizational Psychology

Clemson University (continued)
support: In 2010–11, 20 students received support, including 3 fellowships with full and partial tuition reimbursements available (averaging $6,500 per year), 1 research assistantship with partial tuition reimbursement available (averaging $5,500 per year), 21 teaching assistantships with partial tuition reimbursements available (averaging $11,281 per year); career-related internships or fieldwork, institutionally sponsored loans, scholarships/grants, health care benefits, and unspecified assistantships also available. Support available to part-time students. Financial award application deadline: 3/15; financial award applicants required to submit FAFSA. *Faculty research:* Personnel selection; occupational health; judgment and decision-making; organizational psychology; aging, retirement, and return to work. *Unit head:* Dr. Patrick Raymark, Chair, 864-656-4715, Fax: 864-656-0358, E-mail: praymar@clemson.edu. *Application contact:* Dr. Robert Sinclair, Graduate Program Coordinator, 864-656-3931, Fax: 864-656-0358.

Cleveland State University, College of Graduate Studies, College of Sciences and Health Professions, Department of Psychology, Cleveland, OH 44115. Offers adult development and aging (PhD); clinical psychology (MA); consumer/industrial research (MA); diversity management (MA); experimental research psychology (MA); school psychology (Psy S). *Accreditation:* APA. *Faculty:* 20 full-time (7 women), 16 part-time/adjunct (8 women). *Students:* 63 full-time (45 women), 43 part-time (27 women); includes 15 Black or African American, non-Hispanic/Latino; 1 American Indian or Alaska Native, non-Hispanic/Latino; 3 Asian, non-Hispanic/Latino; 3 Hispanic/Latino, 1 international. Average age 30. 164 applicants, 44% accepted, 62 enrolled. In 2010, 39 master's, 8 other advanced degrees awarded. Terminal master's awarded for partial completion of doctoral program. *Degree requirements:* For master's, comprehensive exam (for some programs), thesis (for some programs); for doctorate, comprehensive exam, thesis/dissertation; for Psy S, internship. *Entrance requirements:* For master's and doctorate, GRE General Test. Additional exam requirements/recommendations for international students: Required—TOEFL (minimum score 525 paper-based; 197 computer-based). *Application deadline:* For fall admission, 2/1 priority date for domestic and international students. Application fee: $30. Electronic applications accepted. *Expenses:* Tuition, state resident: full-time $8447; part-time $469 per credit hour. Tuition, nonresident: full-time $16,020; part-time $890 per credit hour. Required fees: $50. *Financial support:* In 2010–11, 45 students received support. Career-related internships or fieldwork, Federal Work-Study, scholarships/grants, tuition waivers (partial), and unspecified assistantships available. Financial award applicants required to submit FAFSA. *Faculty research:* Cognitive and social psychology, consumer psychology, clinical psychology, school psychology, aging. Total annual research expenditures: $112,607. *Unit head:* Dr. Kathleen M. McNamara, Chairperson, 216-687-2545, Fax: 216-687-9294, E-mail: k.mcnamara@csuohio.edu. *Application contact:* Karen R. Colston, Administrative Coordinator, 216-687-2552, Fax: 216-687-9294, E-mail: k.colston@csuohio.edu.

DePaul University, College of Liberal Arts and Sciences, Department of Psychology, Chicago, IL 60604-2287. Offers clinical psychology (MA, PhD), including child clinical psychology, community clinical psychology; experimental psychology (MA, PhD); general psychology (MS); industrial/organizational psychology (MA, PhD); MA/PhD. *Accreditation:* APA (one or more programs are accredited). *Faculty:* 31 full-time (19 women), 6 part-time/adjunct (4 women). *Students:* 43 full-time (26 women), 57 part-time (39 women); includes 11 Black or African American, non-Hispanic/Latino; 5 Asian, non-Hispanic/Latino; 10 Hispanic/Latino; 4 Two or more races, non-Hispanic/Latino, 2 international. Average age 28. 332 applicants, 14% accepted, 23 enrolled. In 2010, 14 master's, 17 doctorates awarded. *Degree requirements:* For master's, thesis, oral exam; for doctorate, comprehensive exam, thesis/dissertation, oral and written exams. *Entrance requirements:* For master's and doctorate, GRE General Test, GRE Subject Test, 32 quarter hours of course work in psychology, 3 letters of recommendation. Additional exam requirements/recommendations for international students: Required—TOEFL. Application fee: $40. Electronic applications accepted. *Financial support:* In 2010–11, 48 students received support, including 35 research assistantships with full tuition reimbursements available (averaging $11,800 per year), 13 teaching assistantships with full tuition reimbursements available (averaging $11,800 per year); career-related internships or fieldwork, scholarships/grants, traineeships, tuition waivers (full and partial), and unspecified assistantships also available. Financial award application deadline: 1/10. *Faculty research:* Adolescent stress and depression, minority adolescents sexuality, public policy, community influences in child adjustment. *Unit head:* Dr. Christopher B. Keys, Chairman, 773-325-7887, Fax: 773-325-7888. *Application contact:* Alison Pereida Knapp, Graduate Admissions Assistant, 773-325-7887, Fax: 773-325-7888.

Eastern Kentucky University, The Graduate School, College of Arts and Sciences, Department of Psychology, Richmond, KY 40475-3102. Offers clinical psychology (MS); industrial/organizational psychology (MS); school psychology (Psy S). Part-time programs available. *Entrance requirements:* For master's and Psy S, GRE General Test, minimum GPA of 2.5. *Faculty research:* Autism, social psychology, parenting, assessment of depression/anxiety, reading.

Elmhurst College, Graduate Programs, Program in Industrial/Organizational Psychology, Elmhurst, IL 60126-3296. Offers MA. Part-time and evening/weekend programs available. *Faculty:* 1 full-time (0 women), 5 part-time/adjunct (2 women). *Students:* 44 part-time (34 women); includes 7 minority (1 Black or African American, non-Hispanic/Latino; 1 Asian, non-Hispanic/Latino; 4 Hispanic/Latino; 1 Two or more races, non-Hispanic/Latino). Average age 24. 60 applicants, 58% accepted, 20 enrolled. In 2010, 16 master's awarded. *Degree requirements:* For master's, thesis optional. *Entrance requirements:* For master's, GRE General Test, 3 recommendations, resume, statement of purpose. Additional exam requirements/recommendations for international students: Required—TOEFL (minimum score 550 paper-based; 213 computer-based). *Application deadline:* Applications are processed on a rolling basis. Application fee: $0. Electronic applications accepted. *Expenses:* Contact institution. *Financial support:* In 2010–11, 20 students received support. Federal Work-Study and scholarships/grants available. Support available to part-time students. Financial award application deadline: 6/1; financial award applicants required to submit FAFSA. *Unit head:* Elizabeth D. Kuebler, Director of Adult and Graduate Admission, 630-617-3300, Fax: 630-617-5501, E-mail: sal@elmhurst.edu. *Application contact:* Elizabeth D. Kuebler, Director of Adult and Graduate Admission, 630-617-3300, Fax: 630-617-5501, E-mail: sal@elmhurst.edu.

Emporia State University, Graduate School, Teachers College, Department of Psychology, Art Therapy, Rehabilitation and Mental Health Counseling, Program in Psychology, Emporia, KS 66801-5087. Offers general psychology (MS); industrial/organizational psychology (MS). Part-time programs available. *Students:* 15 full-time (9 women), 10 part-time (8 women); includes 2 minority (1 Black or African American, non-Hispanic/Latino; 1 Two or more races, non-Hispanic/Latino), 6 international. 10 applicants, 60% accepted, 5 enrolled. In 2010, 6 master's awarded. *Degree requirements:* For master's, comprehensive exam or thesis, internship. *Entrance requirements:* For master's, GRE General Test or MAT, graduate essay exam, appropriate bachelor's degree, letters of recommendation. Additional exam requirements/recommendations for international students: Required—TOEFL (minimum score 520 paper-based; 133 computer-based; 68 iBT). *Application deadline:* For fall admission, 6/1 priority date for domestic students; for spring admission, 10/1 for domestic students. Applications are processed on a rolling basis. Application fee: $30 ($75 for international students). Electronic applications accepted. *Expenses:* Tuition, state resident: full-time $4382; part-time $183 per credit hour. Tuition, nonresident: full-time $13,572; part-time $566 per credit hour. Required fees: $1022; $62 per credit hour. Tuition and fees vary according to course level, course load and campus/location. *Financial support:* Career-related internships or fieldwork, Federal Work-Study, institutionally sponsored loans, health care benefits, and unspecified assistantships available. Financial award application deadline: 3/15; financial award applicants required to submit FAFSA. *Faculty research:* Driving under the influence (DUI) personality, lifestyles and imposter phenomenon. *Unit head:* Dr. Brian W. Schrader, Chair, 620-341-5317, E-mail: bschrade@emporia.edu. *Application contact:* Mary Sewell, Admissions Coordinator, 800-950-GRAD, Fax: 620-341-5909, E-mail: msewell@emporia.edu.

Fairfield University, Graduate School of Education and Allied Professions, Department of Psychological and Educational Consultation, Fairfield, CT 06824-5195. Offers applied psychology (MA), including foundations of advanced psychology, human services, industrial/organizational; educational technology (MA); school library media specialist (MA); school psychology (MA, CAS); special education (MA, CAS). Part-time and evening/weekend programs available. *Faculty:* 6 full-time (2 women), 7 part-time/adjunct (4 women). *Students:* 52 full-time (46 women), 144 part-time (120 women); includes 2 Black or African American, non-Hispanic/Latino; 1 American Indian or Alaska Native, non-Hispanic/Latino; 2 Asian, non-Hispanic/Latino; 14 Hispanic/Latino, 2 international. 136 applicants, 63% accepted, 59 enrolled. In 2010, 44 master's, 14 other advanced degrees awarded. *Degree requirements:* For master's, comprehensive exam, thesis optional. *Entrance requirements:* For master's, PRAXIS I (PPST), minimum QPA of 3.0, 2 recommendations, resume. Additional exam requirements/recommendations for international students: Required—TOEFL (minimum score 550 paper-based; 213 computer-based; 84 iBT). Application fee: $60. Electronic applications accepted. *Expenses:* Tuition: Part-time $600 per hour. Part-time tuition and fees vary according to degree level and program. *Financial support:* Unspecified assistantships available. Financial award applicants required to submit FAFSA. *Faculty research:* Child neuropsychology, disabilities, effect of pre-treatment orientation on treatment, autism, technology in business and classroom, collaboration with schools, communities and industry. *Unit head:* Dr. David Zera, Chair, 203-254-4250, Fax: 203-254-4047, E-mail: dzera@fairfield.edu. *Application contact:* Marianne Gumpper, Director of Graduate and Continuing Studies Admissions, 203-254-4184, Fax: 203-254-4073, E-mail: gradadmis@fairfield.edu.

Fairleigh Dickinson University, College at Florham, Maxwell Becton College of Arts and Sciences, Department of Psychology, Program in Industrial/Organizational Psychology, Madison, NJ 07940-1099. Offers MA, MA/MBA. *Students:* 7 full-time (5 women), 1 (woman) part-time, 1 international. Average age 24. 20 applicants, 70% accepted, 4 enrolled. In 2010, 8 master's awarded. *Entrance requirements:* For master's, GRE General Test. *Application deadline:* Applications are processed on a rolling basis. Application fee: $40. *Application contact:* Susan Brooman, University Director, Graduate Admissions, 973-443-8905, Fax: 973-443-8088, E-mail: grad@fdu.edu.

Florida Institute of Technology, Graduate Programs, College of Psychology and Liberal Arts, School of Psychology, Melbourne, FL 32901-6975. Offers applied behavior analysis (MS); applied behavior analysis and organizational behavior management (MS); behavior analysis (PhD); clinical psychology (Psy D); industrial/organizational psychology (MS, PhD); organizational behavior management (MS). *Accreditation:* APA (one or more programs are accredited). Part-time programs available. *Faculty:* 21 full-time (10 women), 6 part-time/adjunct (2 women). *Students:* 220 full-time (167 women), 11 part-time (10 women); includes 25 minority (5 Black or African American, non-Hispanic/Latino; 4 Asian, non-Hispanic/Latino; 16 Hispanic/Latino), 22 international. Average age 27. 378 applicants, 42% accepted, 77 enrolled. In 2010, 57 master's, 13 doctorates awarded. Terminal master's awarded for partial completion of doctoral program. *Degree requirements:* For master's, comprehensive exam (for some programs), thesis (for some programs), BCBA certification, final exam; for doctorate, comprehensive exam, thesis/dissertation, internship, full time resident of school for 4 years (8 semesters, 3 summers). *Entrance requirements:* For master's, GRE General Test, 3 letters of recommendation, minimum GPA of 3.0, resume, statement of objectives; for doctorate, GRE General Test, GRE Subject Test (psychology), 3 letters of recommendation, minimum GPA of 3.2, resume, statement of objectives. Additional exam requirements/recommendations for international students: Required—TOEFL (minimum score 550 paper-based; 213 computer-based; 79 iBT). *Application deadline:* For fall admission, 4/1 for international students; for spring admission, 9/30 for international students. Applications are processed on a rolling basis. Application fee: $50. Electronic applications accepted. *Expenses:* Tuition: Part-time $1040 per credit hour. Tuition and fees vary according to campus/location. *Financial support:* In 2010–11, 4 fellowships with full and partial tuition reimbursements (averaging $3,775 per year), 32 research assistantships with full and partial tuition reimbursements (averaging $5,602 per year), 8 teaching assistantships with full and partial tuition reimbursements (averaging $4,570 per year) were awarded; career-related internships or fieldwork, institutionally sponsored loans, tuition waivers (partial), unspecified assistantships, and tuition remissions also available. Support available to part-time students. Financial award application deadline: 3/1; financial award applicants required to submit FAFSA. *Faculty research:* Addictions, neuropsychology, child abuse, assessment, psychological trauma. Total annual research expenditures: $1.8 million. *Unit head:* Dr. Mary Beth Kenkel, Dean, 321-674-8142, Fax: 321-674-7105, E-mail: mkenkel@fit.edu. *Application contact:* Cheryl A. Brown, Associate Director of Graduate Admissions, 321-674-7581, Fax: 321-723-9468, E-mail: cbrown@fit.edu.

The George Washington University, Columbian College of Arts and Sciences, Department of Organizational Sciences and Communication, Washington, DC 20052. Offers human resources management (MA); industrial/organizational psychology (PhD); organizational management (MA). Part-time and evening/weekend programs available. *Faculty:* 10 full-time (7 women), 19 part-time/adjunct (11 women). *Students:* 20 full-time (11 women), 48 part-time (42 women); includes 6 Black or African American, non-Hispanic/Latino; 2 Asian, non-Hispanic/Latino; 6 Hispanic/Latino, 6 international. Average age 29. 72 applicants, 88% accepted, 20 enrolled. In 2010, 31 master's awarded. *Degree requirements:* For master's, comprehensive exam. *Entrance requirements:* For master's, GRE General Test, minimum GPA of 3.0. Additional exam requirements/recommendations for international students: Required—TOEFL (minimum score 500 paper-based; 213 computer-based; 80 iBT). *Application deadline:* For fall admission, 1/15 priority date for domestic and international students; for spring admission, 10/1 priority date for domestic students, 9/1 priority date for international students. Applications are processed on a rolling basis. Application fee: $75. Electronic applications accepted. *Financial support:* Federal Work-Study and institutionally sponsored loans available. *Unit head:* Dr. David Costanza, Acting Director, 202-994-1875, Fax: 202-994-1881, E-mail: dconstanz@gwu.edu. *Application contact:* Information Contact, 202-994-1880, Fax: 202-994-1881.

Georgia Institute of Technology, Graduate Studies and Research, College of Sciences, School of Psychology, Atlanta, GA 30332-0001. Offers human computer interaction (MSHCI); psychology (MS, MS Psy, PhD), including engineering psychology (PhD), experimental psychology (PhD), industrial/organizational psychology (PhD). Terminal master's awarded for partial completion of doctoral program. *Degree requirements:* For master's, thesis; for doctorate, thesis/dissertation. *Entrance requirements:* For master's and doctorate, GRE General Test, GRE Subject Test, minimum GPA of 3.0. Additional exam requirements/recommendations for international students: Required—TOEFL. Electronic applications accepted. *Faculty research:* Experimental, industrial-organizational, and engineering psychology; cognitive aging and processes; leadership; human factors.

Goddard College, Graduate Division, Master of Arts in Psychology and Counseling Program, Plainfield, VT 05667-9432. Offers organizational development (MA); psychology and counseling (MA); sexual orientation (MA). Part-time programs available. Postbaccalaureate distance learning degree programs offered (minimal on-campus study). *Degree requirements:* For master's, thesis. *Entrance requirements:* For master's, recent undergraduate degree in psychology or closely related field (preparatory semester at Goddard can substitute), 3 letters of recommendation, interview. Electronic applications accepted.

Graduate School and University Center of the City University of New York, Graduate Studies, Program in Psychology, New York, NY 10016-4039. Offers basic applied neurocognition (PhD); biopsychology (PhD); clinical psychology (PhD); developmental psychology (PhD); environmental psychology (PhD); experimental psychology (PhD); industrial psychology (PhD); learning processes (PhD); neuropsychology (PhD); psychology (PhD); social personality (PhD). *Degree requirements:* For doctorate, one foreign language, thesis/dissertation. *Entrance requirements:* For doctorate, GRE General Test. Additional exam requirements/recommendations for international students: Required—TOEFL. Electronic applications accepted.

Grand Canyon University, College of Doctoral Studies, Phoenix, AZ 85017-1097. Offers business administration (DBA); general psychology (PhD), including cognition and instruction, industrial and organizational psychology; organizational leadership (Ed D, PhD), including behavioral health (PhD), education and effective schools (PhD), higher education (PhD), instructional leadership (PhD), organizational development (Ed D). *Faculty:* 2 full-time (1 woman), 12 part-time/adjunct (5 women). *Students:* 968 part-time (711 women); includes 316 minority (283 Black or African American, non-Hispanic/Latino; 12 American Indian or Alaska Native, non-Hispanic/Latino; 3 Asian, non-Hispanic/Latino; 11 Hispanic/Latino; 1 Native Hawaiian or other Pacific Islander, non-Hispanic/Latino; 6 Two or more races, non-Hispanic/Latino). *Degree requirements:* For doctorate, comprehensive exam, thesis/dissertation. *Entrance requirements:* For doctorate, minimum GPA of 3.4 on earned advanced degree from regionally-accredited institution; transcripts; goals statement. Application fee: $0. *Unit head:* Dr. Hank Radda, Dean, 602-639-7255, E-mail: hank.radda@gcu.edu. *Application contact:* Hector Leal, Associate Vice President of Internet Enrollment, 800-639-7144, E-mail: hector.leal@.gcu.edu.

Hofstra University, College of Liberal Arts and Sciences, Program in Applied Organizational Psychology, Hempstead, NY 11549. Offers PhD. *Students:* 19 full-time (11 women), 11 part-time (7 women); includes 10 minority (6 Black or African American, non-Hispanic/Latino; 4 Asian, non-Hispanic/Latino), 2 international. Average age 30. 20 applicants, 50% accepted, 10 enrolled. In 2010, 8 doctorates awarded. *Degree requirements:* For doctorate, comprehensive exam, thesis/dissertation. *Entrance requirements:* For doctorate, GRE, 2 letters of recommendation; Essay; Interview. Additional exam requirements/recommendations for international students: Required—TOEFL (minimum score 550 paper-based; 213 computer-based; 80 iBT). *Application deadline:* For fall admission, 2/1 for domestic and international students. Application fee: $70 ($75 for international students). Electronic applications accepted. *Expenses:* Tuition: Full-time $18,000; part-time $1000 per credit hour. Required fees: $970; $145 per term. Tuition and fees vary according to program. *Financial support:* In 2010–11, 21 students received support, including 21 fellowships with full and partial tuition reimbursements available (averaging $6,979 per year); research assistantships with full and partial tuition reimbursements available, career-related internships or fieldwork, Federal Work-Study, institutionally sponsored loans, scholarships/grants, tuition waivers (full and partial), and unspecified assistantships also available. Support available to part-time students. Financial award applicants required to submit FAFSA. *Faculty research:* Customer satisfaction, personnel selection and decision-making, team effectiveness, occupational health, positive organizational behavior. *Unit head:* Dr. Terri Shapiro, Associate Director, 516-463-6345, Fax: 516-463-7306, E-mail: psytzs@hofstra.edu. *Application contact:* Carol Drummer, Dean of Graduate Admissions, 516-463-4876, Fax: 516-463-4664, E-mail: gradstudent@hofstra.edu.

Hofstra University, College of Liberal Arts and Sciences, Program in Industrial/Organizational Psychology, Hempstead, NY 11549. Offers MA. Part-time and evening/weekend programs available. *Students:* 48 full-time (32 women), 12 part-time (8 women); includes 15 minority (6 Black or African American, non-Hispanic/Latino; 7 Asian, non-Hispanic/Latino; 2 Hispanic/Latino), 2 international. Average age 24. 60 applicants, 82% accepted, 28 enrolled. In 2010, 20 master's awarded. *Degree requirements:* For master's, comprehensive exam, thesis optional, internship. *Entrance requirements:* For master's, GRE General Test, minimum GPA of 3.0; essay; interview. Additional exam requirements/recommendations for international students: Required—TOEFL (minimum score 550 paper-based; 213 computer-based; 80 iBT). Application fee: $70 ($75 for international students). Electronic applications accepted. *Expenses:* Tuition: Full-time $18,000; part-time $1000 per credit hour. Required fees: $970; $145 per term. Tuition and fees vary according to program. *Financial support:* In 2010–11, 15 students received support, including 11 fellowships with full and partial tuition reimbursements available (averaging $5,357 per year); research assistantships with full and partial tuition reimbursements available, Federal Work-Study, institutionally sponsored loans, scholarships/grants, tuition waivers (full and partial), and unspecified assistantships also available. Support available to part-time students. Financial award applicants required to submit FAFSA. *Faculty research:* Selection interviews, positive organizational behavior, occupational health, multi-source feedback, customer service. *Unit head:* Dr. Comila Shahani-Denning, Director, 516-463-6343, Fax: 516-463-6354, E-mail: psyczs@hofstra.edu. *Application contact:* Carol Drummer, Dean of Graduate Admissions, 516-463-4876, Fax: 516-463-4664, E-mail: gradstudent@hofstra.edu.

Illinois Institute of Technology, Graduate College, College of Psychology, Chicago, IL 60616. Offers clinical psychology (PhD); industrial/organizational psychology (PhD); personnel/human resource development (MS); rehabilitation (PhD); rehabilitation counseling (MS). *Accreditation:* APA (one or more programs are accredited); CORE. Part-time and evening/weekend programs available. *Faculty:* 21 full-time (7 women), 6 part-time/adjunct (4 women). *Students:* 160 full-time (111 women), 39 part-time (33 women); includes 36 minority (8 Black or African American, non-Hispanic/Latino; 1 American Indian or Alaska Native, non-Hispanic/Latino; 15 Asian, non-Hispanic/Latino; 12 Hispanic/Latino), 16 international. Average age 29. 253 applicants, 40% accepted, 43 enrolled. In 2010, 31 master's, 14 doctorates awarded. Terminal master's awarded for partial completion of doctoral program. *Degree requirements:* For master's, thesis (for some programs); for doctorate, comprehensive exam, thesis/dissertation, 96-108 credit hours, internship (for clinical and industrial/organizational specializations). *Entrance requirements:* For master's, GRE General Test (minimum score 900 Quantitative and Verbal, 2.5 Analytical Writing), minimum high school GPA of 3.0; at least 18 credit hours of undergraduate study in psychology with at least one course each in experimental psychology and statistics; official transcripts; 3 letters of recommendation; personal statement; for doctorate, GRE General Test (minimum score 1000 Quantitative and Verbal, 3.0 Analytical Writing), minimum high school GPA of 3.0; at least 18 credit hours of undergraduate study in psychology with at least one course each in experimental psychology and statistics; official transcripts; 3 letters of recommendation; personal statement. Additional exam requirements/recommendations for international students: Required—TOEFL (minimum score 550 paper-based; 213 computer-based; 80 iBT); Recommended—IELTS (minimum score 5.5). *Application deadline:* For fall admission, 1/15 for domestic and international students. Application fee: $50. Electronic applications accepted. *Expenses:* Tuition: Full-time $18,576; part-time $1032 per credit hour. Required fees: $583 per semester. One-time fee: $150. Tuition and fees vary according to program and student level. *Financial support:* In 2010–11, 23 research assistantships with full and partial tuition reimbursements (averaging $223 per year) were awarded; fellowships with full and partial tuition reimbursements, career-related internships or fieldwork, Federal Work-Study, institutionally sponsored loans, scholarships/grants, traineeships, health care benefits, tuition waivers (partial), and unspecified assistantships also available. Support available to part-time students. Financial award application deadline: 1/15; financial award applicants required to submit FAFSA. *Faculty research:* Health psychology, behavioral medicine, attachment, child social and emotional development, educational assessment. Total annual research expenditures: $1.6 million. *Unit head:* Dr. M. Ellen Mitchell, Dean, 312-567-3362, Fax: 312-567-3493, E-mail: mitchelle@iit.edu. *Application contact:* Institute of Psychology Graduate Admissions, 312-567-3500, Fax: 312-567-3493, E-mail: psychology@iit.edu.

Illinois State University, Graduate School, College of Arts and Sciences, Department of Psychology, Normal, IL 61790-2200. Offers psychology (MA, MS), including clinical psychology, counseling psychology, developmental psychology, educational psychology, experimental psychology, measurement-evaluation, organizational-industrial psychology; school psychology (PhD, SSP). *Accreditation:* APA. *Degree requirements:* For master's, thesis or alternative; for doctorate, variable foreign language requirement, thesis/dissertation, 2 terms of residency, internship, practicum. *Entrance requirements:* For master's, GRE General Test, GRE Subject Test, minimum GPA of 3.0 in last 60 hours of course work; for doctorate, GRE General Test. *Faculty research:* Comprehensive evaluation system for the central region professional development grant, Illinois school psychology internship consortium, for children's sake.

Indiana University–Purdue University Indianapolis, School of Science, Department of Psychology, Program in Industrial/Organizational Psychology, Indianapolis, IN 46202-2896. Offers MS. *Faculty:* 5 full-time (3 women). *Students:* 11 full-time (8 women), 4 part-time (all women); includes 2 minority (1 Black or African American, non-Hispanic/Latino; 1 Asian, non-Hispanic/Latino), 2 international. Average age 25. 38 applicants, 32% accepted, 7 enrolled. In 2010, 5 master's awarded. *Entrance requirements:* For master's, GRE General Test (minimum score 1100 verbal and quantitative, quantitative 550), minimum undergraduate GPA of 3.0. Application fee: $55 ($65 for international students). *Financial support:* In 2010–11, 12 students received support; fellowships with partial tuition reimbursements available, research assistantships with partial tuition reimbursements available, teaching assistantships with partial tuition reimbursements available, career-related internships or fieldwork, Federal Work-Study, and institutionally sponsored loans available. Financial award application deadline: 3/1; financial award applicants required to submit FAFSA. *Faculty research:* Stereotyping and prejudice biases, performance feedback, personnel psychology, organizational decision-making, counterproductive behaviors. *Unit head:* Dr. J. Gregor Fetterman, Chairman, 317-274-6945, Fax: 317-274-6756, E-mail: gfetter@iupui.edu. *Application contact:* Dr. J. Gregor Fetterman, Chairman, 317-274-6945, Fax: 317-274-6756, E-mail: gfetter@iupui.edu.

Inter American University of Puerto Rico, Metropolitan Campus, Graduate Programs, Program in Psychology, San Juan, PR 00919-1293. Offers counseling psychology (MA, PhD); industrial/organizational psychology (MA, PhD); labor relations (MA); school psychology (MA, PhD). *Degree requirements:* For master's, comprehensive exam. *Entrance requirements:* For master's, GRE or EXADEP, interview. Electronic applications accepted.

Iona College, School of Arts and Science, Department of Psychology, New Rochelle, NY 10801-1890. Offers experimental psychology (MA); industrial-organizational psychology (MA); mental health counseling (MA); psychology (MA); school psychology (MA). Part-time and evening/weekend programs available. *Faculty:* 10 full-time (7 women), 12 part-time/adjunct (7 women). *Students:* 86 full-time (70 women), 36 part-time (30 women); includes 21 minority (6 Black or African American, non-Hispanic/Latino; 1 American Indian or Alaska Native, non-Hispanic/Latino; 2 Asian, non-Hispanic/Latino; 12 Hispanic/Latino), 2 international. Average age 25. 153 applicants, 78% accepted, 50 enrolled. In 2010, 36 master's awarded. *Degree requirements:* For master's, thesis. *Entrance requirements:* For master's, GRE or minimum GPA of 3.0. Additional exam requirements/recommendations for international students: Required—TOEFL (minimum score 550 paper-based; 213 computer-based). *Application deadline:* Applications are processed on a rolling basis. Application fee: $50. Electronic applications accepted. *Expenses:* Tuition: Part-time $830 per credit. Required fees: $225 per credit. *Financial support:* Career-related internships or fieldwork, tuition waivers (partial), and unspecified assistantships available. Support available to part-time students. Financial award application deadline: 4/15; financial award applicants required to submit FAFSA. *Unit head:* Dr. Paul Greene, Chair, 914-633-2048, E-mail: pgreene@iona.edu. *Application contact:* Veronica Jarek-Prinz, Director of Graduate Admissions, 914-633-2420, Fax: 914-633-2277, E-mail: vjarekprinz@iona.edu.

John F. Kennedy University, Graduate School of Professional Psychology, Program in Organizational Psychology, Pleasant Hill, CA 94523-4817. Offers MA, Certificate. Part-time and evening/weekend programs available. *Degree requirements:* For master's, thesis or alternative. *Entrance requirements:* For master's, interview. Additional exam requirements/recommendations for international students: Required—TOEFL.

Kean University, College of Humanities and Social Sciences, Program in Psychology, Union, NJ 07083. Offers human behavior and organizational psychology (MA); psychological services (MA). Part-time and evening/weekend programs available. *Faculty:* 17 full-time (13 women). *Students:* 24 full-time (20 women), 20 part-time (13 women); includes 12 Black or African American, non-Hispanic/Latino; 5 Asian, non-Hispanic/Latino; 5 Hispanic/Latino; 1 Two or more races, non-Hispanic/Latino, 2 international. Average age 27. 41 applicants, 83% accepted, 26 enrolled. In 2010, 18 master's awarded. *Degree requirements:* For master's, comprehensive exam, thesis, research, two semesters advanced seminar. *Entrance requirements:* For master's, GRE General Test, minimum GPA of 3.0, 2 letters of recommendation, interview, 12 credits in behavioral sciences, transcripts. *Application deadline:* For fall admission, 6/1 for domestic students; for spring admission, 11/1 for domestic students. Application fee: $75 ($150 for international students). Electronic applications accepted. *Expenses:* Tuition, state resident: full-time $10,872; part-time $500 per credit. Tuition, nonresident: full-time $14,736; part-time $614 per credit. Required fees: $2740.80; $125 per credit. Part-time tuition and fees vary according to course load and degree level. *Financial support:* In 2010–11, 2 research assistantships with full tuition reimbursements (averaging $3,263 per year) were awarded; unspecified assistantships also available. Financial award applicants required to submit FAFSA. *Unit head:* Dr. Joanne Walsh, Program Coordinator, 908-737-5888, E-mail: jwalsh@kean.edu. *Application contact:* Reenat Hasan, Pre-Admissions Coordinator, 908-737-5923, Fax: 908-737-5925, E-mail: rhasan@exchange.kean.edu.

Lamar University, College of Graduate Studies, College of Arts and Sciences, Department of Psychology, Beaumont, TX 77710. Offers community/clinical psychology (MS); industrial/organizational psychology (MS). Part-time programs available. *Faculty:* 7 full-time (4 women). *Students:* 17 full-time (12 women), 10 part-time (4 women); includes 2 Black or African American, non-Hispanic/Latino; 2 Hispanic/Latino, 1 international. Average age 29. 25 applicants, 60% accepted, 9 enrolled. In 2010, 26 master's awarded. *Degree requirements:* For master's, thesis, practicum. *Entrance requirements:* For master's, GRE General Test, minimum GPA of 2.75 in last 60 hours of undergraduate course work. Additional exam requirements/recommendations for international students: Required—TOEFL. *Application deadline:* For fall admission, 8/1 for domestic students; for spring admission, 12/1 for domestic students. Application fee: $25 ($50 for international students). *Expenses:* Tuition, state resident: full-time $4160; part-time $208 per credit hour. Tuition, nonresident: full-time $10,360; part-time $518 per credit hour. *Financial support:* In 2010–11, 12 students received support, including 3 teaching assistantships (averaging $4,500 per year); fellowships, research assistantships, career-related internships or fieldwork, Federal Work-Study, scholarships/grants, and tuition waivers (partial) also available. Support available to part-time students. Financial award application deadline: 4/1. *Faculty research:* Groupthink, health psychology, school psychology, behavioral neuroscience. *Application contact:* Assistant Dean, 409-880-7978, E-mail: westgate@hal.lamar.edu.

Louisiana State University and Agricultural and Mechanical College, Graduate School, College of Humanities and Social Sciences, Department of Psychology, Baton Rouge, LA 70803. Offers biological psychology (MA, PhD); clinical psychology (MA, PhD); cognitive psychology (MA, PhD); developmental psychology (MA, PhD); industrial/organizational psychology (MA, PhD); school psychology (MA, PhD). PhD programs offered jointly with Southeastern Louisiana University. *Accreditation:* APA (one or more programs are accredited). *Faculty:* 26 full-time (10 women). *Students:* 96 full-time (68 women), 24 part-time (19 women); includes 7 Black or African American, non-Hispanic/Latino; 2 American Indian or Alaska Native, non-Hispanic/Latino; 1 Asian, non-Hispanic/Latino; 5 Hispanic/Latino, 2 international. Average age 27. 289 applicants, 11% accepted, 17 enrolled. In 2010, 16 master's, 11 doctorates awarded. Terminal master's awarded for partial completion of doctoral program. *Degree requirements:* For master's, thesis; for doctorate, thesis/dissertation, 1 year internship. *Entrance requirements:* For master's and doctorate, GRE General Test, minimum GPA of 3.0. Additional exam requirements/recommendations for international students: Required—TOEFL (minimum score 550 paper-based; 213 computer-based; 79 iBT) or IELTS (minimum score 6.5). *Application deadline:* For fall admission, 1/15 for domestic and international students. Applications are processed on a rolling basis. Application fee: $50 ($70 for international students). Electronic applications accepted. *Financial support:* In 2010–11, 115 students received support, including 5 fellowships (averaging $25,207 per year), 25 research assistantships with partial tuition reimbursements available (averaging $18,083 per year), 48 teaching assistantships with partial tuition reimbursements available (averaging $13,043 per year); career-related internships or fieldwork, Federal Work-Study, institutionally sponsored loans, scholarships/grants, health care benefits, and tuition waivers (full and partial) also available. Financial award applicants required to submit FAFSA. *Faculty research:* Clinical psychology, autism, anxiety, addition, neuropsychology, school psychology, cognitive psychology, experimental psychology. Total annual research expenditures: $1.3 million. *Unit head:* Dr. Robert Matthews, Chair, 225-578-8745, Fax: 225-578-4125, E-mail: psmath@lsu.edu. *Application contact:* Dr. Jason Hicks, Coordinator of Graduate Studies, 225-578-4109, Fax: 225-578-4125, E-mail: jhicks@lsu.edu.

Industrial and Organizational Psychology

Louisiana Tech University, Graduate School, College of Education, Department of Behavioral Sciences and Psychology, Ruston, LA 71272. Offers counseling (MA); counseling psychology (PhD); industrial/organizational psychology (MA); special education (MA). *Accreditation:* APA (one or more programs are accredited). Part-time programs available. *Degree requirements:* For master's, thesis or alternative; for doctorate, thesis/dissertation. *Entrance requirements:* For master's and doctorate, GRE General Test.

Marshall University, Academic Affairs Division; College of Liberal Arts, Department of Psychology, Huntington, WV 25755. Offers clinical psychology (MA); general psychology (MA); industrial and organizational psychology (MA); psychology (Psy D). *Accreditation:* APA. *Faculty:* 17 full-time (5 women), 1 (woman) part-time/adjunct. *Students:* 98 full-time (67 women), 32 part-time (26 women); includes 7 Black or African American, non-Hispanic/Latino; 1 Asian, non-Hispanic/Latino; 1 Hispanic/Latino; 1 Native Hawaiian or other Pacific Islander, non-Hispanic/Latino, 4 international. Average age 28. In 2010, 33 master's, 4 doctorates awarded. *Degree requirements:* For master's, thesis optional. *Entrance requirements:* For master's, GRE General Test or MAT. *Application deadline:* For fall admission, 3/1 for domestic students; for spring admission, 11/1 for domestic students. Application fee: $40. *Financial support:* Teaching assistantships with tuition reimbursements available. *Unit head:* Dr. Steven Mewaldt, Chairperson, 304-696-2777, E-mail: mewaldt@marshall.edu. *Application contact:* Graduate Admissions, 304-746-1900, Fax: 304-746-1902, E-mail: services@marshall.edu.

Massachusetts School of Professional Psychology, Graduate Programs, Boston, MA 02132. Offers applied psychology in higher education student personnel administration (MA); clinical psychology (Psy D); counseling psychology (MA); counseling psychology and community mental health (MA); counseling psychology and global mental health (MA); executive coaching (Graduate Certificate); forensic and counseling psychology (MA); leadership psychology (Psy D); organizational psychology (MA); primary care psychology (MA); respecialization in clinical psychology (Certificate); school psychology (Psy D); MA/CAGS. *Accreditation:* APA. *Faculty:* 24 full-time (11 women), 13 part-time/adjunct (9 women). *Students:* 515. Average age 28. *Degree requirements:* For master's, comprehensive exam (for some programs); for doctorate, thesis/dissertation (for some programs). Application fee: $50. Electronic applications accepted. *Expenses:* Tuition: Full-time $32,352; part-time $1011 per credit. Full-time tuition and fees vary according to degree level. *Financial support:* Teaching assistantships, career-related internships or fieldwork available. Financial award applicants required to submit FAFSA. *Unit head:* Dr. Nicholas A. Covino, President, 617-327-6777, Fax: 617-327-4447. *Application contact:* Admissions and Marketing, 617-327-6777 Ext. 210, Fax: 617-327-4447, E-mail: admissions@mspp.edu.

Middle Tennessee State University, College of Graduate Studies, College of Behavioral and Health Sciences, Department of Psychology, Murfreesboro, TN 37132. Offers clinical psychology (MA); experimental psychology (MA); industrial/organizational psychology (MA); psychology (MA); quantitative psychology (MA); school psychology (MA, Ed S). Part-time and evening/weekend programs available. Postbaccalaureate distance learning degree programs offered. *Faculty:* 36 full-time (16 women), 2 part-time/adjunct (0 women). *Students:* 32 full-time (27 women), 84 part-time (58 women); includes 11 Black or African American, non-Hispanic/Latino; 6 Asian, non-Hispanic/Latino; 2 Hispanic/Latino. Average age 26. 251 applicants, 55% accepted. In 2010, 52 master's, 10 other advanced degrees awarded. *Degree requirements:* For master's, variable foreign language requirement, comprehensive exam, thesis (for some programs). *Entrance requirements:* Additional exam requirements/recommendations for international students: Required—TOEFL (minimum score 525 paper-based; 195 computer-based; 71 iBT) or IELTS (minimum score 6). *Application deadline:* For fall admission, 6/1 for domestic and international students. Applications are processed on a rolling basis. Application fee: $25 ($30 for international students). Electronic applications accepted. *Expenses:* Tuition, state resident: full-time $4632. Tuition, nonresident: full-time $11,520. *Financial support:* In 2010–11, 16 students received support. Career-related internships or fieldwork and institutionally sponsored loans available. Support available to part-time students. Financial award application deadline: 5/1; financial award applicants required to submit FAFSA. *Faculty research:* Industrial/organizational, social/personality/sports, counseling/clinical/school, cognitive/language/learning/perception, developmental/aging. *Unit head:* Dr. Dennis Papini, Chair, 615-898-2706, Fax: 615-898-5027, E-mail: dpapini@mtsu.edu. *Application contact:* Dr. Michael Allen, Dean and Vice Provost for Research, 615-898-2840, Fax: 615-904-8020, E-mail: mallen@mtsu.edu.

Minnesota State University Mankato, College of Graduate Studies, College of Social and Behavioral Sciences, Department of Psychology, Mankato, MN 56001. Offers clinical psychology (MA); industrial/organizational psychology (MA); school psychology (Psy D). Part-time programs available. *Students:* 57 full-time (38 women), 1 part-time (0 women). *Degree requirements:* For master's, one foreign language, comprehensive exam, thesis (for some programs). *Entrance requirements:* For master's, GRE General Test, GRE Subject Test (clinical psychology), minimum GPA of 3.0 during previous 2 years, 3 letters of reference. Additional exam requirements/recommendations for international students: Required—TOEFL. *Application deadline:* For fall admission, 1/1 priority date for domestic students. Applications are processed on a rolling basis. Application fee: $40. Electronic applications accepted. *Financial support:* Research assistantships, teaching assistantships with full tuition reimbursements, career-related internships or fieldwork, Federal Work-Study, institutionally sponsored loans, and unspecified assistantships available. Support available to part-time students. Financial award application deadline: 3/15; financial award applicants required to submit FAFSA. *Faculty research:* Professional competency in hospitals, mood disturbance, 360-degree feedback, employee selection, planning fallacy. *Unit head:* Dr. Barry Ries, Chairperson, 507-389-2724. *Application contact:* 507-389-2321, E-mail: grad@mnsu.edu.

Missouri State University, Graduate College, College of Health and Human Services, Department of Psychology, Springfield, MO 65897. Offers psychology (MS), including clinical psychology, experimental psychology, industrial/organizational psychology. *Degree requirements:* For master's, comprehensive exam, thesis. *Entrance requirements:* For master's, GRE General Test, GRE Subject Test, minimum GPA of 3.25 in major, 3.0 overall; 20 hours of course work in psychology (experimental and statistics). Additional exam requirements/recommendations for international students: Required—TOEFL (minimum score 550 paper-based; 213 computer-based; 79 iBT). Electronic applications accepted. *Expenses:* Tuition, state resident: full-time $3348; part-time $186 per credit hour. Tuition, nonresident: full-time $6696; part-time $372 per credit hour. Required fees: $238 per semester. Tuition and fees vary according to course level, course load and program. *Faculty research:* Work-family conflict, child forensic psychology, sports psychology, body image assessment, visual learning.

Montclair State University, The Graduate School, College of Humanities and Social Sciences, Department of Psychology, Montclair, NJ 07043-1624. Offers educational psychology (MA), including child/adolescent clinical psychology, clinical psychology for Spanish/English bilinguals, educational psychology; psychology (MA), including industrial and organizational psychology; school psychology (Certificate). Part-time and evening/weekend programs available. *Faculty:* 25 full-time (11 women), 37 part-time/adjunct (21 women). *Students:* 43 full-time (31 women), 33 part-time (22 women); includes 8 Black or African American, non-Hispanic/Latino; 3 Asian, non-Hispanic/Latino; 10 Hispanic/Latino, 2 international. Average age 26. 117 applicants, 33% accepted, 24 enrolled. In 2010, 23 master's, 1 other advanced degree awarded. *Degree requirements:* For master's, comprehensive exam, thesis or alternative. *Entrance requirements:* For master's, GRE General Test, 2 letters of recommendation. Additional exam requirements/recommendations for international students: Required—TOEFL (minimum iBT score of 83) or IELTS. *Application deadline:* For fall admission, 6/1 for international students; for spring admission, 11/1 for international students. Applications are processed on a rolling basis. Application fee: $60. Electronic applications accepted. *Expenses:* Tuition, state resident: part-time $501.34 per credit. Tuition, nonresident: part-time $773.88 per credit. Required fees: $71.15 per credit. *Financial support:* In 2010–11, 13 research assistantships with full tuition reimbursements (averaging $7,000 per year) were awarded; Federal Work-Study, scholarships/grants, and unspecified assistantships also available. Support available to part-time students. Financial award application deadline: 3/1; financial award applicants required to submit FAFSA. *Faculty research:* Legal decision-making, leadership development, bias and stereotype threat in the selection process, nature of pre-linguistic thought in infants, lateralized cortical contributions to memory, pediatric neuro-imaging, the production and perception of speech, school-based assessment and intervention for bullying, cognitive processes in reading, identification of autism in toddlers. Total annual research expenditures: $300,000. *Unit head:* Dr. Peter Vietze, Chairperson, 973-655-5201. *Application contact:* Amy Aiello, Director of Admissions and Operations, 973-655-5147, Fax: 973-655-7869, E-mail: graduate.school@montclair.edu.

New York University, Graduate School of Arts and Science, Department of Psychology, New York, NY 10012-1019. Offers cognition and perception (PhD); community psychology (PhD); general psychology (MA); industrial/organizational psychology (MA); psychotherapy and psychoanalysis (Advanced Certificate); social/personality psychology (PhD). Part-time programs available. *Students:* 157 full-time (113 women), 257 part-time (175 women); includes 18 Black or African American, non-Hispanic/Latino; 1 American Indian or Alaska Native, non-Hispanic/Latino; 29 Asian, non-Hispanic/Latino; 24 Hispanic/Latino, 64 international. Average age 32. 834 applicants, 39% accepted, 82 enrolled. In 2010, 73 master's, 14 doctorates, 13 other advanced degrees awarded. Terminal master's awarded for partial completion of doctoral program. *Degree requirements:* For master's, comprehensive exam, thesis or alternative; for doctorate, thesis/dissertation. *Entrance requirements:* For master's, GRE General Test, minimum GPA of 3.0; for doctorate, GRE General Test, GRE Subject Test; for Advanced Certificate, doctoral degree, minimum GPA of 3.0. Additional exam requirements/recommendations for international students: Required—TOEFL. *Application deadline:* For fall admission, 12/15 for domestic students. Application fee: $90. *Financial support:* Fellowships with tuition reimbursements, research assistantships with tuition reimbursements, teaching assistantships with tuition reimbursements, career-related internships or fieldwork, Federal Work-Study, institutionally sponsored loans, scholarships/grants, traineeships, health care benefits, and unspecified assistantships available. Financial award application deadline: 12/15; financial award applicants required to submit FAFSA. *Faculty research:* Vision, memory, social cognition, social and cognitive development, relationships. *Unit head:* Madeline Heilman, Director of PhD Program, 212-998-7900, Fax: 212-995-4018, E-mail: psychq@psych.nyu.edu. *Application contact:* Barry Cohen, Director of MA Program, 212-998-7900, Fax: 212-995-4018, E-mail: psychq@psych.nyu.edu.

North Carolina State University, Graduate School, College of Humanities and Social Sciences, Department of Psychology, Raleigh, NC 27695. Offers developmental psychology (PhD); ergonomics and experimental psychology (PhD); industrial/organizational psychology (PhD); psychology in the public interest (PhD); school psychology (PhD). *Accreditation:* APA. *Degree requirements:* For doctorate, comprehensive exam, thesis/dissertation. *Entrance requirements:* For doctorate, GRE General Test, GRE Subject Test (industrial/organizational psychology), MAT (recommended), minimum GPA of 3.0 in major. Electronic applications accepted. *Faculty research:* Cognitive and social development (human factors, families, the workplace, community issues and health, aging).

Northern Kentucky University, Office of Graduate Programs, College of Arts and Sciences, Program in Industrial-Organizational Psychology, Highland Heights, KY 41099. Offers industrial psychology (Certificate); industrial-organizational psychology (MS); occupational health psychology (Certificate); organizational psychology (Certificate). Part-time and evening/weekend programs available. *Faculty:* 4 full-time (2 women), 1 part-time/adjunct (0 women). *Students:* 10 full-time (6 women), 26 part-time (19 women); includes 5 minority (2 Black or African American, non-Hispanic/Latino; 2 Asian, non-Hispanic/Latino; 1 Two or more races, non-Hispanic/Latino), 2 international. Average age 29. 43 applicants, 49% accepted, 14 enrolled. In 2010, 4 master's, 2 other advanced degrees awarded. *Degree requirements:* For master's, thesis optional, capstone. *Entrance requirements:* For master's, GRE (minimum score 450 verbal, 450 quantitative, 3.5 writing), minimum GPA of 3.0, at least 9 semester hours of undergraduate psychology, 1 course in statistics, 3 letters of recommendation, letter of intent. Additional exam requirements/recommendations for international students: Required—TOEFL (minimum score 550 paper-based; 213 computer-based; 79 iBT); Recommended—IELTS (minimum score 6.5). *Application deadline:* For fall admission, 8/1 for domestic students, 6/1 for international students; for spring admission, 12/1 for domestic students, 10/1 for international students. Applications are processed on a rolling basis. Application fee: $40. Electronic applications accepted. *Expenses:* Tuition, state resident: full-time $7254; part-time $403 per credit hour. Tuition, nonresident: full-time $12,492; part-time $694 per credit hour. Tuition and fees vary according to degree level and program. *Financial support:* Unspecified assistantships available. Financial award applicants required to submit FAFSA. *Faculty research:* Attitude development, employee surveys, factor analysis, the effect of gender and racial stereotypes on employment decisions, social conflict and human factors in the workplace, workplace abuse and bullying, psychological testing/measurement, leader social-cognitive skills. *Unit head:* Dr. Philip Moberg, Director, Master's Program, 859-572-1913, Fax: 859-572-6085, E-mail: mobergp1@nku.edu. *Application contact:* Dr. Peg Griffin, Director of Graduate Programs, 859-572-6934, Fax: 859-572-6670, E-mail: griffinp@nku.edu.

Ohio University, Graduate College, College of Arts and Sciences, Department of Psychology, Program in Organizational Psychology, Athens, OH 45701-2979. Offers PhD. *Students:* 12 full-time (4 women), 2 part-time (1 woman), 1 international. 16 applicants, 25% accepted, 3 enrolled. In 2010, 4 doctorates awarded. *Degree requirements:* For doctorate, one foreign language, comprehensive exam, thesis/dissertation. *Entrance requirements:* For doctorate, GRE General Test, GRE Subject Test. Additional exam requirements/recommendations for international students: Required—TOEFL. *Application deadline:* For fall admission, 1/1 for domestic students. Application fee: $50 ($55 for international students). *Financial support:* In 2010–11, 1 fellowship with full tuition reimbursement (averaging $16,400 per year), 2 teaching assistantships with full tuition reimbursements (averaging $12,000 per year) were awarded; research assistantships with full tuition reimbursements, career-related internships or fieldwork, Federal Work-Study, institutionally sponsored loans, tuition waivers (full), and unspecified assistantships also available. Financial award application deadline: 1/15. *Faculty research:* Performance appraisal, job satisfaction, organizational entry, sexual harassment. *Unit head:* Dr. Keith Markman, Associate Professor, 740-593-1083, Fax: 740-593-0579, E-mail: markman@ohio.edu. *Application contact:* Karyl Jones, Administrative Secretary, 740-593-1090, Fax: 740-593-0579, E-mail: psychology@ohio.edu.

Old Dominion University, College of Sciences, Doctoral Program in Psychology, Norfolk, VA 23529. Offers applied experimental psychology (PhD); human factors psychology (PhD); industrial/organizational psychology (PhD). *Faculty:* 21 full-time (9 women). *Students:* 32 full-time (21 women), 12 part-time (8 women); includes 2 minority (1 Black or African American, non-Hispanic/Latino; 1 Hispanic/Latino), 4 international. Average age 29. 59 applicants, 24% accepted, 12 enrolled. In 2010, 1 doctorate awarded. *Degree requirements:* For doctorate, thesis/dissertation, candidacy exam. *Entrance requirements:* For doctorate, GRE General Test, GRE Subject Test, 3 recommendation letters. Additional exam requirements/recommendations for international students: Required—TOEFL (minimum score 550 paper-based). *Application deadline:* For winter admission, 1/5 for domestic and international students. Application fee: $50. Electronic applications accepted. *Expenses:* Tuition, state resident: full-time $8592; part-time $358 per credit. Tuition, nonresident: full-time $21,672; part-time $903 per credit. Required fees: $119 per semester. One-time fee: $50. *Financial support:* In 2010–11, 33 students received support, including 4 fellowships with full tuition reimbursements available (averaging $18,000 per year), 4 research assistantships with full tuition reimbursements available (averaging $12,000 per year), 25 teaching assistantships with full tuition reimbursements available (averaging $12,000 per year). Financial award application deadline: 1/15. *Faculty research:* Human factors, industrial psychology, organizational psychology, applied experimental (health, developmental, quantitative). Total annual research expenditures: $978,563. *Unit head:* Dr. Bryan E. Porter, Graduate Program Director, 757-683-4458, Fax: 757-683-5087, E-mail: bporter@odu.edu. *Application contact:* Dr. Bryan E. Porter, Graduate Program Director, 757-683-4458, Fax: 757-683-5087, E-mail: bporter@odu.edu.

Philadelphia College of Osteopathic Medicine, Graduate and Professional Programs, Department of Psychology, Philadelphia, PA 19131-1694. Offers clinical psychology (Psy D);

counseling and clinical health psychology (MS); organizational leadership and development (MS); psychology (Certificate, Post-Doctoral Certificate); school psychology (MS, Psy D, Ed S). *Accreditation:* APA. *Degree requirements:* For master's, thesis; for doctorate, comprehensive exam, thesis/dissertation, final project, fieldwork. *Entrance requirements:* For master's, GRE or MAT, minimum GPA of 3.0; course work in biology, chemistry, English, physics; for other advanced degree, PRAXIS. *Faculty research:* Depression in primary care, integrated primary care, geriatric mental health.

See Display on page 932 and Close-Up on page 1167.

Pontifical Catholic University of Puerto Rico, College of Graduate Studies in Behavioral Science and Community Affairs, Program in Industrial Psychology (Doctorate), Ponce, PR 00717-0777. Offers PhD. Part-time and evening/weekend programs available. *Entrance requirements:* For doctorate, EXADEP, minimum GPA of 2.75.

Radford University, College of Graduate and Professional Studies, College of Humanities and Behavioral Sciences, Program in Psychology, Radford, VA 24142. Offers clinical psychology (MA, MS); experimental psychology (MA, MS); general psychology (MS); industrial/organizational psychology (MA, MS). Part-time programs available. *Faculty:* 18 full-time (7 women), 4 part-time/adjunct (2 women). *Students:* 41 full-time (29 women); includes 6 minority (4 Black or African American, non-Hispanic/Latino; 1 Asian, non-Hispanic/Latino; 1 Hispanic/Latino). Average age 23. 107 applicants, 71% accepted, 23 enrolled. In 2010, 21 master's awarded. *Degree requirements:* For master's, comprehensive exam, thesis (for some programs). *Entrance requirements:* For master's, GRE, minimum GPA of 3.0; 3 letters of reference; essay. Additional exam requirements/recommendations for international students: Required—TOEFL (minimum score 550 paper-based; 213 computer-based; 79 iBT). *Application deadline:* For fall admission, 2/15 priority date for domestic students, 12/1 for international students; for spring admission, 7/1 for international students. Applications are processed on a rolling basis. Application fee: $50. Electronic applications accepted. *Expenses:* Tuition, state resident: full-time $5746; part-time $239 per credit hour. Tuition, nonresident: full-time $14,174; part-time $591 per credit hour. Required fees: $2634; $111 per credit hour. *Financial support:* In 2010–11, 33 students received support, including 18 research assistantships with partial tuition reimbursements available (averaging $8,000 per year), 14 teaching assistantships with partial tuition reimbursements available (averaging $8,700 per year); career-related internships or fieldwork, institutionally sponsored loans, scholarships/grants, and unspecified assistantships also available. Financial award application deadline: 3/1; financial award applicants required to submit FAFSA. *Unit head:* Dr. Hilary M. Lips, Chair, 540-831-5387, Fax: 540-831-6113, E-mail: hlips@radford.edu. *Application contact:* Rebecca Conner, Graduate Admissions Office, 540-831-5431, Fax: 540-831-6061, E-mail: gradcollege@radford.edu.

Rice University, Graduate Programs, School of Social Sciences, Department of Psychology, Houston, TX 77251-1892. Offers cognitive sciences (MA, PhD); industrial-organizational/social psychology (MA, PhD); psychology (MA, PhD). Terminal master's awarded for partial completion of doctoral program. *Degree requirements:* For master's, thesis; for doctorate, thesis/dissertation. *Entrance requirements:* For doctorate, GRE General Test, minimum GPA of 3.0. Additional exam requirements/recommendations for international students: Required—TOEFL. Electronic applications accepted. *Faculty research:* Cognitive, cognitive neuropsychology, human factors, human-computer interaction, industrial-organizational psychology.

Roosevelt University, Graduate Division, College of Arts and Sciences, Department of Psychology, Program in Industrial/Organizational Psychology, Chicago, IL 60605. Offers MA, PhD.

St. Cloud State University, School of Graduate Studies, College of Social Sciences, Program in Industrial-Organizational Psychology, St. Cloud, MN 56301-4498. Offers MS. *Degree requirements:* For master's, thesis or alternative. *Entrance requirements:* For master's, GRE General Test, minimum GPA of 2.75. Additional exam requirements/recommendations for international students: Required—Michigan English Language Assessment Battery; Recommended—TOEFL (minimum score 550 paper-based; 213 computer-based), IELTS (minimum score 6.5). Electronic applications accepted.

Saint Joseph's University, College of Arts and Sciences, Organization Development and Leadership Programs, Philadelphia, PA 19131-1395. Offers adult learning and training (MS, Certificate); organization dynamics and leadership (MS, Certificate); organizational psychology and development (MS, Certificate). Part-time and evening/weekend programs available. Post-baccalaureate distance learning degree programs offered (no on-campus study). *Faculty:* 1 (woman) full-time, 6 part-time/adjunct (3 women). *Students:* 20 full-time (10 women), 112 part-time (81 women); includes 32 Black or African American, non-Hispanic/Latino; 1 American Indian or Alaska Native, non-Hispanic/Latino; 2 Asian, non-Hispanic/Latino; 6 Hispanic/Latino; 3 Two or more races, non-Hispanic/Latino, 11 international. Average age 36. 57 applicants, 84% accepted, 42 enrolled. In 2010, 23 master's awarded. *Entrance requirements:* For master's, GRE (if GPA less than 2.7), minimum GPA of 2.7, 2 letters of recommendation, resume. Additional exam requirements/recommendations for international students: Required—TOEFL (minimum score 550 paper-based; 213 computer-based; 79 iBT). *Application deadline:* For fall admission, 7/15 priority date for domestic students, 4/15 for international students; for winter admission, 1/15 for international students; for spring admission, 11/15 priority date for domestic students, 10/15 for international students. Applications are processed on a rolling basis. Application fee: $35. Electronic applications accepted. *Expenses:* Tuition: Part-time $729 per credit. Tuition and fees vary according to course load, degree level and program. *Financial support:* Applicants required to submit FAFSA. *Unit head:* Dr. Felice Tilin, Director, 610-660-1575, E-mail: ftilin@sju.edu. *Application contact:* Kate McConnell, Director, Graduate College of Arts and Sciences Admissions and Retention, 610-660-3184, Fax: 610-660-3230, E-mail: kate.mcconnell@sju.edu.

Saint Louis University, Graduate Education, College of Arts and Sciences and Graduate Education, Department of Psychology, St. Louis, MO 63103-2097. Offers clinical psychology (MS-R, PhD); experimental psychology (MS-R, PhD); industrial-organizational psychology (PhD); psychology (PhD). *Accreditation:* APA (one or more programs are accredited). Part-time programs available. *Degree requirements:* For master's, comprehensive exam, thesis; for doctorate, thesis/dissertation, clinical internship (for clinical psychology PhD). *Entrance requirements:* For master's, GRE General Test, interview, letters of recommendation, resume; for doctorate, GRE General Test, interview, letters of recommendation, resumé, transcripts, goal statement. Additional exam requirements/recommendations for international students: Required—TOEFL (minimum score 550 paper-based; 213 computer-based). Electronic applications accepted. *Faculty research:* Violence and trauma; neural basis of learning and memory function; eating disorders; body image and health behavior; prejudice, stereotyping, and victimization; memory, cognitive aging and language processing.

Saint Mary's University, Faculty of Science, Department of Psychology, Halifax, NS B3H 3C3, Canada. Offers applied psychology (M Sc, PhD), including industrial/organizational psychology (M Sc). Part-time programs available. *Degree requirements:* For master's, thesis, 500-hour internship; for doctorate, comprehensive exam, thesis/dissertation, research project. *Entrance requirements:* For master's and doctorate, GRE General Test. *Faculty research:* Assessment, health psychology, social psychology, cognition.

St. Mary's University, Graduate School, Department of Psychology, Program in Industrial/Organizational Psychology, San Antonio, TX 78228-8507. Offers MA, MS. Part-time programs available. *Degree requirements:* For master's, comprehensive exam, thesis optional. *Entrance requirements:* For master's, GRE General Test. Additional exam requirements/recommendations for international students: Required—TOEFL (minimum score 550 paper-based; 213 computer-based; 80 iBT). Electronic applications accepted.

San Diego State University, Graduate and Research Affairs, College of Sciences, Department of Psychology, San Diego, CA 92182. Offers clinical psychology (MS, PhD); industrial and organizational psychology (MS); program evaluation (MS); psychology (MA). PhD offered jointly with University of California, San Diego. *Accreditation:* APA (one or more programs are accredited). Terminal master's awarded for partial completion of doctoral program. *Degree requirements:* For master's, thesis, oral exam; for doctorate, thesis/dissertation. *Entrance requirements:* For master's, GRE General Test, GRE Subject Test, 3 letters of recommendation; for doctorate, GRE General Test, GRE Subject Test, minimum GPA of 3.0, 3 letters of recommendation. Additional exam requirements/recommendations for international students: Required—TOEFL. Electronic applications accepted.

San Francisco State University, Division of Graduate Studies, College of Behavioral and Social Sciences, Department of Psychology, San Francisco, CA 94132-1722. Offers clinical psychology (MS); developmental psychology (MA); industrial/organizational psychology (MS); psychological research (MA); school psychology (MS); social psychology (MA). *Financial support:* Teaching assistantships available. Financial award application deadline: 3/1. *Unit head:* Dr. Julia Lewis, Chair, 415-338-7555, E-mail: jmlewis@sfsu.edu. *Application contact:* Leslye M. Tinson, Assistant to the Chair, 415-338-7555, E-mail: ltinson@sfsu.edu.

San Jose State University, Graduate Studies and Research, College of Social Sciences, Department of Psychology, San Jose, CA 95192-0001. Offers clinical psychology (MS); experimental psychology (MA); industrial/organizational psychology (MS); psychology (MA). *Degree requirements:* For master's, comprehensive exam, thesis (for some programs). *Entrance requirements:* For master's, GRE General Test, minimum GPA of 3.0. Electronic applications accepted. *Faculty research:* Drug and alcohol abuse, neurohormonal mechanisms in motion sickness, behavior modification, sleep research, genetics.

Seattle Pacific University, Industrial Organizational Psychology Program, Seattle, WA 98119-1997. Offers MA, PhD. *Faculty:* 7 full-time (2 women), 2 part-time/adjunct (0 women). *Students:* 44 full-time (35 women), 30 part-time (24 women); includes 19 minority (5 Black or African American, non-Hispanic/Latino; 8 Asian, non-Hispanic/Latino; 1 Hispanic/Latino; 5 Two or more races, non-Hispanic/Latino), 2 international. Average age 29. 74 applicants, 39% accepted, 29 enrolled. In 2010, 16 master's awarded. *Degree requirements:* For master's, research project; for doctorate, thesis/dissertation, field placement. *Entrance requirements:* Additional exam requirements/recommendations for international students: Required—TOEFL (minimum score 550 paper-based; 213 computer-based). *Application deadline:* For fall admission, 2/15 for domestic and international students. Application fee: $50. Electronic applications accepted. *Financial support:* In 2010–11, 44 students received support. Applicants required to submit FAFSA. *Unit head:* Dr. Robert B. McKenna, Chair, 206-281-2629, E-mail: rmckenna@spu.edu. *Application contact:* The Graduate Center, 206-281-2091.

Southern Illinois University Edwardsville, Graduate School, School of Education, Department of Psychology, Program in Industrial-Organizational Psychology, Edwardsville, IL 62026-0001. Offers MA. Part-time programs available. *Students:* 15 full-time (9 women), 12 part-time (10 women); includes 4 minority (1 Black or African American, non-Hispanic/Latino; 3 Hispanic/Latino), 1 international. Average age 26. In 2010, 11 master's awarded. *Degree requirements:* For master's, thesis. *Entrance requirements:* For master's, GRE. Additional exam requirements/recommendations for international students: Required—TOEFL (minimum score 550 paper-based; 213 computer-based; 79 iBT), IELTS (minimum score 6.5). *Application deadline:* For fall admission, 2/1 for domestic and international students. Application fee: $30. Electronic applications accepted. *Expenses:* Tuition, state resident: full-time $6012; part-time $1503 per semester. Tuition, nonresident: full-time $15,030; part-time $3758 per semester. Required fees: $1711; $675 per semester. *Financial support:* Career-related internships or fieldwork, Federal Work-Study, institutionally sponsored loans, scholarships/grants, traineeships, and unspecified assistantships available. Support available to part-time students. Financial award application deadline: 3/1; financial award applicants required to submit FAFSA. *Unit head:* Dr. Cynthia Nordstrom, Director, 618-650-2202, E-mail: cnordst@siue.edu. *Application contact:* Dr. Cynthia Nordstrom, Director, 618-650-2202, E-mail: cnordst@siue.edu.

Springfield College, Graduate Programs, Programs in Psychology and Counseling, Springfield, MA 01109-3797. Offers athletic counseling (M Ed, MS, CAGS); industrial/organizational psychology (M Ed, MS, CAGS); marriage and family therapy (M Ed, MS, CAGS); mental health counseling (M Ed, MS, CAGS); school guidance and counseling (M Ed, MS, CAGS); student personnel in higher education (M Ed, MS, CAGS). Part-time programs available. *Degree requirements:* For master's, research project, portfolio. *Entrance requirements:* Additional exam requirements/recommendations for international students: Required—TOEFL (minimum score 550 paper-based; 213 computer-based). Electronic applications accepted.

Teachers College, Columbia University, Graduate Faculty of Education, Department of Organization and Leadership, Program in Social and Organizational Psychology, New York, NY 10027-6696. Offers change leadership (MA); social-organizational psychology (MA). *Faculty:* 8 full-time (5 women), 22 part-time/adjunct (10 women). *Students:* 122 full-time (71 women), 113 part-time (85 women); includes 59 minority (11 Black or African American, non-Hispanic/Latino; 20 Asian, non-Hispanic/Latino; 23 Hispanic/Latino; 1 Native Hawaiian or other Pacific Islander, non-Hispanic/Latino; 4 Two or more races, non-Hispanic/Latino), 40 international. Average age 28. 202 applicants, 62% accepted, 69 enrolled. In 2010, 111 master's awarded. Terminal master's awarded for partial completion of doctoral program. *Degree requirements:* For master's, comprehensive exam. *Entrance requirements:* For master's, GRE, MAT, or GMAT, minimum GPA of 3.0. *Application deadline:* For fall admission, 1/15 priority date for domestic students. Application fee: $65. Electronic applications accepted. *Expenses:* Tuition: Full-time $28,272; part-time $1178 per credit. Required fees: $756; $378 per semester. *Financial support:* Fellowships, research assistantships, career-related internships or fieldwork, Federal Work-Study, institutionally sponsored loans, and tuition waivers (full and partial) available. Support available to part-time students. Financial award application deadline: 2/1. *Faculty research:* Conflict resolution, human resource and organization development, management competence, organizational culture, leadership. *Unit head:* Dr. W. Warner Burke, Director of the Graduate Programs in Social-Organizational Psychology, 212-678-3831, E-mail: wwb3@columbia.edu. *Application contact:* Lynda Hallmark, Program Manager of the Social-Organizational Psychology Program, 212-678-3273, Fax: 212-678-3273, E-mail: hallmark@tc.edu.

Temple University, College of Education, Department of Psychological Studies in Education, Program in Adult and Organizational Development, Philadelphia, PA 19122-6096. Offers Ed M. Part-time and evening/weekend programs available. *Students:* 2 full-time (both women), 17 part-time (14 women); includes 6 Black or African American, non-Hispanic/Latino. 17 applicants, 53% accepted, 7 enrolled. In 2010, 15 master's awarded. *Degree requirements:* For master's, thesis or alternative. *Entrance requirements:* For master's, GRE General Test or MAT, minimum GPA of 3.0. Additional exam requirements/recommendations for international students: Required—TOEFL (minimum score 550 paper-based; 213 computer-based; 79 iBT). *Application deadline:* For fall admission, 6/1 for domestic students, 12/15 for international students; for spring admission, 11/1 for domestic students, 8/1 for international students. Applications are processed on a rolling basis. Application fee: $50. Electronic applications accepted. *Financial support:* Fellowships, research assistantships, teaching assistantships available. Financial award application deadline: 1/15; financial award applicants required to submit FAFSA. *Unit head:* Dr. Joseph Folger, Head, 215-204-1890, E-mail: joseph.folger@temple.edu. *Application contact:* Dr. Margo Greicar, Director for Graduate Academic & Student Affairs, 215-204-8011, Fax: 215-204-4383, E-mail: margo.greicar@temple.edu.

Texas A&M University, College of Liberal Arts, Department of Psychology, College Station, TX 77843. Offers behavioral and cellular neuroscience (PhD); clinical psychology (PhD); cognitive psychology (PhD); developmental psychology (PhD); industrial/organizational psychology (PhD); social psychology (PhD). *Accreditation:* APA. *Faculty:* 39. *Students:* 91 full-time (57 women), 14 part-time (11 women); includes 7 Black or African American, non-Hispanic/Latino; 8 Asian, non-Hispanic/Latino; 17 Hispanic/Latino, 7 international. In 2010, 12 doctorates awarded. *Degree requirements:* For doctorate, comprehensive exam (for some programs), thesis/dissertation. *Entrance requirements:* For doctorate, GRE General Test. Additional exam requirements/recommendations for international students: Required—TOEFL.

Industrial and Organizational Psychology

Texas A&M University (continued)
Application deadline: For fall admission, 1/5 for domestic and international students. Application fee: $50 ($75 for international students). Electronic applications accepted. *Financial support:* Fellowships with partial tuition reimbursements, research assistantships with partial tuition reimbursements, teaching assistantships with partial tuition reimbursements, career-related internships or fieldwork, institutionally sponsored loans, health care benefits, and unspecified assistantships available. Financial award application deadline: 1/5; financial award applicants required to submit FAFSA. *Unit head:* Ludy T. Benjamin, Head, 979-845-2540, Fax: 979-845-4727, E-mail: lbenjamin@tamu.edu. *Application contact:* Julie Austin, Graduate Admissions Supervisor, 979-458-1710, Fax: 979-845-4727, E-mail: gradadv@psyc.tamu.edu.

Union Institute & University, Programs in Psychology and Counseling, Brattleboro, VT 05301. Offers clinical mental health counseling (MA); clinical psychology (Psy D); counseling psychology (MA); counselor education and supervision (CAGS); developmental psychology (MA); educational psychology (MA); human development and wellness (CAGS); organizational psychology (MA); psychology education (CAGS). Psy D offered in Ohio and Vermont. Postbaccalaureate distance learning degree programs offered (minimal on-campus study). *Faculty:* 6 full-time (4 women), 17 part-time/adjunct (6 women). *Students:* 93 full-time (66 women), 11 part-time (10 women); includes 14 minority (6 Black or African American, non-Hispanic/Latino; 1 Asian, non-Hispanic/Latino; 7 Hispanic/Latino). Average age 44. In 2010, 21 master's awarded. *Degree requirements:* For master's, thesis, internship (depending on concentration); for doctorate, thesis/dissertation, internship, practicum. *Application deadline:* Applications are processed on a rolling basis. Application fee: $50. Electronic applications accepted. *Expenses:* Tuition: Full-time $16,430; part-time $685 per credit hour. Required fees: $174; $44 per term. Tuition and fees vary according to course load, degree level and program. *Financial support:* Federal Work-Study available. Financial award applicants required to submit FAFSA. *Unit head:* Dr. Bill Lax, Dean, 802-254-0152, E-mail: bill.lax@myunion.edu. *Application contact:* Diane Robinson, Director of Admissions, 888-828-8575, E-mail: diane.robinson@myunion.edu.

University at Albany, State University of New York, College of Arts and Sciences, Department of Psychology, Albany, NY 12222-0001. Offers autism (Certificate); biopsychology (PhD); clinical psychology (PhD); general/experimental psychology (PhD); industrial/organizational psychology (PhD); psychology (MA); social/personality psychology (PhD). *Accreditation:* APA (one or more programs are accredited). *Degree requirements:* For doctorate, thesis/dissertation. *Entrance requirements:* For doctorate, GRE General Test, GRE Subject Test. Additional exam requirements/recommendations for international students: Required—TOEFL (minimum score 550 paper-based; 213 computer-based). Electronic applications accepted.

The University of Akron, Graduate School, Buchtel College of Arts and Sciences, Department of Psychology, Program in Industrial/Organizational Psychology, Akron, OH 44325. Offers MA, PhD. *Students:* 29 full-time (21 women), 7 part-time (6 women); includes 2 Black or African American, non-Hispanic/Latino; 3 Asian, non-Hispanic/Latino; 1 Two or more races, non-Hispanic/Latino, 1 international. Average age 24. 62 applicants, 0% accepted, 0 enrolled. In 2010, 5 master's, 6 doctorates awarded. Terminal master's awarded for partial completion of doctoral program. *Degree requirements:* For master's, thesis optional, thesis or specialty exam; for doctorate, one foreign language, comprehensive exam, thesis/dissertation. *Entrance requirements:* For master's, GRE General Test, minimum GPA of 2.75, three letters of recommendation, personal statement, curriculum vitae; for doctorate, GRE General Test, minimum graduate GPA of 3.25, three letters of recommendation, personal statement, curriculum vitae. Additional exam requirements/recommendations for international students: Required—TOEFL (minimum score 550 paper-based; 213 computer-based; 79 iBT). *Application deadline:* For fall admission, 1/15 for domestic and international students. Application fee: $30 ($40 for international students). Electronic applications accepted. *Expenses:* Tuition, state resident: full-time $6800; part-time $378 per credit hour. Tuition, nonresident: full-time $11,644; part-time $647 per credit hour. Required fees: $1265. One-time fee: $30 full-time. *Financial support:* Fellowships with full tuition reimbursements, research assistantships with full tuition reimbursements, teaching assistantships with full tuition reimbursements available. *Faculty research:* Personnel selection, performance management, leadership, self-regulation, affect. *Unit head:* Dr. Rosalie Hall, Coordinator, 330-972-8375, E-mail: rhall@uakron.edu. *Application contact:* Dr. Rosalie Hall, Coordinator, 330-972-8375, E-mail: rhall@uakron.edu.

The University of Alabama in Huntsville, School of Graduate Studies, College of Liberal Arts, Department of Psychology, Huntsville, AL 35899. Offers experimental psychology (MA); industrial and organizational psychology (MA). Part-time and evening/weekend programs available. *Faculty:* 7 full-time (4 women). *Students:* 6 full-time (3 women), 4 part-time (3 women). Average age 24. 9 applicants, 56% accepted, 3 enrolled. In 2010, 6 master's awarded. *Degree requirements:* For master's, comprehensive exam, thesis or alternative, oral and written exams. *Entrance requirements:* For master's, GRE General Test, 15 hours of course work in psychology, minimum GPA of 3.25, sample of written work. Additional exam requirements/recommendations for international students: Required—TOEFL (minimum score 500 paper-based; 173 computer-based; 62 iBT). *Application deadline:* For fall admission, 7/15 for domestic students, 4/1 for international students; for spring admission, 11/30 for domestic students, 9/1 for international students. Applications are processed on a rolling basis. Application fee: $40 ($50 for international students). Electronic applications accepted. *Expenses:* Tuition, state resident: full-time $7250; part-time $407.75 per credit hour. Tuition, nonresident: full-time $17,358; part-time $970.05 per credit hour. Required fees: $246.80 per semester. Tuition and fees vary according to course load and program. *Financial support:* In 2010–11, 8 students received support, including 2 teaching assistantships with full tuition reimbursements available (averaging $8,460 per year); career-related internships or fieldwork, Federal Work-Study, institutionally sponsored loans, scholarships/grants, health care benefits, tuition waivers (full), and unspecified assistantships also available. Support available to part-time students. Financial award application deadline: 4/1; financial award applicants required to submit FAFSA. *Faculty research:* Personal and social cognition, development and aging, human factors, perception, biological psychology: hormones and behavior. Total annual research expenditures: $228,509. *Unit head:* Dr. Jeffrey Neuschatz, Assistant Chair, 256-824-2321, Fax: 256-824-2387, E-mail: neuschaj@uah.edu. *Application contact:* Kathy Biggs, Graduate Studies Admissions Manager, 256-824-6199, Fax: 256-824-6405, E-mail: deangrad@uah.edu.

University of Baltimore, Graduate School, The Yale Gordon College of Liberal Arts, Program in Applied Psychology, Baltimore, MD 21201-5779. Offers applied psychology (MS), including counseling, industrial and organizational psychology, psychological applications. Part-time and evening/weekend programs available. *Degree requirements:* For master's, thesis optional. *Entrance requirements:* For master's, GRE, minimum GPA of 3.0. Additional exam requirements/recommendations for international students: Required—TOEFL (minimum score 550 paper-based; 213 computer-based). Electronic applications accepted. *Expenses:* Contact institution. *Faculty research:* Participatory decision making, counter productive workplace behavior, organizational consulting, substance abuse treatment, cognitive functioning in head injured.

University of Central Florida, College of Sciences, Department of Psychology, Program in Industrial/Organizational Psychology, Orlando, FL 32816. Offers MS, PhD. Part-time and evening/weekend programs available. *Students:* 70 full-time (42 women), 9 part-time (6 women); includes 7 Black or African American, non-Hispanic/Latino; 5 Asian, non-Hispanic/Latino; 9 Hispanic/Latino; 4 international. Average age 27. 84 applicants, 29% accepted, 14 enrolled. In 2010, 18 master's awarded. *Degree requirements:* For master's, comprehensive exam, thesis, practicum. *Entrance requirements:* For master's, GRE General Test, minimum GPA of 3.0 in last 60 hours, resume. Additional exam requirements/recommendations for international students: Required—TOEFL. *Application deadline:* For fall admission, 2/1 for domestic students. Application fee: $30. Electronic applications accepted. *Expenses:* Tuition, state resident: part-time $256.56 per credit hour. Tuition, nonresident: part-time $1011.52 per credit hour. Part-time tuition and fees vary according to program. *Financial support:* In 2010–11, 53 students received support, including 6 fellowships (averaging $9,400 per year), 27 research assistantships with partial tuition reimbursements available (averaging $11,400 per year), 37 teaching assistantships (averaging $7,200 per year); career-related internships or fieldwork, Federal Work-Study, institutionally sponsored loans, tuition waivers (partial), and unspecified assistantships also available. Financial award application deadline: 3/1; financial award applicants required to submit FAFSA. *Faculty research:* Sports psychology, electronic selection systems, team training, stress effects, psychometrics. *Unit head:* Program Director. *Application contact:* Program Director.

University of Connecticut, Graduate School, College of Liberal Arts and Sciences, Department of Psychology, Storrs, CT 06269. Offers behavioral neuroscience (PhD); biopsychology (PhD); clinical psychology (MA, PhD); cognition and instruction (PhD); developmental psychology (MA, PhD); ecological psychology (PhD); experimental psychology (PhD); general psychology (MA, PhD); health psychology (Graduate Certificate); industrial/organizational psychology (PhD); language and cognition (PhD); neuroscience (PhD); occupational health psychology (Graduate Certificate); social psychology (MA, PhD). *Accreditation:* APA. Terminal master's awarded for partial completion of doctoral program. *Degree requirements:* For master's, comprehensive exam; for doctorate, thesis/dissertation. *Entrance requirements:* For master's and doctorate, GRE General Test, GRE Subject Test. Additional exam requirements/recommendations for international students: Required—TOEFL (minimum score 550 paper-based; 213 computer-based). Electronic applications accepted.

University of Detroit Mercy, College of Liberal Arts and Education, Department of Psychology, Program in Industrial/Organizational Psychology, Detroit, MI 48221. Offers MA. *Entrance requirements:* For master's, GRE General Test, minimum GPA of 3.0.

University of Guelph, Graduate Studies, College of Social and Applied Human Sciences, Department of Psychology, Guelph, ON N1G 2W1, Canada. Offers applied social psychology (MA, PhD); clinical psychology applied development emphasis (PhD); clinical psychology applied developmental emphasis (MA); industrial/organizational psychology (MA, PhD); neuroscience and applied cognitive science (MA, PhD). *Degree requirements:* For master's, thesis; for doctorate, comprehensive exam, thesis/dissertation. *Entrance requirements:* For master's, GRE General Test, GRE Subject Test, minimum B+ average during previous 2 years of course work; for doctorate, GRE General Test, GRE Subject Test, minimum A- average. Additional exam requirements/recommendations for international students: Required—TOEFL (minimum score 89 iBT). Electronic applications accepted. *Faculty research:* Organizational psychology, reading comprehension and mathematical ability, drug addiction and relapse, gender issues and culture, memory, clinical psychology.

University of Houston, College of Liberal Arts and Social Sciences, Department of Psychology, Houston, TX 77204. Offers clinical psychology (PhD); developmental psychology (PhD); industrial/organizational psychology (PhD); psychology (MA); social psychology (PhD). *Accreditation:* APA (one or more programs are accredited). *Faculty:* 28 full-time (12 women), 7 part-time/adjunct (4 women). *Students:* 117 full-time (86 women), 22 part-time (16 women); includes 7 Black or African American, non-Hispanic/Latino; 10 Asian, non-Hispanic/Latino; 16 Hispanic/Latino; 4 Two or more races, non-Hispanic/Latino, 17 international. Average age 27. 460 applicants, 6% accepted, 28 enrolled. In 2010, 19 master's, 20 doctorates awarded. *Degree requirements:* For master's, comprehensive exam, thesis; for doctorate, comprehensive exam, thesis/dissertation. *Entrance requirements:* For master's, GRE General Test, career statement, 3 letters of recommendation; for doctorate, GRE General Test, 3 letters of recommendation. Additional exam requirements/recommendations for international students: Required—TOEFL (minimum score 550 paper-based; 79 iBT). *Application deadline:* For fall admission, 12/15 for domestic and international students. Application fee: $40 ($75 for international students). Electronic applications accepted. *Expenses:* Tuition, state resident: full-time $8592; part-time $358 per credit hour. Tuition, nonresident: full-time $16,032; part-time $668 per credit hour. Required fees: $2889. Tuition and fees vary according to course load and program. *Financial support:* In 2010–11, 23 fellowships with full tuition reimbursements (averaging $2,828 per year), 39 research assistantships with full tuition reimbursements (averaging $7,864 per year), 62 teaching assistantships with full tuition reimbursements (averaging $9,312 per year) were awarded; career-related internships or fieldwork, Federal Work-Study, institutionally sponsored loans, scholarships/grants, health care benefits, and unspecified assistantships also available. Support available to part-time students. Financial award application deadline: 2/1; financial award applicants required to submit FAFSA. *Faculty research:* Health psychology, depression, child/family process, organizational effectiveness, close relationships. *Unit head:* Dr. David Francis, Chairperson, 713-743-7036, Fax: 713-743-8588, E-mail: dfrancis@uh.edu. *Application contact:* Patti Tolar, Academic Affairs Coordinator, 713-743-5544, Fax: 713-743-8588, E-mail: ptolar@uh.edu.

University of Maryland, Baltimore County, Graduate School, College of Arts, Humanities and Social Sciences, Department of Psychology, Program in Industrial Organizational Psychology, Rockville, MD 20850. Offers MPS. Part-time and evening/weekend programs available. *Faculty:* 2 full-time (1 woman), 5 part-time/adjunct (2 women). *Students:* 10 full-time (6 women), 27 part-time (21 women); includes 5 Black or African American, non-Hispanic/Latino; 2 Asian, non-Hispanic/Latino; 9 Hispanic/Latino, 1 international. Average age 28. 49 applicants, 59% accepted, 14 enrolled. *Entrance requirements:* Additional exam requirements/recommendations for international students: Required—TOEFL. *Application deadline:* For fall admission, 3/1 for domestic students, 1/1 for international students. Application fee: $50. Electronic applications accepted. *Unit head:* Dr. Diane Alonso, Program Director, 301-738-6318, E-mail: dalonso@umbc.edu. *Application contact:* Sonya Crosby, Assistant Director, 301-738-6184, E-mail: scrosby@umbc.edu.

University of Maryland, College Park, Academic Affairs, College of Behavioral and Social Sciences, Department of Psychology, College Park, MD 20742. Offers clinical psychology (PhD); developmental psychology (PhD); experimental psychology (PhD); industrial psychology (MA, MS, PhD); social psychology (PhD). *Accreditation:* APA (one or more programs are accredited). *Faculty:* 70 full-time (34 women), 16 part-time/adjunct (10 women). *Students:* 83 full-time (63 women), 6 part-time (4 women); includes 4 Black or African American, non-Hispanic/Latino; 6 Asian, non-Hispanic/Latino; 6 Hispanic/Latino, 13 international. 653 applicants, 4% accepted, 13 enrolled. In 2010, 8 master's, 18 doctorates awarded. *Degree requirements:* For master's, thesis; for doctorate, variable foreign language requirement, comprehensive exam, thesis/dissertation. *Entrance requirements:* For master's and doctorate, GRE General Test, GRE Subject Test, minimum GPA of 3.5, research and/or work experience, 3 letters of recommendation. *Application deadline:* For fall admission, 12/1 for domestic and international students. Applications are processed on a rolling basis. Application fee: $75. Electronic applications accepted. *Expenses:* Tuition, state resident: part-time $471 per credit hour. Tuition, nonresident: part-time $1016 per credit hour. Required fees: $337 per term. *Financial support:* In 2010–11, 14 fellowships with full and partial tuition reimbursements (averaging $20,179 per year), 5 research assistantships (averaging $18,414 per year), 54 teaching assistantships (averaging $17,209 per year) were awarded; career-related internships or fieldwork, Federal Work-Study, and scholarships/grants also available. Support available to part-time students. Financial award applicants required to submit FAFSA. *Faculty research:* Social stereotyping and prejudice, anxiety disorders, auditory neuroethology, counseling and social psychology. Total annual research expenditures: $4 million. *Unit head:* Thomas S. Wallsten, Chair, 301-405-3562, Fax: 301-314-9566, E-mail: twallst@umd.edu. *Application contact:* Dean of Graduate School, 301-405-0358, Fax: 301-314-9305.

University of Minnesota, Twin Cities Campus, Graduate School, College of Liberal Arts, Department of Psychology, Program in Industrial/Organizational Psychology, Minneapolis, MN 55455-0213. Offers PhD. *Degree requirements:* For doctorate, comprehensive exam, thesis/dissertation. *Entrance requirements:* For doctorate, GRE General Test, GRE Subject Test (recommended), 12 credits of upper-level psychology courses, including a course in statistics or psychological measurement. Additional exam requirements/recommendations for international students: Required—TOEFL (minimum score 550 paper-based; 213 computer-based; 79 iBT).

University of Missouri–St. Louis, College of Arts and Sciences, Department of Psychology, St. Louis, MO 63121. Offers behavioral neuroscience (PhD); clinical community psychology (PhD); clinical psychology respecialization (Certificate); general psychology (MA); industrial/organizational psychology (PhD); trauma studies (Certificate). *Accreditation:* APA (one or more programs are accredited). Evening/weekend programs available. *Faculty:* 19 full-time (9 women), 5 part-time/adjunct (3 women). *Students:* 44 full-time (34 women), 35 part-time (25 women); includes 7 minority (1 Black or African American, non-Hispanic/Latino; 1 American Indian or Alaska Native, non-Hispanic/Latino; 3 Asian, non-Hispanic/Latino; 2 Hispanic/Latino). Average age 27. 220 applicants, 10% accepted, 18 enrolled. In 2010, 10 master's, 6 doctorates awarded. Terminal master's awarded for partial completion of doctoral program. *Degree requirements:* For master's, thesis; for doctorate, thesis/dissertation. *Entrance requirements:* For master's, GRE General Test, 3 letters of recommendation; for doctorate, GRE General Test, GRE Subject Test, 3 letters of recommendation. Additional exam requirements/recommendations for international students: Required—TOEFL (minimum score 550 paper-based; 213 computer-based). *Application deadline:* For fall admission, 1/15 for domestic and international students. Application fee: $35 ($40 for international students). Electronic applications accepted. *Expenses:* Tuition, state resident: full-time $5522; part-time $306.80 per credit hour. Tuition, nonresident: full-time $14,253; part-time $792.10 per credit hour. Required fees: $658; $49 per credit hour. One-time fee: $12. Tuition and fees vary according to program. *Financial support:* In 2010–11, 5 research assistantships with full and partial tuition reimbursements (averaging $13,352 per year), 26 teaching assistantships with full and partial tuition reimbursements (averaging $11,000 per year) were awarded; fellowships with full tuition reimbursements also available. Financial award applicants required to submit FAFSA. *Faculty research:* Bereavement and loss, neuroscience, post-traumatic stress disorder, conflict and negotiation, social psychology. *Unit head:* Dr. George Taylor, Chair, 314-516-5391, Fax: 314-516-5392, E-mail: umslpsychology@msx.umsl.edu. *Application contact:* 314-516-5458, Fax: 314-516-6996, E-mail: gradadm@umsl.edu.

University of Nebraska at Omaha, Graduate Studies, College of Arts and Sciences, Department of Psychology, Omaha, NE 68182. Offers developmental psychology (PhD); industrial/organizational psychology (MS, PhD); psychobiology (PhD); psychology (MA); school psychology (MS, Ed S). Part-time programs available. *Faculty:* 18 full-time (8 women). *Students:* 50 full-time (38 women), 41 part-time (32 women); includes 9 minority (2 Black or African American, non-Hispanic/Latino; 1 American Indian or Alaska Native, non-Hispanic/Latino; 1 Asian, non-Hispanic/Latino; 5 Hispanic/Latino), 2 international. Average age 26. 92 applicants, 39% accepted, 34 enrolled. In 2010, 17 master's, 2 doctorates, 6 other advanced degrees awarded. *Degree requirements:* For master's, comprehensive exam, thesis (for some programs). *Entrance requirements:* For master's, GRE General Test, GRE Subject Test, previous course work in psychology, including statistics and a laboratory course; minimum GPA of 3.0, 3 letters of recommendation; for doctorate, GRE General Test. Additional exam requirements/recommendations for international students: Required—TOEFL (minimum score 500 paper-based; 173 computer-based; 61 iBT). *Application deadline:* For fall admission, 1/5 for domestic students. Application fee: $45. Electronic applications accepted. *Financial support:* In 2010–11, 66 students received support; fellowships, research assistantships with tuition reimbursements available, teaching assistantships with tuition reimbursements available, career-related internships or fieldwork, Federal Work-Study, institutionally sponsored loans, scholarships/grants, tuition waivers (partial), and unspecified assistantships available. Support available to part-time students. Financial award application deadline: 3/1; financial award applicants required to submit FAFSA. *Unit head:* Dr. Brigette Ryalls, Chairperson, 402-554-2592. *Application contact:* Dr. Joseph Brown, Student Contact, 402-554-2592.

University of New Haven, Graduate School, College of Arts and Sciences, Program in Industrial and Organizational Psychology, West Haven, CT 06516-1916. Offers conflict management (MA); human resource management (MA); industrial organizational psychology (MA); organizational development (MA); psychology of conflict management (Certificate). Part-time and evening/weekend programs available. *Students:* 75 full-time (54 women), 29 part-time (19 women); includes 7 Black or African American, non-Hispanic/Latino; 1 American Indian or Alaska Native, non-Hispanic/Latino; 1 Asian, non-Hispanic/Latino; 4 Hispanic/Latino, 13 international. Average age 28. 70 applicants, 100% accepted, 33 enrolled. In 2010, 44 master's, 1 other advanced degree awarded. *Degree requirements:* For master's, thesis or alternative. *Entrance requirements:* Additional exam requirements/recommendations for international students: Required—TOEFL (minimum score 520 paper-based; 190 computer-based; 70 iBT); Recommended—IELTS (minimum score 5.5). *Application deadline:* For fall admission, 5/31 for international students; for winter admission, 10/15 for international students; for spring admission, 1/15 for international students. Applications are processed on a rolling basis. Application fee: $50. Electronic applications accepted. *Expenses:* Contact institution. *Financial support:* Research assistantships with partial tuition reimbursements, teaching assistantships with partial tuition reimbursements, career-related internships or fieldwork, Federal Work-Study, scholarships/grants, tuition waivers, and unspecified assistantships available. Support available to part-time students. Financial award applicants required to submit FAFSA. *Unit head:* Dr. Stuart D. Sidle, Coordinator, 203-932-7341. *Application contact:* Eloise Gormley, Information Contact, 203-932-7449.

The University of North Carolina at Charlotte, Graduate School, College of Arts and Sciences, Department of Psychology, Charlotte, NC 28223-0001. Offers community/clinical psychology (MA); health psychology (PhD); industrial/organizational psychology (MA); organizational science (PhD). Part-time programs available. *Faculty:* 27 full-time (11 women), 1 part-time/adjunct (0 women). *Students:* 67 full-time (50 women), 18 part-time (14 women); includes 19 minority (8 Black or African American, non-Hispanic/Latino; 3 Asian, non-Hispanic/Latino; 4 Hispanic/Latino; 1 Native Hawaiian or other Pacific Islander, non-Hispanic/Latino; 3 Two or more races, non-Hispanic/Latino), 3 international. Average age 29. 317 applicants, 9% accepted, 21 enrolled. In 2010, 14 master's, 1 doctorate awarded. *Degree requirements:* For master's, thesis; for doctorate, thesis/dissertation. *Entrance requirements:* For master's, GRE General Test, GRE Subject Test, minimum GPA of 3.0 in undergraduate major, 2.8 overall. Additional exam requirements/recommendations for international students: Required—TOEFL (minimum score 557 paper-based; 220 computer-based; 83 iBT). *Application deadline:* Applications are processed on a rolling basis. Application fee: $55. Electronic applications accepted. *Expenses:* Tuition, state resident: full-time $3464. Tuition, nonresident: full-time $14,297. Required fees: $2094. Tuition and fees vary according to course load. *Financial support:* In 2010–11, 44 students received support, including 12 research assistantships (averaging $14,191 per year), 31 teaching assistantships (averaging $10,710 per year); career-related internships or fieldwork, Federal Work-Study, institutionally sponsored loans, scholarships/grants, and administrative assistantships also available. Support available to part-time students. Financial award application deadline: 4/1; financial award applicants required to submit FAFSA. *Faculty research:* Health psychology, industrial-organizational psychology, cognitive science. Total annual research expenditures: $435,127. *Unit head:* Dr. Brian L. Cutler, Chair, 704-687-4731, Fax: 704-687-3096, E-mail: blcutler@uncc.edu. *Application contact:* Kathy B. Giddings, Director of Graduate Admissions, 704-687-5503, Fax: 704-687-3279, E-mail: gradadm@uncc.edu.

University of Oklahoma, College of Arts and Sciences, Department of Psychology, Program in Psychology, Norman, OK 73019-0390. Offers industrial and organizational psychology (MS, PhD); psychology (MS, PhD). *Students:* 68 full-time (27 women), 8 part-time (5 women); includes 7 minority (2 Black or African American, non-Hispanic/Latino; 2 American Indian or Alaska Native, non-Hispanic/Latino; 3 Asian, non-Hispanic/Latino), 5 international. Average age 26. 75 applicants, 20% accepted, 14 enrolled. In 2010, 6 master's, 11 doctorates awarded. *Entrance requirements:* Additional exam requirements/recommendations for international students: Required—TOEFL (minimum score 550 paper-based; 213 computer-based; 79 iBT). *Application deadline:* For fall admission, 4/1 priority date for domestic students, 4/1 for international students; for spring admission, 11/1 for domestic students, 9/1 for international students. Applications are processed on a rolling basis. Application fee: $40 ($90 for international students). Electronic applications accepted. *Expenses:* Tuition, state resident: full-time $3893; part-time $162.20 per credit hour. Tuition, nonresident: full-time $14,167; part-time $590.30 per credit hour. Required fees: $2523; $94.60 per credit hour. Tuition and fees vary according to course load and degree level. *Financial support:* Institutionally sponsored loans, scholarships/grants, health care benefits, and unspecified assistantships available. Financial award applicants required to submit FAFSA. *Faculty research:* Leadership, self concept, basic memory findings, human performance, multivariate statistics. *Unit head:* Dr. Jorge Mendoza, Chair, 405-325-4511, Fax: 405-325-4737, E-mail: jmendoza@ou.edu. *Application contact:* Kathryn Paine, Graduate Admissions Coordinator, 405-325-4512, Fax: 405-325-4737, E-mail: kpaine@ou.edu.

University of Phoenix, School of Advanced Studies, Phoenix, AZ 85034-7209. Offers business administration (DBA); education (Ed D); educational leadership (Ed D), including curriculum and instruction, educational technology; health administration (DHA); higher education administration (PhD); industrial organizational psychology (PhD); nursing (PhD); organizational leadership and technology (DM), including information systems and technology, organizational leadership. Evening/weekend programs available. Postbaccalaureate distance learning degree programs offered. *Students:* 6,882 full-time (4,598 women); includes 2,871 minority (2,251 Black or African American, non-Hispanic/Latino; 50 American Indian or Alaska Native, non-Hispanic/Latino; 133 Asian, non-Hispanic/Latino; 378 Hispanic/Latino; 46 Native Hawaiian or other Pacific Islander, non-Hispanic/Latino; 13 Two or more races, non-Hispanic/Latino), 375 international. Average age 46. *Degree requirements:* For doctorate, thesis/dissertation. *Entrance requirements:* For doctorate, master's degree from accredited university, minimum master's GPA of 3.0, 3 years' professional work experience, laptop computer, membership in research library. Additional exam requirements/recommendations for international students: Required—TOEFL (minimum paper score 550, computer score 213, iBT 79), Test of English for International Communication, or IELTS. *Application deadline:* Applications are processed on a rolling basis. Application fee: $45. Electronic applications accepted. *Expenses:* Contact institution. *Financial support:* Scholarships/grants available. Financial award applicants required to submit FAFSA. *Unit head:* Dr. Jeremy Moreland, Dean/Executive Director, 480-557-3231, E-mail: jeremy.moreland@phoenix.edu. *Application contact:* Dr. Jeremy Moreland, Dean/Executive Director, 480-557-3231, E-mail: jeremy.moreland@phoenix.edu.

University of Phoenix–Chattanooga Campus, College of Social Services, Chattanooga, TN 37421-3707. Offers industrial/organizational psychology (PhD); psychology (MSP). Postbaccalaureate distance learning degree programs offered.

University of Phoenix–Milwaukee Campus, College of Social Sciences, Milwaukee, WI 53045. Offers industrial/organizational psychology (PhD); psychology (MS).

University of Phoenix–Washington D.C. Campus, College of Social Sciences, Washington, DC 20001. Offers industrial/organizational psychology (PhD); psychology (MS).

University of Puerto Rico, Río Piedras, College of Social Sciences, Department of Psychology, San Juan, PR 00931-3300. Offers clinical psychology (MA); industrial organizational psychology (MA); investigative academic psychology (MA); psychology (PhD); social-community psychology (MA). Part-time programs available. *Degree requirements:* For master's, comprehensive exam, thesis; for doctorate, comprehensive exam, thesis/dissertation, internship. *Entrance requirements:* For master's, GRE or PAEG, interview, minimum GPA of 3.0; for doctorate, GRE or PAEG, interview, master's degree, minimum GPA of 3.0. *Faculty research:* Intervention on Depressed Latino Youth, biosychosocial training.

University of South Africa, College of Economic and Management Sciences, Pretoria, South Africa. Offers accounting (D Admin, D Com); accounting science (DA); auditing (D Admin, D Com); business administration (M Tech); business economics (D Admin); business leadership (DBL); business management (D Admin, D Com); economic management analysis (M Tech); economics (D Admin, D Com, PhD); human resource development (M Tech); industrial psychology (D Admin, D Com, PhD); logistics (D Com); marketing (M Tech); public administration (D Admin, D Com, DPA, PhD); public management (M Tech); quantitative management (D Admin, D Com); real estate (M Tech); statistics (D Admin, PhD); tourism management (D Admin, D Com); transport economics (D Admin, D Com).

University of South Africa, College of Human Sciences, Pretoria, South Africa. Offers adult education (M Ed); African languages (MA, PhD); African politics (MA, PhD); Afrikaans (MA, PhD); ancient history (MA, PhD); ancient Near Eastern studies (MA, PhD); anthropology (MA, PhD); applied linguistics (MA); Arabic (MA, PhD); archaeology (MA); art history (MA); Biblical archaeology (MA); Biblical studies (M Th, D Th, PhD); Christian spirituality (M Th, D Th); church history (M Th, D Th); classical studies (MA, PhD); clinical psychology (MA); communication (MA, PhD); comparative education (M Ed, Ed D); consulting psychology (D Admin, D Com, PhD); curriculum studies (M Ed, Ed D); development studies (M Admin, MA, D Admin, PhD); didactics (M Ed, Ed D); education (M Tech); education management (M Ed, Ed D); educational psychology (M Ed); English (MA); environmental education (M Ed); French (MA, PhD); German (MA, PhD); Greek (MA); guidance and counseling (M Ed); health studies (MA, PhD), including health sciences education (MA), health services management (MA), medical and surgical nursing science (critical care general) (MA), midwifery and neonatal nursing science (MA), trauma and emergency care (MA); history (MA, PhD); history of education (Ed D); inclusive education (M Ed, Ed D); information and communications technology policy and regulation (MA); information science (MA, MIS, PhD); international politics (MA, PhD); Islamic studies (MA, PhD); Italian (MA, PhD); Judaica (MA, PhD); linguistics (MA, PhD); mathematical education (M Ed); mathematics education (MA); missiology (M Th, D Th); modern Hebrew (MA, PhD); musicology (MA, MMus, D Mus, PhD); natural science education (M Ed); New Testament (M Th, D Th); Old Testament (D Th); pastoral therapy (M Th, D Th); philosophy (MA); philosophy of education (M Ed, Ed D); politics (MA, PhD); Portuguese (MA, PhD); practical theology (M Th, D Th); psychology (MA, MS, PhD); psychology of education (M Ed, Ed D); public health (MA); religious studies (MA, D Th, PhD); Romance languages (MA); Russian (MA, PhD); Semitic languages (MA, PhD); social behavior studies in HIV/AIDS (MA); social science (mental health) (MA); social science in development studies (MA); social science in psychology (MA); social science in social work (MA); social science in sociology (MA); social work (MSW, DSW, PhD); socio-education (M Ed, Ed D); sociolinguistics (MA); sociology (MA, PhD); Spanish (MA, PhD); systematic theology (M Th, D Th); TESOL (teaching English to speakers of other languages) (MA); theological ethics (M Th, D Th); theory of literature (MA, PhD); urban ministries (D Th); urban ministry (M Th).

University of South Florida, Graduate School, College of Arts and Sciences, Department of Psychology, Tampa, FL 33620-9951. Offers clinical psychology (PhD); cognitive and neural sciences (PhD); industrial-organizational psychology (PhD). *Accreditation:* APA. *Faculty:* 17 full-time (4 women). *Students:* 101 full-time (55 women), 24 part-time (16 women); includes 3 Black or African American, non-Hispanic/Latino; 9 Asian, non-Hispanic/Latino; 8 Hispanic/Latino; 1 Two or more races, non-Hispanic/Latino, 12 international. Average age 28. 452 applicants, 8% accepted, 22 enrolled. In 2010, 11 doctorates awarded. *Degree requirements:* For doctorate, comprehensive exam, thesis/dissertation, internship. *Entrance requirements:* For doctorate, GRE General Test, minimum GPA of 3.0 in last 60 hours of course work. Additional exam requirements/recommendations for international students: Required—TOEFL (minimum score 550 paper-based; 213 computer-based). *Application deadline:* For fall admission, 12/1 for domestic and international students. Application fee: $30. Electronic applications accepted. *Expenses:* Contact institution. *Financial support:* In 2010–11, 18 research assistantships (averaging $13,719 per year), 63 teaching assistantships with tuition reimbursements (averaging $13,724 per year) were awarded; tuition waivers (partial) and unspecified assistantships also available. Financial award applicants required to submit FAFSA. *Faculty research:* Clinical, cognitive, neuroscience, social, industrial/organizational. Total annual research expenditures: $3.5 million. *Unit head:* Michael Brannick, Chairperson, 813-974-0478, Fax: 813-974-4617, E-mail: mbrannick@usf.edu. *Application contact:* William Sacco, Program Director, 813-974-0375, Fax: 813-974-4617, E-mail: sacco@cas.usf.edu.

The University of Tennessee, Graduate School, College of Business Administration, Program in Industrial and Organizational Psychology, Knoxville, TN 37996. Offers PhD. *Degree*

Industrial and Organizational Psychology

The University of Tennessee (continued)
requirements: For doctorate, thesis/dissertation. *Entrance requirements:* For doctorate, GRE General Test, minimum GPA of 2.7. Additional exam requirements/recommendations for international students: Required—TOEFL. Electronic applications accepted. *Expenses:* Tuition, state resident: full-time $7440; part-time $414 per credit hour. Tuition, nonresident: full-time $22,478; part-time $1250 per credit hour. Required fees: $922; $43 per credit hour. Tuition and fees vary according to program.

The University of Tennessee at Chattanooga, Graduate School, College of Arts and Sciences, Department of Psychology, Chattanooga, TN 37403. Offers industrial/organizational psychology (MS); research psychology (MS). Part-time and evening/weekend programs available. *Faculty:* 6 full-time (1 woman). *Students:* 46 full-time (27 women), 6 part-time (3 women); includes 6 minority (3 Black or African American, non-Hispanic/Latino; 1 Asian, non-Hispanic/Latino; 1 Hispanic/Latino; 1 Two or more races, non-Hispanic/Latino), 1 international. Average age 25. 60 applicants, 70% accepted, 32 enrolled. In 2010, 24 master's awarded. *Degree requirements:* For master's, thesis (for some programs), practicum (industrial/organizational psychology). *Entrance requirements:* For master's, GRE General Test, minimum GPA of 2.5 on all undergraduate coursework or 3.0 in senior year. Additional exam requirements/recommendations for international students: Required—TOEFL (minimum score 550 paper-based; 213 computer-based; 79 iBT), IELTS (minimum score 6). *Application deadline:* For fall admission, 8/1 priority date for domestic students, 6/1 for international students; for spring admission, 12/1 priority date for domestic students, 10/1 for international students. Applications are processed on a rolling basis. Application fee: $35. Electronic applications accepted. *Financial support:* In 2010–11, 20 research assistantships with full and partial tuition reimbursements (averaging $5,500 per year) were awarded; career-related internships or fieldwork, scholarships/grants, and unspecified assistantships also available. Support available to part-time students. *Faculty research:* Decision processes, philosophical psychology, memory, social cognition, employee selection. Total annual research expenditures: $35,031. *Unit head:* Dr. Paul J. Watson, Department Head, 423-425-4262, Fax: 423-425-4284, E-mail: paul-watson@utc.edu. *Application contact:* Dr. Jerald Ainsworth, Dean of Graduate Studies, 423-425-4478, Fax: 423-425-5223, E-mail: jerald-ainsworth@utc.edu.

The University of Texas at Arlington, Graduate School, College of Science, Department of Psychology, Arlington, TX 76019. Offers experimental psychology (PhD); health psychology (PhD); industrial organizational psychology (MS); psychology (MS). Part-time programs available. *Faculty:* 21 full-time (8 women), 1 part-time/adjunct (0 women). *Students:* 62 full-time (41 women), 10 part-time (7 women); includes 5 Black or African American, non-Hispanic/Latino; 2 Asian, non-Hispanic/Latino; 6 Hispanic/Latino, 7 international. 72 applicants, 90% accepted, 22 enrolled. In 2010, 16 master's, 6 doctorates awarded. Terminal master's awarded for partial completion of doctoral program. *Degree requirements:* For master's, comprehensive exam or thesis; for doctorate, thesis/dissertation (for some programs). *Entrance requirements:* For master's and doctorate, GRE General Test, minimum GPA of 3.0 in last 60 hours of course work. Additional exam requirements/recommendations for international students: Required—TOEFL (minimum score 550 paper-based; 213 computer-based). *Application deadline:* For fall admission, 6/15 for domestic students. Applications are processed on a rolling basis. Application fee: $35 ($50 for international students). *Expenses:* Tuition, state resident: full-time $7500. Tuition, nonresident: full-time $13,080. International tuition: $13,250 full-time. *Financial support:* In 2010–11, 4 fellowships (averaging $1,000 per year), 2 research assistantships with tuition reimbursements (averaging $15,000 per year), 28 teaching assistantships with tuition reimbursements (averaging $15,000 per year) were awarded; career-related internships or fieldwork, Federal Work-Study, institutionally sponsored loans, scholarships/grants, traineeships, tuition waivers (partial), and unspecified assistantships also available. Financial award application deadline: 6/1; financial award applicants required to submit FAFSA. *Unit head:* Dr. Robert Gatchel, Chair, 817-272-2281, Fax: 817-272-2364, E-mail: gatchel@uta.edu. *Application contact:* Dr. Jared Kenworthy, Graduate Advisor, Psychological Sciences, 817-272-2281, Fax: 817-272-2364, E-mail: kenworthy@uta.edu.

University of Tulsa, Graduate School, College of Arts and Sciences, Department of Psychology, Program in Industrial/Organizational Psychology, Tulsa, OK 74104-3189. Offers MA, PhD, JD/MA. Part-time programs available. *Faculty:* 6 full-time (2 women). *Students:* 19 full-time (13 women), 5 part-time (4 women); includes 1 Black or African American, non-Hispanic/Latino; 1 American Indian or Alaska Native, non-Hispanic/Latino; 1 Asian, non-Hispanic/Latino; 1 Hispanic/Latino, 2 international. Average age 25. 47 applicants, 49% accepted, 7 enrolled. In 2010, 4 master's, 2 doctorates awarded. Terminal master's awarded for partial completion of doctoral program. *Degree requirements:* For master's, comprehensive exam, thesis (for some programs), 200 hour internship; for doctorate, comprehensive exam, thesis/dissertation. *Entrance requirements:* For master's and doctorate, GRE General Test. Additional exam requirements/recommendations for international students: Required—TOEFL (minimum score 575 paper-based; 231 computer-based; 91 iBT), IELTS (minimum score 6.5). *Application deadline:* For fall admission, 1/15 for domestic and international students. Application fee: $40. Electronic applications accepted. *Expenses:* Tuition: Full-time $16,902; part-time $939 per credit hour. Required fees: $1020; $4 per credit hour. Tuition and fees vary according to course load. *Financial support:* In 2010–11, 19 students received support, including 4 fellowships with full and partial tuition reimbursements available (averaging $4,187 per year), 1 research assistantship with full and partial tuition reimbursement available (averaging $14,400 per year), 17 teaching assistantships with full and partial tuition reimbursements available (averaging $11,710 per year); career-related internships or fieldwork, Federal Work-Study, scholarships/grants, health care benefits, tuition waivers (full and partial), and unspecified assistantships also available. Support available to part-time students. Financial award application deadline: 2/1; financial award applicants required to submit FAFSA. *Faculty research:* Personnel testing and selection, training, performance appraisal, organizational development, job attitudes and motivation, leadership. Total annual research expenditures: $1 million. *Unit head:* Dr. Robert Tett, Director, 918-631-2737, Fax: 918-631-2833, E-mail: robert-tett@utulsa.edu. *Application contact:* Information Contact, 800-882-4723, E-mail: grad@utulsa.edu.

University of West Florida, College of Arts and Sciences: Arts, Department of Psychology, Pensacola, FL 32514-5750. Offers counseling (MA); counseling-licensed mental health counselor (MA); general (MA); industrial-organizational (MA). Part-time programs available. *Faculty:* 10 full-time (4 women), 1 part-time/adjunct (0 women). *Students:* 67 full-time (45 women), 39 part-time (30 women); includes 16 minority (5 Black or African American, non-Hispanic/Latino; 2 Asian, non-Hispanic/Latino; 5 Hispanic/Latino; 1 Native Hawaiian or other Pacific Islander, non-Hispanic/Latino; 3 Two or more races, non-Hispanic/Latino), 4 international. Average age 26. 143 applicants, 53% accepted, 32 enrolled. In 2010, 34 master's awarded. *Degree requirements:* For master's, thesis (for some programs). *Entrance requirements:* For master's, GRE General Test, GRE Subject Test, minimum GPA of 3.0. Additional exam requirements/recommendations for international students: Required—TOEFL (minimum score 550 paper-based; 213 computer-based). *Application deadline:* For fall admission, 6/1 for domestic students, 5/15 for international students; for spring admission, 10/1 for domestic and international students. Applications are processed on a rolling basis. Application fee: $30. *Expenses:* Tuition, state resident: full-time $4982; part-time $208 per credit hour. Tuition, nonresident: full-time $20,059; part-time $836 per credit hour. Required fees: $1365; $57 per credit hour. *Financial support:* In 2010–11, 19 fellowships with partial tuition reimbursements (averaging $1,090 per year), 30 research assistantships with partial tuition reimbursements (averaging $3,500 per year), 5 teaching assistantships with partial tuition reimbursements (averaging $4,552 per year) were awarded; career-related internships or fieldwork and unspecified assistantships also available. Financial award application deadline: 4/15; financial award applicants required to submit FAFSA. *Faculty research:* Prose recall, brain imaging, peak performance, biofeedback and pain control, comparable worth. Total annual research expenditures: $15,000. *Unit head:* Dr. Laura L. K. Bryan, Chairperson, 850-474-3493. *Application contact:* Terry McCray, Assistant Director of Graduate Admissions, 850-473-7718, Fax: 850-473-7714, E-mail: gradadmissions@uwf.edu.

University of Wisconsin–Oshkosh, The Office of Graduate Studies, College of Letters and Science, Department of Psychology, Oshkosh, WI 54901. Offers experimental psychology (MS); industrial/organizational psychology (MS). *Degree requirements:* For master's, thesis. *Entrance requirements:* For master's, GRE, 10 semester hours of undergraduate course work in psychology. Additional exam requirements/recommendations for international students: Required—TOEFL (minimum score 550 paper-based; 213 computer-based; 79 iBT). Electronic applications accepted. *Faculty research:* Performance evaluation, training, biological bases of behavior, tactile perception, aging.

Valdosta State University, Department of Psychology and Counseling, Valdosta, GA 31698. Offers clinical/counseling psychology (MS); industrial/organizational psychology (MS); school counseling (M Ed, Ed S); school psychology (Ed S). Part-time and evening/weekend programs available. *Faculty:* 19 full-time (6 women). *Students:* 65 full-time (47 women), 41 part-time (35 women); includes 38 minority (29 Black or African American, non-Hispanic/Latino; 3 Asian, non-Hispanic/Latino; 4 Hispanic/Latino; 2 Two or more races, non-Hispanic/Latino). Average age 27. 61 applicants, 51% accepted, 27 enrolled. In 2010, 43 master's awarded. *Degree requirements:* For master's, thesis or alternative, comprehensive written and/or oral exams; for Ed S, thesis. *Entrance requirements:* For master's and Ed S, GRE General Test or MAT. Additional exam requirements/recommendations for international students: Required—TOEFL (minimum score 523 paper-based; 193 computer-based). *Application deadline:* For fall admission, 7/1 for domestic and international students; for spring admission, 11/15 for domestic and international students. Applications are processed on a rolling basis. Application fee: $35. Electronic applications accepted. *Expenses:* Tuition, state resident: full-time $5256; part-time $197 per credit hour. Tuition, nonresident: full-time $14,490; part-time $710 per credit hour. Required fees: $855 per semester. Tuition and fees vary according to course load and campus/location. *Financial support:* In 2010–11, 6 students received support, including 2 research assistantships with full tuition reimbursements available (averaging $3,652 per year); institutionally sponsored loans and unspecified assistantships also available. Support available to part-time students. Financial award application deadline: 7/1; financial award applicants required to submit FAFSA. *Faculty research:* Using Bender-Gestalt to predict graphomotor dimensions of the draw-a-person test, neurobehavioral hemispheric dominance. *Unit head:* Dr. Robert Bauer, Chair, 229-333-5930, Fax: 229-259-5576, E-mail: bbauer@valdosta.edu. *Application contact:* Rebecca Waters, Coordinator of Graduate Admissions, 229-333-5694, Fax: 229-245-3853, E-mail: rlwaters@valdosta.edu.

Walden University, Graduate Programs, School of Psychology, Minneapolis, MN 55401. Offers clinical child psychology (Post-Doctoral Certificate); clinical psychology (MS, Post-Doctoral Certificate), including counseling (MS); counseling psychology (Post-Doctoral Certificate); forensic psychology (MS), including forensic psychology in the community, general program, mental health applications, program planning and evaluation in forensic settings, psychology and legal systems; general psychology (Post-Doctoral Certificate); health psychology (Post-Doctoral Certificate); organizational psychology (Post-Doctoral Certificate); organizational psychology and development (Postbaccalaureate Certificate); psychology (MS, PhD), including clinical psychology (PhD), counseling psychology (PhD), crisis management and response (MS), general program (MS), general psychology (PhD), health psychology, leadership development and coaching (MS), media psychology (MS), organizational psychology (PhD), organizational psychology and development (MS), organizational psychology and nonprofit management (MS), program evaluation and research (MS), psychology of culture (MS), psychology, public administration, and social change (MS), social psychology (MS), terrorism and security (MS); teaching online (Post-Master's Certificate). Part-time and evening/weekend programs available. Postbaccalaureate distance learning degree programs offered (minimal on-campus study). *Faculty:* 41 full-time (25 women), 254 part-time/adjunct (131 women). *Students:* 3,463 full-time (2,737 women), 1,400 part-time (1,130 women); includes 1,491 Black or African American, non-Hispanic/Latino; 59 American Indian or Alaska Native, non-Hispanic/Latino; 89 Asian, non-Hispanic/Latino; 283 Hispanic/Latino; 76 Two or more races, non-Hispanic/Latino, 126 international. Average age 40. In 2010, 559 master's, 100 doctorates awarded. Terminal master's awarded for partial completion of doctoral program. *Degree requirements:* For master's, thesis optional; for doctorate, thesis/dissertation, residency. *Entrance requirements:* For master's, bachelor's degree or equivalent in related field; minimum GPA of 2.5; official transcripts; goal statement; access to computer and Internet; for doctorate, master's degree or equivalent in related field; minimum GPA of 3.0; 3 years of related professional/academic experience (preferred). Additional exam requirements/recommendations for international students: Required—TOEFL (minimum score 550 paper-based; 213 computer-based), IELTS (minimum score 6.5), TOEFL (minimum score 550 paper-based; 213 computer-based), IELTS (minimum score 6.5), or Michigan English Language Assessment Battery (minimum score 82). *Application deadline:* Applications are processed on a rolling basis. Application fee: $50. Electronic applications accepted. *Expenses:* Tuition: Full-time $10,274; part-time $445 per credit. Tuition and fees vary according to course load, degree level and program. *Financial support:* In 2010–11, 1 fellowship was awarded; Federal Work-Study, scholarships/grants, unspecified assistantships, and family tuition reduction, active duty/veteran tuition reduction, group tuition reduction, interest-free payment plans also available. Support available to part-time students. Financial award applicants required to submit FAFSA. *Unit head:* Dr. Melanie Storms, Associate Dean, 800-925-3368. *Application contact:* Jennifer Hall, Vice President of Enrollment Management, 866-4-WALDEN, E-mail: info@waldenu.edu.

Wayne State University, College of Liberal Arts and Sciences, Department of Psychology, Program in Industrial and Organizational Psychology, Detroit, MI 48202. Offers MA, MS, PhD. *Accreditation:* APA (one or more programs are accredited). *Students:* 3 full-time (0 women), 18 part-time (13 women); includes 2 Black or African American, non-Hispanic/Latino; 1 Asian, non-Hispanic/Latino; 1 Hispanic/Latino, 2 international. Average age 28. 28 applicants, 39% accepted, 9 enrolled. In 2010, 9 master's awarded. *Degree requirements:* For doctorate, thesis/dissertation. *Entrance requirements:* For doctorate, GRE General Test, GRE Subject Test. Additional exam requirements/recommendations for international students: Required—TOEFL (minimum score 550 paper-based; 213 computer-based); Recommended—TWE (minimum score 6). *Application deadline:* For fall admission, 2/1 for domestic students, 6/1 for international students; for winter admission, 10/1 for international students; for spring admission, 2/1 for international students. Applications are processed on a rolling basis. Application fee: $30 ($50 for international students). Electronic applications accepted. *Expenses:* Tuition, state resident: full-time $7662; part-time $478.85 per credit hour. Tuition, nonresident: full-time $16,920; part-time $1057.55 per credit hour. Required fees: $571.20; $35.70 per credit hour. $188.05 per semester. Tuition and fees vary according to course load and program. *Financial support:* Application deadline: 2/1. *Unit head:* Douglas Whitman, Chair, 313-577-2803, Fax: 313-577-7636, E-mail: dwhitman@wayne.edu. *Application contact:* Dr. Melissa Kaplan-Estrin, Graduate Director, 313-577-2824, Fax: 313-577-7636, E-mail: mkestrin@sun.science.wayne.edu.

West Chester University of Pennsylvania, Office of Graduate Studies, College of Arts and Sciences, Department of Psychology, West Chester, PA 19383. Offers clinical mental health (Certificate); clinical psychology (MA); general psychology (MA); industrial psychology (MA). Part-time and evening/weekend programs available. *Students:* 79 full-time (56 women), 33 part-time (22 women); includes 16 minority (4 Black or African American, non-Hispanic/Latino; 1 American Indian or Alaska Native, non-Hispanic/Latino; 5 Asian, non-Hispanic/Latino; 6 Hispanic/Latino), 4 international. Average age 27. 192 applicants, 53% accepted, 40 enrolled. In 2010, 43 master's, 4 other advanced degrees awarded. *Degree requirements:* For master's, comprehensive exam, thesis (for some programs). *Entrance requirements:* For master's, GRE General Test or MAT, minimum GPA of 3.0, 3.25 in psychology; three letters of reference. Additional exam requirements/recommendations for international students: Required—TOEFL (minimum score 550 paper-based; 213 computer-based; 80 iBT). *Application deadline:* For fall admission, 4/15 priority date for domestic students, 3/15 for international students; for spring admission, 10/15 for domestic students, 9/1 for international students. Applications are processed on a rolling basis. Application fee: $35. Electronic applications accepted. *Expenses:* Tuition, state resident: full-time $6966; part-time $387 per credit. Tuition, nonresident: full-time $11,146; part-time $619 per credit. Required fees: $1614.40; $133.24 per credit. Part-time tuition and fees vary according to campus/location. *Financial support:* Unspecified assistantships available. Support available to part-time students. Financial award application deadline: 2/15; financial award applicants required to submit FAFSA. *Faculty research:* Animal learning and cognition. *Unit head:* Dr. Loretta Rieser-Danner, Acting Chairperson, 610-436-3106, E-mail: lrieser-danner@wcupa.edu. *Application contact:* Dr. Julian Azorlosa, Graduate Coordinator, 610-738-0430, E-mail: jazorlosa@wcupa.edu.

Western Kentucky University, Graduate Studies, College of Education and Behavioral Sciences, Department of Psychology, Bowling Green, KY 42101. Offers clinical psychology (MA); experimental psychology (MA); general psychology (MA); industrial/organizational psychology (MA); school psychology (Ed S). *Degree requirements:* For master's, comprehensive exam, thesis (for some programs); for Ed S, thesis, oral exam. *Entrance requirements:* For master's, GRE General Test; for Ed S, GRE General Test, minimum GPA of 3.5. Additional exam requirements/recommendations for international students: Required—TOEFL (minimum score 555 paper-based; 213 computer-based; 79 iBT). *Faculty research:* Neural regeneration, enhancing mobility in the elderly, improvement in visual processing in older adults, lifespan development.

Western Michigan University, Graduate College, College of Arts and Sciences, Department of Psychology, Kalamazoo, MI 49008. Offers behavior analysis (MA, PhD); clinical psychology (PhD); industrial/organizational psychology (MA). *Accreditation:* APA (one or more programs are accredited). *Degree requirements:* For master's, variable foreign language requirement, thesis, oral exams; for doctorate, 2 foreign languages, comprehensive exam, thesis/dissertation, oral exams. *Entrance requirements:* For master's and doctorate, GRE General Test.

Wright State University, School of Graduate Studies, College of Science and Mathematics, Department of Psychology, Program in Human Factors and Industrial/Organizational Psychology, Dayton, OH 45435. Offers MS, PhD. *Degree requirements:* For master's, thesis; for doctorate, thesis/dissertation.

Xavier University, College of Social Sciences, Health and Education, Department of Psychology, Cincinnati, OH 45207. Offers clinical psychology (Psy D); psychology (MA), including general experimental psychology, industrial-organizational psychology. *Accreditation:* APA (one or more programs are accredited). *Faculty:* 16 full-time (8 women), 5 part-time/adjunct (2 women). *Students:* 87 full-time (65 women), 26 part-time (21 women); includes 11 minority (4 Black or African American, non-Hispanic/Latino; 1 American Indian or Alaska Native, non-Hispanic/Latino; 3 Asian, non-Hispanic/Latino; 3 Hispanic/Latino), 2 international. Average age 27. 292 applicants, 22% accepted, 25 enrolled. In 2010, 26 master's, 16 doctorates awarded. *Degree requirements:* For master's, one foreign language, comprehensive exam, thesis, internship; for doctorate, one foreign language, comprehensive exam, thesis/dissertation, internship. *Entrance requirements:* For master's and doctorate, GRE. Additional exam requirements/recommendations for international students: Required—TOEFL, IELTS. *Application deadline:* For fall admission, 12/15 for domestic and international students. Application fee: $35. Electronic applications accepted. *Expenses:* Contact institution. *Financial support:* In 2010–11, 54 students received support, including 41 research assistantships with partial tuition reimbursements available, 13 teaching assistantships with partial tuition reimbursements available; scholarships/grants and unspecified assistantships also available. Financial award application deadline: 3/1; financial award applicants required to submit FAFSA. *Faculty research:* Older adults, clinical child and adolescent issues, personnel selection and employee behavior, at-risk youth, sexual abuse. *Unit head:* Dr. Karl Stukenberg, Chair, 513-745-1041, Fax: 513-745-3327, E-mail: stukenb@xavier.edu. *Application contact:* Margaret Maybury, Assistant Director, Enrollment and Student Services, 513-745-1053, Fax: 513-745-3347, E-mail: maybury@xavier.edu.

Marriage and Family Therapy

Abilene Christian University, Graduate School, College of Biblical Studies, Program in Marriage and Family Therapy, Abilene, TX 79699-9100. Offers MMFT. *Accreditation:* AAMFT/COAMFTE. *Faculty:* 2 full-time (both women), 5 part-time/adjunct (2 women). *Students:* 34 full-time (24 women); includes 3 Black or African American, non-Hispanic/Latino; 1 Asian, non-Hispanic/Latino; 1 Hispanic/Latino, 1 international. 45 applicants, 56% accepted, 13 enrolled. In 2010, 19 master's awarded. *Degree requirements:* For master's, comprehensive exam. *Entrance requirements:* For master's, GRE General Test, interview. Additional exam requirements/recommendations for international students: Required—TOEFL (minimum score 550 paper-based; 213 computer-based). *Application deadline:* For fall admission, 4/1 priority date for domestic students; for spring admission, 11/1 for domestic students. Applications are processed on a rolling basis. Application fee: $40. Electronic applications accepted. *Expenses:* Tuition: Full-time $12,906; part-time $717 per hour. Required fees: $1250; $61.50 per unit. *Financial support:* In 2010–11, 33 students received support; teaching assistantships, career-related internships or fieldwork available. Support available to part-time students. Financial award application deadline: 4/1; financial award applicants required to submit FAFSA. *Faculty research:* Overeating variables, family systems, intervention strategies. *Unit head:* Dr. Jaime Goff, Chairperson, 325-674-3778, Fax: 325-674-3749, E-mail: jaime.goff@acu.edu. *Application contact:* David Pittman, Graduate Admissions Counselor, 325-674-2656, Fax: 325-674-6717, E-mail: gradinfo@acu.edu.

Adler Graduate School, Program in Adlerian Counseling and Psychotherapy, Richfield, MN 55423. Offers art therapy (MA); clinical mental health counseling (MA); marriage and family therapy (MA); non-clinical Adlerian studies (MA); online Adlerian studies (MA); organizational wellness and transformation (MA); parent coaching (Certificate); personal and professional life coaching (Certificate); school counseling (MA). Part-time and evening/weekend programs available. *Faculty:* 11 full-time (4 women), 48 part-time/adjunct (28 women). *Students:* 442 part-time (361 women). Average age 37. *Degree requirements:* For master's, thesis or alternative, 500-700 hour internship (depending on license choice). *Entrance requirements:* For master's, minimum undergraduate GPA of 3.0, 12 credits of course work in psychology or related field. *Application deadline:* Applications are processed on a rolling basis. Application fee: $50. *Expenses:* Tuition: Part-time $455 per credit. *Financial support:* Career-related internships or fieldwork and tuition waivers available. Support available to part-time students. Financial award applicants required to submit FAFSA. *Unit head:* Dr. Dan Haugen, President, 612-861-7554 Ext. 107, Fax: 612-861-7559, E-mail: haugen@alfredadler.edu. *Application contact:* Evelyn B. Haas, Director of Student Services and Admissions, 612-861-7554 Ext. 103, Fax: 612-861-7559, E-mail: ev@alfredadler.edu.

Adler School of Professional Psychology, Programs in Psychology, Chicago, IL 60602. Offers advanced Adlerian psychotherapy (Certificate); art therapy (MA); clinical neuropsychology (Certificate); clinical psychology (Psy D); community psychology (MA); counseling and organizational psychology (MA); counseling psychology (MA); forensic psychology (MA); gerontological counseling (MA); marriage and family counseling (MA); marriage and family therapy (Certificate); organizational psychology (MA); police psychology (MA); rehabilitation counseling (MA); sport and health psychology (MA); substance abuse counseling (Certificate); Psy D/Certificate; Psy D/MACAT; Psy D/MACP; Psy D/MAMFC; Psy D/MASAC. *Accreditation:* APA. Part-time and evening/weekend programs available. Postbaccalaureate distance learning degree programs offered (minimal on-campus study). *Faculty:* 40 full-time (18 women), 61 part-time/adjunct (31 women). *Students:* 688 full-time (532 women), 142 part-time (110 women). Average age 27.Terminal master's awarded for partial completion of doctoral program. *Degree requirements:* For master's, thesis or alternative, oral exam, practicum; for doctorate, thesis/dissertation, clinical exam, internship, oral exam, practicum, written qualifying exam. *Entrance requirements:* For master's, 12 semester hours in psychology, minimum GPA of 3.0; for doctorate, 18 semester hours in psychology, minimum GPA of 3.25; for Certificate, appropriate master's or doctoral degree. Additional exam requirements/recommendations for international students: Required—TOEFL (minimum score 550 paper-based; 213 computer-based; 79 iBT). *Application deadline:* For fall admission, 2/15 priority date for domestic students, 12/1 priority date for international students. Applications are processed on a rolling basis. Application fee: $50. Electronic applications accepted. *Financial support:* Career-related internships or fieldwork, Federal Work-Study, scholarships/grants, and tuition waivers (full and partial) available. Support available to part-time students. Financial award application deadline: 5/15; financial award applicants required to submit FAFSA. *Application contact:* Michelle Brice, Director of Admissions, 312-662-4113, Fax: 312-662-4199, E-mail: admissions@adler.edu.

See Display on page 912 and Close-Up on page 1119.

Alliant International University–Irvine, California School of Professional Psychology, Program in Marital and Family Therapy, Irvine, CA 92612. Offers MA, Psy D. *Accreditation:* AAMFT/COAMFTE. Part-time programs available. *Degree requirements:* For doctorate, thesis/dissertation. *Entrance requirements:* For master's, minimum GPA of 3.0, letters of recommendation, interview; for doctorate, letters of recommendation, minimum GPA of 3.0, interview. Additional exam requirements/recommendations for international students: Required—TOEFL (minimum score 600 paper-based; 250 computer-based), TWE (minimum score 5). Electronic applications accepted. *Faculty research:* Chemical dependency, observational research.

Alliant International University–Los Angeles, California School of Professional Psychology, Program in Marital and Family Therapy, Alhambra, CA 91803-1360. Offers biofeedback (MA); chemical dependency (MA); gerontology (MA); Latin American family therapy (MA). *Accreditation:* AAMFT/COAMFTE.

Alliant International University–Sacramento, California School of Professional Psychology, Program in Marital and Family Therapy, Sacramento, CA 95825. Offers MA. *Accreditation:* AAMFT/COAMFTE. *Entrance requirements:* For master's, minimum GPA of 3.0, letters of recommendation, interview. Additional exam requirements/recommendations for international students: Required—TOEFL (minimum score 600 paper-based; 250 computer-based), TWE (minimum score 5). Electronic applications accepted. *Faculty research:* Couples therapy, marital myths, cross-cultural issues.

Alliant International University–San Diego, California School of Professional Psychology, Program in Marital and Family Therapy, San Diego, CA 92131-1799. Offers MA, Psy D. *Accreditation:* AAMFT/COAMFTE. Part-time programs available. *Degree requirements:* For doctorate, thesis/dissertation. *Entrance requirements:* For master's and doctorate, minimum GPA of 3.0, letters of recommendation, interview. Additional exam requirements/recommendations for international students: Required—TOEFL (minimum score 600 paper-based; 250 computer-based), TWE (minimum score 5). Electronic applications accepted. *Faculty research:* Chemical dependency, women's issues, emotionally focused therapy, couple relationships, work/family/parenting.

Amridge University, Graduate and Professional Programs, Montgomery, AL 36117. Offers behavioral leadership and management (MA); Biblical exposition (MA); biblical studies (MA, PhD); family therapy (D Min); historical and theological studies (MA); leadership and management (MS); marriage and family therapy (M Div, MA, PhD); ministerial leadership (M Div, MS); pastoral counseling (M Div, MS); practical ministry (MA); professional counseling (M Div, MA, PhD); theology (D Min). Part-time and evening/weekend programs available. Postbaccalaureate distance learning degree programs offered (no on-campus study). *Faculty:* 39 full-time (6 women), 39 part-time/adjunct (5 women). *Students:* 119 full-time (54 women), 260 part-time (149 women); includes 160 minority (153 Black or African American, non-Hispanic/Latino; 1 Asian, non-Hispanic/Latino; 6 Hispanic/Latino). Average age 35. *Degree requirements:* For master's, one foreign language, comprehensive exam (for some programs), thesis (for some programs); for doctorate, comprehensive exam (for some programs), thesis/dissertation; for M Div, comprehensive exam (for some programs). *Entrance requirements:* For M Div, master's, and doctorate, GRE General Test or MAT. Additional exam requirements/recommendations for international students: Required—TOEFL. *Application deadline:* For fall admission, 9/1 priority date for domestic students; for spring admission, 1/1 priority date for domestic students. Applications are processed on a rolling basis. Application fee: $75. Electronic applications accepted. *Financial support:* Federal Work-Study and scholarships/grants available. Support available to part-time students. Financial award applicants required to submit FAFSA. *Faculty research:* Homiletics, hermeneutics, ancient Near Eastern history. *Unit head:* Director of Enrollment Management, 800-351-4040 Ext. 7513, Fax: 334-387-3878. *Application contact:* Ora Davis, Admissions Officer, 334-387-3877 Ext. 7524, Fax: 334-387-3878, E-mail: admissions@amridgeuniversity.edu.

Antioch University New England, Graduate School, Department of Applied Psychology, Program in Marriage and Family Therapy, Keene, NH 03431-3552. Offers MA, PhD. *Accreditation:* AAMFT/COAMFTE. *Degree requirements:* For master's, internship, practicum. *Entrance requirements:* For master's, previous course work and work experience in psychology; resume; 3 letters of recommendation. Additional exam requirements/recommendations for international students: Required—TOEFL (minimum score 600 paper-based; 250 computer-based). Electronic applications accepted. *Expenses:* Contact institution. *Faculty research:* Use of reflective team model in case teaching and in organizational consulting, executive mentoring and coaching.

Appalachian State University, Cratis D. Williams Graduate School, Department of Human Development and Psychological Counseling, Boone, NC 28608. Offers clinical mental health counseling (MA); college student development (MA); marriage and family therapy (MA); school counseling (MA). *Accreditation:* AAMFT/COAMFTE; ACA; NCATE. Part-time programs available. *Faculty:* 14 full-time (9 women), 7 part-time/adjunct (all women). *Students:* 140 full-time (101 women), 25 part-time (20 women); includes 8 Black or African American, non-Hispanic/Latino; 1 Asian, non-Hispanic/Latino; 1 Hispanic/Latino; 1 Two or more races, non-Hispanic/Latino. 233 applicants, 53% accepted, 74 enrolled. In 2010, 53 master's awarded. *Degree requirements:* For master's, comprehensive exam (for some programs), thesis optional, internships. *Entrance requirements:* For master's, GRE General Test, 3 letters of recommendation. Additional exam requirements/recommendations for international students: Required—TOEFL (minimum score 570 paper-based; 230 computer-based; 79 iBT), IELTS (minimum score 6.5). *Application deadline:* For fall admission, 2/1 priority date for domestic students, 2/1 for international students; for spring admission, 2/1 for international students. Applications are processed on a rolling basis. Application fee: $55. Electronic applications accepted. *Expenses:* Tuition, state resident: full-time $3428; part-time $428 per unit. Tuition, nonresident: full-time $14,518; part-time $1814 per unit. Required fees: $2320; $344 per unit. Tuition and fees vary according to campus/location. *Financial support:* In 2010–11, 20 research assistantships (averaging $8,000 per year), 7 teaching assistantships (averaging $8,000 per year) were awarded; fellowships, career-related internships or fieldwork, Federal Work-Study, scholarships/grants, and unspecified assistantships also available. Financial award application deadline: 4/1; financial

Marriage and Family Therapy

Appalachian State University (continued)
award applicants required to submit FAFSA. *Faculty research:* Multicultural counseling, addictions counseling, play therapy, expressive arts, child and adolescent therapy, sexual abuse counseling. *Unit head:* Dr. Lee Baruth, Chairman, 828-262-2055, E-mail: baruthlg@appstate.edu. *Application contact:* Sandy Krause, Director of Admissions and Recruiting, 828-262-2130, Fax: 828-262-2709, E-mail: krausesl@appstate.edu.

Argosy University, Atlanta, College of Psychology and Behavioral Sciences, Atlanta, GA 30328. Offers clinical psychology (MA, Psy D, Postdoctoral Respecialization Certificate), including child and family psychology (Psy D), general adult clinical (Psy D), health psychology (Psy D), neuropsychology/geropsychology (Psy D); community counseling (MA), including marriage and family therapy; counselor education and supervision (Ed D); forensic psychology (MA); industrial organizational psychology (MA); marriage and family therapy (Certificate); sport-exercise psychology (MA). *Accreditation:* APA.

See Close-Up on page 1121.

Argosy University, Chicago, College of Psychology and Behavioral Sciences, Doctoral Program in Clinical Psychology, Chicago, IL 60601. Offers child and adolescent psychology (Psy D); client-centered and experiential psychotherapies (Psy D); diversity and multicultural psychology (Psy D); family psychology (Psy D); forensic psychology (Psy D); health psychology (Psy D); neuropsychology (Psy D); organizational consulting (Psy D); psychoanalytic psychology (Psy D); psychology and spirituality (Psy D). *Accreditation:* APA.

See Close-Up on page 1123.

Argosy University, Denver, College of Psychology and Behavioral Sciences, Denver, CO 80231. Offers clinical mental health counseling (MA); clinical psychology (MA, Psy D); counseling psychology (Ed D); counselor education and supervision (Ed D); forensic psychology (MA); industrial organizational psychology (MA); marriage and family therapy (MA, DMFT).

See Close-Up on page 1127.

Argosy University, Hawai'i, College of Psychology and Behavioral Sciences, Program in Marriage and Family Therapy, Honolulu, HI 96813. Offers MA.

See Close-Up on page 1129.

Argosy University, Inland Empire, College of Psychology and Behavioral Sciences, San Bernardino, CA 92408. Offers clinical psychology/marriage and family therapy (MA); counseling psychology (Ed D); counseling psychology/marriage and family therapy (MA); forensic psychology (MA); industrial organizational psychology (MA); sport-exercise psychology (MA).

See Close-Up on page 1131.

Argosy University, Los Angeles, College of Psychology and Behavioral Sciences, Santa Monica, CA 90045. Offers clinical psychology/marriage and family therapy (MA); counseling psychology (Ed D); counseling psychology/marriage and family therapy (MA); forensic psychology (MA).

See Close-Up on page 1133.

Argosy University, Orange County, College of Psychology and Behavioral Sciences, Program in Clinical Psychology, Orange, CA 92868. Offers child and adolescent psychology (Psy D); forensic psychology (Psy D); marriage and family therapy (MA). *Accreditation:* APA.

See Close-Up on page 1137.

Argosy University, Orange County, College of Psychology and Behavioral Sciences, Program in Counseling Psychology, Orange, CA 92868. Offers counseling psychology (Ed D); marriage and family therapy (MA).

See Close-Up on page 1137.

Argosy University, Salt Lake City, College of Psychology and Behavioral Sciences, Draper, UT 84020. Offers counseling psychology (Ed D); counselor education and supervision (Ed D); forensic psychology (MA); marriage and family therapy (MA, DMFT); mental health counseling (MA).

See Close-Up on page 1141.

Argosy University, San Diego, College of Psychology and Behavioral Sciences, San Diego, CA 92108. Offers clinical psychology/marriage and family therapy (MA); counseling psychology (Ed D); counseling psychology/marriage and family therapy (MA); forensic psychology (MA).

See Close-Up on page 1143.

Argosy University, Sarasota, College of Psychology and Behavioral Sciences, Sarasota, FL 34235. Offers community counseling (MA); counseling psychology (Ed D); counselor education and supervision (Ed D); forensic psychology (MA); marriage and family therapy (MA); mental health counseling (MA); pastoral community counseling (Ed D).

See Close-Up on page 1147.

Argosy University, Schaumburg, College of Psychology and Behavioral Sciences, Schaumburg, IL 60173-5403. Offers clinical health psychology (Post-Graduate Certificate); clinical psychology (MA, Psy D), including child and family psychology (Psy D), clinical health psychology (Psy D), diversity and multicultural psychology (Psy D), forensic psychology (Psy D), neuropsychology (Psy D); community counseling (MA); counseling psychology (Ed D), including counselor education and supervision; counselor education and supervision (Ed D); forensic psychology (Post-Graduate Certificate); industrial organizational psychology (MA). *Accreditation:* ACA; APA.

See Close-Up on page 1149.

Argosy University, Tampa, College of Psychology and Behavioral Sciences, Program in Clinical Psychology, Tampa, FL 33607. Offers clinical psychology (MA, Psy D), including child and adolescent psychology (Psy D), geropsychology (Psy D), marriage/couples and family therapy (Psy D), neuropsychology (Psy D). *Accreditation:* APA.

See Close-Up on page 1153.

Argosy University, Twin Cities, College of Psychology and Behavioral Sciences, Eagan, MN 55121. Offers clinical psychology (MA, Psy D), including child and family psychology (Psy D), forensic psychology (Psy D), health and neuropsychology (Psy D), trauma (Psy D); forensic counseling (Post-Graduate Certificate); forensic psychology (MA); industrial organizational psychology (MA); marriage and family therapy (MA, DMFT), including forensic counseling (MA). *Accreditation:* AAMFT; AAMFT/COAMFTE; APA.

See Close-Up on page 1155.

Argosy University, Washington DC, College of Psychology and Behavioral Sciences, Arlington, VA 22209. Offers clinical psychology (MA, Psy D), including child and family psychology (Psy D), diversity and multicultural psychology (Psy D), forensic psychology (Psy D), health and neuropsychology (Psy D); community counseling (MA); counseling psychology (Ed D), including counselor education and supervision; counselor education and supervision (Ed D); forensic psychology (MA). *Accreditation:* APA.

See Close-Up on page 1157.

Arizona State University, College of Liberal Arts and Sciences, School of Social and Family Dynamics, Tempe, AZ 85287-3701. Offers family and human development (MS, PhD); infant-family practice (MAS); marriage and family therapy (MAS); sociology (MA, PhD). *Faculty:* 60 full-time (39 women), 2 part-time/adjunct (both women). *Students:* 91 full-time (82 women), 32 part-time (27 women); includes 28 minority (3 Black or African American, non-Hispanic/Latino; 2 American Indian or Alaska Native, non-Hispanic/Latino; 4 Asian, non-Hispanic/Latino; 17 Hispanic/Latino; 1 Native Hawaiian or other Pacific Islander, non-Hispanic/Latino; 1 Two or more races, non-Hispanic/Latino), 10 international. Average age 27. 186 applicants, 38% accepted, 44 enrolled. In 2010, 32 master's, 7 doctorates awarded. Terminal master's awarded for partial completion of doctoral program. *Degree requirements:* For master's, thesis or alternative, interactive Program of Study (iPOS) submitted before completing 50 percent of required credit hours; for doctorate, thesis/dissertation, interactive Program of Study (iPOS) submitted before completing 50 percent of required credit hours. *Entrance requirements:* For master's and doctorate, GRE, minimum GPA of 3.0 or equivalent in last 2 years of work leading to bachelor's degree. Additional exam requirements/recommendations for international students: Required—TOEFL, IELTS, or Pearson Test of English. *Application deadline:* For fall admission, 1/15 for domestic and international students. Application fee: $70 ($90 for international students). Electronic applications accepted. *Expenses:* Contact institution. *Financial support:* In 2010–11, 22 research assistantships with full and partial tuition reimbursements (averaging $14,111 per year), 27 teaching assistantships with full and partial tuition reimbursements (averaging $12,750 per year) were awarded; fellowships with full tuition reimbursements, career-related internships or fieldwork, Federal Work-Study, institutionally sponsored loans, scholarships/grants, and tuition waivers (full and partial) also available. Financial award application deadline: 3/1; financial award applicants required to submit FAFSA. Total annual research expenditures: $4.2 million. *Unit head:* Dr. Richard Fabes, Director, 480-965-4892, E-mail: rf@asu.edu. *Application contact:* Graduate Admissions, 480-965-6113.

Azusa Pacific University, School of Behavioral and Applied Sciences, Department of Graduate Psychology, Azusa, CA 91702-7000. Offers clinical psychology (MA, Psy D), including family therapy (MA). *Accreditation:* APA (one or more programs are accredited). Part-time and evening/weekend programs available. *Faculty:* 14 full-time (8 women), 2 part-time/adjunct (1 woman). *Students:* 186 full-time (134 women), 45 part-time (35 women); includes 68 minority (14 Black or African American, non-Hispanic/Latino; 26 Asian, non-Hispanic/Latino; 27 Hispanic/Latino; 1 Native Hawaiian or other Pacific Islander, non-Hispanic/Latino), 11 international. Average age 30. In 2010, 73 master's, 16 doctorates awarded. *Degree requirements:* For master's, comprehensive exam, 250 hours of clinical experience, individual and group therapy. *Entrance requirements:* For master's, interview, minimum GPA of 3.0, Minnesota Multiphasic Personality Inventory. Additional exam requirements/recommendations for international students: Required—TOEFL (minimum score 600 paper-based). *Application deadline:* For fall admission, 6/30 priority date for domestic students. Applications are processed on a rolling basis. Application fee: $45 ($65 for international students). *Unit head:* Dr. Robert Welsh, Chair, 626-815-5008. *Application contact:* Linda Witte, Graduate Admissions Office, 626-969-3434.

Barry University, School of Education, Program in Marital, Couple and Family Counseling/Therapy, Miami Shores, FL 33161-6695. Offers MS, Ed S. Part-time and evening/weekend programs available. *Degree requirements:* For master's, comprehensive exam, scholarly paper; for Ed S, comprehensive exam. *Entrance requirements:* For master's, GRE General Test or MAT, minimum GPA of 3.0; for Ed S, GRE General Test, minimum GPA of 3.0. Electronic applications accepted.

Bayamón Central University, Graduate Programs, Program in Education, Bayamón, PR 00960-1725. Offers administration and supervision (MA Ed); commercial education (MA Ed); elementary education (K–3) (MA Ed); family counseling (Graduate Certificate); guidance and counseling (MA Ed); pre-elementary teacher (MA Ed); rehabilitation counseling (MA Ed); special education (MA Ed), including attention deficit disorder, education of the autistic, learning disabilities. Part-time and evening/weekend programs available. *Degree requirements:* For master's, comprehensive exam. *Entrance requirements:* For master's, EXADEP, bachelor's degree in education or related field.

Bethel Seminary, Graduate and Professional Programs, St. Paul, MN 55112-6998. Offers Anglican studies (Certificate); applied ministry (MA, Certificate); biblical studies (Certificate); children's and family ministry (MACFM); Christian education (MACE); Christian thought (MACT); community ministry leadership (MA, Certificate); global and contextual studies (MA); Greek and Hebrew language track (M Div); Greek language track (M Div); Hebrew language track (M Div); lay ministry (Certificate); marriage and family therapy (MAMFT, Certificate); men's ministry leadership (Certificate); ministry (D Min); ministry leadership (Certificate); spiritual formation (Certificate); theological studies (MATS, Certificate); transformational leadership (MATL, Certificate); young life youth ministry (Certificate). *Accreditation:* ACIPE; ATS (one or more programs are accredited). Part-time and evening/weekend programs available. Postbaccalaureate distance learning degree programs offered (minimal on-campus study). *Faculty:* 26 full-time (3 women), 74 part-time/adjunct (29 women). *Students:* 729 full-time (275 women), 274 part-time (118 women); includes 75 minority (34 Black or African American, non-Hispanic/Latino; 1 American Indian or Alaska Native, non-Hispanic/Latino; 12 Asian, non-Hispanic/Latino; 16 Hispanic/Latino; 1 Native Hawaiian or other Pacific Islander, non-Hispanic/Latino; 11 Two or more races, non-Hispanic/Latino), 16 international. Average age 38. 525 applicants, 76% accepted, 265 enrolled. In 2010, 149 master's, 13 doctorates awarded. *Degree requirements:* For master's, variable foreign language requirement, thesis (for some programs); for doctorate, thesis/dissertation; for M Div, one foreign language. *Entrance requirements:* For M Div and master's, letters of reference, transcripts, personal statement; for doctorate, M Div, letters of reference, organizational support. Additional exam requirements/recommendations for international students: Required—TOEFL (minimum score 550 paper-based; 213 computer-based; 87 iBT). *Application deadline:* For fall admission, 8/1 priority date for domestic students, 3/1 for international students; for winter admission, 12/1 priority date for domestic students; for spring admission, 3/1 priority date for domestic students. Applications are processed on a rolling basis. Application fee: $20. Electronic applications accepted. *Financial support:* In 2010–11, 655 students received support, including 18 teaching assistantships; career-related internships or fieldwork, Federal Work-Study, scholarships/grants, and tuition waivers (full) also available. Financial award application deadline: 7/15; financial award applicants required to submit FAFSA. *Faculty research:* Nature of theology, ethics, Biblical commentaries, nature of God, science and theology. *Unit head:* Dr. David Ridder, Vice President and Dean, 651-638-6553. *Application contact:* Joseph V. Dworak, Director of Admissions, 651-638-6288, Fax: 651-638-6002, E-mail: j-dworak@bethel.edu.

Briercrest Seminary, Graduate Programs, Program in Christian Ministries, Caronport, SK S0H 0S0, Canada. Offers leadership (MA); marriage and family counseling (MA); missions (MA); pastoral counseling (MA); worship (MA); youth and family ministry (MA). Part-time programs available. *Degree requirements:* For master's, comprehensive exam, thesis optional. *Entrance requirements:* Additional exam requirements/recommendations for international students: Required—TOEFL (minimum score 550 paper-based; 213 computer-based).

Brigham Young University, Graduate Studies, College of Family, Home, and Social Sciences, Marriage and Family Therapy Program, Provo, UT 84602. Offers MS, PhD. *Faculty:* 8 full-time (1 woman), 4 part-time/adjunct (3 women). *Students:* 40 full-time (23 women); includes 4 Black or African American, non-Hispanic/Latino; 1 American Indian or Alaska Native, non-Hispanic/Latino; 1 Asian, non-Hispanic/Latino; 4 Hispanic/Latino, 1 international. Average age 28. 75 applicants, 19% accepted, 14 enrolled. In 2010, 8 master's, 2 doctorates awarded. *Degree requirements:* For master's, comprehensive exam, thesis; for doctorate, comprehensive exam, thesis/dissertation. *Entrance requirements:* For master's and doctorate, GRE General Test, GRE Writing Test, minimum GPA of 3.0 in last 60 hours of course work. Additional exam requirements/recommendations for international students: Required—TOEFL. *Application deadline:* For fall admission, 12/1 for domestic and international students. Application fee: $50. Electronic applications accepted. *Expenses:* Tuition: Full-time $5580; part-time $310 per credit hour. Tuition and fees vary according to program and student's religious affiliation. *Financial support:* In 2010–11, 33 students received support, including 33 research assistantships with full and partial tuition reimbursements available (averaging $12,900 per year); fellowships, teaching assistantships, career-related internships or fieldwork, scholarships/grants, and tuition waivers (partial) also available. *Faculty research:* Therapy processes and outcome, preparation for marriage, family relationships across the life cycle, adjustment to medical illnesses, health-care costs, health family processes. Total annual research expenditures: $10,000. *Unit head:* Dr. Leslie L. Feinauer, Program Director, 801-422-5680, Fax: 801-422-0163, E-mail: leslie_feinauer@byu.edu. *Application contact:* Linda Kader, Program Secretary, 801-422-5680, Fax: 801-422-0163, E-mail: linda_kader@byu.edu.

California Lutheran University, Graduate Studies, Department of Psychology, Thousand Oaks, CA 91360-2787. Offers clinical psychology (MS, Psy D); marital and family therapy (MS). Part-time programs available. *Faculty:* 3 full-time (2 women), 12 part-time/adjunct (10 women). *Students:* 178 full-time (152 women), 11 part-time (9 women); includes 67 minority (5 Black or African American, non-Hispanic/Latino; 1 American Indian or Alaska Native, non-Hispanic/Latino; 7 Asian, non-Hispanic/Latino; 46 Hispanic/Latino; 1 Native Hawaiian or other Pacific Islander, non-Hispanic/Latino; 7 Two or more races, non-Hispanic/Latino), 5 international. Average age 31. 224 applicants, 67% accepted, 103 enrolled. In 2010, 68 master's awarded. *Degree requirements:* For master's, thesis or comprehensive exams; for doctorate, internship. *Entrance requirements:* For master's, GRE General Test, interview, minimum GPA of 3.0. *Application deadline:* For fall admission, 2/15 priority date for domestic students. Applications are processed on a rolling basis. Application fee: $50. *Unit head:* Dr. Mindy Puopolo, Director, 805-493-3528. *Application contact:* 805-493-3127, Fax: 805-493-3542, E-mail: clugrad@clunet.edu.

California State University, Chico, Graduate School, College of Behavioral and Social Sciences, Department of Psychology, Program in Marriage and Family Therapy, Chico, CA 95929-0722. Offers MS. *Students:* 28 full-time (25 women), 6 part-time (3 women); includes 1 American Indian or Alaska Native, non-Hispanic/Latino; 2 Asian, non-Hispanic/Latino; 3 Hispanic/Latino. Average age 32. 36 applicants, 69% accepted, 15 enrolled. In 2010, 21 master's awarded. *Degree requirements:* For master's, thesis or alternative. *Entrance requirements:* For master's, GRE General Test or MAT, 3 letters of recommendation on departmental form. Additional exam requirements/recommendations for international students: Required—TOEFL (minimum score 550 paper-based; 213 computer-based; 80 iBT), IELTS (minimum score 6.5). *Application deadline:* For fall admission, 3/1 for domestic and international students. Application fee: $55. *Unit head:* Dr. Linda Kline, Graduate Coordinator, 530-898-6263. *Application contact:* Dr. Linda Kline, Graduate Coordinator, 530-898-6263.

California State University, Dominguez Hills, College of Professional Studies, School of Health and Human Services, Program in Marital and Family Therapy, Carson, CA 90747-0001. Offers MS. Part-time and evening/weekend programs available. *Faculty:* 2 full-time (both women), 3 part-time/adjunct (all women). *Students:* 88 full-time (74 women), 55 part-time (44 women); includes 46 Black or African American, non-Hispanic/Latino; 4 Asian, non-Hispanic/Latino; 41 Hispanic/Latino, 2 international. Average age 37. 83 applicants, 52% accepted, 34 enrolled. In 2010, 30 master's awarded. *Degree requirements:* For master's, comprehensive exam. *Entrance requirements:* For master's, minimum GPA of 3.0. *Application deadline:* For fall admission, 8/1 for domestic students; for spring admission, 12/15 for domestic students. Applications are processed on a rolling basis. Application fee: $55. Electronic applications accepted. *Faculty research:* Sociology of the family, clinical psychology theory, employee assistance programs, race and sport, secondary trauma. *Unit head:* Dr. Michele Shaw, Coordinator, 310-243-2693, E-mail: mlinden@csudh.edu. *Application contact:* Brandy McLelland, Interim Director, Student Information Services, 310-243-3645, E-mail: bmclelland@csudh.edu.

California State University, Fresno, Division of Graduate Studies, School of Education and Human Development, Department of Counseling and Special Education, Program in Marriage and Family Therapy, Fresno, CA 93740-8027. Offers MS. *Accreditation:* ACA. Part-time and evening/weekend programs available. *Degree requirements:* For master's, thesis or alternative. *Entrance requirements:* For master's, GRE General Test, MAT, minimum GPA of 3.0. Additional exam requirements/recommendations for international students: Required—TOEFL. Electronic applications accepted. *Faculty research:* Child abuse prevention, early childhood education.

California State University, Long Beach, Graduate Studies, College of Education, Department of Advanced Studies in Education and Counseling, Master of Science in Counseling Program, Long Beach, CA 90840. Offers marriage and family therapy (MS); school counseling (MS); student development in higher education (MS). *Accreditation:* NCATE. *Students:* 147 full-time (112 women), 62 part-time (45 women); includes 26 Black or African American, non-Hispanic/Latino; 2 American Indian or Alaska Native, non-Hispanic/Latino; 30 Asian, non-Hispanic/Latino; 80 Hispanic/Latino, 6 international. Average age 29. In 2010, 63 master's awarded. *Degree requirements:* For master's, comprehensive exam or thesis. *Application deadline:* For fall admission, 3/1 for domestic students. Applications are processed on a rolling basis. Application fee: $55. Electronic applications accepted. *Financial support:* Federal Work-Study, institutionally sponsored loans, and scholarships/grants available. Financial award application deadline: 3/2. *Unit head:* Dr. Jennifer Coots, Chair, 562-985-4517, Fax: 562-985-4534, E-mail: jcoots@csulb.edu. *Application contact:* Dr. Bita Ghafoori, Assistant Chair, 562-985-7864, Fax: 562-985-4534, E-mail: bghafoor@csulb.edu.

California State University, Northridge, Graduate Studies, College of Education, Department of Educational Psychology and Counseling, Northridge, CA 91330. Offers counseling (MS), including career counseling, college counseling and student services, marriage and family therapy, school counseling, school psychology; educational psychology (MA Ed), including development, learning, and instruction, early childhood education. *Accreditation:* ACA (one or more programs are accredited); NCATE. Part-time and evening/weekend programs available. *Entrance requirements:* For master's, GRE General Test or minimum GPA of 3.0. Additional exam requirements/recommendations for international students: Required—TOEFL.

Cambridge College, School of Psychology and Counseling, Cambridge, MA 02138-5304. Offers addiction counseling (M Ed); alcohol and drug counseling (Certificate); counseling psychology (M Ed, CAGS); counseling psychology: forensic counseling (M Ed); marriage and family therapy (M Ed); mental health and addiction counseling (M Ed); mental health counseling (M Ed); mental health counseling for school guidance counselors (Post Master's Certificate); psychological studies (M Ed); school adjustment and mental health counseling (M Ed); school adjustment, mental health and addiction counseling (M Ed); school guidance counselor (M Ed); trauma studies (Certificate). Part-time and evening/weekend programs available. *Faculty:* 4 full-time (2 women), 83 part-time/adjunct (48 women). *Students:* 436 full-time (351 women), 351 part-time (274 women); includes 321 Black or African American, non-Hispanic/Latino; 3 American Indian or Alaska Native, non-Hispanic/Latino; 4 Asian, non-Hispanic/Latino; 87 Hispanic/Latino; 4 Two or more races, non-Hispanic/Latino, 6 international. Average age 37. In 2010, 284 master's, 16 other advanced degrees awarded. *Degree requirements:* For master's and other advanced degree, thesis, practicum/internship. *Entrance requirements:* For master's, resume, 2 professional references; for other advanced degree, official transcripts, documents for transfer credit evaluation, resume, written personal statement/essay, 2 professional references, health insurance, immunizations form. Additional exam requirements/recommendations for international students: Required—TOEFL (minimum score 550 paper-based; 213 computer-based; 79 iBT); Recommended—IELTS (minimum score 6). *Application deadline:* Applications are processed on a rolling basis. Application fee: $30. Electronic applications accepted. *Expenses:* Contact institution. *Financial support:* Career-related internships or fieldwork, Federal Work-Study, and scholarships/grants available. Financial award applicants required to submit FAFSA. *Faculty research:* Trauma, drug and alcohol counseling, cross-cultural issues, school counseling, trauma in schools. *Unit head:* Dr. Niti Seth, Dean, 617-873-0208, Fax: 617-349-3561, E-mail: nseth@cambridgecollege.edu. *Application contact:* Elaine M. Lapomardo, Dean of Enrollment Management, 617-873-0274, Fax: 617-349-3561, E-mail: elaine.lapomardo@cambridgecollege.edu.

Capella University, School of Human Services, Minneapolis, MN 55402. Offers addictions counseling (Certificate); counseling studies (MS, PhD); criminal justice (MS, PhD, Certificate); diversity studies (Certificate); general human services (MS, PhD); health care administration (MS, PhD, Certificate); management of nonprofit agencies (MS, PhD, Certificate); marital

couple and family counseling/therapy (MS); marriage and family services (Certificate); mental health counseling (MS); professional counseling (Certificate); social and community services (MS, PhD, Certificate). Part-time and evening/weekend programs available. Postbaccalaureate distance learning degree programs offered (minimal on-campus study). Terminal master's awarded for partial completion of doctoral program. *Degree requirements:* For master's, thesis optional, integrative project; for doctorate, comprehensive exam, thesis/dissertation. *Entrance requirements:* Additional exam requirements/recommendations for international students: Required—TOEFL (minimum score 550 paper-based; 213 computer-based), TWE (minimum score 4). Electronic applications accepted. *Expenses:* Tuition: Full-time $11,880; part-time $440 per credit hour. *Faculty research:* Compulsive and addictive behaviors, substance abuse, assessment of psychopathology and neuropsychology.

Carlos Albizu University, Miami Campus, Graduate Programs, Miami, FL 33172-2209. Offers clinical psychology (Psy D); entrepreneurship (MBA); exceptional student education (MS); industrial/organizational psychology (MS); marriage and family therapy (MS); mental health counseling (MS); nonprofit management (MBA); organizational management (MBA); psychology (MS); school counseling (MS); teaching English as a second language (MS). *Accreditation:* APA. Part-time and evening/weekend programs available. *Faculty:* 21 full-time (12 women), 37 part-time/adjunct (18 women). *Students:* 496 full-time (400 women), 242 part-time (192 women); includes 590 minority (58 Black or African American, non-Hispanic/Latino; 2 American Indian or Alaska Native, non-Hispanic/Latino; 5 Asian, non-Hispanic/Latino; 523 Hispanic/Latino; 2 Two or more races, non-Hispanic/Latino), 15 international. Average age 36. 141 applicants, 84% accepted, 118 enrolled. In 2010, 159 master's, 20 doctorates awarded. Terminal master's awarded for partial completion of doctoral program. *Degree requirements:* For master's, one foreign language, comprehensive exam, integrative project (MBA), research project (exceptional student education, teaching English as a second language); for doctorate, one foreign language, comprehensive exam, internship, project. *Entrance requirements:* For master's, 3 letters of recommendation, interview, minimum GPA of 3.0, resume, statement of purpose, official transcripts; for doctorate, 3 letters of recommendation, minimum GPA of 3.0, resume, interview. *Application deadline:* For fall admission, 8/1 priority date for domestic students; for spring admission, 11/30 priority date for domestic students. Applications are processed on a rolling basis. Application fee: $50. Electronic applications accepted. *Expenses:* Tuition: Full-time $9360; part-time $520 per credit. Required fees: $298 per term. Tuition and fees vary according to course load, degree level and program. *Financial support:* In 2010–11, 106 students received support. Federal Work-Study, scholarships/grants, and tuition discounts available. Financial award application deadline: 6/1; financial award applicants required to submit FAFSA. *Faculty research:* Psychotherapy, forensic psychology, neuropsychology, marketing strategy, entrepreneurship, special education. *Unit head:* Dr. Carmen S. Roca, Chancellor, 305-593-1223 Ext. 120, Fax: 305-629-8052, E-mail: croca@albizu.edu. *Application contact:* Vanessa Almendarez, Secretary, 305-593-1223 Ext. 137, Fax: 305-593-1854, E-mail: valmendarez@albizu.edu.

Central Connecticut State University, School of Graduate Studies, School of Education and Professional Studies, Department of Counseling and Family Therapy, New Britain, CT 06050-4010. Offers marriage and family therapy (MS); professional counseling (MS, Certificate); school counseling (MS); student development in higher education (MS). *Accreditation:* AAMFT/COAMFTE; ACA. Part-time and evening/weekend programs available. *Faculty:* 8 full-time (4 women), 16 part-time/adjunct (12 women). *Students:* 143 full-time (118 women), 223 part-time (188 women); includes 77 minority (39 Black or African American, non-Hispanic/Latino; 2 American Indian or Alaska Native, non-Hispanic/Latino; 4 Asian, non-Hispanic/Latino; 31 Hispanic/Latino; 1 Two or more races, non-Hispanic/Latino), 4 international. Average age 34. 295 applicants, 48% accepted, 119 enrolled. In 2010, 71 master's awarded. *Degree requirements:* For master's, comprehensive exam, thesis or alternative; for Certificate, qualifying exam. *Entrance requirements:* For master's, minimum undergraduate GPA of 2.7. Additional exam requirements/recommendations for international students: Required—TOEFL. *Application deadline:* For fall admission, 5/1 for domestic students. Applications are processed on a rolling basis. Application fee: $50. Electronic applications accepted. *Expenses:* Tuition, area resident: Full-time $5012; part-time $470 per credit. Tuition, state resident: full-time $7518; part-time $482 per credit. Tuition, nonresident: full-time $13,962; part-time $482 per credit. Required fees: $3772. One-time fee: $62 part-time. *Financial support:* In 2010–11, 52 students received support, including 14 research assistantships; career-related internships or fieldwork, Federal Work-Study, scholarships/grants, and unspecified assistantships also available. Support available to part-time students. Financial award application deadline: 2/15; financial award applicants required to submit FAFSA. *Faculty research:* Elementary/secondary school counseling, marriage/family therapy, rehabilitation counseling, counseling in higher educational settings. *Unit head:* Dr. Connie Tait, Chair, 860-832-2154. *Application contact:* Dr. Connie Tait, Chair, 860-832-2154.

Chapman University, Graduate Studies, Schmid College of Science, Marriage and Family Therapy Program, Orange, CA 92866. Offers MA. *Accreditation:* AAMFT/COAMFTE. Part-time and evening/weekend programs available. *Faculty:* 12 full-time (5 women), 8 part-time/adjunct (5 women). *Students:* 44 full-time (42 women), 27 part-time (21 women); includes 19 minority (2 Black or African American, non-Hispanic/Latino; 1 American Indian or Alaska Native, non-Hispanic/Latino; 6 Asian, non-Hispanic/Latino; 9 Hispanic/Latino; 1 Two or more races, non-Hispanic/Latino), 1 international. Average age 27. 119 applicants, 24% accepted, 17 enrolled. In 2010, 20 master's awarded. *Degree requirements:* For master's, comprehensive exam, thesis optional. *Entrance requirements:* For master's, GRE, minimum undergraduate GPA of 2.5. Additional exam requirements/recommendations for international students: Required—TOEFL (minimum score 550 paper-based; 213 computer-based; 80 iBT). *Application deadline:* For fall admission, 3/1 for domestic students; for spring admission, 11/1 for domestic students. Application fee: $55. Electronic applications accepted. *Expenses:* Contact institution. *Financial support:* Fellowships, Federal Work-Study and scholarships/grants available. Financial award applicants required to submit FAFSA. *Unit head:* Dr. Georg Eifert, Associate Dean, 714-997-6776, E-mail: eifert@chapman.edu. *Application contact:* Serena Healey, Admissions Assistant, 714-744-7620, E-mail: healey@chapman.edu.

Chatham University, Program in Counseling Psychology, Pittsburgh, PA 15232-2826. Offers child, adolescent and family (MSCP); counseling psychology (Psy D); health and holistic (MSCP); infant mental health (MSCP); organization and supervision (MSCP); sport and exercise (MSCP). Part-time and evening/weekend programs available. *Degree requirements:* For master's, thesis optional, supervised internship; for doctorate, thesis/dissertation, internship. *Entrance requirements:* For master's, minimum GPA of 3.0; 2 letters of recommendation; resume; prerequisite coursework in statistics, biology, and psychology; for doctorate, GRE. Additional exam requirements/recommendations for international students: Required—TOEFL (minimum score 600 paper-based; 250 computer-based; 100 iBT), IELTS (minimum score 6.5), TWE. Electronic applications accepted. *Faculty research:* Trauma and recovery, hypnosis, psychospiritual dimensions of healing, psychotherapy of schizophrenia.

The Chicago School of Professional Psychology at Downtown Los Angeles, Program in Clinical Psychology, Los Angeles, CA 90017. Offers applied behavior analysis (MA); clinical psychology (Psy D); marital and family therapy (MA).

The Chicago School of Professional Psychology at Irvine, Program in Marital and Family Therapy, Irvine, CA 92612. Offers clinical psychology (MA), including marital and family therapy; management practice (Psy D); psychodynamic psychotherapy (Psy D).

The Chicago School of Professional Psychology at Westwood, Program in Clinical Psychology, Los Angeles, CA 90024. Offers marital and family therapy (MA).

The Chicago School of Professional Psychology at Westwood, Program in Marital and Family Therapy, Los Angeles, CA 90024. Offers management practice (Psy D); psychodynamic psychotherapy (Psy D).

Marriage and Family Therapy

Christian Theological Seminary, Graduate and Professional Programs, Indianapolis, IN 46208-3301. Offers educational and arts ministries (MA); marriage and family therapy (MA); pastoral care and counseling (D Min); psychotherapy and faith (MA); theological studies (MTS); theology (M Div). *Accreditation:* AAMFT/COAMFTE (one or more programs are accredited); ACIPE; ATS. Part-time programs available. Terminal master's awarded for partial completion of doctoral program. *Degree requirements:* For master's, comprehensive exam (for some programs), thesis (for some programs); for doctorate, comprehensive exam, thesis/dissertation; for M Div, comprehensive exam, thesis/dissertation (for some programs), missionary and cross-cultural experience. *Entrance requirements:* For master's, GRE General Test, MAT; for doctorate, M Div. Electronic applications accepted. *Faculty research:* Faith formation, peer learning post graduation.

The College of New Jersey, Graduate Division, School of Education, Department of Counselor Education, Program in Marriage and Family Therapy, Ewing, NJ 08628. Offers Ed S. Part-time programs available. *Students:* 11 part-time (9 women); includes 2 Black or African American, non-Hispanic/Latino; 2 Hispanic/Latino. 11 applicants, 45% accepted, 4 enrolled. In 2010, 5 Ed Ss awarded. *Entrance requirements:* For degree, previous master's degree or higher. Additional exam requirements/recommendations for international students: Required—TOEFL. *Application deadline:* For fall admission, 2/1 priority date for domestic students; for spring admission, 10/1 priority date for domestic students. Applications are processed on a rolling basis. Application fee: $70. *Financial support:* Tuition waivers (partial) and unspecified assistantships available. Financial award application deadline: 5/1; financial award applicants required to submit FAFSA. *Unit head:* Dr. Charlene Alderfer, Coordinator, 609-771-2136, Fax: 609-637-5116, E-mail: alderfer@tcnj.edu. *Application contact:* Susan L. Hydro, Assistant Dean, Office of Graduate Studies, 609-771-2300, Fax: 609-637-5105, E-mail: graduate@tcnj.edu.

The College of William and Mary, School of Education, Program in Counselor Education, Williamsburg, VA 23187-8795. Offers community and addictions counseling (M Ed); community counseling (M Ed); counselor education (PhD); family counseling (M Ed); school counseling (M Ed). *Accreditation:* ACA; NCATE. Part-time and evening/weekend programs available. *Faculty:* 6 full-time (3 women), 7 part-time/adjunct (6 women). *Students:* 68 full-time (59 women), 8 part-time (4 women); includes 16 minority (9 Black or African American, non-Hispanic/Latino; 2 Asian, non-Hispanic/Latino; 3 Hispanic/Latino; 2 Two or more races, non-Hispanic/Latino), 2 international. Average age 29. 148 applicants, 41% accepted, 31 enrolled. In 2010, 27 master's, 1 doctorate awarded. *Degree requirements:* For doctorate, comprehensive exam, thesis/dissertation. *Entrance requirements:* For master's, GRE, minimum GPA of 3.0; for doctorate, GRE, minimum GPA of 3.5. Additional exam requirements/recommendations for international students: Required—TOEFL. *Application deadline:* For fall admission, 1/15 for domestic and international students. Application fee: $50. Electronic applications accepted. *Expenses:* Tuition, state resident: full-time $6400; part-time $345 per credit hour. Tuition, nonresident: full-time $19,720; part-time $920 per credit hour. Required fees: $4368. *Financial support:* In 2010–11, 54 students received support, including 1 fellowship with full tuition reimbursement available (averaging $20,000 per year), 48 research assistantships with full tuition reimbursements available (averaging $13,000 per year); career-related internships or fieldwork, Federal Work-Study, institutionally sponsored loans, scholarships/grants, and unspecified assistantships also available. Financial award application deadline: 1/15; financial award applicants required to submit FAFSA. *Faculty research:* Sexuality, multicultural education, substance abuse, transpersonal psychology. *Unit head:* Dr. Charles McAdams, Area Coordinator, 757-221-2338, E-mail: crmcad@wm.edu. *Application contact:* Dorothy Smith Osborne, Assistant Dean for Admission, 757-221-2317, Fax: 757-221-2293, E-mail: dsosbo@wm.edu.

Converse College, School of Education and Graduate Studies, Education Specialist Program, Spartanburg, SC 29302-0006. Offers administration and supervision (Ed S); curriculum and instruction (Ed S); marriage and family therapy (Ed S). *Accreditation:* AAMFT/COAMFTE. Part-time programs available. *Entrance requirements:* For degree, GRE or MAT (marriage and family therapy), minimum GPA of 3.0. Electronic applications accepted. *Expenses:* Tuition: Part-time $365 per credit hour.

Denver Seminary, Graduate and Professional Programs, Littleton, CO 80120. Offers apologetics (Certificate); biblical studies (MA); Christian formation and soul care (MA, Certificate); Christian studies (MA, Certificate); church and parachurch leadership (D Min); counseling licensure (MA); counseling ministry (MA); intercultural ministry (Certificate); leadership (MA, Certificate); marriage and family counseling (D Min); pastoral ministry (D Min); philosophy of religion (MA); spiritual guidance (Certificate); theology (M Div, Certificate); worship (Certificate); youth and family ministry (MA). *Accreditation:* ACA; ACIPE; ATS (one or more programs are accredited). Part-time and evening/weekend programs available. Postbaccalaureate distance learning degree programs offered. *Degree requirements:* For master's, 2 foreign languages, thesis (for some programs); for doctorate, 2 foreign languages, thesis/dissertation; for M Div, 2 foreign languages. *Entrance requirements:* For M Div, minimum undergraduate GPA of 2.5; for master's, minimum undergraduate GPA of 3.0; for doctorate, M Div, 3 years of ministry experience. Additional exam requirements/recommendations for international students: Required—TOEFL (minimum score 575 paper-based; 233 computer-based; 90 iBT). Electronic applications accepted.

Dominican University of California, Graduate Programs, School of Education and Counseling Psychology, Department of Counseling Psychology, San Rafael, CA 94901-2298. Offers MFT, MS. Part-time programs available. *Faculty:* 3 full-time (2 women), 9 part-time/adjunct (7 women). *Students:* 55 full-time (52 women), 39 part-time (33 women); includes 15 minority (3 Black or African American, non-Hispanic/Latino; 1 American Indian or Alaska Native, non-Hispanic/Latino; 9 Hispanic/Latino; 2 Two or more races, non-Hispanic/Latino), 4 international. Average age 38. 59 applicants, 54% accepted, 23 enrolled. In 2010, 20 master's awarded. *Degree requirements:* For master's, comprehensive exam (for some programs), thesis (for some programs). *Entrance requirements:* For master's, minimum GPA of 3.0 for last 60 units. Additional exam requirements/recommendations for international students: Required—TOEFL (minimum score 550 paper-based; 213 computer-based; 80 iBT), IELTS. *Application deadline:* For fall admission, 6/15 priority date for domestic and international students; for spring admission, 11/15 priority date for domestic and international students. Applications are processed on a rolling basis. Application fee: $40. Electronic applications accepted. *Expenses:* Contact institution. *Financial support:* In 2010–11, 39 students received support, including 38 fellowships (averaging $2,704 per year); career-related internships or fieldwork, scholarships/grants, traineeships, health care benefits, tuition waivers (partial), and tuition discounts also available. Support available to part-time students. Financial award application deadline: 3/2; financial award applicants required to submit FAFSA. *Unit head:* Dr. Charles R. Billings, Chair, 415-485-3263. *Application contact:* Moriah Dunning, Associate Director of Graduate Admissions, 415-485-3246, Fax: 415-485-3214, E-mail: moriah.dunning@dominican.edu.

Drexel University, College of Nursing and Health Professions, Program in Couples and Family Therapy, Philadelphia, PA 19104-2875. Offers couples and family therapy (PhD); family therapy (MFT). *Accreditation:* AAMFT/COAMFTE (one or more programs are accredited). Part-time programs available. Terminal master's awarded for partial completion of doctoral program. *Degree requirements:* For master's, comprehensive exam, thesis; for doctorate, thesis/dissertation, qualifying exam. *Entrance requirements:* For master's, GRE General Test or MAT, minimum GPA of 2.75; for doctorate, GRE General Test, minimum GPA of 3.0. Electronic applications accepted. *Faculty research:* Family assessment, gender issues, chronic illness, early intervention.

East Carolina University, Graduate School, College of Human Ecology, Department of Child Development and Family Relations, Greenville, NC 27858-4353. Offers child development and family relations (MS); marriage and family therapy (MS). *Accreditation:* AAMFT/COAMFTE. Part-time programs available. *Degree requirements:* For master's, comprehensive exam, thesis optional. *Expenses:* Tuition, state resident: full-time $3130; part-time $391.25 per credit hour. Tuition, nonresident: full-time $13,817; part-time $1727.13 per credit hour. Required fees: $1916; $239.50 per credit hour. Tuition and fees vary according to campus/location and program. *Faculty research:* Child care quality, mental health delivery systems for children, family violence.

Eastern Nazarene College, Adult and Graduate Studies, Program in Marriage and Family Therapy, Quincy, MA 02170. Offers MS. Part-time and evening/weekend programs available. *Entrance requirements:* For master's, 3 letters of recommendation, resume. Additional exam requirements/recommendations for international students: Required—TOEFL (minimum score 550 paper-based).

Eastern University, Palmer Theological Seminary, Program in Ministry, St. Davids, PA 19087-3696. Offers marriage and family (D Min). Part-time programs available. *Degree requirements:* For doctorate, thesis/dissertation. *Entrance requirements:* For doctorate, 3 years of experience, involvement in ministry, church endorsement. *Expenses:* Contact institution.

East Tennessee State University, School of Graduate Studies, College of Education, Department of Human Development and Learning, Johnson City, TN 37614. Offers advanced practitioner (M Ed); community agency counseling (M Ed, MA); comprehensive concentration (M Ed); counseling (M Ed, MA); early childhood (PhD); early childhood education (M Ed, MA); early childhood general (M Ed); early childhood special education (M Ed); early childhood teaching (M Ed); elementary and secondary (school counseling) (M Ed, MA); marriage and family therapy (M Ed, MA); modified concentration (M Ed). *Accreditation:* ACA; NCATE. Part-time programs available. *Faculty:* 21 full-time (13 women). *Students:* 102 full-time (84 women), 45 part-time (44 women); includes 11 minority (7 Black or African American, non-Hispanic/Latino; 4 Two or more races, non-Hispanic/Latino), 5 international. Average age 33. 143 applicants, 46% accepted, 45 enrolled. In 2010, 48 master's awarded. Terminal master's awarded for partial completion of doctoral program. *Degree requirements:* For master's, comprehensive exam, thesis optional, internship, student teaching, culminating experience; for doctorate, comprehensive exam, thesis/dissertation, research apprenticeship. *Entrance requirements:* For master's, GRE General Test, minimum GPA of 3.0; for doctorate, GRE General Test, professional resume, master's degree in early childhood or related field, interview. Additional exam requirements/recommendations for international students: Required—TOEFL (minimum score 550 paper-based; 213 computer-based; 79 iBT). *Application deadline:* For fall admission, 2/1 priority date for domestic and international students. Application fee: $25 ($35 for international students). Electronic applications accepted. *Financial support:* In 2010–11, 12 research assistantships with full tuition reimbursements (averaging $5,500 per year) were awarded; teaching assistantships with full tuition reimbursements, career-related internships or fieldwork, institutionally sponsored loans, scholarships/grants, traineeships, and unspecified assistantships also available. Financial award application deadline: 7/1; financial award applicants required to submit FAFSA. *Faculty research:* Drug and alcohol abuse, marriage and family counseling, severe mental retardation, parenting of children with disabilities. Total annual research expenditures: $405,136. *Unit head:* Dr. Patricia Robertson, Chair, 423-439-7693, Fax: 423-439-7790, E-mail: robertpe@etsu.edu. *Application contact:* Admissions and Records Clerk, 423-439-4221, Fax: 423-439-5624, E-mail: gradsch@etsu.edu.

Edgewood College, Program in Marriage and Family Therapy, Madison, WI 53711-1997. Offers MS. *Accreditation:* AAMFT/COAMFTE. Part-time and evening/weekend programs available. *Students:* 30 full-time (25 women), 17 part-time (16 women); includes 5 minority (2 Asian, non-Hispanic/Latino; 1 Hispanic/Latino; 1 Native Hawaiian or other Pacific Islander, non-Hispanic/Latino; 1 Two or more races, non-Hispanic/Latino), 1 international. Average age 31. In 2010, 13 master's awarded. *Degree requirements:* For master's, research project. *Entrance requirements:* For master's, minimum GPA of 2.75, 2 letters of reference, interviews. Additional exam requirements/recommendations for international students: Required—TOEFL (minimum score 213 computer-based). *Application deadline:* For fall admission, 3/1 for domestic students. Application fee: $25. Electronic applications accepted. *Expenses:* Tuition: Part-time $719 per credit hour. *Unit head:* Dr. Peter Fabian, Chair, 608-663-2233, Fax: 608-663-3291, E-mail: fabian@edgewood.edu. *Application contact:* Joann Eastman, Admissions Counselor, 608-663-3250, Fax: 608-663-2214, E-mail: gps@edgewood.edu.

Evangelical Theological Seminary, Graduate and Professional Programs, Myerstown, PA 17067-1212. Offers Biblical studies (MAR); congregational ministry (M Div); global and contextual studies (M Div, MAR); historical and theological studies (MAR); interdisciplinary studies (MAR); marriage and family counseling (M Div); marriage and family therapy (MA); New Testament (MAR); Old Testament (MAR); spiritual formation (MAR); teaching ministry (M Div); youth ministry (M Div). *Accreditation:* ATS (one or more programs are accredited). Part-time programs available. Postbaccalaureate distance learning degree programs offered (minimal on-campus study). *Degree requirements:* For master's, 2 foreign languages; for M Div, 2 foreign languages, ministry internship. *Entrance requirements:* For M Div and master's, minimum GPA of 2.5. Additional exam requirements/recommendations for international students: Required—TOEFL (minimum score 550 paper-based; 213 computer-based). *Faculty research:* Literary form and structure within the Hebrew and Greek scriptures, Wesley studies, esoteric biblical languages, the Mosaic law and the Christian, ethics.

Fairfield University, Graduate School of Education and Allied Professions, Department of Marriage and Family Therapy, Fairfield, CT 06824-5195. Offers family studies (MA); marriage and family therapy (MA). *Accreditation:* AAMFT/COAMFTE. Part-time and evening/weekend programs available. *Faculty:* 3 full-time (all women), 5 part-time/adjunct (3 women). *Students:* 28 full-time (23 women), 55 part-time (51 women); includes 1 Black or African American, non-Hispanic/Latino; 3 Hispanic/Latino. Average age 39. 38 applicants, 53% accepted, 8 enrolled. In 2010, 17 master's awarded. *Degree requirements:* For master's, comprehensive exam. *Entrance requirements:* For master's, minimum QPA of 3.0, 2 recommendations, resume. Additional exam requirements/recommendations for international students: Required—TOEFL (minimum score 550 paper-based; 213 computer-based; 84 iBT). *Application deadline:* For fall admission, 4/15 for domestic and international students; for spring admission, 10/1 for domestic and international students. Application fee: $60. Electronic applications accepted. *Expenses:* Tuition: Part-time $600 per hour. Part-time tuition and fees vary according to degree level and program. *Financial support:* Unspecified assistantships available. Financial award applicants required to submit FAFSA. *Faculty research:* Diversity and multiculturalism, accreditation, professional ethics, program development and alumni engagement, international family therapy. *Unit head:* Dr. Rona Preli, Chair, 203-254-4000 Ext. 2475, Fax: 203-254-4047, E-mail: rpreli@fairfield.edu. *Application contact:* Marianne Gumpper, Director of Graduate and Continuing Studies Admissions, 203-254-4184, Fax: 203-254-4073, E-mail: gradadmis@fairfield.edu.

Florida Atlantic University, College of Education, Department of Counselor Education, Boca Raton, FL 33431-0991. Offers counselor education (M Ed, PhD, Ed S); marriage and family therapy (Ed S); mental health counseling (M Ed, Ed S); rehabilitation counseling (M Ed); school counseling (M Ed, Ed S). *Accreditation:* ACA; NCATE. Part-time and evening/weekend programs available. *Faculty:* 10 full-time (5 women), 1 (woman) part-time/adjunct. *Students:* 75 full-time (60 women), 82 part-time (68 women); includes 46 minority (22 Black or African American, non-Hispanic/Latino; 4 Asian, non-Hispanic/Latino; 20 Hispanic/Latino), 1 international. Average age 32. 118 applicants, 35% accepted, 37 enrolled. In 2010, 51 master's, 1 doctorate awarded. *Degree requirements:* For Ed S, departmental qualifying exam. *Entrance requirements:* For master's, GRE General Test, minimum GPA of 3.0 during previous 2 years; for Ed S, GRE General Test, minimum graduate GPA of 3.25. Additional exam requirements/recommendations for international students: Required—TOEFL. *Application deadline:* For fall admission, 3/1 for domestic students, 2/1 for international students; for spring admission, 9/15 for domestic students, 7/1 for international students. Applications are processed on a rolling basis. Application fee: $30. *Expenses:* Tuition, area resident: Part-time $319.96 per credit. Tuition, state resident: part-time $319.96 per credit. Tuition, nonresident: part-time $926.42 per credit. *Financial support:* Research assistantships with partial tuition reimbursements, teaching assistantships, career-related internships or fieldwork, scholarships/grants, and unspecified assistantships available. *Faculty research:* Brief therapy, psychological type, marriage and family counseling, international programs, integrated services. *Unit head:* Dr. Irene Johnson, Chair, 561-297-

2136, Fax: 561-297-2309. *Application contact:* Darlene Epperson, Office Assistant, 561-297-3601, Fax: 561-297-2309, E-mail: frederic@fau.edu.

Florida State University, The Graduate School, College of Human Sciences, Department of Family and Child Sciences, Tallahassee, FL 32306. Offers family and child sciences (MS); family relations (PhD); marriage and family therapy (PhD). *Accreditation:* AAMFT/COAMFTE. Part-time programs available. *Faculty:* 13 full-time (8 women). *Students:* 36 full-time (27 women), 15 part-time (13 women); includes 12 Black or African American, non-Hispanic/Latino; 1 Asian, non-Hispanic/Latino; 4 Hispanic/Latino, 1 international. 43 applicants, 28% accepted, 10 enrolled. In 2010, 6 master's, 9 doctorates awarded. *Degree requirements:* For master's, comprehensive exam, thesis optional; for doctorate, thesis/dissertation, preliminary examination; clinical examination (for marriage and family therapy). *Entrance requirements:* For master's and doctorate, GRE General Test, minimum GPA of 3.0. Additional exam requirements/recommendations for international students: Required—TOEFL (minimum score 80 iBT). *Application deadline:* For fall admission, 7/1 for domestic students, 5/1 for international students; for spring admission, 11/1 priority date for domestic students, 10/1 priority date for international students. Application fee: $30. Electronic applications accepted. *Expenses:* Tuition, state resident: full-time $8238.24. *Financial support:* In 2010–11, 33 students received support, including 2 fellowships with full tuition reimbursements available (averaging $15,000 per year), 6 research assistantships with full tuition reimbursements available (averaging $16,000 per year), 31 teaching assistantships with full tuition reimbursements available (averaging $16,000 per year); career-related internships or fieldwork, Federal Work-Study, institutionally sponsored loans, scholarships/grants, health care benefits, and unspecified assistantships also available. Financial award application deadline: 1/5; financial award applicants required to submit FAFSA. *Faculty research:* Family therapy, parent-child relations, distressed families and foster care, marital processes, relational interventions. *Unit head:* Dr. Kay Pasley, Chair, 850-644-3217, Fax: 850-644-3439, E-mail: kpasley@admin.fsu.edu. *Application contact:* Bethany Lowe, Academic Support Assistant, 850-644-3217, Fax: 850-644-3439, E-mail: blowe@fsu.edu.

Fresno Pacific University, Fresno Pacific Biblical Seminary, Program in Marriage, Family, and Child Counseling, Fresno, CA 93702-4709. Offers MAMFCC, Diploma. *Degree requirements:* For master's, thesis or alternative. *Entrance requirements:* For master's, GRE General Test, MAT. Additional exam requirements/recommendations for international students: Required—TOEFL (minimum score 550 paper-based; 213 computer-based).

Friends University, Graduate School, Wichita, KS 67213. Offers accounting (MBA); business administration (MBA); business law (MBL); Christian ministry (MACM); family therapy (MSFT); global leadership and management (MA); health care leadership (MHCL); management information systems (MMIS); operations management (MSOM); organization development (MSOD); teaching (MAT). Part-time and evening/weekend programs available. Post-baccalaureate distance learning degree programs offered (minimal on-campus study). *Faculty:* 14 full-time (5 women), 2 part-time/adjunct (1 woman). *Students:* 166 full-time (122 women), 507 part-time (290 women); includes 134 minority (64 Black or African American, non-Hispanic/Latino; 6 American Indian or Alaska Native, non-Hispanic/Latino; 24 Asian, non-Hispanic/Latino; 30 Hispanic/Latino; 1 Native Hawaiian or other Pacific Islander, non-Hispanic/Latino; 9 Two or more races, non-Hispanic/Latino). Average age 38. 445 applicants, 69% accepted, 236 enrolled. In 2010, 345 master's awarded. *Degree requirements:* For master's, research project. *Entrance requirements:* Additional exam requirements/recommendations for international students: Required—TOEFL (minimum score 560 paper-based; 220 computer-based). *Application deadline:* Applications are processed on a rolling basis. Application fee: $45 ($65 for international students). Electronic applications accepted. Tuition and fees vary according to course load, campus/location and program. *Financial support:* Applicants required to submit FAFSA. *Unit head:* Dr. Evelyn Hume, Dean, 800-794-6945 Ext. 5859, Fax: 316-295-5040, E-mail: evelyn_hume@friends.edu. *Application contact:* Jeanette Hanson, Executive Director of Adult Recruitment, 800-794-6945, Fax: 316-295-5050, E-mail: jeanette@friends.edu.

Fuller Theological Seminary, Graduate School of Psychology, Department of Marriage and Family Therapy, Pasadena, CA 91182. Offers family studies (MA); marital and family therapy (MS); marriage and family enrichment (Certificate). *Degree requirements:* For master's, practicum. *Entrance requirements:* For master's, GRE General Test. Additional exam requirements/recommendations for international students: Required—TOEFL. *Expenses:* Contact institution. *Faculty research:* Marital intimacy, sex-roles, psychoanalytical theory, men's issues.

Geneva College, Program in Counseling, Beaver Falls, PA 15010-3599. Offers marriage and family (MA); mental health (MA); school counseling (MA). *Accreditation:* ACA. Part-time and evening/weekend programs available. *Degree requirements:* For master's, comprehensive exam, internship. *Entrance requirements:* For master's, GRE General Test or MAT, minimum GPA of 3.0 (preferred), letters of recommendation, faith statement. Additional exam requirements/recommendations for international students: Required—TOEFL. Electronic applications accepted.

George Fox University, School of Education, Graduate Department of Counseling, Newberg, OR 97132-2697. Offers clinical mental health counseling (MA); marriage, couple and family counseling (MA, Certificate); mental health trauma (Certificate); school counseling (MA, Certificate); school psychology (Certificate, Ed S). Part-time programs available. *Faculty:* 9 full-time (3 women), 7 part-time/adjunct (4 women). *Students:* 119 full-time (95 women), 115 part-time (93 women); includes 34 minority (9 Black or African American, non-Hispanic/Latino; 5 American Indian or Alaska Native, non-Hispanic/Latino; 8 Asian, non-Hispanic/Latino; 10 Hispanic/Latino; 1 Native Hawaiian or other Pacific Islander, non-Hispanic/Latino; 1 Two or more races, non-Hispanic/Latino). Average age 34. 114 applicants, 55% accepted, 45 enrolled. In 2010, 66 master's, 3 other advanced degrees awarded. *Degree requirements:* For master's, clinical project. *Entrance requirements:* For master's, MAT or GRE, bachelor's degree from regionally-accredited college or university, minimum cumulative GPA of 3.0, 1 professional and 1 academic reference, resume, on-campus interview. Additional exam requirements/recommendations for international students: Required—TOEFL (minimum score 577 paper-based; 233 computer-based; 90 iBT), IELTS (minimum score 7). *Application deadline:* For fall admission, 5/30 for domestic and international students; for winter admission, 11/1 for domestic and international students; for spring admission, 2/28 for domestic and international students. Applications are processed on a rolling basis. Application fee: $40. Electronic applications accepted. *Expenses:* Contact institution. *Financial support:* Career-related internships or fieldwork available. *Unit head:* Dr. Richard Shaw, Associate Professor of Marriage and Family Therapy/Chair, 503-554-6142, E-mail: rshaw@georgefox.edu. *Application contact:* Kathy Grant, Admissions Counselor, 800-493-4937, Fax: 503-554-6111, E-mail: counseling@georgefox.edu.

Grand Canyon University, College of Nursing and Health Sciences, Phoenix, AZ 85017-1097. Offers addiction counseling (MS); health care administration (MS); health care informatics (MS); marriage and family therapy (MS); professional counseling (MS); public health (MS). Part-time and evening/weekend programs available. Postbaccalaureate distance learning degree programs offered (no on-campus study). *Faculty:* 2 full-time (1 woman), 54 part-time/adjunct (36 women). *Students:* 2 full-time (both women), 1,818 part-time (1,476 women); includes 414 minority (346 Black or African American, non-Hispanic/Latino; 14 American Indian or Alaska Native, non-Hispanic/Latino; 4 Asian, non-Hispanic/Latino; 29 Hispanic/Latino; 3 Native Hawaiian or other Pacific Islander, non-Hispanic/Latino; 18 Two or more races, non-Hispanic/Latino), 1 international. Average age 44. In 2010, 103 master's awarded. *Entrance requirements:* For master's, undergraduate degree with minimum GPA of 2.8. Additional exam requirements/recommendations for international students: Required—TOEFL (minimum score 575 paper-based; 233 computer-based; 90 iBT), IELTS (minimum score 7). *Application deadline:* For fall admission, 8/21 for domestic students, 7/2 for international students; for spring admission, 12/24 for domestic students, 11/1 for international students. Application fee: $0. *Financial support:* Federal Work-Study available. Support available to part-time students. Financial award applicants required to submit FAFSA. *Unit head:* Dr. Mark Wooden, Dean, 602-639-6815, E-mail: mark.wooden@gcu.edu. *Application contact:* Andrea Wolochuk, Information Contact, 602-639-6429, E-mail: awolochuk@gcu.edu.

Harding University, College of Bible and Religion, Program in Marriage and Family Therapy, Searcy, AR 72149-0001. Offers marriage and family therapy (MS); mental health counseling (MS). Part-time programs available. *Faculty:* 4 full-time (0 women), 4 part-time/adjunct (1 woman). *Students:* 29 full-time (19 women), 3 part-time (all women); includes 2 Black or African American, non-Hispanic/Latino; 1 Hispanic/Latino. Average age 27. 27 applicants, 70% accepted, 19 enrolled. In 2010, 13 master's awarded. *Degree requirements:* For master's, comprehensive exam, 15-month practicum. *Entrance requirements:* For master's, GRE General Test, minimum undergraduate GPA of 2.75, graduate 3.0. *Application deadline:* For fall admission, 4/1 priority date for domestic students. Applications are processed on a rolling basis. Application fee: $40. *Expenses:* Tuition: Full-time $10,098; part-time $561 per credit hour. Required fees: $22.50 per credit hour. *Financial support:* In 2010–11, 6 students received support. Scholarships/grants available. *Faculty research:* Forgiveness, substance abuse, post traumatic stress disorder. *Unit head:* Dr. Lewis L. Moore, Chairman, 501-279-4347, Fax: 501-279-4417, E-mail: lmoore@harding.edu. *Application contact:* Ruth Ann Dawson, Office Manager, 501-279-4347, Fax: 501-279-4417, E-mail: radawson@harding.edu.

Hardin-Simmons University, Graduate School, Cynthia Ann Parker College of Liberal Arts, Department of Psychology, Program in Family Psychology, Abilene, TX 79698-0001. Offers MA. Part-time programs available. *Faculty:* 6 full-time (2 women). *Students:* 14 full-time (11 women), 3 part-time (all women); includes 1 Black or African American, non-Hispanic/Latino; 1 Hispanic/Latino. Average age 27. 14 applicants, 57% accepted, 8 enrolled. In 2010, 9 master's awarded. *Degree requirements:* For master's, comprehensive exam, clinical experience, project. *Entrance requirements:* For master's, minimum undergraduate GPA of 3.0 in major, 2.7 overall; 21 semester hours of course work in psychology, 18 of those in upper division classes; writing sample; letters of recommendation. Additional exam requirements/recommendations for international students: Required—TOEFL (minimum score 550 paper-based; 213 computer-based; 75 iBT). *Application deadline:* For fall admission, 8/15 priority date for domestic students, 4/1 for international students; for spring admission, 1/5 priority date for domestic students, 9/1 for international students. Applications are processed on a rolling basis. Application fee: $50. *Expenses:* Tuition: Full-time $12,150; part-time $675 per credit hour. Required fees: $650; $110 per semester. Tuition and fees vary according to degree level. *Financial support:* In 2010–11, 16 fellowships (averaging $600 per year) were awarded; career-related internships or fieldwork and scholarships/grants also available. Support available to part-time students. Financial award application deadline: 6/30; financial award applicants required to submit FAFSA. *Faculty research:* Family stress management, spirituality in marriage, intimacy and sexuality in marriage, sex education in the church, role of faith in marital satisfaction. *Unit head:* Dr. Sue Lucas, Director, 325-670-1538, Fax: 325-670-1458, E-mail: slucas@hsutx.edu. *Application contact:* Dr. Nancy Kucinski, Dean of Graduate Studies, 325-670-1298, Fax: 325-670-1564, E-mail: gradoff@hsutx.edu.

Hofstra University, School of Education, Health, and Human Services, Programs in Counseling, Hempstead, NY 11549. Offers counseling (MS Ed, PD); creative arts therapy (MA); gerontology (MS, Advanced Certificate); marriage and family therapy (MA); mental health counseling (MA); rehabilitation counseling (MS Ed, CAS, PD); rehabilitation counseling in mental health (MS Ed, CAS); school counselor-bilingual extension (Advanced Certificate). Part-time and evening/weekend programs available. *Students:* 145 full-time (132 women), 80 part-time (74 women); includes 41 minority (23 Black or African American, non-Hispanic/Latino; 5 Asian, non-Hispanic/Latino; 11 Hispanic/Latino; 1 Native Hawaiian or other Pacific Islander, non-Hispanic/Latino; 1 Two or more races, non-Hispanic/Latino), 8 international. Average age 30. 187 applicants, 63% accepted, 67 enrolled. In 2010, 79 master's, 1 other advanced degree awarded. *Degree requirements:* For master's, comprehensive exam (for some programs), thesis (for some programs), internship, practicum, student teaching, seminars. *Entrance requirements:* For master's, GRE, interview, letters of recommendation, portfolio, essay, professional experience, certification; for other advanced degree, GRE, interview, letters of recommendation, essay, professional experience, resume, master's degree. Additional exam requirements/recommendations for international students: Required—TOEFL (minimum score 550 paper-based; 213 computer-based; 80 iBT). *Application deadline:* Applications are processed on a rolling basis. Application fee: $70 ($75 for international students). Electronic applications accepted. *Expenses:* Tuition: Full-time $18,000; part-time $1000 per credit hour. Required fees: $970; $145 per term. Tuition and fees vary according to program. *Financial support:* In 2010–11, 102 students received support, including 27 fellowships with full and partial tuition reimbursements available (averaging $2,466 per year), 4 research assistantships with full and partial tuition reimbursements available (averaging $14,567 per year); career-related internships or fieldwork, Federal Work-Study, institutionally sponsored loans, scholarships/grants, tuition waivers (full and partial), unspecified assistantships, and scholarships also available. Support available to part-time students. Financial award applicants required to submit FAFSA. *Faculty research:* Bereavement, loss, and trauma counseling, creativity for non-artists. *Unit head:* Dr. Darra Pace, Chairperson, 516-463-6476, Fax: 516-463-6415, E-mail: cprdzp@hofstra.edu. *Application contact:* Carol Drummer, Dean of Graduate Admissions, 516-463-4876, Fax: 516-463-4664, E-mail: gradstudent@hofstra.edu.

Hope International University, School of Graduate and Professional Studies, Program in Marriage and Family Therapy, Fullerton, CA 92831-3138. Offers MA, MFT. *Accreditation:* AAMFT/COAMFTE. *Degree requirements:* For master's, comprehensive exam, thesis (for some programs), final exam, practicum. *Entrance requirements:* For master's, minimum GPA of 3.0, interview, bachelor's degree, 2 references. Additional exam requirements/recommendations for international students: Required—TOEFL (minimum score 550 paper-based; 213 computer-based; 86 iBT); Recommended—IELTS (minimum score 6.5). Electronic applications accepted. *Expenses:* Contact institution.

Idaho State University, Office of Graduate Studies, Kasiska College of Health Professions, Department of Counseling, Pocatello, ID 83209-8120. Offers counseling (M Coun, Ed S), including marriage and family counseling (M Coun), mental health counseling (M Coun), school counseling (M Coun), student affairs and college counseling (M Coun); counselor education and counseling (PhD). *Accreditation:* ACA (one or more programs are accredited). Part-time programs available. *Degree requirements:* For master's, comprehensive exam, thesis, 4 semesters resident graduate study, practicum/internship; for doctorate, comprehensive exam, thesis/dissertation, 3 semesters internship, 4 consecutive semesters doctoral-level study on campus; for Ed S, comprehensive exam, thesis, case studies, oral exam. *Entrance requirements:* For master's, GRE General Test, MAT, minimum GPA of 3.0, bachelors degree, interview, 3 letters of recommendation; for doctorate, GRE General Test, MAT, minimum graduate GPA of 3.0, resume, interview, counseling license, master's degree; for Ed S, GRE General Test, minimum graduate GPA of 3.0, master's degree in counseling, 3 letters of recommendation, 2 years work experience. Additional exam requirements/recommendations for international students: Required—TOEFL (minimum score 600 paper-based; 213 computer-based; 80 iBT). Electronic applications accepted. *Faculty research:* Group counseling, multicultural counseling, family counseling, child therapy, supervision.

Indiana University–Purdue University Fort Wayne, School of Education, Department of Professional Studies, Fort Wayne, IN 46805-1499. Offers counselor education (MS Ed); educational leadership (MS Ed); marriage and family therapy (MS Ed); school counseling (MS Ed); special education (MS Ed, Certificate). Part-time programs available. *Faculty:* 10 full-time (5 women). *Students:* 3 full-time (all women), 156 part-time (124 women); includes 20 minority (10 Black or African American, non-Hispanic/Latino; 1 American Indian or Alaska Native, non-Hispanic/Latino; 8 Hispanic/Latino; 1 Two or more races, non-Hispanic/Latino), 1 international. Average age 33. 83 applicants, 63% accepted, 51 enrolled. In 2010, 58 master's awarded. *Degree requirements:* For master's, comprehensive exam, practicum, internship, portfolio. *Entrance requirements:* For master's, minimum GPA of 2.5, three professional letters of recommendation. Additional exam requirements/recommendations for international students: Required—TOEFL (minimum score 550 paper-based; 213 computer-based; 77 iBT). *Application deadline:* For fall admission, 4/1 priority date for domestic and international students. Applications are processed on a rolling basis. Application fee: $55. *Expenses:* Tuition, state resident: full-time $4824; part-time $268 per credit. Tuition, nonresident: full-time $11,625; part-time

Marriage and Family Therapy

Indiana University–Purdue University Fort Wayne (continued)
$646 per credit. Required fees: $555; $30.85 per credit. Tuition and fees vary according to course load. *Financial support:* In 2010–11, 1 teaching assistantship with partial tuition reimbursement (averaging $12,740 per year) was awarded; research assistantships with partial tuition reimbursements, scholarships/grants also available. Support available to part-time students. Financial award application deadline: 3/1; financial award applicants required to submit FAFSA. *Unit head:* Dr. James Burg, Interim Chair, 260-481-5406, Fax: 260-481-5408, E-mail: burgj@ipfw.edu. *Application contact:* Vicky L. Schmidt, Graduate Recorder, 260-481-6450, Fax: 260-481-5408, E-mail: schmidt@ipfw.edu.

Indiana Wesleyan University, Graduate School, College of Arts and Sciences, Marion, IN 46953. Offers addictions counseling (MS); clinical mental health counseling (MS); community counseling (MS); marriage and family therapy (MS); school counseling (MS); student development counseling and administration (MS). *Accreditation:* ACA. Part-time programs available. *Degree requirements:* For master's, thesis or alternative. *Entrance requirements:* For master's, GRE General Test. Additional exam requirements/recommendations for international students: Required—TOEFL. Electronic applications accepted. *Expenses:* Contact institution. *Faculty research:* Community counseling, multicultural counseling, addictions.

Instituto Tecnologico de Santo Domingo, Graduate School, Area of Humanities and Social Sciences, Santo Domingo, Dominican Republic. Offers accounting (Certificate); adult education (Certificate); applied linguistics (MA); economics (MA); education (M Ed); educational psychology (MA, Certificate); gender and development (MA, Certificate); humanistic studies (MA); international marketing management (Certificate); international relations in the Caribbean basin (Certificate); intervention systems in family therapy (MA); linguistic and literary communication (Certificate); pedagogical support (MA); social science education (M Ed); sustainable human development (MA); terminal illness and death psychology (Certificate); youth and adult education (M Ed).

Iona College, School of Arts and Science, Department of Family and Pastoral Counseling, New Rochelle, NY 10801-1890. Offers marriage and family therapy (MS, Certificate). *Accreditation:* AAMFT/COAMFTE. Part-time and evening/weekend programs available. *Faculty:* 4 full-time (0 women), 1 (woman) part-time/adjunct. *Students:* 30 full-time (23 women), 10 part-time (all women); includes 15 minority (7 Black or African American, non-Hispanic/Latino; 8 Hispanic/Latino). Average age 33. 49 applicants, 57% accepted, 15 enrolled. In 2010, 20 master's, 1 other advanced degree awarded. *Degree requirements:* For master's, thesis, project. *Entrance requirements:* For master's, draw-a-person test, sentence completion test, interview, minimum GPA of 3.0. *Application deadline:* Applications are processed on a rolling basis. Application fee: $50. Electronic applications accepted. *Expenses:* Contact institution. *Financial support:* Career-related internships or fieldwork, tuition waivers (partial), and unspecified assistantships available. Support available to part-time students. Financial award application deadline: 4/15; financial award applicants required to submit FAFSA. *Faculty research:* Marriage counseling. *Unit head:* Jerry Rubino, Chair, 914-633-2418, E-mail: jrubino@iona.edu. *Application contact:* Veronica Jarek-Prinz, Director of Graduate Admissions, 914-633-2420, Fax: 914-633-2277, E-mail: vjarekprinz@iona.edu.

John Brown University, Graduate Counseling Programs, Siloam Springs, AR 72761-2121. Offers community counseling (MS); marriage and family therapy (MS); school counseling (MS). *Accreditation:* NCATE. Part-time and evening/weekend programs available. *Degree requirements:* For master's, practica or internships. *Entrance requirements:* For master's, GRE (minimum score of 1000), recommendation forms from three people, 200-word essay describing professional plans and reason for seeking acceptance. Additional exam requirements/recommendations for international students: Required—TOEFL (minimum score 550 paper-based; 173 computer-based; 70 iBT). Electronic applications accepted.

Johnson University, Department of Marriage and Family Therapy, Knoxville, TN 37998-1001. Offers marriage and family therapy/professional counseling (MA). *Degree requirements:* For master's, variable foreign language requirement, comprehensive exam, thesis (for some programs), internship (500 client contact hours). *Entrance requirements:* For master's, interview, minimum GPA of 3.0, 20 credits of course work in psychology, 15 credits of course work in Bible. Additional exam requirements/recommendations for international students: Required—TOEFL. *Expenses:* Tuition: Full-time $8300; part-time $320 per credit hour. Required fees: $800; $32 per hour. Part-time tuition and fees vary according to course load and program.

Kansas State University, Graduate School, College of Human Ecology, Program in Human Ecology, Manhattan, KS 66506. Offers apparel and textiles (PhD); family life education and consultation (PhD); food service and hospitality management (PhD); lifespan and human development (PhD); marriage and family therapy (PhD); personal financial planning (PhD). *Degree requirements:* For doctorate, thesis/dissertation. Electronic applications accepted.

Kansas State University, Graduate School, College of Human Ecology, School of Family Studies and Human Services, Manhattan, KS 66506. Offers communication sciences and disorders (MS); early childhood education (MS); family studies (MS); life span human development (MS); marriage and family therapy (MS). *Accreditation:* AAMFT/COAMFTE; ASHA. Part-time programs available. *Degree requirements:* For master's, thesis or alternative, oral exam, residency. *Entrance requirements:* For master's, GRE, minimum GPA of 3.0 in last 2 years of undergraduate study. Additional exam requirements/recommendations for international students: Required—TOEFL (minimum score 600 paper-based; 250 computer-based). Electronic applications accepted. *Faculty research:* Health and security of military families, personal and family risk assessment and evaluation, disorders of communication and swallowing, families and health.

Kean University, College of Humanities and Social Sciences, Program in Marriage and Family Therapy, Union, NJ 07083. Offers Diploma. Part-time and evening/weekend programs available. *Faculty:* 17 full-time (13 women). *Students:* 6 full-time (all women), 18 part-time (13 women); includes 5 Black or African American, non-Hispanic/Latino; 2 Hispanic/Latino, 1 international. Average age 30. 16 applicants, 81% accepted, 11 enrolled. In 2010, 5 Diplomas awarded. *Degree requirements:* For Diploma, comprehensive exam, thesis, internship, practicum. *Entrance requirements:* For degree, GRE General Test, minimum GPA of 3.0, 3 letters of recommendation, 12 credits in psychology, interview, transcripts. *Application deadline:* For fall admission, 6/1 for domestic students; for spring admission, 11/1 for domestic students. Application fee: $75 ($150 for international students). Electronic applications accepted. *Expenses:* Tuition, state resident: full-time $10,872; part-time $500 per credit. Tuition, nonresident: full-time $14,736; part-time $614 per credit. Required fees: $2740.80; $125 per credit. Part-time tuition and fees vary according to course load and degree level. *Financial support:* In 2010–11, 1 research assistantship with full tuition reimbursement (averaging $3,263 per year) was awarded; unspecified assistantships also available. Financial award applicants required to submit FAFSA. *Unit head:* Dr. Muriel B. Singer, Program Coordinator, 908-737-5886, E-mail: msinger@kean.edu. *Application contact:* Ann-Marie Kay, Assistant Director of Graduate Admissions, 908-737-5922, Fax: 908-737-5925, E-mail: akay@kean.edu.

Kutztown University of Pennsylvania, College of Education, Program in Counseling Psychology, Kutztown, PA 19530-0730. Offers agency counseling (MA); marital and family therapy (MA). Part-time and evening/weekend programs available. *Faculty:* 8 full-time (3 women). *Students:* 28 full-time (25 women), 26 part-time (23 women); includes 5 minority (3 Black or African American, non-Hispanic/Latino; 2 American Indian or Alaska Native, non-Hispanic/Latino). Average age 27. 36 applicants, 47% accepted, 11 enrolled. In 2010, 10 master's awarded. *Degree requirements:* For master's, comprehensive exam, thesis optional. *Entrance requirements:* For master's, GRE General Test, interview. Additional exam requirements/recommendations for international students: Required—TOEFL (minimum score 550 paper-based; 79 iBT). *Application deadline:* For fall admission, 2/1 for domestic and international students; for spring admission, 8/1 for domestic and international students. Application fee: $35. Electronic applications accepted. *Expenses:* Tuition, state resident:

full-time $6966; part-time $387 per credit. Tuition, nonresident: full-time $11,146; part-time $619 per credit hour. Required fees: $1499; $54 per credit. $68 per year. *Financial support:* Career-related internships or fieldwork, Federal Work-Study, scholarships/grants, and unspecified assistantships available. Financial award application deadline: 3/1; financial award applicants required to submit FAFSA. *Faculty research:* Family addictions. *Unit head:* Dr. Deborah Barlieb, Chairperson, 610-683-4204, Fax: 610-683-1585, E-mail: barlieb@kutztown.edu. *Application contact:* Kelly D. Burr, Associate Director, Graduate Admissions, 610-683-4200, Fax: 610-683-1393, E-mail: graduate@kutztown.edu.

Lancaster Bible College, Graduate School, Lancaster, PA 17601-5036. Offers adult ministries (MA); Bible (MA); children and family ministry (MA); consulting resource teacher (M Ed); elementary school counseling (M Ed); leadership (PhD); leadership studies (MA); marriage and family counseling (MA); mental health counseling (MA); pastoral studies (MA); secondary school counseling (M Ed); student ministry (MA). Part-time and evening/weekend programs available. *Faculty:* 8 full-time (1 woman), 5 part-time/adjunct (1 woman). *Students:* 94 full-time (47 women), 89 part-time (45 women); includes 21 minority (15 Black or African American, non-Hispanic/Latino; 5 Asian, non-Hispanic/Latino; 1 Hispanic/Latino). Average age 36. *Degree requirements:* For master's, comprehensive exam (for some programs), thesis (for some programs). *Entrance requirements:* For master's, bachelor's degree with a minimum of 30 credits of course work in Bible, minimum undergraduate GPA of 3.0, interview. Additional exam requirements/recommendations for international students: Required—TOEFL. *Application deadline:* Applications are processed on a rolling basis. Application fee: $25. *Expenses:* Tuition: Part-time $1491 per course. Required fees: $35 per semester. *Financial support:* In 2010–11, 31 students received support; teaching assistantships, scholarships/grants and unspecified assistantships available. Support available to part-time students. Financial award application deadline: 6/1; financial award applicants required to submit FAFSA. *Unit head:* Dr. Gary Bredfeldt, Associate Vice President/Dean of iLead Center, 717-560-8297, Fax: 717-560-8236. *Application contact:* Mark Wilson, Admissions Counselor, 717-560-8229, E-mail: mwilson@lbc.edu.

La Salle University, School of Arts and Sciences, Program in Psychology, Philadelphia, PA 19141-1199. Offers clinical psychology (Psy D); family psychology (Psy D); rehabilitation psychology (Psy D). *Accreditation:* AAMFT/COAMFTE. Part-time and evening/weekend programs available. *Entrance requirements:* For doctorate, GRE, minimum GPA of 3.0. *Expenses:* Contact institution. *Faculty research:* Cognitive therapy, attribution theory, treatment of addiction.

Lee University, Graduate Studies in Counseling, Cleveland, TN 37320-3450. Offers college student development (MS); holistic child development (MS); marriage and family therapy (MS); school counseling (MS). Part-time programs available. *Faculty:* 7 full-time (3 women), 6 part-time/adjunct (2 women). *Students:* 74 full-time (64 women), 36 part-time (30 women); includes 2 Black or African American, non-Hispanic/Latino; 2 American Indian or Alaska Native, non-Hispanic/Latino; 1 Asian, non-Hispanic/Latino; 2 Hispanic/Latino; 1 Native Hawaiian or other Pacific Islander, non-Hispanic/Latino, 4 international. Average age 27. 53 applicants, 91% accepted, 34 enrolled. In 2010, 19 master's awarded. *Degree requirements:* For master's, variable foreign language requirement, comprehensive exam, thesis, internship. *Entrance requirements:* For master's, GRE General Test or MAT, minimum undergraduate GPA of 3.0, 3 letters of recommendation, interview. Additional exam requirements/recommendations for international students: Required—TOEFL (minimum score 450 paper-based; 45 computer-based). *Application deadline:* For fall admission, 4/1 priority date for domestic and international students; for spring admission, 10/1 priority date for domestic and international students. Applications are processed on a rolling basis. Application fee: $25. *Expenses:* Tuition: Full-time $12,120; part-time $506 per credit hour. Required fees: $560; $305 per semester. Part-time tuition and fees vary according to course load and campus/location. *Financial support:* Teaching assistantships, career-related internships or fieldwork, Federal Work-Study, institutionally sponsored loans, scholarships/grants, and unspecified assistantships available. Financial award application deadline: 3/1; financial award applicants required to submit FAFSA. *Unit head:* Dr. Trevor Milliron, Director, 423-614-8126, Fax: 423-614-8129, E-mail: tmilliron@leeuniversity.edu. *Application contact:* Vicki Glasscock, Graduate Admissions Director, 423-614-8059, E-mail: vglasscock@leeunIversity.edu.

Lewis & Clark College, Graduate School of Education and Counseling, Department of Counseling Psychology, Program in Marriage, Couple and Family Therapy, Portland, OR 97219-7899. Offers MA, MS. Part-time and evening/weekend programs available. *Faculty:* 2 full-time (1 woman), 3 part-time/adjunct (2 women). *Students:* 37 full-time (31 women), 15 part-time (14 women); includes 1 Black or African American, non-Hispanic/Latino; 2 Asian, non-Hispanic/Latino; 2 Hispanic/Latino; 3 Two or more races, non-Hispanic/Latino, 1 international. Average age 28. 80 applicants, 43% accepted, 13 enrolled. In 2010, 13 master's awarded. *Degree requirements:* For master's, thesis (MS). *Entrance requirements:* For master's, GRE General Test, minimum undergraduate GPA of 2.75. Additional exam requirements/recommendations for international students: Required—TOEFL (minimum score 575 paper-based; 233 computer-based). *Application deadline:* For fall admission, 2/1 priority date for domestic and international students. Application fee: $50. Electronic applications accepted. *Expenses:* Tuition: Part-time $713 per semester hour. Tuition and fees vary according to course level and campus/location. *Financial support:* In 2010–11, 13 students received support. Career-related internships or fieldwork, Federal Work-Study, institutionally sponsored loans, scholarships/grants, health care benefits, and tuition waivers (partial) available. Support available to part-time students. Financial award application deadline: 3/1; financial award applicants required to submit FAFSA. *Unit head:* Dr. Teresa McDowell, Program Coordinator, 503-768-6060, Fax: 503-768-6005, E-mail: teresamc@lclark.edu. *Application contact:* Becky Haas, Director of Admissions, 503-768-6200, Fax: 503-768-6205, E-mail: gseadmit@lclark.edu.

Loyola Marymount University, College of Fine Arts, Department of Marital and Family Therapy, Program in Marital and Family Therapy, Los Angeles, CA 90045-. Offers MA. *Faculty:* 4 full-time (3 women), 15 part-time/adjunct (12 women). *Students:* 48 full-time (47 women); includes 3 Black or African American, non-Hispanic/Latino; 7 Asian, non-Hispanic/Latino; 7 Hispanic/Latino; 3 Two or more races, non-Hispanic/Latino, 2 international. Average age 32. 59 applicants, 44% accepted, 22 enrolled. In 2010, 16 master's awarded. *Degree requirements:* For master's, thesis, 840-hour internship. *Entrance requirements:* For master's, MAT, art portfolio, interview, autobiographical essay. Additional exam requirements/recommendations for international students: Required—TOEFL (minimum score 600 paper-based; 250 computer-based; 100 iBT). *Application deadline:* For fall admission, 1/4 priority date for domestic students. Application fee: $50. Electronic applications accepted. *Expenses:* Contact institution. *Financial support:* In 2010–11, 44 students received support, including 2 research assistantships (averaging $1,440 per year); career-related internships or fieldwork, institutionally sponsored loans, scholarships/grants, and unspecified assistantships also available. Financial award application deadline: 2/9; financial award applicants required to submit FAFSA. *Unit head:* Dr. Debra B. Linesch, Chair, 310-338-7674, E-mail: dlinesch@lmu.edu. *Application contact:* Chake H. Kouyoumjian, Associate Dean of Graduate Studies, 310-338-2721, Fax: 310-338-6086, E-mail: ckouyoum@lmu.edu.

Maryville University of Saint Louis, School of Health Professions, Program in Rehabilitation Counseling, St. Louis, MO 63141-7299. Offers marriage and family therapy (MARC); music therapy (MARC); rehabilitation counseling (CAGS); substance abuse (MARC). *Accreditation:* CORE. Part-time and evening/weekend programs available. *Students:* 21 full-time (16 women), 29 part-time (21 women); includes 11 minority (all Black or African American, non-Hispanic/Latino). Average age 33. In 2010, 19 master's awarded. *Degree requirements:* For master's, internship, seminar. *Entrance requirements:* For master's, minimum cumulative GPA of 3.0, 2 letters of recommendation, interview. Additional exam requirements/recommendations for international students: Required—TOEFL (minimum score 550 paper-based). *Application deadline:* For fall admission, 1/15 for domestic students; for spring admission, 10/1 for domestic students. Application fee: $40 ($60 for international students). Electronic applications accepted. *Expenses:* Tuition: Full-time $21,100; part-time $633.50 per credit hour. Required fees: $150 per semester.

Financial support: Career-related internships or fieldwork, Federal Work-Study, and campus employment available. Financial award application deadline: 3/1; financial award applicants required to submit FAFSA. *Unit head:* Dr. Michael Kiener, Interim Director, 314-529-9443, Fax: 314-529-9495, E-mail: mkiener@maryville.edu. *Application contact:* Dr. Michael Kiener, Interim Director, 314-529-9443, Fax: 314-529-9495, E-mail: mkiener@maryville.edu.

Mercy College, School of Social and Behavioral Sciences, Program in Counseling, Dobbs Ferry, NY 10522-1189. Offers alcohol and substance abuse counseling (Certificate); counseling (MS); family counseling (Certificate). Part-time and evening/weekend programs available. Postbaccalaureate distance learning degree programs offered (no on-campus study). *Students:* 118 full-time (101 women), 207 part-time (183 women); includes 90 Black or African American, non-Hispanic/Latino; 1 American Indian or Alaska Native, non-Hispanic/Latino; 3 Asian, non-Hispanic/Latino; 127 Hispanic/Latino; 5 Two or more races, non-Hispanic/Latino. Average age 34. 194 applicants, 50% accepted, 74 enrolled. In 2010, 77 master's, 17 other advanced degrees awarded. *Degree requirements:* For master's, comprehensive exam. *Entrance requirements:* For master's, interview, two professional letters of recommendation, minimum undergraduate GPA of 3.0, resume. Additional exam requirements/recommendations for international students: Required—TOEFL (minimum score 600 paper-based; 250 computer-based; 100 iBT), IELTS (minimum score 8). *Application deadline:* For fall admission, 8/1 for international students. Applications are processed on a rolling basis. Application fee: $40. Electronic applications accepted. *Expenses:* Tuition: Full-time $13,572; part-time $754 per credit hour. Required fees: $130 per term. *Financial support:* Career-related internships or fieldwork, Federal Work-Study, scholarships/grants, and unspecified assistantships available. Support available to part-time students. Financial award applicants required to submit FAFSA. *Faculty research:* Ethics, drug abuse problems, human development, domestic violence. *Unit head:* Dr. Arthur McCann, Assistant Professor, Psychology and Behavioral Science, 914-674-7670, E-mail: amccann@mercy.edu. *Application contact:* Allison Gurdineer, Senior Associate Director of Recruitment, 914-674-7601, E-mail: agurdineer@mercy.edu.

Mercy College, School of Social and Behavioral Sciences, Program in Marriage and Family Therapy, Dobbs Ferry, NY 10522-1189. Offers MS. Part-time and evening/weekend programs available. *Students:* 21 full-time (18 women), 46 part-time (38 women); includes 24 Black or African American, non-Hispanic/Latino; 1 Asian, non-Hispanic/Latino; 15 Hispanic/Latino, 2 international. Average age 35. 67 applicants, 31% accepted, 17 enrolled. In 2010, 9 master's awarded. *Degree requirements:* For master's, practicum, research project. *Entrance requirements:* For master's, current resume, interview with program director, written recommendations from 2 instructors. Additional exam requirements/recommendations for international students: Required—TOEFL (minimum score 600 paper-based; 250 computer-based; 100 iBT), IELTS (minimum score 8). *Application deadline:* For fall admission, 8/1 for international students. Applications are processed on a rolling basis. Application fee: $40. Electronic applications accepted. *Expenses:* Tuition: Full-time $13,572; part-time $754 per credit hour. Required fees: $130 per term. *Financial support:* Career-related internships or fieldwork, Federal Work-Study, scholarships/grants, and unspecified assistantships available. Support available to part-time students. Financial award applicants required to submit FAFSA. *Unit head:* Evan Imber-Black, Program Director, 914-674-7800, E-mail: eimberblack@mercy.edu. *Application contact:* Allison Gurdineer, Senior Associate Director of Recruitment, 914-674-7601, E-mail: agurdineer@mercy.edu.

Messiah College, Program in Counseling, Grantham, PA 17027. Offers clinical mental health counseling (MAC); counseling (CAGS); marriage, couple, and family counseling (MAC); school counseling (MAC). Part-time programs available. *Entrance requirements:* For master's, minimum undergraduate cumulative GPA of 3.0, 2 recommendations, resume or curriculum vitae, interview; for CAGS, bachelor's degree, minimum undergraduate cumulative GPA of 3.0, essay, two recommendations, resume or curriculum vitae, interview. *Application deadline:* Applications are processed on a rolling basis. Application fee: $30. Electronic applications accepted. *Financial support:* Applicants required to submit FAFSA. *Unit head:* Dr. John Addleman, Director, 717-796-1800 Ext. 2980, Fax: 717-691-2386, E-mail: jaddlemn@messiah.edu. *Application contact:* Dr. John Addleman, Director, 717-796-1800 Ext. 2980, Fax: 717-691-2386, E-mail: jaddlemn@messiah.edu.

Michigan State University, The Graduate School, College of Social Science, Department of Family and Child Ecology, East Lansing, MI 48824. Offers child development (MA); community services (MS); family and child ecology (PhD); family studies (MA); marriage and family therapy (MA); youth development (MA). *Accreditation:* AAMFT/COAMFTE (one or more programs are accredited). *Entrance requirements:* For master's, GRE General Test, minimum GPA of 3.0 in last 2 years of undergraduate course work, 3 letters of recommendation; for doctorate, GRE General Test, minimum GPA of 3.0, 3 letters of recommendation, background in behavioral sciences. Additional exam requirements/recommendations for international students: Required—TOEFL. Electronic applications accepted.

Mid-America Christian University, Program in Counseling, Oklahoma City, OK 73170-4504. Offers marital and family therapy (MS); pastoral/spiritual direction (MS); professional counselor (MS). *Entrance requirements:* For master's, MAT, bachelor's degree from a regionally accredited college or university, minimum overall cumulative GPA of 2.75 of bachelor course work. Additional exam requirements/recommendations for international students: Required—TOEFL (minimum score 550 paper-based; 213 computer-based).

Minnesota State University Mankato, College of Graduate Studies, College of Education, Department of Counseling and Student Personnel, Mankato, MN 56001. Offers college student affairs (MS); counselor education and supervision (Ed D); marriage and family counseling (Certificate); mental health counseling (MS); professional school counseling (MS). *Accreditation:* ACA (one or more programs are accredited); NCATE. *Students:* 78 full-time (64 women), 35 part-time (25 women). *Degree requirements:* For master's, comprehensive exam, thesis or alternative. *Entrance requirements:* For master's, GRE General Test or MAT (if GPA less than 3.0 for last 2 years), minimum GPA of 3.0 during previous 2 years, 3 letters of reference. Additional exam requirements/recommendations for international students: Required—TOEFL. *Application deadline:* For fall admission, 1/15 priority date for domestic students. Applications are processed on a rolling basis. Application fee: $40. Electronic applications accepted. *Financial support:* Research assistantships with full tuition reimbursements, teaching assistantships with full tuition reimbursements, career-related internships or fieldwork, Federal Work-Study, institutionally sponsored loans, and unspecified assistantships available. Support available to part-time students. Financial award application deadline: 3/15; financial award applicants required to submit FAFSA. *Unit head:* Dr. Jacqueline Lewis, Chairperson, 507-389-5658. *Application contact:* 507-389-2321, E-mail: grad@mnsu.edu.

Mississippi College, Graduate School, School of Education, Department of Psychology and Counseling, Clinton, MS 39058. Offers counseling (Ed S); marriage and family counseling (MS); mental health counseling (MS); school counseling (M Ed). Part-time programs available. *Degree requirements:* For master's and Ed S, comprehensive exam, thesis optional. *Entrance requirements:* For master's, GRE or NTE. Additional exam requirements/recommendations for international students: Recommended—IELTS. Electronic applications accepted.

Montclair State University, The Graduate School, College of Humanities and Social Sciences, Center for Child Advocacy, Montclair, NJ 07043-1624. Offers child advocacy (MA, Certificate); public child welfare (MA). Part-time and evening/weekend programs available. Postbaccalaureate distance learning degree programs offered. *Faculty:* 3 full-time (all women), 3 part-time/adjunct (0 women). *Students:* 11 full-time (all women); 121 part-time (111 women); includes 38 Black or African American, non-Hispanic/Latino; 1 American Indian or Alaska Native, non-Hispanic/Latino; 2 Asian, non-Hispanic/Latino; 21 Hispanic/Latino, 1 international. Average age 34. 66 applicants, 94% accepted, 53 enrolled. In 2010, 21 master's, 53 other advanced degrees awarded. *Degree requirements:* For master's, comprehensive exam (for some programs), thesis (for some programs). *Entrance requirements:* For master's, GRE, 2 letters of recommendation. Additional exam requirements/recommendations for international students: Required—TOEFL (minimum iBT score of 83) or IELTS. Application fee: $60.

Expenses: Tuition, state resident: part-time $501.34 per credit. Tuition, nonresident: part-time $773.88 per credit. Required fees: $71.15 per credit. *Financial support:* In 2010–11, 2 research assistantships with full tuition reimbursements (averaging $7,000 per year) were awarded; Federal Work-Study, scholarships/grants, and unspecified assistantships also available. Support available to part-time students. Financial award application deadline: 3/1; financial award applicants required to submit FAFSA. *Unit head:* Dr. Robert McCormick, Head, 973-655-4188. *Application contact:* Amy Aiello, Director of Graduate Admissions and Operations, 973-655-5147, Fax: 973-655-7869, E-mail: graduate.school@montclair.edu.

Montclair State University, The Graduate School, College of Humanities and Social Sciences, Department of Psychology, Montclair, NJ 07043-1624. Offers educational psychology (MA), including child/adolescent clinical psychology, clinical psychology for Spanish/English bilinguals, educational psychology; psychology (MA), including industrial and organizational psychology; school psychology (Certificate). Part-time and evening/weekend programs available. *Faculty:* 25 full-time (11 women), 37 part-time/adjunct (21 women). *Students:* 43 full-time (31 women), 33 part-time (22 women); includes 8 Black or African American, non-Hispanic/Latino; 3 Asian, non-Hispanic/Latino; 10 Hispanic/Latino, 2 international. Average age 26. 117 applicants, 33% accepted, 24 enrolled. In 2010, 23 master's, 1 other advanced degree awarded. *Degree requirements:* For master's, comprehensive exam, thesis or alternative. *Entrance requirements:* For master's, GRE General Test, 2 letters of recommendation. Additional exam requirements/recommendations for international students: Required—TOEFL (minimum iBT score of 83) or IELTS. *Application deadline:* For fall admission, 6/1 for international students; for spring admission, 11/1 for international students. Applications are processed on a rolling basis. Application fee: $60. Electronic applications accepted. *Expenses:* Tuition, state resident: part-time $501.34 per credit. Tuition, nonresident: part-time $773.88 per credit. Required fees: $71.15 per credit. *Financial support:* In 2010–11, 13 research assistantships with full tuition reimbursements (averaging $7,000 per year) were awarded; Federal Work-Study, scholarships/grants, and unspecified assistantships also available. Support available to part-time students. Financial award application deadline: 3/1; financial award applicants required to submit FAFSA. *Faculty research:* Legal decision-making, leadership development, bias and stereotype threat in the selection process, nature of pre-linguistic thought in infants, lateralized cortical contributions to memory, pediatric neuro-imaging, the production and perception of speech, school-based assessment and intervention for bullying, cognitive processes in reading, identification of autism in toddlers. Total annual research expenditures: $300,000. *Unit head:* Dr. Peter Vietze, Chairperson, 973-655-5201. *Application contact:* Amy Aiello, Director of Admissions and Operations, 973-655-5147, Fax: 973-655-7869, E-mail: graduate.school@montclair.edu.

Mount St. Mary's College, Graduate Division, Program in Counseling Psychology, Los Angeles, CA 90049-1599. Offers counseling psychology (MS); marriage and family therapy (MS); psychology (MS). Part-time and evening/weekend programs available. *Degree requirements:* For master's, research project. *Entrance requirements:* For master's, minimum GPA of 3.0.

Northcentral University, Graduate Studies, Prescott Valley, AZ 86314. Offers business (MBA, DBA, PhD, CAGS); education (M Ed, Ed D, PhD, CAGS); marriage and family therapy (MA, PhD); psychology (MA, PhD, CAGS). Evening/weekend programs available. Postbaccalaureate distance learning degree programs offered (no on-campus study). *Faculty:* 18 full-time (7 women), 449 part-time/adjunct (199 women). *Students:* 8,363 full-time (4,501 women); includes 896 minority (606 Black or African American, non-Hispanic/Latino; 35 American Indian or Alaska Native, non-Hispanic/Latino; 92 Asian, non-Hispanic/Latino; 142 Hispanic/Latino; 13 Native Hawaiian or other Pacific Islander, non-Hispanic/Latino; 8 Two or more races, non-Hispanic/Latino). Average age 43. In 2010, 367 master's, 150 doctorates, 33 other advanced degrees awarded. *Entrance requirements:* For master's, bachelor's degree from regionally-accredited institution, current resume; for doctorate and CAGS, master's degree from regionally-accredited university. Additional exam requirements/recommendations for international students: Required—TOEFL (minimum score 95 computer-based), IELTS (minimum score 7), Pearson Test of English (minimum score: 65). *Application deadline:* Applications are processed on a rolling basis. Application fee: $75. *Financial support:* Scholarships/grants available. *Unit head:* Dr. Clinton D. Gardner, President and Provost, 888-327-2877, Fax: 928-759-6381, E-mail: president@ncu.edu. *Application contact:* Kevin Lustig, Vice President, Enrollment Services, 480-478-7490, Fax: 928-759-6285, E-mail: klustig@ncu.edu.

North Dakota State University, College of Graduate and Interdisciplinary Studies, College of Human Development and Education, Department of Child Development and Family Science, Fargo, ND 58108. Offers child development and family science (MS); couple and family therapy (MS); family financial planning (MS); gerontology (MS, PhD). *Accreditation:* AAMFT/COAMFTE. Part-time and evening/weekend programs available. Postbaccalaureate distance learning degree programs offered (no on-campus study). *Faculty:* 12 full-time (7 women). *Students:* 30 full-time (27 women), 20 part-time (19 women); includes 2 Black or African American, non-Hispanic/Latino, 2 international. 26 applicants, 62% accepted, 13 enrolled. *Degree requirements:* For master's, thesis or alternative; for doctorate, thesis/dissertation. *Entrance requirements:* Additional exam requirements/recommendations for international students: Required—TOEFL (minimum score 525 paper-based; 197 computer-based; 71 iBT). *Application deadline:* For fall admission, 2/1 for domestic and international students; for spring admission, 10/1 for domestic and international students. Application fee: $45 ($60 for international students). *Financial support:* In 2010–11, 17 students received support, including research assistantships with full tuition reimbursements available (averaging $3,000 per year), 17 teaching assistantships with full tuition reimbursements available (averaging $3,000 per year); career-related internships or fieldwork, Federal Work-Study, institutionally sponsored loans, and tuition waivers (full) also available. Financial award application deadline: 4/1. *Faculty research:* Family therapy, resilience, parenting, adolescent development, mental health. Total annual research expenditures: $333,582. *Unit head:* Dr. James Deal, Head, 701-231-7568, Fax: 701-231-9645, E-mail: jim_deal@ndsu.edu. *Application contact:* Theresa Anderson, Administrative Assistant, 701-231-8628, Fax: 701-231-9645, E-mail: theresa.anderson@ndsu.edu.

Northern Kentucky University, Office of Graduate Programs, College of Informatics, Program in Communication, Highland Heights, KY 41099. Offers communication (MA); communication teaching (Certificate); documentary studies (Certificate); public relations (Certificate); relationships (Certificate). Part-time and evening/weekend programs available. *Faculty:* 7 full-time (3 women), 1 part-time/adjunct (0 women). *Students:* 10 full-time (4 women), 36 part-time (15 women); includes 7 minority (3 Black or African American, non-Hispanic/Latino; 2 Asian, non-Hispanic/Latino; 2 Hispanic/Latino). Average age 29. 29 applicants, 62% accepted, 14 enrolled. In 2010, 11 master's, 2 other advanced degrees awarded. *Degree requirements:* For master's, thesis (for some programs), capstone experience, internship. *Entrance requirements:* For master's, GRE, minimum GPA of 3.0, 3 letters of recommendation, letter of intent. Additional exam requirements/recommendations for international students: Required—TOEFL (minimum score 550 paper-based; 213 computer-based; 79 iBT); Recommended—IELTS (minimum score 6.5). *Application deadline:* For fall admission, 2/1 for domestic students, 6/1 for international students; for spring admission, 7/1 for domestic students, 10/1 for international students. Applications are processed on a rolling basis. Application fee: $40. Electronic applications accepted. *Expenses:* Tuition, state resident: full-time $7254; part-time $403 per credit hour. Tuition, nonresident: full-time $12,492; part-time $694 per credit hour. Tuition and fees vary according to degree level and program. *Financial support:* Unspecified assistantships available. Financial award applicants required to submit FAFSA. *Faculty research:* Business/organizational communication, interpersonal/relational communication, public relations, communication teaching/pedagogy, media (production, criticism, popular culture). Total annual research expenditures: $29,000. *Unit head:* Dr. Jimmy Manning, Director, 859-572-1329, E-mail: manningj1@nku.edu. *Application contact:* Dr. Peg Griffin, Director of Graduate Programs, 859-572-6934, Fax: 859-572-6670, E-mail: griffinp@nku.edu.

Northwestern University, The Graduate School, Program in Marital and Family Therapy, Evanston, IL 60208. Offers MS. *Accreditation:* AAMFT/COAMFTE. *Entrance requirements:*

Marriage and Family Therapy

Northwestern University (continued)

For master's, GRE General Test. *Faculty research:* Marital and family therapy training, gender, psychotherapy outcome, adolescents and pre-school children at risk, families.

Northwest Nazarene University, Graduate Studies, Program in Counselor Education, Nampa, ID 83686-5897. Offers community counseling (MS); marriage and family counseling (MS); school counseling (MS). *Faculty:* 5 full-time (3 women), 4 part-time/adjunct (2 women). *Students:* 83 full-time (64 women), 16 part-time (10 women); includes 7 minority (1 Black or African American, non-Hispanic/Latino; 4 Asian, non-Hispanic/Latino; 2 Hispanic/Latino), 1 international. In 2010, 33 master's awarded. Application fee: $25. *Unit head:* Dr. Brenda Freeman, Chair, 208-467-8428, Fax: 208-467-8339. *Application contact:* Judy Bassett, Program Assistant, 208-467-8345, Fax: 208-467-8339, E-mail: jbassett@nnu.edu.

Notre Dame de Namur University, Division of Academic Affairs, College of Arts and Sciences, Department of Art Therapy Psychology, Belmont, CA 94002-1908. Offers art therapy (MA); marriage and family therapy (MA). Part-time programs available. *Faculty:* 4 full-time (3 women), 8 part-time/adjunct (7 women). *Students:* 38 full-time (all women), 74 part-time (72 women); includes 33 minority (3 Black or African American, non-Hispanic/Latino; 10 Asian, non-Hispanic/Latino; 16 Hispanic/Latino; 2 Native Hawaiian or other Pacific Islander, non-Hispanic/Latino; 2 Two or more races, non-Hispanic/Latino), 8 international. Average age 33. 82 applicants, 40% accepted, 31 enrolled. In 2010, 28 master's awarded. *Degree requirements:* For master's, thesis, oral presentation, portfolio. *Entrance requirements:* For master's, interview, minimum GPA of 2.5. Additional exam requirements/recommendations for international students: Required—TOEFL (minimum score 550 paper-based; 213 computer-based; 79 iBT). *Application deadline:* For fall admission, 8/1 priority date for domestic students; for spring admission, 12/1 priority date for domestic students. Applications are processed on a rolling basis. Application fee: $60. Electronic applications accepted. *Expenses:* Tuition: Full-time $14,220; part-time $790 per credit. Required fees: $35 per semester. Tuition and fees vary according to program. *Financial support:* Career-related internships or fieldwork available. Support available to part-time students. Financial award applicants required to submit FAFSA. *Unit head:* Dr. Richard Carolan, Chair, 650-508-3556, Fax: 650-508-3736. *Application contact:* Candace Hallmark, Associate Director of Admissions, 650-508-3600, Fax: 650-508-3426, E-mail: grad.admit@ndnu.edu.

Notre Dame de Namur University, Division of Academic Affairs, College of Arts and Sciences, Department of Clinical Psychology and Gerontology, Program in Clinical Psychology: Marital and Family Therapy, Belmont, CA 94002-1908. Offers MS. *Entrance requirements:* Additional exam requirements/recommendations for international students: Required—TOEFL (minimum score 550 paper-based; 213 computer-based; 79 iBT). Application fee: $60. *Expenses:* Tuition: Full-time $14,220; part-time $790 per credit. Required fees: $35 per semester. Tuition and fees vary according to program. *Unit head:* Dr. Nusha Askari, 650-508-3728, E-mail: naskari@ndnu.edu. *Application contact:* Candace Hallmark, Associate Director of Admissions, 650-508-3600, Fax: 650-508-3426, E-mail: grad.admit@ndnu.edu.

Nova Southeastern University, Graduate School of Humanities and Social Sciences, Department of Family Therapy, Doctor of Marriage and Family Therapy Program, Fort Lauderdale, FL 33314-7796. Offers DMFT. Part-time programs available. *Faculty:* 11 full-time (6 women), 15 part-time/adjunct (12 women). *Students:* 8 full-time (7 women), 4 part-time (all women); includes 4 Black or African American, non-Hispanic/Latino; 1 Hispanic/Latino. Average age 38. 12 applicants, 33% accepted, 2 enrolled. *Degree requirements:* For doctorate, thesis/dissertation or alternative, portfolio. *Entrance requirements:* For doctorate, minimum GPA of 3.5, interview, master's degree in related field, samples of written work. Additional exam requirements/recommendations for international students: Required—TOEFL. *Application deadline:* For fall admission, 4/1 priority date for domestic and international students. Applications are processed on a rolling basis. Application fee: $50. Electronic applications accepted. *Financial support:* In 2010–11, 1 research assistantship (averaging $15,000 per year) was awarded; career-related internships or fieldwork, Federal Work-Study, scholarships/grants, and unspecified assistantships also available. Financial award applicants required to submit CSS PROFILE. *Faculty research:* Diversity, family business, brief therapy, medical family therapy, human sexuality, family therapy in schools. *Unit head:* Dr. Tommie Boyd, Chair, 954-262-3027, Fax: 954-262-3968, E-mail: tommie@nova.edu. *Application contact:* Marcia Arango, Student Recruitment Coordinator, 954-262-3006, Fax: 954-262-3968, E-mail: marango@nsu.nova.edu.

Nova Southeastern University, Graduate School of Humanities and Social Sciences, Department of Family Therapy, Master's Program in Family Therapy, Fort Lauderdale, FL 33314-7796. Offers family studies (Certificate); family systems healthcare (Certificate); family therapy (MS). *Accreditation:* AAMFT/COAMFTE (one or more programs are accredited). Part-time programs available. *Faculty:* 11 full-time (7 women), 14 part-time/adjunct (10 women). *Students:* 90 full-time (82 women), 46 part-time (44 women); includes 30 Black or African American, non-Hispanic/Latino; 5 Asian, non-Hispanic/Latino; 26 Hispanic/Latino, 11 international. Average age 29. 121 applicants, 55% accepted, 43 enrolled. In 2010, 46 master's awarded. *Degree requirements:* For master's, comprehensive exam. *Entrance requirements:* For master's, minimum GPA of 3.0, interview, writing sample. Additional exam requirements/recommendations for international students: Required—TOEFL. *Application deadline:* For fall admission, 4/1 priority date for domestic students, 4/1 for international students; for spring admission, 1/4 priority date for domestic students, 1/4 for international students. Applications are processed on a rolling basis. Application fee: $50. Electronic applications accepted. *Financial support:* Career-related internships or fieldwork, Federal Work-Study, and scholarships/grants available. Financial award application deadline: 4/1; financial award applicants required to submit CSS PROFILE. *Faculty research:* Cross-cultural counseling, family business, medical family therapy, brief therapy, diversity, family therapy in schools. *Unit head:* Dr. Tommie Boyd, Chair, 954-262-3027, Fax: 954-262-3968, E-mail: tommie@nova.edu. *Application contact:* Marcia Arango, Student Recruitment Coordinator, 954-262-3006, Fax: 954-262-3968, E-mail: marango@nsu.nova.edu.

Nova Southeastern University, Graduate School of Humanities and Social Sciences, Department of Family Therapy, PhD Program in Family Therapy, Fort Lauderdale, FL 33314-7796. Offers PhD. *Accreditation:* AAMFT/COAMFTE. Part-time programs available. *Faculty:* 11 full-time (6 women), 14 part-time/adjunct (11 women). *Students:* 76 full-time (67 women), 33 part-time (29 women); includes 34 Black or African American, non-Hispanic/Latino; 1 Asian, non-Hispanic/Latino; 12 Hispanic/Latino; 1 Two or more races, non-Hispanic/Latino, 12 international. Average age 35. 37 applicants, 70% accepted, 19 enrolled. In 2010, 8 doctorates awarded. *Degree requirements:* For doctorate, thesis/dissertation, portfolio. *Entrance requirements:* For doctorate, master's degree in related field, minimum GPA of 3.5, interview, writing sample. Additional exam requirements/recommendations for international students: Required—TOEFL. *Application deadline:* For fall admission, 4/1 priority date for domestic and international students. Application fee: $50. Electronic applications accepted. *Financial support:* In 2010–11, 63 students received support, including 8 research assistantships (averaging $15,000 per year); career-related internships or fieldwork, Federal Work-Study, scholarships/grants, and unspecified assistantships also available. Financial award application deadline: 4/1. *Faculty research:* Medical family therapy, brief therapy, family business, diversity, human sexuality and therapy, family therapy in schools. *Unit head:* Dr. Tommie Boyd, Chair, 954-262-3027, Fax: 954-262-3968, E-mail: tommie@nova.edu. *Application contact:* Marcia Arango, Student Recruitment Coordinator, 954-262-3006, Fax: 954-262-3968, E-mail: marango@nsu.nova.edu.

Nyack College, Alliance Graduate School of Counseling, Nyack, NY 10960-3698. Offers marriage and family therapy (MA); mental health counseling (MA). Part-time programs available. *Students:* 66 full-time (59 women), 190 part-time (154 women); includes 182 minority (103 Black or African American, non-Hispanic/Latino; 30 Asian, non-Hispanic/Latino; 40 Hispanic/Latino; 9 Two or more races, non-Hispanic/Latino), 7 international. Average age 40. In 2010, 50 master's awarded. *Degree requirements:* For master's, comprehensive exam, counselor-in-training therapy, internship, CPCE exam. *Entrance requirements:* Additional exam

requirements/recommendations for international students: Required—TOEFL (minimum score 220 computer-based; 83 iBT). *Application deadline:* Applications are processed on a rolling basis. Application fee: $35. Electronic applications accepted. *Expenses:* Contact institution. *Unit head:* Dr. Carol Robles, Director, 845-770-5730, Fax: 845-348-3923. *Application contact:* Traci Piescki, Director of Admissions, 800-541-6891, Fax: 845-348-3912, E-mail: admissions.grad@nyack.edu.

Oklahoma State University, College of Human Sciences, Department of Human Development and Family Science, Stillwater, OK 74078. Offers human development and family science (MS, PhD), including family financial planning (MS), human environmental sciences (PhD); marriage and family therapy (MS). *Accreditation:* AAMFT/COAMFTE (one or more programs are accredited). Postbaccalaureate distance learning degree programs offered. *Faculty:* 29 full-time (20 women), 4 part-time/adjunct (all women). *Students:* 35 full-time (30 women), 33 part-time (26 women); includes 5 Black or African American, non-Hispanic/Latino; 3 American Indian or Alaska Native, non-Hispanic/Latino; 2 Hispanic/Latino, 7 international. Average age 31. 78 applicants, 31% accepted, 19 enrolled. In 2010, 21 master's, 4 doctorates awarded. *Degree requirements:* For master's, thesis (for some programs); for doctorate, comprehensive exam, thesis/dissertation. *Entrance requirements:* For master's and doctorate, GRE or GMAT. Additional exam requirements/recommendations for international students: Required—TOEFL (minimum score 550 paper-based; 79 iBT). *Application deadline:* For fall admission, 3/1 priority date for international students; for spring admission, 8/1 priority date for international students. Applications are processed on a rolling basis. Application fee: $40 ($75 for international students). Electronic applications accepted. *Expenses:* Tuition, state resident: full-time $3716; part-time $154.85 per credit hour. Tuition, nonresident: full-time $14,892; part-time $621 per credit hour. Required fees: $2044; $85.20 per credit hour. One-time fee: $50. Tuition and fees vary according to course load and campus/location. *Financial support:* In 2010–11, 26 research assistantships (averaging $8,826 per year), 21 teaching assistantships (averaging $8,143 per year) were awarded; career-related internships or fieldwork, Federal Work-Study, scholarships/grants, health care benefits, tuition waivers (partial), and unspecified assistantships also available. Support available to part-time students. Financial award application deadline: 3/1; financial award applicants required to submit FAFSA. *Faculty research:* Family relations and child development, consequences of adolescent parenting, family stress and coping, impacts of sexual abuse on families, children's social cognition and self-competence, gerontology and health care. *Unit head:* Dr. Sue Williams, Head, 405-744-5057, Fax: 405-744-2800. *Application contact:* Dr. Gordon Emslie, Dean, 405-744-6368, Fax: 405-744-0355, E-mail: grad-i@okstate.edu.

Oral Roberts University, School of Theology and Missions, Tulsa, OK 74171. Offers biblical literature (MA), including advanced languages, Judaic-Christian studies; Christian counseling (MA), including marriage and family therapy; divinity (M Div); missions (MA); practical theology (MA); theological/historical studies (MA); theology (D Min). Part-time programs available. Postbaccalaureate distance learning degree programs offered (minimal on-campus study). *Degree requirements:* For master's, thesis (for some programs), practicum/internship; for doctorate, thesis/dissertation, applied research project; for M Div, one foreign language, field experience. *Entrance requirements:* For M Div and master's, GRE General Test or MAT, minimum GPA of 2.5; for doctorate, M Div, minimum GPA of 3.0, 3 years of full-time ministry experience. Additional exam requirements/recommendations for international students: Required—TOEFL (minimum score 550 paper-based; 213 computer-based; 79 iBT). Electronic applications accepted.

Ottawa University, Graduate Studies-Arizona, Program in Professional Counseling, Ottawa, KS 66067-3399. Offers Christian counseling (MA); expressive arts therapy (MA); marriage and family therapy (MA); treatment of trauma, abuse and deprivation (MA). Programs offered in Mesa, Phoenix, Tempe and West Valley, AZ. Part-time and evening/weekend programs available. Postbaccalaureate distance learning degree programs offered. *Degree requirements:* For master's, comprehensive exam, thesis or alternative, field experience, practicum. *Entrance requirements:* For master's, minimum undergraduate GPA of 3.0; course work in theories of personality, abnormal psychology, and human growth and development. Additional exam requirements/recommendations for international students: Required—TOEFL (minimum score 550 paper-based; 213 computer-based).

Our Lady of Holy Cross College, Program in Education and Counseling, New Orleans, LA 70131-7399. Offers administration and supervision (M Ed); curriculum and instruction (M Ed); marriage and family counseling (MA); school counseling (M Ed, MA). *Accreditation:* ACA; NCATE. Part-time and evening/weekend programs available. *Degree requirements:* For master's, thesis. *Entrance requirements:* For master's, GRE General Test, minimum GPA of 2.7.

Our Lady of the Lake University of San Antonio, School of Professional Studies, Program in Psychology, San Antonio, TX 78207-4689. Offers counseling psychology (MS, Psy D); marriage and family therapy (MS); school psychology (MS). *Accreditation:* APA (one or more programs are accredited). Part-time and evening/weekend programs available. *Students:* 118 full-time (97 women), 94 part-time (85 women); includes 119 minority (20 Black or African American, non-Hispanic/Latino; 2 Asian, non-Hispanic/Latino; 90 Hispanic/Latino; 2 Native Hawaiian or other Pacific Islander, non-Hispanic/Latino; 5 Two or more races, non-Hispanic/Latino), 5 international. Average age 30. In 2010, 842 master's, 4 doctorates awarded. *Degree requirements:* For master's, comprehensive exam, thesis optional, practicum; for doctorate, thesis/dissertation, internship, qualifying exam. *Entrance requirements:* For master's and doctorate, GRE General Test or MAT, interview. Additional exam requirements/recommendations for international students: Required—TOEFL. *Application deadline:* For fall admission, 3/1 priority date for domestic and international students. Applications are processed on a rolling basis. Application fee: $25 ($50 for international students). Electronic applications accepted. *Expenses:* Tuition: Full-time $13,500; part-time $750 per contact hour. Required fees: $330. Tuition and fees vary according to course level, degree level and campus/location. *Financial support:* Research assistantships, teaching assistantships, career-related internships or fieldwork available. Support available to part-time students. Financial award application deadline: 4/15. *Faculty research:* Marriage and family therapy, supervision, cross-cultural counseling, violence. *Unit head:* Dr. Joan Biever, Chair, 210-434-6711, E-mail: jbiever@lake.ollusa.edu. *Application contact:* 210-434-6711, Fax: 210-431-4036, E-mail: gradadm@lake.ollusa.edu.

Pacific Lutheran University, Division of Graduate Studies, Division of Social Sciences, Program in Marriage and Family Therapy, Tacoma, WA 98447. Offers MA. *Accreditation:* AAMFT/COAMFTE. *Degree requirements:* For master's, thesis optional, clinical competency. *Entrance requirements:* For master's, GRE. Additional exam requirements/recommendations for international students: Required—TOEFL (minimum score 550 paper-based; 213 computer-based). Electronic applications accepted.

Pacific Oaks College, Graduate School, Program in Marriage and Family Therapy, Pasadena, CA 91103. Offers marriage, family and child counseling (MA). Part-time and evening/weekend programs available. *Degree requirements:* For master's, thesis. *Entrance requirements:* For master's, interview. Additional exam requirements/recommendations for international students: Required—TOEFL (minimum score 550 paper-based; 213 computer-based). *Faculty research:* Family systems, cross-cultural development, therapeutic intervention and Latino families, battered women.

Palm Beach Atlantic University, School of Education and Behavioral Studies, West Palm Beach, FL 33416-4708. Offers counseling psychology (MSCP), including addictions/mental health, marriage and family therapy, mental health counseling, school guidance counseling. Part-time and evening/weekend programs available. *Faculty:* 13 full-time (3 women), 10 part-time/adjunct (5 women). *Students:* 250 full-time (209 women), 61 part-time (47 women); includes 63 Black or African American, non-Hispanic/Latino; 2 Asian, non-Hispanic/Latino; 37 Hispanic/Latino; 1 Native Hawaiian or other Pacific Islander, non-Hispanic/Latino, 7 international. Average age 35. 108 applicants, 92% accepted, 83 enrolled. In 2010, 96 master's awarded. *Entrance requirements:* For master's, GRE, minimum GPA of 3.0. Additional exam requirements/recommendations for international students: Required—TOEFL (minimum score 550 paper-based; 213 computer-based). *Application deadline:* For fall admission, 7/15 priority date for domestic students; for spring admission, 11/15 priority date for domestic students. Applications are processed on a rolling basis. Application fee: $45. Electronic applications accepted. *Expenses:* Tuition: Full-time $8280; part-time $460 per credit hour. Required fees: $99 per semester. Tuition and fees vary according to course load, degree level and campus/location. *Financial support:* Applicants required to submit FAFSA. *Unit head:* Dr. Lisa Stubbs, Program Director, 561-803-2286. *Application contact:* Graduate Admissions, 888-468-6722, E-mail: grad@pba.edu.

Pepperdine University, Graduate School of Education and Psychology, Division of Psychology, MA Program in Clinical Psychology (Day Format), Malibu, CA 90263. Offers marriage and family therapy (MA). *Faculty:* 50 full-time (29 women), 114 part-time/adjunct (68 women). *Students:* 91 full-time (79 women); includes 22 minority (7 Black or African American, non-Hispanic/Latino; 1 American Indian or Alaska Native, non-Hispanic/Latino; 7 Asian, non-Hispanic/Latino; 7 Native Hawaiian or other Pacific Islander, non-Hispanic/Latino). 204 applicants, 36% accepted, 44 enrolled. *Entrance requirements:* For master's, GRE (taken within last five years) or MAT (taken within last two years), two professional recommendations, two- to five-page typed personal statement. Additional exam requirements/recommendations for international students: Required—TOEFL. *Application deadline:* For fall admission, 2/1 for domestic students. Application fee: $55. *Unit head:* Duncan Wigg, Director, 949-223-2522, E-mail: duncan.wigg@pepperdine.edu. *Application contact:* Deanna Schwartz, Psychology Admissions Manager, 310-568-5777, E-mail: deanna.lazaro@pepperdine.edu.

Pepperdine University, Graduate School of Education and Psychology, Division of Psychology, MA Program in Clinical Psychology (Evening Format), Malibu, CA 90263. Offers marriage and family therapy (MA). *Accreditation:* APA. Part-time and evening/weekend programs available. *Faculty:* 50 full-time (29 women), 114 part-time/adjunct (68 women). *Students:* 197 full-time (171 women), 355 part-time (309 women); includes 150 minority (48 Black or African American, non-Hispanic/Latino; 3 American Indian or Alaska Native, non-Hispanic/Latino; 38 Asian, non-Hispanic/Latino; 58 Hispanic/Latino; 2 Native Hawaiian or other Pacific Islander, non-Hispanic/Latino; 1 Two or more races, non-Hispanic/Latino), 4 international. 246 applicants, 75% accepted, 147 enrolled. *Entrance requirements:* For master's, GRE (taken within last five years) or MAT (taken within last two years), two professional recommendations, two- to five-page typed personal statement. Additional exam requirements/recommendations for international students: Required—TOEFL. *Application deadline:* For fall admission, 6/1 priority date for domestic students; for spring admission, 10/1 priority date for domestic students. Applications are processed on a rolling basis. Application fee: $55. *Financial support:* Research assistantships, teaching assistantships available. Financial award application deadline: 7/1; financial award applicants required to submit FAFSA. *Unit head:* Duncan Wigg, Director, 949-223-2522, E-mail: duncan.wigg@pepperdine.edu. *Application contact:* Deanna Schwartz, Psychology Admissions Manager, 310-568-5777, E-mail: deanna.lazaro@pepperdine.edu.

Phillips Graduate Institute, Programs in Marriage and Family Therapy, School Counseling and School Psychology, Encino, CA 91316-1509. Offers marriage and family therapy (MA); school counseling (MA); school psychology (MA). Evening/weekend programs available. *Degree requirements:* For master's, comprehensive exam, thesis. *Entrance requirements:* For master's, minimum GPA of 2.5. *Faculty research:* Integration of interpersonal psychological theory, systems approach, firsthand experiential learning.

Purdue University, Graduate School, College of Consumer and Family Sciences, Department of Child Development and Family Studies, West Lafayette, IN 47907. Offers developmental studies (MS, PhD); family studies (MS, PhD); marriage and family therapy (MS, PhD). *Accreditation:* AAMFT/COAMFTE (one or more programs are accredited). Part-time programs available. Terminal master's awarded for partial completion of doctoral program. *Degree requirements:* For master's, thesis; for doctorate, thesis/dissertation. *Entrance requirements:* For master's and doctorate, GRE General Test. Additional exam requirements/recommendations for international students: Required—TWE. Electronic applications accepted. *Faculty research:* Inclusion of children with special needs, families as learning environments, relationships in child care, work-family relations, AIDS prevention.

Purdue University Calumet, Graduate Studies Office, School of Liberal Arts and Social Sciences, Department of Behavioral Sciences, Hammond, IN 46323-2094. Offers child development and family studies (MS); marriage and family therapy (MS). *Accreditation:* AAMFT/COAMFTE. Part-time programs available. *Faculty:* 3 full-time (1 woman), 2 part-time/adjunct (0 women). *Students:* 18 full-time (16 women), 2 part-time (both women); includes 1 Black or African American, non-Hispanic/Latino; 1 Hispanic/Latino. 35 applicants, 26% accepted, 9 enrolled. In 2010, 4 master's awarded. *Degree requirements:* For master's, thesis. *Entrance requirements:* For master's, GRE, interview. Additional exam requirements/recommendations for international students: Required—TOEFL. *Application deadline:* For fall admission, 1/28 for domestic and international students. Application fee: $50. *Expenses:* Tuition, state resident: full-time $6867. Tuition, nonresident: full-time $14,157. *Financial support:* In 2010–11, 3 research assistantships with full tuition reimbursements (averaging $3,500 per year), 20 teaching assistantships with full tuition reimbursements (averaging $3,500 per year) were awarded; career-related internships or fieldwork and unspecified assistantships also available. Financial award application deadline: 3/1. *Faculty research:* Substance abuse, sexual abuse, couple therapy, professional issues, adolescent therapy. *Unit head:* Dr. Anne Edwards, Interim Head, 219-989-2863, E-mail: edwardsa@purduecal.edu. *Application contact:* Dr. Joseph Wetchler, Program Director, 219-989-2587, E-mail: wetchler@purduecal.edu.

Reformed Theological Seminary–Jackson Campus, Graduate and Professional Programs, Jackson, MS 39209-3099. Offers Bible, theology, and missions (Certificate); biblical studies (MA); Christian education (M Div, MA); counseling (M Div); divinity (M Div, Diploma); marriage and family therapy (MA); ministry (D Min); missions (M Div, MA, D Min); New Testament (Th M); Old Testament (Th M); theological studies (MA); theology (Th M); M Div/MA. *Accreditation:* AAMFT/COAMFTE (one or more programs are accredited); ATS (one or more programs are accredited). *Degree requirements:* For master's, thesis (for some programs), fieldwork; for doctorate, 2 foreign languages, thesis/dissertation; for M Div, 2 foreign languages, thesis/dissertation (for some programs). *Entrance requirements:* For M Div and master's, minimum GPA of 2.6; for doctorate, minimum GPA of 3.0. Additional exam requirements/recommendations for international students: Required—TOEFL.

Regis University, College for Professional Studies, School of Education and Counseling, Department of Counseling, Denver, CO 80221-1099. Offers community counseling (MAC); counseling children and adolescents (Post-Graduate Certificate); marriage and family therapy (MA, Post-Graduate Certificate); transformative counseling (Post-Graduate Certificate). Program offered in Henderson and Las Vegas (Summerlin), NV. *Accreditation:* ACA. Part-time and evening/weekend programs available. *Degree requirements:* For master's, internships, practicum. *Entrance requirements:* For master's, interview, 2 recommendations, resume, criminal background check. Additional exam requirements/recommendations for international students: Required—TOEFL (minimum score 213 computer-based), TWE (minimum score 5). *Expenses:* Contact institution. *Faculty research:* Group development, counselor education, counsel and therapy, influence of technology on psychology, dream finding groups, adult development, depression.

Richmont Graduate University, Graduate Programs, Atlanta, GA 30327. Offers Christian psychological studies (MS); marriage and family therapy (MA); professional counseling (MA).

St. Cloud State University, School of Graduate Studies, College of Education, Department of Educational Leadership and Community Psychology, Program in Marriage and Family Therapy, St. Cloud, MN 56301-4498. Offers MS. *Accreditation:* AAMFT/COAMFTE. *Entrance requirements:* Additional exam requirements/recommendations for international students: Required—Michigan English Language Assessment Battery; Recommended—TOEFL (minimum score 550 paper-based; 213 computer-based), IELTS (minimum score 6.5). Electronic applications accepted.

Saint Joseph College, Department of Marriage and Family Therapy, West Hartford, CT 06117-2700. Offers MA. *Accreditation:* AAMFT/COAMFTE. Part-time and evening/weekend programs available. *Students:* 9 full-time (8 women), 37 part-time (35 women); includes 3 Black or African American, non-Hispanic/Latino. *Degree requirements:* For master's, comprehensive exam, thesis or alternative. *Entrance requirements:* For master's, 2 letters of recommendation. *Application deadline:* Applications are processed on a rolling basis. Application fee: $50. Electronic applications accepted. *Expenses:* Tuition: Full-time $11,340; part-time $630 per credit. Required fees: $540; $30 per credit. Tuition and fees vary according to course load, campus/location and program. *Financial support:* Career-related internships or fieldwork and unspecified assistantships available. Support available to part-time students. Financial award applicants required to submit FAFSA. *Application contact:* Graduate Admissions Office, 860-231-5261, E-mail: graduate@sjc.edu.

Saint Louis University, Graduate Education, College of Education and Public Service and Graduate Education, Department of Counseling and Family Therapy, St. Louis, MO 63103-2097. Offers counseling and family therapy (PhD); human development counseling (MA); marriage and family therapy (Certificate); school counseling (MA, MA-R). *Accreditation:* AAMFT/COAMFTE; NCATE. Part-time programs available. *Degree requirements:* For master's, comprehensive exam, thesis (for some programs); for doctorate, comprehensive exam, thesis/dissertation, preliminary oral and written exams. *Entrance requirements:* For master's, GRE General Test, letters of recommendation, resume; for doctorate, GRE General Test, letters of recommendation, resumé, transcripts, goal statement. Additional exam requirements/recommendations for international students: Required—TOEFL (minimum score 550 paper-based; 213 computer-based). Electronic applications accepted. *Faculty research:* Medical family therapy/collaborative health care multicultural counseling, mental health needs of diverse, minority, or immigrant/refugee populations, divorce, aging families.

Saint Mary's College of California, Kalmanovitz School of Education, Program in Counseling, Moraga, CA 94556. Offers general counseling (MA); marital and family therapy (MA); school counseling (MA). Part-time and evening/weekend programs available. *Faculty:* 6 full-time (5 women), 16 part-time/adjunct (13 women). *Students:* 29 full-time (10 women), 158 part-time (86 women); includes 56 minority (14 Black or African American, non-Hispanic/Latino; 1 American Indian or Alaska Native, non-Hispanic/Latino; 13 Asian, non-Hispanic/Latino; 21 Hispanic/Latino; 6 Native Hawaiian or other Pacific Islander, non-Hispanic/Latino; 1 Two or more races, non-Hispanic/Latino). Average age 32. In 2010, 33 master's awarded. *Degree requirements:* For master's, thesis or alternative. *Entrance requirements:* For master's, interview, minimum GPA of 3.0. *Application deadline:* Applications are processed on a rolling basis. Application fee: $50. *Financial support:* In 2010–11, 5 students received support. Career-related internships or fieldwork and Federal Work-Study available. Support available to part-time students. Financial award application deadline: 2/15; financial award applicants required to submit FAFSA. *Faculty research:* Counselor training effectiveness, multicultural development, empathy, the interface of spirituality and psychotherapy, gender issues. *Unit head:* Dr. Laura Heid, Director, 925-631-4293, Fax: 925-376-8379, E-mail: lheid@stmarys.ca.edu. *Application contact:* Jane Joyce, Coordinator, Recruitment and Admissions, 925-631-4700, Fax: 925-376-8379, E-mail: soereq@stmarys-ca.edu.

St. Mary's University, Graduate School, Department of Counseling and Human Services, Program in Marriage and Family Therapy, San Antonio, TX 78228-8507. Offers MA, PhD. Part-time programs available. *Degree requirements:* For master's, comprehensive exam, thesis optional, internship; for doctorate, comprehensive exam, thesis/dissertation, internship. *Entrance requirements:* For master's, GRE, MAT; for doctorate, GRE, master's degree, work experience, letters of recommendation. Additional exam requirements/recommendations for international students: Required—TOEFL (minimum score 550 paper-based; 213 computer-based; 80 iBT). Electronic applications accepted.

Saint Mary's University of Minnesota, Schools of Graduate and Professional Programs, Graduate School of Health and Human Services, Marriage and Family Therapy Program, Winona, MN 55987-1399. Offers marriage and family therapy (MA, Certificate); play therapy (Certificate). *Accreditation:* AAMFT/COAMFTE. *Unit head:* Dr. Steve W. Peltier, Director, 612-728-5140, Fax: 612-728-5121, E-mail: speltier@smumn.edu. *Application contact:* Yasin Alsaidi, Director of Admissions for Graduate and Professional Programs, 612-728-5207, Fax: 612-728-5121, E-mail: yalsaidi@smumn.edu.

Saint Paul University, Faculty of Human Sciences, Program in Counseling and Spirituality, Ottawa, ON K1S 1C4, Canada. Offers individual or marital/couple counseling (MA); spiritual care (MA). Part-time programs available. *Degree requirements:* For master's, research project or thesis. *Entrance requirements:* For master's, honors BA in human sciences, minimum B average, 12 theology credits.

St. Thomas University, Biscayne College, Department of Social Sciences and Counseling, Program in Marriage and Family Therapy, Miami Gardens, FL 33054-6459. Offers MS, Post-Master's Certificate. Part-time and evening/weekend programs available. *Degree requirements:* For master's, comprehensive exam. *Entrance requirements:* For master's, interview, minimum GPA of 3.0 or GRE. Additional exam requirements/recommendations for international students: Required—TOEFL. Electronic applications accepted.

San Francisco State University, Division of Graduate Studies, College of Health and Human Services, Department of Counseling, San Francisco, CA 94132-1722. Offers counseling (MS); marriage, family, and child counseling (MSC); rehabilitation counseling (MS). *Accreditation:* ACA (one or more programs are accredited). Part-time programs available. *Application deadline:* Applications are processed on a rolling basis. *Unit head:* Dr. Robert Williams, Chair, 415-338-2005. *Application contact:* Couryll Pineda, Academic Office Coordinator, 415-338-2005, E-mail: counsel@sfsu.edu.

Saybrook University, Graduate College of Psychology and Humanistic Studies, San Francisco, CA 94111-1920. Offers clinical psychology (Psy D); human science (MA, PhD), including consciousness and spirituality, humanistic and transpersonal psychology, integrative health studies, organizational systems, social transformation, transformative social change (MA); organizational systems (MA, PhD), including consciousness and spirituality, humanistic and transpersonal psychology, integrative health studies, leadership of sustainable systems (MA), organizational systems, social transformation; psychology (MA, PhD), including clinical psychology (PhD), consciousness and spirituality, creativity studies (MA), humanistic and transpersonal psychology, integrative health studies, Jungian studies, marriage and family therapy (MA), organizational systems, social transformation. Postbaccalaureate distance learning degree programs offered (minimal on-campus study). *Faculty:* 15 full-time (5 women), 83 part-time/adjunct (34 women). *Students:* 479 full-time (333 women); includes 30 Black or African American, non-Hispanic/Latino; 1 American Indian or Alaska Native, non-Hispanic/Latino; 13 Asian, non-Hispanic/Latino; 18 Hispanic/Latino, 18 international. Average age 43. 280 applicants, 52% accepted, 105 enrolled. In 2010, 28 master's, 43 doctorates awarded. Terminal master's awarded for partial completion of doctoral program. *Degree requirements:* For master's, thesis or alternative; for doctorate, thesis/dissertation. *Entrance requirements:* Additional exam requirements/recommendations for international students: Required—TOEFL (minimum score 580 paper-based; 237 computer-based; 93 iBT). *Application deadline:* For fall admission, 6/1 priority date for domestic students; for spring admission, 12/16 priority date for domestic students. Application fee: $50. Electronic applications accepted. *Financial support:* In 2010–11, 335 students received support. Scholarships/grants available. Financial award applicants required to submit FAFSA. *Faculty research:* Humanistic theory, health studies, organizational systems, consciousness and spirituality, social transformation. Total annual research expenditures: $90,000. *Unit head:* Mark Schulman, President, 800-825-4480, Fax: 415-433-9271. *Application contact:* Director of Admissions, 800-825-4480, Fax: 415-433-9271, E-mail: admissions@saybrook.edu.

The School of Professional Psychology at Forest Institute, Graduate Programs, Springfield, MO 65807. Offers applied behavior analysis (MS); clinical psychology (MA, Psy D); counseling

Marriage and Family Therapy

The School of Professional Psychology at Forest Institute (continued)

psychology (MA); marriage and family therapy (MA, PGC). *Accreditation:* AAMFT/COAMFTE; APA (one or more programs are accredited). *Faculty:* 17 full-time (8 women), 18 part-time/adjunct (10 women). *Students:* 214 full-time (144 women), 46 part-time (35 women); includes 35 minority (11 Black or African American, non-Hispanic/Latino; 9 American Indian or Alaska Native, non-Hispanic/Latino; 5 Asian, non-Hispanic/Latino; 10 Hispanic/Latino), 3 international. Average age 28. 176 applicants, 69% accepted, 45 enrolled. In 2010, 35 master's, 31 doctorates awarded. Terminal master's awarded for partial completion of doctoral program. *Degree requirements:* For master's, thesis, practicum; for doctorate, comprehensive exam, thesis/dissertation, internship, practicum. *Entrance requirements:* For master's, GRE General Test, interview, minimum GPA of 3.0, 12 hours in psychology; for doctorate, GRE General Test, interview, minimum GPA of 3.0, 18 hours in psychology. Additional exam requirements/recommendations for international students: Required—TOEFL (minimum score 550 paper-based; 213 computer-based). *Application deadline:* For fall admission, 1/15 priority date for domestic and international students; for spring admission, 8/1 priority date for domestic and international students. Applications are processed on a rolling basis. Application fee: $50. Electronic applications accepted. *Financial support:* In 2010–11, 59 students received support; fellowships with partial tuition reimbursements available, teaching assistantships, career-related internships or fieldwork, Federal Work-Study, scholarships/grants, tuition waivers (partial), and unspecified assistantships available. Financial award applicants required to submit FAFSA. *Faculty research:* Forensics/corrections, marriage and family therapy, child and adolescent, integrated health care, neuropsychology. *Unit head:* Dr. Mark E. Skrade, President, 417-823-3477, Fax: 417-823-3442, E-mail: mskrade@forest.edu. *Application contact:* Bethany Ritter, Admissions Counselor, 417-823-3477, Fax: 417-823-3442, E-mail: britter@forest.edu.

Seattle Pacific University, MS in Marriage and Family Therapy Program, Seattle, WA 98119-1997. Offers marriage and family therapy (MS); medical family therapy (Certificate). *Accreditation:* AAMFT/COAMFTE. Part-time programs available. *Faculty:* 6 full-time (4 women), 6 part-time/adjunct (4 women). *Students:* 54 full-time (44 women), 23 part-time (19 women); includes 6 minority (2 Asian, non-Hispanic/Latino; 1 Hispanic/Latino; 3 Two or more races, non-Hispanic/Latino). Average age 31. 118 applicants, 31% accepted, 36 enrolled. In 2010, 28 master's awarded. *Degree requirements:* For master's, thesis optional, internship, clinical portfolio. *Entrance requirements:* For master's, GRE General Test or MAT. Additional exam requirements/recommendations for international students: Required—TOEFL (minimum score 550 paper-based; 213 computer-based). *Application deadline:* For fall admission, 1/15 for domestic students, 2/1 for international students. Applications are processed on a rolling basis. Application fee: $50. Electronic applications accepted. *Expenses:* Contact institution. *Financial support:* In 2010–11, 51 students received support; fellowships, Federal Work-Study available. Financial award applicants required to submit FAFSA. *Faculty research:* Roles of therapists, models of collaboration, medical and mental health theories of marriage and family therapy. *Unit head:* Dr. Claudia Grauf-Grounds, Chair, 206-281-2632, Fax: 206-281-2695, E-mail: claudiagg@spu.edu. *Application contact:* Dr. Claudia Grauf-Grounds, Chair, 206-281-2632, Fax: 206-281-2695, E-mail: claudiagg@spu.edu.

Seton Hall University, College of Education and Human Services, Department of Professional Psychology and Family Therapy, Program in Marriage and Family Therapy, South Orange, NJ 07079-2697. Offers MS, PhD, Ed S. *Accreditation:* AAMFT/COAMFTE. *Degree requirements:* For master's, comprehensive exam, case study; for Ed S, comprehensive exam, internship. *Entrance requirements:* For master's, GRE; for Ed S, GRE or MAT, interview. *Faculty research:* Family systems.

Seton Hill University, Program in Marriage and Family Therapy, Greensburg, PA 15601. Offers MA. *Accreditation:* AAMFT/COAMFTE. Part-time and evening/weekend programs available. *Faculty:* 3 full-time (2 women), 10 part-time/adjunct (7 women). *Students:* 32 full-time (23 women), 14 part-time (13 women); includes 1 Black or African American, non-Hispanic/Latino. Average age 30. 83 applicants, 41% accepted, 17 enrolled. In 2010, 11 master's awarded. *Entrance requirements:* For master's, minimum GPA of 3.0, 12 credits of course work in psychology, 3 letters of recommendation, interview. Additional exam requirements/recommendations for international students: Required—TOEFL (minimum score 650 paper-based; 280 computer-based), IELTS (minimum score 7). *Application deadline:* For fall admission, 8/15 priority date for domestic students; for spring admission, 12/15 for domestic students. Applications are processed on a rolling basis. Application fee: $35. Electronic applications accepted. *Expenses:* Tuition: Full-time $13,050; part-time $725 per credit. Required fees: $700; $34 per credit. $50 per semester. Tuition and fees vary according to course load and program. *Financial support:* Scholarships/grants, tuition waivers (partial), and unspecified assistantships available. Support available to part-time students. Financial award application deadline: 8/15; financial award applicants required to submit FAFSA. *Faculty research:* Clinical competence with LGBTQ adolescents, African-American youth coming out experience, training the self as the therapist, multicultural competencies. *Unit head:* Dr. Rebecca Harvey, Director, 724-552-0339, E-mail: harvey@setonhill.edu. *Application contact:* Laurel Komarny, Program Counselor, 724-838-4209, Fax: 724-830-1891, E-mail: 1komarny@setonhill.edu.

Shippensburg University of Pennsylvania, School of Graduate Studies, College of Education and Human Services, Department of Counseling, Shippensburg, PA 17257-2299. Offers Adlerian studies (Certificate); advanced study in counseling (Certificate); alcohol and drug counseling (Certificate); counseling (M Ed, MS), including clinical mental health counseling (MS), college counseling (MS), college student personnel services (MS), elementary school counseling (M Ed), secondary school counseling (MS); couple and family counseling (Certificate). *Accreditation:* ACA (one or more programs are accredited); NCATE. Part-time and evening/weekend programs available. *Faculty:* 8 full-time (4 women), 5 part-time/adjunct (3 women). *Students:* 79 full-time (66 women), 105 part-time (92 women); includes 28 minority (20 Black or African American, non-Hispanic/Latino; 3 Asian, non-Hispanic/Latino; 4 Hispanic/Latino; 1 Two or more races, non-Hispanic/Latino), 2 international. Average age 29. 129 applicants, 45% accepted, 43 enrolled. In 2010, 45 master's awarded. *Degree requirements:* For master's, fieldwork, research project, internship, candidacy. *Entrance requirements:* For master's, GRE or MAT (mental health, student personnel, and college counseling applicants if GPA is less than 2.75), minimum GPA of 2.75 (3.0 for M Ed), resume, 3 letters of recommendation, supplemental data forms, one year of relevant work experience, on-campus interview, autobiographical statement. Additional exam requirements/recommendations for international students: Required—TOEFL (minimum score 580 paper-based; 237 computer-based); Recommended—IELTS (minimum score 6). *Application deadline:* For fall admission, 3/1 for international students; for spring admission, 7/1 for international students. Applications are processed on a rolling basis. Application fee: $30. Electronic applications accepted. *Expenses:* Tuition, state resident: full-time $6966. Tuition, nonresident: full-time $11,146. Required fees: $1802. *Financial support:* In 2010–11, 49 research assistantships with full tuition reimbursements (averaging $5,000 per year) were awarded; career-related internships or fieldwork, scholarships/grants, unspecified assistantships, and resident hall director and student payroll positions also available. Support available to part-time students. Financial award application deadline: 3/1; financial award applicants required to submit FAFSA. *Unit head:* Dr. Jan Arminio, Chairperson, 717-477-1668, Fax: 717-477-4016, E-mail: jlarmi@ship.edu. *Application contact:* Jeremy R. Goshorn, Associate Dean of Graduate Admissions, 717-477-1231, Fax: 717-477-4016, E-mail: jrgoshorn@ship.edu.

Sioux Falls Seminary, Graduate and Professional Programs, Program in Marriage and Family Therapy, Sioux Falls, SD 57105-1599. Offers MA. *Entrance requirements:* For master's, minimum GPA of 3.0.

Sonoma State University, School of Social Sciences, Department of Counseling, Rohnert Park, CA 94928. Offers counseling (MA); marriage, family, and child counseling (MA); pupil personnel services (MA). *Accreditation:* ACA. Part-time programs available. *Faculty:* 6 full-time (4 women), 5 part-time/adjunct (3 women). *Students:* 57 full-time (45 women), 40 part-time (33 women); includes 1 Black or African American, non-Hispanic/Latino; 1 American Indian or Alaska Native, non-Hispanic/Latino; 4 Asian, non-Hispanic/Latino; 12 Hispanic/Latino; 4 Two or more races, non-Hispanic/Latino, 1 international. Average age 32. 158 applicants, 26% accepted, 15 enrolled. In 2010, 21 master's awarded. *Degree requirements:* For master's, internship. *Entrance requirements:* For master's, minimum GPA of 3.0. Additional exam requirements/recommendations for international students: Required—TOEFL (minimum score 500 paper-based; 173 computer-based). *Application deadline:* For fall admission, 11/30 for domestic students. Application fee: $55. *Financial support:* Career-related internships or fieldwork available. Financial award application deadline: 3/2; financial award applicants required to submit FAFSA. *Unit head:* Dr. Adam Hill, Program Coordinator, 707-664-2340, E-mail: adam.hill@sonoma.edu. *Application contact:* Jaymala Madathil, Administrative Analyst, 707-664-4067, Fax: 707-664-2038, E-mail: jaymala.madathil@sonoma.edu.

Southeastern Louisiana University, College of Education and Human Development, Department of Counseling and Human Development, Hammond, LA 70402. Offers counselor education (M Ed), including community counseling, marriage and family therapy, school counseling, substance abuse counseling. *Accreditation:* ACA; NCATE. Part-time programs available. *Faculty:* 7 full-time (5 women). *Students:* 62 full-time (58 women), 47 part-time (44 women); includes 26 minority (21 Black or African American, non-Hispanic/Latino; 1 American Indian or Alaska Native, non-Hispanic/Latino; 1 Asian, non-Hispanic/Latino; 2 Hispanic/Latino; 1 Two or more races, non-Hispanic/Latino). Average age 29. 50 applicants, 52% accepted, 16 enrolled. In 2010, 22 master's awarded. *Degree requirements:* For master's, comprehensive exam, 100-hour practicum, 600-hour internship. *Entrance requirements:* For master's, GRE (verbal and quantitative). Additional exam requirements/recommendations for international students: Required—TOEFL (minimum score 500 paper-based; 173 computer-based; 61 iBT). *Application deadline:* For fall admission, 7/15 priority date for domestic students, 6/1 priority date for international students; for spring admission, 12/1 priority date for domestic students, 10/1 priority date for international students. Applications are processed on a rolling basis. Application fee: $20 ($30 for international students). Electronic applications accepted. *Expenses:* Tuition, state resident: full-time $3533. Tuition, nonresident: full-time $12,002. Required fees: $907. Tuition and fees vary according to degree level. *Financial support:* In 2010–11, 5 students received support. Career-related internships or fieldwork, Federal Work-Study, institutionally sponsored loans, unspecified assistantships, and administrative assistantships available. Support available to part-time students. Financial award application deadline: 5/1; financial award applicants required to submit FAFSA. *Faculty research:* Play therapy, grief and loss, addictions, gratitude, couples relationships enrichment/spirituality. *Unit head:* Dr. June Williams, Interim Department Head, 985-549-2309, Fax: 985-549-3758, E-mail: jwilliams@selu.edu. *Application contact:* Sandra Meyers, Graduate Admissions Analyst, 985-549-2066, Fax: 985-549-5632, E-mail: admissions@selu.edu.

Southern California Seminary, Graduate and Professional Programs, El Cajon, CA 92019. Offers Biblical studies (MABS); counseling psychology (MACP); marriage and family therapy (MAMFT); psychology (Psy D); religious studies (MRS); theology (M Div). Part-time and evening/weekend programs available. Postbaccalaureate distance learning degree programs offered (minimal on-campus study). *Students:* 37 full-time (8 women), 80 part-time (37 women); includes 55 minority (20 Black or African American, non-Hispanic/Latino; 14 Asian, non-Hispanic/Latino; 16 Hispanic/Latino; 1 Native Hawaiian or other Pacific Islander, non-Hispanic/Latino; 4 Two or more races, non-Hispanic/Latino), 5 international. Average age 41. In 2010, 7 first professional degrees, 50 master's, 4 doctorates awarded. *Degree requirements:* For master's, thesis (for some programs); for doctorate, thesis/dissertation; for M Div, 2 foreign languages. *Entrance requirements:* For doctorate, master's degree in psychology. Additional exam requirements/recommendations for international students: Required—TOEFL (minimum score 550 paper-based). *Application deadline:* For fall admission, 8/13 for domestic and international students; for spring admission, 12/11 for domestic students, 12/15 for international students. Applications are processed on a rolling basis. Application fee: $31 ($126 for international students). Electronic applications accepted. *Expenses:* Tuition: Part-time $339 per unit. Part-time tuition and fees vary according to degree level, campus/location and program. *Financial support:* In 2010–11, 14 students received support. Federal Work-Study, scholarships/grants, and tuition waivers (partial) available. Financial award application deadline: 3/1; financial award applicants required to submit FAFSA. *Unit head:* Dr. Chuck Emert, Vice-President of Academics, 619-201-8995, Fax: 619-201-8975. *Application contact:* Thomas Pittman, Admissions Officer and Director of Student Services, 888-389-7244, Fax: 619-201-8975, E-mail: thpittman@socalsem.edu.

Southern Nazarene University, Graduate College, School of Psychology, Bethany, OK 73008. Offers counseling psychology (MSCP); marriage and family therapy (MA). *Degree requirements:* For master's, thesis optional. *Entrance requirements:* For master's, English proficiency exam, minimum GPA of 3.0 in last 60 hours/major, 2.7 overall. *Expenses:* Tuition: Part-time $575 per credit hour.

Springfield College, Graduate Programs, Programs in Psychology and Counseling, Springfield, MA 01109-3797. Offers athletic counseling (M Ed, MS, CAGS); industrial/organizational psychology (M Ed, MS, CAGS); marriage and family therapy (M Ed, MS, CAGS); mental health counseling (M Ed, MS, CAGS); school guidance and counseling (M Ed, MS, CAGS); student personnel in higher education (M Ed, MS, CAGS). Part-time programs available. *Degree requirements:* For master's, research project, portfolio. *Entrance requirements:* Additional exam requirements/recommendations for international students: Required—TOEFL (minimum score 550 paper-based; 213 computer-based). Electronic applications accepted.

Stephens College, Division of Graduate and Continuing Studies, Programs in Counseling, Columbia, MO 65215-0002. Offers counseling (M Ed), including marriage and family therapy, professional counseling, school counseling. Part-time and evening/weekend programs available. *Faculty:* 1 (woman) full-time, 13 part-time/adjunct (10 women). *Students:* 130 full-time (114 women), 22 part-time (all women); includes 12 Black or African American, non-Hispanic/Latino; 1 American Indian or Alaska Native, non-Hispanic/Latino; 3 Asian, non-Hispanic/Latino; 3 Hispanic/Latino; 1 Two or more races, non-Hispanic/Latino. Average age 34. 52 applicants, 44% accepted, 23 enrolled. In 2010, 31 master's awarded. *Degree requirements:* For master's, thesis. *Entrance requirements:* For master's, minimum GPA of 3.0 in last 60 hours. Additional exam requirements/recommendations for international students: Required—TOEFL (minimum score 213 computer-based). *Application deadline:* For fall admission, 7/25 priority date for domestic and international students; for winter admission, 12/1 priority date for domestic and international students; for spring admission, 4/25 priority date for domestic and international students. Applications are processed on a rolling basis. Application fee: $40. Electronic applications accepted. *Financial support:* In 2010–11, 62 students received support. Scholarships/grants and unspecified assistantships available. Financial award application deadline: 12/5; financial award applicants required to submit FAFSA. *Unit head:* Dr. Linda Thompson, Program Chair, 800-388-7579. *Application contact:* Jennifer Deaver, Assistant Director of Marketing and Recruitment, 800-388-7579, E-mail: online@stephens.edu.

Stetson University, College of Arts and Sciences, Division of Education, Department of Counselor Education, DeLand, FL 32723. Offers marriage and family therapy (MS); mental health counseling (MS); school guidance and family consultation (MS). *Accreditation:* ACA. Evening/weekend programs available. *Students:* 66 full-time (56 women), 11 part-time (10 women); includes 8 Black or African American, non-Hispanic/Latino; 1 Asian, non-Hispanic/Latino; 10 Hispanic/Latino, 2 international. Average age 31. In 2010, 22 master's awarded. *Entrance requirements:* For master's, GRE General Test. *Application deadline:* For fall admission, 3/1 priority date for domestic students; for spring admission, 11/1 for domestic students. Applications are processed on a rolling basis. Application fee: $25. *Unit head:* Dr. Brigid Noonan-Klima, Chair, 386-822-8992. *Application contact:* Diana Belian, Office of Graduate Studies, 386-822-7075, Fax: 386-822-7388, E-mail: dbelian@stetson.edu.

Syracuse University, College of Human Ecology, Program in Marriage and Family Therapy, Syracuse, NY 13244. Offers MA. *Accreditation:* AAMFT/COAMFTE. Part-time programs available. *Students:* 37 full-time (33 women), 20 part-time (17 women); includes 17 minority

(10 Black or African American, non-Hispanic/Latino; 1 American Indian or Alaska Native, non-Hispanic/Latino; 4 Hispanic/Latino; 2 Two or more races, non-Hispanic/Latino), 4 international. Average age 30. 48 applicants, 85% accepted, 23 enrolled. In 2010, 19 master's awarded. *Entrance requirements:* For master's, GRE General Test. Additional exam requirements/recommendations for international students: Required—TOEFL (minimum score 100 iBT). *Application deadline:* For fall admission, 3/15 priority date for domestic students, 2/15 priority date for international students. Application fee: $75. Electronic applications accepted. *Expenses:* Tuition: Part-time $1162 per credit. *Financial support:* Fellowships with full tuition reimbursements, research assistantships with full and partial tuition reimbursements, teaching assistantships with full and partial tuition reimbursements, tuition waivers (partial) available. Financial award application deadline: 1/1; financial award applicants required to submit FAFSA. *Unit head:* Dr. Thomas DeLara, Chair, 315-443-9403, E-mail: inquire@hshp.syr.edu. *Application contact:* Kathy Pittsn, Information Contact, 315-443-5555, E-mail: inquire@hshp.syr.edu.

Texas Tech University, Graduate School, College of Human Sciences, Department of Applied and Professional Studies, Lubbock, TX 79409. Offers family and consumer sciences education (MS, PhD); marriage and family therapy (MS, PhD); personal financial planning (MS, PhD); JD/MS; MS/MBA; MS/MS. Part-time programs available. *Faculty:* 19 full-time (12 women), 1 part-time/adjunct (0 women). *Students:* 122 full-time (60 women), 62 part-time (28 women); includes 10 Black or African American, non-Hispanic/Latino; 3 American Indian or Alaska Native, non-Hispanic/Latino; 1 Asian, non-Hispanic/Latino; 21 Hispanic/Latino, 23 international. Average age 29. 169 applicants, 56% accepted, 59 enrolled. In 2010, 53 master's, 15 doctorates awarded. Terminal master's awarded for partial completion of doctoral program. *Degree requirements:* For master's, comprehensive exam (for some programs), thesis or alternative; for doctorate, comprehensive exam, thesis/dissertation. *Entrance requirements:* For master's and doctorate, GRE General Test. Additional exam requirements/recommendations for international students: Required—TOEFL (minimum score 550 paper-based; 213 computer-based; 79 iBT). *Application deadline:* For fall admission, 6/1 priority date for domestic students, 1/15 priority date for international students; for spring admission, 9/1 priority date for domestic students, 6/15 priority date for international students. Applications are processed on a rolling basis. Application fee: $50 ($75 for international students). Electronic applications accepted. *Expenses:* Tuition, state resident: full-time $5495.76; part-time $228.99 per credit hour. Tuition, nonresident: full-time $12,936; part-time $538.99 per credit hour. Required fees: $2674; $36 per credit hour. $905 per semester. *Financial support:* In 2010–11, 60 students received support, including 13 research assistantships with partial tuition reimbursements available (averaging $2,975 per year), 16 teaching assistantships with partial tuition reimbursements available (averaging $3,290 per year). Financial award application deadline: 4/15; financial award applicants required to submit FAFSA. *Faculty research:* Addiction and recovery studies; marriage and family therapy with an emphasis in domestic violence and medical family therapy; personal financial planning including financial literacy, charitable financial planning, financial risk tolerance, and retirement planning. Total annual research expenditures: $678,503. *Unit head:* Dr. Vickie Hampton, Chair, 806-742-5050, Fax: 806-742-5033, E-mail: vickie.hampton@ttu.edu. *Application contact:* Dr. Vickie Hampton, Chair, 806-742-5050, Fax: 806-742-5033, E-mail: vickie.hampton@ttu.edu.

Texas Wesleyan University, Graduate Programs, Programs in Education, Fort Worth, TX 76105-1536. Offers education (M Ed, Ed D); marriage and family therapy (MSMFT); professional counseling (MA); school counseling (MS). Part-time and evening/weekend programs available. Postbaccalaureate distance learning degree programs offered (no on-campus study). *Entrance requirements:* For master's, GRE General Test, minimum GPA of 3.0 in final 60 hours of undergraduate course work, interview. Tuition and fees vary according to course level, degree level and program. *Faculty research:* Teacher effectiveness, bilingual education, analytic teaching.

Texas Woman's University, Graduate School, College of Professional Education, Department of Family Sciences, Denton, TX 76201. Offers child development (MS); counseling and development (MS); early childhood development and education (PhD); early childhood education (M Ed, MA, MS); family studies (MS, PhD); family therapy (MS, PhD). *Accreditation:* ACA (one or more programs are accredited). Part-time and evening/weekend programs available. *Faculty:* 22 full-time (17 women). *Students:* 106 full-time (103 women), 327 part-time (303 women); includes 118 Black or African American, non-Hispanic/Latino; 2 American Indian or Alaska Native, non-Hispanic/Latino; 12 Asian, non-Hispanic/Latino; 50 Hispanic/Latino, 20 international. Average age 36. 243 applicants, 58% accepted, 109 enrolled. In 2010, 86 master's, 14 doctorates awarded. Terminal master's awarded for partial completion of doctoral program. *Degree requirements:* For master's, portfolio; for doctorate, comprehensive exam, thesis/dissertation. *Entrance requirements:* For master's, interview, letter of intent, curriculum vitae, minimum GPA of 3.25 on last 60 hours (MS in family therapy); for doctorate, interview, minimum GPA of 3.5 in last 60 hours of course work (family therapy), letter of intent, curriculum vitae. Additional exam requirements/recommendations for international students: Required—TOEFL (minimum score 550 paper-based; 213 computer-based; 79 iBT). *Application deadline:* For fall admission, 2/15 priority date for domestic students, 3/1 for international students; for spring admission, 9/15 priority date for domestic students, 8/1 for international students. Applications are processed on a rolling basis. Application fee: $50 ($75 for international students). Electronic applications accepted. *Expenses:* Tuition, state resident: full-time $3834; part-time $213 per credit hour. Tuition, nonresident: full-time $9468; part-time $526 per credit hour. Required fees: $1247; $220 per credit hour. *Financial support:* In 2010–11, 100 students received support, including 21 research assistantships (averaging $12,942 per year), 2 teaching assistantships (averaging $12,942 per year); career-related internships or fieldwork, Federal Work-Study, institutionally sponsored loans, scholarships/grants, traineeships, health care benefits, and unspecified assistantships also available. Support available to part-time students. Financial award application deadline: 3/1; financial award applicants required to submit FAFSA. *Faculty research:* Parenting/parent education, military families, play therapy, family sexuality, diversity, healthy relationships/healthy marriages, childhood obesity, male communication. Total annual research expenditures: $26,116. *Unit head:* Dr. Larry LeFlore, Chair, 940-898-2685, Fax: 940-898-2676, E-mail: famsci@twu.edu. *Application contact:* Dr. Samuel Wheeler, Assistant Director of Admissions, 940-898-3188, Fax: 940-898-3081, E-mail: wheelersr@twu.edu.

Thomas Jefferson University, Jefferson College of Health Professions, Couple and Family Therapy Department, Philadelphia, PA 19107. Offers family therapy (MS).

Trevecca Nazarene University, Graduate Division, Graduate Psychology Programs, Major in Marriage and Family Therapy, Nashville, TN 37210-2877. Offers MMFT. Part-time and evening/weekend programs available. *Students:* 92 full-time (75 women), 14 part-time (12 women); includes 16 Black or African American, non-Hispanic/Latino; 1 American Indian or Alaska Native, non-Hispanic/Latino; 2 Hispanic/Latino; 1 Two or more races, non-Hispanic/Latino. In 2010, 19 master's awarded. *Degree requirements:* For master's, comprehensive exam, practicum. *Entrance requirements:* For master's, GRE General Test or MAT, minimum GPA of 2.7, letters of reference. Additional exam requirements/recommendations for international students: Required—TOEFL (minimum score 550 paper-based; 213 computer-based). *Application deadline:* Applications are processed on a rolling basis. Application fee: $25. *Expenses:* Contact institution. *Financial support:* Applicants required to submit FAFSA. *Unit head:* Dr. Peter Wilson, Director of Graduate Psychology Program, 615-248-1384, Fax: 615-248-1662, E-mail: admissions_psy@trevecca.edu. *Application contact:* Heather Ambrefe, Administrative Assistant, 615-248-1384, Fax: 615-248-1662, E-mail: admissions_psy@trevecca.edu.

Universidad de las Americas, A.C., Program in Psychology, Mexico City, Mexico. Offers family therapy (MA).

The University of Akron, Graduate School, College of Education, Department of Counseling, Program in Marriage and Family Therapy, Akron, OH 44325. Offers MA, MS. *Accreditation:* AAMFT/COAMFTE; ACA. *Students:* 47 full-time (41 women), 31 part-time (25 women); includes 11 Black or African American, non-Hispanic/Latino; 1 Asian, non-Hispanic/Latino; 2 Hispanic/Latino. Average age 31. 50 applicants, 66% accepted, 23 enrolled. In 2010, 15 master's awarded. *Degree requirements:* For master's, comprehensive exam. *Entrance requirements:* For master's, minimum GPA of 2.75, three letters of recommendation, department supplemental form, interview. Additional exam requirements/recommendations for international students: Required—TOEFL (minimum score 550 paper-based; 213 computer-based; 79 iBT). *Application deadline:* For fall admission, 3/15 for domestic and international students; for spring admission, 10/1 for domestic and international students. Application fee: $30 ($40 for international students). Electronic applications accepted. *Expenses:* Tuition, state resident: full-time $6800; part-time $378 per credit hour. Tuition, nonresident: full-time $11,644; part-time $647 per credit hour. Required fees: $1265. One-time fee: $30 full-time. *Unit head:* Dr. Patricia Parr, Coordinator, 330-972-8151, E-mail: pparr@uakron.edu. *Application contact:* Dr. Patricia Parr, Coordinator, 330-972-8151, E-mail: pparr@uakron.edu.

University of Arkansas at Little Rock, Graduate School, College of Professional Studies, School of Social Work, Program in Marriage and Family Therapy, Little Rock, AR 72204-1099. Offers Graduate Certificate.

University of Central Florida, College of Education, Department of Educational and Human Sciences, Program in Marriage and Family Therapy, Orlando, FL 32816. Offers MA, Certificate. *Students:* 48 full-time (42 women), 23 part-time (20 women); includes 3 Black or African American, non-Hispanic/Latino; 3 Asian, non-Hispanic/Latino; 14 Hispanic/Latino. Average age 27. 58 applicants, 47% accepted, 14 enrolled. In 2010, 12 master's, 7 other advanced degrees awarded. *Expenses:* Tuition, state resident: part-time $256.56 per credit hour. Tuition, nonresident: part-time $1011.52 per credit hour. Part-time tuition and fees vary according to program. *Financial support:* In 2010–11, 9 students received support, including 4 fellowships (averaging $3,500 per year), 6 research assistantships (averaging $4,000 per year).

University of Florida, Graduate School, College of Education, Department of Counselor Education, Gainesville, FL 32611. Offers marriage and family counseling (M Ed, MAE, Ed D, PhD, Ed S); mental health counseling (M Ed, MAE, Ed D, PhD, Ed S); school counseling and guidance (M Ed, MAE, Ed D, PhD, Ed S). *Accreditation:* ACA (one or more programs are accredited); NCATE. Part-time programs available. *Faculty:* 25 full-time (13 women). *Students:* 227 full-time (194 women), 56 part-time (47 women); includes 28 Black or African American, non-Hispanic/Latino; 15 Asian, non-Hispanic/Latino; 43 Hispanic/Latino, 14 international. Average age 27. 165 applicants, 51% accepted, 48 enrolled. In 2010, 36 master's, 16 doctorates awarded. Terminal master's awarded for partial completion of doctoral program. *Degree requirements:* For master's, thesis optional; for doctorate, comprehensive exam, thesis/dissertation. *Entrance requirements:* For master's and doctorate, GRE General Test, minimum GPA of 3.0 (undergraduate), 3.5 (graduate); for Ed S, GRE General Test. Additional exam requirements/recommendations for international students: Required—TOEFL (minimum score 550 paper-based; 213 computer-based; 80 iBT), IELTS (minimum score 6). *Application deadline:* Applications are processed on a rolling basis. Application fee: $30. Electronic applications accepted. *Expenses:* Tuition, state resident: full-time $10,915.92. Tuition, nonresident: full-time $28,309. *Financial support:* In 2010–11, 41 students received support, including 2 fellowships, 23 research assistantships (averaging $16,762 per year), 16 teaching assistantships (averaging $11,939 per year); career-related internships or fieldwork and unspecified assistantships also available. Financial award applicants required to submit FAFSA. *Unit head:* Dr. Harry M. Daniels, Chairman, 352-273-4321, Fax: 352-846-2697, E-mail: harryd@coe.ufl.edu. *Application contact:* Dr. Peter Sherrard, Coordinator, 352-273-4339 Ext. 234, Fax: 352-846-2697, E-mail: psherrard@coe.ufl.edu.

University of Guelph, Graduate Studies, College of Social and Applied Human Sciences, Department of Family Relations and Applied Nutrition, Guelph, ON N1G 2W1, Canada. Offers applied nutrition (MAN); family relations and human development (M Sc, PhD), including applied human nutrition, couple and family therapy (M Sc), family relations and human development. *Accreditation:* AAMFT/COAMFTE (one or more programs are accredited). Part-time programs available. *Degree requirements:* For master's, thesis (for some programs); for doctorate, comprehensive exam, thesis/dissertation. *Entrance requirements:* For master's, minimum B+ average; for doctorate, master's degree in family relations and human development or related field with a minimum B+ average or master's degree in applied human nutrition. Additional exam requirements/recommendations for international students: Required—TOEFL (minimum score 600 paper-based; 250 computer-based). Electronic applications accepted. *Faculty research:* Child and adolescent development, social gerontology, family roles and relations, couple and family therapy, applied human nutrition.

University of Houston–Clear Lake, School of Human Sciences and Humanities, Programs in Human Sciences, Houston, TX 77058-1098. Offers behavioral sciences (MA), including criminology, cross cultural studies, general psychology, sociology; clinical psychology (MA); criminology (MA); cross cultural studies (MA); family therapy (MA); fitness and human performance (MA); school psychology (MA). *Accreditation:* AAMFT/COAMFTE. Part-time and evening/weekend programs available. Postbaccalaureate distance learning degree programs offered (minimal on-campus study). *Degree requirements:* For master's, thesis or alternative. *Entrance requirements:* For master's, GRE General Test. Additional exam requirements/recommendations for international students: Required—TOEFL (minimum score 550 paper-based; 213 computer-based). Electronic applications accepted. *Faculty research:* Smoking cessation, adolescent sexuality, white collar crime, serial murder, human factors/human computer interaction.

University of La Verne, College of Arts and Sciences, Department of Psychology, Programs in Counseling, La Verne, CA 91750-4443. Offers counseling (MS), including student services; marriage and family therapy (MS). Part-time programs available. *Faculty:* 13 full-time (6 women), 25 part-time/adjunct (17 women). *Students:* 36 full-time (33 women), 52 part-time (46 women); includes 54 minority (16 Black or African American, non-Hispanic/Latino; 3 Asian, non-Hispanic/Latino; 35 Hispanic/Latino). Average age 29. In 2010, 36 master's awarded. *Degree requirements:* For master's, thesis, competency exam, personal psychotherapy. *Entrance requirements:* For master's, minimum undergraduate GPA of 3.0; 3 letters of recommendations; interview. Additional exam requirements/recommendations for international students: Required—TOEFL (minimum score 600 paper-based; 250 computer-based). *Application deadline:* Applications are processed on a rolling basis. Application fee: $50. *Expenses:* Contact institution. *Financial support:* Career-related internships or fieldwork, institutionally sponsored loans, and scholarships/grants available. Financial award application deadline: 3/2; financial award applicants required to submit FAFSA. *Unit head:* Patricia Long, 909-593-3511 Ext. 4091, E-mail: plong@laverne.edu. *Application contact:* Barbara Cox, Program and Admission Specialist, 909-593-3511 Ext. 4004, Fax: 909-392-2761, E-mail: gradadmission@laverne.edu.

University of Louisiana at Monroe, Graduate School, College of Education and Human Development, Department of Educational Leadership and Counseling, Program in Marriage and Family Therapy, Monroe, LA 71209-0001. Offers MA, PhD. *Accreditation:* AAMFT/COAMFTE (one or more programs are accredited); ACA. Part-time and evening/weekend programs available. *Faculty:* 6 full-time (1 woman), 2 part-time/adjunct (0 women). *Students:* 52 full-time (39 women), 18 part-time (9 women); includes 7 Black or African American, non-Hispanic/Latino; 1 American Indian or Alaska Native, non-Hispanic/Latino; 2 Asian, non-Hispanic/Latino, 1 international. Average age 31. In 2010, 18 master's, 5 doctorates awarded. *Degree requirements:* For master's, thesis optional; for doctorate, comprehensive exam, thesis/dissertation, clinical experience. *Entrance requirements:* For master's, GRE General Test, minimum GPA of 2.8; for doctorate, GRE General Test, minimum GPA of 3.5. Additional exam requirements/recommendations for international students: Required—TOEFL (minimum score 500 paper-based; 173 computer-based; 61 iBT). *Application deadline:* For fall admission, 8/24 priority date for domestic students, 7/1 for international students; for winter admission, 12/14 priority date for domestic students; for spring admission, 1/19 for domestic students, 11/1 for international students. Applications are processed on a rolling basis. Application fee: $20 ($30 for international students). Electronic applications accepted. *Expenses:* Tuition, state

Marriage and Family Therapy

University of Louisiana at Monroe (continued)
resident: full-time $2991; part-time $197 per credit hour. Tuition, nonresident: full-time $2991; part-time $197 per credit hour. International tuition: $10,288 full-time. *Financial support:* Career-related internships or fieldwork, Federal Work-Study, and unspecified assistantships available. Financial award application deadline: 4/1; financial award applicants required to submit FAFSA. *Faculty research:* Family systems, substance abuse. Total annual research expenditures: $20,000. *Unit head:* Dr. Lamar Woodham, Program Director, 318-362-3008, Fax: 318-342-3131, E-mail: woodham@ulm.edu. *Application contact:* Dr. Harper Gaushell, Admissions Coordinator, 318-343-8441, Fax: 318-342-3131, E-mail: gaushell@ulm.edu.

University of Louisville, Graduate School, Raymond A. Kent School of Social Work, Louisville, KY 40292-0001. Offers marriage and family therapy (PMC), including mental health; social work (MSSW, PhD), including alcohol and drug counseling (MSSW), gerontology (MSSW), marriage and family (PhD), school social work (MSSW). *Accreditation:* AAMFT/COAMFTE; CSWE (one or more programs are accredited). Part-time and evening/weekend programs available. *Faculty:* 23 full-time (15 women), 38 part-time/adjunct (21 women). *Students:* 259 full-time (209 women), 71 part-time (60 women); includes 84 minority (66 Black or African American, non-Hispanic/Latino; 1 American Indian or Alaska Native, non-Hispanic/Latino; 3 Asian, non-Hispanic/Latino; 6 Hispanic/Latino; 8 Two or more races, non-Hispanic/Latino), 7 international. Average age 32. 249 applicants, 78% accepted, 141 enrolled. In 2010, 141 master's, 7 doctorates awarded. *Degree requirements:* For doctorate, comprehensive exam, thesis/dissertation. *Entrance requirements:* For master's, GRE or minimum GPA of 2.75; for doctorate, GRE General Test, interview, writing sample. Additional exam requirements/recommendations for international students: Required—TOEFL (minimum score 550 paper-based; 213 computer-based; 79 iBT). *Application deadline:* For fall admission, 7/31 for domestic and international students. Applications are processed on a rolling basis. Application fee: $50. Electronic applications accepted. *Expenses:* Tuition, state resident: full-time $9144; part-time $508 per credit hour. Tuition, nonresident: full-time $19,026; part-time $1057 per credit hour. Tuition and fees vary according to program and reciprocity agreements. *Financial support:* In 2010–11, 70 students received support, including 9 research assistantships with full tuition reimbursements available (averaging $19,000 per year), 1 teaching assistantship (averaging $19,000 per year); Federal Work-Study, institutionally sponsored loans, scholarships/grants, health care benefits, and unspecified assistantships also available. Support available to part-time students. Financial award application deadline: 5/15; financial award applicants required to submit FAFSA. *Faculty research:* Child welfare, substance abuse, gerontology, family functioning, health behavior. Total annual research expenditures: $2.8 million. *Unit head:* Dr. Terry Singer, Dean, 502-852-6402, Fax: 502-852-0422, E-mail: terry.singer@louisville.edu. *Application contact:* Libby Leggett, Director, Graduate Admissions, 502-852-3101, Fax: 502-852-6536, E-mail: gradadm@louisville.edu.

University of Mary Hardin-Baylor, Graduate Studies in Counseling and Psychology, Belton, TX 76513. Offers clinical mental health counseling (MA); marriage and family Christian counseling (MA); psychology and counseling (MA); school counseling and psychology (MA). Part-time and evening/weekend programs available. *Faculty:* 7 full-time (4 women). *Students:* 33 full-time (23 women), 18 part-time (10 women); includes 11 minority (6 Black or African American, non-Hispanic/Latino; 4 Hispanic/Latino; 1 Two or more races, non-Hispanic/Latino), 1 international. Average age 29. 46 applicants, 50% accepted, 19 enrolled. In 2010, 44 master's awarded. *Degree requirements:* For master's, comprehensive exam. *Entrance requirements:* For master's, GRE General Test, minimum GPA of 3.0 in last 60 hours or 2.75 overall. *Application deadline:* For fall admission, 6/1 priority date for domestic students; for spring admission, 11/1 for domestic students. Applications are processed on a rolling basis. Application fee: $35 ($135 for international students). Electronic applications accepted. *Financial support:* Research assistantships with full tuition reimbursements, Federal Work-Study and scholarships (for some active duty military personnel only) available. Support available to part-time students. Financial award applicants required to submit FAFSA. *Unit head:* Dr. Isaac Gusukuma, Interim Graduate Program Director, 254-295-5017, E-mail: isaac.gusukuma@umhb.edu. *Application contact:* Dr. Isaac Gusukuma, Interim Graduate Program Director, 254-295-5017, E-mail: isaac.gusukuma@umhb.edu.

University of Maryland, College Park, Academic Affairs, School of Public Health, Department of Family Science, College Park, MD 20742. Offers family studies (PhD); marriage and family therapy (MS); maternal and child health (PhD). *Accreditation:* AAMFT/COAMFTE. Part-time and evening/weekend programs available. *Faculty:* 22 full-time (17 women), 14 part-time/adjunct (13 women). *Students:* 51 full-time (45 women), 1 (woman) part-time; includes 15 minority (10 Black or African American, non-Hispanic/Latino; 2 Asian, non-Hispanic/Latino; 3 Hispanic/Latino), 6 international. 150 applicants, 11% accepted, 16 enrolled. In 2010, 12 master's, 2 doctorates awarded. *Degree requirements:* For master's, thesis or alternative; for doctorate, comprehensive exam, thesis/dissertation, oral defense. *Entrance requirements:* For master's, GRE General Test, minimum GPA of 3.0, 3 letters of recommendation; for doctorate, GRE General Test, minimum GPA of 3.0, 3 letters of recommendation, research sample. *Application deadline:* For fall admission, 12/15 for domestic and international students. Applications are processed on a rolling basis. Application fee: $75. Electronic applications accepted. *Expenses:* Tuition, state resident: part-time $471 per credit hour. Tuition, nonresident: part-time $1016 per credit hour. Required fees: $337 per term. *Financial support:* In 2010–11, 2 fellowships with full and partial tuition reimbursements (averaging $18,673 per year), 1 research assistantship (averaging $15,878 per year), 36 teaching assistantships (averaging $16,148 per year) were awarded; career-related internships or fieldwork, Federal Work-Study, and scholarships/grants also available. Support available to part-time students. Financial award applicants required to submit FAFSA. *Faculty research:* Family life quality, interracial couples, child support, homeless families, family and child well-being. Total annual research expenditures: $1.1 million. *Unit head:* Elaine Anderson, Chairman, 301-405-4009, Fax: 301-314-9161, E-mail: eanders@umd.edu. *Application contact:* Dr. Charles A. Caramello, Dean of Graduate School, 301-405-0358, Fax: 301-314-9305.

University of Massachusetts Boston, Office of Graduate Studies, Graduate College of Education, Counseling and School Psychology Department, Program in Family Therapy, Boston, MA 02125-3393. Offers M Ed, CAGS. *Accreditation:* AAMFT/COAMFTE.

University of Miami, Graduate School, School of Education, Department of Educational and Psychological Studies, Program in Counseling, Coral Gables, FL 33124. Offers counseling and research (MS Ed); Latino mental health (Certificate); marriage and family therapy (MS Ed); mental health counseling (MS Ed). Part-time and evening/weekend programs available. *Faculty:* 8 full-time (3 women). *Students:* 48 full-time (42 women), 8 part-time (7 women); includes 24 minority (4 Black or African American, non-Hispanic/Latino; 1 Asian, non-Hispanic/Latino; 18 Hispanic/Latino; 1 Two or more races, non-Hispanic/Latino), 6 international. Average age 25. 130 applicants, 44% accepted, 24 enrolled. In 2010, 15 master's awarded. *Degree requirements:* For master's, comprehensive exam, personal growth experience. *Entrance requirements:* For master's, GRE General Test. Additional exam requirements/recommendations for international students: Required—TOEFL (minimum score 550 paper-based; 80 iBT); Recommended—IELTS (minimum score 6.5). *Application deadline:* For fall admission, 3/15 for domestic students. Application fee: $65. Electronic applications accepted. *Financial support:* In 2010–11, 21 students received support. Career-related internships or fieldwork, institutionally sponsored loans, scholarships/grants, and unspecified assistantships available. Support available to part-time students. Financial award application deadline: 3/1; financial award applicants required to submit FAFSA. *Faculty research:* Cocaine recidivism, HIV, non-traditional families, health psychology, diversity. *Unit head:* Dr. Stephanie Schmitz, Assistant Clinical Professor and Program Director, 305-284-4829, Fax: 305-284-3003, E-mail: sschmitz@miami.edu. *Application contact:* Lois Heffernan, Graduate Admissions Coordinator, 305-284-2167, Fax: 305-284-3003, E-mail: lheffernan@miami.edu.

University of Minnesota, Twin Cities Campus, Graduate School, College of Education and Human Development, Department of Family Social Science, Minneapolis, MN 55455-0213. Offers marriage and family therapy (MA, PhD). *Accreditation:* AAMFT/COAMFTE (one or more programs are accredited). *Faculty:* 15 full-time (11 women). *Students:* 54 full-time (44 women), 13 part-time (10 women); includes 3 Black or African American, non-Hispanic/Latino; 2 American Indian or Alaska Native, non-Hispanic/Latino; 1 Hispanic/Latino, 13 international. Average age 34. 35 applicants, 49% accepted, 10 enrolled. In 2010, 3 master's, 9 doctorates awarded. *Degree requirements:* For master's, thesis; for doctorate, thesis/dissertation. *Entrance requirements:* For master's and doctorate, GRE General Test, minimum undergraduate GPA of 3.0 (preferred). Additional exam requirements/recommendations for international students: Required—TOEFL. *Application deadline:* For fall admission, 12/15 for domestic students. Application fee: $55 ($75 for international students). *Financial support:* In 2010–11, 2 fellowships (averaging $22,500 per year), 43 research assistantships (averaging $26,645 per year), 17 teaching assistantships (averaging $26,645 per year) were awarded; career-related internships or fieldwork, Federal Work-Study, institutionally sponsored loans, and tuition waivers (partial) also available. Financial award application deadline: 6/30; financial award applicants required to submit FAFSA. *Faculty research:* Families and diversity, families and health, families and economic well-being, individuals and relationships across the lifespan. Total annual research expenditures: $795,206. *Unit head:* Dr. Jan McCulloch, Head, 612-624-1208, Fax: 612-625-4227, E-mail: jmccullo@che.umn.edu. *Application contact:* Roberta Daigle, Information Contact, 612-625-3116, E-mail: rdaigle@che.umn.edu.

University of Mobile, Graduate Programs, Program in Religious Studies, Mobile, AL 36613. Offers biblical/theological studies (MA); marriage and family counseling (MA). Part-time and evening/weekend programs available. *Faculty:* 6 full-time (0 women). *Students:* 12 full-time (7 women), 53 part-time (41 women); includes 34 Black or African American, non-Hispanic/Latino; 3 American Indian or Alaska Native, non-Hispanic/Latino, 2 international. Average age 34. 18 applicants, 94% accepted, 16 enrolled. In 2010, 10 master's awarded. *Degree requirements:* For master's, 2 foreign languages, comprehensive exam, thesis optional. *Entrance requirements:* For master's, GRE General Test. Additional exam requirements/recommendations for international students: Required—TOEFL (minimum score 550 paper-based; 213 computer-based; 80 iBT). *Application deadline:* For fall admission, 8/3 priority date for domestic students; for spring admission, 12/23 for domestic students. Applications are processed on a rolling basis. Application fee: $40 ($50 for international students). *Expenses:* Tuition: Full-time $3915; part-time $435 per credit hour. Required fees: $63 per semester. *Financial support:* Federal Work-Study available. Support available to part-time students. Financial award application deadline: 8/1. *Unit head:* Dr. Cecil Taylor, Dean, School of Christian Studies, 251-442-2255, Fax: 251-442-2523, E-mail: ctaylor@mail.umobile.edu. *Application contact:* Tammy C. Eubanks, Administrative Assistant to Dean of Graduate Programs, 251-442-2270, Fax: 251-442-2523, E-mail: teubanks@umobile.edu.

University of Montevallo, College of Education, Program in Counseling, Montevallo, AL 35115. Offers community counseling (M Ed); marriage and family (M Ed); school counseling (M Ed). *Accreditation:* ACA; NCATE. Part-time and evening/weekend programs available. *Students:* 44 full-time (34 women), 42 part-time (35 women); includes 11 minority (10 Black or African American, non-Hispanic/Latino; 1 American Indian or Alaska Native, non-Hispanic/Latino), 1 international. In 2010, 21 master's awarded. *Entrance requirements:* For master's, GRE General Test or MAT, minimum undergraduate GPA of 2.75 in last 60 hours or 2.5 overall, interview. Additional exam requirements/recommendations for international students: Required—TOEFL (minimum score 550 paper-based). *Application deadline:* For fall admission, 7/15 for domestic students; for spring admission, 11/15 for domestic students. Application fee: $25. *Expenses:* Tuition, state resident: full-time $6264; part-time $261 per credit hour. Tuition, nonresident: full-time $12,528; part-time $502 per credit hour. Required fees: $251 per semester. *Financial support:* Federal Work-Study, scholarships/grants, and unspecified assistantships available. *Unit head:* Dr. Leland Doebler, Chair, 205-665-6380. *Application contact:* Dr. Leland Doebler, Chair, 205-665-6380.

University of Nebraska–Lincoln, Graduate College, College of Education and Human Sciences, Department of Child, Youth and Family Studies, Lincoln, NE 68588. Offers child development/early childhood education (MS, PhD); child, youth and family studies (MS); family and consumer sciences education (MS, PhD); family financial planning (MS); family science (MS, PhD); gerontology (PhD); human sciences (PhD), including child, youth and family studies, gerontology, medical family therapy; marriage and family therapy (MS); medical family therapy (PhD); youth development (MS). *Accreditation:* AAMFT/COAMFTE (one or more programs are accredited). Postbaccalaureate distance learning degree programs offered. *Degree requirements:* For master's, thesis optional. *Entrance requirements:* For master's, GRE. Additional exam requirements/recommendations for international students: Required—TOEFL (minimum score 550 paper-based; 213 computer-based). Electronic applications accepted. *Faculty research:* Marriage and family therapy, child development/early childhood education, family financial management.

University of Nevada, Las Vegas, Graduate College, Greenspun College of Urban Affairs, Department of Marriage and Family Therapy, Las Vegas, NV 89154-3045. Offers MS. *Accreditation:* AAMFT/COAMFTE; ACA. Part-time programs available. *Faculty:* 4 full-time (2 women). *Students:* 28 full-time (23 women), 17 part-time (15 women); includes 17 minority (1 Black or African American, non-Hispanic/Latino; 6 Hispanic/Latino; 1 Native Hawaiian or other Pacific Islander, non-Hispanic/Latino; 9 Two or more races, non-Hispanic/Latino), 4 international. Average age 31. 56 applicants, 45% accepted, 20 enrolled. In 2010, 16 master's awarded. *Degree requirements:* For master's, comprehensive exam (for some programs), thesis (for some programs). *Entrance requirements:* For master's, GRE General Test. Additional exam requirements/recommendations for international students: Required—TOEFL (minimum score 550 paper-based; 213 computer-based; 80 iBT), IELTS (minimum score 7). *Application deadline:* For fall admission, 3/7 priority date for domestic and international students. Applications are processed on a rolling basis. Application fee: $60 ($95 for international students). Electronic applications accepted. *Expenses:* Tuition, area resident: Part-time $239.50 per credit. Tuition, state resident: part-time $239.50 per credit. Tuition, nonresident: part-time $503 per credit. Required fees: $108 per semester. Tuition and fees vary according to course load, program and reciprocity agreements. *Financial support:* In 2010–11, 4 students received support, including 4 research assistantships with partial tuition reimbursements available (averaging $10,000 per year); institutionally sponsored loans, scholarships/grants, health care benefits, and unspecified assistantships also available. Financial award application deadline: 3/1. *Faculty research:* Treatment of infidelity in couples therapy; impact of technology (Internet, social media, texting, etc.) on relationships; social justice issues and practices with sexual and gender minority individuals; sex therapy; eco-sustainability, green family living and family therapy. *Unit head:* Dr. Gerald Weeks, Chair/Professor, 702-895-1392, Fax: 702-895-1869, E-mail: gerald.weeks@unlv.edu. *Application contact:* Graduate College Admissions Evaluator, 702-895-3320, Fax: 702-895-4180, E-mail: gradcollege@unlv.edu.

University of New Hampshire, Graduate School, School of Health and Human Services, Department of Family Studies, Durham, NH 03824. Offers family studies (MS); marriage and family therapy (MS). Program offered in fall only. *Accreditation:* AAMFT/COAMFTE. Part-time programs available. *Faculty:* 9 full-time (6 women). *Students:* 17 full-time (15 women), 6 part-time (5 women); includes 1 Hispanic/Latino, 1 international. Average age 30. 26 applicants, 65% accepted, 12 enrolled. In 2010, 10 master's awarded. *Degree requirements:* For master's, thesis or alternative. *Entrance requirements:* For master's, GRE General Test. Additional exam requirements/recommendations for international students: Required—TOEFL (minimum score 550 paper-based; 213 computer-based; 80 iBT). *Application deadline:* For fall admission, 5/15 priority date for domestic students, 4/1 for international students. Applications are processed on a rolling basis. Application fee: $65. Electronic applications accepted. *Financial support:* In 2010–11, 11 students received support, including 5 teaching assistantships; fellowships, research assistantships, career-related internships or fieldwork, Federal Work-Study, scholarships/grants, and tuition waivers (full and partial) also available. Support available to part-time students. Financial award application deadline: 2/15. *Unit head:* Dr. Kerry Kazura, Chairperson, 603-862-2135. *Application contact:* Matty Leighton, Administrative Assistant, 603-862-5021, E-mail: family.studies@unh.edu.

The University of North Carolina at Greensboro, Graduate School, School of Education, Department of Counseling and Educational Development, Greensboro, NC 27412-5001. Offers advanced school counseling (PMC); counseling and counselor education (PhD); counseling and educational development (MS); couple and family counseling (PMC); school counseling (PMC); MS/Ed S. *Accreditation:* ACA (one or more programs are accredited); NCATE. *Degree requirements:* For master's, comprehensive exam, practicum, internship; for doctorate, comprehensive exam, thesis/dissertation. *Entrance requirements:* For master's, doctorate, and PMC, GRE General Test. Additional exam requirements/recommendations for international students: Required—TOEFL. Electronic applications accepted. *Faculty research:* Gerontology, invitational theory, career development, marriage and family therapy, drug and alcohol abuse prevention.

University of Phoenix–Central Valley Campus, College of Human Services, Fresno, CA 93720-1562. Offers marriage, family and child therapy (MSC).

University of Phoenix–Las Vegas Campus, College of Human Services, Las Vegas, NV 89128. Offers marriage, family, and child therapy (MSC); mental health counseling (MSC); school counseling (MSC). Postbaccalaureate distance learning degree programs offered. *Entrance requirements:* For master's, minimum undergraduate GPA of 2.5, 3 years of work experience. Additional exam requirements/recommendations for international students: Required—TOEFL (minimum score 550 paper-based; 213 computer-based; 79 iBT). Electronic applications accepted.

University of Phoenix–Puerto Rico Campus, College of Human Services, Guaynabo, PR 00968. Offers marriage and family counseling (MSC); mental health counseling (MSC). Evening/weekend programs available. *Degree requirements:* For master's, thesis (for some programs). *Entrance requirements:* For master's, Counselor Preparation Comprehensive Examination, minimum undergraduate GPA of 2.5, 3 years work experience. Additional exam requirements/recommendations for international students: Required—TOEFL (minimum score 550 paper-based; 213 computer-based; 79 iBT). Electronic applications accepted.

University of Phoenix–Southern California Campus, College of Social Sciences, Costa Mesa, CA 92626. Offers administration of justice and security (MS); community counseling (MSC); marriage, family and child therapy (MSC); mental health counseling (MSC); psychology (MS); school counseling (MSC). Evening/weekend programs available. *Degree requirements:* For master's, thesis (for some programs). *Entrance requirements:* For master's, minimum undergraduate GPA of 3.0, 3 years work experience. Additional exam requirements/recommendations for international students: Required—TOEFL (minimum score 550 paper-based; 213 computer-based; 79 iBT). Electronic applications accepted.

University of Rochester, School of Medicine and Dentistry, Graduate Programs in Medicine and Dentistry, Department of Psychiatry, Rochester, NY 14627. Offers marriage and family therapy (MS). *Accreditation:* AAMFT/COAMFTE. Part-time programs available. *Degree requirements:* For master's, projects. *Entrance requirements:* For master's, GRE General Test.

University of St. Thomas, Graduate Studies, Graduate School of Professional Psychology, St. Paul, MN 55105-1096. Offers counseling psychology (MA, Psy D); marriage and family psychology (MA, Certificate). *Accreditation:* APA. Part-time and evening/weekend programs available. *Faculty:* 11 full-time (5 women), 13 part-time/adjunct (6 women). *Students:* 68 full-time (54 women), 141 part-time (113 women); includes 5 Black or African American, non-Hispanic/Latino; 13 Asian, non-Hispanic/Latino; 3 Hispanic/Latino, 4 international. Average age 29. 578 applicants, 42% accepted. In 2010, 22 master's, 11 doctorates awarded. *Degree requirements:* For master's, comprehensive exam, practicum; for doctorate, comprehensive exam, thesis/dissertation, qualifying exam, practicum, internship. *Entrance requirements:* For master's, GRE, minimum GPA of 2.75, letters of recommendation, personal statement; for doctorate, GRE, minimum GPA of 3.2, letters of recommendation, personal statement. Additional exam requirements/recommendations for international students: Required—TOEFL (minimum score 550 paper-based; 213 computer-based; 80 iBT). *Application deadline:* For fall admission, 3/1 priority date for domestic students; for winter admission, 2/1 priority date for domestic students; for spring admission, 9/15 priority date for domestic students, 3/1 for international students. Application fee: $50. *Expenses:* Contact institution. *Financial support:* In 2010–11, 2 fellowships (averaging $5,000 per year) were awarded; research assistantships, institutionally sponsored loans and scholarships/grants also available. Support available to part-time students. Financial award application deadline: 8/1; financial award applicants required to submit FAFSA. *Faculty research:* Elderly, eating disorders, anxiety, family. *Unit head:* Dr. Christopher S. Vye, Associate Dean, 651-962-4666, Fax: 651-962-4666, E-mail: bnolan@stthomas.edu. *Application contact:* Laurie Dupont, Administrative Assistant, 651-962-4669, Fax: 651-962-4651, E-mail: ldupont@stthomas.edu.

University of San Diego, School of Leadership and Education Sciences, Program in Marital and Family Therapy, San Diego, CA 92110-2492. Offers MA. *Accreditation:* AAMFT/COAMFTE. *Faculty:* 4 full-time (2 women), 10 part-time/adjunct (6 women). *Students:* 54 full-time (47 women), 7 part-time (all women); includes 2 Black or African American, non-Hispanic/Latino; 1 Asian, non-Hispanic/Latino; 15 Hispanic/Latino; 2 Two or more races, non-Hispanic/Latino, 1 international. Average age 26. 114 applicants, 50% accepted, 27 enrolled. In 2010, 29 master's awarded. *Degree requirements:* For master's, comprehensive exam. *Entrance requirements:* For master's, GRE General Test or MAT, minimum GPA of 3.0, 3 letters of recommendation, resume. Additional exam requirements/recommendations for international students: Required—TOEFL (minimum score 580 paper-based; 237 computer-based; 83 iBT), TWE. *Application deadline:* For fall admission, 3/1 for domestic and international students; for spring admission, 10/15 for domestic and international students. Application fee: $45. *Expenses:* Tuition: Full-time $21,744; part-time $1208 per unit. Required fees: $224. Full-time tuition and fees vary according to course load and degree level. *Financial support:* In 2010–11, 49 students received support. Career-related internships or fieldwork, Federal Work-Study, institutionally sponsored loans, scholarships/grants, unspecified assistantships, and stipends available. Support available to part-time students. Financial award application deadline: 4/1; financial award applicants required to submit FAFSA. *Faculty research:* Child and family interventions and assessment strategies, collaboration between family therapists and medical professionals, family therapy training and supervision, health care reform, premarital counseling. *Unit head:* Dr. Todd M. Edwards, Director, 619-260-5963, Fax: 619-260-6835, E-mail: tedwards@sandiego.edu. *Application contact:* Stephen Pultz, Director of Admissions and Enrollment, 619-260-4506, Fax: 619-260-6836, E-mail: admissions@sandiego.edu.

University of San Francisco, School of Education, Department of Counseling Psychology, San Francisco, CA 94117-1080. Offers counseling (MA), including educational counseling, life transitions counseling, marital and family therapy; counseling psychology (Ed D). *Faculty:* 7 full-time (3 women), 37 part-time/adjunct (26 women). *Students:* 300 full-time (240 women), 14 part-time (10 women); includes 119 minority (14 Black or African American, non-Hispanic/Latino; 43 Asian, non-Hispanic/Latino; 46 Hispanic/Latino; 16 Two or more races, non-Hispanic/Latino), 7 international. Average age 31. 439 applicants, 58% accepted, 142 enrolled. In 2010, 138 master's awarded. *Degree requirements:* For doctorate, thesis/dissertation. *Entrance requirements:* For doctorate, GRE General Test. Application fee: $55 ($65 for international students). *Expenses:* Tuition: Full-time $20,070; part-time $1115 per credit hour. Tuition and fees vary according to course load, degree level and program. *Financial support:* In 2010–11, 245 students received support; fellowships, research assistantships, teaching assistantships available. Financial award application deadline: 3/2; financial award applicants required to submit FAFSA. *Unit head:* Dr. Brian Gerrard, Chair, 415-422-6868. *Application contact:* Beth Teague, Associate Director of Graduate Outreach, 415-422-5467, E-mail: schoolofeducation@usfca.edu.

University of Southern California, Graduate School, Rossier School of Education, Master's Programs in Education, Los Angeles, CA 90089-4038. Offers educational counseling (ME); marriage, family and child counseling (MMFT); postsecondary administration and student affairs [PASA] (ME); school counseling (ME); teaching (online) (MAT); teaching and teaching credential (MAT); teaching English to speakers of other languages (MAT). Part-time and evening/weekend programs available. Postbaccalaureate distance learning degree programs offered (no on-campus study). *Faculty:* 26 full-time (17 women), 24 part-time/adjunct (14 women). *Students:* 1,142 full-time (836 women), 329 part-time (245 women); includes 712 minority (199 Black or African American, non-Hispanic/Latino; 5 American Indian or Alaska Native, non-Hispanic/Latino; 210 Asian, non-Hispanic/Latino; 247 Hispanic/Latino; 5 Native Hawaiian or other Pacific Islander, non-Hispanic/Latino; 46 Two or more races, non-Hispanic/Latino), 34 international. 1,282 applicants, 67% accepted, 484 enrolled. In 2010, 228 master's awarded. *Degree requirements:* For master's, thesis optional. *Entrance requirements:* For master's, GRE (for all programs except MAT). Additional exam requirements/recommendations for international students: Required—TOEFL (minimum score 250 computer-based; 100 iBT). *Application deadline:* For fall admission, 1/5 priority date for domestic and international students. Application fee: $85. Electronic applications accepted. *Expenses:* Tuition: Full-time $31,240; part-time $1420 per unit. Required fees: $600. One-time fee: $35 full-time. Full-time tuition and fees vary according to degree level and program. *Financial support:* Career-related internships or fieldwork, Federal Work-Study, scholarships/grants, traineeships, and unspecified assistantships available. Support available to part-time students. Financial award application deadline: 4/10; financial award applicants required to submit FAFSA. *Faculty research:* College access and equity, preparing teachers for culturally diverse populations, sociocultural basis of learning as mediated by instruction with focus on reading and literacy in English learners, social and political aspects of teaching and learning English, school counselor development and training. *Unit head:* Dr. Arman Davtyan, Director of Master's Programs, 213-740-3540, E-mail: armandav@usc.edu. *Application contact:* Michael Bryant Jackson, 213-740-0224, Fax: 213-740-9433, E-mail: michaebj@usc.edu.

University of Southern Mississippi, Graduate School, College of Education and Psychology, Department of Child and Family Studies, Hattiesburg, MS 39406-0001. Offers child and family studies (MS); marriage and family therapy (MS). *Accreditation:* AAMFT/COAMFTE. Part-time programs available. *Faculty:* 7 full-time (3 women). *Students:* 26 full-time (all women), 32 part-time (31 women); includes 12 Black or African American, non-Hispanic/Latino; 2 Asian, non-Hispanic/Latino. Average age 29. 61 applicants, 48% accepted, 29 enrolled. In 2010, 17 master's awarded. *Degree requirements:* For master's, comprehensive exam, thesis optional. *Entrance requirements:* For master's, GRE General Test, minimum GPA of 2.75 on last 60 hours. Additional exam requirements/recommendations for international students: Required—TOEFL. *Application deadline:* For fall admission, 3/1 priority date for domestic students, 3/1 for international students; for spring admission, 1/1 priority date for domestic and international students. Applications are processed on a rolling basis. Application fee: $50. Electronic applications accepted. *Financial support:* In 2010–11, 21 students received support, including 3 research assistantships with full tuition reimbursements available (averaging $7,200 per year); fellowships, career-related internships or fieldwork, Federal Work-Study, institutionally sponsored loans, scholarships/grants, health care benefits, and unspecified assistantships also available. Financial award application deadline: 3/15; financial award applicants required to submit FAFSA. *Faculty research:* School food service, teen pregnancy, diet and cholesterol metabolism. *Unit head:* Dr. Jeff Hinton, Interim Chair, 601-266-4679, Fax: 601-266-4680, E-mail: jeff.hinton@usm.edu. *Application contact:* Dr. Jeff Hinton, Interim Chair, 601-266-4679, Fax: 601-266-4680, E-mail: jeff.hinton@usm.edu.

The University of Texas at Tyler, College of Education and Psychology, Department of Psychology and Counseling, Tyler, TX 75799-0001. Offers clinical psychology (MS), including neuropsychology, school psychology; counseling psychology (MA), including general, marriage and family; interdisciplinary studies (MSIS); school counseling (MA). Part-time and evening/weekend programs available. *Degree requirements:* For master's, comprehensive exam, thesis optional. *Entrance requirements:* For master's, GRE General Test, minimum GPA of 3.0. Additional exam requirements/recommendations for international students: Required—TOEFL (minimum score 79 computer-based). Electronic applications accepted. *Faculty research:* Neuropsychology, child abuse, psychometric properties of psychological instruments, maternal behavior, clinical practice issues, victimization of women, post-traumatic stress disorder.

The University of Winnipeg, Faculty of Theology, Winnipeg, MB R3B 2E9, Canada. Offers marriage and family therapy (MMFT, Certificate); sacred theology (STM); theology (M Div). *Accreditation:* AAMFT/COAMFTE; ATS. Part-time programs available. *Degree requirements:* For M Div, thesis/dissertation optional.

University of Wisconsin–Milwaukee, Graduate School, School of Social Welfare, Department of Social Work, Milwaukee, WI 53201-0413. Offers applied gerontology (Certificate); marriage and family therapy (Certificate); non-profit management (Certificate); social work (MSW, PhD). *Accreditation:* CSWE. Part-time programs available. *Faculty:* 19 full-time (10 women). *Students:* 214 full-time (196 women), 109 part-time (97 women); includes 35 Black or African American, non-Hispanic/Latino; 1 American Indian or Alaska Native, non-Hispanic/Latino; 6 Asian, non-Hispanic/Latino; 5 Hispanic/Latino. Average age 30. 351 applicants, 55% accepted, 95 enrolled. In 2010, 105 master's awarded. *Degree requirements:* For master's, thesis or alternative. *Entrance requirements:* For doctorate, GRE, bachelor's degree. Additional exam requirements/recommendations for international students: Required—TOEFL (minimum score 550 paper-based; 79 iBT), IELTS (minimum score 6.5). *Application deadline:* For fall admission, 1/1 priority date for domestic students; for spring admission, 9/1 for domestic students. Applications are processed on a rolling basis. Application fee: $56 ($96 for international students). Electronic applications accepted. *Financial support:* In 2010–11, 5 fellowships, 4 research assistantships, 3 teaching assistantships were awarded; career-related internships or fieldwork, health care benefits, unspecified assistantships, and project assistantships also available. Support available to part-time students. Financial award application deadline: 4/15; financial award applicants required to submit FAFSA. *Unit head:* Deborah Padgett, Representative—MSW, 414-229-4851, Fax: 414-229-5311, E-mail: dpadgett@uwm.edu. *Application contact:* Steve McMurtry, Representative—PhD, 414-229-2249, Fax: 414-229-6967, E-mail: mcmurtry@uwm.edu.

University of Wisconsin–Stout, Graduate School, College of Human Development, Program in Marriage and Family Therapy, Menomonie, WI 54751. Offers MS. *Accreditation:* AAMFT/COAMFTE. Part-time programs available. *Degree requirements:* For master's, thesis or alternative. *Entrance requirements:* For master's, minimum GPA of 2.75. Additional exam requirements/recommendations for international students: Required—TOEFL (minimum score 500 paper-based; 173 computer-based; 61 iBT). Electronic applications accepted. *Faculty research:* Abuse, addiction, resilience, diversity, narrative therapy.

Utah State University, School of Graduate Studies, College of Education and Human Services, Department of Family, Consumer, and Human Development, Logan, UT 84322. Offers family and human development (MFHD); family, consumer, and human development (MS, PhD), including adolescence/youth (MS), adult development/aging (MS), consumer science (MS), infancy/childhood (MS), marriage and family relations (MS), marriage and family therapy (MS). *Accreditation:* AAMFT/COAMFTE (one or more programs are accredited). Part-time and evening/weekend programs available. Postbaccalaureate distance learning degree programs offered (minimal on-campus study). *Degree requirements:* For master's, thesis; for doctorate, comprehensive exam, thesis/dissertation, competencies. *Entrance requirements:* For master's, GRE General Test or MAT, minimum GPA of 3.0, 3 letters of recommendation; for doctorate, GRE, minimum GPA of 3.0, 3 letters of recommendation. Additional exam requirements/recommendations for international students: Required—TOEFL. Electronic applications accepted. *Faculty research:* Marriage and family relations, adolescent problem behavior, family financial management, early literacy, mental health in the elderly, parent child attachment.

Valdosta State University, Department of Sociology, Anthropology, and Criminal Justice, Valdosta, GA 31698. Offers criminal justice (MS); marriage and family therapy (MS); sociology (MS). *Accreditation:* AAMFT/COAMFTE. Part-time and evening/weekend programs available. *Faculty:* 18 full-time (9 women). *Students:* 3 full-time (2 women), 11 part-time (8 women); includes 6 minority (4 Black or African American, non-Hispanic/Latino; 1 American Indian or

Marriage and Family Therapy

Valdosta State University (continued)
Alaska Native, non-Hispanic/Latino; 1 Asian, non-Hispanic/Latino). Average age 25. 6 applicants, 83% accepted, 5 enrolled. In 2010, 8 master's awarded. *Degree requirements:* For master's, thesis or alternative, comprehensive written and/or oral exams. *Entrance requirements:* For master's, GRE General Test or MAT (sociology, marriage and family therapy), minimum GPA of 2.5. Additional exam requirements/recommendations for international students: Required—TOEFL (minimum score 523 paper-based; 193 computer-based). *Application deadline:* For fall admission, 7/1 for domestic and international students; for spring admission, 11/15 for domestic and international students. Applications are processed on a rolling basis. Application fee: $35. Electronic applications accepted. *Expenses:* Tuition, state resident: full-time $5256; part-time $197 per credit hour. Tuition, nonresident: full-time $14,490; part-time $710 per credit hour. Required fees: $855 per semester. Tuition and fees vary according to course load and campus/location. *Financial support:* In 2010–11, 5 students received support, including 5 research assistantships with full tuition reimbursements available (averaging $3,652 per year); career-related internships or fieldwork, institutionally sponsored loans, scholarships/grants, and unspecified assistantships also available. Support available to part-time students. Financial award application deadline: 7/1; financial award applicants required to submit FAFSA. *Faculty research:* Police-civilian ride-along project. *Unit head:* Dr. Mike Capece, Acting Head, 229-333-5943, Fax: 229-333-5492. *Application contact:* Misty Lamb, Admissions Specialist, 229-333-5694, Fax: 229-245-3853, E-mail: mllamb@valdosta.edu.

Virginia Polytechnic Institute and State University, Graduate School, College of Liberal Arts and Human Sciences, Department of Human Development, Blacksburg, VA 24061. Offers gerontology (Certificate); human development (MS, PhD); marriage and family therapy (Certificate). *Accreditation:* AAMFT/COAMFTE (one or more programs are accredited). *Faculty:* 21 full-time (18 women), 1 part-time/adjunct (0 women). *Students:* 56 full-time (42 women), 67 part-time (50 women); includes 16 Black or African American, non-Hispanic/Latino; 2 Asian, non-Hispanic/Latino; 1 Hispanic/Latino, 9 international. Average age 34. 91 applicants, 35% accepted, 29 enrolled. In 2010, 23 master's, 10 doctorates awarded. *Degree requirements:* For master's, comprehensive exam (for some programs), thesis (for some programs); for doctorate, comprehensive exam (for some programs), thesis/dissertation (for some programs). *Entrance requirements:* For master's and doctorate, GRE. Additional exam requirements/recommendations for international students: Required—TOEFL (minimum score 550 paper-based; 213 computer-based). *Application deadline:* For fall admission, 7/1 for domestic and international students; for spring admission, 12/1 for domestic and international students. Applications are processed on a rolling basis. Application fee: $65. Electronic applications accepted. *Expenses:* Tuition, state resident: full-time $9399; part-time $488 per credit hour. Tuition, nonresident: full-time $17,854; part-time $957.75 per credit hour. Required fees: $1534. Full-time tuition and fees vary according to program. *Financial support:* In 2010–11, 3 research assistantships with full tuition reimbursements (averaging $16,075 per year), 5 teaching assistantships with full tuition reimbursements (averaging $12,538 per year) were awarded; career-related internships or fieldwork, Federal Work-Study, scholarships/grants, health care benefits, and unspecified assistantships also available. Financial award application deadline: 1/15. *Faculty research:* Stress management, children's play, dual-career families, social cognition, relationships of elderly. Total annual research expenditures: $810,437. *Unit head:* Dr. Sharron E. Jarrott, UNIT HEAD, 540-231-4794, Fax: 540-231-7012, E-mail: sjarrott@vt.edu. *Application contact:* Mark Benson, Contact, 540-231-5720, Fax: 540-231-7012, E-mail: mbenson@vt.edu.

Walden University, Graduate Programs, School of Counseling and Social Service, Minneapolis, MN 55401. Offers career counseling (MS); counselor education and supervision (PhD), including consultation, counseling and social change, forensic mental health counseling, general program, nonprofit management and leadership, trauma and crisis; human services (PhD), including clinical social work, counseling, criminal justice, disaster, crisis and intervention, family studies and intervention strategies, general program, human services administration, public health, self-designed, social policy analysis and planning; marriage, couple, and family counseling (MS), including forensic counseling, trauma and crisis counseling; mental health counseling (MS), including forensic counseling. Part-time and evening/weekend programs available. Postbaccalaureate distance learning degree programs offered (minimal on-campus study). *Faculty:* 25 full-time (17 women), 241 part-time/adjunct (162 women). *Students:* 2,687 full-time (2,269 women), 536 part-time (473 women); includes 1,582 minority (1,319 Black or African American, non-Hispanic/Latino; 34 American Indian or Alaska Native, non-Hispanic/Latino; 29 Asian, non-Hispanic/Latino; 142 Hispanic/Latino; 58 Two or more races, non-Hispanic/Latino), 47 international. Average age 38. In 2010, 182 master's, 8 doctorates awarded. *Degree requirements:* For master's, residency (for some programs); for doctorate, thesis/dissertation, residency. *Entrance requirements:* For master's, bachelor's degree or equivalent in related field, minimum GPA of 2.5; for doctorate, master's degree or equivalent in related field; minimum GPA of 3.0; official transcripts; three years' related professional/academic experience (preferred); access to computer and Internet. Additional exam requirements/recommendations for international students: Required—TOEFL (minimum score 550 paper-based; 213 computer-based), IELTS (minimum score 6.5), TOEFL (minimum score 550 paper-based; 213 computer-based), IELTS (minimum score 6.5), or Michigan English Language Assessment Battery (minimum score 82). *Application deadline:* Applications are processed on a rolling basis. Application fee: $50. Electronic applications accepted. *Expenses:* Tuition: Full-time $10,274; part-time $445 per credit. Tuition and fees vary according to course load, degree level and program. *Financial support:* Fellowships, Federal Work-Study, scholarships/grants, unspecified assistantships, and family tuition reduction, active duty/veteran tuition reduction, group tuition reduction, interest-free payment plans available. Support available to part-time students. Financial award applicants required to submit FAFSA. *Unit head:* Dr. Savitri Dixon-Saxon, Associate Dean, 800-925-3368. *Application contact:* Jennifer Hall, Vice President of Enrollment Management, 866-4-WALDEN, E-mail: info@waldenu.edu.

Wesley Biblical Seminary, Graduate Programs, Jackson, MS 39206. Offers apologetics (MA); Biblical studies (MA); Christian studies (MA); evangelism (M Div); family life ministry (M Div); honors research (M Div); missions (M Div); pastoral ministry (M Div); teaching (M Div); theological studies (MA). *Accreditation:* ATS. Part-time programs available. *Degree requirements:* For master's, thesis. *Entrance requirements:* Additional exam requirements/recommendations for international students: Required—TOEFL. Electronic applications accepted. *Faculty research:* Patristics, missiology, culture, hermeneutics.

Western Kentucky University, Graduate Studies, College of Education and Behavioral Sciences, Department of Counseling and Student Affairs, Bowling Green, KY 42101. Offers counseling (MA Ed), including marriage and family therapy, mental health counseling; school counseling (P-12) (MA Ed); student affairs in higher education (MA Ed). *Accreditation:* ACA; NCATE. Part-time and evening/weekend programs available. *Degree requirements:* For master's, comprehensive exam, thesis optional. *Entrance requirements:* For master's, GRE General Test. Additional exam requirements/recommendations for international students: Required—TOEFL (minimum score 555 paper-based; 213 computer-based; 79 iBT). *Faculty research:* Counselor education, research for residential workers.

Western Seminary–Sacramento Campus, Program in Marital and Family Therapy, Sacramento, CA 95821. Offers MA. *Entrance requirements:* For master's, essays, undergraduate transcripts, 4 recommendations. Additional exam requirements/recommendations for international students: Required—TOEFL.

Western Seminary–San Jose Campus, Graduate Programs, Los Gatos, CA 95032-4520. Offers Biblical and theological studies (MA); exposition ministry (M Div); marital and family therapy (MA); ministry and leadership (MA); open track (M Div); pastoral ministry (M Div); theology (Graduate Diploma). Postbaccalaureate distance learning degree programs offered. *Degree requirements:* For master's, 2 foreign languages; for M Div, 3 foreign languages. *Entrance requirements:* For M Div, minimum GPA of 2.5; for master's, minimum GPA of 3.0. *Expenses:* Tuition: Part-time $445 per unit.

Psychoanalysis and Psychotherapy

Adler Graduate School, Program in Adlerian Counseling and Psychotherapy, Richfield, MN 55423. Offers art therapy (MA); clinical mental health counseling (MA); marriage and family therapy (MA); non-clinical Adlerian studies (MA); online Adlerian studies (MA); organizational wellness and transformation (MA); parent coaching (Certificate); personal and professional life coaching (Certificate); school counseling (MA). Part-time and evening/weekend programs available. *Faculty:* 11 full-time (4 women), 48 part-time/adjunct (28 women). *Students:* 442 part-time (361 women). Average age 37. *Degree requirements:* For master's, thesis or alternative, 500-700 hour internship (depending on license choice). *Entrance requirements:* For master's, minimum undergraduate GPA of 3.0, 12 credits of course work in psychology or related field. *Application deadline:* Applications are processed on a rolling basis. Application fee: $50. *Expenses:* Tuition: Part-time $455 per credit. *Financial support:* Career-related internships or fieldwork and tuition waivers available. Support available to part-time students. Financial award applicants required to submit FAFSA. *Unit head:* Dr. Dan Haugen, President, 612-861-7554 Ext. 107, Fax: 612-861-7559, E-mail: haugen@alfredadler.edu. *Application contact:* Evelyn B. Haas, Director of Student Services and Admissions, 612-861-7554 Ext. 103, Fax: 612-861-7559, E-mail: ev@alfredadler.edu.

Adler School of Professional Psychology, Programs in Psychology, Chicago, IL 60602. Offers advanced Adlerian psychotherapy (Certificate); art therapy (MA); clinical neuropsychology (Certificate); clinical psychology (Psy D); community psychology (MA); counseling and organizational psychology (MA); counseling psychology (MA); forensic psychology (MA); gerontological counseling (MA); marriage and family counseling (MA); marriage and family therapy (Certificate); organizational psychology (MA); police psychology (MA); rehabilitation counseling (MA); sport and health psychology (MA); substance abuse counseling (Certificate); Psy D/Certificate; Psy D/MACAT; Psy D/MACP; Psy D/MAMFC; Psy D/MASAC. *Accreditation:* APA. Part-time and evening/weekend programs available. Postbaccalaureate distance learning degree programs offered (minimal on-campus study). *Faculty:* 40 full-time (18 women), 61 part-time/adjunct (31 women). *Students:* 688 full-time (532 women), 142 part-time (110 women). Average age 27. Terminal master's awarded for partial completion of doctoral program. *Degree requirements:* For master's, thesis or alternative, oral exam, practicum; for doctorate, thesis/dissertation, clinical exam, internship, oral exam, practicum, written qualifying exam. *Entrance requirements:* For master's, 12 semester hours in psychology, minimum GPA of 3.0; for doctorate, 18 semester hours in psychology, minimum GPA of 3.25; for Certificate, appropriate master's or doctoral degree. Additional exam requirements/recommendations for international students: Required—TOEFL (minimum score 550 paper-based; 213 computer-based; 79 iBT). *Application deadline:* For fall admission, 2/15 priority date for domestic students, 12/1 priority date for international students. Applications are processed on a rolling basis. Application fee: $50. Electronic applications accepted. *Financial support:* Career-related internships or fieldwork, Federal Work-Study, scholarships/grants, and tuition waivers (full and partial) available. Support available to part-time students. Financial award application deadline: 5/15; financial award applicants required to submit FAFSA. *Application contact:* Michelle Brice, Director of Admissions, 312-662-4113, Fax: 312-662-4199, E-mail: admissions@adler.edu.

See Display on page 912 and Close-Up on page 1119.

Argosy University, Chicago, College of Psychology and Behavioral Sciences, Doctoral Program in Clinical Psychology, Chicago, IL 60601. Offers child and adolescent psychology (Psy D); client-centered and experiential psychotherapies (Psy D); diversity and multicultural psychology (Psy D); family psychology (Psy D); forensic psychology (Psy D); health psychology (Psy D); neuropsychology (Psy D); organizational consulting (Psy D); psychoanalytic psychology (Psy D); psychology and spirituality (Psy D). *Accreditation:* APA.

See Close-Up on page 1123.

Boston Graduate School of Psychoanalysis, Master's, Certificate, and Doctoral Programs, Brookline, MA 02446-4602. Offers MA, Psya D, Certificate. Part-time programs available. *Faculty:* 11 full-time (7 women), 16 part-time/adjunct (8 women). *Students:* 17 full-time (14 women), 80 part-time (59 women); includes 2 Black or African American, non-Hispanic/Latino; 5 Asian, non-Hispanic/Latino; 6 Hispanic/Latino, 14 international. 10 applicants, 70% accepted, 5 enrolled. In 2010, 8 master's, 3 doctorates awarded. Terminal master's awarded for partial completion of doctoral program. *Degree requirements:* For master's and Certificate, thesis; for doctorate, thesis/dissertation. *Entrance requirements:* For master's and doctorate, interview, BA, personal statement, writing sample, 3 letters of recommendation; for Certificate, interview, MA, personal statement, writing sample, 3 letters of recommendation. Additional exam requirements/recommendations for international students: Required—TOEFL (minimum score 550 paper-based; 213 computer-based; 79 iBT). *Application deadline:* For fall admission, 4/15 priority date for domestic and international students; for spring admission, 11/15 priority date for domestic and international students. Applications are processed on a rolling basis. Application fee: $100. *Expenses:* Tuition: Full-time $13,500; part-time $500 per credit. Required fees: $50; $860 per semester. *Financial support:* In 2010–11, 17 students received support. Career-related internships or fieldwork and unspecified assistantships available. Financial award applicants required to submit FAFSA. *Faculty research:* The effect of extra-analytic contact on the analysis, psychoanalytic intervention with schizophrenia, emotional learning in the classroom, psychoanalytic techniques in the geriatric setting, addictions research. *Unit head:* Dr. Jane Snyder, President, 617-277-3915, E-mail: snyderj@bgsp.edu. *Application contact:* Stephanie Woolbert, Admissions Coordinator, 617-277-3915, Fax: 617-277-0312, E-mail: bgsp@bgsp.edu.

Boston Graduate School of Psychoanalysis, Master's Program—New York, New York, NY 10011. Offers MA. Part-time programs available. *Faculty:* 12 full-time (10 women), 11 part-time/adjunct (7 women). *Students:* 8 full-time (4 women), 24 part-time (16 women). 16 applicants, 100% accepted, 13 enrolled. In 2010, 4 master's awarded. *Degree requirements:* For master's, thesis. *Entrance requirements:* For master's, interview, BA, writing sample. *Application deadline:* Applications are processed on a rolling basis. Application fee: $100. *Expenses:* Tuition: Full-time $13,500; part-time $500 per credit. Required fees: $50; $860 per semester. *Financial support:* Career-related internships or fieldwork available. Financial award applicants required to submit FAFSA. *Unit head:* Dr. Mimi Crowell, Dean, 212-260-7050, Fax: 212-228-6410, E-mail: bgsp-ny.registrar@bgsp.edu. *Application contact:* Stephen Guttman, Registrar, 212-260-7050, Fax: 212-228-6410, E-mail: bgsp-ny.registrar@bgsp.edu.

Boston Graduate School of Psychoanalysis, Programs in Psychoanalysis and Culture, Brookline, MA 02446-4602. Offers MA, Psya D. Part-time programs available. *Faculty:* 2

full-time (1 woman), 20 part-time/adjunct (6 women). *Students:* 2 full-time (1 woman), 12 part-time (7 women); includes 1 Black or African American, non-Hispanic/Latino, 2 international. 11 applicants, 82% accepted, 6 enrolled. In 2010, 1 master's, 1 doctorate awarded. *Degree requirements:* For doctorate, thesis/dissertation. *Entrance requirements:* For master's and doctorate, interview, BA, writing sample, letters of reference, transcripts. Additional exam requirements/recommendations for international students: Required—TOEFL (minimum score 550 paper-based; 213 computer-based; 79 iBT). *Application deadline:* For fall admission, 4/15 priority date for domestic and international students; for spring admission, 11/15 priority date for domestic and international students. Applications are processed on a rolling basis. Application fee: $100. *Expenses:* Tuition: Full-time $13,500; part-time $500 per credit. Required fees: $50; $860 per semester. *Financial support:* In 2010–11, 3 students received support. Unspecified assistantships available. Financial award applicants required to submit FAFSA. *Faculty research:* Institutional violence, developmental impulse control, psychodynamics of murderers, community violence, psychodynamics in the Salem Witch Trials. *Unit head:* Dr. Siamak Movahedi, Director, 617-277-3915, E-mail: bgsp@bgsp.edu. *Application contact:* Stephanie Woolbert, Admissions Coordinator, 617-277-3915, Fax: 617-277-0312, E-mail: admissions@bgsp.edu.

Naropa University, Graduate Programs, Program in Contemplative Psychotherapy, Boulder, CO 80302-6697. Offers MA. *Faculty:* 1 full-time (0 women), 7 part-time/adjunct (4 women). *Students:* 80 full-time (46 women), 3 part-time (all women); includes 6 minority (2 Black or African American, non-Hispanic/Latino; 2 Hispanic/Latino; 2 Two or more races, non-Hispanic/Latino), 1 international. Average age 34. 70 applicants, 70% accepted, 34 enrolled. In 2010, 14 master's awarded. *Degree requirements:* For master's, thesis, internship. *Entrance requirements:* For master's, in-person interview, resume, 3 letters of recommendation, statement of interest. Additional exam requirements/recommendations for international students: Required—TOEFL (minimum score 600 paper-based; 250 computer-based). *Application deadline:* For fall admission, 1/15 priority date for domestic and international students. Applications are processed on a rolling basis. Application fee: $60. Electronic applications accepted. *Expenses:* Tuition: Full-time $17,820; part-time $810 per credit. Required fees: $305 per semester. Tuition and fees vary according to course load, program and reciprocity agreements. *Financial support:* In 2010–11, 22 students received support, including 2 research assistantships with partial tuition reimbursements available (averaging $3,000 per year), teaching assistantships with partial tuition reimbursements available (averaging $3,000 per year); career-related internships or fieldwork, Federal Work-Study, scholarships/grants, health care benefits, tuition waivers (partial), and unspecified assistantships also available. Support available to part-time students. Financial award application deadline: 3/1; financial award applicants required to submit FAFSA. *Unit head:* Dr. MacAndrew Jack, Director, Graduate School of Psychology, 303-245-4752, E-mail: mjack@naropa.edu. *Application contact:* Roslynn Regnery, Graduate Admissions Counselor, 303-54603598, Fax: 303-546-3583, E-mail: rregnery@naropa.edu.

Naropa University, Graduate Programs, Program in Somatic Counseling Psychology, Concentration in Body Psychotherapy, Boulder, CO 80302-6697. Offers MA. Part-time programs available. *Faculty:* 2 full-time (1 woman), 13 part-time/adjunct (10 women). *Students:* 27 full-time (21 women), 4 part-time (all women); includes 4 minority (3 Hispanic/Latino; 1 Two or more races, non-Hispanic/Latino), 4 international. Average age 33. 31 applicants, 61% accepted, 14 enrolled. In 2010, 5 master's awarded. *Degree requirements:* For master's, comprehensive exam, thesis, internship, fieldwork, portfolio. *Entrance requirements:* For master's, interview; body-mind discipline; course work in psychology, anatomy; resume, 3 letters of recommendation. Additional exam requirements/recommendations for international students: Required—TOEFL (minimum score 600 paper-based; 250 computer-based). *Application deadline:* For fall admission, 1/15 priority date for domestic and international students. Applications are processed on a rolling basis. Application fee: $60. Electronic applications accepted. *Expenses:* Tuition: Full-time $17,820; part-time $810 per credit. Required fees: $305 per semester. Tuition and fees vary according to course load, program and reciprocity agreements. *Financial support:* In 2010–11, 8 students received support, including research assistantships with partial tuition reimbursements available (averaging $1,500 per year); teaching assistantships with partial tuition reimbursements available, career-related internships or fieldwork, Federal Work-Study, scholarships/grants, health care benefits, tuition waivers (partial), and unspecified assistantships also available. Support available to part-time students. Financial award application deadline: 3/1; financial award applicants required to submit FAFSA. *Unit head:* Dr. MacAndrew Jack, Director, Graduate School of Psychology, 303-245-4752, E-mail: mjack@naropa.edu. *Application contact:* Roslynn Regnery, Graduate Admissions Counselor, 303-546-3598, Fax: 303-546-3583, E-mail: rregnery@naropa.edu.

New York University, Graduate School of Arts and Science, Department of Psychology, New York, NY 10012-1019. Offers cognition and perception (PhD); community psychology (PhD); general psychology (MA); industrial/organizational psychology (MA); psychotherapy and psychoanalysis (Advanced Certificate); social/personality psychology (PhD). Part-time programs available. *Students:* 157 full-time (113 women), 257 part-time (175 women); includes 18 Black or African American, non-Hispanic/Latino; 1 American Indian or Alaska Native, non-Hispanic/Latino; 29 Asian, non-Hispanic/Latino; 24 Hispanic/Latino, 64 international. Average age 32.

834 applicants, 39% accepted, 82 enrolled. In 2010, 73 master's, 14 doctorates, 13 other advanced degrees awarded. Terminal master's awarded for partial completion of doctoral program. *Degree requirements:* For master's, comprehensive exam, thesis or alternative; for doctorate, thesis/dissertation. *Entrance requirements:* For master's, GRE General Test, minimum GPA of 3.0; for doctorate, GRE General Test, GRE Subject Test; for Advanced Certificate, doctoral degree, minimum GPA of 3.0. Additional exam requirements/recommendations for international students: Required—TOEFL. *Application deadline:* For fall admission, 12/15 for domestic students. Application fee: $90. *Financial support:* Fellowships with tuition reimbursements, research assistantships with tuition reimbursements, teaching assistantships with tuition reimbursements, career-related internships or fieldwork, Federal Work-Study, institutionally sponsored loans, scholarships/grants, traineeships, health care benefits, and unspecified assistantships available. Financial award application deadline: 12/15; financial award applicants required to submit FAFSA. *Faculty research:* Vision, memory, social cognition, social and cognitive development, relationships. *Unit head:* Madeline Heilman, Director of PhD Program, 212-998-7900, Fax: 212-995-4018, E-mail: psychq@psych.nyu.edu. *Application contact:* Barry Cohen, Director of MA Program, 212-998-7900, Fax: 212-995-4018, E-mail: psychq@psych.nyu.edu.

Prescott College, Graduate Programs, Program in Counseling and Psychology, Prescott, AZ 86301. Offers adventure-based psychotherapy (MA); counseling psychology (MA); ecopsychology (MA); ecotherapy (MA); equine-assisted mental health (MA); expressive arts therapy (MA); somatic psychology (MA); student-directed independent study (MA). Part-time programs available. Postbaccalaureate distance learning degree programs offered (minimal on-campus study). *Faculty:* 3 full-time (all women), 25 part-time/adjunct (18 women). *Students:* 71 full-time (55 women), 59 part-time (50 women); includes 16 minority (4 Black or African American, non-Hispanic/Latino; 2 American Indian or Alaska Native, non-Hispanic/Latino; 1 Asian, non-Hispanic/Latino; 3 Hispanic/Latino; 1 Native Hawaiian or other Pacific Islander, non-Hispanic/Latino; 5 Two or more races, non-Hispanic/Latino), 5 international. Average age 38. 107 applicants, 79% accepted, 54 enrolled. In 2010, 23 master's awarded. *Degree requirements:* For master's, thesis, fieldwork or internship, practicum. *Entrance requirements:* For master's, 2 letters of recommendation, resume. Additional exam requirements/recommendations for international students: Required—TOEFL (minimum score 500 paper-based; 173 computer-based). *Application deadline:* For fall admission, 4/15 priority date for domestic and international students; for spring admission, 9/15 priority date for domestic and international students. Applications are processed on a rolling basis. Application fee: $40. Electronic applications accepted. *Expenses:* Tuition: Full-time $15,600; part-time $650 per credit. Required fees: $50 per term. One-time fee: $190. Tuition and fees vary according to course load and degree level. *Financial support:* Career-related internships or fieldwork, Federal Work-Study, and scholarships/grants available. Financial award applicants required to submit FAFSA. *Unit head:* Camille Smith, Chair, 602-373-3881, Fax: 928-776-5151, E-mail: csmith@prescott.edu. *Application contact:* Kerstin Alicki, Admissions Counselor, 877-412-8705, Fax: 928-277-4695, E-mail: admissions@prescott.edu.

Regent University, Graduate School, School of Communication and the Arts, Virginia Beach, VA 23464-9800. Offers acting (MFA); cinema arts/television arts (MA); communication (MA, PhD); digital media (MA); directing for cinema/television (MA, MFA); editing for cinema/television (MA); journalism (MA); producing for cinema/television (MA, MFA); script and screenwriting (MFA); theatre (MA). Part-time programs available. Postbaccalaureate distance learning degree programs offered (minimal on-campus study). *Faculty:* 29 full-time (4 women), 25 part-time/adjunct (5 women). *Students:* 93 full-time (48 women), 167 part-time (80 women); includes 45 Black or African American, non-Hispanic/Latino; 2 American Indian or Alaska Native, non-Hispanic/Latino; 3 Asian, non-Hispanic/Latino; 9 Hispanic/Latino, 11 international. Average age 32. 247 applicants, 45% accepted, 65 enrolled. In 2010, 82 master's, 17 doctorates awarded. *Degree requirements:* For master's, thesis or alternative; for doctorate, thesis/dissertation. *Entrance requirements:* For master's, GRE General Test or MAT, minimum undergraduate GPA of 3.0, writing sample, computer literacy survey, recommendation, resume, interview, audition (MFA programs); for doctorate, GRE General Test, minimum graduate GPA of 3.0, writing sample, computer literacy survey, recommendation, interview, transcripts. Additional exam requirements/recommendations for international students: Required—TOEFL (minimum score 577 paper-based; 233 computer-based). *Application deadline:* For fall admission, 3/1 priority date for domestic students; for spring admission, 10/1 priority date for domestic students. Applications are processed on a rolling basis. Application fee: $50. Electronic applications accepted. *Expenses:* Contact institution. *Financial support:* Fellowships with full and partial tuition reimbursements, career-related internships or fieldwork, scholarships/grants, tuition waivers (full and partial), and unspecified assistantships available. Support available to part-time students. Financial award application deadline: 9/1; financial award applicants required to submit FAFSA. *Faculty research:* Southern gospel music, education and entertainment, celebrities and the media, journalism and ethics, C. S. Lewis. *Unit head:* Dr. Emmanuel Ayee, Interim Dean, 757-352-4945, Fax: 757-352-4291, E-mail: eayee@regent.edu. *Application contact:* Matthew Chadwick, Director of Enrollment Support Services, 800-373-5504, Fax: 757-352-4381, E-mail: admissions@regent.edu.

Rehabilitation Counseling

Adler School of Professional Psychology, Programs in Psychology, Chicago, IL 60602. Offers advanced Adlerian psychotherapy (Certificate); art therapy (MA); clinical neuropsychology (Certificate); clinical psychology (Psy D); community psychology (MA); counseling and organizational psychology (MA); counseling psychology (MA); forensic psychology (MA); gerontological counseling (MA); marriage and family counseling (MA); marriage and family therapy (Certificate); organizational psychology (MA); police psychology (MA); rehabilitation counseling (MA); sport and health psychology (MA); substance abuse counseling (Certificate); Psy D/Certificate; Psy D/MACAT; Psy D/MACP; Psy D/MAMFC; Psy D/MASAC. *Accreditation:* APA. Part-time and evening/weekend programs available. Postbaccalaureate distance learning degree programs offered (minimal on-campus study). *Faculty:* 40 full-time (18 women), 61 part-time/adjunct (31 women). *Students:* 688 full-time (532 women), 142 part-time (110 women). Average age 27. Terminal master's awarded for partial completion of doctoral program. *Degree requirements:* For master's, thesis or alternative, oral exam, practicum; for doctorate, thesis/dissertation, clinical exam, internship, oral exam, practicum, written qualifying exam. *Entrance requirements:* For master's, 12 semester hours in psychology, minimum GPA of 3.0; for doctorate, 18 semester hours in psychology, minimum GPA of 3.25; for Certificate, appropriate master's or doctoral degree. Additional exam requirements/recommendations for international students: Required—TOEFL (minimum score 550 paper-based; 213 computer-based; 79 iBT). *Application deadline:* For fall admission, 2/15 priority date for domestic students, 12/1 priority date for international students. Applications are processed on a rolling basis. Application fee: $50. Electronic applications accepted. *Financial support:* Career-related internships or fieldwork, Federal Work-Study, scholarships/grants, and tuition waivers (full and partial) available. Support available to part-time students. Financial award application deadline: 5/15; financial award applicants required to submit FAFSA. *Application contact:* Michelle Brice, Director of Admissions, 312-662-4113, Fax: 312-662-4199, E-mail: admissions@adler.edu.

See Display on page 912 and Close-Up on page 1119.

Arkansas State University, Graduate School, College of Education, Department of Psychology and Counseling, Jonesboro, State University, AR 72467. Offers college student personnel services (MS); mental health counseling (Certificate); psychology and counseling (Ed S);

rehabilitation counseling (MRC); school counseling (MSE); student affairs (Certificate). *Accreditation:* ACA (one or more programs are accredited); CORE (one or more programs are accredited); NCATE. Part-time programs available. *Faculty:* 11 full-time (6 women), 6 part-time/adjunct (2 women). *Students:* 40 full-time (27 women), 87 part-time (69 women); includes 38 minority (37 Black or African American, non-Hispanic/Latino; 1 Two or more races, non-Hispanic/Latino), 1 international. Average age 34. 55 applicants, 56% accepted, 28 enrolled. In 2010, 24 master's, 19 other advanced degrees awarded. *Degree requirements:* For master's and other advanced degree, comprehensive exam, thesis or alternative. *Entrance requirements:* For master's, GRE General Test or MAT (MSE), appropriate bachelor's degree, interview, letters of reference, official transcripts, immunization records, written statement, 2-3 page autobiography; for other advanced degree, GRE General Test, interview, master's degree, letters of reference, official transcript, personal statement, immunization records. Additional exam requirements/recommendations for international students: Required—TOEFL (minimum score 550 paper-based; 213 computer-based; 79 iBT), IELTS (minimum score 6), PTE: Pearson Test of English Academic (56). *Application deadline:* Applications are processed on a rolling basis. Application fee: $30 ($40 for international students). Electronic applications accepted. *Expenses:* Tuition, state resident: full-time $3888; part-time $216 per credit hour. Tuition, nonresident: full-time $9918; part-time $551 per credit hour. International tuition: $8376 full-time. Required fees: $932; $49 per credit hour. $25 per term. One-time fee: $30. Tuition and fees vary according to course load and program. *Financial support:* In 2010–11, 25 students received support; teaching assistantships, career-related internships or fieldwork, scholarships/grants, and unspecified assistantships available. Financial award application deadline: 7/1; financial award applicants required to submit FAFSA. *Unit head:* Dr. Loretta McGregor, Chair, 870-972-3064, Fax: 870-972-3962, E-mail: lmcgregor@astate.edu. *Application contact:* Dr. Andrew Sustich, Dean of the Graduate School, 870-972-3029, Fax: 870-972-3857, E-mail: sustich@astate.edu.

Assumption College, Graduate School, Rehabilitation Counseling Program, Worcester, MA 01609-1296. Offers MA, CAGS. *Accreditation:* CORE. Part-time and evening/weekend programs available. Postbaccalaureate distance learning degree programs offered (minimal on-campus study). *Faculty:* 1 full-time (0 women), 20 part-time/adjunct (11 women). *Students:* 29 full-time (24 women), 64 part-time (57 women); includes 16 minority (6 Black or African American,

Rehabilitation Counseling

Assumption College (continued)
non-Hispanic/Latino; 1 American Indian or Alaska Native, non-Hispanic/Latino; 2 Asian, non-Hispanic/Latino; 7 Hispanic/Latino), 1 international. Average age 27. 59 applicants, 64% accepted. In 2010, 38 master's, 11 other advanced degrees awarded. *Degree requirements:* For master's, comprehensive exam, internship, practicum. *Entrance requirements:* For master's and CAGS, 3 letters of recommendation, resume, interview, essay. Additional exam requirements/recommendations for international students: Required—TOEFL (minimum score 540 paper-based; 200 computer-based; 76 iBT), IELTS (minimum score 6). *Application deadline:* For fall admission, 6/1 priority date for domestic students, 5/1 priority date for international students; for spring admission, 11/1 priority date for domestic students, 9/1 priority date for international students. Applications are processed on a rolling basis. Application fee: $30. Electronic applications accepted. *Expenses:* Tuition: Part-time $503 per credit. Required fees: $20 per semester. One-time fee: $100. Part-time tuition and fees vary according to campus/location. *Financial support:* In 2010–11, 22 students received support, including 22 fellowships with full and partial tuition reimbursements available (averaging $4,904 per year); scholarships/grants and traineeships also available. Financial award application deadline: 6/1; financial award applicants required to submit FAFSA. *Faculty research:* Job placement for severe disabilities, vocational counseling, conflict resolution, health issues in mental illness. *Unit head:* A. Lee Pearson, Director, 508-767-7063, Fax: 508-798-2872, E-mail: lpearson@assumption.edu. *Application contact:* Daniel Provost, Assistant Director of Graduate Student Services, 508-767-7426, Fax: 508-767-7030, E-mail: dprovost@assumption.edu.

Auburn University, Graduate School, College of Education, Department of Special Education, Rehabilitation, Counseling and School Psychology, Auburn University, AL 36849. Offers collaborative teacher special education (M Ed, MS); early childhood special education (M Ed, MS); rehabilitation counseling (M Ed, MS, PhD). *Accreditation:* CORE; NCATE. Part-time programs available. *Faculty:* 20 full-time (13 women), 8 part-time/adjunct (6 women). *Students:* 149 full-time (117 women), 94 part-time (78 women); includes 56 Black or African American, non-Hispanic/Latino; 1 American Indian or Alaska Native, non-Hispanic/Latino; 2 Asian, non-Hispanic/Latino; 4 Hispanic/Latino, 4 international. Average age 31. 226 applicants, 51% accepted, 87 enrolled. In 2010, 48 master's, 20 doctorates awarded. *Degree requirements:* For master's, thesis (for some programs); for doctorate, thesis/dissertation. *Entrance requirements:* For master's, GRE General Test; for doctorate, GRE General Test, interview. *Application deadline:* For fall admission, 7/7 for domestic students; for spring admission, 11/24 for domestic students. Applications are processed on a rolling basis. Application fee: $50 ($60 for international students). Electronic applications accepted. *Expenses:* Tuition, state resident: full-time $7002. Tuition, nonresident: full-time $21,898. International tuition: $22,116 full-time. Required fees: $892. Tuition and fees vary according to course load and program. *Financial support:* Research assistantships, teaching assistantships, Federal Work-Study available. Support available to part-time students. Financial award application deadline: 3/15; financial award applicants required to submit FAFSA. *Faculty research:* Emotional conflict/behavior disorders, gifted and talented, learning disabilities, mental retardation, multi-handicapped. *Unit head:* Dr. E. Davis Martin, Head, 334-844-7676. *Application contact:* Dr. George Flowers, Dean of the Graduate School, 334-844-2125.

Barry University, School of Education, Program in Rehabilitation Counseling, Miami Shores, FL 33161-6695. Offers MS, Ed S. Part-time and evening/weekend programs available. *Degree requirements:* For master's, comprehensive exam, scholarly paper; for Ed S, comprehensive exam. *Entrance requirements:* For master's, GRE General Test or MAT, minimum GPA of 3.0; for Ed S, GRE General Test, minimum GPA of 3.0. Electronic applications accepted.

Bayamón Central University, Graduate Programs, Program in Education, Bayamón, PR 00960-1725. Offers administration and supervision (MA Ed); commercial education (MA Ed); elementary education (K–3) (MA Ed); family counseling (Graduate Certificate); guidance and counseling (MA Ed); pre-elementary teacher (MA Ed); rehabilitation counseling (MA Ed); special education (MA Ed), including attention deficit disorder, education of the autistic, learning disabilities. Part-time and evening/weekend programs available. *Degree requirements:* For master's, comprehensive exam. *Entrance requirements:* For master's, EXADEP, bachelor's degree in education or related field.

Bowling Green State University, Graduate College, College of Education and Human Development, School of Education and Intervention Services, Intervention Services Division, Program in Rehabilitation Counseling, Bowling Green, OH 43403. Offers MRC. *Accreditation:* CORE. Part-time programs available. *Degree requirements:* For master's, thesis or alternative. *Entrance requirements:* For master's, GRE General Test, interview. Additional exam requirements/recommendations for international students: Required—TOEFL. Electronic applications accepted. *Faculty research:* Depression, disability management, schizophrenia, job analysis, rehabilitation counseling curriculum.

California State University, Fresno, Division of Graduate Studies, School of Education and Human Development, Department of Counseling and Special Education, Rehabilitation Counseling Program, Fresno, CA 93740-8027. Offers MS. *Accreditation:* CORE. Part-time and evening/weekend programs available. *Degree requirements:* For master's, thesis optional. *Entrance requirements:* For master's, GRE General Test, MAT, minimum GPA of 2.75. Additional exam requirements/recommendations for international students: Required—TOEFL. Electronic applications accepted. *Faculty research:* Aging, career development, job retention, rehabilitation administration.

California State University, Los Angeles, Graduate Studies, Charter College of Education, Division of Special Education and Counseling, Los Angeles, CA 90032-8530. Offers counseling (MS), including applied behavior analysis, community college counseling, rehabilitation counseling, school counseling and school psychology; special education (MA, PhD). *Accreditation:* ACA. Part-time and evening/weekend programs available. *Faculty:* 18 full-time (12 women), 14 part-time/adjunct (12 women). *Students:* 362 full-time (295 women), 334 part-time (268 women); includes 417 minority (36 Black or African American, non-Hispanic/Latino; 65 Asian, non-Hispanic/Latino; 309 Hispanic/Latino; 7 Two or more races, non-Hispanic/Latino), 31 international. Average age 34. 152 applicants, 99% accepted, 136 enrolled. In 2010, 177 master's awarded. *Entrance requirements:* For master's, minimum GPA of 2.75 in last 90 units of course work, teaching certificate. Additional exam requirements/recommendations for international students: Required—TOEFL (minimum score 500 paper-based; 173 computer-based). *Application deadline:* For fall admission, 5/1 for domestic and international students. Applications are processed on a rolling basis. Application fee: $55. Electronic applications accepted. *Financial support:* Career-related internships or fieldwork and Federal Work-Study available. Support available to part-time students. Financial award application deadline: 3/1. *Unit head:* Dr. Diane Fazzi, Chair, 323-343-4400, Fax: 323-343-5605, E-mail: dfazzi@calstatela.edu. *Application contact:* Dr. Alan Muchlinski, Dean of Graduate Studies, 323-343-3820, Fax: 323-343-5653, E-mail: amuchli@exchange.calstatela.edu.

California State University, San Bernardino, Graduate Studies, College of Education, Program in Educational Psychology and Counseling, San Bernardino, CA 92407-2397. Offers correctional and alternative education (MA); counseling and guidance (MS); rehabilitation counseling (MA). *Accreditation:* NCATE. Part-time and evening/weekend programs available. *Degree requirements:* For master's, comprehensive exam, thesis or alternative, counselor preparation comprehensive examination. *Entrance requirements:* For master's, minimum GPA of 3.0 in education.

California State University, San Bernardino, Graduate Studies, College of Education, Programs in Special Education and Rehabilitation Counseling, San Bernardino, CA 92407-2397. Offers rehabilitation counseling (MA); special education (MA). *Accreditation:* CORE; NCATE. Part-time and evening/weekend programs available. *Degree requirements:* For master's, thesis or alternative, advancement to candidacy. *Entrance requirements:* For master's, minimum GPA of 3.0 in education.

Central Connecticut State University, School of Graduate Studies, School of Education and Professional Studies, Department of Counseling and Family Therapy, New Britain, CT 06050-4010. Offers marriage and family therapy (MS); professional counseling (MS, Certificate); school counseling (MS); student development in higher education (MS). *Accreditation:* AAMFT/COAMFTE; ACA. Part-time and evening/weekend programs available. *Faculty:* 8 full-time (4 women), 16 part-time/adjunct (12 women). *Students:* 143 full-time (118 women), 223 part-time (188 women); includes 77 minority (39 Black or African American, non-Hispanic/Latino; 2 American Indian or Alaska Native, non-Hispanic/Latino; 4 Asian, non-Hispanic/Latino; 31 Hispanic/Latino; 1 Two or more races, non-Hispanic/Latino), 4 international. Average age 34. 295 applicants, 48% accepted, 119 enrolled. In 2010, 71 master's awarded. *Degree requirements:* For master's, comprehensive exam, thesis or alternative; for Certificate, qualifying exam. *Entrance requirements:* For master's, minimum undergraduate GPA of 2.7. Additional exam requirements/recommendations for international students: Required—TOEFL. *Application deadline:* For fall admission, 5/1 for domestic students. Applications are processed on a rolling basis. Application fee: $50. Electronic applications accepted. *Expenses:* Tuition; area resident: Full-time $5012; part-time $470 per credit. Tuition, state resident: full-time $7518; part-time $482 per credit. Tuition, nonresident: full-time $13,962; part-time $482 per credit. Required fees: $3772. One-time fee: $62 part-time. *Financial support:* In 2010–11, 52 students received support, including 14 research assistantships; career-related internships or fieldwork, Federal Work-Study, scholarships/grants, and unspecified assistantships also available. Support available to part-time students. Financial award application deadline: 2/15; financial award applicants required to submit FAFSA. *Faculty research:* Elementary/secondary school counseling, marriage/family therapy, rehabilitation counseling, counseling in higher educational settings. *Unit head:* Dr. Connie Tait, Chair, 860-832-2154. *Application contact:* Dr. Connie Tait, Chair, 860-832-2154.

Coppin State University, Division of Graduate Studies, Division of Arts and Sciences, Department of Applied Psychology and Rehabilitation Counseling, Program in Rehabilitation Counseling, Baltimore, MD 21216-3698. Offers M Ed. *Accreditation:* CORE. Part-time programs available. *Degree requirements:* For master's, comprehensive exam (for some programs), thesis optional, internship, clinical requirements. *Entrance requirements:* For master's, GRE General Test, interview, minimum GPA of 3.0.

East Carolina University, Graduate School, School of Allied Health Sciences, Program in Rehabilitation Studies, Greenville, NC 27858-4353. Offers rehabilitation counseling (MS); substance abuse and clinical counseling (MS); vocational evaluation (MS). *Accreditation:* CORE. Part-time and evening/weekend programs available. *Degree requirements:* For master's, comprehensive exam, thesis or alternative, internship. *Entrance requirements:* For master's, GRE General Test or MAT. Additional exam requirements/recommendations for international students: Required—TOEFL. *Expenses:* Tuition, state resident: full-time $3130; part-time $391.25 per credit hour. Tuition, nonresident: full-time $13,817; part-time $1727.13 per credit hour. Required fees: $1916; $239.50 per credit hour. Tuition and fees vary according to campus/location and program.

East Central University, School of Graduate Studies, Department of Human Resources, Ada, OK 74820-6899. Offers administration (MSHR); counseling (MSHR); criminal justice (MSHR); rehabilitation counseling (MSHR). *Accreditation:* CORE. Part-time and evening/weekend programs available. *Degree requirements:* For master's, thesis optional. *Entrance requirements:* For master's, GRE General Test, MAT, minimum GPA of 2.5. Electronic applications accepted.

Edinboro University of Pennsylvania, School of Education, Department of Professional Studies, Edinboro, PA 16444. Offers counseling (MA), including community counseling, elementary guidance, rehabilitation counseling, secondary guidance, student personnel services; educational leadership (M Ed), including elementary school administration, secondary school administration; educational psychology (M Ed); educational specialist school psychology (MS); elementary principal (Certificate); elementary school guidance counselor (Certificate); K-12 school administration (Certificate); letter of eligibility (Certificate); reading (M Ed); reading specialist (Certificate); school psychology (Certificate); school supervision (Certificate), including music, special education. Part-time and evening/weekend programs available. *Faculty:* 24 full-time (18 women), 9 part-time/adjunct (5 women). *Students:* 181 full-time (144 women), 736 part-time (581 women); includes 32 minority (23 Black or African American, non-Hispanic/Latino; 3 American Indian or Alaska Native, non-Hispanic/Latino; 1 Asian, non-Hispanic/Latino; 5 Hispanic/Latino). Average age 32. In 2010, 318 master's, 49 other advanced degrees awarded. *Degree requirements:* For master's, thesis or alternative, competency exam; for Certificate, thesis or alternative. *Entrance requirements:* For master's and Certificate, GRE or MAT, minimum QPA of 2.5. *Application deadline:* Applications are processed on a rolling basis. Application fee: $30. Electronic applications accepted. *Expenses:* Tuition, state resident: full-time $6966; part-time $387 per credit. Tuition, nonresident: full-time $11,146; part-time $619 per credit. Required fees: $2401.70; $96.25 per credit. *Financial support:* In 2010–11, 60 research assistantships with full and partial tuition reimbursements (averaging $4,050 per year) were awarded; career-related internships or fieldwork, Federal Work-Study, scholarships/grants, and unspecified assistantships also available. Support available to part-time students. Financial award application deadline: 2/15; financial award applicants required to submit FAFSA. *Unit head:* Dr. Salene Cowher, Program Head, Counseling, 814-732-1116, E-mail: scowher@edinboro.edu. *Application contact:* Dr. Andrew Pushchack, Program Head, Educational Leadership, 814-732-1548, E-mail: apushchack@edinboro.edu.

Emporia State University, Graduate School, Teachers College, Department of Psychology, Art Therapy, Rehabilitation and Mental Health Counseling, Program in Rehabilitation Counseling, Emporia, KS 66801-5087. Offers MS. *Accreditation:* CORE. Part-time programs available. *Students:* 13 full-time (11 women), 10 part-time (8 women); includes 5 minority (2 Black or African American, non-Hispanic/Latino; 3 Hispanic/Latino). 2 applicants, 100% accepted, 2 enrolled. In 2010, 4 master's awarded. *Degree requirements:* For master's, comprehensive exam or thesis, practicum. *Entrance requirements:* For master's, GRE or MAT, graduate essay exam, appropriate bachelor's degree, interview, letters of recommendation. *Application deadline:* For fall admission, 8/15 priority date for domestic students. Applications are processed on a rolling basis. Application fee: $30 ($75 for international students). Electronic applications accepted. *Expenses:* Tuition, state resident: full-time $4382; part-time $183 per credit hour. Tuition, nonresident: full-time $13,572; part-time $566 per credit hour. Required fees: $1022; $62 per credit hour. Tuition and fees vary according to course level, course load and campus/location. *Financial support:* Career-related internships or fieldwork, Federal Work-Study, institutionally sponsored loans, health care benefits, and unspecified assistantships available. Financial award application deadline: 3/15; financial award applicants required to submit FAFSA. *Unit head:* Dr. James Costello, Graduate Co-Coordinator, 620-341-5791, E-mail: jcostell@emporia.edu. *Application contact:* Dr. James Costello, Graduate Co-Coordinator, 620-341-5791, E-mail: jcostell@emporia.edu.

Florida Atlantic University, College of Education, Department of Counselor Education, Boca Raton, FL 33431-0991. Offers counselor education (M Ed, PhD, Ed S); marriage and family therapy (Ed S); mental health counseling (M Ed, Ed S); rehabilitation counseling (M Ed); school counseling (M Ed, Ed S). *Accreditation:* ACA; NCATE. Part-time and evening/weekend programs available. *Faculty:* 10 full-time (5 women), 1 (woman) part-time/adjunct. *Students:* 75 full-time (60 women), 82 part-time (68 women); includes 46 minority (22 Black or African American, non-Hispanic/Latino; 4 Asian, non-Hispanic/Latino; 20 Hispanic/Latino), 1 international. Average age 32. 118 applicants, 35% accepted, 37 enrolled. In 2010, 51 master's, 1 doctorate awarded. *Degree requirements:* For Ed S, departmental qualifying exam. *Entrance requirements:* For master's, GRE General Test, minimum GPA of 3.0 during previous 2 years; for Ed S, GRE General Test, minimum graduate GPA of 3.25. Additional exam requirements/recommendations for international students: Required—TOEFL. *Application deadline:* For fall admission, 3/1 for domestic students, 2/1 for international students; for spring admission, 9/15 for domestic students, 7/1 for international students. Applications are processed on a rolling basis. Application fee: $30. *Expenses:* Tuition, area resident: Part-time $319.96 per credit. Tuition, state resident: part-time $319.96 per credit. Tuition, nonresident: part-time $926.42 per credit. *Financial* *support:* Research assistantships with partial tuition reimbursements, teaching assistantships, career-related internships or fieldwork, scholarships/grants, and unspecified assistantships available. *Faculty research:* Brief therapy, psychological type, marriage and family counseling, international programs, integrated services. *Unit head:* Dr. Irene Johnson, Chair, 561-297-2136, Fax: 561-297-2309. *Application contact:* Darlene Epperson, Office Assistant, 561-297-3601, Fax: 561-297-2309, E-mail: frederic@fau.edu.

Florida International University, College of Education, Department of Educational Leadership and Policy Studies, Miami, FL 33199. Offers adult education (MS); adult education in human resource development (Ed D); clinical mental health counseling (MS); conflict resolution and consensus building (Certificate); counselor education (MS); educational administration and supervision (Ed D); educational leadership (MS, Certificate, Ed S); higher education (Ed D); higher education administration (MS); human resource development (MS); instruction in urban settings (MS); international/intercultural education (MS); learning technologies (MS); multicultural-bilingual (MS); multicultural-TESOL (MS); recreation and sport management (MS); recreation therapy (MS); rehabilitation counseling (MS); school counseling (MS); school psychology (Ed S); urban education (MS). Part-time and evening/weekend programs available. *Students:* 164 full-time (124 women), 308 part-time (234 women); includes 107 Black or African American, non-Hispanic/Latino; 3 American Indian or Alaska Native, non-Hispanic/Latino; 8 Asian, non-Hispanic/Latino; 223 Hispanic/Latino, 12 international. Average age 31. 544 applicants, 41% accepted, 197 enrolled. In 2010, 123 master's, 5 doctorates, 16 other advanced degrees awarded. *Degree requirements:* For doctorate, thesis/dissertation. *Entrance requirements:* For master's, minimum GPA of 3.0; for doctorate and other advanced degree, GRE General Test. Additional exam requirements/recommendations for international students: Required—TOEFL (minimum score 550 paper-based; 213 computer-based; 80 iBT), IELTS (minimum score 6.3). *Application deadline:* For fall admission, 6/1 priority date for domestic students, 4/1 for international students; for winter admission, 10/1 priority date for domestic students, 9/1 for international students; for spring admission, 3/1 priority date for domestic students, 2/1 for international students. Applications are processed on a rolling basis. Application fee: $30. Electronic applications accepted. *Financial support:* Fellowships, research assistantships with full and partial tuition reimbursements, teaching assistantships with full and partial tuition reimbursements, Federal Work-Study and tuition waivers (full and partial) available. Support available to part-time students. Financial award applicants required to submit FAFSA. *Unit head:* Dr. Patricia Barbetta, Dean of Graduate Studies, 305-348-2835, Fax: 305-348-2081, E-mail: barbetta@fiu.edu. *Application contact:* Nanett Rojas, Graduate Admission, 305-348-7442, Fax: 305-348-7441, E-mail: nanett.rojas@fiu.edu.

Florida State University, The Graduate School, College of Education, School of Teacher Education, Program in Special Education, Tallahassee, FL 32306. Offers emotional disturbance/learning disabilities (MS); mental retardation (MS); rehabilitation counseling (MS, PhD, Ed S); special education (PhD, Ed S); visual disabilities (MS). *Accreditation:* CORE. *Faculty:* 10 full-time (8 women). *Students:* 41 full-time (35 women), 57 part-time (54 women); includes 13 minority (3 Black or African American, non-Hispanic/Latino; 1 American Indian or Alaska Native, non-Hispanic/Latino; 2 Asian, non-Hispanic/Latino; 7 Hispanic/Latino), 2 international. Average age 31. 69 applicants, 74% accepted, 29 enrolled. In 2010, 64 master's, 2 doctorates awarded. *Degree requirements:* For master's, comprehensive exam, thesis optional; for doctorate, comprehensive exam, thesis/dissertation; for Ed S, comprehensive exam. *Entrance requirements:* For master's, doctorate, and Ed S, GRE General Test, minimum GPA of 3.0. Additional exam requirements/recommendations for international students: Required—TOEFL (minimum score 550 paper-based; 213 computer-based; 80 iBT); Recommended—TWE. *Application deadline:* For fall admission, 7/1 for domestic and international students; for winter admission, 11/1 for domestic and international students; for spring admission, 3/1 for domestic and international students. Applications are processed on a rolling basis. Application fee: $30. Electronic applications accepted. *Expenses:* Tuition, state resident: full-time $8238.24. *Financial support:* Fellowships with full and partial tuition reimbursements, research assistantships with full and partial tuition reimbursements, teaching assistantships with full and partial tuition reimbursements, career-related internships or fieldwork and traineeships available. Financial award applicants required to submit FAFSA. *Unit head:* Dr. Mary Frances Hanline, Chair, 850-644-4880, Fax: 850-644-8715, E-mail: mhanline@fsu.edu. *Application contact:* Harriet Kasper, Program Assistant, 850-644-2122, Fax: 850-644-7736, E-mail: hkasper@fsu.edu.

Fort Valley State University, College of Graduate Studies and Extended Education, Department of Counseling Psychology, Program in Rehabilitation Counseling, Fort Valley, GA 31030. Offers MS. *Accreditation:* CORE. Part-time programs available. *Degree requirements:* For master's, comprehensive exam (for some programs), thesis optional. *Entrance requirements:* For master's, GRE General Test or MAT.

The George Washington University, Graduate School of Education and Human Development, Department of Counseling/Human and Organizational Studies, Programs in Counseling: School, Community and Rehabilitation, Washington, DC 20052. Offers community counseling (MA Ed); rehabilitation counseling (MA Ed); school counseling (MA Ed). School counseling program also offered in Alexandria, VA. *Accreditation:* ACA; CORE; NCATE. *Students:* 65 full-time (60 women), 51 part-time (40 women); includes 18 Black or African American, non-Hispanic/Latino; 1 American Indian or Alaska Native, non-Hispanic/Latino; 5 Asian, non-Hispanic/Latino; 6 Hispanic/Latino; 1 Two or more races, non-Hispanic/Latino, 3 international. Average age 31. 120 applicants, 97% accepted, 50 enrolled. In 2010, 57 master's awarded. *Degree requirements:* For master's, comprehensive exam. *Entrance requirements:* For master's, GRE General Test or MAT, minimum GPA of 2.75. *Application deadline:* For fall admission, 1/15 priority date for domestic students; for spring admission, 10/1 for domestic students. Applications are processed on a rolling basis. Application fee: $75. *Financial support:* In 2010–11, 27 students received support; fellowships, research assistantships, teaching assistantships, career-related internships or fieldwork, Federal Work-Study, and tuition waivers (full and partial) available. *Faculty research:* Adjustment to disability, head injury rehabilitation, cross-cultural counseling. *Application contact:* Sarah Lang, Director of Graduate Admissions, 202-994-1447, Fax: 202-994-7207, E-mail: slang@gwu.edu.

Georgia State University, College of Education, Department of Counseling and Psychological Services, Program in Rehabilitation Counseling, Atlanta, GA 30302-3083. Offers MS. *Accreditation:* CORE. Part-time and evening/weekend programs available. *Degree requirements:* For master's, comprehensive exam. *Entrance requirements:* For master's, GRE General Test, minimum GPA of 2.5. *Faculty research:* Catastrophic injuries, private sector rehabilitation, closed head injuries, persons with multiple handicaps.

Hofstra University, School of Education, Health, and Human Services, Programs in Counseling, Hempstead, NY 11549. Offers counseling (MS Ed, PD); creative arts therapy (MA); gerontology (MS, Advanced Certificate); marriage and family therapy (MA); mental health counseling (MA); rehabilitation counseling (MS Ed, CAS, PD); rehabilitation counseling in mental health (MS Ed, CAS); school counselor-bilingual extension (Advanced Certificate). Part-time and evening/weekend programs available. *Students:* 145 full-time (132 women), 80 part-time (74 women); includes 41 minority (23 Black or African American, non-Hispanic/Latino; 5 Asian, non-Hispanic/Latino; 11 Hispanic/Latino; 1 Native Hawaiian or other Pacific Islander, non-Hispanic/Latino; 1 Two or more races, non-Hispanic/Latino), 8 international. Average age 30. 187 applicants, 63% accepted, 67 enrolled. In 2010, 79 master's, 1 other advanced degree awarded. *Degree requirements:* For master's, comprehensive exam (for some programs), thesis (for some programs), internship, practicum, student teaching, seminars. *Entrance requirements:* For master's, GRE, interview, letters of recommendation, portfolio, essay, professional experience, certification; for other advanced degree, GRE, interview, letters of recommendation, essay, professional experience, resume, master's degree. Additional exam requirements/recommendations for international students: Required—TOEFL (minimum score 550 paper-based; 213 computer-based; 80 iBT). *Application deadline:* Applications are processed on a rolling basis. Application fee: $70 ($75 for international students). Electronic applications accepted. *Expenses:* Tuition: Full-time $18,000; part-time $1000 per credit hour. Required fees: $970; $145 per term. Tuition and fees vary according to program. *Financial support:* In

2010–11, 102 students received support, including 27 fellowships with full and partial tuition reimbursements available (averaging $2,466 per year), 4 research assistantships with full and partial tuition reimbursements available (averaging $14,567 per year); career-related internships or fieldwork, Federal Work-Study, institutionally sponsored loans, scholarships/grants, tuition waivers (full and partial), unspecified assistantships, and scholarships also available. Support available to part-time students. Financial award applicants required to submit FAFSA. *Faculty research:* Bereavement, loss, and trauma counseling, creativity for non-artists. *Unit head:* Dr. Darra Pace, Chairperson, 516-463-6476, Fax: 516-463-6415, E-mail: cprdzp@hofstra.edu. *Application contact:* Carol Drummer, Dean of Graduate Admissions, 516-463-4876, Fax: 516-463-4664, E-mail: gradstudent@hofstra.edu.

Hunter College of the City University of New York, Graduate School, School of Education, Department of Educational Foundations and Counseling Programs, Program in Rehabilitation Counseling, New York, NY 10021-5085. Offers MS Ed. *Accreditation:* CORE. *Faculty:* 15 full-time (9 women), 67 part-time/adjunct (42 women). *Students:* 27 full-time (22 women), 57 part-time (44 women); includes 27 Black or African American, non-Hispanic/Latino; 5 Asian, non-Hispanic/Latino; 23 Hispanic/Latino, 1 international. Average age 35. 39 applicants, 44% accepted, 12 enrolled. In 2010, 21 master's awarded. *Degree requirements:* For master's, thesis, seminar. *Entrance requirements:* For master's, interview, minimum GPA of 2.7, recommendations. Additional exam requirements/recommendations for international students: Required—TOEFL, TWE. *Application deadline:* For fall admission, 4/1 for domestic students, 2/1 for international students; for spring admission, 11/1 for domestic students, 9/1 for international students. Applications are processed on a rolling basis. Application fee: $125. *Financial support:* Federal Work-Study and tuition waivers (partial) available. Support available to part-time students. *Unit head:* Dr. Arnold Wolf, Adviser, 212-772-4616, E-mail: awo@hunter.cuny.edu. *Application contact:* William Zlata, Director for Graduate Admissions, 212-772-4482, Fax: 212-650-3336, E-mail: admissions@hunter.cuny.edu.

Illinois Institute of Technology, Graduate College, College of Psychology, Chicago, IL 60616. Offers clinical psychology (PhD); industrial/organizational psychology (PhD); personnel/human resource development (MS); rehabilitation (PhD); rehabilitation counseling (MS). *Accreditation:* APA (one or more programs are accredited); CORE. Part-time and evening/weekend programs available. *Faculty:* 21 full-time (7 women), 6 part-time/adjunct (4 women). *Students:* 160 full-time (111 women), 39 part-time (33 women); includes 36 minority (8 Black or African American, non-Hispanic/Latino; 1 American Indian or Alaska Native, non-Hispanic/Latino; 15 Asian, non-Hispanic/Latino; 12 Hispanic/Latino), 16 international. Average age 29. 253 applicants, 40% accepted, 43 enrolled. In 2010, 31 master's, 14 doctorates awarded. Terminal master's awarded for partial completion of doctoral program. *Degree requirements:* For master's, thesis (for some programs); for doctorate, comprehensive exam, thesis/dissertation, 96-108 credit hours, internship (for clinical and industrial/organizational specializations). *Entrance requirements:* For master's, GRE General Test (minimum score 900 Quantitative and Verbal, 2.5 Analytical Writing), minimum high school GPA of 3.0; at least 18 credit hours of undergraduate study in psychology with at least one course each in experimental psychology and statistics; official transcripts; 3 letters of recommendation; personal statement; for doctorate, GRE General Test (minimum score 1000 Quantitative and Verbal, 3.0 Analytical Writing), minimum high school GPA of 3.0; at least 18 credit hours of undergraduate study in psychology with at least one course each in experimental psychology and statistics; official transcripts; 3 letters of recommendation; personal statement. Additional exam requirements/recommendations for international students: Required—TOEFL (minimum score 550 paper-based; 213 computer-based; 80 iBT); Recommended—IELTS (minimum score 5.5). *Application deadline:* For fall admission, 1/15 for domestic and international students. Application fee: $50. Electronic applications accepted. *Expenses:* Tuition: Full-time $18,576; part-time $1032 per credit hour. Required fees: $583 per semester. One-time fee: $150. Tuition and fees vary according to program and student level. *Financial support:* In 2010–11, 23 research assistantships with full and partial tuition reimbursements (averaging $223 per year) were awarded; fellowships with full and partial tuition reimbursements, career-related internships or fieldwork, Federal Work-Study, institutionally sponsored loans, scholarships/grants, traineeships, health care benefits, tuition waivers (partial), and unspecified assistantships also available. Support available to part-time students. Financial award application deadline: 1/15; financial award applicants required to submit FAFSA. *Faculty research:* Health psychology, behavioral medicine, attachment, child social and emotional development, educational assessment. Total annual research expenditures: $1.6 million. *Unit head:* Dr. M. Ellen Mitchell, Dean, 312-567-3362, Fax: 312-567-3493, E-mail: mitchelle@iit.edu. *Application contact:* Institute of Psychology Graduate Admissions, 312-567-3500, Fax: 312-567-3493, E-mail: psychology@iit.edu.

Indiana University–Purdue University Indianapolis, School of Science, Department of Psychology, Indianapolis, IN 46202-3275. Offers clinical rehabilitation psychology (MS); industrial/organizational psychology (MS); psychobiology of addictions (MS, PhD). *Accreditation:* APA (one or more programs are accredited). *Faculty:* 10 full-time (2 women). *Students:* 51 full-time (43 women), 11 part-time (10 women); includes 4 minority (2 Black or African American, non-Hispanic/Latino; 2 Asian, non-Hispanic/Latino), 3 international. Average age 28. 116 applicants, 25% accepted, 18 enrolled. In 2010, 11 master's, 4 doctorates awarded. Terminal master's awarded for partial completion of doctoral program. *Degree requirements:* For master's, thesis; for doctorate, thesis/dissertation. *Entrance requirements:* For master's, GRE General Test, minimum undergraduate GPA of 3.0; for doctorate, GRE General Test, GRE Subject Test (clinical rehabilitation psychology), minimum undergraduate GPA of 3.2. *Application deadline:* For fall admission, 1/1 priority date for domestic students. Application fee: $55 ($65 for international students). *Financial support:* In 2010–11, 5 fellowships with partial tuition reimbursements (averaging $12,218 per year), 23 teaching assistantships with partial tuition reimbursements (averaging $7,553 per year) were awarded; research assistantships with partial tuition reimbursements, career-related internships or fieldwork, Federal Work-Study, and institutionally sponsored loans also available. Financial award application deadline: 3/1; financial award applicants required to submit FAFSA. *Faculty research:* Psychiatric rehabilitation, chronic stress, neurological research, language and cognitive development in infants, alcoholism and psychopathology. *Unit head:* Dr. J. Gregor Fetterman, Chairman, 317-274-6945, Fax: 317-274-6756, E-mail: gfetter@iupui.edu. *Application contact:* Dr. J. Gregor Fetterman, Chairman, 317-274-6945, Fax: 317-274-6756, E-mail: gfetter@iupui.edu.

Jackson State University, Graduate School, College of Education and Human Development, Department of School, Community and Rehabilitation Counseling, Jackson, MS 39217. Offers community and agency counseling (MS); guidance and counseling (MS, MS Ed); rehabilitation counseling (MS Ed). *Accreditation:* ACA; CORE (one or more programs are accredited); NCATE. Part-time and evening/weekend programs available. *Faculty:* 9 full-time (6 women), 1 part-time/adjunct (0 women). *Students:* 48 full-time (38 women), 94 part-time (80 women); includes 136 Black or African American, non-Hispanic/Latino, 1 international. Average age 36. In 2010, 31 master's awarded. *Degree requirements:* For master's, comprehensive exam, thesis. *Entrance requirements:* For master's, GRE General Test. Additional exam requirements/recommendations for international students: Required—TOEFL (minimum score 520 paper-based; 195 computer-based; 67 iBT). *Application deadline:* For fall admission, 3/1 priority date for domestic students, 2/1 for international students; for spring admission, 10/1 for domestic and international students. Applications are processed on a rolling basis. Application fee: $25. *Expenses:* Tuition, state resident: full-time $5050; part-time $281 per credit hour. Tuition, nonresident: full-time $12,380; part-time $689 per credit hour. *Financial support:* Career-related internships or fieldwork, Federal Work-Study, scholarships/grants, and unspecified assistantships available. Support available to part-time students. Financial award application deadline: 3/1; financial award applicants required to submit FAFSA. *Unit head:* Dr. Jean Farish-Jackson, Chair, 601-979-2361, Fax: 601-979-2213, E-mail: jfjackso@jsums.edu. *Application contact:* Sharlene Wilson, Director of Graduate Admissions, 601-979-2455, Fax: 601-979-4325, E-mail: sharlene.f.wilson@jsums.edu.

Kent State University, Graduate School of Education, Health, and Human Services, School of Lifespan Development and Educational Sciences, Program in Rehabilitation Counseling, Kent, OH 44242-0001. Offers M Ed, Ed S. *Accreditation:* CORE (one or more programs are

Rehabilitation Counseling

Kent State University *(continued)*
accredited). *Faculty:* 2 full-time (1 woman), 5 part-time/adjunct (3 women). *Students:* 19 full-time (15 women), 26 part-time (21 women); includes 5 Black or African American, non-Hispanic/Latino; 2 Asian, non-Hispanic/Latino, 2 international. 19 applicants, 42% accepted. In 2010, 11 master's awarded. *Degree requirements:* For master's, thesis (for some programs). *Entrance requirements:* For degree, GRE General Test. Additional exam requirements/recommendations for international students: Required—TOEFL. *Application deadline:* Applications are processed on a rolling basis. Application fee: $30 ($60 for international students). Electronic applications accepted. *Expenses:* Tuition, state resident: full-time $7866; part-time $437 per credit hour. Tuition, nonresident: full-time $14,022; part-time $779 per credit hour. *Financial support:* In 2010–11, research assistantships with full tuition reimbursements (averaging $8,313 per year); Federal Work-Study, scholarships/grants, unspecified assistantships, and 2 administrative assistantships (averaging $8,313 per year) also available. Financial award application deadline: 4/1; financial award applicants required to submit FAFSA. *Unit head:* Dr. Phillip Rumrill, Coordinator, 330-672-0600, E-mail: prumrill@kent.edu. *Application contact:* Nancy Miller, Academic Program Coordinator, Office of Graduate Student Services, 330-672-2576, Fax: 330-672-9162, E-mail: ogs@kent.edu.

Langston University, School of Education and Behavioral Sciences, Langston, OK 73050. Offers bilingual/multicultural (M Ed); elementary education (M Ed); English as a second language (M Ed); rehabilitation counseling (M Sc); urban education (M Ed). *Accreditation:* CORE; NCATE (one or more programs are accredited). Part-time programs available. *Degree requirements:* For master's, comprehensive exam, thesis optional. *Entrance requirements:* For master's, GRE, writing skills test, minimum GPA of 2.5, 3 letters of recommendation. Additional exam requirements/recommendations for international students: Required—TOEFL, TWE. *Faculty research:* Bilingual/multicultural education, financing post-secondary education.

La Salle University, School of Arts and Sciences, Program in Psychology, Philadelphia, PA 19141-1199. Offers clinical psychology (Psy D); family psychology (Psy D); rehabilitation psychology (Psy D). *Accreditation:* AAMFT/COAMFTE. Part-time and evening/weekend programs available. *Entrance requirements:* For doctorate, GRE, minimum GPA of 3.0. *Expenses:* Contact institution. *Faculty research:* Cognitive therapy, attribution theory, treatment of addiction.

Louisiana State University Health Sciences Center, School of Allied Health Professions, Department of Rehabilitation Counseling, New Orleans, LA 70112-2262. Offers MHS. *Accreditation:* CORE. *Faculty:* 4 full-time (1 woman). *Students:* 32 full-time (27 women), 2 part-time (1 woman); includes 16 minority (10 Black or African American, non-Hispanic/Latino; 4 Asian, non-Hispanic/Latino; 2 Hispanic/Latino). Average age 24. 22 applicants, 91% accepted, 20 enrolled. In 2010, 9 master's awarded. *Degree requirements:* For master's, clinical internship. *Entrance requirements:* For master's, GRE General Test, minimum GPA of 2.5, 2 letters of recommendation. *Application deadline:* For fall admission, 4/15 priority date for domestic students. Applications are processed on a rolling basis. Application fee: $50. *Financial support:* In 2010–11, 20 students received support, including 22 fellowships with full tuition reimbursements available (averaging $6,000 per year). Financial award application deadline: 4/15. *Faculty research:* Job placement, clinical judgment, counseling process, consumer satisfaction, vocational assessment. Total annual research expenditures: $10,000. *Unit head:* Dr. John Dolan, Head, 504-568-4315, Fax: 504-568-4324, E-mail: jdolan@lsuhsc.edu. *Application contact:* Yudialys Delgado Stoute, Student Affairs Director, 504-568-4253, Fax: 504-568-3185, E-mail: ydelga@lsuhsc.edu.

Maryville University of Saint Louis, School of Health Professions, Program in Rehabilitation Counseling, St. Louis, MO 63141-7299. Offers marriage and family therapy (MARC); music therapy (MARC); rehabilitation counseling (CAGS); substance abuse (MARC). *Accreditation:* CORE. Part-time and evening/weekend programs available. *Students:* 21 full-time (16 women), 29 part-time (21 women); includes 11 minority (all Black or African American, non-Hispanic/Latino). Average age 33. In 2010, 19 master's awarded. *Degree requirements:* For master's, internship, seminar. *Entrance requirements:* For master's, minimum cumulative GPA of 3.0, 2 letters of recommendation, interview. Additional exam requirements/recommendations for international students: Required—TOEFL (minimum score 550 paper-based). *Application deadline:* For fall admission, 1/15 for domestic students; for spring admission, 10/1 for domestic students. Application fee: $40 ($60 for international students). Electronic applications accepted. *Expenses:* Tuition: Full-time $21,100; part-time $633.50 per credit hour. Required fees: $150 per semester. *Financial support:* Career-related internships or fieldwork, Federal Work-Study, and campus employment available. Financial award application deadline: 3/1; financial award applicants required to submit FAFSA. *Unit head:* Dr. Michael Kiener, Interim Director, 314-529-9443, Fax: 314-529-9495, E-mail: mkiener@maryville.edu. *Application contact:* Dr. Michael Kiener, Interim Director, 314-529-9443, Fax: 314-529-9495, E-mail: mkiener@maryville.edu.

Michigan State University, The Graduate School, College of Education, Department of Counseling, Educational Psychology and Special Education, East Lansing, MI 48824. Offers counseling (MA); educational psychology and educational technology (PhD); educational technology (MA); measurement and quantitative methods (PhD); rehabilitation counseling (MA); rehabilitation counselor education (PhD); school psychology (MA, PhD, Ed S); special education (MA, PhD). *Accreditation:* APA (one or more programs are accredited); CORE (one or more programs are accredited). Part-time programs available. *Entrance requirements:* Additional exam requirements/recommendations for international students: Required—TOEFL. Electronic applications accepted.

Minnesota State University Mankato, College of Graduate Studies, College of Allied Health and Nursing, Program in Rehabilitation Counseling, Mankato, MN 56001. Offers MS. *Accreditation:* CORE. *Students:* 17 full-time (16 women), 10 part-time (3 women). *Degree requirements:* For master's, comprehensive exam. *Entrance requirements:* For master's, GRE General Test, minimum GPA of 3.0 during previous 2 years, references. *Application deadline:* For fall admission, 3/1 priority date for domestic students. Applications are processed on a rolling basis. Application fee: $40. *Financial support:* Research assistantships with full tuition reimbursements, teaching assistantships with full tuition reimbursements available. Financial award application deadline: 3/15; financial award applicants required to submit FAFSA. *Unit head:* Dr. Renee Shellum, Graduate Coordinator, 507-389-5842. *Application contact:* 507-389-2321, E-mail: grad@mnsu.edu.

Montana State University Billings, College of Allied Health Professions, Department of Rehabilitation and Human Services, Billings, MT 59101-0298. Offers MSRC. *Accreditation:* CORE. Part-time programs available. *Degree requirements:* For master's, thesis or professional paper and/or field experience. *Entrance requirements:* For master's, GRE General Test or MAT, minimum GPA of 3.0.

North Carolina Agricultural and Technical State University, Graduate School, School of Education, Department of Human Development and Services, Greensboro, NC 27411. Offers adult education (MS); counselor education (MS); human resources-agency counseling (MS); human resources-rehabilitation counseling (MS); leadership studies (PhD); school administration (MS). *Accreditation:* ACA. Part-time and evening/weekend programs available. *Degree requirements:* For master's, comprehensive exam, thesis, qualifying exam. *Entrance requirements:* For master's, GRE General Test, minimum GPA of 3.0.

Northeastern Illinois University, Graduate College, College of Education, Department of Counselor Education, Chicago, IL 60625-4699. Offers guidance and counseling (MA), including career development, community and family counseling, elementary school counseling, rehabilitation counseling, secondary school counseling. *Accreditation:* ACA. Part-time and evening/weekend programs available. *Faculty:* 9 full-time (5 women), 2 part-time/adjunct (1 woman). *Students:* 38 full-time (26 women), 160 part-time (120 women); includes 34 minority (9 Black or African American, non-Hispanic/Latino; 1 American Indian or Alaska Native, non-Hispanic/Latino; 6 Asian, non-Hispanic/Latino; 17 Hispanic/Latino; 1 Native Hawaiian or other

Pacific Islander, non-Hispanic/Latino), 3 international. Average age 42. 140 applicants, 68% accepted, 65 enrolled. In 2010, 75 master's awarded. *Degree requirements:* For master's, comprehensive exam, thesis or alternative, internship, practicum. *Entrance requirements:* For master's, GRE, minimum GPA of 2.75, workshop. Additional exam requirements/recommendations for international students: Required—TOEFL (minimum score 550 paper-based; 213 computer-based; 79 iBT). *Application deadline:* For fall admission, 4/1 priority date for domestic students; for spring admission, 8/15 for domestic students. Applications are processed on a rolling basis. Application fee: $30. Electronic applications accepted. *Financial support:* In 2010–11, 31 students received support, including 5 research assistantships with full and partial tuition reimbursements available (averaging $6,600 per year); career-related internships or fieldwork, Federal Work-Study, institutionally sponsored loans, scholarships/grants, tuition waivers (full and partial), and unspecified assistantships also available. Support available to part-time students. *Faculty research:* Psychological factors of the visually impaired, reclaiming self through art, ego development, multicultural counseling, family therapy. *Unit head:* Dr. Charles Pistorio, Department Chair. *Application contact:* Dr. Charles Pistorio, Department Chair.

Ohio University, Graduate College, Gladys W. and David H. Patton College of Education and Human Services, Department of Counseling and Higher Education, Athens, OH 45701-2979. Offers college student personnel (M Ed); community/agency counseling (M Ed); counselor education (PhD); higher education (PhD); rehabilitation counseling (M Ed); school counseling (M Ed). *Accreditation:* ACA; CORE. Part-time and evening/weekend programs available. *Students:* 146 full-time (105 women), 41 part-time (24 women); includes 36 minority (22 Black or African American, non-Hispanic/Latino; 1 Asian, non-Hispanic/Latino; 6 Hispanic/Latino; 1 Native Hawaiian or other Pacific Islander, non-Hispanic/Latino; 6 Two or more races, non-Hispanic/Latino), 8 international. 125 applicants, 58% accepted, 49 enrolled. In 2010, 82 master's, 9 doctorates awarded. *Degree requirements:* For master's, comprehensive exam (for some programs), thesis or alternative; for doctorate, comprehensive exam, thesis/dissertation. *Entrance requirements:* For master's, GRE General Test or MAT (if GPA less than 2.9), 3 letters of reference; for doctorate, GRE General Test, work experience, minimum GPA of 3.4. Additional exam requirements/recommendations for international students: Required—TOEFL (minimum score 550 paper-based; 80 iBT) or IELTS (minimum score 6.5). *Application deadline:* For fall admission, 1/15 for domestic and international students. Application fee: $50 ($55 for international students). Electronic applications accepted. *Financial support:* Research assistantships with full tuition reimbursements, teaching assistantships with full tuition reimbursements, Federal Work-Study, institutionally sponsored loans, tuition waivers (partial), and unspecified assistantships available. Financial award application deadline: 1/15. *Faculty research:* Youth violence, gender studies, student affairs, chemical dependency, disabilities issues. Total annual research expenditures: $527,983. *Unit head:* Dr. Tracy Leinbaugh, Chair, 740-593-0846, Fax: 740-593-0477, E-mail: leinbaug@ohio.edu. *Application contact:* Floyd J. Doney, Director of Student Affairs, 740-593-4400, Fax: 740-593-9310, E-mail: doney@ohio.edu.

Pontifical Catholic University of Puerto Rico, College of Graduate Studies in Behavioral Science and Community Affairs, Program in Rehabilitation Counseling, Ponce, PR 00717-0777. Offers MA. *Accreditation:* CORE. Part-time programs available. *Degree requirements:* For master's, thesis. *Entrance requirements:* For master's, EXADEP, GRE General Test, 3 letters of recommendation, interview, minimum GPA of 2.75.

St. Cloud State University, School of Graduate Studies, College of Education, Department of Counselor Education, Higher Education, and Educational Psychology, Program in Rehabilitation Counseling, St. Cloud, MN 56301-4498. Offers MS. *Accreditation:* CORE. *Degree requirements:* For master's, comprehensive exam (for some programs), thesis or alternative. *Entrance requirements:* For master's, GRE General Test, minimum GPA of 2.75. Additional exam requirements/recommendations for international students: Required—Michigan English Language Assessment Battery; Recommended—TOEFL (minimum score 550 paper-based; 213 computer-based), IELTS (minimum score 6.5). Electronic applications accepted.

St. John's University, The School of Education, Department of Human Services and Counseling, Queens, NY 11439. Offers bilingual school counseling (MS Ed); bilingual/multicultural education/teaching English to speakers of other languages (MS Ed); literacy (MS Ed, PhD, Adv C), including literacy (PhD), literacy B-6 or 5-12 (Adv C), teaching literacy 5-12 (MS Ed), teaching literacy B-12 (MS Ed), teaching literacy B-6 (MS Ed); mental health counseling (MS Ed); school counseling (MS Ed); teaching children with disabilities in childhood education (MS Ed). Part-time and evening/weekend programs available. *Students:* 189 full-time (171 women), 334 part-time (300 women); includes 161 minority (32 Black or African American, non-Hispanic/Latino; 20 Asian, non-Hispanic/Latino; 103 Hispanic/Latino; 2 Native Hawaiian or other Pacific Islander, non-Hispanic/Latino; 4 Two or more races, non-Hispanic/Latino), 20 international. Average age 28. 337 applicants, 77% accepted, 152 enrolled. In 2010, 132 master's, 3 other advanced degrees awarded. *Degree requirements:* For master's, comprehensive exam, thesis, internship. *Entrance requirements:* For master's, minimum GPA of 3.0, 2 letters of recommendation, interview; for doctorate, MAT, GRE General Test (analytical), official transcript showing conferral of degree with minimum GPA of 3.2, 2 letters of recommendation, statement of goals, resume, evidence of teaching experience; for Adv C, statement of goals, official transcript showing conferral of degree with minimum GPA of 3.0, 2 letters of recommendation, interview. Additional exam requirements/recommendations for international students: Required—TOEFL (minimum score 600 paper-based; 250 computer-based; 100 iBT), IELTS (minimum score 5.5). *Application deadline:* For fall admission, 8/17 for domestic students, 5/1 priority date for international students; for spring admission, 1/5 for domestic students, 11/1 priority date for international students. Applications are processed on a rolling basis. Application fee: $70. Electronic applications accepted. *Expenses:* Tuition: Full-time $17,100; part-time $950 per credit. Required fees: $340; $170 per semester. Tuition and fees vary according to program. *Financial support:* Research assistantships, career-related internships or fieldwork and scholarships/grants available. Support available to part-time students. Financial award application deadline: 3/1; financial award applicants required to submit FAFSA. *Faculty research:* Assisting troubled children and teens with substance abuse, truancy, and coping skills; literacy development for ESL learners; investigating Caribbean and Creole language and culture. *Unit head:* Dr. Francine Guastello, Acting Chair, 718-990-1475, Fax: 718-990-1614, E-mail: guastelf@stjohns.edu. *Application contact:* Dr. Kelly K. Ronayne, Associate Dean for Graduate Admissions, 718-990-2303, Fax: 718-990-2343, E-mail: graded@stjohns.edu.

Salve Regina University, Graduate Studies, Program in Rehabilitation Counseling, Newport, RI 02840-4192. Offers mental health counseling (CAGS); rehabilitation counseling (MA). *Accreditation:* CORE. Part-time and evening/weekend programs available. *Entrance requirements:* For master's, GMAT, GRE General Test or MAT. Additional exam requirements/recommendations for international students: Required—TOEFL (minimum score 600 paper-based; 250 computer-based; 100 iBT) or IELTS. Electronic applications accepted. *Expenses:* Tuition: Full-time $7740; part-time $430 per credit. Required fees: $40 per semester. Tuition and fees vary according to course level and degree level.

San Diego State University, Graduate and Research Affairs, College of Education, Department of Administration, Rehabilitation and Post-Secondary Education, San Diego, CA 92182. Offers educational leadership in post-secondary education (MA); rehabilitation counseling (MS), including deafness. Evening/weekend programs available. Postbaccalaureate distance learning degree programs offered. *Degree requirements:* For master's, comprehensive exam (for some programs), thesis (for some programs). *Entrance requirements:* For master's, GRE General Test, letters of reference. Additional exam requirements/recommendations for international students: Required—TOEFL. Electronic applications accepted. *Faculty research:* Rehabilitation in cultural diversity, distance learning technology.

San Francisco State University, Division of Graduate Studies, College of Health and Human Services, Department of Counseling, San Francisco, CA 94132-1722. Offers counseling (MS); marriage, family, and child counseling (MSC); rehabilitation counseling (MS). *Accreditation:* ACA (one or more programs are accredited). Part-time programs available. *Application deadline:*

Applications are processed on a rolling basis. *Unit head:* Dr. Robert Williams, Chair, 415-338-2005. *Application contact:* Couryll Pineda, Academic Office Coordinator, 415-338-2005, E-mail: counsel@sfsu.edu.

South Carolina State University, School of Graduate Studies, Department of Human Services, Orangeburg, SC 29117-0001. Offers rehabilitation counseling (MA). *Accreditation:* CORE. Part-time and evening/weekend programs available. *Degree requirements:* For master's, comprehensive exam (for some programs), departmental qualifying exam, internship. *Entrance requirements:* For master's, GRE, MAT, minimum GPA of 2.7. Electronic applications accepted. *Faculty research:* Handicap, disability, rehabilitation evaluation, vocation.

Southern Illinois University Carbondale, Graduate School, College of Education, Rehabilitation Institute, Carbondale, IL 62901-4701. Offers behavioral analysis and therapy (MS); communication disorders and sciences (MS); rehabilitation (Rh D); rehabilitation administration and services (MS); rehabilitation counseling (MS). *Accreditation:* CORE. Part-time programs available. *Degree requirements:* For master's, thesis; for doctorate, thesis/dissertation. *Entrance requirements:* For master's, GRE; for doctorate, GRE or MAT, minimum GPA of 3.25. Additional exam requirements/recommendations for international students: Required—TOEFL. *Faculty research:* Professional ethics.

Southern University and Agricultural and Mechanical College, Graduate School, College of Sciences, Department of Psychology, Program in Rehabilitation Counseling, Baton Rouge, LA 70813. Offers MS. *Accreditation:* CORE. *Degree requirements:* For master's, comprehensive exam, thesis optional. *Entrance requirements:* For master's, GMAT or GRE General Test. Additional exam requirements/recommendations for international students: Required—TOEFL. *Faculty research:* Cultural diversity, professional preparation and participation of minorities, needs and satisfaction of students with disabilities, prediction model for rehabilitation outcome, diabetes.

Springfield College, Graduate Programs, Programs in Rehabilitation Counseling and Services, Springfield, MA 01109-3797. Offers alcohol rehabilitation/substance abuse counseling (M Ed, MS); deaf counseling (M Ed, MS); developmental disabilities (M Ed, MS); general counseling and casework (M Ed, MS); psychiatric rehabilitation/mental health counseling (M Ed, MS); special services (M Ed, MS). *Accreditation:* CORE (one or more programs are accredited). Part-time programs available. *Degree requirements:* For master's, comprehensive exam. *Entrance requirements:* Additional exam requirements/recommendations for international students: Required—TOEFL (minimum score 550 paper-based; 213 computer-based). Electronic applications accepted.

Teachers College, Columbia University, Graduate Faculty of Education, Department of Health and Behavior Studies, Program in Guidance and Rehabilitation, New York, NY 10027-6696. Offers MA. *Expenses:* Tuition: Full-time $28,272; part-time $1178 per credit. Required fees: $756; $378 per semester. *Unit head:* Prof. Linda Hickson, Program Coordinator, 212-678-3880. *Application contact:* Elizabeth Puleio, Admissions Contact, 212-678-3710.

Texas Tech University Health Sciences Center, School of Allied Health Sciences, Program in Rehabilitation Counseling, Lubbock, TX 79430. Offers MRC. *Accreditation:* CORE. Part-time programs available. *Faculty:* 4 full-time (3 women). *Students:* 29 full-time (25 women), 63 part-time (47 women); includes 16 Black or African American, non-Hispanic/Latino; 1 Asian, non-Hispanic/Latino; 17 Hispanic/Latino. Average age 38. 57 applicants, 82% accepted, 47 enrolled. In 2010, 27 master's awarded. *Entrance requirements:* Additional exam requirements/recommendations for international students: Required—TOEFL. *Application deadline:* For fall admission, 6/1 for domestic students; for spring admission, 10/1 for domestic students. Application fee: $35. Electronic applications accepted. *Financial support:* Career-related internships or fieldwork and institutionally sponsored loans available. *Unit head:* Dr. Robin Satterwhite, Chair, 806-743-2263, Fax: 806-743-3249, E-mail: robin.satterwhite@ttuhsc.edu. *Application contact:* Jeri Moravcik, Assistant Director of Admissions and Student Affairs, 806-743-3220, Fax: 806-743-2994, E-mail: jeri.moravcik@ttuhsc.edu.

Thomas University, Department of Human Services, Thomasville, GA 31792-7499. Offers community counseling (MSCC); rehabilitation counseling (MRC). *Accreditation:* CORE. Part-time programs available. *Entrance requirements:* For master's, resume, 3 academic/professional references. Additional exam requirements/recommendations for international students: Required—TOEFL (minimum score 600 paper-based; 250 computer-based). Electronic applications accepted.

Troy University, Graduate School, College of Education, Program in Counseling and Psychology, Troy, AL 36082. Offers agency counseling (Ed S); clinical mental health (MS); community counseling (MS, Ed S); corrections counseling (MS); rehabilitation counseling (MS); school psychology (MS, Ed S); school psychometry (MS); social service counseling (MS); student affairs counseling (MS); substance abuse counseling (MS). *Accreditation:* ACA; CORE; NCATE. Part-time and evening/weekend programs available. *Students:* 419 full-time (338 women), 720 part-time (603 women); includes 696 minority (592 Black or African American, non-Hispanic/Latino; 8 American Indian or Alaska Native, non-Hispanic/Latino; 4 Asian, non-Hispanic/Latino; 46 Hispanic/Latino; 46 Two or more races, non-Hispanic/Latino). Average age 33. 326 applicants, 90% accepted. In 2010, 198 master's, 1 other advanced degree awarded. *Degree requirements:* For master's, comprehensive exam, thesis. *Entrance requirements:* For master's, MAT, minimum GPA of 2.5. Additional exam requirements/recommendations for international students: Required—TOEFL (minimum score 523 paper-based; 193 computer-based; 70 iBT), IELTS (minimum score 6). *Application deadline:* Applications are processed on a rolling basis. Application fee: $50. Electronic applications accepted. *Expenses:* Tuition, state resident: full-time $4428; part-time $246 per credit hour. Tuition, nonresident: full-time $8856; part-time $492 per credit hour. Required fees: $432; $24 per credit hour. $50 per term. Tuition and fees vary according to program. *Unit head:* Dr. Andrew Creamer, Chair, 334-670-3350, Fax: 334-670-32961, E-mail: drcreamer@troy.edu. *Application contact:* Brenda K. Campbell, Director of Graduate Admissions, 334-670-3178, Fax: 334-670-3733, E-mail: bcamp@troy.edu.

University at Albany, State University of New York, School of Education, Department of Educational and Counseling Psychology, Program in Rehabilitation Counseling, Albany, NY 12222-0001. Offers counseling psychology (MS). Evening/weekend programs available. *Entrance requirements:* For master's, GRE General Test. Additional exam requirements/recommendations for international students: Required—TOEFL (minimum score 550 paper-based; 213 computer-based). Electronic applications accepted.

University at Buffalo, the State University of New York, Graduate School, Graduate School of Education, Department of Counseling, School, and Educational Psychology, Buffalo, NY 14260. Offers counseling/school psychology (PhD); counselor education (PhD); educational psychology (MA, PhD); general education (Ed M); mental health counseling (MS); rehabilitation counseling (MS); school counseling (Ed M, Certificate); Singapore school counseling (Ed M). *Accreditation:* CORE (one or more programs are accredited). Part-time programs available. Postbaccalaureate distance learning degree programs offered (no on-campus study). *Faculty:* 21 full-time (12 women), 30 part-time/adjunct (26 women). *Students:* 156 full-time (125 women), 112 part-time (87 women); includes 25 Black or African American, non-Hispanic/Latino; 3 American Indian or Alaska Native, non-Hispanic/Latino; 2 Asian, non-Hispanic/Latino; 8 Hispanic/Latino, 24 international. Average age 30. 403 applicants, 40% accepted, 108 enrolled. In 2010, 35 master's, 12 doctorates, 19 other advanced degrees awarded. *Degree requirements:* For master's, comprehensive exam (for some programs), thesis (for some programs); for doctorate, comprehensive exam, thesis/dissertation. *Entrance requirements:* For master's and doctorate, GRE General Test, interview, letters of reference. Additional exam requirements/recommendations for international students: Required—TOEFL (minimum score 79 iBT). *Application deadline:* For fall admission, 2/1 priority date for domestic and international students. Application fee: $50. Electronic applications accepted. *Financial support:* In 2010–11, 10 fellowships with full tuition reimbursements (averaging $9,474 per year), 24 research assistantships with full tuition reimbursements (averaging $9,301 per year) were awarded; teaching assistantships with tuition reimbursements, career-related internships or fieldwork, Federal Work-Study, institutionally sponsored loans, and unspecified assistantships also available. Financial award application deadline: 2/1; financial award applicants required to submit FAFSA. *Faculty research:* Multicultural counseling, class size effects, good work in counseling, eating disorders, outcome assessment, change agents and therapeutic factors in group counseling. *Unit head:* Dr. Timothy Janikowski, Chair, 716-645-2484, Fax: 716-645-6616, E-mail: tjanikow@buffalo.edu. *Application contact:* Rochelle Cohen, Admissions Assistant, 716-645-2110, Fax: 716-645-7937, E-mail: recohen@buffalo.edu.

The University of Arizona, College of Education, Department of Disability and Psychoeducational Studies, Program in Rehabilitation, Tucson, AZ 85721. Offers MA, PhD. *Faculty:* 17 full-time (9 women). *Students:* 43 full-time (32 women), 15 part-time (13 women); includes 11 Black or African American, non-Hispanic/Latino; 1 American Indian or Alaska Native, non-Hispanic/Latino; 8 Hispanic/Latino; 3 Two or more races, non-Hispanic/Latino, 2 international. Average age 41. 35 applicants, 60% accepted, 11 enrolled. In 2010, 19 master's, 4 doctorates awarded. *Entrance requirements:* For master's, GMAT, 3 letters of recommendation, statement of purpose; for doctorate, GMAT, 3 letters of recommendation. Additional exam requirements/recommendations for international students: Required—TOEFL (minimum score 550 paper-based; 213 computer-based; 79 iBT). *Application deadline:* For fall admission, 2/15 for domestic students, 12/1 for international students. Application fee: $65. Electronic applications accepted. *Expenses:* Tuition, state resident: full-time $7692. *Financial support:* In 2010–11, 4 research assistantships with full tuition reimbursements (averaging $12,828 per year), 4 teaching assistantships with full tuition reimbursements (averaging $12,378 per year) were awarded. *Unit head:* Dr. Linda R. Shaw, Department Head, 520-621-7822, Fax: 520-621-3821, E-mail: lshaw@email.arizona.edu. *Application contact:* Cecilia Carlon, Coordinator, 520-621-7822, Fax: 520-621-3821, E-mail: ccarlon@email.arizona.edu.

University of Arkansas, Graduate School, College of Education and Health Professions, Department of Rehabilitation, Human Resources and Communication Disorders, Program in Rehabilitation, Fayetteville, AR 72701-1201. Offers MS, PhD. *Accreditation:* CORE (one or more programs are accredited). Part-time programs available. *Students:* 28 full-time (20 women), 22 part-time (15 women); includes 11 minority (7 Black or African American, non-Hispanic/Latino; 2 American Indian or Alaska Native, non-Hispanic/Latino; 1 Asian, non-Hispanic/Latino; 1 Hispanic/Latino), 1 international. 20 applicants, 100% accepted. In 2010, 15 master's, 5 doctorates awarded. *Degree requirements:* For doctorate, thesis/dissertation. *Entrance requirements:* For doctorate, GRE General Test. *Application deadline:* For fall admission, 4/1 for international students; for spring admission, 10/1 for international students. Applications are processed on a rolling basis. Application fee: $40 ($50 for international students). Electronic applications accepted. *Financial support:* In 2010–11, 3 fellowships with tuition reimbursements, 6 research assistantships were awarded; teaching assistantships, career-related internships or fieldwork and Federal Work-Study also available. Support available to part-time students. Financial award application deadline: 4/1; financial award applicants required to submit FAFSA. *Unit head:* Dr. Fran Hagstrom, Department Chairperson, 479-575-4758, Fax: 479-575-2492, E-mail: fhagstr@uark.edu. *Application contact:* Dr. Brent Williams, Graduate Coordinator, 479-575-4758, E-mail: btwilli@uark.edu.

University of Arkansas at Little Rock, Graduate School, College of Education, Department of Counseling, Adult and Rehabilitation Education, Little Rock, AR 72204-1099. Offers adult education (M Ed); counselor education (M Ed), including school counseling; orientation and mobility of the blind (Graduate Certificate); rehabilitation counseling (MA, Graduate Certificate); rehabilitation of the blind (MA). *Accreditation:* CORE; NCATE. Part-time programs available. *Entrance requirements:* For master's, interview, minimum GPA of 2.75. *Faculty research:* Low vision, orientation and mobility instruction.

The University of Iowa, Graduate College, College of Education, Department of Counseling, Rehabilitation, and Student Development, Iowa City, IA 52242-1316. Offers administration and research (PhD); community/rehabilitation counseling (MA); counselor education and supervision (PhD); rehabilitation counselor education (PhD); school counseling (MA); student development (MA, PhD). *Accreditation:* ACA (one or more programs are accredited); CORE (one or more programs are accredited). *Degree requirements:* For master's, thesis optional, exam; for doctorate, comprehensive exam, thesis/dissertation. *Entrance requirements:* For master's and doctorate, GRE General Test, minimum GPA of 3.0. Additional exam requirements/recommendations for international students: Required—TOEFL (minimum score 550 paper-based; 213 computer-based; 81 iBT). Electronic applications accepted.

The University of Kansas, Graduate Studies, College of Liberal Arts and Sciences, Department of Psychology, Lawrence, KS 66045. Offers clinical child psychology (MA, PhD); clinical health and rehabilitation (PhD); cognitive psychology (PhD); developmental psychology (PhD); quantitative psychology (PhD); social psychology (MA). *Accreditation:* APA (one or more programs are accredited). *Faculty:* 27 full-time (8 women), 9 part-time/adjunct (4 women). *Students:* 122 full-time (87 women), 1 (woman) part-time; includes 17 minority (4 Black or African American, non-Hispanic/Latino; 8 Asian, non-Hispanic/Latino; 4 Hispanic/Latino; 1 Native Hawaiian or other Pacific Islander, non-Hispanic/Latino), 9 international. Average age 28. 348 applicants, 11% accepted, 25 enrolled. In 2010, 16 master's, 16 doctorates awarded. *Degree requirements:* For master's, thesis; for doctorate, variable foreign language requirement, comprehensive exam, thesis/dissertation. *Entrance requirements:* For doctorate, GRE General Test, minimum GPA of 3.0; undergraduate degree with 15 hours of course work in psychology, curriculum vitae, writing sample (clinical program only). Additional exam requirements/recommendations for international students: Required—TOEFL. *Application deadline:* For fall admission, 12/1 for domestic and international students. Application fee: $55 ($65 for international students). Electronic applications accepted. *Expenses:* Tuition, state resident: full-time $7092; part-time $295.50 per credit hour. Tuition, nonresident: full-time $16,590; part-time $691.25 per credit hour. Required fees: $858; $71.49 per credit hour. Tuition and fees vary according to course load, campus/location and program. *Financial support:* Fellowships with full tuition reimbursements, research assistantships with partial tuition reimbursements, teaching assistantships with full and partial tuition reimbursements, career-related internships or fieldwork and unspecified assistantships available. Financial award application deadline: 12/1; financial award applicants required to submit FAFSA. *Faculty research:* Information processing in depression, rape and other forms of sexual coercion, motions on physical function, processes of memory and understanding text, social stigmas and hostile group environments. *Unit head:* Dr. Ruth Ann Atchley, Chair, 785-864-9821, Fax: 785-864-5696, E-mail: ratchley@ku.edu. *Application contact:* Cathy L. O'Keefe, Graduate Admissions Officer, 785-864-4195, Fax: 785-864-5696, E-mail: psycgrad@ku.edu.

University of Kentucky, Graduate School, College of Education, Program in Special Education, Lexington, KY 40506-0032. Offers early childhood special education (MS Ed); rehabilitation counseling (MRC); special education (MS Ed); special education leadership personnel preparation (Ed D). *Accreditation:* CORE; NCATE. Terminal master's awarded for partial completion of doctoral program. *Degree requirements:* For master's, comprehensive exam, thesis optional; for doctorate, comprehensive exam, thesis/dissertation. *Entrance requirements:* For master's, GRE General Test, minimum undergraduate GPA of 2.75; for doctorate, GRE General Test, minimum graduate GPA of 3.0. Additional exam requirements/recommendations for international students: Required—TOEFL (minimum score 550 paper-based; 213 computer-based). Electronic applications accepted. *Faculty research:* Applied behavior analysis applications in special education, single subject research design in classroom settings, transition research across life span, rural special education personnel.

University of Louisiana at Lafayette, College of Liberal Arts, Department of Psychology, Program in Rehabilitation Counseling, Lafayette, LA 70504. Offers MS. *Entrance requirements:* For master's, GRE General Test, minimum GPA of 3.0. Additional exam requirements/recommendations for international students: Required—TOEFL (minimum score 550 paper-

Rehabilitation Counseling

University of Louisiana at Lafayette (continued)
based; 213 computer-based). Electronic applications accepted. *Faculty research:* Vocational assessment, psychology.

University of Maryland, College Park, Academic Affairs, College of Education, Department of Counseling and Personnel Services, College Park, MD 20742. Offers college student personnel (M Ed, MA); college student personnel administration (PhD); community counseling (CAGS); community/career counseling (M Ed, MA); counseling and personnel services (M Ed, MA, PhD), including art therapy (M Ed), college student personnel (M Ed), counseling and personnel services (PhD), counseling psychology (M Ed), mental health counseling (M Ed), school counseling (M Ed); counseling psychology (PhD); counselor education (PhD); rehabilitation counseling (M Ed, MA, AGSC); school counseling (M Ed, MA); school psychology (M Ed, MA, PhD). *Accreditation:* ACA (one or more programs are accredited); APA (one or more programs are accredited); CORE (one or more programs are accredited); NCATE. Part-time and evening/weekend programs available. Postbaccalaureate distance learning degree programs offered (no on-campus study). *Faculty:* 33 full-time (18 women), 1 (woman) part-time/adjunct. *Students:* 136 full-time (105 women), 16 part-time (11 women); includes 23 Black or African American, non-Hispanic/Latino; 19 Asian, non-Hispanic/Latino; 12 Hispanic/Latino; 5 Two or more races, non-Hispanic/Latino, 11 international. 407 applicants, 11% accepted, 25 enrolled. In 2010, 38 master's, 15 doctorates, 4 other advanced degrees awarded. *Degree requirements:* For master's, thesis (for some programs); for doctorate, thesis/dissertation. *Entrance requirements:* For master's, GRE General Test or MAT, minimum GPA of 3.0, 3 letters of recommendation; for doctorate, GRE General Test or MAT, minimum GPA of 3.5, 3 letters of recommendation. Additional exam requirements/recommendations for international students: Required—TOEFL. *Application deadline:* For fall admission, 12/15 for domestic and international students; for spring admission, 6/1 for international students. Applications are processed on a rolling basis. Application fee: $75. Electronic applications accepted. *Expenses:* Tuition, state resident: part-time $471 per credit hour. Tuition, nonresident: part-time $1016 per credit hour. Required fees: $337 per term. *Financial support:* In 2010–11, 15 fellowships with partial tuition reimbursements (averaging $11,738 per year), 3 research assistantships (averaging $17,258 per year), 83 teaching assistantships with tuition reimbursements (averaging $16,131 per year) were awarded; career-related internships or fieldwork, Federal Work-Study, and scholarships/grants also available. Support available to part-time students. Financial award applicants required to submit FAFSA. *Faculty research:* Educational psychology, counseling, health. Total annual research expenditures: $838,213. *Unit head:* Dr. Dennis Kivlighan, Chair, 301-405-2858, E-mail: dennisk@umd.edu. *Application contact:* Dean of Graduate School, 301-405-0358.

University of Maryland Eastern Shore, Graduate Programs, Department of Rehabilitation Services, Princess Anne, MD 21853-1299. Offers rehabilitation counseling (MS). *Accreditation:* CORE. Part-time and evening/weekend programs available. *Degree requirements:* For master's, internship. *Entrance requirements:* For master's, interview. Additional exam requirements/recommendations for international students: Required—TOEFL (minimum score 213 computer-based; 80 iBT). Electronic applications accepted. *Faculty research:* Long-term rehabilitation training.

University of Massachusetts Boston, Office of Graduate Studies, Graduate College of Education, Counseling and School Psychology Department, Program in Rehabilitation Counseling, Boston, MA 02125-3393. Offers M Ed, CAGS. *Accreditation:* CORE.

University of Medicine and Dentistry of New Jersey, School of Health Related Professions, Department of Psychiatric Rehabilitation and Counseling Professions, Program in Psychiatric Rehabilitation, Newark, NJ 07107-1709. Offers MS, PhD. *Accreditation:* CORE. Part-time and evening/weekend programs available. Postbaccalaureate distance learning degree programs offered (minimal on-campus study). *Students:* 12 part-time (5 women); includes 1 Black or African American, non-Hispanic/Latino; 1 Hispanic/Latino. Average age 41. 23 applicants, 70% accepted, 11 enrolled. In 2010, 5 master's awarded. *Entrance requirements:* For master's, Bachelors Degree, All transcripts, 2 letters, interview, statement of interest in Psych Rehab; for doctorate, GRE General Test, Bachelors Degree*, All transcripts, 3 letters, personal goals, significant experience in Psych Rehab. Additional exam requirements/recommendations for international students: Required—TOEFL (minimum score 500 paper-based; 79 iBT). *Application deadline:* For fall admission, 6/1 for domestic students, 3/1 for international students; for spring admission, 11/15 for domestic students, 7/1 for international students. Applications are processed on a rolling basis. Application fee: $75. Electronic applications accepted. *Financial support:* Traineeships available. *Unit head:* Dr. Carlos W. Pratt, Program Director, 908-889-2461, E-mail: pratt@umdnj.edu. *Application contact:* Douglas Lomonaco, Assistant Dean, 973-972-5454, Fax: 973-972-7463, E-mail: shrpadm@umdnj.edu.

University of Medicine and Dentistry of New Jersey, School of Health Related Professions, Department of Psychiatric Rehabilitation and Counseling Professions, Program in Rehabilitation Counseling, Newark, NJ 07107-1709. Offers psychiatric rehabilitation (MS); vocational rehabilitation (MS). Programs offered at Scotch Plains and Stratford campuses. *Accreditation:* CORE. Part-time and evening/weekend programs available. *Students:* 8 full-time (all women), 46 part-time (36 women); includes 14 Black or African American, non-Hispanic/Latino; 4 Asian, non-Hispanic/Latino; 9 Hispanic/Latino, 2 international. Average age 33. 19 applicants, 68% accepted, 12 enrolled. In 2010, 20 master's awarded. *Degree requirements:* For master's, internship, practicum. *Entrance requirements:* For master's, Bachelors transcript, 2 letters, interview, personal goals statement. Additional exam requirements/recommendations for international students: Required—TOEFL (minimum score 500 paper-based; 79 iBT). *Application deadline:* For fall admission, 6/15 for domestic students, 3/1 for international students; for winter admission, 4/15 for domestic students; for spring admission, 11/15 for domestic students, 7/1 for international students. Applications are processed on a rolling basis. Application fee: $75. Electronic applications accepted. *Unit head:* Dr. Janice Oursler, 856-566-2785, E-mail: ms-crc@umdnj.edu. *Application contact:* Douglas Lomonaco, Assistant Dean, 973-972-5454, Fax: 973-972-7463, E-mail: shrpadm@umdnj.edu.

University of Memphis, Graduate School, College of Education, Department of Counseling, Educational Psychology and Research, Memphis, TN 38152. Offers counseling (MS, Ed D), including community counseling (MS), rehabilitation counseling (MS), school counseling (MS); counseling psychology (PhD); educational psychology and research (MS, PhD), including educational psychology, educational research. *Accreditation:* ACA (one or more programs are accredited); APA (one or more programs are accredited); CORE (one or more programs are accredited); NCATE. *Faculty:* 26 full-time (13 women), 9 part-time/adjunct (5 women). *Students:* 95 full-time (73 women), 104 part-time (81 women); includes 56 Black or African American, non-Hispanic/Latino; 3 American Indian or Alaska Native, non-Hispanic/Latino; 1 Asian, non-Hispanic/Latino; 2 Hispanic/Latino, 5 international. Average age 33. 118 applicants, 63% accepted, 36 enrolled. In 2010, 46 master's, 14 doctorates awarded. *Degree requirements:* For master's, comprehensive exam, thesis or alternative; for doctorate, comprehensive exam, thesis/dissertation. *Entrance requirements:* For master's, GRE General Test or MAT, minimum GPA of 2.5; for doctorate, GRE General Test. *Application deadline:* For fall admission, 10/1 for domestic students; for spring admission, 4/1 for domestic students. Application fee: $35 ($60 for international students). *Financial support:* In 2010–11, 130 students received support; fellowships with full tuition reimbursements available, research assistantships with full tuition reimbursements available, teaching assistantships with full tuition reimbursements available, career-related internships or fieldwork, Federal Work-Study, scholarships/grants, and unspecified assistantships available. Financial award application deadline: 2/15; financial award applicants required to submit FAFSA. *Faculty research:* Anger management, aging and disability, supervision, multicultural counseling. *Unit head:* Dr. Douglas C. Strohmer, Chair, 901-678-2841, Fax: 901-678-5114. *Application contact:* Dr. Ernest A. Rakow, Associate Dean of Administration and Graduate Programs, 901-678-2399, Fax: 901-678-4778.

University of Nevada, Las Vegas, Graduate College, College of Education, Department of Counselor Education, Las Vegas, NV 89154-3066. Offers clinical mental health counseling (MS); community mental health counseling (Advanced Certificate); rehabilitation counseling (Advanced Certificate); school counseling (M Ed). *Faculty:* 7 full-time (2 women), 10 part-time/adjunct (7 women). *Students:* 62 full-time (54 women), 60 part-time (53 women); includes 50 minority (8 Black or African American, non-Hispanic/Latino; 1 American Indian or Alaska Native, non-Hispanic/Latino; 2 Asian, non-Hispanic/Latino; 17 Hispanic/Latino; 1 Native Hawaiian or other Pacific Islander, non-Hispanic/Latino; 21 Two or more races, non-Hispanic/Latino), 1 international. Average age 33. 102 applicants, 82% accepted, 58 enrolled. In 2010, 24 master's, 4 other advanced degrees awarded. *Degree requirements:* For master's, comprehensive exam (for some programs), thesis (for some programs); for Advanced Certificate, thesis (for some programs). *Entrance requirements:* Additional exam requirements/recommendations for international students: Required—TOEFL (minimum score 550 paper-based; 213 computer-based; 80 iBT), IELTS (minimum score 7). *Application deadline:* For fall admission, 2/1 priority date for domestic and international students. Applications are processed on a rolling basis. Application fee: $60 ($95 for international students). Electronic applications accepted. *Expenses:* Tuition, area resident: Part-time $239.50 per credit. Tuition, state resident: part-time $239.50 per credit. Tuition, nonresident: part-time $503 per credit. Required fees: $108 per semester. Tuition and fees vary according to course load, program and reciprocity agreements. *Financial support:* In 2010–11, 10 students received support, including 6 research assistantships with partial tuition reimbursements available (averaging $10,000 per year), 4 teaching assistantships with partial tuition reimbursements available (averaging $10,000 per year); institutionally sponsored loans, scholarships/grants, health care benefits, and unspecified assistantships also available. Financial award application deadline: 3/1. *Faculty research:* Multicultural issues in counseling, counseling with returning veterans, counseling depression and suicide, effective play therapy, ethics and counseling. Total annual research expenditures: $4,627. *Unit head:* Dr. Jesse Brinson, Interim Chair/ Associate Professor, 702-895-1390, Fax: 702-895-5550, E-mail: brinson@unlv.nevada.edu. *Application contact:* Graduate College Admissions Evaluator, 702-895-3320, Fax: 702-895-4180, E-mail: gradcollege@unlv.edu.

The University of North Carolina at Chapel Hill, School of Medicine and Graduate School, Graduate Programs in Medicine, Chapel Hill, NC 27599. Offers allied health sciences (MPT, MS, Au D, DPT, PhD), including human movement science (MS, PhD), occupational science (MS, PhD), physical therapy (MPT, MS, DPT), rehabilitation counseling and psychology (MS), speech and hearing sciences (MS, Au D, PhD); biochemistry and biophysics (MS, PhD); bioinformatics and computational biology (PhD); biomedical engineering (MS, PhD); cell and developmental biology (PhD); cell and molecular physiology (PhD); genetics and molecular biology (PhD); microbiology and immunology (MS, PhD), including immunology, microbiology; neurobiology (PhD); pathology and laboratory medicine (PhD), including experimental pathology; pharmacology (PhD); MD/PhD. Postbaccalaureate distance learning degree programs offered. Terminal master's awarded for partial completion of doctoral program. *Degree requirements:* For master's, comprehensive exam; for doctorate, thesis/dissertation. Electronic applications accepted. *Expenses:* Contact institution.

The University of North Carolina at Chapel Hill, School of Medicine and Graduate School, Graduate Programs in Medicine, Department of Allied Health Sciences, Division of Rehabilitation Counseling and Psychology, Chapel Hill, NC 27599. Offers MS. *Accreditation:* CORE. *Degree requirements:* For master's, comprehensive exam, thesis or alternative, internship. *Entrance requirements:* For master's, GRE. Additional exam requirements/recommendations for international students: Required—TOEFL (minimum score 550 paper-based; 79 computer-based). *Faculty research:* Motor development, motor control; treatment of sports/orthopedic patient problems; movement in older adults; postural control across the lifespan; research in clinical practice; fetal, preterm, and infant movement; functional assessment across the lifespan.

University of Northern Colorado, Graduate School, College of Natural and Health Sciences, School of Human Sciences, Program in Rehabilitation, Greeley, CO 80639. Offers human rehabilitation (PhD); rehabilitation counseling (MA). *Accreditation:* CORE (one or more programs are accredited). Part-time programs available. *Faculty:* 3 full-time (2 women). *Students:* 16 full-time (13 women), 6 part-time (5 women); includes 4 Black or African American, non-Hispanic/Latino; 1 Asian, non-Hispanic/Latino; 2 Hispanic/Latino, 4 international. Average age 33. 12 applicants, 100% accepted, 9 enrolled. In 2010, 5 master's awarded. *Degree requirements:* For master's, comprehensive exam, thesis or alternative; for doctorate, comprehensive exam, thesis/dissertation. *Entrance requirements:* For master's, GRE General Test or MAT, 2 letters of recommendation; for doctorate, GRE General Test, 2 letters of recommendation. *Application deadline:* Applications are processed on a rolling basis. Application fee: $50 ($60 for international students). Electronic applications accepted. *Expenses:* Tuition, state resident: full-time $6199; part-time $344 per credit hour. Tuition, nonresident: full-time $14,834; part-time $824 per credit hour. Required fees: $1091; $60.60 per credit hour. Tuition and fees vary according to course load, degree level and program. *Financial support:* Fellowships, research assistantships, teaching assistantships, unspecified assistantships available. Financial award application deadline: 3/1; financial award applicants required to submit FAFSA. *Unit head:* Dr. Joe Ososkie, Program Coordinator, 970-351-2403. *Application contact:* Linda Sisson, Graduate Student Admission Coordinator, 970-351-1807, Fax: 970-351-2371, E-mail: linda.sisson@unco.edu.

University of North Florida, Brooks College of Health, Department of Public Health, Jacksonville, FL 32224. Offers aging services (Certificate); community health (MPH); geriatric management (MSH); health administration (MHA); rehabilitation counseling (MS). *Accreditation:* CEPH. Part-time and evening/weekend programs available. *Faculty:* 17 full-time (10 women), 3 part-time/adjunct (1 woman). *Students:* 108 full-time (84 women), 77 part-time (50 women); includes 13 Black or African American, non-Hispanic/Latino; 2 American Indian or Alaska Native, non-Hispanic/Latino; 9 Asian, non-Hispanic/Latino; 10 Hispanic/Latino; 2 Two or more races, non-Hispanic/Latino, 8 international. Average age 32. 219 applicants, 37% accepted, 54 enrolled. In 2010, 43 master's awarded. *Degree requirements:* For master's, thesis optional. *Entrance requirements:* For master's, GRE General Test (MSH, MS, MPH); GMAT or GRE General Test (MHA), minimum GPA of 3.0 in last 60 hours. Additional exam requirements/recommendations for international students: Required—TOEFL (minimum score 500 paper-based; 173 computer-based). *Application deadline:* For fall admission, 7/1 priority date for domestic students, 5/1 for international students; for spring admission, 11/1 priority date for domestic students, 10/1 for international students. Applications are processed on a rolling basis. Application fee: $30. Electronic applications accepted. *Expenses:* Tuition, state resident: full-time $7646.40; part-time $318.60 per credit hour. Tuition, nonresident: full-time $23,502; part-time $979.24 per credit hour. Required fees: $1208.88; $50.37 per credit hour. Tuition and fees vary according to course load and program. *Financial support:* In 2010–11, 39 students received support, including 1 teaching assistantship (averaging $1,004 per year); research assistantships, career-related internships or fieldwork, Federal Work-Study, scholarships/grants, and tuition waivers (partial) also available. Support available to part-time students. Financial award application deadline: 4/1; financial award applicants required to submit FAFSA. *Faculty research:* Dietary supplements; alcohol, tobacco, and other drug use prevention; turnover among health professionals; aging; psychosocial aspects of disabilities. Total annual research expenditures: $225,351. *Unit head:* Dr. JoAnn Nolin, Chair, 904-620-2840, Fax: 904-620-2848, E-mail: jnolin@unf.edu. *Application contact:* Heather Kenney, Director of Advising, 904-620-2810, Fax: 904-620-1030, E-mail: heather.kenney@unf.edu.

University of North Texas, Toulouse Graduate School, College of Public Affairs and Community Service, Department of Rehabilitation, Social Work, and Addictions, Denton, TX 76203. Offers rehabilitation counseling (MS). *Accreditation:* CORE. Part-time and evening/weekend programs available. Postbaccalaureate distance learning degree programs offered (no on-campus study). *Degree requirements:* For master's, comprehensive exam, thesis optional, 100 hour practicum, 600 hour internship. *Entrance requirements:* For master's, GRE General Test or 2 years experience, minimum overall GPA of 2.8, 3.0 in last 60 hours. Additional exam requirements/recommendations for international students: Recommended—TOEFL (minimum score 550 paper-based; 213 computer-based; 79 iBT). *Application deadline:* Applications are processed on a rolling basis. Electronic applications accepted. *Expenses:* Tuition, state resident: full-time $4298; part-time $239 per credit hour. Tuition, nonresident: full-time $10,782; part-time $549 per credit hour. Required fees: $1292; $270 per credit hour. *Financial support:* Career-related internships or fieldwork, Federal Work-Study, institutionally sponsored loans, and scholarships/grants available. Financial award application deadline: 4/15; financial award applicants required to submit FAFSA. *Faculty research:* Resiliency, multiculturalism, substance abuse and co-existing disabilities, social work pedagogy, spiritual aspects of disability and aging. *Application contact:* Program Coordinator, 940-565-4054, Fax: 940-369-8649.

University of Pittsburgh, School of Health and Rehabilitation Sciences, Master's Programs in Health and Rehabilitation Sciences, Pittsburgh, PA 15260. Offers health and rehabilitation sciences (MS), including clinical dietetics and nutrition, health care supervision and management, health information systems, occupational therapy, physical therapy, rehabilitation counseling, rehabilitation science and technology, sports medicine, wellness and human performance. *Accreditation:* APTA. Part-time and evening/weekend programs available. *Faculty:* 23 full-time (12 women), 4 part-time/adjunct (2 women). *Students:* 117 full-time (81 women), 41 part-time (27 women); includes 19 minority (8 Black or African American, non-Hispanic/Latino; 7 Asian, non-Hispanic/Latino; 1 Hispanic/Latino; 3 Two or more races, non-Hispanic/Latino), 67 international. Average age 28. 337 applicants, 64% accepted, 100 enrolled. In 2010, 110 master's awarded. *Degree requirements:* For master's, comprehensive exam (for some programs), thesis optional. *Entrance requirements:* For master's, NA, minimum GPA of 3.0. Additional exam requirements/recommendations for international students: Required—TOEFL, IELTS. *Application deadline:* For fall admission, 1/31 for international students; for spring admission, 7/31 for international students. Applications are processed on a rolling basis. Application fee: $50. Electronic applications accepted. *Expenses:* Contact institution. *Financial support:* Research assistantships, teaching assistantships, Federal Work-Study, institutionally sponsored loans, traineeships, and unspecified assistantships available. Financial award applicants required to submit FAFSA. *Faculty research:* Assistive technology, seating and wheeled mobility, cellular neurophysiology, low back syndrome, augmentative communication. Total annual research expenditures: $7.8 million. *Unit head:* Dr. Clifford E. Brubaker, Dean, 412-383-6560, Fax: 412-383-6535, E-mail: cliffb@pitt.edu. *Application contact:* Shameem Gangjee, Director of Admissions, 412-383-6558, Fax: 412-383-6535, E-mail: admissions@shrs.pitt.edu.

University of Puerto Rico, Río Piedras, College of Social Sciences, Graduate School of Rehabilitation Counseling, San Juan, PR 00931-3300. Offers MRC. *Accreditation:* CORE. Part-time programs available. *Degree requirements:* For master's, comprehensive exam, thesis, internship. *Entrance requirements:* For master's, GRE or PAEG, interview, minimum GPA of 3.0, letter of recommendation.

The University of Scranton, College of Graduate and Continuing Education, Department of Counseling and Human Services, Program in Rehabilitation Counseling, Scranton, PA 18510. Offers MS. *Accreditation:* CORE. Part-time and evening/weekend programs available. *Students:* 38 full-time (27 women), 4 part-time (3 women); includes 3 Black or African American, non-Hispanic/Latino; 1 Hispanic/Latino. Average age 27. 23 applicants, 43% accepted. In 2010, 16 master's awarded. *Degree requirements:* For master's, comprehensive exam, capstone experience. *Entrance requirements:* For master's, minimum GPA of 2.75. Additional exam requirements/recommendations for international students: Required—TOEFL (minimum score 500 paper-based; 173 computer-based), IELTS (minimum score 5.5). *Application deadline:* For fall admission, 3/1 for domestic students. Application fee: $0. *Financial support:* Teaching assistantships, career-related internships or fieldwork and Federal Work-Study available. Support available to part-time students. Financial award application deadline: 3/1. *Unit head:* Dr. Lori Bruch, Program Director, 570-941-4308, Fax: 570-941-5882, E-mail: bruchl1@scranton.edu. *Application contact:* Joseph M. Roback, Director of Admissions, 570-941-4385, Fax: 570-941-5928, E-mail: robackj2@scranton.edu.

University of South Alabama, Graduate School, College of Education, Department of Professional Studies, Mobile, AL 36688-0002. Offers community counseling (MS); educational media (M Ed, MS); instructional design and development (MS, PhD); rehabilitation counseling (MS); school counseling (M Ed); school psychometry (M Ed). *Accreditation:* NCATE. Part-time programs available. *Faculty:* 17 full-time (8 women). *Students:* 104 full-time (86 women), 93 part-time (73 women); includes 52 minority (46 Black or African American, non-Hispanic/Latino; 2 American Indian or Alaska Native, non-Hispanic/Latino; 3 Hispanic/Latino; 1 Native Hawaiian or other Pacific Islander, non-Hispanic/Latino), 5 international. 76 applicants, 49% accepted, 32 enrolled. In 2010, 5 master's, 10 doctorates awarded. *Degree requirements:* For master's, comprehensive exam. *Entrance requirements:* For master's, GRE General Test or MAT, minimum GPA of 3.0. *Application deadline:* For fall admission, 6/15 priority date for domestic students; for spring admission, 11/1 priority date for domestic students. Applications are processed on a rolling basis. Application fee: $35. *Expenses:* Tuition, state resident: part-time $300 per credit hour. Tuition, nonresident: part-time $600 per credit hour. Required fees: $150 per semester. *Financial support:* In 2010–11, 5 research assistantships were awarded; career-related internships or fieldwork also available. Support available to part-time students. Financial award application deadline: 4/1. *Faculty research:* Agency counseling, rehabilitation counseling, school psychometry. *Unit head:* Dr. Charles Guest, Chair, 251-380-2861. *Application contact:* Dr. Abigail Baxter, Director of Graduate Studies, 251-380-6310.

University of South Carolina, School of Medicine and The Graduate School, Graduate Programs in Medicine, Program in Rehabilitation Counseling, Columbia, SC 29208. Offers psychiatric rehabilitation (Certificate); rehabilitation counseling (MRC). *Accreditation:* CORE. Part-time and evening/weekend programs available. *Degree requirements:* For master's, comprehensive exam, internship, practicum. *Entrance requirements:* For master's and Certificate, GRE General Test or GMAT. Electronic applications accepted. *Expenses:* Contact institution. *Faculty research:* Quality of life, alcohol dependency, technology for disabled, psychiatric rehabilitation, women with disabilities.

University of Southern Maine, School of Education and Human Development, Program in Counselor Education, Portland, ME 04104-9300. Offers clinical mental health (MS); counseling (CAS); mental health rehabilitation technician/community (Certificate); rehabilitation counseling (MS); school counseling (MS). *Accreditation:* ACA (one or more programs are accredited); CORE; Teacher Education Accreditation Council. Part-time and evening/weekend programs available. *Faculty:* 9 full-time (5 women), 3 part-time/adjunct (1 woman). *Students:* 52 full-time (45 women), 88 part-time (63 women); includes 8 minority (1 Black or African American, non-Hispanic/Latino; 2 American Indian or Alaska Native, non-Hispanic/Latino; 2 Asian, non-Hispanic/Latino; 3 Hispanic/Latino). 103 applicants, 58% accepted, 47 enrolled. In 2010, 39 master's, 1 other advanced degree awarded. *Degree requirements:* For master's, comprehensive exam, thesis or alternative; for other advanced degree, thesis or alternative. *Entrance requirements:* For master's, GRE General Test or MAT, interview; for other advanced degree, master's degree. Additional exam requirements/recommendations for international students: Required—TOEFL (minimum score 550 paper-based; 213 computer-based; 79 iBT). *Application deadline:* For fall admission, 11/15 for domestic students. Application fee: $65. Electronic applications accepted. *Financial support:* In 2010–11, 15 students received support, including 5 research assistantships with partial tuition reimbursements available (averaging $4,500 per year); career-related internships or fieldwork, Federal Work-Study, institutionally sponsored loans, scholarships/grants, and unspecified assistantships also available. Support available to part-time students. Financial award application deadline: 3/1; financial award applicants required to submit FAFSA. *Faculty research:* Counselor licensure. *Unit head:* Dr. E. Michael Brady, Chair, Human Resource Development Department, 207-780-5316, Fax: 207-780-5043, E-mail: mbrady@usm.maine.edu. *Application contact:* Mary Sloan, Director of Graduate Admissions, 207-780-4386, Fax: 207-780-4969, E-mail: msloan@usm.maine.edu.

University of South Florida, Graduate School, College of Behavioral and Community Sciences, Department of Rehabilitation and Mental Health Counseling, Tampa, FL 33620-9951. Offers MA. *Accreditation:* CORE. Part-time and evening/weekend programs available. *Faculty:* 4 full-time (0 women), 3 part-time/adjunct (all women). *Students:* 85 full-time (72 women), 73 part-time (58 women); includes 8 Black or African American, non-Hispanic/Latino; 5 Asian, non-Hispanic/Latino; 28 Hispanic/Latino, 1 international. Average age 31. 107 applicants, 46% accepted, 26 enrolled. In 2010, 29 master's awarded. *Degree requirements:* For master's, comprehensive exam, thesis. *Entrance requirements:* For master's, GRE General Test, minimum GPA of 3.0 in last 60 hours. Additional exam requirements/recommendations for international students: Required—TOEFL (minimum score 550 paper-based; 213 computer-based), TWE. *Application deadline:* For fall admission, 2/15 for domestic students, 1/2 for international students; for spring admission, 10/15 for domestic students, 6/1 for international students. Application fee: $30. Electronic applications accepted. *Financial support:* Application deadline: 6/30. *Faculty research:* Allied health, multiculturalism, couples therapy, addictions. *Unit head:* Charotte G. Dixon, Director, 813-974-2855, Fax: 813-974-8080, E-mail: dixon@chuma1.cas.usf.edu. *Application contact:* Gary DuDell, Director, 813-974-1257, Fax: 813-974-8080, E-mail: gdudell@cas.usf.edu.

The University of Tennessee, Graduate School, College of Education, Health and Human Sciences, Department of Educational Psychology and Counseling, Knoxville, TN 37996. Offers adult education (MS); applied educational psychology (MS); collaborative learning (Ed D); college student personnel (MS); mental health counseling (MS); rehabilitation counseling (MS); school counseling (MS). *Accreditation:* ACA (one or more programs are accredited); CORE (one or more programs are accredited); NCATE. Part-time and evening/weekend programs available. *Degree requirements:* For master's, thesis optional. *Entrance requirements:* For master's, GRE General Test, minimum GPA of 2.7. Additional exam requirements/recommendations for international students: Required—TOEFL. Electronic applications accepted. *Expenses:* Tuition, state resident: full-time $7440; part-time $414 per credit hour. Tuition, nonresident: full-time $22,478; part-time $1250 per credit hour. Required fees: $922; $43 per credit hour. Tuition and fees vary according to program.

The University of Texas at El Paso, Graduate School, College of Health Sciences, Rehabilitation Counseling Program, El Paso, TX 79968-0001. Offers MRC. *Degree requirements:* For master's, thesis optional. *Entrance requirements:* For master's, GRE, minimum GPA of 3.0, statement of professional goals, letters of recommendation. Additional exam requirements/recommendations for international students: Required—TOEFL; Recommended—IELTS. *Application deadline:* For fall admission, 8/1 for domestic students, 3/1 for international students; for spring admission, 11/1 for domestic students, 9/1 for international students. Applications are processed on a rolling basis. Application fee: $45 ($80 for international students). Electronic applications accepted. *Financial support:* Fellowships with partial tuition reimbursements, research assistantships with partial tuition reimbursements, teaching assistantships with partial tuition reimbursements, institutionally sponsored loans, scholarships/grants, health care benefits, tuition waivers (partial), and unspecified assistantships available. Support available to part-time students. Financial award application deadline: 3/15; financial award applicants required to submit FAFSA. *Unit head:* Dr. Timothy Tansey, Program Director, 915-747-7233, E-mail: tntansey@utep.edu. *Application contact:* Dr. Patricia D. Witherspoon, Dean of the Graduate School, 915-747-5491, Fax: 915-747-5788, E-mail: withersp@utep.edu.

The University of Texas–Pan American, College of Health Sciences and Human Services, Department of Rehabilitation, Edinburg, TX 78539. Offers rehabilitation counseling (MS, PhD). *Accreditation:* CORE. Part-time and evening/weekend programs available. *Degree requirements:* For master's, comprehensive exam, thesis optional. *Entrance requirements:* For master's, minimum GPA of 3.0. *Faculty research:* Attitudes and disability, substance abuse, multicultural counseling, Hispanics and disability, Social Security beneficiary characteristics.

The University of Texas Southwestern Medical Center at Dallas, Southwestern School of Health Professions, Rehabilitation Counseling Psychology Program, Dallas, TX 75390. Offers MRC. *Accreditation:* CORE. *Degree requirements:* For master's, thesis. *Entrance requirements:* For master's, GRE General Test, minimum GPA of 3.0. *Application deadline:* For fall admission, 5/1 for domestic students. Applications are processed on a rolling basis. Application fee: $0. Electronic applications accepted. *Financial support:* Career-related internships or fieldwork and institutionally sponsored loans available. Financial award application deadline: 3/1; financial award applicants required to submit FAFSA. *Faculty research:* Psychophysiology of stress and emotion, psychosocial rehabilitation, assessment of learning disabilities. *Unit head:* Dr. Cheryl Silver, Chair, 214-648-1740, Fax: 214-648-1076, E-mail: cheryl.silver@utsouthwestern.edu. *Application contact:* Lisa Halliburton, Department Administrator, 214-648-1544, Fax: 214-648-1076, E-mail: wanda.madyun@utsouthwestern.edu.

University of Wisconsin–Madison, Graduate School, School of Education, Department of Rehabilitation Psychology and Special Education, Program in Rehabilitation Psychology, Madison, WI 53706-1380. Offers MA, MS, PhD. *Accreditation:* CORE (one or more programs are accredited). *Degree requirements:* For doctorate, thesis/dissertation. *Application deadline:* For fall admission, 2/15 for domestic and international students; for spring admission, 10/15 for domestic and international students. Application fee: $56. *Expenses:* Tuition, state resident: full-time $9887; part-time $617.96 per credit. Tuition, nonresident: full-time $24,054; part-time $1503.40 per credit. Required fees: $67.63 per credit. Tuition and fees vary according to reciprocity agreements. *Financial support:* Fellowships with full tuition reimbursements, research assistantships with full tuition reimbursements, teaching assistantships with full tuition reimbursements, project assistantships available. *Unit head:* Dr. David Rosenthal, Chair, 608-263-5860, E-mail: drosenthal@education.wisc.edu. *Application contact:* Dr. David Rosenthal, Chair, 608-263-5860, E-mail: drosenthal@education.wisc.edu.

University of Wisconsin–Stout, Graduate School, College of Human Development, Program in Vocational Rehabilitation, Menomonie, WI 54751. Offers MS. *Accreditation:* CORE. Part-time programs available. Postbaccalaureate distance learning degree programs offered (no on-campus study). *Degree requirements:* For master's, comprehensive exam or thesis. *Entrance requirements:* For master's, minimum GPA of 2.75. Additional exam requirements/recommendations for international students: Required—TOEFL (minimum score 500 paper-based; 173 computer-based; 61 iBT). Electronic applications accepted. *Faculty research:* Aging/gerontology, athletics, neuropsychology, recreation, transition to work.

Utah State University, School of Graduate Studies, College of Education and Human Services, Department of Special Education and Rehabilitation, Program in Rehabilitation Counselor Education, Logan, UT 84322. Offers MRC. *Accreditation:* CORE. Part-time programs available. Postbaccalaureate distance learning degree programs offered (minimal on-campus study). *Degree requirements:* For master's, internship. *Entrance requirements:* For master's, GRE General Test, minimum GPA of 3.0. Additional exam requirements/recommendations for international students: Required—TOEFL (minimum score 550 paper-based; 213 computer-based). Electronic applications accepted. *Expenses:* Contact institution. *Faculty research:* Distance education, Hispanic rehabilitation, transition from school to work.

Virginia Commonwealth University, Graduate School, School of Allied Health Professions, Department of Rehabilitation Counseling, Richmond, VA 23284-9005. Offers MS, CPC. *Accreditation:* CORE (one or more programs are accredited). *Faculty:* 6 full-time (2 women). *Students:* 80 full-time (65 women), 76 part-time (59 women); includes 57 minority (45 Black or African American, non-Hispanic/Latino; 1 Asian, non-Hispanic/Latino; 6 Hispanic/Latino; 1 Native Hawaiian or other Pacific Islander, non-Hispanic/Latino; 4 Two or more races, non-Hispanic/Latino), 1 international. 37 applicants, 51% accepted, 16 enrolled. In 2010, 37 master's, 4 other advanced degrees awarded. *Entrance requirements:* For master's, GRE General Test or MAT. Additional exam requirements/recommendations for international students: Required—TOEFL (minimum score 600 paper-based; 250 computer-based; 100 iBT). *Application deadline:* For fall admission, 6/1 for domestic students; for spring admission, 10/1 for domestic students. Applications are processed on a rolling basis. Application fee: $50. Electronic applications accepted. *Expenses:* Tuition, state resident: full-time $4308; part-time $479 per credit hour. Tuition, nonresident: full-time $8942; part-time $994 per credit hour. Required fees: $2000; $85 per credit hour. Tuition and fees vary according to course level, course load, degree level, campus/location and program. *Financial support:* Fellowships, research assistantships, teaching assistantships, career-related internships or fieldwork and tuition waivers (full and partial) available. Financial award application deadline: 3/1; financial award applicants required to submit FAFSA. *Faculty research:* Substance abuse/addictions, lifelong disabilities,

Rehabilitation Counseling

Virginia Commonwealth University (continued)
consumer empowerment, counseling models, adjustment to disability. *Unit head:* Dr. Allen N. Lewis, Chair, 804-828-1132, Fax: 801-828-1321, E-mail: anlewis@vcu.edu. *Application contact:* Dr. Amy J. Armstrong, Vice Chair, 804-828-1132, Fax: 804-828-1321, E-mail: ajarmstr@vcu.edu.

Wayne State University, College of Education, Division of Theoretical and Behavioral Foundations, Detroit, MI 48202. Offers counseling (M Ed, MA, Ed D, PhD, Ed S); education evaluation and research (M Ed, Ed D, PhD); educational psychology (M Ed, Ed D, PhD, Ed S); educational sociology (M Ed, Ed D, PhD, Ed S); history and philosophy of education (M Ed, Ed D, PhD); rehabilitation counseling and community inclusion (MA, Ed S); school and community psychology (MA, Ed S); school clinical psychology (Ed S). *Accreditation:* ACA (one or more programs are accredited); CORE (one or more programs are accredited). Evening/weekend programs available. *Faculty:* 100 full-time (50 women), 60 part-time/adjunct (35 women). *Students:* 193 full-time (156 women), 202 part-time (164 women); includes 168 minority (150 Black or African American, non-Hispanic/Latino; 3 American Indian or Alaska Native, non-Hispanic/Latino; 8 Asian, non-Hispanic/Latino; 5 Hispanic/Latino; 2 Two or more races, non-Hispanic/Latino), 17 international. Average age 36. 97 applicants, 55% accepted, 35 enrolled. In 2010, 42 master's, 9 doctorates, 2 other advanced degrees awarded. *Degree requirements:* For doctorate, thesis/dissertation. *Entrance requirements:* For master's, GRE; for doctorate, GRE, interview, minimum GPA of 3.0, curriculum vitae, references. Additional exam requirements/recommendations for international students: Required—TOEFL (minimum score 550 paper-based; 213 computer-based), TWE (minimum score 6). *Application deadline:* For fall admission, 7/1 for domestic students, 6/1 for international students; for winter admission, 10/1 for international students; for spring admission, 2/1 for international students. Application fee: $20 ($30 for international students). Electronic applications accepted. *Expenses:* Tuition, state resident: full-time $7662; part-time $478.85 per credit hour. Tuition, nonresident: full-time $16,920; part-time $1057.55 per credit hour. Required fees: $571.20; $35.70 per credit hour. $188.05 per semester. Tuition and fees vary according to course load and program. *Financial support:* In 2010–11, 2 fellowships with tuition reimbursements (averaging $16,875 per year), 3 research assistantships with tuition reimbursements (averaging $17,785 per year), 1 teaching assistantship (averaging $15,181 per year) were awarded; career-related internships or fieldwork, Federal Work-Study, and institutionally sponsored loans also available. *Faculty research:* Adolescents at risk, supervision of counseling. *Unit head:* Dr. JoAnne Holbert, Assistant Dean, 313-577-1721, E-mail: jholbert@wayne.edu. *Application contact:* Janice Green, Assistant Dean, 313-577-1605, E-mail: jwgreen@wayne.edu.

Western Michigan University, Graduate College, College of Health and Human Services, Department of Blindness and Low Vision Studies, Kalamazoo, MI 49008. Offers orientation and mobility (MA); orientation and mobility of children (MA); vision rehabilitation teaching (MA). *Accreditation:* CORE.

Western Oregon University, Graduate Programs, College of Education, Division of Special Education, Program in Rehabilitation Counseling, Monmouth, OR 97361-1394. Offers MS. *Accreditation:* CORE. *Degree requirements:* For master's, thesis optional, oral exam, portfolio. *Entrance requirements:* For master's, interview, minimum GPA of 3.0. Additional exam requirements/recommendations for international students: Required—TOEFL (minimum score 550 paper-based; 213 computer-based; 79 iBT), IELTS (minimum score 6.5). *Faculty research:* Deafness, rehabilitation counseling.

Western Washington University, Graduate School, Woodring College of Education, Program in Rehabilitation Counseling, Bellingham, WA 98225-5996. Offers MA. *Accreditation:* CORE. Part-time and evening/weekend programs available. Postbaccalaureate distance learning degree programs offered (minimal on-campus study). *Degree requirements:* For master's, research project. *Entrance requirements:* For master's, GRE General Test or MAT, minimum GPA of 3.0 in last 60 semester hours or last 90 quarter hours of course work. Additional exam requirements/recommendations for international students: Required—TOEFL (minimum score 567 paper-based; 227 computer-based). Electronic applications accepted. *Faculty research:* Employment issues for individuals with significant disabilities, research and statistics techniques, rehabilitation counselor education.

West Virginia University, College of Human Resources and Education, Department of Counseling, Rehabilitation Counseling, and Counseling Psychology, Program in Rehabilitation Counseling, Morgantown, WV 26506. Offers MS. *Accreditation:* CORE. Part-time programs available. Postbaccalaureate distance learning degree programs offered (minimal on-campus study). *Degree requirements:* For master's, content exams. *Entrance requirements:* For master's, GRE General Test, minimum GPA of 2.5, interview. Additional exam requirements/recommendations for international students: Required—TOEFL (minimum score 550 paper-based; 213 computer-based; 65 iBT). Electronic applications accepted. *Faculty research:* Work adjustment, job modification for the handicapped, computer resource networks, vocational evaluation.

Wilberforce University, Program in Rehabilitation Counseling, Wilberforce, OH 45384. Offers MS. *Entrance requirements:* For master's, bachelor's degree, 3 letters of recommendation, interview. Additional exam requirements/recommendations for international students: Required—TOEFL.

Winston-Salem State University, Program in Rehabilitation Counseling, Winston-Salem, NC 27110-0003. Offers MRC. Part-time programs available. Postbaccalaureate distance learning degree programs offered (minimal on-campus study). *Degree requirements:* For master's, thesis optional. *Entrance requirements:* For master's, GRE, 3 letters of recommendation. Electronic applications accepted. *Faculty research:* Drug addiction, recovery, HIV/AIDS interventions.

Wright State University, School of Graduate Studies, College of Education and Human Services, Department of Human Services, Program in Rehabilitation Counseling, Dayton, OH 45435. Offers chemical dependency (MRC); severe disabilities (MRC). *Accreditation:* CORE. *Degree requirements:* For master's, comprehensive exam. *Entrance requirements:* For master's, GRE General Test, MAT, interview. Additional exam requirements/recommendations for international students: Required—TOEFL.

School Psychology

Abilene Christian University, Graduate School, College of Arts and Sciences, Department of Psychology, Program in School Psychology, Abilene, TX 79699-9100. Offers Specialist. *Students:* 12 full-time (8 women), 8 part-time (6 women); includes 3 Black or African American, non-Hispanic/Latino. 119 applicants, 8% accepted, 6 enrolled. *Entrance requirements:* Additional exam requirements/recommendations for international students: Required—TOEFL (minimum score 550 paper-based; 213 computer-based). *Application deadline:* For fall admission, 4/1 priority date for domestic students; for spring admission, 11/1 for domestic students. Applications are processed on a rolling basis. Application fee: $40. Electronic applications accepted. *Expenses:* Tuition: Full-time $12,906; part-time $717 per hour. Required fees: $1250; $61.50 per unit. *Financial support:* In 2010–11, 8 students received support. Federal Work-Study available. Support available to part-time students. Financial award application deadline: 4/1; financial award applicants required to submit FAFSA. *Unit head:* Dr. Jennifer Shewmaker, Graduate Advisor, 325-674-2381, Fax: 325-674-6968, E-mail: jennifer.shewmaker@acu.edu. *Application contact:* David Pittman, Graduate Admissions Counselor, 325-674-2656, Fax: 325-674-6717, E-mail: gradinfo@acu.edu.

Adelphi University, Derner Institute of Advanced Psychological Studies, Program in School Psychology, Garden City, NY 11530-0701. Offers MA. Part-time programs available. *Students:* 36 full-time (33 women), 27 part-time (24 women); includes 13 minority (6 Black or African American, non-Hispanic/Latino; 1 Asian, non-Hispanic/Latino; 5 Hispanic/Latino; 1 Native Hawaiian or other Pacific Islander, non-Hispanic/Latino). Average age 25. In 2010, 28 master's awarded. *Degree requirements:* For master's, comprehensive exam. *Entrance requirements:* For master's, minimum GPA of 3.0; 15 credits of course work in psychology including general psychology, developmental child or adolescent psychology, abnormal personality in school psychology, tests and measurements, statistics; 3 letters of recommendation. Additional exam requirements/recommendations for international students: Required—TOEFL (minimum score 550 paper-based; 213 computer-based; 80 iBT). *Application deadline:* For fall admission, 5/1 for domestic students, 4/1 for international students. Application fee: $50. Electronic applications accepted. *Financial support:* Research assistantships with full and partial tuition reimbursements, career-related internships or fieldwork, Federal Work-Study, institutionally sponsored loans, and unspecified assistantships available. *Unit head:* Dr. Ionas Sapountzis, 516-877-4743, E-mail: isapountzis@adelphi.edu. *Application contact:* Christine Murphy, Director of Admissions, 516-877-3050, Fax: 516-877-3039, E-mail: graduateadmissions@adelphi.edu.

Alabama Agricultural and Mechanical University, School of Graduate Studies, School of Education, Department of Counseling and Special Education, Huntsville, AL 35811. Offers communicative disorders (M Ed, MS); psychology and counseling (MS, Ed S), including clinical psychology (MS), counseling and guidance, counseling psychology (MS), personnel management (MS), psychometry (MS), school psychology (MS); special education (M Ed, MS). *Accreditation:* CORE; NCATE. Part-time and evening/weekend programs available. *Degree requirements:* For master's, comprehensive exam. *Entrance requirements:* For master's, GRE General Test. Additional exam requirements/recommendations for international students: Required—TOEFL (minimum score 500 paper-based; 173 computer-based; 61 iBT). *Faculty research:* Increasing numbers of minorities in special education and speech-language pathology.

Alfred University, Graduate School, Program in School Psychology, Alfred, NY 14802-1205. Offers school counseling (MS Ed, CAS); school psychology (MA, Psy D, CAS). *Accreditation:* APA. *Degree requirements:* For master's, internship; for doctorate, thesis/dissertation, internship. *Entrance requirements:* For master's and doctorate, GRE General Test. Additional exam requirements/recommendations for international students: Required—TOEFL (minimum score 590 paper-based; 243 computer-based; 90 iBT); Recommended—IELTS (minimum score 6.5). Electronic applications accepted. *Faculty research:* Family processes, alternative assessment approaches, behavior disorders in children, parent involvement, school psychology training issues.

Alliant International University–Irvine, Graduate School of Education, Educational Psychology Programs, Irvine, CA 92612. Offers educational psychology (Psy D); pupil personnel services (Credential); school psychology (MA). Part-time programs available. *Degree requirements:* For doctorate, thesis/dissertation. *Entrance requirements:* For master's, minimum GPA of 3.0, letters of recommendation; for doctorate, interview, minimum GPA of 3.0, letters of recommendation. Additional exam requirements/recommendations for international students: Required—TOEFL (minimum score 550 paper-based; 213 computer-based), TWE (minimum score 5). *Faculty research:* School based mental health.

Alliant International University–Los Angeles, Graduate School of Education, Educational Psychology Programs, Alhambra, CA 91803-1360. Offers educational psychology (Psy D); pupil personnel services (Credential); school psychology (MA). Part-time programs available. *Degree requirements:* For doctorate, thesis/dissertation. *Entrance requirements:* For master's, minimum GPA of 3.0, letters of recommendation; for doctorate, interview, minimum GPA of 3.0, letters of recommendation. Additional exam requirements/recommendations for international students: Required—TOEFL (minimum score 550 paper-based; 213 computer-based), TWE (minimum score 5). Electronic applications accepted. *Faculty research:* Early identification and intervention with high-risk preschoolers, pediatric neuropsychology, interpersonal violence, ADHD, learning theories.

Alliant International University–San Diego, Graduate School of Education, Educational Psychology Programs, San Diego, CA 92131-1799. Offers educational psychology (Psy D); pupil personnel services (Credential); school psychology (MA); student personnel services (Certificate). Part-time programs available. *Degree requirements:* For doctorate, thesis/dissertation. *Entrance requirements:* For master's, minimum GPA of 3.0, letters of recommendation; for doctorate, interview, letters of recommendation. Additional exam requirements/recommendations for international students: Required—TOEFL (minimum score 550 paper-based; 213 computer-based), TWE (minimum score 5). Electronic applications accepted.

Alliant International University–San Francisco, Graduate School of Education, Educational Psychology Programs, San Francisco, CA 94133-1221. Offers educational psychology (Psy D); pupil personnel services (Credential); school psychology (MA). Part-time programs available. *Degree requirements:* For doctorate, thesis/dissertation. *Entrance requirements:* For master's, minimum GPA of 3.0, letters of recommendation; for doctorate, interview, minimum GPA of 3.0, letters of recommendation. Additional exam requirements/recommendations for international students: Required—TOEFL (minimum score 550 paper-based; 213 computer-based), TWE (minimum score 5). Electronic applications accepted. *Faculty research:* Social skills, ADHD, effects of sightedness on areas of knowledge.

Andrews University, School of Graduate Studies, School of Education, Department of Educational and Counseling Psychology, Program in School Counseling, Berrien Springs, MI 49104. Offers MA. *Degree requirements:* For master's, thesis optional. *Entrance requirements:* For master's, GRE. Additional exam requirements/recommendations for international students: Required—TOEFL (minimum score 550 paper-based).

Andrews University, School of Graduate Studies, School of Education, Department of Educational and Counseling Psychology, Program in School Psychology, Berrien Springs, MI 49104. Offers Ed S. Part-time programs available. *Entrance requirements:* Additional exam requirements/recommendations for international students: Required—TOEFL (minimum score 550 paper-based).

Appalachian State University, Cratis D. Williams Graduate School, Department of Human Development and Psychological Counseling, Boone, NC 28608. Offers clinical mental health counseling (MA); college student development (MA); marriage and family therapy (MA); school counseling (MA). *Accreditation:* AAMFT/COAMFTE; ACA; NCATE. Part-time programs available. *Faculty:* 14 full-time (9 women), 7 part-time/adjunct (all women). *Students:* 140 full-time (101 women), 25 part-time (20 women); includes 8 Black or African American, non-Hispanic/Latino; 1 Asian, non-Hispanic/Latino; 1 Hispanic/Latino; 1 Two or more races, non-Hispanic/Latino. 233 applicants, 53% accepted, 74 enrolled. In 2010, 53 master's awarded. *Degree requirements:* For master's, comprehensive exam (for some programs), thesis optional, internships. *Entrance* *requirements:* For master's, GRE General Test, 3 letters of recommendation. Additional exam requirements/recommendations for international students: Required—TOEFL (minimum score 570 paper-based; 230 computer-based; 79 iBT), IELTS (minimum score 6.5). *Application deadline:* For fall admission, 2/1 priority date for domestic students, 2/1 for international students; for spring admission, 2/1 for international students. Applications are processed on a rolling basis. Application fee: $55. Electronic applications accepted. *Expenses:* Tuition, state resident: full-time $3428; part-time $428 per unit. Tuition, nonresident: full-time $14,518; part-time $1814 per unit. Required fees: $2320; $344 per unit. Tuition and fees vary according to campus/location. *Financial support:* In 2010–11, 20 research assistantships (averaging $8,000 per year), 7 teaching assistantships (averaging $8,000 per year) were awarded; fellowships, career-related internships or fieldwork, Federal Work-Study, scholarships/grants, and unspecified assistantships also available. Financial award application deadline: 4/1; financial award applicants required to submit FAFSA. *Faculty research:* Multicultural counseling, addictions counseling, play therapy, expressive arts, child and adolescent therapy, sexual abuse counseling. *Unit head:* Dr. Lee Baruth, Chairman, 828-262-2055, E-mail: baruthlg@appstate.edu. *Application contact:* Sandy Krause, Director of Admissions and Recruiting, 828-262-2130, Fax: 828-262-2709, E-mail: krausesl@appstate.edu.

Arcadia University, Graduate Studies, Department of Psychology, Glenside, PA 19038-3295. Offers community counseling (MACP); school counseling (MACP). Part-time programs available. *Faculty:* 4 full-time (2 women), 6 part-time/adjunct (4 women). *Students:* 32 full-time (30 women), 37 part-time (32 women); includes 11 minority (6 Black or African American, non-Hispanic/Latino; 1 Asian, non-Hispanic/Latino; 3 Hispanic/Latino; 1 Two or more races, non-Hispanic/Latino). Average age 27. In 2010, 11 master's awarded. *Degree requirements:* For master's, practicum. *Entrance requirements:* For master's, GRE General Test or MAT. *Application deadline:* Applications are processed on a rolling basis. Application fee: $50. *Expenses:* Contact institution. *Financial support:* Research assistantships, career-related internships or fieldwork and unspecified assistantships available. Support available to part-time students. Financial award application deadline: 8/15. *Unit head:* Dr. Eleonora Bartoli, Director, 215-572-4693. *Application contact:* 215-572-2925, Fax: 215-572-2126, E-mail: grad@arcadia.edu.

Argosy University, Dallas, College of Education, Farmers Branch, TX 75244. Offers educational administration (MA Ed); educational leadership (Ed D); higher and postsecondary education (MA Ed); instructional leadership (MA Ed); school psychology (MA).

See Close-Up on page 1125.

Argosy University, Hawai'i, College of Education, Program in School Psychology, Honolulu, HI 96813. Offers MA.

See Close-Up on page 1129.

Argosy University, Phoenix, College of Education, Program in School Psychology, Phoenix, AZ 85021. Offers MA, Psy D.

See Close-Up on page 1139.

Argosy University, Sarasota, College of Education, Sarasota, FL 34235. Offers community college executive leadership (Ed D); educational leadership (MA Ed, Ed D, Ed S), including higher education administration (Ed D), K-12 education (Ed D); school counseling (MA, Ed S); school psychology (MA); teaching and learning (MA Ed, Ed D, Ed S), including education technology (Ed D), higher education (Ed D), K-12 education (Ed D).

Arkansas State University, Graduate School, College of Education, Department of Psychology and Counseling, Jonesboro, State University, AR 72467. Offers college student personnel services (MS); mental health counseling (Certificate); psychology and counseling (Ed S); rehabilitation counseling (MRC); school counseling (MSE); student affairs (Certificate). *Accreditation:* ACA (one or more programs are accredited); CORE (one or more programs are accredited); NCATE. Part-time programs available. *Faculty:* 11 full-time (6 women), 6 part-time/adjunct (2 women). *Students:* 40 full-time (27 women), 87 part-time (69 women); includes 38 minority (37 Black or African American, non-Hispanic/Latino; 1 Two or more races, non-Hispanic/Latino), 1 international. Average age 34. 55 applicants, 56% accepted, 28 enrolled. In 2010, 24 master's, 19 other advanced degrees awarded. *Degree requirements:* For master's and other advanced degree, comprehensive exam, thesis or alternative. *Entrance requirements:* For master's, GRE General Test or MAT (MSE), appropriate bachelor's degree, interview, letters of reference, official transcripts, immunization records, written statement, 2-3 page autobiography; for other advanced degree, GRE General Test, interview, master's degree, letters of reference, official transcript, personal statement, immunization records. Additional exam requirements/recommendations for international students: Required—TOEFL (minimum score 550 paper-based; 213 computer-based; 79 iBT), IELTS (minimum score 6), PTE: Pearson Test of English Academic (56). *Application deadline:* Applications are processed on a rolling basis. Application fee: $30 ($40 for international students). Electronic applications accepted. *Expenses:* Tuition, state resident: full-time $3888; part-time $216 per credit hour. Tuition, nonresident: full-time $9918; part-time $551 per credit hour. International tuition: $8376 full-time. Required fees: $932; $49 per credit hour. $25 per term. One-time fee: $30. Tuition and fees vary according to course load and program. *Financial support:* In 2010–11, 25 students received support; teaching assistantships, career-related internships or fieldwork, scholarships/grants, and unspecified assistantships available. Financial award application deadline: 7/1; financial award applicants required to submit FAFSA. *Unit head:* Dr. Loretta McGregor, Chair, 870-972-3064, Fax: 870-972-3962, E-mail: lmcgregor@astate.edu. *Application contact:* Dr. Andrew Sustich, Dean of the Graduate School, 870-972-3029, Fax: 870-972-3857, E-mail: sustich@astate.edu.

Assumption College, Graduate School, School Counseling Program, Worcester, MA 01609-1296. Offers MA, CAGS. Part-time and evening/weekend programs available. *Faculty:* 4 full-time (1 woman), 7 part-time/adjunct (3 women). *Students:* 57 full-time (45 women), 23 part-time (19 women); includes 4 minority (1 Black or African American, non-Hispanic/Latino; 3 Hispanic/Latino). Average age 24. 65 applicants, 82% accepted. In 2010, 27 master's, 2 other advanced degrees awarded. *Degree requirements:* For master's, comprehensive exam, internship; for CAGS, comprehensive exam. *Entrance requirements:* For master's, 3 letters of recommendation, resume, interview, essay; for CAGS, 3 letters of recommendation, resume, essay, interview. Additional exam requirements/recommendations for international students: Required—TOEFL (minimum score 540 paper-based; 200 computer-based; 76 iBT), IELTS (minimum score 6). *Application deadline:* For fall admission, 6/1 priority date for domestic students, 5/1 priority date for international students; for spring admission, 11/1 priority date for domestic students, 9/1 priority date for international students. Applications are processed on a rolling basis. Application fee: $30. Electronic applications accepted. *Expenses:* Tuition: Part-time $503 per credit. Required fees: $20 per semester. One-time fee: $100. Part-time tuition and fees vary according to campus/location. *Financial support:* Tuition waivers (partial) available. Financial award application deadline: 6/1; financial award applicants required to submit FAFSA. *Unit head:* Dr. Mary Ann Mariani, Director, 508-767-7087, Fax: 508-767-7263, E-mail: mmariani@assumption.edu. *Application contact:* Daniel Provost, Assistant Director of Graduate Student Services, 508-767-7426, Fax: 508-767-7030, E-mail: dprovost@assumption.edu.

Azusa Pacific University, School of Education, Department of School Counseling and School Psychology, Program in Educational Psychology, Azusa, CA 91702-7000. Offers MA. *Students:* 35 full-time (28 women), 35 part-time (26 women); includes 34 minority (8 Black or African American, non-Hispanic/Latino; 1 Asian, non-Hispanic/Latino; 25 Hispanic/Latino), 1 international. Average age 31. In 2010, 31 master's awarded. *Unit head:* Dr. Pedro Olvera, Director, 626-815-6000 Ext. 5351, E-mail: rfall@apu.edu. *Application contact:* Dr. Lewis Bonney, Chair, 626-815-5351, E-mail: lbonney@apu.edu.

Ball State University, Graduate School, Teachers College, Department of Educational Psychology, Program in School Psychology, Muncie, IN 47306-1099. Offers MA, PhD, Ed S. *Accreditation:* APA (one or more programs are accredited); NCATE. *Students:* 25 full-time (22 women), 54 part-time (42 women); includes 1 Black or African American, non-Hispanic/Latino; 1 Hispanic/Latino, 4 international. Average age 26. 122 applicants, 14% accepted, 14 enrolled. In 2010, 8 master's, 3 doctorates, 8 other advanced degrees awarded. *Degree requirements:* For doctorate, thesis/dissertation; for Ed S, thesis. *Entrance requirements:* For master's and Ed S, GRE General Test; for doctorate, GRE General Test, interview, minimum graduate GPA of 3.2. Application fee: $50. *Expenses:* Tuition, state resident: full-time $6160; part-time $299 per credit hour. Tuition, nonresident: full-time $16,020; part-time $783 per credit hour. Required fees: $2278; $95 per credit hour. *Financial support:* In 2010–11, 26 teaching assistantships with tuition reimbursements (averaging $10,004 per year) were awarded. Financial award application deadline: 3/1. *Unit head:* Lisa Huffman, Head, 785-285-8500, Fax: 785-285-3653. *Application contact:* Dr. David McIntosh, Associate Provost for Research and Dean of the Graduate School.

Barry University, School of Arts and Sciences, Department of Psychology, Miami Shores, FL 33161-6695. Offers clinical psychology (MS); school psychology (MS, SSP). Part-time and evening/weekend programs available. *Degree requirements:* For master's, thesis, practicum. *Entrance requirements:* For master's, GRE General Test, minimum GPA of 3.0, course work in psychology. Electronic applications accepted. *Faculty research:* Closed head injury, memory and aging, infant/mother interaction, evolutionary aspects of behavior, gender roles.

See Display on page 916 and Close-Up on page 1159.

Boston University, School of Education, Boston, MA 02215. Offers counseling (Ed M, CAGS), including community, school, sport psychology; counseling psychology (Ed D); curriculum and teaching (Ed M, Ed D, CAGS), including early childhood (Ed D), educational media and technology (Ed D), English and language arts (Ed D), mathematics (Ed D), physical education and coaching (Ed D), science (Ed D), social studies education (Ed D), special education (Ed D); developmental studies (Ed D), including literacy and language, reading education; developmental studies in literacy and language education (Ed M, CAGS); early childhood education (Ed M, CAGS); education of the deaf (Ed M, CAGS); educational leadership and development (Ed D), including educational administration (Ed M, Ed D, CAGS), higher education administration (Ed M, Ed D, CAGS); educational media and technology (Ed M, CAGS); elementary education (Ed M); English and language arts (Ed M, CAGS); English education (MAT); health education (Ed M, CAGS); Latin and classical studies (MAT); mathematics education (Ed M, MAT, CAGS); mathematics for teaching (MMT); modern foreign language education (MAT), including French, Spanish; physical education and coaching (Ed M, CAGS); policy, planning, and administration (Ed M, CAGS), including community education leadership, educational administration (Ed M, Ed D, CAGS), higher education administration (Ed M, Ed D, CAGS); reading education (Ed M, CAGS); science education (Ed M, MAT, CAGS), including biology (MAT), chemistry (MAT), earth science (MAT), general science (MAT), physics (MAT); social studies education (Ed M, MAT, CAGS), including history (MAT), political science (MAT); special education (Ed M, Ed D, CAGS), including disability studies (Ed M), moderate disabilities (Ed M), severe disabilities (Ed M), special education administration (Ed M); teaching English as a second language (Ed M, CAGS). Part-time programs available. *Faculty:* 57 full-time, 39 part-time/adjunct. *Students:* 245 full-time (191 women), 376 part-time (274 women); includes 83 minority (14 Black or African American, non-Hispanic/Latino; 2 American Indian or Alaska Native, non-Hispanic/Latino; 28 Asian, non-Hispanic/Latino; 31 Hispanic/Latino; 2 Native Hawaiian or other Pacific Islander, non-Hispanic/Latino; 6 Two or more races, non-Hispanic/Latino), 79 international. Average age 30. 1,270 applicants, 66% accepted, 292 enrolled. In 2010, 273 master's, 15 doctorates, 7 other advanced degrees awarded. Terminal master's awarded for partial completion of doctoral program. *Degree requirements:* For master's, thesis (for some programs); for doctorate, comprehensive exam, thesis/dissertation; for CAGS, comprehensive exam. *Entrance requirements:* For master's and CAGS, GRE General Test or Miller Analogies Test (MAT); for doctorate, GRE General Test. Additional exam requirements/recommendations for international students: Required—TOEFL, IELTS. *Application deadline:* For fall admission, 1/15 priority date for domestic and international students; for spring admission, 9/15 priority date for domestic and international students. Applications are processed on a rolling basis. Application fee: $70. Electronic applications accepted. *Expenses:* Tuition: Full-time $39,314; part-time $1228 per credit. Required fees: $40 per semester. *Financial support:* In 2010–11, 276 students received support, including 31 fellowships with full tuition reimbursements available, 16 research assistantships, 26 teaching assistantships with partial tuition reimbursements available; career-related internships or fieldwork, Federal Work-Study, and scholarships/grants also available. Support available to part-time students. Financial award applicants required to submit FAFSA. *Faculty research:* Deaf studies, social emotional learning, civic engagement and education, STEM education, pre-college educational pipelines. Total annual research expenditures: $2.6 million. *Unit head:* Dr. Hardin Coleman, Dean, 617-353-3213. *Application contact:* Dana Fernandez, Director of Enrollment, 617-353-4237, Fax: 617-353-8937, E-mail: sedgrad@bu.edu.

Bowling Green State University, Graduate College, College of Education and Human Development, School of Education and Intervention Services, Intervention Services Division, Program in School Psychology, Bowling Green, OH 43403. Offers M Ed, Sp Ed. *Accreditation:* NCATE. Part-time programs available. *Degree requirements:* For master's, thesis or alternative, internship. *Entrance requirements:* For master's, GRE General Test. Additional exam requirements/recommendations for international students: Required—TOEFL. Electronic applications accepted. *Faculty research:* Family therapists/multicultural issues, pre-school readiness skills, family relations, multifaceted evaluation, multidisciplinary decision-making.

Brigham Young University, Graduate Studies, David O. McKay School of Education, Department of Counseling Psychology and Special Education, Provo, UT 84602-1001. Offers counseling psychology (PhD); school psychology (Ed S); special education (MS). Part-time programs available. *Faculty:* 12 full-time (7 women), 7 part-time/adjunct (2 women). *Students:* 61 full-time (41 women), 19 part-time (17 women); includes 1 Black or African American, non-Hispanic/Latino; 2 American Indian or Alaska Native, non-Hispanic/Latino; 3 Asian, non-Hispanic/Latino; 1 Hispanic/Latino; 2 Native Hawaiian or other Pacific Islander, non-Hispanic/Latino, 6 international. Average age 30. 91 applicants, 19% accepted, 17 enrolled. In 2010, 14 master's, 6 doctorates, 10 other advanced degrees awarded. *Degree requirements:* For master's, comprehensive exam, thesis; for doctorate, comprehensive exam, thesis/dissertation. *Entrance requirements:* For master's and doctorate, GRE General Test, minimum GPA of 3.0 in last 60 hours of undergraduate coursework. Additional exam requirements/recommendations for international students: Required—TOEFL (minimum score 580 paper-based; 237 computer-based), IELTS (minimum score 7). *Application deadline:* For fall admission, 1/15 for domestic and international students. Application fee: $50. Electronic applications accepted. *Expenses:* Tuition: Full-time $5580; part-time $310 per credit hour. Tuition and fees vary according to program and student's religious affiliation. *Financial support:* In 2010–11, 53 students received support, including 42 research assistantships with partial tuition reimbursements available (averaging $6,715 per year), 4 teaching assistantships with partial tuition reimbursements available (averaging $6,778 per year); institutionally sponsored loans and tuition waivers (partial) also available. Financial award application deadline: 3/15. *Faculty research:* Group psychotherapy, career development of Native Americans, multicultural psychology, gender issues in education, crisis management in schools. *Unit head:* Dr. Timothy B. Smith, Professor and Development Chair, 801-422-3857, Fax: 801-422-0198. *Application contact:* Diane E. Hancock, Department Secretary, 801-422-3859, Fax: 801-422-0198, E-mail: diane_hancock@byu.edu.

Brooklyn College of the City University of New York, Division of Graduate Studies, School of Education, Program in School Psychologist, Brooklyn, NY 11210-2889. Offers school psychologist (MS Ed, CAS); school psychologist-bilingual (CAS). Part-time and evening/weekend programs available. *Students:* 45 full-time (39 women), 43 part-time (40 women); includes 34 minority (15 Black or African American, non-Hispanic/Latino; 3 Asian, non-Hispanic/Latino; 16 Hispanic/Latino). Average age 27. 177 applicants, 38% accepted, 38 enrolled. In 2010, 18 master's, 28 CASs awarded. *Degree requirements:* For master's, internship. *Entrance requirements:* For master's, interview, previous course work in education and psychology, teaching certificate, resume, 2 letters of recommendation; for CAS, master's degree, teaching

School Psychology

Brooklyn College of the City University of New York (continued)
experience. Additional exam requirements/recommendations for international students: Required—TOEFL (minimum score 500 paper-based; 173 computer-based; 61 iBT). *Application deadline:* For fall admission, 3/1 priority date for domestic students, 2/1 priority date for international students. Applications are processed on a rolling basis. Application fee: $125. Electronic applications accepted. *Expenses:* Tuition, state resident: full-time $7360; part-time $310 per credit hour. Tuition, nonresident: full-time $13,800; part-time $575 per credit hour. Required fees: $190 per semester. *Financial support:* Career-related internships or fieldwork, Federal Work-Study, institutionally sponsored loans, and scholarships/grants available. Support available to part-time students. Financial award application deadline: 5/1; financial award applicants required to submit FAFSA. *Unit head:* Prof. Florence Rubinson, Program Head, 718-951-5876, E-mail: rubinson@brooklyn.cuny.edu. *Application contact:* Hernan Sierra, Graduate Admissions Coordinator, 718-951-4536, Fax: 718-951-4506, E-mail: grads@brooklyn.cuny.edu.

Bucknell University, Graduate Studies, College of Arts and Sciences, Department of Education, Specialization in School Psychology, Lewisburg, PA 17837. Offers MS Ed. *Degree requirements:* For master's, thesis or alternative. *Entrance requirements:* For master's, GRE General Test, minimum GPA of 2.8. Additional exam requirements/recommendations for international students: Required—TOEFL. *Expenses:* Tuition: Full-time $36,992; part-time $4624 per course.

California Baptist University, Program in Education, Riverside, CA 92504-3206. Offers educational leadership for faith-based instruction (MS); educational leadership for public institutions (MS); educational technology (MS); instructional computer applications (MS); international education (MS); reading (MS); school counseling (MS); school psychology (MS); special education (MS); special education in mild/moderate disabilities (MS); special education in moderate/severe disabilities (MS); teaching (MS); teaching and learning (MS Ed). Part-time programs available. *Faculty:* 15 full-time (10 women), 8 part-time/adjunct (6 women). *Students:* 69 full-time (55 women), 346 part-time (279 women); includes 148 minority (32 Black or African American, non-Hispanic/Latino; 4 American Indian or Alaska Native, non-Hispanic/Latino; 11 Asian, non-Hispanic/Latino; 97 Hispanic/Latino; 3 Native Hawaiian or other Pacific Islander, non-Hispanic/Latino; 1 Two or more races, non-Hispanic/Latino). 134 applicants, 100% accepted, 118 enrolled. In 2010, 53 master's awarded. *Degree requirements:* For master's, comprehensive exam (for some programs), thesis optional. *Entrance requirements:* For master's, minimum undergraduate GPA of 2.75, 12 semester hours of pre-requisite course work in education. Additional exam requirements/recommendations for international students: Required—TOEFL (minimum score 575 paper-based; 230 computer-based; 89 iBT). *Application deadline:* For fall admission, 8/1 priority date for domestic students, 7/1 for international students; for spring admission, 12/1 priority date for domestic students, 10/15 priority date for international students. Applications are processed on a rolling basis. Application fee: $45. Electronic applications accepted. *Expenses:* Tuition: Full-time $8532; part-time $474 per unit. Required fees: $355 per semester. One-time fee: $45 full-time. Tuition and fees vary according to course load and program. *Financial support:* Career-related internships or fieldwork, Federal Work-Study, and scholarships/grants available. Support available to part-time students. Financial award applicants required to submit FAFSA. *Unit head:* Dr. Mary Crist, Dean, School of Education, 951-343-4313, Fax: 951-343-4516, E-mail: mcrist@calbaptist.edu. *Application contact:* Gail Ronveaux, Dean of Graduate Enrollment, 951-343-5045, Fax: 951-343-5095, E-mail: graduateadmissions@calbaptist.edu.

California State University, Los Angeles, Graduate Studies, Charter College of Education, Division of Special Education and Counseling, Los Angeles, CA 90032-8530. Offers counseling (MS), including applied behavior analysis, community college counseling, rehabilitation counseling, school counseling and school psychology; special education (MA, PhD). *Accreditation:* ACA. Part-time and evening/weekend programs available. *Faculty:* 18 full-time (12 women), 14 part-time/adjunct (12 women). *Students:* 362 full-time (295 women), 334 part-time (268 women); includes 417 minority (36 Black or African American, non-Hispanic/Latino; 65 Asian, non-Hispanic/Latino; 309 Hispanic/Latino; 7 Two or more races, non-Hispanic/Latino), 31 international. Average age 34. 152 applicants, 99% accepted, 136 enrolled. In 2010, 177 master's awarded. *Entrance requirements:* For master's, minimum GPA of 2.75 in last 90 units of course work, teaching certificate. Additional exam requirements/recommendations for international students: Required—TOEFL (minimum score 500 paper-based; 173 computer-based). *Application deadline:* For fall admission, 5/1 for domestic and international students. Applications are processed on a rolling basis. Application fee: $55. Electronic applications accepted. *Financial support:* Career-related internships or fieldwork and Federal Work-Study available. Support available to part-time students. Financial award application deadline: 3/1. *Unit head:* Dr. Diane Fazzi, Chair, 323-343-4400, Fax: 323-343-5605, E-mail: dfazzi@calstatela.edu. *Application contact:* Dr. Alan Muchlinski, Dean of Graduate Studies, 323-343-3820, Fax: 323-343-5653, E-mail: amuchli@exchange.calstatela.edu.

California State University, Northridge, Graduate Studies, College of Education, Department of Educational Psychology and Counseling, Northridge, CA 91330. Offers counseling (MS), including career counseling, college counseling and student services, marriage and family therapy, school counseling, school psychology; educational psychology (MA Ed), including development, learning, and instruction, early childhood education. *Accreditation:* ACA (one or more programs are accredited); NCATE. Part-time and evening/weekend programs available. *Entrance requirements:* For master's, GRE General Test or minimum GPA of 3.0. Additional exam requirements/recommendations for international students: Required—TOEFL.

California State University, Sacramento, Graduate Studies, College of Education, Department of Special Education, Rehabilitation, and School Psychology, Sacramento, CA 95819. Offers school psychology (MS); special education (MA); vocational rehabilitation (MS). *Accreditation:* CORE. Part-time programs available. *Degree requirements:* For master's, thesis or alternative, writing proficiency exam. *Entrance requirements:* For master's, minimum GPA of 2.5. Additional exam requirements/recommendations for international students: Required—TOEFL. Electronic applications accepted.

California University of Pennsylvania, School of Graduate Studies and Research, College of Education and Human Services, Program in School Psychology, California, PA 15419-1394. Offers MS. *Accreditation:* NCATE. Part-time and evening/weekend programs available. *Degree requirements:* For master's, comprehensive exam, thesis optional, internship. *Entrance requirements:* For master's, MAT or GRE, minimum GPA of 3.0, work experience in psychology, letters of reference. Additional exam requirements/recommendations for international students: Required—TOEFL (minimum score 550 paper-based; 213 computer-based; 80 iBT). Electronic applications accepted.

Cambridge College, School of Education, Cambridge, MA 02138-5304. Offers autism specialist (M Ed); autism/behavior analyst (M Ed); behavior analyst (Post-Master's Certificate); behavioral management (M Ed); early childhood teacher (M Ed); education specialist in curriculum and instruction (CAGS); educational leadership (Ed D); elementary teacher (M Ed); English as a second language (M Ed, Certificate); general science (M Ed); health education (Post-Master's Certificate); health/family and consumer sciences (M Ed); history (M Ed); individualized (M Ed); information technology literacy (M Ed); instructional technology (M Ed); interdisciplinary studies (M Ed); library teacher (M Ed); literacy education (M Ed); mathematics (M Ed); mathematics specialist (Certificate); middle school mathematics and science (M Ed); school administration (M Ed, CAGS); school guidance counselor (M Ed); school nurse education (M Ed); school social worker/school adjustment counselor (M Ed); special education administrator (CAGS); special education/moderate disabilities (M Ed); teaching skills and methodologies (M Ed). Part-time and evening/weekend programs available. Postbaccalaureate distance learning degree programs offered (minimal on-campus study). *Faculty:* 8 full-time (2 women), 245 part-time/adjunct (166 women). *Students:* 846 full-time (664 women), 930 part-time (714 women); includes 972 minority (802 Black or African American, non-Hispanic/Latino; 3 American Indian or Alaska Native, non-Hispanic/Latino; 18 Asian, non-Hispanic/Latino; 148 Hispanic/Latino; 1 Two or more races, non-Hispanic/Latino), 23 international. Average age 38. In 2010, 724 master's, 162 other advanced degrees awarded. *Degree requirements:* For master's, thesis, internship/practicum (licensure program only); for doctorate, thesis/dissertation; for other advanced degree, thesis. *Entrance requirements:* For master's, interview, resume, documentation of licensure, 2 professional references; for doctorate, official transcripts, interview, resume, documentation of licensure (if any), written personal statement/essay, portfolio of scholarly and professional work, qualifying assessment, 2 professional references, health insurance, immunizations form; for other advanced degree, official transcripts, interview, resume, documentation of licensure (if any), written personal statement/essay, 2 professional references, health insurance, immunizations form. Additional exam requirements/recommendations for international students: Required—TOEFL (minimum score 550 paper-based; 213 computer-based; 79 iBT); Recommended—IELTS (minimum score 6). *Application deadline:* Applications are processed on a rolling basis. Application fee: $30. Electronic applications accepted. *Expenses:* Contact institution. *Financial support:* Career-related internships or fieldwork, Federal Work-Study, and scholarships/grants available. Financial award applicants required to submit FAFSA. *Faculty research:* Adult education, accelerated learning, mathematics education, brain compatible learning, special education and law. *Unit head:* Dr. N. Alan Sheppard, Interim Associate Dean, 617-873-0619, E-mail: alan.sheppard@cambridgecollege.edu. *Application contact:* Elaine M. Lapomardo, Dean of Enrollment Management, 617-873-0274, Fax: 617-349-3561, E-mail: elaine.lapomardo@cambridgecollege.edu.

Cambridge College, School of Psychology and Counseling, Cambridge, MA 02138-5304. Offers addiction counseling (M Ed); alcohol and drug counseling (Certificate); counseling psychology (M Ed, CAGS); counseling psychology: forensic counseling (M Ed); marriage and family therapy (M Ed); mental health and addiction counseling (M Ed); mental health counseling (M Ed); mental health counseling for school guidance counselors (Post Master's Certificate); psychological studies (M Ed); school adjustment and mental health counseling (M Ed); school adjustment, mental health and addiction counseling (M Ed); school guidance counselor (M Ed); trauma studies (Certificate). Part-time and evening/weekend programs available. *Faculty:* 4 full-time (2 women), 83 part-time/adjunct (48 women). *Students:* 436 full-time (351 women), 351 part-time (274 women); includes 321 Black or African American, non-Hispanic/Latino; 3 American Indian or Alaska Native, non-Hispanic/Latino; 4 Asian, non-Hispanic/Latino; 87 Hispanic/Latino; 4 Two or more races, non-Hispanic/Latino, 6 international. Average age 37. In 2010, 284 master's, 16 other advanced degrees awarded. *Degree requirements:* For master's and other advanced degree, thesis, practicum/internship. *Entrance requirements:* For master's, resume, 2 professional references; for other advanced degree, official transcripts, documents for transfer credit evaluation, resume, written personal statement/essay, 2 professional references, health insurance, immunizations form. Additional exam requirements/recommendations for international students: Required—TOEFL (minimum score 550 paper-based; 213 computer-based; 79 iBT); Recommended—IELTS (minimum score 6). *Application deadline:* Applications are processed on a rolling basis. Application fee: $30. Electronic applications accepted. *Expenses:* Contact institution. *Financial support:* Career-related internships or fieldwork, Federal Work-Study, and scholarships/grants available. Financial award applicants required to submit FAFSA. *Faculty research:* Trauma, drug and alcohol counseling, cross-cultural issues, school counseling, trauma in schools. *Unit head:* Dr. Niti Seth, Dean, 617-873-0208, Fax: 617-349-3561, E-mail: nseth@cambridgecollege.edu. *Application contact:* Elaine M. Lapomardo, Dean of Enrollment Management, 617-873-0274, Fax: 617-349-3561, E-mail: elaine.lapomardo@cambridgecollege.edu.

Canisius College, Graduate Division, School of Education and Human Services, Programs in Counseling and Human Services, Buffalo, NY 14208-1098. Offers community mental health counseling (MS); school agency counseling (MS). *Accreditation:* ACA. Part-time and evening/weekend programs available. *Faculty:* 5 full-time (3 women), 18 part-time/adjunct (13 women). *Students:* 144 full-time (113 women), 50 part-time (42 women); includes 35 minority (28 Black or African American, non-Hispanic/Latino; 4 Asian, non-Hispanic/Latino; 2 Hispanic/Latino; 1 Two or more races, non-Hispanic/Latino), 3 international. Average age 27. 128 applicants, 84% accepted, 51 enrolled. In 2010, 40 master's awarded. *Degree requirements:* For master's, thesis, research project. *Entrance requirements:* For master's, GRE if cumulative GPA less than 2.7, transcripts, two letters of recommendation, interview. Additional exam requirements/recommendations for international students: Required—TOEFL. *Application deadline:* Applications are processed on a rolling basis. Application fee: $25. Electronic applications accepted. *Expenses:* Tuition: Part-time $694 per credit hour. Required fees: $11 per credit hour. $90 per semester. *Financial support:* Research assistantships, career-related internships or fieldwork, Federal Work-Study, scholarships/grants, tuition waivers (partial), and unspecified assistantships available. Support available to part-time students. Financial award application deadline: 7/1; financial award applicants required to submit FAFSA. *Faculty research:* Impact of trauma on adults, long term psych-social impact on police officers. *Unit head:* Dr. Christine Moll, Chair, 716-888-3287, E-mail: moll@canisius.edu. *Application contact:* Jim Bagwell, Director of Graduate Recruitment and Admissions, 716-888-2544, E-mail: bagwellj@canisius.edu.

Capella University, Harold Abel School of Psychology, Minneapolis, MN 55402. Offers child and adolescent development (MS); clinical psychology (MS, Psy D); counseling psychology (MS); educational psychology (MS, PhD); evaluation, research, and measurement (MS); general psychology (MS, PhD); industrial/organizational psychology (MS, PhD); leadership coaching psychology (MS); organizational leader development (MS); school psychology (MS); sport psychology (MS). Part-time and evening/weekend programs available. Postbaccalaureate distance learning degree programs offered (minimal on-campus study). Terminal master's awarded for partial completion of doctoral program. *Degree requirements:* For master's, thesis optional, project; for doctorate, thesis/dissertation. *Entrance requirements:* For degree, master's degree in school psychology. Additional exam requirements/recommendations for international students: Required—TOEFL (minimum score 550 paper-based; 213 computer-based), TWE (minimum score 4); Recommended—IELTS. Electronic applications accepted. *Expenses:* Tuition: Full-time $11,880; part-time $440 per credit hour.

Carlos Albizu University, Miami Campus, Graduate Programs, Miami, FL 33172-2209. Offers clinical psychology (Psy D); entrepreneurship (MBA); exceptional student education (MS); industrial/organizational psychology (MS); marriage and family therapy (MS); mental health counseling (MS); nonprofit management (MBA); organizational management (MBA); psychology (MS); school counseling (MS); teaching English as a second language (MS). *Accreditation:* APA. Part-time and evening/weekend programs available. *Faculty:* 21 full-time (12 women), 37 part-time/adjunct (18 women). *Students:* 496 full-time (400 women), 242 part-time (192 women); includes 590 minority (58 Black or African American, non-Hispanic/Latino; 2 American Indian or Alaska Native, non-Hispanic/Latino; 5 Asian, non-Hispanic/Latino; 523 Hispanic/Latino; 2 Two or more races, non-Hispanic/Latino), 15 international. Average age 36. 141 applicants, 84% accepted, 118 enrolled. In 2010, 159 master's, 20 doctorates awarded. Terminal master's awarded for partial completion of doctoral program. *Degree requirements:* For master's, one foreign language, comprehensive exam, integrative project (MBA), research project (exceptional student education, teaching English as a second language); for doctorate, one foreign language, comprehensive exam, internship, project. *Entrance requirements:* For master's, 3 letters of recommendation, interview, minimum GPA of 3.0, resume, statement of purpose, official transcripts; for doctorate, 3 letters of recommendation, minimum GPA of 3.0, resume, interview. *Application deadline:* For fall admission, 8/1 priority date for domestic students; for spring admission, 11/30 priority date for domestic students. Applications are processed on a rolling basis. Application fee: $50. Electronic applications accepted. *Expenses:* Tuition: Full-time $9360; part-time $520 per credit. Required fees: $298 per term. Tuition and fees vary according to course load, degree level and program. *Financial support:* In 2010–11, 106 students received support. Federal Work-Study, scholarships/grants, and tuition discounts available. Financial award application deadline: 6/1; financial award applicants required to submit FAFSA. *Faculty research:* Psychotherapy, forensic psychology, neuropsychology, marketing strategy, entrepreneurship, special education. *Unit head:* Dr. Carmen S. Roca, Chancellor, 305-593-1223 Ext. 120, Fax: 305-629-8052, E-mail: croca@albizu.edu. *Application contact:* Vanessa Almendarez, Secretary, 305-593-1223 Ext. 137, Fax: 305-593-1854, E-mail: valmendarez@albizu.edu.

Central Connecticut State University, School of Graduate Studies, School of Education and Professional Studies, Department of Counseling and Family Therapy, New Britain, CT 06050-4010. Offers marriage and family therapy (MS); professional counseling (MS, Certificate); school counseling (MS); student development in higher education (MS). *Accreditation:* AAMFT/COAMFTE; ACA. Part-time and evening/weekend programs available. *Faculty:* 8 full-time (4 women), 16 part-time/adjunct (12 women). *Students:* 143 full-time (118 women), 223 part-time (188 women); includes 77 minority (39 Black or African American, non-Hispanic/Latino; 2 American Indian or Alaska Native, non-Hispanic/Latino; 4 Asian, non-Hispanic/Latino; 31 Hispanic/Latino; 1 Two or more races, non-Hispanic/Latino), 4 international. Average age 34. 295 applicants, 48% accepted, 119 enrolled. In 2010, 71 master's awarded. *Degree requirements:* For master's, comprehensive exam, thesis or alternative; for Certificate, qualifying exam. *Entrance requirements:* For master's, minimum undergraduate GPA of 2.7. Additional exam requirements/recommendations for international students: Required—TOEFL. *Application deadline:* For fall admission, 5/1 for domestic students. Applications are processed on a rolling basis. Application fee: $50. Electronic applications accepted. *Expenses:* Tuition, area resident: Full-time $5012; part-time $470 per credit. Tuition, state resident: full-time $7518; part-time $482 per credit. Tuition, nonresident: full-time $13,962; part-time $482 per credit. Required fees: $3772. One-time fee: $62 part-time. *Financial support:* In 2010–11, 52 students received support, including 14 research assistantships; career-related internships or fieldwork, Federal Work-Study, scholarships/grants, and unspecified assistantships also available. Support available to part-time students. Financial award application deadline: 2/15; financial award applicants required to submit FAFSA. *Faculty research:* Elementary/secondary school counseling, marriage/family therapy, rehabilitation counseling, counseling in higher educational settings. *Unit head:* Dr. Connie Tait, Chair, 860-832-2154. *Application contact:* Dr. Connie Tait, Chair, 860-832-2154.

Central Michigan University, College of Graduate Studies, College of Humanities and Social and Behavioral Sciences, Department of Psychology, Program in School Psychology, Mount Pleasant, MI 48859. Offers PhD, S Psy S. *Accreditation:* APA. *Students:* 19 full-time (17 women), 26 part-time (24 women); includes 1 Hispanic/Latino, 1 international. Average age 28. In 2010, 5 other advanced degrees awarded. *Degree requirements:* For doctorate, thesis/dissertation; for S Psy S, thesis. *Entrance requirements:* For doctorate, GRE. *Application deadline:* For fall admission, 1/15 for domestic and international students. Application fee: $35 ($45 for international students). Electronic applications accepted. *Expenses:* Tuition, state resident: full-time $8208; part-time $456 per credit hour. Tuition, nonresident: full-time $13,788; part-time $766 per credit hour. One-time fee: $25. *Financial support:* Fellowships with tuition reimbursements, research assistantships with tuition reimbursements, teaching assistantships with tuition reimbursements, career-related internships or fieldwork, Federal Work-Study, unspecified assistantships, and out-of-state merit awards, non-resident graduate awards available. *Faculty research:* Psychology and education foundations, psychology and education assessment, intervention strategies. *Unit head:* Dr. Hajime Otani, Chairperson, 989-774-6494, Fax: 989-774-2553, E-mail: otani1h@cmich.edu. *Application contact:* Dr. Sandra Morgan, Graduate Coordinator, 989-774-6484, Fax: 989-774-2553, E-mail: morga1sk@cmich.edu.

Central Washington University, Graduate Studies and Research, College of the Sciences, Department of Psychology, Program in School Psychology, Ellensburg, WA 98926. Offers M Ed. *Degree requirements:* For master's, thesis, internship. *Entrance requirements:* For master's, GRE General Test, minimum GPA of 3.0. Additional exam requirements/recommendations for international students: Required—TOEFL (minimum score 550 paper-based; 213 computer-based; 79 iBT). Electronic applications accepted.

Chapman University, Graduate Studies, College of Educational Studies, Program in Education: Cultural and Curricular Studies, Orange, CA 92866. Offers cultural and curricular studies (PhD); disability studies (PhD); school psychology (PhD). Part-time and evening/weekend programs available. *Faculty:* 23 full-time (15 women), 31 part-time/adjunct (22 women). *Students:* 2 full-time (both women), 58 part-time (46 women); includes 26 minority (3 Black or African American, non-Hispanic/Latino; 2 American Indian or Alaska Native, non-Hispanic/Latino; 11 Asian, non-Hispanic/Latino; 9 Hispanic/Latino; 1 Two or more races, non-Hispanic/Latino), 1 international. Average age 37. 45 applicants, 58% accepted, 18 enrolled. In 2010, 4 doctorates awarded. *Degree requirements:* For doctorate, thesis/dissertation. *Entrance requirements:* For doctorate, GRE. Additional exam requirements/recommendations for international students: Required—TOEFL (minimum score 550 paper-based; 213 computer-based; 80 iBT). *Application deadline:* For fall admission, 2/28 priority date for domestic students. Application fee: $60. Electronic applications accepted. *Financial support:* Fellowships, Federal Work-Study and scholarships/grants available. *Unit head:* Dr. Joel Colbert, Director, 714-744-7076. *Application contact:* Becky Campbell, School Psychology/Counseling and PhD Admission Coordinator, 714-628-7263, E-mail: rcampbel@chapman.edu.

Chapman University, Graduate Studies, College of Educational Studies, Program in Education: School Psychology, Orange, CA 92866. Offers PhD. Part-time and evening/weekend programs available. *Faculty:* 24 full-time (15 women), 25 part-time/adjunct (16 women). *Students:* 1 (woman) full-time, 9 part-time (6 women); includes 3 Asian, non-Hispanic/Latino. Average age 39. 2 applicants, 100% accepted, 2 enrolled. *Degree requirements:* For doctorate, thesis/dissertation. *Entrance requirements:* Additional exam requirements/recommendations for international students: Required—TOEFL. Application fee: $55. *Financial support:* Fellowships, Federal Work-Study and scholarships/grants available. *Unit head:* Dr. Joel Colbert, Director, 714-744-7076. *Application contact:* Maureen Rika Judd, Graduate Admission Counselor, 714-997-6786, Fax: 714-997-6713, E-mail: rjudd@chapman.edu.

Chapman University, Graduate Studies, College of Educational Studies, Program in School Psychology, Orange, CA 92866. Offers MA, Credential, Ed S. Part-time and evening/weekend programs available. *Faculty:* 23 full-time (15 women), 31 part-time/adjunct (22 women). *Students:* 39 full-time (34 women), 16 part-time (14 women); includes 22 minority (1 Black or African American, non-Hispanic/Latino; 8 Asian, non-Hispanic/Latino; 12 Hispanic/Latino; 1 Native Hawaiian or other Pacific Islander, non-Hispanic/Latino). Average age 26. 79 applicants, 30% accepted, 17 enrolled. In 2010, 36 master's awarded. *Degree requirements:* For master's, comprehensive exam, 450 hours practicum; 1200 hours internship. *Entrance requirements:* For master's, GRE, CBEST, minimum undergraduate GPA of 2.75. Additional exam requirements/recommendations for international students: Required—TOEFL (minimum score 550 paper-based; 213 computer-based; 80 iBT). *Application deadline:* For fall admission, 2/1 priority date for domestic students. Application fee: $60. Electronic applications accepted. *Expenses:* Contact institution. *Financial support:* Fellowships, Federal Work-Study and scholarships/grants available. Financial award applicants required to submit FAFSA. *Unit head:* Dr. Michael Hass, Coordinator, 714-997-6781, E-mail: hass@chapman.edu. *Application contact:* Becky Campbell, School Psychology/Counseling and PhD Admission Coordinator, 714-628-7263, E-mail: rcampbel@chapman.edu.

The Chicago School of Professional Psychology, Program in School Psychology, Chicago, IL 60610. Offers Ed S. Part-time programs available. *Entrance requirements:* For degree, GRE (recommended), minimum GPA of 3.2 (recommended); completion of one course in statistics or research methods and one course in psychology. Additional exam requirements/recommendations for international students: Required—TOEFL (minimum score 550 paper-based; 213 computer-based; 79 iBT).

The Chicago School of Professional Psychology at Grayslake, Program in School Psychology, Grayslake, IL 60030. Offers Ed S.

The Citadel, The Military College of South Carolina, Citadel Graduate College, Department of Psychology, Program in School Psychology, Charleston, SC 29409. Offers Ed S. *Accreditation:* NCATE. Part-time and evening/weekend programs available. *Faculty:* 10 full-time (3 women), 2 part-time/adjunct (1 woman). *Students:* 39 full-time (37 women), 19 part-time (17 women); includes 3 Black or African American, non-Hispanic/Latino; 1 Asian, non-Hispanic/Latino; 1 Hispanic/Latino. Average age 27. In 2010, 2 Ed Ss awarded. *Degree requirements:* For Ed S, comprehensive exam, thesis, internship. *Entrance requirements:* For degree, GRE (minimum score 1000) or MAT with prior permission (minimum score 410), minimum undergraduate GPA of 3.0, 2 letters of reference. Additional exam requirements/recommendations for international students: Required—TOEFL (minimum score 550 paper-based; 213 computer-based). *Application deadline:* For fall admission, 3/15 for domestic students. Application fee: $30. Electronic applications accepted. *Expenses:* Tuition, state resident: part-time $460 per credit hour. Tuition, nonresident: part-time $756 per credit hour. Required fees: $40 per term. *Financial support:* Research assistantships, career-related internships or fieldwork, health care benefits, and unspecified assistantships available. Support available to part-time students. Financial award application deadline: 7/1; financial award applicants required to submit FAFSA. *Faculty research:* Childhood depression, violence against women, developmental disorders, eyewitness testimony. *Unit head:* Dr. Kerry S. Lassiter, Coordinator, 843-953-6740, Fax: 843-953-6769, E-mail: kerry.lassiter@citadel.edu. *Application contact:* Dr. Steve A. Nida, Associate Provost, The Citadel Graduate College, 843-953-5089, Fax: 843-953-7630, E-mail: cgc@citadel.edu.

City University of Seattle, Graduate Division, Albright School of Education, Bellevue, WA 98005. Offers administrator certification (Certificate); curriculum and instruction (M Ed); elementary education (MIT); guidance and counseling (M Ed); leadership (M Ed); leadership and school counseling (M Ed); reading and literacy (M Ed); special education (MIT); superintendent certification (Certificate). Part-time and evening/weekend programs available. Postbaccalaureate distance learning degree programs offered (no on-campus study). *Entrance requirements:* Additional exam requirements/recommendations for international students: Required—TOEFL (minimum score 540 paper-based; 207 computer-based); Recommended—IELTS. Electronic applications accepted. *Expenses:* Contact institution.

Cleveland State University, College of Graduate Studies, College of Sciences and Health Professions, Department of Psychology, Cleveland, OH 44115. Offers adult development and aging (PhD); clinical psychology (MA); consumer/industrial research (MA); diversity management (MA); experimental research psychology (MA); school psychology (Psy S). *Accreditation:* APA. *Faculty:* 20 full-time (7 women), 16 part-time/adjunct (8 women). *Students:* 63 full-time (45 women), 43 part-time (27 women); includes 15 Black or African American, non-Hispanic/Latino; 1 American Indian or Alaska Native, non-Hispanic/Latino; 3 Asian, non-Hispanic/Latino; 3 Hispanic/Latino, 1 international. Average age 30. 164 applicants, 44% accepted, 62 enrolled. In 2010, 39 master's, 8 other advanced degrees awarded. Terminal master's awarded for partial completion of doctoral program. *Degree requirements:* For master's, comprehensive exam (for some programs), thesis (for some programs); for doctorate, comprehensive exam, thesis/dissertation; for Psy S, internship. *Entrance requirements:* For master's and doctorate, GRE General Test. Additional exam requirements/recommendations for international students: Required—TOEFL (minimum score 525 paper-based; 197 computer-based). *Application deadline:* For fall admission, 2/1 priority date for domestic and international students. Application fee: $30. Electronic applications accepted. *Expenses:* Tuition, state resident: full-time $8447; part-time $469 per credit hour. Tuition, nonresident: full-time $16,020; part-time $890 per credit hour. Required fees: $50. *Financial support:* In 2010–11, 45 students received support. Career-related internships or fieldwork, Federal Work-Study, scholarships/grants, tuition waivers (partial), and unspecified assistantships available. Financial award applicants required to submit FAFSA. *Faculty research:* Cognitive and social psychology, consumer psychology, clinical psychology, school psychology, aging. Total annual research expenditures: $112,607. *Unit head:* Dr. Kathleen M. McNamara, Chairperson, 216-687-2545, Fax: 216-687-9294, E-mail: k.mcnamara@csuohio.edu. *Application contact:* Karen R. Colston, Administrative Coordinator, 216-687-2552, Fax: 216-687-9294, E-mail: k.colston@csuohio.edu.

The College of New Rochelle, Graduate School, Division of Human Services, Program in Community-School Psychology, New Rochelle, NY 10805-2308. Offers MS. *Degree requirements:* For master's, comprehensive exam, clinical fieldwork, journal. *Entrance requirements:* For master's, interview, minimum GPA of 3.0, course work in psychology, sample of written work.

College of St. Joseph, Graduate Programs, Division of Psychology and Human Services, Program in School Guidance Counseling, Rutland, VT 05701-3899. Offers MS. Part-time and evening/weekend programs available. *Faculty:* 4 full-time (1 woman), 8 part-time/adjunct (4 women). *Students:* 8 full-time (7 women), 7 part-time (all women). Average age 30. 7 applicants, 100% accepted, 7 enrolled. In 2010, 2 master's awarded. *Degree requirements:* For master's, comprehensive exam, thesis optional. *Entrance requirements:* For master's, PRAXIS I, 2 letters of reference, interview. *Application deadline:* Applications are processed on a rolling basis. Application fee: $35. Electronic applications accepted. *Expenses:* Tuition: Full-time $14,200; part-time $400 per credit hour. Required fees: $45 per semester. *Financial support:* Unspecified assistantships available. Financial award application deadline: 3/1. *Unit head:* Dr. Craig Knapp, Chair, 802-773-5900 Ext. 3219, Fax: 802-776-5258, E-mail: cknapp@csj.edu. *Application contact:* Alan Young, Dean of Admissions, 802-773-5900 Ext. 3227, Fax: 802-776-5310, E-mail: alanyoung@csj.edu.

The College of Saint Rose, Graduate Studies, School of Education, Educational and School Psychology Department, Albany, NY 12203-1419. Offers applied technology education (MS Ed); educational psychology (MS Ed); school psychology (MS, Certificate). Part-time and evening/weekend programs available. *Entrance requirements:* For master's, minimum undergraduate GPA of 3.0. Additional exam requirements/recommendations for international students: Required—TOEFL (minimum score 550 paper-based; 213 computer-based). Electronic applications accepted.

The College of William and Mary, School of Education, Program in School Psychology, Williamsburg, VA 23187-8795. Offers M Ed, Ed S. *Accreditation:* NCATE. *Faculty:* 4 full-time (2 women), 2 part-time/adjunct (both women). *Students:* 22 full-time (20 women), 12 part-time (11 women); includes 1 Black or African American, non-Hispanic/Latino. Average age 27. 87 applicants, 41% accepted, 22 enrolled. In 2010, 12 master's, 9 other advanced degrees awarded. *Degree requirements:* For Ed S, internship. *Entrance requirements:* For master's, GRE, minimum GPA of 3.0; for Ed S, GRE, minimum GPA of 3.5. Additional exam requirements/recommendations for international students: Required—TOEFL. *Application deadline:* For fall admission, 1/15 for domestic and international students. Application fee: $50. Electronic applications accepted. *Expenses:* Tuition, state resident: full-time $6400; part-time $345 per credit hour. Tuition, nonresident: full-time $19,720; part-time $920 per credit hour. Required fees: $4368. *Financial support:* In 2010–11, 22 students received support, including 19 research assistantships (averaging $13,000 per year); career-related internships or fieldwork, Federal Work-Study, institutionally sponsored loans, scholarships/grants, and unspecified assistantships also available. Financial award application deadline: 1/15; financial award applicants required to submit FAFSA. *Faculty research:* Home schooling, gifted preschoolers, inclusive schools, ability testing. *Unit head:* Dr. Sandra J. Ward, Associate Dean, 757-221-2326, E-mail: scbrub@wm.edu. *Application contact:* Dorothy Smith Osborne, Assistant Dean for Admission, 757-221-2317, Fax: 757-221-2293, E-mail: dsosbo@wm.edu.

Duquesne University, School of Education, Department of Counseling, Psychology, and Special Education, Program in School Psychology, Pittsburgh, PA 15282-0001. Offers child psychology (MS Ed); school psychology (PhD, CAGS). Part-time and evening/weekend programs available. *Faculty:* 6 full-time (4 women). *Students:* 85 full-time (72 women), 7 part-time (6 women); includes 4 Black or African American, non-Hispanic/Latino; 1 Asian, non-Hispanic/Latino; 1 Hispanic/Latino, 3 international. Average age 31. 112 applicants, 39% accepted, 21 enrolled. In 2010, 24 master's, 4 doctorates, 9 other advanced degrees awarded. *Degree requirements:* For master's, thesis optional; for doctorate, thesis/dissertation. *Entrance requirements:* For master's, MAT, minimum GPA of 3.0; for doctorate, GRE, 3 letters of reference, letter of intent; for CAGS, MAT, interview. Additional exam requirements/recommendations for international students: Required—TOEFL (minimum score 550 paper-based; 80 computer-based). *Application deadline:* For fall admission, 3/1 priority date for domestic students. Applications are processed on a rolling basis. Application fee: $0. Electronic applications accepted. *Expenses:* Tuition: Part-time $884 per credit. Required fees: $84 per credit. Tuition and fees vary according to course load. *Financial support:* Research assistant-

School Psychology

Duquesne University (continued)
ships, Federal Work-Study available. Support available to part-time students. *Unit head:* Dr. Laura Crothers, Associate Professor, 412-396-1409, Fax: 412-396-1340, E-mail: crothersl@duq.edu. *Application contact:* Michael Dolinger, Director of Student and Academic Services, 412-396-6647, Fax: 412-396-5585, E-mail: dolingerm@duq.edu.

East Carolina University, Graduate School, Thomas Harriot College of Arts and Sciences, Department of Psychology, Program in School Psychology, Greenville, NC 27858-4353. Offers MA/CAS. *Accreditation:* NCATE. Part-time and evening/weekend programs available. *Expenses:* Tuition, state resident: full-time $3130; part-time $391.25 per credit hour. Tuition, nonresident: full-time $13,817; part-time $1727.13 per credit hour. Required fees: $1916; $239.50 per credit hour. Tuition and fees vary according to campus/location and program.

Eastern Illinois University, Graduate School, College of Sciences, Charleston, IL 61920-3099. Offers biological sciences (MS); chemistry (MS); communication disorders and sciences (MS); economics (MA); mathematics and computer science (MA), including mathematics, mathematics education; natural sciences (MS); political science (MA); psychology (MA, SSP), including clinical psychology (MA), school psychology (SSP). Part-time programs available. *Degree requirements:* For SSP, thesis. *Entrance requirements:* For degree, GRE General Test.

Eastern Illinois University, Graduate School, College of Sciences, Department of Psychology, Program in School Psychology, Charleston, IL 61920-3099. Offers SSP. *Accreditation:* NCATE. *Degree requirements:* For SSP, thesis. *Entrance requirements:* For degree, GRE General Test.

Eastern Kentucky University, The Graduate School, College of Arts and Sciences, Department of Psychology, Richmond, KY 40475-3102. Offers clinical psychology (MS); industrial/organizational psychology (MS); school psychology (Psy S). Part-time programs available. *Entrance requirements:* For master's and Psy S, GRE General Test, minimum GPA of 2.5. *Faculty research:* Autism, social psychology, parenting, assessment of depression/anxiety, reading.

Eastern University, Department of Counseling Psychology, St. Davids, PA 19087-3696. Offers community/clinical counseling (MA); school counseling (MA, Certificate); school psychology (MS, Certificate). *Degree requirements:* For master's, internship. *Entrance requirements:* For master's, minimum GPA of 2.5. Additional exam requirements/recommendations for international students: Required—TOEFL.

Eastern Washington University, Graduate Studies, College of Education and Human Development, Program in School Psychology, Cheney, WA 99004-2431. Offers MS. *Degree requirements:* For master's, comprehensive exam, thesis or alternative. *Entrance requirements:* For master's, GRE General Test, minimum GPA of 3.0.

Eastern Washington University, Graduate Studies, College of Social and Behavioral Sciences, Department of Psychology, Cheney, WA 99004-2431. Offers clinical psychology (MS); experimental psychology (MS); psychology (MS); school psychology (MS). *Degree requirements:* For master's, comprehensive exam, thesis or alternative. *Entrance requirements:* For master's, GRE General Test, minimum GPA of 3.0.

Edinboro University of Pennsylvania, School of Education, Department of Professional Studies, Edinboro, PA 16444. Offers counseling (MA), including community counseling, elementary guidance, rehabilitation counseling, secondary guidance, student personnel services; educational leadership (M Ed), including elementary school administration, secondary school administration; educational psychology (M Ed); educational specialist school psychology (MS); elementary principal (Certificate); elementary school guidance counselor (Certificate); K-12 school administration (Certificate); letter of eligibility (Certificate); reading (M Ed); reading specialist (Certificate); school psychology (Certificate); school supervision (Certificate), including music, special education. Part-time and evening/weekend programs available. *Faculty:* 24 full-time (18 women), 9 part-time/adjunct (5 women). *Students:* 181 full-time (144 women), 736 part-time (581 women); includes 32 minority (23 Black or African American, non-Hispanic/Latino; 3 American Indian or Alaska Native, non-Hispanic/Latino; 1 Asian, non-Hispanic/Latino; 5 Hispanic/Latino). Average age 32. In 2010, 318 master's, 49 other advanced degrees awarded. *Degree requirements:* For master's, thesis or alternative, competency exam; for Certificate, thesis or alternative. *Entrance requirements:* For master's and Certificate, GRE or MAT, minimum QPA of 2.5. *Application deadline:* Applications are processed on a rolling basis. Application fee: $30. Electronic applications accepted. *Expenses:* Tuition, state resident: full-time $6966; part-time $387 per credit. Tuition, nonresident: full-time $11,146; part-time $619 per credit. Required fees: $2401.70; $96.25 per credit. *Financial support:* In 2010–11, 60 research assistantships with full and partial tuition reimbursements (averaging $4,050 per year) were awarded; career-related internships or fieldwork, Federal Work-Study, scholarships/grants, and unspecified assistantships also available. Support available to part-time students. Financial award application deadline: 2/15; financial award applicants required to submit FAFSA. *Unit head:* Dr. Salene Cowher, Program Head, Counseling, 814-732-1116, E-mail: scowher@edinboro.edu. *Application contact:* Dr. Andrew Pushchack, Program Head, Educational Leadership, 814-732-1548, E-mail: apushchack@edinboro.edu.

Emporia State University, Graduate School, Teachers College, Department of Psychology, Art Therapy, Rehabilitation and Mental Health Counseling, Program in School Psychology, Emporia, KS 66801-5087. Offers MS, Ed S. *Accreditation:* NCATE. Part-time programs available. *Students:* 15 full-time (11 women), 6 part-time (4 women); includes 2 minority (1 Black or African American, non-Hispanic/Latino; 1 Two or more races, non-Hispanic/Latino). 9 applicants, 56% accepted; 5 enrolled. In 2010, 5 master's, 11 other advanced degrees awarded. *Degree requirements:* For master's, comprehensive exam or thesis, internship; for Ed S, comprehensive exam, thesis or alternative, internship. *Entrance requirements:* For master's, GRE General Test or MAT, graduate essay exam, appropriate bachelor's degree, teacher certification, letters of recommendation; for Ed S, GRE, graduate essay exam, letters of recommendation, teacher certification. Additional exam requirements/recommendations for international students: Required—TOEFL (minimum score 520 paper-based; 133 computer-based; 68 iBT). *Application deadline:* For fall admission, 8/15 priority date for domestic students. Applications are processed on a rolling basis. Application fee: $30 ($75 for international students). Electronic applications accepted. *Expenses:* Tuition, state resident: full-time $4382; part-time $183 per credit hour. Tuition, nonresident: full-time $13,572; part-time $566 per credit hour. Required fees: $1022; $62 per credit hour. Tuition and fees vary according to course level, course load and campus/location. *Financial support:* Career-related internships or fieldwork, Federal Work-Study, institutionally sponsored loans, health care benefits, and unspecified assistantships available. Financial award application deadline: 3/15; financial award applicants required to submit FAFSA. *Unit head:* Dr. Brian W. Schrader, Chair, 620-341-5317, E-mail: bschrade@emporia.edu. *Application contact:* Mary Sewell, Admissions Coordinator, 800-950-GRAD, Fax: 620-341-5909, E-mail: msewell@emporia.edu.

Evangel University, School Counseling Program, Springfield, MO 65802. Offers MS. Part-time programs available. *Faculty:* 2 full-time (both women), 5 part-time/adjunct (3 women). *Students:* 25 full-time (19 women), 68 part-time (55 women). Average age 32. 17 applicants, 94% accepted, 14 enrolled. In 2010, 9 master's awarded. *Degree requirements:* For master's, comprehensive exam (for some programs), thesis or alternative. *Entrance requirements:* For master's, MAT (preferred) or GRE, teaching certificate. Additional exam requirements/recommendations for international students: Required—TOEFL (minimum score 550 paper-based; 213 computer-based). *Application deadline:* For fall admission, 7/15 priority date for domestic and international students; for spring admission, 11/15 priority date for domestic and international students. Applications are processed on a rolling basis. Application fee: $25. Electronic applications accepted. *Financial support:* In 2010–11, 2 students received support. Career-related internships or fieldwork, scholarships/grants, and unspecified assistantships available. Support available to part-time students. Financial award application deadline: 3/1; financial award applicants required to submit FAFSA. *Unit head:* Debbie Bicket, Chair, 417-865-2815 Ext. 8567, Fax: 417-575-5484, E-mail: bicketd@evangel.edu. *Application contact:*

Charity H. Fahlstrom, Admissions Representative, Graduate and Professional Studies Admissions, 417-865-2815 Ext. 7227, Fax: 417-575-5484, E-mail: fahlstromc@evangel.edu.

Fairfield University, Graduate School of Education and Allied Professions, Department of Psychological and Educational Consultation, Fairfield, CT 06824-5195. Offers applied psychology (MA), including foundations of advanced psychology, human services, industrial/organizational; educational technology (MA); school library media specialist (MA); school psychology (MA, CAS); special education (MA, CAS). Part-time and evening/weekend programs available. *Faculty:* 6 full-time (2 women), 7 part-time/adjunct (4 women). *Students:* 52 full-time (46 women), 144 part-time (120 women); includes 2 Black or African American, non-Hispanic/Latino; 1 American Indian or Alaska Native, non-Hispanic/Latino; 2 Asian, non-Hispanic/Latino; 14 Hispanic/Latino, 2 international. 136 applicants, 63% accepted, 59 enrolled. In 2010, 44 master's, 14 other advanced degrees awarded. *Degree requirements:* For master's, comprehensive exam, thesis optional. *Entrance requirements:* For master's, PRAXIS I (PPST), minimum QPA of 3.0, 2 recommendations, resume. Additional exam requirements/recommendations for international students: Required—TOEFL (minimum score 550 paper-based; 213 computer-based; 84 iBT). Application fee: $60. Electronic applications accepted. *Expenses:* Tuition: Part-time $600 per hour. Part-time tuition and fees vary according to degree level and program. *Financial support:* Unspecified assistantships available. Financial award applicants required to submit FAFSA. *Faculty research:* Child neuropsychology, disabilities, effect of pre-treatment orientation on treatment, autism, technology in business and classroom, collaboration with schools, communities and industry. *Unit head:* Dr. David Zera, Chair, 203-254-4250, Fax: 203-254-4047, E-mail: dzera@fairfield.edu. *Application contact:* Marianne Gumpper, Director of Graduate and Continuing Studies Admissions, 203-254-4184, Fax: 203-254-4073, E-mail: gradadmis@fairfield.edu.

Fairleigh Dickinson University, Metropolitan Campus, University College: Arts, Sciences, and Professional Studies, School of Psychology, Program in School Psychology, Teaneck, NJ 07666-1914. Offers MA, Psy D. *Students:* 95 full-time (66 women), 3 part-time (2 women). Average age 30. 55 applicants, 67% accepted, 21 enrolled. In 2010, 4 master's, 11 doctorates awarded. *Application deadline:* Applications are processed on a rolling basis. Application fee: $40. *Application contact:* Susan Brooman, University Director of Graduate Admissions, 201-692-2554, Fax: 201-692-2560, E-mail: globaleducation@fdu.edu.

Florida Agricultural and Mechanical University, Division of Graduate Studies, Research, and Continuing Education, College of Arts and Sciences, Department of Psychology, Program in School Psychology, Tallahassee, FL 32307-3200. Offers MS. *Accreditation:* NCATE. *Degree requirements:* For master's, thesis. *Entrance requirements:* For master's, GRE General Test, minimum GPA of 3.0, letters of recommendation (3). Additional exam requirements/recommendations for international students: Required—TOEFL.

Florida International University, College of Education, Department of Educational Leadership and Policy Studies, Miami, FL 33199. Offers adult education (MS); adult education in human resource development (Ed D); clinical mental health counseling (MS); conflict resolution and consensus building (Certificate); counselor education (MS); educational administration and supervision (Ed D); educational leadership (MS, Certificate, Ed S); higher education (Ed D); higher education administration (MS); human resource development (MS); instruction in urban settings (MS); international/intercultural education (MS); learning technologies (MS); multicultural-bilingual (MS); multicultural-TESOL (MS); recreation and sport management (MS); recreation therapy (MS); rehabilitation counseling (MS); school counseling (MS); school psychology (Ed S); urban education (MS). Part-time and evening/weekend programs available. *Students:* 164 full-time (124 women), 308 part-time (234 women); includes 107 Black or African American, non-Hispanic/Latino; 3 American Indian or Alaska Native, non-Hispanic/Latino; 8 Asian, non-Hispanic/Latino; 223 Hispanic/Latino, 12 international. Average age 31. 544 applicants, 41% accepted, 197 enrolled. In 2010, 123 master's, 5 doctorates, 16 other advanced degrees awarded. *Degree requirements:* For doctorate, thesis/dissertation. *Entrance requirements:* For master's, minimum GPA of 3.0; for doctorate and other advanced degree, GRE General Test. Additional exam requirements/recommendations for international students: Required—TOEFL (minimum score 550 paper-based; 213 computer-based; 80 iBT), IELTS (minimum score 6.3). *Application deadline:* For fall admission, 6/1 priority date for domestic students, 4/1 for international students; for winter admission, 10/1 priority date for domestic students, 9/1 for international students; for spring admission, 3/1 priority date for domestic students, 2/1 for international students. Applications are processed on a rolling basis. Application fee: $30. Electronic applications accepted. *Financial support:* Fellowships, research assistantships with full and partial tuition reimbursements, teaching assistantships with full and partial tuition reimbursements, Federal Work-Study and tuition waivers (full and partial) available. Support available to part-time students. Financial award applicants required to submit FAFSA. *Unit head:* Dr. Patricia Barbetta, Dean of Graduate Studies, 305-348-2835, Fax: 305-348-2081, E-mail: barbetta@fiu.edu. *Application contact:* Nanett Rojas, Graduate Admission, 305-348-7442, Fax: 305-348-7441, E-mail: nanett.rojas@fiu.edu.

Florida State University, The Graduate School, College of Education, Department of Educational Psychology and Learning Systems, Program in School Psychology, Tallahassee, FL 32306. Offers MS, Ed S. *Faculty:* 2 full-time (both women), 1 (woman) part-time/adjunct. *Students:* 64 full-time (52 women), 22 part-time (16 women); includes 24 minority (9 Black or African American, non-Hispanic/Latino; 1 American Indian or Alaska Native, non-Hispanic/Latino; 4 Asian, non-Hispanic/Latino; 10 Hispanic/Latino), 2 international. Average age 27. 99 applicants, 28% accepted, 13 enrolled. In 2010, 10 master's, 10 other advanced degrees awarded. *Degree requirements:* For master's, comprehensive exam; for Ed S, comprehensive exam, thesis. *Entrance requirements:* For master's and Ed S, GRE General Test, minimum GPA of 3.0. Additional exam requirements/recommendations for international students: Required—TOEFL (minimum score 550 paper-based; 213 computer-based; 80 iBT); Recommended—TWE. *Application deadline:* For fall admission, 2/1 for domestic and international students. Applications are processed on a rolling basis. Application fee: $30. Electronic applications accepted. *Expenses:* Tuition, state resident: full-time $8238.24. *Financial support:* Fellowships with full and partial tuition reimbursements, research assistantships with full and partial tuition reimbursements, teaching assistantships with full and partial tuition reimbursements, career-related internships or fieldwork available. Financial award applicants required to submit FAFSA. *Faculty research:* Practitioner-scholar models, cultural diversity in populations. *Unit head:* Dr. Briley Proctor, Program Leader, 850-644-3742, Fax: 850-644-8776, E-mail: bproctor@fsu.edu. *Application contact:* Terri Wehnert, Program Assistant, 850-644-8046, Fax: 850-644-8776, E-mail: tmpowell@fsu.edu.

Fordham University, Graduate School of Education, Division of Psychological and Educational Services, New York, NY 10023. Offers counseling and personnel services (MSE, Adv C); counseling psychology (PhD); educational psychology (MSE, PhD); school psychology (PhD); urban and urban bilingual school psychology (Adv C). *Accreditation:* APA (one or more programs are accredited); NCATE. *Degree requirements:* For doctorate, thesis/dissertation. *Entrance requirements:* For doctorate, GRE General Test.

Fort Hays State University, Graduate School, College of Arts and Sciences, Department of Psychology, Program in School Psychology, Hays, KS 67601-4099. Offers Ed S. *Accreditation:* NCATE. *Degree requirements:* For Ed S, comprehensive exam, thesis. *Entrance requirements:* Additional exam requirements/recommendations for international students: Required—TOEFL (minimum score 550 paper-based; 213 computer-based). Electronic applications accepted.

Francis Marion University, Graduate Programs, Department of Psychology, Florence, SC 29502-0547. Offers applied psychology (MS), including clinical/counseling, school psychology; school psychology (SSP). Part-time and evening/weekend programs available. *Faculty:* 10 full-time (4 women), 5 part-time/adjunct (4 women). *Students:* 17 full-time (16 women), 26 part-time (25 women); includes 6 Black or African American, non-Hispanic/Latino. Average age 25. 44 applicants, 61% accepted, 14 enrolled. In 2010, 9 master's awarded. *Degree requirements:* For master's, internship. *Entrance requirements:* For master's, GRE General Test. *Application deadline:* For fall admission, 3/15 for domestic students; for spring admission,

10/15 for domestic students. Applications are processed on a rolling basis. Application fee: $30. *Expenses:* Tuition, state resident: full-time $8667; part-time $433.35 per credit hour. Tuition, nonresident: full-time $17,334; part-time $866.70 per credit hour. Required fees: $335; $12.25 per credit hour. $30 per semester. *Financial support:* In 2010–11, 13 students received support, including 2 research assistantships (averaging $7,000 per year), 3 teaching assistantships (averaging $8,000 per year); career-related internships or fieldwork, unspecified assistantships, and scholarships with out-of-state waivers also available. Support available to part-time students. Financial award application deadline: 3/1; financial award applicants required to submit FAFSA. *Faculty research:* Parenting and family relationships, child development, applied behavioral analysis, posttraumatic stress disorder, clinical psychology in adults. *Unit head:* Dr. John R. Hester, Chair, 843-661-1635, Fax: 843-661-1628. *Application contact:* Jennifer Taylor, Administrative Assistant, 843-661-1378, Fax: 843-661-1628.

Fresno Pacific University, Graduate Programs, School of Education, Fresno, CA 93702-4709. Offers administration (MA Ed), including administrative services; foundations, curriculum and teaching (MA Ed), including curriculum and teaching, school library and information technology; language, literacy, and culture (MA Ed), including bilingual/cross-cultural education, language development, multilingual contexts, reading; mathematics/science/computer education (MA Ed), including educational technology, integrated mathematics/science education, mathematics education; pupil personnel services (MA Ed), including school counseling, school psychology; special education (MA Ed), including mild/moderate, moderate/severe, physical and health impairments. Part-time and evening/weekend programs available. *Degree requirements:* For master's, thesis (for some programs). *Entrance requirements:* For master's, interview; GMAT, GRE, MAT, or 6 units of course work with a faculty recommendation. Additional exam requirements/recommendations for international students: Required—TOEFL (minimum score 550 paper-based; 213 computer-based). Electronic applications accepted.

Fresno Pacific University, Graduate Programs, School of Education, Division of Pupil Personnel Services, Program in School Psychology, Fresno, CA 93702-4709. Offers MA Ed. Part-time and evening/weekend programs available. *Degree requirements:* For master's, thesis or alternative. *Entrance requirements:* Additional exam requirements/recommendations for international students: Required—TOEFL (minimum score 550 paper-based; 213 computer-based).

Gallaudet University, The Graduate School, Washington, DC 20002-3625. Offers administration (MS); audiology (Au D, PhD); change leadership in education (Ed S); clinical psychology (PhD); deaf education (Ed D, PhD); deaf education: advanced studies (MA); deaf education: special programs in deaf education (MA); deaf history (Certificate); deaf studies (MA); education: teacher preparation (MA, MA Missions), including deaf education (MA), early childhood education and deaf education (MA), elementary education and deaf education (MA Missions), secondary education and deaf education (MA); hearing, speech and language sciences (MS); international development (MA); interpretation (MA, PhD); leadership (Certificate); leisure services administration (MS); linguistics (MA, PhD); management (Certificate); mental health counseling (MA); school counseling (MA); school counseling (summer session) (MA); school psychology (Psy S); sign language teaching (MA); social work (MSW); special education administration (PhD); speech-language pathology (PhD). Part-time programs available. *Faculty:* 116 full-time (86 women). *Students:* 291 full-time (224 women), 122 part-time (97 women); includes 142 minority (36 Black or African American, non-Hispanic/Latino; 3 American Indian or Alaska Native, non-Hispanic/Latino; 13 Asian, non-Hispanic/Latino; 29 Hispanic/Latino; 61 Two or more races, non-Hispanic/Latino), 28 international. Average age 30. 442 applicants, 52% accepted, 145 enrolled. In 2010, 116 master's, 17 doctorates, 16 other advanced degrees awarded. Terminal master's awarded for partial completion of doctoral program. *Degree requirements:* For master's, comprehensive exam (for some programs), thesis optional; for doctorate, comprehensive exam, thesis/dissertation. *Entrance requirements:* For master's and doctorate, GRE General Test or MAT, letters of recommendation, interviews, goals statement, ASL proficiency interview, written English competency. Additional exam requirements/recommendations for international students: Required—TOEFL. *Application deadline:* For fall admission, 2/15 for domestic students. Applications are processed on a rolling basis. Application fee: $50. Electronic applications accepted. *Expenses:* Tuition: Full-time $11,930; part-time $663 per credit. Required fees: $188 per semester. *Financial support:* In 2010–11, 219 students received support; fellowships, research assistantships, teaching assistantships, career-related internships or fieldwork, Federal Work-Study, scholarships/grants, tuition waivers (partial), and unspecified assistantships available. Support available to part-time students. Financial award applicants required to submit FAFSA. *Faculty research:* Bimodal bilingualism development, audiology, telecommunications access, early childhood education, linguistics, visual language and visual learning, rehabilitation and hearing enhancement. *Unit head:* Dr. Carol J. Erting, Dean, 202-651-5520, Fax: 202-651-5027, E-mail: carol.erting@gallaudet.edu. *Application contact:* Wednesday Luria, Coordinator of Prospective Graduate Student Services, 202-651-5400, Fax: 202-651-5295, E-mail: graduate.school@gallaudet.edu.

Gardner-Webb University, Graduate School, School of Psychology, Program in School Counseling, Boiling Springs, NC 28017. Offers MA. *Accreditation:* NCATE. Part-time and evening/weekend programs available. *Faculty:* 6 full-time (3 women). *Students:* 37 part-time (31 women); includes 9 Black or African American, non-Hispanic/Latino; 1 Asian, non-Hispanic/Latino. Average age 32. In 2010, 14 master's awarded. *Degree requirements:* For master's, comprehensive exam. *Entrance requirements:* For master's, GRE General Test, MAT, minimum GPA of 2.7. *Application deadline:* For fall admission, 7/1 priority date for domestic students. Applications are processed on a rolling basis. Application fee: $40. Electronic applications accepted. *Expenses:* Tuition: Part-time $325 per credit hour. *Financial support:* Unspecified assistantships available. *Unit head:* Dr. David Carscaddon, Coordinator, 704-406-4437, Fax: 704-406-4329, E-mail: ppartin@gardner-webb.edu. *Application contact:* Office of Graduate Admisisons, 877-498-4723, Fax: 704-406-3895, E-mail: gradinfo@gardner-webb.edu.

George Fox University, School of Education, Graduate Department of Counseling, Newberg, OR 97132-2697. Offers clinical mental health counseling (MA); marriage, couple and family counseling (MA, Certificate); mental health trauma (Certificate); school counseling (MA, Certificate); school psychology (Certificate, Ed S). Part-time programs available. *Faculty:* 9 full-time (3 women), 7 part-time/adjunct (4 women). *Students:* 119 full-time (95 women), 115 part-time (93 women); includes 34 minority (9 Black or African American, non-Hispanic/Latino; 5 American Indian or Alaska Native, non-Hispanic/Latino; 8 Asian, non-Hispanic/Latino; 10 Hispanic/Latino; 1 Native Hawaiian or other Pacific Islander, non-Hispanic/Latino; 1 Two or more races, non-Hispanic/Latino). Average age 34. 114 applicants, 55% accepted, 45 enrolled. In 2010, 66 master's, 3 other advanced degrees awarded. *Degree requirements:* For master's, clinical project. *Entrance requirements:* For master's, MAT or GRE, bachelor's degree from regionally-accredited college or university, minimum cumulative GPA of 3.0, 1 professional and 1 academic reference, resume, on-campus interview. Additional exam requirements/recommendations for international students: Required—TOEFL (minimum score 577 paper-based; 233 computer-based; 90 iBT), IELTS (minimum score 7). *Application deadline:* For fall admission, 5/30 for domestic and international students; for winter admission, 11/1 for domestic and international students; for spring admission, 2/28 for domestic and international students. Applications are processed on a rolling basis. Application fee: $40. Electronic applications accepted. *Expenses:* Contact institution. *Financial support:* Career-related internships or fieldwork available. *Unit head:* Dr. Richard Shaw, Associate Professor of Marriage and Family Therapy/Chair, 503-554-6142, E-mail: rshaw@georgefox.edu. *Application contact:* Kathy Grant, Admissions Counselor, 800-493-4937, Fax: 503-554-6111, E-mail: counseling@georgefox.edu.

George Mason University, College of Humanities and Social Sciences, Department of Psychology, Program in School Psychology, Fairfax, VA 22030. Offers Certificate. *Accreditation:* NCATE. *Faculty:* 48 full-time (20 women), 14 part-time/adjunct (8 women). *Students:* 7 part-time (all women); includes 1 Hispanic/Latino; 1 Two or more races, non-Hispanic/Latino. Average age 27. 3 applicants, 67% accepted, 1 enrolled. In 2010, 7 Certificates awarded. *Entrance requirements:* Additional exam requirements/recommendations for international students: Required—TOEFL (minimum score 570 paper-based; 230 computer-based; 88 iBT). *Application deadline:* For fall admission, 1/15 for domestic students. Application fee: $100. Electronic applications accepted. *Expenses:* Tuition, state resident: full-time $8192; part-time $440 per credit hour. Tuition, nonresident: full-time $22,952; part-time $1055 per credit hour. Required fees: $2364; $99 per credit hour. *Financial support:* Federal Work-Study, unspecified assistantships, and health care benefits (full-time research or teaching assistantship recipients) available. Support available to part-time students. Financial award application deadline: 3/1; financial award applicants required to submit FAFSA. *Faculty research:* Psychological and educational assessment of children and adults, cognitive processing-based academic instruction, theories of measurement of intelligence, fair assessment of culturally and linguistically diverse population. *Unit head:* Darby Wiggins, Coordinator, 703-993-1548, E-mail: dwiggin3@gmu.edu. *Application contact:* Darby Wiggins, Information Contact, 703-993-1548, E-mail: dwiggin3@gmu.edu.

Georgian Court University, School of Arts and Sciences, Lakewood, NJ 08701-2697. Offers biology (MA); Catholic school leadership (Certificate); clinical mental health counseling (MA); holistic health studies (MA); mathematics (MA); pastoral ministry (Certificate); religious education (Certificate); school psychology (Certificate); theology (MA, Certificate). Part-time and evening/weekend programs available. *Faculty:* 19 full-time (11 women), 7 part-time/adjunct (5 women). *Students:* 61 full-time (59 women), 143 part-time (113 women); includes 20 minority (5 Black or African American, non-Hispanic/Latino; 3 Asian, non-Hispanic/Latino; 11 Hispanic/Latino; 1 Two or more races, non-Hispanic/Latino), 1 international. Average age 39. 139 applicants, 59% accepted, 50 enrolled. In 2010, 5 master's awarded. *Degree requirements:* For master's, comprehensive exam (for some programs), thesis (for some programs). *Entrance requirements:* For master's, GRE, MAT, or NTE/PRAXIS, 3 letters of recommendation. Additional exam requirements/recommendations for international students: Required—TOEFL (minimum score 550 paper-based; 213 computer-based). *Application deadline:* For fall admission, 8/1 priority date for domestic students, 4/1 for international students; for spring admission, 1/1 priority date for domestic students, 7/1 for international students. Applications are processed on a rolling basis. Application fee: $40. Electronic applications accepted. *Expenses:* Tuition: Full-time $12,510; part-time $695 per credit. Required fees: $416 per year. Tuition and fees vary according to campus/location and program. *Financial support:* Scholarships/grants, health care benefits, and unspecified assistantships available. Financial award application deadline: 4/15; financial award applicants required to submit FAFSA. *Unit head:* Dr. Linda James, Dean, 732-987-2617, Fax: 732-987-2007. *Application contact:* Patrick Givens, Assistant Director of Admissions, 732-987-2736, Fax: 732-987-2084, E-mail: graduateadmissions@georgian.edu.

Georgia Southern University, Jack N. Averitt College of Graduate Studies, College of Education, Department of Leadership, Technology, and Human Development, Program in School Psychology, Statesboro, GA 30460. Offers M Ed, Ed S. *Accreditation:* NCATE. Part-time and evening/weekend programs available. *Students:* 31 full-time (29 women), 25 part-time (21 women); includes 13 Black or African American, non-Hispanic/Latino; 3 Hispanic/Latino. Average age 29. 11 applicants, 64% accepted, 4 enrolled. In 2010, 28 master's, 12 other advanced degrees awarded. *Degree requirements:* For Ed S, comprehensive exam. *Entrance requirements:* For degree, GRE General Test or MAT, minimum graduate GPA of 3.25, letters of reference, interview. Additional exam requirements/recommendations for international students: Required—TOEFL (minimum score 550 paper-based; 213 computer-based; 80 iBT). *Application deadline:* For fall admission, 3/1 priority date for domestic and international students; for spring admission, 10/1 priority date for domestic students, 10/1 for international students. Applications are processed on a rolling basis. Application fee: $50. Electronic applications accepted. *Expenses:* Tuition, state resident: full-time $6000; part-time $250 per semester hour. Tuition, nonresident: full-time $23,976; part-time $999 per semester hour. Required fees: $1644. *Financial support:* In 2010–11, 44 students received support, including research assistantships with partial tuition reimbursements available (averaging $7,200 per year), teaching assistantships with partial tuition reimbursements available (averaging $7,200 per year); career-related internships or fieldwork, Federal Work-Study, scholarships/grants, tuition waivers (partial), and unspecified assistantships also available. Support available to part-time students. Financial award application deadline: 4/15; financial award applicants required to submit FAFSA. *Unit head:* Dr. Terry Diamanduros, Coordinator, 912-478-1548, Fax: 912-478-7104, E-mail: tdiamanduros@georgiasouthern.edu. *Application contact:* Dr. Charles Ziglar, Coordinator for Graduate Student Recruitment, 912-478-5635, Fax: 912-478-0740, E-mail: gradadmissions@georgiasouthern.edu.

Georgia State University, College of Education, Department of Counseling and Psychological Services, Program in School Psychology, Atlanta, GA 30302-3083. Offers M Ed, PhD, Ed S. *Accreditation:* APA (one or more programs are accredited); NCATE. *Degree requirements:* For master's, comprehensive exam; for doctorate, comprehensive exam, thesis/dissertation. *Entrance requirements:* For master's, GRE General Test, minimum GPA of 2.5; for doctorate, GRE General Test, minimum GPA of 3.3; for Ed S, GRE General Test, minimum graduate GPA of 3.25. *Faculty research:* School reform, reading (early intervention), school violence.

Grand Valley State University, College of Education, Program in School Counseling, Allendale, MI 49401-9403. Offers M Ed. Part-time programs available. *Degree requirements:* For master's, thesis or project. *Entrance requirements:* For master's, GRE General Test or minimum GPA of 3.0. Additional exam requirements/recommendations for international students: Required—TOEFL. Electronic applications accepted. *Faculty research:* Multicultural issues in counselor education, use of technology in counseling programs.

Hofstra University, College of Liberal Arts and Sciences, Program in School-Community Psychology, Hempstead, NY 11549. Offers Psy D. *Students:* 43 full-time (36 women), 9 part-time (8 women); includes 8 minority (3 Asian, non-Hispanic/Latino; 5 Hispanic/Latino), 1 international. Average age 26. 74 applicants, 35% accepted, 10 enrolled. In 2010, 10 doctorates awarded. *Degree requirements:* For doctorate, comprehensive exam, thesis/dissertation. *Entrance requirements:* For doctorate, GRE General Test, GRE Subject Test (Psychology), Interview; 3 letters of recommendation; Essay. Additional exam requirements/recommendations for international students: Required—TOEFL (minimum score 550 paper-based; 213 computer-based; 80 iBT). *Application deadline:* For fall admission, 1/15 for domestic and international students. Application fee: $70 ($75 for international students). Electronic applications accepted. *Expenses:* Tuition: Full-time $18,000; part-time $1000 per credit hour. Required fees: $970; $145 per term. Tuition and fees vary according to program. *Financial support:* In 2010–11, 29 students received support, including 19 fellowships with full and partial tuition reimbursements available (averaging $6,153 per year), 1 research assistantship with full and partial tuition reimbursement available (averaging $9,000 per year); Federal Work-Study, institutionally sponsored loans, scholarships/grants, tuition waivers (full and partial), and unspecified assistantships also available. Support available to part-time students. Financial award applicants required to submit FAFSA. *Faculty research:* Cross-cultural psychology, school psychology, childhood and adult trauma, positive psychology, autism spectrum disorders. *Unit head:* Dr. Robert Motta, Program Director, 516-463-5029, Fax: 516-463-6052, E-mail: psyrwm@hofstra.edu. *Application contact:* Carol Drummer, Dean of Graduate Admissions, 516-463-4876, Fax: 516-463-4664, E-mail: gradstudent@hofstra.edu.

Howard University, School of Education, Department of Human Development and Psychoeducational Studies, Program in School Psychology, Washington, DC 20059-0002. Offers M Ed, PhD. MA and PhD offered through the Graduate School of Arts and Sciences. *Accreditation:* NCATE. *Faculty:* 2 full-time (0 women), 1 part-time/adjunct (0 women). *Students:* 36 full-time (28 women), 15 part-time (14 women); includes 43 Black or African American, non-Hispanic/Latino, 8 international. Average age 32. 30 applicants, 80% accepted, 15 enrolled. In 2010, 7 master's, 2 doctorates awarded. *Degree requirements:* For master's, comprehensive exam, thesis (MA), expository writing exam, practicum; for doctorate, one foreign language, comprehensive exam, thesis/dissertation, expository writing exam, internship. *Entrance requirements:* For master's, GRE General Test, minimum GPA of 2.7; for doctorate, GRE General Test, minimum GPA of 3.4. Additional exam requirements/recommendations for international students: Required—TOEFL (minimum score 550 paper-based). *Application deadline:* For fall admission, 2/15 priority date for domestic students; for spring admission, 11/1 for domestic students. Applications are processed on a rolling basis. Application fee: $45. Electronic applications accepted. *Financial support:* In 2010–11, 4 students received support, including 4

School Psychology

Howard University (continued)
research assistantships with full and partial tuition reimbursements available (averaging $9,527 per year); fellowships with full and partial tuition reimbursements available, career-related internships or fieldwork, Federal Work-Study, institutionally sponsored loans, scholarships/grants, and unspecified assistantships also available. Financial award application deadline: 3/15; financial award applicants required to submit FAFSA. *Faculty research:* Psychopathology, maltreatment abuse and neglect, children exposed to political unrest, family conflict and community violence. *Unit head:* Dr. Salman M. Elbedour, Professor/Coordinator, 202-806-6412, Fax: 202-806-5205, E-mail: selbedour@howard.edu. *Application contact:* Frazier Tate-Jackson, Administration Assistant, Department of HDPES, 202-806-7350, Fax: 202-806-5205, E-mail: fjackson@howard.edu.

Humboldt State University, Academic Programs, College of Professional Studies, Department of Psychology, Arcata, CA 95521-8299. Offers psychology (MA), including academic research, counseling, school psychology. *Students:* 45 full-time (31 women), 12 part-time (8 women); includes 12 minority (2 Asian, non-Hispanic/Latino; 7 Hispanic/Latino; 3 Two or more races, non-Hispanic/Latino). Average age 28. 35 applicants, 86% accepted, 9 enrolled. In 2010, 24 master's awarded. *Degree requirements:* For master's, thesis. *Entrance requirements:* For master's, appropriate bachelor's degree, minimum GPA of 2.5. Additional exam requirements/recommendations for international students: Required—TOEFL (minimum score 500 paper-based; 173 computer-based). *Application deadline:* For fall admission, 2/1 for domestic students, 2/15 for international students. Applications are processed on a rolling basis. Application fee: $55. Tuition and fees vary according to program. *Financial support:* Career-related internships or fieldwork available. Financial award application deadline: 3/1; financial award applicants required to submit FAFSA. *Faculty research:* School psychology, counseling, eating disorders, mood induction, depression. *Unit head:* Dr. Gregg Gold, Chair, 707-826-3740, Fax: 707-826-4993, E-mail: gjg14@humboldt.edu. *Application contact:* Dr. Chris Aberson, Coordinator, 707-826-3670, Fax: 707-826-4993, E-mail: cla18@humboldt.edu.

Idaho State University, Office of Graduate Studies, College of Education, Department of Educational Learning and Development, Pocatello, ID 83209-8059. Offers human exceptionality (M Ed); school psychology (Ed S); special education (Ed S). Part-time programs available. *Degree requirements:* For master's, comprehensive exam, thesis (for some programs), oral thesis defense or written comprehensive exam and oral exam; for Ed S, comprehensive exam, thesis (for some programs), oral exam, specialist paper or portfolio. *Entrance requirements:* For master's, GRE or MAT, minimum undergraduate GPA of 3.0, bachelor's degree, professional experience in an educational context; for Ed S, GRE or MAT, master's degree in related field. Additional exam requirements/recommendations for international students: Required—TOEFL (minimum score 550 paper-based; 213 computer-based; 80 iBT). Electronic applications accepted. *Faculty research:* Literacy, school psychology, special education.

Idaho State University, Office of Graduate Studies, Kasiska College of Health Professions, Department of Counseling, Pocatello, ID 83209-8120. Offers counseling (M Coun, Ed S), including marriage and family counseling (M Coun), mental health counseling (M Coun), school counseling (M Coun), student affairs and college counseling (M Coun); counselor education and counseling (PhD). *Accreditation:* ACA (one or more programs are accredited). Part-time programs available. *Degree requirements:* For master's, comprehensive exam, thesis, 4 semesters resident graduate study, practicum/internship; for doctorate, comprehensive exam, thesis/dissertation, 3 semesters internship, 4 consecutive semesters doctoral-level study on campus; for Ed S, comprehensive exam, thesis, case studies, oral exam. *Entrance requirements:* For master's, GRE General Test, MAT, minimum GPA of 3.0, bachelors degree, interview, 3 letters of recommendation; for doctorate, GRE General Test, MAT, minimum graduate GPA of 3.0, resume, interview, counseling license, master's degree; for Ed S, GRE General Test, minimum graduate GPA of 3.0, master's degree in counseling, 3 letters of recommendation, 2 years work experience. Additional exam requirements/recommendations for international students: Required—TOEFL (minimum score 600 paper-based; 213 computer-based; 80 iBT). Electronic applications accepted. *Faculty research:* Group counseling, multicultural counseling, family counseling, child therapy, supervision.

Illinois State University, Graduate School, College of Arts and Sciences, Department of Psychology, Program in School Psychology, Normal, IL 61790-2200. Offers PhD, SSP. *Accreditation:* APA (one or more programs are accredited); NCATE (one or more programs are accredited). *Degree requirements:* For doctorate, variable foreign language requirement, thesis/dissertation, 2 terms of residency, internship, practicum. *Entrance requirements:* For doctorate, GRE General Test.

Immaculata University, College of Graduate Studies, Department of Psychology, Immaculata, PA 19345. Offers clinical psychology (Psy D); counseling psychology (MA, Certificate), including school guidance counselor (Certificate), school psychologist (Certificate). *Accreditation:* APA. Part-time and evening/weekend programs available. *Students:* 123 full-time (100 women), 201 part-time (159 women). Average age 34. 83 applicants, 76% accepted, 55 enrolled. In 2010, 37 master's, 13 doctorates awarded. Terminal master's awarded for partial completion of doctoral program. *Degree requirements:* For master's, comprehensive exam, thesis optional; for doctorate, comprehensive exam, thesis/dissertation. *Entrance requirements:* For master's, GRE General Test or MAT, minimum GPA of 3.0; for doctorate, GRE General Test or MAT, minimum GPA of 3.5. Additional exam requirements/recommendations for international students: Required—TOEFL, IELTS. *Application deadline:* Applications are processed on a rolling basis. Application fee: $50. Electronic applications accepted. *Financial support:* Application deadline: 5/1. *Faculty research:* Supervision ethics, psychology of teaching, gender. *Unit head:* Dr. Jed A. Yalof, Chair, 610-647-4400 Ext. 3503, Fax: 610-993-8550, E-mail: jyalof@immaculata.edu. *Application contact:* Office of Graduate Admission, 610-647-4400 Ext. 3211, Fax: 610-993-8550, E-mail: graduate@immaculata.edu.

Indiana State University, College of Graduate and Professional Studies, College of Education, Department of Communication Disorders, Counseling and School and Educational Psychology, Terre Haute, IN 47809. Offers counseling psychology (MS, PhD); counselor education (PhD); mental health counseling (MS); school counseling (M Ed); school psychology (PhD, Ed S); MA/MS. *Accreditation:* ACA; NCATE. Part-time and evening/weekend programs available. *Degree requirements:* For master's, thesis optional; for doctorate, thesis/dissertation, research tools proficiency tests. *Entrance requirements:* For master's, GRE General Test or MAT, minimum undergraduate GPA of 2.75; for doctorate, GRE General Test, master's degree, minimum undergraduate GPA of 3.5. Electronic applications accepted. *Faculty research:* Vocational development supervision.

Indiana University Bloomington, School of Education, Department of Counseling and Educational Psychology, Bloomington, IN 47405-1006. Offers counseling (MS, PhD, Ed S); counselor education (MS, Ed S); educational psychology (MS, PhD); inquiry methodology (PhD); learning and developmental sciences (MS, PhD); school psychology (PhD, Ed S). *Accreditation:* ACA (one or more programs are accredited); APA (one or more programs are accredited); NCATE. Terminal master's awarded for partial completion of doctoral program. *Degree requirements:* For master's, thesis optional; for doctorate, thesis/dissertation; for Ed S, comprehensive exam or project. *Entrance requirements:* For master's, doctorate, and Ed S, GRE General Test. Additional exam requirements/recommendations for international students: Required—TOEFL. *Application deadline:* Applications are processed on a rolling basis. Application fee: $55 ($65 for international students). Electronic applications accepted. *Financial support:* Fellowships with partial tuition reimbursements, research assistantships with partial tuition reimbursements, teaching assistantships with partial tuition reimbursements, career-related internships or fieldwork, Federal Work-Study, institutionally sponsored loans, scholarships/grants, and unspecified assistantships available. Support available to part-time students. Financial award application deadline: 1/1; financial award applicants required to submit FAFSA. *Faculty research:* Counseling psychology, inquiry methodology, school psychology, learning sciences, human development, educational psychology. *Unit head:* Dr. Joyce Alexander,

Chairperson, 812-856-8300, Fax: 812-856-8333, E-mail: cep@indiana.edu. *Application contact:* Jessica Durnal, Student Services Specialist, 812-856-8300, Fax: 812-856-8333, E-mail: cep@indiana.edu.

Indiana University of Pennsylvania, School of Graduate Studies and Research, College of Education and Educational Technology, Department of Educational and School Psychology, Program in School Psychology, Indiana, PA 15705-1087. Offers D Ed, Certificate. *Accreditation:* NCATE. Part-time and evening/weekend programs available. *Faculty:* 7 full-time (1 woman). *Students:* 14 full-time (all women), 54 part-time (39 women); includes 5 minority (2 Black or African American, non-Hispanic/Latino; 1 Asian, non-Hispanic/Latino; 2 Hispanic/Latino), 1 international. Average age 32. 38 applicants, 26% accepted, 10 enrolled. In 2010, 6 doctorates, 15 other advanced degrees awarded. *Degree requirements:* For doctorate, comprehensive exam, thesis/dissertation. *Entrance requirements:* For doctorate, GRE General Test, GRE Subject Test, 2 letters of recommendation. Additional exam requirements/recommendations for international students: Required—TOEFL. *Application deadline:* For fall admission, 1/10 for domestic students. Applications are processed on a rolling basis. Application fee: $40. *Financial support:* In 2010–11, 2 fellowships with full tuition reimbursements (averaging $3,250 per year), 13 research assistantships with full and partial tuition reimbursements (averaging $4,553 per year), 1 teaching assistantship with partial tuition reimbursement (averaging $10,983 per year) were awarded; career-related internships or fieldwork and Federal Work-Study also available. Support available to part-time students. Financial award application deadline: 3/15; financial award applicants required to submit FAFSA. *Unit head:* Dr. John Quirk, Graduate Coordinator, 724-357-3785. *Application contact:* Dr. Edward Nardi, Interim Associate Dean, 724-357-2480, Fax: 724-357-5595, E-mail: ewnardi@iup.edu.

Inter American University of Puerto Rico, Metropolitan Campus, Graduate Programs, Program in Psychology, San Juan, PR 00919-1293. Offers counseling psychology (MA, PhD); industrial/organizational psychology (MA, PhD); labor relations (MA); school psychology (MA, PhD). *Degree requirements:* For master's, comprehensive exam. *Entrance requirements:* For master's, GRE or EXADEP, interview. Electronic applications accepted.

Inter American University of Puerto Rico, San Germán Campus, Graduate Studies Center, Program in Psychology, San Germán, PR 00683-5008. Offers counseling psychology (MA, PhD); school psychology (MA, PhD). Part-time and evening/weekend programs available. *Degree requirements:* For master's, comprehensive exam, thesis; for doctorate, comprehensive exam, thesis/dissertation. *Entrance requirements:* For master's, GRE General Test or EXADEP, minimum GPA of 3.0; for doctorate, GRE, EXADEP, or MAT, minimum GPA of 3.0. *Expenses:* Tuition: Part-time $202 per credit. Required fees: $258 per semester.

Iona College, School of Arts and Science, Department of Psychology, New Rochelle, NY 10801-1890. Offers experimental psychology (MA); industrial-organizational psychology (MA); mental health counseling (MA); psychology (MA); school psychology (MA). Part-time and evening/weekend programs available. *Faculty:* 10 full-time (7 women), 12 part-time/adjunct (7 women). *Students:* 86 full-time (70 women), 36 part-time (30 women); includes 21 minority (6 Black or African American, non-Hispanic/Latino; 1 American Indian or Alaska Native, non-Hispanic/Latino; 2 Asian, non-Hispanic/Latino; 12 Hispanic/Latino), 2 international. Average age 25. 153 applicants, 78% accepted, 50 enrolled. In 2010, 36 master's awarded. *Degree requirements:* For master's, thesis. *Entrance requirements:* For master's, GRE or minimum GPA of 3.0. Additional exam requirements/recommendations for international students: Required—TOEFL (minimum score 550 paper-based; 213 computer-based). *Application deadline:* Applications are processed on a rolling basis. Application fee: $50. Electronic applications accepted. *Expenses:* Tuition: Part-time $830 per credit. Required fees: $225 per credit. *Financial support:* Career-related internships or fieldwork, tuition waivers (partial), and unspecified assistantships available. Support available to part-time students. Financial award application deadline: 4/15; financial award applicants required to submit FAFSA. *Unit head:* Dr. Paul Greene, Chair, 914-633-2048, E-mail: pgreene@iona.edu. *Application contact:* Veronica Jarek-Prinz, Director of Graduate Admissions, 914-633-2420, Fax: 914-633-2277, E-mail: vjarekprinz@iona.edu.

James Madison University, The Graduate School, College of Integrated Science and Technology, Department of Graduate Psychology, Program in Combined-Integrated Clinical and School Psychology, Harrisonburg, VA 22807. Offers Psy D. Part-time and evening/weekend programs available. *Students:* 20 full-time (16 women); includes 2 minority (1 Black or African American, non-Hispanic/Latino; 1 Asian, non-Hispanic/Latino), 3 international. Average age 27. In 2010, 4 doctorates awarded. *Degree requirements:* For doctorate, thesis/dissertation, 12-month internship. *Entrance requirements:* For doctorate, GRE General Test, GRE Subject Test (advanced psychology), 3 letters of recommendation. Additional exam requirements/recommendations for international students: Required—TOEFL. *Application deadline:* For fall admission, 2/1 for domestic students. Applications are processed on a rolling basis. Application fee: $55. Electronic applications accepted. *Financial support:* In 2010–11, 17 students received support. 17 doctoral assistantships ($14,500) available. Financial award application deadline: 3/1; financial award applicants required to submit FAFSA. *Unit head:* Dr. Gregg R. Henriques, Program Director, 540-568-7857, E-mail: henrigg@jmu.edu. *Application contact:* Dr. Gregg R. Henriques, Program Director, 540-568-7857, E-mail: henrigg@jmu.edu.

James Madison University, The Graduate School, College of Integrated Science and Technology, Department of Graduate Psychology, Program in School Psychology, Harrisonburg, VA 22807. Offers school counseling (Ed S); school psychology (MA). *Accreditation:* APA (one or more programs are accredited); NCATE (one or more programs are accredited). Part-time and evening/weekend programs available. *Students:* 16 full-time (14 women), 10 part-time (8 women); includes 6 minority (3 Black or African American, non-Hispanic/Latino; 1 Asian, non-Hispanic/Latino; 1 Hispanic/Latino; 1 Two or more races, non-Hispanic/Latino). Average age 27. In 2010, 9 master's, 11 other advanced degrees awarded. *Degree requirements:* For master's, comprehensive exam; for Ed S, thesis, research project, 10-month internship. *Entrance requirements:* For master's, GRE General Test, interview, 3 letters of recommendation. Additional exam requirements/recommendations for international students: Required—TOEFL. *Application deadline:* For fall admission, 2/1 priority date for domestic students. Applications are processed on a rolling basis. Application fee: $55. Electronic applications accepted. *Financial support:* In 2010–11, 10 students received support, including 1 teaching assistantship with full tuition reimbursement available (averaging $8,664 per year); career-related internships or fieldwork, Federal Work-Study, and 9 graduate assistantships ($7382) also available. Financial award application deadline: 3/1; financial award applicants required to submit FAFSA. *Unit head:* Dr. Patricia J. Warner, Program Director, 540-568-3358, E-mail: warnerpj@jmu.edu. *Application contact:* Dr. Patricia J. Warner, Program Director, 540-568-3358, E-mail: warnerpj@jmu.edu.

The Johns Hopkins University, School of Education, Department of Counseling and Human Services, Baltimore, MD 21218. Offers clinical community counseling (Certificate); clinical supervision (Certificate); counseling (MS, CAGS), including clinical community counseling (MS), school counseling (MS); play therapy (Certificate). Part-time and evening/weekend programs available. *Faculty:* 4 full-time (2 women), 36 part-time/adjunct (20 women). *Students:* 93 full-time (78 women), 297 part-time (269 women); includes 141 minority (83 Black or African American, non-Hispanic/Latino; 17 Asian, non-Hispanic/Latino; 31 Hispanic/Latino; 10 Two or more races, non-Hispanic/Latino), 5 international. Average age 31. 186 applicants, 57% accepted, 72 enrolled. In 2010, 100 master's, 40 other advanced degrees awarded. *Degree requirements:* For master's, comprehensive exam. *Entrance requirements:* For master's, bachelor's degree, minimum undergraduate GPA of 3.0, 3 letters of recommendation, curriculum vitae/resume, group interview; for other advanced degree, master's degree, minimum undergraduate GPA of 3.0, 3 letters of recommendation, curriculum vitae/resume, interview. Additional exam requirements/recommendations for international students: Required—TOEFL (minimum score 600 paper-based; 250 computer-based; 100 iBT). *Application deadline:* For fall admission, 3/1 for domestic students, 5/1 for international students; for spring admission, 10/1 for domestic students, 10/15 for international students. Applications are processed on a rolling basis. Application fee: $80. Electronic applications accepted. *Financial support:*

Scholarships/grants available. Support available to part-time students. Financial award application deadline: 6/1; financial award applicants required to submit FAFSA. *Faculty research:* College access of low-income students and students-of-color; multicultural counseling training; domestic violence, resilience, and traumatic stress; application of behaviorally-based and ethical practices to criminal justice setting and systems. *Unit head:* Dr. Cheryl Holcomb-McCoy, Chair, 410-516-7928, Fax: 410-516-3939, E-mail: counseling@jhu.edu. *Application contact:* Jennifer Shaffer, Director of Admissions, 410-516-9797 Ext. 410, Fax: 410-516-9799, E-mail: educationinfo@jhu.edu.

Kean University, College of Humanities and Social Sciences, Program in School Psychology, Union, NJ 07083. Offers Diploma. Part-time and evening/weekend programs available. *Faculty:* 17 full-time (13 women). *Students:* 22 full-time (19 women), 6 part-time (all women); includes 1 Black or African American, non-Hispanic/Latino; 7 Hispanic/Latino, 1 international. Average age 24. 29 applicants, 62% accepted, 14 enrolled. In 2010, 9 Diplomas awarded. *Degree requirements:* For Diploma, comprehensive exam, practicum, externship. *Entrance requirements:* For degree, GRE General Test, minimum GPA of 3.0, interview, 3 letters of recommendation, prerequisites in psychology, official transcripts from all institutions attended. *Application deadline:* For fall admission, 3/15 for domestic students. Application fee: $75 ($150 for international students). Electronic applications accepted. *Expenses:* Tuition, state resident: full-time $10,872; part-time $500 per credit. Tuition, nonresident: full-time $14,736; part-time $614 per credit. Required fees: $2740.80; $125 per credit. Part-time tuition and fees vary according to course load and degree level. *Financial support:* In 2010–11, 6 research assistantships with full tuition reimbursements (averaging $3,263 per year) were awarded; unspecified assistantships also available. Financial award applicants required to submit FAFSA. *Unit head:* Dr. Frank Gardner, Program Coordinator, 908-737-5862, E-mail: fgardner@kean.edu. *Application contact:* Ann-Marie Kay, Assistant Director for Graduate Admissions, 908-737-5922, Fax: 908-737-5925, E-mail: akay@kean.edu.

Kean University, Nathan Weiss Graduate College, Program in School and Clinical Psychology, Union, NJ 07083. Offers Psy D. Evening/weekend programs available. *Faculty:* 3 full-time (1 woman). *Students:* 17 full-time (16 women); includes 1 Black or African American, non-Hispanic/Latino, 1 international. Average age 26. 20 applicants, 55% accepted, 8 enrolled. *Degree requirements:* For doctorate, comprehensive exam, thesis/dissertation, externship. *Entrance requirements:* For doctorate, GRE General Test (minimum score 500 verbal, 500 quantitative, 4.0 writing), GRE Subject Test in psychology taken within the last 5 years (minimum score 550), minimum undergraduate GPA of 3.3, graduate 3.5; 3 letters of recommendation (at least one from a professor); personal interview; prerequisite coursework in theories of personality, abnormal psychology, tests and measurements, statistics, and experimental psychology; personal statement; 3 letters of recommendation. *Application deadline:* For fall admission, 1/30 for domestic students. Application fee: $75 ($150 for international students). Electronic applications accepted. *Expenses:* Contact institution. *Financial support:* In 2010–11, 13 research assistantships with full tuition reimbursements (averaging $3,263 per year) were awarded; unspecified assistantships also available. Financial award applicants required to submit FAFSA. *Unit head:* Dr. Frank Gardner, Program Coordinator, 908-737-5862, E-mail: fgardner@kean.edu. *Application contact:* Reenat Hasan, Pre-Admissions Coordinator, 908-737-5923, Fax: 908-737-5925, E-mail: hasanr@kean.edu.

Keene State College, School of Professional and Graduate Studies, Keene, NH 03435. Offers curriculum and instruction (M Ed); education leadership (PMC); educational leadership (M Ed); school counselor (M Ed, PMC); special education (M Ed); teacher certification (Post-baccalaureate Certificate). *Accreditation:* NCATE. Part-time and evening/weekend programs available. *Faculty:* 11 full-time (7 women), 5 part-time/adjunct (3 women). *Students:* 25 full-time (19 women), 74 part-time (56 women); includes 1 Asian, non-Hispanic/Latino. Average age 32. 49 applicants, 71% accepted, 25 enrolled. In 2010, 43 master's, 17 other advanced degrees awarded. *Entrance requirements:* For master's, PRAXIS I, resume; minimum GPA of 2.5. Additional exam requirements/recommendations for international students: Required—TOEFL (minimum score 550 paper-based; 173 computer-based; 61 iBT). *Application deadline:* For fall admission, 4/1 for domestic students; for spring admission, 12/1 for domestic students. Applications are processed on a rolling basis. Application fee: $40. Electronic applications accepted. *Expenses:* Tuition, state resident: full-time $7650; part-time $352 per credit. Tuition, nonresident: full-time $15,820; part-time $380 per credit. Required fees: $2490; $218 per credit. Tuition and fees vary according to course load. *Financial support:* Research assistantships, career-related internships or fieldwork, Federal Work-Study, institutionally sponsored loans, and unspecified assistantships available. Support available to part-time students. Financial award application deadline: 3/1; financial award applicants required to submit FAFSA. *Unit head:* Dr. Melinda Treadwell, Dean, 603-358-2220. *Application contact:* Peggy Richmond, Director of Admissions, 603-358-2276, Fax: 603-358-2767, E-mail: admissions@keene.edu.

Kent State University, Graduate School of Education, Health, and Human Services, School of Lifespan Development and Educational Sciences, Program in School Psychology, Kent, OH 44242-0001. Offers M Ed, PhD, Ed S. *Accreditation:* APA; NCATE. *Faculty:* 4 full-time (1 woman), 2 part-time/adjunct (both women). *Students:* 53 full-time (46 women), 2 part-time (both women); includes 3 Black or African American, non-Hispanic/Latino; 2 Hispanic/Latino. 57 applicants, 26% accepted. In 2010, 17 master's, 4 doctorates, 19 other advanced degrees awarded. *Degree requirements:* For doctorate, comprehensive exam, thesis/dissertation. *Entrance requirements:* For master's and doctorate, GRE General Test; for Ed S, GRE General Test, MAT or minimum graduate GPA of 3.5. Additional exam requirements/recommendations for international students: Required—TOEFL. *Application deadline:* For fall admission, 6/15 for domestic students; for spring admission, 10/15 for domestic students. Application fee: $30 ($60 for international students). Electronic applications accepted. *Expenses:* Tuition, state resident: full-time $7866; part-time $437 per credit hour. Tuition, nonresident: full-time $14,022; part-time $779 per credit hour. *Financial support:* In 2010–11, fellowships with full tuition reimbursements (averaging $10,952 per year), 1 research assistantship with full tuition reimbursement (averaging $8,313 per year) were awarded; teaching assistantships with full tuition reimbursements, Federal Work-Study, scholarships/grants, unspecified assistantships, and 11 administrative assistantships (averaging $9,046 per year) also available. Financial award application deadline: 4/1; financial award applicants required to submit FAFSA. *Faculty research:* Special education policy and practice, treatment fidelity, school-based consultation. *Unit head:* Dr. Richard Cowan, Coordinator, 330-672-4450, E-mail: rcowan1@kent.edu. *Application contact:* Nancy Miller, Academic Program Coordinator, Office of Graduate Student Services, 330-672-2576, Fax: 330-672-9162, E-mail: ogs@kent.edu.

La Sierra University, School of Education, Department of School Psychology and Counseling, Riverside, CA 92515. Offers counseling (MA); educational psychology (Ed S); school psychology (Ed S). Part-time and evening/weekend programs available. *Degree requirements:* For master's, thesis optional; for Ed S, practicum (educational psychology). *Entrance requirements:* For master's, California Basic Educational Skills Test, NTE, minimum GPA of 3.0; for Ed S, minimum GPA of 3.3. *Faculty research:* Equivalent score scales, self perception.

Lehigh University, College of Education, Program in School Psychology, Bethlehem, PA 18015. Offers PhD, Ed S. *Accreditation:* APA (one or more programs are accredited). Part-time programs available. *Faculty:* 6 full-time (4 women). *Students:* 35 full-time (31 women), 12 part-time (8 women); includes 6 minority (3 Black or African American, non-Hispanic/Latino; 3 Asian, non-Hispanic/Latino). Average age 27. 86 applicants, 13% accepted, 7 enrolled. In 2010, 3 doctorates, 3 other advanced degrees awarded. *Degree requirements:* For doctorate, comprehensive exam, thesis/dissertation, internship, research qualifying exam; for Ed S, comprehensive exam, internship. *Entrance requirements:* For doctorate, GRE General Test, minimum GPA of 3.0, 2 letters of recommendation (at least one academic); for Ed S, GRE General Test, minimum GPA of 3.0. Additional exam requirements/recommendations for international students: Required—TOEFL (minimum score 600 paper-based; 250 computer-based; 93 iBT). *Application deadline:* For fall admission, 1/1 for domestic and international students. Application fee: $65. Electronic applications accepted. *Financial support:* In 2010–11, 23 students received support, including 19 research assistantships (averaging $16,000 per year); fellowships, career-related internships or fieldwork, Federal Work-Study, institutionally sponsored loans, tuition waivers (full and partial), and unspecified assistantships also available. Financial award application deadline: 1/31. *Faculty research:* Applied behavior analysis, developmental disabilities, at-risk students, learning and behavior problems, pediatric psychology. *Unit head:* Dr. Patricia R. Manz, Coordinator, 610-758-5656, Fax: 610-758-6223, E-mail: phm3@lehigh.edu. *Application contact:* Sharon Y. Warden, Coordinator, 610-758-3256, Fax: 610-758-6223, E-mail: sy00@lehigh.edu.

Lenoir-Rhyne University, Graduate Programs, School of Counseling and Human Services, Program in School Counseling, Hickory, NC 28601. Offers MA. Part-time and evening/weekend programs available. *Degree requirements:* For master's, comprehensive exam, thesis optional. *Entrance requirements:* For master's, GRE General Test, minimum undergraduate GPA of 2.7, graduate 3.0; writing sample. Additional exam requirements/recommendations for international students: Required—TOEFL (minimum score 600 paper-based). Electronic applications accepted.

Lesley University, Graduate School of Arts and Social Sciences, Program in Counseling Psychology, Cambridge, MA 02138-2790. Offers professional counseling (MA); school counseling (MA). Part-time and evening/weekend programs available. Postbaccalaureate distance learning degree programs offered (no on-campus study). Terminal master's awarded for partial completion of doctoral program. *Degree requirements:* For master's, internship, practicum. *Entrance requirements:* For master's, MAT. Additional exam requirements/recommendations for international students: Required—TOEFL (minimum score 550 paper-based; 213 computer-based; 80 iBT).

Lewis & Clark College, Graduate School of Education and Counseling, Department of Counseling Psychology, Program in School Psychology, Portland, OR 97219-7899. Offers Ed S. Part-time and evening/weekend programs available. *Faculty:* 2 full-time (1 woman), 7 part-time/adjunct (4 women). *Students:* 16 full-time (15 women), 33 part-time (28 women); includes 1 Black or African American, non-Hispanic/Latino; 1 Hispanic/Latino; 3 Two or more races, non-Hispanic/Latino. Average age 30. 44 applicants, 70% accepted, 17 enrolled. *Entrance requirements:* Additional exam requirements/recommendations for international students: Required—TOEFL (minimum score 575 paper-based; 233 computer-based). *Application deadline:* For fall admission, 2/1 for domestic and international students. Application fee: $50. Electronic applications accepted. *Expenses:* Tuition: Part-time $713 per semester hour. Tuition and fees vary according to course level and campus/location. *Financial support:* In 2010–11, 9 students received support. Career-related internships or fieldwork, Federal Work-Study, institutionally sponsored loans, scholarships/grants, health care benefits, and tuition waivers (partial) available. Support available to part-time students. Financial award application deadline: 3/1; financial award applicants required to submit FAFSA. *Unit head:* Dr. Peter Mortola, Program Coordinator, 503-768-6060, Fax: 503-768-6065, E-mail: cpsy@lclark.edu. *Application contact:* Becky Haas, Director of Admissions, 503-768-6200, Fax: 503-768-6205, E-mail: gseadmit@lclark.edu.

Lewis & Clark College, Graduate School of Education and Counseling, Department of Educational Leadership, Program in School Counseling, Portland, OR 97219-7899. Offers M Ed. Part-time and evening/weekend programs available. *Faculty:* 1 (woman) full-time, 10 part-time/adjunct (7 women). *Students:* 72 full-time (53 women), 9 part-time (5 women); includes 3 Black or African American, non-Hispanic/Latino; 2 American Indian or Alaska Native, non-Hispanic/Latino; 5 Asian, non-Hispanic/Latino; 8 Hispanic/Latino; 1 Two or more races, non-Hispanic/Latino, 1 international. Average age 31. 73 applicants, 71% accepted, 43 enrolled. In 2010, 26 master's awarded. *Entrance requirements:* For master's, minimum undergraduate GPA of 2.75. Additional exam requirements/recommendations for international students: Required—TOEFL (minimum score 575 paper-based; 233 computer-based). *Application deadline:* For fall admission, 2/1 for domestic and international students. Application fee: $50. Electronic applications accepted. *Expenses:* Tuition: Part-time $713 per semester hour. Tuition and fees vary according to course level and campus/location. *Financial support:* In 2010–11, 9 students received support. Career-related internships or fieldwork, Federal Work-Study, institutionally sponsored loans, scholarships/grants, health care benefits, and tuition waivers (partial) available. Support available to part-time students. Financial award application deadline: 3/1; financial award applicants required to submit FAFSA. *Unit head:* Dr. Danielle Torres, Coordinator, 503-768-6140, Fax: 503-768-6085, E-mail: schcoun@lclark.edu. *Application contact:* Becky Haas, Director of Admissions, 503-768-6200, Fax: 503-768-6205, E-mail: gseadmit@lclark.edu.

Lindenwood University, Graduate Programs, School of Education, St. Charles, MO 63301-1695. Offers education (MA); educational administration (MA, Ed D, Ed S); instructional leadership (Ed D, Ed S); library media (MA); professional and school counseling (MA); professional counseling (MA); school administration (Ed S); school counseling (MA); teaching (MA). Part-time and evening/weekend programs available. *Faculty:* 33 full-time (13 women), 176 part-time/adjunct (83 women). *Students:* 543 full-time (389 women), 1,827 part-time (1,426 women); includes 510 minority (478 Black or African American, non-Hispanic/Latino; 3 American Indian or Alaska Native, non-Hispanic/Latino; 14 Asian, non-Hispanic/Latino; 14 Hispanic/Latino; 1 Two or more races, non-Hispanic/Latino), 20 international. Average age 35. 248 applicants, 120 enrolled. In 2010, 730 master's, 62 doctorates, 67 other advanced degrees awarded. *Degree requirements:* For master's, thesis (for some programs); for doctorate, thesis/dissertation, minimum GPA of 3.0; for Ed S, comprehensive exam, project, minimum GPA of 3.0. *Entrance requirements:* For master's, interview, minimum GPA of 3.0, writing sample, letter of recommendation; for doctorate, GRE, minimum graduate GPA of 3.4, resume, interview, writing sample, 4 letters of recommendation; for Ed S, master's degree in education, relevant work experience. Additional exam requirements/recommendations for international students: Required—TOEFL (minimum score 550 paper-based; 213 computer-based; 80 iBT). *Application deadline:* For fall admission, 8/27 priority date for domestic and international students; for spring admission, 1/28 priority date for domestic and international students. Applications are processed on a rolling basis. Application fee: $30 ($100 for international students). Electronic applications accepted. *Expenses:* Tuition: Full-time $13,260; part-time $380 per credit hour. Required fees: $340. One-time fee: $30. Tuition and fees vary according to course level and course load. *Financial support:* In 2010–11, 177 students received support. Career-related internships or fieldwork, institutionally sponsored loans, tuition waivers (partial), and unspecified assistantships available. Financial award application deadline: 6/30; financial award applicants required to submit FAFSA. *Unit head:* Dr. Cynthia Bice, Dean, 636-949-4618, Fax: 636-949-4197, E-mail: cbice@lindenwood.edu. *Application contact:* Brett Barger, Dean of Evening Admissions and Extension Campuses, 636-949-4934, Fax: 636-949-4109, E-mail: adultadmissions@lindenwood.edu.

Long Island University, Brooklyn Campus, School of Education, Department of Human Development and Leadership, Program in School Psychology, Brooklyn, NY 11201-8423. Offers MS Ed. Part-time and evening/weekend programs available. *Degree requirements:* For master's, thesis optional. *Entrance requirements:* For master's, 2 letters of recommendation. Additional exam requirements/recommendations for international students: Required—TOEFL (minimum score 500 paper-based; 173 computer-based). Electronic applications accepted.

Long Island University, Westchester Graduate Campus, Programs in Education-School Counselor and School Psychology, Purchase, NY 10577. Offers school counselor (MS Ed); school psychologist (MS Ed). Part-time and evening/weekend programs available.

Louisiana State University and Agricultural and Mechanical College, Graduate School, College of Humanities and Social Sciences, Department of Psychology, Baton Rouge, LA 70803. Offers biological psychology (MA, PhD); clinical psychology (MA, PhD); cognitive psychology (MA, PhD); developmental psychology (MA, PhD); industrial/organizational psychology (MA, PhD); school psychology (MA, PhD). PhD programs offered jointly with Southeastern Louisiana University. *Accreditation:* APA (one or more programs are accredited). *Faculty:* 26 full-time (10 women). *Students:* 96 full-time (68 women), 24 part-time (19 women); includes 7 Black or African American, non-Hispanic/Latino; 2 American Indian or Alaska

School Psychology

Louisiana State University and Agricultural and Mechanical College (continued)

Native, non-Hispanic/Latino; 1 Asian, non-Hispanic/Latino; 5 Hispanic/Latino, 2 international. Average age 27. 289 applicants, 11% accepted, 17 enrolled. In 2010, 16 master's, 11 doctorates awarded. Terminal master's awarded for partial completion of doctoral program. *Degree requirements:* For master's, thesis; for doctorate, thesis/dissertation, 1 year internship. *Entrance requirements:* For master's and doctorate, GRE General Test, minimum GPA of 3.0. Additional exam requirements/recommendations for international students: Required—TOEFL (minimum score 550 paper-based; 213 computer-based; 79 iBT) or IELTS (minimum score 6.5). *Application deadline:* For fall admission, 1/15 for domestic and international students. Applications are processed on a rolling basis. Application fee: $50 ($70 for international students). Electronic applications accepted. *Financial support:* In 2010–11, 115 students received support, including 5 fellowships (averaging $25,207 per year), 25 research assistantships with partial tuition reimbursements available (averaging $18,083 per year), 48 teaching assistantships with partial tuition reimbursements available (averaging $13,043 per year); career-related internships or fieldwork, Federal Work-Study, institutionally sponsored loans, scholarships/grants, health care benefits, and tuition waivers (full and partial) also available. Financial award applicants required to submit FAFSA. *Faculty research:* Clinical psychology, autism, anxiety, addition, neuropsychology, school psychology, cognitive psychology, experimental psychology. Total annual research expenditures: $1.3 million. *Unit head:* Dr. Robert Matthews, Chair, 225-578-8745, Fax: 225-578-4125, E-mail: psmath@lsu.edu. *Application contact:* Dr. Jason Hicks, Coordinator of Graduate Studies, 225-578-4109, Fax: 225-578-4125, E-mail: jhicks@lsu.edu.

Louisiana State University in Shreveport, College of Education and Human Development, Program in School Psychology, Shreveport, LA 71115-2399. Offers SSP. *Students:* 16 full-time (13 women), 4 part-time (3 women); includes 3 minority (2 Black or African American, non-Hispanic/Latino; 1 Hispanic/Latino), 1 international. Average age 30. 15 applicants, 93% accepted, 8 enrolled. In 2010, 8 SSPs awarded. *Entrance requirements:* For degree, GRE General Test, minimum GPA of 2.75. Additional exam requirements/recommendations for international students: Required—TOEFL (minimum score 500 paper-based; 173 computer-based; 61 iBT). *Application deadline:* For fall admission, 6/30 for domestic and international students; for spring admission, 11/30 for domestic and international students. Applications are processed on a rolling basis. Application fee: $10 ($20 for international students). *Expenses:* Tuition, state resident: full-time $3272; part-time $181.80 per credit hour. Tuition, nonresident: full-time $7902; part-time $471.19 per credit hour. Required fees: $850; $47 per credit hour. *Financial support:* In 2010–11, 2 research assistantships with partial tuition reimbursements (averaging $10,000 per year) were awarded. Financial award applicants required to submit FAFSA. *Unit head:* Dr. Kevin Jones, Program Director, 318-797-5050, Fax: 318-798-4171, E-mail: ssp@lsus.edu. *Application contact:* Yvonne Yarbrough, Secretary, Graduate Studies, 318-797-5247, Fax: 318-798-4120, E-mail: yyarbrou@lsus.edu.

Loyola Marymount University, School of Education, Department of Educational Support Services, Program in School Psychology, Los Angeles, CA 90045. Offers MA. Part-time and evening/weekend programs available. *Faculty:* 11 full-time (6 women), 26 part-time/adjunct (19 women). *Students:* 48 full-time (44 women); includes 2 Black or African American, non-Hispanic/Latino; 5 Asian, non-Hispanic/Latino; 11 Hispanic/Latino; 3 Two or more races, non-Hispanic/Latino. Average age 25. 52 applicants, 60% accepted, 18 enrolled. In 2010, 17 master's awarded. *Degree requirements:* For master's, comprehensive exam. *Entrance requirements:* For master's, GRE, CBEST, 3 letters of recommendation, letter of intent. Additional exam requirements/recommendations for international students: Required—TOEFL (minimum score 600 paper-based; 250 computer-based; 100 iBT). *Application deadline:* For fall admission, 2/8 for domestic students. Application fee: $50. Electronic applications accepted. *Financial support:* In 2010–11, 42 students received support, including 7 research assistantships (averaging $1,320 per year); scholarships/grants and unspecified assistantships also available. Support available to part-time students. Financial award application deadline: 2/5; financial award applicants required to submit FAFSA. Total annual research expenditures: $75,545. *Unit head:* Dr. Brian Leung, Chair/Director, 310-338-1707, E-mail: bleung@lmu.edu. *Application contact:* Chake H. Kouyoumjian, Director, Graduate Admissions, 310-338-2721, Fax: 310-338-6086, E-mail: ckouyoum@lmu.edu.

Loyola University Chicago, School of Education, Program in School Psychology, Chicago, IL 60660. Offers PhD, Ed S. PhD offered through the Graduate School. Part-time and evening/weekend programs available. *Faculty:* 7 full-time (5 women), 6 part-time/adjunct (3 women). *Students:* 71. Average age 28. 52 applicants, 52% accepted, 27 enrolled. In 2010, 8 doctorates, 12 other advanced degrees awarded. Terminal master's awarded for partial completion of doctoral program. *Degree requirements:* For doctorate, comprehensive exam, thesis/dissertation. *Entrance requirements:* For doctorate, GRE, interview, letters of recommendation, minimum GPA of 3.0. Additional exam requirements/recommendations for international students: Required—TOEFL (minimum score 550 paper-based; 213 computer-based; 79 iBT). *Application deadline:* For fall admission, 12/1 for domestic and international students. Application fee: $50. Electronic applications accepted. *Expenses:* Tuition: Full-time $14,940; part-time $830 per credit hour. Required fees: $87 per semester. Part-time tuition and fees vary according to course load and program. *Financial support:* In 2010–11, 2 fellowships (averaging $14,000 per year), 9 research assistantships with full tuition reimbursements (averaging $11,000 per year) were awarded; institutionally sponsored loans, scholarships/grants, and tuition waivers (full and partial) also available. Financial award application deadline: 2/15. *Faculty research:* Learning theory and teaching, school reform, instructional intervention, violence prevention, mental health programming in schools and communities. *Unit head:* Dr. Pamela Fenning, Director, 312-915-6803, E-mail: pfennin@luc.edu. *Application contact:* Marie Rosin-Dittmar, Information Contact, 312-915-6800, E-mail: schleduc@luc.edu.

Lynchburg College, Graduate Studies, School of Education and Human Development, M Ed Program in School Counseling, Lynchburg, VA 24501-3199. Offers M Ed. Part-time and evening/weekend programs available. *Faculty:* 6 full-time (4 women). *Students:* 10 full-time (5 women), 8 part-time (7 women); includes 3 minority (all Black or African American, non-Hispanic/Latino). Average age 28. 21 applicants, 33% accepted. In 2010, 9 master's awarded. *Degree requirements:* For master's, comprehensive exam, completion of counseling internship. *Entrance requirements:* For master's, GRE, official transcripts, personal essay, 3 letters of recommendation. Additional exam requirements/recommendations for international students: Required—TOEFL (minimum score 530 paper-based; 197 computer-based; 71 iBT), IELTS (minimum score 6.5). *Application deadline:* For fall admission, 7/31 for domestic students, 6/1 for international students; for spring admission, 11/30 for domestic students, 10/15 for international students. Applications are processed on a rolling basis. Application fee: $30. Electronic applications accepted. *Expenses:* Tuition: Full-time $7200; part-time $400 per credit hour. Required fees: $20; $5.10 per credit hour. $15 per term. Tuition and fees vary according to degree level and program. *Financial support:* Fellowships, research assistantships, Federal Work-Study, scholarships/grants, health care benefits, and unspecified assistantships available. Support available to part-time students. Financial award application deadline: 7/31; financial award applicants required to submit FAFSA. *Unit head:* Dr. Jeanne Booth, Associate Professor and Coordinator, School Counseling Program, 434-544-8551, E-mail: booth@lynchburg.edu. *Application contact:* Dr. Jeanne Booth, Associate Professor and Coordinator, School Counseling Program, 434-544-8551, E-mail: booth@lynchburg.edu.

Marist College, Graduate Programs, School of Social and Behavioral Sciences, Poughkeepsie, NY 12601-1387. Offers education (M Ed, MA); mental health counseling (MA); school psychology (MA, Adv C). Part-time and evening/weekend programs available. *Degree requirements:* For master's, thesis optional. *Entrance requirements:* For master's, GRE General Test, letters of recommendation, minimum undergraduate GPA of 3.0, interview. Additional exam requirements/recommendations for international students: Required—TOEFL (minimum score 550 paper-based; 213 computer-based; 80 iBT); Recommended—IELTS (minimum score 6.5). Electronic applications accepted. *Faculty research:* AIDS prevention, educational intervention, humanistic counseling research, aging and development, neuroimaging.

Marshall University, Academic Affairs Division, Graduate School of Education and Professional Development, Program in School Psychology, Huntington, WV 25755. Offers Ed S. *Accreditation:* NCATE. Part-time and evening/weekend programs available. *Students:* 34 full-time (28 women), 12 part-time (9 women); includes 1 Black or African American, non-Hispanic/Latino; 1 Asian, non-Hispanic/Latino. Average age 28. In 2010, 15 Ed Ss awarded. *Entrance requirements:* For degree, master's degree in psychology. Application fee: $40. *Financial support:* Career-related internships or fieldwork and tuition waivers (full) available. Support available to part-time students. Financial award applicants required to submit FAFSA. *Unit head:* Dr. Fred Kreig, Program Director, 304-746-2067, E-mail: fkreig@marshall.edu. *Application contact:* Information Contact, 304-746-1900, Fax: 304-746-1902, E-mail: services@marshall.edu.

Marywood University, Academic Affairs, Reap College of Education and Human Development, Department of Psychology and Counseling, Program in School Psychology, Scranton, PA 18509-1598. Offers Ed S. *Entrance requirements:* Additional exam requirements/recommendations for international students: Required—TOEFL (minimum score 550 paper-based; 213 computer-based; 79 iBT). Electronic applications accepted. *Expenses:* Tuition: Part-time $735 per credit. Required fees: $470 per semester. Tuition and fees vary according to degree level and campus/location.

Massachusetts School of Professional Psychology, Graduate Programs, Boston, MA 02132. Offers applied psychology in higher education student personnel administration (MA); clinical psychology (Psy D); counseling psychology (MA); counseling psychology and community mental health (MA); counseling psychology and global mental health (MA); executive coaching (Graduate Certificate); forensic and counseling psychology (MA); leadership psychology (Psy D); organizational psychology (MA); primary care psychology (MA); respecialization in clinical psychology (Certificate); school psychology (Psy D); MA/CAGS. *Accreditation:* APA. *Faculty:* 24 full-time (11 women), 13 part-time/adjunct (9 women). *Students:* 515. Average age 28. *Degree requirements:* For master's, comprehensive exam (for some programs); for doctorate, thesis/dissertation (for some programs). Application fee: $50. Electronic applications accepted. *Expenses:* Tuition: Full-time $32,352; part-time $1011 per credit. Full-time tuition and fees vary according to degree level. *Financial support:* Teaching assistantships, career-related internships or fieldwork available. Financial award applicants required to submit FAFSA. *Unit head:* Dr. Nicholas A. Covino, President, 617-327-6777, Fax: 617-327-4447. *Application contact:* Admissions and Marketing, 617-327-6777 Ext. 210, Fax: 617-327-4447, E-mail: admissions@mspp.edu.

McGill University, Faculty of Graduate and Postdoctoral Studies, Faculty of Education, Department of Educational and Counseling Psychology, Montréal, QC H3A 2T5, Canada. Offers counseling psychology (MA, PhD); educational psychology (M Ed, MA, PhD); school/applied child psychology and applied developmental psychology (M Ed, MA, PhD, Diploma), including school psychology. *Accreditation:* APA.

McNeese State University, Doré School of Graduate Studies, Burton College of Education, Department of Teacher Education, Program in School Counseling, Lake Charles, LA 70609. Offers grades K-12 (Postbaccalaureate Certificate); school counseling (M Ed). *Accreditation:* NCATE. Evening/weekend programs available. *Faculty:* 1 (woman) full-time, 1 (woman) part-time/adjunct. *Students:* 9 full-time (7 women), 22 part-time (19 women); includes 7 minority (all Black or African American, non-Hispanic/Latino). In 2010, 8 master's awarded. *Entrance requirements:* For master's, GRE, 18 hours in professional education. *Application deadline:* For fall admission, 5/15 priority date for domestic and international students; for spring admission, 10/15 priority date for domestic and international students. Applications are processed on a rolling basis. Application fee: $20 ($30 for international students). Tuition and fees vary according to course load. *Financial support:* Application deadline: 5/1. *Unit head:* Dr. Royce Zant, Head, 337-475-5404, Fax: 337-475-5398, E-mail: rzant@mcneese.edu. *Application contact:* Dr. George F. Mead, Interim Dean of Dore' School of Graduate Studies, 337-475-5396, Fax: 337-475-5397, E-mail: admissions@mcneese.edu.

Mercy College, School of Social and Behavioral Sciences, Program in School Psychology, Dobbs Ferry, NY 10522-1189. Offers MS. Part-time and evening/weekend programs available. *Students:* 39 full-time (34 women), 17 part-time (16 women); includes 12 Black or African American, non-Hispanic/Latino; 1 Asian, non-Hispanic/Latino; 21 Hispanic/Latino, 2 international. Average age 29. 74 applicants, 47% accepted, 24 enrolled. In 2010, 6 master's awarded. *Degree requirements:* For master's, practica, fieldwork, internship, integrative project. *Entrance requirements:* For master's, current resume; interview; written recommendation from 3 instructors; bachelor's degree with a major in psychology, sociology, behavioral science, or education. Additional exam requirements/recommendations for international students: Required—TOEFL (minimum score 600 paper-based; 250 computer-based; 100 iBT), IELTS (minimum score 8). *Application deadline:* For fall admission, 8/1 for international students. Applications are processed on a rolling basis. Application fee: $40. Electronic applications accepted. *Expenses:* Tuition: Full-time $13,572; part-time $754 per credit hour. Required fees: $130 per term. *Financial support:* Career-related internships or fieldwork, Federal Work-Study, scholarships/grants, and unspecified assistantships available. Support available to part-time students. Financial award applicants required to submit FAFSA. *Faculty research:* Consultation, effective intervention and prevention practices, psychology. *Unit head:* Dr. Jeffrey Cohen, Program Director, 914-674-7503, E-mail: jcohen@mercy.edu. *Application contact:* Allison Gurdineer, Senior Associate Director of Recruitment, 914-674-7601, E-mail: agurdineer@mercy.edu.

Miami University, Graduate School, School of Education and Allied Professions, Department of Educational Psychology, Oxford, OH 45056. Offers educational psychology (M Ed); instructional design and technology (M Ed, MA); school psychology (MS, Ed S); special education (M Ed). *Accreditation:* NCATE. *Students:* 40 full-time (36 women), 49 part-time (40 women); includes 6 minority (2 Black or African American, non-Hispanic/Latino; 2 Asian, non-Hispanic/Latino; 2 Two or more races, non-Hispanic/Latino), 20 international. Average age 28. In 2010, 36 master's awarded. *Entrance requirements:* For master's, GRE General Test or MAT, minimum undergraduate GPA of 3.0 during previous 2 years or 2.75 overall; for Ed S, GRE General Test or MAT. Additional exam requirements/recommendations for international students: Required—TOEFL. Application fee: $50. *Expenses:* Tuition, state resident: full-time $11,616; part-time $484 per credit hour. Tuition, nonresident: full-time $25,656; part-time $1069 per credit hour. Required fees: $528. *Financial support:* Fellowships with full tuition reimbursements, research assistantships with full tuition reimbursements, teaching assistantships with full tuition reimbursements, career-related internships or fieldwork, Federal Work-Study, health care benefits, tuition waivers (full), and unspecified assistantships available. Financial award application deadline: 3/1. *Unit head:* Dr. Nelda Cambron-McCabe, Chair, 513-529-6836, Fax: 513-529-6621, E-mail: cambron@muohio.edu. *Application contact:* Jennifer Turner, Administrative Assistant, 513-529-6621, Fax: 513-529-3646, E-mail: hillje@muohio.edu.

Michigan State University, The Graduate School, College of Education, Department of Counseling, Educational Psychology and Special Education, East Lansing, MI 48824. Offers counseling (MA); educational psychology and educational technology (PhD); educational technology (MA); measurement and quantitative methods (PhD); rehabilitation counseling (MA); rehabilitation counselor education (PhD); school psychology (MA, PhD, Ed S); special education (MA, PhD). *Accreditation:* APA (one or more programs are accredited); CORE (one or more programs are accredited). Part-time programs available. *Entrance requirements:* Additional exam requirements/recommendations for international students: Required—TOEFL. Electronic applications accepted.

Middle Tennessee State University, College of Graduate Studies, College of Behavioral and Health Sciences, Department of Psychology, Murfreesboro, TN 37132. Offers clinical psychology (MA); experimental psychology (MA); industrial/organizational psychology (MA); psychology (MA); quantitative psychology (MA); school psychology (MA, Ed S). Part-time and evening/weekend programs available. Postbaccalaureate distance learning degree programs offered. *Faculty:* 36 full-time (16 women), 2 part-time/adjunct (0 women). *Students:* 32 full-time (27 women), 84 part-time (58 women); includes 11 Black or African American, non-Hispanic/Latino; 6 Asian, non-Hispanic/Latino; 2 Hispanic/Latino. Average age 26. 251 applicants, 55%

accepted. In 2010, 52 master's, 10 other advanced degrees awarded. *Degree requirements:* For master's, variable foreign language requirement, comprehensive exam, thesis (for some programs). *Entrance requirements:* Additional exam requirements/recommendations for international students: Required—TOEFL (minimum score 525 paper-based; 195 computer-based; 71 iBT) or IELTS (minimum score 6). *Application deadline:* For fall admission, 6/1 for domestic and international students. Applications are processed on a rolling basis. Application fee: $25 ($30 for international students). Electronic applications accepted. *Expenses:* Tuition, state resident: full-time $4632. Tuition, nonresident: full-time $11,520. *Financial support:* In 2010–11, 16 students received support. Career-related internships or fieldwork and institutionally sponsored loans available. Support available to part-time students. Financial award application deadline: 5/1; financial award applicants required to submit FAFSA. *Faculty research:* Industrial/organizational, social/personality/sports, counseling/clinical/school, cognitive/language/learning/perception, developmental/aging. *Unit head:* Dr. Dennis Papini, Chair, 615-898-2706, Fax: 615-898-5027, E-mail: dpapini@mtsu.edu. *Application contact:* Dr. Michael Allen, Dean and Vice Provost for Research, 615-898-2840, Fax: 615-904-8020, E-mail: mallen@mtsu.edu.

Middle Tennessee State University, College of Graduate Studies, College of Education, Department of Educational Leadership, Program in Professional Counseling, Murfreesboro, TN 37132. Offers curriculum and instruction (Ed S), including school psychology; mental health counseling (M Ed); school counseling (M Ed). *Accreditation:* ACA; NCATE. Part-time and evening/weekend programs available. Postbaccalaureate distance learning degree programs offered. *Students:* 7 part-time (6 women). 35 applicants, 69% accepted. In 2010, 15 master's awarded. *Degree requirements:* For master's, comprehensive exam. *Entrance requirements:* For master's, GRE or MAT. Additional exam requirements/recommendations for international students: Required—TOEFL (minimum score 525 paper-based; 195 computer-based; 71 iBT) or IELTS (minimum score 6). *Application deadline:* For fall admission, 6/1 for domestic and international students. Applications are processed on a rolling basis. Application fee: $25 ($30 for international students). Electronic applications accepted. *Expenses:* Tuition, state resident: full-time $4632. Tuition, nonresident: full-time $11,520. *Financial support:* Application deadline: 5/1. *Application contact:* Dr. Michael Allen, Dean and Vice Provost for Research, 615-898-2840, Fax: 615-904-8020, E-mail: mallen@mtsu.edu.

Millersville University of Pennsylvania, College of Graduate and Professional Studies, School of Education, Department of Psychology, Program in Psychology, Millersville, PA 17551-0302. Offers clinical psychology (MS); school psychology (MS). Part-time programs available. *Faculty:* 19 full-time (13 women), 8 part-time/adjunct (5 women). *Students:* 53 full-time (45 women), 41 part-time (34 women); includes 3 Black or African American, non-Hispanic/Latino; 1 Hispanic/Latino, 3 international. Average age 28. 65 applicants, 78% accepted, 30 enrolled. In 2010, 23 master's awarded. *Degree requirements:* For master's, comprehensive exam, thesis optional. *Entrance requirements:* For master's, GRE, 3 letters of recommendation; interview (in-person). Additional exam requirements/recommendations for international students: Required—TOEFL (minimum score 500 paper-based; 183 computer-based; 65 iBT) or IELTS (minimum score 6). *Application deadline:* For fall admission, 1/15 for domestic and international students; for winter admission, 10/1 for domestic and international students; for spring admission, 10/1 for domestic and international students. Application fee: $40 ($50 for international students). Electronic applications accepted. *Expenses:* Tuition, state resident: full-time $6966; part-time $387 per credit. Tuition, nonresident: full-time $11,146; part-time $619 per credit. Required fees: $1829.50; $88 per credit. One-time fee: $60 part-time. Tuition and fees vary according to course load. *Financial support:* In 2010–11, 35 students received support, including 35 research assistantships with full and partial tuition reimbursements available (averaging $4,997 per year); institutionally sponsored loans and unspecified assistantships also available. Support available to part-time students. Financial award application deadline: 3/15; financial award applicants required to submit FAFSA. *Faculty research:* Parenting and alcohol risk, time perceptions, time management, stress and coping, autism and behavioral disorders. *Unit head:* Dr. Claudia Haferkamp, Director of Clinical Psychology Program, 717-872-3826, Fax: 717-871-2480, E-mail: claudia.haferkamp@millersville.edu. *Application contact:* Dr. Victor S. DeSantis, Dean of Graduate and Professional Studies, 717-872-3099, Fax: 717-872-3453, E-mail: victor.desantis@millersville.edu.

Millersville University of Pennsylvania, College of Graduate and Professional Studies, School of Education, Department of Psychology, Program in School Counseling, Millersville, PA 17551-0302. Offers M Ed. *Accreditation:* NCATE. Part-time programs available. *Faculty:* 19 full-time (13 women), 8 part-time/adjunct (5 women). *Students:* 11 full-time (9 women), 27 part-time (19 women); includes 1 Asian, non-Hispanic/Latino; 1 Hispanic/Latino. Average age 30. 24 applicants, 46% accepted, 7 enrolled. In 2010, 14 master's awarded. *Degree requirements:* For master's, comprehensive exam, thesis optional. *Entrance requirements:* For master's, GRE, 3 letters of recommendation, interview (in-person). Additional exam requirements/recommendations for international students: Required—TOEFL (minimum score 500 paper-based; 183 computer-based; 65 iBT) or IELTS (minimum score 6). *Application deadline:* For fall admission, 1/15 for domestic and international students; for winter admission, 10/1 for domestic and international students; for spring admission, 10/1 for domestic and international students. Application fee: $40 ($50 for international students). Electronic applications accepted. *Expenses:* Tuition, state resident: full-time $6966; part-time $387 per credit. Tuition, nonresident: full-time $11,146; part-time $619 per credit. Required fees: $1829.50; $88 per credit. One-time fee: $60 part-time. Tuition and fees vary according to course load. *Financial support:* In 2010–11, 9 students received support, including 9 research assistantships with full and partial tuition reimbursements available (averaging $5,167 per year); institutionally sponsored loans and unspecified assistantships also available. Support available to part-time students. Financial award application deadline: 3/15; financial award applicants required to submit FAFSA. *Faculty research:* Solution-focused counseling, sustainability, technology in counseling. *Unit head:* Dr. Nadine E. Garner, Coordinator, 717-872-3097, Fax: 717-871-2480, E-mail: nadine.garner@millersville.edu. *Application contact:* Dr. Victor S. DeSantis, Dean of Graduate and Professional Studies, 717-872-3099, Fax: 717-872-3453, E-mail: victor.desantis@millersville.edu.

Minnesota State University Mankato, College of Graduate Studies, College of Social and Behavioral Sciences, Department of Psychology, Mankato, MN 56001. Offers clinical psychology (MA); industrial/organizational psychology (MA); school psychology (Psy D). Part-time programs available. *Students:* 57 full-time (38 women), 1 part-time (0 women). *Degree requirements:* For master's, one foreign language, comprehensive exam, thesis (for some programs). *Entrance requirements:* For master's, GRE General Test, GRE Subject Test (clinical psychology), minimum GPA of 3.0 during previous 2 years, 3 letters of reference. Additional exam requirements/recommendations for international students: Required—TOEFL. *Application deadline:* For fall admission, 1/1 priority date for domestic students. Applications are processed on a rolling basis. Application fee: $40. Electronic applications accepted. *Financial support:* Research assistantships, teaching assistantships with full tuition reimbursements, career-related internships or fieldwork, Federal Work-Study, institutionally sponsored loans, and unspecified assistantships available. Support available to part-time students. Financial award application deadline: 3/15; financial award applicants required to submit FAFSA. *Faculty research:* Professional competency in hospitals, mood disturbance, 360-degree feedback, employee selection, planning fallacy. *Unit head:* Dr. Barry Ries, Chairperson, 507-389-2724. *Application contact:* 507-389-2321, E-mail: grad@mnsu.edu.

Minnesota State University Moorhead, Graduate Studies, College of Social and Natural Sciences, Program in School Psychology, Moorhead, MN 56563-0002. Offers MS, Psy S. *Accreditation:* NCATE (one or more programs are accredited). *Degree requirements:* For master's, thesis, final oral and written comprehensive exams. *Entrance requirements:* For master's, GRE General Test, interview, minimum GPA of 3.0, 3 letters of recommendation; for Psy S, MS in school psychology. Additional exam requirements/recommendations for international students: Required—TOEFL (minimum score 550 paper-based; 213 computer-based). Electronic applications accepted.

Minot State University, Graduate School, Program in School Psychology, Minot, ND 58707-0002. Offers Ed Sp. *Entrance requirements:* For degree, GRE General Test, minimum GPA of

3.0. Additional exam requirements/recommendations for international students: Required—TOEFL. *Faculty research:* Oppositional defiance disorder and autism, experimental psychology, statistical genetics, adults with developmental disabilities, psychopharmacology.

Mississippi State University, College of Education, Department of Counseling and Educational Psychology, Mississippi State, MS 39762. Offers college/postsecondary student counseling and personnel services (PhD); counselor education (MS); counselor education/student counseling and guidance services (PhD); education (Ed S), including counselor education, school psychology; educational psychology (MS, PhD). *Accreditation:* ACA (one or more programs are accredited); APA; CORE (one or more programs are accredited); NCATE. Part-time programs available. Postbaccalaureate distance learning degree programs offered (minimal on-campus study). *Faculty:* 15 full-time (12 women), 1 (woman) part-time/adjunct. *Students:* 126 full-time (103 women), 104 part-time (91 women); includes 71 minority (62 Black or African American, non-Hispanic/Latino; 2 American Indian or Alaska Native, non-Hispanic/Latino; 4 Asian, non-Hispanic/Latino; 1 Hispanic/Latino; 1 Native Hawaiian or other Pacific Islander, non-Hispanic/Latino; 1 Two or more races, non-Hispanic/Latino), 6 international. Average age 32. 161 applicants, 70% accepted, 74 enrolled. In 2010, 49 master's, 3 doctorates, 8 other advanced degrees awarded. Terminal master's awarded for partial completion of doctoral program. *Degree requirements:* For master's, comprehensive exam, thesis optional; for doctorate, thesis/dissertation, comprehensive oral and written exam. *Entrance requirements:* For master's, GRE, minimum QPA of 3.0; for doctorate, GRE, interview, minimum GPA of 3.4; for Ed S, GRE, MS in counseling or related field. Additional exam requirements/recommendations for international students: Required—TOEFL (minimum score 475 paper-based; 153 computer-based; 53 iBT); Recommended—IELTS (minimum score 4.5). *Application deadline:* For fall admission, 2/1 priority date for domestic and international students. Applications are processed on a rolling basis. Application fee: $40. Electronic applications accepted. *Expenses:* Tuition, state resident: full-time $2730.50; part-time $304 per credit hour. Tuition, nonresident: full-time $6901; part-time $767 per credit hour. *Financial support:* In 2010–11, 1 research assistantship (averaging $9,207 per year), 12 teaching assistantships with full tuition reimbursements (averaging $9,326 per year) were awarded; career-related internships or fieldwork, Federal Work-Study, institutionally sponsored loans, and unspecified assistantships also available. Financial award application deadline: 2/1; financial award applicants required to submit FAFSA. *Faculty research:* HIV-AIDS in college population, substance abuse in youth and college students, ADHD and conduct disorders in youth, assessment and identification of early childhood disabilities, assessment and vocational transition of the disabled. *Unit head:* Dr. Daniel Wong, Professor/Head, 662-325-7928, Fax: 662-325-3263, E-mail: dwong@colled.msstate.edu. *Application contact:* Dr. Tony Doggett, Associate Professor and Graduate Coordinator, 662-325-3312, Fax: 662-325-3263, E-mail: tdoggett@colled.msstate.edu.

Montana State University, College of Graduate Studies, College of Education, Health, and Human Development, Department of Education, Bozeman, MT 59717. Offers adult and higher education (Ed D); curriculum and instruction (M Ed, Ed D), including professional educator (M Ed), technology education (M Ed); education (M Ed), including adult and higher education, educational leadership, school counseling; educational leadership (Ed D, Ed S). *Accreditation:* Teacher Education Accreditation Council. Part-time programs available. Postbaccalaureate distance learning degree programs offered (minimal on-campus study). *Faculty:* 24 full-time (16 women), 9 part-time/adjunct (4 women). *Students:* 13 full-time (10 women), 235 part-time (135 women); includes 20 minority (11 American Indian or Alaska Native, non-Hispanic/Latino; 1 Asian, non-Hispanic/Latino; 2 Hispanic/Latino; 6 Two or more races, non-Hispanic/Latino), 2 international. Average age 37. 95 applicants, 69 enrolled. In 2010, 75 master's, 9 doctorates, 3 other advanced degrees awarded. *Degree requirements:* For master's, comprehensive exam; for doctorate, comprehensive exam, thesis/dissertation. *Entrance requirements:* For master's, GRE, 3 letters of reference, essays, BA transcripts; for doctorate, GRE, MAT, 3 letters of reference, essay, BA and M Ed transcripts; for Ed S, PRAXIS. Additional exam requirements/recommendations for international students: Required—TOEFL (minimum score 550 paper-based; 213 computer-based). *Application deadline:* For fall admission, 7/15 priority date for domestic students, 5/15 priority date for international students; for spring admission, 12/1 priority date for domestic students, 10/1 priority date for international students. Applications are processed on a rolling basis. Application fee: $30. Electronic applications accepted. *Expenses:* Tuition, state resident: full-time $5553.90. Tuition, nonresident: full-time $14,646. Required fees: $1233. *Financial support:* In 2010–11, 16 students received support, including 3 research assistantships with full and partial tuition reimbursements available (averaging $2,400 per year), 12 teaching assistantships with full and partial tuition reimbursements available (averaging $7,000 per year); career-related internships or fieldwork, Federal Work-Study, scholarships/grants, health care benefits, tuition waivers (partial), and unspecified assistantships also available. Financial award application deadline: 3/1; financial award applicants required to submit FAFSA. *Faculty research:* Critical literacy; standards-based education; school improvement, organizational change, leadership in rural education, leadership in Indian education; student Learning; multicultural/culturally responsive education for social justice Native American indigenous education, community-centered education teacher preparation. Total annual research expenditures: $2.3 million. *Unit head:* Dr. Jayne Downey, Department Head, 406-994-7426, Fax: 406-994-3261, E-mail: jdowney@montana.edu. *Application contact:* Dr. Carl A. Fox, Vice Provost for Graduate Education, 406-994-4145, Fax: 406-994-7433, E-mail: gradstudy@montana.edu.

Montclair State University, The Graduate School, College of Humanities and Social Sciences, Department of Psychology, Montclair, NJ 07043-1624. Offers educational psychology (MA), including child/adolescent clinical psychology, clinical psychology for Spanish/English bilinguals, educational psychology; psychology (MA), including industrial and organizational psychology; school psychology (Certificate). Part-time and evening/weekend programs available. *Faculty:* 25 full-time (11 women), 37 part-time/adjunct (21 women). *Students:* 43 full-time (31 women), 33 part-time (22 women); includes 8 Black or African American, non-Hispanic/Latino; 3 Asian, non-Hispanic/Latino; 10 Hispanic/Latino, 2 international. Average age 26. 117 applicants, 33% accepted, 24 enrolled. In 2010, 23 master's, 1 other advanced degree awarded. *Degree requirements:* For master's, comprehensive exam, thesis or alternative. *Entrance requirements:* For master's, GRE General Test, 2 letters of recommendation. Additional exam requirements/recommendations for international students: Required—TOEFL (minimum iBT score of 83) or IELTS. *Application deadline:* For fall admission, 6/1 for international students; for spring admission, 11/1 for international students. Applications are processed on a rolling basis. Application fee: $60. Electronic applications accepted. *Expenses:* Tuition, state resident: part-time $501.34 per credit. Tuition, nonresident: part-time $773.88 per credit. Required fees: $71.15 per credit. *Financial support:* In 2010–11, 13 research assistantships with full tuition reimbursements (averaging $7,000 per year) were awarded; Federal Work-Study, scholarships/grants, and unspecified assistantships also available. Support available to part-time students. Financial award application deadline: 3/1; financial award applicants required to submit FAFSA. *Faculty research:* Legal decision-making, leadership development, bias and stereotype threat in the selection process, nature of pre-linguistic thought in infants, lateralized cortical contributions to memory, pediatric neuro-imaging, the production and perception of speech, school-based assessment and intervention for bullying, cognitive processes in reading, identification of autism in toddlers. Total annual research expenditures: $300,000. *Unit head:* Dr. Peter Vietze, Chairperson, 973-655-5201. *Application contact:* Amy Aiello, Director of Admissions and Operations, 973-655-5147, Fax: 973-655-7869, E-mail: graduate.school@montclair.edu.

Mount Saint Vincent University, Graduate Programs, Faculty of Education, Program in School Psychology, Halifax, NS B3M 2J6, Canada. Offers MASP. *Degree requirements:* For master's, thesis, 500 hour practicum. *Entrance requirements:* For master's, bachelor's degree in psychology or equivalent, related work experience. Electronic applications accepted. *Faculty research:* Relationship between cognitive and emotional development, expression of emotions, cognitive-behavioral constituents of racism.

National-Louis University, National College of Education, Chicago, IL 60603. Offers administration and supervision (M Ed, Ed D, CAS, Ed S); curriculum and instruction (M Ed, MS Ed, CAS); early childhood administration (M Ed, CAS); early childhood education (M Ed,

School Psychology

National-Louis University (continued)
MAT, MS Ed, CAS); education (Ed D); educational psychology/human learning and development (M Ed, MS Ed, CAS, Ed S); elementary education (MAT); interdisciplinary curriculum and instruction (M Ed); mathematics education (M Ed, MS Ed, CAS); reading and language (M Ed, MS Ed, CAS); school psychology (M Ed, Ed S); science education (M Ed, MS Ed, CAS); secondary education (MAT); special education (M Ed, MAT, CAS); technology in education (M Ed, CAS). *Accreditation:* NCATE. Part-time and evening/weekend programs available. *Students:* 501 full-time (370 women), 2,650 part-time (2,011 women); includes 572 minority (258 Black or African American, non-Hispanic/Latino; 2 American Indian or Alaska Native, non-Hispanic/Latino; 60 Asian, non-Hispanic/Latino; 210 Hispanic/Latino; 6 Native Hawaiian or other Pacific Islander, non-Hispanic/Latino; 36 Two or more races, non-Hispanic/Latino), 4 international. Average age 34. In 2010, 1,711 master's, 76 doctorates, 86 other advanced degrees awarded. *Degree requirements:* For doctorate, comprehensive exam, thesis/dissertation. *Entrance requirements:* For master's, MAT or GRE, minimum GPA of 3.0; for doctorate, GRE General Test, minimum GPA of 3.25, interview, resume, writing sample, 4 recommendations. Additional exam requirements/recommendations for international students: Required—TOEFL (minimum score 550 paper-based; 213 computer-based; 79 iBT). *Application deadline:* Applications are processed on a rolling basis. Application fee: $40. *Financial support:* Fellowships, research assistantships, teaching assistantships, career-related internships or fieldwork, Federal Work-Study, institutionally sponsored loans, and scholarships/grants available. Support available to part-time students. Financial award applicants required to submit FAFSA. *Unit head:* Dr. Alison Hilsabeck, Dean, 312-361-3580, Fax: 312-261-2580, E-mail: ahilsabeck@nl.edu. *Application contact:* Dr. George Valcourt, Vice President of Enrollment and Student Services, 312-261-3550, Fax: 312-261-3550, E-mail: george.valcourt@nl.edu.

National University, Academic Affairs, School of Education, Department of School Counseling and Psychology, La Jolla, CA 92037-1011. Offers educational counseling (MS); school psychology (MS). Part-time and evening/weekend programs available. Postbaccalaureate distance learning degree programs offered (no on-campus study). *Faculty:* 9 full-time (4 women), 172 part-time/adjunct (99 women). *Students:* 522 full-time (426 women), 649 part-time (517 women); includes 882 minority (133 Black or African American, non-Hispanic/Latino; 303 American Indian or Alaska Native, non-Hispanic/Latino; 86 Asian, non-Hispanic/Latino; 342 Hispanic/Latino; 5 Native Hawaiian or other Pacific Islander, non-Hispanic/Latino; 13 Two or more races, non-Hispanic/Latino). Average age 34. 581 applicants, 100% accepted, 380 enrolled. In 2010, 207 master's awarded. *Degree requirements:* For master's, thesis (for some programs). *Entrance requirements:* For master's, interview, minimum GPA of 2.5. Additional exam requirements/recommendations for international students: Required—TOEFL (minimum score 550 paper-based; 213 computer-based; 79 iBT), IELTS (minimum score 6). *Application deadline:* Applications are processed on a rolling basis. Application fee: $60 ($65 for international students). Electronic applications accepted. *Expenses:* Tuition: Full-time $9450; part-time $350 per unit. Required fees: $350 per unit. One-time fee: $60. *Financial support:* Career-related internships or fieldwork, institutionally sponsored loans, scholarships/grants, and tuition waivers (partial) available. Support available to part-time students. Financial award application deadline: 6/30; financial award applicants required to submit FAFSA. *Unit head:* Dr. Susan Eldred, Chair, 858-642-8372, Fax: 858-642-8724, E-mail: seldred@nu.edu. *Application contact:* Dominick Giovanniello, Associate Regional Dean—San Diego, 800-NAT-UNIV, Fax: 858-541-7792, E-mail: dgiovann@nu.edu.

New Jersey City University, Graduate Studies and Continuing Education, William J. Maxwell College of Arts and Sciences, Program in Educational Psychology, Jersey City, NJ 07305-1597. Offers educational psychology (MA); school psychology (PD). Part-time and evening/weekend programs available. *Degree requirements:* For PD, summer internship or externship. *Entrance requirements:* For master's, GRE General Test or MAT; for PD, GRE General Test. Additional exam requirements/recommendations for international students: Required—TOEFL.

New Jersey City University, Graduate Studies and Continuing Education, William J. Maxwell College of Arts and Sciences, Program in School Psychology, Jersey City, NJ 07305-1597. Offers PD. Part-time and evening/weekend programs available. *Entrance requirements:* Additional exam requirements/recommendations for international students: Required—TOEFL.

New Mexico Highlands University, Graduate Studies, School of Education, Las Vegas, NM 87701. Offers curriculum and instruction (MA); education (MA), including counseling, school counseling; educational leadership (MA); exercise and sport sciences (MA), including human performance and sport, sports administration, teacher education; guidance and counseling (MA), including professional counseling, rehabilitation counseling, school counseling; special education (MA), including). Part-time programs available. *Faculty:* 23 full-time (16 women). *Students:* 129 full-time (100 women), 254 part-time (202 women); includes 6 Black or African American, non-Hispanic/Latino; 25 American Indian or Alaska Native, non-Hispanic/Latino; 2 Asian, non-Hispanic/Latino; 197 Hispanic/Latino; 3 Two or more races, non-Hispanic/Latino, 9 international. Average age 38. 128 applicants, 98% accepted, 109 enrolled. In 2010, 110 master's awarded. *Degree requirements:* For master's, comprehensive exam, thesis or alternative. *Entrance requirements:* For master's, minimum undergraduate GPA of 3.0. Additional exam requirements/recommendations for international students: Required—TOEFL (minimum score 540 paper-based; 207 computer-based). *Application deadline:* For fall admission, 8/1 priority date for domestic students. Applications are processed on a rolling basis. Application fee: $15. *Expenses:* Tuition, state resident: full-time $2544. Required fees: $624; $132 per credit hour. *Financial support:* In 2010–11, 12 students received support. Career-related internships or fieldwork, Federal Work-Study, institutionally sponsored loans, scholarships/grants, traineeships, tuition waivers (partial), and unspecified assistantships available. Support available to part-time students. Financial award application deadline: 3/1; financial award applicants required to submit FAFSA. *Faculty research:* Teaching the United States Constitution, middle school curriculum, integrated computer applications for pre-service classroom teachers, adolescent literacy, narrative cognitive modes in NM multicultural setting. *Unit head:* Dr. Michael Anderson, Interim Dean, 505-454-3213, E-mail: mfanderson@nmhu.edu. *Application contact:* Diane Trujillo, Administrative Assistant for Graduate Studies, 505-454-3266, Fax: 505-426-2117, E-mail: dtrujillo@nmhu.edu.

New Mexico State University, Graduate School, College of Education, Department of Counseling and Educational Psychology, Las Cruces, NM 88003-8001. Offers counseling and guidance (MA); counseling psychology (PhD); school psychology (Ed S). *Accreditation:* ACA; APA (one or more programs are accredited); NCATE. Part-time programs available. *Faculty:* 11 full-time (7 women), 2 part-time/adjunct (1 woman). *Students:* 69 full-time (54 women), 35 part-time (28 women); includes 52 minority (3 Black or African American, non-Hispanic/Latino; 2 American Indian or Alaska Native, non-Hispanic/Latino; 2 Asian, non-Hispanic/Latino; 44 Hispanic/Latino; 1 Two or more races, non-Hispanic/Latino), 2 international. Average age 30. 135 applicants, 89% accepted, 40 enrolled. In 2010, 11 master's, 4 doctorates, 7 other advanced degrees awarded. *Degree requirements:* For master's, comprehensive exam, thesis optional, internship; for doctorate, comprehensive exam, thesis/dissertation, internship; for Ed S, thesis or alternative, internship. *Entrance requirements:* For master's, doctorate, and Ed S, GRE General Test, minimum GPA of 3.0. *Application deadline:* For fall admission, 12/15 for domestic students; for spring admission, 4/1 priority date for domestic students. Application fee: $30 ($50 for international students). Electronic applications accepted. *Expenses:* Tuition, state resident: full-time $4536; part-time $242 per credit. Tuition, nonresident: full-time $15,816; part-time $712 per credit. Required fees: $636 per term. *Financial support:* In 2010–11, 15 research assistantships with partial tuition reimbursements (averaging $10,567 per year), 30 teaching assistantships with partial tuition reimbursements (averaging $6,880 per year) were awarded; fellowships with partial tuition reimbursements, career-related internships or fieldwork, Federal Work-Study, institutionally sponsored loans, scholarships/grants, traineeships, health care benefits, and unspecified assistantships also available. Support available to part-time students. Financial award application deadline: 4/1. *Faculty research:* Multicultural counseling, integrative health psychology group, career development school counseling. *Unit head:* Dr. Michael Waldo, Head, 575-646-2121, Fax: 575-646-8035, E-mail: miwaldo@nmsu.edu. *Application contact:* Elena Luna, Coordinator, 575-646-3498, Fax: 575-646-7721, E-mail: rosluna@nmsu.edu.

Niagara University, Graduate Division of Education, Concentration in School Psychology, Niagara Falls, Niagara University, NY 14109. Offers MS, Certificate. *Students:* 19 full-time (14 women), 11 part-time (9 women); includes 1 Black or African American, non-Hispanic/Latino. Average age 25. In 2010, 10 master's, 10 other advanced degrees awarded. *Entrance requirements:* Additional exam requirements/recommendations for international students: Required—TOEFL. *Expenses:* Tuition: Full-time $13,230; part-time $735 per credit hour. Required fees: $50. One-time fee: $120 full-time. *Unit head:* Dr. Kristine Augustyniak, Chair, 716-286-8548, E-mail: kma@niagara.edu. *Application contact:* Carlos Tejada, Associate Dean for Graduate Recruitment, 716-286-8769, Fax: 716-286-8170.

Nicholls State University, Graduate Studies, College of Education, Department of Psychology and Counselor Education, Thibodaux, LA 70310. Offers psychological counseling (MA); school psychology (SSP). *Accreditation:* NCATE. Part-time and evening/weekend programs available. *Degree requirements:* For master's, comprehensive exam; for SSP, comprehensive exam, internship. *Entrance requirements:* For master's, GRE General Test. Electronic applications accepted.

North Carolina State University, Graduate School, College of Humanities and Social Sciences, Department of Psychology, Raleigh, NC 27695. Offers developmental psychology (PhD); ergonomics and experimental psychology (PhD); industrial/organizational psychology (PhD); psychology in the public interest (PhD); school psychology (PhD). *Accreditation:* APA. *Degree requirements:* For doctorate, comprehensive exam, thesis/dissertation. *Entrance requirements:* For doctorate, GRE General Test, GRE Subject Test (industrial/organizational psychology), MAT (recommended), minimum GPA of 3.0 in major. Electronic applications accepted. *Faculty research:* Cognitive and social development (human factors, families, the workplace, community issues and health, aging).

Northeastern University, Bouvé College of Health Sciences Graduate School, Department of Counseling and Applied Educational Psychology, Program in School Psychology, Boston, MA 02115-5096. Offers MS, PhD, CAGS. *Accreditation:* APA (one or more programs are accredited). Part-time programs available. *Faculty:* 4 full-time (2 women), 3 part-time/adjunct (all women). *Students:* 107 full-time (87 women), 11 part-time (8 women). Average age 29. 153 applicants, 41% accepted, 22 enrolled. In 2010, 109 master's awarded. *Degree requirements:* For doctorate, comprehensive exam, thesis/dissertation, qualifying exams; for CAGS, comprehensive exam. *Entrance requirements:* For master's, GRE General Test; for doctorate, GRE General Test, school psychologist certificate; for CAGS, GRE General Test or MAT, MS in school psychology or related field. Additional exam requirements/recommendations for international students: Required—TOEFL (minimum score 100 iBT). *Application deadline:* For fall admission, 5/1 for domestic students. Application fee: $50. Electronic applications accepted. *Financial support:* Research assistantships, teaching assistantships, career-related internships or fieldwork, Federal Work-Study, tuition waivers (partial), and unspecified assistantships available. Financial award application deadline: 3/1; financial award applicants required to submit FAFSA. *Faculty research:* Multicultural education, early intervention. *Unit head:* Louis J. Kruger, Director, 617-373-5897, E-mail: l.kruger@neu.edu. *Application contact:* Margaret Schnabel, Director of Graduate Admissions, 617-373-2708, E-mail: bouvegrad@neu.edu.

Northern Arizona University, Graduate College, College of Education, Department of Educational Psychology, Flagstaff, AZ 86011. Offers counseling (MA); educational psychology (PhD), including counseling psychology, learning and instruction, school psychology; human relations (M Ed); school counseling (M Ed); school psychology (MA, Certificate); student affairs (M Ed). Part-time programs available. Postbaccalaureate distance learning degree programs offered. *Faculty:* 19 full-time (9 women). *Students:* 230 full-time (176 women), 217 part-time (167 women); includes 168 minority (27 Black or African American, non-Hispanic/Latino; 19 American Indian or Alaska Native, non-Hispanic/Latino; 8 Asian, non-Hispanic/Latino; 105 Hispanic/Latino; 2 Native Hawaiian or other Pacific Islander, non-Hispanic/Latino; 7 Two or more races, non-Hispanic/Latino), 2 international. 736 applicants, 84% accepted. In 2010, 194 master's, 6 doctorates awarded. Terminal master's awarded for partial completion of doctoral program. *Degree requirements:* For master's, internship (for some programs); for doctorate, comprehensive exam, thesis/dissertation, internship. *Entrance requirements:* Additional exam requirements/recommendations for international students: Required—TOEFL (minimum score 550 paper-based; 213 computer-based; 80 iBT), IELTS (minimum score 7). *Application deadline:* For fall admission, 9/15 for domestic students; for spring admission, 1/15 for domestic students. Applications are processed on a rolling basis. Application fee: $65. Electronic applications accepted. *Financial support:* In 2010–11, 20 students received support, including 1 research assistantship with partial tuition reimbursement available (averaging $10,222 per year), 14 teaching assistantships with partial tuition reimbursements available (averaging $9,660 per year); career-related internships or fieldwork, Federal Work-Study, scholarships/grants, health care benefits, tuition waivers (full and partial), and unspecified assistantships also available. Financial award applicants required to submit FAFSA. *Unit head:* Dr. Kathy Bohan, Chair, 928-523-0362, Fax: 928-523-9284, E-mail: kathy.bohan@nau.edu. *Application contact:* Hope DeMello, Administrative Assistant, 928-523-7103, Fax: 928-523-9284, E-mail: eps@nau.edu.

Northwest Nazarene University, Graduate Studies, Program in Counselor Education, Nampa, ID 83686-5897. Offers community counseling (MS); marriage and family counseling (MS); school counseling (MS). *Faculty:* 5 full-time (3 women), 4 part-time/adjunct (2 women). *Students:* 83 full-time (64 women), 16 part-time (10 women); includes 7 minority (1 Black or African American, non-Hispanic/Latino; 4 Asian, non-Hispanic/Latino; 2 Hispanic/Latino), 1 international. In 2010, 33 master's awarded. Application fee: $25. *Unit head:* Dr. Brenda Freeman, Chair, 208-467-8428, Fax: 208-467-8339. *Application contact:* Judy Bassett, Program Assistant, 208-467-8345, Fax: 208-467-8339, E-mail: jbassett@nnu.edu.

Nova Southeastern University, Center for Psychological Studies, Specialist Program in School Psychology, Fort Lauderdale, FL 33314-7796. Offers Psy S. Evening/weekend programs available. Postbaccalaureate distance learning degree programs offered. *Faculty:* 6 full-time (3 women), 16 part-time/adjunct (10 women). *Students:* 60 full-time (51 women), 65 part-time (57 women); includes 29 Black or African American, non-Hispanic/Latino; 4 Asian, non-Hispanic/Latino; 23 Hispanic/Latino; 1 Native Hawaiian or other Pacific Islander, non-Hispanic/Latino, 4 international. Average age 32. 110 applicants, 50% accepted, 37 enrolled. In 2010, 34 Psy Ss awarded. *Degree requirements:* For Psy S, comprehensive exam, internship. *Entrance requirements:* Additional exam requirements/recommendations for international students: Required—TOEFL (minimum score 530 paper-based; 213 computer-based). *Application deadline:* For fall admission, 2/22 priority date for domestic and international students; for winter admission, 6/30 priority date for domestic and international students. Applications are processed on a rolling basis. Application fee: $50. Electronic applications accepted. *Financial support:* In 2010–11, 1 teaching assistantship was awarded; research assistantships, career-related internships or fieldwork, Federal Work-Study, scholarships/grants, and unspecified assistantships also available. *Unit head:* Karen S. Grosby, Dean, 954-262-5701, Fax: 954-262-3859. *Application contact:* Carlos Perez, Enrollment Management, 954-262-5790, Fax: 954-262-3893, E-mail: cpsinfo@cps.nova.edu.

Oregon State University–Cascades, Program in Counseling, Bend, OR 97701. Offers community counseling (MS); school counseling (MS).

Ottawa University, Graduate Studies-Arizona, Program in Education, Ottawa, KS 66067-3399. Offers community college counseling (MA); curriculum and instruction (MA); early childhood (MA); education intervention (MA); education leadership (MA); education technology (MA); Montessori early childhood education (MA); Montessori elementary education (MA); professional development (MA); school guidance counseling (MA); special education—cross categorical (MA). Programs offered in Mesa, Phoenix, Tempe and West Valley, AZ. *Accreditation:* NCATE. Part-time programs available. *Degree requirements:* For master's, thesis or alternative. *Entrance requirements:* For master's, minimum undergraduate GPA of 3.0, copy of current state certification or teaching license. Additional exam requirements/recommendations for international students: Required—TOEFL (minimum score 550 paper-based; 213 computer-based). Electronic applications accepted. *Expenses:* Contact institution.

Our Lady of the Lake University of San Antonio, School of Professional Studies, Program in Psychology, San Antonio, TX 78207-4689. Offers counseling psychology (MS, Psy D); marriage and family therapy (MS); school psychology (MS). *Accreditation:* APA (one or more programs are accredited). Part-time and evening/weekend programs available. *Students:* 118 full-time (97 women), 94 part-time (85 women); includes 119 minority (20 Black or African American, non-Hispanic/Latino; 2 Asian, non-Hispanic/Latino; 90 Hispanic/Latino; 2 Native Hawaiian or other Pacific Islander, non-Hispanic/Latino; 5 Two or more races, non-Hispanic/Latino), 5 international. Average age 30. In 2010, 842 master's, 4 doctorates awarded. *Degree requirements:* For master's, comprehensive exam, thesis optional, practicum; for doctorate, thesis/dissertation, internship, qualifying exam. *Entrance requirements:* For master's and doctorate, GRE General Test or MAT, interview. Additional exam requirements/recommendations for international students: Required—TOEFL. *Application deadline:* For fall admission, 3/1 priority date for domestic and international students. Applications are processed on a rolling basis. Application fee: $25 ($50 for international students). Electronic applications accepted. *Expenses:* Tuition: Full-time $13,500; part-time $750 per contact hour. Required fees: $330. Tuition and fees vary according to course level, degree level and campus/location. *Financial support:* Research assistantships, teaching assistantships, career-related internships or fieldwork available. Support available to part-time students. Financial award application deadline: 4/15. *Faculty research:* Marriage and family therapy, supervision, cross-cultural counseling, violence. *Unit head:* Dr. Joan Biever, Chair, 210-434-6711, E-mail: jbiever@lake.ollusa.edu. *Application contact:* 210-434-6711, Fax: 210-431-4036, E-mail: gradadm@lake.ollusa.edu.

Pace University, Dyson College of Arts and Sciences, Department of Psychology, Program in School-Clinical Child Psychology, New York, NY 10038. Offers school psychology (MS Ed); school-clinical psychology (Psy D). *Accreditation:* APA (one or more programs are accredited). Terminal master's awarded for partial completion of doctoral program. *Degree requirements:* For master's, comprehensive exam, qualifying exams, internship; for doctorate, comprehensive exam, qualifying exams, externship, internship, project. *Entrance requirements:* For master's, GRE General Test, GRE Subject Test, interview; for doctorate, GRE General Test, GRE Subject Test (psychology), interview, transcripts, 3 letters of reference. Additional exam requirements/recommendations for international students: Required—TOEFL. Electronic applications accepted.

Penn State University Park, Graduate School, College of Education, Department of Educational and School Psychology and Special Education, State College, University Park, PA 16802-1503. Offers M Ed, MS, PhD.

Philadelphia College of Osteopathic Medicine, Graduate and Professional Programs, Department of Psychology, Philadelphia, PA 19131-1694. Offers clinical psychology (Psy D); counseling and clinical health psychology (MS); organizational leadership and development (MS); psychology (Certificate, Post-Doctoral Certificate); school psychology (MS, Psy D, Ed S). *Accreditation:* APA. *Degree requirements:* For master's, thesis; for doctorate, comprehensive exam, thesis/dissertation, final project, fieldwork. *Entrance requirements:* For master's, GRE or MAT, minimum GPA of 3.0; course work in biology, chemistry, English, physics; for other advanced degree, PRAXIS. *Faculty research:* Depression in primary care, integrated primary care, geriatric mental health.

See Display on page 932 and Close-Up on page 1167.

Phillips Graduate Institute, Programs in Marriage and Family Therapy, School Counseling and School Psychology, Encino, CA 91316-1509. Offers marriage and family therapy (MA); school counseling (MA); school psychology (MA). Evening/weekend programs available. *Degree requirements:* For master's, comprehensive exam, thesis. *Entrance requirements:* For master's, minimum GPA of 2.5. *Faculty research:* Integration of interpersonal psychological theory, systems approach, firsthand experiential learning.

Pittsburg State University, Graduate School, College of Education, Department of Psychology and Counseling, Program in School Psychology, Pittsburg, KS 66762. Offers Ed S. *Accreditation:* NCATE. *Degree requirements:* For Ed S, thesis or alternative. *Entrance requirements:* For degree, GRE General Test, minimum GPA of 3.0.

Purdue University Calumet, Graduate Studies Office, School of Education, Program in Counseling, Hammond, IN 46323-2094. Offers human services (MS Ed); mental health counseling (MS Ed); school counseling (MS Ed). *Entrance requirements:* Additional exam requirements/recommendations for international students: Required—TOEFL. Application fee: $30. *Expenses:* Tuition, state resident: full-time $6867. Tuition, nonresident: full-time $14,157. *Financial support:* Application deadline: 3/1. *Unit head:* Dr. Robert Colon, Director, Graduate Studies in Education, 219-989-2867, E-mail: colon2@purduecal.edu. *Application contact:* Dr. Lisa Hollingsworth, Program Chair, 219-989-2789, E-mail: hollings@purduecal.edu.

Queens College of the City University of New York, Division of Graduate Studies, Division of Education, Department of Educational and Community Programs, Program in School Psychology, Flushing, NY 11367-1597. Offers MS Ed, AC. Ms Ed offered jointly with Graduate School and University Center of the City University of New York. Part-time programs available. *Faculty:* 4 full-time (3 women). *Students:* 26 full-time (25 women), 67 part-time (64 women); includes 4 Black or African American, non-Hispanic/Latino; 7 Asian, non-Hispanic/Latino; 13 Hispanic/Latino. 156 applicants, 31% accepted, 34 enrolled. In 2010, 33 master's awarded. *Degree requirements:* For master's, internship, research project; for AC, thesis optional, internship. *Entrance requirements:* For master's, minimum GPA of 3.0; for AC, master's degree or equivalent. Additional exam requirements/recommendations for international students: Required—TOEFL. *Application deadline:* For fall admission, 4/1 for domestic students; for spring admission, 11/1 for domestic students. Applications are processed on a rolling basis. Application fee: $125. *Financial support:* Career-related internships or fieldwork, Federal Work-Study, institutionally sponsored loans, and tuition waivers (partial) available. Support available to part-time students. Financial award application deadline: 4/1; financial award applicants required to submit FAFSA. *Unit head:* Dr. Marion Fish, Coordinator/Graduate Adviser, 718-997-5230. *Application contact:* Mario Caruso, Director of Graduate Admissions, 718-997-5200, Fax: 718-997-5193, E-mail: graduate_admissions@qc.edu.

Quincy University, Program in Counseling, Quincy, IL 62301-2699. Offers education (MS Ed), including clinical mental health counseling, school counseling. Part-time and evening/weekend programs available. *Faculty:* 2 full-time (1 woman). *Students:* 2 full-time (both women), 17 part-time (15 women); includes 1 Black or African American, non-Hispanic/Latino; 1 Two or more races, non-Hispanic/Latino. In 2010, 17 master's awarded. *Degree requirements:* For master's, comprehensive exam, practicum, internship. *Entrance requirements:* For master's, MAT or GRE. Additional exam requirements/recommendations for international students: Required—TOEFL (minimum score 550 paper-based). *Application deadline:* Applications are processed on a rolling basis. Application fee: $25. Electronic applications accepted. *Expenses:* Tuition: Full-time $8880; part-time $370 per semester hour. Required fees: $360; $15 per semester hour. Tuition and fees vary according to course load, campus/location and program. *Financial support:* Available to part-time students. Applicants required to submit FAFSA. *Unit head:* Dr. Kenneth Oliver, Director, 217-228-5432 Ext. 3113, E-mail: oliveke@quincy.edu. *Application contact:* Jennifer Bang, Coordinator of Adult Studies, 217-228-5404, Fax: 217-228-5479, E-mail: admissions@quincy.edu.

Radford University, College of Graduate and Professional Studies, College of Education and Human Development, Department of Counselor Education, Radford, VA 24142. Offers community counseling (MS); school counseling (MS); student affairs—administration (MS); student affairs—counseling (MS). *Accreditation:* ACA; NCATE. Part-time and evening/weekend programs available. *Faculty:* 8 full-time (5 women), 19 part-time/adjunct (12 women). *Students:* 60 full-time (44 women), 43 part-time (35 women); includes 6 minority (3 Black or African American, non-Hispanic/Latino; 1 American Indian or Alaska Native, non-Hispanic/Latino; 1 Asian, non-Hispanic/Latino; 1 Hispanic/Latino). Average age 29. 56 applicants, 82% accepted, 23 enrolled. In 2010, 32 master's awarded. *Degree requirements:* For master's, comprehensive exam, thesis optional. *Entrance requirements:* For master's, GRE or MAT, minimum GPA of 2.75, 3 letters of reference. Additional exam requirements/recommendations for international students: Required—TOEFL (minimum score 550 paper-based; 213 computer-based; 79 iBT). *Application deadline:* For fall admission, 2/15 priority date for domestic students, 12/1 for international students; for spring admission, 7/1 for international students. Applications are processed on a rolling basis. Application fee: $50. Electronic applications accepted. *Expenses:* Tuition, state resident: full-time $5746; part-time $239 per credit hour. Tuition, nonresident: full-time $14,174; part-time $591 per credit hour. Required fees: $2634; $111 per credit hour. *Financial support:* In 2010–11, 26 students received support, including 12 research assistantships with partial tuition reimbursements available (averaging $8,000 per year), 8 teaching assistantships with partial tuition reimbursements available (averaging $8,700 per year); career-related internships or fieldwork, Federal Work-Study, institutionally sponsored loans, scholarships/grants, and unspecified assistantships also available. Financial award application deadline: 3/1; financial award applicants required to submit FAFSA. *Unit head:* Dr. Alan Forrest, Chair, 540-831-5487, Fax: 540-831-6755, E-mail: aforrest@radford.edu. *Application contact:* Rebecca Conner, Graduate Admissions, 540-831-5431, Fax: 540-831-6061, E-mail: gradcollege@radford.edu.

Radford University, College of Graduate and Professional Studies, College of Humanities and Behavioral Sciences, Program in School Psychology, Radford, VA 24142. Offers Ed S. *Accreditation:* NCATE. *Faculty:* 18 full-time (7 women), 4 part-time/adjunct (2 women). *Students:* 24 full-time (23 women), 6 part-time (3 women); includes 4 minority (3 Black or African American, non-Hispanic/Latino; 1 Asian, non-Hispanic/Latino). Average age 25. 25 applicants, 64% accepted, 9 enrolled. In 2010, 6 Ed Ss awarded. *Degree requirements:* For Ed S, comprehensive exam. *Entrance requirements:* For degree, GRE, minimum GPA of 3.0; 2 letters of reference; essay. Additional exam requirements/recommendations for international students: Required—TOEFL (minimum score 550 paper-based; 213 computer-based; 79 iBT). *Application deadline:* For fall admission, 2/15 priority date for domestic students, 12/1 for international students; for spring admission, 7/1 for international students. Applications are processed on a rolling basis. Application fee: $50. Electronic applications accepted. *Expenses:* Tuition, state resident: full-time $5746; part-time $239 per credit hour. Tuition, nonresident: full-time $14,174; part-time $591 per credit hour. Required fees: $2634; $111 per credit hour. *Financial support:* In 2010–11, 15 students received support, including 11 research assistantships with partial tuition reimbursements available (averaging $8,000 per year), 2 teaching assistantships (averaging $8,700 per year); career-related internships or fieldwork, Federal Work-Study, institutionally sponsored loans, scholarships/grants, and unspecified assistantships also available. Financial award application deadline: 3/1; financial award applicants required to submit FAFSA. *Unit head:* Dr. Jayne Bucy, Coordinator, 540-831-5341, Fax: 540-831-6113, E-mail: jebucy@radford.edu. *Application contact:* Rebecca Conner, Graduate Admissions, 540-831-5431, Fax: 540-831-6061, E-mail: gradcollege@radford.edu.

Rhode Island College, School of Graduate Studies, Feinstein School of Education and Human Development, Department of Counseling, Educational Leadership, and School Psychology, Providence, RI 02908-1991. Offers agency counseling (MA); co-occurring disorders (MA, CGS); educational leadership (M Ed); educational psychology (MA); mental health counseling (CAGS); school counseling (MA, CAGS); school psychology (CAGS). *Accreditation:* NCATE. Part-time and evening/weekend programs available. *Faculty:* 10 full-time (5 women), 12 part-time/adjunct (7 women). *Students:* 31 full-time (26 women), 137 part-time (101 women); includes 13 minority (9 Black or African American, non-Hispanic/Latino; 2 Asian, non-Hispanic/Latino; 2 Hispanic/Latino). Average age 34. In 2010, 43 master's, 21 other advanced degrees awarded. *Degree requirements:* For master's and other advanced degree, comprehensive exam (for some programs), thesis (for some programs). *Entrance requirements:* For master's, GRE General Test or MAT, undergraduate transcripts; minimum undergraduate GPA of 3.0; for other advanced degree, GRE or MAT (for most programs), undergraduate transcripts; minimum undergraduate GPA of 3.0; copy of teaching certificate (when applicable); 3 letters of recommendation; current resume. Additional exam requirements/recommendations for international students: Recommended—TOEFL (minimum score 550 paper-based; 213 computer-based; 79 iBT). *Application deadline:* For fall admission, 3/1 for domestic students; for spring admission, 11/1 for domestic students. Applications are processed on a rolling basis. Application fee: $50. *Expenses:* Tuition, state resident: full-time $8208; part-time $342 per credit hour. Tuition, nonresident: full-time $16,080; part-time $670 per credit hour. Required fees: $554; $20 per credit. $72 per term. *Financial support:* Teaching assistantships with full tuition reimbursements, career-related internships or fieldwork, Federal Work-Study, scholarships/grants, health care benefits, and unspecified assistantships available. Support available to part-time students. Financial award application deadline: 5/15; financial award applicants required to submit FAFSA. *Unit head:* Dr. Monica Darcy, Chair, 401-456-8023. *Application contact:* Graduate Studies, 401-456-8700.

Rider University, Department of Graduate Education, Leadership and Counseling, Program in School Psychology, Lawrenceville, NJ 08648-3001. Offers Certificate, Ed S. *Entrance requirements:* For degree, GRE or MAT, resume, 2 professional references, interview, 1 year of counseling experience. Additional exam requirements/recommendations for international students: Required—TOEFL (minimum score 550 paper-based; 213 computer-based). *Expenses:* Tuition: Full-time $29,870; part-time $667.34 per credit. Required fees: $350; $11.60 per credit. Part-time tuition and fees vary according to program. *Faculty research:* Prenatal factors on child development, child abuse developmental assessments.

Roberts Wesleyan College, Division of Social Sciences, Rochester, NY 14624-1997. Offers counseling in ministry (MA); school counseling (MS); school psychology (MS).

Rowan University, Graduate School, College of Education, Department of Special Educational Services/Instruction, Program in School Psychology, Glassboro, NJ 08028-1701. Offers MA, Ed S. *Accreditation:* NCATE. Part-time and evening/weekend programs available. *Students:* 48 full-time (41 women), 39 part-time (34 women); includes 3 Black or African American, non-Hispanic/Latino; 9 Asian, non-Hispanic/Latino; 5 Hispanic/Latino. Average age 26. 36 applicants, 97% accepted, 26 enrolled. In 2010, 43 master's awarded. *Degree requirements:* For master's, comprehensive exam, thesis; for Ed S, thesis or alternative. *Entrance requirements:* For master's and Ed S, GRE General Test, GRE Subject Test, interview, minimum GPA of 3.0. Additional exam requirements/recommendations for international students: Required—TOEFL. *Application deadline:* For fall admission, 10/15 for domestic students; for winter admission, 12/1 priority date for domestic students; for spring admission, 4/1 priority date for domestic students. Applications are processed on a rolling basis. Application fee: $65 ($200 for international students). Electronic applications accepted. *Expenses:* Tuition, area resident: Part-time $602 per semester hour. Tuition, nonresident: part-time $602 per semester hour. Required fees: $100 per semester hour. One-time fee: $10 part-time. *Financial support:* Career-related internships or fieldwork, scholarships/grants, and unspecified assistantships available. Support available to part-time students. *Unit head:* Dr. Horacio Sosa, Dean, College of Graduate and Continuing Education, 856-256-4747, Fax: 856-256-5638, E-mail: sosa@rowan.edu. *Application contact:* Karen Haynes, Graduate Coordinator, 856-256-4052, Fax: 856-256-4436, E-mail: haynes@rowan.edu.

Rutgers, The State University of New Jersey, New Brunswick, Graduate School of Applied and Professional Psychology, Program in School Psychology, Piscataway, NJ 08854-8097. Offers Psy M, Psy D. *Accreditation:* APA (one or more programs are accredited). *Faculty:* 6 full-time (5 women), 4 part-time/adjunct (all women). *Students:* 59 (49 women); includes 5 Black or African American, non-Hispanic/Latino; 2 Asian, non-Hispanic/Latino. Average age 28. 91 applicants, 27% accepted, 18 enrolled. In 2010, 8 master's, 10 doctorates awarded. *Degree requirements:* For doctorate, comprehensive exam, thesis/dissertation, 1 year internship. *Entrance requirements:* For doctorate, GRE General Test, GRE Subject Test, bachelor's degree in psychology or equivalent. Additional exam requirements/recommendations for international students: Required—TOEFL. *Application deadline:* For fall admission, 1/5 for domestic

School Psychology

Rutgers, The State University of New Jersey, New Brunswick (continued)
students. Application fee: $60. Electronic applications accepted. *Expenses:* Contact institution. *Financial support:* In 2010–11, 16 students received support, including 10 fellowships with tuition reimbursements available (averaging $6,350 per year), 1 teaching assistantship with tuition reimbursement available (averaging $14,000 per year); research assistantships with tuition reimbursements available, career-related internships or fieldwork, Federal Work-Study, institutionally sponsored loans, scholarships/grants, and unspecified assistantships also available. Financial award application deadline: 3/15; financial award applicants required to submit FAFSA. *Faculty research:* Consultation, program evaluation, applied educational psychology, exceptional children, crisis intervention. Total annual research expenditures: $350,000. *Unit head:* Dr. Susan G. Forman, Chairman, 732-445-2000 Ext. 119, Fax: 732-445-4888, E-mail: schpsyd@rci.rutgers.edu. *Application contact:* Kathy McLean, Administrative Assistant, 732-445-2000 Ext. 104, Fax: 732-445-4888, E-mail: schpsyd@rci.rutgers.edu.

St. John's University, St. John's College of Liberal Arts and Sciences, Department of Psychology, Program in School Psychology, Queens, NY 11439. Offers MS, Psy D. Part-time programs available. *Students:* 97 full-time (83 women), 66 part-time (60 women); includes 28 minority (5 Black or African American, non-Hispanic/Latino; 7 Asian, non-Hispanic/Latino; 15 Hispanic/Latino; 1 Two or more races, non-Hispanic/Latino), 5 international. Average age 26. 177 applicants, 43% accepted, 37 enrolled. In 2010, 33 master's, 26 doctorates awarded. *Degree requirements:* For master's, comprehensive exam, thesis optional; for doctorate, comprehensive exam, thesis/dissertation, internship, externship. *Entrance requirements:* For master's, GRE General Test, GRE Subject Test, minimum GPA of 3.0, 2 writing samples; for doctorate, GRE General Test, GRE Subject Test, interview, minimum GPA of 3.0. Additional exam requirements/recommendations for international students: Required—TOEFL (minimum score 600 paper-based; 250 computer-based; 100 iBT), IELTS (minimum score 5.5). *Application deadline:* For fall admission, 1/15 for domestic students, 1/15 priority date for international students. Applications are processed on a rolling basis. Application fee: $70. Electronic applications accepted. *Expenses:* Contact institution. *Financial support:* Fellowships, research assistantships, career-related internships or fieldwork, scholarships/grants, and unspecified assistantships available. Support available to part-time students. Financial award application deadline: 3/1; financial award applicants required to submit FAFSA. *Faculty research:* Therapeutic alliance, intelligence testing, multicultural assessment, neuropsychological assessment, adolescent suicide. *Unit head:* Dr. Dawn Flanagan, Director, 718-990-1551, E-mail: flanagad@stjohns.edu. *Application contact:* Kathleen Davis, Director of Graduate Admission, 718-990-1601, Fax: 718-990-5686, E-mail: gradhelp@stjohns.edu.

San Diego State University, Graduate and Research Affairs, College of Education, Department of Counseling and School Psychology, San Diego, CA 92182. Offers MS. *Accreditation:* NCATE. Evening/weekend programs available. *Degree requirements:* For master's, comprehensive exam (for some programs), thesis (for some programs). *Entrance requirements:* For master's, GRE General Test, interview, letters of reference. Additional exam requirements/recommendations for international students: Required—TOEFL. Electronic applications accepted. *Faculty research:* Multicultural and cross-cultural counseling and training, AIDS counseling.

San Francisco State University, Division of Graduate Studies, College of Behavioral and Social Sciences, Department of Psychology, San Francisco, CA 94132-1722. Offers clinical psychology (MS); developmental psychology (MA); industrial/organizational psychology (MS); psychological research (MA); school psychology (MS); social psychology (MA). *Financial support:* Teaching assistantships available. Financial award application deadline: 3/1. *Unit head:* Dr. Julia Lewis, Chair, 415-338-7555, E-mail: jmlewis@sfsu.edu. *Application contact:* Leslye M. Tinson, Assistant to the Chair, 415-338-7555, E-mail: ltinson@sfsu.edu.

Seattle University, College of Education, Program in Counseling and School Psychology, Seattle, WA 98122-1090. Offers MA, Certificate, Ed S. *Accreditation:* NCATE. Part-time and evening/weekend programs available. *Degree requirements:* For master's, comprehensive exam. *Entrance requirements:* For master's, interview; GRE, MAT, or minimum GPA of 3.0; related work experience. Additional exam requirements/recommendations for international students: Required—TOEFL.

Seton Hall University, College of Education and Human Services, Department of Professional Psychology and Family Therapy, Program in School Psychology, South Orange, NJ 07079-2697. Offers Ed S. *Degree requirements:* For Ed S, comprehensive exam, thesis, internship. *Entrance requirements:* For degree, GRE or MAT, interview. *Faculty research:* Family systems, ethical behavior, childhood depression.

Southeast Missouri State University, School of Graduate Studies, Department of Educational Leadership and Counseling, Counseling Program, Cape Girardeau, MO 63701-4799. Offers career counseling (MA); community counseling (MA); counseling education (Ed S); mental health counseling (MA); school counseling (MA), including elementary counseling, secondary counseling. *Accreditation:* ACA; NCATE. Part-time and evening/weekend programs available. Postbaccalaureate distance learning degree programs offered. *Faculty:* 12 full-time (6 women). *Students:* 29 full-time (26 women), 53 part-time (48 women); includes 5 minority (3 Black or African American, non-Hispanic/Latino; 1 American Indian or Alaska Native, non-Hispanic/Latino; 1 Hispanic/Latino), 1 international. Average age 33. 31 applicants, 94% accepted, 20 enrolled. In 2010, 16 master's, 7 other advanced degrees awarded. *Degree requirements:* For master's, comprehensive exam, portfolio, oral exam, minimum GPA of 3.25; for Ed S, oral exam, minimum GPA of 3.25. *Entrance requirements:* For master's, GRE General Test or MAT, minimum undergraduate GPA of 3.0; 18 undergraduate hours in social science including statistics; teaching certification for school counselor or evidence of competency; for Ed S, GRE General Test or MAT, master's degree; teacher certification; recommendations. Additional exam requirements/recommendations for international students: Required—TOEFL (minimum score 550 paper-based; 213 computer-based; 79 iBT); Recommended—IELTS (minimum score 6). *Application deadline:* For fall admission, 8/1 for domestic students, 6/1 for international students; for spring admission, 11/21 for domestic students, 10/1 for international students. Applications are processed on a rolling basis. Application fee: $25 ($35 for international students). Electronic applications accepted. *Expenses:* Tuition, state resident: full-time $4698; part-time $261 per credit hour. Tuition, nonresident: full-time $8379; part-time $465.50 per credit hour. *Financial support:* In 2010–11, 8 students received support. Career-related internships or fieldwork, Federal Work-Study, institutionally sponsored loans, scholarships/grants, tuition waivers (full), and unspecified assistantships available. Financial award application deadline: 6/30; financial award applicants required to submit FAFSA. *Faculty research:* Counselor development, marriage and family counseling, multicultural counseling. *Unit head:* Dr. David Stader, 573-651-2417, E-mail: dstader@semo.edu. *Application contact:* Gail Amick, Administrative Secretary, 573-651-2049, Fax: 573-651-2001, E-mail: gamick@semo.edu.

Southern Connecticut State University, School of Graduate Studies, School of Education, Department of Counseling and School Psychology, New Haven, CT 06515-1355. Offers community counseling (MS); counseling (Diploma); school counseling (MS); school psychology (MS, Diploma). *Accreditation:* ACA (one or more programs are accredited); NCATE. *Faculty:* 9 full-time (7 women). *Students:* 100 full-time (86 women), 56 part-time (41 women); includes 11 Black or African American, non-Hispanic/Latino; 3 Asian, non-Hispanic/Latino; 8 Hispanic/Latino; 1 Two or more races, non-Hispanic/Latino, 1 international. 368 applicants, 20% accepted, 64 enrolled. In 2010, 43 master's, 14 other advanced degrees awarded. *Degree requirements:* For master's, comprehensive exam. *Entrance requirements:* For master's, interview, previous course work in behavioral sciences, minimum QPA of 2.7. *Application deadline:* For fall admission, 1/15 for domestic students; for spring admission, 10/15 for domestic students. Application fee: $50. Electronic applications accepted. *Expenses:* Tuition, state resident: full-time $5137; part-time $518 per credit. Tuition, nonresident: part-time $542 per credit. Required fees: $4008; $55 per semester. Tuition and fees vary according to program. *Financial support:* Teaching assistantships, career-related internships or fieldwork available. Financial award application deadline: 4/15; financial award applicants required to submit FAFSA. *Unit head:* Dr. Patricia DeBarbieri, Chairperson, 203-392-5483, E-mail: debarbierip1@southernct.edu. *Application contact:* Dr. Louisa Foss, Graduate Coordinator, 203-392-5154, E-mail: fossl1@southernct.edu.

Southern Illinois University Edwardsville, Graduate School, School of Education, Department of Psychology, Program in School Psychology, Edwardsville, IL 62026. Offers SD. *Accreditation:* NCATE. Part-time programs available. *Students:* 9 part-time (all women). Average age 26. 10 applicants, 0% accepted. In 2010, 10 SDs awarded. *Degree requirements:* For SD, thesis. *Entrance requirements:* For degree, GRE. Additional exam requirements/recommendations for international students: Required—TOEFL (minimum score 550 paper-based; 213 computer-based; 79 iBT), IELTS (minimum score 6.5). *Application deadline:* For spring admission, 2/1 for domestic and international students. Application fee: $30. Electronic applications accepted. *Expenses:* Tuition, state resident: full-time $6012; part-time $1503 per semester. Tuition, nonresident: full-time $15,030; part-time $3758 per semester. Required fees: $1711; $675 per semester. *Financial support:* Fellowships, research assistantships, teaching assistantships, career-related internships or fieldwork, Federal Work-Study, institutionally sponsored loans, scholarships/grants, traineeships, and unspecified assistantships available. Support available to part-time students. Financial award application deadline: 3/1; financial award applicants required to submit FAFSA. *Unit head:* Dr. Emily Krohn, Director, 618-650-2202, E-mail: ekrohn@siue.edu. *Application contact:* Dr. Emily Krohn, Director, 618-650-2202, E-mail: ekrohn@siue.edu.

Southwestern Oklahoma State University, College of Professional and Graduate Studies, School of Behavioral Sciences and Education, Specialization in School Psychology, Weatherford, OK 73096-3098. Offers MS.

State University of New York at Oswego, Graduate Studies, School of Education, Department of Counseling and Psychological Services, Program in School Psychology, Oswego, NY 13126. Offers MS, CAS, MS/CAS. *Faculty:* 8 full-time (5 women), 6 part-time/adjunct (3 women). *Students:* 23 full-time (21 women), 12 part-time (10 women); includes 3 minority (1 American Indian or Alaska Native, non-Hispanic/Latino; 2 Hispanic/Latino). Average age 31. 48 applicants, 69% accepted. In 2010, 8 master's, 1 other advanced degree awarded. *Degree requirements:* For master's, comprehensive exam, thesis optional, fieldwork; for CAS, thesis, fieldwork. *Entrance requirements:* For master's, GRE General Test, interview, minimum GPA of 3.0; for CAS, GRE General Test, interview, MA or MS, minimum GPA of 3.0. Additional exam requirements/recommendations for international students: Required—TOEFL (minimum score 560 paper-based; 220 computer-based). *Application deadline:* For fall admission, 2/1 for domestic and international students. Application fee: $50. *Expenses:* Tuition, state resident: full-time $8370; part-time $349 per credit hour. Tuition, nonresident: full-time $13,780; part-time $574 per credit hour. Required fees: $853; $22.59 per credit hour. *Financial support:* In 2010–11, 8 students received support, including 1 fellowship with full tuition reimbursement available (averaging $5,100 per year), 7 teaching assistantships with partial tuition reimbursements available (averaging $3,800 per year); career-related internships or fieldwork, Federal Work-Study, institutionally sponsored loans, scholarships/grants, health care benefits, and unspecified assistantships also available. Support available to part-time students. Financial award application deadline: 4/1; financial award applicants required to submit FAFSA. *Faculty research:* Psychological applications in education and human services, evaluation of standard tests for admissions criteria. *Unit head:* Dr. James McDougal, Coordinator, 315-312-4051, E-mail: james.mcdougal@oswego.edu. *Application contact:* Dr. David W. King, Dean of Graduate Studies, 315-312-3152, Fax: 315-312-3228, E-mail: dking@oswego.edu.

State University of New York at Plattsburgh, Faculty of Arts and Science, Department of Psychology, Plattsburgh, NY 12901-2681. Offers school psychology (MA, CAS). Part-time programs available. *Degree requirements:* For master's, thesis, internship. *Entrance requirements:* For master's, GRE General Test, minimum GPA of 3.0. Additional exam requirements/recommendations for international students: Required—TOEFL (minimum score 550 paper-based; 213 computer-based; 79 iBT). *Faculty research:* Alzheimer's disease, adolescent behavior, intellectual assessment, learning disabilities, reading skill acquisition.

Stephen F. Austin State University, Graduate School, College of Education, Department of Human Services, Nacogdoches, TX 75962. Offers counseling (MA); school psychology (MA); special education (M Ed); speech pathology (MS). *Accreditation:* ACA (one or more programs are accredited); ASHA (one or more programs are accredited); CORE; NCATE. *Degree requirements:* For master's, comprehensive exam, thesis (for some programs). *Entrance requirements:* For master's, GRE General Test, minimum GPA of 2.8. Additional exam requirements/recommendations for international students: Required—TOEFL.

Syracuse University, College of Arts and Sciences, Program in School Psychology, Syracuse, NY 13244. Offers PhD. *Accreditation:* APA. *Students:* 16 full-time (15 women), 1 international. Average age 26. 40 applicants, 10% accepted, 4 enrolled. *Degree requirements:* For doctorate, comprehensive exam, thesis/dissertation. *Entrance requirements:* For doctorate, GRE General Test, GRE Subject Test. Additional exam requirements/recommendations for international students: Required—TOEFL (minimum score 100 iBT). *Application deadline:* For fall admission, 1/1 priority date for domestic and international students. Application fee: $75. Electronic applications accepted. *Expenses:* Tuition: Part-time $1162 per credit. *Financial support:* Fellowships with full tuition reimbursements, research assistantships with full tuition reimbursements, teaching assistantships with full tuition reimbursements available. Financial award application deadline: 1/1; financial award applicants required to submit FAFSA. *Unit head:* Dr. Tanya Eckert, Graduate Director, 315-443-2354, Fax: 315-443-4085, E-mail: taeckert@syr.edu. *Application contact:* Sue Bova, Information Contact, 315-443-1050, E-mail: skbova@syr.edu.

Syracuse University, School of Education, Program in School Counseling, Syracuse, NY 13244. Offers MS, CAS. *Students:* 18 full-time (17 women), 10 part-time (9 women); includes 3 minority (2 Black or African American, non-Hispanic/Latino; 1 Hispanic/Latino), 1 international. Average age 26. 29 applicants, 45% accepted, 7 enrolled. In 2010, 5 master's awarded. *Entrance requirements:* For master's, GRE General Test or MAT, group interview. Additional exam requirements/recommendations for international students: Required—TOEFL (minimum score 100 iBT). *Application deadline:* For fall admission, 2/1 priority date for domestic and international students; for spring admission, 10/15 priority date for domestic and international students. Applications are processed on a rolling basis. Application fee: $75. Electronic applications accepted. *Expenses:* Tuition: Part-time $1162 per credit. *Financial support:* Fellowships with full tuition reimbursements, research assistantships with full and partial tuition reimbursements, teaching assistantships with full and partial tuition reimbursements available. Financial award application deadline: 1/1; financial award applicants required to submit FAFSA. *Unit head:* Dr. Dennis Gilbride, Chair, 315-443-2266, Fax: 315-443-5732, E-mail: ddgilbr@syr.edu. *Application contact:* Liza Rochelson, Graduate Recruiter, School of Education, 315-443-2505, E-mail: e-gradrcrt@syr.edu.

Tarleton State University, College of Graduate Studies, College of Education, Department of Psychology and Counseling, Stephenville, TX 76402. Offers counseling and psychology (M Ed), including counseling, counseling psychology, educational psychology; educational administration (M Ed); secondary education (Certificate); special education (Certificate). Part-time and evening/weekend programs available. Postbaccalaureate distance learning degree programs offered (minimal on-campus study). *Degree requirements:* For master's, comprehensive exam, thesis optional. *Entrance requirements:* For master's, GRE General Test, minimum GPA of 3.0. Additional exam requirements/recommendations for international students: Required—TOEFL (minimum score 550 paper-based; 213 computer-based; 80 iBT). Electronic applications accepted.

Teachers College, Columbia University, Graduate Faculty of Education, Department of Health and Behavior Studies, Program in Applied Educational Psychology–School Psychology, New York, NY 10027. Offers Ed M, MA, Ed D, PhD. *Accreditation:* APA (one or more programs are accredited). *Faculty:* 4 full-time (2 women), 12 part-time/adjunct (10 women). *Students:* 47

full-time (43 women), 49 part-time (42 women); includes 19 minority (4 Black or African American, non-Hispanic/Latino; 6 Asian, non-Hispanic/Latino; 4 Hispanic/Latino; 3 Native Hawaiian or other Pacific Islander, non-Hispanic/Latino; 2 Two or more races, non-Hispanic/Latino), 5 international. Average age 26. 143 applicants, 29% accepted, 22 enrolled. In 2010, 123 master's, 3 doctorates awarded. *Degree requirements:* For master's, project; for doctorate, comprehensive exam, thesis/dissertation. *Entrance requirements:* For master's, GRE General Test (for Ed M); for doctorate, GRE General Test. *Application deadline:* For fall admission, 12/15 for domestic students. Application fee: $65. *Expenses:* Tuition: Full-time $28,272; part-time $1178 per credit. Required fees: $756; $378 per semester. *Financial support:* Fellowships, research assistantships, career-related internships or fieldwork, Federal Work-Study, institutionally sponsored loans, and tuition waivers (full and partial) available. Support available to part-time students. Financial award application deadline: 2/1; financial award applicants required to submit FAFSA. *Faculty research:* Psychoeducational assessment, observation and concept acquisition in young children, reading, mathematical thinking, memory. *Unit head:* Prof. Marla Brassard, Chair, 212-678-3942, E-mail: brassard@tc.edu. *Application contact:* Prof. Marla Brassard, Chair, 212-678-3942, E-mail: brassard@tc.edu.

Temple University, College of Education, Department of Psychological Studies in Education, Program in School Psychology, Philadelphia, PA 19122-6096. Offers Ed M, PhD. *Accreditation:* APA (one or more programs are accredited). Part-time and evening/weekend programs available. *Students:* 45 full-time (38 women), 11 part-time (7 women); includes 6 Black or African American, non-Hispanic/Latino; 1 American Indian or Alaska Native, non-Hispanic/Latino; 3 Asian, non-Hispanic/Latino; 1 Hispanic/Latino. In 2010, 19 master's, 4 doctorates awarded. Terminal master's awarded for partial completion of doctoral program. *Degree requirements:* For master's, thesis or alternative; for doctorate, thesis/dissertation. *Entrance requirements:* For master's and doctorate, GRE General Test, GRE Subject Test, minimum GPA of 3.0. Additional exam requirements/recommendations for international students: Required—TOEFL (minimum score 550 paper-based; 213 computer-based; 79 iBT). *Application deadline:* For fall admission, 1/1 for domestic students, 12/15 for international students. Application fee: $50. Electronic applications accepted. *Financial support:* Fellowships, research assistantships with full tuition reimbursements, teaching assistantships with full tuition reimbursements available. Financial award application deadline: 1/15; financial award applicants required to submit FAFSA. *Unit head:* Dr. Catherine Fiorello, Head, 215-204-6254, E-mail: catherine.fiorello@temple.edu. *Application contact:* Dr. Margo Greicar, Director for Graduate Academic & Student Affairs, 215-204-8011, Fax: 215-204-4383, E-mail: margo.greicar@temple.edu.

Tennessee State University, The School of Graduate Studies and Research, College of Education, Department of Psychology, Nashville, TN 37209-1561. Offers counseling and guidance (MS), including counseling, elementary school counseling, organizational counseling, secondary school counseling; counseling psychology (PhD); psychology (MS, PhD); school psychology (MS, PhD). *Accreditation:* APA. *Degree requirements:* For doctorate, thesis/dissertation (for some programs). *Entrance requirements:* For master's, GRE General Test or MAT; for doctorate, GRE General Test or MAT, minimum GPA of 3.25, work experience. Electronic applications accepted.

Texas A&M University, College of Education and Human Development, Department of Educational Psychology, College Station, TX 77843. Offers bilingual education (M Ed, PhD); cognition, creativity, instruction and development (MS, PhD); counseling psychology (PhD); educational psychology (PhD); educational technology (PhD); research, measurement and statistics (MS); research, measurement, and statistics (PhD); school psychology (PhD); special education (M Ed, PhD). *Accreditation:* APA (one or more programs are accredited). Part-time and evening/weekend programs available. Postbaccalaureate distance learning degree programs offered (no on-campus study). *Faculty:* 49. *Students:* 160 full-time (123 women), 147 part-time (120 women); includes 106 minority (24 Black or African American, non-Hispanic/Latino; 16 Asian, non-Hispanic/Latino; 66 Hispanic/Latino), 45 international. In 2010, 36 master's, 31 doctorates awarded. *Degree requirements:* For master's, thesis optional; for doctorate, thesis/dissertation. *Entrance requirements:* For master's and doctorate, GRE General Test. Additional exam requirements/recommendations for international students: Required—TOEFL. Application fee: $50 ($75 for international students). Electronic applications accepted. *Financial support:* In 2010–11, fellowships (averaging $12,000 per year), research assistantships (averaging $9,000 per year), teaching assistantships (averaging $9,000 per year) were awarded; career-related internships or fieldwork, institutionally sponsored loans, scholarships/grants, and unspecified assistantships also available. Financial award applicants required to submit FAFSA. *Unit head:* Dr. Victor Willson, Head, 979-845-1800. *Application contact:* Carol A. Wagner, Director of Advising, 979-845-1833, Fax: 979-862-1256, E-mail: epsyadvisor@tamu.edu.

Texas State University–San Marcos, Graduate School, College of Education, Department of Counseling, Leadership, Adult Education, and School Psychology, Program in School Psychology, San Marcos, TX 78666. Offers SSP. Part-time programs available. *Faculty:* 5 full-time (3 women), 1 part-time/adjunct (0 women). *Students:* 43 full-time (36 women), 20 part-time (16 women); includes 1 Black or African American, non-Hispanic/Latino; 4 Asian, non-Hispanic/Latino; 8 Hispanic/Latino. Average age 26. 40 applicants, 63% accepted, 11 enrolled. *Entrance requirements:* Additional exam requirements/recommendations for international students: Required—TOEFL (minimum score 550 paper-based; 213 computer-based; 78 iBT). *Application deadline:* For fall admission, 2/15 for domestic and international students; for spring admission, 10/15 for domestic students, 10/1 for international students. Applications are processed on a rolling basis. Application fee: $40 ($90 for international students). Electronic applications accepted. *Expenses:* Tuition, state resident: full-time $6024; part-time $251 per credit hour. Tuition, nonresident: full-time $13,536; part-time $564 per credit hour. Required fees: $1776; $50 per credit hour. $306 per semester. *Financial support:* In 2010–11, 45 students received support, including 4 research assistantships (averaging $3,322 per year), 9 teaching assistantships (averaging $1,696 per year); career-related internships or fieldwork, Federal Work-Study, and institutionally sponsored loans also available. Support available to part-time students. Financial award application deadline: 4/1; financial award applicants required to submit FAFSA. *Unit head:* Dr. Jon Lasser, Graduate Advisor, 512-245-3083, Fax: 512-245-8872, E-mail: lasser@txstate.edu. *Application contact:* Dr. J. Michael Willoughby, Dean of Graduate School, 512-245-2581, Fax: 512-245-8365, E-mail: gradcollege@txstate.edu.

Texas Woman's University, Graduate School, College of Arts and Sciences, Department of Psychology and Philosophy, Denton, TX 76201. Offers counseling psychology (MA, PhD); school psychology (PhD, SSP). *Accreditation:* APA (one or more programs are accredited). *Faculty:* 16 full-time (9 women). *Students:* 81 full-time (72 women), 52 part-time (46 women); includes 11 Black or African American, non-Hispanic/Latino; 1 American Indian or Alaska Native, non-Hispanic/Latino; 6 Asian, non-Hispanic/Latino; 13 Hispanic/Latino, 1 international. Average age 30. 169 applicants, 27% accepted, 33 enrolled. In 2010, 15 master's, 9 doctorates awarded. Terminal master's awarded for partial completion of doctoral program. *Degree requirements:* For master's, thesis; for doctorate, comprehensive exam, thesis/dissertation, internship, residency. *Entrance requirements:* For master's, GRE (preferred minimum score 500 Verbal, 500 Quantitative, 4 Analytical), BA/BS or 18 hours in psychology; minimum GPA of 3.0, 3.5 in undergraduate psychology classes; 3 letters of reference; curriculum vitae; essays; for doctorate, GRE (preferred minimum score 500 Verbal, 500 Quantitative, 4 Analytical), 3 letters of reference, minimum GPA of 3.5 overall and in psychology undergraduate classes, BS/BA in psychology or 18 hours of required psychology classes, curriculum vitae, essays. Additional exam requirements/recommendations for international students: Required—TOEFL (minimum score 550 paper-based; 213 computer-based; 79 iBT). *Application deadline:* For fall admission, 12/15 priority date for domestic and international students. Applications are processed on a rolling basis. Application fee: $50 ($75 for international students). Electronic applications accepted. *Expenses:* Tuition, state resident: full-time $3834; part-time $213 per credit hour. Tuition, nonresident: full-time $9468; part-time $526 per credit hour. Required fees: $1247; $220 per credit hour. *Financial support:* In 2010–11, 49 students received support, including 29 research assistantships (averaging $10,746 per year), 9 teaching assistantships (averaging $10,746 per year); career-related internships or fieldwork, Federal Work-Study, institutionally sponsored loans, scholarships/grants, traineeships, health care benefits, and unspecified

assistantships also available. Support available to part-time students. Financial award application deadline: 3/1; financial award applicants required to submit FAFSA. *Faculty research:* Women's anger, school neuropsychological theory and assessment, body image dysfunction, traumatic stress, classical ethics, mental health and behavioral needs of adolescents in alternative education. *Unit head:* Dr. Dan Miller, Chair, 940-898-2303, Fax: 940-898-2301, E-mail: dmiller@twu.edu. *Application contact:* Dr. Samuel Wheeler, Assistant Director of Admissions, 940-898-3188, Fax: 940-898-3081, E-mail: wheelersr@twu.edu.

Towson University, Program in School Psychology, Towson, MD 21252-0001. Offers CAS. Part-time and evening/weekend programs available. *Students:* 11 full-time (all women), 2 part-time (both women); includes 3 minority (all Black or African American, non-Hispanic/Latino). Average age 26. In 2010, 12 CASs awarded. *Application deadline:* For fall admission, 1/15 for domestic students. Application fee: $50. Electronic applications accepted. *Expenses:* Tuition, state resident: part-time $324 per credit. Tuition, nonresident: part-time $681 per credit. Required fees: $95 per term. *Financial support:* In 2010–11, 5 students received support, including 5 fellowships with full tuition reimbursements available (averaging $4,000 per year); Federal Work-Study and unspecified assistantships also available. Financial award application deadline: 4/1; financial award applicants required to submit FAFSA. *Faculty research:* Cognitive behavior, issues affecting the aging, relaxation hypnosis and imagery, lesbian and gay issues. *Unit head:* Dr. Susan Bartels, Graduate Program Director, 410-704-3070, Fax: 410-704-3800, E-mail: sbartels@towson.edu. *Application contact:* 410-704-2501, Fax: 410-704-4675, E-mail: grads@towson.edu.

Trinity University, Department of Education, Program in School Psychology, San Antonio, TX 78212-7200. Offers MA. *Accreditation:* NCATE. *Entrance requirements:* For master's, GRE General Test, minimum GPA of 3.0, interview.

Troy University, Graduate School, College of Education, Program in Counseling and Psychology, Troy, AL 36082. Offers agency counseling (Ed S); clinical mental health (MS); community counseling (MS, Ed S); corrections counseling (MS); rehabilitation counseling (MS); school psychology (MS, Ed S); school psychometry (MS); social service counseling (MS); student affairs counseling (MS); substance abuse counseling (MS). *Accreditation:* ACA; CORE; NCATE. Part-time and evening/weekend programs available. *Students:* 419 full-time (338 women), 720 part-time (603 women); includes 696 minority (592 Black or African American, non-Hispanic/Latino; 8 American Indian or Alaska Native, non-Hispanic/Latino; 4 Asian, non-Hispanic/Latino; 46 Hispanic/Latino; 46 Two or more races, non-Hispanic/Latino). Average age 33. 326 applicants, 90% accepted. In 2010, 198 master's, 1 other advanced degree awarded. *Degree requirements:* For master's, comprehensive exam, thesis. *Entrance requirements:* For master's, MAT, minimum GPA of 2.5. Additional exam requirements/recommendations for international students: Required—TOEFL (minimum score 523 paper-based; 193 computer-based; 70 iBT), IELTS (minimum score 6). *Application deadline:* Applications are processed on a rolling basis. Application fee: $50. Electronic applications accepted. *Expenses:* Tuition, state resident: full-time $4428; part-time $246 per credit hour. Tuition, nonresident: full-time $8856; part-time $492 per credit hour. Required fees: $432; $24 per credit hour. $50 per term. Tuition and fees vary according to program. *Unit head:* Dr. Andrew Creamer, Chair, 334-670-3350, Fax: 334-670-32961, E-mail: drcreamer@troy.edu. *Application contact:* Brenda K. Campbell, Director of Graduate Admissions, 334-670-3178, Fax: 334-670-3733, E-mail: bcamp@troy.edu.

Tufts University, Graduate School of Arts and Sciences, Department of Education, Program in School Psychology, Medford, MA 02155. Offers MA, Ed S. *Entrance requirements:* For master's, GRE General Test. Additional exam requirements/recommendations for international students: Required—TOEFL (minimum score 550 paper-based; 213 computer-based; 80 iBT). Electronic applications accepted. *Expenses:* Tuition: Full-time $39,624; part-time $3962 per course. Required fees: $40 per year. Full-time tuition and fees vary according to degree level, program and student level. Part-time tuition and fees vary according to course load.

Union College, Graduate Programs, Department of Psychology, Barbourville, KY 40906-1499. Offers clinical psychology (MA); counseling psychology (MA); school psychology (MA).

University at Albany, State University of New York, School of Education, Department of Educational and Counseling Psychology, Albany, NY 12222-0001. Offers counseling psychology (MS, PhD, CAS); educational psychology (Ed D); educational psychology and statistics (MS); measurements and evaluation (Ed D); rehabilitation counseling (MS), including counseling psychology; school counselor (CAS); school psychology (Psy D, CAS); special education (MS); statistics and research design (Ed D). *Accreditation:* APA (one or more programs are accredited). Evening/weekend programs available. *Degree requirements:* For doctorate, thesis/dissertation. *Entrance requirements:* For doctorate, GRE General Test. Additional exam requirements/recommendations for international students: Required—TOEFL (minimum score 550 paper-based; 213 computer-based). Electronic applications accepted.

The University of Akron, Graduate School, College of Education, Department of Counseling, Program in Classroom Guidance for Teachers, Akron, OH 44325. Offers MA, MS. *Accreditation:* NCATE. *Students:* 3 part-time (all women); includes 1 Hispanic/Latino. Average age 29. *Degree requirements:* For master's, comprehensive exam. *Entrance requirements:* For master's, minimum GPA of 2.75, interview, letters of recommendation, criminal background check, resume. Additional exam requirements/recommendations for international students: Required—TOEFL (minimum score 550 paper-based; 213 computer-based; 79 iBT). *Application deadline:* For fall admission, 3/15 for domestic and international students; for spring admission, 10/1 for domestic and international students. Application fee: $30 ($40 for international students). Electronic applications accepted. *Expenses:* Tuition, state resident: full-time $6800; part-time $378 per credit hour. Tuition, nonresident: full-time $11,644; part-time $647 per credit hour. Required fees: $1265. One-time fee: $30 full-time. *Unit head:* Dr. Cynthia Reynolds, Coordinator, 330-972-6748, E-mail: creynol@uakron.edu. *Application contact:* Dr. Cynthia Reynolds, Coordinator, 330-972-6748, E-mail: creynol@uakron.edu.

University of Alberta, Faculty of Graduate Studies and Research, Department of Educational Psychology, Edmonton, AB T6G 2E1, Canada. Offers counseling psychology (M Ed, PhD); educational psychology (M Ed, PhD); instructional technology (M Ed); school counseling (M Ed); school psychology (M Ed, PhD); special education (M Ed, PhD); special education-deafness studies (M Ed); teaching English as a second language (M Ed). Part-time programs available. *Degree requirements:* For master's, thesis optional; for doctorate, comprehensive exam, thesis/dissertation. *Entrance requirements:* For master's and doctorate, minimum GPA of 3.0. Additional exam requirements/recommendations for international students: Required—TOEFL. *Faculty research:* Human learning, development and assessment.

The University of Arizona, College of Education, Department of Disability and Psychoeducational Studies, Program in School Psychology, Tucson, AZ 85721. Offers PhD, Ed S. Part-time programs available. *Students:* 36 full-time (31 women), 12 part-time (11 women); includes 4 Black or African American, non-Hispanic/Latino; 9 Hispanic/Latino; 1 Two or more races, non-Hispanic/Latino, 3 international. Average age 32. *Entrance requirements:* For doctorate, GRE General Test; for Ed S, minimum GPA of 3.5, 3 letters of recommendation, curriculum vitae, writing sample. *Application deadline:* For fall admission, 1/10 for domestic students, 12/1 for international students. *Expenses:* Tuition, state resident: full-time $7692. *Unit head:* Dr. Linda R. Shaw, Department Head, 520-621-7822, Fax: 520-621-3821, E-mail: lshaw@email.arizona.edu. *Application contact:* Cecilia Carlon, Coordinator, 520-621-7822, Fax: 520-621-3821, E-mail: ccarlon@email.arizona.edu.

The University of British Columbia, Faculty of Education, Department of Educational and Counseling Psychology, and Special Education, Vancouver, BC V6T 1Z1, Canada. Offers counseling psychology (M Ed, MA, PhD); development, learning and culture (PhD); guidance studies (Diploma); human development, learning and culture (M Ed, MA); measurement and evaluation and research methodology (M Ed); measurement, evaluation and research methodology (MA); measurement, evaluation, and research methodology (PhD); school

School Psychology

The University of British Columbia (continued)

psychology (M Ed, MA, PhD); special education (M Ed, MA, PhD, Diploma). Part-time programs available. *Degree requirements:* For master's, thesis (for some programs); for doctorate, comprehensive exam, thesis/dissertation. *Entrance requirements:* For master's, GRE General Test (counseling psychology MA); for doctorate, GRE General Test. Additional exam requirements/recommendations for international students: Required—TOEFL. Electronic applications accepted. Tuition charges are reported in Canadian dollars. *Expenses:* Tuition, area resident: Full-time $4179 Canadian dollars. International tuition: $7344 Canadian dollars full-time. *Faculty research:* Women, family, social problems, career transition, stress and coping problems.

University of Calgary, Faculty of Graduate Studies, Faculty of Education, Division of Applied Psychology, Calgary, AB T2N 1N4, Canada. Offers counseling psychology (M Ed, M Sc, PhD); human development and learning (M Ed, M Sc, PhD); school psychology (M Ed, M Sc, PhD); special education (M Ed, M Sc, PhD). Part-time programs available. *Degree requirements:* For master's, thesis (for some programs), final oral exam; for doctorate, thesis/dissertation, candidacy exam, final oral exam. *Entrance requirements:* For master's, minimum GPA of 3.0, 3 letters of reference; for doctorate, minimum GPA of 3.5, 3 letters of reference. *Faculty research:* Counselor education, family life studies, learning and cognition.

University of California, Riverside, Graduate Division, Graduate School of Education, Riverside, CA 92521-0102. Offers autism (M Ed); curriculum and instruction (MA, PhD); diversity and equity (M Ed); educational psychology (MA, PhD); general education (M Ed); higher education administration and policy (M Ed, PhD); reading (M Ed); school psychology (PhD); special education (M Ed, MA, PhD). *Faculty:* 23 full-time (12 women), 8 part-time/adjunct (5 women). *Students:* 171 full-time (123 women); includes 9 Black or African American, non-Hispanic/Latino; 1 American Indian or Alaska Native, non-Hispanic/Latino; 18 Asian, non-Hispanic/Latino; 19 Hispanic/Latino, 5 international. Average age 31. 165 applicants, 66% accepted, 80 enrolled. In 2010, 67 master's, 14 doctorates awarded. Terminal master's awarded for partial completion of doctoral program. *Degree requirements:* For master's, comprehensive exams or thesis (MA), case study or analytical report (M Ed); for doctorate, thesis/dissertation, written and oral qualifying exams, college teaching practicum. *Entrance requirements:* For master's, GRE General Test, GRE Subject Test, CBEST, CSET, minimum GPA of 3.2; for doctorate, GRE General Test, GRE Subject Test, master's degree (desirable), minimum GPA of 3.2. Additional exam requirements/recommendations for international students: Required—TOEFL (minimum score 550 paper-based; 213 computer-based; 80 iBT), IELTS (minimum score 7). *Application deadline:* For fall admission, 9/1 for domestic students, 4/1 for international students; for winter admission, 12/1 for domestic students, 7/1 for international students; for spring admission, 3/1 for domestic students, 10/1 for international students. Applications are processed on a rolling basis. Application fee: $80 ($100 for international students). Electronic applications accepted. *Financial support:* In 2010–11, 53 students received support, including 30 fellowships with full and partial tuition reimbursements available (averaging $29,836 per year), 24 research assistantships with full and partial tuition reimbursements available (averaging $14,239 per year), 1 teaching assistantship with full and partial tuition reimbursement available (averaging $16,969 per year); career-related internships or fieldwork, Federal Work-Study, institutionally sponsored loans, scholarships/grants, and unspecified assistantships also available. Financial award application deadline: 1/5. *Faculty research:* Responsiveness to intervention, faculty core, response to intervention of English language learners, advanced modeling techniques, study on social capital, trust, and motivation. Total annual research expenditures: $4.4 million. *Unit head:* Prof. John Levin, Interim Dean, 951-827-5802, Fax: 951-827-3942, E-mail: john.levin@ucr.edu. *Application contact:* Prof. John Wills, Graduate Advisor for Admission, 951-827-6362, Fax: 951-827-3291, E-mail: edgrad@ucr.edu.

University of California, Santa Barbara, Graduate Division, Gevirtz Graduate School of Education, Santa Barbara, CA 93106-9490. Offers counseling, clinical and school psychology (PhD), including clinical psychology, counseling psychology, school psychology; education (M Ed, MA, PhD), including child and adolescent development (MA, PhD), cultural perspectives and comparative education (MA, PhD), educational leadership and organizations (MA, PhD), research methodology (MA, PhD), special education disabilities and risk studies (MA), special education, disabilities and risk studies (PhD), teaching (M Ed), teaching and learning (MA, PhD); educational leadership (Ed D); school psychology (M Ed); MA/PhD. *Accreditation:* APA (one or more programs are accredited). Postbaccalaureate distance learning degree programs offered (minimal on-campus study). *Faculty:* 40 full-time (22 women), 5 part-time/adjunct (1 woman). *Students:* 411 full-time (325 women); includes 19 Black or African American, non-Hispanic/Latino; 3 American Indian or Alaska Native, non-Hispanic/Latino; 59 Asian, non-Hispanic/Latino; 67 Hispanic/Latino. Average age 29. 683 applicants, 38% accepted, 154 enrolled. In 2010, 128 master's, 58 doctorates awarded. Terminal master's awarded for partial completion of doctoral program. *Degree requirements:* For master's, comprehensive exam (for some programs), thesis (for some programs); for doctorate, comprehensive exam (for some programs), thesis/dissertation. *Entrance requirements:* For master's and doctorate, GRE. Additional exam requirements/recommendations for international students: Required—TOEFL (minimum score 550 paper-based; 80 iBT), IELTS (minimum score 7). Application fee: $70 ($90 for international students). Electronic applications accepted. *Financial support:* In 2010–11, 269 students received support, including 222 fellowships with partial tuition reimbursements available (averaging $5,615 per year), 75 research assistantships with full tuition reimbursements available (averaging $6,470 per year), 65 teaching assistantships with partial tuition reimbursements available (averaging $7,059 per year); career-related internships or fieldwork also available. Financial award applicants required to submit FAFSA. *Faculty research:* Needs of diverse students, school accountability and leadership, school violence, language learning and literacy, science/math education. Total annual research expenditures: $3.1 million. *Unit head:* Carol North Dixon, Graduate Advisor, 805-893-2185, E-mail: dixon@education.ucsb.edu. *Application contact:* Kathryn Marie Tucciarone, Student Affairs Officer, 805-893-2137, Fax: 805-893-2588, E-mail: katiet@education.ucsb.edu.

University of Central Arkansas, Graduate School, College of Health and Behavioral Sciences, Department of Counseling and Psychology, Program in School Psychology, Conway, AR 72035-0001. Offers MS, PhD. *Accreditation:* APA; NCATE. *Students:* 13 full-time (10 women), 1 (woman) part-time; includes 2 minority (both Black or African American, non-Hispanic/Latino). Average age 26. 11 applicants, 64% accepted, 7 enrolled. In 2010, 13 master's awarded. Terminal master's awarded for partial completion of doctoral program. *Degree requirements:* For master's, comprehensive exam, thesis optional; for doctorate, comprehensive exam, thesis/dissertation. *Entrance requirements:* For master's, GRE General Test, minimum GPA of 2.7; for doctorate, GRE General Test. Additional exam requirements/recommendations for international students: Required—TOEFL (minimum score 550 paper-based; 213 computer-based). *Application deadline:* For fall admission, 3/1 priority date for domestic and international students; for spring admission, 10/1 for domestic and international students. Applications are processed on a rolling basis. Application fee: $25 ($50 for international students). *Financial support:* Career-related internships or fieldwork, Federal Work-Study, scholarships/grants, tuition waivers (partial), and unspecified assistantships available. Financial award application deadline: 2/15; financial award applicants required to submit FAFSA. *Unit head:* Dr. Joan Simon, Coordinator, 501-450-5405. *Application contact:* Susan Wood, Administrative Assistant, 501-450-3124, Fax: 501-450-5678, E-mail: swood@uca.edu.

University of Central Florida, College of Education, Department of Educational and Human Sciences, Program in School Psychology, Orlando, FL 32816. Offers Ed S. Part-time and evening/weekend programs available. *Students:* 41 full-time (36 women), 1 (woman) part-time; includes 3 Black or African American, non-Hispanic/Latino; 1 Asian, non-Hispanic/Latino; 3 Hispanic/Latino. Average age 25. 41 applicants, 41% accepted, 16 enrolled. In 2010, 14 Ed Ss awarded. *Degree requirements:* For Ed S, thesis or alternative, practicum, internship. *Entrance requirements:* For degree, GRE General Test, minimum GPA of 3.0, resume, interview. Additional exam requirements/recommendations for international students: Required—TOEFL. *Application deadline:* For fall admission, 3/1 for domestic students. Application fee: $30. Electronic applications accepted. *Expenses:* Tuition, state resident: part-time $256.56 per credit hour. Tuition, nonresident: part-time $1011.52 per credit hour. Part-time tuition and fees vary according to program. *Financial support:* In 2010–11, 10 students received support, including 1 fellowship (averaging $10,000 per year), 4 research assistantships with partial tuition reimbursements available (averaging $5,700 per year), 5 teaching assistantships with partial tuition reimbursements available (averaging $3,200 per year); career-related internships or fieldwork, Federal Work-Study, institutionally sponsored loans, tuition waivers (partial), and unspecified assistantships also available. Financial award application deadline: 3/1; financial award applicants required to submit FAFSA.

University of Cincinnati, Graduate School, College of Education, Criminal Justice, and Human Services, Division of Human Services, Program in School Psychology, Cincinnati, OH 45221. Offers PhD, Ed S. *Accreditation:* NCATE. Part-time programs available. *Degree requirements:* For doctorate, comprehensive exam, thesis/dissertation. *Entrance requirements:* For doctorate, GRE General Test, GRE Subject Test. Additional exam requirements/recommendations for international students: Required—TOEFL (minimum score 520 paper-based; 190 computer-based; 68 iBT), OEPT. Electronic applications accepted. *Faculty research:* School psychology services delivery, direct assessment and intervention.

University of Colorado Denver, School of Education and Human Development, Program in Counseling Psychology and Counselor Education, Denver, CO 80217-3364. Offers school counseling (MA). *Accreditation:* ACA; NCATE. Part-time and evening/weekend programs available. *Students:* 183 full-time (159 women), 40 part-time (38 women); includes 5 Black or African American, non-Hispanic/Latino; 1 American Indian or Alaska Native, non-Hispanic/Latino; 6 Asian, non-Hispanic/Latino; 10 Hispanic/Latino, 4 international. Average age 30. 90 applicants, 54% accepted, 31 enrolled. In 2010, 43 master's awarded. *Degree requirements:* For master's, thesis or alternative, 63-66 hours. *Entrance requirements:* For master's, GRE, letters of recommendation, interview, resume. Additional exam requirements/recommendations for international students: Required—TOEFL (minimum score 525 paper-based; 197 computer-based). *Application deadline:* For fall admission, 1/15 for domestic students; for spring admission, 9/15 for domestic students. Application fee: $50 ($75 for international students). Electronic applications accepted. *Expenses:* Contact institution. *Financial support:* Research assistantships, Federal Work-Study and scholarships/grants available. Financial award application deadline: 4/1; financial award applicants required to submit FAFSA. *Faculty research:* Spiritual issues in counseling, multicultural and diversity issues in counseling, adolescent suicide, career development. *Unit head:* Dr. Marsha Wiggins, Division Coordinator, 303-315-6332, E-mail: marsha.wiggins@ucdenver.edu. *Application contact:* Student Services Coordinator, 303-315-6300, Fax: 303-315-6311, E-mail: education@ucdenver.edu.

University of Colorado Denver, School of Education and Human Development, Programs in Educational and School Psychology, Denver, CO 80217. Offers educational psychology (MA), including educational assessment, human development, human learning, individually structured, partner schools, research and evaluation; school psychology (Ed S). Part-time and evening/weekend programs available. *Students:* 123 full-time (111 women), 57 part-time (51 women); includes 4 Black or African American, non-Hispanic/Latino; 1 American Indian or Alaska Native, non-Hispanic/Latino; 5 Asian, non-Hispanic/Latino; 8 Hispanic/Latino, 5 international. Average age 30. 97 applicants, 79% accepted, 54 enrolled. In 2010, 62 master's, 14 other advanced degrees awarded. *Degree requirements:* For master's, recommended plan of study includes 9 hours of core courses, embedded within a minimum of 36 to 38 hours of relevant coursework; for Ed S, comprehensive exam, minimum of 75 semester hours (61 hours of coursework, 6 of 500-hour practicum in field, and 8 of 1200-hour internship); Praxis II. *Entrance requirements:* For master's, GRE if undergraduate GPA below 2.75, resume, written statement, letters of recommendation, transcripts; for Ed S, GRE, resume, written statement, letters of recommendation, transcripts. Additional exam requirements/recommendations for international students: Required—TOEFL. *Application deadline:* For fall admission, 4/15 for domestic students; for spring admission, 9/15 for domestic students. Application fee: $50 ($75 for international students). Electronic applications accepted. *Expenses:* Contact institution. *Financial support:* Application deadline: 4/1. *Faculty research:* Crisis response and intervention, school violence prevention; immigrant experience, educational environments for English language learners, culturally competent assessment and intervention, child and youth suicide. *Application contact:* Student Services Center, 303-315-6300, Fax: 303-315-6311, E-mail: education@ucdenver.edu.

University of Connecticut, Graduate School, Neag School of Education, Department of Educational Psychology, Program in School Psychology, Storrs, CT 06269. Offers MA, PhD, Post-Master's Certificate. *Accreditation:* APA; NCATE. Terminal master's awarded for partial completion of doctoral program. *Degree requirements:* For master's, comprehensive exam, thesis or alternative; for doctorate, thesis/dissertation. *Entrance requirements:* For doctorate, GRE General Test. Additional exam requirements/recommendations for international students: Required—TOEFL (minimum score 550 paper-based; 213 computer-based). Electronic applications accepted.

University of Dayton, Graduate School, School of Education and Allied Professions, Department of Counselor Education and Human Services, Dayton, OH 45469-1300. Offers college student personnel (MS Ed); community counseling (MS Ed); higher education administration (MS Ed); human services (MS Ed); school counseling (MS Ed); school psychology (MS Ed, Ed S). *Accreditation:* ACA; NCATE. Part-time and evening/weekend programs available. *Faculty:* 12 full-time (9 women), 32 part-time/adjunct (18 women). *Students:* 269 full-time (219 women), 180 part-time (150 women); includes 84 minority (69 Black or African American, non-Hispanic/Latino; 2 American Indian or Alaska Native, non-Hispanic/Latino; 8 Asian, non-Hispanic/Latino; 3 Hispanic/Latino; 2 Two or more races, non-Hispanic/Latino), 2 international. Average age 32. 246 applicants, 48% accepted, 89 enrolled. In 2010, 157 master's, 10 Ed Ss awarded. *Degree requirements:* For master's, comprehensive exam (for some programs), thesis (for some programs), exit exam. *Entrance requirements:* For master's, MAT or GRE (if GPA less than 2.75), interview, writing sample. Additional exam requirements/recommendations for international students: Required—TOEFL (minimum score 550 paper-based; 213 computer-based; 80 iBT). *Application deadline:* For fall admission, 4/10 for domestic students, 3/1 priority date for international students; for winter admission, 9/10 for domestic students, 7/1 priority date for international students; for spring admission, 1/10 for domestic students, 1/1 priority date for international students. Application fee: $0 ($50 for international students). Electronic applications accepted. *Expenses:* Tuition: Full-time $7800; part-time $650 per credit hour. *Financial support:* In 2010–11, 7 research assistantships with full tuition reimbursements (averaging $8,400 per year) were awarded; career-related internships or fieldwork, institutionally sponsored loans, health care benefits, and unspecified assistantships also available. Financial award applicants required to submit FAFSA. *Faculty research:* Anger as part of the grief process, inclusion of children with severe disabilities, comparisons of school counselors in Bosnia and the U. S., graduate and professional student socialization, use of cohort groups in doctoral programs, bullying in schools, impact of space on learning, sophomore experience. *Unit head:* Dr. Alan Demmitt, Chairperson, 937-229-3644, Fax: 937-229-1055. *Application contact:* Alexander Popovski, Associate Director of Graduate and International Admissions, 937-229-2357, Fax: 937-229-4729, E-mail: alex.popovski@notes.udayton.edu.

University of Delaware, College of Human Services, Education and Public Policy and Department of Individual and Family Studies, Program in Counseling in Higher Education, Newark, DE 19716. Offers M Ed, MA. *Accreditation:* NCATE. *Degree requirements:* For master's, comprehensive exam. *Entrance requirements:* For master's, GRE (quantitative and verbal), on-campus interview, letters of recommendation. Additional exam requirements/recommendations for international students: Required—TOEFL (minimum score 600 paper-based). Electronic applications accepted. *Faculty research:* Counseling outcomes, student culture, group counseling.

University of Delaware, College of Human Services, Education and Public Policy, School of Education, Newark, DE 19716. Offers education (PhD); educational leadership (Ed D); higher education (M Ed); instruction (MI); reading (M Ed); school leadership (M Ed); school psychology (MA, Ed S); teaching English as a second language (TESL) (MA). *Accreditation:* NCATE. Part-time and evening/weekend programs available. Terminal master's awarded for partial completion of doctoral program. *Degree requirements:* For master's, comprehensive exam (for some programs), thesis (for some programs); for doctorate, comprehensive exam (for some programs), thesis/dissertation. *Entrance requirements:* For master's and doctorate, GRE, 3 letters of recommendation. Additional exam requirements/recommendations for international students: Required—TOEFL (minimum score 600 paper-based; 250 computer-based). Electronic applications accepted. *Faculty research:* Teacher education; curriculum theory and development; community based education models, educational leadership.

University of Denver, Morgridge College of Education, Denver, CO 80208. Offers counseling psychology (MA, PhD); curriculum and instruction (MA, PhD, Certificate), including curriculum leadership (MA, PhD); educational administration and policy studies (Certificate); educational psychology (MA, PhD, Ed S), including child and family studies (MA, PhD), quantitative research methods (MA, PhD), school psychology (PhD, Ed S); higher education and adult studies (MA, PhD); library and information science (MLIS); library and information sciences (Certificate); school administration (PhD). *Accreditation:* ALA; APA (one or more programs are accredited). Part-time and evening/weekend programs available. Postbaccalaureate distance learning degree programs offered (no on-campus study). *Faculty:* 48 full-time (33 women), 68 part-time/adjunct (52 women). *Students:* 405 full-time (311 women), 423 part-time (326 women); includes 171 minority (53 Black or African American, non-Hispanic/Latino; 5 American Indian or Alaska Native, non-Hispanic/Latino; 17 Asian, non-Hispanic/Latino; 88 Hispanic/Latino; 8 Two or more races, non-Hispanic/Latino), 19 international. Average age 33. 934 applicants, 66% accepted, 381 enrolled. In 2010, 203 master's, 59 doctorates, 108 other advanced degrees awarded. Terminal master's awarded for partial completion of doctoral program. *Degree requirements:* For master's, comprehensive exam; for doctorate, 2 foreign languages, comprehensive exam, thesis/dissertation. *Entrance requirements:* For master's and doctorate, GRE General Test or GMAT. Additional exam requirements/recommendations for international students: Required—TOEFL (minimum score 550 paper-based; 80 iBT). *Application deadline:* Applications are processed on a rolling basis. Application fee: $60. Electronic applications accepted. *Expenses:* Tuition: Full-time $35,604; part-time $29,670 per year. Required fees: $687 per year. Tuition and fees vary according to program. *Financial support:* In 2010–11, 1 research assistantship with full and partial tuition reimbursement (averaging $18,297 per year), 26 teaching assistantships with full and partial tuition reimbursements (averaging $12,341 per year) were awarded; career-related internships or fieldwork, Federal Work-Study, institutionally sponsored loans, scholarships/grants, and unspecified assistantships also available. Support available to part-time students. Financial award application deadline: 3/1; financial award applicants required to submit FAFSA. *Faculty research:* Parkinson's disease, personnel training, development and assessments, gifted education, service-learning, transportation, public schools. *Unit head:* Dr. Gregory M. Anderson, Dean, 303-871-3665, E-mail: gregory.m.anderson@du.edu. *Application contact:* Janet Erickson, Director of Graduate Admission, 303-871-2485, E-mail: edinfo@du.edu.

University of Detroit Mercy, College of Liberal Arts and Education, Department of Psychology, Program in School Psychology, Detroit, MI 48221. Offers Spec.

University of Florida, Graduate School, College of Education, Department of Educational Psychology, Gainesville, FL 32611. Offers educational psychology (M Ed, MAE, Ed D, PhD, Ed S); research and evaluation methodology (M Ed, MAE, Ed D, PhD, Ed S); school psychology (M Ed, MAE, Ed D, PhD, Ed S). *Accreditation:* NCATE. *Faculty:* 25 full-time (13 women). *Students:* 84 full-time (63 women), 30 part-time (19 women); includes 14 Black or African American, non-Hispanic/Latino; 1 American Indian or Alaska Native, non-Hispanic/Latino; 5 Asian, non-Hispanic/Latino; 11 Hispanic/Latino, 20 international. Average age 31. 110 applicants, 29% accepted, 15 enrolled. In 2010, 13 master's, 10 doctorates awarded. Terminal master's awarded for partial completion of doctoral program. *Degree requirements:* For master's, thesis (MAE); for doctorate, variable foreign language requirement, thesis/dissertation. *Entrance requirements:* For master's and doctorate, GRE General Test, minimum GPA of 3.0; for Ed S, GRE General Test. Additional exam requirements/recommendations for international students: Required—TOEFL (minimum score 550 paper-based; 213 computer-based; 80 iBT), IELTS (minimum score 6). *Application deadline:* For fall admission, 6/1 priority date for domestic students. Applications are processed on a rolling basis. Application fee: $30. Electronic applications accepted. *Expenses:* Tuition, state resident: full-time $10,915.92. Tuition, nonresident: full-time $28,309. *Financial support:* In 2010–11, 54 students received support, including 3 fellowships, 35 research assistantships (averaging $18,039 per year), 16 teaching assistantships (averaging $7,210 per year); career-related internships or fieldwork and unspecified assistantships also available. Financial award application deadline: 4/30; financial award applicants required to submit FAFSA. *Faculty research:* School improvement, teaching and learning, item response theory. *Unit head:* Dr. Patricia T. Ashton, Program Head, 352-273-4348, Fax: 352-392-5929, E-mail: pashton@ufl.edu. *Application contact:* Dr. Patricia T. Ashton, Program Head, 352-273-4348, Fax: 352-392-5929, E-mail: pashton@ufl.edu.

University of Hartford, College of Arts and Sciences, Department of Psychology, Program in School Psychology, West Hartford, CT 06117-1599. Offers MS. *Accreditation:* NCATE. Part-time programs available. *Degree requirements:* For master's, comprehensive exam. *Entrance requirements:* For master's, GRE General Test, GRE Subject Test, minimum GPA of 3.0, 3 letters of recommendation. Additional exam requirements/recommendations for international students: Required—TOEFL (minimum score 550 paper-based; 213 computer-based). Electronic applications accepted. *Faculty research:* Family therapy, child developments, clinical supervision.

University of Houston–Clear Lake, School of Human Sciences and Humanities, Programs in Human Sciences, Houston, TX 77058-1098. Offers behavioral sciences (MA), including criminology, cross cultural studies, general psychology, sociology; clinical psychology (MA); criminology (MA); cross cultural studies (MA); family therapy (MA); fitness and human performance (MA); school psychology (MA). *Accreditation:* AAMFT/COAMFTE. Part-time and evening/weekend programs available. Postbaccalaureate distance learning degree programs offered (minimal on-campus study). *Degree requirements:* For master's, thesis or alternative. *Entrance requirements:* For master's, GRE General Test. Additional exam requirements/recommendations for international students: Required—TOEFL (minimum score 550 paper-based; 213 computer-based). Electronic applications accepted. *Faculty research:* Smoking cessation, adolescent sexuality, white collar crime, serial murder, human factors/human computer interaction.

University of Houston–Victoria, School of Arts and Sciences, Program in Psychology, Victoria, TX 77901-4450. Offers counseling psychology (MA); school psychology (MA). Part-time and evening/weekend programs available. Postbaccalaureate distance learning degree programs offered (minimal on-campus study). *Faculty:* 6 full-time (4 women). *Students:* 43 full-time (33 women), 64 part-time (56 women); includes 34 Black or African American, non-Hispanic/Latino; 2 Asian, non-Hispanic/Latino; 23 Hispanic/Latino; 2 Two or more races, non-Hispanic/Latino. Average age 33. 61 applicants, 77% accepted, 35 enrolled. In 2010, 9 master's awarded. *Degree requirements:* For master's, project or thesis. *Entrance requirements:* For master's, GRE General Test. Additional exam requirements/recommendations for international students: Required—TOEFL (minimum score 550 paper-based; 213 computer-based). *Application deadline:* For fall admission, 6/1 for international students; for spring admission, 10/1 for international students. Applications are processed on a rolling basis. Application fee: $0. Electronic applications accepted. *Expenses:* Tuition, state resident: full-time $4050; part-time $225 per credit hour. Tuition, nonresident: full-time $8730; part-time $485 per credit hour. Required fees: $810; $54 per credit hour. Tuition and fees vary according to course load. *Financial support:* In 2010–11, research assistantships with partial tuition reimbursements (averaging $2,000 per year), teaching assistantships with partial tuition reimbursements (averaging $2,000 per year) were awarded; Federal Work-Study, scholarships/grants, and unspecified assistantships also available. Support available to part-time students. Financial award application deadline: 4/15; financial award applicants required to submit FAFSA. *Unit head:* Dr. Rick Harrington, Chair, 361-570-4205, Fax: 361-570-4229, E-mail: harringtonr@uhv.edu. *Application contact:* Tracey Fox, Director of Services, 361-570-4233, Fax: 361-580-5507, E-mail: admissions@uhv.edu.

University of Idaho, College of Graduate Studies, College of Education, Department of Leadership and Counseling, Program in School Psychology, Moscow, ID 83844-2282. Offers Ed S. *Accreditation:* NCATE. *Students:* 18 full-time, 11 part-time. Average age 31. In 2010, 5 Ed Ss awarded. *Application deadline:* For fall admission, 8/1 for domestic students; for spring admission, 12/15 for domestic students. Applications are processed on a rolling basis. Application fee: $60. Electronic applications accepted. *Expenses:* Tuition, nonresident: part-time $580 per credit. Required fees: $306 per credit. *Financial support:* Applicants required to submit FAFSA. *Unit head:* Dr. Russell A. Joki, Chair, 208-364-4099, E-mail: rjoki@uidaho.edu. *Application contact:* Dr. Russell A. Joki, Chair, 208-364-4099, E-mail: rjoki@uidaho.edu.

The University of Iowa, Graduate College, College of Education, Department of Psychological and Quantitative Foundations, Iowa City, IA 52242-1316. Offers counseling psychology (PhD); educational measurement and statistics (MA, PhD); educational psychology (MA, PhD); school psychology (PhD, Ed S); JD/PhD. *Accreditation:* APA. *Degree requirements:* For master's, thesis optional, exam; for doctorate, comprehensive exam, thesis/dissertation; for Ed S, exam. *Entrance requirements:* For master's, doctorate, and Ed S, GRE General Test, minimum GPA of 3.0. Additional exam requirements/recommendations for international students: Required—TOEFL (minimum score 550 paper-based; 213 computer-based; 81 iBT). Electronic applications accepted.

The University of Kansas, Graduate Studies, School of Education, Department of Psychology and Research in Education, Program in School Psychology, Lawrence, KS 66045. Offers PhD, Ed S. *Accreditation:* APA (one or more programs are accredited); NCATE. *Students:* 35 full-time (24 women), 1 (woman) part-time; includes 2 minority (1 Asian, non-Hispanic/Latino; 1 Hispanic/Latino), 2 international. Average age 27. 39 applicants, 49% accepted, 11 enrolled. In 2010, 1 doctorate, 10 other advanced degrees awarded. *Degree requirements:* For doctorate, comprehensive exam, thesis/dissertation; for Ed S, comprehensive exam. *Entrance requirements:* For doctorate, GRE General Test; for Ed S, GRE General Test, minimum GPA of 3.0. Additional exam requirements/recommendations for international students: Required—TOEFL. *Application deadline:* For fall admission, 12/15 for domestic and international students. Application fee: $55 ($65 for international students). Electronic applications accepted. *Expenses:* Tuition, state resident: full-time $7092; part-time $295.50 per credit hour. Tuition, nonresident: full-time $16,590; part-time $691.25 per credit hour. Required fees: $858; $71.49 per credit hour. Tuition and fees vary according to course load, campus/location and program. *Financial support:* Fellowships, research assistantships with full and partial tuition reimbursements, teaching assistantships with full and partial tuition reimbursements available. Financial award application deadline: 2/1. *Faculty research:* Classroom management, anxiety in children and youth, child behavior and learning problems, behavioral and personality assessment, home/school/community partnerships. *Unit head:* Patricia A. Lowe, Director of Training, 785-864-9710, Fax: 785-864-3820, E-mail: tlowe@ku.edu. *Application contact:* Admissions Coordinator, 785-864-3931, Fax: 785-864-3820, E-mail: preadmit@ku.edu.

University of Kentucky, Graduate School, College of Education, Program in Educational and Counseling Psychology, Lexington, KY 40506-0032. Offers counseling psychology (MS Ed, PhD, Ed S); educational and counseling psychology (MS Ed); educational psychology (Ed D, PhD, Ed S); school psychometrist and school psychology (MA Ed). *Accreditation:* APA (one or more programs are accredited); NCATE. *Degree requirements:* For master's, comprehensive exam, thesis optional; for doctorate, comprehensive exam, thesis/dissertation; for Ed S, comprehensive exam. *Entrance requirements:* For master's, GRE General Test, minimum undergraduate GPA of 2.75; for doctorate, GRE General Test, minimum graduate GPA of 3.0; for Ed S, GRE General Test. Additional exam requirements/recommendations for international students: Required—TOEFL (minimum score 550 paper-based; 213 computer-based). Electronic applications accepted.

University of Louisiana at Monroe, Graduate School, College of Education and Human Development, Department of Psychology, Program in School Psychology, Monroe, LA 71209-0001. Offers MS, SSP. *Accreditation:* NCATE. *Faculty:* 2 full-time (both women), 2 part-time/adjunct (1 woman). *Students:* 7 full-time (all women), 2 part-time (0 women); includes 2 Black or African American, non-Hispanic/Latino. Average age 29. In 2010, 3 other advanced degrees awarded. *Degree requirements:* For SSP, comprehensive exam, thesis, field and practicum experience (400 hours), internship (1250 hours). *Entrance requirements:* For master's, GRE, minimum cumulative GPA of 2.75; for SSP, GRE General Test, minimum GPA of 3.25. Additional exam requirements/recommendations for international students: Required—TOEFL (minimum score 500 paper-based; 173 computer-based; 61 iBT). *Application deadline:* For fall admission, 8/24 priority date for domestic students, 7/1 for international students; for winter admission, 12/14 priority date for domestic students; for spring admission, 1/19 for domestic students, 11/1 for international students. Applications are processed on a rolling basis. Application fee: $20 ($30 for international students). Electronic applications accepted. *Expenses:* Tuition, state resident: full-time $2991; part-time $197 per credit hour. Tuition, nonresident: full-time $2991; part-time $197 per credit hour. International tuition: $10,288 full-time. *Financial support:* Career-related internships or fieldwork, Federal Work-Study, and unspecified assistantships available. Financial award application deadline: 4/1; financial award applicants required to submit FAFSA. *Unit head:* Dr. Veronica Lewis, Coordinator, 818-342-1332, E-mail: vlewis@ulm.edu. *Application contact:* Dr. Veronica Lewis, Coordinator, 818-342-1332, E-mail: vlewis@ulm.edu.

University of Manitoba, Faculty of Graduate Studies, Faculty of Arts, Department of Psychology, Winnipeg, MB R3T 2N2, Canada. Offers clinical psychology (PhD); psychology (MA, PhD); school psychology (MA). *Accreditation:* APA (one or more programs are accredited). *Degree requirements:* For master's, thesis; for doctorate, one foreign language, thesis/dissertation. *Entrance requirements:* For master's and doctorate, GRE General Test.

University of Mary, School of Education and Behavioral Sciences, Department of Behavioral Sciences, Bismarck, ND 58504-9652. Offers addiction counseling (MSC); community counseling (MSC); school counseling (MSC); student affairs counseling (MSC). Part-time programs available. Postbaccalaureate distance learning degree programs offered (minimal on-campus study). *Faculty:* 11 part-time/adjunct (8 women). *Students:* 32 full-time (21 women), 25 part-time (21 women); includes 4 Black or African American, non-Hispanic/Latino; 1 American Indian or Alaska Native, non-Hispanic/Latino. Average age 32. 27 applicants, 100% accepted, 27 enrolled. In 2010, 14 master's awarded. *Degree requirements:* For master's, thesis, internship. *Entrance requirements:* For master's, coursework/experience in psychology, statistics, minimum GPA of 3.0. Additional exam requirements/recommendations for international students: Required—TOEFL (minimum score 500 paper-based; 197 computer-based; 71 iBT). *Application deadline:* For fall admission, 8/1 priority date for domestic students. Application fee: $40. *Expenses:* Tuition: Full-time $10,800; part-time $450 per credit. Tuition and fees vary according to course load, degree level, program and student level. *Financial support:* Application deadline: 8/1. *Unit head:* James Renner, Program Director for Counseling Graduate Studies, 701-355-8177, Fax: 701-255-7687, E-mail: jrenner@umary.edu. *Application contact:* Jeanette Shaeffer, Accelerated and Distance Education Administrative Assistant, 701-355-8128, Fax: 701-255-7687, E-mail: jgschae@umary.edu.

University of Mary Hardin-Baylor, Graduate Studies in Counseling and Psychology, Belton, TX 76513. Offers clinical mental health counseling (MA); marriage and family Christian counseling (MA); psychology and counseling (MA); school counseling and psychology (MA). Part-time and evening/weekend programs available. *Faculty:* 7 full-time (4 women). *Students:* 33 full-time (23 women), 18 part-time (10 women); includes 11 minority (6 Black or African American, non-Hispanic/Latino; 4 Hispanic/Latino; 1 Two or more races, non-Hispanic/Latino), 1 international. Average age 29. 46 applicants, 50% accepted, 19 enrolled. In 2010, 44 master's awarded. *Degree requirements:* For master's, comprehensive exam. *Entrance requirements:* For master's, GRE General Test, minimum GPA of 3.0 in last 60 hours or 2.75 overall. *Application deadline:* For fall admission, 6/1 priority date for domestic students; for

School Psychology

University of Mary Hardin-Baylor (continued)

spring admission, 11/1 for domestic students. Applications are processed on a rolling basis. Application fee: $35 ($135 for international students). Electronic applications accepted. *Financial support:* Research assistantships with full tuition reimbursements, Federal Work-Study and scholarships (for some active duty military personnel only) available. Support available to part-time students. Financial award applicants required to submit FAFSA. *Unit head:* Dr. Isaac Gusukuma, Interim Graduate Program Director, 254-295-5017, E-mail: isaac.gusukuma@umhb.edu. *Application contact:* Dr. Isaac Gusukuma, Interim Graduate Program Director, 254-295-5017, E-mail: isaac.gusukuma@umhb.edu.

University of Maryland, College Park, Academic Affairs, College of Education, Department of Counseling and Personnel Services, College Park, MD 20742. Offers college student personnel (M Ed, MA); college student personnel administration (PhD); community counseling (CAGS); community/career counseling (M Ed, MA); counseling and personnel services (M Ed, MA, PhD), including art therapy (M Ed), college student personnel (M Ed), counseling and personnel services (PhD), counseling psychology (M Ed), mental health counseling (M Ed), school counseling (M Ed); counseling psychology (PhD); counselor education (PhD); rehabilitation counseling (M Ed, MA, AGSC); school counseling (M Ed, MA); school psychology (M Ed, MA, PhD). *Accreditation:* ACA (one or more programs are accredited); APA (one or more programs are accredited); CORE (one or more programs are accredited); NCATE. Part-time and evening/weekend programs available. Postbaccalaureate distance learning degree programs offered (no on-campus study). *Faculty:* 33 full-time (18 women), 1 (woman) part-time/adjunct. *Students:* 136 full-time (105 women), 16 part-time (11 women); includes 23 Black or African American, non-Hispanic/Latino; 19 Asian, non-Hispanic/Latino; 12 Hispanic/Latino; 5 Two or more races, non-Hispanic/Latino, 11 international. 407 applicants, 11% accepted, 25 enrolled. In 2010, 38 master's, 15 doctorates, 4 other advanced degrees awarded. *Degree requirements:* For master's, thesis (for some programs); for doctorate, thesis/dissertation. *Entrance requirements:* For master's, GRE General Test or MAT, minimum GPA of 3.0, 3 letters of recommendation; for doctorate, GRE General Test or MAT, minimum GPA of 3.5, 3 letters of recommendation. Additional exam requirements/recommendations for international students: Required—TOEFL. *Application deadline:* For fall admission, 12/15 for domestic and international students; for spring admission, 6/1 for international students. Applications are processed on a rolling basis. Application fee: $75. Electronic applications accepted. *Expenses:* Tuition, state resident: part-time $471 per credit hour. Tuition, nonresident: part-time $1016 per credit hour. Required fees: $337 per term. *Financial support:* In 2010–11, 15 fellowships with partial tuition reimbursements (averaging $11,738 per year), 3 research assistantships (averaging $17,258 per year), 83 teaching assistantships with tuition reimbursements (averaging $16,131 per year) were awarded; career-related internships or fieldwork, Federal Work-Study, and scholarships/grants also available. Support available to part-time students. Financial award applicants required to submit FAFSA. *Faculty research:* Educational psychology, counseling, health. Total annual research expenditures: $838,213. *Unit head:* Dr. Dennis Kivlighan, Chair, 301-405-2858, E-mail: dennisk@umd.edu. *Application contact:* Dean of Graduate School, 301-405-0358.

University of Massachusetts Amherst, Graduate School, School of Education, Program in School Psychology, Amherst, MA 01003. Offers M Ed, PhD, CAGS. *Accreditation:* APA; NCATE. Part-time programs available. *Students:* 16 full-time (14 women); includes 1 minority (Asian, non-Hispanic/Latino), 1 international. Average age 28. 42 applicants, 29% accepted, 4 enrolled. In 2010, 8 doctorates awarded. Terminal master's awarded for partial completion of doctoral program. *Degree requirements:* For doctorate, comprehensive exam, thesis/dissertation. *Entrance requirements:* For doctorate, 3 letters of recommendation. Additional exam requirements/recommendations for international students: Required—TOEFL (minimum score 550 paper-based; 213 computer-based; 80 iBT), IELTS (minimum score 6.5). *Application deadline:* For fall admission, 1/15 for domestic and international students. Applications are processed on a rolling basis. Application fee: $50 ($65 for international students). Electronic applications accepted. *Expenses:* Tuition, state resident: full-time $2640. Required fees: $8282. One-time fee: $357 full-time. *Financial support:* Fellowships, research assistantships, teaching assistantships, career-related internships or fieldwork, Federal Work-Study, scholarships/grants, traineeships, health care benefits, tuition waivers (full), and unspecified assistantships available. Support available to part-time students. Financial award application deadline: 1/15; financial award applicants required to submit FAFSA. *Unit head:* Dr. Linda L. Griffin, Graduate Program Director, 413-545-6984, Fax: 413-545-1523. *Application contact:* Jean M. Ames, Supervisor of Admissions, 413-545-0722, Fax: 413-577-0010, E-mail: gradadm@grad.umass.edu.

University of Massachusetts Boston, Office of Graduate Studies, Graduate College of Education, Counseling and School Psychology Department, Program in School Guidance Counseling, Boston, MA 02125-3393. Offers M Ed, CAGS.

University of Massachusetts Boston, Office of Graduate Studies, Graduate College of Education, Counseling and School Psychology Department, Program in School Psychology, Boston, MA 02125-3393. Offers M Ed, CAGS. Part-time and evening/weekend programs available. *Degree requirements:* For master's, comprehensive exam, practicum, final project; for CAGS, comprehensive exam. *Entrance requirements:* For master's, GRE General Test or MAT, minimum GPA of 3.0; for CAGS, minimum GPA of 2.75. *Faculty research:* School psychology services, assessment of children, cultural and gender differences on psychological adjustment to disabilities.

University of Memphis, Graduate School, College of Arts and Sciences, Department of Psychology, Memphis, TN 38152-3230. Offers psychology (MS, PhD), including clinical (PhD), experimental (PhD), general psychology (MS), school (PhD); school psychology (MA, Ed S); MS/PhD. *Faculty:* 28 full-time (9 women), 4 part-time/adjunct (0 women). *Students:* 114 full-time (81 women), 21 part-time (15 women); includes 14 Black or African American, non-Hispanic/Latino; 1 American Indian or Alaska Native, non-Hispanic/Latino; 4 Asian, non-Hispanic/Latino; 3 Hispanic/Latino; 4 Two or more races, non-Hispanic/Latino, 7 international. Average age 27. 220 applicants, 15% accepted, 29 enrolled. In 2010, 31 master's, 9 doctorates awarded. *Degree requirements:* For master's, comprehensive exam (for some programs), thesis (for some programs), 37 credit hours (MA); 33 credit hours with thesis or 36 with exam (MS); for doctorate, comprehensive exam (for some programs), thesis/dissertation, 80 semester hours, major area paper; clinical: 1 year placement and 1 year internship; internship (school psychology). *Entrance requirements:* For master's, GRE; for doctorate, GRE (minimum combined score of 1100), minimum GPA of 2.75, 18 hours of undergraduate psychology courses, transcripts, personal statement, letters of recommendation; for Ed S, GRE (minimum combined score of 1100), minimum GPA of 2.75, 18 hours of undergraduate psychology courses, letters of recommendation. Additional exam requirements/recommendations for international students: Required—TOEFL (minimum score 550 paper-based; 210 computer-based; 79 iBT). *Application deadline:* For fall admission, 12/5 for domestic students. Applications are processed on a rolling basis. Application fee: $35 ($60 for international students). Electronic applications accepted. *Financial support:* In 2010–11, 66 students received support; fellowships with full tuition reimbursements available, research assistantships with full tuition reimbursements available, teaching assistantships with full tuition reimbursements available, Federal Work-Study, scholarships/grants, tuition waivers (partial), and unspecified assistantships available. Financial award application deadline: 2/15; financial award applicants required to submit FAFSA. *Faculty research:* Clinical health; school, child and family psychology; psychotherapy; cognitive and behavioral neuroscience; industrial-organizational psychology. *Unit head:* Dr. Robert Cohen, Coordinator of Graduate Programs, 901-678-4679, Fax: 901-678-2579, E-mail: rcohen@memphis.edu. *Application contact:* Lynell Connable, Graduate Secretary, 901-678-4340, Fax: 901-678-2579, E-mail: dconnabl@memphis.edu.

University of Minnesota, Twin Cities Campus, Graduate School, College of Education and Human Development, Department of Educational Psychology, Program in School Psychology, Minneapolis, MN 55455-0213. Offers MA, PhD, Ed S. *Accreditation:* APA. *Students:* 51 full-time (40 women), 15 part-time (all women); includes 1 Black or African American, non-Hispanic/Latino; 3 Asian, non-Hispanic/Latino; 2 Hispanic/Latino, 2 international. Average age 28. 72 applicants, 32% accepted, 11 enrolled. In 2010, 10 master's, 5 doctorates, 8 other advanced degrees awarded. *Unit head:* Dr. Susan Hupp, Chair, 612-624-1003, Fax: 612-624-8241, E-mail: shupp@umn.edu. *Application contact:* Dr. Jennifer Engler, Assistant Dean, 612-626-2887, Fax: 612-626-7496, E-mail: engle009@umn.edu.

University of Minnesota, Twin Cities Campus, Graduate School, College of Education and Human Development, Institute of Child Development, Minneapolis, MN 55455-0213. Offers child psychology (MA, PhD); early childhood education (M Ed, MA, PhD); school psychology (MA, PhD). *Faculty:* 17 full-time (8 women). *Students:* 94 full-time (87 women), 28 part-time (26 women); includes 2 Black or African American, non-Hispanic/Latino; 3 American Indian or Alaska Native, non-Hispanic/Latino; 3 Asian, non-Hispanic/Latino; 5 Hispanic/Latino, 12 international. Average age 30. 133 applicants, 32% accepted, 29 enrolled. In 2010, 38 master's, 12 doctorates awarded. *Financial support:* In 2010–11, 20 fellowships (averaging $22,273 per year), 24 research assistantships with full tuition reimbursements (averaging $26,645 per year), 32 teaching assistantships with full tuition reimbursements (averaging $28,128 per year) were awarded. *Faculty research:* Developmental affective and cognitive neuroscience; developmental psychopathology; intervention and prevention science; social and emotional development; cognitive, language, and perceptual development. Total annual research expenditures: $5.2 million. *Unit head:* Dr. Megan Gunnar, Director, 612-624-2846, Fax: 612-624-6373, E-mail: gunnar@umn.edu. *Application contact:* Dr. Jennifer Engler, Assistant Dean, 612-626-2887, Fax: 612-626-7496, E-mail: engle009@umn.edu.

University of Minnesota, Twin Cities Campus, Graduate School, College of Liberal Arts, Department of Psychology, Minneapolis, MN 55455-0213. Offers biological psychopathology (PhD); clinical psychology (PhD); cognitive and biological psychology (PhD); counseling psychology (PhD); industrial/organizational psychology (PhD); personality, individual differences, and behavior genetics (PhD); quantitative/psychometric methods (PhD); school psychology (PhD); social psychology (PhD). *Accreditation:* APA. *Degree requirements:* For doctorate, comprehensive exam, thesis/dissertation. *Entrance requirements:* For doctorate, GRE General Test, GRE Subject Test (recommended), 12 credits of upper-level psychology courses, including a course in statistics or psychological measurement. Additional exam requirements/recommendations for international students: Required—TOEFL (minimum score 79 iBT).

University of Missouri, Graduate School, College of Education, Department of Educational, School, and Counseling Psychology, Columbia, MO 65211. Offers counseling psychology (M Ed, MA, PhD, Ed S); educational psychology (M Ed, MA, PhD, Ed S); learning and instruction (M Ed); school psychology (M Ed, MA, PhD, Ed S). *Accreditation:* APA (one or more programs are accredited). Part-time programs available. *Degree requirements:* For doctorate, thesis/dissertation. *Entrance requirements:* For master's, doctorate, and Ed S, GRE General Test, minimum GPA of 3.0. Additional exam requirements/recommendations for international students: Required—TOEFL (minimum score 580 paper-based; 237 computer-based; 92 iBT).

University of Missouri–St. Louis, College of Education, Division of Educational Psychology, Research, and Evaluation, St. Louis, MO 63121. Offers program evaluation and assessment (Certificate); school psychology (Ed S). *Faculty:* 10 full-time (3 women), 9 part-time/adjunct (3 women). *Students:* 16 full-time (13 women), 8 part-time (1 woman); includes 3 minority (2 Black or African American, non-Hispanic/Latino; 1 Asian, non-Hispanic/Latino), 2 international. Average age 26. 29 applicants, 52% accepted, 8 enrolled. In 2010, 7 Ed Ss awarded. *Degree requirements:* For other advanced degree, internship. *Entrance requirements:* For degree, GRE General Test, 2-4 letters of recommendation, personal interview. Additional exam requirements/recommendations for international students: Recommended—TOEFL (minimum score 550 paper-based; 213 computer-based). *Application deadline:* For fall admission, 3/1 for domestic and international students. Application fee: $35 ($40 for international students). Electronic applications accepted. *Expenses:* Tuition, state resident: full-time $5522; part-time $306.80 per credit hour. Tuition, nonresident: full-time $14,253; part-time $792.10 per credit hour. Required fees: $658; $49 per credit hour. One-time fee: $12. Tuition and fees vary according to program. *Financial support:* In 2010–11, 1 research assistantship (averaging $5,625 per year), 1 teaching assistantship (averaging $10,380 per year) were awarded. Financial award application deadline: 4/1; financial award applicants required to submit FAFSA. *Faculty research:* Child/adolescent psychology, quantitative and qualitative methodology, evaluation processes, measurement and assessment. *Unit head:* Dr. Matthew Keefer, Chairperson, 314-516-5783, Fax: 314-516-5784, E-mail: keefer@umsl.edu. *Application contact:* 314-516-5458, Fax: 314-516-6996, E-mail: gradadm@umsl.edu.

The University of Montana, Graduate School, College of Arts and Sciences, Department of Psychology, Program in School Psychology, Missoula, MT 59812-0002. Offers MA, PhD, Ed S. *Degree requirements:* For master's, oral exam, professional paper; for Ed S, thesis. *Entrance requirements:* For master's, GRE General Test, GRE Subject Test, minimum GPA of 3.25 during previous 2 years; for Ed S, GRE General Test. Additional exam requirements/recommendations for international students: Required—TOEFL. *Faculty research:* Child development and creativity, psychological measurement.

University of Nebraska at Kearney, College of Graduate Study, College of Education, Department of Counseling and School Psychology, Kearney, NE 68849-0001. Offers counseling (MS Ed, Ed S); school psychology (Ed S). *Accreditation:* ACA; NCATE. Part-time and evening/weekend programs available. *Degree requirements:* For master's, thesis optional; for Ed S, thesis. *Entrance requirements:* For master's and Ed S, interview. Additional exam requirements/recommendations for international students: Required—TOEFL (minimum score 550 paper-based; 213 computer-based). Electronic applications accepted. *Faculty research:* Multicultural counseling and diversity issues, team decision making, adult development, women's issues, brief therapy.

University of Nebraska at Omaha, Graduate Studies, College of Arts and Sciences, Department of Psychology, Omaha, NE 68182. Offers developmental psychology (PhD); industrial/organizational psychology (MS, PhD); psychobiology (PhD); psychology (MA); school psychology (MS, Ed S). Part-time programs available. *Faculty:* 18 full-time (8 women). *Students:* 50 full-time (38 women), 41 part-time (32 women); includes 9 minority (2 Black or African American, non-Hispanic/Latino; 1 American Indian or Alaska Native, non-Hispanic/Latino; 1 Asian, non-Hispanic/Latino; 5 Hispanic/Latino), 2 international. Average age 26. 92 applicants, 39% accepted, 34 enrolled. In 2010, 17 master's, 2 doctorates, 6 other advanced degrees awarded. *Degree requirements:* For master's, comprehensive exam, thesis (for some programs). *Entrance requirements:* For master's, GRE General Test, GRE Subject Test, previous course work in psychology, including statistics and a laboratory course; minimum GPA of 3.0, 3 letters of recommendation; for doctorate, GRE General Test. Additional exam requirements/recommendations for international students: Required—TOEFL (minimum score 500 paper-based; 173 computer-based; 61 iBT). *Application deadline:* For fall admission, 1/5 for domestic students. Application fee: $45. Electronic applications accepted. *Financial support:* In 2010–11, 66 students received support; fellowships, research assistantships with tuition reimbursements available, teaching assistantships with tuition reimbursements available, career-related internships or fieldwork, Federal Work-Study, institutionally sponsored loans, scholarships/grants, tuition waivers (partial), and unspecified assistantships available. Support available to part-time students. Financial award application deadline: 3/1; financial award applicants required to submit FAFSA. *Unit head:* Dr. Brigette Ryalls, Chairperson, 402-554-2592. *Application contact:* Dr. Joseph Brown, Student Contact, 402-554-2592.

University of Nebraska–Lincoln, Graduate College, College of Education and Human Sciences, Department of Educational Psychology, Lincoln, NE 68588. Offers cognition, learning and development (MA); counseling psychology (MA); educational psychology (MA, Ed S); psychological studies in education (PhD), including cognition, learning and development, counseling psychology, quantitative, qualitative, and psychometric methods, school psychology; quantitative, qualitative, and psychometric methods (MA); school psychology (MA, Ed S).

Accreditation: APA (one or more programs are accredited); NCATE. *Degree requirements:* For master's, thesis optional. *Entrance requirements:* For master's, GRE General Test. Additional exam requirements/recommendations for international students: Required—TOEFL (minimum score 500 paper-based; 173 computer-based). Electronic applications accepted. *Faculty research:* Measurement and assessment, metacognition, academic skills, child development, multicultural education and counseling.

The University of North Carolina at Chapel Hill, Graduate School, School of Education, Program in School Psychology, Chapel Hill, NC 27599. Offers M Ed, MA, PhD. *Accreditation:* APA (one or more programs are accredited); NCATE. *Degree requirements:* For master's, comprehensive exam, thesis (for some programs); for doctorate, comprehensive exam, thesis/dissertation. *Entrance requirements:* For master's and doctorate, GRE General Test, minimum GPA of 3.0 during last 2 years of undergraduate course work. Additional exam requirements/recommendations for international students: Required—TOEFL (minimum score 550 paper-based; 79 computer-based). Electronic applications accepted.

The University of North Carolina at Greensboro, Graduate School, School of Education, Department of Counseling and Educational Development, Greensboro, NC 27412-5001. Offers advanced school counseling (PMC); counseling and counselor education (PhD); counseling and educational development (MS); couple and family counseling (PMC); school counseling (PMC); MS/Ed S. *Accreditation:* ACA (one or more programs are accredited); NCATE. *Degree requirements:* For master's, comprehensive exam, practicum, internship; for doctorate, comprehensive exam, thesis/dissertation. *Entrance requirements:* For master's, doctorate, and PMC, GRE General Test. Additional exam requirements/recommendations for international students: Required—TOEFL. Electronic applications accepted. *Faculty research:* Gerontology, invitational theory, career development, marriage and family therapy, drug and alcohol abuse prevention.

University of Northern Colorado, Graduate School, College of Education and Behavioral Sciences, Department of Counselor Education and Supervision, Program in School Psychology, Greeley, CO 80639. Offers PhD, Ed S. *Accreditation:* APA (one or more programs are accredited); NCATE. Part-time and evening/weekend programs available. *Faculty:* 6 full-time (3 women). *Students:* 14 full-time (12 women), 9 part-time (7 women). Average age 27. 28 applicants, 86% accepted, 7 enrolled. In 2010, 7 doctorates, 17 other advanced degrees awarded. *Degree requirements:* For doctorate, comprehensive exam, thesis/dissertation; for Ed S, comprehensive exam. *Entrance requirements:* For doctorate, GRE General Test, curriculum vitae, 3 letters of recommendation. *Application deadline:* For fall admission, 1/1 for domestic and international students. Applications are processed on a rolling basis. Application fee: $50 ($60 for international students). Electronic applications accepted. *Expenses:* Tuition, state resident: full-time $6199; part-time $344 per credit hour. Tuition, nonresident: full-time $14,834; part-time $824 per credit hour. Required fees: $1091; $60.60 per credit hour. Tuition and fees vary according to course load, degree level and program. *Financial support:* Fellowships, research assistantships, teaching assistantships, unspecified assistantships available. Financial award application deadline: 3/1; financial award applicants required to submit FAFSA. *Unit head:* Diane Greenshields, Program Coordinator, 970-351-2731, Fax: 970-351-2625. *Application contact:* Linda Sisson, Graduate Student Admission Coordinator, 970-351-1807, Fax: 970-351-2371, E-mail: linda.sisson@unco.edu.

University of Northern Iowa, Graduate College, College of Education, Department of Educational Psychology and Foundations, Cedar Falls, IA 50614. Offers educational psychology (MAE); professional development for teachers (MAE); school psychology (Ed S). Part-time and evening/weekend programs available. *Students:* 21 full-time (15 women), 17 part-time (15 women); includes 1 minority (Black or African American, non-Hispanic/Latino), 5 international. 48 applicants, 50% accepted, 14 enrolled. In 2010, 25 master's, 6 other advanced degrees awarded. *Degree requirements:* For master's, comprehensive exam (for some programs), thesis or alternative; for Ed S, thesis or alternative. *Entrance requirements:* For master's, GRE General Test, minimum GPA of 3.0; for Ed S, GRE General Test. Additional exam requirements/recommendations for international students: Required—TOEFL (minimum score 500 paper-based; 180 computer-based; 61 iBT). *Application deadline:* For fall admission, 8/1 priority date for domestic students. Applications are processed on a rolling basis. Application fee: $50 ($70 for international students). Electronic applications accepted. *Financial support:* Career-related internships or fieldwork, Federal Work-Study, scholarships/grants, and tuition waivers (full and partial) available. Support available to part-time students. Financial award application deadline: 2/1. *Unit head:* Dr. Radhi Al-Mabuk, Interim Head, 319-273-2609, Fax: 319-273-7732, E-mail: radhi.al-mabuk@uni.edu. *Application contact:* Laurie S. Russell, Record Analyst, 319-273-2623, Fax: 319-273-2885, E-mail: laurie.russell@uni.edu.

University of Northern Iowa, Graduate College, College of Social and Behavioral Sciences, School of Applied Human Sciences, Cedar Falls, IA 50614. Offers counseling (MA, MAE), including mental health counseling (MA), school counseling (MAE); mental health counseling (MA); school counseling (MAE). Part-time programs available. *Students:* 52 full-time (40 women), 43 part-time (37 women); includes 7 minority (4 Black or African American, non-Hispanic/Latino; 1 Asian, non-Hispanic/Latino; 2 Hispanic/Latino), 4 international. 75 applicants, 35% accepted, 17 enrolled. In 2010, 22 master's awarded. *Degree requirements:* For master's, comprehensive exam, thesis (for some programs). *Entrance requirements:* Additional exam requirements/recommendations for international students: Required—TOEFL (minimum score 550 paper-based; 213 computer-based; 79 iBT). *Application deadline:* For fall admission, 2/1 for domestic students, 4/1 priority date for international students; for winter admission, 10/1 priority date for international students. Application fee: $50 ($70 for international students). Electronic applications accepted. *Financial support:* Unspecified assistantships available. Financial award application deadline: 2/1; financial award applicants required to submit FAFSA. *Unit head:* Jan Bartlett, Coordinator, 319-273-7979, E-mail: jan.bartlett@uni.edu. *Application contact:* Laurie S. Russell, Record Analyst, 319-273-2623, Fax: 319-273-2885, E-mail: laurie.russell@uni.edu.

University of North Texas, Toulouse Graduate School, College of Education, Department of Educational Psychology, Program in School Psychology, Denton, TX 76203. Offers MS. *Degree requirements:* For master's, comprehensive exam, thesis optional, school psychology licensure. *Entrance requirements:* For master's, GRE General Test, undergraduate major in psychology; minimum GPA of 2.8, 3.0 in psychology. Additional exam requirements/recommendations for international students: Recommended—TOEFL (minimum score 550 paper-based; 213 computer-based; 79 iBT). *Expenses:* Tuition, state resident: full-time $4298; part-time $239 per credit hour. Tuition, nonresident: full-time $10,782; part-time $549 per credit hour. Required fees: $1292; $270 per credit hour. *Financial support:* Application deadline: 4/15. *Faculty research:* Minority families, behavioral assessment in natural settings. *Application contact:* Administrative Assistant, 940-565-3486.

University of Phoenix–Denver Campus, College of Education, Lone Tree, CO 80124-5453. Offers administration and supervision (MAEd); curriculum instruction (MAEd); elementary teacher education (MAEd); school counseling (MSC); secondary teacher education (MAEd). Evening/weekend programs available. *Degree requirements:* For master's, thesis (for some programs). *Entrance requirements:* For master's, minimum undergraduate GPA of 2.5, 3 years work experience. Additional exam requirements/recommendations for international students: Required—TOEFL (minimum score 550 paper-based; 213 computer-based; 79 iBT). Electronic applications accepted.

University of Phoenix–Las Vegas Campus, College of Education, Las Vegas, NV 89128. Offers administration and supervision (MA Ed); curriculum and instruction (MA Ed); school counseling (MSC); teacher education-elementary licensure (MA Ed). Evening/weekend programs available. *Degree requirements:* For master's, thesis (for some programs). *Entrance requirements:* For master's, minimum undergraduate GPA of 2.5, 3 years of work experience. Additional exam requirements/recommendations for international students: Required—TOEFL (minimum score 550 paper-based; 213 computer-based; 79 iBT). Electronic applications accepted.

University of Phoenix–Puerto Rico Campus, College of Education, Guaynabo, PR 00968. Offers administration and supervision (MA Ed); early childhood education (MA Ed); school counselor (MSC). Evening/weekend programs available. *Degree requirements:* For master's, thesis (for some programs). *Entrance requirements:* For master's, minimum undergraduate GPA of 2.5, 3 years work experience. Additional exam requirements/recommendations for international students: Required—TOEFL (minimum score 550 paper-based; 213 computer-based; 79 iBT). Electronic applications accepted.

University of Phoenix–Southern California Campus, College of Social Sciences, Costa Mesa, CA 92626. Offers administration of justice and security (MS); community counseling (MSC); marriage, family and child therapy (MSC); mental health counseling (MSC); psychology (MS); school counseling (MSC). Evening/weekend programs available. *Degree requirements:* For master's, thesis (for some programs). *Entrance requirements:* For master's, minimum undergraduate GPA of 3.0, 3 years work experience. Additional exam requirements/recommendations for international students: Required—TOEFL (minimum score 550 paper-based; 213 computer-based; 79 iBT). Electronic applications accepted.

University of Phoenix–Southern Colorado Campus, College of Education, Colorado Springs, CO 80919-2335. Offers administration and supervision (MA Ed); curriculum and instruction (MA Ed); elementary teacher education (MA Ed); principal licensure certification (Certificate); school counseling (MSC); secondary teacher education (MA Ed). Evening/weekend programs available. *Degree requirements:* For master's, thesis (for some programs). *Entrance requirements:* For master's, minimum undergraduate GPA of 2.5, 3 years of work experience. Additional exam requirements/recommendations for international students: Required—TOEFL (minimum score 550 paper-based; 213 computer-based; 79 iBT). Electronic applications accepted.

University of Phoenix–Utah Campus, College of Education, Salt Lake City, UT 84123-4617. Offers administration and supervision (MA Ed); curriculum and instruction (MA Ed); elementary teacher education (MA Ed); school counseling (MSC); secondary teacher education (MA Ed); special education (MA Ed). Evening/weekend programs available. *Degree requirements:* For master's, thesis (for some programs). *Entrance requirements:* For master's, minimum undergraduate GPA of 2.5, 3 years work experience. Additional exam requirements/recommendations for international students: Required—TOEFL (minimum score 550 paper-based; 213 computer-based; 79 iBT). Electronic applications accepted.

University of Rhode Island, Graduate School, College of Arts and Sciences, Department of Psychology, Kingston, RI 02881. Offers behavioral science (PhD); clinical psychology (MA, PhD); school psychology (MS, PhD). *Accreditation:* APA (one or more programs are accredited). Part-time programs available. *Faculty:* 20 full-time (10 women). *Students:* 75 full-time (56 women), 32 part-time (28 women); includes 24 minority (12 Black or African American, non-Hispanic/Latino; 4 Asian, non-Hispanic/Latino; 7 Hispanic/Latino; 1 Two or more races, non-Hispanic/Latino), 6 international. In 2010, 16 master's, 14 doctorates awarded. *Degree requirements:* For master's, comprehensive exam, thesis optional; for doctorate, thesis/dissertation. *Entrance requirements:* For master's and doctorate, GRE, 3 letters of recommendation. Additional exam requirements/recommendations for international students: Required—TOEFL (minimum score 550 paper-based; 213 computer-based). Application fee: $65. Electronic applications accepted. *Expenses:* Tuition, state resident: full-time $9588; part-time $533 per credit hour. Tuition, nonresident: full-time $22,968; part-time $1276 per credit hour. Required fees: $1282; $68 per semester. Tuition and fees vary according to program. *Financial support:* In 2010–11, 5 research assistantships with full and partial tuition reimbursements (averaging $2,927 per year), 20 teaching assistantships with full and partial tuition reimbursements (averaging $12,479 per year) were awarded. Financial award applicants required to submit FAFSA. Total annual research expenditures: $193,164. *Unit head:* Dr. Patricia Morokoff, Chairperson, 401-874-4239, Fax: 401-874-2157, E-mail: morokoff@uri.edu. *Application contact:* Dr. Patricia Morokoff, Chairperson, 401-874-4239, Fax: 401-874-2157, E-mail: morokoff@uri.edu.

University of South Alabama, Graduate School, College of Education, Department of Professional Studies, Mobile, AL 36688-0002. Offers community counseling (MS); educational media (M Ed, MS); instructional design and development (MS, PhD); rehabilitation counseling (MS); school counseling (M Ed); school psychometry (M Ed). *Accreditation:* NCATE. Part-time programs available. *Faculty:* 17 full-time (8 women). *Students:* 104 full-time (86 women), 93 part-time (73 women); includes 52 minority (46 Black or African American, non-Hispanic/Latino; 2 American Indian or Alaska Native, non-Hispanic/Latino; 3 Hispanic/Latino; 1 Native Hawaiian or other Pacific Islander, non-Hispanic/Latino), 5 international. 76 applicants, 49% accepted, 32 enrolled. In 2010, 5 master's, 10 doctorates awarded. *Degree requirements:* For master's, comprehensive exam. *Entrance requirements:* For master's, GRE General Test or MAT, minimum GPA of 3.0. *Application deadline:* For fall admission, 6/15 priority date for domestic students; for spring admission, 11/1 priority date for domestic students. Applications are processed on a rolling basis. Application fee: $35. *Expenses:* Tuition, state resident: part-time $300 per credit hour. Tuition, nonresident: part-time $600 per credit hour. Required fees: $150 per semester. *Financial support:* In 2010–11, 5 research assistantships were awarded; career-related internships or fieldwork also available. Support available to part-time students. Financial award application deadline: 4/1. *Faculty research:* Agency counseling, rehabilitation counseling, school psychometry. *Unit head:* Dr. Charles Guest, Chair, 251-380-2861. *Application contact:* Dr. Abigail Baxter, Director of Graduate Studies, 251-380-6310.

University of South Carolina, The Graduate School, College of Arts and Sciences, Department of Psychology, Program in School Psychology, Columbia, SC 29208. Offers PhD. *Accreditation:* APA; NCATE. *Degree requirements:* For doctorate, thesis/dissertation. *Entrance requirements:* For doctorate, GRE General Test, minimum GPA of 3.0. Additional exam requirements/recommendations for international students: Required—TOEFL. Electronic applications accepted. *Faculty research:* Preschool services, families and diversity life satisfaction, ADHD intervention, attachment.

University of Southern Maine, School of Education and Human Development, Program in School Psychology, Portland, ME 04104-9300. Offers school psychology (MS, Psy D). Part-time and evening/weekend programs available. *Faculty:* 3 full-time (2 women), 1 (woman) part-time/adjunct. *Students:* 16 full-time (13 women), 8 part-time (6 women). 13 applicants, 69% accepted, 4 enrolled. In 2010, 2 master's, 7 doctorates awarded. Terminal master's awarded for partial completion of doctoral program. *Degree requirements:* For master's, comprehensive exam, thesis or alternative, portfolio; for doctorate, comprehensive exam, thesis/dissertation, dissertation defense. *Entrance requirements:* For master's, GRE General Test or MAT, interview; for doctorate, GRE General Test, interview. Additional exam requirements/recommendations for international students: Required—TOEFL (minimum score 550 paper-based; 213 computer-based; 79 iBT). *Application deadline:* For fall admission, 12/1 for domestic students. Application fee: $65. Electronic applications accepted. *Financial support:* In 2010–11, 12 students received support, including 8 research assistantships with partial tuition reimbursements available (averaging $4,500 per year); career-related internships or fieldwork, Federal Work-Study, institutionally sponsored loans, scholarships/grants, and unspecified assistantships also available. Support available to part-time students. Financial award application deadline: 3/1; financial award applicants required to submit FAFSA. *Unit head:* Dr. E. Michael Brady, Chair, Human Resource Development Department, 207-780-5316, Fax: 207-780-5043, E-mail: mbrady@usm.maine.edu. *Application contact:* Mary Sloan, Director of Graduate Admissions, 207-780-4386, Fax: 207-780-4969, E-mail: msloan@usm.maine.edu.

University of Southern Mississippi, Graduate School, College of Education and Psychology, Department of Psychology, Hattiesburg, MS 39406-0001. Offers clinical psychology (MA, PhD); counseling psychology (MA, PhD); experimental psychology (MA, PhD); school psychology (MA, PhD). *Accreditation:* APA (one or more programs are accredited). *Faculty:* 32 full-time (9 women). *Students:* 98 full-time (75 women), 42 part-time (33 women); includes 8 Black or African American, non-Hispanic/Latino; 3 Asian, non-Hispanic/Latino; 5 Hispanic/Latino, 7 international. Average age 29. 219 applicants, 16% accepted, 31 enrolled. In 2010, 27 master's,

School Psychology

University of Southern Mississippi *(continued)*
13 doctorates awarded. Terminal master's awarded for partial completion of doctoral program. *Degree requirements:* For master's, comprehensive exam, thesis; for doctorate, comprehensive exam, thesis/dissertation. *Entrance requirements:* For master's, GRE General Test, minimum GPA of 3.0; for doctorate, GRE General Test, interview, minimum GPA of 3.5. Additional exam requirements/recommendations for international students: Required—TOEFL, IELTS. *Application deadline:* For fall admission, 3/1 priority date for domestic students, 3/1 for international students. Applications are processed on a rolling basis. Application fee: $50. *Financial support:* In 2010–11, 48 research assistantships with full tuition reimbursements (averaging $8,802 per year), 48 teaching assistantships with full tuition reimbursements (averaging $6,500 per year) were awarded; career-related internships or fieldwork, Federal Work-Study, institutionally sponsored loans, scholarships/grants, health care benefits, and unspecified assistantships also available. Financial award application deadline: 3/15; financial award applicants required to submit FAFSA. *Faculty research:* Dolphin cognition, sleep, neuropsychology, health-related behaviors, psychopathology. Total annual research expenditures: $101,200. *Unit head:* Dr. Joesph Olmi, Chair, 601-266-4177, Fax: 601-266-5580. *Application contact:* Susan King, Graduate Secretary, 601-266-4177, Fax: 601-266-5580.

University of South Florida, Graduate School, College of Education, Department of Psychological and Social Foundations, Tampa, FL 33620-9951. Offers college student affairs (M Ed); counselor education (MA, PhD, Ed S); interdisciplinary (PhD, Ed S); school psychology (PhD, Ed S). Part-time and evening/weekend programs available. *Faculty:* 22 full-time (13 women), 6 part-time/adjunct (4 women). *Students:* 179 full-time (140 women), 72 part-time (59 women); includes 58 minority (25 Black or African American, non-Hispanic/Latino; 6 Asian, non-Hispanic/Latino; 25 Hispanic/Latino; 2 Two or more races, non-Hispanic/Latino; 6 international. Average age 30. 207 applicants, 53% accepted, 87 enrolled. In 2010, 55 master's, 10 doctorates, 9 other advanced degrees awarded. *Degree requirements:* For master's, comprehensive exam, thesis (for some programs); for doctorate, comprehensive exam, thesis/dissertation, multiple research methods; philosophies of inquiry (for some programs). *Entrance requirements:* For master's, GRE General Test, minimum GPA of 3.5 in last 60 hours of course work; for doctorate, GRE General Test, MAT, minimum GPA of 3.5 in last 60 hours of course work; for Ed S, GRE General Test. Additional exam requirements/recommendations for international students: Required—TOEFL (minimum score 550 paper-based; 213 computer-based; 79 iBT). *Application deadline:* For fall admission, 1/1 for domestic students, 1/2 for international students. Application fee: $30. Electronic applications accepted. *Financial support:* In 2010–11, 47 students received support, including 6 fellowships with full tuition reimbursements available (averaging $10,000 per year), 6 research assistantships with full tuition reimbursements available (averaging $15,000 per year), 21 teaching assistantships with full tuition reimbursements available (averaging $10,200 per year); career-related internships or fieldwork, scholarships/grants, and unspecified assistantships also available. Financial award application deadline: 1/1; financial award applicants required to submit CSS PROFILE. *Faculty research:* College student affairs, counselor education, educational psychology, school psychology, social foundations. Total annual research expenditures: $4.2 million. *Unit head:* Dr. Herbert Exum, Chairperson, 813-974-8395, Fax: 813-974-5814, E-mail: exum@tempest.coedu.usf.edu. *Application contact:* Dr. Kathy Bradley, Program Director, School Psychology, 813-974-9486, Fax: 813-974-5814, E-mail: kbradley@usf.edu.

The University of Tennessee, Graduate School, College of Education, Health and Human Sciences, Program in Education, Knoxville, TN 37996. Offers art education (MS); counseling education (PhD); cultural studies in education (PhD); curriculum (MS, Ed S); curriculum, educational research and evaluation (Ed D, PhD); early childhood education (PhD); early childhood special education (MS); education of deaf and hard of hearing (MS); educational administration and policy studies (Ed D, PhD); educational administration and supervision (Ed S); educational psychology (Ed D, PhD); elementary education (MS, Ed S); elementary teaching (MS); English education (MS, Ed S); exercise science (PhD); foreign language/ESL education (MS, Ed S); instructional technology (MS, Ed D, PhD, Ed S); literacy, language and

ESL education (PhD); literacy, language education, and ESL education (Ed D); mathematics education (MS, Ed S); modified and comprehensive special education (MS); reading education (MS, Ed S); school counseling (Ed S); school psychology (PhD, Ed S); science education (MS, Ed S); secondary teaching (MS); social foundations (MS); social science education (MS, Ed S); socio-cultural foundations of sports and education (PhD); special education (Ed S); teacher education (Ed D, PhD). *Accreditation:* NCATE. Part-time and evening/weekend programs available. *Degree requirements:* For master's and Ed S, thesis optional; for doctorate, variable foreign language requirement, thesis/dissertation. *Entrance requirements:* For master's, minimum GPA of 2.7; for doctorate and Ed S, GRE General Test, minimum GPA of 2.7. Additional exam requirements/recommendations for international students: Required—TOEFL. Electronic applications accepted. *Expenses:* Tuition, state resident: full-time $7440; part-time $414 per credit hour. Tuition, nonresident: full-time $22,478; part-time $1250 per credit hour. Required fees: $922; $43 per credit hour. Tuition and fees vary according to program.

The University of Tennessee at Chattanooga, Graduate School, College of Health, Education and Professional Studies, Graduate Studies Division of Education, Program for Educational Specialist, Chattanooga, TN 37403-2598. Offers educational technology (Ed S); school psychology (Ed S). Part-time and evening/weekend programs available. *Faculty:* 4 full-time (0 women), 1 part-time/adjunct. *Students:* 22 full-time (19 women), 22 part-time (19 women); includes 5 minority (4 Black or African American, non-Hispanic/Latino; 1 Two or more races, non-Hispanic/Latino). Average age 38. 6 applicants, 100% accepted, 6 enrolled. In 2010, 20 Ed Ss awarded. *Degree requirements:* For Ed S, internship. *Entrance requirements:* For degree, GRE (minimum score 1350), letters of reference. Additional exam requirements/recommendations for international students: Required—TOEFL (minimum score 550 paper-based; 213 computer-based; 79 iBT), IELTS (minimum score 6). *Application deadline:* For fall admission, 8/1 priority date for domestic students, 6/1 for international students; for spring admission, 12/1 priority date for domestic students, 10/1 for international students. Applications are processed on a rolling basis. Application fee: $35. Electronic applications accepted. *Financial support:* In 2010–11, 5 research assistantships with full and partial tuition reimbursements (averaging $5,500 per year) were awarded; career-related internships or fieldwork, scholarships/grants, and unspecified assistantships also available. Support available to part-time students. *Faculty research:* Educational technology, using technology in the classroom, interactive media, distance learning, instructional design technological implementation. *Unit head:* Dr. Lloyd D. Davis, Coordinator, 423-425-4161, Fax: 423-425-5380, E-mail: lloyd-davis@utc.edu. *Application contact:* Dr. Jerald Ainsworth, Dean of Graduate Studies, 423-425-4478, Fax: 423-425-5223, E-mail: jerald-ainsworth@utc.edu.

The University of Texas at Austin, Graduate School, College of Education, Department of Educational Psychology, Austin, TX 78712-1111. Offers academic educational psychology (M Ed, MA); counseling psychology (PhD); counselor education (M Ed); human development and culture (PhD); learning, cognition and instruction (PhD); quantitative methods (PhD); school psychology (PhD). *Accreditation:* APA (one or more programs are accredited). *Degree requirements:* For master's, thesis optional; for doctorate, thesis/dissertation. *Entrance requirements:* For master's and doctorate, GRE General Test, 3 letters of recommendation. Additional exam requirements/recommendations for international students: Required—TOEFL.

The University of Texas at San Antonio, College of Education and Human Development, Department of Educational Psychology, San Antonio, TX 78249-0617. Offers school psychology (MA). Part-time and evening/weekend programs available. *Faculty:* 8 full-time (6 women), 1 (woman) part-time/adjunct. *Students:* 27 full-time (25 women), 18 part-time (16 women); includes 23 minority (2 Black or African American, non-Hispanic/Latino; 19 Hispanic/Latino; 2 Two or more races, non-Hispanic/Latino). Average age 29. 46 applicants, 93% accepted, 38 enrolled. *Degree requirements:* For master's, comprehensive exam (for some programs), thesis (for some programs), practicum, internship. *Entrance requirements:* Additional exam requirements/recommendations for international students: Required—TOEFL (minimum score 500 paper-based; 173 computer-based; 61 iBT), IELTS (minimum score 5). *Application deadline:* For fall admission, 7/1 for domestic students, 4/1 for international students; for spring admission,

11/1 for domestic students, 9/1 for international students. Applications are processed on a rolling basis. Application fee: $45 ($80 for international students). Electronic applications accepted. *Expenses:* Tuition, state resident: full-time $4172; part-time $231.75 per credit hour. Tuition, nonresident: full-time $15,332; part-time $851.75 per credit hour. *Financial support:* In 2010–11, 9 research assistantships (averaging $9,407 per year) were awarded; scholarships/grants, tuition waivers, and unspecified assistantships also available. Support available to part-time students. *Unit head:* Dr. Norma Guerra, Department Chair, 210-458-2650, Fax: 210-458-2019, E-mail: norma.guerra@utsa.edu. *Application contact:* Veronica Ramirez, Assistant Dean, 210-458-2408, Fax: 210-458-4332, E-mail: graduatestudies@utsa.edu.

See Display on page 1098 and Close-Up on page 1185.

The University of Texas at Tyler, College of Education and Psychology, Department of Psychology and Counseling, Tyler, TX 75799-0001. Offers clinical psychology (MS), including neuropsychology, school psychology; counseling psychology (MA), including general, marriage and family; interdisciplinary studies (MSIS); school counseling (MA). Part-time and evening/weekend programs available. *Degree requirements:* For master's, comprehensive exam, thesis optional. *Entrance requirements:* For master's, GRE General Test, minimum GPA of 3.0. Additional exam requirements/recommendations for international students: Required—TOEFL (minimum score 79 computer-based). Electronic applications accepted. *Faculty research:* Neuropsychology, child abuse, psychometric properties of psychological instruments, maternal behavior, clinical practice issues, victimization of women, post-traumatic stress disorder.

The University of Texas–Pan American, College of Education, Department of Educational Psychology, Edinburg, TX 78539. Offers counseling (M Ed); educational diagnostician (M Ed); gifted education (M Ed); school psychology (MA); special education (M Ed). Part-time and evening/weekend programs available. *Degree requirements:* For master's, comprehensive exam (for some programs), thesis (for some programs). *Entrance requirements:* For master's, GRE General Test, interview. *Faculty research:* Reading instruction, assessment practice, behavior interventions consultation, mental retardation.

University of the Pacific, School of Education, Department of Educational and School Psychology, Stockton, CA 95211-0197. Offers educational psychology (MA, Ed D); school psychology (Ed S). *Accreditation:* NCATE. *Faculty:* 5 full-time (3 women). *Students:* 16 full-time (13 women), 13 part-time (9 women); includes 2 Black or African American, non-Hispanic/Latino; 4 Asian, non-Hispanic/Latino; 7 Hispanic/Latino. Average age 28. 21 applicants, 76% accepted, 7 enrolled. In 2010, 7 master's, 1 doctorate awarded. *Degree requirements:* For master's, thesis; for doctorate, thesis/dissertation. *Entrance requirements:* For master's and doctorate, GRE General Test, GRE Subject Test. Additional exam requirements/recommendations for international students: Required—TOEFL (minimum score 475 paper-based; 150 computer-based). *Application deadline:* For fall admission, 3/1 priority date for domestic students; for spring admission, 10/1 priority date for domestic students. Applications are processed on a rolling basis. Application fee: $75. *Financial support:* In 2010–11, 6 teaching assistantships were awarded. Financial award application deadline: 3/1; financial award applicants required to submit FAFSA. *Unit head:* Dr. Linda Webster, Chairperson, 209-946-2559, E-mail: lwebster@pacific.edu. *Application contact:* Office of Graduate Admissions, 209-946-2344.

The University of Toledo, College of Graduate Studies, Judith Herb College of Education, Health Science and Human Service, Department of School Psychology, Legal Specialties and Counselor Education, Toledo, OH 43606-3390. Offers counselor education (MA, PhD, Ed S), including community counseling (MA), counselor education (Ed S), counselor education and supervision (PhD); school psychology (MA, Ed S), including school counseling (MA), school psychology (Ed S). Part-time programs available. *Faculty:* 14. *Students:* 64 full-time (46 women), 62 part-time (48 women); includes 13 Black or African American, non-Hispanic/Latino; 1 Asian, non-Hispanic/Latino; 5 Hispanic/Latino, 3 international. Average age 31. 91 applicants, 54% accepted, 42 enrolled. In 2010, 45 master's, 3 doctorates, 4 other advanced degrees awarded. *Degree requirements:* For master's, comprehensive exam, thesis or alternative; for doctorate, comprehensive exam, thesis/dissertation; for Ed S, thesis optional. *Entrance requirements:* For master's and Ed S, GRE or other qualifying exams required vary by program. A minimum 2.70 cumulative GPA all previous academic work. Two/Three Letters of Recommendation (as required per program). ; for doctorate, GRE or other qualifying exams required vary by program. A minimum 2.70 cumulative GPA all previous academic work. Two/Three Letters of Recommendation (as required per program). . Additional exam requirements/recommendations for international students: Required—TOEFL (minimum score 550 paper-based; 213 computer-based; 80 iBT), IELTS (minimum score 6.5). *Application deadline:* For fall admission, 1/15 priority date for domestic and international students. Applications are processed on a rolling basis. Application fee: $45 ($75 for international students). Electronic applications accepted. *Expenses:* Tuition, state resident: full-time $11,426; part-time $476 per credit hour. Tuition, nonresident: full-time $21,660; part-time $903 per credit hour. One-time fee: $62. *Financial support:* Research assistantships with tuition reimbursements, teaching assistantships with tuition reimbursements, career-related internships or fieldwork, Federal Work-Study, institutionally sponsored loans, scholarships/grants, tuition waivers (full and partial), and unspecified assistantships available. *Unit head:* Dr. Martin Ritchie, Chair, 419-530-4775, E-mail: martin.ritchie@utoledo.edu. *Application contact:* Graduate School Office, 419-530-4723, Fax: 419-530-4724, E-mail: grdsch@utnet.utoledo.edu.

University of Utah, Graduate School, College of Education, Department of Educational Psychology, Salt Lake City, UT 84112. Offers counseling psychology (PhD); educational psychology (MA); instructional design and educational technology (M Ed); learning and cognition (MS, PhD); professional counseling (MS); professional psychology (M Ed); reading and literacy (M Ed, PhD); school counseling (M Ed, MS); school psychology (MS, PhD); statistics (M Stat). *Accreditation:* APA (one or more programs are accredited). Evening/weekend programs available. Postbaccalaureate distance learning degree programs offered (minimal on-campus study). *Faculty:* 20 full-time (10 women), 6 part-time/adjunct (4 women). *Students:* 119 full-time (96 women), 105 part-time (72 women); includes 25 minority (1 American Indian or Alaska Native, non-Hispanic/Latino; 6 Asian, non-Hispanic/Latino; 13 Hispanic/Latino; 1 Native Hawaiian or other Pacific Islander, non-Hispanic/Latino; 4 Two or more races, non-Hispanic/Latino), 3 international. Average age 33. 238 applicants, 34% accepted, 60 enrolled. In 2010, 40 master's, 18 doctorates awarded. *Degree requirements:* For master's, variable foreign language requirement, comprehensive exam, thesis (for some programs); for doctorate, variable foreign language requirement, thesis/dissertation, oral exam. *Entrance requirements:* For master's and doctorate, GRE General Test, minimum GPA of 3.0. Additional exam requirements/recommendations for international students: Required—TOEFL (minimum score 500 paper-based; 173 computer-based). *Application deadline:* For fall admission, 4/1 for domestic and international students; for spring admission, 11/1 for domestic and international students. Application fee: $55 ($65 for international students). *Expenses:* Contact institution. *Financial support:* In 2010–11, 90 students received support, including 45 fellowships with full and partial tuition reimbursements available (averaging $11,500 per year), 13 research assistantships with full and partial tuition reimbursements available (averaging $11,500 per year), 32 teaching assistantships with full and partial tuition reimbursements available (averaging $11,500 per year); career-related internships or fieldwork, Federal Work-Study, institutionally sponsored loans, scholarships/grants, and unspecified assistantships also available. Financial award application deadline: 2/1; financial award applicants required to submit FAFSA. *Faculty research:* Autism, computer technology and instruction, cognitive behavior, aging, group counseling. Total annual research expenditures: $902,082. *Unit head:* Dr. Elaine Clark, Chair, 801-581-7148, Fax: 801-581-5566, E-mail: clark@ed.utah.edu. *Application contact:* Kendra Lee Wiebke, Academic Program Specialist, 801-581-7148, Fax: 801-581-5566, E-mail: kendra.wiebke@utah.edu.

University of Virginia, Curry School of Education, Department of Human Services, Program in Clinical and School Psychology, Charlottesville, VA 22903. Offers PhD. *Students:* 29 full-time (25 women); includes 4 Black or African American, non-Hispanic/Latino; 1 Asian, non-Hispanic/Latino; 1 Hispanic/Latino; 1 Two or more races, non-Hispanic/Latino. Average age 27. 130 applicants, 8% accepted, 7 enrolled. In 2010, 9 doctorates awarded. *Unit head:* Dr. Peter L. Sheras, Director of Clinical Training, 434-924-0795, E-mail: pls@virginia.edu. *Application contact:* Lynn Renfroe, Information Contact, 434-924-6254, E-mail: ldr9t@virginia.edu.

University of Virginia, Curry School of Education, Program in Education, Charlottesville, VA 22903. Offers administration and supervision (PhD); applied developmental science (PhD); counselor education (PhD); curriculum and instruction (PhD); early childhood-developmental risk (MT); education evaluation (PhD); educational psychology (PhD); educational research (PhD); elementary (MT, PhD); English education (MT, PhD); foreign language education (MT); higher education (PhD); instructional technology (PhD); kinesiology (MT, PhD); math education (PhD); reading education (PhD); research statistics and evaluation (PhD); school psychology (PhD); science education (PhD); social studies education (MT, PhD); special education (PhD); world languages education (MT). *Students:* 490 full-time (371 women), 70 part-time (42 women); includes 83 minority (36 Black or African American, non-Hispanic/Latino; 2 American Indian or Alaska Native, non-Hispanic/Latino; 26 Asian, non-Hispanic/Latino; 16 Hispanic/Latino; 1 Native Hawaiian or other Pacific Islander, non-Hispanic/Latino; 2 Two or more races, non-Hispanic/Latino), 24 international. Average age 27. 289 applicants, 55% accepted, 85 enrolled. In 2010, 135 master's, 60 doctorates awarded. *Degree requirements:* For master's, comprehensive exam (for some programs), field project; for doctorate, comprehensive exam, thesis/dissertation. *Entrance requirements:* For doctorate, GRE General Test. Additional exam requirements/recommendations for international students: Required—TOEFL (minimum score 600 paper-based; 250 computer-based; 90 iBT), IELTS (minimum score 7). *Application deadline:* Applications are processed on a rolling basis. Application fee: $60. Electronic applications accepted. *Financial support:* Fellowships, research assistantships, teaching assistantships available. Financial award application deadline: 1/5; financial award applicants required to submit FAFSA.

University of Washington, Graduate School, College of Education, Program in Educational Psychology, Seattle, WA 98195. Offers educational psychology (PhD); human development and cognition (M Ed); learning sciences (M Ed, PhD); measurement, statistics and research design (M Ed); school psychology (M Ed). *Accreditation:* APA. *Degree requirements:* For master's, thesis optional; for doctorate, thesis/dissertation. *Entrance requirements:* For master's and doctorate, GRE General Test, minimum GPA of 3.0. Additional exam requirements/recommendations for international students: Required—TOEFL.

University of Wisconsin–Eau Claire, College of Arts and Sciences, Department of Psychology, Eau Claire, WI 54702-4004. Offers school psychology (MSE, Ed S). Part-time programs available. *Faculty:* 18 full-time (9 women). *Students:* 14 full-time (13 women), 10 part-time (6 women), 1 international. Average age 28. 25 applicants, 28% accepted, 5 enrolled. In 2010, 8 master's, 6 other advanced degrees awarded. *Degree requirements:* For master's, comprehensive exam, thesis, National Certified School Psychologist Professional Exam, written exam, externship. *Entrance requirements:* For master's, GRE, minimum undergraduate GPA of 3.0; courses in exceptional children and youth, statistics, psychopathology, and theories of counseling. Additional exam requirements/recommendations for international students: Required—TOEFL (minimum score 550 paper-based; 213 computer-based; 79 iBT); Recommended—IELTS (minimum score 7). *Application deadline:* For fall admission, 3/1 priority date for domestic and international students. Applications are processed on a rolling basis. Application fee: $56. *Expenses:* Tuition, state resident: full-time $7001; part-time $389 per credit. Tuition, nonresident: full-time $16,771; part-time $932 per credit. Required fees: $1057; $58.49 per credit. *Financial support:* In 2010–11, 15 students received support, including 6 fellowships (averaging $993 per year); Federal Work-Study and unspecified assistantships also available. Financial award application deadline: 3/1; financial award applicants required to submit FAFSA. *Unit head:* Dr. Lori Bica, Chair, 715-836-5733, Fax: 715-836-2214, E-mail: bicala@uwec.edu. *Application contact:* Dr. Barbara Lozar, Professor, 715-836-5733, E-mail: lozarb@uwec.edu.

University of Wisconsin–La Crosse, Office of University Graduate Studies, College of Liberal Studies, Department of Psychology, Program in School Psychology, La Crosse, WI 54601-3742. Offers MS Ed, Ed S. *Students:* 24 full-time (22 women), 34 part-time (30 women); includes 2 minority (1 Hispanic/Latino; 1 Two or more races, non-Hispanic/Latino). Average age 26. 56 applicants, 39% accepted, 12 enrolled. In 2010, 20 master's awarded. *Degree requirements:* For master's, comprehensive exam, thesis. *Entrance requirements:* For master's, GRE, 3 letters of recommendation, writing sample, resume. Additional exam requirements/recommendations for international students: Required—TOEFL (minimum score 550 paper-based; 213 computer-based; 79 iBT). *Application deadline:* For fall admission, 1/15 priority date for domestic and international students. Application fee: $56. Electronic applications accepted. *Expenses:* Tuition, state resident: full-time $7121; part-time $395.61 per credit. Tuition, nonresident: full-time $16,891; part-time $938.41 per credit. Part-time tuition and fees vary according to course load, program and reciprocity agreements. *Financial support:* In 2010–11, 6 research assistantships with partial tuition reimbursements (averaging $7,256 per year) were awarded; Federal Work-Study, scholarships/grants, health care benefits, and tuition waivers (partial) also available. Support available to part-time students. Financial award application deadline: 3/15; financial award applicants required to submit FAFSA. *Unit head:* Dr. Rob Dixon, Program Director, 608-785-6893, Fax: 608-785-8443, E-mail: dixon.rob@uwlax.edu. *Application contact:* Kathryn Kiefer, Director of Admissions, 608-785-8939, E-mail: admissions@uwlac.edu.

University of Wisconsin–Milwaukee, Graduate School, School of Education, Program in School Psychology, Milwaukee, WI 53201-0413. Offers PhD, Ed S. *Accreditation:* APA. *Students:* 12 full-time (all women), 11 part-time (8 women); includes 1 Hispanic/Latino. Average age 26. 18 applicants, 83% accepted. In 2010, 7 doctorates awarded. *Application deadline:* Applications are processed on a rolling basis. Application fee: $56 ($96 for international students). Electronic applications accepted. *Financial support:* Applicants required to submit FAFSA. *Unit head:* Anthony A. Hains, Representative, 414-229-4590, E-mail: aahains@uwm.edu. *Application contact:* General Information Contact, 414-229-4982, Fax: 414-229-6967, E-mail: gradschool@uwm.edu.

University of Wisconsin–River Falls, Outreach and Graduate Studies, College of Education and Professional Studies, Department of Counseling and School Psychology, River Falls, WI 54022. Offers counseling (MSE); school psychology (MSE, Ed S). Part-time programs available. *Entrance requirements:* For master's, minimum GPA of 2.75, resume, 3 letters of reference, vita. Additional exam requirements/recommendations for international students: Required—TOEFL (minimum score 500 paper-based; 65 iBT), IELTS (minimum score 5.5). Electronic applications accepted.

University of Wisconsin–Stout, Graduate School, School of Education, Program in School Psychology, Menomonie, WI 54751. Offers MS Ed, Ed S. Part-time programs available. *Degree requirements:* For master's and Ed S, thesis. *Entrance requirements:* For master's, minimum GPA of 3.0; for Ed S, minimum GPA of 3.25. Additional exam requirements/recommendations for international students: Required—TOEFL (minimum score 500 paper-based; 173 computer-based; 61 iBT). Electronic applications accepted. *Faculty research:* Intelligence assessment, eating disorders, intervention models, resilience, school violence.

University of Wisconsin–Superior, Graduate Division, Department of Counseling and Psychological Professions, Superior, WI 54880-4500. Offers community counseling (MSE); human relations (MSE); school counseling (MSE). Part-time and evening/weekend programs available. *Degree requirements:* For master's, position paper, practicum. *Entrance requirements:* For master's, GRE and/or MAT, minimum GPA of 2.75. Electronic applications accepted. *Faculty research:* Women and power, intrafamily dynamics.

University of Wisconsin–Whitewater, School of Graduate Studies, College of Education, Department of Counselor Education, Whitewater, WI 53190-1790. Offers community counseling (MS Ed); higher education (MS Ed); school counseling (MS Ed). *Accreditation:* ACA; NCATE. Part-time and evening/weekend programs available. *Degree requirements:* For master's, thesis

School Psychology

University of Wisconsin–Whitewater (continued)

or alternative. *Entrance requirements:* For master's, resume, 2 letters of reference. Additional exam requirements/recommendations for international students: Required—TOEFL (minimum score 550 paper-based; 213 computer-based). Electronic applications accepted. *Faculty research:* Alcohol and other drugs, counseling effectiveness, teacher mentoring.

University of Wisconsin–Whitewater, School of Graduate Studies, College of Letters and Sciences, Department of Psychology, Program in School Psychology, Whitewater, WI 53190-1790. Offers Ed S. Part-time and evening/weekend programs available. Postbaccalaureate distance learning degree programs offered (no on-campus study). *Degree requirements:* For Ed S, specialist project. *Entrance requirements:* For degree, master's degree in school psychology from an accredited school. Additional exam requirements/recommendations for international students: Required—TOEFL (minimum score 550 paper-based; 213 computer-based). Electronic applications accepted.

Utah State University, School of Graduate Studies, College of Education and Human Services, Department of Psychology, Logan, UT 84322. Offers clinical/counseling/school psychology (PhD); research and evaluation methodology (PhD); school counseling (MS); school psychology (MS). *Accreditation:* APA (one or more programs are accredited). Part-time and evening/weekend programs available. Postbaccalaureate distance learning degree programs offered (no on-campus study). Terminal master's awarded for partial completion of doctoral program. *Degree requirements:* For master's, thesis (for some programs); for doctorate, thesis/dissertation. *Entrance requirements:* For master's, GRE General Test (school psychology), MAT (school counseling), minimum GPA of 3.5; for doctorate, GRE General Test, minimum GPA of 3.5. Additional exam requirements/recommendations for international students: Required—TOEFL. *Faculty research:* Hearing loss detection in infancy, ADHD, eating disorders, domestic violence, neuropsychology, bilingual/Spanish speaking students/parents.

Valdosta State University, Department of Psychology and Counseling, Valdosta, GA 31698. Offers clinical/counseling psychology (MS); industrial/organizational psychology (MS); school counseling (M Ed, Ed S); school psychology (Ed S). Part-time and evening/weekend programs available. *Faculty:* 19 full-time (6 women). *Students:* 65 full-time (47 women), 41 part-time (35 women); includes 38 minority (29 Black or African American, non-Hispanic/Latino; 3 Asian, non-Hispanic/Latino; 4 Hispanic/Latino; 2 Two or more races, non-Hispanic/Latino). Average age 27. 61 applicants, 51% accepted, 27 enrolled. In 2010, 43 master's awarded. *Degree requirements:* For master's, thesis or alternative, comprehensive written and/or oral exams; for Ed S, thesis. *Entrance requirements:* For master's and Ed S, GRE General Test or MAT. Additional exam requirements/recommendations for international students: Required—TOEFL (minimum score 523 paper-based; 193 computer-based). *Application deadline:* For fall admission, 7/1 for domestic and international students; for spring admission, 11/15 for domestic and international students. Applications are processed on a rolling basis. Application fee: $35. Electronic applications accepted. *Expenses:* Tuition, state resident: full-time $5256; part-time $197 per credit hour. Tuition, nonresident: full-time $14,490; part-time $710 per credit hour. Required fees: $855 per semester. Tuition and fees vary according to course load and campus/location. *Financial support:* In 2010–11, 6 students received support, including 2 research assistantships with full tuition reimbursements available (averaging $3,652 per year); institutionally sponsored loans and unspecified assistantships also available. Support available to part-time students. Financial award application deadline: 7/1; financial award applicants required to submit FAFSA. *Faculty research:* Using Bender-Gestalt to predict graphomotor dimensions of the draw-a-person test, neurobehavioral hemispheric dominance. *Unit head:* Dr. Robert Bauer, Chair, 229-333-5930, Fax: 229-259-5576, E-mail: bbauer@valdosta.edu. *Application contact:* Rebecca Waters, Coordinator of Graduate Admissions, 229-333-5694, Fax: 229-245-3853, E-mail: rlwaters@valdosta.edu.

Valparaiso University, Graduate School, Department of Education, Program in School Psychology, Valparaiso, IN 46383. Offers M Ed/Ed S. Part-time and evening/weekend programs available. *Students:* 14 full-time (12 women), 10 part-time (all women); includes 2 minority (1 Black or African American, non-Hispanic/Latino; 1 Hispanic/Latino), 1 international. Average age 28. *Entrance requirements:* Additional exam requirements/recommendations for international students: Required—TOEFL (minimum score 550 paper-based; 213 computer-based; 80 iBT). *Application deadline:* For fall admission, 3/1 priority date for domestic students. Applications are processed on a rolling basis. Application fee: $30 ($50 for international students). Electronic applications accepted. *Expenses:* Tuition: Full-time $9540; part-time $530 per credit hour. Required fees: $292; $95 per semester. Tuition and fees vary according to program. *Financial support:* Unspecified assistantships available. Support available to part-time students. Financial award applicants required to submit FAFSA. *Unit head:* Dr. Christina Grabarek, Coordinator, 219-464-5790, Fax: 219-464-6720, E-mail: christina.grabarek@valpo.edu. *Application contact:* Laura Groth, Coordinator of Student Services and Support, 219-464-5313, Fax: 219-464-5381, E-mail: laura.groth@valpo.edu.

Washington State University, Graduate School, College of Education, Department of Educational Leadership and Counseling Psychology, Program in Counseling Psychology, Pullman, WA 99164. Offers counseling psychology (Ed M, MA, PhD); school psychologist (Certificate). *Accreditation:* APA (one or more programs are accredited). *Faculty:* 18. *Students:* 54 full-time (41 women), 6 part-time (2 women); includes 7 minority (3 Asian, non-Hispanic/Latino; 4 Hispanic/Latino), 7 international. Average age 29. 319 applicants, 5% accepted, 15 enrolled. In 2010, 7 master's, 8 doctorates awarded. Terminal master's awarded for partial completion of doctoral program. *Degree requirements:* For master's, comprehensive exam (for some programs), thesis (for some programs), oral or written exam; for doctorate, comprehensive exam, thesis/dissertation, oral and written exam. *Entrance requirements:* For master's and doctorate, GRE General Test, minimum GPA of 3.0, 3 letters of recommendation. Additional exam requirements/recommendations for international students: Required—TOEFL (minimum score 550 paper-based; 213 computer-based). *Application deadline:* For fall admission, 2/1 for domestic and international students. Application fee: $50. Electronic applications accepted. *Expenses:* Tuition, state resident: full-time $8552; part-time $443 per credit. Tuition, nonresident: full-time $21,650; part-time $1083 per credit. Required fees: $846. *Financial support:* In 2010–11, 4 research assistantships with partial tuition reimbursements (averaging $18,204 per year), 31 teaching assistantships with partial tuition reimbursements (averaging $18,204 per year) were awarded; career-related internships or fieldwork, Federal Work-Study, institutionally sponsored loans, scholarships/grants, tuition waivers (partial), and unspecified assistantships also available. Financial award application deadline: 4/1; financial award applicants required to submit FAFSA. *Faculty research:* Hypnosis supervision, multicultural counseling, American Indian mental health, eating disorders. Total annual research expenditures: $934,000. *Unit head:* Dr. Kelly Ward, Chair, 509-335-9117, Fax: 509-335-7977, E-mail: kaward@wsu.edu. *Application contact:* Graduate School Admissions, 800-GRADWSU, Fax: 509-335-1949, E-mail: gradsch@wsu.edu.

Wayne State University, College of Education, Division of Theoretical and Behavioral Foundations, Detroit, MI 48202. Offers counseling (M Ed, MA, Ed D, PhD, Ed S); education evaluation and research (M Ed, Ed D, PhD); educational psychology (M Ed, Ed D, PhD, Ed S); educational sociology (M Ed, Ed D, PhD, Ed S); history and philosophy of education (M Ed, Ed D, PhD); rehabilitation counseling and community inclusion (MA, Ed S); school and community psychology (MA, Ed S); school clinical psychology (Ed S). *Accreditation:* ACA (one or more programs are accredited); CORE (one or more programs are accredited). Evening/weekend programs available. *Faculty:* 100 full-time (50 women), 60 part-time/adjunct (35 women). *Students:* 193 full-time (156 women), 202 part-time (164 women); includes 168 minority (150 Black or African American, non-Hispanic/Latino; 3 American Indian or Alaska Native, non-Hispanic/Latino; 8 Asian, non-Hispanic/Latino; 5 Hispanic/Latino; 2 Two or more races, non-Hispanic/Latino), 17 international. Average age 36. 97 applicants, 55% accepted, 35 enrolled. In 2010, 42 master's, 9 doctorates, 2 other advanced degrees awarded. *Degree requirements:* For doctorate, thesis/dissertation. *Entrance requirements:* For master's, GRE; for doctorate, GRE, interview, minimum GPA of 3.0, curriculum vitae, references. Additional exam requirements/recommendations for international students: Required—TOEFL (minimum score 550 paper-based; 213 computer-based), TWE (minimum score 6). *Application deadline:* For fall admission, 7/1 for domestic students, 6/1 for international students; for winter admission, 10/1 for international students; for spring admission, 2/1 for international students. Application fee: $20 ($30 for international students). Electronic applications accepted. *Expenses:* Tuition, state resident: full-time $7662; part-time $478.85 per credit hour. Tuition, nonresident: full-time $16,920; part-time $1057.55 per credit hour. Required fees: $571.20; $35.70 per credit hour. $188.05 per semester. Tuition and fees vary according to course load and program. *Financial support:* In 2010–11, 2 fellowships with tuition reimbursements (averaging $16,875 per year), 3 research assistantships with tuition reimbursements (averaging $17,785 per year), 1 teaching assistantship (averaging $15,181 per year) were awarded; career-related internships or fieldwork, Federal Work-Study, and institutionally sponsored loans also available. *Faculty research:* Adolescents at risk, supervision of counseling. *Unit head:* Dr. JoAnne Holbert, Assistant Dean, 313-577-1721, E-mail: jholbert@wayne.edu. *Application contact:* Janice Green, Assistant Dean, 313-577-1605, E-mail: jwgreen@wayne.edu.

Western Carolina University, Graduate School, College of Education and Allied Professions, Department of Human Services, Program in Counseling, Cullowhee, NC 28723. Offers community counseling (M Ed, MS); school counseling (MA Ed). *Accreditation:* ACA. Part-time and evening/weekend programs available. *Degree requirements:* For master's, comprehensive exam, thesis or alternative. *Entrance requirements:* For master's, GRE General Test, appropriate undergraduate degree with minimum GPA of 3.0, 3 recommendations, writing sample, resume. Additional exam requirements/recommendations for international students: Required—TOEFL (minimum score 550 paper-based; 270 computer-based; 79 iBT). *Faculty research:* Marital and family development, spirituality in counseling, home school law, sexuality education, family functioning models.

Western Carolina University, Graduate School, College of Education and Allied Professions, Department of Psychology, Cullowhee, NC 28723. Offers general psychology (MA); school psychology (MA). Part-time programs available. *Degree requirements:* For master's, comprehensive exam, thesis. *Entrance requirements:* For master's, GRE General Test, appropriate undergraduate degree, interview, 3 letters of recommendation. Additional exam requirements/recommendations for international students: Required—TOEFL (minimum score 550 paper-based; 270 computer-based; 79 iBT). *Faculty research:* Five-factor model of personality, evolutionary psychology, stress and worry, body image and physical attractiveness, moral decision-making, memory, learning styles.

Western Illinois University, School of Graduate Studies, College of Arts and Sciences, Department of Psychology, Macomb, IL 61455-1390. Offers clinical/community mental health (MS); general psychology (MS); psychology (MS, SSP); school psychology (SSP). Part-time programs available. *Students:* 44 full-time (31 women), 15 part-time (7 women); includes 4 minority (1 American Indian or Alaska Native, non-Hispanic/Latino; 3 Asian, non-Hispanic/Latino), 2 international. Average age 26. 94 applicants, 34% accepted. In 2010, 11 master's, 8 other advanced degrees awarded. *Degree requirements:* For master's, comprehensive exam (for some programs), thesis or alternative. *Entrance requirements:* For master's and SSP, GRE General Test. Additional exam requirements/recommendations for international students: Required—TOEFL (minimum score 550 paper-based; 213 computer-based; 80 iBT). *Application deadline:* Applications are processed on a rolling basis. Application fee: $30. Electronic applications accepted. *Expenses:* Tuition, state resident: full-time $6370; part-time $265.40 per credit hour. Tuition, nonresident: full-time $12,740; part-time $530.80 per credit hour. Required fees: $75.67 per credit hour. *Financial support:* In 2010–11, 37 students received support, including 37 research assistantships with full tuition reimbursements available (averaging $7,280 per year). Financial award applicants required to submit FAFSA. *Unit head:* Dr. Steven Dworkin, Chairperson, 309-298-1593. *Application contact:* Evelyn Hoing, Assistant Director of Graduate Studies, 309-298-1806, Fax: 309-298-2345, E-mail: grad-office@wiu.edu.

Western Kentucky University, Graduate Studies, College of Education and Behavioral Sciences, Department of Psychology, Bowling Green, KY 42101. Offers clinical psychology (MA); experimental psychology (MA); general psychology (MA); industrial/organizational psychology (MA); school psychology (Ed S). *Degree requirements:* For master's, comprehensive exam, thesis (for some programs); for Ed S, thesis, oral exam. *Entrance requirements:* For master's, GRE General Test; for Ed S, GRE General Test, minimum GPA of 3.5. Additional exam requirements/recommendations for international students: Required—TOEFL (minimum score 555 paper-based; 213 computer-based; 79 iBT). *Faculty research:* Neural regeneration, enhancing mobility in the elderly, improvement in visual processing in older adults, lifespan development.

Western New Mexico University, Graduate Division, School of Education, Silver City, NM 88062-0680. Offers bilingual education (MAT); counseling (MA); educational leadership (MA); elementary education (MAT); reading (MAT); school psychology (MA); secondary education (MAT); special education (MAT); TESOL (teaching English to speakers of other languages) (MAT). *Accreditation:* NCATE. *Degree requirements:* For master's, comprehensive exam. *Entrance requirements:* For master's, GRE General Test, GRE Subject Test, minimum GPA of 3.2 in last 64 hours of undergraduate study. Additional exam requirements/recommendations for international students: Required—TOEFL (minimum score 550 paper-based; 213 computer-based). Electronic applications accepted.

Wichita State University, Graduate School, College of Education, Department of Counseling, Educational and School Psychology, Wichita, KS 67260. Offers counseling (M Ed); educational psychology (M Ed); school psychology (Ed S). *Accreditation:* NCATE. Part-time and evening/weekend programs available. *Unit head:* Dr. Marlene Schommer-Aikins, Chairperson, 316-978-3326, Fax: 316-978-3102, E-mail: marlene.schommer-aikins@wichita.edu. *Application contact:* Dr. Marlene Schommer-Aikins, Chairperson, 316-978-3326, Fax: 316-978-3102, E-mail: marlene.schommer-aikins@wichita.edu.

Worcester State University, Graduate Studies, Department of Education, Program in School Psychology, Worcester, MA 01602-2597. Offers M Ed, CAGS. *Faculty:* 11 full-time (9 women), 22 part-time/adjunct (8 women). *Students:* 17 full-time (all women), 5 part-time (all women); includes 1 Black or African American, non-Hispanic/Latino; 2 Hispanic/Latino; 1 Two or more races, non-Hispanic/Latino, 1 international. Average age 27. 18 applicants, 94% accepted, 7 enrolled. In 2010, 9 master's, 9 other advanced degrees awarded. *Degree requirements:* For master's, comprehensive exam (for some programs), thesis optional. *Entrance requirements:* Additional exam requirements/recommendations for international students: Required—TOEFL (minimum score 500 paper-based; 61 iBT). *Application deadline:* For fall admission, 3/15 priority date for domestic and international students. Applications are processed on a rolling basis. Application fee: $40. Electronic applications accepted. *Expenses:* Tuition, state resident: full-time $2700; part-time $150 per credit. Tuition, nonresident: full-time $2700; part-time $150 per credit. Required fees: $2016; $112 per credit. *Financial support:* Career-related internships or fieldwork, scholarships/grants, and unspecified assistantships available. Financial award application deadline: 3/1; financial award applicants required to submit FAFSA. *Unit head:* Dr. Diane Tighe Cooke, Coordinator, 508-929-8673, Fax: 508-929-8164, E-mail: dcooke@worcester.edu. *Application contact:* Sara Grady, Assistant Dean of Graduate and Continuing Education, 508-929-8787, Fax: 508-929-8100, E-mail: sara.grady@worcester.edu.

Yeshiva University, Ferkauf Graduate School of Psychology, Program in School/Clinical-Child Psychology, New York, NY 10033-3201. Offers Psy D. *Accreditation:* APA. Part-time programs available. *Degree requirements:* For doctorate, comprehensive exam, thesis/

dissertation. *Entrance requirements:* For doctorate, GRE General Test. *Faculty research:* Testing, early childhood intervention, child and adolescent psychotherapy, clinical child psychology.

Youngstown State University, Graduate School, Beeghly College of Education, Department of Counseling, Youngstown, OH 44555-0001. Offers community counseling (MS Ed); school counseling (MS Ed). *Accreditation:* ACA; NCATE. Part-time and evening/weekend programs available. *Degree requirements:* For master's, comprehensive exam. *Entrance requirements:* For master's, MAT, interview, minimum GPA of 2.7. Additional exam requirements/recommendations for international students: Required—TOEFL. *Faculty research:* Suicide, euthanasia, ethical issues, marriage and family.

Social Psychology

Adler School of Professional Psychology, Programs in Psychology, Chicago, IL 60602. Offers advanced Adlerian psychotherapy (Certificate); art therapy (MA); clinical neuropsychology (Certificate); clinical psychology (Psy D); community psychology (MA); counseling and organizational psychology (MA); counseling psychology (MA); forensic psychology (MA); gerontological counseling (MA); marriage and family counseling (MA); marriage and family therapy (Certificate); organizational psychology (MA); police psychology (MA); rehabilitation counseling (MA); sport and health psychology (MA); substance abuse counseling (Certificate); Psy D/Certificate; Psy D/MACAT; Psy D/MACP; Psy D/MAMFC; Psy D/MASAC. *Accreditation:* APA. Part-time and evening/weekend programs available. Postbaccalaureate distance learning degree programs offered (minimal on-campus study). *Faculty:* 40 full-time (18 women), 61 part-time/adjunct (31 women). *Students:* 688 full-time (532 women), 142 part-time (110 women). Average age 27.Terminal master's awarded for partial completion of doctoral program. *Degree requirements:* For master's, thesis or alternative, oral exam, practicum; for doctorate, thesis/dissertation, clinical exam, internship, oral exam, practicum, written qualifying exam. *Entrance requirements:* For master's, 12 semester hours in psychology, minimum GPA of 3.0; for doctorate, 18 semester hours in psychology, minimum GPA of 3.25; for Certificate, appropriate master's or doctoral degree. Additional exam requirements/recommendations for international students: Required—TOEFL (minimum score 550 paper-based; 213 computer-based; 79 iBT). *Application deadline:* For fall admission, 2/15 priority date for domestic students, 12/1 priority date for international students. Applications are processed on a rolling basis. Application fee: $50. Electronic applications accepted. *Financial support:* Career-related internships or fieldwork, Federal Work-Study, scholarships/grants, and tuition waivers (full and partial) available. Support available to part-time students. Financial award application deadline: 5/15; financial award applicants required to submit FAFSA. *Application contact:* Michelle Brice, Director of Admissions, 312-662-4113, Fax: 312-662-4199, E-mail: admissions@adler.edu.

See Display on page 912 and Close-Up on page 1119.

Alvernia University, Graduate Studies, Department of Psychology and Counseling, Reading, PA 19607-1799. Offers community counseling (MA). *Entrance requirements:* For master's, GRE or MAT.

American University, College of Arts and Sciences, Department of Psychology, Washington, DC 22016-8062. Offers behavior, cognition, and neuroscience (PhD), including psychology; clinical psychology (PhD), including psychology; psychology (MA), including experimental/biological psychology, general psychology, personality/social psychology. *Accreditation:* APA. Part-time programs available. *Faculty:* 19 full-time (7 women), 6 part-time/adjunct (4 women). *Students:* 65 full-time (51 women), 47 part-time (41 women); includes 16 minority (4 Black or African American, non-Hispanic/Latino; 3 Asian, non-Hispanic/Latino; 9 Hispanic/Latino), 3 international. Average age 28. 445 applicants, 19% accepted, 36 enrolled. In 2010, 35 master's, 11 doctorates awarded. *Degree requirements:* For master's, comprehensive exam, thesis or alternative; for doctorate, comprehensive exam, thesis/dissertation, tools of research. *Entrance requirements:* For master's, GRE General Test, GRE Subject Test, recommendations; for doctorate, GRE General Test, GRE Subject Test. Additional exam requirements/recommendations for international students: Required—TOEFL. Application fee: $80. *Financial support:* Fellowships, research assistantships, teaching assistantships, career-related internships or fieldwork, Federal Work-Study, institutionally sponsored loans, tuition waivers (full and partial), and unspecified assistantships available. Support available to part-time students. Financial award application deadline: 2/1. *Faculty research:* Anxiety disorders, cognitive assessment, neuropsychology, conditioning and learning, psychopharmacology. *Unit head:* Dr. Anthony Riley, Chair, 202-885-1720, E-mail: alriley@american.edu. *Application contact:* Sara Holland, Senior Administrative Assistant, 202-885-1717, Fax: 202-885-1023, E-mail: holland@american.edu.

Andrews University, School of Graduate Studies, School of Education, Department of Educational and Counseling Psychology, Program in Community Counseling, Berrien Springs, MI 49104. Offers MA. *Degree requirements:* For master's, thesis optional. *Entrance requirements:* For master's, GRE. Additional exam requirements/recommendations for international students: Required—TOEFL (minimum score 550 paper-based).

Arcadia University, Graduate Studies, Department of Psychology, Glenside, PA 19038-3295. Offers community counseling (MACP); school counseling (MACP). Part-time programs available. *Faculty:* 4 full-time (2 women), 6 part-time/adjunct (4 women). *Students:* 32 full-time (30 women), 37 part-time (32 women); includes 11 minority (6 Black or African American, non-Hispanic/Latino; 1 Asian, non-Hispanic/Latino; 3 Hispanic/Latino; 1 Two or more races, non-Hispanic/Latino). Average age 27. In 2010, 11 master's awarded. *Degree requirements:* For master's, practicum. *Entrance requirements:* For master's, GRE General Test or MAT. *Application deadline:* Applications are processed on a rolling basis. Application fee: $50. *Expenses:* Contact institution. *Financial support:* Research assistantships, career-related internships or fieldwork and unspecified assistantships available. Support available to part-time students. Financial award application deadline: 8/15. *Unit head:* Dr. Eleonora Bartoli, Director, 215-572-4693. *Application contact:* 215-572-2925, Fax: 215-572-2126, E-mail: grad@arcadia.edu.

Argosy University, Atlanta, College of Psychology and Behavioral Sciences, Atlanta, GA 30328. Offers clinical psychology (MA, Psy D, Postdoctoral Respecialization Certificate), including child and family psychology (Psy D), general adult clinical (Psy D), health psychology (Psy D), neuropsychology/geropsychology (Psy D); community counseling (MA), including marriage and family therapy; counselor education and supervision (Ed D); forensic psychology (MA); industrial organizational psychology (MA); marriage and family therapy (Certificate); sport-exercise psychology (MA). *Accreditation:* APA.

See Close-Up on page 1121.

Argosy University, Chicago, College of Psychology and Behavioral Sciences, Chicago, IL 60601. Offers clinical psychology (MA, Psy D), including child and adolescent psychology (Psy D), client-centered and experiential psychotherapies (Psy D), diversity and multicultural psychology (Psy D), family psychology (Psy D), forensic psychology (Psy D), health psychology (Psy D), neuropsychology (Psy D), organizational consulting (Psy D), psychoanalytic psychology (Psy D), psychology and spirituality (Psy D); community counseling (MA); counseling psychology (Ed D), including counselor education and supervision; counselor education and supervision (Ed D); industrial organizational psychology (MA). *Accreditation:* APA (one or more programs are accredited). Postbaccalaureate distance learning degree programs offered (minimal on-campus study).

See Close-Up on page 1123.

Argosy University, Dallas, College of Psychology and Behavioral Sciences, Program in Community Counseling, Farmers Branch, TX 75244. Offers MA.

See Close-Up on page 1125.

Argosy University, Sarasota, College of Psychology and Behavioral Sciences, Sarasota, FL 34235. Offers community counseling (MA); counseling psychology (Ed D); counselor education and supervision (Ed D); forensic psychology (MA); marriage and family therapy (MA); mental health counseling (MA); pastoral community counseling (Ed D).

See Close-Up on page 1147.

Argosy University, Schaumburg, College of Psychology and Behavioral Sciences, Schaumburg, IL 60173-5403. Offers clinical health psychology (Post-Graduate Certificate); clinical psychology (MA, Psy D), including child and family psychology (Psy D), clinical health psychology (Psy D), diversity and multicultural psychology (Psy D), forensic psychology (Psy D), neuropsychology (Psy D); community counseling (MA); counseling psychology (Ed D), including counselor education and supervision; counselor education and supervision (Ed D); forensic psychology (Post-Graduate Certificate); industrial organizational psychology (MA). *Accreditation:* ACA; APA.

See Close-Up on page 1149.

Argosy University, Washington DC, College of Psychology and Behavioral Sciences, Arlington, VA 22209. Offers clinical psychology (MA, Psy D), including child and family psychology (Psy D), diversity and multicultural psychology (Psy D), forensic psychology (Psy D), health and neuropsychology (Psy D); community counseling (MA); counseling psychology (Ed D), including counselor education and supervision; counselor education and supervision (Ed D); forensic psychology (MA). *Accreditation:* APA.

See Close-Up on page 1157.

Arizona State University, College of Liberal Arts and Sciences, Department of Psychology, Tempe, AZ 85287-1104. Offers behavioral neuroscience (PhD); clinical psychology (PhD); cognition, action and perception (PhD); developmental psychology (PhD); quantitative psychology (PhD); social psychology (PhD). *Accreditation:* APA. *Faculty:* 72 full-time (36 women), 9 part-time/adjunct (6 women). *Students:* 113 full-time (79 women), 17 part-time (12 women); includes 24 minority (2 Black or African American, non-Hispanic/Latino; 10 Asian, non-Hispanic/Latino; 10 Hispanic/Latino; 2 Two or more races, non-Hispanic/Latino), 9 international. Average age 28. 519 applicants, 8% accepted, 30 enrolled. In 2010, 19 doctorates awarded. *Degree requirements:* For doctorate, comprehensive exam, thesis/dissertation, interactive Program of Study (iPOS) submitted before completing 50 percent of required credit hours. *Entrance requirements:* For doctorate, GRE General Test, GRE Subject Test, minimum GPA of 3.0 or equivalent in last 2 years of work leading to bachelor's degree. Additional exam requirements/recommendations for international students: Required—TOEFL, IELTS, or Pearson Test of English. *Application deadline:* For fall admission, 12/15 for domestic and international students. Application fee: $70 ($90 for international students). Electronic applications accepted. *Expenses:* Tuition, state resident: full-time $8510; part-time $608 per credit. Tuition, nonresident: full-time $16,542; part-time $919 per credit. Required fees: $339; $110 per credit. Part-time tuition and fees vary according to course load. *Financial support:* In 2010–11, 58 research assistantships with tuition reimbursements (averaging $15,281 per year), 48 teaching assistantships with tuition reimbursements (averaging $15,062 per year) were awarded; fellowships with full tuition reimbursements, career-related internships or fieldwork, Federal Work-Study, institutionally sponsored loans, scholarships/grants, and tuition waivers (full and partial) also available. Financial award application deadline: 3/1; financial award applicants required to submit FAFSA. Total annual research expenditures: $9.4 million. *Unit head:* Dr. Keith Crnic, Chair, 480-965-3061, E-mail: keith.crnic@asu.edu. *Application contact:* Graduate Admissions, 480-965-6113.

Ball State University, Graduate School, Teachers College, Department of Counseling Psychology and Guidance Services, Program in Social Psychology, Muncie, IN 47306-1099. Offers MA. *Faculty:* 12. *Students:* 6 full-time (3 women), 3 part-time (0 women), 1 international. Average age 24. 55 applicants, 13% accepted, 3 enrolled. In 2010, 5 master's awarded. *Entrance requirements:* For master's, GRE General Test. Application fee: $50. *Expenses:* Tuition, state resident: full-time $6160; part-time $299 per credit hour. Tuition, nonresident: full-time $16,020; part-time $783 per credit hour. Required fees: $2278; $95 per credit hour. *Financial support:* Application deadline: 3/1. *Unit head:* Dr. Sharon Bowman, Head, 765-285-8040, Fax: 765-285-2067, E-mail: sbowman@bsu.edu. *Application contact:* Dr. Michael White, Associate Provost for Research and Dean of the Graduate School.

Bethel University, Graduate School, Program in Counseling Psychology, St. Paul, MN 55112-6999. Offers child and adolescent and community counseling (MA). Part-time and evening/weekend programs available. *Faculty:* 5 full-time (2 women), 11 part-time/adjunct (4 women). *Students:* 84 full-time (72 women), 3 part-time (all women); includes 1 Black or African American, non-Hispanic/Latino; 1 Asian, non-Hispanic/Latino; 1 Hispanic/Latino; 4 Two or more races, non-Hispanic/Latino. Average age 32. 42 applicants, 100% accepted, 41 enrolled. In 2010, 32 master's awarded. *Degree requirements:* For master's, comprehensive exam, thesis optional, practicum. *Entrance requirements:* For master's, MAT, minimum GPA of 3.0, course work in psychology and statistics, letters of reference. Additional exam requirements/recommendations for international students: Required—TOEFL (minimum score 550 paper-based; 213 computer-based; 80 iBT). *Application deadline:* For fall admission, 5/1 priority date for domestic students. Applications are processed on a rolling basis. Electronic applications accepted. *Expenses:* Tuition: Full-time $5400; part-time $450 per credit. Tuition and fees vary according to course level, course load, degree level and program. *Financial support:* Applicants required to submit FAFSA. *Unit head:* Dr. Diane Dahl, Assistant Dean, 651-635-8000, Fax: 651-635-8004, E-mail: diane-dahl@bethel.edu. *Application contact:* Paul Ives, Director of Admissions, 651-635-8000, Fax: 651-635-8004, E-mail: gs@bethel.edu.

Boston University, School of Education, Boston, MA 02215. Offers counseling (Ed M, CAGS), including community, school, sport psychology; counseling psychology (Ed D); curriculum and teaching (Ed M, Ed D, CAGS), including early childhood (Ed D), educational media and technology (Ed D), English and language arts (Ed D), mathematics (Ed D), physical education and coaching (Ed D), science (Ed D), social studies education (Ed D), special education (Ed D); developmental studies (Ed D), including literacy and language, reading education; developmental studies in literacy and language education (Ed M, CAGS); early childhood education (Ed M, CAGS); education of the deaf (Ed M, CAGS); educational leadership and development (Ed D), including educational administration (Ed M, Ed D, CAGS), higher education administration (Ed M, Ed D, CAGS); educational media and technology (Ed M, CAGS); elementary education (Ed M); English and language arts (Ed M, CAGS); English education (MAT); health education (Ed M, CAGS); Latin and classical studies (MAT); mathematics education (Ed M, MAT, CAGS); mathematics for teaching (MMT); modern foreign language education (MAT), including French, Spanish; physical education and coaching (Ed M, CAGS); policy, planning, and administration (Ed M, CAGS), including community education leadership, educational administration (Ed M, Ed D, CAGS), higher education administration (Ed M, Ed D,

Social Psychology

Boston University (continued)

CAGS); reading education (Ed M, CAGS); science education (Ed M, MAT, CAGS), including biology (MAT), chemistry (MAT), earth science (MAT), general science (MAT), physics (MAT); social studies education (Ed M, MAT, CAGS), including history (MAT), political science (MAT); special education (Ed M, Ed D, CAGS), including disability studies (Ed M), moderate disabilities (Ed M), severe disabilities (Ed M), special education administration (Ed M); teaching English as a second language (Ed M, CAGS). Part-time programs available. *Faculty:* 57 full-time, 39 part-time/adjunct. *Students:* 245 full-time (191 women), 376 part-time (274 women); includes 83 minority (14 Black or African American, non-Hispanic/Latino; 2 American Indian or Alaska Native, non-Hispanic/Latino; 28 Asian, non-Hispanic/Latino; 31 Hispanic/Latino; 2 Native Hawaiian or other Pacific Islander, non-Hispanic/Latino; 6 Two or more races, non-Hispanic/Latino), 79 international. Average age 30. 1,270 applicants, 66% accepted, 292 enrolled. In 2010, 273 master's, 15 doctorates, 7 other advanced degrees awarded. Terminal master's awarded for partial completion of doctoral program. *Degree requirements:* For master's, thesis (for some programs); for doctorate, comprehensive exam, thesis/dissertation; for CAGS, comprehensive exam. *Entrance requirements:* For master's and CAGS, GRE General Test or Miller Analogies Test (MAT); for doctorate, GRE General Test. Additional exam requirements/recommendations for international students: Required—TOEFL, IELTS. *Application deadline:* For fall admission, 1/15 priority date for domestic and international students; for spring admission, 9/15 priority date for domestic and international students. Applications are processed on a rolling basis. Application fee: $70. Electronic applications accepted. *Expenses:* Tuition: Full-time $39,314; part-time $1228 per credit. Required fees: $40 per semester. *Financial support:* In 2010–11, 276 students received support, including 31 fellowships with full tuition reimbursements available, 16 research assistantships, 26 teaching assistantships with partial tuition reimbursements available; career-related internships or fieldwork, Federal Work-Study, and scholarships/grants also available. Support available to part-time students. Financial award applicants required to submit FAFSA. *Faculty research:* Deaf studies, social emotional learning, civic engagement and education, STEM education, pre-college educational pipelines. Total annual research expenditures: $2.6 million. *Unit head:* Dr. Hardin Coleman, Dean, 617-353-3213. *Application contact:* Dana Fernandez, Director of Enrollment, 617-353-4237, Fax: 617-353-8937, E-mail: sedgrad@bu.edu.

Bowling Green State University, Graduate College, College of Arts and Sciences, Department of Sociology, Bowling Green, OH 43403. Offers demography and population studies (MA); social psychology (MA); sociology (PhD). Part-time programs available. *Degree requirements:* For master's, thesis or alternative; for doctorate, comprehensive exam, thesis/dissertation. *Entrance requirements:* For master's and doctorate, GRE General Test. Additional exam requirements/recommendations for international students: Required—TOEFL. Electronic applications accepted. *Faculty research:* Applied demography, criminology and deviance, family studies, population studies, social psychology.

Brandeis University, Graduate School of Arts and Sciences, Department of Psychology, Waltham, MA 02454-9110. Offers brain, body and behavior (PhD); cognitive neuroscience (PhD); general psychology (MA); social/developmental psychology (PhD). Part-time programs available. *Faculty:* 17 full-time (4 women), 2 part-time/adjunct (1 woman). *Students:* 47 full-time (32 women); includes 2 Asian, non-Hispanic/Latino, 12 international. 164 applicants, 27% accepted, 24 enrolled. In 2010, 8 master's, 4 doctorates awarded. Terminal master's awarded for partial completion of doctoral program. *Degree requirements:* For master's, thesis; for doctorate, comprehensive exam, thesis/dissertation. *Entrance requirements:* For master's and doctorate, GRE General Test, GRE Subject Test (recommended), 3 letters of recommendation, statement of purpose. Additional exam requirements/recommendations for international students: Required—TOEFL (minimum score 600 paper-based; 250 computer-based; 100 iBT); Recommended—IELTS (minimum score 7). *Application deadline:* For fall admission, 1/15 priority date for domestic and international students. Applications are processed on a rolling basis. Application fee: $75. Electronic applications accepted. *Financial support:* In 2010–11, 16 fellowships with full tuition reimbursements (averaging $20,000 per year), 3 research assistantships with full tuition reimbursements (averaging $20,000 per year), 9 teaching assistantships with partial tuition reimbursements (averaging $3,200 per year) were awarded; institutionally sponsored loans, scholarships/grants, health care benefits, tuition waivers (full and partial), and unspecified assistantships also available. Support available to part-time students. Financial award application deadline: 4/15; financial award applicants required to submit FAFSA. *Faculty research:* Cognitive neuroscience, social developmental psychology, brain body and behavior. *Unit head:* Prof. Paul DiZio, Director of Graduate Studies, 781-736-3300, Fax: 781-736-3291, E-mail: dizio@brandeis.edu. *Application contact:* Phil Gnatowski, Department Administrator, 781-736-3303, Fax: 781-736-3291, E-mail: gnat@brandeis.edu.

Brigham Young University, Graduate Studies, College of Family, Home, and Social Sciences, Department of Psychology, Provo, UT 84602. Offers clinical psychology (PhD); general psychology (MS); psychology (PhD), including applied social psychology, behavioral neuroscience. *Accreditation:* APA (one or more programs are accredited). *Faculty:* 32 full-time (6 women), 4 part-time/adjunct (2 women). *Students:* 82 full-time (27 women); includes 3 Black or African American, non-Hispanic/Latino; 1 American Indian or Alaska Native, non-Hispanic/Latino; 6 Asian, non-Hispanic/Latino; 5 Hispanic/Latino; 68 Native Hawaiian or other Pacific Islander, non-Hispanic/Latino, 8 international. Average age 26. 91 applicants, 25% accepted, 18 enrolled. In 2010, 12 master's, 18 doctorates awarded. *Degree requirements:* For master's, thesis; for doctorate, comprehensive exam, thesis/dissertation, publishable paper. *Entrance requirements:* For master's and doctorate, GRE General Test, minimum GPA of 3.0 in last 60 hours of upper division course work. Additional exam requirements/recommendations for international students: Required—TOEFL. *Application deadline:* For fall admission, 1/5 for domestic students. Application fee: $50. Electronic applications accepted. *Expenses:* Tuition: Full-time $5580; part-time $310 per credit hour. Tuition and fees vary according to program and student's religious affiliation. *Financial support:* In 2010–11, 82 students received support, including 20 research assistantships with partial tuition reimbursements available (averaging $10,000 per year), 30 teaching assistantships with partial tuition reimbursements available (averaging $10,000 per year); fellowships, career-related internships or fieldwork, scholarships/grants, tuition waivers (partial), and unspecified assistantships also available. Financial award application deadline: 5/31. *Faculty research:* Psychotherapy process, Alzheimer's disease/dementia, psychology and law, health, psychology, developmental. Total annual research expenditures: $1 million. *Unit head:* Dr. Ramona Hopkins, Chair, 801-422-1170, Fax: 801-422-0602, E-mail: ramona_hopkins@byu.edu. *Application contact:* Karen A. Christensen, Coordinator of Student Programs, 801-422-4560, Fax: 801-422-0602, E-mail: karen@byu.edu.

Brock University, Faculty of Graduate Studies, Faculty of Social Sciences, Program in Psychology, St. Catharines, ON L2S 3A1, Canada. Offers behavioral neuroscience (MA, PhD); life span development (MA, PhD); social personality (MA, PhD). Part-time programs available. *Degree requirements:* For master's, thesis; for doctorate, thesis/dissertation. *Entrance requirements:* For master's, GRE, honors degree; for doctorate, GRE, master's degree. Additional exam requirements/recommendations for international students: Required—TOEFL (minimum score 550 paper-based; 213 computer-based; 80 iBT), IELTS (minimum score 6.5), TWE (minimum score 4). Electronic applications accepted. *Faculty research:* Social personality, behavioral neuroscience, life-span development.

Brooklyn College of the City University of New York, Division of Graduate Studies, Department of Psychology, Program in Industrial and Organizational Psychology, Brooklyn, NY 11210-2889. Offers human relations (MA); organizational behavior (MA). *Students:* 6 full-time (5 women), 100 part-time (78 women); includes 63 minority (42 Black or African American, non-Hispanic/Latino; 8 Asian, non-Hispanic/Latino; 13 Hispanic/Latino), 10 international. Average age 30. 93 applicants, 69% accepted, 41 enrolled. In 2010, 39 master's awarded. *Degree requirements:* For master's, comprehensive exam, thesis. *Entrance requirements:* For master's, 2 letters of recommendation. Additional exam requirements/recommendations for international students: Required—TOEFL (minimum score 520 paper-based; 190 computer-based; 69 iBT). *Application deadline:* For fall admission, 3/1 priority date for domestic students, 2/1 for international students. Applications are processed on a rolling basis. Electronic applications accepted. *Expenses:* Tuition, state resident: full-time $7360; part-time $310 per credit hour. Tuition, nonresident: full-time $13,800; part-time $575 per credit hour. Required fees: $190 per semester. *Unit head:* Benzion Chanowitz, Graduate Advisor, 718-951-5601, E-mail: bchanowitz@brooklyn.cuny.edu. *Application contact:* Hernan Sierra, Graduate Admissions Coordinator, 718-951-4536, Fax: 718-951-4506, E-mail: grads@brooklyn.cuny.edu.

Brown University, Graduate School, Department of Psychology, Providence, RI 02912. Offers behavioral neuroscience (PhD); cognitive processes (PhD); sensation and perception (PhD); social/developmental (PhD); MS/PhD. *Degree requirements:* For doctorate, thesis/dissertation. *Entrance requirements:* For doctorate, GRE General Test, GRE Subject Test.

California Institute of Integral Studies, School of Professional Psychology, San Francisco, CA 94103. Offers clinical psychology (Psy D); community mental health (MA); drama therapy (MA); expressive arts therapy (MA); integral counseling psychology (MA); integral counseling psychology-weekend (MA); somatic psychology (MA). *Accreditation:* APA. Part-time and evening/weekend programs available. *Students:* 651 full-time (476 women), 74 part-time (62 women); includes 146 minority (32 Black or African American, non-Hispanic/Latino; 1 American Indian or Alaska Native, non-Hispanic/Latino; 53 Asian, non-Hispanic/Latino; 43 Hispanic/Latino; 17 Two or more races, non-Hispanic/Latino), 52 international. Average age 37. 556 applicants, 72% accepted, 247 enrolled. In 2010, 148 master's, 27 doctorates awarded. *Degree requirements:* For doctorate, comprehensive exam, thesis/dissertation. *Entrance requirements:* For master's, minimum GPA of 3.0, letters of recommendation, writing sample; for doctorate, GRE, MA in psychology or social work with appropriate practical experience for advanced standing, or BA with a minimum GPA of 3.1; letters of recommendation; writing sample. Additional exam requirements/recommendations for international students: Required—TOEFL. *Application deadline:* For fall admission, 2/1 priority date for domestic and international students; for spring admission, 10/15 priority date for domestic and international students. Applications are processed on a rolling basis. Application fee: $65. Electronic applications accepted. *Expenses:* Tuition: Full-time $15,660; part-time $870 per semester hour. Required fees: $95 per semester. *Financial support:* Research assistantships with tuition reimbursements, teaching assistantships with tuition reimbursements, career-related internships or fieldwork, Federal Work-Study, scholarships/grants, and tuition waivers (partial) available. Support available to part-time students. Financial award application deadline: 4/15; financial award applicants required to submit FAFSA. *Faculty research:* Transpersonal psychology, somatic psychology, expressive arts therapy, drama therapy, community mental health, ecopsychology. *Application contact:* David Townes, Senior Admissions Counselor, 415-575-6152, Fax: 415-575-1268, E-mail: dtownes@ciis.edu.

California State University, Fullerton, Graduate Studies, College of Humanities and Social Sciences, Department of Psychology, Fullerton, CA 92834-9480. Offers clinical/community psychology (MS); psychology (MA). Part-time programs available. *Students:* 67 full-time (49 women), 9 part-time (5 women); includes 2 Black or African American, non-Hispanic/Latino; 5 Asian, non-Hispanic/Latino; 8 Hispanic/Latino; 3 Two or more races, non-Hispanic/Latino, 2 international. Average age 25. 169 applicants, 22% accepted, 37 enrolled. In 2010, 33 master's awarded. *Degree requirements:* For master's, thesis. *Entrance requirements:* For master's, GRE General Test, GRE Subject Test, undergraduate major in psychology or related field. Application fee: $55. *Financial support:* Career-related internships or fieldwork, Federal Work-Study, institutionally sponsored loans, and scholarships/grants available. Support available to part-time students. Financial award application deadline: 3/1; financial award applicants required to submit FAFSA. *Unit head:* Dr. Daniel Kee, Chair, 657-278-3514. *Application contact:* Admissions/Applications, 657-278-2371.

Canisius College, Graduate Division, School of Education and Human Services, Programs in Counseling and Human Services, Buffalo, NY 14208-1098. Offers community mental health counseling (MS); school agency counseling (MS). *Accreditation:* ACA. Part-time and evening/weekend programs available. *Faculty:* 5 full-time (3 women), 18 part-time/adjunct (13 women). *Students:* 144 full-time (113 women), 50 part-time (42 women); includes 35 minority (28 Black or African American, non-Hispanic/Latino; 4 Asian, non-Hispanic/Latino; 2 Hispanic/Latino; 1 Two or more races, non-Hispanic/Latino), 3 international. Average age 27. 128 applicants, 84% accepted, 51 enrolled. In 2010, 40 master's awarded. *Degree requirements:* For master's, thesis, research project. *Entrance requirements:* For master's, GRE if cumulative GPA less than 2.7, transcripts, two letters of recommendation, interview. Additional exam requirements/recommendations for international students: Required—TOEFL. *Application deadline:* Applications are processed on a rolling basis. Application fee: $25. Electronic applications accepted. *Expenses:* Tuition: Part-time $694 per credit hour. Required fees: $11 per credit hour. $90 per semester. *Financial support:* Research assistantships, career-related internships or fieldwork, Federal Work-Study, scholarships/grants, tuition waivers (partial), and unspecified assistantships available. Support available to part-time students. Financial award application deadline: 7/1; financial award applicants required to submit FAFSA. *Faculty research:* Impact of trauma on adults, long term psych-social impact on police officers. *Unit head:* Dr. Christine Moll, Chair, 716-888-3287, E-mail: moll@canisius.edu. *Application contact:* Jim Bagwell, Director of Graduate Recruitment and Admissions, 716-888-2544, E-mail: bagwellj@canisius.edu.

Carnegie Mellon University, College of Humanities and Social Sciences, Department of Psychology, Program in Social/Personality/Health Psychology, Pittsburgh, PA 15213-3891. Offers PhD. *Degree requirements:* For doctorate, comprehensive exam, thesis/dissertation. *Entrance requirements:* For doctorate, GRE General Test. Additional exam requirements/recommendations for international students: Required—TOEFL.

Central Connecticut State University, School of Graduate Studies, School of Arts and Sciences, Department of Psychology, New Britain, CT 06050-4010. Offers community psychology (MA); general psychology (MA); health psychology (MA). Part-time and evening/weekend programs available. *Faculty:* 20 full-time (12 women), 22 part-time/adjunct (6 women). *Students:* 26 full-time (20 women), 25 part-time (20 women); includes 6 minority (1 Black or African American, non-Hispanic/Latino; 4 Hispanic/Latino; 1 Two or more races, non-Hispanic/Latino). Average age 26. 65 applicants, 57% accepted, 19 enrolled. In 2010, 7 master's awarded. *Degree requirements:* For master's, comprehensive exam, thesis or alternative. *Entrance requirements:* For master's, minimum undergraduate GPA of 2.7, essay. Additional exam requirements/recommendations for international students: Required—TOEFL. *Application deadline:* For fall admission, 4/25 for domestic students; for spring admission, 12/1 for domestic students. Applications are processed on a rolling basis. Application fee: $50. Electronic applications accepted. *Expenses:* Tuition, area resident: Full-time $5012; part-time $470 per credit. Tuition, state resident: full-time $7518; part-time $482 per credit. Tuition, nonresident: full-time $13,962; part-time $482 per credit. Required fees: $3772. One-time fee: $62 part-time. *Financial support:* In 2010–11, 8 students received support, including 4 research assistantships; career-related internships or fieldwork, Federal Work-Study, scholarships/grants, and unspecified assistantships also available. Support available to part-time students. Financial award application deadline: 2/15; financial award applicants required to submit FAFSA. *Faculty research:* Clinical psychology, general psychology, child development, cognitive development, drugs/behavior. *Unit head:* Dr. Laura Bowman, Chair, 860-832-3100. *Application contact:* Dr. Laura Bowman, Chair, 860-832-3100.

Claremont Graduate University, Graduate Programs, School of Behavioral and Organizational Sciences, Department of Psychology, Claremont, CA 91711-6160. Offers advanced study in evaluation (Certificate); cognitive psychology (MA, PhD); developmental psychology (MA, PhD); evaluation and applied research methods (MA, PhD); health behavior research and evaluation (MA, PhD); human resource development and evaluation (MA); industrial/organizational psychology (MA, PhD); organizational behavior (MA, PhD); organizational psychology (MA, PhD); social psychology (MA, PhD); MBA/PhD. Part-time programs available. *Faculty:* 15 full-time (6 women), 5 part-time/adjunct (2 women). *Students:* 248 full-time (169 women), 15 part-time (9 women); includes 68 minority (14 Black or African American, non-

Hispanic/Latino; 1 American Indian or Alaska Native, non-Hispanic/Latino; 27 Asian, non-Hispanic/Latino; 19 Hispanic/Latino; 2 Native Hawaiian or other Pacific Islander, non-Hispanic/Latino; 5 Two or more races, non-Hispanic/Latino), 29 international. Average age 30. In 2010, 45 master's, 21 doctorates, 4 other advanced degrees awarded. Terminal master's awarded for partial completion of doctoral program. *Entrance requirements:* For master's and doctorate, GRE General Test. Additional exam requirements/recommendations for international students: Required—TOEFL (minimum score 550 paper-based; 213 computer-based; 80 iBT). *Application deadline:* For fall admission, 1/15 priority date for domestic students. Applications are processed on a rolling basis. Application fee: $60. Electronic applications accepted. *Expenses:* Tuition: Full-time $35,748; part-time $1554 per unit. Required fees: $215 per semester. *Financial support:* Fellowships, research assistantships, teaching assistantships, Federal Work-Study, institutionally sponsored loans, scholarships/grants, and tuition waivers (full and partial) available. Support available to part-time students. Financial award application deadline: 2/15; financial award applicants required to submit FAFSA. *Faculty research:* Social intervention, diversity in organizations, eyewitness memory, aging and cognition, drug policy. *Unit head:* Stewart Donaldson, Dean, 909-607-9001, Fax: 909-621-8905, E-mail: stewart.donaldson@cgu.edu. *Application contact:* Paul Thomas, Director, External Affairs, 909-607-9016, Fax: 909-621-8905, E-mail: paul.thomas@cgu.edu.

Clark University, Graduate School, Department of Psychology, Program in Social-Personality Psychology, Worcester, MA 01610-1477. Offers PhD. *Students:* 11 full-time (6 women), 3 international. Average age 31. *Degree requirements:* For doctorate, thesis/dissertation. *Entrance requirements:* For doctorate, GRE General Test. Additional exam requirements/recommendations for international students: Required—TOEFL. *Application deadline:* For fall admission, 12/28 priority date for domestic students. Applications are processed on a rolling basis. Application fee: $50. *Expenses:* Tuition: Full-time $37,000; part-time $1156 per credit hour. Required fees: $30; $1156 per credit hour. *Financial support:* In 2010–11, fellowships with full tuition reimbursements (averaging $15,700 per year), research assistantships with full tuition reimbursements (averaging $15,700 per year), teaching assistantships with full tuition reimbursements (averaging $15,700 per year) were awarded; tuition waivers (full) also available. *Faculty research:* Development of psychological processes in sociocultural context, conceptualizing and reasoning, symbolization, psychotherapy, metaphor, emotions and personalities. *Unit head:* Dr. Joseph deRivera, Director, 508-793-7274. *Application contact:* Peggy Moskowitz, Graduate School Secretary, 508-793-7274, Fax: 508-793-7265, E-mail: psychology@clarku.edu.

The College of New Rochelle, Graduate School, Division of Human Services, Program in Community-School Psychology, New Rochelle, NY 10805-2308. Offers MS. *Degree requirements:* For master's, comprehensive exam, clinical fieldwork, journal. *Entrance requirements:* For master's, interview, minimum GPA of 3.0, course work in psychology, sample of written work.

College of St. Joseph, Graduate Programs, Division of Psychology and Human Services, Program in Community Counseling, Rutland, VT 05701-3899. Offers MS. Part-time and evening/weekend programs available. *Faculty:* 4 full-time (1 woman), 6 part-time/adjunct (3 women). *Students:* 1 (woman) full-time, 4 part-time (all women). Average age 39. 2 applicants, 50% accepted, 0 enrolled. In 2010, 2 master's awarded. *Degree requirements:* For master's, comprehensive exam, thesis optional. *Entrance requirements:* For master's, 2 letters of reference, interview. *Application deadline:* Applications are processed on a rolling basis. Application fee: $35. Electronic applications accepted. *Expenses:* Tuition: Full-time $14,200; part-time $400 per credit hour. Required fees: $45 per semester. *Financial support:* Career-related internships or fieldwork, Federal Work-Study, and unspecified assistantships available. Support available to part-time students. Financial award application deadline: 3/1. *Unit head:* Dr. Craig Knapp, Chair, 802-773-5900 Ext. 3219, Fax: 802-776-5258, E-mail: cknapp@csj.edu. *Application contact:* Alan Young, Dean of Admissions, 802-773-5900 Ext. 3227, Fax: 802-776-5310, E-mail: alanyoung@csj.edu.

Columbia University, Graduate School of Arts and Sciences, Division of Natural Sciences, Department of Psychology, New York, NY 10027. Offers experimental psychology (M Phil, MA, PhD); psychobiology (M Phil, MA, PhD); social psychology (M Phil, MA, PhD); JD/MA; JD/PhD; MD/PhD. *Degree requirements:* For master's, thesis; for doctorate, thesis/dissertation. *Entrance requirements:* For master's and doctorate, GRE General Test. Additional exam requirements/recommendations for international students: Required—TOEFL.

Cornell University, Graduate School, Graduate Fields of Arts and Sciences, Field of Psychology, Ithaca, NY 14853-0001. Offers biopsychology (PhD); human experimental psychology (PhD); personality and social psychology (PhD). *Faculty:* 40 full-time (15 women). *Students:* 39 full-time (25 women); includes 1 Black or African American, non-Hispanic/Latino; 4 Asian, non-Hispanic/Latino; 2 Hispanic/Latino, 13 international. Average age 27. 273 applicants, 5% accepted, 10 enrolled. In 2010, 4 doctorates awarded. *Degree requirements:* For doctorate, comprehensive exam, thesis/dissertation, 2 semesters of teaching experience. *Entrance requirements:* For doctorate, GRE General Test, 3 letters of recommendation. Additional exam requirements/recommendations for international students: Required—TOEFL (minimum score 550 paper-based; 213 computer-based; 77 iBT). *Application deadline:* For fall admission, 12/15 for domestic students. Application fee: $80. Electronic applications accepted. *Expenses:* Tuition: Full-time $29,500. Required fees: $76. Tuition and fees vary according to degree level and program. *Financial support:* In 2010–11, 12 fellowships with full tuition reimbursements, 2 research assistantships with full tuition reimbursements, 23 teaching assistantships with full tuition reimbursements were awarded; institutionally sponsored loans, scholarships/grants, health care benefits, tuition waivers (full and partial), and unspecified assistantships also available. Financial award applicants required to submit FAFSA. *Faculty research:* Sensory and perceptual systems, social cognition, cognitive development, quantitative and computational modeling, behavioral neuroscience. *Unit head:* Director of Graduate Studies, 607-255-6364, Fax: 607-255-8433. *Application contact:* Graduate Field Assistant, 607-255-3834, Fax: 607-255-8433, E-mail: psychapp@cornell.edu.

Cornell University, Graduate School, Graduate Fields of Arts and Sciences, Field of Sociology, Ithaca, NY 14853-0001. Offers economy and society (MA, PhD); gender and life course (MA, PhD); methodology (MA, PhD); organizations (MA, PhD); policy analysis (MA, PhD); political sociology/social movements (MA, PhD); racial and ethnic relations (MA, PhD); social networks (MA, PhD); social psychology (MA, PhD); social stratification (MA, PhD). *Faculty:* 33 full-time (12 women). *Students:* 36 full-time (18 women); includes 4 Asian, non-Hispanic/Latino, 9 international. Average age 29. 187 applicants, 7% accepted, 9 enrolled. In 2010, 3 master's, 2 doctorates awarded. Terminal master's awarded for partial completion of doctoral program. *Degree requirements:* For master's, thesis; for doctorate, thesis/dissertation, 1 year of teaching experience. *Entrance requirements:* For master's and doctorate, GRE General Test, 2 letters of recommendation, writing sample. Additional exam requirements/recommendations for international students: Required—TOEFL (minimum score 550 paper-based; 213 computer-based; 77 iBT). *Application deadline:* For fall admission, 1/15 for domestic students. Application fee: $80. Electronic applications accepted. *Expenses:* Tuition: Full-time $29,500. Required fees: $76. Tuition and fees vary according to degree level and program. *Financial support:* In 2010–11, 13 fellowships with full tuition reimbursements, 7 research assistantships with full tuition reimbursements, 14 teaching assistantships with full tuition reimbursements were awarded; institutionally sponsored loans, scholarships/grants, health care benefits, tuition waivers (full and partial), and unspecified assistantships also available. Financial award applicants required to submit FAFSA. *Faculty research:* Comparative societal analysis, work and family, simulations, social class and mobility, racial segregation and inequality. *Unit head:* Director of Graduate Studies, 607-255-4266. *Application contact:* Graduate Field Assistant, 607-255-4266, E-mail: sociology@cornell.edu.

Creighton University, Graduate School, College of Arts and Sciences, Department of Education, Program in Counselor Education, Omaha, NE 68178-0001. Offers college student affairs (MS); community counseling (MS); elementary school guidance (MS); secondary school guidance (MS). Part-time and evening/weekend programs available. *Faculty:* 13 full-time (8 women). *Students:* 5 full-time (4 women), 31 part-time (25 women); includes 5 minority (1 Black or African American, non-Hispanic/Latino; 1 American Indian or Alaska Native, non-Hispanic/Latino; 2 Hispanic/Latino; 1 Native Hawaiian or other Pacific Islander, non-Hispanic/Latino), 3 international. Average age 32. 12 applicants, 83% accepted, 10 enrolled. In 2010, 15 master's awarded. *Degree requirements:* For master's, comprehensive exam. *Entrance requirements:* For master's, GRE General Test, resume, 3 letters of recommendation, personal statement. Additional exam requirements/recommendations for international students: Required—TOEFL (minimum score 550 paper-based; 213 computer-based; 80 iBT). *Application deadline:* For fall admission, 7/1 for domestic students, 3/1 for international students; for winter admission, 10/1 for domestic students, 7/1 for international students; for spring admission, 3/1 for domestic students, 9/1 for international students. Applications are processed on a rolling basis. Application fee: $50. Electronic applications accepted. *Expenses:* Tuition: Full-time $12,168; part-time $676 per credit hour. Required fees: $131 per semester. Tuition and fees vary according to program. *Financial support:* Scholarships/grants available. Support available to part-time students. Financial award applicants required to submit FAFSA. *Unit head:* Dr. Debra L. Ponec, Associate Professor of Education, 402-280-2557, E-mail: dlponec@creighton.edu. *Application contact:* Taunya Plater, Senior Program Coordinator, 402-280-2870, Fax: 402-280-2899, E-mail: taunyaplater@creighton.edu.

DePaul University, College of Liberal Arts and Sciences, Department of Psychology, Chicago, IL 60604-2287. Offers clinical psychology (MA, PhD), including child clinical psychology, community clinical psychology; experimental psychology (MA, PhD); general psychology (MS); industrial/organizational psychology (MA, PhD); MA/PhD. *Accreditation:* APA (one or more programs are accredited). *Faculty:* 31 full-time (19 women), 6 part-time/adjunct (4 women). *Students:* 43 full-time (26 women), 57 part-time (39 women); includes 11 Black or African American, non-Hispanic/Latino; 5 Asian, non-Hispanic/Latino; 10 Hispanic/Latino; 4 Two or more races, non-Hispanic/Latino, 2 international. Average age 28. 332 applicants, 14% accepted, 23 enrolled. In 2010, 14 master's, 17 doctorates awarded. *Degree requirements:* For master's, thesis, oral exam; for doctorate, comprehensive exam, thesis/dissertation, oral and written exams. *Entrance requirements:* For master's and doctorate, GRE General Test, GRE Subject Test, 32 quarter hours of course work in psychology, 3 letters of recommendation. Additional exam requirements/recommendations for international students: Required—TOEFL. Application fee: $40. Electronic applications accepted. *Financial support:* In 2010–11, 48 students received support, including 35 research assistantships with full tuition reimbursements available (averaging $11,800 per year), 13 teaching assistantships with full tuition reimbursements available (averaging $11,800 per year); career-related internships or fieldwork, scholarships/grants, traineeships, tuition waivers (full and partial), and unspecified assistantships also available. Financial award application deadline: 1/10. *Faculty research:* Adolescent stress and depression, minority adolescents sexuality, public policy, community influences in child adjustment. *Unit head:* Dr. Christopher B. Keys, Chairman, 773-325-7887, Fax: 773-325-7888. *Application contact:* Alison Pereida Knapp, Graduate Admissions Assistant, 773-325-7887, Fax: 773-325-7888.

Eastern Michigan University, Graduate School, College of Education, Department of Leadership and Counseling, Programs in Counseling, Ypsilanti, MI 48197. Offers college counseling (MA); community counseling (MA); helping interventions in a multicultural society (Graduate Certificate); school counseling (MA); school counselor (MA); school counselor licensure (Post Master's Certificate). Part-time and evening/weekend programs available. *Students:* 19 full-time (17 women), 104 part-time (90 women); includes 31 minority (27 Black or African American, non-Hispanic/Latino; 1 American Indian or Alaska Native, non-Hispanic/Latino; 1 Asian, non-Hispanic/Latino; 1 Hispanic/Latino; 1 Two or more races, non-Hispanic/Latino), 4 international. Average age 32. In 2010, 28 master's, 4 other advanced degrees awarded. *Degree requirements:* For master's, comprehensive exam, internship. *Entrance requirements:* Additional exam requirements/recommendations for international students: Required—TOEFL. *Application deadline:* For fall admission, 5/1 for domestic and international students; for winter admission, 9/15 for domestic and international students; for spring admission, 2/10 for domestic and international students. Applications are processed on a rolling basis. Application fee: $35. *Financial support:* Fellowships, research assistantships with full tuition reimbursements, teaching assistantships with full tuition reimbursements, career-related internships or fieldwork, Federal Work-Study, institutionally sponsored loans, scholarships/grants, tuition waivers (partial), and unspecified assistantships available. Support available to part-time students. Financial award applicants required to submit FAFSA. *Application contact:* Dr. Dibya Choudhuri, Coordinator of Advising, 734-487-0255, Fax: 734-487-4608, E-mail: dchoudhur@emich.edu.

Eastern University, Department of Counseling Psychology, St. Davids, PA 19087-3696. Offers community/clinical counseling (MA); school counseling (MA, Certificate); school psychology (MS, Certificate). *Degree requirements:* For master's, internship. *Entrance requirements:* For master's, minimum GPA of 2.5. Additional exam requirements/recommendations for international students: Required—TOEFL.

Florida Agricultural and Mechanical University, Division of Graduate Studies, Research, and Continuing Education, College of Arts and Sciences, Department of Psychology, Program in Community Psychology, Tallahassee, FL 32307-3200. Offers MS. *Degree requirements:* For master's, thesis, internship. *Entrance requirements:* For master's, GRE General Test, minimum GPA of 3.0, letters of recommendation (3). Additional exam requirements/recommendations for international students: Required—TOEFL. *Faculty research:* African-American personality and mental health, racism in the socialization of black children.

Florida State University, The Graduate School, College of Arts and Sciences, Department of Psychology, Program in Social Psychology, Tallahassee, FL 32306. Offers PhD. *Faculty:* 5 full-time (3 women). *Students:* 21 full-time (11 women), 1 part-time (0 women); includes 2 Asian, non-Hispanic/Latino; 2 Hispanic/Latino. Average age 24. 134 applicants, 4% accepted, 4 enrolled. In 2010, 5 doctorates awarded. Terminal master's awarded for partial completion of doctoral program. *Degree requirements:* For doctorate, thesis/dissertation, preliminary exam. *Entrance requirements:* For doctorate, GRE General Test (suggested minimum total score of 1100), minimum GPA of 3.0, research experience, letters of recommendation. Additional exam requirements/recommendations for international students: Required—TOEFL (minimum score 550 paper-based; 213 computer-based; 80 iBT). *Application deadline:* For fall admission, 12/15 for domestic and international students. Application fee: $30. *Expenses:* Tuition, state resident: full-time $8238.24. *Financial support:* In 2010–11, 21 students received support, including 3 fellowships with full tuition reimbursements available (averaging $20,000 per year), 7 research assistantships with full tuition reimbursements available (averaging $20,000 per year), 11 teaching assistantships with full tuition reimbursements available (averaging $16,500 per year); Federal Work-Study, institutionally sponsored loans, scholarships/grants, traineeships, and unspecified assistantships also available. *Faculty research:* The self, prejudice, stereotyping. Total annual research expenditures: $727,461. *Unit head:* Dr. Roy Baumeister, Director, 850-644-4200, Fax: 850-644-7739, E-mail: baumeister@psy.fsu.edu. *Application contact:* Cherie P. Miller, Graduate Program Assistant, 850-644-2499, Fax: 850-644-7739, E-mail: grad-info@psy.fsu.edu.

Future Generations Graduate School, Program in Applied Community Change and Conservation, Franklin, WV 26807. Offers MA.

The George Washington University, Columbian College of Arts and Sciences, Department of Psychology, Washington, DC 20052. Offers applied social psychology (PhD); clinical psychology (PhD); cognitive neuroscience (PhD). *Accreditation:* APA. Part-time and evening/weekend programs available. *Faculty:* 26 full-time (14 women), 14 part-time/adjunct (9 women). *Students:* 131 full-time (103 women), 75 part-time (55 women); includes 14 Black or African American, non-Hispanic/Latino; 2 American Indian or Alaska Native, non-Hispanic/Latino; 18 Asian, non-Hispanic/Latino; 16 Hispanic/Latino, 4 international. Average age 29. 797 applicants, 6% accepted, 9 enrolled. In 2010, 41 doctorates awarded. *Degree requirements:* For doctorate, thesis/dissertation or alternative, general exam. *Entrance requirements:* For doctorate, GRE General Test, minimum GPA of 3.0. Additional exam requirements/recommendations for inter-

Social Psychology

The George Washington University (continued)

national students: Required—TOEFL (minimum score 550 paper-based; 213 computer-based; 80 iBT). *Application deadline:* For fall admission, 1/15 for domestic and international students. Application fee: $75. *Financial support:* In 2010–11, 62 students received support; fellowships with tuition reimbursements available, teaching assistantships with tuition reimbursements available, career-related internships or fieldwork, Federal Work-Study, and tuition waivers available. *Unit head:* Dr. Paul Poppen, Chair, 202-994-6324, E-mail: pjp@gwu.edu. *Application contact:* Information Contact, 202-994-6320, Fax: 202-994-1602, E-mail: psydept@gwu.edu.

The George Washington University, Graduate School of Education and Human Development, Department of Counseling/Human and Organizational Studies, Programs in Counseling: School, Community and Rehabilitation, Washington, DC 20052. Offers community counseling (MA Ed); rehabilitation counseling (MA Ed); school counseling (MA Ed). School counseling program also offered in Alexandria, VA. *Accreditation:* ACA; CORE; NCATE. *Students:* 65 full-time (60 women), 51 part-time (40 women); includes 18 Black or African American, non-Hispanic/Latino; 1 American Indian or Alaska Native, non-Hispanic/Latino; 5 Asian, non-Hispanic/Latino; 6 Hispanic/Latino; 1 Two or more races, non-Hispanic/Latino, 3 international. Average age 31. 120 applicants, 97% accepted, 50 enrolled. In 2010, 57 master's awarded. *Degree requirements:* For master's, comprehensive exam. *Entrance requirements:* For master's, GRE General Test or MAT, minimum GPA of 2.75. *Application deadline:* For fall admission, 1/15 priority date for domestic students; for spring admission, 10/1 for domestic students. Applications are processed on a rolling basis. Application fee: $75. *Financial support:* In 2010–11, 27 students received support; fellowships, research assistantships, teaching assistantships, career-related internships or fieldwork, Federal Work-Study, and tuition waivers (full and partial) available. *Faculty research:* Adjustment to disability, head injury rehabilitation, cross-cultural counseling. *Application contact:* Sarah Lang, Director of Graduate Admissions, 202-994-1447, Fax: 202-994-7207, E-mail: slang@gwu.edu.

Graduate School and University Center of the City University of New York, Graduate Studies, Program in Psychology, New York, NY 10016-4039. Offers basic applied neurocognition (PhD); biopsychology (PhD); clinical psychology (PhD); developmental psychology (PhD); environmental psychology (PhD); experimental psychology (PhD); industrial psychology (PhD); learning processes (PhD); neuropsychology (PhD); psychology (PhD); social personality (PhD). *Degree requirements:* For doctorate, one foreign language, thesis/dissertation. *Entrance requirements:* For doctorate, GRE General Test. Additional exam requirements/recommendations for international students: Required—TOEFL. Electronic applications accepted.

Harvard University, Graduate School of Arts and Sciences, Department of Psychology, Cambridge, MA 02138. Offers psychology (PhD), including behavior and decision analysis, cognition, developmental psychology, experimental psychology, personality, psychobiology, psychopathology; social psychology (PhD). *Accreditation:* APA. *Degree requirements:* For doctorate, thesis/dissertation, general exams. *Entrance requirements:* For doctorate, GRE General Test. Additional exam requirements/recommendations for international students: Required—TOEFL. *Expenses:* Tuition: Full-time $34,976. Required fees: $1166. Full-time tuition and fees vary according to program.

Hofstra University, College of Liberal Arts and Sciences, Program in School-Community Psychology, Hempstead, NY 11549. Offers Psy D. *Students:* 43 full-time (36 women), 9 part-time (8 women); includes 8 minority (3 Asian, non-Hispanic/Latino; 5 Hispanic/Latino), 1 international. Average age 26. 74 applicants, 35% accepted, 10 enrolled. In 2010, 10 doctorates awarded. *Degree requirements:* For doctorate, comprehensive exam, thesis/dissertation. *Entrance requirements:* For doctorate, GRE General Test, GRE Subject Test (Psychology), Interview; 3 letters of recommendation; Essay. Additional exam requirements/recommendations for international students: Required—TOEFL (minimum score 550 paper-based; 213 computer-based; 80 iBT). *Application deadline:* For fall admission, 1/15 for domestic and international students. Application fee: $70 ($75 for international students). Electronic applications accepted. *Expenses:* Tuition: Full-time $18,000; part-time $1000 per credit hour. Required fees: $970; $145 per term. Tuition and fees vary according to program. *Financial support:* In 2010–11, 29 students received support, including 19 fellowships with full and partial tuition reimbursements available (averaging $6,153 per year), 1 research assistantship with full and partial tuition reimbursement available (averaging $9,000 per year); Federal Work-Study, institutionally sponsored loans, scholarships/grants, tuition waivers (full and partial), and unspecified assistantships also available. Support available to part-time students. Financial award applicants required to submit FAFSA. *Faculty research:* Cross-cultural psychology, school psychology, childhood and adult trauma, positive psychology, autism spectrum disorders. *Unit head:* Dr. Robert Motta, Program Director, 516-463-5029, Fax: 516-463-6052, E-mail: psyrwm@hofstra.edu. *Application contact:* Carol Drummer, Dean of Graduate Admissions, 516-463-4876, Fax: 516-463-4664, E-mail: gradstudent@hofstra.edu.

Howard University, Graduate School, Department of Psychology, Washington, DC 20059-0002. Offers clinical psychology (PhD); developmental psychology (PhD); experimental psychology (PhD); neuropsychology (PhD); personality psychology (PhD); psychology (MS); social psychology (PhD). *Accreditation:* APA (one or more programs are accredited). Part-time programs available. *Degree requirements:* For master's, thesis; for doctorate, comprehensive exam, thesis/dissertation, qualifying exam. *Entrance requirements:* For master's, GRE General Test, minimum GPA of 2.5, bachelor's degree in psychology or related field; for doctorate, GRE General Test, minimum GPA of 3.0. *Faculty research:* Personality and psychophysiology, educational and social development of African-American children, child and adult psychopathology.

Hunter College of the City University of New York, Graduate School, School of Arts and Sciences, Department of Psychology, New York, NY 10021-5085. Offers animal behavior and conservation (MA); applied and evaluative psychology (MA); biopsychology and behavioral neuroscience (PhD); biopsychology and comparative psychology (MA); social, cognitive, and developmental psychology (MA). Part-time and evening/weekend programs available. *Faculty:* 9 full-time (1 woman), 1 part-time/adjunct (0 women). *Students:* 10 full-time (7 women), 79 part-time (61 women); includes 3 Black or African American, non-Hispanic/Latino; 7 Asian, non-Hispanic/Latino; 9 Hispanic/Latino, 2 international. Average age 27. 151 applicants, 34% accepted, 21 enrolled. In 2010, 13 master's awarded. *Degree requirements:* For master's, comprehensive exam, thesis. *Entrance requirements:* For master's, GRE General Test, minimum 12 credits of course work in psychology, including statistics and experimental psychology; 2 letters of recommendation. Additional exam requirements/recommendations for international students: Required—TOEFL. *Application deadline:* For fall admission, 4/1 for domestic students, 2/1 for international students; for spring admission, 11/1 for domestic students, 9/1 for international students. Applications are processed on a rolling basis. Application fee: $125. *Financial support:* Federal Work-Study, scholarships/grants, and tuition waivers (partial) available. Support available to part-time students. *Faculty research:* Personality, cognitive and linguistic development, hormonal and neural control of behavior, gender and culture, social cognition of health and attitudes. *Unit head:* Dr. Jeffrey Parsons, Chairperson, 212-772-5550, Fax: 212-772-5620, E-mail: jeffrey.parsons@hunter.cuny.edu. *Application contact:* Martin Braun, Acting Program Director, 212-772-4482, Fax: 212-650-3336, E-mail: cbraun@hunter.cuny.edu.

Indiana University Bloomington, University Graduate School, College of Arts and Sciences, Department of Psychological and Brain Sciences, Bloomington, IN 47405-7000. Offers biology and behavior (PhD); clinical science (PhD); cognitive psychology (PhD); developmental psychology (PhD); psychological and brain sciences (MA); social psychology (PhD). *Accreditation:* APA (one or more programs are accredited). *Faculty:* 53 full-time (16 women). *Students:* 85 full-time (45 women), 1 (woman) part-time; includes 13 minority (3 Black or African American, non-Hispanic/Latino; 3 Asian, non-Hispanic/Latino; 6 Hispanic/Latino; 1 Two or more races, non-Hispanic/Latino), 19 international. Average age 28. 363 applicants, 10% accepted, 20 enrolled. In 2010, 3 master's, 17 doctorates awarded. *Degree requirements:* For doctorate, comprehensive exam, thesis/dissertation, 1st and 2nd year projects, 1 year as associate instructor, qualifying exam, student teaching. *Entrance requirements:* For doctorate, GRE. Additional exam requirements/recommendations for international students: Required—TOEFL (minimum score 550 paper-based; 213 computer-based). *Application deadline:* For fall admission, 12/15 for domestic students, 12/1 for international students. Application fee: $55 ($65 for international students). Electronic applications accepted. *Financial support:* In 2010–11, 32 fellowships with full tuition reimbursements (averaging $23,580 per year), 7 research assistantships with full tuition reimbursements (averaging $17,850 per year), 7 teaching assistantships with full tuition reimbursements (averaging $17,850 per year) were awarded; scholarships/grants, health care benefits, and unspecified assistantships also available. *Unit head:* Dr. Linda B. Smith, Chair, 812-855-3991, Fax: 812-855-4691, E-mail: smith4@indiana.edu. *Application contact:* Patricia G. Crouch, Academic Services Coordinator, 812-855-4528, Fax: 812-855-4691, E-mail: pcrouch@indiana.edu.

Indiana Wesleyan University, Graduate School, College of Arts and Sciences, Marion, IN 46953. Offers addictions counseling (MS); clinical mental health counseling (MS); community counseling (MS); marriage and family therapy (MS); school counseling (MS); student development counseling and administration (MS). *Accreditation:* ACA. Part-time programs available. *Degree requirements:* For master's, thesis or alternative. *Entrance requirements:* For master's, GRE General Test. Additional exam requirements/recommendations for international students: Required—TOEFL. Electronic applications accepted. *Expenses:* Contact institution. *Faculty research:* Community counseling, multicultural counseling, addictions.

Iowa State University of Science and Technology, Graduate College, College of Liberal Arts and Sciences, Department of Psychology, Ames, IA 50011. Offers cognitive psychology (PhD); counseling psychology (PhD); social psychology (PhD). *Accreditation:* APA. *Faculty:* 34 full-time (14 women), 1 part-time/adjunct (0 women). *Students:* 73 full-time (42 women), 27 part-time (18 women); includes 8 Black or African American, non-Hispanic/Latino; 4 Asian, non-Hispanic/Latino; 4 Hispanic/Latino, 17 international. 88 applicants, 13% accepted, 9 enrolled. In 2010, 4 doctorates awarded. *Degree requirements:* For doctorate, comprehensive exam, thesis/dissertation. *Entrance requirements:* For doctorate, GRE General Test, GRE Subject Test (psychology), 3 letters of recommendation. Additional exam requirements/recommendations for international students: Required—TOEFL (minimum score 560 paper-based; 79 iBT), IELTS (minimum score 6.5). *Application deadline:* For fall admission, 1/2 priority date for domestic and international students. Application fee: $30 ($70 for international students). Electronic applications accepted. *Financial support:* In 2010–11, fellowships with full tuition reimbursements (averaging $14,055 per year), 7 research assistantships with full tuition reimbursements (averaging $13,169 per year), 57 teaching assistantships with full tuition reimbursements (averaging $9,432 per year) were awarded; scholarships/grants, health care benefits, and unspecified assistantships also available. *Faculty research:* Counseling psychology, cognitive psychology, social psychology, health psychology, psychology and public policy. *Unit head:* Carolyn Cutrona, Chair, 515-294-0283, Fax: 515-294-6424, E-mail: ccutrona@iastate.edu. *Application contact:* Ann Schmidt, Graduate Admissions Secretary, 515-294-1743, Fax: 515-294-6424, E-mail: psychadm@iastate.edu.

Lamar University, College of Graduate Studies, College of Arts and Sciences, Department of Psychology, Beaumont, TX 77710. Offers community/clinical psychology (MS); industrial/organizational psychology (MS). Part-time programs available. *Faculty:* 7 full-time (4 women). *Students:* 17 full-time (12 women), 10 part-time (4 women); includes 2 Black or African American, non-Hispanic/Latino; 2 Hispanic/Latino, 1 international. Average age 29. 25 applicants, 60% accepted, 9 enrolled. In 2010, 26 master's awarded. *Degree requirements:* For master's, thesis, practicum. *Entrance requirements:* For master's, GRE General Test, minimum GPA of 2.75 in last 60 hours of undergraduate course work. Additional exam requirements/recommendations for international students: Required—TOEFL. *Application deadline:* For fall admission, 8/1 for domestic students; for spring admission, 12/1 for domestic students. Application fee: $25 ($50 for international students). *Expenses:* Tuition, state resident: full-time $4160; part-time $208 per credit hour. Tuition, nonresident: full-time $10,360; part-time $518 per credit hour. *Financial support:* In 2010–11, 12 students received support, including 3 teaching assistantships (averaging $4,500 per year); fellowships, research assistantships, career-related internships or fieldwork, Federal Work-Study, scholarships/grants, and tuition waivers (partial) also available. Support available to part-time students. Financial award application deadline: 4/1. *Faculty research:* Groupthink, health psychology, school psychology, behavioral neuroscience. *Application contact:* Assistant Dean, 409-880-7978, E-mail: westgate@hal.lamar.edu.

Lenoir-Rhyne University, Graduate Programs, School of Counseling and Human Services, Programs in Counseling, Hickory, NC 28601. Offers agency counseling (MA); community counseling (MA). Part-time and evening/weekend programs available. *Degree requirements:* For master's, comprehensive exam, thesis optional. *Entrance requirements:* For master's, GRE General Test, writing sample, minimum undergraduate GPA of 2.7, minimum graduate GPA of 3.0. Additional exam requirements/recommendations for international students: Required—TOEFL (minimum score 600 paper-based). Electronic applications accepted.

Lesley University, Graduate School of Arts and Social Sciences, Cambridge, MA 02138-2790. Offers clinical mental health counseling (MA), including expressive therapies counseling, holistic counseling, school and community counseling; counseling psychology (MA, CAGS), including professional counseling (MA), school counseling (MA); creative arts in learning (CAGS); creative writing (MFA); ecological teaching and learning (MS); environmental education (MS); expressive therapies (MA, PhD, CAGS), including art (MA), dance (MA), expressive therapies, music (MA); independent studies (CAGS); independent study (MA); intercultural relations (MA, CAGS); interdisciplinary studies (MA), including individualized studies, integrative holistic health, women's studies; urban environmental leadership (MA); visual arts (MFA). Part-time and evening/weekend programs available. Postbaccalaureate distance learning degree programs offered (minimal on-campus study). *Degree requirements:* For master's, internship, practicum, thesis (expressive therapies); for doctorate, thesis/dissertation, arts apprenticeship, field placement; for CAGS, thesis, internship (counseling psychology, expressive therapies). *Entrance requirements:* For master's, MAT (counseling psychology), interview, writing samples, art portfolio; for doctorate, GRE or MAT; for CAGS, interview, master's degree. Additional exam requirements/recommendations for international students: Required—TOEFL (minimum score 550 paper-based; 213 computer-based; 80 iBT). Electronic applications accepted. *Faculty research:* Psychotherapy and culture; psychotherapy and psychological trauma; women's issues in art, teaching and psychotherapy; community based art, psycho-spiritual inquiry.

Lewis & Clark College, Graduate School of Education and Counseling, Department of Counseling Psychology, Program in Community Counseling, Portland, OR 97219-7899. Offers MA, MS. Part-time and evening/weekend programs available. *Faculty:* 5 full-time (4 women), 13 part-time/adjunct (9 women). *Students:* 88 full-time (69 women), 22 part-time (15 women); includes 4 Asian, non-Hispanic/Latino; 5 Hispanic/Latino; 6 Two or more races, non-Hispanic/Latino, 2 international. Average age 32. 104 applicants, 56% accepted, 28 enrolled. In 2010, 39 master's awarded. *Degree requirements:* For master's, thesis (MS). *Entrance requirements:* For master's, GRE General Test, minimum undergraduate GPA of 2.75. Additional exam requirements/recommendations for international students: Required—TOEFL (minimum score 575 paper-based; 233 computer-based). *Application deadline:* For fall admission, 2/1 priority date for domestic and international students; for spring admission, 10/1 priority date for domestic and international students. Application fee: $50. Electronic applications accepted. *Expenses:* Tuition: Part-time $713 per semester hour. Tuition and fees vary according to course level and campus/location. *Financial support:* In 2010–11, 10 students received support. Career-related internships or fieldwork, Federal Work-Study, institutionally sponsored loans, scholarships/grants, and health care benefits available. Support available to part-time students. Financial award application deadline: 3/1; financial award applicants required to submit FAFSA. *Unit head:* Dr. Amy Rees-Turyn, Program Coordinator, 503-768-6060, Fax: 503-768-6065, E-mail: cpsy@lclark.edu. *Application contact:* Becky Haas, Director of Admissions, 503-768-6200, Fax: 503-768-6205, E-mail: gseadmit@lclark.edu.

Loyola University Chicago, Graduate School, Department of Psychology, Program in Applied Social Psychology, Chicago, IL 60660. Offers MA, PhD. *Faculty:* 7 full-time (3 women), 2 part-time/adjunct (1 woman). *Students:* 36 full-time (28 women), 2 part-time (both women); includes 8 minority (2 Black or African American, non-Hispanic/Latino; 1 Asian, non-Hispanic/Latino; 3 Hispanic/Latino; 2 Two or more races, non-Hispanic/Latino), 3 international. Average age 30. 70 applicants, 19% accepted, 6 enrolled. In 2010, 8 master's, 5 doctorates awarded. Terminal master's awarded for partial completion of doctoral program. *Degree requirements:* For master's, thesis; for doctorate, comprehensive exam, thesis/dissertation, internship. *Entrance requirements:* For master's and doctorate, GRE General Test, GRE Subject Test, sample of written work. *Application deadline:* For fall admission, 1/15 for domestic and international students. Applications are processed on a rolling basis. Application fee: $50. *Expenses:* Tuition: Full-time $14,940; part-time $830 per credit hour. Required fees: $87 per semester. Part-time tuition and fees vary according to course load and program. *Financial support:* In 2010–11, 1 fellowship with tuition reimbursement (averaging $14,000 per year), 5 research assistantships with tuition reimbursements (averaging $14,000 per year), 1 teaching assistantship (averaging $14,000 per year) were awarded; career-related internships or fieldwork, Federal Work-Study, and scholarships/grants also available. Financial award application deadline: 1/15; financial award applicants required to submit FAFSA. *Faculty research:* Program evaluation, attitudes and prejudice, psychological well-being, mass media, groups and organizations and communities. Total annual research expenditures: $200,000. *Unit head:* Dr. Scott Tindale, 773-508-3014. *Application contact:* Dr. Scott Tindale, 773-508-3014.

Loyola University Chicago, School of Education, Program in Community Counseling, Chicago, IL 60660. Offers M Ed, MA. MA offered through the Graduate School. Part-time programs available. *Faculty:* 5 full-time (4 women), 4 part-time/adjunct (2 women). *Students:* 36. Average age 25. 70 applicants, 80% accepted, 20 enrolled. In 2010, 15 master's awarded. *Degree requirements:* For master's, comprehensive exam. *Entrance requirements:* For master's, GRE General Test, minimum GPA of 3.0, letters of recommendation, resume. Additional exam requirements/recommendations for international students: Required—TOEFL (minimum score 550 paper-based; 213 computer-based; 80 iBT). *Application deadline:* For fall admission, 1/1 for domestic and international students. Application fee: $50. Electronic applications accepted. *Expenses:* Tuition: Full-time $14,940; part-time $830 per credit hour. Required fees: $87 per semester. Part-time tuition and fees vary according to course load and program. *Financial support:* Fellowships with full tuition reimbursements, research assistantships with full tuition reimbursements, teaching assistantships with full tuition reimbursements, career-related internships or fieldwork and Federal Work-Study available. Financial award application deadline: 2/1; financial award applicants required to submit FAFSA. *Faculty research:* Career development, prevention, group counseling, family therapy, multicultural counseling. *Unit head:* Dr. Anita Thomas, Director, 312-915-7403, E-mail: athoma9@luc.edu. *Application contact:* Marie Rosin-Dittmar, Information Contact, 312-915-6800, E-mail: schleduc@luc.edu.

Lynchburg College, Graduate Studies, School of Education and Human Development, Lynchburg, VA 24501-3199. Offers clinical mental health counseling (M Ed); community counseling (M Ed); counselor education (M Ed), including community counseling; curriculum and instruction (M Ed); educational leadership (M Ed); reading (M Ed); school counseling (M Ed); science education (M Ed); special education (M Ed), including autism spectrum disorder, early childhood special education, mental retardation, teaching children with learning disabilities, teaching the emotionally disturbed. Part-time and evening/weekend programs available. *Degree requirements:* For master's, comprehensive exam. *Entrance requirements:* For master's, GRE, minimum undergraduate GPA of 3.0. Additional exam requirements/recommendations for international students: Required—TOEFL. *Expenses:* Tuition: Full-time $7200; part-time $400 per credit hour. Required fees: $20; $5.10 per credit hour. $15 per term. Tuition and fees vary according to degree level and program.

Martin University, Division of Psychology, Indianapolis, IN 46218-3867. Offers community psychology (MS). Part-time and evening/weekend programs available. *Degree requirements:* For master's, thesis. *Entrance requirements:* For master's, GRE General Test, GRE Subject Test.

Memorial University of Newfoundland, School of Graduate Studies, Department of Psychology, St. John's, NL A1C 5S7, Canada. Offers applied social psychology (MASP); experimental psychology (M Sc, PhD). Part-time programs available. *Degree requirements:* For master's, workterms (MASP), thesis (M Sc); for doctorate, comprehensive exam, thesis/dissertation, oral thesis defense. *Entrance requirements:* For master's, GRE, honors bachelor's degree of high second class standing or equivalent; for doctorate, GRE, master's or honors degree. Electronic applications accepted. *Faculty research:* Behavioral neuroscience, cognition, theory and research on abnormal behavior.

Missouri State University, Graduate College, College of Education, Department of Counseling, Leadership, and Special Education, Program in Counseling, Springfield, MO 65897. Offers counseling (MS), including community agency counseling, elementary school counseling, secondary school counseling. Part-time and evening/weekend programs available. *Degree requirements:* For master's, comprehensive exam, thesis or alternative. *Entrance requirements:* For master's, GRE or MAT, minimum GPA of 2.75. Additional exam requirements/recommendations for international students: Required—TOEFL (minimum score 550 paper-based; 213 computer-based; 79 iBT). Electronic applications accepted. *Expenses:* Tuition: state resident: full-time $3348; part-time $186 per credit hour. Tuition, nonresident: full-time $6696; part-time $372 per credit hour. Required fees: $238 per semester. Tuition and fees vary according to course level, course load and program.

Montclair State University, The Graduate School, College of Education and Human Services, Department of Counseling, Human Development, and Educational Leadership, Montclair, NJ 07043-1624. Offers advanced counseling (Certificate); certified alcohol and drug counselor (Certificate); counseling (MA), including addictions counseling, community counseling, school counseling, student affairs; counselor education (PhD); director of school counseling services (Certificate); educational leadership (MA), including adult and organizational learning, educational leadership; principal (Certificate); school business administrator (Certificate); school counselor (Certificate); substance awareness coordinator (Certificate); supervisor (Certificate). *Accreditation:* NCATE. Part-time and evening/weekend programs available. *Faculty:* 18 full-time (12 women), 37 part-time/adjunct (26 women). *Students:* 169 full-time (125 women), 385 part-time (281 women); includes 51 Black or African American, non-Hispanic/Latino; 13 Asian, non-Hispanic/Latino; 49 Hispanic/Latino; 1 Native Hawaiian or other Pacific Islander, non-Hispanic/Latino; 1 Two or more races, non-Hispanic/Latino, 4 international. Average age 31. 270 applicants, 57% accepted, 124 enrolled. In 2010, 172 master's, 13 other advanced degrees awarded. *Degree requirements:* For master's, comprehensive exam, thesis or alternative; for doctorate, comprehensive exam, thesis/dissertation. *Entrance requirements:* For master's, GRE General Test, interview, 2 letters of recommendation; for doctorate, GRE General Test, interview, 3 letters of recommendation. Additional exam requirements/recommendations for international students: Required—TOEFL (minimum iBT score of 83) or IELTS. *Application deadline:* For fall admission, 6/1 for international students; for spring admission, 10/1 for international students. Applications are processed on a rolling basis. Application fee: $60. Electronic applications accepted. *Expenses:* Tuition, state resident: part-time $501.34 per credit. Tuition, nonresident: part-time $773.88 per credit. Required fees: $71.15 per credit. *Financial support:* In 2010–11, 10 research assistantships with full tuition reimbursements (averaging $7,000 per year), 4 teaching assistantships (averaging $15,000 per year) were awarded; Federal Work-Study, scholarships/grants, and unspecified assistantships also available. Support available to part-time students. Financial award application deadline: 3/1; financial award applicants required to submit FAFSA. *Faculty research:* Multicultural counseling competence and training; adoption triad adjustment, issues and counseling; substance abuse treatment with underserved populations; role of data in school change; adult development: pedagogical issues for adult students and special populations. *Unit head:* Dr. Larry Burlew, Chairperson, 973-655-7611. *Application contact:* Amy Aiello, Director of Graduate Admissions and Operations, 973-655-5147, Fax: 973-655-7869, E-mail: graduate.school@montclair.edu.

Montclair State University, The Graduate School, College of Humanities and Social Sciences, Department of Psychology, Montclair, NJ 07043-1624. Offers educational psychology (MA), including child/adolescent clinical psychology, clinical psychology for Spanish/English bilinguals, educational psychology; psychology (MA), including industrial and organizational psychology; school psychology (Certificate). Part-time and evening/weekend programs available. *Faculty:* 25 full-time (11 women), 37 part-time/adjunct (21 women). *Students:* 43 full-time (31 women), 33 part-time (22 women); includes 8 Black or African American, non-Hispanic/Latino; 3 Asian, non-Hispanic/Latino; 10 Hispanic/Latino, 2 international. Average age 26. 117 applicants, 33% accepted, 24 enrolled. In 2010, 23 master's, 1 other advanced degree awarded. *Degree requirements:* For master's, comprehensive exam, thesis or alternative. *Entrance requirements:* For master's, GRE General Test, 2 letters of recommendation. Additional exam requirements/recommendations for international students: Required—TOEFL (minimum iBT score of 83) or IELTS. *Application deadline:* For fall admission, 6/1 for international students; for spring admission, 11/1 for international students. Applications are processed on a rolling basis. Application fee: $60. Electronic applications accepted. *Expenses:* Tuition, state resident: part-time $501.34 per credit. Tuition, nonresident: part-time $773.88 per credit. Required fees: $71.15 per credit. *Financial support:* In 2010–11, 13 research assistantships with full tuition reimbursements (averaging $7,000 per year) were awarded; Federal Work-Study, scholarships/grants, and unspecified assistantships also available. Support available to part-time students. Financial award application deadline: 3/1; financial award applicants required to submit FAFSA. *Faculty research:* Legal decision-making, leadership development, bias and stereotype threat in the selection process, nature of pre-linguistic thought in infants, lateralized cortical contributions to memory, pediatric neuro-imaging, the production and perception of speech, school-based assessment and intervention for bullying, cognitive processes in reading, identification of autism in toddlers. Total annual research expenditures: $300,000. *Unit head:* Dr. Peter Vietze, Chairperson, 973-655-5201. *Application contact:* Amy Aiello, Director of Admissions and Operations, 973-655-5147, Fax: 973-655-7869, E-mail: graduate.school@montclair.edu.

Mount Aloysius College, Program in Community Counseling, Cresson, PA 16630-1999. Offers MS. Part-time programs available.

Mount Mary College, Graduate Programs, Program in Community Counseling, Milwaukee, WI 53222-4597. Offers community counseling (MS); pastoral counseling (MS); school counseling (MS). Part-time and evening/weekend programs available. *Degree requirements:* For master's, comprehensive exam, thesis or alternative. *Entrance requirements:* For master's, minimum GPA of 3.0. Additional exam requirements/recommendations for international students: Required—TOEFL (minimum score 500 paper-based; 173 computer-based). *Faculty research:* Cognitive behavioral interventions for depression, eating disorders and compliance.

Naropa University, Graduate Programs, Program in Transpersonal Psychology, Ecopsychology Concentration, Boulder, CO 80302-6697. Offers MA. Part-time and evening/weekend programs available. Postbaccalaureate distance learning degree programs offered (minimal on-campus study). *Faculty:* 1 full-time (0 women), 13 part-time/adjunct (7 women). *Students:* 23 part-time (17 women); includes 3 minority (1 Black or African American, non-Hispanic/Latino; 2 Two or more races, non-Hispanic/Latino), 1 international. Average age 38. 26 applicants, 77% accepted, 14 enrolled. In 2010, 10 master's awarded. *Degree requirements:* For master's, thesis, service learning. *Entrance requirements:* For master's, interview (by phone or in-person), technology form, resume, 3 letters of recommendation, letter of interest. Additional exam requirements/recommendations for international students: Required—TOEFL (minimum score 600 paper-based; 250 computer-based). *Application deadline:* For fall admission, 1/15 priority date for domestic and international students. Applications are processed on a rolling basis. Application fee: $60. Electronic applications accepted. *Expenses:* Tuition: Full-time $17,820; part-time $810 per credit. Required fees: $305 per semester. Tuition and fees vary according to course load, program and reciprocity agreements. *Financial support:* In 2010–11, 2 students received support. Career-related internships or fieldwork, Federal Work-Study, scholarships/grants, health care benefits, and tuition waivers (partial) available. Support available to part-time students. Financial award application deadline: 3/1; financial award applicants required to submit FAFSA. *Unit head:* Dr. MacAndrew Jack, Director, Graduate School of Psychology, 303-245-4752, E-mail: mjack@naropa.edu. *Application contact:* Krista Stuchlik, Senior Graduate Admissions Counselor, 303-546-3528, Fax: 303-546-3583, E-mail: kstuchlik@naropa.edu.

New York University, Graduate School of Arts and Science, Department of Psychology, New York, NY 10012-1019. Offers cognition and perception (PhD); community psychology (PhD); general psychology (MA); industrial/organizational psychology (MA); psychotherapy and psychoanalysis (Advanced Certificate); social/personality psychology (PhD). Part-time programs available. *Students:* 157 full-time (113 women), 257 part-time (175 women); includes 18 Black or African American, non-Hispanic/Latino; 1 American Indian or Alaska Native, non-Hispanic/Latino; 29 Asian, non-Hispanic/Latino; 24 Hispanic/Latino, 64 international. Average age 32. 834 applicants, 39% accepted, 82 enrolled. In 2010, 73 master's, 14 doctorates, 13 other advanced degrees awarded. Terminal master's awarded for partial completion of doctoral program. *Degree requirements:* For master's, comprehensive exam, thesis or alternative; for doctorate, thesis/dissertation. *Entrance requirements:* For master's, GRE General Test, minimum GPA of 3.0; for doctorate, GRE General Test, GRE Subject Test; for Advanced Certificate, doctoral degree, minimum GPA of 3.0. Additional exam requirements/recommendations for international students: Required—TOEFL. *Application deadline:* For fall admission, 12/15 for domestic students. Application fee: $90. *Financial support:* Fellowships with tuition reimbursements, research assistantships with tuition reimbursements, teaching assistantships with tuition reimbursements, career-related internships or fieldwork, Federal Work-Study, institutionally sponsored loans, scholarships/grants, traineeships, health care benefits, and unspecified assistantships available. Financial award application deadline: 12/15; financial award applicants required to submit FAFSA. *Faculty research:* Vision, memory, social cognition, social and cognitive development, relationships. *Unit head:* Madeline Heilman, Director of PhD Program, 212-998-7900, Fax: 212-995-4018, E-mail: psychq@psych.nyu.edu. *Application contact:* Barry Cohen, Director of MA Program, 212-998-7900, Fax: 212-995-4018, E-mail: psychq@psych.nyu.edu.

Norfolk State University, School of Graduate Studies, School of Liberal Arts, Department of Psychology, Program in Community/Clinical Psychology, Norfolk, VA 23504. Offers MA. *Degree requirements:* For master's, comprehensive exam, thesis or alternative. *Entrance requirements:* For master's, minimum GPA of 2.7.

North Carolina Central University, Division of Academic Affairs, School of Education, Department of Counselor Education, Durham, NC 27707-3129. Offers career counseling (MA); community agency counseling (MA); school counseling (MA). *Accreditation:* ACA; NCATE. Part-time and evening/weekend programs available. *Degree requirements:* For master's, comprehensive exam, thesis or alternative. *Entrance requirements:* For master's, GRE, minimum GPA of 3.0 in major, 2.5 overall. Additional exam requirements/recommendations for international students: Required—TOEFL. *Faculty research:* Becoming a leader, skill building in academia.

North Carolina State University, Graduate School, College of Education, Department of Curriculum and Instruction, Program in Agency Counseling, Raleigh, NC 27695. Offers M Ed, MS. *Degree requirements:* For master's, thesis optional. *Entrance requirements:* For master's, GRE General Test or MAT, minimum GPA of 3.0 in major. Electronic applications accepted. *Faculty research:* Cross-cultural issues, non-cognitive variables, achievement gaps, identity development, counseling supervision.

North Dakota State University, College of Graduate and Interdisciplinary Studies, College of Science and Mathematics, Department of Psychology, Fargo, ND 58108. Offers clinical psychology (MS); cognitive and visual neuroscience (PhD); health and social psychology (PhD); psychology (MS). *Faculty:* 18 full-time (4 women), 2 part-time/adjunct (1 woman). *Students:* 20 full-time (11 women), 3 part-time (0 women); includes 1 Two or more races, non-Hispanic/Latino, 2 international. Average age 24. 41 applicants, 27% accepted, 6 enrolled. In 2010, 7 master's, 2 doctorates awarded. *Degree requirements:* For master's, thesis; for

Social Psychology

North Dakota State University (continued)
doctorate, thesis/dissertation. *Entrance requirements:* For master's and doctorate, GRE General Test, GRE Subject Test. Additional exam requirements/recommendations for international students: Required—TOEFL (minimum score 525 paper-based; 197 computer-based; 71 iBT). *Application deadline:* For fall admission, 3/1 for domestic and international students. Application fee: $45 ($60 for international students). Electronic applications accepted. *Financial support:* In 2010–11, 2 fellowships with full tuition reimbursements (averaging $16,000 per year), 23 research assistantships with full tuition reimbursements (averaging $16,000 per year), 11 teaching assistantships with full tuition reimbursements (averaging $6,000 per year) were awarded; career-related internships or fieldwork, Federal Work-Study, institutionally sponsored loans, tuition waivers (full and partial), and unspecified assistantships also available. Support available to part-time students. Financial award application deadline: 3/1. *Faculty research:* Cognition science, neuropsychology, group behavior, applied behavior analysis, behavior therapy. Total annual research expenditures: $2 million. *Unit head:* Dr. Paul D. Rokke, Chair, 701-231-8622, Fax: 701-231-8426, E-mail: paul.rokke@ndsu.edu. *Application contact:* Dr. Paul D. Rokke, Chair, 701-231-8622, Fax: 701-231-8426, E-mail: paul.rokke@ndsu.edu.

Northern Kentucky University, Office of Graduate Programs, College of Education and Human Services, Program in Community Counseling, Highland Heights, KY 41099. Offers clinical mental health counseling (MA); college student development administration (Certificate); community counseling (Certificate). Part-time and evening/weekend programs available. *Faculty:* 12 full-time (7 women), 1 part-time/adjunct (0 women). *Students:* 17 full-time (16 women), 24 part-time (19 women). Average age 32. 36 applicants, 61% accepted, 19 enrolled. In 2010, 12 master's, 6 other advanced degrees awarded. *Degree requirements:* For master's, comprehensive exam, internship. *Entrance requirements:* For master's, GRE, minimum GPA of 2.75, 3 letters of reference, criminal background check (state and federal), resume. Additional exam requirements/recommendations for international students: Required—TOEFL (minimum score 550 paper-based; 213 computer-based; 79 iBT); Recommended—IELTS (minimum score 6.5). *Application deadline:* For fall admission, 7/1 for domestic students, 6/1 priority date for international students; for spring admission, 11/1 for domestic students, 10/1 priority date for international students. Applications are processed on a rolling basis. Application fee: $40. Electronic applications accepted. *Expenses:* Tuition, state resident: full-time $7254; part-time $403 per credit hour. Tuition, nonresident: full-time $12,492; part-time $694 per credit hour. Tuition and fees vary according to degree level and program. *Financial support:* Applicants required to submit FAFSA. *Faculty research:* Ethical decision-making in counseling, clinical supervision in counseling, expectations about counseling inventory development. *Unit head:* Dr. Jacqueline Smith, Director, 859-572-6149, E-mail: smithjac@nku.edu. *Application contact:* Dr. Peg Griffin, Director, Graduate Programs, 859-572-6934, Fax: 859-572-6670, E-mail: griffinp@nku.edu.

North Georgia College & State University, Graduate Studies, Program in Community Counseling, Dahlonega, GA 30597. Offers MS. Part-time and evening/weekend programs available. *Degree requirements:* For master's, one foreign language, thesis optional. *Entrance requirements:* For master's, GRE General Test, minimum GPA of 3.0, 3 letters of recommendation, interview. Electronic applications accepted. *Expenses:* Tuition, state resident: full-time $4704; part-time $196 per credit hour. Tuition, nonresident: full-time $18,770; part-time $783 per credit hour. Required fees: $1718; $671 per semester. Tuition and fees vary according to course load, degree level and program.

Northwestern University, The Graduate School, Judd A. and Marjorie Weinberg College of Arts and Sciences, Department of Psychology, Evanston, IL 60208. Offers brain, behavior and cognition (PhD); clinical psychology (PhD); cognitive psychology (PhD); personality (PhD); social psychology (PhD); JD/PhD. Admissions and degrees offered through The Graduate School. *Accreditation:* APA (one or more programs are accredited). Part-time programs available. *Degree requirements:* For doctorate, thesis/dissertation. *Entrance requirements:* For doctorate, GRE General Test, GRE Subject Test. Additional exam requirements/recommendations for international students: Required—TOEFL. Electronic applications accepted. *Faculty research:* Memory and higher order cognition, anxiety and depression, effectiveness of psychotherapy, social cognition, molecular basis of memory.

Northwest Nazarene University, Graduate Studies, Program in Counselor Education, Nampa, ID 83686-5897. Offers community counseling (MS); marriage and family counseling (MS); school counseling (MS). *Faculty:* 5 full-time (3 women), 4 part-time/adjunct (2 women). *Students:* 83 full-time (64 women), 16 part-time (10 women); includes 7 minority (1 Black or African American, non-Hispanic/Latino; 4 Asian, non-Hispanic/Latino; 2 Hispanic/Latino), 1 international. In 2010, 33 master's awarded. Application fee: $25. *Unit head:* Dr. Brenda Freeman, Chair, 208-467-8428, Fax: 208-467-8339. *Application contact:* Judy Bassett, Program Assistant, 208-467-8345, Fax: 208-467-8339, E-mail: jbassett@nnu.edu.

The Ohio State University, Graduate School, College of Arts and Sciences, Division of Social and Behavioral Sciences, Department of Psychology, Columbus, OH 43210. Offers behavioral neuroscience (PhD); clinical psychology (PhD); cognitive psychology (PhD); developmental psychology (PhD); mental retardation and developmental disabilities (PhD); psychology (MA); quantitative psychology (PhD); social psychology (PhD). *Accreditation:* APA (one or more programs are accredited). *Faculty:* 60. *Students:* 106 full-time (65 women), 42 part-time (31 women); includes 5 Black or African American, non-Hispanic/Latino; 1 American Indian or Alaska Native, non-Hispanic/Latino; 5 Asian, non-Hispanic/Latino; 10 Hispanic/Latino; 3 Two or more races, non-Hispanic/Latino, 23 international. Average age 27. In 2010, 21 master's, 22 doctorates awarded. *Degree requirements:* For doctorate, thesis/dissertation. *Entrance requirements:* For master's and doctorate, GRE General Test. Additional exam requirements/recommendations for international students: Required—TOEFL (minimum score 600 paper-based; 250 computer-based). *Application deadline:* For fall admission, 12/31 for domestic students, 11/30 for international students. Applications are processed on a rolling basis. Application fee: $40 ($50 for international students). Electronic applications accepted. *Expenses:* Tuition, state resident: full-time $10,605. Tuition, nonresident: full-time $26,535. Tuition and fees vary according to course load and program. *Financial support:* Fellowships, research assistantships, teaching assistantships available. *Unit head:* Dr. Richard Petty, Chair, 614-292-1640, E-mail: petty.1@osu.edu. *Application contact:* 614-292-9444, Fax: 614-292-3895, E-mail: domestic.grad@osu.edu.

Oregon State University–Cascades, Program in Counseling, Bend, OR 97701. Offers community counseling (MS); school counseling (MS).

Pittsburg State University, Graduate School, College of Education, Department of Psychology and Counseling, Program in Counselor Education, Pittsburg, KS 66762. Offers community counseling (MS); school counseling (MS). *Accreditation:* ACA; NCATE. *Degree requirements:* For master's, thesis or alternative. *Entrance requirements:* For master's, GRE General Test, minimum GPA of 2.8.

Queen's University at Kingston, School of Graduate Studies and Research, Faculty of Arts and Sciences, Department of Psychology, Kingston, ON K7L 3N6, Canada. Offers brain behavior and cognitive science (MA, PhD); clinical psychology (MA, PhD); developmental psychology (MA, PhD); social personality psychology (MA, PhD). *Accreditation:* APA (one or more programs are accredited). *Degree requirements:* For master's, thesis; for doctorate, comprehensive exam, thesis/dissertation. *Entrance requirements:* For master's and doctorate, GRE General Test. Additional exam requirements/recommendations for international students: Required—TOEFL. *Faculty research:* Human development, social, personality, behavioral neuroscience, forensic.

Regent University, Graduate School, School of Psychology and Counseling, Virginia Beach, VA 23464-9800. Offers clinical psychology (MA, Psy D); counseling studies (CAGS); counselor education and supervision (PhD); human services counseling (MA), including community counseling, school counseling; M Div/MA; M Ed/MA; MBA/MA. PhD program offered online only. *Accreditation:* ACA; APA (one or more programs are accredited). Part-time and evening/weekend programs available. Postbaccalaureate distance learning degree programs offered (minimal on-campus study). *Faculty:* 31 full-time (16 women), 23 part-time/adjunct (14 women). *Students:* 235 full-time (190 women), 203 part-time (158 women); includes 104 Black or African American, non-Hispanic/Latino; 7 Asian, non-Hispanic/Latino; 11 Hispanic/Latino, 13 international. Average age 35. 436 applicants, 49% accepted, 111 enrolled. In 2010, 82 master's, 57 doctorates awarded. *Degree requirements:* For master's, thesis or alternative, internship, practicum, written competency exam; for doctorate, thesis/dissertation or alternative. *Entrance requirements:* For master's, GRE General Test including writing exam, minimum undergraduate GPA of 2.75, 3 recommendations, resume, transcripts, writing sample; for doctorate, GRE General Test including writing exam, GRE Subject Test, minimum undergraduate GPA of 3.0, 3.5 (PhD), 10-15 minute VHS tape demonstrating counseling skills, writing sample, 3 recommendations, resume. Additional exam requirements/recommendations for international students: Required—TOEFL (minimum score 577 paper-based; 233 computer-based). *Application deadline:* For fall admission, 4/1 priority date for domestic students; for spring admission, 11/1 priority date for domestic students. Applications are processed on a rolling basis. Application fee: $50. Electronic applications accepted. *Expenses:* Contact institution. *Financial support:* Research assistantships with full and partial tuition reimbursements, teaching assistantships with full and partial tuition reimbursements, career-related internships or fieldwork, scholarships/grants, and tuition waivers (full and partial) available. Support available to part-time students. Financial award application deadline: 9/1; financial award applicants required to submit FAFSA. *Faculty research:* Marriage enrichment, AIDS counseling, troubled youth, faith and learning, trauma. *Unit head:* Dr. William Hathaway, Acting Dean, 757-352-4294, Fax: 757-352-4282, E-mail: willhat@regent.edu. *Application contact:* Matthew Chadwick, Director of Enrollment Support Services, 800-373-5504, Fax: 757-352-4381, E-mail: admissions@regent.edu.

Regis University, College for Professional Studies, School of Education and Counseling, Department of Counseling, Denver, CO 80221-1099. Offers community counseling (MAC); counseling children and adolescents (Post-Graduate Certificate); marriage and family therapy (MA, Post-Graduate Certificate); transformative counseling (Post-Graduate Certificate). Program offered in Henderson and Las Vegas (Summerlin), NV. *Accreditation:* ACA. Part-time and evening/weekend programs available. *Degree requirements:* For master's, internships, practicum. *Entrance requirements:* For master's, interview, 2 recommendations, resume, criminal background check. Additional exam requirements/recommendations for international students: Required—TOEFL (minimum score 213 computer-based), TWE (minimum score 5). *Expenses:* Contact institution. *Faculty research:* Group development, counselor education, counsel and therapy, influence of technology on psychology, dream finding groups, adult development, depression.

Rutgers, The State University of New Jersey, Newark, Graduate School, Program in Psychology, Newark, NJ 07102. Offers cognitive neuroscience (PhD); cognitive science (PhD); perception (PhD); psychobiology (PhD); social cognition (PhD). *Faculty:* 15 full-time (5 women), 6 part-time/adjunct (all women). *Students:* 23 full-time (19 women), 2 part-time (1 woman); includes 3 Black or African American, non-Hispanic/Latino; 1 Asian, non-Hispanic/Latino; 2 Hispanic/Latino. 48 applicants, 17% accepted, 6 enrolled. In 2010, 4 doctorates awarded. *Degree requirements:* For doctorate, comprehensive exam, thesis/dissertation. *Entrance requirements:* For doctorate, GRE General Test, GRE Subject Test, minimum undergraduate B average. *Application deadline:* For fall admission, 2/1 for domestic students; for spring admission, 11/1 for domestic students. Application fee: $60. Electronic applications accepted. *Expenses:* Tuition, state resident: part-time $600 per credit. Tuition, nonresident: full-time $10,694. *Financial support:* In 2010–11, 16 students received support, including 9 fellowships with full and partial tuition reimbursements available (averaging $18,000 per year), 8 teaching assistantships with full and partial tuition reimbursements available (averaging $23,112 per year); career-related internships or fieldwork, health care benefits, and minority scholarships also available. Financial award application deadline: 2/1. *Faculty research:* Visual perception (luminance, motion), neuroendocrine mechanisms in behavior (reproduction, pain), attachment theory, connectionist modeling of cognition. *Unit head:* Dr. Kenneth Kressel, Director, 973-353-5440 Ext. 232, Fax: 973-353-1171, E-mail: kkressel@andromeda.rutgers.edu. *Application contact:* Jason Hand, Director of Admissions, 973-353-5205, Fax: 973-353-1440.

See Display on page 991 and Close-Up on page 1169.

Rutgers, The State University of New Jersey, New Brunswick, Graduate School-New Brunswick, Program in Psychology, Piscataway, NJ 08854-8097. Offers behavioral neuroscience (PhD); clinical psychology (PhD); cognitive psychology (PhD); interdisciplinary health psychology (PhD); social psychology (PhD). *Accreditation:* APA. *Degree requirements:* For doctorate, comprehensive exam, thesis/dissertation. *Entrance requirements:* For doctorate, GRE General Test, 3 letters of recommendation. Additional exam requirements/recommendations for international students: Required—TOEFL (minimum score 577 paper-based; 233 computer-based). Electronic applications accepted. *Expenses:* Tuition, state resident: full-time $7200; part-time $600 per credit. Tuition, nonresident: full-time $11,124; part-time $927 per credit. *Faculty research:* Learning and memory, behavioral ecology, hormones and behavior, psychopharmacology, anxiety disorders.

Sage Graduate School, Graduate School, School of Health Sciences, Department of Psychology, Program in Counseling and Community Psychology, Troy, NY 12180-4115. Offers MA. *Faculty:* 3 full-time (all women), 8 part-time/adjunct (7 women). *Students:* 31 full-time (30 women), 37 part-time (32 women); includes 8 minority (5 Black or African American, non-Hispanic/Latino; 1 Asian, non-Hispanic/Latino; 2 Hispanic/Latino). Average age 29. 62 applicants, 44% accepted, 13 enrolled. In 2010, 22 master's awarded. *Degree requirements:* For master's, externship, internship, thesis or research seminar. *Entrance requirements:* For master's, minimum undergraduate GPA of 3.0, interview. *Application deadline:* Applications are processed on a rolling basis. Application fee: $40. *Expenses:* Tuition: Full-time $10,980; part-time $610 per credit hour. Tuition and fees vary according to course load, degree level and program. *Unit head:* Dr. Esther Haskevitz, Interim Dean, School of Health Sciences, 518-244-2296, Fax: 518-244-4571, E-mail: haskve@sage.edu. *Application contact:* Dr. Jean Poppei, Director, 518-244-2076, Fax: 518-244-4545, E-mail: poppej@sage.edu.

St. Bonaventure University, School of Graduate Studies, School of Education, Program in Counselor Education, St. Bonaventure, NY 14778-2284. Offers community mental health counseling (MS Ed); school counseling (MS Ed); school counselor (Adv C). *Accreditation:* ACA. Part-time and evening/weekend programs available. *Faculty:* 4 full-time (1 woman), 8 part-time/adjunct (3 women). *Students:* 115 full-time (94 women), 24 part-time (17 women); includes 8 minority (4 Black or African American, non-Hispanic/Latino; 4 Hispanic/Latino), 2 international. Average age 29. 110 applicants, 65% accepted, 50 enrolled. In 2010, 23 master's, 8 Adv Cs awarded. *Degree requirements:* For master's, comprehensive exam, thesis optional, completion of internship, submission of porfolio. *Entrance requirements:* For master's, interview, writing sample, minimum undergraduate GPA of 3.0, references. Additional exam requirements/recommendations for international students: Required—TOEFL (minimum score 550 paper-based; 213 computer-based). *Application deadline:* For fall admission, 8/15 priority date for domestic students, 2/1 priority date for international students; for spring admission, 10/15 priority date for domestic students, 7/1 priority date for international students. Applications are processed on a rolling basis. Application fee: $30. Electronic applications accepted. *Expenses:* Tuition: Part-time $670 per credit hour. *Financial support:* In 2010–11, 5 research assistantships with full and partial tuition reimbursements were awarded; career-related internships or fieldwork, Federal Work-Study, scholarships/grants, health care benefits, tuition waivers (partial), and unspecified assistantships also available. Support available to part-time students. Financial award application deadline: 4/15; financial award applicants required to submit FAFSA. *Unit head:* Dr. Craig Zuckerman, Director, 716-375-2374, Fax: 716-375-2360, E-mail: czuck@sbu.edu. *Application contact:* Bruce Campbell, Director of Graduate Admissions, 716-375-2429, E-mail: gradsch@sbu.edu.

St. Cloud State University, School of Graduate Studies, College of Education, Department of Educational Leadership and Community Psychology, Program in Community Counseling, St. Cloud, MN 56301-4498. Offers MS. *Degree requirements:* For master's, comprehensive exam (for some programs), thesis or alternative. *Entrance requirements:* For master's, GRE General Test, minimum GPA of 2.75. Additional exam requirements/recommendations for international students: Required—Michigan English Language Assessment Battery; Recommended—TOEFL (minimum score 550 paper-based; 213 computer-based), IELTS (minimum score 6.5). Electronic applications accepted.

Saint Joseph College, Department of Counselor Education, West Hartford, CT 06117-2700. Offers community counseling (MA); school counseling (MA). Part-time and evening/weekend programs available. *Students:* 57 full-time (54 women), 80 part-time (70 women); includes 1 Black or African American, non-Hispanic/Latino; 4 Hispanic/Latino; 1 Two or more races, non-Hispanic/Latino. *Degree requirements:* For master's, comprehensive exam, thesis optional. *Entrance requirements:* For master's, 2 letters of recommendation. *Application deadline:* Applications are processed on a rolling basis. Application fee: $50. Electronic applications accepted. *Expenses:* Tuition: Full-time $11,340; part-time $630 per credit. Required fees: $540; $30 per credit. Tuition and fees vary according to course load, campus/location and program. *Financial support:* Career-related internships or fieldwork and unspecified assistantships available. Support available to part-time students. Financial award applicants required to submit FAFSA. *Application contact:* Graduate Admissions Office, 860-231-5261, E-mail: graduate@sjc.edu.

Saint Martin's University, Graduate Programs, Program in Counseling Psychology, Lacey, WA 98503. Offers MAC. Part-time and evening/weekend programs available. *Faculty:* 3 full-time (2 women), 3 part-time/adjunct (all women). *Students:* 40 full-time (29 women), 58 part-time (52 women); includes 4 Black or African American, non-Hispanic/Latino; 4 American Indian or Alaska Native, non-Hispanic/Latino; 5 Asian, non-Hispanic/Latino; 5 Hispanic/Latino; 1 Two or more races, non-Hispanic/Latino, 5 international. Average age 36. 24 applicants, 79% accepted, 18 enrolled. In 2010, 17 master's awarded. *Degree requirements:* For master's, clinical experience, interview. *Entrance requirements:* For master's, BA in psychology or related field, clinical experience. Additional exam requirements/recommendations for international students: Required—TOEFL. *Application deadline:* For fall admission, 7/1 for domestic students, 2/15 for international students; for spring admission, 11/1 priority date for domestic students, 7/1 for international students. Applications are processed on a rolling basis. Application fee: $35. *Financial support:* In 2010–11, 97 students received support. Career-related internships or fieldwork, Federal Work-Study, and institutionally sponsored loans available. Support available to part-time students. Financial award application deadline: 3/1; financial award applicants required to submit FAFSA. *Faculty research:* Alcohol studies, clinical effectiveness, social justice, parent adolescent interaction. *Unit head:* Dr. Godfrey J. Ellis, Director, 360-438-4560, E-mail: gellis@stmartin.edu. *Application contact:* Sandy Brandt, Administrative Assistant, 360-438-4560, E-mail: sbrandt@stmartin.edu.

St. Mary's University, Graduate School, Department of Counseling and Human Services, Program in Community Counseling, San Antonio, TX 78228-8507. Offers MA. Part-time programs available. *Degree requirements:* For master's, comprehensive exam, internship. *Entrance requirements:* For master's, GRE, GMAT. Additional exam requirements/recommendations for international students: Required—TOEFL (minimum score 550 paper-based; 213 computer-based; 80 iBT). Electronic applications accepted.

San Francisco State University, Division of Graduate Studies, College of Behavioral and Social Sciences, Department of Psychology, San Francisco, CA 94132-1722. Offers clinical psychology (MS); developmental psychology (MA); industrial/organizational psychology (MS); psychological research (MA); school psychology (MS); social psychology (MA). *Financial support:* Teaching assistantships available. Financial award application deadline: 3/1. *Unit head:* Dr. Julia Lewis, Chair, 415-338-7555, E-mail: jmlewis@sfsu.edu. *Application contact:* Leslye M. Tinson, Assistant to the Chair, 415-338-7555, E-mail: ltinson@sfsu.edu.

Southeastern Louisiana University, College of Education and Human Development, Department of Counseling and Human Development, Hammond, LA 70402. Offers counselor education (M Ed), including community counseling, marriage and family therapy, school counseling, substance abuse counseling. *Accreditation:* ACA; NCATE. Part-time programs available. *Faculty:* 7 full-time (5 women). *Students:* 62 full-time (58 women), 47 part-time (44 women); includes 26 minority (21 Black or African American, non-Hispanic/Latino; 1 American Indian or Alaska Native, non-Hispanic/Latino; 1 Asian, non-Hispanic/Latino; 2 Hispanic/Latino; 1 Two or more races, non-Hispanic/Latino). Average age 29. 50 applicants, 52% accepted, 16 enrolled. In 2010, 22 master's awarded. *Degree requirements:* For master's, comprehensive exam, 100-hour practicum, 600-hour internship. *Entrance requirements:* For master's, GRE (verbal and quantitative). Additional exam requirements/recommendations for international students: Required—TOEFL (minimum score 500 paper-based; 173 computer-based; 61 iBT). *Application deadline:* For fall admission, 7/15 priority date for domestic students, 6/1 priority date for international students; for spring admission, 12/1 priority date for domestic students, 10/1 priority date for international students. Applications are processed on a rolling basis. Application fee: $20 ($30 for international students). Electronic applications accepted. *Expenses:* Tuition, state resident: full-time $3533. Tuition, nonresident: full-time $12,002. Required fees: $907. Tuition and fees vary according to degree level. *Financial support:* In 2010–11, 5 students received support. Career-related internships or fieldwork, Federal Work-Study, institutionally sponsored loans, unspecified assistantships, and administrative assistantships available. Support available to part-time students. Financial award application deadline: 5/1; financial award applicants required to submit FAFSA. *Faculty research:* Play therapy, grief and loss, addictions, gratitude, couples relationships enrichment/spirituality. *Unit head:* Dr. June Williams, Interim Department Head, 985-549-2309, Fax: 985-549-3758, E-mail: jwilliams@selu.edu. *Application contact:* Sandra Meyers, Graduate Admissions Analyst, 985-549-2066, Fax: 985-549-5632, E-mail: admissions@selu.edu.

Southeast Missouri State University, School of Graduate Studies, Department of Educational Leadership and Counseling, Counseling Program, Cape Girardeau, MO 63701-4799. Offers career counseling (MA); community counseling (MA); counseling education (Ed S); mental health counseling (MA); school counseling (MA), including elementary counseling, secondary counseling. *Accreditation:* ACA; NCATE. Part-time and evening/weekend programs available. Postbaccalaureate distance learning degree programs offered. *Faculty:* 12 full-time (6 women). *Students:* 29 full-time (26 women), 53 part-time (48 women); includes 5 minority (3 Black or African American, non-Hispanic/Latino; 1 American Indian or Alaska Native, non-Hispanic/Latino; 1 Hispanic/Latino), 1 international. Average age 33. 31 applicants, 94% accepted, 20 enrolled. In 2010, 16 master's, 7 other advanced degrees awarded. *Degree requirements:* For master's, comprehensive exam, portfolio, oral exam, minimum GPA of 3.25; for Ed S, oral exam, minimum GPA of 3.25. *Entrance requirements:* For master's, GRE General Test or MAT, minimum undergraduate GPA of 3.0; 18 undergraduate hours in social science including statistics; teaching certification for school counselor or evidence of competency; for Ed S, GRE General Test or MAT, master's degree; teacher certification; recommendations. Additional exam requirements/recommendations for international students: Required—TOEFL (minimum score 550 paper-based; 213 computer-based; 79 iBT); Recommended—IELTS (minimum score 6). *Application deadline:* For fall admission, 8/1 for domestic students, 6/1 for international students; for spring admission, 11/21 for domestic students, 10/1 for international students. Applications are processed on a rolling basis. Application fee: $25 ($35 for international students). Electronic applications accepted. *Expenses:* Tuition, state resident: full-time $4698; part-time $261 per credit hour. Tuition, nonresident: full-time $8379; part-time $465.50 per credit hour. *Financial support:* In 2010–11, 8 students received support. Career-related internships or fieldwork, Federal Work-Study, institutionally sponsored loans, scholarships/grants, tuition waivers (full), and unspecified assistantships available. Financial award application deadline: 6/30; financial award applicants required to submit FAFSA. *Faculty research:* Counselor development, marriage and family counseling, multicultural counseling. *Unit head:* Dr. David Stader, 573-651-2417, E-mail: dstader@semo.edu. *Application contact:* Gail Amick, Administrative Secretary, 573-651-2049, Fax: 573-651-2001, E-mail: gamick@semo.edu.

Southwestern College, Program in Transformational Ecopsychology, Santa Fe, NM 87502-4788. Offers Certificate. *Entrance requirements:* For degree, 3 letters of reference, interview.

Springfield College, Graduate Programs, Program in Human Services, Springfield, MA 01109-3797. Offers human services (MS), including community counseling psychology, mental health counseling, organizational management and leadership. Part-time programs available. *Degree requirements:* For master's, comprehensive exam, thesis (for some programs), research project. *Entrance requirements:* For master's, GRE. Additional exam requirements/recommendations for international students: Required—TOEFL (minimum score 550 paper-based; 213 computer-based). Electronic applications accepted. *Expenses:* Contact institution.

Stony Brook University, State University of New York, Graduate School, College of Arts and Sciences, Department of Psychology, Program in Social and Health Psychology, Stony Brook, NY 11794. Offers PhD. *Students:* 17 full-time (12 women); includes 1 Asian, non-Hispanic/Latino; 4 Hispanic/Latino, 2 international. Average age 28. 85 applicants, 6% accepted, 1 enrolled. In 2010, 6 doctorates awarded. *Degree requirements:* For doctorate, thesis/dissertation. *Entrance requirements:* For doctorate, GRE General Test, GRE Subject Test. Additional exam requirements/recommendations for international students: Required—TOEFL. *Application deadline:* For fall admission, 1/15 for domestic students. Application fee: $100. *Expenses:* Tuition, state resident: full-time $8370; part-time $349 per credit. Tuition, nonresident: full-time $13,780; part-time $574 per credit. Required fees: $994. *Unit head:* Dr. Marci Lobel, Head, 631-632-7651, E-mail: marci.lobel@stonybrook.edu. *Application contact:* Dr. Marci Lobel, Head, 631-632-7651, E-mail: marci.lobel@stonybrook.edu.

Syracuse University, College of Arts and Sciences, Program in Social Psychology, Syracuse, NY 13244. Offers PhD. Part-time programs available. *Students:* 5 full-time (4 women), 1 international. Average age 25. 42 applicants, 2% accepted, 1 enrolled. *Degree requirements:* For doctorate, thesis/dissertation. *Entrance requirements:* For doctorate, GRE General Test, GRE Subject Test (recommended). Additional exam requirements/recommendations for international students: Required—TOEFL (minimum score 100 iBT). *Application deadline:* For fall admission, 1/10 priority date for domestic and international students. Application fee: $75. Electronic applications accepted. *Expenses:* Tuition: Part-time $1162 per credit. *Financial support:* Fellowships, research assistantships, teaching assistantships available. Financial award application deadline: 1/1. *Unit head:* Dr. Joshua Smyth, Graduate Director, 315-443-3723, Fax: 315-443-4085, E-mail: jmsmyth@syr.edu. *Application contact:* Sue Bova, Information Contact, 315-443-1050, E-mail: skbova@syr.edu.

Teachers College, Columbia University, Graduate Faculty of Education, Department of Organization and Leadership, Program in Social and Organizational Psychology, New York, NY 10027-6696. Offers change leadership (MA); social-organizational psychology (MA). *Faculty:* 8 full-time (5 women), 22 part-time/adjunct (10 women). *Students:* 122 full-time (71 women), 113 part-time (85 women); includes 59 minority (11 Black or African American, non-Hispanic/Latino; 20 Asian, non-Hispanic/Latino; 23 Hispanic/Latino; 1 Native Hawaiian or other Pacific Islander, non-Hispanic/Latino; 4 Two or more races, non-Hispanic/Latino), 40 international. Average age 28. 202 applicants, 62% accepted, 69 enrolled. In 2010, 111 master's awarded. Terminal master's awarded for partial completion of doctoral program. *Degree requirements:* For master's, comprehensive exam. *Entrance requirements:* For master's, GRE, MAT, or GMAT, minimum GPA of 3.0. *Application deadline:* For fall admission, 1/15 priority date for domestic students. Application fee: $65. Electronic applications accepted. *Expenses:* Tuition: Full-time $28,272; part-time $1178 per credit. Required fees: $756; $378 per semester. *Financial support:* Fellowships, research assistantships, career-related internships or fieldwork, Federal Work-Study, institutionally sponsored loans, and tuition waivers (full and partial) available. Support available to part-time students. Financial award application deadline: 2/1. *Faculty research:* Conflict resolution, human resource and organization development, management competence, organizational culture, leadership. *Unit head:* Dr. W. Warner Burke, Director of the Graduate Programs in Social-Organizational Psychology, 212-678-3831, E-mail: wwb3@columbia.edu. *Application contact:* Lynda Hallmark, Program Manager of the Social-Organizational Psychology Program, 212-678-3273, Fax: 212-678-3273, E-mail: hallmark@tc.edu.

Temple University, College of Liberal Arts, Department of Psychology, Philadelphia, PA 19122-6096. Offers brain and cognitive sciences (PhD); clinical psychology (PhD); developmental psychology (PhD); psychology (MA); social psychology (PhD). *Accreditation:* APA. *Faculty:* 29 full-time (11 women). *Students:* 88 full-time (69 women), 14 part-time (12 women); includes 1 Black or African American, non-Hispanic/Latino; 1 American Indian or Alaska Native, non-Hispanic/Latino; 4 Asian, non-Hispanic/Latino; 2 Hispanic/Latino, 6 international. 538 applicants, 6% accepted, 16 enrolled. In 2010, 10 master's, 15 doctorates awarded. *Degree requirements:* For doctorate, thesis/dissertation. *Entrance requirements:* For doctorate, GRE General Test, minimum GPA of 3.0. Additional exam requirements/recommendations for international students: Required—TOEFL (minimum score 550 paper-based; 213 computer-based; 79 iBT). *Application deadline:* For fall admission, 12/15 for domestic and international students. Application fee: $50. Electronic applications accepted. *Financial support:* Fellowships, research assistantships, teaching assistantships, career-related internships or fieldwork, Federal Work-Study, institutionally sponsored loans, and unspecified assistantships available. Financial award application deadline: 12/15; financial award applicants required to submit FAFSA. Total annual research expenditures: $4 million. *Unit head:* Dr. Marsha Weinraub, Chair, 215-204-7321, Fax: 215-204-5539, E-mail: mweinrau@temple.edu. *Application contact:* Dr. Marsha Weinraub, Chair, 215-204-7321, Fax: 215-204-5539, E-mail: mweinrau@temple.edu.

Texas A&M University, College of Liberal Arts, Department of Psychology, College Station, TX 77843. Offers behavioral and cellular neuroscience (PhD); clinical psychology (PhD); cognitive psychology (PhD); developmental psychology (PhD); industrial/organizational psychology (PhD); social psychology (PhD). *Accreditation:* APA. *Faculty:* 39. *Students:* 91 full-time (57 women), 14 part-time (11 women); includes 7 Black or African American, non-Hispanic/Latino; 8 Asian, non-Hispanic/Latino; 17 Hispanic/Latino, 7 international. In 2010, 12 doctorates awarded. *Degree requirements:* For doctorate, comprehensive exam (for some programs), thesis/dissertation. *Entrance requirements:* For doctorate, GRE General Test. Additional exam requirements/recommendations for international students: Required—TOEFL. *Application deadline:* For fall admission, 1/5 for domestic and international students. Application fee: $50 ($75 for international students). Electronic applications accepted. *Financial support:* Fellowships with partial tuition reimbursements, research assistantships with partial tuition reimbursements, teaching assistantships with partial tuition reimbursements, career-related internships or fieldwork, institutionally sponsored loans, health care benefits, and unspecified assistantships available. Financial award application deadline: 1/5; financial award applicants required to submit FAFSA. *Unit head:* Ludy T. Benjamin, Head, 979-845-2540, Fax: 979-845-4727, E-mail: lbenjamin@tamu.edu. *Application contact:* Julie Austin, Graduate Admissions Supervisor, 979-458-1710, Fax: 979-845-4727, E-mail: gradadv@psyc.tamu.edu.

Texas Christian University, College of Science and Engineering, Department of Psychology, Fort Worth, TX 76129-0002. Offers experimental psychology (PhD), including cognitive psychology, learning, neuropsychology, social psychology; psychology (MA, MS). In 2010, 7 master's, 3 doctorates awarded. Terminal master's awarded for partial completion of doctoral program. *Degree requirements:* For master's, thesis; for doctorate, thesis/dissertation. *Entrance requirements:* For master's and doctorate, GRE General Test. Additional exam requirements/recommendations for international students: Required—TOEFL. *Application deadline:* For fall admission, 3/1 for domestic and international students; for spring admission, 12/1 for domestic students. Applications are processed on a rolling basis. Application fee: $50. Electronic applications accepted. *Expenses:* Tuition: Full-time $18,720; part-time $1040 per credit hour. Tuition and fees vary according to course load and program. *Financial support:* In 2010–11, 20 students received support; teaching assistantships with full tuition reimbursements available, unspecified assistantships available. Financial award application deadline: 3/1. *Unit head:* Dr.

Social Psychology

Texas Christian University *(continued)*
Charles Lord, Coordinator of Graduate Studies, 817-257-7410, Fax: 817-257-7681, E-mail: c.lord@tcu.edu. *Application contact:* Tami Joyce, Department Manager, 817-257-7410, Fax: 817-257-7681, E-mail: t.joyce@tcu.edu.

Thomas University, Department of Human Services, Thomasville, GA 31792-7499. Offers community counseling (MSCC); rehabilitation counseling (MRC). *Accreditation:* CORE. Part-time programs available. *Entrance requirements:* For master's, resume, 3 academic/professional references. Additional exam requirements/recommendations for international students: Required—TOEFL (minimum score 600 paper-based; 250 computer-based). Electronic applications accepted.

Troy University, Graduate School, College of Education, Program in Counseling and Psychology, Troy, AL 36082. Offers agency counseling (Ed S); clinical mental health (MS); community counseling (MS, Ed S); corrections counseling (MS); rehabilitation counseling (MS); school psychology (MS, Ed S); school psychometry (MS); social service counseling (MS); student affairs counseling (MS); substance abuse counseling (MS). *Accreditation:* ACA; CORE; NCATE. Part-time and evening/weekend programs available. *Students:* 419 full-time (338 women), 720 part-time (603 women); includes 696 minority (592 Black or African American, non-Hispanic/Latino; 8 American Indian or Alaska Native, non-Hispanic/Latino; 4 Asian, non-Hispanic/Latino; 46 Hispanic/Latino; 46 Two or more races, non-Hispanic/Latino). Average age 33. 326 applicants, 90% accepted. In 2010, 198 master's, 1 other advanced degree awarded. *Degree requirements:* For master's, comprehensive exam, thesis. *Entrance requirements:* For master's, MAT, minimum GPA of 2.5. Additional exam requirements/recommendations for international students: Required—TOEFL (minimum score 523 paper-based; 193 computer-based; 70 iBT), IELTS (minimum score 6). *Application deadline:* Applications are processed on a rolling basis. Application fee: $50. Electronic applications accepted. *Expenses:* Tuition, state resident: full-time $4428; part-time $246 per credit hour. Tuition, nonresident: full-time $8856; part-time $492 per credit hour. Required fees: $432; $24 per credit hour. $50 per term. Tuition and fees vary according to program. *Unit head:* Dr. Andrew Creamer, Chair, 334-670-3350, Fax: 334-670-32961, E-mail: drcreamer@troy.edu. *Application contact:* Brenda K. Campbell, Director of Graduate Admissions, 334-670-3178, Fax: 334-670-3733, E-mail: bcamp@troy.edu.

Université du Québec à Rimouski, Graduate Programs, Program in Psychosocial Studies, Rimouski, QC G5L 3A1, Canada. Offers MA.

Université Laval, Faculty of Social Sciences, School of Psychology, Programs in Psychology, Québec, QC G1K 7P4, Canada. Offers clinical psychology (PhD); community psychology (PhD); psychology (PhD, Psy D). *Degree requirements:* For doctorate, comprehensive exam, thesis/dissertation. *Entrance requirements:* For doctorate, comprehension of written English, knowledge of French, interview. Electronic applications accepted.

University at Albany, State University of New York, College of Arts and Sciences, Department of Psychology, Albany, NY 12222-0001. Offers autism (Certificate); biopsychology (PhD); clinical psychology (PhD); general/experimental psychology (PhD); industrial/organizational psychology (PhD); psychology (MA); social/personality psychology (PhD). *Accreditation:* APA (one or more programs are accredited). *Degree requirements:* For doctorate, thesis/dissertation. *Entrance requirements:* For doctorate, GRE General Test, GRE Subject Test. Additional exam requirements/recommendations for international students: Required—TOEFL (minimum score 550 paper-based; 213 computer-based). Electronic applications accepted.

University at Buffalo, the State University of New York, Graduate School, College of Arts and Sciences, Department of Psychology, Buffalo, NY 14260. Offers behavioral neuroscience (PhD); clinical psychology (PhD); cognitive psychology (PhD); general psychology (MA); social-personality psychology (PhD). *Accreditation:* APA (one or more programs are accredited). *Faculty:* 26 full-time (8 women), 10 part-time/adjunct (5 women). *Students:* 88 full-time (60 women), 6 part-time (4 women); includes 21 minority (2 Black or African American, non-Hispanic/Latino; 2 American Indian or Alaska Native, non-Hispanic/Latino; 7 Asian, non-Hispanic/Latino; 9 Hispanic/Latino; 1 Two or more races, non-Hispanic/Latino), 11 international. Average age 27. 367 applicants, 12% accepted, 21 enrolled. In 2010, 14 master's, 6 doctorates awarded. Terminal master's awarded for partial completion of doctoral program. *Degree requirements:* For master's, project; for doctorate, thesis/dissertation. *Entrance requirements:* For master's and doctorate, GRE General Test. Additional exam requirements/recommendations for international students: Required—TOEFL (minimum score 550 paper-based; 213 computer-based; 79 iBT). *Application deadline:* For fall admission, 12/1 for domestic and international students. Application fee: $75. Electronic applications accepted. *Financial support:* In 2010–11, 65 students received support, including 8 fellowships with full tuition reimbursements available (averaging $13,700 per year), 16 research assistantships with full tuition reimbursements available (averaging $13,700 per year), 38 teaching assistantships with full tuition reimbursements available (averaging $13,700 per year); career-related internships or fieldwork, Federal Work-Study, institutionally sponsored loans, scholarships/grants, and tuition waivers (partial) also available. Financial award application deadline: 12/1; financial award applicants required to submit FAFSA. *Faculty research:* Neural, endocrine, and molecular bases of behavior; adult mood and anxiety disorders; relationship dysfunction; attention deficit/hyperactivity disorder; psycho-linguistics. Total annual research expenditures: $7.9 million. *Unit head:* Dr. Paul A. Luce, Chair, 716-645-3650 Ext. 203, Fax: 716-645-3801, E-mail: psychair@acsu.buffalo.edu. *Application contact:* Mary Claire Schnepf, Coordinator of Admissions, 716-645-3660, Fax: 716-645-3801, E-mail: psych@abuffalo.edu.

The University of Akron, Graduate School, College of Education, Department of Counseling, Program in Community Counseling, Akron, OH 44325. Offers MA, MS. *Accreditation:* ACA; NCATE. *Students:* 45 full-time (38 women), 29 part-time (27 women); includes 9 Black or African American, non-Hispanic/Latino, 3 international. Average age 30. 45 applicants, 44% accepted, 12 enrolled. In 2010, 17 master's awarded. *Degree requirements:* For master's, comprehensive exam. *Entrance requirements:* For master's, minimum GPA of 2.75, letters of recommendation, interview. Additional exam requirements/recommendations for international students: Required—TOEFL (minimum score 550 paper-based; 213 computer-based; 79 iBT). *Application deadline:* Applications are processed on a rolling basis. Application fee: $30 ($40 for international students). Electronic applications accepted. *Expenses:* Tuition, state resident: full-time $6800; part-time $378 per credit hour. Tuition, nonresident: full-time $11,644; part-time $647 per credit hour. Required fees: $1265. One-time fee: $30 full-time. *Unit head:* Dr. Robert Schwartz, Coordinator, 330-972-8155, E-mail: rcs@uakron.edu. *Application contact:* Dr. Robert Schwartz, Coordinator, 330-972-8155, E-mail: rcs@uakron.edu.

University of Alaska Anchorage, College of Arts and Sciences, Department of Psychology, Anchorage, AK 99508. Offers clinical psychology (MS); clinical-community psychology with rural-indigenous emphasis (PhD). Part-time programs available. *Degree requirements:* For master's, thesis. *Entrance requirements:* For master's, GRE General Test, GRE Subject Test, interview, references; for doctorate, interview, bachelor's or master's degree in psychology. Additional exam requirements/recommendations for international students: Required—TOEFL (minimum score 550 paper-based; 213 computer-based). *Faculty research:* Substance abuse, childhood autism, biofeedback, psychological assessment, mental health in Native Alaskans.

University of Alaska Fairbanks, College of Liberal Arts, Department of Psychology, Fairbanks, AK 99775-6480. Offers clinical-community psychology (PhD), including rural cross-cultural emphasis. Program offered jointly with University of Alaska Anchorage. *Faculty:* 8 full-time (5 women). *Students:* 2 full-time (both women), 28 part-time (25 women); includes 9 minority (2 American Indian or Alaska Native, non-Hispanic/Latino; 2 Hispanic/Latino; 5 Two or more races, non-Hispanic/Latino), 1 international. Average age 31. 36 applicants, 39% accepted, 12 enrolled. *Degree requirements:* For doctorate, comprehensive exam, thesis/dissertation, oral exam, oral defense. *Entrance requirements:* For doctorate, disclosure statement. Additional exam requirements/recommendations for international students: Required—TOEFL (minimum

score 550 paper-based; 213 computer-based; 80 iBT). *Application deadline:* For fall admission, 12/15 for domestic and international students. Application fee: $60. *Expenses:* Tuition, state resident: full-time $5688; part-time $316 per credit. Tuition, nonresident: full-time $11,628; part-time $646 per credit. Required fees: $289 per semester. Tuition and fees vary according to course load and reciprocity agreements. *Financial support:* In 2010–11, 7 research assistantships with tuition reimbursements (averaging $16,679 per year), 6 teaching assistantships with tuition reimbursements (averaging $17,997 per year) were awarded; fellowships with tuition reimbursements, career-related internships or fieldwork, Federal Work-Study, scholarships/grants, health care benefits, and unspecified assistantships also available. Support available to part-time students. Financial award application deadline: 7/1; financial award applicants required to submit FAFSA. *Faculty research:* Clinical and community psychology; rural, indigenous, and cultural psychology. Total annual research expenditures: $42,389. *Unit head:* Dr. Dani Sheppard, Department Chair, 907-474-7007, Fax: 907-474-5781, E-mail: fypsych@uaf.edu. *Application contact:* Dr. Dani Sheppard, Department Chair, 907-474-7007, Fax: 907-474-5781, E-mail: fypsych@uaf.edu.

University of Alaska Fairbanks, School of Education, Program in Counseling, Fairbanks, AK 99775-7520. Offers counseling (M Ed), including community counseling, school counseling. *Students:* 22 full-time (15 women), 46 part-time (37 women); includes 9 minority (3 Black or African American, non-Hispanic/Latino; 3 American Indian or Alaska Native, non-Hispanic/Latino; 1 Hispanic/Latino; 2 Two or more races, non-Hispanic/Latino), 1 international. Average age 36. 52 applicants, 63% accepted, 29 enrolled. In 2010, 21 master's awarded. *Degree requirements:* For master's, comprehensive exam, thesis, oral defense. *Entrance requirements:* For master's, 1 year teaching or administrative experience. *Application deadline:* For fall admission, 6/1 for domestic students, 3/1 for international students; for spring admission, 10/15 for domestic students, 9/1 for international students. Applications are processed on a rolling basis. Application fee: $60. Electronic applications accepted. *Expenses:* Tuition, state resident: full-time $5688; part-time $316 per credit. Tuition, nonresident: full-time $11,628; part-time $646 per credit. Required fees: $289 per semester. Tuition and fees vary according to course load and reciprocity agreements. *Financial support:* In 2010–11, 2 teaching assistantships with tuition reimbursements (averaging $13,330 per year) were awarded; fellowships with tuition reimbursements, career-related internships or fieldwork, Federal Work-Study, scholarships/grants, health care benefits, and unspecified assistantships also available. Support available to part-time students. Financial award application deadline: 7/1; financial award applicants required to submit FAFSA. *Unit head:* Dr. Eric C. Madsen, Dean, 907-474-7341, Fax: 907-474-5451, E-mail: fysoed@uaf.edu. *Application contact:* Dr. Eric C. Madsen, Dean, 907-474-7341, Fax: 907-474-5451, E-mail: fysoed@uaf.edu.

The University of British Columbia, Faculty of Arts and Faculty of Graduate Studies, Department of Psychology, Vancouver, BC V6T 1Z4, Canada. Offers behavioral neuroscience (MA, PhD); clinical psychology (MA, PhD); cognitive science (MA, PhD); developmental psychology (MA, PhD); health psychology (MA, PhD); quantitative methods (MA, PhD); social/personality psychology (MA, PhD). *Accreditation:* APA (one or more programs are accredited). Terminal master's awarded for partial completion of doctoral program. *Degree requirements:* For master's, thesis; for doctorate, comprehensive exam, thesis/dissertation. *Entrance requirements:* For master's and doctorate, GRE General Test. Additional exam requirements/recommendations for international students: Required—TOEFL (minimum score 550 paper-based; 230 computer-based; 80 iBT). Electronic applications accepted. Tuition charges are reported in Canadian dollars. *Expenses:* Tuition, area resident: Full-time $4179 Canadian dollars. International tuition: $7344 Canadian dollars full-time. *Faculty research:* Clinical, developmental, social/personality, cognition, behavioral neuroscience.

University of Central Arkansas, Graduate School, College of Health and Behavioral Sciences, Department of Counseling and Psychology, Program in Community Counseling, Conway, AR 72035-0001. Offers MS. *Students:* 19 full-time (16 women), 13 part-time (11 women); includes 2 Black or African American, non-Hispanic/Latino; 1 Asian, non-Hispanic/Latino. Average age 29. In 2010, 10 master's awarded. *Degree requirements:* For master's, comprehensive exam, thesis optional. *Entrance requirements:* For master's, GRE General Test, minimum GPA of 2.7. Additional exam requirements/recommendations for international students: Required—TOEFL (minimum score 550 paper-based; 213 computer-based). *Application deadline:* For fall admission, 3/1 priority date for domestic students; for spring admission, 10/1 priority date for domestic students. Applications are processed on a rolling basis. Application fee: $25 ($50 for international students). *Financial support:* Career-related internships or fieldwork, Federal Work-Study, scholarships/grants, tuition waivers (partial), and unspecified assistantships available. Support available to part-time students. Financial award application deadline: 2/15; financial award applicants required to submit FAFSA. *Unit head:* Dr. Art Gillaspy, Coordinator, 501-450-5410, Fax: 501-450-5424, E-mail: artg@uca.edu. *Application contact:* Susan Wood, Administrative Assistant, 501-450-3124, Fax: 501-450-5678, E-mail: swood@uca.edu.

University of Connecticut, Graduate School, College of Liberal Arts and Sciences, Department of Psychology, Storrs, CT 06269. Offers behavioral neuroscience (PhD); biopsychology (PhD); clinical psychology (MA, PhD); cognition and instruction (PhD); developmental psychology (MA, PhD); ecological psychology (PhD); experimental psychology (PhD); general psychology (MA, PhD); health psychology (Graduate Certificate); industrial/organizational psychology (PhD); language and cognition (PhD); neuroscience (PhD); occupational health psychology (Graduate Certificate); social psychology (MA, PhD). *Accreditation:* APA. Terminal master's awarded for partial completion of doctoral program. *Degree requirements:* For master's, comprehensive exam; for doctorate, thesis/dissertation. *Entrance requirements:* For master's and doctorate, GRE General Test, GRE Subject Test. Additional exam requirements/recommendations for international students: Required—TOEFL (minimum score 550 paper-based; 213 computer-based). Electronic applications accepted.

University of Dayton, Graduate School, School of Education and Allied Professions, Department of Counselor Education and Human Services, Dayton, OH 45469-1300. Offers college student personnel (MS Ed); community counseling (MS Ed); higher education administration (MS Ed); human services (MS Ed); school counseling (MS Ed); school psychology (MS Ed, Ed S). *Accreditation:* ACA; NCATE. Part-time and evening/weekend programs available. *Faculty:* 12 full-time (9 women), 32 part-time/adjunct (18 women). *Students:* 269 full-time (219 women), 180 part-time (150 women); includes 84 minority (69 Black or African American, non-Hispanic/Latino; 2 American Indian or Alaska Native, non-Hispanic/Latino; 8 Asian, non-Hispanic/Latino; 3 Hispanic/Latino; 2 Two or more races, non-Hispanic/Latino), 2 international. Average age 32. 246 applicants, 48% accepted, 89 enrolled. In 2010, 157 master's, 10 Ed Ss awarded. *Degree requirements:* For master's, comprehensive exam (for some programs), thesis (for some programs), exit exam. *Entrance requirements:* For master's, MAT or GRE (if GPA less than 2.75), interview, writing sample. Additional exam requirements/recommendations for international students: Required—TOEFL (minimum score 550 paper-based; 213 computer-based; 80 iBT). *Application deadline:* For fall admission, 4/10 for domestic students, 3/1 priority date for international students; for winter admission, 9/10 for domestic students, 7/1 priority date for international students; for spring admission, 1/10 for domestic students, 1/1 priority date for international students. Application fee: $0 ($50 for international students). Electronic applications accepted. *Expenses:* Tuition: Full-time $7800; part-time $650 per credit hour. *Financial support:* In 2010–11, 7 research assistantships with full tuition reimbursements (averaging $8,400 per year) were awarded; career-related internships or fieldwork, institutionally sponsored loans, health care benefits, and unspecified assistantships also available. Financial award applicants required to submit FAFSA. *Faculty research:* Anger as part of the grief process, inclusion of children with severe disabilities, comparisons of school counselors in Bosnia and the U. S., graduate and professional student socialization, use of cohort groups in doctoral programs, bullying in schools, impact of space on learning, sophomore experience. *Unit head:* Dr. Alan Demmitt, Chairperson, 937-229-3644, Fax: 937-229-1055. *Application contact:* Alexander Popovski, Associate Director of Graduate and International Admissions, 937-229-2357, Fax: 937-229-4729, E-mail: alex.popovski@notes.udayton.edu.

University of Delaware, College of Arts and Sciences, Department of Psychology, Newark, DE 19716. Offers behavioral neuroscience (PhD); clinical psychology (PhD); cognitive psychology (PhD); social psychology (PhD). *Accreditation:* APA. *Degree requirements:* For doctorate, thesis/dissertation. *Entrance requirements:* For doctorate, GRE General Test. Additional exam requirements/recommendations for international students: Required—TOEFL (minimum score 600 paper-based; 250 computer-based). Electronic applications accepted. *Faculty research:* Emotion development, neural and cognitive aspects of memory, neural control of feeding, intergroup relations, social cognition and communication.

University of Denver, Division of Arts, Humanities and Social Sciences, Department of Psychology, Denver, CO 80208. Offers affective science (PhD); affective/social psychology (PhD); clinical child psychology (PhD); developmental cognitive neuroscience (PhD); developmental psychology (PhD). Incidental Master's program available. *Accreditation:* APA. *Faculty:* 18 full-time (8 women), 5 part-time/adjunct (4 women). *Students:* 32 full-time (31 women), 2 part-time (1 woman); includes 6 minority (3 Asian, non-Hispanic/Latino; 2 Hispanic/Latino; 1 Two or more races, non-Hispanic/Latino), 2 international. Average age 26. 320 applicants, 5% accepted, 13 enrolled. In 2010, 6 doctorates awarded. Terminal master's awarded for partial completion of doctoral program. *Degree requirements:* For doctorate, one foreign language, comprehensive exam (for some programs), thesis/dissertation. *Entrance requirements:* For doctorate, GRE General Test. Additional exam requirements/recommendations for international students: Required—TOEFL (minimum score 550 paper-based; 80 iBT). *Application deadline:* For fall admission, 12/1 for domestic students. Applications are processed on a rolling basis. Application fee: $60. Electronic applications accepted. *Expenses:* Tuition: Full-time $35,604; part-time $29,670 per year. Required fees: $687 per year. Tuition and fees vary according to program. *Financial support:* In 2010–11, 12 research assistantships with full and partial tuition reimbursements (averaging $15,500 per year), 22 teaching assistantships with full and partial tuition reimbursements (averaging $16,773 per year) were awarded; career-related internships or fieldwork, Federal Work-Study, institutionally sponsored loans, scholarships/grants, and unspecified assistantships also available. Support available to part-time students. Financial award application deadline: 1/1; financial award applicants required to submit FAFSA. *Faculty research:* Developmental neuropsychology, self-esteem and peer relationships, child abuse and neglect, marital and family interactions, adolescent peer and romantic relationships. *Unit head:* Dr. Rob Roberts, Chair, 303-871-3792, Fax: 303-871-4747. *Application contact:* Paula Plank-Houghtaling, Graduate Secretary, 303-871-3803, Fax: 303-871-4747, E-mail: info@psy.du.edu.

University of Florida, Graduate School, College of Liberal Arts and Sciences, Department of Psychology, Gainesville, FL 32611. Offers behavior analysis (PhD); behavioral neuroscience (MS, PhD); cognitive and sensory processes (PhD); counseling psychology (PhD); developmental psychology (PhD); social psychology (MS, PhD); JD/PhD. *Faculty:* 29 full-time (10 women). *Students:* 106 full-time (82 women), 14 part-time (7 women); includes 3 Black or African American, non-Hispanic/Latino; 2 American Indian or Alaska Native, non-Hispanic/Latino; 7 Asian, non-Hispanic/Latino; 12 Hispanic/Latino, 11 international. Average age 27. 614 applicants, 7% accepted, 36 enrolled. In 2010, 25 master's, 13 doctorates awarded. *Degree requirements:* For master's, comprehensive exam, thesis or alternative; for doctorate, comprehensive exam, thesis/dissertation. *Entrance requirements:* For master's and doctorate, GRE General Test, minimum GPA of 3.0. Additional exam requirements/recommendations for international students: Required—TOEFL (minimum score 550 paper-based; 213 computer-based; 80 iBT), IELTS (minimum score 6). *Application deadline:* For fall admission, 12/9 priority date for domestic students, 12/9 for international students. Applications are processed on a rolling basis. Application fee: $30. Electronic applications accepted. *Expenses:* Tuition, state resident: full-time $10,915.92. Tuition, nonresident: full-time $28,309. *Financial support:* In 2010–11, 105 students received support, including 19 fellowships, 24 research assistantships (averaging $18,742 per year), 62 teaching assistantships (averaging $19,797 per year); career-related internships or fieldwork and unspecified assistantships also available. Financial award application deadline: 12/9; financial award applicants required to submit FAFSA. *Faculty research:* Behavior analysis, behavioral and cognitive neuroscience, counseling, developmental psychology, social psychology. Total annual research expenditures: $2.7 million. *Unit head:* Dr. Neil E. Rowland, Chair, 352-273-2128, Fax: 352-392-7985, E-mail: nrowland@ufl.edu. *Application contact:* Dr. Clive D. Wynne, Graduate Coordinator, 352-392-0601, Fax: 352-392-7985, E-mail: wynne@ufl.edu.

University of Guelph, Graduate Studies, College of Social and Applied Human Sciences, Department of Psychology, Guelph, ON N1G 2W1, Canada. Offers applied social psychology (MA, PhD); clinical psychology applied development emphasis (PhD); clinical psychology applied developmental emphasis (MA); industrial/organizational psychology (MA, PhD); neuroscience and applied cognitive science (MA, PhD). *Degree requirements:* For master's, thesis; for doctorate, comprehensive exam, thesis/dissertation. *Entrance requirements:* For master's, GRE General Test, GRE Subject Test, minimum B+ average during previous 2 years of course work; for doctorate, GRE General Test, GRE Subject Test, minimum A- average. Additional exam requirements/recommendations for international students: Required—TOEFL (minimum score 89 iBT). Electronic applications accepted. *Faculty research:* Organizational psychology, reading comprehension and mathematical ability, drug addiction and relapse, gender issues and culture, memory, clinical psychology.

University of Hawaii at Manoa, Graduate Division, College of Social Sciences, Department of Psychology, Honolulu, HI 96822. Offers clinical psychology (PhD); community and cultural psychology (PhD); community and culture (MA); psychology (MA, PhD, Graduate Certificate). *Accreditation:* APA (one or more programs are accredited). Part-time programs available. *Faculty:* 35 full-time (12 women), 2 part-time/adjunct (1 woman). *Students:* 75 full-time (56 women), 17 part-time (12 women); includes 34 minority (1 Black or African American, non-Hispanic/Latino; 1 American Indian or Alaska Native, non-Hispanic/Latino; 12 Asian, non-Hispanic/Latino; 3 Hispanic/Latino; 6 Native Hawaiian or other Pacific Islander, non-Hispanic/Latino; 11 Two or more races, non-Hispanic/Latino), 13 international. Average age 31. 203 applicants, 10% accepted, 17 enrolled. In 2010, 9 master's, 4 doctorates awarded. Terminal master's awarded for partial completion of doctoral program. *Degree requirements:* For master's, comprehensive exam, thesis; for doctorate, comprehensive exam, thesis/dissertation. *Entrance requirements:* For master's and doctorate, GRE General Test, GRE Subject Test. Additional exam requirements/recommendations for international students: Required—TOEFL (minimum score 600 paper-based; 250 computer-based; 100 iBT), IELTS (minimum score 7). *Application deadline:* For fall admission, 1/1 for domestic and international students. Application fee: $60. *Financial support:* In 2010–11, 13 fellowships (averaging $6,425 per year), 42 research assistantships (averaging $14,690 per year), 14 teaching assistantships (averaging $14,802 per year) were awarded; career-related internships or fieldwork, institutionally sponsored loans, and tuition waivers (full and partial) also available. Financial award application deadline: 1/1. *Faculty research:* Cross-cultural psychology, health psychology, marine mammals, child/adult psychopathology. Total annual research expenditures: $1.3 million. *Application contact:* Charlene Baker, Graduate Chair, 808-956-8414, Fax: 808-956-4700, E-mail: bakercha@hawaii.edu.

University of Houston, College of Liberal Arts and Social Sciences, Department of Psychology, Houston, TX 77204. Offers clinical psychology (PhD); developmental psychology (PhD); industrial/organizational psychology (PhD); psychology (MA); social psychology (PhD). *Accreditation:* APA (one or more programs are accredited). *Faculty:* 28 full-time (12 women), 7 part-time/adjunct (4 women). *Students:* 117 full-time (86 women), 22 part-time (16 women); includes 7 Black or African American, non-Hispanic/Latino; 10 Asian, non-Hispanic/Latino; 16 Hispanic/Latino; 4 Two or more races, non-Hispanic/Latino, 17 international. Average age 27. 460 applicants, 6% accepted, 28 enrolled. In 2010, 19 master's, 20 doctorates awarded. *Degree requirements:* For master's, comprehensive exam, thesis; for doctorate, comprehensive exam, thesis/dissertation. *Entrance requirements:* For master's, GRE General Test, career statement, 3 letters of recommendation; for doctorate, GRE General Test, 3 letters of recommendation. Additional exam requirements/recommendations for international students: Required—TOEFL (minimum score 550 paper-based; 79 iBT). *Application deadline:* For fall

admission, 12/15 for domestic and international students. Application fee: $40 ($75 for international students). Electronic applications accepted. *Expenses:* Tuition, state resident: full-time $8592; part-time $358 per credit hour. Tuition, nonresident: full-time $16,032; part-time $668 per credit hour. Required fees: $2889. Tuition and fees vary according to course load and program. *Financial support:* In 2010–11, 23 fellowships with full tuition reimbursements (averaging $2,828 per year), 39 research assistantships with full tuition reimbursements (averaging $7,864 per year), 62 teaching assistantships with full tuition reimbursements (averaging $9,312 per year) were awarded; career-related internships or fieldwork, Federal Work-Study, institutionally sponsored loans, scholarships/grants, health care benefits, and unspecified assistantships also available. Support available to part-time students. Financial award application deadline: 2/1; financial award applicants required to submit FAFSA. *Faculty research:* Health psychology, depression, child/family process, organizational effectiveness, close relationships. *Unit head:* Dr. David Francis, Chairperson, 713-743-7036, Fax: 713-743-8588, E-mail: dfrancis@uh.edu. *Application contact:* Patti Tolar, Academic Affairs Coordinator, 713-743-5544, Fax: 713-743-8588, E-mail: ptolar@uh.edu.

The University of Iowa, Graduate College, College of Education, Department of Counseling, Rehabilitation, and Student Development, Iowa City, IA 52242-1316. Offers administration and research (PhD); community/rehabilitation counseling (MA); counselor education and supervision (PhD); rehabilitation counselor education (PhD); school counseling (MA); student development (MA, PhD). *Accreditation:* ACA (one or more programs are accredited); CORE (one or more programs are accredited). *Degree requirements:* For master's, thesis optional, exam; for doctorate, comprehensive exam, thesis/dissertation. *Entrance requirements:* For master's and doctorate, GRE General Test, minimum GPA of 3.0. Additional exam requirements/recommendations for international students: Required—TOEFL (minimum score 550 paper-based; 213 computer-based; 81 iBT). Electronic applications accepted.

The University of Kansas, Graduate Studies, College of Liberal Arts and Sciences, Department of Psychology, Lawrence, KS 66045. Offers clinical child psychology (MA, PhD); clinical health and rehabilitation (PhD); cognitive psychology (PhD); developmental psychology (PhD); quantitative psychology (PhD); social psychology (MA). *Accreditation:* APA (one or more programs are accredited). *Faculty:* 27 full-time (8 women), 9 part-time/adjunct (4 women). *Students:* 122 full-time (87 women), 1 (woman) part-time; includes 17 minority (4 Black or African American, non-Hispanic/Latino; 8 Asian, non-Hispanic/Latino; 4 Hispanic/Latino; 1 Native Hawaiian or other Pacific Islander, non-Hispanic/Latino), 9 international. Average age 28. 348 applicants, 11% accepted, 25 enrolled. In 2010, 16 master's, 16 doctorates awarded. *Degree requirements:* For master's, thesis; for doctorate, variable foreign language requirement, comprehensive exam, thesis/dissertation. *Entrance requirements:* For doctorate, GRE General Test, minimum GPA of 3.0; undergraduate degree with 15 hours of course work in psychology, curriculum vitae, writing sample (clinical program only). Additional exam requirements/recommendations for international students: Required—TOEFL. *Application deadline:* For fall admission, 12/1 for domestic and international students. Application fee: $55 ($65 for international students). Electronic applications accepted. *Expenses:* Tuition, state resident: full-time $7092; part-time $295.50 per credit hour. Tuition, nonresident: full-time $16,590; part-time $691.25 per credit hour. Required fees: $858; $71.49 per credit hour. Tuition and fees vary according to course load, campus/location and program. *Financial support:* Fellowships with full tuition reimbursements, research assistantships with partial tuition reimbursements, teaching assistantships with full and partial tuition reimbursements, career-related internships or fieldwork and unspecified assistantships available. Financial award application deadline: 12/1; financial award applicants required to submit FAFSA. *Faculty research:* Information processing in depression, rape and other forms of sexual coercion, motions on physical function, processes of memory and understanding text, social stigmas and hostile group environments. *Unit head:* Dr. Ruth Ann Atchley, Chair, 785-864-9821, Fax: 785-864-5696, E-mail: ratchley@ku.edu. *Application contact:* Cathy L. O'Keefe, Graduate Admissions Officer, 785-864-4195, Fax: 785-864-5696, E-mail: psycgrad@ku.edu.

University of La Verne, College of Arts and Sciences, Department of Psychology, Program in Clinical-Community Psychology, La Verne, CA 91750-4443. Offers Psy D. Part-time programs available. *Faculty:* 13 full-time (6 women), 25 part-time/adjunct (17 women). *Students:* 65 full-time (56 women), 26 part-time (17 women); includes 48 minority (11 Black or African American, non-Hispanic/Latino; 11 Asian, non-Hispanic/Latino; 26 Hispanic/Latino). Average age 28. In 2010, 8 doctorates awarded. *Degree requirements:* For doctorate, thesis/dissertation, clinical internship, competency exams, practicum, personal psychotherapy. *Entrance requirements:* For doctorate, minimum GPA of 3.0 undergraduate, 3.5 graduate; 3 letters of recommendation; curriculum vitae. Additional exam requirements/recommendations for international students: Required—TOEFL (minimum score 600 paper-based; 250 computer-based). *Application deadline:* For fall admission, 1/15 for domestic and international students. Application fee: $75. *Expenses:* Contact institution. *Financial support:* Career-related internships or fieldwork, institutionally sponsored loans, scholarships/grants, and unspecified assistantships available. Financial award application deadline: 3/2; financial award applicants required to submit FAFSA. *Unit head:* Dr. Jerry Kernes, Chairperson, 909-593-3511 Ext. 4414, E-mail: jkernes@laverne.edu. *Application contact:* Barbara Cox, Admissions Information Specialist, 909-593-3511 Ext. 4004, Fax: 909-392-2761, E-mail: gradadmission@laverne.edu.

University of Mary, School of Education and Behavioral Sciences, Department of Behavioral Sciences, Bismarck, ND 58504-9652. Offers addiction counseling (MSC); community counseling (MSC); school counseling (MSC); student affairs counseling (MSC). Part-time programs available. Postbaccalaureate distance learning degree programs offered (minimal on-campus study). *Faculty:* 11 part-time/adjunct (8 women). *Students:* 32 full-time (21 women), 25 part-time (21 women); includes 4 Black or African American, non-Hispanic/Latino; 1 American Indian or Alaska Native, non-Hispanic/Latino. Average age 32. 27 applicants, 100% accepted, 27 enrolled. In 2010, 14 master's awarded. *Degree requirements:* For master's, thesis, internship. *Entrance requirements:* For master's, coursework/experience in psychology, statistics, minimum GPA of 3.0. Additional exam requirements/recommendations for international students: Required—TOEFL (minimum score 500 paper-based; 197 computer-based; 71 iBT). *Application deadline:* For fall admission, 8/1 priority date for domestic students. Application fee: $40. *Expenses:* Tuition: Full-time $10,800; part-time $450 per credit. Tuition and fees vary according to course load, degree level, program and student level. *Financial support:* Application deadline: 8/1. *Unit head:* James Renner, Program Director for Counseling Graduate Studies, 701-355-8177, Fax: 701-255-7687, E-mail: jrenner@umary.edu. *Application contact:* Jeanette Shaeffer, Accelerated and Distance Education Administrative Assistant, 701-355-8128, Fax: 701-255-7687, E-mail: jgschae@umary.edu.

University of Maryland, College Park, Academic Affairs, College of Behavioral and Social Sciences, Department of Psychology, College Park, MD 20742. Offers clinical psychology (PhD); developmental psychology (PhD); experimental psychology (PhD); industrial psychology (MA, MS, PhD); social psychology (PhD). *Accreditation:* APA (one or more programs are accredited). *Faculty:* 70 full-time (34 women), 16 part-time/adjunct (10 women). *Students:* 83 full-time (63 women), 6 part-time (4 women); includes 4 Black or African American, non-Hispanic/Latino; 6 Asian, non-Hispanic/Latino; 6 Hispanic/Latino, 13 international. 653 applicants, 4% accepted, 13 enrolled. In 2010, 8 master's, 18 doctorates awarded. *Degree requirements:* For master's, thesis; for doctorate, variable foreign language requirement, comprehensive exam, thesis/dissertation. *Entrance requirements:* For master's and doctorate, GRE General Test, GRE Subject Test, minimum GPA of 3.5, research and/or work experience, 3 letters of recommendation. *Application deadline:* For fall admission, 12/1 for domestic and international students. Applications are processed on a rolling basis. Application fee: $75. Electronic applications accepted. *Expenses:* Tuition, state resident: part-time $471 per credit hour. Tuition, nonresident: part-time $1016 per credit hour. Required fees: $337 per term. *Financial support:* In 2010–11, 14 fellowships with full and partial tuition reimbursements (averaging $20,179 per year), 5 research assistantships (averaging $18,414 per year), 54 teaching assistantships (averaging $17,209 per year) were awarded; career-related internships or fieldwork, Federal Work-Study, and scholarships/grants also available. Support available to part-time students. Financial award applicants required to submit FAFSA. *Faculty research:* Social stereotyping

Social Psychology

University of Maryland, College Park (continued)

and prejudice, anxiety disorders, auditory neuroethology, counseling and social psychology. Total annual research expenditures: $4 million. *Unit head:* Thomas S. Wallsten, Chair, 301-405-3562, Fax: 301-314-9566, E-mail: twallst@umd.edu. *Application contact:* Dean of Graduate School, 301-405-0358, Fax: 301-314-9305.

University of Massachusetts Amherst, Graduate School, College of Natural Sciences, Department of Psychology, Amherst, MA 01003. Offers clinical psychology (MS, PhD); cognitive psychology (MS, PhD); developmental science (MS, PhD); psychology of peace and violence (MS, PhD); social psychology (MS, PhD). *Accreditation:* APA (one or more programs are accredited). *Faculty:* 47 full-time (23 women). *Students:* 54 full-time (42 women), 6 part-time (4 women); includes 16 minority (3 Black or African American, non-Hispanic/Latino; 6 Asian, non-Hispanic/Latino; 4 Hispanic/Latino; 3 Two or more races, non-Hispanic/Latino), 3 international. Average age 29. 435 applicants, 4% accepted, 8 enrolled. In 2010, 12 master's, 16 doctorates awarded. Terminal master's awarded for partial completion of doctoral program. *Degree requirements:* For master's, thesis; for doctorate, comprehensive exam, thesis/dissertation. *Entrance requirements:* For master's and doctorate, GRE General Test, 3 letters of recommendation. Additional exam requirements/recommendations for international students: Required—TOEFL (minimum score 550 paper-based; 213 computer-based; 80 iBT), IELTS (minimum score 6.5). *Application deadline:* For fall admission, 12/1 for domestic and international students. Applications are processed on a rolling basis. Application fee: $50 ($65 for international students). Electronic applications accepted. *Expenses:* Tuition, state resident: full-time $2640. Required fees: $8282. One-time fee: $357 full-time. *Financial support:* In 2010–11, 8 fellowships with full tuition reimbursements (averaging $12,569 per year), 41 research assistantships with full tuition reimbursements (averaging $10,714 per year), 55 teaching assistantships with full tuition reimbursements (averaging $10,951 per year) were awarded; career-related internships or fieldwork, Federal Work-Study, scholarships/grants, traineeships, health care benefits, tuition waivers (full), and unspecified assistantships also available. Support available to part-time students. Financial award application deadline: 12/1; financial award applicants required to submit FAFSA. *Unit head:* Dr. Linda M. Isbell, Graduate Program Director, 413-545-2503, Fax: 413-545-0996. *Application contact:* Jean M. Ames, Supervisor of Admissions, 413-545-0722, Fax: 413-577-0010, E-mail: gradadm@grad.umass.edu.

University of Massachusetts Lowell, College of Arts and Sciences, Department of Psychology, Lowell, MA 01854-2881. Offers community social psychology (MA). Part-time programs available. *Degree requirements:* For master's, thesis optional. *Entrance requirements:* For master's, GRE General Test or MAT. Electronic applications accepted. *Faculty research:* Domestic violence, youth sports, teen pregnancy, substance abuse, family and work roles.

University of Michigan, Horace H. Rackham School of Graduate Studies, College of Literature, Science, and the Arts, Department of Psychology, Ann Arbor, MI 48109. Offers biopsychology (PhD); clinical psychology (PhD); cognition and perception (PhD); developmental psychology (PhD); personality and social contexts (PhD); social psychology (PhD). *Accreditation:* APA. *Faculty:* 83 full-time (39 women), 30 part-time/adjunct (14 women). *Students:* 132 full-time (92 women); includes 13 Black or African American, non-Hispanic/Latino; 2 American Indian or Alaska Native, non-Hispanic/Latino; 18 Asian, non-Hispanic/Latino; 7 Hispanic/Latino; 2 Two or more races, non-Hispanic/Latino, 20 international. Average age 27. 608 applicants, 6% accepted, 24 enrolled. In 2010, 28 doctorates awarded. *Degree requirements:* For doctorate, comprehensive exam, thesis/dissertation, oral defense of dissertation, preliminary exam. *Entrance requirements:* For doctorate, GRE General Test. Additional exam requirements/recommendations for international students: Required—TOEFL. *Application deadline:* For fall admission, 12/1 for domestic and international students. Application fee: $65 ($75 for international students). Electronic applications accepted. *Expenses:* Tuition, state resident: full-time $17,784; part-time $1116 per credit hour. Tuition, nonresident: full-time $35,944; part-time $2125 per credit hour. International tuition: $35,994 full-time. Required fees: $95 per semester. Tuition and fees vary according to course load, degree level and program. *Financial support:* In 2010–11, 118 students received support, including 55 fellowships with full tuition reimbursements available (averaging $20,900 per year), 15 research assistantships with full tuition reimbursements available (averaging $25,950 per year), 52 teaching assistantships with full tuition reimbursements available (averaging $22,670 per year); career-related internships or fieldwork also available. Financial award application deadline: 4/15. Total annual research expenditures: $7.4 million. *Unit head:* Prof. Theresa Lee, Chair, 734-764-7429. *Application contact:* Laurie Brannan, Psychology Student Academic Affairs, 731-764-2580, Fax: 734-615-7584, E-mail: psych.saa@umich.edu.

University of Minnesota, Twin Cities Campus, Graduate School, College of Liberal Arts, Department of Psychology, Program in Social Psychology, Minneapolis, MN 55455-0213. Offers PhD. *Degree requirements:* For doctorate, comprehensive exam, thesis/dissertation. *Entrance requirements:* For doctorate, GRE General Test, GRE Subject Test (recommended), 12 credits of upper-level psychology courses, including a course in statistics or psychological measurement. Additional exam requirements/recommendations for international students: Required—TOEFL (minimum score 550 paper-based; 213 computer-based; 79 iBT).

University of Missouri–Kansas City, College of Arts and Sciences, Department of Psychology, Kansas City, MO 64110-2499. Offers clinical psychology (PhD); community psychology (PhD); health psychology (PhD); psychology (MA). PhD (interdisciplinary) offered through the School of Graduate Studies. *Accreditation:* APA. *Faculty:* 14 full-time (10 women), 4 part-time/adjunct (3 women). *Students:* 17 full-time (11 women), 7 part-time (all women); includes 1 Black or African American, non-Hispanic/Latino; 1 Asian, non-Hispanic/Latino; 3 Hispanic/Latino. Average age 30. 89 applicants, 9% accepted, 6 enrolled. In 2010, 6 master's, 4 doctorates awarded. Terminal master's awarded for partial completion of doctoral program. *Degree requirements:* For master's, thesis; for doctorate, comprehensive exam, thesis/dissertation, residency. *Entrance requirements:* For master's, GRE, minimum GPA of 3.5, letter of recommendation; for doctorate, GRE, minimum GPA of 3.25. Additional exam requirements/recommendations for international students: Required—TOEFL (minimum score 550 paper-based; 213 computer-based; 80 iBT). *Application deadline:* For fall admission, 1/15 for domestic and international students. Applications are processed on a rolling basis. Application fee: $45 ($50 for international students). Electronic applications accepted. *Expenses:* Tuition, state resident: full-time $5522.40; part-time $306.80 per credit hour. Tuition, nonresident: full-time $7128; part-time $792 per credit hour. Required fees: $261.15 per term. *Financial support:* In 2010–11, 18 research assistantships (averaging $11,778 per year), 6 teaching assistantships (averaging $11,500 per year) were awarded; career-related internships or fieldwork, Federal Work-Study, and institutionally sponsored loans also available. Support available to part-time students. Financial award application deadline: 3/1; financial award applicants required to submit FAFSA. *Faculty research:* HIV/AIDS research group, psycho-oncology, sensory and cognitive neuroscience, cognitive psychophysiology, obesity and related metabolic disorders. Total annual research expenditures: $933,609. *Unit head:* Dr. Tamera Murdock, Chairperson/Professor, 816-235-1318, Fax: 816-235-1062, E-mail: murdockt@umkc.edu. *Application contact:* Dr. Lisa Terre, Director, Graduate Programs, 816-235-1318, Fax: 816-235-1062, E-mail: terrel@umkc.edu.

University of Missouri–St. Louis, College of Arts and Sciences, Department of Psychology, St. Louis, MO 63121. Offers behavioral neuroscience (PhD); clinical community psychology (PhD); clinical psychology respecialization (Certificate); general psychology (MA); industrial/organizational psychology (PhD); trauma studies (Certificate). *Accreditation:* APA (one or more programs are accredited). Evening/weekend programs available. *Faculty:* 19 full-time (9 women), 5 part-time/adjunct (3 women). *Students:* 44 full-time (34 women), 35 part-time (25 women); includes 7 minority (1 Black or African American, non-Hispanic/Latino; 1 American Indian or Alaska Native, non-Hispanic/Latino; 3 Asian, non-Hispanic/Latino; 2 Hispanic/Latino). Average age 27. 220 applicants, 10% accepted, 18 enrolled. In 2010, 10 master's, 6 doctorates awarded. Terminal master's awarded for partial completion of doctoral program. *Degree requirements:* For master's, thesis; for doctorate, thesis/dissertation. *Entrance requirements:* For master's, GRE General Test, 3 letters of recommendation; for doctorate, GRE General Test, GRE Subject Test, 3 letters of recommendation. Additional exam requirements/recommendations for international students: Required—TOEFL (minimum score 550 paper-based; 213 computer-based). *Application deadline:* For fall admission, 1/15 for domestic and international students. Application fee: $35 ($40 for international students). Electronic applications accepted. *Expenses:* Tuition, state resident: full-time $5522; part-time $306.80 per credit hour. Tuition, nonresident: full-time $14,253; part-time $792.10 per credit hour. Required fees: $658; $49 per credit hour. One-time fee: $12. Tuition and fees vary according to program. *Financial support:* In 2010–11, 5 research assistantships with full and partial tuition reimbursements (averaging $13,352 per year), 26 teaching assistantships with full and partial tuition reimbursements (averaging $11,000 per year) were awarded; fellowships with full tuition reimbursements also available. Financial award applicants required to submit FAFSA. *Faculty research:* Bereavement and loss, neuroscience, post-traumatic stress disorder, conflict and negotiation, social psychology. *Unit head:* Dr. George Taylor, Chair, 314-516-5391, Fax: 314-516-5392, E-mail: umslpsychology@msx.umsl.edu. *Application contact:* 314-516-5458, Fax: 314-516-6996, E-mail: gradadm@umsl.edu.

University of Missouri–St. Louis, College of Education, Division of Counseling, St. Louis, MO 63121. Offers community counseling (M Ed); elementary school counseling (M Ed); secondary school counseling (M Ed). *Accreditation:* ACA; NCATE. Part-time and evening/weekend programs available. *Faculty:* 7 full-time (3 women), 11 part-time/adjunct (7 women). *Students:* 50 full-time (44 women), 165 part-time (135 women); includes 40 minority (33 Black or African American, non-Hispanic/Latino; 2 Asian, non-Hispanic/Latino; 5 Hispanic/Latino), 4 international. Average age 31. 97 applicants, 52% accepted, 32 enrolled. In 2010, 61 master's awarded. *Degree requirements:* For master's, comprehensive exam. *Entrance requirements:* For master's, 3 letters of recommendation. Additional exam requirements/recommendations for international students: Required—TOEFL (minimum score 550 paper-based; 213 computer-based). *Application deadline:* For fall admission, 6/1 for domestic and international students; for spring admission, 10/1 for domestic and international students. Application fee: $35 ($40 for international students). Electronic applications accepted. *Expenses:* Tuition, state resident: full-time $5522; part-time $306.80 per credit hour. Tuition, nonresident: full-time $14,253; part-time $792.10 per credit hour. Required fees: $658; $49 per credit hour. One-time fee: $12. Tuition and fees vary according to program. *Financial support:* In 2010–11, 1 research assistantship with full and partial tuition reimbursement (averaging $12,240 per year), 1 teaching assistantship with full and partial tuition reimbursement (averaging $10,381 per year) were awarded. Financial award application deadline: 4/1; financial award applicants required to submit FAFSA. *Faculty research:* Vocational interests, self-concept, decision-making factors, developmental differences. *Unit head:* Dr. Mark Pope, Chair, 314-516-5782. *Application contact:* 314-516-5458, Fax: 314-516-6996, E-mail: gradadm@umsl.edu.

University of Montevallo, College of Education, Program in Counseling, Montevallo, AL 35115. Offers community counseling (M Ed); marriage and family (M Ed); school counseling (M Ed). *Accreditation:* ACA; NCATE. Part-time and evening/weekend programs available. *Students:* 44 full-time (34 women), 42 part-time (35 women); includes 11 minority (10 Black or African American, non-Hispanic/Latino; 1 American Indian or Alaska Native, non-Hispanic/Latino), 1 international. In 2010, 21 master's awarded. *Entrance requirements:* For master's, GRE General Test or MAT, minimum undergraduate GPA of 2.75 in last 60 hours or 2.5 overall, interview. Additional exam requirements/recommendations for international students: Required—TOEFL (minimum score 550 paper-based). *Application deadline:* For fall admission, 7/15 for domestic students; for spring admission, 11/15 for domestic students. Application fee: $25. *Expenses:* Tuition, state resident: full-time $6264; part-time $261 per credit hour. Tuition, nonresident: full-time $12,528; part-time $502 per credit hour. Required fees: $251 per semester. *Financial support:* Federal Work-Study, scholarships/grants, and unspecified assistantships available. *Unit head:* Dr. Leland Doebler, Chair, 205-665-6380. *Application contact:* Dr. Leland Doebler, Chair, 205-665-6380.

University of Nebraska–Lincoln, Graduate College, College of Arts and Sciences, Department of Psychology, Lincoln, NE 68588. Offers biopsychology (PhD); clinical psychology (PhD); cognitive psychology (PhD); developmental psychology (PhD); psychology (MA); social/personality psychology (PhD); JD/MA; JD/PhD. *Accreditation:* APA (one or more programs are accredited). *Degree requirements:* For master's, thesis optional; for doctorate, comprehensive exam, thesis/dissertation. *Entrance requirements:* For master's and doctorate, GRE General Test. Additional exam requirements/recommendations for international students: Required—TOEFL (minimum score 550 paper-based; 213 computer-based). Electronic applications accepted. *Faculty research:* Law and psychology, rural mental health, chronic mental illness, neuropsychology, child clinical psychology.

University of Nevada, Reno, Graduate School, Interdisciplinary Program in Social Psychology, Reno, NV 89557. Offers PhD. *Degree requirements:* For doctorate, one foreign language, thesis/dissertation. *Entrance requirements:* For doctorate, GRE General Test, GRE Subject Test (psychology or sociology), minimum GPA of 3.0. Additional exam requirements/recommendations for international students: Required—TOEFL (minimum score 500 paper-based; 173 computer-based; 61 iBT), IELTS (minimum score 6). Electronic applications accepted. *Expenses:* Tuition, state resident: full-time $2219; part-time $246 per credit. Tuition, nonresident: part-time $510 per credit. International tuition: $9009 full-time. Required fees: $59 per term. One-time fee: $101. Tuition and fees vary according to course load. *Faculty research:* Social psychological theory, social psychology of law.

University of New Haven, Graduate School, College of Arts and Sciences, Program in Community Psychology, West Haven, CT 06516-1916. Offers applications of psychology (Certificate); community clinical services (MA); forensic psychology (Certificate). Part-time and evening/weekend programs available. *Students:* 22 full-time (19 women), 11 part-time (7 women); includes 6 Black or African American, non-Hispanic/Latino; 2 Hispanic/Latino, 2 international. Average age 29. 29 applicants, 100% accepted, 12 enrolled. In 2010, 24 master's awarded. *Degree requirements:* For master's, thesis or alternative. *Entrance requirements:* Additional exam requirements/recommendations for international students: Required—TOEFL (minimum score 520 paper-based; 190 computer-based; 70 iBT); Recommended—IELTS (minimum score 5.5). *Application deadline:* For fall admission, 5/31 for international students; for winter admission, 10/15 for international students; for spring admission, 1/15 for international students. Applications are processed on a rolling basis. Application fee: $50. Electronic applications accepted. *Financial support:* Research assistantships with partial tuition reimbursements, teaching assistantships with partial tuition reimbursements, career-related internships or fieldwork, Federal Work-Study, scholarships/grants, tuition waivers, and unspecified assistantships available. Support available to part-time students. Financial award application deadline: 5/1; financial award applicants required to submit FAFSA. *Unit head:* Dr. Michael A. Morris, Coordinator, 203-932-7281. *Application contact:* Eloise Gormley, Director of Graduate Admissions, 203-932-7449, Fax: 203-932-7137, E-mail: gradinfo@newhaven.edu.

The University of North Carolina at Chapel Hill, Graduate School, College of Arts and Sciences, Department of Psychology, Chapel Hill, NC 27599. Offers biological psychology (PhD); clinical psychology (PhD); cognitive psychology (PhD); developmental psychology (PhD); quantitative psychology (PhD); social psychology (PhD). *Accreditation:* APA. *Degree requirements:* For doctorate, comprehensive exam, thesis/dissertation. *Entrance requirements:* For doctorate, GRE General Test, minimum GPA of 3.0. Electronic applications accepted. *Faculty research:* Expressed emotion, cognitive development, social cognitive neuroscience, human memory personality.

The University of North Carolina at Charlotte, Graduate School, College of Arts and Sciences, Department of Psychology, Charlotte, NC 28223-0001. Offers community/clinical psychology (MA); health psychology (PhD); industrial/organizational psychology (MA); organizational science (PhD). Part-time programs available. *Faculty:* 27 full-time (11 women), 1 part-time/adjunct (0 women). *Students:* 67 full-time (50 women), 18 part-time (14 women); includes 19 minority (8 Black or African American, non-Hispanic/Latino; 3 Asian, non-Hispanic/

Latino; 4 Hispanic/Latino; 1 Native Hawaiian or other Pacific Islander, non-Hispanic/Latino; 3 Two or more races, non-Hispanic/Latino), 3 international. Average age 29. 317 applicants, 9% accepted, 21 enrolled. In 2010, 14 master's, 1 doctorate awarded. *Degree requirements:* For master's, thesis; for doctorate, thesis/dissertation. *Entrance requirements:* For master's, GRE General Test, GRE Subject Test, minimum GPA of 3.0 in undergraduate major, 2.8 overall. Additional exam requirements/recommendations for international students: Required—TOEFL (minimum score 557 paper-based; 220 computer-based; 83 iBT). *Application deadline:* Applications are processed on a rolling basis. Application fee: $55. Electronic applications accepted. *Expenses:* Tuition, state resident: full-time $3464. Tuition, nonresident: full-time $14,297. Required fees: $2094. Tuition and fees vary according to course load. *Financial support:* In 2010–11, 44 students received support, including 12 research assistantships (averaging $14,191 per year), 31 teaching assistantships (averaging $10,710 per year); career-related internships or fieldwork, Federal Work-Study, institutionally sponsored loans, scholarships/grants, and administrative assistantships also available. Support available to part-time students. Financial award application deadline: 4/1; financial award applicants required to submit FAFSA. *Faculty research:* Health psychology, industrial-organizational psychology, cognitive science. Total annual research expenditures: $435,127. *Unit head:* Dr. Brian L. Cutler, Chair, 704-687-4731, Fax: 704-687-3096, E-mail: blcutler@uncc.edu. *Application contact:* Kathy B. Giddings, Director of Graduate Admissions, 704-687-5503, Fax: 704-687-3279, E-mail: gradadm@uncc.edu.

The University of North Carolina at Charlotte, Graduate School, College of Arts and Sciences, Department of Sociology, Charlotte, NC 28223-0001. Offers health research (MA); mathematical sociology and quantitative methods (MA); organizations, occupations, and work (MA); political sociology (MA); race and gender (MA); social psychology (MA); social theory (MA); sociology of education (MA); stratification (MA). Part-time and evening/weekend programs available. *Faculty:* 18 full-time (10 women). *Students:* 11 full-time (7 women), 14 part-time (8 women); includes 6 minority (4 Black or African American, non-Hispanic/Latino; 2 Asian, non-Hispanic/Latino). Average age 29. 20 applicants, 60% accepted, 8 enrolled. In 2010, 2 master's awarded. *Degree requirements:* For master's, thesis or alternative, thesis or comprehensive exam. *Entrance requirements:* For master's, GRE or MAT, minimum GPA of 3.0 in last 2 years, 2.75 overall. Additional exam requirements/recommendations for international students: Required—TOEFL (minimum score 557 paper-based; 220 computer-based; 83 iBT). *Application deadline:* For fall admission, 7/1 for domestic students, 5/1 for international students; for spring admission, 11/1 for domestic students, 10/1 for international students. Applications are processed on a rolling basis. Application fee: $55. Electronic applications accepted. *Expenses:* Tuition, state resident: full-time $3464. Tuition, nonresident: full-time $14,297. Required fees: $2094. Tuition and fees vary according to course load. *Financial support:* In 2010–11, 6 students received support, including 1 fellowship (averaging $60,000 per year), 1 research assistantship (averaging $9,000 per year), 1 teaching assistantship (averaging $9,000 per year); career-related internships or fieldwork, institutionally sponsored loans, scholarships/grants, and unspecified assistantships also available. Support available to part-time students. Financial award application deadline: 4/1; financial award applicants required to submit FAFSA. *Faculty research:* Social psychology, sociology of education, social gerontology, quantitative methodology, medical sociology. Total annual research expenditures: $61,382. *Unit head:* Dr. Lisa Rachotte, Chair, 704-687-2288, Fax: 704-687-3091, E-mail: lrashott@uncc.edu. *Application contact:* Kathy B. Giddings, Director of Graduate Admissions, 704-687-5503, Fax: 704-687-3279, E-mail: gradadm@uncc.edu.

The University of North Carolina at Greensboro, Graduate School, College of Arts and Sciences, Department of Psychology, Greensboro, NC 27412-5001. Offers clinical psychology (MA, PhD); cognitive psychology (MA, PhD); developmental psychology (MA, PhD); social psychology (MA, PhD). *Accreditation:* APA (one or more programs are accredited). Terminal master's awarded for partial completion of doctoral program. *Degree requirements:* For master's, comprehensive exam, thesis; for doctorate, one foreign language, thesis/dissertation, preliminary exam. *Entrance requirements:* For master's and doctorate, GRE General Test. Additional exam requirements/recommendations for international students: Required—TOEFL. Electronic applications accepted. *Faculty research:* Sensory and perceptual determinants; evoked potential: disorders, deafness, and development.

University of Oklahoma, Jeannine Rainbolt College of Education, Department of Educational Psychology, Program in Community Counseling, Norman, OK 73019. Offers M Ed. *Students:* 32 full-time (27 women), 2 part-time (1 woman); includes 8 minority (2 Black or African American, non-Hispanic/Latino; 2 American Indian or Alaska Native, non-Hispanic/Latino; 1 Asian, non-Hispanic/Latino; 2 Hispanic/Latino; 1 Two or more races, non-Hispanic/Latino). Average age 25. 11 applicants, 0% accepted, 0 enrolled. In 2010, 13 master's awarded. Terminal master's awarded for partial completion of doctoral program. *Degree requirements:* For master's, comprehensive exam. *Entrance requirements:* For master's, GRE General Test, minimum GPA of 3.0. Additional exam requirements/recommendations for international students: Required—TOEFL (minimum score 550 paper-based; 213 computer-based; 79 iBT). *Application deadline:* For fall admission, 1/31 for domestic students, 4/1 for international students; for spring admission, 11/1 for domestic students, 9/1 for international students. Applications are processed on a rolling basis. Application fee: $40 ($90 for international students). Electronic applications accepted. *Expenses:* Tuition, state resident: full-time $3893; part-time $162.20 per credit hour. Tuition, nonresident: full-time $14,167; part-time $590.30 per credit hour. Required fees: $2523; $94.60 per credit hour. Tuition and fees vary according to course load and degree level. *Financial support:* In 2010–11, 24 students received support. Career-related internships or fieldwork, Federal Work-Study, scholarships/grants, health care benefits, and unspecified assistantships available. Support available to part-time students. Financial award application deadline: 3/1; financial award applicants required to submit FAFSA. *Faculty research:* Domestic violence, marriage and family, multicultural, training and supervision, trauma. *Unit head:* Dr. Terri K. Debacker, Chair, 405-325-1068, Fax: 405-325-6655, E-mail: debacker@ou.edu. *Application contact:* Rashida Y. Douglas, Graduate Programs Officer, 405-325-4525, Fax: 405-325-6655, E-mail: ryd618@ou.edu.

University of Oregon, Graduate School, College of Arts and Sciences, Department of Psychology, Eugene, OR 97403. Offers clinical psychology (PhD); cognitive psychology (MA, MS, PhD); developmental psychology (MA, MS, PhD); physiological psychology (MA, MS, PhD); psychology (MA, MS, PhD); social/personality psychology (MA, MS, PhD). *Accreditation:* APA (one or more programs are accredited). Terminal master's awarded for partial completion of doctoral program. *Degree requirements:* For doctorate, thesis/dissertation. *Entrance requirements:* For master's, GRE General Test, minimum GPA of 3.0; for doctorate, GRE General Test. Additional exam requirements/recommendations for international students: Required—TOEFL.

University of Phoenix, College of Social Science, Phoenix, AZ 85034-7209. Offers clinical mental health counseling (MSC); community counseling (MSC); psychology (MS). Programs are offered at the online campus. Evening/weekend programs available. Postbaccalaureate distance learning degree programs offered. *Students:* 4,215 full-time (3,585 women); includes 1,544 minority (1,161 Black or African American, non-Hispanic/Latino; 34 American Indian or Alaska Native, non-Hispanic/Latino; 32 Asian, non-Hispanic/Latino; 280 Hispanic/Latino; 22 Native Hawaiian or other Pacific Islander, non-Hispanic/Latino; 15 Two or more races, non-Hispanic/Latino), 85 international. Average age 38. *Entrance requirements:* For master's, minimum undergraduate GPA of 2.5 from accredited university, 3 years of work experience, citizen of the United States or have valid visa. Additional exam requirements/recommendations for international students: Required—TOEFL (minimum paper score 550, computer score 213, iBT 79), Test of English for International Communication, or IELTS. *Application deadline:* Applications are processed on a rolling basis. Application fee: $45. Electronic applications accepted. *Expenses:* Tuition: Full-time $16,440. One-time fee: $45 full-time. Full-time tuition and fees vary according to course load, degree level, campus/location and program. *Financial support:* Scholarships/grants available. Financial award applicants required to submit FAFSA. *Unit head:* Rob Olding, Associate Dean, Human Service/Psychology, 602-551-3073, E-mail: rob.olding@phoenix.edu. *Application contact:* Rob Olding, Associate Dean, Human Service/Psychology, 602-551-3073, E-mail: rob.olding@phoenix.edu.

University of Phoenix–Minneapolis/St. Louis Park Campus, College of Human Services, St. Louis Park, MN 55426. Offers community counseling (MSC).

University of Phoenix–Phoenix Campus, College of Social Sciences, Phoenix, AZ 85040-1958. Offers community counseling (MC); counseling (MSC); psychology (MSP). Evening/weekend programs available. Postbaccalaureate distance learning degree programs offered. *Students:* 181 full-time (140 women); includes 23 minority (7 Black or African American, non-Hispanic/Latino; 2 Asian, non-Hispanic/Latino; 14 Hispanic/Latino), 7 international. Average age 34. *Entrance requirements:* For master's, minimum undergraduate GPA of 2.5 from accredited university, 3 years of work experience, citizen of the United States or have valid visa. Additional exam requirements/recommendations for international students: Required—TOEFL (minimum paper score 500, computer score 213, iBT 79), Test of English for International Communication, or IELTS. *Application deadline:* Applications are processed on a rolling basis. Application fee: $45. Electronic applications accepted. *Expenses:* Tuition: Full-time $13,560. One-time fee: $45 full-time. Full-time tuition and fees vary according to course load, degree level, campus/location and program. *Financial support:* Scholarships/grants available. Financial award applicants required to submit FAFSA. *Unit head:* Dr. Lynn Hall, Dean/Executive Director, 520-247-4364, E-mail: lynn.hall@phoenix.edu. *Application contact:* Campus Information Center, 866-766-0766.

University of Phoenix–Southern California Campus, College of Social Sciences, Costa Mesa, CA 92626. Offers administration of justice and security (MS); community counseling (MSC); marriage, family and child therapy (MSC); mental health counseling (MSC); psychology (MS); school counseling (MSC). Evening/weekend programs available. *Degree requirements:* For master's, thesis (for some programs). *Entrance requirements:* For master's, minimum undergraduate GPA of 3.0, 3 years work experience. Additional exam requirements/recommendations for international students: Required—TOEFL (minimum score 550 paper-based; 213 computer-based; 79 iBT). Electronic applications accepted.

University of Puerto Rico, Río Piedras, College of Social Sciences, Department of Psychology, San Juan, PR 00931-3300. Offers clinical psychology (MA); industrial organizational psychology (MA); investigative academic psychology (MA); psychology (PhD); social-community psychology (MA). Part-time programs available. *Degree requirements:* For master's, comprehensive exam, thesis; for doctorate, comprehensive exam, thesis/dissertation, internship. *Entrance requirements:* For master's, GRE or PAEG, interview, minimum GPA of 3.0; for doctorate, GRE or PAEG, interview, master's degree, minimum GPA of 3.0. *Faculty research:* Intervention on Depressed Latino Youth, biosychosocial training.

University of Rochester, School of Arts and Sciences, Department of Clinical and Social Sciences in Psychology, Rochester, NY 14627. Offers clinical psychology (PhD); developmental psychology (PhD); psychology (MA); social-personality psychology (PhD). *Accreditation:* APA (one or more programs are accredited). Terminal master's awarded for partial completion of doctoral program. *Degree requirements:* For doctorate, thesis/dissertation, qualifying exam. *Entrance requirements:* For doctorate, GRE General Test. Additional exam requirements/recommendations for international students: Required—TOEFL.

The University of Scranton, College of Graduate and Continuing Education, Department of Counseling and Human Services, Program in Community Counseling, Scranton, PA 18510. Offers MS. *Accreditation:* ACA. Part-time and evening/weekend programs available. *Students:* 44 full-time (36 women), 12 part-time (8 women); includes 2 Black or African American, non-Hispanic/Latino; 2 Asian, non-Hispanic/Latino; 1 Hispanic/Latino. Average age 30. 44 applicants, 45% accepted. In 2010, 16 master's awarded. *Degree requirements:* For master's, comprehensive exam, capstone experience. *Entrance requirements:* For master's, minimum GPA of 2.75. Additional exam requirements/recommendations for international students: Required—TOEFL (minimum score 500 paper-based; 173 computer-based), IELTS (minimum score 5.5). *Application deadline:* For fall admission, 3/1 for domestic students. Application fee: $0. *Financial support:* Teaching assistantships, career-related internships or fieldwork and Federal Work-Study available. Support available to part-time students. Financial award application deadline: 3/1. *Unit head:* Dr. Amy Banner, Program Director, 570-941-4129, Fax: 570-941-6492, E-mail: bannera2@scranton.edu. *Application contact:* Joseph M. Roback, Director of Admissions, 570-941-4385, Fax: 570-941-5928, E-mail: robackj2@scranton.edu.

University of South Carolina, The Graduate School, College of Arts and Sciences, Department of Psychology, Program in Clinical/Community Psychology, Columbia, SC 29208. Offers clinical/community psychology (PhD); general psychology (MA). *Accreditation:* APA. *Degree requirements:* For master's, comprehensive exam, thesis; for doctorate, comprehensive exam, thesis/dissertation. *Entrance requirements:* For doctorate, GRE General Test, minimum GPA of 3.2. Additional exam requirements/recommendations for international students: Required—TOEFL. Electronic applications accepted. *Faculty research:* Developmental psychopathology, health disparities, community-level interventions for psychological well being.

University of Southern California, Graduate School, Dana and David Dornsife College of Letters, Arts and Sciences, Department of Psychology, Los Angeles, CA 90089. Offers brain and cognitive science (PhD); clinical science (PhD); developmental psychology (PhD); human behavior (MHB); quantitative methods (PhD); social psychology (PhD). *Accreditation:* APA. *Faculty:* 34 full-time (10 women), 15 part-time/adjunct (9 women). *Students:* 105 full-time (65 women), 3 part-time (all women); includes 32 minority (4 Black or African American, non-Hispanic/Latino; 17 Asian, non-Hispanic/Latino; 9 Hispanic/Latino; 2 Two or more races, non-Hispanic/Latino), 22 international. 543 applicants, 5% accepted, 14 enrolled. In 2010, 17 master's, 12 doctorates awarded. *Degree requirements:* For doctorate, comprehensive exam, thesis/dissertation, one-year internship (for clinical science students). *Entrance requirements:* For doctorate, GRE. Additional exam requirements/recommendations for international students: Recommended—TOEFL (minimum score 600 paper-based; 250 computer-based; 100 iBT). *Application deadline:* For fall admission, 12/1 for domestic and international students. Application fee: $85. Electronic applications accepted. *Expenses:* Tuition: Full-time $31,240; part-time $1420 per unit. Required fees: $600. One-time fee: $35 full-time. Full-time tuition and fees vary according to degree level and program. *Financial support:* In 2010–11, 85 students received support, including 30 fellowships with full tuition reimbursements available (averaging $24,000 per year), 12 research assistantships with full tuition reimbursements available (averaging $19,250 per year), 40 teaching assistantships with full tuition reimbursements available (averaging $19,250 per year); scholarships/grants, traineeships, health care benefits, and unspecified assistantships also available. Financial award application deadline: 12/1. *Faculty research:* Affective neuroscience; children and families; vision, culture and ethnicity; intergroup relations; aggression and violence; language and reading development; substance abuse. *Unit head:* Dr. Margaret Gatz, Chair and Professor, 213-740-2212, Fax: 213-746-9028, E-mail: gatz@usc.edu. *Application contact:* Irene Takaragawa, Graduate Advisor, 213-740-2205, Fax: 213-746-9082, E-mail: itakarag@usc.edu.

The University of Tennessee at Chattanooga, Graduate School, College of Health, Education and Professional Studies, Graduate Studies Division of Education, Program in Counseling, Chattanooga, TN 37403. Offers community counseling (M Ed); school counseling (M Ed). *Faculty:* 3 full-time (all women). *Students:* 22 full-time (21 women), 31 part-time (28 women); includes 5 minority (4 Black or African American, non-Hispanic/Latino; 1 Two or more races, non-Hispanic/Latino). Average age 28. 34 applicants, 50% accepted, 12 enrolled. In 2010, 14 master's awarded. *Degree requirements:* For master's, comprehensive exam. *Entrance requirements:* For master's, MAT or GRE. Additional exam requirements/recommendations for international students: Required—TOEFL (minimum score 550 paper-based; 213 computer-based; 79 iBT), IELTS (minimum score 6). *Application deadline:* For fall admission, 8/1 for domestic students, 6/1 for international students; for spring admission, 12/1 for domestic students, 10/1 for international students. Applications are processed on a rolling basis. Application fee: $35. Electronic applications accepted. *Financial support:* In 2010–11, 4 research assistantships with full and partial tuition reimbursements (averaging $5,500 per year) were awarded; career-related internships or fieldwork, scholarships/grants, and unspecified assistantships also available. Support available to part-time students. *Faculty research:* Play therapy; clinical

Social Psychology

The University of Tennessee at Chattanooga (continued)

supervision; technology in marital infidelity; female inmates and recidivism; grief, loss and trauma in children. *Unit head:* Dr. John Freeman, Head, 423-425-4133, Fax: 423-425-5380, E-mail: john-freeman@utc.edu. *Application contact:* Dr. Jerald Ainsworth, Dean of Graduate Studies, 423-425-4478, Fax: 423-425-4478, E-mail: jerald-ainsworth@utc.edu.

The University of Tennessee at Martin, Graduate Programs, College of Education and Behavioral Sciences, Program in Counseling, Martin, TN 38238. Offers community counseling (MS Ed); school counseling (MS Ed). *Accreditation:* NCATE. Part-time programs available. Postbaccalaureate distance learning degree programs offered. *Students:* 70 (63 women); includes 7 Black or African American, non-Hispanic/Latino; 1 Hispanic/Latino; 1 Two or more races, non-Hispanic/Latino. 39 applicants, 59% accepted, 22 enrolled. In 2010, 16 master's awarded. *Degree requirements:* For master's, comprehensive exam. *Entrance requirements:* For master's, GRE General Test, minimum GPA of 2.5, resume, letters of reference. Additional exam requirements/recommendations for international students: Required—TOEFL (minimum score 525 paper-based; 197 computer-based; 71 iBT). *Application deadline:* For fall admission, 8/1 priority date for domestic students, 7/15 priority date for international students; for spring admission, 12/15 priority date for domestic students, 12/1 priority date for international students. Applications are processed on a rolling basis. Application fee: $30 ($130 for international students). Electronic applications accepted. *Expenses:* Tuition, state resident: full-time $7164; part-time $400 per credit hour. Tuition, nonresident: full-time $19,574; part-time $1090 per credit hour. Required fees: $1044; $60 per credit hour. *Financial support:* Scholarships/grants and unspecified assistantships available. Support available to part-time students. Financial award application deadline: 2/15; financial award applicants required to submit FAFSA. *Unit head:* Staci H. Fuqua, Staff Assistant, 731-881-7163, Fax: 731-881-7975, E-mail: sfuqua@utm.edu. *Application contact:* Linda S. Arant, Student Services Specialist, 731-881-7012, Fax: 731-881-7499, E-mail: larant@utm.edu.

The University of Toledo, College of Graduate Studies, Judith Herb College of Education, Health Science and Human Service, Department of School Psychology, Legal Specialties and Counselor Education, Toledo, OH 43606-3390. Offers counselor education (MA, PhD, Ed S), including community counseling (MA), counselor education (Ed S), counselor education and supervision (PhD); school psychology (MA, Ed S), including school counseling (MA), school psychology (Ed S). Part-time programs available. *Faculty:* 14. *Students:* 64 full-time (46 women), 62 part-time (48 women); includes 13 Black or African American, non-Hispanic/Latino; 1 Asian, non-Hispanic/Latino; 5 Hispanic/Latino, 3 international. Average age 31. 91 applicants, 54% accepted, 42 enrolled. In 2010, 45 master's, 3 doctorates, 4 other advanced degrees awarded. *Degree requirements:* For master's, comprehensive exam, thesis or alternative; for doctorate, comprehensive exam, thesis/dissertation; for Ed S, thesis optional. *Entrance requirements:* For master's and Ed S, GRE or other qualifying exams required vary by program. A minimum 2.70 cumulative GPA all previous academic work. Two/Three Letters of Recommendation (as required per program). ; for doctorate, GRE or other qualifying exams required vary by program. A minimum 2.70 cumulative GPA all previous academic work. Two/Three Letters of Recommendation (as required per program). . Additional exam requirements/recommendations for international students: Required—TOEFL (minimum score 550 paper-based; 213 computer-based; 80 iBT), IELTS (minimum score 6.5). *Application deadline:* For fall admission, 1/15 priority date for domestic and international students. Applications are processed on a rolling basis. Application fee: $45 ($75 for international students). Electronic applications accepted. *Expenses:* Tuition, state resident: full-time $11,426; part-time $476 per credit hour. Tuition, nonresident: full-time $21,660; part-time $903 per credit hour. One-time fee: $62. *Financial support:* Research assistantships with tuition reimbursements, teaching assistantships with tuition reimbursements, career-related internships or fieldwork, Federal Work-Study, institutionally sponsored loans, scholarships/grants, tuition waivers (full and partial), and unspecified assistantships available. *Unit head:* Dr. Martin Ritchie, Chair, 419-530-4775, E-mail: martin.ritchie@utoledo.edu. *Application contact:* Graduate School Office, 419-530-4723, Fax: 419-530-4724, E-mail: grdsch@utnet.utoledo.edu.

University of Victoria, Faculty of Graduate Studies, Faculty of Education, Department of Educational Psychology and Leadership Studies, Victoria, BC V8W 2Y2, Canada. Offers aboriginal communities counseling (M Ed); counseling (M Ed, MA); educational psychology (M Ed, MA, PhD), including counseling psychology (M Ed, MA), leadership studies (PhD), learning and development (MA, PhD), measurement and evaluation, special education (M Ed, MA); leadership studies (M Ed, MA). Part-time programs available. *Degree requirements:* For master's, thesis (for some programs), comprehensive exam (M Ed); for doctorate, comprehensive exam, thesis/dissertation, candidacy exam. *Entrance requirements:* For master's, 2 years of work experience in a relevant field; for doctorate, GRE, 2 years of work experience in a relevant field, minimum B average. Additional exam requirements/recommendations for international students: Required—TOEFL (minimum score 575 paper-based; 233 computer-based), IELTS (minimum score 7). *Faculty research:* Learning and development (child, adolescent and adult), special education and exceptional children.

University of Victoria, Faculty of Graduate Studies, Faculty of Social Sciences, Department of Psychology, Victoria, BC V8W 2Y2, Canada. Offers clinical psychology (PhD); clinical psychology (neuropsychology) (M Sc); cognition and brain science (M Sc, PhD); experimental neuropsychology (M Sc, PhD); individualized study (M Sc, PhD); life span development psychology (PhD); life span developmental psychology (M Sc); social psychology (M Sc, PhD). *Accreditation:* APA (one or more programs are accredited). *Degree requirements:* For master's, thesis; for doctorate, thesis/dissertation, candidacy exam. *Entrance requirements:* For master's and doctorate, GRE General Test. Additional exam requirements/recommendations for international students: Required—TOEFL (minimum score 600 paper-based; 250 computer-based). Electronic applications accepted. *Faculty research:* Life span development psychology and aging, behavioral neuroscience, cognitive psychology, behavioral psychology, environmental psychology.

University of Washington, Graduate School, College of Arts and Sciences, Department of Psychology, Seattle, WA 98195. Offers animal behavior (PhD); child psychology (PhD); clinical psychology (PhD); cognition and perception (PhD); developmental psychology (PhD); quantitative psychology (PhD); social psychology and personality (PhD). *Accreditation:* APA. *Degree requirements:* For doctorate, thesis/dissertation. *Entrance requirements:* For doctorate, GRE General Test, minimum GPA of 3.0. Electronic applications accepted. *Faculty research:* Addictive behaviors, artificial intelligence, child psychopathology, mechanisms and development of vision, physiology of ingestive behaviors.

University of Windsor, Faculty of Graduate Studies, Faculty of Arts and Social Sciences, Department of Psychology, Windsor, ON N9B 3P4, Canada. Offers adult clinical (MA, PhD); applied social psychology (MA, PhD); child clinical (MA, PhD); clinical neuropsychology (MA, PhD). *Accreditation:* APA (one or more programs are accredited). *Degree requirements:* For master's, thesis; for doctorate, comprehensive exam, thesis/dissertation. *Entrance requirements:* For master's, GRE General Test, GRE Subject Test in psychology, minimum B average; for doctorate, GRE General Test, GRE Subject Test in psychology, master's degree. Additional exam requirements/recommendations for international students: Required—TOEFL (minimum score 600 paper-based; 250 computer-based). Electronic applications accepted. *Faculty research:* Gambling, suicidology, emotional competence, psychotherapy and trauma.

University of Wisconsin–Madison, Graduate School, College of Letters and Science, Department of Psychology, Program in Social and Personality Psychology, Madison, WI 53706-1380. Offers PhD. *Degree requirements:* For doctorate, comprehensive exam, thesis/dissertation. *Entrance requirements:* For doctorate, GRE General Test, minimum undergraduate GPA of 3.0. Additional exam requirements/recommendations for international students: Required—TOEFL. Electronic applications accepted. *Expenses:* Tuition, state resident: full-time $9887; part-time $617.96 per credit. Tuition, nonresident: full-time $24,054; part-time $1503.40 per credit. Required fees: $67.63 per credit. Tuition and fees vary according to reciprocity agreements.

University of Wisconsin–Milwaukee, Graduate School, School of Education, Department of Educational Psychology, Milwaukee, WI 53201-0413. Offers counseling (school, community) (MS); counseling psychology (PhD); learning and development (MS); research methodology (MS, PhD); school psychology (PhD). *Accreditation:* APA. Part-time programs available. *Faculty:* 22 full-time (14 women). *Students:* 158 full-time (130 women), 62 part-time (48 women); includes 14 Black or African American, non-Hispanic/Latino; 8 Asian, non-Hispanic/Latino; 5 Hispanic/Latino, 10 international. Average age 30. 278 applicants, 41% accepted. In 2010, 69 master's, 8 doctorates awarded. *Degree requirements:* For master's, comprehensive exam, thesis; for doctorate, thesis/dissertation. *Entrance requirements:* For master's, minimum GPA of 3.0; for doctorate, GRE General Test, minimum GPA of 3.0. Additional exam requirements/recommendations for international students: Required—TOEFL (minimum score 550 paper-based; 79 iBT), IELTS (minimum score 6.5). *Application deadline:* For fall admission, 1/1 priority date for domestic students; for spring admission, 9/1 for domestic students. Applications are processed on a rolling basis. Application fee: $56 ($96 for international students). Electronic applications accepted. *Financial support:* In 2010–11, 14 fellowships, 1 research assistantship, 8 teaching assistantships were awarded; career-related internships or fieldwork, health care benefits, unspecified assistantships, and project assistantships also available. Support available to part-time students. Financial award application deadline: 4/15; financial award applicants required to submit FAFSA. *Unit head:* Nadya Fouad, Graduate Program Representative, 414-229-4599, Fax: 414-229-4939, E-mail: nadya@uwm.edu. *Application contact:* General Information Contact, 414-229-4982, Fax: 414-229-6967, E-mail: gradschool@uwm.edu.

University of Wisconsin–Superior, Graduate Division, Department of Counseling and Psychological Professions, Superior, WI 54880-4500. Offers community counseling (MSE); human relations (MSE); school counseling (MSE). Part-time and evening/weekend programs available. *Degree requirements:* For master's, position paper, practicum. *Entrance requirements:* For master's, GRE and/or MAT, minimum GPA of 2.75. Electronic applications accepted. *Faculty research:* Women and power, intrafamily dynamics.

University of Wisconsin–Whitewater, School of Graduate Studies, College of Education, Department of Counselor Education, Whitewater, WI 53190-1790. Offers community counseling (MS Ed); higher education (MS Ed); school counseling (MS Ed). *Accreditation:* ACA; NCATE. Part-time and evening/weekend programs available. *Degree requirements:* For master's, thesis or alternative. *Entrance requirements:* For master's, resume, 2 letters of reference. Additional exam requirements/recommendations for international students: Required—TOEFL (minimum score 550 paper-based; 213 computer-based). Electronic applications accepted. *Faculty research:* Alcohol and other drugs, counseling effectiveness, teacher mentoring.

Virginia Commonwealth University, Graduate School, College of Humanities and Sciences, Department of Psychology, Program in General Psychology, Richmond, VA 23284-9005. Offers biopsychology (PhD); developmental psychology (PhD); social psychology (PhD). *Students:* 22 full-time (16 women), 9 part-time (4 women); includes 6 minority (4 Black or African American, non-Hispanic/Latino; 1 Asian, non-Hispanic/Latino; 1 Hispanic/Latino), 1 international. 68 applicants, 6% accepted, 1 enrolled. In 2010, 3 doctorates awarded. *Degree requirements:* For doctorate, thesis/dissertation. *Entrance requirements:* For doctorate, GRE General Test. Additional exam requirements/recommendations for international students: Required—TOEFL (minimum score 600 paper-based; 250 computer-based; 100 iBT); Recommended—IELTS (minimum score 6.5). *Application deadline:* For fall admission, 12/15 for domestic students. Application fee: $50. Electronic applications accepted. *Expenses:* Tuition, state resident: full-time $4308; part-time $479 per credit hour. Tuition, nonresident: full-time $8942; part-time $994 per credit hour. Required fees: $2000; $85 per credit hour. Tuition and fees vary according to course level, course load, degree level, campus/location and program. *Financial support:* Fellowships, research assistantships, teaching assistantships, Federal Work-Study, institutionally sponsored loans, and scholarships/grants available. Support available to part-time students. *Faculty research:* Biopsychology, developmental and social psychology. *Unit head:* Dr. Michael Southam-Gerow, Director, Graduate Programs in Psychology, 804-828-1193, Fax: 804-828-2237, E-mail: masouthamger@vcu.edu. *Application contact:* Dr. Joseph Porter, Director, Biopsychology Division, 804-828-0096, Fax: 804-828-2237, E-mail: jporter@vcu.edu.

Walden University, Graduate Programs, School of Psychology, Minneapolis, MN 55401. Offers clinical child psychology (Post-Doctoral Certificate); clinical psychology (MS, Post-Doctoral Certificate), including counseling (MS); counseling psychology (Post-Doctoral Certificate); forensic psychology (MS), including forensic psychology in the community, general program, mental health applications, program planning and evaluation in forensic settings, psychology and legal systems; general psychology (Post-Doctoral Certificate); health psychology (Post-Doctoral Certificate); organizational psychology (Post-Doctoral Certificate); organizational psychology and development (Postbaccalaureate Certificate); psychology (MS, PhD), including clinical psychology (PhD), counseling psychology (PhD), crisis management and response (MS), general program (MS), general psychology (PhD), health psychology, leadership development and coaching (MS), media psychology (MS), organizational psychology (PhD), organizational psychology and development (MS), organizational psychology and nonprofit management (MS), program evaluation and research (MS), psychology of culture (MS), psychology, public administration, and social change (MS), social psychology (MS), terrorism and security (MS); teaching online (Post-Master's Certificate). Part-time and evening/weekend programs available. Postbaccalaureate distance learning degree programs offered (minimal on-campus study). *Faculty:* 41 full-time (25 women), 254 part-time/adjunct (131 women). *Students:* 3,463 full-time (2,737 women), 1,400 part-time (1,130 women); includes 1,491 Black or African American, non-Hispanic/Latino; 59 American Indian or Alaska Native, non-Hispanic/Latino; 89 Asian, non-Hispanic/Latino; 283 Hispanic/Latino; 76 Two or more races, non-Hispanic/Latino, 126 international. Average age 40. In 2010, 559 master's, 100 doctorates awarded. Terminal master's awarded for partial completion of doctoral program. *Degree requirements:* For master's, thesis optional; for doctorate, thesis/dissertation, residency. *Entrance requirements:* For master's, bachelor's degree or equivalent in related field; minimum GPA of 2.5; official transcripts; goal statement; access to computer and Internet; for doctorate, master's degree or equivalent in related field; minimum GPA of 3.0; 3 years of related professional/academic experience (preferred). Additional exam requirements/recommendations for international students: Required—TOEFL (minimum score 550 paper-based; 213 computer-based), IELTS (minimum score 6.5), TOEFL (minimum score 550 paper-based; 213 computer-based), IELTS (minimum score 6.5), or Michigan English Language Assessment Battery (minimum score 82). *Application deadline:* Applications are processed on a rolling basis. Application fee: $50. Electronic applications accepted. *Expenses:* Tuition: Full-time $10,274; part-time $445 per credit. Tuition and fees vary according to course load, degree level and program. *Financial support:* In 2010–11, 1 fellowship was awarded; Federal Work-Study, scholarships/grants, unspecified assistantships, and family tuition reduction, active duty/veteran tuition reduction, group tuition reduction, interest-free payment plans also available. Support available to part-time students. Financial award applicants required to submit FAFSA. *Unit head:* Dr. Melanie Storms, Associate Dean, 800-925-3368. *Application contact:* Jennifer Hall, Vice President of Enrollment Management, 866-4-WALDEN, E-mail: info@waldenu.edu.

Washington State University, Graduate School, College of Liberal Arts, Department of Sociology, Pullman, WA 99164. Offers crime and deviance (MA, PhD); environments, community and demographics (MA, PhD); institutions and social organizations (MA, PhD); political sociology (MA, PhD); social inequality (MA, PhD); social psychology and life course (MA, PhD). *Faculty:* 22 full-time (14 women), 8 part-time/adjunct (3 women). *Students:* 42 full-time (23 women), 2 part-time (both women); includes 1 Black or African American, non-Hispanic/Latino; 1 American Indian or Alaska Native, non-Hispanic/Latino, 4 international. Average age 30. 71 applicants, 13% accepted, 9 enrolled. In 2010, 7 master's, 4 doctorates awarded. Terminal master's awarded for partial completion of doctoral program. *Degree requirements:* For master's, thesis; for doctorate, comprehensive exam, thesis/dissertation. *Entrance requirements:* For master's, GRE General Test, minimum GPA of 3.0; for doctorate, GRE General Test, MA in sociology, minimum GPA of 3.0. Additional exam requirements/

recommendations for international students: Required—TOEFL (minimum score 550 paper-based). *Application deadline:* For fall admission, 1/15 priority date for domestic students, 1/15 for international students. Application fee: $50. Electronic applications accepted. *Expenses:* Tuition, state resident: full-time $8552; part-time $443 per credit. Tuition, nonresident: full-time $21,650; part-time $1083 per credit. Required fees: $846. *Financial support:* In 2010–11, 5 research assistantships with tuition reimbursements (averaging $12,749 per year), 36 teaching assistantships with tuition reimbursements (averaging $12,749 per year) were awarded; fellowships with tuition reimbursements, Federal Work-Study, institutionally sponsored loans, scholarships/grants, health care benefits, and unspecified assistantships also available. Support available to part-time students. Financial award application deadline: 4/1; financial award applicants required to submit FAFSA. *Faculty research:* Crime/deviance, environmental sociology, social inequality, social psychology, gender. Total annual research expenditures: $101,888. *Unit head:* Dr. Gregory Hooks, Chair, 509-335-4595, Fax: 509-335-6419, E-mail: hooks@mail.wsu.edu. *Application contact:* Dr. Tom Rotolo, Director of Graduate Studies, 509-335-4595, Fax: 509-335-6419, E-mail: rotolo@wsu.edu.

Washington University in St. Louis, Graduate School of Arts and Sciences, Department of Psychology, St. Louis, MO 63130-4899. Offers clinical psychology (PhD); general experimental psychology (PhD); social psychology (PhD). *Accreditation:* APA. Terminal master's awarded for partial completion of doctoral program. *Degree requirements:* For doctorate, thesis/dissertation. *Entrance requirements:* For doctorate, GRE General Test. Electronic applications accepted.

Western Carolina University, Graduate School, College of Education and Allied Professions, Department of Human Services, Program in Counseling, Cullowhee, NC 28723. Offers community counseling (M Ed, MS); school counseling (MA Ed). *Accreditation:* ACA. Part-time and evening/weekend programs available. *Degree requirements:* For master's, comprehensive exam, thesis or alternative. *Entrance requirements:* For master's, GRE General Test, appropriate undergraduate degree with minimum GPA of 3.0, 3 recommendations, writing sample, resume. Additional exam requirements/recommendations for international students: Required—TOEFL (minimum score 550 paper-based; 270 computer-based; 79 iBT). *Faculty research:* Marital and family development, spirituality in counseling, home school law, sexuality education, family functioning models.

Western Connecticut State University, Division of Graduate Studies and External Programs, School of Professional Studies, Department of Education and Educational Psychology, Program in Community Counseling, Danbury, CT 06810-6885. Offers MS. *Accreditation:* ACA. Part-time programs available. *Students:* 4 full-time (2 women), 39 part-time (32 women); includes 5 minority (1 Black or African American, non-Hispanic/Latino; 1 Asian, non-Hispanic/Latino; 3 Hispanic/Latino). Average age 35. In 2010, 3 master's awarded. *Degree requirements:* For master's, practicum, internship, completion of program in 6 years. *Entrance requirements:* For master's, minimum GPA of 2.8, 3 letters of reference, interview, 9 hours of psychology. Additional exam requirements/recommendations for international students: Recommended—TOEFL (minimum score 550 paper-based; 213 computer-based; 79 iBT), IELTS (minimum score 6). *Application deadline:* For fall admission, 8/5 priority date for domestic students; for spring admission, 1/5 for domestic students. Applications are processed on a rolling basis. Application fee: $50. *Expenses:* Tuition, state resident: full-time $5012; part-time $417 per credit hour. Tuition, nonresident: full-time $13,962; part-time $423 per credit hour. Required fees: $3886. Full-time tuition and fees vary according to course load, degree level and program. *Financial support:* In 2010–11, 1 student received support. Scholarships/grants available. Financial award application deadline: 5/1; financial award applicants required to submit FAFSA. *Unit head:* Dr. Mike Gilles, Clinical Mental Health Counseling Coordinator, 203-837-8513, Fax: 203-837-8413, E-mail: gillesm@wcsu.edu. *Application contact:* Chris Shankle, Associate Director of Graduate Admissions, 203-837-9005, Fax: 203-837-8326, E-mail: shanklec@wcsu.edu.

Western Illinois University, School of Graduate Studies, College of Arts and Sciences, Department of Psychology, Macomb, IL 61455-1390. Offers clinical/community mental health (MS); general psychology (MS); psychology (MS, SSP); school psychology (SSP). Part-time programs available. *Students:* 44 full-time (31 women), 15 part-time (7 women); includes 4 minority (1 American Indian or Alaska Native, non-Hispanic/Latino; 3 Asian, non-Hispanic/Latino), 2 international. Average age 26. 94 applicants, 34% accepted. In 2010, 11 master's, 8 other advanced degrees awarded. *Degree requirements:* For master's, comprehensive exam (for some programs), thesis or alternative. *Entrance requirements:* For master's and SSP, GRE General Test. Additional exam requirements/recommendations for international students: Required—TOEFL (minimum score 550 paper-based; 213 computer-based; 80 iBT). *Application deadline:* Applications are processed on a rolling basis. Application fee: $30. Electronic applications accepted. *Expenses:* Tuition, state resident: full-time $6370; part-time $265.40 per credit hour. Tuition, nonresident: full-time $12,740; part-time $530.80 per credit hour. Required fees: $75.67 per credit hour. *Financial support:* In 2010–11, 37 students received support, including 37 research assistantships with full tuition reimbursements available (averaging $7,280 per year). Financial award applicants required to submit FAFSA. *Unit head:* Dr. Steven Dworkin, Chairperson, 309-298-1593. *Application contact:* Evelyn Hoing, Assistant Director of Graduate Studies, 309-298-1806, Fax: 309-298-2345, E-mail: grad-office@wiu.edu.

Wichita State University, Graduate School, Fairmount College of Liberal Arts and Sciences, Department of Psychology, Wichita, KS 67260. Offers clinical (PhD); community (PhD); human factors (PhD). *Accreditation:* APA. Part-time programs available. *Unit head:* Dr. Alex Chaparro, Chair, 316-978-3170, Fax: 316-978-3006, E-mail: alex.chaparro@wichita.edu. *Application contact:* Dr. Robert Zettle, Graduate Coordinator, 316-978-3170, E-mail: robert.zettle@wichita.edu.

Wilfrid Laurier University, Faculty of Graduate and Postdoctoral Studies, Faculty of Science, Department of Psychology, Waterloo, ON N2L 3C5, Canada. Offers behavioral neuroscience (M Sc, PhD); cognitive neuroscience (M Sc, PhD); community psychology (MA, PhD); social and developmental psychology (MA, PhD). Part-time programs available. *Faculty:* 32 full-time (12 women), 8 part-time/adjunct (1 woman). *Students:* 68 full-time (49 women), 4 part-time (3 women), 2 international. 94 applicants, 51% accepted, 27 enrolled. In 2010, 27 master's, 5 doctorates awarded. *Degree requirements:* For master's, thesis; for doctorate, thesis/dissertation. *Entrance requirements:* For master's, GRE General Test, honors BA or the equivalent in psychology, minimum B average in undergraduate course work; for doctorate, GRE General Test, master's degree, minimum A- average. Additional exam requirements/recommendations for international students: Required—TOEFL (minimum score 89 iBT). *Application deadline:* For fall admission, 1/15 priority date for domestic and international students. Application fee: $100. Electronic applications accepted. Tuition and fees charges are reported in Canadian dollars. *Expenses:* Tuition, area resident: Full-time $15,300 Canadian dollars; part-time $1200 Canadian dollars per credit. International tuition: $21,300 Canadian dollars full-time. Required fees: $650 Canadian dollars; $100 Canadian dollars per credit. Tuition and fees vary according to course load, degree level, campus/location and program. *Financial support:* In 2010–11, 116 fellowships, 116 teaching assistantships were awarded; career-related internships or fieldwork, scholarships/grants, health care benefits, and unspecified assistantships also available. *Faculty research:* Brain and cognition, community psychology, social and developmental psychology. *Unit head:* Dr. Alexandra Gottardo, Graduate Coordinator, 519-884-0710 Ext. 2169, Fax: 519-746-7605, E-mail: agottard@wlu.ca. *Application contact:* Rosemary Springett, Graduate Admissions and Records Officer, 519-884-0710 Ext. 3078, Fax: 519-884-1020, E-mail: gradstudies@wlu.ca.

Wilmington University, College of Social and Behavioral Sciences, New Castle, DE 19720-6491. Offers administration of human services (MS); administration of justice (MS); community counseling (MS). *Accreditation:* ACA. Part-time and evening/weekend programs available. *Entrance requirements:* Additional exam requirements/recommendations for international students: Required—TOEFL (minimum score 500 paper-based; 173 computer-based). Electronic applications accepted. *Expenses:* Tuition: Full-time $7110; part-time $395 per credit hour. Tuition and fees vary according to campus/location.

Yale University, Graduate School of Arts and Sciences, Department of Psychology, New Haven, CT 06520. Offers behavioral neuroscience (PhD); clinical psychology (PhD); cognitive psychology (PhD); developmental psychology (PhD); social/personality psychology (PhD). *Accreditation:* APA. *Degree requirements:* For doctorate, thesis/dissertation. *Entrance requirements:* For doctorate, GRE General Test.

Sport Psychology

Adler School of Professional Psychology, Programs in Psychology, Chicago, IL 60602. Offers advanced Adlerian psychotherapy (Certificate); art therapy (MA); clinical neuropsychology (Certificate); clinical psychology (Psy D); community psychology (MA); counseling and organizational psychology (MA); counseling psychology (MA); forensic psychology (MA); gerontological counseling (MA); marriage and family counseling (MA); marriage and family therapy (Certificate); organizational psychology (MA); police psychology (MA); rehabilitation counseling (MA); sport and health psychology (MA); substance abuse counseling (Certificate); Psy D/Certificate; Psy D/MACAT; Psy D/MACP; Psy D/MAMFC; Psy D/MASAC. *Accreditation:* APA. Part-time and evening/weekend programs available. Postbaccalaureate distance learning degree programs offered (minimal on-campus study). *Faculty:* 40 full-time (18 women), 61 part-time/adjunct (31 women). *Students:* 688 full-time (532 women), 142 part-time (110 women). Average age 27.Terminal master's awarded for partial completion of doctoral program. *Degree requirements:* For master's, thesis or alternative, oral exam, practicum; for doctorate, thesis/dissertation, clinical exam, internship, oral exam, practicum, written qualifying exam. *Entrance requirements:* For master's, 12 semester hours in psychology, minimum GPA of 3.0; for doctorate, 18 semester hours in psychology, minimum GPA of 3.25; for Certificate, appropriate master's or doctoral degree. Additional exam requirements/recommendations for international students: Required—TOEFL (minimum score 550 paper-based; 213 computer-based; 79 iBT). *Application deadline:* For fall admission, 2/15 priority date for domestic students, 12/1 priority date for international students. Applications are processed on a rolling basis. Application fee: $50. Electronic applications accepted. *Financial support:* Career-related internships or fieldwork, Federal Work-Study, scholarships/grants, and tuition waivers (full and partial) available. Support available to part-time students. Financial award application deadline: 5/15; financial award applicants required to submit FAFSA. *Application contact:* Michelle Brice, Director of Admissions, 312-662-4113, Fax: 312-662-4199, E-mail: admissions@adler.edu.

See Display on page 912 and Close-Up on page 1119.

Argosy University, Atlanta, College of Psychology and Behavioral Sciences, Atlanta, GA 30328. Offers clinical psychology (MA, Psy D, Postdoctoral Respecialization Certificate), including child and family psychology (Psy D), general adult clinical (Psy D), health psychology (Psy D), neuropsychology/geropsychology (Psy D); community counseling (MA), including marriage and family therapy; counselor education and supervision (Ed D); forensic psychology (MA); industrial organizational psychology (MA); marriage and family therapy (Certificate); sport-exercise psychology (MA). *Accreditation:* APA.

See Close-Up on page 1121.

Argosy University, Inland Empire, College of Psychology and Behavioral Sciences, San Bernardino, CA 92408. Offers clinical psychology/marriage and family therapy (MA); counseling psychology (Ed D); counseling psychology/marriage and family therapy (MA); forensic psychology (MA); industrial organizational psychology (MA); sport-exercise psychology (MA).

See Close-Up on page 1131.

Argosy University, Orange County, College of Psychology and Behavioral Sciences, Program in Sport-Exercise Psychology, Orange, CA 92868. Offers MA.

See Close-Up on page 1137.

Argosy University, Phoenix, College of Psychology and Behavioral Sciences, Program in Clinical Psychology, Phoenix, AZ 85021. Offers clinical psychology (MA); neuropsychology (Psy D); sports-exercise psychology (Psy D). *Accreditation:* APA (one or more programs are accredited).

See Close-Up on page 1139.

Argosy University, Phoenix, College of Psychology and Behavioral Sciences, Program in Sport–Exercise Psychology, Phoenix, AZ 85021. Offers MA.

See Close-Up on page 1139.

Argosy University, San Francisco Bay Area, College of Psychology and Behavioral Sciences, Alameda, CA 94501. Offers clinical psychology (MA, Psy D); counseling psychology (MA, Ed D); forensic psychology (MA); sport-exercise psychology (MA). *Accreditation:* APA (one or more programs are accredited).

See Close-Up on page 1145.

Barry University, School of Human Performance and Leisure Sciences, Programs in Movement Science, Specialization in Sport and Exercise Psychology, Miami Shores, FL 33161-6695. Offers MS. *Entrance requirements:* For master's, GRE.

Boston University, School of Education, Boston, MA 02215. Offers counseling (Ed M, CAGS), including community, school, sport psychology; counseling psychology (Ed D); curriculum and teaching (Ed M, Ed D, CAGS), including early childhood (Ed D), educational media and technology (Ed D), English and language arts (Ed D), mathematics (Ed D), physical education and coaching (Ed D), science (Ed D), social studies education (Ed D), special education (Ed D); developmental studies (Ed D), including literacy and language, reading education; developmental studies in literacy and language education (Ed M, CAGS); early childhood education (Ed M, CAGS); education of the deaf (Ed M, CAGS); educational leadership and development (Ed D), including educational administration (Ed M, Ed D, CAGS), higher education administration (Ed M, Ed D, CAGS); educational media and technology (Ed M, CAGS); elementary education (Ed M); English and language arts (Ed M, CAGS); English education (MAT); health education (Ed M, CAGS); Latin and classical studies (MAT); mathematics education (Ed M, MAT, CAGS); mathematics for teaching (MMT); modern foreign language education (MAT), including French, Spanish; physical education and coaching (Ed M, CAGS); policy, planning, and administration (Ed M, CAGS), including community education leadership, educational administration (Ed M, Ed D, CAGS), higher education administration (Ed M, Ed D, CAGS); reading education (Ed M, CAGS); science education (Ed M, MAT, CAGS), including

Sport Psychology

Boston University *(continued)*

biology (MAT), chemistry (MAT), earth science (MAT), general science (MAT), physics (MAT); social studies education (Ed M, MAT, CAGS), including history (MAT), political science (MAT); special education (Ed M, Ed D, CAGS), including disability studies (Ed M), moderate disabilities (Ed M), severe disabilities (Ed M), special education administration (Ed M); teaching English as a second language (Ed M, CAGS). Part-time programs available. *Faculty:* 57 full-time, 39 part-time/adjunct. *Students:* 245 full-time (191 women), 376 part-time (274 women); includes 83 minority (14 Black or African American, non-Hispanic/Latino; 2 American Indian or Alaska Native, non-Hispanic/Latino; 28 Asian, non-Hispanic/Latino; 31 Hispanic/Latino; 2 Native Hawaiian or other Pacific Islander, non-Hispanic/Latino; 6 Two or more races, non-Hispanic/Latino), 79 international. Average age 30. 1,270 applicants, 66% accepted, 292 enrolled. In 2010, 273 master's, 15 doctorates, 7 other advanced degrees awarded. Terminal master's awarded for partial completion of doctoral program. *Degree requirements:* For master's, thesis (for some programs); for doctorate, comprehensive exam, thesis/dissertation; for CAGS, comprehensive exam. *Entrance requirements:* For master's and CAGS, GRE General Test or Miller Analogies Test (MAT); for doctorate, GRE General Test. Additional exam requirements/recommendations for international students: Required—TOEFL, IELTS. *Application deadline:* For fall admission, 1/15 priority date for domestic and international students; for spring admission, 9/15 priority date for domestic and international students. Applications are processed on a rolling basis. Application fee: $70. Electronic applications accepted. *Expenses:* Tuition: Full-time $39,314; part-time $1228 per credit. Required fees: $40 per semester. *Financial support:* In 2010–11, 276 students received support, including 31 fellowships with full tuition reimbursements available, 16 research assistantships, 26 teaching assistantships with partial tuition reimbursements available; career-related internships or fieldwork, Federal Work-Study, and scholarships/grants also available. Support available to part-time students. Financial award applicants required to submit FAFSA. *Faculty research:* Deaf studies, social emotional learning, civic engagement and education, STEM education, pre-college educational pipelines. Total annual research expenditures: $2.6 million. *Unit head:* Dr. Hardin Coleman, Dean, 617-353-3213. *Application contact:* Dana Fernandez, Director of Enrollment, 617-353-4237, Fax: 617-353-8937, E-mail: sedgrad@bu.edu.

California State University, East Bay, Office of Academic Programs and Graduate Studies, College of Education and Allied Studies, Department of Kinesiology, Hayward, CA 94542-3000. Offers exercise physiology (MS); humanities/cultural studies (MS); professional perspectives (MS); skill acquisition/sport psychology (MS). *Faculty:* 6 full-time (3 women). *Students:* 17 full-time (12 women), 14 part-time (6 women); includes 15 minority (3 Black or African American, non-Hispanic/Latino; 1 American Indian or Alaska Native, non-Hispanic/Latino; 5 Asian, non-Hispanic/Latino; 5 Hispanic/Latino; 1 Two or more races, non-Hispanic/Latino). Average age 31. 31 applicants, 74% accepted, 10 enrolled. In 2010, 16 master's awarded. *Degree requirements:* For master's, exam or thesis. *Entrance requirements:* For master's, BA in kinesiology or related discipline, minimum major course work GPA of 3.0. Additional exam requirements/recommendations for international students: Required—TOEFL (minimum score 550 paper-based; 213 computer-based). *Application deadline:* For fall admission, 6/30 for domestic and international students. Applications are processed on a rolling basis. Application fee: $55. Electronic applications accepted. *Financial support:* Fellowships, Federal Work-Study, institutionally sponsored loans, and scholarships/grants available. Support available to part-time students. Financial award application deadline: 3/2; financial award applicants required to submit FAFSA. *Unit head:* Dr. Penny McCullagh, Chair, 510-885-3061, Fax: 510-885-2423, E-mail: penny.mccullagh@csueastbay.edu. *Application contact:* Dr. Donna Wiley, Interim Associate Director, 510-885-2928, Fax: 510-885-4777, E-mail: donna.wiley@csueastbay.edu.

California State University, Fresno, Division of Graduate Studies, College of Health and Human Services, Department of Kinesiology, Fresno, CA 93740-8027. Offers exercise science (MA); sport psychology (MA). Part-time and evening/weekend programs available. *Degree requirements:* For master's, thesis or alternative. *Entrance requirements:* For master's, GRE General Test, minimum GPA of 2.7. Additional exam requirements/recommendations for international students: Required—TOEFL. Electronic applications accepted. *Faculty research:* Refugee education, homeless, geriatrics, fitness.

California State University, Long Beach, Graduate Studies, College of Health and Human Services, Department of Kinesiology, Long Beach, CA 90840. Offers adapted physical education (MA); coaching and student athlete development (MA); exercise physiology and nutrition (MS); exercise science (MS); individualized studies (MA); kinesiology (MA); pedagogical studies (MA); sport and exercise psychology (MS); sport management (MA); sports medicine and injury studies (MS). Part-time programs available. *Faculty:* 11 full-time (4 women), 5 part-time/adjunct (all women). *Students:* 38 full-time (18 women), 23 part-time (14 women); includes 5 Black or African American, non-Hispanic/Latino; 1 American Indian or Alaska Native, non-Hispanic/Latino; 9 Asian, non-Hispanic/Latino; 7 Hispanic/Latino, 9 international. Average age 27. 209 applicants, 45% accepted, 30 enrolled. In 2010, 89 master's awarded. *Degree requirements:* For master's, oral and written comprehensive exams or thesis. *Entrance requirements:* For master's, GRE General Test, minimum GPA of 2.75 during previous 2 years of course work. *Application deadline:* For fall admission, 6/1 for domestic students. Applications are processed on a rolling basis. Application fee: $55. Electronic applications accepted. *Financial support:* Federal Work-Study, institutionally sponsored loans, and scholarships/grants available. Financial award application deadline: 3/2. *Faculty research:* Pulmonary functioning, feedback and practice structure, strength training, history and politics of sports, special population research issues. *Unit head:* Dr. Sharon R. Guthrie, Chair, 562-985-7487, Fax: 562-985-8067, E-mail: guthrie@csulb.edu. *Application contact:* Dr. Grant Hill, Graduate Advisor, 562-985-8856, Fax: 562-985-8067, E-mail: ghill@csulb.edu.

California University of Pennsylvania, School of Graduate Studies and Research, College of Education and Human Services, Program in Exercise Science and Health Promotion, California, PA 15419-1394. Offers performance enhancement and injury prevention (MS); rehabilitation science (MS); sport psychology (MS); wellness and fitness (MS). Part-time and evening/weekend programs available. Postbaccalaureate distance learning degree programs offered (no on-campus study). *Degree requirements:* For master's, comprehensive exam, thesis optional. *Entrance requirements:* For master's, minimum QPA of 3.0. Additional exam requirements/recommendations for international students: Required—TOEFL (minimum score 550 paper-based; 213 computer-based; 80 iBT). Electronic applications accepted. *Expenses:* Contact institution. *Faculty research:* Reducing obesity in children, sport performance, creating unique biomechanical assessment techniques, Web-based training for fitness professionals, Webcams.

Capella University, Harold Abel School of Psychology, Minneapolis, MN 55402. Offers child and adolescent development (MS); clinical psychology (MS, Psy D); counseling psychology (MS); educational psychology (MS, PhD); evaluation, research, and measurement (MS); general psychology (MS, PhD); industrial/organizational psychology (MS, PhD); leadership coaching psychology (MS); organizational leader development (MS); school psychology (MS); sport psychology (MS). Part-time and evening/weekend programs available. Postbaccalaureate distance learning degree programs offered (minimal on-campus study). Terminal master's awarded for partial completion of doctoral program. *Degree requirements:* For master's, thesis optional, project; for doctorate, thesis/dissertation. *Entrance requirements:* For degree, master's degree in school psychology. Additional exam requirements/recommendations for international students: Required—TOEFL (minimum score 550 paper-based; 213 computer-based), TWE (minimum score 4); Recommended—IELTS. Electronic applications accepted. *Expenses:* Tuition: Full-time $11,880; part-time $440 per credit hour.

Chatham University, Program in Counseling Psychology, Pittsburgh, PA 15232-2826. Offers child, adolescent and family (MSCP); counseling psychology (Psy D); health and holistic (MSCP); infant mental health (MSCP); organization and supervision (MSCP); sport and exercise (MSCP). Part-time and evening/weekend programs available. *Degree requirements:* For master's, thesis optional, supervised internship; for doctorate, thesis/dissertation, internship.

Entrance requirements: For master's, minimum GPA of 3.0; 2 letters of recommendation; resume; prerequisite coursework in statistics, biology, and psychology; for doctorate, GRE. Additional exam requirements/recommendations for international students: Required—TOEFL (minimum score 600 paper-based; 250 computer-based; 100 iBT), IELTS (minimum score 6.5), TWE. Electronic applications accepted. *Faculty research:* Trauma and recovery, hypnosis, psychospiritual dimensions of healing, psychotherapy of schizophrenia.

Cleveland State University, College of Graduate Studies, College of Education and Human Services, Department of Health, Physical Education, Recreation and Dance, Cleveland, OH 44115. Offers community health education (M Ed); exercise science (M Ed); human performance (M Ed); physical education pedagogy (M Ed); public health (MPH); school health education (M Ed); sport and exercise psychology (M Ed); sports management (M Ed). Part-time programs available. *Faculty:* 7 full-time (4 women), 6 part-time/adjunct (3 women). *Students:* 33 full-time (16 women), 66 part-time (45 women); includes 20 Black or African American, non-Hispanic/Latino; 1 Asian, non-Hispanic/Latino; 1 Hispanic/Latino, 11 international. Average age 31. 80 applicants, 66% accepted, 31 enrolled. In 2010, 30 master's awarded. *Degree requirements:* For master's, comprehensive exam, thesis optional. *Entrance requirements:* For master's, GRE General Test or MAT (if undergraduate GPA less than 2.75), minimum undergraduate GPA of 2.75. Additional exam requirements/recommendations for international students: Required—TOEFL (minimum score 525 paper-based; 197 computer-based), IELTS (minimum score 6). *Application deadline:* For fall admission, 7/15 priority date for domestic students; for spring admission, 12/15 priority date for domestic students. Applications are processed on a rolling basis. Application fee: $30. Electronic applications accepted. *Expenses:* Tuition, state resident: full-time $8447; part-time $469 per credit hour. Tuition, nonresident: full-time $16,020; part-time $890 per credit hour. Required fees: $50. *Financial support:* In 2010–11, 6 research assistantships with full and partial tuition reimbursements (averaging $3,480 per year), 1 teaching assistantship with full and partial tuition reimbursement (averaging $3,480 per year) were awarded; career-related internships or fieldwork, tuition waivers (full), and unspecified assistantships also available. Financial award application deadline: 3/15. *Faculty research:* Bone density, marketing fitness centers, motor development of disabled, online learning and survey research. *Unit head:* Dr. Sheila M. Patterson, Chairperson, 216-687-4870, Fax: 216-687-5410, E-mail: s.m.patterson@csuohio.edu. *Application contact:* Deborah L. Brown, Interim Assistant Director, Graduate Admissions, 216-523-7572, Fax: 216-687-5400, E-mail: d.l.brown@csuohio.edu.

Eastern Washington University, Graduate Studies, College of Education and Human Development, Department of Physical Education, Health and Recreation, Cheney, WA 99004-2431. Offers exercise science (MS); sport and exercise psychology (MS); sports administration/pedagogy (MS). *Degree requirements:* For master's, comprehensive exam, thesis or alternative. *Entrance requirements:* For master's, minimum GPA of 3.0.

Florida State University, The Graduate School, College of Education, Department of Educational Psychology and Learning Systems, Program in Educational Psychology, Tallahassee, FL 32306. Offers learning and cognition (MS, PhD, Ed S); sports psychology (MS, PhD). *Faculty:* 6 full-time (3 women). *Students:* 53 full-time (33 women), 19 part-time (13 women); includes 16 minority (9 Black or African American, non-Hispanic/Latino; 1 American Indian or Alaska Native, non-Hispanic/Latino; 1 Asian, non-Hispanic/Latino; 5 Hispanic/Latino), 16 international. Average age 29. 97 applicants, 46% accepted, 20 enrolled. In 2010, 15 master's, 7 doctorates awarded. *Degree requirements:* For master's, comprehensive exam, thesis optional; for doctorate, comprehensive exam, thesis/dissertation. *Entrance requirements:* For master's and doctorate, GRE General Test, minimum GPA of 3.0. Additional exam requirements/recommendations for international students: Required—TOEFL (minimum score 550 paper-based; 213 computer-based; 80 iBT). *Application deadline:* For fall admission, 7/1 for domestic and international students; for winter admission, 11/1 for domestic and international students; for spring admission, 3/1 for domestic and international students. Applications are processed on a rolling basis. Application fee: $30. Electronic applications accepted. *Expenses:* Tuition, state resident: full-time $8238.24. *Financial support:* In 2010–11, 5 fellowships with full and partial tuition reimbursements, 30 research assistantships with full and partial tuition reimbursements, 43 teaching assistantships with full and partial tuition reimbursements were awarded; career-related internships or fieldwork also available. Financial award application deadline: 1/15; financial award applicants required to submit FAFSA. *Faculty research:* Learning and cognition, skill acquisition, self-perception, processes of motivation. *Unit head:* Dr. Susan Losh, Program Leader, 850-644-8776, Fax: 850-644-8776, E-mail: slosh@fsu.edu. *Application contact:* Peggy Lollie, Program Assistant, 850-644-8786, Fax: 850-644-8776, E-mail: plollie@fsu.edu.

John F. Kennedy University, Graduate School of Professional Psychology, Program in Sport Psychology, Pleasant Hill, CA 94523-4817. Offers MA. Part-time and evening/weekend programs available. *Degree requirements:* For master's, thesis or alternative. *Entrance requirements:* For master's, interview. Additional exam requirements/recommendations for international students: Required—TOEFL.

Memorial University of Newfoundland, School of Graduate Studies, School of Human Kinetics and Recreation, St. John's, NL A1C 5S7, Canada. Offers administration, curriculum and supervision (MPE); biomechanics/ergonomics (MS Kin); exercise and work physiology (MS Kin); sport psychology (MS Kin). Part-time programs available. *Degree requirements:* For master's, thesis optional, seminars, thesis presentations. *Entrance requirements:* For master's, bachelor's degree in a related field, minimum B average. Electronic applications accepted. *Faculty research:* Administration, sociology of sports, kinesiology, physiology/recreation.

Purdue University, Graduate School, College of Liberal Arts, Department of Health and Kinesiology, West Lafayette, IN 47907. Offers exercise, human physiology of movement and sport (PhD); health and fitness (MS); health promotion (MS); health promotion and disease prevention (PhD); movement and sport science (MS); pedagogy and administration (MS); pedagogy of physical activity and health (PhD); psychology of sport and exercise, and motor behavior (PhD). Part-time programs available. *Degree requirements:* For master's, thesis (for some programs); for doctorate, thesis/dissertation. *Entrance requirements:* For master's and doctorate, GRE General Test. Additional exam requirements/recommendations for international students: Required—TOEFL. Electronic applications accepted. *Faculty research:* Wellness, motivation, teaching effectiveness, learning and development.

Queen's University at Kingston, School of Graduate Studies and Research, School of Kinesiology and Health Studies, Kingston, ON K7L 3N6, Canada. Offers applied exercise science (PhD); biomechanics/ergonomics (M Sc); exercise physiology (M Sc); social psychology of sport and exercise rehabilitation (MA); sociology of sport (MA). Part-time programs available. *Degree requirements:* For master's, thesis (for some programs); for doctorate, comprehensive exam, thesis/dissertation. *Entrance requirements:* For master's and doctorate, minimum B+ average. Additional exam requirements/recommendations for international students: Required—TOEFL. Electronic applications accepted. *Faculty research:* Expert performance ergonomics, obesity research, pregnancy and exercise, gender and sport participation.

Southern Connecticut State University, School of Graduate Studies, School of Education, Department of Exercise Science, New Haven, CT 06515-1355. Offers human performance (MS); physical education (MS); school health education (MS); sport psychology (MS). Part-time and evening/weekend programs available. *Faculty:* 16 full-time (7 women). *Students:* 9 full-time (6 women), 16 part-time (7 women); includes 1 Black or African American, non-Hispanic/Latino; 2 Hispanic/Latino. 89 applicants, 16% accepted, 9 enrolled. In 2010, 9 master's awarded. *Degree requirements:* For master's, thesis or alternative. *Entrance requirements:* For master's, interview. *Application deadline:* For fall admission, 7/15 priority date for domestic students. Applications are processed on a rolling basis. Application fee: $50. Electronic applications accepted. *Expenses:* Tuition, state resident: full-time $5137; part-time $518 per credit. Tuition, nonresident: part-time $542 per credit. Required fees: $4008; $55 per semester. Tuition and fees vary according to program. *Financial support:* Application deadline: 4/15. *Unit head:* Dr. Daniel Swartz, Chairperson, 203-392-8721, Fax: 203-392-6911, E-mail: swartzd1@

southernct.edu. *Application contact:* Dr. Robert Axtell, Coordinator, 203-392-6037, Fax: 203-392-6093, E-mail: axtell@southernct.edu.

Springfield College, Graduate Programs, Programs in Exercise Science and Sport Studies, Springfield, MA 01109-3797. Offers athletic training (MS); exercise physiology (MS), including clinical exercise physiology, science and research; exercise science and sport studies (PhD); health promotion and disease prevention (MS); sport psychology (MS). Part-time programs available. Terminal master's awarded for partial completion of doctoral program. *Degree requirements:* For master's, comprehensive exam, research project or thesis; for doctorate, comprehensive exam, thesis/dissertation. *Entrance requirements:* For master's and doctorate, GRE General Test. Additional exam requirements/recommendations for international students: Required—TOEFL (minimum score 550 paper-based; 213 computer-based). Electronic applications accepted.

Springfield College, Graduate Programs, Programs in Psychology and Counseling, Springfield, MA 01109-3797. Offers athletic counseling (M Ed, MS, CAGS); industrial/organizational psychology (M Ed, MS, CAGS); marriage and family therapy (M Ed, MS, CAGS); mental health counseling (M Ed, MS, CAGS); school guidance and counseling (M Ed, MS, CAGS); student personnel in higher education (M Ed, MS, CAGS). Part-time programs available. *Degree requirements:* For master's, research project, portfolio. *Entrance requirements:* Additional exam requirements/recommendations for international students: Required—TOEFL (minimum score 550 paper-based; 213 computer-based). Electronic applications accepted.

University of Denver, Graduate School of Professional Psychology, Denver, CO 80208. Offers clinical psychology (Psy D); forensic psychology (MA); international disaster psychology (MA); psychology (MA); sport and performance psychology (MA). *Accreditation:* APA. *Faculty:* 15 full-time (8 women), 24 part-time/adjunct (11 women). *Students:* 209 full-time (170 women), 36 part-time (25 women); includes 26 minority (7 Black or African American, non-Hispanic/Latino; 2 American Indian or Alaska Native, non-Hispanic/Latino; 5 Asian, non-Hispanic/Latino; 9 Hispanic/Latino; 3 Two or more races, non-Hispanic/Latino), 4 international. Average age 26. 612 applicants, 30% accepted, 124 enrolled. In 2010, 74 master's, 38 doctorates awarded. *Degree requirements:* For master's, comprehensive exam (for some programs); for doctorate, comprehensive exam (for some programs), paper, clinical internship. *Entrance requirements:* For master's and doctorate, GRE General Test. Additional exam requirements/recommendations for international students: Required—TOEFL (minimum score 550 paper-based; 80 iBT). Application fee: $60. Electronic applications accepted. *Expenses:* Tuition: Full-time $35,604; part-time $29,670 per year. Required fees: $687 per year. Tuition and fees vary according to program. *Financial support:* In 2010–11, 38 teaching assistantships with full and partial tuition reimbursements (averaging $2,952 per year) were awarded; career-related internships or fieldwork, Federal Work-Study, institutionally sponsored loans, scholarships/grants, unspecified assistantships, and clinical assistantships also available. Support available to part-time students. Financial award application deadline: 3/1; financial award applicants required to submit FAFSA. *Unit head:* Dr. Peter Buirski, Dean, 303-871-2382, E-mail: pbuirski@du.edu. *Application contact:* Admissions Counselor, 303-871-3736, Fax: 303-871-7656, E-mail: gsppinfo@du.edu.

The University of Iowa, Graduate College, College of Liberal Arts and Sciences, Department of Health and Sport Studies, Iowa City, IA 52242-1316. Offers psychology of sport and physical activity (MA, PhD); sports studies (MA, PhD). *Degree requirements:* For master's, thesis optional, exam; for doctorate, comprehensive exam, thesis/dissertation. *Entrance requirements:* For master's and doctorate, GRE General Test, minimum GPA of 3.0. Additional exam requirements/recommendations for international students: Required—TOEFL (minimum score 600 paper-based; 250 computer-based; 100 iBT). Electronic applications accepted.

University of Rhode Island, Graduate School, College of Human Science and Services, Department of Kinesiology, Kingston, RI 02881. Offers cultural studies of sport and physical culture (MS); exercise science (MS); physical education pedagogy (MS); psychosocial/behavioral aspects of physical activity (MS). *Accreditation:* NCATE. Part-time programs available. *Faculty:* 14 full-time (8 women). *Students:* 11 full-time (5 women), 7 part-time (5 women); includes 1 minority (Hispanic/Latino). In 2010, 8 master's awarded. *Degree requirements:* For master's, thesis optional. *Entrance requirements:* For master's, GRE, 2 letters of recommendation. Additional exam requirements/recommendations for international students: Required—TOEFL (minimum score 550 paper-based; 213 computer-based). *Application deadline:* For fall admission, 4/15 for domestic students, 2/1 for international students; for spring admission, 11/15 for domestic students, 7/15 for international students. Application fee: $65. Electronic applications accepted. *Expenses:* Tuition, state resident: full-time $9588; part-time $533 per credit hour. Tuition, nonresident: full-time $22,968; part-time $1276 per credit hour. Required fees: $1282; $68 per semester. Tuition and fees vary according to program. *Financial support:* In 2010–11, 4 teaching assistantships with full and partial tuition reimbursements (averaging $7,939 per year) were awarded. Financial award application deadline: 4/15; financial award applicants required to submit FAFSA. *Faculty research:* Strength training and older adults, interventions to promote a healthy lifestyle as well as analysis of the psychosocial outcomes of those interventions, effects of exercise and nutrition on skeletal muscle of aging healthy adults with CVD and other metabolic related diseases, physical activity and fitness of deaf children and youth. Total annual research expenditures: $117,153. *Unit head:* Dr. Deborah Riebe, Chair, 401-874-5444, Fax: 401-874-4215, E-mail: debriebe@uri.edu. *Application contact:* Dr. Lori Ciccomascolo, Director of Graduate Studies, 401-874-5454, Fax: 401-874-4215, E-mail: lecicco@uri.edu.

The University of Texas at Austin, Graduate School, College of Education, Department of Kinesiology and Health Education, Austin, TX 78712-1111. Offers behavioral health (PhD); exercise and sport psychology (M Ed, MA); health education (M Ed, MA, Ed D, PhD); kinesiology (M Ed, MA). Part-time programs available. Terminal master's awarded for partial completion of doctoral program. *Degree requirements:* For master's, thesis (for some programs); for doctorate, thesis/dissertation. *Entrance requirements:* For master's and doctorate, GRE General Test. Additional exam requirements/recommendations for international students: Required—TOEFL. Electronic applications accepted. *Faculty research:* Health promotion, human performance and exercise biochemistry, motor behavior and biomechanics, sport management, aging and pediatric development.

West Virginia University, School of Physical Education, Morgantown, WV 26506. Offers athletic coaching education (MS); athletic training (MS); physical education/teacher education (MS, PhD), including curriculum and instruction (PhD), motor behavior (PhD), physical education supervision (PhD); sport and exercise psychology (PhD); sport management (MS). *Degree requirements:* For doctorate, comprehensive exam, thesis/dissertation, oral exam. *Entrance requirements:* For master's, GRE or MAT, minimum GPA of 3.0; for doctorate, GRE General Test or MAT, minimum GPA of 3.5. Additional exam requirements/recommendations for international students: Required—TOEFL (minimum score 550 paper-based; 213 computer-based). Electronic applications accepted. *Faculty research:* Sport psychosociology, teacher education, exercise psychology, counseling.

Thanatology

Brooklyn College of the City University of New York, Division of Graduate Studies, Department of Health and Nutrition Science, Program in Community Health, Brooklyn, NY 11210-2889. Offers community health education (MA); computer science and health science (MS); health care management (MPH); health care policy and administration (MPH); thanatology (MA). *Accreditation:* CEPH. *Students:* 3 full-time (all women), 47 part-time (40 women); includes 35 minority (26 Black or African American, non-Hispanic/Latino; 5 Asian, non-Hispanic/Latino; 4 Hispanic/Latino), 2 international. Average age 35. 20 applicants, 85% accepted, 11 enrolled. In 2010, 13 master's awarded. *Degree requirements:* For master's, thesis or alternative. *Entrance requirements:* For master's, 2 letters of recommendation, essay. Additional exam requirements/recommendations for international students: Required—TOEFL. *Application deadline:* For fall admission, 3/1 priority date for domestic students, 2/1 priority date for international students; for spring admission, 11/1 priority date for domestic students, 10/1 priority date for international students. Applications are processed on a rolling basis. Application fee: $125. Electronic applications accepted. *Expenses:* Tuition, state resident: full-time $7360; part-time $310 per credit hour. Tuition, nonresident: full-time $13,800; part-time $575 per credit hour. Required fees: $190 per semester. *Financial support:* Federal Work-Study, institutionally sponsored loans, and scholarships/grants available. Support available to part-time students. Financial award application deadline: 5/1; financial award applicants required to submit FAFSA. *Faculty research:* Diet restriction, religious practices in bereavement, diabetes, stress management, palliative care. *Unit head:* Dr. Elizabeth Eastwood, Graduate Deputy Chairperson, 718-951-5026, Fax: 718-951-4670, E-mail: eastwood@brooklyn.cuny.edu. *Application contact:* Hernan Sierra, Graduate Admissions Coordinator, 718-951-4536, Fax: 718-951-4506, E-mail: grads@brooklyn.cuny.edu.

Hood College, Graduate School, Programs in Human Sciences, Frederick, MD 21701-8575. Offers human sciences (MA), including psychology; thanatology (MA, Certificate). Part-time and evening/weekend programs available. *Faculty:* 5 full-time (3 women), 7 part-time/adjunct (4 women). *Students:* 19 full-time (13 women), 66 part-time (60 women); includes 13 Black or African American, non-Hispanic/Latino; 2 American Indian or Alaska Native, non-Hispanic/Latino; 1 Asian, non-Hispanic/Latino; 2 Hispanic/Latino; 1 Two or more races, non-Hispanic/Latino, 2 international. Average age 34. 40 applicants, 85% accepted, 19 enrolled. In 2010, 40 master's, 27 other advanced degrees awarded. *Degree requirements:* For master's, comprehensive exam, capstone/research project. *Entrance requirements:* For master's, minimum GPA of 2.75. Additional exam requirements/recommendations for international students: Required—TOEFL (minimum score 575 paper-based; 231 computer-based; 89 iBT). *Application deadline:* For fall admission, 7/15 for domestic and international students; for spring admission, 12/15 for domestic and international students. Applications are processed on a rolling basis. Application fee: $35. Electronic applications accepted. *Expenses:* Tuition: Full-time $6480; part-time $360 per credit. Required fees: $100; $50 per term. *Financial support:* Applicants required to submit FAFSA. *Faculty research:* Mind-body medicine and multicultural healing, the New Orleans jazz funeral, death practices in African-American culture, bereavement theories and gender differences, Piaget's theory of cognitive development as a formal mathematical model. *Unit head:* Dr. Terry Martin, Director, 301-696-3759, Fax: 301-696-3597, E-mail: tmartin@hood.edu. *Application contact:* Dr. Allen P. Flora, Dean of Graduate School, 301-696-3811, Fax: 301-696-3597, E-mail: gofurther@hood.edu.

Southwestern College, Program in Grief, Loss and Trauma Counseling, Santa Fe, NM 87502-4788. Offers MA, Certificate. Part-time and evening/weekend programs available. Postbaccalaureate distance learning degree programs offered (minimal on-campus study). *Entrance requirements:* For master's, interview, references, resume; for Certificate, 3 letters of reference, interview.

Transpersonal and Humanistic Psychology

Atlantic University, Program in Transpersonal Studies, Virginia Beach, VA 23451-2061. Offers MA. Part-time and evening/weekend programs available. Postbaccalaureate distance learning degree programs offered (no on-campus study). *Faculty:* 23 part-time/adjunct (10 women). *Students:* 174 part-time (122 women); includes 8 minority (3 Black or African American, non-Hispanic/Latino; 3 Asian, non-Hispanic/Latino; 2 Hispanic/Latino), 5 international. Average age 46. 109 applicants, 33% accepted, 36 enrolled. In 2010, 15 master's awarded. *Degree requirements:* For master's, thesis. *Entrance requirements:* For master's, minimum undergraduate GPA of 2.5. Additional exam requirements/recommendations for international students: Required—TOEFL (minimum score 550 paper-based; 213 computer-based). *Application deadline:* Applications are processed on a rolling basis. Application fee: $50. Electronic applications accepted. *Expenses:* Required fees: $795 per course. One-time fee: $50 part-time. *Unit head:* Kevin J. Todeschi, Chief Executive Officer, 757-631-8101, Fax: 757-631-8096. *Application contact:* Candis Collins, Director of Admissions, 757-631-8101, Fax: 757-631-8096, E-mail: candis.collins@atlanticuniv.edu.

Institute of Transpersonal Psychology, Global Online Programs, Palo Alto, CA 94303. Offers psychology (PhD); transpersonal psychology (MTP); transpersonal studies (Certificate). Postbaccalaureate distance learning degree programs offered (minimal on-campus study). Terminal master's awarded for partial completion of doctoral program. *Degree requirements:* For master's, thesis (for some programs); for doctorate, thesis/dissertation. *Entrance requirements:* For master's and doctorate, bachelor's degree. Additional exam requirements/recommendations for international students: Required—TOEFL. *Expenses:* Contact institution.

Institute of Transpersonal Psychology, Low-Residency Programs, Palo Alto, CA 94303. Offers counseling psychology (online) (MA); spiritual guidance (MA); women's spirituality (MA). Postbaccalaureate distance learning degree programs offered (minimal on-campus study).

Institute of Transpersonal Psychology, Residential Programs, Palo Alto, CA 94303. Offers counseling psychology (MA); spiritually oriented clinical psychology (Psy D); transpersonal psychology (MA, PhD). Part-time and evening/weekend programs available. Terminal master's

Transpersonal and Humanistic Psychology

Institute of Transpersonal Psychology (continued)
awarded for partial completion of doctoral program. *Degree requirements:* For doctorate, thesis/dissertation. *Entrance requirements:* For master's and doctorate, bachelor's degree.

John F. Kennedy University, Graduate School of Holistic Studies, Department of Counseling Psychology, Program in Counseling Psychology, Pleasant Hill, CA 94523-4817. Offers holistic studies (MA); somatic psychology (MA); transpersonal psychology (MA). Part-time and evening/weekend programs available. *Degree requirements:* For master's, thesis or alternative. *Entrance requirements:* For master's, interview. Additional exam requirements/recommendations for international students: Required—TOEFL.

Kona University, Program in Transpersonal Psychology, Kailua-Kona, HI 96740. Offers MTP. *Degree requirements:* For master's, capstone electronic portfolio project/practicum. *Entrance requirements:* For master's, undergraduate degree or equivalent with minimum GPA of 3.0 from accredited U.S. college or university; official transcripts; 2 letters of recommendation; resume or curriculum vitae; personal statement; telephone interview. Additional exam requirements/recommendations for international students: Required—TOEFL (minimum score 577 paper-based; 233 computer-based; 90 iBT), IELTS (minimum score 6.5), TWE (minimum score 4.5). Electronic applications accepted.

Michigan School of Professional Psychology, MA and PsyD Programs in Clinical Psychology, Farmington Hills, MI 48334. Offers MA, Psy D. Part-time programs available. *Faculty:* 7 full-time (3 women), 20 part-time/adjunct (11 women). *Students:* 120 full-time (92 women), 18 part-time (16 women); includes 29 minority (22 Black or African American, non-Hispanic/Latino; 4 Asian, non-Hispanic/Latino; 3 Hispanic/Latino). 126 applicants, 75% accepted, 77 enrolled. In 2010, 41 master's, 20 doctorates awarded. *Degree requirements:* For master's, thesis, practicum; for doctorate, comprehensive exam, thesis/dissertation, internship, practicum. *Entrance requirements:* For master's, undergraduate degree from accredited institution with minimum GPA of 2.5; major in psychology, social work, counseling or equivalent; for doctorate, undergraduate degree from accredited institution with minimum GPA of 2.5; graduate degree from accredited institution with minimum GPA of 3.25; undergraduate or graduate degree in psychology, social work, counseling or equivalent; 500 practicum hours or equivalent field experience. Additional exam requirements/recommendations for international students: Required—TOEFL (minimum score 550 paper-based; 213 computer-based; 79 iBT). *Application deadline:* Applications are processed on a rolling basis. *Financial support:* In 2010–11, 6 students received support, including 3 research assistantships (averaging $12,000 per year), 1 teaching assistantship (averaging $12,000 per year); career-related internships or fieldwork, institutionally sponsored loans, and scholarships/grants also available. Financial award application deadline: 6/30; financial award applicants required to submit FAFSA. *Faculty research:* Qualitative research, existential, phenomenological psychology, clinical practice, humanistic. *Unit head:* Dr. Kerry Moustakas, President, 248-476-1122, Fax: 248-476-1125. *Application contact:* Amanda Ming, Admissions and Recruitment Coordinator, 248-476-1122 Ext. 117, Fax: 248-476-1125, E-mail: aming@mispp.edu.

Naropa University, Graduate Programs; Program in Transpersonal Counseling Psychology, Boulder, CO 80302-6697. Offers art therapy (MA); counseling psychology (MA); wilderness therapy (MA). *Faculty:* 8 full-time (5 women), 27 part-time/adjunct (20 women). *Students:* 159 full-time (121 women), 70 part-time (54 women); includes 25 minority (2 Black or African American, non-Hispanic/Latino; 3 American Indian or Alaska Native, non-Hispanic/Latino; 2 Asian, non-Hispanic/Latino; 10 Hispanic/Latino; 8 Two or more races, non-Hispanic/Latino), 6 international. Average age 30. 237 applicants, 53% accepted, 84 enrolled. In 2010, 53 master's awarded. *Degree requirements:* For master's, internships. *Entrance requirements:* For master's, in-person interview, course work in psychology, 3 letters of recommendation, resume. Additional exam requirements/recommendations for international students: Required—TOEFL (minimum score 600 paper-based; 250 computer-based). *Application deadline:* For fall admission, 1/15 priority date for domestic and international students. Applications are processed on a rolling basis. Application fee: $60. Electronic applications accepted. *Expenses:* Tuition: Full-time $17,820; part-time $810 per credit. Required fees: $305 per semester. Tuition and fees vary according to course load, program and reciprocity agreements. *Financial support:* In 2010–11, 67 students received support, including 21 research assistantships with partial tuition reimbursements available (averaging $2,692 per year), 4 teaching assistantships with partial tuition reimbursements available (averaging $2,866 per year); career-related internships or fieldwork, Federal Work-Study, scholarships/grants, health care benefits, tuition waivers (partial), and unspecified assistantships also available. Support available to part-time students. Financial award application deadline: 3/1; financial award applicants required to submit FAFSA. *Unit head:* Dr. MacAndrew Jack, Director, Graduate School of Psychology. *Application contact:* Office of Admissions, 303-546-3572, Fax: 303-546-3583, E-mail: admissions@naropa.edu.

Naropa University, Graduate Programs, Program in Transpersonal Psychology, Boulder, CO 80302-6697. Offers ecopsychology (MA); transpersonal psychology (MA). Part-time and evening/weekend programs available. Postbaccalaureate distance learning degree programs offered (minimal on-campus study). *Faculty:* 1 full-time (0 women), 13 part-time/adjunct (7 women). *Students:* 1 full-time (0 women), 12 part-time (11 women); includes 2 minority (1 Hispanic/Latino; 1 Two or more races, non-Hispanic/Latino). Average age 45. 17 applicants, 59% accepted, 4 enrolled. In 2010, 5 master's awarded. *Degree requirements:* For master's, thesis, service learning. *Entrance requirements:* For master's, interview (by phone or in-person), technology form, resume, letter of interest, 3 letters of recommendation. Additional exam requirements/recommendations for international students: Required—TOEFL (minimum score 600 paper-based; 250 computer-based). *Application deadline:* For fall admission, 1/15 for domestic and international students. Applications are processed on a rolling basis. Application fee: $60. Electronic applications accepted. *Expenses:* Tuition: Full-time $17,820; part-time $810 per credit. Required fees: $305 per semester. Tuition and fees vary according to course load, program and reciprocity agreements. *Financial support:* In 2010–11, 3 students received support. Career-related internships or fieldwork, Federal Work-Study, scholarships/grants, health care benefits, and tuition waivers (partial) available. Support available to part-time students. Financial award application deadline: 3/1; financial award applicants required to submit FAFSA. *Unit head:* Dr. MacAndrew Jack, Director, Graduate School of Psychology, 303-245-4752, E-mail: mjack@naropa.edu. *Application contact:* Office of Admissions, 303-546-3572, Fax: 303-546-3583, E-mail: admissions@naropa.edu.

Saybrook University, Graduate College of Psychology and Humanistic Studies, San Francisco, CA 94111-1920. Offers clinical psychology (Psy D); human science (MA, PhD), including consciousness and spirituality, humanistic and transpersonal psychology, integrative health studies, organizational systems, social transformation, transformative social change (MA); organizational systems (MA, PhD), including consciousness and spirituality, humanistic and transpersonal psychology, integrative health studies, leadership of sustainable systems (MA), organizational systems, social transformation; psychology (MA, PhD), including clinical psychology (PhD), consciousness and spirituality, creativity studies (MA), humanistic and transpersonal psychology, integrative health studies, Jungian studies, marriage and family therapy (MA), organizational systems, social transformation. Postbaccalaureate distance learning degree programs offered (minimal on-campus study). *Faculty:* 15 full-time (5 women), 83 part-time/adjunct (34 women). *Students:* 479 full-time (333 women); includes 30 Black or African American, non-Hispanic/Latino; 1 American Indian or Alaska Native, non-Hispanic/Latino; 13 Asian, non-Hispanic/Latino; 18 Hispanic/Latino, 18 international. Average age 43. 280 applicants, 52% accepted, 105 enrolled. In 2010, 28 master's, 43 doctorates awarded. Terminal master's awarded for partial completion of doctoral program. *Degree requirements:* For master's, thesis or alternative; for doctorate, thesis/dissertation. Additional exam requirements/recommendations for international students: Required—TOEFL (minimum score 580 paper-based; 237 computer-based; 93 iBT). *Application deadline:* For fall admission, 6/1 priority date for domestic students; for spring admission, 12/16 priority date for domestic students. Application fee: $50. Electronic applications accepted. *Financial support:* In 2010–11, 335 students received support. Scholarships/grants available. Financial award applicants required to submit FAFSA. *Faculty research:* Humanistic theory, health studies, organizational systems, consciousness and spirituality, social transformation. Total annual research expenditures: $90,000. *Unit head:* Mark Schulman, President, 800-825-4480, Fax: 415-433-9271. *Application contact:* Director of Admissions, 800-825-4480, Fax: 415-433-9271, E-mail: admissions@saybrook.edu.

Seattle University, College of Arts and Sciences, Department of Psychology, Seattle, WA 98122-1090. Offers existential and phenomenological therapeutic psychology (MA Psych). *Degree requirements:* For master's, thesis. *Entrance requirements:* For master's, interview, minimum GPA of 3.0, previous undergraduate course work in psychology. *Faculty research:* Healing, transformations in relationships, therapy, dialogical research.

ADELPHI UNIVERSITY

Derner Institute of Advanced Psychological Studies

Programs of Study

The Gordon F. Derner Institute of Advanced Psychological Studies offers a Ph.D. program in clinical psychology and Master of Arts programs in general psychology, school psychology, and mental health counseling. There are also several postgraduate programs.

The Ph.D. program in clinical psychology emphasizes a psychodynamic approach to human behavior and prepares graduates for community practice. The program encompasses research; theory; psychological, biological, and social bases of behavior; and extensive clinical practice in psychodiagnostics and psychotherapy. Four years of full-time study, supervised research, a one-year full-time internship, and a dissertation are required. The clinical psychology program has been accredited by the American Psychological Association (APA) since 1957.

The Master of Arts in general psychology enables students to advance their exploration of human personality, psychodynamics, developmental and social psychology, and psychoanalytic theory. It requires the completion of a 36-credit course of study, which can be completed in one year of full-time study or two years of part-time study. Concentrations are offered in preclinical, forensic psychology, or industrial organizational psychology.

The Master of Arts in school psychology is a 72-credit program that can be completed in three years of full-time study or four years of part-time study. The program enables students to practice in a school setting using integrated skills, such as providing comprehensive psychoeducational evaluations and school consultations. The school practice core culminates with a full-time internship in a public school working under the supervision of a certified school psychologist.

The Master of Arts in mental health counseling is a graduate training program designed to help students acquire knowledge and the clinical skills to become competent mental health counselors. The program is designed to help students acquire competency in the diagnosis and treatment of mental disorders, the ability to facilitate client growth, development, and respect for the ethics and standards of practice endorsed by the mental health counseling profession. The 60-credit curriculum, including an internship, is designed to be completed in two years. The program complies with all standards for state and national accrediting groups. After licensure, mental health counselors may work in a variety of settings, such as hospitals, clinics, and private practice.

The Respecialization Certificate Program in clinical psychology equips doctoral-level psychologists to make a career shift into clinical psychology for community practice. The program focuses on academic work and intensive clinical training, and requires two years of full-time study, supervised clinical practice, and a one-year full-time internship. Graduates of this program earn a Certificate of Respecialization in Clinical Psychology, which is recognized by the American Psychological Association.

Postgraduate programs are available for students who have already earned a Ph.D. in clinical psychology or are licensed mental health professionals—psychiatrists, social workers, and psychiatric nurses—who wish to expand the focus of their practice. Adelphi's postgraduate programs include psychoanalysis and psychotherapy; child, adolescent, and family psychotherapy; group psychotherapy; couple therapy; and psychodynamic school psychology.

Research Facilities

Clinical facilities on campus include the Psychological Services Center and the Postgraduate Psychotherapy Center. Clinical facilities are also located in many neighboring hospitals, public schools, and agencies. Research facilities include the University library and computing center and a number of Institute research laboratories.

Financial Aid

Adelphi University offers a wide variety of federal aid programs; state grants; scholarship and fellowship programs; on- and off-campus employment; teaching, research, and clinical assistantships; and paid field placements.

Cost of Study

In 2011–12, tuition for full-time study (12–17 credits) is $35,300 per year for doctoral study in the Derner Institute of Advanced Psychological Studies. Tuition for part-time study (1–11 credits) is $930 per credit hour for master's degree programs. University fees range from about $315 to $550 per semester.

Living and Housing Costs

The University assists single and married students in finding suitable accommodations whenever possible. The cost of living is dependent upon location and the number of rooms rented.

Location

Adelphi University is located in Nassau County on Long Island, part of the New York City metropolitan area. Students can draw upon the city's cultural and social resources as well as the University's own extensive program in the arts.

The University

Adelphi University is set within a beautifully landscaped campus of 75 acres in the attractive residential community of Garden City, Long Island.

Applying

Application requirements can be found at http://derner.adelphi.edu/graduate (master's programs), http://derner.adelphi.edu/doctoral (doctoral program), http://derner.adelphi.edu/postgraduate (postgraduate programs), and http://derner.adelphi.edu/respecialization (respecialization program).

Correspondence and Information

Dr. Jacques P. Barber, Dean
Derner Institute of Advanced Psychological Studies
Adelphi University
Garden City, New York 11530
Phone: 800-ADELPHI (toll-free)
Fax: 516-877-3093
E-mail: admissions@adelphi.edu
Web site: http://derner.adelphi.edu

Adelphi University

FULL-TIME FACULTY AND THEIR RESEARCH

Jean Lau Chin, Professor; Ed.D., Columbia Teachers College. School psychology, psychology of women, diversity in clinical practice.

Robert Bornstein, Professor; Ph.D., SUNY at Buffalo. Personality disorders and assessment, unconscious processes, interpersonal dependency.

Wilma S. Bucci, Professor; Ph.D., NYU. Psychoanalytic and psycholinguistic research.

Francine Conway, Associate Professor; Ph.D., Adelphi. Aging, emotions, and health studies.

Rebecca C. Curtis, Professor; Ph.D., Columbia. Social/clinical interface, psychotherapy research, self-defeating behavior.

Laura M. DeRose, Assistant Professor; Ph.D., Columbia. Developmental psychology, pubertal development and adjustment during early adolescence.

Jennifer Durham, Assistant Professor; Ph.D., Rutgers. Social justice in mental health, closing the achievement gap, couple and family therapy.

Kate Fiori, Assistant Professor, Ph.D., Michigan. Developmental psychology, adult development and aging.

Jerold Gold, Chair of Undergraduate Psychology; Ph.D., Adelphi. Interpersonal psychoanalysis, personality theory, psychotheory integration.

Patrick Grehan, Assistant Professor; Ph.D., Hofstra. School psychology, emotional intelligence, psychotherapy integration.

Mark Hilsenroth, Professor; Ph.D., Tennessee. Psychodiagnostics.

Jonathan Jackson, Director of Clinical Training and Director, Psychological Services Clinic; Ph.D., NYU. Psychotherapy and psychoanalysis.

Lawrence Josephs, Professor; Ph.D., Tennessee; ABPP. Psychoanalysis, psychotherapy, self-psychology.

Morton Kissen, Professor; Ph.D., New School; ABPP. Object relations theory, projective testing, diagnostic issues.

Karen Lombardi, Professor; Ph.D., NYU. Child clinical psychology, psychoanalytic-developmental psychology, fairy tales and myths.

Robert Mendelsohn, Professor; Ph.D., Massachusetts; ABPP. Short-term psychotherapy, psychoanalytic theory.

Joseph W. Newirth, Professor; Ph.D., Massachusetts; ABPP. Psychoanalysis, object relations theory, disorders of self.

Michael O'Loughlin, Professor, Ph.D., Columbia Teachers College. Child psychotherapy, multicultural issues in school psychology.

Coleman Paul, Professor; Ph.D., Wayne State. Behavior modification, stimulus control, computer technology in psychology.

Susan Petry, Professor; Ph.D., Columbia. Sensation and perception.

Louis H. Primavera, Professor; Ph.D., CUNY. Psychological studies, personality.

Patrick L. Ross, Professor and Special Assistant to the Dean; Ph.D., Johns Hopkins. Statistics, data processing.

Ionas Sapountzis, Associate Professor; Ph.D., NYU. Childhood development, integrating treatment modalities.

Carolyn Springer, Associate Professor; Ph.D., NYU. Statistics.

Janice M. Steil, Professor; Ph.D., Columbia. Social psychology, psychology of injustice and women's issues.

Kate A. Szymanski, Associate Professor; Ph.D., Northeastern. Small groups, social loafing, intrinsic/extrinsic motivation.

Joel Weinberger, Professor; Ph.D., New School. Human motivation.

Adelphi's campus in historic Garden City, Long Island, New York.

A registered arboretum, Adelphi is truly a green campus.

ADLER SCHOOL OF PROFESSIONAL PSYCHOLOGY

Graduate Programs

Programs of Study

Founded in 1952, Adler School of Professional Psychology is the oldest independent school of psychology in North America. The School is named after Alfred Adler (1870–1937), the first community psychologist, whose theories and teachings of psychology emphasize the uniqueness of every individual's relationship with society. Adler School is committed to continuing Adler's work by producing socially responsible graduates, providing holistic services to individuals and communities, and promoting social justice. Students come from all over the world to study in a collaborative atmosphere with accomplished clinical faculty. The School offers both campus-based and online classes to accommodate recent college graduates and working professionals.

The School was named a recipient of the 2007 American Psychological Association Board of Educational Affairs Award for Innovative Practices in Graduate Education in Psychology. The School takes pride in this recognition of its commitment to educate and train socially responsible psychologists through innovative programs that combine service learning and course work that enables graduates to address a broad range of social issues that impact the clients they serve.

The Adler School of Professional Psychology offers the following degree programs:

The Doctor of Psychology (Psy.D.) in Clinical Psychology program follows a scholar-practitioner based training model. This program prepares graduates to conduct clinical interviews and psychological testing, create treatment plans, consult and collaborate with physicians and other professionals, and provide multiple forms of therapy to alleviate mental illness, behavioral problems, and emotional distress. The Adler School has received national recognition for also preparing students for socially responsible clinical practice with a focus on the broader social and systemic factors of human dysfunction. Upon completing foundational course work, students have the opportunity to be placed in internships at prestigious clinics, hospitals, mental health centers, and government agencies. Adler School also offers a variety of concentrations and tracks including child and adolescent psychology, military clinical psychology, neuropsychology, and trauma. The Doctor of Psychology in Clinical Psychology program is accredited by the Committee on Accreditation of the American Psychological Association (APA), 750 First Street NE, Washington, D.C. 20002-4242; phone: 202-336-5510; Web site: http://www.apa.org/ed/accreditation.

The Master of Arts in Counseling Psychology program provides a foundation in the theories and methods of counseling psychology and hands-on, practical, supervised training with an emphasis on socially responsible practice. This broad-based program usually takes two years of full-time study and is offered part-time in an online/blended format. Graduates are prepared for entry-level professional work in a variety of public- and private-sector human services agencies and organizations.

The Master of Arts in Marriage and Family Counseling program prepares entry-level counselors to specialize in working with couples and families. Students complete course work and practicum experiences focused on the understanding and integration of individual lifestyle dynamics with marital and family systems. Graduates have a theoretical understanding of individual marital and family systems, including developmental issues and major variations, assessment skills in lifestyle and systemic diagnosis, and intervention skills based on major models of marital and family therapy, with the theory and methods of individual psychology as the foundation.

The Master of Arts in Counseling Psychology: Art Therapy program combines the theories and techniques of individual psychology with education and clinical training. The program, approved by the American Art Therapy Association, requires 65 credit hours of courses, including 700 hours of clinical practicum experience under at least partial supervision of a registered art therapist (ATR). The program provides students with the academic and predegree clinical experiences required to apply for registration as an art therapist as well as sit for the Licensed Professional Counselor (LPC) examination in the state of Illinois.

The Master of Arts in Counseling and Organizational Psychology program combines the theories and skills of counseling psychology with organizational theory, design, and development to prepare graduates for positions in business and industry, especially in organizational psychology and the related areas of talent management, team building, performance enhancement, executive coaching, organizational development, training, and employee assistance. This one-of-a-kind program prepares graduates to sit for state-level licensure as a master's-level counselor. Graduates are trained to assess and provide intervention in organizational settings at the individual level (personal selection, leadership development, executive coaching, career assessment, and counseling), work group level (team assessment, team issue resolution, and team building), and organizational level (talent audits, needs analysis, strategic planning, and organizational design and development).

The Master of Arts in Gerontological Counseling program is designed to provide students with the course work and practical training to work with older adults. Students are exposed to the impact of biological, psychological, and sociocultural factors on the aging process in order to gain a holistic understanding of the needs and issues of older adults. With the increasing number of older adults, the U.S. Department of Labor projects faster than average growth in employment for individuals with a master's degree. Completion of foundational course work, specialized studies, and supervised training ensures graduates are prepared to work in a variety of human services agencies and organizations with older adults who will have an appreciation for the value of psychology in promoting their quality of life.

The Master of Arts in Rehabilitation Counseling degree is designed to prepare students to become certified rehabilitation counselors (CRC). Rehabilitation counselors work with individuals who have mental, emotional, or physical handicaps, helping them to lead self-sufficient lives. Counselors determine the training and support their clients need to deal with the effects of their conditions. Rehabilitation counselors are employed by publicly funded agencies, schools, and medical facilities. Counselors evaluate clients and arrange for rehabilitation programs that may include medical care, psychological counseling, occupational therapy, and job placement.

The Master of Arts in Counseling Psychology with a specialization in forensic psychology program prepares graduates for a highly specialized career that integrates knowledge of human behavior with active participation in the criminal justice system. Specialized course work exposes students to the predominant theories and techniques of forensic evaluation, including the determination of a defendant's competency to stand trial, sanity at the time of an offense, and qualification for the death penalty in the event of a conviction for a capital crime. Students also develop a comprehensive understanding of the techniques associated with the forensic practitioner's involvement in criminal investigations; activities such as forensic hypnosis, offender and geographic profiling, and the ongoing review of police interview and witness identification procedures. Students are introduced to such specialized topics as the psychological effects of incarceration, jury selection, the evaluation of sexually dangerous persons, and the psychosocial development of the criminal personality type.

The Master of Arts in Counseling Psychology with a specialization in sport and health psychology program prepares graduates to address individual and systemic issues that affect sport performance and health. These areas overlap in the types of interventions used to produce positive changes (goal-setting and self-monitoring to improve consistency of practice or to lose weight). Sport and health goals also share the influence of various social and community factors (coaches, family members, culture, access to facilities). This unique program provides training and understanding of assessment, intervention, and analysis of systems that will allow graduates to work within communities, schools, and professional organizations to address the diverse needs of people with varying ages, health issues, and athletic accomplishments.

The Master of Arts in Police Psychology program is designed for field officers, supervisory personnel, command members, and those interested in a career in law enforcement. The program blends numerous areas within the discipline of psychology with pragmatic applications to patrol, operational, and managerial concerns that arise daily in the field of law enforcement. This degree is not designed to teach students to conduct therapy or engage in psychological testing. There are no clinical hours required or practicum to complete. Rather, the program teaches students the practical applications of psychology to the field of law enforcement. Core professors and adjunct faculty members all have extensive experience in clinical psychology and/or law enforcement.

The Master of Arts in Criminology program, offered completely online, prepares practitioners to examine the causes and consequences of criminal behavior, understand the intricacies and challenges of modern-day criminal justice systems, and apply theoretical skills to address those challenges. Graduates complete their studies ready to develop intervention and prevention strategies that are practical, effective, socially responsible, and sustainable.

Research Facilities

The Sol and Elaine Mosak Library provides resources and services to foster the educational and intellectual inquiry of students and faculty members. In addition to its major holdings in Adlerian-oriented materials, the library contains a wide variety of materials in mental health and related disciplines. The library has a collection of more than 12,000 volumes, subscribes to more than 150 professional journals, and has an extensive collection of more than 1,000 audiotapes and videotapes.

The library's CD-ROM indexes facilitate research by extending its reach to the larger research community. Through interlibrary loans, cooperative agreements with local libraries, and membership in ILLINET, OCLC, and NLM-Docline, students have computer access to learning materials from all over the country.

Financial Aid

Adler School is approved by the U.S. Department of Education to participate in the Federal Family Education Loan Program and Federal Work-Study Program. The School offers a number of scholarships to students based on financial need, academic achievement, service to the community, and availability of funds.

Cost of Study

Tuition on the Chicago campus for 2011–12 is $980 per credit hour for M.A. programs and $1095 per credit hour for the doctorate program. Tuition costs for each year vary depending on whether the student enrolls full-time or part-time. Full-time students enroll for 8 or more credit hours per term. Courses are offered during fall, spring, and summer semesters.

Living and Housing Costs

The School does not provide housing but assists students in securing off-campus housing. Students typically live in apartments in the Chicago area. Living expenses vary considerably according to standard of living, housing, and transportation.

Student Group

Adler School's commitment to social responsibility draws students from all over the world to study in a collaborative atmosphere with accomplished faculty members. The School attracts both recent college graduates and working professionals and offers significant cultural diversity by attracting the best students in the world. The Adler Student Association represents many different countries and encourages students to celebrate their heritage through on- and off-campus learning activities.

Location

Conveniently located in downtown Chicago, Illinois and Vancouver, British Columbia, both campuses are easily accessible by public transportation and provide students with a culturally diverse learning environment as well as hundreds of opportunities for clinical training across the United States and Canada.

The School

Founded in 1952 by Rudolf Dreikurs, M.D., the Adler School is committed to continuing the work of Alfred Adler, the first community psychologist. In addition to preparing individuals for the general practice of clinical psychology, Adler School also offers a community service practicum. Available in the first-year curriculum, this unique practicum allows students to get involved in community organizing, volunteer projects, political initiatives, advocacy, and public policy analysis.

The Adler Institutes for Social Change advance social justice for underserved and disadvantaged communities through applied research, community outreach, and public awareness initiatives. There are also two other institutes on campus: the Institute on Social Exclusion and the Institute on Public Safety and Social Justice.

Applying

All applicants must have at least a bachelor's degree from an accredited college or university. Applicants to the master's programs should ideally have a GPA of 3.0 or higher (on a 4.0 scale) and at least 12 credits of course work in psychology. Applicants to the doctoral program preferably have a GPA of 3.25 or higher (on a 4.0 scale) and at least 18 credits of course work in psychology. Applications are accepted for the fall and winter terms on a rolling basis. The priority deadline for the Psy.D. program is February 15. Applicants are strongly encouraged to begin the preliminary application process at least three months before they plan to begin taking classes.

Correspondence and Information

Adler School of Professional Psychology
Admissions Office
17 North Deaborn Street
Chicago, Illinois 60602

Phone: 312-662-4100
Fax: 312-662-4099
E-mail: admissions@adler.edu
Web site: http://www.adler.edu

Adler School of Professional Psychology

THE FACULTY

With an average class size of fewer than 12 students, faculty mentorship plays a very important role in the learning process at Adler School. Faculty members are licensed professionals who combine clinical practice with their instructional duties. Many hold or have held leadership positions in professional organizations, and most present workshops and seminars throughout the United States, Europe, Canada, and other countries. Adler School faculty members have a broad range of interest and specializations offering students a variety of expertise in the field of psychology.

ARGOSY UNIVERSITY.

ARGOSY UNIVERSITY, ATLANTA

College of Psychology and Behavioral Sciences

Programs of Study

Argosy University, Atlanta, offers the Postdoctoral Respecialization Certificate in Clinical Psychology, the Master of Arts (M.A.) degree in Clinical Psychology, Community Counseling, Forensic Psychology, Industrial Organizational Psychology, and Sport-Exercise Psychology; the Doctor of Education (Ed.D.) degree in Counselor Education and Supervision; and the Doctor of Psychology (Psy.D.) degree in Clinical Psychology. Students completing a program may wish to become licensed professionals. Argosy University, Atlanta does not guarantee third-party certification/licensure. Outside agencies control the requirements for taking and passing certification/licensing exams and are subject to change without notice to Argosy University, Atlanta.

The Postdoctoral Respecialization Certificate in Clinical Psychology is designed for qualified individuals with doctoral degrees in areas of psychology other than clinical psychology. It provides the opportunity to obtain clinical knowledge and skills through class work and through fieldwork experiences. Coursework and clinical training experiences are designed to enable program participants to seek licensure in clinical psychology.

The Master of Arts (M.A.) in Clinical Psychology program is designed to educate and train students to enter professional careers as master's-level practitioners. The program provides the theoretical and clinical elements necessary for graduates to be effective members of a mental health team. It introduces students to basic clinical skills that integrate individual and group theoretical foundations of applied psychology into appropriate client interaction and intervention skills. In addition, it offers excellent preparation for those considering application to the doctor of Psychology (Psy.D.) in Clinical Psychology program.

The Master of Arts (M.A.) in Community Counseling program is designed to provide students with a solid foundation for the practice of professional counseling. The program's curriculum integrates theoretical and conceptual foundations of professional counseling with training in appropriate client intervention and advocacy skills. The program emphasizes the development of attitudes, knowledge, and skills that are essential for professional counselors committed to the ethical provision of quality services. The program is committed to educating and training students to enter a professional career as master's-level counseling practitioners who can function ethically and effectively as skilled professionals with demonstrated knowledge of social and cultural diversity. Since licensing may change and often varies from state to state, students should verify the current requirements of the state in which they plan to become licensed.

The Master of Arts (M.A.) in Forensic Psychology program is designed to educate and train individuals who are currently working, or wish to work, in fields that utilize the study and practice of forensic psychology, such as law enforcement, legal and organizational consultation, and program analysis. The curriculum provides for an understanding of theory, training, and practice of forensic psychology and to emphasize the development of students who are committed to the ethical provision of high-quality services to diverse clients and organizations. The program maintains policies and delivery formats suitable for working adults.

The Master of Arts (M.A.) in Industrial Organizational Psychology program is designed to apply the knowledge of industrial organizational psychology to issues involving individuals and groups in organizational and work settings. This program prepares students for careers in areas such as compensation, training, data analysis, consultation, statistical decision making, organizational development, leadership, and human resource management. The curriculum is competency based, focusing on the outcomes of training and on the knowledge, skills, and behavior necessary to function as a master's-level professional in the field.

The Master of Arts (M.A.) in Sport-Exercise Psychology program is designed to educate and train students to be capable and ethical performance enhancement specialists. This two-year degree is geared for students seeking employment in private practice, athletic departments, coaching, exercise/health, and education, as well as those who will ultimately pursue a doctoral degree. The goals include developing student competencies in theoretical foundations, helping relationships, individual and group skills, normal and abnormal behavior, sport sciences, research and evaluation, diversity, and professional identity. Based on the educational requirements outlined by the Association for Applied Sport Psychology (AASP), the curriculum is designed to provide students with a foundation in applied sport psychology; an understanding of normal and abnormal psychological functioning; and a knowledge base in the physiological, motor, and psychosocial aspects of sport behavior. Graduates are eligible to apply for provisional status as an AASP-certified consultant.

The Doctor of Education (Ed.D.) in Counselor Education and Supervision program aligns with the master's-level counselor education programs in order to encourage entry-level counseling students to work toward becoming doctoral-level advanced practitioners, educators, and supervisors. The program prepares counselors for a variety of settings by providing the advanced skills and knowledge necessary to provide leadership and advocacy, as well as serve in supervisory, training, and teaching positions in the counseling profession. The program can also help current practitioners with existing master's-level preparation advance their careers by providing expanded opportunities to compete in the marketplace, on par with the growing number of doctoral-level counseling practitioners.

The Doctor of Psychology (Psy.D.) in Clinical Psychology program at Argosy University, Atlanta has been accredited by the American Psychological Association since 1994. The program utilizes a practitioner-scholar model of professional training and is designed to educate and train students to function effectively as clinical psychologists. The curriculum provides for the meaningful integration of theory, training, and practice. The emphasis of the program is upon the development of knowledge, skills, and attitudes that are essential for professional psychologists who are committed to the ethical provision of quality services. The degree program is designed to provide students with well-rounded generalist training in clinical psychology; however, students may choose an optional concentration in child and adolescent psychology, general adult clinical, health psychology, or neuropsychology/geropsychology. The two-year practicum training sequence involves a diagnostic/assessment practicum and a therapy practicum. Practicum training sites are developed and coordinated by the program's training office and include a range of clinical settings throughout the metro-Atlanta area. The research component of the program prepares students to anchor their work firmly in the empirical methods and findings of psychology and critically evaluate theoretical and clinical propositions. The clinical and research activities and interests of faculty members expose students to diverse theoretical perspectives and enhance the teaching, clinical supervision, and research guidance they offer.

Research Facilities

Argosy University libraries provide curriculum support and educational resources, including current text materials, diagnostic training documents, reference materials and databases, journals and dissertations, and major and current titles in program areas. There is an online public-access catalog of library resources available throughout the Argosy University system. Students have remote access to the campus library database, enabling them to study and conduct research at home. Academic databases offer dissertation abstracts, academic journals, and professional periodicals. All library computers are Internet accessible. Software applications include Word, Excel, PowerPoint, SPSS, and various test-scoring programs.

Financial Aid

Financial aid is available to those who qualify. Argosy University, Atlanta, offers access to federal and state aid programs, merit-based awards, grants, loans, and a work-study program. As a first step, students should complete the Free Application for Federal Student Aid (FAFSA). Prospective students can apply electronically at http://www.fafsa.ed.gov or at the campus.

Cost of Study

Tuition varies by program. Students should contact Argosy University, Atlanta, for tuition information.

Living and Housing Costs

Students typically live in apartments in the metropolitan Atlanta area. Living expenses vary according to each student's preferred standard of living, housing, and transportation. The University does not offer or operate student housing. Most Argosy University students are full-time working professionals who live within driving distance of the campus. Several nearby hotels offer special rates for those who commute from long distances. The Admissions Department also maintains a list of housing options, including contact information for University students who wish to share housing. For more information, students should contact the Admissions Department.

Student Group

Admission to Argosy University, Atlanta, is selective to ensure a dynamic and engaged student body. The University encourages diversity in academic and employment backgrounds and promotes integration of the student body into professional life through established connections with local and national professional associations. Argosy University offers a professionally oriented education with rich opportunities to gain practical experience in class, field placements, and internships. Full-time students and working professionals can gain the extensive knowledge and range of skills necessary for effective performance in their chosen field.

Student Outcomes

Students can register with Argosy University's online career-services system and use select services from a distance, such as degree-specific career e-mail lists, national job posts, and virtual job fairs. Students should contact the University for more information.

Location

Argosy University, Atlanta, is housed in a modern building in Sandy Springs, a northern suburb of Atlanta. The campus features a café and outdoor lakeside terrace. Beyond the college, students will find a selection of housing options. This major metropolitan area offers many social and recreational opportunities, from clubs and concerts to galleries and museums, from a growing restaurant scene to Braves baseball games and rollerblading in Piedmont Park. The many hospitals, clinics, agencies, and educational institutions in the Atlanta area provide varied opportunities for student training. Atlanta's business environment includes technology companies such as EarthLink and Macquarium as well as corporate giants such as the Coca-Cola Company, CNN, Delta Air Lines, AT&T, and Georgia Pacific.

The University

Argosy University is a private institution with nineteen locations across the nation. Argosy University, Atlanta, provides a career resources office, an academic resources center, and extensive information access for research. It offers the resources of a large university plus the friendliness and personal attention of a small campus. The innovative programs feature dynamic, relevant, and practical curricula delivered in flexible class formats. Students enjoy scheduling options that make it easier to fit school into their busy lives, choosing from day and evening courses, on campus or online. Many students find a combination of class formats to be an ideal way of continuing their education while meeting family and professional demands.

Argosy University is accredited by the Higher Learning Commission and a member of the North Central Association, 230 South LaSalle Street, Suite 7-500, Chicago, Illinois 60604-1413; 800-621-7440 (toll-free); http://www.ncahlc.org.

Applying

Argosy University, Atlanta, accepts students year-round on a rolling admissions basis, depending on availability of required courses. Applications for admission are available online or by contacting the campus.

Correspondence and Information

Argosy University, Atlanta
980 Hammond Drive, Suite 100
Atlanta, Georgia 30328
Phone: 770-671-1200
        888-671-4777 (toll-free)
Fax: 770-671-0476
E-mail: auadmissions@argosy.edu
Web site: http://www.argosy.edu/atlanta

Argosy University, Atlanta

THE FACULTY

The Argosy University faculty is comprised of working professionals who are eager to help students succeed. Members bring real-world experience and the latest practice innovations to the academic setting. The diverse faculty members of the College of Psychology and Behavioral Sciences are widely recognized for contributions to the field. Many are published scholars, and most hold doctoral degrees. They are committed to providing a substantive education that combines comprehensive knowledge with critical skills and practical workplace relevance. Above all, faculty members are committed to their students' personal and professional development.

ARGOSY UNIVERSITY, CHICAGO

College of Psychology and Behavioral Sciences

Programs of Study

Argosy University, Chicago, offers the Graduate Certificate in Psychoanalytic Psychology; the Master of Arts (M.A.) degree in Clinical Psychology, Forensic Psychology, Industrial Organizational Psychology, Marriage and Family Therapy, and Community Counseling; the Doctor of Education (Ed.D.) degree in Counselor Education and Supervision; and the Doctor of Psychology (Psy.D.) degree in Clinical Psychology. Students completing a program may wish to become licensed professionals. Argosy University, Chicago does not guarantee third-party certification/licensure. Outside agencies control the requirements for taking and passing certification/licensing exams and are subject to change without notice to Argosy University, Chicago.

The Graduate Certificate in Psychoanalytic Psychology is designed to provide specialized training in psychoanalytic psychology for post-master's and doctoral clinicians with relevant background and experience. The certificate is designed to meet the need for education and training in assessment, intervention, and supervision within a broad psychoanalytic model. The curriculum provides a firm grounding in major theoretical paradigms with special attention to those that are current and emerging.

The Master of Arts (M.A.) in Clinical Psychology program is designed to prepare students for admission into the Doctor of Psychology (Psy.D.) in Clinical Psychology program and does not prepare student to receive a license at the master's level. The program is designed to introduce students to basic clinical skills that integrate individual, couples/family, and group theoretical foundations of applied psychology. Students are also exposed to various assessment and intervention skills necessary when working with clients. The program can be completed in as little as two years, but must be completed within five years. Admission to the program or completion of the master's degree does not guarantee admission into the Psy.D. in Clinical Psychology program. However, if admitted to the doctoral program, up to 43 credit hours from the M.A. program will apply toward the Psy.D. curriculum.

The Master of Arts (M.A.) in Forensic Psychology program is designed to educate and train individuals who are currently working, or wish to work, in fields that utilize the study and practice of forensic psychology, such as law enforcement, legal and organizational consultation, and program analysis. The curriculum is designed to provide for an understanding of theory, training, and practice of forensic psychology and to emphasize the development of students who are committed to the ethical provision of high-quality services to diverse clients and organizations. The program maintains policies and delivery formats suitable for working adults.

The Master of Arts (M.A.) in Industrial Organizational Psychology program is designed to apply the knowledge of industrial organizational psychology to issues involving individuals and groups in organizational and work settings. This program is designed to prepare students for careers in areas such as compensation, training, data analysis, consultation, statistical decision making, organizational development, leadership, and human resource management. The curriculum is competency based, focusing on the outcomes of training and on the knowledge, skills, and behavior necessary to function as a master's-level professional in the field.

The Master of Arts (M.A.) in Marriage and Family Therapy program strives to educate and train marriage and family therapists with the extensive knowledge and range of skills necessary to function effectively in their profession. The program introduces basic skills that integrate systemic theoretical foundations of marriage and family therapy into appropriate client interaction and intervention skills. The program is designed to emphasize the development of attitudes, knowledge, and skills essential in the formation of marriage and family therapists who are committed to the ethical provision of quality services, with demonstrated knowledge of social and cultural diversity. The curriculum that integrates basic therapy and practicum/field experience into appropriate client interaction and intervention skills for utilization in a wide variety of settings.

The Master of Arts in Community Counseling program is accredited by the Council for Accreditation for Counseling and Related Programs (CACREP), a specialized accrediting body recognized by the Council for Higher Education Accreditation (CHEA).

The Doctor of Education (Ed.D.) in Counselor Education and Supervision program aligns with the master's-level counselor education programs in order to encourage entry-level counseling students to work toward becoming doctoral-level advanced practitioners, educators, and supervisors. The program is designed to prepare counselors for a variety of settings by providing the advanced skills and knowledge necessary to provide leadership and advocacy, as well as serve in supervisory, training, and teaching positions in the counseling profession.

The Ed.D. in Counselor Education and Supervision program is designed to help current practitioners with existing master's-level preparation to advance their careers. This doctoral degree can provide expanded opportunities to compete in the marketplace, on par with the growing number of doctoral-level counseling practitioners.

The Doctor of Psychology (Psy.D.) in Clinical Psychology program has been designed to educate and train students to function effectively as clinical psychologists. The curriculum is designed to provide for the meaningful integration of theory, training, and practice. The program is designed to emphasize the development of attitudes, knowledge, and skills essential in the formation of professional psychologists who are committed to the ethical provision of quality services. This program can be completed in as little as four years, but must be completed in seven years; most students complete it in five or six years. Graduates are qualified for positions as licensed clinical psychologists (provided they pass the appropriate licensure examination). The program is offered in a traditional, though flexible format with classes meeting in the mornings, afternoons and evenings. Students enrolled in the program may complete one of the following optional concentrations: child and adolescent psychology, client-centered and experiential psychotherapies, diversity and multicultural psychology, family psychology, forensic psychology, health psychology, neuropsychology, organizational consulting, psychoanalytic psychology, and psychology and spirituality.

Research Facilities

Argosy University libraries provide curriculum support and educational resources, including current text materials, diagnostic training documents, reference materials and databases, journals and dissertations, and major and current titles in program areas. There is an online public-access catalog of library resources available throughout the Argosy University system. Students have remote access to the campus library database, enabling them to study and conduct research at home. Academic databases offer dissertation abstracts, academic journals, and professional periodicals. All library computers are Internet accessible. Software applications include Word, Excel, PowerPoint, SPSS, and various test-scoring programs.

Financial Aid

Financial aid is available to those who qualify. Argosy University, Chicago, offers access to federal and state aid programs, merit-based awards, grants, loans, and a work-study program. As a first step, students should complete the Free Application for Federal Student Aid (FAFSA). Prospective students can apply electronically at http://www.fafsa.ed.gov or at the campus.

Cost of Study

Tuition varies by program. Students should contact Argosy University, Chicago for tuition information.

Living and Housing Costs

Students typically live in apartments in the metropolitan Chicago area. Living expenses vary according to each student's preferred standard of living, housing, and transportation. The University does not offer or operate student housing. Most of the students are full-time working professionals who live within driving distance of the campus. Several nearby hotels offer special rates for those who commute from long distances. The Admissions Department also maintains a list of housing options, including contact information for university students who wish to share housing. For more information, students should contact the Admissions Department.

Student Group

Admission to Argosy University, Chicago, is selective to ensure a dynamic and engaged student body. The University encourages diversity in academic and employment backgrounds and promotes integration of the student body into professional life through established connections with local and national professional associations. Argosy University offers a professionally oriented education with rich opportunities to gain practical experience in class, field placements, and internships. Full-time students and working professionals gain the extensive knowledge and range of skills necessary for effective performance in their chosen fields.

Student Outcomes

Students can register with the University's online career-services system and use select services from a distance, such as degree-specific career e-mail lists, national job posts, and virtual job fairs. Students should contact the University for more information.

Location

Chicago is a city of world-class status and beauty, drawing visitors from around the globe. Argosy University, Chicago, sits in the heart of The Loop, the city's business and entertainment center. Located on the shores of Lake Michigan, Chicago is home to world-champion sports teams, an internationally acclaimed symphony orchestra, renowned architecture, and a variety of history and art museums. Recreational opportunities include hiking and cycling on miles of lakefront trails, golfing, and shopping. Chicago's business environment includes a broad array of companies including Boeing and Pepsi America. The commercial banking headquarters of JP Morgan Chase is also located in Chicago.

The University

Argosy University is a private institution with nineteen locations across the nation. Argosy University, Chicago, provides a career services office, an academic resources center, and extensive information access for research. It offers the resources of a large university plus the friendliness and personal attention of a small campus. Argosy University, Chicago, is closely associated with the Schaumburg, Illinois, campus, located 45 minutes from downtown Chicago.

The innovative programs feature dynamic, relevant, and practical curricula delivered in flexible class formats. Students enjoy scheduling options that make it easier to fit school into their busy lives, choosing from day and evening courses, on campus or online. Many students find a combination of class formats to be an ideal way of continuing their education while meeting family and professional demands.

Argosy University is accredited by the Higher Learning Commission and a member of the North Central Association, 230 South LaSalle Street, Suite 7-500, Chicago, Illinois 60604-1413; 800-621-7440 (toll-free); http://www.ncahlc.org.

Applying

Argosy University, Chicago, accepts students year-round on a rolling admissions basis, depending on availability of required courses. Applications for admission are available online or by contacting the campus.

Correspondence and Information

Argosy University, Chicago
225 North Michigan Avenue, Suite 1300
Chicago, Illinois 60601

Phone: 312-777-7600
800-626-4123 (toll-free)
Fax: 312-777-7748
E-mail: auadmissions@argosy.edu
Web site: http://www.argosy.edu/chicago

Argosy University, Chicago

THE FACULTY

The Argosy University faculty is comprised of working professionals who are eager to help students succeed. Members bring real-world experience and the latest practice innovations to the academic setting. The diverse faculty members of the College of Psychology and Behavioral Sciences are widely recognized for contributions to the field. Many are published scholars, and most hold doctoral degrees. They are committed to providing a substantive education that combines comprehensive knowledge with critical skills and practical workplace relevance. Above all, faculty members are committed to their students' personal and professional development.

ARGOSY UNIVERSITY.

ARGOSY UNIVERSITY, DALLAS

College of Psychology and Behavioral Sciences

Programs of Study
Argosy University, Dallas, offers the Master of Arts (M.A.) degree in Clinical Psychology, Community Counseling, Forensic Psychology, and Industrial Organizational Psychology; the Doctor of Education (Ed.D.) degree in Counselor Education and Supervision; and the Doctor of Psychology (Psy.D.) degree in Clinical Psychology. Students completing a program may wish to become licensed professionals. Argosy University, Dallas does not guarantee third-party certification/licensure. Outside agencies control the requirements for taking and passing certification/licensing exams and are subject to change without notice to Argosy University, Dallas.

The Master of Arts (M.A.) in Clinical Psychology program is designed to educate and train students to enter professional careers as master's-level practitioners. The program provides the theoretical and clinical elements necessary for graduates to be effective members of a mental health team. It is designed to introduce students to basic clinical skills that integrate individual and group theoretical foundations of applied psychology into appropriate client interaction and intervention skills. In addition, it offers excellent preparation for those considering application to the Psy.D. in Clinical Psychology program. Specific objectives of the program include: entry-level preparation of practitioners capable of delivering effective and ethical diagnostic and therapeutic services to diverse populations of clients in need of such treatment; students who will demonstrate their knowledge and competence in addressing the needs, values, and experiences of people from diverse populations by recognizing and distinguishing people from such subpopulations, differentiating their experiences, and prioritizing their needs; training entry-level practitioners capable of evaluating the effectiveness of their services and enhance their careers through the existing and evolving body of knowledge and methods in the practice and science of psychology; the education of students familiar with the current body of knowledge in cognitive-affective, biological, and sociocultural bases of human behavior; the development of entry-level practitioners capable of assuming leadership in both the health-care delivery system and in the training of mental health professionals; and eligibility for licensure.

The Master of Arts (M.A.) in Community Counseling program is designed to prepare students for the practice of professional counseling. The program promotes the development of attitudes, knowledge, and skills essential to becoming thoughtful, skilled, and ethical professionals who can provide counseling services in a wide variety of government, community, and private settings. Graduates meet the academic requirements for one or more Texas state license exams.

The Master of Arts (M.A.) in Forensic Psychology program is designed to educate and train individuals who are currently working, or wish to work, in fields that utilize the study and practice of forensic psychology, such as to law enforcement, legal and organizational consultation, and program analysis. The curriculum is designed to provide for an understanding of theory, training, and practice of forensic psychology and to emphasize the development of students who are committed to the ethical provision of high-quality services to diverse clients and organizations. The program maintains policies and delivery formats suitable for working adults.

The Master of Arts (M.A.) in Industrial Organizational Psychology program is designed to apply the knowledge of industrial organizational psychology to issues involving individuals and groups in organizational and work settings. This program is designed to prepare students for careers in areas such as compensation, training, data analysis, consultation, statistical decision making, organizational development, leadership, and human resource management. The curriculum is competency based, focusing on the outcomes of training and on the knowledge, skills, and behavior necessary to function as a master's-level professional in the field.

The Doctor of Education (Ed.D.) in Counselor Education and Supervision program aligns with the master's-level counselor education programs in order to encourage entry-level counseling students to work toward becoming doctoral-level advanced practitioners, educators, and supervisors. The program is designed to prepare counselors for a variety of settings by providing the advanced skills and knowledge necessary to provide leadership and advocacy, as well as serve in supervisory, training, and teaching positions in the counseling profession. The program can also help current practitioners with existing master's-level preparation advance their careers by providing expanded opportunities to compete in the marketplace, on par with the growing number of doctoral-level counseling practitioners.

The Doctor of Psychology in Clinical Psychology program (Psy.D.) has been designed to educate and train students to function effectively as clinical psychologists. The curriculum provides for the meaningful integration of theory, training, and practice. The program is designed to emphasize the development of knowledge, skills, and attitudes essential in the formation of professional psychologists who are committed to the ethical provision of quality services.

Research Facilities
Argosy University libraries provide curriculum support and educational resources, including current text materials, diagnostic training documents, reference materials and databases, journals and dissertations, and major and current titles in program areas. There is an online public-access catalog of library resources available throughout the Argosy University system. Students have remote access to the campus library database, enabling them to study and conduct research at home. Academic databases offer dissertation abstracts, academic journals, and professional periodicals. All library computers are Internet accessible. Software applications include Word, Excel, PowerPoint, SPSS, and various test-scoring programs.

Financial Aid
Financial aid is available to those who qualify. Argosy University, Dallas, offers access to federal and state aid programs, merit-based awards, grants, loans, and a work-study program. As a first step, students should complete the Free Application for Federal Student Aid (FAFSA). Prospective students can apply electronically at http://www.fafsa.ed.gov or at the campus.

Cost of Study
Tuition varies by program. Students should contact Argosy University, Dallas, for tuition information.

Living and Housing Costs
Students typically live in apartments in the metropolitan Dallas area. Living expenses vary according to each student's preferred standard of living, housing, and transportation. The University does not offer or operate student housing. Most of the students are full-time working professionals who live within driving distance of the campus. Several nearby hotels offer special rates for those who commute from long distances. The Admissions Department also maintains a list of housing options, including contact information, for University students who wish to share housing. For more information, students should contact the Admissions Department.

Student Group
Admission to Argosy University, Dallas, is selective to ensure a dynamic and engaged student body. The University encourages diversity in academic and employment backgrounds and promotes integration of the student body into professional life through established connections with local and national professional associations. Argosy University offers a professionally oriented education with rich opportunities to gain practical experience in class, field placements, and internships. Full-time students and working professionals gain the extensive knowledge and range of skills necessary for effective performance in their chosen fields.

Student Outcomes
Students can register with the University's online career-services system and use select services from a distance, such as degree-specific career e-mail lists, national job posts, and virtual job fairs. Students should contact the University for more information.

Location
Argosy University, Dallas, offers a north-central location in Dallas, with easy access to freeways, neighboring colleges and universities, libraries, shops, restaurants, theaters, art museums, and other tourist attractions. The business environment in the Dallas–Fort Worth metropolitan area includes a broad array of companies, such as Lockheed Martin Corporation, Baylor University Medical System, and Southwest Airlines.

The University
Argosy University is a private institution with nineteen locations across the nation. Argosy University, Dallas, provides a career resources office, an academic resources center, and extensive information access for research. It offers the resources of a large university, plus the friendliness and personal attention of a small campus.

Argosy University, Dallas, offers the unique opportunity to take one class at a time, with each class lasting for one month. Students are never required to study for multiple exams at the same time. New classes start each month. This flexible format lets students begin working on a graduate degree without waiting for the traditional semester to start.

Argosy University is accredited by the Higher Learning Commission and a member of the North Central Association, 230 South LaSalle Street, Suite 7-500, Chicago, Illinois 60604-1413; 800-621-7440 (toll-free); http://www.ncahlc.org.

Applying
Argosy University, Dallas, accepts students year-round on a rolling admissions basis, depending on availability of required courses. Applications for admission are available online or by contacting the campus.

Correspondence and Information
Argosy University, Dallas
5001 Lyndon B. Johnson Freeway
Heritage Square
Farmers Branch, Texas 75244
Phone: 214-890-9900
          866-954-9900 (toll-free)
Fax: 214-378-8555
E-mail: http://auadmissions@argosy.edu
Web site: http://www.argosy.edu/dallas

Argosy University, Dallas

THE FACULTY

The Argosy University faculty is comprised of working professionals who are eager to help students succeed. Members bring real-world experience and the latest practice innovations to the academic setting. The diverse faculty members of the College of Psychology and Behavioral Sciences are widely recognized for contributions to the field. Many are published scholars, and most hold doctoral degrees. They are committed to providing a substantive education that combines comprehensive knowledge with critical skills and practical workplace relevance. Above all, faculty members are committed to their students' personal and professional development.

ARGOSY UNIVERSITY

ARGOSY UNIVERSITY, DENVER

College of Psychology and Behavioral Sciences

Programs of Study

Argosy University, Denver, offers the Master of Arts (M.A.) degree in Forensic Psychology, Industrial Organizational Psychology, Clinical Mental Health Counseling, and Marriage and Family Therapy; the Doctor of Marriage and Family Therapy (D.M.F.T.) degree; the Doctor of Education (Ed.D.) degree in Counseling Psychology, and Counselor Education and Supervision. Students completing a program may wish to become licensed professionals. Argosy University, Denver does not guarantee third-party certification/licensure. Outside agencies control the requirements for taking and passing certification/licensing exams and are subject to change without notice to Argosy University, Denver.

The Master of Arts (M.A.) in Forensic Psychology program is designed to educate and train individuals who are currently working, or wish to work, in fields that utilize the study and practice of forensic psychology, such as law enforcement, legal and organizational consultation, and program analysis. The curriculum is designed to provide for an understanding of theory, training, and practice of forensic psychology and to emphasize the development of students who are committed to the ethical provision of high-quality services to diverse clients and organizations. The program maintains policies and delivery formats suitable for working adults.

The Master of Arts (M.A.) in Industrial Organizational Psychology program is designed to apply the knowledge of industrial organizational psychology to issues involving individuals and groups in organizational and work settings. This program is designed to prepare students for careers in areas such as compensation, training, data analysis, consultation, statistical decision making, organizational development, leadership, and human resource management. The curriculum is competency based, focusing on the outcomes of training and on the knowledge, skills, and behavior necessary to function as a master's-level professional in the field.

The Master of Arts (M.A.) in Clinical Mental Health Counseling program offers human services providers the extensive knowledge and range of skills necessary to serve effectively in the profession. Courses and curricula are designed to parallel prevailing licensure and certification requirements as closely as possible. Because of variations among states, each student should check with regional authorities to confirm such requirements.

The Master of Arts (M.A.) in Marriage and Family Therapy program strives to educate and train marriage and family therapists with the extensive knowledge and range of skills necessary to function effectively in their profession. The program introduces basic skills that integrate systemic theoretical foundations of marriage and family therapy into appropriate client interaction and intervention skills. The program is designed to emphasize the development of attitudes, knowledge, and skills essential in the formation of marriage and family therapists who are committed to the ethical provision of quality services, with demonstrated knowledge of social and cultural diversity. The curriculum that integrates basic therapy and practicum/field experience into appropriate client interaction and intervention skills for utilization in a wide variety of settings. Marriage and family therapy is recognized by the Public Health Service Act as one of the five core mental health professions, and the National Institute of Mental Health accepts marriage and family therapists as qualified mental health professionals.

The Doctor of Marriage and Family Therapy (D.M.F.T.) degree program is a 60-credit-hour terminal, practice-oriented degree. The program builds upon students' prior learning and professional experience by expanding and deepening their knowledge of human development, family dynamics, systemic thinking, interactional theories, traditional and contemporary marriage and family therapy theories and practices, and cultural contexts. The D.M.F.T. program curriculum provides opportunities for advanced study and research of systemic concepts and methods as applied to clinical work with children, couples, individuals, and families as well as larger systems of organizations and communities. In addition to the continuing development of clinical skills, the curriculum includes the development of skills related to leadership and service to the field in the areas of teaching and supervision. The D.M.F.T. program curriculum is generally designed to meet the American Association for Marriage and Family Therapy (AAMFT) requirements to become an approved supervisor. (Those students who are already AAMFT-approved supervisors may petition for an alternate learning experience equivalent to the 9 credit hours devoted to training and supervision.)

The Doctor of Education (Ed.D.) in Counseling Psychology program has been designed to emphasize the development of attitudes, knowledge, and skills essential for professionals who are committed to the ethical provision of quality services. The curriculum is designed to provide for the meaningful integration of theory, training, and practice. Specific objectives of the program include the following: training practitioners capable of delivering effective treatment to diverse populations in need of such treatment; the development of counseling psychologists who understand the biological, psychological, and sociological bases of human functioning; training practitioners who are capable of exercising leadership both in the health-care delivery system and in training mental health professionals; the preparation of counseling psychologists capable of expanding their role within society; and the education of practitioners capable of working with other disciplines as part of a professional team.

The Doctor of Education (Ed.D.) in Counselor Education and Supervision program aligns with the master's-level counselor education programs in order to encourage entry-level counseling students to work toward becoming doctoral-level advanced practitioners, educators, and supervisors. The program is designed to prepare counselors for a variety of settings by providing the advanced skills and knowledge necessary to provide leadership and advocacy, as well as serve in supervisory, training, and teaching positions in the counseling profession. The program can also help current practitioners with existing master's-level preparation advance their careers by providing expanded opportunities to compete in the marketplace, on par with the growing number of doctoral-level counseling practitioners.

Research Facilities

Argosy University libraries provide curriculum support and educational resources, including current text materials, diagnostic training documents, reference materials and databases, journals and dissertations, and major and current titles in program areas. There is an online public-access catalog of library resources available throughout the Argosy University system. Students have remote access to the campus library database, enabling them to study and conduct research at home. Academic databases offer dissertation abstracts, academic journals, and professional periodicals. All library computers are Internet accessible. Software applications include Word, Excel, PowerPoint, SPSS, and various test-scoring programs.

Financial Aid

Financial aid is available to those who qualify. Argosy University, Denver, offers access to federal and state aid programs, merit-based awards, grants, loans, and a work-study program. As a first step, students should complete the Free Application for Federal Student Aid (FAFSA). Prospective students can apply electronically at http://www.fafsa.ed.gov or at the campus.

Cost of Study

Tuition varies by program. Students should contact Argosy University, Denver, for tuition information.

Living and Housing Costs

Students typically live in apartments in the metropolitan Denver area. Living expenses vary according to each student's preferred standard of living, housing, and transportation. The University does not offer or operate student housing. Most of the students are full-time working professionals who live within driving distance of the campus. Several nearby hotels offer special rates for those who commute from long distances. The Admissions Department also maintains a list of housing options, including contact information for University students who wish to share housing. For more information, students should contact the Admissions Department.

Student Group

Admission to Argosy University, Denver, is selective to ensure a dynamic and engaged student body. The University encourages diversity in academic and employment backgrounds and promotes integration of the student body into professional life through established connections with local and national professional associations. Argosy University offers a professionally oriented education with rich opportunities to gain practical experience in class, field placements, and internships. Full-time students and working professionals gain the extensive knowledge and range of skills necessary for effective performance in their chosen fields.

Student Outcomes

Students can register with the University's online career-services system and use select services from a distance, such as degree-specific career e-mail lists, national job posts, and virtual job fairs. Students should contact the University for more information.

Location

Argosy University, Denver, is conveniently located at 7600 East Eastman Avenue in Denver, Colorado. The campus is close to a variety of local libraries, shops, restaurants, theaters, and art museums. Denver's thriving professional organizations, major corporations, high-tech companies, hospitals, schools, clinics, and social service agencies can also provide varied training opportunities for students.

The University

Argosy University is a private institution with nineteen locations across the nation. Argosy University, Denver, provides a career resources office, an academic resources center, and extensive information access for research. It offers the resources of a large university plus the friendliness and personal attention of a small campus.

The innovative programs feature dynamic, relevant, and practical curricula delivered in flexible class formats. Students enjoy scheduling options that make it easier to fit school into their busy lives, choosing from day and evening courses, on campus or online. Many students find a combination of class formats to be an ideal way of continuing their education while meeting family and professional demands.

Argosy University is accredited by the Higher Learning Commission and a member of the North Central Association, 230 South LaSalle Street, Suite 7-500, Chicago, Illinois 60604-1413; 800-621-7440 (toll-free); http://www.ncahlc.org.

Applying

Argosy University, Denver, accepts students year-round on a rolling admissions basis, depending on availability of required courses. Applications for admission are available online or by contacting the campus.

Correspondence and Information

Argosy University, Denver
7600 East Eastman Avenue
Denver, Colorado 80213
Phone: 303-923-4110
    866-431-5981 (toll-free)
Fax: 303-248-2600
E-mail: auadmissions@argosy.edu
Web site: http://www.argosy.edu/denver

Argosy University, Denver

THE FACULTY

The Argosy University faculty is comprised of working professionals who are eager to help students succeed. Members bring real-world experience and the latest practice innovations to the academic setting. The diverse faculty members of the College of Psychology and Behavioral Sciences are widely recognized for contributions to the field. Many are published scholars, and most hold doctoral degrees. They are committed to providing a substantive education that combines comprehensive knowledge with critical skills and practical workplace relevance. Above all, faculty members are committed to their students' personal and professional development.

ARGOSY UNIVERSITY

ARGOSY UNIVERSITY, HAWAI'I

College of Psychology and Behavioral Sciences

Programs of Study

Argosy University, Hawai'i, offers the Master of Arts (M.A.) degree in Clinical Psychology, Forensic Psychology, and Marriage and Family Therapy; the Master of Science (M.S.) in Psychopharmacology; the Doctor of Education (Ed.D.) degree in Counseling Psychology and Counselor Education and Supervision; and the Doctor of Psychology (Psy.D.) degree in Clinical Psychology. Students completing a program may wish to become licensed professionals. Argosy University, Hawai'i does not guarantee third-party certification/licensure. Outside agencies control the requirements for taking and passing certification/licensing exams and are subject to change without notice to Argosy University, Hawai'i.

Both by virtue of the location of Hawai'i and by the specific design of the faculty, a central focus of education at Argosy University, Hawai'i is relevance to social issues, to social justice, and to all manner of human diversity and difference. Attention to issues of human diversity occurs throughout the curriculum and within a number of additional learning opportunities outside of the classroom. Work with diverse and marginalized populations is a major focus of the teaching, scholarship, and clinical practice of all of the core faculty members at Argosy University, Hawai'i. The faculty is committed to mentoring students who will provide effective and relevant services to underserved populations.

The Master of Arts (M.A.) in Clinical Psychology program is designed as both a terminal degree and for those who plan to pursue doctoral study. The program provides a solid core of basic psychology, as well as a strong clinical orientation, with an emphasis in psychological assessment. The curriculum provides the theoretical and clinical elements to allow students to become effective members of mental health teams.

The Master of Arts (M.A.) in Forensic Psychology program is designed to educate and train individuals who are currently working, or wish to work, in fields that utilize the study and practice of forensic psychology, such as law enforcement, legal and organizational consultation, and program analysis. The curriculum provides for an understanding of theory, training, and practice of forensic psychology and to emphasize the development of students who are committed to the ethical provision of high-quality services to diverse clients and organizations. The program maintains policies and delivery formats suitable for working adults.

The Master of Arts (M.A.) in Marriage and Family Therapy program recognizes the need to provide marriage and family therapists with the extensive knowledge and range of skills necessary to function effectively in their profession. The program introduces basic skills that integrate systemic theoretical foundations of marriage and family therapy into appropriate client interaction and intervention skills. The program emphasizes the development of attitudes, knowledge, and skills essential in the formation of marriage and family therapists who are committed to the ethical provision of quality services. The curriculum integrates basic therapy and practicum/field experience into appropriate client interaction and intervention skills for utilization in a wide variety of settings. Marriage and family therapy is recognized by the Public Health Service Act as one of the five core mental health professions, and the National Institute of Mental Health accepts marriage and family therapists as qualified mental health professionals.

The Master of Science (M.S.) in Psychopharmacology program incorporates course work and clinical practice to train postdoctoral psychologists to prescribe medications independently, appropriately, effectively, and safely. It is a 32-credit-hour program with a practicum component requiring treatment of 100 patients. Upon successful completion of the program, students will have the education and experience to prescribe psychopharmacological medications consistent with state and federal laws, and work collaboratively with physicians, nurses, and other health-care providers in order to coordinate care. This program is intended to prepare students for the Psychopharmacology Exam for Psychologists (PEP).

The Doctor of Education (Ed.D.) in Counseling Psychology degree program (with an optional concentration in Counselor Education and Supervision) is designed to meet the special requirements of working professionals who want to develop their knowledge and skills to handle the changing needs of modern organizations. The program is structured to provide working professionals with the opportunity to pursue their personal and professional goals through the completion of a graduate program.

The Doctor of Education (Ed.D.) in Counselor Education and Supervision program aligns with the master's-level counselor education programs in order to encourage entry-level counseling students to work toward becoming doctoral-level advanced practitioners, educators, and supervisors. The program prepares counselors for a variety of settings by providing the advanced skills and knowledge necessary to provide leadership and advocacy, as well as serve in supervisory, training, and teaching positions in the counseling profession. The program can also help current practitioners with existing master's-level preparation advance their careers by providing expanded opportunities to compete in the marketplace, on par with the growing number of doctoral-level counseling practitioners.

The Doctor of Psychology (Psy.D.) in Clinical Psychology program is designed to prepare students for both contemporary and emerging roles in the practice of professional psychology. Students are trained to be practitioner-scholars who are skilled in local and contextual investigation and problem solving. The school offers a generalist program that supports the development of core competencies in psychological assessment, intervention, consultation/education, and management/supervision. The curriculum provides for the meaningful integration of theory, research, and practice. The doctoral degree program emphasizes the acquisition of attitudes, knowledge bases, and skills essential for professional psychologists who are committed to the provision of ethical quality services. Program requirements include course work, two years of practicum, advanced practicum (optional) and practicum seminar groups, a Clinical Research Project, and a one-year, full-time predoctoral internship (or its equivalent). Argosy University, Hawai'i maintains an internship consortium for its doctoral degree program students, which is listed with the Association of Psychology Postdoctoral and Internship Centers (APPIC).

Research Facilities

Argosy University libraries provide curriculum support and educational resources, including current text materials, diagnostic training documents, reference materials and databases, journals and dissertations, and major and current titles in program areas. There is an online public-access catalog of library resources available throughout the Argosy University system. Students have remote access to the campus library database, enabling them to study and conduct research at home. Academic databases offer dissertation abstracts, academic journals, and professional periodicals. All library computers are Internet accessible. Software applications include Word, Excel, PowerPoint, SPSS, and various test-scoring programs.

Financial Aid

Financial aid is available to those who qualify. Argosy University, Hawai'i, offers access to federal and state aid programs, merit-based awards, grants, loans, and a work-study program. As a first step, students should complete the Free Application for Federal Student Aid (FAFSA). Prospective students can apply electronically at http://www.fafsa.ed.gov or at the campus.

Cost of Study

Tuition varies by program. Students should contact Argosy University, Hawai'i, for tuition information.

Living and Housing Costs

Students typically live in apartments in the metropolitan Honolulu area. Living expenses vary according to each student's preferred standard of living, housing, and transportation. The University does not offer or operate student housing. Most of the students are full-time working professionals who live within driving distance of the campus. Several nearby hotels offer special rates for those who commute from long distances. The Admissions Department also maintains a list of housing options, including contact information for University students who wish to share housing. For more information, students should contact the Admissions Department.

Student Group

Admission to Argosy University, Hawai'i, is selective to ensure a dynamic and engaged student body. The University encourages diversity in academic and employment backgrounds and promotes integration of the student body into professional life through established connections with local and national professional associations. Argosy University offers a professionally oriented education with rich opportunities to gain practical experience in class, field placements, and internships. Full-time students and working professionals gain the extensive knowledge and range of skills necessary for effective performance in their chosen fields.

Student Outcomes

Students can register with the University's online career-services system and use select services from a distance, such as degree-specific career e-mail lists, national job posts, and virtual job fairs. Students should contact the University for more information.

Location

Argosy University, Hawai'i, is located in downtown Honolulu on Oahu. Additional satellite locations on Maui and in Hilo on the island of Hawaii offer programs to communities on the neighboring islands. These locations connect the campus to Hawaii and to the local and native communities of the Pacific Islands and the Pacific Rim. Students enjoy the cultural and recreational opportunities that these locations provide. University faculty and staff members often work in cooperation with the Hawaiian community to create an educational focus on social issues, human diversity, and programs that make a difference to underserved populations.

Honolulu's business environment includes a broad array of companies. The area's largest employers include Bank of Hawaii, Queens Medical Center, and the U.S. government. Many businesses in the metropolitan area provide varied opportunities for student training.

The University

Argosy University is a private institution with nineteen locations across the nation. Argosy University, Hawai'i, provides a career resources office, an academic resources center, and extensive information access for research. It offers the resources of a large university plus the friendliness and personal attention of a small campus.

The innovative programs feature dynamic, relevant, and practical curricula delivered in flexible class formats. Students enjoy scheduling options that make it easier to fit school into their busy lives, choosing from day and evening courses, on campus or online. Many students find a combination of class formats to be an ideal way of continuing their education while meeting family and professional demands.

Argosy University is accredited by the Higher Learning Commission and a member of the North Central Association, 230 South LaSalle Street, Suite 7-500, Chicago, Illinois 60604-1413; 800-621-7440 (toll-free); http://www.ncahlc.org.

Applying

Argosy University, Hawai'i, accepts students year-round on a rolling admissions basis, depending on availability of required courses. Applications for admission are available online or by contacting the campus.

Correspondence and Information

Argosy University, Hawai'i
400 ASB Tower
1001 Bishop Street
Honolulu, Hawaii 96813

Phone: 808-536-5555
888-323-2777 (toll-free)
Fax: 808-536-5505
E-mail: auadmissions@argosy.edu
Web site: http://www.argosy.edu/hawaii

Argosy University, Hawai'i

THE FACULTY

The Argosy University faculty is comprised of working professionals who are eager to help students succeed. Members bring real-world experience and the latest practice innovations to the academic setting. The diverse faculty members of the College of Psychology and Behavioral Sciences are widely recognized for contributions to the field. Many are published scholars, and most hold doctoral degrees. They are committed to providing a substantive education that combines comprehensive knowledge with critical skills and practical workplace relevance. Above all, faculty members are committed to their students' personal and professional development.

ARGOSY UNIVERSITY

ARGOSY UNIVERSITY, INLAND EMPIRE

College of Psychology and Behavioral Sciences

Programs of Study

Argosy University, Inland Empire, offers the Master of Arts (M.A.) degree in Clinical Psychology/Marriage and Family Therapy, Counseling Psychology/Marriage and Family Therapy, Forensic Psychology, Industrial Organizational Psychology, and Sport-Exercise Psychology; and the Doctor of Education (Ed.D.) degree in Counseling Psychology. Students completing a program may wish to become licensed professionals. Argosy University, Inland Empire does not guarantee third-party certification/licensure. Outside agencies control the requirements for taking and passing certification/licensing exams and are subject to change without notice to Argosy University, Inland Empire.

The Master of Arts (M.A.) in Clinical Psychology/Marriage and Family Therapy program is designed for students who wish to pursue the Clinical Psychology track while receiving graduate-level training in the core curricular areas, including supervised clinical practice, required for licensure as a marriage and family therapist in California. (Licensing requirements differ from state to state, so students should verify the current licensing requirements of the state in which they plan to become licensed.) The program emphasizes a practitioner-oriented philosophy and integrates applied theory and field experience. The curriculum shares a common core with most of the first- and second-year course offerings of the doctorate in clinical psychology; refer to the campus-specific program descriptions for details.

The Master of Arts (M.A.) in Counseling Psychology/Marriage and Family Therapy program is designed to prepare students to practice and pursue licensure in California as Marriage and Family Therapists (MFT). The program provides the necessary theoretical and practical elements to allow students to become effective members of a mental health team. It introduces students to skills that integrate individual and group theoretical foundations of counseling psychology into appropriate client interaction and intervention.

The Master of Arts (M.A.) in Forensic Psychology program is designed to educate and train individuals who are currently working, or wish to work, in fields that utilize the study and practice of forensic psychology, such as law enforcement, legal and organizational consultation, and program analysis. The curriculum provides for an understanding of theory, training, and practice of forensic psychology and to emphasize the development of students who are committed to the ethical provision of high-quality services to diverse clients and organizations. The program maintains policies and delivery formats suitable for working adults.

The Master of Arts (M.A.) in Industrial Organizational Psychology program is designed to apply the knowledge of industrial organizational psychology to issues involving individuals and groups in organizational and work settings. This program prepares students for careers in areas such as compensation, training, data analysis, consultation, statistical decision making, organizational development, leadership, and human resource management. The curriculum is competency based, focusing on the outcomes of training and on the knowledge, skills, and behavior necessary to function as a master's-level professional in the field.

The Master of Arts (M.A.) in Sport-Exercise Psychology program is designed to educate and train students to be capable and ethical performance enhancement specialists. This two-year degree is geared for students seeking employment in private practice, athletic departments, coaching, exercise/health, and education, as well as those who will ultimately pursue a doctoral degree. The goals include developing student competencies in theoretical foundations, helping relationships, individual and group skills, normal and abnormal behavior, sport sciences, research and evaluation, diversity, and professional identity. Based on the educational requirements outlined by the Association for Applied Sport Psychology (AASP), the curriculum is designed to provide students with a foundation in applied sport psychology; an understanding of normal and abnormal psychological functioning; and a knowledge base in the physiological, motor, and psychosocial aspects of sport behavior. Graduates are eligible to apply for provisional status as an AASP-certified consultant.

The Doctor of Education (Ed.D.) in Counseling Psychology program embraces a range of relevant theory and techniques applicable in the three major areas of counseling psychology: the remedial (assisting in remedying problems in living), the preventive (anticipating, circumventing, and forestalling difficulties that may arise in the future), and the educative and developmental (discovering and developing potentialities). The program focuses on normal individuals and developmental life stage challenges; assets, strengths, and positive mental health; relatively brief interventions; and context, sociocultural/political influences, diversity, and person-environment interactions rather than exclusive emphasis on the individual.

Research Facilities

Argosy University libraries provide curriculum support and educational resources, including current text materials, diagnostic training documents, reference materials and databases, journals and dissertations, and major and current titles in program areas. There is an online public-access catalog of library resources available throughout the Argosy University system. Students have remote access to the campus library database, enabling them to study and conduct research at home. Academic databases offer dissertation abstracts, academic journals, and professional periodicals. All library computers are Internet accessible. Software applications include Word, Excel, PowerPoint, SPSS, and various test-scoring programs.

Financial Aid

Financial aid is available to those who qualify. Argosy University, Inland Empire, offers access to federal and state aid programs, merit-based awards, grants, loans, and a work-study program. As a first step, students should complete the Free Application for Federal Student Aid (FAFSA). Prospective students can apply electronically at http://www.fafsa.ed.gov or at the campus.

Cost of Study

Tuition varies by program. Students should contact Argosy University, Inland Empire, for tuition information.

Living and Housing Costs

Students typically live in apartments in the San Bernardino metropolitan area. Living expenses vary according to each student's preferred standard of living, housing, and transportation. The University does not offer or operate student housing. Most of the students are full-time working professionals who live within driving distance of the campus. Several nearby hotels offer special rates for those who commute from long distances. The Admissions Department also maintains a list of housing options, including contact information for University students who wish to share housing. For more information, students should contact the Admissions Department.

Student Group

Admission to Argosy University, Inland Empire, is selective to ensure a dynamic and engaged student body. The University encourages diversity in academic and employment backgrounds and promotes integration of the student body into professional life through established connections with local and national professional associations. Argosy University offers a professionally oriented education with rich opportunities to gain practical experience in class, field placements, and internships. Full-time students and working professionals gain the extensive knowledge and range of skills necessary for effective performance in their chosen field.

Student Outcomes

Students can register with the University's online career-services system and use select services from a distance, such as degree-specific career e-mail lists, national job posts, and virtual job fairs. Students should contact the University for more information.

Location

Argosy University's Inland Empire facility features classrooms, computer labs, a resource center with Internet access, a student lounge, staff and faculty offices, and proximity to the region's many cultural and recreational attractions. The University provides a supportive educational environment with convenient class options that enable students to earn a degree while fulfilling other life responsibilities. All of the programs are thoroughly oriented to the real working world. Argosy University focuses on developing technical proficiency in each student's field as well as an overall professional career approach.

The University

Argosy University is a private institution with nineteen locations across the nation. Argosy University, Inland Empire, provides a career resources office, an academic resources center, and extensive information access for research. It offers the resources of a large university plus the friendliness and personal attention of a small campus.

The innovative programs feature dynamic, relevant, and practical curricula delivered in flexible class formats. Students enjoy scheduling options that make it easier to fit school into their busy lives, choosing from day and evening courses, on campus or online. Many students find a combination of class formats to be an ideal way of continuing their education while meeting family and professional demands.

Argosy University is accredited by the Higher Learning Commission and a member of the North Central Association, 230 South LaSalle Street, Suite 7-500, Chicago, Illinois 60602-1413; 800-621-7440 (toll-free); http://www.ncahlc.org.

Applying

Argosy University, Inland Empire, accepts students year-round on a rolling admissions basis, depending on availability of required courses. Applications for admission are available online or by contacting the campus.

Correspondence and Information

Argosy University, Inland Empire
3401 Centre Lake Drive, Suite 200
Ontario, California 91761
Phone: 909-472-0800
　　　　866-217-9075 (toll-free)
Fax: 909-915-3810
E-mail: auadmissions@argosy.edu
Web site: http://www.argosy.edu/inlandempire

Argosy University, Inland Empire

THE FACULTY

The Argosy University faculty is comprised of working professionals who are eager to help students succeed. Members bring real-world experience and the latest practice innovations to the academic setting. The diverse faculty members of the College of Psychology and Behavioral Sciences are widely recognized for contributions to the field. Many are published scholars, and most hold doctoral degrees. They are committed to providing a substantive education that combines comprehensive knowledge with critical skills and practical workplace relevance. Above all, faculty members are committed to their students' personal and professional development.

ARGOSY UNIVERSITY.

ARGOSY UNIVERSITY, LOS ANGELES

College of Psychology and Behavioral Sciences

Programs of Study

Argosy University, Los Angeles, offers the Master of Arts (M.A.) degree in Clinical Psychology/Marriage and Family Therapy, Counseling Psychology/Marriage and Family Therapy, and Forensic Psychology; and the Doctor of Education (Ed.D.) degree in Counseling Psychology. Students completing a program may wish to become licensed professionals. Argosy University, Los Angeles does not guarantee third-party certification/licensure. Outside agencies control the requirements for taking and passing certification/licensing exams and are subject to change without notice to Argosy University, Los Angeles.

The M.A. in Clinical Psychology/Marriage and Family Therapy program is designed for students who wish to pursue the Clinical Psychology track while receiving graduate-level training in the core curricular areas, including supervised clinical practice, required for licensure as a marriage and family therapist in California. (Licensing requirements differ from state to state, so students should verify the current licensing requirements of the state in which they plan to become licensed.) The program emphasizes a practitioner-oriented philosophy and integrates applied theory and field experience. The curriculum shares a common core with most of the first- and second-year course offerings of the doctorate in clinical psychology; refer to the campus-specific program descriptions for details.

The Master of Arts (M.A.) in Counseling Psychology/Marriage and Family Therapy program is designed to prepare students to practice and pursue licensure in California as Marriage and Family Therapists (MFT). The program is designed to provide the necessary theoretical and practical elements to allow students to become effective members of a mental health team. The program introduces students to skills that integrate individual and group theoretical foundations of counseling psychology into appropriate client interaction and intervention.

The Master of Arts (M.A.) in Forensic Psychology program is designed to educate and train individuals who are currently working, or wish to work, in fields that utilize the study and practice of forensic psychology, such as law enforcement, legal and organizational consultation, and program analysis. The curriculum is designed to provide for an understanding of theory, training, and practice of forensic psychology and to emphasize the development of students who are committed to the ethical provision of high-quality services to diverse clients and organizations. The program maintains policies and delivery formats suitable for working adults.

The Doctor of Education (Ed.D.) in Counseling Psychology program embraces a range of relevant theory and techniques applicable in the three major areas of counseling psychology: the remedial (assisting in remedying problems in living), the preventive (anticipating, circumventing, and forestalling difficulties that may arise in the future), and the educative and developmental (discovering and developing potentialities). The program focuses on normal individuals and developmental life stage challenges; assets, strengths, and positive mental health; relatively brief interventions; and context, sociocultural/political influences, diversity, and person-environment interactions rather than exclusive emphasis on the individual.

Research Facilities

Argosy University libraries provide curriculum support and educational resources, including current text materials, diagnostic training documents, reference materials and databases, journals and dissertations, and major and current titles in program areas. There is an online public-access catalog of library resources available throughout the Argosy University system. Students have remote access to the campus library database, enabling them to study and conduct research at home. Academic databases offer dissertation abstracts, academic journals, and professional periodicals. All library computers are Internet accessible. Software applications include Word, Excel, PowerPoint, SPSS, and various test-scoring programs.

Financial Aid

Financial aid is available to those who qualify. Argosy University, Los Angeles, offers access to federal and state aid programs, merit-based awards, grants, loans, and a work-study program. As a first step, students should complete the Free Application for Federal Student Aid (FAFSA). Prospective students can apply electronically at http://www.fafsa.ed.gov or at the campus.

Cost of Study

Tuition varies by program. Students should contact Argosy University, Los Angeles, for tuition information.

Living and Housing Costs

Students typically live in apartments in the metropolitan Santa Monica area. Living expenses vary according to each student's preferred standard of living, housing, and transportation. The University does not offer or operate student housing. Most Argosy University students are full-time working professionals who live within driving distance of the campus. Several nearby hotels offer special rates for those who commute from long distances. The Admissions Department also maintains a list of housing options, including contact information for University students who wish to share housing. For more information, students should contact the Admissions Department.

Student Group

Admission to Argosy University, Los Angeles, is selective to ensure a dynamic and engaged student body. The University encourages diversity in academic and employment backgrounds and promotes integration of the student body into professional life through established connections with local and national professional associations. Argosy University offers a professionally oriented education with rich opportunities to gain practical experience in class, field placements, and internships. Full-time students and working professionals gain the extensive knowledge and range of skills necessary for effective performance in their chosen fields.

Student Outcomes

Students can register with the University's online career-services system and use select services from a distance, such as degree-specific career e-mail lists, national job posts, and virtual job fairs. Students should contact the University for more information.

Location

Argosy University, Los Angeles, is conveniently located just minutes from Los Angeles International Airport and the Pacific coast, near the interchange between I-405 and I-105. The business environment in the Los Angeles metropolitan area offers a broad array of companies, including a proliferation of entertainment, technology, and software firms. Among the principal employers in the area are Yahoo!, MTV Networks, RAND Corporation, and Symantec Corporation. The many businesses in the area provide varied opportunities for student training.

The University

Argosy University is a private institution with nineteen locations across the nation. Argosy University, Los Angeles, provides students with a career resources office, an academic resources center, and extensive information access for research. It offers the resources of a large university plus the friendliness and personal attention of a small campus.

The innovative programs feature dynamic, relevant, and practical curricula delivered in flexible class formats. Students enjoy scheduling options that make it easier to fit school into their busy lives, choosing from day and evening courses, on campus or online. Many students find a combination of class formats to be an ideal way of continuing their education while meeting family and professional demands.

Argosy University is accredited by the Higher Learning Commission and a member of the North Central Association, 230 South LaSalle Street, Suite 7-500, Chicago, Illinois 60604-1413; 800-621-7440 (toll-free); http://www.ncahlc.org.

Applying

Argosy University, Los Angeles, accepts students year-round on a rolling admissions basis, depending on availability of required courses. Applications for admission are available online or by contacting the campus.

Correspondence and Information

Argosy University, Los Angeles
5230 Pacific Concourse
Los Angeles, California 90045
Phone: 310-866-4000
        866-505-0332 (toll-free)
Fax: 310-399-1804
E-mail: auadmissions@argosy.edu
Web site: http://www.argosy.edu/losangeles

Argosy University, Los Angeles

THE FACULTY

The Argosy University faculty is comprised of working professionals who are eager to help students succeed. Members bring real-world experience and the latest practice innovations to the academic setting. The diverse faculty members of the College of Psychology and Behavioral Sciences are is widely recognized for contributions to the field. Many are published scholars, and most hold doctoral degrees. They are committed to providing a substantive education that combines comprehensive knowledge with critical skills and practical workplace relevance. Above all, faculty members are committed to their students' personal and professional development.

ARGOSY UNIVERSITY, NASHVILLE

College of Psychology and Behavioral Sciences

ARGOSY UNIVERSITY

Programs of Study
Argosy University, Nashville, offers the Master of Arts (M.A.) degree in Mental Health Counseling and the Doctor of Education (Ed.D.) degree in Counselor Education and Supervision. Students completing a program may wish to become licensed professionals. Argosy University, Nashville does not guarantee third-party certification/licensure. Outside agencies control the requirements for taking and passing certification/licensing exams and are subject to change without notice to Argosy University, Nashville

The Master of Arts (M.A.) in Mental Health Counseling program is a 60-credit-hour program to provide students with a solid foundation and prepare them to enter a professional career as masters-level counseling practitioners who can function ethically and effectively with demonstrated knowledge of social and cultural diversity. The program's curriculum is designed to integrate the theoretical and conceptual foundations of mental health counseling with training in appropriate client intervention and therapy skills. In addition, the curriculum integrates counseling skills, theoretical foundations of mental health counseling, and field experience into a set of professional competencies that students can utilize with diverse client populations in a wide variety of settings. The program emphasizes the development of attitudes, knowledge, and skills that are essential for mental health counselors who are committed to the ethical provision of quality services. Students completing this program meet the academic requirements toward licensure as a Licensed Professional Counselor (LPC) and Licensed Professional Counselor–Mental Health Services Provider (LPC–MHSP) in Tennessee.

The Doctor of Education (Ed.D.) in Counselor Education and Supervision program aligns with the master's-level counselor education programs in order to encourage entry-level counseling students to work toward becoming doctoral-level advanced practitioners, educators, and supervisors. The program is designed to prepare counselors for a variety of settings by providing the advanced skills and knowledge necessary to provide leadership and advocacy, as well as serve in supervisory, training, and teaching positions in the counseling profession. The program can also help current practitioners with existing master's-level preparation advance their careers by providing expanded opportunities to compete in the marketplace, on par with the growing number of doctoral-level counseling practitioners.

Research Facilities
Argosy University libraries provide curriculum support and educational resources, including current text materials, diagnostic training documents, reference materials and databases, journals and dissertations, and major and current titles in program areas. There is an online public-access catalog of library resources available throughout the Argosy University system. Students have remote access to the campus library database, enabling them to study and conduct research at home. Academic databases offer dissertation abstracts, academic journals, and professional periodicals. All library computers are Internet accessible. Software applications include Word, Excel, PowerPoint, SPSS, and various test-scoring programs.

Financial Aid
Financial aid is available to those who qualify. Argosy University, Nashville, offers access to federal and state aid programs, merit-based awards, grants, loans, and a work-study program. As a first step, students should complete the Free Application for Federal Student Aid (FAFSA). Prospective students can apply electronically at http://www.fafsa.ed.gov or at the campus.

Cost of Study
Tuition varies by program. Students should contact Argosy University, Nashville, for tuition information.

Living and Housing Costs
Students typically live in apartments in the metropolitan Nashville area. Living expenses vary according to each student's preferred standard of living, housing, and transportation. The University does not offer or operate student housing. Most of the students are full-time working professionals who live within driving distance of the campus. Several nearby hotels offer special rates for those who commute from long distances. The Admissions Department also maintains a list of housing options, including contact information for University students who wish to share housing. For more information, students should contact the Admissions Department.

Student Group
Admission to Argosy University, Nashville, is selective to ensure a dynamic and engaged student body. The University encourages diversity in academic and employment backgrounds and promotes integration of the student body into professional life through established connections with local and national professional associations. Argosy University offers a professionally oriented education with rich opportunities to gain practical experience in class, field placements, and internships. Full-time students and working professionals gain the extensive knowledge and range of skills necessary for effective performance in their chosen field.

Student Outcomes
Students can register with the University's online career-services system and use select services from a distance, such as degree-specific career e-mail lists, national job posts, and virtual job fairs. Students should contact the University for more information.

Location
Argosy University, Nashville, is located at 100 Centerview Drive in Nashville, Tennessee. This city offers a variety of recreational activities, including the ballet and symphony, the newly established Frist Museum of Art, and professional sports. Nashville is known as Music City, USA, and is home to the Country Music Hall of Fame. The business environment includes companies such as Moses Cone Health Systems, Inc., and Novant Health, Inc.

The University
Argosy University is a private institution with nineteen locations across the nation. Argosy University, Nashville, provides a career resources office, an academic resources center, and extensive information access for research. It offers the resources of a large university plus the friendliness and personal attention of a small campus.

The innovative programs feature dynamic, relevant, and practical curricula delivered in flexible class formats. Students enjoy scheduling options that make it easier to fit school into their busy lives, choosing from day and evening courses, on campus or online. Many students find a combination of class formats to be an ideal way of continuing their education while meeting family and professional demands.

Argosy University, Nashville, is authorized by the Tennessee Higher Education Commission, Parkway Towers, Suite 1900, 404 James Robertson Parkway, Nashville, Tennessee 37243; 615-741-3605. This authorization must be renewed each year and is based on an evaluation against minimum standards concerning quality of education, ethical business practices, health and safety, and fiscal responsibility. Argosy University is accredited by the Higher Learning Commission and a member of the North Central Association, 230 South LaSalle Street, Suite 7-500, Chicago, Illinois 60604-1413; 800-621-7440 (toll-free); http://www.ncahlc.org.

Applying
Argosy University, Nashville, accepts students year-round on a rolling admissions basis, depending on availability of required courses. Applications for admission are available online or by contacting the campus.

Correspondence and Information
Argosy University, Nashville
100 Centerview Drive, Suite 225
Nashville, Tennessee 37214
Phone: 615-525-2800
          866-833-6598 (toll-free)
Fax: 615-525-2900
E-mail: auadmissions@argosy.edu
Web site: http://www.argosy.edu/nashville

Argosy University, Nashville

THE FACULTY

The Argosy University faculty is comprised of working professionals who are eager to help students succeed. Members bring real-world experience and the latest practice innovations to the academic setting. The diverse faculty members of the College of Psychology and Behavioral Sciences are widely recognized for contributions to the field. Many are published scholars, and most hold doctoral degrees. They are committed to providing a substantive education that combines comprehensive knowledge with critical skills and practical workplace relevance. Above all, faculty members are committed to their students' personal and professional development.

ARGOSY UNIVERSITY, ORANGE COUNTY

ARGOSY UNIVERSITY.

College of Psychology and Behavioral Sciences

Programs of Study

Argosy University, Orange County, offers the Master of Arts (M.A.) degree in Clinical Psychology/Marriage and Family Therapy, Counseling Psychology/Marriage and Family Therapy, Forensic Psychology, and Sport-Exercise Psychology; the Doctor of Education (Ed.D.) degree in Counseling Psychology; and the Doctor of Psychology (Psy.D.) degree in Clinical Psychology. Students completing a program may wish to become licensed professionals. Argosy University, Orange County does not guarantee third-party certification/licensure. Outside agencies control the requirements for taking and passing certification/licensing exams and are subject to change without notice to Argosy University, Orange County.

The M.A. in Clinical Psychology/Marriage and Family Therapy program is designed for students who wish to pursue the Clinical Psychology track while receiving graduate-level training in the core curricular areas, including supervised clinical practice, required for licensure as a marriage and family therapist in California. (Licensing requirements differ from state to state, so students should verify the current licensing requirements of the state in which they plan to become licensed.) The program emphasizes a practitioner-oriented philosophy and integrates applied theory and field experience. The curriculum shares a common core with most of the first- and second-year course offerings of the doctorate in clinical psychology; refer to the campus-specific program descriptions for details.

The Master of Arts (M.A.) in Counseling Psychology/Marriage and Family Therapy program is designed to prepare students to practice and pursue licensure in California as Marriage and Family Therapists (MFT). The program is designed to provide the necessary theoretical and practical elements to allow students to become effective members of a mental health team. The program introduces students to skills that integrate individual and group theoretical foundations of counseling psychology into appropriate client interaction and intervention.

The Master of Arts (M.A.) in Forensic Psychology program is designed to educate and train individuals who are currently working, or wish to work, in fields that utilize the study and practice of forensic psychology, such as law enforcement, legal and organizational consultation, and program analysis. The curriculum is designed to provide for an understanding of theory, training, and practice of forensic psychology and to emphasize the development of students who are committed to the ethical provision of high-quality services to diverse clients and organizations. The program maintains policies and delivery formats suitable for working adults.

The Master of Arts (M.A.) in Sport-Exercise Psychology program is designed to educate and train students to be capable and ethical performance enhancement specialists. This two-year degree is geared for students seeking employment in private practice, athletic departments, coaching, exercise/health, and education, as well as those who will ultimately pursue a doctoral degree. The goals include developing student competencies in theoretical foundations, helping relationships, individual and group skills, normal and abnormal behavior, sport sciences, research and evaluation, diversity, and professional identity. Based on the educational requirements outlined by the Association for Applied Sport Psychology (AASP), the curriculum is designed to provide students with a foundation in applied sport psychology; an understanding of normal and abnormal psychological functioning; and a knowledge base in the physiological, motor, and psychosocial aspects of sport behavior. Graduates are eligible to apply for provisional status as an AASP-certified consultant.

The Doctor of Education (Ed.D.) in Counseling Psychology program embraces a range of relevant theory and techniques applicable in the three major areas of counseling psychology: the remedial (assisting in remedying problems in living), the preventive (anticipating, circumventing, and forestalling difficulties that may arise in the future), and the educative and developmental (discovering and developing potentialities). The program focuses on normal individuals and developmental life stage challenges; assets, strengths, and positive mental health; relatively brief interventions; and context, sociocultural/political influences, diversity, and person-environment interactions rather than exclusive emphasis on the individual.

The Doctor of Psychology (Psy.D.) in Clinical Psychology program has been designed to educate and train students to function effectively as clinical psychologists. The curriculum is designed to provide for the meaningful integration of theory, training, and practice. The program is designed to emphasize the development of attitudes, knowledge, and skills essential in the formation of professional psychologists who are committed to the ethical provision of quality services. Specific objectives of the program include preparation of practitioners capable of ethically delivering diagnostic and therapeutic services, with strong foundational knowledge and the ability to apply it to clinical practice, a commitment to lifelong learning, and understanding and respect for the relevance of diversity and the ability to deliver psychological services to diverse populations.

Research Facilities

Argosy University libraries provide curriculum support and educational resources, including current text materials, diagnostic training documents, reference materials and databases, journals and dissertations, and major and current titles in program areas. There is an online public-access catalog of library resources available throughout the Argosy University system. Students have remote access to the campus library database, enabling them to study and conduct research at home. Academic databases offer dissertation abstracts, academic journals, and professional periodicals. All library computers are Internet accessible. Software applications include Word, Excel, PowerPoint, SPSS, and various test-scoring programs.

Financial Aid

Financial aid is available to those who qualify. Argosy University, Orange County, offers access to federal and state aid programs, merit-based awards, grants, loans, and a work-study program. As a first step, students should complete the Free Application for Federal Student Aid (FAFSA). Prospective students can apply electronically at http://www.fafsa.ed.gov or at the campus.

Cost of Study

Tuition varies by program. Students should contact Argosy University, Orange County, for tuition information.

Living and Housing Costs

Students typically live in apartments in the Santa Ana metropolitan area. Living expenses vary according to each student's preferred standard of living, housing, and transportation. The University does not offer or operate student housing. Most Argosy University students are full-time working professionals who live within driving distance of the campus. Several nearby hotels offer special rates for those who commute from long distances. The Admissions Department also maintains a list of housing options, including contact information for University students who wish to share housing. For more information, students should contact the Admissions Department.

Student Group

Admission to Argosy University, Orange County, is selective to ensure a dynamic and engaged student body. The University encourages diversity in academic and employment backgrounds and promotes integration of the student body into professional life through established connections with local and national professional associations. Argosy University offers a professionally oriented education with rich opportunities to gain practical experience in class, field placements, and internships. Full-time students and working professionals gain the extensive knowledge and range of skills necessary for effective performance in their chosen field.

Student Outcomes

Students can register with Argosy University's online career-services system and use select services from a distance, such as degree-specific career e-mail lists, national job posts, and virtual job fairs. Students should contact the University for more information.

Location

Argosy University, Orange County, attracts students from Southern California as well as around the country and the world. Orange County features a temperate climate, sunny beaches, and a host of cultural and entertainment options. The campus is located approximately 30 miles south of downtown Los Angeles, 90 miles north of San Diego, and just minutes from one of the many freeways that connect the Southern California basin. Regional parks and preserved lands provide opportunities for hiking, biking, riding, and other recreational activities. Whether it's ultra-chic Newport Beach, artsy Laguna Beach, or unspoiled Catalina Island, Orange County's oceanside personalities are as varied as the people who visit the area.

Orange County's business environment includes a broad array of companies. The area's largest employers include Ingram Micro Inc., Orange County Register, ITT Industries, and OneSource.

The University

Argosy University is a private institution with nineteen locations across the nation. Argosy University, Orange County, provides a career resources office, an academic resources center, and extensive information access for research. It offers the resources of a large university plus the friendliness and personal attention of a small campus. The innovative programs feature dynamic, relevant, and practical curricula delivered in flexible class formats. Students enjoy scheduling options that make it easier to fit school into their busy lives, choosing from day and evening courses, on campus or online. Many students find a combination of class formats to be an ideal way of continuing their education while meeting family and professional demands.

Argosy University is accredited by the Higher Learning Commission and a member of the North Central Association, 230 South LaSalle Street, Suite 7-500, Chicago, Illinois 60602-1413; 800-621-7440 (toll-free); http://www.ncahlc.org.

Applying

Argosy University, Orange County, accepts students year-round on a rolling admissions basis, depending on availability of required courses. Applications for admission are available online or by contacting the campus.

Correspondence and Information

Argosy University, Orange County
601 South Lewis Street
Orange, California 92868
Phone: 714-620-3700
        800-716-9598 (toll-free)
Fax: 714-620-3800
E-mail: auadmissions@argosy.edu
Web site: http://www.argosy.edu/orangecounty/

Argosy University, Orange County

THE FACULTY

The Argosy University faculty is comprised of working professionals who are eager to help students succeed. Members bring real-world experience and the latest practice innovations to the academic setting. The diverse faculty members of the College of Psychology and Behavioral Sciences are widely recognized for contributions to the field. Many are published scholars, and most hold doctoral degrees. They are committed to providing a substantive education that combines comprehensive knowledge with critical skills and practical workplace relevance. Above all, faculty members are committed to their students' personal and professional development.

ARGOSY UNIVERSITY.

ARGOSY UNIVERSITY, PHOENIX

College of Psychology and Behavioral Sciences

Programs of Study

Argosy University, Phoenix, offers the Master of Arts (M.A.) degree in Clinical Psychology, Forensic Psychology, Clinical Mental Health Counseling, Industrial Organizational Psychology, and Sport-Exercise Psychology; and the Doctor of Psychology (Psy.D.) degree in Clinical Psychology. Students completing a program may wish to become licensed. Argosy University, Phoenix does not guarantee third-party certification/licensure. Outside agencies control the requirements for taking and passing certification/ licensing exams and are subject to change without notice to Argosy University, Phoenix.

The Master of Arts (M.A.) in Clinical Psychology program is designed to educate and train students to enter professional careers as master's-level practitioners. The program provides the theoretical and clinical elements necessary for graduates to be effective members of a mental health team. It is designed to introduce students to basic clinical skills that integrate individual and group theoretical foundations of applied psychology into appropriate client interaction and intervention skills. In addition, it offers excellent preparation for those considering application to the Psy.D. in Clinical Psychology program. Specific objectives of the program include demonstrated competence in the following areas: effective assessment services in a manner consistent with professional standards, by identifying the strengths and problems of clients and accurately communicating findings in a professional manner; delivery of effective interventions in a manner consistent with professional standards, by utilizing a theoretical model and applying appropriate therapeutic interventions; application of the relevant body of knowledge in the areas of psychology that form the foundation of psychological practice, by applying relevant concepts; relationship skills, by working effectively with clients, colleagues, supervisors, and others; and provision of professional services to clients from diverse backgrounds by integrating information about and appreciation of diversity into assessment and intervention.

The Master of Arts (M.A.) in Forensic Psychology program is designed to educate and train individuals who are currently working, or wish to work, in fields that utilize the study and practice of forensic psychology, such as law enforcement, legal and organizational consultation, and program analysis. The curriculum is designed to provide for an understanding of theory, training, and practice of forensic psychology and to emphasize the development of students who are committed to the ethical provision of high-quality services to diverse clients and organizations. The program maintains policies and delivery formats suitable for working adults.

The Master of Arts (M.A.) in Clinical Mental Health Counseling program is designed to provide students a solid foundation for the eventual practice of mental health counseling. The program introduces basic counseling skills that integrate individual and group theoretical foundations of professional counseling into appropriate client interaction and intervention skills. The program emphasizes the development of attitudes, knowledge, and skills essential to professional counselors who are committed to the ethical provision of quality services. Students also have the option to enroll in a modified program that includes a concentration in Forensic Counseling.

The Master of Arts (M.A.) in Industrial Organizational Psychology program is designed to apply the knowledge of industrial organizational psychology to issues involving individuals and groups in organizational and work settings. This program is designed to prepare students for careers in areas such as compensation, training, data analysis, consultation, statistical decision making, organizational development, leadership, and human resource management. The curriculum is competency based, focusing on the outcomes of training and on the knowledge, skills, and behavior necessary to function as a master's-level professional in the field.

The Master of Arts (M.A.) in Sport-Exercise Psychology program is designed to educate and train students to be capable and ethical performance enhancement specialists. This two-year degree is geared for students seeking employment in private practice, athletic departments, coaching, exercise/health, and education, as well as those who will ultimately pursue a doctoral degree. The goals include developing student competencies in theoretical foundations, helping relationships, individual and group skills, normal and abnormal behavior, sport sciences, research and evaluation, diversity, and professional identity. Based on the educational requirements outlined by the Association for Applied Sport Psychology (AASP), the curriculum is designed to provide students with a foundation in applied sport psychology; an understanding of normal and abnormal psychological functioning; and a knowledge base in the physiological, motor, and psychosocial aspects of sport behavior. Graduates are eligible to apply for provisional status as an AASP-certified consultant.

The Doctor of Psychology (Psy.D.) in Clinical Psychology program has been designed to educate and train students to function effectively as clinical psychologists. The curriculum is designed to provide a meaningful integration of theory, training, and practice. The program is designed to emphasize the development of attitudes, knowledge, and skills essential in the formation of professional psychologists who are committed to the ethical provision of quality services. Specific objectives of the program include preparation of practitioners capable of ethically delivering diagnostic and therapeutic services, with strong foundational knowledge and the ability to apply it to clinical practice, a commitment to lifelong learning, and understanding and respect for the relevance of diversity and the ability to deliver psychological services to diverse populations.

Research Facilities

Argosy University libraries provide curriculum support and educational resources, including current text materials, diagnostic training documents, reference materials and databases, journals and dissertations, and major and current titles in program areas. There is an online public-access catalog of library resources available throughout the Argosy University system. Students have remote access to the campus library database, enabling them to study and conduct research at home. Academic databases offer dissertation abstracts, academic journals, and professional periodicals. All library computers are Internet accessible. Software applications include Word, Excel, PowerPoint, SPSS, and various test-scoring programs.

Financial Aid

Financial aid is available to those who qualify. Argosy University, Phoenix, offers access to federal and state aid programs, merit-based awards, grants, loans, and a work-study program. As a first step, students should complete the Free Application for Federal Student Aid (FAFSA). Prospective students can apply electronically at http://www.fafsa.ed.gov or at the campus.

Cost of Study

Tuition varies by program. Students should contact Argosy University, Phoenix, for tuition information.

Living and Housing Costs

Students typically live in apartments in the metropolitan Phoenix area. Living expenses vary according to each student's preferred standard of living, housing, and transportation. The University does not offer or operate student housing. Most Argosy University students are full-time working professionals who live within driving distance of the campus. Several nearby hotels offer special rates for those who commute from long distances. The Admissions Department also maintains a list of housing options, including contact information for University students who wish to share housing. For more information, students should contact the Admissions Department.

Student Group

Admission to Argosy University, Phoenix, is selective to ensure a dynamic and engaged student body. The University encourages diversity in academic and employment backgrounds and promotes integration of the student body into professional life through established connections with local and national professional associations. Argosy University offers a professionally oriented education with rich opportunities to gain practical experience in class, field placements, and internships. Full-time students and working professionals gain the extensive knowledge and range of skills necessary for effective performance in their chosen field.

Student Outcomes

Students can register with Argosy University's online career-services system and use select services from a distance, such as degree-specific career e-mail lists, national job posts, and virtual job fairs. Students should contact the University for more information.

Location

Argosy University, Phoenix, offers a quality education in an intimate, small-group setting. The campus is located near I-17, close to shops, restaurants, and recreational areas. Phoenix is home to several major league sports teams, and the city offers an array of cultural activities ranging from opera and theatre to science museums. The multi-cultural environment of Arizona, coupled with Argosy University's professional training affiliations throughout the state, creates an exciting opportunity for students to work with urban, rural, and culturally diverse populations.

The business environment in Phoenix includes a wide variety of companies such as Intel and Go Daddy Group, an Internet company. Wells Fargo, Home Depot, Lowe's, and Wal-Mart also represent some of the area's largest employers.

The University

Argosy University is a private institution with nineteen locations across the nation. Argosy University, Phoenix, provides a career resources office, an academic resources center, and extensive information access for research. It offers the resources of a large university plus the friendliness and personal attention of a small campus. The innovative programs feature dynamic, relevant, and practical curricula delivered in flexible class formats. Students enjoy scheduling options that make it easier to fit school into their busy lives, choosing from day and evening courses, on campus or online. Many students find a combination of class formats to be an ideal way of continuing their education while meeting family and professional demands.

Argosy University is accredited by the Higher Learning Commission and a member of the North Central Association, 230 South LaSalle Street, Suite 7-500, Chicago, Illinois 60602-1413; 800-621-7440 (toll-free); http://www.ncahlc.org.

Applying

Argosy University, Phoenix, accepts students year-round on a rolling admissions basis, depending on availability of required courses. Applications for admission are available online or by contacting the campus.

Correspondence and Information

Argosy University, Phoenix
2233 West Dunlap Avenue
Phoenix, Arizona 85021

Phone: 602-216-2600
   866-216-2777 (toll-free)
Fax: 602-216-2601
E-mail: auadmissions@argosy.edu
Web site: http://www.argosy.edu/phoenix/

Argosy University, Phoenix

THE FACULTY

The Argosy University faculty is comprised of working professionals who are eager to help students succeed. Members bring real-world experience and the latest practice innovations to the academic setting. The diverse faculty members of the College of Psychology and Behavioral Sciences are widely recognized for contributions to the field. Many are published scholars, and most hold doctoral degrees. They are committed to providing a substantive education that combines comprehensive knowledge with critical skills and practical workplace relevance. Above all, faculty members are committed to their students' personal and professional development.

ARGOSY UNIVERSITY

ARGOSY UNIVERSITY, SALT LAKE CITY

College of Psychology and Behavioral Sciences

Programs of Study

Argosy University, Salt Lake City, offers the Master of Arts (M.A.) degree in Forensic Psychology, Marriage and Family Therapy, and Mental Health Counseling; the Doctor of Education (Ed.D.) degree in Counselor Education and Supervision; and the Doctor of Marriage and Family Therapy (D.M.F.T.) degree. Students completing a program may wish to become licensed professionals. Argosy University, Salt Lake City does not guarantee third-party certification/licensure. Outside agencies control the requirements for taking and passing certification/licensing exams and are subject to change without notice to Argosy University, Salt Lake City.

The Master of Arts (M.A.) in Forensic Psychology program is designed to educate and train individuals who are currently working, or wish to work, in fields that utilize the study and practice of forensic psychology, such as law enforcement, legal and organizational consultation, and program analysis. The curriculum provides for an understanding of theory, training, and practice of forensic psychology and to emphasize the development of students who are committed to the ethical provision of high-quality services to diverse clients and organizations. The program maintains policies and delivery formats suitable for working adults.

The Master of Arts (M.A.) in Marriage and Family Therapy program recognizes the need to provide marriage and family therapists with the extensive knowledge and range of skills necessary to function effectively in their profession. The program introduces basic skills that integrate systemic theoretical foundations of marriage and family therapy into appropriate client interaction and intervention skills. The program emphasizes the development of attitudes, knowledge, and skills essential in the formation of marriage and family therapists who are committed to the ethical provision of quality services, with demonstrated knowledge of social and cultural diversity. The program has been developed by the school faculty members to provide working students with the opportunity to pursue personal and professional goals through completion of a master's program.

The Master of Arts (M.A.) in Mental Health Counseling program is designed to provide students with a sound foundation for the eventual practice of mental health counseling. The program introduces basic counseling skills that integrate individual and group theoretical foundations of professional counseling into appropriate client interaction and intervention skills. It emphasizes the development of attitudes, knowledge, and skills essential in the formation of professional counselors who are committed to the ethical provision of quality services.

The Doctor of Education (Ed.D.) in Counselor Education and Supervision program aligns with the master's-level counselor education programs in order to encourage entry-level counseling students to work toward becoming doctoral-level advanced practitioners, educators, and supervisors. The program prepares counselors for a variety of settings by providing the advanced skills and knowledge necessary to provide leadership and advocacy, as well as serve in supervisory, training, and teaching positions in the counseling profession.

The Doctor of Marriage and Family Therapy (D.M.F.T.) degree program is a 60-credit-hour terminal, practice-oriented degree. The program builds upon students' prior learning and professional experience by expanding and deepening their knowledge of human development, family dynamics, systemic thinking, interactional theories, traditional and contemporary marriage and family therapy theories and practices, and cultural contexts. The D.M.F.T. program curriculum provides opportunities for advanced study and research of systemic concepts and methods as applied to clinical work with children, couples, individuals, and families as well as larger systems of organizations and communities. In addition to the continuing development of clinical skills, the curriculum includes the development of skills related to leadership and service to the field in the areas of teaching and supervision. The D.M.F.T. program curriculum is generally designed to meet the American Association for Marriage and Family Therapy (AAMFT) requirements to become an approved supervisor. (Those students who are already AAMFT-approved supervisors may petition for an alternate learning experience equivalent to the 9 credit hours devoted to training and supervision.)

Research Facilities

Argosy University libraries provide curriculum support and educational resources, including current text materials, diagnostic training documents, reference materials and databases, journals and dissertations, and major and current titles in program areas. There is an online public-access catalog of library resources available throughout the Argosy University system. Students have remote access to their campus library database, enabling them to study and conduct research at home. Academic databases offer dissertation abstracts, academic journals, and professional periodicals. All library computers are Internet accessible. Software applications include Word, Excel, PowerPoint, SPSS, and various test-scoring programs.

Financial Aid

Financial aid is available to those who qualify. Argosy University, Salt Lake City, offers access to federal and state aid programs, merit-based awards, grants, loans, and a work-study program. As a first step, students should complete the Free Application for Federal Student Aid (FAFSA). Prospective students can apply electronically at http://www.fafsa.ed.gov or at the campus.

Cost of Study

Tuition varies by program. Students should contact Argosy University, Salt Lake City, for tuition information.

Living and Housing Costs

Students typically live in apartments in the metropolitan Salt Lake City area. Living expenses vary according to each student's preferred standard of living, housing, and transportation. The University does not offer or operate student housing. Most of the students are full-time working professionals who live within driving distance of the campus. Several nearby hotels offer special rates for those who commute from long distances. The Admissions Department also maintains a list of housing options, including contact information for University students who wish to share housing. For more information, students should contact the Admissions Department.

Student Group

Admission to Argosy University, Salt Lake City, is selective to ensure a dynamic and engaged student body. The University encourages diversity in academic and employment backgrounds and promotes integration of the student body into professional life through established connections with local and national professional associations. Argosy University offers a professionally oriented education with rich opportunities to gain practical experience in class, field placements, and internships. Full-time students and working professionals gain the extensive knowledge and range of skills necessary for effective performance in their chosen field.

Student Outcomes

Students can register with Argosy University's online career-services system and use select services from a distance, such as degree-specific career e-mail lists, national job posts, and virtual job fairs. Students should contact the University for more information.

Location

Argosy University, Salt Lake City, offers a quality education in an intimate, small-group setting. Argosy University, Salt Lake City, is conveniently located in Draper, Utah, nestled in the Wasatch Mountains about 20 miles south of Salt Lake City. The area's business climate and numerous hospitals, schools, clinics, and social service agencies can provide many training opportunities for students.

The University

Argosy University is a private institution with nineteen locations across the nation. Argosy University, Salt Lake City, provides a career resources office, an academic resources center, and extensive information access for research. It offers the resources of a large university plus the friendliness and personal attention of a small campus. The innovative programs feature dynamic, relevant, and practical curricula delivered in flexible class formats. Students enjoy scheduling options that make it easier to fit school into their busy lives, choosing from day and evening courses, on campus or online. Many students find a combination of class formats to be an ideal way of continuing their education while meeting family and professional demands.

Argosy University is accredited by the Higher Learning Commission, a member of the North Central Association, 230 South LaSalle Street, Suite 7-500, Chicago, Illinois 60604-1413; 800-621-7440 (toll-free); http://www.ncahlc.org.

Applying

Argosy University, Salt Lake City, accepts students on a rolling admissions basis year-round, depending on availability of required courses. Applications for admission may be obtained online or by contacting the campus.

Correspondence and Information

Argosy University, Salt Lake City
121 Election Road, Suite 300
Draper, Utah 84020
Phone: 801-601-5000
        888-639-4756 (toll-free)
Fax: 801-601-4990
E-mail: auadmissions@argosy.edu
Web site: http://www.argosy.edu/saltlakecity

Argosy University, Salt Lake City

THE FACULTY

The Argosy University faculty is comprised of working professionals who are eager to help students succeed. Members bring real-world experience and the latest practice innovations to the academic setting. The diverse faculty members of the College of Psychology and Behavioral Sciences are widely recognized for contributions to the field. Many are published scholars, and most hold doctoral degrees. They are committed to providing a substantive education that combines comprehensive knowledge with critical skills and practical workplace relevance. Above all, faculty members are committed to their students' personal and professional development.

ARGOSY UNIVERSITY

ARGOSY UNIVERSITY, SAN DIEGO

College of Psychology and Behavioral Sciences

Programs of Study

Argosy University, San Diego, offers the Master of Arts (M.A.) degree in Counseling Psychology/Marriage and Family Therapy, and Forensic Psychology; and the Doctor of Education (Ed.D.) degree in Counseling Psychology. Students completing a program may wish to become licensed professionals. Argosy University, San Diego does not guarantee third-party certification/licensure. Outside agencies control the requirements for taking and passing certification/licensing exams and are subject to change without notice to Argosy University, San Diego.

The Master of Arts (M.A.) in Counseling Psychology/Marriage and Family Therapy program is designed to prepare students to practice and pursue licensure in California as Marriage and Family Therapists (MFT). The program is designed to provide the necessary theoretical and practical elements to allow students to become effective members of a mental health team. The program introduces students to skills that integrate individual and group theoretical foundations of counseling psychology into appropriate client interaction and intervention.

The Master of Arts (M.A.) in Forensic Psychology program is designed to educate and train individuals who are currently working, or wish to work, in fields that utilize the study and practice of forensic psychology, such as law enforcement, legal and organizational consultation, and program analysis. The curriculum is designed to provide for an understanding of theory, training, and practice of forensic psychology and to emphasize the development of students who are committed to the ethical provision of high-quality services to diverse clients and organizations. The program maintains policies and delivery formats suitable for working adults.

The Doctor of Education (Ed.D.) in Counseling Psychology program embraces a range of relevant theory and techniques applicable in the three major areas of counseling psychology: the remedial (assisting in remedying problems in living), the preventive (anticipating, circumventing, and forestalling difficulties that may arise in the future), and the educative and developmental (discovering and developing potentialities). The program focuses on normal individuals and developmental life stage challenges; assets, strengths, and positive mental health; relatively brief interventions; and context, sociocultural/political influences, diversity, and person-environment interactions rather than exclusive emphasis on the individual.

Research Facilities

Argosy University libraries provide curriculum support and educational resources, including current text materials, diagnostic training documents, reference materials and databases, journals and dissertations, and major and current titles in program areas. There is an online public-access catalog of library resources available throughout the Argosy University system. Students have remote access to the campus library database, enabling them to study and conduct research at home. Academic databases offer dissertation abstracts, academic journals, and professional periodicals. All library computers are Internet accessible. Software applications include Word, Excel, PowerPoint, SPSS, and various test-scoring programs.

Financial Aid

Financial aid is available to those who qualify. Argosy University, San Diego, offers access to federal and state aid programs, merit-based awards, grants, loans, and a work-study program. As a first step, students should complete the Free Application for Federal Student Aid (FAFSA). Prospective students can apply electronically at http://www.fafsa.ed.gov or at the campus.

Cost of Study

Tuition varies by program. Students should contact Argosy University, San Diego, for tuition information.

Living and Housing Costs

Students typically live in apartments in the San Diego metropolitan area. Living expenses vary according to each student's preferred standard of living, housing, and transportation. The University does not offer or operate student housing. Most of the students are full-time working professionals who live within driving distance of the campus. Several nearby hotels offer special rates for those who commute from long distances. The Admissions Department also maintains a list of housing options, including contact information for University students who wish to share housing. For more information, students should contact the Admissions Department.

Student Group

Admission to Argosy University, San Diego, is selective to ensure a dynamic and engaged student body. The University encourages diversity in academic and employment backgrounds and promotes integration of the student body into professional life through established connections with local and national professional associations. Argosy University offers a professionally oriented education with rich opportunities to gain practical experience in class, field placements, and internships. Full-time students and working professionals gain the extensive knowledge and range of skills necessary for effective performance in their chosen field.

Student Outcomes

Students can register with the University's online career-services system and use select services from a distance, such as degree-specific career e-mail lists, national job posts, and virtual job fairs. Students should contact the University for more information.

Location

San Diego, southern California's second-largest city, offers an ideal climate year-round, 70 miles of beautiful beaches, colorful neighborhoods, and a dynamic downtown district. Argosy University, San Diego, provides classrooms, a library resource center, a student lounge, staff and faculty offices, and other amenities. The area offers numerous attractions, including the famous San Diego Zoo, San Diego Wild Animal Park, and SeaWorld. San Diego's business environment includes several Fortune 500 companies such as QUALCOMM and Pfizer, Inc., and a concentration of technology companies.

The University

Argosy University is a private institution with nineteen locations across the nation. Argosy University, San Diego, provides a career resources office, an academic resources center, and extensive information access for research. It offers the resources of a large university plus the friendliness and personal attention of a small campus.

The innovative programs feature dynamic, relevant, and practical curricula delivered in flexible class formats. Students enjoy scheduling options that make it easier to fit school into their busy lives, choosing from day and evening courses, on campus or online. Many students find a combination of class formats to be an ideal way of continuing their education while meeting family and professional demands.

Argosy University is accredited by the Higher Learning Commission and a member of the North Central Association, 230 South LaSalle Street, Suite 7-500, Chicago, Illinois 60604-1413; 800-621-7440 (toll-free); http://www.ncahlc.org.

Applying

Argosy University, San Diego, accepts students year-round on a rolling admissions basis, depending on availability of required courses. Applications for admission are available online or by contacting the campus.

Correspondence and Information

Argosy University, San Diego
1615 Murray Canyon Road
Suite 100
San Diego, California 92108
Phone: 619-321-3000
         866-505-0333 (toll-free)
Fax: 619-321-3005
E-mail: auadmissions@argosy.edu
Web site: http://www.argosy.edu/sandiego/

Argosy University, San Diego

THE FACULTY

The Argosy University faculty is comprised of working professionals who are eager to help students succeed. Members bring real-world experience and the latest practice innovations to the academic setting. The diverse faculty members of the College of Psychology and Behavioral Sciences are widely recognized for contributions to the field. Many are published scholars, and most hold doctoral degrees. They are committed to providing a substantive education that combines comprehensive knowledge with critical skills and practical workplace relevance. Above all, faculty members are committed to their students' personal and professional development.

ARGOSY UNIVERSITY.

ARGOSY UNIVERSITY, SAN FRANCISCO BAY AREA
College of Psychology and Behavioral Sciences

Programs of Study

Argosy University, San Francisco Bay Area, offers the Master of Arts (M.A.) degree in Clinical Psychology/Marriage and Family Therapy, Counseling Psychology, Counseling Psychology/Marriage and Family Therapy, and Forensic Psychology; the Doctor of Education (Ed.D.) degree in Counseling Psychology; and the Doctor of Psychology (Psy.D.) degree in Clinical Psychology. Students completing a program may wish to become licensed professionals. Argosy University, San Francisco Bay Area does not guarantee third-party certification/licensure. Outside agencies control the requirements for taking and passing certification/licensing exams and are subject to change without notice to Argosy University, San Francisco Bay Area.

The M.A. in Clinical Psychology/Marriage and Family Therapy program is designed for students who wish to pursue the Clinical Psychology track while receiving graduate-level training in the core curricular areas, including supervised clinical practice, required for licensure as a marriage and family therapist in California. (Licensing requirements differ from state to state, so students should verify the current licensing requirements of the state in which they plan to become licensed.) The program emphasizes a practitioner-oriented philosophy and integrates applied theory and field experience.

The M.A. in Counseling Psychology program is designed to provide students with a sound foundation for the eventual practice of mental health counseling. The program emphasizes the development of attitudes, knowledge, and skills essential in the formation of professionals who are committed to the ethical provision of quality services. The program prepares students to enter a professional career as master's-level counseling practitioners who can perform ethically and effectively as skilled professionals with demonstrated knowledge of social and cultural diversity.

The Master of Arts (M.A.) in Counseling Psychology/Marriage and Family Therapy program is designed to prepare students to practice and pursue licensure in California as Marriage and Family Therapists (MFT). The program is designed to provide the necessary theoretical and practical elements to allow students to become effective members of a mental health team. The program introduces students to skills that integrate individual and group theoretical foundations of counseling psychology into appropriate client interaction and intervention.

The Master of Arts (M.A.) in Forensic Psychology program is designed to educate and train individuals who are currently working, or wish to work, in fields that utilize the study and practice of forensic psychology, such as law enforcement, legal and organizational consultation, and program analysis. The curriculum is designed to provide for an understanding of theory, training, and practice of forensic psychology and to emphasize the development of students who are committed to the ethical provision of high-quality services to diverse clients and organizations. The program maintains policies and delivery formats suitable for working adults.

The Doctor of Education (Ed.D.) in Counseling Psychology program emphasizes the development of attitudes, knowledge, and skills essential in the formation of professionals who are committed to the ethical provision of quality services. The curriculum is designed to provide for the meaningful integration of theory, training, and practice.

The Doctor of Psychology (Psy.D.) in Clinical Psychology program has been designed to educate and train students to function effectively as clinical psychologists. The curriculum provides for the meaningful integration of theory, training, and practice. The program emphasizes the development of attitudes, knowledge, and skills essential in the formation of professional psychologists who are committed to the ethical provision of quality services.

Research Facilities

Argosy University libraries provide curriculum support and educational resources, including current text materials, diagnostic training documents, reference materials and databases, journals and dissertations, and major and current titles in program areas. There is an online public-access catalog of library resources available throughout the Argosy University system. Students have remote access to the campus library database, enabling them to study and conduct research at home. Academic databases offer dissertation abstracts, academic journals, and professional periodicals. All library computers are Internet accessible. Software applications include Word, Excel, PowerPoint, SPSS, and various test-scoring programs.

Financial Aid

Financial aid is available to those who qualify. Argosy University, San Francisco Bay Area, offers access to federal and state aid programs, merit-based awards, grants, loans, and a work-study program. As a first step, students should complete the Free Application for Federal Student Aid (FAFSA). Prospective students can apply electronically at http://www.fafsa.ed.gov or at the campus.

Cost of Study

Tuition varies by program. Students should contact Argosy University, San Francisco Bay Area for tuition information.

Living and Housing Costs

Students typically live in apartments in the San Francisco metropolitan area. Living expenses vary according to each student's preferred standard of living, housing, and transportation. The University does not offer or operate student housing. Most Argosy University students are full-time working professionals who live within driving distance of the campus. Several nearby hotels offer special rates for those who commute from long distances. The Admissions Department also maintains a list of housing options, including contact information for University students who wish to share housing. For more information, students should contact the Admissions Department.

Student Group

Admission to Argosy University, San Francisco Bay Area, is selective to ensure a dynamic and engaged student body. The University encourages diversity in academic and employment backgrounds and promotes integration of the student body into professional life through established connections with local and national professional associations. Argosy University offers a professionally oriented education with rich opportunities to gain practical experience in class, field placements, and internships. Full-time students and working professionals gain the extensive knowledge and range of skills necessary for effective performance in their chosen field.

Student Outcomes

Students can register with Argosy University's online career-services system and use select services from a distance, such as degree-specific career e-mail lists, national job posts, and virtual job fairs. Students should contact the University for more information.

Location

Located in northern California, Argosy University, San Francisco Bay Area, attracts students from the immediate area as well as from around the country and the world. In July 2007, the University moved to its new location at 1005 Atlantic Avenue, Alameda, California. The energy in San Francisco is contagious. Numerous surveys rank San Francisco as one of the most wired cities in the world, thanks to its high concentration of computer-savvy citizens and businesses.

Many educational institutions and agencies in the area provide varied opportunities for student training. The Bay Area and nearby Silicon Valley are home to leading new media companies such as Pixar, ILM, and Sega. A who's who of technology companies call the Bay Area home, including Apple, Cisco, Hewlett-Packard, Intel, Oracle, and Sun Microsystems. The Bay Area also is the home of traditional companies such as BankAmerica, Chevron, Levi-Strauss, Safeway, and Wells Fargo.

The University

Argosy University is a private institution with nineteen locations across the nation. Argosy University, San Francisco Bay Area, provides a career resources office, an academic resources center, and extensive information access for research. It offers the resources of a large university plus the friendliness and personal attention of a small campus. The innovative programs feature dynamic, relevant, and practical curricula delivered in flexible class formats. Students enjoy scheduling options that make it easier to fit school into their busy lives, choosing from day and evening courses, on campus or online. Many students find a combination of class formats to be an ideal way of continuing their education while meeting family and professional demands.

Argosy University is accredited by the Higher Learning Commission and a member of the North Central Association, 230 South LaSalle Street, Suite 7-500, Chicago, Illinois 60604-1413; 800-621-7440 (toll-free); http://www.ncahlc.org.

Applying

Argosy University, San Francisco Bay Area, accepts students year-round on a rolling admissions basis, depending on availability of required courses. Applications for admission are available online or by contacting the campus.

Correspondence and Information

Argosy University, San Francisco Bay Area
1005 Atlantic Avenue
Alameda, California 94501
Phone: 510-215-4700
          866-215-2777 (toll free)
Fax: 510-215-0299
E-mail: auadmissions@argosy.edu
Web site: http://www.argosy.edu/sanfrancisco

Argosy University, San Francisco Bay Area

THE FACULTY

The Argosy University faculty is comprised of working professionals who are eager to help students succeed. Members bring real-world experience and the latest practice innovations to the academic setting. The diverse faculty members of the College of Psychology and Behavioral Sciences are widely recognized for contributions to the field. Many are published scholars, and most hold doctoral degrees. They are committed to providing a substantive education that combines comprehensive knowledge with critical skills and practical workplace relevance. Above all, faculty members are committed to their students' personal and professional development.

ARGOSY UNIVERSITY.

ARGOSY UNIVERSITY, SARASOTA

College of Psychology and Behavioral Sciences

Programs of Study

Argosy University, Sarasota, offers the Master of Arts (M.A.) degree in Community Counseling, Forensic Psychology, Industrial Organizational Psychology, Marriage and Family Therapy, and Mental Health Counseling; and the Doctor of Education (Ed.D.) degree in Counseling Psychology, Counselor Education and Supervision, and Pastoral Community Counseling. Students completing a program may wish to become licensed professionals. Argosy University, Sarasota does not guarantee third-party certification/licensure. Outside agencies control the requirements for taking and passing certification/licensing exams and are subject to change without notice to Argosy University, Sarasota.

The Master of Arts (M.A.) in Community Counseling is a 48-credit-hour program designed to provide students with a solid foundation for the practice of professional counseling. The program's curriculum integrates theoretical and conceptual foundations of professional counseling with training in appropriate client intervention and advocacy skills. The program emphasizes the development of attitudes, knowledge, and skills that are essential for professional counselors committed to the ethical provision of quality services. Students completing this program meet the academic requirements toward licensure in Alabama, Georgia, and other states (because licensure requirements vary from state to state, students should verify the current licensing requirements for the state in which they plan to practice).

The Master of Arts (M.A.) in Forensic Psychology program is designed to educate and train individuals who are currently working, or wish to work, in fields that utilize the study and practice of forensic psychology, such as law enforcement, legal and organizational consultation, and program analysis. The curriculum provides for an understanding of theory, training, and practice of forensic psychology and to emphasize the development of students who are committed to the ethical provision of high-quality services to diverse clients and organizations. The program maintains policies and delivery formats suitable for working adults.

The Master of Arts (M.A.) in Industrial Organizational Psychology program is designed to apply the knowledge of industrial organizational psychology to issues involving individuals and groups in organizational and work settings. This program prepares students for careers in areas such as compensation, training, data analysis, consultation, statistical decision making, organizational development, leadership, and human resource management. The curriculum is competency based, focusing on the outcomes of training and on the knowledge, skills, and behavior necessary to function as a master's-level professional in the field.

The Master of Arts (M.A.) in Marriage and Family Therapy program recognizes the need to provide marriage and family therapists with the extensive knowledge and range of skills necessary to function effectively in their profession. The program introduces basic skills that integrate systemic theoretical foundations of marriage and family therapy into appropriate client interaction and intervention skills. The program emphasizes the development of attitudes, knowledge, and skills essential in the formation of marriage and family therapists who are committed to the ethical provision of quality services, with demonstrated knowledge of social and cultural diversity.

The Master of Arts (M.A.) in Mental Health Counseling program is designed to provide students with a sound foundation for the eventual practice of mental health counseling. The program introduces students to basic counseling skills that integrate individual and group theoretical foundations of mental health counseling into appropriate client interaction and intervention skills. The program emphasizes the development of attitudes, knowledge, and skills essential in the formation of mental health counselors who are committed to the ethical provision of quality services.

The Doctor of Education (Ed.D.) in Counseling Psychology program is designed to meet the special requirements of working professionals who want to develop their knowledge and skills to handle the changing needs of modern organizations. The program is designed to provide working professionals with the opportunity to pursue their personal and professional goals through the completion of a graduate program.

The Doctor of Education (Ed.D.) in Counselor Education and Supervision program aligns with the master's-level counselor education programs in order to encourage entry-level counseling students to work toward becoming doctoral-level advanced practitioners, educators, and supervisors. The program prepares counselors for a variety of settings by providing the advanced skills and knowledge necessary to provide leadership and advocacy, as well as serve in supervisory, training, and teaching positions in the counseling profession.

The Doctor of Education (Ed.D.) in Pastoral Community Counseling program is based on the fundamental belief that religious and spiritual communities provide a unique opportunity for human growth and development. The program is designed to provide leaders in religious communities with an opportunity for personal and professional development, directed toward making a significant contribution to their community and to society. The program integrates the engagement of knowledge, the development of skills, reflective practice, and research in a manner that prepares the pastoral counselor to address individual and communal development in an ethically responsible fashion.

Research Facilities

Argosy University libraries provide curriculum support and educational resources, including current text materials, diagnostic training documents, reference materials and databases, journals and dissertations, and major and current titles in program areas. There is an online public-access catalog of library resources available throughout the Argosy University system. Students have remote access to the campus library database, enabling them to study and conduct research at home. Academic databases offer dissertation abstracts, academic journals, and professional periodicals. All library computers are Internet accessible. Software applications include Word, Excel, PowerPoint, SPSS, and various test-scoring programs.

Financial Aid

Financial aid is available to those who qualify. Argosy University, Sarasota, offers access to federal and state aid programs, merit-based awards, grants, loans, and a work-study program. As a first step, students should complete the Free Application for Federal Student Aid (FAFSA). Prospective students can apply electronically at http://www.fafsa.ed.gov or at the campus.

Cost of Study

Tuition varies by program. Students should contact Argosy University, Sarasota, for tuition information.

Living and Housing Costs

Students typically live in apartments in the metropolitan Sarasota area. Living expenses vary according to each student's preferred standard of living, housing, and transportation. The University does not offer or operate student housing. Most of the students are full-time working professionals who live within driving distance of the campus. Several nearby hotels offer special rates for those who commute from long distances to attend scheduled weeklong in-residence sessions. The Admissions Department also maintains a list of housing options, including contact information for University students who wish to share housing. For more information, students should contact the Admissions Department.

Student Group

Admission to Argosy University, Sarasota, is selective to ensure a dynamic and engaged student body. The University encourages diversity in academic and employment backgrounds and promotes integration of the student body into professional life through established connections with local and national professional associations. Argosy University offers a professionally oriented education with rich opportunities to gain practical experience in class, field placements, and internships. Full-time students and working professionals gain the extensive knowledge and range of skills necessary for effective performance in their chosen fields.

Student Outcomes

Students can register with the University's online career-services system and use select services from a distance, such as degree-specific career e-mail lists, national job posts, and virtual job fairs. Students should contact the University for more information.

Location

Located in northeast Sarasota, the campus is specifically designed for postsecondary and graduate-level instruction through a unique combination of in-residence course work, tutorials, and online study courses. Several programs are off-site tutorials and intensive one-week classroom sessions. Students may also complete up to 49 percent of the work in some degree programs via online courses that allow interaction with faculty members and classmates from any Internet connection.

Sarasota is recognized as Florida's cultural coast and is home to a professional symphony, ballet, and opera as well as dozens of theaters and art galleries. Well-known vacation attractions such as Disney World, Busch Gardens–Tampa, and the city of Miami are within a few hours' drive. The area enjoys mild winters and endless summer beauty.

The business sector in the Gulf Coast community helps make it one of the top 20 places to live and work. ASO Corporation, Nelson Publishing, and Select Technology Group are among the numerous companies headquartered in Sarasota County. The area's top employers include Sarasota Memorial Hospital and Publix Supermarkets.

The University

Argosy University is a private institution with nineteen locations across the nation. Argosy University, Sarasota, provides a career resources office, an academic resources center, and extensive information access for research. It offers the resources of a large university plus the friendliness and personal attention of a small campus.

The innovative programs feature dynamic, relevant, and practical curricula delivered in flexible class formats. Students enjoy scheduling options that make it easier to fit school into their busy lives, choosing from day and evening courses, on campus or online. Many students find a combination of class formats to be an ideal way of continuing their education while meeting family and professional demands.

Argosy University is accredited by the Higher Learning Commission, a member of the North Central Association, 230 South LaSalle Street, Suite 7-500, Chicago, Illinois 60604-1413; 800-621-7440 (toll-free); http://www.ncahlc.org.

Applying

Argosy University, Sarasota, accepts students year-round on a rolling admissions basis, depending on availability of required courses. Applications for admission are available online or by contacting the campus.

Correspondence and Information

Argosy University, Sarasota
5250 17th Street
Sarasota, Florida 34235

Phone: 941-379-0404
        800-331-5995 (toll-free)
Fax: 941-371-8910
E-mail: auadmissions@argosy.edu
Web site: http://www.argosy.edu/sarasota

Argosy University, Sarasota

THE FACULTY

The Argosy University faculty is comprised of working professionals who are eager to help students succeed. Members bring real-world experience and the latest practice innovations to the academic setting. The diverse faculty members of the College of Psychology and Behavioral Sciences are widely recognized for contributions to the field. Many are published scholars, and most hold doctoral degrees. They are committed to providing a substantive education that combines comprehensive knowledge with critical skills and practical workplace relevance. Above all, faculty members are committed to their students' personal and professional development.

ARGOSY UNIVERSITY.

ARGOSY UNIVERSITY, SCHAUMBURG

College of Psychology and Behavioral Sciences

Programs of Study
Argosy University, Schaumburg, offers the Master of Arts (M.A.) degree in Clinical Psychology, Community Counseling, and Industrial Organizational Psychology; the Doctor of Education (Ed.D.) degree in Counseling Psychology and Counselor Education and Supervision; and the Doctor of Psychology (Psy.D.) degree in Clinical Psychology. Students completing a program may wish to become licensed professionals. Argosy University, Schaumburg does not guarantee third-party certification/licensure. Outside agencies control the requirements for taking and passing certification/licensing exams and are subject to change without notice to Argosy University, Schaumburg.

The Master of Arts (M.A.) in Clinical Psychology program is designed to educate and train students to enter professional careers as master's-level practitioners. The program provides the theoretical and clinical elements necessary for graduates to be effective members of a mental health team. It introduces students to basic clinical skills that integrate individual and group theoretical foundations of applied psychology into appropriate client interaction and intervention skills. In addition, it offers excellent preparation for those considering application to the Psy.D. in Clinical Psychology program.

The Master of Arts (M.A.) in Community Counseling program is designed to provide students with a sound foundation for eventual practice of professional counseling. The program introduces students to basic counseling skills that integrate individual and group theoretical foundations of professional counseling into appropriate client interaction and intervention skills. The program emphasizes the development of attitudes, knowledge, and skills essential in the formation of professional counselors who are committed to the ethical provision of quality services. The program is committed to educating and training students to enter a professional career as master's-level counseling practitioners who can function ethically and effectively as skilled professionals with demonstrated knowledge of social and cultural diversity. Students are prepared for licensure as professional counselors in the state of Illinois; however, alumni serve clients throughout North America.

The Master of Arts (M.A.) in Industrial Organizational Psychology program is designed to apply the knowledge of industrial organizational psychology to issues involving individuals and groups in organizational and work settings. This program prepares students for careers in areas such as compensation, training, data analysis, consultation, statistical decision making, organizational development, leadership, and human resource management. The curriculum is competency based, focusing on the outcomes of training and on the knowledge, skills, and behavior necessary to function as a master's-level professional in the field. This is an interdisciplinary program that combines the expertise of the faculty in the College of Psychology and Behavioral Sciences and the College of Business.

The Doctor of Education (Ed.D.) in Counseling Psychology program is designed to meet the special requirements of working professionals who want to develop their knowledge and skills to handle the changing needs of modern organizations. The program is structured to provide working professionals with the opportunity to pursue their personal and professional goals through the completion of a graduate program.

The Doctor of Education (Ed.D.) in Counselor Education and Supervision program aligns with the master's-level counselor education programs in order to encourage entry-level counseling students to work toward becoming doctoral-level advanced practitioners, educators, and supervisors. The program prepares counselors for a variety of settings by providing the advanced skills and knowledge necessary to provide leadership and advocacy, as well as serve in supervisory, training, and teaching positions in the counseling profession.

The Doctor of Psychology (Psy.D.) in Clinical Psychology program has been designed to educate and train students to function effectively as clinical psychologists. The curriculum provides for the meaningful integration of theory, training, and practice. The program emphasizes the development of attitudes, knowledge, and skills essential in the formation of professional psychologists who are committed to the ethical provision of quality services.

Research Facilities
Argosy University libraries provide curriculum support and educational resources, including current text materials, diagnostic training documents, reference materials and databases, journals and dissertations, and major and current titles in program areas. There is an online public-access catalog of library resources available throughout the Argosy University system. Students have remote access to the campus library database, enabling them to study and conduct research at home. Academic databases offer dissertation abstracts, academic journals, and professional periodicals. All library computers are Internet accessible. Software applications include Word, Excel, PowerPoint, SPSS, and various test-scoring programs.

Financial Aid
Financial aid is available to those who qualify. Argosy University, Schaumburg, offers access to federal and state aid programs, merit-based awards, grants, loans, and a work-study program. As a first step, students should complete the Free Application for Federal Student Aid (FAFSA). Prospective students can apply electronically at http://www.fafsa.ed.gov or at the campus.

Cost of Study
Tuition varies by program. Students should contact Argosy University, Schaumburg, for tuition information.

Living and Housing Costs
Students typically live in apartments in the metropolitan Chicago area. Living expenses vary according to each student's preferred standard of living, housing, and transportation. The University does not offer or operate student housing. Most Argosy University students are full-time working professionals who live within driving distance of the campus. Several nearby hotels offer special rates for those who commute from long distances. The Admissions Department also maintains a list of housing options, including contact information for University students who wish to share housing. For more information, students should contact the Admissions Department.

Student Group
Admission to Argosy University, Schaumburg, is selective to ensure a dynamic and engaged student body. The University encourages diversity in academic and employment backgrounds and promotes integration of the student body into professional life through established connections with local and national professional associations. Argosy University offers a professionally oriented education with rich opportunities to gain practical experience in class, field placements, and internships. Full-time students and working professionals gain the extensive knowledge and range of skills necessary for effective performance in their chosen field.

Student Outcomes
Students can register with Argosy University's online career-services system and use select services from a distance, such as degree-specific career e-mail lists, national job posts, and virtual job fairs. Students should contact the University for more information.

Location
Argosy University, Schaumburg, is located in the northwest suburban area, approximately 45 minutes from downtown Chicago. The University's small size offers a highly personal atmosphere and flexible programs tailored to students' needs. Visitors to Chicago experience a range of attractions to stimulate both intellectual and recreational pursuits. Located on the shores of Lake Michigan in the Midwest, Chicago is home to world-champion sports teams, an internationally acclaimed symphony orchestra, renowned architecture, and nearly 3 million residents. Among the variety of history and art museums in the city, the Chicago Cultural Center offers more than 600 art programs and exhibits each year. Recreational opportunities include hiking and cycling on miles of lakefront trails, golfing, and shopping

Many facilities and agencies in the area provide opportunities for student training. Schaumburg's thriving business environment includes 5,000 businesses that employ 80,000 people. The area's largest employers are Motorola, Experian, Cingular, and IBM.

The University
Argosy University is a private institution with nineteen locations across the nation. Argosy University, Schaumburg, provides a career resources office, an academic resources center, and extensive information access for research. It offers the resources of a large university plus the friendliness and personal attention of a small campus. The innovative programs feature dynamic, relevant, and practical curricula delivered in flexible class formats. Students enjoy scheduling options that make it easier to fit school into their busy lives, choosing from day and evening courses, on campus or online. Many students find a combination of class formats to be an ideal way of continuing their education while meeting family and professional demands.

Argosy University is accredited by the Higher Learning Commission and a member of the North Central Association, 230 South LaSalle Street, Suite 7-500, Chicago, Illinois 60602-1413; 800-621-7440 (toll-free); http://www.ncahlc.org.

Applying
Argosy University, Schaumburg, accepts students year-round on a rolling admissions basis, depending on availability of required courses. Applications for admission are available online or by contacting the campus.

Correspondence and Information
Argosy University, Schaumburg
999 North Plaza Drive, Suite 111
Schaumburg, Illinois 60173-5403
Phone: 847-969-4900
    866-290-2777 (toll-free)
Fax: 847-969-4998
E-mail: auadmissions@argosy.edu
Web site: http://www.argosy.edu/schaumburg

Argosy University, Schaumburg

THE FACULTY

The Argosy University faculty is comprised of working professionals who are eager to help students succeed. Members bring real-world experience and the latest practice innovations to the academic setting. The diverse faculty members of the College of Psychology and Behavioral Sciences are widely recognized for contributions to the field. Many are published scholars, and most hold doctoral degrees. They are committed to providing a substantive education that combines comprehensive knowledge with critical skills and practical workplace relevance. Above all, faculty members are committed to their students' personal and professional development.

ARGOSY UNIVERSITY.

ARGOSY UNIVERSITY, SEATTLE

College of Psychology and Behavioral Sciences

Programs of Study
Argosy University, Seattle, offers the Master of Arts (M.A.) degree in Clinical Psychology, Counseling Psychology, and Forensic Psychology; the Doctor of Education (Ed.D.) degree in Counseling Psychology, and the Doctor of Psychology (Psy.D.) degree in Clinical Psychology. Students completing a program may wish to become licensed professionals. Argosy University, Seattle does not guarantee third-party certification/licensure. Outside agencies control the requirements for taking and passing certification/licensing exams and are subject to change without notice to Argosy University, Seattle.

The Master of Arts (M.A.) in Clinical Psychology program is designed to educate and train students to enter professional careers as master's-level practitioners. The program provides the theoretical and clinical elements necessary for graduates to be effective members of a mental health team. It introduces students to basic clinical skills that integrate individual and group theoretical foundations of applied psychology into appropriate client interaction and intervention skills.

The Master of Arts (M.A.) in Counseling Psychology program is designed to provide students with a sound foundation for the eventual practice of mental health counseling. The program emphasizes the development of attitudes, knowledge, and skills essential in the formation of professionals who are committed to the ethical provision of quality services. It prepares students to enter a professional career as master's-level counseling practitioners who can perform ethically and effectively as skilled professionals with demonstrated knowledge of social and cultural diversity. Curriculum is designed to integrate basic counseling skills, theoretical foundations of professional counseling, and practicum field experience into appropriate client interaction and intervention skills for application in a wide variety of settings with diverse client populations. Since licensing may change and often varies from state to state, students should verify the current requirements of the state in which they plan to become licensed.

The Master of Arts (M.A.) in Forensic Psychology program is designed to educate and train individuals who are currently working, or wish to work, in fields that utilize the study and practice of forensic psychology, such as law enforcement, legal and organizational consultation, and program analysis. The curriculum provides for an understanding of theory, training, and practice of forensic psychology and to emphasize the development of students who are committed to the ethical provision of high-quality services to diverse clients and organizations. The program maintains policies and delivery formats suitable for working adults.

The Doctor of Education (Ed.D.) in Counseling Psychology program emphasizes the development of attitudes, knowledge, and skills essential for professionals who are committed to the ethical provision of quality services. The curriculum provides for the meaningful integration of theory, training, and practice.

The Doctor of Psychology (Psy.D.) in Clinical Psychology program utilizes a practitioner-scholar model of professional training and is designed to educate and train students to function effectively as clinical psychologists. The curriculum provides for the meaningful integration of theory, training, and practice. The program is competency-based and emphasizes the development of attitudes, knowledge, and skills essential to the training of clinical psychologists committed to the ethical provision of quality services to diverse populations. Students are prepared through the formal curriculum, which exposes them to the practice of professional psychology in both its breadth and depth. Concomitant professional development is supported through mentoring relationships with practitioner-scholar faculty who embody the integration of knowledge and skills with the ethical and professional attitudes required of clinical psychologists.

Research Facilities
Argosy University libraries provide curriculum support and educational resources, including current text materials, diagnostic training documents, reference materials and databases, journals and dissertations, and major and current titles in program areas. There is an online public-access catalog of library resources available throughout the Argosy University system. Students have full remote access to the campus library database, enabling them to study and conduct research at home. Academic databases offer dissertation abstracts, academic journals, and professional periodicals. All library computers are Internet accessible. Software applications include Word, Excel, PowerPoint, SPSS, and various test-scoring programs.

Financial Aid
Financial aid is available to those who qualify. Argosy University, Seattle, offers access to federal and state aid programs, merit-based awards, grants, loans, and a work-study program. As a first step, students should complete the Free Application for Federal Student Aid (FAFSA). Prospective students can apply electronically at http://www.fafsa.ed.gov or at the campus.

Cost of Study
Tuition varies by program. Students should contact Argosy University, Seattle, for tuition information.

Living and Housing Costs
Students typically live in apartments in the metropolitan Seattle area. Living expenses vary according to each student's preferred standard of living, housing, and transportation. The University does not offer or operate student housing. Most of the students are full-time working professionals who live within driving distance of the campus. Several nearby hotels offer special rates for those who commute from long distances. The Admissions Department also maintains a list of housing options, including contact information, for University students who wish to share housing. For more information, students should contact the Admissions Department.

Student Group
Admission to Argosy University, Seattle, is selective to ensure a dynamic and engaged student body. The University encourages diversity in academic and employment backgrounds and promotes integration of the student body into professional life through established connections with local and national professional associations. Argosy University offers a professionally oriented education with rich opportunities to gain practical experience in class, field placements, and internships. Full-time students and working professionals gain the extensive knowledge and range of skills necessary for effective performance in their chosen fields.

Student Outcomes
Students can register with the University's online career-services system and use select services from a distance, such as degree-specific career e-mail lists, national job posts, and virtual job fairs. Students should contact the University for more information.

Location
Argosy University, Seattle, aspires to provide a supportive, collaborative, and engaging yet challenging learning environment. Easily reached through the King County Public Transportation System, the campus sits in proximity to local libraries, shops, restaurants, theaters, and art museums. Seattle offers numerous historical and multicultural museums, a symphony, ballet, and many theater companies. The city is home to several major-league sports teams and offers a myriad of outdoor recreational opportunities, such as camping, hiking, fishing, skiing, and rock climbing. Seattle's business environment encompasses a wide range of industries and features such giants as Microsoft, Boeing, and Alaska Air Group. The Port of Seattle and the University of Washington are also among the area's largest employers.

The University
Argosy University is a private institution with nineteen locations across the nation. Argosy University, Seattle, provides a career resources office, an academic resources center, and extensive information access for research. It offers the resources of a large university, plus the friendliness and personal attention of a small campus.

The innovative programs feature dynamic, relevant, and practical curricula delivered in flexible class formats. Students enjoy scheduling options that make it easier to fit school into their busy lives, choosing from day and evening courses, on campus or online. Many students find a combination of class formats to be an ideal way of continuing their education while meeting family and professional demands.

Argosy University is accredited by the Higher Learning Commission and a member of the North Central Association, 230 South LaSalle Street, Suite 7-500, Chicago, Illinois 60604-1413; 800-621-7440 (toll-free); http://www.ncahlc.org.

Applying
Argosy University, Seattle, accepts students year-round on a rolling admissions basis, depending on availability of required courses. Applications for admission are available online or by contacting the campus.

Correspondence and Information
Argosy University, Seattle
2601-A Elliott Avenue
Seattle, Washington 98121
Phone: 206-283-4500
          888-283-2777 (toll-free)
Fax: 206-283-5777
E-mail: auadmissions@argosy.edu
Web site: http://www.argosy.edu/seattle

Argosy University, Seattle

THE FACULTY

The Argosy University faculty is comprised of working professionals who are eager to help students succeed. Members bring real-world experience and the latest practice innovations to the academic setting. The diverse faculty members of the College of Psychology and Behavioral Sciences are widely recognized for contributions to the field. Many are published scholars, and most hold doctoral degrees. They are committed to providing a substantive education that combines comprehensive knowledge with critical skills and practical workplace relevance. Above all, faculty members are committed to their students' personal and professional development.

ARGOSY UNIVERSITY.

ARGOSY UNIVERSITY, TAMPA

College of Psychology and Behavioral Sciences

Programs of Study	Argosy University, Tampa, offers the Master of Arts (M.A.) degree in Clinical Psychology, Industrial Organizational Psychology, Marriage and Family Therapy, and Mental Health Counseling; the Doctor of Education (Ed.D.) degree in Counselor Education and Supervision; and the Doctor of Psychology (Psy.D.) degree in Clinical Psychology. Students completing a program may wish to become licensed professionals. Argosy University, Tampa does not guarantee third-party certification/licensure. Outside agencies control the requirements for taking and passing certification/licensing exams and are subject to change without notice to Argosy University, Tampa.
	The Master of Arts (M.A.) in Clinical Psychology program is designed to meet the needs of both those students seeking a terminal degree at the master's level and those who plan to pursue a doctoral degree. The terminal master's degree is not, however, license-eligible in the state of Florida. The master's degree provides students a strong clinical orientation with an emphasis in psychological assessment. The master's program offers several unique advantages to those individuals who hope to subsequently pursue a doctoral degree. Admission to the master's program or completion of the master's degree does not guarantee admission to the Psy.D. in clinical psychology program.
	The Master of Arts (M.A.) in Industrial Organizational Psychology program is designed to apply the knowledge of industrial organizational psychology to issues involving individuals and groups in organizational and work settings. This program prepares students for careers in areas such as compensation, training, data analysis, consultation, statistical decision making, organizational development, leadership, and human resource management. The curriculum is competency based, focusing on the outcomes of training and on the knowledge, skills, and behavior necessary to function as a master's-level professional in the field.
	The Master of Arts (M.A.) in Marriage and Family Therapy program recognizes the need to provide marriage and family therapists with the extensive knowledge and range of skills necessary to function effectively in their profession. The program introduces basic skills that integrate systemic theoretical foundations of marriage and family therapy into appropriate client interaction and intervention skills.
	The Master of Arts (M.A.) in Mental Health Counseling program recognizes the need to provide counseling professionals with the extensive knowledge, range of skills, and attitudes necessary to function effectively in their professions. The program introduces students to basic counseling skills that integrate individual and group theoretical foundations of counseling into appropriate client interaction and intervention skills. The program emphasizes formation of professional counselors committed to the ethical provision of quality services.
	The Doctor of Education (Ed.D.) in Counselor Education and Supervision program aligns with the master's-level counselor education programs in order to encourage entry-level counseling students to work toward becoming doctoral-level advanced practitioners, educators, and supervisors. The program prepares counselors for a variety of settings by providing the advanced skills and knowledge necessary to provide leadership and advocacy, as well as serve in supervisory, training, and teaching positions in the counseling profession.
	The Doctor of Psychology (Psy.D.) in Clinical Psychology program has been designed to educate and train students to function effectively as clinical psychologists. The curriculum provides for the meaningful integration of theory, training, and practice. The program emphasizes the development of attitudes, knowledge, and skills essential in the formation of professional psychologists who are committed to the ethical provision of quality services.
Research Facilities	Argosy University libraries provide curriculum support and educational resources, including current text materials, diagnostic training documents, reference materials and databases, journals and dissertations, and major and current titles in program areas. There is an online public-access catalog of library resources available throughout the Argosy University system. Students have remote access to the campus library database, enabling them to study and conduct research at home. Academic databases offer dissertation abstracts, academic journals, and professional periodicals. All library computers are Internet accessible. Software applications include Word, Excel, PowerPoint, SPSS, and various test-scoring programs.
Financial Aid	Financial aid is available to those who qualify. Argosy University, Tampa, offers access to federal and state aid programs, merit-based awards, grants, loans, and a work-study program. As a first step, students should complete the Free Application for Federal Student Aid (FAFSA). Prospective students can apply electronically at http://www.fafsa.ed.gov or at the campus.
Cost of Study	Tuition varies by program. Students should contact Argosy University, Tampa, for tuition information.
Living and Housing Costs	Students typically live in apartments in the metropolitan Tampa area. Living expenses vary according to each student's preferred standard of living, housing, and transportation. The University does not offer or operate student housing. Most of the students are full-time working professionals who live within driving distance of the campus. Several nearby hotels offer special rates for those who commute from long distances. The Admissions Department also maintains a list of housing options, including contact information, for University students who wish to share housing. For more information, students should contact the Admissions Department.
Student Group	Admission to Argosy University, Tampa, is selective to ensure a dynamic and engaged student body. The University encourages diversity in academic and employment backgrounds and promotes integration of the student body into professional life through established connections with local and national professional associations. Argosy University offers a professionally oriented education with rich opportunities to gain practical experience in class, field placements, and internships. Full-time students and working professionals gain the extensive knowledge and range of skills necessary for effective performance in their chosen fields.
Student Outcomes	Students can register with the University's online career-services system and use select services from a distance, such as degree-specific career e-mail lists, national job posts, and virtual job fairs. Students should contact the University for more information.
Location	Located in sunny Florida, Argosy University, Tampa, attracts a diverse student population from throughout the United States, the Caribbean, Europe, Africa, and Asia. Tampa's central location affords students the opportunity to work for major corporations and hear speakers of international acclaim. The school offers rigorous programs of study in a supportive, collaborative environment. The campus sits within an hour's drive of some of the most popular tourist destinations in the world, including the Disney theme parks, Busch Gardens, and the Florida Gulf Coast beaches. Major-league sporting events, concerts, theaters, and world-renowned restaurants are also within easy reach. Tampa combines the opportunities of a large city with the friendliness of a small town.
	The Tampa-St. Petersburg-Clearwater metropolitan area offers a diversified economic base fueled by a broad array of companies, including Verizon Communications and JP Morgan Chase. In addition, Tampa serves as headquarters for three Fortune 100 companies—OSI Restaurant Partners; TECO, an energy provider; and Raymond James Financial.
The University	Argosy University is a private institution with nineteen locations across the nation. Argosy University, Tampa, provides a network of resources, including a career resources office, an academic resources center, and extensive information access for research. It offers the resources of a large university, plus the friendliness and personal attention of a small campus.
	The innovative programs feature dynamic, relevant, and practical curricula delivered in flexible class formats. Students enjoy scheduling options that make it easier to fit school into their busy lives, choosing from day and evening courses, on campus or online. Many students find a combination of class formats to be an ideal way of continuing their education while meeting family and professional demands.
	Argosy University is accredited by the Higher Learning Commission and a member of the North Central Association, 230 South LaSalle Street, Suite 7-500, Chicago, Illinois 60604-1413; 800-621-7440 (toll-free); http://www.ncahlc.org.
Applying	Argosy University, Tampa, accepts students year-round on a rolling admissions basis, depending on availability of required courses. Applications for admission are available online or by contacting the campus.
Correspondence and Information	Argosy University, Tampa 1403 North Howard Avenue Tampa, Florida 33607 Phone: 813-393-5290 800-850-6488 (toll-free) Fax: 813-874-1989 E-mail: auadmissions@argosy.edu Web site: http://www.argosy.edu/tampa

Argosy University, Tampa

THE FACULTY

The Argosy University faculty is comprised of working professionals who are eager to help students succeed. Members bring real-world experience and the latest practice innovations to the academic setting. The diverse faculty members of the College of Psychology and Behavioral Sciences are widely recognized for contributions to the field. Many are published scholars, and most hold doctoral degrees. They are committed to providing a substantive education that combines comprehensive knowledge with critical skills and practical workplace relevance. Above all, faculty members are committed to their students' personal and professional development.

ARGOSY UNIVERSITY

ARGOSY UNIVERSITY, TWIN CITIES

College of Psychology and Behavioral Sciences

Programs of Study

Argosy University, Twin Cities, offers the Master of Arts (M.A.) degree in Clinical Psychology, Forensic Psychology, Industrial Organizational Psychology, and Marriage and Family Therapy; the Doctor of Marriage and Family Therapy (D.M.F.T.) degree; and the Doctor of Psychology (Psy.D.) degree in Clinical Psychology. Students completing a program may wish to become licensed professionals. Argosy University, Twin Cities does not guarantee third-party certification/licensure. Outside agencies control the requirements for taking and passing certification/licensing exams and are subject to change without notice to Argosy University, Twin Cities.

The Master of Arts (M.A.) in Clinical Psychology program is designed to prepare students with the clinical knowledge and skills required to serve the mental health needs of individuals and groups. Students develop proficiency in clinical observation, assessment, appropriate intervention, and evaluation. The program emphasizes a practitioner-oriented philosophy and integrates applied theory, research, and field experience. It is designed for students who are interested in a terminal degree and practice as a master's-level clinician, or for students planning to transfer to the Psy.D. program.

The Master of Arts (M.A.) in Forensic Psychology program is designed to provide course work in forensic psychology for application to law enforcement, legal and organizational consultation, and program analysis. The program is designed to meet growing needs of the legal and criminal justice systems for professional counseling within victim assistance programs, probation and parole offices, court-mandated treatment programs, jails, and prisons. With the exception of the practicum component, courses are offered on weekends, allowing students to continue full-time employment while enrolled in this program.

The Master of Arts (M.A.) in Industrial Organizational Psychology program is designed to apply the knowledge of industrial organizational psychology to issues involving individuals and groups in organizational and work settings. This program prepares students for careers in areas such as compensation, training, data analysis, consultation, statistical decision making, organizational development, leadership, and human resource management. The curriculum is competency based, focusing on the outcomes of training and on the knowledge, skills, and behavior necessary to function as a master's-level professional in the field.

The Master of Arts (M.A.) in Marriage and Family Therapy program is designed to develop the theoretical and clinical elements required to provide effective counseling to individuals, couples, families, and groups. The program introduces basic counseling skills that incorporate foundations of applied psychology and systems theory into the development of appropriate clinical relationships. Course work in addiction studies and substance-abuse counseling prepares students to work with families affected by this burgeoning problem. An optional concentration in forensic counseling is available. Marriage and family therapy is recognized by the Public Health Service Act as one of the five core mental health professions, and the National Institute of Mental Health accepts marriage and family therapists as qualified mental health professionals. The program is offered through weekend courses to allow concurrent employment.

The Doctor of Marriage and Family Therapy (D.M.F.T.) is a practice-oriented degree for licensed marriage and family therapists or professionals who can meet state requirements for licensure as a marriage and family therapist, meeting the Commission on Accreditation of Marriage and Family Therapy Education (COAMFTE) criteria for clinical practice prior to admission. The program seeks to build upon students' prior learning and professional experience by expanding and deepening their knowledge of human development, family dynamics, systemic thinking, interactional theories, traditional and contemporary marriage and family therapy theories and practices, and the cultural contexts within which these are embedded.

The Doctor of Psychology (Psy.D.) in Clinical Psychology program is designed to prepare students to deliver basic diagnostic and therapeutic services to diverse populations, including individuals, groups, and families. By integrating theory, training, research, and practice, students develop and apply the clinical skills of observation, assessment, intervention, and evaluation. Optional concentrations are available in child and family psychology, forensic psychology, health psychology, marriage/couple and family therapy, or neuropsychology. The program prepares graduates for positions in traditional settings, including, but not limited to, independent practice, mental health centers, hospitals, medical centers, and managed-care systems. Graduates are encouraged to utilize clinical skills in innovative ways to become more competitive. Eventual positions may include consulting in various corporate, governmental, academic, multimedia, law, scientific, marketing, and industrial settings. The Doctor of Psychology in clinical psychology program at Argosy University, Twin Cities, is accredited by the Committee on Accreditation of the American Psychological Association (APA) (750 First Street NE, Washington, D.C. 20002-4242; 202-336-5510).

Research Facilities

Argosy University libraries provide curriculum support and educational resources, including current text materials, diagnostic training documents, reference materials and databases, journals and dissertations, and major and current titles in program areas. There is an online public-access catalog of library resources available throughout the Argosy University system. Students have remote access to the campus library database, enabling them to study and conduct research at home. Academic databases offer dissertation abstracts, academic journals, and professional periodicals. All library computers are Internet accessible. Software applications include Word, Excel, PowerPoint, SPSS, and various test-scoring programs.

Financial Aid

Financial aid is available to those who qualify. Argosy University, Twin Cities, offers access to federal and state aid programs, merit-based awards, grants, loans, and a work-study program. As a first step, students should complete the Free Application for Federal Student Aid (FAFSA). Prospective students can apply electronically at http://www.fafsa.ed.gov or at the campus.

Cost of Study

Tuition varies by program. Students should contact Argosy University, Twin Cities, for tuition information.

Living and Housing Costs

Students typically live in apartments in the metropolitan Twin Cities area. Living expenses vary according to each student's preferred standard of living, housing, and transportation. The University does not offer or operate student housing. Most Argosy University students are full-time working professionals who live within driving distance of the campus. Several nearby hotels offer special rates for those who commute from long distances. The Admissions Department also maintains a list of housing options, including contact information for University students who wish to share housing. For more information, students should contact the Admissions Department.

Student Group

Admission to Argosy University, Twin Cities, is selective to ensure a dynamic and engaged student body. The University encourages diversity in academic and employment backgrounds and promotes integration of the student body into professional life through established connections with local and national professional associations. Argosy University offers a professionally oriented education with rich opportunities to gain practical experience in class, field placements, and internships. Full-time students and working professionals gain the extensive knowledge and range of skills necessary for effective performance in their chosen field.

Student Outcomes

Students can register with Argosy University's online career-services system and use select services from a distance, such as degree-specific career e-mail lists, national job posts, and virtual job fairs. Students should contact the University for more information.

Location

Argosy University, Twin Cities, offers rigorous academics in a supportive environment. The campus is nestled in a parklike suburban setting within 10 miles of the airport and the Mall of America. Students enjoy the convenience of nearby shops, restaurants, and housing and easy freeway access. The neighboring Eagan Community Center offers many amenities, including walking trails, a fitness center, meeting rooms, and an outdoor amphitheater. The twin cities of Minneapolis and St. Paul have been rated by popular magazines as one of the most livable metropolitan areas in the country. With a population of 2.5 million, the area offers an abundance of recreational activities. Year-round outdoor activities and nationally acclaimed venues for theater, art, music, and professional sports teams attract residents and visitors alike. The Minneapolis-St. Paul metropolitan area offers a diversified economic base fueled by a broad array of companies. Among the numerous publicly traded companies headquartered in the area are Target, UnitedHealth Group, 3M, General Mills, and US Bancorp.

The University

Argosy University is a private institution with nineteen locations across the nation. Argosy University, Twin Cities, provides a career resources office, an academic resources center, and extensive information access for research. It offers the resources of a large university plus the friendliness and personal attention of a small campus. The innovative programs feature dynamic, relevant, and practical curricula delivered in flexible class formats. Students enjoy scheduling options that make it easier to fit school into their busy lives, choosing from day and evening courses, on campus or online. Many students find a combination of class formats to be an ideal way of continuing their education while meeting family and professional demands.

Argosy University is accredited by the Higher Learning Commission, a member of the North Central Association, 230 South LaSalle Street, Suite 7-500, Chicago, Illinois 60604-1413; 800-621-7440 (toll-free); http://www.ncahlc.org.

Applying

Argosy University, Twin Cities, accepts students on a rolling admissions basis year-round, depending on availability of required courses. Applications for admission may be obtained online or by contacting the campus.

Correspondence and Information

Argosy University, Twin Cities
1515 Central Parkway
Eagan, Minnesota 55121
Phone: 651-846-2882
      888-844-2004 (toll-free)
Fax: 651-994-7956
E-mail: auadmissions@argosy.edu
Web site: http://www.argosy.edu/twincities

Argosy University, Twin Cities

THE FACULTY

The Argosy University faculty is comprised of working professionals who are eager to help students succeed. Members bring real-world experience and the latest practice innovations to the academic setting. The diverse faculty members of the College of Psychology and Behavioral Sciences are widely recognized for contributions to the field. Many are published scholars, and most hold doctoral degrees. They are committed to providing a substantive education that combines comprehensive knowledge with critical skills and practical workplace relevance. Above all, faculty members are committed to their students' personal and professional development.

ARGOSY UNIVERSITY

ARGOSY UNIVERSITY, WASHINGTON D.C.

College of Psychology and Behavioral Sciences

Programs of Study

Argosy University, Washington D.C., offers the Master of Arts (M.A.) degree in Clinical Psychology, Community Counseling, and Forensic Psychology; the Doctor of Education (Ed.D.) degree in Counselor Education and Supervision, and Counseling Psychology; and the Doctor of Psychology (Psy.D.) degree in Clinical Psychology. Students completing a program may wish to become licensed professionals. Argosy University, Washington D.C. does not guarantee third-party certification/licensure. Outside agencies control the requirements for taking and passing certification/licensing exams and are subject to change without notice to Argosy University, Washington D.C.

The Master of Arts (M.A.) in Clinical Psychology program is designed to meet the needs of both those students seeking a terminal degree at the master's level and those who eventually plan to pursue a doctoral degree. The master's degree provides students a strong clinical orientation as well as an emphasis in psychological assessment. The program has been structured to educate and train students so they might either be prepared to enter a doctoral program in clinical psychology or enter a professional career as master's-level practitioners. The program provides a strong background in assessment and introduces students to basic clinical interventions skills. Students also receive an introduction to scientific methodology and the bases of scientific psychology.

The Master of Arts (M.A.) in Community Counseling program is designed to provide students with a sound foundation for the practice of community counseling, with a multifaceted focus on developmental and preventive mental health services. The program introduces students to the basic skills of counseling, integrating individual, group, family, and organizational interventions. It emphasizes development of the attitudes, knowledge, and skills required for the ethical provision of quality professional counseling services. As such, the program is committed to educating and training students to enter the counseling profession as ethical, effective, skilled, and culturally competent practitioners, able to work in a variety of settings with diverse client populations. The curriculum integrates foundational counseling skills, counseling theories, and clinical field experiences taught by experienced practitioners.

The Master of Arts (M.A.) in Forensic Psychology program is designed to educate and train individuals who are currently working, or wish to work, in fields that utilize the study and practice of forensic psychology, such as law enforcement, legal and organizational consultation, and program analysis. The curriculum provides for an understanding of theory, training, and practice of forensic psychology and to emphasize the development of students who are committed to the ethical provision of high-quality services to diverse clients and organizations. The program maintains policies and delivery formats suitable for working adults.

The Doctor of Education (Ed.D.) in Counselor Education and Supervision program aligns with the master's-level counselor education programs in order to encourage entry-level counseling students to work toward becoming doctoral-level advanced practitioners, educators, and supervisors. The program prepares counselors for a variety of settings by providing the advanced skills and knowledge necessary to provide leadership and advocacy, as well as serve in supervisory, training, and teaching positions in the counseling profession. The program can also help current practitioners with existing master's-level preparation advance their careers by providing expanded opportunities to compete in the marketplace, on par with the growing number of doctoral-level counseling practitioners.

The Doctor of Education (Ed.D.) in Counseling Psychology program is designed to meet the special requirements of working professionals who want to develop their knowledge and skills to handle the changing needs of modern organizations. The program is structured to provide working professionals with the opportunity to pursue their personal and professional goals through the completion of a graduate program. An optional concentration in counselor education and supervision is also available.

The Doctor of Psychology (Psy.D.) in Clinical Psychology program has been designed to educate and train students to function effectively as clinical psychologists. The curriculum provides for the meaningful integration of theory, training, and practice. The program emphasizes the development of attitudes, knowledge, and skills essential in the formation of professional psychologists who are committed to the ethical provision of quality services.

Research Facilities

Argosy University libraries provide curriculum support and educational resources, including current text materials, diagnostic training documents, reference materials and databases, journals and dissertations, and major and current titles in program areas. There is an online public-access catalog of library resources available throughout the Argosy University system. Students have remote access to the campus library database, enabling them to study and conduct research at home. Academic databases offer dissertation abstracts, academic journals, and professional periodicals. All library computers are Internet accessible. Software applications include Word, Excel, PowerPoint, SPSS, and various test-scoring programs.

Financial Aid

Financial aid is available to those who qualify. Argosy University, Washington D.C., offers access to federal and state aid programs, merit-based awards, grants, loans, and a work-study program. As a first step, students should complete the Free Application for Federal Student Aid (FAFSA). Prospective students can apply electronically at http://www.fafsa.ed.gov or at the campus.

Cost of Study

Tuition varies by program. Students should contact Argosy University, Washington D.C., for tuition information.

Living and Housing Costs

Students typically live in apartments in the metropolitan Washington, D.C., area. Living expenses vary according to each student's preferred standard of living, housing, and transportation. The University does not offer or operate student housing. Most Argosy University students are full-time working professionals who live within driving distance of the campus. Several nearby hotels offer special rates for those who commute from long distances. The Admissions Department also maintains a list of housing options, including contact information for University students who wish to share housing. For more information, students should contact the Admissions Department.

Student Group

Admission to Argosy University, Washington D.C., is selective to ensure a dynamic and engaged student body. The University encourages diversity in academic and employment backgrounds and promotes integration of the student body into professional life through established connections with local and national professional associations. Argosy University offers a professionally oriented education with rich opportunities to gain practical experience in class, field placements, and internships. Full-time students and working professionals gain the extensive knowledge and range of skills necessary for effective performance in their chosen field.

Student Outcomes

Students can register with Argosy University's online career-services system and use select services from a distance, such as degree-specific career e-mail lists, national job posts, and virtual job fairs. Students should contact the University for more information.

Location

Argosy University, Washington D.C., is located in suburban Arlington, Virginia. The school provides easy access to most major highways in area and is accessible by public transportation. With its proximity to Georgetown, students enjoy access to the many diverse attractions of the D.C. area. Additional campus space is located at the Art Institute of Washington Building (1820 Fort Myer Drive). The university houses administrative space and seven classrooms at this location. Perhaps best known as the home of the Pentagon and Arlington National Cemetery, Arlington, Virginia, is one of the most highly educated areas in the nation. It is also one of the most diverse. Major employers in the region include MCI Telecommunications Corporation; Bell Atlantic Network Services, Inc.; and Gannett/USA Today Company, Inc.

The University

Argosy University is a private institution with nineteen locations across the nation. Argosy University, Washington D.C., provides a career resources office, an academic resources center, and extensive information access for research. It offers the resources of a large university plus the friendliness and personal attention of a small campus. The innovative programs feature dynamic, relevant, and practical curricula delivered in flexible class formats. Students enjoy scheduling options that make it easier to fit school into their busy lives, choosing from day and evening courses, on campus or online. Many students find a combination of class formats to be an ideal way of continuing their education while meeting family and professional demands.

Argosy University is accredited by the Higher Learning Commission, a member of the North Central Association, 230 South LaSalle Street, Suite 7-500, Chicago, Illinois 60604-1413; 800-621-7440 (toll-free); http://www.ncahlc.org.

Applying

Argosy University, Washington D.C., accepts students year-round on a rolling admissions basis, depending on availability of required courses. Applications for admission are available online or by contacting the campus.

Correspondence and Information

Argosy University, Washington D.C.
1550 Wilson Boulevard, Suite 600
Arlington, Virginia 22209
Phone: 703-526-5800
          866-703-2777 (toll-free)
Fax: 703-243-8973
E-mail: auadmissions@argosy.edu
Web site: http://www.argosy.edu/washingtondc

Argosy University, Washington DC

THE FACULTY

The Argosy University faculty is comprised of working professionals who are eager to help students succeed. Members bring real-world experience and the latest practice innovations to the academic setting. The diverse faculty members of the College of Psychology and Behavioral Sciences are widely recognized for contributions to the field. Many are published scholars, and most hold doctoral degrees. They are committed to providing a substantive education that combines comprehensive knowledge with critical skills and practical workplace relevance. Above all, faculty members are committed to their students' personal and professional development.

BARRY UNIVERSITY

Graduate Programs in Psychology

Programs of Study	Barry University in Miami Shores, Florida, offers the Master of Science in clinical psychology, the Master of Science and Specialist degrees in school psychology, and the Master of Science in movement science with a specialization in sport and exercise psychology.
	The Master of Science in clinical psychology program employs the scientist/practitioner model of training with faculty actively involved in research and clinical practice. This offers students the opportunity to obtain the theoretical, scientific, and clinical experience necessary to enter into the practice of mental health evaluation and treatment of diverse populations. The program also prepares students for doctoral-level training.
	Clinical psychology students can choose from two tracks. The 36-credit option prepares students for application to doctoral programs, while the 60-credit option prepares students to sit for licensing as mental health counselors in the state of Florida. The license qualifies students to engage in private practice and to seek employment with public or private mental health organizations, social service agencies, government and private research teams, and community colleges. The program provides high-quality academic instruction, research experience, and supervised clinical training at a variety of mental health centers.
	In the second year, all full-time students enroll in a 165-hour clinical psychology practicum that requires one day per week of supervised clinical work in a mental health setting, with a minimum of 40 client contact hours. In the practicum students learn and practice diagnostic and therapeutic skills. The clinical psychology internship offered in the third year of the 60-credit option is a full-time, supervised clinical experience that requires a minimum of 1,000 hours. Under supervision in a mental health facility, students perform a variety of clinically related activities that a licensed professional with a master's degree in clinical psychology would be expected to perform. The clinical experience includes a minimum of 240 direct client contact hours.
	To accommodate working professionals, all courses are offered in the evening. The 30-credit option can be completed in two years of full-time study, while the 60-credit option can be completed in three years.
	Barry's school psychology program includes the Master of Science degree in psychology and Specialist in School Psychology (S.S.P.), equivalent to an Ed.S. degree. The program is designed to meet the needs of a broad group of students, including recent graduates with bachelor's degrees and experienced teachers and mental health professionals who are interested in a career upgrade. The student is awarded an M.S. degree after completion of 30 credits and can advance to the specialist program. The master's is a prerequisite for the specialist degree, and many students earn both at Barry. However, for students who already have a master's in psychology or a related field, a program adviser can customize a course sequence, which can reduce the total number of credits needed to graduate.
	The 71-credit school psychology program satisfies the academic requirements set by the National Association of School Psychologists (NASP). Following the internship, students are prepared to meet licensure requirements for the private practice of school psychology as set forth by the State of Florida, as well as certification requirements as set forth by the Florida State Board of Education. The school psychology program is approved by the Florida Department of Education and by the National Association of School Psychologists.
	Graduate courses are offered in the evening. Field placement and internship courses, which occur near the completion of training, require daytime availability. The program can be completed in three years of full-time study.
	Barry University offers the only master's degree in sport and exercise psychology in South Florida. The 36-credit master's in movement science with a specialization in sport and exercise psychology focuses on understanding and analyzing the psychological mechanisms and consequences of human movement in sport, physical education, and exercise contexts.
	This program prepares students for careers in teaching, coaching, research, and fitness leadership with an emphasis on psychological principles. The program allows students to explore a variety of research methodologies, while emphasizing hands-on assignments and applied techniques that directly benefit members of the community. Students can choose from a thesis or practicum track. Courses are offered in the evenings and on weekends.
Research Facilities	Graduate psychology programs are supported by evaluation, testing, and computer facilities including an electrophysiology lab, clinical training labs, a graduate research lab, and a performance behavior lab. In addition, the Monsignor William Barry Memorial Library houses more than 950,000 items and participates in regional and state library networks.
Financial Aid	A limited number of graduate assistantships are available. Compensation each semester includes approximately $1500 and tuition remission for one course. The time commitment is 15 hours per week. Normally, positions are awarded for a full academic year, and students are notified of their assistantship in the spring.
	Barry participates in the full array of federal and state financial aid programs. Full-time Florida teachers may receive at least a 20 percent tuition discount under Barry's Professional Recognition Scholarship Program.
Cost of Study	Graduate tuition is $905 per credit for the 2011–12 academic year. Additional course fees may be required.
Living and Housing Costs	Campus housing for full-time graduate students is limited. Barry provides assistance in locating off-campus housing.
Location	The University's 122-acre campus is in Miami Shores, Florida, just a few miles from the ocean, between the cities of Miami and Fort Lauderdale. South Florida offers a dynamic multicultural environment and opportunities in its arts and entertainment, international business, education, medical, nonprofit, professional sports, and tourism sectors. The climate allows for year-round sports and recreation. Students can also experience exciting nightlife and cultural events.
The University	Founded in 1940 by the Adrian Dominican Sisters, Barry University is the second-largest private, Catholic university in the southeastern United States. In the fall 2010 semester, 8,995 students were enrolled, including more than 4,000 graduate students. *U.S. News & World Report* recently ranked Barry among the top 20 schools nationwide for campus diversity. With a 15:1 student-faculty ratio, students receive personal attention from distinguished professors. The University's local partnerships ensure that students gain professional experience before graduation.
Applying	To apply, students must submit the completed application, nonrefundable $30 application fee, official transcripts from all universities and colleges attended, a statement of purpose, letters of recommendation, and GRE scores. International students must also submit TOEFL scores. For specific requirements, please contact the program directly.

Correspondence and Information

Clinical Psychology Program
Dr. Lenore Szuchman, Chair
Department of Psychology
College of Arts and Sciences
Barry University
11300 NE Second Avenue
Miami Shores, Florida 33161-6695
Phone: 305-899-3278
Fax: 305-899-3279
E-mail: lszuchman@mail.barry.edu
Web site: http://www.barry.edu/psychologyclinical

School Psychology Program
Dr. M. Sylvia Fernandez, Chair
Department of Counseling
Adrian Dominican School of Education
Barry University
11300 NE Second Avenue
Miami Shores, Florida 33161-6695
Phone: 305-899-4868
Fax: 305-899-3718
E-mail: smfernandez@mail.barry.edu
Web site: http://www.barry.edu/psychologyssp

Sport and Exercise Psychology Program
Dr. Gualberto Cremades, Coordinator
School of Human Performance and Leisure Sciences
Barry University
11300 NE Second Avenue
Miami Shores, Florida 33161-6695
Phone: 305-899-4846
Fax: 305-899-4809
E-mail: gcremades@mail.barry.edu
Web site: http://www.barry.edu/sportexercisepsychology

Barry University

THE FACULTY AND THEIR RESEARCH

Clinical Psychology Program

Lenore Szuchman, Professor and Department Chair; Ph.D., Florida International, 1990. Cognition and social cognition in older adults, advice.

Frank Muscarella, Professor and Program Director; Ph.D., Louisville, 1991. Evolutionary psychology, human sexuality.

Linda Bacheller, Assistant Professor; Psy.D., J.D., Widener, 2006. In-home psychotherapy, children and adolescent mental health, adolescents within the juvenile justice system.

Michael A. DeDonno, Assistant Professor; Ph.D., Case Western Reserve, 2008. Perceived time pressure and the Iowa gambling task, judgment and decision-making, personality and individual differences, how personality differences affect risk-taking preferences.

David M. Feldman, Assistant Professor; Ph.D., Gallaudet, 2004. Deafness and aging, forensic psychology and sexual offenders.

Pamela Hall, Assistant Professor; Ph.D. Ohio State, 1992. Effect of music on memory and the relationship between music and psychological arousal, the benefits of service learning on college student development.

Stephen W. Koncsol, Associate Professor; Ph.D., Rutgers, 1976. Cultural conceptions of mental illness, dyadic communication failures, marital satisfaction/dissatisfaction.

Guillermo Wated, Assistant Professor; Ph.D., Florida International, 2002. Employee attitudes, counterproductive behavior, cultural factors in organizations.

School Psychology Program

M. Sylvia Fernandez, Professor and Chair; Ph.D., Southern Illinois. Multicultural issues in counseling and related disciplines, counselor education and credentialing, clinical supervision.

Jeffrey Guterman, Associate Professor; Ph.D., Nova Southeastern. Professional identity, integrative counseling models, the application of postmodern theories to counseling.

James Rudes, Associate Professor; Ph.D., Nova Southeastern. Postmodern theory, social constructionism, narrative practices, reflecting teams, supervision.

Karen Shatz, Assistant Professor; Ph.D., Nova Southeastern. Phenomenological experiences of loss, immigration issues in counseling, postmodern supervision.

Agnes E. Shine, Associate Professor; Ph.D., Ball State. Neuropsychological issues with children, traumatic brain injury, learning disabilities.

Richard M. Tureen, Associate Professor; Ph.D., Nova Southeastern. Postmodernism, narrative therapy, solution-focused therapy, systems theory, neuroscience applications to therapy.

Sport and Exercise Psychology Program

Gualberto Cremades, Program Coordinator; Ph.D., Ed.D., Houston. Psycho-physiological aspects of human performance using electroencephalography (EEG) recordings to measure brain wave activity and electromyography (EMG) to measure muscle activation.

BAYLOR UNIVERSITY

Department of Psychology and Neuroscience

Programs of Study

The Department of Psychology and Neuroscience is dedicated to the creation and dissemination of knowledge in the psychological sciences, fostering an environment conducive to creative scholarship and learning and the application of knowledge to the betterment and service of society. Through a program that combines course work and research, students have an outstanding record of achieving academic and professional success, while faculty members are active in publishing scholarly work, obtaining and maintaining extramural funding, and serving the broader community. The Department offers two doctoral degrees: Psy.D. and Ph.D.

The Doctor of Psychology (Psy.D.) in clinical psychology, one of only two clinical psychology programs nationwide to be ranked by *U.S. News & World Report*, currently maintains the longest history of continuous accreditation by the American Psychological Association (APA) among Psy.D. programs. Its primary goal is to develop clinical psychologists with the conceptual and clinical competencies necessary to deliver psychological services in an effective and responsible manner, including establishment of collaborative relationships with others, psychological assessment and intervention/treatment, research and outcome evaluation, consultation and education, management and supervision, and a commitment to lifelong learning, which enables students to adapt to new opportunities and knowledge in professional psychology.

The Psy.D. program follows a scholar-professional training model that emphasizes the interdependence between science and practice, recognizing their equal contributions to training in professional psychology. Major components of the program include a rigorous, broadly based curriculum in clinical psychology; extensive practicum experience in a variety of community-based clinical settings; experience in a clinically applied research laboratory, including completion of a dissertation; and completion of an APA-approved internship in clinical psychology. The program involves four years of intensive year-round training on campus followed by a year-long internship. Students typically take two courses plus a practicum each term (fall, spring, and summer). Each student works 20 hours a week in a supervised practicum setting for the first three years and in a clinically applied research laboratory for the fourth year.

The Ph.D. program follows a research-intensive apprenticeship model in which students develop skills in research methodology, statistics, psychology, neuroscience, and other content areas. The Ph.D. program has three tracks: **behavioral neuroscience, general experimental, and social psychology.** All Ph.D. students begin by taking a set of general core classes representing the breadth of the discipline of psychology. Differences in the tracks occur in the specialty core, which is composed of course work specific to behavioral neuroscience, experimental psychology, or social psychology. Upon acceptance to doctoral candidacy, students then complete a set of doctoral and elective classes. **Behavioral neuroscience** as a discipline emphasizes the relationship between brain and behavior. Faculty members have both behavioral interests (animal learning and behavior, personality and impulsive/aggressive behavior, addiction and treatment of addiction, and memory and cognition) and interests in molecular aspects of neuroscience (psychopharmacology and electrophysiology). **General experimental psychology** as a discipline is concerned with employing empirical principles and procedures in the study of psychological phenomena. Specific faculty research areas include memory and cognition, quantitative psychology, social, and sensation and perception. **Social psychology** as a discipline examines how the power of the situation and relatively stable personality dimensions influence individual behavior, cognition, and emotion. Faculty research areas include interpersonal relations, positive psychology, personality, and the psychology of religion. The Ph.D. program is designed so that the requirements can be completed in four to five years.

Research Facilities

The Department is housed in the 508,000-square-foot Baylor Sciences Building. The Baylor Psychology Clinic, conveniently located in downtown Waco for community access, is involved in the assessment, research, evaluation, and treatment of psychological disorders. Faculty members lead clinical laboratories that focus on specialized topics, including play therapy and the assessment of children, cognitive-behavioral therapy, behavioral medicine, hypnosis, prayer, neuropsychology, addictions, and the neurology of impulsive and aggressive behaviors. The Baylor Sciences Building includes five multidisciplinary research Centers on Pre-health Education, Drug Discovery, Molecular Biosciences, Reservoir and Aquatic Systems Research, and Scientific Analysis and Computing. Students find a truly exceptional facility, one characterized by the finest instructional and laboratory space, all indicative of Baylor's unwavering commitment to the best in science education.

Financial Aid

In the first three years of the program, Psy.D. students receive approximately $24,000 per year in the form of practicum salaries, tuition remission, and a stipend; in the fourth year, they receive stipends of $18,000 plus full tuition. Though admissions decisions and funding decisions are considered separately in the Ph.D. program, most students receive full support. This is given in the form of tuition waivers for standard graduate course loads and stipends for teaching assistantships. Student funding is granted for one year only, with no guarantee of future funding. Rarely, however, has a student in good standing been denied continuing support for the duration of a reasonable term of study (e.g., five years). In addition, students can compete for supplemental scholarships offered by the Graduate School. Some students receive $1000 to $4000 annually in supplemental scholarships.

Cost of Study

In 2011–12, tuition is $1197 per academic credit, plus a general student fee of $123 per credit ($1107 if enrolled in 12 or more credits). Most students received a tuition waiver ($26,894 for 24 hours per year) and teaching assistantship ($19,000). The majority of teaching assistantships are eligible for an insurance subsidy from the graduate school that covers all but $200 of the annual fee for student health insurance or 50 percent of family coverage.

Living and Housing Costs

On-campus housing is available on a limited basis for graduate students. Most graduate students opt to live in affordable off-campus apartments or duplexes near campus. More housing details are available on the Graduate School Web site: http://www.baylor.edu/graduate.

Student Group

Approximately 60 students are enrolled in the Department's graduate programs each year, encompassing a wide range of backgrounds. The majority hold undergraduate degrees in psychology, but a few hold degrees in other fields, including science and business.

Student Outcomes

Clinical students have completed one-year internship programs in clinical centers in some of the finest universities and hospitals in the nation, including a large number of Veterans' Administration hospitals. Upon graduation, they establish themselves in a range of fields as scientists, academics, clinicians, and teachers. Ph.D. graduates find great success as faculty members, postdoctoral fellows, and researchers in excellent universities, medical schools, government agencies, and industry.

Location

Situated between Austin and Dallas–Fort Worth, Waco offers something for everyone. It is home to many museums, including the Texas Ranger Hall of Fame, as well as a symphony orchestra, theaters, and many heritage festivals. Outdoor lovers can enjoy the 416-acre Cameron Park and Lake Waco, while fine dining and shopping abound in Waco's recently restored warehouse district.

The University and The Department

Chartered in 1845, Baylor University is the oldest institution of higher learning in Texas and the largest Baptist university in the world. While remaining true to its Christian heritage, it has grown to almost 14,000 students, who come from all fifty states and seventy other countries and are enrolled in nearly 250 degree programs. Baylor is one of ten Texas colleges with a Phi Beta Kappa chapter, and it is the only school to meet the highest criteria set by the American Council of Trustees and Alumni.

The Baylor University Department of Psychology and Neuroscience is a vibrant and busy department, with more than 800 undergraduate majors, 60 or more doctoral students, 19 tenure system faculty members, and 4 instructors/lecturers, along with a wide range of intriguing and cutting-edge laboratories. This is an exciting time for the Department, with a recent move to the Baylor Science Building, one of the most outstanding facilities in the country.

Applying

Prospective students are required to submit an application for admission, a supplemental application form, a professional statement, official college transcripts showing a minimum 3.0 GPA and at least 12 hours of psychology work, official GRE scores (subject exam not required), and three letters of reference, including at least one from a psychology professor. For Psy.D. applications, all materials must be received by the Baylor Graduate School Admission Office by January 2. The Ph.D. application deadline is February 15. Interviews are conducted with most students in late February/early March, and students are chosen for admission in early April.

Correspondence and Information

Laura Sumrall, Graduate Studies Coordinator
Department of Psychology and Neuroscience
Baylor University
One Bear Place, #97334
Waco, Texas 76798-7334

Phone: 254-710-2961
Fax: 254-710-3033
E-mail: laura_sumrall@baylor.edu
Web site: http://www.baylor.edu/psychologyneuroscience/splash.php

Baylor University

THE FACULTY AND THEIR RESEARCH

L. Joseph Achor, Associate Professor; Ph.D., California, Irvine. Perceptual processes, sensory neurophysiology.

Helen Benedict, Professor and Clinical Training Director; Ph.D., Yale. Play therapy, child clinical assessment, intellectual assessment, learning disabilities, developmental psychopathology.

Jaime Diaz-Granados, Associate Professor and Department Chair; Ph.D., Texas at Austin. Developmental and neurobehavioral aspects of alcohol addiction and abuse.

Sara Dolan, Assistant Professor; Ph.D., Iowa. Neuropsychology, addictions research, psychological assessment, PTSD.

Gary Elkins, Professor and Clinical Psychology Program Director; Ph.D., Texas A&M. Behavioral medicine, clinical hypnosis, cognitive-behavioral therapy, menopausal symptoms, psycho-oncology, and health psychology.

Michael Frisch, Professor; Ph.D., Kansas. Depression, anxiety, relationship problems, quality of life assessment and intervention, cognitive-behavior therapy, psychopathology in literature, clinical practice and supervision, empirically supported treatments, treatment manuals, psychotherapy integration.

N. Bradley Keele, Associate Professor; Ph.D., Texas Medical Branch–Galveston. Neurobiology of complex emotional behaviors, cellular and molecular mechanisms of excitability and epilepsy, functional role of limbic system neuronal excitability in emotional behavior.

Roger Kirk, Distinguished Professor; Ph.D., Ohio State. Statistics, experimental design, multivariate methods.

Christine Limbers; Assistant Professor; Ph.D., Texas A&M. Child mental health, pediatric health psychology, child assessment and psychopathology.

Joaquin Lugo, Assistant Professor; Ph.D., South Carolina. Developmental epilepsy, relationship between epilepsy and autism, and neural mechanisms underlying learning and memory in zebrafish larvae.

Renee Michalski, Lecturer; Ph.D., Baylor. Individuals' reactions to critical incidents and traumatic events, PTSD, neurophysiological basis of behavior.

Jim Patton, Professor; Ph.D., Baylor. Biological bases of psychopathology.

Hugh Riley, Senior Lecturer; Ph.D., Baylor. Developmental aspects of drug withdrawal, nicotine and alcohol interaction.

Tamara Rowatt, Senior Lecturer; Ph.D., Louisville. Social psychology, personal relationships, social rejection.

Wade C. Rowatt, Associate Professor and Graduate Program Director; Ph.D., Louisville. Social-personality psychology, psychology of religion, positive psychology.

Keith Sanford, Associate Professor; Ph.D., Michigan State. Marital and family psychology, communication and cognition in intimate relationships, adult attachment, construction and validation of assessment instruments.

Matthew Stanford, Professor; Ph.D., Baylor. Neuropsychology, psychophysiology, neurobehavioral substrates of impulsivity and aggression.

Jo-Ann Tsang, Assistant Professor; Ph.D., Kansas. Social psychology, including gratitude, forgiveness, moral rationalization, psychology of religion, and prejudice.

Charles A. Weaver III, Professor; Ph.D., Colorado at Boulder. Meta-memory and meta-cognition, autobiographical memory, language, reading.

FELICIAN COLLEGE

Program in Counseling Psychology

Program of Study

The Master of Arts in counseling psychology program is designed to train students to become knowledgeable, skillful, ethical counselors able to assist individuals in need of professional counseling services.

Graduates will be prepared to focus on psychological counseling for individuals, couples, families, and groups. In line with Franciscan mission and in keeping with the most current trends in psychology, Felician College has developed a unique approach to preparing professional counselors by placing an emphasis on mindfulness, spiritual development, and empowering the potential of others. Upon successful completion of the program, students will be qualified to seek employment as counselors in hospitals, schools, clinics, private group practices, and other settings in the community.

The Master of Arts in counseling psychology consists of 60 credits. The program conforms to the licensing expectations of the New Jersey Professional Counselor Licensing Law, and adheres to the accrediting guidelines of CACREP (Council for Accreditation of Counseling and Related Educational Programs), the professional accrediting body for counseling programs.

Research Facilities

The College Library is a two-story building that serves the needs of students, faculty and staff members, and alumni with more than 110,000 books and over 800 periodical subscriptions. This collection is enhanced by large holdings of materials in microform, which can be used on the library's reader/printer equipment. With its computers linked to information services such as Dialog and OCLC, and as a member of the New Jersey Library Network and VALE, the library locates and obtains information, journal articles, and books not available in its collection from sources all over the country. Computerized databases can also be accessed directly by users through the online FirstSearch workstation, where up-to-date information on 40 million books and an index of 15,000 periodicals is available. The library is also connected to the Internet and has several CD-ROM workstations. Through EBSCOhost, Bell & Howell's ProQuest, CINAHL, and other services, students and faculty and staff members have access to numerous online journal indexes—as well as articles from thousands of periodicals—from anywhere on the campus computer network or from their home computers. An experienced staff of professional librarians is available to assist users.

The College's computer facilities include an academic and administrative network, four computerized labs, a computerized learning center, and two computer centers that are available for students, with a total of about 200 computers available for student/faculty member use. All classrooms, offices, and facilities are wired for Internet and e-mail.

Financial Aid

To qualify for financial aid, a student must complete the Free Application for Federal Student Aid (FAFSA).

Cost of Study

In 2011–12, graduate tuition is $875 per credit. Fees are additional.

Living and Housing Costs

Students are housed in two dormitories on the Rutherford campus, Milton and Elliott Halls. Both buildings have housing organized around student suites containing semiprivate baths. On-campus room and board is approximately $10,750 per year. On-campus housing is not available to married students.

Student Group

Felician College enrolls approximately 2,300 students. In fall 2010, there were approximately 350 students enrolled in graduate programs.

Location

Felician College's Lodi campus is located on the banks of the Saddle River on a beautifully landscaped campus of 27 acres and offers a collegiate setting in suburban Bergen County, within easy driving distance of New York City. The Felician College Rutherford Campus is set on 10.5 beautifully landscaped acres in the heart of the historic community of Rutherford, New Jersey. Only 15 minutes from the Lodi campus, the Rutherford complex contains student residences, classroom buildings, a student center, and a gymnasium. The campus is a short distance from downtown Rutherford, where there are many shops and businesses of interest to students. Regular shuttle bus service between the two campuses is a quick 10-minute ride that turns two campuses into a one-campus home for the students.

The College

Felician College, a coeducational liberal arts college, is a Catholic, independent institution for students representing diverse religious, racial, and ethnic backgrounds. The College operates on two campuses in Lodi and Rutherford, New Jersey. The College is one of the institutions of higher learning conducted by the Felician Sisters in the United States. Its mission is to provide a values-oriented education based in the liberal arts while it prepares students for meaningful lives and careers in contemporary society. To meet the needs of students and to provide personal enrichment courses to matriculated and nonmatriculated students, Felician College offers day, evening, and weekend programs. The College is accredited by the Middle States Association of Colleges and Schools and carries program accreditation from the Commission on Collegiate Nursing Education, the International Assembly for Collegiate Business Education, and the Teacher Education Accreditation Council.

Applying

Applicants should complete the application for adult and graduate admission and submit it along with the $40 application fee; transcript(s) from all undergraduate and/or graduate institutions previously attended; scores from GRE or MAT; two letters of reference; and a personal statement. An interview and additional information may be required.

Correspondence and Information

Office of Adult and Graduate Admission
Felician College
262 South Main Street
Lodi, New Jersey 07644-2117
Phone: 201-559-6077
Fax: 201-559-6138
E-mail: adultandgraduate@felician.edu
Web site: http://www.felician.edu/

Felician College

THE FACULTY

For specific information regarding the faculty of Felician College, prospective students should visit the College's Web site at http://www.felician.edu/.

Felician College offers an innovative master's degree program in counseling psychology and other professional areas.

Felician College allows students to work full-time and pursue their graduate degree with convenient class times.

HOLY FAMILY UNIVERSITY

Graduate Program in Counseling Psychology

Programs of Study	Counseling psychology is a field of study that examines the emotional, vocational, and social well-being of individuals at all stages of their lives. Students in Holy Family's graduate counseling psychology program develop an advanced understanding of human behavior throughout the lifespan; sensitivity to the differences inherent in different cultural, ethnic, and social groups; and mastery of counseling guidance theories and client evaluation skills.
	The M.S. degree in counseling psychology at Holy Family University is designed for part-time students who can, under ordinary circumstances, complete the program in three to four years.
	Several concentrations are available, allowing students to focus their studies on the area that interests them most. These include counseling in student affairs in higher education, clinical mental health counseling, family and marital counseling, school counseling (Pennsylvania certification in elementary, secondary, or dual-school counseling), and pastoral counseling. The University also offers two postgraduate programs: a licensure program for practicing master's-level counselors and a school counseling certification program for those with a master's degree wishing to become certified as an elementary or secondary school guidance counselor.
	All concentrations in the graduate counseling psychology program fulfill the educational requirements for licensure as a professional counselor in Pennsylvania, Delaware, and New Jersey.
Research Facilities	Holy Family University's Newtown Center for Counseling Studies and Services provides facilities for students to gain clinical experience. The center includes video- and audio-equipped training areas for play therapy and group psychotherapy, an observation room for monitoring individual and group counseling practice sessions, and individual offices for therapy simulation.
	The Learning Resource Center (LRC) is an extension of the Northeast Philadelphia campus library. Staffed by library professionals, the LRC meets the research, information, and technology/audiovisual needs of students and faculty at the Newtown location. Staff members offer individualized research instruction as well as formal, in-depth research sessions.
	The LRC supports academic programs at Newtown through online research databases, print periodicals, books, and other media. Special collections include children's literature, curriculum materials, and an extensive collection of counseling psychology audiovisual materials. Holdings are supplemented by intercampus and interlibrary loan services.
Financial Aid	Holy Family is committed to helping adults further their education by consistently maintaining competitive tuition rates. Most graduate students are eligible for Federal Stafford Loans when attending with a half-time enrollment status (6 graduate credits) or greater. For more information, potential students may contact the Financial Aid Office via e-mail at finaid@holyfamily.edu or by phone at 267-341-3233.
Cost of Study	Tuition for Holy Family's traditional graduate programs is $630 per credit hour.
Living and Housing Costs	Holy Family University does not provide graduate student housing; however, there are numerous housing options available in the nearby area.
Student Group	Approximately 150 students, all studying part-time, are enrolled in the graduate counseling psychology program. These students see counseling not as a profession but as a way of living, in which they are committed to social justice, empathy, and life-long learning. This involves connection with all of humanity while maintaining individuality.
Student Outcomes	With the range of concentrations offered, Holy Family's program has produced graduates who work as professional counselors in varied environments, including community, school, family and marital, higher education, and pastoral settings.
Location	Classes meet at the Newtown campus of Holy Family University, which occupies 79 acres in suburban Bucks County, Pennsylvania. The building contains the administrative service area; faculty offices; the Center for Graduate Programs in Counseling Psychology; ten classrooms and laboratories, including two mixed-use labs, a science lab, and a nursing lab; the Learning Resource Center; a chapel; the student services office; and a commons dining area.
The University	Holy Family University prides itself on programs that offer students real-world experience. This focus on preparedness and student outcomes is designed to help graduates stand out, with distinction.
	Respect for the individual, the dignity of the human person—these values are taught, lived, and form the foundation of Holy Family University. Concern for moral values and social justice guides the University's programs and enriches the student's education and experience.
Applying	Holy Family University has a rolling admissions policy, with the majority of students enrolling in the fall semester and a limited number in the spring. Applicants must possess a baccalaureate degree from an accredited college or university, and an undergraduate cumulative grade-point average of 3.0 or better or satisfactory GRE or MAT scores. To be reviewed for admission, applicants must submit official transcripts, two letters of recommendation, a personal statement, and test scores if requested.
	Applicants will be considered based on their academic ability, expression of interests and goals, life experience, and personal interview.
	Prior to admission, selected applicants will be invited to complete a personal interview. Notification of acceptance usually is completed within two weeks of the personal interview.
Correspondence and Information	Graduate Admissions Office Holy Family University 9801 Frankford Avenue Philadelphia, Pennsylvania 19114 Phone: 267-341-3327 Fax: 215-637-1478 E-mail: gradstudy@holyfamily.edu Web site: http://my.holyfamily.edu/grad/programs/psych_main.asp

Holy Family University

THE FACULTY AND THEIR RESEARCH

Ellen Brown, Assistant Professor; Ed.D., Temple, 2007. Academic integrity and ethical decision making among students and faculty, student-athletes and academic support, program assessment.

James Huber, Assistant Professor; Ph.D., Virginia Tech, 1989. Resiliency, stress management, couple communication, grief counseling, marriage and family therapy education.

Rochelle Robbins, Associate Professor; Ph.D., SUNY at Stony Brook, 1994. Improving quality of life for persons suffering from dementia, institutional assessment in higher education.

Diane Shea, Assistant Professor; Ph.D., Walden, 2006. Relationship between psychology and spirituality.

PHILADELPHIA COLLEGE
OF OSTEOPATHIC MEDICINE

*Graduate Programs in Clinical Psychology, Counseling and
Clinical Health Psychology, and School Psychology*

Programs of Study

Philadelphia College of Osteopathic Medicine (PCOM) offers nine graduate programs taught by an internationally-renowned, highly credentialed faculty. All faculty members in PCOM's psychology department are teaching faculty members who work closely with students to help them achieve their professional goals. Students often have the opportunity to coauthor scholarly papers, books, and professional presentations with faculty members. PCOM has one of the only psychology departments in the country that provides a standardized patient program. The standardized patient program presents authentic clinical learning and skills situations in which "patients" simulate mental health conditions. Students conduct sessions with the patients, which are videotaped and reviewed by the faculty members to help train and assess students' skills. Students in the psychology program also have the opportunity for clinical experience at any of the College's urban health-care centers.

The 89-credit Psy.D. in clinical psychology program is designed to be completed in five years, including course work, practicum, internship, and dissertation. Graduates of this program are prepared to assume responsibilities in a broad range of clinical settings. Post-doctoral certificates in clinical health psychology and clinical neuropsychology will each provide one year (16 and 19 credits respectively) of post-doctoral specialty training to doctoral-level psychologists. The 61-credit Psy.D. in school psychology program takes three to five years to complete. The fourteen-month, 37-credit M.S. in school psychology program prepares paraprofessionals in community and school settings to provide mental health services to children, youth, and families. This program, taken in sequence with the Ed.S. degree program, leads to certification in school psychology. The three-year, 45-credit Ed.S. program provides students with the knowledge and skills to assume the role of a school psychologist in diverse settings. The two-year, 48-credit M.S. in counseling and clinical health psychology program trains graduates to provide evaluation, counseling, and therapy services to clients in a variety of clinical settings. There is also a 60-credit addictions and offenders counseling track for the M.S. degree. M.S. graduates may also take 12 additional credits offered by PCOM and earn a Certificate of Advanced Graduate Study to meet the education requirements of the licensed professional counseling (LPC) credential in Pennsylvania. The 36-credit M.S. in organizational development and leadership (ODL) program uses a unique combination of organizational theory and individual self-discovery to provide an essential leadership perspective in creating organizational change. Designed for the working professional, all classes for the M.S., Ed.S., and Psy.D. programs are held in the evening and on weekends.

Research Facilities

The academic facilities at PCOM include state-of-the-art amphitheaters and classroom facilities; computer laboratories with extensive software, including PsycLIT and SPSS; a comfortable, sophisticated library with online access to electronic textbooks, journals, databases, and Internet guides; and access to the digital library and statistical programs through the Internet.

Financial Aid

The Financial Aid Office at PCOM offers financial assistance to students through the Federal Direct Loan program, institutional grants, and various alternative private loan programs.

Cost of Study

In 2011–12, the direct tuition costs of attending PCOM (including tuition, fees, books, and supplies) for the year are approximately $21,420 for counseling and clinical health psychology M.S. students, $20,870 for school psychology M.S. students, $14,000 for ODL M.S. students, $15,520 for Ed.S. students, $29,490 for clinical psychology Psy.D. students, and $27,420 for school psychology Psy.D. students.

Living and Housing Costs

Students live off-campus within the Philadelphia metropolitan and suburban areas, as there is no on-campus housing. Room and board costs vary by each student's individual preferences.

Student Group

The programs seek a diverse group of students who are committed to excellence. The Psy.D. in clinical psychology program recruits in-practice professionals who have earned master's degrees in psychology, social work, counseling, psychiatric nursing, or a related field and are working in human services. This population brings to their studies a high level of maturity, established skills, diverse backgrounds, and a strong motivation to succeed. The Psy.D. in school psychology program recruits working school psychologists who want to be leaders in psychoeducational and mental health services to children, youth, and families. Students entering the Ed.S. program typically have completed master's degrees in psychology or education and have been working with school-aged children in some capacity. Candidates for the M.S. programs typically are working professionals and have bachelor's degrees in varying fields, having completed specific prerequisite courses. For 2010, the clinical psychology Psy.D. class had 27 entering students (selected from a pool of 123), with 67 percent women, 14.8 percent members of minority groups, and an average age of 29. The Psy.D. in school psychology program had a class of 18 students (selected from a pool of 23), with 81 percent women, 31 percent members of minority groups, and an average age of 33. The M.S. program in counseling and clinical health psychology totaled 40 students (selected from a pool of 120), with 77.5 percent women, 10 percent members of minority groups, and an average age of 26. The Ed.S. program in school psychology numbered 19 students (selected from a pool of 29), with 84 percent women, 26 percent members of minority groups, and an average age of 28. The M.S. program in school psychology had 23 new students, (selected from a pool of 47), with 87 percent women, 43 percent members of minority groups, and an average age of 26. The M.S. program in organizational development and leadership enrolled 21 new students (selected from a pool of 35), with 71 percent women, 86 percent members of minority groups, and an average age of 35.

Location

Located on City Avenue in Philadelphia, PCOM's 21-acre campus is minutes away from Fairmount Park, Philadelphia's historic district, art museums, theaters, restaurants, and professional sports complexes. Its renovated facilities include two large lecture halls, small classrooms, labs for teaching and research, and scenic landscaping, all in a suburban setting. PCOM also has four health-care centers in Philadelphia and one in LaPorte, Pennsylvania.

The College and The Programs

PCOM, which was chartered in 1899, enrolls approximately 2,200 students in its various programs across both the Philadelphia and Georgia campuses. The clinical and teaching facility in Philadelphia makes an ideal home for psychology graduate programs. The graduate psychology programs at PCOM are accredited by the Department of Education of the Commonwealth of Pennsylvania and the Middle States Association of Colleges and Schools. The clinical psychology Psy.D. program is accredited by the American Psychological Association and fulfills the requirements of the National Register for Healthcare Providers in Psychology. Clinical Psy.D. graduates qualify to take the Examination for Professional Practice of Psychology Licensure in Pennsylvania and New Jersey. The curriculum provides school psychology Psy.D. students with the knowledge and skills to assume the role of a school psychologist, practice in a variety of settings, and be prepared for eligibility for National Certification and for Pennsylvania licensure. The school psychology Psy.D. program has been approved by the National Association of School Psychologists. The M.S. program plus 12 credits has been designed to fulfill the Licensed Professional Counselor curriculum requirements in Pennsylvania.

Applying

Clinical psychology M.S. applicants need to have a baccalaureate degree from a regionally accredited institution, with basic psychology course work (introduction to psychology, abnormal psychology or psychopathology, and statistics). Psy.D. in clinical psychology applicants must have completed a master's degree in psychology or a related field at a regionally accredited institution and also completed developmental psychology, theories of personality, abnormal psychology or psychopathology, and statistics. Candidates for the post-doctoral certificate programs must have completed a doctoral degree in clinical psychology at a regionally accredited institution. Applicants to the M.S. in school psychology need to have a baccalaureate degree in psychology, education, or a related field from a regionally accredited institution and must have completed 6 credits each of English and math, abnormal psychology/psychopathology, or exceptional children and child psychology/adolescent psychology. Nine additional credits in psychology must also have been completed. Applicants to either M.S. program in school or counseling and clinical health psychology must have taken the GRE or MAT exam. Applicants to the ODL program must have completed a bachelor's degree from a regionally accredited institution. Applicants to the Ed.S. program must have a master's degree in school psychology or a related field and must submit test scores from the GRE Psychology Subtest #81 and have successfully passed the Praxis I exam. Applicants to the Psy.D. in school psychology program must have a master's and specialist degree in school psychology and must be a licensed school psychologist. Candidates must also submit scores from the Praxis II School Psychology Specialty exam. All applicants to Psychology Department programs must submit official college transcripts from all schools attended and three letters of recommendation with accompanying recommendation forms, along with a $50 application fee. (The ODL program requires only one recommendation letter and form.) All programs utilize a rolling admissions policy. Finalists for all programs interview with the Admissions Committee and are then notified in writing of the committee's decision.

Correspondence and Information

Office of Admissions
Philadelphia College of Osteopathic Medicine
4170 City Avenue
Philadelphia, Pennsylvania 19131-1694

Phone: 215-871-6700
          800-999-6998 (toll-free)
Fax: 215-871-6719
E-mail: gradadmissions@pcom.edu
Web site: http://www.pcom.edu

Philadelphia College of Osteopathic Medicine

THE FACULTY AND THEIR RESEARCH

Robert A. DiTomasso, Ph.D., ABPP, Professor; Chair, Department of Psychology; and Director, Institutional Outcomes Assessment. Dr. DiTomasso has extensive teaching experience and has published dozens of chapters, articles, reviews, and books. He specializes in behavioral medicine, the cognitive behavioral treatment of anxiety and stress-related medical disorders, research design, psychometrics, methodology, program evaluation, and primary-care consultation. He also specializes in patient nonadherence to medical advice and instrument development for cognitive distortions, anger, health risk behaviors, and patient satisfaction with medical services.

Stephanie Felgoise, Ph.D., ABPP, Professor; Vice Chair, Department of Psychology; and Director, Clinical Psy.D. Program. Dr. Felgoise has coauthored numerous national conference presentations and publications in psycho-oncology, sexual health and dysfunction, and coping and adjustment with chronic medical illness. Other interests include behavioral medicine, social problem solving, caregiver issues, and diversity issues in health care.

Michael Ascher, Ph.D., Clinical Professor. Dr. Ascher has done extensive research on the treatment of anxiety disorders (particularly agoraphobia, obsessive compulsive disorder, panic disorders, and phobias) within the context of behavior therapy. In addition, he has researched investor anxiety, including the emotional difficulties experienced by the average retail stock market investor, and the psychogenic disorders of sleep.

Jeffrey Branch, Ed.D., Adjunct Assistant Professor. Dr. Branch has extensive experience in organizational consultation and has held various leadership positions. His research and teaching expertise includes the intentional design and engagement of mentoring and coaching practices as a multidimensional curricular and cocurricular teaching and learning strategy to promote practitioner development.

Virginia Burks Salzer, Ph.D., Research Associate Professor. Dr. Salzer's research interests include social information processing in the development of children's aggressive behavior, linkages between family and children's peer systems, comorbidity of children's externalizing and internalizing disorders, and impact of parental psychopathology and the development of childhood disorders.

Stacey C. Cahn, Ph.D., Assistant Professor. Dr. Cahn's area of expertise is broadly clinical health psychology, including eating disorders, as well as the areas of sleep, depression in heart disease, and aging.

William Clinton, M.A., Program Director, Organizational Development and Leadership Program. Mr. Clinton has extensive experience in organizational consultation and has held various leadership positions. His specialty is in training practitioners to become effective leaders who implement change in organizational settings.

Terri Erbacher, Ph.D., Clinical Assistant Professor. Dr. Erbacher is a certified school psychologist and licensed psychologist. Her specific population and program expertise includes nonpublic elementary and secondary schools, autistic support, learning support, early intervention, and supervision of school psychology interns.

Jessica Glass Kendorski, Ph.D., NCSP, Assistant Professor and Director, Clinical Training (School Psychology). Dr. Glass is a certified school psychologist. Her clinical experiences and research interests include data-based assessment and interventions in the residential and school settings, specifically, response to intervention, curriculum-based measurement, positive behavior support, and applied behavior analysis. She has extensive experience in supporting the emotional, social, and behavioral needs of children diagnosed with developmental disabilities.

Barbara Golden, Psy.D., ABPP, Associate Professor and Director, Clinical Services. Dr. Golden's experience includes clinical service, administration, supervision, consultation, and education. Her primary areas of interest and research are in behavioral medicine, including nonpharmacological pain management, stress management, and somatization disorder, as well as in psychology and primary-care medicine.

Elizabeth Gosch, Ph.D., ABPP, Professor and Director, M.S. Program in Counseling and Clinical Health Psychology. One of Dr. Gosch's primary areas of expertise is psychotherapy with children and adolescents. Her major research interest concerns the processes and effectiveness of psychotherapy with differing populations. She has published and lectured internationally on the cognitive behavioral treatment of anxiety in children.

Lisa Hain, Psy.D., NCSP, Assistant Professor. Dr. Hain's clinical experience and research interests include utilizing principles of neuropsychology in the practice of school psychology in identifying cognitively-based as well as emotionally-based disabilities affecting children and adolescents using a brain-behavior model in assessment, interpretation, and intervention.

Petra Kottsieper, Ph.D., Assistant Professor. Dr. Kottsieper's main research interests include forensic psychology, therapeutic process, mental health services research, professional development, ethics, and psychiatric rehabilitation for individuals with serious mental illnesses. Much of her clinical work has focused on the empirically-supported treatment and assessment of serious mental illnesses, co-occurring disorders (including developmental disabilities and substance misuse issues), and forensic issues.

Donald Masey, Psy.D., Clinical Assistant Professor. Dr. Masey's research interests include memory and aging, psychological assessment, hospital practice for psychologists, practice models and issues in professional psychology, medical psychology, adult learning disabilities, and adult ADHD.

George McCloskey, Ph.D., Associate Professor and Director of Research (School Psychology). Dr. McCloskey has accumulated a broad range of work experiences in the field of psychology over the last twenty-five years, including research, clinical work, administration, teaching, and business. His research and interests include neuropsychological process and learning, psychological and educational assessment and intervention, reading achievement, ADHD, executive dysfunction, memory problems, and expression disability.

Rosemary Mennuti, Ed.D., NCSP, Professor and Director, School Psychology Program. Dr. Mennuti has extensive experience as a school psychologist and in teaching. She has lectured and published in the areas of moral development, eating disorders, and therapist self-disclosure. Other areas of interest include female development, CBT in schools, and relational cultural theory in practice.

Susan Panichelli Mindel, Ph.D., Assistant Professor and Director of Research (Clinical Psychology). Dr. Mindel has extensive experience in the delivery of cognitive-behavioral empirically-supported treatments in children and adolescents. Her research interests include issues in clinical child psychology, with an emphasis on the prevention and treatment of anxiety disorders as well as diagnostic differences and treatment of subtypes of ADHD.

Stephen Poteau, Ph.D., Assistant Professor. Dr. Poteau's research interests include the implicit measurement of cognitive processes/implicit cognition, terror management theory, and social cognition/psychology.

Bradley Rosenfield, Psy.D., Assistant Professor. Dr. Rosenfield's research interests include cognitive behavioral therapy for adult ADHD, human-animal interactions, depressive disorders, somatic disorders, anxiety disorders, single session treatment for panic attacks, the social psychology of terrorism, multicultural counseling, communication skills, and treating difficult patients.

Matthew Schure, Ph.D., President and Chief Executive Officer. Dr. Schure's major areas of interest include personality correlates of learning, such as self-esteem, level of aspiration, and locus of control. In addition, he has done extensive research on community mental health interventions and family dynamics, including the outcome of dysfunctional parenting and parental rejection.

Marsha S. Singer, Ph.D., Clinical Assistant Professor and Associate Director, M.S. Program in Counseling and Clinical Health Psychology. Dr. Singer's main professional interest is clinical health psychology. She is very interested in the role of cultural, spiritual, and other psychosocial factors in health behavior and patient attitudes. She is also interested in the role of family members as social supports in medical and mental health settings.

Diane Smallwood, Psy.D., NCSP, Professor and Director, Ed.S. program. In addition to school-based work experience, for the past twenty years, Dr. Smallwood has been involved in leadership activities at both the state and national levels. Her professional interests include school crisis prevention, intervention, and response; social-emotional learning; classroom resiliency; bullying and violence in schools; and translating research to practice.

Takako Suzuki, Ph.D., Assistant Professor; Assistant Director of Clinical Services (Center for Brief Therapy); and Clinical Coordinator, Center for Academic Resources and Educational Services (CARES). Dr. Suzuki's major areas of interest include CBT of mood and anxiety disorders; multicultural issues such as development of cultural identity, acculturation process, and issues with expatriates; religion and spirituality; and emotional intelligence and development of empathy.

Shannon Sweitzer, Ph.D., NCSP, Clinical Assistant Professor. Dr. Sweitzer's research interests include cognitive deficits associated with childhood depression, childcare staff consultation, and training to develop environments that foster healthy social and emotional behaviors.

Yuma I. Tomes, Ph.D., Associate Professor and Director, M.S. Program in School Psychology. Dr. Tomes has accumulated a diverse range of work experiences in the field of psychology and education over the last ten years. He brings a unique perspective of clinical, teaching, research, and administrative experience to his position at PCOM. Dr. Tomes has worked as a psychologist in urban school districts. His major areas of interest are cross-cultural psychology, multicultural assessment, cognitive/learning styles, cognition and learning theories, psychological/educational assessments, consultation, and developmental issues.

Beverly White, Psy.D., Clinical Assistant Professor. Dr. White has worked extensively with traumatized children and adolescents. She has published and has research interests in the areas of psychological assessment, dreams in CBT-oriented treatment, and crisis/trauma, post-traumatic stress, and CBT interventions. Other research interests include right/left-hemisphere performance and malfunction and multicultural issues.

Bruce Zahn, Ed.D., ABPP, Professor and Director of Clinical Training (Clinical Psychology). Dr. Zahn has published on cognitive behavioral therapy, childhood sexual abuse, multimodal therapy programs for adolescents, and psychological functioning in survivors of traumatic brain injury. His areas of expertise include geropsychology, behavioral medicine, cognitive behavioral therapy, self-esteem, group therapy, and supervision. Dr. Zahn's mentoring and research interests are in the areas of psychological testing (including projective personality assessment), post-traumatic stress disorder, managed-care issues, and chronic mental illness.

RUTGERS, THE STATE UNIVERSITY OF NEW JERSEY, NEWARK

Graduate Program in Psychology
Concentrations in Cognitive Neuroscience, Perception,
Biopsychology, Developmental Psychology, and Social Psychology

Programs of Study

Students entering the graduate program in psychology can take courses of study leading to a Ph.D. in psychology with specializations in biopsychology, cognitive neuroscience, cognitive science, perception, developmental psychology, and social psychology. Current research in the biopsychology of emotion and adaptive behavior focuses on the motivational, evolutionary, and developmental mechanisms underlying behavior. Research in cognitive neuroscience offers training in neuroimaging methods, concepts, and experimental paradigms. The neuroimaging research focus includes studies in motion and event perception, learning and memory, and how humans process rewards and punishments. Research in the area of cognitive science offers training in the computational and experimental study of cognitive processes. The curriculum provides basic instruction in computational and mathematical modeling methods, with a focus on connectionist systems, learning, memory, and categorization. The perception specialization offers training in the experimental study of motion and color perception as well as many advanced areas within vision science. The social psychology concentration focuses on attachment theory, the mediation of social and interpersonal conflict, aggression, violence and bullying, interracial feedback, social support, and the methods and techniques used most commonly in these areas.

Students are encouraged to take advantage of training opportunities in the adjacent Center for Molecular and Behavioral Neuroscience, the College of Business (Information Sciences), the College of Nursing, the Department of Biological Sciences, the University of Medicine and Dentistry of New Jersey (UMDNJ), and the New Jersey Institute of Technology as well as adjunct courses listed in related areas (such as linguistics, philosophy, or cognitive science) on the New Brunswick campus. A written qualifying examination is given after the completion of basic course work at the end of the second year. Upon satisfactory completion of these requirements, students advance to candidacy for the Ph.D. degree and must submit a thesis proposal, carry out their thesis research, and then defend their dissertation.

Research Facilities

The Department of Psychology occupies about 80,000 square feet on the first, third, fourth, and fifth floors of Smith Hall. The department has its own servers (http://www.psych.rutgers.edu), computing laboratory, and a series of individual laboratories for neurophysiological, neuroanatomical, and neuropharmacological research. There are more than 16,000 square feet for animal holding and testing.

The Rutgers University Brain Imaging Center (RUBIC) is a 2,500-square-foot state-of-the-art imaging center that serves the psychology and neurosciences departments of all three Rutgers campuses (http://www.rubic.rutgers.edu). In addition to the scan room, RUBIC has rooms available to prepare experiments, interview participants, and analyze data. The facility is staffed with an MR physicist and technicians. RUBIC uses a 3T Siemens TRIO for scanning both humans and animals. A 28-node Ravana computing cluster is used for RUMBA (Rutgers University Mind Brain Analysis, http://www.rumba.rutgers.edu). An Eyelink-1000 is available for the collection of eye movement data while scanning. A BIOPAC MP150 system is available for recording skin conductance. Software available includes E-Prime as well as open-source options such as PyEPL. And a number of fiber optic response options are utilized, including response pads and trackballs.

Financial Aid

Students accepted into the program receive a full stipend and tuition remission through a wide range of scholarships, fellowships, and assistantships offered by the Rutgers Graduate School to full-time Ph.D. students whose records demonstrate superior academic achievement and scholarly promise. Stipends range up to $20,000 plus tuition remission for fellowships and $21,400 for teaching or graduate assistantships. They may be renewed for one or more years depending on the availability of funds and the academic standing of the student. Students who are members of minority groups may also be eligible to receive additional support through the Minority Biomedical Research Support Program and other programs. Students also receive financial support from the Department of Psychology to attend conferences.

Cost of Study

Tuition for the 2010–11 academic year was about $16,200 (for New Jersey residents) and about $24,300 for out-of-state residents; graduate students receive tuition remission along with their source of support.

Living and Housing Costs

Graduate student housing is available in Talbott Apartments and University Square Apartments. Costs range from $8700 for an academic year lease to $11,500 for a calendar year lease for a single room in either a 3-person or 4-person shared apartment. A limited number of family apartment options are available for married/domestic partners and students with children in University-owned brownstones.

Student Group

There are currently 25 full-time graduate doctoral students carrying out research in the Department of Psychology. The faculty-student ratio of 1:2 affords ample opportunity for students to interact with faculty members. Students in the Department of Psychology are represented in policy decisions and are actively involved in the selection of new students.

Location

Rutgers' Newark campus is conveniently located in the center of a diverse and thriving educational, professional, and cultural community in the downtown area of New Jersey's largest city. Newark is also at the center of the nation's largest concentration of pharmaceutical industries. The campus is a modern complex serving more than 10,000 students and 500 faculty members. Rutgers-Newark is easily accessible by car or mass transit and is approximately 20 minutes by rail from midtown Manhattan. A free campus shuttle bus links the campus with the city's mass transit centers during the evening hours. The Department of Psychology is located one block from the University's jogging track, fully equipped gymnasium, and swimming pool.

The University

Rutgers, The State University of New Jersey, with more than 47,000 students on campuses in Camden, Newark, and New Brunswick, is one of the major state universities in the nation. The Newark campus is part of a complex of higher education institutions that includes the New Jersey Institute of Technology and the University of Medicine and Dentistry of New Jersey.

Applying

Students apply to enter the program on a full-time basis. Students should apply to the Department of Psychology and mention the area of study they are most interested in. Applications can be submitted at http://gradstudy.rutgers.edu/. The application deadline for the fall semester is January 15 and for the spring semester, November 1. Students should include scores for the General GRE and the Subject GRE in their area of interest.

Correspondence and Information

Kenneth Kressel, Ph.D., Director of Graduate Programs in Psychology
Department of Psychology
301 Smith Hall
Rutgers, The State University of New Jersey
101 Warren Street
Newark, New Jersey 07102
Phone: 973-353-5440 Ext. 232
Fax: 973-353-1171
E-mail: gradprogram@psychology.rutgers.edu
Web site: http://www.psych.rutgers.edu

Rutgers, The State University of New Jersey, Newark

THE FACULTY AND THEIR RESEARCH

Colin G. Beer, D.Phil., Oxford. Ethology, communication, and social development of birds; historical and philosophical aspects of ethology; comparative psychology.

Paul Boxer, Ph.D., Bowling Green. Aggression and violence, social development, contextual influences on behavior.

Mei-Fang Cheng, Ph.D., Bryn Mawr. Neuroethology; neurobiological study of vocal behavior and self-stimulation; mechanism and function of brain injury–induced neurogenesis in adult animals.

Mauricio Delgado, Ph.D., Pittsburgh. Behavioral and neural correlates of reward-related processing, with an emphasis on how the affective properties of outcomes or feedback influence choice behavior; using neuroimaging and behavioral and psychophysiological methods.

Alan Gilchrist, Ph.D., Rutgers. Visual cognition, surface-color perception, art and perception.

Stephen José Hanson, Ph.D., Arizona State. Learning and memory, connectionist models, categorization, cognitive science.

Kent D. Harber, Ph.D., Stanford. Interracial feedback biases; social support and coping; emotion and social perception.

Barry R. Komisaruk, Ph.D., Rutgers. Neurophysiological, functional neuroanatomical, and neuropharmacological study of endogenous pain-blocking mechanisms related to sexual behavior and parturition in mammals, including humans; brain, spinal cord, autonomic, and peripheral nerve mechanisms, using functional magnetic resonance imaging (fMRI).

Ken Kressel, Ph.D., Columbia. Social and interpersonal conflict, mediation of conflict, conflict dynamics in organizational settings.

Vanessa LoBue, Ph.D., Virginia. Infant and child development, emotional development.

Luis M. Rivera, Ph.D., Massachusetts Amherst. Implicit stereotyping and prejudice, self-image motivation, implicit social cognition.

Maggie Shiffrar, Ph.D., Stanford. Visual motion perception; object recognition.

Harold I. Siegel, Ph.D., Rutgers. Attachment theory; adult attachment; attitudes toward mother and other adult relationships, attachment and sexual offenders.

Elizabeth Tricomi, Ph.D., Pittsburgh. Functional neuroimaging of learning and decision making, social and affective influences on reward processing and valuation, neural basis of goal-directed behavior.

Gretchen Van de Walle, Ph.D., Cornell. Conceptual understanding of physical objects and numbers and the interaction between conceptual development and linguistic abilities, particularly the relationship between children's ability to categorize and label classes of objects.

SouthUniversity℠

SOUTH UNIVERSITY

Columbia Campus
Professional Counseling Program

Program of Study	The Master of Arts in professional counseling degree program at South University is intended to meet the local and regional need for qualified professional counselors. The emphasis of the program is on community and agency counseling. The program is designed to enable program graduates to achieve all initial eligibility criteria to become certified as a National Certified Counselor (NCC) by the National Board for Certified Counselors (NBCC) and licensed in the state of South Carolina. The delivery structure of the program gives students the ability to balance the rigors of work and home while pursuing their master's degree. Students can complete one or two courses each term, with each quarter lasting ten weeks. Students select from the convenient Saturday sessions that meet once per week or attend two evenings during the week.
	Students are taught via two primary modes of instruction. The majority of the program involves didactic and experiential classroom instruction, supplemented by computer-based assignments, including the use of Internet technology. The second mode of instruction focuses on supervised field experiences. Students are placed in community counseling settings (while on internship) and practice counseling under the supervision of an on-site supervisor. Students in field placements also receive weekly individual and group supervision from qualified faculty supervisors.
Research Facilities	Along with classrooms and offices, the campus includes a bookstore, student lounge, and career services center. Students may retrieve periodicals in paper or electronic form. The South University Library provides in-library and remote access to electronic databases. Both bibliographic and full-text databases are available via EBSCOhost (e.g., Academic Search Premier, SocINDEX, PsycINFO, PsycARTICLES, and Mental Measurements Yearbook), the search and retrieval system of EBSCO Information Services, and via the Library and Information Resources Network (e.g., Infotrac and ProQuest databases). Infotrac databases include counseling sources such as Expanded Academic ASAP, Academic OneFile, and InfotracOneFile. ProQuest databases include counseling sources such as ProQuest Psychology Journals and ProQuest Research Library. Internet access is available on all computers throughout the campus.
Financial Aid	A wide range of financial aid options is available to students who qualify. The Columbia campus of South University offers access to federal and state aid, including grants, loans, and work-study programs. Eligible students may apply for veterans' educational benefits and are encouraged to investigate the availability of grants and scholarships through community resources. As a first step, students should complete the Free Application for Federal Student Aid (FAFSA). Students may apply electronically at http://www.fafsa.ed.gov or through the program. Applications should be submitted promptly to receive consideration for the maximum amount of aid.
Cost of Study	Tuition information for the professional counseling program may be obtained by contacting the Admissions Department at South University's Columbia campus.
Living and Housing Costs	South University does not offer or operate student housing. Students in the professional counseling program typically live in apartments in the Columbia area. Students who commute from long distances can arrange to stay at nearby hotels that offer long-term rates. More information may be obtained by contacting the Admissions Department.
Student Group	The Columbia campus of South University has a diverse student body enrolled in both day and evening classes. Students are primarily commuters who live within 50 miles of the city.
Student Outcomes	The South University Career Services Department has been established to assist currently enrolled students in developing their career plans and reaching their employment goals. Career services include, but are not limited to, one-on-one career counseling, special career-related workshops and programs, coaching for resume and cover letter development, and resume referral to employers.
Location	South University recently relocated its Columbia campus to the growing east side of Columbia, just minutes from downtown. The campus is conveniently located at 9 Science Court.
	The campus surroundings are highlighted by a natural wooded landscape and vast green space featuring a tranquil campus courtyard. Convenient to malls, shopping, and the growing east side of Columbia, the new campus location provides easier access to students throughout the greater Columbia area.
The University	South University is accredited by the Commission on Colleges of the Southern Association of Colleges and Schools (SACS) to award associate, baccalaureate, master's, and doctoral degrees. Students should contact the Commission on Colleges at 1866 Southern Lane, Decatur, Georgia 30033-4097 or call 404-679-4500 for questions about the accreditation of South University.
Applying	Students are accepted into the Master of Arts in professional counseling degree program every academic quarter. Entrance into the program is gained through a formal application review and interview process. Acceptance is competitive and based on the admission committee's evaluation of the applicant's academic background and personal motivation. Application packets are available by contacting the South University Admissions Department (866-629-3031, toll-free) or visiting the University's Web site (http://www.southuniversity.edu).
Correspondence and Information	Applications for admission to the South University Master of Arts in professional counseling program are available by contacting: Professional Counseling Program South University 9 Science Court Columbia, South Carolina 29203 Phone: 803-799-9082 866-629-3031 (toll-free) Fax: 803-935-4382 E-mail: coladmis@southuniversity.edu Web site: http://www.southuniversity.edu See suprograms.info for program duration; tuition, fees, and other costs; median debt; federal salary data; alumni success; and other important information. http://www.southuniversity.edu/programs-info/form/

South University

THE FACULTY

One of the most outstanding aspects of South University's professional counseling program is the dedication of the faculty members and their ability to cultivate a supportive learning environment. Faculty members are committed to their roles as mentors, teachers, and co-learners. They are also dedicated to the training of students who can assume positions of leadership within the counseling field. A current list of program faculty members appears in the South University catalog, which is available on the South University Web site (http://www.southuniversity.edu).

SouthUniversity℠

SOUTH UNIVERSITY

Montgomery Campus
Professional Counseling Program

Program of Study

The Master of Arts in professional counseling degree program at South University is intended to meet the local and regional need for qualified professional counselors. The emphasis of the program is on community and agency counseling. The program is designed to enable program graduates to achieve all initial eligibility criteria to become certified as a National Certified Counselor (NCC) by the National Board for Certified Counselors (NBCC) and licensed in the state of Alabama. The delivery structure of the program gives students the ability to balance the rigors of work and home while pursuing their master's degree. Students can complete two courses each term, with each quarter lasting eleven weeks. Classes meet on Saturdays from 8:30 a.m. to 5 p.m.

Students are taught via two primary modes of instruction. The majority of the program involves didactic and experiential classroom instruction, supplemented by computer-based assignments, including the use of Internet technology. The second mode of instruction focuses on supervised field experiences. Students are placed in community counseling settings (during practicum and internship) and practice counseling under the supervision of an on-site supervisor. Students in field placements also receive weekly individual and group supervision from qualified faculty supervisors.

Research Facilities

South University in Montgomery is located in a modern 26,000-square-foot, two-story building on a campus of almost 4 acres. The campus includes computer and health professions labs, classrooms, a library, a student lounge, a bookstore, and faculty and administrative offices.

The South University library has wireless technology throughout, comfortable seating, and quiet study space. The South University library provides in-library and remote access to electronic databases. Both bibliographic and full-text databases are available via EBSCOhost (e.g., Academic Search Premier, SocINDEX, PsycINFO, PsycARTICLES, and Mental Measurements Yearbook), the search and retrieval system of EBSCO Information Services, and via the Library and Information Resources Network (e.g., Infotrac and ProQuest databases). Infotrac databases include counseling sources such as Expanded Academic ASAP, Academic OneFile, and InfotracOneFile. ProQuest databases include counseling sources such as ProQuest Psychology Journals and ProQuest Research Library. Also for student use, the library has a modern computer lab with eleven workstations, each with Internet access, online database services, an office suite, tutorials, and class-support software.

Financial Aid

A wide range of financial aid options is available to students who qualify. The Montgomery campus of South University offers access to federal and state aid, including grants, loans, and work-study programs. Eligible students may apply for veterans' educational benefits and are encouraged to investigate the availability of grants and scholarships through community resources. As a first step, students should complete the Free Application for Federal Student Aid (FAFSA). Students may apply electronically at http://www.fafsa.ed.gov or through the program. Applications should be submitted promptly to receive consideration for the maximum amount of aid.

Cost of Study

Tuition information for the professional counseling program may be obtained by contacting the admissions department at South University.

Living and Housing Costs

South University does not offer or operate student housing. Students in the professional counseling program typically live in private housing in the Montgomery area. Students who commute from long distances can arrange to stay at nearby hotels that offer long-term rates. More information may be obtained by contacting the admissions department.

Student Group

South University in Montgomery has a diverse student body enrolled in both day and evening classes. Students are primarily commuters who live within 50 miles of the city.

Student Outcomes

The South University career services department has been established to assist currently enrolled students in developing their career plans and reaching their employment goals. Career services include, but are not limited to, one-on-one career counseling, special career-related workshops and programs, coaching for resume and cover letter development, and resume referral to employers.

Location

South University is located on the rapidly growing east side of Alabama's capital city. As the state capital, Montgomery is a hub of government, banking, and law as well as a state center for culture and entertainment. Montgomery is situated in the middle of the southeastern U.S. and is less than a 3-hour drive from Atlanta and the Gulf of Mexico.

The University

South University is accredited by the Commission on Colleges of the Southern Association of Colleges and Schools (SACS) to award associate, baccalaureate, master's, and doctoral degrees. Students should contact the Commission on Colleges at 1866 Southern Lane, Decatur, Georgia 30033-4097 or call 404-679-4500 with questions about the accreditation of South University.

Applying

Students may be accepted into the Master of Arts in professional counseling degree program every academic quarter. Entrance into the program is gained through a formal application review and interview process. Acceptance is competitive and based on the admission committee's evaluation of the applicant's academic background (completed bachelor's degree with a cumulative minimum GPA of 2.7) and personal motivation. Application packets are available by contacting the South University admissions department or visiting the University's Web site.

Correspondence and Information

Applications for admission to the South University Master of Arts in professional counseling program are available by contacting:
Professional Counseling Program
South University
5355 Vaughn Road
Montgomery, Alabama 36116
Phone: 334-395-8800
          866-629-2962 (toll-free)
Fax: 334-395-8859
E-mail: mtgadmis@southuniversity.edu
Web site: http://www.southuniversity.edu
See suprograms.info for program duration; tuition, fees, and other costs; median debt; federal salary data; alumni success; and other important information. http://www.southuniversity.edu/programs-info/form/

South University

THE FACULTY

One of the most outstanding aspects of South University's professional counseling program is the dedication of the faculty members and their ability to cultivate a supportive learning environment. Faculty members are committed to their roles as mentors, teachers, and co-learners. They are also dedicated to the education of students who can assume positions of leadership within the counseling field. A current list of program faculty members is available at the South University Web site (http://www.southuniversity.edu).

SouthUniversity℠

SOUTH UNIVERSITY

Novi Campus
Professional Counseling Program

Program of Study

The Master of Arts in professional counseling degree program at South University is intended to meet the local and regional need for qualified professional counselors. The emphasis of the program is on community and agency counseling. The program is designed to enable its graduates to achieve all initial eligibility criteria to become certified as National Certified Counselors (NCC) by the National Board for Certified Counselors (NBCC) and licensed in the state of Michigan. The delivery structure of the program gives students the ability to balance the rigors of work and home while pursuing their master's degree. Students can complete one or two courses each term, with each quarter lasting ten weeks. Students select from the convenient Saturday sessions that meet once per week or attend two evenings during the week.

Students are taught via two primary modes of instruction. The majority of the program involves didactic and experiential classroom instruction, supplemented by computer-based assignments, including the use of Internet technology. The second mode of instruction focuses on supervised field experiences. Students are placed in community counseling settings (while on internship) and practice counseling under the supervision of an on-site supervisor. Students in field placements also receive weekly individual and group supervision from qualified faculty supervisors.

Research Facilities

Along with classrooms and offices, the campus includes a bookstore, student lounge, and career services center. Students may retrieve periodicals in paper or electronic form. The South University Library provides in-library and remote access to electronic databases. Both bibliographic and full-text databases are available via EBSCOhost (e.g., Academic Search Premier, SocINDEX, PsycINFO, PsycARTICLES, and Mental Measurements Yearbook), the search and retrieval system of EBSCO Information Services, and via the Library and Information Resources Network (e.g., Infotrac and ProQuest databases). Infotrac databases include counseling sources such as Expanded Academic ASAP, Academic OneFile, and InfotracOneFile. ProQuest databases include counseling sources such as ProQuest Psychology Journals and ProQuest Research Library. Internet access is available on all computers throughout the campus.

Financial Aid

A wide range of financial aid options is available to students who qualify. The Novi campus of South University offers access to federal and state programs, including grants, loans, and work-study programs. Eligible students may apply for veterans' educational benefits and are encouraged to investigate the availability of grants and scholarships through community resources. As a first step, students should complete the Free Application for Federal Student Aid (FAFSA). Students may apply electronically at http://www.fafsa.ed.gov or through the program. Applications should be submitted promptly to receive consideration for the maximum amount of aid.

Cost of Study

Tuition information for the professional counseling program may be obtained by contacting the Admissions Department at South University's Novi campus.

Living and Housing Costs

South University does not offer or operate student housing. Professional counseling program students typically live in apartments in the Novi area. Students who commute from long distances can arrange to stay at nearby hotels that offer long-term rates. More information is available by contacting the Admissions Department.

Student Group

The Novi campus of South University has a diverse student body enrolled in both day and evening classes. Students are primarily commuters who live within 50 miles of the city.

Student Outcomes

The South University Career Services Department has been established to assist currently enrolled students in developing their career plans and reaching their employment goals. Career services include, but are not limited to, one-on-one career counseling, special career-related workshops and programs, coaching for resume and cover letter development, and resume referral to employers.

Location

South University's Novi campus occupies more than 30,000 square feet of a new building located at 4155 Twelve Mile Road, Novi, Michigan 48377. The campus features spacious classrooms, a computer lab, nursing lab, health science lab, and physical therapy lab. The campus is located northwest of Detroit near the Ann Arbor, Michigan area.

The University

South University is accredited by the Commission on Colleges, Southern Association of Colleges and Schools (SACS), to award associate, baccalaureate, master's, and doctoral degrees. For questions about the accreditation of South University, contact the Commission on Colleges at 1866 Southern Lane, Decatur, Georgia 30033-4097; phone 404-679-4500.

South University in Novi is licensed under the laws of the Michigan Department of Energy, Labor, and Economic Growth to award baccalaureate and master's degrees.

Applying

Students are accepted into the Master of Arts in professional counseling degree program every academic quarter. Entrance into the program is gained through a formal application review and interview process. Acceptance is competitive and based on the admission committee's evaluation of the applicant's academic background and personal motivation. Application packets are available by contacting the South University Admissions Department (866-629-3031, toll-free) or visiting the University's Web site (http://www.southuniversity.edu).

Correspondence and Information

Applications for admission to the South University Master of Arts in professional counseling program are available by contacting:
Professional Counseling Program
South University
41555 Twelve Mile Road
Novi, Michigan 48377
Phone: 248-675-0200
        877-693-2085 (toll-free)
Fax: 248-675-0190
E-mail: sunovadmis@southuniversity.edu
Web site: http://www.southuniversity.edu

See suprograms.info for program duration; tuition, fees, and other costs; median debt; federal salary data; alumni success; and other important information. (http://www.southuniversity.edu/programs-info/form/)

South University

THE FACULTY

One of the most outstanding aspects of South University's professional counseling program is the dedication of the faculty members and their ability to cultivate a supportive learning environment. Faculty members are committed to their roles as mentors, teachers, and co-learners. They are also dedicated to the training of students who can assume positions of leadership within the counseling field. A current list of program faculty members appears in the South University catalog, which is available on the South University Web site (http://www.southuniversity.edu).

South University–Novi is located in Novi, Michigan, a suburb of northwest Detroit, convenient to shopping, restaurants, and cultural and entertainment venues.

SouthUniversity℠

SOUTH UNIVERSITY

Richmond Campus
Professional Counseling Program

Program of Study	The Master of Arts in Professional Counseling degree program at South University is intended to meet the local and regional need for qualified professional counselors. The emphasis of the program is on community and agency counseling. The program is designed to enable program graduates to achieve all initial eligibility criteria to become certified as a National Certified Counselor (NCC) by the National Board for Certified Counselors (NBCC) and licensed in their state. The delivery structure of the program gives students the ability to balance the rigors of work and home while pursuing their master's degree. Students can complete two courses each term (or more with approval), with each quarter lasting ten weeks. Class meetings are generally held on Saturdays between 8:30 a.m. and 12 noon as well as some weeknights.

Students are taught via two primary modes of instruction. The majority of the program involves didactic and experiential classroom instruction, supplemented by computer-based assignments, including the use of Internet technology. The second mode of instruction focuses on supervised field experiences. Students are placed in community counseling settings (while on internship) and practice counseling under the supervision of an on-site supervisor. Students in field placements also receive weekly individual and group supervision from qualified faculty supervisors. |
Research Facilities	The South University Library provides in-library and remote access to electronic databases. Both bibliographic and full-text databases are available via EBSCOhost (e.g., Academic Search Premier, SocINDEX, PsycINFO, PsycARTICLES, and Mental Measurements Yearbook), the search and retrieval system of EBSCO Information Services, and via the Library and Information Resources Network (e.g., Infotrac and ProQuest databases). Infotrac databases include counseling sources such as Expanded Academic ASAP, Academic OneFile, and InfotracOneFile. ProQuest databases include counseling sources such as ProQuest Psychology Journals and ProQuest Research Library.
Financial Aid	A wide range of financial aid options is available to students who qualify. The Richmond campus of South University offers access to federal and state aid, including grants, loans, and work-study programs. Eligible students may apply for veterans' educational benefits and are encouraged to investigate the availability of grants and scholarships through community resources. As a first step, students should complete the Free Application for Federal Student Aid (FAFSA). Students may apply electronically at http://www.fafsa.ed.gov or through the program. Applications should be submitted promptly to receive consideration for the maximum amount of aid.
Cost of Study	Tuition information for the Professional Counseling Program may be obtained by contacting the Admissions Department at South University's Richmond campus.
Living and Housing Costs	South University–Richmond does not offer or operate student housing. Students in the professional counseling program typically live in apartments in the Richmond area. Students who commute from long distances can arrange to stay at nearby hotels that offer long-term rates. More information may be obtained by contacting the Admissions Department.
Student Group	The Richmond campus of South University has a diverse student body enrolled in both day and evening classes. Students consist of commuters who live within 50 miles of the city.
Student Outcomes	The South University Career Services Department has been established to assist currently enrolled students in developing their career plans and reaching their employment goals. Career services include, but are not limited to, one-on-one career counseling, special career-related workshops and programs, coaching for resume and cover letter development, and resume referral to employers.
Location	South University–Richmond, one of South University's newest campus locations, occupies approximately 30,000 square feet of classroom, computer lab, library, and office space in Glen Allen, Virginia. The campus is located in the West Broad Village development in the Short Pump area.
The University	South University is accredited by the Commission on Colleges of the Southern Association of Colleges and Schools (SACS) to award associate, baccalaureate, master's, and doctoral degrees. Students should contact the Commission on Colleges at 1866 Southern Lane, Decatur, Georgia 30033-4097 or call 404-679-4500 for questions about the accreditation of South University. South University–Richmond is certified by the State Council of Higher Education in Virginia.
Applying	Students are accepted into the Master of Arts in Professional Counseling degree program every academic quarter. Entrance into the program is gained through a formal application review and interview process. Acceptance is competitive and based on the admission committee's evaluation of the applicant's academic background (completed bachelor's degree with a cumulative minimum GPA of 2.7) and personal motivation. Application packets are available by contacting the South University Admissions Department or visiting the University's Web site.
Correspondence and Information	Applications for admission to the South University Master of Arts in Professional Counseling program are available by contacting:

Professional Counseling Program
South University
2151 Old Brick Road
Glen Allen, Virginia 23060
Phone: 804-727-6800
　　　　888-422-5076 (toll-free)
Fax: 804-727-6790
E-mail: suriadm@southuniversity.edu
Web site: http://www.southuniversity.edu

See suprograms.info for program duration; tuition, fees, and other costs; median debt; federal salary data; alumni success; and other important information. http://www.southuniversity.edu/programs-info/form/ |

South University

THE FACULTY

One of the most outstanding aspects of South University's Professional Counseling Program is the dedication of the faculty members and their ability to cultivate a supportive learning environment. Faculty members are committed to their roles as mentors, teachers, and co-learners. They are also dedicated to the training of students who can assume positions of leadership within the counseling field. A current list of program faculty members appears in the South University catalog, which is available on the South University Web site (http://www.southuniversity.edu).

South University—Richmond Campus.

SouthUniversity℠

SOUTH UNIVERSITY

Savannah Campus
Professional Counseling Program

Program of Study	The Master of Arts in professional counseling degree program at South University is intended to meet the local and regional need for qualified professional counselors. The emphasis of the program is on community and agency counseling. The program is designed to enable program graduates to achieve all initial eligibility criteria to become certified as a National Certified Counselor (NCC) by the National Board for Certified Counselors (NBCC) and licensed in their state. The delivery structure of the program gives students the ability to balance the rigors of work and home while pursuing their master's degree. Students can complete two courses each term (or more with approval), with each quarter lasting ten weeks. Class meetings are generally held Saturdays between 8:30 a.m. and 12 noon as well as some weeknights.
	Students are taught via two primary modes of instruction. The majority of the program involves didactic and experiential classroom instruction, supplemented by computer-based assignments, including the use of Internet technology. The second mode of instruction focuses on supervised field experiences. Students are placed in community counseling settings (during internship) and practice counseling under the supervision of an on-site supervisor. Students in field placements also receive weekly individual and group supervision from qualified faculty supervisors.
Research Facilities	In 2000, the 25,000-square-foot Health Professions building was opened on the Savannah campus to house classroom, computer, and lab facilities for graduate programs within the College of Health Professions. A student lounge and administrative offices are also located in this building. In 2007, a new library facility was opened that provides comfortable study space for students, wireless capabilities for laptop network connectivity, and reference and interlibrary loan services. The South University Library also provides in-library and remote access to electronic databases. Both bibliographic and full-text databases are available via EBSCOhost (e.g., Academic Search Premier, SocINDEX, PsycINFO, PsycARTICLES, and Mental Measurements Yearbook), the search and retrieval system of EBSCO Information Services, and via the Library and Information Resources Network (e.g., Infotrac and ProQuest databases). Infotrac databases include counseling sources such as Expanded Academic ASAP, Academic OneFile, and InfotracOneFile. ProQuest databases include counseling sources such as ProQuest Psychology Journals and ProQuest Research Library.
Financial Aid	A wide range of financial aid options is available to students who qualify. The Savannah campus of South University offers access to federal and state programs, including grants, loans, and work-study programs. Eligible students may apply for veterans' educational benefits and are encouraged to investigate the availability of grants and scholarships through community resources. As a first step, students should complete the Free Application for Federal Student Aid (FAFSA). Students may apply electronically at http://www.fafsa.ed.gov or through the campus Director of Financial Aid. Applications should be submitted promptly to receive consideration for the maximum amount of aid.
Cost of Study	Tuition information for the professional counseling program may be obtained by contacting the Admissions Department at South University's Savannah campus.
Living and Housing Costs	South University offers school-sponsored student housing at its Savannah, Georgia, campus in conjunction with a local apartment complex. Students who commute from long distances can arrange to stay at nearby hotels that offer long-term rates. More information may be obtained by contacting the Director of Student Housing at 912-201-8000.
Student Group	The Savannah campus of South University has a diverse student body enrolled in both day and evening classes. Students consist of commuters who live within 50 miles of the city, as well as those from other areas of the United States (e.g., California, Ohio, Pennsylvania, Connecticut) who have moved to Savannah to pursue a degree in professional counseling.
Student Outcomes	The South University Career Services Department has been established to assist currently enrolled students in developing their career plans and reaching their employment goals. Career services include, but are not limited to, one-on-one career counseling, special career-related workshops and programs, coaching for resume and cover letter development, and resume referral to employers.
Location	Located on the south side of the historic city of Savannah, the campus is situated on 9 acres of land. It is convenient to the city's bustling midtown section and a full range of educational and cultural activities. The Atlantic Ocean and recreational amenities of Tybee Island, including beaches and numerous outdoor activities, are just a short drive away. In addition, the campus is located just a short drive from Hilton Head Island and Charleston, South Carolina.
The University	South University is accredited by the Commission on Colleges of the Southern Association of Colleges and Schools (SACS) to award associate, baccalaureate, master's, and doctoral degrees. Students should contact the Commission on Colleges at 1866 Southern Lane, Decatur, Georgia 30033-4097 or call 404-679-4500 with questions about the accreditation of South University.
Applying	Students are accepted into the Master of Arts in professional counseling degree program twice per year (fall and spring quarters). Entrance into the program is gained through a formal application review and interview process. Acceptance is competitive and based on the admission committee's evaluation of the applicant's academic background (completed bachelor's degree with a cumulative minimum GPA of 2.7) and personal motivation. Application packets are available by contacting the South University Admissions Department or visiting the University's Web site.
Correspondence and Information	Applications for admission to the South University Master of Arts in professional counseling program are available by contacting:

Professional Counseling Program
South University
709 Mall Boulevard
Savannah, Georgia 31406-4805

Phone: 912-201-8000
     866-629-2901 (toll-free)
Fax: 912-201-8070
E-mail: savadmis@southuniversity.edu
Web site: http://www.southuniversity.edu

South University

THE FACULTY

One of the most outstanding aspects of South University's professional counseling program is the dedication of the faculty members and their ability to cultivate a supportive learning environment. Faculty members are committed to their roles as mentors, teachers, and co-learners. They are also dedicated to the training of students who can assume positions of leadership within the counseling field. A current list of program faculty members is available at the South University Web site (http://www.southuniversity.edu).

South University is located on the south side of historic Savannah, Georgia.

SouthUniversity℠

SOUTH UNIVERSITY

Virginia Beach Campus
Professional Counseling Program

Program of Study

The Master of Arts in Professional Counseling degree program at South University is intended to meet the local and regional need for qualified professional counselors. The emphasis of the program is on community and agency counseling. The program is designed to enable program graduates to achieve all initial eligibility criteria to become certified as a National Certified Counselor (NCC) by the National Board for Certified Counselors (NBCC) and licensed in their state. The delivery structure of the program gives students the ability to balance the rigors of work and home while pursuing their master's degree. Students can complete two courses each term (or more with approval), with each quarter lasting ten weeks. Class meetings are generally held on Saturdays between 8:30 a.m. and 12 noon as well as some weeknights from 6 to 9:30 p.m.

Students are taught via two primary modes of instruction. The majority of the program involves didactic and experiential classroom instruction, supplemented by computer-based assignments, including the use of Internet technology. The second mode of instruction focuses on supervised field experiences. Students are placed in community counseling settings (during internship) and practice counseling under the supervision of an on-site supervisor. Students in field placements also receive weekly individual and group supervision from qualified faculty supervisors.

Research Facilities

The South University Library provides in-library and remote access to electronic databases. Both bibliographic and full-text databases are available via EBSCOhost (e.g., Academic Search Premier, SocINDEX, PsycINFO, PsycARTICLES, and Mental Measurements Yearbook), the search and retrieval system of EBSCO Information Services, and via the Library and Information Resources Network (e.g., Infotrac and ProQuest databases). Infotrac databases include counseling sources such as Expanded Academic ASAP, Academic OneFile, and InfotracOneFile. ProQuest databases include counseling sources such as ProQuest Psychology Journals and ProQuest Research Library.

Financial Aid

A wide range of financial aid options is available to students who qualify. The Virginia Beach campus of South University offers access to federal and state programs, including grants, loans, and work-study programs. Eligible students may apply for veterans' educational benefits and are encouraged to investigate the availability of grants and scholarships through community resources. As a first step, students should complete the Free Application for Federal Student Aid (FAFSA). Students may apply electronically at http://www.fafsa.ed.gov or through the campus Director of Financial Aid. Applications should be submitted promptly to receive consideration for the maximum amount of aid.

Cost of Study

Tuition information for the Professional Counseling Program may be obtained by contacting the Admissions Department at South University's Virginia Beach campus.

Living and Housing Costs

South University does not offer or operate student housing. Students in the professional counseling program typically live in apartments in the Virginia Beach area. Students who commute from long distances can arrange to stay at nearby hotels that offer long-term rates. More information may be obtained by contacting the Admissions Department.

Student Group

The Virginia Beach campus of South University has a diverse student body enrolled in both day and evening classes. Students consist of commuters who live within 50 miles of the city.

Student Outcomes

The South University Career Services Department has been established to assist currently enrolled students in developing their career plans and reaching their employment goals. Career services include, but are not limited to, one-on-one career counseling, special career-related workshops and programs, coaching for resume and cover letter development, and resume referral to employers.

Location

South University–Virginia Beach is located in 32,600 square feet of space in the attractive and convenient Convergence Center in Virginia Beach's popular Central Business District. The Virginia Beach campus features a distance learning center, a library, a bookstore, on-site security, student and faculty lounges, as well as health-science labs.

The University

South University is accredited by the Commission on Colleges of the Southern Association of Colleges and Schools (SACS) to award associate, baccalaureate, master's, and doctoral degrees. Students should contact the Commission on Colleges at 1866 Southern Lane, Decatur, Georgia 30033-4097 or call 404-679-4500 with questions about the accreditation of South University. South University–Virginia Beach is certified by the State Council of Higher Education in Virginia.

Applying

Students are accepted into the Master of Arts in Professional Counseling degree program twice per year (fall and spring quarters). Entrance into the program is gained through a formal application review and interview process. Acceptance is competitive and based on the admission committee's evaluation of the applicant's academic background (completed bachelor's degree with a cumulative minimum GPA of 2.7) and personal motivation. Application packets are available by contacting the South University Admissions Department or visiting the University's Web site.

Correspondence and Information

Applications for admission to the South University Master of Arts in Professional Counseling program are available by contacting:

Professional Counseling Program
South University
301 Bendix Road
Virginia Beach, Virginia 23452
Phone: 757-493-6900
      877-206-1845(toll-free)
Fax: 757-493-6990
E-mail: suvbadm@southuniversity.edu
Web site: http://www.southuniversity.edu

South University

THE FACULTY

One of the most outstanding aspects of South University's Professional Counseling Program is the dedication of the faculty members and their ability to cultivate a supportive learning environment. Faculty members are committed to their roles as mentors, teachers, and co-learners. They are also dedicated to the training of students who can assume positions of leadership within the counseling field. A current list of program faculty members is available at the South University Web site (http://www.southuniversity.edu).

South University–Virginia Beach.

SouthUniversity℠

SOUTH UNIVERSITY

West Palm Beach Campus
Professional Counseling Program

Program of Study

The Master of Arts in professional counseling degree program at South University is intended to meet the local and regional need for qualified professional counselors. The emphasis of the program is on community and agency counseling. The program is designed to enable program graduates to achieve all initial eligibility criteria to become certified as a National Certified Counselor (NCC) by the National Board for Certified Counselors (NBCC) and licensed in the state of Florida. The delivery structure of the program gives students the ability to balance the rigors of work and home while pursuing their master's degree. Students can complete two to three courses each term, with each quarter lasting ten weeks. Class meetings are generally held Saturdays between 8:30 a.m. and 5 p.m. as well as some weeknights from 6 to 9:30 p.m.

Students are taught via two primary modes of instruction. The majority of the program involves didactic and experiential classroom instruction, supplemented by computer-based assignments, including the use of Internet technology. The second mode of instruction focuses on supervised field experiences. Students are placed in community counseling settings (during practicum and internship) and practice counseling under the supervision of an on-site supervisor. Students in field placements also receive weekly individual and group supervision from qualified faculty supervisors.

Research Facilities

The South University library has wireless technology throughout, comfortable seating, and quiet study space. The South University library provides in-library and remote access to electronic databases. Both bibliographic and full-text databases are available via EBSCOhost (e.g., Academic Search Premier, SocINDEX, PsycINFO, PsycARTICLES, and Mental Measurements Yearbook), the search and retrieval system of EBSCO Information Services, and via the Library and Information Resources Network (e.g., Infotrac and ProQuest databases). Infotrac databases include counseling sources such as Expanded Academic ASAP, Academic OneFile, and InfotracOneFile. ProQuest databases include counseling sources such as ProQuest Psychology Journals and ProQuest Research Library. Also for student use, the library has a modern computer lab with ten workstations, each with Internet access, online database services, an office suite, tutorials, and class-support software.

Financial Aid

A wide range of financial aid options is available to students who qualify. The West Palm Beach campus of South University offers access to federal and state programs, including grants, loans, and work-study programs. Eligible students may apply for veterans' educational benefits and are encouraged to investigate the availability of grants and scholarships through community resources. As a first step, students should complete the Free Application for Federal Student Aid (FAFSA). Students may apply electronically at http://www.fafsa.ed.gov or through the campus Director of Financial Aid. Applications should be submitted promptly to receive consideration for the maximum amount of aid.

Cost of Study

Tuition information for the professional counseling program may be obtained by contacting the Admissions Department at South University's West Palm Beach campus.

Living and Housing Costs

South University does not offer or operate student housing at its West Palm Beach campus. Students in the professional counseling program typically live in homes or apartments in or near the West Palm Beach area. Students who commute from long distances may arrange to stay at nearby hotels that offer long-term rates. More information may be obtained by contacting the Admissions Department.

Student Group

The West Palm Beach campus of South University has a diverse student body enrolled in both day and evening classes. Students are primarily commuters who live within 50 miles of the city.

Student Outcomes

The South University Career Services Department has been established to assist currently enrolled students in developing their career plans and reaching their employment goals. Career services include, but are not limited to, one-on-one career counseling, special career-related workshops and programs, coaching for resume and cover letter development, and resume referral to employers.

Location

In 2010, South University–West Palm Beach moved into a new University Centre facility in Royal Palm Beach, Florida, to better serve students and the broader community in the Palm Beach County area. The facility features a hurricane-resistant infrastructure and includes several large labs, lecture halls, a library, and seminar rooms.

The University

South University is accredited by the Commission on Colleges of the Southern Association of Colleges and Schools (SACS) to award associate, baccalaureate, master's, and doctoral degrees. Students should contact the Commission on Colleges at 1866 Southern Lane, Decatur, Georgia 30033-4097 or call 404-679-4500 with questions about the accreditation of South University.

Applying

Students are accepted into the Master of Arts in professional counseling degree program every academic quarter. Entrance into the program is gained through a formal application review and interview process. Acceptance is competitive and based on the admission committee's evaluation of the applicant's academic background (completed bachelor's degree with a cumulative minimum GPA of 2.7) and personal motivation. Application packets are available by contacting the South University Admissions Department or visiting the University's Web site.

Correspondence and Information

Applications for admission to the South University Master of Arts in professional counseling program are available by contacting:

Professional Counseling Program
South University
University Centre
9801 Belvedere Road
Royal Palm Beach, Florida 33411
Phone: 561-273-6500
        866-629-2902 (toll-free)
Fax: 561-273-6420
Web site: http://www.southuniversity.edu

South University

THE FACULTY

One of the most outstanding aspects of South University's professional counseling program is the dedication of the faculty members and their ability to cultivate a supportive learning environment. Faculty members are committed to their roles as mentors, teachers, and co-learners. They are also dedicated to the training of students who can assume positions of leadership within the counseling field. A current list of program faculty members appears in the South University catalog, which is available on the South University Web site (http://www.southuniversity.edu).

South University–West Palm Beach campus.

THE UNIVERSITY OF TEXAS AT SAN ANTONIO

M.A. in School Psychology Program

Programs of Study

The Master of Arts in School Psychology program within the Department of Educational Psychology provides students with the academic and practical training needed to become a licensed specialist in school psychology by the Texas State Board of Examiners of Psychologists. The program includes course work and field-based experiences related to psychological assessment, intervention, development, psychopathology, research, statistics, and professional issues. Candidates for the Master of Arts degree in school psychology must earn a minimum of 66 semester credit hours. Students will also complete a full-time internship in a school setting. Due to the clinical nature of this program and the number of hours required, the degree does not have a thesis option.

Common roles and functions of the school psychologist include psychological assessment, counseling, consultation, crisis intervention, research, and program evaluation. School psychology has been identified by the U.S. Department of Labor as a specialization that is likely to have faster than average employment growth. Texas has been identified as a state that will soon experience one of the most serious shortages of school psychologists.

Research Facilities

The Psychological Assessment and Consultation Center within the Department of Educational Psychology provides access to testing materials, work areas, books, and testing rooms for students within the Master of Arts in school psychology program.

Financial Aid

Applicants are strongly encouraged to complete the FAFSA (Free Application for Federal Student Aid) at http://www.fafsa.ed.gov. Additional financial aid information can be found at http://www.graduateschool.utsa.edu/prospective_students/detail/financing_your_future.

In addition, the College of Education and Human Development offers graduate assistantship positions that average 19 hours of work per week.

Cost of Study

In the 2010–11 academic year, tuition and fees for a full-time graduate degree student (9 semester hours) were approximately $3149 per semester for Texas residents and $8783 per semester for nonresidents. Some courses and programs have additional fees. Please view the following Web sites for more information: http://www.utsa.edu/fiscalservices/tuition.html and http://www.graduateschool.utsa.edu/prospective_students/detail/graduate_tuition_and_fees.

Living and Housing Costs

University on-campus housing is available and includes apartment-style living at four complexes—Chisholm Hall, University Oaks, Laurel Village, and Chaparral Village. Off-campus housing is also available and includes many apartments adjacent to the University as well as a large number located within a 5-mile drive. The rate for a one-bedroom apartment is approximately $500 per month.

Student Group

In the 2010 fall semester, the University enrolled more than 30,000 students, of whom more than 4,000 were graduate students. Currently, the Master of Arts in school psychology program has over 50 active enrolled students with a large percentage of both women and minorities represented.

Location

San Antonio, with a population of 1.5 million, is one of the nation's major metropolitan areas. As the home of the Alamo and numerous other missions built by the Franciscans, the city is historically and culturally diverse. The Guadalupe Cultural Arts Center, McNay Art Museum, the San Antonio Museum of Art, and the Witte Museum enrich the city. The performing arts are represented by the San Antonio Symphony, the annual Tejano Music Festival and Tejano Music Awards, and performances by opera and ballet companies. Also notable are Sea World, Six Flags Fiesta Texas, Brackenridge Park, the Botanical Gardens, and the downtown Riverwalk. The San Antonio Zoo has the third-largest collection in North America. A city landmark is the Tower of the Americas, which was built for the 1968 World's Fair. San Antonio is home to the National Basketball Association's Spurs, league champions in 2000, 2003, 2005, and 2007. Numerous nearby lakes allow almost year-round outdoor activity, and the beaches of the Texas Gulf coast are within a 2-hour drive. San Antonio is home to numerous festivals throughout the year, including the Fiesta San Antonio and the Rodeo with activities such as parades, fairs, and concerts.

The University

The University was founded in 1969 and has since become a comprehensive metropolitan institution. Its research expenditures place it in the top 25 percent of public universities in Texas. The University has entered a new building and recruitment phase with a view to greatly expand the research efforts in engineering and the sciences. UTSA Roadrunners football is slated to compete as an NCAA Division I FCS independent in August 2011 and is expected to transition to the Division I FBS by 2013.

Applying

Applicants may apply through the UTSA Graduate School at http://www.graduateschool.utsa.edu. Please send all USPS mail (transcripts, etc.) to: The University of Texas at San Antonio, Attn: The Graduate School, One UTSA Circle, San Antonio, Texas 78249.

For detailed admission requirements, contact the College of Education and Human Development at 210-458-4370 or at education@utsa.edu.

Correspondence and Information

For application information:
The Graduate School
The University of Texas at San Antonio
One UTSA Circle
San Antonio, Texas 78249
Phone: 210-458-4330
Web site: http://www.graduateschool.utsa.edu

For program information:
Department of Educational Psychology
The University of Texas at San Antonio
One UTSA Circle
San Antonio, Texas 78249
Phone: 210-458-2721
E-mail: education@utsa.edu
Web site: http://education.utsa.edu/educational_psychology

The University of Texas at San Antonio

THE FACULTY AND THEIR RESEARCH

Additional information on faculty within the Department of Educational Psychology can be found at: http://education.utsa.edu/educational_psychology/faculty/.

Felicia Castro-Villarreal, Assistant Professor; Ph.D., Oklahoma State.
Norma S. Guerra, Associate Professor; Ph.D., Texas A&M.
Nancy K. Martin, Professor; Ed.D., Texas Tech.
Patricia McGee, Associate Professor; Ph.D., Texas at Austin.
Sharon L. Nichols, Associate Professor; Ph.D., Arizona.
Carolyn Orange, Professor; Ph.D., Washington (St. Louis).
Patricia D. Quijada, Assistant Professor; Ph.D., Wisconsin–Madison.
Billie Jo Rodriguez, Assistant Professor; Ph.D., Oregon.
Daniel Sass, Assistant Professor; Ph.D., Wisconsin–Milwaukee.
Paul A. Schutz, Professor; Ph.D., Texas at Austin.
Jeremy R. Sullivan, Associate Professor; Ph.D., Texas A&M.
Suzanne M. Winter, Associate Professor; Ph.D., Texas at Austin.

Section 25
Public, Regional, and Industrial Affairs

This section contains a directory of institutions offering graduate work in public, regional, and industrial affairs, followed by in-depth entries submitted by institutions that chose to prepare detailed program descriptions. Additional information about programs listed in the directory but not augmented by an in-depth entry may be obtained by writing directly to the dean of a graduate school or chair of a department at the address given in the directory.

For programs offering related work, see also in this book *Architecture, Area and Cultural Studies, Criminology and Forensics, Economics, Humanities, Political Science and International Affairs,* and *Sociology, Anthropology, and Archaeology.* In the other guides in this series:

Graduate Programs in the Physical Sciences, Mathematics, Agricultural Sciences, the Environment & Natural Resources
See *Environmental Sciences and Management*
Graduate Programs in Engineering & Applied Sciences
See *Management of Engineering and Technology*
Graduate Programs in Business, Education, Health, Information Studies, Law & Social Work
See *Business Administration and Management, Law,* and *Public Health*

CONTENTS

Program Directories

Close-Ups and Displays

See also:

Disability Studies

Brandeis University, The Heller School for Social Policy and Management, Program in Social Policy, Waltham, MA 02454-9110. Offers assets and inequalities (PhD); children, youth and families (PhD); global health and development (PhD); health and behavioral health (PhD). *Faculty:* 36 full-time, 107 part-time/adjunct. *Students:* 64 full-time (34 women), 82 part-time (72 women), 17 international. Average age 32. 105 applicants, 51% accepted, 23 enrolled. In 2010, 8 doctorates awarded. *Degree requirements:* For doctorate, thesis/dissertation, qualifying paper, 2-year residency. *Entrance requirements:* For doctorate, GRE General Test, 3 letters of recommendation, statement of purpose, writing sample, at least 3-5 years of professional experience. Additional exam requirements/recommendations for international students: Required—TOEFL (minimum score 600 paper-based; 250 computer-based; 100 iBT). *Application deadline:* For fall admission, 1/2 for domestic and international students. Application fee: $55. Electronic applications accepted. *Financial support:* In 2010–11, 15 fellowships with full tuition reimbursements (averaging $20,000 per year) were awarded; scholarships/grants, traineeships, health care benefits, tuition waivers (full and partial), and unspecified assistantships also available. Financial award application deadline: 1/2. *Faculty research:* Health; mental health; substance abuse; children, youth, and families; aging; international and community development; disabilities; work and inequality; and hunger and poverty. *Unit head:* Dr. Christine Bishop, Program Director, 781-736-3942, E-mail: bishop@brandeis.edu. *Application contact:* Elizabeth Cole, Assistant Director for Admissions and Financial Aid, 781-736-2647, E-mail: elcole@brandeis.edu.

Brock University, Faculty of Graduate Studies, Faculty of Social Sciences, Program in Applied Disability Studies, St. Catharines, ON L2S 3A1, Canada. Offers MA, MADS, Diploma. Part-time programs available. *Degree requirements:* For master's, thesis (for some programs). *Entrance requirements:* For master's, honors degree. Additional exam requirements/recommendations for international students: Required—TOEFL (minimum score 550 paper-based; 213 computer-based; 80 iBT), IELTS (minimum score 6.5). Electronic applications accepted.

Chapman University, Graduate Studies, College of Educational Studies, Program in Education: Disability Studies, Orange, CA 92866. Offers PhD. *Faculty:* 24 full-time (15 women), 25 part-time/adjunct (16 women). *Students:* 20 part-time (16 women); includes 1 Black or African American, non-Hispanic/Latino; 1 American Indian or Alaska Native, non-Hispanic/Latino; 3 Asian, non-Hispanic/Latino; 1 Hispanic/Latino. Average age 39. 12 applicants, 75% accepted, 6 enrolled. *Degree requirements:* For doctorate, thesis/dissertation. *Financial support:* Federal Work-Study and scholarships/grants available. *Unit head:* Dr. Joel Colbert, Director, 714-744-7076. *Application contact:* Maureen Rika Judd, Graduate Admission Counselor, 714-997-6786, Fax: 714-997-6713, E-mail: rjudd@chapman.edu.

Syracuse University, School of Education, Program in Disability Studies, Syracuse, NY 13244. Offers CAS. Part-time programs available. *Students:* 3 part-time (all women). Average age 36. 11 applicants, 91% accepted, 0 enrolled. *Entrance requirements:* Additional exam requirements/recommendations for international students: Required—TOEFL (minimum score 100 iBT). *Application deadline:* For fall admission, 2/1 priority date for domestic and international students; for spring admission, 10/15 priority date for domestic and international students. Applications are processed on a rolling basis. Application fee: $75. Electronic applications accepted. *Expenses:* Tuition: Part-time $1162 per credit. *Financial support:* Application deadline: 1/1. *Unit head:* Dr. Steve Taylor, Program Coordinator, 315-443-4484, E-mail: staylo01@syr.edu. *Application contact:* Liza Rochelson, Graduate Recruiter, School of Education, 315-443-2505, E-mail: e-gradrcrt@syr.edu.

University of Hawaii at Manoa, Graduate Division, College of Education, Program in Disability and Diversity Studies, Honolulu, HI 96822. Offers Graduate Certificate. Part-time programs available. *Faculty:* 5 full-time (3 women). *Students:* 2 full-time (both women), 4 part-time (1 woman); includes 2 minority (1 Black or African American, non-Hispanic/Latino; 1 Asian, non-Hispanic/Latino), 2 international. Average age 37. 11 applicants, 64% accepted, 4 enrolled. In 2010, 3 Graduate Certificates awarded. *Entrance requirements:* Additional exam requirements/recommendations for international students: Required—TOEFL (minimum score 500 paper-based; 173 computer-based; 61 iBT), IELTS (minimum score 5). *Application deadline:* For fall admission, 2/1 for domestic students, 1/15 for international students. Application fee: $60. *Financial support:* In 2010–11, 3 students received support, including 3 research assistantships (averaging $17,964 per year); fellowships also available. Total annual research expenditures: $12.4 million. *Application contact:* Norma Jean Stodden, Director, 808-956-4454, Fax: 808-956-3162, E-mail: nhemphil@hawaii.edu.

University of Illinois at Chicago, Graduate College, College of Applied Health Sciences, Department of Disability and Human Development, Chicago, IL 60607-7128. Offers disability and human development (MS); disability studies (PhD). *Accreditation:* AOTA. Part-time programs available. *Degree requirements:* For master's, thesis optional; for doctorate, thesis/dissertation. *Entrance requirements:* For master's and doctorate, GRE General Test. Additional exam requirements/recommendations for international students: Required—TOEFL. Electronic applications accepted. *Faculty research:* Emerging trends in disability, demography and financial structure of disability services, aging and disability, empowerment of people with disabilities, health promotion in disabilities.

University of Manitoba, Faculty of Graduate Studies, Interdisciplinary Programs, Program in Disability Studies, Winnipeg, MB R3T 2N2, Canada. Offers M Sc, MA.

University of Northern British Columbia, Office of Graduate Studies, Prince George, BC V2N 4Z9, Canada. Offers business administration (Diploma); community health science (M Sc); disability management (MA); education (M Ed); first nations studies (MA); gender studies (MA); history (MA); interdisciplinary studies (MA); international studies (MA); mathematical, computer and physical sciences (M Sc); natural resources and environmental studies (M Sc, MA, MNRES, PhD); political science (MA); psychology (M Sc, PhD); social work (MSW). Part-time and evening/weekend programs available. Postbaccalaureate distance learning degree programs offered (no on-campus study). *Degree requirements:* For master's, thesis; for doctorate, thesis/dissertation. *Entrance requirements:* For master's, GRE, minimum B average in undergraduate course work; for doctorate, candidacy exam, minimum A average in graduate course work.

Utah State University, School of Graduate Studies, College of Education and Human Services, Department of Special Education and Rehabilitation, Logan, UT 84322. Offers disability disciplines (PhD); rehabilitation counselor education (MRC); special education (M Ed, MS, Ed S). *Accreditation:* NCATE (one or more programs are accredited). Part-time programs available. Postbaccalaureate distance learning degree programs offered (minimal on-campus study). *Degree requirements:* For master's, thesis (for some programs), internships (for some programs); for doctorate, comprehensive exam, thesis/dissertation. *Entrance requirements:* For master's and doctorate, GRE General Test, minimum GPA of 3.0. Additional exam requirements/recommendations for international students: Required—TOEFL (minimum score 550 paper-based; 213 computer-based). Electronic applications accepted. *Faculty research:* Applied behavior analysis, effective instructional practices, early childhood teacher training research, distance education, multicultural rehabilitation.

York University, Faculty of Graduate Studies, Faculty of Health, Program in Critical Disability Studies, Toronto, ON M3J 1P3, Canada. Offers MA, PhD. *Degree requirements:* For master's, thesis or alternative. *Entrance requirements:* Additional exam requirements/recommendations for international students: Required—TOEFL (minimum score 600 paper-based; 250 computer-based). Electronic applications accepted.

Emergency Management

Adelphi University, University College, Graduate Certificate in Emergency Management Program, Garden City, NY 11530-0701. Offers Certificate. Part-time and evening/weekend programs available. *Faculty:* 1 full-time (0 women), 22 part-time/adjunct (9 women). *Students:* 8 part-time (4 women). Average age 35. 10 applicants, 50% accepted, 2 enrolled. In 2010, 5 Certificates awarded. *Application deadline:* For fall admission, 5/1 for international students; for spring admission, 12/1 for international students. Applications are processed on a rolling basis. Application fee: $50. Electronic applications accepted. *Financial support:* Research assistantships with partial tuition reimbursements, Federal Work-Study and institutionally sponsored loans available. *Faculty research:* Emergency nursing, disaster management, disaster preparedness. *Unit head:* Shawn O'Riley, Executive Director, 516-877-3412, E-mail: ucinfo@adelphi.edu. *Application contact:* Christine Murphy, Director of Admissions, 516-877-3050, Fax: 516-877-3039, E-mail: graduateadmissions@adelphi.edu.

American Public University System, AMU/APU Graduate Programs, Charles Town, WV 25414. Offers accounting (MBA); administration and supervision (M Ed); air warfare (MA Military Studies); asymmetrical warfare (MA Military Studies); criminal justice (MA); emergency and disaster management (MA); entrepreneurship (MBA); environmental policy and management (MS); finance (MBA); general (MBA); global business management (MBA); guidance and counseling (M Ed); history (MA); homeland security (MA); homeland security resource allocation (MBA); humanities (MA); information technology (MS); information technology management (MBA); intelligence studies (MA); international relations and conflict resolution (MA); joint warfare (MA Military Studies); land warfare (MA Military Studies); legal studies (MA); management (MA), including defense mangement, general, human resource management, organizational leadership, public administration; marketing (MBA); military history (MA); national security studies (MA); naval warfare (MA Military Studies); nonprofit management (MBA); political science (MA); psychology (MA); public administration (MA); public health (MA); security management (MA); space studies (MS); sports management (MS); strategic leadership (MA Military Studies); teaching (M Ed), including elementary, secondary social sciences; transportation and logistics management (MA). Programs offered via distance learning only. Part-time and evening/weekend programs available. Postbaccalaureate distance learning degree programs offered (no on-campus study). *Faculty:* 253 full-time (134 women), 1,208 part-time/adjunct (570 women). *Students:* 956 full-time (422 women), 8,476 part-time (2,821 women); includes 2,511 minority (1,218 Black or African American, non-Hispanic/Latino; 68 American Indian or Alaska Native, non-Hispanic/Latino; 219 Asian, non-Hispanic/Latino; 705 Hispanic/Latino; 46 Native Hawaiian or other Pacific Islander, non-Hispanic/Latino; 255 Two or more races, non-Hispanic/Latino), 107 international. Average age 35. 9,550 applicants, 100% accepted. In 2010, 1,688 master's awarded. *Degree requirements:* For master's, comprehensive exam or practicum. *Entrance requirements:* For master's, official transcript showing earned bachelor's degree from institution accredited by recognized accrediting body. Additional exam requirements/recommendations for international students: Required—TOEFL (minimum score 550 paper-based; 213 computer-based), IELTS (minimum score 6.5). *Application deadline:* Applications are processed on a rolling basis. Application fee: $0. Electronic applications accepted. *Financial support:* Applicants required to submit FAFSA. *Faculty research:* Military history, criminal justice, management performance, national security. *Unit head:* Dr. Frank McCluskey, Provost, 877-468-6268, Fax: 304-724-3780. *Application contact:* Terry Grant, Director of Enrollment Management, 877-468-6268, Fax: 304-724-3780, E-mail: info@apus.edu.

Anna Maria College, Graduate Division, Program in Emergency Management, Paxton, MA 01612. Offers MS, Graduate Certificate. Part-time and evening/weekend programs available. *Degree requirements:* For master's, thesis. *Entrance requirements:* For master's, minimum GPA of 2.7. Additional exam requirements/recommendations for international students: Required—TOEFL (minimum score 500 paper-based). Electronic applications accepted.

Arkansas Tech University, Graduate College, College of Applied Sciences, Russellville, AR 72801. Offers emergency management (MS); engineering (M Engr); information technology (MS). Part-time programs available. *Students:* 86 full-time (24 women), 53 part-time (21 women); includes 14 minority (5 Black or African American, non-Hispanic/Latino; 2 American Indian or Alaska Native, non-Hispanic/Latino; 1 Asian, non-Hispanic/Latino; 4 Hispanic/Latino; 2 Two or more races, non-Hispanic/Latino), 60 international. Average age 31. In 2010, 44 master's awarded. *Degree requirements:* For master's, comprehensive exam (for some programs), thesis (for some programs), internship. *Entrance requirements:* For master's, GRE General Test. Additional exam requirements/recommendations for international students: Required—TOEFL (minimum score 550 paper-based; 213 computer-based; 79 iBT), IELTS (minimum score 6). *Application deadline:* For fall admission, 3/1 priority date for domestic students, 5/1 priority date for international students; for spring admission, 10/1 priority date for domestic and international students. Applications are processed on a rolling basis. Application fee: $0 ($30 for international students). Electronic applications accepted. *Expenses:* Tuition, state resident: full-time $4680; part-time $195 per credit hour. Tuition, nonresident: full-time $9360; part-time $390 per credit hour. Required fees: $714; $14 per credit hour. One-time fee: $326 part-time. Tuition and fees vary according to course load. *Financial support:* In 2010–11, teaching assistantships with full tuition reimbursements (averaging $4,000 per year); research assistantships, career-related internships or fieldwork, Federal Work-Study, scholarships/grants, health care benefits, and unspecified assistantships also available. Support available to part-time students. Financial award application deadline: 4/15; financial award applicants required to submit FAFSA. *Unit head:* Dr. William Hoefler, Dean, 479-968-0353 Ext. 501, E-mail: whoeflerjr@atu.edu. *Application contact:* Dr. Mary B. Gunter, Dean of Graduate College, 479-968-0398, Fax: 479-964-0542, E-mail: graduate.school@atu.edu.

Benedictine University, Graduate Programs, Program in Public Health, Lisle, IL 60532-0900. Offers administration of health care institutions (MPH); dietetics (MPH); disaster management (MPH); health education (MPH); health information systems (MPH); MBA/MPH; MPH/MS. Part-time and evening/weekend programs available. Postbaccalaureate distance learning degree programs offered. *Faculty:* 2 full-time (0 women), 8 part-time/adjunct (3 women). *Students:* 105 full-time (80 women), 401 part-time (313 women); includes 192 minority (121 Black or African American, non-Hispanic/Latino; 1 American Indian or Alaska Native, non-Hispanic/Latino; 48 Asian, non-Hispanic/Latino; 21 Hispanic/Latino; 1 Native Hawaiian or other Pacific Islander, non-Hispanic/Latino), 10 international. Average age 33. 293 applicants, 89% accepted, 145 enrolled. In 2010, 106 master's awarded. *Entrance requirements:* For master's, MAT, GRE, or GMAT. Additional exam requirements/recommendations for international students: Required—

TOEFL (minimum score 550 paper-based; 213 computer-based). *Application deadline:* For fall admission, 9/1 for domestic students; for winter admission, 12/1 for domestic students; for spring admission, 2/15 for domestic students. Application fee: $40. *Financial support:* Career-related internships or fieldwork and health care benefits available. Support available to part-time students. *Unit head:* Dr. Alan Gorr, Director, 630-829-6566, Fax: 630-960-1126, E-mail: agorr@ben.edu. *Application contact:* Kari Gibbons, Director, Admissions, 630-829-6200, Fax: 630-829-6584, E-mail: kgibbons@ben.edu.

Boston University, School of Medicine, Division of Graduate Medical Sciences, Program in Healthcare Emergency Management, Boston, MA 02215. Offers MS. *Faculty:* 3 full-time (0 women), 4 part-time/adjunct (2 women). *Students:* 5 full-time (2 women), 11 part-time (3 women); includes 4 Black or African American, non-Hispanic/Latino; 1 Asian, non-Hispanic/Latino. 16 applicants, 100% accepted, 12 enrolled. In 2010, 3 master's awarded. *Entrance requirements:* For master's, GRE. Additional exam requirements/recommendations for international students: Required—TOEFL. *Application deadline:* Applications are processed on a rolling basis. Application fee: $75. Electronic applications accepted. *Expenses:* Tuition: Full-time $39,314; part-time $1228 per credit. Required fees: $40 per semester. *Financial support:* Applicants required to submit FAFSA. *Unit head:* Dr. Kevin Thomas, Director, 617-414-2316, Fax: 617-414-2332, E-mail: kipthoma@bu.edu. *Application contact:* Patricia Jones, Program Manager and Admissions Director, 617-414-2315, E-mail: psterlin@bu.edu.

California State University, Long Beach, Graduate Studies, College of Health and Human Services, Department of Criminal Justice, Long Beach, CA 90840. Offers criminal justice (MS); emergency services administration (MS). Part-time programs available. *Faculty:* 5 full-time (1 woman), 2 part-time/adjunct (0 women). *Students:* 17 full-time (11 women), 11 part-time (8 women); includes 2 Black or African American, non-Hispanic/Latino; 5 Asian, non-Hispanic/Latino; 4 Hispanic/Latino, 4 international. Average age 26. 66 applicants, 35% accepted, 12 enrolled. In 2010, 50 master's awarded. *Degree requirements:* For master's, comprehensive course or thesis. *Entrance requirements:* For master's, minimum GPA of 3.0. *Application deadline:* For fall admission, 5/1 for domestic students. Applications are processed on a rolling basis. Application fee: $55. Electronic applications accepted. *Financial support:* Federal Work-Study, institutionally sponsored loans, and scholarships/grants available. Financial award application deadline: 3/2. *Unit head:* Dr. Henry F. Fradella, Chair, 562-985-2669, Fax: 562-985-8086, E-mail: hfradell@csulb.edu. *Application contact:* Dr. Connie Estrada Ireland, Graduate Advisor, 562-985-8711, Fax: 562-985-8086, E-mail: cireland@csulb.edu.

Capella University, School of Public Service Leadership, Minneapolis, MN 55402. Offers criminal justice (MS, PhD); emergency management (MS, PhD); general human services (MS, PhD); general public administration (MPA, DPA); gerontology (MS); health care administration (MS, PhD); health management and policy (MSPH); management of nonprofit agencies (MS, PhD); nurse educator (MS); public safety leadership (MS, PhD); social and community services (MS, PhD); social behavioral sciences (MSPH). *Expenses:* Tuition: Full-time $11,880; part-time $440 per credit hour.

Drexel University, College of Nursing and Health Professions, Emergency and Public Safety Services Program, Philadelphia, PA 19104-2875. Offers MS. Part-time and evening/weekend programs available. *Degree requirements:* For master's, comprehensive exam. *Entrance requirements:* For master's, GRE General Test, minimum GPA of 2.75.

Florida Institute of Technology, Graduate Programs, Extended Studies Division, Melbourne, FL 32901-6975. Offers acquisition and contract management (MS); aerospace engineering (MS); business administration (MBA); computer information systems (MS); computer science (MS); electrical engineering (MS); engineering management (MS); human resources management (MS); logistics management (MS), including humanitarian and disaster relief logistics; management (MS), including acquisition and contract management, e-business, human resources management, information systems, logistics management, management, transportation management; material acquisition management (MS); mechanical engineering (MS); operations research (MS); project management (MS), including information systems, operations research; public administration (MPA); quality management (MS); software engineering (MS); space systems (MS); space systems management (MS); systems management (MS), including information systems, operations research. Part-time and evening/weekend programs available. Postbaccalaureate distance learning degree programs offered (no on-campus study). *Faculty:* 11 full-time (3 women), 118 part-time/adjunct (24 women). *Students:* 69 full-time (23 women), 907 part-time (369 women); includes 385 minority (242 Black or African American, non-Hispanic/Latino; 15 American Indian or Alaska Native, non-Hispanic/Latino; 44 Asian, non-Hispanic/Latino; 52 Hispanic/Latino; 3 Native Hawaiian or other Pacific Islander, non-Hispanic/Latino; 29 Two or more races, non-Hispanic/Latino), 17 international. 517 applicants, 49% accepted, 245 enrolled. In 2010, 430 degrees awarded. *Degree requirements:* For master's, comprehensive exam (for some programs), capstone course. *Entrance requirements:* For master's, GMAT or resume showing 8 years of supervised experience, minimum GPA of 3.0, 2 letters of recommendation, resume. Additional exam requirements/recommendations for international students: Required—TOEFL (minimum score 550 paper-based; 213 computer-based; 79 iBT). *Application deadline:* For fall admission, 4/1 for international students; for spring admission, 9/30 for international students. Applications are processed on a rolling basis. Application fee: $50. Electronic applications accepted. *Expenses:* Contact institution. *Financial support:* Application deadline: 3/1. *Unit head:* Dr. Theodore Richardson, Senior Associate Dean, 321-674-8123, Fax: 321-674-7597, E-mail: trichardson@fit.edu. *Application contact:* Carolyn Farrior, Director of Graduate Admissions, Online Learning and Off-Campus Programs, 321-674-7118, Fax: 321-674-8216, E-mail: cfarrior@fit.edu.

Fordham University, Graduate School of Arts and Sciences, Program in International Humanitarian Action, New York, NY 10458. Offers MA. Program offered in collaboration with the Institute for International Humanitarian Affairs (IIHA). *Entrance requirements:* For master's, official transcripts, 3 letters of recommendation, resume, statement of interest. Electronic applications accepted.

George Mason University, College of Humanities and Social Sciences, Department of Public and International Affairs, Fairfax, VA 22030. Offers association management (Certificate); biodefense (MS, PhD); emergency management and homeland security (Certificate); nonprofit management (Certificate); political science (MA, PhD); public administration (MPA); public management (Certificate). *Accreditation:* NASPAA (one or more programs are accredited). *Faculty:* 38 full-time (14 women), 31 part-time/adjunct (8 women). *Students:* 134 full-time (76 women), 319 part-time (176 women); includes 63 minority (29 Black or African American, non-Hispanic/Latino; 9 Asian, non-Hispanic/Latino; 21 Hispanic/Latino; 1 Native Hawaiian or other Pacific Islander, non-Hispanic/Latino; 3 Two or more races, non-Hispanic/Latino), 16 international. Average age 31. 574 applicants, 58% accepted, 144 enrolled. In 2010, 140 master's, 3 doctorates, 11 other advanced degrees awarded. *Entrance requirements:* For master's, GRE General Test, minimum GPA of 3.0 in last 60 hours of course work. Additional exam requirements/recommendations for international students: Required—TOEFL (minimum score 570 paper-based; 230 computer-based; 88 iBT). *Application deadline:* For fall admission, 3/1 priority date for domestic students; for spring admission, 10/15 for domestic students. Application fee: $100. Electronic applications accepted. *Expenses:* Tuition, state resident: full-time $8192; part-time $440 per credit hour. Tuition, nonresident: full-time $22,952; part-time $1055 per credit hour. Required fees: $2364; $99 per credit hour. *Financial support:* In 2010–11, 30 students received support, including 3 fellowships with full tuition reimbursements available (averaging $18,000 per year), 10 research assistantships with full and partial tuition reimbursements available (averaging $12,271 per year), 18 teaching assistantships with full and partial tuition reimbursements available (averaging $10,428 per year); career-related internships or fieldwork, Federal Work-Study, scholarships/grants, unspecified assistantships, and health care benefits (full-time research or teaching assistantship recipients) also available. Financial award application deadline: 3/1; financial award applicants required to submit FAFSA. *Faculty research:* The Rehnquist Court and economic liberties; intersection of economic development with high-tech industry, telecommunications, and entrepreneurism; political economy of development; violence, terrorism and U. S. foreign policy; international security issues. Total annual research expenditures: $696,997. *Unit head:* Dr. Priscilla Regan, Chair, 703-993-1419, Fax: 703-993-1399, E-mail: pregan@gmu.edu. *Application contact:* Peg Koback, Information Contact, 703-993-9466, E-mail: mkoback@gmu.edu.

The George Washington University, School of Medicine and Health Sciences, Health Sciences Programs, Washington, DC 20052. Offers adult nurse practitioner (MSN, Post Master's Certificate); clinical practice management (MSHS); clinical research administration (MSHS); clinical research administration for nurses (MSN); emergency services management (MSHS); end-of-life care (MSHS, MSN); family nurse practitioner (MSN, Post Master's Certificate); immunohematology (MSHS); nursing (DNP); nursing leadership and management (MSN); physical therapy (DPT); physician assistant (MSHS); MSHS/MPH. Postbaccalaureate distance learning degree programs offered (no on-campus study). *Students:* 252 full-time (194 women), 328 part-time (238 women); includes 66 Black or African American, non-Hispanic/Latino; 4 American Indian or Alaska Native, non-Hispanic/Latino; 42 Asian, non-Hispanic/Latino; 24 Hispanic/Latino; 6 Native Hawaiian or other Pacific Islander, non-Hispanic/Latino, 38 international. Average age 32. 1,127 applicants, 49% accepted, 218 enrolled. In 2010, 171 master's, 52 doctorates, 71 other advanced degrees awarded. *Entrance requirements:* Additional exam requirements/recommendations for international students: Required—TOEFL (minimum score 550 paper-based; 213 computer-based). *Application deadline:* Applications are processed on a rolling basis. Application fee: $75. *Expenses:* Contact institution. *Unit head:* Jean E. Johnson, Senior Associate Dean, 202-994-3725, E-mail: jejohns@gwu.edu. *Application contact:* Joke Ogundiran, Director of Admission, 202-994-1668, Fax: 202-994-0870, E-mail: jokeogun@gwu.edu.

Georgia State University, Andrew Young School of Policy Studies, Department of Public Management and Policy, Atlanta, GA 30303. Offers disaster management (Certificate); nonprofit management (Certificate); planning and economic development (Certificate); public administration (MPA), including criminal justice, management and finance, nonprofit management, planning and economic development, policy analysis and evaluation, public health; public policy (MPP, PhD), including disaster policy (MPP), nonprofit policy (MPP), planning and economic development policy (MPP), public finance policy (MPP), social policy (MPP); JD/MPA. *Accreditation:* NASPAA (one or more programs are accredited). Part-time and evening/weekend programs available. Terminal master's awarded for partial completion of doctoral program. *Degree requirements:* For master's, thesis optional; for doctorate, comprehensive exam, thesis/dissertation. *Entrance requirements:* For master's and doctorate, GRE General Test. Additional exam requirements/recommendations for international students: Required—TOEFL. Electronic applications accepted. *Faculty research:* Public management, policy analysis, public finance, planning and economic development, nonprofit leadership and policy.

Grand Canyon University, College of Business, Phoenix, AZ 85017-1097. Offers accounting (MBA); corporate business administration (MBA); disaster preparedness and crisis management (MBA); executive fire service leadership (MS); finance (MBA); general management (MBA); government and policy (MPA); health care management (MPA); health systems management (MBA); human resource management (MBA); innovation (MBA); leadership (MBA, MS); management of information system (MBA); marketing (MBA); project-based (MBA); six sigma (MBA); strategic human resource management (MBA). *Accreditation:* ACBSP. Part-time and evening/weekend programs available. Postbaccalaureate distance learning degree programs offered (no on-campus study). *Faculty:* 8 full-time (3 women), 147 part-time/adjunct (49 women). *Students:* 1 full-time (0 women), 2,121 part-time (1,165 women); includes 341 minority (249 Black or African American, non-Hispanic/Latino; 17 American Indian or Alaska Native, non-Hispanic/Latino; 15 Asian, non-Hispanic/Latino; 29 Hispanic/Latino; 4 Native Hawaiian or other Pacific Islander, non-Hispanic/Latino; 27 Two or more races, non-Hispanic/Latino), 20 international. Average age 38. In 2010, 569 master's awarded. *Entrance requirements:* For master's, equivalent of two years full-time professional work experience. Additional exam requirements/recommendations for international students: Required—TOEFL (minimum score 575 paper-based; 233 computer-based; 90 iBT), IELTS (minimum score 7). *Application deadline:* For fall admission, 8/21 for domestic students, 7/2 for international students; for spring admission, 12/24 for domestic students, 11/1 for international students. Applications are processed on a rolling basis. Application fee: $0. Electronic applications accepted. *Financial support:* Federal Work-Study available. Support available to part-time students. Financial award applicants required to submit FAFSA. *Unit head:* Kim Donaldson, Dean, 602-639-6597, E-mail: kdonaldson@gcu.edu. *Application contact:* Matt Tidwell, Enrollment Manager, 602-639-6020, E-mail: mtidwell@gcu.edu.

Indiana University of Pennsylvania, School of Graduate Studies and Research, College of Natural Sciences and Mathematics, Science for Disaster Response Program, Indiana, PA 15705-1087. Offers MS. *Students:* 2 full-time (1 woman), 3 part-time (0 women). Average age 34. In 2010, 1 master's awarded. Application fee: $40. *Unit head:* Dr. Roberta Eddy, Director, 724-357-4482, E-mail: roberta.eddy@iup.edu. *Application contact:* Dr. Jacqueline Gorman, Dean's Associate, 724-357-2609, E-mail: jgorman@iup.edu.

Jacksonville State University, College of Graduate Studies and Continuing Education, College of Arts and Sciences, Institute for Emergency Preparedness, Jacksonville, AL 36265-1602. Offers emergency management (MS, D Sc). Part-time and evening/weekend programs available. *Degree requirements:* For master's, comprehensive exam, thesis (for some programs). Electronic applications accepted.

The Johns Hopkins University, School of Nursing, Nurse Practitioner Program, Baltimore, MD 21218-2699. Offers adult acute/critical care (MSN, Certificate); adult and pediatric primary care (MSN); adult or pediatric primary care (Certificate); emergency preparedness/disaster response (Certificate); family primary care (MSN, Certificate); women's health (Certificate). *Accreditation:* AACN; NLN (one or more programs are accredited). Part-time programs available. *Faculty:* 9 full-time (all women), 10 part-time/adjunct (all women). *Students:* 42 full-time (40 women), 91 part-time (87 women); includes 47 minority (15 Black or African American, non-Hispanic/Latino; 15 Asian, non-Hispanic/Latino; 8 Hispanic/Latino; 2 Native Hawaiian or other Pacific Islander, non-Hispanic/Latino; 7 Two or more races, non-Hispanic/Latino), 3 international. Average age 30. 232 applicants, 83% accepted, 29 enrolled. In 2010, 5 master's, 2 other advanced degrees awarded. *Degree requirements:* For master's, thesis optional, scholarly project or portfolio. *Entrance requirements:* For master's, GRE, interview, minimum GPA of 3.0, BSN, Maryland RN license. Additional exam requirements/recommendations for international students: Required—TOEFL (minimum score 550 paper-based; 213 computer-based). *Application deadline:* For fall admission, 3/1 priority date for domestic and international students; for spring admission, 7/1 priority date for domestic and international students. Application fee: $75. Electronic applications accepted. *Expenses:* Contact institution. *Financial support:* In 2010–11, 25 students received support. Federal Work-Study, scholarships/grants, traineeships, and tuition waivers (partial) available. Support available to part-time students. Financial award application deadline: 3/1; financial award applicants required to submit FAFSA. *Faculty research:* Community outreach, primary care of underserved populations, substance-abusing individuals, childhood violence, women's health. *Unit head:* Dr. Julie A. Stanik-Hutt, Director, Master's Programs, 410-502-0184, Fax: 410-955-7463, E-mail: jstanik1@son.jhmi.edu. *Application contact:* Mary O'Rourke, Director of Admissions/Student Services, 410-955-7548, Fax: 410-614-7086, E-mail: orourke@son.jhmi.edu.

Lynn University, College of Liberal Education, Boca Raton, FL 33431-5598. Offers applied psychology (MS); criminal justice administration (MS); emergency planning and administration (MS, Certificate). Part-time and evening/weekend programs available. Postbaccalaureate distance learning degree programs offered. *Entrance requirements:* For master's, GRE, resume, 2 letters of recommendation, minimum undergraduate GPA of 3.0. Additional exam requirements/recommendations for international students: Required—TOEFL (minimum score 550 paper-based; 213 computer-based). *Faculty research:* Terrorism, criminological theory, corrections, emergency planning.

Emergency Management

Massachusetts Maritime Academy, Program in Emergency Management, Buzzards Bay, MA 02532-1803. Offers MS.

Millersville University of Pennsylvania, College of Graduate and Professional Studies, School of Humanities and Social Sciences, Center for Disaster Research and Education, Program in Emergency Management, Millersville, PA 17551-0302. Offers MS. Part-time and evening/weekend programs available. Postbaccalaureate distance learning degree programs offered (no on-campus study). *Faculty:* 6 full-time (4 women), 2 part-time/adjunct (1 woman). *Students:* 5 full-time (1 woman), 32 part-time (19 women); includes 1 Black or African American, non-Hispanic/Latino; 1 Asian, non-Hispanic/Latino; 1 Hispanic/Latino, 1 international. Average age 31. 21 applicants, 86% accepted, 14 enrolled. In 2010, 11 master's awarded. *Entrance requirements:* For master's, GRE or MAT (if GPA less than 2.75), 3 letters of recommendation, interview (by telephone), resume. Additional exam requirements/recommendations for international students: Required—TOEFL (minimum score 500 paper-based; 183 computer-based; 65 iBT) or IELTS (minimum score 6). *Application deadline:* For fall admission, 1/15 priority date for domestic and international students; for winter admission, 10/1 priority date for domestic and international students; for spring admission, 10/1 priority date for domestic and international students. Applications are processed on a rolling basis. Application fee: $40 ($50 for international students). Electronic applications accepted. *Expenses:* Tuition, state resident: full-time $6966; part-time $387 per credit. Tuition, nonresident: full-time $11,146; part-time $619 per credit. Required fees: $1829.50; $88 per credit. One-time fee: $60 part-time. Tuition and fees vary according to course load. *Financial support:* In 2010–11, 4 students received support, including 4 research assistantships with full tuition reimbursements available (averaging $5,220 per year); institutionally sponsored loans and unspecified assistantships also available. Support available to part-time students. Financial award application deadline: 3/15; financial award applicants required to submit FAFSA. *Unit head:* Dr. Sepideh Yalda, Coordinator, 717-872-3293, E-mail: syalda@millersville.edu. *Application contact:* Dr. Victor S. DeSantis, Dean of Graduate and Professional Studies, 717-872-3099, Fax: 717-872-3453, E-mail: victor.desantis@millersville.edu.

New Jersey Institute of Technology, Office of Graduate Studies, College of Computing Science, Program in Information Systems, Newark, NJ 07102. Offers business and information systems (MS); emergency management and business continuity (MS); information systems (MS, PhD). Part-time and evening/weekend programs available. *Students:* 86 full-time (26 women), 109 part-time (26 women); includes 23 Black or African American, non-Hispanic/Latino; 30 Asian, non-Hispanic/Latino; 14 Hispanic/Latino, 53 international. Average age 31. 275 applicants, 55% accepted, 69 enrolled. In 2010, 94 master's, 6 doctorates awarded. Terminal master's awarded for partial completion of doctoral program. *Degree requirements:* For master's, thesis optional; for doctorate, thesis/dissertation. *Entrance requirements:* For master's, GRE General Test; for doctorate, GRE General Test, minimum graduate GPA of 3.5. Additional exam requirements/recommendations for international students: Required—TOEFL (minimum score 550 paper-based; 213 computer-based; 79 iBT). *Application deadline:* For fall admission, 6/5 priority date for domestic students, 4/1 for international students; for spring admission, 11/15 for domestic and international students. Applications are processed on a rolling basis. Application fee: $65. Electronic applications accepted. *Expenses:* Tuition, state resident: full-time $14,724; part-time $818 per credit. Tuition, nonresident: full-time $20,304; part-time $1128 per credit. Required fees: $2272; $209 per credit. $103 per semester. One-time fee: $312 full-time; $212 part-time. *Financial support:* Fellowships with full and partial tuition reimbursements, research assistantships with full and partial tuition reimbursements, teaching assistantships with full and partial tuition reimbursements, career-related internships or fieldwork, Federal Work-Study, institutionally sponsored loans, and unspecified assistantships available. Financial award application deadline: 3/15. *Unit head:* Dr. Michael P. Bieber, Associate Chair, 973-596-2681, Fax: 973-596-2986, E-mail: michael.p.bieber@njit.edu. *Application contact:* Kathryn Kelly, Director of Admissions, 973-596-3300, Fax: 973-596-3461, E-mail: admissions@njit.edu.

New York Medical College, School of Health Sciences and Practice, Department of Health Policy and Management, Program in Emergency Preparedness, Valhalla, NY 10595-1691. Offers Graduate Certificate. Program offered in conjunction with NYMCs Center for Disaster Medicine. Electronic applications accepted.

North Dakota State University, College of Graduate and Interdisciplinary Studies, College of Arts, Humanities and Social Sciences, Department of Sociology, Anthropology, and Emergency Management, Fargo, ND 58108. Offers emergency management (MS, PhD); social science (MA, MS); sociology (MS). Part-time programs available. *Faculty:* 8 full-time (3 women), 5 part-time/adjunct (2 women). *Students:* 27 full-time (14 women), 14 part-time (4 women); includes 2 Black or African American, non-Hispanic/Latino; 1 American Indian or Alaska Native, non-Hispanic/Latino; 1 Asian, non-Hispanic/Latino; 1 Hispanic/Latino, 2 international. Average age 27. 15 applicants, 60% accepted, 7 enrolled. In 2010, 9 master's awarded. *Degree requirements:* For master's, thesis; for doctorate, comprehensive exam, thesis/dissertation. *Entrance requirements:* For master's, GRE (emergency management), course work in sociology, minimum GPA of 3.2; for doctorate, GRE, minimum GPA of 3.2. Additional exam requirements/recommendations for international students: Required—TOEFL. *Application deadline:* For fall admission, 4/1 priority date for domestic students. Applications are processed on a rolling basis. Application fee: $45 ($60 for international students). *Financial support:* In 2010–11, 7 research assistantships with full tuition reimbursements (averaging $6,156 per year), 7 teaching assistantships with full tuition reimbursements (averaging $3,078 per year) were awarded; fellowships, career-related internships or fieldwork, Federal Work-Study, institutionally sponsored loans, and tuition waivers (full) also available. Support available to part-time students. Financial award application deadline: 4/15. *Faculty research:* Medical sociology, demography, ethnology, archaeology. Total annual research expenditures: $75,000. *Unit head:* Dr. Daniel J. Klenow, Chair, 701-231-8657, Fax: 701-231-1047, E-mail: daniel.klenow@ndsu.edu. *Application contact:* Dr. Daniel J. Klenow, Chair, 701-231-8657, Fax: 701-231-1047, E-mail: daniel.klenow@ndsu.edu.

Oklahoma State University, College of Arts and Sciences, Department of Political Science, Stillwater, OK 74078. Offers fire and emergency management administration (MS, PhD); political science (MA). *Faculty:* 18 full-time (7 women), 7 part-time/adjunct (0 women). *Students:* 46 full-time (11 women), 86 part-time (20 women); includes 5 Black or African American, non-Hispanic/Latino; 5 American Indian or Alaska Native, non-Hispanic/Latino; 5 Hispanic/Latino, 24 international. Average age 35. 106 applicants, 45% accepted, 31 enrolled. In 2010, 23 master's awarded. *Degree requirements:* For master's, comprehensive exam, thesis or creative component; for doctorate, comprehensive exam, thesis/dissertation. *Entrance requirements:* For master's, GRE; for doctorate, GRE. Additional exam requirements/recommendations for international students: Required—TOEFL (minimum score 550 paper-based; 79 iBT). *Application deadline:* For fall admission, 3/1 priority date for international students; for spring admission, 8/1 priority date for international students. Applications are processed on a rolling basis. Application fee: $40 ($75 for international students). Electronic applications accepted. *Expenses:* Tuition, state resident: full-time $3716; part-time $154.85 per credit hour. Tuition, nonresident: full-time $14,892; part-time $621 per credit hour. Required fees: $2044; $85.20 per credit hour. One-time fee: $50. Tuition and fees vary according to course load and campus/location. *Financial support:* In 2010–11, 7 research assistantships (averaging $11,416 per year), 14 teaching assistantships (averaging $7,891 per year) were awarded; career-related internships or fieldwork, Federal Work-Study, scholarships/grants, health care benefits, tuition waivers (partial), and unspecified assistantships also available. Support available to part-time students. Financial award application deadline: 3/1; financial award applicants required to submit FAFSA. *Faculty research:* Fire and emergency management, environmental dispute resolution, voting and elections, women and politics, urban politics. *Unit head:* Dr. James Scott, Head, 405-744-5569, Fax: 405-744-6534. *Application contact:* Dr. Gordon Emslie, Dean, 405-744-6368, Fax: 405-744-0355, E-mail: grad-i@okstate.edu.

Park University, College of Graduate and Professional Studies, Kansas City, MO 54105. Offers adult education (M Ed); at-risk students (M Ed); disaster and emergency management (MPA); educational administration (M Ed); entrepreneurship (MBA); general business (MBA); general education (M Ed); government/business relations (MPA); healthcare/services management (MBA, MPA); international business (MBA); K-12 certification (MAT); management information systems (MBA); management of information systems (MPA); middle school certification (MAT); multi-cultural education (M Ed); nonprofit management (MPA); public management (MPA); school law (M Ed); secondary school certification (MAT); special education (M Ed). Part-time and evening/weekend programs available. Postbaccalaureate distance learning degree programs offered (no on-campus study). *Degree requirements:* For master's, comprehensive exam, thesis (for some programs). *Entrance requirements:* For master's, GRE, GMAT, teacher certification (M Ed). Additional exam requirements/recommendations for international students: Required—TOEFL (minimum score 550 paper-based). Electronic applications accepted. *Faculty research:* Literacy, leadership, brain based research, multicultural education, diversity.

Philadelphia University, School of Science and Health, Program in Disaster Medicine and Management, Philadelphia, PA 19144. Offers MS. Postbaccalaureate distance learning degree programs offered (minimal on-campus study).

Royal Roads University, Graduate Studies, Peace and Conflict Studies Program, Victoria, BC V9B 5Y2, Canada. Offers conflict analysis (G Dip); conflict analysis and management (MA); disaster and emergency management (MA); human security and peacebuilding (MA). Postbaccalaureate distance learning degree programs offered (minimal on-campus study). *Degree requirements:* For master's, thesis. *Entrance requirements:* For master's, 5-7 years of related work experience. Additional exam requirements/recommendations for international students: Required—TOEFL (paper-based 570; computer-based 233) or IELTS (paper-based 7) (recommended). Electronic applications accepted. *Faculty research:* Conflict analysis, ethno-political conflict reconciliation, international relations, displaced persons.

San Diego State University, Graduate and Research Affairs, College of Health and Human Services, Graduate School of Public Health, San Diego, CA 92182. Offers environmental health (MPH); epidemiology (MPH, PhD), including biostatistics (MPH); global emergency preparedness and response (MS); global health (PhD); health behavior (PhD); health promotion (MPH); health services administration (MPH); toxicology (MS); MPH/MA; MSW/MPH. *Accreditation:* ABET (one or more programs are accredited); CAHME (one or more programs are accredited); CEPH (one or more programs are accredited). Part-time programs available. *Degree requirements:* For master's, comprehensive exam (for some programs), thesis (for some programs); for doctorate, thesis/dissertation. *Entrance requirements:* For master's, GMAT (MPH in health services administration), GRE General Test; for doctorate, GRE General Test. Additional exam requirements/recommendations for international students: Required—TOEFL. *Faculty research:* Evaluation of tobacco, AIDS prevalence and prevention, mammography, infant death project, Alzheimer's in elderly Chinese.

TUI University, College of Health Sciences, Program in Health Sciences, Cypress, CA 90630. Offers clinical research administration (MS, Certificate); emergency and disaster management (MS, Certificate); environmental health science (Certificate); health care administration (PhD); health care management (MS), including health informatics; health education (MS, Certificate); health informatics (Certificate); health sciences (PhD); international health (MS); international health: educator or researcher option (PhD); international health: practitioner option (PhD); law and expert witness studies (MS, Certificate); public health (MS); quality assurance (Certificate). Part-time and evening/weekend programs available. Postbaccalaureate distance learning degree programs offered (no on-campus study). *Students:* 322 full-time (170 women), 709 part-time (357 women). 227 applicants, 80% accepted, 164 enrolled. In 2010, 366 master's, 29 doctorates awarded. *Degree requirements:* For doctorate, comprehensive exam, thesis/dissertation, defense of dissertation. *Entrance requirements:* For master's, minimum GPA of 2.5 (students with GPA 3.0 or greater may transfer up to 30% of graduate level credits); for doctorate, minimum GPA of 3.4, curriculum vitae, course work in research methods or statistics. Additional exam requirements/recommendations for international students: Required—TOEFL. *Application deadline:* For fall admission, 10/3 for domestic and international students; for winter admission, 12/22 for domestic and international students; for spring admission, 4/3 for domestic and international students. Applications are processed on a rolling basis. Application fee: $75. Electronic applications accepted. *Expenses:* Tuition: Full-time $11,040; part-time $345 per semester hour. *Unit head:* Dr. Michaela Tanasescu, Dean, 714-816-0366, Fax: 714-226-9844, E-mail: infocoe@tuiu.edu. *Application contact:* Wei Ren-Finaly, Registrar, 800-375-9878, Fax: 714-827-7407, E-mail: registration@tuiu.edu.

Université de Montréal, Faculty of Medicine, Programs in Environment and Prevention, Montréal, QC H3C 3J7, Canada. Offers environment, health and disaster management (DESS). Electronic applications accepted. *Faculty research:* Health, environment, pollutants, protection, waste.

University of Central Florida, College of Health and Public Affairs, Department of Public Administration, Orlando, FL 32816. Offers emergency management and homeland security (Certificate); non-profit management (MNM, Certificate); public administration (MPA, Certificate); research administration (MS); urban and regional planning (Certificate). *Accreditation:* NASPAA. Part-time and evening/weekend programs available. *Faculty:* 14 full-time (5 women), 9 part-time/adjunct (3 women). *Students:* 103 full-time (70 women), 271 part-time (208 women); includes 125 minority (85 Black or African American, non-Hispanic/Latino; 1 American Indian or Alaska Native, non-Hispanic/Latino; 13 Asian, non-Hispanic/Latino; 22 Hispanic/Latino; 2 Native Hawaiian or other Pacific Islander, non-Hispanic/Latino; 2 Two or more races, non-Hispanic/Latino), 8 international. Average age 31. 258 applicants, 69% accepted, 138 enrolled. In 2010, 101 master's, 25 other advanced degrees awarded. *Degree requirements:* For master's, comprehensive exam, thesis or alternative, research report. *Entrance requirements:* For master's, GRE General Test. *Application deadline:* For fall admission, 7/1 for domestic students; for spring admission, 12/1 for domestic students. Application fee: $30. Electronic applications accepted. *Expenses:* Tuition, state resident: part-time $256.56 per credit hour. Tuition, nonresident: part-time $1011.52 per credit hour. Part-time tuition and fees vary according to program. *Financial support:* In 2010–11, 13 students received support, including 1 fellowship with partial tuition reimbursement available (averaging $10,000 per year), 11 research assistantships with partial tuition reimbursements available (averaging $5,900 per year), 2 teaching assistantships with partial tuition reimbursements available (averaging $7,100 per year); career-related internships or fieldwork, Federal Work-Study, institutionally sponsored loans, tuition waivers (partial), and unspecified assistantships also available. Financial award application deadline: 3/1; financial award applicants required to submit FAFSA. *Unit head:* Dr. Mary Ann Feldheim, Chair, 407-823-3693, Fax: 407-823-5651, E-mail: mfeldhei@mail.ucf.edu. *Application contact:* Dr. Mary Ann Feldheim, Chair, 407-823-3693, Fax: 407-823-5651, E-mail: mfeldhei@mail.ucf.edu.

University of Colorado Denver, School of Public Affairs, Department of Criminology and Criminal Justice, Denver, CO 80217. Offers criminal justice (MCJ), including criminal justice, domestic violence, emergency management and homeland security. Part-time and evening/weekend programs available. *Faculty:* 7 full-time (4 women), 3 part-time/adjunct (2 women). *Students:* 35 full-time (23 women), 26 part-time (20 women); includes 3 Black or African American, non-Hispanic/Latino; 2 American Indian or Alaska Native, non-Hispanic/Latino; 3 Asian, non-Hispanic/Latino; 11 Hispanic/Latino, 1 international. Average age 31. 45 applicants, 80% accepted, 15 enrolled. In 2010, 28 master's awarded. *Degree requirements:* For master's, thesis or alternative, 36-39 semester credit hours. *Entrance requirements:* For master's, GRE, recommendations, official transcripts, current resume. Additional exam requirements/recommendations for international students: Required—TOEFL (minimum score 525 paper-based; 197 computer-based). *Application deadline:* For fall admission, 3/15 priority date for domestic students; for spring admission, 10/15 priority date for domestic students. Application fee: $50 ($75 for international students). Electronic applications accepted. *Expenses:* Contact institution. *Financial support:* Federal Work-Study and scholarships/grants available. Support available to part-time students. Financial award application deadline: 4/1; financial award applicants required to submit FAFSA. *Faculty research:* White collar crime, women and the criminal justice system, applied family violence issues, intimate partner violence and domestic violence interventions, juvenile delinquency. *Unit head:* Dr. Mary Dodge, Director, 303-315-2086, Fax: 303-315-2229, E-mail: mary.dodge@ucdenver.edu. *Application contact:* Brendan Hardy, Criminal Justice Coordinator, 303-315-2227, Fax: 303-315-2229, E-mail: brendan.hardy@ucdenver.edu.

University of Colorado Denver, School of Public Affairs, Program in Public Affairs and Administration, Denver, CO 80127. Offers public administration (MPA), including domestic violence, emergency management and homeland security, environmental policy, management and law, homeland security and defense, local government, nonprofit management, public administration; public affairs (PhD). *Accreditation:* NASPAA. Part-time and evening/weekend programs available. Postbaccalaureate distance learning degree programs offered (no on-campus study). *Faculty:* 19 full-time (9 women), 14 part-time/adjunct (5 women). *Students:* 317 full-time (181 women), 167 part-time (100 women); includes 15 Black or African American, non-Hispanic/Latino; 2 American Indian or Alaska Native, non-Hispanic/Latino; 18 Asian, non-Hispanic/Latino; 29 Hispanic/Latino; 1 Two or more races, non-Hispanic/Latino, 36 international. Average age 30. 270 applicants, 66% accepted, 118 enrolled. In 2010, 119 master's, 4 doctorates awarded. *Degree requirements:* For master's, thesis or alternative, 36-39 credit hours; for doctorate, comprehensive exam, thesis/dissertation, minimum of 66 semester hours, including at least 30 hours of doctoral dissertation credits. *Entrance requirements:* For master's and doctorate, GRE, resume, essay, transcripts, recommendations. Additional exam requirements/recommendations for international students: Required—TOEFL (minimum score 550 paper-based; 223 computer-based). *Application deadline:* For fall admission, 2/1 for domestic students; for spring admission, 10/15 priority date for domestic students. Application fee: $50 ($75 for international students). Electronic applications accepted. *Expenses:* Contact institution. *Financial support:* Fellowships with partial tuition reimbursements, research assistantships with partial tuition reimbursements, teaching assistantships with partial tuition reimbursements, Federal Work-Study and scholarships/grants available. Support available to part-time students. Financial award application deadline: 4/1; financial award applicants required to submit FAFSA. *Faculty research:* Housing, education and the social and economic issues of vulnerable populations; nonprofit governance and management; education finance, effectiveness and reform; P-20 (preschool through graduate school) education initiatives; municipal government accountability. *Unit head:* Dr. Mary Guy, Program Director, 303-315-2007, Fax: 303-315-2229, E-mail: mary.guy@ucdenver.edu. *Application contact:* Annie Davies, Director of Marketing, Community Outreach and Alumni Affairs, 303-315-2896, Fax: 303-315-2229, E-mail: annie.davies@ucdenver.edu.

University of Denver, University College, Denver, CO 80208. Offers arts and culture (MLS, Certificate), including art, literature, and culture, arts development and program management (Certificate), creative writing; environmental policy and management (MAS, Certificate), including energy and sustainability (Certificate), environmental assessment of nuclear power (Certificate), environmental health and safety (Certificate), environmental management, natural resource management (Certificate); geographic information systems (MAS, Certificate); global affairs (MLS, Certificate), including translation studies, world history and culture; healthcare leadership (MPH, Certificate), including healthcare policy, law, and ethics, medical and healthcare information technologies, strategic management of healthcare; information and communications technology (MCIS, Certificate), including database design and administration (Certificate), geographic information systems (MCIS), information security systems security (Certificate), information systems security (MCIS), project management (MCIS, MPS, Certificate), software design and administration (Certificate), software design and programming (MCIS), technology management, telecommunications technology (MCIS), Web design and development; leadership and organizations (MPS, Certificate), including human capital in organizations, philanthropic leadership, project management (MCIS, MPS, Certificate), strategic innovation and change; organizational and professional communication (MPS, Certificate), including alternative dispute resolution, organizational communication, organizational development and training, public relations and marketing; security management (MAS, Certificate), including emergency planning and response, information security (MAS), organizational security; strategic human resource management (MPS, Certificate), including global human resources (MPS), human resource management and development (MPS). Part-time and evening/weekend programs available. Postbaccalaureate distance learning degree programs offered (no on-campus study). *Faculty:* 7 full-time (2 women), 212 part-time/adjunct (83 women). *Students:* 52 full-time (19 women), 1,044 part-time (625 women); includes 196 minority (81 Black or African American, non-Hispanic/Latino; 7 American Indian or Alaska Native, non-Hispanic/Latino; 30 Asian, non-Hispanic/Latino; 66 Hispanic/Latino; 3 Native Hawaiian or other Pacific Islander, non-Hispanic/Latino; 9 Two or more races, non-Hispanic/Latino), 76 international. Average age 36. 488 applicants, 91% accepted, 339 enrolled. In 2010, 286 master's, 130 other advanced degrees awarded. *Entrance requirements:* Additional exam requirements/recommendations for international students: Required—TOEFL (minimum score 550 paper-based; 80 iBT). *Application deadline:* For fall admission, 6/22 priority date for domestic students, 6/10 priority date for international students; for winter admission, 9/15 priority date for domestic students, 9/6 priority date for international students; for spring admission, 2/3 priority date for domestic students, 12/15 priority date for international students. Applications are processed on a rolling basis. Application fee: $75. Electronic applications accepted. *Expenses:* Contact institution. *Financial support:* Applicants required to submit FAFSA. *Unit head:* Dr. James Davis, Dean, 303-871-2291, Fax: 303-871-4047, E-mail: jdavis@du.edu. *Application contact:* Information Contact, 303-871-3155, Fax: 303-871-4047, E-mail: ucolinfo@du.edu.

University of Hawaii at Manoa, Graduate Division, College of Social Sciences, Department of Urban and Regional Planning, Program in Disaster Preparedness and Emergency Management, Honolulu, HI 96822. Offers Graduate Certificate. Part-time programs available. *Students:* 11 full-time (10 women), 3 part-time (2 women); includes 4 minority (1 Black or African American, non-Hispanic/Latino; 1 Asian, non-Hispanic/Latino; 1 Native Hawaiian or other Pacific Islander, non-Hispanic/Latino; 1 Two or more races, non-Hispanic/Latino), 7 international. Average age 31. 18 applicants, 83% accepted, 11 enrolled. In 2010, 7 Graduate Certificates awarded. *Entrance requirements:* Additional exam requirements/recommendations for international students: Required—TOEFL (minimum score 500 paper-based; 173 computer-based; 61 iBT), IELTS (minimum score 5). *Application deadline:* For fall admission, 3/1 for domestic and international students; for spring admission, 9/1 for domestic and international students. Application fee: $60. *Financial support:* In 2010–11, 1 fellowship (averaging $7,470 per year), 5 research assistantships (averaging $17,788 per year), 1 teaching assistantship (averaging $14,382 per year) were awarded. *Application contact:* Karl Kim, Graduate Chair, 808-956-7280, Fax: 808-956-6870, E-mail: karlk@hawaii.edu.

University of Medicine and Dentistry of New Jersey, UMDNJ–School of Public Health (UMDNJ, Rutgers, NJIT) Piscataway/New Brunswick Campus, Piscataway, NJ 08854. Offers biostatistics (MPH, MS, Dr PH, PhD); clinical epidemiology (Certificate); environmental and occupational health (MPH, Dr PH, PhD, Certificate); epidemiology (MPH, Dr PH, PhD); general public health (Certificate); health education and behavioral science (MPH, Dr PH, PhD); health systems and policy (MPH, PhD); public health preparedness (Certificate); DO/MPH; JD/MPH; MD/MPH; MPH/MBA; MPH/MSPA; MS/MPH; Psy D/MPH. *Accreditation:* CEPH. Part-time and evening/weekend programs available. *Degree requirements:* For master's, thesis, internship; for doctorate, comprehensive exam, thesis/dissertation. *Entrance requirements:* For master's, GRE General Test; for doctorate, GRE General Test, MPH (Dr PH); MA, MPH, or MS (PhD). Additional exam requirements/recommendations for international students: Required—TOEFL. *Application deadline:* For fall admission, 5/1 for domestic students; for spring admission, 10/1 for domestic students. Application fee: $115. Electronic applications accepted. *Unit head:* Tina Greco, Program Coordinator, 732-235-4646, Fax: 732-235-5476, E-mail: grecotm@umdnj.edu. *Application contact:* Janet Zamorski, Staff Assistant, 732-235-4646, E-mail: zamorsja@umdnj.edu.

University of Nevada, Las Vegas, Graduate College, Greenspun College of Urban Affairs, School of Environmental and Public Affairs, Las Vegas, NV 89154-4030. Offers crisis and emergency management (MS); environmental science (MS, PhD); non-profit management (Certificate); public administration (MPA); public affairs (PhD); public management (Certificate). Part-time programs available. *Faculty:* 6 full-time (2 women). *Students:* 55 full-time (27 women), 95 part-time (55 women); includes 63 minority (17 Black or African American, non-Hispanic/Latino; 2 American Indian or Alaska Native, non-Hispanic/Latino; 5 Asian, non-Hispanic/Latino; 20 Hispanic/Latino; 19 Two or more races, non-Hispanic/Latino), 8 international. Average age 35. 67 applicants, 72% accepted, 35 enrolled. In 2010, 61 master's, 2 doctorates, 24 other advanced degrees awarded. *Degree requirements:* For master's, comprehensive exam (for some programs), thesis; for doctorate, comprehensive exam (for some programs), thesis/dissertation. *Entrance requirements:* Additional exam requirements/recommendations for international students: Required—TOEFL (minimum score 550 paper-based; 213 computer-based; 80 iBT), IELTS (minimum score 7). *Application deadline:* For fall admission, 2/15 priority date for domestic and international students; for spring admission, 11/15 priority date for domestic and international students. Applications are processed on a rolling basis. Application fee: $60 ($95 for international students). Electronic applications accepted. *Expenses:* Tuition, area resident: Part-time $239.50 per credit. Tuition, state resident: part-time $239.50 per credit. Tuition, nonresident: part-time $503 per credit. Required fees: $108 per semester. Tuition and fees vary according to course load, program and reciprocity agreements. *Financial support:* In 2010–11, 9 students received support, including 6 research assistantships with partial tuition reimbursements available (averaging $13,850 per year), 3 teaching assistantships with partial tuition reimbursements available (averaging $10,666 per year); institutionally sponsored loans, scholarships/grants, health care benefits, and unspecified assistantships also available. Financial award application deadline: 3/1. *Faculty research:* Environmental decision-making and management; budgeting and human resource/workforce management; urban design, sustainability and governance; participatory simulation modeling of environmental issues; public and non-profit management. Total annual research expenditures: $1.1 million. *Unit head:* Dr. Ed Weber, Chair/Associate Professor, 702-895-4440, Fax: 702-895-4436, E-mail: edward.weber@unlv.edu. *Application contact:* Graduate College Admissions Evaluator, 702-895-3320, Fax: 702-895-4180, E-mail: gradcollege@unlv.edu.

University of New Haven, Graduate School, Henry C. Lee College of Criminal Justice and Forensic Sciences, Program in Fire Science, West Haven, CT 06516-1916. Offers emergency management (Certificate); fire administration (MS); fire science technology (Certificate); fire/arson investigation (MS, Certificate); forensic science/fire science (Certificate); public safety management (MS, Certificate). Part-time and evening/weekend programs available. *Students:* 3 full-time (0 women), 15 part-time (3 women); includes 1 Black or African American, non-Hispanic/Latino, 1 international. Average age 38. 6 applicants, 100% accepted, 4 enrolled. In 2010, 4 master's, 3 other advanced degrees awarded. *Degree requirements:* For master's, thesis or alternative. *Entrance requirements:* Additional exam requirements/recommendations for international students: Required—TOEFL (minimum score 520 paper-based; 190 computer-based; 70 iBT); Recommended—IELTS (minimum score 5.5). *Application deadline:* For fall admission, 5/31 for international students; for winter admission, 10/15 for international students; for spring admission, 1/15 for international students. Applications are processed on a rolling basis. Application fee: $50. Electronic applications accepted. *Financial support:* Research assistantships with partial tuition reimbursements, teaching assistantships with partial tuition reimbursements, career-related internships or fieldwork, Federal Work-Study, scholarships/grants, tuition waivers, and unspecified assistantships available. Support available to part-time students. Financial award applicants required to submit FAFSA. *Unit head:* Robert E. Massicotte, Director, 203-932-7424. *Application contact:* Eloise Gormley, Director of Graduate Admissions, 203-932-7449, Fax: 203-932-7137, E-mail: gradinfo@newhaven.edu.

The University of North Carolina at Charlotte, Graduate School, College of Arts and Sciences, Department of Political Science, Charlotte, NC 28223-0001. Offers emergency management (Certificate); non-profit management (Certificate); public administration (MPA, PhD), including arts administration (MPA), emergency management (MPA), non-profit management (MPA), public finance (MPA), urban management and policy (PhD); public finance (Certificate); public policy (PhD); urban management and policy (Certificate). *Accreditation:* NASPAA. Part-time and evening/weekend programs available. *Faculty:* 19 full-time (8 women), 3 part-time/adjunct (2 women). *Students:* 51 full-time (37 women), 75 part-time (49 women); includes 32 minority (26 Black or African American, non-Hispanic/Latino; 1 Asian, non-Hispanic/Latino; 2 Hispanic/Latino; 3 Two or more races, non-Hispanic/Latino), 11 international. Average age 29. 99 applicants, 72% accepted, 42 enrolled. In 2010, 15 master's, 5 doctorates awarded. *Degree requirements:* For master's, thesis or alternative; for doctorate, thesis/dissertation. *Entrance requirements:* For master's, GRE General Test or MAT, minimum GPA of 3.0 in undergraduate major, 2.75 overall. Additional exam requirements/recommendations for international students: Required—TOEFL (minimum score 557 paper-based; 220 computer-based; 83 iBT). *Application deadline:* For fall admission, 7/1 for domestic students, 5/1 for international students; for spring admission, 11/1 for domestic students, 10/1 for international students. Applications are processed on a rolling basis. Application fee: $55. Electronic applications accepted. *Expenses:* Tuition, state resident: full-time $3464. Tuition, nonresident: full-time $14,297. Required fees: $2094. Tuition and fees vary according to course load. *Financial support:* In 2010–11, 22 students received support, including 16 research assistantships (averaging $6,943 per year), 6 teaching assistantships (averaging $9,380 per year); career-related internships or fieldwork, Federal Work-Study, institutionally sponsored loans, scholarships/grants, unspecified assistantships, and administrative assistantship also available. Support available to part-time students. Financial award application deadline: 4/1; financial award applicants required to submit FAFSA. *Faculty research:* Terrorism, public administration, nonprofit and arts administration, educational policy, social policy. Total annual research expenditures: $242,404. *Unit head:* Dr. Theodore S. Arrington, Chair, 704-687-2571, Fax: 704-687-3497, E-mail: tarrngtn@uncc.edu. *Application contact:* Kathy B. Giddings, Director of Graduate Admissions, 704-687-5503, Fax: 704-687-3279, E-mail: gradadm@uncc.edu.

University of Rochester, School of Nursing, Rochester, NY 14642. Offers acute care nurse practitioner (MS); adult nurse practitioner (MS); adult psychiatric mental health nurse practitioner (MS); adult/geriatric nurse practitioner (MS); care of children and families/pediatric nurse practitioner (MS); care of children and families/pediatric nurse practitioner with pediatric behavioral health (MS); care of children and families/pediatric nurse practitioner/neonatal nurse practitioner (MS); child and adolescent psychiatric mental health nurse practitioner (MS); clinical nurse leader (MS); disaster response and emergency preparedness (MS); family nurse practitioner (MS); health care organization management and leadership (MS); health practice research (PhD); health promotion, education and technology (MS); nursing (Certificate). *Accreditation:* AACN; NLN (one or more programs are accredited). Part-time programs available. Postbaccalaureate distance learning degree programs offered (minimal on-campus study). Terminal master's awarded for partial completion of doctoral program. *Degree requirements:* For master's, comprehensive exam or thesis; for doctorate, thesis/dissertation. *Entrance requirements:* For master's, BS in nursing, minimum GPA of 3.0, course work in statistics; for doctorate, GRE General Test, MS in nursing, minimum GPA of 3.5; for Certificate, MS in nursing. Additional exam requirements/recommendations for international students: Recommended—TOEFL (minimum score 560 paper-based; 230 computer-based; 88 iBT). *Faculty research:* Clinical research in aging, managing asthma in children, interventions to improve outcomes in critically ill children and their mothers, nurse home visitation studies, medical device evaluation, critical care clinical studies, high risk behavior and prevention, palliative care, pregnancy-related weight gain.

Virginia Commonwealth University, Graduate School, College of Humanities and Sciences, Wilder School of Government and Public Affairs, Program in Homeland Security and Emergency Preparedness, Richmond, VA 23284-9005. Offers MA, Graduate Certificate. Postbaccalaureate distance learning degree programs offered. *Students:* 12 full-time (8 women), 23 part-time (12 women); includes 13 minority (12 Black or African American, non-Hispanic/Latino; 1 Asian, non-Hispanic/Latino). 35 applicants, 54% accepted, 13 enrolled. In 2010, 10 master's, 7 other advanced degrees awarded. *Entrance requirements:* For master's, GRE, GMAT, MAT or LSAT, minimum GPA of 2.7; for Graduate Certificate, minimum GPA of 2.7. Additional exam requirements/recommendations for international students: Required—TOEFL (minimum score

Emergency Management

Virginia Commonwealth University (continued)
600 paper-based; 250 computer-based; 100 iBT); Recommended—IELTS (minimum score 6.5). *Application deadline:* For fall admission, 7/15 for domestic students; for spring admission, 10/1 for domestic students. Application fee: $50. Electronic applications accepted. *Expenses:* Tuition, state resident: full-time $4308; part-time $479 per credit hour. Tuition, nonresident: full-time $8942; part-time $994 per credit hour. Required fees: $2000; $85 per credit hour. Tuition and fees vary according to course level, course load, degree level, campus/location and program. *Unit head:* Dr. John Aughenbaugh, Program Chair. *Application contact:* Lisbeth Dannenbrink, Student Contact, 804-828-6837, E-mail: lddannenbrin@vcu.edu.

Walden University, Graduate Programs, School of Counseling and Social Service, Minneapolis, MN 55401. Offers career counseling (MS); counselor education and supervision (PhD), including consultation, counseling and social change, forensic mental health counseling, general program, nonprofit management and leadership, trauma and crisis; human services (PhD), including clinical social work, counseling, criminal justice, disaster, crisis and intervention, family studies and intervention strategies, general program, human services administration, public health, self-designed, social policy analysis and planning; marriage, couple, and family counseling (MS), including forensic counseling, trauma and crisis counseling; mental health counseling (MS), including forensic counseling. Part-time and evening/weekend programs available. Postbaccalaureate distance learning degree programs offered (minimal on-campus study). *Faculty:* 25 full-time (17 women), 241 part-time/adjunct (162 women). *Students:* 2,687 full-time (2,269 women), 536 part-time (473 women); includes 1,582 minority (1,319 Black or African American, non-Hispanic/Latino; 34 American Indian or Alaska Native, non-Hispanic/Latino; 29 Asian, non-Hispanic/Latino; 142 Hispanic/Latino; 58 Two or more races, non-Hispanic/Latino), 47 international. Average age 38. In 2010, 182 master's, 8 doctorates awarded. *Degree requirements:* For master's, residency (for some programs); for doctorate, thesis/dissertation, residency. *Entrance requirements:* For master's, bachelor's degree or equivalent in related field, minimum GPA of 2.5; for doctorate, master's degree or equivalent in related field; minimum GPA of 3.0; official transcripts; three years' related professional/academic experience (preferred); access to computer and Internet. Additional exam requirements/recommendations for international students: Required—TOEFL (minimum score 550 paper-based; 213 computer-based), IELTS (minimum score 6.5), TOEFL (minimum score 550 paper-based; 213 computer-based), IELTS (minimum score 6.5), or Michigan English Language Assessment Battery (minimum score 82). *Application deadline:* Applications are processed on a rolling basis. Application fee: $50. Electronic applications accepted. *Expenses:* Tuition: Full-time $10,274; part-time $445 per credit. Tuition and fees vary according to course load, degree level and program. *Financial support:* Fellowships, Federal Work-Study, scholarships/grants, unspecified assistantships, and family tuition reduction, active duty/veteran tuition reduction, group tuition reduction, interest-free payment plans available. Support available to part-time students. Financial award applicants required to submit FAFSA. *Unit head:* Dr. Savitri Dixon-Saxon, Associate Dean, 800-925-3368. *Application contact:* Jennifer Hall, Vice President of Enrollment Management, 866-4-WALDEN, E-mail: info@waldenu.edu.

Walden University, Graduate Programs, School of Public Policy and Administration, Minneapolis, MN 55401. Offers criminal justice (MPA); emergency management (MPA); government management (Postbaccalaureate Certificate); health policy (MPA); homeland security policy (MPA); homeland security policy and coordination (MPA); interdisciplinary policy studies (MPA); international nongovernmental organizations (ngos) (MPA); law and public policy (MPA); local government management for sustainable communities (MPA); nonprofit management (Postbaccalaureate Certificate); nonprofit management and leadership (MPA, MS); policy analysis (MPA); public management and leadership (MPA); public policy and administration (MPA, PhD), including criminal justice (PhD), emergency management (PhD), health policy (PhD), health services (PhD), homeland security policy (PhD), homeland security policy and coordination (PhD), interdisciplinary policy studies (PhD), international nongovernmental organizations (PhD), law and public policy (PhD), local government management for sustainable communities (PhD), nonprofit management and leadership (PhD), policy analysis (PhD), public management and leadership (PhD), terrorism, mediation, and peace (PhD); terrorism, mediation, and peace (MPA). Part-time and evening/weekend programs available. Postbaccalaureate distance learning degree programs offered (minimal on-campus study). *Faculty:* 10 full-time (5 women), 117 part-time/adjunct (49 women). *Students:* 1,408 full-time (901 women), 599 part-time (392 women); includes 1,022 Black or African American, non-Hispanic/Latino; 11 American Indian or Alaska Native, non-Hispanic/Latino; 37 Asian, non-Hispanic/Latino; 64 Hispanic/Latino; 26 Two or more races, non-Hispanic/Latino, 47 international. Average age 40. In 2010, 311 master's, 23 doctorates awarded. *Degree requirements:* For doctorate, thesis/dissertation, residency. *Entrance requirements:* For master's, bachelor's degree or equivalent in related field, minimum GPA of 2.5; for doctorate, master's degree or equivalent in related field; minimum GPA of 3.0; official transcripts; three years of related professional/academic experience (preferred); access to computer and Internet. Additional exam requirements/recommendations for international students: Required—TOEFL (minimum score 550 paper-based; 213 computer-based), IELTS (minimum score 6.5), TOEFL (minimum score 550 paper-based; 213 computer-based), IELTS (minimum score 6.5), or Michigan English Language Assessment Battery (minimum score 82). *Application deadline:* Applications are processed on a rolling basis. Application fee: $50. Electronic applications accepted. *Expenses:* Tuition: Full-time $10,274; part-time $445 per credit. Tuition and fees vary according to course load, degree level and program. *Financial support:* Fellowships with tuition reimbursements, Federal Work-Study, scholarships/grants, unspecified assistantships, and family tuition reduction, active duty/veteran tuition reduction, group tuition reduction, interest-free payment plans available. Support available to part-time students. Financial award applicants required to submit FAFSA. *Unit head:* Dr. Mark Gordon, Associate Dean, 800-925-3368. *Application contact:* Jennifer Hall, Vice President of Enrollment Management, 866-4-WALDEN, E-mail: info@waldenu.edu.

West Chester University of Pennsylvania, Office of Graduate Studies, College of Health Sciences, Department of Health, West Chester, PA 19383. Offers emergency preparedness (Certificate); health care management (MPH, Certificate), including administration (MPH), community (MPH), environment (MPH), health care management (Certificate), integrative (MPH), nutrition (MPH); integrative health (Certificate); school health (M Ed). *Accreditation:* CEPH. Part-time and evening/weekend programs available. *Students:* 84 full-time (61 women), 97 part-time (75 women); includes 66 minority (53 Black or African American, non-Hispanic/Latino; 2 American Indian or Alaska Native, non-Hispanic/Latino; 9 Asian, non-Hispanic/Latino; 2 Hispanic/Latino), 20 international. Average age 30. 114 applicants, 81% accepted, 48 enrolled. In 2010, 57 master's, 9 other advanced degrees awarded. *Degree requirements:* For master's, thesis (for some programs), minimum GPA of 3.0. *Entrance requirements:* For master's, one-page statement of career objectives, two letters of reference. Additional exam requirements/recommendations for international students: Required—TOEFL (minimum score 550 paper-based; 213 computer-based; 80 iBT). *Application deadline:* For fall admission, 4/15 priority date for domestic students, 3/15 for international students; for spring admission, 10/15 for domestic students, 9/1 for international students. Applications are processed on a rolling basis. Application fee: $35. Electronic applications accepted. *Expenses:* Tuition, state resident: full-time $6966; part-time $387 per credit. Tuition, nonresident: full-time $11,146; part-time $619 per credit. Required fees: $1614.40; $133.24 per credit. Part-time tuition and fees vary according to campus/location. *Financial support:* Unspecified assistantships available. Support available to part-time students. Financial award application deadline: 2/15; financial award applicants required to submit FAFSA. *Faculty research:* Health school communities, community health issues and evidence-based programs, environment and health, nutrition and health, integrative health. *Unit head:* Dr. Bethann Cinelli, Chair, 610-436-2267, E-mail: bcinelli@wcupa.edu. *Application contact:* Dr. Lynn Carson, Graduate Coordinator, 610-436-2138, E-mail: lcarson@wcupa.edu.

York University, Faculty of Graduate Studies, Atkinson Faculty of Liberal and Professional Studies, Program in Disaster and Emergency Management, Toronto, ON M3J 1P3, Canada. Offers MA.

Homeland Security

American Public University System, AMU/APU Graduate Programs, Charles Town, WV 25414. Offers accounting (MBA); administration and supervision (M Ed); air warfare (MA Military Studies); asymmetrical warfare (MA Military Studies); criminal justice (MA); emergency and disaster management (MA); entrepreneurship (MBA); environmental policy and management (MS); finance (MBA); general (MBA); global business management (MBA); guidance and counseling (M Ed); history (MA); homeland security (MA); homeland security resource allocation (MBA); humanities (MA); information technology (MS); information technology management (MBA); intelligence studies (MA); international relations and conflict resolution (MA); joint warfare (MA Military Studies); land warfare (MA Military Studies); legal studies (MA); management (MA), including defense mangement, general, human resource management, organizational leadership, public administration; marketing (MBA); military history (MA); national security studies (MA); naval warfare (MA Military Studies); nonprofit management (MA); political science (MA); psychology (MA); public administration (MA); public health (MA); security management (MA); space studies (MS); sports management (MS); strategic leadership (MA Military Studies); teaching (M Ed), including elementary, secondary social sciences; transportation and logistics management (MA). Programs offered via distance learning only. Part-time and evening/weekend programs available. Postbaccalaureate distance learning degree programs offered (no on-campus study). *Faculty:* 253 full-time (134 women), 1,208 part-time/adjunct (570 women). *Students:* 956 full-time (422 women), 8,476 part-time (2,821 women); includes 2,511 minority (1,218 Black or African American, non-Hispanic/Latino; 68 American Indian or Alaska Native, non-Hispanic/Latino; 219 Asian, non-Hispanic/Latino; 705 Hispanic/Latino; 46 Native Hawaiian or other Pacific Islander, non-Hispanic/Latino; 255 Two or more races, non-Hispanic/Latino), 107 international. Average age 35. 9,550 applicants, 100% accepted. In 2010, 1,688 master's awarded. *Degree requirements:* For master's, comprehensive exam or practicum. *Entrance requirements:* For master's, official transcript showing earned bachelor's degree from institution accredited by recognized accrediting body. Additional exam requirements/recommendations for international students: Required—TOEFL (minimum score 550 paper-based; 213 computer-based), IELTS (minimum score 6.5). *Application deadline:* Applications are processed on a rolling basis. Application fee: $0. Electronic applications accepted. *Financial support:* Applicants required to submit FAFSA. *Faculty research:* Military history, criminal justice, management performance, national security. *Unit head:* Dr. Frank McCluskey, Provost, 877-468-6268, Fax: 304-724-3780. *Application contact:* Terry Grant, Director of Enrollment Management, 877-468-6268, Fax: 304-724-3780, E-mail: info@apus.edu.

Chaminade University of Honolulu, Graduate Services, Program in Criminal Justice Administration, Honolulu, HI 96816-1578. Offers criminal justice administration (MSCJA); homeland security (Certificate). Part-time and evening/weekend programs available. Postbaccalaureate distance learning degree programs offered (no on-campus study). *Degree requirements:* For master's, thesis optional. *Entrance requirements:* For master's, minimum undergraduate GPA of 3.0, 3 letters of recommendation. Additional exam requirements/recommendations for international students: Required—TOEFL (minimum score 550 paper-based). Electronic applications accepted. *Faculty research:* Penology, juvenile delinquency, multicultural and ethnic diversity in criminology, law enforcement administration and training, homeland security.

Drexel University, School of Technology and Professional Studies, Philadelphia, PA 19104-2875. Offers construction management (MS); engineering technology (MS); food science (MS); hospitality management (MS); professional studies: creativity studies (MS); professional studies: e-learning leadership (MS); professional studies: homeland security management (MS); project management (MS); property management (MS); sport management (MS). Postbaccalaureate distance learning degree programs offered.

Fairleigh Dickinson University, Metropolitan Campus, Anthony J. Petrocelli College of Continuing Studies, School of Administrative Science, Program in Homeland Security, Teaneck, NJ 07666-1914. Offers MSHS. *Students:* 9 full-time (3 women), 41 part-time (9 women). Average age 37. 19 applicants, 89% accepted, 13 enrolled. In 2010, 6 master's awarded. *Application deadline:* Applications are processed on a rolling basis. Application fee: $40. *Application contact:* Susan Brooman, University Director of Graduate Admissions, 201-692-2554, Fax: 201-692-2560, E-mail: globaleducation@fdu.edu.

George Mason University, College of Humanities and Social Sciences, Department of Public and International Affairs, Fairfax, VA 22030. Offers association management (Certificate); biodefense (MS, PhD); emergency management and homeland security (Certificate); nonprofit management (Certificate); political science (MA, PhD); public administration (MPA); public management (Certificate). *Accreditation:* NASPAA (one or more programs are accredited). *Faculty:* 38 full-time (14 women), 31 part-time/adjunct (8 women). *Students:* 134 full-time (76 women), 319 part-time (176 women); includes 63 minority (29 Black or African American, non-Hispanic/Latino; 9 Asian, non-Hispanic/Latino; 21 Hispanic/Latino; 1 Native Hawaiian or other Pacific Islander, non-Hispanic/Latino; 3 Two or more races, non-Hispanic/Latino), 16 international. Average age 31. 574 applicants, 58% accepted, 144 enrolled. In 2010, 140 master's, 3 doctorates, 11 other advanced degrees awarded. *Entrance requirements:* For master's, GRE General Test, minimum GPA of 3.0 in last 60 hours of course work. Additional exam requirements/recommendations for international students: Required—TOEFL (minimum score 570 paper-based; 230 computer-based; 88 iBT). *Application deadline:* For fall admission, 3/1 priority date for domestic students; for spring admission, 10/15 for domestic students. Application fee: $100. Electronic applications accepted. *Expenses:* Tuition, state resident: full-time $8192; part-time $440 per credit hour. Tuition, nonresident: full-time $22,952; part-time $1055 per credit hour. Required fees: $2364; $99 per credit hour. *Financial support:* In 2010–11, 30 students received support, including 3 fellowships with full tuition reimbursements available (averaging $18,000 per year), 10 research assistantships with full and partial tuition reimbursements available (averaging $12,271 per year), 18 teaching assistantships with full and partial tuition reimbursements available (averaging $10,428 per year); career-related internships or fieldwork, Federal Work-Study, scholarships/grants, unspecified assistantships, and health care benefits (full-time research or teaching assistantship recipients) also available. Financial award application deadline: 3/1; financial award applicants required to submit FAFSA. *Faculty research:* The Rehnquist Court and economic liberties; intersection of economic development with high-tech industry, telecommunications, and entrepreneurism; political economy of development; violence, terrorism and U. S. foreign policy; international security issues. Total annual research expenditures: $696,997. *Unit head:* Dr. Priscilla Regan, Chair, 703-993-1419, Fax: 703-993-1399, E-mail: pregan@gmu.edu. *Application contact:* Peg Koback, Information Contact, 703-993-9466, E-mail: mkoback@gmu.edu.

Henley-Putnam University, Program in Terrorism and Counterterrorism Studies, San Jose, CA 95110. Offers MS. Part-time programs available. Postbaccalaureate distance learning degree programs offered.

The Johns Hopkins University, Zanvyl Krieger School of Arts and Sciences, Advanced Academic Programs, Program in Government, Baltimore, MD 21218-2699. Offers government (MA); national securities study (Certificate); MA/MBA. Part-time and evening/weekend programs available. *Faculty:* 4 full-time (2 women), 35 part-time/adjunct (5 women). *Students:* 249 full-time (110 women), 215 part-time (90 women); includes 103 minority (26 Black or African American, non-Hispanic/Latino; 3 American Indian or Alaska Native, non-Hispanic/Latino; 29 Asian, non-Hispanic/Latino; 36 Hispanic/Latino; 9 Two or more races, non-Hispanic/Latino), 9 international. Average age 28. 144 applicants, 73% accepted, 92 enrolled. In 2010, 89 master's awarded. *Degree requirements:* For master's, thesis. *Entrance requirements:* For master's, minimum GPA of 3.0. Additional exam requirements/recommendations for international students: Required—TOEFL (minimum score 250 computer-based; 100 iBT). *Application deadline:* For fall admission, 5/31 priority date for domestic students, 4/30 priority date for international students; for spring admission, 10/31 priority date for domestic and international students. Applications are processed on a rolling basis. Application fee: $75. Electronic applications accepted. *Financial support:* Applicants required to submit FAFSA. *Unit head:* Dr. Kathy Wagner, Associate Program Chair, 202-452-1953, E-mail: kwagner@jhu.edu. *Application contact:* Valana M. McMickens, Admissions Manager, 202-452-1941, Fax: 202-452-1970, E-mail: aapadmissions@jhu.edu.

Long Island University at Riverhead, Homeland Security Management Institute, Riverhead, NY 11901. Offers MS, Advanced Certificate. Part-time programs available. Postbaccalaureate distance learning degree programs offered (no on-campus study). *Faculty:* 2 full-time (0 women), 10 part-time/adjunct (1 woman). *Students:* 5 full-time (0 women), 107 part-time (17 women); includes 8 Black or African American, non-Hispanic/Latino; 1 American Indian or Alaska Native, non-Hispanic/Latino; 2 Asian, non-Hispanic/Latino; 5 Hispanic/Latino. 48 applicants, 56% accepted, 23 enrolled. In 2010, 11 master's, 36 other advanced degrees awarded. *Degree requirements:* For master's, thesis. *Entrance requirements:* For master's, minimum GPA of 3.0, 2 letters of reference. *Application deadline:* Applications are processed on a rolling basis. Application fee: $0. Electronic applications accepted. *Expenses:* Tuition: Part-time $982 per credit. *Financial support:* In 2010–11, 105 students received support. Career-related internships or fieldwork and scholarships/grants available. Support available to part-time students. Financial award applicants required to submit FAFSA. *Unit head:* Dr. Vincent E. Henry, Unit Head, 631-287-8010, Fax: 631-287-8130, E-mail: vincent.henry@liu.edu. *Application contact:* Andrea Borra, Admissions Counselor, 631-287-8010 Ext. 8326, Fax: 631-287-8253, E-mail: andrea.borra@liu.edu.

Monmouth University, The Graduate School, Department of Criminal Justice, West Long Branch, NJ 07764-1898. Offers criminal justice administration (MA, Certificate); homeland security (MA, Certificate). Part-time and evening/weekend programs available. *Faculty:* 4 full-time (0 women), 6 part-time/adjunct (3 women). *Students:* 26 full-time (11 women), 19 part-time (9 women); includes 3 Black or African American, non-Hispanic/Latino; 1 Asian, non-Hispanic/Latino; 6 Hispanic/Latino, 1 international. Average age 27. 35 applicants, 94% accepted, 20 enrolled. In 2010, 12 master's awarded. *Degree requirements:* For master's, comprehensive exam, thesis or alternative. *Entrance requirements:* For master's, minimum GPA of 3.0 in major, 2.5 overall. Additional exam requirements/recommendations for international students: Required—TOEFL (minimum score 550 paper-based; 213 computer-based; 79 iBT), IELTS (minimum score 5) or Michigan English Language Assessment Battery (minimum score 77), Cambridge A, B, C. *Application deadline:* For fall admission, 7/15 priority date for domestic students, 6/1 for international students; for spring admission, 11/15 priority date for domestic students, 11/1 for international students. Applications are processed on a rolling basis. Application fee: $50. Electronic applications accepted. *Expenses:* Tuition: Full-time $19,572; part-time $816 per credit. Required fees: $628; $157 per semester. *Financial support:* In 2010–11, 30 students received support, including 30 fellowships (averaging $1,840 per year), 2 research assistantships (averaging $422 per year); career-related internships or fieldwork, scholarships/grants, and unspecified assistantships also available. Support available to part-time students. Financial award applicants required to submit FAFSA. *Faculty research:* Violent crimes, criminal pathology, terrorism, computer crime, comparative criminal justice systems. *Unit head:* Dr. Gregory Coram, Director, 732-571-3448, Fax: 732-263-5148, E-mail: coram@monmouth.edu. *Application contact:* Kevin Roane, Director, Office of Graduate Admission, 732-571-3452, Fax: 732-263-5123, E-mail: gradadm@monmouth.edu.

National Defense University, College of International Security Affairs, Washington, DC 20319-5066. Offers strategic security studies (MA), including conflict management, counterterrorism, homeland defense/ security, international security studies. Part-time and evening/weekend programs available. *Degree requirements:* For master's, thesis. *Entrance requirements:* Additional exam requirements/recommendations for international students: Required—TOEFL.

National University, Academic Affairs, School of Engineering and Technology, Department of Applied Engineering, La Jolla, CA 92037-1011. Offers database administration (MS); engineering management (MS); environmental engineering (MS); homeland security and safety engineering (MS); system engineering (MS); wireless communications (MS). Part-time and evening/weekend programs available. Postbaccalaureate distance learning degree programs offered (no on-campus study). *Faculty:* 6 full-time (1 woman), 69 part-time/adjunct (12 women). *Students:* 82 full-time (16 women), 153 part-time (35 women); includes 87 minority (18 Black or African American, non-Hispanic/Latino; 1 American Indian or Alaska Native, non-Hispanic/Latino; 34 Asian, non-Hispanic/Latino; 28 Hispanic/Latino; 2 Native Hawaiian or other Pacific Islander, non-Hispanic/Latino; 4 Two or more races, non-Hispanic/Latino), 60 international. Average age 31. 166 applicants, 100% accepted, 106 enrolled. In 2010, 79 master's awarded. *Degree requirements:* For master's, thesis. *Entrance requirements:* For master's, interview, minimum GPA of 2.5. Additional exam requirements/recommendations for international students: Required—TOEFL (minimum score 550 paper-based; 213 computer-based; 79 iBT), IELTS (minimum score 6). *Application deadline:* Applications are processed on a rolling basis. Application fee: $60 ($65 for international students). Electronic applications accepted. *Expenses:* Tuition: Full-time $9450; part-time $350 per unit. Required fees: $350 per unit. One-time fee: $60. *Financial support:* Career-related internships or fieldwork, institutionally sponsored loans, scholarships/grants, and tuition waivers (partial) available. Support available to part-time students. Financial award application deadline: 6/30; financial award applicants required to submit FAFSA. *Unit head:* Dr. Shekar Viswanathan, Chair and Associate Professor, 858-309-8416, Fax: 858-309-3420, E-mail: sviswana@nu.edu. *Application contact:* Dominick Giovanniello, Associate Regional Dean—San Diego, 800-NAT-UNIV, Fax: 858-541-7792, E-mail: dgiovann@nu.edu.

Notre Dame College, Graduate Studies, South Euclid, OH 44121-4293. Offers accounting (Certificate); creative critical thinking (M Ed); financial services management (Certificate); information systems (Certificate); learning disabilities (M Ed); management (Certificate); paralegal (Certificate); pastoral ministry (Certificate); reading (M Ed); security policy studies (MA); teacher education (Certificate). Part-time and evening/weekend programs available. *Degree requirements:* For master's, thesis. *Entrance requirements:* For master's, GRE General Test, MAT, minimum GPA of 2.75, valid teaching certificate. *Faculty research:* Cognitive psychology, teaching critical thinking in the classroom.

Pace University, Dyson College of Arts and Sciences, Department of Public Administration, New York, NY 10038. Offers environmental management (MPA); government management (MPA); health care administration (MPA); management for public safety and homeland security (MA); nonprofit management (MPA); JD/MPA. Offered at White Plains, NY location only. Part-time and evening/weekend programs available. *Degree requirements:* For master's, capstone project. *Entrance requirements:* For master's, GRE General Test. Additional exam requirements/recommendations for international students: Required—TOEFL. Electronic applications accepted.

Penn State University Park, Graduate School, College of Information Sciences and Technology, State College, University Park, PA 16802-1503. Offers MPS, MS, PhD. *Students:* 95 full-time (39 women), 9 part-time (2 women). Average age 29. 183 applicants, 17% accepted, 24 enrolled. In 2010, 9 master's, 14 doctorates awarded. *Entrance requirements:* Additional exam requirements/recommendations for international students: Required—TOEFL (minimum score 550 paper-based; 213 computer-based; 80 iBT). *Application deadline:* Applications are processed on a rolling basis. Application fee: $65. Electronic applications accepted. *Financial support:* Fellowships, research assistantships, teaching assistantships available. Financial award applicants required to submit FAFSA. *Unit head:* Dr. David L. Hall, Interim Dean, 814-863-3528, Fax: 814-865-5604, E-mail: dlh28@psu.edu. *Application contact:* Cynthia E. Nicosia, Director, Graduate Enrollment Services, 814-865-1795, Fax: 814-865-4627, E-mail: cey1@psu.edu.

Saint Joseph's University, College of Arts and Sciences, Programs in Public Safety and Management, Philadelphia, PA 19131-1395. Offers homeland security (MS, Certificate); public safety management (MS, Certificate). Part-time and evening/weekend programs available. *Faculty:* 1 full-time (0 women), 3 part-time/adjunct (0 women). *Students:* 48 part-time (3 women); includes 8 Black or African American, non-Hispanic/Latino; 1 Asian, non-Hispanic/Latino; 2 Hispanic/Latino. Average age 38. 11 applicants, 100% accepted, 6 enrolled. In 2010, 23 master's awarded. *Entrance requirements:* For master's, GRE (if GPA less than 2.75), minimum GPA of 2.75, 2 letters of recommendation, resume. Additional exam requirements/recommendations for international students: Required—TOEFL (minimum score 550 paper-based; 213 computer-based; 79 iBT). *Application deadline:* For fall admission, 7/15 priority date for domestic students, 4/15 for international students; for winter admission, 1/15 for international students; for spring admission, 11/15 priority date for domestic students, 10/15 for international students. Applications are processed on a rolling basis. Application fee: $35. Electronic applications accepted. *Expenses:* Tuition: Part-time $729 per credit. Tuition and fees vary according to course load, degree level and program. *Financial support:* Applicants required to submit FAFSA. *Unit head:* Patricia Griffin, Director, 610-660-1294, E-mail: pgriffin@sju.edu. *Application contact:* Kate McConnell, Assistant Director of Graduate Admissions, 610-660-3184, Fax: 610-660-3230, E-mail: kate.mcconnell@sju.edu.

Salve Regina University, Graduate Studies, Program in International Relations, Newport, RI 02840-4192. Offers homeland security (Certificate); international relations (MA, Certificate). Part-time and evening/weekend programs available. Postbaccalaureate distance learning degree programs offered (minimal on-campus study). *Entrance requirements:* For master's, GMAT, GRE General Test, MAT or LSAT. Additional exam requirements/recommendations for international students: Required—TOEFL (minimum score 600 paper-based; 250 computer-based; 100 iBT) or IELTS. Electronic applications accepted. *Expenses:* Tuition: Full-time $7740; part-time $430 per credit. Required fees: $40 per semester. Tuition and fees vary according to course level and degree level.

Salve Regina University, Graduate Studies, Programs in Administration of Justice, Newport, RI 02840-4192. Offers justice and homeland security (MS); law enforcement leadership (MS). Part-time and evening/weekend programs available. *Entrance requirements:* For master's, GMAT, GRE General Test, or MAT. Additional exam requirements/recommendations for international students: Required—TOEFL (minimum score 600 paper-based; 250 computer-based; 100 iBT). Electronic applications accepted. *Expenses:* Tuition: Full-time $7740; part-time $430 per credit. Required fees: $40 per semester. Tuition and fees vary according to course level and degree level.

Texas A&M University, Bush School of Government and Public Service, College Station, TX 77843. Offers advanced international affairs (Certificate); China studies (Certificate); homeland security (Certificate); international affairs (MPIA); national security affairs (Certificate); nonprofit management (Certificate); public service and administration (MPSA). *Accreditation:* NASPAA. *Faculty:* 45. *Students:* 215 full-time (98 women), 93 part-time (32 women); includes 20 Black or African American, non-Hispanic/Latino; 2 American Indian or Alaska Native, non-Hispanic/Latino; 14 Asian, non-Hispanic/Latino; 30 Hispanic/Latino, 15 international. Average age 24. In 2010, 93 master's awarded. *Degree requirements:* For master's, summer internship. *Entrance requirements:* For master's, GRE (preferred) or GMAT. *Application deadline:* For fall admission, 1/24 for domestic and international students. Application fee: $50 ($75 for international students). Electronic applications accepted. *Financial support:* In 2010–11, fellowships (averaging $11,000 per year), research assistantships (averaging $11,250 per year) were awarded; career-related internships or fieldwork, Federal Work-Study, and institutionally sponsored loans also available. Financial award application deadline: 2/1; financial award applicants required to submit FAFSA. *Faculty research:* Public policy, presidential studies, public leadership, economic policy, social policy. *Unit head:* Ryan C. Crocker, Dean, 979-862-8007, E-mail: rcrocker@bushschool.tamu.edu. *Application contact:* Kathryn Meyer, Director of Recruiting, 979-458-4767, Fax: 979-845-4155, E-mail: kmeyer@bushschool.tamu.edu.

Thomas Edison State College, Heavin School of Arts and Sciences, Program in Homeland Security, Trenton, NJ 08608-1176. Offers Graduate Certificate. Part-time programs available. Postbaccalaureate distance learning degree programs offered (no on-campus study). *Students:* 30 part-time (10 women); includes 3 Black or African American, non-Hispanic/Latino; 1 Asian, non-Hispanic/Latino; 3 Hispanic/Latino. Average age 40. In 2010, 5 Graduate Certificates awarded. *Entrance requirements:* Additional exam requirements/recommendations for international students: Required—TOEFL (minimum score 550 paper-based; 213 computer-based; 79 iBT). *Application deadline:* For fall admission, 8/15 priority date for domestic and international students; for winter admission, 11/15 priority date for domestic and international students; for spring admission, 2/15 priority date for domestic and international students. Applications are processed on a rolling basis. Application fee: $75. Electronic applications accepted. *Financial support:* Applicants required to submit FAFSA. *Unit head:* Dr. Susan Davenport, Dean, Heavin School of Arts and Sciences, 609-984-1130, Fax: 609-984-0740, E-mail: info@tesc.edu. *Application contact:* David Hoftiezer, Director of Admissions, 888-442-8372, Fax: 609-984-8447, E-mail: admissions@tesc.edu.

Tiffin University, Program in Criminal Justice, Tiffin, OH 44883-2161. Offers crime analysis (MSCJ); criminal behavior (MSCJ); forensic psychology (MSCJ); homeland security administration (MSCJ); justice administration (MSCJ). Part-time and evening/weekend programs available. Postbaccalaureate distance learning degree programs offered (no on-campus study). *Faculty:* 13 full-time (3 women), 20 part-time/adjunct (9 women). *Students:* 120 full-time (84 women), 312 part-time (205 women). Average age 31. 185 applicants, 58% accepted, 104 enrolled. In 2010, 340 master's awarded. *Degree requirements:* For master's, thesis optional. *Entrance requirements:* For master's, minimum undergraduate GPA of 2.5, work experience. Additional exam requirements/recommendations for international students: Required—TOEFL (minimum score 550 paper-based; 213 computer-based). *Application deadline:* For fall admission, 9/3 for domestic students, 8/1 for international students; for spring admission, 1/9 priority date for domestic students, 12/1 for international students. Applications are processed on a rolling basis. Application fee: $0. Electronic applications accepted. *Financial support:* In 2010–11, 64 students received support. Available to part-time students. Application deadline: 7/31. *Faculty research:* Terrorism, intelligence, homeland security, guns and crime. *Unit head:* Dr. Tim Shaw, Dean of Criminal Justice and Social Sciences, 419-448-3305, Fax: 419-443-5002, E-mail: shawta@tiffin.edu. *Application contact:* Kristi Krintzline, Director of Graduate Admissions, 800-968-6446 Ext. 3445, Fax: 419-443-5002, E-mail: krintzlineka@tiffin.edu.

Towson University, Program in Integrated Homeland Security Management, Towson, MD 21252-0001. Offers integrated homeland security management (MS); security assessment and management (Certificate). Part-time and evening/weekend programs available. *Students:* 4 full-time (3 women), 41 part-time (19 women); includes 14 minority (10 Black or African American, non-Hispanic/Latino; 2 American Indian or Alaska Native, non-Hispanic/Latino; 2 Hispanic/Latino). Average age 32. In 2010, 14 master's, 13 other advanced degrees awarded. *Entrance requirements:* For master's, BA in related field, 3 years related work experience, resume. Application fee: $50. *Expenses:* Tuition, state resident: part-time $324 per credit.

Homeland Security

Towson University (continued)
Tuition, nonresident: part-time $681 per credit. Required fees: $95 per term. *Financial support:* Application deadline: 4/1. *Unit head:* Dr. Mike O'Leary, Graduate Program Director, 410-704-4757, E-mail: moleary@towson.edu, *Application contact:* The Graduate School, 410-704-2501, Fax: 410-704-4675, E-mail: grads@towson.edu.

University of Central Florida, College of Health and Public Affairs, Department of Public Administration, Orlando, FL 32816. Offers emergency management and homeland security (Certificate); non-profit management (MNM, Certificate); public administration (MPA, Certificate); research administration (MS); urban and regional planning (Certificate). *Accreditation:* NASPAA. Part-time and evening/weekend programs available. *Faculty:* 14 full-time (5 women), 9 part-time/adjunct (3 women). *Students:* 103 full-time (70 women), 271 part-time (208 women); includes 125 minority (85 Black or African American, non-Hispanic/Latino; 1 American Indian or Alaska Native, non-Hispanic/Latino; 13 Asian, non-Hispanic/Latino; 22 Hispanic/Latino; 2 Native Hawaiian or other Pacific Islander, non-Hispanic/Latino; 2 Two or more races, non-Hispanic/Latino), 8 international. Average age 31. 258 applicants, 69% accepted, 138 enrolled. In 2010, 101 master's, 25 other advanced degrees awarded. *Degree requirements:* For master's, comprehensive exam, thesis or alternative, research report. *Entrance requirements:* For master's, GRE General Test. *Application deadline:* For fall admission, 7/1 for domestic students; for spring admission, 12/1 for domestic students. Application fee: $30. Electronic applications accepted. *Expenses:* Tuition, state resident: part-time $256.56 per credit hour. Tuition, nonresident: part-time $1011.52 per credit hour. Part-time tuition and fees vary according to program. *Financial support:* In 2010–11, 13 students received support, including 1 fellowship with partial tuition reimbursement available (averaging $10,000 per year), 11 research assistantships with partial tuition reimbursements available (averaging $5,900 per year), 2 teaching assistantships with partial tuition reimbursements available (averaging $7,100 per year); career-related internships or fieldwork, Federal Work-Study, institutionally sponsored loans, tuition waivers (partial), and unspecified assistantships also available. Financial award application deadline: 3/1; financial award applicants required to submit FAFSA. *Unit head:* Dr. Mary Ann Feldheim, Chair, 407-823-3693, Fax: 407-823-5651, E-mail: mfeldhei@mail.ucf.edu. *Application contact:* Dr. Mary Ann Feldheim, Chair, 407-823-3693, Fax: 407-823-5651, E-mail: mfeldhei@mail.ucf.edu.

University of Colorado Denver, School of Public Affairs, Program in Public Affairs and Administration, Denver, CO 80127. Offers public administration (MPA), including domestic violence, emergency management and homeland security, environmental policy, management and law, homeland security and defense, local government, nonprofit management, public administration; public affairs (PhD). *Accreditation:* NASPAA. Part-time and evening/weekend programs available. Postbaccalaureate distance learning degree programs offered (no on-campus study). *Faculty:* 19 full-time (9 women), 14 part-time/adjunct (5 women). *Students:* 317 full-time (181 women), 167 part-time (100 women); includes 15 Black or African American, non-Hispanic/Latino; 2 American Indian or Alaska Native, non-Hispanic/Latino; 18 Asian, non-Hispanic/Latino; 29 Hispanic/Latino; 1 Two or more races, non-Hispanic/Latino, 36 international. Average age 30. 270 applicants, 66% accepted, 118 enrolled. In 2010, 119 master's, 4 doctorates awarded. *Degree requirements:* For master's, thesis or alternative, 36-39 credit hours; for doctorate, comprehensive exam, thesis/dissertation, minimum of 66 semester hours, including at least 30 hours of doctoral dissertation credits. *Entrance requirements:* For master's and doctorate, GRE, resume, essay, transcripts, recommendations. Additional exam requirements/recommendations for international students: Required—TOEFL (minimum score 550 paper-based; 223 computer-based). *Application deadline:* For fall admission, 2/1 for domestic students; for spring admission, 10/15 priority date for domestic students. Application fee: $50 ($75 for international students). Electronic applications accepted. *Expenses:* Contact institution. *Financial support:* Fellowships with partial tuition reimbursements, research assistantships with partial tuition reimbursements, teaching assistantships with partial tuition reimbursements, Federal Work-Study and scholarships/grants available. Support available to part-time students. Financial award application deadline: 4/1; financial award applicants required to submit FAFSA. *Faculty research:* Housing, education and the social and economic issues of vulnerable populations; nonprofit governance and management; education finance, effectiveness and reform; P-20 (preschool through graduate school) education initiatives; municipal government accountability. *Unit head:* Dr. Mary Guy, Program Director, 303-315-2007, Fax: 303-315-2229, E-mail: mary.guy@ucdenver.edu. *Application contact:* Annie Davies, Director of Marketing, Community Outreach and Alumni Affairs, 303-315-2896, Fax: 303-315-2229, E-mail: annie.davies@ucdenver.edu.

University of Connecticut, Graduate School, Center for Continuing Studies, Program in Homeland Security Leadership, Storrs, CT 06269. Offers MPS.

University of Denver, Josef Korbel School of International Studies, Denver, CO 80208. Offers conflict resolution (MA); development practice (MDP); global finance, trade and economic integration (MA); global health affairs (Certificate); homeland security (Certificate); humanitarian assistance (Certificate); international development (MA); international human rights (MA); international security (MA); international studies (MA, PhD). Part-time programs available. *Faculty:* 33 full-time (13 women), 38 part-time/adjunct (11 women). *Students:* 461 full-time (279 women), 52 part-time (27 women); includes 71 minority (8 Black or African American, non-Hispanic/Latino; 3 American Indian or Alaska Native, non-Hispanic/Latino; 25 Asian, non-Hispanic/Latino; 25 Hispanic/Latino; 2 Native Hawaiian or other Pacific Islander, non-Hispanic/Latino; 8 Two or more races, non-Hispanic/Latino), 42 international. Average age 28. 1,056 applicants, 69% accepted, 259 enrolled. In 2010, 230 master's, 5 doctorates, 42 other advanced degrees awarded. *Degree requirements:* For master's, one foreign language, thesis; for doctorate, one foreign language, thesis/dissertation. *Entrance requirements:* For master's and doctorate, GRE General Test. Additional exam requirements/recommendations for international students: Required—TOEFL (minimum score 587 paper-based; 95 iBT). *Application deadline:* For fall admission, 1/15 priority date for domestic students, 12/15 priority date for international students; for winter admission, 10/15 priority date for domestic and international students. Applications are processed on a rolling basis. Application fee: $60. Electronic applications accepted. *Expenses:* Tuition: Full-time $35,604; part-time $29,670 per year. Required fees: $687 per year. Tuition and fees vary according to program. *Financial support:* In 2010–11, 1 teaching assistantship with partial tuition reimbursement (averaging $9,999 per year) was awarded; career-related internships or fieldwork, Federal Work-Study, institutionally sponsored loans, scholarships/grants, and unspecified assistantships also available. Support available to part-time students. Financial award applicants required to submit FAFSA. *Faculty research:* Human rights and international security, international politics and economics, economic-social and political development, international technology analysis and management. *Unit head:* Ambassador Christopher R. Hill, Dean, 303-871-2539, Fax: 303-871-2124, E-mail: christopher.r.hill@du.edu. *Application contact:* Brad Miller, Director of Graduate Admissions and Financial Aid, 303-871-2989, Fax: 303-871-2124, E-mail: korbeladm@du.edu.

University of New Haven, Graduate School, Henry C. Lee College of Criminal Justice and Forensic Sciences, National Security and Public Safety Program, West Haven, CT 06516-1916. Offers information protection and security (MS); national security (Certificate); national security administration (Certificate). Part-time and evening/weekend programs available. *Students:* 36 full-time (15 women), 38 part-time (17 women); includes 7 Black or African American, non-Hispanic/Latino; 2 American Indian or Alaska Native, non-Hispanic/Latino; 2 Asian, non-Hispanic/Latino; 10 Hispanic/Latino, 6 international. Average age 32. 27 applicants, 96% accepted, 19 enrolled. In 2010, 28 master's awarded. *Entrance requirements:* Additional exam requirements/recommendations for international students: Required—TOEFL (minimum score 520 paper-based; 190 computer-based; 70 iBT); Recommended—IELTS (minimum score 5.5). *Application deadline:* For fall admission, 5/31 for international students; for winter admission, 10/15 for international students; for spring admission, 1/15 for international students. Applications are processed on a rolling basis. Application fee: $50. Electronic applications accepted. *Financial support:* Research assistantships with partial tuition reimbursements, teaching assistantships with partial tuition reimbursements, career-related internships or fieldwork, Federal Work-Study, scholarships/grants, tuition waivers, and unspecified assistantships available. Support available to part-time students. Financial award applicants required to submit FAFSA. *Unit head:* Dr. William L. Tafoya, Dean, 203-932-7260. *Application contact:* Eloise Gormley, Director of Graduate Admissions, 203-932-7449, Fax: 203-932-7137, E-mail: gradinfo@newhaven.edu.

University of Southern California, Graduate School, School of Policy, Planning, and Development, Public Policy Programs, Los Angeles, CA 90089. Offers homeland security and public policy (Graduate Certificate); public policy (MPP, Graduate Certificate); MPP/JD. Part-time programs available. *Faculty:* 51 full-time (12 women), 100 part-time/adjunct (30 women). *Students:* 111 full-time (65 women), 7 part-time (4 women); includes 51 minority (6 Black or African American, non-Hispanic/Latino; 17 Asian, non-Hispanic/Latino; 24 Hispanic/Latino; 4 Two or more races, non-Hispanic/Latino), 15 international. 275 applicants, 74% accepted, 61 enrolled. In 2010, 32 master's, 1 other advanced degree awarded. Terminal master's awarded for partial completion of doctoral program. *Degree requirements:* For master's, practicum. *Entrance requirements:* For master's, GRE. Additional exam requirements/recommendations for international students: Required—TOEFL (minimum score 600 paper-based; 250 computer-based; 100 iBT). *Application deadline:* For fall admission, 12/15 priority date for domestic and international students; for spring admission, 11/1 for domestic and international students. Applications are processed on a rolling basis. Application fee: $85. Electronic applications accepted. *Expenses:* Tuition: Full-time $31,240; part-time $1420 per unit. Required fees: $600. One-time fee: $35 full-time. Full-time tuition and fees vary according to degree level and program. *Financial support:* In 2010–11, 73 students received support, including 2 research assistantships with full tuition reimbursements available (averaging $14,709 per year); scholarships/grants and tuition waivers (full and partial) also available. Financial award application deadline: 12/15; financial award applicants required to submit CSS PROFILE or FAFSA. *Faculty research:* Urban political economy, community and economic development, environmental policy, transportation policy, housing policy. Total annual research expenditures: $6.2 million. *Unit head:* Dr. Gary Painter, Director, 213-740-8754, Fax: 213-740-7573, E-mail: gpainter@usc.edu. *Application contact:* Marisol R. Gonzalez, Director of Recruitment and Admission, 213-740-0550, Fax: 213-740-7573, E-mail: marisolr@usc.edu.

The University of Texas at El Paso, Graduate School, Institute for Policy and Economic Development, El Paso, TX 79968-0001. Offers border administration (Certificate); homeland security (Certificate); intelligence and national security (MS, Certificate); leadership studies (MA); public administration (MPA). *Accreditation:* NASPAA. Part-time and evening/weekend programs available. *Students:* 187 (57 women); includes 19 Black or African American, non-Hispanic/Latino; 1 American Indian or Alaska Native, non-Hispanic/Latino; 5 Asian, non-Hispanic/Latino; 99 Hispanic/Latino, 5 international. 142 applicants, 77% accepted. In 2010, 76 master's awarded. *Degree requirements:* For master's, thesis optional. *Entrance requirements:* For master's, GRE, statement of purpose, letters of recommendation. Additional exam requirements/recommendations for international students: Required—TOEFL; Recommended—IELTS. *Application deadline:* For fall admission, 8/1 for domestic students, 3/1 for international students; for spring admission, 10/1 for domestic students, 9/1 for international students. Applications are processed on a rolling basis. Application fee: $45 ($80 for international students). Electronic applications accepted. *Financial support:* Fellowships with partial tuition reimbursements, research assistantships with partial tuition reimbursements, teaching assistantships with partial tuition reimbursements, institutionally sponsored loans, scholarships/grants, health care benefits, tuition waivers (partial), and unspecified assistantships available. Support available to part-time students. Financial award application deadline: 3/15; financial award applicants required to submit FAFSA. *Unit head:* Dr. Dennis Soden, Director, 915-747-7974, Fax: 915-747-7948, E-mail: desoden@utep.edu. *Application contact:* Dr. Patricia D. Witherspoon, Dean of the Graduate School, 915-747-5491, Fax: 915-747-5788, E-mail: withersp@utep.edu.

The University of Toledo, College of Graduate Studies, College of Medicine and Life Sciences, Department of Public Health and Preventative Medicine, Toledo, OH 43606-3390. Offers biostatistics and epidemiology (Certificate); contemporary gerontological practice (Certificate); environmental and occupational health and safety (MPH), including public health; epidemiology (MPH, Certificate); health administration (MPH); health promotion (MPH); nutrition (MPH); occupational health (MSOH, Certificate); MD/MPH. Part-time programs available. *Faculty:* 5. *Students:* 98 full-time (69 women), 42 part-time (28 women); includes 20 Black or African American, non-Hispanic/Latino; 8 Asian, non-Hispanic/Latino; 4 Hispanic/Latino, 3 international. Average age 29. 132 applicants, 75% accepted, 70 enrolled. In 2010, 44 master's, 28 other advanced degrees awarded. *Degree requirements:* For master's, thesis or alternative. *Entrance requirements:* For master's, GRE (international applicants only), Minimum undergraduate GPA of 3.0. Three letters of recommendation, a statement of purpose and transcripts from all prior institutions attended; for Certificate, GRE, Minimum undergraduate GPA of 3.0. Three letters of recommendation, a statement of purpose and transcripts from all prior institutions attended. Additional exam requirements/recommendations for international students: Required—TOEFL (minimum score 550 paper-based; 213 computer-based; 80 iBT), IELTS (minimum score 6.5). *Application deadline:* For fall admission, 6/15 for domestic students, 3/15 for international students; for spring admission, 10/15 for domestic students, 2/15 for international students. Applications are processed on a rolling basis. Application fee: $45 ($75 for international students). Electronic applications accepted. *Expenses:* Tuition, state resident: full-time $11,426; part-time $476 per credit hour. Tuition, nonresident: full-time $21,660; part-time $903 per credit hour. One-time fee: $62. *Financial support:* In 2010–11, 14 research assistantships with full tuition reimbursements (averaging $10,000 per year) were awarded; Federal Work-Study, institutionally sponsored loans, scholarships/grants, tuition waivers (full and partial), and unspecified assistantships also available. *Unit head:* Dr. Sheryl A. Milz, Chair, 419-383-3976, Fax: 419-383-6140, E-mail: sheryl.milz@utoledo.edu. *Application contact:* Joan Mulligan, Admissions Analyst, 419-383-4186, Fax: 419-383-6140, E-mail: joan.mulligan@utoledo.edu.

Upper Iowa University, Online Master's Programs, Fayette, IA 52142-1857. Offers accounting (MBA); corporate financial management (MBA); global business (MBA); health and human services (MPA); higher education administration (MHEA); homeland security (MPA); human resources management (MBA); justice administration (MPA); organizational development (MBA); public personnel management (MPA); quality management (MBA). MBA also available at Madison, WI campus. Part-time programs available. Postbaccalaureate distance learning degree programs offered (no on-campus study). *Degree requirements:* For master's, research project. *Entrance requirements:* For master's, GMAT, GRE, or minimum GPA of 2.7 during last 60 hours. Additional exam requirements/recommendations for international students: Required—TOEFL (minimum score 570 paper-based; 230 computer-based). Electronic applications accepted. *Faculty research:* Total quality management, CQI, teams, organization culture and climate, management.

Virginia Commonwealth University, Graduate School, College of Humanities and Sciences, Wilder School of Government and Public Affairs, Program in Homeland Security and Emergency Preparedness, Richmond, VA 23284-9005. Offers MA, Graduate Certificate. Postbaccalaureate distance learning degree programs offered. *Students:* 12 full-time (8 women), 23 part-time (12 women); includes 13 minority (12 Black or African American, non-Hispanic/Latino; 1 Asian, non-Hispanic/Latino). 35 applicants, 54% accepted, 13 enrolled. In 2010, 10 master's, 7 other advanced degrees awarded. *Entrance requirements:* For master's, GRE, GMAT, MAT or LSAT, minimum GPA of 2.7; for Graduate Certificate, minimum GPA of 2.7. Additional exam requirements/recommendations for international students: Required—TOEFL (minimum score 600 paper-based; 250 computer-based; 100 iBT); Recommended—IELTS (minimum score 6.5). *Application deadline:* For fall admission, 7/15 for domestic students; for spring admission, 10/1 for domestic students. Application fee: $50. Electronic applications accepted. *Expenses:* Tuition, state resident: full-time $4308; part-time $479 per credit hour. Tuition, nonresident: full-time $8942; part-time $994 per credit hour. Required fees: $2000; $85 per credit hour. Tuition and fees vary according to course level, course load, degree level, campus/location and program. *Unit head:* Dr. John Aughenbaugh, Program Chair. *Application contact:* Lisbeth Dannenbrink, Student Contact, 804-828-6837, E-mail: lddannenbrin@vcu.edu.

Virginia Polytechnic Institute and State University, Graduate School, College of Architecture and Urban Studies, School of Public and International Affairs, Blacksburg, VA 24061. Offers economic development (Certificate); government and international affairs (MPIA, PhD); homeland security policy (Certificate); local government management (Certificate); nonprofit and nongovernmental organization management (Certificate); planning, governance and globalization (PhD); public administration and public affairs (MPA, PhD); urban and regional planning (MURPL). *Accreditation:* ACSP. *Faculty:* 31 full-time (9 women). *Students:* 114 full-time (66 women), 105 part-time (54 women); includes 11 Black or African American, non-Hispanic/Latino; 1 American Indian or Alaska Native, non-Hispanic/Latino; 7 Asian, non-Hispanic/Latino; 8 Hispanic/Latino, 19 international. Average age 31. 166 applicants, 67% accepted, 53 enrolled. In 2010, 41 master's, 3 doctorates awarded. *Degree requirements:* For master's, comprehensive exam (for some programs), thesis (for some programs); for doctorate, comprehensive exam (for some programs), thesis/dissertation (for some programs). *Entrance requirements:* For master's and doctorate, GRE. Additional exam requirements/recommendations for international students: Required—TOEFL (minimum score 550 paper-based; 213 computer-based). *Application deadline:* For fall admission, 7/1 for domestic and international students; for spring admission, 12/1 for domestic and international students. Applications are processed on a rolling basis. Application fee: $65. Electronic applications accepted. *Expenses:* Tuition, state resident: full-time $9399; part-time $488 per credit hour. Tuition, nonresident: full-time $17,854; part-time $957.75 per credit hour. Required fees: $1534. Full-time tuition and fees vary according to program. *Financial support:* In 2010–11, 1 teaching assistantship with full tuition reimbursement (averaging $21,395 per year) was awarded; career-related internships or fieldwork, Federal Work-Study, scholarships/grants, health care benefits, and unspecified assistantships also available. Financial award application deadline: 1/15. *Faculty research:* Design theory, environmental planning, town planning, transportation planning. Total annual research expenditures: $610,749. *Unit head:* Dr. Karen M. Hult, UNIT HEAD, 540-231-5351, Fax: 540-231-9938, E-mail: khult@vt.edu. *Application contact:* Krystal D. Wright, Contact, 540-231-2291, Fax: 540-231-9938, E-mail: garch@vt.edu.

Walden University, Graduate Programs, School of Psychology, Minneapolis, MN 55401. Offers clinical child psychology (Post-Doctoral Certificate); clinical psychology (MS, Post-Doctoral Certificate), including counseling (MS); counseling psychology (Post-Doctoral Certificate); forensic psychology (MS), including forensic psychology in the community, general program, mental health applications, program planning and evaluation in forensic settings, psychology and legal systems; general psychology (Post-Doctoral Certificate); health psychology (Post-Doctoral Certificate); organizational psychology (Post-Doctoral Certificate); organizational psychology and development (Postbaccalaureate Certificate); psychology (MS, PhD), including clinical psychology (PhD), counseling psychology (PhD), crisis management and response (MS), general program (MS), general psychology (PhD), health psychology, leadership development and coaching (MS), media psychology (MS), organizational psychology (PhD), organizational psychology and development (MS), organizational psychology and nonprofit management (MS), program evaluation and research (MS), psychology of culture (MS), psychology, public administration, and social change (MS), social psychology (MS), terrorism and security (MS); teaching online (Post-Master's Certificate). Part-time and evening/weekend programs available. Postbaccalaureate distance learning degree programs offered (minimal on-campus study). *Faculty:* 41 full-time (25 women), 254 part-time/adjunct (131 women). *Students:* 3,463 full-time (2,737 women), 1,400 part-time (1,130 women); includes 1,491 Black or African American, non-Hispanic/Latino; 59 American Indian or Alaska Native, non-Hispanic/Latino; 89 Asian, non-Hispanic/Latino; 283 Hispanic/Latino; 76 Two or more races, non-Hispanic/Latino, 126 international. Average age 40. In 2010, 559 master's, 100 doctorates awarded. Terminal master's awarded for partial completion of doctoral program. *Degree requirements:* For master's, thesis optional; for doctorate, thesis/dissertation, residency. *Entrance requirements:* For master's, bachelor's degree or equivalent in related field; minimum GPA of 2.5; official transcripts; goal statement; access to computer and Internet; for doctorate, master's degree or equivalent in related field; minimum GPA of 3.0; 3 years of related professional/academic experience (preferred). Additional exam requirements/recommendations for international students: Required—TOEFL (minimum score 550 paper-based; 213 computer-based), IELTS (minimum score 6.5), TOEFL (minimum score 550 paper-based; 213 computer-based), IELTS (minimum score 6.5), or Michigan English Language Assessment Battery (minimum score 82). *Application deadline:* Applications are processed on a rolling basis. Application fee: $50. Electronic applications accepted. *Expenses:* Tuition: Full-time $10,274; part-time $445 per credit. Tuition and fees vary according to course load, degree level and program. *Financial support:* In 2010–11, 1 fellowship was awarded; Federal Work-Study, scholarships/grants, unspecified assistantships, and family tuition reduction, active duty/veteran tuition reduction, group tuition reduction, interest-free payment plans also available. Support available to part-time students. Financial award applicants required to submit FAFSA. *Unit head:* Dr. Melanie Storms, Associate Dean, 800-925-3368. *Application contact:* Jennifer Hall, Vice President of Enrollment Management, 866-4-WALDEN, E-mail: info@waldenu.edu.

Walden University, Graduate Programs, School of Public Policy and Administration, Minneapolis, MN 55401. Offers criminal justice (MPA); emergency management (MPA); government management (Postbaccalaureate Certificate); health policy (MPA); homeland security policy (MPA); homeland security policy and coordination (MPA); interdisciplinary policy studies (MPA); international nongovernmental organizations (ngos) (MPA); law and public policy (MPA); local government management for sustainable communities (MPA); nonprofit management (Postbaccalaureate Certificate); nonprofit management and leadership (MPA, MS); policy analysis (MPA); public management and leadership (MPA); public policy and administration (MPA, PhD), including criminal justice (PhD), emergency management (PhD), health policy (PhD), health services (PhD), homeland security policy (PhD), homeland security policy and coordination (PhD), interdisciplinary policy studies (PhD), international nongovernmental organizations (PhD), law and public policy (PhD), local government management for sustainable communities (PhD), nonprofit management and leadership (PhD), policy analysis (PhD), public management and leadership (PhD), terrorism, mediation, and peace (PhD); terrorism, mediation, and peace (MPA). Part-time and evening/weekend programs available. Postbaccalaureate distance learning degree programs offered (minimal on-campus study). *Faculty:* 10 full-time (5 women), 117 part-time/adjunct (49 women). *Students:* 1,408 full-time (901 women), 599 part-time (392 women); includes 1,022 Black or African American, non-Hispanic/Latino; 11 American Indian or Alaska Native, non-Hispanic/Latino; 37 Asian, non-Hispanic/Latino; 64 Hispanic/Latino; 26 Two or more races, non-Hispanic/Latino, 47 international. Average age 40. In 2010, 311 master's, 23 doctorates awarded. *Degree requirements:* For doctorate, thesis/dissertation, residency. *Entrance requirements:* For master's, bachelor's degree or equivalent in related field, minimum GPA of 2.5; for doctorate, master's degree or equivalent in related field; minimum GPA of 3.0; official transcripts; three years of related professional/academic experience (preferred); access to computer and Internet. Additional exam requirements/recommendations for international students: Required—TOEFL (minimum score 550 paper-based; 213 computer-based), IELTS (minimum score 6.5), TOEFL (minimum score 550 paper-based; 213 computer-based), IELTS (minimum score 6.5), or Michigan English Language Assessment Battery (minimum score 82). *Application deadline:* Applications are processed on a rolling basis. Application fee: $50. Electronic applications accepted. *Expenses:* Tuition: Full-time $10,274; part-time $445 per credit. Tuition and fees vary according to course load, degree level and program. *Financial support:* Fellowships with tuition reimbursements, Federal Work-Study, scholarships/grants, unspecified assistantships, and family tuition reduction, active duty/veteran tuition reduction, group tuition reduction, interest-free payment plans available. Support available to part-time students. Financial award applicants required to submit FAFSA. *Unit head:* Dr. Mark Gordon, Associate Dean, 800-925-3368. *Application contact:* Jennifer Hall, Vice President of Enrollment Management, 866-4-WALDEN, E-mail: info@waldenu.edu.

Wayland Baptist University, Graduate Programs, Program in Counseling, Plainview, TX 79072-6998. Offers counseling (MA); government administration (MPA); homeland security (MPA); justice administration (MPA). Part-time and evening/weekend programs available. Postbaccalaureate distance learning degree programs offered. *Degree requirements:* For master's, comprehensive exam. *Entrance requirements:* For master's, GRE, MAT. Additional exam requirements/recommendations for international students: Required—TOEFL (minimum score 500 paper-based; 173 computer-based; 61 iBT). Electronic applications accepted.

Western Kentucky University, Graduate Studies, Ogden College of Science and Engineering, Department of Physics and Astronomy, Bowling Green, KY 42101. Offers homeland security sciences (MS); physics (MA Ed).

Wilmington University, College of Business, New Castle, DE 19720-6491. Offers business administration (MBA); finance (MBA); health care administration (MBA, MS); homeland security (MBA, MS); human resource management (MS); management (MS); management information systems (MBA); organizational leadership (MS); public administration (MS); transportation and logistics (MBA, MS). Part-time and evening/weekend programs available. *Entrance requirements:* Additional exam requirements/recommendations for international students: Required—TOEFL (minimum score 500 paper-based; 173 computer-based). Electronic applications accepted. *Expenses:* Tuition: Full-time $7110; part-time $395 per credit hour. Tuition and fees vary according to campus/location.

Industrial and Labor Relations

Bernard M. Baruch College of the City University of New York, Zicklin School of Business, Zicklin Executive Programs, Baruch Executive Master of Science in Industrial and Labor Relations Program, New York, NY 10010-5585. Offers MS. Part-time and evening/weekend programs available. *Entrance requirements:* For master's, professional experience in HR or labor relations. Additional exam requirements/recommendations for international students: Required—TOEFL. *Expenses:* Contact institution.

Carnegie Mellon University, College of Humanities and Social Sciences, Department of History, Pittsburgh, PA 15213-3891. Offers African and African-American diaspora (PhD); culture and power (PhD); gender and the family (PhD); history (MA, MS); history and policy (MA); labor and politics (PhD); science, technology, medicine and environment (PhD). Part-time programs available. *Degree requirements:* For doctorate, oral and written comprehensive exams, dissertation defense. *Entrance requirements:* For doctorate, GRE General Test. Additional exam requirements/recommendations for international students: Required—TOEFL. Electronic applications accepted. *Faculty research:* Anthropology and history, African American history, technology/environment, cultural history analysis.

Case Western Reserve University, Weatherhead School of Management, Department of Marketing and Policy Studies, Division of Labor and Human Resource Policy, Cleveland, OH 44106. Offers MBA. Part-time and evening/weekend programs available. *Entrance requirements:* For master's, GMAT. *Faculty research:* Strategic human resource management, negotiations and conflict management, human resources in high performance organizations, international human resources management, union management relations and collective bargaining.

Cleveland State University, Cleveland-Marshall College of Law, Cleveland, OH 44115. Offers business law (JD); civil litigation and dispute resolution (JD); criminal law (JD); employment labor law (JD); international and comparative law (JD); law (LL M); JD/MAES; JD/MBA; JD/MPA; JD/MSES; JD/MUPDD. *Accreditation:* ABA. Part-time and evening/weekend programs available. *Faculty:* 45 full-time (22 women), 33 part-time/adjunct (7 women). *Students:* 453 full-time (176 women), 157 part-time (73 women); includes 58 Black or African American, non-Hispanic/Latino; 1 American Indian or Alaska Native, non-Hispanic/Latino; 10 Asian, non-Hispanic/Latino; 13 Hispanic/Latino, 7 international. Average age 26. 1,765 applicants, 36% accepted, 195 enrolled. In 2010, 183 first professional degrees, 3 master's awarded. *Degree requirements:* For master's, thesis (for graduates of U.S. law schools); for JD, 90 credits (41 in required courses). *Entrance requirements:* For JD, LSAT, bachelor's degree; for master's, JD or LL B. Additional exam requirements/recommendations for international students: Required—TOEFL (minimum score 600 paper-based; 250 computer-based; 100 iBT). *Application deadline:* For fall admission, 5/1 for domestic and international students. Applications are processed on a rolling basis. Application fee: $0. Electronic applications accepted. *Expenses:* Contact institution. *Financial support:* In 2010–11, 206 students received support, including 23 fellowships (averaging $2,400 per year), 50 research assistantships (averaging $900 per year), 8 teaching assistantships with partial tuition reimbursements available (averaging $1,650 per year); career-related internships or fieldwork, Federal Work-Study, scholarships/grants, tuition waivers (full and partial), and unspecified assistantships also available. Support available to part-time students. Financial award application deadline: 5/1; financial award applicants required to submit FAFSA. *Faculty research:* Health law, international law, constitutional law, commercial law, business organizations. *Unit head:* Phyllis L. Crocker, Dean, 216-687-2300, Fax: 216-687-6881, E-mail: phyllis.crocker@law.csuohio.edu. *Application contact:* Christopher Lucak, Assistant Dean for Admissions, 216-687-4692, Fax: 216-687-6881, E-mail: christopher.lucak@law.csuohio.edu.

Cleveland State University, College of Graduate Studies, Nance College of Business Administration, Department of Management and Labor Relations, Cleveland, OH 44115. Offers labor relations and human resources (MLRHR). Part-time programs available. *Faculty:* 9 full-time (4 women), 10 part-time/adjunct (3 women). *Students:* 29 full-time (22 women), 40 part-time (28 women); includes 9 Black or African American, non-Hispanic/Latino; 1 Asian, non-Hispanic/Latino; 1 Hispanic/Latino; 1 Two or more races, non-Hispanic/Latino, 17 international. Average age 29. 95 applicants, 67% accepted, 24 enrolled. In 2010, 16 master's awarded. *Entrance requirements:* For master's, GMAT or GRE. Additional exam requirements/recommendations for international students: Required—TOEFL (minimum score 525 paper-based; 197 computer-based). *Application deadline:* For fall admission, 7/15 for domestic students; for spring admission, 12/15 for domestic students. Applications are processed on a rolling basis. Application fee: $30. Electronic applications accepted. *Expenses:* Tuition, state resident: full-time $8447; part-time $469 per credit hour. Tuition, nonresident: full-time $16,020; part-time $890 per credit hour. Required fees: $50. *Financial support:* In 2010–11, 3 research assistantships with full and partial tuition reimbursements (averaging $6,960 per year) were awarded; career-related internships or fieldwork, tuition waivers (full), and unspecified assistantships also available. Financial award applicants required to submit FAFSA. *Unit head:* Dr. Jeffrey C. Susbauer, Chairperson, 216-687-4747, Fax: 216-687-4708, E-mail: j.susbauer@csuohio.edu. *Application contact:* Dr. W. Benoy Joseph, Associate Dean, 216-687-2019, Fax: 216-687-9354, E-mail: w.joseph@csuohio.edu.

Cornell University, Graduate School, Graduate Fields of Industrial and Labor Relations, Ithaca, NY 14853. Offers collective bargaining, labor law and labor history (MILR, MPS, MS, PhD); economic and social statistics (MILR); human resource studies (MILR, MPS, MS, PhD); industrial and labor relations problems (MILR, MPS, MS, PhD); international and comparative

Industrial and Labor Relations

Cornell University (continued)
labor (MILR, MPS, MS, PhD); labor economics (MILR, MPS, MS, PhD); organizational behavior (MILR, MPS, MS, PhD). *Faculty:* 52 full-time (17 women). *Students:* 165 full-time (100 women); includes 13 Black or African American, non-Hispanic/Latino; 1 American Indian or Alaska Native, non-Hispanic/Latino; 15 Asian, non-Hispanic/Latino; 7 Hispanic/Latino, 60 international. Average age 29. 340 applicants, 29% accepted, 87 enrolled. In 2010, 68 master's, 3 doctorates awarded. *Degree requirements:* For master's, thesis (MS); for doctorate, comprehensive exam, thesis/dissertation, teaching experience. *Entrance requirements:* For master's and doctorate, GMAT or GRE General Test, 2 academic recommendations. Additional exam requirements/recommendations for international students: Required—TOEFL (minimum score 550 paper-based; 213 computer-based; 77 iBT). Application fee: $70. Electronic applications accepted. *Expenses:* Contact institution. *Financial support:* In 2010–11, 73 students received support, including 14 fellowships with full tuition reimbursements available, 26 research assistantships with full tuition reimbursements available, 30 teaching assistantships with full tuition reimbursements available; institutionally sponsored loans, scholarships/grants, health care benefits, tuition waivers (full and partial), and unspecified assistantships also available. Financial award applicants required to submit FAFSA. *Unit head:* Director of Graduate Studies, 607-255-1522. *Application contact:* Graduate Field Assistant, 607-255-1522, E-mail: ilrgradapplicant@cornell.edu.

See Close-Up on page 1265.

Georgetown University, Graduate School of Arts and Sciences, Department of Economics, Washington, DC 20057. Offers econometrics (PhD); economic development (PhD); economic theory (PhD); industrial organization (PhD); international macro and finance (PhD); international trade (PhD); labor economics (PhD); macroeconomics (PhD); public economics and political economics (PhD); MA/PhD; MS/MA. *Degree requirements:* For doctorate, comprehensive exam, thesis/dissertation. *Entrance requirements:* For doctorate, GRE General Test. Additional exam requirements/recommendations for international students: Required—TOEFL. *Faculty research:* International economics, economic development.

Indiana University of Pennsylvania, School of Graduate Studies and Research, College of Health and Human Services, Department of Industrial and Labor Relations, Indiana, PA 15705-1087. Offers MA. Part-time and evening/weekend programs available. *Faculty:* 4 full-time (1 woman). *Students:* 41 full-time (23 women), 12 part-time (5 women); includes 4 minority (2 Black or African American, non-Hispanic/Latino; 1 Hispanic/Latino; 1 Two or more races, non-Hispanic/Latino), 1 international. Average age 27. 62 applicants, 66% accepted, 35 enrolled. In 2010, 44 master's awarded. *Degree requirements:* For master's, thesis optional. *Entrance requirements:* For master's, 2 letters of recommendation. Additional exam requirements/recommendations for international students: Required—TOEFL. *Application deadline:* For fall admission, 7/1 priority date for domestic students; for spring admission, 11/1 for domestic students. Applications are processed on a rolling basis. Application fee: $40. *Financial support:* In 2010–11, 12 research assistantships with full and partial tuition reimbursements (averaging $4,770 per year) were awarded; fellowships, career-related internships or fieldwork and Federal Work-Study also available. Support available to part-time students. Financial award application deadline: 3/15; financial award applicants required to submit FAFSA. *Faculty research:* Conflict resolution, labor-management cooperation, unemployment compensation, public sector labor relations, employee discipline. *Unit head:* Dr. Jennie K. Bullard, Chairperson and Graduate Coordinator, 724-357-4470, E-mail: jbullard@iup.edu. *Application contact:* Dr. Jacqueline Beck, Associate Dean, 724-357-2560, E-mail: jbeck@iup.edu.

Inter American University of Puerto Rico, Metropolitan Campus, Graduate Programs, Program in Labor Relations, San Juan, PR 00919-1293. Offers MA. *Degree requirements:* For master's, comprehensive exam. *Entrance requirements:* For master's, GRE or EXADEP, interview. Electronic applications accepted.

Inter American University of Puerto Rico, Metropolitan Campus, Graduate Programs, Program in Psychology, San Juan, PR 00919-1293. Offers counseling psychology (MA, PhD); industrial/organizational psychology (MA, PhD); labor relations (MA); school psychology (MA, PhD). *Degree requirements:* For master's, comprehensive exam. *Entrance requirements:* For master's, GRE or EXADEP, interview. Electronic applications accepted.

Loyola University Chicago, Graduate School of Business, Institute of Human Resources and Employee Relations, Chicago, IL 60660. Offers MSHR. Part-time programs available. *Entrance requirements:* For master's, GMAT or GRE General Test, letters of recommendation. Additional exam requirements/recommendations for international students: Required—TOEFL (minimum score 550 paper-based; 213 computer-based; 80 iBT). *Expenses:* Contact institution. *Faculty research:* Human resource management, labor relations, global human resource management, organizational development, compensation.

McMaster University, School of Graduate Studies, Faculty of Social Sciences, Program in Labour Studies, Hamilton, ON L8S 4M2, Canada. Offers work and society (MA).

Memorial University of Newfoundland, School of Graduate Studies, Interdisciplinary Program in Employment Relations, St. John's, NL A1C 5S7, Canada. Offers MER. Part-time programs available. *Degree requirements:* For master's, major supervised paper. *Entrance requirements:* For master's, undergraduate degree in related field, minimum B average. Electronic applications accepted.

Michigan State University, The Graduate School, College of Social Science, School of Labor and Industrial Relations, East Lansing, MI 48824. Offers human resources and labor relations (MLRHR); industrial relations and human resources (PhD). *Entrance requirements:* Additional exam requirements/recommendations for international students: Required—TOEFL.

New York Institute of Technology, Graduate Division, School of Management, Program in Human Resources Management and Labor Relations, Old Westbury, NY 11568-8000. Offers human resources administration (Advanced Certificate); human resources management and labor relations (MS); labor relations (Advanced Certificate). Part-time and evening/weekend programs available. *Students:* 41 full-time (28 women), 62 part-time (44 women); includes 30 minority (16 Black or African American, non-Hispanic/Latino; 5 Asian, non-Hispanic/Latino; 9 Hispanic/Latino), 28 international. Average age 31. In 2010, 27 master's, 3 other advanced degrees awarded. *Degree requirements:* For master's, comprehensive exam, thesis optional. *Entrance requirements:* For master's, GRE, minimum QPA of 2.85, interview, 2 letters of recommendation. *Application deadline:* For fall admission, 7/1 priority date for domestic students; for spring admission, 12/1 priority date for domestic students. Applications are processed on a rolling basis. Application fee: $50. Electronic applications accepted. *Expenses:* Tuition: Part-time $835 per credit. *Financial support:* Fellowships, research assistantships, career-related internships or fieldwork, institutionally sponsored loans, and tuition waivers (full and partial) available. Support available to part-time students. Financial award applicants required to submit FAFSA. *Faculty research:* Ethics in industrial relations, employee relations, public sector labor relations, benefits. *Unit head:* William Ninehan, Director, 646-273-6071, Fax: 516-686-7425, E-mail: wninehan@nyit.edu. *Application contact:* Dr. Jacquelyn Nealon, Vice President for Enrollment Services, 516-686-7925, Fax: 516-686-7597, E-mail: jnealon@nyit.edu.

The Ohio State University, Graduate School, Max M. Fisher College of Business, Program in Labor and Human Resources, Columbus, OH 43210. Offers MLHR, PhD. *Faculty:* 28. *Students:* 80 full-time (60 women), 40 part-time (31 women); includes 8 Black or African American, non-Hispanic/Latino; 4 Asian, non-Hispanic/Latino; 3 Hispanic/Latino; 4 Two or more races, non-Hispanic/Latino, 23 international. Average age 28. In 2010, 34 master's, 2 doctorates awarded. *Degree requirements:* For master's, thesis optional; for doctorate, thesis/dissertation. *Entrance requirements:* For master's and doctorate, GRE General Test. Additional exam requirements/recommendations for international students: Recommended—TOEFL (minimum score 600 paper-based; 250 computer-based). *Application deadline:* For fall admission, 8/15 priority date for domestic students, 7/1 priority date for international students; for winter admission, 12/1 priority date for domestic students, 11/1 priority date for international students; for spring admission, 3/1 priority date for domestic students, 2/1 priority date for international students. Applications are processed on a rolling basis. Application fee: $40 ($50 for international students). Electronic applications accepted. *Expenses:* Tuition, state resident: full-time $10,605. Tuition, nonresident: full-time $26,535. Tuition and fees vary according to course load and program. *Financial support:* Fellowships, research assistantships, teaching assistantships, Federal Work-Study and institutionally sponsored loans available. Support available to part-time students. *Unit head:* Robert L. Heneman, Graduate Studies Committee Chair, 614-292-4587, Fax: 614-292-9006, E-mail: heneman.1@osu.edu. *Application contact:* 614-292-9444, Fax: 614-292-3895, E-mail: domestic.grad@osu.edu.

Penn State University Park, Graduate School, College of the Liberal Arts, Department of Labor Studies and Employment Relations, State College, University Park, PA 16802-1503. Offers MPS, MS. Postbaccalaureate distance learning degree programs offered.

Queen's University at Kingston, School of Graduate Studies and Research, School of Industrial Relations, Kingston, ON K7L 3N6, Canada. Offers MIR. Part-time programs available. *Degree requirements:* For master's, research essay, skill seminars and modules. *Entrance requirements:* For master's, course work in micro-economics, macro-economics, and quantitative statistics. Additional exam requirements/recommendations for international students: Required—TOEFL (minimum score 600 paper-based; 250 computer-based). *Faculty research:* Collective bargaining and labor law, personnel and human relations, labor market analysis and policy, change management, teams.

Rutgers, The State University of New Jersey, New Brunswick, School of Management and Labor Relations, Program in Industrial Relations and Human Resources, Piscataway, NJ 08854-8097. Offers PhD. Part-time programs available. *Faculty:* 17 full-time (7 women). *Students:* 12 full-time (5 women); includes 1 Black or African American, non-Hispanic/Latino; 8 Asian, non-Hispanic/Latino. Average age 35. 31 applicants, 23% accepted, 5 enrolled. In 2010, 1 doctorate awarded. *Degree requirements:* For doctorate, comprehensive exam, thesis/dissertation. *Entrance requirements:* For doctorate, GRE or GMAT, 3 letters of recommendation. Additional exam requirements/recommendations for international students: Required—TOEFL (minimum score 575 paper-based; 233 computer-based; 91 iBT). *Application deadline:* For fall admission, 2/1 for domestic and international students. Application fee: $60. Electronic applications accepted. *Expenses:* Tuition, state resident: full-time $7200; part-time $600 per credit. Tuition, nonresident: full-time $11,124; part-time $927 per credit. *Financial support:* In 2010–11, 10 students received support, including teaching assistantships with full tuition reimbursements available (averaging $23,842 per year); health care benefits and tuition waivers (full and partial) also available. Financial award application deadline: 2/1. *Faculty research:* Strategic human resources, labor relations, organizational change, worker representation. Total annual research expenditures: $2 million. *Unit head:* Douglas Kruse, Professor/Director, 732-445-5991, Fax: 732-445-2830, E-mail: dkruse@smlr.rutgers.edu. *Application contact:* Rebecca A. Tinkhorn, Administrative Assistant, 732-445-5974, Fax: 732-445-2830, E-mail: jeriksen@rci.rutgers.edu.

Rutgers, The State University of New Jersey, New Brunswick, School of Management and Labor Relations, Program in Labor and Employment Relations, Piscataway, NJ 08854-8097. Offers MLER. Part-time programs available. Postbaccalaureate distance learning degree programs offered. *Faculty:* 15 full-time (8 women), 3 part-time/adjunct (2 women). *Students:* 40 full-time (26 women), 35 part-time (22 women); includes 21 Black or African American, non-Hispanic/Latino; 1 American Indian or Alaska Native, non-Hispanic/Latino; 13 Asian, non-Hispanic/Latino; 3 Hispanic/Latino, 9 international. Average age 30. 27 applicants, 70% accepted, 18 enrolled. In 2010, 36 master's awarded. *Degree requirements:* For master's, thesis optional. *Entrance requirements:* For master's, GRE General Test. Additional exam requirements/recommendations for international students: Required—TOEFL. *Application deadline:* For fall admission, 7/1 priority date for domestic students, 3/1 priority date for international students; for spring admission, 12/1 priority date for domestic students, 7/1 priority date for international students. Applications are processed on a rolling basis. Application fee: $50. Electronic applications accepted. *Expenses:* Contact institution. *Financial support:* In 2010–11, 9 students received support, including 17 fellowships (averaging $1,500 per year); career-related internships or fieldwork and Federal Work-Study also available. Support available to part-time students. Financial award application deadline: 3/1; financial award applicants required to submit FAFSA. *Faculty research:* Labor history, women and work, labor education, comparative labor movements, labor involvement and corporate decision making. *Unit head:* Amy Marchitto, Coordinator, 732-932-8559, Fax: 732-932-8677, E-mail: marchitto@smlr.rutgers.edu. *Application contact:* Amy Marchitto, Coordinator, 732-932-8559, Fax: 732-932-8677, E-mail: marchitto@smlr.rutgers.edu.

State University of New York Empire State College, Graduate Studies, Program in Labor and Policy Studies, Saratoga Springs, NY 12866-4391. Offers MA. Part-time and evening/weekend programs available. Postbaccalaureate distance learning degree programs offered (minimal on-campus study). *Degree requirements:* For master's, thesis, exam. *Entrance requirements:* Additional exam requirements/recommendations for international students: Required—TOEFL (minimum score 600 paper-based; 280 computer-based). Electronic applications accepted. *Faculty research:* Work and technology, collective bargaining, labor law, human resources management, trade union governance.

Université de Montréal, Faculty of Arts and Sciences, School of Industrial Relations, Montréal, QC H3C 3J7, Canada. Offers M Sc, PhD, DESS. Part-time programs available. *Degree requirements:* For master's, thesis; for doctorate, thesis/dissertation, general exam. *Entrance requirements:* For master's, BS in industrial relations. Electronic applications accepted. *Faculty research:* Labor law, health and safety at work, stress, job satisfaction, labor economics.

Université du Québec à Trois-Rivières, Graduate Programs, Program in Labor Relations, Trois-Rivières, QC G9A 5H7, Canada. Offers DESS.

Université du Québec à Trois-Rivières, Graduate Programs, Program in Labor Relations, Trois-Rivières, QC G9A 5H7, Canada. Offers DESS.

Université du Québec en Outaouais, Graduate Programs, Department of Industrial Relations, Gatineau, QC J8X 3X7, Canada. Offers M Sc, MA, PhD, Diploma. Part-time programs available. *Students:* 45 full-time, 24 part-time, 5 international. *Degree requirements:* For master's, thesis (for some programs), internship (for some programs); for doctorate, thesis/dissertation. *Entrance requirements:* For master's, appropriate bachelor's degree, proficiency in French; for doctorate, appropriate master's degree, proficiency in French. *Application deadline:* For fall admission, 6/1 for domestic students, 3/1 for international students; for winter admission, 11/1 for domestic students, 10/1 for international students. Application fee: $30 Canadian dollars. *Financial support:* Fellowships, research assistantships, teaching assistantships available. *Unit head:* Christiane Labelle, Director, 819-595-3900 Ext. 1780, Fax: 819-773-1788, E-mail: christiane.labelle@uqo.ca. *Application contact:* Registrar's Office, 819-773-1850, Fax: 819-773-1835, E-mail: registraire@uqo.ca.

Université Laval, Faculty of Social Sciences, Department of Industrial Relations, Programs in Industrial Relations, Québec, QC G1K 7P4, Canada. Offers MA, PhD. Terminal master's awarded for partial completion of doctoral program. *Degree requirements:* For master's, thesis (for some programs); for doctorate, comprehensive exam, thesis/dissertation. *Entrance requirements:* For master's and doctorate, knowledge of French, comprehension of written English. Electronic applications accepted.

University of Alberta, Faculty of Graduate Studies and Research, Doctoral Program in Business, Edmonton, AB T6G 2E1, Canada. Offers accounting (PhD); finance (PhD); human resources/industrial relations (PhD); management science (PhD); marketing (PhD); organizational analysis (PhD); MBA/PhD. *Accreditation:* AACSB. Part-time programs available. *Degree requirements:* For doctorate, comprehensive exam, thesis/dissertation. *Entrance requirements:* For doctorate, GMAT. Additional exam requirements/recommendations for international students: Required—TOEFL (minimum score 550 paper-based; 213 computer-based). Electronic applications accepted. *Faculty research:* Accounting, capital markets and corporate finance, organizational change and human resource management, marketing, strategic management.

University of California, Berkeley, Graduate Division, Haas School of Business, PhD in Business Administration Program, Berkeley, CA 94720-1500. Offers accounting (PhD); business and public policy (PhD); finance (PhD); management of organizations (PhD); marketing (PhD); operations management (PhD); real estate (PhD). *Accreditation:* AACSB. *Students:* 78 full-time (25 women); includes 12 Asian, non-Hispanic/Latino; 2 Hispanic/Latino, 32 international. Average age 30. 526 applicants, 7% accepted, 17 enrolled. In 2010, 17 doctorates awarded. *Degree requirements:* For doctorate, comprehensive exam, thesis/dissertation, written preliminary exams, oral qualifying exam. *Entrance requirements:* For doctorate, GMAT or GRE, minimum GPA of 3.0 in undergraduate and graduate coursework. Additional exam requirements/recommendations for international students: Required—TOEFL (minimum score 570 paper-based; 230 computer-based; 70 iBT), IELTS (minimum score 7). *Application deadline:* For fall admission, 12/10 for domestic and international students. Application fee: $70 ($90 for international students). Electronic applications accepted. *Financial support:* In 2010–11, 63 students received support, including 58 fellowships with full and partial tuition reimbursements available (averaging $26,000 per year); research assistantships with full and partial tuition reimbursements available, teaching assistantships with full and partial tuition reimbursements available, scholarships/grants, health care benefits, tuition waivers (full), unspecified assistantships, and transit pass, travel grants also available. Financial award application deadline: 12/10; financial award applicants required to submit FAFSA. *Faculty research:* Accounting, business and public policy, finance, management of organizations, marketing, operations and information technology management, real estate526. *Unit head:* Dr. Sunil Dutta, Director, 510-642-1229, Fax: 510-643-4255, E-mail: .kimg@haas.berkeley.edu. *Application contact:* Kim Guilfoyle, Director, Student Affairs, 510-642-3944, Fax: 510-643-4255, E-mail: kimg@haas.berkeley.edu.

University of Cincinnati, Graduate School, McMicken College of Arts and Sciences, Center for Organizational Leadership, Program in Labor and Employment Relations, Cincinnati, OH 45221. Offers MALER. Part-time and evening/weekend programs available. *Degree requirements:* For master's, thesis or alternative, final experience project. *Entrance requirements:* For master's, minimum undergraduate GPA of 3.0. Additional exam requirements/recommendations for international students: Required—TOEFL (minimum score 560 paper-based). Electronic applications accepted. *Faculty research:* Human resource management, diversity, leadership.

University of Cincinnati, Graduate School, McMicken College of Arts and Sciences, Department of Economics, Cincinnati, OH 45221. Offers applied economics (MA); labor and employment relations (MALER). Part-time and evening/weekend programs available. Electronic applications accepted.

University of Illinois at Urbana–Champaign, Graduate College, School of Labor and Employment Relations, Champaign, IL 61820. Offers human resources and industrial relations (MHRIR, PhD); MHRIR/JD; MHRIR/MBA. Part-time programs available. *Faculty:* 15 full-time (4 women). *Students:* 169 full-time (117 women), 24 part-time (11 women); includes 40 minority (15 Black or African American, non-Hispanic/Latino; 16 Asian, non-Hispanic/Latino; 7 Hispanic/Latino; 2 Two or more races, non-Hispanic/Latino), 66 international. 262 applicants, 43% accepted, 63 enrolled. In 2010, 99 master's, 1 doctorate awarded. Terminal master's awarded for partial completion of doctoral program. *Entrance requirements:* For master's and doctorate, GRE or GMAT, minimum GPA of 3.0. Additional exam requirements/recommendations for international students: Required—TOEFL (minimum score 590 paper-based; 243 computer-based; 96 iBT) or IELTS (minimum score 6.5). Application fee: $75 ($90 for international students). Electronic applications accepted. *Financial support:* In 2010–11, 8 fellowships, 10 research assistantships, 4 teaching assistantships were awarded; tuition waivers (full and partial) also available. *Unit head:* Dr. Joel E. Cutcher-Gershenfeld, Dean, 217-333-1482, Fax: 217-244-9290, E-mail: joelcg@illinois.edu. *Application contact:* Elizabeth Barker, Director of Student Services, 217-333-2381, Fax: 217-244-9290, E-mail: ebarker@illinois.edu.

University of Massachusetts Amherst, Graduate School, College of Social and Behavioral Sciences, The Labor Center, Amherst, MA 01003. Offers labor studies (MS); union leadership and administration (MS). Part-time programs available. Postbaccalaureate distance learning degree programs offered (minimal on-campus study). *Faculty:* 3 full-time (2 women). *Students:* 19 full-time (7 women), 53 part-time (23 women); includes 20 minority (6 Black or African American, non-Hispanic/Latino; 6 Asian, non-Hispanic/Latino; 8 Hispanic/Latino). Average age 37. 38 applicants, 84% accepted, 16 enrolled. In 2010, 18 master's awarded. *Degree requirements:* For master's, thesis or alternative. *Entrance requirements:* Additional exam requirements/recommendations for international students: Required—TOEFL (minimum score 550 paper-based; 213 computer-based; 80 iBT), IELTS (minimum score 6.5). *Application deadline:* For fall admission, 2/1 for domestic and international students; for spring admission, 10/1 for domestic and international students. Applications are processed on a rolling basis. Application fee: $50 ($65 for international students). Electronic applications accepted. *Expenses:* Tuition, state resident: full-time $2640. Required fees: $8282. One-time fee: $357 full-time. *Financial support:* In 2010–11, 10 teaching assistantships with full tuition reimbursements (averaging $5,266 per year) were awarded; fellowships, research assistantships, career-related internships or fieldwork, Federal Work-Study, scholarships/grants, traineeships, health care benefits, tuition waivers (full), and unspecified assistantships also available. Support available to part-time students. Financial award application deadline: 2/1; financial award applicants required to submit FAFSA. *Unit head:* Dr. Eve Weinbaum, Graduate Program Director, 413-545-4875, Fax: 413-545-0110. *Application contact:* Jean M. Ames, Supervisor of Admissions, 413-545-0722, Fax: 413-577-0010, E-mail: gradadm@grad.umass.edu.

University of Minnesota, Twin Cities Campus, Carlson School of Management, Program in Human Resources and Industrial Relations, Minneapolis, MN 55455-0213. Offers MA, PhD. *Accreditation:* AACSB. Part-time and evening/weekend programs available. *Faculty:* 11 full-time (6 women), 6 part-time/adjunct (1 woman). *Students:* 196 full-time (138 women), 92 part-time (68 women); includes 13 Black or African American, non-Hispanic/Latino; 18 Asian, non-Hispanic/Latino; 5 Hispanic/Latino, 62 international. Average age 26. 306 applicants, 44% accepted, 85 enrolled. In 2010, 96 master's, 5 doctorates awarded. Terminal master's awarded for partial completion of doctoral program. *Degree requirements:* For master's, thesis optional; for doctorate, thesis/dissertation. *Entrance requirements:* For master's, GMAT or GRE General Test; for doctorate, GRE General Test. Additional exam requirements/recommendations for international students: Required—TOEFL (minimum score 580 paper-based; 85 iBT). *Application deadline:* For fall admission, 6/15 for domestic and international students; for spring admission, 10/15 for domestic and international students. Applications are processed on a rolling basis. Application fee: $75 ($95 for international students). *Expenses:* Contact institution. *Financial support:* In 2010–11, 60 students received support, including 39 fellowships with partial tuition reimbursements available (averaging $6,500 per year), 14 research assistantships with full and partial tuition reimbursements available (averaging $12,500 per year), 7 teaching assistantships with full tuition reimbursements available (averaging $9,000 per year); career-related internships or fieldwork, Federal Work-Study, institutionally sponsored loans, and tuition waivers (full and partial) also available. Support available to part-time students. Financial award application deadline: 2/1; financial award applicants required to submit FAFSA. *Faculty research:* Staffing, training, and development; compensation and benefits; organization theory; collective bargaining. Total annual research expenditures: $200,000. *Unit head:* Theresa Glomb, Director of Graduate Studies, 612-624-4863, Fax: 612-624-8360, E-mail: tglomb@umn.edu. *Application contact:* Christina Hill, Admissions Coordinator, 612-624-5704, Fax: 612-624-8360, E-mail: hill1312@umn.edu.

University of New Haven, Graduate School, School of Business, Program in Public Administration, West Haven, CT 06516-1916. Offers personnel and labor relations (MPA); public administration (MPA, Certificate), including city management (MPA), community-clinical services (MPA), health care management (MPA), long-term health care (MPA), personnel and labor relations (MPA), public administration (Certificate), public management (Certificate), public personnel management (Certificate); MBA/MPA. Part-time and evening/weekend programs available. *Students:* 37 full-time (19 women), 33 part-time (18 women); includes 15 Black or African American, non-Hispanic/Latino; 1 Asian, non-Hispanic/Latino; 4 Hispanic/Latino, 9 international. Average age 33. 51 applicants, 100% accepted, 35 enrolled. In 2010, 14 master's, 4 other advanced degrees awarded. *Degree requirements:* For master's, thesis or alternative. *Entrance requirements:* Additional exam requirements/recommendations for international students: Required—TOEFL (minimum score 520 paper-based; 190 computer-based; 70 iBT); Recommended—IELTS (minimum score 5.5). *Application deadline:* For fall admission, 5/31 for international students; for winter admission, 10/15 for international students; for spring admission, 1/15 for international students. Applications are processed on a rolling basis. Application fee: $50. Electronic applications accepted. *Expenses:* Contact institution. *Financial support:* Research assistantships with partial tuition reimbursements, teaching assistantships with partial tuition reimbursements, career-related internships or fieldwork, Federal Work-Study, scholarships/grants, tuition waivers, and unspecified assistantships available. Support available to part-time students. Financial award application deadline: 5/1; financial award applicants required to submit FAFSA. *Unit head:* Charles Coleman, Chairman, 203-932-7375. *Application contact:* Eloise Gormley, Director of Graduate Admissions, 203-932-7449, Fax: 203-932-7137, E-mail: gradinfo@newhaven.edu.

University of New Mexico, Graduate School, College of Arts and Sciences, Department of Economics, Albuquerque, NM 87131-2039. Offers environmental/natural resources (MA, PhD); international/development (MA, PhD); labor/human resources (MA, PhD); public finance (MA, PhD). Part-time programs available. *Faculty:* 26 full-time (9 women), 7 part-time/adjunct (1 woman). *Students:* 47 full-time (14 women), 17 part-time (5 women); includes 2 American Indian or Alaska Native, non-Hispanic/Latino; 2 Asian, non-Hispanic/Latino; 8 Hispanic/Latino, 18 international. Average age 34. 75 applicants, 51% accepted, 15 enrolled. In 2010, 14 master's, 1 doctorate awarded. Terminal master's awarded for partial completion of doctoral program. *Degree requirements:* For master's, comprehensive exam, thesis (for some programs); for doctorate, comprehensive exam, thesis/dissertation. *Entrance requirements:* For master's and doctorate, GRE General Test, 3 letters of recommendation, letter of intent. Additional exam requirements/recommendations for international students: Required—TOEFL (minimum score 520 paper-based; 190 computer-based; 68 iBT). *Application deadline:* For fall admission, 3/1 priority date for domestic students, 3/1 for international students. Applications are processed on a rolling basis. Application fee: $50. Electronic applications accepted. *Expenses:* Tuition, state resident: full-time $5991; part-time $251 per credit hour. Tuition, nonresident: full-time $14,405; part-time $800.20 per credit hour. Tuition and fees vary according to course level, course load, program and reciprocity agreements. *Financial support:* In 2010–11, 47 students received support, including 3 fellowships with tuition reimbursements available (averaging $3,611 per year), 14 research assistantships with tuition reimbursements available (averaging $7,791 per year), 15 teaching assistantships (averaging $7,467 per year); career-related internships or fieldwork, Federal Work-Study, scholarships/grants, health care benefits, and unspecified assistantships also available. Support available to part-time students. Financial award application deadline: 3/1; financial award applicants required to submit FAFSA. *Faculty research:* Core theory, econometrics, public finance, international/development economics, labor/human resource economics, environmental/natural resource economics. Total annual research expenditures: $1.8 million. *Unit head:* Dr. Robert Berrens, Chair, 505-277-5304, Fax: 505-277-9445, E-mail: rberrens@unm.edu. *Application contact:* Shoshana Handel, Academic Advisor, 505-277-3056, Fax: 505-277-9445, E-mail: shandel@unm.edu.

University of North Texas, Toulouse Graduate School, College of Arts and Sciences, Department of Economics, Denton, TX 76203. Offers economic research (MS); economics (MA, MS); labor and industrial relations (MS). Part-time and evening/weekend programs available. *Degree requirements:* For master's, comprehensive exam, thesis (for some programs). *Entrance requirements:* For master's, GMAT, GRE General Test, minimum GPA of 3.0, 2 letters of recommendation, 500-word essay. Additional exam requirements/recommendations for international students: Recommended—TOEFL (minimum score 550 paper-based; 213 computer-based). *Expenses:* Tuition, state resident: full-time $4298; part-time $239 per credit hour. Tuition, nonresident: full-time $10,782; part-time $549 per credit hour. Required fees: $1292; $270 per credit hour. *Financial support:* Fellowships with partial tuition reimbursements, research assistantships with partial tuition reimbursements, teaching assistantships with partial tuition reimbursements, career-related internships or fieldwork, Federal Work-Study, and institutionally sponsored loans available. Support available to part-time students. Financial award application deadline: 4/1. *Faculty research:* Econometrics, international trade and development, immigration, telecommunications, micro enterprise development. *Application contact:* Graduate Adviser, 940-565-3442, Fax: 940-565-4426, E-mail: tieslau@unt.edu.

University of Rhode Island, Graduate School, Labor Research Center, Kingston, RI 02881. Offers labor relations and human resources (MS); MS/JD. Part-time and evening/weekend programs available. *Faculty:* 1 full-time (0 women), 3 part-time/adjunct (2 women). *Students:* 24 full-time (20 women), 31 part-time (23 women); includes 14 minority (5 Black or African American, non-Hispanic/Latino; 1 Hispanic/Latino; 8 Native Hawaiian or other Pacific Islander, non-Hispanic/Latino), 3 international. In 2010, 8 master's awarded. *Entrance requirements:* For master's, GRE, MAT, GMAT, or LSAT, 2 letters of recommendation. Additional exam requirements/recommendations for international students: Required—TOEFL (minimum score 550 paper-based; 213 computer-based). *Application deadline:* For fall admission, 7/15 for domestic students, 2/1 for international students; for spring admission, 11/15 for domestic students, 7/15 for international students. Application fee: $65. Electronic applications accepted. *Expenses:* Tuition, state resident: full-time $9588; part-time $533 per credit hour. Tuition, nonresident: full-time $22,968; part-time $1276 per credit hour. Required fees: $1282; $68 per semester. Tuition and fees vary according to program. *Financial support:* In 2010–11, 2 teaching assistantships with full tuition reimbursements (averaging $13,894 per year) were awarded; institutionally sponsored loans also available. Financial award application deadline: 2/1; financial award applicants required to submit FAFSA. *Unit head:* Dr. Richard W. Scholl, Director, 401-874-4347, Fax: 401-874-2954, E-mail: rscholl@uri.edu. *Application contact:* Dr. Richard W. Scholl, Director, 401-874-4347, Fax: 401-874-2954, E-mail: rscholl@uri.edu.

University of Saskatchewan, College of Graduate Studies and Research, Edwards School of Business, Department of Industrial Relations and Organizational Behavior, Saskatoon, SK S7N 5A2, Canada. Offers M Sc. Part-time programs available. *Degree requirements:* For master's, thesis. *Entrance requirements:* For master's, GMAT. Additional exam requirements/recommendations for international students: Required—TOEFL.

University of Toronto, School of Graduate Studies, Social Sciences Division, Centre for Industrial Relations and Human Resources, Toronto, ON M5S 1A1, Canada. Offers MHRIR, PhD. Part-time programs available. *Degree requirements:* For doctorate, thesis/dissertation. *Entrance requirements:* For master's, GRE or GMAT (for applicants who completed degree outside of Canada), minimum B+ in final 2 years of bachelor's degree completion, 2 letters of reference, resume; for doctorate, GRE or GMAT, MIR degree or equivalent, minimum B+ average, 3 letters of reference, resumé. Additional exam requirements/recommendations for international students: Required—TOEFL (minimum score 600 paper-based; 250 computer-based), TWE (minimum score 5), Michigan English Language Assessment Battery, IELTS, or COPE. *Expenses:* Contact institution.

University of Wisconsin–Milwaukee, Graduate School, College of Letters and Sciences, Interdepartmental Program in Human Resources and Labor Relations, Milwaukee, WI 53201-0413. Offers human resources and labor relations (MHRLR); international human resources and labor relations (Certificate); mediation and negotiation (Certificate). Part-time programs available. *Students:* 17 full-time (13 women), 30 part-time (23 women); includes 5 Black or African American, non-Hispanic/Latino; 1 American Indian or Alaska Native, non-Hispanic/Latino, 5 international. Average age 30. 38 applicants, 58% accepted, 8 enrolled. In 2010, 20 master's awarded. *Entrance requirements:* For master's, GMAT or GRE General Test. Additional exam requirements/recommendations for international students: Required—TOEFL (minimum

Industrial and Labor Relations

University of Wisconsin–Milwaukee (continued)
score 550 paper-based; 79 iBT), IELTS (minimum score 6.5). *Application deadline:* For fall admission, 1/1 priority date for domestic students; for spring admission, 9/1 for domestic students. Applications are processed on a rolling basis. Application fee: $56 ($96 for international students). Electronic applications accepted. *Financial support:* Career-related internships or fieldwork available. Support available to part-time students. Financial award application deadline: 4/15; financial award applicants required to submit FAFSA. *Unit head:* Susan M. Donohue-Davies, Representative, 414-299-4009, Fax: 414-229-5915, E-mail: suedono@uwm.edu. *Application contact:* General Information Contact, 414-229-4982, Fax: 414-229-6967, E-mail: gradschool@uwm.edu.

West Virginia University, College of Business and Economics, Program in Industrial Relations, Morgantown, WV 26506. Offers MSIR. *Accreditation:* AACSB. *Entrance requirements:* For master's, GRE or GMAT, minimum GPA of 3.0. Additional exam requirements/recommendations for international students: Required—TOEFL. Electronic applications accepted. *Faculty research:* Labor relations, mediation, leadership, benefits.

Philanthropic Studies

Indiana University–Purdue University Indianapolis, School of Liberal Arts, Department of Philanthropic Studies, Indianapolis, IN 46202. Offers MA, XMA, PhD. *Faculty:* 52 full-time, 10 part-time/adjunct. *Students:* 54 full-time (37 women), 28 part-time (27 women); includes 17 minority (10 Black or African American, non-Hispanic/Latino; 1 American Indian or Alaska Native, non-Hispanic/Latino; 4 Asian, non-Hispanic/Latino; 1 Hispanic/Latino; 1 Two or more races, non-Hispanic/Latino), 11 international. Average age 37. 39 applicants, 46% accepted, 17 enrolled. In 2010, 37 master's awarded. *Degree requirements:* For master's, thesis optional; for doctorate, thesis/dissertation. *Entrance requirements:* For master's, GRE General Test (minimum score 500 quantitative, 500 verbal, 4.5 analytical writing), minimum undergraduate GPA of 3.0; for doctorate, GRE General Test (minimum score: 500 quantitative, 500 verbal, 4.5 analytical writing), minimum GPA of 3.0, master's degree. *Application deadline:* For fall admission, 1/15 for domestic students, 1/1 for international students. Application fee: $55 ($65 for international students). *Financial support:* In 2010–11, 1 fellowship with partial tuition reimbursement (averaging $16,500 per year), 3 teaching assistantships (averaging $5,567 per year) were awarded; research assistantships with partial tuition reimbursements, career-related internships or fieldwork, Federal Work-Study, institutionally sponsored loans, and scholarships/grants also available. Financial award application deadline: 3/1; financial award applicants required to submit FAFSA. *Unit head:* Robert W. White, Dean, School of Liberal Arts, 317-274-8448. *Application contact:* Student Services, 317-274-4200, E-mail: maphil@iupui.edu.

Saint Mary's University of Minnesota, Schools of Graduate and Professional Programs, Graduate School of Business and Technology, Philanthropy and Development Program, Winona, MN 55987-1399. Offers MA. *Unit head:* Dr. Gary Kelsey, Director, 612-867-8663, E-mail: gkelsey@smumn.edu. *Application contact:* Jami Spitzer, Information Contact, 507-457-7500, E-mail: jspitzer@smumn.edu.

Public Administration

Adelphi University, University College, Graduate Certificate in Emergency Management Program, Garden City, NY 11530-0701. Offers Certificate. Part-time and evening/weekend programs available. *Faculty:* 1 full-time (0 women), 22 part-time/adjunct (9 women). *Students:* 8 part-time (4 women). Average age 35. 10 applicants, 50% accepted, 2 enrolled. In 2010, 5 Certificates awarded. *Application deadline:* For fall admission, 5/1 for international students; for spring admission, 12/1 for international students. Applications are processed on a rolling basis. Application fee: $50. Electronic applications accepted. *Financial support:* Research assistantships with partial tuition reimbursements, Federal Work-Study and institutionally sponsored loans available. *Faculty research:* Emergency nursing, disaster management, disaster preparedness. *Unit head:* Shawn O'Riley, Executive Director, 516-877-3412, E-mail: ucinfo@adelphi.edu. *Application contact:* Christine Murphy, Director of Admissions, 516-877-3050, Fax: 516-877-3039, E-mail: graduateadmissions@adelphi.edu.

Albany State University, College of Arts and Humanities, Program in Public Administration, Albany, GA 31705-2717. Offers community and economic development administration (MPA); criminal justice administration (MPA); fiscal management (MPA); general management (MPA); health administration and policy (MPA); human resources management (MPA); public policy (MPA); water resource management and policy (MPA). *Accreditation:* NASPAA. *Faculty:* 3 full-time (1 woman), 2 part-time/adjunct (0 women). *Students:* 13 full-time (7 women), 49 part-time (32 women); includes 60 Black or African American, non-Hispanic/Latino, 1 international. Average age 34. 18 applicants, 78% accepted, 12 enrolled. In 2010, 12 master's awarded. *Degree requirements:* For master's, professional public service internship, professional portfolio, capstone research project. *Entrance requirements:* For master's, GRE, MAT, or GMAT, baccalaureate degree from accredited college or university, two letters of recommendation, ASU medical and immunization form. *Application deadline:* For fall admission, 7/15 for domestic students, 5/15 for international students; for spring admission, 11/15 for domestic students, 9/15 for international students. Applications are processed on a rolling basis. Application fee: $20. Electronic applications accepted. *Expenses:* Tuition, state resident: full-time $3060; part-time $170 per credit hour. Tuition, nonresident: full-time $12,204; part-time $678 per credit hour. Required fees: $1160. Part-time tuition and fees vary according to course load. *Financial support:* Application deadline: 4/15. *Faculty research:* Public policy, strategic public human resources and human capital management, diversity management in the public sector and collective bargaining and labor relations in the public sector, e-government and public sector information systems, public administration pedagogy and business process modeling simulation, community development, nonprofit organizations, civic engagement and civic participation, healthcare disparities among minorities, poverty. Total annual research expenditures: $250. *Unit head:* Dr. Peter Ngwafu, Director, 229-430-4760, Fax: 229-430-7895, E-mail: peter.ngwafu@asurams.edu. *Application contact:* Dr. Rani George, Dean, Graduate School, 229-430-5118, Fax: 229-430-6398, E-mail: rani.george@asurams.edu.

Albany State University, College of Sciences and Health Professions, Department of Criminal Justice and Forensic Science, Albany, GA 31705-2717. Offers criminal justice (MS), including corrections, forensic science, law enforcement, public administration. Postbaccalaureate distance learning degree programs offered (no on-campus study). *Faculty:* 6 full-time (0 women), 2 part-time/adjunct (0 women). *Students:* 14 full-time (11 women), 41 part-time (30 women); includes 51 Black or African American, non-Hispanic/Latino. Average age 33. 20 applicants, 100% accepted, 14 enrolled. In 2010, 6 master's awarded. *Degree requirements:* For master's, comprehensive exam, thesis optional. *Entrance requirements:* For master's, GRE General Test or MAT. *Application deadline:* For fall admission, 7/15 for domestic students, 5/15 for international students; for spring admission, 11/15 for domestic students, 9/15 for international students. Applications are processed on a rolling basis. Application fee: $20. Electronic applications accepted. *Expenses:* Tuition, state resident: full-time $3060; part-time $170 per credit hour. Tuition, nonresident: full-time $12,204; part-time $678 per credit hour. Required fees: $1160. Part-time tuition and fees vary according to course load. *Financial support:* Application deadline: 4/15. *Faculty research:* Gang-related research, HIV-related research, behavioral-related research. Total annual research expenditures: $65,000. *Unit head:* Dr. Charles Ochie, Chair, 229-430-4864, Fax: 229-430-1676, E-mail: charles.ochie@asurams.edu. *Application contact:* Dr. Rani George, Dean, Graduate School, 229-430-5118, Fax: 229-430-6398, E-mail: rani.george@asurams.edu.

American International College, School of Business Administration, Program in Public Administration, Springfield, MA 01109-3189. Offers MPA. Part-time and evening/weekend programs available. *Degree requirements:* For master's, comprehensive exam (for some programs), thesis (for some programs), oral exam, practicum. *Entrance requirements:* Additional exam requirements/recommendations for international students: Required—TOEFL. Electronic applications accepted.

American Public University System, AMU/APU Graduate Programs, Charles Town, WV 25414. Offers accounting (MBA); administration and supervision (M Ed); air warfare (MA Military Studies); asymmetrical warfare (MA Military Studies); criminal justice (MA); emergency and disaster management (MA); entrepreneurship (MBA); environmental policy and management (MS); finance (MBA); general (MBA); global business management (MBA); guidance and counseling (M Ed); history (MA); homeland security (MA); homeland security resource allocation (MBA); humanities (MA); information technology (MS); information technology management (MBA); intelligence studies (MA); international relations and conflict resolution (MA); joint warfare (MA Military Studies); land warfare (MA Military Studies); legal studies (MA); management (MA), including defense mangement, general, human resource management, organizational leadership, public administration; marketing (MBA); military history (MA); national security studies (MA); naval warfare (MA Military Studies); nonprofit management (MBA); political science (MA); psychology (MA); public administration (MA); public health (MA); security management (MA); space studies (MS); sports management (MS); strategic leadership (MA Military Studies); teaching (M Ed), including elementary, secondary social sciences; transportation and logistics management (MA). Programs offered via distance learning only. Part-time and evening/weekend programs available. Postbaccalaureate distance learning degree programs offered (no on-campus study). *Faculty:* 253 full-time (134 women), 1,208 part-time/adjunct (570 women). *Students:* 956 full-time (422 women), 8,476 part-time (2,821 women); includes 2,511 minority (1,218 Black or African American, non-Hispanic/Latino; 68 American Indian or Alaska Native, non-Hispanic/Latino; 219 Asian, non-Hispanic/Latino; 705 Hispanic/Latino; 46 Native Hawaiian or other Pacific Islander, non-Hispanic/Latino; 255 Two or more races, non-Hispanic/Latino), 107 international. Average age 35. 9,550 applicants, 100% accepted. In 2010, 1,688 master's awarded. *Degree requirements:* For master's, comprehensive exam or practicum. *Entrance requirements:* For master's, official transcript showing earned bachelor's degree from institution accredited by recognized accrediting body. Additional exam requirements/recommendations for international students: Required—TOEFL (minimum score 550 paper-based; 213 computer-based), IELTS (minimum score 6.5). *Application deadline:* Applications are processed on a rolling basis. Application fee: $0. Electronic applications accepted. *Financial support:* Applicants required to submit FAFSA. *Faculty research:* Military history, criminal justice, management performance, national security. *Unit head:* Dr. Frank McCluskey, Provost, 877-468-6268, Fax: 304-724-3780. *Application contact:* Terry Grant, Director of Enrollment Management, 877-468-6268, Fax: 304-724-3780, E-mail: info@apus.edu.

American University, School of Public Affairs, Department of Public Administration, Program in Public Administration, Washington, DC 20016-8070. Offers MPA, PhD, Certificate. *Accreditation:* NASPAA (one or more programs are accredited). Part-time and evening/weekend programs available. *Degree requirements:* For master's, comprehensive exam; for doctorate, comprehensive exam, thesis/dissertation. *Entrance requirements:* For master's, GRE, statement of purpose; 2 recommendations; for doctorate, GRE, 3 recommendations; for Certificate, bachelor's degree. Additional exam requirements/recommendations for international students: Required—TOEFL.

The American University in Cairo, School of Global Affairs and Public Policy, Department of Public Policy and Administration, Cairo, Egypt. Offers MA, MPA, MPP, Diploma.

American University of Beirut, Graduate Programs, Faculty of Arts and Sciences, Beirut, Lebanon. Offers anthropology (MA); Arabic language and literature (MA); archaeology (MA); biology (MS); chemistry (MS); computational science (MS); computer science (MS); economics (MA); education (MA); English language (MA); English literature (MA); environmental policy planning (MSES); financial economics (MAFE); geology (MS); history (MA); mathematics (MA, MS); Middle Eastern studies (MA); philosophy (MA); physics (MS); political studies (MA); psychology (MA); public administration (MA); sociology (MA); statistics (MA, MS). Part-time programs available. *Faculty:* 229 full-time (98 women), 136 part-time/adjunct (79 women). *Students:* 158 full-time (104 women), 263 part-time (171 women). Average age 25. 356 applicants, 59% accepted, 127 enrolled. In 2010, 57 master's awarded. *Degree requirements:* For master's, one foreign language, comprehensive exam, thesis (for some programs). *Entrance requirements:* For master's, GRE, letter of recommendation. Additional exam requirements/recommendations for international students: Required—TOEFL (minimum score 600 paper-based; 250 computer-based; 97 iBT), IELTS (minimum score 7). *Application deadline:* For fall admission, 4/30 for domestic and international students; for spring admission, 11/1 for domestic and international students. Application fee: $50. *Expenses:* Tuition: Full-time $12,294; part-time $683 per credit. Required fees: $499; $499 per credit. Tuition and fees vary according to course load and program. *Financial support:* In 2010–11, 33 students received support. Career-related internships or fieldwork, institutionally sponsored loans, scholarships/grants, health care benefits, and unspecified assistantships available. Financial award application deadline: 2/4; financial award applicants required to submit FAFSA. *Faculty research:* Modern and contemporary world theatre; mineralogy, petrology, and geochemistry; cell differentiation and transformation; combinatorial technologies; philosophy of action; continental philosophy; Phoenician epigraphy; nascent complex societies and urbanism; the economies of the Arab world; environmental economics; tectonophysics; host-parasite interactions; innate immunity; insect-plant interactions; history of the Ottoman archives; decentralization; transparency and corruption. Total annual research expenditures: $622,243. *Unit head:* Dr. Patrick McGreevy, Dean, 961-137-4374 Ext. 3800, Fax: 961-174-4461, E-mail: pm07@aub.edu.lb. *Application contact:* Dr. Salim Kanaan, Director, Admissions Office, 961-135-0000 Ext. 2594, Fax: 961-175-0775, E-mail: sk00@aub.edu.lb.

American University of Sharjah, Graduate Programs, Sharjah, United Arab Emirates. Offers business (EMBA, GEMPA, MBA); chemical engineering (MS Ch E); civil engineering (MSCE); computer engineering (MS); electrical engineering (MSEE); mechanical engineering (MSME); mechatronics engineering (MS); public administration (MPA); teaching English to speakers of other languages (MA); translation and interpreting (MA); urban planning (MUP). Part-time and evening/weekend programs available. *Entrance requirements:* For master's, GMAT (MBA). Additional exam requirements/recommendations for international students: Required—TOEFL (minimum score 550 paper-based; 213 computer-based; 80 iBT), TWE (minimum score 5). Electronic applications accepted. *Faculty research:* Chemical engineering, civil engineering, computer engineering, electrical engineering, linguistics, translation.

Andrew Jackson University, Jeffrey D. Rubenstein College of Criminal Justice, Program in Public Administration, Birmingham, AL 35244. Offers MPA. Part-time and evening/weekend programs available. Postbaccalaureate distance learning degree programs offered (no on-campus study). *Entrance requirements:* For master's, course work in calculus, statistics. Additional exam requirements/recommendations for international students: Required—TOEFL (minimum score 550 paper-based; 213 computer-based). Electronic applications accepted.

Angelo State University, College of Graduate Studies, College of Liberal and Fine Arts, Department of Political Science and Criminal Justice, San Angelo, TX 76909. Offers public administration (MPA). Part-time and evening/weekend programs available. *Faculty:* 3 full-time (0 women). *Students:* 3 full-time (2 women), 5 part-time (2 women); includes 3 Hispanic/Latino. Average age 26. 4 applicants, 50% accepted, 2 enrolled. In 2010, 1 master's awarded. *Degree requirements:* For master's, comprehensive exam. *Entrance requirements:* Additional exam requirements/recommendations for international students: Required—TOEFL or IELTS. *Application deadline:* For fall admission, 7/15 priority date for domestic students, 6/10 for international students; for spring admission, 12/1 priority date for domestic students, 11/1 for international students. Applications are processed on a rolling basis. Application fee: $40 ($50 for international students). Electronic applications accepted. *Expenses:* Tuition, state resident: full-time $4560; part-time $152 per credit hour. Tuition, nonresident: full-time $13,860; part-time $462 per credit hour. Required fees: $2132. Tuition and fees vary according to course load. *Financial support:* Career-related internships or fieldwork, Federal Work-Study, and scholarships/grants available. Support available to part-time students. Financial award application deadline: 3/1; financial award applicants required to submit FAFSA. *Unit head:* Dr. Edward C. Olson, Department Head, 325-942-2262 Ext. 275, Fax: 325-942-2307, E-mail: ed.olson@angelo.edu. *Application contact:* Dr. Jack Barbour, Graduate Advisor, 325-942-2262 Ext. 282, Fax: 325-942-2307, E-mail: jack.barbour@angelo.edu.

Anna Maria College, Graduate Division, Program in Public Administration, Paxton, MA 01612. Offers MPA.

Appalachian State University, Cratis D. Williams Graduate School, Department of Government and Justice Studies, Boone, NC 28608. Offers criminal justice (MS); political science (MA), including American government, environmental politics and policy analysis, international relations; public administration (MPA), including public management, town, city and county management. Part-time programs available. Postbaccalaureate distance learning degree programs offered (no on-campus study). *Faculty:* 24 full-time (5 women), 3 part-time/adjunct (2 women). *Students:* 72 full-time (29 women), 53 part-time (25 women); includes 6 Black or African American, non-Hispanic/Latino; 1 Asian, non-Hispanic/Latino; 3 Hispanic/Latino; 1 Two or more races, non-Hispanic/Latino. 86 applicants, 86% accepted, 58 enrolled. In 2010, 49 master's awarded. *Degree requirements:* For master's, variable foreign language requirement, comprehensive exam, thesis optional. *Entrance requirements:* For master's, GRE General Test, 3 letters of recommendation. Additional exam requirements/recommendations for international students: Required—TOEFL (minimum score 570 paper-based; 230 computer-based; 79 iBT), IELTS (minimum score 6.5). *Application deadline:* For fall admission, 7/1 for domestic students, 2/1 for international students; for spring admission, 11/1 for domestic students, 7/1 for international students. Applications are processed on a rolling basis. Application fee: $55. Electronic applications accepted. *Expenses:* Tuition, state resident: full-time $3428; part-time $428 per unit. Tuition, nonresident: full-time $14,518; part-time $1814 per unit. Required fees: $2320; $344 per unit. Tuition and fees vary according to campus/location. *Financial support:* In 2010–11, 20 research assistantships (averaging $8,000 per year) were awarded; fellowships, teaching assistantships, career-related internships or fieldwork, Federal Work-Study, scholarships/grants, and unspecified assistantships also available. Financial award application deadline: 4/1; financial award applicants required to submit FAFSA. *Faculty research:* Campaign finance, emerging democracies, bureaucratic politics, judicial behavior, administration of justice. Total annual research expenditures: $143,000. *Unit head:* Dr. Brian Ellison, Chairperson, 828-262-3085, E-mail: ellisonba@appstate.edu. *Application contact:* Sandy Krause, Director of Admissions and Recruiting, 828-262-2130, Fax: 828-262-2709, E-mail: krausesl@appstate.edu.

Argosy University, Chicago, College of Business, Chicago, IL 60601. Offers accounting (DBA); customized professional concentration (MBA, DBA); finance (MBA); fraud examination (MBA); global business sustainability (DBA); healthcare administration (MBA); information systems (DBA); information systems management (MBA); international business (MBA, DBA); management (MBA, MSM, DBA); marketing (MBA, DBA); organizational leadership (Ed D); public administration (MBA); sustainable management (MBA). Postbaccalaureate distance learning degree programs offered (minimal on-campus study).

Argosy University, Dallas, College of Business, Farmers Branch, TX 75244. Offers accounting (DBA, AGC); corporate compliance (MBA, Graduate Certificate); customized professional concentration (MBA); finance (MBA, Graduate Certificate); fraud examination (MBA, Graduate Certificate); global business sustainability (DBA, AGC); healthcare administration (Graduate Certificate); healthcare management (MBA); information systems (MBA, DBA, AGC); information systems management (Graduate Certificate); international business (MBA, DBA, AGC, Graduate Certificate); management (MBA, DBA, AGC, Graduate Certificate); marketing (MBA, DBA, AGC, Graduate Certificate); public administration (MBA, Graduate Certificate); sustainable management (MBA, Graduate Certificate).

Argosy University, Denver, College of Business, Denver, CO 80231. Offers accounting (DBA); corporate compliance (MBA); customized professional concentration (MBA, DBA); finance (MBA); fraud examination (MBA); global business sustainability (DBA); healthcare administration (MBA); information systems (DBA); information systems management (MBA); international business (MBA, DBA); management (MBA, MSM, DBA); marketing (MBA, DBA); organizational leadership (Ed D); public administration (MBA); sustainable management (MBA).

Argosy University, Inland Empire, College of Business, San Bernardino, CA 92408. Offers accounting (DBA); corporate compliance (MBA); customized professional concentration (MBA, DBA); finance (MBA); fraud examination (MBA); global business sustainability (DBA); healthcare administration (MBA); information systems (DBA); information systems management (MBA); international business (MBA, DBA); management (MBA, MSM, DBA); marketing (MBA, DBA); organizational leadership (Ed D); public administration (MBA); sustainable management (MBA).

Argosy University, Los Angeles, College of Business, Santa Monica, CA 90045. Offers accounting (DBA); corporate compliance (MBA); customized professional concentration (MBA, DBA); finance (MBA); fraud examination (MBA); global business sustainability (DBA); healthcare administration (MBA); information systems (DBA); information systems management (MBA); international business (MBA, DBA); management (MBA, MSM, DBA); marketing (MBA, DBA); organizational leadership (Ed D); public administration (MBA); sustainable management (MBA).

Argosy University, Orange County, College of Business, Orange, CA 92868. Offers accounting (DBA, Adv C); corporate compliance (MBA); customized professional concentration (MBA, DBA); finance (MBA, Certificate); fraud examination (MBA); global business sustainability (DBA); healthcare administration (MBA, Certificate); information systems (DBA, Adv C, Certificate); information systems management (MBA); international business (MBA, DBA, Adv C, Certificate); management (MBA, MSM, DBA, Adv C); marketing (MBA, DBA, Adv C, Certificate); organizational leadership (Ed D); public administration (MBA, Certificate); sustainable management (MBA).

Argosy University, Phoenix, College of Business, Phoenix, AZ 85021. Offers accounting (DBA); corporate compliance (MBA); customized professional concentration (MBA, DBA); finance (MBA); fraud examination (MBA); global business sustainability (DBA); healthcare administration (MBA); information systems (DBA); information systems management (MBA); international business (MBA, DBA); management (MBA, DBA); marketing (MBA, DBA); public administration (MBA); sustainable management (MBA).

Argosy University, Salt Lake City, College of Business, Draper, UT 84020. Offers accounting (DBA); corporate compliance (MBA); customized professional concentration (MBA, DBA); finance (MBA); fraud examination (MBA); global business sustainability (DBA); healthcare administration (MBA); information systems (DBA); information systems management (MBA); international business (MBA, DBA); management (MBA, DBA); marketing (MBA, DBA); public administration (MBA); sustainable management (MBA).

Argosy University, San Diego, College of Business, San Diego, CA 92108. Offers accounting (DBA); corporate compliance (MBA); customized professional concentration (MBA, DBA); finance (MBA); fraud examination (MBA); global business sustainability (DBA); information systems (DBA); information systems management (MBA); international business (MBA, DBA); management (MBA, MSM, DBA); marketing (MBA, DBA); organizational leadership (Ed D); public administration (MBA).

Argosy University, San Francisco Bay Area, College of Business, Alameda, CA 94501. Offers accounting (DBA); corporate compliance (MBA); customized professional concentration (MBA, DBA); finance (MBA); fraud examination (MBA); global business sustainability (DBA); healthcare administration (MBA); information systems (DBA); information systems management (MBA); international business (MBA, DBA); management (MBA, MSM, DBA); marketing (MBA, DBA); organizational leadership (Ed D); public administration (MBA); sustainable management (MBA).

Argosy University, Sarasota, College of Business, Sarasota, FL 34235. Offers accounting (DBA, Adv C); corporate compliance (MBA, DBA, Certificate); customized professional concentration (MBA, DBA); finance (MBA, Certificate); fraud examination (MBA, Certificate); global business sustainability (DBA, Adv C); healthcare administration (MBA, Certificate); information systems (DBA, Adv C, Certificate); information systems management (MBA); international business (MBA, DBA, Adv C, Certificate); management (MBA, MSM, DBA, Adv C, Certificate); marketing (MBA, DBA, Adv C, Certificate); organizational leadership (Ed D); public administration (MBA, Certificate); sustainable management (MBA, Certificate).

Argosy University, Schaumburg, College of Business, Schaumburg, IL 60173-5403. Offers accounting (DBA, Adv C); customized professional concentration (MBA, DBA); finance (MBA, Certificate); fraud examination (MBA); global business sustainability (DBA); healthcare administration (MBA, Certificate); information systems (DBA, Adv C, Certificate); information systems management (MBA); international business (MBA, DBA, Adv C, Certificate); management (MBA, MSM, DBA, Adv C, Certificate); marketing (MBA, DBA, Adv C, Certificate); organizational leadership (Ed D); public administration (MBA); sustainable management (MBA).

Argosy University, Seattle, College of Business, Seattle, WA 98121. Offers accounting (DBA); corporate compliance (MBA); customized professional concentration (MBA, DBA); finance (MBA); fraud examination (MBA); global business sustainability (DBA); healthcare administration (MBA); information systems (DBA); information systems management (MBA); international business (MBA, DBA); management (MBA, MSM, DBA); marketing (MBA, DBA); organizational leadership (Ed D); public administration (MBA); sustainable management (MBA).

Argosy University, Tampa, College of Business, Tampa, FL 33607. Offers accounting (DBA); corporate compliance (MBA); customized professional concentration (MBA, DBA); finance (MBA); fraud examination (MBA); global business sustainability (DBA); healthcare administration (MBA); information systems (DBA); information systems management (MBA); international business (MBA, DBA); management (MBA, MSM, DBA); marketing (MBA, DBA); organizational leadership (Ed D); public administration (MBA); sustainable management (MBA).

Argosy University, Twin Cities, College of Business, Eagan, MN 55121. Offers accounting (DBA); customized professional concentration (MBA, DBA); finance (MBA); fraud examination (MBA); global business sustainability (DBA); healthcare administration (MBA); information systems (DBA); information systems management (MBA); international business (MBA, DBA); management (MBA, MSM, DBA); marketing (MBA, DBA); organizational leadership (Ed D); public administration (MBA); sustainable management (MBA).

Argosy University, Washington DC, College of Business, Arlington, VA 22209. Offers accounting (DBA); customized professional concentration (MBA, DBA); finance (MBA); fraud examination (MBA); global business sustainability (DBA); healthcare administration (MBA); information systems (DBA); information systems management (MBA); international business (MBA, DBA, Certificate); management (MBA, MSM, DBA); marketing (MBA, DBA, Certificate); organizational leadership (Ed D); public administration (MBA); sustainable management (MBA).

Arkansas State University, Graduate School, College of Humanities and Social Sciences, Department of Political Science, Jonesboro, State University, AR 72467. Offers political science (MA); political science education (SCCT); public administration (MPA). *Accreditation:* NASPAA (one or more programs are accredited). Part-time programs available. *Faculty:* 8 full-time (3 women), 1 (woman) part-time/adjunct. *Students:* 26 full-time (13 women), 24 part-time (8 women); includes 14 minority (13 Black or African American, non-Hispanic/Latino; 1 American Indian or Alaska Native, non-Hispanic/Latino), 9 international. Average age 29. 36 applicants, 78% accepted, 21 enrolled. In 2010, 16 master's awarded. *Degree requirements:* For master's, comprehensive exam, thesis or alternative; for SCCT, comprehensive exam. *Entrance requirements:* For master's, GRE General Test or MAT, GMAT, appropriate bachelor's degree, letters of recommendation, official transcripts, immunization records, statement of purpose; for SCCT, GRE General Test or MAT, GMAT, interview, master's degree, official transcript, letters of recommendation, immunization records. Additional exam requirements/recommendations for international students: Required—TOEFL (minimum score 550 paper-based; 213 computer-based; 79 iBT), IELTS (minimum score 6), PTE: Pearson Test of English Academic (56). *Application deadline:* For fall admission, 7/1 for domestic and international students; for spring admission, 11/15 for domestic students, 11/14 for international students. Applications are processed on a rolling basis. Application fee: $30 ($40 for international students). Electronic applications accepted. *Expenses:* Tuition, state resident: full-time $3888; part-time $216 per credit hour. Tuition, nonresident: full-time $9918; part-time $551 per credit hour. International tuition: $8376 full-time. Required fees: $932; $49 per credit hour. $25 per term. One-time fee: $30. Tuition and fees vary according to course load and program. *Financial support:* In 2010–11, 15 students received support; teaching assistantships, career-related internships or fieldwork, scholarships/grants, and unspecified assistantships available. Financial award application deadline: 7/1; financial award applicants required to submit FAFSA. *Unit head:* Dr. Richard Wang, Chair, 870-972-3048, Fax: 870-972-2720, E-mail: rwang@astate.edu. *Application contact:* Dr. Andrew Sustich, Dean of the Graduate School, 870-972-3029, Fax: 870-972-3857, E-mail: sustich@astate.edu.

Auburn University, Graduate School, College of Liberal Arts, Department of Political Science, Program in Public Administration, Auburn University, AL 36849. Offers MPA, PhD, MPA/MCP. PhD offered jointly with Auburn University Montgomery. *Accreditation:* NASPAA (one or more

Public Administration

Auburn University (continued)
programs are accredited). Part-time programs available. *Faculty:* 21 full-time (5 women), 5 part-time/adjunct (1 woman). *Students:* 27 full-time (14 women), 43 part-time (22 women); includes 12 Black or African American, non-Hispanic/Latino; 1 Asian, non-Hispanic/Latino; 1 Hispanic/Latino, 6 international. Average age 35. 58 applicants, 53% accepted, 14 enrolled. In 2010, 20 master's, 6 doctorates awarded. *Degree requirements:* For master's, internship or research project; for doctorate, thesis/dissertation. *Entrance requirements:* For master's, GRE General Test, sample of written work; for doctorate, GRE General Test. *Application deadline:* For fall admission, 7/7 for domestic students; for spring admission, 11/24 for domestic students. Applications are processed on a rolling basis. Application fee: $50 ($60 for international students). Electronic applications accepted. *Expenses:* Tuition, state resident: full-time $7002. Tuition, nonresident: full-time $21,898. International tuition: $22,116 full-time. Required fees: $892. Tuition and fees vary according to course load and program. *Financial support:* Fellowships, research assistantships, teaching assistantships, career-related internships or fieldwork and Federal Work-Study available. Support available to part-time students. Financial award application deadline: 3/15; financial award applicants required to submit FAFSA. *Faculty research:* Privatization studies, policy evolution, water resources, election administration. *Unit head:* Dr. Caleb Clark, Head, 334-844-5371. *Application contact:* Dr. George Flowers, Dean of the Graduate School, 334-844-2125.

Auburn University Montgomery, School of Sciences, Department of Public Administration and Political Science, Montgomery, AL 36124-4023. Offers MPA, MPS, PhD. PhD offered jointly with Auburn University. *Accreditation:* NASPAA (one or more programs are accredited). Part-time and evening/weekend programs available. *Degree requirements:* For master's, comprehensive exam; for doctorate, thesis/dissertation. *Entrance requirements:* For master's, GRE General Test or MAT; for doctorate, GRE General Test. Electronic applications accepted.

Azusa Pacific University, School of Business and Management, Azusa, CA 91702-7000. Offers business administration (MBA); diversity for strategic advantage (MA); entrepreneurship (MBA); finance (MBA); human and organizational development (MA); human resources and organizational development (MBA); human resources management (MA); international business (MBA); marketing (MBA); non-profit management (MA); organizational development and change (MA); performance improvement (MA); public administration (MA); strategic management (MBA). Part-time and evening/weekend programs available. *Faculty:* 19 full-time (5 women), 2 part-time/adjunct (1 woman). *Students:* 75 full-time (41 women), 96 part-time (46 women); includes 65 minority (15 Black or African American, non-Hispanic/Latino; 15 Asian, non-Hispanic/Latino; 34 Hispanic/Latino; 1 Native Hawaiian or other Pacific Islander, non-Hispanic/Latino), 17 international. Average age 30. In 2010, 82 master's awarded. *Degree requirements:* For master's, thesis (for some programs), final project. *Entrance requirements:* For master's, GMAT, minimum GPA of 3.0. Additional exam requirements/recommendations for international students: Required—TOEFL (minimum score 600 paper-based). *Application deadline:* For fall admission, 8/15 priority date for domestic students. Applications are processed on a rolling basis. Application fee: $45 ($65 for international students). *Expenses:* Contact institution. *Financial support:* Scholarships/grants available. *Faculty research:* Gender issues, financial risk, leadership and ethics, marketing strategy. *Unit head:* Dr. Ilene Bezjian, Dean, 626-815-3090, Fax: 626-815-3802, E-mail: ibezjian@apu.edu. *Application contact:* Dr. Ilene Bezjian, Dean, 626-815-3090, Fax: 626-815-3802, E-mail: ibezjian@apu.edu.

Ball State University, Graduate School, College of Sciences and Humanities, Department of Political Science, Program in Public Administration, Muncie, IN 47306-1099. Offers criminal justice (MPA); public administration (MPA), including criminal justice. *Faculty:* 16. *Students:* 11 full-time (4 women), 20 part-time (11 women); includes 1 Black or African American, non-Hispanic/Latino, 1 international. Average age 28. 15 applicants, 73% accepted, 7 enrolled. In 2010, 11 master's awarded. *Entrance requirements:* For master's, GRE General Test. Application fee: $50. *Expenses:* Tuition, state resident: full-time $6160; part-time $299 per credit hour. Tuition, nonresident: full-time $16,020; part-time $783 per credit hour. Required fees: $2278; $95 per credit hour. *Financial support:* Career-related internships or fieldwork available. Financial award application deadline: 3/1. *Faculty research:* Employment training programs, personnel and labor relations, planning. *Unit head:* Dr. Joseph Losco, Director, 765-285-8800, Fax: 765-285-5345. *Application contact:* Dr. Gary Crawley, Associate Provost for Research and Dean of the Graduate School, 765-285-8785, E-mail: gcrawley@bsu.edu.

Barry University, School of Adult and Continuing Education, Program in Public Administration, Miami Shores, FL 33161-6695. Offers MPA. Part-time and evening/weekend programs available. *Entrance requirements:* For master's, GMAT, GRE or MAT, recommendations. Electronic applications accepted.

Baylor University, Graduate School, College of Arts and Sciences, Department of Political Science, Waco, TX 76798. Offers international studies (MA); political science (MA, PhD); public policy and administration (MPPA); JD/MPPA. *Students:* 29 full-time (8 women), 1 part-time (0 women), 3 international. In 2010, 6 master's, 3 doctorates awarded. *Entrance requirements:* For master's, GRE General Test. *Application deadline:* Applications are processed on a rolling basis. Application fee: $25. *Financial support:* Research assistantships, career-related internships or fieldwork, Federal Work-Study, and institutionally sponsored loans available. Financial award application deadline: 3/1. *Unit head:* Dr. David Corey, Graduate Program Director, 254-710-3161, Fax: 254-710-3122, E-mail: david_d_corey@baylor.edu. *Application contact:* Jenice Langston, Administrative Assistant, 254-710-3161, Fax: 254-710-3870, E-mail: jenice_langston@baylor.edu.

Belhaven University, School of Business, Jackson, MS 39202-1789. Offers business administration (MBA); leadership (MSL); public administration (MPA). MBA program also offered in Houston, TX, Memphis, TN and Orlando, FL. Evening/weekend programs available. *Faculty:* 13 full-time (3 women), 24 part-time/adjunct (6 women). *Students:* 316 full-time (231 women), 39 part-time (25 women); includes 15 Black or African American, non-Hispanic/Latino; 1 Hispanic/Latino. Average age 36. 329 applicants, 54% accepted, 124 enrolled. In 2010, 103 master's awarded. *Degree requirements:* For master's, comprehensive exam (for some programs), thesis (for some programs). *Entrance requirements:* For master's, GMAT, GRE General Test or MAT, minimum GPA of 2.8. *Application deadline:* Applications are processed on a rolling basis. Application fee: $25. Electronic applications accepted. *Expenses:* Tuition: Full-time $6456; part-time $538 per credit hour. Tuition and fees vary according to campus/location. *Financial support:* Applicants required to submit FAFSA. *Unit head:* Dr. Ralph Mason, Dean, 601-968-8949, Fax: 601-968-8951, E-mail: cmason@belhaven.edu. *Application contact:* Dr. Audrey Kelleher, Vice President of Adult and Graduate Marketing and Development, 407-804-1424, Fax: 407-620-5210, E-mail: akelleher@belhaven.edu.

Bellevue University, Graduate School, Bellevue, NE 68005-3098. Offers acquisition and contract management (MS); business administration (MBA); clinical counseling (MS); computer information systems (MS); healthcare administration (MA, MHA, MS), including healthcare administration (MHA), human services (MA, MS); human capital management (MS, PhD); instructional design and development (MS); leadership (MA); management (MA); management information systems (MS); organizational performance (MS); public administration (MPA); public health (MPH); security management (MS). Part-time and evening/weekend programs available. Postbaccalaureate distance learning degree programs offered (no on-campus study). *Degree requirements:* For master's, thesis or project. *Entrance requirements:* For master's, minimum GPA of 2.5 in last 60 hours. Additional exam requirements/recommendations for international students: Required—TOEFL (minimum score 538 paper-based; 200 computer-based).

Bernard M. Baruch College of the City University of New York, School of Public Affairs, Program in Public Administration, New York, NY 10010-5585. Offers health care policy (MPA); nonprofit administration (MPA); policy analysis and evaluation (MPA); public management (MPA); MS/MPA. *Accreditation:* NASPAA. Part-time and evening/weekend programs available. *Faculty:* 71 full-time (27 women), 51 part-time/adjunct (23 women). *Students:* 180 full-time (125 women), 491 part-time (327 women); includes 152 Black or African American, non-Hispanic/Latino; 2 American Indian or Alaska Native, non-Hispanic/Latino; 68 Asian, non-Hispanic/Latino; 107 Hispanic/Latino; 18 Two or more races, non-Hispanic/Latino. Average age 33. 482 applicants, 68% accepted, 233 enrolled. In 2010, 203 master's awarded. *Degree requirements:* For master's, thesis, capstone. *Entrance requirements:* For master's, GRE General Test. Additional exam requirements/recommendations for international students: Required—TOEFL. *Application deadline:* For fall admission, 4/1 priority date for domestic and international students; for spring admission, 11/15 priority date for domestic and international students. Applications are processed on a rolling basis. Application fee: $125. Electronic applications accepted. *Expenses:* Contact institution. *Financial support:* In 2010–11, 31 students received support, including 8 fellowships (averaging $1,500 per year), 23 research assistantships (averaging $12,000 per year); career-related internships or fieldwork, Federal Work-Study, scholarships/grants, tuition waivers (partial), and unspecified assistantships also available. Support available to part-time students. Financial award application deadline: 5/15; financial award applicants required to submit FAFSA. *Faculty research:* Urbanization, population and poverty in the developing world, housing and community development, labor unions and housing, government-nongovernment relations, immigration policy, social network analysis, cross-sectoral governance, comparative healthcare systems, program evaluation, social welfare policy, health outcomes, educational policy and leadership, transnationalism, infant health, welfare reform, racial/ethnic disparities in health, urban politics, homelessness, race and ethnic relations. Total annual research expenditures: $2.6 million. *Unit head:* David Birdsell, Dean, 646-660-6700, Fax: 646-660-6721, E-mail: david.birdsell@baruch.cuny.edu. *Application contact:* Michael J. Lovaglio, Director of Student Affairs and Graduate Admissions, 646-660-6750, Fax: 646-660-6751, E-mail: michael.lovaglio@baruch.cuny.edu.

Boise State University, Graduate College, College of Social Sciences and Public Affairs, Department of Public Policy and Administration, Boise, ID 83725-0399. Offers environmental and natural resources policy and administration (MPA); general public administration (MPA); state and local government policy and administration (MPA). *Accreditation:* NASPAA. Part-time programs available. *Degree requirements:* For master's, comprehensive exam, directed research project, internship. *Entrance requirements:* For master's, GRE General Test, minimum GPA of 3.0. Additional exam requirements/recommendations for international students: Required—TOEFL. Electronic applications accepted.

Boston University, School of Education, Boston, MA 02215. Offers counseling (Ed M, CAGS), including community, school, sport psychology; counseling psychology (Ed D); curriculum and teaching (Ed M, Ed D, CAGS), including early childhood (Ed D), educational media and technology (Ed D), English and language arts (Ed D), mathematics (Ed D), physical education and coaching (Ed D), science (Ed D), social studies education (Ed D), special education (Ed D); developmental studies (Ed D), including literacy and language, reading education; developmental studies in literacy and language education (Ed M, CAGS); early childhood education (Ed M, CAGS); education of the deaf (Ed M, CAGS); educational leadership and development (Ed D), including educational administration (Ed M, Ed D, CAGS), higher education administration (Ed M, Ed D, CAGS); educational media and technology (Ed M, CAGS); elementary education (Ed M); English and language arts (Ed M, CAGS); English education (MAT); health education (Ed M, CAGS); Latin and classical studies (MAT); mathematics education (Ed M, MAT, CAGS); mathematics for teaching (MMT); modern foreign language education (MAT), including French, Spanish; physical education and coaching (Ed M, CAGS); policy, planning, and administration (Ed M, CAGS), including community education leadership, educational administration (Ed M, Ed D, CAGS), higher education administration (Ed M, Ed D, CAGS); reading education (Ed M, CAGS); science education (Ed M, MAT, CAGS), including biology (MAT), chemistry (MAT), earth science (MAT), general science (MAT), physics (MAT); social studies education (Ed M, MAT, CAGS), including history (MAT), political science (MAT); special education (Ed M, Ed D, CAGS), including disability studies (Ed M), moderate disabilities (Ed M), severe disabilities (Ed M), special education administration (Ed M); teaching English as a second language (Ed M, CAGS). Part-time programs available. *Faculty:* 57 full-time, 39 part-time/adjunct. *Students:* 245 full-time (191 women), 376 part-time (274 women); includes 83 minority (14 Black or African American, non-Hispanic/Latino; 2 American Indian or Alaska Native, non-Hispanic/Latino; 28 Asian, non-Hispanic/Latino; 31 Hispanic/Latino; 2 Native Hawaiian or other Pacific Islander, non-Hispanic/Latino; 6 Two or more races, non-Hispanic/Latino), 79 international. Average age 30. 1,270 applicants, 66% accepted, 292 enrolled. In 2010, 273 master's, 15 doctorates, 7 other advanced degrees awarded. Terminal master's awarded for partial completion of doctoral program. *Degree requirements:* For master's, thesis (for some programs); for doctorate, comprehensive exam, thesis/dissertation; for CAGS, comprehensive exam. *Entrance requirements:* For master's and CAGS, GRE General Test or Miller Analogies Test (MAT); for doctorate, GRE General Test. Additional exam requirements/recommendations for international students: Required—TOEFL, IELTS. *Application deadline:* For fall admission, 1/15 priority date for domestic and international students; for spring admission, 9/15 priority date for domestic and international students. Applications are processed on a rolling basis. Application fee: $70. Electronic applications accepted. *Expenses:* Tuition: Full-time $39,314; part-time $1228 per credit. Required fees: $40 per semester. *Financial support:* In 2010–11, 276 students received support, including 31 fellowships with full tuition reimbursements available, 16 research assistantships, 26 teaching assistantships with partial tuition reimbursements available; career-related internships or fieldwork, Federal Work-Study, and scholarships/grants also available. Support available to part-time students. Financial award applicants required to submit FAFSA. *Faculty research:* Deaf studies, social emotional learning, civic engagement and education, STEM education, pre-college educational pipelines. Total annual research expenditures: $2.6 million. *Unit head:* Dr. Hardin Coleman, Dean, 617-353-3213. *Application contact:* Dana Fernandez, Director of Enrollment, 617-353-4237, Fax: 617-353-8937, E-mail: sedgrad@bu.edu.

Bowie State University, Graduate Programs, Program in Public Administration, Bowie, MD 20715-9465. Offers MPA. Part-time and evening/weekend programs available. *Degree requirements:* For master's, comprehensive exam. *Entrance requirements:* For master's, minimum undergraduate GPA of 2.5. Electronic applications accepted. *Expenses:* Tuition, state resident: full-time $4080; part-time $340 per credit. Tuition, nonresident: full-time $7752; part-time $646 per credit. Required fees: $2128; $340 per credit.

Bowling Green State University, Graduate College, College of Arts and Sciences, Department of Political Science, Program in Public Administration, Bowling Green, OH 43403. Offers MPA. *Degree requirements:* For master's, comprehensive exam or thesis, experiential paper for all non-thesis students. *Entrance requirements:* For master's, GRE General Test. Additional exam requirements/recommendations for international students: Required—TOEFL. Electronic applications accepted. *Faculty research:* Public sector labor relations, administrative law, sexual harassment and violence in the public workplace.

Bridgewater State University, School of Graduate Studies, School of Arts and Sciences, Department of Political Science, Program in Public Administration, Bridgewater, MA 02325-0001. Offers MPA. *Accreditation:* NASPAA. *Entrance requirements:* For master's, GRE General Test.

Brigham Young University, Graduate Studies, Marriott School of Management, Executive Master of Public Administration Program, Provo, UT 84602. Offers EMPA, JD/MPA. *Accreditation:* NASPAA (one or more programs are accredited). Part-time and evening/weekend programs available. *Faculty:* 11 full-time (2 women), 3 part-time/adjunct (0 women). *Students:* 137 part-time (48 women); includes 2 Black or African American, non-Hispanic/Latino; 3 American Indian or Alaska Native, non-Hispanic/Latino; 12 Asian, non-Hispanic/Latino; 4 Hispanic/Latino. Average age 37. 69 applicants, 75% accepted, 48 enrolled. In 2010, 43 master's awarded. *Application deadline:* For fall admission, 5/1 for domestic students. Application fee: $50. Electronic applications accepted. *Expenses:* Contact institution. *Financial support:* In 2010–11, 13 students received support. Application deadline: 6/15. *Unit head:* Dr. David W. Hart, Director, 801-422-7391, Fax: 801-422-0311, E-mail: mpa@byu.edu. *Application contact:*

Catherine L. Cooper, Director of Student Services, 801-422-9173, Fax: 801-422-0311, E-mail: mpa@byu.edu.

Brigham Young University, Graduate Studies, Marriott School of Management, Master of Public Administration Program, Provo, UT 84602. Offers finance (MPA); human resources (MPA); local government (MPA); nonprofit management (MPA); JD/MPA. *Faculty:* 12 full-time (1 woman), 5 part-time/adjunct (0 women). *Students:* 121 full-time (58 women); includes 3 Black or African American, non-Hispanic/Latino; 1 American Indian or Alaska Native, non-Hispanic/Latino; 11 Asian, non-Hispanic/Latino; 8 Hispanic/Latino. Average age 27. 137 applicants, 64% accepted, 61 enrolled. In 2010, 47 master's awarded. *Entrance requirements:* For master's, GRE, GMAT, minimum GPA of 3.0. Additional exam requirements/recommendations for international students: Required—TOEFL (minimum score 580 paper-based; 85 iBT), IELTS (minimum score 7). *Application deadline:* For fall admission, 2/1 for domestic and international students. Application fee: $50. Electronic applications accepted. *Expenses:* Tuition: Full-time $5580; part-time $310 per credit hour. Tuition and fees vary according to program and student's religious affiliation. *Financial support:* In 2010–11, 73 students received support. Career-related internships or fieldwork and scholarships/grants available. Financial award application deadline: 4/15; financial award applicants required to submit FAFSA. *Faculty research:* Taxes, budgeting, nonprofit, ethics, decision modeling, work balance, organizational behavior. *Unit head:* Dr. David W. Hart, Director, 801-422-4221, Fax: 801-422-0311, E-mail: mpa@byu.edu. *Application contact:* Catherine Cooper, Director of Student Services, 801-422-4221, E-mail: mpa@byu.edu.

California Baptist University, Program in Public Administration, Riverside, CA 92504-3206. Offers MPA. Part-time programs available. *Faculty:* 1 (woman) full-time. *Students:* 34 full-time (22 women), 18 part-time (11 women); includes 11 Black or African American, non-Hispanic/Latino; 2 Asian, non-Hispanic/Latino; 12 Hispanic/Latino; 1 Two or more races, non-Hispanic/Latino, 2 international. 21 applicants, 95% accepted, 18 enrolled. In 2010, 34 master's awarded. *Degree requirements:* For master's, thesis optional. *Entrance requirements:* For master's, minimum GPA of 2.75. Additional exam requirements/recommendations for international students: Required—TOEFL (minimum score 575 paper-based; 230 computer-based; 89 iBT). *Application deadline:* For fall admission, 8/1 priority date for domestic students, 7/1 for international students; for spring admission, 12/1 priority date for domestic students, 10/15 for international students. Applications are processed on a rolling basis. Application fee: $45. Electronic applications accepted. *Expenses:* Tuition: Full-time $8532; part-time $474 per unit. Required fees: $355 per semester. One-time fee: $45 full-time. Tuition and fees vary according to course load and program. *Financial support:* Federal Work-Study and scholarships/grants available. Support available to part-time students. Financial award applicants required to submit FAFSA. *Unit head:* Dr. Elaine Ahumada, Director, 951-343-4306, Fax: 951-343-4661, E-mail: eahumada@calbaptist.edu. *Application contact:* Gail Ronveaux, Dean of Graduate Enrollment, 951-343-5045, Fax: 951-343-5095, E-mail: graduateadmissions@calbaptist.edu.

California Lutheran University, Graduate Studies, Program in Public Policy and Administration, Thousand Oaks, CA 91360-2787. Offers MPPA. *Faculty:* 1 full-time (0 women), 6 part-time/adjunct (4 women). *Students:* 30 full-time (13 women), 42 part-time (27 women); includes 25 minority (5 Black or African American, non-Hispanic/Latino; 2 Asian, non-Hispanic/Latino; 16 Hispanic/Latino; 2 Two or more races, non-Hispanic/Latino), 12 international. Average age 34. 30 applicants, 77% accepted, 16 enrolled. In 2010, 26 master's awarded. *Degree requirements:* For master's, comprehensive exam, thesis or project, internship. *Entrance requirements:* For master's, GMAT or GRE General Test, interview, minimum GPA of 3.0. *Application deadline:* Applications are processed on a rolling basis. Application fee: $50. *Expenses:* Contact institution. *Unit head:* Dr. Herbert Gooch, Director, 805-493-3348. *Application contact:* 805-493-3127, Fax: 805-493-3542, E-mail: clugrad@clunet.edu.

California State Polytechnic University, Pomona, Academic Affairs, College of Letters, Arts, and Social Sciences, Program in Public Administration, Pomona, CA 91768-2557. Offers MPA. *Accreditation:* NASPAA. Part-time programs available. *Students:* 8 full-time (5 women), 62 part-time (37 women); includes 42 minority (7 Black or African American, non-Hispanic/Latino; 9 Asian, non-Hispanic/Latino; 25 Hispanic/Latino; 1 Two or more races, non-Hispanic/Latino), 2 international. Average age 32. 99 applicants, 41% accepted, 20 enrolled. In 2010, 15 master's awarded. *Degree requirements:* For master's, thesis or alternative. *Entrance requirements:* For master's, GRE General Test. *Application deadline:* For fall admission, 5/1 priority date for domestic students; for winter admission, 10/15 priority date for domestic students; for spring admission, 1/20 priority date for domestic students. Applications are processed on a rolling basis. Application fee: $55. Electronic applications accepted. *Expenses:* Tuition, state resident: full-time $5386; part-time $2850 per year. Tuition, nonresident: full-time $12,082; part-time $248 per credit. Required fees: $577; $248 per credit. $577 per year. Tuition and fees vary according to course load and program. *Unit head:* Dr. Sandra M. Emerson, Graduate Coordinator, 909-869-3879, E-mail: smemerson@csupomona.edu. *Application contact:* Scott J. Duncan, Director, Admissions, 909-869-3258, Fax: 909-869-4529, E-mail: sjduncan@csupomona.edu.

California State University, Bakersfield, Division of Graduate Studies, School of Business and Public Administration, Program in Public Administration, Bakersfield, CA 93311. Offers MPA. *Accreditation:* NASPAA. *Degree requirements:* For master's, thesis or alternative. *Entrance requirements:* For master's, GRE, minimum GPA of 2.75.

California State University, Chico, Graduate School, College of Behavioral and Social Sciences, Department of Political Science, Program in Public Administration, Chico, CA 95929-0722. Offers health administration (MPA); local government management (MPA); public administration (MPA). *Accreditation:* NASPAA. Part-time programs available. *Students:* 28 full-time (13 women), 23 part-time (12 women); includes 4 Black or African American, non-Hispanic/Latino; 1 American Indian or Alaska Native, non-Hispanic/Latino; 5 Asian, non-Hispanic/Latino; 10 Hispanic/Latino, 4 international. Average age 31. 45 applicants, 71% accepted, 18 enrolled. In 2010, 9 master's awarded. *Entrance requirements:* For master's, 2 letters of recommendation. Additional exam requirements/recommendations for international students: Required—TOEFL (minimum score 550 paper-based; 213 computer-based; 80 iBT), IELTS (minimum score 6.5). *Application deadline:* For fall admission, 3/1 priority date for domestic students, 3/1 for international students; for spring admission, 9/15 priority date for domestic students, 9/15 for international students. Applications are processed on a rolling basis. Application fee: $55. Electronic applications accepted. *Financial support:* Fellowships, career-related internships or fieldwork available. *Unit head:* Dr. Donna Kemp, Graduate Coordinator, 530-898-5734. *Application contact:* Dr. Donna Kemp, Graduate Coordinator, 530-898-5734.

California State University, Dominguez Hills, College of Business Administration and Public Policy, Program in Public Administration, Carson, CA 90747-0001. Offers MPA. *Accreditation:* NASPAA. Part-time and evening/weekend programs available. Postbaccalaureate distance learning degree programs offered (no on-campus study). *Faculty:* 7 full-time (6 women), 10 part-time/adjunct (5 women). *Students:* 31 full-time (21 women), 58 part-time (45 women); includes 26 Black or African American, non-Hispanic/Latino; 2 American Indian or Alaska Native, non-Hispanic/Latino; 8 Asian, non-Hispanic/Latino; 14 Hispanic/Latino; 2 Two or more races, non-Hispanic/Latino, 1 international. Average age 37. 344 applicants, 22% accepted, 17 enrolled. In 2010, 72 master's awarded. *Degree requirements:* For master's, thesis or alternative, capstone project. *Entrance requirements:* For master's, GRE, minimum GPA of 2.75. Additional exam requirements/recommendations for international students: Required—TOEFL (minimum score 550 paper-based; 213 computer-based; 79 iBT). *Application deadline:* For fall admission, 4/1 for domestic and international students; for spring admission, 11/1 for domestic students, 10/1 for international students. Application fee: $55. *Faculty research:* Applied public management. *Unit head:* Dr. Kaye Bragg, Interim Chair, 310-243-2356, E-mail: kbragg@csudh.edu. *Application contact:* Eileen Hall, Graduate Advisor, 310-243-3465, E-mail: ehall@csudh.edu.

California State University, East Bay, Office of Academic Programs and Graduate Studies, College of Letters, Arts, and Social Sciences, Department of Public Affairs and Administration, Hayward, CA 94542-3000. Offers health care administration (MS); public administration (MPA). Part-time and evening/weekend programs available. *Faculty:* 8 full-time (4 women), 9 part-time/adjunct (1 woman). *Students:* 48 full-time (30 women), 241 part-time (162 women); includes 116 minority (36 Black or African American, non-Hispanic/Latino; 1 American Indian or Alaska Native, non-Hispanic/Latino; 46 Asian, non-Hispanic/Latino; 24 Hispanic/Latino; 4 Native Hawaiian or other Pacific Islander, non-Hispanic/Latino; 5 Two or more races, non-Hispanic/Latino), 28 international. Average age 34. 223 applicants, 49% accepted, 59 enrolled. In 2010, 119 master's awarded. *Degree requirements:* For master's, comprehensive exam or thesis. *Entrance requirements:* For master's, minimum GPA of 2.5. Additional exam requirements/recommendations for international students: Required—TOEFL (minimum score 550 paper-based; 213 computer-based). *Application deadline:* For fall admission, 6/30 for domestic and international students. Application fee: $55. Electronic applications accepted. *Financial support:* Fellowships, teaching assistantships, career-related internships or fieldwork, Federal Work-Study, institutionally sponsored loans, and scholarships/grants available. Support available to part-time students. Financial award application deadline: 3/2; financial award applicants required to submit FAFSA. *Unit head:* Dr. Toni Fogarty, Chair, 510-885-2268, Fax: 510-885-3726, E-mail: toni.fogarty@csueastbay.edu. *Application contact:* Dr. Donna Wiley, Interim Associate Director, 510-885-2928, Fax: 510-885-4777, E-mail: donna.wiley@csueastbay.edu.

California State University, Fresno, Division of Graduate Studies, College of Social Sciences, Department of Political Science, Program in Public Administration, Fresno, CA 93740-8027. Offers MPA. *Accreditation:* NASPAA. Part-time and evening/weekend programs available. *Degree requirements:* For master's, thesis or alternative. *Entrance requirements:* For master's, GRE General Test or GMAT, minimum GPA of 3.0. Additional exam requirements/recommendations for international students: Required—TOEFL. Electronic applications accepted.

California State University, Fullerton, Graduate Studies, College of Humanities and Social Sciences, Division of Politics, Administration, and Justice, Fullerton, CA 92834-9480. Offers political science (MA); public administration (MPA). *Accreditation:* NASPAA (one or more programs are accredited). Part-time programs available. *Students:* 27 full-time (16 women), 123 part-time (60 women); includes 5 Black or African American, non-Hispanic/Latino; 28 Asian, non-Hispanic/Latino; 38 Hispanic/Latino; 6 Two or more races, non-Hispanic/Latino, 4 international. Average age 31. 223 applicants, 31% accepted, 45 enrolled. In 2010, 57 master's awarded. *Degree requirements:* For master's, comprehensive exam, project or thesis. *Entrance requirements:* For master's, minimum GPA of 2.5 in last 60 units of course work, 12 units of course work in social sciences. Application fee: $55. *Financial support:* Career-related internships or fieldwork, Federal Work-Study, institutionally sponsored loans, and scholarships/grants available. Support available to part-time students. Financial award application deadline: 3/1; financial award applicants required to submit FAFSA. *Faculty research:* Emergency management plans. *Unit head:* Dr. Phil Gianos, Chair, 657-278-3521. *Application contact:* Admissions/Applications, 657-278-2371.

California State University, Long Beach, Graduate Studies, College of Health and Human Services, Graduate Center for Public Policy and Administration, Long Beach, CA 90840. Offers MPA. *Accreditation:* NASPAA. Part-time and evening/weekend programs available. *Faculty:* 6 full-time (2 women), 5 part-time/adjunct (1 woman). *Students:* 55 full-time (34 women), 174 part-time (109 women); includes 16 Black or African American, non-Hispanic/Latino; 4 American Indian or Alaska Native, non-Hispanic/Latino; 34 Asian, non-Hispanic/Latino; 76 Hispanic/Latino, 5 international. Average age 32. 301 applicants, 40% accepted, 84 enrolled. In 2010, 119 master's awarded. *Degree requirements:* For master's, comprehensive exam. *Entrance requirements:* For master's, minimum GPA of 2.75. *Application deadline:* For fall admission, 7/1 for domestic students. Applications are processed on a rolling basis. Application fee: $55. Electronic applications accepted. *Financial support:* Fellowships, career-related internships or fieldwork, Federal Work-Study, institutionally sponsored loans, and scholarships/grants available. Financial award application deadline: 3/2. *Faculty research:* Transportation access, air quality controls, coastal issues, intergovernmental relations. *Unit head:* Dr. Walter Frank Baber, Director, 562-985-4178, Fax: 562-985-4672, E-mail: wbaber@csulb.edu. *Application contact:* Dr. Walter Frank Baber, Director, 562-985-4178, Fax: 562-985-4672, E-mail: wbaber@csulb.edu.

California State University, Los Angeles, Graduate Studies, College of Natural and Social Sciences, Department of Political Science, Los Angeles, CA 90032-8530. Offers political science (MA); public administration (MS). Part-time and evening/weekend programs available. *Faculty:* 18 full-time (16 women), 4 part-time/adjunct (1 woman). *Students:* 21 full-time (12 women), 83 part-time (45 women); includes 68 minority (6 Black or African American, non-Hispanic/Latino; 8 Asian, non-Hispanic/Latino; 54 Hispanic/Latino), 6 international. Average age 30. 61 applicants, 95% accepted, 32 enrolled. In 2010, 39 master's awarded. *Degree requirements:* For master's, comprehensive exam or thesis. *Entrance requirements:* Additional exam requirements/recommendations for international students: Required—TOEFL (minimum score 500 paper-based; 173 computer-based). *Application deadline:* For fall admission, 5/1 for domestic and international students. Applications are processed on a rolling basis. Application fee: $55. Electronic applications accepted. *Financial support:* Career-related internships or fieldwork and Federal Work-Study available. Support available to part-time students. Financial award application deadline: 3/1. *Faculty research:* Government; public policy and law; international, political, and economic relations; comparative politics. *Unit head:* Dr. Scott Bowman, Chair, 323-343-2248, Fax: 323-343-6452, E-mail: sbowman@calstatela.edu. *Application contact:* Dr. Alan Muchlinski, Dean of Graduate Studies, 323-343-3820, Fax: 323-343-5653, E-mail: amuchli@exchange.calstatela.edu.

California State University, Northridge, Graduate Studies, The Tseng College of Extended Learning, Northridge, CA 91330. Offers knowledge management (MKM); public administration (MPA); taxation (MS). *Entrance requirements:* For master's, GRE (if cumulative undergraduate GPA less than 3.0).

California State University, Sacramento, Graduate Studies, College of Social Sciences and Interdisciplinary Studies, Program in Public Policy and Administration, Sacramento, CA 95819. Offers MPPA. Part-time programs available. *Degree requirements:* For master's, thesis or alternative, writing proficiency exam. *Entrance requirements:* For master's, GRE General Test. Additional exam requirements/recommendations for international students: Required—TOEFL. Electronic applications accepted.

California State University, San Bernardino, Graduate Studies, College of Business and Public Administration, Program in Public Administration, San Bernardino, CA 92407-2397. Offers MPA. *Accreditation:* NASPAA. Part-time and evening/weekend programs available. *Degree requirements:* For master's, comprehensive exam, advancement to candidacy.

California State University, Stanislaus, College of Humanities and Social Sciences, Program in Public Administration (MPA), Turlock, CA 95382. Offers MPA. *Accreditation:* NASPAA. Part-time and evening/weekend programs available. *Faculty:* 8. *Students:* 21 full-time (11 women), 72 part-time (45 women); includes 43 minority (2 Black or African American, non-Hispanic/Latino; 1 American Indian or Alaska Native, non-Hispanic/Latino; 12 Asian, non-Hispanic/Latino; 25 Hispanic/Latino; 3 Two or more races, non-Hispanic/Latino), 1 international. Average age 31. 57 applicants, 65% accepted, 27 enrolled. In 2010, 23 master's awarded. *Degree requirements:* For master's, comprehensive exam, thesis or alternative. *Entrance requirements:* For master's, minimum GPA of 2.7, 3 letters of reference, personal statement. Additional exam requirements/recommendations for international students: Required—TOEFL (minimum score 550 paper-based; 213 computer-based), ELPT (minimum score: 954). *Application deadline:* For fall admission, 5/1 for domestic students; for spring admission, 1/7 for domestic students. Application fee: $55. Electronic applications accepted. Tuition and fees vary according to program. *Financial support:* Fellowships, career-related internships or fieldwork and Federal Work-Study available. Financial award application deadline: 3/1; financial award applicants required to submit FAFSA. *Faculty research:* Blogging in the Middle East, incumbency and electoral competitiveness, legislative acceptance of gubernatorial budget proposals. *Unit head:* Dr. Stephen Routh, MPA Department Chair, 209-667-3388, Fax: 209-667-3724, E-mail:

Public Administration

California State University, Stanislaus (continued)
srouth@csustan.edu. *Application contact:* Graduate School, 209-667-3129, Fax: 209-664-7025, E-mail: graduate_school@csustan.edu.

Capella University, School of Public Service Leadership, Minneapolis, MN 55402. Offers criminal justice (MS, PhD); emergency management (MS, PhD); general human services (MS, PhD); general public administration (MPA, DPA); gerontology (MS); health care administration (MS, PhD); health management and policy (MSPH); management of nonprofit agencies (MS, PhD); nurse educator (MS); public safety leadership (MS, PhD); social and community services (MS, PhD); social behavioral sciences (MSPH). *Expenses:* Tuition: Full-time $11,880; part-time $440 per credit hour.

Carleton University, Faculty of Graduate Studies, Faculty of Public Affairs and Management, School of Public Policy and Administration, Ottawa, ON K1S 5B6, Canada. Offers public administration (MA, DPA); public policy (PhD). Part-time programs available. *Degree requirements:* For master's, thesis optional; for doctorate, one foreign language, comprehensive exam, thesis/dissertation. *Entrance requirements:* For master's, GRE, honors degree; for doctorate, master's degree. Additional exam requirements/recommendations for international students: Required—TOEFL. *Faculty research:* Canadian public administration and policy, development administration, public policy analysis, public management.

Carnegie Mellon University, H. John Heinz III College, School of Public Policy and Management, Master of Public Management Program, Pittsburgh, PA 15213-3891. Offers MPM. Part-time and evening/weekend programs available. *Degree requirements:* For master's, internship. *Entrance requirements:* For master's, undergraduate degree; five years of full-time, relevant work experience.

Central Michigan University, Central Michigan University Off-Campus Programs, Program in Administration, Mount Pleasant, MI 48859. Offers acquisitions administration (MSA, Certificate); general administration (MSA, Certificate); health services administration (MSA, Certificate); human resources administration (MSA, Certificate); information resource management (MSA, Certificate); international administration (MSA, Certificate); leadership (MSA, Certificate); public administration (MSA, Certificate); vehicle design and manufacturing administration (Certificate). Part-time and evening/weekend programs available. Postbaccalaureate distance learning degree programs offered (no on-campus study). *Students:* Average age 38. *Entrance requirements:* For master's, minimum GPA of 2.7 in major. *Application deadline:* Applications are processed on a rolling basis. Application fee: $50. Electronic applications accepted. *Expenses:* Tuition, state resident: full-time $8208; part-time $456 per credit hour. Tuition, nonresident: full-time $13,788; part-time $766 per credit hour. One-time fee: $25. *Financial support:* Scholarships/grants available. Support available to part-time students. Financial award applicants required to submit FAFSA. *Unit head:* Dr. Nana Korsah, Director, MSA Programs, 989-774-6525, E-mail: korsa1na@cmich.edu. *Application contact:* 877-268-4636, E-mail: cmuoffcampus@cmich.edu.

Central Michigan University, Central Michigan University Off-Campus Programs, Program in Public Administration, Mount Pleasant, MI 48859. Offers public management (MPA); state and local government (MPA). *Accreditation:* NASPAA. Part-time and evening/weekend programs available. *Entrance requirements:* For master's, minimum GPA of 2.8. Additional exam requirements/recommendations for international students: Required—TOEFL. Electronic applications accepted. *Expenses:* Tuition, state resident: full-time $8208; part-time $456 per credit hour. Tuition, nonresident: full-time $13,788; part-time $766 per credit hour. One-time fee: $25. *Financial support:* Scholarships/grants available. Support available to part-time students. *Unit head:* Dr. Lawrence Sych, Program Director, 989-774-3316, E-mail: sych1l@cmich.edu. *Application contact:* 877-268-4636, E-mail: cmuoffcampus@cmich.edu.

Central Michigan University, College of Graduate Studies, College of Humanities and Social and Behavioral Sciences, Department of Political Science, Program in Public Administration, Mount Pleasant, MI 48859. Offers professional development in public administration (Graduate Certificate); public administration (MPA), including cognate courses option; public management (MPA); state and local government (MPA). Part-time programs available. *Faculty:* 11 full-time (2 women), 1 part-time/adjunct (0 women). *Students:* 10 full-time (2 women), 12 part-time (5 women); includes 1 American Indian or Alaska Native, non-Hispanic/Latino; 1 Asian, non-Hispanic/Latino, 4 international. Average age 32. *Degree requirements:* For master's, thesis or alternative. *Application deadline:* For fall admission, 6/1 for international students; for spring admission, 10/1 for international students. Applications are processed on a rolling basis. Application fee: $35 ($45 for international students). Electronic applications accepted. *Expenses:* Tuition, state resident: full-time $8208; part-time $456 per credit hour. Tuition, nonresident: full-time $13,788; part-time $766 per credit hour. One-time fee: $25. *Financial support:* Fellowships with tuition reimbursements, career-related internships or fieldwork, Federal Work-Study, unspecified assistantships, and out-of-state merit awards, non-resident graduate awards available. *Unit head:* Dr. Orlando J. Perez, Chairperson, 989-774-3442, Fax: 989-774-1136, E-mail: perez1oj@cmich.edu. *Application contact:* Laura Orta, Assistant Director of Graduate Programs, 989-774-2391, Fax: 989-774-1136, E-mail: orta1lj@cmich.edu.

Central Michigan University, College of Graduate Studies, Interdisciplinary Administration Programs, Mount Pleasant, MI 48859. Offers acquisitions administration (MSA, Graduate Certificate); general administration (MSA, Graduate Certificate); health services administration (MSA, Graduate Certificate); human resource administration (Graduate Certificate); human resources administration (MSA); information resource management (MSA, Graduate Certificate); international administration (MSA, Graduate Certificate); leadership (MSA, Graduate Certificate); organizational communication (MSA, Graduate Certificate); public administration (MSA, Graduate Certificate); recreation and park administration (MSA); sport administration (MSA). *Accreditation:* AACSB. Part-time and evening/weekend programs available. Postbaccalaureate distance learning degree programs offered (no on-campus study). *Students:* 102 full-time (50 women), 77 part-time (51 women); includes 10 Black or African American, non-Hispanic/Latino; 3 American Indian or Alaska Native, non-Hispanic/Latino; 5 Asian, non-Hispanic/Latino; 65 international. Average age 29. *Degree requirements:* For master's, thesis or alternative. *Entrance requirements:* For master's, bachelor's degree with minimum GPA of 2.7. *Application deadline:* For fall admission, 6/1 for international students; for spring admission, 10/1 for international students. Applications are processed on a rolling basis. Application fee: $35 ($45 for international students). Electronic applications accepted. *Expenses:* Tuition, state resident: full-time $8208; part-time $456 per credit hour. Tuition, nonresident: full-time $13,788; part-time $766 per credit hour. One-time fee: $25. *Financial support:* Fellowships with tuition reimbursements, research assistantships with tuition reimbursements, career-related internships or fieldwork, Federal Work-Study, unspecified assistantships, and out-of-state merit awards, non-resident graduate awards available. *Faculty research:* Interdisciplinary studies in acquisitions administration, health services administration, sport administration, recreation and park administration, and international administration. *Unit head:* Dr. Nana Korash, Director, 989-774-6525, Fax: 989-774-2575, E-mail: msa@cmich.edu. *Application contact:* Denise Schafer, Coordinator, 989-774-4373, Fax: 989-774-2575, E-mail: schaf1dr@cmich.edu.

Cheyney University of Pennsylvania, School of Education and Professional Studies, Program in Public Administration, Cheyney, PA 19319. Offers MPA. *Expenses:* Tuition, state resident: full-time $3483; part-time $2322 per semester. Tuition, nonresident: full-time $5573; part-time $3714 per semester. Required fees: $270 per semester. Tuition and fees vary according to course load.

City College of the City University of New York, Graduate School, College of Liberal Arts and Science, Division of Social Science, New York, NY 10031-9198. Offers economics (MA); international relations (MA); psychology (MA, PhD), including clinical psychology (PhD), experimental cognition (PhD), general psychology (MA), mental health counseling (MA); public service management (MPA); sociology (MA). Part-time programs available. *Entrance requirements:* For master's, GRE. Additional exam requirements/recommendations for international students: Required—TOEFL (minimum score 500 paper-based; 61 iBT). Electronic applications accepted.

Clark Atlanta University, School of Arts and Sciences, Department of Public Administration, Atlanta, GA 30314. Offers MPA. *Accreditation:* NASPAA. Part-time programs available. *Faculty:* 2 full-time (0 women), 1 (woman) part-time/adjunct. *Students:* 15 full-time (9 women), 22 part-time (15 women); includes 32 Black or African American, non-Hispanic/Latino. Average age 28. 17 applicants, 88% accepted, 12 enrolled. In 2010, 14 master's awarded. *Degree requirements:* For master's, one foreign language, thesis or alternative. *Entrance requirements:* For master's, GRE General Test, minimum GPA of 2.5. Additional exam requirements/recommendations for international students: Required—TOEFL (minimum score 500 paper-based; 173 computer-based; 61 iBT). *Application deadline:* For fall admission, 4/1 for domestic and international students; for spring admission, 11/1 for domestic and international students. Applications are processed on a rolling basis. Application fee: $40 ($55 for international students). *Expenses:* Tuition: Full-time $12,942; part-time $719 per credit hour. Required fees: $710; $355 per semester. *Financial support:* Scholarships/grants and unspecified assistantships available. Financial award application deadline: 4/30; financial award applicants required to submit FAFSA. *Faculty research:* Nutrition education, Africa. *Unit head:* Dr. Ron Finnell, Chairperson, 404-880-6651, E-mail: rfinnell@cau.edu. *Application contact:* Michelle Clark-Davis, Graduate Program Admissions, 404-880-6605, E-mail: cauadmissions@cau.edu.

Clark University, Graduate School, College of Professional and Continuing Education, Program in Public Administration, Worcester, MA 01610-1477. Offers MPA, Certificate. Part-time and evening/weekend programs available. *Students:* 30 full-time (19 women), 19 part-time (11 women); includes 2 Black or African American, non-Hispanic/Latino; 2 Asian, non-Hispanic/Latino; 1 Hispanic/Latino, 9 international. Average age 30. 31 applicants, 100% accepted, 24 enrolled. In 2010, 23 master's awarded. *Degree requirements:* For master's, thesis optional. *Entrance requirements:* For master's, GMAT or GRE General Test. *Application deadline:* Applications are processed on a rolling basis. Application fee: $50. Electronic applications accepted. *Expenses:* Tuition: Full-time $37,000; part-time $1156 per credit hour. Required fees: $30; $1156 per credit hour. *Financial support:* Career-related internships or fieldwork available. Support available to part-time students. *Unit head:* Max E. Hess, Director of Graduate Studies, 508-793-7217, Fax: 508-793-7232. *Application contact:* Julia Parent, Director of Marketing, Communications, and Admissions, 508-793-7217, Fax: 508-793-7232, E-mail: jparent@clarku.edu.

Clemson University, Graduate School, Program in Public Administration, Clemson, SC 29634. Offers MPA. Part-time and evening/weekend programs available. Postbaccalaureate distance learning degree programs offered. *Faculty:* 11 full-time (2 women). *Students:* 11 full-time (7 women), 23 part-time (12 women); includes 3 Black or African American, non-Hispanic/Latino. Average age 32. 29 applicants, 66% accepted, 11 enrolled. In 2010, 10 master's awarded. *Entrance requirements:* For master's, GRE, 2 letters of recommendation. Additional exam requirements/recommendations for international students: Required—TOEFL. *Application deadline:* For fall admission, 6/1 for domestic students; for spring admission, 11/1 for domestic students. Applications are processed on a rolling basis. Application fee: $70 ($80 for international students). Electronic applications accepted. *Expenses:* Contact institution. *Financial support:* In 2010–11, 1 student received support. Institutionally sponsored loans available. Financial award applicants required to submit FAFSA. *Faculty research:* Strategic planning in public administration, evaluation of public projects. *Unit head:* Dr. Catherine Watt, Coordinator, 864-656-0847, E-mail: cwatt@strom.clemson.edu. *Application contact:* Angela Guido, Information Contact, 864-656-3233, E-mail: nangela@clemson.edu.

Cleveland State University, College of Graduate Studies, Maxine Goodman Levin College of Urban Affairs, Program in Public Administration, Cleveland, OH 44115. Offers geographic information systems (Certificate); local and urban management (Certificate); non-profit management (Certificate); public administration (MPA); urban real estate development (Certificate); JD/MPA. *Accreditation:* NASPAA. Part-time and evening/weekend programs available. *Faculty:* 26 full-time (10 women), 14 part-time/adjunct (8 women). *Students:* 36 full-time (22 women), 70 part-time (41 women); includes 26 Black or African American, non-Hispanic/Latino; 1 American Indian or Alaska Native, non-Hispanic/Latino; 1 Asian, non-Hispanic/Latino; 2 Hispanic/Latino; 1 Two or more races, non-Hispanic/Latino, 4 international. Average age 36. 82 applicants, 41% accepted, 15 enrolled. In 2010, 37 master's, 8 other advanced degrees awarded. *Degree requirements:* For master's, thesis or alternative, capstone course. *Entrance requirements:* For master's, GRE General Test (minimum 40th percentile verbal and quantitative, 4.0 writing), minimum GPA of 3.0. Additional exam requirements/recommendations for international students: Required—TOEFL (minimum score 525 paper-based; 197 computer-based; 65 iBT). *Application deadline:* For fall admission, 7/15 priority date for domestic students, 5/15 for international students; for spring admission, 11/1 for international students. Applications are processed on a rolling basis. Application fee: $30. Electronic applications accepted. *Expenses:* Tuition, state resident: full-time $8447; part-time $469 per credit hour. Tuition, nonresident: full-time $16,020; part-time $890 per credit hour. Required fees: $50. *Financial support:* In 2010–11, 10 students received support, including 7 research assistantships with full and partial tuition reimbursements available (averaging $6,960 per year), 3 teaching assistantships with full and partial tuition reimbursements available (averaging $6,960 per year); career-related internships or fieldwork, institutionally sponsored loans, tuition waivers (full and partial), and unspecified assistantships also available. Financial award application deadline: 3/1; financial award applicants required to submit FAFSA. *Faculty research:* Health care administration, public management, economic development, city management, nonprofit management. *Unit head:* Dr. Jennifer Alexander, Director, 216-687-5011, Fax: 216-687-2013, E-mail: j.k.alexander@csuohio.edu. *Application contact:* Joan Demko, Graduate Academic Support Specialist, 216-523-7522, Fax: 216-687-5398, E-mail: urbanprograms@csuohio.edu.

The College at Brockport, State University of New York, School of Education and Human Services, Department of Public Administration, Brockport, NY 14420-2997. Offers arts administration (AGC); nonprofit management (AGC); public administration (MPA), including general public administration, health care management, nonprofit management, public safety. *Accreditation:* NASPAA. Part-time and evening/weekend programs available. *Students:* 26 full-time (17 women), 80 part-time (64 women); includes 12 Black or African American, non-Hispanic/Latino; 2 Asian, non-Hispanic/Latino; 5 Hispanic/Latino. 48 applicants, 79% accepted, 27 enrolled. In 2010, 49 master's, 2 other advanced degrees awarded. *Degree requirements:* For master's, thesis or alternative. *Entrance requirements:* For master's, GRE or minimum GPA of 3.0, letters of recommendation, statement of objectives; current resume. Additional exam requirements/recommendations for international students: Required—TOEFL (minimum score 550 paper-based; 213 computer-based; 79 iBT). *Application deadline:* For fall admission, 3/1 priority date for domestic and international students; for spring admission, 10/1 priority date for domestic and international students. Application fee: $50. Electronic applications accepted. *Financial support:* In 2010–11, teaching assistantships with full tuition reimbursements (averaging $6,000 per year); Federal Work-Study, scholarships/grants, and unspecified assistantships also available. Support available to part-time students. Financial award application deadline: 3/15; financial award applicants required to submit FAFSA. *Faculty research:* E-government, performance management, nonprofits and policy implementation, Medicaid and disabilities. *Unit head:* Dr. Ed Downey, Chairperson, 585-395-2375, Fax: 585-395-2172, E-mail: edowney@brockport.edu. *Application contact:* Dr. Ed Downey, Chairperson, 585-395-2375, Fax: 585-395-2172, E-mail: edowney@brockport.edu.

College of Charleston, Graduate School, School of Humanities and Social Sciences, Program in Public Administration, Charleston, SC 29424-0001. Offers MPA. Program offered jointly with University of South Carolina. *Accreditation:* NASPAA. Part-time and evening/weekend programs available. *Faculty:* 15 full-time (7 women), 5 part-time/adjunct (1 woman). *Students:* 37 full-time (23 women), 24 part-time (16 women); includes 8 minority (5 Black or African American, non-Hispanic/Latino; 3 Hispanic/Latino), 1 international. Average age 28. 45 applicants, 62% accepted, 27 enrolled. In 2010, 23 master's awarded. *Degree requirements:* For master's, thesis optional, internship, capstone seminar. *Entrance requirements:* For master's, GRE General Test, previous course work in statistics, 3 letters of recommendation, minimum GPA of 3.0. Additional exam requirements/recommendations for international students: Required—TOEFL (minimum score 81 iBT). *Application deadline:* For fall admission, 7/1 for domestic students; for spring admission, 11/1 for domestic students. Applications are processed on a rolling basis. Application fee: $45. Electronic applications accepted. *Financial support:* In 2010–11, 6 research assistantships (averaging $12,400 per year) were awarded; career-related internships or fieldwork, Federal Work-Study, scholarships/grants, and unspecified assistantships also available. Support available to part-time students. Financial award application deadline: 4/1; financial award applicants required to submit FAFSA. *Faculty research:* Local government, environmental policy, budgeting, ethics. *Unit head:* Dr. Kendra Stewart, Acting Director, 843-953-5724, Fax: 843-953-8140, E-mail: stewartk@cofc.edu. *Application contact:* Susan Hallatt, Director of Graduate Admissions, 843-953-5614, Fax: 843-953-1434, E-mail: hallatts@cofc.edu.

College of Saint Elizabeth, Program in Justice Studies, Morristown, NJ 07960-6989. Offers justice administration and public service (MA). Part-time and evening/weekend programs available. *Faculty:* 1 full-time (0 women), 2 part-time/adjunct (both women). *Students:* 3 full-time (2 women), 13 part-time (9 women); includes 5 Black or African American, non-Hispanic/Latino; 2 Hispanic/Latino. Average age 33. 10 applicants, 80% accepted, 7 enrolled. In 2010, 1 master's awarded. *Degree requirements:* For master's, thesis or alternative. *Entrance requirements:* Additional exam requirements/recommendations for international students: Required—TOEFL (minimum score 550 paper-based). *Application deadline:* Applications are processed on a rolling basis. Application fee: $35. Electronic applications accepted. *Expenses:* Tuition: Part-time $857 per credit. Required fees: $70 per credit. *Financial support:* Unspecified assistantships available. Support available to part-time students. Financial award applicants required to submit FAFSA. *Unit head:* Dr. James Ford, Associate Professor, 973-290-4324, E-mail: jford@cse.edu. *Application contact:* Dean Donna Tatarka, Dean of Admission, 973-290-4705, Fax: 973-290-4710, E-mail: dtatarka@cse.edu.

Columbia University, School of International and Public Affairs, Program in Public Policy and Administration, New York, NY 10027. Offers MPA, JD/MPA, MPA/MS, MPH/MPA. *Entrance requirements:* For master's, GRE General Test. Additional exam requirements/recommendations for international students: Required—TOEFL (minimum score 600 paper-based; 250 computer-based; 100 iBT). Electronic applications accepted.

Columbus State University, Graduate Studies, College of Letters and Sciences, Master of Public Administration Program, Columbus, GA 31907-5645. Offers justice administration (MPA). Part-time and evening/weekend programs available. *Faculty:* 6 full-time (1 woman), 13 part-time/adjunct (0 women). *Students:* 112 full-time (36 women), 204 part-time (56 women); includes 99 minority (86 Black or African American, non-Hispanic/Latino; 2 American Indian or Alaska Native, non-Hispanic/Latino; 7 Hispanic/Latino; 4 Two or more races, non-Hispanic/Latino), 2 international. Average age 40. 77 applicants, 79% accepted, 53 enrolled. In 2010, 116 master's awarded. *Entrance requirements:* For master's, GRE General Test, minimum GPA of 2.75. Additional exam requirements/recommendations for international students: Required—TOEFL (minimum score 550 paper-based; 213 computer-based; 79 iBT). *Application deadline:* For fall admission, 6/30 for domestic students, 5/1 for international students; for spring admission, 11/1 for domestic and international students. Applications are processed on a rolling basis. Application fee: $30. Electronic applications accepted. *Expenses:* Tuition, state resident: full-time $5573; part-time $232 per semester hour. Tuition, nonresident: full-time $13,968; part-time $582 per semester hour. Required fees: $1300; $650 per semester. Tuition and fees vary according to degree level and program. *Financial support:* In 2010–11, 66 students received support, including 6 research assistantships with partial tuition reimbursements available (averaging $3,000 per year); career-related internships or fieldwork, Federal Work-Study, institutionally sponsored loans, scholarships/grants, tuition waivers (partial), and unspecified assistantships also available. Support available to part-time students. Financial award application deadline: 5/1; financial award applicants required to submit FAFSA. *Unit head:* Dr. Tom Dolan, Director, 706-565-7875, E-mail: dolan_thomas@colstate.edu. *Application contact:* Katie Thornton, Graduate Admissions Specialist, 706-568-2035, Fax: 706-568-2462, E-mail: thornton_katie@colstate.edu.

Concordia University, School of Graduate Studies, Faculty of Arts and Science, Department of Political Science, Montréal, QC H3G 1M8, Canada. Offers political science (PhD); public policy and public administration (MA), including geography. *Degree requirements:* For master's, one foreign language, comprehensive exam, thesis optional, internship. *Entrance requirements:* For master's, honors degree or equivalent. Additional exam requirements/recommendations for international students: Required—TOEFL. *Faculty research:* International public policy and administration, Quebec public administration, public policy and social/political theory, geography and public policy, public administration and decision making.

Concordia University Wisconsin, Graduate Programs, School of Business and Legal Studies, MBA Program, Mequon, WI 53097-2402. Offers finance (MBA); health care administration (MBA); human resource management (MBA); international business (MBA); international business-bilingual English/Chinese (MBA); management (MBA); management information systems (MBA); managerial communications (MBA); marketing (MBA); public administration (MBA); risk management (MBA). Postbaccalaureate distance learning degree programs offered (minimal on-campus study). *Degree requirements:* For master's, comprehensive exam, thesis or alternative. *Entrance requirements:* Additional exam requirements/recommendations for international students: Required—TOEFL. *Expenses:* Contact institution.

Cumberland University, Program in Public Service Administration, Lebanon, TN 37087. Offers MS. Part-time and evening/weekend programs available. *Degree requirements:* For master's, comprehensive exam. *Entrance requirements:* For master's, MAT, 3 letters of recommendation. Additional exam requirements/recommendations for international students: Required—TOEFL (minimum score 500 paper-based; 173 computer-based).

Dalhousie University, Faculty of Management, School of Public Administration, Halifax, NS B3H 3J5, Canada. Offers management (MPA); public administration (MPA, GDPA); LL B/MPA; MLIS/MPA. Part-time programs available. *Entrance requirements:* For master's, GMAT. Additional exam requirements/recommendations for international students: Required—TOEFL, IELTS, CANTEST, CAEL, or Michigan English Language Assessment Battery. Electronic applications accepted. *Expenses:* Contact institution. *Faculty research:* Municipal management, policy and program management, environmental policy, economic and social policy, business and government.

DePaul University, School of Public Service, Chicago, IL 60604. Offers financial administration management (Certificate); health administration (Certificate); health law and policy (MS); international public services (MS); leadership and policy studies (MS); metropolitan planning (Certificate); public administration (MPA); public service management (MS), including association management, fundraising and philanthropy, healthcare administration, higher education administration, metropolitan planning; public services (Certificate); JD/MS. Part-time and evening/weekend programs available. Postbaccalaureate distance learning degree programs offered (minimal on-campus study). *Faculty:* 14 full-time (3 women), 43 part-time/adjunct (24 women). *Students:* 372 full-time (256 women), 324 part-time (237 women); includes 156 Black or African American, non-Hispanic/Latino; 33 Asian, non-Hispanic/Latino; 65 Hispanic/Latino; 18 Two or more races, non-Hispanic/Latino, 18 international. Average age 26. 162 applicants, 100% accepted, 94 enrolled. In 2010, 108 master's awarded. *Degree requirements:* For master's, thesis or integrative seminar. *Entrance requirements:* For master's, minimum GPA of 2.7. Additional exam requirements/recommendations for international students: Required—TOEFL (minimum score 550 paper-based; 213 computer-based; 80 iBT), IELTS (minimum score 6.5). *Application deadline:* Applications are processed on a rolling basis. Application fee: $40. Electronic applications accepted. *Financial support:* In 2010–11, 60 students received support, including 3 research assistantships with full tuition reimbursements available (averaging $7,000 per year); career-related internships or fieldwork, Federal Work-Study, institutionally

sponsored loans, scholarships/grants, tuition waivers (partial), and unspecified assistantships also available. Support available to part-time students. Financial award application deadline: 7/1; financial award applicants required to submit FAFSA. *Faculty research:* Government financing, transportation, leadership, health care, volunteerism and organizational behavior, non-profit organizations. Total annual research expenditures: $20,000. *Unit head:* Dr. J. Patrick Murphy, Director, 312-362-5608, Fax: 312-362-5506, E-mail: jpmurphy@depaul.edu. *Application contact:* Megan B. Balderston, Director of Admissions and Marketing, 312-362-5565, Fax: 312-362-5506, E-mail: pubserv@depaul.edu.

DeVry University, Keller Graduate School of Management, Downers Grove, IL 60515. Offers accounting and financial management (MAFM); business administration (MBA); human resources management (MHRM); information systems management (MISM); network and communications management (MNCM); project management (MPM); public administration (MPA).

Drake University, College of Business and Public Administration, Des Moines, IA 50311-4516. Offers M Acc, MBA, MFM, MPA, JD/MBA, JD/MPA, Pharm D/MBA, Pharm D/MPA. *Accreditation:* AACSB. Part-time and evening/weekend programs available. *Degree requirements:* For master's, comprehensive exam (for some programs), thesis (for some programs), internships. *Entrance requirements:* For master's, GMAT, letters of recommendation, resume. Additional exam requirements/recommendations for international students: Required—TOEFL (minimum score 550 paper-based; 213 computer-based). Electronic applications accepted. *Expenses:* Contact institution. *Faculty research:* Venture capital, online commerce, professional ethics, process improvement, project management.

Duquesne University, Graduate School of Liberal Arts, Graduate Center for Social and Public Policy, Pittsburgh, PA 15282-0001. Offers conflict resolution and peace studies (Certificate); social and public policy (MA, Certificate). Part-time and evening/weekend programs available. *Faculty:* 15 full-time (3 women), 1 (woman) part-time/adjunct. *Students:* 52 full-time (26 women), 9 part-time (4 women); includes 1 Black or African American, non-Hispanic/Latino, 5 international. Average age 27. 38 applicants, 95% accepted, 17 enrolled. In 2010, 11 master's awarded. *Degree requirements:* For master's, thesis. *Entrance requirements:* For master's, GRE General Test. Additional exam requirements/recommendations for international students: Required—TOEFL. *Application deadline:* For fall admission, 4/30 priority date for domestic and international students; for spring admission, 11/1 priority date for domestic and international students. Applications are processed on a rolling basis. Electronic applications accepted. *Expenses:* Tuition: Part-time $884 per credit. Required fees: $84 per credit. Tuition and fees vary according to course load. *Financial support:* In 2010–11, 20 students received support, including 12 research assistantships with full and partial tuition reimbursements available (averaging $9,000 per year). 4 teaching assistantships with full and partial tuition reimbursements available (averaging $9,000 per year); career-related internships or fieldwork, institutionally sponsored loans, scholarships/grants, tuition waivers (full and partial), and unspecified assistantships also available. Support available to part-time students. Financial award application deadline: 5/1. *Faculty research:* Program evaluation, environmental policy, criminal justice policy, health care policy. Total annual research expenditures: $30,000. *Unit head:* Dr. Joseph Yenerall, Director, 412-396-6485, Fax: 412-396-5265, E-mail: socialpolicy@duq.edu. *Application contact:* Dr. Joseph Yenerall, Assistant to the Dean, 412-396-6485.

East Carolina University, Graduate School, Thomas Harriot College of Arts and Sciences, Department of Political Science, Greenville, NC 27858-4353. Offers public administration (MPA). *Accreditation:* NASPAA. Part-time and evening/weekend programs available. *Degree requirements:* For master's, one foreign language, comprehensive exam. *Entrance requirements:* For master's, GRE General Test. Additional exam requirements/recommendations for international students: Required—TOEFL. *Expenses:* Tuition, state resident: full-time $3130; part-time $391.25 per credit hour. Tuition, nonresident: full-time $13,817; part-time $1727.13 per credit hour. Required fees: $1916; $239.50 per credit hour. Tuition and fees vary according to campus/location and program.

Eastern Kentucky University, The Graduate School, College of Arts and Sciences, Department of Government, Program in General Public Administration, Richmond, KY 40475-3102. Offers community development (MPA); community health administration (MPA); general public administration (MPA). *Accreditation:* NASPAA. Part-time and evening/weekend programs available. *Entrance requirements:* For master's, GRE General Test, minimum GPA of 2.5.

Eastern Michigan University, Graduate School, College of Arts and Sciences, Department of Political Science, Programs in Public Administration, Ypsilanti, MI 48197. Offers local government management (Graduate Certificate); management of public healthcare services (Graduate Certificate); public administration (MPA, Graduate Certificate); public budget management (Graduate Certificate); public land planning (Graduate Certificate); public management (Graduate Certificate); public personnel management (Graduate Certificate); public policy analysis (Graduate Certificate). *Accreditation:* NASPAA. *Students:* 28 full-time (18 women), 124 part-time (64 women); includes 50 minority (40 Black or African American, non-Hispanic/Latino; 1 American Indian or Alaska Native, non-Hispanic/Latino; 1 Asian, non-Hispanic/Latino; 6 Hispanic/Latino; 2 Two or more races, non-Hispanic/Latino), 5 international. Average age 34. In 2010, 17 master's, 17 other advanced degrees awarded. Application fee: $35. *Unit head:* Dr. Joseph Ohren, Program Director, 734-487-2522, Fax: 734-487-3340, E-mail: joseph.ohren@emich.edu. *Application contact:* Dr. Joseph Ohren, Program Director, 734-487-2522, Fax: 734-487-3340, E-mail: joseph.ohren@emich.edu.

Eastern Washington University, Graduate Studies, College of Business and Public Administration, Program in Public Administration, Cheney, WA 99004-2431. Offers MPA, MBA/MPA, MPA/MSW, MPA/MURP. Part-time and evening/weekend programs available. *Degree requirements:* For master's, comprehensive exam, thesis optional. *Entrance requirements:* For master's, minimum GPA of 3.0.

The Evergreen State College, Graduate Programs, Program in Public Administration, Olympia, WA 98505. Offers MPA. Part-time and evening/weekend programs available. *Faculty:* 8 full-time (3 women), 4 part-time/adjunct (1 woman). *Students:* 73 full-time (53 women), 79 part-time (48 women); includes 13 Black or African American, non-Hispanic/Latino; 26 American Indian or Alaska Native, non-Hispanic/Latino; 6 Asian, non-Hispanic/Latino; 10 Hispanic/Latino; 5 Native Hawaiian or other Pacific Islander, non-Hispanic/Latino. Average age 36. 122 applicants, 71% accepted, 65 enrolled. In 2010, 54 master's awarded. *Degree requirements:* For master's, 6 credit capstone course or 8 credit thesis. *Entrance requirements:* For master's, minimum GPA of 3.0 in last 90 quarter hours toward BA/BS; 4 quarter credits in statistics within past 5 years; evidence of writing, analytical, and general communication skills at appropriate level for graduate study. Additional exam requirements/recommendations for international students: Required—TOEFL (minimum score 600 paper-based; 250 computer-based; 100 iBT). *Application deadline:* For fall admission, 3/3 priority date for domestic and international students. Applications are processed on a rolling basis. Application fee: $50. Electronic applications accepted. *Expenses:* Contact institution. *Financial support:* In 2010–11, 51 students received support, including 8 fellowships (averaging $2,398 per year); career-related internships or fieldwork, Federal Work-Study, scholarships/grants, tuition waivers (partial), and unspecified assistantships also available. Support available to part-time students. Financial award application deadline: 3/15; financial award applicants required to submit FAFSA. *Faculty research:* Fair housing, democratic governance, energy/public/environmental policy, tribal/community/economic development, tribal governance, nonprofit administration, international administration, organizational theory, management science, culture and dynamic of public organization, leadership and decision-making process. *Unit head:* Dr. Lee Lyttle, MPA Program Director, 360-867-6678, E-mail: lyttlel@evergreen.edu. *Application contact:* Randee Gibbons, Associate MPA Program Director, 360-867-6554, E-mail: gibbonsr@evergreen.edu.

Fairleigh Dickinson University, College at Florham, Anthony J. Petrocelli College of Continuing Studies, Public Administration Institute, Program in Public Administration, Madison, NJ 07940-1099. Offers MPA. *Students:* 1 applicant, 0% accepted, 0 enrolled. Application fee:

Public Administration

Fairleigh Dickinson University, College at Florham *(continued)*
$40. *Unit head:* Dr. William Roberts, Head, 973-443-8500. *Application contact:* Susan Brooman, University Director, Graduate Admissions, 973-443-8905, Fax: 973-443-8088, E-mail: grad@fdu.edu.

Fairleigh Dickinson University, Metropolitan Campus, Anthony J. Petrocelli College of Continuing Studies, Public Administration Institute, Program in Public Administration, Teaneck, NJ 07666-1914. Offers MPA, Certificate. *Students:* 116 full-time (49 women), 123 part-time (64 women), 97 international. Average age 32. 165 applicants, 76% accepted, 56 enrolled. In 2010, 104 master's awarded. *Application deadline:* Applications are processed on a rolling basis. Application fee: $40. *Unit head:* Dr. William Roberts, Director, 201-692-2000. *Application contact:* Dr. William Roberts, Director, 201-692-2000.

Florida Agricultural and Mechanical University, Division of Graduate Studies, Research, and Continuing Education, College of Arts and Sciences, Division of History and Political Sciences, Program in Applied Social Science, Tallahassee, FL 32307-3200. Offers African American history (MASS); criminal justice (MASS); economics (MASS); history (MASS); political science (MASS); public administration (MASS); public management (MASS); social work (MASS); sociology (MASS). Part-time programs available. *Degree requirements:* For master's, thesis optional. *Entrance requirements:* For master's, GRE General Test, minimum GPA of 3.0. *Faculty research:* Southern history, black history, election trends, presidential history.

Florida Atlantic University, College of Design and Social Inquiry, School of Public Administration, Boca Raton, FL 33431-0991. Offers MNM, MPA, PhD. *Accreditation:* NASPAA (one or more programs are accredited). Part-time and evening/weekend programs available. *Faculty:* 13 full-time (4 women), 2 part-time/adjunct (0 women). *Students:* 41 full-time (22 women), 82 part-time (47 women); includes 40 minority (24 Black or African American, non-Hispanic/Latino; 2 Asian, non-Hispanic/Latino; 12 Hispanic/Latino; 2 Two or more races, non-Hispanic/Latino), 6 international. Average age 34, 87 applicants, 43% accepted, 25 enrolled. In 2010, 30 master's, 4 doctorates awarded. *Degree requirements:* For master's, thesis optional; for doctorate, comprehensive exam, thesis/dissertation. *Entrance requirements:* For master's, GRE General Test, minimum GPA of 3.0; for doctorate, GRE General Test, faculty reference, scholarly writing samples, letters of recommendation. Additional exam requirements/recommendations for international students: Required—TOEFL. *Application deadline:* For fall admission, 7/1 priority date for domestic students, 2/15 for international students; for spring admission, 11/1 for domestic students, 7/15 for international students. Applications are processed on a rolling basis. Application fee: $30. *Expenses:* Tuition, area resident: Part-time $319.96 per credit. Tuition, state resident: part-time $319.96 per credit. Tuition, nonresident: part-time $926.42 per credit. *Financial support:* Fellowships with full tuition reimbursements, research assistantships with partial tuition reimbursements, teaching assistantships with partial tuition reimbursements, career-related internships or fieldwork, Federal Work-Study, institutionally sponsored loans, and tuition waivers (partial) available. Support available to part-time students. Financial award application deadline: 4/1. *Faculty research:* Public finance and budgeting, public management, evaluation, criminal justice, postmodern public administration. *Unit head:* Dr. Khi Thai, Director, 954-762-5650, Fax: 954-762-5693, E-mail: thai@fau.edu. *Application contact:* Dr. Khi Thai, Director, 954-762-5650, Fax: 954-762-5693, E-mail: thai@fau.edu.

Florida Gulf Coast University, College of Professional Studies, Program in Public Administration, Fort Myers, FL 33965-6565. Offers criminal justice (MPA); environmental policy (MPA); general public administration (MPA); management (MPA). *Accreditation:* NASPAA. Part-time programs available. *Faculty:* 35 full-time (15 women), 34 part-time/adjunct (12 women). *Students:* 71 full-time (46 women), 20 part-time (11 women); includes 10 Black or African American, non-Hispanic/Latino; 1 American Indian or Alaska Native, non-Hispanic/Latino; 7 Hispanic/Latino, 2 international. Average age 31. 46 applicants, 67% accepted, 26 enrolled. In 2010, 11 master's awarded. *Entrance requirements:* For master's, GRE General Test, MAT, minimum GPA of 3.0. Additional exam requirements/recommendations for international students: Required—TOEFL (minimum score 550 paper-based; 213 computer-based). *Application deadline:* For fall admission, 7/1 priority date for domestic students; for spring admission, 11/15 for domestic students. Applications are processed on a rolling basis. Application fee: $30. Electronic applications accepted. *Expenses:* Tuition, state resident: part-time $322.08 per credit hour. Tuition, nonresident: part-time $1117.08 per credit hour. *Financial support:* In 2010–11, 5 research assistantships were awarded; career-related internships or fieldwork and tuition waivers (full and partial) also available. Support available to part-time students. *Faculty research:* Personnel, public policy, public finance, housing policy. *Unit head:* Terry Busson, Chair, 239-590-7704, E-mail: tbusson@fgcu.edu. *Application contact:* Roger Green, Information Contact, 239-590-7838, Fax: 239-590-7846.

Florida Institute of Technology, Graduate Programs, Extended Studies Division, Melbourne, FL 32901-6975. Offers acquisition and contract management (MS); aerospace engineering (MS); business administration (MBA); computer information systems (MS); computer science (MS); electrical engineering (MS); engineering management (MS); human resources management (MS); logistics management (MS), including humanitarian and disaster relief logistics; management (MS), including acquisition and contract management, e-business, human resources management, information systems, logistics management, management, transportation management; material acquisition management (MS); mechanical engineering (MS); operations research (MS); project management (MS), including information systems, operations research; public administration (MPA); quality management (MS); software engineering (MS); space systems (MS); space systems management (MS); systems management (MS), including information systems, operations research. Part-time and evening/weekend programs available. Postbaccalaureate distance learning degree programs offered (no on-campus study). *Faculty:* 11 full-time (3 women), 118 part-time/adjunct (24 women). *Students:* 69 full-time (23 women), 907 part-time (369 women); includes 385 minority (242 Black or African American, non-Hispanic/Latino; 15 American Indian or Alaska Native, non-Hispanic/Latino; 44 Asian, non-Hispanic/Latino; 52 Hispanic/Latino; 3 Native Hawaiian or other Pacific Islander, non-Hispanic/Latino; 29 Two or more races, non-Hispanic/Latino), 17 international. 517 applicants, 49% accepted, 245 enrolled. In 2010, 430 degrees awarded. *Degree requirements:* For master's, comprehensive exam (for some programs), capstone course. *Entrance requirements:* For master's, GMAT or resume showing 8 years of supervised experience, minimum GPA of 3.0, 2 letters of recommendation, resume. Additional exam requirements/recommendations for international students: Required—TOEFL (minimum score 550 paper-based; 213 computer-based; 79 iBT). *Application deadline:* For fall admission, 4/1 for international students; for spring admission, 9/30 for international students. Applications are processed on a rolling basis. Application fee: $50. Electronic applications accepted. *Expenses:* Contact institution. *Financial support:* Application deadline: 3/1. *Unit head:* Dr. Theodore Richardson, Senior Associate Dean, 321-674-8123, Fax: 321-674-7597, E-mail: trichardson@fit.edu. *Application contact:* Carolyn Farrior, Director of Graduate Admissions, Online Learning and Off-Campus Programs, 321-674-7118, Fax: 321-674-8216, E-mail: cfarrior@fit.edu.

Florida International University, College of Arts and Sciences, Department of Public Administration, Miami, FL 33199. Offers public administration (MPA); public management (PhD). *Accreditation:* NASPAA (one or more programs are accredited). Part-time and evening/weekend programs available. *Faculty:* 10 full-time (6 women), 4 part-time/adjunct (2 women). *Students:* 120 full-time (80 women), 156 part-time (104 women); includes 70 Black or African American, non-Hispanic/Latino; 1 American Indian or Alaska Native, non-Hispanic/Latino; 5 Asian, non-Hispanic/Latino; 143 Hispanic/Latino, 10 international. Average age 33. 259 applicants, 53% accepted, 133 enrolled. In 2010, 66 master's awarded. *Degree requirements:* For doctorate, comprehensive exam, thesis/dissertation. *Entrance requirements:* For master's, minimum undergraduate GPA of 3.0 in upper-level coursework, 1 letter of recommendation, letter of intent; for doctorate, GRE, minimum undergraduate GPA of 3.0 in upper-level coursework, 3 letters of recommendation, samples of scholarly written work, interview (when student lives within 50 miles of campus). Additional exam requirements/recommendations for international students: Required—TOEFL (minimum score 550 paper-based; 80 iBT). *Application*

deadline: For fall admission, 6/1 for domestic students, 4/1 for international students; for spring admission, 10/1 for domestic students, 9/1 for international students. Applications are processed on a rolling basis. Application fee: $30. Electronic applications accepted. *Financial support:* Institutionally sponsored loans and scholarships/grants available. Financial award application deadline: 3/1; financial award applicants required to submit FAFSA. *Unit head:* Dr. Meredith Newman, Chair, 305-348-5890, Fax: 305-348-5848, E-mail: meredith.newman@fiu.edu. *Application contact:* Liga Replogle, Student Services Coordinator, 305-348-5890, Fax: 305-348-5848, E-mail: liga.replogle@fiu.edu.

Florida State University, The Graduate School, College of Social Sciences and Public Policy, Reubin O'D. Askew School of Public Administration and Policy, Tallahassee, FL 32306-2250. Offers MPA, PhD, Certificate, JD/MPA, MPA/MSC, MPA/MSP, MPA/MSW. *Accreditation:* NASPAA (one or more programs are accredited). Part-time and evening/weekend programs available. *Faculty:* 11 full-time (1 woman), 13 part-time/adjunct (5 women). *Students:* 72 full-time (27 women), 120 part-time (64 women); includes 42 minority (27 Black or African American, non-Hispanic/Latino; 2 Asian, non-Hispanic/Latino; 11 Hispanic/Latino; 1 Native Hawaiian or other Pacific Islander, non-Hispanic/Latino; 1 Two or more races, non-Hispanic/Latino), 45 international. Average age 25. 193 applicants, 84% accepted, 82 enrolled. In 2010, 34 master's, 9 doctorates awarded. *Degree requirements:* For master's, action report; for doctorate, comprehensive exam, thesis/dissertation. *Entrance requirements:* For master's, GRE General Test, GMAT, MAT, LSAT, minimum undergraduate upper-division GPA of 3.0; for doctorate, GRE General Test (minimum score of 1100); GMAT, MAT, LSAT, minimum undergraduate GPA of 3.0, graduate 3.5. Additional exam requirements/recommendations for international students: Required—TOEFL (minimum score 550 paper-based; 213 computer-based; 80 iBT), IELTS (minimum score 6.5), Michigan English Language Assessment Battery (minimum score 77). *Application deadline:* For fall admission, 7/1 for domestic students, 5/1 for international students; for spring admission, 11/1 for domestic students, 9/1 for international students. Applications are processed on a rolling basis. Application fee: $30. Electronic applications accepted. *Expenses:* Tuition, state resident: full-time $8238.24. *Financial support:* In 2010–11, 38 students received support, including 18 fellowships with full tuition reimbursements available (averaging $18,000 per year), 21 research assistantships with full tuition reimbursements available (averaging $15,000 per year), 3 teaching assistantships with full tuition reimbursements available (averaging $12,000 per year); career-related internships or fieldwork, Federal Work-Study, institutionally sponsored loans, scholarships/grants, tuition waivers (full), and unspecified assistantships also available. Support available to part-time students. Financial award application deadline: 2/1. *Faculty research:* Financial management, human resource management, policy, strategic management, organizations, nonprofit management. *Unit head:* Dr. William Earle Klay, Director, 850-644-3525, Fax: 850-644-7617, E-mail: eklay@fsu.edu. *Application contact:* Velda Williams, Academic Program Specialist, 850-644-3060, Fax: 850-644-7617, E-mail: vwilliams3@fsu.edu.

Framingham State University, Division of Graduate and Continuing Education, Program in Public Administration, Framingham, MA 01701-9101. Offers MA. Part-time and evening/weekend programs available.

Gannon University, School of Graduate Studies, College of Engineering and Business, School of Business, Program in Public Administration, Erie, PA 16541-0001. Offers MPA, Certificate. Part-time and evening/weekend programs available. *Students:* 20 full-time (5 women), 15 part-time (11 women); includes 4 minority (3 Black or African American, non-Hispanic/Latino; 1 Hispanic/Latino), 6 international. Average age 31. 36 applicants, 92% accepted, 6 enrolled. In 2010, 16 master's awarded. *Degree requirements:* For master's, thesis or alternative, research project. *Entrance requirements:* For master's, GRE or GMAT. Additional exam requirements/recommendations for international students: Required—TOEFL (minimum score 79 iBT). *Application deadline:* Applications are processed on a rolling basis. Application fee: $25. Electronic applications accepted. *Expenses:* Tuition: Full-time $14,670; part-time $815 per credit. Required fees: $430; $18 per credit. Tuition and fees vary according to class time, course load, degree level, campus/location and program. *Financial support:* Career-related internships or fieldwork, scholarships/grants, and unspecified assistantships available. Support available to part-time students. Financial award application deadline: 7/1; financial award applicants required to submit FAFSA. *Unit head:* Dr. Duane Prokop, Director, 814-871-7576, E-mail: prokop001@gannon.edu. *Application contact:* Kara Morgan, Assistant Director of Graduate Admissions, 814-871-5831, Fax: 814-871-5827, E-mail: graduate@gannon.edu.

George Mason University, College of Humanities and Social Sciences, Department of Public and International Affairs, Fairfax, VA 22030. Offers association management (Certificate); biodefense (MS, PhD); emergency management and homeland security (Certificate); nonprofit management (Certificate); political science (MA, PhD); public administration (MPA); public management (Certificate). *Accreditation:* NASPAA (one or more programs are accredited). *Faculty:* 38 full-time (14 women), 31 part-time/adjunct (8 women). *Students:* 134 full-time (76 women), 319 part-time (176 women); includes 63 minority (29 Black or African American, non-Hispanic/Latino; 9 Asian, non-Hispanic/Latino; 21 Hispanic/Latino; 1 Native Hawaiian or other Pacific Islander, non-Hispanic/Latino; 3 Two or more races, non-Hispanic/Latino), 16 international. Average age 31. 574 applicants, 58% accepted, 144 enrolled. In 2010, 140 master's, 3 doctorates, 11 other advanced degrees awarded. *Entrance requirements:* For master's, GRE General Test, minimum GPA of 3.0 in last 60 hours of course work. Additional exam requirements/recommendations for international students: Required—TOEFL (minimum score 570 paper-based; 230 computer-based; 88 iBT). *Application deadline:* For fall admission, 3/1 priority date for domestic students; for spring admission, 10/15 for domestic students. Application fee: $100. Electronic applications accepted. *Expenses:* Tuition, state resident: full-time $8192; part-time $440 per credit hour. Tuition, nonresident: full-time $22,952; part-time $1055 per credit hour. Required fees: $2364; $99 per credit hour. *Financial support:* In 2010–11, 30 students received support, including 3 fellowships with full tuition reimbursements available (averaging $18,000 per year), 10 research assistantships with full and partial tuition reimbursements available (averaging $12,271 per year), 18 teaching assistantships with full and partial tuition reimbursements available (averaging $10,428 per year); career-related internships or fieldwork, Federal Work-Study, scholarships/grants, unspecified assistantships, and health care benefits (full-time research or teaching assistantship recipients) also available. Financial award application deadline: 3/1; financial award applicants required to submit FAFSA. *Faculty research:* The Rehnquist Court and economic liberties; intersection of economic development with high-tech industry, telecommunications, and entrepreneurism; political economy of development; violence, terrorism and U. S. foreign policy; international security issues. Total annual research expenditures: $696,997. *Unit head:* Dr. Priscilla Regan, Chair, 703-993-1419, Fax: 703-993-1399, E-mail: pregan@gmu.edu. *Application contact:* Peg Koback, Information Contact, 703-993-9466, E-mail: mkoback@gmu.edu.

The George Washington University, Columbian College of Arts and Sciences, Trachtenberg School of Public Policy and Public Administration, Washington, DC 20052. Offers public administration (MPA), including budget and public finance, managing state and local governments; JD/MPP; MPA/JD; PhD/MPP. Part-time and evening/weekend programs available. *Faculty:* 37 full-time (13 women), 19 part-time/adjunct (10 women). *Students:* 286 full-time (182 women), 163 part-time (123 women); includes 18 Black or African American, non-Hispanic/Latino; 1 American Indian or Alaska Native, non-Hispanic/Latino; 30 Asian, non-Hispanic/Latino; 12 Hispanic/Latino; 1 Native Hawaiian or other Pacific Islander, non-Hispanic/Latino. Average age 26. 1,102 applicants, 49% accepted, 146 enrolled. In 2010, 113 master's awarded. *Entrance requirements:* For master's, GRE General Test, minimum GPA of 3.0. Additional exam requirements/recommendations for international students: Required—TOEFL (minimum score 600 paper-based; 250 computer-based; 100 iBT). *Application deadline:* For fall admission, 1/15 priority date for domestic and international students; for spring admission, 10/1 priority date for domestic students, 9/1 priority date for international students. Application fee: $60. Electronic applications accepted. *Financial support:* In 2010–11, 65 students received support; fellowships, research assistantships, teaching assistantships available. Financial award application deadline: 1/15. *Faculty research:* Education policy, budget and finance, health policy, regulatory policy. *Unit head:* Dr. Kathyrn E. Newcomer, Director, 202-994-3959, Fax: 202-994-3959, E-mail: newcomer@gwu.edu. *Application contact:* Bethany Pope, Program Coordinator, 202-994-6295, Fax: 202-994-6295, E-mail: tspppa@gwu.edu.

Georgia College & State University, Graduate School, College of Arts and Sciences, Department of Government and Sociology, Program in Public Administration, Milledgeville, GA 31061. Offers MPA. *Accreditation:* NASPAA. Part-time and evening/weekend programs available. *Students:* 14 full-time (9 women), 90 part-time (65 women); includes 37 minority (29 Black or African American, non-Hispanic/Latino; 1 American Indian or Alaska Native, non-Hispanic/Latino; 2 Asian, non-Hispanic/Latino; 1 Hispanic/Latino; 4 Two or more races, non-Hispanic/Latino), 2 international. Average age 30. 40 applicants, 93% accepted, 34 enrolled. In 2010, 35 master's awarded. *Degree requirements:* For master's, thesis optional, capstone project or internship. *Entrance requirements:* For master's, GRE General Test or MAT. Additional exam requirements/recommendations for international students: Recommended—TOEFL (minimum score 550 paper-based; 213 computer-based; 79 iBT), IELTS. *Application deadline:* For fall admission, 7/1 priority date for domestic students, 4/1 priority date for international students; for spring admission, 11/15 priority date for domestic students, 9/1 priority date for international students. Applications are processed on a rolling basis. Application fee: $40. Electronic applications accepted. *Expenses:* Tuition, state resident: full-time $4806; part-time $267 per hour. Tuition, nonresident: full-time $17,802; part-time $989 per hour. Tuition and fees vary according to course load. *Financial support:* In 2010–11, 14 research assistantships were awarded; career-related internships or fieldwork and unspecified assistantships also available. Support available to part-time students. Financial award application deadline: 3/1; financial award applicants required to submit FAFSA. *Unit head:* Dr. Jerry Herbel, Graduate Coordinator, 478-445-7393, E-mail: mpa@gcsu.edu. *Application contact:* Dr. Jerry Herbel, Graduate Coordinator, 478-445-7393, E-mail: mpa@gcsu.edu.

Georgia Southern University, Jack N. Averitt College of Graduate Studies, College of Liberal Arts and Social Sciences, Department of Political Science, Statesboro, GA 30460. Offers public administration (MPA). Part-time and evening/weekend programs available. *Students:* 29 full-time (17 women), 18 part-time (11 women); includes 11 Black or African American, non-Hispanic/Latino; 1 Asian, non-Hispanic/Latino; 3 Hispanic/Latino, 1 international. Average age 26. 21 applicants, 90% accepted, 14 enrolled. In 2010, 16 master's awarded. *Degree requirements:* For master's, comprehensive exam. *Entrance requirements:* For master's, GRE General Test, letters of reference, resume. Additional exam requirements/recommendations for international students: Required—TOEFL (minimum score 550 paper-based; 213 computer-based; 80 iBT). *Application deadline:* For fall admission, 3/1 priority date for domestic and international students; for spring admission, 10/1 priority date for domestic students, 10/1 for international students. Applications are processed on a rolling basis. Application fee: $50. Electronic applications accepted. *Expenses:* Tuition, state resident: full-time $6000; part-time $250 per semester hour. Tuition, nonresident: full-time $23,976; part-time $999 per semester hour. Required fees: $1644. *Financial support:* In 2010–11, 35 students received support, including research assistantships with partial tuition reimbursements available (averaging $7,200 per year), teaching assistantships with partial tuition reimbursements available (averaging $7,200 per year); Federal Work-Study, scholarships/grants, tuition waivers (partial), and unspecified assistantships also available. Support available to part-time students. Financial award application deadline: 4/15; financial award applicants required to submit FAFSA. *Faculty research:* Challenges in motivating the public sector employee, nonprofit management and innovation, decision-making on the U. S. Supreme Court, separation of powers and strategic decision making, environmental policy, tragedy in politics, specialized courts, territorial disputes and conflict, media and politics, criminal justice administration, budgeting and financial management, EEO and diversity management, employee motivation and executive compensation, public and nonprofit governance and management. Total annual research expenditures: $18,611. *Unit head:* Dr. Richard Pacelle, Chair, 912-478-5698, Fax: 912-478-5348, E-mail: rpacelle@georgiasouthern.edu. *Application contact:* Dr. Charles Ziglar, Coordinator for Graduate Student Recruitment, 912-478-5635, Fax: 912-478-0740, E-mail: gradadmissions@georgiasouthern.edu.

Georgia State University, Andrew Young School of Policy Studies, Department of Public Management and Policy, Atlanta, GA 30303. Offers disaster management (Certificate); nonprofit management (Certificate); planning and economic development (Certificate); public administration (MPA), including criminal justice, management and finance, nonprofit management, planning and economic development, policy analysis and evaluation, public health; public policy (MPP, PhD), including disaster policy (MPP), nonprofit policy (MPP), planning and economic development policy (MPP), public finance policy (MPP), social policy (MPP); JD/MPA. *Accreditation:* NASPAA (one or more programs are accredited). Part-time and evening/weekend programs available. Terminal master's awarded for partial completion of doctoral program. *Degree requirements:* For master's, thesis optional; for doctorate, comprehensive exam, thesis/dissertation. *Entrance requirements:* For master's and doctorate, GRE General Test. Additional exam requirements/recommendations for international students: Required—TOEFL. Electronic applications accepted. *Faculty research:* Public management, policy analysis, public finance, planning and economic development, nonprofit leadership and policy.

Golden Gate University, Ageno School of Business, San Francisco, CA 94105-2968. Offers accounting (MBA); business administration (EMBA, MBA, PMBA, DBA); finance (MBA, MS, Certificate); financial planning (MS, Certificate); healthcare information systems (Certificate); human resource management (MBA, MS); human resources management (Certificate); information systems (MS); information technology (MBA); information technology management (Certificate); integrated marketing and communications (MS, Certificate); international business (MBA); management (MBA); marketing (MBA, MS, Certificate); operations supply chain management (Certificate); psychology (MA, Certificate); public administration (EMPA); public relations (MS, Certificate); technical market analysis (Certificate); JD/MBA. Part-time and evening/weekend programs available. *Faculty:* 16 full-time (4 women), 241 part-time/adjunct (72 women). *Students:* 421 full-time (235 women), 744 part-time (425 women); includes 526 minority (114 Black or African American, non-Hispanic/Latino; 2 American Indian or Alaska Native, non-Hispanic/Latino; 296 Asian, non-Hispanic/Latino; 73 Hispanic/Latino; 29 Native Hawaiian or other Pacific Islander, non-Hispanic/Latino; 12 Two or more races, non-Hispanic/Latino), 100 international. Average age 32. 681 applicants, 78% accepted, 270 enrolled. In 2010, 550 master's, 13 doctorates awarded. *Degree requirements:* For doctorate, thesis/dissertation. *Entrance requirements:* For master's, GMAT (MBA), minimum GPA of 2.5 (MS). Additional exam requirements/recommendations for international students: Required—TOEFL. *Application deadline:* For fall admission, 5/15 for domestic and international students; for winter admission, 1/15 for domestic and international students; for spring admission, 9/15 for domestic and international students. Applications are processed on a rolling basis. Application fee: $70 ($110 for international students). Electronic applications accepted. *Expenses:* Contact institution. *Financial support:* Career-related internships or fieldwork, Federal Work-Study, institutionally sponsored loans, and scholarships/grants available. Support available to part-time students. Financial award applicants required to submit FAFSA. *Unit head:* Dr. Paul Fouts, Dean, 415-442-7026, Fax: 415-442-6579. *Application contact:* Angela Melero, Enrollment Services, 415-442-7800, Fax: 415-442-7807, E-mail: info@ggu.edu.

Governors State University, College of Business and Public Administration, Program in Public Administration, University Park, IL 60466-0975. Offers MPA. *Accreditation:* NASPAA. Part-time and evening/weekend programs available. *Degree requirements:* For master's, comprehensive exam, thesis or alternative, internship or previous work in field. *Entrance requirements:* For master's, minimum GPA of 2.5. *Expenses:* Tuition, state resident: full-time $5400; part-time $225 per credit hour. Tuition, nonresident: full-time $16,200; part-time $675 per credit hour. Required fees: $1358; $46 per credit hour. $126 per term. Tuition and fees vary according to degree level and program. *Faculty research:* State and local politics.

Grambling State University, School of Graduate Studies and Research, College of Arts and Sciences, Program in Public Administration, Grambling, LA 71270. Offers health service administration (MPA); human resource management (MPA); public management (MPA); state and local government (MPA). *Accreditation:* NASPAA. Part-time programs available. *Degree requirements:* For master's, comprehensive exam (for some programs), thesis optional. *Entrance requirements:* For master's, GRE, minimum GPA of 2.75 on last degree. Additional exam requirements/recommendations for international students: Required—TOEFL (minimum score 500 paper-based; 173 computer-based; 61 iBT). Electronic applications accepted.

Grand Canyon University, College of Business, Phoenix, AZ 85017-1097. Offers accounting (MBA); corporate business administration (MBA); disaster preparedness and crisis management (MBA); executive fire service leadership (MS); finance (MBA); general management (MBA); government and policy (MPA); health care management (MPA); health systems management (MBA); human resource management (MBA); innovation (MBA); leadership (MBA, MS); management of information system (MBA); marketing (MBA); project-based (MBA); six sigma (MBA); strategic human resource management (MBA). *Accreditation:* ACBSP. Part-time and evening/weekend programs available. Postbaccalaureate distance learning degree programs offered (no on-campus study). *Faculty:* 8 full-time (3 women), 147 part-time/adjunct (49 women). *Students:* 1 full-time (0 women), 2,121 part-time (1,165 women); includes 341 minority (249 Black or African American, non-Hispanic/Latino; 17 American Indian or Alaska Native, non-Hispanic/Latino; 15 Asian, non-Hispanic/Latino; 29 Hispanic/Latino; 4 Native Hawaiian or other Pacific Islander, non-Hispanic/Latino; 27 Two or more races, non-Hispanic/Latino), 20 international. Average age 38. In 2010, 569 master's awarded. *Entrance requirements:* For master's, equivalent of two years full-time professional work experience. Additional exam requirements/recommendations for international students: Required—TOEFL (minimum score 575 paper-based; 233 computer-based; 90 iBT), IELTS (minimum score 7). *Application deadline:* For fall admission, 8/21 for domestic students, 7/2 for international students; for spring admission, 12/24 for domestic students, 11/1 for international students. Applications are processed on a rolling basis. Application fee: $0. Electronic applications accepted. *Financial support:* Federal Work-Study available. Support available to part-time students. Financial award applicants required to submit FAFSA. *Unit head:* Kim Donaldson, Dean, 602-639-6597, E-mail: kdonaldson@gcu.edu. *Application contact:* Matt Tidwell, Enrollment Manager, 602-639-6020, E-mail: mtidwell@gcu.edu.

Grand Valley State University, College of Community and Public Service, School of Public and Nonprofit Administration, Allendale, MI 49401-9403. Offers MHA, MPA. *Accreditation:* NASPAA. Part-time and evening/weekend programs available. Electronic applications accepted. *Faculty research:* Comparative urban systems, ethics and public management, local economic development, public and nonprofit boards and governance.

Hamline University, School of Business, St. Paul, MN 55104-1284. Offers business (MBA); nonprofit management (MA); public administration (MA, DPA); JD/MA; JD/MBA; LL M/MA; LL M/MBA; MA/MA; MBA/MA. Part-time and evening/weekend programs available. *Faculty:* 20 full-time (8 women), 42 part-time/adjunct (12 women). *Students:* 509 full-time (234 women), 130 part-time (74 women); includes 102 minority (55 Black or African American, non-Hispanic/Latino; 6 American Indian or Alaska Native, non-Hispanic/Latino; 29 Asian, non-Hispanic/Latino; 10 Hispanic/Latino; 2 Two or more races, non-Hispanic/Latino), 66 international. Average age 32. 244 applicants, 73% accepted, 139 enrolled. In 2010, 293 master's, 3 doctorates awarded. *Degree requirements:* For master's, thesis (for some programs); for doctorate, comprehensive exam, thesis/dissertation. *Entrance requirements:* For master's, personal statement, official transcripts, curriculum vitae, letters of recommendation, writing sample; for doctorate, personal statement, curriculum vitae, official transcripts, letters of recommendation, writing sample. Additional exam requirements/recommendations for international students: Required—TOEFL (minimum score 80 iBT). *Application deadline:* For fall admission, 6/1 for international students; for spring admission, 10/1 for international students. Applications are processed on a rolling basis. Application fee: $0. Electronic applications accepted. *Expenses:* Tuition: Full-time $7248; part-time $453 per credit hour. Required fees: $7 per credit hour. One-time fee: $210. Tuition and fees vary according to degree level, campus/location and program. *Financial support:* Federal Work-Study and scholarships/grants available. Support available to part-time students. Financial award applicants required to submit FAFSA. *Faculty research:* Liberal arts-based business programs, experiential learning, organizational process/politics, gender differences, social equity. *Unit head:* Nancy Hellerud, Interim Dean, 651-523-2284, Fax: 651-523-3098, E-mail: nhellerud@gw.hamline.edu. *Application contact:* Rae A. Lenway, Director, Graduate Recruitment and Admission, 651-523-2900, Fax: 651-523-3058, E-mail: rlenway@gw.hamline.edu.

Harrisburg University of Science and Technology, Program in Project Management, Harrisburg, PA 17101. Offers construction services (MS); governmental services (MS); information technology (MS). Part-time and evening/weekend programs available. *Faculty:* 1 full-time (0 women), 3 part-time/adjunct (0 women). *Students:* 11 part-time (2 women); includes 1 Black or African American, non-Hispanic/Latino; 1 Asian, non-Hispanic/Latino; 1 Hispanic/Latino, 1 international. Average age 30. 24 applicants, 75% accepted. In 2010, 7 master's awarded. *Entrance requirements:* For master's, BS, BBA. Additional exam requirements/recommendations for international students: Required—TOEFL (minimum score 520 paper-based; 200 computer-based; 80 iBT). *Application deadline:* For fall admission, 8/1 priority date for domestic students, 7/1 priority date for international students. Applications are processed on a rolling basis. Application fee: $0. Electronic applications accepted. *Expenses:* Tuition: Full-time $19,500; part-time $700 per credit hour. *Financial support:* Scholarships/grants available. Financial award applicants required to submit FAFSA. *Unit head:* Dr. Amjad Umar, Director and Professor, 717-901-5141, Fax: 717-901-3141, E-mail: aumar@harrisburgu.edu. *Application contact:* Timothy Dawson, Information Contact, 717-901-5158, Fax: 717-901-3158, E-mail: admissions@harrisburgu.edu.

Harvard University, John F. Kennedy School of Government, Lucius N. Littauer Mid-Career Program in Public Administration, Cambridge, MA 02138. Offers MPA. *Students:* 171 full-time (61 women), 7 part-time (2 women); includes 4 Black or African American, non-Hispanic/Latino; 4 American Indian or Alaska Native, non-Hispanic/Latino; 2 Asian, non-Hispanic/Latino; 8 Hispanic/Latino; 4 Two or more races, non-Hispanic/Latino, 85 international. Average age 40. 603 applicants, 47% accepted, 178 enrolled. In 2010, 174 master's awarded. *Entrance requirements:* For master's, GMAT or GRE General Test, minimum 7 years of professional experience. Additional exam requirements/recommendations for international students: Required—TOEFL (minimum score 600 paper-based; 250 computer-based; 100 iBT), TWE. *Application deadline:* For fall admission, 12/2 for domestic students. Applications are processed on a rolling basis. Application fee: $100. Electronic applications accepted. *Expenses:* Contact institution. *Financial support:* Fellowships, Federal Work-Study, institutionally sponsored loans, scholarships/grants, health care benefits, and unspecified assistantships available. Financial award application deadline: 3/25; financial award applicants required to submit CSS PROFILE or FAFSA. *Unit head:* Amy Davies, Director, 617-496-1100, E-mail: amy_davies@harvard.edu. *Application contact:* 617-495-1155, E-mail: admissions@hks.harvard.edu.

Harvard University, John F. Kennedy School of Government, Master in Public Administration/International Development Program, Cambridge, MA 02138. Offers MPAID. *Students:* 130 full-time (58 women), 2 part-time (both women); includes 1 Black or African American, non-Hispanic/Latino; 9 Asian, non-Hispanic/Latino, 87 international. Average age 29. 371 applicants, 26% accepted, 69 enrolled. In 2010, 58 master's awarded. *Entrance requirements:* For master's, GMAT or GRE General Test (for joint Business School applicants), one course each in microeconomics and macroeconomics; two college-level calculus courses (one must contain multivariable calculus); bachelor's degree; 2-3 years of professional experience in development (strongly encouraged). Additional exam requirements/recommendations for international students: Required—TOEFL (minimum score 600 paper-based; 250 computer-based; 100 iBT). *Application deadline:* For fall admission, 12/2 for domestic students. Application fee: $100. Electronic applications accepted. *Expenses:* Tuition: Full-time $34,976. Required fees: $1166. Full-time tuition and fees vary according to program. *Financial support:* Fellowships, research assistantships, teaching assistantships, career-related internships or fieldwork, Federal Work-Study, institutionally sponsored loans, scholarships/grants, health care benefits, and unspecified assistantships available. Financial award application deadline: 2/6; financial award applicants required to submit CSS PROFILE or FAFSA. *Unit head:* Carol Finney, Director,

Public Administration

Harvard University (continued)
617-495-7799, E-mail: carol_finney@harvard.edu. *Application contact:* 617-495-2133, E-mail: mpaid_program@hks.harvard.edu.

Harvard University, John F. Kennedy School of Government, Program in Public Administration, Cambridge, MA 02138. Offers MPA. *Students:* 162 full-time (55 women), 4 part-time (0 women); includes 3 Black or African American, non-Hispanic/Latino; 10 Asian, non-Hispanic/Latino; 9 Hispanic/Latino; 8 Two or more races, non-Hispanic/Latino, 81 international. Average age 31. 159 applicants, 62% accepted, 71 enrolled. In 2010, 99 master's awarded. *Entrance requirements:* For master's, GMAT or GRE General Test, minimum of 3 years of work experience. Additional exam requirements/recommendations for international students: Required—TOEFL (minimum score 600 paper-based; 250 computer-based; 100 iBT), TWE. *Application deadline:* For fall admission, 12/2 for domestic students. Application fee: $100. Electronic applications accepted. *Expenses:* Tuition: Full-time $34,976. Required fees: $1166. Full-time tuition and fees vary according to program. *Financial support:* Fellowships, research assistantships, teaching assistantships, career-related internships or fieldwork, Federal Work-Study, institutionally sponsored loans, scholarships/grants, health care benefits, and unspecified assistantships available. Financial award application deadline: 2/6; financial award applicants required to submit CSS PROFILE or FAFSA. *Unit head:* Amy Davies, Director, 617-496-1100, E-mail: amy_davies@harvard.edu. *Application contact:* 617-495-1155.

Hodges University, Graduate Programs, Naples, FL 34119. Offers business administration (MBA); computer information technology (MS); criminal justice (MCJ); education (MPS); information systems management (MIS); interdisciplinary (MPS); legal studies (MS); management (MSM); mental health counseling (MS); psychology (MPS); public administration (MPA). Part-time and evening/weekend programs available. Postbaccalaureate distance learning degree programs offered (no on-campus study). *Faculty:* 25 full-time (9 women), 5 part-time/adjunct (4 women). *Students:* 27 full-time (15 women), 228 part-time (146 women); includes 76 minority (35 Black or African American, non-Hispanic/Latino; 5 Asian, non-Hispanic/Latino; 36 Hispanic/Latino). Average age 36. 92 applicants, 91% accepted, 81 enrolled. In 2010, 92 master's awarded. *Degree requirements:* For master's, comprehensive exam (for some programs), thesis (for some programs). *Entrance requirements:* For master's, in-house entrance exam. *Application deadline:* Applications are processed on a rolling basis. Application fee: $50. Electronic applications accepted. *Expenses:* Tuition: Full-time $16,605; part-time $615 per credit hour. Required fees: $190 per trimester. *Financial support:* In 2010–11, 200 students received support. Federal Work-Study and scholarships/grants available. Financial award application deadline: 7/9; financial award applicants required to submit FAFSA. *Unit head:* Terry McMahan, President, 239-513-1122, Fax: 239-598-6253, E-mail: tmcmahan@hodges.edu. *Application contact:* Rita Lampus, Vice President of Student Enrollment Management, 239-513-1122, Fax: 239-598-6253, E-mail: rlampus@hodges.edu.

Hood College, Graduate School, Department of Economics and Management, Frederick, MD 21701-8575. Offers accounting (MBA); administration and management (MBA); finance (MBA); human resource management (MBA); information systems (MBA); marketing (MBA); public management (MBA). *Accreditation:* ACBSP. Part-time and evening/weekend programs available. *Faculty:* 4 full-time (1 woman), 9 part-time/adjunct (1 woman). *Students:* 16 full-time (9 women), 127 part-time (65 women); includes 17 Black or African American, non-Hispanic/Latino; 9 Asian, non-Hispanic/Latino; 5 Hispanic/Latino; 1 Two or more races, non-Hispanic/Latino, 10 international. Average age 32. 60 applicants, 62% accepted, 25 enrolled. In 2010, 56 master's awarded. *Degree requirements:* For master's, capstone/final research project. *Entrance requirements:* For master's, minimum GPA of 2.75, resume, letters of recommendation. Additional exam requirements/recommendations for international students: Required—TOEFL (minimum score 575 paper-based; 231 computer-based; 89 iBT). *Application deadline:* For fall admission, 7/15 for domestic and international students; for spring admission, 12/15 for domestic and international students. Applications are processed on a rolling basis. Application fee: $35. Electronic applications accepted. *Expenses:* Tuition: Full-time $6480; part-time $360 per credit. Required fees: $100; $50 per term. *Financial support:* Applicants required to submit FAFSA. *Faculty research:* Corporate strategy and sustainable competitive advantages, business ethics, entrepreneurship, investments management, economic development. *Unit head:* Dr. Anita Jose, Program Director, 301-696-3691, Fax: 301-696-3597, E-mail: jose@hood.edu. *Application contact:* Dr. Allen P. Flora, Dean of Graduate School, 301-696-3811, Fax: 301-696-3597, E-mail: gofurther@hood.edu.

Howard University, Graduate School, Department of Political Science, Program in Public Administration, Washington, DC 20059-0002. Offers MAPA. *Accreditation:* NASPAA. Part-time programs available. *Degree requirements:* For master's, comprehensive exam. *Entrance requirements:* For master's, GRE General Test, minimum GPA of 3.0.

Idaho State University, Office of Graduate Studies, College of Arts and Sciences, Department of Political Science, Program in Public Administration, Pocatello, ID 83209-8073. Offers MPA. Part-time programs available. *Degree requirements:* For master's, comprehensive exam, thesis optional, public service internship. *Entrance requirements:* For master's, GRE General Test, course work in humanities and social sciences, 3 letters of recommendation. Additional exam requirements/recommendations for international students: Required—TOEFL (minimum score 550 paper-based; 213 computer-based; 80 iBT). Electronic applications accepted. *Faculty research:* Constitutional law, policy theory, public administration, international affairs.

Illinois Institute of Technology, Stuart School of Business, Program in Public Administration, Chicago, IL 60661. Offers MPA, JD/MPA, MBA/MPA. Part-time and evening/weekend programs available. *Faculty:* 37 full-time (4 women), 21 part-time/adjunct (5 women). *Students:* 60 full-time (29 women), 42 part-time (25 women); includes 17 minority (12 Black or African American, non-Hispanic/Latino; 2 Asian, non-Hispanic/Latino; 1 Hispanic/Latino; 2 Two or more races, non-Hispanic/Latino), 54 international. Average age 32. 157 applicants, 94% accepted, 58 enrolled. In 2010, 104 master's awarded. *Entrance requirements:* Additional exam requirements/recommendations for international students: Required—TOEFL (minimum score 600 paper-based; 85 iBT); Recommended—IELTS (minimum score 7). *Application deadline:* For fall admission, 8/1 for domestic students, 5/1 for international students; for spring admission, 12/15 for domestic students, 10/15 for international students. Applications are processed on a rolling basis. Application fee: $75. Electronic applications accepted. *Expenses:* Tuition: Full-time $18,576; part-time $1032 per credit hour. Required fees: $583 per semester. One-time fee: $150. Tuition and fees vary according to program and student level. *Financial support:* Fellowships with partial tuition reimbursements, Federal Work-Study, institutionally sponsored loans, scholarships/grants, and health care benefits available. Support available to part-time students. Financial award applicants required to submit FAFSA. *Faculty research:* Comparative public administration and policy, migration and ethnic politics, social dimension and impact of science and technology, urban politics, urban ethnography. *Unit head:* Dr. Roland Calia, Senior Lecturer, 312-906-5181, Fax: 312-906-6549, E-mail: rcalia@stuart.iit.edu. *Application contact:* Deborah Gibson, Director, Graduate Admission, 866-472-3448, Fax: 312-567-3138, E-mail: inquiry.grad@iit.edu.

Indiana State University, College of Graduate and Professional Studies, College of Arts and Sciences, Department of Political Science, Terre Haute, IN 47809. Offers political science (MA, MS); public administration (MPA). *Degree requirements:* For master's, thesis (for some programs). *Entrance requirements:* For master's, GRE or minimum undergraduate GPA of 2.75, 18 semester hours of course work in political science. Additional exam requirements/recommendations for international students: Required—TOEFL (minimum score 550 paper-based). Electronic applications accepted.

Indiana University Bloomington, School of Public and Environmental Affairs, Public Affairs Programs, Bloomington, IN 47405-7000. Offers comparative and international affairs (MPA); economic development (MPA); energy (MPA); environmental policy (PhD); environmental policy and natural resource management (MPA); information systems (MPA); local government management (MPA); nonprofit management (MPA, Certificate); policy analysis (MPA); public finance (PhD); public financial administration (MPA); public management (MPA, PhD); public policy analysis (PhD); specialized public affairs (MPA); sustainability and sustainable development (MPA); JD/MPA; MPA/MIS; MPA/MLS; MSES/MPA. *Accreditation:* NASPAA (one or more programs are accredited). Part-time programs available. *Faculty:* 31 full-time, 15 part-time/adjunct. *Students:* 466 full-time (261 women); includes 11 Black or African American, non-Hispanic/Latino; 2 American Indian or Alaska Native, non-Hispanic/Latino; 42 Asian, non-Hispanic/Latino; 1 Hispanic/Latino, 65 international. Average age 26. 650 applicants, 218 enrolled. In 2010, 166 master's, 10 doctorates awarded. *Degree requirements:* For master's, core classes, capstone; for doctorate, comprehensive exam, thesis/dissertation. *Entrance requirements:* For master's, GRE General Test or GMAT, official transcripts, 3 letters of recommendation, resume, personal statement, departmental questions; for doctorate, GRE General Test or LSAT, official transcripts, 3 letters of recommendation, resume or curriculum vitae, statement of purpose. Additional exam requirements/recommendations for international students: Required—TOEFL (minimum score 600 paper-based; 96 iBT); Recommended—IELTS (minimum score 7). *Application deadline:* For fall admission, 5/1 priority date for domestic students, 12/1 priority date for international students. Applications are processed on a rolling basis. Application fee: $55 ($65 for international students). Electronic applications accepted. *Financial support:* Fellowships with partial tuition reimbursements, research assistantships with partial tuition reimbursements, teaching assistantships with partial tuition reimbursements, career-related internships or fieldwork, Federal Work-Study, scholarships/grants, health care benefits, unspecified assistantships, and Service Corps programs available. Financial award application deadline: 2/1; financial award applicants required to submit FAFSA. *Faculty research:* Comparative and international affairs, environmental policy and resource management, policy analysis, public finance, public management, urban management, nonprofit management, energy policy, social policy, public finance. *Unit head:* Jennifer Forney, Director of Graduate Student Services, 812-855-9485, Fax: 812-856-3665, E-mail: speampo@indiana.edu. *Application contact:* Audrey Whitaker, Admissions Assistant, 812-855-2840, E-mail: speaapps@indiana.edu.

See Close-Up on page 1271.

Indiana University Kokomo, School of Public and Environmental Affairs, Kokomo, IN 46904-9003. Offers public management (MS, Graduate Certificate). *Students:* 11 full-time (6 women), 33 part-time (21 women); includes 10 minority (6 Black or African American, non-Hispanic/Latino; 1 Asian, non-Hispanic/Latino; 2 Hispanic/Latino; 1 Two or more races, non-Hispanic/Latino), 1 international. Average age 39. 14 applicants, 100% accepted, 12 enrolled. In 2010, 19 master's, 5 other advanced degrees awarded. *Application deadline:* For fall admission, 8/1 priority date for domestic students; for spring admission, 12/9 priority date for domestic students. Application fee: $40 ($50 for international students). *Unit head:* Dr. Robert Dibie, Assistant Dean, 765-455-9417, Fax: 765-455-9537, E-mail: iuadmis@iuk.edu. *Application contact:* Susan Wilson, Information Contact, 765-455-9330.

Indiana University Northwest, School of Public and Environmental Affairs, Gary, IN 46408-1197. Offers criminal justice (MPA); environmental affairs (Graduate Certificate); health services administration (MPA); human services administration (MPA); nonprofit management (Graduate Certificate); public management (MPA, Graduate Certificate). *Accreditation:* NASPAA (one or more programs are accredited). Part-time programs available. *Faculty:* 5 full-time (3 women). *Students:* 9 full-time (6 women), 127 part-time (96 women); includes 96 minority (81 Black or African American, non-Hispanic/Latino; 1 American Indian or Alaska Native, non-Hispanic/Latino; 2 Asian, non-Hispanic/Latino; 10 Hispanic/Latino; 2 Two or more races, non-Hispanic/Latino). Average age 38. 43 applicants, 95% accepted, 40 enrolled. In 2010, 37 master's, 24 other advanced degrees awarded. *Entrance requirements:* For master's, GRE General Test or GMAT, letters of recommendation. *Application deadline:* For fall admission, 8/15 priority date for domestic students. Applications are processed on a rolling basis. Application fee: $25. *Financial support:* Career-related internships or fieldwork, Federal Work-Study, and tuition waivers (partial) available. Support available to part-time students. Financial award application deadline: 3/1. *Faculty research:* Employment in income security policies, evidence in criminal justice, equal employment law, social welfare policy and welfare reform, public finance in developing countries. *Unit head:* George Assibey-Mensah, Interim Dean/Division Director, 219-980-6695, Fax: 219-980-6737. *Application contact:* Sandra Hall Smith, Secretary, 219-980-6695, Fax: 219-980-6737, E-mail: shsmith@iun.edu.

Indiana University–Purdue University Indianapolis, School of Public and Environmental Affairs, Indianapolis, IN 46202. Offers criminal justice and public safety (MSCJPS); public affairs (MPA), including criminal justice, nonprofit management, policy analysis, public management; public management (Graduate Certificate); JD/MPA; MATS/MM; MLS/NMC; MLS/PMC. *Accreditation:* CAHME (one or more programs are accredited); NASPAA. Part-time and evening/weekend programs available. Postbaccalaureate distance learning degree programs offered (no on-campus study). *Faculty:* 23 full-time (7 women). *Students:* 81 full-time (47 women), 205 part-time (142 women); includes 30 Black or African American, non-Hispanic/Latino; 6 Asian, non-Hispanic/Latino; 8 Hispanic/Latino, 9 international. Average age 31. 217 applicants, 73% accepted, 136 enrolled. In 2010, 77 degrees awarded. *Entrance requirements:* For master's, GRE General Test, GMAT or LSAT, minimum GPA of 3.0 (preferred). Additional exam requirements/recommendations for international students: Required—All international applicants to IUPUI whose native language is not English must demonstrate proficiency in English as a second language through an accepted examination and an accepted score. *Application deadline:* For fall admission, 5/15 priority date for domestic students; for spring admission, 2/15 priority date for domestic students. Applications are processed on a rolling basis. Application fee: $50 ($65 for international students). Electronic applications accepted. *Financial support:* In 2010–11, 1 fellowship with full tuition reimbursement (averaging $14,000 per year), 4 research assistantships with full tuition reimbursements (averaging $12,000 per year) were awarded; teaching assistantships, career-related internships or fieldwork, Federal Work-Study, institutionally sponsored loans, and scholarships/grants also available. Support available to part-time students. Financial award application deadline: 3/1; financial award applicants required to submit FAFSA. *Faculty research:* Nonprofit and public management, public policy, urban and environmental policy, disaster preparedness and recovery, vehicular safety, homicide, and offender rehabilitation and re-entry. Total annual research expenditures: $1.6 million. *Unit head:* Dr. Terry L. Baumer, Executive Associate Dean, 317-274-2016, Fax: 317-274-5153.

Indiana University South Bend, School of Public and Environmental Affairs, South Bend, IN 46634-7111. Offers health systems administration and policy (MPA); health systems management (Certificate); nonprofit management (Certificate); public and community services administration and policy (MPA); public management (Certificate); urban affairs (Certificate). *Accreditation:* NASPAA. Part-time and evening/weekend programs available. *Faculty:* 4 full-time (1 woman). *Students:* 1 full-time (0 women), 9 part-time (7 women); includes 1 minority (Black or African American, non-Hispanic/Latino). Average age 43. 2 applicants, 0% accepted, 0 enrolled. In 2010, 11 master's awarded. *Entrance requirements:* For master's, GRE General Test, minimum undergraduate GPA of 2.5. *Application deadline:* For fall admission, 7/1 priority date for domestic students; for spring admission, 11/1 for domestic students. Applications are processed on a rolling basis. Application fee: $50 ($60 for international students). *Financial support:* Fellowships, research assistantships, career-related internships or fieldwork, Federal Work-Study, and institutionally sponsored loans available. Support available to part-time students. Financial award application deadline: 3/1; financial award applicants required to submit FAFSA. *Unit head:* Leda M. Hall, Dean, 574-520-4803. *Application contact:* Leda M. Hall, Dean, 574-520-4803.

Institute of Public Administration, Programs in Public Administration, Dublin, Ireland. Offers healthcare management (MA); local government management (MA); public management (MA, Diploma).

Instituto Tecnológico y de Estudios Superiores de Monterrey, Campus Ciudad Juárez, Program in Applied Public Management, Ciudad Juárez, Mexico. Offers MPM.

Iowa State University of Science and Technology, Graduate College, College of Liberal Arts and Sciences, Department of Political Science, Ames, IA 50011. Offers political science (MA); public administration (MPA); JD/MA. JD/MA offered jointly with Drake University. *Accreditation:* NASPAA. *Faculty:* 15 full-time (3 women), 6 part-time/adjunct (2 women). *Students:* 45 full-time (21 women), 62 part-time (20 women); includes 6 Black or African American, non-Hispanic/Latino; 5 Asian, non-Hispanic/Latino; 1 Hispanic/Latino, 14 international. 37 applicants, 78% accepted, 19 enrolled. In 2010, 16 master's awarded. *Degree requirements:* For master's, thesis (for some programs). *Entrance requirements:* For master's, GRE General Test, GMAT or LSAT. Additional exam requirements/recommendations for international students: Required—TOEFL (minimum score 570 paper-based; 80 iBT), IELTS (minimum score 6.5). *Application deadline:* For fall admission, 1/1 priority date for domestic and international students; for spring admission, 10/1 for domestic and international students. Applications are processed on a rolling basis. Application fee: $40 ($90 for international students). Electronic applications accepted. *Financial support:* In 2010–11, 18 research assistantships with full and partial tuition reimbursements (averaging $4,063 per year), 3 teaching assistantships with full and partial tuition reimbursements (averaging $6,713 per year) were awarded; fellowships, scholarships/grants, health care benefits, and unspecified assistantships also available. *Unit head:* Dr. James M. McCormick, Chair, 515-294-8682, Fax: 515-294-1003, E-mail: polsc@iastate.edu. *Application contact:* Dr. Mack Shelley, Director of Graduate Education, 515-294-1075, E-mail: polsci@iastate.edu.

Jackson State University, Graduate School, College of Public Service, Department of Public Policy and Administration, Jackson, MS 39217. Offers MPPA, PhD. *Accreditation:* NASPAA (one or more programs are accredited). Evening/weekend programs available. *Faculty:* 4 full-time (1 woman), 3 part-time/adjunct (all women). *Students:* 25 full-time (19 women), 71 part-time (48 women); includes 84 Black or African American, non-Hispanic/Latino, 3 international. Average age 36. In 2010, 15 master's, 2 doctorates awarded. *Degree requirements:* For master's, comprehensive exam, thesis optional; for doctorate, comprehensive exam, thesis/dissertation. *Entrance requirements:* For master's, GRE General Test; for doctorate, GRE, GMAT, MAT. Additional exam requirements/recommendations for international students: Required—TOEFL (minimum score 520 paper-based; 195 computer-based; 67 iBT). *Application deadline:* For fall admission, 3/1 for domestic and international students; for spring admission, 10/1 for domestic and international students. Application fee: $25. *Expenses:* Tuition, state resident: full-time $5050; part-time $281 per credit hour. Tuition, nonresident: full-time $12,380; part-time $689 per credit hour. *Financial support:* Career-related internships or fieldwork, Federal Work-Study, scholarships/grants, tuition waivers (full and partial), and unspecified assistantships available. Support available to part-time students. Financial award application deadline: 3/1; financial award applicants required to submit FAFSA. *Unit head:* Dr. Curtina Moreland-Young, Interim Chair, 601-432-6277, Fax: 601-432-6322, E-mail: ppa@jsums.edu. *Application contact:* Sharlene Wilson, Director of Graduate Admissions, 601-979-2455, Fax: 601-979-4325, E-mail: sharlene.f.wilson@jsums.edu.

James Madison University, The Graduate School, College of Arts and Letters, Department of Political Science, Program in Public Administration, Harrisonburg, VA 22807. Offers MPA. Part-time programs available. *Students:* 17 full-time (6 women), 27 part-time (12 women); includes 4 minority (3 Black or African American, non-Hispanic/Latino; 1 Hispanic/Latino), 1 international. Average age 27. In 2010, 9 master's awarded. *Degree requirements:* For master's, comprehensive exam. *Entrance requirements:* For master's, GMAT or GRE General Test. Additional exam requirements/recommendations for international students: Required—TOEFL. *Application deadline:* For fall admission, 5/1 priority date for domestic students; for spring admission, 9/1 priority date for domestic students. Applications are processed on a rolling basis. Application fee: $55. Electronic applications accepted. *Financial support:* In 2010–11, 9 students received support. Application deadline: 3/1. *Unit head:* Dr. Jessica Adolino, Department Chair, 540-568-6149, E-mail: adolinjr@jmu.edu. *Application contact:* Dr. B. Douglas Skelley, Director, 540-568-6149, E-mail: skellebd@jmu.edu.

John Jay College of Criminal Justice of the City University of New York, Graduate Studies, Program in Public Administration, New York, NY 10019-1093. Offers MPA. *Accreditation:* NASPAA. Part-time and evening/weekend programs available. *Degree requirements:* For master's, thesis or alternative. *Entrance requirements:* For master's, minimum B average. Additional exam requirements/recommendations for international students: Required—TOEFL (minimum score 500 paper-based; 173 computer-based).

Kansas State University, Graduate School, College of Arts and Sciences, Department of Political Science, Manhattan, KS 66506. Offers political science (MA), including international service, political science; public administration (MPA). Part-time programs available. *Degree requirements:* For master's, thesis or alternative. *Entrance requirements:* For master's, GRE (recommended), minimum GPA of 3.0. Additional exam requirements/recommendations for international students: Required—TOEFL (minimum score 550 paper-based; 213 computer-based). Electronic applications accepted. *Faculty research:* Armed conflict, civil military relations, comparative public administration and policy, electoral competition, legislative studies.

Kean University, College of Business and Public Management, Program in Public Administration, Union, NJ 07083. Offers environmental management (MPA); health services administration (MPA); non-profit management (MPA); public administration (MPA). *Accreditation:* NASPAA. Part-time and evening/weekend programs available. *Faculty:* 7 full-time (4 women). *Students:* 61 full-time (41 women), 82 part-time (48 women); includes 61 Black or African American, non-Hispanic/Latino; 7 Asian, non-Hispanic/Latino; 19 Hispanic/Latino, 5 international. Average age 31. 70 applicants, 76% accepted, 36 enrolled. In 2010, 44 master's awarded. *Degree requirements:* For master's, thesis, internship, research seminar. *Entrance requirements:* For master's, minimum GPA of 3.0, 2 letters of recommendation, interview, writing sample, transcripts. *Application deadline:* For fall admission, 6/1 for domestic students; for spring admission, 11/1 for domestic students. Application fee: $75 ($150 for international students). Electronic applications accepted. *Expenses:* Tuition, state resident: full-time $10,872; part-time $500 per credit. Tuition, nonresident: full-time $14,736; part-time $614 per credit. Required fees: $2740.80; $125 per credit. Part-time tuition and fees vary according to course load and degree level. *Financial support:* In 2010–11, 11 research assistantships with full tuition reimbursements (averaging $3,263 per year) were awarded; unspecified assistantships also available. Financial award applicants required to submit FAFSA. *Unit head:* Dr. Patricia Moore, Program Coordinator, 908-737-4314, E-mail: pmoore@kean.edu. *Application contact:* Reenat Hasan, Pre-Admissions Coordinator, 908-737-5923, Fax: 908-737-5925, E-mail: hasanr@kean.edu.

Kennesaw State University, College of Humanities and Social Sciences, Program in Public Administration, Kennesaw, GA 30144-5591. Offers MPA. *Accreditation:* NASPAA. Part-time and evening/weekend programs available. *Students:* 51 full-time (29 women), 58 part-time (40 women); includes 37 minority (31 Black or African American, non-Hispanic/Latino; 4 Hispanic/Latino; 2 Two or more races, non-Hispanic/Latino), 7 international. Average age 30. 60 applicants, 67% accepted, 34 enrolled. In 2010, 32 master's awarded. *Entrance requirements:* For master's, GRE General Test, minimum GPA of 2.75. Additional exam requirements/recommendations for international students: Required—TOEFL (minimum score 550 paper-based; 213 computer-based; 80 iBT), IELTS (minimum score 6). *Application deadline:* For fall admission, 7/1 for domestic and international students; for winter admission, 12/1 for domestic and international students; for spring admission, 5/1 for domestic students, 8/1 for international students. Applications are processed on a rolling basis. Application fee: $60. Electronic applications accepted. *Expenses:* Tuition, state resident: full-time $5500; part-time $225 per credit hour. Tuition, nonresident: full-time $16,100; part-time $813 per credit hour. Required fees: $673 per semester. *Financial support:* In 2010–11, 2 research assistantships with full tuition reimbursements (averaging $4,000 per year) were awarded; Federal Work-Study also available. Support available to part-time students. Financial award application deadline: 6/15; financial award applicants required to submit FAFSA. *Unit head:* Dr. Andrew Ewoh, Director, 770-423-6246, E-mail: aewoh@kennesaw.edu. *Application contact:* Tamara Hutto, Admissions Counselor, 770-420-4377, Fax: 770-423-6885, E-mail: ksugrad@kennesaw.edu.

Kent State University, College of Arts and Sciences, Department of Political Science, Program in Public Administration, Kent, OH 44242-0001. Offers MPA. *Accreditation:* NASPAA. *Degree requirements:* For master's, thesis optional, public sector internship. *Entrance requirements:* For master's, GRE General Test, minimum GPA of 2.75. Additional exam requirements/recommendations for international students: Required—TOEFL. Electronic applications accepted. *Expenses:* Tuition, state resident: full-time $7866; part-time $437 per credit hour. Tuition, nonresident: full-time $14,022; part-time $779 per credit hour.

Kentucky State University, College of Professional Studies, Frankfort, KY 40601. Offers business administration (MBA), including accounting, finance, management, marketing; public administration (MPA), including human resource management, international administration and development, management information systems, nonprofit management; special education (MA). Part-time and evening/weekend programs available. Postbaccalaureate distance learning degree programs offered (minimal on-campus study). *Faculty:* 12 full-time (4 women), 2 part-time/adjunct (both women). *Students:* 88 full-time (57 women), 79 part-time (42 women); includes 104 minority (101 Black or African American, non-Hispanic/Latino; 1 Asian, non-Hispanic/Latino; 2 Hispanic/Latino), 2 international. Average age 34. 124 applicants, 62% accepted, 45 enrolled. In 2010, 38 master's awarded. *Degree requirements:* For master's, comprehensive exam, thesis optional. *Entrance requirements:* For master's, GMAT, GRE. Additional exam requirements/recommendations for international students: Required—TOEFL (minimum score 525 paper-based; 173 computer-based). *Application deadline:* Applications are processed on a rolling basis. Application fee: $30 ($100 for international students). Electronic applications accepted. *Expenses:* Tuition, state resident: full-time $5886; part-time $352 per credit hour. Tuition, nonresident: full-time $9054; part-time $528 per credit hour. Required fees: $450; $26 per credit hour. *Financial support:* In 2010–11, 46 students received support, including 4 research assistantships (averaging $10,975 per year); career-related internships or fieldwork, scholarships/grants, tuition waivers (partial), and unspecified assistantships also available. Financial award application deadline: 4/15; financial award applicants required to submit FAFSA. *Unit head:* Dr. Gashaw Lake, Dean, 502-597-6105, Fax: 502-597-6715, E-mail: gashaw.lake@kysu.edu. *Application contact:* Dr. Titilayo Ufomata, Acting Director of Graduate Studies, 502-597-6443, E-mail: titilayo.ufomata@kysu.edu.

Kutztown University of Pennsylvania, College of Liberal Arts and Sciences, Program in Public Administration, Kutztown, PA 19530-0730. Offers MPA. Part-time and evening/weekend programs available. *Faculty:* 3 full-time (1 woman). *Students:* 17 full-time (9 women), 28 part-time (18 women); includes 11 minority (8 Black or African American, non-Hispanic/Latino; 1 American Indian or Alaska Native, non-Hispanic/Latino; 2 Hispanic/Latino), 3 international. Average age 31. 30 applicants, 63% accepted, 14 enrolled. In 2010, 2 master's awarded. *Degree requirements:* For master's, comprehensive exam, thesis optional. *Entrance requirements:* For master's, GRE General Test. Additional exam requirements/recommendations for international students: Required—TOEFL (minimum score 550 paper-based; 79 iBT). *Application deadline:* For fall admission, 8/15 priority date for domestic and international students; for spring admission, 12/15 priority date for domestic and international students. Applications are processed on a rolling basis. Application fee: $35. Electronic applications accepted. *Expenses:* Tuition, state resident: full-time $6966; part-time $387 per credit. Tuition, nonresident: full-time $11,146; part-time $619 per credit hour. Required fees: $1499; $54 per credit. $68 per year. *Financial support:* Career-related internships or fieldwork, Federal Work-Study, scholarships/grants, and unspecified assistantships available. Financial award application deadline: 3/1; financial award applicants required to submit FAFSA. *Faculty research:* Structure of code enforcement offices in smaller developing communities. *Unit head:* Dr. Thomas Stewart, Chairperson, 610-683-4517, Fax: 610-683-4603, E-mail: stewart@kutztown.edu. *Application contact:* Kelly D. Burr, Associate Director, Graduate Admissions, 610-683-4200, Fax: 610-683-1393, E-mail: graduate@kutztown.edu.

Lamar University, College of Graduate Studies, College of Arts and Sciences, Department of Political Science, Beaumont, TX 77710. Offers public administration (MPA). Part-time programs available. *Faculty:* 4 full-time (0 women). *Students:* 4 full-time (2 women), 9 part-time (4 women); includes 4 Black or African American, non-Hispanic/Latino; 1 Hispanic/Latino, 2 international. Average age 29. 6 applicants, 50% accepted, 2 enrolled. In 2010, 4 master's awarded. *Entrance requirements:* For master's, GRE General Test. Additional exam requirements/recommendations for international students: Required—TOEFL. *Application deadline:* For fall admission, 8/1 for domestic students; for spring admission, 12/1 for domestic students. Applications are processed on a rolling basis. Application fee: $25 ($50 for international students). *Expenses:* Tuition, state resident: full-time $4160; part-time $208 per credit hour. Tuition, nonresident: full-time $10,360; part-time $518 per credit hour. *Financial support:* Fellowships, research assistantships, teaching assistantships, career-related internships or fieldwork, Federal Work-Study, and institutionally sponsored loans available. Financial award application deadline: 4/1. *Faculty research:* Political activities of administrators, administrative response to hurricane Rita, budgeting, environmental politics, urban planning. *Unit head:* Dr. Glenn Utter, Chair, 409-880-8526, Fax: 409-880-8710. *Application contact:* Dr. Terri Davis, Director, 409-880-8533, Fax: 409-880-1710, E-mail: davistb@hal.lamar.edu.

Lewis University, College of Arts and Sciences, Program in Organizational Leadership, Romeoville, IL 60446. Offers higher education/student services (MA); organizational management (MA); public administration (MA); training and development (MA). Part-time and evening/weekend programs available. Postbaccalaureate distance learning degree programs offered (no on-campus study). *Faculty:* 2 full-time (0 women), 9 part-time/adjunct (2 women). *Students:* 18 full-time (8 women), 151 part-time (111 women); includes 44 Black or African American, non-Hispanic/Latino; 1 Asian, non-Hispanic/Latino; 11 Hispanic/Latino. Average age 36. In 2010, 51 master's awarded. *Entrance requirements:* For master's, bachelor's degree, at least 25 years of age, minimum of 3 years of work experience, minimum GPA of 3.0, letter of recommendation, interview. Additional exam requirements/recommendations for international students: Required—TOEFL (minimum score 550 paper-based; 213 computer-based). *Application deadline:* For fall admission, 5/1 priority date for international students; for spring admission, 11/15 priority date for international students. Applications are processed on a rolling basis. Application fee: $40. Electronic applications accepted. *Expenses:* Tuition: Full-time $13,320; part-time $740 per credit hour. Tuition and fees vary according to program. *Financial support:* Federal Work-Study, scholarships/grants, tuition waivers, and unspecified assistantships available. Financial award application deadline: 5/1; financial award applicants required to submit FAFSA. *Unit head:* Dr. Rich Walsh, Director, 815-838-0500, E-mail: walshri@lewisu.edu. *Application contact:* Julie Nickel, Assistant Director, Graduate and Adult Admission, 815-836-5574, Fax: 815-836-5578, E-mail: nickelju@lewisu.edu.

Lincoln University, School of Graduate Studies and Continuing Education, Jefferson City, MO 65102. Offers business administration (MBA), including accounting, entrepreneurship, management, public administration and policy; educational leadership (Ed S), including elementary leadership, secondary leadership, superintendency; guidance and counseling (M Ed), including community/agency counseling, elementary school, secondary school; history (MA); school administration and supervision (M Ed), including elementary school administration, secondary school administration, special education administration; school teaching (M Ed), including elementary school teaching, secondary school teaching; social science (MA), including history, political science, sociology; sociology (MA); sociology/criminal justice (MA). Part-time and evening/weekend programs available. *Degree requirements:* For master's and Ed S, comprehensive exam, thesis optional. *Entrance requirements:* For master's and Ed S, GRE, MAT or GMAT, minimum GPA of 2.75 in major, 2.5 overall; 3 letters of recommendation; minimum C average in English composition; personal statement of purpose. Additional exam requirements/recommendations for international students: Required—TOEFL (minimum score 500 paper-based; 173 computer-based; 61 iBT). *Faculty research:* Suicide prevention.

Lindenwood University, Graduate Programs, School of Business and Entrepreneurship, St. Charles, MO 63301-1695. Offers accounting (MBA, MS); business administration (MBA); entrepreneurial studies (MBA, MS); finance (MBA, MS); human resource management (MBA); human resources (MS); international business (MBA, MS); management (MBA, MS);

Public Administration

Lindenwood University (continued)
management information systems (MBA, MS); marketing (MBA, MS); public management (MBA, MS); sport management (MA). *Accreditation:* ACBSP. Part-time and evening/weekend programs available. *Faculty:* 20 full-time (8 women), 17 part-time/adjunct (5 women). *Students:* 179 full-time (73 women), 184 part-time (87 women); includes 27 minority (20 Black or African American, non-Hispanic/Latino; 3 Asian, non-Hispanic/Latino; 4 Hispanic/Latino), 146 international. Average age 28. 149 applicants, 73 enrolled. In 2010, 142 master's awarded. *Degree requirements:* For master's, comprehensive exam (for some programs), thesis (for some programs). *Entrance requirements:* For master's, interview, minimum GPA of 3.0, letter of recommendation. Additional exam requirements/recommendations for international students: Required—TOEFL (minimum score 550 paper-based; 213 computer-based; 80 iBT). *Application deadline:* For fall admission, 7/30 priority date for domestic students, 9/16 priority date for international students; for winter admission, 12/15 priority date for domestic and international students; for spring admission, 2/25 priority date for domestic students, 2/11 priority date for international students. Applications are processed on a rolling basis. Application fee: $30 ($100 for international students). Electronic applications accepted. *Expenses:* Tuition: Full-time $13,260; part-time $380 per credit hour. Required fees: $340. One-time fee: $30. Tuition and fees vary according to course level and course load. *Financial support:* In 2010–11, 209 students received support. Career-related internships or fieldwork, Federal Work-Study, institutionally sponsored loans, and tuition waivers (partial) available. Financial award application deadline: 6/30; financial award applicants required to submit FAFSA. *Unit head:* Roger Ellis, Dean, 636-949-4839, E-mail: rellis@lindenwood.edu. *Application contact:* Brett Barger, Dean of Evening Admissions and Extension Campuses, 636-949-4934, Fax: 636-949-4109, E-mail: adultadmissions@lindenwood.edu.

Lindenwood University, Graduate Programs, School of Human Services, St. Charles, MO 63301-1695. Offers nonprofit administration (MA); public administration (MPA). Part-time programs available. *Faculty:* 2 full-time (1 woman), 9 part-time/adjunct (4 women). *Students:* 7 full-time (3 women), 22 part-time (19 women); includes 7 Black or African American, non-Hispanic/Latino. Average age 33. *Degree requirements:* For master's, minimum cumulative GPA of 3.0, directed internship, capstone project. *Entrance requirements:* Additional exam requirements/recommendations for international students: Required—TOEFL (minimum score 550 paper-based; 213 computer-based; 80 iBT). *Application deadline:* For fall admission, 8/27 priority date for domestic and international students; for spring admission, 1/28 priority date for domestic and international students. Applications are processed on a rolling basis. Application fee: $30 ($100 for international students). Electronic applications accepted. *Expenses:* Tuition: Full-time $13,260; part-time $380 per credit hour. Required fees: $340. One-time fee: $30. Tuition and fees vary according to course level and course load. *Financial support:* Career-related internships or fieldwork, institutionally sponsored loans, tuition waivers, and unspecified assistantships available. Financial award application deadline: 6/30; financial award applicants required to submit FAFSA. *Unit head:* Carla Mueller, Dean, 636-949-4731, E-mail: cmueller@lindenwood.edu. *Application contact:* Brett Barger, Dean of Evening Admissions and Extension Campuses, 636-949-4934, Fax: 636-949-4109, E-mail: adultadmissions@lindenwood.edu.

Long Island University, Brooklyn Campus, School of Business, Public Administration and Information Sciences, Program in Public Administration, Brooklyn, NY 11201-8423. Offers MPA. *Accreditation:* NASPAA. Part-time and evening/weekend programs available. *Entrance requirements:* For master's, GMAT or GRE Subject Test, 2 letters of recommendation. Additional exam requirements/recommendations for international students: Required—TOEFL (minimum score 500 paper-based; 173 computer-based). Electronic applications accepted.

Long Island University, C.W. Post Campus, College of Management, Department of Health Care and Public Administration, Brookville, NY 11548-1300. Offers gerontology (Certificate); health care administration (MPA); health care administration/gerontology (MPA); nonprofit management (MPA, Certificate); public administration (MPA). *Accreditation:* NASPAA (one or more programs are accredited). Part-time and evening/weekend programs available. *Degree requirements:* For master's, thesis. *Entrance requirements:* For master's, GMAT, minimum GPA of 2.5; for Certificate, minimum GPA of 2.5. Electronic applications accepted. *Faculty research:* Critical issues in sexuality, social work in religious communities, gerontological social work.

Long Island University, Rockland Graduate Campus, Graduate School, Programs in Health and Public Administration, Orangeburg, NY 10962. Offers gerontology (Advanced Certificate); health administration (MPA); public administration (MPA). Part-time and evening/weekend programs available. *Faculty:* 1 full-time (0 women), 5 part-time/adjunct (3 women). *Students:* 2 full-time (both women), 22 part-time (16 women). In 2010, 9 master's awarded. *Degree requirements:* For master's, thesis. *Entrance requirements:* For master's, college transcripts, letters of recommendation, personal statement, resume. *Application deadline:* Applications are processed on a rolling basis. Application fee: $30. *Expenses:* Tuition: Part-time $1028 per credit. Required fees: $340 per semester. *Financial support:* Applicants required to submit FAFSA. *Unit head:* Prof. Patricia Latona, Program Director, 845-359-7200 Ext. 5410, Fax: 845-359-7248, E-mail: patricia.latona@liu.edu. *Application contact:* Carolyn Reiter, Admissions Manager, 845-359-7200 Ext. 5417, Fax: 845-359-7248, E-mail: carolyn.reiter@liu.edu.

Louisiana State University and Agricultural and Mechanical College, Graduate School, E. J. Ourso College of Business, Public Administration Institute, Baton Rouge, LA 70803. Offers MPA, JD/MPA. Part-time programs available. *Faculty:* 6 full-time (2 women). *Students:* 67 full-time (41 women), 70 part-time (44 women); includes 44 Black or African American, non-Hispanic/Latino; 1 American Indian or Alaska Native, non-Hispanic/Latino; 6 Asian, non-Hispanic/Latino; 1 Hispanic/Latino; 1 Two or more races, non-Hispanic/Latino, 4 international. Average age 29. 54 applicants, 91% accepted, 13 enrolled. In 2010, 30 master's awarded. *Degree requirements:* For master's, comprehensive exam. *Entrance requirements:* For master's, GRE General Test, minimum GPA of 3.0. Additional exam requirements/recommendations for international students: Required—TOEFL (minimum score 550 paper-based; 213 computer-based; 79 iBT) or IELTS (minimum score 6.5). *Application deadline:* For fall admission, 1/25 priority date for domestic students, 5/15 for international students; for spring admission, 10/15 for international students. Applications are processed on a rolling basis. Application fee: $50 ($70 for international students). Electronic applications accepted. *Financial support:* In 2010–11, 95 students received support, including 5 research assistantships with full and partial tuition reimbursements available (averaging $12,480 per year), 9 teaching assistantships with partial tuition reimbursements available (averaging $13,824 per year); Federal Work-Study, scholarships/grants, health care benefits, and unspecified assistantships also available. Support available to part-time students. Financial award applicants required to submit FAFSA. *Faculty research:* Policy analysis, health care policy, financial and budget analysis. Total annual research expenditures: $240,278. *Unit head:* Dr. James A. Richardson, Director, 225-578-6745, Fax: 225-578-9078, E-mail: parich@lsu.edu. *Application contact:* Dr. James A. Richardson, Director, 225-578-6745, Fax: 225-578-9078, E-mail: parich@lsu.edu.

Louisiana State University and Agricultural and Mechanical College, Graduate School, Manship School of Mass Communication, Baton Rouge, LA 70803. Offers MMC, PhD. *Accreditation:* ACEJMC. Part-time programs available. Postbaccalaureate distance learning degree programs offered (minimal on-campus study). *Faculty:* 26 full-time (14 women). *Students:* 53 full-time (32 women), 17 part-time (11 women); includes 10 Black or African American, non-Hispanic/Latino; 2 American Indian or Alaska Native, non-Hispanic/Latino; 2 Hispanic/Latino; 2 Two or more races, non-Hispanic/Latino, 4 international. Average age 30. 77 applicants, 40% accepted, 14 enrolled. In 2010, 20 master's, 1 doctorate awarded. *Degree requirements:* For master's, thesis; for doctorate, thesis/dissertation. *Entrance requirements:* For master's, GRE General Test, minimum GPA of 3.0. Additional exam requirements/recommendations for international students: Required—TOEFL (minimum score 550 paper-based; 213 computer-based; 79 iBT) or IELTS (minimum score 6.5). *Application deadline:* For fall admission, 1/25 priority date for domestic students, 5/15 for international students; for spring admission, 10/15 for international students. Applications are processed on a rolling basis. Application fee: $50 ($70 for international students). Electronic applications accepted. *Financial support:* In 2010–11, 57 students received support, including 2 fellowships (averaging $23,089 per year), 29 research assistantships with full and partial tuition reimbursements available (averaging $16,224 per year), 10 teaching assistantships with full and partial tuition reimbursements available (averaging $18,180 per year); career-related internships or fieldwork, Federal Work-Study, institutionally sponsored loans, scholarships/grants, health care benefits, tuition waivers (full and partial), and unspecified assistantships also available. Support available to part-time students. Financial award application deadline: 3/1; financial award applicants required to submit FAFSA. *Faculty research:* Media effects, political communication, new media technologies, persuasive communication, journalism processes and practice. Total annual research expenditures: $14,696. *Unit head:* Dr. John Maxwell Hamilton, Dean, 225-578-2002, Fax: 225-578-2125, E-mail: jhamilt@lsu.edu. *Application contact:* Dr. Amy L. Reynolds, Associate Dean of Graduate Studies and Research, 225-578-9294, Fax: 225-578-2125, E-mail: areynolds@lsu.edu.

Marist College, Graduate Programs, School of Management, Program in Public Administration, Poughkeepsie, NY 12601-1387. Offers MPA. Part-time and evening/weekend programs available. Postbaccalaureate distance learning degree programs offered (no on-campus study). *Entrance requirements:* For master's, GRE General Test, resume. Additional exam requirements/recommendations for international students: Required—TOEFL (minimum score 550 paper-based; 213 computer-based; 80 iBT); Recommended—IELTS (minimum score 6.5). Electronic applications accepted. *Faculty research:* Public policy analysis, health administration.

Marquette University, Graduate School, Program in Public Service, Milwaukee, WI 53201-1881. Offers criminal justice administration (MLS); dispute resolution (MDR, MLS); engineering (MLS); health care administration (MLS); law enforcement leadership and management (Certificate); leadership studies (Certificate); non-profit sector (MLS); public service (MAPS, MLS); sports leadership (MLS). Part-time and evening/weekend programs available. Postbaccalaureate distance learning degree programs offered (no on-campus study). *Faculty:* 3 full-time (2 women), 29 part-time/adjunct (11 women). *Students:* 27 full-time (13 women), 134 part-time (84 women); includes 29 minority (21 Black or African American, non-Hispanic/Latino; 1 American Indian or Alaska Native, non-Hispanic/Latino; 1 Asian, non-Hispanic/Latino; 6 Hispanic/Latino), 1 international. Average age 38. 108 applicants, 78% accepted, 36 enrolled. In 2010, 11 master's, 12 Certificates awarded. *Degree requirements:* For master's, comprehensive exam (for some programs). *Entrance requirements:* For master's, GRE General Test (preferred), GMAT, or LSAT, official transcripts from all current and previous colleges/universities except Marquette, three letters of recommendation, statement of purpose. Additional exam requirements/recommendations for international students: Required—TOEFL. *Application deadline:* Applications are processed on a rolling basis. Application fee: $50. Electronic applications accepted. *Expenses:* Tuition: Full-time $16,290; part-time $905 per credit hour. Tuition and fees vary according to program. *Financial support:* In 2010–11, 1 fellowship, 1 research assistantship were awarded; teaching assistantships. Financial award application deadline: 2/15. *Unit head:* Dr. Johnette Caulfield, Adjunct Assistant Professor and Director of Graduate Programs, 414-288-5556, E-mail: jay.caulfield@marquette.edu. *Application contact:* Erin Fox, Assistant Director for Recruitment, 414-288-5319, Fax: 414-288-1902, E-mail: erin.fox@marquette.edu.

Marylhurst University, Department of Business Administration, Marylhurst, OR 97036-0261. Offers finance (MBA); general management (MBA); government policy and administration (MBA); green development (MBA); health care management (MBA); marketing (MBA); natural and organic resources (MBA); nonprofit management (MBA); organizational behavior (MBA); real estate (MBA); renewable energy (MBA); sustainable business (MBA). Part-time and evening/weekend programs available. Postbaccalaureate distance learning degree programs offered (no on-campus study). *Faculty:* 3 full-time (0 women), 36 part-time/adjunct (6 women). *Students:* 27 full-time (13 women), 727 part-time (373 women); includes 167 minority (47 Black or African American, non-Hispanic/Latino; 6 American Indian or Alaska Native, non-Hispanic/Latino; 36 Asian, non-Hispanic/Latino; 51 Hispanic/Latino; 6 Native Hawaiian or other Pacific Islander, non-Hispanic/Latino; 21 Two or more races, non-Hispanic/Latino), 7 international. Average age 38. 262 applicants, 91% accepted, 194 enrolled. In 2010, 289 master's awarded. *Degree requirements:* For master's, comprehensive exam, capstone course. *Entrance requirements:* For master's, GMAT (if GPA less than 3.0 and fewer than 5 years of work experience), interview, resume, 2 letters of recommendation. Additional exam requirements/recommendations for international students: Recommended—TOEFL (minimum score 550 paper-based; 213 computer-based; 80 iBT). *Application deadline:* For fall admission, 9/11 priority date for domestic and international students; for winter admission, 12/15 priority date for domestic and international students; for spring admission, 3/15 priority date for domestic students, 3/17 priority date for international students. Applications are processed on a rolling basis. Application fee: $50. Electronic applications accepted. *Expenses:* Tuition: Full-time $13,932; part-time $516 per credit. Tuition and fees vary according to course load and program. *Financial support:* Scholarships/grants available. Support available to part-time students. Financial award applicants required to submit FAFSA. *Unit head:* Bob Hanks, Director of Business and Real Estate Programs, 503-636-8141, Fax: 503-697-5597, E-mail: mba@marylhurst.edu. *Application contact:* Maruska Lynch, Graduate Admissions Specialist, 800-634-9982 Ext. 6322, Fax: 503-699-6320, E-mail: admissions@marylhurst.edu.

Marywood University, Academic Affairs, College of Health and Human Services, Department of Nursing and Public Administration, Program in Public Administration, Scranton, PA 18509-1598. Offers nonprofit management (MPA). *Entrance requirements:* Additional exam requirements/recommendations for international students: Required—TOEFL (minimum score 550 paper-based; 213 computer-based; 79 iBT). Electronic applications accepted. *Expenses:* Tuition: Part-time $735 per credit. Required fees: $470 per semester. Tuition and fees vary according to degree level and campus/location.

McMaster University, School of Graduate Studies, Faculty of Social Sciences, Department of Political Science, Hamilton, ON L8S 4M2, Canada. Offers international relations (PhD); political science (MA); public and the global economy (MA); public policy (PhD); public policy and administration (MA). MA program in public policy and administration offered jointly with University of Guelph. Part-time programs available. *Degree requirements:* For master's, thesis or alternative. *Entrance requirements:* For master's, minimum B+ average. Additional exam requirements/recommendations for international students: Required—TOEFL (minimum score 580 paper-based; 237 computer-based). *Faculty research:* Organizational theory, internationalization of public policy, water resource policies, political interest intermediation, comparative politics.

Metropolitan College of New York, Program in Public Administration, New York, NY 10013. Offers MPA. Evening/weekend programs available. *Degree requirements:* For master's, thesis. *Entrance requirements:* For master's, appropriate work experience, interview, minimum GPA of 2.7, internship or job in administrative setting. Additional exam requirements/recommendations for international students: Required—TOEFL (minimum score 600 paper-based; 220 computer-based). Electronic applications accepted. *Expenses:* Contact institution. *Faculty research:* Transnational politics and culture, women and social policy, confidentiality in the human services, concepts of marginality, ethics in social policy.

Metropolitan State University, College of Management, St. Paul, MN 55106-5000. Offers business administration (MBA, DBA); information assurance security (Graduate Certificate); management information systems (MMIS); MIS generalist (Graduate Certificate); MIS systems analysis and design (Graduate Certificate); nonprofit management (MPNA); project management (Graduate Certificate); public administration (MPNA). Part-time and evening/weekend programs available. *Students:* 158 full-time (74 women), 217 part-time (114 women); includes 31 Black or African American, non-Hispanic/Latino; 26 Asian, non-Hispanic/Latino; 10 Hispanic/Latino; 6 Two or more races, non-Hispanic/Latino, 47 international. Average age 35. In 2010, 100 master's, 7 other advanced degrees awarded. *Degree requirements:* For master's, thesis optional, computer language (MMIS). *Entrance requirements:* For master's, GMAT (MBA), resume. Additional exam requirements/recommendations for international students: Required—TOEFL (minimum score 550 paper-based; 213 computer-based). *Application deadline:* For fall admission, 7/15 for international students; for winter admission, 11/15 for international students;

for spring admission, 3/15 for international students. Applications are processed on a rolling basis. Application fee: $20. Electronic applications accepted. *Expenses:* Tuition, state resident: full-time $5827; part-time $291 per credit hour. Tuition, nonresident: full-time $11,654; part-time $583 per credit hour. Required fees: $10 per credit hour. Tuition and fees vary according to degree level. *Financial support:* Research assistantships with partial tuition reimbursements, career-related internships or fieldwork and Federal Work-Study available. Support available to part-time students. Financial award applicants required to submit FAFSA. *Faculty research:* Yugoslav economic system, workers' cooperatives, participative management and job enrichment, global business systems. *Unit head:* Dr. Paul Huo, Graduate Director, 612-659-7271, Fax: 612-659-7268, E-mail: carol.bormann.young@metrostate.edu. *Application contact:* Gloria B. Marcus, Recruiter/Admissions Adviser, 612-659-7258, Fax: 612-659-7268, E-mail: gloria.marcus@metrostate.edu.

Mid-America Christian University, Program in Public Administration, Oklahoma City, OK 73170-4504. Offers MA. *Entrance requirements:* For master's, bachelor's degree from a regionally accredited college or university, minimum overall cumulative GPA of 2.75 of bachelor course work. Additional exam requirements/recommendations for international students: Required—TOEFL (minimum score 550 paper-based; 213 computer-based).

Midwestern State University, Graduate Studies, College of Health Sciences and Human Services, Program in Health Services and Public Administration, Wichita Falls, TX 76308. Offers health services administration (MHA); public administration (MPA); public administration (administrative justice) (MPA); public administration (health services administration) with certificate (MPA); public administration (health services) (MPA). Part-time and evening/weekend programs available. *Faculty:* 4 full-time (2 women), 1 (woman) part-time/adjunct. *Students:* 12 full-time (8 women), 46 part-time (21 women); includes 7 Black or African American, non-Hispanic/Latino; 2 Asian, non-Hispanic/Latino; 1 Hispanic/Latino, 18 international. Average age 32. 31 applicants, 52% accepted, 6 enrolled. In 2010, 12 master's awarded. *Degree requirements:* For master's, comprehensive exam, thesis. *Entrance requirements:* For master's, GRE. Additional exam requirements/recommendations for international students: Required—TOEFL (minimum score 550 paper-based; 213 computer-based). *Application deadline:* For fall admission, 7/1 priority date for domestic students, 4/1 for international students; for spring admission, 11/1 priority date for domestic students, 8/1 for international students. Applications are processed on a rolling basis. Application fee: $35 ($50 for international students). Electronic applications accepted. *Expenses:* Tuition, state resident: full-time $1620; part-time $90 per credit hour. Tuition, nonresident: full-time $2160; part-time $120 per credit hour. International tuition: $7200 full-time. *Financial support:* In 2010–11, 13 students received support; teaching assistantships with partial tuition reimbursements available, career-related internships or fieldwork, Federal Work-Study, institutionally sponsored loans, scholarships/grants, tuition waivers (partial), and unspecified assistantships available. Support available to part-time students. Financial award application deadline: 3/1; financial award applicants required to submit FAFSA. *Faculty research:* Universal service policy, telehealth, bullying, healthcare financial management, public health ethics. *Unit head:* Dr. Kirk Harlow, Acting Chair, 940-397-4745, Fax: 940-397-6291, E-mail: kirk.harlow@mwsu.edu. *Application contact:* 800-842-1922, Fax: 940-397-4672, E-mail: admissions@mwsu.edu.

Minnesota State University Mankato, College of Graduate Studies, College of Social and Behavioral Sciences, Department of Government, Program in Public Administration, Mankato, MN 56001. Offers MPA. *Students:* 18 full-time (11 women), 55 part-time (27 women). *Degree requirements:* For master's, one foreign language, comprehensive exam, thesis or alternative. *Entrance requirements:* For master's, minimum GPA of 3.0 during previous 2 years. Additional exam requirements/recommendations for international students: Required—TOEFL. *Application deadline:* For fall admission, 3/1 priority date for domestic students. Applications are processed on a rolling basis. Application fee: $40. Electronic applications accepted. *Financial support:* Research assistantships with full tuition reimbursements, teaching assistantships with full tuition reimbursements, unspecified assistantships available. Financial award application deadline: 3/15; financial award applicants required to submit FAFSA. *Unit head:* Dr. Scott Granberg-Rademacker, Graduate Coordinator, 507-389-6939. *Application contact:* 507-389-2321, E-mail: grad@mnsu.edu.

Minnesota State University Moorhead, Graduate Studies, College of Social and Natural Sciences, Program in Public, Human Services, and Health Administration, Moorhead, MN 56563-0002. Offers MS. Part-time and evening/weekend programs available. *Degree requirements:* For master's, final oral exam, final project paper or thesis. *Entrance requirements:* For master's, GRE General Test, minimum GPA of 2.75. Additional exam requirements/recommendations for international students: Required—TOEFL (minimum score 550 paper-based; 213 computer-based). Electronic applications accepted.

Mississippi State University, College of Arts and Sciences, Department of Political Science and Public Administration, Mississippi State, MS 39762. Offers political science (MA); public policy and administration (MPPA, PhD). *Accreditation:* NASPAA (one or more programs are accredited). Evening/weekend programs available. Postbaccalaureate distance learning degree programs offered (no on-campus study). *Faculty:* 13 full-time (4 women). *Students:* 61 full-time (31 women), 47 part-time (26 women); includes 37 minority (33 Black or African American, non-Hispanic/Latino; 1 American Indian or Alaska Native, non-Hispanic/Latino; 1 Asian, non-Hispanic/Latino; 1 Hispanic/Latino; 1 Two or more races, non-Hispanic/Latino), 4 international. Average age 30. 60 applicants, 62% accepted, 26 enrolled. In 2010, 32 master's, 2 doctorates awarded. *Degree requirements:* For master's, thesis optional, comprehensive oral or written exam; for doctorate, thesis/dissertation, comprehensive oral and written exam. *Entrance requirements:* For master's, GRE, minimum GPA of 3.0 on the last two years of undergraduate courses or graduate work; for doctorate, GRE General Test, minimum graduate GPA of 3.35. Additional exam requirements/recommendations for international students: Required—TOEFL (minimum score 600 paper-based; 250 computer-based; 100 iBT); Recommended—IELTS (minimum score 7.5). *Application deadline:* For fall admission, 8/1 priority date for domestic students, 5/1 for international students; for spring admission, 12/1 priority date for domestic students, 9/1 for international students. Applications are processed on a rolling basis. Application fee: $40. Electronic applications accepted. *Expenses:* Tuition, state resident: full-time $2730.50; part-time $304 per credit hour. Tuition, nonresident: full-time $6901; part-time $767 per credit hour. *Financial support:* In 2010–11, 3 research assistantships (averaging $10,144 per year), 8 teaching assistantships with full tuition reimbursements (averaging $10,138 per year) were awarded; Federal Work-Study, institutionally sponsored loans, scholarships/grants, and unspecified assistantships also available. Financial award application deadline: 4/1; financial award applicants required to submit FAFSA. *Faculty research:* American politics, international relations, state and local government, comparative government, public administration. Total annual research expenditures: $1.2 million. *Unit head:* Dr. K. C. Morrison, Department Head, 662-325-2711, Fax: 662-325-2716, E-mail: kcmorrison@ps.msstate.edu. *Application contact:* Dr. Edward French, Assistant Professor and Graduate Coordinator, 662-325-2711, Fax: 662-325-2716, E-mail: efrench@ps.msstate.edu.

Missouri State University, Graduate College, College of Humanities and Public Affairs, Department of Political Science, Program in Public Administration, Springfield, MO 65897. Offers MPA. *Accreditation:* NASPAA. Part-time programs available. *Degree requirements:* For master's, comprehensive exam, thesis or alternative, internship. *Entrance requirements:* For master's, GRE, minimum GPA of 3.0. Additional exam requirements/recommendations for international students: Required—TOEFL (minimum score 550 paper-based; 213 computer-based; 79 iBT). Electronic applications accepted. *Expenses:* Tuition, state resident: full-time $3348; part-time $186 per credit hour. Tuition, nonresident: full-time $6696; part-time $372 per credit hour. Required fees: $238 per semester. Tuition and fees vary according to course level, course load and program. *Faculty research:* Public management, environmental policy, health care policy, law and religion.

Missouri State University, Graduate College, Interdisciplinary Program in Administrative Studies, Springfield, MO 65897. Offers applied communication (MS); criminal justice (MS); environmental management (MS); project management (MS); sports management (MS). Part-time and evening/weekend programs available. Postbaccalaureate distance learning degree programs offered (no on-campus study). *Degree requirements:* For master's, comprehensive exam, thesis or alternative. *Entrance requirements:* For master's, GRE, GMAT, 3 years of work experience. Additional exam requirements/recommendations for international students: Required—TOEFL (minimum score 550 paper-based; 213 computer-based; 79 iBT). Electronic applications accepted. *Expenses:* Tuition, state resident: full-time $3348; part-time $186 per credit hour. Tuition, nonresident: full-time $6696; part-time $372 per credit hour. Required fees: $238 per semester. Tuition and fees vary according to course level, course load and program.

Montana State University, College of Graduate Studies, College of Letters and Science, Department of Political Science, Bozeman, MT 59717. Offers public administration (MPA). Program offered jointly with The University of Montana. Part-time programs available. *Faculty:* 7 full-time (4 women), 1 part-time/adjunct (0 women). *Students:* 16 full-time (14 women), 21 part-time (10 women), 2 international. Average age 29. 24 applicants, 63% accepted, 12 enrolled. In 2010, 8 master's awarded. *Degree requirements:* For master's, comprehensive exam, thesis (for some programs). *Entrance requirements:* For master's, GRE General Test. Additional exam requirements/recommendations for international students: Required—TOEFL (minimum score 550 paper-based; 213 computer-based). *Application deadline:* For fall admission, 7/15 priority date for domestic students, 5/15 priority date for international students; for spring admission, 12/1 priority date for domestic students, 10/1 priority date for international students. Applications are processed on a rolling basis. Application fee: $30. Electronic applications accepted. *Expenses:* Tuition, state resident: full-time $5553.90. Tuition, nonresident: full-time $14,646. Required fees: $1233. *Financial support:* In 2010–11, 2 students received support; research assistantships, teaching assistantships, tuition waivers (full and partial) and unspecified assistantships available. Financial award application deadline: 3/1; financial award applicants required to submit FAFSA. *Faculty research:* National resource policy, political economy of agriculture, qualitative methods, organizational theory. Total annual research expenditures: $162,814. *Unit head:* Dr. Jerry Johnson, Head, 406-994-5164, Fax: 406-994-6692, E-mail: jdj@montana.edu. *Application contact:* Dr. Carl A. Fox, Vice Provost for Graduate Education, 406-994-4145, Fax: 406-994-7433, E-mail: gradstudy@montana.edu.

Montana State University Billings, College of Arts and Sciences, Program in Public Administration, Billings, MT 59101-0298. Offers MPA.

Monterey Institute of International Studies, Graduate School of International Policy and Management, Program in International Public Administration, Monterey, CA 93940-2691. Offers MPA. *Degree requirements:* For master's, one foreign language. *Entrance requirements:* For master's, minimum GPA of 3.0, proficiency in a foreign language. Additional exam requirements/recommendations for international students: Required—TOEFL (minimum score 550 paper-based; 213 computer-based; 80 iBT). Electronic applications accepted. *Expenses:* Tuition: Full-time $32,000; part-time $1525 per credit hour. Required fees: $56.

Morehead State University, Graduate Programs, Institute for Regional Analysis and Public Policy, Morehead, KY 40351. Offers public administration (MPA). *Entrance requirements:* For master's, GRE. Additional exam requirements/recommendations for international students: Required—TOEFL (minimum score 500 paper-based). Electronic applications accepted.

National University, Academic Affairs, College of Letters and Sciences, Department of Professional Studies, La Jolla, CA 92037-1011. Offers forensic science (MFS), including criminalistics and investigation; public administration (MPA), including alternative dispute resolution, human resource management, organizational leadership, public finance. Part-time and evening/weekend programs available. Postbaccalaureate distance learning degree programs offered (no on-campus study). *Faculty:* 10 full-time (3 women), 110 part-time/adjunct (22 women). *Students:* 189 full-time (117 women), 284 part-time (167 women); includes 259 minority (101 Black or African American, non-Hispanic/Latino; 2 American Indian or Alaska Native, non-Hispanic/Latino; 33 Asian, non-Hispanic/Latino; 104 Hispanic/Latino; 7 Native Hawaiian or other Pacific Islander, non-Hispanic/Latino; 12 Two or more races, non-Hispanic/Latino). Average age 38. 305 applicants, 100% accepted, 192 enrolled. In 2010, 160 master's awarded. *Degree requirements:* For master's, thesis. *Entrance requirements:* For master's, interview, minimum GPA of 2.5. Additional exam requirements/recommendations for international students: Required—TOEFL (minimum score 550 paper-based; 213 computer-based; 79 iBT), IELTS (minimum score 6). *Application deadline:* Applications are processed on a rolling basis. Application fee: $60 ($65 for international students). Electronic applications accepted. *Expenses:* Tuition: Full-time $9450; part-time $350 per unit. Required fees: $350 per unit. One-time fee: $60. *Financial support:* Career-related internships or fieldwork, institutionally sponsored loans, scholarships/grants, and tuition waivers (partial) available. Support available to part-time students. Financial award application deadline: 6/30; financial award applicants required to submit FAFSA. *Unit head:* James G. Larsen, Associate Professor and Chair, 858-642-8418, Fax: 858-642-8715, E-mail: jlarson@nu.edu. *Application contact:* Dominick Giovanniello, Associate Regional Dean—San Diego, 800-NAT-UNIV, Fax: 858-541-7792, E-mail: dgiovann@nu.edu.

National University of Singapore, Lee Kuan Yew School of Public Policy, Singapore, Singapore. Offers MPA, MPM, MPP, PhD.

New York University, Robert F. Wagner Graduate School of Public Service, Executive Master of Public Administration Program, New York, NY 10012-1019. Offers nurse leader (EMPA); public administration (EMPA); MSW/EMPA. *Accreditation:* AACSB. Part-time and evening/weekend programs available. *Faculty:* 10 full-time (3 women), 3 part-time/adjunct (all women). *Students:* 22 full-time (13 women), 84 part-time (57 women); includes 9 Black or African American, non-Hispanic/Latino; 12 Asian, non-Hispanic/Latino; 2 Hispanic/Latino, 10 international. Average age 40. 101 applicants, 74% accepted, 51 enrolled. In 2010, 39 master's awarded. *Entrance requirements:* For master's, minimum undergraduate GPA of 3.0. Additional exam requirements/recommendations for international students: Required—TOEFL (minimum score 600 paper-based; 250 computer-based; 100 iBT), IELTS (minimum score 7.5), TWE (minimum score 4). *Application deadline:* For fall admission, 5/15 for domestic students; for spring admission, 11/15 for domestic students. Applications are processed on a rolling basis. Application fee: $80. Electronic applications accepted. *Expenses:* Contact institution. *Financial support:* In 2010–11, 7 students received support, including 7 fellowships (averaging $9,306 per year); research assistantships with full and partial tuition reimbursements available, institutionally sponsored loans, scholarships/grants, health care benefits, and unspecified assistantships also available. Support available to part-time students. Financial award application deadline: 1/4; financial award applicants required to submit FAFSA. *Unit head:* David Elcott, Director, 212-992-9894, Fax: 212-995-4164, E-mail: david.elcott@nyu.edu. *Application contact:* Christopher Alexander, Administrative Aide, Enrollment, 212-998-7414, Fax: 212-995-4611, E-mail: wagner.admissions@nyu.edu.

New York University, Robert F. Wagner Graduate School of Public Service, Program in Public Administration, New York, NY 10012-1019. Offers public administration (PhD); public and nonprofit management and policy (MPA, Advanced Certificate), including developmental administration (Advanced Certificate), financial management and public finance, human resources management (Advanced Certificate), international administration (Advanced Certificate), management (MPA), management for public and nonprofit organizations (Advanced Certificate), public policy analysis, quantitative analysis and computer applications (Advanced Certificate), urban public policy (Advanced Certificate); JD/MPA; MBA/MPA; MPA/MA. *Accreditation:* NASPAA (one or more programs are accredited). Part-time and evening/weekend programs available. *Faculty:* 32 full-time (13 women), 41 part-time/adjunct (22 women). *Students:* 400 full-time (301 women), 206 part-time (156 women); includes 43 Black or African American, non-Hispanic/Latino; 58 Asian, non-Hispanic/Latino; 36 Hispanic/Latino, 65 international. Average age 28. 1,230 applicants, 54% accepted, 219 enrolled. In 2010, 210 master's, 5 doctorates awarded. *Degree requirements:* For master's, thesis or alternative, capstone end event; for doctorate, one foreign language, thesis/dissertation. *Entrance requirements:* For master's, minimum undergraduate GPA of 3.0; for doctorate, GMAT or GRE

New York University (continued)
General Test, minimum GPA of 3.5. Additional exam requirements/recommendations for international students: Required—TOEFL (minimum score 600 paper-based; 250 computer-based; 100 iBT), IELTS (minimum score 7.5), TWE (minimum score 4). *Application deadline:* For fall admission, 1/15 for domestic students, 1/4 for international students; for spring admission, 11/15 for domestic students, 10/1 for international students. Applications are processed on a rolling basis. Application fee: $80. Electronic applications accepted. *Expenses:* Contact institution. *Financial support:* In 2010–11, 176 students received support, including 171 fellowships (averaging $14,022 per year), 5 research assistantships with full tuition reimbursements available (averaging $22,440 per year); career-related internships or fieldwork, Federal Work-Study, institutionally sponsored loans, scholarships/grants, health care benefits, and unspecified assistantships also available. Support available to part-time students. Financial award application deadline: 1/5; financial award applicants required to submit FAFSA. *Unit head:* Katty Jones, Director, Program Services, 212-998-7411, Fax: 212-995-4164, E-mail: katty.jones@nyu.edu. *Application contact:* Christopher Alexander, Administrative Aide, Enrollment, 212-998-7414, Fax: 212-995-4611, E-mail: wagner.admissions@nyu.edu.

North Carolina Central University, Division of Academic Affairs, College of Behavioral and Social Sciences, Department of Public Administration, Durham, NC 27707-3129. Offers MPA. Part-time and evening/weekend programs available. *Degree requirements:* For master's, one foreign language, comprehensive exam, thesis or alternative. *Entrance requirements:* For master's, GRE, minimum GPA of 3.0 in major, 2.5 overall. Additional exam requirements/recommendations for international students: Required—TOEFL. *Faculty research:* Racial diversity and community policing, economic development, issues in urban transportation.

North Carolina State University, Graduate School, College of Humanities and Social Sciences, School of Public and International Affairs, Program in Public Administration, Raleigh, NC 27695. Offers MPA, PhD. *Accreditation:* NASPAA. *Degree requirements:* For master's, thesis optional; for doctorate, thesis/dissertation. *Entrance requirements:* For master's, GRE General Test, minimum GPA of 3.0 during previous 2 years; for doctorate, GRE General Test. Electronic applications accepted. *Faculty research:* Public budgeting, human resources, public information technology, nonprofit management, environmental policy.

Northeastern University, College of Social Sciences and Humanities, Department of Political Science, Boston, MA 02115-5096. Offers political science (MA); public administration (MPA, Certificate), including development administration (MPA), health administration and policy (MPA), state and local government (MPA), urban studies (Certificate); public and international affairs (PhD). Part-time and evening/weekend programs available. *Faculty:* 22 full-time (4 women), 10 part-time/adjunct (1 woman). *Students:* 64 full-time (30 women), 12 part-time (7 women). Average age 30. 132 applicants, 47% accepted, 23 enrolled. In 2010, 21 master's, 3 doctorates awarded. *Degree requirements:* For master's, thesis optional; for doctorate, thesis/dissertation. *Entrance requirements:* For master's, GRE General Test. Additional exam requirements/recommendations for international students: Required—TOEFL. *Application deadline:* Applications are processed on a rolling basis. Application fee: $50. *Financial support:* In 2010–11, 12 fellowships, 1 research assistantship with tuition reimbursement, 17 teaching assistantships with tuition reimbursements (averaging $14,035 per year) were awarded; career-related internships or fieldwork, Federal Work-Study, tuition waivers (full and partial), and unspecified assistantships also available. Support available to part-time students. Financial award application deadline: 2/1; financial award applicants required to submit FAFSA. *Faculty research:* Presidency, public opinion, Congress, democratization, national identity. *Unit head:* Dr. John Portz, Chair, 617-373-2796, Fax: 617-373-5311, E-mail: gradpolisci@neu.edu. *Application contact:* Brynn Thompson, Graduate Programs Assistant, 617-373-4404, Fax: 617-373-5311, E-mail: gradpolisci@neu.edu.

Northeastern University, College of Social Sciences and Humanities, School of Public Policy and Urban Affairs, Program in Public Administration, Boston, MA 02115-5096. Offers development administration (MPA); health administration and policy (MPA); state and local government (MPA); urban studies (Certificate). *Accreditation:* NASPAA (one or more programs are accredited). Part-time and evening/weekend programs available. *Faculty:* 22 full-time (4 women), 10 part-time/adjunct (1 woman). *Students:* 74 full-time (48 women), 44 part-time (30 women). 149 applicants, 77% accepted, 56 enrolled. In 2010, 18 master's awarded. *Degree requirements:* For master's, thesis optional. *Entrance requirements:* For master's, GRE General Test. Additional exam requirements/recommendations for international students: Required—TOEFL. *Application deadline:* For fall admission, 2/1 priority date for domestic students, 5/1 for international students. Applications are processed on a rolling basis. Application fee: $50. *Financial support:* In 2010–11, 2 research assistantships with tuition reimbursements (averaging $14,035 per year) were awarded; teaching assistantships with tuition reimbursements, career-related internships or fieldwork, Federal Work-Study, tuition waivers (full and partial), and unspecified assistantships also available. Support available to part-time students. Financial award application deadline: 2/1; financial award applicants required to submit FAFSA. *Faculty research:* National health care, Third World development, leadership and ethics, science and technology, budgeting. *Unit head:* Dr. Ronald D. Hedlund, Graduate Coordinator, 617-373-2796, Fax: 617-373-5311, E-mail: gradpolisci@neu.edu. *Application contact:* Brynn Thompson, Graduate Programs Assistant, 617-373-4404, Fax: 617-373-5311, E-mail: gradpolisci@neu.edu.

Northern Arizona University, Graduate College, College of Social and Behavioral Sciences, Department of Politics and International Affairs, Flagstaff, AZ 86011. Offers political science (MA, PhD); public administration (MPA); public management (Certificate). Part-time programs available. *Faculty:* 23 full-time (8 women). *Students:* 37 full-time (13 women), 39 part-time (26 women); includes 20 minority (3 Black or African American, non-Hispanic/Latino; 5 American Indian or Alaska Native, non-Hispanic/Latino; 4 Asian, non-Hispanic/Latino; 7 Hispanic/Latino; 1 Two or more races, non-Hispanic/Latino), 7 international. Average age 34. 47 applicants, 81% accepted, 27 enrolled. In 2010, 9 master's, 6 doctorates, 5 other advanced degrees awarded. *Degree requirements:* For master's, comprehensive exam (for some programs), thesis optional; for doctorate, one foreign language, comprehensive exam, thesis/dissertation. *Entrance requirements:* For master's, GRE (70th percentile ranking in each testing area preferred); for doctorate, GRE (minimum 70th percentile in each testing area preferred). Additional exam requirements/recommendations for international students: Required—TOEFL (minimum score 550 paper-based; 213 computer-based; 80 iBT), IELTS (minimum score 7). *Application deadline:* For fall admission, 2/1 priority date for domestic and international students. Applications are processed on a rolling basis. Application fee: $65. Electronic applications accepted. *Financial support:* In 2010–11, 1 fellowship, 13 teaching assistantships with partial tuition reimbursements (averaging $11,300 per year) were awarded; career-related internships or fieldwork, Federal Work-Study, scholarships/grants, health care benefits, tuition waivers (full and partial), and unspecified assistantships also available. Financial award applicants required to submit FAFSA. *Unit head:* Dr. Frederic Solop, Chair, 928-523-3135, Fax: 928-523-6777, E-mail: fred.solop@nau.edu. *Application contact:* Julie Hammond, Administrative Assistant, 928-523-6544, Fax: 928-523-6777, E-mail: political.science@nau.edu.

Northern Illinois University, Graduate School, College of Liberal Arts and Sciences, Department of Political Science, Division of Public Administration, De Kalb, IL 60115-2854. Offers MPA. *Accreditation:* NASPAA. Part-time and evening/weekend programs available. *Faculty:* 5 full-time (1 woman), 3 part-time/adjunct (1 woman). *Students:* 34 full-time (15 women), 36 part-time (13 women); includes 4 Black or African American, non-Hispanic/Latino; 1 Hispanic/Latino, 1 international. Average age 31. 59 applicants, 69% accepted, 26 enrolled. In 2010, 37 master's awarded. *Degree requirements:* For master's, comprehensive exam, internship, research paper. *Entrance requirements:* For master's, GRE General Test, minimum GPA of 2.75, 9 hours in social science. Additional exam requirements/recommendations for international students: Required—TOEFL (minimum score 550 paper-based; 213 computer-based). *Application deadline:* For fall admission, 3/1 priority date for domestic students, 5/1 for international students; for spring admission, 10/1 priority date for domestic students, 10/1 for international students. Applications are processed on a rolling basis. Application fee: $30. Electronic applications accepted. *Expenses:* Tuition, state resident: full-time $7200; part-time $300 per credit hour. Tuition, nonresident: full-time $14,400; part-time $600 per credit hour. Required fees: $79 per credit hour. *Financial support:* In 2010–11, 4 teaching assistantships were awarded; fellowships with full tuition reimbursements, research assistantships with full tuition reimbursements, career-related internships or fieldwork, Federal Work-Study, scholarships/grants, tuition waivers (full), and unspecified assistantships also available. Support available to part-time students. Financial award applicants required to submit FAFSA. *Faculty research:* Urban service and management, manpower public policy, performance appraisal, bureaucratic politics. *Unit head:* Dr. Gerald Gabris, Acting Director, 815-753-6140, Fax: 815-753-2539, E-mail: ggabris@niu.edu. *Application contact:* Samantha Fisher, Program Coordinator, 815-753-6149, E-mail: samfisher@niu.edu.

Northern Kentucky University, Office of Graduate Programs, College of Arts and Sciences, Program in Public Administration, Highland Heights, KY 41099. Offers non-profit management (Certificate); public administration (MPA). *Accreditation:* NASPAA. Part-time and evening/weekend programs available. *Faculty:* 5 full-time (2 women), 1 (woman) part-time/adjunct. *Students:* 12 full-time (5 women), 89 part-time (50 women); includes 19 minority (17 Black or African American, non-Hispanic/Latino; 1 Asian, non-Hispanic/Latino; 1 Hispanic/Latino), 1 international. Average age 34. 45 applicants, 62% accepted, 24 enrolled. In 2010, 20 master's, 7 other advanced degrees awarded. *Degree requirements:* For master's, capstone. *Entrance requirements:* For master's, GRE, GMAT or MAT, 2 letters of recommendation, writing sample, minimum GPA of 2.75, essay, resume (for those in-career). Additional exam requirements/recommendations for international students: Required—TOEFL (minimum score 550 paper-based; 213 computer-based; 79 iBT); Recommended—IELTS (minimum score 6.5). *Application deadline:* For fall admission, 7/1 for domestic students, 6/1 for international students; for spring admission, 12/1 for domestic students, 10/1 for international students. Applications are processed on a rolling basis. Application fee: $40. Electronic applications accepted. *Expenses:* Tuition, state resident: full-time $7254; part-time $403 per credit hour. Tuition, nonresident: full-time $12,492; part-time $694 per credit hour. Tuition and fees vary according to degree level and program. *Financial support:* Unspecified assistantships available. Financial award applicants required to submit FAFSA. *Faculty research:* Non-profit management, human resource management, local government, budgeting and finance, urban planning. *Unit head:* Dr. Shamima Ahmed, Director, 859-572-6402, Fax: 859-572-6184, E-mail: ahmed@nku.edu. *Application contact:* Beth Devantier, MPA Coordinator, 859-572-5326, Fax: 859-572-6184, E-mail: devantier@nku.edu.

Northern Michigan University, College of Graduate Studies, College of Arts and Sciences, Department of Political Science and Public Administration, Marquette, MI 49855-5301. Offers public administration (MPA). Part-time programs available. *Degree requirements:* For master's, thesis or alternative. *Entrance requirements:* For master's, minimum GPA of 3.0.

North Georgia College & State University, Graduate Studies, Program in Public Administration, Dahlonega, GA 30597. Offers MPA. Part-time and evening/weekend programs available. Postbaccalaureate distance learning degree programs offered. *Degree requirements:* For master's, thesis optional, internship. *Entrance requirements:* For master's, GMAT or GRE General Test, minimum undergraduate GPA of 2.75, 3 letters of recommendation. Electronic applications accepted. *Expenses:* Tuition, state resident: full-time $4704; part-time $196 per credit hour. Tuition, nonresident: full-time $18,770; part-time $783 per credit hour. Required fees: $1718; $671 per semester. Tuition and fees vary according to course load, degree level and program.

Northwestern University, School of Continuing Studies, Program in Public Policy and Administration, Evanston, IL 60208. Offers MA. Postbaccalaureate distance learning degree programs offered.

Norwich University, School of Graduate and Continuing Studies, Program in Business Continuity, Northfield, VT 05663. Offers consultancy project (MS); continuity of government operations (MS); private sector continuity of operations (MS). *Expenses:* Tuition: Full-time $17,380; part-time $645 per credit. Tuition and fees vary according to program. *Unit head:* Dr. William Clements, Vice President of Academic Affairs and Dean of the School of Graduate and Continuing Studies, 802-485-2730. *Application contact:* Allison Crownson, Director of Admissions and Retention, 802-485-2720, Fax: 802-485-2533.

Norwich University, School of Graduate and Continuing Studies, Program in Public Administration, Northfield, VT 05663. Offers continuity of government operations (MPA); criminal justice (MPA); fiscal management (MPA); leadership (MPA); organizational leadership (MPA); public works administration (MPA). Evening/weekend programs available. *Faculty:* 12 part-time/adjunct (5 women). *Students:* 64 full-time (21 women); includes 4 Black or African American, non-Hispanic/Latino; 2 Two or more races, non-Hispanic/Latino. Average age 37. 189 applicants, 81% accepted. In 2010, 64 master's awarded. *Entrance requirements:* Additional exam requirements/recommendations for international students: Required—TOEFL (minimum score 550 paper-based; 212 computer-based; 83 iBT). *Application deadline:* For fall admission, 8/10 for domestic and international students; for winter admission, 11/7 for domestic and international students; for spring admission, 2/6 for domestic and international students. Application fee: $50. *Expenses:* Tuition: Full-time $17,380; part-time $645 per credit. Tuition and fees vary according to program. *Financial support:* Scholarships/grants available. Financial award applicants required to submit FAFSA. *Unit head:* Donal Hartman, Program Director, 802-485-2567, Fax: 802-485-2533, E-mail: dhartman@norwich.edu. *Application contact:* Chris Ormsby, Associate Program Director, 802-249-7809, Fax: 802-485-2533, E-mail: cormsby@norwich.edu.

Notre Dame de Namur University, Division of Academic Affairs, School of Business and Management, Department of Public Administration, Belmont, CA 94002-1908. Offers human resource management (MPA); public administration (MPA); public affairs administration (MPA). Part-time and evening/weekend programs available. *Faculty:* 3 full-time (1 woman), 4 part-time/adjunct (2 women). *Students:* 13 full-time (11 women), 41 part-time (34 women); includes 4 Black or African American, non-Hispanic/Latino; 4 Asian, non-Hispanic/Latino; 12 Hispanic/Latino; 1 Native Hawaiian or other Pacific Islander, non-Hispanic/Latino, 10 international. Average age 32. 35 applicants, 49% accepted, 14 enrolled. In 2010, 13 master's awarded. *Entrance requirements:* For master's, interview, minimum GPA of 2.5. Additional exam requirements/recommendations for international students: Required—TOEFL (minimum score 550 paper-based; 213 computer-based; 79 iBT). *Application deadline:* For fall admission, 8/1 priority date for domestic students; for spring admission, 12/1 priority date for domestic students. Applications are processed on a rolling basis. Application fee: $60. Electronic applications accepted. *Expenses:* Tuition: Full-time $14,220; part-time $790 per credit. Required fees: $35 per semester. Tuition and fees vary according to program. *Financial support:* Available to part-time students. Applicants required to submit FAFSA. *Unit head:* Jordan Holtzman, Director, 650-508-3637, E-mail: jholtzman@ndnu.edu. *Application contact:* Candace Hallmark, Associate Director of Admissions, 650-508-3600, Fax: 650-508-3426, E-mail: grad.admit@ndnu.edu.

Nova Southeastern University, H. Wayne Huizenga School of Business and Entrepreneurship, Program in Public Administration, Fort Lauderdale, FL 33314-7796. Offers MPA. Part-time and evening/weekend programs available. Postbaccalaureate distance learning degree programs offered (minimal on-campus study). *Faculty:* 2 full-time (0 women), 10 part-time/adjunct (1 woman). *Students:* 6 full-time (2 women), 188 part-time (116 women); includes 110 Black or African American, non-Hispanic/Latino; 30 Hispanic/Latino, 1 international. Average age 35. 99 applicants, 75% accepted, 55 enrolled. In 2010, 67 master's awarded. *Degree requirements:* For master's, thesis or alternative. *Entrance requirements:* For master's, work experience. Additional exam requirements/recommendations for international students: Required—TOEFL (minimum score 550 paper-based; 213 computer-based; 79 iBT), IELTS (minimum score 6). *Application deadline:* For fall admission, 8/15 priority date for domestic students, 8/15 for international students; for winter admission, 12/10 for domestic and international students; for spring admission, 2/10 for domestic and international students. Applications are processed on a rolling basis. Application fee: $50. Electronic applications accepted. *Financial support:*

Career-related internships or fieldwork, Federal Work-Study, and institutionally sponsored loans available. Financial award applicants required to submit FAFSA. *Unit head:* Dr. Preston Jones, Executive Associate Dean, 954-262-5127, Fax: 954-262-3960, E-mail: prestonj@huizenga.nova.edu. *Application contact:* Karen Goldberg, Associate Director of Recruitment and Special Events, 954-262-5039, Fax: 954-262-3822, E-mail: karen@nova.edu.

Oakland University, Graduate Study and Lifelong Learning, College of Arts and Sciences, Department of Political Science, Rochester, MI 48309-4401. Offers public administration (MPA). *Accreditation:* NASPAA. Part-time and evening/weekend programs available. *Entrance requirements:* For master's, minimum GPA of 3.0 for unconditional admission. Additional exam requirements/recommendations for international students: Required—TOEFL (minimum score 550 paper-based; 213 computer-based). Electronic applications accepted.

The Ohio State University, Graduate School, John Glenn School of Public Affairs, Columbus, OH 43210. Offers public administration (MA, MPA); public policy and management (PhD). *Accreditation:* NASPAA (one or more programs are accredited). Part-time programs available. *Faculty:* 14. *Students:* 82 full-time (37 women), 114 part-time (72 women); includes 13 Black or African American, non-Hispanic/Latino; 7 Asian, non-Hispanic/Latino; 5 Hispanic/Latino; 4 Two or more races, non-Hispanic/Latino, 15 international. Average age 32. In 2010, 55 master's, 1 doctorate awarded. *Degree requirements:* For doctorate, thesis/dissertation. *Entrance requirements:* For master's, GMAT, GRE General Test (MPA), minimum GPA of 3.0 (MA); for doctorate, GRE General Test. Additional exam requirements/recommendations for international students: Recommended—TOEFL (minimum score 573 paper-based; 230 computer-based). *Application deadline:* For fall admission, 8/15 priority date for domestic students, 7/1 priority date for international students; for winter admission, 12/1 priority date for domestic students, 11/1 priority date for international students; for spring admission, 3/1 priority date for domestic students, 2/1 priority date for international students. Applications are processed on a rolling basis. Application fee: $40 ($50 for international students). Electronic applications accepted. *Expenses:* Tuition, state resident: full-time $10,605. Tuition, nonresident: full-time $26,535. Tuition and fees vary according to course load and program. *Financial support:* Fellowships, research assistantships, teaching assistantships, Federal Work-Study, institutionally sponsored loans, and unspecified assistantships available. Support available to part-time students. *Unit head:* Charles R. Wise, Graduate Studies Committee Chair, 614-292-8696, Fax: 614-292-4868, E-mail: wise.983@osu.edu. *Application contact:* 614-292-9444, Fax: 614-292-3895, E-mail: domestic.grad@osu.edu.

Ohio University, Graduate College, Voinovich School of Leadership and Public Affairs, Athens, OH 45701-2979. Offers public administration (MPA). *Faculty:* 7 full-time (5 women), 1 part-time/adjunct (0 women). *Students:* 33 full-time (17 women), 1 (woman) part-time; includes 3 minority (1 Black or African American, non-Hispanic/Latino; 1 Hispanic/Latino; 1 Two or more races, non-Hispanic/Latino), 1 international. 65 applicants, 83% accepted, 12 enrolled. Application fee: $50 ($55 for international students). Electronic applications accepted. *Unit head:* Dr. Mark Weinberg, Head, 740-593-4390, Fax: 740-593-9758, E-mail: weinberm@ohio.edu. *Application contact:* Dr. Judith Millesen, MPA Director, 740-593-4381, E-mail: millesen@ohio.edu.

Old Dominion University, College of Business and Public Administration, Doctoral Program in Public Administration and Urban Policy, Norfolk, VA 23529. Offers PhD. Part-time and evening/weekend programs available. *Faculty:* 7 full-time (2 women). *Students:* 11 full-time (8 women), 22 part-time (11 women); includes 7 minority (6 Black or African American, non-Hispanic/Latino; 1 Hispanic/Latino), 5 international. Average age 38. 27 applicants, 44% accepted, 10 enrolled. In 2010, 3 doctorates awarded. *Degree requirements:* For doctorate, comprehensive exam, thesis/dissertation. *Entrance requirements:* For doctorate, GMAT, GRE General Test, master's degree, minimum graduate GPA of 3.25. Additional exam requirements/recommendations for international students: Required—TOEFL (minimum score 550 paper-based; 213 computer-based; 79 iBT). *Application deadline:* For fall admission, 3/15 priority date for domestic and international students. Application fee: $50. Electronic applications accepted. *Expenses:* Tuition, state resident: full-time $8592; part-time $358 per credit. Tuition, nonresident: full-time $21,672; part-time $903 per credit. Required fees: $119 per semester. One-time fee: $50. *Financial support:* In 2010–11, 8 students received support, including 4 fellowships with full tuition reimbursements available (averaging $7,500 per year), 12 research assistantships with partial tuition reimbursements available (averaging $6,000 per year), 4 teaching assistantships with tuition reimbursements available (averaging $7,500 per year); unspecified assistantships also available. Financial award application deadline: 3/15; financial award applicants required to submit FAFSA. *Faculty research:* Educational needs and program development, policy analysis and administration, excellence norms for cooperative education programs. Total annual research expenditures: $60,000. *Unit head:* Dr. John C. Morris, Graduate Program Director, 757-683-3961, Fax: 757-683-4886, E-mail: jcmorris@odu.edu. *Application contact:* Megan S. Jones, Graduate Program Manager, 757-683-3961, Fax: 757-683-4886, E-mail: mmjones@odu.edu.

Old Dominion University, College of Business and Public Administration, MBA Program, Norfolk, VA 23529. Offers business and economic forecasting (MBA); financial analysis and valuation (MBA); information technology and enterprise integration (MBA); international business (MBA); maritime and port management (MBA); public administration (MBA). *Accreditation:* AACSB. Part-time and evening/weekend programs available. *Faculty:* 66 full-time (15 women), 6 part-time/adjunct (1 woman). *Students:* 74 full-time (32 women), 166 part-time (62 women); includes 45 minority (21 Black or African American, non-Hispanic/Latino; 1 American Indian or Alaska Native, non-Hispanic/Latino; 8 Asian, non-Hispanic/Latino; 10 Hispanic/Latino; 1 Native Hawaiian or other Pacific Islander, non-Hispanic/Latino; 4 Two or more races, non-Hispanic/Latino), 19 international. Average age 31. 169 applicants, 52% accepted, 61 enrolled. In 2010, 100 master's awarded. *Entrance requirements:* For master's, GMAT, letter of reference, resume, coursework in calculus, essay. Additional exam requirements/recommendations for international students: Required—TOEFL (minimum score 550 paper-based; 213 computer-based; 80 iBT). *Application deadline:* For fall admission, 6/1 priority date for domestic students, 4/15 priority date for international students; for spring admission, 11/1 priority date for domestic students, 10/1 priority date for international students. Applications are processed on a rolling basis. Application fee: $50. Electronic applications accepted. *Expenses:* Tuition, state resident: full-time $8592; part-time $358 per credit. Tuition, nonresident: full-time $21,672; part-time $903 per credit. Required fees: $119 per semester. One-time fee: $50. *Financial support:* In 2010–11, 44 students received support, including 90 research assistantships with partial tuition reimbursements available (averaging $3,200 per year); career-related internships or fieldwork, scholarships/grants, and unspecified assistantships also available. Support available to part-time students. Financial award application deadline: 2/15; financial award applicants required to submit FAFSA. *Faculty research:* International business, buyer behavior, financial markets, strategy, operations research. *Unit head:* Dr. Larry Filer, Graduate Program Director, 757-683-3585, Fax: 757-683-5750, E-mail: mbainfo@odu.edu. *Application contact:* Shanna Wood, MBA Program Manager, 757-683-3585, Fax: 757-683-5750, E-mail: mbainfo@odu.edu.

Old Dominion University, College of Business and Public Administration, Program in Public Administration, Norfolk, VA 23529. Offers MPA. *Accreditation:* NASPAA. Part-time and evening/weekend programs available. *Faculty:* 7 full-time (2 women), 10 part-time/adjunct (7 women). *Students:* 43 full-time (29 women), 88 part-time (50 women); includes 47 minority (35 Black or African American, non-Hispanic/Latino; 2 American Indian or Alaska Native, non-Hispanic/Latino; 2 Asian, non-Hispanic/Latino; 6 Hispanic/Latino; 2 Two or more races, non-Hispanic/Latino), 4 international. Average age 34. 49 applicants, 78% accepted, 27 enrolled. In 2010, 39 master's awarded. *Degree requirements:* For master's, thesis optional, capstone seminar. *Entrance requirements:* For master's, GRE. Additional exam requirements/recommendations for international students: Required—TOEFL (minimum score 550 paper-based; 213 computer-based; 79 iBT). *Application deadline:* For fall admission, 7/15 for domestic students; for spring admission, 11/15 for domestic students. Applications are processed on a rolling basis. Application fee: $50. Electronic applications accepted. *Expenses:* Tuition, state resident: full-time $8592; part-time $358 per credit. Tuition, nonresident: full-time $21,672; part-time $903 per credit. Required fees: $119 per semester. One-time fee: $50. *Financial support:* In 2010–11, 5 students received support, including 6 research assistantships with partial tuition reimbursements available (averaging $6,400 per year); unspecified assistantships also available. Financial award application deadline: 2/15; financial award applicants required to submit FAFSA. *Faculty research:* Environmental administration, personnel policy analysis, urban administration. *Unit head:* Dr. William M. Leavitt, Graduate Program Director, 757-683-5695, Fax: 757-683-5639, E-mail: padmgpd@odu.edu. *Application contact:* Megan S. Jones, Graduate Program Manager, 757-683-3961, Fax: 757-683-4886, E-mail: mmjones@odu.edu.

Pace University, Dyson College of Arts and Sciences, Department of Public Administration, New York, NY 10038. Offers environmental management (MPA); government management (MPA); health care administration (MPA); management for public safety and homeland security (MA); nonprofit management (MPA); JD/MPA. Offered at White Plains, NY location only. Part-time and evening/weekend programs available. *Degree requirements:* For master's, capstone project. *Entrance requirements:* For master's, GRE General Test. Additional exam requirements/recommendations for international students: Required—TOEFL. Electronic applications accepted.

Park University, College of Graduate and Professional Studies, Kansas City, MO 54105. Offers adult education (M Ed); at-risk students (M Ed); disaster and emergency management (MPA); educational administration (M Ed); entrepreneurship (MBA); general business (MBA); general education (M Ed); government/business relations (MPA); healthcare/services management (MBA, MPA); international business (MBA); K-12 certification (MAT); management information systems (MBA); management of information systems (MPA); middle school certification (MAT); multi-cultural education (M Ed); nonprofit management (MPA); public management (MPA); school law (M Ed); secondary school certification (MAT); special education (M Ed). Part-time and evening/weekend programs available. Postbaccalaureate distance learning degree programs offered (no on-campus study). *Degree requirements:* For master's, comprehensive exam, thesis (for some programs). *Entrance requirements:* For master's, GRE, GMAT, teacher certification (M Ed). Additional exam requirements/recommendations for international students: Required—TOEFL (minimum score 550 paper-based). Electronic applications accepted. *Faculty research:* Literacy, leadership, brain based research, multicultural education, diversity.

Pepperdine University, School of Public Policy, Malibu, CA 90263. Offers American politics (MPP); economics (MPP); international relations (MPP); public policy (MPP); state and local policy (MPP). *Faculty:* 7 full-time (2 women), 10 part-time/adjunct (0 women). *Students:* 123 full-time (72 women), 4 part-time (all women); includes 36 minority (11 Black or African American, non-Hispanic/Latino; 2 American Indian or Alaska Native, non-Hispanic/Latino; 11 Asian, non-Hispanic/Latino; 9 Hispanic/Latino; 3 Two or more races, non-Hispanic/Latino), 13 international. 168 applicants, 93% accepted, 66 enrolled. In 2010, 50 master's awarded. *Entrance requirements:* For master's, GRE or GMAT, 2 letters of recommendation, resume, two essays. Additional exam requirements/recommendations for international students: Required—TOEFL. *Application deadline:* For fall admission, 5/1 for domestic students. Applications are processed on a rolling basis. Application fee: $50. Electronic applications accepted. *Financial support:* Institutionally sponsored loans and scholarships/grants available. Financial award application deadline: 5/1; financial award applicants required to submit FAFSA. *Unit head:* Dr. James R. Wilburn, Dean, 310-506-7490, Fax: 310-506-7494, E-mail: james.wilburn@pepperdine.edu. *Application contact:* Melinda E. van Hemert, Director of Recruitment and Career Services, 310-506-7492, Fax: 310-506-7494, E-mail: melinda.vanhemert@pepperdine.edu.

Pontifical Catholic University of Puerto Rico, College of Graduate Studies in Behavioral Science and Community Affairs, Program in Public Administration, Ponce, PR 00717-0777. Offers MSS. Part-time and evening/weekend programs available. *Degree requirements:* For master's, thesis. *Entrance requirements:* For master's, EXADEP, 3 letters of recommendation, interview, minimum GPA of 2.75.

Portland State University, Graduate Studies, College of Urban and Public Affairs, Hatfield School of Government, Division of Public Administration, Portland, OR 97207-0751. Offers public administration (MPA); public administration and policy (PhD). *Accreditation:* NASPAA (one or more programs are accredited). Part-time and evening/weekend programs available. *Faculty:* 16 full-time (8 women), 12 part-time/adjunct (6 women). *Students:* 93 full-time (53 women), 145 part-time (88 women); includes 32 minority (7 Black or African American, non-Hispanic/Latino; 4 American Indian or Alaska Native, non-Hispanic/Latino; 11 Asian, non-Hispanic/Latino; 4 Hispanic/Latino; 1 Native Hawaiian or other Pacific Islander, non-Hispanic/Latino; 5 Two or more races, non-Hispanic/Latino), 10 international. Average age 34. 144 applicants, 75% accepted, 69 enrolled. In 2010, 86 master's, 14 doctorates awarded. *Degree requirements:* For master's, internship (MPA), practicum (MPH); for doctorate, comprehensive exam, thesis/dissertation, residency. *Entrance requirements:* For master's, GRE, minimum GPA of 3.0 in upper-division course work or 2.75 overall, 3 recommendation forms, resume; for doctorate, GRE General Test, minimum GPA of 2.75. Additional exam requirements/recommendations for international students: Required—TOEFL (minimum score 550 paper-based; 213 computer-based). *Application deadline:* For fall admission, 4/1 for domestic students, 3/1 for international students; for winter admission, 9/1 for domestic students, 8/1 for international students; for spring admission, 11/1 for domestic and international students. Application fee: $50. *Expenses:* Tuition, state resident: full-time $8505; part-time $315 per credit. Tuition, nonresident: full-time $13,284; part-time $492 per credit. Required fees: $1482; $21 per credit. $99 per term. One-time fee: $120. Part-time tuition and fees vary according to course load and program. *Financial support:* In 2010–11, 2 research assistantships with full tuition reimbursements (averaging $7,686 per year) were awarded; teaching assistantships, career-related internships or fieldwork, Federal Work-Study, scholarships/grants, tuition waivers (partial), and unspecified assistantships also available. Support available to part-time students. Financial award application deadline: 3/1; financial award applicants required to submit FAFSA. *Faculty research:* Public budgeting, program evaluation, nonprofit management, natural resources policy and administration. Total annual research expenditures: $466,642. *Unit head:* Dr. Sherril Gelmon, Chair, 503-725-3920, Fax: 503-725-8250, E-mail: gelmons@pdx.edu. *Application contact:* Dr. Sherril Gelmon, Chair, 503-725-3920, Fax: 503-725-8250, E-mail: gelmons@pdx.edu.

Regent University, Graduate School, Robertson School of Government, Virginia Beach, VA 23464. Offers American government (MA); international politics (MA); political theory (MA); public administration (MA); JD/MA; M Div/MA; M Ed/MA; MBA/MA. Part-time and evening/weekend programs available. Postbaccalaureate distance learning degree programs offered (minimal on-campus study). *Faculty:* 6 full-time (1 woman), 11 part-time/adjunct (2 women). *Students:* 91 full-time (57 women), 62 part-time (37 women); includes 41 Black or African American, non-Hispanic/Latino; 3 Asian, non-Hispanic/Latino; 7 Hispanic/Latino, 1 international. Average age 30. 149 applicants, 61% accepted, 40 enrolled. In 2010, 59 master's awarded. *Degree requirements:* For master's, thesis optional, internship. *Entrance requirements:* For master's, GRE General Test or LSAT, minimum undergraduate GPA of 3.0, writing sample, resume, interview, references. Additional exam requirements/recommendations for international students: Required—TOEFL (minimum score 577 paper-based; 233 computer-based). *Application deadline:* For fall admission, 5/1 priority date for domestic students; for spring admission, 11/1 priority date for domestic students. Applications are processed on a rolling basis. Application fee: $50. Electronic applications accepted. *Expenses:* Contact institution. *Financial support:* Career-related internships or fieldwork, scholarships/grants, tuition waivers (full and partial), and unspecified assistantships available. Support available to part-time students. Financial award application deadline: 9/1; financial award applicants required to submit FAFSA. *Faculty research:* Education reform, political character issues, social capital concerns, administrative ethics, Biblical law and public policy. *Unit head:* Dr. Gary Roberts, Interim Dean, 757-352-4962, Fax: 757-352-4735, E-mail: garyrob@regent.edu. *Application contact:* Matthew Chadwick, Director of Enrollment Support Services, 800-373-5504, Fax: 757-352-4381, E-mail: admissions@regent.edu.

Public Administration

Rhode Island College, School of Graduate Studies, Faculty of Arts and Sciences, Department of Political Science, Providence, RI 02908-1991. Offers public administration (MPA). Part-time and evening/weekend programs available. *Faculty:* 2 full-time (0 women). *Entrance requirements:* For master's, GRE, GMAT, or MAT. Additional exam requirements/recommendations for international students: Recommended—TOEFL (minimum score 550 paper-based; 213 computer-based; 79 iBT). *Application deadline:* For fall admission, 3/1 for domestic students; for spring admission, 11/1 for domestic students. Applications are processed on a rolling basis. *Expenses:* Tuition, state resident: full-time $8208; part-time $342 per credit hour. Tuition, nonresident: full-time $16,080; part-time $670 per credit hour. Required fees: $554; $20 per credit. $72 per term. *Financial support:* Career-related internships or fieldwork, Federal Work-Study, scholarships/grants, health care benefits, and unspecified assistantships available. Support available to part-time students. Financial award application deadline: 5/15; financial award applicants required to submit FAFSA. *Unit head:* Dr. Thomas Schmeling, Chair, 401-456-8056. *Application contact:* Graduate Studies, 401-456-8700.

Roger Williams University, Feinstein College of Arts and Sciences, Program in Public Administration, Bristol, RI 02809. Offers MPA. Part-time and evening/weekend programs available. Postbaccalaureate distance learning degree programs offered (minimal on-campus study). *Degree requirements:* For master's, internship/research project. *Entrance requirements:* For master's, 2 letters of recommendation, curriculum vitae/resume. Additional exam requirements/recommendations for international students: Recommended—IELTS. Electronic applications accepted. *Expenses:* Contact institution.

Roosevelt University, Graduate Division, College of Arts and Sciences, Department of Political Science and Public Administration, Program in Public Administration, Chicago, IL 60605. Offers MPA. Part-time and evening/weekend programs available. *Degree requirements:* For master's, thesis optional. *Entrance requirements:* For master's, minimum undergraduate GPA of 3.0. *Faculty research:* Health policy issues, environmental policy, local government administration.

Rutgers, The State University of New Jersey, Camden, Graduate School of Arts and Sciences, Department of Public Policy and Administration, Camden, NJ 08102. Offers education policy and leadership (MPA); international public service and development (MPA); public management (MPA); JD/MPA; MPA/MA. *Accreditation:* NASPAA. Part-time and evening/weekend programs available. *Faculty:* 17 full-time (7 women), 3 part-time/adjunct (1 woman). *Students:* 75 full-time (45 women), 49 part-time (26 women); includes 38 Black or African American, non-Hispanic/Latino; 1 American Indian or Alaska Native, non-Hispanic/Latino; 5 Asian, non-Hispanic/Latino; 11 Hispanic/Latino. Average age 32. 132 applicants, 73% accepted, 58 enrolled. In 2010, 44 master's awarded. *Degree requirements:* For master's, directed study, research workshop, 42 credits. *Entrance requirements:* For master's, GRE General Test, GMAT or LSAT, 3 letters of recommendation; resume. Additional exam requirements/recommendations for international students: Required—TOEFL (minimum score 550 paper-based; 213 computer-based), IELTS. *Application deadline:* For fall admission, 5/1 priority date for domestic students; for spring admission, 12/1 priority date for domestic students. Applications are processed on a rolling basis. Application fee: $65. Electronic applications accepted. *Expenses:* Tuition, state resident: full-time $4963; part-time $319 per credit. Tuition, nonresident: full-time $10,493; part-time $680 per credit. *Financial support:* In 2010–11, 97 students received support, including 3 fellowships with partial tuition reimbursements available (averaging $3,500 per year), 1 research assistantship with full tuition reimbursement available (averaging $26,000 per year); career-related internships or fieldwork, Federal Work-Study, scholarships/grants, and tuition waivers (partial) also available. Financial award application deadline: 3/15; financial award applicants required to submit FAFSA. *Faculty research:* Nonprofit management, county and municipal administration, health and human services, government communication, administrative law, educational finance. Total annual research expenditures: $8.8 million. *Unit head:* Dr. Robyne Turner, Chair, 856-225-2982, Fax: 856-225-6559, E-mail: rsturner@camden.rutgers.edu. *Application contact:* Sandra J. Cheesman, Department Administrator, 856-225-6860, Fax: 856-225-6559, E-mail: scheesma@camden.rutgers.edu.

Rutgers, The State University of New Jersey, Newark, Graduate School, Program in Public Administration, Newark, NJ 07102. Offers health care administration (MPA); human resources administration (MPA); public administration (PhD); public management (MPA); public policy analysis (MPA); urban systems and issues (MPA). *Accreditation:* NASPAA (one or more programs are accredited). Part-time and evening/weekend programs available. *Faculty:* 9 full-time (3 women). *Students:* 19 full-time (12 women), 24 part-time (11 women); includes 10 Black or African American, non-Hispanic/Latino; 14 Asian, non-Hispanic/Latino; 3 Hispanic/Latino. 46 applicants, 24% accepted, 6 enrolled. In 2010, 8 doctorates awarded. *Degree requirements:* For master's, comprehensive exam, thesis or alternative; for doctorate, thesis/dissertation. *Entrance requirements:* For master's, GRE, minimum undergraduate B average; for doctorate, GRE, MPA, minimum B average. *Application deadline:* For fall admission, 7/1 priority date for domestic students; for spring admission, 12/1 for domestic students. Applications are processed on a rolling basis. Application fee: $60. Electronic applications accepted. *Expenses:* Tuition, state resident: part-time $600 per credit. Tuition, nonresident: full-time $10,694. *Financial support:* In 2010–11, 3 fellowships (averaging $18,000 per year), 11 teaching assistantships with full and partial tuition reimbursements (averaging $23,112 per year) were awarded; career-related internships or fieldwork also available. Support available to part-time students. Financial award application deadline: 3/1. *Faculty research:* Government finance, municipal and state government, public productivity. *Unit head:* Dr. Norma Riccucci, Chairman and Director, 973-353-5093 Ext. 16, E-mail: riccucci@andromeda.rutgers.edu. *Application contact:* Gail Daniels, Assistant Dean for Student Services, 201-973-5093 Ext. 11, E-mail: gaild@andromeda.rutgers.edu.

Sage Graduate School, Graduate School, School of Management, Program in Organization Management, Troy, NY 12180-4115. Offers organization management (MS); public administration (MS). Part-time and evening/weekend programs available. *Faculty:* 4 full-time (2 women), 8 part-time/adjunct (3 women). *Students:* 9 full-time (5 women), 43 part-time (29 women); includes 12 minority (10 Black or African American, non-Hispanic/Latino; 1 Asian, non-Hispanic/Latino; 1 Hispanic/Latino). Average age 32. 26 applicants, 69% accepted, 15 enrolled. In 2010, 19 master's awarded. *Degree requirements:* For master's, capstone seminar. *Entrance requirements:* For master's, minimum GPA of 2.75. Additional exam requirements/recommendations for international students: Required—TOEFL (minimum score 550 paper-based; 213 computer-based). *Application deadline:* Applications are processed on a rolling basis. Application fee: $40. *Expenses:* Tuition: Full-time $10,980; part-time $610 per credit hour. Tuition and fees vary according to course load, degree level and program. *Financial support:* Fellowships, research assistantships, Federal Work-Study, scholarships/grants, tuition waivers (partial), and unspecified assistantships available. Support available to part-time students. Financial award application deadline: 3/1; financial award applicants required to submit FAFSA. *Unit head:* Dr. Daniel Robeson, Dean, School of Management, 518-292-8637, Fax: 518-292-1964, E-mail: robesd@sage.edu. *Application contact:* Wendy D. Diefendorf, Director of Graduate and Adult Admission, 518-244-2443, Fax: 518-244-6880, E-mail: diefew@sage.edu.

Saginaw Valley State University, College of Arts and Behavioral Sciences, Program in Administrative Science, University Center, MI 48710. Offers MA. Part-time and evening/weekend programs available. *Students:* 23 full-time (12 women), 42 part-time (28 women); includes 12 Black or African American, non-Hispanic/Latino; 1 American Indian or Alaska Native, non-Hispanic/Latino; 1 Asian, non-Hispanic/Latino; 4 Hispanic/Latino, 2 international. Average age 33. 35 applicants, 83% accepted, 22 enrolled. In 2010, 22 master's awarded. *Degree requirements:* For master's, thesis optional. *Entrance requirements:* For master's, minimum GPA of 3.0 in social sciences, 2.75 overall. Additional exam requirements/recommendations for international students: Required—TOEFL. *Application deadline:* Applications are processed on a rolling basis. Application fee: $25. Electronic applications accepted. *Expenses:* Tuition, state resident: full-time $7902. *Financial support:* In 2010–11, 2 fellowships with partial tuition reimbursements, 1 research assistantship with full tuition reimbursement (averaging $5,000 per year) were awarded; Federal Work-Study also available. Support available to part-time students. Financial award application deadline: 4/1; financial award applicants required to submit FAFSA. *Unit head:* Mark Nicol, MAS Graduate Coordinator/Instructor of Political Science, 989-964-2605, E-mail: nlnicol@svsu.edu. *Application contact:* Mark Nicol, MAS Graduate Coordinator/Instructor of Political Science, 989-964-2605, E-mail: nlnicol@svsu.edu.

Saint Louis University, Graduate Education, College of Education and Public Service, Department of Public Policy Studies, St. Louis, MO 63103-2097. Offers geographic information systems (Certificate); organizational development (Certificate); public administration (MAPA); public policy analysis (PhD); urban affairs (MAUA); urban planning and real estate development (MUPRED). *Accreditation:* NASPAA. Part-time programs available. *Degree requirements:* For master's, comprehensive exam (for some programs), thesis (for some programs); for doctorate, comprehensive exam, thesis/dissertation, preliminary exams. *Entrance requirements:* For master's, GMAT, GRE General Test, or LSAT, letters of recommendation, resume; for doctorate, GMAT, GRE General Test, or LSAT, letters of recommendation, resumé, interview, transcripts, goal statement. Additional exam requirements/recommendations for international students: Required—TOEFL (minimum score 525 paper-based; 194 computer-based). Electronic applications accepted. *Faculty research:* Urban politics, brown fields, e-government, and administration, evaluation research, community development, electronic government and governance.

St. Mary's University, Graduate School, Department of Political Science, Program in Public Administration, San Antonio, TX 78228-8507. Offers inter-American administration (MPA); public management (MPA); JD/MPA. Part-time programs available. Postbaccalaureate distance learning degree programs offered (no on-campus study). *Degree requirements:* For master's, comprehensive exam, internship. *Entrance requirements:* For master's, GRE General Test. Additional exam requirements/recommendations for international students: Required—TOEFL (minimum score 550 paper-based; 213 computer-based; 80 iBT). Electronic applications accepted. *Faculty research:* Voting rights, natural resources, urban policy.

St. Thomas University, School of Business, Department of Management, Miami Gardens, FL 33054-6459. Offers accounting (MBA); general management (MSM, Certificate); health management (MBA, MSM, Certificate); human resource management (MBA, MSM, Certificate); international business (MBA, MIB, MSM, Certificate); justice administration (MSM, Certificate); management accounting (MSM, Certificate); public management (MSM, Certificate); sports administration (MS). Part-time and evening/weekend programs available. *Degree requirements:* For master's, comprehensive exam. *Entrance requirements:* For master's, interview, minimum GPA of 3.0 or GMAT. Additional exam requirements/recommendations for international students: Required—TOEFL (minimum score 550 paper-based; 213 computer-based; 79 iBT). Electronic applications accepted.

Sam Houston State University, College of Humanities and Social Sciences, Department of Political Science, Huntsville, TX 77341. Offers political science (MA); public administration (MPA). Evening/weekend programs available. *Faculty:* 8 full-time (5 women). *Students:* 10 full-time (7 women), 25 part-time (20 women); includes 4 Black or African American, non-Hispanic/Latino; 2 Hispanic/Latino, 2 international. Average age 33. 18 applicants, 94% accepted, 13 enrolled. In 2010, 9 master's awarded. *Degree requirements:* For master's, thesis or alternative. *Entrance requirements:* For master's, GRE General Test. Additional exam requirements/recommendations for international students: Required—TOEFL (minimum score 550 paper-based; 213 computer-based; 79 iBT). *Application deadline:* For fall admission, 8/1 for domestic students; for spring admission, 12/1 for domestic students. Applications are processed on a rolling basis. Application fee: $20. *Expenses:* Tuition, state resident: full-time $1363; part-time $163 per credit hour. Tuition, nonresident: full-time $3856; part-time $473 per credit hour. *Financial support:* Research assistantships, teaching assistantships, career-related internships or fieldwork and institutionally sponsored loans available. Support available to part-time students. Financial award application deadline: 5/31; financial award applicants required to submit FAFSA. *Unit head:* Dr. Rhonda Callaway, Chair, 936-294-4108, Fax: 936-294-4172, E-mail: rlc005@shsu.edu. *Application contact:* Dr. Tamara Waggener, Advisor, 936-294-1466, E-mail: pol_taw@shsu.edu.

San Diego State University, Graduate and Research Affairs, College of Professional Studies and Fine Arts, School of Public Affairs, Program in Public Administration, San Diego, CA 92182. Offers MPA. *Accreditation:* NASPAA. Part-time programs available. *Entrance requirements:* For master's, GRE General Test, 2 letters of reference. Additional exam requirements/recommendations for international students: Required—TOEFL. Electronic applications accepted.

San Francisco State University, Division of Graduate Studies, College of Behavioral and Social Sciences, Public Administration Program, San Francisco, CA 94132-1722. Offers nonprofit administration (MPA); policy making and analysis (MPA); public management (MPA); urban administration (MPA). *Accreditation:* NASPAA. *Unit head:* Dr. Genie Stowers, Chair, 415-817-4457, Fax: 415-338-1980, E-mail: gstowers@sfsu.edu. *Application contact:* Bridget McCracken, Director of Academic Services, 415-817-4455, E-mail: mpa@sfsu.edu.

San Jose State University, Graduate Studies and Research, College of Social Sciences, Department of Political Science, San Jose, CA 95192-0001. Offers public administration (MPA). *Accreditation:* NASPAA. Part-time and evening/weekend programs available. *Degree requirements:* For master's, comprehensive exam, thesis or alternative. *Entrance requirements:* For master's, GRE Subject Test. Additional exam requirements/recommendations for international students: Required—TOEFL (minimum score 575 paper-based). Electronic applications accepted. *Faculty research:* Modern political philosophy, international relations in the Middle East, public policy, American public policy, political parties and political reform.

Savannah State University, Master of Public Administration Program, Savannah, GA 31404. Offers MPA. *Accreditation:* NASPAA. Part-time programs available. *Faculty:* 5 full-time (2 women). *Students:* 15 full-time (11 women), 15 part-time (10 women); includes 28 minority (all Black or African American, non-Hispanic/Latino). Average age 29. In 2010, 7 master's awarded. *Degree requirements:* For master's, major paper, oral exam, public service internship. *Entrance requirements:* For master's, GRE General Test. Additional exam requirements/recommendations for international students: Required—TOEFL. *Application deadline:* For fall admission, 7/1 priority date for domestic students, 7/1 for international students; for spring admission, 10/31 priority date for domestic students, 10/1 for international students. Applications are processed on a rolling basis. Application fee: $25. *Expenses:* Tuition, state resident: full-time $4042. Tuition, nonresident: full-time $15,028. Required fees: $1350. *Financial support:* Career-related internships or fieldwork, Federal Work-Study, institutionally sponsored loans, scholarships/grants, and unspecified assistantships available. Financial award applicants required to submit FAFSA. *Faculty research:* Community development, human resources, leadership, conflict resolution. *Unit head:* Dr. Ronald Bailey, Interim Chair, 912-358-2331, E-mail: baileyr@savannahstate.edu. *Application contact:* Dr. Emily Crawford, Interim Dean of Graduate Studies, 912-358-4182, Fax: 912-356-2299, E-mail: crawford@savannahstate.edu.

Seattle University, College of Arts and Sciences, Institute of Public Service, Seattle, WA 98122-1090. Offers MPA. *Accreditation:* NASPAA. *Degree requirements:* For master's, thesis or alternative. *Entrance requirements:* For master's, minimum GPA of 3.0, 1 year work experience. *Faculty research:* Housing, experiential learning, citizenship education.

Seton Hall University, College of Arts and Sciences, Department of Public and Healthcare Administration, South Orange, NJ 07079-2697. Offers healthcare administration (MHA, Graduate Certificate); public administration (MPA, Graduate Certificate), including health policy and management (MPA), nonprofit organization management, public service: leadership, governance, and policy. *Accreditation:* NASPAA. Part-time and evening/weekend programs available. Postbaccalaureate distance learning degree programs offered (minimal on-campus study). *Degree requirements:* For master's, thesis or alternative, internship or practicum. *Entrance requirements:* Additional exam requirements/recommendations for international students: Required—TOEFL. Electronic applications accepted.

Shenandoah University, School of Education and Human Development, Winchester, VA 22601-5195. Offers administrative leadership (D Ed); advanced professional teaching English to speakers of other languages (Certificate); education (MSE); elementary education (Certificate); middle school education (Certificate); organizational leadership (MS, D Prof); professional studies (Certificate), including administration and supervision, ESL teacher education, reading specialist, special education; professional teaching English to speakers of other languages (Certificate); public management (Certificate); school reform (Certificate); secondary education (Certificate). *Accreditation:* Teacher Education Accreditation Council. Part-time and evening/weekend programs available. Postbaccalaureate distance learning degree programs offered (minimal on-campus study). *Faculty:* 14 full-time (8 women), 25 part-time/adjunct (20 women). *Students:* 22 full-time (14 women), 369 part-time (267 women); includes 27 minority (12 Black or African American, non-Hispanic/Latino; 4 Asian, non-Hispanic/Latino; 10 Hispanic/Latino; 1 Two or more races, non-Hispanic/Latino), 13 international. Average age 38. 270 applicants, 91% accepted, 187 enrolled. In 2010, 111 master's, 7 doctorates, 45 other advanced degrees awarded. *Degree requirements:* For master's, comprehensive exam (for some programs), thesis (for some programs), internship; for doctorate, comprehensive exam, thesis/dissertation; for Certificate, full time teaching in area for 1 year. *Entrance requirements:* For master's, minimum GPA of 3.0 or satisfactory GRE, 3 letters of recommendation, valid teaching license, writing sample; for doctorate, minimum graduate GPA of 3.5, 3 years of teaching experience, 3 letters of recommendation, writing samples, interview, resume; for Certificate, minimum undergraduate GPA of 3.0, essay, 3 letters of recommendation. Additional exam requirements/recommendations for international students: Required—TOEFL (minimum score 550 paper-based; 213 computer-based; 79 iBT), IELTS (minimum score 6.5), Sakae Institute of Study Abroad (550). *Application deadline:* For fall admission, 7/1 for domestic and international students; for spring admission, 10/15 for domestic and international students. Application fee: $30. Electronic applications accepted. *Expenses:* Tuition: Full-time $17,352; part-time $723 per credit. Tuition and fees vary according to course load and program. *Financial support:* Application deadline: 3/15. *Unit head:* Dr. Steven E. Humphries, Director, 540-535-3574, E-mail: shumphri@su.edu. *Application contact:* David Anthony, Dean of Admissions, 540-665-4581, Fax: 540-665-4627, E-mail: admit@su.edu.

Shippensburg University of Pennsylvania, School of Graduate Studies, College of Arts and Sciences, Department of Political Science, Shippensburg, PA 17257-2299. Offers public administration (MPA). Part-time and evening/weekend programs available. *Faculty:* 4 full-time (2 women). *Students:* 10 full-time (4 women), 31 part-time (13 women); includes 10 minority (7 Black or African American, non-Hispanic/Latino; 2 Asian, non-Hispanic/Latino; 1 Hispanic/Latino), 1 international. Average age 30. 26 applicants, 77% accepted, 9 enrolled. In 2010, 20 master's awarded. *Degree requirements:* For master's, thesis optional, thesis or internship, candidacy. *Entrance requirements:* For master's, GRE (if GPA less than 2.75), resume, 2-3 page writing sample, 6 credits of course work in political science or public administration. Additional exam requirements/recommendations for international students: Required—TOEFL (minimum score 580 paper-based; 237 computer-based); Recommended—IELTS (minimum score 6). *Application deadline:* For fall admission, 3/1 for international students; for spring admission, 7/1 for international students. Applications are processed on a rolling basis. Application fee: $30. Electronic applications accepted. *Expenses:* Tuition, state resident: full-time $6966. Tuition, nonresident: full-time $11,146. Required fees: $1802. *Financial support:* In 2010–11, 4 research assistantships with full tuition reimbursements (averaging $5,000 per year) were awarded; career-related internships or fieldwork, scholarships/grants, unspecified assistantships, and resident hall director and student payroll positions also available. Support available to part-time students. Financial award application deadline: 3/1; financial award applicants required to submit FAFSA. *Unit head:* Dr. Sara Grove, Chairperson, 717-477-1718, Fax: 717-477-4030, E-mail: sagrov@ship.edu. *Application contact:* Jeremy R. Goshorn, Associate Dean of Graduate Admissions, 717-477-1231, Fax: 717-477-4016, E-mail: jrgoshorn@ship.edu.

Sojourner-Douglass College, Graduate Program, Baltimore, MD 21205-1814. Offers human services (MASS); public administration (MASS); urban education (reading) (MASS). Part-time and evening/weekend programs available. *Degree requirements:* For master's, comprehensive exam, written proposal oral defense. *Entrance requirements:* For master's, Graduate Examination.

Sonoma State University, School of Social Sciences, Department of Political Science, Rohnert Park, CA 94928. Offers public administration (MPA). Part-time and evening/weekend programs available. *Faculty:* 3 full-time (1 woman), 3 part-time/adjunct (all women). *Students:* 1 (woman) full-time, 53 part-time (31 women); includes 18 minority (4 Black or African American, non-Hispanic/Latino; 4 Asian, non-Hispanic/Latino; 5 Hispanic/Latino; 1 Native Hawaiian or other Pacific Islander, non-Hispanic/Latino; 4 Two or more races, non-Hispanic/Latino). Average age 34. 22 applicants, 86% accepted, 10 enrolled. In 2010, 7 master's awarded. *Degree requirements:* For master's, thesis or alternative. *Entrance requirements:* For master's, GRE General Test, minimum GPA of 3.0. Additional exam requirements/recommendations for international students: Required—TOEFL (minimum score 500 paper-based; 173 computer-based). *Application deadline:* For fall admission, 11/30 for domestic students; for spring admission, 8/31 for domestic students. Application fee: $55. *Financial support:* Research assistantships, teaching assistantships, career-related internships or fieldwork and Federal Work-Study available. Support available to part-time students. Financial award application deadline: 3/2; financial award applicants required to submit FAFSA. *Unit head:* Dr. Robert McNamara, Chair, 707-664-2676. *Application contact:* Dr. David McCuan, Graduate Program Coordinator, 707-664-2179, Fax: 707-664-3920, E-mail: david.mccuan@sonoma.edu.

Southeast Missouri State University, School of Graduate Studies, Department of Political Science, Philosophy and Religion, Cape Girardeau, MO 63701-4799. Offers public administration (MPA). Part-time and evening/weekend programs available. *Faculty:* 6 full-time (0 women). *Students:* 6 full-time (2 women), 21 part-time (13 women); includes 6 minority (4 Black or African American, non-Hispanic/Latino; 1 Hispanic/Latino; 1 Native Hawaiian or other Pacific Islander, non-Hispanic/Latino), 2 international. Average age 28. 22 applicants, 100% accepted, 12 enrolled. In 2010, 5 master's awarded. *Degree requirements:* For master's, internship, thesis or other capstone experience. *Entrance requirements:* For master's, minimum undergraduate GPA of 2.7; statement of objectives; resume; 2 letters of evaluation. Additional exam requirements/recommendations for international students: Required—TOEFL (minimum score 600 paper-based; 213 computer-based; 79 iBT); Recommended—IELTS (minimum score 6). *Application deadline:* For fall admission, 8/1 for domestic students, 6/1 for international students; for spring admission, 11/21 for domestic students, 10/1 for international students. Applications are processed on a rolling basis. Application fee: $25 ($35 for international students). Electronic applications accepted. *Expenses:* Tuition, state resident: full-time $4698; part-time $261 per credit hour. Tuition, nonresident: full-time $8379; part-time $465.50 per credit hour. *Financial support:* In 2010–11, 13 students received support, including 1 teaching assistantship with full tuition reimbursement available (averaging $7,600 per year); career-related internships or fieldwork, Federal Work-Study, institutionally sponsored loans, scholarships/grants, tuition waivers (full), and unspecified assistantships also available. Financial award application deadline: 6/30; financial award applicants required to submit FAFSA. *Faculty research:* American political institutions, state and local government, non-profit management. *Unit head:* Dr. Hamner Hill, Chairperson, 573-651-2816, Fax: 573-651-2695, E-mail: hhill@semo.edu. *Application contact:* Gail Amick, Administrative Secretary, 573-651-2049, Fax: 573-651-2001, E-mail: gamick@semo.edu.

Southern Arkansas University–Magnolia, Graduate Programs, Magnolia, AR 71753. Offers agriculture (MS); business administration (MBA); computer and information sciences (MS); education (M Ed), including counseling and development, curriculum and instruction emphasis, educational administration and supervision, elementary education, middle level emphasis, reading emphasis, secondary education, TESOL emphasis; kinesiology (M Ed); library media and information specialist (M Ed); mental health and clinical counseling (MS); public administration (MPA); school counseling (M Ed); teaching (MAT). *Accreditation:* NCATE. Part-time and evening/weekend programs available. *Faculty:* 32 full-time (16 women), 6 part-time/

adjunct (5 women). *Students:* 71 full-time (43 women), 364 part-time (275 women); includes 109 Black or African American, non-Hispanic/Latino; 1 American Indian or Alaska Native, non-Hispanic/Latino; 3 Asian, non-Hispanic/Latino, 19 international. Average age 33. 107 applicants, 71% accepted, 69 enrolled. In 2010, 157 master's awarded. *Degree requirements:* For master's, comprehensive exam, thesis optional. *Entrance requirements:* For master's, GRE, MAT or GMAT, minimum GPA of 2.75. *Application deadline:* For fall admission, 7/31 for domestic students; for winter admission, 12/1 for domestic students; for spring admission, 12/1 for domestic students. Applications are processed on a rolling basis. Application fee: $25. *Expenses:* Tuition, state resident: part-time $221 per hour. Tuition, nonresident: part-time $325 per hour. *Financial support:* Career-related internships or fieldwork, Federal Work-Study, scholarships/grants, tuition waivers (full), and unspecified assistantships available. Financial award applicants required to submit FAFSA. *Faculty research:* Alternative certification for teachers, supervision of instruction, instructional leadership, counseling. *Unit head:* Dr. Kim Bloss, Dean, Graduate Studies, 870-235-4150, Fax: 870-235-5227, E-mail: kkbloss@saumag.edu. *Application contact:* Dr. Kim Bloss, Dean, Graduate Studies, 870-235-4150, Fax: 870-235-5227, E-mail: kkbloss@saumag.edu.

Southern Illinois University Carbondale, Graduate School, College of Liberal Arts, Department of Political Science, Public Administration Program, Carbondale, IL 62901-4701. Offers MPA, JD/MPA. *Accreditation:* NASPAA. Part-time programs available. *Degree requirements:* For master's, thesis or alternative. *Entrance requirements:* For master's, minimum GPA of 2.7. Additional exam requirements/recommendations for international students: Required—TOEFL. *Faculty research:* Natural resources and environmental management, intergovernmental relations, state mandates, rural administration, economic development policy, nonprofit management.

Southern Illinois University Edwardsville, Graduate School, College of Arts and Sciences, Department of Public Administration and Policy Analysis, Edwardsville, IL 62026. Offers public administration (MPA). *Accreditation:* NASPAA. Part-time and evening/weekend programs available. *Faculty:* 6 full-time (2 women). *Students:* 57 full-time (37 women), 76 part-time (44 women); includes 48 minority (41 Black or African American, non-Hispanic/Latino; 2 Asian, non-Hispanic/Latino; 2 Hispanic/Latino; 3 Two or more races, non-Hispanic/Latino), 9 international. Average age 26. 83 applicants, 88% accepted. In 2010, 52 master's awarded. *Degree requirements:* For master's, comprehensive exam, final exam. *Entrance requirements:* Additional exam requirements/recommendations for international students: Required—TOEFL (minimum score 550 paper-based; 213 computer-based; 79 iBT), IELTS (minimum score 6.5). *Application deadline:* For fall admission, 7/22 for domestic students, 6/1 for international students; for spring admission, 12/9 for domestic students, 10/1 for international students. Applications are processed on a rolling basis. Application fee: $30. Electronic applications accepted. *Expenses:* Tuition, state resident: full-time $6012; part-time $1503 per semester. Tuition, nonresident: full-time $15,030; part-time $3758 per semester. Required fees: $1711; $675 per semester. *Financial support:* In 2010–11, research assistantships with full tuition reimbursements (averaging $8,064 per year), 32 teaching assistantships with full tuition reimbursements (averaging $8,064 per year) were awarded; fellowships with full tuition reimbursements, career-related internships or fieldwork, Federal Work-Study, institutionally sponsored loans, scholarships/grants, traineeships, and unspecified assistantships also available. Support available to part-time students. Financial award application deadline: 3/1; financial award applicants required to submit FAFSA. *Unit head:* Dr. T. R. Carr, Chair, 618-650-3762, E-mail: tcarr@siue.edu. *Application contact:* Dr. Drew Dolan, Program Director, 618-650-3762, E-mail: ddolan@siue.edu.

Southern University and Agricultural and Mechanical College, Graduate School, Nelson Mandela School of Public Policy and Urban Affairs, Department of Public Administration, Baton Rouge, LA 70813. Offers MPA. *Accreditation:* NASPAA. Part-time and evening/weekend programs available. *Degree requirements:* For master's, thesis. *Entrance requirements:* For master's, GRE General Test. Additional exam requirements/recommendations for international students: Required—TOEFL (minimum score 525 paper-based; 193 computer-based). *Faculty research:* Fiscal policy, public finance policy and practitioner interests; minority politics, healthcare and political economy.

Southern Utah University, College of Humanities and Social Sciences, Program in Public Administration, Cedar City, UT 84720-2498. Offers MS. *Faculty:* 5 full-time (0 women), 2 part-time/adjunct (1 woman). *Students:* 8 full-time (3 women), 34 part-time (8 women); includes 1 Black or African American, non-Hispanic/Latino; 1 Asian, non-Hispanic/Latino; 2 Hispanic/Latino; 2 Native Hawaiian or other Pacific Islander, non-Hispanic/Latino. 20 applicants, 95% accepted, 16 enrolled. In 2010, 11 master's awarded. *Application deadline:* Applications are processed on a rolling basis. Application fee: $50 ($65 for international students). Electronic applications accepted. *Unit head:* Dr. James McDonald, Dean, 435-586-7898, Fax: 435-865-8193, E-mail: mcdonaldj@suu.edu. *Application contact:* Sandi Levy, Administrative Assistant, 435-865-8420, Fax: 435-586-1925.

State University of New York at Binghamton, Graduate School, College of Community and Public Affairs, Department of Public Administration, Binghamton, NY 13902-6000. Offers MPA. *Faculty:* 7 full-time (4 women). *Students:* 56 full-time (35 women), 29 part-time (20 women); includes 8 Black or African American, non-Hispanic/Latino; 2 Asian, non-Hispanic/Latino; 3 Hispanic/Latino, 10 international. Average age 29. 81 applicants, 68% accepted, 29 enrolled. In 2010, 35 master's awarded. Application fee: $60. *Financial support:* In 2010–11, 13 students received support, including 1 fellowship with full tuition reimbursement available (averaging $10,000 per year), 1 teaching assistantship with full tuition reimbursement available (averaging $10,000 per year); career-related internships or fieldwork, Federal Work-Study, institutionally sponsored loans, scholarships/grants, health care benefits, and unspecified assistantships also available. Financial award application deadline: 2/15; financial award applicants required to submit FAFSA. *Unit head:* Dr. Kristina Lambright, Chairperson, 607-777-9186, E-mail: klambrig@binghamton.edu. *Application contact:* Catherine Smith, Recruiting and Admissions Coordinator, 607-777-2151, Fax: 607-777-2501, E-mail: cmsmith@binghamton.edu.

Stephen F. Austin State University, Graduate School, College of Liberal Arts, Department of Political Science and Geography, Nacogdoches, TX 75962. Offers public administration (MPA). *Degree requirements:* For master's, thesis optional. *Entrance requirements:* For master's, GRE General Test. Additional exam requirements/recommendations for international students: Required—TOEFL.

Strayer University, Graduate Studies, Washington, DC 20005-2603. Offers accounting (MS); acquisition (MBA); business administration (MBA); communications technology (MS); educational management (M Ed); finance (MBA); health services administration (MHSA); hospitality and tourism management (MBA); human resource management (MBA); information systems (MS), including computer security management, decision support system management, enterprise resource management, network management, software engineering management, systems development management; management (MBA); management information systems (MS); marketing (MBA); professional accounting (MS), including accounting information systems, controllership, taxation; public administration (MPA); supply chain management (MBA); technology in education (M Ed). Programs also offered at campus locations in Birmingham, AL; Chamblee, GA; Cobb County, GA; Morrow, GA; White Marsh, MD; Charleston, SC; Columbia, SC; Greensboro, NC; Greenville, SC; Lexington, KY; Louisville, KY; Nashville, TN; North Raleigh, NC; Washington, DC. Part-time and evening/weekend programs available. Postbaccalaureate distance learning degree programs offered (minimal on-campus study). *Degree requirements:* For master's, thesis. *Entrance requirements:* For master's, GMAT, GRE General Test, bachelor's degree from an accredited college or university, minimum undergraduate GPA of 2.75. Electronic applications accepted.

Suffolk University, Sawyer Business School, Department of Public Administration, Boston, MA 02108-2770. Offers nonprofit management (MPA); public administration (CASPA); state and local government (MPA); JD/MPA; MPA/MS. *Accreditation:* NASPAA (one or more programs are accredited). Part-time and evening/weekend programs available. *Faculty:* 9 full-time (4 women), 5 part-time/adjunct (2 women). *Students:* 30 full-time (17 women), 102 part-time (65

Public Administration

Suffolk University (continued)
women); includes 12 Black or African American, non-Hispanic/Latino; 1 American Indian or Alaska Native, non-Hispanic/Latino; 3 Asian, non-Hispanic/Latino; 8 Hispanic/Latino; 2 Two or more races, non-Hispanic/Latino, 5 international. Average age 31. 76 applicants, 87% accepted, 28 enrolled. In 2010, 62 master's awarded. *Entrance requirements:* Additional exam requirements/recommendations for international students: Required—TOEFL (minimum score 550 paper-based; 213 computer-based; 80 iBT). *Application deadline:* For fall admission, 6/15 priority date for domestic students, 6/15 for international students; for spring admission, 11/1 priority date for domestic students, 11/1 for international students. Applications are processed on a rolling basis. Application fee: $50. Electronic applications accepted. *Expenses:* Contact institution. *Financial support:* In 2010–11, 93 students received support, including 52 fellowships with full and partial tuition reimbursements available (averaging $9,356 per year); career-related internships or fieldwork and Federal Work-Study also available. Support available to part-time students. Financial award application deadline: 4/1; financial award applicants required to submit FAFSA. *Faculty research:* Local government, health care, federal policy, mental health, HIV/AIDS. *Unit head:* Dr. Richard Beinecke, Chair, 617-573-8062, Fax: 617-227-4618, E-mail: rbeineck@suffolk.edu. *Application contact:* Judith Reynolds, Director of Graduate Admissions, 617-573-8302, Fax: 617-305-1733, E-mail: grad.admission@suffolk.edu.

Sul Ross State University, School of Arts and Sciences, Department of Behavioral and Social Sciences, Program in Public Administration, Alpine, TX 79832. Offers MA. Part-time and evening/weekend programs available. *Entrance requirements:* For master's, GRE General Test, minimum GPA of 2.5 in last 60 hours of undergraduate work. *Faculty research:* Local government, state government, personnel, volunteer fire departments, rural health.

Syracuse University, Maxwell School of Citizenship and Public Affairs, Executive Master of Public Administration Program, Syracuse, NY 13244. Offers EMPA. Part-time programs available. *Students:* 47 full-time (13 women), 23 part-time (10 women); includes 3 minority (all Black or African American, non-Hispanic/Latino), 46 international. Average age 40. 76 applicants, 57% accepted, 27 enrolled. In 2010, 56 master's awarded. *Entrance requirements:* For master's, 7 years of mid-career experience. Additional exam requirements/recommendations for international students: Required—TOEFL (minimum score 100 iBT). *Application deadline:* For fall admission, 2/1 priority date for domestic and international students; for spring admission, 8/15 priority date for domestic and international students. Applications are processed on a rolling basis. Application fee: $75. Electronic applications accepted. *Expenses:* Tuition: Part-time $1162 per credit. *Financial support:* Application deadline: 2/1. *Unit head:* Steve Lux, Director, 315-443-3759. *Application contact:* Margaret Lane, Assistant Director, 315-443-8708, E-mail: melane@syr.edu.

Syracuse University, Maxwell School of Citizenship and Public Affairs, International Relations/Public Administration Joint Program, Syracuse, NY 13244. Offers MPA/MA. *Students:* 32 full-time (19 women), 2 part-time (1 woman); includes 6 minority (2 Black or African American, non-Hispanic/Latino; 4 Asian, non-Hispanic/Latino), 2 international. Average age 26. 66 applicants, 65% accepted, 19 enrolled. *Entrance requirements:* Additional exam requirements/recommendations for international students: Required—TOEFL (minimum score 100 iBT). *Application deadline:* For fall admission, 2/1 priority date for domestic and international students. Application fee: $75. Electronic applications accepted. *Expenses:* Tuition: Part-time $1162 per credit. *Financial support:* Fellowships with full tuition reimbursements, research assistantships with full and partial tuition reimbursements, teaching assistantships with full and partial tuition reimbursements available. Financial award application deadline: 1/1; financial award applicants required to submit FAFSA. *Unit head:* Donald Planty, Chair and Ambassador, 315-443-2306. *Application contact:* Nell Silva Bartkowiak, Director, International Relations, 315-443-9340, E-mail: nsbartko@syr.edu.

Syracuse University, Maxwell School of Citizenship and Public Affairs, Program in Public Administration, Syracuse, NY 13244. Offers EMPA, MPA, PhD, CAS, MPA/MA. *Accreditation:* NASPAA (one or more programs are accredited). Part-time programs available. *Students:* 121 full-time (66 women), 17 part-time (8 women); includes 31 minority (9 Black or African American, non-Hispanic/Latino; 11 Asian, non-Hispanic/Latino; 11 Hispanic/Latino), 33 international. Average age 29. 538 applicants, 48% accepted, 92 enrolled. In 2010, 32 master's, 4 doctorates, 8 other advanced degrees awarded. *Degree requirements:* For doctorate, comprehensive exam, thesis/dissertation. *Entrance requirements:* For master's, GRE General Test (MPA), 7 years of work experience (EMPA); for doctorate, GRE General Test. Additional exam requirements/recommendations for international students: Required—TOEFL (minimum score 100 iBT). *Application deadline:* For fall admission, 2/1 priority date for domestic and international students. Application fee: $75. Electronic applications accepted. *Expenses:* Tuition: Part-time $1162 per credit. *Financial support:* Fellowships with full tuition reimbursements, research assistantships with full and partial tuition reimbursements, teaching assistantships with full and partial tuition reimbursements, scholarships/grants and unspecified assistantships available. Financial award application deadline: 1/1; financial award applicants required to submit FAFSA. *Unit head:* Dr. Stuart Bretschneider, Chair, 315-443-4000, Fax: 315-443-5330, E-mail: sibretsc@syr.edu. *Application contact:* Christine Omolino, Associate Director, 315-443-3712, Fax: 315-443-5330, E-mail: comolino@syr.edu.

Syracuse University, Maxwell School of Citizenship and Public Affairs, Program in Public Management and Policy, Syracuse, NY 13244. Offers CAS. Part-time programs available. *Entrance requirements:* For degree, matriculated graduate student status. Additional exam requirements/recommendations for international students: Required—TOEFL (minimum score 100 iBT). *Application deadline:* For fall admission, 2/1 priority date for domestic and international students. Application fee: $75. Electronic applications accepted. *Expenses:* Tuition: Part-time $1162 per credit. *Unit head:* Margaret Lane, Director, Executive Education, 315-443-2878, Fax: 315-443-3385, E-mail: meland@syr.edu. *Application contact:* Margaret Lane, Director, Executive Education, 315-443-2878, Fax: 315-443-3385, E-mail: meland@syr.edu.

Tennessee State University, The School of Graduate Studies and Research, Institute of Government, Nashville, TN 37209-1561. Offers public administration (MPA, PhD). *Accreditation:* NASPAA (one or more programs are accredited). Part-time and evening/weekend programs available. *Degree requirements:* For master's, comprehensive exam, thesis optional; for doctorate, comprehensive exam, thesis/dissertation. *Entrance requirements:* For master's, GRE General Test, minimum GPA of 2.5, writing sample; for doctorate, GRE General Test, minimum GPA of 3.25, writing sample. *Faculty research:* Total quality management and process improvement, national health care policy and administration, starting non-profit ventures, public service ethics, state education financing across the U.S. public.

Texas A&M International University, Office of Graduate Studies and Research, College of Arts and Sciences, Department of Social Sciences, Laredo, TX 78041-1900. Offers history (MA); political science (MA); public administration (MPA). *Faculty:* 8 full-time (3 women). *Students:* 4 full-time (2 women), 52 part-time (27 women); includes 1 Asian, non-Hispanic/Latino; 52 Hispanic/Latino, 1 international. Average age 30. 35 applicants, 74% accepted, 19 enrolled. In 2010, 10 master's awarded. *Degree requirements:* For master's, thesis (for some programs). *Entrance requirements:* For master's, GRE General Test. Additional exam requirements/recommendations for international students: Required—TOEFL (minimum score 550 paper-based; 213 computer-based). *Application deadline:* For fall admission, 4/30 priority date for domestic students; for spring admission, 11/30 for domestic students, 10/1 for international students. Applications are processed on a rolling basis. Application fee: $25. *Financial support:* In 2010–11, 14 students received support, including 7 research assistantships. Financial award application deadline: 11/1. *Unit head:* Dr. Mohammed Ben-Ruwin, Chair, 956-328-2632, E-mail: mbenruwin@tamiu.edu. *Application contact:* Suzanne Hansen-Alford, Director of Admissions, 956-326-3023, Fax: 956-326-3021, E-mail: graduateschool@tamiu.edu.

Texas A&M University, Bush School of Government and Public Service, College Station, TX 77843. Offers advanced international affairs (Certificate); China studies (Certificate); homeland security (Certificate); international affairs (MRIA); national security affairs (Certificate); nonprofit management (Certificate); public service and administration (MPSA). *Accreditation:* NASPAA. *Faculty:* 45. *Students:* 215 full-time (98 women), 93 part-time (32 women); includes 20 Black or African American, non-Hispanic/Latino; 2 American Indian or Alaska Native, non-Hispanic/Latino; 14 Asian, non-Hispanic/Latino; 30 Hispanic/Latino, 15 international. Average age 24. In 2010, 93 master's awarded. *Degree requirements:* For master's, summer internship. *Entrance requirements:* For master's, GRE (preferred) or GMAT. *Application deadline:* For fall admission, 1/24 for domestic and international students. Application fee: $50 ($75 for international students). Electronic applications accepted. *Financial support:* In 2010–11, fellowships (averaging $11,000 per year), research assistantships (averaging $11,250 per year) were awarded; career-related internships or fieldwork, Federal Work-Study, and institutionally sponsored loans also available. Financial award application deadline: 2/1; financial award applicants required to submit FAFSA. *Faculty research:* Public policy, presidential studies, public leadership, economic policy, social policy. *Unit head:* Ryan C. Crocker, Dean, 979-862-8007, E-mail: rcrocker@bushschool.tamu.edu. *Application contact:* Kathryn Meyer, Director of Recruiting, 979-458-4767, Fax: 979-845-4155, E-mail: kmeyer@bushschool.tamu.edu.

Texas A&M University–Corpus Christi, Graduate Studies and Research, College of Liberal Arts, Corpus Christi, TX 78412-5503. Offers English (MA); history (MA); psychology (MA); public administration (MPA); studio arts (MA, MFA). Part-time and evening/weekend programs available. *Degree requirements:* For master's, comprehensive exam, thesis (for some programs). *Entrance requirements:* For master's, GRE General Test. Additional exam requirements/recommendations for international students: Required—TOEFL. Electronic applications accepted.

Texas Southern University, School of Public Affairs, Program in Public Administration, Houston, TX 77004-4584. Offers MPA. *Faculty:* 8 full-time (2 women), 5 part-time/adjunct (0 women). *Students:* 125 full-time (63 women), 18 part-time (11 women); includes 131 Black or African American, non-Hispanic/Latino; 6 Asian, non-Hispanic/Latino; 5 Hispanic/Latino, 1 international. Average age 32. 89 applicants, 100% accepted, 79 enrolled. In 2010, 33 master's awarded. *Degree requirements:* For master's, comprehensive exam, thesis optional. *Entrance requirements:* For master's, GRE General Test, minimum GPA of 2.5. Additional exam requirements/recommendations for international students: Required—TOEFL. *Application deadline:* For fall admission, 7/1 for domestic and international students; for spring admission, 11/1 for domestic and international students. Applications are processed on a rolling basis. Application fee: $50 ($75 for international students). Electronic applications accepted. *Expenses:* Tuition, state resident: full-time $1875; part-time $100 per credit hour. Tuition, nonresident: full-time $6641; part-time $343 per credit hour. Tuition and fees vary according to course level, course load and degree level. *Financial support:* In 2010–11, 1 research assistantship (averaging $1,500 per year), 17 teaching assistantships (averaging $2,894 per year) were awarded; fellowships, career-related internships or fieldwork, scholarships/grants, and unspecified assistantships also available. Financial award application deadline: 5/1. *Unit head:* Dr. Franklin Jones, Chair, 713-313-7313, E-mail: jones_fd@tsu.edu. *Application contact:* Dr. Franklin Jones, Chair, 713-313-7313, E-mail: jones_fd@tsu.edu.

Texas State University–San Marcos, Graduate School, College of Liberal Arts, Department of Political Science, Program in Public Administration, San Marcos, TX 78666. Offers MPA. *Accreditation:* NASPAA. Part-time and evening/weekend programs available. *Faculty:* 11 full-time (6 women). *Students:* 39 full-time (19 women), 132 part-time (74 women); includes 82 minority (22 Black or African American, non-Hispanic/Latino; 3 Asian, non-Hispanic/Latino; 52 Hispanic/Latino; 5 Two or more races, non-Hispanic/Latino). Average age 30. 44 applicants, 86% accepted, 28 enrolled. In 2010, 32 master's awarded. *Degree requirements:* For master's, comprehensive exam, applied research project. *Entrance requirements:* For master's, GRE General Test, minimum GPA of 2.75 in last 60 hours of course work. Additional exam requirements/recommendations for international students: Required—TOEFL (minimum score 550 paper-based; 213 computer-based; 78 iBT), TWE. *Application deadline:* For fall admission, 6/15 priority date for domestic students, 6/1 priority date for international students; for spring admission, 10/15 priority date for domestic students, 10/1 priority date for international students. Applications are processed on a rolling basis. Application fee: $40 ($90 for international students). Electronic applications accepted. *Expenses:* Tuition, state resident: full-time $6024; part-time $251 per credit hour. Tuition, nonresident: full-time $13,536; part-time $564 per credit hour. Required fees: $1776; $50 per credit hour. $306 per semester. *Financial support:* In 2010–11, 63 students received support, including 12 teaching assistantships (averaging $5,217 per year); research assistantships, career-related internships or fieldwork, Federal Work-Study, institutionally sponsored loans, scholarships/grants, and unspecified assistantships also available. Support available to part-time students. Financial award application deadline: 4/1; financial award applicants required to submit FAFSA. *Unit head:* Dr. Patricia Shields, Graduate Advisor, 512-245-7582, Fax: 512-245-7815, E-mail: ps07@txstate.edu. *Application contact:* Dr. J. Michael Willoughby, Dean of Graduate School, 512-245-2581, Fax: 512-245-8365, E-mail: gradcollege@txstate.edu.

Thomas Edison State College, School of Business and Management, Program in Public Service Leadership, Trenton, NJ 08608-1176. Offers Graduate Certificate. Part-time programs available. Postbaccalaureate distance learning degree programs offered (no on-campus study). *Students:* 4 part-time (1 woman); includes 2 Black or African American, non-Hispanic/Latino. Average age 42. *Entrance requirements:* Additional exam requirements/recommendations for international students: Required—TOEFL (minimum score 550 paper-based; 213 computer-based; 79 iBT). *Application deadline:* For fall admission, 8/15 priority date for domestic and international students; for winter admission, 11/15 priority date for domestic and international students; for spring admission, 2/15 priority date for domestic and international students. Applications are processed on a rolling basis. Application fee: $75. Electronic applications accepted. *Financial support:* Applicants required to submit FAFSA. *Unit head:* Dr. Susan Gilbert, Dean, School of Business and Management, 609-984-1130, Fax: 609-984-3898, E-mail: info@tesc.edu. *Application contact:* David Hoftiezer, Director of Admissions, 888-442-8372, Fax: 609-984-8447, E-mail: admissions@tesc.edu.

Troy University, Graduate School, College of Arts and Sciences, Program in Public Administration, Troy, AL 36082. Offers education (MPA); environmental management (MPA); government contracting (MPA); health care administration (MPA); justice administration (MPA); national security affairs (MPA); nonprofit management (MPA); public human resources management (MPA); public management (MPA). *Accreditation:* NASPAA. Part-time and evening/weekend programs available. Postbaccalaureate distance learning degree programs offered (no on-campus study). *Degree requirements:* For master's, capstone course, research methodologies course. *Entrance requirements:* For master's, GRE, MAT or GMAT, minimum undergraduate GPA of 2.5, letter of recommendation, essay. Additional exam requirements/recommendations for international students: Required—TOEFL (minimum score 523 paper-based; 193 computer-based; 70 iBT), IELTS (minimum score 6). *Application deadline:* Applications are processed on a rolling basis. Application fee: $50. Electronic applications accepted. *Expenses:* Tuition, state resident: full-time $4428; part-time $246 per credit hour. Tuition, nonresident: full-time $8856; part-time $492 per credit hour. Required fees: $432; $24 per credit hour. $50 per term. Tuition and fees vary according to program. *Financial support:* Available to part-time students. Applicants required to submit FAFSA. *Unit head:* Dr. Ellen Rosell, Chairman, 334-670-3758, Fax: 334-670-5647, E-mail: erosell@troy.edu. *Application contact:* Brenda K. Campbell, Director of Graduate Admissions, 334-670-3178, Fax: 334-670-3733, E-mail: bcamp@troy.edu.

Troy University, Graduate School, College of Business, Program in Management, Troy, AL 36082. Offers applied management (MSM); healthcare management (MSM); human resources management (MSM); information systems (MSM); international hospitality management (MSM); international management (MSM); leadership and organizational effectiveness (MSM); public management (MS, MSM). *Accreditation:* ACBSP. Evening/weekend programs available. *Students:* 101 full-time (62 women), 398 part-time (249 women); includes 308 minority (278 Black or African American, non-Hispanic/Latino; 8 American Indian or Alaska Native, non-Hispanic/Latino; 8 Asian, non-Hispanic/Latino; 13 Hispanic/Latino; 1 Two or more races, non-Hispanic/Latino). Average age 35. 218 applicants, 80% accepted. In 2010, 314 master's awarded. *Degree requirements:* For master's, Graduate Educational Testing Service Major Field Test, capstone exam, minimum GPA of 3.0. *Entrance requirements:* For master's, GMAT (minimum score 500) or GRE General Test (minimum score 900), minimum GPA of 2.5, bachelor's degree, letter of recommendation. Additional exam requirements/recommendations for international students: Required—TOEFL (minimum score 523 paper-based; 193 computer-based; 70 iBT), IELTS, or ACT compass ESL (minimum Listening, Reading, and Grammar score: 270). *Application deadline:* Applications are processed on a rolling basis. Application fee: $50. Electronic applications accepted. *Expenses:* Contact institution. *Unit head:* Dr. Henry M. Findley, Interim Chair/Professor, 334-670-3271, Fax: 334-670-3599, E-mail: hfindley@troy.edu. *Application contact:* Brenda K. Campbell, Director of Graduate Admissions, 334-670-3178, Fax: 334-670-3733, E-mail: bcamp@troy.edu.

Troy University, Graduate School, College of Education, Program in Postsecondary Education, Troy, AL 36082. Offers adult education (M Ed); biology (M Ed); criminal justice (M Ed); English (M Ed); foundations of education (M Ed); general science (M Ed); higher education administration (M Ed); history (M Ed); instructional technology (M Ed); mathematics (M Ed); music industry (M Ed); physical fitness (M Ed); political science (M Ed); public administration (M Ed); social science (M Ed); teaching English (M Ed). *Accreditation:* NCATE. Part-time and evening/weekend programs available. *Students:* 314 full-time (247 women), 153 part-time (122 women); includes 255 minority (242 Black or African American, non-Hispanic/Latino; 3 American Indian or Alaska Native, non-Hispanic/Latino; 5 Asian, non-Hispanic/Latino; 5 Hispanic/Latino). Average age 34. 223 applicants, 89% accepted. In 2010, 364 master's awarded. *Degree requirements:* For master's, comprehensive exam, thesis. *Entrance requirements:* For master's, MAT (minimum score 385), minimum GPA of 2.5. Additional exam requirements/recommendations for international students: Required—TOEFL (minimum score 523 paper-based; 193 computer-based; 70 iBT), IELTS, or ACT compass ESL (minimum Listening, Reading, and Grammar score: 270). *Application deadline:* Applications are processed on a rolling basis. Application fee: $50. Electronic applications accepted. *Expenses:* Tuition, state resident: full-time $4428; part-time $246 per credit hour. Tuition, nonresident: full-time $8856; part-time $492 per credit hour. Required fees: $432; $24 per credit hour. $50 per term. Tuition and fees vary according to program. *Financial support:* Available to part-time students. Applicants required to submit FAFSA. *Unit head:* Dr. Andrew Creamer, Chair, 334-670-3350, Fax: 334-670-3296, E-mail: drcreamer@troy.edu. *Application contact:* Brenda K. Campbell, Director of Graduate Admissions, 334-670-3178, Fax: 334-670-3733, E-mail: bcamp@troy.edu.

Tufts University, Graduate School of Arts and Sciences, Graduate Certificate Programs, Program Evaluation Program, Medford, MA 02155. Offers Certificate. Part-time and evening/weekend programs available. Electronic applications accepted. *Expenses:* Contact institution.

TUI University, College of Business Administration, Program in Business Administration, Cypress, CA 90630. Offers business administration (PhD); conflict and negotiation management (MBA); criminal justice administration (MBA); entrepreneurship (MBA); finance (MBA); general management (MBA); government accounting (MBA); human resource management (MBA); information security and digital assurance management (MBA); information technology management (MBA); international business (MBA); logistics management (MBA); marketing (MBA); project management (MBA); public management (MBA); quality management (MBA); strategic leadership (MBA). Part-time and evening/weekend programs available. Post-baccalaureate distance learning degree programs offered (no on-campus study). *Students:* 741 full-time (200 women), 1,585 part-time (410 women). 379 applicants, 81% accepted, 300 enrolled. In 2010, 752 master's, 28 doctorates awarded. *Degree requirements:* For doctorate, comprehensive exam, thesis/dissertation, defense of dissertation. *Entrance requirements:* For master's, minimum GPA of 2.5 (students with GPA 3.0 or greater may transfer up to 30% of graduate level credits); for doctorate, minimum GPA of 3.4, curriculum vitae, course work in research methods or statistics. Additional exam requirements/recommendations for international students: Required—TOEFL. *Application deadline:* For fall admission, 10/3 for domestic and international students; for winter admission, 12/22 for domestic and international students; for spring admission, 4/3 for domestic and international students. Applications are processed on a rolling basis. Application fee: $75. Electronic applications accepted. *Expenses:* Tuition: Full-time $11,040; part-time $345 per semester hour. *Unit head:* Paul Watkins, Dean, College of Business Administration, 800-375-9878, E-mail: pwatkins@tuiu.edu. *Application contact:* Wei Ren-Finaly, Registrar, 800-375-9878, Fax: 714-827-7407, E-mail: registration@tuiu.edu.

Université de Moncton, Faculty of Arts and Social Sciences, Department of Public Administration, Moncton, NB E1A 3E9, Canada. Offers MPA, LL B/MPA. Part-time and evening/weekend programs available. *Degree requirements:* For master's, one foreign language. *Entrance requirements:* For master's, minimum GPA of 3.0. *Faculty research:* Public sector reform, privatization, economic modeling, public policy.

Université de Sherbrooke, Faculty of Administration, Program in Public Management, Sherbrooke, QC J1K 2R1, Canada. Offers M Adm. *Faculty:* 7 full-time (2 women), 5 part-time/adjunct (3 women). *Students:* 26 full-time (9 women). Average age 25. 95 applicants, 67% accepted, 26 enrolled. In 2010, 29 master's awarded. *Degree requirements:* For master's, one foreign language, thesis. *Entrance requirements:* For master's, bachelor degree in related field Minimum GPA 3/4.3. *Application deadline:* For fall admission, 4/30 for domestic students, 1/15 for international students. Applications are processed on a rolling basis. Application fee: $70. Electronic applications accepted. *Unit head:* Prof. Julien Bilodeau, Director, Graduate programs in business, 819-821-8000 Ext. 62355. *Application contact:* Marie-Claude Drouin, Programs director's assistant, 819-821-8000 Ext. 63301.

Université du Québec à Montréal, Graduate Programs, Program in Urban Analysis and Management, Montréal, QC H3C 3P8, Canada. Offers MA. Program offered jointly with Université du Québec, École nationale d'administration publique and Université du Québec, Institut National de la Recherche Scientifique. Part-time programs available. *Entrance requirements:* For master's, appropriate bachelor's degree or equivalent and proficiency in French.

Université du Québec, École nationale d'administration publique, Graduate Program in Public Administration, Diploma Program in Public Administration, Quebec, QC G1K 9E5, Canada. Offers Diploma.

Université du Québec, École nationale d'administration publique, Graduate Program in Public Administration, Doctorate Program in Public Administration, Quebec, QC G1K 9E5, Canada. Offers PhD.

University at Albany, State University of New York, Nelson A. Rockefeller College of Public Affairs and Policy, Department of Public Administration and Policy, Albany, NY 12222-0001. Offers administrative behavior (PhD); comparative and development administration (MPA, PhD); human resources (MPA); legislative administration (MPA); nonprofit leadership and management (Certificate); planning and policy analysis (CAS); policy analysis (MPA); program analysis and evaluation (PhD); public affairs and policy (MA); public finance (MPA, PhD); public management (MPA, PhD); women and public policy (Certificate); JD/MPA. JD/MPA offered jointly with Albany Law School. *Accreditation:* NASPAA (one or more programs are accredited). *Degree requirements:* For doctorate, one foreign language, thesis/dissertation. *Entrance requirements:* For doctorate, GRE General Test. Additional exam requirements/recommendations for international students: Required—TOEFL (minimum score 550 paper-based; 213 computer-based). Electronic applications accepted.

The University of Akron, Graduate School, Buchtel College of Arts and Sciences, Department of Public Administration and Urban Studies, Program in Public Administration, Akron, OH 44325. Offers MPA, JD/MPA. *Accreditation:* NASPAA. *Faculty:* 9 full-time (5 women), 7 part-time/adjunct (3 women). *Students:* 52 full-time (30 women), 46 part-time (25 women); includes 29 minority (22 Black or African American, non-Hispanic/Latino; 1 American Indian or Alaska Native, non-Hispanic/Latino; 1 Asian, non-Hispanic/Latino; 4 Hispanic/Latino; 1 Two or more races, non-Hispanic/Latino), 18 international. Average age 38. 76 applicants, 84% accepted, 33 enrolled. In 2010, 38 master's awarded. *Degree requirements:* For master's, thesis optional. *Entrance requirements:* For master's, GRE, GMAT, LSAT, MAT (if undergraduate cumulative GPA less than 3.0), minimum GPA of 3.0, resume, one page personal essay. Additional exam requirements/recommendations for international students: Required—TOEFL (minimum score 550 paper-based; 213 computer-based; 79 iBT). *Application deadline:* For fall admission, 7/1 for domestic and international students; for spring admission, 11/15 for domestic and international students. Application fee: $30 ($40 for international students). Electronic applications accepted. *Expenses:* Tuition, state resident: full-time $6800; part-time $378 per credit hour. Tuition, nonresident: full-time $11,644; part-time $647 per credit hour. Required fees: $1265. One-time fee: $30 full-time. *Unit head:* Dr. Raymond Cox, Chair, 330-972-7616, E-mail: rcox@uakron.edu. *Application contact:* Dr. Raymond Cox, Chair, 330-972-7616, E-mail: rcox@uakron.edu.

The University of Alabama, Graduate School, College of Arts and Sciences, Department of Political Science, Tuscaloosa, AL 35487. Offers political science (MA, PhD); public administration (MPA). Part-time programs available. *Faculty:* 12 full-time (4 women), 1 part-time/adjunct (0 women). *Students:* 52 full-time (20 women), 32 part-time (18 women); includes 14 minority (6 Black or African American, non-Hispanic/Latino; 1 American Indian or Alaska Native, non-Hispanic/Latino; 2 Asian, non-Hispanic/Latino; 3 Hispanic/Latino; 2 Two or more races, non-Hispanic/Latino), 4 international. Average age 28. 57 applicants, 51% accepted, 16 enrolled. In 2010, 11 master's, 4 doctorates awarded. Terminal master's awarded for partial completion of doctoral program. *Degree requirements:* For master's, thesis optional; for doctorate, comprehensive exam, thesis/dissertation. *Entrance requirements:* For master's and doctorate, GRE (minimum score: 1000), minimum undergraduate GPA of 3.0. Additional exam requirements/recommendations for international students: Required—TOEFL. *Application deadline:* For fall admission, 6/30 for domestic and international students; for spring admission, 10/15 for domestic and international students. Applications are processed on a rolling basis. Application fee: $50 ($60 for international students). Electronic applications accepted. *Expenses:* Tuition, state resident: full-time $7900. Tuition, nonresident: full-time $20,500. *Financial support:* In 2010–11, 15 students received support, including teaching assistantships with full tuition reimbursements available (averaging $10,908 per year); fellowships, career-related internships or fieldwork and Federal Work-Study also available. Financial award application deadline: 2/15. *Faculty research:* American politics, comparative politics, international relations, public administration, political theory. Total annual research expenditures: $167,549. *Unit head:* Dr. Carol A. Cassel, Chair and Professor, 205-348-5981, Fax: 205-348-5298, E-mail: ccassel@tenhoor.as.ua.edu. *Application contact:* Dr. Joseph Smith, Graduate Advisor, 205-348-3806, Fax: 205-348-5248, E-mail: josmith@bama.ua.edu.

The University of Alabama at Birmingham, College of Arts and Sciences, Program in Public Administration, Birmingham, AL 35294. Offers MPA. *Accreditation:* NASPAA. *Students:* 26 full-time (12 women), 34 part-time (30 women); includes 19 minority (all Black or African American, non-Hispanic/Latino), 2 international. Average age 28. 26 applicants, 81% accepted, 14 enrolled. In 2010, 20 master's awarded. *Entrance requirements:* For master's, GRE General Test or MAT. *Application deadline:* Applications are processed on a rolling basis. Electronic applications accepted. *Expenses:* Tuition, state resident: full-time $5482. Tuition, nonresident: full-time $12,430. Tuition and fees vary according to program. *Financial support:* Fellowships, career-related internships or fieldwork available. *Unit head:* Dr. Wendy Gunther-Canada, Chair, 205-934-8674. *Application contact:* Julie Bryant, Director of Graduate Admissions, 205-934-8227, Fax: 205-934-8413, E-mail: jbryant@uab.edu.

University of Alaska Anchorage, College of Business and Public Policy, Program in Public Administration, Anchorage, AK 99508. Offers MPA. Part-time programs available. *Degree requirements:* For master's, comprehensive exam, thesis or alternative, capstone project. *Entrance requirements:* For master's, GRE General Test. Additional exam requirements/recommendations for international students: Required—TOEFL (minimum score 550 paper-based; 213 computer-based). *Faculty research:* Policy analysis, policy and administration issues in the North, hypothetical government policies, public management in health care.

University of Alaska Southeast, Graduate Programs, Program in Public Administration, Juneau, AK 99801. Offers MPA. Part-time and evening/weekend programs available. Post-baccalaureate distance learning degree programs offered (no on-campus study). *Degree requirements:* For master's, capstone course or thesis. *Entrance requirements:* For master's, minimum GPA of 3.0, curriculum vitae, letters of reference. Electronic applications accepted. *Faculty research:* Democratic governance, public administrative theory, local government.

The University of Arizona, Eller College of Management, School of Public Administration and Policy, Tucson, AZ 85721. Offers public administration (MPA); public administration and policy (PhD). *Accreditation:* NASPAA. *Students:* 64 full-time (38 women), 22 part-time (11 women); includes 2 Black or African American, non-Hispanic/Latino; 1 American Indian or Alaska Native, non-Hispanic/Latino; 2 Asian, non-Hispanic/Latino; 15 Hispanic/Latino; 8 Two or more races, non-Hispanic/Latino, 5 international. Average age 31. 76 applicants, 70% accepted, 27 enrolled. In 2010, 23 master's awarded. *Degree requirements:* For master's, internship of 400 hours; for doctorate, comprehensive exam, thesis/dissertation. *Entrance requirements:* For doctorate, GMAT or GRE, minimum graduate GPA of 3.5, letter of interest, 3 letters of recommendation, resume. Additional exam requirements/recommendations for international students: Required—TOEFL (minimum score 650 paper-based; 280 computer-based; 115 iBT). *Application deadline:* For fall admission, 2/15 priority date for domestic students, 2/15 for international students. Applications are processed on a rolling basis. Application fee: $75. Electronic applications accepted. *Expenses:* Contact institution. *Financial support:* In 2010–11, 1 research assistantship with full tuition reimbursement (averaging $9,429 per year) was awarded; teaching assistantships with full tuition reimbursements, career-related internships or fieldwork, scholarships/grants, health care benefits, tuition waivers (full and partial), and unspecified assistantships also available. Financial award application deadline: 4/15. Total annual research expenditures: $18,581. *Unit head:* Dr. H. Brinton Milward, Director, 520-621-7476, Fax: 520-626-5549, E-mail: bmilward@eller.arizona.edu. *Application contact:* Pamela Adams, Administrative Associate, 520-621-3128, Fax: 520-621-5549.

University of Arkansas, Graduate School, J. William Fulbright College of Arts and Sciences, Department of Political Science, Program in Public Administration, Fayetteville, AR 72701-1201. Offers MPA. *Students:* 12 full-time (5 women), 6 part-time (2 women); includes 3 minority (1 Black or African American, non-Hispanic/Latino; 1 Asian, non-Hispanic/Latino; 1 Hispanic/Latino), 3 international. 11 applicants, 64% accepted. In 2010, 10 master's awarded. *Degree requirements:* For master's, comprehensive exam, thesis or alternative. *Entrance requirements:* For master's, GRE General Test. *Application deadline:* For fall admission, 4/1 for international students; for spring admission, 10/1 for international students. Applications are processed on a rolling basis. Application fee: $40 ($50 for international students). Electronic applications accepted. *Financial support:* In 2010–11, 2 research assistantships, 1 teaching assistantship were awarded; fellowships with tuition reimbursements, career-related internships or fieldwork and Federal Work-Study also available. Support available to part-time students. Financial award application deadline: 4/1; financial award applicants required to submit FAFSA. *Unit head:* Dr. Margaret Reid, Graduate Coordinator, 479-575-3356, Fax: 479-575-6432, E-mail: mreid@uark.edu. *Application contact:* Dr. Andrew Dowdle, Graduate Coordinator, 479-575-3356, Fax: 479-575-6432, E-mail: adowdle@uark.edu.

University of Arkansas at Little Rock, Graduate School, College of Professional Studies, Program in Public Administration, Little Rock, AR 72204-1099. Offers MPA. *Accreditation:* NASPAA. Part-time and evening/weekend programs available. *Degree requirements:* For master's, comprehensive exam. *Entrance requirements:* For master's, GRE General Test or MAT, minimum GPA of 2.7. *Faculty research:* State and local administration, nonprofit management.

University of Baltimore, Graduate School, The Yale Gordon College of Liberal Arts, Doctoral Program in Public Administration, Baltimore, MD 21201-5779. Offers DPA. Part-time and evening/weekend programs available. *Degree requirements:* For doctorate, thesis/dissertation.

Public Administration

University of Baltimore (continued)
Entrance requirements: For doctorate, GRE. Additional exam requirements/recommendations for international students: Required—TOEFL.

University of Baltimore, Graduate School, The Yale Gordon College of Liberal Arts, Master's Program in Public Administration, Baltimore, MD 21201-5779. Offers MPA, JD/MPA. *Accreditation:* NASPAA. Part-time and evening/weekend programs available. Postbaccalaureate distance learning degree programs offered (minimal on-campus study). *Entrance requirements:* For master's, interview, minimum GPA of 3.0. Additional exam requirements/recommendations for international students: Required—TOEFL (minimum score 550 paper-based; 213 computer-based). Electronic applications accepted. *Expenses:* Contact institution. *Faculty research:* Welfare policy, public administration ethics, bureaucratic politics, public sector budgeting, program evaluation.

University of Central Florida, College of Health and Public Affairs, Department of Public Administration, Orlando, FL 32816. Offers emergency management and homeland security (Certificate); non-profit management (MNM, Certificate); public administration (MPA, Certificate); research administration (MS); urban and regional planning (Certificate). *Accreditation:* NASPAA. Part-time and evening/weekend programs available. *Faculty:* 14 full-time (5 women), 9 part-time/adjunct (3 women). *Students:* 103 full-time (70 women), 271 part-time (208 women); includes 125 minority (85 Black or African American, non-Hispanic/Latino; 1 American Indian or Alaska Native, non-Hispanic/Latino; 13 Asian, non-Hispanic/Latino; 22 Hispanic/Latino; 2 Native Hawaiian or other Pacific Islander, non-Hispanic/Latino; 2 Two or more races, non-Hispanic/Latino), 8 international. Average age 31. 258 applicants, 69% accepted, 138 enrolled. In 2010, 101 master's, 25 other advanced degrees awarded. *Degree requirements:* For master's, comprehensive exam, thesis or alternative, research report. *Entrance requirements:* For master's, GRE General Test. *Application deadline:* For fall admission, 7/1 for domestic students; for spring admission, 12/1 for domestic students. Application fee: $30. Electronic applications accepted. *Expenses:* Tuition, state resident: part-time $256.56 per credit hour. Tuition, nonresident: part-time $1011.52 per credit hour. Part-time tuition and fees vary according to program. *Financial support:* In 2010–11, 13 students received support, including 1 fellowship with partial tuition reimbursement available (averaging $10,000 per year), 11 research assistantships with partial tuition reimbursements available (averaging $5,900 per year), 2 teaching assistantships with partial tuition reimbursements available (averaging $7,100 per year); career-related internships or fieldwork, Federal Work-Study, institutionally sponsored loans, tuition waivers (partial), and unspecified assistantships also available. Financial award application deadline: 3/1; financial award applicants required to submit FAFSA. *Unit head:* Dr. Mary Ann Feldheim, Chair, 407-823-3693, Fax: 407-823-5651, E-mail: mfeldhei@mail.ucf.edu. *Application contact:* Dr. Mary Ann Feldheim, Chair, 407-823-3693, Fax: 407-823-5651, E-mail: mfeldhei@mail.ucf.edu.

University of Colorado at Colorado Springs, Graduate School of Public Affairs, Colorado Springs, CO 80933-7150. Offers criminal justice (MCJ); public administration (MPA). Part-time and evening/weekend programs available. *Faculty:* 7 full-time (2 women). *Students:* 14 full-time (9 women), 3 part-time (1 woman); includes 1 Black or African American, non-Hispanic/Latino; 2 Asian, non-Hispanic/Latino; 4 Hispanic/Latino. Average age 34. 56 applicants, 88% accepted. In 2010, 18 master's awarded. *Degree requirements:* For master's, thesis optional, internship (if no experience), capstone project. *Entrance requirements:* For master's, GRE General Test, GMAT, LSAT, minimum GPA of 3.0. *Application deadline:* For fall admission, 6/1 priority date for domestic students; for spring admission, 11/1 priority date for domestic students. Applications are processed on a rolling basis. Application fee: $60 ($75 for international students). *Expenses:* Contact institution. *Financial support:* Career-related internships or fieldwork, Federal Work-Study, and scholarships/grants available. Support available to part-time students. Financial award application deadline: 3/1; financial award applicants required to submit FAFSA. Total annual research expenditures: $16,459. *Unit head:* Dr. Terry Schwartz, Dean, 719-255-4047, Fax: 719-255-4183, E-mail: tschwart@uccs.edu. *Application contact:* Mary Lou Kartis, Program Assistant, 719-255-4182, Fax: 719-255-4183, E-mail: mkartis@uccs.edu.

University of Colorado Denver, School of Public Affairs, Program in Public Affairs and Administration, Denver, CO 80127. Offers public administration (MPA), including domestic violence, emergency management and homeland security, environmental policy, management and law, homeland security and defense, local government, nonprofit management, public administration; public affairs (PhD). *Accreditation:* NASPAA. Part-time and evening/weekend programs available. Postbaccalaureate distance learning degree programs offered (no on-campus study). *Faculty:* 19 full-time (9 women), 14 part-time/adjunct (5 women). *Students:* 317 full-time (181 women), 167 part-time (100 women); includes 15 Black or African American, non-Hispanic/Latino; 2 American Indian or Alaska Native, non-Hispanic/Latino; 18 Asian, non-Hispanic/Latino; 29 Hispanic/Latino; 1 Two or more races, non-Hispanic/Latino, 36 international. Average age 30. 270 applicants, 66% accepted, 118 enrolled. In 2010, 119 master's, 4 doctorates awarded. *Degree requirements:* For master's, thesis or alternative, 36-39 credit hours; for doctorate, comprehensive exam, thesis/dissertation, minimum of 66 semester hours, including at least 30 hours of doctoral dissertation credits. *Entrance requirements:* For master's and doctorate, GRE, resume, essay, transcripts, recommendations. Additional exam requirements/recommendations for international students: Required—TOEFL (minimum score 550 paper-based; 223 computer-based). *Application deadline:* For fall admission, 2/1 for domestic students; for spring admission, 10/15 priority date for domestic students. Application fee: $50 ($75 for international students). Electronic applications accepted. *Expenses:* Contact institution. *Financial support:* Fellowships with partial tuition reimbursements, research assistantships with partial tuition reimbursements, teaching assistantships with partial tuition reimbursements, Federal Work-Study and scholarships/grants available. Support available to part-time students. Financial award application deadline: 4/1; financial award applicants required to submit FAFSA. *Faculty research:* Housing, education and the social and economic issues of vulnerable populations; nonprofit governance and management; education finance, effectiveness and reform; P-20 (preschool through graduate school) education initiatives; municipal government accountability. *Unit head:* Dr. Mary Guy, Program Director, 303-315-2007, Fax: 303-315-2229, E-mail: mary.guy@ucdenver.edu. *Application contact:* Annie Davies, Director of Marketing, Community Outreach and Alumni Affairs, 303-315-2896, Fax: 303-315-2229, E-mail: annie.davies@ucdenver.edu.

University of Connecticut, Graduate School, College of Liberal Arts and Sciences, Department of Public Policy, Field of Public Administration, Storrs, CT 06269. Offers nonprofit management (Graduate Certificate); public administration (MPA); public financial management (Graduate Certificate); JD/MPA; MPA/MSW. *Accreditation:* NASPAA. *Degree requirements:* For master's, comprehensive exam, internship. *Entrance requirements:* For master's, GRE General Test. Additional exam requirements/recommendations for international students: Required—TOEFL (minimum score 550 paper-based; 213 computer-based). Electronic applications accepted.

University of Dayton, Graduate School, College of Arts and Sciences, Program in Public Administration, Dayton, OH 45469-1300. Offers MPA. *Accreditation:* NASPAA. Part-time and evening/weekend programs available. *Faculty:* 5 full-time (2 women), 5 part-time/adjunct (2 women). *Students:* 20 full-time (16 women), 12 part-time (5 women); includes 6 minority (4 Black or African American, non-Hispanic/Latino; 2 Hispanic/Latino). Average age 32. 10 applicants, 60% accepted, 6 enrolled. In 2010, 15 master's awarded. *Degree requirements:* For master's, internship or public service project. *Entrance requirements:* For master's, GRE General Test. Additional exam requirements/recommendations for international students: Required—TOEFL (minimum score 550 paper-based; 213 computer-based; 80 iBT). *Application deadline:* For fall admission, 4/1 priority date for domestic students, 3/1 priority date for international students; for winter admission, 7/1 priority date for international students; for spring admission, 1/1 priority date for international students. Applications are processed on a rolling basis. Application fee: $0 ($50 for international students). Electronic applications accepted. *Expenses:* Tuition: Full-time $7800; part-time $650 per credit hour. *Financial support:* In 2010–11, 4 research assistantships with full tuition reimbursements (averaging $10,795 per year) were awarded; career-related internships or fieldwork, institutionally sponsored loans, health care benefits, and unspecified assistantships also available. Financial award applicants required to submit FAFSA. *Faculty research:* Ethics, leadership, state government, environmental policy, welfare reforms, state legislatures. *Unit head:* Dr. Nancy Miller, Interim Director, MPA Program, 937-229-3626, Fax: 937-229-1400, E-mail: grant.neeley@notes.udayton.edu. *Application contact:* Alexander Popovski, Associate Director of Graduate and International Admissions, 937-229-2357, Fax: 937-229-4729, E-mail: alex.popovski@notes.udayton.edu.

University of Delaware, College of Human Services, Education and Public Policy, School of Public Policy and Administration, Program in Public Administration, Newark, DE 19716. Offers MPA. *Accreditation:* NASPAA. Part-time and evening/weekend programs available. *Degree requirements:* For master's, internship or thesis. *Entrance requirements:* For master's, GRE General Test. Additional exam requirements/recommendations for international students: Required—TOEFL. Electronic applications accepted. *Faculty research:* State and local management, community development and nonprofit leadership, drug and alcohol epidemiology, fiscal and financial policy, transportation impacts and management.

See Display on next page and Close-Up on page 1273.

University of Evansville, Center for Adult Education, Evansville, IN 47722. Offers public service administration (MS). Part-time and evening/weekend programs available. *Faculty:* 4 full-time (2 women), 7 part-time/adjunct (3 women). *Students:* 62 full-time (45 women), 2 part-time (0 women); includes 10 minority (all Black or African American, non-Hispanic/Latino), 1 international. Average age 36. 24 applicants, 96% accepted, 19 enrolled. In 2010, 31 master's awarded. *Entrance requirements:* For master's, GRE or MAT, minimum undergraduate GPA of 3.0, resume, minimum of 3 years work experience, 2 letters of reference. Additional exam requirements/recommendations for international students: Required—TOEFL (minimum score 570 paper-based; 88 iBT). *Application deadline:* For fall admission, 7/15 priority date for domestic students; for spring admission, 11/30 priority date for domestic students. Applications are processed on a rolling basis. Application fee: $35. *Expenses:* Tuition: Full-time $7830. Tuition and fees vary according to course load and program. *Financial support:* In 2010–11, 10 students received support. Unspecified assistantships available. Financial award application deadline: 6/1; financial award applicants required to submit FAFSA. *Unit head:* Carla Doty, Director, 812-488-2981, Fax: 812-488-2432, E-mail: cd39@evansville.edu. *Application contact:* Carla Doty, Director, 812-488-2981, Fax: 812-488-2432, E-mail: cd39@evansville.edu.

The University of Findlay, Graduate and Professional Studies, College of Business, Findlay, OH 45840-3653. Offers health care management (MBA); hospitality management (MBA); organizational leadership (MBA); public management (MBA). Part-time and evening/weekend programs available. Postbaccalaureate distance learning degree programs offered (no on-campus study). *Faculty:* 20 full-time (5 women), 6 part-time/adjunct (0 women). *Students:* 25 full-time (11 women), 239 part-time (112 women); includes 15 minority (5 Black or African American, non-Hispanic/Latino; 9 Asian, non-Hispanic/Latino; 1 Hispanic/Latino), 98 international. Average age 25. 93 applicants, 86% accepted, 70 enrolled. In 2010, 283 master's awarded. *Degree requirements:* For master's, thesis, cumulative project. *Entrance requirements:* For master's, GMAT or GRE, minimum undergraduate GPA of 3.0. Additional exam requirements/recommendations for international students: Required—TOEFL (minimum score 550 paper-based; 213 computer-based; 80 iBT). *Application deadline:* Applications are processed on a rolling basis. Application fee: $25. Electronic applications accepted. *Expenses:* Contact institution. *Financial support:* In 2010–11, 8 research assistantships with full and partial tuition reimbursements (averaging $4,200 per year) were awarded; career-related internships or fieldwork, Federal Work-Study, health care benefits, and unspecified assistantships also available. Financial award application deadline: 4/1; financial award applicants required to submit FAFSA. *Faculty research:* Health care management, operations and logistics management. *Unit head:* Dr. Paul Sears, Dean, College of Business, 419-434-4704, Fax: 419-434-4822. *Application contact:* Heather Riffle, Assistant Director, Graduate and Professional Studies, 419-434-4640, Fax: 419-434-5517, E-mail: riffle@findlay.edu.

University of Georgia, School of Public and International Affairs, Department of Public Administration and Policy, Athens, GA 30602. Offers public administration (MPA, PhD). *Accreditation:* NASPAA (one or more programs are accredited). *Faculty:* 16 full-time (2 women), 1 part-time/adjunct (0 women). *Students:* 136 full-time (68 women), 51 part-time (32 women); includes 27 Black or African American, non-Hispanic/Latino; 4 American Indian or Alaska Native, non-Hispanic/Latino; 6 Asian, non-Hispanic/Latino; 1 Hispanic/Latino; 1 Two or more races, non-Hispanic/Latino, 22 international. 309 applicants, 37% accepted, 58 enrolled. In 2010, 68 master's, 3 doctorates awarded. *Degree requirements:* For master's, internship; for doctorate, thesis/dissertation. *Entrance requirements:* For master's and doctorate, GRE General Test. *Application deadline:* For fall admission, 7/1 priority date for domestic students; for spring admission, 11/15 for domestic students. Application fee: $50. Electronic applications accepted. *Expenses:* Tuition, state resident: full-time $7200; part-time $344 per credit hour. Tuition, nonresident: full-time $21,900; part-time $944 per credit hour. Tuition and fees vary according to course load and program. *Financial support:* Fellowships, research assistantships, teaching assistantships, unspecified assistantships available. *Unit head:* Dr. J. Edward Kellough, Head, 706-542-2057, E-mail: kellough@uga.edu. *Application contact:* Dr. Vicky M. Wilkins, Graduate Coordinator, 706-542-2648, Fax: 706-583-4421, E-mail: vwilkins@uga.edu.

University of Guam, Office of Graduate Studies, School of Business and Public Administration, Public Administration Program, Mangilao, GU 96923. Offers MPA. *Entrance requirements:* For master's, GRE General Test. Additional exam requirements/recommendations for international students: Required—TOEFL.

University of Guelph, Graduate Studies, College of Social and Applied Human Sciences, Department of Political Science, Guelph, ON N1G 2W1, Canada. Offers comparative politics (MA); international development (MA); political science (MA); public policy and public administration (MA); the Americas (Canada emphasis) (MA). MA in public policy and public administration offered in collaboration with Department of Political Science of McMaster University. *Degree requirements:* For master's, thesis or paper. *Entrance requirements:* For master's, minimum B average during previous 2 years of course work, 4 year Honours Degree in Political Science. Additional exam requirements/recommendations for international students: Required—TOEFL. Electronic applications accepted. *Faculty research:* Political ethics, constitutional power.

University of Hawaii at Manoa, Graduate Division, College of Social Sciences, Department of Public Administration, Honolulu, HI 96822. Offers MPA, Graduate Certificate. Part-time programs available. *Faculty:* 9 full-time (3 women). *Students:* 24 full-time (13 women), 28 part-time (18 women); includes 21 minority (11 Asian, non-Hispanic/Latino; 8 Native Hawaiian or other Pacific Islander, non-Hispanic/Latino; 2 Two or more races, non-Hispanic/Latino), 12 international. Average age 35. 83 applicants, 58% accepted, 40 enrolled. In 2010, 26 master's, 2 other advanced degrees awarded. *Degree requirements:* For master's, thesis optional, practicum. *Entrance requirements:* Additional exam requirements/recommendations for international students: Required—TOEFL (minimum score 540 paper-based; 207 computer-based; 76 iBT), IELTS (minimum score 5). *Application deadline:* For fall admission, 3/1 for domestic and international students. Application fee: $60. *Financial support:* In 2010–11, 8 fellowships (averaging $745 per year), 1 teaching assistantship (averaging $14,382 per year) were awarded; career-related internships or fieldwork, Federal Work-Study, institutionally sponsored loans, and tuition waivers (full and partial) also available. Support available to part-time students. *Faculty research:* Public sector finance and the budget process, collaboration between sectors, organizational problem solving and communication processes, system reform in government organizations, public policy analysis. *Application contact:* Richard Pratt, Graduate Chair, 808-956-8260, Fax: 808-956-9571, E-mail: pratt@hawaii.edu.

University of Houston, College of Liberal Arts and Social Sciences, Department of Political Science, Houston, TX 77204. Offers political science (MA, PhD); public administration (MA). Part-time programs available. *Faculty:* 19 full-time (3 women), 7 part-time/adjunct (1 woman).

Students: 61 full-time (29 women), 63 part-time (33 women); includes 12 Black or African American, non-Hispanic/Latino; 1 American Indian or Alaska Native, non-Hispanic/Latino; 3 Asian, non-Hispanic/Latino; 10 Hispanic/Latino; 2 Two or more races, non-Hispanic/Latino, 21 international. Average age 32. 128 applicants, 40% accepted, 32 enrolled. In 2010, 12 master's, 6 doctorates awarded. Terminal master's awarded for partial completion of doctoral program. *Degree requirements:* For master's, thesis optional; for doctorate, thesis/dissertation. *Entrance requirements:* For master's and doctorate, GRE. Additional exam requirements/recommendations for international students: Required—TOEFL (minimum score 550 paper-based; 213 computer-based; 79 iBT). *Application deadline:* For fall admission, 2/15 for domestic and international students; for spring admission, 10/1 for domestic and international students. Application fee: $0 ($75 for international students). *Expenses:* Tuition, state resident: full-time $8592; part-time $358 per credit hour. Tuition, nonresident: full-time $16,032; part-time $668 per credit hour. Required fees: $2889. Tuition and fees vary according to course load and program. *Financial support:* In 2010–11, 3 fellowships with full tuition reimbursements (averaging $2,500 per year), 1 research assistantship with full tuition reimbursement (averaging $10,400 per year), 26 teaching assistantships with full tuition reimbursements (averaging $11,168 per year) were awarded; career-related internships or fieldwork, Federal Work-Study, institutionally sponsored loans, scholarships/grants, health care benefits, and unspecified assistantships also available. Support available to part-time students. Financial award application deadline: 2/1. *Faculty research:* American politics, political theory, judicial process, public policy, comparative politics. *Unit head:* Dr. Gregory Weiher, Chairperson, 713-743-3890, Fax: 713-743-3927, E-mail: gweiher@uh.edu. *Application contact:* Edward Manouelian, Graduate Advisor, 713-743-3939, E-mail: eemanoue@central.uh.edu.

University of Idaho, College of Graduate Studies, College of Letters, Arts and Social Sciences, Department of Political Science and Public Affairs Research, Program in Public Administration, Moscow, ID 83844-2282. Offers MPA. *Students:* 3 full-time, 8 part-time. Average age 36. In 2010, 5 master's awarded. *Entrance requirements:* For master's, minimum GPA of 2.8. *Application deadline:* For fall admission, 8/1 for domestic students; for spring admission, 12/15 for domestic students. Applications are processed on a rolling basis. Application fee: $60. Electronic applications accepted. *Expenses:* Tuition, nonresident: part-time $580 per credit. Required fees: $306 per credit. *Financial support:* Applicants required to submit FAFSA. *Unit head:* Dr. Donald W. Crowley, Chair, 208-885-6328. *Application contact:* Dr. Donald W. Crowley, Chair, 208-885-6328.

University of Illinois at Chicago, Graduate College, College of Urban Planning and Public Affairs, Program in Public Administration, Chicago, IL 60607-7128. Offers MPA, PhD. *Accreditation:* NASPAA (one or more programs are accredited). Part-time and evening/weekend programs available. Terminal master's awarded for partial completion of doctoral program. *Degree requirements:* For master's, internship/project. *Entrance requirements:* For master's, GRE General Test, minimum GPA of 3.0. Additional exam requirements/recommendations for international students: Required—TOEFL. Electronic applications accepted. *Faculty research:* Public management, economic development, public personnel.

University of Illinois at Springfield, Graduate Programs, College of Public Affairs and Administration, Program in Public Administration, Springfield, IL 62703-5407. Offers MPA, DPA. *Accreditation:* NASPAA. Part-time and evening/weekend programs available. Post-baccalaureate distance learning degree programs offered (no on-campus study). *Degree requirements:* For master's, thesis or seminar; for doctorate, comprehensive exam, thesis/dissertation. *Entrance requirements:* For master's, minimum undergraduate GPA of 2.5, resume, career goals statement; for doctorate, GRE, minimum graduate GPA of 3.25; writing sample; 3 letters of reference; interview. Additional exam requirements/recommendations for international students: Required—TOEFL (minimum score 550 paper-based; 213 computer-based). Electronic applications accepted. *Expenses:* Tuition, state resident: full-time $6774; part-time $282.25 per credit hour. Tuition, nonresident: full-time $15,078; part-time $628.25 per credit hour. Required fees: $15.25 per credit hour. $492 per term.

The University of Kansas, Graduate Studies, College of Liberal Arts and Sciences, Department of Public Administration, Lawrence, KS 66045-3129. Offers MPA, PhD, JD/MPA, MUP/MPA.

Accreditation: NASPAA. Part-time and evening/weekend programs available. *Faculty:* 12 full-time (5 women). *Students:* 50 full-time (19 women), 82 part-time (46 women); includes 19 minority (9 Black or African American, non-Hispanic/Latino; 1 Asian, non-Hispanic/Latino; 7 Hispanic/Latino; 2 Two or more races, non-Hispanic/Latino), 5 international. Average age 35. 111 applicants, 43% accepted, 37 enrolled. In 2010, 40 master's, 2 doctorates awarded. Terminal master's awarded for partial completion of doctoral program. *Degree requirements:* For master's, comprehensive exam; for doctorate, comprehensive exam, thesis/dissertation. *Entrance requirements:* For master's and doctorate, GRE General Test. Additional exam requirements/recommendations for international students: Required—TOEFL. *Application deadline:* For fall admission, 7/1 for domestic students, 5/1 for international students; for spring admission, 11/15 for domestic students, 10/1 for international students. Application fee: $55 ($65 for international students). Electronic applications accepted. *Expenses:* Tuition, state resident: full-time $7092; part-time $295.50 per credit hour. Tuition, nonresident: full-time $16,590; part-time $691.25 per credit hour. Required fees: $858; $71.49 per credit hour. Tuition and fees vary according to course load, campus/location and program. *Financial support:* Fellowships, research assistantships with full and partial tuition reimbursements, teaching assistantships with full and partial tuition reimbursements, career-related internships or fieldwork, institutionally sponsored loans, scholarships/grants, and unspecified assistantships available. Financial award application deadline: 2/1. *Faculty research:* Local government, administrative ethics, nonprofit management, policy studies, law and public administration, finance, budgeting. *Unit head:* Marilu Goodyear, Chair, 785-864-3527, Fax: 785-864-5208, E-mail: padept@ku.edu. *Application contact:* Jim Hummert, Administrative Director, 785-864-9097, Fax: 785-864-5208, E-mail: rhummert@ku.edu.

University of Kentucky, Graduate School, Program in Public Administration, Lexington, KY 40506-0032. Offers MPA, MPP, PhD. *Accreditation:* NASPAA (one or more programs are accredited). *Degree requirements:* For master's, comprehensive exam; for doctorate, comprehensive exam, thesis/dissertation. *Entrance requirements:* For master's, GMAT or GRE General Test, minimum undergraduate GPA of 2.75; for doctorate, GMAT or GRE General Test, minimum graduate GPA of 3.0. Additional exam requirements/recommendations for international students: Required—TOEFL (minimum score 550 paper-based; 213 computer-based). Electronic applications accepted. *Faculty research:* Public financial management, education finance and policy, health finance and policy, welfare policy, program evaluation.

University of La Verne, College of Business and Public Management, Doctoral Program in Public Administration, La Verne, CA 91750-4443. Offers DPA. Part-time programs available. *Faculty:* 34 full-time (12 women), 36 part-time/adjunct (9 women). *Students:* 62 full-time (32 women), 45 part-time (21 women); includes 57 minority (21 Black or African American, non-Hispanic/Latino; 7 Asian, non-Hispanic/Latino; 29 Hispanic/Latino), 7 international. Average age 42. In 2010, 6 doctorates awarded. *Degree requirements:* For doctorate, thesis/dissertation. *Entrance requirements:* For doctorate, MAT, GMAT or GRE, minimum undergraduate GPA of 3.25, interview, 3 letters of recommendation. Additional exam requirements/recommendations for international students: Required—TOEFL (minimum score 550 paper-based; 213 computer-based). Application fee: $75. *Expenses:* Contact institution. *Financial support:* Institutionally sponsored loans available. Financial award application deadline: 3/2; financial award applicants required to submit FAFSA. *Unit head:* Dr. Suzanne Beaumaster, Chairperson, 909-593-3511 Ext. 4817, E-mail: sbeaumaster@laverne.edu. *Application contact:* Erma Cross, Program and Admission Specialist, 909-593-3511 Ext. 4948, Fax: 909-392-2761, E-mail: ecross@laverne.edu.

University of La Verne, College of Business and Public Management, Master's Program in Public Administration, La Verne, CA 91750-4443. Offers MPA. *Accreditation:* NASPAA. Part-time programs available. *Faculty:* 34 full-time (12 women), 36 part-time/adjunct (9 women). *Students:* 60 full-time (39 women), 38 part-time (25 women); includes 70 minority (9 Black or African American, non-Hispanic/Latino; 10 Asian, non-Hispanic/Latino; 51 Hispanic/Latino). Average age 32. In 2010, 24 master's awarded. *Entrance requirements:* For master's, minimum undergraduate GPA of 2.75, 2 letters of recommendation, resume. Additional exam requirements/recommendations for international students: Required—TOEFL (minimum score 550 paper-

Public Administration

University of La Verne (continued)

based; 213 computer-based). *Application deadline:* Applications are processed on a rolling basis. Application fee: $50. *Expenses:* Contact institution. *Financial support:* Fellowships, research assistantships available. Financial award application deadline: 3/2; financial award applicants required to submit FAFSA. *Unit head:* Dr. Jack Meek, Chairperson, 909-593-3511 Ext. 4941, E-mail: jmeek@laverne.edu. *Application contact:* Connie Hamlow, Program and Admission Specialist, 909-593-3511 Ext. 4819, Fax: 909-392-2761, E-mail: cbpm@laverne.edu.

University of Louisville, Graduate School, College of Arts and Sciences, Department of Urban and Public Affairs, Louisville, KY 40208. Offers public administration (MPA), including human resources management, non-profit management, public policy and administration; urban and public affairs (PhD), including urban planning and development, urban policy and administration; urban planning (MUP), including administration of planning organizations, housing and community development, land use and environmental planning, spatial analysis. Part-time and evening/weekend programs available. *Faculty:* 22 full-time (7 women), 8 part-time/adjunct (1 woman). *Students:* 73 full-time (36 women), 31 part-time (18 women); includes 11 Black or African American, non-Hispanic/Latino; 2 Asian, non-Hispanic/Latino; 2 Hispanic/Latino; 1 Native Hawaiian or other Pacific Islander, non-Hispanic/Latino; 2 Two or more races, non-Hispanic/Latino, 11 international. Average age 31. 96 applicants, 67% accepted, 37 enrolled. In 2010, 28 master's, 5 doctorates awarded. Terminal master's awarded for partial completion of doctoral program. *Degree requirements:* For master's, internship; for doctorate, comprehensive exam, thesis/dissertation. *Entrance requirements:* For master's, GRE General Test, minimum GPA of 3.0; for doctorate, GRE General Test, master's degree in appropriate field. Additional exam requirements/recommendations for international students: Required—TOEFL (minimum score 550 paper-based; 213 computer-based; 79 iBT). *Application deadline:* For fall admission, 7/15 for domestic students; for spring admission, 11/15 for domestic students. Applications are processed on a rolling basis. Application fee: $50. Electronic applications accepted. *Expenses:* Tuition, state resident: full-time $9144; part-time $508 per credit hour. Tuition, nonresident: full-time $19,026; part-time $1057 per credit hour. Tuition and fees vary according to program and reciprocity agreements. *Financial support:* In 2010–11, 23 students received support; fellowships, research assistantships, health care benefits available. Financial award application deadline: 3/1. *Faculty research:* Housing and community development, performance-based budgeting, environmental policy and natural hazards, sustainability, real estate development, comparative urban development. *Unit head:* Dr. David Simpson, Chair, 502-852-8019, Fax: 502-852-4558, E-mail: dave.simpson@louisville.edu. *Application contact:* Patty Sarley, Graduate Student Advisor, 502-852-7914, Fax: 502-852-4558, E-mail: plclea01@louisville.edu.

University of Maine, Graduate School, College of Business, Public Policy and Health, Department of Public Administration, Orono, ME 04469. Offers MPA, PhD. *Accreditation:* NASPAA. Part-time and evening/weekend programs available. *Faculty:* 4 full-time (1 woman), 1 part-time/adjunct (0 women). *Students:* 20 full-time (11 women), 16 part-time (10 women); includes 2 minority (both American Indian or Alaska Native, non-Hispanic/Latino), 2 international. Average age 36. 12 applicants, 67% accepted, 6 enrolled. In 2010, 10 degrees awarded. *Entrance requirements:* For master's, GMAT or GRE General Test. Additional exam requirements/recommendations for international students: Required—TOEFL. *Application deadline:* Applications are processed on a rolling basis. Application fee: $65. Electronic applications accepted. *Expenses:* Tuition, state resident: full-time $400. Tuition, nonresident: full-time $1050. *Financial support:* In 2010–11, 1 teaching assistantship with tuition reimbursement (averaging $12,790 per year) was awarded; career-related internships or fieldwork, Federal Work-Study, institutionally sponsored loans, tuition waivers (full and partial), and unspecified assistantships also available. Support available to part-time students. Financial award application deadline: 3/1. *Faculty research:* Organization theory, personnel administration, public budgeting and finance, policy analysis, environmental policy, community policy and development. *Unit head:* Dr. Carolyn Ball, Chairperson, 207-581-4142, Fax: 207-581-3039. *Application contact:* Scott G. Delcourt, Associate Dean of the Graduate School, 207-581-3291, Fax: 207-581-3232, E-mail: graduate@maine.edu.

University of Management and Technology, Program in Management, Arlington, VA 22209. Offers acquisition management (MS, AC); general management (MS); project management (MS, AC); public administration (MPA, MS, AC). Part-time and evening/weekend programs available. Postbaccalaureate distance learning degree programs offered (no on-campus study). *Entrance requirements:* For master's, 3 recommendations, resume. Additional exam requirements/recommendations for international students: Required—TOEFL (minimum score 550 paper-based; 213 computer-based). Electronic applications accepted.

University of Manitoba, Faculty of Graduate Studies, Faculty of Arts, Department of Political Studies, Program in Public Administration, Winnipeg, MB R3T 2N2, Canada. Offers MPA. Program offered jointly with The University of Winnipeg. *Degree requirements:* For master's, thesis or alternative.

University of Maryland, College Park, Academic Affairs, Joint Program in Business and Management/Public Policy, College Park, MD 20742. Offers MBA/MPM. *Accreditation:* AACSB. *Students:* 13 full-time (5 women), 2 part-time (0 women); includes 4 minority (1 Black or African American, non-Hispanic/Latino; 2 Asian, non-Hispanic/Latino; 1 Two or more races, non-Hispanic/Latino). 45 applicants, 20% accepted, 6 enrolled. *Application deadline:* For fall admission, 12/15 for domestic students, 2/1 for international students; for spring admission, 10/15 for domestic students, 6/1 for international students. Applications are processed on a rolling basis. Application fee: $75. Electronic applications accepted. *Expenses:* Tuition, state resident: part-time $471 per credit hour. Tuition, nonresident: part-time $1016 per credit hour. Required fees: $337 per term. *Financial support:* In 2010–11, 2 fellowships with full and partial tuition reimbursements (averaging $13,807 per year), 7 teaching assistantships (averaging $15,250 per year) were awarded; research assistantships. Financial award applicants required to submit FAFSA. *Unit head:* Dr. Charles Caramello, Dean of the Graduate School, 301-405-0358, Fax: 301-314-9305, E-mail: ccaramel@umd.edu. *Application contact:* Dean of Graduate School, 301-405-0358, Fax: 301-314-9305.

University of Maryland, College Park, Academic Affairs, School of Public Policy, Joint Program in Public Policy/Law, College Park, MD 20742. Offers JD/MPM. *Students:* 7 full-time (2 women), 1 (woman) part-time; includes 1 minority (Black or African American, non-Hispanic/Latino). 29 applicants, 45% accepted, 4 enrolled. *Application deadline:* For fall admission, 4/1 for domestic students, 2/1 for international students; for spring admission, 10/15 for domestic students, 6/1 for international students. Applications are processed on a rolling basis. Application fee: $75. Electronic applications accepted. *Expenses:* Tuition, state resident: part-time $471 per credit hour. Tuition, nonresident: part-time $1016 per credit hour. Required fees: $337 per term. *Financial support:* In 2010–11, 2 teaching assistantships (averaging $16,543 per year) were awarded. Financial award applicants required to submit FAFSA. *Application contact:* Dr. Charles A. Caramello, Dean of Graduate School, 301-405-0358, Fax: 301-314-9305, E-mail: ccaramel@umd.edu.

University of Maryland, College Park, Academic Affairs, School of Public Policy, Public Management Program, College Park, MD 20742. Offers MPM. *Accreditation:* NASPAA. *Students:* 60 full-time (12 women), 36 part-time (23 women); includes 15 minority (8 Black or African American, non-Hispanic/Latino; 5 Asian, non-Hispanic/Latino; 2 Hispanic/Latino), 56 international. 69 applicants, 51% accepted, 21 enrolled. In 2010, 44 master's awarded. *Degree requirements:* For master's, internship. *Entrance requirements:* For master's, GRE General Test, minimum GPA of 3.0. Additional exam requirements/recommendations for international students: Required—TOEFL. *Application deadline:* For fall admission, 4/1 for domestic students, 2/1 for international students; for spring admission, 10/15 for domestic students, 6/1 for international students. Applications are processed on a rolling basis. Application fee: $75. Electronic applications accepted. *Expenses:* Tuition, state resident: part-time $471 per credit hour. Tuition, nonresident: part-time $1016 per credit hour. Required fees: $337 per term. *Financial support:* In 2010–11, 2 teaching assistantships (averaging $15,023 per year) were awarded. Financial award applicants required to submit FAFSA. *Faculty research:* International security, economic policy, financial management, social policy. *Unit head:* Donald Kettl, Dean, 301-405-6356, E-mail: kettl@umd.edu. *Application contact:* Dr. Charles A. Caramello, Dean of Graduate School, 301-405-0358, Fax: 301-314-9305, E-mail: ccaramel@umd.edu.

University of Massachusetts Amherst, Graduate School, College of Social and Behavioral Sciences, Center for Public Policy and Administration, Amherst, MA 01003. Offers MPPA, MPH/MPPA. Part-time programs available. *Students:* 28 full-time (16 women), 11 part-time (8 women); includes 2 minority (1 Asian, non-Hispanic/Latino; 1 Hispanic/Latino), 6 international. Average age 33. 87 applicants, 78% accepted, 17 enrolled. In 2010, 17 master's awarded. *Degree requirements:* For master's, thesis or alternative. *Entrance requirements:* For master's, GRE General Test. Additional exam requirements/recommendations for international students: Required—TOEFL (minimum score 550 paper-based; 213 computer-based; 80 iBT), IELTS (minimum score 6.5). *Application deadline:* For fall admission, 2/1 for domestic and international students. Applications are processed on a rolling basis. Application fee: $50 ($65 for international students). Electronic applications accepted. *Expenses:* Tuition, state resident: full-time $2640. Required fees: $8282. One-time fee: $357 full-time. *Financial support:* In 2010–11, 2 fellowships with full tuition reimbursements (averaging $3,750 per year), 23 research assistantships with full tuition reimbursements (averaging $6,584 per year) were awarded; teaching assistantships, career-related internships or fieldwork, Federal Work-Study, scholarships/grants, traineeships, health care benefits, tuition waivers (full), and unspecified assistantships also available. Support available to part-time students. Financial award application deadline: 2/1; financial award applicants required to submit FAFSA. *Unit head:* Dr. M. V. Lee Badgett, Graduate Program Director, 413-545-3956, Fax: 413-545-1108. *Application contact:* Jean M. Ames, Supervisor of Admissions, 413-545-0722, Fax: 413-577-0010, E-mail: gradadm@grad.umass.edu.

University of Memphis, Graduate School, College of Arts and Sciences, Division of Public and Nonprofit Administration, Memphis, TN 38152. Offers nonprofit administration (MPA); public management and policy (MPA); urban management and planning (MPA). *Accreditation:* NASPAA. Part-time and evening/weekend programs available. Postbaccalaureate distance learning degree programs offered (minimal on-campus study). *Faculty:* 5 full-time (2 women), 1 (woman) part-time/adjunct. *Students:* 18 full-time (15 women), 43 part-time (33 women); includes 35 Black or African American, non-Hispanic/Latino; 1 Hispanic/Latino; 1 Two or more races, non-Hispanic/Latino. Average age 34. 32 applicants, 88% accepted, 9 enrolled. In 2010, 17 master's awarded. *Degree requirements:* For master's, comprehensive exam, thesis or alternative, internship. *Entrance requirements:* For master's, GRE General Test, GMAT, or MAT, minimum GPA of 3.0. Additional exam requirements/recommendations for international students: Required—TOEFL. *Application deadline:* For fall admission, 7/1 for domestic students, 5/15 for international students; for spring admission, 12/1 for domestic students, 9/15 for international students. Applications are processed on a rolling basis. Application fee: $35 ($60 for international students). *Financial support:* In 2010–11, 37 students received support; fellowships, research assistantships with full tuition reimbursements available, career-related internships or fieldwork, Federal Work-Study, scholarships/grants, and unspecified assistantships available. Support available to part-time students. Financial award application deadline: 2/15; financial award applicants required to submit FAFSA. *Faculty research:* Nonprofit organization governance, local government management, community collaboration, urban problems, accountability. *Unit head:* Dr. Charles Menifield, Director, 901-678-5527, Fax: 901-678-2981, E-mail: cmenifld@memphis.edu. *Application contact:* Dr. Charles Menifield, Graduate Admissions Coordinator, 901-678-3360, Fax: 901-678-2981, E-mail: cmenifld@memphis.edu.

University of Michigan–Dearborn, College of Arts, Sciences, and Letters, Master of Public Administration Program, Dearborn, MI 48128. Offers assessment and evaluation (Certificate); nonprofit leadership (Certificate); public administration (MPA). Part-time and evening/weekend programs available. *Faculty:* 3 full-time (1 woman), 9 part-time/adjunct (2 women). *Students:* 21 full-time (13 women), 59 part-time (44 women); includes 26 minority (20 Black or African American, non-Hispanic/Latino; 1 American Indian or Alaska Native, non-Hispanic/Latino; 2 Asian, non-Hispanic/Latino; 1 Hispanic/Latino; 1 Native Hawaiian or other Pacific Islander, non-Hispanic/Latino; 1 Two or more races, non-Hispanic/Latino). Average age 35. 36 applicants, 86% accepted, 31 enrolled. In 2010, 22 master's awarded. *Degree requirements:* For master's, assessment seminar. *Entrance requirements:* For master's, GRE or minimum undergraduate GPA of 3.0, 3 letters of recommendation. Additional exam requirements/recommendations for international students: Required—TOEFL, TWE. *Application deadline:* For fall admission, 8/1 for domestic students, 4/1 for international students; for winter admission, 12/1 for domestic students, 11/1 for international students; for spring admission, 4/1 for domestic students, 3/1 for international students. Applications are processed on a rolling basis. Application fee: $60. *Financial support:* Career-related internships or fieldwork and Federal Work-Study available. Support available to part-time students. Financial award applicants required to submit FAFSA. *Faculty research:* Federal, state, and local agency management; independent sector management; educational administration. *Unit head:* Dr. Paul Draus, Director, 313-583-6539, Fax: 313-583-6700, E-mail: draus@umich.edu. *Application contact:* Carol Ligienza, Graduate Programs Coordinator, 313-593-1183, Fax: 313-583-6700, E-mail: caslgrad@umd.umich.edu.

University of Michigan–Flint, Graduate Programs, Program in Public Administration, Flint, MI 48502-1950. Offers MPA. Part-time programs available. *Degree requirements:* For master's, thesis or alternative, internship. *Entrance requirements:* For master's, minimum GPA of 3.0, 1 course each in American government, microeconomics and statistics. Additional exam requirements/recommendations for international students: Required—TOEFL (minimum score 550 paper-based; 220 computer-based), IELTS (minimum score 6.5). Electronic applications accepted. *Expenses:* Contact institution.

University of Missouri–Kansas City, Henry W. Bloch School of Management, Kansas City, MO 64110-2499. Offers accounting (MS); business administration (MBA); entrepreneurship and innovation (PhD); public affairs (MPA, PhD); JD/MBA; LL M/MPA. PhD (interdisciplinary) offered through the School of Graduate Studies. *Accreditation:* AACSB; NASPAA. Part-time and evening/weekend programs available. *Faculty:* 49 full-time (16 women), 21 part-time/adjunct (5 women). *Students:* 280 full-time (134 women), 435 part-time (193 women); includes 91 minority (44 Black or African American, non-Hispanic/Latino; 19 Asian, non-Hispanic/Latino; 23 Hispanic/Latino; 5 Two or more races, non-Hispanic/Latino), 50 international. Average age 30. 426 applicants, 255 enrolled. In 2010, 254 master's awarded. Terminal master's awarded for partial completion of doctoral program. *Entrance requirements:* For master's, GMAT, GRE, 2 writing essays, 2 references and support of employer; for doctorate, GRE, minimum GPA of 3.0. Additional exam requirements/recommendations for international students: Required—TOEFL (minimum score 550 paper-based; 213 computer-based; 80 iBT). *Application deadline:* For fall admission, 5/1 priority date for domestic and international students; for spring admission, 10/1 priority date for domestic and international students. Applications are processed on a rolling basis. Application fee: $45 ($50 for international students). Electronic applications accepted. *Expenses:* Tuition, state resident: full-time $5522.40; part-time $306.80 per credit hour. Tuition, nonresident: full-time $7128; part-time $792 per credit hour. Required fees: $261.15 per term. *Financial support:* In 2010–11, 26 research assistantships with partial tuition reimbursements (averaging $7,767 per year), 5 teaching assistantships with partial tuition reimbursements (averaging $8,430 per year) were awarded; career-related internships or fieldwork, Federal Work-Study, institutionally sponsored loans, scholarships/grants, tuition waivers (full and partial), and unspecified assistantships also available. Support available to part-time students. Financial award application deadline: 3/1; financial award applicants required to submit FAFSA. *Faculty research:* Entrepreneurship, finance, non-profit, risk management. *Unit head:* Dr. Teng-Kee Tan, Dean, 816-235-2215, Fax: 816-235-2206. *Application contact:* 816-235-1111, E-mail: admit@umkc.edu.

University of Missouri–St. Louis, College of Arts and Sciences, Department of Political Science, St. Louis, MO 63121. Offers American politics (MA); comparative politics (MA); international politics (MA); political process and behavior (MA); political science (PhD); public administration and public policy (MA); urban and regional politics (MA). Part-time and evening/

weekend programs available. *Faculty:* 18 full-time (7 women), 1 (woman) part-time/adjunct. *Students:* 15 full-time (7 women), 39 part-time (21 women); includes 13 minority (8 Black or African American, non-Hispanic/Latino; 2 American Indian or Alaska Native, non-Hispanic/Latino; 3 Asian, non-Hispanic/Latino), 3 international. Average age 35. 43 applicants, 47% accepted, 10 enrolled. In 2010, 4 master's, 5 doctorates awarded. Terminal master's awarded for partial completion of doctoral program. *Degree requirements:* For master's, thesis optional; for doctorate, thesis/dissertation. *Entrance requirements:* For master's, GRE General Test, 2 letters of recommendation; for doctorate, GRE General Test, 3 letters of recommendation. Additional exam requirements/recommendations for international students: Required—TOEFL (minimum score 550 paper-based; 213 computer-based). *Application deadline:* For fall admission, 2/15 priority date for domestic and international students; for spring admission, 10/15 priority date for domestic and international students. Applications are processed on a rolling basis. Application fee: $35 ($40 for international students). Electronic applications accepted. *Expenses:* Tuition, state resident: full-time $5522; part-time $306.80 per credit hour. Tuition, nonresident: full-time $14,253; part-time $792.10 per credit hour. Required fees: $658; $49 per credit hour. One-time fee: $12. Tuition and fees vary according to program. *Financial support:* In 2010–11, 8 research assistantships with full and partial tuition reimbursements (averaging $1,110 per year), 6 teaching assistantships with full and partial tuition reimbursements (averaging $10,800 per year) were awarded; fellowships, career-related internships or fieldwork also available. Support available to part-time students. Financial award application deadline: 3/15; financial award applicants required to submit FAFSA. *Faculty research:* Public policy, urban politics and administration, American government. *Unit head:* Dr. Kenneth Thomas, Director of Graduate Studies, 314-516-5521, Fax: 314-516-5268, E-mail: umslpolisci@umsl.edu. *Application contact:* 314-516-5458, Fax: 314-516-6996, E-mail: gradadm@umsl.edu.

University of Missouri–St. Louis, Graduate School, Program in Public Policy Administration, St. Louis, MO 63121. Offers health policy (MPPA); local government management (MPPA); managing human resources and organization (MPPA); nonprofit organization management (MPPA); nonprofit organization management and leadership (Certificate); policy research and analysis (MPPA). *Accreditation:* NASPAA. Part-time and evening/weekend programs available. *Faculty:* 9 full-time (4 women), 8 part-time/adjunct (6 women). *Students:* 36 full-time (21 women), 59 part-time (33 women); includes 17 minority (13 Black or African American, non-Hispanic/Latino; 2 American Indian or Alaska Native, non-Hispanic/Latino; 1 Asian, non-Hispanic/Latino; 1 Hispanic/Latino), 11 international. Average age 31. 60 applicants, 68% accepted, 24 enrolled. In 2010, 23 master's, 17 Certificates awarded. *Entrance requirements:* For master's, 3 letters of recommendation. Additional exam requirements/recommendations for international students: Required—TOEFL (minimum score 550 paper-based; 213 computer-based). *Application deadline:* For fall admission, 7/1 priority date for domestic and international students; for spring admission, 12/1 priority date for domestic and international students. Applications are processed on a rolling basis. Application fee: $35 ($40 for international students). Electronic applications accepted. *Expenses:* Tuition, state resident: full-time $5522; part-time $306.80 per credit hour. Tuition, nonresident: full-time $14,253; part-time $792.10 per credit hour. Required fees: $658; $49 per credit hour. One-time fee: $12. Tuition and fees vary according to program. *Financial support:* In 2010–11, 3 research assistantships with full and partial tuition reimbursements (averaging $12,000 per year) were awarded; career-related internships or fieldwork also available. Financial award application deadline: 4/1; financial award applicants required to submit FAFSA. *Faculty research:* Urban policy, public finance, evaluation. *Unit head:* Dr. Brady Baybeck, Director, 314-516-5145, Fax: 314-516-5210, E-mail: baybeck@umsl.edu. *Application contact:* 314-516-5458, Fax: 314-516-6996, E-mail: gradadm@umsl.edu.

The University of Montana, Graduate School, College of Arts and Sciences, Department of Political Science, Program in Public Administration, Missoula, MT 59812-0002. Offers MPA, JD/MPA. MPA offered jointly with Montana State University. *Degree requirements:* For master's, professional paper. *Entrance requirements:* For master's, GRE General Test.

University of Nebraska at Omaha, Graduate Studies, College of Public Affairs and Community Service, School of Public Administration, Omaha, NE 68182. Offers public administration (MPA, PhD); public management (Certificate); urban studies (MS). *Accreditation:* NASPAA (one or more programs are accredited). Part-time and evening/weekend programs available. Postbaccalaureate distance learning degree programs offered (no on-campus study). *Faculty:* 14 full-time (6 women). *Students:* 36 full-time (21 women), 156 part-time (79 women); includes 13 minority (9 Black or African American, non-Hispanic/Latino; 1 Asian, non-Hispanic/Latino; 3 Hispanic/Latino), 12 international. Average age 33. 125 applicants, 46% accepted, 47 enrolled. In 2010, 63 master's, 1 doctorate, 2 other advanced degrees awarded. *Degree requirements:* For master's, comprehensive exam (for some programs), thesis (for some programs); for doctorate, comprehensive exam, thesis/dissertation. *Entrance requirements:* For master's, GRE General Test, minimum GPA of 3.0, letters of recommendation; for doctorate, GRE General Test, master's degree, minimum graduate GPA of 3.35, resume. Additional exam requirements/recommendations for international students: Required—TOEFL (minimum score 550 paper-based; 213 computer-based; 80 iBT). *Application deadline:* For fall admission, 6/1 for domestic students; for spring admission, 10/1 for domestic students. Applications are processed on a rolling basis. Application fee: $45. Electronic applications accepted. *Financial support:* In 2010–11, 91 students received support; research assistantships with tuition reimbursements available, career-related internships or fieldwork, Federal Work-Study, institutionally sponsored loans, scholarships/grants, tuition waivers (partial), and unspecified assistantships available. Support available to part-time students. Financial award application deadline: 3/1. *Unit head:* Dr. John Bartle, Director, 402-554-2625. *Application contact:* Meagan Van Gelder, Student Contact, 402-554-2341, Fax: 402-554-3143, E-mail: graduate@unomaha.edu.

University of Nevada, Las Vegas, Graduate College, Greenspun College of Urban Affairs, School of Environmental and Public Affairs, Las Vegas, NV 89154-4030. Offers crisis and emergency management (MS); environmental science (MS, PhD); non-profit management (Certificate); public administration (MPA); public affairs (PhD); public management (Certificate). Part-time programs available. *Faculty:* 6 full-time (2 women). *Students:* 55 full-time (27 women), 95 part-time (55 women); includes 63 minority (17 Black or African American, non-Hispanic/Latino; 2 American Indian or Alaska Native, non-Hispanic/Latino; 5 Asian, non-Hispanic/Latino; 20 Hispanic/Latino; 19 Two or more races, non-Hispanic/Latino), 8 international. Average age 35. 67 applicants, 72% accepted, 35 enrolled. In 2010, 61 master's, 2 doctorates, 24 other advanced degrees awarded. *Degree requirements:* For master's, comprehensive exam (for some programs), thesis; for doctorate, comprehensive exam (for some programs), thesis/dissertation. *Entrance requirements:* Additional exam requirements/recommendations for international students: Required—TOEFL (minimum score 550 paper-based; 213 computer-based; 80 iBT), IELTS (minimum score 7). *Application deadline:* For fall admission, 2/15 priority date for domestic and international students; for spring admission, 11/15 priority date for domestic and international students. Applications are processed on a rolling basis. Application fee: $60 ($95 for international students). Electronic applications accepted. *Expenses:* Tuition, area resident: Part-time $239.50 per credit. Tuition, state resident: part-time $239.50 per credit. Tuition, nonresident: part-time $503 per credit. Required fees: $108 per semester. Tuition and fees vary according to course load, program and reciprocity agreements. *Financial support:* In 2010–11, 9 students received support, including 6 research assistantships with partial tuition reimbursements available (averaging $13,850 per year), 3 teaching assistantships with partial tuition reimbursements available (averaging $10,666 per year); institutionally sponsored loans, scholarships/grants, health care benefits, and unspecified assistantships also available. Financial award application deadline: 3/1. *Faculty research:* Environmental decision-making and management; budgeting and human resource/workforce management; urban design, sustainability and governance; participatory simulation modeling of environmental issues; public and nonprofit management. Total annual research expenditures: $1.1 million. *Unit head:* Dr. Ed Weber, Chair/Associate Professor, 702-895-4440, Fax: 702-895-4436, E-mail: edward.weber@unlv.edu. *Application contact:* Graduate College Admissions Evaluator, 702-895-3320, Fax: 702-895-4180, E-mail: gradcollege@unlv.edu.

University of Nevada, Reno, Graduate School, College of Liberal Arts, Department of Political Science, Program in Public Administration and Policy, Reno, NV 89557. Offers public administration (MPA). *Degree requirements:* For master's, comprehensive exam, oral exam/thesis or professional paper. *Entrance requirements:* For master's, GRE General Test, GMAT, or LSAT, minimum GPA of 2.75. Additional exam requirements/recommendations for international students: Required—TOEFL (minimum score 500 paper-based; 173 computer-based; 61 iBT), IELTS (minimum score 6). Electronic applications accepted. *Expenses:* Tuition, state resident: full-time $2219; part-time $246 per credit. Tuition, nonresident: part-time $510 per credit. International tuition: $9009 full-time. Required fees: $59 per term. One-time fee: $101. Tuition and fees vary according to course load. *Faculty research:* Administrative processes and problems, public policy issues.

University of New Brunswick Fredericton, School of Graduate Studies, Faculty of Business Administration, Fredericton, NB E3B 5A3, Canada. Offers business administration (MBA); engineering management (MBA); entrepreneurship (MBA); sports and recreation management (MBA); MBA/LL B. Part-time programs available. *Faculty:* 23 full-time (3 women), 5 part-time/adjunct (2 women). *Students:* 43 full-time (18 women), 35 part-time (20 women). In 2010, 29 master's awarded. *Degree requirements:* For master's, thesis optional. *Entrance requirements:* For master's, GMAT (550 minimum score), minimum GPA of 3.0; 3-5 years work experience. Additional exam requirements/recommendations for international students: Required—TOEFL (minimum score 580 paper-based; 92 iBT), IELTS (minimum score 7), TOEFL or IELTS. *Application deadline:* For fall admission, 3/1 priority date for domestic students. Applications are processed on a rolling basis. Application fee: $50 Canadian dollars. *Expenses:* Tuition, area resident: Full-time $3708; part-time $927 per term. International tuition: $6300 full-time. Required fees: $50 per term. *Financial support:* In 2010–11, 4 research assistantships (averaging $4,500 per year), 13 teaching assistantships (averaging $2,250 per year) were awarded. *Faculty research:* Accounting and auditing practices, human resource management, the non-profit sector, marketing, strategic management, entrepreneurship, investment practices, supply chain management, and operations management. *Unit head:* Judy Roy, Director of Graduate Studies, 506-458-7307, Fax: 506-453-3561, E-mail: jroy@unb.ca. *Application contact:* Marilyn Davis, Acting Graduate Secretary, 506-453-4766, Fax: 506-453-3561, E-mail: mbacontact@unb.ca.

University of New Hampshire, Center for Graduate and Professional Studies, Manchester, NH 03101. Offers business administration (MBA); counseling (M Ed); education (M Ed, MAT); educational administration and supervision (M Ed, Ed S); industrial statistics (Certificate); public administration (MPA); public health (MPH, Certificate); social work (MSW); software systems engineering (Certificate). Part-time and evening/weekend programs available. *Students:* 97 full-time (65 women), 159 part-time (85 women); includes 20 minority (11 Black or African American, non-Hispanic/Latino; 1 American Indian or Alaska Native, non-Hispanic/Latino; 6 Asian, non-Hispanic/Latino; 2 Hispanic/Latino), 2 international. 119 applicants, 71% accepted, 61 enrolled. In 2010, 79 master's, 1 other advanced degree awarded. *Degree requirements:* For master's, thesis or alternative. *Entrance requirements:* Additional exam requirements/recommendations for international students: Required—TOEFL (minimum score 550 paper-based; 213 computer-based; 80 iBT). *Application deadline:* For fall admission, 6/1 for domestic students, 4/1 for international students; for spring admission, 12/1 for domestic students. Applications are processed on a rolling basis. Application fee: $65. Electronic applications accepted. *Financial support:* In 2010–11, 21 students received support, including 1 fellowship, 1 teaching assistantship; research assistantships, Federal Work-Study, scholarships/grants, health care benefits, and unspecified assistantships also available. Support available to part-time students. Financial award application deadline: 3/1; financial award applicants required to submit FAFSA. *Unit head:* Kate Ferreira, Director, 603-641-4313, E-mail: unhm.gradcenter@unh.edu. *Application contact:* Graduate Admissions Office, 603-862-3000, Fax: 603-862-0275, E-mail: grad.school@unh.edu.

University of New Hampshire, Graduate School, College of Liberal Arts, Department of Political Science, Program in Public Administration, Durham, NH 03824. Offers MPA. Part-time programs available. *Faculty:* 15 full-time. *Students:* 20 full-time (7 women), 40 part-time (22 women); includes 1 Black or African American, non-Hispanic/Latino, 1 international. Average age 36. 37 applicants, 84% accepted, 21 enrolled. In 2010, 11 master's awarded. *Entrance requirements:* For master's, GMAT or GRE General Test. Additional exam requirements/recommendations for international students: Required—TOEFL (minimum score 550 paper-based; 213 computer-based; 80 iBT). *Application deadline:* For fall admission, 6/1 priority date for domestic students, 4/1 for international students; for spring admission, 12/1 for domestic students. Applications are processed on a rolling basis. Application fee: $65. Electronic applications accepted. *Financial support:* In 2010–11, 4 students received support, including 1 fellowship, 3 teaching assistantships; research assistantships, career-related internships or fieldwork, Federal Work-Study, scholarships/grants, and tuition waivers (full and partial) also available. Support available to part-time students. Financial award application deadline: 2/15. *Unit head:* Dr. Dante Scala, Chairperson, 603-862-3225. *Application contact:* Janis Marshal, Administrative Assistant, 603-862-1750, E-mail: mpa.ma.political.science.grad@unh.edu.

University of New Haven, Graduate School, Henry C. Lee College of Criminal Justice and Forensic Sciences, National Security and Public Safety Program, West Haven, CT 06516-1916. Offers information protection and security (MS); national security (Certificate); national security administration (Certificate). Part-time and evening/weekend programs available. *Students:* 36 full-time (15 women), 38 part-time (17 women); includes 7 Black or African American, non-Hispanic/Latino; 2 American Indian or Alaska Native, non-Hispanic/Latino; 2 Asian, non-Hispanic/Latino; 10 Hispanic/Latino, 6 international. Average age 32. 27 applicants, 96% accepted, 19 enrolled. In 2010, 28 master's awarded. *Entrance requirements:* Additional exam requirements/recommendations for international students: Required—TOEFL (minimum score 520 paper-based; 190 computer-based; 70 iBT); Recommended—IELTS (minimum score 5.5). *Application deadline:* For fall admission, 5/31 for international students; for winter admission, 10/15 for international students; for spring admission, 1/15 for international students. Applications are processed on a rolling basis. Application fee: $50. Electronic applications accepted. *Financial support:* Research assistantships with partial tuition reimbursements, teaching assistantships with partial tuition reimbursements, career-related internships or fieldwork, Federal Work-Study, scholarships/grants, tuition waivers, and unspecified assistantships available. Support available to part-time students. Financial award applicants required to submit FAFSA. *Unit head:* Dr. William L. Tafoya, Dean, 203-932-7260. *Application contact:* Eloise Gormley, Director of Graduate Admissions, 203-932-7449, Fax: 203-932-7137, E-mail: gradinfo@newhaven.edu.

University of New Haven, Graduate School, Henry C. Lee College of Criminal Justice and Forensic Sciences, Program in Fire Science, West Haven, CT 06516-1916. Offers emergency management (Certificate); fire administration (MS); fire science technology (Certificate); fire/arson investigation (MS, Certificate); forensic science/fire science (Certificate); public safety management (MS, Certificate). Part-time and evening/weekend programs available. *Students:* 3 full-time (0 women), 15 part-time (3 women); includes 1 Black or African American, non-Hispanic/Latino, 1 international. Average age 38. 6 applicants, 100% accepted, 4 enrolled. In 2010, 4 master's, 3 other advanced degrees awarded. *Degree requirements:* For master's, thesis or alternative. *Entrance requirements:* Additional exam requirements/recommendations for international students: Required—TOEFL (minimum score 520 paper-based; 190 computer-based; 70 iBT); Recommended—IELTS (minimum score 5.5). *Application deadline:* For fall admission, 5/31 for international students; for winter admission, 10/15 for international students; for spring admission, 1/15 for international students. Applications are processed on a rolling basis. Application fee: $50. Electronic applications accepted. *Financial support:* Research assistantships with partial tuition reimbursements, teaching assistantships with partial tuition reimbursements, career-related internships or fieldwork, Federal Work-Study, scholarships/grants, tuition waivers, and unspecified assistantships available. Support available to part-time students. Financial award applicants required to submit FAFSA. *Unit head:* Robert E. Massicotte, Director, 203-932-7424. *Application contact:* Eloise Gormley, Director of Graduate Admissions, 203-932-7449, Fax: 203-932-7137, E-mail: gradinfo@newhaven.edu.

Public Administration

University of New Haven, Graduate School, School of Business, Program in Public Administration, West Haven, CT 06516-1916. Offers personnel and labor relations (MPA); public administration (MPA, Certificate), including city management (MPA), community-clinical services (MPA), health care management (MPA), long-term health care (MPA), personnel and labor relations (MPA), public administration (Certificate), public management (Certificate), public personnel management (Certificate); MBA/MPA. Part-time and evening/weekend programs available. *Students:* 37 full-time (19 women), 33 part-time (18 women); includes 15 Black or African American, non-Hispanic/Latino; 1 Asian, non-Hispanic/Latino; 4 Hispanic/Latino, 9 international. Average age 33. 51 applicants, 100% accepted, 35 enrolled. In 2010, 14 master's, 4 other advanced degrees awarded. *Degree requirements:* For master's, thesis or alternative. *Entrance requirements:* Additional exam requirements/recommendations for international students: Required—TOEFL (minimum score 520 paper-based; 190 computer-based; 70 iBT); Recommended—IELTS (minimum score 5.5). *Application deadline:* For fall admission, 5/31 for international students; for winter admission, 10/15 for international students; for spring admission, 1/15 for international students. Applications are processed on a rolling basis. Application fee: $50. Electronic applications accepted. *Expenses:* Contact institution. *Financial support:* Research assistantships with partial tuition reimbursements, teaching assistantships with partial tuition reimbursements, career-related internships or fieldwork, Federal Work-Study, scholarships/grants, tuition waivers, and unspecified assistantships available. Support available to part-time students. Financial award application deadline: 5/1; financial award applicants required to submit FAFSA. *Unit head:* Charles Coleman, Chairman, 203-932-7375. *Application contact:* Eloise Gormley, Director of Graduate Admissions, 203-932-7449, Fax: 203-932-7137, E-mail: gradinfo@newhaven.edu.

University of New Mexico, Graduate School, School of Public Administration, Albuquerque, NM 87131-2039. Offers MPA, JD/MPA, MPA/MCRP, MSN/MPA. *Accreditation:* NASPAA (one or more programs are accredited). Part-time and evening/weekend programs available. Post-baccalaureate distance learning degree programs offered (no on-campus study). *Faculty:* 10 full-time (3 women), 3 part-time/adjunct (1 woman). *Students:* 60 full-time (35 women), 159 part-time (100 women); includes 138 minority (6 Black or African American, non-Hispanic/Latino; 32 American Indian or Alaska Native, non-Hispanic/Latino; 5 Asian, non-Hispanic/Latino; 88 Hispanic/Latino; 1 Native Hawaiian or other Pacific Islander, non-Hispanic/Latino; 6 Two or more races, non-Hispanic/Latino), 4 international. Average age 35. 145 applicants, 57% accepted, 64 enrolled. In 2010, 31 master's awarded. *Degree requirements:* For master's, thesis optional, professional paper. *Entrance requirements:* For master's, minimum GPA of 3.0, 3 letters of recommendation, resume, letter of intent. Additional exam requirements/recommendations for international students: Required—TOEFL (minimum score 520 paper-based; 190 computer-based; 68 iBT). *Application deadline:* For fall admission, 6/1 for domestic students, 3/1 for international students; for spring admission, 11/1 for domestic students, 8/1 for international students. Application fee: $50. Electronic applications accepted. *Expenses:* Tuition, state resident: full-time $5991; part-time $251 per credit hour. Tuition, nonresident: full-time $14,405; part-time $800.20 per credit hour. Tuition and fees vary according to course level, course load, program and reciprocity agreements. *Financial support:* In 2010-11, 104 students received support, including 2 fellowships with tuition reimbursements available (averaging $5,400 per year), 3 research assistantships with tuition reimbursements available (averaging $7,171 per year); career-related internships or fieldwork, scholarships/grants, health care benefits, and unspecified assistantships also available. Financial award application deadline: 3/31; financial award applicants required to submit FAFSA. *Faculty research:* Human resources, health care policy and management, privatization, program evaluation, comparative administration, budget and finance. Total annual research expenditures: $65,961. *Unit head:* Dr. Uday Desai, Director, 505-277-1092, Fax: 505-277-2529, E-mail: ucdesai@unm.edu. *Application contact:* Kristen L. Cole, Department Administrator, 505-277-9196, Fax: 505-277-2529, E-mail: klcole@unm.edu.

University of New Orleans, Graduate School, College of Liberal Arts, Department of Political Science, Program in Public Administration, New Orleans, LA 70148. Offers MPA. *Degree requirements:* For master's, thesis. *Entrance requirements:* For master's, GRE General Test. Additional exam requirements/recommendations for international students: Required—TOEFL (minimum score 550 paper-based; 213 computer-based; 79 iBT). Electronic applications accepted.

The University of North Carolina at Chapel Hill, Graduate School, School of Government, Chapel Hill, NC 27599. Offers MPA, JD/MPA, MPA/MRP, MPA/MSW. *Accreditation:* NASPAA. *Faculty:* 15 full-time (3 women), 2 part-time/adjunct (both women). *Students:* 43 full-time (27 women); includes 9 minority (8 Black or African American, non-Hispanic/Latino; 1 Hispanic/Latino). Average age 25. 98 applicants, 34% accepted, 24 enrolled. In 2010, 18 master's awarded. *Degree requirements:* For master's, comprehensive exam. *Entrance requirements:* For master's, GRE General Test, minimum GPA of 3.0. Additional exam requirements/recommendations for international students: Required—TOEFL. *Application deadline:* For fall admission, 1/1 priority date for domestic students. Applications are processed on a rolling basis. Application fee: $60. Electronic applications accepted. *Financial support:* In 2010-11, 35 students received support, including fellowships with full tuition reimbursements available (averaging $7,000 per year), 25 research assistantships with full tuition reimbursements available (averaging $5,000 per year), 1 teaching assistantship with full tuition reimbursement available (averaging $7,000 per year); career-related internships or fieldwork, Federal Work-Study, and scholarships/grants also available. Financial award application deadline: 3/1; financial award applicants required to submit FAFSA. *Faculty research:* Local government management, nonprofit management. *Unit head:* Dr. David N. Ammons, Director, 919-962-7696, Fax: 919-962-8271, E-mail: ammons@iogmail.iog.unc.edu. *Application contact:* Jessica C. Russell, Admissions Coordinator, 919-962-0425, Fax: 919-962-8271, E-mail: mpastaff@iogmail.iog.unc.edu.

The University of North Carolina at Charlotte, Graduate School, College of Arts and Sciences, Department of Political Science, Charlotte, NC 28223-0001. Offers emergency management (Certificate); non-profit management (Certificate); public administration (MPA, PhD), including arts administration (MPA), emergency management (MPA), non-profit management (MPA), public finance (MPA), urban management and policy (PhD); public finance (Certificate); public policy (PhD); urban management and policy (Certificate). *Accreditation:* NASPAA. Part-time and evening/weekend programs available. *Faculty:* 19 full-time (8 women), 3 part-time/adjunct (2 women). *Students:* 51 full-time (37 women), 75 part-time (49 women); includes 32 minority (26 Black or African American, non-Hispanic/Latino; 1 Asian, non-Hispanic/Latino; 2 Hispanic/Latino; 3 Two or more races, non-Hispanic/Latino), 11 international. Average age 29. 99 applicants, 72% accepted, 42 enrolled. In 2010, 15 master's, 5 doctorates awarded. *Degree requirements:* For master's, thesis or alternative; for doctorate, thesis/dissertation. *Entrance requirements:* For master's, GRE General Test or MAT, minimum GPA of 3.0 in undergraduate major, 2.75 overall. Additional exam requirements/recommendations for international students: Required—TOEFL (minimum score 557 paper-based; 220 computer-based; 83 iBT). *Application deadline:* For fall admission, 7/1 for domestic students, 5/1 for international students; for spring admission, 11/1 for domestic students, 10/1 for international students. Applications are processed on a rolling basis. Application fee: $55. Electronic applications accepted. *Expenses:* Tuition, state resident: full-time $3464. Tuition, nonresident: full-time $14,297. Required fees: $2094. Tuition and fees vary according to course load. *Financial support:* In 2010-11, 22 students received support, including 16 research assistantships (averaging $6,943 per year), 6 teaching assistantships (averaging $9,380 per year); career-related internships or fieldwork, Federal Work-Study, institutionally sponsored loans, scholarships/grants, unspecified assistantships, and administrative assistantship also available. Support available to part-time students. Financial award application deadline: 4/1; financial award applicants required to submit FAFSA. *Faculty research:* Terrorism, public administration, nonprofit and arts administration, educational policy, social policy. Total annual research expenditures: $242,404. *Unit head:* Dr. Theodore S. Arrington, Chair, 704-687-2571, Fax: 704-687-3497, E-mail: tarrngtn@uncc.edu. *Application contact:* Kathy B. Giddings, Director of Graduate Admissions, 704-687-5503, Fax: 704-687-3279, E-mail: gradadm@uncc.edu.

The University of North Carolina at Pembroke, Graduate Studies, Public Administration Program, Pembroke, NC 28372-1510. Offers MPA. Part-time and evening/weekend programs available. *Degree requirements:* For master's, comprehensive exam, thesis optional. *Entrance requirements:* For master's, GRE General Test or MAT, minimum GPA of 3.0 in major, 2.5 overall; interview. Additional exam requirements/recommendations for international students: Required—TOEFL.

The University of North Carolina Wilmington, College of Arts and Sciences, Department of Public and International Affairs, Wilmington, NC 28403-3297. Offers MPA. *Accreditation:* NASPAA. Part-time programs available. *Faculty:* 13 full-time (3 women). *Students:* 31 full-time (16 women), 43 part-time (25 women); includes 8 minority (2 Black or African American, non-Hispanic/Latino; 2 Asian, non-Hispanic/Latino; 1 Hispanic/Latino; 1 Native Hawaiian or other Pacific Islander, non-Hispanic/Latino; 2 Two or more races, non-Hispanic/Latino), 2 international. Average age 32. 48 applicants, 83% accepted, 35 enrolled. In 2010, 17 master's awarded. *Degree requirements:* For master's, comprehensive exam, thesis or alternative, practicum. *Entrance requirements:* For master's, GRE, GMAT. Additional exam requirements/recommendations for international students: Required—TOEFL (minimum score 550 paper-based; 217 computer-based; 79 iBT), IELTS (minimum score 6.5). *Application deadline:* For fall admission, 4/15 for domestic students; for spring admission, 9/1 for domestic students. Application fee: $60. *Financial support:* In 2010-11, 9 teaching assistantships with full and partial tuition reimbursements (averaging $9,500 per year) were awarded. Financial award application deadline: 3/15. *Unit head:* Dr. Roger Lowery, Chair, 910-962-3225, E-mail: lowery@uncw.edu. *Application contact:* Dr. Mark Imperial, Graduate Coordinator, 910-962-7928, E-mail: imperialm@uncw.edu.

University of North Dakota, Graduate School, College of Business and Public Administration, Department of Public Administration, Grand Forks, ND 58202. Offers MPA. *Accreditation:* NASPAA. Part-time programs available. Postbaccalaureate distance learning degree programs offered (minimal on-campus study). *Faculty:* 9 full-time (1 woman), 1 part-time/adjunct (0 women). *Students:* 16 full-time (10 women), 44 part-time (17 women); includes 6 minority (1 Black or African American, non-Hispanic/Latino; 3 American Indian or Alaska Native, non-Hispanic/Latino; 2 Hispanic/Latino), 1 international. Average age 31. 42 applicants, 74% accepted, 26 enrolled. In 2010, 12 master's awarded. *Degree requirements:* For master's, comprehensive exam, thesis or alternative, final exam. *Entrance requirements:* For master's, GRE General Test, GMAT or LSAT, minimum GPA of 3.0. Additional exam requirements/recommendations for international students: Required—TOEFL (minimum score 550 paper-based; 213 computer-based; 79 iBT), IELTS (minimum score 6.5). *Application deadline:* For fall admission, 8/1 priority date for domestic students, 5/1 priority date for international students; for spring admission, 12/1 priority date for domestic students, 9/1 priority date for international students. Applications are processed on a rolling basis. Application fee: $35. Electronic applications accepted. *Expenses:* Tuition, state resident: full-time $5857; part-time $306.74 per credit. Tuition, nonresident: full-time $15,666; part-time $729.77 per credit. Required fees: $53.42 per credit. Tuition and fees vary according to course load, program and reciprocity agreements. *Financial support:* In 2010-11, 7 students received support; fellowships with full and partial tuition reimbursements available, research assistantships with full and partial tuition reimbursements available, teaching assistantships with full and partial tuition reimbursements available, Federal Work-Study, institutionally sponsored loans, scholarships/grants, health care benefits, tuition waivers (full and partial), and unspecified assistantships available. Support available to part-time students. Financial award application deadline: 3/15; financial award applicants required to submit FAFSA. *Unit head:* Dr. Jason Jensen, Director, 701-777-3831, Fax: 701-777-5099, E-mail: jason_jensen2@und.nodak.edu. *Application contact:* Matt Anderson, Admissions Specialist, 701-777-2947, Fax: 701-777-3619, E-mail: matthew.anderson@gradschool.und.edu.

University of North Florida, College of Arts and Sciences, Department of Political Science and Public Administration, Jacksonville, FL 32224. Offers nonprofit management (Graduate Certificate); public administration (MPA). *Accreditation:* NASPAA. Part-time programs available. *Faculty:* 11 full-time (3 women), 1 part-time/adjunct (0 women). *Students:* 27 full-time (15 women), 48 part-time (27 women); includes 11 Black or African American, non-Hispanic/Latino; 3 Asian, non-Hispanic/Latino; 7 Hispanic/Latino; 1 Native Hawaiian or other Pacific Islander, non-Hispanic/Latino; 2 Two or more races, non-Hispanic/Latino, 1 international. Average age 30. 38 applicants, 55% accepted, 13 enrolled. In 2010, 27 master's awarded. *Degree requirements:* For master's, thesis or alternative, internship. *Entrance requirements:* For master's, GRE General Test, minimum GPA of 3.0 in last 60 hours, 2 letters of recommendation, interview. Additional exam requirements/recommendations for international students: Required—TOEFL (minimum score 500 paper-based; 173 computer-based; 61 iBT). *Application deadline:* For fall admission, 7/1 priority date for domestic students, 5/1 for international students; for spring admission, 11/1 priority date for domestic students, 10/1 for international students. Applications are processed on a rolling basis. Application fee: $30. Electronic applications accepted. *Expenses:* Tuition, state resident: full-time $7646.40; part-time $318.60 per credit hour. Tuition, nonresident: full-time $23,502; part-time $979.24 per credit hour. Required fees: $1208.88; $50.37 per credit hour. Tuition and fees vary according to course load and program. *Financial support:* In 2010-11, 20 students received support, including 1 research assistantship (averaging $2,354 per year), 2 teaching assistantships (averaging $3,667 per year); career-related internships or fieldwork, Federal Work-Study, scholarships/grants, tuition waivers (partial), and unspecified assistantships also available. Financial award application deadline: 4/1; financial award applicants required to submit FAFSA. *Faculty research:* America's usage of the Internet, use of information communication technologies by educators and children. Total annual research expenditures: $23,372. *Unit head:* Dr. Matthew T. Corrigan, Chair, 904-620-2977, Fax: 904-620-2979, E-mail: mcorriga@unf.edu. *Application contact:* Lillith Richardson, Assistant Director, The Graduate School, 904-620-1360, Fax: 907-620-1362, E-mail: graduateschool@unf.edu.

University of North Texas, Toulouse Graduate School, College of Public Affairs and Community Service, Department of Public Administration, Denton, TX 76203. Offers public administration (MPA); public administration and management (PhD). *Accreditation:* NASPAA. Part-time and evening/weekend programs available. *Degree requirements:* For master's, comprehensive exam, thesis optional, paid internship; for doctorate, comprehensive exam, thesis/dissertation. *Entrance requirements:* For master's, GRE General Test or GMAT, minimum GPA of 3.0 on last 60 hours; for doctorate, GRE General Test, minimum GPA of 3.2 on last 60 hours. Additional exam requirements/recommendations for international students: Required—TOEFL (minimum score 550 paper-based; 213 computer-based; 79 iBT). *Application deadline:* Applications are processed on a rolling basis. Electronic applications accepted. *Expenses:* Tuition, state resident: full-time $4298; part-time $239 per credit hour. Tuition, nonresident: full-time $10,782; part-time $549 per credit hour. Required fees: $1292; $270 per credit hour. *Financial support:* Fellowships with partial tuition reimbursements, research assistantships with partial tuition reimbursements, teaching assistantships with partial tuition reimbursements, career-related internships or fieldwork, Federal Work-Study, institutionally sponsored loans, and tuition waivers (full and partial) available. Support available to part-time students. Financial award applicants required to submit FAFSA. *Faculty research:* Municipal management, government financial management, public/private cooperation, emergency administration and planning, nonprofit management.

University of Oklahoma, College of Arts and Sciences, Department of Political Science, Program in Public Administration, Norman, OK 73019-0390. Offers MPA. Part-time and evening/weekend programs available. *Students:* 59 full-time (40 women), 156 part-time (64 women); includes 61 minority (26 Black or African American, non-Hispanic/Latino; 10 American Indian or Alaska Native, non-Hispanic/Latino; 12 Asian, non-Hispanic/Latino; 7 Hispanic/Latino; 6 Two or more races, non-Hispanic/Latino), 9 international. Average age 31. 92 applicants, 90% accepted, 59 enrolled. In 2010, 74 master's awarded. *Entrance requirements:* For master's, minimum GPA of 2.75 or GRE. Additional exam requirements/recommendations for international students: Required—TOEFL (minimum score 600 paper-based; 250 computer-based; 79 iBT). *Application deadline:* For fall admission, 2/1 for domestic and international students;

for spring admission, 10/1 for domestic students, 9/1 for international students. Application fee: $40 ($90 for international students). Electronic applications accepted. *Expenses:* Tuition, state resident: full-time $3893; part-time $162.20 per credit hour. Tuition, nonresident: full-time $14,167; part-time $590.30 per credit hour. Required fees: $2523; $94.60 per credit hour. Tuition and fees vary according to course load and degree level. *Financial support:* In 2010–11, 59 students received support. *Faculty research:* Risk perception, education diversity policy, health policy, public sector contracting, citizen participation. *Unit head:* Greg Russell, Department Chair, 405-325-5517, Fax: 405-325-3733, E-mail: grussell@ou.edu. *Application contact:* Deborah Snider, Academic Counselor, 405-325-6432, Fax: 405-325-3733, E-mail: dsnider@ou.edu.

University of Ottawa, Faculty of Graduate and Postdoctoral Studies, Interdisciplinary Programs, Ottawa, ON K1N 6N5, Canada. Offers e-business (Certificate); e-commerce (Certificate); finance (Certificate); health services and policies research (Diploma); population health (PhD); population health risk assessment and management (Certificate); public management and governance (Certificate); systems science (Certificate).

University of Pennsylvania, School of Arts and Sciences, Fels Institute of Government, Philadelphia, PA 19104. Offers MGA. Part-time and evening/weekend programs available. *Students:* 57 full-time (23 women), 69 part-time (39 women); includes 12 Black or African American, non-Hispanic/Latino; 3 Asian, non-Hispanic/Latino; 4 Hispanic/Latino, 13 international. 476 applicants, 44% accepted, 99 enrolled. In 2010, 48 master's awarded. *Entrance requirements:* For master's, GRE. Additional exam requirements/recommendations for international students: Required—TOEFL or IELTS. *Application deadline:* For fall admission, 1/15 for domestic students. Applications are processed on a rolling basis. Application fee: $70. *Expenses:* Tuition: Full-time $25,660; part-time $4758 per course. Required fees: $2152; $270 per course. Tuition and fees vary according to course load, degree level and program. *Financial support:* Fellowships, institutionally sponsored loans and scholarships/grants available. Financial award application deadline: 1/15; financial award applicants required to submit FAFSA. *Unit head:* David B. Thornburgh, Director, 215-898-2600. *Application contact:* Ilene Ford, Administrative Coordinator, 215-898-2600, Fax: 215-898-6238, E-mail: felsinstitute@sas.upenn.edu.

University of Phoenix, School of Business, Phoenix, AZ 85034-7209. Offers accounting (MBA, MSA); business administration (MBA); energy management (MBA); global management (MBA); health care management (MBA); human resources management (MM); international management (MM); management (MM); marketing (MBA); project management (MBA); public administration (MPA); technology management (MBA). Programs are offered at the online campus. Evening/weekend programs available. Postbaccalaureate distance learning degree programs offered. *Students:* 20,237 full-time (12,641 women); includes 6,424 minority (4,376 Black or African American, non-Hispanic/Latino; 150 American Indian or Alaska Native, non-Hispanic/Latino; 546 Asian, non-Hispanic/Latino; 1,137 Hispanic/Latino; 155 Native Hawaiian or other Pacific Islander, non-Hispanic/Latino; 60 Two or more races, non-Hispanic/Latino), 1,149 international. Average age 39. *Entrance requirements:* For master's, minimum undergraduate GPA of 2.5 from accredited university, 3 years of work experience, citizen of the United States or have valid visa. Additional exam requirements/recommendations for international students: Required—TOEFL (minimum paper score 550, computer score 213, iBT 79), Test of English for International Communication, or IELTS. *Application deadline:* Applications are processed on a rolling basis. Application fee: $45. Electronic applications accepted. *Expenses:* Tuition: Full-time $16,440. One-time fee: $45 full-time. Full-time tuition and fees vary according to course load, degree level, campus/location and program. *Financial support:* Scholarships/grants available. Financial award applicants required to submit FAFSA. *Unit head:* Dr. Bill Berry, Director, 480-557-1824, E-mail: bill.berry@phoenix.edu. *Application contact:* Dr. Bill Berry, Director, 480-557-1824, E-mail: bill.berry@phoenix.edu.

University of Phoenix–Atlanta Campus, School of Business, Sandy Springs, GA 30350-4153. Offers accounting (MBA); business administration (MBA); global management (MBA); human resources management (MBA, MM); management (MM); marketing (MBA); public administration (MM). Evening/weekend programs available. Postbaccalaureate distance learning degree programs offered. *Degree requirements:* For master's, thesis (for some programs). *Entrance requirements:* For master's, minimum undergraduate GPA of 3.0, 3 years of work experience. Additional exam requirements/recommendations for international students: Required—TOEFL (minimum score 550 paper-based; 213 computer-based; 79 iBT).

University of Phoenix–Augusta Campus, School of Business, Augusta, GA 30909-4583. Offers accounting (MBA); business administration (MBA); business and management (MBA, MM); global management (MBA); human resources management (MBA, MM); management (MM); marketing (MBA); public administration (MBA, MM). Postbaccalaureate distance learning degree programs offered.

University of Phoenix–Austin Campus, School of Business, Austin, TX 78759. Offers accounting (MBA); business administration (MBA); business and management (MBA); e-business (MBA); global management (MBA); human resources management (MBA, MM); management (MM); marketing (MBA); public administration (MBA). Postbaccalaureate distance learning degree programs offered.

University of Phoenix–Birmingham Campus, College of Graduate Business and Management, Birmingham, AL 35244. Offers accounting (MBA); business administration (MBA); global management (MBA); human resources management (MBA, MM); management (MM); marketing (MBA); public administration (MM).

University of Phoenix–Central Florida Campus, School of Business, Maitland, FL 32751-7057. Offers accounting (MBA); business administration (MBA); business and management (MM); global management (MBA); human resources management (MBA, MM); management (MM); marketing (MBA); public administration (MBA, MM). Evening/weekend programs available. *Degree requirements:* For master's, thesis (for some programs). *Entrance requirements:* For master's, minimum undergraduate GPA of 3.0, 3 years work experience. Additional exam requirements/recommendations for international students: Required—TOEFL (minimum score 550 paper-based; 213 computer-based; 79 iBT). Electronic applications accepted.

University of Phoenix–Central Valley Campus, School of Business, Fresno, CA 93720-1562. Offers accounting (MBA); business administration (MBA); global management (MBA); human resources management (MBA, MM); management (MM); marketing (MBA); public administration (MBA, MM).

University of Phoenix–Chattanooga Campus, School of Business, Chattanooga, TN 37421-3707. Offers accounting (MBA); business administration (MBA); business and management (MBA); global management (MBA); human resources management (MBA, MM); management (MM); marketing (MBA); public administration (MBA, MM). Postbaccalaureate distance learning degree programs offered.

University of Phoenix–Cheyenne Campus, School of Business, Cheyenne, WY 82009. Offers global management (MBA); human resources management (MBA, MM); management (MM); marketing (MBA); public administration (MBA, MM). Postbaccalaureate distance learning degree programs offered.

University of Phoenix–Cincinnati Campus, School of Business, West Chester, OH 45069-4875. Offers accounting (MBA); business administration (MBA); global management (MBA); human resources management (MBA, MM); management (MM); marketing (MBA); public administration (MM). Evening/weekend programs available. *Degree requirements:* For master's, thesis (for some programs). *Entrance requirements:* For master's, minimum undergraduate GPA of 3.0, 3 years of work experience. Additional exam requirements/recommendations for international students: Required—TOEFL (minimum score 550 paper-based; 213 computer-based; 79 iBT). Electronic applications accepted.

University of Phoenix–Cleveland Campus, School of Business, Independence, OH 44131-2194. Offers accounting (MBA); business administration (MBA); global management (MBA); human resources management (MBA, MM); management (MM); marketing (MBA); public administration (MBA, MM). Evening/weekend programs available. Postbaccalaureate distance learning degree programs offered (no on-campus study). *Degree requirements:* For master's, thesis (for some programs). *Entrance requirements:* For master's, minimum undergraduate GPA of 3.0, 3 years of work experience. Additional exam requirements/recommendations for international students: Required—TOEFL (minimum score 550 paper-based; 213 computer-based; 79 iBT). Electronic applications accepted.

University of Phoenix–Columbus Georgia Campus, School of Business, Columbus, GA 31904-6321. Offers accounting (MBA); business administration (MBA); global management (MBA); human resources management (MBA, MM); management (MM); marketing (MBA); public administration (MBA). Evening/weekend programs available. *Degree requirements:* For master's, thesis (for some programs). *Entrance requirements:* For master's, minimum undergraduate GPA of 3.0, 3 years of work experience. Additional exam requirements/recommendations for international students: Required—TOEFL (minimum score 550 paper-based; 213 computer-based; 79 iBT). Electronic applications accepted.

University of Phoenix–Columbus Ohio Campus, School of Business, Columbus, OH 43240-4032. Offers accounting (MBA); business administration (MBA); global management (MBA); human resources management (MBA, MM); management (MM); marketing (MBA); public administration (MM). Evening/weekend programs available. Postbaccalaureate distance learning degree programs offered. *Degree requirements:* For master's, thesis (for some programs). *Entrance requirements:* For master's, minimum undergraduate GPA of 3.0, 3 years of work experience. Additional exam requirements/recommendations for international students: Required—TOEFL (minimum score 550 paper-based; 213 computer-based; 79 iBT). Electronic applications accepted.

University of Phoenix–Dallas Campus, School of Business, Dallas, TX 75251-2009. Offers accounting (MBA); business administration (MBA); global management (MBA); human resources management (MBA, MM); management (MM); marketing (MBA); public administration (MBA, MM). Evening/weekend programs available. Postbaccalaureate distance learning degree programs offered. *Degree requirements:* For master's, thesis (for some programs). *Entrance requirements:* For master's, 3 years of work experience, minimum undergraduate GPA of 3.0. Additional exam requirements/recommendations for international students: Required—TOEFL (minimum score 550 paper-based; 213 computer-based; 79 iBT). Electronic applications accepted.

University of Phoenix–Denver Campus, School of Business, Lone Tree, CO 80124-5453. Offers accountancy (MSA); accounting (MBA); business administration (MBA); e-business (MBA); global management (MBA); human resources management (MBA, MM); management (MM); marketing (MBA); public administration (MBA, MM). Evening/weekend programs available. Postbaccalaureate distance learning degree programs offered. *Degree requirements:* For master's, thesis (for some programs). *Entrance requirements:* For master's, minimum undergraduate GPA of 3.0, 3 years work experience. Additional exam requirements/recommendations for international students: Required—TOEFL (minimum score 550 paper-based; 213 computer-based; 79 iBT). Electronic applications accepted.

University of Phoenix–Des Moines Campus, School of Business, Des Moines, IA 50266. Offers accounting (MBA); business administration (MBA); global management (MBA); human resources management (MBA, MM); management (MM); marketing (MBA); public administration (MBA, MM). Postbaccalaureate distance learning degree programs offered.

University of Phoenix–Eastern Washington Campus, School of Business, Spokane Valley, WA 99212-2531. Offers accounting (MBA); business administration (MBA); human resources management (MBA); marketing (MBA); public administration (MBA). Evening/weekend programs available. *Degree requirements:* For master's, thesis (for some programs). *Entrance requirements:* For master's, minimum undergraduate GPA of 3.0, 3 years of work experience. Additional exam requirements/recommendations for international students: Required—TOEFL (minimum score 550 paper-based; 213 computer-based; 79 iBT). Electronic applications accepted.

University of Phoenix–Harrisburg Campus, School of Business, Harrisburg, PA 17112. Offers accounting (MBA); business administration (MBA); business and management (MBA); global management (MBA); human resources management (MBA, MM); management (MM); marketing (MBA); public administration (MBA, MM). Postbaccalaureate distance learning degree programs offered.

University of Phoenix–Hawaii Campus, School of Business, Honolulu, HI 96813-4317. Offers accounting (MBA); business administration (MBA); global management (MBA); human resources management (MBA, MM); management (MM); marketing (MBA); public administration (MBA, MM). Evening/weekend programs available. *Degree requirements:* For master's, thesis (for some programs). *Entrance requirements:* For master's, minimum undergraduate GPA of 3.0, 3 years of work experience. Additional exam requirements/recommendations for international students: Required—TOEFL (minimum score 550 paper-based; 213 computer-based; 79 iBT). Electronic applications accepted.

University of Phoenix–Houston Campus, School of Business, Houston, TX 77079-2004. Offers accounting (MBA); business administration (MBA); global management (MBA); human resources management (MBA, MM); management (MM); marketing (MBA); public administration (MBA, MM). Evening/weekend programs available. Postbaccalaureate distance learning degree programs offered. *Degree requirements:* For master's, thesis (for some programs). *Entrance requirements:* For master's, 3 years of work experience, minimum undergraduate GPA of 3.0. Additional exam requirements/recommendations for international students: Required—TOEFL (minimum score 550 paper-based; 213 computer-based; 79 iBT). Electronic applications accepted.

University of Phoenix–Idaho Campus, School of Business, Meridian, ID 83642-3014. Offers accounting (MBA); administration (MBA); global management (MBA); human resources management (MBA, MM); management (MM); marketing (MBA); public administration (MM). Evening/weekend programs available. Postbaccalaureate distance learning degree programs offered. *Degree requirements:* For master's, thesis (for some programs). *Entrance requirements:* For master's, 3 years of work experience, minimum undergraduate GPA of 3.0. Additional exam requirements/recommendations for international students: Required—TOEFL (minimum score 550 paper-based; 213 computer-based). Electronic applications accepted.

University of Phoenix–Indianapolis Campus, School of Business, Indianapolis, IN 46250-932. Offers accounting (MBA); business administration (MBA); global management (MBA); human resources management (MBA, MM); management (MM); marketing (MBA); public administration (MM). Evening/weekend programs available. *Degree requirements:* For master's, thesis (for some programs). *Entrance requirements:* For master's, minimum undergraduate GPA of 3.0, 3 years of work experience. Additional exam requirements/recommendations for international students: Required—TOEFL (minimum score 550 paper-based; 213 computer-based). Electronic applications accepted.

University of Phoenix–Jersey City Campus, School of Business, Jersey City, NJ 07310. Offers accounting (MBA); business administration (MBA); global management (MBA); human resources management (MBA, MM); management (MM); marketing (MBA); public administration (MBA, MM).

University of Phoenix–Kansas City Campus, School of Business, Kansas City, MO 64131-4517. Offers accounting (MBA); business administration (MBA); global management (MBA); human resources management (MBA, MM); management (MM); marketing (MBA); public administration (MBA). Evening/weekend programs available. *Degree requirements:* For master's,

Public Administration

University of Phoenix–Kansas City Campus (continued)
thesis (for some programs). *Entrance requirements:* For master's, minimum undergraduate GPA of 3.0, 3 years of work experience. Additional exam requirements/recommendations for international students: Required—TOEFL (minimum score 550 paper-based; 213 computer-based). Electronic applications accepted.

University of Phoenix–Las Vegas Campus, School of Business, Las Vegas, NV 89128. Offers accounting (MBA); business administration (MBA); global management (MBA); human resources management (MBA, MM); management (MM); marketing (MBA); public administration (MM). Evening/weekend programs available. Postbaccalaureate distance learning degree programs offered (no on-campus study). *Degree requirements:* For master's, thesis (for some programs). *Entrance requirements:* For master's, minimum undergraduate GPA of 3.0, 3 years of work experience. Additional exam requirements/recommendations for international students: Required—TOEFL (minimum score 550 paper-based; 213 computer-based; 79 iBT). Electronic applications accepted.

University of Phoenix–Louisiana Campus, School of Business, Metairie, LA 70001-2082. Offers accounting (MBA); business administration (MBA); global management (MBA); human resources management (MBA, MM); management (MM); marketing (MBA); public administration (MBA). Evening/weekend programs available. *Degree requirements:* For master's, thesis (for some programs). *Entrance requirements:* For master's, minimum undergraduate GPA of 3.0, 3 years work experience. Additional exam requirements/recommendations for international students: Required—TOEFL (minimum score 550 paper-based; 213 computer-based; 79 iBT). Electronic applications accepted.

University of Phoenix–Madison Campus, School of Business, Madison, WI 53718-2416. Offers accounting (MBA); business and management (MBA); e-business (MBA); global management (MBA); human resources management (MBA, MM); management (MM); marketing (MBA); public administration (MBA).

University of Phoenix–Maryland Campus, School of Business, Columbia, MD 21045-5424. Offers accounting (MBA); business administration (MBA); e-business (MBA); global management (MBA); human resources management (MBA, MM); management (MM); marketing (MBA); public administration (MBA, MM). Evening/weekend programs available. *Degree requirements:* For master's, thesis (for some programs). *Entrance requirements:* For master's, minimum undergraduate GPA of 3.0, 3 years of work experience. Additional exam requirements/recommendations for international students: Required—TOEFL (minimum score 550 paper-based; 213 computer-based; 79 iBT). Electronic applications accepted.

University of Phoenix–Memphis Campus, School of Business, Cordova, TN 38018. Offers accounting (MBA); business and management (MBA); e-business (MBA); global management (MBA); human resources management (MBA, MM); management (MM); marketing (MBA); public administration (MBA, MM).

University of Phoenix–Milwaukee Campus, School of Business, Milwaukee, WI 53045. Offers accounting (MS); business administration (MBA, DBA); human resources management (MM); management (MM); organizational leadership (DM); public administration (MPA).

University of Phoenix–Minneapolis/St. Louis Park Campus, School of Business, St. Louis Park, MN 55426. Offers accounting (MBA); business administration (MBA); global management (MBA); human resources management (MBA); management (MM); marketing (MBA); public administration (MBA).

University of Phoenix–Northern Nevada Campus, School of Business, Reno, NV 89521-5862. Offers accounting (MBA); business administration (MBA); global management (MBA); human resources management (MBA, MM); management (MM); marketing (MBA); public administration (MBA, MM).

University of Phoenix–Northern Virginia Campus, School of Business, Reston, VA 20190. Offers business administration (MBA); public accounting (MPA). Evening/weekend programs available. Postbaccalaureate distance learning degree programs offered. *Students:* 135 full-time (50 women); includes 43 Black or African American, non-Hispanic/Latino; 3 Asian, non-Hispanic/Latino; 3 Hispanic/Latino, 6 international. Average age 40. *Entrance requirements:* For master's, minimum undergraduate GPA of 2.5 from an accredited university, 3 years of work experience, must be a citizen of the United States or have a valid visa. Specific requirements may vary by program. Additional exam requirements/recommendations for international students: Required—TOEFL (minimum score 213 paper, 79 iBT), TOEIC, IELTS or Berlitz. *Application deadline:* Applications are processed on a rolling basis. Application fee: $45. Electronic applications accepted. *Expenses:* Tuition: Full-time $16,440. One-time fee: $45 full-time. Full-time tuition and fees vary according to course load, degree level, campus/location and program. *Financial support:* Scholarships/grants available. Financial award applicants required to submit FAFSA. *Unit head:* Erik Greenberg, Campus Director, 703-376-6150, E-mail: erik.greenberg@phoenix.edu. *Application contact:* Erik Greenberg, Campus Director, 703-376-6150, E-mail: erik.greenberg@phoenix.edu.

University of Phoenix–North Florida Campus, School of Business, Jacksonville, FL 32216-0959. Offers accounting (MBA); business administration (MBA); global management (MBA); human resources management (MBA, MM); management (MM); marketing (MBA); public administration (MBA, MM). Evening/weekend programs available. *Degree requirements:* For master's, thesis (for some programs). *Entrance requirements:* For master's, minimum undergraduate GPA of 3.0, 3 years work experience. Additional exam requirements/recommendations for international students: Required—TOEFL (minimum score 550 paper-based; 213 computer-based; 79 iBT). Electronic applications accepted.

University of Phoenix–Northwest Arkansas Campus, School of Business, Rogers, AR 72756-9615. Offers accounting (MBA); business and management (MBA); global management (MBA); human resources management (MBA, MM); management (MM); marketing (MBA); public administration (MBA, MM).

University of Phoenix–Omaha Campus, School of Business, Omaha, NE 68154-5240. Offers accounting (MBA); business and management (MBA); global management (MBA); human resources management (MBA, MM); management (MM); marketing (MBA); public administration (MBA, MM).

University of Phoenix–Oregon Campus, School of Business, Tigard, OR 97223. Offers accounting (MBA); business administration (MBA); global management (MBA); human resource management (MM); human resources management (MBA); management (MM); marketing (MBA); public administration (MM). Evening/weekend programs available. *Degree requirements:* For master's, thesis (for some programs). *Entrance requirements:* For master's, minimum undergraduate GPA of 3.0, 3 years of work experience. Additional exam requirements/recommendations for international students: Required—TOEFL (minimum score 550 paper-based; 213 computer-based; 79 iBT). Electronic applications accepted.

University of Phoenix–Philadelphia Campus, School of Business, Wayne, PA 19087-2121. Offers accounting (MBA); business administration (MBA); global management (MBA); human resources management (MBA, MM); management (MM); marketing (MBA); public administration (MM). Evening/weekend programs available. *Degree requirements:* For master's, thesis (for some programs). *Entrance requirements:* For master's, minimum undergraduate GPA of 3.0, 3 years work experience. Additional exam requirements/recommendations for international students: Required—TOEFL (minimum score 550 paper-based; 213 computer-based; 79 iBT). Electronic applications accepted.

University of Phoenix–Pittsburgh Campus, School of Business, Pittsburgh, PA 15276. Offers accounting (MBA); business administration (MBA); global management (MBA); human resources management (MBA, MM); management (MM); marketing (MBA); public administration (MBA, MM). Evening/weekend programs available. *Degree requirements:* For master's, thesis (for some programs). *Entrance requirements:* For master's, minimum undergraduate GPA of 3.0, 3 years work experience. Additional exam requirements/recommendations for international students: Required—TOEFL (minimum score 550 paper-based; 213 computer-based; 79 iBT). Electronic applications accepted.

University of Phoenix–Richmond Campus, School of Business, Richmond, VA 23230. Offers accounting (MBA); business administration (MBA); global management (MBA); human resources management (MBA, MM); management (MM); marketing (MBA); public administration (MBA, MM). Evening/weekend programs available. *Degree requirements:* For master's, thesis (for some programs). *Entrance requirements:* For master's, minimum undergraduate GPA of 3.0, 3 years work experience. Additional exam requirements/recommendations for international students: Required—TOEFL (minimum score 550 paper-based; 213 computer-based; 79 iBT). Electronic applications accepted.

University of Phoenix–Sacramento Valley Campus, School of Business, Sacramento, CA 95833-3632. Offers accounting (MBA); business administration (MBA); global management (MBA); human resources management (MBA, MM); management (MM); marketing (MBA); public administration (MBA, MM). Evening/weekend programs available. *Degree requirements:* For master's, thesis (for some programs). *Entrance requirements:* For master's, minimum undergraduate GPA of 3.0, 3 years work experience. Additional exam requirements/recommendations for international students: Required—TOEFL (minimum score 550 paper-based; 213 computer-based; 79 iBT). Electronic applications accepted.

University of Phoenix–St. Louis Campus, School of Business, St. Louis, MO 63043-4828. Offers accounting (MBA); business administration (MBA); global management (MBA); human resources management (MBA, MM); management (MM); marketing (MBA); public administration (MM). Evening/weekend programs available. *Degree requirements:* For master's, thesis (for some programs). *Entrance requirements:* For master's, 3 years of work experience, minimum undergraduate GPA of 3.0. Additional exam requirements/recommendations for international students: Required—TOEFL (minimum score 550 paper-based; 213 computer-based; 79 iBT). Electronic applications accepted.

University of Phoenix–San Antonio Campus, School of Business, San Antonio, TX 78230. Offers accounting (MBA); business administration (MBA); e-business (MBA); global management (MBA); human resources management (MBA, MM); management (MM); marketing (MBA); public administration (MBA, MM).

University of Phoenix–San Diego Campus, School of Business, San Diego, CA 92123. Offers accounting (MBA); business administration (MBA); global management (MBA); human resources management (MBA, MM); management (MM); marketing (MBA); public administration (MBA). Evening/weekend programs available. *Degree requirements:* For master's, thesis (for some programs). *Entrance requirements:* For master's, 3 years of work experience, minimum undergraduate GPA of 3.0. Additional exam requirements/recommendations for international students: Required—TOEFL (minimum score 550 paper-based; 213 computer-based; 79 iBT). Electronic applications accepted.

University of Phoenix–Savannah Campus, School of Business, Savannah, GA 31405-7400. Offers accounting (MBA); business administration (MBA); global management (MBA); human resources management (MBA, MM); management (MM); marketing (MBA); public administration (MBA, MM).

University of Phoenix–Southern Colorado Campus, School of Business, Colorado Springs, CO 80919-2335. Offers accounting (MBA); business administration (MBA); global management (MBA); human resources management (MBA, MM); management (MM); marketing (MBA); public administration (MM). Evening/weekend programs available. *Degree requirements:* For master's, thesis (for some programs). *Entrance requirements:* For master's, minimum undergraduate GPA of 3.0, 3 years of work experience. Additional exam requirements/recommendations for international students: Required—TOEFL (minimum score 550 paper-based; 213 computer-based; 79 iBT). Electronic applications accepted.

University of Phoenix–South Florida Campus, School of Business, Fort Lauderdale, FL 33309. Offers accounting (MBA); business administration (MBA); global management (MBA); human resource management (MBA); human resources management (MM); management (MM); marketing (MBA); public administration (MBA, MM). Evening/weekend programs available. *Degree requirements:* For master's, thesis (for some programs). *Entrance requirements:* For master's, minimum undergraduate GPA of 3.0, 3 years work experience. Additional exam requirements/recommendations for international students: Required—TOEFL (minimum score 550 paper-based; 213 computer-based; 79 iBT). Electronic applications accepted.

University of Phoenix–Springfield Campus, School of Business, Springfield, MO 65804-7211. Offers accounting (MBA); business administration (MBA); global management (MBA); human resources management (MBA, MM); management (MM); marketing (MBA); public administration (MBA, MM).

University of Phoenix–Washington D.C. Campus, School of Business, Washington, DC 20001. Offers accountancy (MS); business administration (MBA, DBA); human resources management (MM); management (MM); organizational leadership (DM); public administration (MPA).

University of Phoenix–West Florida Campus, School of Business, Temple Terrace, FL 33637. Offers accounting (MBA); business administration (MBA); global management (MBA); human resources management (MBA, MM); management (MM); marketing (MBA); public administration (MBA, MM). Evening/weekend programs available. *Degree requirements:* For master's, thesis (for some programs). *Entrance requirements:* For master's, 3 years of work experience, minimum undergraduate GPA of 3.0. Additional exam requirements/recommendations for international students: Required—TOEFL (minimum score 550 paper-based; 213 computer-based; 79 iBT). Electronic applications accepted.

University of Pittsburgh, Graduate School of Public and International Affairs, Division of Public and Urban Affairs, Pittsburgh, PA 15260. Offers policy research and analysis (MPA); public and nonprofit management (MPA); urban and regional affairs (MPA); JD/MPA; MPA/MPIA; MPH/MPA; MSIS/MPA; MSW/MPA. Part-time and evening/weekend programs available. *Faculty:* 30 full-time (12 women), 67 part-time/adjunct (25 women). *Students:* 61 full-time (29 women), 22 part-time (16 women); includes 4 Black or African American, non-Hispanic/Latino; 1 Asian, non-Hispanic/Latino; 1 Hispanic/Latino, 8 international. Average age 25. 119 applicants, 76% accepted, 38 enrolled. In 2010, 24 master's awarded. *Degree requirements:* For master's, thesis optional, internship, capstone seminar. *Entrance requirements:* For master's, GRE General Test, 3 letters of recommendation, resume; minimum GPA of 3.2 (recommended). Additional exam requirements/recommendations for international students: Required—TOEFL (minimum score 550 paper-based; 213 computer-based; 80 iBT), TWE (minimum score 4); Recommended—IELTS (minimum score 7). *Application deadline:* For fall admission, 2/1 for domestic students, 1/15 for international students; for spring admission, 11/1 for domestic students, 8/1 for international students. Application fee: $50. Electronic applications accepted. *Expenses:* Tuition, state resident: full-time $17,304; part-time $701 per credit. Tuition, nonresident: full-time $29,554; part-time $1210 per credit. Required fees: $740; $214 per term. Tuition and fees vary according to program. *Financial support:* In 2010–11, 18 students received support. Scholarships/grants, tuition waivers (full and partial), unspecified assistantships, and student employment available. Financial award application deadline: 2/1. *Faculty research:* Disaster response management, government regulation of health and safety risks, comparative regional governance, nonprofit management, environmental policy, housing policy, strategic management. Total annual research expenditures: $892,349. *Unit head:* Dr. David Y. Miller, Director, Public and Urban Affairs Division, 412-648-7606, Fax: 412-648-2605, E-mail: dymiller@pitt.edu. *Application contact:* Elizabeth A. Hruby, Graduate Enrollment Counselor, 412-648-7640, Fax: 412-648-7641, E-mail: eah44@pitt.edu.

University of Pittsburgh, Graduate School of Public and International Affairs, Doctoral Program in Public and International Affairs, Pittsburgh, PA 15260. Offers development policy (PhD); foreign and security policy (PhD); international political economy (PhD); public administration (PhD); public policy (PhD). *Accreditation:* NASPAA. Part-time programs available. *Faculty:* 30 full-time (12 women), 67 part-time/adjunct (25 women). *Students:* 43 full-time (18 women), 3 part-time (2 women); includes 3 minority (2 Black or African American, non-Hispanic/Latino; 1 Asian, non-Hispanic/Latino), 19 international. Average age 30. 105 applicants, 11% accepted, 6 enrolled. In 2010, 11 doctorates awarded. Terminal master's awarded for partial completion of doctoral program. *Degree requirements:* For doctorate, comprehensive exam, thesis/dissertation, mid-term evaluation, preliminary exam, annual review. *Entrance requirements:* For doctorate, GRE, 3 letters of recommendation, resume, minimum GPA of 3.0 (recommended), writing sample. Additional exam requirements/recommendations for international students: Required—TOEFL (minimum score 600 paper-based; 250 computer-based; 100 iBT), TWE (minimum score 4); Recommended—IELTS (minimum score 7). *Application deadline:* For fall admission, 2/1 for domestic students, 1/15 for international students. Application fee: $50. Electronic applications accepted. *Expenses:* Tuition, state resident: full-time $17,304; part-time $701 per credit. Tuition, nonresident: full-time $29,554; part-time $1210 per credit. Required fees: $740; $214 per term. Tuition and fees vary according to program. *Financial support:* In 2010–11, 10 students received support, including 10 fellowships (averaging $41,325 per year). Financial award application deadline: 2/1. *Faculty research:* International political economy, international development, public administration, public policy, foreign policy, international security policy. Total annual research expenditures: $893,349. *Unit head:* Dr. Kevin P. Kearns, Program Coordinator, 412-648-7621, Fax: 412-648-2605, E-mail: kkearns@pitt.edu. *Application contact:* Julie Korade, Program Administrator/Graduate Enrollment Counselor, 412-648-7640, Fax: 412-648-7641, E-mail: korade@pitt.edu.

University of Puerto Rico, Río Piedras, College of Social Sciences, School of Public Administration, San Juan, PR 00931-3300. Offers MPA. *Accreditation:* NASPAA. Part-time programs available. *Degree requirements:* For master's, comprehensive exam, thesis. *Entrance requirements:* For master's, GRE or PAEG, interview, minimum GPA of 3.0, letter of recommendation.

University of Regina, Faculty of Graduate Studies and Research, Johnson-Shoyama Graduate School of Public Policy, Regina, SK S4S 0A2, Canada. Offers economic analysis for public policy (Master's Certificate); health systems management (Master's Certificate); health systems research (MPP); non-profit management (Master's Certificate); public management (MPA, Master's Certificate); public policy (MPA, MPP, PhD); public policy analysis (Master's Certificate). Part-time programs available. *Faculty:* 7 full-time (3 women). *Students:* 60 full-time (28 women), 71 part-time (36 women). 101 applicants, 72% accepted. In 2010, 48 master's awarded. *Degree requirements:* For master's, thesis; for doctorate, thesis/dissertation. *Entrance requirements:* For doctorate, master's degree, intended research program in an area of public policy. Additional exam requirements/recommendations for international students: Required—TOEFL (minimum score 580 paper-based; 80 iBT), GRE. *Application deadline:* For fall admission, 2/1 for domestic and international students. Application fee: $100. Electronic applications accepted. *Expenses:* Contact institution. *Financial support:* In 2010–11, 11 fellowships (averaging $18,000 per year), 2 research assistantships (averaging $16,500 per year), 15 teaching assistantships (averaging $6,759 per year) were awarded; scholarships/grants also available. Financial award application deadline: 6/15. *Faculty research:* Governance and administration, public finance, public policy analysis, non-governmental organizations and alternative service delivery, micro-economics for policy analysis. *Unit head:* Dr. Michael Atkinson, Director, 306-996-1984, Fax: 306-585-5461, E-mail: michael.atkinson@usask.ca. *Application contact:* Elaine Groenendyk, Program Advisor, 306-585-5462, Fax: 306-585-5461, E-mail: elaine.groenendyk@uregina.ca.

University of Rhode Island, Graduate School, College of Arts and Sciences, Department of Political Science, Kingston, RI 02881. Offers political science (MA), including American politics, comparative government, international relations, public policy; public policy and administration (MPA); MLIS/MPA. Part-time programs available. *Faculty:* 10 full-time (4 women). *Students:* 17 full-time (10 women), 31 part-time (19 women); includes 10 minority (4 Black or African American, non-Hispanic/Latino; 1 Asian, non-Hispanic/Latino; 5 Hispanic/Latino). In 2010, 22 master's awarded. *Degree requirements:* For master's, comprehensive exam (for some programs), thesis optional. *Entrance requirements:* For master's, GRE, GMAT or MAT, 2 letters of recommendation. Additional exam requirements/recommendations for international students: Required—TOEFL (minimum score 550 paper-based; 213 computer-based). *Application deadline:* For fall admission, 2/1 for international students; for spring admission, 7/15 for international students. Application fee: $65. Electronic applications accepted. *Expenses:* Tuition, state resident: full-time $9588; part-time $533 per credit hour. Tuition, nonresident: full-time $22,968; part-time $1276 per credit hour. Required fees: $1282; $68 per semester. Tuition and fees vary according to program. *Financial support:* In 2010–11, 4 teaching assistantships with full tuition reimbursements (averaging $9,263 per year) were awarded. Financial award applicants required to submit FAFSA. *Unit head:* Dr. Gerry Tyler, Department Chair, 401-874-4053, Fax: 401-874-4072, E-mail: gtyler@uri.edu. *Application contact:* Dr. Gerry Tyler, Department Chair, 401-874-4053, Fax: 401-874-4072, E-mail: gtyler@uri.edu.

University of San Francisco, School of Business and Professional Studies, Program in Public Administration, Concentration in Public Administration, San Francisco, CA 94117-1080. Offers MPA. Part-time and evening/weekend programs available. *Faculty:* 3 full-time (1 woman), 4 part-time/adjunct (all women). *Students:* 100 full-time (64 women), 1 (woman) part-time; includes 56 minority (15 Black or African American, non-Hispanic/Latino; 2 American Indian or Alaska Native, non-Hispanic/Latino; 18 Asian, non-Hispanic/Latino; 18 Hispanic/Latino; 3 Two or more races, non-Hispanic/Latino), 3 international. Average age 33. 107 applicants, 84% accepted, 60 enrolled. In 2010, 42 master's awarded. *Entrance requirements:* For master's, minimum GPA of 3.0. Application fee: $55 ($65 for international students). *Expenses:* Tuition: Full-time $20,070; part-time $1115 per credit hour. Tuition and fees vary according to course load, degree level and program. *Financial support:* In 2010–11, 74 students received support. Application deadline: 3/2. *Unit head:* Dr. Maurice Penner, Director, 415-422-2142. *Application contact:* 415-422-6000, E-mail: graduate@usfca.edu.

University of South Africa, College of Economic and Management Sciences, Pretoria, South Africa. Offers accounting (D Admin, D Com); accounting science (DA); auditing (D Admin, D Com); business administration (M Tech); business economics (D Admin); business leadership (DBL); business management (D Admin, D Com); economic management analysis (M Tech); economics (D Admin, D Com, PhD); human resource development (M Tech); industrial psychology (D Admin, D Com, PhD); logistics (D Com); marketing (M Tech); public administration (D Admin, D Com, DPA, PhD); public management (M Tech); quantitative management (D Admin, D Com); real estate (M Tech); statistics (D Admin, PhD); tourism management (D Admin, D Com); transport economics (D Admin, D Com).

University of South Alabama, Graduate School, College of Arts and Sciences, Department of Political Science and Criminal Justice, Mobile, AL 36688-0002. Offers public administration (MPA). Part-time and evening/weekend programs available. *Faculty:* 10 full-time (1 woman), 1 part-time/adjunct (0 women). *Students:* 31 full-time (19 women), 13 part-time (11 women); includes 16 minority (13 Black or African American, non-Hispanic/Latino; 2 American Indian or Alaska Native, non-Hispanic/Latino; 1 Hispanic/Latino), 3 international. 34 applicants, 62% accepted, 16 enrolled. In 2010, 3 master's awarded. *Degree requirements:* For master's, comprehensive exam, thesis optional. *Entrance requirements:* For master's, GRE, minimum GPA of 3.0. Additional exam requirements/recommendations for international students: Required—TOEFL. *Application deadline:* For fall admission, 7/15 priority date for domestic students, 6/15 priority date for international students; for spring admission, 12/1 priority date for domestic students, 11/1 priority date for international students. Applications are processed on a rolling basis. Application fee: $35. *Expenses:* Tuition, state resident: part-time $300 per credit hour. Tuition, nonresident: part-time $600 per credit hour. Required fees: $150 per semester. *Financial support:* Research assistantships, career-related internships or fieldwork

available. Support available to part-time students. Financial award application deadline: 4/1. *Unit head:* Dr. Sam Fisher, Director, 251-460-7204. *Application contact:* Dr. Sam Fisher, Director, 251-460-7204.

University of South Carolina, The Graduate School, College of Arts and Sciences, Department of Political Science, Program in Public Administration, Columbia, SC 29208. Offers MPA, JD/MPA, MSW/MPA. MPA offered jointly with Clemson University, The Graduate School of the College of Charleston. *Accreditation:* NASPAA. Part-time and evening/weekend programs available. *Degree requirements:* For master's, capstone seminar. *Entrance requirements:* For master's, GRE General Test, minimum GPA of 3.0. Additional exam requirements/recommendations for international students: Required—TOEFL. Electronic applications accepted. *Faculty research:* Public policy, organizational theory, personnel administration, budgeting, finance.

The University of South Dakota, Graduate School, College of Arts and Sciences, Department of Political Science, Vermillion, SD 57069-2390. Offers American political institutions (PhD); political science (MA); public administration (MPA, PhD); public policy (PhD); JD/MA; JD/MPA. *Accreditation:* NASPAA (one or more programs are accredited). Part-time programs available. Postbaccalaureate distance learning degree programs offered. *Degree requirements:* For master's, comprehensive exam, thesis (for some programs). *Entrance requirements:* For master's, GRE or LSAT (MPA), GRE General Test (MA), minimum GPA of 2.7. Additional exam requirements/recommendations for international students: Required—TOEFL (minimum score 550 paper-based; 213 computer-based; 79 iBT). Electronic applications accepted.

University of Southern California, Graduate School, School of Policy, Planning, and Development, Master of Public Administration Program, Los Angeles, CA 90089. Offers nonprofit management and policy (Graduate Certificate); political management (Graduate Certificate); public administration (MPA); public management (Graduate Certificate); MPA/JD; MPA/M Pl; MPA/MA; MPA/MAJCS; MPA/MS; MPA/MSW. *Accreditation:* NASPAA (one or more programs are accredited). Part-time and evening/weekend programs available. Postbaccalaureate distance learning degree programs offered (minimal on-campus study). *Faculty:* 51 full-time (12 women), 100 part-time/adjunct (30 women). *Students:* 171 full-time (117 women), 37 part-time (16 women); includes 79 minority (14 Black or African American, non-Hispanic/Latino; 29 Asian, non-Hispanic/Latino; 31 Hispanic/Latino; 5 Two or more races, non-Hispanic/Latino), 37 international. 297 applicants, 64% accepted, 90 enrolled. In 2010, 71 master's awarded. Terminal master's awarded for partial completion of doctoral program. *Degree requirements:* For master's, capstone, internship. *Entrance requirements:* For master's, GRE, GMAT. Additional exam requirements/recommendations for international students: Required—TOEFL (minimum score 600 paper-based; 250 computer-based; 100 iBT). *Application deadline:* For fall admission, 12/15 priority date for domestic and international students; for spring admission, 11/1 for domestic and international students. Applications are processed on a rolling basis. Application fee: $85. Electronic applications accepted. *Expenses:* Tuition: Full-time $31,240; part-time $1420 per unit. Required fees: $600. One-time fee: $35 full-time. Full-time tuition and fees vary according to degree level and program. *Financial support:* In 2010–11, 99 students received support, including 2 research assistantships with full tuition reimbursements available (averaging $19,612 per year); scholarships/grants and tuition waivers (full and partial) also available. Financial award application deadline: 12/15. *Faculty research:* Collaborative governance and decision-making, nonprofit management, environmental management, institutional analysis, local government, civic engagement. Total annual research expenditures: $6.2 million. *Unit head:* Dr. Shui Yan Tang, Director, 213-740-0379, Fax: 213-740-0001, E-mail: stang@usc.edu. *Application contact:* Marisol R. Gonzalez, Director of Recruitment and Admission, 213-740-0550, Fax: 213-740-7573, E-mail: marisolr@usc.edu.

University of Southern Indiana, Graduate Studies, College of Liberal Arts, Program in Public Administration, Evansville, IN 47712-3590. Offers MPA. Part-time and evening/weekend programs available. *Faculty:* 3 full-time (1 woman). *Students:* 1 (woman) full-time, 22 part-time (14 women); includes 1 American Indian or Alaska Native, non-Hispanic/Latino; 1 Asian, non-Hispanic/Latino. Average age 32. 5 applicants, 100% accepted, 5 enrolled. In 2010, 8 master's awarded. *Entrance requirements:* For master's, GMAT or GRE, 2 letters of reference, analytical writing sample, minimum GPA of 2.7. Additional exam requirements/recommendations for international students: Required—TOEFL (minimum score 550 paper-based; 213 computer-based; 79 iBT), IELTS (minimum score 6). *Application deadline:* For fall admission, 8/15 priority date for domestic students, 3/1 priority date for international students. Applications are processed on a rolling basis. Application fee: $25. Electronic applications accepted. *Expenses:* Tuition, state resident: full-time $4823; part-time $267.95 per credit hour. Tuition, nonresident: full-time $9515; part-time $528.62 per credit hour. Required fees: $220; $22.75 per term. Tuition and fees vary according to course load and reciprocity agreements. *Financial support:* In 2010–11, 4 students received support. Federal Work-Study, scholarships/grants, tuition waivers (full and partial), and unspecified assistantships available. Financial award application deadline: 3/1; financial award applicants required to submit FAFSA. *Unit head:* Dr. Matthew Hanka, Director, 812-461-5204, E-mail: mjhanka@usi.edu. *Application contact:* Dr. Matthew Hanka, Director, 812-461-5204, E-mail: mjhanka@usi.edu.

University of South Florida, Graduate School, College of Arts and Sciences, Department of Government and International Affairs, Tampa, FL 33620-9951. Offers government (PhD); Latin American Caribbean and Latino Studies (MA); political science (MA); public administration (MPA). Part-time and evening/weekend programs available. *Faculty:* 5 full-time (1 woman), 1 part-time/adjunct (0 women). *Students:* 57 full-time (35 women), 84 part-time (42 women); includes 23 Black or African American, non-Hispanic/Latino; 1 American Indian or Alaska Native, non-Hispanic/Latino; 4 Asian, non-Hispanic/Latino; 18 Hispanic/Latino, 2 international. Average age 32. 151 applicants, 38% accepted, 41 enrolled. In 2010, 31 master's awarded. *Degree requirements:* For master's, comprehensive exam, thesis; for doctorate, comprehensive exam, thesis/dissertation. *Entrance requirements:* For master's, GRE (minimum score 470 verbal, 470 quantitative), minimum GPA of 3.0 in last 60 hours of course work. Additional exam requirements/recommendations for international students: Required—TOEFL (minimum score 550 paper-based; 213 computer-based). *Application deadline:* For fall admission, 2/15 for domestic students, 1/2 for international students; for spring admission, 10/15 for domestic students, 6/1 for international students. Applications are processed on a rolling basis. Application fee: $30. Electronic applications accepted. *Financial support:* In 2010–11, 12 teaching assistantships with tuition reimbursements (averaging $15,000 per year) were awarded; unspecified assistantships also available. Financial award application deadline: 4/1. *Unit head:* Dr. Mohsen Milani, Chairperson, 813-974-2384, Fax: 813-974-0832, E-mail: milani@chuma1.cas.usf.edu. *Application contact:* Dr. Stephen Tauber, Graduate Coordinator, 813-974-0781, Fax: 813-974-0832, E-mail: stauber@chuma1.cas.usf.edu.

The University of Tennessee, Graduate School, College of Arts and Sciences, Department of Political Science, Program in Public Administration, Knoxville, TN 37996. Offers MPA, JD/MPA. *Accreditation:* NASPAA. Part-time programs available. *Degree requirements:* For master's, thesis or alternative. *Entrance requirements:* For master's, GRE General Test, minimum GPA of 2.7. Additional exam requirements/recommendations for international students: Required—TOEFL. Electronic applications accepted. *Expenses:* Tuition, state resident: full-time $7440; part-time $414 per credit hour. Tuition, nonresident: full-time $22,478; part-time $1250 per credit hour. Required fees: $922; $43 per credit hour. Tuition and fees vary according to program.

The University of Tennessee at Chattanooga, Graduate School, College of Arts and Sciences, Department of Political Science, Chattanooga, TN 37403. Offers local government management (MPA); non profit management (MPA); public administration (MPA); public administration and non-profit management (Postbaccalaureate Certificate). Part-time and evening/weekend programs available. *Faculty:* 4 full-time (0 women). *Students:* 11 full-time (8 women), 18 part-time (10 women); includes 2 minority (both Black or African American, non-Hispanic/Latino). Average age 28. 32 applicants, 66% accepted, 17 enrolled. In 2010, 21 master's, 1 other advanced degree awarded. *Degree requirements:* For master's, comprehensive

Public Administration

The University of Tennessee at Chattanooga (continued)
exam, thesis or alternative, internship. *Entrance requirements:* For master's, GRE General Test. Additional exam requirements/recommendations for international students: Required—TOEFL (minimum score 550 paper-based; 213 computer-based; 79 iBT), IELTS (minimum score 6). *Application deadline:* For fall admission, 8/1 priority date for domestic students, 6/1 for international students; for spring admission, 12/1 priority date for domestic students, 10/1 for international students. Applications are processed on a rolling basis. Application fee: $35. Electronic applications accepted. *Financial support:* In 2010–11, 6 research assistantships with full and partial tuition reimbursements (averaging $5,500 per year) were awarded; career-related internships or fieldwork, scholarships/grants, and unspecified assistantships also available. Support available to part-time students. *Faculty research:* Organizational cultures and renewal, management theory, public policy, policy analysis, nonprofit organization. Total annual research expenditures: $35,240. *Unit head:* Dr. Fouad M. Moughrabi, Head, 423-425-4281, Fax: 423-425-2373, E-mail: fouad-moughrabi@utc.edu. *Application contact:* Dr. Jerald Ainsworth, Dean of Graduate Studies, 423-425-4478, Fax: 423-425-5223, E-mail: jerald-ainsworth@utc.edu.

The University of Texas at Arlington, Graduate School, School of Urban and Public Affairs, Program in Public Administration, Arlington, TX 76019. Offers MPA. *Accreditation:* NASPAA. Part-time and evening/weekend programs available. Postbaccalaureate distance learning degree programs offered (no on-campus study). *Students:* 95 full-time (50 women), 117 part-time (74 women); includes 95 minority (50 Black or African American, non-Hispanic/Latino; 2 American Indian or Alaska Native, non-Hispanic/Latino; 6 Asian, non-Hispanic/Latino; 31 Hispanic/Latino; 1 Native Hawaiian or other Pacific Islander, non-Hispanic/Latino; 5 Two or more races, non-Hispanic/Latino). 87 applicants, 90% accepted, 62 enrolled. *Degree requirements:* For master's, comprehensive exam, thesis or alternative. *Entrance requirements:* For master's, GRE General Test. Additional exam requirements/recommendations for international students: Required—TOEFL (minimum score 550 paper-based; 213 computer-based). *Application deadline:* For fall admission, 6/1 for domestic students, 4/1 for international students; for spring admission, 10/15 for domestic students, 9/15 for international students. Applications are processed on a rolling basis. Application fee: $35 ($50 for international students). Electronic applications accepted. *Expenses:* Tuition, state resident: full-time $7500. Tuition, nonresident: full-time $13,080. International tuition: $13,250 full-time. *Financial support:* In 2010–11, 6 students received support, including 1 research assistantship (averaging $750 per year); fellowships, career-related internships or fieldwork also available. Financial award application deadline: 6/1; financial award applicants required to submit FAFSA. *Faculty research:* Environment, statistics, public administration, social welfare, economic development, economics, budgeting, planning. Total annual research expenditures: $53,550. *Unit head:* Dr. David Coursey, Program Director, 817-272-4061, Fax: 817-272-5008, E-mail: dcoursey@uta.edu. *Application contact:* Tangie Fields, Academic Advisor, 817-272-3340, Fax: 817-272-5008, E-mail: nfields@uta.edu.

The University of Texas at Brownsville, Graduate Studies, College of Liberal Arts, Program in Public Policy and Management, Brownsville, TX 78520-4991. Offers MPPM. *Degree requirements:* For master's, thesis. *Entrance requirements:* For master's, GRE, 2 letters of recommendation.

The University of Texas at El Paso, Graduate School, Institute for Policy and Economic Development, El Paso, TX 79968-0001. Offers border administration (Certificate); homeland security (Certificate); intelligence and national security (MS, Certificate); leadership studies (MA); public administration (MPA). *Accreditation:* NASPAA. Part-time and evening/weekend programs available. *Students:* 187 (57 women); includes 19 Black or African American, non-Hispanic/Latino; 1 American Indian or Alaska Native, non-Hispanic/Latino; 5 Asian, non-Hispanic/Latino; 99 Hispanic/Latino, 5 international. 142 applicants, 77% accepted. In 2010, 76 master's awarded. *Degree requirements:* For master's, thesis optional. *Entrance requirements:* For master's, GRE, statement of purpose, letters of recommendation. Additional exam requirements/recommendations for international students: Required—TOEFL; Recommended—IELTS. *Application deadline:* For fall admission, 8/1 for domestic students, 3/1 for international students; for spring admission, 10/1 for domestic students, 9/1 for international students. Applications are processed on a rolling basis. Application fee: $45 ($80 for international students). Electronic applications accepted. *Financial support:* Fellowships with partial tuition reimbursements, research assistantships with partial tuition reimbursements, teaching assistantships with partial tuition reimbursements, institutionally sponsored loans, scholarships/grants, health care benefits, tuition waivers (partial), and unspecified assistantships available. Support available to part-time students. Financial award application deadline: 3/15; financial award applicants required to submit FAFSA. *Unit head:* Dr. Dennis Soden, Director, 915-747-7974, Fax: 915-747-7948, E-mail: desoden@utep.edu. *Application contact:* Dr. Patricia D. Witherspoon, Dean of the Graduate School, 915-747-5491, Fax: 915-747-5788, E-mail: withersp@utep.edu.

The University of Texas at San Antonio, College of Public Policy, Department of Public Administration, San Antonio, TX 78249-0617. Offers MPA. *Accreditation:* NASPAA. Part-time and evening/weekend programs available. *Faculty:* 9 full-time (4 women), 2 part-time/adjunct (0 women). *Students:* 48 full-time (29 women), 111 part-time (68 women); includes 103 minority (15 Black or African American, non-Hispanic/Latino; 4 Asian, non-Hispanic/Latino; 78 Hispanic/Latino; 1 Native Hawaiian or other Pacific Islander, non-Hispanic/Latino; 5 Two or more races, non-Hispanic/Latino), 4 international. Average age 31. 66 applicants, 76% accepted, 38 enrolled. In 2010, 48 master's awarded. *Degree requirements:* For master's, comprehensive exam (for some programs), thesis (for some programs). *Entrance requirements:* For master's, GMAT or GRE General Test, undergraduate course work in American government, economics, and research methods; minimum GPA of 3.0 on last 60 hours. Additional exam requirements/recommendations for international students: Required—TOEFL (minimum score 500 paper-based; 173 computer-based; 61 iBT), IELTS (minimum score 5). *Application deadline:* For fall admission, 7/1 for domestic students, 4/1 for international students; for spring admission, 11/1 for domestic students, 9/1 for international students. Applications are processed on a rolling basis. Application fee: $45 ($80 for international students). Electronic applications accepted. *Expenses:* Tuition, state resident: full-time $4172; part-time $231.75 per credit hour. Tuition, nonresident: full-time $15,332; part-time $851.75 per credit hour. *Financial support:* In 2010–11, 14 students received support, including 33 research assistantships (averaging $12,402 per year); career-related internships or fieldwork, scholarships/grants, tuition waivers, and unspecified assistantships also available. Support available to part-time students. *Faculty research:* Politics-administration relationship process models for decision-making, homeland security, bureaucratic politics, institutional determinants of public policy. Total annual research expenditures: $11,307. *Unit head:* Dr. Christopher Reddick, Department Chair, 210-458-2501, Fax: 210-458-2536, E-mail: chris.reddick@utsa.edu. *Application contact:* Veronica Ramirez, Assistant Dean of the Graduate School, 210-458-4330, Fax: 210-458-4332, E-mail: graduatestudies@utsa.edu.

The University of Texas at Tyler, College of Arts and Sciences, Department of Social Sciences, Tyler, TX 75799-0001. Offers criminal justice (MS); public administration (MPA); sociology (MS). Part-time and evening/weekend programs available. *Degree requirements:* For master's, comprehensive exam, thesis optional. *Entrance requirements:* For master's, GRE General Test, minimum GPA of 3.0. Additional exam requirements/recommendations for international students: Required—TOEFL (minimum score 79 computer-based). *Faculty research:* Urban segregation, minority business, violent crime, gender discrimination.

The University of Texas–Pan American, College of Social and Behavioral Sciences, Program in Public Administration, Edinburg, TX 78539. Offers MPA. Part-time and evening/weekend programs available. *Degree requirements:* For master's, comprehensive exam (for some programs), thesis optional. *Entrance requirements:* For master's, GRE General Test. Additional exam requirements/recommendations for international students: Required—TOEFL. Electronic applications accepted. *Faculty research:* Immigration policy reform, agriculture food policy, social service delivery systems, community development, social welfare policy reform, urban/city management.

University of the District of Columbia, School of Business and Public Administration, Program in Public Administration, Washington, DC 20008-1175. Offers MPA. Part-time and evening/weekend programs available. *Degree requirements:* For master's, comprehensive exam, thesis optional. *Entrance requirements:* For master's, GMAT or GRE General Test, writing proficiency exam. *Expenses:* Tuition, state resident: full-time $7580; part-time $421 per credit. Tuition, nonresident: full-time $14,580; part-time $810 per credit. Required fees: $620; $30 per credit. One-time fee: $100 part-time. *Faculty research:* Government management, public personnel management, urban management, management information systems, public financial management.

University of the Virgin Islands, Graduate Programs, Division of Humanities and Social Sciences, Saint Thomas, VI 00802-9990. Offers MPA. Part-time and evening/weekend programs available. *Degree requirements:* For master's, comprehensive exam, thesis or alternative. *Entrance requirements:* For master's, GMAT, GRE, minimum GPA of 2.5. Additional exam requirements/recommendations for international students: Required—TOEFL (minimum score 550 paper-based; 213 computer-based). *Faculty research:* Ethical issues of arbitration, spiritual leadership, accountability.

The University of Toledo, College of Graduate Studies, College of Language, Literature and Social Sciences, Department of Political Science and Public Administration, Toledo, OH 43606-3390. Offers health care administration (Certificate); management of non-profit organizations (Certificate); political science (MA); public administration (MPA), including health care policy, municipal administration, public administration. Part-time programs available. *Faculty:* 9. *Students:* 21 full-time (11 women), 13 part-time (8 women); includes 7 minority (5 Black or African American, non-Hispanic/Latino; 2 Hispanic/Latino), 2 international. Average age 30. 34 applicants, 59% accepted, 16 enrolled. In 2010, 14 master's, 7 other advanced degrees awarded. *Degree requirements:* For master's, thesis. *Entrance requirements:* For master's, GRE General Test, A minimum 2.7 cumulative point-hour ratio (on a 4.0 scale) for all previous academic work, a statement of purpose, 3 letters of recommendation and transcripts from all prior institutions attended; for Certificate, A minimum 2.7 cumulative point-hour ratio (on a 4.0 scale) for all previous academic work, a statement of purpose, 3 letters of recommendation and transcripts from all prior institutions attended. Additional exam requirements/recommendations for international students: Required—TOEFL (minimum score 550 paper-based; 213 computer-based; 80 iBT), IELTS (minimum score 6.5). *Application deadline:* For fall admission, 1/15 priority date for domestic and international students. Applications are processed on a rolling basis. Application fee: $45 ($75 for international students). Electronic applications accepted. *Expenses:* Tuition, state resident: full-time $11,426; part-time $476 per credit hour. Tuition, nonresident: full-time $21,660; part-time $903 per credit hour. One-time fee: $62. *Financial support:* Research assistantships with tuition reimbursements, teaching assistantships with tuition reimbursements, career-related internships or fieldwork, Federal Work-Study, institutionally sponsored loans, scholarships/grants, tuition waivers (full), and unspecified assistantships available. Support available to part-time students. *Faculty research:* Economic development, health care, Third World, criminal justice, Eastern Europe. *Unit head:* Dr. Mark E. Denham, Chair, 419-530-4151, E-mail: mark.denham@utoledo.edu. *Application contact:* Graduate School Office, 419-530-4723, Fax: 419-530-4724, E-mail: grdsch@utnet.utoledo.edu.

University of Utah, Graduate School, College of Social and Behavioral Science, Department of Political Science, Program in Public Administration, Salt Lake City, UT 84112. Offers Exec MPA, MPA, JD/MPA, MHA/MPA, MPA/Ed D, MPA/MPH, MPA/MSW, MPA/PhD. *Accreditation:* NASPAA (one or more programs are accredited). Part-time and evening/weekend programs available. *Students:* 47 full-time (22 women), 79 part-time (36 women); includes 18 minority (1 Black or African American, non-Hispanic/Latino; 1 American Indian or Alaska Native, non-Hispanic/Latino; 4 Asian, non-Hispanic/Latino; 9 Hispanic/Latino; 1 Native Hawaiian or other Pacific Islander, non-Hispanic/Latino; 2 Two or more races, non-Hispanic/Latino), 2 international. Average age 34. 165 applicants, 79% accepted, 105 enrolled. In 2010, 60 master's awarded. *Degree requirements:* For master's, internship, thesis or research paper. *Entrance requirements:* For master's, GMAT, GRE General Test, LSAT, MAT, minimum GPA of 3.2. Additional exam requirements/recommendations for international students: Required—TOEFL (minimum score 580 paper-based; 237 computer-based; 92 iBT). *Application deadline:* For fall admission, 2/15 priority date for domestic and international students. Application fee: $55 ($65 for international students). *Expenses:* Contact institution. *Financial support:* In 2010–11, 14 students received support; research assistantships with full tuition reimbursements available, career-related internships or fieldwork available. Financial award application deadline: 3/15; financial award applicants required to submit FAFSA. *Faculty research:* Non-profit organizations, health policy, environmental policy, law and legal, human resource management, local government, e-government, conflict resolution, organization theory and behavior. *Unit head:* Dr. Christopher A. Simon, MPA program director, 801-581-6781, E-mail: simon@cppa.utah.edu. *Application contact:* Melissa Hall, Program Manager, 801-585-7985, Fax: 801-585-6492, E-mail: melissa.hall@cppa.utah.edu.

University of Vermont, Graduate College, College of Agriculture and Life Sciences, Department of Community Development and Applied Economics, Program in Public Administration, Burlington, VT 05405. Offers MPA. *Students:* 35 (16 women); includes 2 Asian, non-Hispanic/Latino; 1 Hispanic/Latino. 38 applicants, 76% accepted, 9 enrolled. In 2010, 19 master's awarded. *Entrance requirements:* For master's, GRE General Test. Additional exam requirements/recommendations for international students: Required—TOEFL (minimum score 550 paper-based; 213 computer-based; 80 iBT). *Application deadline:* For fall admission, 4/1 priority date for domestic students. Applications are processed on a rolling basis. Application fee: $40. Electronic applications accepted. *Expenses:* Tuition, state resident: part-time $537 per credit hour. Tuition, nonresident: part-time $1355 per credit hour. *Financial support:* Fellowships, teaching assistantships available. Financial award application deadline: 3/1. *Unit head:* Dr. Chris Koliba, Coordinator, 802-656-2606. *Application contact:* Dr. Chris Koliba, Coordinator, 802-656-2606.

University of Victoria, Faculty of Graduate Studies, Faculty of Human and Social Development, School of Public Administration, Victoria, BC V8W 2Y2, Canada. Offers dispute resolution (MADR); public administration (MPA, PhD); MPA/LL B. Part-time and evening/weekend programs available. Postbaccalaureate distance learning degree programs offered. *Degree requirements:* For master's, thesis (for some programs), report; for doctorate, thesis/dissertation, candidacy exam. *Entrance requirements:* For master's, GMAT or GRE General Test, professional resume; for doctorate, GMAT or GRE General Test. Additional exam requirements/recommendations for international students: Required—TOEFL (minimum score 610 paper-based; 255 computer-based). Electronic applications accepted. *Faculty research:* Policy analysis, local government, performance management, energy markets, labor markets.

University of Washington, Graduate School, Daniel J. Evans School of Public Affairs, Seattle, WA 98195. Offers public administration (MPA); public policy and management (PhD); JD/MPA; MPA/MAIS; MPA/MPH; MPA/MS; MPA/MUP. *Accreditation:* NASPAA. Part-time and evening/weekend programs available. *Degree requirements:* For master's, thesis, internship or cooperative experience. *Entrance requirements:* For master's and doctorate, GRE General Test, minimum GPA of 3.0. Additional exam requirements/recommendations for international students: Required—TOEFL (minimum score 580 paper-based; 237 computer-based; 92 iBT). Electronic applications accepted. *Faculty research:* Environmental policy, education and social policy, nonprofit management, international affairs, urban and regional development.

University of West Florida, College of Arts and Sciences: Arts, Department of Government, Pensacola, FL 32514-5750. Offers political science (MA), including public administration, security and diplomacy. Part-time and evening/weekend programs available. *Faculty:* 3 full-time (1 woman), 1 part-time/adjunct (0 women). *Students:* 12 full-time (5 women), 10 part-time (7 women); includes 3 minority (1 Hispanic/Latino; 1 Native Hawaiian or other Pacific Islander, non-Hispanic/Latino; 1 Two or more races, non-Hispanic/Latino). Average age 28. 15 applicants, 87% accepted, 6 enrolled. In 2010, 5 master's awarded. *Degree requirements:* For master's, thesis or alternative. *Entrance requirements:* For master's, GRE General Test, minimum GPA of 3.0. Additional exam requirements/recommendations for international students: Required—TOEFL (minimum score 550 paper-based; 213 computer-based). *Application deadline:* For fall admission, 6/1 for domestic students, 5/15 for international students; for spring admission, 10/1 for domestic and international students. Applications are processed on a rolling basis. Application fee: $30. *Expenses:* Tuition, state resident: full-time $4982; part-time $208 per credit hour. Tuition, nonresident: full-time $20,059; part-time $836 per credit hour. Required fees: $1365; $57 per credit hour. *Financial support:* In 2010–11, 14 fellowships with partial tuition reimbursements (averaging $134 per year), 5 research assistantships (averaging $3,280 per year), 2 teaching assistantships with partial tuition reimbursements (averaging $5,000 per year) were awarded; unspecified assistantships also available. Financial award application deadline: 4/15; financial award applicants required to submit FAFSA. *Faculty research:* Political campaigns, elections, law enforcement, growth management. *Unit head:* Dr. Alfred Cuzan, Chairperson, 850-474-2337, E-mail: govt@uwf.edu. *Application contact:* Terry McCray, Assistant Director of Graduate Admissions, 850-473-7718, Fax: 850-473-7714, E-mail: gradadmissions@uwf.edu.

University of West Florida, College of Professional Studies, Department of Professional and Community Leadership, Program in Administration, Pensacola, FL 32514-5750. Offers acquisition and contract administration (MSA); biomedical/pharmaceutical (MSA); criminal justice administration (MSA); database administration (MSA); education leadership (MSA); healthcare administration (MSA); human performance technology (MSA); leadership (MSA); nursing administration (MSA); public administration (MSA); software engineering administration (MSA). Part-time and evening/weekend programs available. Postbaccalaureate distance learning degree programs offered (no on-campus study). *Students:* 26 full-time (24 women), 185 part-time (115 women); includes 30 Black or African American, non-Hispanic/Latino; 1 American Indian or Alaska Native, non-Hispanic/Latino; 5 Asian, non-Hispanic/Latino; 13 Hispanic/Latino; 1 Native Hawaiian or other Pacific Islander, non-Hispanic/Latino, 2 international. Average age 34. 139 applicants, 70% accepted, 80 enrolled. In 2010, 60 master's awarded. *Entrance requirements:* For master's, GRE General Test, letter of intent, names of references. Additional exam requirements/recommendations for international students: Required—TOEFL (minimum score 550 paper-based; 213 computer-based). *Application deadline:* For fall admission, 6/1 for domestic students, 5/15 for international students; for spring admission, 10/1 for domestic and international students. Applications are processed on a rolling basis. Application fee: $30. *Expenses:* Tuition, state resident: full-time $4982; part-time $208 per credit hour. Tuition, nonresident: full-time $20,059; part-time $836 per credit hour. Required fees: $1365; $57 per credit hour. *Financial support:* Unspecified assistantships available. Financial award application deadline: 4/15; financial award applicants required to submit FAFSA. *Unit head:* Dr. Karen Rasmussen, Chairperson, 850-474-2301, Fax: 850-474-2804, E-mail: krasmuss@uwf.edu. *Application contact:* Terry McCray, Assistant Director of Graduate Admissions, 850-473-7718, Fax: 850-473-7714, E-mail: gradadmissions@uwf.edu.

University of West Georgia, College of Arts and Sciences, Department of Political Science and Planning, Carrollton, GA 30118. Offers political science (Certificate); public administration (MPA); public management (Certificate); rural and small town planning (MS). *Accreditation:* NASPAA (one or more programs are accredited). Part-time programs available. *Faculty:* 5 full-time (0 women). *Students:* 19 full-time (5 women), 22 part-time (11 women); includes 11 Black or African American, non-Hispanic/Latino; 1 Native Hawaiian or other Pacific Islander, non-Hispanic/Latino. Average age 33. 26 applicants, 58% accepted, 6 enrolled. In 2010, 10 master's, 5 other advanced degrees awarded. *Degree requirements:* For master's, exit paper. *Entrance requirements:* For master's, GRE General Test. Additional exam requirements/recommendations for international students: Required—TOEFL. *Application deadline:* For fall admission, 7/17 priority date for domestic students; for spring admission, 11/20 for domestic students. Applications are processed on a rolling basis. Application fee: $30. Electronic applications accepted. *Expenses:* Tuition, state resident: full-time $4130; part-time $173 per semester hour. Tuition, nonresident: full-time $16,524; part-time $689 per semester hour. Required fees: $1586; $44.01 per semester hour. $397 per semester. Tuition and fees vary according to program. *Financial support:* In 2010–11, 4 students received support, including 4 research assistantships with partial tuition reimbursements available (averaging $3,000 per year); career-related internships or fieldwork and unspecified assistantships also available. Support available to part-time students. Financial award application deadline: 7/1; financial award applicants required to submit FAFSA. *Faculty research:* State and local government, environmental health, administrative studies. *Unit head:* Dr. Robert M. Schaefer, Chair, 678-839-6504, Fax: 678-839-5009, E-mail: rschaefe@westga.edu. *Application contact:* Dr. Charles W. Clark, Dean, 678-839-6419, E-mail: cclark@westga.edu.

The University of Winnipeg, Graduate Studies, Program in Public Administration, Winnipeg, MB R3B 2E9, Canada. Offers MPA. Program offered jointly with University of Manitoba. Part-time programs available. *Degree requirements:* For master's, comprehensive exam, thesis optional. *Entrance requirements:* For master's, minimum GPA of 3.0 in last 60 credit hours. *Faculty research:* Policy evaluation, federalism, administrative innovation, administrative ethics, economic development/administration.

University of Wisconsin–Milwaukee, Graduate School, College of Letters and Sciences, Interdepartmental Program in Public Administration, Milwaukee, WI 53201-0413. Offers MPA, MPA/MUP. Part-time programs available. *Faculty:* 11 full-time (2 women). *Students:* 10 full-time (5 women), 11 part-time (3 women); includes 4 Black or African American, non-Hispanic/Latino; 1 American Indian or Alaska Native, non-Hispanic/Latino; 2 Asian, non-Hispanic/Latino. Average age 33. 32 applicants, 63% accepted, 7 enrolled. In 2010, 16 master's awarded. *Degree requirements:* For master's, thesis or alternative. *Entrance requirements:* For master's, GRE General Test, minimum GPA of 3.0. Additional exam requirements/recommendations for international students: Required—TOEFL (minimum score 550 paper-based; 79 iBT), IELTS (minimum score 6.5). *Application deadline:* For fall admission, 1/1 priority date for domestic students; for spring admission, 9/1 for domestic students. Applications are processed on a rolling basis. Application fee: $56 ($96 for international students). Electronic applications accepted. *Financial support:* Career-related internships or fieldwork and unspecified assistantships available. Support available to part-time students. Financial award application deadline: 4/15; financial award applicants required to submit FAFSA. *Unit head:* John Bohte, Representative, 414-229-4209, Fax: 414-229-5021, E-mail: jbohte@uwm.edu. *Application contact:* General Information Contact, 414-229-4982, Fax: 414-229-6967, E-mail: gradschool@uwm.edu.

University of Wisconsin–Oshkosh, The Office of Graduate Studies, College of Letters and Science, Department of Public Administration, Oshkosh, WI 54901. Offers general agency (MPA); health care (MPA). Part-time and evening/weekend programs available. *Degree requirements:* For master's, thesis or alternative. *Entrance requirements:* For master's, public service-related experience, resume, sample of written work. Additional exam requirements/recommendations for international students: Required—TOEFL (minimum score 550 paper-based; 213 computer-based; 79 iBT). Electronic applications accepted. *Faculty research:* Drug policy, local government state revenues and expenditures, health care regulation.

University of Wyoming, College of Arts and Sciences, Department of Political Science, Program in Public Administration, Laramie, WY 82070. Offers MPA. Part-time programs available. Postbaccalaureate distance learning degree programs offered (minimal on-campus study). *Degree requirements:* For master's, comprehensive exam (for some programs), thesis (for some programs). *Entrance requirements:* For master's, GRE General Test, minimum GPA of 3.0. Additional exam requirements/recommendations for international students: Required—TOEFL (minimum score 525 paper-based; 195 computer-based). Electronic applications accepted. *Faculty research:* Public policy, public ethics, administrative theory, natural resource policy.

Upper Iowa University, Online Master's Programs, Fayette, IA 52142-1857. Offers accounting (MBA); corporate financial management (MBA); global business (MBA); health and human services (MPA); higher education administration (MHEA); homeland security (MPA); human resources management (MBA); justice administration (MPA); organizational development (MBA); public personnel management (MPA); quality management (MBA). MBA also available at Madison, WI campus. Part-time programs available. Postbaccalaureate distance learning degree programs offered (no on-campus study). *Degree requirements:* For master's, research project. *Entrance requirements:* For master's, GMAT, GRE, or minimum GPA of 2.7 during last 60 hours. Additional exam requirements/recommendations for international students: Required—TOEFL (minimum score 570 paper-based; 230 computer-based). Electronic applications accepted. *Faculty research:* Total quality management, CQI, teams, organization culture and climate, management.

Villanova University, Graduate School of Liberal Arts and Sciences, Department of Political Science, Program in Public Administration, Villanova, PA 19085-1699. Offers MPA. *Accreditation:* NASPAA. Part-time and evening/weekend programs available. *Faculty:* 6 full-time (3 women), 2 part-time/adjunct (1 woman). *Students:* 45 full-time (28 women), 14 part-time (4 women); includes 11 minority (8 Black or African American, non-Hispanic/Latino; 2 Asian, non-Hispanic/Latino; 1 Hispanic/Latino), 3 international. Average age 30. 34 applicants, 82% accepted, 15 enrolled. In 2010, 22 master's awarded. *Degree requirements:* For master's, comprehensive exam. *Entrance requirements:* For master's, GRE General Test, minimum GPA of 3.0. Additional exam requirements/recommendations for international students: Required—TOEFL. *Application deadline:* For fall admission, 3/1 priority date for domestic and international students; for spring admission, 11/15 priority date for domestic and international students. Applications are processed on a rolling basis. Application fee: $50. Electronic applications accepted. *Expenses:* Tuition: Part-time $700 per credit. Part-time tuition and fees vary according to degree level and program. *Financial support:* Career-related internships or fieldwork, scholarships/grants, and unspecified assistantships available. Financial award application deadline: 3/15; financial award applicants required to submit FAFSA. *Unit head:* Dr. Markus Kreuzer, Director, 610-519-4710. *Application contact:* Dr. Adele Lindenmeyr.

Virginia Commonwealth University, Graduate School, College of Humanities and Sciences, Wilder School of Government and Public Affairs, Department of Political Science and Public Administration, Richmond, VA 23284-9005. Offers public administration (MPA); public management (CPM). *Accreditation:* NASPAA (one or more programs are accredited). Part-time programs available. *Students:* 33 full-time (23 women), 62 part-time (43 women); includes 31 minority (28 Black or African American, non-Hispanic/Latino; 1 Asian, non-Hispanic/Latino; 1 Hispanic/Latino; 1 Two or more races, non-Hispanic/Latino). 74 applicants, 68% accepted, 34 enrolled. In 2010, 37 master's awarded. *Entrance requirements:* For master's, GRE, GMAT or LSAT. Additional exam requirements/recommendations for international students: Required—TOEFL (minimum score 600 paper-based; 250 computer-based; 100 iBT); Recommended—IELTS (minimum score 6.5). *Application deadline:* For fall admission, 7/15 for domestic students; for spring admission, 10/1 for domestic students. Applications are processed on a rolling basis. Application fee: $50. Electronic applications accepted. *Expenses:* Tuition, state resident: full-time $4308; part-time $479 per credit hour. Tuition, nonresident: full-time $8942; part-time $994 per credit hour. Required fees: $2000; $85 per credit hour. Tuition and fees vary according to course level, course load, degree level, campus/location and program. *Financial support:* Fellowships, career-related internships or fieldwork, Federal Work-Study, institutionally sponsored loans, and tuition waivers (full and partial) available. Support available to part-time students. Financial award application deadline: 3/1. *Faculty research:* Environmental policy, executive leadership, human resource management, local government management, nonprofit management, public financial management, public policy analysis and evaluation. *Unit head:* Dr. Niraj Verma, Director, L. Douglas Wilder School of Government and Public Affairs, 804-828-2292. *Application contact:* Lisbeth D. Dannenbrink, Recruitment Contact, 804-828-6837, E-mail: lddannenbrin@vcu.edu.

Virginia Polytechnic Institute and State University, Graduate School, College of Architecture and Urban Studies, Center for Public Administration and Policy, Blacksburg, VA 24061. Offers Certificate. *Accreditation:* NASPAA. *Students:* 63 full-time (30 women), 112 part-time (48 women); includes 25 Black or African American, non-Hispanic/Latino; 6 Asian, non-Hispanic/Latino; 3 Hispanic/Latino, 12 international. Average age 36. 80 applicants, 64% accepted, 29 enrolled. *Entrance requirements:* Additional exam requirements/recommendations for international students: Required—TOEFL (minimum score 550 paper-based; 213 computer-based). *Application deadline:* For fall admission, 7/1 for domestic and international students; for spring admission, 12/1 for domestic and international students. Applications are processed on a rolling basis. Application fee: $65. Electronic applications accepted. *Expenses:* Tuition, state resident: full-time $9399; part-time $488 per credit hour. Tuition, nonresident: full-time $17,854; part-time $957.75 per credit hour. Required fees: $1534. Full-time tuition and fees vary according to program. *Financial support:* Career-related internships or fieldwork, Federal Work-Study, scholarships/grants, health care benefits, and unspecified assistantships available. Financial award application deadline: 1/15. *Faculty research:* Public administration theory, strategic management, ethics, the Constitution, computer-assisted creativity. *Unit head:* Dr. Brian J. Cook, UNIT HEAD, 540-231-3438, Fax: 540-231-7067, E-mail: brian_j_cook@vt.edu. *Application contact:* Laura French, Contact, 703-231-5133, Fax: 540-231-7067, E-mail: lhf@vt.edu.

Virginia Polytechnic Institute and State University, Graduate School, College of Architecture and Urban Studies, School of Public and International Affairs, Blacksburg, VA 24061. Offers economic development (Certificate); government and international affairs (MPIA, PhD); homeland security policy (Certificate); local government management (Certificate); nonprofit and nongovernmental organization management (Certificate); planning, governance and globalization (PhD); public administration and public affairs (MPA, PhD); urban and regional planning (MURPL). *Accreditation:* ACSP. *Faculty:* 31 full-time (9 women). *Students:* 114 full-time (66 women), 105 part-time (54 women); includes 11 Black or African American, non-Hispanic/Latino; 1 American Indian or Alaska Native, non-Hispanic/Latino; 7 Asian, non-Hispanic/Latino; 8 Hispanic/Latino, 19 international. Average age 31. 166 applicants, 67% accepted, 53 enrolled. In 2010, 41 master's, 3 doctorates awarded. *Degree requirements:* For master's, comprehensive exam (for some programs), thesis (for some programs); for doctorate, comprehensive exam (for some programs), thesis/dissertation (for some programs). *Entrance requirements:* For master's and doctorate, GRE. Additional exam requirements/recommendations for international students: Required—TOEFL (minimum score 550 paper-based; 213 computer-based). *Application deadline:* For fall admission, 7/1 for domestic and international students; for spring admission, 12/1 for domestic and international students. Applications are processed on a rolling basis. Application fee: $65. Electronic applications accepted. *Expenses:* Tuition, state resident: full-time $9399; part-time $488 per credit hour. Tuition, nonresident: full-time $17,854; part-time $957.75 per credit hour. Required fees: $1534. Full-time tuition and fees vary according to program. *Financial support:* In 2010–11, 1 teaching assistantship with full tuition reimbursement (averaging $21,395 per year) was awarded; career-related internships or fieldwork, Federal Work-Study, scholarships/grants, health care benefits, and unspecified assistantships also available. Financial award application deadline: 1/15. *Faculty research:* Design theory, environmental planning, town planning, transportation planning. Total annual research expenditures: $610,749. *Unit head:* Dr. Karen M. Hult, UNIT HEAD, 540-231-5351, Fax: 540-231-9938, E-mail: khult@vt.edu. *Application contact:* Krystal D. Wright, Contact, 540-231-2291, Fax: 540-231-9938, E-mail: garch@vt.edu.

Virginia Polytechnic Institute and State University, Graduate School, Intercollege, Certificate Programs, Blacksburg, VA 24061. Offers collaborative community leadership (Certificate); future professoriate (Certificate); geospatial information technology (Certificate); international research and development (Certificate); macromolecular interfaces with life sciences (Certificate); qualitative resource assessment (Certificate). *Students:* 61 part-time (29 women); includes 9 Black or African American, non-Hispanic/Latino; 2 Asian, non-Hispanic/Latino; 1 Hispanic/Latino, 2 international. Average age 40. 51 applicants, 96% accepted, 32 enrolled. In 2010, 135 Certificates awarded. *Entrance requirements:* Additional exam requirements/recommendations for international students: Required—TOEFL (minimum score 550 paper-based; 213 computer-based). *Application deadline:* For fall admission, 7/1 for domestic and

Public Administration

Virginia Polytechnic Institute and State University (continued)
international students; for spring admission, 12/1 for domestic and international students. Application fee: $65. *Expenses:* Tuition, state resident: full-time $9399; part-time $488 per credit hour. Tuition, nonresident: full-time $17,854; part-time $957.75 per credit hour. Required fees: $1534. Full-time tuition and fees vary according to program. *Financial support:* Career-related internships or fieldwork, Federal Work-Study, scholarships/grants, health care benefits, and unspecified assistantships available. *Unit head:* By Program. *Application contact:* By Program.

Walden University, Graduate Programs, School of Public Policy and Administration, Minneapolis, MN 55401. Offers criminal justice (MPA); emergency management (MPA); government management (Postbaccalaureate Certificate); health policy (MPA); homeland security policy (MPA); homeland security policy and coordination (MPA); interdisciplinary policy studies (MPA); international nongovernmental organizations (ngos) (MPA); law and public policy (MPA); local government management for sustainable communities (MPA); nonprofit management (Postbaccalaureate Certificate); nonprofit management and leadership (MPA, MS); policy analysis (MPA); public management and leadership (MPA); public policy and administration (MPA, PhD), including criminal justice (PhD), emergency management (PhD), health policy (PhD), health services (PhD), homeland security policy (PhD), homeland security policy and coordination (PhD), interdisciplinary policy studies (PhD), international nongovernmental organizations (PhD), law and public policy (PhD), local government management for sustainable communities (PhD), nonprofit management and leadership (PhD), policy analysis (PhD), public management and leadership (PhD), terrorism, mediation, and peace (PhD); terrorism, mediation, and peace (MPA). Part-time and evening/weekend programs available. Postbaccalaureate distance learning degree programs offered (minimal on-campus study). *Faculty:* 10 full-time (5 women), 117 part-time/adjunct (49 women). *Students:* 1,408 full-time (901 women), 599 part-time (392 women); includes 1,022 Black or African American, non-Hispanic/Latino; 11 American Indian or Alaska Native, non-Hispanic/Latino; 37 Asian, non-Hispanic/Latino; 64 Hispanic/Latino; 26 Two or more races, non-Hispanic/Latino, 47 international. Average age 40. In 2010, 311 master's, 23 doctorates awarded. *Degree requirements:* For doctorate, thesis/dissertation, residency. *Entrance requirements:* For master's, bachelor's degree or equivalent in related field, minimum GPA of 2.5; for doctorate, master's degree or equivalent in related field; minimum GPA of 3.0; official transcripts; three years of related professional/academic experience (preferred); access to computer and Internet. Additional exam requirements/recommendations for international students: Required—TOEFL (minimum score 550 paper-based; 213 computer-based), IELTS (minimum score 6.5), TOEFL (minimum score 550 paper-based; 213 computer-based), IELTS (minimum score 6.5), or Michigan English Language Assessment Battery (minimum score 82). *Application deadline:* Applications are processed on a rolling basis. Application fee: $50. Electronic applications accepted. *Expenses:* Tuition: Full-time $10,274; part-time $445 per credit. Tuition and fees vary according to course load, degree level and program. *Financial support:* Fellowships with tuition reimbursements, Federal Work-Study, scholarships/grants, unspecified assistantships, and family tuition reduction, active duty/veteran tuition reduction, group tuition reduction, interest-free payment plans available. Support available to part-time students. Financial award applicants required to submit FAFSA. *Unit head:* Dr. Mark Gordon, Associate Dean, 800-925-3368. *Application contact:* Jennifer Hall, Vice President of Enrollment Management, 866-4-WALDEN, E-mail: info@waldenu.edu.

Washington Adventist University, Program in Public Administration, Takoma Park, MD 20912. Offers MPA. Part-time programs available.

Wayland Baptist University, Graduate Programs, Program in Counseling, Plainview, TX 79072-6998. Offers counseling (MA); government administration (MPA); homeland security (MPA); justice administration (MPA). Part-time and evening/weekend programs available. Postbaccalaureate distance learning degree programs offered. *Degree requirements:* For master's, comprehensive exam. *Entrance requirements:* For master's, GRE, MAT. Additional exam requirements/recommendations for international students: Required—TOEFL (minimum score 500 paper-based; 173 computer-based; 61 iBT). Electronic applications accepted.

Wayne State University, College of Liberal Arts and Sciences, Department of Political Science, Program in Public Administration, Detroit, MI 48202. Offers criminal justice (MPA); public administration (MPA). *Accreditation:* NASPAA. Evening/weekend programs available. *Faculty:* 16 full-time (5 women), 2 part-time/adjunct (1 woman). *Students:* 15 full-time (9 women), 67 part-time (45 women); includes 27 minority (22 Black or African American, non-Hispanic/Latino; 1 American Indian or Alaska Native, non-Hispanic/Latino; 2 Asian, non-Hispanic/Latino; 2 Hispanic/Latino), 1 international. Average age 32. 47 applicants, 70% accepted, 22 enrolled. In 2010, 24 master's awarded. *Entrance requirements:* For master's, GRE General Test. Additional exam requirements/recommendations for international students: Required—TOEFL (minimum score 550 paper-based; 213 computer-based); Recommended—TWE (minimum score 6). *Application deadline:* For fall admission, 7/1 for domestic students, 6/1 for international students; for winter admission, 10/1 for international students; for spring admission, 2/1 for international students. Applications are processed on a rolling basis. Application fee: $30 ($50 for international students). Electronic applications accepted. *Expenses:* Tuition, state resident: full-time $7662; part-time $478.85 per credit hour. Tuition, nonresident: full-time $16,920; part-time $1057.55 per credit hour. Required fees: $571.20; $35.70 per credit hour. $188.05 per semester. Tuition and fees vary according to course load and program. *Faculty research:* Urban politics, urban education, state administration. *Unit head:* John Strate, Director, 313-577-2639, E-mail: jstrate@wayne.edu. *Application contact:* Ewa Golebiowska, Associate Professor, 313-577-2630, Fax: 313-993-3435, E-mail: ewa_golebiowska@wayne.edu.

Webster University, George Herbert Walker School of Business and Technology, Department of Management, St. Louis, MO 63119-3194. Offers business and organizational security management (MA); computer resources and information management (MA); environmental management (MS); government contracting (Certificate); health care management (MA); health services management (MA); human resources development (MA); human resources management (MA); management (DM); management and leadership (MA); marketing (MA); nonprofit management (Certificate); procurement and acquisitions management (MA); public administration (MA); quality management (MA); space systems operations management (MS); telecommunications management (MA). *Accreditation:* ACBSP. Part-time and evening/weekend programs available. Postbaccalaureate distance learning degree programs offered (no on-campus study). *Degree requirements:* For master's, thesis (for some programs); for doctorate, thesis/dissertation, written exam. *Entrance requirements:* For doctorate, GMAT, 3 years of work experience, MBA. Additional exam requirements/recommendations for international students: Required—TOEFL. *Expenses:* Tuition: Part-time $585 per credit hour. Tuition and fees vary according to degree level, campus/location and program.

West Chester University of Pennsylvania, Office of Graduate Studies, College of Business and Public Affairs, Department of Political Science, West Chester, PA 19383. Offers general public administration (MPA); human resource management (MPA, Certificate); non profit administration (Certificate); nonprofit administration (MPA); public administration (Certificate). Part-time and evening/weekend programs available. *Students:* 22 full-time (12 women), 39 part-time (31 women); includes 16 minority (12 Black or African American, non-Hispanic/Latino; 4 Hispanic/Latino), 2 international. Average age 31. 41 applicants, 88% accepted, 17 enrolled. In 2010, 22 master's awarded. *Degree requirements:* For master's, capstone project. *Entrance requirements:* For master's and Certificate, statement of professional goals, resume, two letters of reference. Additional exam requirements/recommendations for international students: Required—TOEFL (minimum score 550 paper-based; 213 computer-based; 80 iBT). *Application deadline:* For fall admission, 4/15 priority date for domestic students, 3/15 for international students; for spring admission, 10/15 for domestic students, 9/1 for international students. Applications are processed on a rolling basis. Application fee: $35. Electronic applications accepted. *Expenses:* Tuition, state resident: full-time $6966; part-time $387 per credit. Tuition, nonresident: full-time $11,146; part-time $619 per credit. Required fees: $1614.40; $133.24 per credit. Part-time tuition and fees vary according to campus/location. *Financial support:* Unspecified assistantships available. Support available to part-time students. Financial award application deadline: 2/15; financial award applicants required to submit FAFSA. *Faculty research:* Public policy, economic development, public opinion, urban politics, public administration. *Unit head:* Dr. Christopher Fiorentino, Dean, College of Business and Public Affairs, 610-436-2930, E-mail: cfiorentino@wcupa.edu. *Application contact:* Dr. Lorraine Bernotsky, Graduate Coordinator, 610-738-0576, E-mail: lbernotsky@wcupa.edu.

Western International University, Graduate Programs in Business, Master of Public Administration Program, Phoenix, AZ 85021-2718. Offers MPA. Part-time and evening/weekend programs available. Postbaccalaureate distance learning degree programs offered (no on-campus study). *Entrance requirements:* For master's, minimum GPA of 2.75. Additional exam requirements/recommendations for international students: Required—TOEFL (minimum score 550 paper-based; 213 computer-based; 79 iBT), TWE (minimum score 5), or IELTS (minimum score 6.5). Electronic applications accepted.

Western Kentucky University, Graduate Studies, Potter College of Arts and Letters, Department of Political Science, Bowling Green, KY 42101. Offers MPA. *Accreditation:* NASPAA. Part-time and evening/weekend programs available. *Degree requirements:* For master's, comprehensive exam, final exam. *Entrance requirements:* For master's, GRE General Test, minimum GPA of 2.75. Additional exam requirements/recommendations for international students: Required—TOEFL (minimum score 555 paper-based; 213 computer-based; 79 iBT). *Faculty research:* Role of non-profits, comparative policy analysis, social welfare policy, rural administration, ethics and bureaucracy.

Western Michigan University, Graduate College, College of Arts and Sciences, Department of Political Science, Program in International Development Administration, Kalamazoo, MI 49008. Offers MDA.

Western Michigan University, Graduate College, College of Arts and Sciences, School of Public Affairs and Administration, Kalamazoo, MI 49008. Offers health care administration (Graduate Certificate); nonprofit leadership and administration (Graduate Certificate); public administration (MPA, PhD). *Accreditation:* NASPAA (one or more programs are accredited). *Degree requirements:* For doctorate, thesis/dissertation, oral exams. *Entrance requirements:* For doctorate, GRE General Test.

West Virginia University, Eberly College of Arts and Sciences, School of Applied Social Sciences, Division of Public Administration, Morgantown, WV 26506. Offers legal studies (MLS); public administration (MPA); JD/MPA; MSW/MPA. *Accreditation:* NASPAA. Part-time programs available. *Degree requirements:* For master's, internship. *Entrance requirements:* For master's, GRE General Test, minimum GPA of 2.75. Additional exam requirements/recommendations for international students: Required—TOEFL. Electronic applications accepted. *Faculty research:* Public management and organization, conflict resolution, work satisfaction, health administration, social policy and welfare.

Wichita State University, Graduate School, Fairmount College of Liberal Arts and Sciences, Hugo Wall School of Urban and Public Affairs, Wichita, KS 67260. Offers public administration (MPA). *Accreditation:* NASPAA. Part-time programs available. *Unit head:* Dr. Nancy McCarthy Snyder, Director, 316-978-7240, Fax: 316-978-6533, E-mail: nancy.mccarthy-snyder@wichita.edu. *Application contact:* Dr. Samuel Yeager, Graduate Coordinator, 316-978-7240, E-mail: sam.yeager@wichita.edu.

Widener University, College of Arts and Sciences, Program in Public Administration, Chester, PA 19013-5792. Offers MPA, Psy D/MPA. Part-time and evening/weekend programs available. *Faculty:* 1 full-time (0 women), 3 part-time/adjunct (0 women). *Students:* 1 (woman) full-time, 29 part-time (20 women); includes 8 Black or African American, non-Hispanic/Latino; 1 American Indian or Alaska Native, non-Hispanic/Latino; 1 Asian, non-Hispanic/Latino; 1 Hispanic/Latino. Average age 31. 21 applicants, 86% accepted. In 2010, 9 master's awarded. *Degree requirements:* For master's, thesis or comprehensive exam. *Entrance requirements:* For master's, minimum undergraduate GPA of 3.0. *Application deadline:* For fall admission, 8/1 priority date for domestic students; for spring admission, 12/1 priority date for domestic students. Applications are processed on a rolling basis. Application fee: $25 ($300 for international students). Electronic applications accepted. *Expenses:* Contact institution. *Financial support:* In 2010–11, 8 students received support. Career-related internships or fieldwork and institutionally sponsored loans available. Support available to part-time students. Financial award application deadline: 5/1. *Faculty research:* Intergovernmental relations, nonprofit organizations, public policy, political economy, bureaucratic politics. *Unit head:* Dr. James E. Vike, Director, 610-499-1120, Fax: 610-499-4603, E-mail: james.vike@widener.edu. *Application contact:* Christine M. Weist, Assistant to Associate Provost for Graduate Studies, 610-499-4351, Fax: 610-499-4277, E-mail: christine.m.weist@widener.edu.

Wilmington University, College of Business, New Castle, DE 19720-6491. Offers business administration (MBA); finance (MBA); health care administration (MBA, MS); homeland security (MBA, MS); human resource management (MS); management (MS); management information systems (MBA); organizational leadership (MS); public administration (MS); transportation and logistics (MBA, MS). Part-time and evening/weekend programs available. *Entrance requirements:* Additional exam requirements/recommendations for international students: Required—TOEFL (minimum score 500 paper-based; 173 computer-based). Electronic applications accepted. *Expenses:* Tuition: Full-time $7110; part-time $395 per credit hour. Tuition and fees vary according to campus/location.

Wright State University, School of Graduate Studies, College of Liberal Arts, Department of Urban Affairs and Geography, Dayton, OH 45435. Offers public administration (MPA). *Accreditation:* NASPAA. *Degree requirements:* For master's, thesis optional. *Entrance requirements:* For master's, interview, minimum GPA of 2.7. Additional exam requirements/recommendations for international students: Required—TOEFL. *Faculty research:* Strategic planning, economic development, housing and public management.

York University, Faculty of Graduate Studies, Atkinson Faculty of Liberal and Professional Studies, Program in Public Policy, Administration and Law, Toronto, ON M3J 1P3, Canada. Offers MPPAL.

York University, Faculty of Graduate Studies, Schulich School of Business, Toronto, ON M3J 1P3, Canada. Offers administration (PhD); business (MBA); finance (MF); international business (IMBA); public administration (MPA); MBA/JD; MBA/MA; MBA/MFA. Part-time and evening/weekend programs available. *Degree requirements:* For master's, advanced proficiency in a second language, work term (IMBA); for doctorate, comprehensive exam, thesis/dissertation. *Entrance requirements:* For master's, GMAT, minimum GPA of 3.0; for doctorate, GMAT, minimum GPA of 3.3. Electronic applications accepted.

Public Affairs

American University, School of Communication, Program in Journalism and Public Affairs, Washington, DC 20016-8001. Offers broadcast journalism (MA), including economic communication, international journalism, public policy journalism; interactive journalism (MA); print journalism (MA), including economic communication, international journalism, public policy journalism. *Accreditation:* ACEJMC. *Faculty:* 13 full-time (5 women), 4 part-time/adjunct (all women). *Students:* 39 full-time (29 women). 169 applicants, 74% accepted, 37 enrolled. In 2010, 40 master's awarded. *Degree requirements:* For master's, comprehensive exam, thesis or alternative. *Entrance requirements:* For master's, GRE General Test. Additional exam requirements/recommendations for international students: Required—TOEFL (minimum score 600 paper-based; 250 computer-based; 100 iBT), IELTS (minimum score 7). *Application deadline:* For fall admission, 2/1 priority date for domestic students, 4/1 priority date for international students. Applications are processed on a rolling basis. Application fee: $50. Electronic applications accepted. *Financial support:* In 2010–11, 3 fellowships with full and partial tuition reimbursements (averaging $27,000 per year), 14 research assistantships with partial tuition reimbursements (averaging $7,000 per year), 3 teaching assistantships with partial tuition reimbursements (averaging $7,000 per year) were awarded; career-related internships or fieldwork, Federal Work-Study, institutionally sponsored loans, scholarships/grants, tuition waivers (partial), and unspecified assistantships also available. Financial award application deadline: 2/1; financial award applicants required to submit FAFSA. *Faculty research:* Government and media effects of journalistic practices and policies, race and gender and the media, investigative reporting, computer assisted reporting. *Unit head:* Prof. Jill Olmsted, Division Director, 202-885-2010, E-mail: jolmste@american.edu. *Application contact:* Sharmeen Ahsan-Bracciale, Graduate Admissions Office, 202-885-2040, Fax: 202-885-2019, E-mail: sharmeen@american.edu.

Arizona State University, College of Public Programs, School of Public Affairs, Phoenix, AZ 85004-0687. Offers public administration (nonprofit administration) (MPA); public administration (urban management) (MPA); public affairs (PhD); public policy (MPP); MPA/MSW. *Accreditation:* NASPAA (one or more programs are accredited). Part-time and evening/weekend programs available. *Faculty:* 19 full-time (7 women), 1 part-time/adjunct (0 women). *Students:* 149 full-time (96 women), 106 part-time (62 women); includes 62 minority (14 Black or African American, non-Hispanic/Latino; 5 American Indian or Alaska Native, non-Hispanic/Latino; 9 Asian, non-Hispanic/Latino; 32 Hispanic/Latino; 2 Two or more races, non-Hispanic/Latino), 34 international. Average age 32. 227 applicants, 71% accepted, 87 enrolled. In 2010, 68 master's, 4 doctorates awarded. Terminal master's awarded for partial completion of doctoral program. *Degree requirements:* For master's, thesis or alternative, policy analysis or capstone project; interactive Program of Study (iPOS) submitted before completing 50 percent of required credit hours; for doctorate, comprehensive exam, thesis/dissertation, interactive Program of Study (iPOS) submitted before completing 50 percent of required credit hours. *Entrance requirements:* For master's, GRE, minimum GPA of 3.0 or equivalent in last 2 years of work leading to bachelor's degree; for doctorate, GRE, minimum GPA of 3.0 or equivalent in last 2 years of work leading to bachelor's degree, 3 letters of recommendation, resume, statement of goals, samples of research reports. Additional exam requirements/recommendations for international students: Required—TOEFL (minimum score 600 paper-based; 213 computer-based; 100 iBT), IELTS (minimum score 6.5). *Application deadline:* For fall admission, 1/15 for domestic and international students. Application fee: $70 ($90 for international students). Electronic applications accepted. *Expenses:* Contact institution. *Financial support:* In 2010–11, 16 research assistantships with full and partial tuition reimbursements (averaging $14,106 per year), 2 teaching assistantships with full and partial tuition reimbursements (averaging $9,913 per year) were awarded; fellowships with full tuition reimbursements, career-related internships or fieldwork, Federal Work-Study, institutionally sponsored loans, scholarships/grants, and tuition waivers (full and partial) also available. Financial award application deadline: 3/1; financial award applicants required to submit FAFSA. Total annual research expenditures: $621,146. *Unit head:* Dr. Jonathan Koppell, Director, 602-496-1101, E-mail: koppell@asu.edu. *Application contact:* Graduate Admissions, 480-965-6113.

Clemson University, Graduate School, Program in International Family and Community Studies, Clemson, SC 29634. Offers PhD. *Faculty:* 6 full-time (2 women), 8 part-time/adjunct. *Students:* 12 full-time (11 women), 5 part-time (4 women); includes 2 Black or African American, non-Hispanic/Latino; 1 Asian, non-Hispanic/Latino, 5 international. Average age 36. 20 applicants, 20% accepted, 4 enrolled. In 2010, 2 doctorates awarded. *Degree requirements:* For doctorate, thesis/dissertation. *Entrance requirements:* For doctorate, GRE General Test. Additional exam requirements/recommendations for international students: Required—TOEFL. *Application deadline:* Applications are processed on a rolling basis. Application fee: $70 ($80 for international students). Electronic applications accepted. *Expenses:* Contact institution. *Financial support:* In 2010–11, 12 students received support, including 1 fellowship with full and partial tuition reimbursement available (averaging $4,000 per year), 17 research assistantships with partial tuition reimbursements available (averaging $13,914 per year); career-related internships or fieldwork, institutionally sponsored loans, scholarships/grants, health care benefits, and unspecified assistantships also available. Support available to part-time students. *Unit head:* Dr. Gary B. Melton, Director, 864-656-6271. *Application contact:* Information Contact, 864-656-3195, E-mail: gradapp@clemson.edu.

Concordia University, School of Graduate Studies, Faculty of Arts and Science, School of Community and Public Affairs, Montréal, QC H3G 1M8, Canada. Offers community economic development (Diploma).

Cornell University, Graduate School, Graduate Fields of Arts and Sciences, Field of Public Affairs, Ithaca, NY 14853-0001. Offers public affairs (MPA); public policy (MPA). *Faculty:* 96 full-time (30 women). *Students:* 234 full-time (134 women); includes 13 Black or African American, non-Hispanic/Latino; 14 Asian, non-Hispanic/Latino; 12 Hispanic/Latino, 119 international. Average age 25. 447 applicants, 55% accepted, 139 enrolled. In 2010, 68 master's awarded. *Degree requirements:* For master's, thesis, research project, paper. *Entrance requirements:* For master's, GRE General Test, 2 letters of recommendation. Additional exam requirements/recommendations for international students: Required—TOEFL (minimum score 550 paper-based; 213 computer-based; 77 iBT). *Application deadline:* Applications are processed on a rolling basis. Application fee: $80. Electronic applications accepted. *Expenses:* Tuition: Full-time $29,500. Required fees: $76. Tuition and fees vary according to degree level and program. *Financial support:* In 2010–11, 16 fellowships with full tuition reimbursements, 2 research assistantships with full tuition reimbursements, 2 teaching assistantships with full tuition reimbursements were awarded; institutionally sponsored loans, scholarships/grants, health care benefits, tuition waivers (full and partial), and unspecified assistantships also available. Financial award applicants required to submit FAFSA. *Unit head:* Director of Graduate Studies, 607-255-8018, Fax: 607-255-5240. *Application contact:* Graduate Field Assistant, 607-255-8018, Fax: 607-255-5240, E-mail: cipa@cornell.edu.

DePaul University, School of Public Service, Chicago, IL 60604. Offers financial administration management (Certificate); health administration (Certificate); health law and policy (MS); international public services (MS); leadership and policy studies (MS); metropolitan planning (Certificate); public administration (MPA); public service management (MS), including association management, fundraising and philanthropy, healthcare administration, higher education administration, metropolitan planning; public services (Certificate); JD/MS. Part-time and evening/weekend programs available. Postbaccalaureate distance learning degree programs offered (minimal on-campus study). *Faculty:* 14 full-time (3 women), 43 part-time/adjunct (24 women). *Students:* 372 full-time (256 women), 324 part-time (237 women); includes 156 Black or African American, non-Hispanic/Latino; 33 Asian, non-Hispanic/Latino; 65 Hispanic/Latino; 18 Two or more races, non-Hispanic/Latino, 18 international. Average age 26. 162 applicants, 100% accepted, 94 enrolled. In 2010, 108 master's awarded. *Degree requirements:* For master's, thesis or integrative seminar. *Entrance requirements:* For master's, minimum GPA of 2.7. Additional exam requirements/recommendations for international students: Required—

TOEFL (minimum score 550 paper-based; 213 computer-based; 80 iBT), IELTS (minimum score 6.5). *Application deadline:* Applications are processed on a rolling basis. Application fee: $40. Electronic applications accepted. *Financial support:* In 2010–11, 60 students received support, including 3 research assistantships with full tuition reimbursements available (averaging $7,000 per year); career-related internships or fieldwork, Federal Work-Study, institutionally sponsored loans, scholarships/grants, tuition waivers (partial), and unspecified assistantships also available. Support available to part-time students. Financial award application deadline: 7/1; financial award applicants required to submit FAFSA. *Faculty research:* Government financing, transportation, leadership, health care, volunteerism and organizational behavior, non-profit organizations. Total annual research expenditures: $20,000. *Unit head:* Dr. J. Patrick Murphy, Director, 312-362-5608, Fax: 312-362-5506, E-mail: jpmurphy@depaul.edu. *Application contact:* Megan B. Balderston, Director of Admissions and Marketing, 312-362-5565, Fax: 312-362-5506, E-mail: pubserv@depaul.edu.

George Mason University, College of Humanities and Social Sciences, Department of Public and International Affairs, Fairfax, VA 22030. Offers association management (Certificate); biodefense (MS, PhD); emergency management and homeland security (Certificate); nonprofit management (Certificate); political science (MA, PhD); public administration (MPA); public management (Certificate). *Accreditation:* NASPAA (one or more programs are accredited). *Faculty:* 38 full-time (14 women), 31 part-time/adjunct (8 women). *Students:* 134 full-time (76 women), 319 part-time (176 women); includes 63 minority (29 Black or African American, non-Hispanic/Latino; 9 Asian, non-Hispanic/Latino; 21 Hispanic/Latino; 1 Native Hawaiian or other Pacific Islander, non-Hispanic/Latino; 3 Two or more races, non-Hispanic/Latino), 16 international. Average age 31. 574 applicants, 58% accepted, 144 enrolled. In 2010, 140 master's, 3 doctorates, 11 other advanced degrees awarded. *Entrance requirements:* For master's, GRE General Test, minimum GPA of 3.0 in last 60 hours of course work. Additional exam requirements/recommendations for international students: Required—TOEFL (minimum score 570 paper-based; 230 computer-based; 88 iBT). *Application deadline:* For fall admission, 3/1 priority date for domestic students; for spring admission, 10/15 for domestic students. Application fee: $100. Electronic applications accepted. *Expenses:* Tuition, state resident: full-time $8192; part-time $440 per credit hour. Tuition, nonresident: full-time $22,952; part-time $1055 per credit hour. Required fees: $2364; $99 per credit hour. *Financial support:* In 2010–11, 30 students received support, including 3 fellowships with full tuition reimbursements available (averaging $18,000 per year), 10 research assistantships with full and partial tuition reimbursements available (averaging $12,271 per year), 18 teaching assistantships with full and partial tuition reimbursements available (averaging $10,428 per year); career-related internships or fieldwork, Federal Work-Study, scholarships/grants, unspecified assistantships, and health care benefits (full-time research or teaching assistantship recipients) also available. Financial award application deadline: 3/1; financial award applicants required to submit FAFSA. *Faculty research:* The Rehnquist Court and economic liberties; intersection of economic development with high-tech industry, telecommunications, and entrepreneurism; political economy of development; violence, terrorism and U. S. foreign policy; international security issues. Total annual research expenditures: $696,997. *Unit head:* Dr. Priscilla Regan, Chair, 703-993-1419, Fax: 703-993-1399, E-mail: pregan@gmu.edu. *Application contact:* Peg Koback, Information Contact, 703-993-9466, E-mail: mkoback@gmu.edu.

The George Washington University, Columbian College of Arts and Sciences, School of Media and Public Affairs, Washington, DC 20052. Offers MA. *Faculty:* 24 full-time (7 women), 16 part-time/adjunct (5 women). *Students:* 22 full-time (14 women), 17 part-time (15 women); includes 1 Black or African American, non-Hispanic/Latino; 3 Asian, non-Hispanic/Latino; 1 Hispanic/Latino, 5 international. Average age 26. 119 applicants, 55% accepted, 21 enrolled. In 2010, 11 master's awarded. *Degree requirements:* For master's, thesis optional. *Entrance requirements:* For master's, GRE General Test. Additional exam requirements/recommendations for international students: Required—TOEFL (minimum score 550 paper-based; 213 computer-based; 80 iBT). *Application deadline:* For fall admission, 4/1 priority date for domestic students, 1/15 priority date for international students; for spring admission, 10/1 priority date for domestic students, 9/1 priority date for international students. Applications are processed on a rolling basis. Application fee: $75. Electronic applications accepted. *Financial support:* In 2010–11, fellowships with tuition reimbursements (averaging $10,000 per year), teaching assistantships with tuition reimbursements (averaging $5,000 per year) were awarded. Financial award application deadline: 1/15. *Unit head:* Lee W. Huebner, Director, 202-994-6227, E-mail: huebner@gwu.edu. *Application contact:* Information Contact, 202-994-6227, Fax: 202-994-5806, E-mail: smpa@gwu.edu.

Indiana University Bloomington, School of Public and Environmental Affairs, Public Affairs Programs, Bloomington, IN 47405-7000. Offers comparative and international affairs (MPA); economic development (MPA); energy (MPA); environmental policy (PhD); environmental policy and natural resource management (MPA); information systems (MPA); local government management (MPA); nonprofit management (MPA, Certificate); policy analysis (MPA); public finance (PhD); public financial administration (MPA); public management (MPA, PhD); public policy analysis (PhD); specialized public affairs (MPA); sustainability and sustainable development (MPA); JD/MPA; MPA/MIS; MPA/MLS; MSES/MPA. *Accreditation:* NASPAA (one or more programs are accredited). Part-time programs available. *Faculty:* 31 full-time, 15 part-time/adjunct. *Students:* 466 full-time (261 women); includes 11 Black or African American, non-Hispanic/Latino; 2 American Indian or Alaska Native, non-Hispanic/Latino; 42 Asian, non-Hispanic/Latino; 1 Hispanic/Latino, 65 international. Average age 26. 650 applicants, 218 enrolled. In 2010, 166 master's, 10 doctorates awarded. *Degree requirements:* For master's, core classes, capstone; for doctorate, comprehensive exam, thesis/dissertation. *Entrance requirements:* For master's, GRE General Test or GMAT, official transcripts, 3 letters of recommendation, resume, personal statement, departmental questions; for doctorate, GRE General Test or LSAT, official transcripts, 3 letters of recommendation, resume or curriculum vitae, statement of purpose. Additional exam requirements/recommendations for international students: Required—TOEFL (minimum score 600 paper-based; 96 iBT); Recommended—IELTS (minimum score 7). *Application deadline:* For fall admission, 5/1 priority date for domestic students, 12/1 priority date for international students. Applications are processed on a rolling basis. Application fee: $55 ($65 for international students). Electronic applications accepted. *Financial support:* Fellowships with partial tuition reimbursements, research assistantships with partial tuition reimbursements, teaching assistantships with partial tuition reimbursements, career-related internships or fieldwork, Federal Work-Study, scholarships/grants, health care benefits, unspecified assistantships, and Service Corps programs available. Financial award application deadline: 2/1; financial award applicants required to submit FAFSA. *Faculty research:* Comparative and international affairs, environmental policy and resource management, policy analysis, public finance, public management, urban management, nonprofit management, energy policy, social policy, public finance. *Unit head:* Jennifer Forney, Director of Graduate Student Services, 812-855-9485, Fax: 812-856-3665, E-mail: speampo@indiana.edu. *Application contact:* Audrey Whitaker, Admissions Assistant, 812-855-2840, E-mail: speaapps@indiana.edu.

See Close-Up on page 1271.

Indiana University Northwest, School of Public and Environmental Affairs, Gary, IN 46408-1197. Offers criminal justice (MPA); environmental affairs (Graduate Certificate); health services administration (MPA); human services administration (MPA); nonprofit management (Graduate Certificate); public management (MPA, Graduate Certificate). *Accreditation:* NASPAA (one or more programs are accredited). Part-time programs available. *Faculty:* 5 full-time (3 women). *Students:* 9 full-time (6 women), 127 part-time (96 women); includes 96 minority (81 Black or African American, non-Hispanic/Latino; 1 American Indian or Alaska Native, non-Hispanic/Latino; 2 Asian, non-Hispanic/Latino; 10 Hispanic/Latino; 2 Two or more races, non-Hispanic/Latino). Average age 38. 43 applicants, 95% accepted, 40 enrolled. In 2010, 37 master's, 24 other advanced degrees awarded. *Entrance requirements:* For master's, GRE General Test or GMAT, letters of recommendation. *Application deadline:* For fall admission, 8/15 priority date

Public Affairs

Indiana University Northwest (continued)

for domestic students. Applications are processed on a rolling basis. Application fee: $25. *Financial support:* Career-related internships or fieldwork, Federal Work-Study, and tuition waivers (partial) available. Support available to part-time students. Financial award application deadline: 3/1. *Faculty research:* Employment in income security policies, evidence in criminal justice, equal employment law, social welfare policy and welfare reform, public finance in developing countries. *Unit head:* George Assibey-Mensah, Interim Dean/Division Director, 219-980-6695, Fax: 219-980-6737. *Application contact:* Sandra Hall Smith, Secretary, 219-980-6695, Fax: 219-980-6737, E-mail: shsmith@iun.edu.

Indiana University of Pennsylvania, School of Graduate Studies and Research, College of Humanities and Social Sciences, Department of Political Science, Program in Public Affairs, Indiana, PA 15705-1087. Offers MA. Part-time programs available. *Faculty:* 8 full-time (4 women). *Students:* 12 full-time (5 women), 3 part-time (2 women); includes 1 minority (Black or African American, non-Hispanic/Latino), 5 international. Average age 28. 13 applicants, 77% accepted, 9 enrolled. In 2010, 7 master's awarded. *Degree requirements:* For master's, thesis optional. *Entrance requirements:* For master's, GRE, 2 letters of recommendation. Additional exam requirements/recommendations for international students: Required—TOEFL. *Application deadline:* For fall admission, 7/1 priority date for domestic students; for spring admission, 11/1 for domestic students. Applications are processed on a rolling basis. Application fee: $40. *Financial support:* In 2010–11, 9 research assistantships with full and partial tuition reimbursements (averaging $3,627 per year) were awarded. Financial award application deadline: 3/15; financial award applicants required to submit FAFSA. *Unit head:* Dr. Susan Martin, Graduate Coordinator, 724-357-2776, E-mail: susan.martin@iup.edu. *Application contact:* Dr. David Chambers, Graduate Coordinator, 724-357-2776, E-mail: chambers@iup.edu.

Indiana University–Purdue University Fort Wayne, Division of Public and Environmental Affairs, Fort Wayne, IN 46805-1499. Offers public affairs (MPA); public management (MPM, Certificate). *Accreditation:* NASPAA (one or more programs are accredited). Part-time programs available. *Faculty:* 9 full-time (3 women). *Students:* 14 full-time (9 women), 33 part-time (21 women); includes 5 minority (3 Black or African American, non-Hispanic/Latino; 1 Hispanic/Latino; 1 Two or more races, non-Hispanic/Latino), 4 international. Average age 31. 21 applicants, 95% accepted, 20 enrolled. In 2010, 13 master's, 2 Certificates awarded. *Degree requirements:* For master's, internship. *Entrance requirements:* For master's, GRE General Test or GMAT, minimum GPA of 3.0, 3 letters of reference. Additional exam requirements/recommendations for international students: Required—TOEFL (minimum score 550 paper-based; 213 computer-based; 77 iBT). *Application deadline:* Applications are processed on a rolling basis. Application fee: $55. *Expenses:* Tuition, state resident: full-time $4824; part-time $268 per credit. Tuition, nonresident: full-time $11,625; part-time $646 per credit. Required fees: $555; $30.85 per credit. Tuition and fees vary according to course load. *Financial support:* In 2010–11, 1 teaching assistantship with partial tuition reimbursement (averaging $12,740 per year) was awarded; career-related internships or fieldwork and scholarships/grants also available. Support available to part-time students. Financial award application deadline: 3/1; financial award applicants required to submit FAFSA. *Faculty research:* Physician assisted suicide, serious crime and minorities, healthcare costs. *Unit head:* Dr. Jane Grant, Chair, 260-481-6349, Fax: 260-481-6346, E-mail: grant@ipfw.edu. *Application contact:* Dr. Brian L. Fife, Director of Graduate Studies, 260-481-6961, Fax: 260-481-6346, E-mail: fifeb@ipfw.edu.

Indiana University–Purdue University Indianapolis, School of Public and Environmental Affairs, Indianapolis, IN 46202. Offers criminal justice and public safety (MSCJPS); public affairs (MPA), including criminal justice, nonprofit management, policy analysis, public management; public management (Graduate Certificate); JD/MPA; MATS/MM; MLS/NMC; MLS/PMC. *Accreditation:* CAHME (one or more programs are accredited); NASPAA. Part-time and evening/weekend programs available. Postbaccalaureate distance learning degree programs offered (no on-campus study). *Faculty:* 23 full-time (7 women). *Students:* 81 full-time (47 women), 205 part-time (142 women); includes 30 Black or African American, non-Hispanic/Latino; 6 Asian, non-Hispanic/Latino; 8 Hispanic/Latino, 9 international. Average age 31. 217 applicants, 73% accepted, 136 enrolled. In 2010, 77 degrees awarded. *Entrance requirements:* For master's, GRE General Test, GMAT or LSAT, minimum GPA of 3.0 (preferred). Additional exam requirements/recommendations for international students: Required—All international applicants to IUPUI whose native language is not English must demonstrate proficiency in English as a second language through an accepted examination and an accepted score. *Application deadline:* For fall admission, 5/15 priority date for domestic students; for spring admission, 2/15 priority date for domestic students. Applications are processed on a rolling basis. Application fee: $50 ($65 for international students). Electronic applications accepted. *Financial support:* In 2010–11, 1 fellowship with full tuition reimbursement (averaging $14,000 per year), 4 research assistantships with full tuition reimbursements (averaging $12,000 per year) were awarded; teaching assistantships, career-related internships or fieldwork, Federal Work-Study, institutionally sponsored loans, and scholarships/grants also available. Support available to part-time students. Financial award application deadline: 3/1; financial award applicants required to submit FAFSA. *Faculty research:* Nonprofit and public management, public policy, urban and environmental policy, disaster preparedness and recovery, vehicular safety, homicide, and offender rehabilitation and re-entry. Total annual research expenditures: $1.6 million. *Unit head:* Dr. Terry L. Baumer, Executive Associate Dean, 317-274-2016, Fax: 317-274-5153.

Indiana University South Bend, School of Public and Environmental Affairs, South Bend, IN 46634-7111. Offers health systems administration and policy (MPA); health systems management (Certificate); nonprofit management (Certificate); public and community services administration and policy (MPA); public management (Certificate); urban affairs (Certificate). *Accreditation:* NASPAA. Part-time and evening/weekend programs available. *Faculty:* 4 full-time (1 woman). *Students:* 1 full-time (0 women), 9 part-time (7 women); includes 1 minority (Black or African American, non-Hispanic/Latino). Average age 43. 2 applicants, 0% accepted, 0 enrolled. In 2010, 11 master's awarded. *Entrance requirements:* For master's, GRE General Test, minimum undergraduate GPA of 2.5. *Application deadline:* For fall admission, 7/1 priority date for domestic students; for spring admission, 11/1 for domestic students. Applications are processed on a rolling basis. Application fee: $50 ($60 for international students). *Financial support:* Fellowships, research assistantships, career-related internships or fieldwork, Federal Work-Study, and institutionally sponsored loans available. Support available to part-time students. Financial award application deadline: 3/1; financial award applicants required to submit FAFSA. *Unit head:* Leda M. Hall, Dean, 574-520-4803. *Application contact:* Leda M. Hall, Dean, 574-520-4803.

The Institute of World Politics, Graduate Programs in National Security, Intelligence, and International Affairs, Washington, DC 20036. Offers American foreign policy (Certificate); comparative political culture (Certificate); counterintelligence (Certificate); democracy building (Certificate); intelligence (Certificate); international politics (Certificate); national security affairs (Certificate); public diplomacy and political warfare (Certificate); statecraft and national security affairs (MA); statecraft and world politics (MA); strategic intelligence studies (MA). Part-time and evening/weekend programs available. *Degree requirements:* For master's, comprehensive exam, thesis optional. *Entrance requirements:* For master's, GRE General Test. Additional exam requirements/recommendations for international students: Required—TOEFL. Electronic applications accepted. *Faculty research:* Intelligence, national security, statecraft.

Jackson State University, Graduate School, College of Public Service, Jackson, MS 39217. Offers MPPA, MS, PhD. *Faculty:* 45 full-time (23 women), 9 part-time/adjunct (5 women). *Students:* 358 full-time (286 women), 222 part-time (163 women); includes 480 minority (473 Black or African American, non-Hispanic/Latino; 5 Asian, non-Hispanic/Latino; 2 Hispanic/Latino), 18 international. Average age 35. In 2010, 113 master's, 7 doctorates awarded. *Degree requirements:* For master's, comprehensive exam. *Entrance requirements:* For master's, GRE General Test. Additional exam requirements/recommendations for international students: Required—TOEFL. *Application deadline:* For fall admission, 3/1 for domestic and international students; for spring admission, 10/1 for domestic and international students. Application fee: $25. *Expenses:* Tuition, state resident: full-time $5050; part-time $281 per credit hour. Tuition, nonresident: full-time $12,380; part-time $689 per credit hour. *Financial support:* Career-related internships or fieldwork, Federal Work-Study, scholarships/grants, tuition waivers (full), and unspecified assistantships available. Support available to part-time students. Financial award application deadline: 3/1; financial award applicants required to submit FAFSA. *Unit head:* Dr. Mario Azevedo, Interim Dean, 601-979-8836, Fax: 601-979-8837, E-mail: deanofcps@jsums.edu. *Application contact:* Sharlene Wilson, Director of Graduate Admissions, 601-979-2455, Fax: 601-979-4325, E-mail: sharlene.f.wilson@jsums.edu.

McMaster University, School of Graduate Studies, Faculty of Social Sciences, Department of Political Science, Hamilton, ON L8S 4M2, Canada. Offers international relations (PhD); political science (MA); public and the global economy (MA); public policy (PhD); public policy and administration (MA). MA program in public policy and administration offered jointly with University of Guelph. Part-time programs available. *Degree requirements:* For master's, thesis or alternative. *Entrance requirements:* For master's, minimum B+ average. Additional exam requirements/recommendations for international students: Required—TOEFL (minimum score 580 paper-based; 237 computer-based). *Faculty research:* Organizational theory, internationalization of public policy, water resource policies, political interest intermediation, comparative politics.

Murray State University, College of Humanities and Fine Arts, Department of Government, Laws and International Affairs, Program in Public Administration, Murray, KY 42071. Offers public affairs (MPA). Part-time programs available. Postbaccalaureate distance learning degree programs offered (minimal on-campus study). *Degree requirements:* For master's, capstone course. *Entrance requirements:* For master's, GRE General Test. Additional exam requirements/recommendations for international students: Required—TOEFL.

National University of Singapore, Lee Kuan Yew School of Public Policy, Singapore, Singapore. Offers MPA, MPM, MPP, PhD.

New Mexico Highlands University, Graduate Studies, College of Arts and Sciences, Department of History, Political Science, and Languages and Culture, Las Vegas, NM 87701. Offers MA. Program is interdisciplinary. *Faculty:* 8 full-time (4 women). *Students:* 9 full-time (5 women), 10 part-time (4 women); includes 10 Hispanic/Latino, 5 international. Average age 32. 12 applicants, 100% accepted, 11 enrolled. In 2010, 2 master's awarded. *Degree requirements:* For master's, comprehensive exam, thesis or alternative. *Entrance requirements:* Additional exam requirements/recommendations for international students: Required—TOEFL (minimum score 540 paper-based; 207 computer-based). *Application deadline:* For fall admission, 8/1 priority date for domestic students. Applications are processed on a rolling basis. Application fee: $15. *Expenses:* Tuition, state resident: full-time $2544. Required fees: $624; $132 per credit hour. *Financial support:* In 2010–11, 8 students received support. Career-related internships or fieldwork, Federal Work-Study, institutionally sponsored loans, scholarships/grants, traineeships, tuition waivers (full and partial), and unspecified assistantships available. Support available to part-time students. Financial award application deadline: 3/1. *Unit head:* Dr. Peter Linder, 505-454-3423, E-mail: linderpeter@nmhu.edu. *Application contact:* Diane Trujillo, Administrative Assistant, Graduate Studies, 505-454-3266, Fax: 505-426-2117, E-mail: dtrujillo@nmhu.edu.

Northeastern University, College of Social Sciences and Humanities, Department of Political Science, Boston, MA 02115-5096. Offers political science (MA); public administration (MPA, Certificate), including development administration (MPA), health administration and policy (MPA), state and local government (MPA), urban studies (Certificate); public and international affairs (PhD). Part-time and evening/weekend programs available. *Faculty:* 22 full-time (4 women), 10 part-time/adjunct (1 woman). *Students:* 64 full-time (30 women), 12 part-time (7 women). Average age 30. 132 applicants, 47% accepted, 23 enrolled. In 2010, 21 master's, 3 doctorates awarded. *Degree requirements:* For master's, thesis optional; for doctorate, thesis/dissertation. *Entrance requirements:* For master's, GRE General Test. Additional exam requirements/recommendations for international students: Required—TOEFL. *Application deadline:* Applications are processed on a rolling basis. Application fee: $50. *Financial support:* In 2010–11, 12 fellowships, 1 research assistantship with tuition reimbursement, 17 teaching assistantships with tuition reimbursements (averaging $14,035 per year) were awarded; career-related internships or fieldwork, Federal Work-Study, tuition waivers (full and partial), and unspecified assistantships also available. Support available to part-time students. Financial award application deadline: 2/1; financial award applicants required to submit FAFSA. *Faculty research:* Presidency, public opinion, Congress, democratization, national identity. *Unit head:* Dr. John Portz, Chair, 617-373-2796, Fax: 617-373-5311, E-mail: gradpolisci@neu.edu. *Application contact:* Brynn Thompson, Graduate Programs Assistant, 617-373-4404, Fax: 617-373-5311, E-mail: gradpolisci@neu.edu.

Notre Dame de Namur University, Division of Academic Affairs, School of Business and Management, Department of Public Administration, Belmont, CA 94002-1908. Offers human resource management (MPA); public administration (MPA); public affairs administration (MPA). Part-time and evening/weekend programs available. *Faculty:* 3 full-time (1 woman), 4 part-time/adjunct (2 women). *Students:* 13 full-time (11 women), 41 part-time (34 women); includes 4 Black or African American, non-Hispanic/Latino; 4 Asian, non-Hispanic/Latino; 12 Hispanic/Latino; 1 Native Hawaiian or other Pacific Islander, non-Hispanic/Latino, 10 international. Average age 32. 35 applicants, 49% accepted, 14 enrolled. In 2010, 13 master's awarded. *Entrance requirements:* For master's, interview, minimum GPA of 2.5. Additional exam requirements/recommendations for international students: Required—TOEFL (minimum score 550 paper-based; 213 computer-based; 79 iBT). *Application deadline:* For fall admission, 8/1 priority date for domestic students; for spring admission, 12/1 priority date for domestic students. Applications are processed on a rolling basis. Application fee: $60. Electronic applications accepted. *Expenses:* Tuition: Full-time $14,220; part-time $790 per credit. Required fees: $35 per semester. Tuition and fees vary according to program. *Financial support:* Available to part-time students. Applicants required to submit FAFSA. *Unit head:* Jordan Holtzman, Director, 650-508-3637, E-mail: jholtzman@ndnu.edu. *Application contact:* Candace Hallmark, Associate Director of Admissions, 650-508-3600, Fax: 650-508-3426, E-mail: grad.admit@ndnu.edu.

The Ohio State University, Graduate School, John Glenn School of Public Affairs, Columbus, OH 43210. Offers public administration (MA, MPA); public policy and management (PhD). *Accreditation:* NASPAA (one or more programs are accredited). Part-time programs available. *Faculty:* 14. *Students:* 82 full-time (37 women), 114 part-time (72 women); includes 13 Black or African American, non-Hispanic/Latino; 7 Asian, non-Hispanic/Latino; 5 Hispanic/Latino; 4 Two or more races, non-Hispanic/Latino, 15 international. Average age 32. In 2010, 55 master's, 1 doctorate awarded. *Degree requirements:* For doctorate, thesis/dissertation. *Entrance requirements:* For master's, GMAT, GRE General Test (MPA), minimum GPA of 3.0 (MA); for doctorate, GRE General Test. Additional exam requirements/recommendations for international students: Recommended—TOEFL (minimum score 573 paper-based; 230 computer-based). *Application deadline:* For fall admission, 8/15 priority date for domestic students, 7/1 priority date for international students; for winter admission, 12/1 priority date for domestic students, 11/1 priority date for international students; for spring admission, 3/1 priority date for domestic students, 2/1 priority date for international students. Applications are processed on a rolling basis. Application fee: $40 ($50 for international students). Electronic applications accepted. *Expenses:* Tuition, state resident: full-time $10,605. Tuition, nonresident: full-time $26,535. Tuition and fees vary according to course load and program. *Financial support:* Fellowships, research assistantships, teaching assistantships, Federal Work-Study, institutionally sponsored loans, and unspecified assistantships available. Support available to part-time students. *Unit head:* Charles R. Wise, Graduate Studies Committee Chair, 614-292-8696, Fax: 614-292-4868, E-mail: wise.983@osu.edu. *Application contact:* 614-292-9444, Fax: 614-292-3895, E-mail: domestic.grad@osu.edu.

Park University, College of Graduate and Professional Studies, Kansas City, MO 54105. Offers adult education (M Ed); at-risk students (M Ed); disaster and emergency management

(MPA); educational administration (M Ed); entrepreneurship (MBA); general business (MBA); general education (M Ed); government/business relations (MPA); healthcare/services management (MBA, MPA); international business (MBA); K-12 certification (MAT); management information systems (MBA); management of information systems (MPA); middle school certification (MAT); multi-cultural education (M Ed); nonprofit management (MPA); public management (MPA); school law (M Ed); secondary school certification (MAT); special education (M Ed). Part-time and evening/weekend programs available. Postbaccalaureate distance learning degree programs offered (no on-campus study). *Degree requirements:* For master's, comprehensive exam, thesis (for some programs). *Entrance requirements:* For master's, GRE, GMAT, teacher certification (M Ed). Additional exam requirements/recommendations for international students: Required—TOEFL (minimum score 550 paper-based). Electronic applications accepted. *Faculty research:* Literacy, leadership, brain based research, multicultural education, diversity.

Penn State Harrisburg, Graduate School, School of Public Affairs, Middletown, PA 17057-4898. Offers MA, MHA, MPA, PhD, MPA/JD. *Accreditation:* NASPAA. *Unit head:* Dr. Steven A. Peterson, Director, 717-948-6154, E-mail: sap12@psu.edu. *Application contact:* Robert Coffman, Director of Admissions, 717-948-6250, Fax: 717-948-6325, E-mail: ric1@psu.edu.

Princeton University, Graduate School, Program in Population Studies, Princeton, NJ 08544-1019. Offers demography (PhD, Certificate); economics and demography (PhD); public affairs and demography (PhD); sociology and demography (PhD). *Degree requirements:* For doctorate, thesis/dissertation. *Entrance requirements:* For doctorate, GRE General Test. Additional exam requirements/recommendations for international students: Required—TOEFL (minimum score 600 paper-based; 250 computer-based). Electronic applications accepted. *Faculty research:* Models, fertility, infant and child mortality, migration.

Princeton University, Graduate School, Woodrow Wilson School of Public and International Affairs, Princeton, NJ 08544-1019. Offers public affairs (MPA, PhD); public policy (MPP); JD/MPA. JD/MPA offered jointly with Columbia University, New York University, Stanford University. Terminal master's awarded for partial completion of doctoral program. *Degree requirements:* For master's, internship; for doctorate, one foreign language, thesis/dissertation. *Entrance requirements:* For master's, GRE General Test, original policy memo; for doctorate, GRE General Test. Additional exam requirements/recommendations for international students: Required—TOEFL (minimum score 600 paper-based; 250 computer-based). Electronic applications accepted.

Texas A&M University, Bush School of Government and Public Service, College Station, TX 77843. Offers advanced international affairs (Certificate); China studies (Certificate); homeland security (Certificate); international affairs (MPIA); national security affairs (Certificate); nonprofit management (Certificate); public service and administration (MPSA). *Accreditation:* NASPAA. *Faculty:* 45. *Students:* 215 full-time (98 women), 93 part-time (32 women); includes 20 Black or African American, non-Hispanic/Latino; 2 American Indian or Alaska Native, non-Hispanic/Latino; 14 Asian, non-Hispanic/Latino; 30 Hispanic/Latino, 15 international. Average age 24. In 2010, 93 master's awarded. *Degree requirements:* For master's, summer internship. *Entrance requirements:* For master's, GRE (preferred) or GMAT. *Application deadline:* For fall admission, 1/24 for domestic and international students. Application fee: $50 ($75 for international students). Electronic applications accepted. *Financial support:* In 2010–11, fellowships (averaging $11,000 per year), research assistantships (averaging $11,250 per year) were awarded; career-related internships or fieldwork, Federal Work-Study, and institutionally sponsored loans also available. Financial award application deadline: 2/1; financial award applicants required to submit FAFSA. *Faculty research:* Public policy, presidential studies, public leadership, economic policy, social policy. *Unit head:* Ryan C. Crocker, Dean, 979-862-8007, E-mail: rcrocker@bushschool.tamu.edu. *Application contact:* Kathryn Meyer, Director of Recruiting, 979-458-4767, Fax: 979-845-4155, E-mail: kmeyer@bushschool.tamu.edu.

The University of Alabama in Huntsville, School of Graduate Studies, College of Liberal Arts, Program in Public Affairs, Huntsville, AL 35899. Offers MA. Part-time and evening/weekend programs available. *Faculty:* 5 full-time (4 women), 1 part-time/adjunct (0 women). *Students:* 12 full-time (10 women), 24 part-time (12 women); includes 5 minority (3 Black or African American, non-Hispanic/Latino; 1 Asian, non-Hispanic/Latino; 1 Two or more races, non-Hispanic/Latino), 1 international. Average age 30. 16 applicants, 88% accepted, 9 enrolled. In 2010, 5 master's awarded. *Degree requirements:* For master's, comprehensive exam, thesis or alternative, oral and written exams. *Entrance requirements:* For master's, GRE General Test, minimum GPA of 3.0. Additional exam requirements/recommendations for international students: Required—TOEFL (minimum score 500 paper-based; 173 computer-based; 62 iBT). *Application deadline:* For fall admission, 7/15 for domestic students, 4/1 for international students; for spring admission, 11/30 for domestic students, 9/1 for international students. Applications are processed on a rolling basis. Application fee: $40 ($50 for international students). Electronic applications accepted. *Expenses:* Tuition, state resident: full-time $7250; part-time $407.75 per credit hour. Tuition, nonresident: full-time $17,358; part-time $970.05 per credit hour. Required fees: $246.80 per semester. Tuition and fees vary according to course load and program. *Financial support:* In 2010–11, 2 students received support. Career-related internships or fieldwork, Federal Work-Study, institutionally sponsored loans, scholarships/grants, health care benefits, tuition waivers (full), and unspecified assistantships available. Support available to part-time students. Financial award application deadline: 4/1; financial award applicants required to submit FAFSA. *Faculty research:* Public policy, public management professions, intergovernmental relations, international politics. Total annual research expenditures: $93,994. *Unit head:* Dr. Kathleen H. Hawk, Chair, Political Science and Sociology, 256-824-2315, Fax: 256-824-6949, E-mail: hawkk@email.uah.edu. *Application contact:* Kathy Biggs, Graduate Studies Admissions Manager, 256-824-6199, Fax: 256-824-6405, E-mail: deangrad@uah.edu.

University of Arkansas at Little Rock, Graduate School, Clinton School of Public Service, Little Rock, AR 72204-1099. Offers MPS, Graduate Certificate.

University of Central Florida, College of Health and Public Affairs, Program in Public Affairs, Orlando, FL 32816. Offers PhD. Part-time and evening/weekend programs available. *Faculty:* 2 full-time (0 women). *Students:* 51 full-time (23 women), 44 part-time (25 women); includes 9 Black or African American, non-Hispanic/Latino; 3 Asian, non-Hispanic/Latino; 7 Hispanic/Latino, 16 international. Average age 38. 50 applicants, 54% accepted, 22 enrolled. In 2010, 9 doctorates awarded. *Degree requirements:* For doctorate, thesis/dissertation, candidacy and qualifying exams. *Entrance requirements:* For doctorate, GRE General Test or minimum GPA of 3.0 during final 60 hours. Additional exam requirements/recommendations for international students: Required—TOEFL. *Application deadline:* For fall admission, 2/7 priority date for domestic students. Application fee: $30. Electronic applications accepted. *Expenses:* Tuition, state resident: part-time $256.56 per credit hour. Tuition, nonresident: part-time $1011.52 per credit hour. Part-time tuition and fees vary according to program. *Financial support:* In 2010–11, 28 students received support, including 9 fellowships with partial tuition reimbursements available (averaging $7,800 per year), 7 research assistantships with partial tuition reimbursements available (averaging $4,700 per year), 22 teaching assistantships with partial tuition reimbursements available (averaging $6,100 per year); career-related internships or fieldwork, Federal Work-Study, institutionally sponsored loans, tuition waivers (partial), and unspecified assistantships also available. Financial award application deadline: 3/1; financial award applicants required to submit FAFSA. *Unit head:* Dr. Ronnie Korosec, Interim Director, 407-823-5732, Fax: 407-823-0822, E-mail: ronnie@ucf.edu. *Application contact:* Dr. Ronnie Korosec, Interim Director, 407-823-5732, Fax: 407-823-0822, E-mail: ronnie@ucf.edu.

University of Colorado at Colorado Springs, Graduate School of Public Affairs, Colorado Springs, CO 80933-7150. Offers criminal justice (MCJ); public administration (MPA). Part-time and evening/weekend programs available. *Faculty:* 7 full-time (2 women). *Students:* 14 full-time (9 women), 3 part-time (1 woman); includes 1 Black or African American, non-Hispanic/Latino; 2 Asian, non-Hispanic/Latino; 4 Hispanic/Latino. Average age 34. 56 applicants, 88% accepted. In 2010, 18 master's awarded. *Degree requirements:* For master's, thesis optional, internship (if no experience), capstone project. *Entrance requirements:* For master's, GRE General Test, GMAT, LSAT, minimum GPA of 3.0. *Application deadline:* For fall admission, 6/1 priority date for domestic students; for spring admission, 11/1 priority date for domestic students. Applications are processed on a rolling basis. Application fee: $60 ($75 for international students). *Expenses:* Contact institution. *Financial support:* Career-related internships or fieldwork, Federal Work-Study, and scholarships/grants available. Support available to part-time students. Financial award application deadline: 3/1; financial award applicants required to submit FAFSA. Total annual research expenditures: $16,459. *Unit head:* Dr. Terry Schwartz, Dean, 719-255-4047, Fax: 719-255-4183, E-mail: tschwart@uccs.edu. *Application contact:* Mary Lou Kartis, Program Assistant, 719-255-4182, Fax: 719-255-4183, E-mail: mkartis@uccs.edu.

University of Colorado Denver, School of Public Affairs, Program in Public Affairs and Administration, Denver, CO 80127. Offers public administration (MPA), including domestic violence, emergency management and homeland security, environmental policy, management and law, homeland security and defense, local government, nonprofit management, public administration; public affairs (PhD). *Accreditation:* NASPAA. Part-time and evening/weekend programs available. Postbaccalaureate distance learning degree programs offered (no on-campus study). *Faculty:* 19 full-time (9 women), 14 part-time/adjunct (5 women). *Students:* 317 full-time (181 women), 167 part-time (100 women); includes 15 Black or African American, non-Hispanic/Latino; 2 American Indian or Alaska Native, non-Hispanic/Latino; 18 Asian, non-Hispanic/Latino; 29 Hispanic/Latino; 1 Two or more races, non-Hispanic/Latino, 36 international. Average age 30. 270 applicants, 66% accepted, 118 enrolled. In 2010, 119 master's, 4 doctorates awarded. *Degree requirements:* For master's, thesis or alternative, 36-39 credit hours; for doctorate, comprehensive exam, thesis/dissertation, minimum of 66 semester hours, including at least 30 hours of doctoral dissertation credits. *Entrance requirements:* For master's and doctorate, GRE, resume, essay, transcripts, recommendations. Additional exam requirements/recommendations for international students: Required—TOEFL (minimum score 550 paper-based; 223 computer-based). *Application deadline:* For fall admission, 2/1 for domestic students; for spring admission, 10/15 priority date for domestic students. Application fee: $50 ($75 for international students). Electronic applications accepted. *Expenses:* Contact institution. *Financial support:* Fellowships with partial tuition reimbursements, research assistantships with partial tuition reimbursements, teaching assistantships with partial tuition reimbursements, Federal Work-Study and scholarships/grants available. Support available to part-time students. Financial award application deadline: 4/1; financial award applicants required to submit FAFSA. *Faculty research:* Housing, education and the social and economic issues of vulnerable populations; nonprofit governance and management; education finance, effectiveness and reform; P-20 (preschool through graduate school) education initiatives; municipal government accountability. *Unit head:* Dr. Mary Guy, Program Director, 303-315-2007, Fax: 303-315-2229, E-mail: mary.guy@ucdenver.edu. *Application contact:* Annie Davies, Director of Marketing, Community Outreach and Alumni Affairs, 303-315-2896, Fax: 303-315-2229, E-mail: annie.davies@ucdenver.edu.

University of Florida, Graduate School, College of Liberal Arts and Sciences, Department of Political Science, Gainesville, FL 32611. Offers international development policy and administration (MA, Certificate); international relations (MA, MAT); political campaigning (MA, Certificate); political science (MA, MAT, PhD); public affairs (MA, Certificate); JD/MA. *Faculty:* 27 full-time (9 women), 3 part-time/adjunct (1 woman). *Students:* 115 full-time (43 women), 23 part-time (13 women); includes 6 Black or African American, non-Hispanic/Latino; 3 Asian, non-Hispanic/Latino; 10 Hispanic/Latino, 25 international. Average age 27. 185 applicants, 48% accepted, 35 enrolled. In 2010, 28 master's, 11 doctorates awarded. Terminal master's awarded for partial completion of doctoral program. *Degree requirements:* For master's, variable foreign language requirement, comprehensive exam (for some programs), thesis or alternative, internship (for some programs); for doctorate, variable foreign language requirement, comprehensive exam, thesis/dissertation. *Entrance requirements:* For master's and doctorate, GRE General Test, minimum GPA of 3.0. Additional exam requirements/recommendations for international students: Required—TOEFL (minimum score 550 paper-based; 213 computer-based; 80 iBT), IELTS (minimum score 6). *Application deadline:* For fall admission, 1/1 priority date for domestic students, 1/1 for international students. Applications are processed on a rolling basis. Application fee: $30. Electronic applications accepted. *Expenses:* Tuition, state resident: full-time $10,915.92. Tuition, nonresident: full-time $28,309. *Financial support:* In 2010–11, 104 students received support, including 50 fellowships, 13 research assistantships (averaging $15,878 per year), 41 teaching assistantships (averaging $16,099 per year); career-related internships or fieldwork, Federal Work-Study, institutionally sponsored loans, and unspecified assistantships also available. Financial award application deadline: 1/15; financial award applicants required to submit FAFSA. *Faculty research:* American political institutions, comparative democratization, political theory and judgment, religion and politics, theories of international relations. *Unit head:* Dr. Michael D. Martinez, Chair, 352-273-2363, Fax: 352-392-8127, E-mail: martinez@ufl.edu. *Application contact:* Dr. Dan O'Neill, Interim Graduate Coordinator, 352-273-2386, Fax: 352-392-8127, E-mail: doneill@ufl.edu.

University of Idaho, College of Graduate Studies, College of Letters, Arts and Social Sciences, Department of Political Science and Public Affairs Research, Moscow, ID 83844-2282. Offers political science (MA, PhD); public administration (MPA). *Faculty:* 6 full-time. *Students:* 11 full-time, 12 part-time. Average age 36. In 2010, 7 master's, 1 doctorate awarded. *Degree requirements:* For doctorate, thesis/dissertation. *Entrance requirements:* For master's, minimum GPA of 2.8; for doctorate, minimum undergraduate GPA of 2.8, 3.0 graduate. *Application deadline:* For fall admission, 8/1 for domestic students; for spring admission, 12/15 for domestic students. Applications are processed on a rolling basis. Application fee: $60. Electronic applications accepted. *Expenses:* Tuition, nonresident: part-time $580 per credit. Required fees: $306 per credit. *Financial support:* Research assistantships, teaching assistantships available. Financial award applicants required to submit FAFSA. *Unit head:* Dr. Donald W. Crowley, Chair, 208-885-6328. *Application contact:* Dr. Donald W. Crowley, Chair, 208-885-6328.

University of Louisville, Graduate School, College of Arts and Sciences, Department of Urban and Public Affairs, Louisville, KY 40208. Offers public administration (MPA), including human resources management, non-profit management, public policy and administration; urban and public affairs (PhD), including urban planning and development, urban policy and administration; urban planning (MUP), including administration of planning organizations, housing and community development, land use and environmental planning, spatial analysis. Part-time and evening/weekend programs available. *Faculty:* 22 full-time (7 women), 8 part-time/adjunct (1 woman). *Students:* 73 full-time (36 women), 31 part-time (18 women); includes 11 Black or African American, non-Hispanic/Latino; 2 Asian, non-Hispanic/Latino; 2 Hispanic/Latino; 1 Native Hawaiian or other Pacific Islander, non-Hispanic/Latino; 2 Two or more races, non-Hispanic/Latino, 11 international. Average age 31. 96 applicants, 67% accepted, 37 enrolled. In 2010, 28 master's, 5 doctorates awarded. Terminal master's awarded for partial completion of doctoral program. *Degree requirements:* For master's, internship; for doctorate, comprehensive exam, thesis/dissertation. *Entrance requirements:* For master's, GRE General Test, minimum GPA of 3.0; for doctorate, GRE General Test, master's degree in appropriate field. Additional exam requirements/recommendations for international students: Required—TOEFL (minimum score 550 paper-based; 213 computer-based; 79 iBT). *Application deadline:* For fall admission, 7/15 for domestic students; for spring admission, 11/15 for domestic students. Applications are processed on a rolling basis. Application fee: $50. Electronic applications accepted. *Expenses:* Tuition, state resident: full-time $9144; part-time $508 per credit hour. Tuition, nonresident: full-time $19,026; part-time $1057 per credit hour. Tuition and fees vary according to program and reciprocity agreements. *Financial support:* In 2010–11, 23 students received support; fellowships, research assistantships, health care benefits available. Financial award application deadline: 3/1. *Faculty research:* Housing and community development, performance-based budgeting, environmental policy and natural hazards, sustainability, real estate development, comparative urban development. *Unit head:* Dr. David Simpson, Chair, 502-852-8019, Fax: 502-852-4558, E-mail: dave.simpson@louisville.edu. *Application contact:* Patty Sarley, Graduate Student Advisor, 502-852-7914, Fax: 502-852-4558, E-mail: plclea01@louisville.edu.

University of Massachusetts Boston, Office of Graduate Studies, John W. McCormack Graduate School of Policy Studies, Program in Public Affairs, Boston, MA 02125-3393. Offers

Public Affairs

University of Massachusetts Boston (continued)
MS. Part-time and evening/weekend programs available. *Degree requirements:* For master's, final project. *Entrance requirements:* For master's, GRE General Test or MAT, minimum GPA of 2.75. *Faculty research:* Leadership and policy implementation, public management, disability; human services and sound policy.

University of Minnesota, Twin Cities Campus, Graduate School, Hubert H. Humphrey School of Public Affairs, Program in Public Affairs, Minneapolis, MN 55455-0213. Offers MPA. *Accreditation:* NASPAA. Part-time and evening/weekend programs available. *Entrance requirements:* For master's, 10 years of work experience, minimum undergraduate GPA of 3.0. Additional exam requirements/recommendations for international students: Required—TOEFL (minimum score 600 paper-based; 250 computer-based; 100 iBT). Electronic applications accepted. *Expenses:* Contact institution. *Faculty research:* Public and non-profit leadership and management, social policy, urban and regional planning, economic and community development, foreign policy and international affairs.

University of Missouri, Graduate School, Harry S Truman School of Public Affairs, Columbia, MO 65211. Offers MPA. *Accreditation:* NASPAA. *Entrance requirements:* For master's, GRE General Test, minimum GPA of 3.0. Additional exam requirements/recommendations for international students: Required—TOEFL (minimum score 550 paper-based; 213 computer-based; 79 iBT).

University of Missouri–Kansas City, Henry W. Bloch School of Management, Kansas City, MO 64110-2499. Offers accounting (MS); business administration (MBA); entrepreneurship and innovation (PhD); public affairs (MPA, PhD); JD/MBA; LL M/MPA. PhD (interdisciplinary) offered through the School of Graduate Studies. *Accreditation:* AACSB; NASPAA. Part-time and evening/weekend programs available. *Faculty:* 49 full-time (16 women), 21 part-time/adjunct (5 women). *Students:* 280 full-time (134 women), 435 part-time (193 women); includes 91 minority (44 Black or African American, non-Hispanic/Latino; 19 Asian, non-Hispanic/Latino; 23 Hispanic/Latino; 5 Two or more races, non-Hispanic/Latino), 50 international. Average age 30. 426 applicants, 255 enrolled. In 2010, 254 master's awarded. Terminal master's awarded for partial completion of doctoral program. *Entrance requirements:* For master's, GMAT, GRE, 2 writing essays, 2 references and support of employer; for doctorate, GRE, minimum GPA of 3.0. Additional exam requirements/recommendations for international students: Required—TOEFL (minimum score 550 paper-based; 213 computer-based; 80 iBT). *Application deadline:* For fall admission, 5/1 priority date for domestic and international students; for spring admission, 10/1 priority date for domestic and international students. Applications are processed on a rolling basis. Application fee: $45 ($50 for international students). Electronic applications accepted. *Expenses:* Tuition, state resident: full-time $5522.40; part-time $306.80 per credit hour. Tuition, nonresident: full-time $7128; part-time $792 per credit hour. Required fees: $261.15 per term. *Financial support:* In 2010–11, 26 research assistantships with partial tuition reimbursements (averaging $7,767 per year), 5 teaching assistantships with partial tuition reimbursements (averaging $8,430 per year) were awarded; career-related internships or fieldwork, Federal Work-Study, institutionally sponsored loans, scholarships/grants, tuition waivers (full and partial), and unspecified assistantships also available. Support available to part-time students. Financial award application deadline: 3/1; financial award applicants required to submit FAFSA. *Faculty research:* Entrepreneurship, finance, non-profit, risk management. *Unit head:* Dr. Teng-Kee Tan, Dean, 816-235-2215, Fax: 816-235-2206. *Application contact:* 816-235-1111, E-mail: admit@umkc.edu.

University of Nevada, Las Vegas, Graduate College, Greenspun College of Urban Affairs, School of Environmental and Public Affairs, Las Vegas, NV 89154-4030. Offers crisis and emergency management (MS); environmental science (MS, PhD); non-profit management (Certificate); public administration (MPA); public affairs (PhD); public management (Certificate). Part-time programs available. *Faculty:* 6 full-time (2 women). *Students:* 55 full-time (27 women), 95 part-time (55 women); includes 63 minority (17 Black or African American, non-Hispanic/Latino; 2 American Indian or Alaska Native, non-Hispanic/Latino; 5 Asian, non-Hispanic/Latino; 20 Hispanic/Latino; 19 Two or more races, non-Hispanic/Latino), 8 international. Average age 35. 67 applicants, 72% accepted, 35 enrolled. In 2010, 61 master's, 2 doctorates, 24 other advanced degrees awarded. *Degree requirements:* For master's, comprehensive exam (for some programs), thesis; for doctorate, comprehensive exam (for some programs), thesis/dissertation. *Entrance requirements:* Additional exam requirements/recommendations for international students: Required—TOEFL (minimum score 550 paper-based; 213 computer-based; 80 iBT), IELTS (minimum score 7). *Application deadline:* For fall admission, 2/15 priority date for domestic and international students; for spring admission, 11/15 priority date for domestic and international students. Applications are processed on a rolling basis. Application fee: $60 ($95 for international students). Electronic applications accepted. *Expenses:* Tuition, area resident: Part-time $239.50 per credit. Tuition, state resident: part-time $239.50 per credit. Tuition, nonresident: part-time $503 per credit. Required fees: $108 per semester. Tuition and fees vary according to course load, program and reciprocity agreements. *Financial support:* In 2010–11, 9 students received support, including 6 research assistantships with partial tuition reimbursements available (averaging $13,850 per year), 3 teaching assistantships with partial tuition reimbursements available (averaging $10,666 per year); institutionally sponsored loans, scholarships/grants, health care benefits, and unspecified assistantships also available. Financial award application deadline: 3/1. *Faculty research:* Environmental decision-making and management; budgeting and human resource/workforce management; urban design, sustainability and governance; participatory simulation modeling of environmental issues; public and non-profit management. Total annual research expenditures: $1.1 million. *Unit head:* Dr. Ed Weber, Chair/Associate Professor, 702-895-4440, Fax: 702-895-4436, E-mail: edward.weber@unlv.edu. *Application contact:* Graduate College Admissions Evaluator, 702-895-3320, Fax: 702-895-4180, E-mail: gradcollege@unlv.edu.

The University of North Carolina at Greensboro, Graduate School, College of Arts and Sciences, Department of Political Science, Greensboro, NC 27412-5001. Offers nonprofit management (Certificate); public affairs (MPA); urban and economic development (Certificate). *Accreditation:* NASPAA. *Degree requirements:* For master's, comprehensive exam. *Entrance requirements:* For master's, GRE General Test. Additional exam requirements/recommendations for international students: Required—TOEFL. Electronic applications accepted. *Faculty research:* U.S. Constitution, Canadian parliament, public management, ethical challenge of public service.

University of San Francisco, College of Arts and Sciences, Graduate Program in Public Affairs and Practical Politics, San Francisco, CA 94117-1080. Offers MPA. *Students:* 22 full-time (12 women); includes 11 minority (2 Black or African American, non-Hispanic/Latino; 5 Asian, non-Hispanic/Latino; 4 Hispanic/Latino), 1 international. 42 applicants, 81% accepted, 22 enrolled. *Degree requirements:* For master's, internship, capstone project. *Expenses:* Tuition: Full-time $20,070; part-time $1115 per credit hour. Tuition and fees vary according to course load, degree level and program. *Financial support:* In 2010–11, 20 students received support. Scholarships/grants available. *Unit head:* Prof. Corey Cook, Program Advisor, 415-422-5101. *Application contact:* Information Contact, 415-422-5135, Fax: 415-422-2217, E-mail: asgraduate@usfca.edu.

University of Saskatchewan, College of Graduate Studies and Research, School of Public Policy, Saskatoon, SK S7N 5A2, Canada. Offers MIT, MPA, MPP, PhD.

The University of Texas at Arlington, Graduate School, School of Urban and Public Affairs, Program in Urban and Public Affairs, Arlington, TX 76019. Offers PhD. Part-time and evening/weekend programs available. *Faculty:* 7 full-time (4 women). *Students:* 37 full-time (15 women), 59 part-time (30 women); includes 32 minority (23 Black or African American, non-Hispanic/Latino; 1 Asian, non-Hispanic/Latino; 7 Hispanic/Latino; 1 Two or more races, non-Hispanic/Latino), 10 international. Average age 30. 34 applicants, 47% accepted, 12 enrolled. In 2010, 3 doctorates awarded. *Degree requirements:* For doctorate, comprehensive exam, thesis/dissertation. *Entrance requirements:* For doctorate, GRE General Test. *Application deadline:* For fall admission, 2/1 for domestic and international students. Application fee: $35 ($50 for

international students). Electronic applications accepted. *Expenses:* Tuition, state resident: full-time $7500. Tuition, nonresident: full-time $13,080. International tuition: $13,250 full-time. *Financial support:* In 2010–11, 2 students received support, including 4 fellowships (averaging $1,000 per year), 6 research assistantships (averaging $4,500 per year), 2 teaching assistantships with full tuition reimbursements available (averaging $18,000 per year). Financial award application deadline: 6/1; financial award applicants required to submit FAFSA. *Faculty research:* Environment urban policy personnel, research theoretical foundations, urban problems. *Unit head:* Dr. Maria Martinez-Cosio, Program Director/Academic Advisor, 817-272-3302, Fax: 817-272-5008, E-mail: mcosio@uta.edu. *Application contact:* Maria Martinez-Cosio, Academic Advisor, 817-272-3302, Fax: 817-272-5008, E-mail: mcosio@uta.edu.

The University of Texas at Austin, Graduate School, Lyndon B. Johnson School of Public Affairs, Austin, TX 78712-1111. Offers global policy studies (MGPS); public affairs (MP Aff); public policy (PhD); JD/MP Aff; MBA/MP Aff; MP Aff/MA; MP Aff/MSE. *Accreditation:* NASPAA (one or more programs are accredited). Part-time programs available. *Degree requirements:* For master's, thesis, summer internship; for doctorate, thesis/dissertation. *Entrance requirements:* For master's, GRE General Test; for doctorate, GRE General Test, master's degree in policy-related field. Additional exam requirements/recommendations for international students: Required—TOEFL. Electronic applications accepted. *Faculty research:* Human resource development, health and social policy, philanthropy and community service, ethical leadership, urban and international policy, science and technology policy.

The University of Texas at Dallas, School of Economic, Political and Policy Sciences, Program in Public Affairs, Richardson, TX 75080. Offers MPA, PhD. *Accreditation:* NASPAA. Part-time and evening/weekend programs available. *Faculty:* 6 full-time (2 women), 3 part-time/adjunct (2 women). *Students:* 38 full-time (20 women), 103 part-time (49 women); includes 49 minority (25 Black or African American, non-Hispanic/Latino; 1 American Indian or Alaska Native, non-Hispanic/Latino; 5 Asian, non-Hispanic/Latino; 17 Hispanic/Latino; 1 Two or more races, non-Hispanic/Latino), 9 international. Average age 37. 67 applicants, 66% accepted, 34 enrolled. In 2010, 37 master's, 33 doctorates awarded. *Degree requirements:* For master's, internship; for doctorate, thesis/dissertation. *Entrance requirements:* For master's and doctorate, GRE (minimum combined score of 1000 on verbal and quantitative), minimum GPA of 3.0 in upper-level course work in field. Additional exam requirements/recommendations for international students: Required—TOEFL (minimum score 550 paper-based; 215 computer-based). *Application deadline:* For fall admission, 7/15 for domestic students, 5/1 priority date for international students; for spring admission, 11/15 for domestic students, 9/1 priority date for international students. Applications are processed on a rolling basis. Application fee: $50 ($100 for international students). Electronic applications accepted. *Expenses:* Tuition, state resident: full-time $10,248; part-time $569 per credit hour. Tuition, nonresident: full-time $18,544; part-time $1030 per credit hour. Tuition and fees vary according to course load. *Financial support:* In 2010–11, 47 students received support, including 1 research assistantship with partial tuition reimbursement available (averaging $10,800 per year), 6 teaching assistantships with partial tuition reimbursements available (averaging $11,550 per year); career-related internships or fieldwork, Federal Work-Study, institutionally sponsored loans, and scholarships/grants also available. Support available to part-time students. Financial award application deadline: 4/30; financial award applicants required to submit FAFSA. *Faculty research:* Corporate citizenship and urban problem solving, policy analysis, presidential decision-making, hazardous material safety, emergency management. *Unit head:* Dr. Richard Scotch, Director, 972-883-2922, Fax: 972-883-2735, E-mail: richard.scotch@utdallas.edu. *Application contact:* Dr. Jeremy L. Hall, Assistant Program Head, 972-883-5347, Fax: 972-883-2735, E-mail: jeremy.hall@utdallas.edu.

See Close-Up on page 811.

University of Washington, Graduate School, Daniel J. Evans School of Public Affairs, Seattle, WA 98195. Offers public administration (MPA); public policy and management (PhD); JD/MPA; MPA/MAIS; MPA/MPH; MPA/MS; MPA/MUP. *Accreditation:* NASPAA. Part-time and evening/weekend programs available. *Degree requirements:* For master's, thesis, internship or cooperative experience. *Entrance requirements:* For master's and doctorate, GRE General Test, minimum GPA of 3.0. Additional exam requirements/recommendations for international students: Required—TOEFL (minimum score 580 paper-based; 237 computer-based; 92 iBT). Electronic applications accepted. *Faculty research:* Environmental policy, education and social policy, nonprofit management, international affairs, urban and regional development.

University of Waterloo, Graduate Studies, Faculty of Arts, Department of Anthropology, Waterloo, ON N2L 3G1, Canada. Offers anthropology (MA); public issues (MA). *Entrance requirements:* Additional exam requirements/recommendations for international students: Required—TOEFL. Electronic applications accepted. *Faculty research:* Applied socio-cultural anthropology and archaeology.

University of Wisconsin–Madison, Graduate School, College of Letters and Science, Robert M. La Follette School of Public Affairs, Public Policy and Administration Program, Madison, WI 53706-1380. Offers international public affairs (MPIA); public affairs (MPA). Part-time programs available. Electronic applications accepted. *Expenses:* Tuition, state resident: full-time $9887; part-time $617.96 per credit. Tuition, nonresident: full-time $24,054; part-time $1503.40 per credit. Required fees: $67.63 per credit. Tuition and fees vary according to reciprocity agreements.

Virginia Commonwealth University, Graduate School, College of Humanities and Sciences, Wilder School of Government and Public Affairs, Richmond, VA 23284-9005. Offers MA, MPA, MS, MURP, PhD, CASR, CCJA, CPM, CURP, Certificate, Graduate Certificate, JD/MURP, MSW/Certificate. *Students:* 1,004 full-time (558 women), 1,058 part-time (655 women); includes 434 minority (259 Black or African American, non-Hispanic/Latino; 6 American Indian or Alaska Native, non-Hispanic/Latino; 88 Asian, non-Hispanic/Latino; 53 Hispanic/Latino; 3 Native Hawaiian or other Pacific Islander, non-Hispanic/Latino; 25 Two or more races, non-Hispanic/Latino), 117 international. *Expenses:* Tuition, state resident: full-time $4308; part-time $479 per credit hour. Tuition, nonresident: full-time $8942; part-time $994 per credit hour. Required fees: $2000; $85 per credit hour. Tuition and fees vary according to course level, course load, degree level, campus/location and program. *Unit head:* Dr. Niraj Verma, Director, L. Douglas Wilder School of Government and Public Affairs, 804-828-2292. *Application contact:* Dr. Niraj Verma, Director, L. Douglas Wilder School of Government and Public Affairs, 804-828-2292.

Virginia Polytechnic Institute and State University, Graduate School, College of Architecture and Urban Studies, School of Public and International Affairs, Blacksburg, VA 24061. Offers economic development (Certificate); government and international affairs (MPIA, PhD); homeland security policy (Certificate); local government management (Certificate); nonprofit and nongovernmental organization management (Certificate); planning, governance and globalization (PhD); public administration and public affairs (MPA, PhD); urban and regional planning (MURPL). *Accreditation:* ACSP. *Faculty:* 31 full-time (9 women). *Students:* 114 full-time (66 women), 105 part-time (54 women); includes 11 Black or African American, non-Hispanic/Latino; 1 American Indian or Alaska Native, non-Hispanic/Latino; 7 Asian, non-Hispanic/Latino; 8 Hispanic/Latino, 19 international. Average age 31. 166 applicants, 67% accepted, 53 enrolled. In 2010, 41 master's, 3 doctorates awarded. *Degree requirements:* For master's, comprehensive exam (for some programs), thesis (for some programs); for doctorate, comprehensive exam (for some programs), thesis/dissertation (for some programs). *Entrance requirements:* For master's and doctorate, GRE. Additional exam requirements/recommendations for international students: Required—TOEFL (minimum score 550 paper-based; 213 computer-based). *Application deadline:* For fall admission, 7/1 for domestic and international students; for spring admission, 12/1 for domestic and international students. Applications are processed on a rolling basis. Application fee: $65. Electronic applications accepted. *Expenses:* Tuition, state resident: full-time $9399; part-time $488 per credit hour. Tuition, nonresident: full-time $17,854; part-time $957.75 per credit hour. Required fees: $1534. Full-time tuition and fees vary according to program. *Financial support:* In 2010–11, 1 teaching assistantship with full tuition reimbursement (averaging $21,395 per year) was awarded; career-related internships or fieldwork, Federal Work-Study, scholarships/grants, health care benefits, and unspecified assistantships also available. Financial award application deadline: 1/15. *Faculty research:* Design theory, environmental planning, town planning, transportation planning. Total annual research expenditures: $610,749. *Unit head:* Dr. Karen M. Hult, UNIT HEAD, 540-231-5351, Fax: 540-231-9938, E-mail: khult@vt.edu. *Application contact:* Krystal D. Wright, Contact, 540-231-2291, Fax: 540-231-9938, E-mail: garch@vt.edu.

Washington State University Vancouver, Graduate Programs, Program in Public Affairs, Vancouver, WA 98686. Offers MPA. Part-time and evening/weekend programs available. *Faculty:* 6. *Students:* 2 full-time (both women), 20 part-time (13 women); includes 1 American Indian or Alaska Native, non-Hispanic/Latino; 1 Hispanic/Latino, 1 international. *Degree requirements:* For master's, comprehensive exam, thesis (for some programs). *Entrance requirements:* For master's, GRE, minimum GPA of 3.0, resume, 3 references. Additional exam requirements/recommendations for international students: Required—TOEFL (minimum score 550 paper-based; 213 computer-based). *Application deadline:* For fall admission, 1/10 priority date for domestic students, 1/10 for international students; for spring admission, 7/1 priority date for domestic students, 7/1 for international students. Application fee: $50. *Financial support:* Federal Work-Study and unspecified assistantships available. Financial award application deadline: 2/15. *Unit head:* Dr. Dana Baker, Director, 360-546-9125, Fax: 360-546-9074, E-mail: bakerdl@vancouver.wsu.edu. *Application contact:* Marie Loudermilk, 360-546-9640, E-mail: loudermilk@vancouver.wsu.edu.

West Chester University of Pennsylvania, Office of Graduate Studies, College of Business and Public Affairs, West Chester, PA 19383. Offers MA, MBA, MPA, MS, MSA, MSW, Certificate. Part-time and evening/weekend programs available. *Students:* 134 full-time (97 women), 186 part-time (106 women); includes 57 minority (42 Black or African American, non-Hispanic/Latino; 1 American Indian or Alaska Native, non-Hispanic/Latino; 4 Asian, non-Hispanic/Latino; 10 Hispanic/Latino), 6 international. Average age 30. 237 applicants, 92% accepted, 98 enrolled. In 2010, 113 master's, 19 other advanced degrees awarded. *Degree requirements:* For master's, comprehensive exam (for some programs), thesis (for some programs). *Entrance requirements:* Additional exam requirements/recommendations for international students: Required—TOEFL (minimum score 550 paper-based; 213 computer-based; 80 iBT). *Application deadline:* For fall admission, 4/15 priority date for domestic students, 3/15 for international students; for spring admission, 10/15 for domestic students, 9/1 for international students. Applications are processed on a rolling basis. Application fee: $35. Electronic applications accepted. *Expenses:* Tuition, state resident: full-time $6966; part-time $387 per credit. Tuition, nonresident: full-time $11,146; part-time $619 per credit. Required fees: $1614.40; $133.24 per credit. Part-time tuition and fees vary according to campus/location. *Financial support:* Career-related internships or fieldwork and unspecified assistantships available. Support available to part-time students. Financial award application deadline: 2/15; financial award applicants required to submit FAFSA. *Unit head:* Dr. Christopher Fiorentino, Dean, 610-436-2824, E-mail: cfiorentino@wcupa.edu. *Application contact:* Office of Graduate Studies, 610-436-2943, Fax: 610-436-2763, E-mail: gradstudy@wcupa.edu.

Western Carolina University, Graduate School, College of Arts and Sciences, Department of Political Science and Public Affairs, Cullowhee, NC 28723. Offers MPA. Part-time and evening/weekend programs available. *Degree requirements:* For master's, comprehensive exam. *Entrance requirements:* For master's, GRE General Test, appropriate undergraduate degree, 3 letters of recommendation. Additional exam requirements/recommendations for international students: Required—TOEFL (minimum score 550 paper-based; 270 computer-based; 79 iBT). *Faculty research:* Press-government relations, comparative governments, gender in politics, Latin American political systems, foreign policy, trust in government, zoning.

Western Michigan University, Graduate College, College of Arts and Sciences, School of Public Affairs and Administration, Kalamazoo, MI 49008. Offers health care administration (Graduate Certificate); nonprofit leadership and administration (Graduate Certificate); public administration (MPA, PhD). *Accreditation:* NASPAA (one or more programs are accredited). *Degree requirements:* For doctorate, thesis/dissertation, oral exams. *Entrance requirements:* For doctorate, GRE General Test.

York University, Faculty of Graduate Studies, Glendon College, Program in Public and International Affairs, Toronto, ON M3J 1P3, Canada. Offers MA.

Public Policy

Albany State University, College of Arts and Humanities, Program in Public Administration, Albany, GA 31705-2717. Offers community and economic development administration (MPA); criminal justice administration (MPA); fiscal management (MPA); general management (MPA); health administration and policy (MPA); human resources management (MPA); public policy (MPA); water resource management and policy (MPA). *Accreditation:* NASPAA. *Faculty:* 3 full-time (1 woman), 2 part-time/adjunct (0 women). *Students:* 13 full-time (7 women), 49 part-time (32 women); includes 60 Black or African American, non-Hispanic/Latino, 1 international. Average age 34. 18 applicants, 78% accepted, 12 enrolled. In 2010, 12 master's awarded. *Degree requirements:* For master's, professional public service internship, professional portfolio, capstone research project. *Entrance requirements:* For master's, GRE, MAT, or GMAT, baccalaureate degree from accredited college or university, two letters of recommendation, ASU medical and immunization form. *Application deadline:* For fall admission, 7/15 for domestic students, 5/15 for international students; for spring admission, 11/15 for domestic students, 9/15 for international students. Applications are processed on a rolling basis. Application fee: $20. Electronic applications accepted. *Expenses:* Tuition, state resident: full-time $3060; part-time $170 per credit hour. Tuition, nonresident: full-time $12,204; part-time $678 per credit hour. Required fees: $1160. Part-time tuition and fees vary according to course load. *Financial support:* Application deadline: 4/15. *Faculty research:* Public policy, strategic public human resources and human capital management, diversity management in the public sector and collective bargaining and labor relations in the public sector, e-government and public sector information systems, public administration pedagogy and business process modeling simulation, community development, nonprofit organizations, civic engagement and civic participation, healthcare disparities among minorities, poverty. Total annual research expenditures: $250. *Unit head:* Dr. Peter Ngwafu, Director, 229-430-4760, Fax: 229-430-7895, E-mail: peter.ngwafu@asurams.edu. *Application contact:* Dr. Rani George, Dean, Graduate School, 229-430-5118, Fax: 229-430-6398, E-mail: rani.george@asurams.edu.

American University, School of Public Affairs, Department of Public Administration, Program in Public Policy, Washington, DC 20016-8070. Offers MPP, MPP/JD, MPP/LL M. *Degree requirements:* For master's, comprehensive exam. *Entrance requirements:* For master's, GRE, 2 recommendations. Additional exam requirements/recommendations for international students: Required—TOEFL.

The American University in Cairo, School of Global Affairs and Public Policy, Department of Public Policy and Administration, Cairo, Egypt. Offers MA, MPA, MPP, Diploma.

The American University of Paris, Graduate Programs, Paris, France. Offers cross-cultural and sustainable business management (MA); cultural translation (MA); global communications (MA); global communications and civil society (MA); international affairs, conflict resolution and civil society development (MA); Middle East and Islamic studies (MA); Middle East and Islamic studies and international affairs (MA); public policy and international affairs (MA); public policy and international law (MA). *Faculty:* 14 full-time (3 women). *Students:* 151 full-time (110 women), 56 part-time (43 women). 271 applicants, 83% accepted, 104 enrolled. In 2010, 67 master's awarded. *Degree requirements:* For master's, thesis. *Entrance requirements:* For master's, minimum undergraduate GPA of 3.0. Additional exam requirements/recommendations for international students: Recommended—IELTS. *Application deadline:* For fall admission, 4/15 priority date for international students; for spring admission, 11/15 priority date for international students. Applications are processed on a rolling basis. Application fee: $75. Electronic applications accepted. *Financial support:* Scholarships/grants available. Financial award applicants required to submit FAFSA. *Unit head:* Dr. Celeste Schenck, President, 33-1 40 62 06 59, E-mail: president@aup.fr. *Application contact:* International Admissions Counselor, 33-1 40 62 07 20, Fax: 33-1 47 05 34 32, E-mail: admissions@aup.edu.

Arizona State University, College of Public Programs, School of Public Affairs, Phoenix, AZ 85004-0687. Offers public administration (nonprofit administration) (MPA); public administration (urban management) (MPA); public affairs (PhD); public policy (MPP); MPA/MSW. *Accreditation:* NASPAA (one or more programs are accredited). Part-time and evening/weekend programs available. *Faculty:* 19 full-time (7 women), 1 part-time/adjunct (0 women). *Students:* 149 full-time (96 women), 106 part-time (62 women); includes 62 minority (14 Black or African American, non-Hispanic/Latino; 5 American Indian or Alaska Native, non-Hispanic/Latino; 9 Asian, non-Hispanic/Latino; 32 Hispanic/Latino; 2 Two or more races, non-Hispanic/Latino), 34 international. Average age 32. 227 applicants, 71% accepted, 87 enrolled. In 2010, 68 master's, 4 doctorates awarded. Terminal master's awarded for partial completion of doctoral program. *Degree requirements:* For master's, thesis or alternative, policy analysis or capstone project; interactive Program of Study (iPOS) submitted before completing 50 percent of required credit hours; for doctorate, comprehensive exam, thesis/dissertation, interactive Program of Study (iPOS) submitted before completing 50 percent of required credit hours. *Entrance requirements:* For master's, GRE, minimum GPA of 3.0 or equivalent in last 2 years of work leading to bachelor's degree; for doctorate, GRE, minimum GPA of 3.0 or equivalent in last 2 years of work leading to bachelor's degree, 3 letters of recommendation, resume, statement of goals, samples of research reports. Additional exam requirements/recommendations for international students: Required—TOEFL (minimum score 600 paper-based; 213 computer-based; 100 iBT), IELTS (minimum score 6.5). *Application deadline:* For fall admission, 1/15 for domestic and international students. Application fee: $70 ($90 for international students). Electronic applications accepted. *Expenses:* Contact institution. *Financial support:* In 2010–11, 16 research assistantships with full and partial tuition reimbursements (averaging $14,106 per year), 2 teaching assistantships with full and partial tuition reimbursements (averaging $9,913 per year) were awarded; fellowships with full tuition reimbursements, career-related internships or fieldwork, Federal Work-Study, institutionally sponsored loans, scholarships/grants, and tuition waivers (full and partial) also available. Financial award application deadline: 3/1; financial award applicants required to submit FAFSA. Total annual research expenditures: $621,146. *Unit head:* Dr. Jonathan Koppell, Director, 602-496-1101, E-mail: koppell@asu.edu. *Application contact:* Graduate Admissions, 480-965-6113.

Arizona State University, Sandra Day O'Connor College of Law, Tempe, AZ 85287-7906. Offers biotechnology and genomics (LL M); global legal studies (LL M); law (JD); law (customized) (LL M); legal studies (MLS); tribal policy, law and government (LL M); JD/MBA; JD/MD; JD/PhD. JD/MD offered jointly with Mayo Medical School. *Accreditation:* ABA. *Faculty:* 63 full-time (20 women), 29 part-time/adjunct (4 women). *Students:* 643 full-time (286 women), 14 part-time (6 women); includes 161 minority (19 Black or African American, non-Hispanic/Latino; 36 American Indian or Alaska Native, non-Hispanic/Latino; 25 Asian, non-Hispanic/Latino; 70 Hispanic/Latino; 11 Two or more races, non-Hispanic/Latino), 8 international. Average age 28. 2,457 applicants, 24% accepted, 191 enrolled. In 2010, 167 first professional degrees awarded. *Degree requirements:* For JD, comprehensive exam, paper. *Entrance requirements:* For JD, LSAT, bachelor's degree; for master's, bachelor's degree; JD (for LL M). Additional exam requirements/recommendations for international students: Required—TOEFL (minimum score 550 paper-based; 80 iBT). *Application deadline:* For fall admission, 11/15 priority date for domestic and international students; for spring admission, 2/1 for domestic and international students. Applications are processed on a rolling basis. Application fee: $60. Electronic applications accepted. *Expenses:* Contact institution. *Financial support:* In 2010–11, 280 students received support; research assistantships, teaching assistantships, career-related internships or fieldwork, Federal Work-Study, institutionally sponsored loans, scholarships/grants, tuition waivers (full and partial), and unspecified assistantships available. Financial award application deadline: 3/15; financial award applicants required to submit FAFSA. *Faculty research:* Emerging technologies and the law, Indian law, law and philosophy, international law, intellectual property. Total annual research expenditures: $524,024. *Unit head:* Dean Paul Schiff Berman, Dean/Professor, 480-965-6188, Fax: 480-965-6521, E-mail: paul.berman@asu.edu. *Application contact:* Chitra Damania, Director of Operations, 480-965-1474, Fax: 480-727-7930, E-mail: law.admissions@asu.edu.

Baylor University, Graduate School, College of Arts and Sciences, Department of Political Science, Waco, TX 76798. Offers international studies (MA); political science (MA, PhD); public policy and administration (MPPA); JD/MPPA. *Students:* 29 full-time (8 women), 1 part-time (0 women), 3 international. In 2010, 6 master's, 3 doctorates awarded. *Entrance requirements:* For master's, GRE General Test. *Application deadline:* Applications are processed on a rolling basis. Application fee: $25. *Financial support:* Research assistantships, career-related internships or fieldwork, Federal Work-Study, and institutionally sponsored loans available. Financial award application deadline: 3/1. *Unit head:* Dr. David Corey, Graduate Program Director, 254-710-3161, Fax: 254-710-3122, E-mail: david_d_corey@baylor.edu. *Application contact:* Jenice Langston, Administrative Assistant, 254-710-3161, Fax: 254-710-3870, E-mail: jenice_langston@baylor.edu.

Bernard M. Baruch College of the City University of New York, School of Public Affairs, Program in Public Administration, New York, NY 10010-5585. Offers health care policy (MPA); nonprofit administration (MPA); policy analysis and evaluation (MPA); public management (MPA); MS/MPA. *Accreditation:* NASPAA. Part-time and evening/weekend programs available. *Faculty:* 71 full-time (27 women), 51 part-time/adjunct (23 women). *Students:* 180 full-time (125 women), 491 part-time (327 women); includes 152 Black or African American, non-Hispanic/Latino; 2 American Indian or Alaska Native, non-Hispanic/Latino; 68 Asian, non-Hispanic/Latino; 107 Hispanic/Latino; 18 Two or more races, non-Hispanic/Latino. Average age 33. 482 applicants, 68% accepted, 233 enrolled. In 2010, 203 master's awarded. *Degree requirements:* For master's, thesis, capstone. *Entrance requirements:* For master's, GRE General Test. Additional exam requirements/recommendations for international students: Required—TOEFL. *Application deadline:* For fall admission, 4/1 priority date for domestic and international students; for spring admission, 11/15 priority date for domestic and international students. Applications are processed on a rolling basis. Application fee: $125. Electronic applications accepted. *Expenses:* Contact institution. *Financial support:* In 2010–11, 31 students received support, including 8 fellowships (averaging $1,500 per year), 23 research assistantships (averaging $12,000 per year); career-related internships or fieldwork, Federal Work-Study, scholarships/grants, tuition waivers (partial), and unspecified assistantships also available. Support available to part-time students. Financial award application deadline: 5/15; financial award applicants required to submit FAFSA. *Faculty research:* Urbanization, population and

Public Policy

Bernard M. Baruch College of the City University of New York (continued)
poverty in the developing world, housing and community development, labor unions and housing, government-nongovernment relations, immigration policy, social network analysis, cross-sectoral governance, comparative healthcare systems, program evaluation, social welfare policy, health outcomes, educational policy and leadership, transnationalism, infant health, welfare reform, racial/ethnic disparities in health, urban politics, homelessness, race and ethnic relations. Total annual research expenditures: $2.6 million. *Unit head:* David Birdsell, Dean, 646-660-6700, Fax: 646-660-6721, E-mail: david.birdsell@baruch.cuny.edu. *Application contact:* Michael J. Lovaglio, Director of Student Affairs and Graduate Admissions, 646-660-6750, Fax: 646-660-6751, E-mail: michael.lovaglio@baruch.cuny.edu.

Boise State University, Graduate College, College of Social Sciences and Public Affairs, Department of Public Policy and Administration, Boise, ID 83725-0399. Offers environmental and natural resources policy and administration (MPA); general public administration (MPA); state and local government policy and administration (MPA). *Accreditation:* NASPAA. Part-time programs available. *Degree requirements:* For master's, comprehensive exam, directed research project, internship. *Entrance requirements:* For master's, GRE General Test, minimum GPA of 3.0. Additional exam requirements/recommendations for international students: Required—TOEFL. Electronic applications accepted.

Boston University, School of Education, Boston, MA 02215. Offers counseling (Ed M, CAGS), including community, school, sport psychology; counseling psychology (Ed D); curriculum and teaching (Ed M, Ed D, CAGS), including early childhood (Ed D), educational media and technology (Ed D), English and language arts (Ed D), mathematics (Ed D), physical education and coaching (Ed D), science (Ed D), social studies education (Ed D), special education (Ed D); developmental studies (Ed D), including literacy and language, reading education; developmental studies in literacy and language education (Ed M, CAGS); early childhood education (Ed M, CAGS); education of the deaf (Ed M, CAGS); educational leadership and development (Ed D), including educational administration (Ed M, Ed D, CAGS), higher education administration (Ed M, Ed D, CAGS); educational media and technology (Ed M, CAGS); elementary education (Ed M); English and language arts (Ed M, CAGS); English education (MAT); health education (Ed M, CAGS); Latin and classical studies (MAT); mathematics education (Ed M, MAT, CAGS); mathematics for teaching (MMT); modern foreign language education (MAT), including French, Spanish; physical education and coaching (Ed M, CAGS); policy, planning, and administration (Ed M, CAGS), including community education leadership, educational administration (Ed M, Ed D, CAGS), higher education administration (Ed M, Ed D, CAGS); reading education (Ed M, CAGS); science education (Ed M, MAT, CAGS), including biology (MAT), chemistry (MAT), earth science (MAT), general science (MAT), physics (MAT); social studies education (Ed M, MAT, CAGS), including history (MAT), political science (MAT); special education (Ed M, Ed D, CAGS), including disability studies (Ed M), moderate disabilities (Ed M), severe disabilities (Ed M), special education administration (Ed M); teaching English as a second language (Ed M, CAGS). Part-time programs available. *Faculty:* 57 full-time, 39 part-time/adjunct. *Students:* 245 full-time (191 women), 376 part-time (274 women); includes 83 minority (14 Black or African American, non-Hispanic/Latino; 2 American Indian or Alaska Native, non-Hispanic/Latino; 28 Asian, non-Hispanic/Latino; 31 Hispanic/Latino; 2 Native Hawaiian or other Pacific Islander, non-Hispanic/Latino; 6 Two or more races, non-Hispanic/Latino), 79 international. Average age 30. 1,270 applicants, 66% accepted, 292 enrolled. In 2010, 273 master's, 15 doctorates, 7 other advanced degrees awarded. Terminal master's awarded for partial completion of doctoral program. *Degree requirements:* For master's, thesis (for some programs); for doctorate, comprehensive exam, thesis/dissertation; for CAGS, comprehensive exam. *Entrance requirements:* For master's and CAGS, GRE General Test or Miller Analogies Test (MAT); for doctorate, GRE General Test. Additional exam requirements/recommendations for international students: Required—TOEFL, IELTS. *Application deadline:* For fall admission, 1/15 priority date for domestic and international students; for spring admission, 9/15 priority date for domestic and international students. Applications are processed on a rolling basis. Application fee: $70. Electronic applications accepted. *Expenses:* Tuition: Full-time $39,314; part-time $1228 per credit. Required fees: $40 per semester. *Financial support:* In 2010–11, 276 students received support, including 31 fellowships with full tuition reimbursements available, 16 research assistantships, 26 teaching assistantships with partial tuition reimbursements available; career-related internships or fieldwork, Federal Work-Study, and scholarships/grants also available. Support available to part-time students. Financial award applicants required to submit FAFSA. *Faculty research:* Deaf studies, social emotional learning, civic engagement and education, STEM education, pre-college educational pipelines. Total annual research expenditures: $2.6 million. *Unit head:* Dr. Hardin Coleman, Dean, 617-353-3213. *Application contact:* Dana Fernandez, Director of Enrollment, 617-353-4237, Fax: 617-353-8937, E-mail: sedgrad@bu.edu.

Brandeis University, Graduate School of Arts and Sciences, Joint Master's Programs in Women's and Gender Studies, Waltham, MA 02454-9110. Offers anthropology and women's and gender studies (MA); English and women's and gender studies (MA); music and women's and gender studies (MA); Near Eastern and Judaic studies and women's and gender studies (MA); public policy and women's and gender studies (MA); sociology and women's and gender studies (MA); sustainable international development and women's/gender studies (MA). Part-time programs available. *Degree requirements:* For master's, thesis. *Entrance requirements:* For master's, GRE, sample of written work, resume. Additional exam requirements/recommendations for international students: Required—TOEFL (minimum score 600 paper-based; 250 computer-based; 100 iBT); Recommended—IELTS (minimum score 7). Electronic applications accepted.

Brandeis University, The Heller School for Social Policy and Management, Program in Public Policy, Waltham, MA 02454-9110. Offers aging (MPP); behavioral health (MPP); children, youth and families (MPP); general social policy (MPP); health (MPP); poverty alleviation and development (MPP); MPP/MA. *Faculty:* 36 full-time, 107 part-time/adjunct. *Students:* 45 full-time (36 women); includes 2 Black or African American, non-Hispanic/Latino; 5 Asian, non-Hispanic/Latino; 4 Hispanic/Latino. Average age 26. 136 applicants, 61% accepted, 26 enrolled. In 2010, 18 master's awarded. *Degree requirements:* For master's, thesis. *Entrance requirements:* For master's, GRE, 3 letters of recommendation, statement of purpose, 3 to 5 years of professional experience. Additional exam requirements/recommendations for international students: Required—TOEFL (minimum score 600 paper-based; 250 computer-based; 100 iBT). *Application deadline:* For fall admission, 3/15 for domestic and international students. Applications are processed on a rolling basis. Application fee: $55. Electronic applications accepted. *Financial support:* Scholarships/grants and tuition waivers (full and partial) available. Financial award application deadline: 3/15; financial award applicants required to submit FAFSA. *Faculty research:* Health and behavioral health, children and families, disabilities, aging policy, substance abuse, work, inequality and social change, women/gender, poverty alleviation. *Unit head:* Dr. Michael Doonan, Program Director, 781-736-4831, E-mail: doonan@brandeis.edu. *Application contact:* Shana Mongan, Admissions Officer, 781-736-4229, E-mail: mongan@brandeis.edu.

Brigham Young University, Graduate Studies, College of Family, Home, and Social Sciences, Public Policy Program, Provo, UT 84602. Offers MPP, JD/MPP. *Faculty:* 4 full-time (0 women), 3 part-time/adjunct (1 woman). *Students:* 18 full-time (7 women); includes 2 minority (both Hispanic/Latino). Average age 26. 22 applicants, 82% accepted, 11 enrolled. In 2010, 4 master's awarded. *Degree requirements:* For master's, internship. *Entrance requirements:* For master's, GRE. Additional exam requirements/recommendations for international students: Required—TOEFL (minimum score 580 paper-based; 237 computer-based; 85 iBT). *Application deadline:* For fall admission, 3/1 priority date for domestic and international students. Application fee: $50. Electronic applications accepted. *Expenses:* Tuition: Full-time $5580; part-time $310 per credit hour. Tuition and fees vary according to program and student's religious affiliation. *Financial support:* In 2010–11, 18 students received support, including 7 research assistantships with full and partial tuition reimbursements available (averaging $4,185 per year), 2 teaching assistantships with full and partial tuition reimbursements available (averaging $4,500 per year); fellowships also available. Financial award application deadline: 3/1; financial award applicants required to submit FAFSA. *Faculty research:* Welfare, environment, health policy issues; U. S. elections, family. *Unit head:* Dr. Sven E. Wilson, Graduate Program Director, 801-422-9018, Fax: 801-422-0224, E-mail: sven_wilson@byu.edu. *Application contact:* Jessica A. McArthur, Graduate Secretary, 801-422-7146, Fax: 801-422-0224, E-mail: publicpolicy@byu.edu.

Brock University, Faculty of Graduate Studies, Faculty of Social Sciences, Program in Political Science, St. Catharines, ON L2S 3A1, Canada. Offers Canadian politics (MA); comparative politics (MA); international relations (MA); political theory or philosophy (MA); public policy (MA). Part-time programs available. *Degree requirements:* For master's, thesis optional. *Entrance requirements:* For master's, honors degree. Additional exam requirements/recommendations for international students: Required—TOEFL (minimum score 550 paper-based; 213 computer-based; 80 iBT), IELTS (minimum score 6.5), TWE (minimum score 4). Electronic applications accepted. *Faculty research:* Public administration reform, economic and social justice, politics of societies, Canadian politics, international relations.

Brooklyn College of the City University of New York, Division of Graduate Studies, Department of Political Science, Brooklyn, NY 11210-2889. Offers international affairs (MA); political science (MA, PhD); political science, urban policy and administration (MA). Part-time and evening/weekend programs available. *Students:* 23 full-time (13 women), 219 part-time (124 women); includes 119 minority (92 Black or African American, non-Hispanic/Latino; 12 Asian, non-Hispanic/Latino; 15 Hispanic/Latino), 28 international. Average age 30. 155 applicants, 80% accepted, 88 enrolled. In 2010, 49 master's awarded. *Degree requirements:* For master's, comprehensive exam (for some programs), thesis or alternative, foreign language exam (for international affairs program). *Entrance requirements:* For master's, 2 letters of recommendation, personal statement. Additional exam requirements/recommendations for international students: Required—TOEFL (minimum score 500 paper-based; 173 computer-based; 61 iBT). *Application deadline:* For fall admission, 5/1 for domestic and international students; for spring admission, 12/15 for domestic students, 11/1 for international students. *Expenses:* Tuition, state resident: full-time $7360; part-time $310 per credit hour. Tuition, nonresident: full-time $13,800; part-time $575 per credit hour. Required fees: $190 per semester. *Financial support:* Career-related internships or fieldwork and Federal Work-Study available. Support available to part-time students. Financial award application deadline: 5/1; financial award applicants required to submit FAFSA. *Faculty research:* Ethics and politics, politics of criminal justice, Western Europe, international law and politics, labor politics. *Unit head:* Dr. Paisley Currah, Acting Chairperson, 718-951-5306, E-mail: pcurrah@brooklyn.cuny.edu. *Application contact:* Hernan Sierra, Graduate Admissions Coordinator, 718-951-4536, Fax: 718-951-4506, E-mail: grads@brooklyn.cuny.edu.

Brown University, Graduate School, A. Alfred Taubman Center for Public Policy and American Institutions, Providence, RI 02912. Offers MPA, MPP. *Entrance requirements:* For master's, GRE, 3 letters of recommendation. Additional exam requirements/recommendations for international students: Required—TOEFL.

California Lutheran University, Graduate Studies, Program in Public Policy and Administration, Thousand Oaks, CA 91360-2787. Offers MPPA. *Faculty:* 1 full-time (0 women), 6 part-time/adjunct (4 women). *Students:* 30 full-time (13 women), 42 part-time (27 women); includes 25 minority (5 Black or African American, non-Hispanic/Latino; 2 Asian, non-Hispanic/Latino; 16 Hispanic/Latino; 2 Two or more races, non-Hispanic/Latino), 12 international. Average age 34. 30 applicants, 77% accepted, 16 enrolled. In 2010, 26 master's awarded. *Degree requirements:* For master's, comprehensive exam, thesis or project, internship. *Entrance requirements:* For master's, GMAT or GRE General Test, interview, minimum GPA of 3.0. *Application deadline:* Applications are processed on a rolling basis. Application fee: $50. *Expenses:* Contact institution. *Unit head:* Dr. Herbert Gooch, Director, 805-493-3348. *Application contact:* 805-493-3127, Fax: 805-493-3542, E-mail: clugrad@clunet.edu.

California State University, Long Beach, Graduate Studies, College of Health and Human Services, Graduate Center for Public Policy and Administration, Long Beach, CA 90840. Offers MPA. *Accreditation:* NASPAA. Part-time and evening/weekend programs available. *Faculty:* 6 full-time (2 women), 5 part-time/adjunct (1 woman). *Students:* 55 full-time (34 women), 174 part-time (109 women); includes 16 Black or African American, non-Hispanic/Latino; 4 American Indian or Alaska Native, non-Hispanic/Latino; 34 Asian, non-Hispanic/Latino; 76 Hispanic/Latino, 5 international. Average age 32. 301 applicants, 40% accepted, 84 enrolled. In 2010, 119 master's awarded. *Degree requirements:* For master's, comprehensive exam. *Entrance requirements:* For master's, minimum GPA of 2.75. *Application deadline:* For fall admission, 7/1 for domestic students. Applications are processed on a rolling basis. Application fee: $55. Electronic applications accepted. *Financial support:* Fellowships, career-related internships or fieldwork, Federal Work-Study, institutionally sponsored loans, and scholarships/grants available. Financial award application deadline: 3/2. *Faculty research:* Transportation access, air quality controls, coastal issues, intergovernmental relations. *Unit head:* Dr. Walter Frank Baber, Director, 562-985-4178, Fax: 562-985-4672, E-mail: wbaber@csulb.edu. *Application contact:* Dr. Walter Frank Baber, Director, 562-985-4178, Fax: 562-985-4672, E-mail: wbaber@csulb.edu.

California State University, Monterey Bay, College of Professional Studies, Health, Human Services and Public Policy Department, Seaside, CA 93955-8001. Offers public policy (MPP); social work (MSW). Part-time programs available. *Degree requirements:* For master's, internship. *Entrance requirements:* For master's, GRE, curriculum vitae, recommendations. Additional exam requirements/recommendations for international students: Required—TOEFL (minimum score 525 paper-based; 213 computer-based; 71 iBT). Electronic applications accepted. *Faculty research:* Social policy, health policy, politics and government.

California State University, Sacramento, Graduate Studies, College of Social Sciences and Interdisciplinary Studies, Program in Public Policy and Administration, Sacramento, CA 95819. Offers MPPA. Part-time programs available. *Degree requirements:* For master's, thesis or alternative, writing proficiency exam. *Entrance requirements:* For master's, GRE General Test. Additional exam requirements/recommendations for international students: Required—TOEFL. Electronic applications accepted.

Carleton University, Faculty of Graduate Studies, Faculty of Public Affairs and Management, School of Public Policy and Administration, Ottawa, ON K1S 5B6, Canada. Offers public administration (MA, DPA); public policy (PhD). Part-time programs available. *Degree requirements:* For master's, thesis optional; for doctorate, one foreign language, comprehensive exam, thesis/dissertation. *Entrance requirements:* For master's, GRE, honors degree; for doctorate, master's degree. Additional exam requirements/recommendations for international students: Required—TOEFL. *Faculty research:* Canadian public administration and policy, development administration, public policy analysis, public management.

Carnegie Mellon University, College of Humanities and Social Sciences, Department of Statistics, Pittsburgh, PA 15213-3891. Offers machine learning and statistics (PhD); mathematical finance (PhD); statistics (MS, PhD), including applied statistics (PhD), computational statistics (PhD), theoretical statistics (PhD); statistics and public policy (PhD). Terminal master's awarded for partial completion of doctoral program. *Degree requirements:* For doctorate, comprehensive exam, thesis/dissertation. *Entrance requirements:* For master's and doctorate, GRE General Test. Additional exam requirements/recommendations for international students: Required—TOEFL. *Faculty research:* Stochastic processes, Bayesian statistics, statistical computing, decision theory, psychiatric statistics.

Carnegie Mellon University, Heinz College Australia, Master of Science in Public Policy and Management Program (Adelaide, South Australia), Adelaide, PA 5000, Australia. Offers MS. *Entrance requirements:* For master's, GRE or GMAT, college-level course in advanced algebra/pre-calculus; college-level courses in economics and statistics (recommended). Additional exam requirements/recommendations for international students: Required—TOEFL or IELTS.

Carnegie Mellon University, H. John Heinz III College, School of Public Policy and Management, Master of Science in Public Policy and Management Program, Pittsburgh, PA 15213-3891. Offers MS. Program also offered with second-year study in Washington, DC. *Degree requirements:* For master's, internship. *Entrance requirements:* For master's, GRE or GMAT, college-level course in advanced algebra/pre-calculus; college-level courses in economics and statistics (recommended). Additional exam requirements/recommendations for international students: Required—TOEFL or IELTS. Electronic applications accepted.

Carnegie Mellon University, H. John Heinz III College, School of Public Policy and Management, PhD in Public Policy and Management Program, Pittsburgh, PA 15213-3891. Offers PhD. *Entrance requirements:* For doctorate, GRE or GMAT. Additional exam requirements/recommendations for international students: Required—TOEFL or IELTS.

Central European University, Graduate Studies, School of Social Sciences and Humanities, Budapest, Hungary. Offers economics (MA, PhD); gender studies (MA, PhD); international relations and European studies (MA, PhD); mathematics and its applications (MS, PhD); medieval studies (MA, PhD); nationalism studies (MA, PhD); philosophy (MA, PhD); political science (MA, PhD); public policy (MA, PhD); sociology and social anthropology (MA, PhD). *Faculty:* 90 full-time (29 women), 13 part-time/adjunct (7 women). *Students:* 732 full-time (404 women). Average age 28. 3,639 applicants, 22% accepted, 416 enrolled. In 2010, 278 master's, 16 doctorates awarded. Terminal master's awarded for partial completion of doctoral program. *Degree requirements:* For master's, one foreign language, thesis; for doctorate, one foreign language, comprehensive exam, thesis/dissertation. *Entrance requirements:* For master's, interview; for doctorate, GRE, CEU subject test, interview. Additional exam requirements/recommendations for international students: Required—TOEFL (minimum score 570 paper-based; 230 computer-based); Recommended—IELTS (minimum score 6.5). *Application deadline:* For fall admission, 1/15 priority date for domestic and international students. Application fee: $0. Electronic applications accepted. Tuition and fees charges are reported in euros. *Expenses:* Tuition: Full-time 11,000 euros. Required fees: 250 euros. One-time fee: 200 euros full-time. Tuition and fees vary according to degree level, program, reciprocity agreements and student level. *Financial support:* In 2010–11, 402 students received support, including 416 fellowships with full and partial tuition reimbursements available (averaging $6,200 per year); career-related internships or fieldwork, institutionally sponsored loans, and scholarships/grants also available. Financial award application deadline: 1/5. *Faculty research:* Civil society, fiscal decentralization, party politics, political philosophy (especially liberalism, theory of democracy). Total annual research expenditures: $35,000. *Unit head:* Dr. Katalin Farkas, Provost/Academic Pro Rector, 361-327-3000 Ext. 2227, E-mail: farkask@ceu.hu. *Application contact:* Zsuzsanna Jaszberenyi, Admissions Officer, 361-327-3009, Fax: 361-327-3211, E-mail: admissions@ceu.hu.

Claremont Graduate University, Graduate Programs, Program in Public Policy and Evaluation, Claremont, CA 91711-6160. Offers MA. *Students:* 1 (woman) part-time; includes Hispanic/Latino. Average age 23. *Entrance requirements:* For master's, GRE General Test. Additional exam requirements/recommendations for international students: Required—TOEFL (minimum score 550 paper-based; 213 computer-based; 80 iBT). *Application deadline:* For fall admission, 2/1 priority date for domestic students. Application fee: $60. Electronic applications accepted. *Expenses:* Tuition: Full-time $35,748; part-time $1554 per unit. Required fees: $215 per semester. *Financial support:* Fellowships, Federal Work-Study, institutionally sponsored loans, and scholarships/grants available. Support available to part-time students. Financial award application deadline: 2/15; financial award applicants required to submit FAFSA. *Unit head:* Jean Schroedel, Dean, 909-621-8696, Fax: 909-621-8545, E-mail: jean.schroedel@cgu.edu. *Application contact:* Lesa Hiben, Recruiter and Admissions Coordinator, 909-621-8699, Fax: 909-621-7545, E-mail: lesa.hiben@cgu.edu.

Claremont Graduate University, Graduate Programs, School of Politics and Economics, Department of Economics, Claremont, CA 91711-6160. Offers business and financial economics (MA, PhD); economic development (Certificate); economics (PhD); industrial organization (PhD); international and development economics (PhD); international economics policy and development (MA); international money and finance (PhD); neuroeconomics (PhD); political economy and public policy (MA); public choice and public economics (PhD); MBA/PhD. Part-time programs available. *Faculty:* 8 full-time (0 women), 1 (woman) part-time/adjunct. *Students:* 128 full-time (39 women), 14 part-time (5 women); includes 3 Black or African American, non-Hispanic/Latino; 13 Asian, non-Hispanic/Latino; 5 Hispanic/Latino; 4 Two or more races, non-Hispanic/Latino, 73 international. Average age 32. In 2010, 13 master's, 8 doctorates awarded. *Entrance requirements:* For master's and doctorate, GRE General Test or GMAT. Additional exam requirements/recommendations for international students: Required—TOEFL (minimum score 550 paper-based; 213 computer-based; 80 iBT). *Application deadline:* For fall admission, 2/1 priority date for domestic students. Applications are processed on a rolling basis. Application fee: $60. Electronic applications accepted. *Expenses:* Tuition: Full-time $35,748; part-time $1554 per unit. Required fees: $215 per semester. *Financial support:* Fellowships, research assistantships, teaching assistantships, Federal Work-Study, institutionally sponsored loans, and scholarships/grants available. Support available to part-time students. Financial award application deadline: 2/15; financial award applicants required to submit FAFSA. *Faculty research:* International and financial economics, law and economics, regulation, public choice economics. *Unit head:* Paul Zak, Chair, 909-621-8788, Fax: 909-621-8545, E-mail: paul.zak@cgu.edu. *Application contact:* Lesa Hiben, Admissions Coordinator, 909-621-8699, Fax: 909-621-7545, E-mail: lesa.hiben@cga.edu.

Claremont Graduate University, Graduate Programs, School of Politics and Economics, Department of Politics and Policy, Claremont, CA 91711-6160. Offers American politics (MA, PhD); comparative politics (PhD); international political economy (MA); international studies (MA); political philosophy (PhD); political science (PhD); politics, economics and business (MA); public policy (MA, PhD); world politics (PhD); MBA/PhD. Part-time programs available. *Faculty:* 8 full-time (5 women), 3 part-time/adjunct (0 women). *Students:* 155 full-time (59 women), 15 part-time (6 women); includes 35 minority (5 Black or African American, non-Hispanic/Latino; 9 Asian, non-Hispanic/Latino; 17 Hispanic/Latino; 3 Native Hawaiian or other Pacific Islander, non-Hispanic/Latino; 1 Two or more races, non-Hispanic/Latino), 36 international. Average age 32. In 2010, 16 master's, 21 doctorates awarded. Terminal master's awarded for partial completion of doctoral program. *Entrance requirements:* For master's and doctorate, GRE General Test. Additional exam requirements/recommendations for international students: Required—TOEFL (minimum score 550 paper-based; 213 computer-based; 80 iBT). *Application deadline:* For fall admission, 2/1 priority date for domestic students. Applications are processed on a rolling basis. Application fee: $60. Electronic applications accepted. *Expenses:* Tuition: Full-time $35,748; part-time $1554 per unit. Required fees: $215 per semester. *Financial support:* Fellowships, research assistantships, teaching assistantships, Federal Work-Study, institutionally sponsored loans, and scholarships/grants available. Support available to part-time students. Financial award application deadline: 2/15; financial award applicants required to submit FAFSA. *Faculty research:* Environmental policy, international debt, global democratization, Third World development, public sector discrimination. *Unit head:* Jennifer Merolla, Chair, 909-621-8696, Fax: 909-621-8545, E-mail: jennifer.merolla@cgu.edu. *Application contact:* Lesa Hiben, Admissions Coordinator, 909-621-8699, Fax: 909-621-7545, E-mail: lesa.hiben@cga.edu.

Clemson University, Graduate School, Program in Policy Studies, Clemson, SC 29634. Offers PhD, Certificate. *Faculty:* 25 full-time (5 women), 8 part-time/adjunct (1 woman). *Students:* 17 full-time (7 women), 9 part-time (3 women); includes 1 Black or African American, non-Hispanic/Latino, 6 international. Average age 38. 20 applicants, 65% accepted, 9 enrolled. In 2010, 2 doctorates awarded. *Degree requirements:* For doctorate, thesis/dissertation. *Entrance requirements:* For doctorate, GRE General Test. Additional exam requirements/recommendations for international students: Required—TOEFL. *Application deadline:* Applications are processed on a rolling basis. Application fee: $70 ($80 for international students). Electronic applications accepted. *Expenses:* Tuition, state resident: full-time $6492; part-time $400 per credit hour. Tuition, nonresident: full-time $13,634; part-time $800 per credit hour. Required fees: $262 per semester. Part-time tuition and fees vary according to course load and program. *Financial support:* In 2010–11, 14 students received support, including 14 research assistantships with partial tuition reimbursements available (averaging $13,844 per year), 1 teaching assistantship with partial tuition reimbursement available (averaging $16,925 per year); fellowships with full and partial tuition reimbursements available, career-related internships or fieldwork, institutionally sponsored loans, scholarships/grants, health care benefits, and unspecified assistantships also available. Support available to part-time students. *Unit head:* Dr. Bruce W. Ransom, Coordinator, 864-656-0214, E-mail: bruce@strom.clemson.edu. *Application contact:* Dr. Tristam Aldridge, Interim Associate Dean, 864-656-2561, Fax: 864-656-5344, E-mail: saldrid@clemson.edu.

The College of William and Mary, Faculty of Arts and Sciences, Thomas Jefferson Program in Public Policy, Williamsburg, VA 23187-8795. Offers MPP, JD/MPP, MBA/MPP, MS/MPP. *Faculty:* 2 full-time (1 woman), 23 part-time/adjunct (5 women). *Students:* 35 full-time (18 women); includes 3 minority (1 Black or African American, non-Hispanic/Latino; 1 Asian, non-Hispanic/Latino; 1 Two or more races, non-Hispanic/Latino), 6 international. Average age 25. 95 applicants, 45% accepted, 19 enrolled. In 2010, 27 master's awarded. *Entrance requirements:* For master's, GRE General Test. Additional exam requirements/recommendations for international students: Required—TOEFL (minimum score 600 paper-based; 100 iBT). *Application deadline:* For fall admission, 2/15 priority date for domestic and international students. Application fee: $45. Electronic applications accepted. *Expenses:* Tuition, state resident: full-time $6400; part-time $345 per credit hour. Tuition, nonresident: full-time $19,720; part-time $920 per credit hour. Required fees: $4368. *Financial support:* In 2010–11, 20 research assistantships with partial tuition reimbursements (averaging $7,000 per year), 15 teaching assistantships with partial tuition reimbursements (averaging $8,000 per year) were awarded; career-related internships or fieldwork and unspecified assistantships also available. Financial award application deadline: 2/15; financial award applicants required to submit FAFSA. *Faculty research:* Social policy, international development, health care policy, environmental policy, state and local policy. *Unit head:* Dr. Eric Jensen, Director, 757-221-2384, Fax: 757-221-2390. *Application contact:* Sophie Correll, Administrative Assistant, 757-221-2368, Fax: 757-221-2390, E-mail: sbcorr@wm.edu.

Columbia University, School of International and Public Affairs, Program in Public Policy and Administration, New York, NY 10027. Offers MPA, JD/MPA, MPA/MS, MPH/MPA. *Entrance requirements:* For master's, GRE General Test. Additional exam requirements/recommendations for international students: Required—TOEFL (minimum score 600 paper-based; 250 computer-based; 100 iBT). Electronic applications accepted.

Concordia University, School of Graduate Studies, Faculty of Arts and Science, Department of Political Science, Montréal, QC H3G 1M8, Canada. Offers political science (PhD); public policy and public administration (MA), including geography. *Degree requirements:* For master's, one foreign language, comprehensive exam, thesis optional, internship. *Entrance requirements:* For master's, honors degree or equivalent. Additional exam requirements/recommendations for international students: Required—TOEFL. *Faculty research:* International public policy and administration, Quebec public administration, public policy and social/political theory, geography and public policy, public administration and decision making.

Cornell University, Graduate School, Graduate Fields of Arts and Sciences, Field of Government, Ithaca, NY 14853-0001. Offers American politics (PhD); comparative politics (PhD); international relations (PhD); political methodology (PhD); political thought (PhD); public policy (PhD). *Faculty:* 45 full-time (14 women). *Students:* 74 full-time (40 women); includes 1 Black or African American, non-Hispanic/Latino; 5 Asian, non-Hispanic/Latino; 4 Hispanic/Latino, 22 international. Average age 28. 394 applicants, 9% accepted, 20 enrolled. In 2010, 12 doctorates awarded. *Degree requirements:* For doctorate, comprehensive exam, thesis/dissertation. *Entrance requirements:* For doctorate, GRE General Test, sample of written work, 3 letters of recommendation. Additional exam requirements/recommendations for international students: Required—TOEFL (minimum score 550 paper-based; 213 computer-based; 77 iBT). *Application deadline:* For fall admission, 1/15 for domestic students. Application fee: $80. Electronic applications accepted. *Expenses:* Tuition: Full-time $29,500. Required fees: $76. Tuition and fees vary according to degree level and program. *Financial support:* In 2010–11, 29 fellowships with full tuition reimbursements, 2 research assistantships with full tuition reimbursements, 29 teaching assistantships with full tuition reimbursements were awarded; institutionally sponsored loans, scholarships/grants, health care benefits, tuition waivers (full and partial), and unspecified assistantships also available. Financial award applicants required to submit FAFSA. *Faculty research:* Political theory, American politics, comparative politics, international relations, methodology. *Unit head:* Director of Graduate Studies, 607-255-3567, Fax: 607-255-4530. *Application contact:* Graduate Field Assistant, 607-255-3567, Fax: 607-255-4530, E-mail: cu_govt@cornell.edu.

Cornell University, Graduate School, Graduate Fields of Human Ecology, Field of Policy Analysis and Management, Ithaca, NY 14853-0001. Offers consumer policy (PhD); evaluation (PhD); family and social welfare policy (PhD); health administration (MHA); health management and policy (PhD). *Faculty:* 34 full-time (15 women). *Students:* 73 full-time (39 women); includes 6 Black or African American, non-Hispanic/Latino; 1 American Indian or Alaska Native, non-Hispanic/Latino; 9 Asian, non-Hispanic/Latino; 2 Hispanic/Latino, 9 international. Average age 24. 157 applicants, 43% accepted, 46 enrolled. In 2010, 18 master's, 3 doctorates awarded. *Degree requirements:* For master's, thesis; for doctorate, thesis/dissertation. *Entrance requirements:* For master's, GRE General Test or GMAT, 2 letters of recommendation; for doctorate, GRE General Test, 2 letters of recommendation. Additional exam requirements/recommendations for international students: Required—TOEFL (minimum score 550 paper-based; 213 computer-based; 77 iBT). *Application deadline:* For fall admission, 1/15 for domestic students. Application fee: $70. Electronic applications accepted. *Expenses:* Tuition: Full-time $29,500. Required fees: $76. Tuition and fees vary according to degree level and program. *Financial support:* In 2010–11, 17 students received support, including 4 fellowships with full and partial tuition reimbursements available, 6 research assistantships with full and partial tuition reimbursements available, 11 teaching assistantships with full and partial tuition reimbursements available; institutionally sponsored loans, scholarships/grants, health care benefits, tuition waivers (full and partial), and unspecified assistantships also available. Financial award applicants required to submit FAFSA. *Faculty research:* Health policy, family policy, social welfare policy, program evaluation, consumer policy. *Unit head:* Director of Graduate Studies, 607-255-7772. *Application contact:* Graduate Field Assistant, 607-255-7772, Fax: 607-255-4071, E-mail: pam_phd@cornell.edu.

DePaul University, School of Public Service, Chicago, IL 60604. Offers financial administration management (Certificate); health administration (Certificate); health law and policy (MS); international public services (MS); leadership and policy studies (MS); metropolitan planning (Certificate); public administration (MPA); public service management (MS), including association management, fundraising and philanthropy, healthcare administration, higher education administration, metropolitan planning; public services (Certificate); JD/MS. Part-time and evening/weekend programs available. Postbaccalaureate distance learning degree programs offered (minimal on-campus study). *Faculty:* 14 full-time (3 women), 43 part-time/adjunct (24 women). *Students:* 372 full-time (256 women), 324 part-time (237 women); includes 156 Black or African American, non-Hispanic/Latino; 33 Asian, non-Hispanic/Latino; 65 Hispanic/Latino; 18 Two or more races, non-Hispanic/Latino, 18 international. Average age 26. 162 applicants, 100% accepted, 94 enrolled. In 2010, 108 master's awarded. *Degree requirements:* For master's, thesis or integrative seminar. *Entrance requirements:* For master's, minimum GPA of 2.7. Additional exam requirements/recommendations for international students: Required—TOEFL (minimum score 550 paper-based; 213 computer-based; 80 iBT), IELTS (minimum score 6.5). *Application deadline:* Applications are processed on a rolling basis. Application fee: $40. Electronic applications accepted. *Financial support:* In 2010–11, 60 students received support, including 3 research assistantships with full tuition reimbursements available (averaging $7,000 per year); career-related internships or fieldwork, Federal Work-Study, institutionally sponsored loans, scholarships/grants, tuition waivers (partial), and unspecified assistantships

Public Policy

DePaul University (continued)
also available. Support available to part-time students. Financial award application deadline: 7/1; financial award applicants required to submit FAFSA. *Faculty research:* Government financing, transportation, leadership, health care, volunteerism and organizational behavior, non-profit organizations. Total annual research expenditures: $20,000. *Unit head:* Dr. J. Patrick Murphy, Director, 312-362-5608, Fax: 312-362-5506, E-mail: jpmurphy@depaul.edu. *Application contact:* Megan B. Balderston, Director of Admissions and Marketing, 312-362-5565, Fax: 312-362-5506, E-mail: pubserv@depaul.edu.

Duke University, Graduate School, Duke Sanford Institute of Public Policy, Durham, NC 27708-0243. Offers AM, MPP, PhD, Certificate, JD/AM, JD/MPP, MBA/AM, MBA/MPP, MD/AM, MEM/MPP, MF/MPP. *Faculty:* 42 full-time, 19 part-time/adjunct. *Students:* 157 applicants, 8% accepted, 2 enrolled. *Entrance requirements:* For master's and doctorate, GRE General Test. Additional exam requirements/recommendations for international students: Required—TOEFL, IELTS. *Application deadline:* For fall admission, 12/8 priority date for domestic students, 12/8 for international students. Application fee: $75. Electronic applications accepted. *Financial support:* Career-related internships or fieldwork and Federal Work-Study available. Financial award application deadline: 12/31. *Unit head:* Jacob Vigdor, Director, 919-613-9214. *Application contact:* Jacob Vigdor, Director, 919-613-9214.

Duke University, Graduate School, Program in Public Policy, Durham, NC 27708. Offers PhD. *Faculty:* 42 full-time, 19 part-time/adjunct. *Students:* 18 full-time (16 women); includes 2 Black or African American, non-Hispanic/Latino, 8 international. 157 applicants, 8% accepted, 2 enrolled. *Entrance requirements:* For doctorate, GRE General. Additional exam requirements/recommendations for international students: Required—TOEFL (minimum score 550 paper-based; 213 computer-based; 83 iBT), IELTS. *Application deadline:* For fall admission, 12/8 priority date for domestic and international students. Application fee: $75. Electronic applications accepted. *Financial support:* Fellowships, research assistantships, teaching assistantships available. Financial award application deadline: 12/8. *Unit head:* Jacob Vigdor, Director of Graduate Studies, 919-613-9214, Fax: 919-684-3702, E-mail: patrick.morris@duke.edu. *Application contact:* Elizabeth Hutton, Director of Admissions, 919-684-3913, Fax: 919-684-2277, E-mail: grad-admissions@duke.edu.

Duquesne University, Graduate School of Liberal Arts, Graduate Center for Social and Public Policy, Pittsburgh, PA 15282-0001. Offers conflict resolution and peace studies (Certificate); social and public policy (MA, Certificate). Part-time and evening/weekend programs available. *Faculty:* 15 full-time (3 women), 1 (woman) part-time/adjunct. *Students:* 52 full-time (26 women), 9 part-time (4 women); includes 1 Black or African American, non-Hispanic/Latino, 5 international. Average age 27. 38 applicants, 95% accepted, 17 enrolled. In 2010, 11 master's awarded. *Degree requirements:* For master's, thesis. *Entrance requirements:* For master's, GRE General Test. Additional exam requirements/recommendations for international students: Required—TOEFL. *Application deadline:* For fall admission, 4/30 priority date for domestic and international students; for spring admission, 11/1 priority date for domestic and international students. Applications are processed on a rolling basis. Electronic applications accepted. *Expenses:* Tuition: Part-time $884 per credit. Required fees: $84 per credit. Tuition and fees vary according to course load. *Financial support:* In 2010–11, 20 students received support, including 12 research assistantships with full and partial tuition reimbursements available (averaging $9,000 per year), 4 teaching assistantships with full and partial tuition reimbursements available (averaging $9,000 per year); career-related internships or fieldwork, institutionally sponsored loans, scholarships/grants, tuition waivers (full and partial), and unspecified assistantships also available. Support available to part-time students. Financial award application deadline: 5/1. *Faculty research:* Program evaluation, environmental policy, criminal justice policy, health care policy. Total annual research expenditures: $30,000. *Unit head:* Dr. Joseph Yenerall, Director, 412-396-6485, Fax: 412-396-5265, E-mail: socialpolicy@duq.edu. *Application contact:* Dr. Joseph Yenerall, Assistant to the Dean, 412-396-6485.

Eastern Michigan University, Graduate School, College of Arts and Sciences, Department of Political Science, Programs in Public Administration, Ypsilanti, MI 48197. Offers local government management (Graduate Certificate); management of public healthcare services (Graduate Certificate); public administration (MPA, Graduate Certificate); public budget management (Graduate Certificate); public land planning (Graduate Certificate); public management (Graduate Certificate); public personnel management (Graduate Certificate); public policy analysis (Graduate Certificate). *Accreditation:* NASPAA. *Students:* 28 full-time (18 women), 124 part-time (64 women); includes 50 minority (40 Black or African American, non-Hispanic/Latino; 1 American Indian or Alaska Native, non-Hispanic/Latino; 1 Asian, non-Hispanic/Latino; 6 Hispanic/Latino; 2 Two or more races, non-Hispanic/Latino), 5 international. Average age 34. In 2010, 17 master's, 17 other advanced degrees awarded. Application fee: $35. *Unit head:* Dr. Joseph Ohren, Program Director, 734-487-2522, Fax: 734-487-3340, E-mail: joseph.ohren@emich.edu. *Application contact:* Dr. Joseph Ohren, Program Director, 734-487-2522, Fax: 734-487-3340, E-mail: joseph.ohren@emich.edu.

Florida State University, The Graduate School, College of Social Sciences and Public Policy, Reubin O'D. Askew School of Public Administration and Policy, Tallahassee, FL 32306-2250. Offers MPA, PhD, Certificate, JD/MPA, MPA/MSC, MPA/MSP, MPA/MSW. *Accreditation:* NASPAA (one or more programs are accredited). Part-time and evening/weekend programs available. *Faculty:* 11 full-time (1 woman), 13 part-time/adjunct (5 women). *Students:* 72 full-time (27 women), 120 part-time (64 women); includes 42 minority (27 Black or African American, non-Hispanic/Latino; 2 Asian, non-Hispanic/Latino; 11 Hispanic/Latino; 1 Native Hawaiian or other Pacific Islander, non-Hispanic/Latino; 1 Two or more races, non-Hispanic/Latino), 45 international. Average age 25. 193 applicants, 84% accepted, 82 enrolled. In 2010, 34 master's, 9 doctorates awarded. *Degree requirements:* For master's, action report; for doctorate, comprehensive exam, thesis/dissertation. *Entrance requirements:* For master's, GRE General Test, GMAT, MAT, LSAT, minimum undergraduate upper-division GPA of 3.0; for doctorate, GRE General Test (minimum score of 1100); GMAT; MAT, LSAT, minimum undergraduate GPA of 3.0, graduate 3.5. Additional exam requirements/recommendations for international students: Required—TOEFL (minimum score 550 paper-based; 213 computer-based; 80 iBT), IELTS (minimum score 6.5), Michigan English Language Assessment Battery (minimum score 77). *Application deadline:* For fall admission, 7/1 for domestic students, 5/1 for international students; for spring admission, 11/1 for domestic students, 9/1 for international students. Applications are processed on a rolling basis. Application fee: $30. Electronic applications accepted. *Expenses:* Tuition, state resident: full-time $8238.24. *Financial support:* In 2010–11, 38 students received support, including 18 fellowships with full tuition reimbursements available (averaging $18,000 per year), 21 research assistantships with full tuition reimbursements available (averaging $15,000 per year), 3 teaching assistantships with full tuition reimbursements available (averaging $12,000 per year); career-related internships or fieldwork, Federal Work-Study, institutionally sponsored loans, scholarships/grants, tuition waivers (full), and unspecified assistantships also available. Support available to part-time students. Financial award application deadline: 2/1. *Faculty research:* Financial management, human resource management, policy, strategic management, organizations, nonprofit management. *Unit head:* Dr. William Earle Klay, Director, 850-644-3525, Fax: 850-644-7617, E-mail: eklay@fsu.edu. *Application contact:* Velda Williams, Academic Program Specialist, 850-644-3060, Fax: 850-644-7617, E-mail: vwilliams3@fsu.edu.

Frederick S. Pardee RAND Graduate School, Program in Policy Analysis, Santa Monica, CA 90407-2138. Offers PhD. *Faculty:* 1 full-time (0 women), 142 part-time/adjunct (38 women). *Students:* 102 full-time (44 women); includes 1 Black or African American, non-Hispanic/Latino; 7 Asian, non-Hispanic/Latino; 2 Hispanic/Latino, 43 international. Average age 28. 126 applicants, 24% accepted, 22 enrolled. *Degree requirements:* For doctorate, comprehensive exam, thesis/dissertation. *Entrance requirements:* For doctorate, GMAT or GRE General Test, resume or curriculum vitae, essay, three letters of recommendation. Additional exam requirements/recommendations for international students: Required—TOEFL. *Application deadline:* For fall admission, 1/5 for domestic and international students. Application fee: $50. Electronic applications accepted. *Expenses:* Tuition: Full-time $25,000. Full-time tuition and fees vary according to student level. *Financial support:* Fellowships, research assistantships, teaching assistantships, career-related internships or fieldwork available. *Faculty research:* Education, defense policy, health, labor and population, justice. *Unit head:* Dr. Susan L. Marquis, Dean, 310-393-0411 Ext. 7075, Fax: 310-451-6978. *Application contact:* Dr. Stefanie Stern, Assistant Dean, 310-393-0411 Ext. 8224, Fax: 310-451-6978, E-mail: stern@rand.org.

George Mason University, School of Public Policy, Program in Public Policy, Arlington, VA 22201. Offers MPP, PhD. Part-time programs available. *Faculty:* 66 full-time (24 women), 15 part-time/adjunct (3 women). *Students:* 153 full-time (78 women), 368 part-time (188 women); includes 31 Black or African American, non-Hispanic/Latino; 22 Asian, non-Hispanic/Latino; 24 Hispanic/Latino; 2 Two or more races, non-Hispanic/Latino, 68 international. Average age 31. 508 applicants, 62% accepted, 143 enrolled. In 2010, 133 master's, 15 doctorates awarded. *Degree requirements:* For master's, thesis or alternative; for doctorate, comprehensive exam, thesis/dissertation. *Entrance requirements:* For master's, GRE (for students seeking merit-based scholarships), minimum GPA of 3.0, resume, 2 letters of recommendation, goals statement; for doctorate, GMAT or GRE General Test, resume, writing sample, 2 letters of recommendation. Additional exam requirements/recommendations for international students: Required—TOEFL (minimum score 570 paper-based; 230 computer-based; 88 iBT). *Application deadline:* For fall admission, 6/1 priority date for domestic students, 5/1 priority date for international students; for spring admission, 12/1 priority date for domestic students, 11/1 priority date for international students. Applications are processed on a rolling basis. Application fee: $100. Electronic applications accepted. *Expenses:* Contact institution. *Financial support:* In 2010–11, 42 students received support, including 2 fellowships with full tuition reimbursements available (averaging $18,000 per year), 40 research assistantships with full and partial tuition reimbursements available (averaging $18,153 per year), 2 teaching assistantships with full and partial tuition reimbursements available (averaging $10,408 per year); career-related internships or fieldwork, Federal Work-Study, scholarships/grants, unspecified assistantships, and health care benefits (full-time research or teaching assistantship recipients) also available. Financial award application deadline: 3/1; financial award applicants required to submit FAFSA. *Unit head:* Dr. Catherine Rudder, Director of MPP Program, 703-993-8099, E-mail: spp@gmu.edu. *Application contact:* Tennille Haegele, Director, Graduate Admissions, 703-993-3183, Fax: 703-993-4876, E-mail: thaegele@gmu.edu.

See Close-Up on page 1267.

Georgetown University, Graduate School of Arts and Sciences, The Georgetown Public Policy Institute, Washington, DC 20057. Offers MPM, MPP, MBA/MPP, MPP/JD, MPP/MA, MPP/MS, MPP/PhD. *Entrance requirements:* For master's, GRE General Test, minimum B average. Additional exam requirements/recommendations for international students: Required—TOEFL. *Faculty research:* Social policy, government, private sector.

Georgetown University, Graduate School of Arts and Sciences, School of Continuing Studies, Washington, DC 20057. Offers American studies (MALS); Catholic studies (MALS); classical civilizations (MALS); disability studies (MPS); ethics and the professions (MALS); human resources management (MPS); humanities (MALS); individualized study (MALS); international affairs (MALS); Islam and Muslim-Christian relations (MALS); journalism (MPS); liberal studies (DLS); literature and society (MALS); medieval and early modern European studies (MALS); public relations and corporate communications (MPS); real estate (MPS); religious studies (MALS); social and public policy (MALS); sports industry management (MPS); the theory and practice of American democracy (MALS); visual culture (MALS). *Entrance requirements:* Additional exam requirements/recommendations for international students: Required—TOEFL.

The George Washington University, Columbian College of Arts and Sciences, Trachtenberg School of Public Policy and Public Administration, Washington, DC 20052. Offers public administration (MPA), including budget and public finance, managing state and local governments; JD/MPP; MPA/JD; PhD/MPP. Part-time and evening/weekend programs available. *Faculty:* 37 full-time (13 women), 19 part-time/adjunct (10 women). *Students:* 286 full-time (182 women), 163 part-time (123 women); includes 18 Black or African American, non-Hispanic/Latino; 1 American Indian or Alaska Native, non-Hispanic/Latino; 30 Asian, non-Hispanic/Latino; 12 Hispanic/Latino; 1 Native Hawaiian or other Pacific Islander, non-Hispanic/Latino. Average age 26. 1,102 applicants, 49% accepted, 146 enrolled. In 2010, 113 master's awarded. *Entrance requirements:* For master's, GRE General Test, minimum GPA of 3.0. Additional exam requirements/recommendations for international students: Required—TOEFL (minimum score 600 paper-based; 250 computer-based; 100 iBT). *Application deadline:* For fall admission, 1/15 priority date for domestic and international students; for spring admission, 10/1 priority date for domestic students, 9/1 priority date for international students. Application fee: $60. Electronic applications accepted. *Financial support:* In 2010–11, 65 students received support; fellowships, research assistantships, teaching assistantships available. Financial award application deadline: 1/15. *Faculty research:* Education policy, budget and finance, health policy, regulatory policy. *Unit head:* Dr. Kathyrn E. Newcomer, Director, 202-994-3959, Fax: 202-994-3959, E-mail: newcomer@gwu.edu. *Application contact:* Bethany Pope, Program Coordinator, 202-994-6295, Fax: 202-994-6295, E-mail: tspppa@gwu.edu.

The George Washington University, School of Business, Department of Strategic Management and Public Policy, Washington, DC 20052. Offers MBA, PhD. Part-time and evening/weekend programs available. *Faculty:* 15 full-time (4 women), 6 part-time/adjunct (1 woman). *Students:* 231 full-time (101 women), 4 part-time (1 woman); includes 9 Black or African American, non-Hispanic/Latino; 1 American Indian or Alaska Native, non-Hispanic/Latino; 23 Asian, non-Hispanic/Latino; 6 Hispanic/Latino; 1 Two or more races, non-Hispanic/Latino, 71 international. Average age 28. 574 applicants, 54% accepted. In 2010, 92 master's awarded. *Degree requirements:* For doctorate, thesis/dissertation. *Entrance requirements:* For master's, GMAT; for doctorate, GMAT or GRE. Additional exam requirements/recommendations for international students: Required—TOEFL. *Application deadline:* For fall admission, 4/1 priority date for domestic students; for spring admission, 10/1 for domestic students. Applications are processed on a rolling basis. Application fee: $75. *Financial support:* In 2010–11, 1 student received support; fellowships, teaching assistantships, career-related internships or fieldwork, Federal Work-Study, and institutionally sponsored loans available. Financial award application deadline: 4/1. *Unit head:* Dr. Mark Starik, Chair, 202-994-6677, E-mail: starik@gwu.edu. *Application contact:* Kristin Williams, Asst VP Gradpec Enrlmnt Mgmt, 202-994-0467, Fax: 202-994-0371, E-mail: ksw@gwu.edu.

Georgia Institute of Technology, Graduate Studies and Research, Ivan Allen College of Policy and International Affairs, School of Public Policy, Atlanta, GA 30332-0001. Offers MS Pub P, PhD. Part-time programs available. *Degree requirements:* For master's, professional paper or thesis. *Entrance requirements:* Additional exam requirements/recommendations for international students: Required—TOEFL. Electronic applications accepted. *Faculty research:* National/regional science and technology policy, environmental policy, urban policy and planning, telecommunications policy.

Georgia State University, Andrew Young School of Policy Studies, Department of Public Management and Policy, Atlanta, GA 30303. Offers disaster management (Certificate); non-profit management (Certificate); planning and economic development (Certificate); public administration (MPA), including criminal justice, management and finance, nonprofit management, planning and economic development, policy analysis and evaluation, public health; public policy (MPP, PhD), including disaster policy (MPP), nonprofit policy (MPP), planning and economic development policy (MPP), public finance policy (MPP), social policy (MPP); JD/MPA. *Accreditation:* NASPAA (one or more programs are accredited). Part-time and evening/weekend programs available. Terminal master's awarded for partial completion of doctoral program. *Degree requirements:* For master's, thesis optional; for doctorate, comprehensive exam, thesis/dissertation. *Entrance requirements:* For master's and doctorate, GRE General Test. Additional exam requirements/recommendations for international students: Required—TOEFL. Electronic applications accepted. *Faculty research:* Public management, policy analysis, public finance, planning and economic development, nonprofit leadership and policy.

Graduate School and University Center of the City University of New York, Graduate Studies, Interdisciplinary Studies, New York, NY 10016-4039. Offers language in social context (PhD); medieval studies (PhD); public policy (MA, PhD); urban studies (MA, PhD); women's studies (MA, PhD). Terminal master's awarded for partial completion of doctoral program. *Degree requirements:* For master's, thesis; for doctorate, comprehensive exam, thesis/dissertation. *Entrance requirements:* For master's and doctorate, GRE General Test.

Harvard University, Graduate School of Arts and Sciences and John F. Kennedy School of Government, Committee on Public Policy, Cambridge, MA 02138. Offers PhD. *Degree requirements:* For doctorate, thesis/dissertation, exams. *Entrance requirements:* For doctorate, GRE General Test or GMAT, Harvard MPP degree. Additional exam requirements/recommendations for international students: Required—TOEFL. *Expenses:* Tuition: Full-time $34,976. Required fees: $1166. Full-time tuition and fees vary according to program.

Harvard University, Graduate School of Arts and Sciences, Program in Social Policy, Cambridge, MA 02138. Offers PhD. *Expenses:* Tuition: Full-time $34,976. Required fees: $1166. Full-time tuition and fees vary according to program.

Harvard University, John F. Kennedy School of Government, Doctoral Programs in Government, Cambridge, MA 02138. Offers political economy and government (PhD); public policy (PhD). *Students:* 20 full-time (11 women); includes 3 Two or more races, non-Hispanic/Latino, 6 international. Average age 27. 243 applicants, 7% accepted, 11 enrolled. *Degree requirements:* For doctorate, comprehensive exam, thesis/dissertation. *Entrance requirements:* For doctorate, GRE General Test, course work in macroeconomics, multi-variable calculus. Additional exam requirements/recommendations for international students: Required—TOEFL (minimum score 600 paper-based; 250 computer-based; 100 iBT), TWE. *Application deadline:* For fall admission, 12/2 for domestic students. Application fee: $100. Electronic applications accepted. *Expenses:* Tuition: Full-time $34,976. Required fees: $1166. Full-time tuition and fees vary according to program. *Financial support:* Fellowships, research assistantships, teaching assistantships, Federal Work-Study, institutionally sponsored loans, scholarships/grants, health care benefits, and unspecified assistantships available. *Unit head:* Nicole Tateosian, Director, 617-495-1190, E-mail: nicole_tateosian@harvard.edu. *Application contact:* Nicole Tateosian, Director, 617-495-1190, E-mail: nicole_tateosian@harvard.edu.

Harvard University, John F. Kennedy School of Government, Program in Public Policy, Cambridge, MA 02138. Offers public policy (MPP); JD/MPP; MBA/MPP; MD/MPP. *Accreditation:* NASPAA. *Students:* 416 full-time (192 women), 18 part-time (8 women); includes 24 Black or African American, non-Hispanic/Latino; 3 American Indian or Alaska Native, non-Hispanic/Latino; 40 Asian, non-Hispanic/Latino; 36 Hispanic/Latino; 23 Two or more races, non-Hispanic/Latino, 90 international. Average age 28. 1,753 applicants, 21% accepted, 252 enrolled. In 2010, 182 master's awarded. *Entrance requirements:* For master's, GMAT or GRE General Test. Additional exam requirements/recommendations for international students: Required—TOEFL (minimum score 600 paper-based; 250 computer-based; 100 iBT), TWE. *Application deadline:* For fall admission, 12/2 for domestic students. Application fee: $100. Electronic applications accepted. *Expenses:* Tuition: Full-time $34,976. Required fees: $1166. Full-time tuition and fees vary according to program. *Financial support:* Fellowships, research assistantships, teaching assistantships, career-related internships or fieldwork, Federal Work-Study, institutionally sponsored loans, scholarships/grants, health care benefits, and unspecified assistantships available. Financial award application deadline: 2/6; financial award applicants required to submit CSS PROFILE or FAFSA. *Unit head:* Debra Isaacson, Director, 617-496-8382, E-mail: debra_isaacson@harvard.edu. *Application contact:* 617-495-1155.

Indiana University Bloomington, School of Public and Environmental Affairs, Public Affairs Programs, Bloomington, IN 47405-7000. Offers comparative and international affairs (MPA); economic development (MPA); energy (MPA); environmental policy (PhD); environmental policy and natural resource management (MPA); information systems (MPA); local government management (MPA); nonprofit management (MPA, Certificate); policy analysis (MPA); public finance (PhD); public financial administration (MPA); public management (MPA, PhD); public policy analysis (PhD); specialized public affairs (MPA); sustainability and sustainable development (MPA); JD/MPA; MPA/MIS; MPA/MLS; MSES/MPA. *Accreditation:* NASPAA (one or more programs are accredited). Part-time programs available. *Faculty:* 31 full-time, 15 part-time/adjunct. *Students:* 466 full-time (261 women); includes 11 Black or African American, non-Hispanic/Latino; 2 American Indian or Alaska Native, non-Hispanic/Latino; 42 Asian, non-Hispanic/Latino; 1 Hispanic/Latino, 65 international. Average age 26. 650 applicants, 218 enrolled. In 2010, 166 master's, 10 doctorates awarded. *Degree requirements:* For master's, core classes, capstone; for doctorate, comprehensive exam, thesis/dissertation. *Entrance requirements:* For master's, GRE General Test or GMAT, official transcripts, 3 letters of recommendation, resume, personal statement, departmental questions; for doctorate, GRE General Test or LSAT, official transcripts, 3 letters of recommendation, resume or curriculum vitae, statement of purpose. Additional exam requirements/recommendations for international students: Required—TOEFL (minimum score 600 paper-based; 96 iBT); Recommended—IELTS (minimum score 7). *Application deadline:* For fall admission, 5/1 priority date for domestic students, 12/1 priority date for international students. Applications are processed on a rolling basis. Application fee: $55 ($65 for international students). Electronic applications accepted. *Financial support:* Fellowships with partial tuition reimbursements, research assistantships with partial tuition reimbursements, teaching assistantships with partial tuition reimbursements, career-related internships or fieldwork, Federal Work-Study, scholarships/grants, health care benefits, unspecified assistantships, and Service Corps programs available. Financial award application deadline: 2/1; financial award applicants required to submit FAFSA. *Faculty research:* Comparative and international affairs, environmental policy and resource management, policy analysis, public finance, public management, urban management, nonprofit management, energy policy, social policy, public finance. *Unit head:* Jennifer Forney, Director of Graduate Student Services, 812-855-9485, Fax: 812-856-3665, E-mail: speampo@indiana.edu. *Application contact:* Audrey Whitaker, Admissions Assistant, 812-855-2840, E-mail: speaapps@indiana.edu.

See Close-Up on page 1271.

Indiana University–Purdue University Indianapolis, School of Public and Environmental Affairs, Indianapolis, IN 46202. Offers criminal justice and public safety (MSCJPS); public affairs (MPA), including criminal justice, nonprofit management, policy analysis, public management; public management (Graduate Certificate); JD/MPA; MATS/MM; MLS/NMC; MLS/PMC. *Accreditation:* CAHME (one or more programs are accredited); NASPAA. Part-time and evening/weekend programs available. Postbaccalaureate distance learning degree programs offered (no on-campus study). *Faculty:* 23 full-time (7 women). *Students:* 81 full-time (47 women), 205 part-time (142 women); includes 30 Black or African American, non-Hispanic/Latino; 6 Asian, non-Hispanic/Latino; 8 Hispanic/Latino, 9 international. Average age 31. 217 applicants, 73% accepted, 136 enrolled. In 2010, 77 degrees awarded. *Entrance requirements:* For master's, GRE General Test, GMAT or LSAT, minimum GPA of 3.0 (preferred). Additional exam requirements/recommendations for international students: Required—All international applicants to IUPUI whose native language is not English must demonstrate proficiency in English as a second language through an accepted examination and an accepted score. *Application deadline:* For fall admission, 5/15 priority date for domestic students; for spring admission, 2/15 priority date for domestic students. Applications are processed on a rolling basis. Application fee: $50 ($65 for international students). Electronic applications accepted. *Financial support:* In 2010–11, 1 fellowship with full tuition reimbursement (averaging $14,000 per year), 4 research assistantships with full tuition reimbursements (averaging $12,000 per year) were awarded; teaching assistantships, career-related internships or fieldwork, Federal Work-Study, institutionally sponsored loans, and scholarships/grants also available. Support available to part-time students. Financial award application deadline: 3/1; financial award applicants required to submit FAFSA. *Faculty research:* Nonprofit and public management, public policy, urban and environmental policy, disaster preparedness and recovery, vehicular safety, homicide, and offender rehabilitation and re-entry. Total annual research expenditures: $1.6 million. *Unit head:* Dr. Terry L. Baumer, Executive Associate Dean, 317-274-2016, Fax: 317-274-5153.

The Institute of World Politics, Graduate Programs in National Security, Intelligence, and International Affairs, Washington, DC 20036. Offers American foreign policy (Certificate); comparative political culture (Certificate); counterintelligence (Certificate); democracy building (Certificate); intelligence (Certificate); international politics (Certificate); national security affairs (Certificate); public diplomacy and political warfare (Certificate); statecraft and national security affairs (MA); statecraft and world politics (MA); strategic intelligence studies (MA). Part-time and evening/weekend programs available. *Degree requirements:* For master's, comprehensive exam, thesis optional. *Entrance requirements:* For master's, GRE General Test. Additional exam requirements/recommendations for international students: Required—TOEFL. Electronic applications accepted. *Faculty research:* Intelligence, national security, statecraft.

Jackson State University, Graduate School, College of Public Service, Department of Public Policy and Administration, Jackson, MS 39217. Offers MPPA, PhD. *Accreditation:* NASPAA (one or more programs are accredited). Evening/weekend programs available. *Faculty:* 4 full-time (1 woman), 3 part-time/adjunct (all women). *Students:* 25 full-time (19 women), 71 part-time (48 women); includes 84 Black or African American, non-Hispanic/Latino, 3 international. Average age 36. In 2010, 15 master's, 2 doctorates awarded. *Degree requirements:* For master's, comprehensive exam, thesis optional; for doctorate, comprehensive exam, thesis/dissertation. *Entrance requirements:* For master's, GRE General Test; for doctorate, GRE, GMAT, MAT. Additional exam requirements/recommendations for international students: Required—TOEFL (minimum score 520 paper-based; 195 computer-based; 67 iBT). *Application deadline:* For fall admission, 3/1 for domestic and international students; for spring admission, 10/1 for domestic and international students. Application fee: $25. *Expenses:* Tuition, state resident: full-time $5050; part-time $281 per credit hour. Tuition, nonresident: full-time $12,380; part-time $689 per credit hour. *Financial support:* Career-related internships or fieldwork, Federal Work-Study, scholarships/grants, tuition waivers (full and partial), and unspecified assistantships available. Support available to part-time students. Financial award application deadline: 3/1; financial award applicants required to submit FAFSA. *Unit head:* Dr. Curtina Moreland-Young, Interim Chair, 601-432-6277, Fax: 601-432-6322, E-mail: ppa@jsums.edu. *Application contact:* Sharlene Wilson, Director of Graduate Admissions, 601-979-2455, Fax: 601-979-4325, E-mail: sharlene.f.wilson@jsums.edu.

John Jay College of Criminal Justice of the City University of New York, Graduate Studies, Programs in Criminal Justice, New York, NY 10019-1093. Offers criminal justice (MA, PhD); criminology and deviance (PhD); forensic psychology (PhD); forensic science (PhD); law and philosophy (PhD); organizational behavior (PhD); public policy (PhD). Part-time and evening/weekend programs available. Terminal master's awarded for partial completion of doctoral program. *Degree requirements:* For master's, thesis or alternative; for doctorate, one foreign language, thesis/dissertation. *Entrance requirements:* For master's, GRE General Test, minimum B average; for doctorate, GRE General Test. Additional exam requirements/recommendations for international students: Required—TOEFL (minimum score 500 paper-based; 173 computer-based).

The Johns Hopkins University, Zanvyl Krieger School of Arts and Sciences, Institute for Policy Studies, Baltimore, MD 21218-2699. Offers public policy (MA). *Faculty:* 7 full-time (4 women), 7 part-time/adjunct (3 women). *Students:* 83 full-time (54 women); includes 19 minority (4 Black or African American, non-Hispanic/Latino; 1 American Indian or Alaska Native, non-Hispanic/Latino; 8 Asian, non-Hispanic/Latino; 2 Hispanic/Latino; 4 Two or more races, non-Hispanic/Latino), 23 international. Average age 25. 210 applicants, 43% accepted, 45 enrolled. In 2010, 24 master's awarded. *Degree requirements:* For master's, thesis optional, summer internship. *Entrance requirements:* For master's, GRE General Test. Additional exam requirements/recommendations for international students: Required—TOEFL (minimum score 600 paper-based; 250 computer-based; 100 iBT), IELTS (minimum score 7). *Application deadline:* For fall admission, 1/15 for domestic and international students. Application fee: $75. Electronic applications accepted. *Financial support:* In 2010–11, 50 students received support. Career-related internships or fieldwork, Federal Work-Study, and unspecified assistantships available. Financial award application deadline: 4/15; financial award applicants required to submit FAFSA. *Faculty research:* Housing, criminal justice, human capital investment, nonprofit sector, public finance and infrastructure. *Unit head:* Dr. Carey C. Borkoski, Assistant Director of the Graduate Program, 410-516-4624, Fax: 410-516-8233, E-mail: cborkoski@jhu.edu. *Application contact:* Dr. Carey Borkoski, Assistant Director, 410-516-4624, Fax: 410-516-8233, E-mail: cborkoski@jhu.edu.

Kent State University, College of Arts and Sciences, Department of Political Science, Kent, OH 44242-0001. Offers political science (MA); public administration (MPA); public policy (PhD). Part-time programs available. Postbaccalaureate distance learning degree programs offered. *Degree requirements:* For master's, thesis optional; for doctorate, 2 foreign languages, thesis/dissertation. *Entrance requirements:* For master's, GRE General Test, minimum GPA of 2.75; for doctorate, GRE General Test, minimum GPA of 3.0. Additional exam requirements/recommendations for international students: Required—TOEFL. Electronic applications accepted. *Expenses:* Tuition, state resident: full-time $7866; part-time $437 per credit hour. Tuition, nonresident: full-time $14,022; part-time $779 per credit hour.

Lincoln University, School of Graduate Studies and Continuing Education, Jefferson City, MO 65102. Offers business administration (MBA), including accounting, entrepreneurship, management, public administration and policy; educational leadership (Ed S), including elementary leadership, secondary leadership, superintendency; guidance and counseling (M Ed), including community/agency counseling, elementary school, secondary school; history (MA); school administration and supervision (M Ed), including elementary school administration, secondary school administration, special education administration; school teaching (M Ed), including elementary school teaching, secondary school teaching; social science (MA), including history, political science, sociology; sociology (MA); sociology/criminal justice (MA). Part-time and evening/weekend programs available. *Degree requirements:* For master's and Ed S, comprehensive exam, thesis optional. *Entrance requirements:* For master's and Ed S, GRE, MAT or GMAT, minimum GPA of 2.75 in major, 2.5 overall; 3 letters of recommendation; minimum C average in English composition; personal statement of purpose. Additional exam requirements/recommendations for international students: Required—TOEFL (minimum score 500 paper-based; 173 computer-based; 61 iBT). *Faculty research:* Suicide prevention.

Marylhurst University, Department of Business Administration, Marylhurst, OR 97036-0261. Offers finance (MBA); general management (MBA); government policy and administration (MBA); green development (MBA); health care management (MBA); marketing (MBA); natural and organic resources (MBA); nonprofit management (MBA); organizational behavior (MBA); real estate (MBA); renewable energy (MBA); sustainable business (MBA). Part-time and evening/weekend programs available. Postbaccalaureate distance learning degree programs offered (no on-campus study). *Faculty:* 3 full-time (0 women), 36 part-time/adjunct (6 women). *Students:* 27 full-time (13 women), 727 part-time (373 women); includes 167 minority (47 Black or African American, non-Hispanic/Latino; 6 American Indian or Alaska Native, non-Hispanic/Latino; 36 Asian, non-Hispanic/Latino; 51 Hispanic/Latino; 6 Native Hawaiian or other Pacific Islander, non-Hispanic/Latino; 21 Two or more races, non-Hispanic/Latino), 7 international. Average age 38. 262 applicants, 91% accepted, 194 enrolled. In 2010, 289 master's awarded. *Degree requirements:* For master's, comprehensive exam, capstone course. *Entrance requirements:* For master's, GMAT (if GPA less than 3.0 and fewer than 5 years of work experience), interview, resume, 2 letters of recommendation. Additional exam requirements/recommendations for international students: Recommended—TOEFL (minimum score 550 paper-based; 213 computer-based; 80 iBT). *Application deadline:* For fall admission, 9/11 priority date for domestic and international students; for winter admission, 12/15 priority date for domestic and international students; for spring admission, 3/15 priority date for domestic students, 3/17 priority date for international students. Applications are processed on a rolling basis. Application fee: $50. Electronic applications accepted. *Expenses:* Tuition: Full-time $13,932; part-time $516 per credit. Tuition and fees vary according to course load and program. *Financial support:* Scholarships/grants available. Support available to part-time students. Financial award applicants required to submit FAFSA. *Unit head:* Bob Hanks,

Public Policy

Marylhurst University (continued)

Director of Business and Real Estate Programs, 503-636-8141, Fax: 503-697-5597, E-mail: mba@marylhurst.edu. *Application contact:* Maruska Lynch, Graduate Admissions Specialist, 800-634-9982 Ext. 6322, Fax: 503-699-6320, E-mail: admissions@marylhurst.edu.

McMaster University, School of Graduate Studies, Faculty of Social Sciences, Department of Political Science, Hamilton, ON L8S 4M2, Canada. Offers international relations (PhD); political science (MA); public and the global economy (MA); public policy (PhD); public policy and administration (MA). MA program in public policy and administration offered jointly with University of Guelph. Part-time programs available. *Degree requirements:* For master's, thesis or alternative. *Entrance requirements:* For master's, minimum B+ average. Additional exam requirements/recommendations for international students: Required—TOEFL (minimum score 580 paper-based; 237 computer-based). *Faculty research:* Organizational theory, internationalization of public policy, water resource policies, political interest intermediation, comparative politics.

Mills College, Graduate Studies, Program in Public Policy, Oakland, CA 94613-1000. Offers MPP. *Faculty:* 3 full-time (2 women), 1 part-time/adjunct (0 women). *Students:* 27 full-time (all women); includes 3 Black or African American, non-Hispanic/Latino; 5 Asian, non-Hispanic/Latino; 1 Hispanic/Latino; 3 Two or more races, non-Hispanic/Latino. Average age 28. 57 applicants, 51% accepted, 15 enrolled. In 2010, 4 master's awarded. *Degree requirements:* For master's, thesis. *Application deadline:* For fall admission, 1/15 for domestic students, 1/1 for international students. Application fee: $50. *Expenses:* Tuition: Full-time $28,280; part-time $7070 per course. Required fees: $1058; $1058 per year. Tuition and fees vary according to program. *Financial support:* In 2010–11, 27 students received support, including 27 fellowships (averaging $6,585 per year), 1 teaching assistantship (averaging $1,691 per year); scholarships/grants also available. Financial award applicants required to submit FAFSA. *Unit head:* Carol Chetkovich, Director, 510-430-3370, E-mail: cchetkov@mills.edu. *Application contact:* Jessica King, Graduate Admission Specialist, 510-430-3305, Fax: 510-430-2159, E-mail: grad-studies@mills.edu.

Mississippi State University, College of Arts and Sciences, Department of Political Science and Public Administration, Mississippi State, MS 39762. Offers political science (MA); public policy and administration (MPPA, PhD). *Accreditation:* NASPAA (one or more programs are accredited). Evening/weekend programs available. Postbaccalaureate distance learning degree programs offered (no on-campus study). *Faculty:* 13 full-time (4 women). *Students:* 61 full-time (31 women), 47 part-time (26 women); includes 37 minority (33 Black or African American, non-Hispanic/Latino; 1 American Indian or Alaska Native, non-Hispanic/Latino; 1 Asian, non-Hispanic/Latino; 1 Hispanic/Latino; 1 Two or more races, non-Hispanic/Latino), 4 international. Average age 30. 60 applicants, 62% accepted, 26 enrolled. In 2010, 32 master's, 2 doctorates awarded. *Degree requirements:* For master's, thesis optional, comprehensive oral or written exam; for doctorate, thesis/dissertation, comprehensive oral and written exam. *Entrance requirements:* For master's, GRE, minimum GPA of 3.0 on the last two years of undergraduate courses or graduate work; for doctorate, GRE General Test, minimum graduate GPA of 3.35. Additional exam requirements/recommendations for international students: Required—TOEFL (minimum score 600 paper-based; 250 computer-based; 100 iBT); Recommended—IELTS (minimum score 7.5). *Application deadline:* For fall admission, 8/1 priority date for domestic students, 5/1 for international students; for spring admission, 12/1 priority date for domestic students, 9/1 for international students. Applications are processed on a rolling basis. Application fee: $40. Electronic applications accepted. *Expenses:* Tuition, state resident: full-time $2730.50; part-time $304 per credit hour. Tuition, nonresident: full-time $6901; part-time $767 per credit hour. *Financial support:* In 2010–11, 3 research assistantships (averaging $10,144 per year), 8 teaching assistantships with full tuition reimbursements (averaging $10,138 per year) were awarded; Federal Work-Study, institutionally sponsored loans, scholarships/grants, and unspecified assistantships also available. Financial award application deadline: 4/1; financial award applicants required to submit FAFSA. *Faculty research:* American politics, international relations, state and local government, comparative government, public administration. Total annual research expenditures: $1.2 million. *Unit head:* Dr. K. C. Morrison, Department Head, 662-325-2711, Fax: 662-325-2716, E-mail: kcmorrison@ps.msstate.edu. *Application contact:* Dr. Edward French, Assistant Professor and Graduate Coordinator, 662-325-2711, Fax: 662-325-2716, E-mail: efrench@ps.msstate.edu.

Monmouth University, The Graduate School, Department of Public Policy, West Long Branch, NJ 07764-1898. Offers MA. Part-time and evening/weekend programs available. *Faculty:* 7 full-time (3 women). *Students:* 12 full-time (4 women), 23 part-time (11 women); includes 1 Black or African American, non-Hispanic/Latino; 4 Hispanic/Latino, 1 international. Average age 27. 22 applicants, 91% accepted, 12 enrolled. In 2010, 11 degrees awarded. *Entrance requirements:* For master's, minimum overall GPA of 2.75. Additional exam requirements/recommendations for international students: Required—TOEFL (minimum score 550 paper-based; 213 computer-based; 79 iBT), IELTS (minimum score 5) or Michigan English Language Assessment Battery (minimum score 77), Cambridge A, B, C. *Application deadline:* For fall admission, 7/15 for domestic students, 6/1 for international students; for spring admission, 11/15 for domestic students, 11/1 for international students. Application fee: $50. *Expenses:* Tuition: Full-time $19,572; part-time $816 per credit. Required fees: $628; $157 per semester. *Financial support:* In 2010–11, 23 students received support, including 22 fellowships (averaging $1,505 per year), 4 research assistantships (averaging $7,336 per year); career-related internships or fieldwork, scholarships/grants, and unspecified assistantships also available. Support available to part-time students. Financial award applicants required to submit FAFSA. *Faculty research:* Political theory, international relations and comparative politics, globalization, politics of language, family sociology, race-class-gender studies, U. S. Senate and impact of domestic politics on U. S. foreign policy. *Unit head:* Dr. Kathryn Kloby, Program Director, 732-263-5892, E-mail: kkloby@monmouth.edu. *Application contact:* Kevin Roane, Director, Office of Graduate Admission, 732-571-3452, Fax: 732-263-5123, E-mail: gradadm@monmouth.edu.

Morehead State University, Graduate Programs, College of Business and Public Affairs, School of Public Affairs, Morehead, KY 40351. Offers public policy (MPA). Part-time and evening/weekend programs available. *Degree requirements:* For master's, comprehensive exam, thesis. *Entrance requirements:* For master's, GRE, thesis (two-page paper to be used as writing sample on personal, education or career goals). Additional exam requirements/recommendations for international students: Required—TOEFL (minimum score 500 paper-based; 173 computer-based). Electronic applications accepted.

National-Louis University, College of Arts and Sciences, Chicago, IL 60603. Offers counseling and human services (MS); language and academic development (M Ed, Certificate); psychology (MA, PhD, Certificate); public policy (MA); written communication (MS, Certificate). Part-time and evening/weekend programs available. Postbaccalaureate distance learning degree programs offered (minimal on-campus study). *Students:* 29 full-time (22 women), 489 part-time (405 women); includes 186 minority (137 Black or African American, non-Hispanic/Latino; 8 Asian, non-Hispanic/Latino; 32 Hispanic/Latino; 9 Two or more races, non-Hispanic/Latino), 2 international. Average age 38. In 2010, 245 master's, 9 doctorates, 24 other advanced degrees awarded. *Degree requirements:* For master's and Certificate, comprehensive exam (for some programs), thesis (for some programs); for doctorate, thesis/dissertation. *Entrance requirements:* For master's, MAT or GRE, 3 professional or academic references, interview, minimum GPA of 3.0; for doctorate, GRE General Test, MAT, or Watson-Glaser Critical Thinking Appraisal, three professional or academic references, statement of academic and professional goals, 3 years of experience in field, interview, master's degree, resume, writing sample; for Certificate, GRE, MAT, or Watson-Glaser Critical Thinking Appraisal, three professional or academic references, statement of academic and professional goals, interview, minimum GPA of 3.0. Additional exam requirements/recommendations for international students: Required—Department of Language Studies Assessment or TOEFL (minimum score 550 paper-based; 213 computer-based; 79 iBT). *Application deadline:* Applications are processed on a rolling basis. Application fee: $40. Electronic applications accepted. *Financial support:* Career-related internships or fieldwork, Federal Work-Study, institutionally sponsored loans, scholarships/grants, and tuition waivers available. Support available to part-time students. Financial award applicants required to submit FAFSA. *Unit head:* Dr. Stephen Thompson, Interim Dean, 224-233-2539, Fax: 224-233-2539, E-mail: sthompson@nl.edu. *Application contact:* Dr. George Valcourt, Vice President of Enrollment and Student Services, 888-658-8632, Fax: 312-261-3550, E-mail: george.valcourt@nl.edu.

National University of Singapore, Lee Kuan Yew School of Public Policy, Singapore, Singapore. Offers MPA, MPM, MPP, PhD.

New England College, Program in Public Policy, Henniker, NH 03242-3293. Offers MA. Part-time and evening/weekend programs available. Postbaccalaureate distance learning degree programs offered (no on-campus study). *Degree requirements:* For master's, thesis. *Entrance requirements:* Additional exam requirements/recommendations for international students: Recommended—TOEFL (minimum score 600 paper-based). Electronic applications accepted.

The New School: A University, Milano The New School for Management and Urban Policy, Program in Public and Urban Policy, New York, NY 10011. Offers PhD. Part-time and evening/weekend programs available. *Degree requirements:* For doctorate, thesis/dissertation, qualifying exams. *Entrance requirements:* For doctorate, GRE General Test, MA in political science, urban policy or public policy. Additional exam requirements/recommendations for international students: Required—TOEFL (minimum score 600 paper-based; 250 computer-based; 100 iBT). Electronic applications accepted.

Northeastern University, College of Social Sciences and Humanities, School of Public Policy and Urban Affairs, Program in Law and Public Policy, Boston, MA 02115-5096. Offers MS, PhD, JD/PhD. Part-time and evening/weekend programs available. *Faculty:* 33 full-time (18 women), 18 part-time/adjunct (6 women). *Students:* 40 full-time (21 women), 22 part-time (14 women). Average age 40. 39 applicants, 51% accepted, 6 enrolled. In 2010, 5 master's, 6 doctorates awarded. *Degree requirements:* For master's, comprehensive exam; for doctorate, comprehensive exam, thesis/dissertation. *Entrance requirements:* For master's, GRE General Test; for doctorate, GRE General Test or LSAT. Additional exam requirements/recommendations for international students: Required—TOEFL. *Application deadline:* For fall admission, 2/1 for domestic students. Application fee: $50. *Financial support:* In 2010–11, teaching assistantships with tuition reimbursements (averaging $14,035 per year); fellowships with tuition reimbursements, research assistantships with tuition reimbursements, tuition waivers (full and partial) and unspecified assistantships also available. Financial award application deadline: 2/1; financial award applicants required to submit FAFSA. *Faculty research:* Policy issues in health, crime, and labor; urban studies; education; law and environmental issues; economic development, international trade and law. *Unit head:* Dr. Joan Fitzgerald, Director, 617-373-3644, Fax: 617-373-4691, E-mail: jo.fitzgerald@neu.edu. *Application contact:* Dr. Joan Fitzgerald, Director, 617-373-3644, Fax: 617-373-4691, E-mail: jo.fitzgerald@neu.edu.

Northwestern University, The Graduate School, School of Education and Social Policy, Program in Human Development and Social Policy, Evanston, IL 60208. Offers PhD. Admissions and degrees offered through The Graduate School. *Degree requirements:* For doctorate, comprehensive exam, thesis/dissertation. *Entrance requirements:* For doctorate, GRE General Test. Additional exam requirements/recommendations for international students: Required—TOEFL (minimum score 600 paper-based; 250 computer-based; 100 iBT). Electronic applications accepted. *Faculty research:* Individual development and the personal narrative; the life course and culture; development, intervention and culture; the life course and policy; analysis of policy effects on lives.

Northwestern University, School of Continuing Studies, Program in Public Policy and Administration, Evanston, IL 60208. Offers MA. Postbaccalaureate distance learning degree programs offered.

The Ohio State University, Graduate School, John Glenn School of Public Affairs, Columbus, OH 43210. Offers public administration (MA, MPA); public policy and management (PhD). *Accreditation:* NASPAA (one or more programs are accredited). Part-time programs available. *Faculty:* 14. *Students:* 82 full-time (37 women), 114 part-time (72 women); includes 13 Black or African American, non-Hispanic/Latino; 7 Asian, non-Hispanic/Latino; 5 Hispanic/Latino; 4 Two or more races, non-Hispanic/Latino, 15 international. Average age 32. In 2010, 55 master's, 1 doctorate awarded. *Degree requirements:* For doctorate, thesis/dissertation. *Entrance requirements:* For master's, GMAT, GRE General Test (MPA), minimum GPA of 3.0 (MA); for doctorate, GRE General Test. Additional exam requirements/recommendations for international students: Recommended—TOEFL (minimum score 573 paper-based; 230 computer-based). *Application deadline:* For fall admission, 8/15 priority date for domestic students, 7/1 priority date for international students; for winter admission, 12/1 priority date for domestic students, 11/1 priority date for international students; for spring admission, 3/1 priority date for domestic students, 2/1 priority date for international students. Applications are processed on a rolling basis. Application fee: $40 ($50 for international students). Electronic applications accepted. *Expenses:* Tuition, state resident: full-time $10,605. Tuition, nonresident: full-time $26,535. Tuition and fees vary according to course load and program. *Financial support:* Fellowships, research assistantships, teaching assistantships, Federal Work-Study, institutionally sponsored loans, and unspecified assistantships available. Support available to part-time students. *Unit head:* Charles R. Wise, Graduate Studies Committee Chair, 614-292-8696, Fax: 614-292-4868, E-mail: wise.983@osu.edu. *Application contact:* 614-292-9444, Fax: 614-292-3895, E-mail: domestic.grad@osu.edu.

Pepperdine University, School of Public Policy, Malibu, CA 90263. Offers American politics (MPP); economics (MPP); international relations (MPP); public policy (MPP); state and local policy (MPP). *Faculty:* 7 full-time (2 women), 10 part-time/adjunct (0 women). *Students:* 123 full-time (72 women), 4 part-time (all women); includes 36 minority (11 Black or African American, non-Hispanic/Latino; 2 American Indian or Alaska Native, non-Hispanic/Latino; 11 Asian, non-Hispanic/Latino; 9 Hispanic/Latino; 3 Two or more races, non-Hispanic/Latino), 13 international. 168 applicants, 93% accepted, 66 enrolled. In 2010, 50 master's awarded. *Entrance requirements:* For master's, GRE or GMAT, 2 letters of recommendation, resume, two essays. Additional exam requirements/recommendations for international students: Required—TOEFL. *Application deadline:* For fall admission, 5/1 for domestic students. Applications are processed on a rolling basis. Application fee: $50. Electronic applications accepted. *Financial support:* Institutionally sponsored loans and scholarships/grants available. Financial award application deadline: 5/1; financial award applicants required to submit FAFSA. *Unit head:* Dr. James R. Wilburn, Dean, 310-506-7490, Fax: 310-506-7494, E-mail: james.wilburn@pepperdine.edu. *Application contact:* Melinda E. van Hemert, Director of Recruitment and Career Services, 310-506-7492, Fax: 310-506-7494, E-mail: melinda.vanhemert@pepperdine.edu.

Princeton University, Graduate School, Woodrow Wilson School of Public and International Affairs, Princeton, NJ 08544-1019. Offers public affairs (MPA, PhD); public policy (MPP); JD/MPA. JD/MPA offered jointly with Columbia University, New York University, Stanford University. Terminal master's awarded for partial completion of doctoral program. *Degree requirements:* For master's, internship; for doctorate, one foreign language, thesis/dissertation. *Entrance requirements:* For master's, GRE General Test, original policy memo; for doctorate, GRE General Test. Additional exam requirements/recommendations for international students: Required—TOEFL (minimum score 600 paper-based; 250 computer-based). Electronic applications accepted.

Queen's University at Kingston, School of Graduate Studies and Research, School of Policy Studies, Kingston, ON K7L 3N6, Canada. Offers MIR, MPA. Part-time programs available. *Entrance requirements:* For master's, minimum B+ average. Additional exam requirements/recommendations for international students: Required—TOEFL. *Faculty research:* Public management, social policy, defense management, health policy, the third sector.

Rochester Institute of Technology, Graduate Enrollment Services, College of Liberal Arts, Department of Science, Technology and Society/Public Policy, Rochester, NY 14623-5603.

Offers science, technology and public policy (MS). Part-time programs available. *Students:* 6 full-time (3 women), 6 part-time (3 women), 2 international. Average age 27. 15 applicants, 80% accepted, 4 enrolled. In 2010, 3 master's awarded. *Degree requirements:* For master's, thesis. *Entrance requirements:* For master's, GRE General Test, minimum GPA of 3.0. Additional exam requirements/recommendations for international students: Required—TOEFL (minimum score 570 paper-based; 230 computer-based; 88 iBT) or IELTS (minimum score 6.5). *Application deadline:* For fall admission, 2/15 priority date for domestic and international students; for winter admission, 11/1 for domestic and international students; for spring admission, 2/1 for domestic and international students. Applications are processed on a rolling basis. Electronic applications accepted. *Expenses:* Tuition: Full-time $33,234; part-time $924 per credit hour. Required fees: $219. *Financial support:* In 2010–11, 9 students received support; research assistantships with partial tuition reimbursements available, teaching assistantships with partial tuition reimbursements available, career-related internships or fieldwork, scholarships/grants, and unspecified assistantships available. Support available to part-time students. Financial award applicants required to submit FAFSA. *Faculty research:* Environmental policy, information and communications policy, energy policy, biotechnology policy. *Unit head:* Dr. James Winebrake, Chair, 585-475-4648, Fax: 585-475-2510, E-mail: james.winebrake@rit.edu. *Application contact:* Diane Ellison, Assistant Vice President, Graduate Enrollment Services, 585-475-2229, Fax: 585-475-7164, E-mail: gradinfo@rit.edu.

Rutgers, The State University of New Jersey, Camden, Graduate School of Arts and Sciences, Department of Public Policy and Administration, Camden, NJ 08102. Offers education policy and leadership (MPA); international public service and development (MPA); public management (MPA); JD/MPA; MPA/MA. *Accreditation:* NASPAA. Part-time and evening/weekend programs available. *Faculty:* 17 full-time (7 women), 3 part-time/adjunct (1 woman). *Students:* 75 full-time (45 women), 49 part-time (26 women); includes 38 Black or African American, non-Hispanic/Latino; 1 American Indian or Alaska Native, non-Hispanic/Latino; 5 Asian, non-Hispanic/Latino; 11 Hispanic/Latino. Average age 32. 132 applicants, 73% accepted, 58 enrolled. In 2010, 44 master's awarded. *Degree requirements:* For master's, directed study, research workshop, 42 credits. *Entrance requirements:* For master's, GRE General Test, GMAT or LSAT, 3 letters of recommendation; resume. Additional exam requirements/recommendations for international students: Required—TOEFL (minimum score 550 paper-based; 213 computer-based), IELTS. *Application deadline:* For fall admission, 5/1 priority date for domestic students; for spring admission, 12/1 priority date for domestic students. Applications are processed on a rolling basis. Application fee: $65. Electronic applications accepted. *Expenses:* Tuition, state resident: full-time $4963; part-time $319 per credit. Tuition, nonresident: full-time $10,493; part-time $680 per credit. *Financial support:* In 2010–11, 97 students received support, including 3 fellowships with partial tuition reimbursements available (averaging $3,500 per year), 1 research assistantship with full tuition reimbursement available (averaging $26,000 per year); career-related internships or fieldwork, Federal Work-Study, scholarships/grants, and tuition waivers (partial) also available. Financial award application deadline: 3/15; financial award applicants required to submit FAFSA. *Faculty research:* Nonprofit management, county and municipal administration, health and human services, government communication, administrative law, educational finance. Total annual research expenditures: $8.8 million. *Unit head:* Dr. Robyne Turner, Chair, 856-225-2982, Fax: 856-225-6559, E-mail: rsturner@camden.rutgers.edu. *Application contact:* Sandra J. Cheesman, Department Administrator, 856-225-6860, Fax: 856-225-6559, E-mail: scheesma@camden.rutgers.edu.

Rutgers, The State University of New Jersey, Newark, Graduate School, Program in Public Administration, Newark, NJ 07102. Offers health care administration (MPA); human resources administration (MPA); public administration (PhD); public management (MPA); public policy analysis (MPA); urban systems and issues (MPA). *Accreditation:* NASPAA (one or more programs are accredited). Part-time and evening/weekend programs available. *Faculty:* 9 full-time (3 women). *Students:* 19 full-time (12 women), 24 part-time (11 women); includes 10 Black or African American, non-Hispanic/Latino; 14 Asian, non-Hispanic/Latino; 3 Hispanic/Latino. 46 applicants, 24% accepted, 6 enrolled. In 2010, 8 doctorates awarded. *Degree requirements:* For master's, comprehensive exam, thesis or alternative; for doctorate, thesis/dissertation. *Entrance requirements:* For master's, GRE, minimum undergraduate B average; for doctorate, GRE, MPA, minimum B average. *Application deadline:* For fall admission, 7/1 priority date for domestic students; for spring admission, 12/1 for domestic students. Applications are processed on a rolling basis. Application fee: $60. Electronic applications accepted. *Expenses:* Tuition, state resident: part-time $600 per credit. Tuition, nonresident: full-time $10,694. *Financial support:* In 2010–11, 3 fellowships (averaging $18,000 per year), 11 teaching assistantships with full and partial tuition reimbursements (averaging $23,112 per year) were awarded; career-related internships or fieldwork also available. Support available to part-time students. Financial award application deadline: 3/1. *Faculty research:* Government finance, municipal and state government, public productivity. *Unit head:* Dr. Norma Riccucci, Chairman and Director, 973-353-5093 Ext. 16, E-mail: riccucci@andromeda.rutgers.edu. *Application contact:* Gail Daniels, Assistant Dean for Student Services, 201-973-5093 Ext. 11, E-mail: gaild@andromeda.rutgers.edu.

Rutgers, The State University of New Jersey, New Brunswick, Edward J. Bloustein School of Planning and Public Policy, Doctoral Program in Planning and Public Policy, Piscataway, NJ 08854-8097. Offers PhD. Part-time programs available. *Faculty:* 35 full-time (11 women), 41 part-time/adjunct (16 women). *Students:* 25 full-time (15 women), 30 part-time (17 women); includes 7 Black or African American, non-Hispanic/Latino; 2 Asian, non-Hispanic/Latino; 3 Hispanic/Latino, 8 international. Average age 39. 100 applicants, 13% accepted, 8 enrolled. In 2010, 5 doctorates awarded. *Degree requirements:* For doctorate, comprehensive exam, thesis/dissertation. *Entrance requirements:* For doctorate, GRE, master's degree. Additional exam requirements/recommendations for international students: Required—TOEFL (minimum score 575 paper-based; 245 computer-based; 88 iBT). *Application deadline:* For fall admission, 1/15 for domestic and international students. Application fee: $65. Electronic applications accepted. *Expenses:* Tuition, state resident: full-time $7200; part-time $600 per credit. Tuition, nonresident: full-time $11,124; part-time $927 per credit. *Financial support:* In 2010–11, 28 students received support, including 5 fellowships with full and partial tuition reimbursements available (averaging $15,000 per year), 4 research assistantships with full and partial tuition reimbursements available (averaging $24,000 per year), 1 teaching assistantship with full and partial tuition reimbursement available (averaging $24,000 per year); Federal Work-Study, institutionally sponsored loans, scholarships/grants, health care benefits, tuition waivers (full and partial), and unspecified assistantships also available. Support available to part-time students. Financial award application deadline: 1/15; financial award applicants required to submit FAFSA. *Faculty research:* Housing and community development, land use and transportation, politics and policy analysis, urban and regional economics, international development. *Unit head:* Dr. David Listokin, Director, Doctoral Program in Planning and Public Policy, 732-932-5475 Ext. 550, Fax: 732-932-2253, E-mail: listokin@rci.rutgers.edu. *Application contact:* Steve Weston, Assistant Dean for Student and Academic Services, 732-932-5475 Ext. 753, Fax: 732-932-0934, E-mail: sdweston@rci.rutgers.edu.

Rutgers, The State University of New Jersey, New Brunswick, Edward J. Bloustein School of Planning and Public Policy, Program in Public Policy, Piscataway, NJ 08854-8097. Offers MPAP, MPP, JD/MPAP, MBA/MPP, MCRP/MPP. JD/MPAP offered jointly with Rutgers, The State University of New Jersey, Camden. Part-time and evening/weekend programs available. *Faculty:* 16 full-time (5 women), 2 part-time/adjunct (0 women). *Students:* 80 (39 women); includes 9 Black or African American, non-Hispanic/Latino; 3 Asian, non-Hispanic/Latino; 2 Hispanic/Latino. Average age 23. 130 applicants, 42% accepted, 30 enrolled. In 2010, 25 master's awarded. *Entrance requirements:* For master's, GRE General Test or LSAT(dual law program). Additional exam requirements/recommendations for international students: Required—TOEFL (minimum score 575 paper-based; 245 computer-based; 88 iBT). *Application deadline:* For fall admission, 1/15 for domestic and international students; for spring admission, 11/1 for domestic students. Application fee: $65. Electronic applications accepted. *Expenses:* Tuition, state resident: full-time $7200; part-time $600 per credit. Tuition, nonresident: full-time $11,124; part-time $927 per credit. *Financial support:* In 2010–11, 30 students received support, including

15 fellowships with full and partial tuition reimbursements available (averaging $5,000 per year), 8 research assistantships with full and partial tuition reimbursements available (averaging $24,000 per year), 10 teaching assistantships with full and partial tuition reimbursements available (averaging $24,000 per year); career-related internships or fieldwork, Federal Work-Study, institutionally sponsored loans, and tuition waivers (full and partial) also available. Financial award application deadline: 1/15; financial award applicants required to submit FAFSA. *Faculty research:* Environment, social and health policy, public opinion, economics, education policy, community development. *Unit head:* Dr. Cliff Zukin, Director, 732-932-2499 Ext. 880, Fax: 732-932-1107, E-mail: zukin@rci.rutgers.edu. *Application contact:* Lynn Astorga, Student and Academic Services Assistant, 732-932-5475 Ext. 740, Fax: 732-932-1771, E-mail: lastorga@policy.rutgers.edu.

Saint Louis University, Graduate Education, College of Education and Public Service, Department of Public Policy Studies, St. Louis, MO 63103-2097. Offers geographic information systems (Certificate); organizational development (Certificate); public administration (MAPA); public policy analysis (PhD); urban affairs (MAUA); urban planning and real estate development (MUPRED). *Accreditation:* NASPAA. Part-time programs available. *Degree requirements:* For master's, comprehensive exam (for some programs), thesis (for some programs); for doctorate, comprehensive exam, thesis/dissertation, preliminary exams. *Entrance requirements:* For master's, GMAT, GRE General Test, or LSAT, letters of recommendation, resume; for doctorate, GMAT, GRE General Test, or LSAT, letters of recommendation, resumé, interview, transcripts, goal statement. Additional exam requirements/recommendations for international students: Required—TOEFL (minimum score 525 paper-based; 194 computer-based). Electronic applications accepted. *Faculty research:* Urban politics, brown fields, e-government, and administration, evaluation research, community development, electronic government and governance.

San Francisco State University, Division of Graduate Studies, College of Behavioral and Social Sciences, Public Administration Program, San Francisco, CA 94132-1722. Offers nonprofit administration (MPA); policy making and analysis (MPA); public management (MPA); urban administration (MPA). *Accreditation:* NASPAA. *Unit head:* Dr. Genie Stowers, Chair, 415-817-4457, Fax: 415-338-1980, E-mail: gstowers@sfsu.edu. *Application contact:* Bridget McCracken, Director of Academic Services, 415-817-4455, E-mail: mpa@sfsu.edu.

Seton Hall University, College of Arts and Sciences, Department of Public and Healthcare Administration, Program in Public Administration, South Orange, NJ 07079-2697. Offers nonprofit organization management (MPA). *Accreditation:* NASPAA. Part-time and evening/weekend programs available. *Degree requirements:* For master's, thesis or alternative, internship or practicum. *Entrance requirements:* Additional exam requirements/recommendations for international students: Required—TOEFL.

Simon Fraser University, Graduate Studies, Faculty of Arts and Social Sciences, Public Policy Program, Burnaby, BC V5A 1S6, Canada. Offers MPP. *Degree requirements:* For master's, internship. *Entrance requirements:* For master's, GRE, 3 letters of reference, resume, minimum undergraduate GPA of 3.0. Additional exam requirements/recommendations for international students: Required—TOEFL (minimum score 570 paper-based; 230 computer-based), TWE (minimum score 5). Electronic applications accepted.

Southeastern Louisiana University, College of Arts, Humanities and Social Sciences, Department of Sociology and Criminal Justice, Hammond, LA 70402. Offers applied sociology (MS), including criminal justice, globalization and social diversity, public policy. Part-time and evening/weekend programs available. *Faculty:* 7 full-time (2 women). *Students:* 23 full-time (17 women), 11 part-time (8 women); includes 11 minority (9 Black or African American, non-Hispanic/Latino; 2 Hispanic/Latino), 1 international. Average age 28. 18 applicants, 72% accepted, 12 enrolled. In 2010, 7 master's awarded. *Degree requirements:* For master's, comprehensive exam, thesis (for some programs), internship research (for those who select an internship track). *Entrance requirements:* For master's, GRE General Test (verbal and quantitative), bachelor's degree in sociology, social work, criminal justice or related social science; minimum GPA of 3.0. Additional exam requirements/recommendations for international students: Required—TOEFL (minimum score 500 paper-based; 173 computer-based; 61 iBT). *Application deadline:* For fall admission, 7/15 priority date for domestic students, 6/1 priority date for international students; for spring admission, 12/1 priority date for domestic students, 10/1 priority date for international students. Applications are processed on a rolling basis. Application fee: $20 ($30 for international students). Electronic applications accepted. *Expenses:* Tuition, state resident: full-time $3533. Tuition, nonresident: full-time $12,002. Required fees: $907. Tuition and fees vary according to degree level. *Financial support:* In 2010–11, 4 students received support, including 4 research assistantships (averaging $10,100 per year); Federal Work-Study, institutionally sponsored loans, and scholarships/grants also available. Support available to part-time students. Financial award application deadline: 5/1; financial award applicants required to submit FAFSA. *Faculty research:* Criminology, environmental sociology, globalization, public policy, race and ethnic relations. *Unit head:* Dr. Kenneth Bolton, Department Head, 985-549-2110, Fax: 985-549-5961, E-mail: kbolton@selu.edu. *Application contact:* Sandra Meyers, Graduate Admissions Analyst, 985-549-5620, Fax: 985-549-5632, E-mail: admissions@selu.edu.

Southern New Hampshire University, School of Community Economic Development, Manchester, NH 03106-1045. Offers MA, MBA, MS, PhD. Part-time and evening/weekend programs available. *Degree requirements:* For master's, thesis or alternative, community project; for doctorate, comprehensive exam, thesis/dissertation, community project. *Entrance requirements:* For master's, 2 years of work experience, minimum GPA of 3.0, 2 letters of recommendation, review; for doctorate, 2 years of work experience, minimum GPA of 3.5, 3 letters of recommendation, research samples. Additional exam requirements/recommendations for international students: Required—TOEFL (minimum score 550 paper-based; 300 computer-based; 70 iBT). Electronic applications accepted. *Expenses:* Contact institution.

Southern University and Agricultural and Mechanical College, Graduate School, Nelson Mandela School of Public Policy and Urban Affairs, Program in Public Policy, Baton Rouge, LA 70813. Offers PhD. *Degree requirements:* For doctorate, comprehensive exam, thesis/dissertation. *Entrance requirements:* For doctorate, GRE General Test. Additional exam requirements/recommendations for international students: Required—TOEFL (minimum score 525 paper-based; 193 computer-based).

State University of New York at Binghamton, Graduate School, School of Arts and Sciences, Department of Political Science, Binghamton, NY 13902-6000. Offers political science (MA, PhD); public policy (MA, PhD). *Faculty:* 17 full-time (4 women), 2 part-time/adjunct (1 woman). *Students:* 27 full-time (7 women), 21 part-time (8 women); includes 3 Black or African American, non-Hispanic/Latino, 16 international. Average age 29. 45 applicants, 44% accepted, 9 enrolled. In 2010, 9 master's, 5 doctorates awarded. Terminal master's awarded for partial completion of doctoral program. *Degree requirements:* For master's, thesis or alternative, written exam; for doctorate, 2 foreign languages, thesis/dissertation, written exam. *Entrance requirements:* For master's and doctorate, GRE General Test, GRE Subject Test. Additional exam requirements/recommendations for international students: Required—TOEFL (minimum score 550 paper-based; 213 computer-based; 80 iBT). *Application deadline:* For fall admission, 2/15 priority date for domestic and international students. Applications are processed on a rolling basis. Application fee: $60. Electronic applications accepted. *Financial support:* In 2010–11, 33 students received support, including 1 fellowship with full tuition reimbursement available (averaging $15,000 per year), 3 research assistantships with full tuition reimbursements available (averaging $15,000 per year), 24 teaching assistantships with full tuition reimbursements available (averaging $15,000 per year); career-related internships or fieldwork, Federal Work-Study, institutionally sponsored loans, scholarships/grants, health care benefits, tuition waivers (full), and unspecified assistantships also available. Financial award application deadline: 2/15; financial award applicants required to submit FAFSA. *Unit head:* Dr. David H. Clark, Chairperson, 607-777-6786, E-mail: dclark@binghamton.edu. *Application contact:* Catherine Smith, Recruiting and Admissions Coordinator, 607-777-2151, Fax: 607-777-2501, E-mail: cmsmith@binghamton.edu.

Public Policy

State University of New York Empire State College, Graduate Studies, Program in Business and Policy Studies, Saratoga Springs, NY 12866-4391. Offers MA. Part-time and evening/weekend programs available. Postbaccalaureate distance learning degree programs offered (minimal on-campus study). *Degree requirements:* For master's, thesis, exam. *Entrance requirements:* For master's, proficiency in statistics. Additional exam requirements/recommendations for international students: Required—TOEFL (minimum score 600 paper-based; 280 computer-based). Electronic applications accepted. *Faculty research:* Business history, applied business statistics, labor/management relations, American social problems and business, effect of government economic policies on business.

State University of New York Empire State College, Graduate Studies, Program in Social Policy, Saratoga Springs, NY 12866-4391. Offers MA. Part-time and evening/weekend programs available. Postbaccalaureate distance learning degree programs offered (minimal on-campus study). *Degree requirements:* For master's, thesis, exam. *Entrance requirements:* Additional exam requirements/recommendations for international students: Required—TOEFL (minimum score 600 paper-based; 250 computer-based). Electronic applications accepted. *Faculty research:* Study of culture, society and mass communications, urban culture and policy, social decision making processes.

Stony Brook University, State University of New York, Graduate School, College of Arts and Sciences, Department of Political Science, Program in Public Policy and Urban Development, Stony Brook, NY 11794. Offers MA. *Students:* 42 full-time (16 women), 19 part-time (11 women); includes 8 Black or African American, non-Hispanic/Latino; 7 Asian, non-Hispanic/Latino; 4 Hispanic/Latino; 2 Two or more races, non-Hispanic/Latino, 6 international. In 2010, 37 master's awarded. Application fee: $100. *Expenses:* Tuition, state resident: full-time $8370; part-time $349 per credit. Tuition, nonresident: full-time $13,780; part-time $574 per credit. Required fees: $994. *Unit head:* Dr. Jeffrey Segal, Chair, 631-632-7640. *Application contact:* Director, 631-632-7667, Fax: 631-632-4116, E-mail: charles.taber@stonybrook.edu.

Suffolk University, College of Arts and Sciences, Program in Ethics and Public Policy, Boston, MA 02108-2770. Offers MS. Part-time and evening/weekend programs available. *Faculty:* 5 full-time (2 women). *Students:* 10 full-time (5 women), 5 part-time (2 women). Average age 28. 29 applicants, 72% accepted, 10 enrolled. In 2010, 8 master's awarded. *Degree requirements:* For master's, internship or thesis. *Entrance requirements:* For master's, GRE General Test, MAT, GMAT, statement of professional goals, official transcripts, 2 letters of recommendation, resume. Additional exam requirements/recommendations for international students: Required—TOEFL (minimum score 550 paper-based; 213 computer-based; 80 iBT). *Application deadline:* For fall and spring admission, 6/15 priority date for domestic and international students. Applications are processed on a rolling basis. Application fee: $50. Electronic applications accepted. *Expenses:* Contact institution. *Financial support:* In 2010–11, 13 students received support, including 11 fellowships (averaging $6,264 per year); career-related internships or fieldwork, Federal Work-Study, institutionally sponsored loans, and unspecified assistantships also available. Support available to part-time students. Financial award application deadline: 4/1; financial award applicants required to submit FAFSA. *Faculty research:* History of philosophy, ethics, political philosophy, continental philosophy and phenomenology, applied ethics. *Unit head:* Dr. Greg Fried, Chair of Philosophy Department, 617-573-8109, E-mail: gfried@suffolk.edu. *Application contact:* Judith Reynolds, Director of Graduate Admissions, 617-573-8302, Fax: 617-305-1733, E-mail: grad.admission@suffolk.edu.

Syracuse University, Maxwell School of Citizenship and Public Affairs, Program in Public Management and Policy, Syracuse, NY 13244. Offers CAS. Part-time programs available. *Entrance requirements:* For degree, matriculated graduate student status. Additional exam requirements/recommendations for international students: Required—TOEFL (minimum score 100 iBT). *Application deadline:* For fall admission, 2/1 priority date for domestic and international students. Application fee: $75. Electronic applications accepted. *Expenses:* Tuition: Part-time $1162 per credit. *Unit head:* Margaret Lane, Director, Executive Education, 315-443-2878, Fax: 315-443-3385, E-mail: meland@syr.edu. *Application contact:* Margaret Lane, Director, Executive Education, 315-443-2878, Fax: 315-443-3385, E-mail: meland@syr.edu.

Trinity College, Graduate Programs, Program in Public Policy Studies, Hartford, CT 06106-3100. Offers MA. Part-time and evening/weekend programs available. *Degree requirements:* For master's, thesis optional, departmental qualifying exam. *Entrance requirements:* For master's, minimum GPA of 3.0.

Tufts University, Graduate School of Arts and Sciences, Department of Urban and Environmental Policy and Planning, Medford, MA 02155. Offers community development (MA); environmental policy (MA); health and human welfare (MA); housing policy (MA); international environment/development policy (MA); public policy (MPP); MA/MS; MALD/MA. *Accreditation:* ACSP (one or more programs are accredited). Part-time programs available. *Degree requirements:* For master's, thesis, internship. *Entrance requirements:* For master's, GRE General Test. Additional exam requirements/recommendations for international students: Required—TOEFL (minimum score 550 paper-based; 213 computer-based; 80 iBT). Electronic applications accepted. *Expenses:* Contact institution.

Union Institute & University, Master of Arts Program–Online, Montpelier, VT 05602. Offers creativity studies (MA); education (MA); health and wellness (MA); history and culture (MA); leadership, public policy, and social issues (MA); literature and writing (MA); psychology (MA). Part-time programs available. Postbaccalaureate distance learning degree programs offered (no on-campus study). *Faculty:* 2 full-time (1 woman), 18 part-time/adjunct (11 women). *Students:* 27 full-time (26 women), 119 part-time (98 women); includes 34 minority (25 Black or African American, non-Hispanic/Latino; 3 American Indian or Alaska Native, non-Hispanic/Latino; 6 Hispanic/Latino). Average age 40. In 2010, 26 master's awarded. *Degree requirements:* For master's, thesis. *Application deadline:* Applications are processed on a rolling basis. Application fee: $50. Electronic applications accepted. *Expenses:* Tuition: Full-time $16,430; part-time $685 per credit hour. Required fees: $174; $44 per term. Tuition and fees vary according to course load, degree level and program. *Financial support:* Career-related internships or fieldwork and tuition waivers available. Financial award applicants required to submit FAFSA. *Unit head:* Dr. Brian Webb, Program Director, 802-828-8777, E-mail: brian.webb@tui.edu. *Application contact:* Diane Robinson, Director of Admissions, 888-828-8575, E-mail: diane.robinson@myunion.edu.

Union Institute & University, PhD Program in Interdisciplinary Studies, Cincinnati, OH 45206-1925. Offers ethical and creative leadership (PhD), including Martin Luther King studies; humanities and culture (PhD), including Martin Luther King studies; public policy and social change (PhD), including Martin Luther King studies. Program requires participation in brief on-campus residencies twice each year (January and July). Postbaccalaureate distance learning degree programs offered (minimal on-campus study). *Faculty:* 4 full-time (1 woman), 14 part-time/adjunct (9 women). *Students:* 103 full-time (60 women), 3 part-time (1 woman); includes 42 minority (40 Black or African American, non-Hispanic/Latino; 1 American Indian or Alaska Native, non-Hispanic/Latino; 1 Hispanic/Latino). Average age 46. In 2010, 2 doctorates awarded. *Degree requirements:* For doctorate, comprehensive exam, thesis/dissertation. *Entrance requirements:* For doctorate, master's degree, letters of recommendation, interview. *Application deadline:* Applications are processed on a rolling basis. Application fee: $50. *Expenses:* Tuition: Full-time $16,430; part-time $685 per credit hour. Required fees: $174; $44 per term. Tuition and fees vary according to course load, degree level and program. *Financial support:* Federal Work-Study, scholarships/grants, and tuition waivers (partial) available. Financial award application deadline: 5/1; financial award applicants required to submit FAFSA. *Faculty research:* Social responsibility, ethical leadership, Martin Luther King studies. *Unit head:* Dr. Larry Preston, Dean, 513-861-6400 Ext. 1151, E-mail: larry.preston@myunion.edu. *Application contact:* Michelle Flick, Admissions Counselor, 800-486-3116 Ext. 1225.

Universidad Autonoma de Guadalajara, Graduate Programs, Guadalajara, Mexico. Offers administrative law and justice (LL M); advertising and corporate communications (MA); architecture (M Arch); business (MBA); computational science (MCC); education (Ed M, Ed D); English-Spanish translation (MA); entrepreneurship and management (MBA); integrated management of digital animation (MA); international business (MIB); international corporate law (LL M); internet technologies (MS); manufacturing systems (MMS); occupational health (MS); philosophy (MA, PhD); power electronics (MS); quality systems (MQS); renewable energy (MS); social evaluation of projects (MBA); strategic market research (MBA); tax law (MA); teaching mathematics (MA).

Universidad del Este, Graduate School, Carolina, PR 00984. Offers accounting (MBA); adult education (M Ed); agribusiness (MBA); criminal justice and criminology (MA); curriculum and instruction—early education (M Ed); curriculum and instruction—elementary (M Ed); curriculum and instruction—English (M Ed); curriculum and instruction—Spanish (M Ed); human resources (MBA); information security management (MBA); information technology and Web business development (MBA); management (MBA); public policy (MPA); social work (MA), including clinical social work; special education (M Ed); strategic leadership (MBA).

Université de Montréal, Faculty of Arts and Sciences, Program in Societies, Public Policies and Health, Montréal, QC H3C 3J7, Canada. Offers DESS.

University at Albany, State University of New York, Nelson A. Rockefeller College of Public Affairs and Policy, Department of Public Administration and Policy, Albany, NY 12222-0001. Offers administrative behavior (PhD); comparative and development administration (MPA, PhD); human resources (MPA); legislative administration (MPA); nonprofit leadership and management (Certificate); planning and policy analysis (CAS); policy analysis (MPA); program analysis and evaluation (PhD); public affairs and policy (MA); public finance (MPA, PhD); public management (MPA, PhD); women and public policy (Certificate); JD/MPA. JD/MPA offered jointly with Albany Law School. *Accreditation:* NASPAA (one or more programs are accredited). *Degree requirements:* For doctorate, one foreign language, thesis/dissertation. *Entrance requirements:* For doctorate, GRE General Test. Additional exam requirements/recommendations for international students: Required—TOEFL (minimum score 550 paper-based; 213 computer-based). Electronic applications accepted.

The University of Arizona, Eller College of Management, School of Public Administration and Policy, Tucson, AZ 85721. Offers public administration (MPA); public administration and policy (PhD). *Accreditation:* NASPAA. *Students:* 64 full-time (38 women), 22 part-time (11 women); includes 2 Black or African American, non-Hispanic/Latino; 1 American Indian or Alaska Native, non-Hispanic/Latino; 2 Asian, non-Hispanic/Latino; 15 Hispanic/Latino; 8 Two or more races, non-Hispanic/Latino, 5 international. Average age 31. 76 applicants, 70% accepted, 27 enrolled. In 2010, 23 master's awarded. *Degree requirements:* For master's, internship of 400 hours; for doctorate, comprehensive exam, thesis/dissertation. *Entrance requirements:* For doctorate, GMAT or GRE, minimum graduate GPA of 3.5, letter of interest, 3 letters of recommendation, resume. Additional exam requirements/recommendations for international students: Required—TOEFL (minimum score 650 paper-based; 280 computer-based; 115 iBT). *Application deadline:* For fall admission, 2/15 priority date for domestic students, 2/15 for international students. Applications are processed on a rolling basis. Application fee: $75. Electronic applications accepted. *Expenses:* Contact institution. *Financial support:* In 2010–11, 1 research assistantship with full tuition reimbursement (averaging $9,429 per year) was awarded; teaching assistantships with full tuition reimbursements, career-related internships or fieldwork, scholarships/grants, health care benefits, tuition waivers (full and partial), and unspecified assistantships also available. Financial award application deadline: 4/15. Total annual research expenditures: $18,581. *Unit head:* Dr. H. Brinton Milward, Director, 520-621-7476, Fax: 520-626-5549, E-mail: bmilward@eller.arizona.edu. *Application contact:* Pamela Adams, Administrative Associate, 520-621-3128, Fax: 520-621-5549.

University of Arkansas, Graduate School, Interdisciplinary Program in Public Policy, Fayetteville, AR 72701-1201. Offers PhD. *Students:* 14 full-time (7 women), 45 part-time (27 women); includes 17 minority (13 Black or African American, non-Hispanic/Latino; 3 American Indian or Alaska Native, non-Hispanic/Latino; 1 Hispanic/Latino), 11 international. 12 applicants, 67% accepted. In 2010, 6 doctorates awarded. *Degree requirements:* For doctorate, thesis/dissertation. *Application deadline:* For fall admission, 4/1 for international students; for spring admission, 10/1 for international students. Applications are processed on a rolling basis. Application fee: $40 ($50 for international students). Electronic applications accepted. *Financial support:* In 2010–11, 1 fellowship with tuition reimbursement, 11 research assistantships were awarded; teaching assistantships. Financial award application deadline: 4/1; financial award applicants required to submit FAFSA. *Unit head:* Dr. Brinck Kerr, Head, 479-575-3356, Fax: 479-575-5908, E-mail: jbkerr@uark.edu. *Application contact:* Graduate Admissions, 479-575-6246, Fax: 479-575-5908, E-mail: gradinfo@uark.edu.

University of California, Berkeley, Graduate Division, Graduate School of Public Policy, Berkeley, CA 94720-1500. Offers MPP, PhD, JD/MPP, MPP/MA, MPP/MPH, MPP/MS. *Degree requirements:* For doctorate, thesis/dissertation, qualifying exam. *Entrance requirements:* For master's and doctorate, GRE General Test, minimum GPA of 3.0, 3 letters of recommendation.

University of California, Berkeley, Graduate Division, Haas School of Business, PhD in Business Administration Program, Berkeley, CA 94720-1500. Offers accounting (PhD); business and public policy (PhD); finance (PhD); management of organizations (PhD); marketing (PhD); operations management (PhD); real estate (PhD). *Accreditation:* AACSB. *Students:* 78 full-time (25 women); includes 12 Asian, non-Hispanic/Latino; 2 Hispanic/Latino, 32 international. Average age 30. 526 applicants, 7% accepted, 17 enrolled. In 2010, 17 doctorates awarded. *Degree requirements:* For doctorate, comprehensive exam, thesis/dissertation, written preliminary exams, oral qualifying exam. *Entrance requirements:* For doctorate, GMAT or GRE, minimum GPA of 3.0 in undergraduate and graduate coursework. Additional exam requirements/recommendations for international students: Required—TOEFL (minimum score 570 paper-based; 230 computer-based; 70 iBT), IELTS (minimum score 7). *Application deadline:* For fall admission, 12/10 for domestic and international students. Application fee: $70 ($90 for international students). Electronic applications accepted. *Financial support:* In 2010–11, 63 students received support, including 58 fellowships with full and partial tuition reimbursements available (averaging $26,000 per year); research assistantships with full and partial tuition reimbursements available, teaching assistantships with full and partial tuition reimbursements available, scholarships/grants, health care benefits, tuition waivers (full), unspecified assistantships, and transit pass, travel grants also available. Financial award application deadline: 12/10; financial award applicants required to submit FAFSA. *Faculty research:* Accounting, business and public policy, finance, management of organizations, marketing, operations and information technology management, real estate526. *Unit head:* Dr. Sunil Dutta, Director, 510-642-1229, Fax: 510-643-4255, E-mail: kimg@haas.berkeley.edu. *Application contact:* Kim Guilfoyle, Director, Student Affairs, 510-642-3944, Fax: 510-643-4255, E-mail: kimg@haas.berkeley.edu.

University of California, Los Angeles, Graduate Division, School of Public Affairs, Program in Public Policy, Los Angeles, CA 90095. Offers MPP. *Accreditation:* NASPAA. *Entrance requirements:* For master's, GRE General Test, minimum GPA of 3.0. Additional exam requirements/recommendations for international students: Required—TOEFL. Electronic applications accepted.

University of Chicago, Irving B. Harris Graduate School of Public Policy Studies, Chicago, IL 60637-1513. Offers environmental science and policy (MS); public policy studies (AM, MPP, PhD); JD/MPP; MBA/MPP; MPP/M Div; MPP/MA. Part-time programs available. *Degree requirements:* For doctorate, thesis/dissertation. *Entrance requirements:* Additional exam requirements/recommendations for international students: Required—TOEFL. Electronic applications accepted. *Expenses:* Contact institution. *Faculty research:* Family and child policy, international security, health policy, social policy.

University of Colorado Boulder, Graduate School, College of Arts and Sciences, Department of Political Science, Boulder, CO 80309. Offers international affairs (MA); political science (MA, PhD); public policy (MA). *Faculty:* 27 full-time (9 women). *Students:* 65 full-time (31 women), 2 part-time (0 women); includes 7 minority (2 American Indian or Alaska Native, non-Hispanic/

Latino; 2 Asian, non-Hispanic/Latino; 3 Hispanic/Latino), 7 international. Average age 30. 184 applicants, 15 enrolled. In 2010, 23 master's, 6 doctorates awarded. Terminal master's awarded for partial completion of doctoral program. *Degree requirements:* For master's, comprehensive exam, thesis; for doctorate, one foreign language, thesis/dissertation. *Entrance requirements:* For master's, GRE General Test, minimum undergraduate GPA of 3.0; for doctorate, GRE General Test, minimum GPA of 3.5 (undergraduate), 3.0 (graduate). *Application deadline:* For fall admission, 12/31 priority date for domestic students, 12/31 for international students. Application fee: $50 ($60 for international students). *Financial support:* In 2010–11, 10 fellowships (averaging $2,060 per year), 41 research assistantships (averaging $12,087 per year) were awarded; Federal Work-Study also available. Financial award application deadline: 12/31. *Faculty research:* American government and politics, comparative politics, international relations, public policy, law and politics, political philosophy, empirical theory and methodology. Total annual research expenditures: $92,305.

University of Delaware, College of Human Services, Education and Public Policy, Center for Energy and Environmental Policy, Program in Urban Affairs and Public Policy, Newark, DE 19716. Offers community development and nonprofit leadership (MA); energy and environmental policy (MA); governance, planning and management (PhD); historic preservation (MA); social and urban policy (PhD); technology, environment and society (PhD). Part-time programs available. Terminal master's awarded for partial completion of doctoral program. *Degree requirements:* For master's, analytical paper or thesis; for doctorate, thesis/dissertation. *Entrance requirements:* For master's, GRE General Test, minimum GPA of 3.0; for doctorate, GRE General Test, minimum GPA of 3.5. Additional exam requirements/recommendations for international students: Required—TOEFL. Electronic applications accepted. *Faculty research:* Political economy; social policy analysis; technology and society; historic preservation; urban policy.

University of Denver, Division of Arts, Humanities and Social Sciences, Department of Public Policy, Denver, CO 80208. Offers MPP. *Faculty:* 6 full-time (0 women), 1 (woman) part-time/adjunct. *Students:* 22 full-time (14 women), 2 part-time (1 woman); includes 3 minority (1 American Indian or Alaska Native, non-Hispanic/Latino; 1 Asian, non-Hispanic/Latino; 1 Native Hawaiian or other Pacific Islander, non-Hispanic/Latino). Average age 28. 42 applicants, 88% accepted, 16 enrolled. In 2010, 15 master's awarded. *Degree requirements:* For master's, thesis or alternative, policy memorandum capstone. *Entrance requirements:* For master's, GRE General Test. Additional exam requirements/recommendations for international students: Required—TOEFL (minimum score 570 paper-based; 88 iBT). *Application deadline:* For fall admission, 7/15 priority date for domestic students; for winter admission, 11/15 priority date for domestic students. Applications are processed on a rolling basis. Application fee: $60. Electronic applications accepted. *Expenses:* Tuition: Full-time $35,604; part-time $29,670 per year. Required fees: $687 per year. Tuition and fees vary according to program. *Financial support:* In 2010–11, 4 teaching assistantships with full and partial tuition reimbursements (averaging $3,500 per year) were awarded; Federal Work-Study and unspecified assistantships also available. Financial award application deadline: 3/15. *Unit head:* Richard Caldwell, Co-Director, 303-871-2468, Fax: 303-871-3066, E-mail: richard.caldwell@du.edu. *Application contact:* Information Contact, 303-871-2468, Fax: 303-871-3066, E-mail: ipps@du.edu.

University of Georgia, School of Public and International Affairs, Department of Public Administration and Policy, Athens, GA 30602. Offers public administration (MPA, PhD). *Accreditation:* NASPAA (one or more programs are accredited). *Faculty:* 16 full-time (2 women), 1 part-time/adjunct (0 women). *Students:* 136 full-time (68 women), 51 part-time (32 women); includes 27 Black or African American, non-Hispanic/Latino; 4 American Indian or Alaska Native, non-Hispanic/Latino; 6 Asian, non-Hispanic/Latino; 1 Hispanic/Latino; 1 Two or more races, non-Hispanic/Latino, 22 international. 309 applicants, 37% accepted, 58 enrolled. In 2010, 68 master's, 3 doctorates awarded. *Degree requirements:* For master's, internship; for doctorate, thesis/dissertation. *Entrance requirements:* For master's and doctorate, GRE General Test. *Application deadline:* For fall admission, 7/1 priority date for domestic students; for spring admission, 11/15 for domestic students. Application fee: $50. Electronic applications accepted. *Expenses:* Tuition, state resident: full-time $7200; part-time $344 per credit hour. Tuition, nonresident: full-time $21,900; part-time $944 per credit hour. Tuition and fees vary according to course load and program. *Financial support:* Fellowships, research assistantships, teaching assistantships, unspecified assistantships available. *Unit head:* Dr. J. Edward Kellough, Head, 706-542-2057, E-mail: kellough@uga.edu. *Application contact:* Dr. Vicky M. Wilkins, Graduate Coordinator, 706-542-2648, Fax: 706-583-4421, E-mail: vwilkins@uga.edu.

University of Guelph, Graduate Studies, College of Social and Applied Human Sciences, Department of Political Science, Guelph, ON N1G 2W1, Canada. Offers comparative politics (MA); international development (MA); political science (MA); public policy and public administration (MA); the Americas (Canada emphasis) (MA). MA in public policy and public administration offered in collaboration with Department of Political Science of McMaster University. *Degree requirements:* For master's, thesis or paper. *Entrance requirements:* For master's, minimum B average during previous 2 years of course work, 4 year Honours Degree in Political Science. Additional exam requirements/recommendations for international students: Required—TOEFL. Electronic applications accepted. *Faculty research:* Political ethics, constitutional power.

University of Hawaii at Manoa, Graduate Division, College of Social Sciences, Public Policy Center, Honolulu, HI 96822. Offers Graduate Certificate. Part-time programs available. *Faculty:* 3 full-time (2 women), 2 part-time/adjunct (1 woman). *Students:* 2 full-time (0 women), 2 part-time (1 woman), 1 international. Average age 27. 2 applicants, 50% accepted, 1 enrolled. In 2010, 1 Graduate Certificate awarded. *Entrance requirements:* Additional exam requirements/recommendations for international students: Required—TOEFL (minimum score 500 paper-based; 173 computer-based; 61 iBT), IELTS (minimum score 5). *Application deadline:* For fall admission, 3/1 for domestic students, 2/1 for international students. Application fee: $60. *Financial support:* In 2010–11, 2 fellowships (averaging $5,157 per year), 1 research assistantship (averaging $17,496 per year) were awarded. *Application contact:* Susan Chandler, Interim Director, 808-956-4237, Fax: 808-956-0950, E-mail: chandler@hawaii.edu.

University of Louisville, Graduate School, College of Arts and Sciences, Department of Urban and Public Affairs, Louisville, KY 40208. Offers public administration (MPA), including human resources management, non-profit management, public policy and administration; urban and public affairs (PhD), including urban planning and development, urban policy and administration; urban planning (MUP), including administration of planning organizations, housing and community development, land use and environmental planning, spatial analysis. Part-time and evening/weekend programs available. *Faculty:* 22 full-time (7 women), 8 part-time/adjunct (1 woman). *Students:* 73 full-time (36 women), 31 part-time (18 women); includes 11 Black or African American, non-Hispanic/Latino; 2 Asian, non-Hispanic/Latino; 2 Hispanic/Latino; 1 Native Hawaiian or other Pacific Islander, non-Hispanic/Latino; 2 Two or more races, non-Hispanic/Latino, 11 international. Average age 31. 96 applicants, 67% accepted, 37 enrolled. In 2010, 28 master's, 5 doctorates awarded. Terminal master's awarded for partial completion of doctoral program. *Degree requirements:* For master's, internship; for doctorate, comprehensive exam, thesis/dissertation. *Entrance requirements:* For master's, GRE General Test, minimum GPA of 3.0; for doctorate, GRE General Test, master's degree in appropriate field. Additional exam requirements/recommendations for international students: Required—TOEFL (minimum score 550 paper-based; 213 computer-based; 79 iBT). *Application deadline:* For fall admission, 7/15 for domestic students; for spring admission, 11/15 for domestic students. Applications are processed on a rolling basis. Application fee: $50. Electronic applications accepted. *Expenses:* Tuition, state resident: full-time $9144; part-time $508 per credit hour. Tuition, nonresident: full-time $19,026; part-time $1057 per credit hour. Tuition and fees vary according to program and reciprocity agreements. *Financial support:* In 2010–11, 23 students received support; fellowships, research assistantships, health care benefits available. Financial award application deadline: 3/1. *Faculty research:* Housing and community development, performance-based budgeting, environmental policy and natural hazards, sustainability, real estate development, comparative urban development. *Unit head:* Dr. David Simpson, Chair, 502-852-8019, Fax: 502-852-4558, E-mail: dave.simpson@louisville.edu. *Application contact:* Patty Sarley, Graduate Student Advisor, 502-852-7914, Fax: 502-852-4558, E-mail: plclea01@louisville.edu.

University of Maryland, Baltimore County, Graduate School, College of Arts, Humanities and Social Sciences, Department of Economics, Program in Economic Policy Analysis, Baltimore, MD 21250. Offers MA. Part-time and evening/weekend programs available. *Faculty:* 25 full-time (9 women), 2 part-time/adjunct (0 women). *Students:* 13 full-time (6 women), 8 part-time (1 woman); includes 4 minority (1 American Indian or Alaska Native, non-Hispanic/Latino; 3 Asian, non-Hispanic/Latino), 3 international. Average age 27. 26 applicants, 62% accepted, 9 enrolled. In 2010, 9 master's awarded. *Degree requirements:* For master's, comprehensive exam, capstone research project. *Entrance requirements:* For master's, GRE General Test, undergraduate coursework in economic theory, econometrics, calculus. Additional exam requirements/recommendations for international students: Required—TOEFL (minimum score 80 computer-based). *Application deadline:* For fall admission, 7/1 priority date for domestic students, 3/1 priority date for international students; for spring admission, 1/1 priority date for domestic students, 9/15 priority date for international students. Applications are processed on a rolling basis. Application fee: $45. Electronic applications accepted. *Financial support:* In 2010–11, 5 students received support, including 5 research assistantships with full and partial tuition reimbursements available (averaging $11,324 per year); Federal Work-Study, health care benefits, tuition waivers (full and partial), and unspecified assistantships also available. Support available to part-time students. Financial award application deadline: 4/15; financial award applicants required to submit FAFSA. *Faculty research:* International trade policy analysis, health and hospital policy evaluation, environmental policy analysis, economics of education, economic growth and development. Total annual research expenditures: $70,000. *Unit head:* Prof. David F. Mitch, Professor of Economics and Graduate Director, 410-455-2157, Fax: 410-455-1054, E-mail: mitch@umbc.edu. *Application contact:* Prof. David F. Mitch, Professor of Economics and Graduate Director, 410-455-2157, Fax: 410-455-1054, E-mail: mitch@umbc.edu.

University of Maryland, Baltimore County, Graduate School, College of Arts, Humanities and Social Sciences, Department of Public Policy, Program in Public Policy, Baltimore, MD 21250. Offers economics (PhD); education (MPP, PhD); evaluation (MPP); health (MPP, PhD); management (MPP, PhD); policy history (PhD); urban (MPP, PhD). Part-time and evening/weekend programs available. *Faculty:* 10 full-time (3 women), 2 part-time/adjunct (0 women). *Students:* 62 full-time (37 women), 94 part-time (54 women); includes 39 minority (25 Black or African American, non-Hispanic/Latino; 6 Asian, non-Hispanic/Latino; 2 Hispanic/Latino; 1 Native Hawaiian or other Pacific Islander, non-Hispanic/Latino; 5 Two or more races, non-Hispanic/Latino), 10 international. Average age 36. 102 applicants, 65% accepted, 28 enrolled. In 2010, 20 master's, 8 doctorates awarded. Terminal master's awarded for partial completion of doctoral program. *Degree requirements:* For master's, thesis optional, public analysis paper, internship for pre-service; for doctorate, comprehensive exam, thesis/dissertation, comprehensive and field qualifying exams. *Entrance requirements:* For master's, GRE General Test, 3 academic letters of reference, transcripts, resume; for doctorate, GRE General Test, 3 academic letters of reference, transcripts, resume, research paper. Additional exam requirements/recommendations for international students: Required—TOEFL (minimum score 550 paper-based; 213 computer-based; 80 iBT). *Application deadline:* For fall admission, 1/15 priority date for domestic students, 1/1 priority date for international students; for spring admission, 11/1 priority date for domestic students, 5/1 priority date for international students. Applications are processed on a rolling basis. Application fee: $50. Electronic applications accepted. *Financial support:* In 2010–11, 26 students received support, including fellowships (averaging $3,000 per year), 21 research assistantships with full tuition reimbursements available (averaging $17,400 per year); career-related internships or fieldwork, Federal Work-Study, scholarships/grants, health care benefits, and unspecified assistantships also available. Support available to part-time students. Financial award application deadline: 1/15; financial award applicants required to submit FAFSA. *Faculty research:* Health policy, education policy, urban policy, public management, evaluation and analytical methods. *Unit head:* Dr. Donald Norris, Chair, 410-455-1455, E-mail: norris@umbc.edu. *Application contact:* Sally F. Helms, Administrator of Academic Affairs, 410-455-3202, Fax: 410-455-1172, E-mail: gradposi@umbc.edu.

University of Maryland, College Park, Academic Affairs, A. James Clark School of Engineering and School of Public Policy, Program in Engineering and Public Policy, College Park, MD 20742. Offers MS. *Students:* 8 full-time (3 women), 10 part-time (1 woman); includes 3 minority (1 Asian, non-Hispanic/Latino; 2 Hispanic/Latino), 1 international. 39 applicants, 51% accepted, 9 enrolled. In 2010, 6 master's awarded. *Application deadline:* For fall admission, 4/1 for domestic students, 2/1 for international students; for spring admission, 10/15 for domestic students, 6/1 for international students. Application fee: $75. *Expenses:* Tuition, state resident: part-time $471 per credit hour. Tuition, nonresident: part-time $1016 per credit hour. Required fees: $337 per term. *Unit head:* Dr. Steven Gabriel, Co-Director, 301-405-3242, E-mail: sgabriel@umd.edu. *Application contact:* Dean of the Graduate School, 301-405-0358, Fax: 301-314-9305, E-mail: ccaramel@umd.edu.

University of Maryland, College Park, Academic Affairs, School of Public Policy, Policy Studies Program, College Park, MD 20742. Offers PhD. *Students:* 33 full-time (19 women), 23 part-time (8 women); includes 8 minority (1 Black or African American, non-Hispanic/Latino; 4 Asian, non-Hispanic/Latino; 3 Hispanic/Latino), 24 international. 149 applicants, 7% accepted, 11 enrolled. In 2010, 5 doctorates awarded. *Degree requirements:* For doctorate, comprehensive exam, thesis/dissertation, written and oral exams. *Entrance requirements:* For doctorate, GRE General Test, writing sample. *Application deadline:* For fall admission, 4/1 for domestic students, 2/1 for international students. Applications are processed on a rolling basis. Application fee: $75. Electronic applications accepted. *Expenses:* Tuition, state resident: part-time $471 per credit hour. Tuition, nonresident: part-time $1016 per credit hour. Required fees: $337 per term. *Financial support:* In 2010–11, 5 fellowships with full and partial tuition reimbursements (averaging $11,375 per year), 22 teaching assistantships (averaging $16,313 per year) were awarded. Financial award applicants required to submit FAFSA. *Application contact:* Dr. Charles A. Caramello, Dean of Graduate School, 301-405-0358, Fax: 301-314-9305, E-mail: ccaramel@umd.edu.

University of Maryland, College Park, Academic Affairs, School of Public Policy, Programs in Public Policy, College Park, MD 20742. Offers MPP. *Accreditation:* NASPAA. *Students:* 215 full-time (102 women), 35 part-time (17 women); includes 41 minority (15 Black or African American, non-Hispanic/Latino; 11 Asian, non-Hispanic/Latino; 11 Hispanic/Latino; 4 Two or more races, non-Hispanic/Latino), 22 international. 716 applicants, 55% accepted, 130 enrolled. In 2010, 70 master's awarded. *Entrance requirements:* Additional exam requirements/recommendations for international students: Required—TOEFL. *Application deadline:* For fall admission, 4/1 for domestic students, 2/1 for international students; for spring admission, 10/15 for domestic students, 6/1 for international students. Applications are processed on a rolling basis. Application fee: $75. Electronic applications accepted. *Expenses:* Tuition, state resident: part-time $471 per credit hour. Tuition, nonresident: part-time $1016 per credit hour. Required fees: $337 per term. *Financial support:* In 2010–11, 13 fellowships with full and partial tuition reimbursements (averaging $15,012 per year), 2 research assistantships (averaging $19,347 per year), 104 teaching assistantships (averaging $14,665 per year) were awarded. *Application contact:* Dr. Charles A. Caramello, Dean of Graduate School, 301-405-0358, Fax: 301-314-9305, E-mail: ccaramel@umd.edu.

University of Massachusetts Amherst, Graduate School, College of Social and Behavioral Sciences, Center for Public Policy and Administration, Amherst, MA 01003. Offers MPPA, MPH/MPPA. Part-time programs available. *Students:* 28 full-time (16 women), 11 part-time (8 women); includes 2 minority (1 Asian, non-Hispanic/Latino; 1 Hispanic/Latino), 6 international. Average age 33. 87 applicants, 78% accepted, 17 enrolled. In 2010, 17 master's awarded. *Degree requirements:* For master's, thesis or alternative. *Entrance requirements:* For master's, GRE General Test. Additional exam requirements/recommendations for international students: Required—TOEFL (minimum score 550 paper-based; 213 computer-based; 80 iBT), IELTS (minimum score 6.5). *Application deadline:* For fall admission, 2/1 for domestic and inter-

University of Massachusetts Amherst (continued)
national students. Applications are processed on a rolling basis. Application fee: $50 ($65 for international students). Electronic applications accepted. *Expenses:* Tuition, state resident: full-time $2640. Required fees: $8282. One-time fee: $357 full-time. *Financial support:* In 2010–11, 2 fellowships with full tuition reimbursements (averaging $3,750 per year), 23 research assistantships with full tuition reimbursements (averaging $6,584 per year) were awarded; teaching assistantships, career-related internships or fieldwork, Federal Work-Study, scholarships/grants, traineeships, health care benefits, tuition waivers (full), and unspecified assistantships also available. Support available to part-time students. Financial award application deadline: 2/1; financial award applicants required to submit FAFSA. *Unit head:* Dr. M. V. Lee Badgett, Graduate Program Director, 413-545-3956, Fax: 413-545-1108. *Application contact:* Jean M. Ames, Supervisor of Admissions, 413-545-0722, Fax: 413-577-0010, E-mail: gradadm@grad.umass.edu.

University of Massachusetts Amherst, Graduate School, Interdisciplinary Programs, Program in Public Policy and Business Administration, Amherst, MA 01003. Offers MPPA/MBA. *Accreditation:* AACSB. Part-time programs available. *Students:* 7 full-time (6 women); includes 2 minority (1 Asian, non-Hispanic/Latino; 1 Two or more races, non-Hispanic/Latino). Average age 30. 12 applicants, 50% accepted, 3 enrolled. *Entrance requirements:* Additional exam requirements/recommendations for international students: Required—TOEFL (minimum score 600 paper-based; 250 computer-based; 100 iBT), IELTS (minimum score 7). *Application deadline:* For fall admission, 2/1 for domestic and international students. Applications are processed on a rolling basis. Application fee: $50 ($65 for international students). Electronic applications accepted. *Expenses:* Tuition, state resident: full-time $2640. Required fees: $8282. One-time fee: $357 full-time. *Financial support:* Career-related internships or fieldwork, Federal Work-Study, scholarships/grants, traineeships, health care benefits, tuition waivers (full), and unspecified assistantships available. Support available to part-time students. Financial award application deadline: 2/1; financial award applicants required to submit FAFSA. *Unit head:* Dr. M. V. Lee Badgett, Graduate Program Director, 413-545-3956, Fax: 413-545-1108. *Application contact:* Jean M. Ames, Supervisor of Admissions, 413-545-0722, Fax: 413-577-0010, E-mail: gradadm@grad.umass.edu.

University of Massachusetts Boston, Office of Graduate Studies, John W. McCormack Graduate School of Policy Studies, Program in Public Policy, Boston, MA 02125-3393. Offers PhD. Evening/weekend programs available. *Degree requirements:* For doctorate, comprehensive exam, thesis/dissertation, practicum, oral exam. *Entrance requirements:* For doctorate, GRE General Test. *Faculty research:* Political economy, public managerial control, healthcare policy, planning and public policy theory, economic development.

University of Massachusetts Dartmouth, Graduate School, School of Education, Public Policy, and Civic Engagement, Department of Public Policy, North Dartmouth, MA 02747-2300. Offers environmental policy (Postbaccalaureate Certificate); public policy (MPP). Part-time programs available. Postbaccalaureate distance learning degree programs offered (minimal on-campus study). *Faculty:* 5 full-time (2 women), 1 (woman) part-time/adjunct. *Students:* 13 full-time (7 women), 28 part-time (16 women); includes 1 Black or African American, non-Hispanic/Latino; 1 Hispanic/Latino. Average age 32. 26 applicants, 77% accepted, 7 enrolled. In 2010, 10 master's awarded. *Entrance requirements:* For master's, GRE or GMAT. Additional exam requirements/recommendations for international students: Required—TOEFL (minimum score 500 paper-based; 213 computer-based). *Application deadline:* For fall admission, 4/20 for domestic students, 2/20 for international students; for spring admission, 11/15 for domestic students, 9/15 for international students. Applications are processed on a rolling basis. Application fee: $40 ($60 for international students). Electronic applications accepted. *Expenses:* Tuition, state resident: full-time $2071; part-time $86 per credit. Tuition, nonresident: full-time $8099; part-time $337 per credit. Required fees: $9446; $394 per credit. One-time fee: $75. Part-time tuition and fees vary according to class time, course load, degree level and reciprocity agreements. *Financial support:* In 2010–11, 3 research assistantships with full tuition reimbursements (averaging $5,333 per year) were awarded; Federal Work-Study and unspecified assistantships also available. Support available to part-time students. Financial award application deadline: 3/1. *Faculty research:* Demographic analysis, legal and regulatory framework. Total annual research expenditures: $82,244. *Unit head:* Dr. Michael Goodman, 508-990-9660, E-mail: mgoodman@umassd.edu. *Application contact:* Elan Turcotte-Shamski, Graduate Admissions Officer, 508-999-8604, Fax: 508-999-8183, E-mail: graduate@umassd.edu.

University of Medicine and Dentistry of New Jersey, UMDNJ–School of Public Health (UMDNJ, Rutgers, NJIT) Newark Campus, Newark, NJ 07107-1709. Offers clinical epidemiology (Certificate); dental public health (MPH); general public health (Certificate); public policy and oral health services administration (Certificate); quantitative methods (MPH); urban health (MPH); DMD/MPH; MD/MPH; MS/MPH. *Accreditation:* CEPH. Part-time and evening/weekend programs available. *Degree requirements:* For master's, thesis, internship. *Entrance requirements:* For master's, GRE General Test. Additional exam requirements/recommendations for international students: Required—TOEFL. *Application deadline:* For fall admission, 5/1 for domestic students; for spring admission, 10/1 for domestic students. Application fee: $115. Electronic applications accepted. *Application contact:* Yvette J. Holding-Ford, Information Contact, 973-972-7212, Fax: 973-972-8032, E-mail: holdinys@umdnj.edu.

University of Memphis, Graduate School, College of Arts and Sciences, Division of Public and Nonprofit Administration, Memphis, TN 38152. Offers nonprofit administration (MPA); public management and policy (MPA); urban management and planning (MPA). *Accreditation:* NASPAA. Part-time and evening/weekend programs available. Postbaccalaureate distance learning degree programs offered (minimal on-campus study). *Faculty:* 5 full-time (2 women), 1 (woman) part-time/adjunct. *Students:* 18 full-time (15 women), 43 part-time (33 women); includes 35 Black or African American, non-Hispanic/Latino; 1 Hispanic/Latino; 1 Two or more races, non-Hispanic/Latino. Average age 34. 32 applicants, 88% accepted, 9 enrolled. In 2010, 17 master's awarded. *Degree requirements:* For master's, comprehensive exam, thesis or alternative, internship. *Entrance requirements:* For master's, GRE General Test, GMAT, or MAT, minimum GPA of 3.0. Additional exam requirements/recommendations for international students: Required—TOEFL. *Application deadline:* For fall admission, 7/1 for domestic students, 5/15 for international students; for spring admission, 12/1 for domestic students, 9/15 for international students. Applications are processed on a rolling basis. Application fee: $35 ($60 for international students). *Financial support:* In 2010–11, 37 students received support; fellowships, research assistantships with full tuition reimbursements available, career-related internships or fieldwork, Federal Work-Study, scholarships/grants, and unspecified assistantships available. Support available to part-time students. Financial award application deadline: 2/15; financial award applicants required to submit FAFSA. *Faculty research:* Nonprofit organization governance, local government management, community collaboration, urban problems, accountability. *Unit head:* Dr. Charles Menifield, Director, 901-678-5527, Fax: 901-678-2981, E-mail: cmenifld@memphis.edu. *Application contact:* Dr. Charles Menifield, Graduate Admissions Coordinator, 901-678-3360, Fax: 901-678-2981, E-mail: cmenifld@memphis.edu.

University of Michigan, Horace H. Rackham School of Graduate Studies, College of Literature, Science, and the Arts, Department of Economics, Ann Arbor, MI 48109. Offers applied economics (AM); economics (AM, PhD); public policy and economics (PhD); social work and economics (PhD); JD/PhD; MPP/AM. Terminal master's awarded for partial completion of doctoral program. *Degree requirements:* For doctorate, oral defense of dissertation, preliminary exam. *Entrance requirements:* For master's and doctorate, GRE General Test. Additional exam requirements/recommendations for international students: Required—TOEFL (minimum score 600 paper-based; 250 computer-based; 100 iBT). Electronic applications accepted. *Expenses:* Tuition, state resident: full-time $17,784; part-time $1116 per credit hour. Tuition, nonresident: full-time $35,944; part-time $2125 per credit hour. International tuition: $35,994 full-time. Required fees: $95 per semester. Tuition and fees vary according to course load, degree level and program. *Faculty research:* Economic and econometrical analysis, industrial organization, international trade, public finance, development, health, labor, population standard, macro, theory.

University of Michigan, Horace H. Rackham School of Graduate Studies, College of Literature, Science, and the Arts, Department of Sociology, Ann Arbor, MI 48109. Offers public policy and sociology (PhD); social work and sociology (PhD); sociology (PhD); women's studies and sociology (PhD). *Degree requirements:* For doctorate, comprehensive exam, thesis/dissertation, oral defense of dissertation, preliminary exam. *Entrance requirements:* For doctorate, GRE General Test, letters of recommendation, writing sample. Additional exam requirements/recommendations for international students: Required—TOEFL (minimum score 560 paper-based; 220 computer-based; 84 iBT). Electronic applications accepted. *Expenses:* Tuition, state resident: full-time $17,784; part-time $1116 per credit hour. Tuition, nonresident: full-time $35,944; part-time $2125 per credit hour. International tuition: $35,994 full-time. Required fees: $95 per semester. Tuition and fees vary according to course load, degree level and program. *Faculty research:* Power, history and social change; gender and sexuality; race and ethnicity; economic sociology; social demography.

University of Michigan, Horace H. Rackham School of Graduate Studies, Gerald R. Ford School of Public Policy, Ann Arbor, MI 48109. Offers MPA, MPP, PhD, JD/MPP, MBA/MPP, MD/MPP, MHSA/MPP, MPH/MPP, MPP/AM, MPP/MA, MPP/MS, MPP/MUP, MSW/MPP. Part-time programs available. *Entrance requirements:* For master's, GRE. Additional exam requirements/recommendations for international students: Required—TOEFL (minimum score 600 paper-based; 250 computer-based; 100 iBT). Electronic applications accepted. *Expenses:* Tuition, state resident: full-time $17,784; part-time $1116 per credit hour. Tuition, nonresident: full-time $35,944; part-time $2125 per credit hour. International tuition: $35,994 full-time. Required fees: $95 per semester. Tuition and fees vary according to course load, degree level and program. *Faculty research:* U.S. social policy; international economic policy; quantitative policy analysis; environmental policy; health policy.

University of Michigan–Dearborn, College of Arts, Sciences, and Letters, Master of Public Policy Program, Dearborn, MI 48128. Offers MPP. Part-time and evening/weekend programs available. *Faculty:* 7 full-time (4 women). *Students:* 19 full-time (11 women), 18 part-time (9 women); includes 9 minority (3 Black or African American, non-Hispanic/Latino; 1 Asian, non-Hispanic/Latino; 2 Hispanic/Latino; 1 Native Hawaiian or other Pacific Islander, non-Hispanic/Latino; 2 Two or more races, non-Hispanic/Latino). Average age 31. 22 applicants, 86% accepted, 19 enrolled. In 2010, 6 master's awarded. *Entrance requirements:* For master's, GRE, 2 letters of recommendation. Additional exam requirements/recommendations for international students: Required—TOEFL (minimum score 560 paper-based; 220 computer-based). *Application deadline:* For fall admission, 8/1 for domestic students, 4/1 for international students; for winter admission, 12/1 for domestic students, 11/1 for international students; for spring admission, 4/1 for domestic students, 3/1 for international students. Application fee: $60 ($75 for international students). *Faculty research:* Peace and conflict studies, courts and public policy, public policy and the media. *Unit head:* Dr. Paul Draus, Director, 313-583-6539, Fax: 313-583-6700, E-mail: draus@umd.umich.edu. *Application contact:* Carol Ligienza, Coordinator, CASL Graduate Programs, 313-593-1183, Fax: 313-583-6700, E-mail: caslgrad@umd.umich.edu.

University of Minnesota, Twin Cities Campus, Graduate School, Hubert H. Humphrey School of Public Affairs, Program in Public Policy, Minneapolis, MN 55455-0213. Offers advanced policy analysis methods (MPP); economic and community development (MPP); foreign policy (MPP); public and nonprofit leadership and management (MPP); science technology and environmental policy (MPP); social policy (MPP); women and public policy (MPP); JD/MPP; MPP/MS; MSW/MPP. Part-time programs available. *Degree requirements:* For master's, thesis or alternative, internship or equivalent work experience. *Entrance requirements:* For master's, GRE General Test, minimum undergraduate GPA of 3.0. Additional exam requirements/recommendations for international students: Required—TOEFL (minimum score 600 paper-based; 250 computer-based; 100 iBT). Electronic applications accepted. *Faculty research:* Social policy, public and non-profit management and leadership, community and economic development, foreign policy and international affairs, women and public policy.

University of Missouri–St. Louis, College of Arts and Sciences, Department of Political Science, St. Louis, MO 63121. Offers American politics (MA); comparative politics (MA); international politics (MA); political process and behavior (MA); political science (PhD); public administration and public policy (MA); urban and regional politics (MA). Part-time and evening/weekend programs available. *Faculty:* 18 full-time (7 women), 1 (woman) part-time/adjunct. *Students:* 15 full-time (7 women), 39 part-time (21 women); includes 13 minority (8 Black or African American, non-Hispanic/Latino; 2 American Indian or Alaska Native, non-Hispanic/Latino; 3 Asian, non-Hispanic/Latino), 3 international. Average age 35. 43 applicants, 47% accepted, 10 enrolled. In 2010, 4 master's, 5 doctorates awarded. Terminal master's awarded for partial completion of doctoral program. *Degree requirements:* For master's, thesis optional; for doctorate, thesis/dissertation. *Entrance requirements:* For master's, GRE General Test, 2 letters of recommendation; for doctorate, GRE General Test, 3 letters of recommendation. Additional exam requirements/recommendations for international students: Required—TOEFL (minimum score 550 paper-based; 213 computer-based). *Application deadline:* For fall admission, 2/15 priority date for domestic and international students; for spring admission, 10/15 priority date for domestic and international students. Applications are processed on a rolling basis. Application fee: $35 ($40 for international students). Electronic applications accepted. *Expenses:* Tuition, state resident: full-time $5522; part-time $306.80 per credit hour. Tuition, nonresident: full-time $14,253; part-time $792.10 per credit hour. Required fees: $658; $49 per credit hour. One-time fee: $12. Tuition and fees vary according to program. *Financial support:* In 2010–11, 8 research assistantships with full and partial tuition reimbursements (averaging $1,110 per year), 6 teaching assistantships with full and partial tuition reimbursements (averaging $10,800 per year) were awarded; fellowships, career-related internships or fieldwork also available. Support available to part-time students. Financial award application deadline: 3/15; financial award applicants required to submit FAFSA. *Faculty research:* Public policy, urban politics and administration, American government. *Unit head:* Dr. Kenneth Thomas, Director of Graduate Studies, 314-516-5521, Fax: 314-516-5268, E-mail: umslpolisci@umsl.edu. *Application contact:* 314-516-5458, Fax: 314-516-6996, E-mail: gradadm@umsl.edu.

University of Missouri–St. Louis, Graduate School, Program in Public Policy Administration, St. Louis, MO 63121. Offers health policy (MPPA); local government management (MPPA); managing human resources and organization (MPPA); nonprofit organization management (MPPA); nonprofit organization management and leadership (Certificate); policy research and analysis (MPPA). *Accreditation:* NASPAA. Part-time and evening/weekend programs available. *Faculty:* 9 full-time (4 women), 8 part-time/adjunct (6 women). *Students:* 36 full-time (21 women), 59 part-time (33 women); includes 17 minority (13 Black or African American, non-Hispanic/Latino; 2 American Indian or Alaska Native, non-Hispanic/Latino; 1 Asian, non-Hispanic/Latino; 1 Hispanic/Latino), 11 international. Average age 31. 60 applicants, 68% accepted, 24 enrolled. In 2010, 23 master's, 17 Certificates awarded. *Entrance requirements:* For master's, 3 letters of recommendation. Additional exam requirements/recommendations for international students: Required—TOEFL (minimum score 550 paper-based; 213 computer-based). *Application deadline:* For fall admission, 7/1 priority date for domestic and international students; for spring admission, 12/1 priority date for domestic and international students. Applications are processed on a rolling basis. Application fee: $35 ($40 for international students). Electronic applications accepted. *Expenses:* Tuition, state resident: full-time $5522; part-time $306.80 per credit hour. Tuition, nonresident: full-time $14,253; part-time $792.10 per credit hour. Required fees: $658; $49 per credit hour. One-time fee: $12. Tuition and fees vary according to program. *Financial support:* In 2010–11, 3 research assistantships with full and partial tuition reimbursements (averaging $12,000 per year) were awarded; career-related internships or fieldwork also available. Financial award application deadline: 4/1; financial award applicants required to submit FAFSA. *Faculty research:* Urban policy, public finance, evaluation. *Unit head:* Dr. Brady Baybeck, Director, 314-516-5145, Fax: 314-516-5210, E-mail: baybeck@umsl.edu. *Application contact:* 314-516-5458, Fax: 314-516-6996, E-mail: gradadm@umsl.edu.

University of Nebraska–Lincoln, Graduate College, College of Arts and Sciences, Department of Political Science, Lincoln, NE 68588. Offers political science (MA, PhD); public policy analysis (Graduate Certificate). *Degree requirements:* For master's, thesis optional; for doctorate, variable foreign language requirement, comprehensive exam, thesis/dissertation. *Entrance requirements:* For master's and doctorate, GRE General Test, writing sample. Additional exam requirements/recommendations for international students: Required—TOEFL (minimum score 600 paper-based; 250 computer-based). Electronic applications accepted. *Faculty research:* Public policy; comparative politics; international relations; political theory, behavior, and methodology; American politics.

University of Nevada, Las Vegas, Graduate College, College of Liberal Arts, Department of Political Science, Program in Ethics and Policy Studies, Las Vegas, NV 89154-5029. Offers MA. Part-time programs available. *Faculty:* 2 full-time (0 women), 2 part-time/adjunct (both women). *Students:* 7 part-time (2 women); includes 4 minority (2 Asian, non-Hispanic/Latino; 2 Hispanic/Latino). Average age 33. 1 applicant, 0% accepted, 0 enrolled. In 2010, 1 master's awarded. *Degree requirements:* For master's, thesis. *Entrance requirements:* For master's, GRE General Test. Additional exam requirements/recommendations for international students: Required—TOEFL (minimum score 550 paper-based; 213 computer-based; 80 iBT), IELTS (minimum score 7). Application fee: $60 ($95 for international students). *Expenses:* Tuition, area resident: Part-time $239.50 per credit. Tuition, state resident: part-time $239.50 per credit. Tuition, nonresident: part-time $503 per credit. Required fees: $108 per semester. Tuition and fees vary according to course load, program and reciprocity agreements. *Financial support:* Institutionally sponsored loans, scholarships/grants, health care benefits, and unspecified assistantships available. Financial award application deadline: 3/1. *Faculty research:* Ancient political philosophy, international security, globalization, Islamic law, informal education in Senegal. *Unit head:* Dr. John Tuman, Chair/ Associate Professor, 702-895-5258, Fax: 702-895-1065, E-mail: john.tuman@unlv.edu. *Application contact:* Graduate College Admissions Evaluator, 702-895-3320, Fax: 702-895-4180, E-mail: gradcollege@unlv.edu.

University of New Brunswick Fredericton, School of Graduate Studies, Policy Studies Program, Fredericton, NB E3B 5A3, Canada. Offers people, property and alternative dispute resolution (M Phil); philosophy politics and economics (M Phil); sustainable development (M Phil). Part-time programs available. *Faculty:* 7 full-time (4 women), 8 part-time/adjunct (4 women). *Students:* 4 full-time (2 women), 5 part-time (3 women). In 2010, 3 master's awarded. *Degree requirements:* For master's, thesis, report. *Entrance requirements:* For master's, minimum GPA of 3.5. Additional exam requirements/recommendations for international students: Required—TWE (minimum score 4), TOEFL (minimum score 600 paper-based; 250 computer-based; 100 iBT) or IELTS (minimum score 7). Application fee: $50 Canadian dollars. *Expenses:* Tuition, area resident: Full-time $3708; part-time $927 per term. International tuition: $6300 full-time. Required fees: $50 per term. *Financial support:* In 2010–11, 3 fellowships, research assistantships (averaging $5,600 per year), teaching assistantships (averaging $4,400 per year) were awarded. *Unit head:* Dr. Linda Eyre, Dean of Graduate Studies, 506-447-3044, Fax: 506-453-4817, E-mail: gradidst@unb.ca. *Application contact:* Janet Amurault, Graduate Secretary, 506-458-7558, Fax: 506-453-4817, E-mail: jamiraul@unb.ca.

The University of North Carolina at Chapel Hill, Graduate School, College of Arts and Sciences, Department of Public Policy, Chapel Hill, NC 27599. Offers PhD. *Faculty:* 11 full-time (3 women), 7 part-time/adjunct (2 women). *Students:* 20 full-time; includes 1 minority (Black or African American, non-Hispanic/Latino), 9 international. Average age 35. 33 applicants, 18% accepted, 5 enrolled. In 2010, 3 doctorates awarded. *Degree requirements:* For doctorate, thesis/dissertation. *Entrance requirements:* For doctorate, GRE General Test. *Application deadline:* For fall admission, 1/1 priority date for domestic and international students. Application fee: $60. Electronic applications accepted. *Financial support:* In 2010–11, 4 fellowships with full tuition reimbursements (averaging $17,000 per year), 10 research assistantships with full tuition reimbursements (averaging $11,000 per year), 4 teaching assistantships with full tuition reimbursements (averaging $10,000 per year) were awarded; career-related internships or fieldwork, Federal Work-Study, and stipends also available. *Faculty research:* Environmental policy; energy policy; economic development and science and technology policy; social policy; welfare, education and low-income communities. Total annual research expenditures: $460,000. *Unit head:* Dr. Michael A. Stegman, Chairman, 919-962-6849, Fax: 919-962-5824, E-mail: stegman@email.unc.edu. *Application contact:* Dr. Michael A. Stegman, Chairman, 919-962-6849, Fax: 919-962-5824, E-mail: stegman@email.unc.edu.

The University of North Carolina at Charlotte, Graduate School, College of Arts and Sciences, Department of Political Science, Charlotte, NC 28223-0001. Offers emergency management (Certificate); non-profit management (Certificate); public administration (MPA, PhD), including arts administration (MPA), emergency management (MPA), non-profit management (MPA), public finance (MPA), urban management and policy (PhD); public finance (Certificate); public policy (PhD); urban management and policy (Certificate). *Accreditation:* NASPAA. Part-time and evening/weekend programs available. *Faculty:* 19 full-time (8 women), 3 part-time/adjunct (2 women). *Students:* 51 full-time (37 women), 75 part-time (49 women); includes 32 minority (26 Black or African American, non-Hispanic/Latino; 1 Asian, non-Hispanic/Latino; 2 Hispanic/Latino; 3 Two or more races, non-Hispanic/Latino), 11 international. Average age 29. 99 applicants, 72% accepted, 42 enrolled. In 2010, 15 master's, 5 doctorates awarded. *Degree requirements:* For master's, thesis or alternative; for doctorate, thesis/dissertation. *Entrance requirements:* For master's, GRE General Test or MAT, minimum GPA of 3.0 in undergraduate major, 2.75 overall. Additional exam requirements/recommendations for international students: Required—TOEFL (minimum score 557 paper-based; 220 computer-based; 83 iBT). *Application deadline:* For fall admission, 7/1 for domestic students, 5/1 for international students; for spring admission, 11/1 for domestic students, 10/1 for international students. Applications are processed on a rolling basis. Application fee: $55. Electronic applications accepted. *Expenses:* Tuition, state resident: full-time $3464. Tuition, nonresident: full-time $14,297. Required fees: $2094. Tuition and fees vary according to course load. *Financial support:* In 2010–11, 22 students received support, including 16 research assistantships (averaging $6,943 per year), 6 teaching assistantships (averaging $9,380 per year); career-related internships or fieldwork, Federal Work-Study, institutionally sponsored loans, scholarships/grants, unspecified assistantships, and administrative assistantship also available. Support available to part-time students. Financial award application deadline: 4/1; financial award applicants required to submit FAFSA. *Faculty research:* Terrorism, public administration, nonprofit and arts administration, educational policy, social policy. Total annual research expenditures: $242,404. *Unit head:* Dr. Theodore S. Arrington, Chair, 704-687-2571, Fax: 704-687-3497, E-mail: tarrngtn@uncc.edu. *Application contact:* Kathy B. Giddings, Director of Graduate Admissions, 704-687-5503, Fax: 704-687-3279, E-mail: gradadm@uncc.edu.

University of Northern Iowa, Graduate College, Program in Public Policy, Cedar Falls, IA 50614. Offers MPP. Part-time programs available. *Students:* 23 full-time (8 women), 4 part-time (3 women); includes 4 minority (3 Black or African American, non-Hispanic/Latino; 1 Hispanic/Latino), 3 international. 32 applicants, 66% accepted, 9 enrolled. In 2010, 4 master's awarded. *Degree requirements:* For master's, comprehensive exam (for some programs). *Entrance requirements:* For master's, minimum GPA of 3.0. Additional exam requirements/recommendations for international students: Required—TOEFL (minimum score 500 paper-based; 180 computer-based; 61 iBT). *Application deadline:* For fall admission, 3/1 priority date for domestic students. Applications are processed on a rolling basis. Application fee: $50 ($70 for international students). Electronic applications accepted. *Financial support:* Career-related internships or fieldwork, Federal Work-Study, institutionally sponsored loans, tuition waivers (full), and unspecified assistantships available. Financial award application deadline: 2/1. *Unit head:* Dr. Richard Allen Hays, Director, 319-273-2910, Fax: 319-273-7126, E-mail: allen.hays@uni.edu. *Application contact:* Laurie S. Russell, Record Analyst, 319-273-2623, Fax: 319-273-2885, E-mail: laurie.russell@uni.edu.

University of Oregon, Graduate School, School of Architecture and Allied Arts, Department of Planning, Public Policy, and Management, Program in Public Policy and Management, Eugene, OR 97403. Offers MA, MPA, MS. *Accreditation:* NASPAA. Part-time and evening/weekend programs available. *Degree requirements:* For master's, thesis. *Entrance requirements:* For master's, minimum GPA of 3.0. Additional exam requirements/recommendations for international students: Required—TOEFL. *Faculty research:* Community economic development, families in poverty, health services.

University of Pennsylvania, Wharton School, Department of Business and Public Policy, Philadelphia, PA 19104. Offers MBA, PhD. *Degree requirements:* For doctorate, thesis/dissertation. *Entrance requirements:* For doctorate, GRE General Test. *Expenses:* Tuition: Full-time $25,660; part-time $4758 per course. Required fees: $2152; $270 per course. Tuition and fees vary according to course load, degree level and program. *Faculty research:* International policy, business and government, regulation, urban development and policy, transportation.

University of Pittsburgh, Graduate School of Public and International Affairs, Division of Public and Urban Affairs, Pittsburgh, PA 15260. Offers policy research and analysis (MPA); public and nonprofit management (MPA); urban and regional affairs (MPA); JD/MPA; MPA/MPIA; MPH/MPA; MSIS/MPA; MSW/MPA. Part-time and evening/weekend programs available. *Faculty:* 30 full-time (12 women), 67 part-time/adjunct (25 women). *Students:* 61 full-time (29 women), 22 part-time (16 women); includes 4 Black or African American, non-Hispanic/Latino; 1 Asian, non-Hispanic/Latino; 1 Hispanic/Latino, 8 international. Average age 25. 119 applicants, 76% accepted, 38 enrolled. In 2010, 24 master's awarded. *Degree requirements:* For master's, thesis optional, internship, capstone seminar. *Entrance requirements:* For master's, GRE General Test, 3 letters of recommendation, resume; minimum GPA of 3.2 (recommended). Additional exam requirements/recommendations for international students: Required—TOEFL (minimum score 550 paper-based; 213 computer-based; 80 iBT), TWE (minimum score 4); Recommended—IELTS (minimum score 7). *Application deadline:* For fall admission, 2/1 for domestic students, 1/15 for international students; for spring admission, 11/1 for domestic students, 8/1 for international students. Application fee: $50. Electronic applications accepted. *Expenses:* Tuition, state resident: full-time $17,304; part-time $701 per credit. Tuition, nonresident: full-time $29,554; part-time $1210 per credit. Required fees: $740; $214 per term. Tuition and fees vary according to program. *Financial support:* In 2010–11, 18 students received support. Scholarships/grants, tuition waivers (full and partial), unspecified assistantships, and student employment available. Financial award application deadline: 2/1. *Faculty research:* Disaster response management, government regulation of health and safety risks, comparative regional governance, nonprofit management, environmental policy, housing policy, strategic management. Total annual research expenditures: $892,349. *Unit head:* Dr. David Y. Miller, Director, Public and Urban Affairs Division, 412-648-7606, Fax: 412-648-2605, E-mail: dymiller@pitt.edu. *Application contact:* Elizabeth A. Hruby, Graduate Enrollment Counselor, 412-648-7640, Fax: 412-648-7641, E-mail: eah44@pitt.edu.

University of Pittsburgh, Graduate School of Public and International Affairs, Doctoral Program in Public and International Affairs, Pittsburgh, PA 15260. Offers development policy (PhD); foreign and security policy (PhD); international political economy (PhD); public administration (PhD); public policy (PhD). *Accreditation:* NASPAA. Part-time programs available. *Faculty:* 30 full-time (12 women), 67 part-time/adjunct (25 women). *Students:* 43 full-time (18 women), 3 part-time (2 women); includes 3 minority (2 Black or African American, non-Hispanic/Latino; 1 Asian, non-Hispanic/Latino), 19 international. Average age 30. 105 applicants, 11% accepted, 6 enrolled. In 2010, 11 doctorates awarded. Terminal master's awarded for partial completion of doctoral program. *Degree requirements:* For doctorate, comprehensive exam, thesis/dissertation, mid-term evaluation, preliminary exam, annual review. *Entrance requirements:* For doctorate, GRE, 3 letters of recommendation, resume, minimum GPA of 3.0 (recommended), writing sample. Additional exam requirements/recommendations for international students: Required—TOEFL (minimum score 600 paper-based; 250 computer-based; 100 iBT), TWE (minimum score 4); Recommended—IELTS (minimum score 7). *Application deadline:* For fall admission, 2/1 for domestic students, 1/15 for international students. Application fee: $50. Electronic applications accepted. *Expenses:* Tuition, state resident: full-time $17,304; part-time $701 per credit. Tuition, nonresident: full-time $29,554; part-time $1210 per credit. Required fees: $740; $214 per term. Tuition and fees vary according to program. *Financial support:* In 2010–11, 10 students received support, including 10 fellowships (averaging $41,325 per year). Financial award application deadline: 2/1. *Faculty research:* International political economy, international development, public administration, public policy, foreign policy, international security policy. Total annual research expenditures: $893,349. *Unit head:* Dr. Kevin P. Kearns, Program Coordinator, 412-648-7621, Fax: 412-648-2605, E-mail: kkearns@pitt.edu. *Application contact:* Julie Korade, Program Administrator/Graduate Enrollment Counselor, 412-648-7640, Fax: 412-648-7641, E-mail: korade@pitt.edu.

University of Pittsburgh, Graduate School of Public and International Affairs, Public Policy and Management Program for Mid-Career Professionals, Pittsburgh, PA 15260. Offers development planning (MPPM); international development (MPPM); international political economy (MPPM); international security studies (MPPM); management of non profit organizations (MPPM); metropolitan management and regional development (MPPM); policy analysis and evaluation (MPPM). Part-time programs available. *Faculty:* 30 full-time (12 women), 67 part-time/adjunct (25 women). *Students:* 14 full-time (1 woman), 34 part-time (17 women), 8 international. Average age 38. 31 applicants, 74% accepted, 15 enrolled. In 2010, 14 master's awarded. *Degree requirements:* For master's, thesis optional, capstone seminar. *Entrance requirements:* For master's, 2 letters of recommendation, resume, 5 years of supervisory or budgetary experience. Additional exam requirements/recommendations for international students: Required—TOEFL (minimum score 600 paper-based; 250 computer-based; 100 iBT), TWE (minimum score 4); Recommended—IELTS (minimum score 7). *Application deadline:* For fall admission, 6/1 priority date for domestic students, 2/15 for international students; for spring admission, 1/1 priority date for domestic students, 8/1 for international students. Applications are processed on a rolling basis. Application fee: $50. Electronic applications accepted. *Expenses:* Tuition, state resident: full-time $17,304; part-time $701 per credit. Tuition, nonresident: full-time $29,554; part-time $1210 per credit. Required fees: $740; $214 per term. Tuition and fees vary according to program. *Financial support:* In 2010–11, 14 students received support. Scholarships/grants and tuition waivers (partial) available. Support available to part-time students. Financial award application deadline: 2/1. *Faculty research:* Nonprofit management, urban and regional affairs, policy analysis and evaluation, security and intelligence studies, global political economy, nongovernmental organizations, civil society, development planning and environmental sustainability, human security. Total annual research expenditures: $892,349. *Unit head:* Dr. George Dougherty, Director, Executive Education, 412-648-7603, Fax: 412-648-2605, E-mail: gwdjr@pitt.edu. *Application contact:* Michael T. Rizzi, Associate Director of Student Services, 412-648-7640, Fax: 412-648-7641, E-mail: rizzim@pitt.edu.

University of Puerto Rico, Río Piedras, Graduate School of Planning, San Juan, PR 00931-3300. Offers economic planning systems (MP); environmental planning (MP); social policy and planning (MP); urban and territorial planning (MP). *Accreditation:* ACSP. Part-time programs available. *Degree requirements:* For master's, comprehensive exam, thesis, planning project defense. *Entrance requirements:* For master's, PAEG, GRE, minimum GPA of 3.0, 2 letters of recommendation. *Faculty research:* Municipalities, historic Atlas, Puerto Rico, economic future.

University of Regina, Faculty of Graduate Studies and Research, Johnson-Shoyama Graduate School of Public Policy, Regina, SK S4S 0A2, Canada. Offers economic analysis for public policy (Master's Certificate); health systems management (Master's Certificate); health systems research (MPP); non-profit management (Master's Certificate); public management (MPA, Master's Certificate); public policy (MPA, MPP, PhD); public policy analysis (Master's Certificate). Part-time programs available. *Faculty:* 7 full-time (3 women). *Students:* 60 full-time (28 women), 71 part-time (36 women). 101 applicants, 72% accepted. In 2010, 48 master's awarded. *Degree requirements:* For master's, thesis; for doctorate, thesis/dissertation. *Entrance requirements:* For doctorate, master's degree, intended research program in an area of public policy. Additional exam requirements/recommendations for international students: Required—TOEFL (minimum score 580 paper-based; 80 iBT), GRE. *Application deadline:* For fall admission, 2/1 for domestic and international students. Application fee: $100. Electronic applications

Public Policy

University of Regina *(continued)*
accepted. *Expenses:* Contact institution. *Financial support:* In 2010–11, 11 fellowships (averaging $18,000 per year), 2 research assistantships (averaging $16,500 per year), 15 teaching assistantships (averaging $6,759 per year) were awarded; scholarships/grants also available. Financial award application deadline: 6/15. *Faculty research:* Governance and administration, public finance, public policy analysis, non-governmental organizations and alternative service delivery, micro-economics for policy analysis. *Unit head:* Dr. Michael Atkinson, Director, 306-996-1984, Fax: 306-585-5461, E-mail: michael.atkinson@usask.ca. *Application contact:* Elaine Groenendyk, Program Advisor, 306-585-5462, Fax: 306-585-5461, E-mail: elaine.groenendyk@uregina.ca.

University of Rhode Island, Graduate School, College of Arts and Sciences, Department of Political Science, Kingston, RI 02881. Offers political science (MA), including American politics, comparative government, international relations, public policy; public policy and administration (MPA); MLIS/MPA. Part-time programs available. *Faculty:* 10 full-time (4 women). *Students:* 17 full-time (10 women), 31 part-time (19 women); includes 10 minority (4 Black or African American, non-Hispanic/Latino; 1 Asian, non-Hispanic/Latino; 5 Hispanic/Latino). In 2010, 22 master's awarded. *Degree requirements:* For master's, comprehensive exam (for some programs), thesis optional. *Entrance requirements:* For master's, GRE, GMAT or MAT, 2 letters of recommendation. Additional exam requirements/recommendations for international students: Required—TOEFL (minimum score 550 paper-based; 213 computer-based). *Application deadline:* For fall admission, 2/1 for international students; for spring admission, 7/15 for international students. Application fee: $65. Electronic applications accepted. *Expenses:* Tuition, state resident: full-time $9588; part-time $533 per credit hour. Tuition, nonresident: full-time $22,968; part-time $1276 per credit hour. Required fees: $1282; $68 per semester. Tuition and fees vary according to program. *Financial support:* In 2010–11, 4 teaching assistantships with full tuition reimbursements (averaging $9,263 per year) were awarded. Financial award applicants required to submit FAFSA. *Unit head:* Dr. Gerry Tyler, Department Chair, 401-874-4053, Fax: 401-874-4072, E-mail: gtyler@uri.edu. *Application contact:* Dr. Gerry Tyler, Department Chair, 401-874-4053, Fax: 401-874-4072, E-mail: gtyler@uri.edu.

University of Saskatchewan, College of Graduate Studies and Research, School of Public Policy, Saskatoon, SK S7N 5A2, Canada. Offers MIT, MPA, MPP, PhD.

University of Southern California, Graduate School, School of Policy, Planning, and Development, Doctor of Philosophy in Public Policy and Management Program, Los Angeles, CA 90089. Offers PhD. *Faculty:* 51 full-time (12 women), 100 part-time/adjunct (30 women). *Students:* 9 full-time (5 women); includes 1 minority (Hispanic/Latino), 3 international. 95 applicants, 11% accepted, 6 enrolled. *Degree requirements:* For doctorate, thesis/dissertation. *Entrance requirements:* For doctorate, GRE. Additional exam requirements/recommendations for international students: Required—TOEFL (minimum score 600 paper-based; 250 computer-based; 100 iBT). *Application deadline:* For fall admission, 12/1 for domestic and international students. Application fee: $85. Electronic applications accepted. *Expenses:* Tuition: Full-time $31,240; part-time $1420 per unit. Required fees: $600. One-time fee: $35 full-time. Full-time tuition and fees vary according to degree level and program. *Financial support:* In 2010–11, 24 students received support, including 24 research assistantships with full tuition reimbursements available (averaging $18,024 per year); scholarships/grants and tuition waivers (full and partial) also available. *Faculty research:* Governance: effective institutions, leadership, management, community and economic development, institutional analysis, civic engagement. Total annual research expenditures: $6.2 million. *Unit head:* Dr. Shui Yan Tang, Director, 213-740-0379, Fax: 213-740-0001, E-mail: stang@usc.edu. *Application contact:* Marisol R. Gonzalez, Director of Recruitment and Admission, 213-740-0550, Fax: 213-740-7573, E-mail: marisolr@usc.edu.

University of Southern California, Graduate School, School of Policy, Planning, and Development, Public Policy Programs, Los Angeles, CA 90089. Offers homeland security and public policy (Graduate Certificate); public policy (MPP, Graduate Certificate); MPP/JD. Part-time programs available. *Faculty:* 51 full-time (12 women), 100 part-time/adjunct (30 women). *Students:* 111 full-time (65 women), 7 part-time (4 women); includes 51 minority (6 Black or African American, non-Hispanic/Latino; 17 Asian, non-Hispanic/Latino; 24 Hispanic/Latino; 4 Two or more races, non-Hispanic/Latino), 15 international. 275 applicants, 74% accepted, 61 enrolled. In 2010, 32 master's, 1 other advanced degree awarded. Terminal master's awarded for partial completion of doctoral program. *Degree requirements:* For master's, practicum. *Entrance requirements:* For master's, GRE. Additional exam requirements/recommendations for international students: Required—TOEFL (minimum score 600 paper-based; 250 computer-based; 100 iBT). *Application deadline:* For fall admission, 12/15 priority date for domestic and international students; for spring admission, 11/1 for domestic and international students. Applications are processed on a rolling basis. Application fee: $85. Electronic applications accepted. *Expenses:* Tuition: Full-time $31,240; part-time $1420 per unit. Required fees: $600. One-time fee: $35 full-time. Full-time tuition and fees vary according to degree level and program. *Financial support:* In 2010–11, 73 students received support, including 2 research assistantships with full tuition reimbursements available (averaging $14,709 per year); scholarships/grants and tuition waivers (full and partial) also available. Financial award application deadline: 12/15; financial award applicants required to submit CSS PROFILE or FAFSA. *Faculty research:* Urban political economy, community and economic development, environmental policy, transportation policy, housing policy. Total annual research expenditures: $6.2 million. *Unit head:* Dr. Gary Painter, Director, 213-740-8754, Fax: 213-740-7573, E-mail: gpainter@usc.edu. *Application contact:* Marisol R. Gonzalez, Director of Recruitment and Admission, 213-740-0550, Fax: 213-740-7573, E-mail: marisolr@usc.edu.

University of Southern Maine, Edmund S. Muskie School of Public Service, Doctoral Program in Public Policy, Portland, ME 04104-9300. Offers PhD. Applicants accepted in odd numbered years only. Part-time and evening/weekend programs available. *Degree requirements:* For doctorate, comprehensive exam, thesis/dissertation. *Entrance requirements:* For doctorate, GRE. Additional exam requirements/recommendations for international students: Required—TOEFL. Electronic applications accepted. *Faculty research:* Health policy, community planning and development, education policy, environmental policy.

University of Southern Maine, Edmund S. Muskie School of Public Service, Program in Public Policy and Management, Portland, ME 04104-9300. Offers child and family policy (Certificate); non-profit management (Certificate); public policy and management (MPPM); JD/MPPM. Part-time and evening/weekend programs available. Postbaccalaureate distance learning degree programs offered (minimal on-campus study). *Degree requirements:* For master's, thesis, capstone project, field experience. *Entrance requirements:* For master's, GRE General Test or LSAT. Additional exam requirements/recommendations for international students: Required—TOEFL. Electronic applications accepted. *Faculty research:* Sustainable communities, juvenile justice, program management, nonprofit management.

The University of Texas at Austin, Graduate School, Lyndon B. Johnson School of Public Affairs, Austin, TX 78712-1111. Offers global policy studies (MGPS); public affairs (MP Aff); public policy (PhD); JD/MP Aff; MBA/MP Aff; MP Aff/MA; MP Aff/MSE. *Accreditation:* NASPAA (one or more programs are accredited). Part-time programs available. *Degree requirements:* For master's, thesis, summer internship; for doctorate, thesis/dissertation. *Entrance requirements:* For master's, GRE General Test; for doctorate, GRE General Test, master's degree in policy-related field. Additional exam requirements/recommendations for international students: Required—TOEFL. Electronic applications accepted. *Faculty research:* Human resource development, health and social policy, philanthropy and community service, ethical leadership, urban and international policy, science and technology policy.

The University of Texas at Brownsville, Graduate Studies, College of Liberal Arts, Program in Public Policy and Management, Brownsville, TX 78520-4991. Offers MPPM. *Degree requirements:* For master's, thesis. *Entrance requirements:* For master's, GRE, 2 letters of recommendation.

The University of Texas at Dallas, School of Economic, Political and Policy Sciences, Program in Public Policy and Political Economy, Richardson, TX 75080. Offers international political economy (MS); public policy (MPP); public policy and political economy (PhD). Part-time and evening/weekend programs available. *Faculty:* 19 full-time (5 women), 1 (woman) part-time/adjunct. *Students:* 59 full-time (28 women), 41 part-time (17 women); includes 30 minority (14 Black or African American, non-Hispanic/Latino; 8 Asian, non-Hispanic/Latino; 8 Hispanic/Latino), 17 international. Average age 35. 84 applicants, 48% accepted, 24 enrolled. In 2010, 9 master's, 11 doctorates awarded. *Degree requirements:* For doctorate, thesis/dissertation. *Entrance requirements:* For master's and doctorate, GRE General Test, minimum GPA of 3.0 in upper-level course work in field. Additional exam requirements/recommendations for international students: Required—TOEFL (minimum score 550 paper-based; 215 computer-based). *Application deadline:* For fall admission, 7/15 for domestic students, 5/1 priority date for international students; for spring admission, 11/15 for domestic students, 9/1 priority date for international students. Applications are processed on a rolling basis. Application fee: $50 ($100 for international students). Electronic applications accepted. *Expenses:* Tuition, state resident: full-time $10,248; part-time $569 per credit hour. Tuition, nonresident: full-time $18,544; part-time $1030 per credit hour. Tuition and fees vary according to course load. *Financial support:* In 2010–11, 45 students received support, including 6 research assistantships with partial tuition reimbursements available (averaging $14,850 per year), 14 teaching assistantships with partial tuition reimbursements available (averaging $11,517 per year); career-related internships or fieldwork, Federal Work-Study, institutionally sponsored loans, scholarships/grants, and unspecified assistantships also available. Support available to part-time students. Financial award application deadline: 4/30; financial award applicants required to submit FAFSA. *Faculty research:* Ethnicity, community and local public good provision; community mental health policy; Texas Schools Project; biological and chemical arms control; cross-disciplinary applications of quantitative methodology. *Unit head:* Dr. Paul Jargowski, Program Head, 972-883-2992, Fax: 972-883-6297, E-mail: jargo@utdallas.edu. *Application contact:* Dr. Marie I. Chevrier, Associate Program Head, 972-883-2727, Fax: 972-883-6297, E-mail: chevrier@utdallas.edu.

See Close-Up on page 811.

The University of Texas at El Paso, Graduate School, Institute for Policy and Economic Development, El Paso, TX 79968-0001. Offers border administration (Certificate); homeland security (Certificate); intelligence and national security (MS, Certificate); leadership studies (MA); public administration (MPA). *Accreditation:* NASPAA. Part-time and evening/weekend programs available. *Students:* 187 (57 women); includes 19 Black or African American, non-Hispanic/Latino; 1 American Indian or Alaska Native, non-Hispanic/Latino; 5 Asian, non-Hispanic/Latino; 99 Hispanic/Latino, 5 international. 142 applicants, 77% accepted. In 2010, 76 master's awarded. *Degree requirements:* For master's, thesis optional. *Entrance requirements:* For master's, GRE, statement of purpose, letters of recommendation. Additional exam requirements/recommendations for international students: Required—TOEFL; Recommended—IELTS. *Application deadline:* For fall admission, 8/1 for domestic students, 3/1 for international students; for spring admission, 10/1 for domestic students, 9/1 for international students. Applications are processed on a rolling basis. Application fee: $45 ($80 for international students). Electronic applications accepted. *Financial support:* Fellowships with partial tuition reimbursements, research assistantships with partial tuition reimbursements, teaching assistantships with partial tuition reimbursements, institutionally sponsored loans, scholarships/grants, health care benefits, tuition waivers (partial), and unspecified assistantships available. Support available to part-time students. Financial award application deadline: 3/15; financial award applicants required to submit FAFSA. *Unit head:* Dr. Dennis Soden, Director, 915-747-7974, Fax: 915-747-7948, E-mail: desoden@utep.edu. *Application contact:* Dr. Patricia D. Witherspoon, Dean of the Graduate School, 915-747-5491, Fax: 915-747-5788, E-mail: withersp@utep.edu.

University of the Pacific, McGeorge School of Law, Sacramento, CA 95817. Offers advocacy (JD); criminal justice (JD); experiential law teaching (LL M); intellectual property (JD); international legal studies (JD); international water resources law (LL M, JSD); law (JD); public law and policy (JD); public policy and law (LL M); tax (JD); transnational business practice (LL M); JD/MBA; JD/MPPA. *Accreditation:* ABA. Part-time and evening/weekend programs available. *Faculty:* 49 full-time (22 women), 45 part-time/adjunct (15 women). *Students:* 756 full-time (362 women), 303 part-time (148 women); includes 27 Black or African American, non-Hispanic/Latino; 19 American Indian or Alaska Native, non-Hispanic/Latino; 150 Asian, non-Hispanic/Latino; 60 Hispanic/Latino, 27 international. Average age 27. 3,209 applicants, 42% accepted, 344 enrolled. In 2010, 307 first professional degrees, 36 master's awarded. *Degree requirements:* For master's, thesis (for some programs); for doctorate, thesis/dissertation. *Entrance requirements:* For JD, LSAT; for master's, JD; for doctorate, LL M. Additional exam requirements/recommendations for international students: Required—TOEFL (minimum score 600 paper-based; 250 computer-based; 100 iBT). *Application deadline:* For fall admission, 3/15 priority date for domestic students. Applications are processed on a rolling basis. Application fee: $50. Electronic applications accepted. *Expenses:* Contact institution. *Financial support:* Fellowships, research assistantships, teaching assistantships, career-related internships or fieldwork, Federal Work-Study, institutionally sponsored loans, and scholarships/grants available. Support available to part-time students. Financial award applicants required to submit FAFSA. *Faculty research:* International legal studies, public policy and law, advocacy, intellectual property law, taxation, criminal law. *Unit head:* Elizabeth Rindskopf Parker, Dean, 916-739-7151, E-mail: elizabeth@pacific.edu. *Application contact:* 916-739-7105, Fax: 916-739-7301, E-mail: mcgeorge@pacific.edu.

University of Tulsa, College of Law, Tulsa, OK 74104. Offers American Indian and indigenous law (LL M); American law for foreign lawyers (LL M); comparative and international law (Certificate); entrepreneurial law (Certificate); health law (Certificate); law (JD); Native American law (Certificate); public policy (Certificate); resources, energy, and environmental law (Certificate); JD/M Tax; JD/MA; JD/MBA; JD/MS; JD/MSF. *Accreditation:* ABA. Part-time programs available. *Faculty:* 28 full-time (12 women), 20 part-time/adjunct (5 women). *Students:* 368 full-time (140 women), 38 part-time (18 women); includes 10 Black or African American, non-Hispanic/Latino; 36 American Indian or Alaska Native, non-Hispanic/Latino; 8 Asian, non-Hispanic/Latino; 14 Hispanic/Latino; 12 Two or more races, non-Hispanic/Latino, 1 international. Average age 27. 1,373 applicants, 43% accepted, 146 enrolled. In 2010, 130 first professional degrees, 6 master's awarded. *Entrance requirements:* For JD, LSAT, BS or BA from accredited college/university; for master's, JD or equivalent from non-US university. Additional exam requirements/recommendations for international students: Required—TOEFL (minimum score 570 paper-based; 230 computer-based; 90 iBT), IELTS (minimum score 7). *Application deadline:* For fall admission, 2/1 priority date for domestic and international students. Applications are processed on a rolling basis. Application fee: $30. Electronic applications accepted. *Expenses:* Contact institution. *Financial support:* In 2010–11, 176 students received support. Career-related internships or fieldwork, Federal Work-Study, and scholarships/grants available. Support available to part-time students. Financial award applicants required to submit FAFSA. *Faculty research:* International law, Native American law, criminal law, commercial speech, copyright law. *Unit head:* Janet Levit, Dean, 918-631-2400, Fax: 918-631-3126, E-mail: janet-levit@utulsa.edu. *Application contact:* April M. Fox, Assistant Dean of Admissions and Financial Aid, 918-631-2406, Fax: 918-631-3630, E-mail: april-fox@utulsa.edu.

University of Virginia, Frank Batten Sr. School of Leadership and Public Policy, Program in Public Policy, Charlottesville, VA 22903. Offers MPP. *Students:* 27 full-time (19 women); includes 4 Black or African American, non-Hispanic/Latino; 2 Asian, non-Hispanic/Latino; 2 Hispanic/Latino. Average age 22. In 2010, 29 master's awarded. *Application deadline:* For fall admission, 2/20 for domestic and international students. Application fee: $60. *Unit head:* Dr. Harry Harding, Dean, 434-924-0812, Fax: 434-243-2318. *Application contact:* Howard H. Hoege, Director of Graduate Admissions, 434-243-4383, Fax: 434-243-2318, E-mail: hhh@virginia.edu.

University of Washington, Graduate School, Daniel J. Evans School of Public Affairs, Seattle, WA 98195. Offers public administration (MPA); public policy and management (PhD);

JD/MPA; MPA/MAIS; MPA/MPH; MPA/MS; MPA/MUP. *Accreditation:* NASPAA. Part-time and evening/weekend programs available. *Degree requirements:* For master's, thesis, internship or cooperative experience. *Entrance requirements:* For master's and doctorate, GRE General Test, minimum GPA of 3.0. Additional exam requirements/recommendations for international students: Required—TOEFL (minimum score 580 paper-based; 237 computer-based; 92 iBT). Electronic applications accepted. *Faculty research:* Environmental policy, education and social policy, nonprofit management, international affairs, urban and regional development.

University of Washington, Bothell, Program in Policy Studies, Bothell, WA 98011-8246. Offers MA. Evening/weekend programs available. *Faculty:* 9 full-time (4 women), 2 part-time/adjunct (both women). *Students:* 27 full-time (13 women), 6 part-time (5 women); includes 8 minority (4 Black or African American, non-Hispanic/Latino; 3 Asian, non-Hispanic/Latino; 1 Hispanic/Latino), 2 international. Average age 32. 43 applicants, 63% accepted, 17 enrolled. In 2010, 22 master's awarded. *Degree requirements:* For master's, thesis. *Entrance requirements:* For master's, GRE, 100-level statistics and micro-economics courses. Additional exam requirements/recommendations for international students: Required—TOEFL. *Application deadline:* For fall admission, 3/1 for domestic and international students. Application fee: $65. Electronic applications accepted. *Expenses:* Tuition, state resident: full-time $10,870; part-time $518 per quarter hour. Tuition, nonresident: full-time $24,210; part-time $1153 per quarter hour. Required fees: $495; $24 per quarter hour. Part-time tuition and fees vary according to course load, program and student level. *Financial support:* In 2010–11, 9 students received support, including 5 fellowships (averaging $1,000 per year), 1 research assistantship (averaging $1,000 per year); Federal Work-Study and unspecified assistantships also available. Financial award applicants required to submit FAFSA. *Faculty research:* Policy studies, cultural studies, cultural and environmental politics, disability studies, public policy. *Unit head:* Prof. Bruce Burgett, Director, 425-352-5452, Fax: 425-352-3462, E-mail: bburgett@uwb.edu. *Application contact:* Andrew Bruslétten, Program Manager, 425-352-5427, Fax: 425-352-3462, E-mail: abrusletten@uwb.edu.

Vanderbilt University, Graduate School, Program in Community Research and Action, Nashville, TN 37240-1001. Offers MS, PhD. *Faculty:* 18 full-time (7 women), 4 part-time/adjunct (2 women). *Students:* 25 full-time (13 women), 3 part-time (2 women); includes 3 Black or African American, non-Hispanic/Latino; 2 Two or more races, non-Hispanic/Latino. Average age 32. 75 applicants, 12% accepted, 6 enrolled. In 2010, 6 master's awarded. *Degree requirements:* For master's, thesis; for doctorate, thesis/dissertation, internship, fundable grant proposal. *Entrance requirements:* For doctorate, GRE General Test. Additional exam requirements/recommendations for international students: Required—TOEFL (minimum score 570 paper-based; 230 computer-based; 88 iBT). *Application deadline:* For fall admission, 12/31 for domestic and international students. Application fee: $0. Electronic applications accepted. *Financial support:* Fellowships with tuition reimbursements, research assistantships with full tuition reimbursements, teaching assistantships with full tuition reimbursements, Federal Work-Study, institutionally sponsored loans, scholarships/grants, traineeships, and health care benefits available. Financial award application deadline: 1/15; financial award applicants required to submit CSS PROFILE or FAFSA. *Faculty research:* Applied psychological research, community theory, mental health, public policy, race dynamics. *Unit head:* Joseph Cunningham, Chair, 615-322-6881, Fax: 615-343-2661, E-mail: joe.cunningham@vanderbilt.edu. *Application contact:* Paul Dokecki, Director of Graduate Studies, 615-322-6881, E-mail: paul.r.dokecki@vanderbilt.edu.

Virginia Commonwealth University, Graduate School, College of Humanities and Sciences, Wilder School of Government and Public Affairs, Center for Public Policy, Richmond, VA 23284-9005. Offers public policy and administration (PhD). *Students:* 19 full-time (10 women), 88 part-time (53 women); includes 35 minority (33 Black or African American, non-Hispanic/Latino; 1 Asian, non-Hispanic/Latino; 1 Hispanic/Latino), 16 international. 35 applicants, 63% accepted, 18 enrolled. In 2010, 11 doctorates awarded. *Degree requirements:* For doctorate, thesis/dissertation. *Entrance requirements:* For doctorate, GMAT, GRE General Test, LSAT, or MAT. Additional exam requirements/recommendations for international students: Required—TOEFL (minimum score 600 paper-based; 250 computer-based; 100 iBT); Recommended—IELTS (minimum score 6.5). *Application deadline:* For fall admission, 3/15 for domestic students. Application fee: $50. Electronic applications accepted. *Expenses:* Tuition, state resident: full-time $4308; part-time $479 per credit hour. Tuition, nonresident: full-time $8942; part-time $994 per credit hour. Required fees: $2000; $85 per credit hour. Tuition and fees vary according to course level, course load, degree level, campus/location and program. *Financial support:* Fellowships, career-related internships or fieldwork and Federal Work-Study available. Support available to part-time students. Financial award applicants required to submit FAFSA. *Unit head:* Dr. Carl Ameringer, Program Chair, 804-828-6837, E-mail: ppa@vcu.edu. *Application contact:* Lisbeth D. Dannenbrink, Program Recruitment Contact, 804-828-6837, E-mail: lddannenbrin@vcu.edu.

Virginia Polytechnic Institute and State University, Graduate School, College of Architecture and Urban Studies, Center for Public Administration and Policy, Blacksburg, VA 24061. Offers Certificate. *Accreditation:* NASPAA. *Students:* 63 full-time (30 women), 112 part-time (48 women); includes 25 Black or African American, non-Hispanic/Latino; 6 Asian, non-Hispanic/Latino; 3 Hispanic/Latino, 12 international. Average age 36. 80 applicants, 64% accepted, 29 enrolled. *Entrance requirements:* Additional exam requirements/recommendations for international students: Required—TOEFL (minimum score 550 paper-based; 213 computer-based). *Application deadline:* For fall admission, 7/1 for domestic and international students; for spring admission, 12/1 for domestic and international students. Applications are processed on a rolling basis. Application fee: $65. Electronic applications accepted. *Expenses:* Tuition, state resident: full-time $9399; part-time $488 per credit hour. Tuition, nonresident: full-time $17,854; part-time $957.75 per credit hour. Required fees: $1534. Full-time tuition and fees vary according to program. *Financial support:* Career-related internships or fieldwork, Federal Work-Study, scholarships/grants, health care benefits, and unspecified assistantships available. Financial award application deadline: 1/15. *Faculty research:* Public administration theory, strategic management, ethics, the Constitution, computer-assisted creativity. *Unit head:* Dr. Brian J. Cook, UNIT HEAD, 540-231-3438, Fax: 540-231-7067, E-mail: brian_j_cook@vt.edu. *Application contact:* Laura French, Contact, 703-231-5133, Fax: 540-231-7067, E-mail: lhf@vt.edu.

Virginia Polytechnic Institute and State University, Graduate School, College of Science, Program in Biomedical Technology Development and Management, Blacksburg, VA 24061. Offers MS. *Students:* 5 part-time (4 women); includes 3 Asian, non-Hispanic/Latino. Average age 25. 2 applicants, 100% accepted, 2 enrolled. *Degree requirements:* For master's, comprehensive exam (for some programs), thesis (for some programs). *Entrance requirements:* For master's, GRE. Additional exam requirements/recommendations for international students: Required—TOEFL (minimum score 550 paper-based; 213 computer-based). *Application deadline:* For fall admission, 7/1 for domestic and international students; for spring admission, 12/1 for domestic and international students. Applications are processed on a rolling basis. Application fee: $65. Electronic applications accepted. *Expenses:* Tuition, state resident: full-time $9399; part-time $488 per credit hour. Tuition, nonresident: full-time $17,854; part-time $957.75 per credit hour. Required fees: $1534. Full-time tuition and fees vary according to program. *Financial support:* Career-related internships or fieldwork, Federal Work-Study, scholarships/grants, health care benefits, and unspecified assistantships available. Total annual research expenditures: $289,400. *Unit head:* Dr. Kenneth H. Wong, UNIT HEAD, 703-518-2978, Fax: 540-231-7511, E-mail: khwong@vt.edu. *Application contact:* Jennifer LeFurgy, Contact, 703-518-2710, Fax: 540-231-7511, E-mail: jlefurgy@vt.edu.

Walden University, Graduate Programs, Richard W. Riley College of Education and Leadership, Minneapolis, MN 55401. Offers administrator leadership for teaching and learning (Ed D, Ed S); adult learning (MS), including developmental education, online teaching, teaching adults English as a second language, training and performance management; college teaching and learning (Postbaccalaureate Certificate); curriculum, instruction and assessment (Ed D, Postbaccalaureate Certificate); curriculum, instruction, and professional development (Ed S); early childhood education (birth-grade 3) (MAT); early childhood studies (MS), including administration, management and leadership, early childhood public policy and advocacy, teaching adults in the early childhood field, teaching and diversity; education (MS, PhD), including adolescent literacy and technology (grades 6-12) (MS), adult education leadership (PhD), community college leadership (PhD), curriculum, instruction, and assessment, early childhood education (PhD), educational leadership (MS), educational technology (PhD), elementary reading and literacy (MS), elementary reading and mathematics (MS), emotional/behavioral disorders (K-12) (MS), general program, higher education (PhD), integrating technology in the classroom (MS), K-12 educational leadership (PhD), leadership, policy and change (PhD), learning disabilities (K-12) (MS), learning, instruction and innovation (PhD), literacy and learning in the content areas (MS), mathematics (grades 6-8) (MS), mathematics (grades K-5) (MS), middle level education (grades 5-8) (MS), professional development (MS), science (grades K-8) (MS), self-designed (PhD), special education (PhD), special education (non-licensure) (MS), teacher leadership (grades K-12) (MS), teaching English language learners (grades K-12) (MS); educational leadership and administration (principal preparation) (Ed S); educational technology (Ed S); engaging culturally diverse learners (Postbaccalaureate Certificate); enrollment management and institutional marketing (Postbaccalaureate Certificate); higher education (MS), including college teaching and learning, enrollment management and institutional planning, global higher education, leadership for student success, online and distance learning; higher education and adult learning (Ed D); higher education leadership (Ed D); instructional design (Postbaccalaureate Certificate); instructional design and technology (MS), including general program (MS, PhD), online learning, training and performance improvement; integrating technology in the classroom (Postbaccalaureate Certificate); online learning (Postbaccalaureate Certificate); professional development (Postbaccalaureate Certificate); special education (Ed D, Ed S); special education: emotional/behavioral disorders (K-12) (MAT); special education: learning disabilities (K-12) (MAT); teacher leadership (Ed D, Ed S, Postbaccalaureate Certificate); training and performance management (Postbaccalaureate Certificate). Part-time and evening/weekend programs available. Postbaccalaureate distance learning degree programs offered (minimal on-campus study). *Faculty:* 61 full-time (44 women), 822 part-time/adjunct (539 women). *Students:* 13,130 full-time (10,679 women), 1,719 part-time (1,437 women); includes 5,153 minority (4,233 Black or African American, non-Hispanic/Latino; 89 American Indian or Alaska Native, non-Hispanic/Latino; 161 Asian, non-Hispanic/Latino; 542 Hispanic/Latino; 12 Native Hawaiian or other Pacific Islander, non-Hispanic/Latino; 116 Two or more races, non-Hispanic/Latino), 325 international. Average age 38. In 2010, 4,656 master's, 306 doctorates, 65 other advanced degrees awarded. *Degree requirements:* For doctorate, thesis/dissertation (for some programs), residency; for other advanced degree, residency (for some programs). *Entrance requirements:* For master's, bachelor's degree or equivalent in related field; minimum GPA of 2.5; official transcripts; goal statement; access to computer and Internet; for doctorate, master's degree or equivalent in related field; minimum GPA of 3.0; official transcripts; three years' related professional/academic experience (preferred); access to computer and Internet; for other advanced degree, master's degree or equivalent in related field; minimum GPA of 3.0; 3 years related professional/academic experience (preferred); access to computer and Internet (Ed S). Additional exam requirements/recommendations for international students: Required—TOEFL (minimum score 550 paper-based; 213 computer-based), IELTS (minimum score 6.5), TOEFL (minimum score 550 paper-based; 213 computer-based), IELTS (minimum score 6.5), or Michigan English Language Assessment Battery (minimum score 82). *Application deadline:* Applications are processed on a rolling basis. Application fee: $50. Electronic applications accepted. *Expenses:* Tuition: Full-time $10,274; part-time $445 per credit. Tuition and fees vary according to course load, degree level and program. *Financial support:* In 2010–11, 1 fellowship was awarded; Federal Work-Study, scholarships/grants, unspecified assistantships, and family tuition reduction, active duty/veteran tuition reduction, group tuition reduction, interest-free payment plans also available. Support available to part-time students. Financial award applicants required to submit FAFSA. *Unit head:* Dr. Kate Steffens, Dean, 800-925-3368. *Application contact:* Jennifer Hall, Vice President of Enrollment Management, 866-4-WALDEN, E-mail: info@waldenu.edu.

Walden University, Graduate Programs, School of Counseling and Social Service, Minneapolis, MN 55401. Offers career counseling (MS); counselor education and supervision (PhD), including consultation, counseling and social change, forensic mental health counseling, general program, nonprofit management and leadership, trauma and crisis; human services (PhD), including clinical social work, counseling, criminal justice, disaster, crisis and intervention, family studies and intervention strategies, general program, human services administration, public health, self-designed, social policy analysis and planning; marriage, couple, and family counseling (MS), including forensic counseling, trauma and crisis counseling; mental health counseling (MS), including forensic counseling. Part-time and evening/weekend programs available. Postbaccalaureate distance learning degree programs offered (minimal on-campus study). *Faculty:* 25 full-time (17 women), 241 part-time/adjunct (162 women). *Students:* 2,687 full-time (2,269 women), 536 part-time (473 women); includes 1,582 minority (1,319 Black or African American, non-Hispanic/Latino; 34 American Indian or Alaska Native, non-Hispanic/Latino; 29 Asian, non-Hispanic/Latino; 142 Hispanic/Latino; 58 Two or more races, non-Hispanic/Latino), 47 international. Average age 38. In 2010, 182 master's, 8 doctorates awarded. *Degree requirements:* For master's, residency (for some programs); for doctorate, thesis/dissertation, residency. *Entrance requirements:* For master's, bachelor's degree or equivalent in related field, minimum GPA of 2.5; for doctorate, master's degree or equivalent in related field; minimum GPA of 3.0; official transcripts; three years' related professional/academic experience (preferred); access to computer and Internet. Additional exam requirements/recommendations for international students: Required—TOEFL (minimum score 550 paper-based; 213 computer-based), IELTS (minimum score 6.5), TOEFL (minimum score 550 paper-based; 213 computer-based), IELTS (minimum score 6.5), or Michigan English Language Assessment Battery (minimum score 82). *Application deadline:* Applications are processed on a rolling basis. Application fee: $50. Electronic applications accepted. *Expenses:* Tuition: Full-time $10,274; part-time $445 per credit. Tuition and fees vary according to course load, degree level and program. *Financial support:* Fellowships, Federal Work-Study, scholarships/grants, unspecified assistantships, and family tuition reduction, active duty/veteran tuition reduction, group tuition reduction, interest-free payment plans available. Support available to part-time students. Financial award applicants required to submit FAFSA. *Unit head:* Dr. Savitri Dixon-Saxon, Associate Dean, 800-925-3368. *Application contact:* Jennifer Hall, Vice President of Enrollment Management, 866-4-WALDEN, E-mail: info@waldenu.edu.

Walden University, Graduate Programs, School of Public Policy and Administration, Minneapolis, MN 55401. Offers criminal justice (MPA); emergency management (MPA); government management (Postbaccalaureate Certificate); health policy (MPA); homeland security policy (MPA); homeland security policy and coordination (MPA); interdisciplinary policy studies (MPA); international nongovernmental organizations (ngos) (MPA); law and public policy (MPA); local government management for sustainable communities (MPA); nonprofit management (Postbaccalaureate Certificate); nonprofit management and leadership (MPA, MS); policy analysis (MPA); public management and leadership (MPA); public policy and administration (MPA, PhD), including criminal justice (PhD), emergency management (PhD), health policy (PhD), health services (PhD), homeland security policy (PhD), homeland security policy and coordination (PhD), interdisciplinary policy studies (PhD), international nongovernmental organizations (PhD), law and public policy (PhD), local government management for sustainable communities (PhD), nonprofit management and leadership (PhD), policy analysis (PhD), public management and leadership (PhD), terrorism, mediation, and peace (PhD); terrorism, mediation, and peace (MPA). Part-time and evening/weekend programs available. Postbaccalaureate distance learning degree programs offered (minimal on-campus study). *Faculty:* 10 full-time (5 women), 117 part-time/adjunct (49 women). *Students:* 1,408 full-time (901 women), 599 part-time (392 women); includes 1,022 Black or African American, non-Hispanic/Latino; 11 American Indian or Alaska Native, non-Hispanic/Latino; 37 Asian, non-Hispanic/Latino; 64 Hispanic/Latino; 26 Two or more races, non-Hispanic/Latino, 47 international. Average age 40. In 2010, 311 master's, 23 doctorates awarded. *Degree requirements:* For doctorate, thesis/dissertation, residency. *Entrance requirements:* For master's, bachelor's degree or equivalent in related field, minimum GPA of 2.5; for doctorate, master's degree or equivalent in related field;

Public Policy

Walden University (continued)
minimum GPA of 3.0; official transcripts; three years of related professional/academic experience (preferred); access to computer and Internet. Additional exam requirements/recommendations for international students: Required—TOEFL (minimum score 550 paper-based; 213 computer-based), IELTS (minimum score 6.5), TOEFL (minimum score 550 paper-based; 213 computer-based), IELTS (minimum score 6.5), or Michigan English Language Assessment Battery (minimum score 82). *Application deadline:* Applications are processed on a rolling basis. Application fee: $50. Electronic applications accepted. *Expenses:* Tuition: Full-time $10,274; part-time $445 per credit. Tuition and fees vary according to course load, degree level and program. *Financial support:* Fellowships with tuition reimbursements, Federal Work-Study, scholarships/grants, unspecified assistantships, and family tuition reduction, active duty/veteran tuition reduction, group tuition reduction, interest-free payment plans available. Support available to part-time students. Financial award applicants required to submit FAFSA. *Unit head:* Dr. Mark Gordon, Associate Dean, 800-925-3368. *Application contact:* Jennifer Hall, Vice President of Enrollment Management, 866-4-WALDEN, E-mail: info@waldenu.edu.

Washington State University, Graduate School, College of Liberal Arts, Department of Sociology, Pullman, WA 99164. Offers crime and deviance (MA, PhD); environments, community and demographics (MA, PhD); institutions and social organizations (MA, PhD); political sociology (MA, PhD); social inequality (MA, PhD); social psychology and life course (MA, PhD). *Faculty:* 22 full-time (14 women), 8 part-time/adjunct (3 women). *Students:* 42 full-time (23 women), 2 part-time (both women); includes 1 Black or African American, non-Hispanic/Latino; 1 American Indian or Alaska Native, non-Hispanic/Latino, 4 international. Average age 30. 71 applicants, 13% accepted, 9 enrolled. In 2010, 7 master's, 4 doctorates awarded. Terminal master's awarded for partial completion of doctoral program. *Degree requirements:* For master's, thesis; for doctorate, comprehensive exam, thesis/dissertation. *Entrance requirements:* For master's, GRE General Test, minimum GPA of 3.0; for doctorate, GRE General Test, MA in sociology, minimum GPA of 3.0. Additional exam requirements/recommendations for international students: Required—TOEFL (minimum score 550 paper-based). *Application deadline:* For fall admission, 1/15 priority date for domestic students, 1/15 for international students. Application fee: $50. Electronic applications accepted. *Expenses:* Tuition, state resident: full-time $8552; part-time $443 per credit. Tuition, nonresident: full-time $21,650; part-time $1083 per credit. Required fees: $846. *Financial support:* In 2010–11, 5 research assistantships with tuition reimbursements (averaging $12,749 per year), 36 teaching assistantships with tuition reimbursements (averaging $12,749 per year) were awarded; fellowships with tuition reimbursements, Federal Work-Study, institutionally sponsored loans, scholarships/grants, health care benefits, and unspecified assistantships also available. Support available to part-time students. Financial award application deadline: 4/1; financial award applicants required to submit FAFSA. *Faculty research:* Crime/deviance, environmental sociology, social inequality, social psychology, gender. Total annual research expenditures: $101,888. *Unit head:* Dr. Gregory Hooks, Chair, 509-335-4595, Fax: 509-335-6419, E-mail: hooks@mail.wsu.edu. *Application contact:* Dr. Tom Rotolo, Director of Graduate Studies, 509-335-4595, Fax: 509-335-6419, E-mail: rotolo@wsu.edu.

Washington University in St. Louis, Graduate School of Arts and Sciences, Department of Political Science, Program in Political Economy and Public Policy, St. Louis, MO 63130-4899. Offers MA. *Degree requirements:* For master's, thesis or alternative. *Entrance requirements:* For master's, GRE General Test. Electronic applications accepted.

West Virginia University, Eberly College of Arts and Sciences, Department of Political Science, Morgantown, WV 26506. Offers American public policy and politics (MA); international and comparative public policy and politics (MA); political science (PhD); public policy analysis (PhD). Terminal master's awarded for partial completion of doctoral program. *Degree requirements:* For master's, thesis optional; for doctorate, comprehensive exam, thesis/dissertation. *Entrance requirements:* For master's, GRE General Test, minimum GPA of 2.75; for doctorate, GRE General Test, minimum GPA of 3.0. Additional exam requirements/recommendations for international students: Required—TOEFL. *Faculty research:* Public policy, research methods, foreign policy analysis, judicial politics, environmental and energy policy.

Wilfrid Laurier University, Faculty of Graduate and Postdoctoral Studies, Faculty of Arts and School of Business and Economics, International Public Policy Program, Waterloo, ON N2L 3C5, Canada. Offers global governance (MIPP); human security (MIPP); international economic relations (MIPP); international environmental policy (MIPP). *Faculty:* 17 full-time (8 women). *Students:* 16 full-time (9 women), 2 international. 90 applicants, 30% accepted, 14 enrolled. In 2010, 15 master's awarded. *Entrance requirements:* For master's, honours BA with minimum B average. Additional exam requirements/recommendations for international students: Required—TOEFL (minimum score 89 iBT). *Application deadline:* For fall admission, 2/1 priority date for domestic and international students. Application fee: $100. Electronic applications accepted. Tuition and fees charges are reported in Canadian dollars. *Expenses:* Tuition, area resident: Full-time $15,300 Canadian dollars; part-time $1200 Canadian dollars per credit. International tuition: $21,300 Canadian dollars full-time. Required fees: $650 Canadian dollars; $100 Canadian dollars per credit. Tuition and fees vary according to course load, degree level, campus/location and program. *Financial support:* In 2010–11, 5 fellowships, 5 teaching assistantships were awarded; career-related internships or fieldwork, scholarships/grants, health care benefits, and unspecified assistantships also available. *Faculty research:* International environmental policy, international economic relations, human security, global governance. *Unit head:* Dr. Terry Snodden, Graduate Coordinator, 519-884-0710 Ext. 2945, Fax: 519-884-8854, E-mail: tlevesque@wlu.ca. *Application contact:* Jennifer Williams, Graduate Admissions and Records Officer, 519-884-0710 Ext. 3536, Fax: 519-884-1020, E-mail: gradstudies@wlu.ca.

William Paterson University of New Jersey, College of Humanities and Social Sciences, Wayne, NJ 07470-8420. Offers clinical and counseling psychology (MA); English (MA); history (MA); public policy and international affairs (MA); sociology (MA). Part-time and evening/weekend programs available. Electronic applications accepted.

York University, Faculty of Graduate Studies, Atkinson Faculty of Liberal and Professional Studies, Program in Public Policy, Administration and Law, Toronto, ON M3J 1P3, Canada. Offers MPPAL.

Rural Planning and Studies

Brandon University, Department of Rural Development, Brandon, MB R7A 6A9, Canada. Offers MRD, Diploma. *Degree requirements:* For master's, thesis. *Entrance requirements:* For master's, minimum GPA of 3.0, 2 letters of reference. Additional exam requirements/recommendations for international students: Required—TOEFL (minimum score 580 paper-based). Electronic applications accepted. *Faculty research:* Regional development, healthy communities, economic impact analysis, rural tourism, resource management.

California State University, Chico, Graduate School, College of Behavioral and Social Sciences, Department of Geography and Planning, Program in Rural and Town Planning, Chico, CA 95929-0722. Offers MA. Part-time programs available. *Students:* 6 full-time (2 women), 6 part-time (1 woman). Average age 35. 10 applicants, 80% accepted, 8 enrolled. *Entrance requirements:* For master's, GRE, 2 letters of recommendation. Additional exam requirements/recommendations for international students: Required—TOEFL (minimum score 550 paper-based; 213 computer-based; 80 iBT), IELTS (minimum score 6.5). *Application deadline:* For fall admission, 3/1 priority date for domestic students, 3/1 for international students; for spring admission, 9/15 priority date for domestic students, 9/15 for international students. Applications are processed on a rolling basis. Application fee: $55. Electronic applications accepted. *Unit head:* Dr. Dean Fairbanks, Graduate Coordinator, 530-898-5780. *Application contact:* Dr. Paul Melcon, Graduate Coordinator, 530-898-6871.

Concordia University, School of Graduate Studies, John Molson School of Business, Montréal, QC H3G 1M8, Canada. Offers administration (M Sc, Diploma); aviation management (Certificate, Diploma); business administration (MBA, UA Undergraduate Associate, PhD), including international aviation (UA Undergraduate Associate); chartered accountancy (Diploma); community organizational development (Certificate); event management and fundraising (Certificate); executive business administration (EMBA); investment management (Diploma); investment management option (MBA); management accounting (Certificate); management of healthcare organizations (Certificate); sport administration (Diploma). PhD program offered jointly with HEC Montreal, McGill University, and Université du Québec à Montréal. *Accreditation:* AACSB. Part-time and evening/weekend programs available. *Degree requirements:* For master's, one foreign language, thesis (for some programs), research project; for doctorate, one foreign language, thesis/dissertation; for other advanced degree, one foreign language. *Entrance requirements:* For master's and doctorate, GMAT. Additional exam requirements/recommendations for international students: Required—TOEFL. *Expenses:* Contact institution. *Faculty research:* General business, capital markets, international business.

Cornell University, Graduate School, Graduate Fields of Agriculture and Life Sciences, Field of International Agriculture and Rural Development, Ithaca, NY 14853-0001. Offers international agriculture and development (MPS). *Faculty:* 44 full-time (9 women). *Students:* 31 full-time (12 women); includes 1 Black or African American, non-Hispanic/Latino; 1 Hispanic/Latino, 4 international. Average age 29. 45 applicants, 76% accepted, 29 enrolled. In 2010, 15 master's awarded. *Degree requirements:* For master's, project paper. *Entrance requirements:* For master's, GRE General Test (recommended), 2 years of development experience, 2 letters of recommendation. Additional exam requirements/recommendations for international students: Required—TOEFL (minimum score 550 paper-based; 213 computer-based; 77 iBT). *Application deadline:* For fall admission, 3/1 for domestic students. Application fee: $70. Electronic applications accepted. *Expenses:* Tuition: Full-time $29,500. Required fees: $76. Tuition and fees vary according to degree level and program. *Financial support:* In 2010–11, 12 fellowships with full tuition reimbursements, 1 teaching assistantship with full tuition reimbursement were awarded; research assistantships with full tuition reimbursements, institutionally sponsored loans, scholarships/grants, health care benefits, tuition waivers (full and partial), and unspecified assistantships also available. Financial award applicants required to submit FAFSA. *Unit head:* Director of Graduate Studies, 607-255-3037, Fax: 607-255-1005. *Application contact:* Graduate Field Assistant, 607-255-3035, Fax: 607-255-1005, E-mail: mpsiard@cornell.edu.

Dalhousie University, Faculty of Architecture and Planning, School of Planning, Halifax, NS B3J 2X4, Canada. Offers M Eng, M Plan, MPS. *Degree requirements:* For master's, thesis. *Entrance requirements:* Additional exam requirements/recommendations for international students: Required—TOEFL, IELTS, CANTEST, CAEL, or Michigan English Language Assessment Battery. Electronic applications accepted.

George Mason University, College of Health and Human Services, Department of Health Administration and Policy, Fairfax, VA 22030. Offers health and medical policy (MS); health information systems (Certificate); health systems management (MS); quality improvement and outcomes management in health care systems (Certificate); risk management and patient safety (Certificate); senior housing administration (MS, Certificate). *Accreditation:* CAHME. *Faculty:* 16 full-time (3 women), 11 part-time/adjunct (7 women). *Students:* 28 full-time (18 women), 111 part-time (85 women); includes 56 minority (15 Black or African American, non-Hispanic/Latino; 29 Asian, non-Hispanic/Latino; 9 Hispanic/Latino; 3 Two or more races, non-Hispanic/Latino), 9 international. Average age 32. 89 applicants, 67% accepted, 40 enrolled. In 2010, 28 master's, 7 other advanced degrees awarded. *Degree requirements:* For master's, comprehensive exam, internship. *Entrance requirements:* For master's, GRE, curriculum vitae, 2 letters of recommendation. Additional exam requirements/recommendations for international students: Required—TOEFL (minimum score 570 paper-based; 230 computer-based; 88 iBT). *Application deadline:* For fall admission, 3/1 priority date for domestic students; for spring admission, 11/1 for domestic students. Applications are processed on a rolling basis. Application fee: $100. Electronic applications accepted. *Expenses:* Tuition, state resident: full-time $8192; part-time $440 per credit hour. Tuition, nonresident: full-time $22,952; part-time $1055 per credit hour. Required fees: $2364; $99 per credit hour. *Financial support:* In 2010–11, 6 students received support, including 5 research assistantships with full and partial tuition reimbursements available (averaging $15,000 per year), 1 teaching assistantship (averaging $12,480 per year); career-related internships or fieldwork, Federal Work-Study, scholarships/grants, unspecified assistantships, and health care benefits (full-time research or teaching assistantship recipients) also available. Financial award application deadline: 3/1; financial award applicants required to submit FAFSA. *Faculty research:* Universal health care, publications, relationships between malpractice pressure and rates of cesarean section and VBAC, seniors and Wii gaming, relationships between changes in physician's incomes and practice settings and their care to Medicaid and charity patients. Total annual research expenditures: $838,668. *Unit head:* Dr. P. J. Maddox, Chair, 703-993-1982, E-mail: pmaddox@gmu.edu. *Application contact:* Adam McCutcheon, Office Manager, 703-993-1929, E-mail: amccutch@gmu.edu.

Iowa State University of Science and Technology, Graduate College, College of Liberal Arts and Sciences, Department of History, Ames, IA 50011. Offers agricultural history and rural studies (PhD); history (MA); history of technology and science (MA, PhD). *Faculty:* 18 full-time (5 women). *Students:* 30 full-time (8 women), 18 part-time (5 women); includes 1 Black or African American, non-Hispanic/Latino, 5 international. 31 applicants, 61% accepted, 13 enrolled. In 2010, 5 master's, 3 doctorates awarded. *Degree requirements:* For master's, thesis or alternative; for doctorate, thesis/dissertation. *Entrance requirements:* For master's and doctorate, GRE General Test. Additional exam requirements/recommendations for international students: Required—TOEFL (minimum score 600 paper-based; 79 iBT), IELTS (minimum score 7). *Application deadline:* For fall admission, 1/15 priority date for domestic and international students. Applications are processed on a rolling basis. Application fee: $40 ($90 for international students). Electronic applications accepted. *Financial support:* In 2010–11, 1 research assistantship with full and partial tuition reimbursement (averaging $20,295 per year), 21 teaching assistantships with full and partial tuition reimbursements (averaging $9,263 per year) were awarded; scholarships/grants, health care benefits, and unspecified assistantships also available. *Unit head:* Dr. Charles Dobbs, Chair, 515-294-7266, Fax: 515-294-6390, E-mail: cdobbs@iastate.edu. *Application contact:* Dr. Pamela Riney-Kehrberg, Information Contact, 515-294-1451, Fax: 515-294-6390.

Université Laval, Faculty of Agricultural and Food Sciences, Program in Integrated Rural Development, Québec, QC G1K 7P4, Canada. Offers Diploma. *Entrance requirements:* For degree, good knowledge of French. Electronic applications accepted.

University of Alaska Fairbanks, College of Rural and Community Development, Department of Alaska Native and Rural Development, Fairbanks, AK 99775. Offers rural development

(MA). Part-time programs available. Postbaccalaureate distance learning degree programs offered. *Faculty:* 2 full-time (both women). *Students:* 9 full-time (8 women), 20 part-time (17 women); includes 11 American Indian or Alaska Native, non-Hispanic/Latino; 1 Asian, non-Hispanic/Latino. Average age 40. 16 applicants, 75% accepted, 10 enrolled. In 2010, 4 master's awarded. *Degree requirements:* For master's, comprehensive exam, thesis or alternative. *Entrance requirements:* Additional exam requirements/recommendations for international students: Required—TOEFL (minimum score 550 paper-based; 213 computer-based; 80 iBT). *Application deadline:* For fall admission, 6/1 for domestic students, 3/1 for international students; for spring admission, 10/15 for domestic students, 9/1 for international students. Applications are processed on a rolling basis. Application fee: $60. Electronic applications accepted. *Expenses:* Tuition, state resident: full-time $5688; part-time $316 per credit. Tuition, nonresident: full-time $11,628; part-time $646 per credit. Required fees: $289 per semester. Tuition and fees vary according to course load and reciprocity agreements. *Financial support:* Fellowships, Federal Work-Study, scholarships/grants, and health care benefits available. Support available to part-time students. Financial award application deadline: 2/15; financial award applicants required to submit FAFSA. *Faculty research:* International indigenous leadership development, interrelationships between rural communities and global economy. *Unit head:* Gordon Pullar, Director, 907-474-6528, Fax: 907-474-6325, E-mail: fydanrd@uaf.edu. *Application contact:* Gordon Pullar, Director, 907-474-6528, Fax: 907-474-6325, E-mail: fydanrd@uaf.edu.

University of Guelph, Graduate Studies, Ontario Agricultural College, School of Environmental Design and Rural Development, Interdisciplinary Program in Rural Studies, Guelph, ON N1G 2W1, Canada. Offers PhD. Offered in cooperation with the Department of Food, Agricultural and Resource Economics, and the Department of Geography. Part-time programs available. *Degree requirements:* For doctorate, thesis/dissertation, qualifying exam. *Entrance requirements:* Additional exam requirements/recommendations for international students: Required—TOEFL (minimum score 600 paper-based; 218 computer-based), IELTS (minimum score 7). Electronic applications accepted. *Faculty research:* Sustainable rural communities, human resource development, rural planning and development.

University of Guelph, Graduate Studies, Ontario Agricultural College, School of Environmental Design and Rural Development, Program in Capacity Development and Extension, Guelph, ON N1G 2W1, Canada. Offers M Sc. Part-time programs available. *Degree requirements:* For master's, thesis optional. *Entrance requirements:* For master's, minimum B- average in previous 2 years of course work. Additional exam requirements/recommendations for international students: Required—TOEFL (minimum score 550 paper-based; 213 computer-based; 89 iBT), IELTS (minimum score 6.5). Electronic applications accepted. *Faculty research:* Adult learning in non-formal settings, communication technology for remote areas, rural quality of life.

University of Guelph, Graduate Studies, Ontario Agricultural College, School of Environmental Design and Rural Development, Program in Rural Planning and Development, Guelph, ON N1G 2W1, Canada. Offers international rural planning and development (M Sc); rural planning and development in Canada (M Sc). M Sc offered in cooperation with Departments of Food, Agricultural and Resource Economics; Geography; Land Resource Science; and others by arrangement. Part-time programs available. *Degree requirements:* For master's, thesis or alternative. *Entrance requirements:* For master's, minimum B- average during previous 2 years of course work. Additional exam requirements/recommendations for international students: Required—TOEFL (minimum score 550 paper-based; 213 computer-based), IELTS (minimum score 6.5). Electronic applications accepted. *Faculty research:* Canadian and international rural planning, resource and economic development, tourism.

The University of Montana, Graduate School, College of Arts and Sciences, Department of Geography, Missoula, MT 59812-0002. Offers geography (MA), including cartography and GIS, community and environmental planning. *Entrance requirements:* For master's, GRE General Test. Additional exam requirements/recommendations for international students: Required—TOEFL.

University of West Georgia, College of Arts and Sciences, Department of Political Science and Planning, Carrollton, GA 30118. Offers political science (Certificate); public administration (MPA); public management (Certificate); rural and small town planning (MS). *Accreditation:* NASPAA (one or more programs are accredited). Part-time programs available. *Faculty:* 5 full-time (0 women). *Students:* 19 full-time (5 women), 22 part-time (11 women); includes 11 Black or African American, non-Hispanic/Latino; 1 Native Hawaiian or other Pacific Islander, non-Hispanic/Latino. Average age 33. 26 applicants, 58% accepted, 6 enrolled. In 2010, 10 master's, 5 other advanced degrees awarded. *Degree requirements:* For master's, exit paper. *Entrance requirements:* For master's, GRE General Test. Additional exam requirements/recommendations for international students: Required—TOEFL. *Application deadline:* For fall admission, 7/17 priority date for domestic students; for spring admission, 11/20 for domestic students. Applications are processed on a rolling basis. Application fee: $30. Electronic applications accepted. *Expenses:* Tuition, state resident: full-time $4130; part-time $173 per semester hour. Tuition, nonresident: full-time $16,524; part-time $689 per semester hour. Required fees: $1586; $44.01 per semester hour. $397 per semester. Tuition and fees vary according to program. *Financial support:* In 2010–11, 4 students received support, including 4 research assistantships with partial tuition reimbursements available (averaging $3,000 per year); career-related internships or fieldwork and unspecified assistantships also available. Support available to part-time students. Financial award application deadline: 7/1; financial award applicants required to submit FAFSA. *Faculty research:* State and local government, environmental health, administrative studies. *Unit head:* Dr. Robert M. Schaefer, Chair, 678-839-6504, Fax: 678-839-5009, E-mail: rschaefe@westga.edu. *Application contact:* Dr. Charles W. Clark, Dean, 678-839-6419, E-mail: cclark@westga.edu.

University of Wyoming, College of Arts and Sciences, Department of Geography, Program in Rural Planning and Natural Resources, Laramie, WY 82070. Offers community and regional planning and natural resources (MP). *Degree requirements:* For master's, thesis or alternative. *Entrance requirements:* For master's, GRE General Test, minimum GPA of 3.0. Additional exam requirements/recommendations for international students: Required—TOEFL. *Faculty research:* Rural and small town planning, public land management.

Sustainable Development

American University, School of International Service, Washington, DC 20016-8071. Offers comparative and regional studies (Certificate); cross-cultural communication (Certificate); development management (MS); ethics, peace, and global affairs (MA); European studies (Certificate); global environmental policy (MA, Certificate); international affairs (MA), including comparative and regional studies, environmental policy, international economic policy, international politics, natural resources and sustainable development, U. S. foreign policy; international communication (MA, Certificate); international development (MA, Certificate); international development management (Certificate); international economic policy (Certificate); international economic relations (Certificate); international media (MA); international peace and conflict resolution (MA, Certificate); international relations (PhD); international service (MIS); peace building (Certificate); the Americas (Certificate); United States foreign policy (Certificate); JD/MA. Part-time and evening/weekend programs available. *Faculty:* 91 full-time (35 women), 48 part-time/adjunct (16 women). *Students:* 591 full-time (383 women), 367 part-time (229 women); includes 164 minority (51 Black or African American, non-Hispanic/Latino; 4 American Indian or Alaska Native, non-Hispanic/Latino; 42 Asian, non-Hispanic/Latino; 63 Hispanic/Latino; 4 Two or more races, non-Hispanic/Latino), 94 international. Average age 27. 2,115 applicants, 59% accepted, 360 enrolled. In 2010, 370 master's, 7 doctorates awarded. Terminal master's awarded for partial completion of doctoral program. *Degree requirements:* For master's, one foreign language, comprehensive exam, thesis or alternative; for doctorate, one foreign language, comprehensive exam, thesis/dissertation, research practicum; for Certificate, minimum 15 credit hours related course work. *Entrance requirements:* For master's, GRE, 24 credits of course work in related social sciences, minimum GPA of 3.5, 2 letters of recommendation, bachelor's degree, resume; for doctorate, GRE, 2 letters of recommendation, 24 credits in related social sciences; for Certificate, bachelor's degree. Additional exam requirements/recommendations for international students: Required—TOEFL (minimum score 600 paper-based; 250 computer-based; 100 iBT). *Application deadline:* For fall admission, 1/15 priority date for domestic students; for spring admission, 10/1 priority date for domestic students. Applications are processed on a rolling basis. Application fee: $50. *Financial support:* Career-related internships or fieldwork, Federal Work-Study, and institutionally sponsored loans available. Financial award application deadline: 1/15. *Faculty research:* International intellectual property, international environmental issues, international law and legal order, international telecommunications/technology, international sustainable development. *Unit head:* Dr. Louis W. Goodman, Dean, 202-885-1600, Fax: 202-885-2494. *Application contact:* Yasmin Quianzon, Director of Graduate Admissions and Financial Aid, 202-885-2496, Fax: 202-885-1109.

Appalachian State University, Cratis D. Williams Graduate School, Center for Appalachian Studies, Boone, NC 28608. Offers culture (MA); music (MA); sustainable development (MA). Part-time programs available. *Faculty:* 14 full-time (5 women). *Students:* 25 full-time (15 women), 5 part-time (4 women); includes 1 Hispanic/Latino. 20 applicants, 85% accepted, 12 enrolled. In 2010, 11 master's awarded. *Degree requirements:* For master's, one foreign language, comprehensive exam, thesis optional. *Entrance requirements:* For master's, GRE General Test, 3 letters of recommendation. Additional exam requirements/recommendations for international students: Required—TOEFL (minimum score 570 paper-based; 230 computer-based; 79 iBT), IELTS (minimum score 6.5). *Application deadline:* For fall admission, 7/1 for domestic students, 2/1 for international students; for spring admission, 11/1 for domestic students, 7/1 for international students. Applications are processed on a rolling basis. Application fee: $55. Electronic applications accepted. *Expenses:* Tuition, state resident: full-time $3428; part-time $428 per unit. Tuition, nonresident: full-time $14,518; part-time $1814 per unit. Required fees: $2320; $344 per unit. Tuition and fees vary according to campus/location. *Financial support:* In 2010–11, 8 research assistantships (averaging $8,000 per year) were awarded; fellowships, teaching assistantships, career-related internships or fieldwork, Federal Work-Study, scholarships/grants, and unspecified assistantships also available. Financial award application deadline: 4/1; financial award applicants required to submit FAFSA. *Faculty research:* Appalachian culture, sustainable development, Appalachian music. Total annual research expenditures: $35,275. *Unit head:* Dr. Pat Beaver, Director, 828-262-2550, E-mail: beaverpd@appstate.edu. *Application contact:* Dr. Katherine Ledford, Graduate Program Director, 828-262-4089, E-mail: ledfordke@appstate.edu.

Arizona State University, School of Sustainability, Tempe, AZ 85287-5502. Offers sustainability (MA, MS, PhD); sustainable technology and management (Graduate Certificate). Part-time and evening/weekend programs available. *Faculty:* 9 full-time (3 women). *Students:* 60 full-time (30 women), 26 part-time (12 women); includes 17 minority (2 Black or African American, non-Hispanic/Latino; 4 Asian, non-Hispanic/Latino; 9 Hispanic/Latino; 2 Two or more races, non-Hispanic/Latino), 18 international. Average age 32. 216 applicants, 25% accepted, 30 enrolled. In 2010, 11 master's, 1 doctorate, 3 other advanced degrees awarded. Terminal master's awarded for partial completion of doctoral program. *Degree requirements:* For master's, thesis, interactive Program of Study (iPOS) submitted before completing 50 percent of required credit hours; for doctorate, comprehensive exam, thesis/dissertation, interactive Program of Study (iPOS) submitted before completing 50 percent of required credit hours. *Entrance requirements:* For master's, GRE; for doctorate, GRE, minimum GPA of 3.0 or equivalent in last 2 years of work leading to bachelor's degree. Additional exam requirements/recommendations for international students: Required—TOEFL, IELTS, or Pearson Test of English. *Application deadline:* For fall admission, 7/1 for domestic and international students; for spring admission, 12/1 for domestic and international students. Applications are processed on a rolling basis. Application fee: $70 ($90 for international students). Electronic applications accepted. *Expenses:* Tuition, state resident: full-time $8510; part-time $608 per credit. Tuition, nonresident: full-time $16,542; part-time $919 per credit. Required fees: $339; $110 per credit. Part-time tuition and fees vary according to course load. *Financial support:* In 2010–11, 25 research assistantships with full and partial tuition reimbursements (averaging $16,992 per year), 39 teaching assistantships with full and partial tuition reimbursements (averaging $16,179 per year) were awarded; fellowships with full tuition reimbursements, career-related internships or fieldwork, Federal Work-Study, institutionally sponsored loans, scholarships/grants, and tuition waivers (full and partial) also available. Financial award application deadline: 3/1; financial award applicants required to submit FAFSA. Total annual research expenditures: $1.5 million. *Unit head:* Sander Van Der Leeuw, Dean, 480-965-2975, Fax: 480-965-8087, E-mail: vanderle@asu.edu. *Application contact:* Graduate Admissions, 480-965-6113.

Brandeis University, The Heller School for Social Policy and Management, Program in Nonprofit Management, Waltham, MA 02454-9110. Offers child, youth, and family management (MBA); health care management (MBA); social impact management (MBA); social policy and management (MBA); sustainable development (MBA); MBA/MA; MBA/MD. MBA/MD program offered in conjunction with Tufts University School of Medicine. *Accreditation:* AACSB. Part-time programs available. *Faculty:* 36 full-time, 107 part-time/adjunct. *Students:* 58 full-time (39 women), 5 part-time (3 women); includes 2 Black or African American, non-Hispanic/Latino; 11 Asian, non-Hispanic/Latino; 2 Hispanic/Latino, 4 international. Average age 27. 116 applicants, 57% accepted, 34 enrolled. In 2010, 21 master's awarded. *Degree requirements:* For master's, team consulting project. *Entrance requirements:* For master's, GMAT (preferred) or GRE, 2 letters of recommendation, problem statement analysis, 3-5 years of professional experience. Additional exam requirements/recommendations for international students: Required—TOEFL (minimum score 600 paper-based; 250 computer-based; 100 iBT). *Application deadline:* For fall admission, 3/15 for domestic and international students. Applications are processed on a rolling basis. Application fee: $55. Electronic applications accepted. *Expenses:* Contact institution. *Financial support:* Scholarships/grants and tuition waivers (partial) available. Financial award application deadline: 3/15; financial award applicants required to submit FAFSA. *Faculty research:* Health care; children and families; elder and disabled services; social impact management; organizations in the non-profit, for-profit, or public sector. *Unit head:* Dr. Brenda Anderson, Program Director, 781-736-8423, E-mail: banderson@brandeis.edu. *Application contact:* Shana Mongan, Assistant Director for Admissions and Financial Aid, 781-736-4229, E-mail: mongan@brandeis.edu.

Brandeis University, The Heller School for Social Policy and Management, Program in Sustainable International Development, Waltham, MA 02454-9110. Offers international

Sustainable Development

Brandeis University (continued)
development (MA); sustainable development (MA); MA/JD; MA/MA; MBA/MA. MA/JD program offered in conjunction with Northeastern University School of Law. *Faculty:* 36 full-time, 107 part-time/adjunct. *Students:* 246 full-time (148 women); includes 7 Black or African American, non-Hispanic/Latino; 5 Asian, non-Hispanic/Latino; 7 Hispanic/Latino, 148 international. Average age 30. 772 applicants, 47% accepted, 106 enrolled. In 2010, 68 master's awarded. *Degree requirements:* For master's, 2nd year fieldwork or internship. *Entrance requirements:* For master's, 3 letters of recommendation, curriculum vitae or resume, 3 years of development experience (international experience preferred). Additional exam requirements/recommendations for international students: Required—TOEFL (minimum score 600 paper-based; 250 computer-based; 100 iBT). *Application deadline:* For fall admission, 3/15 for domestic and international students. Applications are processed on a rolling basis. Application fee: $55. Electronic applications accepted. *Expenses:* Contact institution. *Financial support:* In 2010–11, 2 fellowships with full and partial tuition reimbursements (averaging $10,000 per year) were awarded; scholarships/grants and tuition waivers (full and partial) also available. Financial award application deadline: 3/15; financial award applicants required to submit FAFSA. *Faculty research:* Water resource management, human rights, biosphere management, rural development, public policy and governance, gender, conservation, civil society, poverty eradication, project planning and implementation, evaluation, organizational management. *Unit head:* Dr. Laurence R. Simon, Director, 781-736-2770, Fax: 781-736-2774, E-mail: sid@brandeis.edu. *Application contact:* Jamie McCarthy, Admissions Officer, 781-736-3923, E-mail: jamiemcc@brandeis.edu.

California State University, Stanislaus, College of Natural Sciences, Program in Ecology and Sustainability (MS), Turlock, CA 95382. Offers ecological conservation (MS); ecological economics (MS). Part-time programs available. *Faculty:* 9 full-time (3 women), 1 (woman) part-time/adjunct. *Students:* 7 full-time (1 woman), 8 part-time (6 women); includes 6 minority (1 Black or African American, non-Hispanic/Latino; 4 Hispanic/Latino; 1 Two or more races, non-Hispanic/Latino). Average age 33. 10 applicants, 70% accepted, 4 enrolled. *Degree requirements:* For master's, thesis. *Entrance requirements:* For master's, GRE, Minimum GPA of 3.0; 3 letters of recommendation, personal statement. Additional exam requirements/recommendations for international students: Required—TOEFL (minimum score 550 paper-based; 213 computer-based). *Application deadline:* For fall admission, 5/1 for domestic students; for spring admission, 1/7 for domestic students. Application fee: $55. Electronic applications accepted. Tuition and fees vary according to program. *Financial support:* In 2010–11, 4 teaching assistantships (averaging $4,500 per year) were awarded. Financial award application deadline: 3/1; financial award applicants required to submit FAFSA. *Unit head:* Dr. Matthew Cover, Program Director, 209-667-3153, E-mail: mcover@biology.csustan.edu. *Application contact:* Graduate School, 209-667-3129, Fax: 209-664-7025, E-mail: graduate_school@csustan.edu.

The Catholic University of America, School of Architecture and Planning, Washington, DC 20064. Offers architecture studies (MS Arch St); sustainable design (MSSD). Part-time programs available. *Faculty:* 25 full-time (6 women), 38 part-time/adjunct (9 women). *Students:* 116 full-time (55 women), 31 part-time (13 women); includes 11 Black or African American, non-Hispanic/Latino; 6 Asian, non-Hispanic/Latino; 11 Hispanic/Latino, 11 international. Average age 27. 167 applicants, 70% accepted, 56 enrolled. In 2010, 55 master's awarded. *Degree requirements:* For master's, thesis. *Entrance requirements:* For master's, GRE (minimum score: 1000), minimum GPA of 2.8, portfolio, statement of purpose, official copies of academic transcripts, three letters of recommendation. Additional exam requirements/recommendations for international students: Required—TOEFL (minimum score 580 paper-based; 237 computer-based). *Application deadline:* For fall admission, 1/15 priority date for domestic students, 1/15 for international students; for spring admission, 10/15 priority date for domestic students, 10/15 for international students. Applications are processed on a rolling basis. Application fee: $55. Electronic applications accepted. *Expenses:* Contact institution. *Financial support:* Fellowships, research assistantships, teaching assistantships, Federal Work-Study, scholarships/grants, tuition waivers (full and partial), and unspecified assistantships available. Financial award application deadline: 2/1; financial award applicants required to submit FAFSA. *Faculty research:* Architectural history, cultural studies/sacred space, design technologies, digital media, real estate development, urban design. *Unit head:* Randall Ott, Dean, 202-319-5784, Fax: 202-319-2023, E-mail: ott@cua.edu. *Application contact:* Andrew Woodall, Director of Graduate Admissions, 202-319-5057, Fax: 202-319-6533, E-mail: cua-admissions@cua.edu.

City College of the City University of New York, Graduate School, Program in Sustainability in the Urban Environment, New York, NY 10031-9198. Offers MS. *Degree requirements:* For master's, capstone project.

Clarkson University, Graduate School, Institute for a Sustainable Environment, Potsdam, NY 13699. Offers MS, PhD. Part-time programs available. *Faculty:* 4 full-time (2 women). *Students:* 30 full-time (16 women), 1 (woman) part-time, 16 international. Average age 27. 7 applicants, 100% accepted, 7 enrolled. In 2010, 5 master's, 2 doctorates awarded. Terminal master's awarded for partial completion of doctoral program. *Degree requirements:* For master's, thesis; for doctorate, comprehensive exam, thesis/dissertation, departmental qualifying exam. *Entrance requirements:* For master's and doctorate, GRE, transcripts of all college coursework, resume, personal statement, three letters of recommendation. Additional exam requirements/recommendations for international students: Required—TOEFL (minimum score 550 paper-based; 213 computer-based; 80 iBT), IELTS (minimum score 6.5). *Application deadline:* For fall admission, 1/30 priority date for domestic and international students; for spring admission, 9/1 priority date for domestic and international students. Applications are processed on a rolling basis. Application fee: $25 ($35 for international students). Electronic applications accepted. *Expenses:* Tuition: Part-time $1136 per credit hour. *Financial support:* In 2010–11, 29 students received support, including fellowships with full tuition reimbursements available (averaging $21,580 per year), 17 research assistantships with full tuition reimbursements available (averaging $21,580 per year), 10 teaching assistantships with full tuition reimbursements available (averaging $21,580 per year); scholarships/grants, tuition waivers (partial), and unspecified assistantships also available. *Faculty research:* Soil and groundwater remediations, air quality, sustainable energy systems. *Unit head:* Dr. Philip Hopke, Director, 315-268-3856, Fax: 315-268-4291, E-mail: hopkepk@clarkson.edu. *Application contact:* Suzann Cheney, Administrative Secretary, 315-268-3856, Fax: 315-268-4291, E-mail: scheney@clarkson.edu.

Clark University, Graduate School, Department of International Development, Community, and Environment, Worchester, MA 01610-1477. Offers community development and planning (MA); environmental science and policy (MA); geographic information science for development and environment (MA); international development and social change (MA); MA/MBA. *Faculty:* 18 full-time (11 women), 2 part-time/adjunct (1 woman). *Students:* 165 full-time (96 women), 25 part-time (11 women); includes 21 minority (12 Black or African American, non-Hispanic/Latino; 2 Asian, non-Hispanic/Latino; 7 Hispanic/Latino), 72 international. Average age 28. 448 applicants, 71% accepted, 111 enrolled. In 2010, 86 master's awarded. *Degree requirements:* For master's, thesis. *Entrance requirements:* For master's, 3 references, resume or curriculum vitae. Additional exam requirements/recommendations for international students: Required—TOEFL (minimum score 575 paper-based; 233 computer-based; 90 iBT) or IELTS (minimum score 6.5). *Application deadline:* For fall admission, 1/15 for domestic students. Application fee: $50. *Expenses:* Tuition: Full-time $37,000; part-time $1156 per credit hour. Required fees: $30; $1156 per credit hour. *Financial support:* In 2010–11, research assistantships with partial tuition reimbursements (averaging $5,000 per year), teaching assistantships with partial tuition reimbursements (averaging $5,000 per year) were awarded; fellowships with partial tuition reimbursements, institutionally sponsored loans and scholarships/grants also available. *Faculty research:* Community action research, gender analysis, land-use planning, geographic information systems, HIV and AIDS, global health and social justice, environmental health, climate change and sustainability. Total annual research expenditures: $2.3 million. *Unit head:* Dr. William F. Fisher, Director, 508-421-3765, Fax: 508-793-8820, E-mail: wfisher@clarku.edu. *Application contact:* Paula Hall, Department of International Development, Community, and Environment Graduate Admissions Office, 508-793-7201, Fax: 508-793-8820, E-mail: idce@clarku.edu.

Columbia University, Graduate School of Arts and Sciences, Program in Climate and Society, New York, NY 10027. Offers MA.

Columbia University, Graduate School of Arts and Sciences, Program in Sustainable Development, New York, NY 10027. Offers PhD.

Columbia University, School of International and Public Affairs, Program in Development Practice, New York, NY 10027. Offers MPA. Offered through The Earth Institute.

Dominican University of California, Graduate Programs, School of Business and Leadership, Green Business Administration Program, San Rafael, CA 94901-2298. Offers sustainable enterprise (MBA). Part-time and evening/weekend programs available. *Faculty:* 4 full-time (3 women), 12 part-time/adjunct (7 women). *Students:* 56 full-time (30 women), 58 part-time (34 women); includes 28 minority (3 Black or African American, non-Hispanic/Latino; 7 Asian, non-Hispanic/Latino; 11 Hispanic/Latino; 7 Two or more races, non-Hispanic/Latino). Average age 35. 46 applicants, 70% accepted, 21 enrolled. In 2010, 36 master's awarded. *Entrance requirements:* Additional exam requirements/recommendations for international students: Required—TOEFL (minimum score 550 paper-based; 213 computer-based; 80 iBT), IELTS (minimum score 7). *Application deadline:* For fall admission, 6/15 priority date for domestic and international students; for spring admission, 11/15 priority date for domestic and international students. Applications are processed on a rolling basis. Application fee: $40. Electronic applications accepted. *Financial support:* In 2010–11, 43 students received support; fellowships, scholarships/grants available. Financial award application deadline: 3/2; financial award applicants required to submit FAFSA. *Unit head:* Joey Shepp, Director, 415-482-1822, Fax: 415-459-3206, E-mail: joey.shepp@dominican.edu. *Application contact:* Robbie Hayes, Assistant Director, 415-458-3771, Fax: 415-485-3214, E-mail: robbie.hayes@dominican.edu.

Emory University, Laney Graduate School, Program in Development Practice, Atlanta, GA 30322-1100. Offers MDP. *Expenses:* Tuition: Full-time $33,800. Required fees: $1300.

Fashion Institute of Technology, School of Graduate Studies, Program in Sustainable Interior Environments, New York, NY 10001-5992. Offers MA.

See Display on page 107 and Close-Up on page 125.

Florida Atlantic University, College of Design and Social Inquiry, School of Urban and Regional Planning, Boca Raton, FL 33431-0991. Offers economic development and tourism (Certificate); environmental planning (Certificate); sustainable community planning (Certificate); urban and regional planning (MURP); visual planning technology (Certificate). *Accreditation:* ACSP. Part-time and evening/weekend programs available. *Faculty:* 8 full-time (5 women), 2 part-time/adjunct (1 woman). *Students:* 24 full-time (18 women), 12 part-time (1 woman); includes 17 minority (4 Black or African American, non-Hispanic/Latino; 1 American Indian or Alaska Native, non-Hispanic/Latino; 12 Hispanic/Latino), 2 international. Average age 30. 55 applicants, 35% accepted, 12 enrolled. In 2010, 13 master's awarded. *Entrance requirements:* For master's, GRE General Test, minimum GPA of 3.0. Additional exam requirements/recommendations for international students: Required—TOEFL. *Application deadline:* For fall admission, 7/1 priority date for domestic students, 2/15 for international students; for spring admission, 11/1 priority date for domestic students, 7/15 for international students. Applications are processed on a rolling basis. Application fee: $30. *Expenses:* Tuition, area resident: Part-time $319.96 per credit. Tuition, state resident: part-time $319.96 per credit. Tuition, nonresident: part-time $926.42 per credit. *Financial support:* Fellowships with full tuition reimbursements, research assistantships, career-related internships or fieldwork, Federal Work-Study, institutionally sponsored loans, and tuition waivers (partial) available. Financial award application deadline: 4/1. *Faculty research:* Growth management, urban design, computer applications/geographical information systems, environmental planning. *Unit head:* Dr. Jaap Vos, Chair, 954-762-5653, Fax: 954-762-5673, E-mail: jvos@fau.edu. *Application contact:* Dr. Jaap Vos, Chair, 954-762-5653, Fax: 954-762-5673, E-mail: jvos@fau.edu.

George Mason University, Volgenau School of Engineering, Department of Civil, Environmental, and Infrastructure Engineering, Fairfax, VA 22030. Offers civil and infrastructure engineering (MS, PhD); civil infrastructure and security engineering (Certificate); leading technical enterprises (Certificate); sustainability and the environment (Certificate); water resources engineering (Certificate). Part-time and evening/weekend programs available. *Faculty:* 9 full-time (4 women), 18 part-time/adjunct (1 woman). *Students:* 15 full-time (4 women), 62 part-time (13 women); includes 7 Black or African American, non-Hispanic/Latino; 9 Asian, non-Hispanic/Latino; 4 Hispanic/Latino; 2 Two or more races, non-Hispanic/Latino, 6 international. Average age 32. 77 applicants, 70% accepted, 29 enrolled. In 2010, 13 master's, 1 doctorate, 2 other advanced degrees awarded. *Degree requirements:* For master's, thesis (for some programs), 30 credits, departmental seminars; for doctorate, thesis/dissertation, qualifying exams. *Entrance requirements:* For master's, GRE or GMAT. Additional exam requirements/recommendations for international students: Required—TOEFL (minimum score 570 paper-based; 230 computer-based; 88 iBT). *Application deadline:* For fall admission, 3/15 priority date for domestic students, 3/15 for international students; for spring admission, 11/1 for domestic students, 10/1 for international students. Application fee: $100. Electronic applications accepted. *Expenses:* Tuition, state resident: full-time $8192; part-time $440 per credit hour. Tuition, nonresident: full-time $22,952; part-time $1055 per credit hour. Required fees: $2364; $99 per credit hour. *Financial support:* In 2010–11, 13 students received support, including 1 fellowship (averaging $18,000 per year), 2 research assistantships with full and partial tuition reimbursements available (averaging $13,924 per year), 10 teaching assistantships with full and partial tuition reimbursements available (averaging $10,468 per year); career-related internships or fieldwork, Federal Work-Study, scholarships/grants, unspecified assistantships, and health care benefits (full-time research or teaching assistantship recipients) also available. Financial award application deadline: 3/1; financial award applicants required to submit FAFSA. *Faculty research:* Evolutionary design, infrastructure security, intelligent transportation systems, national transportation networks, water quality modeling. Total annual research expenditures: $177,807. *Unit head:* Dr. Michael Bronzini, Chair, 703-993-1504, Fax: 703-993-1521. *Application contact:* Lisa Nolder, Graduate Student Services Director, 703-993-1499, E-mail: snolder@gmu.edu.

Hawai'i Pacific University, College of Natural and Computational Sciences, Program in Global Leadership and Sustainable Development, Honolulu, HI 96813. Offers MA. Part-time and evening/weekend programs available. *Degree requirements:* For master's, thesis. *Entrance requirements:* Additional exam requirements/recommendations for international students: Recommended—TOEFL (minimum score 550 paper-based; 213 computer-based; 80 iBT), TWE (minimum score 5). Electronic applications accepted.

See Close-Up on page 1269.

HEC Montreal, School of Business Administration, Diploma Programs in Administration, Program in Management and Sustainable Development, Montréal, QC H3T 2A7, Canada. Offers Diploma. Part-time programs available. *Students:* 16 full-time (8 women), 59 part-time (31 women). 80 applicants, 70% accepted, 36 enrolled. In 2010, 30 Diplomas awarded. *Degree requirements:* For Diploma, one foreign language. *Application deadline:* For fall admission, 4/15 for domestic students. Application fee: $78. Electronic applications accepted. *Expenses:* Tuition, area resident: Part-time $68.93 per credit. Tuition, state resident: full-time $2481.48; part-time $188.92 per credit. Tuition, nonresident: full-time $6801; part-time $482.06 per course. International tuition: $17,354.16 full-time. Required fees: $1309.50; $30.28 per credit. $93.45 per term. Tuition and fees vary according to degree level and program. *Financial support:* Research assistantships, teaching assistantships available. Financial award application deadline: 9/2. *Unit head:* Silvia Ponce, Director, 514-340-6393, Fax: 514-340-6915, E-mail: silvia.ponce@hec.ca. *Application contact:* Marie Deshaies, Senior Student Advisor, 514-340-6135, Fax: 514-340-6411, E-mail: marie.deshaies@hec.ca.

Sustainable Development

Instituto Centroamericano de Administración de Empresas, Graduate Programs, La Garita, Costa Rica. Offers agribusiness management (MIAM); business administration (EMBA); finance (MBA); real estate management (MGREM); sustainable development (MBA); technology (MBA). *Degree requirements:* For master's, comprehensive exam, essay. *Entrance requirements:* For master's, GMAT or GRE General Test, fluency in Spanish, interview, letters of recommendation, minimum 1 year of work experience. Electronic applications accepted. *Faculty research:* Competitiveness, production.

Instituto Tecnologico de Santo Domingo, Graduate School, Area of Humanities and Social Sciences, Santo Domingo, Dominican Republic. Offers accounting (Certificate); adult education (Certificate); applied linguistics (MA); economics (MA); education (M Ed); educational psychology (MA, Certificate); gender and development (MA, Certificate); humanistic studies (MA); international marketing management (Certificate); international relations in the Caribbean basin (Certificate); intervention systems in family therapy (MA); linguistic and literary communication (Certificate); pedagogical support (MA); social science education (M Ed); sustainable human development (MA); terminal illness and death psychology (Certificate); youth and adult education (M Ed).

Iowa State University of Science and Technology, Graduate College, Interdisciplinary Programs, Program in Sustainable Agriculture, Ames, IA 50011. Offers MS, PhD. *Students:* 35 full-time (21 women), 8 part-time (3 women); includes 3 Black or African American, non-Hispanic/Latino; 2 Asian, non-Hispanic/Latino; 2 Hispanic/Latino, 7 international. In 2010, 4 master's, 3 doctorates awarded. *Degree requirements:* For master's, thesis or alternative; for doctorate, thesis/dissertation. *Entrance requirements:* For master's and doctorate, GRE General Test. Additional exam requirements/recommendations for international students: Required—TOEFL (minimum score 570 paper-based; 80 iBT), IELTS (minimum score 6.5). *Application deadline:* For fall admission, 2/1 for domestic and international students; for spring admission, 6/1 priority date for domestic and international students. Application fee: $40 ($90 for international students). *Financial support:* In 2010–11, 20 research assistantships with full and partial tuition reimbursements (averaging $15,362 per year), 3 teaching assistantships with full and partial tuition reimbursements (averaging $11,088 per year) were awarded. *Unit head:* Dr. Mary Wiedenhoeft, Chair, Supervising Committee, 515-294-6518, E-mail: gpsa@iastate.edu. *Application contact:* Charles Sauer, Information Contact, 515-294-6518, E-mail: gpsa@iastate.edu.

Lesley University, Graduate School of Arts and Social Sciences, Program in Urban Environmental Leadership, Cambridge, MA 02138-2790. Offers MA. *Entrance requirements:* For master's, 2 letters of recommendation, interview.

Lipscomb University, Institute for Sustainable Practice, Nashville, TN 37204-3951. Offers MS. *Faculty:* 1 full-time (0 women), 3 part-time/adjunct (2 women). *Students:* 18 full-time (9 women), 10 part-time (6 women); includes 1 Black or African American, non-Hispanic/Latino; 1 Asian, non-Hispanic/Latino; 1 Hispanic/Latino. Average age 31. 17 applicants, 100% accepted, 17 enrolled. In 2010, 10 master's awarded. *Expenses:* Tuition: Full-time $18,149; part-time $943 per hour. Tuition and fees vary according to program. *Unit head:* G. Dodd Galbreath, Executive Director, 615-966-1771, E-mail: dodd.galbreath@lipscomb.edu. *Application contact:* Aileen Bennett, Program Coordinator, 615-966-1771, E-mail: aileen.bennett@lipscomb.edu.

Marylhurst University, Department of Business Administration, Marylhurst, OR 97036-0261. Offers finance (MBA); general management (MBA); government policy and administration (MBA); green development (MBA); health care management (MBA); marketing (MBA); natural and organic resources (MBA); nonprofit management (MBA); organizational behavior (MBA); real estate (MBA); renewable energy (MBA); sustainable business (MBA). Part-time and evening/weekend programs available. Postbaccalaureate distance learning degree programs offered (no on-campus study). *Faculty:* 3 full-time (0 women), 36 part-time/adjunct (6 women). *Students:* 27 full-time (13 women), 727 part-time (373 women); includes 167 minority (47 Black or African American, non-Hispanic/Latino; 6 American Indian or Alaska Native, non-Hispanic/Latino; 36 Asian, non-Hispanic/Latino; 51 Hispanic/Latino; 6 Native Hawaiian or other Pacific Islander, non-Hispanic/Latino; 21 Two or more races, non-Hispanic/Latino), 7 international. Average age 38. 262 applicants, 91% accepted, 194 enrolled. In 2010, 289 master's awarded. *Degree requirements:* For master's, comprehensive exam, capstone course. *Entrance requirements:* For master's, GMAT (if GPA less than 3.0 and fewer than 5 years of work experience), interview, resume, 2 letters of recommendation. Additional exam requirements/recommendations for international students: Recommended—TOEFL (minimum score 550 paper-based; 213 computer-based; 80 iBT). *Application deadline:* For fall admission, 9/11 priority date for domestic and international students; for winter admission, 12/15 priority date for domestic and international students; for spring admission, 3/15 priority date for domestic students, 3/17 priority date for international students. Applications are processed on a rolling basis. Application fee: $50. Electronic applications accepted. *Expenses:* Tuition: Full-time $13,932; part-time $516 per credit. Tuition and fees vary according to course load and program. *Financial support:* Scholarships/grants available. Support available to part-time students. Financial award applicants required to submit FAFSA. *Unit head:* Bob Hanks, Director of Business and Real Estate Programs, 503-636-8141, Fax: 503-697-5597, E-mail: mba@marylhurst.edu. *Application contact:* Maruska Lynch, Graduate Admissions Specialist, 800-634-9982 Ext. 6322, Fax: 503-699-6320, E-mail: admissions@marylhurst.edu.

Michigan Technological University, Graduate School, Sustainable Futures Institute, Houghton, MI 49931. Offers sustainability (Certificate). Part-time programs available.

Minneapolis College of Art and Design, Certificate Programs, Minneapolis, MN 55404-4347. Offers design (Certificate); fine arts (Certificate); graphic design (Certificate); media (Certificate); sustainable design (Certificate). Part-time programs available. Postbaccalaureate distance learning degree programs offered. *Degree requirements:* For Certificate, final project. *Entrance requirements:* For degree, resume, portfolio, letter of recommendation. Additional exam requirements/recommendations for international students: Required—TOEFL (minimum score 550 paper-based; 213 computer-based; 79 iBT). Electronic applications accepted. *Faculty research:* Visual arts.

New York School of Interior Design, Program in Sustainable Interior Environments, New York, NY 10021-5110. Offers MPS. *Faculty:* 24 part-time/adjunct (10 women). *Students:* 9 full-time (7 women); includes 4 minority (2 Asian, non-Hispanic/Latino; 2 Hispanic/Latino). Average age 27. In 2010, 1 master's awarded. *Entrance requirements:* For master's, first-professional degree in interior design, architecture, or a closely related field; portfolio. Additional exam requirements/recommendations for international students: Required—TOEFL (minimum score 550 paper-based; 213 computer-based; 79 iBT). *Application deadline:* For fall admission, 2/1 priority date for domestic and international students. Applications are processed on a rolling basis. Application fee: $60 ($100 for international students). Electronic applications accepted. *Expenses:* Tuition: Full-time $26,500. Required fees: $335. One-time fee: $60 full-time. *Financial support:* Research assistantships, Federal Work-Study available. Financial award applicants required to submit FAFSA. *Application contact:* Scott Ageloff, Dean, 212-472-1500 Ext. 301, Fax: 212-288-6577, E-mail: sageloff@nysid.edu.

New York University, School of Continuing and Professional Studies, Schack Institute of Real Estate, Program in Real Estate, New York, NY 10012-1019. Offers business of development (MS); finance and investment (MS); global real estate (MS); real estate (Advanced Certificate); strategic real estate management (MS); sustainable development (MS). Part-time and evening/weekend programs available. *Faculty:* 11 full-time (3 women), 74 part-time/adjunct (8 women). *Students:* 94 full-time (17 women), 282 part-time (63 women); includes 16 Black or African American, non-Hispanic/Latino; 2 American Indian or Alaska Native, non-Hispanic/Latino; 30 Asian, non-Hispanic/Latino; 17 Hispanic/Latino, 62 international. Average age 30. 298 applicants, 68% accepted, 111 enrolled. In 2010, 184 master's, 48 other advanced degrees awarded. *Degree requirements:* For master's, thesis, capstone. *Entrance requirements:* For master's, GRE General Test or GMAT (for recent graduates), resume, 2 letters of recommendation, essay, professional experience. Additional exam requirements/recommendations for international students: Required—TOEFL (minimum score 600 paper-based; 250 computer-based; 100 iBT), TWE. *Application deadline:* For fall admission, 2/1 priority date for domestic and international students; for spring admission, 10/15 priority date for domestic students, 8/15 priority date for international students. Applications are processed on a rolling basis. Application fee: $75. Electronic applications accepted. *Financial support:* In 2010–11, 186 students received support, including 186 fellowships (averaging $2,423 per year); scholarships/grants also available. Support available to part-time students. Financial award application deadline: 3/1; financial award applicants required to submit FAFSA. *Faculty research:* Economics and market cycles, international property rights, comparative metropolitan economies, current market trends. *Unit head:* James Stuckey, Divisional Dean, 212-992-3335, Fax: 212-992-3686, E-mail: james.stuckey@nyu.edu. *Application contact:* Jennifer Monahan, Director of Administration and Student Services, 212-992-3335, Fax: 212-992-3686, E-mail: jm189@nyu.edu.

Northern Arizona University, Graduate College, College of Social and Behavioral Sciences, Program in Sustainable Communities, Flagstaff, AZ 86011. Offers MA. Part-time programs available. *Faculty:* 1 (woman) full-time. *Students:* 43 full-time (29 women), 18 part-time (15 women); includes 8 minority (3 American Indian or Alaska Native, non-Hispanic/Latino; 1 Asian, non-Hispanic/Latino; 4 Hispanic/Latino). Average age 40. 38 applicants, 66% accepted, 19 enrolled. In 2010, 11 master's awarded. *Degree requirements:* For master's, thesis. *Entrance requirements:* For master's, minimum GPA of 3.0. Additional exam requirements/recommendations for international students: Required—TOEFL (minimum score 550 paper-based; 213 computer-based; 80 iBT), IELTS (minimum score 7). *Application deadline:* For fall admission, 3/15 priority date for domestic and international students. Applications are processed on a rolling basis. Application fee: $65. Electronic applications accepted. *Financial support:* Federal Work-Study, scholarships/grants, health care benefits, tuition waivers (full and partial), and unspecified assistantships available. Support available to part-time students. Financial award applicants required to submit FAFSA. *Unit head:* Dr. Luis Fernandez, Director, 928-523-2382, Fax: 928-523-2020, E-mail: luis.fernandez@nau.edu. *Application contact:* Tamara Ramirez, Program Coordinator, 928-523-0499, Fax: 928-523-2020, E-mail: sustainable.communities@nau.edu.

Pace University, Pace Law School, White Plains, NY 10603. Offers comparative legal studies (LL M); environmental law (LL M, SJD), including climate change (LL M), land use and sustainability (LL M); law (JD); JD/LL M; JD/MA; JD/MBA; JD/MEM; JD/MPA; JD/MS. JD/MA offered jointly with Sarah Lawrence College; JD/MEM offered jointly with Yale University School of Forestry and Environmental Studies. *Accreditation:* ABA. Part-time programs available. *Faculty:* 41 full-time (18 women), 52 part-time/adjunct (23 women). *Students:* 582 full-time (326 women), 230 part-time (145 women); includes 33 Black or African American, non-Hispanic/Latino; 1 American Indian or Alaska Native, non-Hispanic/Latino; 53 Asian, non-Hispanic/Latino; 49 Hispanic/Latino, 17 international. Average age 26. 3,082 applicants, 38% accepted, 263 enrolled. In 2010, 216 first professional degrees, 20 master's, 1 doctorate awarded. *Degree requirements:* For master's, writing sample; for doctorate, thesis/dissertation, extensive thesis proposal. *Entrance requirements:* LSAT. Additional exam requirements/recommendations for international students: Required—TOEFL (minimum score 600 paper-based; 250 computer-based); Recommended—TWE. *Application deadline:* For fall admission, 3/1 priority date for domestic students; for winter admission, 11/15 priority date for domestic students. Applications are processed on a rolling basis. Application fee: $65. Electronic applications accepted. *Expenses:* Contact institution. *Financial support:* Career-related internships or fieldwork, Federal Work-Study, institutionally sponsored loans, scholarships/grants, and unspecified assistantships available. Support available to part-time students. Financial award application deadline: 2/1; financial award applicants required to submit FAFSA. *Faculty research:* Reform of energy regulations, international law, land use law, prosecutorial misconduct, corporation law, international sale of goods. Total annual research expenditures: $2.2 million. *Unit head:* Michelle S. Simon, Dean, 914-422-4407, E-mail: msimon@law.pace.edu. *Application contact:* Cathy Alexander, Assistant Dean, 914-422-4210, Fax: 914-989-8714, E-mail: calexander@law.pace.edu.

Philadelphia University, School of Architecture, Program in Sustainable Design, Philadelphia, PA 19144. Offers MS.

Pratt Institute, School of Architecture, Environmental Systems Management Program, Brooklyn, NY 11205-3899. Offers MS. Part-time programs available. *Faculty:* 5 part-time/adjunct (3 women). *Students:* 20 full-time (12 women), 13 part-time (7 women); includes 1 Black or African American, non-Hispanic/Latino; 1 Asian, non-Hispanic/Latino; 5 Hispanic/Latino, 3 international. Average age 31. 41 applicants, 85% accepted, 14 enrolled. In 2010, 12 master's awarded. *Degree requirements:* For master's, thesis. *Entrance requirements:* For master's, portfolio or writing sample, letters of recommendation. Additional exam requirements/recommendations for international students: Required—TOEFL (minimum score 550 paper-based; 213 computer-based; 79 iBT). *Application deadline:* For fall admission, 1/5 for domestic and international students; for spring admission, 10/1 for domestic and international students. Application fee: $50 ($90 for international students). Electronic applications accepted. *Expenses:* Tuition: Full-time $22,734; part-time $1263 per credit. Required fees: $1280. *Financial support:* Career-related internships or fieldwork, Federal Work-Study, institutionally sponsored loans, scholarships/grants, and unspecified assistantships available. Support available to part-time students. Financial award application deadline: 2/1; financial award applicants required to submit FAFSA. *Unit head:* Jaime Stein, Chairperson, 718-399-4323, E-mail: jstein9@pratt.edu. *Application contact:* Young Hah, Director of Graduate Admissions, 718-636-3683, Fax: 718-399-4242, E-mail: yhah@pratt.edu.

See Display on page 141 and Close-Up on page 161.

Ramapo College of New Jersey, Master of Arts in Sustainability Studies Program, Mahwah, NJ 07430. Offers MA. Evening/weekend programs available. *Faculty:* 4 part-time/adjunct (1 woman). *Students:* 17 part-time (10 women). Average age 36. 29 applicants, 76% accepted, 17 enrolled. *Degree requirements:* For master's, thesis, summer practicum. *Entrance requirements:* For master's, GRE. Additional exam requirements/recommendations for international students: Required—TOEFL. *Application deadline:* For fall admission, 5/1 priority date for domestic and international students. Applications are processed on a rolling basis. Application fee: $60. Electronic applications accepted. *Expenses:* Tuition, state resident: part-time $525.30 per credit. Tuition, nonresident: part-time $675.20 per credit. Required fees: $107.70 per credit. *Financial support:* In 2010–11, 1 research assistantship was awarded; career-related internships or fieldwork and tuition waivers (full) also available. *Faculty research:* Urban ecology, tropical forest ecology, governance and organizational development, political economy, psycho-social impact assessment of environmental disaster and change. *Unit head:* Dr. Ashwani Vasishth, Director, 201-684-6616, E-mail: vasishth@ramapo.edu. *Application contact:* Dr. Ashwani Vasishth, Director, 201-684-6616, E-mail: vasishth@ramapo.edu.

Rensselaer Polytechnic Institute, Graduate School, School of Humanities, Arts, and Social Sciences, Program in Science and Technology Studies, Troy, NY 12180-3590. Offers design studies (MS, PhD); policy studies (MS, PhD); science studies (MS, PhD); sustainability studies (MS, PhD); technology studies (MS, PhD). *Faculty:* 15 full-time (5 women). *Students:* 20 full-time (5 women), 4 part-time (2 women); includes 2 Black or African American, non-Hispanic/Latino; 1 Asian, non-Hispanic/Latino, 4 international. Average age 27. 19 applicants, 42% accepted, 5 enrolled. In 2010, 2 master's, 1 doctorate awarded. Terminal master's awarded for partial completion of doctoral program. *Degree requirements:* For master's, thesis (for some programs); for doctorate, comprehensive exam, thesis/dissertation. *Entrance requirements:* For master's and doctorate, GRE General Test. Additional exam requirements/recommendations for international students: Required—TOEFL (minimum score 600 paper-based; 250 computer-based). *Application deadline:* For fall admission, 1/15 priority date for domestic students, 1/15 for international students. Applications are processed on a rolling basis. Application fee: $75. Electronic applications accepted. *Expenses:* Tuition: Full-time $39,600; part-time $1650 per credit. Required fees: $1896. *Financial support:* In 2010–11, 22 students received support, including 6 fellowships with tuition reimbursements available (averaging $19,800 per year), 2

Sustainable Development

Rensselaer Polytechnic Institute (continued)
research assistantships with full tuition reimbursements available (averaging $19,800 per year), 11 teaching assistantships with full tuition reimbursements available (averaging $19,800 per year); career-related internships or fieldwork, institutionally sponsored loans, and tuition waivers (partial) also available. Financial award application deadline: 1/15. *Faculty research:* Communities and technology, social dimensions of IT and biotechnology, ethics and policy, design. Total annual research expenditures: $75,000. *Unit head:* Dr. Sharon Anderson-Gold, Chair, 518-276-8837, Fax: 518-276-2659, E-mail: anders@rpi.edu. *Application contact:* Dr. Edward J. Woodhouse, Director of Graduate Studies, 518-276-8506, Fax: 518-276-2659, E-mail: woodhouse@rpi.edu.

Rochester Institute of Technology, Graduate Enrollment Services, Golisano Institute for Sustainability, Rochester, NY 14623-5603. Offers M Arch, PhD. *Students:* 11 full-time (7 women), 1 part-time (0 women); includes 1 Black or African American, non-Hispanic/Latino; 1 Hispanic/Latino, 5 international. Average age 31. 45 applicants, 24% accepted, 6 enrolled. *Degree requirements:* For master's, comprehensive exam, thesis. *Entrance requirements:* For master's, GRE. Additional exam requirements/recommendations for international students: Required—TOEFL (minimum score 600 paper-based; 250 computer-based; 100 iBT) or IELTS (minimum score 6.5). *Application deadline:* For fall admission, 1/15 priority date for domestic and international students. Application fee: $50. *Expenses:* Tuition: Full-time $33,234; part-time $924 per credit hour. Required fees: $219. *Financial support:* In 2010–11, 12 students received support. *Faculty research:* Remanufacturing and resource recovery, sustainable production, sustainable mobility, systems modernization and sustainment, pollution prevention. *Unit head:* Dr. Nabil Nasr, Assistant Provost and Director, 585-475-2602, E-mail: info@sustainability.rit.edu. *Application contact:* Diane Ellison, Assistant Vice President, Graduate Enrollment Services, 585-475-2229, Fax: 585-475-7164, E-mail: gradinfo@rit.edu.

Rollins College, Hamilton Holt School, Program in Civic Urbanism, Winter Park, FL 32789. Offers M Pl. Part-time and evening/weekend programs available. *Faculty:* 2 full-time (0 women). *Students:* 26 part-time (13 women); includes 4 minority (1 Asian, non-Hispanic/Latino; 3 Hispanic/Latino). Average age 32. 44 applicants, 64% accepted, 24 enrolled. *Entrance requirements:* For master's, GRE. Additional exam requirements/recommendations for international students: Required—TOEFL (minimum score 550 paper-based; 213 computer-based; 80 iBT). *Application deadline:* For fall admission, 4/1 for domestic students. Application fee: $50. *Expenses:* Contact institution. *Financial support:* Career-related internships or fieldwork, scholarships/grants, and unspecified assistantships available. Support available to part-time students. Financial award applicants required to submit FAFSA. *Unit head:* Dr. Bruce Stephenson, Chair, 407-646-2232. *Application contact:* Graduate Program Admission, 407-646-2232, Fax: 407-646-1551.

Saybrook University, Graduate College of Psychology and Humanistic Studies, San Francisco, CA 94111-1920. Offers clinical psychology (Psy D); human science (MA, PhD), including consciousness and spirituality, humanistic and transpersonal psychology, integrative health studies, organizational systems, social transformation, transformative social change (MA); organizational systems (MA, PhD), including consciousness and spirituality, humanistic and transpersonal psychology, integrative health studies, leadership of sustainable systems (MA), organizational systems, social transformation; psychology (MA, PhD), including clinical psychology (PhD), consciousness and spirituality, creativity studies (MA), humanistic and transpersonal psychology, integrative health studies, Jungian studies, marriage and family therapy (MA), organizational systems, social transformation. Postbaccalaureate distance learning degree programs offered (minimal on-campus study). *Faculty:* 15 full-time (5 women), 83 part-time/adjunct (34 women). *Students:* 479 full-time (333 women); includes 30 Black or African American, non-Hispanic/Latino; 1 American Indian or Alaska Native, non-Hispanic/Latino; 13 Asian, non-Hispanic/Latino; 18 Hispanic/Latino, 18 international. Average age 43. 280 applicants, 52% accepted, 105 enrolled. In 2010, 28 master's, 43 doctorates awarded. Terminal master's awarded for partial completion of doctoral program. *Degree requirements:* For master's, thesis or alternative; for doctorate, thesis/dissertation. *Entrance requirements:* Additional exam requirements/recommendations for international students: Required—TOEFL (minimum score 580 paper-based; 237 computer-based; 93 iBT). *Application deadline:* For fall admission, 6/1 priority date for domestic students; for spring admission, 12/16 priority date for domestic students. Application fee: $50. Electronic applications accepted. *Financial support:* In 2010–11, 335 students received support. Scholarships/grants available. Financial award applicants required to submit FAFSA. *Faculty research:* Humanistic theory, health studies, organizational systems, consciousness and spirituality, social transformation. Total annual research expenditures: $90,000. *Unit head:* Mark Schulman, President, 800-825-4480, Fax: 415-433-9271. *Application contact:* Director of Admissions, 800-825-4480, Fax: 415-433-9271, E-mail: admissions@saybrook.edu.

SIT Graduate Institute, Graduate Programs, Master's Programs in Intercultural Service, Leadership, and Management, Program in Sustainable Development, Washington, DC 20005. Offers MA. *Expenses:* Tuition: Full-time $35,260; part-time $14,876 per year. Required fees: $1495; $1495 per year. Tuition and fees vary according to class time and campus/location.

Slippery Rock University of Pennsylvania, Graduate Studies (Recruitment), College of Health, Environment, and Science, Department of Geography, Geology, and the Environment, Slippery Rock, PA 16057-1383. Offers sustainable systems (MS). Part-time and evening/weekend programs available. *Faculty:* 3 full-time (1 woman). *Students:* 10 full-time (4 women), 4 part-time (1 woman); includes 1 minority (Hispanic/Latino). Average age 32. 33 applicants, 70% accepted, 13 enrolled. In 2010, 1 master's awarded. *Degree requirements:* For master's, thesis, internship, professional portfolio. *Entrance requirements:* For master's, GRE General Test, minimum GPA of 3.0, two letters of recommendation, writing sample, resume. Additional exam requirements/recommendations for international students: Required—TOEFL (minimum score 550 paper-based; 213 computer-based; 80 iBT). *Application deadline:* For fall admission, 3/1 priority date for domestic students, 5/1 priority date for international students; for spring admission, 11/1 priority date for domestic students, 9/1 priority date for international students. Applications are processed on a rolling basis. Application fee: $25 ($30 for international students). Electronic applications accepted. *Expenses:* Tuition, state resident: full-time $6966; part-time $387 per credit. Tuition, nonresident: full-time $11,146; part-time $619 per credit. Required fees: $2388; $202 per credit. *Financial support:* Career-related internships or fieldwork, Federal Work-Study, institutionally sponsored loans, scholarships/grants, tuition waivers (partial), and unspecified assistantships available. Support available to part-time students. Financial award application deadline: 5/1; financial award applicants required to submit FAFSA. *Faculty research:* Using GIS to integrate the NOAA HYSPLIT model with surfaced-based air quality and mercury deposition data, bedrock geology of the Glenshaw Quadrangle. Total annual research expenditures: $203,915. *Unit head:* Dr. Langdon Smith, Coordinator, 724-738-2389, Fax: 724-738-4217, E-mail: langdon.smith@sru.edu. *Application contact:* Angela Piverotto, Director of Graduate Admissions, 724-738-2051, Fax: 724-738-2146, E-mail: graduate.admissions@sru.edu.

University of Alaska Fairbanks, School of Natural Resources and Agricultural Sciences, Fairbanks, AK 99775-7140. Offers natural resource and sustainability (PhD); natural resource management (MS); natural resource management and geography (MNRM, MS). Part-time programs available. *Faculty:* 37 full-time (12 women), 5 part-time/adjunct (4 women). *Students:* 31 full-time (22 women), 24 part-time (10 women); includes 5 minority (2 American Indian or Alaska Native, non-Hispanic/Latino; 1 Hispanic/Latino; 2 Two or more races, non-Hispanic/Latino), 6 international. Average age 33. 42 applicants, 26% accepted, 8 enrolled. In 2010, 3 master's, 2 doctorates awarded. *Degree requirements:* For master's, comprehensive exam, thesis or alternative. *Entrance requirements:* For master's, GRE General Test. Additional exam requirements/recommendations for international students: Required—TOEFL (minimum score 550 paper-based; 213 computer-based). *Application deadline:* For fall admission, 6/1 for domestic students, 3/1 for international students; for spring admission, 10/15 for domestic students, 9/1 for international students. Applications are processed on a rolling basis. Application fee: $60. Electronic applications accepted. *Expenses:* Tuition, state resident: full-time $5688; part-time $316 per credit. Tuition, nonresident: full-time $11,628; part-time $646 per credit. Required fees: $289 per semester. Tuition and fees vary according to course load and reciprocity agreements. *Financial support:* In 2010–11, 17 research assistantships (averaging $11,187 per year), 4 teaching assistantships (averaging $8,943 per year) were awarded; fellowships, career-related internships or fieldwork, Federal Work-Study, scholarships/grants, health care benefits, and unspecified assistantships also available. Support available to part-time students. Financial award application deadline: 2/15; financial award applicants required to submit FAFSA. *Faculty research:* Conservation biology, soil/water conservation, land use policy and planning in the arctic and subarctic, forest ecosystem management, subarctic agricultural production. Total annual research expenditures: $5.6 million. *Unit head:* Dr. Carol E. Lewis, Dean, 907-474-7083, Fax: 907-474-6567, E-mail: fysnras@uaf.edu. *Application contact:* Veazey David, Director of Enrollment Management, 907-474-5276, Fax: 907-474-6567, E-mail: dave.veazey@alaska.edu.

University of California, Berkeley, UC Berkeley Extension, Certificate Programs in Sustainability Studies, Berkeley, CA 94720-1500. Offers leadership in sustainability and environmental management (Professional Certificate); solar energy and green building (Professional Certificate); sustainable design (Professional Certificate).

University of California, Santa Barbara, Graduate Division, College of Letters and Sciences, Division of Social Sciences, Department of Global and International Studies, Santa Barbara, CA 93106-7065. Offers global culture and religion (MA); global government and human rights (MA); political economy, sustainable development, and the environment (MA). *Faculty:* 14 full-time (5 women), 4 part-time/adjunct (1 woman). *Students:* 37 full-time (25 women); includes 6 Asian, non-Hispanic/Latino; 2 Hispanic/Latino; 1 Native Hawaiian or other Pacific Islander, non-Hispanic/Latino. Average age 28. 55 applicants, 42% accepted, 12 enrolled. In 2010, 14 master's awarded. *Degree requirements:* For master's, one foreign language, thesis or alternative, 2 years of a second language. *Entrance requirements:* For master's, GRE, 2 years of a second language with minimum B grade, 3 letters of recommendation, resume/curriculum vitae. Additional exam requirements/recommendations for international students: Required—TOEFL (minimum score 600 paper-based; 80 iBT), IELTS (minimum score 7). *Application deadline:* For fall admission, 12/15 for domestic and international students. Application fee: $70 ($90 for international students). Electronic applications accepted. *Financial support:* In 2010–11, 36 students received support, including 29 fellowships with partial tuition reimbursements available (averaging $6,805 per year), 31 teaching assistantships with partial tuition reimbursements available (averaging $8,175 per year); career-related internships or fieldwork also available. Financial award application deadline: 12/15; financial award applicants required to submit FAFSA. *Faculty research:* Global culture religion, global governance human rights, political economy, environment, sustainable development. Total annual research expenditures: $240,000. *Unit head:* Prof. Giles Gunn, Chair, 805-893-4299, Fax: 805-893-8003, E-mail: ggunn@global.ucsb.edu. *Application contact:* Jessea Gay Marie, Graduate Program Advisor/Internship Assistance Officer, 805-893-4668, Fax: 805-893-8003, E-mail: gd-global@global.ucsb.edu.

University of Colorado Denver, College of Architecture and Planning, Program in Design and Planning, Denver, CO 80217-3364. Offers history of architecture, landscape and urbanism (PhD); sustainable and healthy environments (PhD). Part-time programs available. *Students:* 25 full-time (15 women), 11 part-time (7 women); includes 2 Black or African American, non-Hispanic/Latino; 1 Asian, non-Hispanic/Latino; 2 Hispanic/Latino, 7 international. Average age 40. 60 applicants, 15% accepted, 6 enrolled. In 2010, 2 doctorates awarded. *Degree requirements:* For doctorate, comprehensive exam, thesis/dissertation. *Entrance requirements:* For doctorate, GRE, minimum undergraduate GPA of 3.0, graduate 3.5; writing sample. Additional exam requirements/recommendations for international students: Required—TOEFL (minimum score 575 paper-based). *Application deadline:* For fall admission, 2/1 for domestic students; for spring admission, 10/1 for domestic students. Application fee: $50 ($75 for international students). Electronic applications accepted. *Expenses:* Contact institution. *Financial support:* Fellowships, research assistantships, teaching assistantships, career-related internships or fieldwork, Federal Work-Study, scholarships/grants, tuition waivers, and unspecified assistantships available. Support available to part-time students. Financial award application deadline: 4/1; financial award applicants required to submit FAFSA. *Faculty research:* Land use and environmental planning and design; design and planning processes and practices; history, theory, and criticism of the built environment. *Unit head:* Dr. Kevin Krizek, Director, 303-556-3282, Fax: 303-556-3687, E-mail: kevin.krizek@colorado.edu. *Application contact:* Michael Harper, Administrative Coordinator, 303-556-6042, Fax: 303-556-3687, E-mail: michael.t.harper@ucdenver.edu.

University of Colorado Denver, College of Engineering and Applied Science, Department of Civil Engineering, Denver, CO 80217-3364. Offers civil engineering (PhD); environmental and sustainability engineering (MS); geographic information systems (MS); geotechnical engineering (MS); hydrology and hydraulics (MS); structural engineering (MS); transportation engineering (MS). Part-time and evening/weekend programs available. *Faculty:* 14 full-time (1 woman), 6 part-time/adjunct (0 women). *Students:* 66 full-time (13 women), 72 part-time (16 women); includes 9 Black or African American, non-Hispanic/Latino; 8 Asian, non-Hispanic/Latino; 11 Hispanic/Latino, 15 international. Average age 32. 72 applicants, 54% accepted, 29 enrolled. In 2010, 14 master's, 3 doctorates awarded. *Degree requirements:* For master's, comprehensive exam, thesis or alternative; for doctorate, comprehensive exam, thesis/dissertation. *Entrance requirements:* For master's, GRE, statement of purpose, transcripts, references; for doctorate, GRE, statement of purpose, transcripts, references, letter of support from faculty stating willingness to serve as dissertation advisor and outlining plan for financial support. Additional exam requirements/recommendations for international students: Required—TOEFL (minimum score 525 paper-based; 197 computer-based). *Application deadline:* For fall admission, 7/15 for domestic students, 6/15 for international students; for spring admission, 12/1 for domestic students, 11/1 for international students. Applications are processed on a rolling basis. Application fee: $50 ($75 for international students). Electronic applications accepted. *Expenses:* Contact institution. *Financial support:* Research assistantships, teaching assistantships, career-related internships or fieldwork and Federal Work-Study available. Financial award application deadline: 4/1; financial award applicants required to submit FAFSA. *Faculty research:* Environmental engineering and sustainable systems, geosynthetics, hydrologic and hydraulic engineering, structural engineering, transportation, transportation energy use and greenhouse gas emissions. *Unit head:* Dr. Nien-Yin Chang, Acting Chair, 303-556-2810, Fax: 303-556-2368, E-mail: nien.chang@ucdenver.edu. *Application contact:* Mindy Gewuerz, Program Assistant, 303-556-6712, Fax: 303-556-2368, E-mail: mindy.gewuerz@ucdenver.edu.

University of Colorado Denver, College of Liberal Arts and Sciences, Department of Anthropology, Denver, CO 80217. Offers archaeological studies (MA); biological anthropology (MA); medical anthropology (MA); sustainable development and political ecology (MA). Part-time and evening/weekend programs available. *Faculty:* 8 full-time (1 woman). *Students:* 16 full-time (12 women), 7 part-time (6 women); includes 1 Hispanic/Latino. Average age 30. 44 applicants, 59% accepted, 9 enrolled. In 2010, 13 master's awarded. *Degree requirements:* For master's, comprehensive exam, thesis or alternative, 30-36 credit hours. *Entrance requirements:* For master's, GRE General Test, minimum GPA of 3.0 for all undergraduate studies, two copies of transcripts from all undergraduate/graduate institutions attended, prior training in anthropology, three letters of recommendation, statement of purpose. Additional exam requirements/recommendations for international students: Required—TOEFL (minimum score 525 paper-based; 197 computer-based). *Application deadline:* For fall admission, 2/15 for domestic students. Applications are processed on a rolling basis. Application fee: $50 ($75 for international students). Electronic applications accepted. *Expenses:* Tuition, state resident: full-time $7332; part-time $355 per credit hour. Tuition, nonresident: full-time $18,990; part-time $1055 per credit hour. Required fees: $998. Tuition and fees vary according to course level, course load, degree level, campus/location, program, reciprocity agreements and student level. *Financial support:* Research assistantships, teaching assistantships, Federal Work-Study available. Financial award application deadline: 4/1; financial award applicants required to submit FAFSA.

Faculty research: Applied medical anthropology, primate social behavior, environmental anthropology, Southwestern and Mexican archaeology, human ecology. *Unit head:* Dr. Steve P. Koester, Chair, 303-556-6795, Fax: 303-556-8501, E-mail: steve.koester@ucdenver.edu. *Application contact:* Connie Turner, Program Assistant, 303-556-3554, Fax: 303-556-8501, E-mail: connie.turner@ucdenver.edu.

University of Connecticut, Graduate School, Center for Continuing Studies, Program in Humanitarian Services Administration, Storrs, CT 06269. Offers MPS. Postbaccalaureate distance learning degree programs offered. *Entrance requirements:* For master's, minimum GPA of 3.0 or greater than 3.0 for the last 2 years of study; 3 letters of reference. Additional exam requirements/recommendations for international students: Required—TOEFL (minimum score 540 paper-based; 207 computer-based).

University of Georgia, School of Ecology, Athens, GA 30602. Offers conservation ecology and sustainable development (MS); ecology (MS, PhD). *Faculty:* 19 full-time (5 women), 4 part-time/adjunct (1 woman). *Students:* 62 full-time (35 women), 19 part-time (10 women); includes 1 Black or African American, non-Hispanic/Latino; 4 Hispanic/Latino; 1 Two or more races, non-Hispanic/Latino, 3 international. 93 applicants, 24% accepted, 14 enrolled. In 2010, 4 master's, 9 doctorates awarded. *Degree requirements:* For master's, thesis; for doctorate, one foreign language, thesis/dissertation. *Entrance requirements:* For master's and doctorate, GRE General Test. *Application deadline:* For fall admission, 7/1 priority date for domestic students; for spring admission, 11/15 for domestic students. Application fee: $50. Electronic applications accepted. *Expenses:* Tuition, state resident: full-time $7200; part-time $344 per credit hour. Tuition, nonresident: full-time $21,900; part-time $944 per credit hour. Tuition and fees vary according to course load and program. *Financial support:* Fellowships, research assistantships, teaching assistantships, unspecified assistantships available. *Unit head:* Dr. John L. Gittleman, Dean, 706-542-2968, Fax: 706-542-4819, E-mail: ecohead@uga.edu. *Application contact:* Dr. James Byers, Graduate Coordinator, 706-338-0012, Fax: 706-542-4819, E-mail: jebyers@uga.edu.

University of Maryland, College Park, Academic Affairs, College of Computer, Mathematical and Natural Sciences, Department of Biology, Program in Sustainable Development and Conservation Biology, College Park, MD 20742. Offers MS. Part-time and evening/weekend programs available. *Students:* 20 full-time (11 women), 3 part-time (2 women); includes 1 Hispanic/Latino, 5 international. 105 applicants, 22% accepted, 13 enrolled. In 2010, 14 master's awarded. *Degree requirements:* For master's, internship, scholarly paper. *Entrance requirements:* For master's, GRE General Test, minimum GPA of 3.0, 3 letters of recommendation. *Application deadline:* For fall admission, 1/15 priority date for domestic students, 2/1 for international students. Applications are processed on a rolling basis. Application fee: $75. Electronic applications accepted. *Expenses:* Tuition, state resident: part-time $471 per credit hour. Tuition, nonresident: part-time $1016 per credit hour. Required fees: $337 per term. *Financial support:* In 2010–11, 14 teaching assistantships (averaging $18,659 per year) were awarded. Financial award application deadline: 2/1; financial award applicants required to submit FAFSA. *Faculty research:* Biodiversity, global change, conservation. *Unit head:* Dr. David W. Inouye, Director, 301-405-9358, Fax: 301-314-9358, E-mail: inouye@umd.edu. *Application contact:* Dean of Graduate School, 301-405-0358, Fax: 301-314-9305.

University of Massachusetts Lowell, James B. Francis College of Engineering, Department of Civil and Environmental Engineering, Lowell, MA 01854-2881. Offers civil and environmental engineering (MS Eng, Certificate); environmental engineering (D Eng); environmental studies (MSES, PhD, Certificate), including environmental engineering (MSES), environmental studies (PhD, Certificate); sustainable infrastructure for developing nations (Certificate). Part-time programs available. *Degree requirements:* For master's, thesis optional. *Entrance requirements:* For master's, GRE General Test. *Faculty research:* Bridge design, traffic control, groundwater remediation, pile capacity.

University of Michigan, School of Natural Resources and Environment, Program in Natural Resources and Environment, Ann Arbor, MI 48109. Offers aquatic sciences: research and management (MS); behavior, education and communication (MS); conservation biology (MS); conservation ecology (MS); environmental informatics (MS); environmental justice (MS); environmental policy and planning (MS); natural resources and environment (PhD); sustainable systems (MS); terrestrial ecosystems (MS); MS/AM; MS/JD; MS/MBA. *Faculty:* 42 full-time, 23 part-time/adjunct. *Students:* 450 full-time (254 women); includes 7 Black or African American, non-Hispanic/Latino; 2 American Indian or Alaska Native, non-Hispanic/Latino; 35 Asian, non-Hispanic/Latino; 13 Hispanic/Latino; 6 Two or more races, non-Hispanic/Latino, 50 international. Average age 27. 692 applicants. In 2010, 133 master's, 11 doctorates awarded. Terminal master's awarded for partial completion of doctoral program. *Degree requirements:* For master's, practicum or group project; for doctorate, comprehensive exam, thesis/dissertation, oral defense of dissertation, preliminary exam. *Entrance requirements:* For master's, GRE General Test; for doctorate, GRE General Test, master's degree. Additional exam requirements/recommendations for international students: Required—TOEFL (minimum score 560 paper-based; 220 computer-based; 84 iBT). *Application deadline:* For fall admission, 1/5 priority date for domestic and international students. Applications are processed on a rolling basis. Application fee: $65 ($75 for international students). Electronic applications accepted. *Expenses:* Tuition, state resident: full-time $17,784; part-time $1116 per credit hour. Tuition, nonresident: full-time $35,944; part-time $2125 per credit hour. International tuition: $35,994 full-time. Required fees: $95 per semester. Tuition and fees vary according to course load, degree level and program. *Financial support:* Fellowships with tuition reimbursements, research assistantships with tuition reimbursements, teaching assistantships with tuition reimbursements, career-related internships or fieldwork, Federal Work-Study, institutionally sponsored loans, scholarships/grants, health care benefits, and unspecified assistantships available. Support available to part-time students. Financial award application deadline: 1/5; financial award applicants required to submit FAFSA. *Faculty research:* Stream ecology, plant-insect interactions, fish biology, resource control and reproductive success, remote sensing, conservation ecology. *Application contact:* Graduate Admissions Team, 734-764-6453, Fax: 734-936-2195, E-mail: snre.admissions@umich.edu.

University of New Brunswick Fredericton, School of Graduate Studies, Policy Studies Program, Fredericton, NB E3B 5A3, Canada. Offers people, property and alternative dispute resolution (M Phil); philosophy politics and economics (M Phil); sustainable development (M Phil). Part-time programs available. *Faculty:* 7 full-time (4 women), 8 part-time/adjunct (4 women). *Students:* 4 full-time (2 women), 5 part-time (3 women). In 2010, 3 master's awarded. *Degree requirements:* For master's, thesis, report. *Entrance requirements:* For master's, minimum GPA of 3.5. Additional exam requirements/recommendations for international students: Required—TWE (minimum score 4), TOEFL (minimum score 600 paper-based; 250 computer-based; 100 iBT) or IELTS (minimum score 7). Application fee: $50 Canadian dollars. *Expenses:* Tuition, area resident: Full-time $3708; part-time $927 per term. International tuition: $6300 full-time. Required fees: $50 per term. *Financial support:* In 2010–11, 3 fellowships, research assistantships (averaging $5,600 per year), teaching assistantships (averaging $4,400 per year) were awarded. *Unit head:* Dr. Linda Eyre, Dean of Graduate Studies, 506-447-3044, Fax: 506-453-4817, E-mail: gradidst@unb.ca. *Application contact:* Janet Amurault, Graduate Secretary, 506-458-7558, Fax: 506-453-4817, E-mail: jamiraul@unb.ca.

University of Southern California, Graduate School, School of Policy, Planning, and Development, Master of Planning Program, Los Angeles, CA 90089. Offers sustainable cities (Graduate Certificate); transportation systems (Graduate Certificate); urban planning (M Pl); M Arch/M Pl; M Pl/MA; M Pl/MS; M Pl/MSW; MBA/M Pl; ML Arch/M Pl; MPA/M Pl. *Accreditation:* ACSP. Part-time programs available. *Faculty:* 51 full-time (12 women), 100 part-time/adjunct (30 women). *Students:* 114 full-time (63 women), 8 part-time (4 women); includes 45 minority (3 Black or African American, non-Hispanic/Latino; 23 Asian, non-Hispanic/Latino; 14 Hispanic/Latino; 5 Two or more races, non-Hispanic/Latino), 15 international. 259 applicants, 71% accepted, 74 enrolled. In 2010, 40 master's awarded. *Degree requirements:* For master's, comprehensive exam, internship. *Entrance requirements:* For master's, GRE, GMAT. Additional exam requirements/recommendations for international students: Required—TOEFL (minimum score 600 paper-based; 250 computer-based; 100 iBT). *Application deadline:* For fall admission, 12/15 priority date for domestic and international students; for spring admission, 11/1 for domestic students, 10/1 for international students. Applications are processed on a rolling basis. Application fee: $85. Electronic applications accepted. *Expenses:* Tuition: Full-time $31,240; part-time $1420 per unit. Required fees: $600. One-time fee: $35 full-time. Full-time tuition and fees vary according to degree level and program. *Financial support:* In 2010–11, 87 students received support, including 2 research assistantships with full tuition reimbursements available (averaging $9,806 per year); scholarships/grants and tuition waivers (full and partial) also available. Financial award application deadline: 12/15; financial award applicants required to submit CSS PROFILE or FAFSA. *Faculty research:* Transportation and infrastructure, comparative international development, healthy communities, social economic development, sustainable community planning. Total annual research expenditures: $6.2 million. *Unit head:* Dr. Tridib Banerjee, Director, Graduate Programs in Urban Planning, 213-740-4724, Fax: 213-740-5379, E-mail: tbanerje@usc.edu. *Application contact:* Marisol R. Gonzalez, Director of Recruitment and Admission, 213-740-0550, Fax: 213-740-7573, E-mail: marisolr@usc.edu.

University of Southern California, Graduate School, Viterbi School of Engineering, Sonny Astani Department of Civil Engineering, Los Angeles, CA 90089. Offers applied mechanics (MS); civil engineering (MS, PhD); computer-aided engineering (ME, Graduate Certificate); construction management (MCM); engineering technology commercialization (Graduate Certificate); environmental engineering (MS, PhD); environmental quality management (ME); structural design (ME); sustainable cities (Graduate Certificate); transportation systems (MS, Graduate Certificate); water and waste management (MS). Part-time and evening/weekend programs available. *Faculty:* 16 full-time (2 women), 35 part-time/adjunct (5 women). *Students:* 190 full-time (52 women), 81 part-time (20 women); includes 54 minority (2 Black or African American, non-Hispanic/Latino; 42 Asian, non-Hispanic/Latino; 9 Hispanic/Latino; 1 Two or more races, non-Hispanic/Latino), 149 international. 541 applicants, 43% accepted, 100 enrolled. In 2010, 74 master's, 10 doctorates awarded. Terminal master's awarded for partial completion of doctoral program. *Degree requirements:* For master's, thesis optional; for doctorate, thesis/dissertation. *Entrance requirements:* For master's and doctorate, GRE General Test. *Application deadline:* For fall admission, 12/1 priority date for domestic and international students; for spring admission, 9/15 for domestic students, 9/15 priority date for international students. Applications are processed on a rolling basis. Application fee: $85. Electronic applications accepted. *Expenses:* Tuition: Full-time $31,240; part-time $1420 per unit. Required fees: $600. One-time fee: $35 full-time. Full-time tuition and fees vary according to degree level and program. *Financial support:* In 2010–11, fellowships with full tuition reimbursements (averaging $30,000 per year), research assistantships with full tuition reimbursements (averaging $20,000 per year), teaching assistantships with full tuition reimbursements (averaging $20,000 per year) were awarded; career-related internships or fieldwork, scholarships/grants, health care benefits, and unspecified assistantships also available. Financial award application deadline: 12/1; financial award applicants required to submit CSS PROFILE or FAFSA. *Faculty research:* Geotechnical engineering, transportation engineering, structural engineering, construction management, environmental engineering, water resources. Total annual research expenditures: $5 million. *Unit head:* Dr. Jean-Pierre Bardet, Chair, 213-740-0603, Fax: 213-744-1426, E-mail: ceedept@usc.edu. *Application contact:* Jennifer A. Gerson, Director of Student Affairs, 213-740-0573, Fax: 213-740-8662, E-mail: jgerson@usc.edu.

University of Washington, Graduate School, College of Forest Resources, Seattle, WA 98195. Offers bioresource science and engineering (MS, PhD); environmental horticulture (MEH); environmental horticulture and urban forestry (MS, PhD); forest ecology (MS, PhD); forest management (MFR); forest soils (MS, PhD); forest systems and bioenergy (MS, PhD); restoration ecology (MS, PhD); social sciences (MS, PhD); sustainable resource management (MS, PhD); wildlife science (MS, PhD); MFR/MAIS; MPA/MS. *Accreditation:* SAF. *Degree requirements:* For master's, thesis (for some programs); for doctorate, comprehensive exam (for some programs), thesis/dissertation. *Entrance requirements:* For master's and doctorate, GRE, minimum GPA of 3.0. Additional exam requirements/recommendations for international students: Required—TOEFL. Electronic applications accepted. *Faculty research:* Ecosystem analysis, silviculture and forest protection, paper science and engineering, environmental horticulture and urban forestry, natural resource policy and economics.

University of Washington, Graduate School, School of Law, Seattle, WA 98195-3020. Offers Asian law (LL M, PhD); intellectual property law and policy (LL M); law (JD); law of sustainable international development (LL M); taxation (LL M); JD/LL M; JD/MA; JD/MAIS; JD/MBA; JD/MPA; JD/MS; JD/PhD. *Accreditation:* ABA. *Degree requirements:* For master's, thesis; for doctorate, thesis/dissertation. *Entrance requirements:* For JD, LSAT; for master's, language proficiency (LL M in Asian law). Additional exam requirements/recommendations for international students: Required—TOEFL. *Expenses:* Contact institution. *Faculty research:* Asian, international and comparative law, intellectual property law, health law, environmental law, taxation.

The University of Western Ontario, Faculty of Graduate Studies, Physical Sciences Division, Department of Earth Sciences, London, ON N6A 5B8, Canada. Offers environment and sustainability (MES); geology (M Sc, PhD); geology and environmental science (M Sc, PhD); geophysics (M Sc, PhD); geophysics and environmental science (M Sc, PhD). *Degree requirements:* For master's, thesis; for doctorate, thesis/dissertation, qualifying exam. *Entrance requirements:* For master's, honors in B Sc; for doctorate, M Sc. Additional exam requirements/recommendations for international students: Required—TOEFL. *Faculty research:* Geophysics, geochemistry, paleontology, sedimentology/stratigraphy, glaciology/quaternary.

University of Wisconsin–Madison, Graduate School, Gaylord Nelson Institute for Environmental Studies, Conservation Biology and Sustainable Development Program, Madison, WI 53706-1380. Offers MS. Part-time programs available. *Faculty:* 3 full-time (1 woman), 15 part-time/adjunct (4 women). *Students:* 26 (22 women); includes 1 Asian, non-Hispanic/Latino. Average age 27. 54 applicants, 35% accepted, 11 enrolled. In 2010, 7 master's awarded. *Degree requirements:* For master's, thesis or alternative, exit seminar. *Entrance requirements:* For master's, GRE General Test. Additional exam requirements/recommendations for international students: Required—TOEFL (minimum score 550 paper-based; 213 computer-based; 80 iBT). *Application deadline:* For fall admission, 1/15 for domestic and international students; for spring admission, 10/15 for domestic and international students. Application fee: $56. Electronic applications accepted. *Expenses:* Tuition, state resident: full-time $9887; part-time $617.96 per credit. Tuition, nonresident: full-time $24,054; part-time $1503.40 per credit. Required fees: $67.63 per credit. Tuition and fees vary according to reciprocity agreements. *Financial support:* In 2010–11, 19 students received support, including 3 fellowships with full tuition reimbursements available (averaging $18,756 per year), 3 research assistantships with full tuition reimbursements available (averaging $14,960 per year), 7 teaching assistantships with full tuition reimbursements available (averaging $9,392 per year); career-related internships or fieldwork, Federal Work-Study, scholarships/grants, health care benefits, unspecified assistantships, and project assistantships also available. Financial award application deadline: 1/2. *Faculty research:* Ornithology, forestry, sociology, rural sociology, plant ecology, biodiversity, sustainability, sustainable development. *Unit head:* Janet M. Silbernagel, Chair, 608-890-2600, Fax: 608-262-2273, E-mail: jmsilber@wisc.edu. *Application contact:* Jim Miller, Student Services Coordinator, 608-263-4373, Fax: 608-262-2273, E-mail: jemiller@wisc.edu.

Walden University, Graduate Programs, School of Public Policy and Administration, Minneapolis, MN 55401. Offers criminal justice (MPA); emergency management (MPA); government management (Postbaccalaureate Certificate); health policy (MPA); homeland security policy (MPA); homeland security policy and coordination (MPA); interdisciplinary policy studies (MPA); international nongovernmental organizations (ngos) (MPA); law and public policy (MPA); local government management for sustainable communities (MPA); nonprofit management (Postbaccalaureate Certificate); nonprofit management and leadership (MPA, MS); policy analysis (MPA); public management and leadership (MPA); public policy and administration (MPA, PhD), including criminal justice (PhD), emergency management (PhD), health policy (PhD), health services (PhD), homeland security policy (PhD), homeland security policy and coordination

Sustainable Development

Walden University *(continued)*
(PhD), interdisciplinary policy studies (PhD), international nongovernmental organizations (PhD), law and public policy (PhD), local government management for sustainable communities (PhD), nonprofit management and leadership (PhD), policy analysis (PhD), public management and leadership (PhD), terrorism, mediation, and peace (PhD); terrorism, mediation and peace (MPA). Part-time and evening/weekend programs available. Postbaccalaureate distance learning degree programs offered (minimal on-campus study). *Faculty:* 10 full-time (5 women), 117 part-time/adjunct (49 women). *Students:* 1,408 full-time (901 women), 599 part-time (392 women); includes 1,022 Black or African American, non-Hispanic/Latino; 11 American Indian or Alaska Native, non-Hispanic/Latino; 37 Asian, non-Hispanic/Latino; 64 Hispanic/Latino; 26 Two or more races, non-Hispanic/Latino, 47 international. Average age 40. In 2010, 311 master's, 23 doctorates awarded. *Degree requirements:* For doctorate, thesis/dissertation, residency. *Entrance requirements:* For master's, bachelor's degree or equivalent in related field, minimum GPA of 2.5; for doctorate, master's degree or equivalent in related field; minimum GPA of 3.0; official transcripts; three years of related professional/academic experience (preferred); access to computer and Internet. Additional exam requirements/recommendations for international students: Required—TOEFL (minimum score 550 paper-based; 213 computer-based), IELTS (minimum score 6.5), TOEFL (minimum score 550 paper-based; 213 computer-based), IELTS (minimum score 6.5), or Michigan English Language Assessment Battery (minimum score 82). *Application deadline:* Applications are processed on a rolling basis. Application fee: $50. Electronic applications accepted. *Expenses:* Tuition: Full-time $10,274; part-time $445 per credit. Tuition and fees vary according to course load, degree level and program. *Financial support:* Fellowships with tuition reimbursements, Federal Work-Study, scholarships/grants, unspecified assistantships, and family tuition reduction, active duty/veteran tuition reduction, group tuition reduction, interest-free payment plans available. Support available to part-time students. Financial award applicants required to submit FAFSA. *Unit head:* Dr. Mark Gordon, Associate Dean, 800-925-3368. *Application contact:* Jennifer Hall, Vice President of Enrollment Management, 866-4-WALDEN, E-mail: info@waldenu.edu.

Wayne State University, College of Engineering, Program in Sustainable Engineering, Detroit, MI 48202. Offers Certificate. *Students:* 19 full-time (1 woman), 24 part-time (5 women); includes 11 minority (5 Black or African American, non-Hispanic/Latino; 6 Asian, non-Hispanic/Latino), 11 international. Average age 34. 27 applicants, 74% accepted, 9 enrolled. *Expenses:* Tuition, state resident: full-time $7662; part-time $478.85 per credit hour. Tuition, nonresident: full-time $16,920; part-time $1057.55 per credit hour. Required fees: $571.20; $35.70 per credit hour. $188.05 per semester. Tuition and fees vary according to course load and program. *Financial support:* In 2010–11, 2 research assistantships (averaging $18,492 per year) were awarded. *Unit head:* Dr. Carol Miller, Chair, 313-577-3789, Fax: 313-577-3881, E-mail: ab1421@wayne.edu. *Application contact:* Dr. Gerald O. Thompkins, Associate Dean, 313-577-3780.

West Chester University of Pennsylvania, Office of Graduate Studies, College of Education, Department of Professional and Secondary Education, West Chester, PA 19383. Offers education for sustainability (Certificate); entrepreneurial education (Certificate); secondary education (M Ed, Teaching Certificate); teaching and learning with technology (Certificate). Part-time and evening/weekend programs available. *Students:* 1 (woman) full-time, 32 part-time (17 women); includes 3 minority (2 Black or African American, non-Hispanic/Latino; 1 Asian, non-Hispanic/Latino). Average age 33. 26 applicants, 73% accepted, 2 enrolled. In 2010, 11 master's, 2 other advanced degrees awarded. *Degree requirements:* For master's, comprehensive exam, thesis (for some programs). *Entrance requirements:* For master's, GRE or MAT, teaching certificate. Additional exam requirements/recommendations for international students: Required—TOEFL (minimum score 550 paper-based; 213 computer-based; 80 iBT). *Application deadline:* For fall admission, 4/15 priority date for domestic students, 3/15 for international students; for spring admission, 10/15 priority date for domestic students, 9/1 for international students. Applications are processed on a rolling basis. Application fee: $35. Electronic applications accepted. *Expenses:* Tuition, state resident: full-time $6966; part-time $387 per credit. Tuition, nonresident: full-time $11,146; part-time $619 per credit. Required fees: $1614.40; $133.24 per credit. Part-time tuition and fees vary according to campus/location. *Financial support:* Unspecified assistantships available. Support available to part-time students. Financial award application deadline: 2/15; financial award applicants required to submit FAFSA. *Faculty research:* Technology integration: preparing our teachers for the twenty-first century. *Unit head:* Dr. John Elmore, Chair, 610-436-3057, E-mail: jelmore@wcupa.edu. *Application contact:* Dr. Cynthia Haggard, Graduate Coordinator, 610-436-6934, E-mail: chaggard@wcupa.edu.

Western Illinois University, School of Graduate Studies, College of Arts and Sciences, Department of Geography, Macomb, IL 61455-1390. Offers community development (Certificate); environmental GIS (Certificate); geography (MA). Part-time programs available. *Students:* 13 full-time (3 women), 5 part-time (4 women); includes 3 minority (1 Black or African American, non-Hispanic/Latino; 1 Asian, non-Hispanic/Latino; 1 Hispanic/Latino), 1 international. Average age 32. 9 applicants, 78% accepted. In 2010, 7 master's, 7 other advanced degrees awarded. *Degree requirements:* For master's, thesis or alternative. *Entrance requirements:* Additional exam requirements/recommendations for international students: Required—TOEFL (minimum score 550 paper-based; 213 computer-based; 80 iBT). *Application deadline:* Applications are processed on a rolling basis. Application fee: $30. Electronic applications accepted. *Expenses:* Tuition, state resident: full-time $6370; part-time $265.40 per credit hour. Tuition, nonresident: full-time $12,740; part-time $530.80 per credit hour. Required fees: $75.67 per credit hour. *Financial support:* In 2010–11, 11 students received support, including 11 research assistantships with full tuition reimbursements available (averaging $7,280 per year). Financial award applicants required to submit FAFSA. *Unit head:* Dr. Sam Thompson, Chairperson, 309-298-1648. *Application contact:* Evelyn Hoing, Assistant Director of Graduate Studies, 309-298-1806, Fax: 309-298-2345, E-mail: grad-office@wiu.edu.

West Virginia University, Davis College of Agriculture, Forestry and Consumer Sciences, Division of Resource Management and Sustainable Development, Program in Resource Management and Sustainable Development, Morgantown, WV 26506. Offers PhD. Part-time programs available. *Degree requirements:* For doctorate, thesis/dissertation. *Entrance requirements:* For doctorate, GRE General Test. Additional exam requirements/recommendations for international students: Required—TOEFL.

Urban and Regional Planning

Alabama Agricultural and Mechanical University, School of Graduate Studies, School of Agricultural and Environmental Sciences, Department of Community Planning and Urban Studies, Huntsville, AL 35811. Offers urban and regional planning (MURP). *Accreditation:* ACSP. Part-time and evening/weekend programs available. *Degree requirements:* For master's, comprehensive exam. *Entrance requirements:* For master's, GRE General Test. Additional exam requirements/recommendations for international students: Required—TOEFL (minimum score 500 paper-based; 173 computer-based; 61 iBT). Electronic applications accepted. *Faculty research:* Urban and rural research, needs assessment and community trends through analysis of social indicators, fiscal impact studies, rural transportation, health care.

American University of Beirut, Graduate Programs, Faculty of Engineering and Architecture, Beirut, Lebanon. Offers applied energy (MME); civil engineering (ME, PhD); electrical and computer engineering (ME, PhD); engineering management (MEM); environmental and water resources (ME); environmental and water resources engineering (PhD); environmental technology (MSES); mechanical engineering (ME, PhD); urban design (MUD); urban planning and policy (MUP). Part-time programs available. *Faculty:* 57 full-time (12 women), 3 part-time/adjunct (0 women). *Students:* 261 full-time (92 women), 58 part-time (20 women). Average age 25. 272 applicants, 79% accepted, 108 enrolled. In 2010, 70 master's, 1 doctorate awarded. *Degree requirements:* For master's, one foreign language, comprehensive exam, thesis (for some programs); for doctorate, one foreign language, comprehensive exam, thesis/dissertation, publications. *Entrance requirements:* For master's, GRE (for electrical and computer engineering), letters of recommendation; for doctorate, GRE, letters of recommendation, master's degree, transcripts, curriculum vitae, interview. Additional exam requirements/recommendations for international students: Required—TOEFL (minimum score 600 paper-based; 250 computer-based; 100 iBT), IELTS (minimum score 7.5). *Application deadline:* For fall admission, 2/5 priority date for domestic and international students; for spring admission, 11/1 priority date for domestic students, 11/1 for international students. Applications are processed on a rolling basis. Application fee: $50. Electronic applications accepted. *Expenses:* Tuition: Full-time $12,294; part-time $683 per credit. Required fees: $499; $499 per credit. Tuition and fees vary according to course load and program. *Financial support:* In 2010–11, 10 fellowships with full tuition reimbursements (averaging $24,800 per year), 33 research assistantships with full tuition reimbursements (averaging $24,800 per year), 70 teaching assistantships with full tuition reimbursements (averaging $9,800 per year) were awarded; career-related internships or fieldwork, institutionally sponsored loans, scholarships/grants, health care benefits, and unspecified assistantships also available. Total annual research expenditures: $586,131. *Unit head:* Fadl H. Moukalled, Acting Dean, 961-135-0000 Ext. 3400, Fax: 961-174-4462, E-mail: memouk@aub.edu.lb. *Application contact:* Dr. Salim Kanaan, Director, Admissions Office, 961-135-0000 Ext. 2594, Fax: 961-175-0775, E-mail: sk00@aub.edu.lb.

American University of Sharjah, Graduate Programs, Sharjah, United Arab Emirates. Offers business (EMBA, GEMPA, MBA); chemical engineering (MS Ch E); civil engineering (MSCE); computer engineering (MS); electrical engineering (MSEE); mechanical engineering (MSME); mechatronics engineering (MS); public administration (MPA); teaching English to speakers of other languages (MA); translation and interpreting (MA); urban planning (MUP). Part-time and evening/weekend programs available. *Entrance requirements:* For master's, GMAT (MBA). Additional exam requirements/recommendations for international students: Required—TOEFL (minimum score 550 paper-based; 213 computer-based; 80 iBT), TWE (minimum score 5). Electronic applications accepted. *Faculty research:* Chemical engineering, civil engineering, computer engineering, electrical engineering, linguistics, translation.

Arizona State University, College of Liberal Arts and Sciences, School of Geographical Sciences, Tempe, AZ 85287-5302. Offers atmospheric science (Graduate Certificate); geographic education (MAS); geographic information systems (MAS); geographical information science (Graduate Certificate); geography (MA, PhD); transportation systems (Graduate Certificate); urban and environmental planning (MUEP). *Faculty:* 34 full-time (9 women), 2 part-time/adjunct (both women). *Students:* 125 full-time (40 women), 47 part-time (25 women); includes 24 minority (4 Black or African American, non-Hispanic/Latino; 1 American Indian or Alaska Native, non-Hispanic/Latino; 1 Asian, non-Hispanic/Latino; 16 Hispanic/Latino; 2 Two or more races, non-Hispanic/Latino), 34 international. Average age 30. 261 applicants, 56% accepted, 79 enrolled. In 2010, 76 master's, 3 doctorates, 13 other advanced degrees awarded. Terminal master's awarded for partial completion of doctoral program. *Degree requirements:* For master's, thesis, interactive Program of Study (iPOS) submitted before completing 50 percent of required credit hours; for doctorate, comprehensive exam, thesis/dissertation, interactive Program of Study (iPOS) submitted before completing 50 percent of required credit hours. *Entrance requirements:* For master's and doctorate, GRE, minimum GPA of 3.0 or equivalent in last 2 years of work leading to bachelor's degree. Additional exam requirements/recommendations for international students: Required—TOEFL, IELTS, or Pearson Test of English. *Application deadline:* For fall admission, 1/15 for domestic and international students. Applications are processed on a rolling basis. Application fee: $70 ($90 for international students). Electronic applications accepted. *Expenses:* Contact institution. *Financial support:* In 2010–11, 25 research assistantships with full and partial tuition reimbursements (averaging $15,546 per year), 50 teaching assistantships with full and partial tuition reimbursements (averaging $10,686 per year) were awarded; fellowships with full tuition reimbursements, career-related internships or fieldwork, Federal Work-Study, institutionally sponsored loans, scholarships/grants, and tuition waivers (full and partial) also available. Financial award application deadline: 3/1; financial award applicants required to submit FAFSA. Total annual research expenditures: $2.6 million. *Unit head:* Dr. Luc Anselin, Chair and Director, 480-965-7533, E-mail: luc.anselin@asu.edu. *Application contact:* Graduate Admissions, 480-965-6113.

Arizona State University, College of Public Programs, School of Community Resources and Development, Phoenix, AZ 85004-0685. Offers community resources and development (PhD); nonprofit leadership and management (Graduate Certificate); nonprofit studies (MNpS); recreation and tourism studies (MS). Part-time and evening/weekend programs available. *Faculty:* 19 full-time (8 women), 2 part-time/adjunct (both women). *Students:* 53 full-time (35 women), 72 part-time (55 women); includes 28 minority (6 Black or African American, non-Hispanic/Latino; 5 American Indian or Alaska Native, non-Hispanic/Latino; 1 Asian, non-Hispanic/Latino; 16 Hispanic/Latino), 12 international. Average age 33. 90 applicants, 73% accepted, 45 enrolled. In 2010, 37 master's, 3 other advanced degrees awarded. Terminal master's awarded for partial completion of doctoral program. *Degree requirements:* For master's, thesis or alternative, interactive Program of Study (iPOS) submitted before completing 50 percent of required credit hours; for doctorate, comprehensive exam, thesis/dissertation, interactive Program of Study (iPOS) submitted before completing 50 percent of required credit hours. *Entrance requirements:* For master's and doctorate, GRE, minimum GPA of 3.0 or equivalent in last 2 years of work leading to bachelor's degree. Additional exam requirements/recommendations for international students: Required—TOEFL, IELTS, or Pearson Test of English. *Application deadline:* For fall admission, 3/1 for domestic and international students; for spring admission, 10/1 for domestic and international students. Application fee: $70 ($90 for international students). Electronic applications accepted. *Expenses:* Contact institution. *Financial support:* In 2010–11, 6 research assistantships with full and partial tuition reimbursements (averaging $8,949 per year), 5 teaching assistantships with full and partial tuition reimbursements (averaging $9,774 per year) were awarded; fellowships with full tuition reimbursements, career-related internships or fieldwork, Federal Work-Study, institutionally sponsored loans, scholarships/grants, and tuition waivers (full and partial) also available. Financial award application deadline: 3/1; financial award applicants required to submit FAFSA. Total annual research expenditures: $2.5 million. *Unit head:* Dr. Kathleen Andereck, Director, 602-496-1056, E-mail: kandereck@asu.edu. *Application contact:* Graduate Admissions, 480-965-6113.

Arizona State University, College of Public Programs, School of Public Affairs, Phoenix, AZ 85004-0687. Offers public administration (nonprofit administration) (MPA); public administration (urban management) (MPA); public affairs (PhD); public policy (MPP); MPA/MSW. *Accreditation:* NASPAA (one or more programs are accredited). Part-time and evening/weekend programs available. *Faculty:* 19 full-time (7 women), 1 part-time/adjunct (0 women). *Students:* 149 full-time (96 women), 106 part-time (62 women); includes 62 minority (14 Black or African American, non-Hispanic/Latino; 5 American Indian or Alaska Native, non-Hispanic/Latino; 9

Asian, non-Hispanic/Latino; 32 Hispanic/Latino; 2 Two or more races, non-Hispanic/Latino), 34 international. Average age 32. 227 applicants, 71% accepted, 87 enrolled. In 2010, 68 master's, 4 doctorates awarded. Terminal master's awarded for partial completion of doctoral program. *Degree requirements:* For master's, thesis or alternative, policy analysis or capstone project; interactive Program of Study (iPOS) submitted before completing 50 percent of required credit hours; for doctorate, comprehensive exam, thesis/dissertation, interactive Program of Study (iPOS) submitted before completing 50 percent of required credit hours. *Entrance requirements:* For master's, GRE, minimum GPA of 3.0 or equivalent in last 2 years of work leading to bachelor's degree; for doctorate, GRE, minimum GPA of 3.0 or equivalent in last 2 years of work leading to bachelor's degree, 3 letters of recommendation, resume, statement of goals, samples of research reports. Additional exam requirements/recommendations for international students: Required—TOEFL (minimum score 600 paper-based; 213 computer-based; 100 iBT), IELTS (minimum score 6.5). *Application deadline:* For fall admission, 1/15 for domestic and international students. Application fee: $70 ($90 for international students). Electronic applications accepted. *Expenses:* Contact institution. *Financial support:* In 2010–11, 16 research assistantships with full and partial tuition reimbursements (averaging $14,106 per year), 2 teaching assistantships with full and partial tuition reimbursements (averaging $9,913 per year) were awarded; fellowships with full tuition reimbursements, career-related internships or fieldwork, Federal Work-Study, institutionally sponsored loans, scholarships/grants, and tuition waivers (full and partial) also available. Financial award application deadline: 3/1; financial award applicants required to submit FAFSA. Total annual research expenditures: $621,146. *Unit head:* Dr. Jonathan Koppell, Director, 602-496-1101, E-mail: koppell@asu.edu. *Application contact:* Graduate Admissions, 480-965-6113.

Auburn University, Graduate School, College of Architecture, Design, and Construction, Program in Community Planning, Auburn University, AL 36849. Offers MCP, MPA/MCP. *Accreditation:* ACSP. Part-time programs available. *Faculty:* 9 full-time (3 women). *Students:* 24 full-time (13 women), 6 part-time (3 women); includes 5 Black or African American, non-Hispanic/Latino, 2 international. Average age 26. 39 applicants, 62% accepted, 10 enrolled. In 2010, 7 master's awarded. *Degree requirements:* For master's, oral exam, project. *Entrance requirements:* For master's, GRE General Test. *Application deadline:* For fall admission, 7/7 for domestic students; for spring admission, 11/24 for domestic students. Applications are processed on a rolling basis. Application fee: $50 ($60 for international students). Electronic applications accepted. *Expenses:* Tuition, state resident: full-time $7002. Tuition, nonresident: full-time $21,898. International tuition: $22,116 full-time. Required fees: $892. Tuition and fees vary according to course load and program. *Financial support:* Federal Work-Study available. Support available to part-time students. Financial award application deadline: 3/15; financial award applicants required to submit FAFSA. *Unit head:* Dr. John J. Pittari, Chair, 334-844-4516. *Application contact:* Dr. George Flowers, Dean of the Graduate School, 334-844-2125.

Ball State University, Graduate School, College of Architecture and Planning, Department of Urban Planning, Muncie, IN 47306-1099. Offers MURP. *Accreditation:* ACSP. *Faculty:* 10. *Students:* 31 full-time (10 women), 10 part-time (4 women); includes 1 Black or African American, non-Hispanic/Latino, 11 international. Average age 25. 64 applicants, 83% accepted, 21 enrolled. In 2010, 11 master's awarded. *Degree requirements:* For master's, thesis. *Entrance requirements:* For master's, writing sample. Application fee: $50. *Expenses:* Tuition, state resident: full-time $6160; part-time $299 per credit hour. Tuition, nonresident: full-time $16,020; part-time $783 per credit hour. Required fees: $2278; $95 per credit hour. *Financial support:* In 2010–11, 11 teaching assistantships with full tuition reimbursements (averaging $6,678 per year) were awarded; research assistantships with full tuition reimbursements, career-related internships or fieldwork also available. Financial award application deadline: 3/1. *Faculty research:* Computer-assisted land-use analysis. *Unit head:* Dr. Michael Burayidi, Interim Chair, 765-285-1963, Fax: 765-285-2648. *Application contact:* Dr. Francis Parker, Director, 765-285-1963, Fax: 765-285-2648, E-mail: fparker@bsu.edu.

Boston University, Metropolitan College, Program in City Planning, Boston, MA 02215. Offers MCP. Part-time and evening/weekend programs available. *Faculty:* 3 full-time (0 women), 14 part-time/adjunct (3 women). *Students:* 16 full-time (6 women), 24 part-time (13 women); includes 9 minority (2 Black or African American, non-Hispanic/Latino; 1 American Indian or Alaska Native, non-Hispanic/Latino; 2 Asian, non-Hispanic/Latino; 4 Hispanic/Latino), 6 international. Average age 27. 22 applicants, 82% accepted, 12 enrolled. In 2010, 11 master's awarded. *Degree requirements:* For master's, thesis optional. *Entrance requirements:* Additional exam requirements/recommendations for international students: Required—TOEFL (minimum score 590 paper-based; 243 computer-based; 84 iBT). *Application deadline:* For fall admission, 7/15 priority date for domestic and international students; for spring admission, 12/15 priority date for domestic students, 11/15 priority date for international students. Applications are processed on a rolling basis. Application fee: $70. Electronic applications accepted. *Expenses:* Tuition: Full-time $39,314; part-time $1228 per credit. Required fees: $40 per semester. *Financial support:* In 2010–11, 3 research assistantships with partial tuition reimbursements (averaging $5,000 per year), 3 teaching assistantships with partial tuition reimbursements (averaging $5,000 per year) were awarded; career-related internships or fieldwork and unspecified assistantships also available. Support available to part-time students. Financial award application deadline: 6/15; financial award applicants required to submit FAFSA. *Faculty research:* Housing, community development and land use planning, environmental management and planning, international comparative development planning. *Unit head:* Dr. Daniel P. LeClair, Chair, 617-353-3025, Fax: 617-358-3595, E-mail: dleclair@bu.edu. *Application contact:* Dr. Enrique R. Silva, Assistant Professor and Faculty Coordinator, 617-358-3264, Fax: 617-358-3595, E-mail: ersilva@bu.edu.

California Polytechnic State University, San Luis Obispo, College of Architecture and Environmental Design, Department of City and Regional Planning, San Luis Obispo, CA 93407. Offers MCRP, MCRP/MS. *Accreditation:* ACSP. Part-time programs available. *Faculty:* 5 full-time (1 woman). *Students:* 53 full-time (32 women); includes 12 minority (9 Asian, non-Hispanic/Latino; 1 Hispanic/Latino; 2 Two or more races, non-Hispanic/Latino). Average age 27. 149 applicants, 32% accepted, 31 enrolled. In 2010, 23 master's awarded. *Degree requirements:* For master's, thesis. *Entrance requirements:* For master's, GRE, minimum GPA of 3.0 in last 90 quarter units. Additional exam requirements/recommendations for international students: Required—TOEFL (minimum score 550 paper-based; 213 computer-based) or IELTS (minimum score 6). *Application deadline:* For fall admission, 2/1 for domestic students, 11/30 for international students; for winter admission, 11/1 for domestic students, 6/30 for international students. Applications are processed on a rolling basis. Application fee: $55. Electronic applications accepted. *Expenses:* Tuition, state resident: full-time $5386; part-time $3124 per year. Tuition, nonresident: full-time $11,160; part-time $248 per unit. Required fees: $2250; $614 per term. One-time fee: $2250 full-time; $1842 part-time. *Financial support:* Research assistantships, career-related internships or fieldwork, Federal Work-Study, institutionally sponsored loans, and unspecified assistantships available. Support available to part-time students. Financial award application deadline: 3/2; financial award applicants required to submit FAFSA. *Faculty research:* Natural hazards, housing, small town and rural planning, planning implementation, subdivision site design, transportation. *Unit head:* Dr. Michael Boswell, Graduate Coordinator, 805-756-2496, Fax: 805-756-1340, E-mail: mboswell@calpoly.edu. *Application contact:* Dr. Michael Boswell, Graduate Coordinator, 805-756-2496, Fax: 805-756-1340, E-mail: mboswell@calpoly.edu.

California State Polytechnic University, Pomona, Academic Affairs, College of Environmental Design, Program in Urban and Regional Planning, Pomona, CA 91768-2557. Offers MURP. *Accreditation:* ACSP. Part-time programs available. *Students:* 32 full-time (13 women), 34 part-time (12 women); includes 35 minority (2 Black or African American, non-Hispanic/Latino; 16 Asian, non-Hispanic/Latino; 14 Hispanic/Latino; 3 Two or more races, non-Hispanic/Latino), 2 international. Average age 30. 119 applicants, 41% accepted, 22 enrolled. In 2010, 29 master's awarded. *Degree requirements:* For master's, thesis or alternative. *Entrance requirements:* For master's, GRE General Test. *Application deadline:* For fall admission, 5/1 priority date for domestic students; for winter admission, 10/15 priority date for domestic students; for spring admission, 1/20 priority date for domestic students. Applications are processed on a rolling basis. Application fee: $55. Electronic applications accepted. *Expenses:* Tuition, state resident: full-time $5386; part-time $2850 per year. Tuition, nonresident: full-time $12,082; part-time $248 per credit. Required fees: $577; $248 per credit. $577 per year. Tuition and fees vary according to course load and program. *Financial support:* Career-related internships or fieldwork, Federal Work-Study, and institutionally sponsored loans available. Support available to part-time students. Financial award application deadline: 3/2; financial award applicants required to submit FAFSA. *Unit head:* Herschel H. Farberow, Graduate Coordinator, 909-869-2716, Fax: 909-869-4688, E-mail: hfarberow@csupomona.edu. *Application contact:* Scott J. Duncan, Director, Admissions, 909-869-3258, Fax: 909-869-4529, E-mail: sjduncan@csupomona.edu.

California State University, Chico, Graduate School, College of Behavioral and Social Sciences, Department of Geography and Planning, Program in Rural and Town Planning, Chico, CA 95929-0722. Offers MA. Part-time programs available. *Students:* 6 full-time (2 women), 6 part-time (1 woman). Average age 35. 10 applicants, 80% accepted, 8 enrolled. *Entrance requirements:* For master's, GRE, 2 letters of recommendation. Additional exam requirements/recommendations for international students: Required—TOEFL (minimum score 550 paper-based; 213 computer-based; 80 iBT), IELTS (minimum score 6.5). *Application deadline:* For fall admission, 3/1 priority date for domestic students, 3/1 for international students; for spring admission, 9/15 priority date for domestic students, 9/15 for international students. Applications are processed on a rolling basis. Application fee: $55. Electronic applications accepted. *Unit head:* Dr. Dean Fairbanks, Graduate Coordinator, 530-898-5780. *Application contact:* Dr. Paul Melcon, Graduate Coordinator, 530-898-6871.

The Catholic University of America, School of Architecture and Planning, Washington, DC 20064. Offers architecture studies (MS Arch St); sustainable design (MSSD). Part-time programs available. *Faculty:* 25 full-time (6 women), 38 part-time/adjunct (9 women). *Students:* 116 full-time (55 women), 31 part-time (13 women); includes 11 Black or African American, non-Hispanic/Latino; 6 Asian, non-Hispanic/Latino; 11 Hispanic/Latino, 11 international. Average age 27. 167 applicants, 70% accepted, 56 enrolled. In 2010, 55 master's awarded. *Degree requirements:* For master's, thesis. *Entrance requirements:* For master's, GRE (minimum score: 1000), minimum GPA of 2.8, portfolio, statement of purpose, official copies of academic transcripts, three letters of recommendation. Additional exam requirements/recommendations for international students: Required—TOEFL (minimum score 580 paper-based; 237 computer-based). *Application deadline:* For fall admission, 1/15 priority date for domestic students, 1/15 for international students; for spring admission, 10/15 priority date for domestic students, 10/15 for international students. Applications are processed on a rolling basis. Application fee: $55. Electronic applications accepted. *Expenses:* Contact institution. *Financial support:* Fellowships, research assistantships, teaching assistantships, Federal Work-Study, scholarships/grants, tuition waivers (full and partial), and unspecified assistantships available. Financial award application deadline: 2/1; financial award applicants required to submit FAFSA. *Faculty research:* Architectural history, cultural studies/sacred space, design technologies, digital media, real estate development, urban design. *Unit head:* Randall Ott, Dean, 202-319-5784, Fax: 202-319-2023, E-mail: ott@cua.edu. *Application contact:* Andrew Woodall, Director of Graduate Admissions, 202-319-5057, Fax: 202-319-6533, E-mail: cua-admissions@cua.edu.

Clark University, Graduate School, Department of International Development, Community, and Environment, Program in Community Development and Planning, Worcester, MA 01610-1477. Offers MA, MA/MBA. *Students:* 26 full-time (16 women), 2 part-time (1 woman); includes 6 minority (2 Black or African American, non-Hispanic/Latino; 1 Asian, non-Hispanic/Latino; 3 Hispanic/Latino), 4 international. Average age 27. 53 applicants, 75% accepted, 19 enrolled. In 2010, 27 master's awarded. *Degree requirements:* For master's, thesis. *Entrance requirements:* For master's, 3 references, resume or curriculum vitae. Additional exam requirements/recommendations for international students: Required—TOEFL (minimum score 575 paper-based; 233 computer-based; 90 iBT) or IELTS (minimum score 6.5). *Application deadline:* For fall admission, 1/15 for domestic students. Application fee: $50. *Expenses:* Tuition: Full-time $37,000; part-time $1156 per credit hour. Required fees: $30; $1156 per credit hour. *Financial support:* In 2010–11, research assistantships with partial tuition reimbursements (averaging $5,000 per year), teaching assistantships with partial tuition reimbursements (averaging $5,000 per year) were awarded; fellowships with partial tuition reimbursements, institutionally sponsored loans and scholarships/grants also available. *Faculty research:* Urban revitalization, youth and gang violence, using GIS to assess the location and need for community *healthy*; amenities, systemic education reform, housing for disabled residents, economic development in neighborhood planning. *Unit head:* Dr. William F. Fisher, Director, 508-421-3765, Fax: 508-793-8820, E-mail: wfisher@clarku.edu. *Application contact:* Paula Hall, IDCE Graduate Admissions, 508-793-7201, Fax: 508-793-8820, E-mail: idce@clarku.edu.

Clemson University, Graduate School, College of Architecture, Arts, and Humanities, Department of Planning and Landscape Architecture, Program in City and Regional Planning, Clemson, SC 29634. Offers developmental planning (MCRP). *Students:* 43 full-time (15 women), 1 part-time (0 women); includes 2 Black or African American, non-Hispanic/Latino; 1 Hispanic/Latino, 4 international. Average age 28. 79 applicants, 65% accepted, 18 enrolled. In 2010, 20 master's awarded. *Degree requirements:* For master's, departmental paper or thesis. *Entrance requirements:* For master's, GRE General Test. Additional exam requirements/recommendations for international students: Required—TOEFL. *Application deadline:* For fall admission, 2/15 priority date for domestic and international students. Applications are processed on a rolling basis. Application fee: $70 ($80 for international students). Electronic applications accepted. *Expenses:* Tuition, state resident: full-time $6492; part-time $400 per credit hour. Tuition, nonresident: full-time $13,634; part-time $800 per credit hour. Required fees: $262 per semester. Part-time tuition and fees vary according to course load and program. *Financial support:* In 2010–11, 30 students received support, including 1 research assistantship with partial tuition reimbursement available (averaging $7,830 per year), 31 teaching assistantships with partial tuition reimbursements available (averaging $4,116 per year); fellowships with full and partial tuition reimbursements available, career-related internships or fieldwork, Federal Work-Study, institutionally sponsored loans, scholarships/grants, health care benefits, and unspecified assistantships also available. Financial award application deadline: 4/15; financial award applicants required to submit FAFSA. *Faculty research:* Coastal planning, regional economic development, health care access. *Unit head:* Dr. Elaine M. Worzala, Chair, 864-656-3657, Fax: 864-656-0204, E-mail: eworzal@clemson.edu. *Application contact:* Dr. Barry C. Nocks, Director, 864-656-3926, Fax: 864-656-7519, E-mail: nocks2@clemson.edu.

Cleveland State University, College of Graduate Studies, Maxine Goodman Levin College of Urban Affairs, Program in Urban Planning, Design, and Development, Cleveland, OH 44115. Offers geographic information systems (Certificate); local and urban management (Certificate); urban economic development (Certificate); urban planning, design, and development (MUPDD); urban real estate development and finance (Certificate); JD/MUPDD. *Accreditation:* ACSP. Part-time and evening/weekend programs available. *Faculty:* 32 full-time (19 women), 8 part-time/adjunct (4 women). *Students:* 30 full-time (10 women), 28 part-time (17 women); includes 6 Black or African American, non-Hispanic/Latino; 3 Hispanic/Latino, 5 international. Average age 38. 72 applicants, 56% accepted, 21 enrolled. In 2010, 24 master's, 9 Certificates awarded. *Degree requirements:* For master's, thesis or alternative, project or thesis. *Entrance requirements:* For master's, GRE General Test (minimum 50th percentile verbal and quantitative, 4.0 analytical writing), minimum GPA of 3.0. Additional exam requirements/recommendations for international students: Required—TOEFL (minimum score 525 paper-based; 197 computer-based; 65 iBT). *Application deadline:* For fall admission, 7/15 priority date for domestic students, 5/15 for international students; for spring admission, 11/1 for international students. Applications are processed on a rolling basis. Application fee: $30. Electronic applications accepted. *Expenses:* Tuition, state resident: full-time $8447; part-time $469 per credit hour. Tuition, nonresident: full-time $16,020; part-time $890 per credit hour. Required fees: $50. *Financial support:* In 2010–11, 15 students received support, including 10 research assistantships with full and partial tuition reimbursements available (averaging $6,960 per year), 5 teaching assistantships with full and partial tuition reimbursements available (averaging $6,960 per year); career-related internships or fieldwork, Federal Work-Study, tuition waivers (full and

Urban and Regional Planning

Cleveland State University (continued)
partial), and unspecified assistantships also available. Support available to part-time students. Financial award application deadline: 3/1. *Faculty research:* Housing and neighborhood development, urban housing policy, environmental sustainability, economic development, metropolitan change, GIS and planning decision support, PPGIS. *Unit head:* Dr. Dennis Keating, Director, 216-687-2298, Fax: 216-687-2013, E-mail: w.keating@csuohio.edu. *Application contact:* Joan Demkow, Graduate Program Coordinator, 216-523-7522, Fax: 216-687-5398, E-mail: urbanprograms@csuohio.edu.

College of Charleston, Graduate School, School of Humanities and Social Sciences, Program in Urban and Regional Planning, Charleston, SC 29424-0001. Offers Certificate. Part-time and evening/weekend programs available. *Faculty:* 15 full-time (7 women), 5 part-time/adjunct (1 woman). *Students:* 2 part-time (both women). Average age 35. 4 applicants, 100% accepted, 2 enrolled. In 2010, 5 Certificates awarded. *Entrance requirements:* Additional exam requirements/recommendations for international students: Required—TOEFL (minimum score 81 iBT). *Application deadline:* For fall admission, 4/1 for domestic students; for spring admission, 11/1 for domestic students. Application fee: $45. Electronic applications accepted. *Unit head:* Dr. Kevin Keenan, Program Director, 843-953-5679, E-mail: keenank@cofc.edu. *Application contact:* Susan Hallatt, Director of Graduate Admissions, 843-953-5614, Fax: 843-953-1434, E-mail: hallatts@cofc.edu.

Columbia University, Graduate School of Architecture, Planning, and Preservation, Program in Urban Planning, New York, NY 10027. Offers MS, PhD, JD/MS, M Arch/MS, MBA/MS, MIA/MS, MPH/MS, MS/MS. PhD offered through the Graduate School of Arts and Sciences. *Accreditation:* ACSP (one or more programs are accredited). *Degree requirements:* For master's, thesis. *Entrance requirements:* For master's, GRE General Test.

Concordia University, School of Graduate Studies, Faculty of Arts and Science, School of Community and Public Affairs, Montréal, QC H3G 1M8, Canada. Offers community economic development (Diploma).

Cornell University, Graduate School, Graduate Fields of Architecture, Art and Planning, Field of City and Regional Planning, Ithaca, NY 14853-0001. Offers city and regional planning (MRP, PhD); environmental planning and design (MRP, PhD); historic preservation planning (MA); international development planning (MRP, PhD); planning theory and systems analysis (MRP, PhD); regional economics and development planning (MRP, PhD); regional science (MRP, PhD); social and health systems planning (MRP, PhD); urban and regional theory (MRP, PhD); urban planning history (MRP, PhD). *Accreditation:* ACSP (one or more programs are accredited). *Faculty:* 31 full-time (10 women). *Students:* 136 full-time (66 women); includes 6 Black or African American, non-Hispanic/Latino; 10 Asian, non-Hispanic/Latino; 9 Hispanic/Latino, 20 international. Average age 27. 452 applicants, 32% accepted, 64 enrolled. In 2010, 42 master's, 4 doctorates awarded. *Degree requirements:* For master's, thesis (MA); for doctorate, comprehensive exam, thesis/dissertation. *Entrance requirements:* For master's and doctorate, GRE General Test, 2 letters of recommendation. Additional exam requirements/recommendations for international students: Required—TOEFL (minimum score 600 paper-based; 250 computer-based; 77 iBT). *Application deadline:* For fall admission, 1/10 for domestic students. Application fee: $70. Electronic applications accepted. *Expenses:* Tuition: Full-time $29,500. Required fees: $76. Tuition and fees vary according to degree level and program. *Financial support:* In 2010–11, 9 fellowships with full tuition reimbursements, 2 research assistantships with full tuition reimbursements, 13 teaching assistantships with full tuition reimbursements were awarded; institutionally sponsored loans, scholarships/grants, health care benefits, tuition waivers (full and partial), and unspecified assistantships also available. Financial award applicants required to submit FAFSA. *Faculty research:* Land use planning, economic development, international development, historic preservation, community development. *Unit head:* Director of Graduate Studies, 607-255-6848, Fax: 607-255-1971. *Application contact:* Graduate Field Assistant, 607-255-6848, Fax: 607-255-1971, E-mail: crp_admissions@cornell.edu.

Cornell University, Graduate School, Graduate Fields of Architecture, Art and Planning, Field of Regional Science, Ithaca, NY 14853-0001. Offers environmental studies (MA, MS, PhD); international spatial problems (MA, MS, PhD); location theory (MA, MS, PhD); multiregional economic analysis (MA, MS, PhD); peace science (MA, MS, PhD); planning methods (MA, MS, PhD); urban and regional economics (MA, MS, PhD). *Faculty:* 22 full-time (6 women). *Students:* 20 full-time (6 women); includes 1 Black or African American, non-Hispanic/Latino, 18 international. Average age 31. 5 applicants, 80% accepted, 4 enrolled. In 2010, 3 doctorates awarded. Terminal master's awarded for partial completion of doctoral program. *Degree requirements:* For master's, thesis; for doctorate, comprehensive exam, thesis/dissertation. *Entrance requirements:* For master's and doctorate, GRE General Test, 2 letters of recommendation. Additional exam requirements/recommendations for international students: Required—TOEFL (minimum score 600 paper-based; 250 computer-based; 77 iBT). *Application deadline:* For fall admission, 1/15 priority date for domestic students. Application fee: $70. Electronic applications accepted. *Expenses:* Tuition: Full-time $29,500. Required fees: $76. Tuition and fees vary according to degree level and program. *Financial support:* In 2010–11, 1 research assistantship with full tuition reimbursement, 2 teaching assistantships with full tuition reimbursements were awarded; fellowships with full tuition reimbursements, institutionally sponsored loans, scholarships/grants, health care benefits, tuition waivers (full and partial), and unspecified assistantships also available. Financial award applicants required to submit FAFSA. *Faculty research:* Urban and regional growth, spatial economics, formation of spatial patterns by socioeconomic systems, non-linear dynamics and complex systems, environmental-economic systems. *Unit head:* Director of Graduate Studies, 607-255-6848, Fax: 607-255-1971. *Application contact:* Graduate Field Assistant, 607-255-6848, Fax: 607-255-1971, E-mail: regsci@cornell.edu.

Dalhousie University, Faculty of Architecture and Planning, School of Planning, Halifax, NS B3J 2X4, Canada. Offers M Eng, M Plan, MPS. *Degree requirements:* For master's, thesis. *Entrance requirements:* Additional exam requirements/recommendations for international students: Required—TOEFL, IELTS, CANTEST, CAEL, or Michigan English Language Assessment Battery. Electronic applications accepted.

Delta State University, Graduate Programs, College of Arts and Sciences, Division of Social Sciences and History, Program in Community Development, Cleveland, MS 38733-0001. Offers MS. Part-time programs available. *Degree requirements:* For master's, thesis or alternative. *Expenses:* Tuition, state resident: full-time $4347; part-time $202 per credit hour. Tuition, nonresident: full-time $12,052; part-time $523 per credit hour. Required fees: $504.

DePaul University, School of Public Service, Chicago, IL 60604. Offers financial administration management (Certificate); health administration (Certificate); health law and policy (MS); international public services (MS); leadership and policy studies (MS); metropolitan planning (Certificate); public administration (MPA); public service management (MS), including association management, fundraising and philanthropy, healthcare administration, higher education administration, metropolitan planning; public services (Certificate); JD/MS. Part-time and evening/weekend programs available. Postbaccalaureate distance learning degree programs offered (minimal on-campus study). *Faculty:* 14 full-time (3 women), 43 part-time/adjunct (24 women). *Students:* 372 full-time (256 women), 324 part-time (237 women); includes 156 Black or African American, non-Hispanic/Latino; 33 Asian, non-Hispanic/Latino; 65 Hispanic/Latino; 18 Two or more races, non-Hispanic/Latino, 18 international. Average age 26. 162 applicants, 100% accepted, 94 enrolled. In 2010, 108 master's awarded. *Degree requirements:* For master's, thesis or integrative seminar. *Entrance requirements:* For master's, minimum GPA of 2.7. Additional exam requirements/recommendations for international students: Required—TOEFL (minimum score 550 paper-based; 213 computer-based; 80 iBT), IELTS (minimum score 6.5). *Application deadline:* Applications are processed on a rolling basis. Application fee: $40. Electronic applications accepted. *Financial support:* In 2010–11, 60 students received support, including 3 research assistantships with full tuition reimbursements available (averaging $7,000 per year); career-related internships or fieldwork, Federal Work-Study, institutionally

sponsored loans, scholarships/grants, tuition waivers (partial), and unspecified assistantships also available. Support available to part-time students. Financial award application deadline: 7/1; financial award applicants required to submit FAFSA. *Faculty research:* Government financing, transportation, leadership, health care, volunteerism and organizational behavior, non-profit organizations. Total annual research expenditures: $20,000. *Unit head:* Dr. J. Patrick Murphy, Director, 312-362-5608, Fax: 312-362-5506, E-mail: jpmurphy@depaul.edu. *Application contact:* Megan B. Balderston, Director of Admissions and Marketing, 312-362-5565, Fax: 312-362-5506, E-mail: pubserv@depaul.edu.

Eastern Kentucky University, The Graduate School, College of Arts and Sciences, Department of Government, Program in General Public Administration, Richmond, KY 40475-3102. Offers community development (MPA); community health administration (MPA); general public administration (MPA). *Accreditation:* NASPAA. Part-time and evening/weekend programs available. *Entrance requirements:* For master's, GRE General Test, minimum GPA of 2.5.

Eastern Michigan University, Graduate School, College of Arts and Sciences, Department of Geography and Geology, Program in Urban and Regional Planning, Ypsilanti, MI 48197. Offers MS. *Students:* 4 full-time (2 women), 17 part-time (7 women); includes 5 minority (3 Black or African American, non-Hispanic/Latino; 1 American Indian or Alaska Native, non-Hispanic/Latino; 1 Two or more races, non-Hispanic/Latino). Average age 36. In 2010, 4 master's awarded. Application fee: $35. *Application contact:* Dr. Norman Tyler, Program Advisor, 734-487-8656, Fax: 734-487-6979, E-mail: norman.tyler@emich.edu.

Eastern Michigan University, Graduate School, College of Arts and Sciences, Department of Political Science, Programs in Public Administration, Ypsilanti, MI 48197. Offers local government management (Graduate Certificate); management of public healthcare services (Graduate Certificate); public administration (MPA, Graduate Certificate); public budget management (Graduate Certificate); public land planning (Graduate Certificate); public management (Graduate Certificate); public personnel management (Graduate Certificate); public policy analysis (Graduate Certificate). *Accreditation:* NASPAA. *Students:* 28 full-time (18 women), 124 part-time (64 women); includes 50 minority (40 Black or African American, non-Hispanic/Latino; 1 American Indian or Alaska Native, non-Hispanic/Latino; 1 Asian, non-Hispanic/Latino; 6 Hispanic/Latino; 2 Two or more races, non-Hispanic/Latino), 5 international. Average age 34. In 2010, 17 master's, 17 other advanced degrees awarded. Application fee: $35. *Unit head:* Dr. Joseph Ohren, Program Director, 734-487-2522, Fax: 734-487-3340, E-mail: joseph.ohren@emich.edu. *Application contact:* Dr. Joseph Ohren, Program Director, 734-487-2522, Fax: 734-487-3340, E-mail: joseph.ohren@emich.edu.

Eastern University, School for Social Change, St. Davids, PA 19087-3696. Offers urban studies (MA), including arts in transformation, community development, youth leadership.

Eastern University, School of Leadership and Development, St. Davids, PA 19087-3696. Offers economic development (MBA), including international development, urban development (MA, MBA); international development (MA), including global development, urban development (MA, MBA); nonprofit management (MS); organizational leadership (MA); M Div/MBA. Part-time and evening/weekend programs available. *Degree requirements:* For master's, thesis (for some programs). *Entrance requirements:* For master's, GMAT (MBA), minimum GPA of 2.5. *Expenses:* Contact institution. *Faculty research:* Micro-level economic development, China welfare and economic development, macroethics, micro- and macro-level economic development in transitional economics, organizational effectiveness.

Eastern Washington University, Graduate Studies, College of Business and Public Administration, Program in Urban and Regional Planning, Cheney, WA 99004-2431. Offers MURP, MPA/MURP. *Accreditation:* ACSP. *Degree requirements:* For master's, comprehensive exam, thesis or alternative. *Entrance requirements:* For master's, minimum GPA of 3.0.

East Tennessee State University, School of Graduate Studies, College of Arts and Sciences, Department of Economics, Finance, and Urban Studies, Johnson City, TN 37614. Offers city management (MCM); not-for-profit (MPA); planning and development (MPA); public financial management (MPA). Part-time programs available. *Faculty:* 1 full-time (0 women). *Students:* 15 full-time (5 women), 8 part-time (4 women); includes 1 Black or African American, non-Hispanic/Latino, 2 international. Average age 30. 19 applicants, 42% accepted, 7 enrolled. In 2010, 14 master's awarded. *Degree requirements:* For master's, comprehensive exam, internship, capstone, research report. *Entrance requirements:* For master's, GRE General Test, minimum GPA of 2.5. Additional exam requirements/recommendations for international students: Required—TOEFL (minimum score 550 paper-based; 213 computer-based; 79 iBT). *Application deadline:* For fall admission, 6/1 priority date for domestic students, 4/30 for international students; for spring admission, 11/1 for domestic students, 9/30 for international students. Application fee: $25 ($35 for international students). Electronic applications accepted. *Financial support:* In 2010–11, 9 research assistantships with full tuition reimbursements (averaging $5,500 per year) were awarded; career-related internships or fieldwork, institutionally sponsored loans, scholarships/grants, and unspecified assistantships also available. Financial award application deadline: 7/1; financial award applicants required to submit FAFSA. Total annual research expenditures: $6,519. *Unit head:* Dr. Weixing Chen, Chair, 423-439-6632, Fax: 423-439-4348, E-mail: chen@etsu.edu. *Application contact:* Dr. Weixing Chen, Chair, 423-439-6632, Fax: 423-439-4348, E-mail: chen@etsu.edu.

Florida Atlantic University, College of Design and Social Inquiry, School of Urban and Regional Planning, Boca Raton, FL 33431-0991. Offers economic development and tourism (Certificate); environmental planning (Certificate); sustainable community planning (Certificate); urban and regional planning (MURP); visual planning technology (Certificate). *Accreditation:* ACSP. Part-time and evening/weekend programs available. *Faculty:* 8 full-time (5 women), 2 part-time/adjunct (1 woman). *Students:* 24 full-time (18 women), 12 part-time (1 woman); includes 17 minority (4 Black or African American, non-Hispanic/Latino; 1 American Indian or Alaska Native, non-Hispanic/Latino; 12 Hispanic/Latino), 2 international. Average age 30. 55 applicants, 35% accepted, 12 enrolled. In 2010, 13 master's awarded. *Entrance requirements:* For master's, GRE General Test, minimum GPA of 3.0. Additional exam requirements/recommendations for international students: Required—TOEFL. *Application deadline:* For fall admission, 7/1 priority date for domestic students, 2/15 for international students; for spring admission, 11/1 priority date for domestic students, 7/15 for international students. Applications are processed on a rolling basis. Application fee: $30. *Expenses:* Tuition, area resident: Part-time $319.96 per credit. Tuition, state resident: part-time $319.96 per credit. Tuition, nonresident: part-time $926.42 per credit. *Financial support:* Fellowships with full tuition reimbursements, research assistantships, career-related internships or fieldwork, Federal Work-Study, institutionally sponsored loans, and tuition waivers (partial) available. Financial award application deadline: 4/1. *Faculty research:* Growth management, urban design, computer applications/geographical information systems, environmental planning. *Unit head:* Dr. Jaap Vos, Chair, 954-762-5653, Fax: 954-762-5673, E-mail: jvos@fau.edu. *Application contact:* Dr. Jaap Vos, Chair, 954-762-5653, Fax: 954-762-5673, E-mail: jvos@fau.edu.

Florida State University, The Graduate School, College of Social Sciences and Public Policy, Department of Urban and Regional Planning, Tallahassee, FL 32306. Offers MSP, PhD, JD/MSP, MA/MSP, MPA/MSP, MPH/MSP, MSD/MSP. *Accreditation:* ACSP (one or more programs are accredited). Part-time programs available. *Faculty:* 12 full-time (4 women), 4 part-time/adjunct (0 women). *Students:* 107 full-time (50 women), 38 part-time (20 women); includes 44 minority (13 Black or African American, non-Hispanic/Latino; 3 American Indian or Alaska Native, non-Hispanic/Latino; 9 Asian, non-Hispanic/Latino; 12 Hispanic/Latino; 7 Two or more races, non-Hispanic/Latino), 7 international. Average age 26. 130 applicants, 58% accepted, 48 enrolled. In 2010, 42 master's, 2 doctorates awarded. *Degree requirements:* For master's, capstone project, internship; for doctorate, thesis/dissertation. *Entrance requirements:* For master's and doctorate, GRE General Test, minimum GPA of 3.0. Additional exam requirements/recommendations for international students: Required—TOEFL (minimum score 550 paper-based; 213 computer-based; 80 iBT); Recommended—IELTS. *Application deadline:* For fall admission, 2/15 priority date for domestic students, 11/15 priority date for international students; for spring admission, 11/1 for domestic students, 9/1 for international students. Applications are processed on a rolling basis. Application fee: $30. Electronic applications accepted. *Expenses:* Tuition, state resident: full-time $8238.24. *Financial support:* In 2010–11, 35 students received support, including 1 fellowship with full tuition reimbursement available (averaging $19,000 per year), 22 research assistantships with full tuition reimbursements available (averaging $7,000 per year), 12 teaching assistantships with full tuition reimbursements available (averaging $13,500 per year); career-related internships or fieldwork, Federal Work-Study, institutionally sponsored loans, and tuition waivers (partial) also available. Financial award application deadline: 2/15; financial award applicants required to submit FAFSA. *Faculty research:* Growth management, environmental planning, developing countries, transportation, sustainable and healthy communities, housing and community development. Total annual research expenditures: $625,000. *Unit head:* Dr. Timothy S. Chapin, Associate Professor and Chairperson, 850-644-4510, Fax: 850-645-4841, E-mail: tchapin@fsu.edu. *Application contact:* Cynthia E. Brown, Admissions Coordinator, 850-644-4510, Fax: 850-644-4841, E-mail: durp@coss.fsu.edu.

Georgia Institute of Technology, Graduate Studies and Research, College of Architecture, City and Regional Planning Program, Atlanta, GA 30332-0001. Offers city and regional planning (PhD); economic development (MCRP); environmental planning and management (MCRP); geographic information systems (MCRP); land and community development (MCRP); land use planning (MCRP); transportation (MCRP); urban design (MCRP); MCP/MSCE. *Accreditation:* ACSP. *Degree requirements:* For master's, thesis, internship. *Entrance requirements:* For master's, GRE General Test, minimum GPA of 2.7. Additional exam requirements/recommendations for international students: Required—TOEFL. Electronic applications accepted.

Georgia State University, Andrew Young School of Policy Studies, Department of Public Management and Policy, Atlanta, GA 30303. Offers disaster management (Certificate); nonprofit management (Certificate); planning and economic development (Certificate); public administration (MPA), including criminal justice, management and finance, nonprofit management, planning and economic development, policy analysis and evaluation, public health; public policy (MPP, PhD), including disaster policy (MPP), nonprofit policy (MPP), planning and economic development policy (MPP), public finance policy (MPP), social policy (MPP); JD/MPA. *Accreditation:* NASPAA (one or more programs are accredited). Part-time and evening/weekend programs available. Terminal master's awarded for partial completion of doctoral program. *Degree requirements:* For master's, thesis optional; for doctorate, comprehensive exam, thesis/dissertation. *Entrance requirements:* For master's and doctorate, GRE General Test. Additional exam requirements/recommendations for international students: Required—TOEFL. Electronic applications accepted. *Faculty research:* Public management, policy analysis, public finance, planning and economic development, nonprofit leadership and policy.

Harvard University, Graduate School of Arts and Sciences, Committee on Architecture, Landscape Architecture, and Urban Planning, Cambridge, MA 02138. Offers architecture (PhD); landscape architecture (PhD); urban planning (PhD). *Degree requirements:* For doctorate, one foreign language, thesis/dissertation, oral exam. *Entrance requirements:* For doctorate, GRE General Test. Additional exam requirements/recommendations for international students: Required—TOEFL. *Expenses:* Tuition: Full-time $34,976. Required fees: $1166. Full-time tuition and fees vary according to program.

Harvard University, Graduate School of Design, Department of Urban Planning and Design, Cambridge, MA 02138. Offers urban planning (MUP); urban planning and design (MAUD, MLAUD). *Accreditation:* ACSP (one or more programs are accredited). *Entrance requirements:* For master's, GRE General Test. Additional exam requirements/recommendations for international students: Required—TOEFL (minimum score 600 paper-based; 250 computer-based; 104 iBT). Electronic applications accepted. *Expenses:* Tuition: Full-time $34,976. Required fees: $1166. Full-time tuition and fees vary according to program.

Hunter College of the City University of New York, Graduate School, School of Arts and Sciences, Department of Urban Affairs and Planning, Program in Urban Planning, New York, NY 10021-5085. Offers MUP, JD/MUP. JD/MUP offered jointly with Brooklyn Law School. *Accreditation:* ACSP. Part-time programs available. *Faculty:* 12 full-time (3 women), 11 part-time/adjunct (5 women). *Students:* 64 full-time (32 women), 61 part-time (26 women); includes 19 Black or African American, non-Hispanic/Latino; 1 American Indian or Alaska Native, non-Hispanic/Latino; 7 Asian, non-Hispanic/Latino; 12 Hispanic/Latino, 4 international. Average age 30. 198 applicants, 31% accepted, 33 enrolled. *Degree requirements:* For master's, planning studio and internship. *Entrance requirements:* For master's, minimum 12 credits of course work in social sciences, 2 letters of recommendation. Additional exam requirements/recommendations for international students: Required—TOEFL. *Application deadline:* For fall admission, 4/1 for domestic students, 2/1 for international students; for spring admission, 11/1 for domestic students, 9/1 for international students. Application fee: $125. *Financial support:* In 2010–11, 4 fellowships with full tuition reimbursements (averaging $9,000 per year), 10 teaching assistantships (averaging $1,200 per year) were awarded; research assistantships, career-related internships or fieldwork, Federal Work-Study, and tuition waivers (partial) also available. Support available to part-time students. *Faculty research:* Community and economic development, transportation planning and policy, geographic information systems, housing, land use. *Unit head:* Dr. Lynn McCormick, Director, 212-772-5733, Fax: 212-772-5593, E-mail: lmccormi@hunter.cuny.edu. *Application contact:* William Zlata, Director for Graduate Admissions, 212-772-4482, Fax: 212-650-3336, E-mail: admissions@hunter.cuny.edu.

Iowa State University of Science and Technology, Graduate College, College of Design, Department of Community and Regional Planning, Ames, IA 50011. Offers community and regional planning (MCRP); transportation (MS); M Arch/MCRP; MBA/MCRP; MCRP/MLA; MCRP/MPA. *Accreditation:* ACSP (one or more programs are accredited). Part-time programs available. *Faculty:* 11 full-time (4 women), 1 part-time/adjunct (0 women). *Students:* 26 full-time (14 women), 26 part-time (9 women); includes 3 Black or African American, non-Hispanic/Latino; 1 Hispanic/Latino, 6 international. Average age 31. 44 applicants, 55% accepted, 16 enrolled. In 2010, 10 master's awarded. *Degree requirements:* For master's, thesis or alternative. *Entrance requirements:* For master's, GRE General Test. Additional exam requirements/recommendations for international students: Required—TOEFL (minimum score 550 paper-based; 79 iBT), IELTS (minimum score 6.5). *Application deadline:* For fall admission, 1/1 priority date for domestic and international students. Applications are processed on a rolling basis. Application fee: $40 ($90 for international students). Electronic applications accepted. *Financial support:* In 2010–11, 3 research assistantships with full and partial tuition reimbursements (averaging $13,788 per year), 13 teaching assistantships with full and partial tuition reimbursements (averaging $3,886 per year) were awarded; career-related internships or fieldwork, institutionally sponsored loans, tuition waivers (partial), and unspecified assistantships also available. Support available to part-time students. Financial award application deadline: 2/1; financial award applicants required to submit FAFSA. *Faculty research:* Economic development, housing, land use, geographic information systems planning in developing nations, regional and community revitalization, transportation planning in developing countries. *Unit head:* Dr. Douglas Johnston, Chair, 515-294-8958, Fax: 515-294-2348, E-mail: landarch@iastate.edu. *Application contact:* Dr. Francis Owusu, Director of Graduate Education, 515-294-7769, E-mail: crp@iastate.edu.

Jackson State University, Graduate School, College of Public Service, Department of Urban and Regional Planning, Jackson, MS 39217. Offers MS, PhD. *Accreditation:* ACSP. *Faculty:* 5 full-time (1 woman), 3 part-time/adjunct (0 women). *Students:* 41 full-time (26 women), 32 part-time (19 women); includes 60 Black or African American, non-Hispanic/Latino, 3 international. Average age 36. In 2010, 4 master's, 2 doctorates awarded. *Degree requirements:* For master's, comprehensive exam. *Entrance requirements:* For master's, GRE General Test. Additional exam requirements/recommendations for international students: Required—TOEFL (minimum score 520 paper-based; 195 computer-based; 67 iBT). *Application deadline:* For fall admission, 3/1 for domestic and international students; for spring admission, 10/1 for domestic and international students. Application fee: $25. *Expenses:* Tuition, state resident: full-time $5050; part-time $281 per credit hour. Tuition, nonresident: full-time $12,380; part-time $689 per credit hour. *Financial support:* Application deadline: 3/1. *Unit head:* Dr. Otha Burton, Chair, 601-432-6865, E-mail: otha.burton@jsums.edu. *Application contact:* Sharlene Wilson, Director of Graduate Admissions, 601-979-2455, Fax: 601-979-4325, E-mail: sharlene.f.wilson@jsums.edu.

John Brown University, Graduate Business Programs, Siloam Springs, AR 72761-2121. Offers business administration (MBA), including international business, leadership and ethics; international community development leadership (MS); leadership and ethics (MS); leadership and higher education (MS). Part-time and evening/weekend programs available. Postbaccalaureate distance learning degree programs offered (minimal on-campus study). *Entrance requirements:* For master's, MAT, GMAT or GRE if undergraduate GPA is less than 3.0, recommendation forms from three people, 200-word essay describing professional plans and reason for seeking acceptance. Additional exam requirements/recommendations for international students: Required—TOEFL (minimum score 550 paper-based; 173 computer-based; 70 iBT). Electronic applications accepted.

Kansas State University, Graduate School, College of Architecture, Planning and Design, Department of Interior Architecture and Product Design, Manhattan, KS 66506. Offers regional and community planning (MRCP). *Accreditation:* ACSP. Part-time and evening/weekend programs available. Postbaccalaureate distance learning degree programs offered (minimal on-campus study). *Degree requirements:* For master's, thesis, oral exam. *Entrance requirements:* For master's, minimum GPA of 3.0, portfolio. Additional exam requirements/recommendations for international students: Required—TOEFL (minimum score 600 paper-based). Electronic applications accepted. *Faculty research:* Planning interior spaces for exhibition; residential and commercial spaces; design of objects such as furniture, lighting, equipment, finishing treatments and accessories.

Lesley University, Graduate School of Arts and Social Sciences, Program in Urban Environmental Leadership, Cambridge, MA 02138-2790. Offers MA. *Entrance requirements:* For master's, 2 letters of recommendation, interview.

Loyola University Chicago, Institute of Pastoral Studies, Program in Social Justice and Community Development, Chicago, IL 60660. Offers community development (MA); social justice (MA); social justice and community development (MA, Certificate); MSW/MA. *Students:* 26 full-time (23 women), 22 part-time (12 women); includes 16 minority (9 Black or African American, non-Hispanic/Latino; 6 Hispanic/Latino; 1 Two or more races, non-Hispanic/Latino), 3 international. Average age 32. 49 applicants, 80% accepted, 25 enrolled. In 2010, 16 master's awarded. *Degree requirements:* For master's, internship. *Expenses:* Tuition: Full-time $14,940; part-time $830 per credit hour. Required fees: $87 per semester. Part-time tuition and fees vary according to course load and program. *Unit head:* Dr. Robert A. Ludwig. *Application contact:* Randy Gibbons, Administrative Assistant, 312-915-7450, Fax: 312-915-7410, E-mail: rgibbon@luc.edu.

Massachusetts Institute of Technology, School of Architecture and Planning, Department of Urban Studies and Planning, Cambridge, MA 02139-4307. Offers city planning (MCP); urban and regional planning (PhD); urban and regional studies (PhD); urban studies and planning (SM). *Accreditation:* ACSP (one or more programs are accredited). *Faculty:* 28 full-time (10 women). *Students:* 201 full-time (120 women); includes 53 minority (10 Black or African American, non-Hispanic/Latino; 2 American Indian or Alaska Native, non-Hispanic/Latino; 22 Asian, non-Hispanic/Latino; 14 Hispanic/Latino; 5 Two or more races, non-Hispanic/Latino), 55 international. Average age 29. 606 applicants, 21% accepted, 95 enrolled. In 2010, 73 master's, 11 doctorates awarded. Terminal master's awarded for partial completion of doctoral program. *Degree requirements:* For master's, thesis; for doctorate, comprehensive exam, thesis/dissertation. *Entrance requirements:* For master's, GRE General Test; for doctorate, GRE General Test (minimum scores: 1200 Verbal and Quantitative combined; 5.0 Analytical Writing). Additional exam requirements/recommendations for international students: Required—TOEFL (minimum score 250 computer-based; 100 iBT), IELTS (minimum score 7). *Application deadline:* For fall admission, 1/3 for domestic and international students. Application fee: $75. Electronic applications accepted. *Expenses:* Tuition: Full-time $38,940; part-time $605 per unit. Required fees: $272. *Financial support:* In 2010–11, 166 students received support, including 81 fellowships with tuition reimbursements available (averaging $23,223 per year), 58 research assistantships with tuition reimbursements available (averaging $18,475 per year), 21 teaching assistantships with tuition reimbursements available (averaging $29,214 per year); career-related internships or fieldwork, Federal Work-Study, institutionally sponsored loans, scholarships/grants, health care benefits, and unspecified assistantships also available. *Faculty research:* City design and sustainable urban development; housing, community, and economic development; environment and energy policy and planning; international development and regional planning; urban and geographic information systems. Total annual research expenditures: $2.7 million. *Unit head:* Prof. Amy Glasmeier, Department Head, 617-253-1907, Fax: 617-253-2654, E-mail: duspinfo@mit.edu. *Application contact:* Graduate Admissions, 617-253-4543, Fax: 617-253-2654, E-mail: duspapply@mit.edu.

McGill University, Faculty of Graduate and Postdoctoral Studies, Faculty of Engineering, School of Urban Planning, Montréal, QC H3A 2T5, Canada. Offers environmental planning (MUP); housing (MUP); transportation (MUP); urban design (MUP); urban planning, policy and design (PhD).

Michigan State University, The Graduate School, College of Agriculture and Natural Resources and College of Social Science, School of Planning, Design and Construction, East Lansing, MI 48824. Offers construction management (MS, PhD); environmental design (MA); interior design and facilities management (MA); international planning studies (MIPS); urban and regional planning (MURP). *Degree requirements:* For master's, thesis or alternative. *Entrance requirements:* Additional exam requirements/recommendations for international students: Required—TOEFL. Electronic applications accepted.

Minnesota State University Mankato, College of Graduate Studies, College of Social and Behavioral Sciences, Department of Urban and Regional Studies, Mankato, MN 56001. Offers local government management (Certificate); urban and regional studies (MA); urban planning (MA, Certificate). *Students:* 19 full-time (4 women), 18 part-time (7 women). *Degree requirements:* For master's, one foreign language, comprehensive exam, thesis or alternative. *Entrance requirements:* For master's, minimum GPA of 3.0 during previous 2 years, 2 letters of recommendation. Additional exam requirements/recommendations for international students: Required—TOEFL. *Application deadline:* For fall admission, 7/1 priority date for domestic students; for spring admission, 11/1 for domestic students. Applications are processed on a rolling basis. Application fee: $40. Electronic applications accepted. *Financial support:* Fellowships with partial tuition reimbursements, research assistantships with full tuition reimbursements, teaching assistantships with full tuition reimbursements, career-related internships or fieldwork, Federal Work-Study, institutionally sponsored loans, and unspecified assistantships available. Support available to part-time students. Financial award application deadline: 3/15; financial award applicants required to submit FAFSA. *Unit head:* Dr. Anthony Filipovitch, Graduate Coordinator, 507-389-1714. *Application contact:* 507-389-2321, E-mail: grad@mnsu.edu.

Missouri State University, Graduate College, College of Natural and Applied Sciences, Department of Geography, Geology, and Planning, Springfield, MO 65897. Offers geospatial sciences (MS); natural and applied science (MNAS), including geography, geology and planning; secondary education (MS Ed), including earth science, geography. Part-time and evening/weekend programs available. *Degree requirements:* For master's, comprehensive exam, thesis (for some programs). *Entrance requirements:* For master's, GRE General Test (MS, MNAS), minimum undergraduate GPA of 3.0 (MS, MNAS), 9-12 teacher certification (MS Ed). Additional exam requirements/recommendations for international students: Required—TOEFL (minimum score 550 paper-based; 213 computer-based; 79 iBT). Electronic applications accepted. *Expenses:* Tuition, state resident: full-time $3348; part-time $186 per credit hour. Tuition,

Urban and Regional Planning

Missouri State University (continued)
nonresident: full-time $6696; part-time $372 per credit hour. Required fees: $238 per semester. Tuition and fees vary according to course level, course load and program. *Faculty research:* Stratigraphy and ancient meteorite impacts, environmental geochemistry of karst, hyperspectral image processing, water quality, small town planning.

Montclair State University, The Graduate School, College of Humanities and Social Sciences, Department of Anthropology, Montclair, NJ 07043-1624. Offers community development (Certificate). Part-time and evening/weekend programs available. *Faculty:* 10 full-time (5 women), 9 part-time/adjunct (6 women). *Students:* 1 (woman) full-time, 2 part-time (1 woman); includes 1 Black or African American, non-Hispanic/Latino. Average age 24. 5 applicants, 80% accepted, 3 enrolled. *Entrance requirements:* Additional exam requirements/recommendations for international students: Required—TOEFL (minimum score: 83 iBT) or IELTS. *Expenses:* Tuition, state resident: part-time $501.34 per credit. Tuition, nonresident: part-time $773.88 per credit. Required fees: $71.15 per credit. *Financial support:* In 2010–11, 1 research assistantship with full tuition reimbursement (averaging $7,000 per year) was awarded; Federal Work-Study, scholarships/grants, and unspecified assistantships also available. Support available to part-time students. Financial award application deadline: 3/1; financial award applicants required to submit FAFSA. *Unit head:* Dr. Francis Rothstein, Chairperson, 973-655-4133, E-mail: brookk@mail.montclair.edu. *Application contact:* Amy Aiello, Director of Graduate Admissions and Operations, 973-655-5147, Fax: 973-655-7869, E-mail: graduate.school@montclair.edu.

Morgan State University, School of Graduate Studies, Institute of Architecture and Planning, Program in City and Regional Planning, Baltimore, MD 21251. Offers MCRP. *Accreditation:* ACSP. *Degree requirements:* For master's, thesis. *Entrance requirements:* Additional exam requirements/recommendations for international students: Required—TOEFL (minimum score 550 paper-based; 213 computer-based). *Faculty research:* Nonprofit organizations, community development, urban design, transportation, international planning.

New York University, Robert F. Wagner Graduate School of Public Service, Program in Urban Planning, New York, NY 10012-1019. Offers housing (Advanced Certificate); public economics (Advanced Certificate); quantitative analysis and computer applications for policy and planning (Advanced Certificate); urban planning (MUP); JD/MUP. *Accreditation:* ACSP (one or more programs are accredited). Part-time and evening/weekend programs available. *Faculty:* 6 full-time (2 women), 11 part-time/adjunct (3 women). *Students:* 87 full-time (50 women), 41 part-time (21 women); includes 5 Black or African American, non-Hispanic/Latino; 14 Asian, non-Hispanic/Latino; 8 Hispanic/Latino, 9 international. Average age 28. 321 applicants, 46% accepted, 46 enrolled. In 2010, 47 master's awarded. *Degree requirements:* For master's, thesis or alternative, end event workshop. *Entrance requirements:* For master's, minimum undergraduate GPA of 3.0. Additional exam requirements/recommendations for international students: Required—TOEFL (minimum score 600 paper-based; 250 computer-based; 100 iBT), IELTS (minimum score 7.5), TWE (minimum score 4). *Application deadline:* For fall admission, 5/15 for domestic students, 1/5 for international students; for spring admission, 11/15 for domestic students, 10/1 for international students. Applications are processed on a rolling basis. Application fee: $80. Electronic applications accepted. *Financial support:* In 2010–11, 40 students received support, including 39 fellowships (averaging $8,876 per year), 1 research assistantship with full tuition reimbursement available (averaging $22,440 per year); career-related internships or fieldwork, Federal Work-Study, institutionally sponsored loans, scholarships/grants, health care benefits, and unspecified assistantships also available. Support available to part-time students. Financial award application deadline: 1/4; financial award applicants required to submit FAFSA. *Unit head:* Prof. Ingrid Gould Ellen, Director, 212-998-7533, Fax: 212-995-4164, E-mail: ingrid.ellen@nyu.edu. *Application contact:* Christopher Alexander, Administrative Aide, Enrollment, 212-998-7414, Fax: 212-995-4611, E-mail: wagner.admissions@nyu.edu.

Northeastern University, College of Social Sciences and Humanities, School of Public Policy and Urban Affairs, Boston, MA 02115-5096. Offers law and public policy (PhD); public administration (MPA, Certificate), including development administration (MPA), health administration and policy (MPA), state and local government (MPA), urban studies (Certificate); urban and regional policy (MURP); JD/PhD. Part-time and evening/weekend programs available. *Faculty:* 8 full-time (3 women), 4 part-time/adjunct (3 women). *Students:* 22 full-time (14 women), 12 part-time (7 women). Average age 27. 51 applicants, 57% accepted, 18 enrolled. *Entrance requirements:* Additional exam requirements/recommendations for international students: Required—TOEFL. *Application deadline:* For fall admission, 2/1 priority date for domestic and international students. Applications are processed on a rolling basis. Application fee: $50. Electronic applications accepted. *Financial support:* Federal Work-Study, scholarships/grants, and tuition waivers available. Financial award application deadline: 2/1; financial award applicants required to submit FAFSA. *Faculty research:* Urban and regional development, housing, transportation and energy, urban sustainability, land use. *Unit head:* Dr. Laurie Dopkins, Graduate Coordinator, 617-373-2889, E-mail: murp@neu.edu. *Application contact:* Jo-Anne Dickinson, Graduate Admissions Contact, 617-373-5990, Fax: 617-373-7281, E-mail: gsas@neu.edu.

The Ohio State University, Graduate School, College of Engineering, Austin E. Knowlton School of Architecture, Columbus, OH 43210. Offers architecture (M Arch); city and regional planning (MCRP, PhD); landscape architecture (M Land Arch). *Accreditation:* ACSP; ASLA. *Faculty:* 35. *Students:* 204 full-time (81 women), 27 part-time (14 women); includes 9 Black or African American, non-Hispanic/Latino; 1 American Indian or Alaska Native, non-Hispanic/Latino; 8 Asian, non-Hispanic/Latino; 8 Hispanic/Latino; 1 Two or more races, non-Hispanic/Latino, 26 international. Average age 28. In 2010, 76 master's, 6 doctorates awarded. *Degree requirements:* For doctorate, thesis/dissertation. *Entrance requirements:* Additional exam requirements/recommendations for international students: Recommended—TOEFL (minimum score 600 paper-based; 250 computer-based). *Application deadline:* For fall admission, 8/15 priority date for domestic students, 7/1 priority date for international students; for winter admission, 12/1 priority date for domestic students, 11/1 priority date for international students; for spring admission, 3/1 priority date for domestic students, 2/1 priority date for international students. Applications are processed on a rolling basis. Application fee: $40 ($50 for international students). Electronic applications accepted. *Expenses:* Tuition, state resident: full-time $10,605. Tuition, nonresident: full-time $26,535. Tuition and fees vary according to course load and program. *Financial support:* Fellowships, research assistantships, Federal Work-Study, institutionally sponsored loans, and unspecified assistantships available. Support available to part-time students. *Unit head:* Ann Pendleton-Jullian, Director, 614-292-9811, Fax: 614-292-7106, E-mail: pendleton-jullia@osu.edu. *Application contact:* 614-292-9444, Fax: 614-292-3895, E-mail: domestic.grad@osu.edu.

Polytechnic Institute of NYU, Department of Civil Engineering, Major in Urban Systems Engineering and Management, Brooklyn, NY 11201-2990. Offers MS. *Students:* 1 (woman) full-time, 3 part-time (2 women); includes 1 Black or African American, non-Hispanic/Latino; 1 Asian, non-Hispanic/Latino, 2 international. Average age 25. 9 applicants, 56% accepted, 2 enrolled. In 2010, 4 master's awarded. *Application deadline:* For fall admission, 7/31 priority date for domestic students, 4/30 priority date for international students; for spring admission, 12/31 priority date for domestic students, 11/30 priority date for international students. Application fee: $75. *Expenses:* Tuition: Full-time $21,492; part-time $1194 per credit. Required fees: $385 per semester. Tuition and fees vary according to course load. *Unit head:* Dr. Lawrence Chiarelli, Head, 718-260-4040, Fax: 718-260-3433, E-mail: lchiarel@poly.edu. *Application contact:* JeanCarlo Bonilla, Director of Graduate Enrollment Management, 718-260-3182, Fax: 718-260-3624, E-mail: gradinfo@poly.edu.

Portland State University, Graduate Studies, College of Urban and Public Affairs, Nohad A. Toulan School of Urban Studies and Planning, Program in Urban and Regional Planning, Portland, OR 97207-0751. Offers MURP. *Accreditation:* ACSP. Part-time programs available. *Faculty:* 19 full-time (4 women), 15 part-time/adjunct (8 women). *Students:* 58 full-time (30 women), 21 part-time (10 women); includes 1 Black or African American, non-Hispanic/Latino; 3 Asian, non-Hispanic/Latino; 4 Hispanic/Latino; 1 Two or more races, non-Hispanic/Latino. Average age 28. 256 applicants, 37% accepted, 32 enrolled. In 2010, 39 master's awarded. *Entrance requirements:* For master's, minimum GPA of 2.75, 3 letters of recommendation. Additional exam requirements/recommendations for international students: Required—TOEFL (minimum score 550 paper-based; 213 computer-based). *Application deadline:* For fall admission, 1/15 for domestic and international students. Application fee: $50. *Expenses:* Tuition, state resident: full-time $8505; part-time $315 per credit. Tuition, nonresident: full-time $13,284; part-time $492 per credit. Required fees: $1482; $21 per credit. $99 per term. One-time fee: $120. Part-time tuition and fees vary according to course load and program. *Financial support:* Research assistantships, teaching assistantships, career-related internships or fieldwork, Federal Work-Study, and unspecified assistantships available. Support available to part-time students. Financial award application deadline: 3/1; financial award applicants required to submit FAFSA. *Faculty research:* Policy planning and administration, community development, land-use and environment, transportation, urban and regional analysis. Total annual research expenditures: $2 million. *Unit head:* Dr. Ethan P. Seltzer, Director, 503-725-4045, E-mail: seltzere@pdx.edu. *Application contact:* Tracy Braden, Office Coordinator, 503-725-4015, Fax: 503-725-8770, E-mail: tbraden@pdx.edu.

Pratt Institute, School of Architecture, Program in City and Regional Planning, Brooklyn, NY 11205-3899. Offers MSCRP. *Accreditation:* ACSP. Part-time programs available. *Faculty:* 2 full-time (1 woman), 9 part-time/adjunct (3 women). *Students:* 70 full-time (32 women), 13 part-time (12 women); includes 9 Black or African American, non-Hispanic/Latino; 3 Asian, non-Hispanic/Latino; 6 Hispanic/Latino, 5 international. Average age 29. 121 applicants, 69% accepted, 23 enrolled. In 2010, 16 master's awarded. *Degree requirements:* For master's, thesis. *Entrance requirements:* For master's, writing sample, bachelor's degree, transcripts, letters of recommendation, portfolio. Additional exam requirements/recommendations for international students: Required—TOEFL (minimum score 550 paper-based; 213 computer-based; 79 iBT). *Application deadline:* For fall admission, 1/5 for domestic and international students; for spring admission, 10/1 for domestic and international students. Applications are processed on a rolling basis. Application fee: $50 ($90 for international students). Electronic applications accepted. *Expenses:* Tuition: Full-time $22,734; part-time $1263 per credit. Required fees: $1280. *Financial support:* Career-related internships or fieldwork, Federal Work-Study, institutionally sponsored loans, scholarships/grants, health care benefits, and unspecified assistantships available. Support available to part-time students. Financial award application deadline: 2/1; financial award applicants required to submit FAFSA. *Faculty research:* Advocacy planning, community development, comprehensive physical planning, transportation planning, real estate development. *Unit head:* John Shapiro, Chairperson, 718-399-4391, E-mail: jshapir6@pratt.edu. *Application contact:* Young Hah, Director of Graduate Admissions, 718-636-3683, Fax: 718-399-4242, E-mail: yhah@pratt.edu.

See Display on page 141 and Close-Up on page 161.

Queen's University at Kingston, School of Graduate Studies and Research, School of Urban and Regional Planning, Kingston, ON K7L 3N6, Canada. Offers M Pl. Part-time programs available. *Degree requirements:* For master's, thesis optional. *Entrance requirements:* Additional exam requirements/recommendations for international students: Required—TOEFL (minimum score 580 paper-based; 237 computer-based). *Faculty research:* Housing, real estate development, human services, environmental services, land use planning.

Rutgers, The State University of New Jersey, New Brunswick, Edward J. Bloustein School of Planning and Public Policy, Doctoral Program in Planning and Public Policy, Piscataway, NJ 08854-8097. Offers PhD. Part-time programs available. *Faculty:* 35 full-time (11 women), 41 part-time/adjunct (16 women). *Students:* 25 full-time (15 women), 30 part-time (17 women); includes 7 Black or African American, non-Hispanic/Latino; 2 Asian, non-Hispanic/Latino; 3 Hispanic/Latino, 8 international. Average age 39. 100 applicants, 13% accepted, 8 enrolled. In 2010, 5 doctorates awarded. *Degree requirements:* For doctorate, comprehensive exam, thesis/dissertation. *Entrance requirements:* For doctorate, GRE, master's degree. Additional exam requirements/recommendations for international students: Required—TOEFL (minimum score 575 paper-based; 245 computer-based; 88 iBT). *Application deadline:* For fall admission, 1/15 for domestic and international students. Application fee: $65. Electronic applications accepted. *Expenses:* Tuition, state resident: full-time $7200; part-time $600 per credit. Tuition, nonresident: full-time $11,124; part-time $927 per credit. *Financial support:* In 2010–11, 28 students received support, including 5 fellowships with full and partial tuition reimbursements available (averaging $15,000 per year), 4 research assistantships with full and partial tuition reimbursements available (averaging $24,000 per year), 1 teaching assistantship with full and partial tuition reimbursement available (averaging $24,000 per year); Federal Work-Study, institutionally sponsored loans, scholarships/grants, health care benefits, tuition waivers (full and partial), and unspecified assistantships also available. Support available to part-time students. Financial award application deadline: 1/15; financial award applicants required to submit FAFSA. *Faculty research:* Housing and community development, land use and transportation, politics and policy analysis, urban and regional economics, international development. *Unit head:* Dr. David Listokin, Director, Doctoral Program in Planning and Public Policy, 732-932-5475 Ext. 550, Fax: 732-932-2253, E-mail: listokin@rci.rutgers.edu. *Application contact:* Steve Weston, Assistant Dean for Student and Academic Services, 732-932-5475 Ext. 753, Fax: 732-932-0934, E-mail: sdweston@rci.rutgers.edu.

Rutgers, The State University of New Jersey, New Brunswick, Edward J. Bloustein School of Planning and Public Policy, Program in Urban Planning and Policy Development, Piscataway, NJ 08854-8097. Offers MCRP, MCRS, JD/MCRP, MBA/MCRP. *Accreditation:* ACSP (one or more programs are accredited). Part-time and evening/weekend programs available. *Faculty:* 24 full-time (5 women), 3 part-time/adjunct (1 woman). *Students:* 130 full-time (66 women), 46 part-time (21 women); includes 22 Black or African American, non-Hispanic/Latino; 2 American Indian or Alaska Native, non-Hispanic/Latino; 8 Asian, non-Hispanic/Latino; 11 Hispanic/Latino. Average age 26. 325 applicants, 58% accepted, 100 enrolled. In 2010, 52 master's awarded. *Entrance requirements:* For master's, GRE General Test. Additional exam requirements/recommendations for international students: Required—TOEFL (minimum score 575 paper-based; 245 computer-based; 88 iBT). *Application deadline:* For fall admission, 1/15 for domestic and international students; for spring admission, 11/1 for domestic students. Application fee: $65. Electronic applications accepted. *Expenses:* Tuition, state resident: full-time $7200; part-time $600 per credit. Tuition, nonresident: full-time $11,124; part-time $927 per credit. *Financial support:* In 2010–11, 75 students received support, including 20 fellowships with full and partial tuition reimbursements available (averaging $5,000 per year), 16 research assistantships with full tuition reimbursements available (averaging $24,000 per year), 20 teaching assistantships with full tuition reimbursements available (averaging $24,000 per year); career-related internships or fieldwork, Federal Work-Study, scholarships/grants, tuition waivers (full and partial), and unspecified assistantships also available. Financial award application deadline: 1/15; financial award applicants required to submit FAFSA. *Faculty research:* Land use, transportation, housing, environmental planning, urban redevelopment, international development. *Unit head:* Dr. Clinton J. Andrews, Director, 732-932-5975 Ext. 721, Fax: 732-932-2253, E-mail: cja1@rci.rutgers.edu. *Application contact:* Lynn Astorga, Student and Academic Services Assistant, 732-932-5475 Ext. 740, Fax: 732-932-1771, E-mail: lastorga@policy.rutgers.edu.

San Diego State University, Graduate and Research Affairs, College of Professional Studies and Fine Arts, School of Public Affairs, Program in City Planning, San Diego, CA 92182. Offers MCP. Part-time programs available. *Entrance requirements:* For master's, GRE General Test. Additional exam requirements/recommendations for international students: Required—TOEFL. Electronic applications accepted. *Faculty research:* Community development, housing, sustainable development, visioning.

San Jose State University, Graduate Studies and Research, College of Social Sciences, Department of Urban and Regional Planning, San Jose, CA 95192-0001. Offers MUP, Certificate. *Accreditation:* ACSP. Part-time programs available. *Degree requirements:* For master's, comprehensive exam, thesis or alternative. *Entrance requirements:* For master's, GRE, minimum GPA of 3.0. Electronic applications accepted. *Faculty research:* Retirement communities, planning and problems, women in suburbia, influence on urban development, Taiwanese urban development issues.

State University of New York College of Environmental Science and Forestry, Department of Landscape Architecture, Syracuse, NY 13210-2779. Offers community design and planning (MLA, MS); cultural landscape conservation (MLA, MS); landscape and urban ecology (MLA, MS). *Accreditation:* ASLA (one or more programs are accredited). *Degree requirements:* For master's, comprehensive exam (for some programs), thesis (for some programs). *Entrance requirements:* For master's, GRE General Test, minimum GPA of 3.0. Additional exam requirements/recommendations for international students: Required—TOEFL (paper-based 550, computer-based 213, iBT 80) or IELTS (6) or STEP Aiken (Grade 1). *Expenses:* Tuition, state resident: full-time $8370; part-time $349 per credit hour. Tuition, nonresident: full-time $13,780. Required fees: $30.30 per credit hour. $20 per year. *Faculty research:* Site analysis and design, city and regional planning, community environments.

State University of New York College of Environmental Science and Forestry, Program in Environmental Science, Syracuse, NY 13210-2779. Offers environmental and community land planning (MPS, MS, PhD); environmental and natural resources policy (PhD); environmental communication and participatory processes (MPS, MS, PhD); environmental policy and democratic processes (MPS, MS, PhD); environmental systems and risk management (MPS, MS, PhD); water and wetland resource studies (MPS, MS, PhD). Part-time programs available. *Degree requirements:* For master's, thesis (for some programs); for doctorate, comprehensive exam, thesis/dissertation. *Entrance requirements:* For master's and doctorate, GRE General Test, minimum GPA of 3.0. Additional exam requirements/recommendations for international students: Required—TOEFL (minimum score 550 paper-based; 213 computer-based; 80 iBT), IELTS (minimum score 6). *Expenses:* Tuition, state resident: full-time $8370; part-time $349 per credit hour. Tuition, nonresident: full-time $13,780. Required fees: $30.30 per credit hour. $20 per year. *Faculty research:* Environmental education/communications, water resources, land resources, waste management.

Temple University, School of Environmental Design, Department of Community and Regional Planning, Philadelphia, PA 19122-6096. Offers MS. *Accreditation:* ACSP. Part-time and evening/weekend programs available. *Faculty:* 6 full-time (2 women). *Students:* 26 full-time (12 women), 22 part-time (10 women); includes 1 Asian, non-Hispanic/Latino, 2 international. 25 applicants, 84% accepted, 16 enrolled. In 2010, 13 master's awarded. *Entrance requirements:* For master's, GRE or GMAT, 2 letters of recommendation, minimum undergraduate GPA of 3.0. Additional exam requirements/recommendations for international students: Required—TOEFL (minimum score 550 paper-based; 213 computer-based; 79 iBT). *Application deadline:* For fall admission, 7/1 for domestic students, 12/15 for international students; for spring admission, 11/1 for domestic students, 8/1 for international students. Applications are processed on a rolling basis. Application fee: $50. *Financial support:* Application deadline: 1/15. *Unit head:* Dr. Deborah Howe, Chair, 267-468-8301, E-mail: deborah.howe@temple.edu. *Application contact:* Dr. Deborah Howe, Chair, 267-468-8301, E-mail: deborah.howe@temple.edu.

Texas A&M University, College of Architecture, Department of Landscape Architecture and Urban Planning, College Station, TX 77843. Offers land development (MSLD); landscape architecture (MLA); urban and regional science (PhD); urban planning (MUP). *Accreditation:* ACSP (one or more programs are accredited); ASLA (one or more programs are accredited). *Faculty:* 29. *Students:* 166 full-time (69 women), 19 part-time (7 women); includes 18 minority (5 Black or African American, non-Hispanic/Latino; 1 American Indian or Alaska Native, non-Hispanic/Latino; 3 Asian, non-Hispanic/Latino; 9 Hispanic/Latino), 97 international. Average age 31. In 2010, 46 master's, 6 doctorates awarded. Terminal master's awarded for partial completion of doctoral program. *Degree requirements:* For master's, thesis optional, professional internship; for doctorate, comprehensive exam, thesis/dissertation, methods statistics seminar. *Entrance requirements:* For master's, GMAT or GRE General Test, portfolio (MLA), minimum GPA of 3.0; for doctorate, GMAT or GRE General Test. Additional exam requirements/recommendations for international students: Required—TOEFL. *Application deadline:* For fall admission, 2/1 priority date for domestic students; for spring admission, 8/1 for domestic students. Applications are processed on a rolling basis. Application fee: $50 ($75 for international students). Electronic applications accepted. *Financial support:* In 2010–11, fellowships with tuition reimbursements (averaging $1,000 per year), research assistantships with partial tuition reimbursements (averaging $8,100 per year), teaching assistantships with partial tuition reimbursements (averaging $11,250 per year) were awarded; career-related internships or fieldwork, institutionally sponsored loans, and scholarships/grants also available. Financial award application deadline: 4/1; financial award applicants required to submit FAFSA. *Faculty research:* Erosion control/water quality, geographic information systems/spatial information technology, transport hazards, international sustainable development. *Unit head:* Dr. Forster Ndubisi, Head, 979-845-1019, Fax: 979-862-1784. *Application contact:* Thena Morris, Administrative Assistant, 979-845-6582, Fax: 979-845-4491, E-mail: t-morris@tamu.edu.

Texas Southern University, School of Public Affairs, Program in Urban Planning and Environmental Policy, Houston, TX 77004-4584. Offers MS, PhD. *Accreditation:* ACSP. Part-time and evening/weekend programs available. *Faculty:* 4 full-time (2 women). *Students:* 44 full-time (21 women), 35 part-time (20 women); includes 62 Black or African American, non-Hispanic/Latino; 7 Asian, non-Hispanic/Latino; 3 Hispanic/Latino, 1 international. Average age 37. 27 applicants, 100% accepted, 20 enrolled. In 2010, 1 master's, 3 doctorates awarded. *Degree requirements:* For master's, comprehensive exam, thesis optional. *Entrance requirements:* For master's, GRE General Test, minimum GPA of 2.5. Additional exam requirements/recommendations for international students: Required—TOEFL. *Application deadline:* For fall admission, 7/1 priority date for domestic students, 7/1 for international students; for spring admission, 11/1 for domestic and international students. Applications are processed on a rolling basis. Application fee: $50 ($75 for international students). Electronic applications accepted. *Expenses:* Tuition, state resident: full-time $1875; part-time $100 per credit hour. Tuition, nonresident: full-time $6641; part-time $343 per credit hour. Tuition and fees vary according to course level, course load and degree level. *Financial support:* In 2010–11, 6 research assistantships (averaging $4,122 per year), 1 teaching assistantship (averaging $6,000 per year) were awarded; fellowships, career-related internships or fieldwork, Federal Work-Study, and institutionally sponsored loans also available. Financial award application deadline: 5/1; financial award applicants required to submit FAFSA. *Unit head:* Dr. Qisheng Pan, Chair, 713-313-7221, E-mail: taylor_sa@tsu.edu. *Application contact:* Sheila Taylor, Secretary, 713-313-6842, E-mail: randell_bj@tsu.edu.

Tufts University, Graduate School of Arts and Sciences, Department of Urban and Environmental Policy and Planning, Medford, MA 02155. Offers community development (MA); environmental policy (MA); health and human welfare (MA); housing policy (MA); international environment/development policy (MA); public policy (MPP); MA/MS; MALD/MA. *Accreditation:* ACSP (one or more programs are accredited). Part-time programs available. *Degree requirements:* For master's, thesis, internship. *Entrance requirements:* For master's, GRE General Test. Additional exam requirements/recommendations for international students: Required—TOEFL (minimum score 550 paper-based; 213 computer-based; 80 iBT). Electronic applications accepted. *Expenses:* Contact institution.

Université de Montréal, Faculty of Environmental Design and Planning, Montréal, QC H3C 3J7, Canada. Offers environmental design and planning (M Sc A, PhD); environmental planning and design projects (DESS); game design (DESS); urban management for developing countries (DESS); urban planning (M Urb). DESS programs offered jointly with HEC Montreal and École Polytechnique de Montréal. *Accreditation:* ACSP. *Degree requirements:* For doctorate, thesis/dissertation, general exam. Electronic applications accepted. *Expenses:* Contact institution. *Faculty research:* Wayfinding, environmental evaluation, housing studies, urban design, urban and regional planning.

Université du Québec à Rimouski, Graduate Programs, Program in Regional Development, Rimouski, QC G5L 3A1, Canada. Offers MA, PhD, Diploma. PhD offered jointly with Université du Québec à Chicoutimi; Diploma with Université du Québec, École nationale d'administration publique. Part-time programs available. *Degree requirements:* For master's, thesis. *Entrance requirements:* For master's, appropriate bachelor's degree, proficiency in French.

Université du Québec en Outaouais, Graduate Programs, Program in Regional Development, Gatineau, QC J8X 3X7, Canada. Offers MA. *Students:* 69 full-time, 8 part-time, 6 international. *Degree requirements:* For master's, thesis (for some programs). *Application deadline:* For fall admission, 6/1 priority date for domestic students, 3/1 for international students; for winter admission, 11/1 priority date for domestic students, 10/1 for international students. Application fee: $30. *Unit head:* Simard Jean-Franois, Director, 819-595-3900 Ext. 2210, Fax: 819-595-2384, E-mail: jean-francois.simard@uqo.ca. *Application contact:* Registrar's Office, 819-773-1850, Fax: 819-773-1835, E-mail: registraire@uqo.ca.

Université Laval, Faculty of Architecture, Planning and Visual Arts, Department of Regional Planning, Programs in Planning and Regional Development, Québec, QC G1K 7P4, Canada. Offers MATDR, PhD. Terminal master's awarded for partial completion of doctoral program. *Degree requirements:* For master's, thesis (for some programs); for doctorate, comprehensive exam, thesis/dissertation. *Entrance requirements:* For master's and doctorate, knowledge of French and English. Electronic applications accepted.

University at Albany, State University of New York, College of Arts and Sciences, Department of Geography and Planning, Program in Regional Planning, Albany, NY 12222-0001. Offers MRP. *Accreditation:* ACSP. Part-time programs available. *Degree requirements:* For master's, thesis optional. *Entrance requirements:* Additional exam requirements/recommendations for international students: Required—TOEFL (minimum score 550 paper-based; 213 computer-based). Electronic applications accepted. *Faculty research:* Urban planning, Third World development, political and social aspects of planning, urban housing and employment, environmental planning.

University at Buffalo, the State University of New York, Graduate School, School of Architecture and Planning, Department of Urban and Regional Planning, Buffalo, NY 14260. Offers MUP, JD/MUP, M Arch/MUP. *Accreditation:* ACSP. Part-time programs available. *Faculty:* 14 full-time (3 women), 8 part-time/adjunct (2 women). *Students:* 81 full-time (35 women), 13 part-time (7 women); includes 9 Black or African American, non-Hispanic/Latino; 1 American Indian or Alaska Native, non-Hispanic/Latino; 3 Asian, non-Hispanic/Latino; 6 Hispanic/Latino, 20 international. Average age 28. 214 applicants, 39% accepted, 40 enrolled. In 2010, 39 master's awarded. *Degree requirements:* For master's, thesis or alternative, project. *Entrance requirements:* For master's, minimum GPA of 3.0, resume, 3 letters of recommendation. Additional exam requirements/recommendations for international students: Required—TOEFL (minimum score 213 computer-based; 79 iBT), IELTS (minimum score 6.5). *Application deadline:* For fall admission, 3/1 priority date for domestic and international students; for spring admission, 10/31 priority date for domestic students, 10/1 priority date for international students. Applications are processed on a rolling basis. Application fee: $75. Electronic applications accepted. *Financial support:* In 2010–11, 5 fellowships with full tuition reimbursements (averaging $9,600 per year), 15 research assistantships with full and partial tuition reimbursements (averaging $5,044 per year), 14 teaching assistantships with partial tuition reimbursements (averaging $4,800 per year) were awarded; career-related internships or fieldwork, Federal Work-Study, institutionally sponsored loans, scholarships/grants, health care benefits, tuition waivers (partial), and unspecified assistantships also available. Support available to part-time students. Financial award application deadline: 3/1; financial award applicants required to submit FAFSA. *Faculty research:* Community development and urban management, economic and international development, environmental and land use planning, GIS and spatial modeling, urban design and physical planning. Total annual research expenditures: $204,853. *Unit head:* Dr. Ernest Sternberg, Professor and Chair, 716-829-2133 Ext. 109, Fax: 716-829-3256, E-mail: ezs@buffalo.edu. *Application contact:* Donna M. Rogalski, Assistant to the Chair, 716-829-2133 Ext. 109, Fax: 716-829-3256, E-mail: dmr1@buffalo.edu.

The University of Akron, Graduate School, Buchtel College of Arts and Sciences, Department of Geography and Planning, Program in Urban Planning, Akron, OH 44325. Offers MA. *Students:* 13 full-time (5 women), 5 part-time (1 woman); includes 1 Black or African American, non-Hispanic/Latino; 1 Asian, non-Hispanic/Latino, 4 international. Average age 30. 16 applicants, 94% accepted, 6 enrolled. In 2010, 7 master's awarded. *Degree requirements:* For master's, thesis optional. *Entrance requirements:* For master's, two letters of recommendation, statement of purpose. Additional exam requirements/recommendations for international students: Required—TOEFL (minimum score 550 paper-based; 213 computer-based; 79 iBT). *Application deadline:* Applications are processed on a rolling basis. Application fee: $30 ($40 for international students). Electronic applications accepted. *Expenses:* Tuition, state resident: full-time $6800; part-time $378 per credit hour. Tuition, nonresident: full-time $11,644; part-time $647 per credit hour. Required fees: $1265. One-time fee: $30 full-time. *Unit head:* Dr. Linda Barrett, Graduate Director, 330-972-6120. *Application contact:* Dr. Linda Barrett, Graduate Director, 330-972-6120.

The University of Arizona, College of Architecture and Landscape Architecture, Planning Program, Tucson, AZ 85721. Offers MS. *Accreditation:* ACSP. *Faculty:* 2 full-time (1 woman), 1 part-time/adjunct (0 women). *Students:* 21 full-time (8 women), 5 part-time (1 woman); includes 1 Black or African American, non-Hispanic/Latino; 1 Asian, non-Hispanic/Latino; 5 Hispanic/Latino; 1 Two or more races, non-Hispanic/Latino, 3 international. Average age 34. 26 applicants, 77% accepted, 9 enrolled. In 2010, 13 master's awarded. *Entrance requirements:* For master's, GRE, 3 letters of recommendation, letter of intent. Additional exam requirements/recommendations for international students: Required—TOEFL (minimum score 573 paper-based; 233 computer-based; 80 iBT). *Application deadline:* For fall admission, 2/1 for domestic students, 12/1 for international students; for spring admission, 10/1 for domestic students, 6/1 for international students. Application fee: $75. Electronic applications accepted. *Expenses:* Tuition, state resident: full-time $7692. *Financial support:* In 2010–11, 3 research assistantships (averaging $13,290 per year) were awarded; health care benefits and unspecified assistantships also available. Total annual research expenditures: $3,040. *Unit head:* Dr. John Paul Jones, Department Head, 520-621-1652, Fax: 520-621-2889, E-mail: jpjones@email.arizona.edu. *Application contact:* Debi Romero, 520-621-1004, Fax: 520-626-6448, E-mail: dab@ul.arizona.edu.

The University of British Columbia, School of Community and Regional Planning, Vancouver, BC V6T 1Z1, Canada. Offers M Sc P, MAP, PhD. *Accreditation:* ACSP (one or more programs are accredited). *Degree requirements:* For master's, thesis; for doctorate, thesis/dissertation, oral exam. *Entrance requirements:* For master's, GRE (recommended); for doctorate, MCRP or equivalent. Additional exam requirements/recommendations for international students: Required—TOEFL (minimum score 600 paper-based; 250 computer-based). Electronic applications accepted. Tuition charges are reported in Canadian dollars. *Expenses:* Tuition, area resident: Full-time $4179 Canadian dollars. International tuition: $7344 Canadian dollars full-time. *Faculty research:* Natural resources management, international development, urban spatial, urban policy and community development planning.

University of California, Berkeley, Graduate Division, College of Environmental Design, Department of City and Regional Planning, Berkeley, CA 94720-1500. Offers MCP, PhD, JD/MCP, M Arch/MCP, MCP/MPH, MCP/MS, MLA/MCP. JD/MCP offered jointly with University of California, Hastings College of the Law and School of Law. *Accreditation:* ACSP. *Degree requirements:* For master's, professional project or thesis; for doctorate, thesis/dissertation, qualifying exam. *Entrance requirements:* For master's and doctorate, GRE General Test, minimum GPA of 3.0, 3 letters of recommendation. Additional exam requirements/recommendations for international students: Required—TOEFL. *Faculty research:* Housing and project development, physical planning and design, community and economic development, geographic information systems, transportation.

Urban and Regional Planning

University of California, Davis, Graduate Studies, Graduate Group in Community Development, Davis, CA 95616. Offers MS. *Degree requirements:* For master's, comprehensive exam (for some programs), thesis (for some programs). *Entrance requirements:* For master's, GRE General Test, minimum GPA of 3.0. Additional exam requirements/recommendations for international students: Required—TOEFL (minimum score 550 paper-based; 213 computer-based). Electronic applications accepted. *Faculty research:* Globalization; community economic change; urban and regional development; community planning design and sustainability; race, ethnic, and gender roles; community organization and political mobilization.

University of California, Irvine, School of Social Ecology, Department of Planning, Policy and Design, Irvine, CA 92697. Offers planning, policy and design (PhD); urban and regional planning (MURP). *Accreditation:* ACSP (one or more programs are accredited). *Students:* 121 full-time (69 women); includes 36 minority (2 Black or African American, non-Hispanic/Latino; 1 American Indian or Alaska Native, non-Hispanic/Latino; 19 Asian, non-Hispanic/Latino; 14 Hispanic/Latino), 31 international. Average age 28. 252 applicants, 55% accepted, 50 enrolled. In 2010, 29 master's, 9 doctorates awarded. *Degree requirements:* For doctorate, thesis/dissertation, research project. *Entrance requirements:* For master's and doctorate, GRE General Test, minimum GPA of 3.0. Additional exam requirements/recommendations for international students: Required—TOEFL (minimum score 550 paper-based; 213 computer-based). *Application deadline:* For fall admission, 1/15 priority date for domestic and international students. Application fee: $80 ($100 for international students). Electronic applications accepted. *Financial support:* Fellowships with tuition reimbursements, research assistantships with full tuition reimbursements, teaching assistantships with tuition reimbursements, institutionally sponsored loans, traineeships, health care benefits, and unspecified assistantships available. Financial award application deadline: 1/15; financial award applicants required to submit FAFSA. *Faculty research:* Community and social policy, economic development, land-use and growth management, transportation planning, environmental policy. *Unit head:* David L. Feldman, Chair, 949-824-4384, Fax: 949-824-3056, E-mail: feldmand@uci.edu. *Application contact:* Janet Gallagher, Academic Coordinator, 949-824-9849, Fax: 949-824-8566, E-mail: ppd@uci.edu.

University of California, Los Angeles, Graduate Division, School of Public Affairs, Department of Urban Planning, Los Angeles, CA 90095-1656. Offers MA, PhD, JD/MA, MA/MA, MBA/MA. *Accreditation:* ACSP (one or more programs are accredited). *Degree requirements:* For master's, comprehensive exam or thesis; for doctorate, thesis/dissertation, oral and written qualifying exams. *Entrance requirements:* For master's, GRE General Test (recommended); for doctorate, GRE General Test, master's degree in urban planning or related field. Additional exam requirements/recommendations for international students: Required—TOEFL. Electronic applications accepted. *Faculty research:* Industrial hazards, political economy of South and Southeast Asia, historic preservation, flexible production in U.S. and Western Europe, land-use controls.

University of Central Arkansas, Graduate School, College of Liberal Arts, Department of Geography, Conway, AR 72035-0001. Offers community and economic development (MS); geographic information systems (MGIS, Certificate). Part-time programs available. Post-baccalaureate distance learning degree programs offered (minimal on-campus study). *Faculty:* 3 full-time (0 women). *Students:* 4 full-time (1 woman), 11 part-time (1 woman); includes 1 minority (Black or African American, non-Hispanic/Latino). Average age 30. 6 applicants, 100% accepted, 5 enrolled. *Entrance requirements:* Additional exam requirements/recommendations for international students: Required—TOEFL (minimum score 550 paper-based; 213 computer-based). *Application deadline:* For fall admission, 3/1 priority date for domestic and international students; for spring admission, 10/1 priority date for domestic and international students. Applications are processed on a rolling basis. Application fee: $25 ($50 for international students). *Financial support:* Applicants required to submit FAFSA. *Unit head:* Dr. Brooks Green, Chairperson, 501-450-5636, Fax: 501-450-5185, E-mail: brooksg@uca.edu. *Application contact:* Susan Wood, Admissions Assistant, 501-450-3124, Fax: 501-450-5678, E-mail: swood@uca.edu.

University of Central Florida, College of Health and Public Affairs, Department of Public Administration, Orlando, FL 32816. Offers emergency management and homeland security (Certificate); non-profit management (MNM, Certificate); public administration (MPA, Certificate); research administration (MS); urban and regional planning (Certificate). *Accreditation:* NASPAA. Part-time and evening/weekend programs available. *Faculty:* 14 full-time (5 women), 9 part-time/adjunct (3 women). *Students:* 103 full-time (70 women), 271 part-time (208 women); includes 125 minority (85 Black or African American, non-Hispanic/Latino; 1 American Indian or Alaska Native, non-Hispanic/Latino; 13 Asian, non-Hispanic/Latino; 22 Hispanic/Latino; 2 Native Hawaiian or other Pacific Islander, non-Hispanic/Latino; 2 Two or more races, non-Hispanic/Latino), 8 international. Average age 31. 258 applicants, 69% accepted, 138 enrolled. In 2010, 101 master's, 25 other advanced degrees awarded. *Degree requirements:* For master's, comprehensive exam, thesis or alternative, research report. *Entrance requirements:* For master's, GRE General Test. *Application deadline:* For fall admission, 7/1 for domestic students; for spring admission, 12/1 for domestic students. Application fee: $30. Electronic applications accepted. *Expenses:* Tuition, state resident: part-time $256.56 per credit hour. Tuition, nonresident: part-time $1011.52 per credit hour. Part-time tuition and fees vary according to program. *Financial support:* In 2010–11, 13 students received support, including 1 fellowship with partial tuition reimbursement available (averaging $10,000 per year), 11 research assistantships with partial tuition reimbursements available (averaging $5,900 per year), 2 teaching assistantships with partial tuition reimbursements available (averaging $7,100 per year); career-related internships or fieldwork, Federal Work-Study, institutionally sponsored loans, tuition waivers (partial), and unspecified assistantships also available. Financial award application deadline: 3/1; financial award applicants required to submit FAFSA. *Unit head:* Dr. Mary Ann Feldheim, Chair, 407-823-3693, Fax: 407-823-5651, E-mail: mfeldhei@mail.ucf.edu. *Application contact:* Dr. Mary Ann Feldheim, Chair, 407-823-3693, Fax: 407-823-5651, E-mail: mfeldhei@mail.ucf.edu.

University of Cincinnati, Graduate School, College of Design, Architecture, Art, and Planning, School of Planning, Program in Community Planning, Cincinnati, OH 45221. Offers MCP, JD/MCP. *Accreditation:* ACSP. *Degree requirements:* For master's, thesis. *Entrance requirements:* For master's, GRE General Test. Additional exam requirements/recommendations for international students: Required—TOEFL.

University of Colorado Denver, College of Architecture and Planning, Program in Design and Planning, Denver, CO 80217-3364. Offers history of architecture, landscape and urbanism (PhD); sustainable and healthy environments (PhD). Part-time programs available. *Students:* 25 full-time (15 women), 11 part-time (7 women); includes 2 Black or African American, non-Hispanic/Latino; 1 Asian, non-Hispanic/Latino; 2 Hispanic/Latino, 7 international. Average age 40. 60 applicants, 15% accepted, 6 enrolled. In 2010, 2 doctorates awarded. *Degree requirements:* For doctorate, comprehensive exam, thesis/dissertation. *Entrance requirements:* For doctorate, GRE, minimum undergraduate GPA of 3.0, graduate 3.5; writing sample. Additional exam requirements/recommendations for international students: Required—TOEFL (minimum score 575 paper-based). *Application deadline:* For fall admission, 2/1 for domestic students; for spring admission, 10/1 for domestic students. Application fee: $50 ($75 for international students). Electronic applications accepted. *Expenses:* Contact institution. *Financial support:* Fellowships, research assistantships, teaching assistantships, career-related internships or fieldwork, Federal Work-Study, scholarships/grants, tuition waivers, and unspecified assistantships available. Support available to part-time students. Financial award application deadline: 4/1; financial award applicants required to submit FAFSA. *Faculty research:* Land use and environmental planning and design; design and planning processes and practices; history, theory, and criticism of the built environment. *Unit head:* Dr. Kevin Krizek, Director, 303-556-3282, Fax: 303-556-3687, E-mail: kevin.krizek@colorado.edu. *Application contact:* Michael Harper, Administrative Coordinator, 303-556-6042, Fax: 303-556-3687, E-mail: michael.t.harper@ucdenver.edu.

University of Colorado Denver, College of Architecture and Planning, Program in Urban and Regional Planning, Denver, CO 80217-3364. Offers economic and community development planning (MURP); land use and environmental planning (MURP); urban place making (MURP). *Accreditation:* ACSP. Part-time programs available. *Students:* 125 full-time (57 women), 5 part-time (3 women); includes 1 Black or African American, non-Hispanic/Latino; 2 American Indian or Alaska Native, non-Hispanic/Latino; 3 Asian, non-Hispanic/Latino; 8 Hispanic/Latino, 9 international. Average age 30. 145 applicants, 68% accepted, 38 enrolled. In 2010, 47 master's awarded. *Degree requirements:* For master's, thesis optional, minimum of 51 semester hours. *Entrance requirements:* For master's, GRE if GPA below 3.0, writing sample. Additional exam requirements/recommendations for international students: Required—TOEFL (minimum score 550 paper-based; 213 computer-based). *Application deadline:* For fall admission, 2/15 for domestic students; for spring admission, 10/1 for domestic students. Application fee: $50 ($75 for international students). Electronic applications accepted. *Expenses:* Contact institution. *Financial support:* Career-related internships or fieldwork, Federal Work-Study, and scholarships/grants available. Financial award application deadline: 4/1; financial award applicants required to submit FAFSA. *Faculty research:* Physical planning, environmental planning, economic development planning. *Unit head:* Brian Muller, Associate Professor and Chair, 303-556-5967, E-mail: brian.muller@ucdenver.edu. *Application contact:* Brian Muller, Associate Professor and Chair, 303-556-5967, E-mail: brian.muller@ucdenver.edu.

University of Florida, Graduate School, College of Design, Construction and Planning, Department of Urban and Regional Planning, Gainesville, FL 32611. Offers MAURP, JD/MAURP. *Accreditation:* ACSP (one or more programs are accredited). *Faculty:* 8 full-time (4 women), 1 (woman) part-time/adjunct. *Students:* 65 full-time (34 women), 16 part-time (9 women); includes 5 Black or African American, non-Hispanic/Latino; 1 American Indian or Alaska Native, non-Hispanic/Latino; 7 Asian, non-Hispanic/Latino; 8 Hispanic/Latino, 13 international. Average age 28. 96 applicants, 74% accepted, 19 enrolled. In 2010, 22 master's awarded. *Entrance requirements:* For master's, GRE General Test, minimum GPA of 3.0. Additional exam requirements/recommendations for international students: Required—TOEFL (minimum score 550 paper-based; 213 computer-based; 80 iBT), IELTS (minimum score 6). *Application deadline:* For fall admission, 6/1 priority date for domestic students; for spring admission, 10/1 priority date for domestic students. Applications are processed on a rolling basis. Application fee: $30. Electronic applications accepted. *Expenses:* Tuition, state resident: full-time $10,915.92. Tuition, nonresident: full-time $28,309. *Financial support:* In 2010–11, 19 students received support, including 2 fellowships with tuition reimbursements available, 17 research assistantships with tuition reimbursements available (averaging $8,652 per year); career-related internships or fieldwork, Federal Work-Study, and unspecified assistantships also available. Support available to part-time students. Financial award applicants required to submit FAFSA. *Faculty research:* Planning and information systems, urban and environmental design, community and economic development, transportation and growth management. *Unit head:* Dr. Kristin E. Larsen, Chair, 352-392-0997 Ext. 433, Fax: 352-392-3308, E-mail: klarsen@ufl.edu. *Application contact:* Dr. Richard H. Schneider, Graduate Coordinator, 352-392-0997 Ext. 430, Fax: 352-392-3308, E-mail: rschnei@ufl.edu.

University of Hawaii at Manoa, Graduate Division, College of Social Sciences, Department of Urban and Regional Planning, Honolulu, HI 96822. Offers community planning and social policy (MURP); disaster preparedness and emergency management (Graduate Certificate); environmental planning and management (MURP); land use and infrastructure planning (MURP); urban and regional planning (PhD, Graduate Certificate); urban and regional planning in Asia and Pacific (MURP). *Accreditation:* ACSP. Part-time programs available. *Faculty:* 28 full-time (9 women), 11 part-time/adjunct (2 women). *Students:* 63 full-time (35 women), 25 part-time (12 women); includes 24 minority (1 Black or African American, non-Hispanic/Latino; 6 Asian, non-Hispanic/Latino; 1 Hispanic/Latino; 9 Native Hawaiian or other Pacific Islander, non-Hispanic/Latino; 7 Two or more races, non-Hispanic/Latino), 30 international. Average age 33. 89 applicants, 63% accepted, 32 enrolled. In 2010, 30 master's, 3 doctorates, 1 other advanced degree awarded. *Entrance requirements:* For master's, GRE General Test, minimum GPA of 3.0; for doctorate, GRE General Test. Additional exam requirements/recommendations for international students: Required—TOEFL (minimum score 500 paper-based; 173 computer-based; 61 iBT), IELTS (minimum score 5). *Application deadline:* For fall admission, 3/1 for domestic and international students; for spring admission, 9/1 for domestic and international students. Application fee: $60. *Financial support:* In 2010–11, 11 fellowships (averaging $2,314 per year), 28 research assistantships (averaging $16,718 per year), 2 teaching assistantships (averaging $14,382 per year) were awarded; career-related internships or fieldwork, Federal Work-Study, institutionally sponsored loans, and tuition waivers (full) also available. Total annual research expenditures: $423,000. *Application contact:* Dolores Foley, Graduate Chair, 808-956-7381, Fax: 808-956-6870, E-mail: dolores@hawaii.edu.

University of Idaho, College of Graduate Studies, College of Art and Architecture, Moscow, ID 83844-2282. Offers architecture (MS), including community planning, compution and visualization studies, environment and behavior studies, urban design; architecture (professional degree) (M Arch); landscape architecture (MS); studio art (MFA), including graphic design, interactive and information design, interface, painting, printmaking, sculpture; teaching art (MAT). *Accreditation:* NASAD. *Faculty:* 19 full-time, 1 part-time/adjunct. *Students:* 102 full-time, 15 part-time. Average age 27. In 2010, 31 master's awarded. *Application deadline:* For fall admission, 8/1 for domestic students; for spring admission, 12/15 for domestic students. Applications are processed on a rolling basis. Application fee: $60. Electronic applications accepted. *Expenses:* Tuition, nonresident: part-time $580 per credit. Required fees: $306 per credit. *Financial support:* Applicants required to submit FAFSA. *Faculty research:* Sustainability in communities, urban research, virtual technology, bioregional planning, environment and behavior interaction. *Unit head:* Dr. Mark Elison Hoversten, Dean, 208-885-5423, E-mail: caa@uidaho.edu. *Application contact:* Dr. Mark Elison Hoversten, Dean, 208-885-5423, E-mail: caa@uidaho.edu.

University of Idaho, College of Graduate Studies, Department of Bioregional Planning and Community Design, Moscow, ID 83844-2282. Offers MS. *Faculty:* 5 full-time, 1 part-time/adjunct. *Students:* 23 full-time, 2 part-time. Average age 30. In 2010, 3 master's awarded. *Application deadline:* Applications are processed on a rolling basis. Application fee: $60. Electronic applications accepted. *Expenses:* Tuition, nonresident: part-time $580 per credit. Required fees: $306 per credit. *Financial support:* Applicants required to submit FAFSA. *Faculty research:* Environment and behavior interaction, geographic trade, design development, economic development, natural resource policy. *Unit head:* Mark Hoversten, Dean, 208-885-7448, E-mail: bioregionalplanning@uidaho.edu. *Application contact:* Mark Hoversten, Dean, 208-885-7448, E-mail: bioregionalplanning@uidaho.edu.

University of Illinois at Chicago, Graduate College, College of Urban Planning and Public Affairs, Program in Urban Planning and Policy, Chicago, IL 60607-7128. Offers MUPP, PhD. *Accreditation:* ACSP (one or more programs are accredited). Part-time programs available. *Degree requirements:* For master's, thesis or alternative, internship; for doctorate, thesis/dissertation. *Entrance requirements:* For master's and doctorate, GRE General Test, minimum GPA of 2.75, writing sample. Additional exam requirements/recommendations for international students: Required—TOEFL. Electronic applications accepted.

University of Illinois at Urbana–Champaign, Graduate College, College of Fine and Applied Arts, Department of Urban and Regional Planning, Champaign, IL 61820. Offers regional planning (PhD); urban planning (MUP); JD/MUP; M Arch/MUP. *Accreditation:* ACSP (one or more programs are accredited). *Faculty:* 11 full-time (3 women). *Students:* 61 full-time (31 women), 8 part-time (5 women); includes 17 minority (5 Black or African American, non-Hispanic/Latino; 5 Asian, non-Hispanic/Latino; 4 Hispanic/Latino; 3 Two or more races, non-Hispanic/Latino), 20 international. 193 applicants, 21% accepted, 20 enrolled. In 2010, 19 master's, 7 doctorates awarded. *Entrance requirements:* For master's and doctorate, GRE, minimum GPA of 3.0. Additional exam requirements/recommendations for international students: Required—TOEFL (minimum score 610 paper-based; 253 computer-based; 102 iBT). *Application deadline:* Applications are processed on a rolling basis. Application fee: $75 ($90 for international students). Electronic applications accepted. *Financial support:* In 2010–11, 10 fellowships, 28 research assistantships, 17 teaching assistantships were awarded; tuition waivers (full and partial) also available. *Faculty research:* Environmental impact, economic development, firmation technology, planning systems, housing, community participation. *Unit head:* Edward Feser, Head, 217-244-6767, Fax: 217-244-1717, E-mail: feser@illinois.edu. *Application contact:* Jane Terry, Admissions and Records Officer II, 217-244-5401, Fax: 217-244-1717, E-mail: jterry2@illinois.edu.

The University of Iowa, Graduate College, Program in Urban and Regional Planning, Iowa City, IA 52242-1316. Offers MA, MS, JD/MA, MHA/MA, MHA/MS, MS/MA, MS/MS, MSW/MA, MSW/MS. *Accreditation:* ACSP. *Degree requirements:* For master's, thesis optional, portfolio. *Entrance requirements:* For master's, GRE General Test, minimum GPA of 3.0. Additional exam requirements/recommendations for international students: Required—TOEFL (minimum score 600 paper-based; 250 computer-based; 100 iBT). Electronic applications accepted.

The University of Kansas, Graduate Studies, School of Architecture, Design, and Planning, Program in Urban Planning, Lawrence, KS 66045. Offers MUP, JD/MUP, M Arch/MUP, MUP/MA, MUP/MPA. *Accreditation:* ACSP. Part-time programs available. *Faculty:* 5 full-time (2 women), 6 part-time/adjunct (0 women). *Students:* 38 full-time (17 women), 2 part-time (1 woman); includes 5 minority (2 Black or African American, non-Hispanic/Latino; 3 Hispanic/Latino), 6 international. Average age 27. 48 applicants, 83% accepted, 18 enrolled. In 2010, 14 master's awarded. *Degree requirements:* For master's, comprehensive exam, thesis or alternative. *Entrance requirements:* For master's, GRE. Additional exam requirements/recommendations for international students: Required—TOEFL (minimum score 570 paper-based; 230 computer-based). *Application deadline:* For fall admission, 7/1 for domestic students, 6/1 for international students; for spring admission, 12/1 for domestic students, 11/1 for international students. Applications are processed on a rolling basis. Application fee: $55 ($65 for international students). Electronic applications accepted. *Expenses:* Tuition, state resident: full-time $7092; part-time $295.50 per credit hour. Tuition, nonresident: full-time $16,590; part-time $691.25 per credit hour. Required fees: $858; $71.49 per credit hour. Tuition and fees vary according to course load, campus/location and program. *Financial support:* In 2010–11, 5 fellowships (averaging $2,910 per year) were awarded; research assistantships with partial tuition reimbursements, career-related internships or fieldwork also available. Financial award application deadline: 2/1. *Faculty research:* Environmental land use, housing and economic development, community development and transportation, urban mass transportation, urban sprawl. *Unit head:* James M. Mayo, Chair, 785-864-4184, Fax: 785-864-5301, E-mail: jimmayo@ku.edu. *Application contact:* Pat Owens, Administrative Specialist, 785-864-4184, Fax: 785-864-5301, E-mail: ubpl@ku.edu.

University of Louisville, Graduate School, College of Arts and Sciences, Department of Urban and Public Affairs, Louisville, KY 40208. Offers public administration (MPA), including human resources management, non-profit management, public policy and administration; urban and public affairs (PhD), including urban planning and development, urban policy and administration; urban planning (MUP), including administration of planning organizations, housing and community development, land use and environmental planning, spatial analysis. Part-time and evening/weekend programs available. *Faculty:* 22 full-time (7 women), 8 part-time/adjunct (1 woman). *Students:* 73 full-time (36 women), 31 part-time (18 women); includes 11 Black or African American, non-Hispanic/Latino; 2 Asian, non-Hispanic/Latino; 2 Hispanic/Latino; 1 Native Hawaiian or other Pacific Islander, non-Hispanic/Latino; 2 Two or more races, non-Hispanic/Latino, 11 international. Average age 31. 96 applicants, 67% accepted, 37 enrolled. In 2010, 28 master's, 5 doctorates awarded. Terminal master's awarded for partial completion of doctoral program. *Degree requirements:* For master's, internship; for doctorate, comprehensive exam, thesis/dissertation. *Entrance requirements:* For master's, GRE General Test, minimum GPA of 3.0; for doctorate, GRE General Test, master's degree in appropriate field. Additional exam requirements/recommendations for international students: Required—TOEFL (minimum score 550 paper-based; 213 computer-based; 79 iBT). *Application deadline:* For fall admission, 7/15 for domestic students; for spring admission, 11/15 for domestic students. Applications are processed on a rolling basis. Application fee: $50. Electronic applications accepted. *Expenses:* Tuition, state resident: full-time $9144; part-time $508 per credit hour. Tuition, nonresident: full-time $19,026; part-time $1057 per credit hour. Tuition and fees vary according to program and reciprocity agreements. *Financial support:* In 2010–11, 23 students received support; fellowships, research assistantships, health care benefits available. Financial award application deadline: 3/1. *Faculty research:* Housing and community development, performance-based budgeting, environmental policy and natural hazards, sustainability, real estate development, comparative urban development. *Unit head:* Dr. David Simpson, Chair, 502-852-8019, Fax: 502-852-4558, E-mail: dave.simpson@louisville.edu. *Application contact:* Patty Sarley, Graduate Student Advisor, 502-852-7914, Fax: 502-852-4558, E-mail: plclea01@louisville.edu.

University of Manitoba, Faculty of Graduate Studies, Faculty of Architecture, Department of City Planning, Winnipeg, MB R3T 2N2, Canada. Offers MCP. *Accreditation:* ACSP. *Degree requirements:* For master's, thesis.

University of Maryland, College Park, Academic Affairs, School of Architecture, Planning and Preservation, Program in Urban Studies and Planning, College Park, MD 20742. Offers urban and regional planning/design (PhD); urban studies and planning (MCP). *Accreditation:* ACSP. Part-time and evening/weekend programs available. *Faculty:* 8 full-time (1 woman), 3 part-time/adjunct (0 women). *Students:* 56 full-time (29 women), 25 part-time (10 women); includes 11 minority (7 Black or African American, non-Hispanic/Latino; 2 Asian, non-Hispanic/Latino; 1 Hispanic/Latino; 1 Two or more races, non-Hispanic/Latino), 8 international. 229 applicants, 38% accepted, 26 enrolled. In 2010, 15 master's awarded. *Entrance requirements:* For master's and doctorate, GRE General Test, minimum GPA of 3.0, 3 letters of recommendation. Additional exam requirements/recommendations for international students: Required—TOEFL. *Application deadline:* For fall admission, 12/15 for domestic and international students. Applications are processed on a rolling basis. Application fee: $75. Electronic applications accepted. *Expenses:* Tuition, state resident: part-time $471 per credit hour. Tuition, nonresident: part-time $1016 per credit hour. Required fees: $337 per term. *Financial support:* In 2010–11, 6 fellowships with full and partial tuition reimbursements (averaging $11,234 per year), 33 teaching assistantships (averaging $15,815 per year) were awarded; research assistantships, Federal Work-Study and scholarships/grants also available. Support available to part-time students. Financial award applicants required to submit FAFSA. *Faculty research:* Policy analysis, urban planning, program planning and management, economic development planning. Total annual research expenditures: $3,570. *Unit head:* James R. Cohen, Director, 301-405-6795, Fax: 301-314-9583, E-mail: jimcohen@umd.edu. *Application contact:* Dean of Graduate School, 301-405-0358.

University of Massachusetts Amherst, Graduate School, College of Social and Behavioral Sciences, Department of Landscape Architecture and Regional Planning, Program in Landscape Architecture and Regional Planning, Amherst, MA 01003. Offers MLA/MRP. *Accreditation:* ACSP; ASLA. Part-time programs available. *Students:* 9 full-time (6 women), 1 international. Average age 32. 12 applicants, 83% accepted, 4 enrolled. *Entrance requirements:* Additional exam requirements/recommendations for international students: Required—TOEFL (minimum score 550 paper-based; 213 computer-based; 80 iBT), IELTS (minimum score 6.5). *Application deadline:* For fall admission, 2/1 for domestic and international students. Applications are processed on a rolling basis. Application fee: $50 ($65 for international students). Electronic applications accepted. *Expenses:* Tuition, state resident: full-time $2640. Required fees: $8282. One-time fee: $357 full-time. *Financial support:* Fellowships, research assistantships, teaching assistantships, career-related internships or fieldwork, Federal Work-Study, scholarships/grants, traineeships, health care benefits, tuition waivers (full), and unspecified assistantships available. Support available to part-time students. Financial award application deadline: 2/1; financial award applicants required to submit FAFSA. *Unit head:* Dr. Robert L. Ryan, Graduate Program Director, 413-545-2266, Fax: 413-545-1772. *Application contact:* Jean M. Ames, Supervisor of Admissions, 413-545-0721, Fax: 413-577-0010, E-mail: gradadm@grad.umass.edu.

University of Massachusetts Amherst, Graduate School, College of Social and Behavioral Sciences, Department of Landscape Architecture and Regional Planning, Program in Regional Planning, Amherst, MA 01003. Offers MRP, PhD, MLA/MRP. *Accreditation:* ACSP (one or more programs are accredited). Part-time programs available. *Students:* 37 full-time (18 women), 12 part-time (8 women); includes 6 minority (2 Asian, non-Hispanic/Latino; 1 Hispanic/Latino; 3 Two or more races, non-Hispanic/Latino), 10 international. Average age 30. 89 applicants, 60% accepted, 18 enrolled. In 2010, 8 master's, 4 doctorates awarded. Terminal master's awarded for partial completion of doctoral program. *Degree requirements:* For master's, thesis or alternative; for doctorate, comprehensive exam, thesis/dissertation. *Entrance requirements:* For master's and doctorate, GRE General Test. Additional exam requirements/recommendations for international students: Required—TOEFL (minimum score 550 paper-based; 213 computer-based; 80 iBT), IELTS (minimum score 6.5). *Application deadline:* For fall admission, 2/1 for domestic and international students. Applications are processed on a rolling basis. Application fee: $50 ($65 for international students). Electronic applications accepted. *Expenses:* Tuition, state resident: full-time $2640. Required fees: $8282. One-time fee: $357 full-time. *Financial support:* Fellowships, research assistantships, teaching assistantships, career-related internships or fieldwork, Federal Work-Study, scholarships/grants, traineeships, health care benefits, tuition waivers (full), and unspecified assistantships available. Support available to part-time students. Financial award application deadline: 2/1; financial award applicants required to submit FAFSA. *Unit head:* Dr. Mark T. Hamin, Graduate Program Director, 413-545-2266, Fax: 413-545-1772. *Application contact:* Jean M. Ames, Supervisor of Admissions, 413-545-0722, Fax: 413-577-0010, E-mail: gradadm@grad.umass.edu.

University of Memphis, Graduate School, College of Arts and Sciences, Division of City and Regional Planning, Memphis, TN 38152. Offers MCRP. *Accreditation:* ACSP. *Faculty:* 4 full-time (2 women), 1 part-time/adjunct (0 women). *Students:* 14 full-time (5 women), 13 part-time (5 women); includes 6 Black or African American, non-Hispanic/Latino. Average age 30. 20 applicants, 95% accepted, 9 enrolled. In 2010, 6 master's awarded. *Degree requirements:* For master's, comprehensive exam, thesis. *Entrance requirements:* For master's, GRE General Test. *Application deadline:* For fall admission, 7/1 for domestic students; for spring admission, 12/1 for domestic students. Applications are processed on a rolling basis. Application fee: $35 ($60 for international students). *Financial support:* In 2010–11, 14 students received support; research assistantships with full tuition reimbursements available, career-related internships or fieldwork, Federal Work-Study, scholarships/grants, and unspecified assistantships available. Financial award application deadline: 2/15; financial award applicants required to submit FAFSA. *Faculty research:* Growth planning, site design, economic development, housing, smart growth. *Unit head:* Kenneth Reardon, Director and Coordinator of Graduate Studies in Planning, 901-678-2161, Fax: 901-678-4162, E-mail: kreardon@memphis.edu. *Application contact:* Kenneth Reardon, Director and Coordinator of Graduate Studies in Planning, 901-678-2161, Fax: 901-678-4162, E-mail: kreardon@memphis.edu.

University of Memphis, Graduate School, College of Arts and Sciences, Division of Public and Nonprofit Administration, Memphis, TN 38152. Offers nonprofit administration (MPA); public management and policy (MPA); urban management and planning (MPA). *Accreditation:* NASPAA. Part-time and evening/weekend programs available. Postbaccalaureate distance learning degree programs offered (minimal on-campus study). *Faculty:* 5 full-time (2 women), 1 (woman) part-time/adjunct. *Students:* 18 full-time (15 women), 43 part-time (33 women); includes 35 Black or African American, non-Hispanic/Latino; 1 Hispanic/Latino; 1 Two or more races, non-Hispanic/Latino. Average age 34. 32 applicants, 88% accepted, 9 enrolled. In 2010, 17 master's awarded. *Degree requirements:* For master's, comprehensive exam, thesis or alternative, internship. *Entrance requirements:* For master's, GRE General Test, GMAT, or MAT, minimum GPA of 3.0. Additional exam requirements/recommendations for international students: Required—TOEFL. *Application deadline:* For fall admission, 7/1 for domestic students, 5/15 for international students; for spring admission, 12/1 for domestic students, 9/15 for international students. Applications are processed on a rolling basis. Application fee: $35 ($60 for international students). *Financial support:* In 2010–11, 37 students received support; fellowships, research assistantships with full tuition reimbursements available, career-related internships or fieldwork, Federal Work-Study, scholarships/grants, and unspecified assistantships available. Support available to part-time students. Financial award application deadline: 2/15; financial award applicants required to submit FAFSA. *Faculty research:* Nonprofit organization governance, local government management, community collaboration, urban problems, accountability. *Unit head:* Dr. Charles Menifield, Director, 901-678-5527, Fax: 901-678-2981, E-mail: cmenifld@memphis.edu. *Application contact:* Dr. Charles Menifield, Graduate Admissions Coordinator, 901-678-3360, Fax: 901-678-2981, E-mail: cmenifld@memphis.edu.

University of Michigan, Taubman College of Architecture and Urban Planning, Urban and Regional Planning PhD Program, Ann Arbor, MI 48109. Offers PhD. Offered through the Horace H. Rackham School of Graduate Studies. *Degree requirements:* For doctorate, comprehensive exam, thesis/dissertation, 1 interdisciplinary paper, 2 preliminary exams, oral defense of dissertation. *Entrance requirements:* For doctorate, GRE General Test. Additional exam requirements/recommendations for international students: Required—TOEFL (minimum score 560 paper-based; 220 computer-based; 100 iBT). Electronic applications accepted. *Expenses:* Contact institution. *Faculty research:* Urban and regional planning, community and economic development, transportation planning and geological information systems, environmental planning, the built environment, international development and planning.

University of Michigan, Taubman College of Architecture and Urban Planning, Urban and Regional Planning Program, Ann Arbor, MI 48109. Offers real estate development (Certificate); urban planning (MUP); JD/MUP; M Arch/MUP; MBA/MUP; MLA/MUP; MPP/MUP. Offered through the Horace H. Rackham School of Graduate Studies; students in the Certificate program must either be currently enrolled in a graduate program or have earned a master's or PhD degree within the last five years. *Accreditation:* ACSP (one or more programs are accredited). Part-time programs available. *Degree requirements:* For master's, thesis or alternative, professional project, capstone studio. *Entrance requirements:* For master's, GRE General Test, LSAT or GMAT. Additional exam requirements/recommendations for international students: Required—TOEFL (minimum score 600 paper-based; 250 computer-based; 100 iBT). Electronic applications accepted. *Expenses:* Tuition, state resident: full-time $17,784; part-time $1116 per credit hour. Tuition, nonresident: full-time $35,944; part-time $2125 per credit hour. International tuition: $35,994 full-time. Required fees: $95 per semester. Tuition and fees vary according to course load, degree level and program. *Faculty research:* Housing community and economic development; transportation planning; physical planning and urban design; planning in developing countries; land use and environmental planning.

University of Minnesota, Twin Cities Campus, Graduate School, Hubert H. Humphrey School of Public Affairs, Program in Urban and Regional Planning, Minneapolis, MN 55455-0213. Offers environmental planning (MURP); housing and community development (MURP); land use and urban design (MURP); regional, economic and workforce development (MURP); transportation planning (MURP); JD/MURP; MURP/MLA; MURP/MS. *Accreditation:* ACSP (one or more programs are accredited). Part-time programs available. *Degree requirements:* For master's, thesis or alternative, internship or equivalent work experience. *Entrance requirements:* For master's, GRE General Test, minimum undergraduate GPA of 3.0. Additional exam requirements/recommendations for international students: Required—TOEFL (minimum score 600 paper-based; 250 computer-based; 100 iBT). Electronic applications accepted. *Faculty research:* Policy planning, resource allocation planning, regulatory planning, program planning, project planning.

University of Nebraska–Lincoln, Graduate College, College of Agricultural Sciences and Natural Resources, Department of Agricultural Economics, Lincoln, NE 68588. Offers agribusiness (MBA); agricultural economics (MS, PhD); community development (M Ag). *Degree requirements:* For master's, thesis optional; for doctorate, comprehensive exam, thesis/dissertation. *Entrance requirements:* For master's and doctorate, GRE General Test. Additional exam requirements/recommendations for international students: Required—TOEFL (minimum score 550 paper-based; 213 computer-based). Electronic applications accepted. *Faculty*

Urban and Regional Planning

University of Nebraska–Lincoln (continued)
research: Marketing and agribusiness, production economics, resource law, international trade and development, rural policy and revitalization.

University of Nebraska–Lincoln, Graduate College, College of Architecture, Department of Community and Regional Planning, Lincoln, NE 68588. Offers MCRP, JD/MCRP, M Arch/MCRP, MCRP/MSCE. *Accreditation:* ACSP. *Degree requirements:* For master's, thesis optional. *Entrance requirements:* For master's, GRE General Test. Additional exam requirements/recommendations for international students: Required—TOEFL (minimum score 550 paper-based; 213 computer-based). Electronic applications accepted. *Faculty research:* Economic development, community development and improvement, social planning, land use planning, physical planning, environmental planning.

University of New Haven, Graduate School, School of Business, Program in Public Administration, West Haven, CT 06516-1916. Offers personnel and labor relations (MPA); public administration (MPA, Certificate), including city management (MPA), community-clinical services (MPA), health care management (MPA), long-term health care (MPA), personnel and labor relations (MPA), public administration (Certificate), public management (Certificate), public personnel management (Certificate); MBA/MPA. Part-time and evening/weekend programs available. *Students:* 37 full-time (19 women), 33 part-time (18 women); includes 15 Black or African American, non-Hispanic/Latino; 1 Asian, non-Hispanic/Latino; 4 Hispanic/Latino, 9 international. Average age 33. 51 applicants, 100% accepted, 35 enrolled. In 2010, 14 master's, 4 other advanced degrees awarded. *Degree requirements:* For master's, thesis or alternative. *Entrance requirements:* Additional exam requirements/recommendations for international students: Required—TOEFL (minimum score 520 paper-based; 190 computer-based; 70 iBT); Recommended—IELTS (minimum score 5.5). *Application deadline:* For fall admission, 5/31 for international students; for winter admission, 10/15 for international students; for spring admission, 1/15 for international students. Applications are processed on a rolling basis. Application fee: $50. Electronic applications accepted. *Expenses:* Contact institution. *Financial support:* Research assistantships with partial tuition reimbursements, teaching assistantships with partial tuition reimbursements, career-related internships or fieldwork, Federal Work-Study, scholarships/grants, tuition waivers, and unspecified assistantships available. Support available to part-time students. Financial award application deadline: 5/1; financial award applicants required to submit FAFSA. *Unit head:* Charles Coleman, Chairman, 203-932-7375. *Application contact:* Eloise Gormley, Director of Graduate Admissions, 203-932-7449, Fax: 203-932-7137, E-mail: gradinfo@newhaven.edu.

University of New Mexico, Graduate School, School of Architecture and Planning, Program in Community and Regional Planning, Albuquerque, NM 87131-2039. Offers MCRP, MCRP/MA, MPA/MCRP. *Accreditation:* ACSP. Part-time programs available. *Students:* 52 full-time (27 women), 29 part-time (18 women); includes 1 Black or African American, non-Hispanic/Latino; 13 American Indian or Alaska Native, non-Hispanic/Latino; 1 Asian, non-Hispanic/Latino; 15 Hispanic/Latino; 2 Two or more races, non-Hispanic/Latino, 1 international. Average age 32. 58 applicants, 48% accepted, 16 enrolled. In 2010, 12 master's awarded. *Degree requirements:* For master's, thesis. *Entrance requirements:* For master's, minimum GPA of 3.0 in last two years of graduate study, 3 letters of recommendation, letter of intent, resume, copies of all official transcripts. Additional exam requirements/recommendations for international students: Required—TOEFL (minimum score 550 paper-based; 213 computer-based; 79 iBT). *Application deadline:* For fall admission, 1/30 priority date for domestic students, 1/30 for international students. Application fee: $50. Electronic applications accepted. *Expenses:* Tuition, state resident: full-time $5991; part-time $251 per credit hour. Tuition, nonresident: full-time $14,405; part-time $800.20 per credit hour. Tuition and fees vary according to course level, course load, program and reciprocity agreements. *Financial support:* In 2010–11, 64 students received support, including 8 fellowships (averaging $6,238 per year), 4 research assistantships with partial tuition reimbursements available (averaging $10,419 per year), 2 teaching assistantships with partial tuition reimbursements available (averaging $8,837 per year); career-related internships or fieldwork, Federal Work-Study, institutionally sponsored loans, scholarships/grants, health care benefits, tuition waivers (full), and unspecified assistantships also available. Support available to part-time students. Financial award application deadline: 3/1; financial award applicants required to submit FAFSA. *Faculty research:* Community development, urban and ecological design, land economics, community-based planning, environmental dispute resolution, environmental justice, indigenous planning, watershed management. *Unit head:* Dr. Teresa L. Cordova, Program Director, 505-277-3922, Fax: 505-277-0076, E-mail: tcordova@unm.edu. *Application contact:* Beth Rowe, Senior Academic Advisor, 505-277-1303, Fax: 505-277-0076, E-mail: erowe@unm.edu.

University of New Orleans, Graduate School, College of Liberal Arts, School of Urban Planning and Regional Studies, Program in Urban and Regional Planning, New Orleans, LA 70148. Offers MURP. *Accreditation:* ACSP. *Degree requirements:* For master's, thesis. *Entrance requirements:* For master's, GRE General Test. Additional exam requirements/recommendations for international students: Required—TOEFL (minimum score 550 paper-based; 213 computer-based; 79 iBT). Electronic applications accepted. *Faculty research:* Urban economic development, environmental planning and analysis, social and cultural change.

The University of North Carolina at Chapel Hill, Graduate School, College of Arts and Sciences, Department of City and Regional Planning, Chapel Hill, NC 27599-3140. Offers city and regional planning (MCRP); planning (PhD); public policy analysis (PhD); JD/MCRP; MBA/MCRP; MPA/MCRP. *Accreditation:* ACSP (one or more programs are accredited). *Faculty:* 16 full-time (5 women), 6 part-time/adjunct (1 woman). *Students:* 105 full-time (47 women); includes 15 minority (6 Black or African American, non-Hispanic/Latino; 6 Asian, non-Hispanic/Latino; 3 Hispanic/Latino), 5 international. Average age 27. 293 applicants, 26% accepted, 42 enrolled. In 2010, 55 master's, 1 doctorate awarded. *Degree requirements:* For master's, project; for doctorate, comprehensive exam, thesis/dissertation. *Entrance requirements:* For master's and doctorate, GRE General Test. Additional exam requirements/recommendations for international students: Required—TOEFL (minimum score 550 paper-based; 213 computer-based). *Application deadline:* For fall admission, 1/1 priority date for domestic students, 12/1 priority date for international students; for spring admission, 3/15 for domestic and international students. Applications are processed on a rolling basis. Application fee: $77. Electronic applications accepted. *Financial support:* In 2010–11, 54 students received support, including 4 fellowships with full tuition reimbursements available (averaging $20,000 per year), 24 research assistantships with full and partial tuition reimbursements available (averaging $10,000 per year), 26 teaching assistantships with full and partial tuition reimbursements available (averaging $10,700 per year); career-related internships or fieldwork, Federal Work-Study, scholarships/grants, traineeships, health care benefits, and unspecified assistantships also available. Financial award application deadline: 1/1; financial award applicants required to submit FAFSA. *Faculty research:* Developing areas, transportation, affordable housing, growth management, coastal zone management. *Unit head:* Dr. Emil E. Malizla, Chairman, 919-962-4759, Fax: 919-962-5206, E-mail: malizia@email.unc.edu. *Application contact:* Carolyn Turner, Student Services Manager, 919-962-4784, Fax: 919-962-5206, E-mail: turnerc@email.unc.edu.

The University of North Carolina at Charlotte, Graduate School, College of Arts and Sciences, Department of Political Science, Charlotte, NC 28223-0001. Offers emergency management (Certificate); non-profit management (Certificate); public administration (MPA, PhD), including arts administration (MPA), emergency management (MPA), non-profit management (MPA), public finance (MPA), urban management and policy (PhD); public finance (Certificate); public policy (PhD); urban management and policy (Certificate). *Accreditation:* NASPAA. Part-time and evening/weekend programs available. *Faculty:* 19 full-time (8 women), 3 part-time/adjunct (2 women). *Students:* 51 full-time (37 women), 75 part-time (49 women); includes 32 minority (26 Black or African American, non-Hispanic/Latino; 1 Asian, non-Hispanic/Latino; 2 Hispanic/Latino; 3 Two or more races, non-Hispanic/Latino), 11 international. Average age 29. 99 applicants, 72% accepted, 42 enrolled. In 2010, 15 master's, 5 doctorates awarded. *Degree requirements:* For master's, thesis or alternative; for doctorate, thesis/dissertation. *Entrance requirements:* For master's, GRE General Test or MAT, minimum GPA of 3.0 in undergraduate major, 2.75 overall. Additional exam requirements/recommendations for international students: Required—TOEFL (minimum score 557 paper-based; 220 computer-based; 83 iBT). *Application deadline:* For fall admission, 7/1 for domestic students, 5/1 for international students; for spring admission, 11/1 for domestic students, 10/1 for international students. Applications are processed on a rolling basis. Application fee: $55. Electronic applications accepted. *Expenses:* Tuition, state resident: full-time $3464. Tuition, nonresident: full-time $14,297. Required fees: $2094. Tuition and fees vary according to course load. *Financial support:* In 2010–11, 22 students received support, including 16 research assistantships (averaging $6,943 per year), 6 teaching assistantships (averaging $9,380 per year); career-related internships or fieldwork, Federal Work-Study, institutionally sponsored loans, scholarships/grants, unspecified assistantships, and administrative assistantship also available. Support available to part-time students. Financial award application deadline: 4/1; financial award applicants required to submit FAFSA. *Faculty research:* Terrorism, public administration, nonprofit and arts administration, educational policy, social policy. Total annual research expenditures: $242,404. *Unit head:* Dr. Theodore S. Arrington, Chair, 704-687-2571, Fax: 704-687-3497, E-mail: tarrngtn@uncc.edu. *Application contact:* Kathy B. Giddings, Director of Graduate Admissions, 704-687-5503, Fax: 704-687-3279, E-mail: gradadm@uncc.edu.

University of Oklahoma, College of Architecture, Division of Regional and City Planning, Norman, OK 73019-0390. Offers MRCP, MRCP/MLA. *Accreditation:* ACSP (one or more programs are accredited). Part-time programs available. *Faculty:* 2 full-time (1 woman). *Students:* 18 full-time (9 women), 3 part-time (all women); includes 2 minority (1 Black or African American, non-Hispanic/Latino; 1 American Indian or Alaska Native, non-Hispanic/Latino), 5 international. Average age 28. 12 applicants, 92% accepted, 7 enrolled. In 2010, 18 master's awarded. *Degree requirements:* For master's, thesis or alternative, portfolio, project. *Entrance requirements:* For master's, GRE General Test, appropriate bachelor's degree, portfolio. Additional exam requirements/recommendations for international students: Required—TOEFL (minimum score 550 paper-based; 213 computer-based; 79 iBT). *Application deadline:* For fall admission, 4/1 for domestic and international students; for spring admission, 11/1 for domestic students, 9/1 for international students. Applications are processed on a rolling basis. Application fee: $40 ($90 for international students). Electronic applications accepted. *Expenses:* Tuition, state resident: full-time $3893; part-time $162.20 per credit hour. Tuition, nonresident: full-time $14,167; part-time $590.30 per credit hour. Required fees: $2523; $94.60 per credit hour. Tuition and fees vary according to course load and degree level. *Financial support:* In 2010–11, 16 students received support, including 1 research assistantship with partial tuition reimbursement available (averaging $13,500 per year); career-related internships or fieldwork, institutionally sponsored loans, scholarships/grants, tuition waivers (partial), and unspecified assistantships also available. Support available to part-time students. Financial award applicants required to submit FAFSA. *Faculty research:* Built environment and public health, transportation logistics, costs and benefits of sprawl, impediments to affordable housing. *Unit head:* Charles Warnken, Interim Director of Regional and City Planning, 405-325-3871, Fax: 405-325-7558, E-mail: cwarnken@ou.edu. *Application contact:* Charles Warnken, Interim Director of Regional and City Planning, 405-325-3871, Fax: 405-325-7558, E-mail: cwarnken@ou.edu.

University of Oregon, Graduate School, School of Architecture and Allied Arts, Department of Planning, Public Policy, and Management, Program in Community and Regional Planning, Eugene, OR 97403. Offers MCRP. *Accreditation:* ACSP. Part-time programs available. *Degree requirements:* For master's, thesis or alternative. *Entrance requirements:* For master's, minimum GPA of 3.0. Additional exam requirements/recommendations for international students: Required—TOEFL. *Faculty research:* Community economic development, tourism, families in poverty.

University of Pennsylvania, School of Design, Department of City and Regional Planning, Philadelphia, PA 19104. Offers MCP, PhD, Certificate, MSE/MCP. *Accreditation:* ACSP (one or more programs are accredited). *Faculty:* 15 full-time (5 women), 4 part-time/adjunct (0 women). *Students:* 149 full-time (78 women), 10 part-time (6 women); includes 13 Black or African American, non-Hispanic/Latino; 16 Asian, non-Hispanic/Latino; 6 Hispanic/Latino, 10 international. 569 applicants, 35% accepted, 86 enrolled. In 2010, 89 master's, 5 doctorates awarded. *Degree requirements:* For doctorate, thesis/dissertation. *Entrance requirements:* For master's and doctorate, GRE General Test. Additional exam requirements/recommendations for international students: Required—TOEFL. *Application deadline:* For fall admission, 1/2 priority date for domestic students. Application fee: $70. *Expenses:* Tuition: Full-time $25,660; part-time $4758 per course. Required fees: $2152; $270 per course. Tuition and fees vary according to course load, degree level and program. *Financial support:* Fellowships, research assistantships, teaching assistantships, institutionally sponsored loans, scholarships/grants, traineeships, health care benefits, and unspecified assistantships available. *Faculty research:* Growth management, transportation planning, urban simulation modeling, housing, development planning.

University of Pennsylvania, School of Design, Program in Landscape Architecture and Regional Planning, Philadelphia, PA 19104. Offers landscape architecture and regional planning (MLA); landscape studies (Certificate). *Accreditation:* ASLA (one or more programs are accredited). Part-time programs available. *Faculty:* 7 full-time (3 women), 4 part-time/adjunct (2 women). *Students:* 98 full-time (68 women); includes 2 Black or African American, non-Hispanic/Latino; 6 Asian, non-Hispanic/Latino; 2 Hispanic/Latino, 32 international. 274 applicants, 39% accepted, 34 enrolled. In 2010, 46 master's, 6 Certificates awarded. *Degree requirements:* For master's, thesis optional. *Entrance requirements:* For master's, GRE, portfolio. Additional exam requirements/recommendations for international students: Required—TOEFL. *Application deadline:* For fall admission, 1/2 priority date for domestic students. Application fee: $70. *Expenses:* Tuition: Full-time $25,660; part-time $4758 per course. Required fees: $2152; $270 per course. Tuition and fees vary according to course load, degree level and program. *Financial support:* Fellowships, research assistantships, teaching assistantships, career-related internships or fieldwork, Federal Work-Study, and institutionally sponsored loans available. Financial award applicants required to submit FAFSA. *Faculty research:* Early landscape architecture, natural distribution through landslides, urban gardens, landscape registration, watershed studies. *Application contact:* Diane Pringle, Coordinator, 215-898-6591, E-mail: dianep@design.upenn.edu.

University of Pittsburgh, Graduate School of Public and International Affairs, Division of International Development, Pittsburgh, PA 15260. Offers development planning and environmental sustainability (MID); human security (MID); nongovernmental organizations and civil society (MID); MID/JD; MID/MBA; MID/MPH; MID/MPIA; MID/MSIS; MID/MSW. Part-time programs available. *Faculty:* 30 full-time (12 women), 67 part-time/adjunct (25 women). *Students:* 66 full-time (46 women), 7 part-time (5 women); includes 7 minority (1 Black or African American, non-Hispanic/Latino; 3 Asian, non-Hispanic/Latino; 3 Hispanic/Latino), 11 international. Average age 25. 125 applicants, 82% accepted, 39 enrolled. In 2010, 35 master's awarded. *Degree requirements:* For master's, thesis optional, internship, capstone seminar. *Entrance requirements:* For master's, GRE General Test, 3 letters of recommendation; minimum GPA of 3.2 (recommended). Additional exam requirements/recommendations for international students: Required—TOEFL (minimum score 550 paper-based; 213 computer-based; 80 iBT), TWE (minimum score 4); Recommended—IELTS (minimum score 7). *Application deadline:* For fall admission, 2/1 for domestic students, 1/5 for international students; for spring admission, 11/1 for domestic students, 8/1 for international students. Application fee: $50. Electronic applications accepted. *Expenses:* Tuition, state resident: full-time $17,304; part-time $701 per credit. Tuition, nonresident: full-time $29,554; part-time $1210 per credit. Required fees: $740; $214 per term. Tuition and fees vary according to program. *Financial support:* In 2010–11, 28 students received support. Scholarships/grants, tuition waivers (full and partial), unspecified assistantships, and student employment available. Financial award application deadline: 2/1. *Faculty research:* Nongovernmental organizations, religion and civil society, international development, development economics and policy, human rights and development, humanitarian intervention, ethnic conflict and civil war, post-conflict peace-building, corruption and transnational governance, civil society and public affairs, political constraints on rural development. Total annual research expenditures: $892,349. *Unit head:* Dr. Paul J. Nelson, Director, 412-648-7645, Fax: 412-648-2605, E-mail: pjnelson@pitt.edu. *Application contact:* Elizabeth Hruby, Graduate Enrollment Counselor, 412-648-7640, Fax: 412-648-7641, E-mail: eah44@pitt.edu.

University of Pittsburgh, Graduate School of Public and International Affairs, Division of Public and Urban Affairs, Pittsburgh, PA 15260. Offers policy research and analysis (MPA); public and nonprofit management (MPA); urban and regional affairs (MPA); JD/MPA; MPA/MPIA; MPH/MPA; MSIS/MPA; MSW/MPA. Part-time and evening/weekend programs available. *Faculty:* 30 full-time (12 women), 67 part-time/adjunct (25 women). *Students:* 61 full-time (29 women), 22 part-time (16 women); includes 4 Black or African American, non-Hispanic/Latino; 1 Asian, non-Hispanic/Latino; 1 Hispanic/Latino, 8 international. Average age 25. 119 applicants, 76% accepted, 38 enrolled. In 2010, 24 master's awarded. *Degree requirements:* For master's, thesis optional, internship, capstone seminar. *Entrance requirements:* For master's, GRE General Test, 3 letters of recommendation, resume; minimum GPA of 3.2 (recommended). Additional exam requirements/recommendations for international students: Required—TOEFL (minimum score 550 paper-based; 213 computer-based; 80 iBT), TWE (minimum score 4); Recommended—IELTS (minimum score 7). *Application deadline:* For fall admission, 2/1 for domestic students, 1/15 for international students; for spring admission, 11/1 for domestic students, 8/1 for international students. Application fee: $50. Electronic applications accepted. *Expenses:* Tuition, state resident: full-time $17,304; part-time $701 per credit. Tuition, nonresident: full-time $29,554; part-time $1210 per credit. Required fees: $740; $214 per term. Tuition and fees vary according to program. *Financial support:* In 2010–11, 18 students received support. Scholarships/grants, tuition waivers (full and partial), unspecified assistantships, and student employment available. Financial award application deadline: 2/1. *Faculty research:* Disaster response management, government regulation of health and safety risks, comparative regional governance, nonprofit management, environmental policy, housing policy, strategic management. Total annual research expenditures: $892,349. *Unit head:* Dr. David Y. Miller, Director, Public and Urban Affairs Division, 412-648-7606, Fax: 412-648-2605, E-mail: dymiller@pitt.edu. *Application contact:* Elizabeth A. Hruby, Graduate Enrollment Counselor, 412-648-7640, Fax: 412-648-7641, E-mail: eah44@pitt.edu.

University of Puerto Rico, Río Piedras, Graduate School of Planning, San Juan, PR 00931-3300. Offers economic planning systems (MP); environmental planning (MP); social policy and planning (MP); urban and territorial planning (MP). *Accreditation:* ACSP. Part-time programs available. *Degree requirements:* For master's, comprehensive exam, thesis, planning project defense. *Entrance requirements:* For master's, PAEG, GRE, minimum GPA of 3.0, 2 letters of recommendation. *Faculty research:* Municipalities, historic Atlas, Puerto Rico, economic future.

University of Southern California, Graduate School, School of Policy, Planning, and Development, Doctor of Philosophy in Urban Planning and Development Program, Los Angeles, CA 90089. Offers PhD. *Faculty:* 51 full-time (12 women), 100 part-time/adjunct (30 women). *Students:* 4 full-time (3 women); includes 1 minority (Asian, non-Hispanic/Latino), 2 international. 95 applicants, 11% accepted, 4 enrolled. *Degree requirements:* For doctorate, thesis/dissertation. *Entrance requirements:* For doctorate, GRE. Additional exam requirements/recommendations for international students: Required—TOEFL (minimum score 600 paper-based; 250 computer-based; 100 iBT). *Application deadline:* For fall admission, 12/1 for domestic and international students. Application fee: $85. Electronic applications accepted. *Expenses:* Tuition: Full-time $31,240; part-time $1420 per unit. Required fees: $600. One-time fee: $35 full-time. Full-time tuition and fees vary according to degree level and program. *Financial support:* In 2010–11, 24 students received support, including 1 fellowship with full tuition reimbursement available (averaging $19,612 per year), 23 research assistantships with full tuition reimbursements available (averaging $18,024 per year); scholarships/grants and tuition waivers (full and partial) also available. *Faculty research:* Transportation and infrastructure, healthy urban and place development, social economic development, sustainable community planning. Total annual research expenditures: $6.2 million. *Unit head:* Dr. Tridib Banerjee, Director, Graduate Programs in Urban Planning, 213-740-4724, Fax: 213-740-5379, E-mail: tbanerje@usc.edu. *Application contact:* Marisol R. Gonzalez, Director of Recruitment and Admission, 213-740-0550, Fax: 213-740-7573, E-mail: marisolr@usc.edu.

University of Southern California, Graduate School, School of Policy, Planning, and Development, Doctor of Policy, Planning, and Development Program, Los Angeles, CA 90089. Offers DPPD. *Accreditation:* ACSP. Part-time programs available. *Faculty:* 51 full-time (12 women), 100 part-time/adjunct (30 women). *Students:* 17 full-time (7 women), 26 part-time (13 women); includes 17 minority (5 Black or African American, non-Hispanic/Latino; 1 American Indian or Alaska Native, non-Hispanic/Latino; 4 Asian, non-Hispanic/Latino; 6 Hispanic/Latino; 1 Native Hawaiian or other Pacific Islander, non-Hispanic/Latino). 41 applicants, 39% accepted, 13 enrolled. In 2010, 3 doctorates awarded. *Degree requirements:* For doctorate, project. *Entrance requirements:* Additional exam requirements/recommendations for international students: Required—TOEFL (minimum score 600 paper-based; 250 computer-based; 100 iBT). *Application deadline:* For fall admission, 2/1 priority date for domestic and international students. Applications are processed on a rolling basis. Application fee: $85. Electronic applications accepted. *Expenses:* Tuition: Full-time $31,240; part-time $1420 per unit. Required fees: $600. One-time fee: $35 full-time. Full-time tuition and fees vary according to degree level and program. *Faculty research:* Governance: effective institutions, leadership, management, healthy urban and place development, sustainability, community, public policy and planning, societal problem solving and analysis. Total annual research expenditures: $6.2 million. *Unit head:* Dr. Elizabeth Graddy, Vice Dean and Professor, 213-740-5725, Fax: 213-740-5379, E-mail: graddy@usc.edu. *Application contact:* Marisol R. Gonzalez, Director of Recruitment and Admission, 213-740-0550, Fax: 213-740-7573, E-mail: marisolr@usc.edu.

University of Southern California, Graduate School, School of Policy, Planning, and Development, Master of Planning Program, Los Angeles, CA 90089. Offers sustainable cities (Graduate Certificate); transportation systems (Graduate Certificate); urban planning (M Pl); M Arch/M Pl; M Pl/MA; M Pl/MS; M Pl/MSW; MBA/M Pl; ML Arch/M Pl; MPA/M Pl. *Accreditation:* ACSP. Part-time programs available. *Faculty:* 51 full-time (12 women), 100 part-time/adjunct (30 women). *Students:* 114 full-time (63 women), 8 part-time (4 women); includes 45 minority (3 Black or African American, non-Hispanic/Latino; 23 Asian, non-Hispanic/Latino; 14 Hispanic/Latino; 5 Two or more races, non-Hispanic/Latino), 15 international. 259 applicants, 71% accepted, 74 enrolled. In 2010, 40 master's awarded. *Degree requirements:* For master's, comprehensive exam, internship. *Entrance requirements:* For master's, GRE, GMAT. Additional exam requirements/recommendations for international students: Required—TOEFL (minimum score 600 paper-based; 250 computer-based; 100 iBT). *Application deadline:* For fall admission, 12/15 priority date for domestic and international students; for spring admission, 11/1 for domestic students, 10/1 for international students. Applications are processed on a rolling basis. Application fee: $85. Electronic applications accepted. *Expenses:* Tuition: Full-time $31,240; part-time $1420 per unit. Required fees: $600. One-time fee: $35 full-time. Full-time tuition and fees vary according to degree level and program. *Financial support:* In 2010–11, 87 students received support, including 2 research assistantships with full tuition reimbursements available (averaging $9,806 per year); scholarships/grants and tuition waivers (full and partial) also available. Financial award application deadline: 12/15; financial award applicants required to submit CSS PROFILE or FAFSA. *Faculty research:* Transportation and infrastructure, comparative international development, healthy communities, social economic development, sustainable community planning. Total annual research expenditures: $6.2 million. *Unit head:* Dr. Tridib Banerjee, Director, Graduate Programs in Urban Planning, 213-740-4724, Fax: 213-740-5379, E-mail: tbanerje@usc.edu. *Application contact:* Marisol R. Gonzalez, Director of Recruitment and Admission, 213-740-0550, Fax: 213-740-7573, E-mail: marisolr@usc.edu.

University of Southern Maine, Edmund S. Muskie School of Public Service, Program in Community Planning and Development, Portland, ME 04104-9300. Offers MCPD, Certificate; JD/MCPD. Part-time and evening/weekend programs available. *Degree requirements:* For master's, thesis, capstone project, field experience. *Entrance requirements:* For master's, GRE General Test or LSAT. Additional exam requirements/recommendations for international

students: Required—TOEFL. Electronic applications accepted. *Faculty research:* Sustainable communities, ego system management, economic and environmental tradeoffs.

The University of Texas at Arlington, Graduate School, School of Urban and Public Affairs, Program in City and Regional Planning, Arlington, TX 76019. Offers MCRP, M Arch/MCRP. *Accreditation:* ACSP. Part-time and evening/weekend programs available. *Faculty:* 4 full-time (1 woman), 2 part-time/adjunct (both women). *Students:* 31 full-time (14 women), 35 part-time (14 women); includes 18 minority (8 Black or African American, non-Hispanic/Latino; 2 Asian, non-Hispanic/Latino; 8 Hispanic/Latino), 9 international. Average age 35. 32 applicants, 84% accepted, 17 enrolled. In 2010, 15 master's awarded. *Degree requirements:* For master's, comprehensive exam (for some programs), thesis or alternative. *Entrance requirements:* For master's, GRE General Test. Additional exam requirements/recommendations for international students: Required—TOEFL (minimum score 550 paper-based; 213 computer-based). *Application deadline:* For fall admission, 6/1 for domestic students, 4/1 for international students; for spring admission, 10/15 for domestic students, 9/15 for international students. Applications are processed on a rolling basis. Application fee: $35 ($50 for international students). Electronic applications accepted. *Expenses:* Tuition, state resident: full-time $7500. Tuition, nonresident: full-time $13,080. International tuition: $13,250 full-time. *Financial support:* In 2010–11, 6 students received support; fellowships, research assistantships, career-related internships or fieldwork available. Financial award application deadline: 6/1; financial award applicants required to submit FAFSA. *Faculty research:* Urban structure, GIS environmental resolutions, qualitative methods, JTS housing, planning history/theory. Total annual research expenditures: $30,453. *Unit head:* Dr. Ivonne Audirac, Program Director, 817-272-3338, Fax: 817-272-5008, E-mail: audirac@uta.edu. *Application contact:* Tangie Fields, Academic Advisor, 817-272-3340, Fax: 817-272-5008, E-mail: nfields@uta.edu.

The University of Texas at Arlington, Graduate School, School of Urban and Public Affairs, Urban and Public Affairs Division, Arlington, TX 76019. Offers MA, MSSW/MA. Part-time and evening/weekend programs available. Postbaccalaureate distance learning degree programs offered (no on-campus study). *Faculty:* 2 full-time (both women). *Students:* 16 full-time (8 women), 54 part-time (22 women); includes 16 Black or African American, non-Hispanic/Latino; 1 Asian, non-Hispanic/Latino; 5 Hispanic/Latino, 11 international. Average age 25. 10 applicants, 100% accepted, 7 enrolled. In 2010, 3 master's awarded. *Degree requirements:* For master's, thesis or alternative. *Entrance requirements:* For master's, GRE General Test. Additional exam requirements/recommendations for international students: Required—TOEFL (minimum score 550 paper-based; 213 computer-based). *Application deadline:* For fall admission, 6/1 for domestic students, 4/1 for international students; for spring admission, 10/15 for domestic students. Application fee: $35 ($50 for international students). *Expenses:* Tuition, state resident: full-time $7500. Tuition, nonresident: full-time $13,080. International tuition: $13,250 full-time. *Financial support:* In 2010–11, 2 students received support, including 1 research assistantship (averaging $750 per year); career-related internships or fieldwork also available. Financial award application deadline: 6/1; financial award applicants required to submit FAFSA. *Faculty research:* Personnel, non-profit organizational change, welfare policy, urban research. Total annual research expenditures: $33,080. *Unit head:* Dr. Edith Barrett, Graduate Adviser, 817-272-3285, Fax: 817-272-5008, E-mail: ebarrett@uta.edu. *Application contact:* Linda Slaughter, Administrative Clerk, 817-272-3071, Fax: 817-272-5008, E-mail: slaughter@uta.edu.

The University of Texas at Austin, Graduate School, School of Architecture, Program in Community and Regional Planning, Austin, TX 78712-1111. Offers MSCRP, PhD, JD/MSCRP, MSCRP/MA, MSCRP/PhD. *Accreditation:* ACSP. *Degree requirements:* For master's, thesis; for doctorate, thesis/dissertation. *Entrance requirements:* For master's and doctorate, GRE General Test. Electronic applications accepted.

The University of Toledo, College of Graduate Studies, College of Language, Literature and Social Sciences, Department of Geography and Planning, Toledo, OH 43606-3390. Offers geographic information systems and applied geographics (Certificate); geography (MA); planning (MA); spatially-integrated social sciences (PhD). Part-time programs available. *Faculty:* 10. *Students:* 18 full-time (8 women), 9 part-time (5 women), 10 international. Average age 29. 32 applicants, 66% accepted, 18 enrolled. In 2010, 7 master's, 4 other advanced degrees awarded. *Degree requirements:* For master's, comprehensive exam, thesis; for doctorate, thesis/dissertation. *Entrance requirements:* For master's and doctorate, GRE General Test, A minimum 2.7 cumulative point-hour ratio (on a 4.0 scale) for all previous academic work. Three Letters of Recommendation; for Certificate, A minimum 2.7 cumulative point-hour ratio (on a 4.0 scale) for all previous academic work. Three Letters of Recommendation. Additional exam requirements/recommendations for international students: Required—TOEFL (minimum score 550 paper-based; 213 computer-based; 80 iBT), IELTS (minimum score 6.5). *Application deadline:* For fall admission, 1/15 priority date for domestic and international students. Applications are processed on a rolling basis. Application fee: $45 ($75 for international students). Electronic applications accepted. *Expenses:* Tuition, state resident: full-time $11,426; part-time $476 per credit hour. Tuition, nonresident: full-time $21,660; part-time $903 per credit hour. One-time fee: $62. *Financial support:* Research assistantships with full tuition reimbursements, teaching assistantships with full tuition reimbursements, career-related internships or fieldwork, institutionally sponsored loans, scholarships/grants, tuition waivers (full), and unspecified assistantships available. Support available to part-time students. *Unit head:* Dr. Patrick Lawrence, Chair, 419-530-4128, Fax: 419-530-7919, E-mail: patrick.lawrence@utoledo.edu. *Application contact:* Graduate School Office, 419-530-4723, Fax: 419-530-4724, E-mail: grdsch@utnet.utoledo.edu.

University of Toronto, School of Graduate Studies, Social Sciences Division, Department of Geography, Program in Planning, Toronto, ON M5S 1A1, Canada. Offers M Sc Pl, PhD. Part-time programs available. *Degree requirements:* For master's, summer internship. *Entrance requirements:* For master's, bachelor's degree in planning, geography, social science or a closely related professional field, minimum B+ average in final year, 3 letters of reference. *Expenses:* Contact institution.

University of Utah, Graduate School, College of Architecture and Planning, Department of City and Metropolitan Planning, Salt Lake City, UT 84112. Offers city and metropolitan planning (MCMP); metropolitan planning, policy and design (PhD). Part-time programs available. *Faculty:* 16 full-time (6 women), 8 part-time/adjunct (1 woman). *Students:* 54 full-time (17 women), 22 part-time (2 women); includes 4 minority (1 Asian, non-Hispanic/Latino; 1 Hispanic/Latino; 2 Two or more races, non-Hispanic/Latino), 2 international. Average age 32. 78 applicants, 51% accepted, 22 enrolled. In 2010, 18 master's awarded. *Degree requirements:* For master's, thesis or alternative, comprehensive project; for doctorate, thesis/dissertation. *Entrance requirements:* For master's, GRE, minimum undergraduate GPA of 3.0; for doctorate, GRE, minimum GPA of 3.5. Additional exam requirements/recommendations for international students: Required—TOEFL (minimum score 500 paper-based; 173 computer-based). *Application deadline:* For fall admission, 4/1 for domestic and international students; for spring admission, 11/1 for domestic and international students. Applications are processed on a rolling basis. Application fee: $55 ($65 for international students). Electronic applications accepted. *Expenses:* Contact institution. *Financial support:* In 2010–11, 14 students received support, including 4 research assistantships with full and partial tuition reimbursements available, 14 teaching assistantships with full and partial tuition reimbursements available (averaging $5,750 per year); fellowships with full tuition reimbursements available, career-related internships or fieldwork, Federal Work-Study, scholarships/grants, and unspecified assistantships also available. Financial award application deadline: 2/1; financial award applicants required to submit FAFSA. *Faculty research:* Transportation, land use, smart growth, public health, climate change, urban design, sustainable communities, community-based decision-making process, urban morphology, urban design regulation and policy, theory and practice in scenario-planning techniques, service-learning teaching methodologies, interactions between federal environmental policies and state/local community development patterns, values in architecture and planning practices. Total annual research expenditures: $248,190. *Unit head:* Nan Ellin, Chair, 801-585-9354,

Urban and Regional Planning

University of Utah (continued)
E-mail: nan.ellin@utah.edu. *Application contact:* Kassy Keen, Admissions Advisor, 801-581-7175, Fax: 801-581-8217, E-mail: advisor@arch.utah.edu.

University of Virginia, School of Architecture, Department of Urban and Environmental Planning, Charlottesville, VA 22903. Offers MUEP, JD/MUEP. *Accreditation:* ACSP (one or more programs are accredited). *Faculty:* 5 full-time (1 woman). *Students:* 61 full-time (36 women), 1 (woman) part-time; includes 2 Black or African American, non-Hispanic/Latino; 1 Asian, non-Hispanic/Latino; 5 Hispanic/Latino, 5 international. Average age 25. 153 applicants, 50% accepted, 34 enrolled. In 2010, 20 master's awarded. *Entrance requirements:* For master's, GRE General Test, previous course work in statistics, 3 letters of recommendation. Additional exam requirements/recommendations for international students: Required—TOEFL (minimum score 600 paper-based; 250 computer-based; 90 iBT). *Application deadline:* For fall admission, 1/15 for domestic students, 1/16 for international students. Applications are processed on a rolling basis. Application fee: $60. Electronic applications accepted. *Financial support:* Applicants required to submit FAFSA. *Faculty research:* Urban development, land use, environment, policy analysis, historic preservation. *Unit head:* Bruce A. Dotson, Chair, 434-924-1339, Fax: 434-982-2678, E-mail: abd8p@virginia.edu. *Application contact:* Graduate Admissions Officer, 434-924-6442, Fax: 434-982-2678, E-mail: arch-admissions@virginia.edu.

University of Washington, Graduate School, College of Built Environments, Department of Urban Design and Planning, Seattle, WA 98195. Offers strategic planning for critical infrastructures (MSCPI); urban design and planning (PhD); urban planning (MUP). *Accreditation:* ACSP (one or more programs are accredited). *Degree requirements:* For master's, thesis or alternative; for doctorate, thesis/dissertation. *Entrance requirements:* For master's and doctorate, GRE General Test, minimum GPA of 3.0. Additional exam requirements/recommendations for international students: Required—TOEFL. *Faculty research:* Land-use and growth management, urban form and travel behavior, geographic information systems/remote sensing, historic preservation, urban ecology and environmental planning.

University of Waterloo, Graduate Studies, Faculty of Environmental Studies, Program in Local Economic Development, Waterloo, ON N2L 3G1, Canada. Offers MAES. Part-time programs available. *Degree requirements:* For master's, internship, research paper. Electronic applications accepted.

University of Waterloo, Graduate Studies, Faculty of Environmental Studies, School of Planning, Waterloo, ON N2L 3G1, Canada. Offers MA, MAES, MES, PhD. Part-time programs available. *Degree requirements:* For master's, thesis (for some programs); for doctorate, comprehensive exam, thesis/dissertation. *Entrance requirements:* For master's, honors degree, minimum B+ average; for doctorate, master's degree, minimum A- average, resume. Additional exam requirements/recommendations for international students: Required—TOEFL, TWE. Electronic applications accepted. *Faculty research:* Environmental planning, planning for resource development, urban planning and information systems, social planning, urban design.

University of Wisconsin–Madison, Graduate School, College of Letters and Science and College of Agricultural and Life Sciences, Department of Urban and Regional Planning, Madison, WI 53706-1380. Offers MS, PhD. *Accreditation:* ACSP (one or more programs are accredited). Part-time programs available. *Degree requirements:* For master's, thesis optional, internship; for doctorate, thesis/dissertation, 3 preliminary exams. *Entrance requirements:* For master's, GRE, minimum GPA of 3.0, previous course work in statistics; for doctorate, 1 year of experience, master's degree in related field. Electronic applications accepted. *Expenses:* Tuition, state resident: full-time $9887; part-time $617.96 per credit. Tuition, nonresident: full-time $24,054; part-time $1503.40 per credit. Required fees: $67.63 per credit. Tuition and fees vary according to reciprocity agreements. *Faculty research:* Land use, environmental planning, community development, economic development planning.

University of Wisconsin–Milwaukee, Graduate School, School of Architecture and Urban Planning, Department of Urban Planning, Milwaukee, WI 53201-0413. Offers geographic information systems (Certificate); real estate development (Certificate); urban planning (MUP); M Arch/MUP; MPA/MUP; MUP/MS. *Accreditation:* ACSP. Part-time programs available. *Faculty:* 5 full-time (2 women). *Students:* 40 full-time (14 women), 28 part-time (11 women); includes 3 Black or African American, non-Hispanic/Latino; 1 American Indian or Alaska Native, non-Hispanic/Latino; 3 Asian, non-Hispanic/Latino; 1 Hispanic/Latino, 3 international. Average age 29. 75 applicants, 72% accepted, 28 enrolled. In 2010, 21 master's awarded. *Degree requirements:* For master's, comprehensive exam, thesis or alternative. *Entrance requirements:* For master's, GRE General Test. Additional exam requirements/recommendations for international students: Required—TOEFL (minimum score 550 paper-based; 213 computer-based; 79 iBT), IELTS (minimum score 6.5). *Application deadline:* For fall admission, 1/1 priority date for domestic students; for spring admission, 9/1 for domestic students. Applications are processed on a rolling basis. Application fee: $56 ($96 for international students). Electronic applications accepted. *Financial support:* Fellowships, research assistantships, teaching assistantships, career-related internships or fieldwork, health care benefits, and unspecified assistantships available. Support available to part-time students. Financial award application deadline: 4/15; financial award applicants required to submit FAFSA. *Unit head:* Joan Simuncak, Representative, 414-229-4015, Fax: 414-229-6976, E-mail: joanarch@uwm.edu. *Application contact:* General Information Contact, 414-229-4982, Fax: 414-229-6967, E-mail: gradschool@uwm.edu.

Utah State University, School of Graduate Studies, College of Humanities, Arts and Social Sciences, Department of Landscape Architecture and Environmental Planning, Logan, UT 84322. Offers bioregional planning (MS); landscape architecture (MLA). *Accreditation:* ASLA (one or more programs are accredited). *Degree requirements:* For master's, thesis. *Entrance requirements:* For master's, GRE General Test, minimum GPA of 3.0. Additional exam requirements/recommendations for international students: Required—TOEFL. *Faculty research:* Visual resource management, planning for wildlife, agricultural land preservation, watershed planning, community planning and design.

Utah State University, School of Graduate Studies, College of Natural Resources, Department of Environment and Society, Logan, UT 84322. Offers bioregional planning (MS); geography (MA, MS); human dimensions of ecosystem science and management (MS, PhD); recreation resource management (MS, PhD). *Degree requirements:* For master's, comprehensive exam, thesis (for some programs). *Entrance requirements:* For master's and doctorate, GRE General Test, minimum GPA of 3.0. Additional exam requirements/recommendations for international students: Required—TOEFL. Electronic applications accepted. *Faculty research:* Geographic information systems/geographic and environmental education, bioregional planning, natural resource and environmental policy, outdoor recreation and tourism, natural resource and environmental management.

Vanderbilt University, Peabody College, Department of Human and Organizational Development, Nashville, TN 37240-1001. Offers community development and action (M Ed); human development counseling (M Ed). *Accreditation:* ACA; NCATE. Part-time programs available. *Faculty:* 32 full-time (14 women), 20 part-time/adjunct (11 women). *Students:* 82 full-time (67 women), 9 part-time (7 women); includes 18 minority (8 Black or African American, non-Hispanic/Latino; 1 American Indian or Alaska Native, non-Hispanic/Latino; 4 Asian, non-Hispanic/Latino; 4 Hispanic/Latino; 1 Two or more races, non-Hispanic/Latino), 1 international. Average age 27. 161 applicants, 60% accepted, 48 enrolled. In 2010, 45 master's awarded. *Degree requirements:* For master's, comprehensive exam, thesis optional. *Entrance requirements:* For master's, GRE General Test, MAT. Additional exam requirements/recommendations for international students: Required—TOEFL (minimum score 550 paper-based; 213 computer-based). *Application deadline:* For fall admission, 12/31 priority date for domestic and international students; for spring admission, 11/1 priority date for domestic and international students. Applications are processed on a rolling basis. Application fee: $0. Electronic applications accepted. *Financial support:* In 2010–11, 85 students received support, including 20 research assistantships with full and partial tuition reimbursements available, 20 teaching assistantships with full and partial tuition reimbursements available; fellowships with full and partial tuition reimbursements available, Federal Work-Study, institutionally sponsored loans, scholarships/grants, tuition waivers (partial), and unspecified assistantships also available. Support available to part-time students. Financial award application deadline: 2/1; financial award applicants required to submit FAFSA. *Faculty research:* Community psychology, community development and urban policy, counseling and mental health services, organizational development and institutional change; youth physical and behavioral health in schools and communities. *Unit head:* Dr. Marybeth Shinn, Chair, 615-322-6881, Fax: 615-322-1141, E-mail: marybeth.shinn@vanderbilt.edu. *Application contact:* Sherrie Lane, Office Assistant, 615-322-8484, Fax: 615-322-1141, E-mail: sherrie.a.lane@vanderbilt.edu.

Virginia Commonwealth University, Graduate School, College of Humanities and Sciences, Wilder School of Government and Public Affairs, Department of Urban Studies and Planning, Program in Urban and Regional Planning, Richmond, VA 23284-9005. Offers MURP, JD/MURP. *Students:* 54 full-time (28 women), 26 part-time (12 women); includes 22 minority (17 Black or African American, non-Hispanic/Latino; 1 American Indian or Alaska Native, non-Hispanic/Latino; 2 Asian, non-Hispanic/Latino; 1 Hispanic/Latino; 1 Two or more races, non-Hispanic/Latino), 2 international. 59 applicants, 92% accepted, 28 enrolled. In 2010, 34 master's awarded. *Degree requirements:* For master's, thesis optional, internship. *Entrance requirements:* For master's, GRE General Test, GMAT, or LSAT, minimum GPA of 2.7. Additional exam requirements/recommendations for international students: Required—TOEFL (minimum score 600 paper-based; 250 computer-based; 100 iBT); Recommended—IELTS (minimum score 6.5). *Application deadline:* For fall admission, 7/15 for domestic students; for spring admission, 10/1 for domestic students. Applications are processed on a rolling basis. Application fee: $50. Electronic applications accepted. *Expenses:* Tuition, state resident: full-time $4308; part-time $479 per credit hour. Tuition, nonresident: full-time $8942; part-time $994 per credit hour. Required fees: $2000; $85 per credit hour. Tuition and fees vary according to course level, course load, degree level, campus/location and program. *Unit head:* Dr. I-Shian Suen, Program Director, 804-828-2721, E-mail: isuen@vcu.edu. *Application contact:* Dr. I-Shian Suen, Program Director, 804-828-2721, E-mail: isuen@vcu.edu.

Virginia Polytechnic Institute and State University, Graduate School, College of Architecture and Urban Studies, School of Public and International Affairs, Blacksburg, VA 24061. Offers economic development (Certificate); government and international affairs (MPIA, PhD); homeland security policy (Certificate); local government management (Certificate); nonprofit and nongovernmental organization management (Certificate); planning, governance and globalization (PhD); public administration and public affairs (MPA, PhD); urban and regional planning (MURPL). *Accreditation:* ACSP. *Faculty:* 31 full-time (9 women). *Students:* 114 full-time (66 women), 105 part-time (54 women); includes 11 Black or African American, non-Hispanic/Latino; 1 American Indian or Alaska Native, non-Hispanic/Latino; 7 Asian, non-Hispanic/Latino; 8 Hispanic/Latino, 19 international. Average age 31. 166 applicants, 67% accepted, 53 enrolled. In 2010, 41 master's, 3 doctorates awarded. *Degree requirements:* For master's, comprehensive exam (for some programs), thesis (for some programs); for doctorate, comprehensive exam (for some programs), thesis/dissertation (for some programs). *Entrance requirements:* For master's and doctorate, GRE. Additional exam requirements/recommendations for international students: Required—TOEFL (minimum score 550 paper-based; 213 computer-based). *Application deadline:* For fall admission, 7/1 for domestic and international students; for spring admission, 12/1 for domestic and international students. Applications are processed on a rolling basis. Application fee: $65. Electronic applications accepted. *Expenses:* Tuition, state resident: full-time $9399; part-time $488 per credit hour. Tuition, nonresident: full-time $17,854; part-time $957.75 per credit hour. Required fees: $1534. Full-time tuition and fees vary according to program. *Financial support:* In 2010–11, 1 teaching assistantship with full tuition reimbursement (averaging $21,395 per year) was awarded; career-related internships or fieldwork, Federal Work-Study, scholarships/grants, health care benefits, and unspecified assistantships also available. Financial award application deadline: 1/15. *Faculty research:* Design theory, environmental planning, town planning, transportation planning. Total annual research expenditures: $610,749. *Unit head:* Dr. Karen M. Hult, UNIT HEAD, 540-231-5351, Fax: 540-231-9938, E-mail: khult@vt.edu. *Application contact:* Krystal D. Wright, Contact, 540-231-2291, Fax: 540-231-9938, E-mail: garch@vt.edu.

Wayne State University, College of Liberal Arts and Sciences, Department of Urban Studies and Planning, Detroit, MI 48202. Offers MUP. *Accreditation:* ACSP. Evening/weekend programs available. *Faculty:* 8 full-time (3 women), 2 part-time/adjunct (0 women). *Students:* 23 full-time (12 women), 50 part-time (28 women); includes 27 minority (23 Black or African American, non-Hispanic/Latino; 1 Asian, non-Hispanic/Latino; 1 Hispanic/Latino; 1 Native Hawaiian or other Pacific Islander, non-Hispanic/Latino; 1 Two or more races, non-Hispanic/Latino), 3 international. Average age 31. 53 applicants, 53% accepted, 18 enrolled. In 2010, 22 master's awarded. *Degree requirements:* For master's, thesis. *Entrance requirements:* Additional exam requirements/recommendations for international students: Required—TOEFL (minimum score 550 paper-based; 213 computer-based); Recommended—TWE (minimum score 6). *Application deadline:* For fall admission, 7/1 for domestic students, 6/1 for international students; for winter admission, 10/1 for international students; for spring admission, 2/1 for international students. Applications are processed on a rolling basis. Application fee: $30 ($50 for international students). Electronic applications accepted. *Expenses:* Tuition, state resident: full-time $7662; part-time $478.85 per credit hour. Tuition, nonresident: full-time $16,920; part-time $1057.55 per credit hour. Required fees: $571.20; $35.70 per credit hour. $188.05 per semester. Tuition and fees vary according to course load and program. *Unit head:* Robert Thomas, Dean, 313-577-2519, Fax: 313-577-8971, E-mail: aa0817@wayne.edu. *Application contact:* Janet Hankin, Professor, 313-577-0841, E-mail: janet.hankin@wayne.edu.

West Chester University of Pennsylvania, Office of Graduate Studies, College of Business and Public Affairs, Department of Geography and Planning, West Chester, PA 19383. Offers geographic technology (Certificate); geography (MA); regional planning (MPA, MSA); urban regional planning (Certificate). Part-time and evening/weekend programs available. *Students:* 18 full-time (8 women), 18 part-time (6 women); includes 7 minority (6 Black or African American, non-Hispanic/Latino; 1 Hispanic/Latino), 2 international. Average age 28. 18 applicants, 89% accepted, 11 enrolled. In 2010, 8 master's, 6 other advanced degrees awarded. *Degree requirements:* For master's, comprehensive exam, thesis optional. *Entrance requirements:* For master's, GRE, GMAT, or MAT, minimum GPA of 2.8, resume, two letters of recommendation; for Certificate, minimum GPA of 2.8, resume, two letters of recommendation. Additional exam requirements/recommendations for international students: Required—TOEFL (minimum score 550 paper-based; 213 computer-based; 80 iBT). *Application deadline:* For fall admission, 4/15 priority date for domestic students, 3/15 for international students; for spring admission, 10/15 for domestic students, 9/1 for international students. Applications are processed on a rolling basis. Application fee: $35. Electronic applications accepted. *Expenses:* Tuition, state resident: full-time $6966; part-time $387 per credit. Tuition, nonresident: full-time $11,146; part-time $619 per credit. Required fees: $1614.40; $133.24 per credit. Part-time tuition and fees vary according to campus/location. *Financial support:* Unspecified assistantships available. Support available to part-time students. Financial award application deadline: 2/15; financial award applicants required to submit FAFSA. *Faculty research:* Environmental education, land use/suburban planning, landscapes of Catalunya, transportation planning, housing, environmental planning. *Unit head:* Dr. Joan Welch, Chair and Graduate Coordinator for the Geography Programs, 610-436-2940, E-mail: jwelch@wcupa.edu. *Application contact:* Dr. Dottie Ives Dewey, Graduate Coordinator for the Urban and Regional Planning Programs, 610-436-2746, E-mail: divesdewey@wcupa.edu.

West Virginia University, Davis College of Agriculture, Forestry and Consumer Sciences, Division of Resource Management and Sustainable Development, Morgantown, WV 26506. Offers agricultural and extension education (MS, PhD), including agricultural and extension education, teaching vocational-agriculture (MS); agricultural and resource economics (MS); human and community development (PhD); natural resource economics (PhD); resource management (PhD); resource management and sustainable development (PhD). Part-time programs available. *Degree requirements:* For master's, thesis; for doctorate, comprehensive exam, thesis/dissertation. *Entrance requirements:* For master's, GRE General Test. Additional exam requirements/recommendations for international students: Required—TOEFL. *Faculty research:* Environmental economics, energy economics, agriculture.

West Virginia University, Eberly College of Arts and Sciences, Department of Geology and Geography, Program in Geography, Morgantown, WV 26506. Offers energy and environmental resources (MA); geographic information systems (PhD); geography-regional development (PhD); GIS/cartographic analysis (MA); regional development (MA). Part-time programs available. *Degree requirements:* For master's, thesis, oral and written exams; for doctorate, comprehensive exam, thesis/dissertation, oral and written exams. *Entrance requirements:* For master's and doctorate, GRE General Test, minimum GPA of 3.0. Additional exam requirements/recommendations for international students: Required—TOEFL. Electronic applications accepted. *Faculty research:* Space, place and development, geographic information science, environmental geography.

Urban Studies

Azusa Pacific University, Haggard Graduate School of Theology, Program in Pastoral Studies, Concentration in Urban Studies, Azusa, CA 91702-7000. Offers MAPS. *Students:* 1 (woman) full-time, 7 part-time (4 women); includes 6 minority (4 Black or African American, non-Hispanic/Latino; 2 Hispanic/Latino). Average age 41. *Unit head:* Dr. Scott Daniels, ean, 626-387-5750. *Application contact:* Dr. Scott Daniels, ean, 626-387-5750.

Boston University, Metropolitan College, Program in Urban Affairs, Boston, MA 02215. Offers MUA. Part-time and evening/weekend programs available. *Faculty:* 3 full-time (0 women), 14 part-time/adjunct (3 women). *Students:* 1 full-time (0 women), 15 part-time (9 women); includes 6 minority (4 Black or African American, non-Hispanic/Latino; 2 Hispanic/Latino). Average age 36. 14 applicants, 71% accepted, 7 enrolled. In 2010, 6 master's awarded. *Degree requirements:* For master's, thesis optional. *Entrance requirements:* Additional exam requirements/recommendations for international students: Required—TOEFL. *Application deadline:* For fall admission, 7/15 priority date for domestic and international students; for spring admission, 12/15 for domestic students, 11/15 priority date for international students. Applications are processed on a rolling basis. Application fee: $70. Electronic applications accepted. *Expenses:* Tuition: Full-time $39,314; part-time $1228 per credit. Required fees: $40 per semester. *Financial support:* In 2010–11, 3 research assistantships with partial tuition reimbursements (averaging $5,000 per year), 3 teaching assistantships with partial tuition reimbursements (averaging $5,000 per year) were awarded; career-related internships or fieldwork, Federal Work-Study, and unspecified assistantships also available. Support available to part-time students. Financial award application deadline: 6/15; financial award applicants required to submit FAFSA. *Faculty research:* Housing, community development and land use planning, environmental management and planning, international comparative development planning, sustainability. *Unit head:* Dr. Daniel P. LeClair, Chair, 617-353-3025, Fax: 617-358-3595, E-mail: dleclair@bu.edu. *Application contact:* Dr. Enrique Silvia, Assistant Professor, 617-358-2364, E-mail: ersilva@bu.edu.

Brooklyn College of the City University of New York, Division of Graduate Studies, Department of Political Science, Brooklyn, NY 11210-2889. Offers international affairs (MA); political science (MA, PhD); political science, urban policy and administration (MA). Part-time and evening/weekend programs available. *Students:* 23 full-time (13 women), 219 part-time (124 women); includes 119 minority (92 Black or African American, non-Hispanic/Latino; 12 Asian, non-Hispanic/Latino; 15 Hispanic/Latino), 28 international. Average age 30. 155 applicants, 80% accepted, 88 enrolled. In 2010, 49 master's awarded. *Degree requirements:* For master's, comprehensive exam (for some programs), thesis or alternative, foreign language exam (for international affairs program). *Entrance requirements:* For master's, 2 letters of recommendation, personal statement. Additional exam requirements/recommendations for international students: Required—TOEFL (minimum score 500 paper-based; 173 computer-based; 61 iBT). *Application deadline:* For fall admission, 5/1 for domestic and international students; for spring admission, 12/15 for domestic students, 11/1 for international students. *Expenses:* Tuition, state resident: full-time $7360; part-time $310 per credit hour. Tuition, nonresident: full-time $13,800; part-time $575 per credit hour. Required fees: $190 per semester. *Financial support:* Career-related internships or fieldwork and Federal Work-Study available. Support available to part-time students. Financial award application deadline: 5/1; financial award applicants required to submit FAFSA. *Faculty research:* Ethics and politics, politics of criminal justice, Western Europe, international law and politics, labor politics. *Unit head:* Dr. Paisley Currah, Acting Chairperson, 718-951-5306, E-mail: pcurrah@brooklyn.cuny.edu. *Application contact:* Hernan Sierra, Graduate Admissions Coordinator, 718-951-4536, Fax: 718-951-4506, E-mail: grads@brooklyn.cuny.edu.

Cleveland State University, College of Graduate Studies, Maxine Goodman Levin College of Urban Affairs, Program in Urban Studies, Cleveland, OH 44115. Offers geographic information systems (Certificate); local and urban management (Certificate); nonprofit management (Certificate); urban economic development (Certificate); urban real estate development and finance (Certificate); urban studies (MS); urban studies and public affairs (PhD). PhD program offered jointly with The University of Akron. Part-time and evening/weekend programs available. *Faculty:* 26 full-time (10 women), 20 part-time/adjunct (11 women). *Students:* 16 full-time (10 women), 35 part-time (18 women); includes 7 Black or African American, non-Hispanic/Latino, 17 international. Average age 37. 90 applicants, 38% accepted, 18 enrolled. In 2010, 6 master's, 7 doctorates, 6 other advanced degrees awarded. *Degree requirements:* For master's, thesis or alternative, exit project, capstone course; for doctorate, comprehensive exam, thesis/dissertation. *Entrance requirements:* For master's, GRE General Test, minimum GPA of 3.0; for doctorate, GRE General Test, minimum GPA of 3.5. Additional exam requirements/recommendations for international students: Required—TOEFL (minimum score 525 paper-based; 197 computer-based; 65 iBT). *Application deadline:* For fall admission, 7/15 priority date for domestic students, 5/15 for international students; for spring admission, 11/1 for international students. Applications are processed on a rolling basis. Application fee: $30. Electronic applications accepted. *Expenses:* Tuition, state resident: full-time $8447; part-time $469 per credit hour. Tuition, nonresident: full-time $16,020; part-time $890 per credit hour. Required fees: $50. *Financial support:* In 2010–11, 15 students received support, including 11 research assistantships with full tuition reimbursements available (averaging $7,000 per year), 4 teaching assistantships with full and partial tuition reimbursements available (averaging $7,000 per year); career-related internships or fieldwork, Federal Work-Study, institutionally sponsored loans, scholarships/grants, tuition waivers (full and partial), and unspecified assistantships also available. Support available to part-time students. Financial award application deadline: 3/1; financial award applicants required to submit FAFSA. *Faculty research:* Environmental issues, economic development, urban and public policy, public management. *Unit head:* Dr. Sugie Lee, Director, 216-687-2381, Fax: 216-687-9342, E-mail: s.lee56@csuohio.edu. *Application contact:* Joan Demko, Graduate Academic Support Specialist, 216-523-7522, Fax: 216-687-5398, E-mail: urbanprograms@csuohio.edu.

Concordia University, School of Graduate Studies, Faculty of Arts and Science, Department of Geography, Planning and Environment, Montréal, QC H3G 1M8, Canada. Offers environmental impact assessment (Diploma); geography, urban and environmental studies (M Sc).

Eastern University, School for Social Change, St. Davids, PA 19087-3696. Offers urban studies (MA), including arts in transformation, community development, youth leadership.

East Tennessee State University, School of Graduate Studies, College of Arts and Sciences, Department of Economics, Finance, and Urban Studies, Johnson City, TN 37614. Offers city management (MCM); not-for-profit (MPA); planning and development (MPA); public financial management (MPA). Part-time programs available. *Faculty:* 1 full-time (0 women). *Students:* 15 full-time (5 women), 8 part-time (4 women); includes 1 Black or African American, non-Hispanic/Latino, 2 international. Average age 30. 19 applicants, 42% accepted, 7 enrolled. In 2010, 14 master's awarded. *Degree requirements:* For master's, comprehensive exam, internship, capstone, research report. *Entrance requirements:* For master's, GRE General Test, minimum GPA of 2.5. Additional exam requirements/recommendations for international students: Required—TOEFL (minimum score 550 paper-based; 213 computer-based; 79 iBT). *Application deadline:* For fall admission, 6/1 priority date for domestic students, 4/30 for international students; for spring admission, 11/1 for domestic students, 9/30 for international students. Application fee: $25 ($35 for international students). Electronic applications accepted. *Financial support:* In 2010–11, 9 research assistantships with full tuition reimbursements (averaging $5,500 per year) were awarded; career-related internships or fieldwork, institutionally sponsored loans, scholarships/grants, and unspecified assistantships also available. Financial award application deadline: 7/1; financial award applicants required to submit FAFSA. Total annual research expenditures: $6,519. *Unit head:* Dr. Weixing Chen, Chair, 423-439-6632, Fax: 423-439-4348, E-mail: chen@etsu.edu. *Application contact:* Dr. Weixing Chen, Chair, 423-439-6632, Fax: 423-439-4348, E-mail: chen@etsu.edu.

Fordham University, Graduate School of Arts and Sciences, Program in Urban Studies, New York, NY 10458. Offers MA. *Students:* 2 full-time (both women), 10 part-time (5 women); includes 1 Black or African American, non-Hispanic/Latino; 2 Asian, non-Hispanic/Latino; 1 Hispanic/Latino, 3 international. 5 applicants, 100% accepted, 2 enrolled. *Degree requirements:* For master's, internship or field work, research project. *Unit head:* Dr. Rosemary Wakeman, Director, 212-636-7359, E-mail: rwakeman@fordham.edu. *Application contact:* Charlene Dundie, Director of Graduate Admissions, 718-817-4420, Fax: 718-817-3566, E-mail: dundie@fordham.edu.

Graduate School and University Center of the City University of New York, Graduate Studies, Interdisciplinary Studies, New York, NY 10016-4039. Offers language in social context (PhD); medieval studies (PhD); public policy (MA, PhD); urban studies (MA, PhD); women's studies (MA, PhD). Terminal master's awarded for partial completion of doctoral program. *Degree requirements:* For master's, thesis; for doctorate, comprehensive exam, thesis/dissertation. *Entrance requirements:* For master's and doctorate, GRE General Test.

Hunter College of the City University of New York, Graduate School, School of Arts and Sciences, Department of Urban Affairs and Planning, Program in Urban Affairs, New York, NY 10021-5085. Offers urban studies/affairs (MS). Part-time programs available. *Faculty:* 12 full-time (3 women), 11 part-time/adjunct (5 women). *Students:* 18 full-time (14 women), 74 part-time (52 women); includes 28 Black or African American, non-Hispanic/Latino; 6 Asian, non-Hispanic/Latino; 13 Hispanic/Latino, 1 international. Average age 32. 96 applicants, 61% accepted, 36 enrolled. In 2010, 57 master's awarded. *Degree requirements:* For master's, thesis or alternative, 2 formal reports, internship. *Entrance requirements:* For master's, minimum 12 credits of course work in social sciences. Additional exam requirements/recommendations for international students: Required—TOEFL. *Application deadline:* For fall admission, 4/1 priority date for domestic students, 2/1 for international students; for spring admission, 11/1 priority date for domestic students, 9/1 for international students. Applications are processed on a rolling basis. Application fee: $125. *Financial support:* Fellowships, research assistantships, teaching assistantships, career-related internships or fieldwork, Federal Work-Study, scholarships/grants, and unspecified assistantships available. *Faculty research:* Women, tourism, youth, immigration, employment. *Unit head:* Dr. Jill Simone Gross, Director, 212-772-5600, Fax: 212-772-5593, E-mail: igross@hunter.cuny.edu. *Application contact:* William Zlata, Director for Graduate Admissions, 212-772-4482, Fax: 212-650-3336, E-mail: admissions@hunter.cuny.edu.

Le Moyne College, Department of Education, Syracuse, NY 13214. Offers adolescent education (MS Ed, MST); adolescent education/special education (MS Ed, MST); adolescent English (grades 7-12) (MST); adolescent history (grades 7-12) (MST); childhood education (MS Ed); childhood education/special education (MS Ed); elementary education (MS Ed); general professional education (MS Ed); inclusive childhood education (MST); literacy education (birth to grade 6) (MS Ed); literacy education (grades 5-12) (MS Ed); middle child specialist/special education (MS Ed); middle childhood specialist (MS Ed); school building leadership (MS Ed, CAS); school district business leader (MS Ed, CAS); school district leadership (MS Ed, CAS); secondary education (MS Ed); special education (MS Ed); TESOL (teaching English to speakers of other languages) (MS Ed); urban studies (MS Ed). *Accreditation:* Teacher Education Accreditation Council. Part-time and evening/weekend programs available. *Faculty:* 13 full-time (8 women), 54 part-time/adjunct (32 women). *Students:* 30 full-time (21 women), 330 part-time (239 women); includes 28 minority (13 Black or African American, non-Hispanic/Latino; 3 American Indian or Alaska Native, non-Hispanic/Latino; 4 Asian, non-Hispanic/Latino; 8 Hispanic/Latino). Average age 30. 280 applicants, 86% accepted, 231 enrolled. In 2010, 155 master's, 19 CASs awarded. *Degree requirements:* For master's, thesis. *Entrance requirements:* For master's, GRE General Test, bachelor's degree, 2 letters of recommendation, transcripts. Additional exam requirements/recommendations for international students: Required—TOEFL (minimum score 550 paper-based; 213 computer-based; 79 iBT). *Application deadline:* For fall admission, 4/1 priority date for domestic and international students; for spring admission, 10/1 priority date for domestic and international students. Applications are processed on a rolling basis. Application fee: $50. *Expenses:* Contact institution. *Financial support:* In 2010–11, 23 students received support. Career-related internships or fieldwork and health care benefits available. Support available to part-time students. Financial award applicants required to submit FAFSA. *Faculty research:* Recruitment/retention strategies, minority teachers, special education, multiculturalism, literacy, technology, video games learning, autism, school district organization. *Unit head:* Dr. Suzanne L. Gilmour, Chair/Director of Graduate Programs, 315-445-4376, Fax: 315-445-4744, E-mail: gilmous@lemoyne.edu. *Application contact:* Kristen P. Trapasso, Director of Graduate Admission, 315-445-4265, Fax: 315-445-6027, E-mail: trapaskp@lemoyne.edu.

Long Island University, Brooklyn Campus, Richard L. Conolly College of Liberal Arts and Sciences, Department of Urban Studies, Brooklyn, NY 11201-8423. Offers MA. Part-time and evening/weekend programs available. *Degree requirements:* For master's, thesis or alternative. *Entrance requirements:* For master's, 2 letters of recommendation. Additional exam requirements/recommendations for international students: Required—TOEFL (minimum score 500 paper-based; 173 computer-based). Electronic applications accepted.

Loyola University Chicago, Graduate School, Department of Sociology, Chicago, IL 60660. Offers sociology (MA, PhD); urban studies (MA). Part-time and evening/weekend programs available. *Faculty:* 13 full-time (5 women), 3 part-time/adjunct (1 woman). *Students:* 75 full-time (50 women), 18 part-time (12 women); includes 21 minority (8 Black or African American,

Urban Studies

Loyola University Chicago (continued)

non-Hispanic/Latino; 8 Asian, non-Hispanic/Latino; 4 Hispanic/Latino; 1 Two or more races, non-Hispanic/Latino), 8 international. Average age 33. 99 applicants, 46% accepted, 17 enrolled. In 2010, 5 master's, 5 doctorates awarded. Terminal master's awarded for partial completion of doctoral program. *Degree requirements:* For master's, thesis or alternative; for doctorate, comprehensive exam, thesis/dissertation. *Entrance requirements:* For master's and doctorate, GRE General Test. Additional exam requirements/recommendations for international students: Required—TOEFL. *Application deadline:* For fall and winter admission, 2/1 for domestic and international students. Application fee: $0. Electronic applications accepted. *Expenses:* Tuition: Full-time $14,940; part-time $830 per credit hour. Required fees: $87 per semester. Part-time tuition and fees vary according to course load and program. *Financial support:* In 2010–11, 25 students received support, including 10 fellowships with full tuition reimbursements available (averaging $14,000 per year), 5 research assistantships with full tuition reimbursements available (averaging $14,000 per year), 9 teaching assistantships with full tuition reimbursements available (averaging $14,000 per year); career-related internships or fieldwork, Federal Work-Study, health care benefits, tuition waivers (full), and unspecified assistantships also available. Financial award application deadline: 2/1; financial award applicants required to submit FAFSA. *Faculty research:* Religion, knowledge, culture, urban and social policy. Total annual research expenditures: $160,000. *Unit head:* Dr. Rhys Williams, Chair, 773-508-3459, Fax: 773-508-7099, E-mail: rwilliams7s@luc.edu. *Application contact:* Dr. Anne Figert, Graduate Program Director, 773-508-3431, Fax: 773-508-7099, E-mail: afigert@luc.edu.

Massachusetts Institute of Technology, School of Architecture and Planning, Department of Urban Studies and Planning, Cambridge, MA 02139-4307. Offers city planning (MCP); urban and regional planning (PhD); urban and regional studies (PhD); urban studies and planning (SM). *Accreditation:* ACSP (one or more programs are accredited). *Faculty:* 28 full-time (10 women). *Students:* 201 full-time (120 women); includes 53 minority (10 Black or African American, non-Hispanic/Latino; 2 American Indian or Alaska Native, non-Hispanic/Latino; 22 Asian, non-Hispanic/Latino; 14 Hispanic/Latino; 5 Two or more races, non-Hispanic/Latino), 55 international. Average age 29. 606 applicants, 21% accepted, 95 enrolled. In 2010, 73 master's, 11 doctorates awarded. Terminal master's awarded for partial completion of doctoral program. *Degree requirements:* For master's, thesis; for doctorate, comprehensive exam, thesis/dissertation. *Entrance requirements:* For master's, GRE General Test; for doctorate, GRE General Test (minimum scores: 1200 Verbal and Quantitative combined; 5.0 Analytical Writing). Additional exam requirements/recommendations for international students: Required—TOEFL (minimum score 250 computer-based; 100 iBT), IELTS (minimum score 7). *Application deadline:* For fall admission, 1/3 for domestic and international students. Application fee: $75. Electronic applications accepted. *Expenses:* Tuition: Full-time $38,940; part-time $605 per unit. Required fees: $272. *Financial support:* In 2010–11, 166 students received support, including 81 fellowships with tuition reimbursements available (averaging $23,223 per year), 58 research assistantships with tuition reimbursements available (averaging $18,475 per year), 21 teaching assistantships with tuition reimbursements available (averaging $29,214 per year); career-related internships or fieldwork, Federal Work-Study, institutionally sponsored loans, scholarships/grants, health care benefits, and unspecified assistantships also available. *Faculty research:* City design and sustainable urban development; housing, community, and economic development; environment and energy policy and planning; international development and regional planning; urban and geographic information systems. Total annual research expenditures: $2.7 million. *Unit head:* Prof. Amy Glasmeier, Department Head, 617-253-1907, Fax: 617-253-2654, E-mail: duspinfo@mit.edu. *Application contact:* Graduate Admissions, 617-253-4543, Fax: 617-253-2654, E-mail: duspapply@mit.edu.

Minnesota State University Mankato, College of Graduate Studies, College of Social and Behavioral Sciences, Department of Urban and Regional Studies, Mankato, MN 56001. Offers local government management (Certificate); urban and regional studies (MA); urban planning (MA, Certificate). *Students:* 19 full-time (4 women), 18 part-time (7 women). *Degree requirements:* For master's, one foreign language, comprehensive exam, thesis or alternative. *Entrance requirements:* For master's, minimum GPA of 3.0 during previous 2 years, 2 letters of recommendation. Additional exam requirements/recommendations for international students: Required—TOEFL. *Application deadline:* For fall admission, 7/1 priority date for domestic students; for spring admission, 11/1 for domestic students. Applications are processed on a rolling basis. Application fee: $40. Electronic applications accepted. *Financial support:* Fellowships with partial tuition reimbursements, research assistantships with full tuition reimbursements, teaching assistantships with full tuition reimbursements, career-related internships or fieldwork, Federal Work-Study, institutionally sponsored loans, and unspecified assistantships available. Support available to part-time students. Financial award application deadline: 3/15; financial award applicants required to submit FAFSA. *Unit head:* Dr. Anthony Filipovitch, Graduate Coordinator, 507-389-1714. *Application contact:* 507-389-2321, E-mail: grad@mnsu.edu.

Moody Bible Institute, Graduate School, Chicago, IL 60610-3284. Offers biblical studies (MABS, Graduate Certificate); intercultural studies (MAIS, Graduate Certificate); ministry (M Div, M Min); spiritual formation and discipleship (MASF, Graduate Certificate); urban studies (MA, Graduate Certificate). Part-time programs available. *Degree requirements:* For master's, 2 foreign languages, fieldwork (MABS); colloquium, field research project (MA Min). *Entrance requirements:* For master's, 30 hours in Bible/theology, 2 years of ministry experience (MA Min).

New Jersey City University, Graduate Studies and Continuing Education, Debra Cannon Partridge Wolfe College of Education, Department of Educational Leadership, Jersey City, NJ 07305-1597. Offers basics and urban studies (MA); bilingual/bicultural education and English as a second language (MA); educational administration and supervision (MA). Part-time and evening/weekend programs available. *Entrance requirements:* For master's, GRE General Test or MAT. Additional exam requirements/recommendations for international students: Required—TOEFL.

New Jersey Institute of Technology, Office of Graduate Studies, School of Architecture, Program in Urban Systems, Newark, NJ 07102. Offers PhD. Part-time and evening/weekend programs available. *Students:* 14 full-time (8 women), 10 part-time (7 women); includes 2 Black or African American, non-Hispanic/Latino; 1 Asian, non-Hispanic/Latino, 10 international. Average age 42. 27 applicants, 44% accepted, 6 enrolled. In 2010, 3 doctorates awarded. *Entrance requirements:* Additional exam requirements/recommendations for international students: Required—TOEFL (minimum score 550 paper-based; 213 computer-based; 79 iBT). *Application deadline:* For fall admission, 6/5 priority date for domestic students, 4/1 for international students; for spring admission, 11/15 for domestic and international students. Applications are processed on a rolling basis. Application fee: $65. Electronic applications accepted. *Expenses:* Tuition, state resident: full-time $14,724; part-time $818 per credit. Tuition, nonresident: full-time $20,304; part-time $1128 per credit. Required fees: $2272; $209 per credit. $103 per semester. One-time fee: $312 full-time; $212 part-time. *Financial support:* Fellowships with full and partial tuition reimbursements, research assistantships with full and partial tuition reimbursements, teaching assistantships with full and partial tuition reimbursements, career-related internships or fieldwork, Federal Work-Study, institutionally sponsored loans, and unspecified assistantships available. Financial award application deadline: 3/15. *Unit head:* Karen Franck, Director, 973-596-3092, E-mail: karen.a.franck@njit.edu. *Application contact:* Kathryn Kelly, Director of Admissions, 973-596-3300, Fax: 973-596-3461, E-mail: admissions@njit.edu.

The New School: A University, Milano The New School for Management and Urban Policy, Program in Urban Policy Analysis and Management, 72 5th Avenue, NY 10011. Offers MS. *Accreditation:* NASPAA. Part-time programs available. *Degree requirements:* For master's, thesis. *Entrance requirements:* For master's, interview. Additional exam requirements/recommendations for international students: Required—TOEFL (minimum score 600 paper-based; 250 computer-based; 100 iBT). Electronic applications accepted. *Faculty research:* Community and economic development, national urban policy, social welfare policy, management of low-income housing, race and gender issues.

Norfolk State University, School of Graduate Studies, School of Liberal Arts, Department of Sociology, Program in Urban Affairs, Norfolk, VA 23504. Offers MA. Part-time programs available. *Degree requirements:* For master's, thesis. *Entrance requirements:* For master's, minimum GPA of 2.5.

Northeastern University, College of Social Sciences and Humanities, Department of Political Science, Boston, MA 02115-5096. Offers political science (MA); public administration (MPA, Certificate), including development administration (MPA), health administration and policy (MPA), state and local government (MPA), urban studies (Certificate); public and international affairs (PhD). Part-time and evening/weekend programs available. *Faculty:* 22 full-time (4 women), 10 part-time/adjunct (1 woman). *Students:* 64 full-time (30 women), 12 part-time (7 women). Average age 30. 132 applicants, 47% accepted, 23 enrolled. In 2010, 21 master's, 3 doctorates awarded. *Degree requirements:* For master's, thesis optional; for doctorate, thesis/dissertation. *Entrance requirements:* For master's, GRE General Test. Additional exam requirements/recommendations for international students: Required—TOEFL. *Application deadline:* Applications are processed on a rolling basis. Application fee: $50. *Financial support:* In 2010–11, 12 fellowships, 1 research assistantship with tuition reimbursement, 17 teaching assistantships with tuition reimbursements (averaging $14,035 per year) were awarded; career-related internships or fieldwork, Federal Work-Study, tuition waivers (full and partial), and unspecified assistantships also available. Support available to part-time students. Financial award application deadline: 2/1; financial award applicants required to submit FAFSA. *Faculty research:* Presidency, public opinion, Congress, democratization, national identity. *Unit head:* Dr. John Portz, Chair, 617-373-2796, Fax: 617-373-5311, E-mail: gradpolisci@neu.edu. *Application contact:* Brynn Thompson, Graduate Programs Assistant, 617-373-4404, Fax: 617-373-5311, E-mail: gradpolisci@neu.edu.

Northeastern University, College of Social Sciences and Humanities, School of Public Policy and Urban Affairs, Program in Public Administration, Boston, MA 02115-5096. Offers development administration (MPA); health administration and policy (MPA); state and local government (MPA); urban studies (Certificate). *Accreditation:* NASPAA (one or more programs are accredited). Part-time and evening/weekend programs available. *Faculty:* 22 full-time (4 women), 10 part-time/adjunct (1 woman). *Students:* 74 full-time (48 women), 44 part-time (30 women). 149 applicants, 77% accepted, 56 enrolled. In 2010, 18 master's awarded. *Degree requirements:* For master's, thesis optional. *Entrance requirements:* For master's, GRE General Test. Additional exam requirements/recommendations for international students: Required—TOEFL. *Application deadline:* For fall admission, 2/1 priority date for domestic students, 5/1 for international students. Applications are processed on a rolling basis. Application fee: $50. *Financial support:* In 2010–11, 2 research assistantships with tuition reimbursements (averaging $14,035 per year) were awarded; teaching assistantships with tuition reimbursements, career-related internships or fieldwork, Federal Work-Study, tuition waivers (full and partial), and unspecified assistantships also available. Support available to part-time students. Financial award application deadline: 2/1; financial award applicants required to submit FAFSA. *Faculty research:* National health care, Third World development, leadership and ethics, science and technology, budgeting. *Unit head:* Dr. Ronald D. Hedlund, Graduate Coordinator, 617-373-2796, Fax: 617-373-5311, E-mail: gradpolisci@neu.edu. *Application contact:* Brynn Thompson, Graduate Programs Assistant, 617-373-4404, Fax: 617-373-5311, E-mail: gradpolisci@neu.edu.

Old Dominion University, College of Business and Public Administration, Doctoral Program in Public Administration and Urban Policy, Norfolk, VA 23529. Offers PhD. Part-time and evening/weekend programs available. *Faculty:* 7 full-time (2 women). *Students:* 11 full-time (8 women), 22 part-time (11 women); includes 7 minority (6 Black or African American, non-Hispanic/Latino; 1 Hispanic/Latino), 5 international. Average age 38. 27 applicants, 44% accepted, 10 enrolled. In 2010, 3 doctorates awarded. *Degree requirements:* For doctorate, comprehensive exam, thesis/dissertation. *Entrance requirements:* For doctorate, GMAT, GRE General Test, master's degree, minimum graduate GPA of 3.25. Additional exam requirements/recommendations for international students: Required—TOEFL (minimum score 550 paper-based; 213 computer-based; 79 iBT). *Application deadline:* For fall admission, 3/15 priority date for domestic and international students. Application fee: $50. Electronic applications accepted. *Expenses:* Tuition, state resident: full-time $8592; part-time $358 per credit. Tuition, nonresident: full-time $21,672; part-time $903 per credit. Required fees: $119 per semester. One-time fee: $50. *Financial support:* In 2010–11, 8 students received support, including 4 fellowships with full tuition reimbursements available (averaging $7,500 per year), 12 research assistantships with partial tuition reimbursements available (averaging $6,000 per year), 4 teaching assistantships with tuition reimbursements available (averaging $7,500 per year); unspecified assistantships also available. Financial award application deadline: 3/15; financial award applicants required to submit FAFSA. *Faculty research:* Educational needs and program development, policy analysis and administration, excellence norms for cooperative education programs. Total annual research expenditures: $60,000. *Unit head:* Dr. John C. Morris, Graduate Program Director, 757-683-3961, Fax: 757-683-4886, E-mail: jcmorris@odu.edu. *Application contact:* Megan S. Jones, Graduate Program Manager, 757-683-3961, Fax: 757-683-4886, E-mail: mmjones@odu.edu.

Polytechnic Institute of NYU, Department of Civil Engineering, Major in Urban Systems Engineering and Management, Brooklyn, NY 11201-2990. Offers MS. *Students:* 1 (woman) full-time, 3 part-time (2 women); includes 1 Black or African American, non-Hispanic/Latino; 1 Asian, non-Hispanic/Latino, 2 international. Average age 25. 9 applicants, 56% accepted, 2 enrolled. In 2010, 4 master's awarded. *Application deadline:* For fall admission, 7/31 priority date for domestic students, 4/30 priority date for international students; for spring admission, 12/31 priority date for domestic students, 11/30 priority date for international students. Application fee: $75. *Expenses:* Tuition: Full-time $21,492; part-time $1194 per credit. Required fees: $385 per semester. Tuition and fees vary according to course load. *Unit head:* Dr. Lawrence Chiarelli, Head, 718-260-4040, Fax: 718-260-3433, E-mail: lchiarel@poly.edu. *Application contact:* JeanCarlo Bonilla, Director of Graduate Enrollment Management, 718-260-3182, Fax: 718-260-3624, E-mail: gradinfo@poly.edu.

Portland State University, Graduate Studies, College of Urban and Public Affairs, Nohad A. Toulan School of Urban Studies and Planning, Program in Urban Studies, Portland, OR 97207-0751. Offers MUS, PhD. *Faculty:* 19 full-time (4 women), 15 part-time/adjunct (8 women). *Students:* 38 applicants, 47% accepted, 12 enrolled. In 2010, 7 master's awarded. *Degree requirements:* For doctorate, comprehensive exam, thesis/dissertation, residency. *Entrance requirements:* For master's, GRE General Test, minimum GPA of 2.75, 3 letters of recommendation; for doctorate, GRE General Test, minimum GPA of 2.75. Additional exam requirements/recommendations for international students: Required—TOEFL (minimum score 550 paper-based; 213 computer-based). *Application deadline:* For fall admission, 1/15 for domestic and international students; for winter admission, 9/1 for domestic and international students. Application fee: $50. *Expenses:* Tuition, state resident: full-time $8505; part-time $315 per credit. Tuition, nonresident: full-time $13,284; part-time $492 per credit. Required fees: $1482; $21 per credit. $99 per term. One-time fee: $120. Part-time tuition and fees vary according to course load and program. *Financial support:* Research assistantships available. Financial award application deadline: 3/1. *Unit head:* James Strathman, Director, 503-725-4069, E-mail: strathmanj@pdx.edu. *Application contact:* Tracy Braden, Office Coordinator, 503-725-4015, Fax: 503-725-8770, E-mail: tbraden@pdx.edu.

Queens College of the City University of New York, Division of Graduate Studies, Social Science Division, Department of Urban Studies, Flushing, NY 11367-1597. Offers MA. Part-time and evening/weekend programs available. *Faculty:* 12 full-time (4 women). *Students:* 7 full-time (6 women), 166 part-time (121 women); includes 68 Black or African American, non-Hispanic/Latino; 10 Asian, non-Hispanic/Latino; 30 Hispanic/Latino, 7 international. 177 applicants, 56% accepted, 89 enrolled. In 2010, 80 master's awarded. *Degree requirements:* For master's, thesis. *Entrance requirements:* For master's, minimum GPA of 3.0. Additional exam requirements/

recommendations for international students: Required—TOEFL. *Application deadline:* For fall admission, 4/1 for domestic students; for spring admission, 11/1 for domestic students. Applications are processed on a rolling basis. Application fee: $125. *Financial support:* Career-related internships or fieldwork, Federal Work-Study, institutionally sponsored loans, and tuition waivers (partial) available. Support available to part-time students. Financial award application deadline: 4/1; financial award applicants required to submit FAFSA. *Faculty research:* Housing abandonment, industrial rehabilitation of Long Island City, health facilities in Queens County. *Unit head:* Dr. Leonard S. Rodberg, Chairperson, 718-997-5130. *Application contact:* Dr. William Muraskin, Graduate Adviser, 718-997-5130, E-mail: william_muraskin@qc.edu.

Rutgers, The State University of New Jersey, Newark, Graduate School, Program in Public Administration, Newark, NJ 07102. Offers health care administration (MPA); human resources administration (MPA); public administration (PhD); public management (MPA); public policy analysis (MPA); urban systems and issues (MPA). *Accreditation:* NASPAA (one or more programs are accredited). Part-time and evening/weekend programs available. *Faculty:* 9 full-time (3 women). *Students:* 19 full-time (12 women), 24 part-time (11 women); includes 10 Black or African American, non-Hispanic/Latino; 14 Asian, non-Hispanic/Latino; 3 Hispanic/Latino. 46 applicants, 24% accepted, 6 enrolled. In 2010, 8 doctorates awarded. *Degree requirements:* For master's, comprehensive exam, thesis or alternative; for doctorate, thesis/dissertation. *Entrance requirements:* For master's, GRE, minimum undergraduate B average; for doctorate, GRE, MPA, minimum B average. *Application deadline:* For fall admission, 7/1 priority date for domestic students; for spring admission, 12/1 for domestic students. Applications are processed on a rolling basis. Application fee: $60. Electronic applications accepted. *Expenses:* Tuition, state resident: part-time $600 per credit. Tuition, nonresident: full-time $10,694. *Financial support:* In 2010–11, 3 fellowships (averaging $18,000 per year), 11 teaching assistantships with full and partial tuition reimbursements (averaging $23,112 per year) were awarded; career-related internships or fieldwork also available. Support available to part-time students. Financial award application deadline: 3/1. *Faculty research:* Government finance, municipal and state government, public productivity. *Unit head:* Dr. Norma Riccucci, Chairman and Director, 973-353-5093 Ext. 16, E-mail: riccucci@andromeda.rutgers.edu. *Application contact:* Gail Daniels, Assistant Dean for Student Services, 201-973-5093 Ext. 11, E-mail: gaild@andromeda.rutgers.edu.

Rutgers, The State University of New Jersey, Newark, Graduate School, Program in Urban Systems, Newark, NJ 07102. Offers PhD. Program offered jointly with University of Medicine and Dentistry of New Jersey, New Jersey Institute of Technology. *Faculty:* 5 full-time (3 women). *Students:* 15 full-time (13 women), 19 part-time (15 women); includes 16 Black or African American, non-Hispanic/Latino. 19 applicants, 100% accepted, 16 enrolled. In 2010, 2 doctorates awarded. Application fee: $60. *Expenses:* Tuition, state resident: part-time $600 per credit. Tuition, nonresident: full-time $10,694. *Financial support:* In 2010–11, 3 fellowships (averaging $18,000 per year), 9 teaching assistantships with full and partial tuition reimbursements (averaging $23,112 per year) were awarded. *Unit head:* Dr. Alan Sadovnik, Head, 973-353-3532, E-mail: sadovnik@andromeda.rutgers.edu. *Application contact:* Jason Hand, Director of Admissions, 973-353-5205, Fax: 973-353-1440.

Saint Louis University, Graduate Education, College of Education and Public Service, Department of Public Policy Studies, St. Louis, MO 63103-2097. Offers geographic information systems (Certificate); organizational development (Certificate); public administration (MAPA); public policy analysis (PhD); urban affairs (MAUA); urban planning and real estate development (MUPRED). *Accreditation:* NASPAA. Part-time programs available. *Degree requirements:* For master's, comprehensive exam (for some programs), thesis (for some programs); for doctorate, comprehensive exam, thesis/dissertation, preliminary exams. *Entrance requirements:* For master's, GMAT, GRE General Test, or LSAT, letters of recommendation, resume; for doctorate, GMAT, GRE General Test, or LSAT, letters of recommendation, resumé, interview, transcripts, goal statement. Additional exam requirements/recommendations for international students: Required—TOEFL (minimum score 525 paper-based; 194 computer-based). Electronic applications accepted. *Faculty research:* Urban politics, brown fields, e-government, and administration, evaluation research, community development, electronic government and governance.

San Francisco Art Institute, Graduate Program, Department of Urban Studies, San Francisco, CA 94133. Offers MA. *Entrance requirements:* Additional exam requirements/recommendations for international students: Required—TOEFL (minimum score 580 paper-based; 237 computer-based). Electronic applications accepted.

Savannah State University, Master of Science in Urban Studies and Planning Program, Savannah, GA 31404. Offers MS. Part-time programs available. *Faculty:* 1 (woman) full-time, 5 part-time/adjunct (0 women). *Students:* 9 full-time (7 women), 3 part-time (0 women); includes 8 Black or African American, non-Hispanic/Latino; 1 Asian, non-Hispanic/Latino. Average age 34. In 2010, 8 master's awarded. *Degree requirements:* For master's, thesis optional. *Entrance requirements:* For master's, GRE. Additional exam requirements/recommendations for international students: Required—TOEFL. *Application deadline:* For fall admission, 7/1 priority date for domestic students, 5/15 for international students; for spring admission, 10/31 priority date for domestic students, 10/1 for international students. Applications are processed on a rolling basis. Application fee: $25. *Expenses:* Tuition, state resident: full-time $4042. Tuition, nonresident: full-time $15,028. Required fees: $1350. *Financial support:* In 2010–11, 5 students received support, including 1 fellowship (averaging $1,000 per year), 2 research assistantships (averaging $2,000 per year); career-related internships or fieldwork, Federal Work-Study, institutionally sponsored loans, and scholarships/grants also available. Support available to part-time students. Financial award applicants required to submit FAFSA. *Faculty research:* Transportation, political effectiveness, labor, sociology, criminal justice, waste management. *Application contact:* Dr. Rukmana Deden, Graduate Coordinator, 912-356-2982, E-mail: rukmanad@savannahstate.edu.

Simon Fraser University, Graduate Studies, Faculty of Arts and Social Sciences, Urban Studies Program, Burnaby, BC V5A 1S6, Canada. Offers MUS, Graduate Diploma. *Degree requirements:* For master's, project.

Southern Connecticut State University, School of Graduate Studies, School of Arts and Sciences, Program in Urban Studies, New Haven, CT 06515-1355. Offers MS, MSW/MS. Part-time and evening/weekend programs available. *Students:* 4 full-time (1 woman), 8 part-time (4 women); includes 7 Black or African American, non-Hispanic/Latino. 26 applicants, 23% accepted, 4 enrolled. In 2010, 3 master's awarded. *Degree requirements:* For master's, thesis or alternative. *Entrance requirements:* For master's, interview, minimum QPA of 2.5. *Application deadline:* For fall admission, 7/15 priority date for domestic students. Applications are processed on a rolling basis. Application fee: $50. Electronic applications accepted. *Expenses:* Tuition, state resident: full-time $5137; part-time $518 per credit. Tuition, nonresident: part-time $542 per credit. Required fees: $4008; $55 per semester. Tuition and fees vary according to program. *Financial support:* Career-related internships or fieldwork available. Financial award application deadline: 4/15; financial award applicants required to submit FAFSA. *Unit head:* Dr. Eric West, Interim Chair of Geography, 203-392-6693, E-mail: weste1@southernct.edu. *Application contact:* Dr. Eric West, Graduate Coordinator, 203-392-6693.

Temple University, College of Liberal Arts, Department of Geography and Urban Studies, Philadelphia, PA 19122-6096. Offers geography (MA); geography and urban studies (MA); urban studies (MA, PhD). *Faculty:* 25 full-time (16 women). *Students:* 19 full-time (11 women), 12 part-time (6 women); includes 3 Black or African American, non-Hispanic/Latino; 2 Asian, non-Hispanic/Latino; 1 Hispanic/Latino; 3 international. 69 applicants, 41% accepted, 11 enrolled. In 2010, 13 master's awarded. *Degree requirements:* For master's, comprehensive exam, thesis or alternative. *Entrance requirements:* For master's, GRE General Test, minimum GPA of 3.0. Additional exam requirements/recommendations for international students: Required—TOEFL (minimum score 550 paper-based; 213 computer-based; 79 iBT). *Application deadline:* For fall admission, 1/15 for domestic students, 12/15 for international students; for spring admission, 10/15 for domestic students, 8/1 for international students. Applications are processed on a rolling basis. Application fee: $50. Electronic applications accepted. *Financial support:*

Fellowships, teaching assistantships, career-related internships or fieldwork, Federal Work-Study, and tuition waivers (partial) available. Financial award application deadline: 1/15; financial award applicants required to submit FAFSA. *Faculty research:* Environmental issues, urban political economy, poverty and unemployment, neighborhood development, African and Asian urbanization, housing, computer cartography. Total annual research expenditures: $400,000. *Unit head:* Dr. Michele Masucci, Chair, 215-204-7692, Fax: 215-204-7833, E-mail: masucci@temple.edu. *Application contact:* Dr. Michele Masucci, Chair, 215-204-7692, Fax: 215-204-7833, E-mail: masucci@temple.edu.

Tufts University, Graduate School of Arts and Sciences, Department of Urban and Environmental Policy and Planning, Medford, MA 02155. Offers community development (MA); environmental policy (MA); health and human welfare (MA); housing policy (MA); international environment/development policy (MA); public policy (MPP); MA/MS; MALD/MA. *Accreditation:* ACSP (one or more programs are accredited). Part-time programs available. *Degree requirements:* For master's, thesis, internship. *Entrance requirements:* For master's, GRE General Test. Additional exam requirements/recommendations for international students: Required—TOEFL (minimum score 550 paper-based; 213 computer-based; 80 iBT). Electronic applications accepted. *Expenses:* Contact institution.

Université du Québec à Montréal, Graduate Programs, Program in Urban Analysis and Management, Montréal, QC H3C 3P8, Canada. Offers MA. Program offered jointly with Université du Québec, École nationale d'administration publique and Université du Québec, Institut National de la Recherche Scientifique. Part-time programs available. *Entrance requirements:* For master's, appropriate bachelor's degree or equivalent and proficiency in French.

Université du Québec à Montréal, Graduate Programs, Program in Urban Studies, Montréal, QC H3C 3P8, Canada. Offers MA, PhD. Part-time programs available. *Degree requirements:* For doctorate, thesis/dissertation. *Entrance requirements:* For doctorate, appropriate master's degree or equivalent, proficiency in French.

Université du Québec, École nationale d'administration publique, Graduate Program in Public Administration, Program in Urban Analysis and Management, Quebec, QC G1K 9E5, Canada. Offers MAGU. Part-time programs available. *Entrance requirements:* For master's, appropriate bachelor's degree, proficiency in French.

Université du Québec, Institut National de la Recherche Scientifique, Graduate Programs, Research Center—Urbanization, Culture and Society, Québec, QC G1K 9A9, Canada. Offers demography (M Sc, PhD); research and public action (MA); urban studies (M Sc, PhD). Programs given in French. Part-time programs available. *Faculty:* 36. *Students:* 150 full-time (87 women), 13 part-time (5 women), 28 international. Average age 33. In 2010, 12 master's, 8 doctorates awarded. *Degree requirements:* For master's, thesis optional; for doctorate, thesis/dissertation. *Entrance requirements:* For master's, appropriate bachelor's degree, proficiency in French; for doctorate, appropriate master's degree, proficiency in French. *Application deadline:* For fall admission, 3/30 for domestic and international students; for winter admission, 11/1 for domestic and international students; for spring admission, 3/1 for domestic and international students. Application fee: $30. *Financial support:* Fellowships, research assistantships, teaching assistantships available. *Faculty research:* Regional space, urban and metropolitan space, micro-urban space. *Unit head:* Claire Poitras, Director, 514-499-4037, Fax: 514-499-4065, E-mail: claire.poitras@ucs.inrs.ca. *Application contact:* Yvonne Boisvert, Registrar, 418-654-3861, Fax: 418-654-3858, E-mail: registrariat@adm.inrs.ca.

University at Albany, State University of New York, College of Arts and Sciences, Department of Sociology, Albany, NY 12222-0001. Offers demography (Certificate); sociology (MA, PhD); urban policy (Certificate). Terminal master's awarded for partial completion of doctoral program. *Degree requirements:* For master's, thesis; for doctorate, thesis/dissertation, 2 specialization exams, research tool. *Entrance requirements:* For master's and doctorate, GRE General Test. Additional exam requirements/recommendations for international students: Required—TOEFL (minimum score 213 computer-based). Electronic applications accepted. *Faculty research:* Gender and equality, crime and deviance, aging, work and organizations, social demography.

The University of Akron, Graduate School, Buchtel College of Arts and Sciences, Department of Public Administration and Urban Studies, Program in Urban Studies, Akron, OH 44325. Offers urban studies (MA); urban studies and public affairs (PhD). *Students:* 19 full-time (13 women), 29 part-time (18 women); includes 18 Black or African American, non-Hispanic/Latino; 1 Two or more races, non-Hispanic/Latino, 7 international. Average age 40. 20 applicants, 35% accepted, 7 enrolled. In 2010, 2 master's, 7 doctorates awarded. *Degree requirements:* For master's, thesis optional; for doctorate, one foreign language, comprehensive exam, thesis/dissertation. *Entrance requirements:* For master's, GRE, GMAT, LSAT, MAT (if undergraduate cumulative GPA less than 3.0), minimum GPA of 3.0, resume, one page personal essay; for doctorate, GRE General Test, minimum graduate GPA of 3.5, three letters of recommendation, statement of purpose, writing sample. Additional exam requirements/recommendations for international students: Required—TOEFL (minimum score 570 paper-based; 230 computer-based; 88 iBT). *Application deadline:* For fall admission, 7/1 priority date for domestic and international students; for spring admission, 11/15 priority date for domestic students, 11/14 priority date for international students. Applications are processed on a rolling basis. Application fee: $30 ($40 for international students). Electronic applications accepted. *Expenses:* Tuition, state resident: full-time $6800; part-time $378 per credit hour. Tuition, nonresident: full-time $11,644; part-time $647 per credit hour. Required fees: $1265. One-time fee: $30 full-time. *Unit head:* Dr. Raymond Cox, Chair, 330-972-7616, E-mail: rcox@uakron.edu. *Application contact:* Dr. Raymond Cox, Chair, 330-972-7616, E-mail: rcox@uakron.edu.

University of California, Irvine, School of Social Ecology, Department of Planning, Policy and Design, Irvine, CA 92697. Offers planning, policy and design (PhD); urban and regional planning (MURP). *Accreditation:* ACSP (one or more programs are accredited). *Students:* 121 full-time (69 women); includes 36 minority (2 Black or African American, non-Hispanic/Latino; 1 American Indian or Alaska Native, non-Hispanic/Latino; 19 Asian, non-Hispanic/Latino; 14 Hispanic/Latino), 31 international. Average age 28. 252 applicants, 55% accepted, 50 enrolled. In 2010, 29 master's, 9 doctorates awarded. *Degree requirements:* For doctorate, thesis/dissertation, research project. *Entrance requirements:* For master's and doctorate, GRE General Test, minimum GPA of 3.0. Additional exam requirements/recommendations for international students: Required—TOEFL (minimum score 550 paper-based; 213 computer-based). *Application deadline:* For fall admission, 1/15 priority date for domestic and international students. Application fee: $80 ($100 for international students). Electronic applications accepted. *Financial support:* Fellowships with tuition reimbursements, research assistantships with full tuition reimbursements, teaching assistantships with tuition reimbursements, institutionally sponsored loans, traineeships, health care benefits, and unspecified assistantships available. Financial award application deadline: 1/15; financial award applicants required to submit FAFSA. *Faculty research:* Community and social policy, economic development, land-use and growth management, transportation planning, environmental policy. *Unit head:* David L. Feldman, Chair, 949-824-4384, Fax: 949-824-3056, E-mail: feldmand@uci.edu. *Application contact:* Janet Gallagher, Academic Coordinator, 949-824-9849, Fax: 949-824-8566, E-mail: ppd@uci.edu.

University of Central Oklahoma, College of Graduate Studies and Research, College of Liberal Arts, Department of Political Science, Program in Urban Affairs, Edmond, OK 73034-5209. Offers MA. Part-time programs available. *Entrance requirements:* Additional exam requirements/recommendations for international students: Required—TOEFL (minimum score 550 paper-based; 213 computer-based). Electronic applications accepted.

University of Delaware, College of Human Services, Education and Public Policy, Center for Energy and Environmental Policy, Program in Urban Affairs and Public Policy, Newark, DE 19716. Offers community development and nonprofit leadership (MA); energy and environ-

Urban Studies

University of Delaware (continued)
mental policy (MA); governance, planning and management (PhD); historic preservation (MA); social and urban policy (PhD); technology, environment and society (PhD). Part-time programs available. Terminal master's awarded for partial completion of doctoral program. *Degree requirements:* For master's, analytical paper or thesis; for doctorate, thesis/dissertation. *Entrance requirements:* For master's, GRE General Test, minimum GPA of 3.0; for doctorate, GRE General Test, minimum GPA of 3.5. Additional exam requirements/recommendations for international students: Required—TOEFL. Electronic applications accepted. *Faculty research:* Political economy; social policy analysis; technology and society; historic preservation; urban policy.

University of Lethbridge, School of Graduate Studies, Lethbridge, AB T1K 3M4, Canada. Offers accounting (MScM); addictions counseling (M Sc); agricultural biotechnology (M Sc); agricultural studies (M Sc, MA); anthropology (MA); archaeology (MA); art (MA, MFA); biochemistry (M Sc); biological sciences (M Sc); biomolecular science (PhD); biosystems and biodiversity (PhD); Canadian studies (MA); chemistry (M Sc); computer science (M Sc); computer science and geographical information science (M Sc); counseling psychology (M Ed); dramatic arts (MA); earth, space, and physical science (PhD); economics (MA); educational leadership (M Ed); English (MA); environmental science (M Sc); evolution and behavior (PhD); exercise science (M Sc); finance (MScM); French (MA); French/German (MA); French/Spanish (MA); general education (M Ed); general management (MScM); geography (M Sc, MA); German (MA); health science (M Sc); history (MA); human resource management and labour relations (MScM); individualized multidisciplinary (M Sc, MA); information systems (MScM); international management (MScM); kinesiology (M Sc, MA); management (M Sc, MA); marketing (MScM); mathematics (M Sc); music (M Mus, MA); Native American studies (MA); neuroscience (M Sc, PhD); new media (MA); nursing (M Sc); philosophy (MA); physics (M Sc); policy and strategy (MScM); political science (MA); psychology (M Sc, MA); religious studies (MA); social sciences (MA); sociology (MA); theatre and dramatic arts (MFA); theoretical and computational science (PhD); urban and regional studies (MA); women's studies (MA). Part-time and evening/weekend programs available. *Degree requirements:* For doctorate, comprehensive exam, thesis/dissertation. *Entrance requirements:* For master's, GMAT (M Sc in management), bachelor's degree in related field, minimum GPA of 3.0 during previous 20 graded semester courses, 2 years teaching or related experience (M Ed); for doctorate, master's degree, minimum graduate GPA of 3.5. Additional exam requirements/recommendations for international students: Required—TOEFL. *Faculty research:* Movement and brain plasticity, gibberellin physiology, photosynthesis, carbon cycling, molecular properties of main-group ring components.

University of Louisville, Graduate School, College of Arts and Sciences, Department of Urban and Public Affairs, Louisville, KY 40208. Offers public administration (MPA), including human resources management, non-profit management, public policy and administration; urban and public affairs (PhD), including urban planning and development, urban policy and administration; urban planning (MUP), including administration of planning organizations, housing and community development, land use and environmental planning, spatial analysis. Part-time and evening/weekend programs available. *Faculty:* 22 full-time (7 women), 8 part-time/adjunct (1 woman). *Students:* 73 full-time (36 women), 31 part-time (18 women); includes 11 Black or African American, non-Hispanic/Latino; 2 Asian, non-Hispanic/Latino; 2 Hispanic/Latino; 1 Native Hawaiian or other Pacific Islander, non-Hispanic/Latino; 2 Two or more races, non-Hispanic/Latino, 11 international. Average age 31. 96 applicants, 67% accepted, 37 enrolled. In 2010, 28 master's, 5 doctorates awarded. Terminal master's awarded for partial completion of doctoral program. *Degree requirements:* For master's, internship; for doctorate, comprehensive exam, thesis/dissertation. *Entrance requirements:* For master's, GRE General Test, minimum GPA of 3.0; for doctorate, GRE General Test, master's degree in appropriate field. Additional exam requirements/recommendations for international students: Required—TOEFL (minimum score 550 paper-based; 213 computer-based; 79 iBT). *Application deadline:* For fall admission, 7/15 for domestic students; for spring admission, 11/15 for domestic students. Applications are processed on a rolling basis. Application fee: $50. Electronic applications accepted. *Expenses:* Tuition, state resident: full-time $9144; part-time $508 per credit hour. Tuition, nonresident: full-time $19,026; part-time $1057 per credit hour. Tuition and fees vary according to program and reciprocity agreements. *Financial support:* In 2010–11, 23 students received support; fellowships, research assistantships, health care benefits available. Financial award application deadline: 3/1. *Faculty research:* Housing and community development, performance-based budgeting, environmental policy and natural hazards, sustainability, real estate development, comparative urban development. *Unit head:* Dr. David Simpson, Chair, 502-852-8019, Fax: 502-852-4558, E-mail: dave.simpson@louisville.edu. *Application contact:* Patty Sarley, Graduate Student Advisor, 502-852-7914, Fax: 502-852-4558, E-mail: plclea01@louisville.edu.

University of Maryland, Baltimore County, Graduate School, College of Arts, Humanities and Social Sciences, Department of Public Policy, Program in Public Policy, Baltimore, MD 21250. Offers economics (PhD); education (MPP, PhD); evaluation (MPP); health (MPP, PhD); management (MPP, PhD); policy history (PhD); urban (MPP, PhD). Part-time and evening/weekend programs available. *Faculty:* 10 full-time (3 women), 2 part-time/adjunct (0 women). *Students:* 62 full-time (37 women), 94 part-time (54 women); includes 39 minority (25 Black or African American, non-Hispanic/Latino; 6 Asian, non-Hispanic/Latino; 2 Hispanic/Latino; 1 Native Hawaiian or other Pacific Islander, non-Hispanic/Latino; 5 Two or more races, non-Hispanic/Latino), 10 international. Average age 36. 102 applicants, 65% accepted, 28 enrolled. In 2010, 20 master's, 8 doctorates awarded. Terminal master's awarded for partial completion of doctoral program. *Degree requirements:* For master's, thesis optional, public analysis paper, internship for pre-service; for doctorate, comprehensive exam, thesis/dissertation, comprehensive and field qualifying exams. *Entrance requirements:* For master's, GRE General Test, 3 academic letters of reference, transcripts, resume; for doctorate, GRE General Test, 3 academic letters of reference, transcripts, resume, research paper. Additional exam requirements/recommendations for international students: Required—TOEFL (minimum score 550 paper-based; 213 computer-based; 80 iBT). *Application deadline:* For fall admission, 1/15 priority date for domestic students, 1/1 priority date for international students; for spring admission, 11/1 priority date for domestic students, 5/1 priority date for international students. Applications are processed on a rolling basis. Application fee: $50. Electronic applications accepted. *Financial support:* In 2010–11, 26 students received support, including fellowships (averaging $3,000 per year), 21 research assistantships with full tuition reimbursements available (averaging $17,400 per year); career-related internships or fieldwork, Federal Work-Study, scholarships/grants, health care benefits, and unspecified assistantships also available. Support available to part-time students. Financial award application deadline: 1/15; financial award applicants required to submit FAFSA. *Faculty research:* Health policy, education policy, urban policy, public management, evaluation and analytical methods. *Unit head:* Dr. Donald Norris, Chair, 410-455-1455, E-mail: norris@umbc.edu. *Application contact:* Sally F. Helms, Administrator of Academic Affairs, 410-455-3202, Fax: 410-455-1172, E-mail: gradposi@umbc.edu.

University of New Orleans, Graduate School, College of Liberal Arts, School of Urban Planning and Regional Studies, Program in Urban Studies, New Orleans, LA 70148. Offers MS, PhD. *Degree requirements:* For master's, thesis; for doctorate, thesis/dissertation. *Entrance requirements:* For master's, GRE General Test. Additional exam requirements/recommendations for international students: Required—TOEFL (minimum score 550 paper-based; 213 computer-based; 79 iBT). Electronic applications accepted. *Faculty research:* Urban economic development, environmental planning and analysis, social and cultural change.

University of Wisconsin–Milwaukee, Graduate School, College of Letters and Sciences, Department of History, Milwaukee, WI 53201-0413. Offers global history (PhD); history (MA); modern studies (PhD); urban history (PhD). Part-time programs available. *Faculty:* 34 full-time (16 women). *Students:* 29 full-time (12 women), 46 part-time (19 women); includes 1 Black or African American, non-Hispanic/Latino; 2 Hispanic/Latino, 2 international. Average age 32. 80 applicants, 60% accepted, 19 enrolled. In 2010, 25 master's, 1 doctorate awarded. *Degree requirements:* For master's, comprehensive exam, thesis or alternative; for doctorate, thesis/dissertation. *Entrance requirements:* For master's and doctorate, GRE General Test. Additional exam requirements/recommendations for international students: Required—TOEFL (minimum score 550 paper-based; 79 iBT), IELTS (minimum score 6.5). *Application deadline:* For fall admission, 1/1 priority date for domestic students; for spring admission, 9/1 for domestic students. Applications are processed on a rolling basis. Application fee: $56 ($96 for international students). Electronic applications accepted. *Financial support:* In 2010–11, 23 teaching assistantships were awarded; career-related internships or fieldwork and unspecified assistantships also available. Support available to part-time students. Financial award application deadline: 4/15; financial award applicants required to submit FAFSA. Total annual research expenditures: $9,560. *Unit head:* Aims McGuinness, Representative, 414-229-4361, Fax: 414-229-2435, E-mail: smia@uwm.edu. *Application contact:* General Information Contact, 414-229-4982, Fax: 414-229-6967, E-mail: gradschool@uwm.edu.

University of Wisconsin–Milwaukee, Graduate School, College of Letters and Sciences, Interdepartmental Program in Urban Studies, Milwaukee, WI 53201-0413. Offers MS, PhD, MLIS/MS. *Faculty:* 32 full-time (13 women). *Students:* 15 full-time (7 women), 32 part-time (16 women); includes 7 Black or African American, non-Hispanic/Latino; 2 American Indian or Alaska Native, non-Hispanic/Latino; 1 Hispanic/Latino, 4 international. Average age 37. 16 applicants, 56% accepted, 4 enrolled. In 2010, 7 master's, 4 doctorates awarded. *Degree requirements:* For master's, thesis or alternative; for doctorate, thesis/dissertation. *Entrance requirements:* For doctorate, GRE General Test. Additional exam requirements/recommendations for international students: Required—TOEFL (minimum score 550 paper-based; 79 iBT), IELTS (minimum score 6.5). *Application deadline:* For fall admission, 1/1 priority date for domestic students; for spring admission, 9/1 for domestic students. Applications are processed on a rolling basis. Application fee: $56 ($96 for international students). Electronic applications accepted. *Financial support:* In 2010–11, 2 fellowships, 1 research assistantship, 5 teaching assistantships were awarded; career-related internships or fieldwork, unspecified assistantships, and project assistantships also available. Support available to part-time students. Financial award application deadline: 4/15; financial award applicants required to submit FAFSA. Total annual research expenditures: $1,224. *Unit head:* Amanda Seligman, Representative, 414-229-4751, Fax: 414-229-4266, E-mail: seligman@uwm.edu. *Application contact:* General Information Contact, 414-229-4982, Fax: 414-229-6967, E-mail: gradschool@uwm.edu.

Wright State University, School of Graduate Studies, College of Liberal Arts, Department of Urban Affairs and Geography, Dayton, OH 45435. Offers public administration (MPA). *Accreditation:* NASPAA. *Degree requirements:* For master's, thesis optional. *Entrance requirements:* For master's, interview, minimum GPA of 2.7. Additional exam requirements/recommendations for international students: Required—TOEFL. *Faculty research:* Strategic planning, economic development, housing and public management.

Cornell University
ILR School

CORNELL UNIVERSITY

ILR School

Programs of Study

Cornell University and the ILR School are world-renowned global institutions that have earned a reputation for excellence. The School's graduate degree programs provide a broad-based foundation with a specific, intense focus on the interaction between people and organizations in the workplace. ILR's unique depth and breadth sets it apart from other programs. No other educational institution has graduate programs in workplace studies that are as comprehensive, or the number of faculty teaching and doing research on workplace issues in one school. The curriculum is thorough, rigorous, and comprehensive, combining experience and theory in innovative ways. ILR studies many areas that shape the working world and contribute to an organization's success in a global economy. These include human resource management; labor-management relations; labor economics; organizational behavior; international and comparative labor; labor relations, labor law, and history; conflict resolution; management development; diversity management; employment and disability; and social statistics. ILR was the first school to develop a graduate degree program in the study of employment and workplace issues, and its advanced degrees are considered among the best in the world.

ILR offers five top-ranked and highly regarded graduate degree programs. The **Master of Industrial and Labor Relations (M.I.L.R.)** is a two-year, professional, career-focused degree for those interested in putting their education into practice. The M.I.L.R. is specifically for students preparing to enter the workforce or professionals who wish to enhance their education and skills. The **Master of Industrial and Labor Relations/Master of Business Administration (M.I.L.R./M.B.A.)** is a dual-degree program offered jointly by the ILR School and the Samuel Curtis Johnson Graduate School of Management at Cornell, giving graduates a powerful double credential highly valued by employers. The **Master of Industrial and Labor Relations/Master in Management** is a global three-year dual degree that allows students the opportunity for an international experience that will advance their career goals and increase their marketability worldwide with degrees from ILR and ESCP Europe, which includes five fully integrated campuses in Paris, London, Madrid, Berlin, and Torino. The **Master of Science and the Doctor of Philosophy (M.S./Ph.D.)** are excellent for students considering academic or research careers. The ILR graduate field is multidisciplinary, focusing broadly on work and employment relationships from a variety of social science perspectives, including political science, history, sociology, psychology, and economics. Students applying to the M.S./Ph.D. program apply to one of four ILR departments: organizational behavior; human resource studies; labor relations, law, and history; or international and comparative labor. The **Master of Professional Studies in Industrial and Labor Relations (M.P.S.)** is designed for individuals who are already seasoned practitioners and want to expand or advance into a specific competency or upgrade their skills and understanding.

Candidates for the M.I.L.R. degree come from a variety of backgrounds and are interested in preparing for positions in human resource management, labor relations (including collective bargaining), and public policy. The M.I.L.R. reflects the need of future practitioners to become broadly familiar with all major aspects of the field and to become particularly competent in one of five areas: human resources and organizations, collective representation, dispute resolution, international and comparative labor, or labor-market policy. Students complete a minimum of 48 credits in courses and seminars, including required courses in collective bargaining, labor economics, labor and employment law, human resource management, organizational behavior, and statistics. Students have a great deal of flexibility in choosing courses in addition to their required core courses. Courses offered by the ILR School and the thirteen other colleges at Cornell provide opportunity for cross-disciplinary work. Some candidates with a law (J.D.) or M.B.A. degree may be able to obtain an M.I.L.R. degree in two semesters. The M.P.S. degree is limited to individuals with substantive professionally related work experience who wish to update their knowledge of current practices. Applicants for this degree are often sponsored by their governments or organizations. Degree requirements include course work and an M.P.S. project. Students may choose to study part-time in New York City in the M.P.S. New York program or full-time in residence on the Ithaca campus. M.S. and Ph.D. candidates select major and minor subjects from the following areas: collective bargaining, labor law, and labor history; organizational behavior; human resource studies; and international and comparative labor. Minor subjects can also include social statistics and labor economics. Minor subjects in fields outside ILR are encouraged. Each candidate's program is supervised by a special committee of faculty members chosen by the candidate. The average M.S. program requires two years; the doctoral program typically takes an additional three years.

Research Facilities

The ILR School's Catherwood Library, with more than 232,000 volumes, is regarded as the world's most comprehensive source of information on work, employment, and labor issues. Catherwood's Kheel Center for Labor-Management Documentation and Archives ranks as one of three major centers of its type in the country. Catherwood is one of seventeen libraries constituting the Cornell University Library, ranked as one of the ten largest academic research libraries in the United States, with more than 7 million printed volumes, 65,000 journal and newspaper subscriptions, and more than 40,000 networked electronic databases available to users. Networked computer facilities in Catherwood and in other campus libraries are provided for graduate students, and a rapidly expanding array of electronic and full-text resources is available for use outside of the library. Catherwood's programs and services are aimed at providing easy access to its outstanding collections. Library staff members offer seminars and individualized training to acquaint graduate students with the research potential of Catherwood's print and electronic holdings.

Financial Aid

A small number of fellowships may be awarded on a competitive basis by Cornell University and the ILR School for students interested in the M.I.L.R., M.P.S., or dual-degree programs. In addition, the School awards a limited number of merit-based teaching, research, or graduate assistantships to qualified students in their second year of study in the M.I.L.R. degree program. Assistantships require 15–20 hours of work each week in the School's instructional, research, or extension programs. Funding is guaranteed for students accepted in the M.S./Ph.D. programs.

Cost of Study

Tuition is $27,040 for the 2011–12 academic year for both state residents and out-of-state students in the M.I.L.R. and M.P.S. degree programs. Books cost between $900 and $1200 per year; there is also a thesis fee for M.S./Ph.D. students.

Living and Housing Costs

Budgets for single students to live at a modest comfort level average $1200 per month. Married students should expect greater expenses. The largest variable is rent; both University and private housing are available to graduate students.

Student Group

The population of graduate students at Cornell is more than 6,000, representing all regions of the United States and many other countries. Candidates for the M.I.L.R. degree, approximately half of the 180 graduate students in ILR, have a wide variety of academic and employment backgrounds. M.I.L.R. candidates generally choose professional careers, while Ph.D. candidates usually aim for academic appointments.

Student Outcomes

Most students have job offers before graduation, even in tough economies. ILR graduates work in every region of the United States and around the world in business, manufacturing, consulting, technology, not-for-profit, unions, government, and other sectors. The ILR Office of Career Services provides a wide variety of services, including individual advising, workshops, resume reviews, career fairs, networking assistance, job listings, and practice interviews to help students explore their career options and develop effective job-search strategies. The office manages an on-campus recruitment program, with representatives of numerous corporations, labor unions, government agencies, and labor law firms interviewing students for positions in human resources and labor relations. The office also cultivates contacts with alumni and others working in the field. Further career information is available from the Office of Career Services, 201 Ives Hall, Cornell University (phone: 607-255-7816; Web site: http://www.ilr.cornell.edu/careerservices/). A few of the leading employers of M.I.L.R. degree recipients are the AFL-CIO, American Express Company, Citigroup, Dell, General Electric, General Mills, Honeywell, IBM, Microsoft, the National Labor Relations Board (NLRB), and Shell Oil Company. The mean salary for a recent M.I.L.R. graduating class was approximately $73,982. The mean salary for recent M.I.L.R. graduates choosing the corporate sector was $80,857, with a mean signing bonus of $12,065. Those recently completing doctoral degree programs found employment at such places as Cornell, Washington University, the London School of Business, the University of Delaware, Cardiff University in Wales, the University of Michigan, Harvard Business School, and the U.S. Bureau of Labor Statistics.

Location

Ithaca is a university town of nearly 40,000, set in the center of the beautiful Finger Lakes region of upstate New York. The area is rich in outdoor recreational resources for swimming, skiing, and boating. Cornell and neighboring Ithaca College as well as community groups in the creative and performing arts contribute to a lively and diverse cultural life that includes plays, concerts, opera, ballet, and lectures.

The University

The Cornell tradition of graduate education recognizes that each student has different needs, strengths, and goals, and the University makes every effort to accommodate students' specific requirements and incomes. Every member of the social science faculties at Cornell is a potential resource to each ILR graduate student, whatever the field of study, providing intellectual resources that are extensive and cross college boundaries. Distinguished scholars in economics, sociology, and psychology can be found in ILR as well as in appropriate fields in the College of Arts and Sciences, the College of Human Ecology, and the Johnson School of Management; in other professional fields, such as developmental sociology, child development and family relations, agricultural economics, and business law; and in research institutes such as the Southeast Asia and Latin American Centers.

Applying

While a strong background in the social sciences is both appropriate and helpful for advanced work at ILR, those with different backgrounds (engineering, law, business) regularly enroll. The deadlines for fall admission are January 1 and February 15; for spring admission, the deadline is October 15 (M.I.L.R. and M.P.S.only). Ph.D. candidates generally undertake master's thesis research before entering the Ph.D. program. Exceptionally well-qualified applicants may be admitted directly to the doctoral program with only a bachelor's degree. All applicants must take the General Test of the Graduate Record Examinations (GRE) or the Graduate Management Admission Test (GMAT). International students are also required to take the Test of English as a Foreign Language (TOEFL).

Correspondence and Information

ILR Graduate Programs Office
ILR School
218 Ives Hall
Cornell University
Ithaca, New York 14853-3901

Phone: 607-255-1522
E-mail: ilrgradapplicant@cornell.edu
Web site: http://www.ilr.cornell.edu/graddegreeprograms

Cornell University

THE FACULTY

The graduate faculty members at Cornell's ILR School represent a wide spectrum of the social and behavioral sciences—cultural anthropology, economics, history, law, political science, psychology, social psychology, sociology, and statistics—offering courses, advising, consulting, directing research activities, and sharing research opportunities. In addition, students may take courses from and select as advisers other Cornell faculty members in the social sciences, the humanities, mathematics, and engineering.

Department of Labor Relations, Law, and History

Lee H. Adler, Senior Extension Associate; J.D., Golden Gate. Law.
Kate Brofenbrenner, Senior Lecturer and Director of Labor Education Research; Ph.D., Cornell. Labor and industrial relations.
Alex Colvin, Associate Professor; Ph.D., Cornell.
Lance Compa, Senior Lecturer; J.D., Yale. Law.
Maria L. Cook, Associate Professor; Ph.D., Berkeley. Political science.
Jefferson Cowie, Associate Professor; Ph.D., North Carolina at Chapel Hill. History.
Ileen A. DeVault, Professor; Ph.D., Yale. History.
Michael E. Gold, Associate Professor; J.D., Stanford. Law.
Kate Griffith, Assistant Professor; J.D., NYU. Law.
James A. Gross, Professor; Ph.D., Wisconsin. Labor economics and industrial relations.
Richard W. Hurd, Professor; Ph.D., Vanderbilt. Economics.
Lawrence Kahn, Professor; Ph.D., Berkeley. Economics.
Harry C. Katz, Jack Sheinkman Professor in Collective Bargaining and Dean of the ILR School; Ph.D., Berkeley. Economics.
Sarosh C. Kuruvilla, Professor; Ph.D., Iowa. Business administration.
Risa L. Lieberwitz, Professor; J.D., Florida. Law.
David B. Lipsky, Professor; Ph.D., MIT. Economics.
Nicholas Salvatore, Maurice and Hinda Neufeld Founders Professorship in Industrial and Labor Relations; Ph.D., Berkeley. History.
Ronald L. Seeber, Professor; Ph.D., Illinois. Labor and industrial relations.
Lowell Turner, Professor; Ph.D., Berkeley. Political science.

Department of Human Resource Studies

Rosemary Batt, Professor and Alice Cook Professor of Women and Work; Ph.D., MIT. Human resources.
Bradford Bell, Associate Professor; Ph.D., Michigan State. Organizational psychology.
John H. Bishop, Associate Professor; Ph.D., Michigan. Economics.
Diane Burton, Associate Professor, Ph.D., Stanford. Sociology.
Christopher Collins, Associate Professor; Ph.D., Maryland. Organizational behavior.
Lisa Dragoni, Assistant Professor; Ph.D., Maryland. Organizational behavior and human resource management.
Lee D. Dyer, Professor; Ph.D., Wisconsin. Personnel.
Kevin F. Hallock, Professor; Ph.D., Princeton. Economics.
John Hausknecht, Assistant Professor; Ph.D., Penn State. Industrial and organizational psychology.
Beth Livingston, Assistant Professor, Ph.D., Florida. Organizational behavior/management.
Lisa Hisae Nishii, Assistant Professor; Ph.D., Maryland. Organizational psychology.
Patrick M. Wright, Professor; Ph.D., Michigan State. Business administration.

Department of International and Comparative Labor Relations

Rosemary Batt, Professor and Alice Cook Professor of Women and Work; Ph.D., MIT. Human resources.
John H. Bishop, Associate Professor; Ph.D., Michigan. Economics.
George Boyer, Professor; Ph.D., Wisconsin. Economics.

Alex Colvin, Associate Professor; Ph.D., Cornell. Collective bargaining and conflict resolution.
Lance Compa, Senior Lecturer; J.D., Yale. Law.
Maria L. Cook, Associate Professor; Ph.D., Berkeley. Political science.
Gary S. Fields, Professor; Ph.D., Michigan. Economics.
James A. Gross, Professor; Ph.D., Wisconsin. Labor economics and industrial relations.
Sarosh C. Kuruvilla, Professor; Ph.D., Iowa. Business administration.
Lisa Hisae Nishii, Assistant Professor; Ph.D., Maryland. Organizational psychology.
Lowell Turner, Professor; Ph.D., Berkeley. Political science.

Department of Labor Economics

John M. Abowd, Edmund Ezra Day Professor of Industrial and Labor Relations; Ph.D., Chicago. Economics.
Francine D. Blau, Frances Perkins Professor of Industrial and Labor Relations; Ph.D., Harvard. Economics.
George R. Boyer, Professor; Ph.D., Wisconsin. Economics.
Ronald Ehrenberg, Irving M. Ives Professor of Industrial and Labor Relations; Ph.D., Northwestern. Economics.
Gary S. Fields, Professor; Ph.D., Michigan. Economics.
Matthew Freedman, Assistant Professor, Ph.D., Maryland, College Park. Economics.
Kevin F. Hallock, Professor; Ph.D., Princeton. Economics.
Robert M. Hutchens, Professor; Ph.D., Wisconsin. Economics.
George H. Jakubson, Associate Professor; Ph.D., Wisconsin. Economics.
Lawrence M. Kahn, Professor; Ph.D., Berkeley. Economics.
Robert S. Smith, Professor; Ph.D., Stanford. Economics.

Department of Organizational Behavior

Samuel B. Bacharach, Jean McKelvey-Alice Grant Professor of Labor Management Relations; Ph.D., Wisconsin. Sociology.
Marya Besharov, Assistant Professor; Ph.D., Harvard, Organizational behavior.
Jack Goncalo, Assistant Professor; Ph.D., Berkeley. Business administration.
Tove H. Hammer, Professor; Ph.D., Maryland. Industrial organizational psychology.
Edward J. Lawler, Martin P. Catherwood Professor of Industrial and Labor Relations; Ph.D., Wisconsin. Sociology.
Brian Rubineau, Assistant Professor; Ph.D., MIT. Organization studies and economic sociology.
William J. Sonnenstuhl, Associate Professor; Ph.D., NYU. Sociology.
Pamela S. Tolbert, Professor; Ph.D., UCLA. Sociology.
Michele Williams, Assistant Professor; Ph.D., Michigan. Organizational behavior.

Department of Social Statistics

John A. Bunge, Associate Professor; Ph.D., Ohio. Statistics.
Thomas J. DiCiccio, Associate Professor; Ph.D., Waterloo. Statistics.
Paul F. Velleman, Associate Professor; Ph.D., Princeton. Statistics.
Martin T. Wells, Associate Professor; Ph.D., Berkeley. Mathematics.

ILR School at Cornell's Ives Hall.

GEORGE MASON UNIVERSITY

School of Public Policy

School of
Public Policy

Programs of Study

The School of Public Policy (SPP) at George Mason University seeks to prepare its graduates for positions of responsibility in academic institutions, industry, government, and profit and not-for-profit institutions dedicated to the improvement of both the substance and the processes of public policymaking in the United States and abroad. SPP offers the following degree programs: Doctor of Philosophy (Ph.D.) in public policy; Master of Public Policy (M.P.P.); Master of Arts (M.A.) in international commerce and policy; Master of Arts (M.A.) in transportation policy, operations, and logistics; Master of Science (M.S.) in organization development and knowledge management; and Master of Science in new professional studies: peace operations. In conjunction with the master's programs, SPP offers certificate programs in specialized areas of study including culture and values in social policy, global trade management, and national security and public policy.

The School's programs, led by a distinguished faculty, focus on the interplay of culture, organizations, and technology in a quest to find alternative approaches to public policy decisions and policymaking. Teaching and research is focused on, but not limited to, six themes: Governance; International Commerce and Policy; Entrepreneurship; Regional and Economic Development; Science and Technology Policy; and Culture and Values.

The Ph.D. in Public Policy program is distinctive in its emphasis on the combined influence of technology, culture, and institutions on public policy. To investigate the policy issues associated with substantive policy areas, students develop an in-depth understanding of American institutions, values, and culture; competence in research methods and advanced analytical methodologies; and a comparative, international perspective. The M.P.P. provides a degree for aspiring or experienced professionals who seek career advancement through cutting-edge education and training in policy analysis and development in increasingly technical and global environments. Professional certificates are also offered with this program. The M.A. in International Commerce and Policy program is an interdisciplinary course of study that prepares students for careers in the new global economy. Unlike traditional M.B.A. and international affairs programs, the degree is focused on international economic issues such as global trade and investment. Professional certificates are also offered with this program. The M.A. in Transportation Policy, Operations, and Logistics program is designed for students and practicing professionals engaged in planning, regulating, managing, and operating transportation facilities and services. The M.S. in Organization Development and Knowledge Management program is run in an executive format and is designed for professionals with several years of work experience. It provides students with the conceptual tools and practical guidance to foster organizational change. The Peace Operations program offers candidates a focused degree in various aspects of the planning, regulation, management, and conduct of peace operations.

Research Facilities

George Mason University (GMU) Libraries comprise the Fenwick and Johnson Center Libraries on the Fairfax campus and the Arlington and Prince William campus libraries. Fenwick is the main research library and offers access to a large number of electronic resources in addition to more than 600,000 volumes. GMU provides students with e-mail and Internet access and is a member of the Washington Regional Library Consortium, giving students access to 4 million volumes. In addition to research facilities on campus, GMU is a short distance from major research facilities in the Washington, D.C., area, including the Library of Congress, the National Archives, and numerous governmental agencies. Students may visit the GMU Libraries' Web site for more information (http://library.gmu.edu).

SPP's research centers include the Center for Regional Analysis; the International Center for Applied Studies in Information Technology; the Center for Science and Technology Policy; the Center for Transportation Policy, Operations, and Logistics; the Center for the Study of International Medical Policies and Practices; the State Economic Development Center; the Center for Entrepreneurship and Public Policy; the Center for Global Policy; the Center for Aerospace Policy Research; the Terrorism, Transnational Crime, and Corruption Center (TraCCC); the Transportation and Economic Development Research Center; and the Mason Enterprise Center.

Financial Aid

Full-time Ph.D. candidates are eligible for graduate research assistantships. These assistantships offer a stipend of $19,000 and also include tuition waivers. Financial assistance is granted to master's candidates on a limited basis.

Cost of Study

For the 2011–12 academic year, tuition and fees are $661 per credit hour for in-state students and $1200.25 for out-of-state students.

Living and Housing Costs

The cost of living in the northern Virginia/Washington, D.C., area is comparable to that in most major metropolitan centers. Limited on-campus graduate student housing is available on the Fairfax campus; no on-campus housing is available on the Arlington campus. Most graduate students choose to live off campus.

Student Group

In recent years, SPP enrolled approximately 970 students in its various graduate programs. Fifty-three percent were women, 12 percent were members of minority groups, and 11 percent were international students. Fifteen percent were enrolled in the Ph.D. program, and 85 percent were enrolled in the various master's programs. Sixty-eight percent enrolled part-time, while 32 percent enrolled full-time.

Student Outcomes

Upon completion of degree requirements, graduates find employment in academic institutions, federal and state agencies and departments, international businesses and banks, law firms, consulting firms, think tanks, and not-for-profit organizations. Many international students return home to work in the public and private sectors. SPP provides career advisement, internship, and placement support for all students.

Location

Located in Northern Virginia, George Mason is only 15 miles from all the resources of the National Capital Region and the Washington metropolitan area. Washington's libraries, galleries, and museums; Virginia's historic sites; and Fairfax County's high-technology firms are easily accessible. George Mason's 5.2-acre Arlington Campus, which is home to most SPP master's programs, is just minutes to Washington, D.C., by Metrorail.

Applying

Application deadlines for the master's and certificate programs are June 1 for fall and December 1 for spring. International applicant deadlines are one month prior to these dates. For Ph.D. applicants, fall application deadlines are February 1 for international students and March 1 for domestic students. For the spring term, Ph.D. application deadlines are October 1 for international applicants and November 1 for domestic applicants. Students should note that funding is only awarded to full-time Ph.D. students beginning their study in the fall term. All applicants must submit a graduate application and fee, all official university transcripts, a written goals statement, a professional resume, two letters of recommendation, and a writing sample (Ph.D. applicants only). GRE or GMAT scores are required for all Ph.D. candidates and for master's degree applicants who are seeking merit-based funding consideration. International applicants must also submit a TOEFL score. Students should visit http://policy.gmu.edu/admissions for more specific information on application requirements for both the master's and Ph.D. degree programs.

Correspondence and Information

Graduate Admissions
School of Public Policy
George Mason University
3401 Fairfax Drive, MS 3B1
Arlington, Virginia 22201
Phone: 703-993-8099
Fax: 703-993-4876
E-mail: spp@gmu.edu
Web site: http://policy.gmu.edu

George Mason University

CORE FACULTY

Administrative Faculty

Kingsley E. Haynes, University Professor and Dean; Ph.D., Johns Hopkins, 1971.

James H. Finkelstein, Professor and Vice Dean for Administration; Ph.D., Ohio State, 1980.

Jonathan L. Gifford, Professor, Associate Dean for Research, and Program Director for the Transportation, Operations, and Logistics M.A. program; Ph.D., Berkeley, 1983.

Matthys van Schaik, Associate Dean for Academic Affairs; Ph.D., South Carolina, 1995.

The Faculty and Their Research

Zoltan J. Acs, University Professor; Ph.D., The New School, 1980. Mathematical economics, microeconomics, macroeconomics, managerial economics and public policy, the global economic environment, technology management, entrepreneurship and innovation, new venture creation, global and domestic business environment, global and domestic business environment–Web, basic economics–Web.

Mark S. Addleson, Associate Professor; Ph.D., Witwatersrand, 1992. Knowledge management, organizational change, learning organizations, methodology of social inquiry, Austrian economics.

Katrin B. Anacker, Assistant Professor; Ph.D., Ohio State, 2006. City and regional planning, housing, housing policy, urban policy, race and public policy, real estate markets, statistical methods, qualitative methods, research writing.

David J. Armor, Professor of Public Policy; Ph.D., Harvard, 1966. Education policy, military manpower, family policy, welfare policy, civil rights/race relations policy (desegregation, affirmative action), methodology (statistical analysis, survey design).

Philip E. Auerswald, Assistant Professor; Ph.D., Washington (Seattle), 1999. Innovation, entrepreneurship, economics of security, energy policy.

Ann Baker, Associate Professor; Ph.D., Case Western Reserve, 1995. Organization change, group and organization communication to promote innovation, knowledge management, cross-cultural communication.

Kenneth J. Button, University Professor; Ph.D., Loughborough (England), 1981. Transportation economics, transport planning, economics of privatization and regulation, environmental economics, regional economics, urban economics.

Janine Davidson, Assistant Professor of National and Global Security; Ph.D., South Carolina, 2005. International Security, U.S. foreign policy, civil and ethnic conflict, weak and failed states, terrorism.

Desmond Dinan, Professor of Public Policy and Jean Monnet Chair; Ph.D., National University of Ireland, 1985. Global governance; European Union institutions, history, and historiography.

Michael K. Fauntroy, Assistant Professor of Public Policy; Ph.D., Howard, 2001. American government and politics, political parties, race and public policy, civil rights policy, urban policy, District of Columbia governance.

Allison M. Frendak-Blume, Assistant Professor of Public Policy; Ph.D., George Mason, 2004. International peacekeeping, stability and reconstruction operations, post-conflict peacebuilding, conflict analysis and resolution, international supervisory/administrative regimes, U.S. foreign policy, Balkans, Russia/former Soviet Union.

A. Lee Fritschler, Professor of Public Policy; Ph.D., Syracuse, 1965. U.S. national government (executive branch), relationship between the institutions of government, accountability, regulation, federalism, public management, science and public policy, higher education policy, U.S. Postal Service, communications policy.

Stephen S. Fuller, Dwight Schar Faculty Chair and University Professor of Public Policy and Regional Development; Ph.D., Cornell, 1969. Regional economic development; urban development; housing; urban planning; demographics; development of the Washington D.C. area; economic analysis; labor force; forecasting—population, income, employment, real estate development; economic and fiscal impact analyses; economic development in developing countries.

Jonathan L. Gifford, Professor of Public Policy, Associate Dean for Research, and Director, Transportation, Policy, Operations, and Logistics Program; Ph.D., Berkeley, 1983. Transportation policy and planning, infrastructure policy and planning, urban and metropolitan planning and land use, technology standards and public policy, transportation and regional development policy, transportation finance and privatization.

Jack A. Goldstone, Virginia E. Hazel and John T. Hazel, Jr. Professor of Public Policy; Ph.D., Harvard, 1981. Democratization, civil conflict, state failure and reconstruction, long-term social change, sources of economic growth.

David M. Hart, Associate Professor; Ph.D., MIT, 1995. Science and technology policy; business and politics; lobbying and representation; U.S. public policy process; U.S. policy history, especially business, economic, and political history; international migration; entrepreneurship; global governance.

Kingsley E. Haynes, Ruth D. and John T. Hazel M.D. Endowed Chair and Eminent Scholar, Professor and Dean, School of Public Policy; Ph.D., Johns Hopkins, 1971. Regional economic development, infrastructure and transportation policy, resource planning and policy analysis.

Jack C. High, Professor of Public Policy, Economics, and Social Learning; Ph.D., UCLA, 1980. Economic regulation, economic growth, economic history, international trade and investment, international institutions.

Christopher T. Hill, Professor of Public Policy and Technology and Director, Public Policy Doctoral Program; Ph.D., Wisconsin–Madison, 1969. Science, technology, and innovation policy (U.S. and international); climate change policy; research management in higher education, government, and industry.

Andrew Hughes Hallett, Professor of Public Policy and Economics; D.Phil., Oxford, 1976. Open economy macroeconomics; policy coordination and exchange rate management; monetary integration (monetary and fiscal union in Europe); political economy models; fiscal policy; regionalism, policy choice, and reform; the theory of economic policy and institutional design; dynamic games and bargaining models; risk and decisions under uncertainty; commodity markets, financial policy, and strategic trade policy; numerical methods in economics.

Jessica Heineman-Pieper, Assistant Professor of Public Policy; Ph.D., Chicago, 2005. Psychology and the conceptual foundations of science, philosophy of the social sciences, deep democracy, post-development studies, applied ethics, transformation, leadership.

Michael R. Kelley, Professor of Telecommunications; Ph.D., Catholic University, 1970. Telecommunications policy, polices for managing scarce radio frequency spectrum, government organizations and their approach to managing a variety of public assets (oil, gas, fishing, hunting, etc.).

Naoru Koizumi, Assistant Professor; Ph.D. (regional science), Pennsylvania, 2002; Ph.D. (environmental and preventive medicine), Hyogo Medical College, (Japan), 2005. Stochastic modeling, simulation of health care systems, applied statistics in health care, spatial statistics and applications of geographic information systems in public health

Todd M. La Porte, Associate Professor; Ph.D., Yale, 1989. Technologies and organizations; technology and society; technology and politics; technology in politics; technology assessment and policy analysis; information and communications technologies; energy technologies; digital government, both worldwide and in the U.S.; comparative political and economic systems, particularly European; critical infrastructures; large technical systems; high reliability organizations and organizational failure; organization studies; public management and public administration; qualitative methods; data collection methodologies; extreme events; disaster studies; emergency management; space weather.

Siona R. Listokin, Assistant Professor; Ph.D., Berkeley, 2007. Public finance, political economy, retirement and welfare policy, public management, private regulation.

Stuart S. Malawer, Distinguished Service Professor of Law and International Trade; Ph.D., Pennsylvania, 1976; Diploma, Hague Academy of International Law, 1971; J.D., Cornell, 1967. U.S. trade law, U.S. and global trade politics, international trade relations, World Trade Organization, national security law and policy.

Jeremy D. Mayer, Associate Professor and Director, Master of Public Policy Program; Ph.D., Georgetown, 1996. Public opinion, racial politics, foreign policy, presidential elections, statistical methods, survey methods, media politics.

Connie L. McNeely, Associate Professor of Public Policy; Ph.D., Stanford, 1990. Culture and policy; states and society; international development; complex organizations and institutional analysis; comparative education; race, ethnicity, and nations; gender; social theory.

Arnauld Nicogossian, Distinguished Research Professor; M.D., Teheran, 1964; M.S., Ohio State, 1972. Public health policy, program/project management, strategic planning and execution of research and development, global public health and preventative medicine, aerospace medicine, internal medicine.

Todd Olmstead, Assistant Professor; Ph.D., Harvard, 2000. Public policy, health policy, transportation policy, health services research, operations research, statistics, program evaluation.

Wayne D. Perry, Professor of Public Policy and Operations Research; Ph.D., Carnegie Mellon, 1975. Science and technology, defense, international security and arms control, health care, operations research/management science, statistical models, stochastic processes, managerial economics and econometrics, policy analysis, cost-benefit analysis.

John E. Petersen, Professor of Public Policy; Ph.D., Pennsylvania, 1967. Public finance (government finance), both domestic (state, local, federal) and international; international finance and financial institutions.

James P. Pfiffner, University Professor of Public Policy; Ph.D., Wisconsin–Madison, 1975. The presidency, Congress, American national government and policy process, public administration.

Ramkishen S. Rajan, Associate Professor of Public Policy; Ph.D., Claremont, 2000. International economics (open economy macroeconomics, finance, and trade) with particular reference to Asia.

Kenneth A. Reinert, Professor of Public Policy and Director, International Commerce and Policy Program; Ph.D., Maryland, College Park, 1988. International trade policy, international development policy, multilateral development organizations, foreign direct investment.

Hilton L. Root, Professor of Public Policy; Ph.D., Michigan, 1983. International economics; international finance; international development; developing nations; political economy of the design and implementation of development policy, economic policy reform; North-South relations and Asian-Pacific affairs.

Mark J. Rozell, Professor of Public Policy; Ph.D., Virginia, 1987. The presidency, media and politics, religion and politics.

Catherine Rudder, Professor of Public Policy; Ph.D., Ohio State, 1973. American political institutions and politics, Congress, tax policy making, self-regulation, governance, non-profit institutions.

Stephen R. Ruth, Professor; Ph.D., Pennsylvania, 1971. Policy approaches for technology-based learning interventions, information technology diffusion in developing nations, religious/theological issues in public policy formulation, strategic issues in knowledge management implementation.

Laurie A. Schintler, Associate Professor of Public Policy; Ph.D., Illinois at Urbana-Champaign, 1996. Critical infrastructure, transportation, quantitative methods, regional development, geographic information systems.

William Schneider, Hirst Chair in Public Policy; Ph.D., Harvard, 1972. Political science; American politics; public opinion and public policy; news media and public affairs; polling and vote analysis; interviewing and fieldwork; comparative elections and politics; ideology and political movements; presidential politics; race, religion, and gender; the politics of foreign policy and national security.

Louise Shelley, Professor of Public Policy; Ph.D., Pennsylvania, 1977. Transnational crime; terrorism; corruption; human trafficking; illicit trade; Soviet successor states.

Rainer Sommer, Associate Professor of Public Policy and Enterprise Engineering; Ph.D., Columbia Pacific (software engineering), 1991; Ph.D., George Mason (information technology), 1998. Enterprise systems, strategic planning and telecommunications.

Roger R. Stough, Vice President for Research and Economic Development; President, George Mason Intellectual Properties; NOVA Endowed Chair and Professor of Public Policy; Ph.D., Johns Hopkins, 1978. Regional economic development policy and analysis, information technology policy, transportation policy, entrepreneurship.

Tojo J. Thatchenkery, Professor of Organization Development and Director, Organization Development and Knowledge Management; Ph.D., Case Western Reserve, 1994. Organizational learning and development; appreciative intelligence; knowledge management; ethnicity, social capital, and organizational mobility; information communication technology and development of Southeast Asia.

Susan Tolchin, University Professor; Ph.D., NYU, 1968. Public policy theory, federal government (U.S.), federal regulation, ethics.

Matthys van Schaik, Associate Dean for Academic Affairs; Ph.D., South Carolina, 1995. International commerce and research methods.

Janine R. Wedel, Professor; Ph.D., Berkeley, 1985. Governance and privatization of policy, corruption and the state, foreign aid, social networks, eastern Europe, anthropology of public policy.

Selected Affiliated Faculty

Kevin Avruch, Professor of Anthropology; Ph.D., California, San Diego, 1978.

Timothy J. Conlan, Associate Professor of Government and Politics; Ph.D., Harvard, 1981.

George L. Donahue, Professor of Systems Engineering and Operations Research; Ph.D., Oklahoma State, 1972.

Robert L. Dudley, Associate Professor of Government and Politics; Ph.D., Northern Illinois.

Gregory A. Guagnano, Associate Professor of Sociology; Ph.D., California, Davis, 1986.

Hugh Heclo, Robinson Professor of Public Affairs; Ph.D., Yale, 1970.

James T. Hennessey, Chief of Staff; Ph.D., George Mason, 1997.

Julianne G. Mahler, Associate Professor of Government and Politics; Ph.D., SUNY at Buffalo, 1976.

John Paden, Robinson Professor of International Studies; Ph.D., Harvard, 1968.

Priscilla M. Regan, Associate Professor of Government and Politics; Ph.D., Cornell, 1981.

Joseph A. Scimecca, Professor of Sociology; Ph.D., NYU, 1972.

Martin Jay Sherwin, Professor of History; Ph.D., UCLA, 1971.

Edgar H. Sibley, University of Professor of Information and Software Engineering; Sc.D., MIT, 1967.

Instructional and Research Faculty

Brien Benson, Research Associate Professor; Ph.D., George Mason, 1998.

George Cook, Affiliate Professor; A.B., George Washington, 1957.

David F. Davis, Assistant Research Professor; M.S., Naval Postgraduate School, 1981.

Robert L. Deitz, Distinguished Visiting Professor, CIA Officer In Residence; M.P.A., Princeton (Wilson), 1972; J.D. Harvard, 1975.

Michael V. Hayden, Distinguished Visiting Professor; M.A., Duquesne, 1969.

Desmond J. Lugg, Distinguished Research Professor; M.D., Adelaide, 1974.

Monty Marshall, Research Professor; Ph.D., Iowa, 1996.

Arthur S. Melmed, Research Professor; M.S.E.E., Columbia, 1956.

James L. Narel, Academic Director, Peace Operations Policy Program, School of Public Policy; Ph.D., George Mason, 2007.

James Riggle, Research Associate Professor; Ph.D., George Mason, 2002.

Charles Robb, Distinguished Professor of Law and Public Policy; J.D., Virginia, 1973.

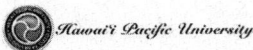

HAWAI'I PACIFIC UNIVERSITY

Master of Arts in Global Leadership and Sustainable Development

Program of Study	Hawai'i Pacific University's (HPU's) Master of Arts in Global Leadership and Sustainable Development (M.A./GLSD) program is designed to prepare students to lead change initiatives in a globalizing world that is increasingly characterized by chaos, complexity, and change. Students learn simultaneously to search for the underlying causes of global environmental, economic, and social problems and how to design and lead responses that produce sustainable outcomes for current and future generations.
	Faculty members who teach in the M.A./GLSD program combine impressive academic credentials, stature in their professional disciplines, and years of actual business and consulting experience. Many have extensive international experience and therefore welcome the diversity that HPU's students bring to the classroom. Graduate students have the benefit of learning from adjunct professors who are part of the local business community—managing partners, vice presidents, and presidents from a wide variety of companies and organizations, both domestic and international. All program faculty members are dedicated to making the HPU experience edifying, challenging, and enjoyable for the student.
	The M.A./GLSD is designed to prepare students to become leaders in all types of organizations, including multinational, governmental, and not-for-profit organizations. The program concentrates on teaching relevant interdisciplinary theories and tools to help professionals succeed in today's fast-paced global economy.
Research Facilities	To support graduate studies, HPU's Meader and Atherton Libraries offer more than 110,000 bound volumes, 350,000 microfiche items, and periodical subscriptions to 1,500 print titles and 30,000 electronic journals. Databases of public and state university libraries, legislative information, and business-oriented statistical data are also available in the library or online. Students can access HPU's library databases, course information, their academic information, and an e-mail account through Pipeline, the University's internal Web site for students. The University's accessible on-campus computer center houses more than 420 computers with specialized software to support graduate academic programs. HPU also provides free Wi-Fi service so students can have wireless access to Pipeline resources anywhere on campus using laptops. A significant number of online courses are available as well.
Financial Aid	The University participates in all federal financial aid programs designated for graduate students. These programs provide aid in the form of subsidized (need-based) and unsubsidized (non-need-based) Federal Stafford Student Loans. Through these loans, funds may be available to cover the student's entire cost of education. To apply for aid, students must submit the Free Application for Federal Student Aid (FAFSA) beginning January 1.
	Hawai'i Pacific University offers institutional graduate scholarships to new, full-time, degree-seeking students. U.S. citizens, permanent residents, and international students who have a demonstrated financial need may apply. HPU's graduate scholarships include the Graduate Trustee Scholarship ($6000 for two semesters), the Graduate Dean Scholarship ($4000 for two semesters), and the Graduate Kokua Scholarship ($2000 for two semesters). Factors that may be considered when evaluating requests are previous academic record, community involvement and service, professional work experience, and achievement.
	In order to be eligible for the best award package, students should apply by HPU's priority deadline of March 1. Applications received after the priority deadline will be awarded on a funds-available basis. Mailing of student award letters usually begins by the end of March. Applicants will be notified by mail as decisions are made.
Cost of Study	Tuition for graduate students enrolled in fall and spring semesters is determined on a per-credit basis; full-time status for a graduate student is nine credits. Tuition for the optional winter and summer sessions is also determined on a per-credit basis. For the 2011–12 academic year, full-time tuition (9 credits) is $13,230 for most graduate degree programs, including the M.A./GLSD program. Other expenses, including books, personal expenses, fees, and a student bus pass, are estimated at $3190.
Living and Housing Costs	Most graduate students live in off-campus housing. The cost to live in off-campus apartments is approximately $12,230 for a double occupancy room.
Student Group	University enrollment currently stands at more than 8,200. HPU is one of the most culturally diverse universities in America with students from all 50 U.S. states and more than 100 countries. HPU strives to maintain a student profile that is one third Hawaii, one third mainland U.S.A., and one third global.
Location	Hawai'i Pacific combines the excitement of an urban, downtown campus with the serenity of a residential campus. The urban campus is ideally located in downtown Honolulu, the business and financial center of the Pacific. The downtown campus comprises six buildings in the center of Honolulu's business district and is home to the College of Business Administration and the College of Humanities and Social Sciences.
	Eight miles away, situated on 135 acres in Kaneohe, the windward Hawai'i Loa campus is the site of the College of Nursing and Health Sciences and the College of Natural and Computational Sciences. The Hawai'i Loa campus has residence halls, dining commons, the Educational Technology Center, a student center, and outdoor recreational facilities, including a soccer field, tennis courts, a softball field, and an exercise room.
	HPU is affiliated with the Oceanic Institute, an applied aquaculture research facility located on a 56-acre site at Makapu'u Point on the windward coast of Oahu, Hawai'i. All three sites are linked by HPU shuttle as well as easily accessed by public transportation.
	Notably, the downtown campus location is within walking distance of shopping and dining. Iolani Palace, the only palace in the U.S., is a few blocks away, as are the State Capitol, City Hall, and the Blaisdell Concert Hall. The Honolulu Academy of Arts, Museum of Contemporary Art, Waikiki Aquarium, Honolulu Zoo, and many other cultural attractions are located nearby.
The University	HPU is a private, nonprofit university with approximately 8,200 students. Founded in 1965, HPU prides itself on maintaining strong academic programs, small class sizes, individual attention to students, and a diverse faculty and student population. HPU is recognized as a "Best Western" college by Princeton Review and a "Best Buy in College Education" by *Barron's* business magazine. HPU offers more than fifty acclaimed undergraduate programs and fourteen distinguished graduate programs. The University has a faculty of more than 500, a student-faculty ratio of 15:1, and an average class size of fewer than 25 students. A wide range of counseling and other student support services are available. There are more than sixty student organizations on campus, including the Graduate Student Organization.
Applying	Students must have a baccalaureate degree from an accredited college or university in the United States or an equivalent degree from another country. Applicants should complete and forward a Graduate Admissions Application, send in the $50 nonrefundable application fee, have official transcripts sent from all colleges or universities previously attended, and forward two letters of recommendation. A resume and a personal statement about the applicant's academic and career goals are required. Applicants who have taken the Graduate Record Examination (GRE) should have their scores sent directly to the Graduate Admissions Office. International students should submit scores from a recognized English proficiency test, such as the TOEFL. Admissions decisions are made on a rolling basis, and applicants are notified between one and two weeks after all documents have been submitted. Applicants are encouraged to submit their applications online.
Correspondence and Information	Graduate Admissions Hawai'i Pacific University 1164 Bishop Street, Suite 911 Honolulu, Hawaii 96813 Phone: 808-544-1135 866-GRAD-HPU (toll-free) Fax: 808-544-0280 E-mail: graduate@hpu.edu Web site: http://www.hpu.edu/hpumaglsd

Hawai'i Pacific University

THE FACULTY AND THEIR RESEARCH

Cheryl Crozier-Garcia, Assistant Professor of Human Resource Management; Ph.D., Walden.
Gerald W. Glover, Professor of Organizational Change; Ph.D., Florida.
John Gutrich, Associate Professor of Environmental Sciences; Ph.D., Ohio State.
Gordon Jones, Professor of Computer Science and Information Systems; Ph.D., New Mexico.
Margo Kitts, Associate Professor of Humanities/Religious Studies; Ph.D., Berkeley.
Ernesto Lucas, Associate Professor of Economics; Ph.D., Hawaii.
Daniel Morgan, Instructor of Sociology; M.A., Miami (Florida).
Regina Ostergaard-Klem, Adjunct Professor of Mathematics; Ph.D., Johns Hopkins.
Catherine Sajna, Assistant Professor of English; M.A., Hawaii at Manoa.
Richard Ward, Associate Professor of Organizational Change; Ed.D., USC.
Arthur Whatley, Professor of Management; Ph.D., North Texas.
Larry Zimmerman, Assistant Professor of Organizational Change; Ph.D., Nebraska–Lincoln.

INDIANA UNIVERSITY BLOOMINGTON

SCHOOL OF PUBLIC AND
ENVIRONMENTAL AFFAIRS
INDIANA UNIVERSITY

School of Public and Environmental Affairs
Public Affairs Graduate Programs

Programs of Study

The School of Public and Environmental Affairs (SPEA) offers the Master of Public Affairs (MPA), the Ph.D. in public policy, and the Ph.D. in public affairs. The two-year, 48-credit hour MPA degree is an interdisciplinary program that equips students with a combination of skills for professional careers in government, nonprofit, and private sectors. The program consists of three components and culminates in a capstone course. The three components are a core curriculum, concentration area(s), and an experiential component. The core courses include public management, statistical analysis, public management economics, law and public affairs, public finance and budgeting, and a capstone project in public and environmental affairs. Many SPEA students choose to pursue more than one concentration. The MPA concentration areas are comparative and international affairs, economic development, environmental policy and natural resource management, local government management, nonprofit management, policy analysis, public financial administration, public management, sustainability and sustainable development, and SPEA's latest addition, energy. To integrate their academic training into a practical framework, students are required to complete an internship or a significant research project in order to satisfy the experiential component of the MPA program. The capstone project serves as the culmination to a student's academic training. Capstone projects are normally a semester-long, detailed analysis of a policy or management issue, often undertaken for a real-world client in the public or nonprofit sector.

MPA dual-degree programs are offered with SPEA's Master of Science in Environmental Science (MSES) and Indiana University's Departments of African American and African Diaspora Studies, African Studies, Central Eurasian Studies, East Asian Studies, Latin American and Caribbean Studies, Russian and East European Studies, and West European Studies, as well as the Schools of Library and Information Science, Law, and Journalism.

The Ph.D. in public affairs is designed to prepare scholars for research and teaching in the multidisciplinary field of public policy and management. The program emphasizes the study of public management and organization, policy analysis, and public finance. The joint Ph.D. in public policy is a collaborative venture with Indiana University's Department of Political Science. This program emphasizes study of the public policy process. Students explore issues regarding policy analysis, government institutions, political behavior, and public affairs.

Research Facilities

Complementing SPEA's own resources, Indiana University maintains eight nationally prominent area studies centers and sixty language programs to facilitate international research and career interests. SPEA has affiliations with several research centers on both the Bloomington and Indianapolis campuses, including the Transportation Research Center; the Institute for Family and Social Responsibility; the Environmental Science Research Center; the Indiana University Research and Teaching Preserve; the Center for the Study of Institutions, Population, and Environmental Change; the Indiana University Public Policy Institute; and the Center for Urban Policy and Environment.

SPEA houses its own newly renovated Information Commons, which provides convenient access to individual and group workstations, student-focused services that support individual and collaborative learning and research, and access to rich library resources shared with the Kelley School of Business. The Indiana University Bloomington Libraries have been recognized by peers as the top university library in the country, according to the Association of College and Research Libraries, 2010.

Financial Aid

Departmental assistance for qualified students is awarded on a competitive basis determined by merit. Awards include fellowships, scholarships, and teaching and research assistantships. Prospective students may apply for merit-based awards by checking the appropriate box on the admission application form. Students may apply for need-based aid through the University's Office of Student Financial Assistance (OSFA).

SPEA hosts a one-of-a-kind, collaborative program called Service Corps, which enables SPEA students to apply their classroom learning directly to the field in both the public and nonprofit sectors. Service Corps is a financial aid mechanism that offers students real-world experience working in an array of governmental and nonprofit agencies while concurrently pursuing their academic plans. The program is a partnership among the University, SPEA, and a number of valued external stakeholders in the community and region. Students are selected for participation during the merit aid allocation process.

SPEA also houses a brand new AmeriCorps VISTA program, in which SPEA graduate students take a hiatus from their studies to serve a one-year term as full-time AmeriCorps VISTA members. Students will have the opportunity to serve at a variety of nonprofit and government agencies working on capacity-building projects. SPEA VISTA Fellows receive 3 credit hours for their year of service, which also fulfills the master's program's experiential requirement. In addition, VISTA members receive receive an annual living allowance, a health benefit, and all benefits associated with AmeriCorps VISTA service, including an education award of $5550. VISTA members gain a civil service benefit, authorizing noncompetitive eligibility for federal jobs extending one year following service.

Cost of Study

In-state residents pay $415 per credit hour and nonresidents pay $902 per credit hour for SPEA's master's programs in 2011–12.

Living and Housing Costs

The 1,200 on-campus apartments for graduate students range in monthly rent from $519 for a furnished efficiency to $1164 for an unfurnished three-bedroom apartment. Rates include all utilities as well as local telephone service, cable TV, and Internet connection. A variety of off-campus apartments and rental houses are available near the University. Rents are generally inexpensive, with the average two-bedroom unit renting for $550 to $800 per month. Free campus and municipal bus systems service most apartment complexes. Recently named the number-one small transit system in North America by the American Public Transportation Association, the Bloomington Transit system provides easy transportation to SPEA and many other areas of Bloomington.

Student Groups

About 320 students are enrolled in the MPA program, with approximately 100 students pursuing the dual MPA/MSES program. SPEA's doctoral programs in public affairs and public policy have close to 70 students combined. About 30 percent of these students are international, more than one half are women, and more than 10 percent are members of underrepresented populations.

SPEA recognizes service in AmeriCorps, Teach for America, and Peace Corps. These volunteers receive a waiver of the experiential component which is a part of the MPA degree program's academic design and a reduction of the total number of credit hours required for degree completion. SPEA also hosts both Peace Corps' Coverdell Fellows/U.S.A., and Master's International (MI) programs. Peace Corps and MI Fellows receive a competitive merit aid package in addition to the benefits described above.

Student Outcomes

SPEA maintains an outstanding placement record, attributed to a well-rounded curriculum, national prestige, and strong alumni support. Within six months of the close of the 2008–09 academic year, approximately 76 percent of students responding to SPEA's annual employment survey indicated that they had procured full-time professional positions or were continuing their education. The SPEA Office of Career Services (OCS) is staffed with professionals who assist graduate students with all of their career development needs. The services offered to students include individual career counseling; on-campus recruiting; a Web-based job listing service, SPEACareers.com; a wide range of employer information sessions; alumni mentoring; user-friendly Web-based career resources; and an extensive career resource library. With so many resources at their disposal, SPEA students annually compete for many of the most prestigious and competitive positions in federal and state government and top-tier nonprofits and foundations. SPEA students are also top candidates for positions with top consulting firms like Booz Allen Hamilton, Crowe Chizek, Deloitte, and Grant Thornton. Some examples of other recent placements include the World Bank, the Environmental Protection Agency, the Department of State, the National Forest Service, the Government Accountability Office, the National Institutes of Health, the National Oceanographic and Atmospheric Institute, the Millennium Challenge Corporation, the Nature Conservancy, the Corporation for National and Community Service, the Bill and Melinda Gates Foundation, the Indiana Department of Environmental Management, the Indiana Office of Management and Budget, and the Indiana Department of Transportation.

In addition, SPEA typically has 5–15 MPA students selected as finalists for the Presidential Management Fellowship Program (PMF), one of the most selective federal programs for graduate students pursuing careers with the federal government.

Location

Bloomington, a college town of 110,000 people, was chosen as one of the top ten college towns in America for its "rich mixture of atmospherics and academia" by Edward Fiske, former education editor of the *New York Times*. It is a culturally vibrant community settled among southern Indiana's rolling hills, just 45 miles south of Indianapolis, the state capital. Mild winters and warm summers are ideal for outdoor recreation in the two state forests, one national forest, three state parks, and an array of lakes and streams that surround Bloomington.

The University and The School

Established in 1820, Indiana University has more than 9,100 graduate students and close to 42,500 students enrolled on the Bloomington campus. SPEA is the top-ranked graduate program on campus. Fifty-five other academic departments are ranked in the top 20 in the country, including music, business, biology, foreign languages, political science, and chemistry. Attractions include nearly 1,000 musical performances each year, with eight full-length operas and professional Broadway plays; the IU Art Museum, designed by I. M. Pei, with more than 30,000 art objects; fifty campus and community volunteer agencies; more than 700 student sports clubs and organizations; two indoor student recreational facilities; and Big Ten athletics. SPEA, founded in 1972, was the first school to combine public management, policy, and administration with the environmental sciences.

Applying

Application files must include the SPEA Admission Application form, transcripts, GRE General Test scores, and three letters of recommendation. Priority is given to applications received by February 1. Students applying for awards must submit a complete application file by the priority deadline, February 1. School visits are encouraged. Applicants can also access the School's Web site at http://www.spea.indiana.edu.

Correspondence and Information

For master's programs:
Master's Program Office
SPEA 260
Indiana University
Bloomington, Indiana 47405

Phone: 812-855-2840
800-765-7755 (toll-free, domestic only)
E-mail: speainfo@indiana.edu
Web site: http://www.spea.indiana.edu

For doctoral programs:
Doctoral Program Office
SPEA 441
Indiana University
Bloomington, Indiana 47405

Phone: 812-855-2457
800-765-7755 (toll-free, domestic only)
E-mail: dpritche@indiana.edu
Web site: http://www.spea.indiana.edu

Indiana University Bloomington

THE FACULTY AND THEIR RESEARCH

Osita G. Afoaku, Ph.D., Washington State, 1991. Human rights, sustainable development, democratization, and state reconstruction in Africa; U.S.-African/Third World relations; UN Security Council reform.

David B. Audretsch, Ph.D., Wisconsin, 1980. Economics policy, entrepreneurship, innovation, globalization, regional economic policy, industrial restructuring and government policy, small enterprises in Europe and the United States.

Matthew R. Auer, Ph.D., Yale, 1996. Intersection of foreign aid and sustainable development, international forest politics, energy efficiency, environmental education.

Mathew Baggetta, Ph.D., Harvard, 2009. Civil society, voluntary associations, civic engagement, social capital.

James Barnes, J.D., Harvard, 1967. Environmental law, domestic and international environmental policy, ethics and the public official, mediation and alternative dispute resolution, law and public policy.

Lisa Blomgren Bingham, J.D., Connecticut, 1979. Collaborative governance, comparative governance, dispute resolution, dispute system design, mediation, administrative law, labor and employment law.

Jennifer N. Brass, Ph.D., Berkeley, 2010. African politics, nongovernmental organizations (NGOs), energy and international development, comparative public administration, governance, civil society, political economy of development.

Sanya Carley, Ph.D., North Carolina at Chapel Hill, 2010. Energy policy and economics, electricity technology innovation policy, applied econometrics, policy instruments.

Joyce Y. Chang, Ph.D. candidate, Indiana, Bloomington; J.D., Ohio State, 2003. Environmental policy, public policy, political theory and methodology, public law.

Melissa A. L. Clark, M.S., Indiana, 1999. Aquatic and terrestrial habitats, Indiana Clean Lakes Program, water resources and water quality, implementing sustainability initiatives on campus and community.

Christopher B. Craft, Ph.D., North Carolina State, 1987. Wetland restoration and ecosystem development; wetlands and water quality; wetlands and climate change, including carbon sequestration and peat accretion.

Brian L. DeLong, M.A., Wake Forest. National and international security policies from an argumentation, rhetorical, and critical cultural perspective.

Sameeksha Desai, Ph.D., George Mason, 2008. Entrepreneurship, innovation, and economic development policy; political economy and allocation of entrepreneurship in areas of political instability, conflict, and disaster; postconflict reconstruction; social entrepreneurship.

Denvil R. Duncan, Ph.D., Georgia State, 2010. Public economics, labor economics, economic development.

Sébastien Dusanter, Ph.D., Université Lille 1(France), 2002. Advancing knowledge of the oxidative capacity of the atmosphere through laboratory studies and field measurements to improve the chemical mechanisms included in atmospheric models to tackle fundamental issues related to climate change and air quality.

Michael A. Edwards, Ph.D., North Dakota State, 1999. Atmospheric chemistry research: mechanistic studies of terpenes reacting with ozone, future regulation of hydrogen storage materials.

Sergio Fernandez, Ph.D., Georgia, 2004. Public management and organization theory, privatization and contracting out, public-sector leadership, organizational change.

Burnell C. Fischer, Ph.D., Purdue, 1974. Forestry, particularly silviculture and urban forestry; growth and development of Central Hardwood forest stands and response to various silvicultural practices; community and urban forestry issues; forest resources policy and state government management; human factors relating to forests and forest products, particularly with regard to collaborative forestry.

Seth Freedman, Ph.D., Maryland, College Park, 2010. Health economics, public economics, labor economics.

Beth Gazley, Ph.D., Georgia, 2004. Nonprofit management and governance, volunteerism, collaboration, intersectoral relations and the role of the voluntary sector in emergency planning.

David Good, Ph.D., Pennsylvania, 1985. Quantitative policy modeling, productivity measurement in public and regulated industries, urban policy analysis.

John D. Graham, Ph.D., Carnegie Mellon, 1983. Government reform, energy and the environment, the future of the automobile in both developed and developing countries.

Kirsten Grønbjerg, Ph.D., Chicago, 1974. Nonprofit and public sector relationships, examining scope and community dimensions of the Indiana nonprofit sector, the American welfare system, nonprofit funding relations, nonprofit data sources.

Hendrik M. Haitjema, Ph.D., Minnesota, 1982. Groundwater flow modeling, including regional groundwater flow systems, conjunctive surface-water and groundwater flow modeling, 3-D groundwater flow, and saltwater intrusion problems, with emphasis on application of analytic functions to modeling groundwater flow, specifically analytic-element method.

Bradley T. Heim, Ph.D., Northwestern, 2002. Behavioral impact of tax policies on labor supply, consumption, income and earnings, employment mode, health insurance purchases, charitable giving, and retirement savings; analysis of labor, business, and household income dynamics.

Diane S. Henshel, Ph.D., Washington (St. Louis), 1987. Sublethal health effects of environmental pollutants, especially pollutant effects on the developing organism, including the effects of polychlorinated dibenzo-p-dioxins (PCDDs) and related congeners on the developing nervous system of birds exposed in the wild and under controlled laboratory conditions.

Monika Herzig, D.M.E., Indiana, 1997. Touring jazz pianist, concert promotion, music industry, jazz education.

Ronald Hites, Ph.D., MIT, 1968. Applying organic analytical chemistry techniques to the analysis of trace levels of toxic pollutants, such as polychlorinated biphenyls and pesticides, with focus on understanding behavior of these compounds in the atmosphere and in the Great Lakes.

Cheryl K. Hughes, M.B.A., Indiana Wesleyan, 2002. Human resource management/training and development.

Christopher Hunt, M.A., Cambridge, 1961. Programming and presentation of the performing and visual arts and entertainment.

Chaman Jain, Ph.D., Indiana, 1975. Governmental and non-profit accounting and reporting, financial management in nonprofit organizations, governmental budgeting and finance, financial (corporate) management.

Craig Johnson, Ph.D., SUNY at Albany, 1993. Capital markets and financial intermediation, financial management, public budgeting and finance, financing e-government, financing economic development, environmental and infrastructure finance.

William W. Jones, M.S., Wisconsin–Madison, 1977. Lake and watershed management, especially diagnosing lake and watershed water-quality problems; preparing management plans to address problems identified; stream ecology.

Haeil Jung, Ph.D., Chicago, 2009. Applied econometrics and program evaluation, crime policy, public policy for low-income families.

Kerry Krutilla, Ph.D., Duke, 1988. Theory and practice of benefit-cost analysis, environmental policy analysis, program evaluation of environmental programs, natural resource management in developing countries.

Marc L. Lame, Ph.D., Arizona State, 1992. Implementation of integrated pest-management programs in schools and day-care facilities.

Leslie Lenkowsky, Ph.D., Harvard, 1982. Nonprofits and public policy, civil society in comparative perspective, institutional grant makers, volunteering and civic engagement, education and social welfare policy, social entrepreneurship.

Alvin (Al) Lyons, Ph.D., Indiana–Purdue at Indianapolis, 2009. Philanthropic studies; nonprofit management, fund development, strategic planning, and board development; social entrepreneurship; programs for nonprofit organizations, with an emphasis on hospitals.

Joyce Y. Man, Ph.D., Johns Hopkins, 1993. Public finance, urban and regional economics, international trade, economic development, public budgeting and financial management.

Michael McGuire, Ph.D., Indiana, 1995. Intergovernmental and interorganizational collaboration and networks, federalism and intergovernmental relations, public management, emergency management.

Vicky J. Meretsky, Ph.D., Arizona, 1995. Ecology and management of rare species, biocomplexity, landscape-level species and community conservation, temporal patterns in biodiversity, integrating ecosystem research and endangered species management within adaptive management.

John L. Mikesell, Ph.D., Illinois, 1969. Governmental finance, especially questions of policy and administration of sales and property taxation; state lotteries; public budgeting; public finance in countries of the former Soviet Union.

Ashlyn Aiko Nelson, Ph.D., Stanford, 2005. Housing finance, education finance, education policy, the mortgage crisis.

Patrick O'Meara, Ph.D., Indiana, 1970. Comparative politics and development, Southern African politics, ethics and politics.

Clinton V. Oster Jr., Ph.D., Harvard, 1978. Aviation safety, airline economics and competition policy, international aviation, aviation infrastructure, environmental and natural resource policy, government regulation, business-government relations.

Elinor Ostrom, Ph.D., UCLA, 1965. Exploring how institutional rules affect the structure of action situations within which individuals face incentives, make choices, and jointly affect each other; problems involving collective goods and common-pool resource systems; how various types of institutions enhance or detract from the capabilities of individuals to achieve equitable, workable, efficient solutions.

James Perry, Ph.D., Syracuse, 1974. Public service motivation, government and civil service reform, public management, public human resource management, national and community service, performance-related pay, public organizational behavior.

Flynn W. Picardal, Ph.D., Arizona, 1992. Bioremediation, environmental microbiology, and biogeochemistry, with a focus on the microbial reduction of iron oxides and nitrate, transformation of metals and chlorinated hydrocarbons, and combined microbial-geochemical interactions.

Maureen A. Pirog, Ph.D., Pennsylvania, 1981. Poverty and income maintenance, child support enforcement, welfare reform, adolescent parenting.

Orville W. Powell, MPA, Penn State, 1963. Local government and the U.S. Constitution.

Daniel Preston, M.A.L.D, Fletcher (Tufts), 2005. Global environment, international affairs, politics, poverty alleviation, corporate and public sector strategy, country competitiveness, financial markets, economic development, education, good governance and public policy.

Jonathan D. Raff, Ph.D., Indiana Bloomington, 2007. Applying interdisciplinary approaches to understand how thermal and photochemical reactions on surfaces affect the fate of pollutants in the environment and impact global climate.

J. C. Randolph, Ph.D., Carleton (Ottawa), 1972. Forest ecology; ecological aspects of global environmental change, with particular interests in forestry and agriculture; applications of geographic information systems (GIS) and remote sensing in environmental and natural resources management; landscape ecology and regional-scale modeling; physiological ecology of woody plants and of small mammals.

David A. Reingold, Ph.D., Chicago, 1996. Urban poverty, economic development, social welfare policy, low-income housing policy and government performance.

Terri L. Renner, M.B.A., Indiana, 1985. Financial management, information systems, entrepreneurship.

Rafael Reuveny, Ph.D., Indiana, 1997. International political economy; globalization; rise and fall of major powers; political conflict and how it interacts with international trade, democracy, and the environment; sustainable development; Middle East political economy.

Kenneth R. Richards, J.D./Ph.D., Pennsylvania, 1997. Domestic and international climate change policy, environmental policy implementation, carbon sequestration economics and law, energy law, U.S. Forest Service organizational design and management.

Evan J. Ringquist, Ph.D., Wisconsin–Madison, 1990. Public policy (environmental, energy, natural resources, and regulation), research methodology, American political institutions.

Justin Ross, Ph.D., West Virginia, 2007. Public economics, urban/regional economics, spatial econometrics, applied microeconomics, quantile regressions, public finance, political economy, game theory.

Todd V. Royer, Ph.D., Idaho State, 1999. Aquatic biogeochemistry, water resources, nutrient and carbon cycling in streams and rivers, water quality and nutrient standards.

Barry Rubin, Ph.D., Wisconsin–Madison, 1977. Urban and regional economic development and impact analysis, quantitative analysis of local government management and labor relations issues, statistics and quantitative methods, econometric modeling, public management information systems, strategic planning and management.

Michael Rushton, Ph.D., British Columbia, 1990. Cultural economics, policy and administration, nonprofit and public organizations and management, tax policy, government funding for the arts and other policies toward nonprofit organizations, cultural districts, the relationships between the arts and economic growth.

Adrian Sargeant, Ph.D., Exeter (England). Nonprofit marketing including the arts, education, health care, and philanthropy; fundraising and philanthropy.

Kristin Seefeldt, Ph.D., Michigan, 2010. Poverty and low-income families in the United States, housing instability, implementation of programs serving low-income families.

Yue (Jen) Shang, Ph.D., Indiana, 2008. Nonprofit marketing, marketing communications for nonprofit organizations, donor behavior, fund development, philanthropic psychology.

Joseph Shaw, Ph.D., Kentucky, 2001. Environmental toxicology, environmental genomics, comparative physiology.

Daniel Simon, Ph.D., Maryland, 1999. Variety of issues linking government policies and firm behavior with individual outcomes and firm performance.

Kosali Simon, Ph.D., Maryland, College Park, 1999. Health economics and policy; impact of state and federal regulations attempting to ease the availability of private and public health insurance for vulnerable populations on health insurance, health, and labor market outcomes.

Nan Stager, M.S., Indiana, 1978. Mediation, negotiation, alternative dispute resolution, public input processes.

Philip S. Stevens, Ph.D., Harvard, 1990. Characterization of chemical mechanisms that influence regional air quality and global climate change.

Anh Tran, Ph.D., Harvard, 2009. Institutions and behavior of bureaucrats, entrepreneurs, and workers in developing countries.

Terry Usrey, M.S., Indiana, 1983. E-government, information technology policy, Information Technology Management.

Henry K. Wakhungu, Ph.D., Indiana, 2004. Development of growth simulation models for sustainable management of indigenous community forests; experimental designs in tropical forestry research; how preservice teachers conceptualize mathematics (philosophically), indexed with mathematics learning and teaching.

Jeffrey R. White, Ph.D., Syracuse, 1984. Environmental biogeochemistry, aquatic chemistry, limnology.

Lois R. Wise, Ph.D., Indiana, 1982. Public management and employment policies and practices.

Wenli Yan, Ph.D., Kentucky, 2008. Public and nonprofit financial management, state and local government finance, quantitative methodology.

C. Kurt Zorn, Ph.D., Syracuse, 1981. State and local finance, transportation safety, economic development, gaming policy.

UNIVERSITY OF DELAWARE

School of Public Policy and Administration

Programs of Study

The School of Public Policy and Administration offers six graduate degree programs: a Master of Public Administration (M.P.A.), a Master of Arts (M.A.) in urban affairs and public policy, a Ph.D. in urban affairs and public policy, a Master of Arts (M.A.) in historic preservation, a Master of Science in Disaster Science and Management, and a Ph.D. in Disaster Science and Management.

The M.P.A. is a 42- or 45-credit, two-year professional degree program that prepares students for leadership positions in public affairs. The M.P.A. program is accredited by the National Association of Schools of Public Affairs and Administration (NASPAA). Students can choose from four options for areas of focus: nonprofit management, public management, policy and program development, or a student-designed area of focus.

The M.A. and Ph.D. in urban affairs and public policy programs are ranked among the top nine programs in the United States. The M.A. is a 36-credit degree program designed for students who are interested in pursuing policy analysis and planning–related careers. The program extends over two years and may include a thesis, an analytical paper, or an internship. M.A. students may choose from the following areas of focus: housing and community development; nonprofits and philanthropy ; historic preservation; health services policy; media and public policy; and urban and regional planning. The Ph.D. is a research-oriented interdisciplinary degree intended for students who have completed master's-level work in urban affairs and public policy or other related social science fields. First-year doctoral seminars are followed by study in a specialization that leads to the preparation of the dissertation proposal. Most students conduct dissertation research in the areas of technology, environment, and society; governance planning and management; social and urban policy; public administration; and urban affairs. All doctoral students collaborate with faculty and staff members on regional, national, and international research on critical urban and policy issues.

The School offers a nationally recognized internship program that places students in paid professional positions in international, national, state, and local government. All students in the School are eligible; the internship is a requirement for preservice M.P.A. students.

The M.A. in historic preservation program is designed to meet the needs of both traditional graduate students and working professionals, with graduates having the skills and knowledge to work with a wide variety of populations and in diverse settings. The M.A. requires 39 credits to graduate.

The M.S. and Ph.D. program in disaster science and management covers the theories, research methodologies, and policies informing efforts focused on emergency preparedness, mitigation, management and response. The M.S. degree requires 30 credits (non-thesis requires 24 credits). The Ph.D. degree requires 42 credits of graduate-level course work beyond the master's degree and 9 credits of dissertation.

Research Facilities

The School is centrally located in its own building, with its own classrooms and student offices. One of the most distinguishing characteristics of the School of Public Policy and Administration is the integration of theory and practice through applied research projects with the affiliated research and public service centers. Some full-time students are awarded research assistantships on projects in these centers.

The Center for Applied Demography and Survey Research provides demographic and survey data and information on important public issues to researchers and policy makers at all levels (http://www.cadsr.udel.edu). The Center for Community Research and Service helps public, nonprofit, and private organizations in Delaware to design, implement, and evaluate policies and programs that address the needs of low- and moderate-income families and communities related to economic development, housing, and social services. The center also focuses on issues that are vital to the physical and emotional well-being of the world's population. These questions concern the delivery and financing of health care and the outcomes of health care provided (http://www.udel.edu/CCRS). The Center for Historic Architecture and Design focuses on shaping historic preservation planning and policy, reconstructing historic landscapes, documenting threatened historic properties, and advocating for the preservation of historic resources (http://www.udel.edu/CHAD). The Institute for Public Administration links the resources of the University of Delaware (UD) with the management and policy information needs of public and nonprofit organizations (http://www.ipa.udel.edu).

Financial Aid

The School has competitive financial aid programs, including fellowships, research assistantships, and scholarships. Aid is awarded on merit and is limited by the various restrictions established by the sources of aid. Stipends for 2011–12 are $16,000 for the full academic year. Additional special assistantships, fellowships, and internships are available to students through the University Graduate Scholar's Program, for both newly admitted and graduate students currently enrolled. Awards are competitive and are based on many criteria, including challenging social, economic, educational, cultural, or other life circumstances; academic achievements; first generation graduate student status; and/or need as determined by federal income guidelines (FAFSA). Funds are also available through the Delaware Legislative Fellows Program.

Cost of Study

In 2011–12, tuition for full-time graduate students is $25,940 per academic year. Part-time students are charged on a per-credit basis. (The 2011–12 rate is $1441 per credit.) Full-time matriculated students are automatically assessed nonrefundable fees of $494 for health and $238 for student-sponsored activities.

Living and Housing Costs

The University provides some graduate apartments, and there is plenty of off-campus housing in the surrounding community in many price ranges. For more information, students should contact the Housing Assignment Services Office (302-831-2491; http://www.udel.edu/has).

Student Group

The School has 64 students in the M.P.A. program, 52 in the M.A. and 44 in the Ph.D. Urban Affairs and Public Policy program, 5 in the M.A. of Historic Preservation program, and 10 in the M.S. and 16 in the Ph.D. Disaster Science and Management program.

Student Outcomes

Graduates find career positions in government and nonprofit organizations and occasionally in the private sector with consulting firms. With UD's proximity to Washington, D.C.; Philadelphia; and New York, many graduates pursue positions in nearby metropolitan areas, as well as positions in state and local government in the region and in the nation. Several recent graduates have been successful in the highly competitive federal Presidential Management Fellowship Program.

Location

Located midway between Philadelphia and Baltimore, the main campus of the University of Delaware is in Newark, conveniently near New York City; Washington, D.C.; and the seashore. A community of 30,000, with a vibrant Main Street of coffeehouses, restaurants, and small shops, Newark is about 14 miles from Wilmington, Delaware's largest city.

The University

The University is a comprehensive land-, sea-, space-, and urban-grant institution of higher education with an enrollment of nearly 3,500 graduate students in 2011–12. The University offers one hundred fifteen programs leading to a master's degree and forty-three programs leading to a doctoral degree. In 2010, the University awarded 251 doctoral degrees and 727 master's degrees.

Applying

The School welcomes informal inquiries. Students seeking financial aid or admission to the Ph.D. program should apply by February 1. For the master's programs, candidates must have an undergraduate GPA above 3.0 (on a 4.0 scale). Admission to the Ph.D. program requires a master's degree with at least a 3.5 GPA. A combined GRE score above 1000 on the math and verbal portions of the exam is normally expected. Complete applications contain three letters of recommendation, a personal statement of academic and career objectives (for the Ph.D., a 1,000-word statement of the applicant's research interest as well), and academic transcripts. For nonnative speakers of English, a demonstrated proficiency in English is required, with a TOEFL score of at least 550 (213 on the computer-based test).

Correspondence and Information

School of Public Policy and Administration Admissions
University of Delaware
Newark, Delaware 19716-7310

Phone: 302-831-1687
Fax: 302-831-3296
E-mail: sppa@udel.edu
Web site: http://www.sppa.udel.edu

University of Delaware

THE FACULTY AND THEIR RESEARCH

At the core of the School of Public Policy and Administration are the dedicated faculty members, who are challenging teachers, seasoned researchers, and experienced practitioners. With interdisciplinary backgrounds as skilled executives, managers, and community leaders, they bring practical experience to the classroom and successfully blend a solid academic base with stimulating practical experience.

David L. Ames, Professor and Director, Center for Historic Architecture and Design; Ph.D., Clark, 1969; ACIP. Historic preservation, urban geography, urban and regional planning.

Maria P. Aristigueta, Professor; Director, School of Public Policy and Administration; and Senior Policy Fellow, Institute for Public Administration; D.P.A., USC, 1997. Administrative behavior, performance management, policy analysis, strategic management.

Deborah A. Auger, Associate Professor and Policy Fellow, Center for Community Research and Service; Ph.D., MIT, 1988. Public policy and administration, nonprofit management, state and local government, U.S. social policy.

Karen A. Curtis, Associate Professor and Policy Scientist, Center for Community Research and Service; Ph.D., Temple, 1984. Nonprofit leadership and management, applied research and public policy analysis, qualitative methods, social and economic opportunity.

Robert B. Denhardt, Visiting Scholar; Ph.D., Kentucky, 1968. Public sector management, strategic planning and public productivity.

Bernard L. Dworsky, Assistant Professor and Policy Scientist, Institute for Public Administration; M.A., Delaware, 1971. Water resources management, planning.

James P. Flynn, Assistant Professor; Director, M.P.A. Program; and Associate Policy Scientist, Institute for Public Administration; Ed.D., Delaware, 1998. Personnel administration, quality improvement initiatives, educational governance, legislative management, professional development, human resources management.

Edward J. Freel, Instructor and Policy Scientist, Institute for Public Administration; M.Ed., Delaware, 1975. Civic education, learning initiatives, public administration.

Audrey L. Helfman, Associate Professor and Director, Organizational and Community Leadership Program; Ph.D., Delaware, 1993. Personnel administration, organizational theory, legislative management, public fiscal analysis, data systems, analytic methods.

Raheemah Jabbar-Bey, Assistant Professor and Assistant Policy Specialist, Center for Community Research and Service; M.A., New Hampshire, 1996. Community and economic development planning, organizational capacity building of nonprofits, urban policy analysis.

Eric D. Jacobson, Associate Professor and Assistant Director, Institute for Public Administration; M.P.A., Delaware, 1981. Public economics, health policy, employee compensation and benefits, tourism development and research, analytical methods.

Janet B. Johnson, Associate Professor, Department of Political Science and International Relations and Senior Research Associate, Center for Energy and Environmental Policy; Ph.D., Cornell, 1978. Subnational politics, environmental policy, research methods, public policy analysis.

Jonathan Justice, Associate Professor; Ph.D., Rutgers, 2003. Public financial management, nongovernmental public administration, urban policy and administration.

Gerald Kauffman, Instructor and Director, Water Resources Agency; M.P.A., Delaware, 2003. Watershed policy, planning, and management; water resources government and finance; water resources engineering; hydrology and hydraulics.

Jerome R. Lewis, Associate Professor and Director, Institute for Public Administration; Ph.D., NYU, 1968. Public administration, personnel management, urban planning, political leadership.

John G. McNutt, Professor; Ph.D., Tennessee, 1991. Technology, nonprofit management, advocacy and government relations, community organization and planning.

Anthony E. Middlebrooks, Associate Professor; Ph.D., Wisconsin, 1999. Leadership formation and development, creativity and leadership, service and social justice, research methods.

James L. Morrison, Professor; Ed.D., Temple, 1971. Telecommunications and consumer policy, consumer environmental issues, consumer protection.

Audrey J. Noble, Assistant Professor; Ph.D., Arizona State, 1994. Qualitative research and evaluation.

Edward J. O'Donnell, Instructor and Senior Policy Advisor, Institute for Public Administration; M.Ed., West Chester, 1975. Growth management, transportation/infrastructure planning, comprehensive planning.

Marian Lief Palley, Professor, Department of Political Science and International Relations; Ph.D., NYU, 1966. American politics and public policy, intergovernmental relations, health and welfare policy.

Steven W. Peuquet, Associate Professor and Director, Center for Community Research and Service; Ph.D., Pennsylvania, 1996. Strategic planning, housing, homelessness, electronic community networks, public policy analysis and evaluation.

Jeffrey A. Raffel, Charles P. Messick Professor of Public Administration and Faculty Associate, Institute for Public Administration; Ph.D., MIT, 1972. Educational policy, policy analysis, urban management.

Edward C. Ratledge, Associate Professor and Director, Center for Applied Demography and Survey Research; M.A., Delaware, 1972. Management information systems, econometrics, criminal justice systems.

Daniel Rich, Professor and Director, Public Policy Program; Ph.D., MIT, 1972. Public policy and public management.

Breck Robinson, Associate Professor and Associate Professor, Institute for Public Administration; Ph.D., Tennessee, 1994. Financial institutions, public policy, real estate finance.

Andrea Sarzynski, Assistant Professor; Ph.D., George Washington, 2006. Urbanization and environmental change; environmental policy and politics; urban and regional planning; science and policymaking.

Rebecca Sheppard, Assistant Professor and Associate Director, Center of Historic Architecture and Design; Ph.D. Delaware, 2009. Historic preservation planning, history of rural landscapes and the built environment, landscape preservation.

Paul L. Solano, Associate Professor; Ph.D., Maryland, 1978. Financial administration and public finance, political economy, health economics.

Karen F. Stein, Associate Professor; Ph.D., Delaware, 1984. Domestic elder abuse and neglect, leadership studies, consumer and family economic policy analysis.

Richard T. Sylves, Professor, Department of Political Science and International Relations, and Fellow, Center for Energy and Environmental Policy; Ph.D., Illinois at Urbana-Champaign, 1977. Energy policy, disaster policy.

Douglas F. Tuttle, Instructor; Internship Coordinator; and Policy Scientist, Institute for Public Administration; M.P.A., Delaware, 1990. State and local government personnel development, strategic planning, emergency service planning and public service quality assessment.

Leland Ware, Louis L. Redding Chair for the Study of Law and Public Policy and Associate Director, School of Public Policy and Administration; J.D., Boston College, 1973. Employment discrimination law, civil rights law, civil procedure.

Robert Warren, Professor and Senior Research Associate, Institute for Public Administration; Ph.D., UCLA, 1964. Urban and regional government, telecommunications policy, urban planning and development, cultural theory.

Margaret G. Wilder, Professor; Ph.D., Michigan, 1983. Community development policy and organizations; economic development policy and planning; housing problems and policy; race, gender, and economic mobility.

Danilo Yanich, Associate Professor; Director, Urban Affairs and Public Policy Program; and Associate Policy Scientist, Center for Community Research and Service; Ph.D., Delaware, 1980. Criminal justice policy, media and public policy, international comparative governance.

Section 26
Social Sciences

This section contains a directory of institutions offering graduate work in social sciences. Additional information about programs listed in the directory may be obtained by writing directly to the dean of a graduate school or chair of a department at the address given in the directory.

For programs offering related work, see also in this book *Area and Cultural Studies, Communication and Media, Criminology and Forensics, Economics, Geography, Family and Consumer Sciences, Political Science and International Affairs, Psychology and Counseling,* and *Sociology, Anthropology, and Archaeology.*

CONTENTS

Program Directory

Social Sciences

Arkansas Tech University, Graduate College, College of Arts and Humanities, Russellville, AR 72801. Offers communication (MLA); English (M Ed, MA); fine arts (MLA); history (MA); multi-media journalism (MA); psychology (MS); social science (MLA); Spanish (MA, MLA); teaching English as a second language (MA, MLA). Part-time programs available. *Students:* 39 full-time (23 women), 87 part-time (69 women); includes 13 minority (3 Black or African American, non-Hispanic/Latino; 1 American Indian or Alaska Native, non-Hispanic/Latino; 1 Asian, non-Hispanic/Latino; 8 Hispanic/Latino), 14 international. Average age 32. In 2010, 54 master's awarded. *Degree requirements:* For master's, comprehensive exam (for some programs), thesis (for some programs), project. *Entrance requirements:* For master's, GRE General Test or MAT. Additional exam requirements/recommendations for international students: Required—TOEFL (minimum score 550 paper-based; 213 computer-based; 79 iBT), IELTS (minimum score 6). *Application deadline:* For fall admission, 3/1 priority date for domestic students, 5/1 priority date for international students; for spring admission, 10/1 priority date for domestic and international students. Applications are processed on a rolling basis. Application fee: $0 ($50 for international students). Electronic applications accepted. *Expenses:* Tuition, state resident: full-time $4680; part-time $195 per credit hour. Tuition, nonresident: full-time $9360; part-time $390 per credit hour. Required fees: $714; $14 per credit hour. One-time fee: $326 part-time. Tuition and fees vary according to course load. *Financial support:* In 2010–11, teaching assistantships with full tuition reimbursements (averaging $4,000 per year); research assistantships, career-related internships or fieldwork, Federal Work-Study, scholarships/grants, health care benefits, and unspecified assistantships also available. Support available to part-time students. Financial award application deadline: 4/15; financial award applicants required to submit FAFSA. *Unit head:* Dr. Micheal Tarver, Dean, 479-968-0274, Fax: 479-964-0812, E-mail: mtarver@atu.edu. *Application contact:* Dr. Mary B. Gunter, Dean of Graduate College, 479-968-0398, Fax: 479-964-0542, E-mail: graduate.school@atu.edu.

California Institute of Technology, Division of the Humanities and Social Sciences, Social Science Program, Pasadena, CA 91125-0001. Offers MS, PhD. *Faculty:* 27 full-time (3 women). *Students:* 34 full-time (8 women); includes 2 minority (both Asian, non-Hispanic/Latino), 18 international. Average age 26. 300 applicants, 10% accepted, 12 enrolled. In 2010, 6 master's, 7 doctorates awarded. Terminal master's awarded for partial completion of doctoral program. *Degree requirements:* For doctorate, thesis/dissertation. *Entrance requirements:* For doctorate, GRE General Test. Additional exam requirements/recommendations for international students: Required—TOEFL (minimum score 90 paper-based; 120 computer-based); Recommended—TWE. *Application deadline:* For fall admission, 12/15 for domestic and international students. Application fee: $80. Electronic applications accepted. *Financial support:* In 2010–11, 35 students received support, including 20 fellowships with tuition reimbursements available (averaging $28,000 per year), 6 research assistantships with tuition reimbursements available (averaging $28,000 per year), 8 teaching assistantships with tuition reimbursements available (averaging $28,000 per year); Federal Work-Study, institutionally sponsored loans, and scholarships/grants also available. *Faculty research:* Individual and group decision making, experimental social science, political science, quantitative history, behavioral economics and neuroscience. *Unit head:* Dr. Jonathan Katz. *Application contact:* Laurel Auchampaugh, Graduate Secretary, 626-395-4206, Fax: 626-405-9841, E-mail: gradsec@hss.caltech.edu.

California State University, Chico, Graduate School, College of Behavioral and Social Sciences, Social Science Program, Chico, CA 95929-0722. Offers social science (MA); social science education (MA). *Students:* 9 full-time (8 women), 9 part-time (6 women); includes 1 Asian, non-Hispanic/Latino; 3 Hispanic/Latino. Average age 33. 12 applicants, 83% accepted, 8 enrolled. In 2010, 8 master's awarded. *Degree requirements:* For master's, thesis or alternative. *Entrance requirements:* For master's, GRE General Test or MAT. Additional exam requirements/recommendations for international students: Required—TOEFL (minimum score 550 paper-based; 213 computer-based; 80 iBT), IELTS (minimum score 6.5). *Application deadline:* For fall admission, 3/1 priority date for domestic students, 3/1 for international students; for spring admission, 9/15 priority date for domestic students, 9/15 for international students. Applications are processed on a rolling basis. Application fee: $55. Electronic applications accepted. *Financial support:* Fellowships, teaching assistantships available. *Unit head:* Dr. Gwen Sheldon, Graduate Coordinator, 530-895-5204. *Application contact:* School of Graduate, International, and Interdisciplinary Studies, 530-898-6880, Fax: 530-898-6889, E-mail: grin@csuchico.edu.

California State University, San Bernardino, Graduate Studies, College of Social and Behavioral Sciences, Program in Social Sciences, San Bernardino, CA 92407-2397. Offers MA. *Degree requirements:* For master's, comprehensive exam or thesis. *Entrance requirements:* For master's, writing exam, minimum GPA of 3.5 in major, 2.5 overall.

California University of Pennsylvania, School of Graduate Studies and Research, College of Liberal Arts, Department of Sociology/Criminal Justice, California, PA 15419-1394. Offers social science—criminal justice (MA). Part-time and evening/weekend programs available. *Degree requirements:* For master's, comprehensive exam, thesis optional. *Entrance requirements:* For master's, MAT, minimum GPA of 3.0. Additional exam requirements/recommendations for international students: Required—TOEFL (minimum score 550 paper-based; 213 computer-based; 80 iBT). Electronic applications accepted. *Faculty research:* Ethics and law, ethics in police practice, law and morality, police policy, St. Thomas Aquinas and crime.

Campbellsville University, College of Arts and Sciences, Campbellsville, KY 42718-2799. Offers social science (MA). Part-time programs available. *Degree requirements:* For master's, comprehensive exam. *Entrance requirements:* For master's, GRE General Test, LSAT, minimum GPA of 2.9. Electronic applications accepted. *Expenses:* Tuition: Full-time $7110; part-time $395 per contact hour. Required fees: $250; $75 per course.

Carnegie Mellon University, College of Humanities and Social Sciences, Department of Social and Decision Sciences, Pittsburgh, PA 15213-3891. Offers behavioral decision research (PhD); behavioral decision research and psychology (PhD); social and decision science (PhD); strategy, entrepeneurship, and technological change (PhD). Terminal master's awarded for partial completion of doctoral program. *Degree requirements:* For doctorate, comprehensive exam, thesis/dissertation, research paper. *Entrance requirements:* For doctorate, GRE General Test. Additional exam requirements/recommendations for international students: Required—TOEFL. Electronic applications accepted. *Faculty research:* Organization theory, political science, sociology, technology studies.

Central European University, Graduate Studies, School of Social Sciences and Humanities, Budapest, Hungary. Offers economics (MA, PhD); gender studies (MA, PhD); international relations and European studies (MA, PhD); mathematics and its applications (MS, PhD); medieval studies (MA, PhD); nationalism studies (MA, PhD); philosophy (MA, PhD); political science (MA, PhD); public policy (MA, PhD); sociology and social anthropology (MA, PhD). *Faculty:* 90 full-time (29 women), 13 part-time/adjunct (7 women). *Students:* 732 full-time (404 women). Average age 28. 3,639 applicants, 22% accepted, 416 enrolled. In 2010, 278 master's, 16 doctorates awarded. Terminal master's awarded for partial completion of doctoral program. *Degree requirements:* For master's, one foreign language, thesis; for doctorate, one foreign language, comprehensive exam, thesis/dissertation. *Entrance requirements:* For master's, interview; for doctorate, GRE, CEU subject test, interview. Additional exam requirements/recommendations for international students: Required—TOEFL (minimum score 570 paper-based; 230 computer-based); Recommended—IELTS (minimum score 6.5). *Application deadline:* For fall admission, 1/15 priority date for domestic and international students. Application fee: $0. Electronic applications accepted. Tuition and fees charges are reported in euros. *Expenses:* Tuition: Full-time 11,000 euros. Required fees: 250 euros. One-time fee: 200 euros full-time. Tuition and fees vary according to degree level, program, reciprocity agreements and student level. *Financial support:* In 2010–11, 402 students received support, including 416 fellowships with full and partial tuition reimbursements available (averaging $6,200 per year); career-related internships or fieldwork, institutionally sponsored loans, and scholarships/grants also available. Financial award application deadline: 1/5. *Faculty research:* Civil society, fiscal decentralization, party politics, political philosophy (especially liberalism, theory of democracy). Total annual research expenditures: $35,000. *Unit head:* Dr. Katalin Farkas, Provost/Academic Pro Rector, 361-327-3000 Ext. 2227, E-mail: farkask@ceu.hu. *Application contact:* Zsuzsanna Jaszberenyi, Admissions Officer, 361-327-3009, Fax: 361-327-3211, E-mail: admissions@ceu.hu.

The Citadel, The Military College of South Carolina, Citadel Graduate College, Department of Political Science and Criminal Justice, Charleston, SC 29409. Offers social science (MA). Part-time and evening/weekend programs available. *Faculty:* 3 full-time (1 woman). *Students:* 4 full-time (3 women), 20 part-time (7 women); includes 3 Black or African American, non-Hispanic/Latino; 1 Hispanic/Latino, 1 international. Average age 32. In 2010, 8 master's awarded. *Entrance requirements:* For master's, GRE (minimum score 900) or MAT (minimum score 396). Additional exam requirements/recommendations for international students: Required—TOEFL (minimum score 550 paper-based; 213 computer-based). *Application deadline:* Applications are processed on a rolling basis. Application fee: $30. Electronic applications accepted. *Expenses:* Tuition, state resident: part-time $460 per credit hour. Tuition, nonresident: part-time $756 per credit hour. Required fees: $40 per term. *Financial support:* Health care benefits and unspecified assistantships available. Support available to part-time students. Financial award application deadline: 7/1; financial award applicants required to submit FAFSA. *Unit head:* Dr. Gardel M. Feurtado, Department Head, 843-953-2037, Fax: 843-953-5066, E-mail: gardel.feurtado@citadel.edu. *Application contact:* Dr. Terry M. Mays, Associate Professor, 843-953-5069, Fax: 843-953-5069, E-mail: terry.mays@citadel.edu.

Clemson University, Graduate School, Program in International Family and Community Studies, Clemson, SC 29634. Offers PhD. *Faculty:* 6 full-time (2 women), 8 part-time/adjunct. *Students:* 12 full-time (11 women), 5 part-time (4 women); includes 2 Black or African American, non-Hispanic/Latino; 1 Asian, non-Hispanic/Latino, 5 international. Average age 36. 20 applicants, 20% accepted, 4 enrolled. In 2010, 2 doctorates awarded. *Degree requirements:* For doctorate, thesis/dissertation. *Entrance requirements:* For doctorate, GRE General Test. Additional exam requirements/recommendations for international students: Required—TOEFL. *Application deadline:* Applications are processed on a rolling basis. Application fee: $70 ($80 for international students). Electronic applications accepted. *Expenses:* Contact institution. *Financial support:* In 2010–11, 12 students received support, including 1 fellowship with full and partial tuition reimbursement available (averaging $4,000 per year), 17 research assistantships with partial tuition reimbursements available (averaging $13,914 per year); career-related internships or fieldwork, institutionally sponsored loans, scholarships/grants, health care benefits, and unspecified assistantships also available. Support available to part-time students. *Unit head:* Dr. Gary B. Melton, Director, 864-656-6271. *Application contact:* Information Contact, 864-656-3195, E-mail: gradapp@clemson.edu.

College of the Humanities and Sciences, Harrison Middleton University, Graduate Program, Tempe, AZ 85282. Offers education (MA, Ed D); humanities (MA); imaginative literature (MA); interdisciplinary studies (DA); jurisprudence (MA); natural science (MA); philosophy and religion (MA); social science (MA). Part-time and evening/weekend programs available. Postbaccalaureate distance learning degree programs offered (no on-campus study). *Faculty:* 17 full-time (7 women), 14 part-time/adjunct (6 women). *Students:* 52 full-time (20 women). In 2010, 4 master's awarded. *Degree requirements:* For master's and doctorate, capstone project. *Entrance requirements:* For doctorate, 3 academic letters of reference, interview. *Application deadline:* Applications are processed on a rolling basis. Application fee: $50. Electronic applications accepted. *Expenses:* Tuition: Part-time $300 per credit hour. One-time fee: $350 part-time. *Faculty research:* Japanese animation, educational leadership, war art, John Muir's wilderness. *Application contact:* Deborah Deacon, Dean of Graduate Studies, 877-248-6724, Fax: 800-762-1622, E-mail: ddeacon@hmu.edu.

Columbia University, Graduate School of Arts and Sciences, Program in Quantitative Methods in the Social Sciences, New York, NY 10027. Offers MA. Part-time programs available.

Eastern Michigan University, Graduate School, College of Arts and Sciences, Department of History and Philosophy, Programs in Social Sciences, Ypsilanti, MI 48197. Offers social science (MA, Graduate Certificate); social science and American culture (MLS). Part-time and evening/weekend programs available. Postbaccalaureate distance learning degree programs offered (minimal on-campus study). *Students:* 4 full-time (3 women), 18 part-time (8 women); includes 3 minority (all Black or African American, non-Hispanic/Latino). Average age 34. In 2010, 6 master's awarded. *Degree requirements:* For master's, thesis optional. *Entrance requirements:* Additional exam requirements/recommendations for international students: Required—TOEFL. *Application deadline:* Applications are processed on a rolling basis. Application fee: $35. *Financial support:* Fellowships, research assistantships with full tuition reimbursements, teaching assistantships with full tuition reimbursements, career-related internships or fieldwork, Federal Work-Study, institutionally sponsored loans, scholarships/grants, tuition waivers (partial), and unspecified assistantships available. Support available to part-time students. Financial award applicants required to submit FAFSA. *Application contact:* Dr. Ronald Delph, Coordinator, 734-487-0053, Fax: 734-487-6835, E-mail: rdelph@emich.edu.

Edinboro University of Pennsylvania, College of Arts and Sciences, Department of History and Anthropology, Edinboro, PA 16444. Offers social sciences (MA). Part-time and evening/weekend programs available. *Faculty:* 7 full-time (4 women). *Students:* 25 full-time (10 women), 12 part-time (7 women); includes 2 Black or African American, non-Hispanic/Latino. Average age 33. In 2010, 12 master's awarded. *Degree requirements:* For master's, thesis or alternative, competency exam. *Entrance requirements:* For master's, GRE or MAT, minimum QPA of 2.5. *Application deadline:* Applications are processed on a rolling basis. Application fee: $30. Electronic applications accepted. *Expenses:* Tuition, state resident: full-time $6966; part-time $387 per credit. Tuition, nonresident: full-time $11,146; part-time $619 per credit. Required fees: $2401.70; $96.25 per credit. *Financial support:* In 2010–11, 10 research assistantships with full and partial tuition reimbursements (averaging $4,050 per year) were awarded; career-related internships or fieldwork, Federal Work-Study, institutionally sponsored loans, scholarships/grants, and unspecified assistantships also available. Support available to part-time students. Financial award application deadline: 2/15; financial award applicants required to submit FAFSA. *Unit head:* Dr. Ron Spiller, Program Head, Social Sciences, 814-732-2966, E-mail: rspiller@edinboro.edu. *Application contact:* Dr. Ron Spiller, Program Head, Social Sciences, 814-732-2966, E-mail: rspiller@edinboro.edu.

Florida Agricultural and Mechanical University, Division of Graduate Studies, Research, and Continuing Education, College of Arts and Sciences, Division of History and Political Sciences, Program in Applied Social Science, Tallahassee, FL 32307-3200. Offers African American history (MASS); criminal justice (MASS); economics (MASS); history (MASS); political science (MASS); public administration (MASS); public management (MASS); social work (MASS); sociology (MASS). Part-time programs available. *Degree requirements:* For master's, thesis optional. *Entrance requirements:* For master's, GRE General Test, minimum GPA of 3.0. *Faculty research:* Southern history, black history, election trends, presidential history.

Graduate Theological Union, Graduate Programs, Berkeley, CA 94709-1212. Offers art and religion (MA, PhD, Th D); biblical languages (MA); biblical studies (MA); Biblical studies (PhD, Th D); Buddhist studies (MA); Christian spirituality (MA, PhD, Th D); cultural and historical studies of religions (MA, PhD, Th D); ethics and social theory (PhD, Th D); history (MA, PhD, Th D); homiletics (MA, PhD, Th D); interdisciplinary studies (PhD, Th D); Jewish studies (MA, PhD, Th D, Certificate); liturgical studies (MA, PhD, Th D); Near Eastern religions (PhD, Th D); Orthodox Christian studies (MA); religion and psychology (MA, PhD, Th D); religion and society/ethics and social theory (MA); systematic and philosophical theology (MA, PhD, Th D). PhD programs in Jewish studies and Near Eastern religions offered jointly with University of California, Berkeley. *Accreditation:* ATS. Terminal master's awarded for partial completion of doctoral program. *Degree requirements:* For master's, one foreign language, thesis; for doctorate, one foreign language, comprehensive exam, thesis/dissertation. *Entrance requirements:* For master's, GRE General Test; for doctorate, GRE General Test, MA or M Div. Additional exam requirements/recommendations for international students: Required—TOEFL. Electronic applications accepted.

Hollins University, Graduate Programs, Program in Liberal Studies, Roanoke, VA 24020-1603. Offers humanities (MALS); interdisciplinary studies (MALS); justice and legal studies (MALS); liberal studies (CAS); social science (MALS); visual and performing arts (MALS). Part-time and evening/weekend programs available. *Degree requirements:* For master's, thesis. *Entrance requirements:* For master's, letters of recommendation, interview. Additional exam requirements/recommendations for international students: Required—TOEFL (minimum score 550 paper-based; 213 computer-based; 79 iBT). Electronic applications accepted. *Faculty research:* Elderly blacks, film, feminist economics, US voting patterns, Wagner, diversity.

Humboldt State University, Academic Programs, College of Arts, Humanities, and Social Sciences, Program in Environment and Community, Arcata, CA 95521-8299. Offers MA. *Students:* 32 full-time (26 women), 11 part-time (all women); includes 10 minority (1 Black or African American, non-Hispanic/Latino; 2 American Indian or Alaska Native, non-Hispanic/Latino; 1 Asian, non-Hispanic/Latino; 2 Hispanic/Latino; 4 Two or more races, non-Hispanic/Latino). Average age 30. 58 applicants, 60% accepted, 20 enrolled. In 2010, 7 master's awarded. *Degree requirements:* For master's, thesis or alternative, qualifying exam. *Entrance requirements:* For master's, minimum GPA of 2.5, 3 letters of recommendation. Additional exam requirements/recommendations for international students: Required—TOEFL (minimum score 500 paper-based; 173 computer-based). *Application deadline:* For fall admission, 3/1 for domestic students, 3/15 for international students. Applications are processed on a rolling basis. Application fee: $55. Tuition and fees vary according to program. *Financial support:* Application deadline: 3/1. *Faculty research:* Geography, political science, ethnic studies, anthropology, economics. *Unit head:* Dr. Noah Zerbe, Chair, 707-826-3911, Fax: 707-826-4496, E-mail: noah.zerbe@humboldt.edu. *Application contact:* Dr. Mark Baker, Coordinator, 717-826-3907, Fax: 707-826-4496, E-mail: j.mark.baker@humboldt.edu.

Indiana University Bloomington, Maurer School of Law, Bloomington, IN 47405-7000. Offers comparative law (MCL); juridical science (SJD); law (JD, LL M); law and social sciences (PhD); legal studies (Certificate); JD/MA; JD/MBA; JD/MLS; JD/MPA; JD/MS; JD/MSES. PhD offered through University Graduate School. *Accreditation:* ABA. *Faculty:* 72 full-time (28 women), 14 part-time/adjunct (4 women). *Students:* 725 full-time (298 women), 37 part-time (13 women); includes 49 Black or African American, non-Hispanic/Latino; 25 Asian, non-Hispanic/Latino; 32 Hispanic/Latino; 5 Two or more races, non-Hispanic/Latino, 129 international. Average age 26. 1,726 applicants, 49% accepted, 248 enrolled. In 2010, 185 first professional degrees, 44 master's, 10 doctorates, 1 other advanced degree awarded. *Degree requirements:* For master's, thesis or practicum; for doctorate, thesis/dissertation (for some programs); for JD, research seminar. *Entrance requirements:* For JD, LSAT; for master's, LSAT, 3 letters of recommendation, law degree or license to practice; for doctorate, LSAT, 3 letters of recommendation, LL M or JD. Additional exam requirements/recommendations for international students: Required—TOEFL (minimum score 560 paper-based; 213 computer-based; 80 iBT). *Application deadline:* For fall admission, 3/1 priority date for domestic and international students. Applications are processed on a rolling basis. Application fee: $55 ($65 for international students). Electronic applications accepted. *Financial support:* In 2010–11, 301 students received support, including 278 fellowships (averaging $16,000 per year), 1 research assistantship (averaging $15,217 per year), 2 teaching assistantships (averaging $14,000 per year); career-related internships or fieldwork, Federal Work-Study, institutionally sponsored loans, scholarships/grants, health care benefits, and unspecified assistantships also available. Financial award application deadline: 3/1; financial award applicants required to submit FAFSA. *Faculty research:* Environmental risk assessment and policy analysis, information privacy and security, judicial independence, accountability, ethics. Total annual research expenditures: $1.4 million. *Unit head:* Lauren K. Robel, Dean, 812-855-8885, Fax: 812-855-7057, E-mail: lrobel@indiana.edu. *Application contact:* Kelly M. Compton, Director of Admissions, 812-855-2704, Fax: 812-855-0555, E-mail: kmcompto@indiana.edu.

The Johns Hopkins University, Bloomberg School of Public Health, Department of Health, Behavior and Society, Baltimore, MD 21218-2699. Offers genetic counseling (Sc M); health education and health communication (MHS); social and behavioral sciences (Dr PH, PhD, Sc D); social factors in health (MHS). *Faculty:* 43 full-time (30 women), 59 part-time/adjunct (40 women). *Students:* 114 full-time (105 women), 5 part-time (all women); includes 43 minority (14 Black or African American, non-Hispanic/Latino; 15 Asian, non-Hispanic/Latino; 6 Hispanic/Latino; 8 Two or more races, non-Hispanic/Latino), 11 international. Average age 28. 227 applicants, 31% accepted, 26 enrolled. In 2010, 21 master's, 10 doctorates awarded. *Degree requirements:* For master's, comprehensive exam (for some programs), thesis (for some programs); for doctorate, comprehensive exam, thesis/dissertation. *Entrance requirements:* For master's, GRE, curriculum vitae, 3 letters of recommendation; for doctorate, GRE, transcripts, curriculum vitae, 3 recommendation letters. Additional exam requirements/recommendations for international students: Required—TOEFL (minimum score 600 paper-based; 250 computer-based; 100 iBT). *Application deadline:* For fall admission, 12/1 for domestic and international students. Applications are processed on a rolling basis. Application fee: $45. Electronic applications accepted. *Financial support:* In 2010–11, 96 students received support, including 17 fellowships with tuition reimbursements available (averaging $23,634 per year), 30 research assistantships (averaging $7,800 per year), 25 teaching assistantships (averaging $2,759 per year); career-related internships or fieldwork, Federal Work-Study, scholarships/grants, traineeships, health care benefits, unspecified assistantships, and stipends also available. Financial award application deadline: 3/15. *Faculty research:* Social determinants of health and structural and community-level inventions to improve health, communication and health education, behavioral and social aspects of genetic counseling. Total annual research expenditures: $6.3 million. *Unit head:* Georgean Smith, Administrator, 410-502-3715, Fax: 410-502-4333, E-mail: gcsmith@jhsph.edu. *Application contact:* Barbara W. Diehl, Senior Academic Program Coordinator, 410-502-4415, Fax: 410-502-4333, E-mail: bdiehl@jhsph.edu.

Lincoln University, School of Graduate Studies and Continuing Education, Jefferson City, MO 65102. Offers business administration (MBA), including accounting, entrepreneurship, management, public administration and policy; educational leadership (Ed S), including elementary leadership, secondary leadership, superintendency; guidance and counseling (M Ed), including community/agency counseling, elementary school, secondary school; history (MA); school administration and supervision (M Ed), including elementary school administration, secondary school administration, special education administration; school teaching (M Ed), including elementary school teaching, secondary school teaching; social science (MA), including history, political science, sociology; sociology (MA); sociology/criminal justice (MA). Part-time and evening/weekend programs available. *Degree requirements:* For master's and Ed S, comprehensive exam, thesis optional. *Entrance requirements:* For master's and Ed S, GRE, MAT or GMAT, minimum GPA of 2.75 in major, 2.5 overall; 3 letters of recommendation; minimum C average in English composition; personal statement of purpose. Additional exam requirements/recommendations for international students: Required—TOEFL (minimum score 500 paper-based; 173 computer-based; 61 iBT). *Faculty research:* Suicide prevention.

Long Island University, Brooklyn Campus, Richard L. Conolly College of Liberal Arts and Sciences, Program in Social Science, Brooklyn, NY 11201-8423. Offers history (MS); United Nations studies (Certificate). Part-time and evening/weekend programs available. *Entrance requirements:* For master's, 2 letters of recommendation. Additional exam requirements/recommendations for international students: Required—TOEFL (minimum score 500 paper-based; 173 computer-based). Electronic applications accepted.

Long Island University, C.W. Post Campus, School of Education, Department of Curriculum and Instruction, Brookville, NY 11548-1300. Offers adolescence education (MS); adolescence education: biology (MS); adolescence education: earth science (MS); adolescence education: English (MS); adolescence education: mathematics (MS); adolescence education: social studies (MS); adolescence education: Spanish (MS); art education (MS); bilingual education (MS); childhood education (MS); early childhood education (MS); middle childhood education (MS); music education (MS); teaching English to speakers of other languages (MS). Part-time and evening/weekend programs available. *Degree requirements:* For master's, comprehensive exam or thesis, student teaching. *Entrance requirements:* For master's, minimum GPA of 2.75 in major, 2.5 overall. Electronic applications accepted. *Faculty research:* Ethics and education, teaching strategies.

Massachusetts Institute of Technology, School of Humanities, Arts, and Social Sciences, Program in Science, Technology, and Society, Cambridge, MA 02139. Offers history, anthropology, and science, technology and society (PhD). *Faculty:* 13 full-time (5 women). *Students:* 28 full-time (17 women); includes 4 minority (1 Black or African American, non-Hispanic/Latino; 1 American Indian or Alaska Native, non-Hispanic/Latino; 1 Asian, non-Hispanic/Latino; 1 Two or more races, non-Hispanic/Latino), 7 international. Average age 30. 146 applicants, 6% accepted, 5 enrolled. In 2010, 1 doctorate awarded. *Degree requirements:* For doctorate, comprehensive exam, thesis/dissertation. *Entrance requirements:* For doctorate, GRE General Test. Additional exam requirements/recommendations for international students: Required—TOEFL (minimum score 577 paper-based; 233 computer-based; 90 iBT), IELTS (minimum score 7). *Application deadline:* For fall admission, 1/1 for domestic and international students. Application fee: $75. Electronic applications accepted. *Expenses:* Tuition: Full-time $38,940; part-time $605 per unit. Required fees: $272. *Financial support:* In 2010–11, 25 students received support, including 19 fellowships with tuition reimbursements available (averaging $31,612 per year), 1 research assistantship (averaging $30,697 per year), 6 teaching assistantships with tuition reimbursements available (averaging $31,405 per year); Federal Work-Study, institutionally sponsored loans, scholarships/grants, traineeships, health care benefits, and unspecified assistantships also available. *Faculty research:* History of science; history of technology; sociology of science and technology; anthropology of science and technology; science, technology, and society; aeronautics and astronautics; humans and automation. Total annual research expenditures: $472,000. *Unit head:* Prof. David A. Mindell, Director, 617-253-4062, Fax: 617-258-8118, E-mail: stsprogram@mit.edu. *Application contact:* Karen Gardner, Academic Administrator, 617-253-9759, Fax: 617-258-8118, E-mail: hasts@mit.edu.

Middle Tennessee State University, College of Graduate Studies, University College, Murfreesboro, TN 37132. Offers M Ed, MPS, MSN, Graduate Certificate. Part-time and evening/weekend programs available. Postbaccalaureate distance learning degree programs offered. *Students:* 1 (woman) full-time, 184 part-time (144 women); includes 28 Black or African American, non-Hispanic/Latino; 1 American Indian or Alaska Native, non-Hispanic/Latino; 3 Hispanic/Latino; 5 Two or more races, non-Hispanic/Latino. Average age 38. 41 applicants, 78% accepted, 32 enrolled. In 2010, 38 master's, 1 other advanced degree awarded. *Entrance requirements:* Additional exam requirements/recommendations for international students: Required—TOEFL (minimum score 525 paper-based; 195 computer-based; 71 iBT) or IELTS (minimum score 6). *Application deadline:* For fall admission, 6/1 for domestic and international students. Applications are processed on a rolling basis. Application fee: $25 ($30 for international students). *Expenses:* Tuition, state resident: full-time $4632. Tuition, nonresident: full-time $11,520. *Financial support:* In 2010–11, 4 students received support. Application deadline: 5/1. *Unit head:* Dr. Mike Boyle, Dean, 615-898-2177, Fax: 615-896-7925, E-mail: mboyle@mtsu.edu. *Application contact:* Dr. Michael Allen, Dean and Vice Provost for Research, 615-898-2840, Fax: 615-904-8020, E-mail: mallen@mtsu.edu.

Mississippi College, Graduate School, College of Arts and Sciences, School of Humanities and Social Sciences, Department of History, Political Science, Administration of Justice, and Paralegal Studies, Clinton, MS 39058. Offers administration of justice (MSS); history (M Ed, MA, MSS); paralegal studies (Certificate); political science (MSS); social sciences (M Ed, MSS). Part-time programs available. *Degree requirements:* For master's, one foreign language, comprehensive exam, thesis (for some programs). *Entrance requirements:* For master's, GRE or NTE, minimum GPA of 2.5. Additional exam requirements/recommendations for international students: Recommended—IELTS. Electronic applications accepted.

Montclair State University, The Graduate School, College of Education and Human Services, Department of Curriculum and Teaching, Montclair, NJ 07043-1624. Offers education (M Ed); educational technology (M Ed); learning disabilities teacher consultant (Certificate); teaching (MAT), including art, biological science, early childhood education (P-3), earth science, elementary education (K-8), English, French, health and physical education, health education, home economics, mathematics, music, physical education, physical science, social studies, Spanish, teacher of ESL, teacher of students with disabilities. Part-time and evening/weekend programs available. *Faculty:* 18 full-time (12 women), 37 part-time/adjunct (26 women). *Students:* 183 full-time (105 women), 176 part-time (136 women); includes 20 Black or African American, non-Hispanic/Latino; 7 Asian, non-Hispanic/Latino; 15 Hispanic/Latino; 2 Two or more races, non-Hispanic/Latino, 6 international. Average age 30. 123 applicants, 56% accepted, 55 enrolled. In 2010, 133 master's, 1 other advanced degree awarded. *Degree requirements:* For master's, comprehensive exam, field experience. *Entrance requirements:* For master's, GRE, 2 letters of recommendation. Additional exam requirements/recommendations for international students: Required—TOEFL (minimum iBT score of 83) or IELTS. *Application deadline:* For fall admission, 2/15 for domestic and international students; for spring admission, 9/15 for domestic and international students. Applications are processed on a rolling basis. Application fee: $60. Electronic applications accepted. *Expenses:* Tuition, state resident: part-time $501.34 per credit. Tuition, nonresident: part-time $773.88 per credit. Required fees: $71.15 per credit. *Financial support:* In 2010–11, 8 research assistantships with full tuition reimbursements (averaging $7,000 per year) were awarded; Federal Work-Study, scholarships/grants, and unspecified assistantships also available. Support available to part-time students. Financial award application deadline: 3/1; financial award applicants required to submit FAFSA. *Faculty research:* Technology in the service of democratic education, case pedagogy in teacher preparation, public education in the United States, school reform: secondary science education, role of teacher learning as an agency of school reform. Total annual research expenditures: $11,313. *Unit head:* Dr. David Schwarzer, Chairperson, 973-655-5187. *Application contact:* Amy Aiello, Director of Graduate Admissions and Operations, 973-655-5147, Fax: 973-655-7869, E-mail: graduate.school@montclair.edu.

The New School: A University, The New School for Social Research, New York, NY 10003. Offers M Phil, MA, MS, DS Sc, PhD. Part-time and evening/weekend programs available. Terminal master's awarded for partial completion of doctoral program. *Degree requirements:* For master's, variable foreign language requirement, exam or thesis; for doctorate, variable foreign language requirement, comprehensive exam, thesis/dissertation, qualifying exam. *Entrance requirements:* For master's, GRE General Test; for doctorate, GRE General Test, MA. Additional exam requirements/recommendations for international students: Required—TOEFL (minimum score 600 paper-based; 250 computer-based; 100 iBT). Electronic applications accepted. *Expenses:* Contact institution. *Faculty research:* Civil society and democracy, international movements of refugees, minority use of health services, memory, morality and genetics.

New York University, Graduate School of Arts and Science, Program in Trauma and Violence Transdisciplinary Studies, New York, NY 10012-1019. Offers MA, Advanced Certificate. *Students:* 3 full-time (all women), 5 part-time (4 women), 2 international. Average age 32. 4 applicants, 100% accepted, 2 enrolled. In 2010, 2 master's, 1 other advanced degree awarded. *Entrance requirements:* Additional exam requirements/recommendations for international students: Required—TOEFL. *Application deadline:* For fall admission, 7/1 priority date for domestic students; for spring admission, 12/1 priority date for domestic students. Application fee: $90. *Financial support:* Application deadline: 7/1. *Unit head:* Judie Alpert, Co-Director, 212-998-8655, Fax: 212-995-4370, E-mail: tvts.info@nyu.edu. *Application contact:* Avital Ronell, Co-Director, 212-998-8655, Fax: 212-995-4370, E-mail: tvts.info@nyu.edu.

Social Sciences

North Dakota State University, College of Graduate and Interdisciplinary Studies, College of Arts, Humanities and Social Sciences, Department of Sociology, Anthropology, and Emergency Management, Fargo, ND 58108. Offers emergency management (MS, PhD); social science (MA, MS); sociology (MS). Part-time programs available. *Faculty:* 8 full-time (3 women), 5 part-time/adjunct (2 women). *Students:* 27 full-time (14 women), 14 part-time (4 women); includes 2 Black or African American, non-Hispanic/Latino; 1 American Indian or Alaska Native, non-Hispanic/Latino; 1 Asian, non-Hispanic/Latino; 1 Hispanic/Latino, 2 international. Average age 27. 15 applicants, 60% accepted, 7 enrolled. In 2010, 9 master's awarded. *Degree requirements:* For master's, thesis; for doctorate, comprehensive exam, thesis/dissertation. *Entrance requirements:* For master's, GRE (emergency management), course work in sociology, minimum GPA of 3.2; for doctorate, GRE, minimum GPA of 3.2. Additional exam requirements/recommendations for international students: Required—TOEFL. *Application deadline:* For fall admission, 4/1 priority date for domestic students. Applications are processed on a rolling basis. Application fee: $45 ($60 for international students). *Financial support:* In 2010–11, 7 research assistantships with full tuition reimbursements (averaging $6,156 per year), 7 teaching assistantships with full tuition reimbursements (averaging $3,078 per year) were awarded; fellowships, career-related internships or fieldwork, Federal Work-Study, institutionally sponsored loans, and tuition waivers (full) also available. Support available to part-time students. Financial award application deadline: 4/15. *Faculty research:* Medical sociology, demography, ethnology, archaeology. Total annual research expenditures: $75,000. *Unit head:* Dr. Daniel J. Klenow, Chair, 701-231-8657, Fax: 701-231-1047, E-mail: daniel.klenow@ndsu.edu. *Application contact:* Dr. Daniel J. Klenow, Chair, 701-231-8657, Fax: 701-231-1047, E-mail: daniel.klenow@ndsu.edu.

Northwestern University, The Graduate School, Interdepartmental Programs, Program in Mathematical Methods in Social Science, Evanston, IL 60208. Offers MS.

Northwestern University, The Graduate School, Program in Law and Social Science, Evanston, IL 60208. Offers Certificate. *Degree requirements:* For Certificate, research project. *Faculty research:* Law and social science.

Nova Southeastern University, Graduate School of Humanities and Social Sciences, Department of Multi-Disciplinary Studies, Fort Lauderdale, FL 33314-7796. Offers college student affairs (MS); college student personnel administration (Certificate); cross-disciplinary studies (MA); national security affairs (MS); qualitative methods (Certificate). Part-time programs available. Postbaccalaureate distance learning degree programs offered (minimal on-campus study). *Faculty:* 1 (woman) full-time, 52 part-time/adjunct (30 women). *Students:* 50 full-time (34 women), 65 part-time (52 women); includes 34 Black or African American, non-Hispanic/Latino; 3 Asian, non-Hispanic/Latino; 25 Hispanic/Latino; 1 Two or more races, non-Hispanic/Latino, 6 international. Average age 32. 76 applicants, 66% accepted, 40 enrolled. In 2010, 27 master's awarded. *Degree requirements:* For master's, comprehensive exam, thesis optional, portfolio. *Entrance requirements:* For master's, interview, minimum GPA of 3.0. Additional exam requirements/recommendations for international students: Required—TOEFL. *Application deadline:* For fall admission, 7/1 priority date for domestic and international students; for winter admission, 11/1 priority date for domestic and international students; for spring admission, 3/1 priority date for domestic and international students. Applications are processed on a rolling basis. Application fee: $50. Electronic applications accepted. *Financial support:* In 2010–11, 1 research assistantship (averaging $15,000 per year) was awarded; career-related internships or fieldwork, Federal Work-Study, institutionally sponsored loans, and scholarships/grants also available. Financial award applicants required to submit CSS PROFILE. *Unit head:* Dr. Judith McKay, Chair, 954-262-3060, Fax: 954-262-3893, E-mail: mckayj@nsu.nova.edu. *Application contact:* Marcia Arango, Student Recruitment Coordinator, 954-262-3006, Fax: 954-262-3968, E-mail: marango@nsu.nova.edu.

Ohio University, Graduate College, College of Arts and Sciences, Program in Social Sciences, Athens, OH 45701-2979. Offers MSS. Part-time and evening/weekend programs available. *Students:* 3 full-time (1 woman), 30 part-time (13 women); includes 2 minority (1 Black or African American, non-Hispanic/Latino; 1 Asian, non-Hispanic/Latino). Average age 39. 3 applicants, 33% accepted, 0 enrolled. In 2010, 16 master's awarded. *Degree requirements:* For master's, oral exam. *Entrance requirements:* For master's, minimum GPA of 2.75. Additional exam requirements/recommendations for international students: Required—TOEFL (minimum score 600 paper-based; 220 computer-based). Application fee: $50 ($55 for international students). Electronic applications accepted. *Financial support:* Institutionally sponsored loans available. Financial award application deadline: 3/15; financial award applicants required to submit FAFSA. *Unit head:* Dr. Katherine Jellison, Director, 740-593-0438, E-mail: jellison@ohio.edu. *Application contact:* Dr. Katherine Jellison, Director, 740-593-0438, E-mail: jellison@ohio.edu.

Queens College of the City University of New York, Division of Graduate Studies, Social Science Division, Program in Social Sciences, Flushing, NY 11367-1597. Offers MASS. Part-time and evening/weekend programs available. *Students:* 4 part-time (2 women); includes 1 Asian, non-Hispanic/Latino, 2 international. *Degree requirements:* For master's, thesis. *Entrance requirements:* For master's, minimum GPA of 3.0. Additional exam requirements/recommendations for international students: Required—TOEFL. *Application deadline:* For fall admission, 4/1 for domestic students; for spring admission, 11/1 for domestic students. Applications are processed on a rolling basis. Application fee: $125. *Financial support:* Career-related internships or fieldwork, Federal Work-Study, institutionally sponsored loans, and tuition waivers (partial) available. Support available to part-time students. Financial award application deadline: 4/1; financial award applicants required to submit FAFSA. *Unit head:* Dr. Martin Hanlon, Graduate Adviser, 718-997-5510, E-mail: martin_hanlon@qc.edu. *Application contact:* Mario Caruso, Director of Graduate Admissions, 718-997-5200, Fax: 718-997-5193, E-mail: graduate_admissions@qc.edu.

St. Edward's University, New College, Program in Liberal Arts, Austin, TX 78704. Offers global issues (MLA); humanities (MLA); liberal arts (Certificate); social sciences (MLA). Part-time and evening/weekend programs available. *Students:* 6 full-time (5 women), 80 part-time (54 women); includes 28 minority (6 Black or African American, non-Hispanic/Latino; 2 Asian, non-Hispanic/Latino; 19 Hispanic/Latino; 1 Two or more races, non-Hispanic/Latino, 1 international. Average age 34. 47 applicants, 68% accepted, 24 enrolled. In 2010, 29 master's awarded. *Degree requirements:* For master's, minimum of 24 resident hours. *Entrance requirements:* For master's, minimum GPA of 2.75 in last 60 hours of course work, interview. Additional exam requirements/recommendations for international students: Required—TOEFL (minimum score 550 paper-based; 213 computer-based; 79 iBT) or IELTS (minimum score 6). *Application deadline:* For fall admission, 7/1 for domestic and international students; for spring admission, 11/1 for domestic and international students. Applications are processed on a rolling basis. Application fee: $45 ($50 for international students). Electronic applications accepted. *Expenses:* Tuition: Full-time $16,200; part-time $900 per credit hour. Required fees: $50 per trimester. Full-time tuition and fees vary according to course load and program. *Financial support:* In 2010–11, 2 students received support. Scholarships/grants available. *Unit head:* Dr. H. Ramsey Fowler, Director, 512-448-8648, Fax: 512-448-8492, E-mail: ramseyf@stewards.edu. *Application contact:* Carrie Martin, Graduate Admission Coordinator, 512-233-1694, Fax: 512-428-1032, E-mail: carriem@stedwards.edu.

Southern University and Agricultural and Mechanical College, Graduate School, College of Arts and Humanities, Department of History, Baton Rouge, LA 70813. Offers social sciences (MA). Part-time programs available. *Degree requirements:* For master's, thesis. *Entrance requirements:* For master's, GRE General Test. Additional exam requirements/recommendations for international students: Required—TOEFL (minimum score 525 paper-based; 193 computer-based).

Stony Brook University, State University of New York, School of Professional Development, Stony Brook, NY 11794. Offers biology-grade 7-12 (MAT); chemistry-grade 7-12 (MAT); coaching (Graduate Certificate); coaching online (Graduate Certificate); computer integrated engineering (Graduate Certificate); earth science-grade 7-12 (MAT); educational computing (Graduate Certificate); educational leadership (Advanced Certificate); English-grade 7-12 (MAT); environmental management (Graduate Certificate); environmental/occupational health and safety (Graduate Certificate); French-grade 7-12 (MAT); German-grade 7-12 (MAT); human resource management (Graduate Certificate); human resource management online (Graduate Certificate); information systems management (Graduate Certificate); Italian-grade 7-12 (MAT); liberal studies (MA); liberal studies online (MAT); mathematics-grade 7-12 (MAT); operation research (Graduate Certificate); physics-grade 7-12 (MAT); professional studies online (MPS); school administration and supervision (Graduate Certificate); school building leadership (Graduate Certificate); school district administration (Graduate Certificate); school district business leadership (Advanced Certificate); school district leadership (Graduate Certificate); social science and the professions (MPS), including environmental waste management, human resource management; social studies-grade 7-12 (MAT); Spanish-grade 7-12 (MAT); waste management (Graduate Certificate). Part-time and evening/weekend programs available. Postbaccalaureate distance learning degree programs offered. *Faculty:* 25 full-time (10 women), 105 part-time/adjunct (40 women). *Students:* 360 full-time (228 women), 1,097 part-time (729 women); includes 180 minority (65 Black or African American, non-Hispanic/Latino; 2 American Indian or Alaska Native, non-Hispanic/Latino; 30 Asian, non-Hispanic/Latino; 81 Hispanic/Latino; 1 Native Hawaiian or other Pacific Islander, non-Hispanic/Latino; 1 Two or more races, non-Hispanic/Latino), 10 international. Average age 28. In 2010, 505 master's, 187 other advanced degrees awarded. *Degree requirements:* For master's, one foreign language, thesis or alternative. *Application deadline:* Applications are processed on a rolling basis. Application fee: $100. *Expenses:* Tuition, state resident: full-time $8370; part-time $349 per credit. Tuition, nonresident: full-time $13,780; part-time $574 per credit. Required fees: $994. *Financial support:* In 2010–11, 1 teaching assistantship was awarded; fellowships, research assistantships, career-related internships or fieldwork also available. Support available to part-time students. *Unit head:* Dr. Paul J. Edelson, Dean, 631-632-7052, Fax: 631-632-9046, E-mail: paul.edelson@stonybrook.edu. *Application contact:* Dr. Paul J. Edelson, Dean, 631-632-7052, Fax: 631-632-9046, E-mail: paul.edelson@stonybrook.edu.

Syracuse University, Maxwell School of Citizenship and Public Affairs, Program in Social Sciences, Syracuse, NY 13244. Offers MS Sc, PhD. Part-time and evening/weekend programs available. Postbaccalaureate distance learning degree programs offered. *Students:* 27 full-time (14 women), 43 part-time (20 women); includes 9 minority (2 Black or African American, non-Hispanic/Latino; 1 American Indian or Alaska Native, non-Hispanic/Latino; 3 Asian, non-Hispanic/Latino; 2 Hispanic/Latino; 1 Two or more races, non-Hispanic/Latino), 8 international. Average age 41. 29 applicants, 41% accepted, 7 enrolled. In 2010, 8 master's, 10 doctorates awarded. *Degree requirements:* For doctorate, thesis/dissertation. *Entrance requirements:* For doctorate, GRE General Test. Additional exam requirements/recommendations for international students: Required—TOEFL (minimum score 100 iBT). *Application deadline:* For fall admission, 3/15 priority date for domestic and international students. Application fee: $75. Electronic applications accepted. *Expenses:*. Tuition: Part-time $1162 per credit. *Financial support:* Fellowships with full tuition reimbursements, research assistantships with full and partial tuition reimbursements, teaching assistantships with full and partial tuition reimbursements available. Financial award application deadline: 1/1. *Unit head:* Dr. Vernon Greene, Chair, 315-443-2275, Fax: 315-443-1463, E-mail: vgreene@maxwell.syr.edu. *Application contact:* Mary Olszewski, Information Contact, 315-443-2275, E-mail: mtolszew@maxwell.syr.edu.

Texas A&M International University, Office of Graduate Studies and Research, College of Arts and Sciences, Department of Social Sciences, Laredo, TX 78041-1900. Offers history (MA); political science (MA); public administration (MPA). *Faculty:* 8 full-time (3 women). *Students:* 4 full-time (2 women), 52 part-time (27 women); includes 1 Asian, non-Hispanic/Latino; 52 Hispanic/Latino, 1 international. Average age 30. 35 applicants, 74% accepted, 19 enrolled. In 2010, 10 master's awarded. *Degree requirements:* For master's, thesis (for some programs). *Entrance requirements:* For master's, GRE General Test. Additional exam requirements/recommendations for international students: Required—TOEFL (minimum score 550 paper-based; 213 computer-based). *Application deadline:* For fall admission, 4/30 priority date for domestic students; for spring admission, 11/30 for domestic students, 10/1 for international students. Applications are processed on a rolling basis. Application fee: $25. *Financial support:* In 2010–11, 14 students received support, including 7 research assistantships. Financial award application deadline: 11/1. *Unit head:* Dr. Mohammed Ben-Ruwin, Chair, 956-328-2632, E-mail: mbenruwin@tamiu.edu. *Application contact:* Suzanne Hansen-Alford, Director of Admissions, 956-326-3023, Fax: 956-326-3021, E-mail: graduateschool@tamiu.edu.

Texas A&M University–Commerce, Graduate School, College of Arts and Sciences, Department of History, Commerce, TX 75429-3011. Offers history (MA, MS); social sciences (M Ed, MS). Part-time programs available. *Degree requirements:* For master's, comprehensive exam, thesis (for some programs). *Entrance requirements:* For master's, GRE General Test. Electronic applications accepted. *Faculty research:* American foreign policy, colonial America, Texas politics, Medieval England.

Towson University, Program in Social Science, Towson, MD 21252-0001. Offers MS. Part-time and evening/weekend programs available. *Students:* 12 full-time (9 women), 19 part-time (11 women); includes 9 minority (6 Black or African American, non-Hispanic/Latino; 1 American Indian or Alaska Native, non-Hispanic/Latino; 1 Asian, non-Hispanic/Latino; 1 Hispanic/Latino), 2 international. Average age 31. In 2010, 9 master's awarded. *Entrance requirements:* For master's, minimum GPA of 3.0, 3 letters of recommendation, letter of intent. Additional exam requirements/recommendations for international students: Required—TOEFL. *Application deadline:* For fall admission, 10/15 priority date for domestic and international students; for spring admission, 4/15 priority date for domestic and international students. Applications are processed on a rolling basis. Application fee: $50. Electronic applications accepted. *Expenses:* Tuition, state resident: part-time $324 per credit. Tuition, nonresident: part-time $681 per credit. Required fees: $95 per term. *Financial support:* Career-related internships or fieldwork, Federal Work-Study, and unspecified assistantships available. Support available to part-time students. Financial award application deadline: 4/1; financial award applicants required to submit FAFSA. *Faculty research:* Race and ethnicity, diplomatic history, sociology methodology, central Asian geography. *Unit head:* Michael Korzi, Graduate Program Director, 410-704-5219, Fax: 410-704-5995, E-mail: mkorzi@towson.edu. *Application contact:* 410-704-2501, Fax: 410-704-4675, E-mail: grads@towson.edu.

University of Atlanta, Graduate Programs, Atlanta, GA 30360. Offers business (MS); business administration (Exec MBA, MBA); computer science (MS); educational leadership (MS, Ed D); healthcare administration (MS, D Sc, Graduate Certificate); information technology for management (Graduate Certificate); international project management (Graduate Certificate); law (JD); managerial science (DBA); project management (Graduate Certificate); social science (MS). Postbaccalaureate distance learning degree programs offered. *Entrance requirements:* For master's, minimum cumulative GPA of 2.5.

University of California, Irvine, School of Social Sciences, Irvine, CA 92697. Offers MA, PhD. *Students:* 372 full-time (158 women), 6 part-time (2 women); includes 101 minority (2 Black or African American, non-Hispanic/Latino; 1 American Indian or Alaska Native, non-Hispanic/Latino; 61 Asian, non-Hispanic/Latino; 31 Hispanic/Latino; 6 Two or more races, non-Hispanic/Latino), 43 international. Average age 28. 848 applicants, 23% accepted, 94 enrolled. In 2010, 64 master's, 34 doctorates awarded. *Degree requirements:* For doctorate, thesis/dissertation. *Entrance requirements:* For master's, GRE, minimum GPA of 3.0; for doctorate, GRE General Test, minimum GPA of 3.0. Additional exam requirements/recommendations for international students: Required—TOEFL (minimum score 550 paper-based; 213 computer-based). *Application deadline:* For fall admission, 1/15 priority date for domestic students, 1/15 for international students. Applications are processed on a rolling basis. Application fee: $80 ($100 for international students). Electronic applications accepted. *Financial support:* Fellowships, research assistantships with full tuition reimbursements, teaching assistantships, institutionally sponsored loans, traineeships, health care benefits, and unspecified assistantships available. Financial award application deadline: 3/1; financial award applicants required to submit FAFSA. *Faculty research:* Mathematical modeling of perception and cognitive processes, economic analysis of transportation, impact of society's political system on its economy, exploration of authority structures and inequality in society. *Unit head:* Prof. Barbara Anne Dosher, Dean, 949-824-6802, Fax: 949-824-3995, E-mail: bdosher@uci.edu. *Application contact:* Prof. Bill M. Maurer, Associate Dean, 949-824-6680, Fax: 949-824-0646, E-mail: wmmaurer@uci.edu.

University of California, Merced, Division of Graduate Studies, School of Social Sciences, Humanities and Arts, Merced, CA 95343. Offers social and cognitive sciences (MA, PhD); world cultures (MA, PhD).

University of California, Santa Barbara, Graduate Division, College of Letters and Sciences, Division of Mathematics, Life, and Physical Sciences, Department of Psychology, Santa Barbara, CA 93106-9660. Offers cognitive science (PhD); psychology (PhD); quantitative methods in the social sciences (PhD). *Faculty:* 33 full-time (10 women). *Students:* 59 full-time (36 women); includes 2 Black or African American, non-Hispanic/Latino; 8 Asian, non-Hispanic/Latino. Average age 27. 240 applicants, 6% accepted, 5 enrolled. In 2010, 8 doctorates awarded. Terminal master's awarded for partial completion of doctoral program. *Degree requirements:* For doctorate, comprehensive exam, thesis/dissertation, teaching assistant training, progress report, papers, mini-convention presentation, 1 quarter of student teaching or teaching assistant class with section lab. *Entrance requirements:* For doctorate, GRE General Test. Additional exam requirements/recommendations for international students: Required—TOEFL (minimum score 550 paper-based; 80 iBT), IELTS (minimum score 7). *Application deadline:* For fall admission, 12/1 for domestic and international students. Application fee: $70 ($90 for international students). Electronic applications accepted. *Financial support:* In 2010–11, 59 students received support, including 60 fellowships with full and partial tuition reimbursements available (averaging $6,819 per year), 29 research assistantships with full and partial tuition reimbursements available (averaging $10,114 per year), 48 teaching assistantships with full and partial tuition reimbursements available (averaging $11,597 per year); tuition waivers (full and partial) also available. Financial award application deadline: 12/15; financial award applicants required to submit FAFSA. *Faculty research:* Social psychology; developmental and evolutionary psychology; neuroscience and behavior; cognition, perception and cognitive neuroscience. Total annual research expenditures: $6 million. *Unit head:* Greg Ashby, Chair, 805-893-2130, Fax: 805-893-4303. *Application contact:* Greg Ashby, Chair, 805-893-2130, Fax: 805-893-4303.

University of California, Santa Barbara, Graduate Division, College of Letters and Sciences, Division of Social Sciences, Department of Communication, Santa Barbara, CA 93106-4020. Offers cognitive science (PhD); feminist studies (PhD); quantitative methods in the social science (PhD); society and technology (PhD); MA/PhD. *Faculty:* 20 full-time (9 women). *Students:* 39 full-time (26 women); includes 3 Black or African American, non-Hispanic/Latino; 5 Asian, non-Hispanic/Latino; 6 Hispanic/Latino. Average age 30. 169 applicants, 6% accepted, 5 enrolled. In 2010, 3 doctorates awarded. Terminal master's awarded for partial completion of doctoral program. *Degree requirements:* For doctorate, comprehensive exam, thesis/dissertation. *Entrance requirements:* For doctorate, GRE. Additional exam requirements/recommendations for international students: Required—TOEFL (minimum score 550 paper-based; 80 iBT), IELTS (minimum score 7). *Application deadline:* For fall admission, 12/1 for domestic and international students. Application fee: $70 ($90 for international students). Electronic applications accepted. *Financial support:* In 2010–11, 39 students received support, including 39 fellowships with full and partial tuition reimbursements available (averaging $6,045 per year), 5 research assistantships with full and partial tuition reimbursements available (averaging $9,646 per year), 29 teaching assistantships with partial tuition reimbursements available (averaging $14,294 per year); career-related internships or fieldwork, health care benefits, and tuition waivers (full and partial) also available. Support available to part-time students. Financial award application deadline: 12/1. *Faculty research:* Interpersonal, intercultural, organizational, health, media. *Unit head:* Prof. Linda L. Putnam, Professor, 805-893-7935, Fax: 805-893-7102, E-mail: lputnam@comm.ucsb.edu. *Application contact:* Nancy Siris-Rawls, Graduate Program Assistant, 805-893-3046, Fax: 805-893-7102, E-mail: nsiris@comm.ucsb.edu.

University of California, Santa Cruz, Division of Graduate Studies, Division of Humanities, Program in the History of Consciousness, Santa Cruz, CA 95064. Offers PhD. *Students:* 29 full-time (13 women), 1 part-time (0 women); includes 8 minority (2 Black or African American, non-Hispanic/Latino; 3 Asian, non-Hispanic/Latino; 3 Hispanic/Latino), 2 international. Average age 32. In 2010, 8 doctorates awarded. *Degree requirements:* For doctorate, one foreign language, thesis/dissertation, qualifying exam. *Entrance requirements:* For doctorate, GRE General Test. Additional exam requirements/recommendations for international students: Required—TOEFL (minimum score 550 paper-based; 220 computer-based; 83 iBT); Recommended—IELTS (minimum score 8). *Application deadline:* For fall admission, 12/10 for domestic and international students. Application fee: $70 ($90 for international students). Electronic applications accepted. *Financial support:* Fellowships, teaching assistantships, institutionally sponsored loans and tuition waivers available. Financial award applicants required to submit FAFSA. *Faculty research:* Interdisciplinary humanities and social sciences, political theory, cultural theory, feminist studies, literary theory. *Unit head:* Anne Spalliero, Graduate Program Coordinator, 831-459-1478, E-mail: amspa@ucsc.edu. *Application contact:* Anne Spalliero, Graduate Program Coordinator, 831-459-1478, E-mail: amspa@ucsc.edu.

University of Chicago, Division of Social Sciences, Committee on Social Thought, Chicago, IL 60637-1513. Offers PhD. *Degree requirements:* For doctorate, one foreign language, thesis/dissertation, exam. *Entrance requirements:* For doctorate, GRE General Test. Additional exam requirements/recommendations for international students: Required—TOEFL, IELTS (minimum score 7). Electronic applications accepted.

University of Chicago, Division of Social Sciences, Master of Arts Program in the Social Sciences, Chicago, IL 60637-1513. Offers AM. Part-time programs available. *Degree requirements:* For master's, thesis. *Entrance requirements:* For master's, GRE General Test. Additional exam requirements/recommendations for international students: Required—TOEFL. Electronic applications accepted.

University of Colorado Denver, College of Liberal Arts and Sciences, Program in Humanities, Denver, CO 80217-3364. Offers community health science (MSS); humanities (MH); international studies (MSS); social science (MSS); society and the environment (MSS); women's and gender studies (MSS). Part-time and evening/weekend programs available. *Students:* 53 full-time (39 women), 35 part-time (22 women); includes 4 Black or African American, non-Hispanic/Latino; 1 American Indian or Alaska Native, non-Hispanic/Latino; 3 Asian, non-Hispanic/Latino; 7 Hispanic/Latino, 1 international. Average age 33. 41 applicants, 54% accepted, 19 enrolled. In 2010, 29 master's awarded. *Degree requirements:* For master's, thesis or alternative, 36 credit hours, project or thesis. *Entrance requirements:* For master's, writing sample, statement of purpose/letter of intent. Additional exam requirements/recommendations for international students: Required—TOEFL (minimum score 525 paper-based). *Application deadline:* For fall admission, 5/15 priority date for domestic students; for spring admission, 10/15 priority date for domestic students. Application fee: $50 ($75 for international students). Electronic applications accepted. *Expenses:* Tuition, state resident: full-time $7332; part-time $355 per credit hour. Tuition, nonresident: full-time $18,990; part-time $1055 per credit hour. Required fees: $998. Tuition and fees vary according to course level, course load, degree level, campus/location, program, reciprocity agreements and student level. *Financial support:* Federal Work-Study and scholarships/grants available. Financial award application deadline: 4/1; financial award applicants required to submit FAFSA. *Faculty research:* Women and gender in the classical Mediterranean, communication theory and democracy, relationship between psychology and philosophy. *Unit head:* Myra Bookman, Associate Director of Humanities and Social Science, 303-556-2496, Fax: 303-556-8100, E-mail: myra.bookman@ucdenver.edu. *Application contact:* Catherine Osmundson, Program Assistant, 303-556-2305, E-mail: catherine.osmundson@ucdenver.edu.

University of Florida, Graduate School, College of Public Health and Health Professions and College of Medicine, Programs in Public Health, Gainesville, FL 32611. Offers biostatistics (MPH); environmental health (MPH); epidemiology (MPH); public health management and policy (MPH); public health practice (MPH); social and behavioral sciences (MPH). *Accreditation:* CEPH. Postbaccalaureate distance learning degree programs offered. *Students:* 127 full-time (85 women), 38 part-time (22 women); includes 21 Black or African American, non-Hispanic/Latino; 19 Asian, non-Hispanic/Latino; 16 Hispanic/Latino, 11 international. Average age 28. 263 applicants, 29% accepted, 48 enrolled. In 2010, 54 master's awarded. *Degree requirements:* For master's, internship. *Entrance requirements:* For master's, GRE General Test, minimum GPA of 3.0. Additional exam requirements/recommendations for international students: Required—TOEFL (minimum score 550 paper-based; 213 computer-based; 80 iBT), IELTS (minimum score 6). Application fee: $30. *Expenses:* Tuition, state resident: full-time $10,915.92. Tuition, nonresident: full-time $28,309. *Financial support:* In 2010–11, 12 students received support, including 4 fellowships, 5 research assistantships (averaging $14,122 per year), 3 teaching assistantships (averaging $12,501 per year). Financial award applicants required to submit FAFSA. *Unit head:* Prof. Mary Peoples-Sheps, Associate Dean for Public Health, 352-273-6084, Fax: 352-273-6448, E-mail: mpeoplessheps@phhp.ufl.edu. *Application contact:* Prof. Mary Peoples-Sheps, Associate Dean for Public Health, 352-273-6084, Fax: 352-273-6448, E-mail: mpeoplessheps@phhp.ufl.edu.

University of Idaho, College of Graduate Studies, College of Natural Resources, Department of Conservation Social Sciences, Moscow, ID 83844-2282. Offers natural resources (MS, PhD). *Faculty:* 13 full-time. *Students:* 16 full-time, 4 part-time. Average age 27. In 2010, 5 master's awarded. *Degree requirements:* For doctorate, thesis/dissertation. *Entrance requirements:* For master's, minimum GPA of 2.8; for doctorate, minimum undergraduate GPA of 2.8, 3.0 graduate. *Application deadline:* For fall admission, 8/1 for domestic students; for spring admission, 12/15 for domestic students. Applications are processed on a rolling basis. Application fee: $60. Electronic applications accepted. *Expenses:* Tuition, nonresident: part-time $580 per credit. Required fees: $306 per credit. *Financial support:* Research assistantships, teaching assistantships available. Financial award applicants required to submit FAFSA. *Faculty research:* Parks, wilderness and protected areas policy, planning and management, recreation and tourism planning, urban and community forestry, resource-based tourism, ecotourism, human dimensions of ecosystem management. *Unit head:* Dr. Larry Young, Department Head, 208-885-7911, E-mail: css@uidaho.edu. *Application contact:* Dr. Larry Young, Department Head, 208-885-7911, E-mail: css@uidaho.edu.

University of Illinois at Springfield, Graduate Programs, College of Education and Human Services, Program in Human Services, Springfield, IL 62703-5407. Offers alcoholism and substance abuse (MA); child and family services (MA); gerontology (MA); social services administration (MA). Part-time and evening/weekend programs available. Postbaccalaureate distance learning degree programs offered (no on-campus study). *Degree requirements:* For master's, internship; project or thesis. *Entrance requirements:* For master's, minimum undergraduate GPA of 3.0, 2 letters of recommendation. Additional exam requirements/recommendations for international students: Required—TOEFL (minimum score 500 paper-based; 176 computer-based; 61 iBT). Electronic applications accepted. *Expenses:* Tuition, state resident: full-time $6774; part-time $282.25 per credit hour. Tuition, nonresident: full-time $15,078; part-time $628.25 per credit hour. Required fees: $15.25 per credit hour. $492 per term.

University of Lethbridge, School of Graduate Studies, Lethbridge, AB T1K 3M4, Canada. Offers accounting (MScM); addictions counseling (M Sc); agricultural biotechnology (M Sc); agricultural studies (M Sc, MA); anthropology (MA); archaeology (MA); art (MA, MFA); biochemistry (M Sc); biological sciences (M Sc); biomolecular science (PhD); biosystems and biodiversity (PhD); Canadian studies (MA); chemistry (M Sc); computer science (M Sc); computer science and geographical information science (M Sc); counseling psychology (M Ed); dramatic arts (MA); earth, space, and physical science (PhD); economics (MA); educational leadership (M Ed); English (MA); environmental science (M Sc); evolution and behavior (PhD); exercise science (M Sc); finance (MScM); French (MA); French/German (MA); French/Spanish (MA); general education (M Ed); general management (MScM); geography (M Sc, MA); German (MA); health science (M Sc); history (MA); human resource management and labour relations (MScM); individualized multidisciplinary (M Sc, MA); information systems (MScM); international management (MScM); kinesiology (M Sc, MA); management (M Sc, MA); marketing (MScM); mathematics (M Sc); music (M Mus, MA); Native American studies (MA); neuroscience (M Sc, PhD); new media (MA); nursing (M Sc); philosophy (MA); physics (M Sc); policy and strategy (MScM); political science (MA); psychology (M Sc, MA); religious studies (MA); social sciences (MA); sociology (MA); theatre and dramatic arts (MFA); theoretical and computational science (PhD); urban and regional studies (MA); women's studies (MA). Part-time and evening/weekend programs available. *Degree requirements:* For doctorate, comprehensive exam, thesis/dissertation. *Entrance requirements:* For master's, GMAT (M Sc in management), bachelor's degree in related field, minimum GPA of 3.0 during previous 20 graded semester courses, 2 years teaching or related experience (M Ed); for doctorate, master's degree, minimum graduate GPA of 3.5. Additional exam requirements/recommendations for international students: Required—TOEFL. *Faculty research:* Movement and brain plasticity, gibberellin physiology, photosynthesis, carbon cycling, molecular properties of main-group ring components.

The University of Manchester, School of Social Sciences, Manchester, United Kingdom. Offers ethnographic documentary (M Phil); interdisciplinary study of culture (PhD); philosophy (PhD); politics (PhD); social anthropology (PhD); social anthropology with visual media (PhD); social change (PhD); social statistics (PhD); sociology (PhD); visual anthropology (M Phil).

University of Maryland, Baltimore County, Graduate School, Program in Gerontology, Baltimore, MD 21201. Offers aging policy for the elderly (PhD); epidemiology of aging (PhD); social, cultural, and behavioral sciences (PhD); MA/PhD; MS/PhD. Part-time programs available. *Faculty:* 19 part-time/adjunct (13 women). *Students:* 12 full-time (10 women), 14 part-time (12 women); includes 4 Black or African American, non-Hispanic/Latino; 1 Asian, non-Hispanic/Latino; 1 Hispanic/Latino, 1 international. Average age 34. 24 applicants, 33% accepted, 5 enrolled. In 2010, 3 doctorates awarded. *Degree requirements:* For doctorate, comprehensive exam, thesis/dissertation. *Entrance requirements:* For doctorate, GRE General Test. Additional exam requirements/recommendations for international students: Required—TOEFL, TWE. *Application deadline:* For spring admission, 1/15 for domestic and international students. Application fee: $45. Electronic applications accepted. *Financial support:* In 2010–11, 4 fellowships with full tuition reimbursements (averaging $21,180 per year), 7 research assistantships with full tuition reimbursements (averaging $21,000 per year), 1 teaching assistantship with full tuition reimbursement (averaging $20,000 per year) were awarded; career-related internships or fieldwork, scholarships/grants, traineeships, health care benefits, tuition waivers (partial), and unspecified assistantships also available. Financial award application deadline: 2/1; financial award applicants required to submit FAFSA. *Faculty research:* Aging and health policy, behavioral aspects of aging, caregiving, epidemiology of aging. Total annual research expenditures: $32.5 million. *Unit head:* Dr. Leslie Morgan, Co-Director, 410-455-2074, Fax: 410-455-1154, E-mail: lmorgan@umbc.edu. *Application contact:* Justine Golden, Academic Coordinator, 410-706-4926, Fax: 410-706-4433, E-mail: jgold002@umaryland.edu.

University of Memphis, Graduate School, School of Public Health, Memphis, TN 38152. Offers biostatistics (MPH); environmental health (MPH); epidemiology (MPH); health systems management (MPH); public health (MHA); social and behavioral sciences (MPH). Part-time and evening/weekend programs available. Postbaccalaureate distance learning degree programs offered. *Faculty:* 5 full-time (2 women), 4 part-time/adjunct (2 women). *Students:* 45 full-time (23 women), 29 part-time (14 women); includes 19 Black or African American, non-Hispanic/Latino; 6 Asian, non-Hispanic/Latino; 2 Hispanic/Latino, 7 international. Average age 32. 57 applicants, 70% accepted, 22 enrolled. In 2010, 17 master's awarded. *Degree requirements:* For master's, comprehensive exam, thesis. *Entrance requirements:* For master's, GRE, letters of recommendation. Additional exam requirements/recommendations for international students: Required—TOEFL. *Application deadline:* For fall admission, 4/1 for domestic students; for spring admission, 11/1 for domestic students. Application fee: $35 ($60 for international students). Electronic applications accepted. *Financial support:* In 2010–11, 46 students received

Social Sciences

University of Memphis (continued)

support; research assistantships with full tuition reimbursements available, Federal Work-Study, scholarships/grants, and unspecified assistantships available. Financial award application deadline: 2/15; financial award applicants required to submit FAFSA. *Faculty research:* Health and medical savings accounts, adoption rates, health informatics, Telehealth technologies, biostatistics, environmental health, epidemiology, health systems management, social and behavioral sciences. *Unit head:* Dr. Lisa M. Klesges, Director, 901-678-4637, E-mail: lmklsges@memphis.edu. *Application contact:* Dr. Lisa M. Klesges, Director, 901-678-4637, E-mail: lmklsges@memphis.edu.

University of Michigan, School of Social Work, Interdisciplinary Program in Social Work and Social Science, Ann Arbor, MI 48109. Offers PhD. Offered through the Horace H. Rackham School of Graduate Studies. *Faculty:* 51 full-time (23 women), 47 part-time/adjunct (32 women). *Students:* 79 full-time (64 women); includes 22 minority (8 Black or African American, non-Hispanic/Latino; 2 American Indian or Alaska Native, non-Hispanic/Latino; 6 Asian, non-Hispanic/Latino; 6 Hispanic/Latino), 15 international. Average age 34. 95 applicants, 9% accepted, 9 enrolled. In 2010, 9 doctorates awarded. *Degree requirements:* For doctorate, thesis/dissertation, oral defense of dissertation, preliminary exam. *Entrance requirements:* For doctorate, GRE General Test. Additional exam requirements/recommendations for international students: Required—TOEFL. *Application deadline:* For fall admission, 12/1 for domestic and international students. Application fee: $65 ($75 for international students). *Expenses:* Tuition, state resident: full-time $17,784; part-time $1116 per credit hour. Tuition, nonresident: full-time $35,944; part-time $2125 per credit hour. International tuition: $35,994 full-time. Required fees: $95 per semester. Tuition and fees vary according to course load, degree level and program. *Financial support:* In 2010–11, 67 students received support, including 15 fellowships with full tuition reimbursements available (averaging $15,200 per year), 14 research assistantships with full tuition reimbursements available (averaging $17,300 per year), 25 teaching assistantships with full tuition reimbursements available (averaging $17,300 per year); career-related internships or fieldwork, Federal Work-Study, scholarships/grants, traineeships, health care benefits, tuition waivers (full and partial), and unspecified assistantships also available. Financial award application deadline: 12/1; financial award applicants required to submit FAFSA. *Faculty research:* Substance abuse, child welfare, mental health, poverty, aging. Total annual research expenditures: $7.1 million. *Unit head:* Dr. Berit Ingersoll-Dayton, Director, 734-763-5768, Fax: 734-615-3192, E-mail: bid@umich.edu. *Application contact:* Graduate Coordinator, 734-647-2554, Fax: 734-615-3192, E-mail: ssw.phd.info@umich.edu.

University of Michigan–Flint, College of Arts and Sciences, Program in Social Sciences, Flint, MI 48502-1950. Offers MA. Part-time programs available. *Entrance requirements:* Additional exam requirements/recommendations for international students: Required—TOEFL (minimum score 560 paper-based; 220 computer-based; 84 iBT), IELTS (minimum score 6.5). *Expenses:* Contact institution.

The University of North Carolina at Charlotte, Graduate School, College of Arts and Sciences, Department of Sociology, Charlotte, NC 28223-0001. Offers health research (MA); mathematical sociology and quantitative methods (MA); organizations, occupations, and work (MA); political sociology (MA); race and gender (MA); social psychology (MA); social theory (MA); sociology of education (MA); stratification (MA). Part-time and evening/weekend programs available. *Faculty:* 18 full-time (10 women). *Students:* 11 full-time (7 women), 14 part-time (8 women); includes 6 minority (4 Black or African American, non-Hispanic/Latino; 2 Asian, non-Hispanic/Latino). Average age 29. 20 applicants, 60% accepted, 8 enrolled. In 2010, 2 master's awarded. *Degree requirements:* For master's, thesis or alternative, thesis or comprehensive exam. *Entrance requirements:* For master's, GRE or MAT, minimum GPA of 3.0 in last 2 years, 2.75 overall. Additional exam requirements/recommendations for international students: Required—TOEFL (minimum score 557 paper-based; 220 computer-based; 83 iBT). *Application deadline:* For fall admission, 7/1 for domestic students, 5/1 for international students; for spring admission, 11/1 for domestic students, 10/1 for international students. Applications are processed on a rolling basis. Application fee: $55. Electronic applications accepted. *Expenses:* Tuition, state resident: full-time $3464. Tuition, nonresident: full-time $14,297. Required fees: $2094. Tuition and fees vary according to course load. *Financial support:* In 2010–11, 6 students received support, including 1 fellowship (averaging $60,000 per year), 1 research assistantship (averaging $9,000 per year), 1 teaching assistantship (averaging $9,000 per year); career-related internships or fieldwork, institutionally sponsored loans, scholarships/grants, and unspecified assistantships also available. Support available to part-time students. Financial award application deadline: 4/1; financial award applicants required to submit FAFSA. *Faculty research:* Social psychology, sociology of education, social gerontology, quantitative methodology, medical sociology. Total annual research expenditures: $61,382. *Unit head:* Dr. Lisa Rachotte, Chair, 704-687-2288, Fax: 704-687-3091, E-mail: lrashott@uncc.edu. *Application contact:* Kathy B. Giddings, Director of Graduate Admissions, 704-687-5503, Fax: 704-687-3279, E-mail: gradadm@uncc.edu.

University of Northern Iowa, Graduate College, College of Social and Behavioral Sciences, Department of Social Science, Cedar Falls, IA 50614. Offers MA. *Students:* 16 part-time (7 women). 2 applicants, 0% accepted, 0 enrolled. In 2010, 12 master's awarded. *Entrance requirements:* For master's, minimum GPA of 3.0. Additional exam requirements/recommendations for international students: Required—TOEFL (minimum score 500 paper-based; 180 computer-based; 61 iBT). Application fee: $50 ($70 for international students). *Unit head:* Dr. Chad Christopher, Coordinator, 319-273-3157, Fax: 319-273-2222, E-mail: chad.christopher@uni.edu. *Application contact:* Laurie S. Russell, Record Analyst, 319-273-2623, Fax: 319-273-2885, E-mail: laurie.russell@uni.edu.

University of Regina, Faculty of Graduate Studies and Research, Faculty of Arts, Department of Sociology and Social Studies, Regina, SK S4S 0A2, Canada. Offers social studies (MA); sociology (MA). Part-time programs available. *Faculty:* 12 full-time (5 women), 1 part-time/adjunct (0 women). *Students:* 7 full-time (3 women), 5 part-time (4 women). 10 applicants, 70% accepted. In 2010, 3 master's awarded. *Degree requirements:* For master's, thesis. *Entrance requirements:* Additional exam requirements/recommendations for international students: Required—TOEFL (minimum score 580 paper-based; 80 iBT). *Application deadline:* Applications are processed on a rolling basis. Application fee: $10 ($100 for international students). Electronic applications accepted. Tuition and fees charges are reported in Canadian dollars. *Expenses:* Tuition, area resident: Full-time $3244.50 Canadian dollars; part-time $180.25 Canadian dollars per credit hour. International tuition: $4744.50 Canadian dollars full-time. Required fees: $494 Canadian dollars; $115.25 Canadian dollars per credit hour. $115.25 Canadian dollars per semester. Tuition and fees vary according to program. *Financial support:* In 2010–11, 1 fellowship (averaging $18,000 per year), 2 research assistantships (averaging $16,500 per year), 2 teaching assistantships (averaging $6,759 per year) were awarded; scholarships/grants also available. Financial award application deadline: 6/15. *Faculty research:* Social justice, international development, globalization, social policy, political economy. *Unit head:* Dr. John Conway, Head, 306-585-4052, Fax: 306-585-4815, E-mail: john.conway@uregina.ca. *Application contact:* Dr. Henry Chow, Graduate Program Coordinator, 306-585-5604, Fax: 306-585-4815, E-mail: henry.chow@uregina.ca.

The University of Texas at Tyler, College of Arts and Sciences, Department of Social Sciences, Tyler, TX 75799-0001. Offers criminal justice (MS); public administration (MPA); sociology (MS). Part-time and evening/weekend programs available. *Degree requirements:* For master's, comprehensive exam, thesis optional. *Entrance requirements:* For master's, GRE General Test, minimum GPA of 3.0. Additional exam requirements/recommendations for international students: Required—TOEFL (minimum score 79 computer-based). *Faculty research:* Urban segregation, minority business, violent crime, gender discrimination.

University of Washington, Graduate School, School of Public Health, Department of Health Services, Seattle, WA 98195. Offers bioinformatics (PhD); cancer prevention and control (PhD); clinical research (MS); community oriented public health practice (MPH); economics or finance (PhD); evaluation sciences (PhD); executive program (MHA); health behavior and health promotion (PhD); health care and population health research (MPH); health policy analysis and process (PhD); health policy and analysis and process (MPH); health services (MS, PhD); health services administration (EMHA, MHA); in residence program (MHA); maternal and child health (MPH, PhD); occupational health (PhD); population health and social determinants (PhD); social and behavioral sciences (MPH); sociology and demography (PhD); JD/MHA; MHA/MBA; MHA/MD; MHA/MPA; MPH/JD; MPH/MD; MPH/MN; MPH/MPA; MPH/MS; MPH/MSD; MPH/MSW; MPH/PhD. Part-time and evening/weekend programs available. Post-baccalaureate distance learning degree programs offered (minimal on-campus study). *Faculty:* 36 full-time (18 women), 59 part-time/adjunct (26 women). *Students:* 107 full-time (82 women), 101 part-time (82 women); includes 1 Black or African American, non-Hispanic/Latino; 1 American Indian or Alaska Native, non-Hispanic/Latino; 27 Asian, non-Hispanic/Latino; 10 Hispanic/Latino, 4 international. Average age 34. 426 applicants, 41% accepted, 106 enrolled. In 2010, 37 master's, 11 doctorates awarded. Terminal master's awarded for partial completion of doctoral program. *Degree requirements:* For master's, thesis (for some programs), practicum (MPH); for doctorate, comprehensive exam, thesis/dissertation. *Entrance requirements:* For master's and doctorate, GRE General Test, minimum GPA of 3.0. Additional exam requirements/recommendations for international students: Required—TOEFL (minimum score 580 paper-based; 237 computer-based; 92 iBT), IELTS (minimum score 7). *Application deadline:* For fall admission, 1/1 for domestic students, 11/1 for international students. Application fee: 75 Albanian leks. Electronic applications accepted. *Financial support:* In 2010–11, 47 students received support, including 10 fellowships with full and partial tuition reimbursements available (averaging $22,000 per year), 10 research assistantships with full and partial tuition reimbursements available (averaging $18,700 per year), 3 teaching assistantships with full and partial tuition reimbursements available (averaging $4,575 per year); institutionally sponsored loans, traineeships, and health care benefits also available. Financial award application deadline: 2/28; financial award applicants required to submit FAFSA. *Faculty research:* Public health practice, health promotion and disease prevention, maternal and child health, organizational behavior and culture, health policy. *Unit head:* Dr. Larry Kessler, Chair, 206-543-2930. *Application contact:* Kitty A. Andert, MPH/MS/PhD Program Manager, 206-616-2926, Fax: 206-543-3964, E-mail: kitander@u.washington.edu.

University of Wisconsin–Madison, Development Studies Program, Madison, WI 53706-1380. Offers PhD. Part-time programs available. *Faculty:* 41 part-time/adjunct (15 women). *Students:* 15 full-time (7 women), 3 part-time (all women); includes 3 Black or African American, non-Hispanic/Latino; 1 Hispanic/Latino, 8 international. 15 applicants, 27% accepted, 2 enrolled. In 2010, 1 doctorate awarded. *Degree requirements:* For doctorate, thesis/dissertation, Preliminary exam. *Entrance requirements:* For doctorate, GRE. Additional exam requirements/recommendations for international students: Required—TOEFL. *Application deadline:* For fall admission, 12/31 for domestic and international students; for spring admission, 9/30 for domestic and international students. Application fee: $56. Electronic applications accepted. *Expenses:* Tuition, state resident: full-time $9887; part-time $617.96 per credit. Tuition, nonresident: full-time $24,054; part-time $1503.40 per credit. Required fees: $67.63 per credit. Tuition and fees vary according to reciprocity agreements. *Financial support:* In 2010–11, 1 fellowship, 1 research assistantship, 5 teaching assistantships were awarded. *Faculty research:* International context: community and economic development, political movements, labor markets, women and gender studies, public policy for land use and environmental management, trade policy. *Unit head:* Dr. Gay Seidman, Professor, 608-262-3412, E-mail: seidman@ssc.wisc.edu. *Application contact:* Christine Elholm, Graduate Coordinator, 608-262-3412, E-mail: caelholm@wisc.edu.

Wilfrid Laurier University, Faculty of Graduate and Postdoctoral Studies, Faculty of Arts, Cultural Analysis and Social Theory Program, Waterloo, ON N2L 3C5, Canada. Offers body politics (MA); cultural representation and social theory (MA); gender, sexuality and embodiment (MA); globalization, identity and social movements (MA). Part-time programs available. *Faculty:* 16 full-time (10 women). *Students:* 9 full-time (6 women), 2 part-time (both women). 23 applicants, 61% accepted, 7 enrolled. In 2010, 4 master's awarded. *Entrance requirements:* For master's, honours BA in humanities, social science or interdisciplinary program with social theory, minimum B+ in final year of full-time study. Additional exam requirements/recommendations for international students: Required—TOEFL (minimum score 89 iBT). *Application deadline:* For fall admission, 2/1 priority date for domestic and international students. Application fee: $100. Electronic applications accepted. Tuition and fees charges are reported in Canadian dollars. *Expenses:* Tuition, area resident: Full-time $15,300 Canadian dollars; part-time $1200 Canadian dollars per credit. International tuition: $21,300 Canadian dollars full-time. Required fees: $650 Canadian dollars; $100 Canadian dollars per credit. Tuition and fees vary according to course load, degree level, campus/location and program. *Financial support:* Career-related internships or fieldwork, scholarships/grants, and unspecified assistantships available. *Faculty research:* Globalization; identity and social movements; body politics: gender, sexuality and embodiment; cultural representation and social theory. *Unit head:* Dr. Jasmin Zine, Director, 519-884-0710 Ext. 3267, Fax: 519-884-8854, E-mail: jzine@wlu.ca. *Application contact:* Jennifer Williams, Graduate Admission and Records Officer, 519-884-0710 Ext. 3536, Fax: 519-884-1020, E-mail: gradstudies@wlu.ca.

Worcester Polytechnic Institute, Graduate Studies, Department of Social Science and Policy Studies, Worcester, MA 01609-2280. Offers interdisciplinary social science (PhD); system dynamics (MS, Graduate Certificate). Part-time and evening/weekend programs available. Postbaccalaureate distance learning degree programs offered (no on-campus study). *Faculty:* 4 full-time (1 woman), 3 part-time/adjunct (0 women). *Students:* 8 part-time (1 woman); includes 1 Hispanic/Latino; 1 Native Hawaiian or other Pacific Islander, non-Hispanic/Latino, 1 international. 23 applicants, 61% accepted, 2 enrolled. In 2010, 2 master's awarded. *Entrance requirements:* For master's, GRE General Test, 3 letters of recommendation. Additional exam requirements/recommendations for international students: Required—TOEFL (minimum score 550 paper-based; 213 computer-based; 79 iBT), IELTS (minimum score 6.5). *Application deadline:* For fall admission, 1/1 priority date for domestic students, 1/15 for international students; for spring admission, 10/1 priority date for domestic students, 10/1 for international students. Applications are processed on a rolling basis. Application fee: $70. Electronic applications accepted. *Expenses:* Tuition: Full-time $20,862; part-time $1159 per term. One-time fee: $15. *Financial support:* Career-related internships or fieldwork, institutionally sponsored loans, scholarships/grants, and unspecified assistantships available. Financial award application deadline: 1/1; financial award applicants required to submit FAFSA. *Faculty research:* Microeconomics, political economy, system dynamics, systems thinking, social simulation. *Unit head:* Dr. James K. Doyle, Head, 508-831-5296, Fax: 508-831-5896, E-mail: doyle@wpi.edu. *Application contact:* Dr. Oleg Pavlov, Graduate Coordinator, 508-831-5296, Fax: 508-831-5896, E-mail: opavlov@wpi.edu.

Worcester Polytechnic Institute, Graduate Studies, Programs in Interdisciplinary Studies, Worcester, MA 01609-2280. Offers bioscience administration (MS); impact engineering (MS); manufacturing engineering management (MS); power systems management (MS); social science (PhD); systems modeling (MS). Part-time and evening/weekend programs available. *Faculty:* 1 part-time/adjunct (0 women). *Students:* 6 full-time (1 woman), 146 part-time (25 women); includes 1 Black or African American, non-Hispanic/Latino; 6 Hispanic/Latino; 11 Native Hawaiian or other Pacific Islander, non-Hispanic/Latino, 1 international. 151 applicants, 76% accepted, 79 enrolled. In 2010, 47 master's awarded. *Degree requirements:* For master's, thesis; for doctorate, comprehensive exam, thesis/dissertation. *Entrance requirements:* For master's and doctorate, 3 letters of recommendation. Additional exam requirements/recommendations for international students: Required—TOEFL (minimum score 550 paper-based; 213 computer-based; 79 iBT), IELTS (minimum score 6.5). *Application deadline:* For fall admission, 1/1 priority date for domestic students, 1/1 for international students; for spring admission, 10/1 priority date for domestic students, 10/1 for international students. Application fee: $70. *Expenses:* Tuition: Full-time $20,862; part-time $1159 per term. One-time fee: $15. *Financial support:* Institutionally sponsored loans, scholarships/grants, and unspecified assistantships available. Financial award application deadline: 1/1; financial award applicants required to submit FAFSA. *Unit head:* Dr. Fred J. Looft, Head, 508-831-5231, Fax: 508-831-5491,

E-mail: fjlooft@wpi.edu. *Application contact:* Lynne Dougherty, Administrative Assistant, 508-831-5301, Fax: 508-831-5717, E-mail: grad@wpi.edu.

Yale University, School of Medicine, Yale School of Public Health, New Haven, CT 06520. Offers applied biostatistics and epidemiology (APMPH); biostatistics (MPH, MS, PhD), including global health (MPH); chronic disease epidemiology (MPH, PhD), including global health (MPH); environmental health sciences (MPH, PhD), including global health (MPH); epidemiology of microbial diseases (MPH, PhD), including global health (MPH); global health (APMPH); health management (MPH), including global health; health policy (MPH), including global health; health policy and administration (APMPH, PhD); occupational and environmental medicine (APMPH); preventive medicine (APMPH); social and behavioral sciences (APMPH, MPH), including global health (MPH); JD/MPH; M Div/MPH; MBA/MPH; MD/MPH; MEM/MPH; MFS/MPH; MPH/MA; MSN/MPH. MS and PhD offered through the Graduate School. *Accreditation:* CEPH. Part-time programs available. *Faculty:* 67 full-time (37 women), 53 part-time/adjunct (18 women). *Students:* 209 full-time (169 women), 8 part-time (4 women); includes 24 Black or African American, non-Hispanic/Latino; 44 Asian, non-Hispanic/Latino; 9 Hispanic/Latino, 21 international. Average age 26. 1,100 applicants, 117 enrolled. In 2010, 124 master's, 8 doctorates awarded. Terminal master's awarded for partial completion of doctoral program. *Degree requirements:* For master's, thesis, summer internship; for doctorate, comprehensive exam, thesis/dissertation, residency. *Entrance requirements:* For master's,

GMAT, GRE, or MCAT, two years of undergraduate coursework in math and science; for doctorate, GRE General Test. Additional exam requirements/recommendations for international students: Required—TOEFL (minimum score 100 iBT). *Application deadline:* For fall admission, 1/15 priority date for domestic and international students. Applications are processed on a rolling basis. Application fee: $115. Electronic applications accepted. *Expenses:* Contact institution. *Financial support:* In 2010–11, 21 fellowships with full tuition reimbursements (averaging $12,560 per year), 4 research assistantships with full tuition reimbursements (averaging $24,910 per year) were awarded; teaching assistantships with full tuition reimbursements, career-related internships or fieldwork, Federal Work-Study, institutionally sponsored loans, scholarships/grants, and tuition waivers (full and partial) also available. Support available to part-time students. Financial award application deadline: 3/1; financial award applicants required to submit FAFSA. *Faculty research:* Genetic and emerging infections epidemiology, virology, cost/quality, vector biology, quantitative methods, aging, asthma, cancer. *Unit head:* Dr. Paul D. Cleary, Dean and Chairman, 203-785-2867, Fax: 203-785-6103, E-mail: paul.cleary@yale.edu. *Application contact:* Jacqui R. Comshaw, Director of Admissions, 203-785-2844, Fax: 203-785-4845, E-mail: ysph.admissions@yale.edu.

York University, Faculty of Graduate Studies, Faculty of Arts, Program in International Development Studies, Toronto, ON M3J 1P3, Canada. Offers MA.

Section 27
Sociology, Anthropology, and Archaeology

This section contains a directory of institutions offering graduate work in sociology, anthropology, and archaeology, followed by an in-depth entry submitted by an institution that chose to prepare a detailed program description. Additional information about programs listed in the directory but not augmented by an in-depth entry may be obtained by writing directly to the dean of a graduate school or chair of a department at the address given in the directory.

For programs offering related work, see also in this book *Area and Cultural Studies, Art and Art History, History, Humanities, Language and Literature,* and *Psychology and Counseling.*

CONTENTS

Program Directories

Close-Ups and Display

See also:

Anthropology

American University, College of Arts and Sciences, Department of Anthropology, Washington, DC 20016-8003. Offers anthropology (PhD); public anthropology (MA, Certificate). Part-time and evening/weekend programs available. *Faculty:* 15 full-time (7 women), 8 part-time/adjunct (4 women). *Students:* 29 full-time (21 women), 60 part-time (47 women); includes 25 minority (14 Black or African American, non-Hispanic/Latino; 4 Asian, non-Hispanic/Latino; 7 Hispanic/Latino), 8 international. Average age 32. 89 applicants, 44% accepted, 16 enrolled. In 2010, 12 master's, 4 doctorates awarded. Terminal master's awarded for partial completion of doctoral program. *Degree requirements:* For master's, comprehensive exam, thesis or alternative; for doctorate, 2 foreign languages, comprehensive exam, thesis/dissertation. *Entrance requirements:* For master's, GRE, sample of written work; for doctorate, GRE, sample of written work, personal statement. Additional exam requirements/recommendations for international students: Required—TOEFL. *Application deadline:* For fall admission, 2/1 for domestic students; for spring admission, 10/1 for domestic students. Application fee: $80. *Financial support:* Fellowships, research assistantships with full and partial tuition reimbursements, teaching assistantships with full and partial tuition reimbursements, career-related internships or fieldwork, Federal Work-Study, institutionally sponsored loans, and unspecified assistantships available. Support available to part-time students. Financial award application deadline: 1/15. *Faculty research:* Poverty and race, lesbian and gay studies, class and culture, developing countries. *Unit head:* Dr. William Leap, Chair, 202-885-1831, Fax: 202-885-1837. *Application contact:* Dr. William Leap, Chair, 202-885-1831, Fax: 202-885-1837.

The American University in Cairo, School of Humanities and Social Sciences, Department of Sociology, Anthropology, Psychology, and Egyptology, Cairo, Egypt. Offers sociology and anthropology (MA). *Degree requirements:* For master's, one foreign language, thesis. *Entrance requirements:* Additional exam requirements/recommendations for international students: Required—English entrance exam and/or TOEFL. Electronic applications accepted. *Faculty research:* Development, gender, sociopolitical economic formulations, social science indigenization, Arab world.

American University of Beirut, Graduate Programs, Faculty of Arts and Sciences, Beirut, Lebanon. Offers anthropology (MA); Arabic language and literature (MA); archaeology (MA); biology (MS); chemistry (MS); computational science (MS); computer science (MS); economics (MA); education (MA); English language (MA); English literature (MA); environmental policy planning (MSES); financial economics (MAFE); geology (MS); history (MA); mathematics (MA, MS); Middle Eastern studies (MA); philosophy (MA); physics (MS); political studies (MA); psychology (MA); public administration (MA); sociology (MA); statistics (MA, MS). Part-time programs available. *Faculty:* 229 full-time (98 women), 136 part-time/adjunct (79 women). *Students:* 158 full-time (104 women), 263 part-time (171 women). Average age 25. 356 applicants, 59% accepted, 127 enrolled. In 2010, 57 master's awarded. *Degree requirements:* For master's, one foreign language, comprehensive exam, thesis (for some programs). *Entrance requirements:* For master's, GRE, letter of recommendation. Additional exam requirements/recommendations for international students: Required—TOEFL (minimum score 600 paper-based; 250 computer-based; 97 iBT), IELTS (minimum score 7). *Application deadline:* For fall admission, 4/30 for domestic and international students; for spring admission, 11/1 for domestic and international students. Application fee: $50. *Expenses:* Tuition: Full-time $12,294; part-time $683 per credit. Required fees: $499; $499 per credit. Tuition and fees vary according to course load and program. *Financial support:* In 2010–11, 33 students received support. Career-related internships or fieldwork, institutionally sponsored loans, scholarships/grants, health care benefits, and unspecified assistantships available. Financial award application deadline: 2/4; financial award applicants required to submit FAFSA. *Faculty research:* Modern and contemporary world theatre; mineralogy, petrology, and geochemistry; cell differentiation and transformation; combinatorial technologies; philosophy of action; continental philosophy; Phoenician epigraphy; nascent complex societies and urbanism; the economies of the Arab world; environmental economics; tectonophysics; host-parasite interactions; innate immunity; insect-plant interactions; history of the Ottoman archives; decentralization; transparency and corruption. Total annual research expenditures: $622,243. *Unit head:* Dr. Patrick McGreevy, Dean, 961-137-4374 Ext. 3800, Fax: 961-174-4461, E-mail: pm07@aub.edu.lb. *Application contact:* Dr. Salim Kanaan, Director, Admissions Office, 961-135-0000 Ext. 2594, Fax: 961-175-0775, E-mail: sk00@aub.edu.lb.

Arizona State University, College of Liberal Arts and Sciences, School of Human Evolution and Social Change, Tempe, AZ 85287-2402. Offers anthropology (PhD); anthropology (archaeology) (PhD); anthropology (bioarchaeology) (PhD); anthropology (museum studies) (MA); anthropology (physical) (PhD); applied mathematics for the life and social sciences (PhD); environmental social science (PhD); environmental social science (urbanism) (PhD); global health (MA); global health (health and culture) (PhD); global health (urbanism) (PhD); immigration studies (Graduate Certificate). *Faculty:* 52 full-time (19 women), 4 part-time/adjunct (2 women). *Students:* 127 full-time (77 women), 52 part-time (37 women); includes 43 minority (8 Black or African American, non-Hispanic/Latino; 4 American Indian or Alaska Native, non-Hispanic/Latino; 4 Asian, non-Hispanic/Latino; 26 Hispanic/Latino; 1 Two or more races, non-Hispanic/Latino), 19 international. Average age 32. 250 applicants, 24% accepted, 25 enrolled. In 2010, 8 master's, 18 doctorates, 7 other advanced degrees awarded. Terminal master's awarded for partial completion of doctoral program. *Degree requirements:* For master's, thesis or alternative, interactive Program of Study (iPOS) submitted before completing 50 percent of required credit hours; for doctorate, comprehensive exam, thesis/dissertation, interactive Program of Study (iPOS) submitted before completing 50 percent of required credit hours. *Entrance requirements:* For master's and doctorate, GRE, minimum GPA of 3.0 or equivalent in last 2 years of work leading to bachelor's degree. Additional exam requirements/recommendations for international students: Required—TOEFL, IELTS, or Pearson Test of English. *Application deadline:* For fall admission, 12/15 for domestic students, 12/1 for international students. Applications are processed on a rolling basis. Application fee: $70 ($90 for international students). Electronic applications accepted. *Expenses:* Tuition, state resident: full-time $8510; part-time $608 per credit. Tuition, nonresident: full-time $16,542; part-time $919 per credit. Required fees: $339; $110 per credit. Part-time tuition and fees vary according to course load. *Financial support:* In 2010–11, 30 research assistantships with full and partial tuition reimbursements (averaging $14,993 per year), 63 teaching assistantships with full and partial tuition reimbursements (averaging $15,266 per year) were awarded; fellowships with full tuition reimbursements, career-related internships or fieldwork, Federal Work-Study, institutionally sponsored loans, scholarships/grants, and tuition waivers (full and partial) also available. Financial award application deadline: 3/1; financial award applicants required to submit FAFSA. Total annual research expenditures: $3.8 million. *Unit head:* Dr. Sander van der Leeuw, Director, 480-965-6214, E-mail: vanderle@asu.edu. *Application contact:* Graduate Admissions, 480-965-6113.

Ball State University, Graduate School, College of Sciences and Humanities, Department of Anthropology, Muncie, IN 47306-1099. Offers MA. *Faculty:* 15. *Students:* 9 full-time (7 women), 24 part-time (13 women); includes 4 minority (1 Black or African American, non-Hispanic/Latino; 1 American Indian or Alaska Native, non-Hispanic/Latino; 1 Asian, non-Hispanic/Latino; 1 Two or more races, non-Hispanic/Latino), 1 international. Average age 29. 14 applicants, 50% accepted, 4 enrolled. In 2010, 10 master's awarded. *Entrance requirements:* For master's, GRE General Test, resume. Application fee: $50. *Expenses:* Tuition, state resident: full-time $6160; part-time $299 per credit hour. Tuition, nonresident: full-time $16,020; part-time $783 per credit hour. Required fees: $2278; $95 per credit hour. *Financial support:* In 2010–11, 6 teaching assistantships with full tuition reimbursements (averaging $9,807 per year) were awarded. Financial award application deadline: 3/1. *Unit head:* Dr. S. Homes Hogue, Chairman, 765-285-1575, Fax: 765-285-2163. *Application contact:* Dr. Robert Morris, Associate Provost for Research and Dean of the Graduate School, 765-285-1300, E-mail: rmorris@bsu.edu.

Biola University, School of Intercultural Studies, La Mirada, CA 90639-0001. Offers anthropology (MA); applied linguistics (MA); Biblical languages and linguistics (MA); intercultural education (PhD); intercultural studies (MAICS); linguistics (Certificate); missiology (D Miss); missions (MA); teaching English to speakers of other languages (MA, Certificate). Part-time and evening/weekend programs available. *Faculty:* 16 full-time (5 women), 6 part-time/adjunct (1 woman). *Students:* 66 full-time (39 women), 126 part-time (72 women); includes 48 minority (6 Black or African American, non-Hispanic/Latino; 40 Asian, non-Hispanic/Latino; 2 Two or more races, non-Hispanic/Latino), 30 international. 136 applicants, 70% accepted, 59 enrolled. In 2010, 27 master's, 10 doctorates awarded. Terminal master's awarded for partial completion of doctoral program. *Degree requirements:* For master's, one foreign language, comprehensive exam; for doctorate, one foreign language, comprehensive exam, thesis/dissertation. *Entrance requirements:* For master's, minimum undergraduate GPA of 3.0; for doctorate, MA, 3 years of ministry experience, minimum graduate GPA of 3.3. Additional exam requirements/recommendations for international students: Required—TOEFL (minimum score 550 paper-based; 213 computer-based). *Application deadline:* For fall admission, 7/1 for domestic students; for spring admission, 1/1 for domestic students. Applications are processed on a rolling basis. Application fee: $45. Electronic applications accepted. *Financial support:* Teaching assistantships, career-related internships or fieldwork, institutionally sponsored loans, and scholarships/grants available. Support available to part-time students. Financial award application deadline: 3/2; financial award applicants required to submit FAFSA. *Unit head:* Dr. Douglas Pennoyer, Dean, 562-903-4844, Fax: 562-903-4748, E-mail: douglas.pennoyer@biola.edu. *Application contact:* Roy M. Allinson, Director of Graduate Admissions, 562-903-4752, Fax: 562-903-4709, E-mail: admissions@biola.edu.

Boston University, Graduate School of Arts and Sciences, Department of Anthropology, Boston, MA 02215. Offers anthropology (PhD); applied anthropology (MA). *Students:* 36 full-time (24 women), 1 (woman) part-time; includes 3 minority (2 Black or African American, non-Hispanic/Latino; 1 Asian, non-Hispanic/Latino), 12 international. Average age 33. 81 applicants, 14% accepted, 4 enrolled. In 2010, 2 master's, 2 doctorates awarded. Terminal master's awarded for partial completion of doctoral program. *Degree requirements:* For master's, one foreign language, thesis or alternative; for doctorate, one foreign language, thesis/dissertation. *Entrance requirements:* For master's and doctorate, GRE General Test, 2 letters of recommendation. Additional exam requirements/recommendations for international students: Required—TOEFL (minimum score 550 paper-based; 213 computer-based). *Application deadline:* For fall admission, 1/1 for domestic and international students. Application fee: $70. *Expenses:* Tuition: Full-time $39,314; part-time $1228 per credit. Required fees: $40 per semester. *Financial support:* In 2010–11, 15 students received support, including 3 fellowships with full tuition reimbursements available (averaging $19,300 per year), 7 teaching assistantships with full tuition reimbursements available (averaging $18,800 per year); Federal Work-Study and unspecified assistantships also available. Support available to part-time students. Financial award application deadline: 1/1; financial award applicants required to submit FAFSA. *Unit head:* Robert Weller, Chairman, 617-353-2195, Fax: 617-353-2610, E-mail: rpweller@bu.edu. *Application contact:* Mark Palmer, Administrator, 617-353-2195, Fax: 617-353-2610, E-mail: palmerm@bu.edu.

Boston University, School of Medicine, Division of Graduate Medical Sciences, Program in Forensic Anthropology, Boston, MA 02215. Offers MS. *Faculty:* 10 full-time (3 women). *Students:* 22 full-time (16 women), 7 part-time (5 women); includes 2 Black or African American, non-Hispanic/Latino; 1 American Indian or Alaska Native, non-Hispanic/Latino; 4 Hispanic/Latino, 1 international. 42 applicants, 62% accepted, 15 enrolled. In 2010, 1 master's awarded. *Entrance requirements:* For master's, GRE. Additional exam requirements/recommendations for international students: Required—TOEFL. *Application deadline:* Applications are processed on a rolling basis. Application fee: $75. Electronic applications accepted. *Expenses:* Tuition: Full-time $39,314; part-time $1228 per credit. Required fees: $40 per semester. *Financial support:* Applicants required to submit FAFSA. *Unit head:* Dr. Tara L. Moore, Co-Director, 617-638-4054, Fax: 617-638-4922, E-mail: tlmoore@bu.edu. *Application contact:* Patty Jones, Executive Financial Coordinator, 617-414-2315, E-mail: psterlin@bu.edu.

Boston University, School of Medicine, Division of Graduate Medical Sciences, Program in Medical Anthropology and Cross Cultural Practice, Boston, MA 02215. Offers MA. *Faculty:* 4 full-time (3 women). *Students:* 10 full-time (all women), 1 (woman) part-time; includes 1 Black or African American, non-Hispanic/Latino; 2 Hispanic/Latino. 17 applicants, 76% accepted, 6 enrolled. *Entrance requirements:* For master's, GRE. Additional exam requirements/recommendations for international students: Required—TOEFL. *Application deadline:* Applications are processed on a rolling basis. Application fee: $75. Electronic applications accepted. *Expenses:* Tuition: Full-time $39,314; part-time $1228 per credit. Required fees: $40 per semester. *Financial support:* Applicants required to submit FAFSA. *Unit head:* Dr. Linda Barnes, Director, 617-414-4534, Fax: 617-414-5511, E-mail: linda.barnes@bmc.org. *Application contact:* Michelle Hall, Associate Director of Admissions, 617-638-5121, Fax: 617-638-5740, E-mail: natashah@bu.edu.

Brandeis University, Graduate School of Arts and Sciences, Department of Anthropology, Waltham, MA 02454. Offers anthropology (MA, PhD); anthropology and women's and gender studies (MA). Part-time programs available. *Faculty:* 8 full-time (4 women), 3 part-time/adjunct (1 woman). *Students:* 43 full-time (30 women), 1 (woman) part-time; includes 4 Hispanic/Latino, 13 international. Average age 34. 40 applicants, 53% accepted, 13 enrolled. In 2010, 6 master's, 2 doctorates awarded. Terminal master's awarded for partial completion of doctoral program. *Degree requirements:* For master's, thesis; for doctorate, one foreign language, comprehensive exam, thesis/dissertation. *Entrance requirements:* For master's, GRE General Test (recommended), sample of written work, resume, letters of recommendation; for doctorate, GRE General Test, sample of written work, resume, letters of recommendation. Additional exam requirements/recommendations for international students: Required—TOEFL (minimum score 600 paper-based; 250 computer-based; 100 iBT); Recommended—IELTS (minimum score 7). *Application deadline:* For fall admission, 1/15 for domestic students. Application fee: $75. Electronic applications accepted. *Financial support:* In 2010–11, 23 students received support, including 12 fellowships with full tuition reimbursements available (averaging $20,000 per year), 11 teaching assistantships with partial tuition reimbursements available (averaging $3,200 per year); research assistantships with partial tuition reimbursements available, career-related internships or fieldwork, scholarships/grants, health care benefits, tuition waivers (full and partial), and unspecified assistantships also available. Support available to part-time students. Financial award application deadline: 4/15; financial award applicants required to submit FAFSA. *Faculty research:* Evolutionary processes, comparative social institutions, systems of meaning, gender studies, sociocultural anthropology, linguistic anthropology, archaeology, and physical anthropology. *Unit head:* Dr. Janet McIntosh, Associate Professor/Director of Graduate Studies, 781-736-2210, Fax: 781-736-2232, E-mail: janetmc@brandeis.edu. *Application contact:* Laurel Carpenter, Academic Administrator, 781-736-2210, Fax: 781-736-2232, E-mail: lcarpenter@brandeis.edu.

Brigham Young University, Graduate Studies, College of Family, Home, and Social Sciences, Department of Anthropology, Provo, UT 84602-1001. Offers MA. *Faculty:* 9 full-time (1 woman). *Students:* 14 full-time (all women), 9 part-time (6 women). Average age 27. 13 applicants, 46% accepted, 6 enrolled. In 2010, 1 master's awarded. *Degree requirements:* For master's, comprehensive exam, thesis. *Entrance requirements:* For master's, GRE General Test, minimum GPA of 3.0 in last 60 hours. Additional exam requirements/recommendations for international students: Required—TOEFL (minimum score 580 paper-based; 237 computer-based). *Application deadline:* For fall admission, 2/1 for domestic and international students. Application fee: $50. Electronic applications accepted. *Expenses:* Tuition: Full-time $5580; part-time $310 per credit hour. Tuition and fees vary according to program and student's religious affiliation. *Financial support:* In 2010–11, 17 students received support, including 12 research assistantships (averaging $8,000 per year), 5 teaching assistantships (averaging $8,000 per year); fellowships, career-related internships or fieldwork, institutionally sponsored loans, and tuition waivers (partial) also available. Financial award application deadline: 3/1;

financial award applicants required to submit FAFSA. *Faculty research:* Archaeology of the Southwest, Near East, and Mesoamerica; Mayan glyphs. Total annual research expenditures: $51,800. *Unit head:* Dr. Charles W. Nuckolls, Chair, 801-422-3058, Fax: 801-422-0021, E-mail: charles_nuckolls@byu.edu. *Application contact:* Dr. John E. Clark, Graduate Coordinator, 801-422-3822, Fax: 801-422-0021, E-mail: john_clark@byu.edu.

Brown University, Graduate School, Department of Anthropology, Providence, RI 02912. Offers anthropology (AM, PhD); museum studies (AM). *Degree requirements:* For doctorate, one foreign language, thesis/dissertation, preliminary exam.

California State University, Bakersfield, Division of Graduate Studies, School of Humanities and Social Sciences, Program in Anthropology, Bakersfield, CA 93311. Offers MA. *Degree requirements:* For master's, thesis optional. *Entrance requirements:* For master's, GRE, minimum GPA of 2.5, 3 letters of recommendation. Additional exam requirements/recommendations for international students: Required—TOEFL (minimum score 550 paper-based; 213 computer-based). *Faculty research:* Human services, social science teaching.

California State University, Chico, Graduate School, College of Behavioral and Social Sciences, Department of Anthropology, Chico, CA 95929-0722. Offers museum studies (MA). *Students:* 22 full-time (19 women), 13 part-time (9 women); includes 1 Asian, non-Hispanic/Latino; 3 Hispanic/Latino, 1 international. Average age 29. 62 applicants, 32% accepted, 17 enrolled. In 2010, 8 master's awarded. *Degree requirements:* For master's, thesis. *Entrance requirements:* For master's, GRE General Test, 2 letters of recommendation. Additional exam requirements/recommendations for international students: Required—TOEFL (minimum score 550 paper-based; 213 computer-based; 80 iBT), IELTS (minimum score 6.5). *Application deadline:* For fall admission, 1/15 for domestic students, 3/1 for international students. Application fee: $55. Electronic applications accepted. *Financial support:* Fellowships, career-related internships or fieldwork available. *Unit head:* Dr. William Collins, Graduate Coordinator, 530-898-4953. *Application contact:* Dr. William Collins, Graduate Coordinator, 530-898-4953.

California State University, East Bay, Office of Academic Programs and Graduate Studies, College of Letters, Arts, and Social Sciences, Department of Anthropology, Hayward, CA 94542-3000. Offers MA. Part-time programs available. *Faculty:* 7 full-time (2 women). *Students:* 10 full-time (7 women), 17 part-time (10 women); includes 8 minority (2 Black or African American, non-Hispanic/Latino; 2 Asian, non-Hispanic/Latino; 3 Hispanic/Latino; 1 Two or more races, non-Hispanic/Latino), 1 international. Average age 32. 27 applicants, 70% accepted, 14 enrolled. In 2010, 10 master's awarded. *Degree requirements:* For master's, one foreign language, comprehensive exam, thesis. *Entrance requirements:* For master's, minimum GPA of 2.5 during previous 2 years of course work. Additional exam requirements/recommendations for international students: Required—TOEFL (minimum score 550 paper-based; 213 computer-based). *Application deadline:* For fall admission, 6/30 for domestic and international students. Applications are processed on a rolling basis. Application fee: $55. Electronic applications accepted. *Financial support:* Fellowships, teaching assistantships, career-related internships or fieldwork, Federal Work-Study, institutionally sponsored loans, and scholarships/grants available. Support available to part-time students. Financial award application deadline: 3/2; financial award applicants required to submit FAFSA. *Unit head:* Prof. Laurie Price, Graduate Coordinator, 510-885-4367, Fax: 510-885-3353, E-mail: laurie.price@csueastbay.edu. *Application contact:* Dr. Donna Wiley, Interim Associate Director, 510-885-2928, Fax: 510-885-4777, E-mail: donna.wiley@csueastbay.edu.

California State University, Fullerton, Graduate Studies, College of Humanities and Social Sciences, Department of Anthropology, Fullerton, CA 92834-9480. Offers MA. Part-time programs available. *Students:* 36 full-time (21 women), 35 part-time (19 women); includes 1 Black or African American, non-Hispanic/Latino; 3 American Indian or Alaska Native, non-Hispanic/Latino; 2 Asian, non-Hispanic/Latino; 14 Hispanic/Latino; 2 Two or more races, non-Hispanic/Latino, 2 international. Average age 32. 68 applicants, 51% accepted, 28 enrolled. In 2010, 14 master's awarded. *Degree requirements:* For master's, project or thesis. *Entrance requirements:* For master's, minimum GPA of 2.5 in last 60 hours of course work. Application fee: $55. *Financial support:* Career-related internships or fieldwork, Federal Work-Study, institutionally sponsored loans, and scholarships/grants available. Support available to part-time students. Financial award application deadline: 3/1; financial award applicants required to submit FAFSA. *Unit head:* Dr. Mitch Avila, Chair, 657-278-2272. *Application contact:* Admissions/Applications, 657-278-2371.

California State University, Long Beach, Graduate Studies, College of Liberal Arts, Department of Anthropology, Long Beach, CA 90840. Offers anthropology (MA); applied anthropology (MA). Part-time programs available. *Faculty:* 9 full-time (4 women), 1 (woman) part-time/adjunct. *Students:* 25 full-time (16 women), 17 part-time (10 women); includes 1 American Indian or Alaska Native, non-Hispanic/Latino; 2 Asian, non-Hispanic/Latino; 8 Hispanic/Latino, 1 international. Average age 30. 61 applicants, 41% accepted, 22 enrolled. In 2010, 12 master's awarded. *Degree requirements:* For master's, one foreign language, comprehensive exam or thesis. *Application deadline:* For fall admission, 4/15 for domestic students. Applications are processed on a rolling basis. Application fee: $55. Electronic applications accepted. *Financial support:* Research assistantships, Federal Work-Study, institutionally sponsored loans, and scholarships/grants available. Financial award application deadline: 3/2. *Faculty research:* Archeology of California, Fiji, and Ireland; cultures of American Indians and Mexico. *Unit head:* Dr. Barbara LeMaster, Chair, 562-985-5171, Fax: 562-985-4379. *Application contact:* Dr. Ron Loewe, Graduate Advisor, 562-985-5034, Fax: 562-985-4379, E-mail: rloewe@csulb.edu.

California State University, Los Angeles, Graduate Studies, College of Natural and Social Sciences, Department of Anthropology, Los Angeles, CA 90032-8530. Offers MA. Part-time and evening/weekend programs available. *Faculty:* 4 full-time (3 women), 1 part-time/adjunct (0 women). *Students:* 24 full-time (14 women), 42 part-time (30 women); includes 19 minority (3 Black or African American, non-Hispanic/Latino; 1 Asian, non-Hispanic/Latino; 13 Hispanic/Latino; 2 Two or more races, non-Hispanic/Latino), 2 international. Average age 31. 22 applicants, 100% accepted, 19 enrolled. In 2010, 11 master's awarded. *Degree requirements:* For master's, one foreign language, comprehensive exam or thesis. *Entrance requirements:* Additional exam requirements/recommendations for international students: Required—TOEFL (minimum score 500 paper-based; 173 computer-based). *Application deadline:* For fall admission, 5/1 for domestic and international students. Applications are processed on a rolling basis. Application fee: $55. *Financial support:* Federal Work-Study available. Support available to part-time students. Financial award application deadline: 3/1. *Faculty research:* Archaeology, folklore, petroglyphs, symbolism, medical anthropology. *Unit head:* Dr. Rene Vellanoweth, Chair, 323-343-2440, Fax: 323-343-2446, E-mail: rvellan@calstatela.edu. *Application contact:* Dr. Alan Muchlinski, Dean of Graduate Studies, 323-343-3820, Fax: 323-343-5653, E-mail: amuchli@exchange.calstatela.edu.

California State University, Northridge, Graduate Studies, College of Social and Behavioral Sciences, Department of Anthropology, Northridge, CA 91330. Offers general anthropology (MA); public archaeology (MA). *Degree requirements:* For master's, thesis or alternative. *Entrance requirements:* For master's, GRE General Test or minimum GPA of 3.0. Additional exam requirements/recommendations for international students: Required—TOEFL.

California State University, Sacramento, Graduate Studies, College of Social Sciences and Interdisciplinary Studies, Department of Anthropology, Sacramento, CA 95819. Offers MA. Part-time programs available. *Degree requirements:* For master's, thesis, departmental qualifying exam, writing proficiency exam. *Entrance requirements:* For master's, minimum GPA of 3.0 during previous 2 years. Additional exam requirements/recommendations for international students: Required—TOEFL. Electronic applications accepted.

Carleton University, Faculty of Graduate Studies, Faculty of Arts and Social Sciences, Department of Sociology and Anthropology, Program in Anthropology, Ottawa, ON K1S 5B6, Canada. Offers MA. *Degree requirements:* For master's, comprehensive exam, thesis optional. *Entrance requirements:* For master's, honors degree. Additional exam requirements/recommendations for international students: Required—TOEFL. *Faculty research:* Culture, symbols and mind, anthropology of signs and symbols, Indigenous studies, anthropology of development and underdevelopment.

Case Western Reserve University, Frances Payne Bolton School of Nursing and Department of Anthropology, Nursing/Anthropology Program, Cleveland, OH 44106. Offers MSN/MA.

Case Western Reserve University, School of Graduate Studies, Department of Anthropology, Cleveland, OH 44106. Offers MA, PhD, MD/MA, MD/PhD, MPH/MA, MSN/MA, PhD/MPH. Part-time programs available. *Faculty:* 10 full-time (5 women), 11 part-time/adjunct (4 women). *Students:* 30 full-time (25 women), 2 part-time (both women); includes 1 Black or African American, non-Hispanic/Latino; 3 Asian, non-Hispanic/Latino, 2 international. Average age 30. 41 applicants, 34% accepted, 10 enrolled. In 2010, 5 master's awarded. Terminal master's awarded for partial completion of doctoral program. *Degree requirements:* For master's, comprehensive exam, thesis optional; for doctorate, one foreign language, thesis/dissertation. *Entrance requirements:* For master's and doctorate, GRE General Test. Additional exam requirements/recommendations for international students: Required—TOEFL (minimum score 550 paper-based; 213 computer-based; 79 iBT). *Application deadline:* For fall admission, 3/1 priority date for domestic students. Applications are processed on a rolling basis. Application fee: $50. Electronic applications accepted. *Financial support:* Research assistantships with tuition reimbursements, teaching assistantships with tuition reimbursements, career-related internships or fieldwork and Federal Work-Study available. Support available to part-time students. Financial award application deadline: 2/15; financial award applicants required to submit FAFSA. *Faculty research:* Medical anthropology, psychological anthropology, cross-cultural aging, physical anthropology, international health. *Unit head:* Lawrence P. Greksa, Chairman, 216-368-2259, Fax: 216-368-5334, E-mail: lawrence.greksa@case.edu. *Application contact:* Kathleen Dowdell, Department Assistant, 216-368-2264, Fax: 216-368-5334, E-mail: kathleen.dowdell@case.edu.

The Catholic University of America, School of Arts and Sciences, Department of Anthropology, Washington, DC 20064. Offers MA. Part-time programs available. *Faculty:* 4 full-time (2 women), 1 part-time/adjunct (0 women). *Students:* 3 full-time (all women), 4 part-time (2 women); includes 1 Asian, non-Hispanic/Latino. Average age 34. 4 applicants, 50% accepted, 2 enrolled. In 2010, 1 master's awarded. *Degree requirements:* For master's, one foreign language, comprehensive exam, thesis or alternative. *Entrance requirements:* For master's, GRE General Test, statement of purpose, official copies of academic transcripts, three letters of recommendation. Additional exam requirements/recommendations for international students: Required—TOEFL (minimum score 580 paper-based; 237 computer-based). *Application deadline:* For fall admission, 4/1 priority date for domestic students, 7/15 for international students; for spring admission, 11/15 priority date for domestic students, 10/15 for international students. Applications are processed on a rolling basis. Application fee: $55. Electronic applications accepted. *Expenses:* Tuition: Full-time $33,580; part-time $1315 per credit hour. Required fees: $80; $40 per semester hour. One-time fee: $425. *Financial support:* Fellowships, research assistantships, teaching assistantships, Federal Work-Study, scholarships/grants, tuition waivers (full and partial), and unspecified assistantships available. Financial award application deadline: 2/1; financial award applicants required to submit FAFSA. *Faculty research:* Medical and applied anthropology, ethnopsychology, Latin American studies, ceramic analysis, economics and ecological anthropology. *Unit head:* Dr. Jon W. Anderson, Chair, 202-319-5080, Fax: 202-319-4782, E-mail: anderson@cua.edu. *Application contact:* Andrew Woodall, Director of Graduate Admissions, 202-319-5057, Fax: 202-319-6533, E-mail: cua-admissions@cua.edu.

Central European University, Graduate Studies, School of Social Sciences and Humanities, Budapest, Hungary. Offers economics (MA, PhD); gender studies (MA, PhD); international relations and European studies (MA, PhD); mathematics and its applications (MS, PhD); medieval studies (MA, PhD); nationalism studies (MA, PhD); philosophy (MA, PhD); political science (MA, PhD); public policy (MA, PhD); sociology and social anthropology (MA, PhD). *Faculty:* 90 full-time (29 women), 13 part-time/adjunct (7 women). *Students:* 732 full-time (404 women). Average age 28. 3,639 applicants, 22% accepted, 416 enrolled. In 2010, 278 master's, 16 doctorates awarded. Terminal master's awarded for partial completion of doctoral program. *Degree requirements:* For master's, one foreign language, thesis; for doctorate, one foreign language, comprehensive exam, thesis/dissertation. *Entrance requirements:* For master's, interview; for doctorate, GRE, CEU subject test, interview. Additional exam requirements/recommendations for international students: Required—TOEFL (minimum score 570 paper-based; 230 computer-based); Recommended—IELTS (minimum score 6.5). *Application deadline:* For fall admission, 1/15 priority date for domestic and international students. Application fee: $0. Electronic applications accepted. Tuition and fees charges are reported in euros. *Expenses:* Tuition: Full-time 11,000 euros. Required fees: 250 euros. One-time fee: 200 euros full-time. Tuition and fees vary according to degree level, program, reciprocity agreements and student level. *Financial support:* In 2010–11, 402 students received support, including 416 fellowships with full and partial tuition reimbursements available (averaging $6,200 per year); career-related internships or fieldwork, institutionally sponsored loans, and scholarships/grants also available. Financial award application deadline: 1/5. *Faculty research:* Civil society, fiscal decentralization, party politics, political philosophy (especially liberalism, theory of democracy). Total annual research expenditures: $35,000. *Unit head:* Dr. Katalin Farkas, Provost/Academic Pro Rector, 361-327-3000 Ext. 2227, E-mail: farkask@ceu.hu. *Application contact:* Zsuzsanna Jaszberenyi, Admissions Officer, 361-327-3009, Fax: 361-327-3211, E-mail: admissions@ceu.hu.

The College of William and Mary, Faculty of Arts and Sciences, Department of Anthropology, Williamsburg, VA 23187-8795. Offers MA, PhD. *Faculty:* 15 full-time (6 women), 3 part-time/adjunct (2 women). *Students:* 33 full-time (24 women); includes 6 minority (1 Black or African American, non-Hispanic/Latino; 2 American Indian or Alaska Native, non-Hispanic/Latino; 2 Hispanic/Latino; 1 Two or more races, non-Hispanic/Latino), 1 international. Average age 30. 77 applicants, 18% accepted, 10 enrolled. In 2010, 6 master's awarded. Terminal master's awarded for partial completion of doctoral program. *Degree requirements:* For master's, thesis, fieldwork; for doctorate, one foreign language, comprehensive exam, thesis/dissertation, fieldwork. *Entrance requirements:* For master's and doctorate, GRE, course work in anthropology or history. Additional exam requirements/recommendations for international students: Required—TOEFL. *Application deadline:* For fall admission, 1/15 for domestic and international students. Application fee: $45. Electronic applications accepted. *Expenses:* Tuition, state resident: full-time $6400; part-time $345 per credit hour. Tuition, nonresident: full-time $19,720; part-time $920 per credit hour. Required fees: $4368. *Financial support:* Research assistantships with full tuition reimbursements, teaching assistantships with full tuition reimbursements, career-related internships or fieldwork, institutionally sponsored loans, and scholarships/grants available. Financial award application deadline: 1/15; financial award applicants required to submit FAFSA. *Faculty research:* Historical archaeology, comparative colonialism, biocultural anthropology, African diaspora, historical archaeology of native America. Total annual research expenditures: $602,664. *Unit head:* Dr. Katie Bragdon, Chair, 757-221-1067, Fax: 757-221-1066, E-mail: bkbrag@wm.edu. *Application contact:* Dr. Martin D. Gallivan, Director of Graduate Studies, 757-221-3622, Fax: 757-221-1066, E-mail: mdgall@wm.edu.

Colorado State University, Graduate School, College of Liberal Arts, Department of Anthropology, Fort Collins, CO 80523-1787. Offers MA. Part-time programs available. *Faculty:* 12 full-time (7 women). *Students:* 22 full-time (11 women), 34 part-time (21 women); includes 2 minority (1 Asian, non-Hispanic/Latino; 1 Hispanic/Latino). Average age 30. 56 applicants, 38% accepted, 15 enrolled. In 2010, 11 master's awarded. *Degree requirements:* For master's, variable foreign language requirement, comprehensive exam, thesis (for some programs), oral exam. *Entrance requirements:* For master's, GRE General Test, minimum GPA of 3.0, BA/BS. Additional exam requirements/recommendations for international students: Required—TOEFL (minimum score 550 paper-based; 213 computer-based; 80 iBT). *Application deadline:* For fall admission, 2/15 priority date for domestic and international students. Applications are processed on a rolling basis. Application fee: $50. Electronic applications accepted. *Expenses:* Tuition,

Anthropology

Colorado State University *(continued)*
state resident: full-time $7434; part-time $413 per credit. Tuition, nonresident: full-time $19,022; part-time $1057 per credit. Required fees: $1729; $88 per credit. *Financial support:* In 2010–11, 16 students received support, including 4 research assistantships with full tuition reimbursements available (averaging $14,056 per year), 12 teaching assistantships with full tuition reimbursements available (averaging $11,303 per year); fellowships, career-related internships or fieldwork, Federal Work-Study, scholarships/grants, and unspecified assistantships also available. Financial award application deadline: 3/1; financial award applicants required to submit FAFSA. *Faculty research:* Archaeology, cultural anthropology, biological anthropology, globalizational development, human ecology. Total annual research expenditures: $85,646. *Unit head:* Dr. Kathleen Sherman, Chair, 970-491-5962, Fax: 970-491-7597, E-mail: kathleen. sherman@colostate.edu. *Application contact:* Rosalie Samaniego, Graduate Contact, 970-491-0930, Fax: 970-491-7597, E-mail: rosalie.samaniego@colostate.edu.

Columbia University, Graduate School of Arts and Sciences, Division of Social Sciences, Department of Anthropology, New York, NY 10027. Offers M Phil, MA, PhD, JD/MA, JD/PhD. Part-time programs available. *Degree requirements:* For master's, one foreign language, 2 research papers; for doctorate, 2 foreign languages, thesis/dissertation. *Entrance requirements:* For master's and doctorate, GRE General Test. Additional exam requirements/recommendations for international students: Required—TOEFL. *Faculty research:* Archaeology, physical anthropology, cultural and linguistic anthropology.

Concordia University, School of Graduate Studies, Faculty of Arts and Science, Department of Sociology and Anthropology, Montréal, QC H3G 1M8, Canada. Offers social and cultural anthropology (MA); sociology (MA). *Degree requirements:* For master's, comprehensive exam or thesis. *Entrance requirements:* For master's, honors degree in sociology or equivalent. *Faculty research:* Community and ethnic relations, popular culture, regional development in Canada, industrial and social movements, social problems and policies.

Cornell University, Graduate School, Graduate Fields of Arts and Sciences, Field of Anthropology, Ithaca, NY 14853-0001. Offers archaeological anthropology (PhD); biological anthropology (PhD); sociocultural anthropology (PhD). *Faculty:* 28 full-time (11 women). *Students:* 51 full-time (36 women); includes 3 Black or African American, non-Hispanic/Latino; 1 American Indian or Alaska Native, non-Hispanic/Latino; 1 Asian, non-Hispanic/Latino; 3 Hispanic/Latino, 17 international. Average age 31. 135 applicants, 9% accepted, 8 enrolled. In 2010, 7 doctorates awarded. *Degree requirements:* For doctorate, one foreign language, comprehensive exam, thesis/dissertation, teaching experience. *Entrance requirements:* For doctorate, GRE General Test, 3 letters of recommendation, sample of written work. Additional exam requirements/recommendations for international students: Required—TOEFL (minimum score 550 paper-based; 213 computer-based; 77 iBT). *Application deadline:* For fall admission, 1/1 for domestic students. Application fee: $80. Electronic applications accepted. *Expenses:* Tuition: Full-time $29,500. Required fees: $76. Tuition and fees vary according to degree level and program. *Financial support:* In 2010–11, 21 fellowships with full tuition reimbursements, 2 research assistantships with full tuition reimbursements, 17 teaching assistantships with full tuition reimbursements were awarded; institutionally sponsored loans, scholarships/grants, health care benefits, tuition waivers (full and partial), and unspecified assistantships also available. Financial award applicants required to submit FAFSA. *Faculty research:* Culture, engaged anthropology, political economy, area studies: Asia, Americas, Europe; interdisciplinary and ethnic studies: Asian-American studies. *Unit head:* Director of Graduate Studies, 607-255-6768. *Application contact:* Graduate Field Assistant, 607-255-6768, E-mail: graduate_anthropology@cornell.edu.

Dalhousie University, Faculty of Arts and Social Science, Department of Sociology and Social Anthropology, Halifax, NS B3H 4R2, Canada. Offers social anthropology (MA, PhD); sociology (MA, PhD). *Entrance requirements:* Additional exam requirements/recommendations for international students: Required—TOEFL, IELTS, CANTEST, CAEL, or Michigan English Language Assessment Battery. Electronic applications accepted. *Faculty research:* Social inequality and social injustice; work, industry, and development (regional and international perspectives); health and illness.

East Carolina University, Graduate School, Thomas Harriot College of Arts and Sciences, Department of Anthropology, Greenville, NC 27858-4353. Offers MA. Part-time programs available. *Degree requirements:* For master's, one foreign language, comprehensive exam, thesis. *Entrance requirements:* For master's, GRE General Test. Additional exam requirements/recommendations for international students: Required—TOEFL. *Expenses:* Tuition, state resident: full-time $3130; part-time $391.25 per credit hour. Tuition, nonresident: full-time $13,817; part-time $1727.13 per credit hour. Required fees: $1916; $239.50 per credit hour. Tuition and fees vary according to campus/location and program.

Eastern New Mexico University, Graduate School, College of Liberal Arts and Sciences, Department of Anthropology and Applied Archaeology, Portales, NM 88130. Offers anthropology (MA). Part-time programs available. *Faculty:* 5 full-time (2 women). *Students:* 14 full-time (6 women), 19 part-time (14 women); includes 4 minority (2 American Indian or Alaska Native, non-Hispanic/Latino; 2 Hispanic/Latino). Average age 31. 13 applicants, 38% accepted, 5 enrolled. In 2010, 3 master's awarded. *Degree requirements:* For master's, variable foreign language requirement, comprehensive exam, thesis. *Entrance requirements:* For master's, minimum GPA of 3.0, letters of recommendation, curriculum vitae, writing sample. Additional exam requirements/recommendations for international students: Required—TOEFL (minimum score 550 paper-based; 213 computer-based; 79 iBT), IELTS (minimum score 6). *Application deadline:* For fall admission, 7/20 priority date for domestic students, 6/20 priority date for international students; for spring admission, 12/15 priority date for domestic students, 11/15 priority date for international students. Applications are processed on a rolling basis. Application fee: $10. Electronic applications accepted. *Expenses:* Tuition, state resident: full-time $3210; part-time $130 per credit hour. Tuition, nonresident: full-time $8652; part-time $360.50 per credit hour. Required fees: $1212; $50.50 per credit hour. Tuition and fees vary according to course load. *Financial support:* In 2010–11, 1 fellowship (averaging $5,312 per year), 19 research assistantships with partial tuition reimbursements (averaging $4,250 per year) were awarded; career-related internships or fieldwork and unspecified assistantships also available. Support available to part-time students. Financial award applicants required to submit FAFSA. *Faculty research:* Paleobotany, remote sensing, conservation archaeology, obsidian hydration. *Unit head:* Dr. David Batten, Interim Graduate Coordinator, 575-562-2750, Fax: 575-562-2555, E-mail: david.batten@enmu.edu. *Application contact:* Barbara Senn, Secretary, 575-562-2206, Fax: 575-562-2555, E-mail: barbara.senn@enmu.edu.

Emory University, Laney Graduate School, Department of Anthropology, Atlanta, GA 30322-1100. Offers PhD. *Degree requirements:* For doctorate, thesis/dissertation, qualifying exams. *Entrance requirements:* For doctorate, GRE General Test. Additional exam requirements/recommendations for international students: Required—TOEFL. Electronic applications accepted. *Expenses:* Tuition: Full-time $33,800. Required fees: $1300. *Faculty research:* Primate behavioral ecology, comparative human biology, human growth and development, medical anthropology, globalization, gender and sexuality.

Florida Atlantic University, Dorothy F. Schmidt College of Arts and Letters, Department of Anthropology, Boca Raton, FL 33431-0991. Offers MA. Part-time programs available. *Faculty:* 9 full-time (4 women), 4 part-time/adjunct (3 women). *Students:* 23 full-time (14 women), 15 part-time (10 women); includes 6 minority (1 Black or African American, non-Hispanic/Latino; 1 Asian, non-Hispanic/Latino; 3 Hispanic/Latino; 1 Two or more races, non-Hispanic/Latino). Average age 31. 30 applicants, 60% accepted, 13 enrolled. In 2010, 8 master's awarded. *Degree requirements:* For master's, one foreign language, thesis. *Entrance requirements:* For master's, GRE General Test, minimum GPA of 3.0. Additional exam requirements/recommendations for international students: Required—TOEFL. *Application deadline:* For fall admission, 7/1 priority date for domestic students, 2/15 for international students; for spring admission, 11/1 for domestic students, 7/15 for international students. Applications are processed on a rolling basis. Application fee: $30. Electronic applications accepted. *Expenses:* Tuition, area resident: Part-time $319.96 per credit. Tuition, state resident: part-time $319.96 per credit. Tuition, nonresident: part-time $926.42 per credit. *Financial support:* Fellowships, research assistantships with tuition reimbursements, teaching assistantships with tuition reimbursements, Federal Work-Study and unspecified assistantships available. *Faculty research:* Archaeological, ethnological, ethnographical, osteological, paleoanthropological, and zoo-archaeological research. *Unit head:* Dr. Michael S. Harris, Chairman, 561-297-3233, Fax: 561-297-0084, E-mail: mharris@fau.edu. *Application contact:* Dr. Emily Stockard, Associate Dean, 561-297-2817, Fax: 561-297-2744, E-mail: stockard@fau.edu.

George Mason University, College of Humanities and Social Sciences, Department of Sociology and Anthropology, Fairfax, VA 22030. Offers anthropology (MA); sociology (MA, PhD). *Faculty:* 26 full-time (11 women), 7 part-time/adjunct (3 women). *Students:* 28 full-time (15 women), 80 part-time (62 women); includes 7 Black or African American, non-Hispanic/Latino; 4 Asian, non-Hispanic/Latino; 9 Hispanic/Latino; 1 Two or more races, non-Hispanic/Latino, 2 international. Average age 32. 99 applicants, 55% accepted, 30 enrolled. In 2010, 7 master's awarded. *Degree requirements:* For master's, thesis; for doctorate, comprehensive exam, thesis/dissertation. *Entrance requirements:* For doctorate, GRE. Additional exam requirements/recommendations for international students: Required—TOEFL (minimum score 570 paper-based; 230 computer-based; 88 iBT). *Application deadline:* For fall admission, 3/1 priority date for domestic students; for spring admission, 10/1 for domestic students. Applications are processed on a rolling basis. Application fee: $100. Electronic applications accepted. *Expenses:* Tuition, state resident: full-time $8192; part-time $440 per credit hour. Tuition, nonresident: full-time $22,952; part-time $1055 per credit hour. Required fees: $2364; $99 per credit hour. *Financial support:* In 2010–11, 19 students received support, including 3 fellowships with full tuition reimbursements available (averaging $18,000 per year), 5 research assistantships with full and partial tuition reimbursements available (averaging $13,169 per year), 12 teaching assistantships with full and partial tuition reimbursements available (averaging $7,268 per year); career-related internships or fieldwork, Federal Work-Study, scholarships/grants, unspecified assistantships, and health care benefits (full-time research or teaching assistantship recipients) also available. Financial award application deadline: 3/1; financial award applicants required to submit FAFSA. *Faculty research:* Africa, American teenagers, black entrepreneurs, human rights, gambling. Total annual research expenditures: $41,941. *Unit head:* Dr. Susan Trencher, Chair, 703-993-1429, E-mail: strenche@gmu.edu. *Application contact:* Amy Best, Associate Professor/Graduate Coordinator, 703-993-1426, E-mail: abest@gmu.edu.

The George Washington University, Columbian College of Arts and Sciences, Department of Anthropology, Washington, DC 20052. Offers anthropology (MA); folklife (MA); hominid paleobiology (MS, PhD); international development (MA). Part-time and evening/weekend programs available. *Faculty:* 14 full-time (5 women), 6 part-time/adjunct (4 women). *Students:* 41 full-time (39 women), 12 part-time (10 women); includes 1 Black or African American, non-Hispanic/Latino; 1 Asian, non-Hispanic/Latino; 2 Hispanic/Latino; 1 Native Hawaiian or other Pacific Islander, non-Hispanic/Latino, 3 international. Average age 27. 62 applicants, 63% accepted, 18 enrolled. In 2010, 11 master's awarded. *Degree requirements:* For master's, one foreign language, comprehensive exam, thesis or alternative. *Entrance requirements:* For master's, GRE General Test, minimum GPA of 3.0. Additional exam requirements/recommendations for international students: Required—TOEFL (minimum score 550 paper-based; 213 computer-based; 80 iBT). *Application deadline:* For fall admission, 1/15 priority date for international students; for spring admission, 9/15 priority date for domestic students, 9/1 priority date for international students. Applications are processed on a rolling basis. Application fee: $75. Electronic applications accepted. *Financial support:* In 2010–11, 8 students received support; fellowships, teaching assistantships, career-related internships or fieldwork and Federal Work-Study available. Financial award application deadline: 1/15. *Unit head:* Catherine J. Allen, Chair, 202-994-7545, E-mail: kitallen@gwu.edu. *Application contact:* Information Contact, 202-994-6075, E-mail: anth@gwu.edu.

Georgia State University, College of Arts and Sciences, Department of Anthropology, Atlanta, GA 30302. Offers MA. Part-time programs available. *Degree requirements:* For master's, one foreign language, thesis or alternative, exam. *Entrance requirements:* For master's, GRE General Test, departmental supplemental form. Additional exam requirements/recommendations for international students: Required—TOEFL. Electronic applications accepted. *Faculty research:* Latin America, medical anthropology, urban anthropology.

Graduate School and University Center of the City University of New York, Graduate Studies, Program in Anthropology, New York, NY 10016-4039. Offers anthropological linguistics (PhD); archaeology (PhD); cultural anthropology (PhD); physical anthropology (PhD). *Degree requirements:* For doctorate, one foreign language, thesis/dissertation. *Entrance requirements:* For doctorate, GRE General Test. Additional exam requirements/recommendations for international students: Required—TOEFL. Electronic applications accepted.

Harvard University, Graduate School of Arts and Sciences, Committee on Middle Eastern Studies, Cambridge, MA 02138. Offers anthropology and Middle Eastern studies (PhD); economics and Middle Eastern studies (PhD); fine arts and Middle Eastern studies (PhD); history and Middle Eastern studies (PhD); regional studies–Middle East (AM). Terminal master's awarded for partial completion of doctoral program. *Degree requirements:* For master's, one foreign language; for doctorate, 2 foreign languages, thesis/dissertation. *Entrance requirements:* For master's, GRE General Test; for doctorate, GRE General Test, 1 year of course work in Middle Eastern regional studies, proficiency in a related language. Additional exam requirements/recommendations for international students: Required—TOEFL. *Expenses:* Tuition: Full-time $34,976. Required fees: $1166. Full-time tuition and fees vary according to program.

Harvard University, Graduate School of Arts and Sciences, Department of Anthropology, Cambridge, MA 02138. Offers archaeology (PhD); biological anthropology (PhD); legal anthropology (AM); medical anthropology (AM); social anthropology (AM, PhD); social change and development (AM). Terminal master's awarded for partial completion of doctoral program. *Degree requirements:* For master's, 2 foreign languages, thesis (for some programs); for doctorate, 2 foreign languages, thesis/dissertation, laboratory and/or fieldwork; general, qualifying, or special exams. *Entrance requirements:* For master's and doctorate, GRE General Test. Additional exam requirements/recommendations for international students: Required—TOEFL. *Expenses:* Tuition: Full-time $34,976. Required fees: $1166. Full-time tuition and fees vary according to program.

Hunter College of the City University of New York, Graduate School, School of Arts and Sciences, Department of Anthropology, New York, NY 10021-5085. Offers MA. Part-time and evening/weekend programs available. *Faculty:* 6 full-time (1 woman), 2 part-time/adjunct (both women). *Students:* 5 full-time (4 women), 46 part-time (29 women); includes 4 Black or African American, non-Hispanic/Latino; 2 American Indian or Alaska Native, non-Hispanic/Latino; 2 Asian, non-Hispanic/Latino; 7 Hispanic/Latino, 2 international. Average age 31. 49 applicants, 57% accepted, 18 enrolled. In 2010, 12 master's awarded. *Degree requirements:* For master's, comprehensive exam, thesis, language or statistics exam. *Entrance requirements:* For master's, GRE General Test, minimum 9 credits of course work in anthropology or a related field. Additional exam requirements/recommendations for international students: Required—TOEFL. *Application deadline:* For fall admission, 4/1 for domestic students, 2/1 for international students; for spring admission, 11/1 for domestic students, 9/1 for international students. Application fee: $125. *Financial support:* Research assistantships, tuition waivers (full and partial) available. *Faculty research:* Primatology, human ecology, archeology, political anthropology, primate and human evolution. *Unit head:* Gregory A. Johnson, Chair, 212-772-5652, Fax: 212-772-5410, E-mail: gjohnson@hunter.cuny.edu. *Application contact:* William Zlata, Director for Graduate Admissions, 212-772-4482, Fax: 212-650-3336, E-mail: admissions@hunter.cuny.edu.

Idaho State University, Office of Graduate Studies, College of Arts and Sciences, Department of Anthropology, Pocatello, ID 83209-8005. Offers MA, MS. Part-time programs available. *Degree requirements:* For master's, one foreign language, comprehensive exam, thesis, 4 semesters foreign language, oral defense. *Entrance requirements:* For master's, GRE General Test, GMAT or MAT, minimum GPA of 3.0 in all upper-division classes, 3 letters of recommendation. Additional exam requirements/recommendations for international students: Required—TOEFL (minimum score 550 paper-based; 213 computer-based; 80 iBT). Electronic applications accepted. *Faculty research:* Native American studies: health care, language/ethnopoetics, prehistory, art, resource environmental management.

Indiana University Bloomington, University Graduate School, College of Arts and Sciences, Department of Anthropology, Bloomington, IN 47405-7000. Offers MA, PhD. *Faculty:* 26 full-time (16 women), 25 part-time/adjunct (9 women). *Students:* 145 full-time (96 women); includes 25 minority (2 Black or African American, non-Hispanic/Latino; 7 American Indian or Alaska Native, non-Hispanic/Latino; 2 Asian, non-Hispanic/Latino; 9 Hispanic/Latino; 5 Two or more races, non-Hispanic/Latino), 12 international. Average age 32. 181 applicants, 19% accepted, 19 enrolled. In 2010, 23 master's, 9 doctorates awarded. Terminal master's awarded for partial completion of doctoral program. *Degree requirements:* For master's, thesis or alternative; for doctorate, one foreign language, comprehensive exam, thesis/dissertation. *Entrance requirements:* For master's and doctorate, GRE General Test, minimum GPA of 3.0. Additional exam requirements/recommendations for international students: Required—TOEFL (minimum score 550 paper-based; 213 computer-based; 79 iBT). *Application deadline:* For fall admission, 1/15 for domestic and international students. Application fee: $55 ($65 for international students). Electronic applications accepted. *Financial support:* In 2010–11, 36 students received support, including 12 fellowships with full tuition reimbursements available (averaging $15,000 per year), 10 research assistantships with full tuition reimbursements available (averaging $11,400 per year), 35 teaching assistantships with full tuition reimbursements available (averaging $14,300 per year); Federal Work-Study, scholarships/grants, health care benefits, and unspecified assistantships also available. Financial award application deadline: 2/15; financial award applicants required to submit FAFSA. *Faculty research:* Ecologic and economic development, symbolism, arts/dance, paleoarchaeology, bioanthropology. Total annual research expenditures: $22.7 million. *Unit head:* Dr. Eduardo S. Brondizio, Chair, 812-855-2555, Fax: 812-855-4358, E-mail: ebrondiz@indiana.edu. *Application contact:* Debra Wilkerson, Secretary, 812-855-1203, Fax: 812-855-4358, E-mail: dwilkers@indiana.edu.

Iowa State University of Science and Technology, Graduate College, College of Liberal Arts and Sciences, Department of Anthropology, Ames, IA 50011. Offers MA. *Faculty:* 9 full-time (4 women), 1 (woman) part-time/adjunct. *Students:* 10 full-time (9 women), 4 part-time (all women); includes 1 American Indian or Alaska Native, non-Hispanic/Latino, 3 international. 11 applicants, 45% accepted, 1 enrolled. In 2010, 3 master's awarded. *Degree requirements:* For master's, thesis. *Entrance requirements:* For master's, GRE General Test. Additional exam requirements/recommendations for international students: Required—TOEFL (minimum score 550 paper-based; 79 iBT), IELTS (minimum score 6.5). *Application deadline:* For fall admission, 1/15 priority date for domestic and international students; for spring admission, 10/1 for domestic and international students. Applications are processed on a rolling basis. Application fee: $40 ($90 for international students). Electronic applications accepted. *Financial support:* In 2010–11, 2 research assistantships with full and partial tuition reimbursements (averaging $5,967 per year), 10 teaching assistantships with full and partial tuition reimbursements (averaging $6,543 per year) were awarded; fellowships, scholarships/grants, health care benefits, and unspecified assistantships also available. *Unit head:* Dr. R. Paul Lasley, Interim Chair, 515-294-8212, Fax: 515-294-1708, E-mail: anthgrad@iastate.edu. *Application contact:* Dr. Jill Pruetz, Director of Graduate Education, 515-294-7139, E-mail: anthgrade@iastate.edu.

The Johns Hopkins University, Zanvyl Krieger School of Arts and Sciences, Department of Anthropology, Baltimore, MD 21218-2699. Offers PhD. *Faculty:* 10 full-time (7 women), 1 part-time/adjunct (0 women). *Students:* 17 full-time (10 women); includes 2 minority (1 Asian, non-Hispanic/Latino; 1 Hispanic/Latino), 9 international. Average age 29. 102 applicants, 4% accepted, 4 enrolled. In 2010, 4 doctorates awarded. *Degree requirements:* For doctorate, one foreign language, thesis/dissertation. *Entrance requirements:* For doctorate, GRE General Test. Additional exam requirements/recommendations for international students: Required—TOEFL, IELTS. *Application deadline:* For fall admission, 1/1 for domestic students, 1/10 for international students. Application fee: $75. Electronic applications accepted. *Financial support:* In 2010–11, 12 fellowships with full and partial tuition reimbursements (averaging $17,500 per year), 10 teaching assistantships with full and partial tuition reimbursements (averaging $17,500 per year) were awarded; research assistantships, career-related internships or fieldwork, Federal Work-Study, and institutionally sponsored loans also available. Financial award application deadline: 4/15; financial award applicants required to submit FAFSA. *Faculty research:* Social and cultural anthropology of complex societies, gender politics, economic anthropology, religion. Total annual research expenditures: $117,673. *Unit head:* Dr. Jane I. Guyer, Chair, 410-516-7272, Fax: 410-516-6080, E-mail: jiguyer@jhu.edu. *Application contact:* Richard Helman, Admissions Coordinator, 410-516-7271, Fax: 410-516-6080, E-mail: rhelman@jhu.edu.

Kent State University, College of Arts and Sciences, Department of Anthropology, Kent, OH 44242-0001. Offers MA. *Degree requirements:* For master's, thesis. *Entrance requirements:* For master's, GRE General Test, minimum GPA of 3.0. Additional exam requirements/recommendations for international students: Required—TOEFL. Electronic applications accepted. *Expenses:* Tuition, state resident: full-time $7866; part-time $437 per credit hour. Tuition, nonresident: full-time $14,022; part-time $779 per credit hour.

Louisiana State University and Agricultural and Mechanical College, Graduate School, College of Humanities and Social Sciences, Department of Geography and Anthropology, Baton Rouge, LA 70803. Offers anthropology (MA); geography (MA, MS, PhD). Part-time programs available. *Faculty:* 30 full-time (11 women), 1 part-time/adjunct (0 women). *Students:* 75 full-time (40 women), 24 part-time (12 women); includes 1 Black or African American, non-Hispanic/Latino; 1 Hispanic/Latino; 2 Two or more races, non-Hispanic/Latino, 24 international. Average age 31. 84 applicants, 67% accepted, 18 enrolled. In 2010, 13 master's, 7 doctorates awarded. Terminal master's awarded for partial completion of doctoral program. *Degree requirements:* For master's, 2 foreign languages, thesis (for some programs); for doctorate, 2 foreign languages, thesis/dissertation. *Entrance requirements:* For master's and doctorate, GRE General Test, minimum GPA of 3.0. Additional exam requirements/recommendations for international students: Required—TOEFL (minimum score 550 paper-based; 213 computer-based; 79 iBT) or IELTS (minimum score 6.5). *Application deadline:* For fall admission, 1/25 priority date for domestic students, 5/15 for international students; for spring admission, 10/15 for international students. Applications are processed on a rolling basis. Application fee: $50 ($70 for international students). Electronic applications accepted. *Financial support:* In 2010–11, 72 students received support, including 3 fellowships with full tuition reimbursements available (averaging $20,126 per year), 29 research assistantships with full and partial tuition reimbursements available (averaging $18,220 per year), 25 teaching assistantships with full and partial tuition reimbursements available (averaging $12,636 per year); career-related internships or fieldwork, health care benefits, and unspecified assistantships also available. Financial award application deadline: 3/1; financial award applicants required to submit FAFSA. *Faculty research:* Cultural, coastal, climate, geographic information systems-geography, cultural, linguistics, archaeology-anthropology. Total annual research expenditures: $731,204. *Unit head:* Dr. Kevin Robbins, Chair, 225-578-5942, Fax: 225-578-4420, E-mail: gachair@lsu.edu. *Application contact:* Dr. Barry Keim, Graduate Adviser, 225-578-6170, Fax: 225-578-4420, E-mail: bkeim@lsu.edu.

McGill University, Faculty of Graduate and Postdoctoral Studies, Faculty of Arts, Department of Anthropology, Montréal, QC H3A 2T5, Canada. Offers anthropology (MA, PhD); medical anthropology (MA).

McGill University, Faculty of Graduate and Postdoctoral Studies, Faculty of Medicine, Department of Social Studies in Medicine, Montréal, QC H3A 2T5, Canada. Offers medical anthropology (MA, PhD); medical history (MA, PhD); medical sociology (MA, PhD).

McMaster University, School of Graduate Studies, Faculty of Social Sciences, Department of Anthropology, Hamilton, ON L8S 4M2, Canada. Offers MA, PhD. Part-time programs available. *Degree requirements:* For master's, thesis or alternative; for doctorate, one foreign language, comprehensive exam, thesis/dissertation, fieldwork. *Entrance requirements:* Additional exam requirements/recommendations for international students: Required—TOEFL (minimum score 580 paper-based; 237 computer-based). *Faculty research:* Medical anthropology, contemporary ethnography in an interdisciplinary perspective, archaeological and social theory, linguistics, folklore.

Memorial University of Newfoundland, School of Graduate Studies, Department of Anthropology, St. John's, NL A1C 5S7, Canada. Offers archaeology and physical anthropology (MA, PhD); social and cultural anthropology (MA, PhD). Part-time programs available. *Degree requirements:* For master's, thesis (for some programs); for doctorate, comprehensive exam, thesis/dissertation, oral defense of thesis. *Entrance requirements:* For master's, 2nd class degree in related field. Electronic applications accepted. *Faculty research:* Early European settlements, ethnoarchaeology, economic/political anthropology, land claims and aboriginal rights, marine anthropology.

Michigan State University, The Graduate School, College of Social Science, Department of Anthropology, East Lansing, MI 48824. Offers anthropology (MA, PhD); professional applications in anthropology (MA). Terminal master's awarded for partial completion of doctoral program. *Degree requirements:* For master's, comprehensive exam (for some programs); for doctorate, annual evaluation. *Entrance requirements:* Additional exam requirements/recommendations for international students: Required—TOEFL. Electronic applications accepted.

Minnesota State University Mankato, College of Graduate Studies, College of Social and Behavioral Sciences, Department of Anthropology, Mankato, MN 56001. Offers MS. Part-time programs available. *Students:* 2 full-time (1 woman), 10 part-time (7 women). *Degree requirements:* For master's, comprehensive exam. *Entrance requirements:* For master's, minimum undergraduate GPA of 3.0 in last 2 years of course work. Additional exam requirements/recommendations for international students: Required—TOEFL. *Application deadline:* For fall admission, 7/1 priority date for domestic students; for spring admission, 11/1 for domestic students. Applications are processed on a rolling basis. Application fee: $40. Electronic applications accepted. *Financial support:* Unspecified assistantships available. Financial award application deadline: 3/15; financial award applicants required to submit FAFSA. *Unit head:* Dr. Paul Brown, Chair, 507-389-6504, Fax: 507-389-6769, E-mail: paul.brown@mnsu.edu. *Application contact:* 507-389-2321, E-mail: grad@mnsu.edu.

Mississippi State University, College of Arts and Sciences, Department of Anthropology and Middle Eastern Cultures, Mississippi State, MS 39762. Offers applied anthropology (MA). Part-time programs available. *Faculty:* 7 full-time (2 women). *Students:* 12 full-time (5 women), 9 part-time (4 women), 1 international. Average age 29. 13 applicants, 77% accepted, 4 enrolled. In 2010, 2 master's awarded. *Degree requirements:* For master's, thesis. *Entrance requirements:* For master's, GRE, minimum GPA of 3.0 on last 60 hours of undergraduate courses. Additional exam requirements/recommendations for international students: Required—TOEFL (minimum score 475 paper-based; 153 computer-based; 53 iBT); Recommended—IELTS (minimum score 4.5). *Application deadline:* For fall admission, 4/15 priority date for domestic students, 4/15 for international students; for spring admission, 11/1 priority date for domestic students, 9/1 for international students. Applications are processed on a rolling basis. Application fee: $40. Electronic applications accepted. *Expenses:* Tuition, state resident: full-time $2730.50; part-time $304 per credit hour. Tuition, nonresident: full-time $6901; part-time $767 per credit hour. *Financial support:* In 2010–11, 4 research assistantships with full and partial tuition reimbursements (averaging $10,728 per year), 5 teaching assistantships with full and partial tuition reimbursements (averaging $9,582 per year) were awarded; Federal Work-Study, institutionally sponsored loans, scholarships/grants, and unspecified assistantships also available. Financial award application deadline: 3/15; financial award applicants required to submit FAFSA. *Faculty research:* Archaeology and bioarchaeology, environmental archaeology, cultural archaeology, research projects in Southeastern archaeology and bioarchaeology. *Unit head:* Dr. Paul F. Jacobs, Professor and Department Head, 662-325-7525, Fax: 662-325-8690, E-mail: pfj1@ra.msstate.edu. *Application contact:* Dr. Evan Peacock, Associate Professor/Graduate Coordinator, 662-325-1663, Fax: 662-325-1967, E-mail: peacock@anthro.msstate.edu.

Missouri State University, Graduate College, College of Humanities and Public Affairs, Department of Sociology, Anthropology, and Criminology, Springfield, MO 65897. Offers applied anthropology (MS); criminology (MS). Part-time programs available. *Degree requirements:* For master's, comprehensive exam. *Entrance requirements:* For master's, GRE, minimum GPA of 3.0. Additional exam requirements/recommendations for international students: Required—TOEFL (minimum score 550 paper-based; 213 computer-based; 79 iBT). Electronic applications accepted. *Expenses:* Tuition, state resident: full-time $3348; part-time $186 per credit hour. Tuition, nonresident: full-time $6696; part-time $372 per credit hour. Required fees: $238 per semester. Tuition and fees vary according to course level, course load and program. *Faculty research:* Youth delinquency, social theory, linguistic anthropology, forensic anthropology, homeland security.

Montclair State University, The Graduate School, College of Humanities and Social Sciences, Department of Anthropology, Montclair, NJ 07043-1624. Offers community development (Certificate). Part-time and evening/weekend programs available. *Faculty:* 10 full-time (5 women), 9 part-time/adjunct (6 women). *Students:* 1 (woman) full-time, 2 part-time (1 woman); includes 1 Black or African American, non-Hispanic/Latino. Average age 24. 5 applicants, 80% accepted, 3 enrolled. *Entrance requirements:* Additional exam requirements/recommendations for international students: Required—TOEFL (minimum score: 83 iBT) or IELTS. *Expenses:* Tuition, state resident: part-time $501.34 per credit. Tuition, nonresident: part-time $773.88 per credit. Required fees: $71.15 per credit. *Financial support:* In 2010–11, 1 research assistantship with full tuition reimbursement (averaging $7,000 per year) was awarded; Federal Work-Study, scholarships/grants, and unspecified assistantships also available. Support available to part-time students. Financial award application deadline: 3/1; financial award applicants required to submit FAFSA. *Unit head:* Dr. Francis Rothstein, Chairperson, 973-655-4133, E-mail: brookk@mail.montclair.edu. *Application contact:* Amy Aiello, Director of Graduate Admissions and Operations, 973-655-5147, Fax: 973-655-7869, E-mail: graduate.school@montclair.edu.

New Mexico Highlands University, Graduate Studies, College of Arts and Sciences, Program in Southwest Studies, Las Vegas, NM 87701. Offers MA, MS. Program is interdisciplinary. Part-time programs available. *Faculty:* 6 full-time (0 women). *Students:* 13 full-time (2 women), 3 part-time (2 women); includes 6 Hispanic/Latino, 9 international. Average age 26. 17 applicants, 100% accepted, 5 enrolled. In 2010, 6 master's awarded. *Degree requirements:* For master's, comprehensive exam, thesis or alternative. *Entrance requirements:* Additional exam requirements/recommendations for international students: Required—TOEFL (minimum score 540 paper-based; 207 computer-based). *Application deadline:* For fall admission, 8/1 priority date for domestic students. Applications are processed on a rolling basis. Application fee: $15. *Expenses:* Tuition, state resident: full-time $2544. Required fees: $624; $132 per credit hour. *Financial support:* In 2010–11, 14 students received support. Career-related internships or fieldwork, Federal Work-Study, institutionally sponsored loans, scholarships/grants, tuition waivers (full and partial), and unspecified assistantships available. Support available to part-time students. Financial award application deadline: 3/1; financial award applicants required to submit FAFSA. *Unit head:* Dr. John Jeffries, Department Head of Computer and Mathematical Sciences, 505-454-3480, E-mail: jjeffries@nmhu.edu. *Application contact:* Diane Trujillo, Administrative Assistant, Graduate Studies, 505-454-3266, Fax: 505-426-2117, E-mail: dtrujillo@nmhu.edu.

New Mexico State University, Graduate School, College of Arts and Sciences, Department of Anthropology, Las Cruces, NM 88003-8001. Offers anthropology (MA). Part-time programs available. *Faculty:* 8 full-time (6 women), 2 part-time/adjunct (1 woman). *Students:* 34 full-time (24 women), 29 part-time (19 women); includes 10 minority (1 Black or African American, non-Hispanic/Latino; 9 Hispanic/Latino), 3 international. Average age 30. 48 applicants, 92%

Anthropology

New Mexico State University *(continued)*
accepted, 23 enrolled. In 2010, 18 master's awarded. *Degree requirements:* For master's, comprehensive exam (for some programs), thesis (for some programs). *Entrance requirements:* For master's, undergraduate research methods and statistics. Additional exam requirements/recommendations for international students: Required—TOEFL. *Application deadline:* For fall admission, 2/15 priority date for domestic and international students; for spring admission, 10/15 priority date for domestic and international students. Applications are processed on a rolling basis. Application fee: $30 ($50 for international students). Electronic applications accepted. *Expenses:* Tuition, state resident: full-time $4536; part-time $242 per credit. Tuition, nonresident: full-time $15,816; part-time $712 per credit. Required fees: $636 per term. *Financial support:* In 2010–11, 2 research assistantships with partial tuition reimbursements (averaging $14,225 per year), 11 teaching assistantships with partial tuition reimbursements (averaging $7,182 per year) were awarded; fellowships, career-related internships or fieldwork, Federal Work-Study, and health care benefits also available. Support available to part-time students. Financial award application deadline: 2/15. *Faculty research:* Native American culture and society, Latin America and border studies, prehistoric and historic archaeology, medical anthropology, applied anthropology. *Unit head:* Dr. Miriam Chaiken, Head, 575-646-2826, Fax: 575-646-3725, E-mail: mchaiken@nmsu.edu. *Application contact:* Coordinator.

The New School: A University, The New School for Social Research, Department of Anthropology, New York, NY 10003. Offers M Phil, MA, DS Sc, PhD. Part-time and evening/weekend programs available. Terminal master's awarded for partial completion of doctoral program. *Degree requirements:* For master's, comprehensive exam; for doctorate, one foreign language, comprehensive exam, thesis/dissertation, 30 credits, including three proseminars. *Entrance requirements:* For master's, GRE General Test; for doctorate, GRE General Test, MA in anthropology. Additional exam requirements/recommendations for international students: Required—TOEFL (minimum score 600 paper-based; 250 computer-based; 100 iBT). Electronic applications accepted. *Faculty research:* Critical theory; modern social and cultural systems; race, class, gender.

New York University, Graduate School of Arts and Science, Department of Anthropology, New York, NY 10012-1019. Offers anthropology (MA, PhD), including archaeological anthropology, linguistic anthropology, physical anthropology, socio-cultural anthropology; anthropology and French studies (PhD); MA/Advanced Certificate; PhD/Advanced Certificate. Part-time programs available. *Faculty:* 22 full-time, 13 part-time/adjunct. *Students:* 72 full-time (50 women), 12 part-time (9 women); includes 6 Asian, non-Hispanic/Latino; 4 Hispanic/Latino, 25 international. Average age 29. 409 applicants, 4% accepted, 12 enrolled. In 2010, 12 master's, 8 doctorates awarded. *Degree requirements:* For master's, thesis; for doctorate, one foreign language, comprehensive exam, thesis/dissertation. *Entrance requirements:* For master's, GRE General Test; for doctorate, GRE General Test, MA or equivalent. Additional exam requirements/recommendations for international students: Required—TOEFL. *Application deadline:* For fall admission, 12/15 priority date for domestic students; 12/15 for international students. Application fee: $90. *Financial support:* Fellowships with tuition reimbursements, research assistantships with tuition reimbursements, teaching assistantships with tuition reimbursements, career-related internships or fieldwork, Federal Work-Study, institutionally sponsored loans, scholarships/grants, health care benefits, and unspecified assistantships available. Financial award application deadline: 12/15; financial award applicants required to submit FAFSA. *Faculty research:* Sociocultural anthropology, archaeology, biological anthropology, linguistic anthropology. *Unit head:* Terry Harrison, Chair, 212-998-8550, Fax: 212-995-4014, E-mail: anthropology@nyu.edu. *Application contact:* Bruce Grant, Director of Graduate Studies, 212-998-8550, Fax: 212-995-4014, E-mail: anthropology@nyu.edu.

North Carolina State University, Graduate School, College of Humanities and Social Sciences, Department of Sociology and Anthropology, Program in Anthropology, Raleigh, NC 27695. Offers bioarchaeology (MA); cultural anthropology (MA); environmental anthropology (MA).

Northern Arizona University, Graduate College, College of Social and Behavioral Sciences, Department of Anthropology, Flagstaff, AZ 86011. Offers archaeology (MA); cultural anthropology (MA); linguistic anthropology (MA). *Faculty:* 17 full-time (7 women). *Students:* 48 full-time (29 women), 14 part-time (8 women); includes 14 minority (3 American Indian or Alaska Native, non-Hispanic/Latino; 8 Hispanic/Latino; 3 Two or more races, non-Hispanic/Latino), 1 international. Average age 35. 100 applicants, 45% accepted, 26 enrolled. In 2010, 25 master's awarded. *Degree requirements:* For master's, thesis (for some programs), internship paper. *Entrance requirements:* For master's, 12 undergraduate hours in anthropology. Additional exam requirements/recommendations for international students: Required—TOEFL (minimum score 550 paper-based; 213 computer-based; 80 iBT), IELTS (minimum score 7). *Application deadline:* For fall admission, 2/15 priority date for domestic and international students. Applications are processed on a rolling basis. Application fee: $65. Electronic applications accepted. *Financial support:* In 2010–11, 1 fellowship (averaging $10,774 per year), 9 teaching assistantships with partial tuition reimbursements (averaging $10,449 per year) were awarded; career-related internships or fieldwork, Federal Work-Study, scholarships/grants, health care benefits, tuition waivers (full and partial), and unspecified assistantships also available. Financial award applicants required to submit FAFSA. *Faculty research:* Economic development, culture change, ethnohistory, archaeology of the Southwest, small town networks and HIV. Total annual research expenditures: $594,266. *Unit head:* Dr. Robert Trotter, Chair/Professor, 928-523-4521, Fax: 928-523-9135, E-mail: robert.trotter@nau.edu. *Application contact:* Pamela Lamb, Administrative Assistant, 928-523-3180, Fax: 928-523-9135, E-mail: anthropology@nau.edu.

Northern Illinois University, Graduate School, College of Liberal Arts and Sciences, Department of Anthropology, De Kalb, IL 60115-2854. Offers MA. Part-time programs available. *Faculty:* 12 full-time (6 women). *Students:* 17 full-time (11 women), 28 part-time (14 women); includes 1 Black or African American, non-Hispanic/Latino; 1 American Indian or Alaska Native, non-Hispanic/Latino; 1 Asian, non-Hispanic/Latino; 4 Hispanic/Latino, 5 international. Average age 31. 32 applicants, 66% accepted, 13 enrolled. In 2010, 13 master's awarded. *Degree requirements:* For master's, one foreign language, comprehensive exam, thesis optional. *Entrance requirements:* For master's, GRE General Test, minimum GPA of 2.75, 15 hours of course work in anthropology, course work in statistics. Additional exam requirements/recommendations for international students: Required—TOEFL (minimum score 550 paper-based; 213 computer-based). *Application deadline:* For fall admission, 6/1 for domestic students, 5/1 for international students; for spring admission, 11/1 for domestic students, 10/1 for international students. Applications are processed on a rolling basis. Application fee: $30. Electronic applications accepted. *Expenses:* Tuition, state resident: full-time $7200; part-time $300 per credit hour. Tuition, nonresident: full-time $14,400; part-time $600 per credit hour. Required fees: $79 per credit hour. *Financial support:* In 2010–11, 2 research assistantships with full tuition reimbursements, 14 teaching assistantships with full tuition reimbursements were awarded; fellowships with full tuition reimbursements, career-related internships or fieldwork, Federal Work-Study, scholarships/grants, tuition waivers (full), and unspecified assistantships also available. Support available to part-time students. Financial award applicants required to submit FAFSA. *Faculty research:* Linguistic anthropology of Oceania, Mayan languages, human paleontology, primate evolution, dental anthropology. *Unit head:* Dr. Judy Ledgerwood, Chair, 815-753-0246, Fax: 815-753-7027, E-mail: jledgerw@niu.edu. *Application contact:* Graduate School Office, 815-753-0395, E-mail: gradsch@niu.edu.

Northwestern University, The Graduate School, Judd A. and Marjorie Weinberg College of Arts and Sciences, Department of Anthropology, Evanston, IL 60208. Offers PhD, JD/PhD. Admissions and degrees offered through The Graduate School. *Degree requirements:* For doctorate, thesis/dissertation. *Entrance requirements:* For doctorate, GRE General Test. Additional exam requirements/recommendations for international students: Required—TOEFL. Electronic applications accepted. *Faculty research:* Archaeology of complex societies, gender, political/urban anthropology, linguistic anthropology, African studies.

The Ohio State University, Graduate School, College of Arts and Sciences, Division of Social and Behavioral Sciences, Department of Anthropology, Columbus, OH 43210. Offers MA, PhD. *Faculty:* 31. *Students:* 27 full-time (20 women), 26 part-time (15 women); includes 1 American Indian or Alaska Native, non-Hispanic/Latino; 1 Asian, non-Hispanic/Latino; 4 Hispanic/Latino, 2 international. Average age 29. In 2010, 7 master's, 5 doctorates awarded. *Degree requirements:* For master's, thesis optional; for doctorate, one foreign language, thesis/dissertation. *Entrance requirements:* For master's and doctorate, GRE General Test. Additional exam requirements/recommendations for international students: Required—TOEFL (minimum score 600 paper-based; 250 computer-based). *Application deadline:* For fall admission, 8/15 priority date for domestic students, 7/1 priority date for international students; for winter admission, 12/1 priority date for domestic students, 11/1 priority date for international students; for spring admission, 3/1 priority date for domestic students, 2/1 priority date for international students. Applications are processed on a rolling basis. Application fee: $40 ($50 for international students). Electronic applications accepted. *Expenses:* Tuition, state resident: full-time $10,605. Tuition, nonresident: full-time $26,535. Tuition and fees vary according to course load and program. *Financial support:* Fellowships, research assistantships, teaching assistantships, Federal Work-Study, institutionally sponsored loans, and unspecified assistantships available. Support available to part-time students. *Unit head:* Dr. Clark S. Larsen, Chair, 614-292-4149, Fax: 614-292-4155, E-mail: larsen.53@osu.edu. *Application contact:* 614-292-9444, Fax: 614-292-3895, E-mail: domestic.grad@osu.edu.

Oregon State University, Graduate School, College of Liberal Arts, Department of Anthropology, Corvallis, OR 97331. Offers anthropology (MAIS); applied anthropology (MA). *Degree requirements:* For master's, one foreign language, thesis. *Entrance requirements:* For master's, minimum GPA of 3.0 in last 90 hours. Additional exam requirements/recommendations for international students: Required—TOEFL. *Faculty research:* Historical anthropology; first American studies; Japanese, Asian, South Pacific, and Native American cultures; business anthropology.

Penn State University Park, Graduate School, College of the Liberal Arts, Department of Anthropology, State College, University Park, PA 16802-1503. Offers MA, PhD.

Portland State University, Graduate Studies, College of Liberal Arts and Sciences, Department of Anthropology, Portland, OR 97207-0751. Offers MA. *Faculty:* 6 full-time (4 women), 4 part-time/adjunct (1 woman). *Students:* 12 full-time (8 women), 18 part-time (13 women); includes 1 minority (Asian, non-Hispanic/Latino), 1 international. Average age 32. 18 applicants, 89% accepted, 9 enrolled. *Degree requirements:* For master's, one foreign language, thesis. *Entrance requirements:* For master's, GRE General Test, minimum GPA of 3.25 in upper-division anthropology course work, 3.0 overall; 3 letters of recommendation. Additional exam requirements/recommendations for international students: Required—TOEFL. *Application deadline:* For fall admission, 2/1 for domestic and international students. Application fee: $50. *Expenses:* Tuition, state resident: full-time $8505; part-time $315 per credit. Tuition, nonresident: full-time $13,284; part-time $492 per credit. Required fees: $1482; $21 per credit. $99 per term. One-time fee: $120. Part-time tuition and fees vary according to course load and program. *Financial support:* In 2010–11, 6 teaching assistantships with full tuition reimbursements (averaging $6,499 per year) were awarded; research assistantships with full tuition reimbursements, career-related internships or fieldwork, Federal Work-Study, and unspecified assistantships also available. Support available to part-time students. Financial award application deadline: 3/1; financial award applicants required to submit FAFSA. *Faculty research:* Forensic anthropology, Northwest Coast prehistory, Native Americans, applied anthropology, urban anthropology. Total annual research expenditures: $464,633. *Unit head:* Dr. Kenneth M. Ames, Chair, 503-725-3081, E-mail: amesk@pdx.edu. *Application contact:* Connie Cash, Office Coordinator, 503-725-3081, Fax: 503-725-3905, E-mail: cashc@pdx.edu.

Portland State University, Graduate Studies, Systems Science Program, Portland, OR 97207-0751. Offers computational intelligence (Certificate); computer modeling and simulation (Certificate); systems science (MS); systems science/anthropology (PhD); systems science/business administration (PhD); systems science/civil engineering (PhD); systems science/economics (PhD); systems science/engineering management (PhD); systems science/general (PhD); systems science/mathematical sciences (PhD); systems science/mechanical engineering (PhD); systems science/psychology (PhD); systems science/sociology (PhD). *Faculty:* 4 full-time (0 women), 1 part-time/adjunct (0 women). *Students:* 15 full-time (4 women), 35 part-time (11 women); includes 1 American Indian or Alaska Native, non-Hispanic/Latino; 1 Asian, non-Hispanic/Latino; 1 Two or more races, non-Hispanic/Latino, 4 international. Average age 39. 8 applicants, 88% accepted, 5 enrolled. In 2010, 2 master's, 4 doctorates awarded. *Degree requirements:* For doctorate, variable foreign language requirement, thesis/dissertation. *Entrance requirements:* For master's, 2 letters of recommendation; for doctorate, GMAT, GRE General Test, minimum undergraduate GPA of 3.0. Additional exam requirements/recommendations for international students: Required—TOEFL. *Application deadline:* For fall admission, 2/1 for domestic students; for spring admission, 11/1 for domestic students. Application fee: $50. *Expenses:* Tuition, state resident: full-time $8505; part-time $315 per credit. Tuition, nonresident: full-time $13,284; part-time $492 per credit. Required fees: $1482; $21 per credit. $99 per term. One-time fee: $120. Part-time tuition and fees vary according to course load and program. *Financial support:* In 2010–11, 1 research assistantship with full tuition reimbursement (averaging $7,704 per year) was awarded; teaching assistantships with full tuition reimbursements, career-related internships or fieldwork, Federal Work-Study, scholarships/grants, and unspecified assistantships also available. Support available to part-time students. Financial award application deadline: 3/1; financial award applicants required to submit FAFSA. *Faculty research:* Systems theory and methodology, artificial intelligence neural networks, information theory, nonlinear dynamics/chaos, modeling and simulation. *Unit head:* George Lendaris, Acting Director, 503-725-4960. *Application contact:* Dawn Sharafi, Administrative Assistant, 503-725-4960, E-mail: dawn@sysc.pdx.edu.

Princeton University, Graduate School, Department of Anthropology, Princeton, NJ 08544-1019. Offers PhD. *Degree requirements:* For doctorate, variable foreign language requirement, thesis/dissertation. *Entrance requirements:* For doctorate, GRE General Test, sample of written work. Additional exam requirements/recommendations for international students: Required—TOEFL (minimum score 600 paper-based; 250 computer-based). Electronic applications accepted. *Faculty research:* Symbolic anthropology, social theory, gender studies, law and society, political and social anthropology.

Purdue University, Graduate School, College of Liberal Arts, Department of Sociology and Anthropology, West Lafayette, IN 47907. Offers anthropology (MS, PhD); sociology (MS, PhD). Terminal master's awarded for partial completion of doctoral program. *Degree requirements:* For doctorate, thesis/dissertation. *Entrance requirements:* For master's and doctorate, GRE General Test. Additional exam requirements/recommendations for international students: Required—TOEFL, TWE. Electronic applications accepted. *Faculty research:* Communiversity survey project, risk, fear, constrained behavior, archaeological services.

Rice University, Graduate Programs, School of Social Sciences, Department of Anthropology, Houston, TX 77251-1892. Offers archaeology (MA, PhD); social-cultural anthropology (MA, PhD). Terminal master's awarded for partial completion of doctoral program. *Degree requirements:* For master's, one foreign language, 3 major papers, dissertation proposal and language exam or thesis; for doctorate, one foreign language, thesis/dissertation. *Entrance requirements:* For master's and doctorate, research proposal. Additional exam requirements/recommendations for international students: Required—TOEFL (minimum score 90 iBT). Electronic applications accepted.

Roosevelt University, Graduate Division, College of Arts and Sciences, Department of Sociology and Anthropology, Chicago, IL 60605. Offers anthropology (MA); sociology (MA). Part-time and evening/weekend programs available. *Degree requirements:* For master's, comprehensive exam, thesis. *Faculty research:* Social theory, urban sociology, gerontology, social organizations.

Rutgers, The State University of New Jersey, New Brunswick, Graduate School-New Brunswick, Program in Anthropology, Piscataway, NJ 08854-8097. Offers MA, PhD. Terminal master's awarded for partial completion of doctoral program. *Degree requirements:* For master's, thesis or alternative; for doctorate, comprehensive exam, thesis/dissertation. *Entrance requirements:* For master's and doctorate, GRE General Test, writing sample. Additional exam requirements/recommendations for international students: Required—TOEFL. Electronic applications accepted. *Expenses:* Tuition, state resident: full-time $7200; part-time $600 per credit. Tuition, nonresident: full-time $11,124; part-time $927 per credit. *Faculty research:* Human evolution, lithic technology, behavioral ecology, ethnicity, gender.

San Diego State University, Graduate and Research Affairs, College of Arts and Letters, Department of Anthropology, San Diego, CA 92182. Offers MA. *Degree requirements:* For master's, one foreign language, thesis. *Entrance requirements:* For master's, GRE General Test, 3 letters of recommendation, typed writing sample. Additional exam requirements/recommendations for international students: Required—TOEFL. Electronic applications accepted. *Faculty research:* Meso-American archaeology, cognitive anthropology, ethnomusicology, primate conservation, biomedical anthropology.

San Francisco State University, Division of Graduate Studies, College of Behavioral and Social Sciences, Department of Anthropology, San Francisco, CA 94132-1722. Offers archaeology (MA); biological/physical anthropology (MA); social/cultural anthropology (MA); visual anthropology (MA). *Faculty research:* Immigration, ethnicity, urban anthropology, Californian and Latin American archaeology. *Unit head:* Dr. Douglass Bailey, Chair, 415-338-1427. *Application contact:* Dr. Mariana Ferreira, Graduate Coordinator, 415-405-2467, E-mail: mariana@sfsu.edu.

San Jose State University, Graduate Studies and Research, College of Social Sciences, Department of Anthropology, San Jose, CA 95192-0001. Offers applied anthropology (MA). *Entrance requirements:* For master's, curriculum vitae or resume, official transcripts, 2 letters of reference.

Simon Fraser University, Graduate Studies, Faculty of Arts and Social Sciences, Department of Sociology and Anthropology, Burnaby, BC V5A 1S6, Canada. Offers anthropology (MA, PhD); sociology (MA, PhD). *Degree requirements:* For master's, thesis (for some programs); for doctorate, thesis/dissertation. *Entrance requirements:* For master's and doctorate, minimum GPA of 3.25. Additional exam requirements/recommendations for international students: Required—TOEFL or IELTS. *Faculty research:* Sociology theory, social and cultural anthropology, political sociology, religion and society, Canadian native peoples.

Sonoma State University, School of Social Sciences, Program in Cultural Resources Management, Rohnert Park, CA 94928. Offers MA. Part-time programs available. *Faculty:* 6 full-time (5 women). *Students:* 1 full-time (0 women), 21 part-time (14 women); includes 4 minority (2 Hispanic/Latino; 1 Native Hawaiian or other Pacific Islander, non-Hispanic/Latino; 1 Two or more races, non-Hispanic/Latino). Average age 31. 13 applicants, 54% accepted, 3 enrolled. In 2010, 8 master's awarded. *Degree requirements:* For master's, thesis. *Entrance requirements:* For master's, minimum GPA of 3.0. Additional exam requirements/recommendations for international students: Required—TOEFL (minimum score 500 paper-based; 173 computer-based). *Application deadline:* For fall admission, 1/31 for domestic students. Application fee: $55. *Financial support:* Career-related internships or fieldwork, scholarships/grants, traineeships, and unspecified assistantships available. Financial award application deadline: 3/2; financial award applicants required to submit FAFSA. *Unit head:* Dr. Karin Jaffe, Chair, Anthropology Department, 707-664-2944, Fax: 707-664-2505, E-mail: jkarin.jaffe@sonoma.edu. *Application contact:* Margaret Purser, Coordinator, 707-664-3164, Fax: 707-664-2505, E-mail: purser@sonoma.edu.

Southern Illinois University Carbondale, Graduate School, College of Liberal Arts, Department of Anthropology, Carbondale, IL 62901-4701. Offers MA, PhD. *Degree requirements:* For master's, one foreign language, thesis; for doctorate, one foreign language, thesis/dissertation. *Entrance requirements:* For master's, GRE General Test, minimum GPA of 2.7; for doctorate, GRE General Test, minimum GPA of 3.25. Additional exam requirements/recommendations for international students: Required—TOEFL. *Faculty research:* Archaeology, human variability, evolution, cultural ecology, social anthropology.

Southern Methodist University, Dedman College, Department of Anthropology, Dallas, TX 75205. Offers anthropology (PhD); medical anthropology (MA). *Faculty:* 15 full-time (8 women), 6 part-time/adjunct (3 women). *Students:* 15 full-time (14 women), 33 part-time (15 women); includes 1 Asian, non-Hispanic/Latino; 3 Hispanic/Latino, 3 international. Average age 32. 21 applicants, 29% accepted, 6 enrolled. In 2010, 7 master's, 2 doctorates awarded. Terminal master's awarded for partial completion of doctoral program. *Degree requirements:* For master's, one foreign language, comprehensive exam, thesis or alternative; for doctorate, one foreign language, comprehensive exam, thesis/dissertation, qualifying exam, defense of dissertation. *Entrance requirements:* For master's and doctorate, GRE General Test, minimum GPA of 3.0. Additional exam requirements/recommendations for international students: Required—TOEFL (minimum score 550 paper-based). *Application deadline:* For fall admission, 2/1 priority date for domestic students; for spring admission, 11/30 priority date for domestic students. Applications are processed on a rolling basis. Application fee: $60. *Financial support:* In 2010–11, 1 fellowship with full and partial tuition reimbursement (averaging $16,000 per year), 3 research assistantships with full tuition reimbursements (averaging $16,000 per year), 4 teaching assistantships with full tuition reimbursements (averaging $16,000 per year) were awarded; Federal Work-Study, institutionally sponsored loans, scholarships/grants, traineeships, tuition waivers (full), and unspecified assistantships also available. Financial award application deadline: 3/1; financial award applicants required to submit FAFSA. *Faculty research:* Health and gender, Paleo-Indians, Mesoamerica, American southwest, migration and ethnicity. Total annual research expenditures: $300,000. *Unit head:* Pamela Carter Hogan, Administrative Assistant to the Chair, 214-768-4152, Fax: 214-768-2906, E-mail: phogan@smu.edu. *Application contact:* Dr. Caroline Brettell, Director of Graduate Studies, 214-768-4254, Fax: 214-768-2906, E-mail: trick@smu.edu.

Stanford University, School of Humanities and Sciences, Department of Anthropological Sciences, Stanford, CA 94305-9991. Offers MA, MS, PhD. Terminal master's awarded for partial completion of doctoral program. *Degree requirements:* For master's, thesis; for doctorate, one foreign language, thesis/dissertation. *Entrance requirements:* For master's and doctorate, GRE General Test. Additional exam requirements/recommendations for international students: Required—TOEFL. Electronic applications accepted. *Expenses:* Tuition: Full-time $38,700; part-time $860 per unit. One-time fee: $200 full-time.

State University of New York at Binghamton, Graduate School, School of Arts and Sciences, Department of Anthropology, Binghamton, NY 13902-6000. Offers MA, PhD. Part-time programs available. *Faculty:* 18 full-time (9 women), 5 part-time/adjunct (1 woman). *Students:* 54 full-time (38 women), 74 part-time (52 women); includes 3 Black or African American, non-Hispanic/Latino; 2 American Indian or Alaska Native, non-Hispanic/Latino; 2 Asian, non-Hispanic/Latino; 5 Hispanic/Latino, 20 international. Average age 32. 83 applicants, 46% accepted, 18 enrolled. In 2010, 24 master's, 9 doctorates awarded. Terminal master's awarded for partial completion of doctoral program. *Degree requirements:* For master's, one foreign language, thesis or alternative, written exam; for doctorate, variable foreign language requirement, thesis/dissertation, oral exam. *Entrance requirements:* For master's and doctorate, GRE General Test, GRE Subject Test. Additional exam requirements/recommendations for international students: Required—TOEFL (minimum score 550 paper-based; 213 computer-based; 80 iBT). *Application deadline:* For fall admission, 4/15 priority date for domestic and international students. Applications are processed on a rolling basis. Application fee: $60. Electronic applications accepted. *Financial support:* In 2010–11, 34 students received support, including 4 fellowships with full tuition reimbursements available (averaging $1,500 per year), 1 research assistantship with full tuition reimbursement available (averaging $15,000 per year), 23 teaching assistantships with full tuition reimbursements available (averaging $15,000 per year); career-related internships or fieldwork, Federal Work-Study, institutionally sponsored loans, scholarships/grants, health care benefits, tuition waivers (full and partial), and unspecified assistantships also available. Financial award application deadline: 2/15; financial award applicants required to submit FAFSA. *Unit head:* Dr. Randall H. McGuire, Chairperson, 607-777-2906, E-mail: rmcguire@binghamton.edu. *Application contact:* Catherine Smtih, Recruiting and Admissions Coordinator, 607-777-2151, Fax: 607-777-2501, E-mail: cmsmith@binghamton.edu.

Stony Brook University, State University of New York, Graduate School, College of Arts and Sciences, Department of Anthropology, Stony Brook, NY 11794. Offers MA, PhD. *Faculty:* 14 full-time (7 women), 1 (woman) part-time/adjunct. *Students:* 42 full-time (32 women), 5 part-time (2 women); includes 1 Black or African American, non-Hispanic/Latino; 2 Asian, non-Hispanic/Latino; 1 Hispanic/Latino, 9 international. Average age 30. 81 applicants, 12% accepted, 7 enrolled. In 2010, 8 master's, 4 doctorates awarded. *Degree requirements:* For master's, thesis, fieldwork; for doctorate, one foreign language, thesis/dissertation, fieldwork. *Entrance requirements:* For master's and doctorate, GRE General Test. Additional exam requirements/recommendations for international students: Required—TOEFL. *Application deadline:* For fall admission, 1/15 for domestic students. Application fee: $100. *Expenses:* Tuition, state resident: full-time $8370; part-time $349 per credit. Tuition, nonresident: full-time $13,780; part-time $574 per credit. Required fees: $994. *Financial support:* In 2010–11, 2 research assistantships, 24 teaching assistantships were awarded; fellowships, career-related internships or fieldwork also available. *Faculty research:* Social and cultural anthropology, cultural history and archaeology, physical anthropology. Total annual research expenditures: $1.1 million. *Unit head:* Prof. Diane M. Doran-Sheehy, Chair, 631-632-9445, E-mail: diane.doran@stonybrook.edu. *Application contact:* Dr. Elizabeth Stone, Director, 631-632-7627, Fax: 631-632-9165, E-mail: elizabeth.stone@stonybrook.edu.

Syracuse University, Maxwell School of Citizenship and Public Affairs, Program in Anthropology, Syracuse, NY 13244. Offers MA, PhD. *Students:* 47 full-time (29 women), 17 part-time (12 women); includes 5 minority (1 Black or African American, non-Hispanic/Latino; 2 Asian, non-Hispanic/Latino; 2 Hispanic/Latino), 13 international. Average age 32. 58 applicants, 21% accepted, 5 enrolled. In 2010, 5 master's, 5 doctorates awarded. *Degree requirements:* For master's, thesis or alternative; for doctorate, one foreign language, thesis/dissertation. *Entrance requirements:* For master's and doctorate, GRE General Test. Additional exam requirements/recommendations for international students: Required—TOEFL (minimum score 100 iBT). *Application deadline:* For fall admission, 12/15 priority date for domestic and international students. Application fee: $75. Electronic applications accepted. *Expenses:* Tuition: Part-time $1162 per credit. *Financial support:* Fellowships with full tuition reimbursements, research assistantships with full and partial tuition reimbursements, teaching assistantships with full and partial tuition reimbursements available. Financial award application deadline: 1/1. *Unit head:* Dr. Christopher DeCorse, Chair, 315-443-4647, Fax: 315-443-4860. *Application contact:* Denise Mallory-Green, Recruiting Contact, 315-443-2200, E-mail: dmbreen@syr.edu.

Teachers College, Columbia University, Graduate Faculty of Education, Department of International and Transcultural Studies, Program in Anthropology and Education, New York, NY 10027-6696. Offers Ed M, MA, Ed D, PhD. *Faculty:* 6 full-time (1 woman), 2 part-time/adjunct (0 women). *Students:* 31 full-time (24 women), 47 part-time (34 women); includes 31 minority (4 Black or African American, non-Hispanic/Latino; 1 American Indian or Alaska Native, non-Hispanic/Latino; 14 Asian, non-Hispanic/Latino; 4 Hispanic/Latino; 8 Two or more races, non-Hispanic/Latino), 14 international. Average age 33. 5 applicants, 80% accepted, 3 enrolled. In 2010, 10 master's, 2 doctorates awarded. *Degree requirements:* For master's, integrative project; for doctorate, variable foreign language requirement, thesis/dissertation. *Entrance requirements:* For master's and doctorate, GRE General Test. Additional exam requirements/recommendations for international students: Required—TOEFL. *Application deadline:* For fall admission, 12/15 for domestic students. Applications are processed on a rolling basis. Application fee: $65. Electronic applications accepted. *Expenses:* Tuition: Full-time $28,272; part-time $1178 per credit. Required fees: $756; $378 per semester. *Financial support:* Career-related internships or fieldwork, Federal Work-Study, institutionally sponsored loans, and tuition waivers (full and partial) available. Support available to part-time students. Financial award application deadline: 2/1; financial award applicants required to submit FAFSA. *Faculty research:* African studies, sociocultural change, education in the developing world, human development in social and cultural contexts, culture and communication theory. *Unit head:* Prof. Lambros Comitas, Program Coordinator, 212-678-4040, E-mail: comitas@tc.edu. *Application contact:* Deanna Ghozati, Assistant Associate Director of Admission, 212-678-3710, Fax: 212-678-4171, E-mail: tcinfo@tc.edu.

Temple University, College of Liberal Arts, Department of Anthropology, Philadelphia, PA 19122-6096. Offers PhD. Part-time and evening/weekend programs available. *Faculty:* 16 full-time (7 women). *Students:* 58 full-time (40 women), 6 part-time (4 women); includes 6 Black or African American, non-Hispanic/Latino; 1 Asian, non-Hispanic/Latino; 7 Hispanic/Latino, 3 international. 71 applicants, 31% accepted, 11 enrolled. In 2010, 4 doctorates awarded. Terminal master's awarded for partial completion of doctoral program. *Degree requirements:* For doctorate, 2 foreign languages, thesis/dissertation. *Entrance requirements:* For doctorate, GRE General Test, minimum GPA of 3.0. Additional exam requirements/recommendations for international students: Required—TOEFL (minimum score 550 paper-based; 213 computer-based; 79 iBT). *Application deadline:* For fall admission, 1/15 for domestic students, 12/15 for international students. Application fee: $50. Electronic applications accepted. *Financial support:* Fellowships, research assistantships, teaching assistantships, career-related internships or fieldwork, Federal Work-Study, and institutionally sponsored loans available. Financial award application deadline: 1/15; financial award applicants required to submit FAFSA. *Faculty research:* Political economy, biocultural adaptation, visual anthropology, critical urban anthropology, archaeology. *Unit head:* Dr. Mindie Lazarus-Black, Chair, 215-204-7577, Fax: 215-204-1410, E-mail: mindielb@temple.edu. *Application contact:* Dr. Mindie Lazarus-Black, Chair, 215-204-7577, Fax: 215-204-1410, E-mail: mindielb@temple.edu.

Texas A&M University, College of Liberal Arts, Department of Anthropology, College Station, TX 77843. Offers MA, PhD. *Faculty:* 23. *Students:* 77 full-time (41 women), 50 part-time (27 women); includes 2 Black or African American, non-Hispanic/Latino; 2 Asian, non-Hispanic/Latino; 5 Hispanic/Latino, 15 international. Average age 33. In 2010, 6 master's awarded. *Degree requirements:* For doctorate, thesis/dissertation. *Entrance requirements:* For master's and doctorate, GRE General Test. Additional exam requirements/recommendations for international students: Required—TOEFL. Application fee: $50 ($75 for international students). *Financial support:* Fellowships, research assistantships, teaching assistantships, career-related internships or fieldwork, Federal Work-Study, and institutionally sponsored loans available. Financial award application deadline: 4/1; financial award applicants required to submit FAFSA. *Faculty research:* Nautical archaeology, archaeological conservation, archaeological palynology, paleoethnobotany, folklore. *Unit head:* Cynthia Werner, Interim Head, 979-845-6355, E-mail: werner@tamu.edu. *Application contact:* Cynthia Werner, Interim Head, 979-845-6355, E-mail: werner@tamu.edu.

Texas State University–San Marcos, Graduate School, College of Liberal Arts, Department of Anthropology, San Marcos, TX 78666. Offers MA. *Faculty:* 14 full-time (6 women). *Students:* 37 full-time (22 women), 7 part-time (3 women); includes 13 minority (1 Black or African American, non-Hispanic/Latino; 1 American Indian or Alaska Native, non-Hispanic/Latino; 10 Hispanic/Latino; 1 Two or more races, non-Hispanic/Latino). Average age 29. 70 applicants, 46% accepted, 21 enrolled. In 2010, 20 master's awarded. *Degree requirements:* For master's, comprehensive exam, thesis. *Entrance requirements:* For master's, GRE (minimum score 1000 verbal and quantitative preferred), minimum GPA of 3.0 in last 60 undergraduate hours. Additional exam requirements/recommendations for international students: Required—TOEFL (minimum score 550 paper-based; 213 computer-based; 78 iBT). *Application deadline:* For fall admission, 3/15 for domestic and international students. Applications are processed on a rolling basis. Application fee: $40 ($90 for international students). Electronic applications accepted. *Expenses:* Tuition, state resident: full-time $6024; part-time $251 per credit hour.

Anthropology

Texas State University–San Marcos (continued)
Tuition, nonresident: full-time $13,536; part-time $564 per credit hour. Required fees: $1776; $50 per credit hour. $306 per semester. *Financial support:* In 2010–11, 31 students received support, including 3 research assistantships (averaging $4,754 per year), 24 teaching assistantships (averaging $1,752 per year); Federal Work-Study, institutionally sponsored loans, scholarships/grants, and unspecified assistantships also available. Support available to part-time students. Financial award application deadline: 4/1; financial award applicants required to submit FAFSA. *Faculty research:* Reu Site Guatemala, Zatopeck Site, Excavation S. Africa, Wilson Pottery Site, El Camino Real Survey, Highland Mesoamerica, herd ranch testing. Total annual research expenditures: $443,376. *Unit head:* Dr. Jon McGee, Chair, 512-245-8272, E-mail: rm08@txstate.edu. *Application contact:* Dr. J. Michael Willoughby, Dean of Graduate School, 512-245-2581, Fax: 512-245-8365, E-mail: gradcollege@txstate.edu.

Texas Tech University, Graduate School, College of Arts and Sciences, Department of Sociology, Anthropology and Social Work, Lubbock, TX 79409. Offers anthropology (MA); sociology (MA). Part-time programs available. *Faculty:* 17 full-time (7 women). *Students:* 30 full-time (18 women), 11 part-time (7 women); includes 2 Black or African American, non-Hispanic/Latino; 1 Asian, non-Hispanic/Latino; 2 Hispanic/Latino; 2 Two or more races, non-Hispanic/Latino, 2 international. Average age 28. 34 applicants, 74% accepted, 14 enrolled. In 2010, 7 master's awarded. *Degree requirements:* For master's, one foreign language, thesis or alternative. *Entrance requirements:* For master's, GRE General Test. Additional exam requirements/recommendations for international students: Required—TOEFL (minimum score 550 paper-based; 213 computer-based; 79 iBT). *Application deadline:* For fall admission, 6/1 priority date for domestic students, 1/15 priority date for international students; for spring admission, 9/1 priority date for domestic students, 6/15 priority date for international students. Applications are processed on a rolling basis. Application fee: $50 ($75 for international students). Electronic applications accepted. *Expenses:* Tuition, state resident: full-time $5495.76; part-time $228.99 per credit hour. Tuition, nonresident: full-time $12,936; part-time $538.99 per credit hour. Required fees: $2674; $36 per credit hour. $905 per semester. *Financial support:* In 2010–11, 24 students received support, including 1 research assistantship with partial tuition reimbursement available (averaging $3,464 per year), 6 teaching assistantships with partial tuition reimbursements available (averaging $3,809 per year). Financial award application deadline: 4/15; financial award applicants required to submit FAFSA. *Faculty research:* Sociology theory, research methods, physical and forensic anthropology, Texas archaeology, Mayan archaeology. Total annual research expenditures: $28,649. *Unit head:* Dr. Jeffrey Payne Williams, Chair and Professor, 806-742-2400, Fax: 806-742-1088, E-mail: jeff.williams@ttu.edu. *Application contact:* Dr. Yung-Mei Tsai, Sociology Program Director, 806-742-2400, Fax: 806-742-1088, E-mail: yung.mei.tsai@ttu.edu.

Trent University, Graduate Studies, Program in Anthropology, Peterborough, ON K9J 7B8, Canada. Offers MA. Part-time programs available. *Degree requirements:* For master's, thesis. *Entrance requirements:* For master's, honors degree. *Faculty research:* Paleoecology, trade and fortification networks, pre-Columbian art.

Tulane University, School of Liberal Arts, Department of Anthropology, New Orleans, LA 70118-5669. Offers MA, PhD. Terminal master's awarded for partial completion of doctoral program. *Degree requirements:* For master's, one foreign language, thesis; for doctorate, 2 foreign languages, thesis/dissertation. *Entrance requirements:* For master's, GRE General Test, minimum B average in undergraduate course work; for doctorate, GRE General Test. Additional exam requirements/recommendations for international students: Required—TOEFL. Electronic applications accepted. *Faculty research:* Linguistics, physical anthropology, sociocultural archaeology, Mesoamerica.

Universidad de las Américas–Puebla, Division of Graduate Studies, School of Social Sciences, Program in Anthropology, Puebla, Mexico. Offers anthropology (MA); archaeology (MA). Part-time and evening/weekend programs available. *Degree requirements:* For master's, one foreign language, thesis. *Entrance requirements:* For master's, bachelor's degree in anthropology or equivalent. *Faculty research:* Archaeology, ethnography, and ethnohistory of Mesoamerica.

Université de Montréal, Faculty of Arts and Sciences, Department of Anthropology, Montréal, QC H3C 3J7, Canada. Offers M Sc, PhD. Part-time programs available. *Degree requirements:* For master's, thesis; for doctorate, thesis/dissertation, general exam. Electronic applications accepted. *Faculty research:* Archaeology, ethnolinguistics, ethnology.

Université Laval, Faculty of Social Sciences, Department of Anthropology, Programs in Anthropology, Québec, QC G1K 7P4, Canada. Offers MA, PhD. Terminal master's awarded for partial completion of doctoral program. *Degree requirements:* For master's, thesis; for doctorate, thesis/dissertation. *Entrance requirements:* For master's, knowledge of French, interview; for doctorate, knowledge of French, comprehensive of written English, knowledge of a third language. Electronic applications accepted.

University at Albany, State University of New York, College of Arts and Sciences, Department of Anthropology, Albany, NY 12222-0001. Offers MA, PhD. Terminal master's awarded for partial completion of doctoral program. *Degree requirements:* For master's, comprehensive exam, thesis; for doctorate, 2 foreign languages, thesis/dissertation, field exams. *Entrance requirements:* For master's and doctorate, GRE. Additional exam requirements/recommendations for international students: Required—TOEFL (minimum score 550 paper-based; 213 computer-based). Electronic applications accepted. *Faculty research:* Economic and ecological anthropology; language, culture, and cognition; symbolic and interpretive anthropology; human evolution, morphology, demography, and medical anthropology; spatial and settlement archaeology.

University at Buffalo, the State University of New York, Graduate School, College of Arts and Sciences, Department of Anthropology, Buffalo, NY 14260. Offers MA, PhD. *Faculty:* 17 full-time (8 women), 5 part-time/adjunct (0 women). *Students:* 96 full-time (61 women), 14 part-time (8 women); includes 2 Black or African American, non-Hispanic/Latino; 1 American Indian or Alaska Native, non-Hispanic/Latino; 2 Asian, non-Hispanic/Latino; 5 Hispanic/Latino, 7 international. Average age 32. 79 applicants, 46% accepted, 28 enrolled. In 2010, 14 master's, 5 doctorates awarded. Terminal master's awarded for partial completion of doctoral program. *Degree requirements:* For master's, project; for doctorate, one foreign language, thesis/dissertation, exam. *Entrance requirements:* For master's, GRE General Test, minimum GPA of 3.0; for doctorate, GRE General Test, minimum GPA of 3.2. Additional exam requirements/recommendations for international students: Required—TOEFL (minimum score 600 paper-based; 250 computer-based; 79 iBT). *Application deadline:* For fall admission, 1/16 priority date for domestic students, 1/15 priority date for international students; for winter admission, 5/1 for domestic students, 3/15 for international students. Applications are processed on a rolling basis. Application fee: $75. Electronic applications accepted. *Financial support:* In 2010–11, 7 fellowships with full tuition reimbursements (averaging $19,616 per year), 14 teaching assistantships with full tuition reimbursements (averaging $13,616 per year) were awarded; career-related internships or fieldwork, Federal Work-Study, and institutionally sponsored loans also available. Financial award application deadline: 1/15; financial award applicants required to submit FAFSA. *Faculty research:* Old and New World archaeology, medical anthropology, primatology/human biology, cognition. Total annual research expenditures: $800,000. *Unit head:* Dr. Peter Biehl, Chair, 716-645-0407, Fax: 716-645-3808. *Application contact:* Margaret M. Kasprzyk, Graduate Coordinator, 716-645-2414 Ext. 104, Fax: 716-645-3808, E-mail: mmk22@buffalo.edu.

The University of Alabama, Graduate School, College of Arts and Sciences, Department of Anthropology, Tuscaloosa, AL 35487. Offers MA, PhD. *Faculty:* 11 full-time (3 women), 2 part-time/adjunct (0 women). *Students:* 30 full-time (19 women), 13 part-time (9 women); includes 5 minority (1 Asian, non-Hispanic/Latino; 4 Hispanic/Latino), 1 international. Average age 29. 42 applicants, 52% accepted, 12 enrolled. In 2010, 6 master's awarded. *Degree requirements:* For master's, one foreign language, comprehensive exam, thesis optional; for doctorate, one foreign language, comprehensive exam, thesis/dissertation. *Entrance requirements:* For master's, GRE; for doctorate, GRE, MA in anthropology. *Application deadline:* For fall admission, 1/31 for domestic and international students. Application fee: $50 ($60 for international students). *Expenses:* Tuition, state resident: full-time $7900. Tuition, nonresident: full-time $20,500. *Financial support:* In 2010–11, 25 students received support, including 4 fellowships with full tuition reimbursements available (averaging $15,000 per year), 1 research assistantship with full tuition reimbursement available (averaging $12,258 per year), 20 teaching assistantships with full tuition reimbursements available (averaging $12,258 per year); Federal Work-Study and health care benefits also available. Financial award application deadline: 1/31. *Faculty research:* Medical anthropology, Southeastern archaeology, physical and cultural anthropology. Total annual research expenditures: $236,044. *Unit head:* Dr. Michael D. Murphy, Chairman/Professor, 205-348-1953, Fax: 205-348-7937, E-mail: mdmurphy@ua.edu. *Application contact:* Dr. Ian Brown, Professor and Director of Graduate Studies, 205-348-9758, Fax: 205-348-7937, E-mail: ibrown@bama.ua.edu.

The University of Alabama at Birmingham, College of Arts and Sciences, Program in Anthropology, Birmingham, AL 35294. Offers MA. Program offered jointly with The University of Alabama (Tuscaloosa). *Students:* 1 (woman) full-time, 1 part-time (0 women). Average age 26. 3 applicants, 100% accepted, 0 enrolled. *Degree requirements:* For master's, one foreign language. *Entrance requirements:* For master's, GRE General Test. *Application deadline:* Applications are processed on a rolling basis. Electronic applications accepted. *Expenses:* Tuition, state resident: full-time $5482. Tuition, nonresident: full-time $12,430. Tuition and fees vary according to program. *Financial support:* Career-related internships or fieldwork, Federal Work-Study, and institutionally sponsored loans available. *Faculty research:* Ethnicity, medical anthropology, primate conservation, pastoral systems, Southeastern archaeology. *Unit head:* Dr. Carolyn Conley, Chair, 205-934-8691, Fax: 205-975-8360. *Application contact:* Julie Bryant, Director of Graduate Admissions, 205-934-8227, Fax: 205-934-8413, E-mail: jbryant@uab.edu.

University of Alaska Anchorage, College of Arts and Sciences, Department of Anthropology, Anchorage, AK 99508. Offers MA. *Degree requirements:* For master's, comprehensive exam, thesis (for some programs), practicum. *Entrance requirements:* For master's, GRE General Test. Additional exam requirements/recommendations for international students: Required—TOEFL (minimum score 550 paper-based; 213 computer-based).

University of Alaska Fairbanks, College of Liberal Arts, Department of Anthropology, Fairbanks, AK 99775-7720. Offers MA, PhD. Part-time programs available. *Faculty:* 10 full-time (2 women). *Students:* 29 full-time (20 women), 18 part-time (14 women); includes 4 minority (1 American Indian or Alaska Native, non-Hispanic/Latino; 1 Hispanic/Latino; 2 Two or more races, non-Hispanic/Latino), 5 international. Average age 34. 19 applicants, 63% accepted, 10 enrolled. In 2010, 4 master's, 3 doctorates awarded. Terminal master's awarded for partial completion of doctoral program. *Degree requirements:* For master's, one foreign language, comprehensive exam, thesis, oral defense; for doctorate, 2 foreign languages, comprehensive exam, thesis/dissertation, oral defense. *Entrance requirements:* For master's and doctorate, GRE General Test. Additional exam requirements/recommendations for international students: Required—TOEFL (minimum score 550 paper-based; 213 computer-based; 80 iBT). *Application deadline:* For fall admission, 6/1 for domestic students, 3/1 for international students; for spring admission, 10/15 for domestic students, 9/1 for international students. Applications are processed on a rolling basis. Application fee: $60. Electronic applications accepted. *Expenses:* Tuition, state resident: full-time $5688; part-time $316 per credit. Tuition, nonresident: full-time $11,628; part-time $646 per credit. Required fees: $289 per semester. Tuition and fees vary according to course load and reciprocity agreements. *Financial support:* In 2010–11, 6 research assistantships with tuition reimbursements (averaging $8,858 per year), 14 teaching assistantships with tuition reimbursements (averaging $8,399 per year) were awarded; fellowships with tuition reimbursements, Federal Work-Study, scholarships/grants, health care benefits, and unspecified assistantships also available. Support available to part-time students. Financial award application deadline: 7/1; financial award applicants required to submit FAFSA. *Faculty research:* Circumpolar archaeology and population biology; rural subsistence; arctic physical, biological and social anthropology; arctic ethnohistory; arctic linguistics. Total annual research expenditures: $417,196. *Unit head:* Joel Irish, Department Chair, 907-474-7288, Fax: 907-474-7453, E-mail: fyanth@uaf.edu. *Application contact:* Joel Irish, Department Chair, 907-474-7288, Fax: 907-474-7453, E-mail: fyanth@uaf.edu.

University of Alberta, Faculty of Graduate Studies and Research, Department of Anthropology, Edmonton, AB T6G 2E1, Canada. Offers MA, PhD. *Degree requirements:* For master's, thesis; for doctorate, one foreign language, thesis/dissertation. *Entrance requirements:* For master's and doctorate, minimum GPA of 7.0 on a 9.0 scale in last 2 years. Additional exam requirements/recommendations for international students: Required—TOEFL. *Faculty research:* Cultural anthropology of North America, South East Asia; physical anthropology in osteology, forensic primatology; archaeology of North America, South America, Old World/Africa.

The University of Arizona, College of Social and Behavioral Sciences, Department of Anthropology, Tucson, AZ 85721. Offers MA, PhD. Part-time programs available. *Faculty:* 19 full-time (9 women), 11 part-time/adjunct (6 women). *Students:* 105 full-time (67 women), 36 part-time (20 women); includes 2 American Indian or Alaska Native, non-Hispanic/Latino; 2 Asian, non-Hispanic/Latino; 5 Hispanic/Latino; 10 Two or more races, non-Hispanic/Latino, 29 international. Average age 34. 179 applicants, 18% accepted, 14 enrolled. In 2010, 16 master's, 13 doctorates awarded. Terminal master's awarded for partial completion of doctoral program. *Degree requirements:* For master's, thesis or alternative; for doctorate, one foreign language, thesis/dissertation. *Entrance requirements:* For master's and doctorate, GRE General Test, minimum GPA of 3.5, 2 letters of recommendation. Additional exam requirements/recommendations for international students: Required—TOEFL (minimum score 550 paper-based; 213 computer-based; 79 iBT). *Application deadline:* For fall admission, 3/1 for domestic and international students. Applications are processed on a rolling basis. Application fee: $65. Electronic applications accepted. *Expenses:* Tuition, state resident: full-time $7692. *Financial support:* In 2010–11, 22 research assistantships (averaging $19,492 per year), 41 teaching assistantships with full tuition reimbursements (averaging $20,044 per year) were awarded; career-related internships or fieldwork, Federal Work-Study, institutionally sponsored loans, scholarships/grants, health care benefits, tuition waivers (full and partial), and unspecified assistantships also available. *Faculty research:* Archaeology of pre-Han China, cultural ecology, health and illness-related behavior, interaction of linguistic and social processes, human growth and development under stress. Total annual research expenditures: $1.8 million. *Unit head:* Dr. Barbara J. Mills, Department Head, 520-621-6298, Fax: 520-621-2088, E-mail: bmills@u.arizona.edu. *Application contact:* Ann Samuelson, 520-626-6027, Fax: 520-621-2088, E-mail: anns@email.arizona.edu.

University of Arkansas, Graduate School, J. William Fulbright College of Arts and Sciences, Department of Anthropology, Fayetteville, AR 72701-1201. Offers MA, PhD. Part-time and evening/weekend programs available. *Students:* 21 full-time (13 women), 33 part-time (17 women); includes 4 minority (all American Indian or Alaska Native, non-Hispanic/Latino), 3 international. 25 applicants, 84% accepted. In 2010, 10 master's, 5 doctorates awarded. *Degree requirements:* For master's, comprehensive exam. *Entrance requirements:* For master's, GRE General Test, minimum GPA of 3.0; for doctorate, GRE General Test. *Application deadline:* For fall admission, 4/1 for international students; for spring admission, 10/1 for international students. Applications are processed on a rolling basis. Application fee: $40 ($50 for international students). Electronic applications accepted. *Financial support:* In 2010–11, 7 fellowships with tuition reimbursements, 5 research assistantships, 21 teaching assistantships were awarded; career-related internships or fieldwork and Federal Work-Study also available. Support available to part-time students. Financial award application deadline: 4/1; financial award applicants required to submit FAFSA. *Unit head:* Dr. Peter Ungar, Department Chairperson, 479-575-2508, Fax: 479-575-6595, E-mail: pungar@uark.edu. *Application contact:* Dr. Mary

Jo Schneider, Graduate Coordinator, 479-575-2508, Fax: 479-575-6595, E-mail: maryjo@uark.edu.

The University of British Columbia, Faculty of Arts, Department of Anthropology, Vancouver, BC V6T 1Z1, Canada. Offers MA, PhD. *Degree requirements:* For master's, thesis; for doctorate, comprehensive exam, thesis/dissertation. *Entrance requirements:* For master's, BA in anthropology or equivalent with minimum B+ average in upper level courses; for doctorate, MA in anthropology or equivalent. Additional exam requirements/recommendations for international students: Required—TOEFL (minimum score 600 paper-based; 250 computer-based; 80 iBT). Electronic applications accepted. Tuition charges are reported in Canadian dollars. *Expenses:* Tuition, area resident: Full-time $4179 Canadian dollars. International tuition: $7344 Canadian dollars full-time. *Faculty research:* Cultures of North America, East Asia, Oceania; museum studies; archaeology.

University of Calgary, Faculty of Graduate Studies, Faculty of Social Sciences, Department of Anthropology, Calgary, AB T2N 1N4, Canada. Offers MA, PhD. *Degree requirements:* For master's, thesis; for doctorate, one foreign language, comprehensive exam, thesis/dissertation, candidacy exam. *Entrance requirements:* Additional exam requirements/recommendations for international students: Required—TOEFL. *Faculty research:* Primatology, culture and society, biosocial anthropology, political anthropology, evolutionary theory.

University of California, Berkeley, Graduate Division, College of Letters and Science, Department of Anthropology, Program in Anthropology, Berkeley, CA 94720-1500. Offers PhD. *Degree requirements:* For doctorate, thesis/dissertation. *Entrance requirements:* For doctorate, GRE General Test, minimum GPA of 3.0, 3 letters of recommendation. Additional exam requirements/recommendations for international students: Required—TOEFL.

University of California, Berkeley, Graduate Division, College of Letters and Science, Department of Anthropology, Program in Medical Anthropology, Berkeley, CA 94720-1500. Offers PhD. Program held jointly with University of California, San Francisco. *Degree requirements:* For doctorate, thesis/dissertation. *Entrance requirements:* For doctorate, GRE General Test, minimum GPA of 3.0, 3 letters of recommendation. Additional exam requirements/recommendations for international students: Required—TOEFL.

University of California, Davis, Graduate Studies, Program in Anthropology, Davis, CA 95616. Offers MA, PhD. Terminal master's awarded for partial completion of doctoral program. *Degree requirements:* For master's, one foreign language; for doctorate, one foreign language, thesis/dissertation. *Entrance requirements:* For master's and doctorate, GRE General Test, minimum GPA of 3.0. Additional exam requirements/recommendations for international students: Required—TOEFL (minimum score 550 paper-based; 213 computer-based). Electronic applications accepted. *Faculty research:* Archaeology, linguistics, biological and sociocultural anthropology.

University of California, Irvine, School of Social Sciences, Department of Anthropology, Irvine, CA 92697. Offers MA, PhD. *Students:* 43 full-time (26 women), 1 part-time (0 women); includes 12 minority (9 Asian, non-Hispanic/Latino; 3 Hispanic/Latino), 5 international. Average age 28. 93 applicants, 22% accepted, 9 enrolled. In 2010, 4 master's, 5 doctorates awarded. *Degree requirements:* For doctorate, thesis/dissertation. *Entrance requirements:* For master's, GRE, minimum GPA of 3.0; for doctorate, GRE General Test, minimum GPA of 3.0. Additional exam requirements/recommendations for international students: Required—TOEFL (minimum score 550 paper-based; 213 computer-based). *Application deadline:* For fall admission, 1/15 priority date for domestic and international students. Applications are processed on a rolling basis. Application fee: $80 ($100 for international students). Electronic applications accepted. *Financial support:* Fellowships, research assistantships with full tuition reimbursements, teaching assistantships, institutionally sponsored loans, traineeships, health care benefits, and unspecified assistantships available. Financial award application deadline: 3/1; financial award applicants required to submit FAFSA. *Faculty research:* Cognitive anthropology, sociology of culture, social structure, family and gender. *Unit head:* Prof. Karen B. Leonard, Chair, 949-824-5136, Fax: 949-824-6046, E-mail: kbleonar@uci.edu. *Application contact:* Leo Chavez, Graduate Advisor, 949-824-4054, Fax: 949-824-0646, E-mail: lchavez@uci.edu.

University of California, Los Angeles, Graduate Division, College of Letters and Science, Department of Anthropology, Los Angeles, CA 90095. Offers MA, PhD. *Faculty:* 29 full-time (14 women). *Students:* 64 full-time (48 women); includes 13 minority (2 Black or African American, non-Hispanic/Latino; 6 Asian, non-Hispanic/Latino; 4 Hispanic/Latino; 1 Two or more races, non-Hispanic/Latino), 8 international. Average age 30. 161 applicants, 12% accepted, 7 enrolled. In 2010, 11 master's, 9 doctorates awarded. Terminal master's awarded for partial completion of doctoral program. *Degree requirements:* For master's, thesis; for doctorate, thesis/dissertation, oral and written qualifying exams. *Entrance requirements:* For master's, GRE General Test, minimum GPA of 3.0, sample of research writing, 3 letters of recommendation; for doctorate, GRE General Test, minimum undergraduate GPA of 3.0, sample of research writing, 3 letters of recommendation. *Application deadline:* For fall admission, 12/15 for domestic students. Application fee: $70 ($90 for international students). Electronic applications accepted. *Financial support:* In 2010–11, 66 fellowships with full and partial tuition reimbursements, 23 research assistantships with full and partial tuition reimbursements, 38 teaching assistantships with full and partial tuition reimbursements were awarded; Federal Work-Study, institutionally sponsored loans, scholarships/grants, health care benefits, tuition waivers (full and partial), and unspecified assistantships also available. Financial award application deadline: 3/1; financial award applicants required to submit FAFSA. *Unit head:* Dr. Carole Browner, Chair, 310-825-4119, E-mail: browner@ucla.edu. *Application contact:* Departmental Office, 310-825-2511, E-mail: awalters@anthro.ucla.edu.

University of California, Riverside, Graduate Division, Department of Anthropology, Riverside, CA 92521-0102. Offers MA, MS, PhD. Part-time programs available. Terminal master's awarded for partial completion of doctoral program. *Degree requirements:* For master's, comprehensive exams or thesis; for doctorate, one foreign language, comprehensive exam, thesis/dissertation, qualifying exams. *Entrance requirements:* For master's and doctorate, GRE General Test, sample of written work, minimum GPA of 3.2, 3 letters of recommendation. Additional exam requirements/recommendations for international students: Required—TOEFL (minimum score 550 paper-based; 213 computer-based; 80 iBT). Electronic applications accepted. *Faculty research:* Transnational processes, border communities, political and cultural ecology, Mesoamerican and Western US archaeology, applied anthropology.

University of California, San Diego, Office of Graduate Studies, Department of Anthropology, La Jolla, CA 92093. Offers PhD. *Degree requirements:* For doctorate, thesis/dissertation. *Entrance requirements:* For doctorate, GRE General Test. Electronic applications accepted.

University of California, San Diego, Office of Graduate Studies, Interdisciplinary Program in Cognitive Science, La Jolla, CA 92093. Offers cognitive science/anthropology (PhD); cognitive science/communication (PhD); cognitive science/computer science and engineering (PhD); cognitive science/linguistics (PhD); cognitive science/neuroscience (PhD); cognitive science/philosophy (PhD); cognitive science/psychology (PhD); cognitive science/sociology (PhD). Admissions offered through affiliated departments. *Degree requirements:* For doctorate, thesis/dissertation. *Entrance requirements:* For doctorate, GRE General Test, acceptance into one of the eight participating departments. *Faculty research:* Language and cognition, philosophy of mind, visual perception, biological anthropology, sociolinguistics.

University of California, San Francisco, Graduate Division, Program in Medical Anthropology, San Francisco, CA 94143. Offers PhD. Program offered jointly with University of California, Berkeley. *Degree requirements:* For doctorate, one foreign language, thesis/dissertation, 3 field statements. *Entrance requirements:* For doctorate, GRE General Test, master's degree in anthropology or a related social or health science. *Faculty research:* Ethnicity, gender, aging, international health, health policy.

University of California, Santa Barbara, Graduate Division, College of Letters and Sciences, Division of Social Sciences, Department of Anthropology, Santa Barbara, CA 93106-2014. Offers archaeology (MA); biosocial anthropology (MA, PhD); sociocultural anthropology (MA, PhD); MA/PhD. *Faculty:* 12 full-time (3 women), 2 part-time/adjunct (both women). *Students:* 51 full-time (34 women); includes 2 Asian, non-Hispanic/Latino; 7 Hispanic/Latino. Average age 31. 47 applicants, 30% accepted, 4 enrolled. In 2010, 6 master's, 9 doctorates awarded. Terminal master's awarded for partial completion of doctoral program. *Degree requirements:* For master's, comprehensive exam (for some programs), thesis (for some programs); for doctorate, comprehensive exam (for some programs), thesis/dissertation. *Entrance requirements:* For master's and doctorate, GRE General Test, statement of purpose, transcripts, writing sample, curriculum vitae. Additional exam requirements/recommendations for international students: Required—TOEFL (minimum score 550 paper-based; 80 iBT), IELTS (minimum score 7). *Application deadline:* For fall admission, 12/1 for domestic and international students. Application fee: $70 ($90 for international students). Electronic applications accepted. *Financial support:* In 2010–11, 48 students received support, including 35 fellowships with full and partial tuition reimbursements available (averaging $5,749 per year), 7 research assistantships with full and partial tuition reimbursements available (averaging $7,287 per year), 37 teaching assistantships with full tuition reimbursements available (averaging $10,042 per year); career-related internships or fieldwork, Federal Work-Study, institutionally sponsored loans, scholarships/grants, traineeships, health care benefits, tuition waivers (full and partial), and unspecified assistantships also available. Support available to part-time students. Financial award application deadline: 12/1; financial award applicants required to submit FAFSA. *Faculty research:* Archaeology, bioarchaeology, biosocial anthropology, evolutionary ecology, evolutionary psychology, sociocultural anthropology. *Unit head:* Prof. Katharina Schreiber, Department Chair, 805-893-2519, Fax: 805-893-8707, E-mail: kschreiber@anth.ucsb.edu. *Application contact:* Robin Roe, Graduate Program Assistant, 805-893-2516, Fax: 805-893-8707, E-mail: roe@anth.ucsb.edu.

University of California, Santa Cruz, Division of Graduate Studies, Division of Social Sciences, Department of Anthropology, Santa Cruz, CA 95064. Offers cultural anthropology (PhD). *Students:* 39 full-time (25 women), 7 part-time (6 women); includes 16 minority (1 American Indian or Alaska Native, non-Hispanic/Latino; 5 Asian, non-Hispanic/Latino; 8 Hispanic/Latino; 2 Two or more races, non-Hispanic/Latino), 3 international. Average age 31. 71 applicants, 18% accepted, 5 enrolled. In 2010, 9 doctorates awarded. *Degree requirements:* For doctorate, thesis/dissertation, qualifying exam. *Entrance requirements:* For doctorate, GRE General Test. Additional exam requirements/recommendations for international students: Required—TOEFL (minimum score 550 paper-based; 220 computer-based; 83 iBT); Recommended—IELTS (minimum score 8). *Application deadline:* For fall admission, 12/15 for domestic and international students. Application fee: $70 ($90 for international students). Electronic applications accepted. *Financial support:* Fellowships, research assistantships, teaching assistantships, institutionally sponsored loans and tuition waivers available. Financial award applicants required to submit FAFSA. *Faculty research:* Culture and power, women's roles, AIDS, folklore. *Unit head:* Allyson Ramage, Graduate Program Coordinator, 831-459-3588, E-mail: aramage@ucsc.edu. *Application contact:* Allyson Ramage, Graduate Program Coordinator, 831-459-3588, E-mail: aramage@ucsc.edu.

University of Central Florida, College of Sciences, Department of Anthropology, Orlando, FL 32816. Offers MA. *Faculty:* 14 full-time (6 women), 1 part-time/adjunct (0 women). *Students:* 32 full-time (21 women), 18 part-time (12 women); includes 1 Black or African American, non-Hispanic/Latino; 6 Hispanic/Latino, 1 international. Average age 31. 51 applicants, 47% accepted, 13 enrolled. In 2010, 15 master's awarded. *Expenses:* Tuition, state resident: part-time $256.56 per credit hour. Tuition, nonresident: part-time $1011.52 per credit hour. Part-time tuition and fees vary according to program. *Financial support:* In 2010–11, 28 students received support, including 3 fellowships with partial tuition reimbursements available (averaging $6,000 per year), 4 research assistantships with partial tuition reimbursements available (averaging $6,100 per year), 24 teaching assistantships with full tuition reimbursements available (averaging $5,700 per year). *Unit head:* Dr. Arlen Chase, Chair, 407-823-2227, Fax: 407-823-3498, E-mail: achase@mail.ucf.edu. *Application contact:* Dr. Arlen Chase, Chair, 407-823-2227, Fax: 407-823-3498, E-mail: achase@mail.ucf.edu.

University of Chicago, Division of Social Sciences, Department of Anthropology, Chicago, IL 60637-1513. Offers PhD. *Degree requirements:* For doctorate, 2 foreign languages, thesis/dissertation, exams. *Entrance requirements:* For doctorate, GRE General Test. Additional exam requirements/recommendations for international students: Required—TOEFL, IELTS (minimum score 7). Electronic applications accepted.

University of Chicago, Division of the Humanities, Department of Linguistics, Chicago, IL 60637-1513. Offers anthropology and linguistics (PhD); linguistics (AM, PhD). Terminal master's awarded for partial completion of doctoral program. *Degree requirements:* For master's, one foreign language, thesis; for doctorate, 2 foreign languages, thesis/dissertation. *Entrance requirements:* For master's and doctorate, GRE General Test. Additional exam requirements/recommendations for international students: Required—TOEFL.

University of Cincinnati, Graduate School, McMicken College of Arts and Sciences, Department of Anthropology, Cincinnati, OH 45221. Offers MA. Part-time programs available. *Degree requirements:* For master's, thesis or alternative. *Entrance requirements:* For master's, GRE General Test. Additional exam requirements/recommendations for international students: Required—TOEFL; Recommended—TWE. Electronic applications accepted. *Faculty research:* Medical anthropology, Mayan prehistory, southwestern U.S. prehistory, skeletal biology and paleoanthropology; immigrants; Mexico.

University of Colorado Boulder, Graduate School, College of Arts and Sciences, Department of Anthropology, Boulder, CO 80309. Offers MA, PhD. *Faculty:* 19 full-time (7 women). *Students:* 54 full-time (34 women), 18 part-time (10 women); includes 9 minority (2 American Indian or Alaska Native, non-Hispanic/Latino; 2 Asian, non-Hispanic/Latino; 5 Hispanic/Latino), 6 international. Average age 30. 106 applicants, 15 enrolled. In 2010, 14 master's, 5 doctorates awarded. *Degree requirements:* For master's, comprehensive exam, thesis or alternative; for doctorate, one foreign language, thesis/dissertation. *Entrance requirements:* For master's, GRE General Test, minimum undergraduate GPA of 3.0; for doctorate, GRE General Test, minimum undergraduate GPA of 3.0, master's degree in anthropology. *Application deadline:* For fall admission, 1/15 for domestic students, 12/1 for international students. Applications are processed on a rolling basis. Application fee: $50 ($60 for international students). Electronic applications accepted. *Financial support:* In 2010–11, 18 fellowships (averaging $4,283 per year), 18 research assistantships (averaging $4,514 per year) were awarded; tuition waivers (full) also available. Financial award application deadline: 1/15. *Faculty research:* Archaeology of ancient Mayan, plains Indians; skeletal biology of ancient Nubians; human biology of modern people of the Amazon; paleontology of early primates. Total annual research expenditures: $316,453.

University of Colorado Denver, College of Liberal Arts and Sciences, Department of Anthropology, Denver, CO 80217. Offers archaeological studies (MA); biological anthropology (MA); medical anthropology (MA); sustainable development and political ecology (MA). Part-time and evening/weekend programs available. *Faculty:* 8 full-time (1 woman). *Students:* 16 full-time (12 women), 7 part-time (6 women); includes 1 Hispanic/Latino. Average age 30. 44 applicants, 59% accepted, 9 enrolled. In 2010, 13 master's awarded. *Degree requirements:* For master's, comprehensive exam, thesis or alternative, 30-36 credit hours. *Entrance requirements:* For master's, GRE General Test, minimum GPA of 3.0 for all undergraduate studies, two copies of transcripts from all undergraduate/graduate institutions attended, prior training in anthropology, three letters of recommendation, statement of purpose. Additional exam requirements/recommendations for international students: Required—TOEFL (minimum score 525 paper-based; 197 computer-based). *Application deadline:* For fall admission, 2/15 for domestic students. Applications are processed on a rolling basis. Application fee: $50 ($75 for international students). Electronic applications accepted. *Expenses:* Tuition, state resident: full-time

Anthropology

University of Colorado Denver (continued)
$7332; part-time $355 per credit hour. Tuition, nonresident: full-time $18,990; part-time $1055 per credit hour. Required fees: $998. Tuition and fees vary according to course level, course load, degree level, campus/location, program, reciprocity agreements and student level. *Financial support:* Research assistantships, teaching assistantships, Federal Work-Study available. Financial award application deadline: 4/1; financial award applicants required to submit FAFSA. *Faculty research:* Applied medical anthropology, primate social behavior, environmental anthropology, Southwestern and Mexican archaeology, human ecology. *Unit head:* Dr. Steve P. Koester, Chair, 303-556-6795, Fax: 303-556-8501, E-mail: steve.koester@ucdenver.edu. *Application contact:* Connie Turner, Program Assistant, 303-556-3554, Fax: 303-556-8501, E-mail: connie.turner@ucdenver.edu.

University of Connecticut, Graduate School, College of Liberal Arts and Sciences, Department of Anthropology, Storrs, CT 06269. Offers MA, PhD. Terminal master's awarded for partial completion of doctoral program. *Degree requirements:* For master's, comprehensive exam; for doctorate, thesis/dissertation. *Entrance requirements:* For master's and doctorate, GRE General Test. Additional exam requirements/recommendations for international students: Required—TOEFL (minimum score 550 paper-based; 213 computer-based). Electronic applications accepted.

University of Denver, Division of Arts, Humanities and Social Sciences, Department of Anthropology, Denver, CO 80208. Offers archaeology (MA); cultural anthropology (MA); museum studies (MA). Part-time programs available. *Faculty:* 8 full-time (4 women). *Students:* 1 (woman) full-time, 17 part-time (12 women); includes 4 minority (2 Black or African American, non-Hispanic/Latino; 1 American Indian or Alaska Native, non-Hispanic/Latino; 1 Hispanic/Latino), 1 international. Average age 26. 45 applicants, 47% accepted, 8 enrolled. In 2010, 11 master's awarded. *Degree requirements:* For master's, comprehensive exam, thesis or alternative, proficiency in foreign language other than English or in quantitative methods. *Entrance requirements:* For master's, GRE General Test. Additional exam requirements/recommendations for international students: Required—TOEFL (minimum score 550 paper-based; 80 iBT). *Application deadline:* Applications are processed on a rolling basis. Application fee: $60. Electronic applications accepted. *Expenses:* Tuition: Full-time $35,604; part-time $29,670 per year. Required fees: $687 per year. Tuition and fees vary according to program. *Financial support:* In 2010–11, 12 teaching assistantships with full and partial tuition reimbursements (averaging $4,667 per year) were awarded; career-related internships or fieldwork, Federal Work-Study, institutionally sponsored loans, scholarships/grants, and unspecified assistantships also available. Support available to part-time students. Financial award application deadline: 3/15; financial award applicants required to submit FAFSA. *Faculty research:* Gender, class, race, ground-penetrating radar, archaeology. *Unit head:* Dr. Dean J. Saitta, Chair, 303-871-2680, E-mail: dsaitta@du.edu. *Application contact:* Carrie Shrader, Assistant to Chair, 303-871-2677, E-mail: anth02@du.edu.

University of Florida, Graduate School, College of Liberal Arts and Sciences, Department of Anthropology, Gainesville, FL 32611. Offers MA, PhD, JD/MA. Part-time programs available. *Faculty:* 19 full-time (6 women), 7 part-time/adjunct (3 women). *Students:* 123 full-time (74 women), 51 part-time (29 women); includes 16 Black or African American, non-Hispanic/Latino; 2 American Indian or Alaska Native, non-Hispanic/Latino; 2 Asian, non-Hispanic/Latino; 16 Hispanic/Latino, 19 international. Average age 34. 174 applicants, 19% accepted, 20 enrolled. In 2010, 11 master's, 30 doctorates awarded. *Degree requirements:* For master's, thesis optional; for doctorate, comprehensive exam, thesis/dissertation. *Entrance requirements:* For master's and doctorate, GRE General Test, minimum GPA of 3.2. Additional exam requirements/recommendations for international students: Required—TOEFL (minimum score 550 paper-based; 213 computer-based; 80 iBT), IELTS (minimum score 6). *Application deadline:* For fall admission, 1/5 for domestic students. Application fee: $30. Electronic applications accepted. *Expenses:* Tuition, state resident: full-time $10,915.92. Tuition, nonresident: full-time $28,309. *Financial support:* In 2010–11, 97 students received support, including 40 fellowships, 19 research assistantships (averaging $19,894 per year), 38 teaching assistantships (averaging $19,561 per year); career-related internships or fieldwork, Federal Work-Study, institutionally sponsored loans, and unspecified assistantships also available. Support available to part-time students. Financial award applicants required to submit FAFSA. *Faculty research:* Social and cultural anthropology, archaeology, anthropological linguistics, physical anthropology. *Unit head:* Dr. Allan F. Burns, Chair, 352-392-2253 Ext. 205, Fax: 352-392-6929, E-mail: afburns@ufl.edu. *Application contact:* Dr. Brenda H. Chalfin, Graduate Coordinator, 352-392-2427 Ext. 306, Fax: 352-392-6929, E-mail: bchalfin@ufl.edu.

University of Georgia, College of Arts and Sciences, Department of Anthropology, Athens, GA 30602. Offers anthropology (MA, PhD); archaeological resource management (MS). *Faculty:* 12 full-time (4 women), 1 (woman) part-time/adjunct. *Students:* 51 full-time (32 women), 7 part-time (3 women); includes 1 Black or African American, non-Hispanic/Latino; 1 Hispanic/Latino; 2 Two or more races, non-Hispanic/Latino, 6 international. 56 applicants, 34% accepted, 14 enrolled. In 2010, 7 master's, 9 doctorates awarded. *Degree requirements:* For master's, one foreign language, thesis; for doctorate, one foreign language, thesis/dissertation. *Entrance requirements:* For master's and doctorate, GRE General Test. *Application deadline:* For fall admission, 7/1 priority date for domestic students; for spring admission, 11/15 for domestic students. Application fee: $50. Electronic applications accepted. *Expenses:* Tuition, state resident: full-time $7200; part-time $344 per credit hour. Tuition, nonresident: full-time $21,900; part-time $944 per credit hour. Tuition and fees vary according to course load and program. *Financial support:* Fellowships, research assistantships, teaching assistantships, unspecified assistantships available. *Unit head:* Dr. Ted Gragson, Head, 706-542-1479, Fax: 706-542-3998, E-mail: tgragso@uga.edu. *Application contact:* Dr. Elizabeth J. Reitz, Graduate Coordinator, 706-542-1464, Fax: 706-542-3998, E-mail: ereitz@uga.edu.

University of Guelph, Graduate Studies, College of Social and Applied Human Sciences, Department of Sociology and Anthropology, Guelph, ON N1G 2W1, Canada. Offers anthropology (MA); crime and criminal justice policy (MA); sociology (MA, PhD). *Degree requirements:* For master's, thesis or major paper; for doctorate, comprehensive exam, thesis/dissertation. *Entrance requirements:* For master's, minimum B+ average during previous 2 years of course work, honors BA or equivalent; for doctorate, must have an MA in Sociology, must have 80% or higher in graduate level studies. Additional exam requirements/recommendations for international students: Required—TOEFL (minimum score 550 paper-based; 213 computer-based; 89 iBT), IELTS (minimum score 6.5), TOEFL or IELTS. Electronic applications accepted. *Faculty research:* Rural and development sociology; education, employment, and the workplace; race, ethnicity, and native studies; criminology and deviance; social psychology.

University of Hawaii at Manoa, Graduate Division, College of Social Sciences, Department of Anthropology, Honolulu, HI 96822. Offers MA, PhD. Part-time programs available. *Faculty:* 31 full-time (8 women), 14 part-time/adjunct (7 women). *Students:* 58 full-time (35 women), 24 part-time (18 women); includes 27 minority (1 Black or African American, non-Hispanic/Latino; 12 Asian, non-Hispanic/Latino; 7 Native Hawaiian or other Pacific Islander, non-Hispanic/Latino; 7 Two or more races, non-Hispanic/Latino), 21 international. Average age 33. 126 applicants, 27% accepted, 17 enrolled. In 2010, 13 master's, 7 doctorates awarded. *Degree requirements:* For master's, thesis optional; for doctorate, comprehensive exam, thesis/dissertation. *Entrance requirements:* For master's and doctorate, GRE General Test. Additional exam requirements/recommendations for international students: Required—TOEFL (minimum score 560 paper-based; 220 computer-based; 83 iBT), IELTS (minimum score 5). *Application deadline:* For fall admission, 1/15 for domestic and international students. Application fee: $60. *Financial support:* In 2010–11, 1 student received support, including 35 fellowships (averaging $2,635 per year), 3 research assistantships (averaging $13,611 per year), 11 teaching assistantships (averaging $15,344 per year); Federal Work-Study, institutionally sponsored loans, and tuition waivers (full) also available. Financial award application deadline: 3/1; financial award applicants required to submit FAFSA. *Faculty research:* Evolution of social complexity, ethnopharmacology, social interaction, faunal analysis, human ecology. Total annual research expenditures: $464,951. *Application contact:* Dr. Geoffrey White, Graduate Chairperson, 808-956-7153, Fax: 808-956-4893, E-mail: bilmes@hawaii.edu.

University of Houston, College of Liberal Arts and Social Sciences, Department of Anthropology, Houston, TX 77204. Offers MA. Part-time programs available. *Faculty:* 7 full-time (3 women). *Students:* 8 full-time (7 women), 13 part-time (10 women); includes 3 Black or African American, non-Hispanic/Latino; 1 American Indian or Alaska Native, non-Hispanic/Latino; 1 Two or more races, non-Hispanic/Latino, 1 international. Average age 32. 11 applicants, 82% accepted, 6 enrolled. In 2010, 7 master's awarded. *Degree requirements:* For master's, comprehensive exam, thesis. *Entrance requirements:* For master's, GRE General Test (minimum 500 verbal, 500 quantitative), minimum GPA of 3.0 in last 60 undergraduate hours. Additional exam requirements/recommendations for international students: Required—TOEFL (minimum score 550 paper-based; 79 computer-based; 79 iBT). *Application deadline:* For fall admission, 2/28 for domestic and international students. Application fee: $0 ($75 for international students). Electronic applications accepted. *Expenses:* Tuition, state resident: full-time $8592; part-time $358 per credit hour. Tuition, nonresident: full-time $16,032; part-time $668 per credit hour. Required fees: $2889. Tuition and fees vary according to course load and program. *Financial support:* In 2010–11, 5 teaching assistantships with full tuition reimbursements (averaging $7,720 per year) were awarded; career-related internships or fieldwork, Federal Work-Study, institutionally sponsored loans, scholarships/grants, health care benefits, and unspecified assistantships also available. Support available to part-time students. Financial award application deadline: 2/1. *Unit head:* Dr. Norris Lang, Chairperson, 713-743-3780, Fax: 713-743-3798, E-mail: nlang@uh.edu. *Application contact:* Dr. Norris Lang, Chairperson, 713-743-3780, Fax: 713-743-3798, E-mail: nlang@uh.edu.

University of Idaho, College of Graduate Studies, College of Letters, Arts and Social Sciences, Department of Sociology, Anthropology and Justice Studies, Moscow, ID 83844-2282. Offers anthropology (MA). *Faculty:* 5 full-time, 2 part-time/adjunct. *Students:* 19 full-time, 9 part-time. Average age 32. In 2010, 2 master's awarded. *Degree requirements:* For master's, one foreign language. *Entrance requirements:* For master's, minimum GPA of 2.8. *Application deadline:* For fall admission, 8/1 for domestic students; for spring admission, 12/15 for domestic students. Applications are processed on a rolling basis. Application fee: $60. Electronic applications accepted. *Expenses:* Tuition, nonresident: part-time $580 per credit. Required fees: $306 per credit. *Financial support:* Research assistantships, teaching assistantships available. Financial award applicants required to submit FAFSA. *Unit head:* Dr. John Mihelich, Chair, 208-885-6751, E-mail: socanth@uidaho.edu. *Application contact:* Dr. John Mihelich, Chair, 208-885-6751, E-mail: socanth@uidaho.edu.

University of Illinois at Chicago, Graduate College, College of Liberal Arts and Sciences, Department of Anthropology, Chicago, IL 60607-7128. Offers anthropology (MA, PhD); environmental and urban geography (MA), including environmental studies, urban geography. Part-time programs available. *Degree requirements:* For doctorate, comprehensive exam. *Entrance requirements:* For master's and doctorate, minimum GPA of 2.75. Additional exam requirements/recommendations for international students: Required—TOEFL. Electronic applications accepted. *Faculty research:* Archaeological, physical, and cultural anthropology.

University of Illinois at Urbana–Champaign, Graduate College, College of Liberal Arts and Sciences, Department of Anthropology, Champaign, IL 61820. Offers MA, PhD. *Faculty:* 27 full-time (12 women). *Students:* 40 full-time (27 women), 17 part-time (13 women); includes 1 Black or African American, non-Hispanic/Latino; 3 Asian, non-Hispanic/Latino; 5 Hispanic/Latino; 1 Native Hawaiian or other Pacific Islander, non-Hispanic/Latino, 11 international. 82 applicants, 5% accepted, 4 enrolled. In 2010, 4 master's, 8 doctorates awarded. Terminal master's awarded for partial completion of doctoral program. *Entrance requirements:* For master's and doctorate, GRE General Test, minimum GPA of 3.0. Additional exam requirements/recommendations for international students: Required—TOEFL (minimum score 550 paper-based; 213 computer-based).. *Application deadline:* Applications are processed on a rolling basis. Application fee: $75 ($90 for international students). Electronic applications accepted. *Financial support:* In 2010–11, 14 fellowships, 21 research assistantships, 26 teaching assistantships were awarded; tuition waivers (full and partial) also available. *Unit head:* Steven R. Leigh, Head, 217-333-3616, Fax: 217-244-3490, E-mail: sleigh@illinois.edu. *Application contact:* Elizabeth M. Spears, Office Support Specialist, 217-244-0296, Fax: 217-244-3490, E-mail: espears@illinois.edu.

University of Indianapolis, Graduate Programs, College of Arts and Sciences, Department of Anthropology, Indianapolis, IN 46227-3697. Offers MS. *Faculty:* 1 full-time (0 women). *Students:* 1 (woman) full-time. Average age 32. *Entrance requirements:* For master's, GRE General Test (minimum score of 500 on both the verbal and quantitative sections), bachelor's degree with major or minor in anthropology or closely-related field; undergraduate or graduate coursework in anthropology and the natural sciences with minimum C grade (ideally, semester in cultural anthropology, biological anthropology, archeology, statistics, and geology); minimum cumulative undergraduate GPA of 3.2. Additional exam requirements/recommendations for international students: Required—TOEFL (minimum score 550 paper-based; 213 computer-based; 79 iBT). Application fee: $30. Tuition and fees vary according to course load, degree level and program. *Unit head:* Dr. Gregory Reinhardt, Chair, 317-788-3440, E-mail: reinhardt@uindy.edu. *Application contact:* Linda Corn, 317-788-3395, E-mail: lcorn@uindy.edu.

The University of Iowa, Graduate College, College of Liberal Arts and Sciences, Department of Anthropology, Iowa City, IA 52242-1316. Offers MA, PhD. *Degree requirements:* For master's, thesis optional, exam; for doctorate, comprehensive exam, thesis/dissertation. *Entrance requirements:* For master's and doctorate, GRE General Test, minimum GPA of 3.0. Additional exam requirements/recommendations for international students: Required—TOEFL (minimum score 550 paper-based; 213 computer-based; 81 iBT). Electronic applications accepted.

The University of Kansas, Graduate Studies, College of Liberal Arts and Sciences, Department of Anthropology, Lawrence, KS 66045. Offers MA, PhD. *Faculty:* 19 full-time (6 women), 17 part-time/adjunct (6 women). *Students:* 58 full-time (36 women), 22 part-time (10 women); includes 7 minority (1 Black or African American, non-Hispanic/Latino; 2 American Indian or Alaska Native, non-Hispanic/Latino; 1 Asian, non-Hispanic/Latino; 1 Hispanic/Latino; 2 Two or more races, non-Hispanic/Latino), 7 international. Average age 31. 51 applicants, 45% accepted, 13 enrolled. In 2010, 6 master's, 5 doctorates awarded. *Degree requirements:* For master's, comprehensive exam (for some programs), thesis; for doctorate, one foreign language, comprehensive exam, thesis/dissertation. *Entrance requirements:* For master's, minimum GPA of 3.2; for doctorate, minimum GPA of 3.5. Additional exam requirements/recommendations for international students: Required—TOEFL. *Application deadline:* For fall admission, 1/5 for domestic and international students. Application fee: $55 ($65 for international students). Electronic applications accepted. *Expenses:* Tuition, state resident: full-time $7092; part-time $295.50 per credit hour. Tuition, nonresident: full-time $16,590; part-time $691.25 per credit hour. Required fees: $858; $71.49 per credit hour. Tuition and fees vary according to course load, campus/location and program. *Financial support:* Fellowships with full tuition reimbursements, research assistantships with full and partial tuition reimbursements, teaching assistantships with full and partial tuition reimbursements, career-related internships or fieldwork, institutionally sponsored loans, and unspecified assistantships available. Financial award application deadline: 1/5; financial award applicants required to submit FAFSA. *Faculty research:* Theoretical and applied anthropology; old and new world archaeology; endangered language documentation and revitalization; bio-cultural medical anthropology; anthropological/molecular genetics; Latin American, African, Asian, European and North American anthropology. *Unit head:* Jane W. Gibson, Chair, 785-864-4103, Fax: 785-864-5224, E-mail: jwgc@ku.edu. *Application contact:* Donald D. Stull, Graduate Coordinator, 785-864-4103, Fax: 785-864-5224, E-mail: stull@ku.edu.

University of Kentucky, Graduate School, College of Arts and Sciences, Program in Anthropology, Lexington, KY 40506-0032. Offers MA, PhD. Part-time programs available. *Degree requirements:* For master's, comprehensive exam, thesis optional; for doctorate, one foreign language, comprehensive exam, thesis/dissertation. *Entrance requirements:* For master's,

GRE General Test, minimum undergraduate GPA of 2.75; for doctorate, GRE General Test, minimum graduate GPA of 3.0. Additional exam requirements/recommendations for international students: Required—TOEFL (minimum score 550 paper-based; 213 computer-based). Electronic applications accepted. *Faculty research:* Applied social anthropology, developmental change, medical anthropology, culture history, ethnohistory.

University of Lethbridge, School of Graduate Studies, Lethbridge, AB T1K 3M4, Canada. Offers accounting (MScM); addictions counseling (M Sc); agricultural biotechnology (M Sc); agricultural studies (M Sc, MA); anthropology (MA); archaeology (MA); art (MA, MFA); biochemistry (M Sc); biological sciences (M Sc); biomolecular science (PhD); biosystems and biodiversity (PhD); Canadian studies (MA); chemistry (M Sc); computer science (M Sc); computer science and geographical information science (M Sc); counseling psychology (M Ed); dramatic arts (MA); earth, space, and physical science (PhD); economics (MA); educational leadership (M Ed); English (MA); environmental science (M Sc); evolution and behavior (PhD); exercise science (M Sc); finance (MScM); French (MA); French/German (MA); French/Spanish (MA); general education (M Ed); general management (MScM); geography (M Sc, MA); German (MA); health science (M Sc); history (MA); human resource management and labour relations (MScM); individualized multidisciplinary (M Sc, MA); information systems (MScM); international management (MScM); kinesiology (M Sc, MA); management (M Sc, MA); marketing (MScM); mathematics (M Sc); music (M Mus, MA); Native American studies (MA); neuroscience (M Sc, PhD); new media (MA); nursing (M Sc); philosophy (MA); physics (M Sc); policy and strategy (MScM); political science (MA); psychology (M Sc, MA); religious studies (MA); social sciences (MA); sociology (MA); theatre and dramatic arts (MFA); theoretical and computational science (PhD); urban and regional studies (MA); women's studies (MA). Part-time and evening/weekend programs available. *Degree requirements:* For doctorate, comprehensive exam, thesis/dissertation. *Entrance requirements:* For master's, GMAT (M Sc in management), bachelor's degree in related field, minimum GPA of 3.0 during previous 20 graded semester courses, 2 years teaching or related experience (M Ed); for doctorate, master's degree, minimum graduate GPA of 3.5. Additional exam requirements/recommendations for international students: Required—TOEFL. *Faculty research:* Movement and brain plasticity, gibberellin physiology, photosynthesis, carbon cycling, molecular properties of main-group ring components.

University of Louisville, Graduate School, College of Arts and Sciences, Department of Anthropology, Louisville, KY 40292-0001. Offers MA. Part-time and evening/weekend programs available. *Faculty:* 10 full-time (5 women), 2 part-time/adjunct (1 woman). *Students:* 7 full-time (4 women), 7 part-time (6 women); includes 1 Hispanic/Latino; 1 Native Hawaiian or other Pacific Islander, non-Hispanic/Latino. Average age 29. 7 applicants, 71% accepted, 4 enrolled. *Degree requirements:* For master's, thesis or internship. *Entrance requirements:* For master's, GRE (minimum Verbal and Quantitative score of 1100). Additional exam requirements/recommendations for international students: Required—TOEFL (minimum score 550 paper-based; 79 iBT). *Application deadline:* For fall admission, 4/1 for domestic and international students; for spring admission, 11/1 for domestic and international students. Application fee: $50. *Expenses:* Tuition, state resident: full-time $9144; part-time $508 per credit hour. Tuition, nonresident: full-time $19,026; part-time $1057 per credit hour. Tuition and fees vary according to program and reciprocity agreements. *Financial support:* In 2010–11, 1 teaching assistantship with full tuition reimbursement (averaging $21,000 per year) was awarded; career-related internships or fieldwork and scholarships/grants also available. *Faculty research:* Evolutionary anthropology, cultural diaspora studies, archaeology, political economy, violence and the state. *Unit head:* Dr. Lisa Markowitz, Chair, 502-852-2426, Fax: 502-852-4560, E-mail: lisam@louisville.edu. *Application contact:* Libby Leggett, Director, Graduate Admissions, 502-852-3101, Fax: 502-852-6536, E-mail: gradadm@louisville.edu.

The University of Manchester, School of Arts, Histories and Cultures, Manchester, United Kingdom. Offers anthropology, media and performance (PhD); applied theatre professional (PhD); archaeology (PhD); art history and visual studies (PhD); arts management and cultural policy (PhD); classics and ancient history (PhD); composition (PhD); creative writing (PhD); drama (PhD); economic and social history (PhD); electroacoustic composition (PhD); English and American studies (PhD); history (PhD); humanitarianism and conflict response (PhD); museology (PhD); music (PhD); musicology (PhD); religions and theology (PhD).

The University of Manchester, School of Social Sciences, Manchester, United Kingdom. Offers ethnographic documentary (M Phil); interdisciplinary study of culture (PhD); philosophy (PhD); politics (PhD); social anthropology (PhD); social anthropology with visual media (PhD); social change (PhD); social statistics (PhD); sociology (PhD); visual anthropology (M Phil).

University of Manitoba, Faculty of Graduate Studies, Faculty of Arts, Department of Anthropology, Winnipeg, MB R3T 2N2, Canada. Offers MA, PhD. *Degree requirements:* For master's, thesis or alternative.

University of Maryland, College Park, Academic Affairs, College of Behavioral and Social Sciences, Department of Anthropology, College Park, MD 20742. Offers applied anthropology (MAA). Part-time and evening/weekend programs available. *Faculty:* 15 full-time (6 women), 3 part-time/adjunct (2 women). *Students:* 29 full-time (22 women), 10 part-time (7 women); includes 6 minority (1 Asian, non-Hispanic/Latino; 4 Hispanic/Latino; 1 Two or more races, non-Hispanic/Latino). 117 applicants, 28% accepted, 14 enrolled. In 2010, 13 master's awarded. *Degree requirements:* For master's, internship. *Entrance requirements:* For master's, GRE General Test, minimum GPA of 3.0, 3 letters of recommendation. Additional exam requirements/recommendations for international students: Required—TOEFL. *Application deadline:* For fall admission, 12/15 for domestic and international students. Applications are processed on a rolling basis. Application fee: $75. Electronic applications accepted. *Expenses:* Tuition, state resident: part-time $471 per credit hour. Tuition, nonresident: part-time $1016 per credit hour. Required fees: $337 per term. *Financial support:* In 2010–11, 6 fellowships with full and partial tuition reimbursements (averaging $11,802 per year), 23 teaching assistantships with tuition reimbursements (averaging $15,375 per year) were awarded; research assistantships, Federal Work-Study and scholarships/grants also available. Support available to part-time students. Financial award applicants required to submit FAFSA. *Faculty research:* Archaeology, human biodiversity, cultural and resource management. Total annual research expenditures: $489,941. *Unit head:* Dr. Paul Shackel, Chair, 301-405-1423, E-mail: pshackel@umd.edu. *Application contact:* Dean of Graduate School, 301-405-0358, Fax: 301-314-9305.

University of Massachusetts Amherst, Graduate School, College of Social and Behavioral Sciences, Department of Anthropology, Amherst, MA 01003. Offers MA, PhD. Part-time programs available. *Faculty:* 24 full-time (12 women). *Students:* 47 full-time (37 women), 25 part-time (18 women); includes 22 minority (7 Black or African American, non-Hispanic/Latino; 3 American Indian or Alaska Native, non-Hispanic/Latino; 2 Asian, non-Hispanic/Latino; 3 Hispanic/Latino; 7 Two or more races, non-Hispanic/Latino), 5 international. Average age 35. 98 applicants, 17% accepted, 9 enrolled. In 2010, 7 master's, 6 doctorates awarded. Terminal master's awarded for partial completion of doctoral program. *Degree requirements:* For master's, thesis or alternative; for doctorate, comprehensive exam, thesis/dissertation. *Entrance requirements:* Additional exam requirements/recommendations for international students: Required—TOEFL (minimum score 550 paper-based; 213 computer-based; 80 iBT), IELTS (minimum score 6.5). *Application deadline:* For fall admission, 1/2 for domestic and international students. Applications are processed on a rolling basis. Application fee: $50 ($65 for international students). Electronic applications accepted. *Expenses:* Tuition, state resident: full-time $2640. Required fees: $8282. One-time fee: $357 full-time. *Financial support:* In 2010–11, 1 fellowship with full tuition reimbursement (averaging $6,757 per year), 9 research assistantships with full tuition reimbursements (averaging $8,531 per year), 30 teaching assistantships with full tuition reimbursements (averaging $10,822 per year) were awarded; career-related internships or fieldwork, Federal Work-Study, scholarships/grants, traineeships, health care benefits, tuition waivers (full), and unspecified assistantships also available. Support available to part-time students. Financial award application deadline: 1/2; financial award applicants required to submit FAFSA. *Unit head:* Dr. Brigitte Holt, Graduate Program Director, 413-545-0935, Fax: 413-545-9494. *Application contact:* Jean M. Ames, Supervisor of Admissions, 413-545-0722, Fax: 413-577-0010, E-mail: gradadm@grad.umass.edu.

University of Memphis, Graduate School, College of Arts and Sciences, Department of Anthropology, Memphis, TN 38152. Offers medical anthropology (MA); urban anthropology (MA). Part-time programs available. *Faculty:* 6 full-time (4 women), 2 part-time/adjunct (1 woman). *Students:* 29 full-time (26 women), 4 part-time (3 women); includes 2 Black or African American, non-Hispanic/Latino; 1 Hispanic/Latino; 1 Two or more races, non-Hispanic/Latino. Average age 27. 23 applicants, 83% accepted, 10 enrolled. In 2010, 7 master's awarded. *Degree requirements:* For master's, comprehensive exam, practicum. *Entrance requirements:* For master's, GRE General Test, minimum GPA of 3.0, letter of intent, 3 letters of recommendation. *Application deadline:* For fall admission, 11/1 priority date for domestic students; for spring admission, 4/1 priority date for domestic students. Application fee: $35 ($60 for international students). Electronic applications accepted. *Financial support:* In 2010–11, 27 students received support; fellowships, research assistantships with full tuition reimbursements available, teaching assistantships with full tuition reimbursements available, career-related internships or fieldwork, Federal Work-Study, scholarships/grants, and unspecified assistantships available. Financial award application deadline: 2/15; financial award applicants required to submit FAFSA. *Faculty research:* Community development, medical anthropology, environmental justice, health disparities, cultural identity and heritage. *Unit head:* Dr. Ruth Beth Finerman, Chair, 901-678-3334, Fax: 901-678-2069, E-mail: finerman@memphis.edu. *Application contact:* Dr. Charles Williams, Coordinator of Graduate Studies, 901-678-3333, Fax: 901-678-0827, E-mail: cwilliam@memphis.edu.

University of Michigan, Horace H. Rackham School of Graduate Studies, College of Literature, Science, and the Arts, Department of Anthropology, Ann Arbor, MI 48109. Offers PhD. *Faculty:* 39 full-time (17 women), 6 part-time/adjunct (3 women). *Students:* 131 full-time (83 women); includes 1 Black or African American, non-Hispanic/Latino; 6 Asian, non-Hispanic/Latino; 13 Hispanic/Latino; 4 Two or more races, non-Hispanic/Latino, 25 international. Average age 28. 273 applicants, 7% accepted, 12 enrolled. In 2010, 12 doctorates awarded. *Degree requirements:* For doctorate, one foreign language, comprehensive exam, thesis/dissertation, oral defense of dissertation, preliminary exam. *Entrance requirements:* For doctorate, GRE General Test. Additional exam requirements/recommendations for international students: Required—TOEFL (minimum score 560 paper-based; 220 computer-based; 84 iBT). *Application deadline:* For fall admission, 12/15 for domestic and international students. Application fee: $65 ($75 for international students). Electronic applications accepted. *Expenses:* Tuition, state resident: full-time $17,784; part-time $1116 per credit hour. Tuition, nonresident: full-time $35,944; part-time $2125 per credit hour. International tuition: $35,994 full-time. Required fees: $95 per semester. Tuition and fees vary according to course load, degree level and program. *Financial support:* In 2010–11, 31 students received support, including 40 fellowships with full tuition reimbursements available (averaging $16,000 per year), 10 research assistantships with full tuition reimbursements available (averaging $17,270 per year), 40 teaching assistantships with full tuition reimbursements available (averaging $17,270 per year); institutionally sponsored loans, scholarships/grants, traineeships, health care benefits, tuition waivers (full), and unspecified assistantships also available. Financial award application deadline: 3/1; financial award applicants required to submit FAFSA. *Faculty research:* Kinship and behavior in wild chimpanzees, paleontological research in the Lower Miocene of Northeast Uganda, long-term fitness consequences of wild chimpanzee behavior, social movements. Total annual research expenditures: $85,748. *Unit head:* Dr. Thomas Fricke, Chair, 734-764-7274, Fax: 734-763-6077. *Application contact:* Michelle O'Donnell, Graduate Admissions Coordinator, 734-936-7933, Fax: 734-763-6077, E-mail: odonnelm@umich.edu.

University of Michigan, Horace H. Rackham School of Graduate Studies, College of Literature, Science, and the Arts, Doctoral Program in Anthropology and History, Ann Arbor, MI 48109. Offers PhD. *Degree requirements:* For doctorate, 2 foreign languages, thesis/dissertation, oral defense of dissertation, preliminary exam. *Entrance requirements:* For doctorate, GRE General Test, writing sample. Additional exam requirements/recommendations for international students: Required—TOEFL. Electronic applications accepted. *Expenses:* Tuition, state resident: full-time $17,784; part-time $1116 per credit hour. Tuition, nonresident: full-time $35,944; part-time $2125 per credit hour. International tuition: $35,994 full-time. Required fees: $95 per semester. Tuition and fees vary according to course load, degree level and program. *Faculty research:* Historical anthropology.

University of Minnesota, Duluth, Graduate School, College of Liberal Arts, Department of Sociology/Anthropology, Duluth, MN 55812-2496. Offers criminology (MA); liberal studies (MLS). Part-time programs available. *Degree requirements:* For master's, thesis or alternative. *Entrance requirements:* For master's, interview, minimum GPA of 3.0, letters of recommendation. Additional exam requirements/recommendations for international students: Required—TOEFL. *Faculty research:* Nature of knowledge, philosophy of science, ecology, cultural studies, language.

University of Minnesota, Twin Cities Campus, Graduate School, College of Liberal Arts, Department of Anthropology, Minneapolis, MN 55455-0213. Offers MA, PhD. Terminal master's awarded for partial completion of doctoral program. *Degree requirements:* For master's, thesis optional; for doctorate, comprehensive exam, thesis/dissertation. *Entrance requirements:* For master's and doctorate, GRE. Electronic applications accepted. *Faculty research:* Psychological/psychoanalytic anthropology, gender and feminist anthropology, economic anthropology, medical anthropology, paleoanthropology.

University of Mississippi, Graduate School, College of Liberal Arts, Department of Sociology and Anthropology, Oxford, University, MS 38677. Offers anthropology (MA); sociology (MA, MSS). *Students:* 32 full-time (15 women), 5 part-time (4 women); includes 12 minority (6 Black or African American, non-Hispanic/Latino; 1 American Indian or Alaska Native, non-Hispanic/Latino; 1 Hispanic/Latino; 1 Native Hawaiian or other Pacific Islander, non-Hispanic/Latino; 3 Two or more races, non-Hispanic/Latino), 1 international. In 2010, 11 master's awarded. *Degree requirements:* For master's, thesis (for some programs). *Entrance requirements:* For master's, GRE General Test, minimum GPA of 3.0. Additional exam requirements/recommendations for international students: Required—TOEFL. *Application deadline:* For fall admission, 4/1 for domestic students; for spring admission, 10/1 for domestic students. Applications are processed on a rolling basis. Application fee: $25. Electronic applications accepted. *Financial support:* Scholarships/grants available. Financial award application deadline: 3/1; financial award applicants required to submit FAFSA. *Unit head:* Dr. Kirsten A. Dellinger, Chairman, 662-915-7421, Fax: 662-915-5372, E-mail: kdelling@olemiss.edu. *Application contact:* Dr. Christy M. Wyandt, Associate Dean, 662-915-7474, Fax: 662-915-7577, E-mail: cwyandt@olemiss.edu.

University of Missouri, Graduate School, College of Arts and Sciences, Department of Anthropology, Columbia, MO 65211. Offers MA, PhD. *Faculty:* 11 full-time (4 women), 3 part-time/adjunct (1 woman). *Students:* 26 full-time (16 women), 16 part-time (8 women); includes 3 minority (1 Asian, non-Hispanic/Latino; 1 Hispanic/Latino; 1 Two or more races, non-Hispanic/Latino), 1 international. Average age 32. 27 applicants, 37% accepted, 7 enrolled. In 2010, 5 master's, 1 doctorate awarded. *Degree requirements:* For master's, thesis (for some programs); for doctorate, one foreign language, comprehensive exam, thesis/dissertation. *Entrance requirements:* For master's, GRE General Test (minimum score 1000 verbal and quantitative), minimum GPA of 3.25 in last 60 hours and in all anthropology courses; for doctorate, GRE General Test (minimum score 1000 verbal and quantitative), minimum GPA of 3.5 in previous graduate work. Additional exam requirements/recommendations for international students: Required—TOEFL (minimum score 500 paper-based; 173 computer-based; 61 iBT), IELTS (minimum score 5.5). *Application deadline:* For fall admission, 1/10 priority date for domestic students; for winter admission, 10/15 for domestic students. Applications are processed on a rolling basis. Application fee: $45 ($60 for international students). Electronic applications accepted. *Financial support:* In 2010–11, 2 fellowships with full tuition reimbursements, 5 research assistantships with full tuition reimbursements, 16 teaching assistantships

Anthropology

University of Missouri (continued)
with full tuition reimbursements were awarded; institutionally sponsored loans, scholarships/grants, health care benefits, and unspecified assistantships also available. Support available to part-time students. *Faculty research:* Social/cultural anthropology, biological anthropology, archaeology. *Unit head:* Dr. R. Lee Lyman, Department Chair, 573-882-4731, E-mail: lymanr@missouri.edu. *Application contact:* Gail Lawrence, 573-882-4731, E-mail: lawrenceag@missouri.edu.

The University of Montana, Graduate School, College of Arts and Sciences, Department of Anthropology, Missoula, MT 59812-0002. Offers anthropology (MA); cultural heritage (MA); cultural heritage studies (PhD); forensic anthropology (MA); historical anthropology (PhD); linguistics (MA). *Degree requirements:* For master's, thesis (for some programs). *Entrance requirements:* For master's, GRE General Test. Additional exam requirements/recommendations for international students: Required—TOEFL. *Faculty research:* Historical preservation, plateau-plains archaeology and ethnohistory.

University of Nebraska–Lincoln, Graduate College, College of Arts and Sciences, Department of Anthropology and Geography, Program in Anthropology, Lincoln, NE 68588. Offers MA. *Degree requirements:* For master's, thesis optional. *Entrance requirements:* For master's, GRE General Test. Additional exam requirements/recommendations for international students: Required—TOEFL (minimum score 500 paper-based; 173 computer-based). Electronic applications accepted. *Faculty research:* Cultural, archaeologic, linguistic, and physical anthropology.

University of Nevada, Las Vegas, Graduate College, College of Liberal Arts, Department of Anthropology and Ethnic Studies, Las Vegas, NV 89154-5003. Offers MA, PhD. Part-time programs available. *Faculty:* 14 full-time (7 women). *Students:* 25 full-time (18 women), 16 part-time (12 women); includes 15 minority (1 Black or African American, non-Hispanic/Latino; 1 Asian, non-Hispanic/Latino; 4 Hispanic/Latino; 9 Two or more races, non-Hispanic/Latino), 2 international. Average age 30. 38 applicants, 50% accepted, 15 enrolled. In 2010, 8 master's, 1 doctorate awarded. *Degree requirements:* For master's, thesis, oral defense of thesis; for doctorate, comprehensive exam, thesis/dissertation, oral defense of dissertation. *Entrance requirements:* For master's and doctorate, GRE General Test. Additional exam requirements/recommendations for international students: Required—TOEFL (minimum score 550 paper-based; 213 computer-based; 80 iBT), IELTS (minimum score 7). *Application deadline:* For fall admission, 2/1 priority date for domestic and international students. Applications are processed on a rolling basis. Application fee: $60 ($95 for international students). Electronic applications accepted. *Expenses:* Tuition, area resident: Part-time $239.50 per credit. Tuition, state resident: part-time $239.50 per credit. Tuition, nonresident: part-time $503 per credit. Required fees: $108 per semester. Tuition and fees vary according to course load, program and reciprocity agreements. *Financial support:* In 2010–11, 15 students received support, including 15 teaching assistantships with partial tuition reimbursements available (averaging $10,800 per year); institutionally sponsored loans, scholarships/grants, health care benefits, and unspecified assistantships also available. Financial award application deadline: 3/1. *Faculty research:* Bio-cultural evolution; foraging to farming transition (old and new world); human nutrition, health, and disease; human growth and development; human love, sexuality and family systems. Total annual research expenditures: $37,385. *Unit head:* Dr. Debra Martin, Chair/Professor, 702-895-1881, Fax: 702-8985-4823, E-mail: debra.martin@unlv.edu. *Application contact:* Graduate College Admissions Evaluator, 702-895-3320, Fax: 702-895-4180, E-mail: gradcollege@unlv.edu.

University of Nevada, Reno, Graduate School, College of Liberal Arts, Department of Anthropology, Reno, NV 89557. Offers MA, PhD. Terminal master's awarded for partial completion of doctoral program. *Degree requirements:* For master's, thesis; for doctorate, thesis/dissertation. *Entrance requirements:* For master's, GRE, minimum GPA of 2.75; for doctorate, GRE, minimum GPA of 3.0. Additional exam requirements/recommendations for international students: Required—TOEFL (minimum score 500 paper-based; 173 computer-based; 61 iBT), IELTS (minimum score 6). Electronic applications accepted. *Expenses:* Tuition, state resident: full-time $2219; part-time $246 per credit. Tuition, nonresident: part-time $510 per credit. International tuition: $9009 full-time. Required fees: $59 per term. One-time fee: $101. Tuition and fees vary according to course load. *Faculty research:* Ethnology, linguistics, cultural/medical/religious/ethnic relations, ecological anthropology, historical anthropology.

University of New Brunswick Fredericton, School of Graduate Studies, Faculty of Arts, Department of Anthropology, Fredericton, NB E3B 5A3, Canada. Offers MA. Part-time programs available. *Faculty:* 7 full-time (6 women), 3 part-time/adjunct (0 women). *Students:* 6 full-time (3 women), 4 part-time (2 women). In 2010, 3 master's awarded. *Degree requirements:* For master's, thesis, proposal. *Entrance requirements:* For master's, minimum GPA of 3.7. Additional exam requirements/recommendations for international students: Required—TOEFL. *Application deadline:* 1/31 for domestic and international students. Application fee: $50 Canadian dollars. *Expenses:* Tuition, area resident: Full-time $3708; part-time $927 per term. International tuition: $6300 full-time. Required fees: $50 per term. *Financial support:* In 2010–11, 2 fellowships (averaging $9,709 per year), 7 research assistantships (averaging $7,214 per year), 4 teaching assistantships (averaging $3,600 per year) were awarded. *Faculty research:* South Asia, anthropology of education, community-based fisheries, biomedical anthropology, archaeology of the Maritimes. *Unit head:* Susan Blair, Director of Graduate Studies, 506-458-7929, Fax: 506-453-5071, E-mail: sblair@unb.ca. *Application contact:* Misty Cormier, Graduate Secretary, 506-453-4975, Fax: 506-453-5071, E-mail: mistyc@unb.ca.

University of New Mexico, Graduate School, College of Arts and Sciences, Department of Anthropology, Albuquerque, NM 87131-2039. Offers MA, MS, PhD. *Faculty:* 31 full-time (14 women), 31 part-time/adjunct (23 women). *Students:* 104 full-time (70 women), 35 part-time (24 women); includes 25 minority (2 American Indian or Alaska Native, non-Hispanic/Latino; 3 Asian, non-Hispanic/Latino; 16 Hispanic/Latino; 1 Native Hawaiian or other Pacific Islander, non-Hispanic/Latino; 3 Two or more races, non-Hispanic/Latino), 5 international. Average age 33. 121 applicants, 18% accepted, 17 enrolled. In 2010, 12 master's, 11 doctorates awarded. Terminal master's awarded for partial completion of doctoral program. *Degree requirements:* For master's, comprehensive exam (for some programs), thesis or alternative, 3 exams; for doctorate, one foreign language, comprehensive exam, thesis/dissertation, proposal, oral defense, skill and/or second language. *Entrance requirements:* For master's and doctorate, GRE General Test, 3 letters of recommendation, letter of interest, transcripts. Additional exam requirements/recommendations for international students: Required—TOEFL (minimum score 550 paper-based; 213 computer-based), IELTS (minimum score 7). *Application deadline:* For fall admission, 1/2 for domestic students, 1/7 for international students. Application fee: $50. Electronic applications accepted. *Expenses:* Tuition, state resident: full-time $5991; part-time $251 per credit hour. Tuition, nonresident: full-time $14,405; part-time $800.20 per credit hour. Tuition and fees vary according to course level, course load, program and reciprocity agreements. *Financial support:* In 2010–11, 104 students received support, including 17 fellowships (averaging $9,268 per year), 22 research assistantships with partial tuition reimbursements available (averaging $10,567 per year), 41 teaching assistantships with partial tuition reimbursements available (averaging $8,608 per year); career-related internships or fieldwork, Federal Work-Study, institutionally sponsored loans, scholarships/grants, traineeships, health care benefits, tuition waivers (partial), and unspecified assistantships also available. Support available to part-time students. Financial award application deadline: 3/1; financial award applicants required to submit FAFSA. *Faculty research:* Ethnology, archaeology, evolutionary anthropology, environment, water and land use, gender and social frameworks, Greater Southwest, Latin America, political economy, public anthropology. Total annual research expenditures: $1.2 million. *Unit head:* Michael W. Graves, Chair, 505-277-4524, Fax: 505-277-0874, E-mail: mwgraves@unm.edu. *Application contact:* Erika E. Gerety, Program Advisement Coordinator, 505-277-2732, Fax: 505-277-0874, E-mail: erika@unm.edu.

The University of North Carolina at Chapel Hill, Graduate School, College of Arts and Sciences, Department of Anthropology, Chapel Hill, NC 27599-3115. Offers MA, PhD. Terminal master's awarded for partial completion of doctoral program. *Degree requirements:* For master's, variable foreign language requirement, thesis; for doctorate, variable foreign language requirement, comprehensive exam, thesis/dissertation. *Entrance requirements:* For master's and doctorate, GRE General Test, minimum GPA of 3.0. Additional exam requirements/recommendations for international students: Required—TOEFL. Electronic applications accepted. *Faculty research:* Archeology, ecology and evolution, medical anthropology, social systems, anthropology of meaning.

University of North Texas, Toulouse Graduate School, College of Public Affairs and Community Service, Department of Anthropology, Denton, TX 76203. Offers applied anthropology (MA, MS). Part-time and evening/weekend programs available. *Degree requirements:* For master's, practicum. *Entrance requirements:* For master's, GRE General Test. Additional exam requirements/recommendations for international students: Recommended—TOEFL (minimum score 550 paper-based; 213 computer-based; 79 iBT). *Application deadline:* Applications are processed on a rolling basis. Electronic applications accepted. *Expenses:* Tuition, state resident: full-time $4298; part-time $239 per credit hour. Tuition, nonresident: full-time $10,782; part-time $549 per credit hour. Required fees: $1292; $270 per credit hour. *Financial support:* Research assistantships, teaching assistantships, career-related internships or fieldwork, Federal Work-Study, and scholarships/grants available. Financial award applicants required to submit FAFSA. *Faculty research:* Cross-cultural/bilingual education in schools, globalization in work teams/business culture, environmental anthropology. *Application contact:* Graduate Adviser, 940-565-4160, Fax: 940-369-7833, E-mail: lhenry@unt.edu.

University of Oklahoma, College of Arts and Sciences, Department of Anthropology, Norman, OK 73019. Offers anthropology (MA, PhD); applied linguistic anthropology (MA). Part-time programs available. *Faculty:* 25 full-time (11 women). *Students:* 40 full-time (22 women), 22 part-time (15 women); includes 9 minority (4 American Indian or Alaska Native, non-Hispanic/Latino; 2 Asian, non-Hispanic/Latino; 2 Hispanic/Latino; 1 Two or more races, non-Hispanic/Latino), 1 international. Average age 32. 35 applicants, 49% accepted, 10 enrolled. In 2010, 11 master's, 1 doctorate awarded. Terminal master's awarded for partial completion of doctoral program. *Degree requirements:* For master's, thesis; for doctorate, thesis/dissertation, departmental qualifying exam. *Entrance requirements:* For master's, GRE, BA with 12 hours in anthropology. Additional exam requirements/recommendations for international students: Required—TOEFL (minimum score 550 paper-based; 213 computer-based; 79 iBT). *Application deadline:* For fall admission, 4/1 for domestic and international students; for spring admission, 11/1 for domestic students, 9/1 for international students. Applications are processed on a rolling basis. Application fee: $40 ($90 for international students). Electronic applications accepted. *Expenses:* Tuition, state resident: full-time $3893; part-time $162.20 per credit hour. Tuition, nonresident: full-time $14,167; part-time $590.30 per credit hour. Required fees: $2523; $94.60 per credit hour. Tuition and fees vary according to course load and degree level. *Financial support:* In 2010–11, 54 students received support, including 3 fellowships (averaging $4,167 per year), 3 research assistantships with partial tuition reimbursements available (averaging $13,423 per year), 20 teaching assistantships with partial tuition reimbursements available (averaging $14,039 per year); career-related internships or fieldwork, Federal Work-Study, scholarships/grants, health care benefits, and unspecified assistantships also available. Financial award applicants required to submit FAFSA. *Faculty research:* Sociocultural anthropology, archeology, linguistic anthropology, biological/medical anthropology, Native America, applied anthropological linguistics. Total annual research expenditures: $1.3 million. *Unit head:* Dr. Susan Vehik, Chair, 405-325-3261, Fax: 405-325-7386, E-mail: svehik@ou.edu. *Application contact:* Keli Mitchell, Staff Assistant, 405-325-3261, Fax: 405-325-7386, E-mail: keli@ou.edu.

University of Oregon, Graduate School, College of Arts and Sciences, Department of Anthropology, Eugene, OR 97403. Offers MA, MS, PhD. Terminal master's awarded for partial completion of doctoral program. *Degree requirements:* For master's, one foreign language; for doctorate, 2 foreign languages, thesis/dissertation. *Entrance requirements:* For master's and doctorate, GRE General Test. Additional exam requirements/recommendations for international students: Required—TOEFL. *Faculty research:* Prehistory, primatology, cultural anthropology of Native Americans, human evolution, Africa.

University of Ottawa, Faculty of Graduate and Postdoctoral Studies, Faculty of Social Sciences, Department of Sociology and Anthropology, Ottawa, ON K1N 6N5, Canada. Offers MA. *Degree requirements:* For master's, thesis or alternative. *Entrance requirements:* For master's, honors bachelor's degree or equivalent, minimum B average. Electronic applications accepted. *Faculty research:* Inter-ethnic relations, development, political policies.

University of Pennsylvania, School of Arts and Sciences, Graduate Group in Anthropology, Philadelphia, PA 19104. Offers AM, MS, PhD. *Faculty:* 24 full-time (10 women), 15 part-time/adjunct (8 women). *Students:* 51 full-time (28 women), 11 part-time (9 women); includes 1 Asian, non-Hispanic/Latino; 2 Hispanic/Latino, 7 international. 243 applicants, 7% accepted, 7 enrolled. In 2010, 6 master's, 7 doctorates awarded. Terminal master's awarded for partial completion of doctoral program. *Degree requirements:* For master's, thesis, final exam; for doctorate, one foreign language, thesis/dissertation, fieldwork, preliminary and final exams. *Entrance requirements:* For doctorate, GRE General Test. Additional exam requirements/recommendations for international students: Required—TOEFL. *Application deadline:* For fall admission, 12/1 priority date for domestic students. Application fee: $70. *Expenses:* Tuition: Full-time $25,660; part-time $4758 per course. Required fees: $2152; $270 per course. Tuition and fees vary according to course load, degree level and program. *Financial support:* Fellowships, teaching assistantships, institutionally sponsored loans, scholarships/grants, traineeships, health care benefits, and unspecified assistantships available. Financial award application deadline: 12/15. *Unit head:* Robert W. Preucel, Department Chair, Anthropology, 215-898-9017, E-mail: rpreucel@sas.upenn.edu. *Application contact:* Robert W. Preucel, Department Chair, Anthropology, 215-898-9017, E-mail: rpreucel@sas.upenn.edu.

University of Pittsburgh, School of Arts and Sciences, Department of Anthropology, Pittsburgh, PA 15260. Offers MA, PhD. Part-time programs available. *Faculty:* 20 full-time (6 women), 3 part-time/adjunct (2 women). *Students:* 64 full-time (38 women), 4 part-time (2 women); includes 1 Black or African American, non-Hispanic/Latino; 3 Hispanic/Latino, 28 international. 144 applicants, 10% accepted, 11 enrolled. In 2010, 2 master's, 6 doctorates awarded. *Degree requirements:* For master's, one foreign language, thesis or alternative; for doctorate, one foreign language, thesis/dissertation. *Entrance requirements:* For master's and doctorate, GRE General Test. Additional exam requirements/recommendations for international students: Required—TOEFL (minimum score 550 paper-based; 213 computer-based), IELTS (minimum score 5.5). *Application deadline:* For fall admission, 1/7 priority date for domestic and international students. Applications are processed on a rolling basis. Application fee: $50. Electronic applications accepted. *Expenses:* Tuition, state resident: full-time $17,304; part-time $701 per credit. Tuition, nonresident: full-time $29,554; part-time $1210 per credit. Required fees: $740; $214 per term. Tuition and fees vary according to program. *Financial support:* In 2010–11, 58 students received support, including 25 fellowships with full tuition reimbursements available (averaging $18,546 per year), 3 research assistantships with full tuition reimbursements available (averaging $6,335 per year), 30 teaching assistantships with full tuition reimbursements available (averaging $15,520 per year); career-related internships or fieldwork, Federal Work-Study, scholarships/grants, health care benefits, tuition waivers (full and partial), and unspecified assistantships also available. Support available to part-time students. Financial award application deadline: 1/7. *Faculty research:* Conflict studies; ethnicity, nationalism, and the state; origins of complex societies; Latin American archaeology; human evolutionary biology. Total annual research expenditures: $46,692. *Unit head:* Dr. Joseph S. Alter, Chair, 412-648-7530, Fax: 412-648-7535, E-mail: jsalter@pitt.edu. *Application contact:* Phyllis J. Deasy, Graduate Coordinator, 412-648-7504, Fax: 412-648-7535, E-mail: pdeasy@pitt.edu.

University of Regina, Faculty of Graduate Studies and Research, Faculty of Arts, Department of Anthropology, Regina, SK S4S 0A2, Canada. Offers MA. Part-time programs available. *Faculty:* 5 full-time (2 women). *Students:* 5 full-time (2 women). 2 applicants, 50% accepted. *Degree requirements:* For master's, thesis. *Entrance requirements:* For master's, writing sample.

Additional exam requirements/recommendations for international students: Required—TOEFL (minimum score 580 paper-based; 80 iBT). *Application deadline:* Applications are processed on a rolling basis. Application fee: $100. Electronic applications accepted. Tuition and fees charges are reported in Canadian dollars. *Expenses:* Tuition, area resident: Full-time $3244.50 Canadian dollars; part-time $180.25 Canadian dollars per credit hour. International tuition: $4744.50 Canadian dollars full-time. Required fees: $494 Canadian dollars; $115.25 Canadian dollars per credit hour. $115.25 Canadian dollars per semester. Tuition and fees vary according to program. *Financial support:* Fellowships, research assistantships, teaching assistantships, scholarships/grants available. Financial award application deadline: 6/15. *Unit head:* Dr. Carlos Londono Sulkin, Head, 306-585-5405, Fax: 306-585-4815, E-mail: carlos.londono@uregina.ca. *Application contact:* Tobias Sperlich, Graduate Program Coordinator, 306-585-4773, Fax: 306-585-4815, E-mail: tobias.sperlich@uregina.ca.

University of Saskatchewan, College of Graduate Studies and Research, College of Arts and Sciences, Department of Religious Studies and Anthropology, Saskatoon, SK S7N 5A2, Canada. Offers MA. *Degree requirements:* For master's, thesis. *Entrance requirements:* Additional exam requirements/recommendations for international students: Required—TOEFL (minimum score 80 iBT); Recommended—IELTS (minimum score 6.5). Electronic applications accepted.

University of South Africa, College of Human Sciences, Pretoria, South Africa. Offers adult education (M Ed); African languages (MA, PhD); African politics (MA, PhD); Afrikaans (MA, PhD); ancient history (MA, PhD); ancient Near Eastern studies (MA, PhD); anthropology (MA, PhD); applied linguistics (MA); Arabic (MA, PhD); archaeology (MA); art history (MA); Biblical archaeology (MA); Biblical studies (M Th, D Th, PhD); Christian spirituality (M Th, D Th); church history (M Th, D Th); classical studies (MA, PhD); clinical psychology (MA); communication (MA, PhD); comparative education (M Ed, Ed D); consulting psychology (D Admin, D Com, PhD); curriculum studies (M Ed, Ed D); development studies (M Admin, MA, D Admin, PhD); didactics (M Ed, Ed D); education (M Tech); education management (M Ed, Ed D); educational psychology (M Ed); English (MA); environmental education (M Ed); French (MA, PhD); German (MA, PhD); Greek (MA); guidance and counseling (M Ed); health studies (MA, PhD), including health sciences education (MA), health services management (MA), medical and surgical nursing science (critical care general) (MA), midwifery and neonatal nursing science (MA), trauma and emergency care (MA); history (MA, PhD); history of education (Ed D); inclusive education (M Ed, Ed D); information and communications technology policy and regulation (MA); information science (MA, MIS, PhD); international politics (MA, PhD); Islamic studies (MA, PhD); Italian (MA, PhD); Judaica (MA, PhD); linguistics (MA, PhD); mathematical education (M Ed); mathematics education (MA); missiology (M Th, D Th); modern Hebrew (MA, PhD); musicology (MA, MMus, D Mus, PhD); natural science education (M Ed); New Testament (M Th, D Th); Old Testament (D Th); pastoral therapy (M Th, D Th); philosophy (MA); philosophy of education (M Ed, Ed D); politics (MA, PhD); Portuguese (MA, PhD); practical theology (M Th, D Th); psychology (MA, MS, PhD); psychology of education (M Ed, Ed D); public health (MA); religious studies (MA, D Th, PhD); Romance languages (MA); Russian (MA, PhD); Semitic languages (MA, PhD); social behavior studies in HIV/AIDS (MA); social science (mental health) (MA); social science in development studies (MA); social science in psychology (MA); social science in social work (MA); social science in sociology (MA); social work (MSW, DSW, PhD); socio-education (M Ed, Ed D); sociolinguistics (MA); sociology (MA, PhD); Spanish (MA, PhD); systematic theology (M Th, D Th); TESOL (teaching English to speakers of other languages) (MA); theological ethics (M Th, D Th); theory of literature (MA, PhD); urban ministries (D Th); urban ministry (M Th).

University of South Carolina, The Graduate School, College of Arts and Sciences, Department of Anthropology, Columbia, SC 29208. Offers MA, PhD. Terminal master's awarded for partial completion of doctoral program. *Degree requirements:* For master's, comprehensive exam, thesis; for doctorate, comprehensive exam, thesis/dissertation. *Entrance requirements:* For master's and doctorate, GRE General Test, letters of reference. Additional exam requirements/recommendations for international students: Required—TOEFL. Electronic applications accepted. *Faculty research:* Biocultural anthropology, archaeology, cultural anthropology.

University of Southern Mississippi, Graduate School, College of Arts and Letters, Department of Anthropology and Sociology, Hattiesburg, MS 39406-0001. Offers anthropology (MA). Part-time programs available. *Faculty:* 8 full-time (5 women). *Students:* 13 full-time (8 women), 15 part-time (11 women); includes 1 Hispanic/Latino; 1 Two or more races, non-Hispanic/Latino. Average age 33. 20 applicants, 55% accepted, 9 enrolled. In 2010, 2 master's awarded. *Degree requirements:* For master's, one foreign language, comprehensive exam, thesis (for some programs). *Entrance requirements:* For master's, GRE General Test, minimum GPA of 2.75 in last 2 years, 3.0 in field of study. Additional exam requirements/recommendations for international students: Required—TOEFL, IELTS. *Application deadline:* For fall admission, 3/15 priority date for domestic students, 3/1 for international students. Applications are processed on a rolling basis. Application fee: $50. *Financial support:* In 2010–11, 8 research assistantships with full tuition reimbursements (averaging $7,500 per year), 6 teaching assistantships with full tuition reimbursements (averaging $7,500 per year) were awarded; career-related internships or fieldwork, Federal Work-Study, institutionally sponsored loans, scholarships/grants, and unspecified assistantships also available. Financial award application deadline: 3/15; financial award applicants required to submit FAFSA. *Faculty research:* Archaeology of North America, historic archaeology, bioarchaeology, ethnography of Europe, ethnography of Africa. *Unit head:* Dr. Amy Miller, Chair, 601-266-4306, Fax: 601-266-6373. *Application contact:* Dr. Marie Danforth, Graduate Coordinator, 601-266-4306, Fax: 601-266-6373, E-mail: marie.danforth@usm.edu.

University of South Florida, Graduate School, College of Arts and Sciences, Department of Anthropology, Tampa, FL 33620-9951. Offers applied anthropology (MA, PhD). Part-time programs available. *Faculty:* 10 full-time (6 women), 1 (woman) part-time/adjunct. *Students:* 99 full-time (65 women), 66 part-time (49 women); includes 15 Black or African American, non-Hispanic/Latino; 1 American Indian or Alaska Native, non-Hispanic/Latino; 5 Asian, non-Hispanic/Latino; 17 Hispanic/Latino; 1 Two or more races, non-Hispanic/Latino, 6 international. Average age 32. 192 applicants, 34% accepted, 37 enrolled. In 2010, 11 master's, 8 doctorates awarded. *Degree requirements:* For master's, comprehensive exam, thesis; for doctorate, one foreign language, comprehensive exam, thesis/dissertation. *Entrance requirements:* For master's and doctorate, GRE General Test, minimum GPA of 3.2, 3 letters of recommendation. Additional exam requirements/recommendations for international students: Required—TOEFL (minimum score 550 paper-based; 213 computer-based). *Application deadline:* For fall admission, 1/15 for domestic students, 1/2 for international students. Application fee: $30. Electronic applications accepted. *Financial support:* In 2010–11, 15 research assistantships (averaging $13,042 per year), 55 teaching assistantships with partial tuition reimbursements (averaging $15,042 per year) were awarded; scholarships/grants and tuition waivers (partial) also available. Financial award application deadline: 1/15; financial award applicants required to submit FAFSA. *Faculty research:* Population genetics, biomedical anthropology, archaeology and culture resource management in the Americas, urban community issues, media and education. Total annual research expenditures: $2.3 million. *Unit head:* Dr. Elizabeth Bird, Chairperson, 813-974-0802, Fax: 813-974-2668, E-mail: ebird@cas.usf.edu. *Application contact:* Nancy Romero-Daza, Director, 813-974-1205, Fax: 813-974-2668, E-mail: daza@cas.usf.edu.

The University of Tennessee, Graduate School, College of Arts and Sciences, Department of Anthropology, Knoxville, TN 37996. Offers archaeology (MA, PhD); biological anthropology (MA, PhD); cultural anthropology (MA, PhD); zoo-archaeology (MA, PhD). *Degree requirements:* For master's, thesis; for doctorate, one foreign language, thesis/dissertation. *Entrance requirements:* For master's and doctorate, GRE General Test, minimum GPA of 2.7. Additional exam requirements/recommendations for international students: Required—TOEFL. Electronic applications accepted. *Expenses:* Tuition, state resident: full-time $7440; part-time $414 per credit hour. Tuition, nonresident: full-time $22,478; part-time $1250 per credit hour. Required fees: $922; $43 per credit hour. Tuition and fees vary according to program.

The University of Texas at Arlington, Graduate School, College of Liberal Arts, Department of Sociology and Anthropology, Program in Anthropology, Arlington, TX 79019. Offers MA. Part-time and evening/weekend programs available. *Faculty:* 5 full-time (3 women), 1 (woman) part-time/adjunct. *Students:* 5 full-time (4 women), 11 part-time (7 women); includes 5 minority (2 Black or African American, non-Hispanic/Latino; 1 American Indian or Alaska Native, non-Hispanic/Latino; 2 Hispanic/Latino). 6 applicants, 50% accepted, 2 enrolled. *Degree requirements:* For master's, comprehensive exam, thesis or alternative. *Entrance requirements:* For master's, GRE General Test, minimum GPA of 3.0, 3 letters of recommendation. Additional exam requirements/recommendations for international students: Required—TOEFL (minimum score 550 paper-based; 213 computer-based). *Application deadline:* For fall admission, 6/15 priority date for domestic students. Applications are processed on a rolling basis. Application fee: $35 ($50 for international students). Electronic applications accepted. *Expenses:* Tuition, state resident: full-time $7500. Tuition, nonresident: full-time $13,080. International tuition: $13,250 full-time. *Financial support:* In 2010–11, 1 fellowship (averaging $500 per year), 2 teaching assistantships (averaging $9,000 per year) were awarded; Federal Work-Study and institutionally sponsored loans also available. Financial award application deadline: 6/1; financial award applicants required to submit FAFSA. *Application contact:* Dr. Joci Ryan, Graduate Advisor, 817-272-3765, Fax: 817-272-3759, E-mail: jcryan@uta.edu.

The University of Texas at Austin, Graduate School, College of Liberal Arts, Department of Anthropology, Austin, TX 78712-1111. Offers archaeology (MA, PhD); folklore and public culture (MA, PhD); linguistic anthropology (MA, PhD); physical anthropology (MA, PhD); social anthropology (MA, PhD). Part-time programs available. Terminal master's awarded for partial completion of doctoral program. *Degree requirements:* For master's, thesis; for doctorate, one foreign language, thesis/dissertation. *Entrance requirements:* For master's and doctorate, GRE General Test. Additional exam requirements/recommendations for international students: Required—TOEFL. Electronic applications accepted.

The University of Texas at San Antonio, College of Liberal and Fine Arts, Department of Anthropology, San Antonio, TX 78249-0617. Offers MA, PhD. Part-time programs available. *Faculty:* 9 full-time (4 women), 1 (woman) part-time/adjunct. *Students:* 30 full-time (18 women), 34 part-time (23 women); includes 15 minority (1 Asian, non-Hispanic/Latino; 11 Hispanic/Latino; 3 Two or more races, non-Hispanic/Latino), 3 international. Average age 30. 45 applicants, 91% accepted, 25 enrolled. In 2010, 1 master's awarded. *Degree requirements:* For master's, one foreign language, comprehensive exam (for some programs), thesis (for some programs); for doctorate, comprehensive exam (for some programs), thesis/dissertation (for some programs). *Entrance requirements:* For master's, GRE General Test, minimum GPA of 3.0 during last 60 hours, 18 hours in major field; for doctorate, GRE. Additional exam requirements/recommendations for international students: Required—TOEFL (minimum score 500 paper-based; 173 computer-based; 61 iBT), IELTS (minimum score 5). *Application deadline:* For fall admission, 7/1 for domestic students, 4/1 for international students; for spring admission, 11/1 for domestic students, 9/1 for international students. Applications are processed on a rolling basis. Application fee: $45 ($80 for international students). Electronic applications accepted. *Expenses:* Tuition, state resident: full-time $4172; part-time $231.75 per credit hour. Tuition, nonresident: full-time $15,332; part-time $851.75 per credit hour. *Financial support:* In 2010–11, 15 students received support, including 15 research assistantships (averaging $15,074 per year), 13 teaching assistantships (averaging $7,569 per year); career-related internships or fieldwork, scholarships/grants, and unspecified assistantships also available. Support available to part-time students. *Faculty research:* Archaeology, ethnohistory, American social history, borderlands history, history of imperialism. Total annual research expenditures: $244,303. *Unit head:* Dr. Laura Levi, Interim Chair, 210-458-4075, Fax: 210-458-7811, E-mail: laura.levi@utsa.edu. *Application contact:* Veronica Ramirez, Assistant Dean of the Graduate School, 210-458-4330, Fax: 210-458-4332, E-mail: graduatestudies@utsa.edu.

University of Toronto, School of Graduate Studies, Social Sciences Division, Department of Anthropology, Toronto, ON M5S 1A1, Canada. Offers M Sc, MA, PhD. Part-time programs available. *Degree requirements:* For master's, research paper; for doctorate, one foreign language, thesis/dissertation, language exam, thesis defense. *Entrance requirements:* For master's, minimum B+ average, 5 full-year anthropology courses, 2 letters of reference, resume; for doctorate, minimum B+ average, master's degree in relevant area, resumé, 2 letters of reference. Additional exam requirements/recommendations for international students: Required—TOEFL (minimum score 580 paper-based), TWE (minimum score 5), Michigan English Language Assessment Battery (minimum score: 85), IELTS (minimum score: 7) or COPE (minimum score: 4).

University of Tulsa, Graduate School, College of Arts and Sciences, Department of Anthropology, Tulsa, OK 74104-3189. Offers MA, JD/MA. Part-time programs available. *Faculty:* 6 full-time (0 women). *Students:* 7 full-time (6 women), 2 part-time (both women); includes 1 minority (Hispanic/Latino). Average age 31. 9 applicants, 67% accepted, 6 enrolled. In 2010, 4 master's awarded. *Degree requirements:* For master's, thesis (for some programs). *Entrance requirements:* For master's, GRE General Test. Additional exam requirements/recommendations for international students: Required—TOEFL (minimum score 575 paper-based; 231 computer-based; 91 iBT), IELTS (minimum score 6.5). *Application deadline:* Applications are processed on a rolling basis. Application fee: $40. Electronic applications accepted. *Expenses:* Tuition: Full-time $16,902; part-time $939 per credit hour. Required fees: $1020; $4 per credit hour. Tuition and fees vary according to course load. *Financial support:* In 2010–11, 6 students received support, including 1 fellowship with full and partial tuition reimbursement available (averaging $14,000 per year), 1 research assistantship with full and partial tuition reimbursement available (averaging $11,942 per year), 4 teaching assistantships with full and partial tuition reimbursements available (averaging $11,942 per year); career-related internships or fieldwork, Federal Work-Study, scholarships/grants, health care benefits, tuition waivers (full and partial), and unspecified assistantships also available. Support available to part-time students. Financial award application deadline: 2/1; financial award applicants required to submit FAFSA. *Faculty research:* Archaeology, cultural anthropology, Native American studies. Total annual research expenditures: $23,073. *Unit head:* Dr. Michael Whalen, Chairperson, 918-631-2370, Fax: 918-631-2540, E-mail: michael-whalen@utulsa.edu. *Application contact:* Dr. George Odell, Advisor, 918-631-3082, Fax: 918-631-2540, E-mail: george-odell@utulsa.edu.

University of Tulsa, Graduate School, Program in Museum Science and Management, Tulsa, OK 74104-3189. Offers anthropology (MA); general (MA); history (MA); Native American (MA). Part-time programs available. *Faculty:* 9 full-time (1 woman). *Students:* 6 full-time (all women); includes 1 minority (Black or African American, non-Hispanic/Latino). Average age 29. 14 applicants, 86% accepted, 6 enrolled. *Degree requirements:* For master's, final semester internship or independent research project. *Entrance requirements:* For master's, GRE General Test. Additional exam requirements/recommendations for international students: Required—TOEFL (minimum score 575 paper-based; 231 computer-based; 91 iBT), IELTS (minimum score 6.5). *Application deadline:* Applications are processed on a rolling basis. Application fee: $40. Electronic applications accepted. *Expenses:* Tuition: Full-time $16,902; part-time $939 per credit hour. Required fees: $1020; $4 per credit hour. Tuition and fees vary according to course load. *Financial support:* In 2010–11, 4 students received support, including 1 research assistantship with full and partial tuition reimbursement available (averaging $5,504 per year), 3 teaching assistantships with full and partial tuition reimbursements available (averaging $13,040 per year); fellowships with full and partial tuition reimbursements available, career-related internships or fieldwork, Federal Work-Study, scholarships/grants, health care benefits, tuition waivers (full and partial), and unspecified assistantships also available. Support available to part-time students. Total annual research expenditures: $12,000. *Unit head:* Dr. Bob Pickering, Senior Curator, 918-596-2706, Fax: 918-596-2770, E-mail: bob-pickering@utulsa.edu. *Application contact:* Graduate School, 918-631-2336, Fax: 918-631-2156, E-mail: grad@utulsa.edu.

University of Utah, Graduate School, College of Humanities, Program in Middle East Studies, Salt Lake City, UT 84112. Offers anthropology (MA); Arabic (MA, PhD); Arabic and linguistics (MA, PhD); Hebrew (MA); history (MA, PhD); Persian (MA, PhD); political science (MA, PhD);

Anthropology

University of Utah (continued)
Turkish (MA). *Students:* 20 full-time (10 women), 15 part-time (5 women), 8 international. Average age 33. 28 applicants, 29% accepted, 3 enrolled. In 2010, 3 master's awarded. Terminal master's awarded for partial completion of doctoral program. *Degree requirements:* For master's, 2 foreign languages, comprehensive exam, thesis optional; for doctorate, 3 foreign languages, comprehensive exam, thesis/dissertation. *Entrance requirements:* For master's, GRE General Test, minimum GPA of 3.2; for doctorate, GRE General Test, MA in Middle East studies or equivalent, minimum GPA of 3.2. Additional exam requirements/recommendations for international students: Required—TOEFL (minimum score 580 paper-based; 237 computer-based; 92 iBT). *Application deadline:* For fall admission, 1/15 priority date for domestic and international students. Application fee: $55 ($65 for international students). Electronic applications accepted. *Expenses:* Tuition, area resident: Part-time $179.19 per credit hour. Tuition, state resident: full-time $4384. Tuition, nonresident: full-time $16,684; part-time $630.67 per credit hour. Required fees: $350 per semester. Tuition and fees vary according to course load, degree level and program. *Financial support:* In 2010–11, 17 students received support, including 11 fellowships with full tuition reimbursements available (averaging $14,000 per year), 6 teaching assistantships with full tuition reimbursements available (averaging $12,000 per year); unspecified assistantships also available. Financial award application deadline: 1/15. *Faculty research:* Arabic linguistics; Islamic studies; Middle Eastern history; political science; Judaic studies; anthropology; Arabic, Persian, Hebrew, and Turkish language and literature. *Application contact:* Peter von Sivers, Director of Graduate Studies, 801-581-8073, Fax: 801-581-6183, E-mail: peter.vonsivers@utah.edu.

University of Utah, Graduate School, College of Social and Behavioral Science, Department of Anthropology, Salt Lake City, UT 84112. Offers M Phil, MA, MS, PhD. Part-time programs available. *Faculty:* 17 full-time (6 women), 2 part-time/adjunct (1 woman). *Students:* 22 full-time (10 women), 19 part-time (12 women). Average age 35. 47 applicants, 45% accepted, 10 enrolled. In 2010, 15 master's awarded. *Degree requirements:* For master's, comprehensive exam, thesis optional; for doctorate, comprehensive exam (for some programs), thesis/dissertation. *Entrance requirements:* For master's, GRE General Test, minimum undergraduate GPA of 3.0; for doctorate, GRE General Test. Additional exam requirements/recommendations for international students: Required—TOEFL (minimum score 500 paper-based; 173 computer-based). *Application deadline:* For fall admission, 1/15 for domestic and international students. Application fee: $55 ($65 for international students). Electronic applications accepted. *Expenses:* Tuition, area resident: Part-time $179.19 per credit hour. Tuition, state resident: full-time $4384. Tuition, nonresident: full-time $16,684; part-time $630.67 per credit hour. Required fees: $350 per semester. Tuition and fees vary according to course load, degree level and program. *Financial support:* In 2010–11, 18 students received support, including 12 fellowships with full tuition reimbursements available, 1 research assistantship with full tuition reimbursement available (averaging $15,000 per year), 16 teaching assistantships with full tuition reimbursements available (averaging $11,000 per year); career-related internships or fieldwork, health care benefits, and unspecified assistantships also available. Financial award application deadline: 2/15. *Faculty research:* Evolutionary ecology, anthropological genetics, hunter-gatherers, North American archaeology. Total annual research expenditures: $370,527. *Unit head:* Dr. Elizabeth A. Cashdan, Chair, 801-581-6251, Fax: 801-581-6252, E-mail: cashdan@anthro.utah.edu. *Application contact:* Ursula E. Hanly, Administrative Assistant, 801-581-6251, Fax: 801-581-6252, E-mail: ursula@anthro.utah.edu.

University of Victoria, Faculty of Graduate Studies, Faculty of Social Sciences, Department of Anthropology, Victoria, BC V8W 2Y2, Canada. Offers MA. Part-time programs available. *Degree requirements:* For master's, comprehensive exam (for some programs), thesis (for some programs). *Entrance requirements:* For master's, minimum B+ average in last 2 years of undergraduate course work, writing sample. Additional exam requirements/recommendations for international students: Required—TOEFL (minimum score 575 paper-based; 233 computer-based), IELTS (minimum score 7).

University of Virginia, College and Graduate School of Arts and Sciences, Department of Anthropology, Charlottesville, VA 22903. Offers MA, PhD. *Faculty:* 20 full-time (10 women). *Students:* 53 full-time (36 women); includes 3 Black or African American, non-Hispanic/Latino; 1 Asian, non-Hispanic/Latino; 2 Hispanic/Latino, 8 international. Average age 30. 82 applicants, 13% accepted, 6 enrolled. In 2010, 12 master's, 7 doctorates awarded. *Degree requirements:* For master's, one foreign language, thesis; for doctorate, 2 foreign languages, thesis/dissertation. *Entrance requirements:* For master's and doctorate, GRE General Test, GRE Subject Test, 3 letters of recommendation. Additional exam requirements/recommendations for international students: Required—TOEFL (minimum score 600 paper-based; 250 computer-based; 90 iBT), IELTS (minimum score 7). *Application deadline:* For fall admission, 12/15 for domestic and international students. Applications are processed on a rolling basis. Application fee: $60. Electronic applications accepted. *Financial support:* Application deadline: 3/15. *Unit head:* Susan McKinnon, Chair, 434-924-7044, Fax: 434-924-1350. *Application contact:* Susan McKinnon, Chair, 434-924-7044, Fax: 434-924-1350.

University of Washington, Graduate School, College of Arts and Sciences, Department of Anthropology, Seattle, WA 98195. Offers MA, PhD. *Faculty:* 24 full-time (13 women), 21 part-time/adjunct (11 women). *Students:* 68 full-time (42 women), 13 part-time (8 women); includes 20 minority (4 Black or African American, non-Hispanic/Latino; 3 American Indian or Alaska Native, non-Hispanic/Latino; 5 Asian, non-Hispanic/Latino; 7 Hispanic/Latino; 1 Native Hawaiian or other Pacific Islander, non-Hispanic/Latino), 11 international. Average age 32. 110 applicants, 12% accepted, 8 enrolled. In 2010, 13 master's, 17 doctorates awarded. Terminal master's awarded for partial completion of doctoral program. *Degree requirements:* For master's, one foreign language, comprehensive exam (for some programs), thesis optional; for doctorate, one foreign language, comprehensive exam (for some programs), thesis/dissertation. *Entrance requirements:* For doctorate, GRE General Test, minimum GPA of 3.6. Additional exam requirements/recommendations for international students: Recommended—TOEFL (minimum score 500 paper-based; 173 computer-based; 61 iBT), IELTS (minimum score 6). *Application deadline:* For fall admission, 12/15 for domestic and international students. Application fee: $75. Electronic applications accepted. *Financial support:* In 2010–11, 2 fellowships with full tuition reimbursements (averaging $12,000 per year), 4 research assistantships with full tuition reimbursements (averaging $13,000 per year), 20 teaching assistantships with full tuition reimbursements (averaging $13,000 per year) were awarded; Federal Work-Study, institutionally sponsored loans, scholarships/grants, traineeships, health care benefits, and unspecified assistantships also available. Financial award application deadline: 1/15; financial award applicants required to submit FAFSA. *Faculty research:* Sociocultural anthropology, biocultural anthropology, archaeology, environmental anthropology, medical anthropology. *Unit head:* Dr. Bettina Shell-Duncan, Chair, 206-543-9607, Fax: 206-543-3285, E-mail: bsd@u.washington.edu. *Application contact:* Catherine M. Zeigler, Graduate Program Assistant, 206-685-1562, Fax: 206-543-3285, E-mail: gradanth@u.washington.edu.

University of Waterloo, Graduate Studies, Faculty of Arts, Department of Anthropology, Waterloo, ON N2L 3G1, Canada. Offers anthropology (MA); public issues (MA). *Entrance requirements:* Additional exam requirements/recommendations for international students: Required—TOEFL. Electronic applications accepted. *Faculty research:* Applied socio-cultural anthropology and archaeology.

The University of Western Ontario, Faculty of Graduate Studies, Social Sciences Division, Department of Anthropology, London, ON N6A 5B8, Canada. Offers MA, PhD. *Degree requirements:* For master's, thesis; for doctorate, thesis/dissertation. *Entrance requirements:* For master's, minimum B average, honors BA. Additional exam requirements/recommendations for international students: Required—TOEFL. Electronic applications accepted. *Faculty research:* Sociocultural anthropology, bioarchaeology, linguistics.

University of West Florida, College of Arts and Sciences: Arts, Division of Anthropology and Archaeology, Pensacola, FL 32514-5750. Offers anthropology (MA); historical archaeology (MA). *Faculty:* 6 full-time (2 women). *Students:* 37 full-time (22 women), 31 part-time (22 women); includes 1 Black or African American, non-Hispanic/Latino; 2 Asian, non-Hispanic/Latino; 3 Hispanic/Latino; 2 Two or more races, non-Hispanic/Latino. Average age 29. 59 applicants, 53% accepted, 13 enrolled. In 2010, 2 master's awarded. *Degree requirements:* For master's, internship or thesis. *Entrance requirements:* For master's, GRE, bachelor's degree in anthropology, minimum GPA of 3.0, 3 letters of recommendation, writing sample. Additional exam requirements/recommendations for international students: Required—TOEFL (minimum score 550 paper-based; 213 computer-based). *Application deadline:* For fall admission, 6/1 for domestic students, 5/15 for international students; for spring admission, 10/1 for domestic and international students. Application fee: $30. *Expenses:* Tuition, state resident: full-time $4982; part-time $208 per credit hour. Tuition, nonresident: full-time $20,059; part-time $836 per credit hour. Required fees: $1365; $57 per credit hour. *Financial support:* In 2010–11, 2 fellowships with partial tuition reimbursements (averaging $3,702 per year), 39 research assistantships with partial tuition reimbursements (averaging $3,500 per year), 7 teaching assistantships with partial tuition reimbursements (averaging $3,760 per year) were awarded; unspecified assistantships also available. Financial award application deadline: 4/15; financial award applicants required to submit FAFSA. *Unit head:* Dr. John Bratten, Interim Chair, 850-857-6278, E-mail: anthropology@uwf.edu. *Application contact:* Terry McCray, Assistant Director of Graduate Admissions, 850-473-7718, Fax: 850-473-7714, E-mail: gradadmissions@uwf.edu.

University of Wisconsin–Madison, Graduate School, College of Letters and Science, Department of Anthropology, Madison, WI 53706-1380. Offers archaeology (PhD); biological anthropology (PhD); cultural anthropology (PhD). Terminal master's awarded for partial completion of doctoral program. *Degree requirements:* For doctorate, thesis/dissertation. *Entrance requirements:* For doctorate, qualifying exam. Electronic applications accepted. *Expenses:* Tuition, state resident: full-time $9887; part-time $617.96 per credit. Tuition, nonresident: full-time $24,054; part-time $1503.40 per credit. Required fees: $67.63 per credit. Tuition and fees vary according to reciprocity agreements. *Faculty research:* Archaeology, biological, anthropology, cultural anthropology.

University of Wisconsin–Milwaukee, Graduate School, College of Letters and Sciences, Department of Anthropology, Milwaukee, WI 53201-0413. Offers anthropology (PhD); museum studies (Certificate). *Faculty:* 18 full-time (8 women). *Students:* 65 full-time (46 women), 31 part-time (24 women); includes 3 Black or African American, non-Hispanic/Latino; 2 Hispanic/Latino, 2 international. Average age 33. 51 applicants, 78% accepted, 16 enrolled. In 2010, 15 master's, 2 doctorates awarded. *Degree requirements:* For master's, thesis or alternative; for doctorate, one foreign language, thesis/dissertation, departmental qualifying exam. *Entrance requirements:* For master's, GRE; for doctorate, GRE, minimum GPA of 3.0, master's degree. Additional exam requirements/recommendations for international students: Required—TOEFL (minimum score 550 paper-based; 79 iBT), IELTS (minimum score 6.5). *Application deadline:* For fall admission, 1/1 priority date for domestic students; for spring admission, 9/1 for domestic students. Applications are processed on a rolling basis. Application fee: $56 ($96 for international students). *Financial support:* In 2010–11, 4 fellowships, 2 research assistantships, 26 teaching assistantships were awarded; career-related internships or fieldwork, unspecified assistantships, and project assistantships also available. Support available to part-time students. Financial award application deadline: 4/15; financial award applicants required to submit FAFSA. Total annual research expenditures: $752,931. *Unit head:* Patrick Gray, Representative, 414-229-4822, Fax: 414-229-5848, E-mail: jpgray@uwm.edu. *Application contact:* General Information Contact, 414-229-4982, Fax: 414-229-6967, E-mail: gradschool@uwm.edu.

University of Wyoming, College of Arts and Sciences, Department of Anthropology, Laramie, WY 82070. Offers MA, PhD. Part-time programs available. Terminal master's awarded for partial completion of doctoral program. *Degree requirements:* For master's, one foreign language, comprehensive exam, thesis optional; for doctorate, one foreign language, comprehensive exam, thesis/dissertation. *Entrance requirements:* For master's and doctorate, GRE General Test, minimum GPA of 3.0. Electronic applications accepted. *Faculty research:* Paleo-Indian archaeology, osteology, faunal analysis, lithic analysis, hunter-gatherers.

Vanderbilt University, Graduate School, Department of Anthropology, Nashville, TN 37240-1001. Offers MA, PhD. *Faculty:* 14 full-time (4 women). *Students:* 32 full-time (18 women), 1 (woman) part-time; includes 3 minority (2 Hispanic/Latino; 1 Two or more races, non-Hispanic/Latino). Average age 31. 67 applicants, 10% accepted, 6 enrolled. In 2010, 1 master's, 2 doctorates awarded. *Degree requirements:* For master's, comprehensive exam, thesis or alternative; for doctorate, one foreign language, comprehensive exam, thesis/dissertation, general, qualifying, and final exams. *Entrance requirements:* For master's and doctorate, GRE General Test. Additional exam requirements/recommendations for international students: Required—TOEFL (minimum score 570 paper-based; 230 computer-based; 88 iBT). *Application deadline:* For fall admission, 1/15 for domestic and international students. Application fee: $0. Electronic applications accepted. *Financial support:* Fellowships with full and partial tuition reimbursements, research assistantships with full tuition reimbursements, teaching assistantships with full tuition reimbursements, career-related internships or fieldwork, Federal Work-Study, institutionally sponsored loans, scholarships/grants, and health care benefits available. Financial award application deadline: 1/15; financial award applicants required to submit CSS PROFILE or FAFSA. *Faculty research:* Archaeology, ethnohistory and ethnography, epigraphy, conflict theory, Latin America. *Unit head:* Sally Miller, 615-343-6120, Fax: 615-343-0230, E-mail: sally.c.miller@vanderbilt.edu. *Application contact:* Dr. John W. Janusek, Director of Graduate Studies, 615-343-6120, Fax: 615-343-0230, E-mail: anthropology@vanderbilt.edu.

Washington State University, Graduate School, College of Liberal Arts, Department of Anthropology, Pullman, WA 99164. Offers archaeology (MA, PhD); cultural anthropology (MA, PhD); evolutionary anthropology (MA, PhD). Part-time programs available. *Faculty:* 20. *Students:* 59 full-time (36 women), 11 part-time (7 women); includes 1 Black or African American, non-Hispanic/Latino; 4 Asian, non-Hispanic/Latino; 1 Hispanic/Latino, 3 international. Average age 32. 93 applicants, 35% accepted, 15 enrolled. In 2010, 14 master's, 5 doctorates awarded. *Degree requirements:* For master's, comprehensive exam (for some programs), thesis, oral exam; for doctorate, comprehensive exam, thesis/dissertation, qualifying, oral, and written exams. *Entrance requirements:* For master's, GRE General Test, curriculum vitae, 3 references; for doctorate, GRE General Test, current curriculum vitae, statement of educational and professional goals, official transcripts of all post-secondary education, three references. Additional exam requirements/recommendations for international students: Required—TOEFL (minimum score 550 paper-based; 213 computer-based), IELTS. *Application deadline:* For fall admission, 1/10 priority date for domestic and international students; for spring admission, 7/1 priority date for domestic and international students. Applications are processed on a rolling basis. Application fee: $50. Electronic applications accepted. *Expenses:* Tuition, state resident: full-time $8552; part-time $443 per credit. Tuition, nonresident: full-time $21,650; part-time $1083 per credit. Required fees: $846. *Financial support:* In 2010–11, 5 research assistantships with full tuition reimbursements (averaging $13,917 per year), 34 teaching assistantships with full tuition reimbursements (averaging $13,056 per year) were awarded; fellowships, Federal Work-Study, scholarships/grants, health care benefits, and tuition waivers (partial) also available. Support available to part-time students. Financial award application deadline: 2/15; financial award applicants required to submit FAFSA. *Faculty research:* Western North America, including Alaska; international development; psychological anthropology; cultural ecology; medical anthropology; power and gender; evolutionary psychology; behavioral ecology; evolutionary cultural anthropology; evolutionary archaeology; paleoanthropology. Total annual research expenditures: $791,000. *Unit head:* Dr. William Andrefsky, Chair, 509-335-3441, Fax: 509-335-3999, E-mail: jmstrunk@wsu.edu. *Application contact:* Graduate School Admissions, 800-GRADWSU, Fax: 509-335-1949, E-mail: gradsch@wsu.edu.

Washington University in St. Louis, Graduate School of Arts and Sciences, Department of Anthropology, St. Louis, MO 63130-4899. Offers PhD. Terminal master's awarded for partial completion of doctoral program. *Degree requirements:* For doctorate, thesis/dissertation. *Entrance requirements:* For doctorate, GRE General Test. Additional exam requirements/

recommendations for international students: Required—TOEFL. Electronic applications accepted. *Faculty research:* Archaeology; physical anthropology; primate studies; sociocultural anthropology; medical anthropology.

Wayne State University, College of Liberal Arts and Sciences, Department of Anthropology, Detroit, MI 48202. Offers MA, PhD. *Faculty:* 20 full-time (10 women), 2 part-time/adjunct (0 women). *Students:* 33 full-time (23 women), 35 part-time (26 women); includes 18 minority (12 Black or African American, non-Hispanic/Latino; 6 Hispanic/Latino). Average age 38. 23 applicants, 61% accepted, 10 enrolled. In 2010, 10 master's, 4 doctorates awarded. *Degree requirements:* For master's, one foreign language, thesis; for doctorate, one foreign language, thesis/dissertation. *Entrance requirements:* Additional exam requirements/recommendations for international students: Required—TOEFL (minimum score 550 paper-based; 213 computer-based); Recommended—TWE (minimum score 6). *Application deadline:* For fall admission, 7/1 for domestic students, 6/1 for international students; for winter admission, 10/1 for international students; for spring admission, 2/1 for international students. Applications are processed on a rolling basis. Application fee: $30 ($50 for international students). Electronic applications accepted. *Expenses:* Tuition, state resident: full-time $7662; part-time $478.85 per credit hour. Tuition, nonresident: full-time $16,920; part-time $1057.55 per credit hour. Required fees: $571.20; $35.70 per credit hour. $188.05 per semester. Tuition and fees vary according to course load and program. *Financial support:* In 2010–11, 2 fellowships with tuition reimbursements (averaging $16,875 per year), 1 research assistantship (averaging $16,425 per year), 6 teaching assistantships (averaging $15,181 per year) were awarded. *Faculty research:* Business anthropology and organizational culture, African and African-American religions, medical anthropology, skeletal epidemiology and forensic anthropology, Latin American anthropology and archaeology. *Unit head:* Dr. Andrea Sankar, Chair, 313-577-2935, Fax: 313-577-5958, E-mail: aa7651@wayne.edu. *Application contact:* Beverly Fogelson, Graduate Director, 313-577-2935, E-mail: bfogelson@wayne.edu.

West Chester University of Pennsylvania, Office of Graduate Studies, College of Arts and Sciences, Department of Anthropology and Sociology, West Chester, PA 19383. Offers gerontology (Certificate); long term health care (MPA, MSA). Part-time and evening/weekend programs available. *Students:* 2 full-time (both women), 4 part-time (all women); includes 3 minority (all Black or African American, non-Hispanic/Latino). Average age 39. 3 applicants, 100% accepted, 1 enrolled. In 2010, 1 other advanced degree awarded. *Degree requirements:* For master's, comprehensive exam. *Entrance requirements:* For master's, MAT, GRE, or GMAT, interview, resume, 2 letters of reference. Additional exam requirements/recommendations for international students: Required—TOEFL (minimum score 550 paper-based; 213 computer-based; 80 iBT). *Application deadline:* For fall admission, 4/15 priority date for domestic students, 3/15 for international students; for spring admission, 10/15 for domestic students, 9/1 for international students. Applications are processed on a rolling basis. Application fee: $35. Electronic applications accepted. *Expenses:* Tuition, state resident: full-time $6966; part-time $387 per credit. Tuition, nonresident: full-time $11,146; part-time $619 per credit. Required fees: $1614.40; $133.24 per credit. Part-time tuition and fees vary according to campus/location. *Financial support:* Unspecified assistantships available. Support available to part-time students. Financial award application deadline: 2/15; financial award applicants required to submit FAFSA. *Faculty research:* West African communities in the U. S., life-long learning and distance education, comparative religions. *Unit head:* Dr. Douglas McConatha, Chair and Graduate Coordinator, 610-436-2556, E-mail: dmcconatha@wcupa.edu. *Application contact:* Dr. Douglas McConatha, Chair and Graduate Coordinator, 610-436-2556, E-mail: dmcconatha@wcupa.edu.

Western Kentucky University, Graduate Studies, Potter College of Arts and Letters, Department of Folk Studies and Anthropology, Bowling Green, KY 42101. Offers folk studies (MA). *Degree requirements:* For master's, comprehensive exam, thesis optional, written exam. *Entrance requirements:* For master's, GRE General Test, minimum GPA of 3.0. Additional exam requirements/recommendations for international students: Required—TOEFL (minimum score 555 paper-based; 213 computer-based; 79 iBT). *Faculty research:* Public folklore, folklore and education, vernacular belief, music and culture, historic presentation.

Western Michigan University, Graduate College, College of Arts and Sciences, Department of Anthropology, Kalamazoo, MI 49008. Offers MA. *Degree requirements:* For master's, comprehensive exam, thesis, written exams.

Western Washington University, Graduate School, College of Humanities and Social Sciences, Department of Anthropology, Bellingham, WA 98225-5996. Offers MA. Part-time programs available. *Degree requirements:* For master's, thesis. *Entrance requirements:* For master's, GRE General Test, minimum GPA of 3.0 in last 60 semester hours or last 90 quarter hours. Additional exam requirements/recommendations for international students: Required—TOEFL (minimum score 567 paper-based; 227 computer-based). Electronic applications accepted. *Faculty research:* Peoples and culture of the Pacific Rim; prehistory of North America; applied health; community-based action research; globalization and human rights.

Wichita State University, Graduate School, Fairmount College of Liberal Arts and Sciences, Department of Anthropology, Wichita, KS 67260. Offers MA. Part-time programs available. *Students:* 22 applicants. *Entrance requirements:* For master's, minimum GPA of 2.75 in last 60 hours and 3.0 in anthropology. *Unit head:* Dr. Peer H. Moore-Jansen, Chair, 316-978-3195, E-mail: pmojan@wichita.edu. *Application contact:* Dr. David Hughes, Graduate Coordinator, 316-978-3195, E-mail: david.hughes@wichita.edu.

Yale University, Graduate School of Arts and Sciences, Department of Anthropology, New Haven, CT 06520. Offers M Phil, MA, PhD. *Degree requirements:* For doctorate, thesis/dissertation. *Entrance requirements:* For master's and doctorate, GRE General Test. *Faculty research:* Linguistics, national identity.

York University, Faculty of Graduate Studies, Faculty of Arts, Program in Social Anthropology, Toronto, ON M3J 1P3, Canada. Offers MA, PhD. Part-time programs available. *Degree requirements:* For master's, thesis or alternative; for doctorate, comprehensive exam, thesis/dissertation. Electronic applications accepted.

Applied Social Research

American University, College of Arts and Sciences, Department of Sociology, Washington, DC 22016-8072. Offers social research (Certificate); sociology (MA). Part-time and evening/weekend programs available. *Faculty:* 15 full-time (10 women), 4 part-time/adjunct (2 women). *Students:* 15 full-time (14 women), 26 part-time (23 women); includes 20 minority (13 Black or African American, non-Hispanic/Latino; 2 Asian, non-Hispanic/Latino; 5 Hispanic/Latino), 2 international. Average age 36. 35 applicants, 69% accepted, 12 enrolled. In 2010, 6 master's awarded. *Degree requirements:* For master's, comprehensive exam, thesis or alternative, tool of research examination. *Entrance requirements:* For master's, GRE; for Certificate, bachelor's degree. Additional exam requirements/recommendations for international students: Required—TOEFL. *Application deadline:* For fall admission, 2/1 for domestic students. Application fee: $80. *Financial support:* Fellowships, research assistantships with full and partial tuition reimbursements, teaching assistantships with full and partial tuition reimbursements, career-related internships or fieldwork, Federal Work-Study, institutionally sponsored loans, tuition waivers (full and partial), and unspecified assistantships available. Support available to part-time students. Financial award application deadline: 2/1; financial award applicants required to submit FAFSA. *Faculty research:* Gender, race, development, applied social policy, political economy. *Unit head:* Dr. Kim M. Blankenship, Chair, 202-885-6211, Fax: 202-885-2477, E-mail: blankens@american.edu. *Application contact:* Dr. Kim M. Blankenship, Chair, 202-885-6211, Fax: 202-885-2477, E-mail: blankens@american.edu.

California State University, Dominguez Hills, College of Natural and Behavioral Sciences, Program in Sociology, Carson, CA 90747-0001. Offers social research (Certificate); sociology (MA). Part-time and evening/weekend programs available. *Faculty:* 3 full-time (all women), 3 part-time/adjunct (1 woman). *Students:* 26 full-time (20 women), 39 part-time (28 women); includes 32 Black or African American, non-Hispanic/Latino; 1 Asian, non-Hispanic/Latino; 18 Hispanic/Latino; 1 Native Hawaiian or other Pacific Islander, non-Hispanic/Latino. Average age 38. 46 applicants, 67% accepted, 16 enrolled. In 2010, 17 master's awarded. *Degree requirements:* For master's, comprehensive exam, thesis. *Entrance requirements:* For master's and Certificate, minimum GPA of 2.85. *Application deadline:* For fall admission, 6/1 for domestic students. Application fee: $55. *Faculty research:* Community studies, social movements, criminology. *Unit head:* Dr. Clare Weber, Chair, 310-243-3458, E-mail: cweber@csudh.edu. *Application contact:* Brandy McLelland, Interim Director, Student Information Services, 310-243-3645, E-mail: bmclelland@csudh.edu.

Concordia University, School of Theology, Irvine, CA 92612-3299. Offers Christian leadership (MA); research in theology (MA); theology and culture (MA). Part-time and evening/weekend programs available. *Faculty:* 8 full-time (1 woman), 2 part-time/adjunct (0 women). *Students:* 30 full-time (3 women), 7 part-time (3 women); includes 5 minority (1 Black or African American, non-Hispanic/Latino; 1 Asian, non-Hispanic/Latino; 3 Hispanic/Latino), 4 international. Average age 34. 11 applicants, 55% accepted, 5 enrolled. In 2010, 2 master's awarded. *Degree requirements:* For master's, project/thesis or vicarage. *Entrance requirements:* For master's, official college transcript(s), statement of intent, 2 references, graduate health form, interview. Additional exam requirements/recommendations for international students: Required—TOEFL. *Application deadline:* For fall admission, 7/1 priority date for domestic students, 6/1 for international students; for spring admission, 11/30 priority date for domestic students, 10/1 for international students. Applications are processed on a rolling basis. Application fee: $50 ($125 for international students). Electronic applications accepted. *Expenses:* Contact institution. *Financial support:* Scholarships/grants and unspecified assistantships available. Financial award applicants required to submit FAFSA. *Unit head:* Rev. Dr. James Bachman, Dean of Graduate Studies, 949-214-3387, E-mail: james.bachman@cui.edu. *Application contact:* Carrie Donohoe, Christ College Program Coordinator, 949-214-3389, E-mail: carrie.donohoe@cui.edu.

Hofstra University, College of Liberal Arts and Sciences, Program in Applied Social Research and Public Policy, Hempstead, NY 11549. Offers MA. Part-time and evening/weekend programs available. *Faculty:* 6 full-time (3 women). *Students:* 8 full-time (6 women), 2 part-time (1 woman); includes 4 minority (2 Black or African American, non-Hispanic/Latino; 2 Hispanic/Latino), 2 international. Average age 28. 6 applicants, 100% accepted, 5 enrolled. In 2010, 1 master's awarded. *Degree requirements:* For master's, comprehensive exam, thesis optional, internship. *Entrance requirements:* For master's, GRE, interview; essay; minimum GPA of 3.0. Additional exam requirements/recommendations for international students: Required—TOEFL (minimum score 550 paper-based; 213 computer-based; 80 iBT). *Application deadline:* Applications are processed on a rolling basis. Application fee: $70 ($75 for international students). Electronic applications accepted. *Expenses:* Tuition: Full-time $18,000; part-time $1000 per credit hour. Required fees: $970; $145 per term. Tuition and fees vary according to program. *Financial support:* In 2010–11, 4 students received support, including 3 fellowships with full and partial tuition reimbursements available (averaging $3,667 per year), 1 research assistantship with full and partial tuition reimbursement available (averaging $167 per year); Federal Work-Study, institutionally sponsored loans, scholarships/grants, tuition waivers (full and partial), unspecified assistantships, and Scholarships also available. Support available to part-time students. Financial award applicants required to submit FAFSA. *Faculty research:* Housing policy, immigration, labor economic policy, education policy, health care policy. *Unit head:* Dr. Marc Silver, Program Director, 516-463-5640, Fax: 516-463-6250, E-mail: socmls@hofstra.edu. *Application contact:* Carol Drummer, Dean of Graduate Admissions, 516-463-4876, Fax: 516-463-4664, E-mail: gradstudent@hofstra.edu.

Hunter College of the City University of New York, Graduate School, School of Arts and Sciences, Department of Sociology, Program in Applied Social Research, New York, NY 10021-5085. Offers MS. Part-time and evening/weekend programs available. *Faculty:* 5 full-time (0 women), 1 part-time/adjunct (0 women). *Students:* 19 full-time (14 women), 26 part-time (18 women); includes 1 American Indian or Alaska Native, non-Hispanic/Latino; 10 Hispanic/Latino, 4 international. Average age 28. 38 applicants, 76% accepted, 18 enrolled. In 2010, 11 master's awarded. *Degree requirements:* For master's, internship, research reports. *Entrance requirements:* For master's, GRE General Test or GMAT, 3 credits of course work in statistics, research methods, background in sociology or related social science. Additional exam requirements/recommendations for international students: Required—TOEFL. *Application deadline:* For fall admission, 4/1 for domestic students, 2/1 for international students; for spring admission, 11/1 for domestic students, 9/1 for international students. Applications are processed on a rolling basis. Application fee: $125. *Financial support:* Fellowships, research assistantships, teaching assistantships, career-related internships or fieldwork, Federal Work-Study, institutionally sponsored loans, scholarships/grants, and tuition waivers (full and partial) available. Support available to part-time students. *Faculty research:* Consumer behavior, new electronic media, voting behavior, policy analysis, sociomedicine. *Unit head:* Dr. Joong-Hwan Oh, Director, 212-772-5643, E-mail: goh@hunter.cuny.edu. *Application contact:* Prof. Howard Lune, Advisor, 212-772-5641, Fax: 212-772-5581, E-mail: hlune@hunter.cuny.edu.

Laurentian University, School of Graduate Studies and Research, Programme in Sociology, Sudbury, ON P3E 2C6, Canada. Offers applied social research (MA). Part-time programs available. *Entrance requirements:* For master's, honors degree in sociology or equivalent. *Faculty research:* Work foundations, managing AIDS organization, tracking laid-off mine workers.

The New School: A University, The New School for Social Research, New York, NY 10003. Offers M Phil, MA, MS, DS Sc, PhD. Part-time and evening/weekend programs available. Terminal master's awarded for partial completion of doctoral program. *Degree requirements:* For master's, variable foreign language requirement, exam or thesis; for doctorate, variable foreign language requirement, comprehensive exam, thesis/dissertation, qualifying exam. *Entrance requirements:* For master's, GRE General Test; for doctorate, GRE General Test, MA. Additional exam requirements/recommendations for international students: Required—TOEFL (minimum score 600 paper-based; 250 computer-based; 100 iBT). Electronic applications accepted. *Expenses:* Contact institution. *Faculty research:* Civil society and democracy, international movements of refugees, minority use of health services, memory, morality and genetics.

Portland State University, Graduate Studies, Graduate School of Social Work, Portland, OR 97207-0751. Offers social work (MSW); social work and social research (PhD). *Accreditation:* CSWE (one or more programs are accredited). Part-time programs available. *Faculty:* 35

Applied Social Research

Portland State University (continued)
full-time (24 women), 22 part-time/adjunct (15 women). *Students:* 393 full-time (313 women), 168 part-time (131 women); includes 124 minority (29 Black or African American, non-Hispanic/Latino; 13 American Indian or Alaska Native, non-Hispanic/Latino; 24 Asian, non-Hispanic/Latino; 43 Hispanic/Latino; 2 Native Hawaiian or other Pacific Islander, non-Hispanic/Latino; 13 Two or more races, non-Hispanic/Latino), 4 international. Average age 35. 598 applicants, 54% accepted, 235 enrolled. In 2010, 158 master's, 4 doctorates awarded. *Degree requirements:* For doctorate, comprehensive exam, thesis/dissertation, residency. *Entrance requirements:* For master's, minimum GPA of 3.0 in upper-division course work or 2.75 overall; for doctorate, GRE General Test, 4 references. Additional exam requirements/recommendations for international students: Required—TOEFL (minimum score 550 paper-based; 213 computer-based). *Application deadline:* For fall admission, 2/1 for domestic and international students. Application fee: $50. *Expenses:* Tuition, state resident: full-time $8505; part-time $315 per credit. Tuition, nonresident: full-time $13,284; part-time $492 per credit. Required fees: $1482; $21 per credit. $99 per term. One-time fee: $120. Part-time tuition and fees vary according to course load and program. *Financial support:* In 2010–11, 10 research assistantships with full tuition reimbursements (averaging $11,972 per year), 1 teaching assistantship with full tuition reimbursement (averaging $13,692 per year) were awarded; career-related internships or fieldwork, Federal Work-Study, scholarships/grants, tuition waivers (partial), and unspecified assistantships also available. Support available to part-time students. Financial award application deadline: 3/1; financial award applicants required to submit FAFSA. *Faculty research:* Child welfare; child mental health; social welfare policies and services; work, family, and dependent care; adult mental health. Total annual research expenditures: $10.5 million. *Unit head:* Dr. Kristine E. Nelson, Dean, 503-725-4712, Fax: 503-725-5545, E-mail: nelsonk@pdx.edu. *Application contact:* Janet Putnam, Director of Student Affairs, 503-725-4712, Fax: 503-725-5545, E-mail: putnamj@pdx.edu.

University of California, Los Angeles, Graduate Division, School of Public Affairs, Los Angeles, CA 90095. Offers MA, MPP, MSW, PhD, JD/MA, JD/MSW, MA/MA, MBA/MA, MD/PhD. *Accreditation:* CSWE. *Degree requirements:* For doctorate, thesis/dissertation, oral and written qualifying exams. *Entrance requirements:* For master's, minimum GPA of 3.0; for doctorate, minimum undergraduate GPA of 3.0. Additional exam requirements/recommendations for international students: Required—TOEFL. Electronic applications accepted.

Virginia Commonwealth University, Graduate School, College of Humanities and Sciences, Wilder School of Government and Public Affairs, Department of Sociology, Richmond, VA 23284-9005. Offers applied social research (CASR); sociology (MS). *Students:* 12 full-time (8 women), 9 part-time (4 women); includes 5 minority (2 Black or African American, non-Hispanic/Latino; 2 Hispanic/Latino; 1 Two or more races, non-Hispanic/Latino), 2 international. 14 applicants, 86% accepted, 8 enrolled. In 2010, 9 master's awarded. *Degree requirements:* For master's, thesis optional. *Entrance requirements:* For master's, GRE General Test. Additional exam requirements/recommendations for international students: Required—TOEFL (minimum score 600 paper-based; 250 computer-based; 100 iBT); Recommended—IELTS (minimum score 6.5). *Application deadline:* For fall admission, 7/15 for domestic students; for spring admission, 10/1 for domestic students. Application fee: $50. Electronic applications accepted. *Expenses:* Tuition, state resident: full-time $4308; part-time $479 per credit hour. Tuition, nonresident: full-time $8942; part-time $994 per credit hour. Required fees: $2000; $85 per credit hour. Tuition and fees vary according to course level, course load, degree level, campus/location and program. *Financial support:* Teaching assistantships, career-related internships or fieldwork, Federal Work-Study, institutionally sponsored loans, and tuition waivers (full and partial) available. Support available to part-time students. *Unit head:* Dr. Niraj Verma, Director, L. Douglas Wilder School of Government and Public Affairs, 804-827-0776, E-mail: nverma2@vcu.edu. *Application contact:* Dr. Sarah Jane Brubaker, Program Chair, 804-827-2400, Fax: 804-828-1027, E-mail: sbrubaker@vcu.edu.

West Virginia University, Eberly College of Arts and Sciences, School of Applied Social Sciences, Department of Sociology, Morgantown, WV 26506. Offers applied social research (MA). Part-time programs available. *Degree requirements:* For master's, thesis or alternative. *Entrance requirements:* For master's, GRE General Test, minimum GPA of 2.75. Additional exam requirements/recommendations for international students: Required—TOEFL. *Faculty research:* Applied sociology, stratification, social/complex organization, research methodology criminology.

Archaeology

American University of Beirut, Graduate Programs, Faculty of Arts and Sciences, Beirut, Lebanon. Offers anthropology (MA); Arabic language and literature (MA); archaeology (MA); biology (MS); chemistry (MS); computational science (MS); computer science (MS); economics (MA); education (MA); English language (MA); English literature (MA); environmental policy planning (MSES); financial economics (MAFE); geology (MS); history (MA); mathematics (MA, MS); Middle Eastern studies (MA); philosophy (MA); physics (MS); political studies (MA); psychology (MA); public administration (MA); sociology (MA); statistics (MA, MS). Part-time programs available. *Faculty:* 229 full-time (98 women), 136 part-time/adjunct (79 women). *Students:* 158 full-time (104 women), 263 part-time (171 women). Average age 25. 356 applicants, 59% accepted, 127 enrolled. In 2010, 57 master's awarded. *Degree requirements:* For master's, one foreign language, comprehensive exam, thesis (for some programs). *Entrance requirements:* For master's, GRE, letter of recommendation. Additional exam requirements/recommendations for international students: Required—TOEFL (minimum score 600 paper-based; 250 computer-based; 97 iBT), IELTS (minimum score 7). *Application deadline:* For fall admission, 4/30 for domestic and international students; for spring admission, 11/1 for domestic and international students. Application fee: $50. *Expenses:* Tuition: Full-time $12,294; part-time $683 per credit. Required fees: $499; $499 per credit. Tuition and fees vary according to course load and program. *Financial support:* In 2010–11, 33 students received support. Career-related internships or fieldwork, institutionally sponsored loans, scholarships/grants, health care benefits, and unspecified assistantships available. Financial award application deadline: 2/4; financial award applicants required to submit FAFSA. *Faculty research:* Modern and contemporary world theatre; mineralogy, petrology, and geochemistry; cell differentiation and transformation; combinatorial technologies; philosophy of action; continental philosophy; Phoenician epigraphy; nascent complex societies and urbanism; the economies of the Arab world; environmental economics; tectonophysics; host-parasite interactions; innate immunity; insect-plant interactions; history of the Ottoman archives; decentralization; transparency and corruption. Total annual research expenditures: $622,243. *Unit head:* Dr. Patrick McGreevy, Dean, 961-137-4374 Ext. 3800, Fax: 961-174-4461, E-mail: pm07@aub.edu.lb. *Application contact:* Dr. Salim Kanaan, Director, Admissions Office, 961-135-0000 Ext. 2594, Fax: 961-175-0775, E-mail: sk00@aub.edu.lb.

Arizona State University, College of Liberal Arts and Sciences, School of Human Evolution and Social Change, Tempe, AZ 85287-2402. Offers anthropology (PhD); anthropology (archaeology) (PhD); anthropology (bioarchaeology) (PhD); anthropology (museum studies) (MA); anthropology (physical) (PhD); applied mathematics for the life and social sciences (PhD); environmental social science (PhD); environmental social science (urbanism) (PhD); global health (MA); global health (health and culture) (PhD); global health (urbanism) (PhD); immigration studies (Graduate Certificate). *Faculty:* 52 full-time (19 women), 4 part-time/adjunct (2 women). *Students:* 127 full-time (77 women), 52 part-time (37 women); includes 43 minority (8 Black or African American, non-Hispanic/Latino; 4 American Indian or Alaska Native, non-Hispanic/Latino; 4 Asian, non-Hispanic/Latino; 26 Hispanic/Latino; 1 Two or more races, non-Hispanic/Latino), 19 international. Average age 32. 250 applicants, 24% accepted, 25 enrolled. In 2010, 8 master's, 18 doctorates, 7 other advanced degrees awarded. Terminal master's awarded for partial completion of doctoral program. *Degree requirements:* For master's, thesis or alternative, interactive Program of Study (iPOS) submitted before completing 50 percent of required credit hours; for doctorate, comprehensive exam, thesis/dissertation, interactive Program of Study (iPOS) submitted before completing 50 percent of required credit hours. *Entrance requirements:* For master's and doctorate, GRE, minimum GPA of 3.0 or equivalent in last 2 years of work leading to bachelor's degree. Additional exam requirements/recommendations for international students: Required—TOEFL, IELTS, or Pearson Test of English. *Application deadline:* For fall admission, 12/15 for domestic students, 12/1 for international students. Applications are processed on a rolling basis. Application fee: $70 ($90 for international students). Electronic applications accepted. *Expenses:* Tuition, state resident: full-time $8510; part-time $608 per credit. Tuition, nonresident: full-time $16,542; part-time $919 per credit. Required fees: $339; $110 per credit. Part-time tuition and fees vary according to course load. *Financial support:* In 2010–11, 30 research assistantships with full and partial tuition reimbursements (averaging $14,993 per year), 63 teaching assistantships with full and partial tuition reimbursements (averaging $15,266 per year) were awarded; fellowships with full tuition reimbursements, career-related internships or fieldwork, Federal Work-Study, institutionally sponsored loans, scholarships/grants, and tuition waivers (full and partial) also available. Financial award application deadline: 3/1; financial award applicants required to submit FAFSA. Total annual research expenditures: $3.8 million. *Unit head:* Dr. Sander van der Leeuw, Director, 480-965-6214, E-mail: vanderle@asu.edu. *Application contact:* Graduate Admissions, 480-965-6113.

Boston University, Graduate School of Arts and Sciences, Department of Archaeology, Boston, MA 02215. Offers archaeological heritage management (MA); archaeology (MA, PhD); geoarchaeology (MA). *Students:* 58 full-time (33 women), 3 part-time (1 woman); includes 5 minority (1 Black or African American, non-Hispanic/Latino; 1 Asian, non-Hispanic/Latino; 1 Hispanic/Latino; 2 Two or more races, non-Hispanic/Latino), 6 international. Average age 30. 107 applicants, 30% accepted, 9 enrolled. In 2010, 2 master's, 1 doctorate awarded. Terminal master's awarded for partial completion of doctoral program. *Degree requirements:* For master's, one foreign language, comprehensive exam, thesis or alternative; for doctorate, 2 foreign languages, comprehensive exam, thesis/dissertation. *Entrance requirements:* For master's, GRE General Test, 3 letters of recommendation; for doctorate, GRE General Test, scholarly writing sample, 3 letters of recommendation. Additional exam requirements/recommendations for international students: Required—TOEFL (minimum score 550 paper-based; 213 computer-based). *Application deadline:* For fall admission, 1/15 for domestic and international students. Application fee: $70. *Expenses:* Tuition: Full-time $39,314; part-time $1228 per credit. Required fees: $40 per semester. *Financial support:* In 2010–11, 26 students received support, including 2 fellowships with full tuition reimbursements available (averaging $19,300 per year), 1 research assistantship with full tuition reimbursement available (averaging $18,800 per year), 7 teaching assistantships with full tuition reimbursements available (averaging $18,800 per year); career-related internships or fieldwork, Federal Work-Study, and unspecified assistantships also available. Support available to part-time students. Financial award application deadline: 1/15; financial award applicants required to submit FAFSA. *Unit head:* Ricardo Elia, Chairman, 617-353-3415, Fax: 617-353-6800, E-mail: elia@bu.edu. *Application contact:* Evelyn Labree, Department Administrator, 617-358-1640, Fax: 617-353-6800, E-mail: labree@bu.edu.

Brown University, Graduate School, Department of Egyptology and Ancient Western Asian Studies, Providence, RI 02912. Offers AM, PhD. *Degree requirements:* For master's, one foreign language, thesis, final exam; for doctorate, 2 foreign languages, comprehensive exam, thesis/dissertation. *Entrance requirements:* For master's and doctorate, GRE General Test.

Brown University, Graduate School, Joukowsky Institute for Archaeology and the Ancient World, Providence, RI 02912. Offers PhD. *Degree requirements:* For doctorate, thesis/dissertation.

Bryn Mawr College, Graduate School of Arts and Sciences, Department of Classical and Near Eastern Archaeology, Bryn Mawr, PA 19010-2899. Offers MA, PhD. Part-time programs available. *Faculty:* 5. *Students:* 17 full-time (11 women), 6 part-time (5 women), 4 international. Average age 29. 44 applicants, 16% accepted, 3 enrolled. In 2010, 4 master's, 1 doctorate awarded. *Degree requirements:* For master's, 2 foreign languages, thesis; for doctorate, 3 foreign languages, comprehensive exam, thesis/dissertation. *Entrance requirements:* For master's and doctorate, GRE General Test. Additional exam requirements/recommendations for international students: Required—TOEFL (minimum score 600 paper-based; 250 computer-based). *Application deadline:* For fall admission, 1/3 for domestic and international students. Application fee: $50. *Financial support:* In 2010–11, 16 fellowships (averaging $16,844 per year), 3 teaching assistantships with partial tuition reimbursements (averaging $14,000 per year) were awarded; Federal Work-Study and scholarships/grants also available. Support available to part-time students. Financial award application deadline: 1/3. *Unit head:* Dr. James C. Wright, Chair, 610-526-5053, E-mail: jwright@brynmawr.edu. *Application contact:* Teri Lobo, Secretary, 610-526-5074, Fax: 610-526-5076, E-mail: lrmiller@brynmawr.edu.

See Display on next page and Close-Up on page 1329.

California State University, Northridge, Graduate Studies, College of Social and Behavioral Sciences, Department of Anthropology, Northridge, CA 91330. Offers general anthropology (MA); public archaeology (MA). *Degree requirements:* For master's, thesis or alternative. *Entrance requirements:* For master's, GRE General Test or minimum GPA of 3.0. Additional exam requirements/recommendations for international students: Required—TOEFL.

Columbia University, Graduate School of Arts and Sciences, Division of Humanities, Department of Art History and Archaeology, New York, NY 10027. Offers archaeology (M Phil, MA, PhD); art history and archaeology (M Phil, MA, PhD); modern art (MA). *Degree requirements:* For master's, 2 foreign languages, thesis; for doctorate, 3 foreign languages, thesis/dissertation. *Entrance requirements:* For master's and doctorate, GRE General Test. Additional exam requirements/recommendations for international students: Required—TOEFL.

Cornell University, Graduate School, Graduate Fields of Arts and Sciences, Field of Archaeology, Ithaca, NY 14853-0001. Offers environmental archaeology (MA); historical archaeology (MA); Latin American archaeology (MA); medieval archaeology (MA); Mediterranean and Near Eastern archaeology (MA); Stone Age archaeology (MA). *Faculty:* 18 full-time (5 women). *Students:* 8 full-time (7 women); includes 1 Hispanic/Latino. Average age 24. 23 applicants, 30% accepted, 3 enrolled. *Degree requirements:* For master's, one foreign language, thesis. *Entrance requirements:* For master's, GRE General Test, 3 letters of recommendation, sample of written work. Additional exam requirements/recommendations for international students: Required—TOEFL (minimum score 550 paper-based; 213 computer-based; 77 iBT). *Application deadline:* For fall admission, 1/15 for domestic students. Application fee: $80. Electronic applications accepted. *Expenses:* Tuition: Full-time $29,500. Required fees: $76.

Tuition and fees vary according to degree level and program. *Financial support:* In 2010–11, 1 fellowship with full tuition reimbursement, 3 teaching assistantships with full tuition reimbursements were awarded; research assistantships with full tuition reimbursements, institutionally sponsored loans, scholarships/grants, health care benefits, tuition waivers (full and partial), and unspecified assistantships also available. Financial award applicants required to submit FAFSA. *Faculty research:* Anatolia, Lydia, Sardis, classical and Hellenistic Greece; science in archaeology; North American Indians; Stone Age Africa; Mayan trade. *Unit head:* Director of Graduate Studies, 607-255-6768, E-mail: blj7@cornell.edu. *Application contact:* Graduate Field Assistant, 607-255-6768, E-mail: dsd6@cornell.edu.

Cornell University, Graduate School, Graduate Fields of Arts and Sciences, Field of History of Art, Archaeology and Visual Studies, Ithaca, NY 14853. Offers American art (PhD); ancient art and archaeology (PhD); Asian art (PhD); Baroque art (PhD); medieval art (PhD); modern art (PhD); Renaissance art (PhD); Southeast Asian art (PhD); theory and criticism (PhD). *Faculty:* 24 full-time (15 women). *Students:* 21 full-time (19 women); includes 1 Black or African American, non-Hispanic/Latino; 2 American Indian or Alaska Native, non-Hispanic/Latino; 1 Hispanic/Latino, 7 international. Average age 31. 71 applicants, 7% accepted, 5 enrolled. In 2010, 2 doctorates awarded. *Degree requirements:* For doctorate, one foreign language, comprehensive exam, thesis/dissertation, general exams in 3 areas. *Entrance requirements:* For doctorate, GRE General Test, sample of written work, 3 letters of recommendation. Additional exam requirements/recommendations for international students: Required—TOEFL (minimum score 550 paper-based; 213 computer-based; 77 iBT). *Application deadline:* For fall admission, 1/15 for domestic students. Application fee: $80. Electronic applications accepted. *Expenses:* Tuition: Full-time $29,500. Required fees: $76. Tuition and fees vary according to degree level and program. *Financial support:* In 2010–11, 8 fellowships with full tuition reimbursements, 11 teaching assistantships with full tuition reimbursements were awarded; research assistantships with full tuition reimbursements, institutionally sponsored loans, scholarships/grants, health care benefits, tuition waivers (full and partial), and unspecified assistantships also available. Financial award applicants required to submit FAFSA. *Unit head:* Director of Graduate Studies, 607-255-4905, Fax: 607-255-0566, E-mail: art_history@cornell.edu. *Application contact:* Graduate Field Assistant, 607-255-4905, Fax: 607-255-0566, E-mail: art_history@cornell.edu.

Florida State University, The Graduate School, College of Arts and Sciences, Department of Classics, Tallahassee, FL 32306-1510. Offers classical archaeology (MA); classical civilization (MA); classics (MA, PhD), including archaeology (PhD), literature and languages (PhD); Greek (MA); Greek and Latin (MA); Latin (MA). Part-time programs available. *Faculty:* 13 full-time (3 women), 1 (woman) part-time/adjunct. *Students:* 43 full-time (22 women); includes 2 Asian, non-Hispanic/Latino; 1 Hispanic/Latino. Average age 24. 54 applicants, 41% accepted, 16 enrolled. In 2010, 15 master's awarded. Terminal master's awarded for partial completion of doctoral program. *Degree requirements:* For master's, 2 foreign languages, comprehensive exam (for some programs), thesis (for some programs); for doctorate, 4 foreign languages, comprehensive exam, thesis/dissertation. *Entrance requirements:* For master's, GRE General Test, minimum GPA of 3.0; for doctorate, GRE General Test, minimum GPA of 3.5. Additional exam requirements/recommendations for international students: Required—TOEFL. *Application deadline:* For fall admission, 1/15 priority date for domestic students, 2/15 for international students. Applications are processed on a rolling basis. Application fee: $30. Electronic applications accepted. *Expenses:* Tuition: state resident: full-time $8238.24. *Financial support:* In 2010–11, 43 students received support, including 4 fellowships with full tuition reimbursements available (averaging $18,000 per year), 2 research assistantships with full tuition reimbursements available (averaging $10,000 per year), 28 teaching assistantships with full tuition reimbursements available (averaging $10,000 per year); Federal Work-Study, institutionally sponsored loans, and tuition waivers (full and partial) also available. Support available to part-time students. Financial award application deadline: 1/15; financial award applicants required to submit FAFSA. *Faculty research:* Greek and Latin literature, classical archaeology, mythology, ancient history, religion. Total annual research expenditures: $100,000. *Unit head:* Dr. John M. Marincola, Chairman, 850-644-0304, Fax: 850-644-4073, E-mail: jmarincola@fsu.edu. *Application contact:* Dr. Allen Romano, Admissions Director, 850-644-0305, Fax: 850-644-4073, E-mail: aromano@fsu.edu.

Gordon-Conwell Theological Seminary, Graduate and Professional Programs, South Hamilton, MA 01982. Offers Biblical languages (MABL); church history (MACH); counseling (MACO); ministry (D Min); missions/evangelism (MAME); New Testament (MANT); Old Testament (MAOT); religion (MAR); theology (M Div, MATH, Th M, Th D). *Accreditation:* ACIPE; ATS (one or more programs are accredited). Part-time and evening/weekend programs available. *Degree requirements:* For master's, one foreign language, thesis optional; for doctorate, 2 foreign languages, thesis/dissertation; for M Div, 2 foreign languages. *Entrance requirements:* For M Div and master's, minimum GPA of 2.5; for doctorate, minimum GPA of 3.0.

Graduate School and University Center of the City University of New York, Graduate Studies, Program in Anthropology, New York, NY 10016-4039. Offers anthropological linguistics (PhD); archaeology (PhD); cultural anthropology (PhD); physical anthropology (PhD). *Degree requirements:* For doctorate, one foreign language, thesis/dissertation. *Entrance requirements:* For doctorate, GRE General Test. Additional exam requirements/recommendations for international students: Required—TOEFL. Electronic applications accepted.

Harvard University, Graduate School of Arts and Sciences, Department of Anthropology, Cambridge, MA 02138. Offers archaeology (PhD); biological anthropology (PhD); legal anthropology (AM); medical anthropology (AM); social anthropology (AM, PhD); social change and development (AM). Terminal master's awarded for partial completion of doctoral program. *Degree requirements:* For master's, 2 foreign languages, thesis (for some programs); for doctorate, 2 foreign languages, thesis/dissertation, laboratory and/or fieldwork; general, qualifying, or special exams. *Entrance requirements:* For master's and doctorate, GRE General Test. Additional exam requirements/recommendations for international students: Required—TOEFL. *Expenses:* Tuition: Full-time $34,976. Required fees: $1166. Full-time tuition and fees vary according to program.

Harvard University, Graduate School of Arts and Sciences, Department of Near Eastern Languages and Civilizations, Cambridge, MA 02138. Offers Akkadian and Sumerian (AM, PhD); Arabic (AM, PhD); Armenian (AM, PhD); biblical history (AM, PhD); Hebrew (AM, PhD); Indo-Muslim culture (AM, PhD); Iranian (AM, PhD); Jewish history and literature (AM, PhD); Persian (AM, PhD); Semitic philology (AM, PhD); Syro-Palestinian archaeology (AM, PhD); Turkish (AM, PhD). *Degree requirements:* For doctorate, variable foreign language requirement, thesis/dissertation, general exams. *Entrance requirements:* For master's, GRE General Test; for doctorate, GRE General Test, proficiency in a Near Eastern language. Additional exam requirements/recommendations for international students: Required—TOEFL. *Expenses:* Tuition: Full-time $34,976. Required fees: $1166. Full-time tuition and fees vary according to program.

Harvard University, Graduate School of Arts and Sciences, Department of the Classics, Cambridge, MA 02138. Offers Byzantine Greek (PhD); classical archaeology (PhD); classical philology (PhD); classical philosophy (PhD); medieval Latin (PhD). *Degree requirements:* For doctorate, 4 foreign languages, thesis/dissertation, preliminary and special exams. *Entrance requirements:* For doctorate, GRE General Test. Additional exam requirements/recommendations for international students: Required—TOEFL. *Expenses:* Tuition: Full-time $34,976. Required fees: $1166. Full-time tuition and fees vary according to program.

Illinois State University, Graduate School, College of Arts and Sciences, Department of Sociology, Program in Historical Archaeology, Normal, IL 61790-2200. Offers MA, MS.

Indiana University of Pennsylvania, School of Graduate Studies and Research, College of Humanities and Social Sciences, Department of Anthropology, Indiana, PA 15705-1087. Offers applied archaeology (MA). *Faculty:* 4 full-time (3 women). *Students:* 30 full-time (17 women), 3 part-time (1 woman); includes 3 minority (2 American Indian or Alaska Native, non-Hispanic/Latino; 1 Hispanic/Latino). Average age 28. 39 applicants, 49% accepted, 19 enrolled. *Degree*

Archaeology

Indiana University of Pennsylvania (continued)
requirements: For master's, thesis and/or internship. *Application deadline:* Applications are processed on a rolling basis. Application fee: $40. Electronic applications accepted. *Financial support:* In 2010–11, 4 research assistantships (averaging $2,970 per year) were awarded; fellowships, unspecified assistantships also available. Financial award application deadline: 3/15. *Unit head:* Dr. Phillip Neusius, Chair, 724-357-2841, Fax: 724-357-7637, E-mail: phillip.neusius@iup.edu. *Application contact:* Dr. Phillip Neusius, Chair, 724-357-2841, Fax: 724-357-7637, E-mail: phillip.neusius@iup.edu.

Massachusetts Institute of Technology, School of Engineering, Department of Materials Science and Engineering, Cambridge, MA 02139. Offers archaeological materials (PhD, Sc D); bio- and polymeric materials (PhD, Sc D); electronic, photonic and magnetic materials (PhD, Sc D); emerging, fundamental and computational studies in materials science (Sc D); emerging, fundamental, and computational studies in materials science (PhD); materials engineering (Mat E); materials science and engineering (M Eng, SM, PhD, Sc D); metallurgical engineering (Met E); structural and environmental materials (PhD, Sc D); SM/MBA. *Faculty:* 34 full-time (8 women). *Students:* 196 full-time (52 women); includes 32 minority (2 Black or African American, non-Hispanic/Latino; 20 Asian, non-Hispanic/Latino; 7 Hispanic/Latino; 3 Two or more races, non-Hispanic/Latino), 113 international. Average age 26. 507 applicants, 15% accepted, 41 enrolled. In 2010, 22 master's, 38 doctorates awarded. Terminal master's awarded for partial completion of doctoral program. *Degree requirements:* For master's and other advanced degree, thesis; for doctorate, comprehensive exam, thesis/dissertation. *Entrance requirements:* For master's, doctorate, and other advanced degree, GRE General Test. Additional exam requirements/recommendations for international students: Required—IELTS (minimum score 7). *Application deadline:* For fall admission, 12/15 for domestic and international students. Application fee: $75. Electronic applications accepted. *Expenses:* Tuition: Full-time $38,940; part-time $605 per unit. Required fees: $272. *Financial support:* In 2010–11, 183 students received support, including 52 fellowships with tuition reimbursements available (averaging $32,695 per year), 124 research assistantships with tuition reimbursements available (averaging $27,409 per year), 8 teaching assistantships with tuition reimbursements available (averaging $31,861 per year); career-related internships or fieldwork, Federal Work-Study, institutionally sponsored loans, scholarships/grants, health care benefits, and unspecified assistantships also available. *Faculty research:* Thermodynamics and kinetics of phase transformations; structure of all materials classes: metals, ceramics, semiconductors, polymers, biomaterials; influence of processing on materials structure; structure property relationships (electrical, magnetic, optical, mechanical); materials in extreme environments. Total annual research expenditures: $28.1 million. *Unit head:* Prof. Edwin L. Thomas, Department Head, 617-253-3300, Fax: 617-252-1775. *Application contact:* Angelita Mireles, Graduate Admissions, 617-253-3302, E-mail: dmse-admissions@mit.edu.

Memorial University of Newfoundland, School of Graduate Studies, Department of Anthropology, St. John's, NL A1C 5S7, Canada. Offers archaeology and physical anthropology (MA, PhD); social and cultural anthropology (MA, PhD). Part-time programs available. *Degree requirements:* For master's, thesis (for some programs); for doctorate, comprehensive exam, thesis/dissertation, oral defense of thesis. *Entrance requirements:* For master's, 2nd class degree in related field. Electronic applications accepted. *Faculty research:* Early European settlements, ethnoarchaeology, economic/political anthropology, land claims and aboriginal rights, marine anthropology.

Michigan Technological University, Graduate School, College of Sciences and Arts, Department of Social Sciences, Program in Industrial Archaeology, Houghton, MI 49931. Offers MS. Part-time programs available. *Degree requirements:* For master's, comprehensive exam, thesis. *Entrance requirements:* For master's, GRE. Additional exam requirements/recommendations for international students: Required—TOEFL (minimum score 550 paper-based; 213 computer-based). Electronic applications accepted.

Michigan Technological University, Graduate School, College of Sciences and Arts, Department of Social Sciences, Program in Industrial Heritage and Archeology, Houghton, MI 49931. Offers PhD. Part-time programs available. *Degree requirements:* For doctorate, comprehensive exam, thesis/dissertation. *Entrance requirements:* Additional exam requirements/recommendations for international students: Required—TOEFL (minimum score 550 paper-based; 213 computer-based). Electronic applications accepted.

Midwestern Baptist Theological Seminary, Graduate and Professional Programs, Kansas City, MO 64118-4697. Offers Biblical archaeology (MA); Biblical languages (MA); Christian education (M Div, MACE); Christian foundations—lay ministry (Graduate Certificate); collegiate ministries (M Div); counseling (MA); educational ministry (D Ed Min); international church planting (M Div); ministry (M Div, D Min); North American church planting (M Div); sacred music (MCM); urban ministry (M Div); worship leadership (M Div); youth ministry (M Div). *Accreditation:* ATS. Part-time programs available. Postbaccalaureate distance learning degree programs offered (minimal on-campus study). *Degree requirements:* For doctorate, thesis/dissertation; for M Div, 2 foreign languages. *Entrance requirements:* For doctorate, MAT. Electronic applications accepted. *Faculty research:* Ministerial studies, Biblical and theological studies, missions, counseling.

New York University, Graduate School of Arts and Science, Institute of Fine Arts, Program in Art History and Archaeology, New York, NY 10012-1019. Offers architectural studies (PhD); art history and archaeology (MA, PhD); classical art and archaeology (PhD); curatorial studies (PhD); East and South Asian art (PhD); Near Eastern art and archaeology (PhD); MA/Diploma; PhD/Certificate. Part-time programs available. *Students:* 243 full-time (192 women), 59 part-time (47 women); includes 2 Black or African American, non-Hispanic/Latino; 20 Asian, non-Hispanic/Latino; 8 Hispanic/Latino, 29 international. Average age 32. 394 applicants, 27% accepted, 57 enrolled. In 2010, 29 master's, 12 doctorates awarded. Terminal master's awarded for partial completion of doctoral program. *Degree requirements:* For master's, 2 foreign languages, thesis or alternative, 2 qualifying papers; for doctorate, 2 foreign languages, thesis/dissertation. *Entrance requirements:* For master's, GRE General Test; for doctorate, GRE General Test, MA. Additional exam requirements/recommendations for international students: Required—TOEFL. *Application deadline:* For fall admission, 12/15 for domestic students. Application fee: $90. *Financial support:* Fellowships with tuition reimbursements, research assistantships with tuition reimbursements, teaching assistantships with tuition reimbursements, career-related internships or fieldwork, Federal Work-Study, and institutionally sponsored loans available. Financial award application deadline: 12/15; financial award applicants required to submit FAFSA. *Unit head:* Patricia Rubin, Chair, 212-992-5800, Fax: 212-992-5807, E-mail: ifa.program@nyu.edu. *Application contact:* Priscilla Saucek, Director of Graduate Studies, 212-992-5800, Fax: 212-992-5807, E-mail: ifa.program@nyu.edu.

Northern Arizona University, Graduate College, College of Social and Behavioral Sciences, Department of Anthropology, Flagstaff, AZ 86011. Offers archaeology (MA); cultural anthropology (MA); linguistic anthropology (MA). *Faculty:* 17 full-time (7 women). *Students:* 48 full-time (29 women), 14 part-time (8 women); includes 14 minority (3 American Indian or Alaska Native, non-Hispanic/Latino; 8 Hispanic/Latino; 3 Two or more races, non-Hispanic/Latino), 1 international. Average age 35. 100 applicants, 45% accepted, 26 enrolled. In 2010, 25 master's awarded. *Degree requirements:* For master's, thesis (for some programs), internship paper. *Entrance requirements:* For master's, 12 undergraduate hours in anthropology. Additional exam requirements/recommendations for international students: Required—TOEFL (minimum score 550 paper-based; 213 computer-based; 80 iBT), IELTS (minimum score 7). *Application deadline:* For fall admission, 2/15 priority date for domestic and international students. Applications are processed on a rolling basis. Application fee: $65. Electronic applications accepted. *Financial support:* In 2010–11, 1 fellowship (averaging $10,774 per year), 9 teaching assistantships with partial tuition reimbursements (averaging $10,449 per year) were awarded; career-related internships or fieldwork, Federal Work-Study, scholarships/grants, health care benefits, tuition waivers (full and partial), and unspecified assistantships also available. Financial award applicants required to submit FAFSA. *Faculty research:* Economic development, culture change, ethnohistory, archaeology of the Southwest, small town networks and HIV. Total annual research expenditures: $594,266. *Unit head:* Dr. Robert Trotter, Chair/Professor, 928-523-4521, Fax: 928-523-9135, E-mail: robert.trotter@nau.edu. *Application contact:* Pamela Lamb, Administrative Assistant, 928-523-3180, Fax: 928-523-9135, E-mail: anthropology@nau.edu.

Northwestern State University of Louisiana, Graduate Studies and Research, Program in Heritage Resources, Natchitoches, LA 71497. Offers MA. *Degree requirements:* For master's, comprehensive exam, thesis or alternative. *Entrance requirements:* For master's, GRE General Test, minimum undergraduate GPA of 2.5.

Princeton University, Graduate School, Department of Art and Archaeology, Princeton, NJ 08544-1019. Offers classical art and archaeology (PhD); East Asian art and archaeology (PhD). *Degree requirements:* For doctorate, 2 foreign languages, thesis/dissertation. *Entrance requirements:* For doctorate, GRE General Test. Additional exam requirements/recommendations for international students: Required—TOEFL (minimum score 600 paper-based; 250 computer-based). Electronic applications accepted.

Rice University, Graduate Programs, School of Social Sciences, Department of Anthropology, Houston, TX 77251-1892. Offers archaeology (MA, PhD); social-cultural anthropology (MA, PhD). Terminal master's awarded for partial completion of doctoral program. *Degree requirements:* For master's, one foreign language, 3 major papers, dissertation proposal and language exam or thesis; for doctorate, one foreign language, thesis/dissertation. *Entrance requirements:* For master's and doctorate, research proposal. Additional exam requirements/recommendations for international students: Required—TOEFL (minimum score 90 iBT). Electronic applications accepted.

St. Cloud State University, School of Graduate Studies, College of Social Sciences, Program in Cultural Resource Management Archeology, St. Cloud, MN 56301-4498. Offers MS. *Entrance requirements:* For master's, GRE General Test, minimum GPA of 2.75. Additional exam requirements/recommendations for international students: Required—Michigan English Language Assessment Battery; Recommended—TOEFL (minimum score 550 paper-based; 213 computer-based).

San Francisco State University, Division of Graduate Studies, College of Behavioral and Social Sciences, Department of Anthropology, San Francisco, CA 94132-1722. Offers archaeology (MA); biological/physical anthropology (MA); social/cultural anthropology (MA); visual anthropology (MA). *Faculty research:* Immigration, ethnicity, urban anthropology, Californian and Latin American archaeology. *Unit head:* Dr. Douglass Bailey, Chair, 415-338-1427. *Application contact:* Dr. Mariana Ferreira, Graduate Coordinator, 415-405-2467, E-mail: mariana@sfsu.edu.

Simon Fraser University, Graduate Studies, Faculty of Arts and Social Sciences, Department of Archaeology, Burnaby, BC V5A 1S6, Canada. Offers MA, PhD. *Degree requirements:* For master's, one foreign language, thesis; for doctorate, one foreign language, thesis/dissertation. *Entrance requirements:* For master's, minimum GPA of 3.0; for doctorate, minimum GPA of 3.5. Additional exam requirements/recommendations for international students: Required—TOEFL or IELTS. *Faculty research:* Ethnology, archaeometry, zooarchaeology, primate behavior, forensic anthropology.

Temple Baptist Seminary, Program in Theology, Chattanooga, TN 37404-3530. Offers biblical languages (M Div); Biblical studies (MABS); Christian education (MACE); English Bible û language tools (M Div); theology (MM, D Min). Part-time and evening/weekend programs available. Postbaccalaureate distance learning degree programs offered (minimal on-campus study). *Degree requirements:* For doctorate, thesis/dissertation; for M Div, proficiency in Greek and Hebrew. *Entrance requirements:* For doctorate, minimum GPA of 3.0, M Div.

Trinity International University, Trinity Evangelical Divinity School, Deerfield, IL 60015-1284. Offers Biblical and Near Eastern archaeology and languages (MA); Christian studies (MA, Certificate); Christian thought (MA); church history (MA, Th M); congregational ministry: pastor-teacher (M Div); congregational ministry: team ministry (M Div); counseling ministries (MA); counseling psychology (MA); cross-cultural ministry (M Div); educational studies (PhD); evangelism (MA); history of Christianity in America (MA); intercultural studies (MA, PhD); leadership and ministry management (D Min); military chaplaincy (D Min); ministry (MA); mission and evangelism (Th M); missions and evangelism (D Min); New Testament (MA, Th M); Old Testament (Th M); Old Testament and Semitic languages (MA); pastoral care (M Div); pastoral care and counseling (D Min); pastoral counseling and psychology (Th M); pastoral theology (Th M); philosophy of religion (MA); preaching (D Min); religion (MA); research ministry (M Div); systematic theology (Th M); theological studies (PhD); urban ministry (MA). *Accreditation:* ATS (one or more programs are accredited). Part-time programs available. Postbaccalaureate distance learning degree programs offered (minimal on-campus study). *Degree requirements:* For master's, comprehensive exam, thesis, fieldwork; for doctorate, comprehensive exam (for some programs), thesis/dissertation; for M Div, 2 foreign languages, fieldwork; for Certificate, comprehensive exam, integrative papers. *Entrance requirements:* For M Div, GRE, MAT; for master's, GRE, MAT, minimum cumulative undergraduate GPA of 3.0; for doctorate, GRE, minimum cumulative graduate GPA of 3.2; for Certificate, GRE, MAT, minimum undergraduate GPA of 2.5. Additional exam requirements/recommendations for international students: Required—TOEFL (minimum score 580 paper-based; 237 computer-based), TWE (minimum score 4). Electronic applications accepted.

Tufts University, Graduate School of Arts and Sciences, Department of Classics, Medford, MA 02155. Offers classical archaeology (MA); classics (MA). Part-time programs available. *Degree requirements:* For master's, 2 foreign languages, comprehensive exam, thesis or alternative. *Entrance requirements:* For master's, GRE General Test, writing sample. Additional exam requirements/recommendations for international students: Required—TOEFL (minimum score 550 paper-based; 213 computer-based; 80 iBT). Electronic applications accepted. *Expenses:* Tuition: Full-time $39,624; part-time $3962 per course. Required fees: $40 per year. Full-time tuition and fees vary according to degree level, program and student level. Part-time tuition and fees vary according to course load.

Universidad de las Américas–Puebla, Division of Graduate Studies, School of Social Sciences, Program in Anthropology, Puebla, Mexico. Offers anthropology (MA); archaeology (MA). Part-time and evening/weekend programs available. *Degree requirements:* For master's, one foreign language, thesis. *Entrance requirements:* For master's, bachelor's degree in anthropology or equivalent. *Faculty research:* Archaeology, ethnography, and ethnohistory of Mesoamerica.

Université Laval, Faculty of Letters, Department of History, Programs in Archaeology, Québec, QC G1K 7P4, Canada. Offers MA, PhD. Terminal master's awarded for partial completion of doctoral program. *Degree requirements:* For master's, thesis; for doctorate, comprehensive exam, thesis/dissertation. *Entrance requirements:* For master's and doctorate, English test, knowledge of French. Electronic applications accepted.

University of Alberta, Faculty of Graduate Studies and Research, Department of History and Classics, Edmonton, AB T6G 2E1, Canada. Offers ancient history (PhD); classical archaeology (MA, PhD); classical literature (PhD); classics (MA); history (MA, PhD). Part-time and evening/weekend programs available. *Degree requirements:* For master's, one foreign language, thesis (for some programs); for doctorate, one foreign language, thesis/dissertation. *Entrance requirements:* For master's, minimum B+ average; for doctorate, minimum A- average. Additional exam requirements/recommendations for international students: Required—TOEFL (minimum score 580 paper-based; 237 computer-based). Electronic applications accepted. *Faculty research:* Western Canada, classical archaeology, Britain, Eastern Europe, East Asia.

The University of British Columbia, Faculty of Arts and Faculty of Graduate Studies, Department of Classical, Near Eastern and Religious Studies, Programmes in Classics, Vancouver, BC V6T 1Z1, Canada. Offers ancient culture, religion, and ethnicity (MA); classical and near eastern archaeology (MA); classics (MA, PhD). Part-time programs available. *Degree requirements:* For master's, 2 foreign languages, thesis or comprehensive exam; for doctorate, 2 foreign languages, comprehensive exam, thesis/dissertation. *Entrance requirements:* For doctorate, MA. Additional exam requirements/recommendations for international students: Required—TOEFL (minimum score 600 paper-based; 250 computer-based), IELTS (minimum score 7.5). Electronic applications accepted. Tuition charges are reported in Canadian dollars. *Expenses:* Tuition, area resident: Full-time $4179 Canadian dollars. International tuition: $7344 Canadian dollars full-time. *Faculty research:* Classical archaeology, ancient historians, late antiquity, ancient prose fiction, epigraphy.

University of Calgary, Faculty of Graduate Studies, Faculty of Social Sciences, Department of Archaeology, Calgary, AB T2N 1N4, Canada. Offers MA, PhD. *Degree requirements:* For master's, thesis; for doctorate, one foreign language, thesis/dissertation, candidacy exam. *Entrance requirements:* For master's, BA or B Sc in anthropology or archaeology; for doctorate, MA in anthropology or archaeology. Additional exam requirements/recommendations for international students: Required—TOEFL. Electronic applications accepted. *Faculty research:* Prehistory, ethnoarchaeology, Africa, Latin America, biological anthropology.

University of California, Berkeley, Graduate Division, College of Letters and Science, Department of Classics, Program in Classical Archaeology, Berkeley, CA 94720-1500. Offers MA, PhD. *Degree requirements:* For master's, one foreign language, thesis, exams; for doctorate, 2 foreign languages, thesis/dissertation, qualifying exam. *Entrance requirements:* For master's and doctorate, GRE General Test, minimum GPA of 3.0, 3 letters of recommendation. Additional exam requirements/recommendations for international students: Required—TOEFL (minimum score 570 paper-based; 230 computer-based), TWE.

University of California, Berkeley, Graduate Division, College of Letters and Science, Group in Ancient History and Mediterranean Archaeology, Berkeley, CA 94720-1500. Offers MA, PhD. *Degree requirements:* For master's, one foreign language, exam or thesis; for doctorate, 2 foreign languages, thesis/dissertation, qualifying exam. *Entrance requirements:* For master's and doctorate, GRE General Test, minimum GPA of 3.0, 3 letters of recommendation. Additional exam requirements/recommendations for international students: Required—TOEFL (minimum score 570 paper-based; 230 computer-based), TWE.

University of California, Los Angeles, Graduate Division, College of Letters and Science, Interdepartmental Program in Archaeology, Los Angeles, CA 90095. Offers MA, PhD. *Students:* 25 full-time (18 women); includes 5 minority (1 Black or African American, non-Hispanic/Latino; 3 Asian, non-Hispanic/Latino; 1 Two or more races, non-Hispanic/Latino), 4 international. Average age 28. 80 applicants, 11% accepted, 6 enrolled. In 2010, 5 master's, 3 doctorates awarded. *Degree requirements:* For master's, one foreign language, comprehensive exam, comprehensive core exam, paper, field experience; for doctorate, 2 foreign languages, thesis/dissertation, oral and written qualifying exams. *Entrance requirements:* For master's, GRE General Test, minimum GPA of 3.0, sample of research writing; for doctorate, GRE General Test, minimum undergraduate GPA of 3.0, sample of research writing, ability to read 1 foreign language. *Application deadline:* For fall admission, 12/15 for domestic and international students. Application fee: $70 ($90 for international students). Electronic applications accepted. *Financial support:* In 2010–11, 21 fellowships with full and partial tuition reimbursements, 8 research assistantships with full and partial tuition reimbursements, 11 teaching assistantships with full and partial tuition reimbursements were awarded; Federal Work-Study, institutionally sponsored loans, scholarships/grants, health care benefits, tuition waivers (full and partial), and unspecified assistantships also available. Financial award application deadline: 3/1; financial award applicants required to submit FAFSA. *Unit head:* Dr. Richard Lesure, Chair, 310-825-4169. *Application contact:* Department Office, 310-825-4169, E-mail: evgenia@ioa.ucla.edu.

University of California, Los Angeles, Graduate Division, College of Letters and Science, Interdepartmental Program in Conservation of Archaeological and Ethnographic Materials, Los Angeles, CA 90095. Offers MA. *Students:* 7 full-time (all women); includes 2 minority (1 Asian, non-Hispanic/Latino; 1 Hispanic/Latino), 1 international. Average age 27. In 2010, 4 master's awarded. Application fee: $70 ($90 for international students). *Financial support:* In 2010–11, 7 fellowships, 7 research assistantships were awarded; teaching assistantships. *Unit head:* Dr. David A. Scott, Chair, 310-794-4855, E-mail: dascott@ucla.edu. *Application contact:* Amber Cordts-Cole, Program Coordinator, 310-825-1711, E-mail: acordts@ucla.edu.

University of California, Santa Barbara, Graduate Division, College of Letters and Sciences, Division of Social Sciences, Department of Anthropology, Santa Barbara, CA 93106-2014. Offers archaeology (MA); biosocial anthropology (MA, PhD); sociocultural anthropology (MA, PhD); MA/PhD. *Faculty:* 12 full-time (3 women), 2 part-time/adjunct (both women). *Students:* 51 full-time (34 women); includes 2 Asian, non-Hispanic/Latino; 7 Hispanic/Latino. Average age 31. 47 applicants, 30% accepted, 4 enrolled. In 2010, 6 master's, 9 doctorates awarded. Terminal master's awarded for partial completion of doctoral program. *Degree requirements:* For master's, comprehensive exam (for some programs), thesis (for some programs); for doctorate, comprehensive exam (for some programs), thesis/dissertation. *Entrance requirements:* For master's and doctorate, GRE General Test, statement of purpose, transcripts, writing sample, curriculum vitae. Additional exam requirements/recommendations for international students: Required—TOEFL (minimum score 550 paper-based; 80 iBT), IELTS (minimum score 7). *Application deadline:* For fall admission, 12/1 for domestic and international students. Application fee: $70 ($90 for international students). Electronic applications accepted. *Financial support:* In 2010–11, 48 students received support, including 35 fellowships with full and partial tuition reimbursements available (averaging $5,749 per year), 7 research assistantships with full and partial tuition reimbursements available (averaging $7,287 per year), 37 teaching assistantships with full tuition reimbursements available (averaging $10,042 per year); career-related internships or fieldwork, Federal Work-Study, institutionally sponsored loans, scholarships/grants, traineeships, health care benefits, tuition waivers (full and partial), and unspecified assistantships also available. Support available to part-time students. Financial award application deadline: 12/1; financial award applicants required to submit FAFSA. *Faculty research:* Archaeology, bioarchaeology, biosocial anthropology, evolutionary ecology, evolutionary psychology, sociocultural anthropology. *Unit head:* Prof. Katharina Schreiber, Department Chair, 805-893-2519, Fax: 805-893-8707, E-mail: kschreiber@anth.ucsb.edu. *Application contact:* Robin Roe, Graduate Program Assistant, 805-893-2516, Fax: 805-893-8707, E-mail: roe@anth.ucsb.edu.

University of Chicago, Division of the Humanities, Department of Classics, Chicago, IL 60637-1513. Offers ancient philosophy (AM, PhD); classical archaeology (AM, PhD); classical languages and literatures (AM, PhD). Terminal master's awarded for partial completion of doctoral program. *Degree requirements:* For master's, one foreign language, thesis; for doctorate, 2 foreign languages, thesis/dissertation. *Entrance requirements:* For master's and doctorate, GRE General Test. Additional exam requirements/recommendations for international students: Required—TOEFL.

University of Colorado Denver, College of Liberal Arts and Sciences, Department of Anthropology, Denver, CO 80217. Offers archaeological studies (MA); biological anthropology (MA); medical anthropology (MA); sustainable development and political ecology (MA). Part-time and evening/weekend programs available. *Faculty:* 8 full-time (1 woman). *Students:* 16 full-time (12 women), 7 part-time (6 women); includes 1 Hispanic/Latino. Average age 30. 44 applicants, 59% accepted, 9 enrolled. In 2010, 13 master's awarded. *Degree requirements:* For master's, comprehensive exam, thesis or alternative, 30-36 credit hours. *Entrance requirements:* For master's, GRE General Test, minimum GPA of 3.0 for all undergraduate studies, two copies of transcripts from all undergraduate/graduate institutions attended, prior training in anthropology, three letters of recommendation, statement of purpose. Additional exam requirements/recommendations for international students: Required—TOEFL (minimum score 525 paper-based; 197 computer-based). *Application deadline:* For fall admission, 2/15 for domestic students. Applications are processed on a rolling basis. Application fee: $50 ($75 for international students). Electronic applications accepted. *Expenses:* Tuition, state resident: full-time $7332; part-time $355 per credit hour. Tuition, nonresident: full-time $18,990; part-time $1055 per credit hour. Required fees: $998. Tuition and fees vary according to course level, course load, degree level, campus/location, program, reciprocity agreements and student level. *Financial support:* Research assistantships, teaching assistantships, Federal Work-Study available. Financial award application deadline: 4/1; financial award applicants required to submit FAFSA. *Faculty research:* Applied medical anthropology, primate social behavior, environmental anthropology, Southwestern and Mexican archaeology, human ecology. *Unit head:* Dr. Steve P. Koester, Chair, 303-556-6795, Fax: 303-556-8501, E-mail: steve.koester@ucdenver.edu. *Application contact:* Connie Turner, Program Assistant, 303-556-3554, Fax: 303-556-8501, E-mail: connie.turner@ucdenver.edu.

University of Denver, Division of Arts, Humanities and Social Sciences, Department of Anthropology, Denver, CO 80208. Offers archaeology (MA); cultural anthropology (MA); museum studies (MA). Part-time programs available. *Faculty:* 8 full-time (4 women). *Students:* 1 (woman) full-time, 17 part-time (12 women); includes 4 minority (2 Black or African American, non-Hispanic/Latino; 1 American Indian or Alaska Native, non-Hispanic/Latino; 1 Hispanic/Latino), 1 international. Average age 26. 45 applicants, 47% accepted, 8 enrolled. In 2010, 11 master's awarded. *Degree requirements:* For master's, comprehensive exam, thesis or alternative, proficiency in foreign language other than English or in quantitative methods. *Entrance requirements:* For master's, GRE General Test. Additional exam requirements/recommendations for international students: Required—TOEFL (minimum score 550 paper-based; 80 iBT). *Application deadline:* Applications are processed on a rolling basis. Application fee: $60. Electronic applications accepted. *Expenses:* Tuition: Full-time $35,604; part-time $29,670 per year. Required fees: $687 per year. Tuition and fees vary according to program. *Financial support:* In 2010–11, 12 teaching assistantships with full and partial tuition reimbursements (averaging $4,667 per year) were awarded; career-related internships or fieldwork, Federal Work-Study, institutionally sponsored loans, scholarships/grants, and unspecified assistantships also available. Support available to part-time students. Financial award application deadline: 3/15; financial award applicants required to submit FAFSA. *Faculty research:* Gender, class, race, ground-penetrating radar, archaeology. *Unit head:* Dr. Dean J. Saitta, Chair, 303-871-2680, E-mail: dsaitta@du.edu. *Application contact:* Carrie Shrader, Assistant to Chair, 303-871-2677, E-mail: anth02@du.edu.

University of Georgia, College of Arts and Sciences, Department of Anthropology, Athens, GA 30602. Offers anthropology (MA, PhD); archaeological resource management (MS). *Faculty:* 12 full-time (4 women), 1 (woman) part-time/adjunct. *Students:* 51 full-time (32 women), 7 part-time (3 women); includes 1 Black or African American, non-Hispanic/Latino; 1 Hispanic/Latino; 2 Two or more races, non-Hispanic/Latino, 6 international. 56 applicants, 34% accepted, 14 enrolled. In 2010, 7 master's, 9 doctorates awarded. *Degree requirements:* For master's, one foreign language, thesis; for doctorate, one foreign language, thesis/dissertation. *Entrance requirements:* For master's and doctorate, GRE General Test. *Application deadline:* For fall admission, 7/1 priority date for domestic students; for spring admission, 11/15 for domestic students. Application fee: $50. Electronic applications accepted. *Expenses:* Tuition, state resident: full-time $7200; part-time $344 per credit hour. Tuition, nonresident: full-time $21,900; part-time $944 per credit hour. Tuition and fees vary according to course load and program. *Financial support:* Fellowships, research assistantships, teaching assistantships, unspecified assistantships available. *Unit head:* Dr. Ted Gragson, Head, 706-542-1479, Fax: 706-542-3998, E-mail: tgragso@uga.edu. *Application contact:* Dr. Elizabeth J. Reitz, Graduate Coordinator, 706-542-1464, Fax: 706-542-3998, E-mail: ereitz@uga.edu.

University of Lethbridge, School of Graduate Studies, Lethbridge, AB T1K 3M4, Canada. Offers accounting (MScM); addictions counseling (M Sc); agricultural biotechnology (M Sc); agricultural studies (M Sc, MA); anthropology (MA); archaeology (MA); art (MA, MFA); biochemistry (M Sc); biological sciences (M Sc); biomolecular science (PhD); biosystems and biodiversity (PhD); Canadian studies (MA); chemistry (M Sc); computer science (M Sc); computer science and geographical information science (M Sc); counseling psychology (M Ed); dramatic arts (MA); earth, space, and physical science (PhD); economics (MA); educational leadership (M Ed); English (MA); environmental science (M Sc); evolution and behavior (PhD); exercise science (M Sc); finance (MScM); French (MA); French/German (MA); French/Spanish (MA); general education (M Ed); general management (MScM); geography (M Sc, MA); German (MA); health science (M Sc); history (MA); human resource management and labour relations (MScM); individualized multidisciplinary (M Sc, MA); information systems (MScM); international management (MScM); kinesiology (M Sc, MA); management (M Sc, MA); marketing (MScM); mathematics (M Sc); music (M Mus, MA); Native American studies (MA); neuroscience (M Sc, PhD); new media (MA); nursing (M Sc); philosophy (MA); physics (M Sc); policy and strategy (MScM); political science (MA); psychology (M Sc, MA); religious studies (MA); social sciences (MA); sociology (MA); theatre and dramatic arts (MFA); theoretical and computational science (PhD); urban and regional studies (MA); women's studies (MA). Part-time and evening/weekend programs available. *Degree requirements:* For doctorate, comprehensive exam, thesis/dissertation. *Entrance requirements:* For master's, GMAT (M Sc in management), bachelor's degree in related field, minimum GPA of 3.0 during previous 20 graded semester courses, 2 years teaching or related experience (M Ed); for doctorate, master's degree, minimum graduate GPA of 3.5. Additional exam requirements/recommendations for international students: Required—TOEFL. *Faculty research:* Movement and brain plasticity, gibberellin physiology, photosynthesis, carbon cycling, molecular properties of main-group ring components.

The University of Manchester, Faculty of Life Sciences, Manchester, United Kingdom. Offers adaptive organismal biology (M Phil, PhD); animal biology (M Phil, PhD); biochemistry (M Phil, PhD); bioinformatics (M Phil, PhD); biomolecular sciences (M Phil, PhD); biotechnology (M Phil, PhD); cell biology (M Phil, PhD); cell matrix research (M Phil, PhD); channels and transporters (M Phil, PhD); developmental biology (M Phil, PhD); Egyptology (M Phil, PhD); environmental biology (M Phil, PhD); evolutionary biology (M Phil, PhD); gene expression (M Phil, PhD); genetics (M Phil, PhD); history of science, technology and medicine (M Phil, PhD); immunology (M Phil, PhD); integrative neurobiology and behavior (M Phil, PhD); membrane trafficking (M Phil, PhD); microbiology (M Phil, PhD); molecular and cellular neuroscience (M Phil, PhD); molecular biology (M Phil, PhD); molecular cancer studies (M Phil, PhD); neuroscience (M Phil, PhD); ophthalmology (M Phil, PhD); optometry (M Phil, PhD); organelle function (M Phil, PhD); pharmacology (M Phil, PhD); physiology (M Phil, PhD); plant sciences (M Phil, PhD); stem cell research (M Phil, PhD); structural biology (M Phil, PhD); systems neuroscience (M Phil, PhD); toxicology (M Phil, PhD).

The University of Manchester, School of Arts, Histories and Cultures, Manchester, United Kingdom. Offers anthropology, media and performance (PhD); applied theatre professional (PhD); archaeology (PhD); art history and visual studies (PhD); arts management and cultural policy (PhD); classics and ancient history (PhD); composition (PhD); creative writing (PhD); drama (PhD); economic and social history (PhD); electroacoustic composition (PhD); English and American studies (PhD); history (PhD); humanitarianism and conflict response (PhD); museology (PhD); music (PhD); musicology (PhD); religions and theology (PhD).

University of Massachusetts Boston, Office of Graduate Studies, College of Liberal Arts, Program in History, Track in Historical Archaeology, Boston, MA 02125-3393. Offers MA. Part-time and evening/weekend programs available. *Degree requirements:* For master's, thesis, oral exams, practicum. *Entrance requirements:* For master's, GRE General Test, minimum GPA of 2.75. *Faculty research:* New World Colonialism, New England archeology, historical and urban archeology, archeological botany, ethnology.

University of Memphis, Graduate School, College of Arts and Sciences, Department of Earth Sciences, Memphis, TN 38152. Offers archaeology (MS); earth sciences (PhD); geographic information systems (Graduate Certificate); geography (MA, MS); geology (MS); geophysics (MS); interdisciplinary (MS). Part-time and evening/weekend programs available. *Faculty:* 15 full-time (3 women), 6 part-time/adjunct (2 women). *Students:* 35 full-time (7 women), 28 part-time (13 women); includes 5 Black or African American, non-Hispanic/Latino; 1 Asian, non-Hispanic/Latino, 15 international. Average age 33. 48 applicants, 69% accepted, 18 enrolled. In 2010, 2 master's, 2 doctorates, 1 other advanced degree awarded. Terminal

Archaeology

University of Memphis (continued)
master's awarded for partial completion of doctoral program. *Degree requirements:* For master's, comprehensive exam, thesis, seminar presentation; for doctorate, thesis/dissertation. *Entrance requirements:* For master's, GRE General Test, 3 letters of recommendation, statement of research interests; for doctorate, GRE General Test, 2 letters of recommendation, resume, personal statement. Additional exam requirements/recommendations for international students: Required—TOEFL (minimum score 550 paper-based; 210 computer-based). *Application deadline:* For fall admission, 1/31 for domestic students; for spring admission, 11/1 for domestic students. Applications are processed on a rolling basis. Application fee: $35 ($60 for international students). Electronic applications accepted. *Financial support:* In 2010–11, 18 students received support; fellowships with full tuition reimbursements available, research assistantships with full tuition reimbursements available, teaching assistantships with full tuition reimbursements available, Federal Work-Study, scholarships/grants, and unspecified assistantships available. Financial award application deadline: 2/15; financial award applicants required to submit FAFSA. *Faculty research:* Hazards, active tectonics, geophysics, hydrology and water resources, spatial analysis. *Unit head:* Dr. M. Jerry Bartholomew, Chair, 901-678-4536, Fax: 901-678-4467, E-mail: jbrthlm1@memphis.edu. *Application contact:* Dr. Arlene Hill, Associate Professor and Graduate Program Coordinator, 901-678-4358, Fax: 901-678-2178, E-mail: dlarsen@memphis.edu.

University of Memphis, Graduate School, College of Communication and Fine Arts, Department of Art, Memphis, TN 38152. Offers art (Graduate Certificate); art history (MA), including Egyptian art and archaeology, general art history; ceramics (MFA); graphic design (MFA); interior design (MFA); painting (MFA); printmaking/photography (MFA); sculpture (MFA). *Accreditation:* NASAD (one or more programs are accredited). *Faculty:* 20 full-time (7 women), 4 part-time/adjunct (2 women). *Students:* 39 full-time (26 women), 10 part-time (8 women); includes 4 Black or African American, non-Hispanic/Latino; 1 Asian, non-Hispanic/Latino, 1 international. Average age 29. 44 applicants, 77% accepted, 22 enrolled. In 2010, 16 master's, 5 other advanced degrees awarded. *Degree requirements:* For master's, 2 foreign languages, comprehensive exam, thesis. *Entrance requirements:* For master's, GRE General Test or MAT, portfolio (MFA). *Application deadline:* For fall admission, 8/1 for domestic students; for spring admission, 12/1 for domestic students. Applications are processed on a rolling basis. Application fee: $35 ($60 for international students). *Financial support:* In 2010–11, 38 students received support; research assistantships with full tuition reimbursements available, teaching assistantships with full tuition reimbursements available, Federal Work-Study, scholarships/grants, and unspecified assistantships available. Financial award application deadline: 2/15; financial award applicants required to submit FAFSA. *Faculty research:* Online collaborative learning, advanced art history studies, electronic publishing/design, studio arts, architectural studies. *Unit head:* Prof. Richard Lou, Chair, 901-678-2216, Fax: 901-678-2735, E-mail: gmyatt@memphis.edu. *Application contact:* Greely Myat, Graduate Studies Coordinator, 901-678-2650.

University of Michigan, Horace H. Rackham School of Graduate Studies, College of Literature, Science, and the Arts, Interdepartmental Program in Classical Art and Archaeology, Ann Arbor, MI 48109. Offers PhD. *Faculty:* 26 full-time (12 women), 1 (woman) part-time/adjunct. *Students:* 28 full-time (19 women); includes 1 Hispanic/Latino, 5 international. Average age 27. 68 applicants, 4% accepted, 3 enrolled. In 2010, 3 doctorates awarded. *Degree requirements:* For doctorate, 4 foreign languages, comprehensive exam, thesis/dissertation, ancient history exam, preliminary exam. *Entrance requirements:* For doctorate, GRE General Test. Additional exam requirements/recommendations for international students: Required—TOEFL (minimum score 560 paper-based; 84 iBT). *Application deadline:* For fall admission, 12/15 for domestic and international students. Application fee: $65 ($75 for international students). Electronic applications accepted. *Expenses:* Tuition, state resident: full-time $17,784; part-time $1116 per credit hour. Tuition, nonresident: full-time $35,944; part-time $2125 per credit hour. International tuition: $35,994 full-time. Required fees: $95 per semester. Tuition and fees vary according to course load, degree level and program. *Financial support:* In 2010–11, 27 students received support, including 16 fellowships with full tuition reimbursements available (averaging $17,000 per year), 1 research assistantship with full tuition reimbursement available (averaging $16,694 per year), 8 teaching assistantships with full tuition reimbursements available (averaging $16,694 per year); career-related internships or fieldwork and health care benefits also available. Financial award application deadline: 4/15. *Faculty research:* Greek art and archaeology, roman art and archaeology, near eastern art and archaeology, archaeological theory and methodology. Total annual research expenditures: $30,880. *Unit head:* Prof. Christopher Ratte, Director, 734-936-3888, Fax: 734-763-8976, E-mail: ratte@umich.edu. *Application contact:* Alexander Zwinak, Graduate Coordinator, 734-764-6323, Fax: 734-763-8976, E-mail: ipcaa.office@umich.edu.

University of Minnesota, Twin Cities Campus, Graduate School, College of Liberal Arts, Department of Classical and Near Eastern Studies, Minneapolis, MN 55455-0213. Offers ancient and medieval art and archaeology (MA, PhD); classics (MA, PhD); Greek (MA, PhD); Latin (MA, PhD); religions in antiquity (MA). Part-time programs available. Terminal master's awarded for partial completion of doctoral program. *Degree requirements:* For master's, 2 foreign languages, comprehensive exam, thesis or alternative; for doctorate, variable foreign language requirement, comprehensive exam, thesis/dissertation. *Entrance requirements:* For master's and doctorate, GRE, 3 letters of recommendation, writing sample, copies of transcripts, personal statement. Additional exam requirements/recommendations for international students: Required—TOEFL. Electronic applications accepted. *Faculty research:* Greek and Latin literature, religions in antiquity, ancient Near East.

University of Missouri, Graduate School, College of Arts and Sciences, Department of Art History and Archaeology, Columbia, MO 65211. Offers MA, PhD. *Faculty:* 10 full-time (5 women). *Students:* 26 full-time (21 women), 1 (woman) part-time; includes 2 minority (1 Hispanic/Latino; 1 Two or more races, non-Hispanic/Latino), 2 international. Average age 30. 33 applicants, 42% accepted, 7 enrolled. In 2010, 4 master's, 1 doctorate awarded. Terminal master's awarded for partial completion of doctoral program. *Degree requirements:* For master's, 2 foreign languages, thesis; for doctorate, 2 foreign languages, thesis/dissertation. *Entrance requirements:* For master's, GRE General Test (minimum score 1000 verbal and quantitative, 4.5 analytical), minimum GPA of 3.0, 3.3 in major field; at least 3 semesters in appropriate foreign language; for doctorate, GRE General Test, minimum GPA of 3.0; MA or equivalent in art history or classical archaeology; master's thesis. Additional exam requirements/recommendations for international students: Required—TOEFL (minimum score 500 paper-based; 173 computer-based; 61 iBT), IELTS (minimum score 5.5). *Application deadline:* For fall admission, 1/18 priority date for domestic students. Applications are processed on a rolling basis. Application fee: $45 ($60 for international students). Electronic applications accepted. *Financial support:* In 2010–11, 4 fellowships with full tuition reimbursements, 13 research assistantships with full tuition reimbursements, 5 teaching assistantships with full tuition reimbursements were awarded; institutionally sponsored loans, health care benefits, and unspecified assistantships also available. *Faculty research:* Classical Mediterranean archaeology, medieval and Renaissance art, art and architecture of modern Europe and the Americas. *Unit head:* Dr. Anne Rudloff Stanton, Department Chair, 573-882-6711, E-mail: stantona@missouri.edu. *Application contact:* Linda Garrison, 573-882-2757, E-mail: garrisonl@missouri.edu.

University of Nebraska–Lincoln, Graduate College, College of Arts and Sciences, Department of Anthropology and Geography, Lincoln, NE 68588. Offers anthropology (MA); geography (MA, PhD); professional archaeology (MA). *Degree requirements:* For master's, thesis optional. *Entrance requirements:* For master's, GRE General Test. Additional exam requirements/recommendations for international students: Required—TOEFL. Electronic applications accepted.

The University of North Carolina at Chapel Hill, Graduate School, College of Arts and Sciences, Department of Classics, Chapel Hill, NC 27599. Offers classical archaeology (MA, PhD); classics (MA, PhD). Terminal master's awarded for partial completion of doctoral program.

Degree requirements: For master's, one foreign language, comprehensive exam, thesis; for doctorate, 2 foreign languages, comprehensive exam, thesis/dissertation. *Entrance requirements:* For master's and doctorate, GRE General Test, minimum GPA of 3.0. Electronic applications accepted.

University of Pennsylvania, School of Arts and Sciences, Graduate Group in Art and Archaeology of the Mediterranean World, Philadelphia, PA 19104. Offers AM, PhD. Part-time programs available. *Faculty:* 17 full-time (8 women), 2 part-time/adjunct (both women). *Students:* 18 full-time (12 women), 5 part-time (4 women), 6 international. 88 applicants, 5% accepted, 4 enrolled. In 2010, 1 doctorate awarded. Terminal master's awarded for partial completion of doctoral program. *Degree requirements:* For master's, 3 foreign languages, thesis, Greek or Latin exam, German and French or Italian exam; for doctorate, 4 foreign languages, thesis/dissertation, Greek or Latin exam, 2nd ancient language exam, German and French or Italian exam. *Entrance requirements:* For master's and doctorate, GRE General Test, knowledge of Greek or Latin and either French, German, or Italian. Additional exam requirements/recommendations for international students: Required—TOEFL. *Application deadline:* For fall admission, 12/1 priority date for domestic students. Application fee: $70. Electronic applications accepted. *Expenses:* Tuition: Full-time $25,660; part-time $4758 per course. Required fees: $2152; $270 per course. Tuition and fees vary according to course load, degree level and program. *Financial support:* Fellowships, institutionally sponsored loans, scholarships/grants, traineeships, health care benefits, and unspecified assistantships available. Financial award application deadline: 12/15. *Unit head:* Robert Ousterhout, Chair of the Graduate Group in Art and Archaeology of the Mediterranean World, 215-898-3249, E-mail: ousterob@sas.upenn.edu. *Application contact:* Robert Ousterhout, Chair of the Graduate Group in Art and Archaeology of the Mediterranean World, 215-898-3249, E-mail: ousterob@sas.upenn.edu.

University of Saskatchewan, College of Graduate Studies and Research, College of Arts and Sciences, Department of Archaeology, Saskatoon, SK S7N 5A2, Canada. Offers MA, PhD. Part-time programs available. *Degree requirements:* For master's, thesis; for doctorate, comprehensive exam (for some programs), thesis/dissertation. *Entrance requirements:* Additional exam requirements/recommendations for international students: Required—TOEFL (minimum score 80 iBT); Recommended—IELTS (minimum score 6.5).

University of South Africa, College of Human Sciences, Pretoria, South Africa. Offers adult education (M Ed); African languages (MA, PhD); African politics (MA, PhD); Afrikaans (MA, PhD); ancient history (MA, PhD); ancient Near Eastern studies (MA, PhD); anthropology (MA, PhD); applied linguistics (MA); Arabic (MA, PhD); archaeology (MA); art history (MA); Biblical archaeology (MA); Biblical studies (M Th, D Th, PhD); Christian spirituality (M Th, D Th); church history (M Th, D Th); classical studies (MA, PhD); clinical psychology (MA); communication (MA, PhD); comparative education (M Ed, Ed D); consulting psychology (D Admin, D Com, PhD); curriculum studies (M Ed, Ed D); development studies (M Admin, MA, D Admin, PhD); didactics (M Ed, Ed D); education (M Tech); education management (M Ed, Ed D); educational psychology (M Ed); English (MA); environmental education (M Ed); French (MA, PhD); German (MA, PhD); Greek (MA); guidance and counseling (M Ed); health studies (MA, PhD), including health sciences education (MA), health services management (MA), medical and surgical nursing science (critical care general) (MA), midwifery and neonatal nursing science (MA), trauma and emergency care (MA); history (MA, PhD); history of education (Ed D); inclusive education (M Ed, Ed D); information and communications technology policy and regulation (MA); information science (MA, MIS, PhD); international politics (MA, PhD); Islamic studies (MA, PhD); Italian (MA, PhD); Judaica (MA, PhD); linguistics (MA, PhD); mathematical education (M Ed); mathematics education (MA); missiology (M Th, D Th); modern Hebrew (MA, PhD); musicology (MA, MMus, D Mus, PhD); natural science education (M Ed); New Testament (M Th, D Th); Old Testament (D Th); pastoral therapy (M Th, D Th); philosophy (MA); philosophy of education (M Ed, Ed D); politics (MA, PhD); Portuguese (MA, PhD); practical theology (M Th, D Th); psychology (MA, MS, PhD); psychology of education (M Ed, Ed D); public health (MA); religious studies (MA, D Th, PhD); Romance languages (MA); Russian (MA, PhD); Semitic languages (MA, PhD); social behavior studies in HIV/AIDS (MA); social science (mental health) (MA); social science in development studies (MA); social science in psychology (MA); social science in social work (MA); social science in sociology (MA); social work (MSW, DSW, PhD); socio-education (M Ed, Ed D); sociolinguistics (MA); sociology (MA, PhD); Spanish (MA, PhD); systematic theology (M Th, D Th); TESOL (teaching English to speakers of other languages) (MA); theological ethics (M Th, D Th); theory of literature (MA, PhD); urban ministries (D Th); urban ministry (M Th).

The University of Tennessee, Graduate School, College of Arts and Sciences, Department of Anthropology, Knoxville, TN 37996. Offers archaeology (MA, PhD); biological anthropology (MA, PhD); cultural anthropology (MA, PhD); zoo-archaeology (MA, PhD). *Degree requirements:* For master's, thesis; for doctorate, one foreign language, thesis/dissertation. *Entrance requirements:* For master's and doctorate, GRE General Test, minimum GPA of 2.7. Additional exam requirements/recommendations for international students: Required—TOEFL. Electronic applications accepted. *Expenses:* Tuition, state resident: full-time $7440; part-time $414 per credit hour. Tuition, nonresident: full-time $22,478; part-time $1250 per credit hour. Required fees: $922; $43 per credit hour. Tuition and fees vary according to program.

The University of Texas at Austin, Graduate School, College of Liberal Arts, Department of Anthropology, Austin, TX 78712-1111. Offers archaeology (MA, PhD); folklore and public culture (MA, PhD); linguistic anthropology (MA, PhD); physical anthropology (MA, PhD); social anthropology (MA, PhD). Part-time programs available. Terminal master's awarded for partial completion of doctoral program. *Degree requirements:* For master's, thesis; for doctorate, one foreign language, thesis/dissertation. *Entrance requirements:* For master's and doctorate, GRE General Test. Additional exam requirements/recommendations for international students: Required—TOEFL. Electronic applications accepted.

University of West Florida, College of Arts and Sciences: Arts, Division of Anthropology and Archaeology, Pensacola, FL 32514-5750. Offers anthropology (MA); historical archaeology (MA). *Faculty:* 6 full-time (2 women). *Students:* 37 full-time (22 women), 31 part-time (22 women); includes 1 Black or African American, non-Hispanic/Latino; 2 Asian, non-Hispanic/Latino; 3 Hispanic/Latino; 2 Two or more races, non-Hispanic/Latino. Average age 29. 59 applicants, 53% accepted, 13 enrolled. In 2010, 2 master's awarded. *Degree requirements:* For master's, internship or thesis. *Entrance requirements:* For master's, GRE, bachelor's degree in anthropology, minimum GPA of 3.0, 3 letters of recommendation, writing sample. Additional exam requirements/recommendations for international students: Required—TOEFL (minimum score 550 paper-based; 213 computer-based). *Application deadline:* For fall admission, 6/1 for domestic students, 5/15 for international students; for spring admission, 10/1 for domestic and international students. Application fee: $30. *Expenses:* Tuition, state resident: full-time $4982; part-time $208 per credit hour. Tuition, nonresident: full-time $20,059; part-time $836 per credit hour. Required fees: $1365; $57 per credit hour. *Financial support:* In 2010–11, 2 fellowships with partial tuition reimbursements (averaging $3,702 per year), 39 research assistantships with partial tuition reimbursements (averaging $3,500 per year), 7 teaching assistantships with partial tuition reimbursements (averaging $3,760 per year) were awarded; unspecified assistantships also available. Financial award application deadline: 4/15; financial award applicants required to submit FAFSA. *Unit head:* Dr. John Bratten, Interim Chair, 850-857-6278, E-mail: anthropology@uwf.edu. *Application contact:* Terry McCray, Assistant Director of Graduate Admissions, 850-473-7718, Fax: 850-473-7714, E-mail: gradadmissions@uwf.edu.

University of Wisconsin–Madison, Graduate School, College of Letters and Science, Department of Anthropology, Madison, WI 53706-1380. Offers archaeology (PhD); biological anthropology (PhD); cultural anthropology (PhD). Terminal master's awarded for partial completion of doctoral program. *Degree requirements:* For doctorate, thesis/dissertation. *Entrance requirements:* For doctorate, qualifying exam. Electronic applications accepted. *Expenses:* Tuition, state resident: full-time $9887; part-time $617.96 per credit. Tuition, nonresident: full-time $24,054; part-time $1503.40 per credit. Required fees: $67.63 per credit.

Tuition and fees vary according to reciprocity agreements. *Faculty research:* Archaeology, biological, anthropology, cultural anthropology.

Washington State University, Graduate School, College of Liberal Arts, Department of Anthropology, Pullman, WA 99164. Offers archaeology (MA, PhD); cultural anthropology (MA, PhD); evolutionary anthropology (MA, PhD). Part-time programs available. *Faculty:* 20. *Students:* 59 full-time (36 women), 11 part-time (7 women); includes 1 Black or African American, non-Hispanic/Latino; 4 Asian, non-Hispanic/Latino; 1 Hispanic/Latino, 3 international. Average age 32. 93 applicants, 35% accepted, 15 enrolled. In 2010, 14 master's, 5 doctorates awarded. *Degree requirements:* For master's, comprehensive exam (for some programs), thesis, oral exam; for doctorate, comprehensive exam, thesis/dissertation, qualifying, oral, and written exams. *Entrance requirements:* For master's, GRE General Test, curriculum vitae, 3 references; for doctorate, GRE General Test, current curriculum vitae, statement of educational and professional goals, official transcripts of all post-secondary education, three references. Additional exam requirements/recommendations for international students: Required—TOEFL (minimum score 550 paper-based; 213 computer-based), IELTS. *Application deadline:* For fall admission, 1/10 priority date for domestic and international students; for spring admission, 7/1 priority date for domestic and international students. Applications are processed on a rolling basis. Application fee: $50. Electronic applications accepted. *Expenses:* Tuition, state resident: full-time $8552; part-time $443 per credit. Tuition, nonresident: full-time $21,650; part-time $1083 per credit. Required fees: $846. *Financial support:* In 2010–11, 5 research assistantships with full tuition reimbursements (averaging $13,917 per year), 34 teaching assistantships with full tuition reimbursements (averaging $13,056 per year) were awarded; fellowships, Federal Work-Study, scholarships/grants, health care benefits, and tuition waivers (partial) also available. Support available to part-time students. Financial award application deadline: 2/15; financial award applicants required to submit FAFSA. *Faculty research:* Western North America, including Alaska; international development; psychological anthropology; cultural ecology; medical anthropology; power and gender; evolutionary psychology; behavioral ecology; evolutionary cultural anthropology; evolutionary archaeology; paleoanthropology. Total annual research expenditures: $791,000. *Unit head:* Dr. William Andrefsky, Chair, 509-335-3441, Fax: 509-335-3999, E-mail: jmstrunk@wsu.edu. *Application contact:* Graduate School Admissions, 800-GRADWSU, Fax: 509-335-1949, E-mail: gradsch@wsu.edu.

Washington University in St. Louis, Graduate School of Arts and Sciences, Department of Art History and Archaeology, St. Louis, MO 63130-4899. Offers art history (MA, PhD); classical archaeology (MA, PhD). *Degree requirements:* For doctorate, 2 foreign languages, comprehensive exam, thesis/dissertation. *Entrance requirements:* For master's and doctorate, GRE General Test, sample of written work. Electronic applications accepted.

Wheaton College, Graduate School, Department of Biblical and Theological Studies, Program in Biblical Archaeology, Wheaton, IL 60187-5593. Offers MA. *Degree requirements:* For master's, thesis or alternative, semester of study in Israel. *Entrance requirements:* For master's, GRE General Test or MAT. Electronic applications accepted.

Wilfrid Laurier University, Faculty of Graduate and Postdoctoral Studies, Faculty of Arts, Department of Archaeology and Classical Studies, Waterloo, ON N2L 3C5, Canada. Offers MA. *Faculty:* 15 full-time (6 women), 3 part-time/adjunct (1 woman). *Students:* 6 full-time (3 women). 14 applicants, 36% accepted, 2 enrolled. *Degree requirements:* For master's, thesis optional. *Entrance requirements:* For master's, minimum B+ average in last two undergraduate years (exclusive of first year level courses in those years). Additional exam requirements/recommendations for international students: Required—TOEFL (minimum score 89 iBT). *Application deadline:* For fall admission, 2/1 priority date for domestic students, 1/1 priority date for international students. Application fee: $100. Electronic applications accepted. Tuition and fees charges are reported in Canadian dollars. *Expenses:* Tuition, area resident: Full-time $15,300 Canadian dollars; part-time $1200 Canadian dollars per credit. International tuition: $21,300 Canadian dollars full-time. Required fees: $650 Canadian dollars; $100 Canadian dollars per credit. Tuition and fees vary according to course load, degree level, campus/location and program. *Financial support:* In 2010–11, 5 fellowships, 5 teaching assistantships were awarded; career-related internships or fieldwork, scholarships/grants, health care benefits, and unspecified assistantships also available. *Faculty research:* History, languages, civilizations, archaeology. *Unit head:* Dr. Gerald Schaus, Graduate Officer, 519-884-0710 Ext. 3302, Fax: 519-883-0991, E-mail: gschaus@wlu.ca. *Application contact:* Jennifer Williams, Graduate Admissions and Records Officer, 519-884-0710 Ext. 3536, Fax: 519-884-1020, E-mail: gradstudies@wlu.ca.

Yale University, Graduate School of Arts and Sciences, Department of Near Eastern Languages and Civilizations, New Haven, CT 06520. Offers Arabic and Islamic studies (MA, PhD); archaeology of the ancient Near East (MA, PhD); Assyriology (MA, PhD); Egyptology (MA, PhD); Graeco-Arabic studies (MA, PhD); Northwest Semitic, Bible, comparative Semitics (MA, PhD). *Degree requirements:* For doctorate, 2 foreign languages, thesis/dissertation. *Entrance requirements:* For doctorate, GRE General Test.

Yale University, Graduate School of Arts and Sciences, Interdisciplinary Program in Archaeological Studies, New Haven, CT 06520. Offers MA. *Degree requirements:* For master's, thesis. *Entrance requirements:* For master's, GRE General Test.

Biological Anthropology

Duke University, Graduate School, Department of Biological Anthropology and Anatomy, Durham, NC 27710. Offers cellular and molecular biology (PhD); gross anatomy and physical anthropology (PhD), including comparative morphology of human and non-human primates, primate social behavior, vertebrate paleontology; neuroanatomy (PhD). *Faculty:* 9 full-time. *Students:* 13 full-time (9 women); includes 1 Black or African American, non-Hispanic/Latino; 2 Hispanic/Latino, 1 international. 54 applicants, 9% accepted, 2 enrolled. In 2010, 2 doctorates awarded. *Degree requirements:* For doctorate, one foreign language, thesis/dissertation. *Entrance requirements:* For doctorate, GRE General Test. Additional exam requirements/recommendations for international students: Required—TOEFL (minimum score 550 paper-based; 213 computer-based; 83 iBT), IELTS (minimum score 7). *Application deadline:* For fall admission, 12/8 priority date for domestic and international students. Application fee: $75. Electronic applications accepted. *Financial support:* Fellowships, teaching assistantships, Federal Work-Study available. Financial award application deadline: 12/31. *Unit head:* Daniel Schmitt, Director of Graduate Studies, 919-684-4124, Fax: 919-684-8542, E-mail: mlsquire@duke.edu. *Application contact:* Elizabeth Hutton, Director of Admissions, 919-684-3913, Fax: 919-684-2277, E-mail: grad-admissions@duke.edu.

Kent State University, School of Biomedical Sciences, Program in Biological Anthropology, Kent, OH 44242-0001. Offers PhD. Offered in cooperation with Northeastern Ohio Universities College of Medicine. *Degree requirements:* For doctorate, thesis/dissertation. *Entrance requirements:* For doctorate, GRE General Test, MA/MS in anthropology or one of the biological science disciplines, letter of recommendation. Electronic applications accepted. *Expenses:* Tuition, state resident: full-time $7866; part-time $437 per credit hour. Tuition, nonresident: full-time $14,022; part-time $779 per credit hour. *Faculty research:* Human evolution, paleodemography, orofacial anatomy, osteology, primate behavior.

Mercyhurst College, Graduate Program, Program in Forensic and Biological Anthropology, Erie, PA 16546. Offers MS. *Entrance requirements:* For master's, GRE or MAT, undergraduate degree in related field, interview. Additional exam requirements/recommendations for international students: Required—TOEFL.

Cultural Anthropology

California Institute of Integral Studies, School of Consciousness and Transformation, San Francisco, CA 94103. Offers creative inquiry/interdisciplinary arts (MFA); cultural anthropology and social transformation (MA); East-West psychology (MA, PhD); integrative health studies (MA); philosophy and religion (MA, PhD), including Asian and comparative studies, philosophy, cosmology, and consciousness, women's spirituality; social and cultural anthropology (PhD); transformative leadership (MA); transformative studies (PhD); writing and consciousness (MFA). Part-time and evening/weekend programs available. Postbaccalaureate distance learning degree programs offered (minimal on-campus study). *Students:* 455 full-time (315 women), 133 part-time (90 women); includes 47 Black or African American, non-Hispanic/Latino; 3 American Indian or Alaska Native, non-Hispanic/Latino; 21 Asian, non-Hispanic/Latino; 41 Hispanic/Latino, 40 international. Average age 37. 265 applicants, 91% accepted, 163 enrolled. In 2010, 64 master's, 22 doctorates awarded. Terminal master's awarded for partial completion of doctoral program. *Degree requirements:* For master's, thesis optional; for doctorate, comprehensive exam, thesis/dissertation, 1 foreign language (Asian comparative studies). *Entrance requirements:* For master's, minimum GPA of 3.0, letters of recommendation, writing sample; for doctorate, master's degree, minimum GPA of 3.0, letters of recommendation, writing sample. Additional exam requirements/recommendations for international students: Required—TOEFL. *Application deadline:* For fall admission, 2/1 priority date for domestic and international students; for spring admission, 10/15 priority date for domestic and international students. Applications are processed on a rolling basis. Application fee: $65. Electronic applications accepted. *Expenses:* Tuition: Full-time $15,660; part-time $870 per semester hour. Required fees: $95 per semester. *Financial support:* In 2010–11, 255 students received support; research assistantships, teaching assistantships, career-related internships or fieldwork, Federal Work-Study, scholarships/grants, and tuition waivers (partial) available. Support available to part-time students. Financial award application deadline: 4/15; financial award applicants required to submit FAFSA. *Faculty research:* Ecology and sustainablility, philosophy and religion, East-West psychology, integrative health, social and cultural anthropology, transformative leadership. *Application contact:* Allyson Werner, Associate Director of Admissions, 415-575-6155, Fax: 415-575-1268.

Concordia University, School of Graduate Studies, Faculty of Arts and Science, Department of Sociology and Anthropology, Montréal, QC H3G 1M8, Canada. Offers social and cultural anthropology (MA); sociology (MA). *Degree requirements:* For master's, comprehensive exam or thesis. *Entrance requirements:* For master's, honors degree in sociology or equivalent. *Faculty research:* Community and ethnic relations, popular culture, regional development in Canada, industrial and social movements, social problems and policies.

Cornell University, Graduate School, Graduate Fields of Arts and Sciences, Field of Anthropology, Ithaca, NY 14853-0001. Offers archaeological anthropology (PhD); biological anthropology (PhD); sociocultural anthropology (PhD). *Faculty:* 28 full-time (11 women). *Students:* 51 full-time (36 women); includes 3 Black or African American, non-Hispanic/Latino; 1 American Indian or Alaska Native, non-Hispanic/Latino; 1 Asian, non-Hispanic/Latino; 3 Hispanic/Latino, 17 international. Average age 31. 135 applicants, 9% accepted, 8 enrolled. In 2010, 7 doctorates awarded. *Degree requirements:* For doctorate, one foreign language, comprehensive exam, thesis/dissertation, teaching experience. *Entrance requirements:* For doctorate, GRE General Test, 3 letters of recommendation, sample of written work. Additional exam requirements/recommendations for international students: Required—TOEFL (minimum score 550 paper-based; 213 computer-based; 77 iBT). *Application deadline:* For fall admission, 1/1 for domestic students. Application fee: $80. Electronic applications accepted. *Expenses:* Tuition: Full-time $29,500. Required fees: $76. Tuition and fees vary according to degree level and program. *Financial support:* In 2010–11, 21 fellowships with full tuition reimbursements, 2 research assistantships with full tuition reimbursements, 17 teaching assistantships with full tuition reimbursements were awarded; institutionally sponsored loans, scholarships/grants, health care benefits, tuition waivers (full and partial), and unspecified assistantships also available. Financial award applicants required to submit FAFSA. *Faculty research:* Culture, engaged anthropology, political economy, area studies: Asia, Americas, Europe; interdisciplinary and ethnic studies: Asian-American studies. *Unit head:* Director of Graduate Studies, 607-255-6768. *Application contact:* Graduate Field Assistant, 607-255-6768, E-mail: graduate_anthropology@cornell.edu.

Duke University, Graduate School, Department of Cultural Anthropology, Durham, NC 27708. Offers physical anthropology (PhD), including comparative morphology of human and non-human primates, primate social behavior; social/cultural anthropology (PhD); JD/AM. *Faculty:* 13 full-time. *Students:* 32 full-time (21 women); includes 3 Black or African American, non-Hispanic/Latino; 2 Asian, non-Hispanic/Latino; 3 Hispanic/Latino, 11 international. 151 applicants, 10% accepted, 5 enrolled. In 2010, 5 doctorates awarded. *Degree requirements:* For doctorate, one foreign language, thesis/dissertation. *Entrance requirements:* For doctorate, GRE General Test. Additional exam requirements/recommendations for international students: Required—TOEFL (minimum score 550 paper-based; 213 computer-based; 83 iBT), IELTS (minimum score 7). *Application deadline:* For fall admission, 12/8 priority date for domestic and international students. Application fee: $75. *Financial support:* Fellowships, research assistantships, teaching assistantships, Federal Work-Study available. Financial award application deadline: 12/8. *Unit head:* Louise Meintjes, Director of Graduate Studies, 919-684-4544, Fax: 919-681-8483, E-mail: kfreeman@duke.edu. *Application contact:* Elizabeth Hutton, Director, Graduate Admissions, 919-684-3913, Fax: 919-684-2277, E-mail: grad-admissions@duke.edu.

Graduate School and University Center of the City University of New York, Graduate Studies, Program in Anthropology, New York, NY 10016-4039. Offers anthropological linguistics

Cultural Anthropology

Graduate School and University Center of the City University of New York (continued)
(PhD); archaeology (PhD); cultural anthropology (PhD); physical anthropology (PhD). *Degree requirements:* For doctorate, one foreign language, thesis/dissertation. *Entrance requirements:* For doctorate, GRE General Test. Additional exam requirements/recommendations for international students: Required—TOEFL. Electronic applications accepted.

Memorial University of Newfoundland, School of Graduate Studies, Department of Anthropology, St. John's, NL A1C 5S7, Canada. Offers archaeology and physical anthropology (MA, PhD); social and cultural anthropology (MA, PhD). Part-time programs available. *Degree requirements:* For master's, thesis (for some programs); for doctorate, comprehensive exam, thesis/dissertation, oral defense of thesis. *Entrance requirements:* For master's, 2nd class degree in related field. Electronic applications accepted. *Faculty research:* Early European settlements, ethnoarchaeology, economic/political anthropology, land claims and aboriginal rights, marine anthropology.

North Carolina State University, Graduate School, College of Humanities and Social Sciences, Department of Sociology and Anthropology, Program in Anthropology, Raleigh, NC 27695. Offers bioarchaeology (MA); cultural anthropology (MA); environmental anthropology (MA).

Northern Arizona University, Graduate College, College of Social and Behavioral Sciences, Department of Anthropology, Flagstaff, AZ 86011. Offers archaeology (MA); cultural anthropology (MA); linguistic anthropology (MA). *Faculty:* 17 full-time (7 women). *Students:* 48 full-time (29 women), 14 part-time (8 women); includes 14 minority (3 American Indian or Alaska Native, non-Hispanic/Latino; 8 Hispanic/Latino; 3 Two or more races, non-Hispanic/Latino), 1 international. Average age 35. 100 applicants, 45% accepted, 26 enrolled. In 2010, 25 master's awarded. *Degree requirements:* For master's, thesis (for some programs), internship paper. *Entrance requirements:* For master's, 12 undergraduate hours in anthropology. Additional exam requirements/recommendations for international students: Required—TOEFL (minimum score 550 paper-based; 213 computer-based; 80 iBT), IELTS (minimum score 7). *Application deadline:* For fall admission, 2/15 priority date for domestic and international students. Applications are processed on a rolling basis. Application fee: $65. Electronic applications accepted. *Financial support:* In 2010–11, 1 fellowship (averaging $10,774 per year), 9 teaching assistantships with partial tuition reimbursements (averaging $10,449 per year) were awarded; career-related internships or fieldwork, Federal Work-Study, scholarships/grants, health care benefits, tuition waivers (full and partial), and unspecified assistantships also available. Financial award applicants required to submit FAFSA. *Faculty research:* Economic development, culture change, ethnohistory, archaeology of the Southwest, small town networks and HIV. Total annual research expenditures: $594,266. *Unit head:* Dr. Robert Trotter, Chair/Professor, 928-523-4521, Fax: 928-523-9135, E-mail: robert.trotter@nau.edu. *Application contact:* Pamela Lamb, Administrative Assistant, 928-523-3180, Fax: 928-523-9135, E-mail: anthropology@nau.edu.

Rice University, Graduate Programs, School of Social Sciences, Department of Anthropology, Houston, TX 77251-1892. Offers archaeology (MA, PhD); social-cultural anthropology (MA, PhD). Terminal master's awarded for partial completion of doctoral program. *Degree requirements:* For master's, one foreign language, 3 major papers, dissertation proposal and language exam or thesis; for doctorate, one foreign language, thesis/dissertation. *Entrance requirements:* For master's and doctorate, research proposal. Additional exam requirements/recommendations for international students: Required—TOEFL (minimum score 90 iBT). Electronic applications accepted.

San Francisco State University, Division of Graduate Studies, College of Behavioral and Social Sciences, Department of Anthropology, San Francisco, CA 94132-1722. Offers archaeology (MA); biological/physical anthropology (MA); social/cultural anthropology (MA); visual anthropology (MA). *Faculty research:* Immigration, ethnicity, urban anthropology, Californian and Latin American archaeology. *Unit head:* Dr. Douglass Bailey, Chair, 415-338-1427. *Application contact:* Dr. Mariana Ferreira, Graduate Coordinator, 415-405-2467, E-mail: mariana@sfsu.edu.

Stanford University, School of Humanities and Sciences, Department of Cultural and Social Anthropology, Stanford, CA 94305-9991. Offers MA, PhD. Terminal master's awarded for partial completion of doctoral program. *Degree requirements:* For master's, thesis; for doctorate, one foreign language, thesis/dissertation. *Entrance requirements:* For master's and doctorate, GRE General Test. Additional exam requirements/recommendations for international students: Required—TOEFL. Electronic applications accepted. *Expenses:* Tuition: Full-time $38,700; part-time $860 per unit. One-time fee: $200 full-time.

University of California, Santa Barbara, Graduate Division, College of Letters and Sciences, Division of Social Sciences, Department of Anthropology, Santa Barbara, CA 93106-2014. Offers archaeology (MA); biosocial anthropology (MA, PhD); sociocultural anthropology (MA, PhD); MA/PhD. *Faculty:* 12 full-time (3 women), 2 part-time/adjunct (both women). *Students:* 51 full-time (34 women); includes 2 Asian, non-Hispanic/Latino; 7 Hispanic/Latino. Average age 31. 47 applicants, 30% accepted, 4 enrolled. In 2010, 6 master's, 9 doctorates awarded. Terminal master's awarded for partial completion of doctoral program. *Degree requirements:* For master's, comprehensive exam (for some programs), thesis (for some programs); for doctorate, comprehensive exam (for some programs), thesis/dissertation. *Entrance requirements:* For master's and doctorate, GRE General Test, statement of purpose, transcripts, writing sample, curriculum vitae. Additional exam requirements/recommendations for international students: Required—TOEFL (minimum score 550 paper-based; 80 iBT), IELTS (minimum score 7). *Application deadline:* For fall admission, 12/1 for domestic and international students. Application fee: $70 ($90 for international students). Electronic applications accepted. *Financial support:* In 2010–11, 48 students received support, including 35 fellowships with full and partial tuition reimbursements available (averaging $5,749 per year), 7 research assistantships with full and partial tuition reimbursements available (averaging $7,287 per year), 37 teaching assistantships with full tuition reimbursements available (averaging $10,042 per year); career-related internships or fieldwork, Federal Work-Study, institutionally sponsored loans, scholarships/grants, traineeships, health care benefits, tuition waivers (full and partial), and unspecified assistantships also available. Support available to part-time students. Financial award application deadline: 12/1; financial award applicants required to submit FAFSA. *Faculty research:* Archaeology, bioarchaeology, biosocial anthropology, evolutionary ecology, evolutionary psychology, sociocultural anthropology. *Unit head:* Prof. Katharina Schreiber, Department Chair, 805-893-2519, Fax: 805-893-8707, E-mail: kschreiber@anth.ucsb.edu. *Application contact:* Robin Roe, Graduate Program Assistant, 805-893-2516, Fax: 805-893-8707, E-mail: roe@anth.ucsb.edu.

University of California, Santa Cruz, Division of Graduate Studies, Division of Social Sciences, Department of Anthropology, Santa Cruz, CA 95064. Offers cultural anthropology (PhD). *Students:* 39 full-time (25 women), 7 part-time (6 women); includes 16 minority (1 American Indian or Alaska Native, non-Hispanic/Latino; 5 Asian, non-Hispanic/Latino; 8 Hispanic/Latino; 2 Two or more races, non-Hispanic/Latino), 3 international. Average age 31. 71 applicants, 18% accepted, 5 enrolled. In 2010, 9 doctorates awarded. *Degree requirements:* For doctorate, thesis/dissertation, qualifying exam. *Entrance requirements:* For doctorate, GRE General Test. Additional exam requirements/recommendations for international students: Required—TOEFL (minimum score 550 paper-based; 220 computer-based; 83 iBT); Recommended—IELTS (minimum score 8). *Application deadline:* For fall admission, 12/15 for domestic and international students. Application fee: $70 ($90 for international students). Electronic applications accepted. *Financial support:* Fellowships, research assistantships, teaching assistantships, institutionally sponsored loans and tuition waivers available. Financial award applicants required to submit FAFSA. *Faculty research:* Culture and power, women's roles, AIDS, folklore. *Unit head:* Allyson Ramage, Graduate Program Coordinator, 831-459-3588, E-mail: aramage@ucsc.edu. *Application contact:* Allyson Ramage, Graduate Program Coordinator, 831-459-3588, E-mail: aramage@ucsc.edu.

University of Denver, Division of Arts, Humanities and Social Sciences, Department of Anthropology, Denver, CO 80208. Offers archaeology (MA); cultural anthropology (MA); museum studies (MA). Part-time programs available. *Faculty:* 8 full-time (4 women). *Students:* 1 (woman) full-time, 17 part-time (12 women); includes 4 minority (2 Black or African American, non-Hispanic/Latino; 1 American Indian or Alaska Native, non-Hispanic/Latino; 1 Hispanic/Latino), 1 international. Average age 26. 45 applicants, 47% accepted, 8 enrolled. In 2010, 11 master's awarded. *Degree requirements:* For master's, comprehensive exam, thesis or alternative, proficiency in foreign language other than English or in quantitative methods. *Entrance requirements:* For master's, GRE General Test. Additional exam requirements/recommendations for international students: Required—TOEFL (minimum score 550 paper-based; 80 iBT). *Application deadline:* Applications are processed on a rolling basis. Application fee: $60. Electronic applications accepted. *Expenses:* Tuition: Full-time $35,604; part-time $29,670 per year. Required fees: $687 per year. Tuition and fees vary according to program. *Financial support:* In 2010–11, 12 teaching assistantships with full and partial tuition reimbursements (averaging $4,667 per year) were awarded; career-related internships or fieldwork, Federal Work-Study, institutionally sponsored loans, scholarships/grants, and unspecified assistantships also available. Support available to part-time students. Financial award application deadline: 3/15; financial award applicants required to submit FAFSA. *Faculty research:* Gender, class, race, ground-penetrating radar, archaeology. *Unit head:* Dr. Dean J. Saitta, Chair, 303-871-2680, E-mail: dsaitta@du.edu. *Application contact:* Carrie Shrader, Assistant to Chair, 303-871-2677, E-mail: anth02@du.edu.

The University of Tennessee, Graduate School, College of Arts and Sciences, Department of Anthropology, Knoxville, TN 37996. Offers archaeology (MA, PhD); biological anthropology (MA, PhD); cultural anthropology (MA, PhD); zoo-archaeology (MA, PhD). *Degree requirements:* For master's, thesis; for doctorate, one foreign language, thesis/dissertation. *Entrance requirements:* For master's and doctorate, GRE General Test, minimum GPA of 2.7. Additional exam requirements/recommendations for international students: Required—TOEFL. Electronic applications accepted. *Expenses:* Tuition, state resident: full-time $7440; part-time $414 per credit hour. Tuition, nonresident: full-time $22,478; part-time $1250 per credit hour. Required fees: $922; $43 per credit hour. Tuition and fees vary according to program.

University of Wisconsin–Madison, Graduate School, College of Letters and Science, Department of Anthropology, Madison, WI 53706-1380. Offers archaeology (PhD); biological anthropology (PhD); cultural anthropology (PhD). Terminal master's awarded for partial completion of doctoral program. *Degree requirements:* For doctorate, thesis/dissertation. *Entrance requirements:* For doctorate, qualifying exam. Electronic applications accepted. *Expenses:* Tuition, state resident: full-time $9887; part-time $617.96 per credit. Tuition, nonresident: full-time $24,054; part-time $1503.40 per credit. Required fees: $67.63 per credit. Tuition and fees vary according to reciprocity agreements. *Faculty research:* Archaeology, biological, anthropology, cultural anthropology.

Washington State University, Graduate School, College of Liberal Arts, Department of Anthropology, Pullman, WA 99164. Offers archaeology (MA, PhD); cultural anthropology (MA, PhD); evolutionary anthropology (MA, PhD). Part-time programs available. *Faculty:* 20. *Students:* 59 full-time (36 women), 11 part-time (7 women); includes 1 Black or African American, non-Hispanic/Latino; 4 Asian, non-Hispanic/Latino; 1 Hispanic/Latino, 3 international. Average age 32. 93 applicants, 35% accepted, 15 enrolled. In 2010, 14 master's, 5 doctorates awarded. *Degree requirements:* For master's, comprehensive exam (for some programs), thesis, oral exam; for doctorate, comprehensive exam, thesis/dissertation, qualifying, oral, and written exams. *Entrance requirements:* For master's, GRE General Test, curriculum vitae, 3 references; for doctorate, GRE General Test, current curriculum vitae, statement of educational and professional goals, official transcripts of all post-secondary education, three references. Additional exam requirements/recommendations for international students: Required—TOEFL (minimum score 550 paper-based; 213 computer-based), IELTS. *Application deadline:* For fall admission, 1/10 priority date for domestic and international students; for spring admission, 7/1 priority date for domestic and international students. Applications are processed on a rolling basis. Application fee: $50. Electronic applications accepted. *Expenses:* Tuition, state resident: full-time $8552; part-time $443 per credit. Tuition, nonresident: full-time $21,650; part-time $1083 per credit. Required fees: $846. *Financial support:* In 2010–11, 5 research assistantships with full tuition reimbursements (averaging $13,917 per year), 34 teaching assistantships with full tuition reimbursements (averaging $13,056 per year) were awarded; fellowships, Federal Work-Study, scholarships/grants, health care benefits, and tuition waivers (partial) also available. Support available to part-time students. Financial award application deadline: 2/15; financial award applicants required to submit FAFSA. *Faculty research:* Western North America, including Alaska; international development; psychological anthropology; cultural ecology; medical anthropology; power and gender; evolutionary psychology; behavioral ecology; evolutionary cultural anthropology; evolutionary archaeology; paleoanthropology. Total annual research expenditures: $791,000. *Unit head:* Dr. William Andrefsky, Chair, 509-335-3441, Fax: 509-335-3999, E-mail: jmstrunk@wsu.edu. *Application contact:* Graduate School Admissions, 800-GRADWSU, Fax: 509-335-1949, E-mail: gradsch@wsu.edu.

Demography and Population Studies

The American University in Cairo, School of Global Affairs and Public Policy, Program in Migration and Refugee Studies, Cairo, Egypt. Offers forced migration and refugee studies (Diploma); migration and refugee studies (MA).

Bowling Green State University, Graduate College, College of Arts and Sciences, Department of Sociology, Bowling Green, OH 43403. Offers demography and population studies (MA); social psychology (MA); sociology (PhD). Part-time programs available. *Degree requirements:* For master's, thesis or alternative; for doctorate, comprehensive exam, thesis/dissertation. *Entrance requirements:* For master's and doctorate, GRE General Test. Additional exam requirements/recommendations for international students: Required—TOEFL. Electronic applications accepted. *Faculty research:* Applied demography, criminology and deviance, family studies, population studies, social psychology.

Cornell University, Graduate School, Graduate Fields of Agriculture and Life Sciences, Field of Development Sociology, Ithaca, NY 14853-0001. Offers community and regional society (MS); community and regional sociology (MPS, PhD); methods of social research (MPS, MS, PhD); population and development (MPS, MS, PhD); rural and environmental sociology (MPS, MS, PhD); state, economy, and society (MPS, MS, PhD). *Faculty:* 22 full-time (7 women). *Students:* 44 full-time (28 women); includes 1 Black or African American, non-Hispanic/Latino; 2 American Indian or Alaska Native, non-Hispanic/Latino; 1 Asian, non-Hispanic/Latino; 1

Hispanic/Latino, 17 international. Average age 31. 73 applicants, 16% accepted, 7 enrolled. In 2010, 4 master's, 3 doctorates awarded. *Degree requirements:* For doctorate, comprehensive exam, thesis/dissertation. *Entrance requirements:* For master's and doctorate, GRE General Test, 3 letters of recommendation. Additional exam requirements/recommendations for international students: Required—TOEFL (minimum score 550 paper-based; 213 computer-based; 77 iBT). *Application deadline:* For fall admission, 1/15 priority date for domestic students. Application fee: $70. Electronic applications accepted. *Expenses:* Tuition: Full-time $29,500. Required fees: $76. Tuition and fees vary according to degree level and program. *Financial support:* In 2010–11, 9 fellowships with full tuition reimbursements, 8 research assistantships with full tuition reimbursements, 16 teaching assistantships with full tuition reimbursements were awarded; institutionally sponsored loans, scholarships/grants, health care benefits, tuition waivers (full and partial), and unspecified assistantships also available. Financial award applicants required to submit FAFSA. *Faculty research:* Demography (population and development), environmental sociology, international and rural community development, political economy and ecology, sustainable agriculture. *Unit head:* Director of Graduate Studies, 607-255-3092, Fax: 607-254-2896. *Application contact:* Graduate Field Assistant, 607-255-3092, Fax: 607-254-2896, E-mail: devsoc@cornell.edu.

Cornell University, Graduate School, Graduate Fields of Arts and Sciences, Field of International Development, Ithaca, NY 14853-0001. Offers development policy (MPS); international nutrition (MPS); international planning (MPS); international population (MPS); science and technology policy (MPS). *Faculty:* 41 full-time (14 women). *Students:* 7 full-time (3 women), 5 international. Average age 28. 36 applicants, 22% accepted, 4 enrolled. In 2010, 7 master's awarded. *Degree requirements:* For master's, project paper. *Entrance requirements:* For master's, GRE General Test (recommended), 2 academic recommendations, 2 years of development experience. Additional exam requirements/recommendations for international students: Required—TOEFL (minimum score 77 iBT). *Application deadline:* Applications are processed on a rolling basis. Application fee: $80. Electronic applications accepted. *Expenses:* Tuition: Full-time $29,500. Required fees: $76. Tuition and fees vary according to degree level and program. *Financial support:* In 2010–11, 1 fellowship with full tuition reimbursement was awarded; research assistantships with full tuition reimbursements, teaching assistantships with full tuition reimbursements, institutionally sponsored loans, scholarships/grants, health care benefits, tuition waivers (full and partial), and unspecified assistantships also available. Financial award applicants required to submit FAFSA. *Faculty research:* Development policy, international nutrition, international planning, science and technology policy, international population. *Unit head:* Director of Graduate Studies, 607-255-3037, Fax: 607-255-1005. *Application contact:* Graduate Field Assistant, 607-255-0831, Fax: 607-255-1005, E-mail: mpsid@cornell.edu.

Emory University, Rollins School of Public Health, Hubert Department of Global Health, Atlanta, GA 30322-1100. Offers global demography (MSPH); global environmental health (MPH); public nutrition (MSPH). *Accreditation:* CEPH. Part-time programs available. *Degree requirements:* For master's, thesis, practicum. *Entrance requirements:* For master's, GRE General Test. Additional exam requirements/recommendations for international students: Required—TOEFL (minimum score 550 paper-based; 213 computer-based; 80 iBT). Electronic applications accepted. *Expenses:* Tuition: Full-time $33,800. Required fees: $1300.

Florida State University, The Graduate School, College of Social Sciences and Public Policy, Center for Demography and Population Health, Tallahassee, FL 32306-2240. Offers MS. *Faculty:* 14 full-time (6 women). *Students:* 10 full-time (6 women), 2 part-time (1 woman); includes 1 Hispanic/Latino; 2 Two or more races, non-Hispanic/Latino, 1 international. Average age 24. 14 applicants, 86% accepted, 9 enrolled. In 2010, 13 master's awarded. *Degree requirements:* For master's, thesis. *Entrance requirements:* For master's, GRE General Test, minimum upper-division GPA of 3.0. Additional exam requirements/recommendations for international students: Required—TOEFL (minimum score 550 paper-based; 213 computer-based; 80 iBT). *Application deadline:* For fall admission, 7/1 for domestic and international students. Application fee: $30. Electronic applications accepted. *Expenses:* Tuition, state resident: full-time $8238.24. *Financial support:* Career-related internships or fieldwork, Federal Work-Study, and institutionally sponsored loans available. Financial award application deadline: 1/31; financial award applicants required to submit FAFSA. *Faculty research:* Aging, family, fertility, health, immigration, mortality. Total annual research expenditures: $14,724. *Unit head:* Dr. Karin L. Brewster, Director, 850-644-7106, Fax: 850-644-8818, E-mail: karin.brewster@fsu.edu. *Application contact:* Dr. Karin L. Brewster, Director, 850-644-7106, Fax: 850-644-8818, E-mail: karin.brewster@fsu.edu.

Harvard University, Harvard School of Public Health, Department of Global Health and Population, Boston, MA 02115-6096. Offers SM, DPH, SD. Part-time programs available. *Faculty:* 39 full-time (9 women), 9 part-time/adjunct (2 women). *Students:* 88 full-time, 2 part-time; includes 18 minority (3 Black or African American, non-Hispanic/Latino; 10 Asian, non-Hispanic/Latino; 1 Hispanic/Latino; 4 Two or more races, non-Hispanic/Latino), 33 international. Average age 28. 243 applicants, 24% accepted, 29 enrolled. In 2010, 29 master's, 4 doctorates awarded. *Degree requirements:* For master's, thesis; for doctorate, thesis/dissertation, qualifying exam. *Entrance requirements:* For master's and doctorate, GRE. Additional exam requirements/recommendations for international students: Required—TOEFL (minimum score 595 paper-based; 240 computer-based; 95 iBT); Recommended—IELTS (minimum score 7). *Application deadline:* For fall admission, 12/15 for domestic and international students. Application fee: $115. Electronic applications accepted. *Expenses:* Tuition: Full-time $34,976. Required fees: $1166. Full-time tuition and fees vary according to program. *Financial support:* Fellowships, research assistantships, teaching assistantships, Federal Work-Study, scholarships/grants, traineeships, tuition waivers (partial), and unspecified assistantships available. Support available to part-time students. Financial award application deadline: 2/8; financial award applicants required to submit FAFSA. *Faculty research:* International health policy, economics, reproductive health, ecology. *Unit head:* Dr. David Bloom, Chair, 617-432-1232, Fax: 617-432-6733, E-mail: dbloom@hsph.harvard.edu. *Application contact:* Vincent W. James, Director of Admissions, 617-432-1031, Fax: 617-432-7080, E-mail: admissions@hsph.harvard.edu.

The Johns Hopkins University, Bloomberg School of Public Health, Department of Population, Family and Reproductive Health, Baltimore, MD 21205. Offers child and adolescent health and development (Dr PH, PhD); demography (MHS); population and health (Dr PH, PhD); population, family and reproductive health (MHS); reproductive, perinatal women's health (Dr PH, PhD). Part-time programs available. *Faculty:* 35 full-time (24 women), 40 part-time/adjunct (25 women). *Students:* 90 full-time (81 women), 6 part-time (3 women); includes 29 minority (14 Black or African American, non-Hispanic/Latino; 8 Asian, non-Hispanic/Latino; 4 Hispanic/Latino; 3 Two or more races, non-Hispanic/Latino), 14 international. Average age 29. 150 applicants, 40% accepted, 33 enrolled. In 2010, 21 master's, 14 doctorates awarded. *Degree requirements:* For master's, essay, fieldwork; for doctorate, thesis/dissertation, 1 year full-time residency, oral and written exams. *Entrance requirements:* For master's and doctorate, GRE General Test, 3 letters of recommendation, curriculum vitae. Additional exam requirements/recommendations for international students: Required—TOEFL (minimum score 600 paper-based; 250 computer-based). *Application deadline:* For fall admission, 1/2 for domestic and international students. Applications are processed on a rolling basis. Application fee: $45. Electronic applications accepted. *Financial support:* In 2010–11, 89 students received support, including 13 fellowships with full and partial tuition reimbursements available (averaging $51,144 per year), 6 research assistantships (averaging $5,760 per year), 10 teaching assistantships (averaging $1,136 per year); Federal Work-Study, institutionally sponsored loans, scholarships/grants, traineeships, health care benefits, and stipends also available. Support available to part-time students. Financial award application deadline: 3/15; financial award applicants required to submit FAFSA. *Faculty research:* Child and adolescent health and development, population and health and reproductive, perinatal and women's health. Total annual research expenditures: $18.8 million. *Unit head:* Dr. Robert Blum, Chair, 410-955-3384, Fax: 410-955-2303, E-mail: rblum@jhsph.edu. *Application contact:* Lauren Ferretti, Academic Coordinator, 410-614-6676, Fax: 410-955-2303, E-mail: lferrett@jhsph.edu.

Princeton University, Graduate School, Department of Sociology, Princeton, NJ 08544-1019. Offers sociology (PhD); sociology and demography (PhD). *Degree requirements:* For doctorate, variable foreign language requirement, thesis/dissertation. *Entrance requirements:* For doctorate, GRE General Test, GRE Subject Test (recommended), sample of written work. Additional exam requirements/recommendations for international students: Required—TOEFL (minimum score 600 paper-based; 250 computer-based). Electronic applications accepted.

Princeton University, Graduate School, Program in Population Studies, Princeton, NJ 08544-1019. Offers demography (PhD, Certificate); economics and demography (PhD); public affairs and demography (PhD); sociology and demography (PhD). *Degree requirements:* For doctorate, thesis/dissertation. *Entrance requirements:* For doctorate, GRE General Test. Additional exam requirements/recommendations for international students: Required—TOEFL (minimum score 600 paper-based; 250 computer-based). Electronic applications accepted. *Faculty research:* Models, fertility, infant and child mortality, migration.

Université de Montréal, Faculty of Arts and Sciences, Department of Demography, Montréal, QC H3C 3J7, Canada. Offers M Sc, PhD. Terminal master's awarded for partial completion of doctoral program. *Degree requirements:* For master's, one foreign language, thesis; for doctorate, one foreign language, thesis/dissertation, general exam. *Entrance requirements:* For master's, minimum GPA of 2.7. Electronic applications accepted. *Faculty research:* Historical demography, population and development, ethnic and linguistic groups, aging of population, family demography.

Université du Québec, Institut National de la Recherche Scientifique, Graduate Programs, Research Center—Urbanization, Culture and Society, Québec, QC G1K 9A9, Canada. Offers demography (M Sc, PhD); research and public action (MA); urban studies (M Sc, PhD). Programs given in French. Part-time programs available. *Faculty:* 36. *Students:* 150 full-time (87 women), 13 part-time (5 women), 28 international. Average age 33. In 2010, 12 master's, 8 doctorates awarded. *Degree requirements:* For master's, thesis optional; for doctorate, thesis/dissertation. *Entrance requirements:* For master's, appropriate bachelor's degree, proficiency in French; for doctorate, appropriate master's degree, proficiency in French. *Application deadline:* For fall admission, 3/30 for domestic and international students; for winter admission, 11/1 for domestic and international students; for spring admission, 3/1 for domestic and international students. Application fee: $30. *Financial support:* Fellowships, research assistantships, teaching assistantships available. *Faculty research:* Regional space, urban and metropolitan space, micro-urban space. *Unit head:* Claire Poitras, Director, 514-499-4037, Fax: 514-499-4065, E-mail: claire.poitras@ucs.inrs.ca. *Application contact:* Yvonne Boisvert, Registrar, 418-654-3861, Fax: 418-654-3858, E-mail: registrariat@adm.inrs.ca.

University at Albany, State University of New York, College of Arts and Sciences, Department of Sociology, Albany, NY 12222-0001. Offers demography (Certificate); sociology (MA, PhD); urban policy (Certificate). Terminal master's awarded for partial completion of doctoral program. *Degree requirements:* For master's, thesis; for doctorate, thesis/dissertation, 2 specialization exams, research tool. *Entrance requirements:* For master's and doctorate, GRE General Test. Additional exam requirements/recommendations for international students: Required—TOEFL (minimum score 213 computer-based). Electronic applications accepted. *Faculty research:* Gender and equality, crime and deviance, aging, work and organizations, social demography.

University of Alberta, Faculty of Graduate Studies and Research, Department of Sociology, Edmonton, AB T6G 2E1, Canada. Offers criminal justice (MA); demography (MA, PhD); sociology (MA, PhD). Part-time programs available. *Degree requirements:* For master's, thesis (for some programs); for doctorate, thesis/dissertation. *Faculty research:* Criminology, knowledge and culture, methods and theory, population studies, stratification.

University of California, Berkeley, Graduate Division, College of Letters and Science, Department of Demography, Berkeley, CA 94720-1500. Offers PhD. *Degree requirements:* For doctorate, thesis/dissertation, qualifying exam. *Entrance requirements:* For doctorate, GRE General Test, minimum GPA of 3.0, 3 letters of recommendation.

University of California, Berkeley, Graduate Division, College of Letters and Science, Group in Sociology and Demography, Berkeley, CA 94720-1500. Offers MA, PhD. *Degree requirements:* For doctorate, thesis/dissertation, qualifying exam. *Entrance requirements:* For master's and doctorate, GRE General Test, minimum GPA of 3.0, 3 letters of recommendation. Electronic applications accepted.

University of California, Irvine, School of Social Sciences and School of Social Ecology, Program in Demographic and Social Analysis, Irvine, CA 92697. Offers MA. *Students:* 14 full-time (11 women); includes 11 minority (9 Asian, non-Hispanic/Latino; 2 Hispanic/Latino), 1 international. Average age 28. 34 applicants, 71% accepted, 14 enrolled. In 2010, 17 master's awarded. *Entrance requirements:* For master's, GRE, minimum GPA of 3.0. Additional exam requirements/recommendations for international students: Required—TOEFL (minimum score 550 paper-based; 213 computer-based). *Application deadline:* For fall admission, 1/15 priority date for domestic and international students. Application fee: $80 ($100 for international students). *Financial support:* Application deadline: 3/1. *Application contact:* Matt Huffman, Associate Professor, 949-824-5341, Fax: 949-824-4717, E-mail: mhuffman@uci.edu.

University of Guelph, Ontario Veterinary College and Graduate Studies, Graduate Programs in Veterinary Sciences, Department of Population Medicine, Guelph, ON N1G 2W1, Canada. Offers epidemiology (M Sc, DV Sc, PhD); health management (DV Sc); population medicine and health management (M Sc); swine health management (M Sc); theriogenology (M Sc, DV Sc). *Degree requirements:* For master's, thesis; for doctorate, comprehensive exam, thesis/dissertation. *Entrance requirements:* Additional exam requirements/recommendations for international students: Required—TOEFL.

University of Hawaii at Manoa, John A. Burns School of Medicine, Department of Public Health Sciences and Epidemiology, Global Health and Population Studies Program, Honolulu, HI 96822. Offers Graduate Certificate. Part-time programs available. *Faculty:* 36 full-time (16 women). *Students:* 67 full-time (53 women), 15 part-time (12 women); includes 41 minority (2 Black or African American, non-Hispanic/Latino; 1 American Indian or Alaska Native, non-Hispanic/Latino; 24 Asian, non-Hispanic/Latino; 8 Native Hawaiian or other Pacific Islander, non-Hispanic/Latino; 6 Two or more races, non-Hispanic/Latino), 15 international. Average age 34. 106 applicants, 59% accepted, 44 enrolled. In 2010, 1 Graduate Certificate awarded. *Entrance requirements:* For degree, GRE General Test. Additional exam requirements/recommendations for international students: Required—TOEFL (minimum score 550 paper-based; 173 computer-based; 79 iBT), IELTS (minimum score 5). *Application deadline:* For fall admission, 1/15 for domestic students, 1/25 for international students; for spring admission, 9/1 for domestic and international students. Application fee: $60. *Financial support:* In 2010–11, 26 fellowships (averaging $1,610 per year), 21 research assistantships (averaging $17,727 per year), 1 teaching assistantship (averaging $14,382 per year) were awarded. *Application contact:* Alan Katz, Information Contact, 808-956-5741, Fax: 808-956-6041, E-mail: katz@hawaii.edu.

University of Pennsylvania, School of Arts and Sciences, Graduate Group in Demography, Philadelphia, PA 19104. Offers AM, PhD. *Faculty:* 39 full-time (16 women), 8 part-time/adjunct (5 women). *Students:* 31 full-time (17 women); includes 4 Asian, non-Hispanic/Latino, 11 international. 34 applicants, 26% accepted, 6 enrolled. In 2010, 5 master's, 6 doctorates awarded. Terminal master's awarded for partial completion of doctoral program. *Degree requirements:* For master's, thesis or alternative; for doctorate, thesis/dissertation. *Entrance requirements:* For master's and doctorate, GRE General Test. Additional exam requirements/recommendations for international students: Required—TOEFL. *Application deadline:* For fall admission, 12/1 priority date for domestic students. Application fee: $70. Electronic applications accepted. *Expenses:* Tuition: Full-time $25,660; part-time $4758 per course. Required fees: $2152; $270 per course. Tuition and fees vary according to course load, degree level and program. *Financial support:* Fellowships, research assistantships, institutionally sponsored

Demography and Population Studies

University of Pennsylvania (continued)
loans, scholarships/grants, traineeships, health care benefits, and unspecified assistantships available. Financial award application deadline: 12/15.

University of Puerto Rico, Medical Sciences Campus, Graduate School of Public Health, Department of Social Sciences, Program in Demography, San Juan, PR 00936-5067. Offers MS. Part-time programs available. *Degree requirements:* For master's, thesis. *Entrance requirements:* For master's, GRE, previous course work in algebra and statistics.

The University of Texas at San Antonio, College of Public Policy, Department of Demography and Organizational Studies, San Antonio, TX 78249-0617. Offers applied demography (PhD). Part-time and evening/weekend programs available. *Faculty:* 6 full-time (2 women), 1 (woman) part-time/adjunct. *Students:* 15 full-time (5 women), 22 part-time (16 women); includes 22 minority (1 Black or African American, non-Hispanic/Latino; 3 Asian, non-Hispanic/Latino; 15 Hispanic/Latino; 3 Two or more races, non-Hispanic/Latino), 6 international. Average age 36. 18 applicants, 61% accepted, 9 enrolled. In 2010, 7 doctorates awarded. *Entrance requirements:* For doctorate, GRE. Additional exam requirements/recommendations for international students: Required—TOEFL (minimum score 500 paper-based; 173 computer-based; 61 iBT), IELTS (minimum score 5). *Application deadline:* For fall admission, 7/1 for domestic students, 4/1 for international students; for spring admission, 11/1 for domestic students, 9/1 for international students. Applications are processed on a rolling basis. Application fee: $45 ($80 for international students). Electronic applications accepted. *Expenses:* Tuition, state resident: full-time $4172; part-time $231.75 per credit hour. Tuition, nonresident: full-time $15,332; part-time $851.75 per credit hour. *Financial support:* In 2010–11, 1 student received support, including 3 research assistantships (averaging $16,000 per year); career-related internships or fieldwork, scholarships/grants, tuition waivers, and unspecified assistantships also available. Support available to part-time students. *Faculty research:* Health disparities, immigration, population estimates and projections, rural development and fertility change, spatial inequality. Total annual research expenditures: $13,776. *Unit head:* Joachim Singelmann, Department Chair, 210-458-3163, Fax: 210-458-3164, E-mail: dem@utsa.edu. *Application contact:* Veronica Ramirez, Assistant Dean of the Graduate School, 210-458-4330, Fax: 210-458-4332, E-mail: graduatestudies@utsa.edu.

University of Washington, Graduate School, School of Public Health, Department of Health Services, Seattle, WA 98195. Offers bioinformatics (PhD); cancer prevention and control (PhD); clinical research (MS); community oriented public health practice (MPH); economics or finance (PhD); evaluation sciences (PhD); executive program (MHA); health behavior and health promotion (PhD); health care and population health research (MPH); health policy analysis and process (PhD); health policy and analysis and process (MPH); health services (MS, PhD); health services administration (EMHA, MHA); in residence program (MHA); maternal and child health (MPH, PhD); occupational health (PhD); population health and social determinants (PhD); social and behavioral sciences (MPH); sociology and demography (PhD); JD/MHA; MHA/MBA; MHA/MD; MHA/MPA; MPH/JD; MPH/MD; MPH/MN; MPH/MPA; MPH/MS; MPH/MSD; MPH/MSW; MPH/PhD. Part-time and evening/weekend programs available. Postbaccalaureate distance learning degree programs offered (minimal on-campus study). *Faculty:* 36 full-time (18 women), 59 part-time/adjunct (26 women). *Students:* 107 full-time (82 women), 101 part-time (82 women); includes 1 Black or African American, non-Hispanic/Latino; 1 American Indian or Alaska Native, non-Hispanic/Latino; 27 Asian, non-Hispanic/Latino; 10 Hispanic/Latino, 4 international. Average age 34. 426 applicants, 41% accepted, 106 enrolled. In 2010, 37 master's, 11 doctorates awarded. Terminal master's awarded for partial completion of doctoral program. *Degree requirements:* For master's, thesis (for some programs), practicum (MPH); for doctorate, comprehensive exam, thesis/dissertation. *Entrance requirements:* For master's and doctorate, GRE General Test, minimum GPA of 3.0. Additional exam requirements/recommendations for international students: Required—TOEFL (minimum score 580 paper-based; 237 computer-based; 92 iBT), IELTS (minimum score 7). *Application deadline:* For fall admission, 1/1 for domestic students, 11/1 for international students. Application fee: 75 Albanian leks. Electronic applications accepted. *Financial support:* In 2010–11, 47 students received support, including 10 fellowships with full and partial tuition reimbursements available (averaging $22,000 per year), 10 research assistantships with full and partial tuition reimbursements available (averaging $18,700 per year), 3 teaching assistantships with full and partial tuition reimbursements available (averaging $4,575 per year); institutionally sponsored loans, traineeships, and health care benefits also available. Financial award application deadline: 2/28; financial award applicants required to submit FAFSA. *Faculty research:* Public health practice, health promotion and disease prevention, maternal and child health, organizational behavior and culture, health policy. *Unit head:* Dr. Larry Kessler, Chair, 206-543-2930. *Application contact:* Kitty A. Andert, MPH/MS/PhD Program Manager, 206-616-2926, Fax: 206-543-3964, E-mail: kitander@u.washington.edu.

Washington State University, Graduate School, College of Liberal Arts, Department of Sociology, Pullman, WA 99164. Offers crime and deviance (MA, PhD); environments, community and demographics (MA, PhD); institutions and social organizations (MA, PhD); political sociology (MA, PhD); social inequality (MA, PhD); social psychology and life course (MA, PhD). *Faculty:* 22 full-time (14 women), 8 part-time/adjunct (3 women). *Students:* 42 full-time (23 women), 2 part-time (both women); includes 1 Black or African American, non-Hispanic/Latino; 1 American Indian or Alaska Native, non-Hispanic/Latino, 4 international. Average age 30. 71 applicants, 13% accepted, 9 enrolled. In 2010, 7 master's, 4 doctorates awarded. Terminal master's awarded for partial completion of doctoral program. *Degree requirements:* For master's, thesis; for doctorate, comprehensive exam, thesis/dissertation. *Entrance requirements:* For master's, GRE General Test, minimum GPA of 3.0; for doctorate, GRE General Test, MA in sociology, minimum GPA of 3.0. Additional exam requirements/recommendations for international students: Required—TOEFL (minimum score 550 paper-based). *Application deadline:* For fall admission, 1/15 priority date for domestic students, 1/15 for international students. Application fee: $50. Electronic applications accepted. *Expenses:* Tuition, state resident: full-time $8552; part-time $443 per credit. Tuition, nonresident: full-time $21,650; part-time $1083 per credit. Required fees: $846. *Financial support:* In 2010–11, 5 research assistantships with tuition reimbursements (averaging $12,749 per year), 36 teaching assistantships with tuition reimbursements (averaging $12,749 per year) were awarded; fellowships with tuition reimbursements, Federal Work-Study, institutionally sponsored loans, scholarships/grants, health care benefits, and unspecified assistantships also available. Support available to part-time students. Financial award application deadline: 4/1; financial award applicants required to submit FAFSA. *Faculty research:* Crime/deviance, environmental sociology, social inequality, social psychology, gender. Total annual research expenditures: $101,888. *Unit head:* Dr. Gregory Hooks, Chair, 509-335-4595, Fax: 509-335-6419, E-mail: hooks@mail.wsu.edu. *Application contact:* Dr. Tom Rotolo, Director of Graduate Studies, 509-335-4595, Fax: 509-335-6419, E-mail: rotolo@wsu.edu.

Rural Sociology

Auburn University, Graduate School, Interdepartmental Programs, Graduate Programs in Sociology and Rural Sociology, Auburn University, AL 36849. Offers rural sociology (MS); sociology (MA, MS). Part-time programs available. *Faculty:* 33 full-time (12 women), 1 (woman) part-time/adjunct. *Students:* 6 full-time (5 women), 5 part-time (3 women); includes 1 Asian, non-Hispanic/Latino, 3 international. Average age 27. 15 applicants, 20% accepted, 2 enrolled. In 2010, 4 master's awarded. *Degree requirements:* For master's, thesis, computer language (MS), foreign language (MA). *Entrance requirements:* For master's, GRE General Test. *Application deadline:* For fall admission, 7/7 for domestic students; for spring admission, 11/24 for domestic students. Applications are processed on a rolling basis. Application fee: $50 ($60 for international students). *Expenses:* Tuition, state resident: full-time $7002. Tuition, nonresident: full-time $21,898. International tuition: $22,116 full-time. Required fees: $892. Tuition and fees vary according to course load and program. *Financial support:* Research assistantships, teaching assistantships available. Financial award application deadline: 3/15; financial award applicants required to submit FAFSA. *Unit head:* Dr. Kelly Alley, Chair, 334-844-5049. *Application contact:* Dr. George Flowers, Dean of the Graduate School, 334-844-4700.

Cornell University, Graduate School, Graduate Fields of Agriculture and Life Sciences, Field of Development Sociology, Ithaca, NY 14853-0001. Offers community and regional society (MS); community and regional sociology (MPS, PhD); methods of social research (MPS, MS, PhD); population and development (MPS, MS, PhD); rural and environmental sociology (MPS, MS, PhD); state, economy, and society (MPS, MS, PhD). *Faculty:* 22 full-time (7 women). *Students:* 44 full-time (28 women); includes 1 Black or African American, non-Hispanic/Latino; 2 American Indian or Alaska Native, non-Hispanic/Latino; 1 Asian, non-Hispanic/Latino; 1 Hispanic/Latino, 17 international. Average age 31. 73 applicants, 16% accepted, 7 enrolled. In 2010, 4 master's, 3 doctorates awarded. *Degree requirements:* For doctorate, comprehensive exam, thesis/dissertation. *Entrance requirements:* For master's and doctorate, GRE General Test, 3 letters of recommendation. Additional exam requirements/recommendations for international students: Required—TOEFL (minimum score 550 paper-based; 213 computer-based; 77 iBT). *Application deadline:* For fall admission, 1/15 priority date for domestic students. Application fee: $70. Electronic applications accepted. *Expenses:* Tuition: Full-time $29,500. Required fees: $76. Tuition and fees vary according to degree level and program. *Financial support:* In 2010–11, 9 fellowships with full tuition reimbursements, 8 research assistantships with full tuition reimbursements, 16 teaching assistantships with full tuition reimbursements were awarded; institutionally sponsored loans, scholarships/grants, health care benefits, tuition waivers (full and partial), and unspecified assistantships also available. Financial award applicants required to submit FAFSA. *Faculty research:* Demography (population and development), environmental sociology, international and rural community development, political economy and ecology, sustainable agriculture. *Unit head:* Director of Graduate Studies, 607-255-3092, Fax: 607-254-2896. *Application contact:* Graduate Field Assistant, 607-255-3092, Fax: 607-254-2896, E-mail: devsoc@cornell.edu.

Iowa State University of Science and Technology, Graduate College, College of Liberal Arts and Sciences, Department of Sociology and College of Agriculture, Program in Rural Sociology, Ames, IA 50011. Offers MS, PhD. *Faculty:* 12 full-time (6 women), 1 (woman) part-time/adjunct. *Students:* 13 full-time (10 women), 12 part-time (7 women); includes 1 Black or African American, non-Hispanic/Latino; 1 Hispanic/Latino, 5 international. 14 applicants, 86% accepted, 4 enrolled. In 2010, 1 doctorate awarded. *Degree requirements:* For master's, thesis; for doctorate, thesis/dissertation. *Entrance requirements:* For master's, GRE General Test; for doctorate, GRE General Test, master's degree. Additional exam requirements/recommendations for international students: Required—TOEFL (minimum score 550 paper-based; 79 iBT), IELTS (minimum score 6.5). *Application deadline:* For fall admission, 1/10 priority date for domestic and international students; for spring admission, 10/1 for domestic and international students. Application fee: $40 ($90 for international students). Electronic applications accepted. *Financial support:* In 2010–11, 7 research assistantships with full and partial tuition reimbursements (averaging $12,671 per year), 1 teaching assistantship with partial tuition reimbursement (averaging $14,130 per year) were awarded; scholarships/grants, health care benefits, and unspecified assistantships also available. *Unit head:* Dr. R. Paul Lasley, Chair, 515-294-2506, Fax: 515-294-8312, E-mail: sociology@iastate.edu. *Application contact:* Dr. Stephen Sapp, Director of Graduate Education, 515-294-1403, E-mail: sociology@iastate.edu.

The Ohio State University, Graduate School, College of Food, Agricultural, and Environmental Sciences, Department of Agricultural, Environmental, and Development Economics, Columbus, OH 43210. Offers agricultural economics and rural sociology (MS, PhD). *Faculty:* 32. *Students:* 64 full-time (28 women), 18 part-time (8 women); includes 2 Black or African American, non-Hispanic/Latino; 7 Asian, non-Hispanic/Latino, 39 international. Average age 28. In 2010, 15 master's, 8 doctorates awarded. *Degree requirements:* For master's, thesis optional; for doctorate, thesis/dissertation. *Entrance requirements:* For master's and doctorate, GRE General Test. Additional exam requirements/recommendations for international students: Required—TOEFL (minimum score 550 paper-based; 213 computer-based), IELTS (minimum score 7), or Michigan English Language Assessment Battery (minimum score 92). *Application deadline:* For fall admission, 8/15 priority date for domestic students, 7/1 priority date for international students; for winter admission, 12/1 priority date for domestic students, 11/1 priority date for international students; for spring admission, 3/1 priority date for domestic students, 2/1 priority date for international students. Applications are processed on a rolling basis. Application fee: $40 ($50 for international students). Electronic applications accepted. *Expenses:* Tuition, state resident: full-time $10,605. Tuition, nonresident: full-time $26,535. Tuition and fees vary according to course load and program. *Financial support:* Fellowships, research assistantships, teaching assistantships, Federal Work-Study and institutionally sponsored loans available. Support available to part-time students. *Unit head:* Tim Haab, Graduate Studies Committee Chair, 614-292-6237, E-mail: haab.1@osu.edu. *Application contact:* Graduate Admissions, 614-292-9444, Fax: 614-292-3895, E-mail: domestic.grad@osu.edu.

The Ohio State University, Graduate School, College of Food, Agricultural, and Environmental Sciences, Department of Human and Community Resource Development, Program in Rural Sociology, Columbus, OH 43210. Offers MS, PhD. *Students:* 15 full-time (11 women), 6 part-time (4 women); includes 2 Black or African American, non-Hispanic/Latino; 2 Hispanic/Latino, 3 international. Average age 31. In 2010, 3 master's, 2 doctorates awarded. *Entrance requirements:* For master's and doctorate, GRE or GMAT. *Application deadline:* Applications are processed on a rolling basis. Application fee: $40 ($50 for international students). Electronic applications accepted. *Expenses:* Tuition, state resident: full-time $10,605. Tuition, nonresident: full-time $26,535. Tuition and fees vary according to course load and program. *Unit head:* Linda M. Lobao, Graduate Studies Committee Chair, 614-292-6394, Fax: 614-292-7007, E-mail: lobao.1@osu.edu. *Application contact:* Graduate Admissions, 614-292-9444, Fax: 614-292-3985, E-mail: domestic.grad@osu.edu.

Penn State University Park, Graduate School, College of Agricultural Sciences, Department of Agricultural Economics and Rural Sociology, State College, University Park, PA 16802-1503. Offers MS, PhD.

South Dakota State University, Graduate School, College of Agriculture and Biological Sciences, Department of Rural Sociology, Brookings, SD 57007. Offers rural sociology (MS); sociology (PhD). Part-time programs available. Postbaccalaureate distance learning degree programs offered. *Degree requirements:* For master's, comprehensive exam (for some programs), thesis, oral and written exams; for doctorate, comprehensive exam, thesis/dissertation, preliminary oral and written exams. *Entrance requirements:* Additional exam requirements/recommendations for international students: Required—TOEFL (minimum score

550 paper-based; 213 computer-based; 79 iBT). *Faculty research:* Demography, rural families, rural development, Native Americans, rural poverty, sociology of agriculture.

University of Alberta, Faculty of Graduate Studies and Research, Department of Rural Economy, Edmonton, AB T6G 2E1, Canada. Offers agricultural economics (M Ag, M Sc, PhD); forest economics (M Ag, M Sc, PhD); rural sociology (M Ag, M Sc); MBA/M Ag. Part-time programs available. *Degree requirements:* For doctorate, thesis/dissertation. *Entrance requirements:* Additional exam requirements/recommendations for international students: Required—TOEFL. *Faculty research:* Agroforestry, development, extension education, marketing and trade, natural resources and environment, policy, production economics.

University of Missouri, Graduate School, College of Agriculture, Food and Natural Resources, Department of Rural Sociology, Columbia, MO 65211. Offers MS, PhD. Part-time programs available. *Faculty:* 6 full-time (2 women), 6 part-time/adjunct (2 women). *Students:* 17 full-time (9 women), 6 part-time (5 women); includes 3 minority (all Black or African American, non-Hispanic/Latino), 6 international. Average age 41. 15 applicants, 53% accepted, 4 enrolled. In 2010, 5 doctorates awarded. *Degree requirements:* For doctorate, comprehensive exam, thesis/dissertation. *Entrance requirements:* For master's and doctorate, GRE General Test, minimum GPA of 3.0. Additional exam requirements/recommendations for international students: Required—TOEFL (minimum score 570 paper-based; 233 computer-based; 89 iBT). *Application deadline:* Applications are processed on a rolling basis. Application fee: $45 ($60 for international students). Electronic applications accepted. *Financial support:* Fellowships with tuition reimbursements, research assistantships with tuition reimbursements, teaching assistantships with tuition reimbursements, institutionally sponsored loans, scholarships/grants, health care benefits, and unspecified assistantships available. Support available to part-time students. *Faculty research:* Rural social organization; social change and development; sociology of agriculture; natural resource management; sociology of consumption, culture and organization; science, technology and society studies; social inequality; survey research; entrepreneurship; state and local public finance; community economics; rural development. *Unit head:* Dr. Mary E. Grigsby, Department Chair, Interim, 573-882-3895, E-mail: grigsbym@missouri.edu. *Application contact:* Carol Swaim, Administrative Assistant, 573-882-7451, E-mail: swaimc@missouri.edu.

The University of Montana, Graduate School, College of Arts and Sciences, Department of Sociology, Missoula, MT 59812-0002. Offers criminology (MA); rural and environmental change (MA); sociology (MA). *Entrance requirements:* For master's, GRE General Test. Additional exam requirements/recommendations for international students: Required—TOEFL. *Faculty research:* Housing, homelessness, hunger, infant mortality, work safety.

University of Wisconsin–Madison, Graduate School, College of Letters and Science, Department of Sociology, Madison, WI 53706-1380. Offers rural sociology (MS); sociology (MS, PhD). Part-time programs available. Terminal master's awarded for partial completion of doctoral program. *Degree requirements:* For master's, thesis, oral exam; for doctorate, thesis/dissertation, preliminary and final oral exams, 4 seminars. *Entrance requirements:* For master's and doctorate, GRE General Test. Additional exam requirements/recommendations for international students: Required—TOEFL. Electronic applications accepted. *Expenses:* Tuition, state resident: full-time $9887; part-time $617.96 per credit. Tuition, nonresident: full-time $24,054; part-time $1503.40 per credit. Required fees: $67.63 per credit. Tuition and fees vary according to reciprocity agreements.

Sociology

Acadia University, Faculty of Arts, Department of Sociology, Wolfville, NS B4P 2R6, Canada. Offers MA. *Faculty:* 9 full-time (6 women), 1 (woman) part-time/adjunct. *Students:* 7 full-time (4 women), 7 part-time (6 women). Average age 25. 16 applicants, 69% accepted, 7 enrolled. In 2010, 2 master's awarded. *Degree requirements:* For master's, thesis. *Entrance requirements:* For master's, honors degree, minimum GPA of 3.25. Additional exam requirements/recommendations for international students: Required—TOEFL (minimum score 580 paper-based; 237 computer-based; 93 iBT), IELTS (minimum score 6.5). *Application deadline:* For fall admission, 2/1 priority date for domestic and international students. Applications are processed on a rolling basis. Application fee: $50. *Financial support:* Research assistantships, teaching assistantships, unspecified assistantships available. Financial award application deadline: 2/1. *Faculty research:* Atlantic cultures, class analysis, gender and women's studies, religion, symbolism, development studies. *Unit head:* Dr. Jim Sacouman, Head, 902-585-1494, Fax: 902-585-1769, E-mail: jim.sacouman@acadiau.ca. *Application contact:* Karen Turner, Administrative Secretary, 902-585-1493, Fax: 902-585-1769, E-mail: karen.turner@acadiau.ca.

American University, College of Arts and Sciences, Department of Sociology, Washington, DC 22016-8072. Offers social research (Certificate); sociology (MA). Part-time and evening/weekend programs available. *Faculty:* 15 full-time (10 women), 4 part-time/adjunct (2 women). *Students:* 15 full-time (14 women), 26 part-time (23 women); includes 20 minority (13 Black or African American, non-Hispanic/Latino; 2 Asian, non-Hispanic/Latino; 5 Hispanic/Latino), 2 international. Average age 36. 35 applicants, 69% accepted, 12 enrolled. In 2010, 6 master's awarded. *Degree requirements:* For master's, comprehensive exam, thesis or alternative, tool of research examination. *Entrance requirements:* For master's, GRE; for Certificate, bachelor's degree. Additional exam requirements/recommendations for international students: Required—TOEFL. *Application deadline:* For fall admission, 2/1 for domestic students. Application fee: $80. *Financial support:* Fellowships, research assistantships with full and partial tuition reimbursements, teaching assistantships with full and partial tuition reimbursements, career-related internships or fieldwork, Federal Work-Study, institutionally sponsored loans, tuition waivers (full and partial), and unspecified assistantships available. Support available to part-time students. Financial award application deadline: 2/1; financial award applicants required to submit FAFSA. *Faculty research:* Gender, race, development, applied social policy, political economy. *Unit head:* Dr. Kim M. Blankenship, Chair, 202-885-6211, Fax: 202-885-2477, E-mail: blankens@american.edu. *Application contact:* Dr. Kim M. Blankenship, Chair, 202-885-6211, Fax: 202-885-2477, E-mail: blankens@american.edu.

The American University in Cairo, School of Humanities and Social Sciences, Department of Sociology, Anthropology, Psychology, and Egyptology, Cairo, Egypt. Offers sociology and anthropology (MA). *Degree requirements:* For master's, one foreign language, thesis. *Entrance requirements:* Additional exam requirements/recommendations for international students: Required—English entrance exam and/or TOEFL. Electronic applications accepted. *Faculty research:* Development, gender, sociopolitical economic formulations, social science indigenization, Arab world.

American University of Beirut, Graduate Programs, Faculty of Arts and Sciences, Beirut, Lebanon. Offers anthropology (MA); Arabic language and literature (MA); archaeology (MA); biology (MS); chemistry (MS); computational science (MS); computer science (MS); economics (MA); education (MA); English language (MA); English literature (MA); environmental policy planning (MSES); financial economics (MAFE); geology (MS); history (MA); mathematics (MA, MS); Middle Eastern studies (MA); philosophy (MA); physics (MS); political studies (MA); psychology (MA); public administration (MA); sociology (MA); statistics (MA, MS). Part-time programs available. *Faculty:* 229 full-time (98 women), 136 part-time/adjunct (79 women). *Students:* 158 full-time (104 women), 263 part-time (171 women). Average age 25. 356 applicants, 59% accepted, 127 enrolled. In 2010, 57 master's awarded. *Degree requirements:* For master's, one foreign language, comprehensive exam, thesis (for some programs). *Entrance requirements:* For master's, GRE, letter of recommendation. Additional exam requirements/recommendations for international students: Required—TOEFL (minimum score 600 paper-based; 250 computer-based; 97 iBT), IELTS (minimum score 7). *Application deadline:* For fall admission, 4/30 for domestic and international students; for spring admission, 11/1 for domestic and international students. Application fee: $50. *Expenses:* Tuition: Full-time $12,294; part-time $683 per credit. Required fees: $499; $499 per credit. Tuition and fees vary according to course load and program. *Financial support:* In 2010–11, 33 students received support. Career-related internships or fieldwork, institutionally sponsored loans, scholarships/grants, health care benefits, and unspecified assistantships available. Financial award application deadline: 2/4; financial award applicants required to submit FAFSA. *Faculty research:* Modern and contemporary world theatre; mineralogy, petrology, and geochemistry; cell differentiation and transformation; combinatorial technologies; philosophy of action; continental philosophy; Phoenician epigraphy; nascent complex societies and urbanism; the economies of the Arab world; environmental economics; tectonophysics; host-parasite interactions; innate immunity; insect-plant interactions; history of the Ottoman archives; decentralization; transparency and corruption. Total annual research expenditures: $622,243. *Unit head:* Dr. Patrick McGreevy, Dean, 961-137-4374 Ext. 3800, Fax: 961-174-4461, E-mail: pm07@aub.edu.lb. *Application contact:* Dr. Salim Kanaan, Director, Admissions Office, 961-135-0000 Ext. 2594, Fax: 961-175-0775, E-mail: sk00@aub.edu.lb.

Arizona State University, College of Liberal Arts and Sciences, School of Social and Family Dynamics, Tempe, AZ 85287-3701. Offers family and human development (MS, PhD); infant-family practice (MAS); marriage and family therapy (MAS); sociology (MA, PhD). *Faculty:* 60 full-time (39 women), 2 part-time/adjunct (both women). *Students:* 91 full-time (82 women), 32 part-time (27 women); includes 28 minority (3 Black or African American, non-Hispanic/Latino; 2 American Indian or Alaska Native, non-Hispanic/Latino; 4 Asian, non-Hispanic/Latino; 17 Hispanic/Latino; 1 Native Hawaiian or other Pacific Islander, non-Hispanic/Latino; 1 Two or more races, non-Hispanic/Latino), 10 international. Average age 27. 186 applicants, 38% accepted, 44 enrolled. In 2010, 32 master's, 7 doctorates awarded. Terminal master's awarded for partial completion of doctoral program. *Degree requirements:* For master's, thesis or alternative, interactive Program of Study (iPOS) submitted before completing 50 percent of required credit hours; for doctorate, thesis/dissertation, interactive Program of Study (iPOS) submitted before completing 50 percent of required credit hours. *Entrance requirements:* For master's and doctorate, GRE, minimum GPA of 3.0 or equivalent in last 2 years of work leading to bachelor's degree. Additional exam requirements/recommendations for international students: Required—TOEFL, IELTS, or Pearson Test of English. *Application deadline:* For fall admission, 1/15 for domestic and international students. Application fee: $70 ($90 for international students). Electronic applications accepted. *Expenses:* Contact institution. *Financial support:* In 2010–11, 22 research assistantships with full and partial tuition reimbursements (averaging $14,111 per year), 27 teaching assistantships with full and partial tuition reimbursements (averaging $12,750 per year) were awarded; fellowships with full tuition reimbursements, career-related internships or fieldwork, Federal Work-Study, institutionally sponsored loans, scholarships/grants, and tuition waivers (full and partial) also available. Financial award application deadline: 3/1; financial award applicants required to submit FAFSA. Total annual research expenditures: $4.2 million. *Unit head:* Dr. Richard Fabes, Director, 480-965-4892, E-mail: rf@asu.edu. *Application contact:* Graduate Admissions, 480-965-6113.

Arkansas State University, Graduate School, College of Humanities and Social Sciences, Department of Criminology, Sociology, and Geography, Jonesboro, State University, AR 72467. Offers criminal justice (MA, Certificate); sociology (MA); sociology education (SCCT). Part-time programs available. *Faculty:* 7 full-time (4 women). *Students:* 14 full-time (all women), 30 part-time (19 women); includes 14 minority (all Black or African American, non-Hispanic/Latino). Average age 33. 35 applicants, 69% accepted, 18 enrolled. In 2010, 10 master's awarded. *Degree requirements:* For master's, one foreign language, comprehensive exam, thesis or alternative; for other advanced degree, comprehensive exam. *Entrance requirements:* For master's, GRE General Test or MAT, appropriate bachelor's degree, letters of recommendation, official transcripts, immunization records; for other advanced degree, GRE General Test or MAT, interview, master's degree, official transcript, immunization records. Additional exam requirements/recommendations for international students: Required—TOEFL (minimum score 550 paper-based; 213 computer-based; 79 iBT), IELTS (minimum score 6), PTE: Pearson Test of English Academic (56). *Application deadline:* For fall admission, 7/1 for domestic and international students; for spring admission, 11/15 for domestic students, 11/14 for international students. Applications are processed on a rolling basis. Application fee: $30 ($40 for international students). Electronic applications accepted. *Expenses:* Tuition, state resident: full-time $3888; part-time $216 per credit hour. Tuition, nonresident: full-time $9918; part-time $551 per credit hour. International tuition: $8376 full-time. Required fees: $932; $49 per credit hour. $25 per term. One-time fee: $30. Tuition and fees vary according to course load and program. *Financial support:* In 2010–11, 14 students received support. Career-related internships or fieldwork, scholarships/grants, and unspecified assistantships available. Financial award application deadline: 7/1; financial award applicants required to submit FAFSA. *Unit head:* Dr. Gretchen Hill, Interim Chair, 870-972-3246, Fax: 870-972-3694, E-mail: ghill@astate.edu. *Application contact:* Dr. Andrew Sustich, Dean of the Graduate School, 870-972-3029, Fax: 870-972-3857, E-mail: sustich@astate.edu.

Auburn University, Graduate School, Interdepartmental Programs, Graduate Programs in Sociology and Rural Sociology, Auburn University, AL 36849. Offers rural sociology (MS); sociology (MA, MS). Part-time programs available. *Faculty:* 33 full-time (12 women), 1 (woman) part-time/adjunct. *Students:* 6 full-time (5 women), 5 part-time (3 women); includes 1 Asian, non-Hispanic/Latino, 3 international. Average age 27. 15 applicants, 20% accepted, 2 enrolled. In 2010, 4 master's awarded. *Degree requirements:* For master's, thesis, computer language (MS), foreign language (MA). *Entrance requirements:* For master's, GRE General Test. *Application deadline:* For fall admission, 7/7 for domestic students; for spring admission, 11/24 for domestic students. Applications are processed on a rolling basis. Application fee: $50 ($60 for international students). *Expenses:* Tuition, state resident: full-time $7002. Tuition, nonresident: full-time $21,898. International tuition: $22,116 full-time. Required fees: $892. Tuition and fees vary according to course load and program. *Financial support:* Research assistantships, teaching assistantships available. Financial award application deadline: 3/15; financial award applicants required to submit FAFSA. *Unit head:* Dr. Kelly Alley, Chair, 334-844-5049. *Application contact:* Dr. George Flowers, Dean of the Graduate School, 334-844-4700.

Ball State University, Graduate School, College of Sciences and Humanities, Department of Sociology, Muncie, IN 47306-1099. Offers MA. *Faculty:* 10. *Students:* 12 full-time (7 women), 8 part-time (7 women); includes 1 Hispanic/Latino; 3 Two or more races, non-Hispanic/Latino, 1 international. Average age 31. 18 applicants, 56% accepted, 7 enrolled. In 2010, 7 master's awarded. *Entrance requirements:* For master's, GRE General Test. Application fee: $50. *Expenses:* Tuition, state resident: full-time $6160; part-time $299 per credit hour. Tuition, nonresident: full-time $16,020; part-time $783 per credit hour. Required fees: $2278; $95 per credit hour. *Financial support:* In 2010–11, 6 teaching assistantships with full tuition reimbursements (averaging $9,108 per year) were awarded; research assistantships with full tuition reimbursements, career-related internships or fieldwork also available. Financial award

Sociology

Ball State University (continued)
application deadline: 3/1. *Faculty research:* Retention policies for secondary education, community mental health. *Unit head:* Roger Wojtkiewicz, Chairman, 765-285-5978, Fax: 765-285-8980, E-mail: rwojtkiew@gw.bsu.edu. *Application contact:* Dr. Rachel Kraus, Director of Graduate Programs, 765-285-5978, Fax: 765-285-8980.

Baylor University, Graduate School, College of Arts and Sciences, Department of Sociology and Anthropology, Waco, TX 76798. Offers applied sociology (PhD); sociology (MA). *Students:* 23 full-time (11 women); includes 8 minority (1 Black or African American, non-Hispanic/Latino; 1 Asian, non-Hispanic/Latino; 3 Hispanic/Latino; 3 Two or more races, non-Hispanic/Latino), 1 international. In 2010, 6 master's, 3 doctorates awarded. *Entrance requirements:* For master's and doctorate, GRE General Test. *Application deadline:* For fall admission, 8/1 for domestic students. Applications are processed on a rolling basis. Application fee: $25. *Financial support:* Research assistantships, teaching assistantships, career-related internships or fieldwork, Federal Work-Study, and institutionally sponsored loans available. *Faculty research:* Community studies, thanatology, sociology of education. *Unit head:* Dr. Roby Driskell, Graduate Program Director, 254-710-3362, Fax: 254-710-3809, E-mail: robyn_driskell@baylor.edu. *Application contact:* Sharon Sloan, Administrative Assistant, 254-710-1165, Fax: 254-710-3870, E-mail: sharon_sloan@baylor.edu.

Boston College, Graduate School of Arts and Sciences, Department of Sociology, Chestnut Hill, MA 02467-3800. Offers MA, PhD, MBA/MA, MBA/PhD. Part-time programs available. Terminal master's awarded for partial completion of doctoral program. *Degree requirements:* For master's, thesis optional; for doctorate, thesis/dissertation. *Entrance requirements:* For master's and doctorate, GRE General Test. Additional exam requirements/recommendations for international students: Required—TOEFL (minimum score 600 paper-based; 250 computer-based; 100 iBT). Electronic applications accepted. *Faculty research:* Sociological theory, social economy, social psychology, political sociology, development modernization.

Boston University, Graduate School of Arts and Sciences, Department of Sociology, Boston, MA 02215. Offers MA, PhD. *Students:* 23 full-time (17 women), 6 part-time (2 women); includes 7 minority (1 Black or African American, non-Hispanic/Latino; 1 Asian, non-Hispanic/Latino; 1 Hispanic/Latino; 2 Native Hawaiian or other Pacific Islander, non-Hispanic/Latino; 2 Two or more races, non-Hispanic/Latino), 3 international. Average age 31. 113 applicants, 19% accepted, 6 enrolled. In 2010, 1 master's, 4 doctorates awarded. Terminal master's awarded for partial completion of doctoral program. *Degree requirements:* For master's, one foreign language, comprehensive exam, thesis; for doctorate, one foreign language, comprehensive exam, thesis/dissertation. *Entrance requirements:* For master's, GRE General Test, sample of written work, 3 letters of recommendation; for doctorate, GRE General Test or MAT, sample of written work, 3 letters of recommendation. Additional exam requirements/recommendations for international students: Required—TOEFL (minimum score 550 paper-based; 213 computer-based). *Application deadline:* For fall admission, 1/15 for domestic and international students. Application fee: $70. Electronic applications accepted. *Expenses:* Tuition: Full-time $39,314; part-time $1228 per credit. Required fees: $40 per semester. *Financial support:* In 2010–11, 9 students received support, including 1 fellowship with full tuition reimbursement available (averaging $19,300 per year), 1 research assistantship with full tuition reimbursement available (averaging $18,800 per year), 4 teaching assistantships with full tuition reimbursements available (averaging $18,800 per year); career-related internships or fieldwork, Federal Work-Study, and scholarships/grants also available. Support available to part-time students. Financial award application deadline: 1/15; financial award applicants required to submit FAFSA. *Unit head:* Nazli Kibria, Chairman, 617-358-0641, Fax: 617-353-4837, E-mail: nkibria@bu.edu. *Application contact:* Kathleen Hennessy, Department Administrator, 617-353-2594, Fax: 617-353-4837, E-mail: kch@bu.edu.

Boston University, Graduate School of Arts and Sciences, Interdisciplinary Program in Sociology and Social Work, Boston, MA 02215. Offers PhD. *Students:* 19 full-time (15 women), 9 part-time (8 women); includes 9 minority (2 Black or African American, non-Hispanic/Latino; 3 Asian, non-Hispanic/Latino; 4 Hispanic/Latino), 2 international. Average age 37. 30 applicants, 30% accepted, 3 enrolled. *Degree requirements:* For doctorate, one foreign language, comprehensive exam, thesis/dissertation, critical essay. *Entrance requirements:* For doctorate, GRE General Test or MAT, sample of written work. Additional exam requirements/recommendations for international students: Required—TOEFL. *Application deadline:* For fall admission, 1/15 for domestic and international students. Application fee: $70. Electronic applications accepted. *Expenses:* Tuition: Full-time $39,314; part-time $1228 per credit. Required fees: $40 per semester. *Financial support:* In 2010–11, 22 students received support, including 2 research assistantships with full tuition reimbursements available (averaging $18,800 per year); career-related internships or fieldwork, Federal Work-Study, and scholarships/grants also available. Support available to part-time students. Financial award application deadline: 1/15; financial award applicants required to submit FAFSA. *Faculty research:* Mental health, child welfare, aging, substance abuse. *Unit head:* Sara Bachman, Director, 617-353-1415, Fax: 617-353-5612, E-mail: sbachman@bu.edu. *Application contact:* Staff Coordinator, 617-353-9675, Fax: 617-353-5612.

Bowling Green State University, Graduate College, College of Arts and Sciences, Department of Sociology, Bowling Green, OH 43403. Offers demography and population studies (MA); social psychology (MA); sociology (PhD). Part-time programs available. *Degree requirements:* For master's, thesis or alternative; for doctorate, comprehensive exam, thesis/dissertation. *Entrance requirements:* For master's and doctorate, GRE General Test. Additional exam requirements/recommendations for international students: Required—TOEFL. Electronic applications accepted. *Faculty research:* Applied demography, criminology and deviance, family studies, population studies, social psychology.

Brandeis University, Graduate School of Arts and Sciences, Department of Sociology, Waltham, MA 02454-9110. Offers Near Eastern and Judaic studies and sociology (PhD); social policy and sociology (PhD); sociology (MA, PhD); sociology and women's and gender studies (MA). Part-time programs available. *Faculty:* 10 full-time (6 women), 1 part-time/adjunct (0 women). *Students:* 21 full-time (17 women), 1 (woman) part-time; includes 2 Black or African American, non-Hispanic/Latino; 2 Hispanic/Latino, 5 international. 116 applicants, 16% accepted, 6 enrolled. In 2010, 4 master's, 1 doctorate awarded. Terminal master's awarded for partial completion of doctoral program. *Degree requirements:* For master's, thesis; for doctorate, thesis/dissertation. *Entrance requirements:* For master's, GRE, resume, letters of recommendation, statement of purpose; for doctorate, GRE, writing sample, resume, letters of recommendation, statement of purpose. Additional exam requirements/recommendations for international students: Required—TOEFL (minimum score 600 paper-based; 250 computer-based; 100 iBT); Recommended—IELTS (minimum score 7). *Application deadline:* For fall admission, 1/15 for domestic and international students. Application fee: $75. Electronic applications accepted. *Financial support:* In 2010–11, 14 students received support, including 13 fellowships with full tuition reimbursements available (averaging $20,000 per year), 1 teaching assistantship with partial tuition reimbursement available (averaging $3,200 per year); scholarships/grants, health care benefits, and tuition waivers (full and partial) also available. Support available to part-time students. Financial award application deadline: 4/15; financial award applicants required to submit FAFSA. *Faculty research:* Social theory and cultural studies; feminist sociology; political sociology; sociology of medicine, health and health care; comparative social structures. *Unit head:* Dr. Wendy Cadge, Director of Graduate Studies, 781-736-2631, Fax: 781-736-2653, E-mail: wcadge@brandeis.edu. *Application contact:* Cheryl Hansen, Graduate Program Administrator, 781-736-2631, Fax: 781-736-2653, E-mail: chansen@brandeis.edu.

Brigham Young University, Graduate Studies, College of Family, Home, and Social Sciences, Department of Sociology, Provo, UT 84602. Offers MS. *Faculty:* 18 full-time (5 women), 2 part-time/adjunct (1 woman). *Students:* 35 full-time (19 women), 1 (woman) part-time, 1 international. Average age 28. 22 applicants, 59% accepted, 13 enrolled. In 2010, 4 master's awarded. Terminal master's awarded for partial completion of doctoral program. *Degree requirements:* For master's, thesis. *Entrance requirements:* For master's, GRE General Test, minimum GPA of 3.0 in last 60 hours, writing sample, bachelor's degree in sociology or related field, 3 letters of recommendation, Honor Code commitment. Additional exam requirements/recommendations for international students: Required—TOEFL. *Application deadline:* For fall admission, 2/1 for domestic and international students. Application fee: $50. Electronic applications accepted. *Expenses:* Tuition: Full-time $5580; part-time $310 per credit hour. Tuition and fees vary according to program and student's religious affiliation. *Financial support:* In 2010–11, 12 research assistantships (averaging $15,750 per year), 12 teaching assistantships (averaging $15,750 per year) were awarded; institutionally sponsored loans and unspecified assistantships also available. Financial award application deadline: 2/1. *Faculty research:* Demography, race and ethnicity, gender, rural and community, international development, comparative family. Total annual research expenditures: $33,500. *Unit head:* Dr. Renata Forste, Department Chair, 801-422-3146, Fax: 801-422-0625, E-mail: renata_forste@byu.edu. *Application contact:* Dr. Carol J. Ward, Graduate Coordinator, 801-422-3047, Fax: 801-422-0625, E-mail: carol.ward@byu.edu.

Brock University, Faculty of Graduate Studies, Faculty of Social Sciences, Program in Critical Sociology, St. Catharines, ON L2S 3A1, Canada. Offers MA.

Brooklyn College of the City University of New York, Division of Graduate Studies, Department of Sociology, Brooklyn, NY 11210-2889. Offers MA, PhD. Part-time and evening/weekend programs available. *Students:* 33 part-time (24 women); includes 21 minority (11 Black or African American, non-Hispanic/Latino; 5 Asian, non-Hispanic/Latino; 5 Hispanic/Latino). Average age 33. 24 applicants, 67% accepted, 8 enrolled. In 2010, 5 master's awarded. *Degree requirements:* For master's, comprehensive exam or research essay. *Entrance requirements:* For master's, 12 upper-level credits in sociology, 2 letters of recommendation, essay. Additional exam requirements/recommendations for international students: Required—TOEFL (minimum score 500 paper-based; 173 computer-based; 61 iBT). *Application deadline:* For fall admission, 3/1 priority date for domestic students, 2/1 priority date for international students; for spring admission, 11/1 priority date for domestic students, 10/1 priority date for international students. Applications are processed on a rolling basis. Application fee: $125. Electronic applications accepted. *Expenses:* Tuition, state resident: full-time $7360; part-time $310 per credit hour. Tuition, nonresident: full-time $13,800; part-time $575 per credit hour. Required fees: $190 per semester. *Financial support:* Career-related internships or fieldwork, Federal Work-Study, institutionally sponsored loans, and scholarships/grants available. Support available to part-time students. Financial award application deadline: 5/1; financial award applicants required to submit FAFSA. *Faculty research:* Urbanization, religion, family, gender, research methods. *Unit head:* Dr. Kenneth Gould, Chairperson, 718-951-5314, E-mail: kgould@brooklyn.cuny.edu. *Application contact:* Hernan Sierra, Graduate Admissions Coordinator, 718-951-4536, Fax: 718-951-4506, E-mail: grads@brooklyn.cuny.edu.

Brown University, Graduate School, Department of Sociology, Program in Sociology, Providence, RI 02912. Offers AM, PhD. *Degree requirements:* For master's, thesis; for doctorate, thesis/dissertation, oral exam. *Entrance requirements:* For master's and doctorate, GRE General Test.

California State University, Bakersfield, Division of Graduate Studies, School of Humanities and Social Sciences, Program in Sociology, Bakersfield, CA 93311. Offers MA.

California State University, Dominguez Hills, College of Natural and Behavioral Sciences, Program in Sociology, Carson, CA 90747-0001. Offers social research (Certificate); sociology (MA). Part-time and evening/weekend programs available. *Faculty:* 3 full-time (all women), 3 part-time/adjunct (1 woman). *Students:* 26 full-time (20 women), 39 part-time (28 women); includes 32 Black or African American, non-Hispanic/Latino; 1 Asian, non-Hispanic/Latino; 18 Hispanic/Latino; 1 Native Hawaiian or other Pacific Islander, non-Hispanic/Latino. Average age 38. 46 applicants, 67% accepted, 16 enrolled. In 2010, 17 master's awarded. *Degree requirements:* For master's, comprehensive exam, thesis. *Entrance requirements:* For master's and Certificate, minimum GPA of 2.85. *Application deadline:* For fall admission, 6/1 for domestic students. Application fee: $55. *Faculty research:* Community studies, social movements, criminology. *Unit head:* Dr. Clare Weber, Chair, 310-243-3458, E-mail: cweber@csudh.edu. *Application contact:* Brandy McLelland, Interim Director, Student Information Services, 310-243-3645, E-mail: bmclelland@csudh.edu.

California State University, Fullerton, Graduate Studies, College of Humanities and Social Sciences, Department of Sociology, Fullerton, CA 92834-9480. Offers MA. Part-time programs available. *Students:* 12 full-time (4 women), 27 part-time (17 women); includes 2 Black or African American, non-Hispanic/Latino; 4 Asian, non-Hispanic/Latino; 9 Hispanic/Latino; 2 Two or more races, non-Hispanic/Latino. Average age 26. 67 applicants, 39% accepted, 18 enrolled. In 2010, 18 master's awarded. *Degree requirements:* For master's, thesis. *Entrance requirements:* For master's, minimum GPA of 3.0 in sociology, 2.5 in last 60 units. Application fee: $55. *Financial support:* Career-related internships or fieldwork, Federal Work-Study, institutionally sponsored loans, and scholarships/grants available. Support available to part-time students. Financial award application deadline: 3/1; financial award applicants required to submit FAFSA. *Faculty research:* Gerontology wellness clinic. *Unit head:* Dr. Dennis Berg, Chair, 657-278-3531. *Application contact:* Admissions/Applications, 657-278-2371.

California State University, Los Angeles, Graduate Studies, College of Natural and Social Sciences, Department of Sociology, Los Angeles, CA 90032-8530. Offers MA. Part-time and evening/weekend programs available. *Faculty:* 5 full-time (2 women), 1 (woman) part-time/adjunct. *Students:* 16 full-time (9 women), 38 part-time (18 women); includes 46 minority (10 Black or African American, non-Hispanic/Latino; 1 American Indian or Alaska Native, non-Hispanic/Latino; 4 Asian, non-Hispanic/Latino; 31 Hispanic/Latino). Average age 31. 29 applicants, 100% accepted, 19 enrolled. In 2010, 7 master's awarded. *Degree requirements:* For master's, comprehensive exam or thesis. *Entrance requirements:* For master's, minimum GPA of 2.5 in last 90 units of course work. Additional exam requirements/recommendations for international students: Required—TOEFL (minimum score 500 paper-based; 173 computer-based). *Application deadline:* For fall admission, 5/1 for domestic and international students. Applications are processed on a rolling basis. Application fee: $55. Electronic applications accepted. *Financial support:* Federal Work-Study available. Support available to part-time students. Financial award application deadline: 3/1. *Faculty research:* Criminal and delinquent careers, family and sex, ethnic minorities, demographic trends, human socialization and aging. *Unit head:* Dr. Steven L. Gordon, Chair, 323-343-2200, Fax: 323-343-5155, E-mail: sgordon@calstatela.edu. *Application contact:* Dr. Alan Muchlinski, Dean of Graduate Studies, 323-343-3820, Fax: 323-343-5653, E-mail: amuchli@exchange.calstatela.edu.

California State University, Northridge, Graduate Studies, College of Social and Behavioral Sciences, Department of Sociology, Northridge, CA 91330. Offers MA. *Accreditation:* CSWE. Part-time and evening/weekend programs available. *Degree requirements:* For master's, thesis or alternative. *Entrance requirements:* For master's, GRE General Test. Additional exam requirements/recommendations for international students: Required—TOEFL. *Faculty research:* Crime and corrections, relationships between adult children and parents.

California State University, Sacramento, Graduate Studies, College of Social Sciences and Interdisciplinary Studies, Department of Sociology, Sacramento, CA 95819. Offers MA. Part-time programs available. *Degree requirements:* For master's, thesis or alternative, writing proficiency exam. *Entrance requirements:* For master's, minimum GPA of 3.0 during previous 2 years. Additional exam requirements/recommendations for international students: Required—TOEFL. Electronic applications accepted.

California State University, San Marcos, College of Arts and Sciences, Program in Sociological Practice, San Marcos, CA 92096-0001. Offers MA. *Degree requirements:* For master's, thesis. *Entrance requirements:* For master's, GRE General Test (recommended), minimum GPA of 3.0 in last 60 units of undergraduate study, minimum GPA of 3.0 in upper division sociology courses. *Faculty research:* Organized crime, juvenile detention, counseling services for minorities, mental-health facilities.

Carleton University, Faculty of Graduate Studies, Faculty of Arts and Social Sciences, Department of Sociology and Anthropology, Program in Sociology, Ottawa, ON K1S 5B6, Canada. Offers MA, PhD. *Degree requirements:* For master's, thesis optional; for doctorate, one foreign language, comprehensive exam, thesis/dissertation. *Entrance requirements:* For master's, honors degree; for doctorate, master's degree. Additional exam requirements/recommendations for international students: Required—TOEFL. *Faculty research:* Canadian society and policy, inequality and mobility, race/ethnic relations, cultural studies, gender studies.

Case Western Reserve University, School of Graduate Studies, Department of Sociology, Cleveland, OH 44106. Offers MA, PhD. *Faculty:* 8 full-time (4 women). *Students:* 33 full-time (23 women), 1 (woman) part-time; includes 2 Black or African American, non-Hispanic/Latino; 1 Asian, non-Hispanic/Latino, 5 international. Average age 33. 26 applicants, 31% accepted, 5 enrolled. In 2010, 5 master's, 3 doctorates awarded. Terminal master's awarded for partial completion of doctoral program. *Degree requirements:* For master's, comprehensive exam; for doctorate, comprehensive exam, thesis/dissertation. *Entrance requirements:* For master's and doctorate, GRE, writing sample, recommendations, letter of intent. Additional exam requirements/recommendations for international students: Required—TOEFL (minimum score 550 paper-based; 213 computer-based; 79 iBT). *Application deadline:* For fall admission, 2/1 priority date for domestic students. Applications are processed on a rolling basis. Application fee: $50. Electronic applications accepted. *Financial support:* Research assistantships, tuition waivers (full and partial) and student employment available. Financial award application deadline:#2/15. *Faculty research:* Sociology of aging and the life course, medical sociology, population and individual health, social inequality, family sociology, and public policy and community action. *Unit head:* Dr. Dale Dannefer, Chair, 216-368-2700, Fax: 216-368-2676, E-mail: dale.dannefer@case.edu. *Application contact:* Prof. Jessica Kelley-Moore, Interim Graduate Director, 216-368-2700, Fax: 216-368-2676, E-mail: jessica.kelley-moore@case.edu.

The Catholic University of America, School of Arts and Sciences, Department of Sociology, Washington, DC 20064. Offers MA. Part-time programs available. *Faculty:* 4 full-time (1 woman). *Students:* 4 full-time (2 women), 1 (woman) part-time. Average age 29. 18 applicants, 56% accepted, 2 enrolled. In 2010, 1 master's awarded. *Degree requirements:* For master's, comprehensive exam, thesis or alternative. *Entrance requirements:* For master's, GRE General Test, statement of purpose, official copies of academic transcripts, three letters of recommendation. Additional exam requirements/recommendations for international students: Required—TOEFL (minimum score 580 paper-based; 237 computer-based). *Application deadline:* For fall admission, 8/1 priority date for domestic students, 7/15 for international students; for spring admission, 12/1 priority date for domestic students, 10/15 for international students. Applications are processed on a rolling basis. Application fee: $55. Electronic applications accepted. *Expenses:* Tuition: Full-time $33,580; part-time $1315 per credit hour. Required fees: $80; $40 per semester hour. One-time fee: $425. *Financial support:* Fellowships, research assistantships, teaching assistantships, Federal Work-Study, scholarships/grants, tuition waivers (full and partial), and unspecified assistantships available. Financial award application deadline: 2/1; financial award applicants required to submit FAFSA. *Faculty research:* Social movements, gender structure, political sociology, race and ethnic relations, evaluation methodologies. Total annual research expenditures: $79,339. *Unit head:* Dr. Bronislaw Misztal, Chair, 202-319-5445, Fax: 202-319-4980, E-mail: misztal@cua.edu. *Application contact:* Andrew Woodall, Director of Graduate Admissions, 202-319-5057, Fax: 202-319-6533, E-mail: cua-admissions@cua.edu.

Central European University, Graduate Studies, School of Social Sciences and Humanities, Budapest, Hungary. Offers economics (MA, PhD); gender studies (MA, PhD); international relations and European studies (MA, PhD); mathematics and its applications (MS, PhD); medieval studies (MA, PhD); nationalism studies (MA, PhD); philosophy (MA, PhD); political science (MA, PhD); public policy (MA, PhD); sociology and social anthropology (MA, PhD). *Faculty:* 90 full-time (29 women), 13 part-time/adjunct (7 women). *Students:* 732 full-time (404 women). Average age 28. 3,639 applicants, 22% accepted, 416 enrolled. In 2010, 278 master's, 16 doctorates awarded. Terminal master's awarded for partial completion of doctoral program. *Degree requirements:* For master's, one foreign language, thesis; for doctorate, one foreign language, comprehensive exam, thesis/dissertation. *Entrance requirements:* For master's, interview; for doctorate, GRE, CEU subject test, interview. Additional exam requirements/recommendations for international students: Required—TOEFL (minimum score 570 paper-based; 230 computer-based); Recommended—IELTS (minimum score 6.5). *Application deadline:* For fall admission, 1/15 priority date for domestic and international students. Application fee: $0. Electronic applications accepted. Tuition and fees charges are reported in euros. *Expenses:* Tuition: Full-time 11,000 euros. Required fees: 250 euros. One-time fee: 200 euros full-time. Tuition and fees vary according to degree level, program, reciprocity agreements and student level. *Financial support:* In 2010–11, 402 students received support, including 416 fellowships with full and partial tuition reimbursements available (averaging $6,200 per year); career-related internships or fieldwork, institutionally sponsored loans, and scholarships/grants also available. Financial award application deadline: 1/5. *Faculty research:* Civil society, fiscal decentralization, party politics, political philosophy (especially liberalism, theory of democracy). Total annual research expenditures: $35,000. *Unit head:* Dr. Katalin Farkas, Provost/Academic Pro Rector, 361-327-3000 Ext. 2227, E-mail: farkask@ceu.hu. *Application contact:* Zsuzsanna Jaszberenyi, Admissions Officer, 361-327-3009, Fax: 361-327-3211, E-mail: admissions@ceu.hu.

City College of the City University of New York, Graduate School, College of Liberal Arts and Science, Division of Social Science, Department of Sociology, New York, NY 10031-9198. Offers MA. *Degree requirements:* For master's, one foreign language, comprehensive exam, thesis. *Entrance requirements:* Additional exam requirements/recommendations for international students: Required—TOEFL (minimum score 500 paper-based; 61 iBT). Electronic applications accepted. *Faculty research:* Urban sociology, criminology and deviance, race and ethnicity.

Clark Atlanta University, School of Arts and Sciences, Department of Sociology, Atlanta, GA 30314. Offers MA. Part-time programs available. *Faculty:* 2 full-time (1 woman). *Students:* 2 full-time (1 woman), 1 (woman) part-time; includes all Black or African American, non-Hispanic/Latino. Average age 26. 10 applicants, 90% accepted, 1 enrolled. In 2010, 1 master's awarded. *Degree requirements:* For master's, one foreign language, comprehensive exam, thesis. *Entrance requirements:* For master's, GRE General Test, minimum GPA of 2.5. Additional exam requirements/recommendations for international students: Required—TOEFL (minimum score 500 paper-based; 173 computer-based; 61 iBT). *Application deadline:* For fall admission, 4/1 for domestic and international students; for spring admission, 11/1 for domestic and international students. Applications are processed on a rolling basis. Application fee: $40 ($55 for international students). Electronic applications accepted. *Expenses:* Tuition: Full-time $12,942; part-time $719 per credit hour. Required fees: $710; $355 per semester. *Financial support:* Scholarships/grants and unspecified assistantships available. Financial award application deadline: 4/30; financial award applicants required to submit FAFSA. *Faculty research:* Gerontology, geriatric education. *Unit head:* Dr. Sandra Taylor, Chairperson, 404-880-8681, E-mail: staylor@cau.edu. *Application contact:* Michelle Clark-Davis, Graduate Program Admissions, 404-880-6605, E-mail: cauadmissions@cau.edu.

Clemson University, Graduate School, College of Business and Behavioral Science, Department of Sociology and Anthropology, Clemson, SC 29634. Offers applied sociology (MS). Part-time programs available. *Faculty:* 15 full-time (10 women). *Students:* 10 full-time (8 women), 3 part-time (1 woman); includes 1 minority (Hispanic/Latino), 2 international. Average age 25. 10 applicants, 60% accepted, 4 enrolled. In 2010, 6 master's awarded. *Degree requirements:* For master's, thesis. *Entrance requirements:* For master's, GRE General Test, minimum GPA of 3.0. Additional exam requirements/recommendations for international students: Required—TOEFL. *Application deadline:* For fall admission, 3/15 priority date for domestic students. Applications are processed on a rolling basis. Application fee: $70 ($80 for international students). Electronic applications accepted. *Expenses:* Contact institution. *Financial support:* In 2010–11, 8 students received support, including 1 research assistantship with

partial tuition reimbursement available (averaging $13,000 per year), 6 teaching assistantships with partial tuition reimbursements available (averaging $10,000 per year); fellowships with full and partial tuition reimbursements available, career-related internships or fieldwork, institutionally sponsored loans, scholarships/grants, health care benefits, and unspecified assistantships also available. Support available to part-time students. Financial award application deadline: 3/15; financial award applicants required to submit FAFSA. *Faculty research:* Organizational and industrial sociology, inequality, sexual abuse and police-community relations, homelessness, emotions. Total annual research expenditures: $69,184. *Unit head:* Dr. Kinly Sturkie, Chair, 864-656-3820, E-mail: dkstr@clemson.edu. *Application contact:* Dr. Brenda Vander Mey, Graduate Coordinator, 864-656-3821, Fax: 864-656-1252, E-mail: vanmey@clemson.edu.

Cleveland State University, College of Graduate Studies, College of Liberal Arts and Social Sciences, Department of Sociology, Cleveland, OH 44115. Offers MA. Part-time and evening/weekend programs available. *Faculty:* 12 full-time (6 women). *Students:* 9 full-time (5 women), 30 part-time (28 women); includes 7 Black or African American, non-Hispanic/Latino; 1 Hispanic/Latino, 1 international. Average age 34. 31 applicants, 42% accepted, 9 enrolled. In 2010, 11 master's awarded. *Entrance requirements:* For master's, minimum GPA of 3.0. Additional exam requirements/recommendations for international students: Required—TOEFL (minimum score 525 paper-based; 197 computer-based). *Application deadline:* For fall admission, 7/15 priority date for domestic students, 1/15 priority date for international students; for spring admission, 12/1 priority date for domestic students, 9/15 priority date for international students. Applications are processed on a rolling basis. Application fee: $30. Electronic applications accepted. *Expenses:* Tuition, state resident: full-time $8447; part-time $469 per credit hour. Tuition, nonresident: full-time $16,020; part-time $890 per credit hour. Required fees: $50. *Financial support:* In 2010–11, 12 students received support, including 3 research assistantships (averaging $9,000 per year), 4 teaching assistantships (averaging $9,000 per year); scholarships/grants, tuition waivers (full and partial), and unspecified assistantships also available. Support available to part-time students. Financial award application deadline: 7/15. *Faculty research:* Criminology, research methods, theory, symbolic interaction. Total annual research expenditures: $45,000. *Unit head:* Dr. Philip Manning, Chair, 216-687-4504, Fax: 216-687-9314, E-mail: p.mannings@csuohio.edu. *Application contact:* Dr. Wendy Regoeczi, Graduate Program Director, 216-687-9349, Fax: 216-687-9314, E-mail: w.regoeczi@csuohio.edu.

Colorado State University, Graduate School, College of Liberal Arts, Department of Sociology, Fort Collins, CO 80523-1784. Offers MA, PhD. *Faculty:* 14 full-time (5 women). *Students:* 21 full-time (15 women), 25 part-time (13 women); includes 2 minority (1 Asian, non-Hispanic/Latino; 1 Hispanic/Latino), 1 international. Average age 32. 40 applicants, 20% accepted, 8 enrolled. In 2010, 4 master's, 2 doctorates awarded. *Degree requirements:* For master's, variable foreign language requirement, comprehensive exam (for some programs), thesis (for some programs); for doctorate, variable foreign language requirement, comprehensive exam, thesis/dissertation (for some programs). *Entrance requirements:* For master's, GRE General Test, minimum GPA of 3.0; BA coursework in sociology, letters of recommendation; for doctorate, GRE General Test, minimum GPA of 3.0, BA and MA coursework in sociology, letters of recommendation, statement of purpose. Additional exam requirements/recommendations for international students: Required—TOEFL (minimum score 550 paper-based; 213 computer-based; 80 iBT). *Application deadline:* For fall admission, 1/15 priority date for domestic and international students. Applications are processed on a rolling basis. Application fee: $50. Electronic applications accepted. *Expenses:* Tuition, state resident: full-time $7434; part-time $413 per credit. Tuition, nonresident: full-time $19,022; part-time $1057 per credit. Required fees: $1729; $88 per credit. *Financial support:* In 2010–11, 22 students received support, including 5 research assistantships (averaging $11,147 per year), 17 teaching assistantships (averaging $12,435 per year); career-related internships or fieldwork, Federal Work-Study, institutionally sponsored loans, scholarships/grants, traineeships, and unspecified assistantships also available. Financial award application deadline: 3/1; financial award applicants required to submit FAFSA. *Faculty research:* Sociology policy analysis, environmental impact, criminology, community development, rural and natural resources. Total annual research expenditures: $325,242. *Unit head:* Dr. Jack Brouillette, Chairman, 970-491-6805, Fax: 970-491-2191, E-mail: jack.brouillette@colostate.edu. *Application contact:* Betty Burkett, Administrative Assistant, 970-491-6044, Fax: 970-491-2191, E-mail: elizabeth.burkett@colostate.edu.

Columbia University, Graduate School of Arts and Sciences, Division of Social Sciences, Department of Sociology, New York, NY 10027. Offers M Phil, MA, PhD, JD/MA, JD/PhD. *Degree requirements:* For master's, 2 research papers; for doctorate, one foreign language, thesis/dissertation. *Entrance requirements:* For master's and doctorate, GRE General Test. Additional exam requirements/recommendations for international students: Required—TOEFL. *Faculty research:* Urban and political studies, sociology of knowledge, organizations.

Concordia University, School of Graduate Studies, Faculty of Arts and Science, Department of Sociology and Anthropology, Montréal, QC H3G 1M8, Canada. Offers social and cultural anthropology (MA); sociology (MA). *Degree requirements:* For master's, comprehensive exam or thesis. *Entrance requirements:* For master's, honors degree in sociology or equivalent. *Faculty research:* Community and ethnic relations, popular culture, regional development in Canada, industrial and social movements, social problems and policies.

Cornell University, Graduate School, Graduate Fields of Agriculture and Life Sciences, Field of Development Sociology, Ithaca, NY 14853-0001. Offers community and regional society (MS); community and regional sociology (MPS, PhD); methods of social research (MPS, MS, PhD); population and development (MPS, MS, PhD); rural and environmental sociology (MPS, MS, PhD); state, economy, and society (MPS, MS, PhD). *Faculty:* 22 full-time (7 women). *Students:* 44 full-time (28 women); includes 1 Black or African American, non-Hispanic/Latino; 2 American Indian or Alaska Native, non-Hispanic/Latino; 1 Asian, non-Hispanic/Latino; 1 Hispanic/Latino, 17 international. Average age 31. 73 applicants, 16% accepted, 7 enrolled. In 2010, 4 master's, 3 doctorates awarded. *Degree requirements:* For doctorate, comprehensive exam, thesis/dissertation. *Entrance requirements:* For master's and doctorate, GRE General Test, 3 letters of recommendation. Additional exam requirements/recommendations for international students: Required—TOEFL (minimum score 550 paper-based; 213 computer-based; 77 iBT). *Application deadline:* For fall admission, 1/15 priority date for domestic students. Application fee: $70. Electronic applications accepted. *Expenses:* Tuition: Full-time $29,500. Required fees: $76. Tuition and fees vary according to degree level and program. *Financial support:* In 2010–11, 9 fellowships with full tuition reimbursements, 8 research assistantships with full tuition reimbursements, 16 teaching assistantships with full tuition reimbursements were awarded; institutionally sponsored loans, scholarships/grants, health care benefits, tuition waivers (full and partial), and unspecified assistantships also available. Financial award applicants required to submit FAFSA. *Faculty research:* Demography (population and development), environmental sociology, international and rural community development, political economy and ecology, sustainable agriculture. *Unit head:* Director of Graduate Studies, 607-255-3092, Fax: 607-254-2896. *Application contact:* Graduate Field Assistant, 607-255-3092, Fax: 607-254-2896, E-mail: devsoc@cornell.edu.

Cornell University, Graduate School, Graduate Fields of Arts and Sciences, Field of Sociology, Ithaca, NY 14853-0001. Offers economy and society (MA, PhD); gender and life course (MA, PhD); methodology (MA, PhD); organizations (MA, PhD); policy analysis (MA, PhD); political sociology/social movements (MA, PhD); racial and ethnic relations (MA, PhD); social networks (MA, PhD); social psychology (MA, PhD); social stratification (MA, PhD). *Faculty:* 33 full-time (12 women). *Students:* 36 full-time (18 women); includes 4 Asian, non-Hispanic/Latino, 9 international. Average age 29. 187 applicants, 7% accepted, 9 enrolled. In 2010, 3 master's, 2 doctorates awarded. Terminal master's awarded for partial completion of doctoral program. *Degree requirements:* For master's, thesis; for doctorate, thesis/dissertation, 1 year of teaching experience. *Entrance requirements:* For master's and doctorate, GRE General Test, 2 letters of recommendation, writing sample. Additional exam requirements/recommendations for international students: Required—TOEFL (minimum score 550 paper-based; 213 computer-based; 77 iBT). *Application deadline:* For fall admission, 1/15 for domestic students. Application fee:

Cornell University (continued)
$80. Electronic applications accepted. *Expenses:* Tuition: Full-time $29,500. Required fees: $76. Tuition and fees vary according to degree level and program. *Financial support:* In 2010–11, 13 fellowships with full tuition reimbursements, 7 research assistantships with full tuition reimbursements, 14 teaching assistantships with full tuition reimbursements were awarded; institutionally sponsored loans, scholarships/grants, health care benefits, tuition waivers (full and partial), and unspecified assistantships also available. Financial award applicants required to submit FAFSA. *Faculty research:* Comparative societal analysis, work and family, simulations, social class and mobility, racial segregation and inequality. *Unit head:* Director of Graduate Studies, 607-255-4266. *Application contact:* Graduate Field Assistant, 607-255-4266, E-mail: sociology@cornell.edu.

Dalhousie University, Faculty of Arts and Social Science, Department of Sociology and Social Anthropology, Halifax, NS B3H 4R2, Canada. Offers social anthropology (MA, PhD); sociology (MA, PhD). *Entrance requirements:* Additional exam requirements/recommendations for international students: Required—TOEFL, IELTS, CANTEST, CAEL, or Michigan English Language Assessment Battery. Electronic applications accepted. *Faculty research:* Social inequality and social injustice; work, industry, and development (regional and international perspectives); health and illness.

DePaul University, College of Liberal Arts and Sciences, Department of Sociology, Chicago, IL 60614. Offers MA. Part-time and evening/weekend programs available. *Faculty:* 21 full-time (12 women), 4 part-time/adjunct (2 women). *Students:* 41 full-time (30 women), 37 part-time (28 women); includes 15 Black or African American, non-Hispanic/Latino; 4 Asian, non-Hispanic/Latino; 12 Hispanic/Latino; 1 Two or more races, non-Hispanic/Latino, 2 international. Average age 28. 34 applicants, 94% accepted, 27 enrolled. In 2010, 22 master's awarded. *Degree requirements:* For master's, thesis or alternative, essay, research project, literature review. *Entrance requirements:* Additional exam requirements/recommendations for international students: Required—TOEFL. *Application deadline:* For fall admission, 8/25 priority date for domestic students; for winter admission, 12/15 priority date for domestic students. Applications are processed on a rolling basis. Application fee: $25. Electronic applications accepted. *Financial support:* In 2010–11, 21 students received support, including 1 research assistantship with full tuition reimbursement available (averaging $7,000 per year); career-related internships or fieldwork and tuition waivers (partial) also available. Financial award application deadline: 6/15. *Faculty research:* Law and society, urban sociology, race/ethnicity, health, social inequality, culture. *Unit head:* Dr. Julie Artis, Chairperson, 773-325-7823, Fax: 773-325-7821, E-mail: jartis@depaul.edu. *Application contact:* Dr. Grace Budrys, Graduate Program Director, 773-325-4433, Fax: 773-325-7821, E-mail: gbudrys@depaul.edu.

Duke University, Graduate School, Department of Sociology, Durham, NC 27708. Offers AM, PhD. *Faculty:* 20 full-time. *Students:* 48 full-time (27 women); includes 6 Black or African American, non-Hispanic/Latino; 1 Asian, non-Hispanic/Latino; 5 Hispanic/Latino, 12 international. 142 applicants, 10% accepted, 7 enrolled. In 2010, 8 master's, 5 doctorates awarded. Terminal master's awarded for partial completion of doctoral program. *Degree requirements:* For doctorate, thesis/dissertation. *Entrance requirements:* For master's and doctorate, GRE General Test. Additional exam requirements/recommendations for international students: Required—TOEFL (minimum score 550 paper-based; 213 computer-based; 83 iBT), IELTS (minimum score 7). *Application deadline:* For fall admission, 12/8 priority date for domestic and international students. Application fee: $75. Electronic applications accepted. *Financial support:* Fellowships, research assistantships, teaching assistantships, Federal Work-Study available. Financial award application deadline: 12/8. *Unit head:* James Moody, Director of Graduate Studies, 919-660-5614, Fax: 919-660-5623, E-mail: jessicae@soc.duke.edu. *Application contact:* Elizabeth Hutton, Director of Admissions, 919-684-3913, Fax: 919-684-2277, E-mail: grad-admissions@duke.edu.

East Carolina University, Graduate School, Thomas Harriot College of Arts and Sciences, Department of Sociology, Greenville, NC 27858-4353. Offers MA. Part-time and evening/weekend programs available. *Degree requirements:* For master's, one foreign language, comprehensive exam, thesis. *Entrance requirements:* For master's, GRE General Test. Additional exam requirements/recommendations for international students: Required—TOEFL. *Expenses:* Tuition, state resident: full-time $3130; part-time $391.25 per credit hour. Tuition, nonresident: full-time $13,817; part-time $1727.13 per credit hour. Required fees: $1916; $239.50 per credit hour. Tuition and fees vary according to campus/location and program.

Eastern Michigan University, Graduate School, College of Arts and Sciences, Department of Sociology, Anthropology and Criminology, Programs in Sociology, Ypsilanti, MI 48197. Offers schools, society and violence (MA); sociology (MA); sociology—family specialty (MA). *Students:* 6 full-time (3 women), 17 part-time (16 women); includes 8 minority (7 Black or African American, non-Hispanic/Latino; 1 Asian, non-Hispanic/Latino). Average age 30. In 2010, 7 master's awarded. Application fee: $35. *Application contact:* Dr. Denise Reiling, Advisor, 734-487-0012, Fax: 734-487-9666, E-mail: dreiling@emich.edu.

East Tennessee State University, School of Graduate Studies, College of Arts and Sciences, Department of Sociology and Anthropology, Johnson City, TN 37614. Offers applied sociology (MA); general sociology (MA). Part-time and evening/weekend programs available. *Faculty:* 10 full-time (3 women). *Students:* 14 full-time (5 women), 3 part-time (2 women); includes 1 minority (Two or more races, non-Hispanic/Latino), 1 international. Average age 27. 14 applicants, 43% accepted, 4 enrolled. In 2010, 6 master's awarded. *Degree requirements:* For master's, comprehensive exam, thesis optional, internship (for non-thesis option). *Entrance requirements:* For master's, GRE General Test, minimum GPA of 3.0 in sociology major. Additional exam requirements/recommendations for international students: Required—TOEFL (minimum score 550 paper-based; 213 computer-based; 79 iBT). *Application deadline:* For fall admission, 6/1 priority date for domestic students, 4/30 for international students; for spring admission, 11/1 for domestic students, 9/30 for international students. Application fee: $25 ($35 for international students). Electronic applications accepted. *Financial support:* In 2010–11, 2 research assistantships with full tuition reimbursements (averaging $6,000 per year), 4 teaching assistantships with full tuition reimbursements (averaging $6,000 per year) were awarded; career-related internships or fieldwork, institutionally sponsored loans, scholarships/grants, tuition waivers (full), and unspecified assistantships also available. Financial award application deadline: 7/1; financial award applicants required to submit FAFSA. *Faculty research:* Biosociology and sex differences, political change in Latin America, medical beliefs and practices in southern Appalachia, Scottish-Irish traditions and Appalachia culture. *Unit head:* Dr. Martha Copp, Graduate Coordinator, 423-439-7056, Fax: 423-439-5313, E-mail: coppm@etsu.edu. *Application contact:* Admissions and Records Clerk, 423-439-4221, Fax: 423-439-5624, E-mail: gradsch@etsu.edu.

Emory University, Laney Graduate School, Department of Sociology, Atlanta, GA 30322-1100. Offers MA, PhD. Terminal master's awarded for partial completion of doctoral program. *Degree requirements:* For master's, thesis optional; for doctorate, comprehensive exam, thesis/dissertation, 2 preliminary exams, research paper, paper presentation. *Entrance requirements:* For doctorate, GRE General Test, minimum GPA of 3.0. Additional exam requirements/recommendations for international students: Required—TOEFL. Electronic applications accepted. *Expenses:* Tuition: Full-time $33,800. Required fees: $1300. *Faculty research:* Political economy and global analysis, culture, social psychology, criminology, stratification.

Fayetteville State University, Graduate School, Program in Sociology, Fayetteville, NC 28301-4298. Offers MA. Part-time and evening/weekend programs available. *Faculty:* 12 full-time (4 women). *Students:* 2 full-time (both women), 14 part-time (13 women); includes 12 Black or African American, non-Hispanic/Latino; 1 Asian, non-Hispanic/Latino. Average age 35. 6 applicants, 100% accepted, 6 enrolled. *Degree requirements:* For master's, comprehensive exam, internship. *Application deadline:* For fall admission, 4/15 for domestic students; for spring admission, 10/15 for domestic students. Applications are processed on a rolling basis. Application fee: $35. Electronic applications accepted. *Unit head:* Dr. Kwaku Twumasi-Ankrah, Chairperson, 910-672-1122, E-mail: kankrah@uncfsu.edu. *Application contact:* Katrina Hoffman, Graduate Admissions Officer, 910-672-1374, Fax: 910-672-1470, E-mail: khoffma1@uncfsu.edu.

Florida Agricultural and Mechanical University, Division of Graduate Studies, Research, and Continuing Education, College of Arts and Sciences, Division of History and Political Sciences, Program in Applied Social Science, Tallahassee, FL 32307-3200. Offers African American history (MASS); criminal justice (MASS); economics (MASS); history (MASS); political science (MASS); public administration (MASS); public management (MASS); social work (MASS); sociology (MASS). Part-time programs available. *Degree requirements:* For master's, thesis optional. *Entrance requirements:* For master's, GRE General Test, minimum GPA of 3.0. *Faculty research:* Southern history, black history, election trends, presidential history.

Florida Atlantic University, Dorothy F. Schmidt College of Arts and Letters, Department of Sociology, Boca Raton, FL 33431-0991. Offers MA. Part-time and evening/weekend programs available. *Faculty:* 17 full-time (10 women), 6 part-time/adjunct (2 women). *Students:* 15 full-time (all women), 1 part-time (0 women); includes 2 minority (1 Black or African American, non-Hispanic/Latino; 1 Hispanic/Latino), 1 international. Average age 30. 16 applicants, 63% accepted, 8 enrolled. In 2010, 10 master's awarded. *Degree requirements:* For master's, thesis optional. *Entrance requirements:* For master's, GRE General Test, minimum GPA of 3.0. Additional exam requirements/recommendations for international students: Required—TOEFL. *Application deadline:* For fall admission, 5/1 priority date for domestic and international students. Applications are processed on a rolling basis. Application fee: $30. Electronic applications accepted. *Expenses:* Tuition, area resident: Part-time $319.96 per credit. Tuition, state resident: part-time $319.96 per credit. Tuition, nonresident: part-time $926.42 per credit. *Financial support:* Teaching assistantships with tuition reimbursements, Federal Work-Study available. *Faculty research:* Gender/race/class, globalization, theory, social control, social movements. *Unit head:* Dr. Farshad A. Araghi, Chair and Associate Professor, 561-297-0261, Fax: 561-297-2511, E-mail: araghi@fau.edu. *Application contact:* Dr. Ann Branaman, Associate Professor, 561-297-3278, Fax: 561-297-2511, E-mail: branaman@fau.edu.

Florida International University, College of Arts and Sciences, Department of Global and Sociocultural Studies, Miami, FL 33199. Offers comparative sociology (MA, PhD). Part-time and evening/weekend programs available. *Faculty:* 24 full-time (12 women), 8 part-time/adjunct (5 women). *Students:* 29 full-time (22 women), 18 part-time (12 women); includes 6 Black or African American, non-Hispanic/Latino; 1 American Indian or Alaska Native, non-Hispanic/Latino; 12 Hispanic/Latino, 8 international. Average age 28. 40 applicants, 18% accepted, 7 enrolled. In 2010, 10 master's, 2 doctorates awarded. *Degree requirements:* For master's, thesis; for doctorate, comprehensive exam, thesis/dissertation. *Entrance requirements:* For master's, GRE General Test, 3 letters of recommendation; minimum undergraduate GPA of 3.25, 3.5 on any previous graduate work; written examples of academic or other relevant professional work; for doctorate, GRE General Test, letter of intent; 3 letters of recommendation; minimum undergraduate GPA of 3.25, 3.5 on any previous graduate work; written examples of academic or other relevant professional work. Additional exam requirements/recommendations for international students: Required—TOEFL (minimum score 550 paper-based; 80 iBT). *Application deadline:* For fall admission, 6/1 for domestic students, 4/1 for international students; for spring admission, 10/1 for domestic students, 9/1 for international students. Applications are processed on a rolling basis. Application fee: $30. Electronic applications accepted. *Financial support:* Institutionally sponsored loans and scholarships/grants available. Financial award application deadline: 3/1; financial award applicants required to submit FAFSA. *Unit head:* Dr. Rod Neumann, Chair, 305-348-2247, Fax: 305-348-3605, E-mail: roderick.neumann@fiu.edu. *Application contact:* Dr. Kathleen Martin, Graduate Program Director, 305-348-2247, Fax: 305-348-7441, E-mail: kathleen.martin@fiu.edu.

Florida State University, The Graduate School, College of Social Sciences and Public Policy, Department of Sociology, Tallahassee, FL 32306. Offers MA, MS, PhD. *Faculty:* 20 full-time (10 women). *Students:* 46 full-time (31 women), 13 part-time (10 women); includes 5 Black or African American, non-Hispanic/Latino; 1 Asian, non-Hispanic/Latino; 2 Hispanic/Latino, 4 international. Average age 27. 64 applicants, 31% accepted, 8 enrolled. In 2010, 11 master's, 7 doctorates awarded. *Degree requirements:* For doctorate, comprehensive exam, thesis/dissertation. *Entrance requirements:* For master's and doctorate, GRE General Test, minimum GPA of 3.0. Additional exam requirements/recommendations for international students: Required—TOEFL (minimum score 550 paper-based; 213 computer-based; 80 iBT). *Application deadline:* For fall admission, 1/10 priority date for domestic students. Applications are processed on a rolling basis. Application fee: $30. Electronic applications accepted. *Expenses:* Tuition, state resident: full-time $8238.24. *Financial support:* In 2010–11, 53 students received support, including 3 fellowships with full tuition reimbursements available (averaging $23,660 per year), 3 research assistantships with full tuition reimbursements available (averaging $18,000 per year), 47 teaching assistantships with full tuition reimbursements available (averaging $18,000 per year); institutionally sponsored loans, scholarships/grants, health care benefits, and unspecified assistantships also available. Financial award application deadline: 1/10; financial award applicants required to submit FAFSA. *Faculty research:* Inequality (gender/race), demography, social psychology, health and aging. Total annual research expenditures: $161,000. *Unit head:* Dr. Isaac Eberstein, Chair, 850-644-6416, Fax: 850-644-6208, E-mail: iebe rstn@fsu.edu. *Application contact:* Dr. John Taylor, Graduate Program Director, 850-644-7109, Fax: 850-644-6208, E-mail: jrtaylor@fsu.edu.

Fordham University, Graduate School of Arts and Sciences, Department of Sociology, New York, NY 10458. Offers MA. Part-time and evening/weekend programs available. *Faculty:* 21 full-time (10 women). *Students:* 16 full-time (10 women), 19 part-time (13 women); includes 1 Black or African American, non-Hispanic/Latino; 1 Asian, non-Hispanic/Latino; 7 Hispanic/Latino, 3 international. Average age 35. 25 applicants, 64% accepted, 4 enrolled. In 2010, 3 master's awarded. Terminal master's awarded for partial completion of doctoral program. *Degree requirements:* For master's, comprehensive exam. *Entrance requirements:* For master's, GRE General Test. Additional exam requirements/recommendations for international students: Required—TOEFL (minimum score 600 paper-based; 250 computer-based). *Application deadline:* For fall admission, 1/4 priority date for domestic students; for spring admission, 11/1 for domestic students. Application fee: $70. Electronic applications accepted. *Financial support:* In 2010–11, 8 students received support, including 2 fellowships with tuition reimbursements available (averaging $19,600 per year), 6 research assistantships with tuition reimbursements available (averaging $18,400 per year); career-related internships or fieldwork, Federal Work-Study, institutionally sponsored loans, tuition waivers (full and partial), and unspecified assistantships also available. Financial award application deadline: 1/4; financial award applicants required to submit FAFSA. *Faculty research:* Social demography, immigration, crime and deviance, religion. *Unit head:* Dr. Greta Gilbertson, Acting Chair, 718-817-3850, Fax: 718-817-3846, E-mail: gilbertson@fordham.edu. *Application contact:* Charlene Dundie, Director of Graduate Admissions, 718-817-4420, Fax: 718-817-3566, E-mail: dundie@fordham.edu.

George Mason University, College of Humanities and Social Sciences, Department of Sociology and Anthropology, Fairfax, VA 22030. Offers anthropology (MA); sociology (MA, PhD). *Faculty:* 26 full-time (11 women), 7 part-time/adjunct (3 women). *Students:* 28 full-time (15 women), 80 part-time (62 women); includes 7 Black or African American, non-Hispanic/Latino; 4 Asian, non-Hispanic/Latino; 9 Hispanic/Latino; 1 Two or more races, non-Hispanic/Latino, 2 international. Average age 32. 99 applicants, 55% accepted, 30 enrolled. In 2010, 7 master's awarded. *Degree requirements:* For master's, thesis; for doctorate, comprehensive exam, thesis/dissertation. *Entrance requirements:* For doctorate, GRE. Additional exam requirements/recommendations for international students: Required—TOEFL (minimum score 570 paper-based; 230 computer-based; 88 iBT). *Application deadline:* For fall admission, 3/1 priority date for domestic students; for spring admission, 10/1 for domestic students. Applications are processed on a rolling basis. Application fee: $100. Electronic applications accepted. *Expenses:* Tuition, state resident: full-time $8192; part-time $440 per credit hour. Tuition, nonresident: full-time $22,952; part-time $1055 per credit hour. Required fees: $2364; $99 per credit hour. *Financial support:* In 2010–11, 19 students received support, including 3 fellowships with full tuition reimbursements available (averaging $18,000 per year), 5 research assistantships with full and partial tuition reimbursements available (averaging $13,169 per year), 12 teaching assistantships with full and partial tuition reimbursements available (averaging $7,268 per year); career-related internships or fieldwork, Federal Work-Study, scholarships/grants, unspecified assistantships, and health care benefits (full-time research or teaching assistantship recipients) also available. Financial award application deadline: 3/1; financial award applicants required to submit FAFSA. *Faculty research:* Africa, American teenagers, black entrepreneurs, human rights, gambling. Total annual research expenditures: $41,941. *Unit head:* Dr. Susan Trencher, Chair, 703-993-1429, E-mail: strenche@gmu.edu. *Application contact:* Amy Best, Associate Professor/Graduate Coordinator, 703-993-1426, E-mail: abest@gmu.edu.

The George Washington University, Columbian College of Arts and Sciences, Department of Sociology, Washington, DC 20052. Offers criminology (MA); sociology (MA). Part-time and evening/weekend programs available. *Faculty:* 12 full-time (7 women), 17 part-time/adjunct (5 women). *Students:* 21 full-time (15 women), 10 part-time (8 women); includes 3 Black or African American, non-Hispanic/Latino; 1 Asian, non-Hispanic/Latino; 1 Hispanic/Latino, 1 international. Average age 26. 49 applicants, 57% accepted, 12 enrolled. In 2010, 7 master's awarded. *Degree requirements:* For master's, comprehensive exam, thesis or alternative. *Entrance requirements:* For master's, GRE General Test, minimum GPA of 3.0. Additional exam requirements/recommendations for international students: Required—TOEFL (minimum score 550 paper-based; 213 computer-based; 80 iBT). *Application deadline:* For fall admission, 6/1 priority date for domestic students, 1/15 priority date for international students; for spring admission, 11/1 priority date for domestic students, 9/1 priority date for international students. Applications are processed on a rolling basis. Application fee: $75. Electronic applications accepted. *Financial support:* In 2010–11, 7 students received support; fellowships with full tuition reimbursements available, teaching assistantships with tuition reimbursements available, career-related internships or fieldwork, Federal Work-Study, and tuition waivers available. Financial award application deadline: 1/15. *Unit head:* Dr. Steven Tuch, Chair, 202-994-7466, E-mail: steven.tuch@gwu.edu. *Application contact:* Information Contact, 202-994-6345, Fax: 202-994-3239, E-mail: soc@gwu.edu.

Georgia Southern University, Jack N. Averitt College of Graduate Studies, College of Liberal Arts and Social Sciences, Department of Sociology and Anthropology, Statesboro, GA 30460. Offers MA. Part-time and evening/weekend programs available. *Students:* 22 full-time (15 women), 10 part-time (5 women); includes 3 Black or African American, non-Hispanic/Latino; 1 American Indian or Alaska Native, non-Hispanic/Latino; 1 Hispanic/Latino; 1 Two or more races, non-Hispanic/Latino. Average age 29. 18 applicants, 78% accepted, 12 enrolled. In 2010, 5 master's awarded. *Degree requirements:* For master's, thesis optional. *Entrance requirements:* For master's, GRE General Test. Additional exam requirements/recommendations for international students: Required—TOEFL (minimum score 550 paper-based; 213 computer-based; 80 iBT). *Application deadline:* For fall admission, 3/1 priority date for domestic and international students; for spring admission, 10/1 priority date for domestic students, 10/1 for international students. Applications are processed on a rolling basis. Application fee: $50. Electronic applications accepted. *Expenses:* Tuition, state resident: full-time $6000; part-time $250 per semester hour. Tuition, nonresident: full-time $23,976; part-time $999 per semester hour. Required fees: $1644. *Financial support:* In 2010–11, 24 students received support, including research assistantships with partial tuition reimbursements available (averaging $7,200 per year), teaching assistantships with partial tuition reimbursements available (averaging $7,200 per year); career-related internships or fieldwork, Federal Work-Study, scholarships/grants, tuition waivers (partial), and unspecified assistantships also available. Support available to part-time students. Financial award application deadline: 4/15; financial award applicants required to submit FAFSA. *Faculty research:* Cultural resource management, historical interpretation, international relations, sociological practice, social psychology. Total annual research expenditures: $341,500. *Unit head:* Dr. Peggy Hargis, Chair, 912-478-5443, Fax: 912-478-0703, E-mail: har_agga@georgiasouthern.edu. *Application contact:* Dr. Charles Ziglar, Coordinator for Graduate Student Recruitment, 912-478-5635, Fax: 912-478-0740, E-mail: gradadmissions@georgiasouthern.edu.

Georgia State University, College of Arts and Sciences, Department of Sociology, Atlanta, GA 30302-3083. Offers MA, PhD. Part-time and evening/weekend programs available. Terminal master's awarded for partial completion of doctoral program. *Degree requirements:* For master's, thesis; for doctorate, comprehensive exam, thesis/dissertation. *Entrance requirements:* For master's, GRE General Test, departmental supplemental form, letters of recommendation; for doctorate, GRE General Test, departmental supplemental form, writing sample, letters of recommendation. Additional exam requirements/recommendations for international students: Required—TOEFL. Electronic applications accepted. *Faculty research:* Family, health, and life course; gender and sexuality; race and urban studies.

Graduate School and University Center of the City University of New York, Graduate Studies, Program in Sociology, New York, NY 10016-4039. Offers PhD. *Degree requirements:* For doctorate, one foreign language, thesis/dissertation. *Entrance requirements:* For doctorate, GRE General Test, writing sample. Additional exam requirements/recommendations for international students: Required—TOEFL. Electronic applications accepted.

Harvard University, Graduate School of Arts and Sciences, Department of Sociology, Cambridge, MA 02138. Offers PhD. *Degree requirements:* For doctorate, thesis/dissertation, oral exams in 2 subfields. *Entrance requirements:* For doctorate, GRE General Test. Additional exam requirements/recommendations for international students: Required—TOEFL. *Expenses:* Tuition: Full-time $34,976. Required fees: $1166. Full-time tuition and fees vary according to program. *Faculty research:* Sociological theory, political theories, quantitative approaches to methodology.

Hofstra University, College of Liberal Arts and Sciences, Program in Applied Social Research and Public Policy, Hempstead, NY 11549. Offers MA. Part-time and evening/weekend programs available. *Faculty:* 6 full-time (3 women). *Students:* 8 full-time (6 women), 2 part-time (1 woman); includes 4 minority (2 Black or African American, non-Hispanic/Latino; 2 Hispanic/Latino), 2 international. Average age 28. 6 applicants, 100% accepted, 5 enrolled. In 2010, 1 master's awarded. *Degree requirements:* For master's, comprehensive exam, thesis optional, internship. *Entrance requirements:* For master's, GRE, interview; essay; minimum GPA of 3.0. Additional exam requirements/recommendations for international students: Required—TOEFL (minimum score 550 paper-based; 213 computer-based; 80 iBT). *Application deadline:* Applications are processed on a rolling basis. Application fee: $70 ($75 for international students). Electronic applications accepted. *Expenses:* Tuition: Full-time $18,000; part-time $1000 per credit hour. Required fees: $970; $145 per term. Tuition and fees vary according to program. *Financial support:* In 2010–11, 4 students received support, including 3 fellowships with full and partial tuition reimbursements available (averaging $3,667 per year), 1 research assistantship with full and partial tuition reimbursement available (averaging $167 per year); Federal Work-Study, institutionally sponsored loans, scholarships/grants, tuition waivers (full and partial), unspecified assistantships, and Scholarships also available. Support available to part-time students. Financial award applicants required to submit FAFSA. *Faculty research:* Housing policy, immigration, labor economic policy, education policy, health care policy. *Unit head:* Dr. Marc Silver, Program Director, 516-463-5640, Fax: 516-463-6250, E-mail: socmls@hofstra.edu. *Application contact:* Carol Drummer, Dean of Graduate Admissions, 516-463-4876, Fax: 516-463-4664, E-mail: gradstudent@hofstra.edu.

Howard University, Graduate School, Department of Health, Human Performance and Leisure Studies, Washington, DC 20059-0002. Offers exercise physiology (MS); health education (MS); sports studies (MS), including sociology of sports, sports management; urban recreation (MS), including leisure studies. Part-time and evening/weekend programs available. *Degree requirements:* For master's, comprehensive exam, thesis. *Entrance requirements:* For master's, BS in human performance or related field. Electronic applications accepted. *Faculty research:* Health promotion, cardiovascular hypertension, physical activity, sport and human rights issues.

Howard University, Graduate School, Department of Sociology and Anthropology, Washington, DC 20059-0002. Offers sociology (MA, PhD). Part-time and evening/weekend programs available. *Degree requirements:* For master's, thesis; for doctorate, one foreign language, comprehensive exam, thesis/dissertation, RCR, writing exam. *Entrance requirements:* For master's, GRE General Test, minimum GPA of 3.0; for doctorate, GRE General Test, minimum GPA of 3.5. Additional exam requirements/recommendations for international students: Required—TOEFL. Electronic applications accepted. *Faculty research:* Medical sociology; criminology; race, class and gender; urban sociology.

Humboldt State University, Academic Programs, College of Arts, Humanities, and Social Sciences, Department of Sociology, Arcata, CA 95521-8299. Offers MA. *Students:* 15 full-time (9 women), 3 part-time (2 women); includes 6 minority (1 American Indian or Alaska Native, non-Hispanic/Latino; 4 Hispanic/Latino; 1 Two or more races, non-Hispanic/Latino). Average age 31. 17 applicants, 88% accepted, 10 enrolled. In 2010, 7 master's awarded. *Degree requirements:* For master's, thesis or alternative, qualifying exam. *Entrance requirements:* For master's, minimum GPA of 2.5, 3 letters of recommendation. Additional exam requirements/recommendations for international students: Required—TOEFL (minimum score 500 paper-based; 173 computer-based). *Application deadline:* For fall admission, 3/15 for domestic students; for spring admission, 12/1 for domestic students. Applications are processed on a rolling basis. Application fee: $55. Tuition and fees vary according to program. *Financial support:* Application deadline: 3/1. *Faculty research:* Sociology of women political activists, environmental dispute resolution, prosocial behavior. *Unit head:* Dr. Mary Virnoche, Chair, 707-826-4569, Fax: 707-826-4418, E-mail: mv23@humboldt.edu. *Application contact:* Dr. Joshua Meisel, Coordinator, 707-826-4446, Fax: 707-826-4418, E-mail: meisel@humboldt.edu.

Hunter College of the City University of New York, Graduate School, School of Arts and Sciences, Department of Sociology, New York, NY 10021-5085. Offers applied social research (MS). *Faculty:* 5 full-time (0 women), 1 part-time/adjunct (0 women). *Students:* 19 full-time (14 women), 26 part-time (18 women); includes 3 Black or African American, non-Hispanic/Latino; 3 Asian, non-Hispanic/Latino; 5 Hispanic/Latino, 4 international. Average age 28. 38 applicants, 76% accepted, 18 enrolled. In 2010, 11 master's awarded. *Degree requirements:* For master's, internship. *Entrance requirements:* For master's, GRE General Test or GMAT, 3 credits of course work in statistics, 2 letters of recommendation. Additional exam requirements/recommendations for international students: Required—TOEFL. *Application deadline:* For fall admission, 4/1 for domestic students, 2/1 for international students; for spring admission, 11/1 for domestic students, 9/1 for international students. Application fee: $125. *Financial support:* Federal Work-Study and tuition waivers (partial) available. Support available to part-time students. *Unit head:* Dr. Robert Perinbanayagaia, Chairperson, 212-772-5585, Fax: 212-772-5645, E-mail: rperinba@hunter.cuny.edu. *Application contact:* Dr. Joong-Hwan Oh, Graduate Adviser, 212-772-5643.

Idaho State University, Office of Graduate Studies, College of Arts and Sciences, Department of Sociology, Pocatello, ID 83209-8114. Offers MA. Part-time programs available. *Degree requirements:* For master's, comprehensive exam, thesis, oral defense of thesis. *Entrance requirements:* For master's, GRE General Test (minimum 40th percentile in one of 3 sections), minimum undergraduate GPA of 3.0, 3 letters of recommendation. Additional exam requirements/recommendations for international students: Required—TOEFL (minimum score 550 paper-based; 213 computer-based; 80 iBT). Electronic applications accepted. *Faculty research:* Terrorism, social organization, family social work.

Illinois State University, Graduate School, College of Arts and Sciences, Department of Sociology, Normal, IL 61790-2200. Offers historical archaeology (MA, MS); sociology (MA, MS). *Degree requirements:* For master's, thesis. *Entrance requirements:* For master's, GRE General Test, GRE Subject Test, minimum GPA of 2.4 in last 60 hours of course work. *Faculty research:* Japanese Saturday school (Kato).

Indiana University Bloomington, University Graduate School, College of Arts and Sciences, Department of Sociology, Bloomington, IN 47405-7000. Offers MA, PhD. *Faculty:* 18 full-time (9 women). *Students:* 87 full-time (53 women), 1 (woman) part-time; includes 21 minority (11 Black or African American, non-Hispanic/Latino; 3 Asian, non-Hispanic/Latino; 6 Hispanic/Latino; 1 Two or more races, non-Hispanic/Latino), 8 international. Average age 29. 138 applicants, 14% accepted, 11 enrolled. In 2010, 10 master's, 9 doctorates awarded. Terminal master's awarded for partial completion of doctoral program. *Degree requirements:* For master's, thesis; for doctorate, comprehensive exam, thesis/dissertation. *Entrance requirements:* For master's and doctorate, GRE General Test. Additional exam requirements/recommendations for international students: Required—TOEFL. *Application deadline:* For fall admission, 1/15 for domestic students, 12/1 for international students. Application fee: $55 ($65 for international students). Electronic applications accepted. *Financial support:* In 2010–11, 14 fellowships with full tuition reimbursements (averaging $20,275 per year), 6 research assistantships with full tuition reimbursements (averaging $14,595 per year), 33 teaching assistantships with full tuition reimbursements (averaging $13,635 per year) were awarded; scholarships/grants, health care benefits, and unspecified assistantships also available. Financial award application deadline: 1/15; financial award applicants required to submit FAFSA. *Faculty research:* Social psychology, political sociology, sociological research methods, stratification/mobility, education. *Unit head:* Prof. Eliza Pavalko, Professor, 812-855-7629, Fax: 812-855-0781, E-mail: epavalko@indiana.edu. *Application contact:* Shana Bergen, Information Contact, 812-855-2924, E-mail: sbergen@indiana.edu.

Indiana University of Pennsylvania, School of Graduate Studies and Research, College of Humanities and Social Sciences, Department of Sociology, Program in Sociology, Indiana, PA 15705-1087. Offers MA. Part-time programs available. *Faculty:* 13 full-time (7 women). *Students:* 21 full-time (17 women), 4 part-time (3 women). Average age 28. 15 applicants, 80% accepted, 9 enrolled. In 2010, 12 master's awarded. *Degree requirements:* For master's, thesis optional. *Entrance requirements:* For master's, GRE, 2 letters of recommendation. Additional exam requirements/recommendations for international students: Required—TOEFL. *Application deadline:* For fall admission, 7/1 priority date for domestic students; for spring admission, 11/1 for domestic students. Applications are processed on a rolling basis. Application fee: $40. *Financial support:* In 2010–11, 11 research assistantships (averaging $5,218 per year) were awarded. Financial award application deadline: 3/15; financial award applicants required to submit FAFSA. *Unit head:* Dr. Valerie Gunter, Graduate Coordinator, 724-357-3931, E-mail: valeriegunter@iup.edu. *Application contact:* Dr. Valerie Gunter, Graduate Coordinator, 724-357-3931, E-mail: valeriegunter@iup.edu.

Indiana University–Purdue University Fort Wayne, College of Arts and Sciences, Department of Sociology, Fort Wayne, IN 46805-1499. Offers sociological practice (MA). Part-time programs available. *Faculty:* 10 full-time (3 women). *Students:* 8 part-time (5 women); includes 3 minority (all Black or African American, non-Hispanic/Latino). Average age 36. 3 applicants, 100% accepted, 1 enrolled. In 2010, 4 master's awarded. *Degree requirements:* For master's, thesis optional, practicum. *Entrance requirements:* For master's, minimum GPA of 3.0, 3 letters of recommendation, essay, interview. Additional exam requirements/recommendations for international students: Required—TOEFL (minimum score 550 paper-based; 213 computer-based; 77 iBT). *Application deadline:* For fall admission, 8/1 for domestic students; for spring admission, 11/1 priority date for domestic students. Applications are processed on a rolling basis. Application fee: $50. *Expenses:* Tuition, state resident: full-time $4824; part-time $268 per credit. Tuition, nonresident: full-time $11,625; part-time $646 per credit. Required fees: $555; $30.85 per credit. Tuition and fees vary according to course load. *Financial support:* Scholarships/grants and unspecified assistantships available. Support available to part-time students. Financial award application deadline: 3/1; financial award applicants required to submit FAFSA. *Faculty research:* Drug war films, barriers to social relationships, tattooing practices. *Unit head:* Dr. Peter Iadicola, Chair, 260-481-6572, Fax: 260-481-0474, E-mail: iadicola@ipfw.edu. *Application contact:* Dr. Anson Shupe, Graduate Program Director, 260-481-6667, Fax: 260-481-0474, E-mail: shupe@ipfw.edu.

Sociology

Indiana University–Purdue University Indianapolis, School of Liberal Arts, Department of Sociology, Indianapolis, IN 46202-2896. Offers family/gender studies (MA); medical sociology (MA); work/occupations (MA). *Faculty:* 17 full-time (8 women). *Students:* 13 full-time (8 women), 9 part-time (5 women); includes 1 minority (Black or African American, non-Hispanic/Latino), 2 international. Average age 30. 16 applicants, 75% accepted, 10 enrolled. In 2010, 9 master's awarded. Application fee: $55 ($65 for international students). *Financial support:* In 2010–11, 2 fellowships (averaging $9,500 per year), 2 teaching assistantships (averaging $6,309 per year) were awarded. *Unit head:* Carrie Foote, Director of Graduate Studies, 317-274-8981, E-mail: sociology@iupui.edu. *Application contact:* Director of Research and Graduate Programs, 317-274-8305.

Iowa State University of Science and Technology, Graduate College, College of Liberal Arts and Sciences, Department of Sociology, Ames, IA 50011. Offers rural sociology (MS, PhD); sociology (MS, PhD). *Faculty:* 33 full-time (17 women), 1 (woman) part-time/adjunct. *Students:* 41 full-time (31 women), 40 part-time (23 women); includes 4 Black or African American, non-Hispanic/Latino; 2 Asian, non-Hispanic/Latino; 1 Hispanic/Latino, 20 international. 57 applicants, 70% accepted, 14 enrolled. In 2010, 6 master's, 8 doctorates awarded. *Degree requirements:* For master's, thesis; for doctorate, thesis/dissertation. *Entrance requirements:* For master's and doctorate, GRE General Test. Additional exam requirements/recommendations for international students: Required—TOEFL (minimum score 550 paper-based; 79 iBT), IELTS (minimum score 6.5). *Application deadline:* For fall admission, 1/10 priority date for domestic and international students; for spring admission, 10/1 for domestic and international students. Application fee: $40 ($90 for international students). Electronic applications accepted. *Financial support:* In 2010–11, 13 research assistantships with full and partial tuition reimbursements (averaging $16,153 per year), 13 teaching assistantships with full and partial tuition reimbursements (averaging $13,228 per year) were awarded; fellowships, scholarships/grants, health care benefits, and unspecified assistantships also available. *Unit head:* Dr. R. Paul Lasley, Chair, 515-294-2506, Fax: 515-294-8312, E-mail: sociology@iastate.edu. *Application contact:* Dr. Stephen Sapp, Director of Graduate Education, 515-294-1403, E-mail: sociology@iastate.edu.

Jackson State University, Graduate School, College of Liberal Arts, Department of Sociology, Jackson, MS 39217. Offers criminology and justice services (MA); sociology (MA). Part-time and evening/weekend programs available. *Faculty:* 6 full-time (4 women), 1 part-time/adjunct (0 women). *Students:* 24 full-time (20 women), 49 part-time (38 women); includes 65 Black or African American, non-Hispanic/Latino. Average age 38. In 2010, 36 master's awarded. *Degree requirements:* For master's, comprehensive exam, thesis or alternative. *Entrance requirements:* For master's, GRE General Test. Additional exam requirements/recommendations for international students: Required—TOEFL (minimum score 520 paper-based; 195 computer-based; 67 iBT). *Application deadline:* For fall admission, 3/1 priority date for domestic students, 3/1 for international students; for spring admission, 10/1 for domestic students. Applications are processed on a rolling basis. Application fee: $25. *Expenses:* Tuition, state resident: full-time $5050; part-time $281 per credit hour. Tuition, nonresident: full-time $12,380; part-time $689 per credit hour. *Financial support:* Career-related internships or fieldwork, Federal Work-Study, scholarships/grants, and unspecified assistantships available. Support available to part-time students. Financial award application deadline: 3/1; financial award applicants required to submit FAFSA. *Unit head:* Dr. Etta F. Morgan, Interim Chair, 601-979-2626, E-mail: etta.faye.morgan@jsums.edu. *Application contact:* Sharlene Wilson, Director of Graduate Admissions, 601-979-2455, Fax: 601-979-4325, E-mail: sharlene.f.wilson@jsums.edu.

The Johns Hopkins University, Bloomberg School of Public Health, Department of Health, Behavior and Society, Baltimore, MD 21218-2699. Offers genetic counseling (Sc M); health education and health communication (MHS); social and behavioral sciences (Dr PH, PhD, Sc D); social factors in health (MHS). *Faculty:* 43 full-time (30 women), 59 part-time/adjunct (40 women). *Students:* 114 full-time (105 women), 5 part-time (all women); includes 43 minority (14 Black or African American, non-Hispanic/Latino; 15 Asian, non-Hispanic/Latino; 6 Hispanic/Latino; 8 Two or more races, non-Hispanic/Latino), 11 international. Average age 28. 227 applicants, 31% accepted, 26 enrolled. In 2010, 21 master's, 10 doctorates awarded. *Degree requirements:* For master's, comprehensive exam (for some programs), thesis (for some programs); for doctorate, comprehensive exam, thesis/dissertation. *Entrance requirements:* For master's, GRE, curriculum vitae, 3 letters of recommendation; for doctorate, GRE, transcripts, curriculum vitae, 3 recommendation letters. Additional exam requirements/recommendations for international students: Required—TOEFL (minimum score 600 paper-based; 250 computer-based; 100 iBT). *Application deadline:* For fall admission, 12/1 for domestic and international students. Applications are processed on a rolling basis. Application fee: $45. Electronic applications accepted. *Financial support:* In 2010–11, 96 students received support, including 17 fellowships with tuition reimbursements available (averaging $23,634 per year), 30 research assistantships (averaging $7,800 per year), 25 teaching assistantships (averaging $2,759 per year); career-related internships or fieldwork, Federal Work-Study, scholarships/grants, traineeships, health care benefits, unspecified assistantships, and stipends also available. Financial award application deadline: 3/15. *Faculty research:* Social determinants of health and structural and community-level inventions to improve health, communication and health education, behavioral and social aspects of genetic counseling. Total annual research expenditures: $6.3 million. *Unit head:* Georgean Smith, Administrator, 410-502-3715, Fax: 410-502-4333, E-mail: gcsmith@jhsph.edu. *Application contact:* Barbara W. Diehl, Senior Academic Program Coordinator, 410-502-4415, Fax: 410-502-4333, E-mail: bdiehl@jhsph.edu.

The Johns Hopkins University, Zanvyl Krieger School of Arts and Sciences, Department of Sociology, Baltimore, MD 21218-2699. Offers PhD. *Faculty:* 13 full-time (7 women), 2 part-time/adjunct (both women). *Students:* 37 full-time (19 women), 1 part-time (0 women); includes 2 Black or African American, non-Hispanic/Latino; 1 Asian, non-Hispanic/Latino; 2 Hispanic/Latino, 15 international. Average age 29. 109 applicants, 7% accepted, 3 enrolled. In 2010, 7 doctorates awarded. *Degree requirements:* For doctorate, one foreign language, thesis/dissertation. *Entrance requirements:* For doctorate, GRE General Test. Additional exam requirements/recommendations for international students: Required—TOEFL (minimum score 600 paper-based; 250 computer-based; 100 iBT), IELTS; Recommended—TWE. *Application deadline:* For fall admission, 12/31 for domestic and international students. Application fee: $75. Electronic applications accepted. *Financial support:* In 2010–11, 2 fellowships with full tuition reimbursements (averaging $15,000 per year), 7 research assistantships with full tuition reimbursements (averaging $15,000 per year), 11 teaching assistantships with full tuition reimbursements (averaging $15,000 per year) were awarded; institutionally sponsored loans, health care benefits, and tuition waivers (partial) also available. Financial award applicants required to submit CSS PROFILE or FAFSA. *Faculty research:* Education, immigration, race and gender, world systems, social policy. Total annual research expenditures: $599,554. *Unit head:* Dr. Karl Alexander, Chair, 410-516-6178, Fax: 410-516-7590, E-mail: karl@jhu.edu. *Application contact:* Linda Burkhardt, Academic Program Coordinator, 410-516-7627, Fax: 410-516-7590, E-mail: lindab@jhu.edu.

Kansas State University, Graduate School, College of Arts and Sciences, Department of Sociology, Anthropology and Social Work, Manhattan, KS 66506. Offers sociology (MA, PhD). Part-time programs available. *Degree requirements:* For master's, thesis or alternative; for doctorate, thesis/dissertation. *Entrance requirements:* For master's, GRE, minimum undergraduate GPA of 3.0; for doctorate, master's degree in sociology. Additional exam requirements/recommendations for international students: Required—TOEFL (minimum score 550 paper-based; 213 computer-based). Electronic applications accepted. *Faculty research:* Rural development, sex and gender, criminology/delinquency, international development/globalization, political sociology/social movements.

Kean University, College of Humanities and Social Sciences, Program in Sociology and Social Justice, Union, NJ 07083. Offers MA. *Faculty:* 12 full-time (6 women). *Students:* 8 full-time (all women), 18 part-time (11 women); includes 10 Black or African American, non-Hispanic/Latino; 1 Asian, non-Hispanic/Latino; 6 Hispanic/Latino, 1 international. Average age 35. 15 applicants, 100% accepted, 10 enrolled. *Degree requirements:* For master's, comprehensive exam, practicum. *Entrance requirements:* For master's, GRE (may be waived if cumulative undergraduate GPA is 3.7 or higher), minimum GPA of 3.0, 2 letters of recommendation, interview, official transcripts from all institutions attended. *Application deadline:* For fall admission, 6/1 for domestic students; for spring admission, 11/1 for domestic students. Application fee: $75 ($150 for international students). Electronic applications accepted. *Expenses:* Tuition, state resident: full-time $10,872; part-time $500 per credit. Tuition, nonresident: full-time $14,736; part-time $614 per credit. Required fees: $2740.80; $125 per credit. Part-time tuition and fees vary according to course load and degree level. *Financial support:* In 2010–11, 1 research assistantship with full tuition reimbursement (averaging $3,263 per year) was awarded; unspecified assistantships also available. Financial award applicants required to submit FAFSA. *Unit head:* Dr. Jose Sanchez, Program Coordinator, 908-737-4053, E-mail: jsanchez@kean.edu. *Application contact:* Steven Koch, Pre-Admissions Coordinator, 908-737-5924, Fax: 908-737-5925, E-mail: skoch@kean.edu.

Kent State University, College of Arts and Sciences, Department of Sociology, Kent, OH 44242-0001. Offers MA, PhD. PhD offered jointly with The University of Akron. Part-time programs available. *Degree requirements:* For master's, thesis optional, monograph option; for doctorate, comprehensive exam, thesis/dissertation. *Entrance requirements:* For master's, GRE General Test or MAT, minimum GPA of 2.75; for doctorate, GRE, minimum GPA of 3.0. Additional exam requirements/recommendations for international students: Required—TOEFL. Electronic applications accepted. *Expenses:* Tuition, state resident: full-time $7866; part-time $437 per credit hour. Tuition, nonresident: full-time $14,022; part-time $779 per credit hour. *Faculty research:* Medical sociology, social psychology, social inequalities.

Lakehead University, Graduate Studies, Faculty of Social Sciences and Humanities, Department of Sociology, Thunder Bay, ON P7B 5E1, Canada. Offers gerontology (MA); health services and policy research (MA); sociology (MA); women's studies (MA). Part-time and evening/weekend programs available. *Degree requirements:* For master's, research project or thesis. *Entrance requirements:* For master's, minimum B average. Additional exam requirements/recommendations for international students: Required—TOEFL. *Faculty research:* Sociology of medicine, cultural and social change, health human resources, gerontology, women's studies.

Laurentian University, School of Graduate Studies and Research, Programme in Sociology, Sudbury, ON P3E 2C6, Canada. Offers applied social research (MA). Part-time programs available. *Entrance requirements:* For master's, honors degree in sociology or equivalent. *Faculty research:* Work foundations, managing AIDS organization, tracking laid-off mine workers.

Lehigh University, College of Arts and Sciences, Department of Sociology and Anthropology, Bethlehem, PA 18015. Offers sociology (MA). Part-time programs available. *Faculty:* 12 full-time (6 women), 1 (woman) part-time/adjunct. *Students:* 11 full-time (9 women), 3 part-time (1 woman); includes 2 minority (1 Black or African American, non-Hispanic/Latino; 1 Asian, non-Hispanic/Latino), 1 international. Average age 26. 28 applicants, 50% accepted, 11 enrolled. In 2010, 4 master's awarded. *Degree requirements:* For master's, comprehensive exam, thesis optional. *Entrance requirements:* For master's, GRE General Test. Additional exam requirements/recommendations for international students: Required—TOEFL (minimum score 650 paper-based; 94 iBT). *Application deadline:* For fall admission, 1/15 priority date for domestic and international students. Application fee: $65. Electronic applications accepted. *Financial support:* In 2010–11, 10 students received support, including 4 fellowships with full tuition reimbursements available, 6 teaching assistantships with full tuition reimbursements available; research assistantships with full tuition reimbursements available, career-related internships or fieldwork, Federal Work-Study, institutionally sponsored loans, scholarships/grants, tuition waivers (full and partial), and unspecified assistantships also available. Support available to part-time students. Financial award application deadline: 1/15. *Faculty research:* Juvenile delinquency, parent-child relations, urban sociology, medical sociology, policy studies. Total annual research expenditures: $289,500. *Unit head:* Dr. Judith N. Lasker, Chair/Professor, 610-758-3811, Fax: 610-758-6552, E-mail: judith.lasker@lehigh.edu. *Application contact:* Prof. James McIntosh, Graduate Program Director, 610-758-3809, Fax: 610-758-6552, E-mail: ijm1@lehigh.edu.

Lincoln University, School of Graduate Studies and Continuing Education, Jefferson City, MO 65102. Offers business administration (MBA), including accounting, entrepreneurship, management, public administration and policy; educational leadership (Ed S), including elementary leadership, secondary leadership, superintendency; guidance and counseling (M Ed), including community/agency counseling, elementary school, secondary school; history (MA); school administration and supervision (M Ed), including elementary school administration, secondary school administration, special education administration; school teaching (M Ed), including elementary school teaching, secondary school teaching; social science (MA), including history, political science, sociology; sociology (MA); sociology/criminal justice (MA). Part-time and evening/weekend programs available. *Degree requirements:* For master's and Ed S, comprehensive exam, thesis optional. *Entrance requirements:* For master's and Ed S, GRE, MAT or GMAT, minimum GPA of 2.75 in major, 2.5 overall; 3 letters of recommendation; minimum C average in English composition; personal statement of purpose. Additional exam requirements/recommendations for international students: Required—TOEFL (minimum score 500 paper-based; 173 computer-based; 61 iBT). *Faculty research:* Suicide prevention.

Louisiana State University and Agricultural and Mechanical College, Graduate School, College of Humanities and Social Sciences, Department of Sociology, Baton Rouge, LA 70803. Offers MA, PhD. Part-time programs available. *Faculty:* 16 full-time (4 women). *Students:* 35 full-time (18 women), 6 part-time (4 women); includes 7 Black or African American, non-Hispanic/Latino; 2 Asian, non-Hispanic/Latino; 2 Hispanic/Latino, 3 international. Average age 30. 50 applicants, 72% accepted, 10 enrolled. In 2010, 4 master's, 5 doctorates awarded. Terminal master's awarded for partial completion of doctoral program. *Degree requirements:* For master's, comprehensive exam, thesis; for doctorate, comprehensive exam, thesis/dissertation. *Entrance requirements:* For master's and doctorate, GRE General Test, minimum GPA of 3.0. Additional exam requirements/recommendations for international students: Required—TOEFL (minimum score 550 paper-based; 213 computer-based; 79 iBT) or IELTS (minimum score 6.5). *Application deadline:* For fall admission, 1/31 priority date for domestic students, 3/31 for international students; for spring admission, 10/15 for international students. Applications are processed on a rolling basis. Application fee: $50 ($70 for international students). Electronic applications accepted. *Financial support:* In 2010–11, 38 students received support, including 5 fellowships (averaging $21,378 per year), 7 research assistantships with partial tuition reimbursements available (averaging $18,789 per year), 17 teaching assistantships with partial tuition reimbursements available (averaging $13,524 per year); Federal Work-Study, scholarships/grants, health care benefits, tuition waivers (full and partial), and unspecified assistantships also available. Support available to part-time students. Financial award application deadline: 3/1; financial award applicants required to submit FAFSA. *Faculty research:* Family, stratification, demography, rural sociology, criminology. Total annual research expenditures: $408,602. *Unit head:* Dr. Wesley Shrum, Chair, 225-578-1645, Fax: 225-578-5102, E-mail: shrum@lsu.edu. *Application contact:* Dr. Yoshinori Kamo, Graduate Adviser, 225-578-5311, Fax: 225-578-5102.

Loyola University Chicago, Graduate School, Department of Sociology, Chicago, IL 60660. Offers sociology (MA, PhD); urban studies (MA). Part-time and evening/weekend programs available. *Faculty:* 13 full-time (5 women), 3 part-time/adjunct (1 woman). *Students:* 75 full-time (50 women), 18 part-time (12 women); includes 21 minority (8 Black or African American, non-Hispanic/Latino; 8 Asian, non-Hispanic/Latino; 4 Hispanic/Latino; 1 Two or more races, non-Hispanic/Latino), 8 international. Average age 33. 99 applicants, 46% accepted, 17 enrolled. In 2010, 5 master's, 5 doctorates awarded. Terminal master's awarded for partial completion of doctoral program. *Degree requirements:* For master's, thesis or alternative; for doctorate, comprehensive exam, thesis/dissertation. *Entrance requirements:* For master's and doctorate, GRE General Test. Additional exam requirements/recommendations for international students: Required—TOEFL. *Application deadline:* For fall and winter admission, 2/1 for domestic and international students. Application fee: $0. Electronic applications accepted. *Expenses:* Tuition: Full-time $14,940; part-time $830 per credit hour. Required fees: $87 per semester. Part-time tuition and fees vary according to course load and program. *Financial support:* In 2010–11, 25 students received support, including 10 fellowships with full tuition reimbursements available (averaging $14,000 per year), 5 research assistantships with full tuition reimbursements available (averaging $14,000 per year), 9 teaching assistantships with full tuition reimbursements available (averaging $14,000 per year); career-related internships or fieldwork, Federal Work-Study, health care benefits, tuition waivers (full), and unspecified assistantships also available. Financial award application deadline: 2/1; financial award applicants required to submit FAFSA. *Faculty research:* Religion, knowledge, culture, urban and social policy. Total annual research expenditures: $160,000. *Unit head:* Dr. Rhys Williams, Chair, 773-508-3459, Fax: 773-508-7099, E-mail: rwilliams7s@luc.edu. *Application contact:* Dr. Anne Figert, Graduate Program Director, 773-508-3431, Fax: 773-508-7099, E-mail: afigert@luc.edu.

Marshall University, Academic Affairs Division, College of Liberal Arts, Department of Sociology and Anthropology, Huntington, WV 25755. Offers sociology (MA). *Faculty:* 8 full-time (1 woman). *Students:* 16 full-time (7 women), 3 part-time (all women); includes 1 Black or African American, non-Hispanic/Latino. Average age 30. In 2010, 3 master's awarded. *Degree requirements:* For master's, thesis optional. Application fee: $40. *Unit head:* Dr. Anders Lind-Laursen, Chairperson, 304-696-6700, E-mail: sociology@marshall.edu. *Application contact:* Information Contact Graduate Admissions, 304-746-1900, Fax: 304-746-1902, E-mail: services@marshall.edu.

McGill University, Faculty of Graduate and Postdoctoral Studies, Faculty of Arts, Department of Sociology, Montréal, QC H3A 2T5, Canada. Offers medical sociology (MA); neo-tropical environment (MA); social statistics (MA); sociology (MA, PhD, Diploma).

McGill University, Faculty of Graduate and Postdoctoral Studies, Faculty of Medicine, Department of Social Studies in Medicine, Montréal, QC H3A 2T5, Canada. Offers medical anthropology (MA, PhD); medical history (MA, PhD); medical sociology (MA, PhD).

McMaster University, School of Graduate Studies, Faculty of Social Sciences, Department of Sociology, Hamilton, ON L8S 4M2, Canada. Offers MA, PhD. Part-time programs available. *Degree requirements:* For master's, thesis; for doctorate, comprehensive exam, thesis/dissertation. *Entrance requirements:* For master's and doctorate, minimum B+ average. Additional exam requirements/recommendations for international students: Required—TOEFL (minimum score 580 paper-based; 237 computer-based). *Faculty research:* Socialization and conversion, ethnic relations, international migration, racism, social implications of the Internet.

Memorial University of Newfoundland, School of Graduate Studies, Department of Sociology, St. John's, NL A1C 5S7, Canada. Offers gender (PhD); maritime sociology (PhD); sociology (M Phil, MA); work and development (PhD). Part-time programs available. *Degree requirements:* For master's, comprehensive exam, thesis optional, program journal (M Phil); for doctorate, one foreign language, comprehensive exam, thesis/dissertation, oral defense of thesis. *Entrance requirements:* For master's, 2nd class degree from university of recognized standing in area of study; for doctorate, MA, M Phil, or equivalent. Electronic applications accepted. *Faculty research:* Work and development, gender, maritime sociology.

Michigan State University, The Graduate School, College of Social Science, Department of Sociology, East Lansing, MI 48824. Offers MA, PhD. Part-time programs available. *Entrance requirements:* Additional exam requirements/recommendations for international students: Required—TOEFL (minimum score 550 paper-based; 213 computer-based), Michigan State University ELT (minimum score 85), Michigan English Language Assessment Battery (minimum score 83). Electronic applications accepted.

Middle Tennessee State University, College of Graduate Studies, College of Liberal Arts, Department of Sociology and Anthropology, Murfreesboro, TN 37132. Offers sociology (MA). Part-time and evening/weekend programs available. Postbaccalaureate distance learning degree programs offered. *Faculty:* 12 full-time (6 women). *Students:* 1 (woman) full-time, 18 part-time (13 women); includes 1 Asian, non-Hispanic/Latino. Average age 30. 14 applicants, 64% accepted, 9 enrolled. In 2010, 9 master's awarded. *Degree requirements:* For master's, comprehensive exam, thesis. *Entrance requirements:* For master's, GRE. Additional exam requirements/recommendations for international students: Required—TOEFL (minimum score 525 paper-based; 195 computer-based; 71 iBT) or IELTS (minimum score 6). *Application deadline:* For fall admission, 6/1 for domestic and international students. Applications are processed on a rolling basis. Application fee: $25 ($30 for international students). Electronic applications accepted. *Expenses:* Tuition, state resident: full-time $4632. Tuition, nonresident: full-time $11,520. *Financial support:* In 2010–11, 8 students received support. Institutionally sponsored loans available. Support available to part-time students. Financial award application deadline: 5/1; financial award applicants required to submit FAFSA. *Faculty research:* Applied sociology, crime/deviance, aging/social gerontology, social organization, social psychology. *Unit head:* Dr. Jackie Eller, Interim Chair, 615-898-2508, Fax: 615-898-5427, E-mail: jaeller@mtsu.edu. *Application contact:* Dr. Michael Allen, Dean and Vice Provost for Research, 615-898-2840, Fax: 615-904-8020, E-mail: mallen@mtsu.edu.

Minnesota State University Mankato, College of Graduate Studies, College of Social and Behavioral Sciences, Department of Sociology and Corrections, Mankato, MN 56001. Offers sociology (MA); sociology: college teaching option (MA); sociology: corrections (MS); sociology: human services planning and administration (MS). Part-time programs available. *Students:* 17 full-time (8 women), 35 part-time (20 women). *Degree requirements:* For master's, comprehensive exam, thesis or alternative. *Entrance requirements:* For master's, minimum GPA of 3.0 during previous 2 years, 3 letters of reference, resume. Additional exam requirements/recommendations for international students: Required—TOEFL. *Application deadline:* For fall admission, 7/1 priority date for domestic students; for spring admission, 11/1 for domestic students. Applications are processed on a rolling basis. Application fee: $40. Electronic applications accepted. *Financial support:* Research assistantships with full tuition reimbursements, teaching assistantships with full tuition reimbursements, career-related internships or fieldwork, Federal Work-Study, institutionally sponsored loans, and unspecified assistantships available. Support available to part-time students. Financial award application deadline: 3/15; financial award applicants required to submit FAFSA. *Faculty research:* Women's suffrage movements. *Unit head:* Dr. Barbara Carson, Chairperson, 507-389-1562. *Application contact:* 507-389-2321, E-mail: grad@mnsu.edu.

Mississippi State University, College of Arts and Sciences, Department of Sociology, Mississippi State, MS 39762. Offers MS, PhD. Part-time programs available. *Faculty:* 16 full-time (8 women), 2 part-time/adjunct (0 women). *Students:* 27 full-time (17 women), 18 part-time (12 women); includes 14 minority (8 Black or African American, non-Hispanic/Latino; 3 American Indian or Alaska Native, non-Hispanic/Latino; 1 Asian, non-Hispanic/Latino; 1 Hispanic/Latino; 1 Two or more races, non-Hispanic/Latino), 8 international. Average age 31. 24 applicants, 67% accepted, 11 enrolled. In 2010, 3 master's, 2 doctorates awarded. *Degree requirements:* For master's, thesis optional, comprehensive oral or written exam; for doctorate, thesis/dissertation, comprehensive oral and written exam. *Entrance requirements:* For master's, minimum GPA of 3.0 on last two years of undergraduate courses or GRE; academic writing sample; for doctorate, GRE, academic writing sample. Additional exam requirements/recommendations for international students: Required—TOEFL (minimum score 550 paper-based). *Application deadline:* For fall admission, 4/15 priority date for domestic students, 5/1 for international students; for spring admission, 10/15 priority date for domestic students, 9/1 for international students. Applications are processed on a rolling basis. Application fee: $40. Electronic applications accepted. *Expenses:* Tuition, state resident: full-time $2730.50; part-time $304 per credit hour. Tuition, nonresident: full-time $6901; part-time $767 per credit hour. *Financial support:* In 2010–11, 11 research assistantships (averaging $11,340 per year), 15 teaching assistantships with tuition reimbursements (averaging $11,748 per year) were awarded; Federal Work-Study, institutionally sponsored loans, scholarships/grants, and unspecified assistantships also available. Financial award application deadline: 3/15; financial award applicants required to submit FAFSA. *Faculty research:* Community and regional development, criminology, natural resource development, family sociology, gender. Total annual research expenditures: $1.4 million. *Unit head:* Dr. R. Gregory Dunaway, Head, 662-325-2495, Fax: 662-325-4564, E-mail: dunaway@soc.msstate.edu. *Application contact:* Dr. Lynne Cossman, Graduate Coordinator, 662-325-2495, Fax: 662-325-4564, E-mail: sociology@soc.msstate.edu.

Montclair State University, The Graduate School, College of Humanities and Social Sciences, Department of Sociology, Montclair, NJ 07043-1624. Offers applied sociology (MA). Part-time and evening/weekend programs available. In 2010, 1 master's awarded. *Degree requirements:* For master's, comprehensive exam, comprehensive project, internship. *Entrance requirements:* For master's, GRE General Test, 2 letters of recommendation. Additional exam requirements/recommendations for international students: Required—TOEFL (minimum score: 83 iBT) or IELTS. *Application deadline:* For fall admission, 6/1 for international students; for spring admission, 10/1 for international students. Applications are processed on a rolling basis. Application fee: $60. Electronic applications accepted. *Expenses:* Tuition, state resident: part-time $501.34 per credit. Tuition, nonresident: part-time $773.88 per credit. Required fees: $71.15 per credit. *Financial support:* In 2010–11, 1 research assistantship with full tuition reimbursement (averaging $7,000 per year) was awarded; Federal Work-Study and scholarships/grants also available. Support available to part-time students. Financial award application deadline: 3/1; financial award applicants required to submit FAFSA. *Unit head:* Dr. Jay Livingston, Chairperson, 973-655-4131. *Application contact:* Amy Aiello, Associate Director of Admissions, 973-655-5147, Fax: 973-655-7869, E-mail: graduate.school@montclair.edu.

Morehead State University, Graduate Programs, Caudill College of Arts, Humanities and Social Sciences, Department of Sociology, Social Work and Criminology, Morehead, KY 40351. Offers criminology (MA); general sociology (MA); gerontology (MA); sociology regional analysis (MA); sociology/chemical dependency (MA). Part-time and evening/weekend programs available. *Degree requirements:* For master's, comprehensive exam, thesis (for some programs). *Entrance requirements:* For master's, GRE General Test, minimum GPA of 3.0 in sociology, 2.75 overall; 18 hours of course work in sociology, writing sample. Additional exam requirements/recommendations for international students: Required—TOEFL (minimum score 500 paper-based; 173 computer-based). Electronic applications accepted. *Faculty research:* Death and dying; aging, drinking, and drugs; economic development; adult children of alcoholics.

Morgan State University, School of Graduate Studies, College of Liberal Arts, Department of Sociology and Anthropology, Baltimore, MD 21251. Offers sociology (MA, MS). Part-time and evening/weekend programs available. *Degree requirements:* For master's, comprehensive exam. *Entrance requirements:* Additional exam requirements/recommendations for international students: Required—TOEFL (minimum score 550 paper-based; 213 computer-based). *Faculty research:* Domestic violence, homelessness, social movements, marriage and family.

The New School: A University, The New School for Social Research, Department of Sociology, New York, NY 10003. Offers sociology (MA, DS Sc, PhD); sociology and historical studies (MA, PhD). Part-time and evening/weekend programs available. Terminal master's awarded for partial completion of doctoral program. *Degree requirements:* For master's, exam; for doctorate, one foreign language, thesis/dissertation, qualifying exam. *Entrance requirements:* For master's, GRE General Test; for doctorate, GRE General Test, MA. Additional exam requirements/recommendations for international students: Required—TOEFL (minimum score 600 paper-based; 250 computer-based; 100 iBT). Electronic applications accepted. *Faculty research:* Media, culture, urban sociology, democratic transitions, critical theory.

New York University, Graduate School of Arts and Science, Department of Sociology, New York, NY 10012-1019. Offers French studies and sociology (PhD); sociology (MA, PhD); JD/MA. Part-time programs available. *Faculty:* 27 full-time (9 women), 1 part-time/adjunct (0 women). *Students:* 71 full-time (35 women), 3 part-time (2 women); includes 5 Black or African American, non-Hispanic/Latino; 4 Asian, non-Hispanic/Latino; 6 Hispanic/Latino, 15 international. Average age 31. 419 applicants, 7% accepted, 14 enrolled. In 2010, 1 master's, 9 doctorates awarded. Terminal master's awarded for partial completion of doctoral program. *Degree requirements:* For master's, thesis or alternative; for doctorate, comprehensive exam, thesis/dissertation. *Entrance requirements:* For master's and doctorate, GRE General Test. Additional exam requirements/recommendations for international students: Required—TOEFL. *Application deadline:* For fall admission, 1/4 priority date for domestic students. Application fee: $90. *Financial support:* Fellowships with tuition reimbursements, research assistantships with tuition reimbursements, teaching assistantships with tuition reimbursements, Federal Work-Study, institutionally sponsored loans, scholarships/grants, health care benefits, and unspecified assistantships available. Financial award application deadline: 1/4; financial award applicants required to submit FAFSA. *Faculty research:* Political sociology and social movements; gender and inequality; deviance, law, and crime; education; stratification and theory. *Unit head:* Jeff Manza, Chair, 212-998-8340, Fax: 212-995-4140, E-mail: gsas.sociology.info@nyu.edu. *Application contact:* Eric Klinenberg, Director of Graduate Studies, 212-998-8340, Fax: 212-995-4140, E-mail: gsas.sociology.info@nyu.edu.

New York University, Steinhardt School of Culture, Education, and Human Development, Department of Humanities and Social Sciences in the Professions, Program in Sociology of Education, New York, NY 10012-1019. Offers education and social policy (MA); sociology of education (MA, PhD), including education policy (MA), social and cultural studies of education (MA). Part-time programs available. *Faculty:* 14 full-time (7 women). *Students:* 31 full-time (23 women), 8 part-time (6 women); includes 6 Black or African American, non-Hispanic/Latino; 3 Asian, non-Hispanic/Latino; 1 Hispanic/Latino, 7 international. Average age 27. 119 applicants, 71% accepted, 24 enrolled. In 2010, 10 master's, 1 doctorate awarded. *Degree requirements:* For master's, thesis (for some programs); for doctorate, thesis/dissertation. *Entrance requirements:* For master's, letters of recommendation; for doctorate, GRE General Test, interview. Additional exam requirements/recommendations for international students: Required—TOEFL. *Application deadline:* For fall admission, 12/1 priority date for domestic and international students; for spring admission, 11/1 for domestic and international students. Applications are processed on a rolling basis. Application fee: $75. Electronic applications accepted. *Financial support:* Fellowships with full and partial tuition reimbursements, Federal Work-Study, institutionally sponsored loans, scholarships/grants, and tuition waivers (partial) available. Support available to part-time students. Financial award application deadline: 2/1; financial award applicants required to submit FAFSA. *Faculty research:* Legal and institutional environments of schools; social inequality; high school reform and achievement; urban schooling, economics and education, educational policy. *Unit head:* Dr. Floyd M. Hammack, Program Director, 212-998-5542, Fax: 212-995-4832, E-mail: fmhl@nyu.edu. *Application contact:* 212-998-5030, Fax: 212-995-4328, E-mail: steinhardt.gradadmissions@nyu.edu.

Norfolk State University, School of Graduate Studies, School of Liberal Arts, Department of Sociology, Program in Applied Sociology, Norfolk, VA 23504. Offers MS. Program offered jointly with Old Dominion University. Part-time programs available.

North Carolina Central University, Division of Academic Affairs, College of Behavioral and Social Sciences, Department of Sociology, Durham, NC 27707-3129. Offers MA. Part-time and evening/weekend programs available. *Degree requirements:* For master's, one foreign language, comprehensive exam, thesis. *Entrance requirements:* For master's, GRE, minimum GPA of 3.0 in major, 2.5 overall. Additional exam requirements/recommendations for international students: Required—TOEFL. *Faculty research:* Urban demography, family, statistical methods.

North Carolina State University, Graduate School, College of Humanities and Social Sciences, Department of Sociology and Anthropology, Program in Sociology, Raleigh, NC 27695. Offers M Soc, MS, PhD. Part-time programs available. *Degree requirements:* For master's, practicum (M Soc), thesis (MS); for doctorate, comprehensive exam, thesis/dissertation. *Entrance requirements:* For master's and doctorate, GRE General Test, sample of written work. Electronic applications accepted. *Faculty research:* Inequity: gender, race and class; crime and social control; work and organizations; rural sociology; family and intimate relations.

Sociology

North Dakota State University, College of Graduate and Interdisciplinary Studies, College of Arts, Humanities and Social Sciences, Department of Sociology, Anthropology, and Emergency Management, Fargo, ND 58108. Offers emergency management (MS, PhD); social science (MA, MS); sociology (MS). Part-time programs available. *Faculty:* 8 full-time (3 women), 5 part-time/adjunct (2 women). *Students:* 27 full-time (14 women), 14 part-time (4 women); includes 2 Black or African American, non-Hispanic/Latino; 1 American Indian or Alaska Native, non-Hispanic/Latino; 1 Asian, non-Hispanic/Latino; 1 Hispanic/Latino, 2 international. Average age 27. 15 applicants, 60% accepted, 7 enrolled. In 2010, 9 master's awarded. *Degree requirements:* For master's, thesis; for doctorate, comprehensive exam, thesis/dissertation. *Entrance requirements:* For master's, GRE (emergency management), course work in sociology, minimum GPA of 3.2; for doctorate, GRE, minimum GPA of 3.2. Additional exam requirements/recommendations for international students: Required—TOEFL. *Application deadline:* For fall admission, 4/1 priority date for domestic students. Applications are processed on a rolling basis. Application fee: $45 ($60 for international students). *Financial support:* In 2010–11, 7 research assistantships with full tuition reimbursements (averaging $6,156 per year), 7 teaching assistantships with full tuition reimbursements (averaging $3,078 per year) were awarded; fellowships, career-related internships or fieldwork, Federal Work-Study, institutionally sponsored loans, and tuition waivers (full) also available. Support available to part-time students. Financial award application deadline: 4/15. *Faculty research:* Medical sociology, demography, ethnology, archaeology. Total annual research expenditures: $75,000. *Unit head:* Dr. Daniel J. Klenow, Chair, 701-231-8657, Fax: 701-231-1047, E-mail: daniel.klenow@ndsu.edu. *Application contact:* Dr. Daniel J. Klenow, Chair, 701-231-8657, Fax: 701-231-1047, E-mail: daniel.klenow@ndsu.edu.

Northeastern University, College of Social Sciences and Humanities, Department of Sociology and Anthropology, Boston, MA 02115-5096. Offers sociology (MA, PhD). Part-time programs available. *Faculty:* 24 full-time (11 women), 6 part-time/adjunct (5 women). *Students:* 62 full-time (47 women), 1 (woman) part-time. 116 applicants, 23% accepted, 10 enrolled. In 2010, 7 master's, 2 doctorates awarded. *Degree requirements:* For master's, thesis; for doctorate, thesis/dissertation, teaching tutorial. *Entrance requirements:* For master's and doctorate, GRE General Test or MAT. Additional exam requirements/recommendations for international students: Required—TOEFL. *Application deadline:* For fall admission, 2/1 for domestic students. Application fee: $50. *Financial support:* In 2010–11, 1 research assistantship with tuition reimbursement, 18 teaching assistantships with tuition reimbursements (averaging $14,035 per year) were awarded; fellowships, career-related internships or fieldwork, tuition waivers (full and partial), and unspecified assistantships also available. Financial award application deadline: 2/1; financial award applicants required to submit FAFSA. *Faculty research:* Globalization and international studies, urban affairs, social justice. *Unit head:* Dr. Steven Vallas, Acting Chair, 617-373-2686, Fax: 617-373-2688, E-mail: gradsoc@neu.edu. *Application contact:* Graduate Programs Assistant, 617-373-2686, Fax: 617-373-2688, E-mail: gradsoc@neu.edu.

Northern Arizona University, Graduate College, College of Social and Behavioral Sciences, Department of Sociology and Social Work, Flagstaff, AZ 86011. Offers applied sociology (MA). Part-time programs available. *Faculty:* 17 full-time (9 women). *Students:* 18 full-time (11 women), 9 part-time (5 women); includes 6 minority (1 Black or African American, non-Hispanic/Latino; 3 American Indian or Alaska Native, non-Hispanic/Latino; 1 Hispanic/Latino; 1 Two or more races, non-Hispanic/Latino), 2 international. Average age 33. 25 applicants, 76% accepted, 12 enrolled. In 2010, 8 master's awarded. *Degree requirements:* For master's, thesis optional, thesis or internship. *Entrance requirements:* For master's, minimum GPA of 3.0. Additional exam requirements/recommendations for international students: Required—TOEFL (minimum score 550 paper-based; 213 computer-based; 80 iBT), IELTS (minimum score 7). *Application deadline:* For fall admission, 2/15 priority date for domestic and international students. Applications are processed on a rolling basis. Application fee: $65. Electronic applications accepted. *Financial support:* In 2010–11, 6 teaching assistantships with partial tuition reimbursements (averaging $10,124 per year) were awarded; career-related internships or fieldwork, Federal Work-Study, scholarships/grants, health care benefits, tuition waivers (full and partial), and unspecified assistantships also available. Support available to part-time students. Financial award applicants required to submit FAFSA. *Faculty research:* Demography, death and dying, criminology, social policy, divorce. *Unit head:* Dr. Kooros Mohit Mahmoudi, Chair, 928-523-6554, Fax: 928-523-6777, E-mail: kooros.mahmoudi@nau.edu. *Application contact:* Hilary McDonald, Administrative Assistant, 928-523-6562, Fax: 928-523-6777, E-mail: ssw@nau.edu.

Northern Illinois University, Graduate School, College of Liberal Arts and Sciences, Department of Sociology, De Kalb, IL 60115-2854. Offers MA. Part-time programs available. *Faculty:* 14 full-time (3 women). *Students:* 18 full-time (13 women), 8 part-time (5 women); includes 1 Black or African American, non-Hispanic/Latino; 1 Hispanic/Latino, 1 international. Average age 26. 31 applicants, 58% accepted, 12 enrolled. In 2010, 9 master's awarded. *Degree requirements:* For master's, comprehensive exam, thesis optional. *Entrance requirements:* For master's, GRE General Test, minimum GPA of 2.75; course work in social theory, social methods, and statistics. Additional exam requirements/recommendations for international students: Required—TOEFL (minimum score 550 paper-based; 213 computer-based). *Application deadline:* For fall admission, 6/1 for domestic students, 5/1 for international students; for spring admission, 11/1 for domestic students, 10/1 for international students. Applications are processed on a rolling basis. Application fee: $30. Electronic applications accepted. *Expenses:* Tuition, state resident: full-time $7200; part-time $300 per credit hour. Tuition, nonresident: full-time $14,400; part-time $600 per credit hour. Required fees: $79 per credit hour. *Financial support:* In 2010–11, 19 research assistantships with full tuition reimbursements were awarded; fellowships with full tuition reimbursements, teaching assistantships with full tuition reimbursements, career-related internships or fieldwork, Federal Work-Study, scholarships/grants, tuition waivers (full), and unspecified assistantships also available. Support available to part-time students. Financial award applicants required to submit FAFSA. *Faculty research:* Welfare reform, interpersonal disputes, multicultural education, race and ethnicism, social control. *Unit head:* Dr. William Minor, Chair, 815-753-1194, Fax: 815-753-6302, E-mail: bminor@niu.edu. *Application contact:* Dr. William Minor, Chair, 815-753-1194, Fax: 815-753-6302, E-mail: bminor@niu.edu.

Northwestern University, The Graduate School, Interdepartmental Programs and Kellogg School of Management, Program in Management and Organizations and Sociology, Evanston, IL 60208. Offers PhD. Program requires admission to both The Graduate School and the Kellogg School of Management. *Degree requirements:* For doctorate, comprehensive exam, thesis/dissertation. *Entrance requirements:* For doctorate, GRE General Test. Additional exam requirements/recommendations for international students: Required—TOEFL. Electronic applications accepted. *Faculty research:* Strategic alliances and organizational competitiveness, institutional change and the information of industries, social capital and the creation of financial capital, negotiation, organizational networks, diversity.

Northwestern University, The Graduate School, Judd A. and Marjorie Weinberg College of Arts and Sciences, Department of Sociology, Evanston, IL 60208. Offers PhD, JD/PhD. Admissions and degrees offered through The Graduate School. *Degree requirements:* For doctorate, thesis/dissertation. *Entrance requirements:* For doctorate, GRE General Test. Additional exam requirements/recommendations for international students: Required—TOEFL. Electronic applications accepted. *Faculty research:* Sociology of culture, social organizations, social inequality, comparative/historical sociology, economic sociology.

The Ohio State University, Graduate School, College of Arts and Sciences, Division of Social and Behavioral Sciences, Department of Sociology, Columbus, OH 43210. Offers MA, PhD. *Faculty:* 41. *Students:* 38 full-time (17 women), 31 part-time (20 women); includes 6 Black or African American, non-Hispanic/Latino; 1 American Indian or Alaska Native, non-Hispanic/Latino; 6 Asian, non-Hispanic/Latino; 3 Hispanic/Latino; 1 Two or more races, non-Hispanic/Latino, 4 international. Average age 29. In 2010, 9 master's, 25 doctorates awarded. *Degree requirements:* For master's, thesis; for doctorate, thesis/dissertation. *Entrance requirements:* For master's and doctorate, GRE General Test. Additional exam requirements/recommendations for international students: Required—TOEFL (minimum score 600 paper-based; 250 computer-based). *Application deadline:* For fall admission, 8/15 priority date for domestic students, 7/1 priority date for international students; for winter admission, 12/1 priority date for domestic students, 11/1 priority date for international students; for spring admission, 3/1 priority date for domestic students, 2/1 priority date for international students. Applications are processed on a rolling basis. Application fee: $40 ($50 for international students). Electronic applications accepted. *Expenses:* Tuition, state resident: full-time $10,605. Tuition, nonresident: full-time $26,535. Tuition and fees vary according to course load and program. *Financial support:* Fellowships, research assistantships, teaching assistantships, Federal Work-Study and institutionally sponsored loans available. Support available to part-time students. *Unit head:* Zhenchao Qian, Chair, 614-688-8612, Fax: 614-292-6687, E-mail: qian.26@sociology.osu.edu. *Application contact:* 614-292-9444, Fax: 614-292-3895, E-mail: domestic.grad@osu.edu.

Ohio University, Graduate College, College of Arts and Sciences, Department of Sociology and Anthropology, Athens, OH 45701-2979. Offers sociology (MA). Part-time programs available. *Students:* 19 full-time (11 women), 6 part-time (5 women); includes 6 minority (3 Black or African American, non-Hispanic/Latino; 2 Hispanic/Latino; 1 Two or more races, non-Hispanic/Latino), 5 international. 28 applicants, 57% accepted, 12 enrolled. In 2010, 14 master's awarded. *Degree requirements:* For master's, thesis or alternative. *Entrance requirements:* For master's, minimum GPA of 3.0; minimum of 20 hours in sociology including statistics, theory, and research methods. Additional exam requirements/recommendations for international students: Required—TOEFL (minimum score 550 paper-based; 80 iBT) or IELTS (minimum score 6.5). *Application deadline:* For fall admission, 6/1 for domestic students, 3/1 priority date for international students; for winter admission, 10/1 for domestic and international students; for spring admission, 1/1 for domestic and international students. Application fee: $50 ($55 for international students). Electronic applications accepted. *Financial support:* Research assistantships with full and partial tuition reimbursements, teaching assistantships with full tuition reimbursements, career-related internships or fieldwork, Federal Work-Study, and unspecified assistantships available. Financial award application deadline: 3/1. *Faculty research:* Criminology/deviance, gender studies, inequality, social psychology and rural poverty. *Unit head:* Dr. Leon Anderson, Department Chair, 740-593-1381, Fax: 740-593-1365, E-mail: andersoe@ohio.edu. *Application contact:* Dr. Cynthia D. Anderson, Graduate Chair, 740-593-1385, Fax: 740-593-1365, E-mail: andersc2@ohio.edu.

Oklahoma City University, Petree College of Arts and Sciences, Division of Sociology and Justice Studies, Oklahoma City, OK 73106-1402. Offers applied sociology (MA), including nonprofit leadership; criminal justice (MCJ). Part-time and evening/weekend programs available. *Degree requirements:* For master's, thesis optional. *Entrance requirements:* For master's, minimum GPA of 3.0, two letters of recommendation. Additional exam requirements/recommendations for international students: Required—TOEFL (minimum score 550 paper-based). *Expenses:* Contact institution. *Faculty research:* Victims, police, corrections, security, women and crime.

Oklahoma State University, College of Arts and Sciences, Department of Sociology, Stillwater, OK 74078. Offers sociology (MS, PhD). *Faculty:* 14 full-time (3 women), 3 part-time/adjunct (2 women). *Students:* 7 full-time (4 women), 27 part-time (16 women); includes 3 Black or African American, non-Hispanic/Latino; 2 American Indian or Alaska Native, non-Hispanic/Latino; 1 Hispanic/Latino, 1 international. Average age 35. 56 applicants, 32% accepted, 5 enrolled. In 2010, 1 master's, 2 doctorates awarded. *Degree requirements:* For master's, thesis; for doctorate, comprehensive exam, thesis/dissertation. *Entrance requirements:* For master's and doctorate, GRE General Test. Additional exam requirements/recommendations for international students: Required—TOEFL (minimum score 550 paper-based; 79 iBT). *Application deadline:* For fall admission, 3/1 priority date for international students; for spring admission, 8/1 priority date for international students. Applications are processed on a rolling basis. Application fee: $40 ($75 for international students). Electronic applications accepted. *Expenses:* Tuition, state resident: full-time $3716; part-time $154.85 per credit hour. Tuition, nonresident: full-time $14,892; part-time $621 per credit hour. Required fees: $2044; $85.20 per credit hour. One-time fee: $50. Tuition and fees vary according to course load and campus/location. *Financial support:* In 2010–11, 1 research assistantship (averaging $3,064 per year), 23 teaching assistantships (averaging $13,944 per year) were awarded; career-related internships or fieldwork, Federal Work-Study, scholarships/grants, health care benefits, tuition waivers (partial), and unspecified assistantships also available. Support available to part-time students. Financial award application deadline: 3/1; financial award applicants required to submit FAFSA. *Faculty research:* Criminology/correction/legal issues; race, ethnicity, and gender in American society; environmental conflict and population problems; international comparative research; social change and social movement in American culture. *Unit head:* Dr. Duane Gill, Head, 405-744-6105, Fax: 405-744-5780. *Application contact:* Dr. Gordon Emslie, Dean, 405-744-6368, Fax: 405-744-0355, E-mail: grad-i@okstate.edu.

Old Dominion University, College of Arts and Letters, Program in Applied Sociology, Norfolk, VA 23529. Offers MA. Part-time and evening/weekend programs available. *Faculty:* 15 full-time (10 women), 1 part-time/adjunct (0 women). *Students:* 13 full-time (9 women), 14 part-time (9 women); includes 6 minority (5 Black or African American, non-Hispanic/Latino; 1 Asian, non-Hispanic/Latino), 1 international. Average age 29. 26 applicants, 65% accepted, 12 enrolled. In 2010, 7 master's awarded. *Degree requirements:* For master's, thesis. *Entrance requirements:* For master's, GRE General Test, minimum GPA of 3.0, 12 credits in criminal justice, sociology, or women's studies. Additional exam requirements/recommendations for international students: Required—TOEFL. *Application deadline:* For fall admission, 3/1 for domestic and international students. Application fee: $50. Electronic applications accepted. *Expenses:* Tuition, state resident: full-time $8592; part-time $358 per credit. Tuition, nonresident: full-time $21,672; part-time $903 per credit. Required fees: $119 per semester. One-time fee: $50. *Financial support:* In 2010–11, fellowships (averaging $2,000 per year), 2 research assistantships (averaging $10,000 per year), 2 teaching assistantships (averaging $10,000 per year) were awarded; career-related internships or fieldwork, scholarships/grants, and unspecified assistantships also available. Financial award application deadline: 2/15; financial award applicants required to submit CSS PROFILE or FAFSA. *Faculty research:* Quantitative methodology, theory, family, gender/class/race, crime. Total annual research expenditures: $350,000. *Unit head:* Dr. Dianne Carmody, Graduate Program Director, 757-683-6801, Fax: 757-683-5634, E-mail: dcarmody@odu.edu. *Application contact:* Dr. Dianne Carmody, Graduate Program Director, 757-683-6801, Fax: 757-683-5634, E-mail: dcarmody@odu.edu.

Oxford Graduate School, Graduate Programs, Dayton, TN 37321-6736. Offers family life education (M Litt); organizational leadership (M Litt); sociological integration of religion and society (D Phil). *Faculty:* 10 full-time (2 women), 22 part-time/adjunct (7 women). *Students:* 105 full-time (40 women). *Application contact:* Joanne Phillips, Information Contact, 423-775-6596, Fax: 423-775-6599, E-mail: oxfordgraduateschool@ogs.edu.

Penn State University Park, Graduate School, College of the Liberal Arts, Department of Sociology, State College, University Park, PA 16802-1503. Offers MA, PhD. *Unit head:* Dr. John D. McCarthy, Head, 814-863-8260, Fax: 814-863-7216, E-mail: jxm516@psu.edu. *Application contact:* Cynthia E. Nicosia, Director, Graduate Enrollment Services, 814-865-1795, Fax: 814-865-4627, E-mail: cey1@psu.edu.

Portland State University, Graduate Studies, College of Liberal Arts and Sciences, Department of Sociology, Portland, OR 97207-0751. Offers MA, MS, PhD. Part-time programs available. *Faculty:* 16 full-time (7 women), 8 part-time/adjunct (3 women). *Students:* 26 full-time (18 women), 10 part-time (7 women); includes 2 Black or African American, non-Hispanic/Latino; 1 Asian, non-Hispanic/Latino; 3 Hispanic/Latino; 1 Two or more races, non-Hispanic/Latino, 2 international. Average age 30. 73 applicants, 32% accepted, 15 enrolled. In 2010, 12 master's awarded. *Degree requirements:* For master's, variable foreign language requirement, thesis, written exam; for doctorate, thesis/dissertation. *Entrance requirements:* For master's, GRE General Test, GRE Subject Test, minimum GPA of 3.0 in upper-division course work or 2.75 overall, 3 letters of recommendation. Additional exam requirements/recommendations for international students: Required—TOEFL (minimum score 550 paper-based; 213 computer-based). *Application deadline:* For fall admission, 1/15 for domestic and international students. Applications are processed on a rolling basis. Application fee: $50. *Expenses:* Tuition, state resident: full-time $8505; part-time $315 per credit. Tuition, nonresident: full-time $13,284; part-time $492 per credit. Required fees: $1482; $21 per credit. $99 per term. One-time fee: $120. Part-time tuition and fees vary according to course load and program. *Financial support:* In 2010–11, 5 research assistantships with full tuition reimbursements (averaging $9,328 per year) were awarded; fellowships with full tuition reimbursements, teaching assistantships with full tuition reimbursements, career-related internships or fieldwork, Federal Work-Study, and unspecified assistantships also available. Support available to part-time students. Financial award application deadline: 3/1; financial award applicants required to submit FAFSA. *Faculty research:* Urban sociology, gender and class, development, social change, race/ethnic/minority relations. Total annual research expenditures: $4.6 million. *Unit head:* Veronica Dujon, Chair, 503-725-3926. *Application contact:* Bahar Jaberi, Information Contact, 503-725-3926.

Portland State University, Graduate Studies, Systems Science Program, Portland, OR 97207-0751. Offers computational intelligence (Certificate); computer modeling and simulation (Certificate); systems science (MS); systems science/anthropology (PhD); systems science/business administration (PhD); systems science/civil engineering (PhD); systems science/economics (PhD); systems science/engineering management (PhD); systems science/general (PhD); systems science/mathematical sciences (PhD); systems science/mechanical engineering (PhD); systems science/psychology (PhD); systems science/sociology (PhD). *Faculty:* 4 full-time (0 women), 1 part-time/adjunct (0 women). *Students:* 15 full-time (4 women), 35 part-time (11 women); includes 1 American Indian or Alaska Native, non-Hispanic/Latino; 1 Asian, non-Hispanic/Latino; 1 Two or more races, non-Hispanic/Latino, 4 international. Average age 39. 8 applicants, 88% accepted, 5 enrolled. In 2010, 2 master's, 4 doctorates awarded. *Degree requirements:* For doctorate, variable foreign language requirement, thesis/dissertation. *Entrance requirements:* For master's, 2 letters of recommendation; for doctorate, GMAT, GRE General Test, minimum undergraduate GPA of 3.0. Additional exam requirements/recommendations for international students: Required—TOEFL. *Application deadline:* For fall admission, 2/1 for domestic students; for spring admission, 11/1 for domestic students. Application fee: $50. *Expenses:* Tuition, state resident: full-time $8505; part-time $315 per credit. Tuition, nonresident: full-time $13,284; part-time $492 per credit. Required fees: $1482; $21 per credit. $99 per term. One-time fee: $120. Part-time tuition and fees vary according to course load and program. *Financial support:* In 2010–11, 1 research assistantship with full tuition reimbursement (averaging $7,704 per year) was awarded; teaching assistantships with full tuition reimbursements, career-related internships or fieldwork, Federal Work-Study, scholarships/grants, and unspecified assistantships also available. Support available to part-time students. Financial award application deadline: 3/1; financial award applicants required to submit FAFSA. *Faculty research:* Systems theory and methodology, artificial intelligence neural networks, information theory, nonlinear dynamics/chaos, modeling and simulation. *Unit head:* George Lendaris, Acting Director, 503-725-4960. *Application contact:* Dawn Sharafi, Administrative Assistant, 503-725-4960, E-mail: dawn@sysc.pdx.edu.

Prairie View A&M University, College of Arts and Sciences, Division of Social Work, Behavioral and Political Science, Prairie View, TX 77446-0519. Offers sociology (MA). Part-time and evening/weekend programs available. *Faculty:* 3 full-time (2 women), 1 part-time/adjunct (0 women). *Students:* 4 full-time (3 women), 17 part-time (15 women); includes 17 Black or African American, non-Hispanic/Latino; 1 Asian, non-Hispanic/Latino; 2 Hispanic/Latino, 1 international. Average age 30. 5 applicants, 100% accepted, 5 enrolled. In 2010, 1 master's awarded. *Degree requirements:* For master's, comprehensive exam, thesis optional. *Entrance requirements:* For master's, GRE General Test. *Application deadline:* Applications are processed on a rolling basis. Application fee: $50. *Expenses:* Tuition, state resident: full-time $3586.14; part-time $119.06 per credit hour. Tuition, nonresident: part-time $511.23 per credit hour. *Financial support:* Federal Work-Study and institutionally sponsored loans available. Financial award application deadline: 4/1; financial award applicants required to submit FAFSA. *Faculty research:* Criminology, political sociology, sociology of education, gender, race, African-American mental health, global development-social movements, African-American status attainment. *Unit head:* Dr. Walle Engedayehu, Division Head, 936-261-3200, Fax: 936-261-3229, E-mail: waengedayehu@pvamu.edu. *Application contact:* Dr. Walle Engedayehu, Division Head, 936-261-3200, Fax: 936-261-3229, E-mail: waengedayehu@pvamu.edu.

Princeton University, Graduate School, Department of Sociology, Princeton, NJ 08544-1019. Offers sociology (PhD); sociology and demography (PhD). *Degree requirements:* For doctorate, variable foreign language requirement, thesis/dissertation. *Entrance requirements:* For doctorate, GRE General Test, GRE Subject Test (recommended), sample of written work. Additional exam requirements/recommendations for international students: Required—TOEFL (minimum score 600 paper-based; 250 computer-based). Electronic applications accepted.

Princeton University, Graduate School, Program in Population Studies, Princeton, NJ 08544-1019. Offers demography (PhD, Certificate); economics and demography (PhD); public affairs and demography (PhD); sociology and demography (PhD). *Degree requirements:* For doctorate, thesis/dissertation. *Entrance requirements:* For doctorate, GRE General Test. Additional exam requirements/recommendations for international students: Required—TOEFL (minimum score 600 paper-based; 250 computer-based). Electronic applications accepted. *Faculty research:* Models, fertility, infant and child mortality, migration.

Purdue University, Graduate School, College of Liberal Arts, Department of Sociology and Anthropology, West Lafayette, IN 47907. Offers anthropology (MS, PhD); sociology (MS, PhD). Terminal master's awarded for partial completion of doctoral program. *Degree requirements:* For doctorate, thesis/dissertation. *Entrance requirements:* For master's and doctorate, GRE General Test. Additional exam requirements/recommendations for international students: Required—TOEFL, TWE. Electronic applications accepted. *Faculty research:* Communiversity survey project, risk, fear, constrained behavior, archaeological services.

Queens College of the City University of New York, Division of Graduate Studies, Social Science Division, Department of Sociology, Flushing, NY 11367-1597. Offers MA. Part-time and evening/weekend programs available. *Faculty:* 26 full-time (9 women). *Students:* 6 full-time (3 women), 37 part-time (22 women); includes 10 Black or African American, non-Hispanic/Latino; 4 Asian, non-Hispanic/Latino; 6 Hispanic/Latino, 10 international. 41 applicants, 78% accepted, 26 enrolled. In 2010, 10 master's awarded. *Degree requirements:* For master's, thesis optional. *Entrance requirements:* For master's, minimum GPA of 3.0. Additional exam requirements/recommendations for international students: Required—TOEFL. *Application deadline:* For fall admission, 4/1 for domestic students; for spring admission, 11/1 for domestic students. Applications are processed on a rolling basis. Application fee: $125. *Financial support:* Career-related internships or fieldwork, Federal Work-Study, institutionally sponsored loans, and tuition waivers (partial) available. Support available to part-time students. Financial award application deadline: 4/1; financial award applicants required to submit FAFSA. *Unit head:* Dr. Andrew Beveridge, Chairperson, 718-997-2800. *Application contact:* Mario Caruso, Director of Graduate Admissions, 718-997-5200, Fax: 718-997-5193, E-mail: graduate_admissions@qc.edu.

Queen's University at Kingston, School of Graduate Studies and Research, Faculty of Arts and Sciences, Department of Sociology, Kingston, ON K7L 3N6, Canada. Offers communication and Information technology (MA, PhD); feminist sociology (MA, PhD); socio-legal studies (MA, PhD); sociological theory (MA, PhD). Part-time programs available. *Degree requirements:* For master's, thesis; for doctorate, comprehensive exam, thesis/dissertation. *Entrance requirements:* For master's, honors bachelors degree in sociology; for doctorate, honors bachelors degree, masters degree in sociology. Additional exam requirements/recommendations for international students: Required—TOEFL. *Faculty research:* Social change and modernization, social control, deviance and criminology, surveillance.

Rice University, Graduate Programs, School of Social Sciences, Department of Sociology, Houston, TX 77251-1892. Offers PhD.

Roosevelt University, Graduate Division, College of Arts and Sciences, Department of Sociology and Anthropology, Chicago, IL 60605. Offers anthropology (MA); sociology (MA). Part-time and evening/weekend programs available. *Degree requirements:* For master's, comprehensive exam, thesis. *Faculty research:* Social theory, urban sociology, gerontology, social organizations.

Rutgers, The State University of New Jersey, New Brunswick, Graduate School-New Brunswick, Program in Sociology, Piscataway, NJ 08854-8097. Offers MA, PhD. Terminal master's awarded for partial completion of doctoral program. *Degree requirements:* For master's, qualifying paper; for doctorate, thesis/dissertation, qualifying exam, qualifying papers. *Entrance requirements:* For master's, GRE General Test; for doctorate, GRE General Test, sample of written work. Additional exam requirements/recommendations for international students: Required—TOEFL. Electronic applications accepted. *Expenses:* Tuition, state resident: full-time $7200; part-time $600 per credit. Tuition, nonresident: full-time $11,124; part-time $927 per credit. *Faculty research:* Comparative-historical, sex and gender, organizations and work, culture and cognition, economics, occupations/professions, religion.

St. John's University, St. John's College of Liberal Arts and Sciences, Department of Sociology and Anthropology, Queens, NY 11439. Offers criminology and justice (MA); sociology (MA). Part-time and evening/weekend programs available. *Students:* 40 full-time (30 women), 30 part-time (17 women); includes 50 minority (24 Black or African American, non-Hispanic/Latino; 5 Asian, non-Hispanic/Latino; 19 Hispanic/Latino; 1 Native Hawaiian or other Pacific Islander, non-Hispanic/Latino; 1 Two or more races, non-Hispanic/Latino), 4 international. Average age 28. 76 applicants, 46% accepted, 28 enrolled. In 2010, 27 master's awarded. *Degree requirements:* For master's, comprehensive exam, thesis optional. *Entrance requirements:* For master's, 18 undergraduate credits in social services, minimum GPA of 3.0. Additional exam requirements/recommendations for international students: Required—TOEFL (minimum score 600 paper-based; 250 computer-based; 100 iBT), IELTS (minimum score 5.5). *Application deadline:* For fall admission, 5/1 priority date for domestic and international students; for spring admission, 11/1 priority date for domestic and international students. Applications are processed on a rolling basis. Application fee: $70. Electronic applications accepted. *Expenses:* Tuition: Full-time $17,100; part-time $950 per credit. Required fees: $340; $170 per semester. Tuition and fees vary according to program. *Financial support:* Research assistantships, career-related internships or fieldwork and scholarships/grants available. Support available to part-time students. Financial award application deadline: 3/1; financial award applicants required to submit FAFSA. *Faculty research:* Community studies and gentrification, global financial crisis, insurance fraud, globalization, immigration and human rights. *Unit head:* Dr. Dawn Esposito, Chair, 718-990-5667, E-mail: espositd@stjohns.edu. *Application contact:* Kathleen Davis, Director of Graduate Admission, 718-990-1601, Fax: 718-990-5686, E-mail: gradhelp@stjohns.edu.

Sam Houston State University, College of Humanities and Social Sciences, Department of Sociology, Huntsville, TX 77341. Offers MA. Part-time programs available. *Faculty:* 7 full-time (5 women). *Students:* 2 full-time (both women), 5 part-time (1 woman); includes 1 Black or African American, non-Hispanic/Latino, 2 international. Average age 32. 4 applicants, 100% accepted, 4 enrolled. In 2010, 3 master's awarded. *Degree requirements:* For master's, thesis optional. *Entrance requirements:* For master's, GRE General Test. Additional exam requirements/recommendations for international students: Required—TOEFL (minimum score 550 paper-based; 213 computer-based; 79 iBT). *Application deadline:* For fall admission, 8/1 for domestic students; for spring admission, 12/1 for domestic students. Applications are processed on a rolling basis. Application fee: $20. *Expenses:* Tuition, state resident: full-time $1363; part-time $163 per credit hour. Tuition, nonresident: full-time $3856; part-time $473 per credit hour. *Financial support:* Teaching assistantships, Federal Work-Study available. Support available to part-time students. Financial award application deadline: 5/31; financial award applicants required to submit FAFSA. *Unit head:* Dr. Alessandro Bonanno, Chair, 936-294-1488, Fax: 963-294-3573, E-mail: soc_aab@shsu.edu. *Application contact:* Dr. Gene Theodori, Director of Graduate Studies, 936-294-4143, E-mail: glt002@shsu.edu.

San Diego State University, Graduate and Research Affairs, College of Arts and Letters, Department of Sociology, San Diego, CA 92182. Offers MA. *Degree requirements:* For master's, thesis. *Entrance requirements:* For master's, GRE General Test, 3 letters of recommendation, writing sample. Additional exam requirements/recommendations for international students: Required—TOEFL. Electronic applications accepted. *Faculty research:* The homeless and mentally ill, medical data relating to the homeless.

San Jose State University, Graduate Studies and Research, College of Social Sciences, Department of Sociology, San Jose, CA 95192-0001. Offers MA. Part-time and evening/weekend programs available. *Degree requirements:* For master's, comprehensive exams or thesis. *Entrance requirements:* For master's, GRE Subject Test, minimum GPA of 3.0. Electronic applications accepted. *Faculty research:* Theory construction, sexuality, sociology of the media, social causes of stress, social change.

Shippensburg University of Pennsylvania, School of Graduate Studies, College of Arts and Sciences, Department of Sociology and Anthropology, Shippensburg, PA 17257-2299. Offers organizational development and leadership (MS), including business, communications, education, environmental management, higher education, historical administration, individual and organizational development, public organizations, social structures and organizations. Part-time and evening/weekend programs available. *Faculty:* 3 full-time (all women). *Students:* 18 full-time (13 women), 46 part-time (33 women); includes 11 minority (6 Black or African American, non-Hispanic/Latino; 3 Asian, non-Hispanic/Latino; 2 Two or more races, non-Hispanic/Latino), 2 international. Average age 32. 56 applicants, 55% accepted, 20 enrolled. In 2010, 28 master's awarded. *Degree requirements:* For master's, capstone experience including internship. *Entrance requirements:* For master's, interview (if GPA less than 2.75), resume, personal goals statement. Additional exam requirements/recommendations for international students: Required—TOEFL (minimum score 580 paper-based; 237 computer-based); Recommended—IELTS (minimum score 6). *Application deadline:* For fall admission, 3/1 for international students; for spring admission, 7/1 for international students. Applications are processed on a rolling basis. Application fee: $30. Electronic applications accepted. *Expenses:* Tuition, state resident: full-time $6966. Tuition, nonresident: full-time $11,146. Required fees: $1802. *Financial support:* In 2010–11, 8 research assistantships with full tuition reimbursements (averaging $5,000 per year) were awarded; career-related internships or fieldwork, scholarships/grants, unspecified assistantships, and resident hall director and student payroll positions also available. Support available to part-time students. Financial award applicants required to submit FAFSA. *Unit head:* Dr. Barbara Denison, Chairperson, 717-477-1735, Fax: 717-477-4011, E-mail: bjdeni@ship.edu. *Application contact:* Jeremy R. Goshorn, Associate Dean of Graduate Admissions, 717-477-1231, Fax: 717-477-4016, E-mail: jrgoshorn@ship.edu.

Simon Fraser University, Graduate Studies, Faculty of Arts and Social Sciences, Department of Sociology and Anthropology, Burnaby, BC V5A 1S6, Canada. Offers anthropology (MA, PhD); sociology (MA, PhD). *Degree requirements:* For master's, thesis (for some programs); for doctorate, thesis/dissertation. *Entrance requirements:* For master's and doctorate, minimum GPA of 3.25. Additional exam requirements/recommendations for international students: Required—TOEFL or IELTS. *Faculty research:* Sociology theory, social and cultural anthropology, political sociology, religion and society, Canadian native peoples.

Southeastern Louisiana University, College of Arts, Humanities and Social Sciences, Department of Sociology and Criminal Justice, Hammond, LA 70402. Offers applied sociology (MS), including criminal justice, globalization and social diversity, public policy. Part-time and evening/weekend programs available. *Faculty:* 7 full-time (2 women). *Students:* 23 full-time (17 women), 11 part-time (8 women); includes 11 minority (9 Black or African American, non-Hispanic/Latino; 2 Hispanic/Latino), 1 international. Average age 28. 18 applicants, 72% accepted, 12 enrolled. In 2010, 7 master's awarded. *Degree requirements:* For master's, comprehensive exam, thesis (for some programs), internship research (for those who select an internship track). *Entrance requirements:* For master's, GRE General Test (verbal and

Sociology

Southeastern Louisiana University (continued)

quantitative), bachelor's degree in sociology, social work, criminal justice or related social science; minimum GPA of 3.0. Additional exam requirements/recommendations for international students: Required—TOEFL (minimum score 500 paper-based; 173 computer-based; 61 iBT). *Application deadline:* For fall admission, 7/15 priority date for domestic students, 6/1 priority date for international students; for spring admission, 12/1 priority date for domestic students, 10/1 priority date for international students. Applications are processed on a rolling basis. Application fee: $20 ($30 for international students). Electronic applications accepted. *Expenses:* Tuition, state resident: full-time $3533. Tuition, nonresident: full-time $12,002. Required fees: $907. Tuition and fees vary according to degree level. *Financial support:* In 2010–11, 4 students received support, including 4 research assistantships (averaging $10,100 per year); Federal Work-Study, institutionally sponsored loans, and scholarships/grants also available. Support available to part-time students. Financial award application deadline: 5/1; financial award applicants required to submit FAFSA. *Faculty research:* Criminology, environmental sociology, globalization, public policy, race and ethnic relations. *Unit head:* Dr. Kenneth Bolton, Department Head, 985-549-2110, Fax: 985-549-5961, E-mail: kbolton@selu.edu. *Application contact:* Sandra Meyers, Graduate Admissions Analyst, 985-549-5620, Fax: 985-549-5632, E-mail: admissions@selu.edu.

Southern Connecticut State University, School of Graduate Studies, School of Arts and Sciences, Department of Sociology, New Haven, CT 06515-1355. Offers MS. Part-time and evening/weekend programs available. *Faculty:* 7 full-time (4 women). *Students:* 5 full-time (4 women), 11 part-time (7 women); includes 1 Black or African American, non-Hispanic/Latino; 1 Asian, non-Hispanic/Latino; 2 Two or more races, non-Hispanic/Latino. 30 applicants, 37% accepted, 9 enrolled. In 2010, 2 master's awarded. *Degree requirements:* For master's, thesis or alternative. *Entrance requirements:* For master's, interview. *Application deadline:* For fall admission, 7/15 priority date for domestic students. Applications are processed on a rolling basis. Application fee: $50. Electronic applications accepted. *Expenses:* Tuition, state resident: full-time $5137; part-time $518 per credit. Tuition, nonresident: part-time $542 per credit. Required fees: $4008; $55 per semester. Tuition and fees vary according to program. *Financial support:* Application deadline: 4/15. *Unit head:* Dr. Jon Bloch, Chairperson, 203-392-5685, Fax: 203-392-5670, E-mail: blochj1@southernct.edu. *Application contact:* Dr. Jessica Kenty-Drane, Graduate Coordinator, 203-392-5689, Fax: 203-392-5670, E-mail: kentydranej1@southernct.edu.

Southern Illinois University Carbondale, Graduate School, College of Liberal Arts, Department of Sociology, Carbondale, IL 62901-4701. Offers MA, PhD. Part-time programs available. *Degree requirements:* For master's, thesis; for doctorate, thesis/dissertation. *Entrance requirements:* For master's, minimum GPA of 2.7; for doctorate, minimum GPA of 3.25. Additional exam requirements/recommendations for international students: Required—TOEFL. *Faculty research:* Deviance, family, social stratification, social change, theory methodology, culture.

Southern Illinois University Edwardsville, Graduate School, College of Arts and Sciences, Department of Sociology and Criminal Justice Studies, Edwardsville, IL 62026-0001. Offers sociology (MA). Part-time programs available. *Faculty:* 14 full-time (8 women). *Students:* 7 full-time (6 women), 20 part-time (15 women); includes 7 minority (4 Black or African American, non-Hispanic/Latino; 2 Hispanic/Latino; 1 Two or more races, non-Hispanic/Latino), 2 international. Average age 26. 23 applicants, 65% accepted. In 2010, 4 master's awarded. *Degree requirements:* For master's, thesis (for some programs), internship. *Entrance requirements:* Additional exam requirements/recommendations for international students: Required—TOEFL (minimum score 550 paper-based; 213 computer-based; 79 iBT), IELTS (minimum score 6.5). *Application deadline:* For fall admission, 7/10 for domestic and international students; for spring admission, 11/15 for domestic and international students. Application fee: $30. Electronic applications accepted. *Expenses:* Tuition, state resident: full-time $6012; part-time $1503 per semester. Tuition, nonresident: full-time $15,030; part-time $3758 per semester. Required fees: $1711; $675 per semester. *Financial support:* In 2010–11, 1 fellowship with full tuition reimbursement (averaging $8,370 per year), 8 teaching assistantships with full tuition reimbursements (averaging $8,064 per year) were awarded; research assistantships with full tuition reimbursements, career-related internships or fieldwork, Federal Work-Study, institutionally sponsored loans, scholarships/grants, traineeships, and unspecified assistantships also available. Support available to part-time students. Financial award application deadline: 3/1; financial award applicants required to submit FAFSA. *Unit head:* Dr. David Kauzlarich, Chair, 618-650-3713, E-mail: dkauzla@siue.edu. *Application contact:* Dr. Florence Maatita, Program Director, 618-650-3287, E-mail: fmaatit@siue.edu.

Stanford University, School of Humanities and Sciences, Department of Sociology, Stanford, CA 94305-9991. Offers PhD. *Degree requirements:* For doctorate, thesis/dissertation, oral exam. *Entrance requirements:* For doctorate, GRE General Test. Additional exam requirements/recommendations for international students: Required—TOEFL. Electronic applications accepted. *Expenses:* Tuition: Full-time $38,700; part-time $860 per unit. One-time fee: $200 full-time.

State University of New York at Binghamton, Graduate School, School of Arts and Sciences, Department of Sociology, Binghamton, NY 13902-6000. Offers MA, PhD. *Faculty:* 15 full-time (7 women), 5 part-time/adjunct (2 women). *Students:* 28 full-time (9 women), 47 part-time (23 women); includes 4 Black or African American, non-Hispanic/Latino; 5 Asian, non-Hispanic/Latino; 4 Hispanic/Latino, 34 international. Average age 34. 45 applicants, 53% accepted, 15 enrolled. In 2010, 4 master's, 8 doctorates awarded. Terminal master's awarded for partial completion of doctoral program. *Degree requirements:* For doctorate, thesis/dissertation. *Entrance requirements:* For master's and doctorate, GRE General Test, GRE Subject Test. Additional exam requirements/recommendations for international students: Required—TOEFL (minimum score 550 paper-based; 213 computer-based; 80 iBT). *Application deadline:* For fall admission, 1/15 priority date for domestic and international students. Applications are processed on a rolling basis. Application fee: $60. Electronic applications accepted. *Financial support:* In 2010–11, 20 students received support, including 2 fellowships with full tuition reimbursements available (averaging $14,700 per year), 16 teaching assistantships with full tuition reimbursements available (averaging $14,700 per year); career-related internships or fieldwork, Federal Work-Study, institutionally sponsored loans, scholarships/grants, health care benefits, tuition waivers (full and partial), and unspecified assistantships also available. Financial award application deadline: 2/15; financial award applicants required to submit FAFSA. *Unit head:* Dr. Ravi Palat, Chairperson, 607-777-4756, E-mail: palat@binghamton.edu. *Application contact:* Catherine Smith, Recruiting and Admissions Coordinator, 607-777-2151, Fax: 607-777-2501, E-mail: cmsmith@binghamton.edu.

State University of New York Institute of Technology, School of Arts and Sciences, Program in Applied Sociology, Utica, NY 13504-3050. Offers MS. Part-time and evening/weekend programs available. *Degree requirements:* For master's, thesis or project. *Entrance requirements:* For master's, minimum GPA of 3.0, letters of recommendation (3). Additional exam requirements/recommendations for international students: Required—TOEFL (minimum score 550 paper-based; 213 computer-based). *Faculty research:* Family violence, race/class/gender, prisoner re-entry, drug abuse, information technology applications.

Stony Brook University, State University of New York, Graduate School, College of Arts and Sciences, Department of Sociology, Stony Brook, NY 11794. Offers MA, PhD. *Faculty:* 14 full-time (3 women), 2 part-time/adjunct (both women). *Students:* 47 full-time (31 women), 5 part-time (all women); includes 5 Black or African American, non-Hispanic/Latino; 2 Asian, non-Hispanic/Latino, 14 international. Average age 33. 84 applicants, 24% accepted, 8 enrolled. In 2010, 6 master's, 2 doctorates awarded. *Degree requirements:* For doctorate, thesis/dissertation, comprehensive exam or professional papers, field exam, teaching practicum. *Entrance requirements:* For doctorate, GRE General Test, minimum GPA of 3.0. Additional exam requirements/recommendations for international students: Required—TOEFL. *Application deadline:* For fall admission, 1/15 for domestic students. Application fee: $60. *Expenses:* Tuition, state resident: full-time $8370; part-time $349 per credit. Tuition, nonresident: full-time $13,780; part-time $574 per credit. Required fees: $994. *Financial support:* In 2010–11, 2 research assistantships, 29 teaching assistantships were awarded; fellowships also available. *Faculty research:* Deviant behavior, history of sociology/social thought, marriage and family sociology, political sociology. Total annual research expenditures: $124,415. *Unit head:* Dr. Ian Roxborough, Chair, 631-632-7700, Fax: 631-632-8203, E-mail: ian.roxborough@stonybrook.edu. *Application contact:* Dr. Timothy P. Moran, Director, 631-632-7700, Fax: 631-632-8203, E-mail: tpmoran@notes.cc.sunysb.edu.

Syracuse University, Maxwell School of Citizenship and Public Affairs, Program in Sociology, Syracuse, NY 13244. Offers MA, PhD. *Students:* 32 full-time (26 women), 7 part-time (all women); includes 11 minority (8 Black or African American, non-Hispanic/Latino; 1 Asian, non-Hispanic/Latino; 2 Hispanic/Latino), 9 international. Average age 32. 50 applicants, 26% accepted, 7 enrolled. In 2010, 5 master's, 1 doctorate awarded. *Degree requirements:* For master's, thesis optional; for doctorate, thesis/dissertation. *Entrance requirements:* For master's and doctorate, GRE General Test. Additional exam requirements/recommendations for international students: Required—TOEFL (minimum score 100 iBT). *Application deadline:* For fall admission, 2/1 priority date for domestic and international students. Application fee: $75. Electronic applications accepted. *Expenses:* Tuition: Part-time $1162 per credit. *Financial support:* Fellowships with full tuition reimbursements, research assistantships with full and partial tuition reimbursements, teaching assistantships with full and partial tuition reimbursements, tuition waivers (full and partial) and unspecified assistantships available. Financial award application deadline: 1/1. *Faculty research:* Qualitative methods and feminist methods, inequality studies, aging and the life course. *Unit head:* Dr. Prema Kurien, Graduate Chair, 315-443-2347, Fax: 315-443-4597, E-mail: sociology@maxwell.syr.edu. *Application contact:* Janet Coria, Recruiting Contact, 315-443-2347, E-mail: jmcoria@syr.edu.

Teachers College, Columbia University, Graduate Faculty of Education, Department of Human Development, Program in Sociology and Education, New York, NY 10027. Offers Ed M, MA, Ed D, PhD. *Faculty:* 3 full-time (1 woman), 2 part-time/adjunct (1 woman). *Students:* 24 full-time (19 women), 56 part-time (43 women); includes 51 minority (26 Black or African American, non-Hispanic/Latino; 10 Asian, non-Hispanic/Latino; 9 Hispanic/Latino; 1 Native Hawaiian or other Pacific Islander, non-Hispanic/Latino; 5 Two or more races, non-Hispanic/Latino), 6 international. Average age 28. 75 applicants, 73% accepted, 26 enrolled. In 2010, 20 master's awarded. *Degree requirements:* For master's, comprehensive exam, exam or essay; for doctorate, thesis/dissertation. *Entrance requirements:* For doctorate, GRE. *Application deadline:* For fall admission, 12/15 for domestic students; for spring admission, 11/1 for domestic students. Applications are processed on a rolling basis. Application fee: $65. Electronic applications accepted. *Expenses:* Tuition: Full-time $28,272; part-time $1178 per credit. Required fees: $756; $378 per semester. *Financial support:* Career-related internships or fieldwork, Federal Work-Study, institutionally sponsored loans, and tuition waivers (full and partial) available. Support available to part-time students. Financial award application deadline: 2/1; financial award applicants required to submit FAFSA. *Faculty research:* Stratification, race and evaluation, desegregation of schools and communities, quantitative research. *Unit head:* Prof. Aaron M. Pallas, Program Coordinator, 212-678-4150, E-mail: amp155@columbia.edu. *Application contact:* Prof. Aaron M. Pallas, Program Coordinator, 212-678-4150, E-mail: amp155@columbia.edu.

Temple University, College of Liberal Arts, Department of Sociology, Philadelphia, PA 19122-6096. Offers MA, PhD. Part-time and evening/weekend programs available. *Faculty:* 19 full-time (8 women). *Students:* 42 full-time (31 women), 3 part-time (all women); includes 2 Black or African American, non-Hispanic/Latino; 3 Asian, non-Hispanic/Latino; 3 Hispanic/Latino; 1 Two or more races, non-Hispanic/Latino, 1 international. 56 applicants, 45% accepted, 9 enrolled. In 2010, 6 master's, 2 doctorates awarded. Terminal master's awarded for partial completion of doctoral program. *Degree requirements:* For doctorate, thesis/dissertation. *Entrance requirements:* For master's and doctorate, GRE General Test, minimum GPA of 3.0. Additional exam requirements/recommendations for international students: Required—TOEFL (minimum score 550 paper-based; 213 computer-based; 79 iBT). *Application deadline:* For fall admission, 1/15 for domestic students, 12/15 for international students. Application fee: $50. Electronic applications accepted. *Financial support:* Fellowships with tuition reimbursements, research assistantships with tuition reimbursements, teaching assistantships with tuition reimbursements, career-related internships or fieldwork, Federal Work-Study, institutionally sponsored loans, and scholarships/grants available. Financial award application deadline: 1/15; financial award applicants required to submit FAFSA. *Faculty research:* International development, race-ethnicity-gender inequality, urban structure, political economy. *Unit head:* Dr. Robert Kaufman, Chair, 215-204-7760, Fax: 215-204-3352, E-mail: soc@temple.edu. *Application contact:* Dr. Robert Kaufman, Chair, 215-204-7760, Fax: 215-204-3352, E-mail: soc@temple.edu.

Texas A&M International University, Office of Graduate Studies and Research, College of Arts and Sciences, Department of Behavioral Sciences, Laredo, TX 78041-1900. Offers counseling psychology (MACP); criminal justice (MS); psychology (MS); sociology (MA). *Faculty:* 9 full-time (5 women), 2 part-time/adjunct (1 woman). *Students:* 12 full-time (8 women), 116 part-time (80 women); includes 1 Black or African American, non-Hispanic/Latino; 1 Asian, non-Hispanic/Latino; 120 Hispanic/Latino, 1 international. Average age 29. 20 applicants, 90% accepted, 10 enrolled. In 2010, 16 master's awarded. *Degree requirements:* For master's, thesis (for some programs). *Entrance requirements:* For master's, GRE General Test. Additional exam requirements/recommendations for international students: Required—TOEFL (minimum score 550 paper-based; 213 computer-based; 79 iBT). *Application deadline:* For fall admission, 4/30 priority date for domestic students; for spring admission, 11/30 for domestic students. Applications are processed on a rolling basis. Application fee: $25. *Financial support:* In 2010–11, 17 students received support, including 2 fellowships, 6 research assistantships; teaching assistantships. Financial award application deadline: 11/1. *Unit head:* Dr. Frances P. Bernat, Chair, 956-326-2475, Fax: 956-326-2474, E-mail: gvillagran@tamiu.edu. *Application contact:* Suzanne Hansen-Alford, Director of Graduate Recruiting, 956-326-3023, Fax: 956-326-3021, E-mail: graduateschool@tamiu.edu.

Texas A&M University, College of Liberal Arts, Department of Sociology, College Station, TX 77843. Offers MS, PhD. *Faculty:* 20. *Students:* 81 full-time (46 women), 24 part-time (11 women); includes 25 Black or African American, non-Hispanic/Latino; 2 American Indian or Alaska Native, non-Hispanic/Latino; 4 Asian, non-Hispanic/Latino; 31 Hispanic/Latino, 9 international. Average age 32. In 2010, 5 master's, 8 doctorates awarded. *Degree requirements:* For master's, thesis or alternative; for doctorate, thesis/dissertation. *Entrance requirements:* For master's and doctorate, GRE General Test. Additional exam requirements/recommendations for international students: Required—TOEFL. *Application deadline:* For fall admission, 1/15 priority date for domestic students; for winter admission, 11/1 priority date for domestic students. Applications are processed on a rolling basis. Application fee: $50 ($75 for international students). Electronic applications accepted. *Financial support:* In 2010–11, fellowships (averaging $12,000 per year), research assistantships (averaging $9,795 per year), teaching assistantships (averaging $9,795 per year) were awarded; institutionally sponsored loans and unspecified assistantships also available. Financial award application deadline: 1/15; financial award applicants required to submit FAFSA. *Faculty research:* Crime, deviance, and law; culture; demography and human ecology; political and economic sociology; racial and ethnic relations; social psychology; Latino sociology; gender; Asian studies. *Unit head:* Mark Fossett, Head, 979-845-5133, Fax: 979-862-4057, E-mail: m-fossett@tamu.edu. *Application contact:* Dr. William Alex McIntosh, Graduate Advisor, 979-862-7948, Fax: 979-862-4057, E-mail: w-mcintosh@tamu.edu.

Texas A&M University–Commerce, Graduate School, College of Arts and Sciences, Department of Sociology and Criminal Justice, Commerce, TX 75429-3011. Offers sociology (MA, MS). Part-time programs available. *Degree requirements:* For master's, comprehensive exam, thesis (for some programs). *Entrance requirements:* For master's, GRE General Test. *Faculty research:* Marriage and family, drugs and society, criminal justice, delinquency.

Texas A&M University–Kingsville, College of Graduate Studies, College of Arts and Sciences, Department of Psychology and Sociology, Kingsville, TX 78363. Offers gerontology

(MS); psychology (MA, MS); sociology (MA, MS). Part-time and evening/weekend programs available. *Degree requirements:* For master's, comprehensive exam, thesis or alternative. *Entrance requirements:* For master's, GRE General Test, minimum GPA of 2.5. Additional exam requirements/recommendations for international students: Required—TOEFL. *Faculty research:* Hispanic female voting behavior, attitudes toward criminal justice, immigration of aged into south Texas, folk medicine.

Texas Southern University, College of Liberal Arts and Behavioral Sciences, Department of Sociology, Houston, TX 77004-4584. Offers MA. Part-time and evening/weekend programs available. *Faculty:* 4 full-time (2 women). *Students:* 18 full-time (13 women), 21 part-time (17 women); includes 37 Black or African American, non-Hispanic/Latino; 2 Asian, non-Hispanic/Latino. Average age 37. 19 applicants, 100% accepted, 15 enrolled. In 2010, 1 master's awarded. *Degree requirements:* For master's, comprehensive exam, thesis. *Entrance requirements:* For master's, GRE General Test, minimum GPA of 2.5. Additional exam requirements/recommendations for international students: Required—TOEFL. *Application deadline:* For fall admission, 7/1 for domestic and international students; for spring admission, 11/1 for domestic and international students. Applications are processed on a rolling basis. Application fee: $50 ($75 for international students). Electronic applications accepted. *Expenses:* Tuition, state resident: full-time $1875; part-time $100 per credit hour. Tuition, nonresident: full-time $6641; part-time $343 per credit hour. Tuition and fees vary according to course level, course load and degree level. *Financial support:* In 2010–11, 1 research assistantship (averaging $8,000 per year), 4 teaching assistantships (averaging $6,150 per year) were awarded; scholarships/grants and unspecified assistantships also available. Financial award application deadline: 5/1. *Faculty research:* Sociocultural systems, ethnic and regional studies, community sociology. *Unit head:* Dr. Earl Wright, Chair, 713-313-4438. *Application contact:* Dr. Gregory Maddox, Dean of the Graduate School, 713-313-7011 Ext. 4410, Fax: 713-639-1876, E-mail: maddox_gh@tsu.edu.

Texas State University–San Marcos, Graduate School, College of Liberal Arts, Department of Sociology, San Marcos, TX 78666. Offers applied sociology (MS); criminal justice (MSIS); sociology (MA). Part-time and evening/weekend programs available. *Faculty:* 13 full-time (8 women), 1 part-time/adjunct (0 women). *Students:* 27 full-time (17 women), 37 part-time (25 women); includes 25 minority (10 Black or African American, non-Hispanic/Latino; 1 Asian, non-Hispanic/Latino; 12 Hispanic/Latino; 2 Two or more races, non-Hispanic/Latino). Average age 30. 36 applicants, 92% accepted, 23 enrolled. In 2010, 6 master's awarded. *Degree requirements:* For master's, comprehensive exam, thesis (for some programs). *Entrance requirements:* For master's, minimum GPA of 3.0 in last 60 hours of course work, 3 letters of reference, letter of intent, personal interview. Additional exam requirements/recommendations for international students: Required—TOEFL (minimum score 550 paper-based; 213 computer-based; 78 iBT). *Application deadline:* For fall admission, 6/15 priority date for domestic students, 6/1 priority date for international students; for spring admission, 10/15 priority date for domestic students, 10/1 priority date for international students. Applications are processed on a rolling basis. Application fee: $40 ($90 for international students). Electronic applications accepted. *Expenses:* Tuition, state resident: full-time $6024; part-time $251 per credit hour. Tuition, nonresident: full-time $13,536; part-time $564 per credit hour. Required fees: $1776; $50 per credit hour. $306 per semester. *Financial support:* In 2010–11, 17 students received support, including 16 teaching assistantships (averaging $5,346 per year); research assistantships, career-related internships or fieldwork, Federal Work-Study, institutionally sponsored loans, scholarships/grants, and unspecified assistantships also available. Support available to part-time students. Financial award application deadline: 4/1; financial award applicants required to submit FAFSA. *Faculty research:* Healthcare models. Total annual research expenditures: $36,716. *Unit head:* Dr. Susan Day, Chair, 512-245-2113, Fax: 512-245-8362, E-mail: sd01@txstate.edu. *Application contact:* Dr. J. Michael Willoughby, Dean of Graduate School, 512-245-2581, Fax: 512-245-8365, E-mail: gradcollege@txstate.edu.

Texas Tech University, Graduate School, College of Arts and Sciences, Department of Sociology, Anthropology and Social Work, Lubbock, TX 79409. Offers anthropology (MA); sociology (MA). Part-time programs available. *Faculty:* 17 full-time (7 women). *Students:* 30 full-time (18 women), 11 part-time (7 women); includes 2 Black or African American, non-Hispanic/Latino; 1 Asian, non-Hispanic/Latino; 2 Hispanic/Latino; 2 Two or more races, non-Hispanic/Latino, 2 international. Average age 28. 34 applicants, 74% accepted, 14 enrolled. In 2010, 7 master's awarded. *Degree requirements:* For master's, one foreign language, thesis or alternative. *Entrance requirements:* For master's, GRE General Test. Additional exam requirements/recommendations for international students: Required—TOEFL (minimum score 550 paper-based; 213 computer-based; 79 iBT). *Application deadline:* For fall admission, 6/1 priority date for domestic students, 1/15 priority date for international students; for spring admission, 9/1 priority date for domestic students, 6/15 priority date for international students. Applications are processed on a rolling basis. Application fee: $50 ($75 for international students). Electronic applications accepted. *Expenses:* Tuition, state resident: full-time $5495.76; part-time $228.99 per credit hour. Tuition, nonresident: full-time $12,936; part-time $538.99 per credit hour. Required fees: $2674; $36 per credit hour. $905 per semester. *Financial support:* In 2010–11, 24 students received support, including 1 research assistantship with partial tuition reimbursement available (averaging $3,464 per year), 6 teaching assistantships with partial tuition reimbursements available (averaging $3,809 per year). Financial award application deadline: 4/15; financial award applicants required to submit FAFSA. *Faculty research:* Sociology theory, research methods, physical and forensic anthropology, Texas archaeology, Mayan archaeology. Total annual research expenditures: $28,649. *Unit head:* Dr. Jeffrey Payne Williams, Chair and Professor, 806-742-2400, Fax: 806-742-1088, E-mail: jeff.williams@ttu.edu. *Application contact:* Dr. Yung-Mei Tsai, Sociology Program Director, 806-742-2400, Fax: 806-742-1088, E-mail: yung.mei.tsai@ttu.edu.

Texas Woman's University, Graduate School, College of Arts and Sciences, Department of Sociology and Social Work, Denton, TX 76201. Offers sociology (MA, PhD). Evening/weekend programs available. *Faculty:* 10 full-time (6 women). *Students:* 12 full-time (10 women), 27 part-time (18 women); includes 7 Black or African American, non-Hispanic/Latino; 1 American Indian or Alaska Native, non-Hispanic/Latino; 6 Hispanic/Latino, 7 international. Average age 38. 20 applicants, 65% accepted, 9 enrolled. In 2010, 3 master's, 6 doctorates awarded. Terminal master's awarded for partial completion of doctoral program. *Degree requirements:* For master's, thesis; for doctorate, one foreign language, comprehensive exam, thesis/dissertation. *Entrance requirements:* For master's, minimum GPA of 3.0, 2 letters of reference, statement of intent; for doctorate, GRE General Test, minimum GPA of 3.5, minimum 12 hours course work in sociology (including graduate statistics and research methods), 3 letters of reference, statement of intent. Additional exam requirements/recommendations for international students: Required—TOEFL (minimum score 550 paper-based; 213 computer-based; 79 iBT). *Application deadline:* For fall admission, 7/1 priority date for domestic students, 3/1 for international students; for spring admission, 12/1 priority date for domestic students, 7/1 for international students. Applications are processed on a rolling basis. Application fee: $50 ($75 for international students). Electronic applications accepted. *Expenses:* Tuition, state resident: full-time $3834; part-time $213 per credit hour. Tuition, nonresident: full-time $9468; part-time $526 per credit hour. Required fees: $1247; $220 per credit hour. *Financial support:* In 2010–11, 22 students received support, including 8 research assistantships (averaging $12,942 per year), 10 teaching assistantships (averaging $12,942 per year); career-related internships or fieldwork, Federal Work-Study, institutionally sponsored loans, scholarships/grants, traineeships, health care benefits, and unspecified assistantships also available. Support available to part-time students. Financial award application deadline: 3/1; financial award applicants required to submit FAFSA. *Faculty research:* Pre-impact evaluation planning for families of law enforcement, disasters, criminology, immigration, sociological theory, race/ethnicity, culture of breast cancer. Total annual research expenditures: $380,914. *Unit head:* Dr. James Williams, Chair, 940-898-2052, Fax: 940-898-2067, E-mail: atilton@twu.edu. *Application contact:* Dr. Samuel Wheeler, Assistant Director of Admissions, 940-898-3188, Fax: 940-898-3081, E-mail: wheelersr@twu.edu.

Tulane University, School of Liberal Arts, Department of Sociology, New Orleans, LA 70118-5669. Offers MA, PhD. Terminal master's awarded for partial completion of doctoral program. *Degree requirements:* For master's, thesis; for doctorate, thesis/dissertation, preliminary exams. *Entrance requirements:* For master's, GRE General Test, minimum B average in undergraduate course work; for doctorate, GRE General Test. Additional exam requirements/recommendations for international students: Required—TOEFL. Electronic applications accepted.

Université de Montréal, Faculty of Arts and Sciences, Department of Sociology, Montréal, QC H3C 3J7, Canada. Offers M Sc, PhD. *Degree requirements:* For master's, thesis; for doctorate, thesis/dissertation, general exam. *Entrance requirements:* For master's, minimum GPA of 3.0; for doctorate, minimum GPA of 3.5, proficiency in French. Electronic applications accepted. *Faculty research:* Sociological theory, economy, state and social movements, work, social politics and health.

Université du Québec à Montréal, Graduate Programs, Program in Social Intervention, Montréal, QC H3C 3P8, Canada. Offers MA. Part-time programs available. *Degree requirements:* For master's, thesis. *Entrance requirements:* For master's, appropriate bachelor's degree or equivalent, proficiency in French.

Université du Québec à Montréal, Graduate Programs, Program in Sociology, Montréal, QC H3C 3P8, Canada. Offers MA, PhD. Part-time programs available. *Degree requirements:* For master's, thesis optional; for doctorate, thesis/dissertation. *Entrance requirements:* For master's, appropriate bachelor's degree or equivalent, proficiency in French; for doctorate, appropriate master's degree or equivalent, proficiency in French.

Université Laval, Faculty of Social Sciences, Department of Sociology, Programs in Sociology, Québec, QC G1K 7P4, Canada. Offers MA, PhD. Terminal master's awarded for partial completion of doctoral program. *Degree requirements:* For master's, thesis; for doctorate, comprehensive exam, thesis/dissertation. *Entrance requirements:* For master's, English exam (comprehension of written English), French exam (for some), knowledge of French; for doctorate, English exam (comprehension of written English), French exam may be required, knowledge of French. Electronic applications accepted.

University at Albany, State University of New York, College of Arts and Sciences, Department of Communication, Albany, NY 12222-0001. Offers communication (MA); sociology and communication (PhD). Part-time programs available. *Degree requirements:* For master's, comprehensive exam, thesis or alternative; for doctorate, comprehensive exam, thesis/dissertation. *Entrance requirements:* For master's, minimum GPA of 3.0; for doctorate, GRE, minimum GPA of 3.0. Additional exam requirements/recommendations for international students: Required—TOEFL (minimum score 550 paper-based; 213 computer-based). Electronic applications accepted. *Faculty research:* Language and social interaction, campaign communication, media agenda-setting, high-speed management, organizational boundary-spanning.

University at Albany, State University of New York, College of Arts and Sciences, Department of Sociology, Albany, NY 12222-0001. Offers demography (Certificate); sociology (MA, PhD); urban policy (Certificate). Terminal master's awarded for partial completion of doctoral program. *Degree requirements:* For master's, thesis; for doctorate, thesis/dissertation, 2 specialization exams, research tool. *Entrance requirements:* For master's and doctorate, GRE General Test. Additional exam requirements/recommendations for international students: Required—TOEFL (minimum score 213 computer-based). Electronic applications accepted. *Faculty research:* Gender and equality, crime and deviance, aging, work and organizations, social demography.

University at Buffalo, the State University of New York, Graduate School, College of Arts and Sciences, Department of Sociology, Buffalo, NY 14260. Offers MA, PhD. Part-time programs available. *Faculty:* 16 full-time (6 women), 4 part-time/adjunct (1 woman). *Students:* 28 full-time (18 women), 26 part-time (12 women); includes 12 minority (4 Black or African American, non-Hispanic/Latino; 6 Asian, non-Hispanic/Latino; 1 Hispanic/Latino; 1 Two or more races, non-Hispanic/Latino), 3 international. Average age 26. 54 applicants, 33% accepted, 9 enrolled. In 2010, 6 master's, 4 doctorates awarded. Terminal master's awarded for partial completion of doctoral program. *Degree requirements:* For master's, project or thesis; for doctorate, thesis/dissertation, qualifying paper. *Entrance requirements:* For master's and doctorate, GRE General Test. Additional exam requirements/recommendations for international students: Required—TOEFL (minimum score 550 paper-based; 213 computer-based; 79 iBT). *Application deadline:* For fall admission, 2/1 priority date for domestic and international students. Applications are processed on a rolling basis. Application fee: $75. Electronic applications accepted. *Financial support:* In 2010–11, 16 students received support, including 3 fellowships with full tuition reimbursements available (averaging $16,400 per year), 1 research assistantship (averaging $8,000 per year), 16 teaching assistantships with full tuition reimbursements available (averaging $13,460 per year); Federal Work-Study and unspecified assistantships also available. Financial award application deadline: 10/5; financial award applicants required to submit FAFSA. *Faculty research:* Theory, culture, sociology of law/criminology, urban sociology, family. Total annual research expenditures: $102,000. *Unit head:* Dr. Robert Granfield, Chair, 716-645-8462, Fax: 716-645-3934, E-mail: rgranfie@buffalo.edu. *Application contact:* Dr. Robert Adelman, Director of Graduate Studies, 716-645-8478, Fax: 716-645-3934, E-mail: adelman4@buffalo.edu.

The University of Akron, Graduate School, Buchtel College of Arts and Sciences, Department of Sociology, Akron, OH 44325. Offers MA, PhD. PhD offered jointly with Kent State University. Part-time programs available. *Faculty:* 14 full-time (8 women), 17 part-time/adjunct (10 women). *Students:* 25 full-time (20 women), 9 part-time (8 women); includes 5 Black or African American, non-Hispanic/Latino; 1 Two or more races, non-Hispanic/Latino, 1 international. Average age 28. 35 applicants, 49% accepted, 9 enrolled. In 2010, 6 master's, 1 doctorate awarded. Terminal master's awarded for partial completion of doctoral program. *Degree requirements:* For master's, thesis optional, oral defense of thesis, paper or oral exam; for doctorate, one foreign language, comprehensive exam, thesis/dissertation. *Entrance requirements:* For master's, GRE General Test, minimum GPA of 3.0, three letters of recommendation, writing sample, statement of purpose outlining educational and career objectives; for doctorate, GRE General Test, minimum GPA of 3.5, three letters of recommendation, writing sample, statement of purpose outlining educational and career objectives. Additional exam requirements/recommendations for international students: Required—TOEFL (minimum score 577 paper-based; 233 computer-based; 90 iBT). *Application deadline:* For fall admission, 1/15 priority date for domestic and international students. Application fee: $30 ($40 for international students). Electronic applications accepted. *Expenses:* Tuition, state resident: full-time $6800; part-time $378 per credit hour. Tuition, nonresident: full-time $11,644; part-time $647 per credit hour. Required fees: $1265. One-time fee: $30 full-time. *Financial support:* In 2010–11, 1 research assistantship with full tuition reimbursement, 22 teaching assistantships with full tuition reimbursements were awarded; career-related internships or fieldwork and Federal Work-Study also available. *Faculty research:* Medical sociology, inequality, social psychology, criminology, mental health. Total annual research expenditures: $752,857. *Unit head:* Dr. Matthew Lee, Interim Chair, 330-972-5357, E-mail: mlee2@uakron.edu. *Application contact:* Dr. Rebecca Erickson, Director of Graduate Studies, 330-972-5157, E-mail: rericks@uakron.edu.

The University of Alabama at Birmingham, College of Arts and Sciences, Program in Medical Sociology, Birmingham, AL 35294. Offers PhD. *Students:* 19 full-time (13 women), 6 part-time (3 women); includes 6 minority (3 Black or African American, non-Hispanic/Latino; 1 American Indian or Alaska Native, non-Hispanic/Latino; 2 Asian, non-Hispanic/Latino), 4 international. Average age 33. 9 applicants, 56% accepted, 2 enrolled. In 2010, 1 doctorate awarded. *Expenses:* Tuition, state resident: full-time $5482. Tuition, nonresident: full-time $12,430. Tuition and fees vary according to program. *Unit head:* Dr. William Cockerham, 205-934-3307. *Application contact:* Julie Bryant, Director of Graduate Admissions, 205-934-8227, Fax: 205-934-8413, E-mail: jbryant@uab.edu.

The University of Alabama at Birmingham, College of Arts and Sciences, Program in Sociology, Birmingham, AL 35294. Offers MA. Evening/weekend programs available. *Students:* 2 full-time (1 woman). Average age 26. 2 applicants, 50% accepted, 1 enrolled. In 2010, 1 master's awarded. *Degree requirements:* For master's, thesis or alternative. *Entrance requirements:* For master's, GRE General Test or MAT. *Application deadline:* Applications are

Sociology

The University of Alabama at Birmingham (continued)

processed on a rolling basis. Application fee: $35 ($60 for international students). Electronic applications accepted. *Expenses:* Tuition, state resident: full-time $5482. Tuition, nonresident: full-time $12,430. Tuition and fees vary according to program. *Financial support:* In 2010–11, 2 fellowships, 3 research assistantships were awarded; career-related internships or fieldwork, Federal Work-Study, and institutionally sponsored loans also available. Financial award application deadline: 3/1. *Faculty research:* Gerontology, applied sociology, urban sociology. *Unit head:* Dr. William Cockerham, Chair, 205-934-3307. *Application contact:* Julie Bryant, Director of Graduate Admissions, 205-934-8227, Fax: 205-934-8413, E-mail: jbryant@uab.edu.

University of Alberta, Faculty of Graduate Studies and Research, Department of Sociology, Edmonton, AB T6G 2E1, Canada. Offers criminal justice (MA); demography (MA, PhD); sociology (MA, PhD). Part-time programs available. *Degree requirements:* For master's, thesis (for some programs); for doctorate, thesis/dissertation. *Faculty research:* Criminology, knowledge and culture, methods and theory, population studies, stratification.

The University of Arizona, College of Social and Behavioral Sciences, Department of Sociology, Tucson, AZ 85721. Offers PhD. *Faculty:* 14 full-time (6 women), 2 part-time/adjunct (1 woman). *Students:* 46 full-time (26 women), 11 part-time (8 women); includes 5 Hispanic/Latino; 2 Two or more races, non-Hispanic/Latino, 3 international. Average age 30. 90 applicants, 7% accepted, 5 enrolled. In 2010, 10 doctorates awarded. *Degree requirements:* For doctorate, thesis/dissertation, 2 preliminary exams. *Entrance requirements:* For doctorate, GRE General Test, 3 letters of recommendation, writing samples. Additional exam requirements/recommendations for international students: Required—TOEFL (minimum score 630 paper-based; 267 computer-based). *Application deadline:* For fall admission, 1/15 for domestic and international students. Applications are processed on a rolling basis. Application fee: $65. Electronic applications accepted. *Expenses:* Tuition, state resident: full-time $7692. *Financial support:* In 2010–11, 7 research assistantships with full tuition reimbursements (averaging $20,117 per year), 43 teaching assistantships with full tuition reimbursements (averaging $20,273 per year) were awarded; institutionally sponsored loans, scholarships/grants, health care benefits, tuition waivers (full), and unspecified assistantships also available. Financial award application deadline: 1/15; financial award applicants required to submit FAFSA. *Faculty research:* Organizations, social psychology, social movement, stratification, religion. Total annual research expenditures: $168,595. *Unit head:* Dr. Albert J. Bergesen, Head, 520-621-3303, Fax: 520-621-9875, E-mail: albert@u.arizona.edu. *Application contact:* Vienna Marum, Information Contact, 520-621-5057, Fax: 520-621-9875, E-mail: vienna@u.arizona.edu.

University of Arkansas, Graduate School, J. William Fulbright College of Arts and Sciences, Department of Sociology, Fayetteville, AR 72701-1201. Offers MA. Part-time programs available. *Students:* 9 full-time (4 women), 13 part-time (10 women); includes 4 minority (1 Black or African American, non-Hispanic/Latino; 2 American Indian or Alaska Native, non-Hispanic/Latino; 1 Hispanic/Latino), 1 international. 14 applicants, 79% accepted. In 2010, 6 master's awarded. *Degree requirements:* For master's, thesis. *Application deadline:* For fall admission, 4/1 for international students; for spring admission, 10/1 for international students. Applications are processed on a rolling basis. Application fee: $40 ($50 for international students). Electronic applications accepted. *Financial support:* In 2010–11, 2 fellowships with tuition reimbursements, 13 research assistantships, 2 teaching assistantships were awarded; career-related internships or fieldwork and Federal Work-Study also available. Support available to part-time students. Financial award application deadline: 4/1; financial award applicants required to submit FAFSA. *Unit head:* Dr. Brent Smith, Department Chairperson, 479-575-3206, Fax: 479-575-7981, E-mail: bls@uark.edu. *Application contact:* Dr. Anna Zajicek, Graduate Coordinator, 479-575-5149, Fax: 479-575-7981, E-mail: azajicek@uark.edu.

The University of British Columbia, Faculty of Arts, Department of Sociology, Vancouver, BC V6T 1Z1, Canada. Offers MA, PhD. *Degree requirements:* For master's, thesis; for doctorate, comprehensive exam, thesis/dissertation. *Entrance requirements:* For master's, BA in sociology or equivalent with minimum B+ average in upper level courses; for doctorate, master's degree in sociology or equivalent. Additional exam requirements/recommendations for international students: Required—TOEFL (minimum score 600 paper-based; 250 computer-based). Electronic applications accepted. Tuition charges are reported in Canadian dollars. *Expenses:* Tuition, area resident: Full-time $4179 Canadian dollars. International tuition: $7344 Canadian dollars full-time. *Faculty research:* Social and cultural theories and methods; gender, race, class and sexuality; environment economy and development politics; law and social movements.

University of Calgary, Faculty of Graduate Studies, Faculty of Social Sciences, Department of Sociology, Calgary, AB T2N 1N4, Canada. Offers MA, PhD. Terminal master's awarded for partial completion of doctoral program. *Degree requirements:* For master's, thesis, prospectus; for doctorate, comprehensive exam, thesis/dissertation, oral and written candidacy exams, prospectus, qualifying paper. *Entrance requirements:* For master's, minimum GPA of 3.2; for doctorate, minimum GPA of 3.5. Additional exam requirements/recommendations for international students: Required—TOEFL or IELTS. Electronic applications accepted. *Faculty research:* Deviance, gender, medical, religion, ethnicity.

University of California, Berkeley, Graduate Division, College of Letters and Science, Department of Sociology, Berkeley, CA 94720-1500. Offers PhD. *Degree requirements:* For doctorate, thesis/dissertation, qualifying exam. *Entrance requirements:* For doctorate, GRE General Test, minimum GPA of 3.0, sample of academic written work, 3 letters of recommendation. Additional exam requirements/recommendations for international students: Required—TOEFL (minimum score 570 paper-based; 230 computer-based) or IELTS. Electronic applications accepted. *Faculty research:* Race, gender, political, stratification theory.

University of California, Davis, Graduate Studies, Program in Sociology, Davis, CA 95616. Offers MA, PhD. Terminal master's awarded for partial completion of doctoral program. *Degree requirements:* For master's, written exam; for doctorate, thesis/dissertation, professional paper, qualifying exam. *Entrance requirements:* For master's and doctorate, GRE General Test, minimum GPA of 3.0, writing sample. Additional exam requirements/recommendations for international students: Required—TOEFL (minimum score 550 paper-based; 213 computer-based). Electronic applications accepted. *Faculty research:* Collective behavior, social movements, comparative sociology, historical sociology, culture development, inequality.

University of California, Irvine, School of Social Sciences, Department of Sociology, Irvine, CA 92697. Offers social networks (PhD); social networks-social science (MA); social science (MA, PhD); sociology and social relations-social science (MA, PhD). *Students:* 76 full-time (40 women), 1 (woman) part-time; includes 22 minority (1 Black or African American, non-Hispanic/Latino; 1 American Indian or Alaska Native, non-Hispanic/Latino; 8 Asian, non-Hispanic/Latino; 11 Hispanic/Latino; 1 Two or more races, non-Hispanic/Latino), 1 international. Average age 28. 167 applicants, 17% accepted, 13 enrolled. In 2010, 8 master's, 5 doctorates awarded. *Degree requirements:* For doctorate, thesis/dissertation. *Entrance requirements:* For master's and doctorate, GRE General Test, minimum GPA of 3.0. *Application deadline:* For fall admission, 1/15 priority date for domestic students, 1/15 for international students. Applications are processed on a rolling basis. Application fee: $80 ($100 for international students). Electronic applications accepted. *Financial support:* Fellowships, research assistantships with full tuition reimbursements, teaching assistantships, institutionally sponsored loans, traineeships, health care benefits, and unspecified assistantships available. Financial award application deadline: 3/1; financial award applicants required to submit FAFSA. *Faculty research:* Cognitive anthropology, sociology of culture, social structure, family and gender. *Unit head:* Prof. Francesca Polletta Polletta, Professor, 949-824-5041, Fax: 949-824-4717, E-mail: polletta@uci.edu. *Application contact:* Jennifer Lee, Associate Professor, 949-824-7011, Fax: 949-824-4717, E-mail: jenlee@uci.edu.

University of California, Los Angeles, Graduate Division, College of Letters and Science, Department of Sociology, Los Angeles, CA 90095. Offers MA, PhD. *Faculty:* 38 full-time (14 women). *Students:* 104 full-time (63 women); includes 41 minority (4 Black or African American, non-Hispanic/Latino; 19 Asian, non-Hispanic/Latino; 17 Hispanic/Latino; 1 Two or more races, non-Hispanic/Latino), 10 international. Average age 29. 243 applicants, 17% accepted, 21 enrolled. In 2010, 16 master's, 9 doctorates awarded. Terminal master's awarded for partial completion of doctoral program. *Degree requirements:* For master's, thesis or alternative, final paper; for doctorate, thesis/dissertation, oral and written qualifying exams. *Entrance requirements:* For master's, GRE General Test, minimum GPA of 3.0, sample of work; for doctorate, GRE General Test, minimum undergraduate GPA of 3.0, sample of work. Additional exam requirements/recommendations for international students: Required—TOEFL. *Application deadline:* For fall admission, 12/1 for domestic and international students. Application fee: $70 ($90 for international students). Electronic applications accepted. *Financial support:* In 2010–11, 72 fellowships with full and partial tuition reimbursements, 39 research assistantships with full and partial tuition reimbursements, 54 teaching assistantships with full and partial tuition reimbursements were awarded; Federal Work-Study, institutionally sponsored loans, scholarships/grants, health care benefits, tuition waivers (full and partial), and unspecified assistantships also available. Financial award application deadline: 3/1; financial award applicants required to submit FAFSA. *Unit head:* Dr. William Roy, Chair, 310-825-3633, E-mail: billroy@soc.ucla.edu. *Application contact:* Department Office, 310-825-1026, E-mail: wendyf@soc.ucla.edu.

University of California, Riverside, Graduate Division, Department of Sociology, Riverside, CA 92521-0102. Offers MA, PhD. *Degree requirements:* For doctorate, thesis/dissertation, 1 quarter of teaching experience, professional paper. *Entrance requirements:* For doctorate, GRE General Test, minimum GPA of 3.2. Additional exam requirements/recommendations for international students: Required—TOEFL (minimum score 550 paper-based; 213 computer-based; 80 iBT). Electronic applications accepted. *Faculty research:* Crime/deviance, race/ethnic relations, family/gender, political economy/globalization, theory.

University of California, San Diego, Office of Graduate Studies, Department of Sociology, La Jolla, CA 92093. Offers science studies (PhD); sociology (PhD). *Degree requirements:* For doctorate, thesis/dissertation. *Entrance requirements:* For doctorate, GRE General Test. Electronic applications accepted.

University of California, San Diego, Office of Graduate Studies, Interdisciplinary Program in Cognitive Science, La Jolla, CA 92093. Offers cognitive science/anthropology (PhD); cognitive science/communication (PhD); cognitive science/computer science and engineering (PhD); cognitive science/linguistics (PhD); cognitive science/neuroscience (PhD); cognitive science/philosophy (PhD); cognitive science/psychology (PhD); cognitive science/sociology (PhD). Admissions offered through affiliated departments. *Degree requirements:* For doctorate, thesis/dissertation. *Entrance requirements:* For doctorate, GRE General Test, acceptance into one of the eight participating departments. *Faculty research:* Language and cognition, philosophy of mind, visual perception, biological anthropology, sociolinguistics.

University of California, San Francisco, Graduate Division, School of Nursing, Department of Social and Behavioral Sciences, San Francisco, CA 94143. Offers sociology (PhD). *Degree requirements:* For doctorate, one foreign language, thesis/dissertation. *Entrance requirements:* For doctorate, GRE General Test. *Faculty research:* Urban social relations; sociology of women's role in healing; sociology of work, occupations, and professions.

University of California, Santa Barbara, Graduate Division, College of Letters and Sciences, Division of Social Sciences, Department of Anthropology, Santa Barbara, CA 93106-2014. Offers archaeology (MA); biosocial anthropology (MA, PhD); sociocultural anthropology (MA, PhD); MA/PhD. *Faculty:* 12 full-time (3 women), 2 part-time/adjunct (both women). *Students:* 51 full-time (34 women); includes 2 Asian, non-Hispanic/Latino; 7 Hispanic/Latino. Average age 31. 47 applicants, 30% accepted, 4 enrolled. In 2010, 6 master's, 9 doctorates awarded. Terminal master's awarded for partial completion of doctoral program. *Degree requirements:* For master's, comprehensive exam (for some programs), thesis (for some programs); for doctorate, comprehensive exam (for some programs), thesis/dissertation. *Entrance requirements:* For master's and doctorate, GRE General Test, statement of purpose, transcripts, writing sample, curriculum vitae. Additional exam requirements/recommendations for international students: Required—TOEFL (minimum score 550 paper-based; 80 iBT), IELTS (minimum score 7). *Application deadline:* For fall admission, 12/1 for domestic and international students. Application fee: $70 ($90 for international students). Electronic applications accepted. *Financial support:* In 2010–11, 48 students received support, including 35 fellowships with full and partial tuition reimbursements available (averaging $5,749 per year), 7 research assistantships with full and partial tuition reimbursements available (averaging $7,287 per year), 37 teaching assistantships with full tuition reimbursements available (averaging $10,042 per year); career-related internships or fieldwork, Federal Work-Study, institutionally sponsored loans, scholarships/grants, traineeships, health care benefits, tuition waivers (full and partial), and unspecified assistantships also available. Support available to part-time students. Financial award application deadline: 12/1; financial award applicants required to submit FAFSA. *Faculty research:* Archaeology, bioarchaeology, biosocial anthropology, evolutionary ecology, evolutionary psychology, sociocultural anthropology. *Unit head:* Prof. Katharina Schreiber, Department Chair, 805-893-2519, Fax: 805-893-8707, E-mail: kschreiber@anth.ucsb.edu. *Application contact:* Robin Roe, Graduate Program Assistant, 805-893-2516, Fax: 805-893-8707, E-mail: roe@anth.ucsb.edu.

University of California, Santa Barbara, Graduate Division, College of Letters and Sciences, Division of Social Sciences, Department of Sociology, Santa Barbara, CA 93106-9430. Offers feminist studies (PhD); global studies (PhD); language, interaction and social organization (PhD); quantitative methods in the social sciences (PhD); technology and society (PhD); MA/PhD. *Faculty:* 35 full-time (14 women). *Students:* 71 full-time (44 women); includes 5 Black or African American, non-Hispanic/Latino; 4 Asian, non-Hispanic/Latino; 21 Hispanic/Latino. Average age 30. 162 applicants, 8% accepted, 6 enrolled. In 2010, 13 doctorates awarded. Terminal master's awarded for partial completion of doctoral program. *Degree requirements:* For doctorate, comprehensive exam, thesis/dissertation. *Entrance requirements:* For doctorate, GRE General Test. Additional exam requirements/recommendations for international students: Required—TOEFL (minimum score 550 paper-based; 80 iBT), IELTS (minimum score 7). *Application deadline:* For fall admission, 12/1 for domestic and international students. Application fee: $70 ($90 for international students). Electronic applications accepted. *Financial support:* In 2010–11, 60 students received support, including 40 fellowships with full and partial tuition reimbursements available (averaging $10,059 per year), 4 research assistantships with full and partial tuition reimbursements available (averaging $10,166 per year), 43 teaching assistantships with full and partial tuition reimbursements available (averaging $11,913 per year); career-related internships or fieldwork, Federal Work-Study, institutionally sponsored loans, scholarships/grants, health care benefits, tuition waivers (full and partial), and unspecified assistantships also available. Financial award application deadline: 12/1. *Faculty research:* Feminist studies/sexualities, race ethnicity, global, culture, conversation analysis. *Unit head:* Prof. Verta Taylor, Chair, 805-893-3118, Fax: 805-893-3324. *Application contact:* Sharon Applegate, Graduate Program Assistant, 805-893-3328, Fax: 805-893-3324, E-mail: grad-soc@soc.ucsb.edu.

University of California, Santa Cruz, Division of Graduate Studies, Division of Social Sciences, Department of Sociology, Santa Cruz, CA 95064. Offers PhD. *Students:* 34 full-time (19 women), 1 (woman) part-time; includes 15 minority (3 Black or African American, non-Hispanic/Latino; 5 Asian, non-Hispanic/Latino; 6 Hispanic/Latino; 1 Two or more races, non-Hispanic/Latino). Average age 35. 111 applicants, 13% accepted, 5 enrolled. In 2010, 5 doctorates awarded. *Degree requirements:* For doctorate, thesis/dissertation, qualifying exam. *Entrance requirements:* For doctorate, GRE General Test. Additional exam requirements/recommendations for international students: Required—TOEFL (minimum score 550 paper-based; 220 computer-based; 83 iBT); Recommended—IELTS (minimum score 8). *Application deadline:* For fall admission, 12/15 for domestic and international students. Application fee: $70 ($90 for international students). Electronic applications accepted. *Financial support:* Fellowships, research assistantships, teaching assistantships, institutionally sponsored loans and tuition waivers available. Financial award applicants required to submit FAFSA. *Faculty research:* Globalization, political economy, and environment; inequality and identity; culture, knowledge, and power. *Unit head:* Ann McCardy, Graduate Program Coordinator, 831-459-3168, E-mail: amccardy@ucsc.edu. *Application contact:* Ann McCardy, Graduate Program Coordinator, 831-459-3168, E-mail: amccardy@ucsc.edu.

University of Central Florida, College of Sciences, Department of Sociology, Orlando, FL 32816. Offers applied sociology (MA); Maya studies (Certificate); sociology (PhD). Part-time and evening/weekend programs available. *Faculty:* 19 full-time (10 women), 7 part-time/adjunct (6 women). *Students:* 46 full-time (35 women), 19 part-time (13 women); includes 6 Black or African American, non-Hispanic/Latino; 1 Asian, non-Hispanic/Latino; 8 Hispanic/Latino; 1 Two or more races, non-Hispanic/Latino, 2 international. Average age 30. 46 applicants, 65% accepted, 20 enrolled. In 2010, 17 master's, 4 doctorates, 2 other advanced degrees awarded. *Degree requirements:* For master's, comprehensive written exam or thesis. *Entrance requirements:* For master's, GRE General Test, minimum GPA of 3.0 in last 60 hours of course work. Additional exam requirements/recommendations for international students: Required—TOEFL. *Application deadline:* For fall admission, 7/15 for domestic students; for spring admission, 12/1 for domestic students. Application fee: $30. Electronic applications accepted. *Expenses:* Tuition, state resident: part-time $256.56 per credit hour. Tuition, nonresident: part-time $1011.52 per credit hour. Part-time tuition and fees vary according to program. *Financial support:* In 2010–11, 36 students received support, including 13 fellowships with partial tuition reimbursements available (averaging $3,700 per year), 6 research assistantships with partial tuition reimbursements available (averaging $5,900 per year), 28 teaching assistantships with partial tuition reimbursements available (averaging $8,100 per year); career-related internships or fieldwork, Federal Work-Study, institutionally sponsored loans, tuition waivers (partial), and unspecified assistantships also available. Financial award application deadline: 3/1; financial award applicants required to submit FAFSA. *Faculty research:* Religious subcultures, attitudes toward abortion, population, sport research, stratification. *Unit head:* Dr. Jay Corzine, Chair, 407-823-2227, Fax: 407-823-5156, E-mail: hcorzine@mail.ucf.edu. *Application contact:* Dr. Jay Corzine, Chair, 407-823-2227, Fax: 407-823-5156, E-mail: hcorzine@mail.ucf.edu.

University of Central Missouri, The Graduate School, College of Health and Human Services, Warrensburg, MO 64093. Offers criminal justice (MS); industrial hygiene (MS); occupational safety management (MS); physical education/exercise and sport science (MS); rural family nursing (MS); social gerontology (MS); sociology (MA); speech language pathology and audiology (MS). *Accreditation:* NCATE. Part-time programs available. Postbaccalaureate distance learning degree programs offered. *Entrance requirements:* Additional exam requirements/recommendations for international students: Required—TOEFL (minimum score 550 paper-based; 79 computer-based). Electronic applications accepted.

University of Chicago, Division of Social Sciences, Department of Sociology, Chicago, IL 60637-1513. Offers PhD. *Degree requirements:* For doctorate, one foreign language, thesis/dissertation, 2 field exams. *Entrance requirements:* For doctorate, GRE General Test. Additional exam requirements/recommendations for international students: Required—TOEFL, IELTS (minimum score 7). Electronic applications accepted.

University of Cincinnati, Graduate School, McMicken College of Arts and Sciences, Department of Sociology, Cincinnati, OH 45221. Offers MA, PhD. Part-time programs available. *Degree requirements:* For master's, thesis; for doctorate, thesis/dissertation. *Entrance requirements:* For master's and doctorate, GRE General Test. Additional exam requirements/recommendations for international students: Required—TOEFL. Electronic applications accepted. *Faculty research:* Work and family, race and urban, health and medicine, social psychology.

University of Colorado at Colorado Springs, College of Letters, Arts and Sciences, Department of Sociology, Colorado Springs, CO 80933-7150. Offers MA. Part-time programs available. *Faculty:* 10 full-time (7 women), 4 part-time/adjunct (3 women). *Students:* 27 full-time (18 women), 8 part-time (7 women); includes 2 Black or African American, non-Hispanic/Latino; 1 Asian, non-Hispanic/Latino; 3 Hispanic/Latino. Average age 30. 24 applicants, 83% accepted, 14 enrolled. In 2010, 11 master's awarded. *Degree requirements:* For master's, thesis optional. *Entrance requirements:* For master's, GRE, minimum GPA of 2.75. *Application deadline:* For fall admission, 7/1 priority date for domestic students; for spring admission, 12/1 for domestic students. Applications are processed on a rolling basis. Application fee: $60 ($75 for international students). *Expenses:* Tuition, state resident: full-time $7916. Tuition, nonresident: full-time $16,610. Tuition and fees vary according to course load, degree level, program, reciprocity agreements and student level. *Financial support:* Teaching assistantships, career-related internships or fieldwork, Federal Work-Study, and scholarships/grants available. Support available to part-time students. Financial award application deadline: 3/1; financial award applicants required to submit FAFSA. *Faculty research:* Environmental justice; gender, race and ethnicity; sport and popular culture; youth and deviant behavior. *Unit head:* Dr. Heather Albanesi, Director of Graduate Studies, 719-255-4137, Fax: 719-255-4450, E-mail: halbanes@uccs.edu. *Application contact:* Rosemary Kelbel, Program Assistant, 719-255-4153, Fax: 719-255-4450, E-mail: rkelbel@uccs.edu.

University of Colorado Boulder, Graduate School, College of Arts and Sciences, Department of Sociology, Boulder, CO 80309. Offers PhD. *Faculty:* 22 full-time (14 women). *Students:* 56 full-time (36 women), 2 part-time (1 woman); includes 7 minority (3 Black or African American, non-Hispanic/Latino; 1 Asian, non-Hispanic/Latino; 3 Hispanic/Latino), 5 international. Average age 31. 116 applicants, 5 enrolled. In 2010, 12 doctorates awarded. *Degree requirements:* For doctorate, comprehensive exam, thesis/dissertation. *Entrance requirements:* For doctorate, GRE General Test, GRE Subject Test, minimum undergraduate GPA of 2.75. *Application deadline:* For fall admission, 1/1 for domestic students, 12/1 for international students. Application fee: $50 ($60 for international students). *Financial support:* In 2010–11, 17 fellowships (averaging $1,388 per year), 29 research assistantships (averaging $8,451 per year) were awarded; Federal Work-Study, institutionally sponsored loans, and scholarships/grants also available. Support available to part-time students. Financial award application deadline: 1/1; financial award applicants required to submit FAFSA. *Faculty research:* Criminology, social control, law delinquency and deviance, population, health studies, gender relations, social stratification, race relations, the environment, institutions and international systems. Total annual research expenditures: $1.8 million.

University of Colorado Denver, College of Liberal Arts and Sciences, Department of Sociology, Denver, CO 80217. Offers MA. Part-time and evening/weekend programs available. *Faculty:* 9 full-time (4 women), 1 (woman) part-time/adjunct. *Students:* 18 full-time (11 women), 2 part-time (1 woman); includes 1 Asian, non-Hispanic/Latino; 1 Hispanic/Latino; 1 Two or more races, non-Hispanic/Latino. Average age 30. 18 applicants, 61% accepted, 7 enrolled. In 2010, 1 master's awarded. *Degree requirements:* For master's, thesis or alternative, 36 credit hours. *Entrance requirements:* For master's, GRE (recommended), minimum combined GPA of 3.3 for all courses taken at undergraduate or graduate level prior to admission, 3.5 for all sociology courses; writing sample; statement of intent. Additional exam requirements/recommendations for international students: Required—TOEFL (minimum score 525 paper-based). *Application deadline:* For fall admission, 2/15 for domestic students. Application fee: $50 ($75 for international students). Electronic applications accepted. *Expenses:* Tuition, state resident: full-time $7332; part-time $355 per credit hour. Tuition, nonresident: full-time $18,990; part-time $1055 per credit hour. Required fees: $998. Tuition and fees vary according to course level, course load, degree level, campus/location, program, reciprocity agreements and student level. *Financial support:* Federal Work-Study, scholarships/grants, and unspecified assistantships available. Financial award application deadline: 4/1; financial award applicants required to submit FAFSA. *Faculty research:* Domestic violence, elderly and housing, family demography, immigrants and immigration, social determinants of health behaviors. *Unit head:* Dr. John Freed, Department Chair, 303-315-2143, E-mail: john.freed@ucdenver.edu. *Application contact:* Rachel Watson, Program Assistant, 303-315-2148, Fax: 303-315-2149, E-mail: rachel.watson@ucdenver.edu.

University of Colorado Denver, College of Liberal Arts and Sciences, Program in Humanities, Denver, CO 80217-3364. Offers community health science (MSS); humanities (MH); international studies (MSS); social science (MSS); society and the environment (MSS); women's and gender studies (MSS). Part-time and evening/weekend programs available. *Students:* 53 full-time (39 women), 35 part-time (22 women); includes 4 Black or African American, non-Hispanic/Latino; 1 American Indian or Alaska Native, non-Hispanic/Latino; 3 Asian, non-Hispanic/Latino; 7 Hispanic/Latino, 1 international. Average age 33. 41 applicants, 54% accepted, 19 enrolled. In 2010, 29 master's awarded. *Degree requirements:* For master's, thesis or alternative, 36 credit hours, project or thesis. *Entrance requirements:* For master's, writing sample, statement of purpose/letter of intent. Additional exam requirements/recommendations for international students: Required—TOEFL (minimum score 525 paper-based). *Application deadline:* For fall admission, 5/15 priority date for domestic students; for spring admission, 10/15 priority date for domestic students. Application fee: $50 ($75 for international students). Electronic applications accepted. *Expenses:* Tuition, state resident: full-time $7332; part-time $355 per credit hour. Tuition, nonresident: full-time $18,990; part-time $1055 per credit hour. Required fees: $998. Tuition and fees vary according to course level, course load, degree level, campus/location, program, reciprocity agreements and student level. *Financial support:* Federal Work-Study and scholarships/grants available. Financial award application deadline: 4/1; financial award applicants required to submit FAFSA. *Faculty research:* Women and gender in the classical Mediterranean, communication theory and democracy, relationship between psychology and philosophy. *Unit head:* Myra Bookman, Associate Director of Humanities and Social Science, 303-556-2496, Fax: 303-556-8100, E-mail: myra.bookman@ucdenver.edu. *Application contact:* Catherine Osmundson, Program Assistant, 303-556-2305, E-mail: catherine.osmundson@ucdenver.edu.

University of Connecticut, Graduate School, College of Liberal Arts and Sciences, Department of Sociology, Storrs, CT 06269. Offers MA, PhD. Terminal master's awarded for partial completion of doctoral program. *Degree requirements:* For master's, comprehensive exam; for doctorate, thesis/dissertation. *Entrance requirements:* For master's and doctorate, GRE General Test. Additional exam requirements/recommendations for international students: Required—TOEFL (minimum score 550 paper-based; 213 computer-based). Electronic applications accepted.

University of Delaware, College of Arts and Sciences, Department of Sociology and Criminology, Newark, DE 19716. Offers criminology (MA, PhD); sociology (MA, PhD). *Degree requirements:* For master's, thesis; for doctorate, comprehensive exam, thesis/dissertation. *Entrance requirements:* For master's and doctorate, GRE, 3 letters of recommendation. Additional exam requirements/recommendations for international students: Required—TOEFL. Electronic applications accepted. *Faculty research:* Sex and gender, criminology/deviance, theory, methods, collective behavior.

University of Florida, Graduate School, College of Liberal Arts and Sciences, Department of Sociology, Gainesville, FL 32611. Offers MA, PhD, JD/MA. *Entrance requirements:* Additional exam requirements/recommendations for international students: Required—TOEFL, IELTS. *Application deadline:* Applications are processed on a rolling basis. Electronic applications accepted. *Expenses:* Tuition, state resident: full-time $10,915.92. Tuition, nonresident: full-time $28,309. *Financial support:* Fellowships, research assistantships, teaching assistantships, career-related internships or fieldwork and unspecified assistantships available. *Unit head:* Dr. Constance Shehan, Chair, 352-392-0265 Ext. 254, Fax: 352-392-6568, E-mail: cshehan@ufl.edu. *Application contact:* Dr. Barbara Zsembik, Graduate Coordinator, 352-392-0265 Ext. 226, Fax: 352-392-6568, E-mail: zsembik@ufl.edu.

University of Georgia, College of Arts and Sciences, Department of Sociology, Athens, GA 30602. Offers MA, PhD. *Faculty:* 16 full-time (5 women). *Students:* 28 full-time (17 women), 4 part-time (all women); includes 1 Black or African American, non-Hispanic/Latino, 2 international. 53 applicants, 15% accepted, 5 enrolled. In 2010, 3 master's, 2 doctorates awarded. *Degree requirements:* For master's, thesis; for doctorate, thesis/dissertation. *Entrance requirements:* For master's and doctorate, GRE General Test. Additional exam requirements/recommendations for international students: Required—TOEFL. *Application deadline:* For fall admission, 2/1 priority date for domestic students, 1/1 for international students. Application fee: $50. Electronic applications accepted. *Expenses:* Tuition, state resident: full-time $7200; part-time $344 per credit hour. Tuition, nonresident: full-time $21,900; part-time $944 per credit hour. Tuition and fees vary according to course load and program. *Financial support:* In 2010–11, 16 students received support, including teaching assistantships with full tuition reimbursements available (averaging $12,220 per year); research assistantships, unspecified assistantships also available. Financial award application deadline: 1/1. *Faculty research:* Race, deviance, gender, culture. *Unit head:* Dr. William Finlay, Head, 706-542-3175, Fax: 706-542-4320, E-mail: wfinlay@uga.edu. *Application contact:* Dr. Linda Renzulli, Graduate Coordinator, 706-542-3213, Fax: 706-542-4320, E-mail: renzulli@uga.edu.

University of Guelph, Graduate Studies, College of Social and Applied Human Sciences, Department of Sociology and Anthropology, Guelph, ON N1G 2W1, Canada. Offers anthropology (MA); crime and criminal justice policy (MA); sociology (MA, PhD). *Degree requirements:* For master's, thesis or major paper; for doctorate, comprehensive exam, thesis/dissertation. *Entrance requirements:* For master's, minimum B+ average during previous 2 years of course work, honors BA or equivalent; for doctorate, must have an MA in Sociology, must have 80% or higher in graduate level studies. Additional exam requirements/recommendations for international students: Required—TOEFL (minimum score 550 paper-based; 213 computer-based; 89 iBT), IELTS (minimum score 6.5), TOEFL or IELTS. Electronic applications accepted. *Faculty research:* Rural and development sociology; education, employment, and the workplace; race, ethnicity, and native studies; criminology and deviance; social psychology.

University of Hawaii at Manoa, Graduate Division, College of Social Sciences, Department of Sociology, Honolulu, HI 96822. Offers sociology (MA, PhD). Part-time programs available. *Faculty:* 23 full-time (11 women), 4 part-time/adjunct (2 women). *Students:* 47 full-time (24 women), 9 part-time (7 women); includes 15 minority (8 Asian, non-Hispanic/Latino; 2 Hispanic/Latino; 1 Native Hawaiian or other Pacific Islander, non-Hispanic/Latino; 4 Two or more races, non-Hispanic/Latino), 28 international. Average age 34. 52 applicants, 62% accepted, 18 enrolled. In 2010, 6 master's, 4 doctorates awarded. *Degree requirements:* For master's, thesis optional; for doctorate, comprehensive exam, thesis/dissertation. *Entrance requirements:* For master's and doctorate, GRE General Test. Additional exam requirements/recommendations for international students: Required—TOEFL (minimum score 500 paper-based; 173 computer-based; 61 iBT), IELTS (minimum score 5). *Application deadline:* For fall admission, 2/1 for domestic and international students; for spring admission, 9/1 for domestic students, 8/15 for international students. Applications are processed on a rolling basis. Application fee: $60. *Financial support:* In 2010–11, 13 fellowships (averaging $2,616 per year), 6 research assistantships (averaging $16,166 per year), 11 teaching assistantships (averaging $15,451 per year) were awarded; Federal Work-Study, institutionally sponsored loans, and tuition waivers (full and partial) also available. *Faculty research:* Comparative sociology of Asia; population studies; crime, law, and deviance; health; aging and medical sociology. Total annual research expenditures: $1.1 million. *Application contact:* Patricia Steinhoff, Graduate Chair, 808-956-7693, Fax: 808-956-3707, E-mail: sunki@hawaii.edu.

University of Houston, College of Liberal Arts and Social Sciences, Department of Sociology, Houston, TX 77204. Offers MA. Part-time programs available. *Faculty:* 9 full-time (4 women), 2 part-time/adjunct (1 woman). *Students:* 19 full-time (13 women), 10 part-time (7 women); includes 3 Black or African American, non-Hispanic/Latino; 1 Asian, non-Hispanic/Latino; 8 Hispanic/Latino; 1 Two or more races, non-Hispanic/Latino, 8 international. Average age 28. 42 applicants, 38% accepted, 11 enrolled. In 2010, 8 master's awarded. *Degree requirements:* For master's, thesis, 4 core courses, 36 hours. *Entrance requirements:* For master's, GRE (minimum score 1000), minimum GPA of 3.0; letters of recommendation, resume. Additional exam requirements/recommendations for international students: Required—TOEFL (minimum score 550 paper-based; 79 iBT). *Application deadline:* For fall admission, 4/1 for domestic and international students; for spring admission, 11/1 for domestic students. Application fee: $75 for international students. Electronic applications accepted. *Expenses:* Tuition, state resident: full-time $8592; part-time $358 per credit hour. Tuition, nonresident: full-time $16,032; part-time

Sociology

University of Houston *(continued)*
$668 per credit hour. Required fees: $2889. Tuition and fees vary according to course load and program. *Financial support:* In 2010–11, 2 research assistantships with full tuition reimbursements (averaging $7,720 per year), 12 teaching assistantships with full tuition reimbursements (averaging $7,793 per year) were awarded; career-related internships or fieldwork, Federal Work-Study, institutionally sponsored loans, scholarships/grants, health care benefits, and unspecified assistantships also available. Support available to part-time students. Financial award application deadline: 2/1; financial award applicants required to submit FAFSA. *Faculty research:* Immigration, public education, HIV/AIDS. *Unit head:* Dr. Xavia Karner, Chairperson, 713-743-3961, Fax: 713-743-3943, E-mail: txkarner@uh.edu. *Application contact:* Dr. Stella Grigorian, Graduate Advisor, 713-743-3960, Fax: 713-743-3943, E-mail: sgrigorian@uh.edu.

University of Houston–Clear Lake, School of Human Sciences and Humanities, Programs in Human Sciences, Houston, TX 77058-1098. Offers behavioral sciences (MA), including criminology, cross cultural studies, general psychology, sociology; clinical psychology (MA); criminology (MA); cross cultural studies (MA); family therapy (MA); fitness and human performance (MA); school psychology (MA). *Accreditation:* AAMFT/COAMFTE. Part-time and evening/weekend programs available. Postbaccalaureate distance learning degree programs offered (minimal on-campus study). *Degree requirements:* For master's, thesis or alternative. *Entrance requirements:* For master's, GRE General Test. Additional exam requirements/recommendations for international students: Required—TOEFL (minimum score 550 paper-based; 213 computer-based). Electronic applications accepted. *Faculty research:* Smoking cessation, adolescent sexuality, white collar crime, serial murder, human factors/human computer interaction.

University of Illinois at Chicago, Graduate College, College of Liberal Arts and Sciences, Department of Sociology, Chicago, IL 60607-7128. Offers MA, PhD. Terminal master's awarded for partial completion of doctoral program. *Degree requirements:* For master's, comprehensive exam, thesis; for doctorate, thesis/dissertation, qualifying exam. *Entrance requirements:* For master's and doctorate, GRE General Test, minimum GPA of 3.0. Additional exam requirements/recommendations for international students: Required—TOEFL. Electronic applications accepted. *Faculty research:* Social psychology, social organization, applied sociology, demography and human ecology.

University of Illinois at Urbana–Champaign, Graduate College, College of Liberal Arts and Sciences, Department of Sociology, Champaign, IL 61820. Offers MA, PhD. *Faculty:* 13 full-time (7 women), 2 part-time/adjunct (1 woman). *Students:* 32 full-time (21 women), 21 part-time (11 women); includes 13 minority (5 Black or African American, non-Hispanic/Latino; 4 Asian, non-Hispanic/Latino; 3 Hispanic/Latino; 1 Two or more races, non-Hispanic/Latino), 20 international. 66 applicants, 17% accepted, 7 enrolled. In 2010, 2 master's, 6 doctorates awarded. *Entrance requirements:* For doctorate, GRE, minimum GPA of 3.0; writing sample. Additional exam requirements/recommendations for international students: Required—TOEFL (minimum score 79 iBT). *Application deadline:* Applications are processed on a rolling basis. Application fee: $75 ($90 for international students). Electronic applications accepted. *Financial support:* In 2010–11, 7 fellowships, 6 research assistantships, 34 teaching assistantships were awarded; tuition waivers (full and partial) also available. *Unit head:* Anna-Maria Marshall, Head, 217-333-1950, Fax: 217-333-5225, E-mail: amarshll@illinois.edu. *Application contact:* Shari Day, Office Manager, 217-244-1809, Fax: 217-333-5225, E-mail: shariday@illinois.edu.

University of Indianapolis, Graduate Programs, College of Arts and Sciences, Department of Social Sciences, Indianapolis, IN 46227-3697. Offers applied sociology (MA). Part-time and evening/weekend programs available. *Faculty:* 4 full-time (1 woman). *Students:* 21 full-time (14 women), 17 part-time (10 women); includes 7 Black or African American, non-Hispanic/Latino; 1 Two or more races, non-Hispanic/Latino, 10 international. Average age 27. In 2010, 6 master's awarded. *Degree requirements:* For master's, thesis optional. *Entrance requirements:* For master's, GRE Subject Test, minimum GPA of 3.0, letter of intent, 3 letters of recommendation. Additional exam requirements/recommendations for international students: Required—TOEFL (minimum score 550 paper-based; 213 computer-based). *Application deadline:* Applications are processed on a rolling basis. Application fee: $30. Electronic applications accepted. Tuition and fees vary according to course load, degree level and program. *Financial support:* Federal Work-Study, scholarships/grants, tuition waivers (full and partial), and unspecified assistantships available. Support available to part-time students. Financial award application deadline: 5/1; financial award applicants required to submit FAFSA. *Unit head:* Dr. James Pennell, Chair, 317-788-3535, Fax: 317-788-3480, E-mail: jpennell@uindy.edu. *Application contact:* Dr. James Pennell, Chair, 317-788-3535, Fax: 317-788-3480, E-mail: jpennell@uindy.edu.

The University of Iowa, Graduate College, College of Liberal Arts and Sciences, Department of Sociology, Iowa City, IA 52242-1316. Offers MA, PhD. *Degree requirements:* For master's, thesis optional, exam; for doctorate, comprehensive exam, thesis/dissertation. *Entrance requirements:* For master's and doctorate, GRE General Test, minimum GPA of 3.0. Additional exam requirements/recommendations for international students: Required—TOEFL (minimum score 600 paper-based; 250 computer-based; 100 iBT). Electronic applications accepted.

The University of Kansas, Graduate Studies, College of Liberal Arts and Sciences, Department of Sociology, Lawrence, KS 66045. Offers MA, PhD. Part-time programs available. *Faculty:* 14 full-time (8 women), 9 part-time/adjunct (5 women). *Students:* 39 full-time (22 women), 4 part-time (all women); includes 2 minority (1 Black or African American, non-Hispanic/Latino; 1 Asian, non-Hispanic/Latino), 4 international. Average age 29. 47 applicants, 55% accepted, 13 enrolled. In 2010, 2 master's, 3 doctorates awarded. *Degree requirements:* For master's, thesis; for doctorate, comprehensive exam, thesis/dissertation. *Entrance requirements:* For master's, GRE General Test, bachelor's degree; minimum GPA of 3.0; 15 credit hours in sociology; 1 course each in sociology theory and sociology statistics; for doctorate, GRE General Test, master's degree in sociology or closely-related field. Additional exam requirements/recommendations for international students: Required—TOEFL: paper, all part scores at least 53; computer, all part scores at least 20; internet, all part scores at least 30 OR IELTS minimum 6.0 total w/no part score below 5.5 OR Degree from institution in U.S. or other English speaking country . *Application deadline:* For fall admission, 12/15 priority date for domestic and international students; for spring admission, 10/15 for domestic and international students. Applications are processed on a rolling basis. Application fee: $55 ($65 for international students). Electronic applications accepted. *Expenses:* Tuition, state resident: full-time $7092; part-time $295.50 per credit hour. Tuition, nonresident: full-time $16,590; part-time $691.25 per credit hour. Required fees: $858; $71.49 per credit hour. Tuition and fees vary according to course load, campus/location and program. *Financial support:* Fellowships with full tuition reimbursements, research assistantships with full tuition reimbursements, teaching assistantships with full and partial tuition reimbursements, scholarships/grants, health care benefits, and unspecified assistantships available. Financial award application deadline: 12/15. *Faculty research:* Family/life course and aging, gender and sexuality, globalization, migration, medicine/health, political sociology, race/ethnicity, social inequality/stratification, culture, religion, economic sociology. *Unit head:* William G. Staples, Chair, 785-864-4111, Fax: 785-864-5280, E-mail: staples@ku.edu. *Application contact:* Shirley Hill, Graduate Director, 785-864-4111, Fax: 785-864-5280, E-mail: hill@ku.edu.

University of Kentucky, Graduate School, College of Arts and Sciences, Program in Sociology, Lexington, KY 40506-0032. Offers MA, PhD. Part-time programs available. *Degree requirements:* For master's, comprehensive exam, thesis optional; for doctorate, comprehensive exam, thesis/dissertation. *Entrance requirements:* For master's, GRE General Test, minimum undergraduate GPA of 2.75; for doctorate, GRE General Test, minimum graduate GPA of 3.0. Additional exam requirements/recommendations for international students: Required—TOEFL (minimum score 550 paper-based; 213 computer-based). Electronic applications accepted. *Faculty research:* Work organizations, social inequalities, rural sociology, criminology/deviance, medical sociology.

University of Lethbridge, School of Graduate Studies, Lethbridge, AB T1K 3M4, Canada. Offers accounting (MScM); addictions counseling (M Sc); agricultural biotechnology (M Sc); agricultural studies (M Sc, MA); anthropology (MA); archaeology (MA); art (MA, MFA); biochemistry (M Sc); biological sciences (M Sc); biomolecular science (PhD); biosystems and biodiversity (PhD); Canadian studies (MA); chemistry (M Sc); computer science (M Sc); computer science and geographical information science (M Sc); counseling psychology (M Ed); dramatic arts (MA); earth, space, and physical science (PhD); economics (MA); educational leadership (M Ed); English (MA); environmental science (M Sc); evolution and behavior (PhD); exercise science (M Sc); finance (MScM); French (MA); French/German (MA); French/Spanish (MA); general education (M Ed); general management (MScM); geography (M Sc, MA); German (MA); health science (M Sc); history (MA); human resource management and labour relations (MScM); individualized multidisciplinary (M Sc, MA); information systems (MScM); international management (MScM); kinesiology (M Sc, MA); management (M Sc, MA); marketing (MScM); mathematics (M Sc); music (M Mus, MA); Native American studies (MA); neuroscience (M Sc, PhD); new media (MA); nursing (M Sc); philosophy (MA); physics (M Sc); policy and strategy (MScM); political science (MA); psychology (M Sc, MA); religious studies (MA); social sciences (MA); sociology (MA); theatre and dramatic arts (MFA); theoretical and computational science (PhD); urban and regional studies (MA); women's studies (MA). Part-time and evening/weekend programs available. *Degree requirements:* For doctorate, comprehensive exam, thesis/dissertation. *Entrance requirements:* For master's, GMAT (M Sc in management), bachelor's degree in related field, minimum GPA of 3.0 during previous 20 graded semester courses, 2 years teaching or related experience (M Ed); for doctorate, master's degree, minimum graduate GPA of 3.5. Additional exam requirements/recommendations for international students: Required—TOEFL. *Faculty research:* Movement and brain plasticity, gibberellin physiology, photosynthesis, carbon cycling, molecular properties of main-group ring components.

University of Louisville, Graduate School, College of Arts and Sciences, Department of Sociology, Louisville, KY 40292. Offers MA. Part-time and evening/weekend programs available. *Faculty:* 17 full-time (9 women). *Students:* 18 full-time (11 women), 16 part-time (10 women); includes 3 Black or African American, non-Hispanic/Latino, 1 international. Average age 31. 35 applicants, 80% accepted, 20 enrolled. In 2010, 5 master's awarded. *Degree requirements:* For master's, thesis optional, thesis or practicum. *Entrance requirements:* For master's, GRE General Test. Additional exam requirements/recommendations for international students: Required—TOEFL. *Application deadline:* For fall admission, 6/1 priority date for domestic students, 6/1 for international students; for spring admission, 10/1 priority date for domestic students, 10/1 for international students. Applications are processed on a rolling basis. Application fee: $50. Electronic applications accepted. *Expenses:* Tuition, state resident: full-time $9144; part-time $508 per credit hour. Tuition, nonresident: full-time $19,026; part-time $1057 per credit hour. Tuition and fees vary according to program and reciprocity agreements. *Financial support:* In 2010–11, 4 students received support, including 1 fellowship with full tuition reimbursement available, 6 teaching assistantships with full tuition reimbursements available. *Faculty research:* Crime/corrections, gender/sexuality, medicine/health, education, urban. *Unit head:* Dr. Cynthia L. Negrey, Chair, 502-852-8023, Fax: 502-852-0099, E-mail: cynthia.negrey@louisville.edu. *Application contact:* Libby Leggett, Director, Graduate Admissions, 502-852-3101, Fax: 502-852-6536, E-mail: gradadm@louisville.edu.

The University of Manchester, School of Social Sciences, Manchester, United Kingdom. Offers ethnographic documentary (M Phil); interdisciplinary study of culture (PhD); philosophy (PhD); politics (PhD); social anthropology (PhD); social anthropology with visual media (PhD); social change (PhD); social statistics (PhD); sociology (PhD); visual anthropology (M Phil).

University of Manitoba, Faculty of Graduate Studies, Faculty of Arts, Department of Sociology, Winnipeg, MB R3T 2N2, Canada. Offers MA, PhD. *Degree requirements:* For master's, thesis.

University of Maryland, Baltimore County, Graduate School, College of Arts, Humanities and Social Sciences, Department of Sociology and Anthropology, Baltimore, MD 21250. Offers applied sociology (MA, Postbaccalaureate Certificate), including applied sociology (MA), nonprofit sector (Postbaccalaureate Certificate). Part-time and evening/weekend programs available. *Faculty:* 16 full-time (10 women), 2 part-time/adjunct (both women). *Students:* 33 full-time (25 women), 23 part-time (19 women); includes 8 Black or African American, non-Hispanic/Latino; 5 Asian, non-Hispanic/Latino; 4 Hispanic/Latino, 1 international. Average age 26. 40 applicants, 93% accepted, 23 enrolled. In 2010, 27 master's awarded. *Degree requirements:* For master's, thesis or alternative. *Entrance requirements:* For master's, minimum GPA of 3.0, undergraduate statistics course. Additional exam requirements/recommendations for international students: Required—TOEFL. *Application deadline:* For fall admission, 7/15 for domestic students; for spring admission, 12/15 for domestic students. Applications are processed on a rolling basis. Application fee: $70. Electronic applications accepted. *Financial support:* In 2010–11, 11 students received support, including 7 research assistantships with full and partial tuition reimbursements available (averaging $12,500 per year), 4 teaching assistantships with full and partial tuition reimbursements available (averaging $12,500 per year); scholarships/grants, health care benefits, unspecified assistantships, and tuition remission also available. Financial award application deadline: 2/14; financial award applicants required to submit FAFSA. *Faculty research:* Sociology of aging, medical sociology, migration. *Unit head:* Dr. J. Kevin Eckert, Chairperson, 410-455-2076, Fax: 410-455-1154, E-mail: eckert@umbc.edu. *Application contact:* Dr. William G. Rothstein, Director, 410-455-2078, Fax: 410-455-1154, E-mail: rothstei@umbc.edu.

University of Maryland, College Park, Academic Affairs, College of Behavioral and Social Sciences, Department of Sociology, College Park, MD 20742. Offers MA, PhD. *Faculty:* 24 full-time (11 women), 7 part-time/adjunct (3 women). *Students:* 71 full-time (45 women), 3 part-time (2 women); includes 7 Black or African American, non-Hispanic/Latino; 4 Asian, non-Hispanic/Latino; 5 Hispanic/Latino; 2 Two or more races, non-Hispanic/Latino, 13 international. 222 applicants, 15% accepted, 11 enrolled. In 2010, 8 master's, 9 doctorates awarded. *Degree requirements:* For master's, thesis; for doctorate, thesis/dissertation, 2 qualifying exams. *Entrance requirements:* For master's, GRE General Test, minimum GPA of 3.0, 3 letters of recommendation; for doctorate, GRE General Test, 3 letters of recommendation. Additional exam requirements/recommendations for international students: Required—TOEFL. *Application deadline:* For fall admission, 2/15 for domestic students, 2/1 for international students. Applications are processed on a rolling basis. Application fee: $75. Electronic applications accepted. *Expenses:* Tuition, state resident: part-time $471 per credit hour. Tuition, nonresident: part-time $1016 per credit hour. Required fees: $337 per term. *Financial support:* In 2010–11, 3 fellowships with partial tuition reimbursements (averaging $8,667 per year), 1 research assistantship (averaging $17,642 per year), 58 teaching assistantships (averaging $15,881 per year) were awarded; Federal Work-Study and scholarships/grants also available. Support available to part-time students. Financial award applicants required to submit FAFSA. *Faculty research:* Social psychology, sociology of work, sociology of the military, population studies, stratification. Total annual research expenditures: $596,155. *Unit head:* Dr. Reeve Vannerman, Chair, 301-405-6892, Fax: 301-314-6892, E-mail: reeve@umd.edu. *Application contact:* Dean of Graduate School, 301-405-0358, Fax: 301-314-9305.

University of Massachusetts Amherst, Graduate School, College of Social and Behavioral Sciences, Department of Sociology, Amherst, MA 01003. Offers MA, PhD. Part-time programs available. *Faculty:* 30 full-time (14 women). *Students:* 51 full-time (35 women), 22 part-time (16 women); includes 20 minority (5 Black or African American, non-Hispanic/Latino; 2 American Indian or Alaska Native, non-Hispanic/Latino; 1 Asian, non-Hispanic/Latino; 10 Hispanic/Latino; 2 Two or more races, non-Hispanic/Latino), 18 international. Average age 32. 64 applicants, 27% accepted, 7 enrolled. In 2010, 4 master's, 4 doctorates awarded. Terminal master's awarded for partial completion of doctoral program. *Degree requirements:* For master's, thesis or alternative; for doctorate, comprehensive exam, thesis/dissertation. *Entrance requirements:* For master's and doctorate, GRE General Test, writing sample, 3 letters of recommendation. Additional exam requirements/recommendations for international students: Required—TOEFL (minimum score 550 paper-based; 213 computer-based; 80 iBT), IELTS (minimum score 6.5). *Application deadline:* For fall admission, 1/15 for domestic and international students. Applications are processed on a rolling basis. Application fee: $50 ($65 for international students). Electronic applications accepted. *Expenses:* Tuition, state resident: full-time $2640. Required fees: $8282. One-time fee: $357 full-time. *Financial support:* In 2010–11, 9 research assistantships with full tuition reimbursements (averaging $7,485 per year), 51 teaching assistantships with full tuition reimbursements (averaging $12,178 per year) were awarded; fellowships, career-related internships or fieldwork, Federal Work-Study, scholarships/grants, traineeships, health care benefits, tuition waivers (full), and unspecified assistantships also available. Support available to part-time students. Financial award application deadline: 1/15; financial award applicants required to submit FAFSA. *Unit head:* Dr. Sanjiv Gupta, Graduate Program Director, 413-545-4057, Fax: 413-545-3204. *Application contact:* Jean M. Ames, Supervisor of Admissions, 413-545-0722, Fax: 413-577-0010, E-mail: gradadm@grad.umass.edu.

University of Massachusetts Boston, Office of Graduate Studies, College of Liberal Arts, Program in Applied Sociology, Boston, MA 02125-3393. Offers MA. Part-time and evening/weekend programs available. *Degree requirements:* For master's, comprehensive exam, thesis. *Entrance requirements:* For master's, GRE or MAT, minimum GPA of 2.75. *Faculty research:* Sociology of education, social deviance and control, women and development, race and ethnic group relations, criminology.

University of Massachusetts Lowell, College of Arts and Sciences, Department of Regional Economic and Social Development, Lowell, MA 01854-2881. Offers MA, Graduate Certificate. Part-time programs available. *Entrance requirements:* For master's, GRE. Electronic applications accepted.

University of Memphis, Graduate School, College of Arts and Sciences, Department of Sociology, Memphis, TN 38152. Offers MA. Part-time programs available. *Faculty:* 6 full-time (3 women). *Students:* 12 full-time (10 women), 4 part-time (3 women); includes 2 Black or African American, non-Hispanic/Latino; 1 Hispanic/Latino. Average age 33. 9 applicants, 89% accepted, 1 enrolled. In 2010, 4 master's awarded. *Degree requirements:* For master's, comprehensive exam, thesis (for some programs). *Entrance requirements:* For master's, GRE General Test, 12 undergraduate hours in sociology. Additional exam requirements/recommendations for international students: Required—TOEFL (minimum score 550 paper-based; 213 computer-based). *Application deadline:* For fall admission, 7/1 for domestic students, 5/1 for international students; for spring admission, 12/1 for domestic students, 9/15 for international students. Applications are processed on a rolling basis. Application fee: $35 ($60 for international students). Electronic applications accepted. *Financial support:* In 2010–11, 12 students received support, including 9 research assistantships with full tuition reimbursements available (averaging $9,600 per year), 1 teaching assistantship with full tuition reimbursement available (averaging $6,000 per year); Federal Work-Study, scholarships/grants, and unspecified assistantships also available. Financial award application deadline: 2/15; financial award applicants required to submit FAFSA. *Faculty research:* Globalization, medical, inequality, religion, urban. *Unit head:* Dr. Martin Levin, Chair, 901-678-2611, Fax: 901-678-2525. *Application contact:* Dr. Larry Petersen, Professor and Graduate Coordinator, 901-678-3341, Fax: 901-678-2525, E-mail: lpetersn@memphis.edu.

University of Miami, Graduate School, College of Arts and Sciences, Department of Sociology, Coral Gables, FL 33124. Offers MA, PhD. Part-time programs available. Terminal master's awarded for partial completion of doctoral program. *Degree requirements:* For master's, thesis; for doctorate, comprehensive exam, thesis/dissertation. *Entrance requirements:* For master's and doctorate, GRE General Test. Additional exam requirements/recommendations for international students: Required—TOEFL (minimum score 515 paper-based; 213 computer-based). Electronic applications accepted. *Faculty research:* Crime, violence, mental health, ethnic relations, health.

University of Miami, Graduate School, School of Education, Department of Educational and Psychological Studies, Program in Community and Social Change, Coral Gables, FL 33124. Offers MS Ed. Part-time and evening/weekend programs available. *Faculty:* 4 full-time (3 women). *Students:* 8 full-time (7 women), 5 part-time (3 women); includes 4 minority (2 Black or African American, non-Hispanic/Latino; 2 Hispanic/Latino). Average age 29. 17 applicants, 94% accepted, 13 enrolled. *Degree requirements:* For master's, comprehensive exam, thesis optional. *Entrance requirements:* For master's, GRE General Test. Additional exam requirements/recommendations for international students: Required—TOEFL (minimum score 550 paper-based; 80 iBT); Recommended—IELTS (minimum score 6.5). *Application deadline:* For fall admission, 3/15 for domestic students. Application fee: $65. Electronic applications accepted. *Financial support:* In 2010–11, 5 students received support. Application deadline: 3/1. *Unit head:* Dr. Laura Kohn-Wood, Associate Department Chairperson and Program Director, 305-284-1316, Fax: 305-284-3003, E-mail: l.kohnwood@miami.edu. *Application contact:* Lois Heffernan, Graduate Admissions Coordinator, 305-284-2167, Fax: 305-284-3003, E-mail: lheffernan@miami.edu.

University of Miami, Graduate School, School of Education, Department of Teaching and Learning, Program in Education and Social Change, Coral Gables, FL 33124. Offers MS Ed. Part-time and evening/weekend programs available. *Students:* 29 part-time (22 women); includes 16 minority (7 Black or African American, non-Hispanic/Latino; 2 Asian, non-Hispanic/Latino; 6 Hispanic/Latino; 1 Two or more races, non-Hispanic/Latino). Average age 23. *Degree requirements:* For master's, electronic portfolio. *Entrance requirements:* For master's, GRE General Test. Additional exam requirements/recommendations for international students: Required—TOEFL (minimum score 550 paper-based; 80 iBT); Recommended—IELTS (minimum score 6.5). Application fee: $65. Electronic applications accepted. *Financial support:* In 2010–11, 2 students received support. Application deadline: 3/1. *Unit head:* Dr. Mary Avalos, Assistant Research Professor and Program Director, 305-284-6467, Fax: 305-284-3003, E-mail: mavalos@miami.edu. *Application contact:* Maria Papazian, Graduate Admissions Coordinator, 305-284-2963, Fax: 305-284-4439, E-mail: m.papazian@miami.edu.

University of Michigan, Horace H. Rackham School of Graduate Studies, College of Literature, Science, and the Arts, Department of Sociology, Ann Arbor, MI 48109. Offers public policy and sociology (PhD); social work and sociology (PhD); sociology (PhD); women's studies and sociology (PhD). *Degree requirements:* For doctorate, comprehensive exam, thesis/dissertation, oral defense of dissertation, preliminary exam. *Entrance requirements:* For doctorate, GRE General Test, letters of recommendation, writing sample. Additional exam requirements/recommendations for international students: Required—TOEFL (minimum score 560 paper-based; 220 computer-based; 84 iBT). Electronic applications accepted. *Expenses:* Tuition, state resident: full-time $17,784; part-time $1116 per credit hour. Tuition, nonresident: full-time $35,944; part-time $2125 per credit hour. International tuition: $35,994 full-time. Required fees: $95 per semester. Tuition and fees vary according to course load, degree level and program. *Faculty research:* Power, history and social change; gender and sexuality; race and ethnicity; economic sociology; social demography.

University of Michigan, Horace H. Rackham School of Graduate Studies, College of Literature, Science, and the Arts, Department of Women's Studies, Ann Arbor, MI 48109. Offers English and women's studies (PhD); history and women's studies (PhD); lesbian, gay, bisexual, transgender, queer (LGBTQ) studies (Certificate); psychology and women's studies (PhD); sociology and women's studies (PhD); women's studies (Certificate). *Faculty:* 77 full-time (71 women). *Students:* 71 full-time (63 women); includes 6 Black or African American, non-Hispanic/Latino; 11 Asian, non-Hispanic/Latino; 7 Hispanic/Latino; 4 Two or more races, non-Hispanic/Latino. Average age 30. 101 applicants, 10% accepted, 9 enrolled. In 2010, 5 doctorates, 8 other advanced degrees awarded. *Degree requirements:* For doctorate, variable foreign language requirement, comprehensive exam (for some programs), thesis/dissertation. *Entrance requirements:* For doctorate, GRE General Test, previous undergraduate course work in women's studies; for Certificate, GRE General Test, previous course work in women's studies. Additional exam requirements/recommendations for international students: Required—TOEFL. *Application deadline:* For fall admission, 12/1 for domestic and international students. Application fee: $65 ($75 for international students). Electronic applications accepted. *Expenses:* Tuition, state resident: full-time $17,784; part-time $1116 per credit hour. Tuition, nonresident: full-time $35,944; part-time $2125 per credit hour. International tuition: $35,994 full-time. Required fees: $95 per semester. Tuition and fees vary according to course load, degree level and program. *Financial support:* In 2010–11, 39 students received support, including 21 fellowships with full tuition reimbursements available (averaging $16,800 per year), 18 teaching assistantships with full tuition reimbursements available (averaging $17,270 per year); career-related internships or fieldwork, institutionally sponsored loans, scholarships/grants, traineeships, health care benefits, and unspecified assistantships also available. *Faculty research:* Gender issues, LGBTQ studies, sexuality, women and science, global feminism. *Unit head:* Elizabeth R. Cole, Chair, Department of Women's Studies, Professor of Women's Studies, Professor of Afroamerican and African Studies, Professor of Psychology, 734-763-2047, Fax: 734-647-4943, E-mail: wsdgradInquiry@umich.edu. *Application contact:* Aimee Germain, Graduate Program Coordinator, 734-763-2047, Fax: 734-647-4943, E-mail: wsdgradinquiry@umich.edu.

University of Minnesota, Duluth, Graduate School, College of Liberal Arts, Department of Sociology/Anthropology, Duluth, MN 55812-2496. Offers criminology (MA); liberal studies (MLS). Part-time programs available. *Degree requirements:* For master's, thesis or alternative. *Entrance requirements:* For master's, interview, minimum GPA of 3.0, letters of recommendation. Additional exam requirements/recommendations for international students: Required—TOEFL. *Faculty research:* Nature of knowledge, philosophy of science, ecology, cultural studies, language.

University of Minnesota, Twin Cities Campus, Graduate School, College of Liberal Arts, Department of Sociology, Minneapolis, MN 55455-0213. Offers MA, PhD. Terminal master's awarded for partial completion of doctoral program. *Degree requirements:* For master's, thesis optional; for doctorate, thesis/dissertation, preliminary written exam, prospectus hearing, final oral defense. *Entrance requirements:* For doctorate, GRE General Test, bachelor's degree, official transcripts, minimum GPA of 3.0, personal statement, three letters of recommendation, writing sample. Additional exam requirements/recommendations for international students: Required—TOEFL (minimum score 550 paper-based; 79 iBT). Electronic applications accepted. *Faculty research:* Organizations, work, and markets; inequality: race, class, and gender; law, crime and deviance; family and life course; political sociology and social movements.

University of Mississippi, Graduate School, College of Liberal Arts, Department of Sociology and Anthropology, Oxford, University, MS 38677. Offers anthropology (MA); sociology (MA, MSS). *Students:* 32 full-time (15 women), 5 part-time (4 women); includes 12 minority (6 Black or African American, non-Hispanic/Latino; 1 American Indian or Alaska Native, non-Hispanic/Latino; 1 Hispanic/Latino; 1 Native Hawaiian or other Pacific Islander, non-Hispanic/Latino; 3 Two or more races, non-Hispanic/Latino), 1 international. In 2010, 11 master's awarded. *Degree requirements:* For master's, thesis (for some programs). *Entrance requirements:* For master's, GRE General Test, minimum GPA of 3.0. Additional exam requirements/recommendations for international students: Required—TOEFL. *Application deadline:* For fall admission, 4/1 for domestic students; for spring admission, 10/1 for domestic students. Applications are processed on a rolling basis. Application fee: $25. Electronic applications accepted. *Financial support:* Scholarships/grants available. Financial award application deadline: 3/1; financial award applicants required to submit FAFSA. *Unit head:* Dr. Kirsten A. Dellinger, Chairman, 662-915-7421, Fax: 662-915-5372, E-mail: kdelling@olemiss.edu. *Application contact:* Dr. Christy M. Wyandt, Associate Dean, 662-915-7474, Fax: 662-915-7577, E-mail: cwyandt@olemiss.edu.

University of Missouri, Graduate School, College of Arts and Sciences, Department of Sociology, Columbia, MO 65211. Offers MA, PhD. *Degree requirements:* For doctorate, one foreign language, comprehensive exam, thesis/dissertation. *Entrance requirements:* For master's and doctorate, GRE General Test, minimum GPA of 3.0; 15 hours of undergraduate sociology with minimum B average, including one course each in sociological theory and basic statistics. Additional exam requirements/recommendations for international students: Required—TOEFL (minimum score 500 paper-based; 173 computer-based; 61 iBT). Electronic applications accepted. *Faculty research:* Culture and identity; political and economic institutions and social movements; social control and deviance; social inequalities.

University of Missouri–Kansas City, College of Arts and Sciences, Department of Sociology, Kansas City, MO 64110-2499. Offers MA, PhD. PhD (interdisciplinary) offered through the School of Graduate Studies. Part-time and evening/weekend programs available. *Faculty:* 13 full-time (7 women), 1 (woman) part-time/adjunct. *Students:* 1 (woman) full-time, 14 part-time (10 women); includes 3 minority (2 Black or African American, non-Hispanic/Latino; 1 Hispanic/Latino), 2 international. Average age 32. 12 applicants, 25% accepted, 1 enrolled. In 2010, 2 master's awarded. *Degree requirements:* For master's, thesis optional. *Entrance requirements:* For master's, GRE, minimum GPA of 3.0 in major, 2.7 overall. Additional exam requirements/recommendations for international students: Required—TOEFL (minimum score 550 paper-based; 213 computer-based; 80 iBT). *Application deadline:* For fall admission, 3/1 for domestic and international students; for spring admission, 11/1 for domestic and international students. Applications are processed on a rolling basis. Application fee: $45 ($50 for international students). Electronic applications accepted. *Expenses:* Tuition, state resident: full-time $5522.40; part-time $306.80 per credit hour. Tuition, nonresident: full-time $7128; part-time $792 per credit hour. Required fees: $261.15 per term. *Financial support:* In 2010–11, 1 research assistantship with full tuition reimbursement (averaging $12,000 per year), 4 teaching assistantships with full and partial tuition reimbursements (averaging $12,000 per year) were awarded; career-related internships or fieldwork, Federal Work-Study, institutionally sponsored loans, and tuition waivers (partial) also available. Support available to part-time students. Financial award application deadline: 3/1; financial award applicants required to submit FAFSA. *Faculty research:* Gerontology, religious movements, urban community and neighborhoods. *Unit head:* Dr. Linda Breytspraak, Chairperson, 816-235-2514, Fax: 816-235-1117. *Application contact:* Dr. Deborah Smith, Graduate Advisor, 816-235-2529, Fax: 816-235-1117, E-mail: smithde@umkc.edu.

The University of Montana, Graduate School, College of Arts and Sciences, Department of Sociology, Missoula, MT 59812-0002. Offers criminology (MA); rural and environmental change (MA); sociology (MA). *Entrance requirements:* For master's, GRE General Test. Additional exam requirements/recommendations for international students: Required—TOEFL. *Faculty research:* Housing, homelessness, hunger, infant mortality, work safety.

University of Nebraska–Lincoln, Graduate College, College of Arts and Sciences, Department of Sociology, Lincoln, NE 68588. Offers MA, PhD. *Degree requirements:* For master's, thesis optional; for doctorate, comprehensive exam, thesis/dissertation. *Entrance requirements:* For master's and doctorate, GRE General Test, writing sample. Additional exam requirements/recommendations for international students: Required—TOEFL (minimum score 550 paper-based; 213 computer-based). Electronic applications accepted. *Faculty research:* Family, deviance and social control, ethnic studies, inequality (gender, race, and class).

University of Nevada, Las Vegas, Graduate College, College of Liberal Arts, Department of Sociology, Las Vegas, NV 89154-5003. Offers MA, PhD. Part-time programs available. *Faculty:* 13 full-time (4 women). *Students:* 32 full-time (22 women), 15 part-time (7 women); includes 25 minority (5 Black or African American, non-Hispanic/Latino; 1 Asian, non-Hispanic/Latino; 4 Hispanic/Latino; 15 Two or more races, non-Hispanic/Latino), 1 international. Average age 34. 31 applicants, 39% accepted, 7 enrolled. In 2010, 2 master's, 2 doctorates awarded. *Degree requirements:* For master's, thesis, oral exams; for doctorate, comprehensive exam, thesis/dissertation, oral exams. *Entrance requirements:* For master's and doctorate, GRE General Test. Additional exam requirements/recommendations for international students: Required—TOEFL (minimum score 550 paper-based; 213 computer-based), IELTS (minimum score 7). *Application deadline:* For fall admission, 12/1 priority date for domestic and international students. Applications are processed on a rolling basis. Application fee: $60 ($95 for international students). Electronic applications accepted. *Expenses:* Tuition, area resident: Part-time $239.50 per credit. Tuition, state resident: part-time $239.50 per credit. Tuition, nonresident:

Sociology

University of Nevada, Las Vegas (continued)
part-time $503 per credit. Required fees: $108 per semester. Tuition and fees vary according to course load, program and reciprocity agreements. *Financial support:* In 2010–11, 28 students received support, including 12 research assistantships with partial tuition reimbursements available (averaging $12,125 per year), 16 teaching assistantships with partial tuition reimbursements available (averaging $12,000 per year); institutionally sponsored loans, scholarships/grants, health care benefits, and unspecified assistantships also available. Financial award application deadline: 3/1. *Faculty research:* Urban and community studies, political sociology and social movements, health and environment, culture, social psychology. Total annual research expenditures: $28,872. *Unit head:* Dr. Dmitri Shalin, Chair/ Professor, 702-895-0259, Fax: 702-895-4800, E-mail: shalin@unlv.nevada.edu. *Application contact:* Graduate College Admissions Evaluator, 702-895-3320, Fax: 702-895-4180, E-mail: gradcollege@unlv.edu.

University of Nevada, Reno, Graduate School, College of Liberal Arts, School of Social Research and Justice Studies, Department of Sociology, Reno, NV 89557. Offers MA. *Degree requirements:* For master's, thesis optional. *Entrance requirements:* For master's, GRE General Test, minimum GPA of 2.75. Additional exam requirements/recommendations for international students: Required—TOEFL (minimum score 500 paper-based; 173 computer-based; 61 iBT), IELTS (minimum score 6). Electronic applications accepted. *Expenses:* Tuition, state resident: full-time $2219; part-time $246 per credit. Tuition, nonresident: part-time $510 per credit. International tuition: $9009 full-time. Required fees: $59 per term. One-time fee: $101. Tuition and fees vary according to course load. *Faculty research:* Statistics, politics and economics, religion and law, industry, theory stratification.

University of New Brunswick Fredericton, School of Graduate Studies, Faculty of Arts, Department of Sociology, Fredericton, NB E3B 5A3, Canada. Offers MA, PhD. Part-time programs available. *Faculty:* 10 full-time (7 women), 2 part-time/adjunct (1 woman). *Students:* 23 full-time (12 women), 6 part-time (4 women). In 2010, 2 master's, 2 doctorates awarded. *Degree requirements:* For master's, thesis; for doctorate, comprehensive exam, thesis/dissertation, 6 courses. *Entrance requirements:* For master's, minimum GPA of 3.5; for doctorate, minimum GPA of 3.0, MA in sociology with thesis or equivalent, curriculum vitae, statement of interest about interview research. Additional exam requirements/recommendations for international students: Required—TOEFL (minimum score 650 paper-based). *Application deadline:* For fall admission, 3/1 priority date for domestic students. Application fee: $50 Canadian dollars. *Expenses:* Tuition, area resident: Full-time $3708; part-time $927 per term. International tuition: $6300 full-time. Required fees: $50 per term. *Financial support:* In 2010–11, teaching assistantships with full tuition reimbursements (averaging $17,000 per year). *Faculty research:* Social policy; media, communication and culture; family and domestic violence; sociology of health and health care. *Unit head:* Dr. Vanda Rideout, Director of Graduate Studies, 506-447-3393, Fax: 506-453-4659, E-mail: vrideout@unb.ca. *Application contact:* Joyce Smith, Acting Graduate Secretary, 506-458-7474, Fax: 506-453-4659, E-mail: socio@unb.ca.

University of New Hampshire, Graduate School, College of Liberal Arts, Department of Sociology, Durham, NH 03824. Offers MA, PhD. Part-time programs available. *Faculty:* 12 full-time. *Students:* 32 full-time (25 women), 8 part-time (7 women); includes 5 minority (1 Black or African American, non-Hispanic/Latino; 4 Hispanic/Latino), 2 international. Average age 31. 47 applicants, 45% accepted, 7 enrolled. In 2010, 2 master's, 3 doctorates awarded. *Degree requirements:* For master's, thesis; for doctorate, one foreign language, thesis/dissertation. *Entrance requirements:* For master's and doctorate, GRE General Test. Additional exam requirements/recommendations for international students: Required—TOEFL (minimum score 550 paper-based; 213 computer-based; 80 iBT). *Application deadline:* For fall admission, 4/1 priority date for domestic students, 4/1 for international students; for spring admission, 12/1 for domestic students. Applications are processed on a rolling basis. Application fee: $65. Electronic applications accepted. *Financial support:* In 2010–11, 23 students received support, including 2 fellowships, 2 research assistantships, 17 teaching assistantships; career-related internships or fieldwork, Federal Work-Study, scholarships/grants, and tuition waivers (full and partial) also available. Support available to part-time students. Financial award application deadline: 2/15. *Faculty research:* Deviance, conflict and control, social psychology, comparative institutional analysis, family. *Unit head:* Dr. Michele Dillon, Chairperson, 603-862-1814. *Application contact:* Deena Peschke, Administrative Assistant, 603-862-2500, E-mail: sociology.dept@unh.edu.

University of New Mexico, Graduate School, College of Arts and Sciences, Department of Sociology, Albuquerque, NM 87131-2039. Offers MA, PhD, MWR/MCRP. Part-time programs available. *Faculty:* 31 full-time (13 women), 27 part-time/adjunct (10 women). *Students:* 31 full-time (18 women), 10 part-time (6 women); includes 2 Black or African American, non-Hispanic/Latino; 1 American Indian or Alaska Native, non-Hispanic/Latino; 5 Hispanic/Latino, 3 international. Average age 34. 36 applicants, 39% accepted, 6 enrolled. In 2010, 2 master's, 3 doctorates awarded. Terminal master's awarded for partial completion of doctoral program. *Degree requirements:* For master's, thesis; for doctorate, comprehensive exam, thesis/dissertation. *Entrance requirements:* For master's and doctorate, GRE General Test, 2 writing samples, 3 letters of reference, letter of intent. Additional exam requirements/recommendations for international students: Required—TOEFL (minimum score 550 paper-based; 213 computer-based; 79 iBT), IELTS (minimum score 7). *Application deadline:* For fall admission, 1/15 priority date for domestic and international students; for spring admission, 9/30 for domestic and international students. Application fee: $50. Electronic applications accepted. *Expenses:* Tuition, state resident: full-time $5991; part-time $251 per credit hour. Tuition, nonresident: full-time $14,405; part-time $800.20 per credit hour. Tuition and fees vary according to course level, course load, program and reciprocity agreements. *Financial support:* In 2010–11, 35 students received support, including 1 fellowship (averaging $13,500 per year), 3 research assistantships (averaging $12,394 per year), 17 teaching assistantships with partial tuition reimbursements available (averaging $13,817 per year); institutionally sponsored loans, scholarships/grants, health care benefits, tuition waivers (partial), and unspecified assistantships also available. Support available to part-time students. Financial award applicants required to submit FAFSA. *Faculty research:* Criminology/deviance, gender, Latin American/comparative sociology, political sociology, race and ethnicity, social movements, religion, social welfare, work/organizations. Total annual research expenditures: $696,098. *Unit head:* Dr. Beverly Burris, Chair, 505-277-2501, Fax: 505-277-8805, E-mail: bburris@unm.edu. *Application contact:* Kaitlin Coalson, Academic Advisor, 505-277-2501, Fax: 505-277-8805, E-mail: kcoalson@unm.edu.

University of New Orleans, Graduate School, College of Liberal Arts, Department of Sociology, New Orleans, LA 70148. Offers MA. Part-time and evening/weekend programs available. *Degree requirements:* For master's, thesis (for some programs). *Entrance requirements:* For master's, GRE General Test. Additional exam requirements/recommendations for international students: Required—TOEFL (minimum score 550 paper-based; 213 computer-based; 79 iBT). Electronic applications accepted. *Faculty research:* Environment and gender.

The University of North Carolina at Chapel Hill, Graduate School, College of Arts and Sciences, Department of Sociology, Chapel Hill, NC 27599. Offers MA, PhD. *Degree requirements:* For master's, comprehensive exam, thesis; for doctorate, comprehensive exam, thesis/dissertation. *Entrance requirements:* For master's and doctorate, GRE General Test, minimum GPA of 3.0. Additional exam requirements/recommendations for international students: Required—TOEFL (minimum score 550 paper-based; 213 computer-based). Electronic applications accepted. *Faculty research:* Comparative historical, work/organizations, religion, demography, stratification.

The University of North Carolina at Charlotte, Graduate School, College of Arts and Sciences, Department of Sociology, Charlotte, NC 28223-0001. Offers health research (MA); mathematical sociology and quantitative methods (MA); organizations, occupations, and work (MA); political sociology (MA); race and gender (MA); social psychology (MA); social theory (MA); sociology of education (MA); stratification (MA). Part-time and evening/weekend programs available. *Faculty:* 18 full-time (10 women). *Students:* 11 full-time (7 women), 14 part-time (8 women); includes 6 minority (4 Black or African American, non-Hispanic/Latino; 2 Asian, non-Hispanic/Latino). Average age 29. 20 applicants, 60% accepted, 8 enrolled. In 2010, 2 master's awarded. *Degree requirements:* For master's, thesis or alternative, thesis or comprehensive exam. *Entrance requirements:* For master's, GRE or MAT, minimum GPA of 3.0 in last 2 years, 2.75 overall. Additional exam requirements/recommendations for international students: Required—TOEFL (minimum score 557 paper-based; 220 computer-based; 83 iBT). *Application deadline:* For fall admission, 7/1 for domestic students, 5/1 for international students; for spring admission, 11/1 for domestic students, 10/1 for international students. Applications are processed on a rolling basis. Application fee: $55. Electronic applications accepted. *Expenses:* Tuition, state resident: full-time $3464. Tuition, nonresident: full-time $14,297. Required fees: $2094. Tuition and fees vary according to course load. *Financial support:* In 2010–11, 6 students received support, including 1 fellowship (averaging $60,000 per year), 1 research assistantship (averaging $9,000 per year), 1 teaching assistantship (averaging $9,000 per year); career-related internships or fieldwork, institutionally sponsored loans, scholarships/grants, and unspecified assistantships also available. Support available to part-time students. Financial award application deadline: 4/1; financial award applicants required to submit FAFSA. *Faculty research:* Social psychology, sociology of education, social gerontology, quantitative methodology, medical sociology. Total annual research expenditures: $61,382. *Unit head:* Dr. Lisa Rachotte, Chair, 704-687-2288, Fax: 704-687-3091, E-mail: lrashott@uncc.edu. *Application contact:* Kathy B. Giddings, Director of Graduate Admissions, 704-687-5503, Fax: 704-687-3279, E-mail: gradadm@uncc.edu.

The University of North Carolina at Greensboro, Graduate School, College of Arts and Sciences, Department of Sociology, Greensboro, NC 27412-5001. Offers criminology (MA); sociology (MA). Part-time programs available. *Degree requirements:* For master's, comprehensive exam, thesis. *Entrance requirements:* For master's, GRE General Test. Additional exam requirements/recommendations for international students: Required—TOEFL. Electronic applications accepted.

The University of North Carolina Wilmington, College of Arts and Sciences, Department of Sociology and Criminology, Wilmington, NC 28403-3297. Offers criminology (MA); public sociology (MA). *Faculty:* 20 full-time (9 women). *Students:* 14 full-time (10 women), 6 part-time (4 women); includes 1 Black or African American, non-Hispanic/Latino. Average age 27. 24 applicants, 42% accepted, 7 enrolled. In 2010, 6 master's awarded. *Degree requirements:* For master's, comprehensive exam, thesis or internship. *Entrance requirements:* Additional exam requirements/recommendations for international students: Required—TOEFL (minimum score 550 paper-based; 217 computer-based; 79 iBT), IELTS (minimum score 6.5). *Application deadline:* For fall admission, 6/15 for domestic students. Application fee: $60. Electronic applications accepted. *Financial support:* In 2010–11, 5 teaching assistantships with full and partial tuition reimbursements (averaging $9,500 per year) were awarded; unspecified assistantships also available. *Unit head:* Dr. Kimberly J. Cook, Chair, 910-962-3785, E-mail: cookk@uncw.edu. *Application contact:* Dr. Michael Maume, Graduate Coordinator, 910-962-7749, E-mail: maumm@uncw.edu.

University of North Dakota, Graduate School, College of Arts and Sciences, Department of Sociology, Grand Forks, ND 58202. Offers MA. *Faculty:* 9 full-time (3 women). *Students:* 4 full-time (3 women), 6 part-time (2 women); includes 2 minority (both American Indian or Alaska Native, non-Hispanic/Latino). Average age 27. 9 applicants, 56% accepted, 5 enrolled. In 2010, 10 master's awarded. *Degree requirements:* For master's, thesis, final examination. *Entrance requirements:* For master's, minimum GPA of 3.0. Additional exam requirements/recommendations for international students: Required—TOEFL (minimum score 550 paper-based; 213 computer-based; 79 iBT), IELTS (minimum score 6.5). *Application deadline:* For fall admission, 8/1 priority date for domestic students, 5/1 priority date for international students; for spring admission, 12/1 priority date for domestic students, 9/1 priority date for international students. Applications are processed on a rolling basis. Application fee: $35. Electronic applications accepted. *Expenses:* Tuition, state resident: full-time $5857; part-time $306.74 per credit. Tuition, nonresident: full-time $15,666; part-time $729.77 per credit. Required fees: $53.42 per credit. Tuition and fees vary according to course load, program and reciprocity agreements. *Financial support:* In 2010–11, 4 students received support, including 4 teaching assistantships with full and partial tuition reimbursements available (averaging $9,632 per year); fellowships with full and partial tuition reimbursements available, research assistantships with full and partial tuition reimbursements available, Federal Work-Study, institutionally sponsored loans, scholarships/grants, health care benefits, tuition waivers (full and partial), and unspecified assistantships also available. Support available to part-time students. Financial award application deadline: 3/15; financial award applicants required to submit FAFSA. *Faculty research:* Criminal justice studies, social psychology, research methods, corrections, social theory. Total annual research expenditures: $180,567. *Unit head:* Dr. Abdallah Badahdah, Graduate Director, 701-777-4424, Fax: 701-777-2468, E-mail: abdallah.badahdah@und.nodak.edu. *Application contact:* Matt Anderson, Admissions Specialist, 701-777-2947, Fax: 701-777-3619, E-mail: matthew.anderson@gradschool.und.edu.

University of Northern Colorado, Graduate School, College of Humanities and Social Sciences, School of Sociology and Criminal Justice, Greeley, CO 80639. Offers criminal justice (MA); sociology (MA). *Faculty:* 11 full-time (6 women). *Students:* 6 full-time (2 women), 6 part-time (3 women); includes 2 Black or African American, non-Hispanic/Latino; 1 American Indian or Alaska Native, non-Hispanic/Latino; 1 Hispanic/Latino, 3 international. Average age 34. 13 applicants, 62% accepted, 0 enrolled. In 2010, 8 master's awarded. *Expenses:* Tuition, state resident: full-time $6199; part-time $344 per credit hour. Tuition, nonresident: full-time $14,834; part-time $824 per credit hour. Required fees: $1091; $60.60 per credit hour. Tuition and fees vary according to course load, degree level and program. *Financial support:* In 2010–11, 2 teaching assistantships (averaging $5,698 per year) were awarded. *Unit head:* Dr. Denise A. Battles, Dean, 970-351-2877, Fax: 970-351-2176. *Application contact:* Linda Sisson, Graduate Student Admission Coordinator, 970-351-1807, Fax: 970-351-2371, E-mail: linda.sisson@unco.edu.

University of Northern Iowa, Graduate College, College of Social and Behavioral Sciences, Department of Sociology, Anthropology and Criminology, Cedar Falls, IA 50614. Offers criminology (MA); sociology (MA). Part-time and evening/weekend programs available. *Students:* 14 full-time (8 women), 5 part-time (3 women); includes 2 minority (1 Black or African American, non-Hispanic/Latino; 1 American Indian or Alaska Native, non-Hispanic/Latino), 1 international. 27 applicants, 48% accepted, 9 enrolled. In 2010, 4 master's awarded. *Degree requirements:* For master's, thesis. *Entrance requirements:* For master's, minimum GPA of 3.0. Additional exam requirements/recommendations for international students: Required—TOEFL (minimum score 500 paper-based; 180 computer-based; 61 iBT). *Application deadline:* For fall admission, 8/1 priority date for domestic students. Applications are processed on a rolling basis. Application fee: $50 ($70 for international students). Electronic applications accepted. *Financial support:* Career-related internships or fieldwork, Federal Work-Study, scholarships/grants, and tuition waivers (full and partial) available. Support available to part-time students. Financial award application deadline: 2/1. *Unit head:* Dr. Kent Sandstrom, Head/Professor, 319-273-2786, Fax: 319-273-7104, E-mail: kent.sandstrom@uni.edu. *Application contact:* Laurie S. Russell, Record Analyst, 319-273-2623, Fax: 319-273-2885, E-mail: laurie.russell@uni.edu.

University of North Texas, Toulouse Graduate School, College of Public Affairs and Community Service, Department of Sociology, Denton, TX 76203. Offers global and comparative (PhD); health and illness (PhD); social stratification and inequality (PhD); sociology (MA, MS). Terminal master's awarded for partial completion of doctoral program. *Degree requirements:* For master's, variable foreign language requirement, comprehensive exam, thesis (for some programs); for doctorate, variable foreign language requirement, comprehensive exam, thesis/dissertation. *Entrance requirements:* For master's, GRE General Test, 4 letters of recommendation; for doctorate, GRE General Test, master's degree, 4 letters of recommendation. Additional exam requirements/recommendations for international students: Required—TOEFL (minimum score 550 paper-based; 213 computer-based; 79 iBT). *Application deadline:* Applications are processed on a rolling basis. Electronic applications accepted. *Expenses:* Tuition, state resident: full-time $4298; part-time $239 per credit hour. Tuition, nonresident: full-time $10,782; part-time $549 per credit hour. Required fees: $1292; $270 per credit hour. *Financial support:* Fellowships, research assistantships, teaching assistantships, career-related internships or fieldwork, Federal Work-Study, institutionally sponsored loans, scholarships/grants, health care benefits, tuition waivers (partial), and unspecified assistantships available. Support available to part-time students. Financial award applicants required to submit FAFSA. *Faculty research:* Health and illness, social inequality, globalization and development, family. *Application contact:* Graduate Adviser, 940-565-2296, Fax: 940-369-7035, E-mail: seward@unt.edu.

University of Notre Dame, Graduate School, College of Arts and Letters, Division of Social Science, Department of Sociology, Notre Dame, IN 46556. Offers PhD. *Degree requirements:* For doctorate, thesis/dissertation, 2 area specialty exams. *Entrance requirements:* For doctorate, GRE General Test, GRE Subject Test (strongly recommended). Additional exam requirements/recommendations for international students: Required—TOEFL (minimum score 600 paper-based; 250 computer-based; 80 iBT). Electronic applications accepted. *Faculty research:* Cultural sociology, development, family, education, historical/comparative sociology.

University of Oklahoma, College of Arts and Sciences, Department of Sociology, Norman, OK 73019. Offers MA, PhD. *Faculty:* 14 full-time (9 women). *Students:* 28 full-time (17 women), 7 part-time (5 women); includes 8 minority (2 Black or African American, non-Hispanic/Latino; 1 American Indian or Alaska Native, non-Hispanic/Latino; 2 Asian, non-Hispanic/Latino; 3 Two or more races, non-Hispanic/Latino), 1 international. Average age 30. 12 applicants, 75% accepted, 6 enrolled. In 2010, 2 master's, 2 doctorates awarded. Terminal master's awarded for partial completion of doctoral program. *Degree requirements:* For master's, thesis or alternative; for doctorate, thesis/dissertation, general exams, qualifying exam. *Entrance requirements:* For master's and doctorate, GRE General Test, 3 letters of recommendation. Additional exam requirements/recommendations for international students: Required—TOEFL (minimum score 550 paper-based; 213 computer-based; 79 iBT). *Application deadline:* For fall admission, 2/15 priority date for domestic students, 2/15 for international students; for spring admission, 11/1 for domestic students, 9/1 for international students. Applications are processed on a rolling basis. Application fee: $40 ($90 for international students). Electronic applications accepted. *Expenses:* Tuition, state resident: full-time $3893; part-time $162.20 per credit hour. Tuition, nonresident: full-time $14,167; part-time $590.30 per credit hour. Required fees: $2523; $94.60 per credit hour. Tuition and fees vary according to course load and degree level. *Financial support:* In 2010–11, 2 fellowships with full tuition reimbursements (averaging $5,000 per year), 27 teaching assistantships with partial tuition reimbursements (averaging $13,969 per year) were awarded; health care benefits and unspecified assistantships also available. Financial award application deadline: 3/15; financial award applicants required to submit FAFSA. *Faculty research:* Criminology, sociology of gender, sociology of family, social stratification, demography. Total annual research expenditures: $10,051. *Unit head:* Dr. Craig St. John, Chair, 405-325-1751, Fax: 405-325-7825, E-mail: cstjohn@ou.edu. *Application contact:* Dr. Amy Kroska, Associate Professor and Director of Graduate Studies, 405-325-1751, Fax: 405-325-7825, E-mail: amykroska@ou.edu.

University of Oregon, Graduate School, College of Arts and Sciences, Department of Sociology, Eugene, OR 97403. Offers MA, MS, PhD. Part-time programs available. Terminal master's awarded for partial completion of doctoral program. *Degree requirements:* For doctorate, thesis/dissertation. *Entrance requirements:* For master's and doctorate, GRE General Test, minimum GPA of 3.0. Additional exam requirements/recommendations for international students: Required—TOEFL. *Faculty research:* Criminology, environment, gender, labor, political economy.

University of Ottawa, Faculty of Graduate and Postdoctoral Studies, Faculty of Social Sciences, Department of Sociology and Anthropology, Ottawa, ON K1N 6N5, Canada. Offers MA. *Degree requirements:* For master's, thesis or alternative. *Entrance requirements:* For master's, honors bachelor's degree or equivalent, minimum B average. Electronic applications accepted. *Faculty research:* Inter-ethnic relations, development, political policies.

University of Pennsylvania, School of Arts and Sciences, Graduate Group in Sociology, Philadelphia, PA 19104. Offers AM, PhD. *Faculty:* 39 full-time (16 women), 8 part-time/adjunct (5 women). *Students:* 42 full-time (33 women), 1 (woman) part-time; includes 5 Black or African American, non-Hispanic/Latino; 1 American Indian or Alaska Native, non-Hispanic/Latino; 2 Asian, non-Hispanic/Latino; 3 Hispanic/Latino, 9 international. 217 applicants, 6% accepted, 5 enrolled. In 2010, 4 master's, 6 doctorates awarded. Terminal master's awarded for partial completion of doctoral program. *Degree requirements:* For master's, thesis or alternative; for doctorate, one foreign language, thesis/dissertation. *Entrance requirements:* For master's and doctorate, GRE General Test. Additional exam requirements/recommendations for international students: Required—TOEFL. *Application deadline:* For fall admission, 12/1 priority date for domestic students. Application fee: $70. Electronic applications accepted. *Expenses:* Tuition: Full-time $25,660; part-time $4758 per course. Required fees: $2152; $270 per course. Tuition and fees vary according to course load, degree level and program. *Financial support:* Fellowships, teaching assistantships, institutionally sponsored loans, scholarships/grants, traineeships, health care benefits, and unspecified assistantships available. Financial award application deadline: 12/15. *Unit head:* Emily Hannum, Graduate Chair, 215-898-9633, E-mail: hannumem@soc.upenn.edu. *Application contact:* Audra Rodgers, Graduate Coordinator, 215-898-5711, E-mail: arodgers@sas.upenn.edu.

University of Pittsburgh, School of Arts and Sciences, Department of Sociology, Pittsburgh, PA 15260. Offers MA, PhD. Part-time programs available. *Faculty:* 16 full-time (9 women). *Students:* 35 full-time (20 women), 3 part-time (2 women); includes 4 Black or African American, non-Hispanic/Latino; 6 Asian, non-Hispanic/Latino; 1 Hispanic/Latino. Average age 28. 93 applicants, 6% accepted, 6 enrolled. In 2010, 1 master's, 2 doctorates awarded. Terminal master's awarded for partial completion of doctoral program. *Degree requirements:* For master's, thesis; for doctorate, comprehensive exam, thesis/dissertation, preliminary exam. *Entrance requirements:* For master's and doctorate, GRE General Test, writing sample. Additional exam requirements/recommendations for international students: Required—TOEFL (minimum score 550 paper-based; 213 computer-based). *Application deadline:* For fall admission, 3/15 priority date for domestic and international students. Application fee: $50. Electronic applications accepted. *Expenses:* Tuition, state resident: full-time $17,304; part-time $701 per credit. Tuition, nonresident: full-time $29,554; part-time $1210 per credit. Required fees: $740; $214 per term. Tuition and fees vary according to program. *Financial support:* In 2010–11, 3 fellowships with full tuition reimbursements, 1 research assistantship with full tuition reimbursement, 19 teaching assistantships with full tuition reimbursements were awarded; scholarships/grants, health care benefits, tuition waivers (partial), and unspecified assistantships also available. Financial award application deadline: 1/15. *Faculty research:* Collective behavior/social movements, comparative sociology/historical sociology, cultural sociology, political sociology, qualitative methodology, quantitative methodology, sex and gender, social change, theory. *Unit head:* Dr. Kathleen Blee, Chairman, 412-648-7584, Fax: 412-648-2799, E-mail: jm2@pitt.edu. *Application contact:* Paulette Jean Hill, Graduate Administrator, 412-648-7585, Fax: 412-648-2799, E-mail: pjh40@pitt.edu.

University of Puerto Rico, Río Piedras, College of Social Sciences, Department of Sociology, San Juan, PR 00931-3300. Offers MA. *Degree requirements:* For master's, comprehensive exam, thesis. *Entrance requirements:* For master's, GRE or PAEG, interview, minimum GPA of 3.0, letter of recommendation.

University of Regina, Faculty of Graduate Studies and Research, Faculty of Arts, Department of Sociology and Social Studies, Regina, SK S4S 0A2, Canada. Offers social studies (MA); sociology (MA). Part-time programs available. *Faculty:* 12 full-time (5 women), 1 part-time/adjunct (0 women). *Students:* 7 full-time (3 women), 5 part-time (4 women). 10 applicants, 70% accepted. In 2010, 3 master's awarded. *Degree requirements:* For master's, thesis. *Entrance requirements:* Additional exam requirements/recommendations for international students: Required—TOEFL (minimum score 580 paper-based; 80 iBT). *Application deadline:* Applications are processed on a rolling basis. Application fee: $10 ($100 for international students). Electronic applications accepted. Tuition and fees charges are reported in Canadian dollars. *Expenses:* Tuition, area resident: Full-time $3244.50 Canadian dollars; part-time $180.25 Canadian dollars per credit hour. International tuition: $4744.50 Canadian dollars full-time. Required fees: $494 Canadian dollars; $115.25 Canadian dollars per credit hour. $115.25 Canadian dollars per semester. Tuition and fees vary according to program. *Financial support:* In 2010–11, 1 fellowship (averaging $18,000 per year), 2 research assistantships (averaging $16,500 per year), 2 teaching assistantships (averaging $6,759 per year) were awarded; scholarships/grants also available. Financial award application deadline: 6/15. *Faculty research:* Social justice, international development, globalization, social policy, political economy. *Unit head:* Dr. John Conway, Head, 306-585-4052, Fax: 306-585-4815, E-mail: john.conway@uregina.ca. *Application contact:* Dr. Henry Chow, Graduate Program Coordinator, 306-585-5604, Fax: 306-585-4815, E-mail: henry.chow@uregina.ca.

University of Saskatchewan, College of Graduate Studies and Research, College of Arts and Sciences, Department of Sociology, Saskatoon, SK S7N 5A2, Canada. Offers MA, PhD. *Degree requirements:* For master's, thesis; for doctorate, comprehensive exam (for some programs), thesis/dissertation. *Entrance requirements:* Additional exam requirements/recommendations for international students: Required—TOEFL (minimum score 80 iBT); Recommended—IELTS (minimum score 6.5). Electronic applications accepted.

University of South Africa, College of Human Sciences, Pretoria, South Africa. Offers adult education (M Ed); African languages (MA, PhD); African politics (MA, PhD); Afrikaans (MA, PhD); ancient history (MA, PhD); ancient Near Eastern studies (MA, PhD); anthropology (MA, PhD); applied linguistics (MA); Arabic (MA, PhD); archaeology (MA); art history (MA); Biblical archaeology (MA); Biblical studies (M Th, D Th, PhD); Christian spirituality (M Th, D Th); church history (M Th, D Th); classical studies (MA, PhD); clinical psychology (MA); communication (MA, PhD); comparative education (M Ed, Ed D); consulting psychology (D Admin, D Com, PhD); curriculum studies (M Ed, Ed D); development studies (M Admin, MA, D Admin, PhD); didactics (M Ed, Ed D); education (M Tech); education management (M Ed, Ed D); educational psychology (M Ed); English (MA); environmental education (M Ed); French (MA, PhD); German (MA, PhD); Greek (MA); guidance and counseling (M Ed); health studies (MA, PhD), including health sciences education (MA), health services management (MA), medical and surgical nursing science (critical care general) (MA), midwifery and neonatal nursing science (MA), trauma and emergency care (MA); history (MA, PhD); history of education (Ed D); inclusive education (M Ed, Ed D); information and communications technology policy and regulation (MA); information science (MA, MIS, PhD); international politics (MA, PhD); Islamic studies (MA, PhD); Italian (MA, PhD); Judaica (MA, PhD); linguistics (MA, PhD); mathematical education (M Ed); mathematics education (MA); missiology (M Th, D Th); modern Hebrew (MA, PhD); musicology (MA, MMus, D Mus, PhD); natural science education (M Ed); New Testament (M Th, D Th); Old Testament (D Th); pastoral therapy (M Th, D Th); philosophy (MA); philosophy of education (M Ed, Ed D); politics (MA, PhD); Portuguese (MA, PhD); practical theology (M Th, D Th); psychology (MA, MS, PhD); psychology of education (M Ed, Ed D); public health (MA); religious studies (MA, D Th, PhD); Romance languages (MA); Russian (MA, PhD); Semitic languages (MA, PhD); social behavior studies in HIV/AIDS (MA); social science (mental health) (MA); social science in development studies (MA); social science in psychology (MA); social science in social work (MA); social science in sociology (MA); social work (MSW, DSW, PhD); socio-education (M Ed, Ed D); sociolinguistics (MA); sociology (MA, PhD); Spanish (MA, PhD); systematic theology (M Th, D Th); TESOL (teaching English to speakers of other languages) (MA); theological ethics (M Th, D Th); theory of literature (MA, PhD); urban ministries (D Th); urban ministry (M Th).

University of South Alabama, Graduate School, College of Arts and Sciences, Department of Sociology, Anthropology and Social Work, Mobile, AL 36688-0002. Offers sociology (MA). Part-time and evening/weekend programs available. *Faculty:* 10 full-time (1 woman). *Students:* 5 full-time (2 women), 2 part-time (both women); includes 1 Black or African American, non-Hispanic/Latino. 3 applicants, 0% accepted, 0 enrolled. *Degree requirements:* For master's, comprehensive exam, thesis optional. *Entrance requirements:* For master's, GRE General Test, minimum GPA of 3.0. Additional exam requirements/recommendations for international students: Required—TOEFL. *Application deadline:* For fall admission, 7/15 priority date for domestic students, 6/15 priority date for international students. Applications are processed on a rolling basis. Application fee: $35. *Expenses:* Tuition, state resident: part-time $300 per credit hour. Tuition, nonresident: part-time $600 per credit hour. Required fees: $150 per semester. *Financial support:* Fellowships, research assistantships available. Financial award application deadline: 4/1. *Faculty research:* Cultural adaptation. *Unit head:* Dr. Roma S. Hanks, Chair, 251-460-6347, Fax: 251-460-7925. *Application contact:* Dr. Nicole Carr, Graduate Coordinator, 251-460-6347, Fax: 251-460-7925, E-mail: ntcarr@jaguar1.usouthal.edu.

University of South Carolina, The Graduate School, College of Arts and Sciences, Department of Sociology, Columbia, SC 29208. Offers MA, PhD. Part-time programs available. Terminal master's awarded for partial completion of doctoral program. *Degree requirements:* For master's, thesis; for doctorate, comprehensive exam, thesis/dissertation. *Entrance requirements:* For master's and doctorate, GRE General Test. Additional exam requirements/recommendations for international students: Required—TOEFL (minimum score 570 paper-based; 230 computer-based; 75 iBT). Electronic applications accepted. *Faculty research:* Social psychology, social inequality.

University of Southern California, Graduate School, Dana and David Dornsife College of Letters, Arts and Sciences, Department of Sociology, Los Angeles, CA 90089. Offers PhD. *Faculty:* 22 full-time (11 women), 2 part-time/adjunct (0 women). *Students:* 34 full-time (19 women); includes 11 minority (1 Black or African American, non-Hispanic/Latino; 1 American Indian or Alaska Native, non-Hispanic/Latino; 3 Asian, non-Hispanic/Latino; 6 Hispanic/Latino), 6 international. 98 applicants, 7% accepted, 3 enrolled. In 2010, 6 doctorates awarded. *Degree requirements:* For doctorate, comprehensive exam, thesis/dissertation. *Entrance requirements:* For doctorate, GRE. Additional exam requirements/recommendations for international students: Required—TOEFL. *Application deadline:* For fall admission, 12/1 for domestic and international students. Application fee: $85. Electronic applications accepted. *Expenses:* Tuition: Full-time $31,240; part-time $1420 per unit. Required fees: $600. One-time fee: $35 full-time. Full-time tuition and fees vary according to degree level and program. *Financial support:* In 2010–11, 28 students received support, including 12 fellowships with full tuition reimbursements available (averaging $23,000 per year), 6 research assistantships with full tuition reimbursements available (averaging $23,000 per year), 10 teaching assistantships with full tuition reimbursements available (averaging $20,000 per year). Financial award application deadline: 12/1; financial award applicants required to submit FAFSA. *Faculty research:* Family, immigration, gender, culture, race. *Unit head:* Dr. Tim Biblarz, Chair, 213-740-3574, Fax: 213-740-3535, E-mail: biblarz@dornsife.usc,edu. *Application contact:* Stachelle L. Overland, Academic Advisor, 213-740-8851, Fax: 213-740-3535, E-mail: overland@dornsife.usc.edu.

University of South Florida, Graduate School, College of Arts and Sciences, Department of Sociology, Tampa, FL 33620-9951. Offers MA, PhD. Part-time programs available. *Faculty:* 6 full-time (4 women). *Students:* 21 full-time (12 women), 5 part-time (3 women); includes 1 Black or African American, non-Hispanic/Latino; 3 Asian, non-Hispanic/Latino; 1 Hispanic/Latino, 1 international. Average age 29. 37 applicants, 43% accepted, 11 enrolled. In 2010, 4 master's awarded. *Degree requirements:* For master's, comprehensive exam, thesis; for doctorate, comprehensive exam, thesis/dissertation. *Entrance requirements:* For master's, GRE General Test, minimum GPA of 3.0 in last 60 hours. Additional exam requirements/recommendations for international students: Required—TOEFL (minimum score 550 paper-based; 213 computer-based). *Application deadline:* For fall admission, 2/15 priority date for domestic students, 1/2 priority date for international students; for spring admission, 10/15 for domestic students, 6/1 priority date for international students. Application fee: $30. Electronic applications accepted. *Financial support:* In 2010–11, 2 research assistantships (averaging $16,000 per year), 16 teaching assistantships with tuition reimbursements (averaging $15,003 per year) were awarded; unspecified assistantships also available. Financial award application

Sociology

University of South Florida (continued)

deadline: 3/1. Total annual research expenditures: $279,530. *Unit head:* Dr. Maralee Mayberry, Chairperson, 813-974-2241, Fax: 813-974-6455, E-mail: mayberry@chuma1.cas.usf.edu. *Application contact:* Dr. Donileen R. Loseke, Program Director, 813-974-2517, Fax: 813-974-6455, E-mail: dloseke@cas.usf.edu.

The University of Tennessee, Graduate School, College of Arts and Sciences, Department of Sociology, Knoxville, TN 37996. Offers criminology (MA, PhD); energy, environment, and resource policy (MA, PhD); political economy (MA, PhD). Part-time programs available. *Degree requirements:* For master's, thesis or alternative; for doctorate, thesis/dissertation. *Entrance requirements:* For master's, GRE General Test, minimum GPA of 3.0; for doctorate, GRE General Test, minimum GPA of 3.5. Additional exam requirements/recommendations for international students: Required—TOEFL. Electronic applications accepted. *Expenses:* Tuition, state resident: full-time $7440; part-time $414 per credit hour. Tuition, nonresident: full-time $22,478; part-time $1250 per credit hour. Required fees: $922; $43 per credit hour. Tuition and fees vary according to program.

The University of Texas at Arlington, Graduate School, College of Liberal Arts, Department of Sociology and Anthropology, Program in Sociology, Arlington, TX 76019. Offers MA. Part-time and evening/weekend programs available. *Faculty:* 10 full-time (6 women). *Students:* 11 full-time (6 women), 15 part-time (10 women); includes 11 minority (6 Black or African American, non-Hispanic/Latino; 2 Asian, non-Hispanic/Latino; 3 Hispanic/Latino), 1 international. 13 applicants, 85% accepted, 8 enrolled. In 2010, 4 master's awarded. *Degree requirements:* For master's, comprehensive exam, thesis or alternative. *Entrance requirements:* For master's, GRE General Test, 12 hours of undergraduate course work in sociology. Additional exam requirements/recommendations for international students: Required—TOEFL (minimum score 550 paper-based; 213 computer-based). *Application deadline:* For fall admission, 6/15 for domestic students. Applications are processed on a rolling basis. Application fee: $35 ($50 for international students). Electronic applications accepted. *Expenses:* Tuition, state resident: full-time $7500. Tuition, nonresident: full-time $13,080. International tuition: $13,250 full-time. *Financial support:* In 2010–11, 3 teaching assistantships (averaging $9,000 per year) were awarded; research assistantships, Federal Work-Study also available. Financial award application deadline: 4/1. *Application contact:* Dr. Bob Kunovich, Graduate Advisor, 817-272-2650, Fax: 817-272-3759, E-mail: kunovich@uta.edu.

The University of Texas at Austin, Graduate School, College of Liberal Arts, Department of Sociology, Austin, TX 78712-1111. Offers MA, PhD. *Degree requirements:* For master's, thesis; for doctorate, thesis/dissertation. *Entrance requirements:* For master's and doctorate, GRE General Test. Additional exam requirements/recommendations for international students: Required—TOEFL. Electronic applications accepted. *Faculty research:* Criminology, demography, Latin America, health, political sociology.

The University of Texas at Dallas, School of Economic, Political and Policy Sciences, Program in Sociology, Richardson, TX 75080. Offers applied sociology (MS). *Faculty:* 3 full-time (0 women). *Students:* 8 full-time (6 women), 4 part-time (1 woman); includes 5 minority (2 Black or African American, non-Hispanic/Latino; 1 Asian, non-Hispanic/Latino; 2 Hispanic/Latino). Average age 34. 14 applicants, 57% accepted, 7 enrolled. In 2010, 10 master's awarded. *Degree requirements:* For master's, internship. *Entrance requirements:* For master's, GRE General Test, minimum GPA of 3.0 in upper-level coursework in field. Additional exam requirements/recommendations for international students: Required—TOEFL (minimum score 550 paper-based; 215 computer-based). *Application deadline:* For fall admission, 7/15 for domestic students, 5/1 priority date for international students; for spring admission, 11/15 for domestic students, 9/1 priority date for international students. Applications are processed on a rolling basis. Application fee: $50 ($100 for international students). Electronic applications accepted. *Expenses:* Tuition, state resident: full-time $10,248; part-time $569 per credit hour. Tuition, nonresident: full-time $18,544; part-time $1030 per credit hour. Tuition and fees vary according to course load. *Financial support:* In 2010–11, 7 students received support; research assistantships with partial tuition reimbursements available, teaching assistantships with partial tuition reimbursements available, career-related internships or fieldwork, Federal Work-Study, institutionally sponsored loans, and scholarships/grants available. Support available to part-time students. Financial award application deadline: 4/30. *Faculty research:* Religion and social change among new immigrants, social identity, inequality. *Unit head:* Dr. Sheryl L. Skaggs, Associate Program Head, 972-883-4460, Fax: 972-883-2735, E-mail: slskaggs@utdallas.edu. *Application contact:* Dr. Sheryl L. Skaggs, Associate Program Head, 972-883-4460, Fax: 972-883-2735, E-mail: slskaggs@utdallas.edu.

See Close-Up on page 811.

The University of Texas at El Paso, Graduate School, College of Liberal Arts, Department of Sociology and Anthropology, El Paso, TX 79968-0001. Offers Latin American and border studies (MA, Certificate); sociology (MA). Part-time and evening/weekend programs available. *Students:* 17 (11 women); includes 3 Black or African American, non-Hispanic/Latino; 10 Hispanic/Latino, 1 international. Average age 34. In 2010, 2 master's awarded. *Degree requirements:* For master's, thesis optional. *Entrance requirements:* For master's, GRE General Test, minimum GPA of 3.0. Additional exam requirements/recommendations for international students: Required—TOEFL. *Application deadline:* For fall admission, 8/15 priority date for domestic students, 3/1 for international students; for spring admission, 12/15 priority date for domestic students, 9/1 for international students. Applications are processed on a rolling basis. Application fee: $15 ($65 for international students). Electronic applications accepted. *Financial support:* In 2010–11, research assistantships with partial tuition reimbursements (averaging $18,625 per year), teaching assistantships with partial tuition reimbursements (averaging $14,900 per year) were awarded; career-related internships or fieldwork, Federal Work-Study, institutionally sponsored loans, and scholarships/grants also available. Financial award application deadline: 3/15; financial award applicants required to submit FAFSA. *Unit head:* Josiah Heyman, Chair, 915-747-5740, E-mail: jmheyman@utep.edu. *Application contact:* Dr. Charles H. Ambler, Dean of the Graduate School, 915-747-5491 Ext. 7886, Fax: 915-747-5788, E-mail: cambler@utep.edu.

The University of Texas at San Antonio, College of Liberal and Fine Arts, Department of Sociology, San Antonio, TX 78249-0617. Offers MS. Part-time and evening/weekend programs available. *Faculty:* 11 full-time (3 women). *Students:* 21 full-time (10 women), 41 part-time (28 women); includes 32 minority (9 Black or African American, non-Hispanic/Latino; 1 American Indian or Alaska Native, non-Hispanic/Latino; 3 Asian, non-Hispanic/Latino; 18 Hispanic/Latino; 1 Two or more races, non-Hispanic/Latino), 4 international. Average age 32. 32 applicants, 81% accepted, 22 enrolled. In 2010, 11 master's awarded. *Degree requirements:* For master's, comprehensive exam (for some programs), thesis (for some programs). *Entrance requirements:* For master's, GRE General Test, undergraduate course work in sociology or related areas. Additional exam requirements/recommendations for international students: Required—TOEFL (minimum score 500 paper-based; 173 computer-based; 61 iBT), IELTS (minimum score 5). *Application deadline:* For fall admission, 7/1 for domestic students, 4/1 for international students; for spring admission, 11/1 for domestic students, 9/1 for international students. Applications are processed on a rolling basis. Application fee: $45 ($80 for international students). Electronic applications accepted. *Expenses:* Tuition, state resident: full-time $4172; part-time $231.75 per credit hour. Tuition, nonresident: full-time $15,332; part-time $851.75 per credit hour. *Financial support:* In 2010–11, 2 students received support, including 10 research assistantships (averaging $9,824 per year); career-related internships or fieldwork, scholarships/grants, and unspecified assistantships also available. Support available to part-time students. *Faculty research:* Social welfare and social policy, violent behavior and homicide, migration and immigration to the U. S./Mexico border, educational experiences of Latino children, sociology of marriage and family. Total annual research expenditures: $21,348. *Unit head:* Dr. Raquel R. Marquez, Chair, 210-458-5606, Fax: 210-458-4619, E-mail: raquel.marquez@utsa.edu. *Application contact:* Veronica Ramirez, Assistant Dean of the Graduate School, 210-458-4330, Fax: 210-458-4332, E-mail: graduatestudies@utsa.edu.

The University of Texas at Tyler, College of Arts and Sciences, Department of Social Sciences, Tyler, TX 75799-0001. Offers criminal justice (MS); public administration (MPA); sociology (MS). Part-time and evening/weekend programs available. *Degree requirements:* For master's, comprehensive exam, thesis optional. *Entrance requirements:* For master's, GRE General Test, minimum GPA of 3.0. Additional exam requirements/recommendations for international students: Required—TOEFL (minimum score 79 computer-based). *Faculty research:* Urban segregation, minority business, violent crime, gender discrimination.

The University of Texas–Pan American, College of Social and Behavioral Sciences, Department of Sociology, Edinburg, TX 78539. Offers MS. Part-time programs available. *Degree requirements:* For master's, thesis or journal article. *Entrance requirements:* For master's, minimum GPA of 3.0, BS of BA in sociology or social science. Additional exam requirements/recommendations for international students: Required—TOEFL (minimum score 500 paper-based). *Faculty research:* Border studies, U.S.-Mexico issues, Mexican-American peoples, aging and gerontology.

The University of Toledo, College of Graduate Studies, College of Language, Literature and Social Sciences, Department of Sociology and Anthropology, Toledo, OH 43606-3390. Offers sociology (MA). Part-time programs available. *Faculty:* 10. *Students:* 11 full-time (7 women), 6 part-time (5 women); includes 6 minority (4 Black or African American, non-Hispanic/Latino; 1 Asian, non-Hispanic/Latino; 1 Hispanic/Latino), 1 international. Average age 32. 8 applicants, 88% accepted, 6 enrolled. In 2010, 6 master's awarded. *Degree requirements:* For master's, thesis or alternative. *Entrance requirements:* For master's, GRE, A minimum 2.7 cumulative point-hour ratio (on a 4.0 scale) for all previous academic work. Three Letters of Recommendation, a statement of purpose, and transcripts from all prior institutions attended. Additional exam requirements/recommendations for international students: Required—TOEFL (minimum score 550 paper-based; 213 computer-based; 80 iBT), IELTS (minimum score 6.5). *Application deadline:* For fall admission, 1/15 priority date for domestic and international students. Applications are processed on a rolling basis. Application fee: $45 ($75 for international students). Electronic applications accepted. *Expenses:* Tuition, state resident: full-time $11,426; part-time $476 per credit hour. Tuition, nonresident: full-time $21,660; part-time $903 per credit hour. One-time fee: $62. *Financial support:* Research assistantships with full tuition reimbursements, teaching assistantships with full tuition reimbursements, career-related internships or fieldwork, Federal Work-Study, institutionally sponsored loans, scholarships/grants, tuition waivers (full and partial), and unspecified assistantships available. Support available to part-time students. *Faculty research:* Medical and social gerontology, population, social movements, socioeconomic development, corporations and work, race and ethnicity. *Unit head:* Dr. Rubin Patterson, Chair, 419-530-7252, Fax: 419-530-8406, E-mail: rubin.patterson@utoledo.edu. *Application contact:* Graduate School Office, 419-530-4723, Fax: 419-530-4724, E-mail: grdsch@utnet.utoledo.edu.

University of Toronto, School of Graduate Studies, Social Sciences Division, Department of Sociology, Toronto, ON M5S 1A1, Canada. Offers M Ed, MA, Ed D, PhD. Part-time programs available. *Degree requirements:* For doctorate, thesis/dissertation. *Entrance requirements:* For master's, GRE (for applicants from non-Canadian universities, recommended for those from Canadian universities), 5 full-year courses in sociology, basic research and statistical skills; 2 letters of reference; for doctorate, GRE (required for applicants from non-Canadian universities; recommended for those from Canadian universities), MA in sociology, minimum A–average, 2 letters of reference.

University of Utah, Graduate School, College of Social and Behavioral Science, Department of Sociology, Salt Lake City, UT 84112-1107. Offers M Stat, MA, MS, PhD. *Faculty:* 11 full-time (7 women), 1 part-time/adjunct (0 women). *Students:* 21 full-time (13 women), 2 part-time (1 woman); includes 1 minority (Native Hawaiian or other Pacific Islander, non-Hispanic/Latino), 6 international. Average age 30. 35 applicants, 20% accepted, 7 enrolled. In 2010, 5 master's, 1 doctorate awarded. *Degree requirements:* For master's, thesis; for doctorate, comprehensive exam, thesis/dissertation. *Entrance requirements:* For master's and doctorate, GRE, minimum undergraduate GPA of 3.0. Additional exam requirements/recommendations for international students: Required—TOEFL (minimum score 550 paper-based; 213 computer-based). *Application deadline:* For fall admission, 2/1 priority date for domestic and international students. Applications are processed on a rolling basis. Application fee: $55 ($65 for international students). *Expenses:* Tuition, area resident: Part-time $179.19 per credit hour. Tuition, state resident: full-time $4384. Tuition, nonresident: full-time $16,684; part-time $630.67 per credit hour. Required fees: $350 per semester. Tuition and fees vary according to course load, degree level and program. *Financial support:* In 2010–11, 1 research assistantship with full tuition reimbursement (averaging $11,500 per year), 23 teaching assistantships with full and partial tuition reimbursements (averaging $11,500 per year) were awarded; Federal Work-Study, scholarships/grants, health care benefits, tuition waivers, and departmental waivers also available. Support available to part-time students. Financial award application deadline: 2/1; financial award applicants required to submit FAFSA. *Faculty research:* Comparative international sociology, population and health, criminology, diversity, demography. Total annual research expenditures: $19,042. *Unit head:* Dr. Jeffrey Kentor, Chair, 801-581-6153, Fax: 801-585-3784, E-mail: kentor@soc.utah.edu. *Application contact:* Dr. Ming Wen, Director of Graduate Studies, 801-581-6153, Fax: 801-585-3784, E-mail: ming.wen@soc.utah.edu.

University of Utah, Graduate School, Interdepartmental Program in Statistics, Salt Lake City, UT 84112-1107. Offers biostatistics (M Stat); econometrics (M Stat); educational psychology (M Stat); mathematics (M Stat); sociology (M Stat); statistics (M Stat). Part-time programs available. *Students:* 28 full-time (11 women), 17 part-time (9 women); includes 2 Black or African American, non-Hispanic/Latino; 2 Asian, non-Hispanic/Latino; 2 Hispanic/Latino, 10 international. Average age 30. 59 applicants, 44% accepted, 12 enrolled. In 2010, 15 master's awarded. *Degree requirements:* For master's, comprehensive exam, projects. *Entrance requirements:* For master's, GRE General Test (sociology and educational psychology), minimum GPA of 3.0; course work in calculus, matrix theory, statistics. Additional exam requirements/recommendations for international students: Required—TOEFL (minimum score 500 paper-based; 173 computer-based). *Application deadline:* For fall admission, 7/1 for domestic students, 4/1 for international students. Applications are processed on a rolling basis. Application fee: $55 ($65 for international students). *Expenses:* Tuition, area resident: Part-time $179.19 per credit hour. Tuition, state resident: full-time $4384. Tuition, nonresident: full-time $16,684; part-time $630.67 per credit hour. Required fees: $350 per semester. Tuition and fees vary according to course load, degree level and program. *Financial support:* Career-related internships or fieldwork available. *Faculty research:* Biostatistics, management, economics, educational psychology, mathematics. *Unit head:* Tariq Mughal, Chair, University Statistics Committee, 801-585-9547, E-mail: tariaq.mughal@business.utah.edu. *Application contact:* Laura Egbert, MSTAT Program Coordinator, 801-585-6853, E-mail: laura.demattia@utah.edu.

University of Victoria, Faculty of Graduate Studies, Faculty of Social Sciences, Department of Sociology, Victoria, BC V8W 2Y2, Canada. Offers MA, PhD. PhD by special arrangement. Part-time programs available. *Degree requirements:* For master's, thesis; for doctorate, thesis/dissertation, candidacy exam. *Entrance requirements:* For master's, minimum B+ average. Additional exam requirements/recommendations for international students: Required—TOEFL (minimum score 575 paper-based; 233 computer-based), IELTS (minimum score 7), TWE (minimum score 4). *Faculty research:* Social and political thought, social justice, health and aging, globalization and social psychology.

University of Virginia, College and Graduate School of Arts and Sciences, Department of Sociology, Charlottesville, VA 22903. Offers MA, PhD. *Faculty:* 16 full-time (7 women), 1 (woman) part-time/adjunct. *Students:* 51 full-time (24 women); includes 2 Black or African American, non-Hispanic/Latino; 2 Asian, non-Hispanic/Latino; 1 Hispanic/Latino, 11 international. Average age 29. 80 applicants, 40% accepted, 13 enrolled. In 2010, 5 master's, 4 doctorates awarded. *Degree requirements:* For master's, thesis; for doctorate, comprehensive exam, thesis/dissertation. *Entrance requirements:* For master's and doctorate, GRE General Test, GRE Subject Test, 2 letters of recommendation. Additional exam requirements/recommendations for international students: Required—TOEFL (minimum score 600 paper-based; 250 computer-based; 90 iBT), IELTS (minimum score 7). *Application deadline:* For fall admission, 1/1 for domestic and international students. Applications are processed on a rolling basis. Application fee: $60. Electronic applications accepted. *Financial support:* Applicants required to submit FAFSA. *Unit head:* Krishan Kumar, Chair, 434-924-7293, Fax: 434-924-7028, E-mail: sociology@virginia.edu. *Application contact:* Paul Kingston, Director, Graduate Admissions Committee, 434-924-6521, E-mail: pwk@virginia.edu.

University of Washington, Graduate School, College of Arts and Sciences, Department of Sociology, Seattle, WA 98195. Offers MA, PhD. *Degree requirements:* For master's, thesis; for doctorate, thesis/dissertation. *Entrance requirements:* For master's and doctorate, GRE General Test, minimum GPA of 3.0. Additional exam requirements/recommendations for international students: Required—TOEFL. Electronic applications accepted. *Faculty research:* Demography, criminology, social psychology, race/ethnicity/inequality, family.

University of Washington, Graduate School, School of Public Health, Department of Health Services, Seattle, WA 98195. Offers bioinformatics (PhD); cancer prevention and control (PhD); clinical research (MS); community oriented public health practice (MPH); economics or finance (PhD); evaluation sciences (PhD); executive program (MHA); health behavior and health promotion (PhD); health care and population health research (MPH); health policy analysis and process (PhD); health policy and analysis and process (MPH); health services (MS, PhD); health services administration (EMHA, MHA); in residence program (MHA); maternal and child health (MPH, PhD); occupational health (PhD); population health and social determinants (PhD); social and behavioral sciences (MPH); sociology and demography (PhD); JD/MHA; MHA/MBA; MHA/MD; MHA/MPA; MPH/JD; MPH/MD; MPH/MN; MPH/MPA; MPH/MS; MPH/MSD; MPH/MSW; MPH/PhD. Part-time and evening/weekend programs available. Post-baccalaureate distance learning degree programs offered (minimal on-campus study). *Faculty:* 36 full-time (18 women), 59 part-time/adjunct (26 women). *Students:* 107 full-time (82 women), 101 part-time (82 women); includes 1 Black or African American, non-Hispanic/Latino; 1 American Indian or Alaska Native, non-Hispanic/Latino; 27 Asian, non-Hispanic/Latino; 10 Hispanic/Latino, 4 international. Average age 34. 426 applicants, 41% accepted, 106 enrolled. In 2010, 37 master's, 11 doctorates awarded. Terminal master's awarded for partial completion of doctoral program. *Degree requirements:* For master's, thesis (for some programs), practicum (MPH); for doctorate, comprehensive exam, thesis/dissertation. *Entrance requirements:* For master's and doctorate, GRE General Test, minimum GPA of 3.0. Additional exam requirements/recommendations for international students: Required—TOEFL (minimum score 580 paper-based; 237 computer-based; 92 iBT), IELTS (minimum score 7). *Application deadline:* For fall admission, 1/1 for domestic students, 11/1 for international students. Application fee: 75 Albanian leks. Electronic applications accepted. *Financial support:* In 2010–11, 47 students received support, including 10 fellowships with full and partial tuition reimbursements available (averaging $22,000 per year), 10 research assistantships with full and partial tuition reimbursements available (averaging $18,700 per year), 3 teaching assistantships with full and partial tuition reimbursements available (averaging $4,575 per year); institutionally sponsored loans, traineeships, and health care benefits also available. Financial award application deadline: 2/28; financial award applicants required to submit FAFSA. *Faculty research:* Public health practice, health promotion and disease prevention, maternal and child health, organizational behavior and culture, health policy. *Unit head:* Dr. Larry Kessler, Chair, 206-543-2930. *Application contact:* Kitty A. Andert, MPH/MS/PhD Program Manager, 206-616-2926, Fax: 206-543-3964, E-mail: kitander@u.washington.edu.

University of Waterloo, Graduate Studies, Faculty of Arts, Department of Sociology, Waterloo, ON N2L 3G1, Canada. Offers MA, PhD. Part-time programs available. *Degree requirements:* For master's, thesis (for some programs); for doctorate, one foreign language, thesis/dissertation. *Entrance requirements:* For master's, honors degree, minimum B+ average, resume, writing sample; for doctorate, master's degree, minimum A- average, resumé, writing sample. Additional exam requirements/recommendations for international students: Required—TOEFL, TWE. Electronic applications accepted. *Faculty research:* Theory, methods, stratification deviance, political sociology.

The University of Western Ontario, Faculty of Graduate Studies, Social Sciences Division, Department of Sociology, London, ON N6A 5B8, Canada. Offers MA, PhD. Terminal master's awarded for partial completion of doctoral program. *Degree requirements:* For master's, thesis (for some programs); for doctorate, one foreign language, comprehensive exam, thesis/dissertation. *Entrance requirements:* For master's, minimum B+ average, honors degree; for doctorate, minimum A- average. Additional exam requirements/recommendations for international students: Required—TOEFL. Electronic applications accepted. *Faculty research:* Social demography, class and change, health and aging, theory, methods.

University of West Florida, College of Professional Studies, Department of Health, Leisure, and Exercise Science, Community Health Education Program, Pensacola, FL 32514-5750. Offers aging studies (MS); health promotion and worksite wellness (MS); psychosocial (MS). Part-time and evening/weekend programs available. *Faculty:* 1 (woman) part-time/adjunct. *Students:* 11 full-time (all women), 4 part-time (2 women); includes 2 Black or African American, non-Hispanic/Latino; 1 Asian, non-Hispanic/Latino; 1 Hispanic/Latino. Average age 33. 10 applicants, 90% accepted, 6 enrolled. In 2010, 5 master's awarded. *Degree requirements:* For master's, thesis or alternative. *Entrance requirements:* For master's, GRE General Test, minimum GPA of 3.0. Additional exam requirements/recommendations for international students: Required—TOEFL (minimum score 550 paper-based; 213 computer-based). *Application deadline:* For fall admission, 6/1 for domestic students, 5/15 for international students; for spring admission, 10/1 for domestic and international students. Applications are processed on a rolling basis. Application fee: $30. *Expenses:* Tuition, state resident: full-time $4982; part-time $208 per credit hour. Tuition, nonresident: full-time $20,059; part-time $836 per credit hour. Required fees: $1365; $57 per credit hour. *Financial support:* Research assistantships, teaching assistantships, unspecified assistantships available. *Unit head:* Dr. John Todorovich, Chairperson, 850-473-7248, Fax: 850-474-2106. *Application contact:* Terry McCray, Assistant Director of Graduate Admissions, 850-473-7718, Fax: 850-473-7714, E-mail: gradadmissions@uwf.edu.

University of West Georgia, College of Arts and Sciences, Department of Sociology and Criminology, Carrollton, GA 30118. Offers criminology (MA); sociology (MA). Part-time and evening/weekend programs available. *Faculty:* 13 full-time (5 women), 5 part-time/adjunct (4 women). *Students:* 10 full-time (5 women), 8 part-time (4 women); includes 5 Black or African American, non-Hispanic/Latino; 1 Hispanic/Latino. Average age 28. 14 applicants, 29% accepted, 1 enrolled. In 2010, 8 master's awarded. *Degree requirements:* For master's, one foreign language, comprehensive exam (for some programs), thesis (for some programs). *Entrance requirements:* For master's, GRE General Test, minimum GPA of 2.5, references, intellectual biography. Additional exam requirements/recommendations for international students: Required—TOEFL. *Application deadline:* For fall admission, 7/17 for domestic students; for spring admission, 11/20 for domestic students. Applications are processed on a rolling basis. Application fee: $30. Electronic applications accepted. *Expenses:* Tuition, state resident: full-time $4130; part-time $173 per semester hour. Tuition, nonresident: full-time $16,524; part-time $689 per semester hour. Required fees: $1586; $44.01 per semester hour. $397 per semester. Tuition and fees vary according to program. *Financial support:* In 2010–11, 8 students received support, including 7 research assistantships with full tuition reimbursements available (averaging $6,000 per year); career-related internships or fieldwork, scholarships/grants, and unspecified assistantships also available. Financial award application deadline: 7/1; financial award applicants required to submit FAFSA. *Faculty research:* Criminology, gangs, courts, policing, ethics, women's studies, methods. *Unit head:* Dr. Laurel Holland, Interim Chair, 678-839-6505, Fax: 678-839-6506, E-mail: lholland@westga.edu. *Application contact:* Dr. Charles W. Clark, Dean, 678-839-6508, E-mail: cclark@westga.edu.

University of Windsor, Faculty of Graduate Studies, Faculty of Arts and Social Sciences, Department of Sociology and Anthropology, Windsor, ON N9B 3P4, Canada. Offers criminology (MA); sociology (MA); sociology-social justice (PhD). Part-time programs available. *Degree*

requirements: For master's, thesis; for doctorate, comprehensive exam, thesis/dissertation. *Entrance requirements:* For master's, minimum B+ average; for doctorate, writing sample, minimum B+ average. Additional exam requirements/recommendations for international students: Required—TOEFL (minimum score 560 paper-based; 220 computer-based). Electronic applications accepted. *Faculty research:* Power and social change; criminology/deviance; social psychology; comparative development; race and ethnic relations; family, sex, and gender, social justice.

University of Wisconsin–Madison, Graduate School, College of Letters and Science, Department of Sociology, Madison, WI 53706-1380. Offers rural sociology (MS); sociology (MS, PhD). Part-time programs available. Terminal master's awarded for partial completion of doctoral program. *Degree requirements:* For master's, thesis, oral exam; for doctorate, thesis/dissertation, preliminary and final oral exams, 4 seminars. *Entrance requirements:* For master's and doctorate, GRE General Test. Additional exam requirements/recommendations for international students: Required—TOEFL. Electronic applications accepted. *Expenses:* Tuition, state resident: full-time $9887; part-time $617.96 per credit. Tuition, nonresident: full-time $24,054; part-time $1503.40 per credit. Required fees: $67.63 per credit. Tuition and fees vary according to reciprocity agreements.

University of Wisconsin–Milwaukee, Graduate School, College of Letters and Sciences, Department of Sociology, Milwaukee, WI 53201-0413. Offers MA. Part-time programs available. *Faculty:* 17 full-time (7 women). *Students:* 18 full-time (10 women), 8 part-time (7 women); includes 2 Black or African American, non-Hispanic/Latino; 1 Asian, non-Hispanic/Latino. Average age 30. 32 applicants, 72% accepted, 13 enrolled. In 2010, 8 master's awarded. *Degree requirements:* For master's, thesis. *Entrance requirements:* For master's, GRE. *Application deadline:* For fall admission, 1/1 priority date for domestic students; for spring admission, 9/1 for domestic students. Applications are processed on a rolling basis. Application fee: $56 ($96 for international students). Electronic applications accepted. *Financial support:* In 2010–11, 1 fellowship, 16 teaching assistantships were awarded; career-related internships or fieldwork, unspecified assistantships, and project assistantships also available. Support available to part-time students. Financial award application deadline: 4/15; financial award applicants required to submit FAFSA. Total annual research expenditures: $104,814. *Unit head:* Pat Rubio Goldsmith, Representative, 414-229-6945, Fax: 847-673-4122, E-mail: goldsmit@uwm.edu. *Application contact:* General Information Contact, 414-229-4982, Fax: 414-229-6967, E-mail: gradschool@uwm.edu.

University of Wyoming, College of Arts and Sciences, Department of Sociology, Laramie, WY 82070. Offers MA. Part-time programs available. *Degree requirements:* For master's, thesis. *Entrance requirements:* For master's, GRE General Test, minimum GPA of 3.0. Additional exam requirements/recommendations for international students: Required—TOEFL (minimum score 525 paper-based). Electronic applications accepted. *Faculty research:* Gender, theory, international studies, law, social inequality.

Utah State University, School of Graduate Studies, College of Humanities, Arts and Social Sciences, Department of Sociology, Logan, UT 84322. Offers MA, MS, MSS, PhD. *Degree requirements:* For master's, thesis; for doctorate, comprehensive exam, thesis/dissertation. *Entrance requirements:* For master's, GRE General Test, minimum GPA of 3.0, recommendation letters; for doctorate, GRE General Test, minimum GPA of 3.0, recommendation letters, transcripts, personal statement, MS degree. Additional exam requirements/recommendations for international students: Required—TOEFL; Recommended—TWE. *Faculty research:* Demography, environmental/natural resource sociology, rural community change, international development, health studies.

Valdosta State University, Department of Sociology, Anthropology, and Criminal Justice, Valdosta, GA 31698. Offers criminal justice (MS); marriage and family therapy (MS); sociology (MS). *Accreditation:* AAMFT/COAMFTE. Part-time and evening/weekend programs available. *Faculty:* 18 full-time (9 women). *Students:* 3 full-time (2 women), 11 part-time (8 women); includes 6 minority (4 Black or African American, non-Hispanic/Latino; 1 American Indian or Alaska Native, non-Hispanic/Latino; 1 Asian, non-Hispanic/Latino). Average age 25. 6 applicants, 83% accepted, 5 enrolled. In 2010, 8 master's awarded. *Degree requirements:* For master's, thesis or alternative, comprehensive written and/or oral exams. *Entrance requirements:* For master's, GRE General Test or MAT (sociology, marriage and family therapy), minimum GPA of 2.5. Additional exam requirements/recommendations for international students: Required—TOEFL (minimum score 523 paper-based; 193 computer-based). *Application deadline:* For fall admission, 7/1 for domestic and international students; for spring admission, 11/15 for domestic and international students. Applications are processed on a rolling basis. Application fee: $35. Electronic applications accepted. *Expenses:* Tuition, state resident: full-time $5256; part-time $197 per credit hour. Tuition, nonresident: full-time $14,490; part-time $710 per credit hour. Required fees: $855 per semester. Tuition and fees vary according to course load and campus/location. *Financial support:* In 2010–11, 5 students received support, including 5 research assistantships with full tuition reimbursements available (averaging $3,652 per year); career-related internships or fieldwork, institutionally sponsored loans, scholarships/grants, and unspecified assistantships also available. Support available to part-time students. Financial award application deadline: 7/1; financial award applicants required to submit FAFSA. *Faculty research:* Police-civilian ride-along project. *Unit head:* Dr. Mike Capece, Acting Head, 229-333-5943, Fax: 229-333-5492. *Application contact:* Misty Lamb, Admissions Specialist, 229-333-5694, Fax: 229-245-3853, E-mail: mllamb@valdosta.edu.

Vanderbilt University, Graduate School, Department of Sociology, Nashville, TN 37240-1001. Offers MA, PhD. *Faculty:* 21 full-time (7 women). *Students:* 26 full-time (20 women), 2 part-time (both women); includes 4 Black or African American, non-Hispanic/Latino; 2 Hispanic/Latino; 1 Two or more races, non-Hispanic/Latino. Average age 28. 194 applicants, 9% accepted, 9 enrolled. In 2010, 3 master's, 2 doctorates awarded. *Degree requirements:* For master's, thesis; for doctorate, comprehensive exam, thesis/dissertation, area, qualifying, and final exams. *Entrance requirements:* For master's and doctorate, GRE General Test. Additional exam requirements/recommendations for international students: Required—TOEFL (minimum score 570 paper-based; 230 computer-based; 88 iBT). *Application deadline:* For fall admission, 1/15 for domestic and international students. Application fee: $0. Electronic applications accepted. *Financial support:* Fellowships with full tuition reimbursements, research assistantships, teaching assistantships with full tuition reimbursements, Federal Work-Study, institutionally sponsored loans, scholarships/grants, and health care benefits available. Financial award application deadline: 1/15; financial award applicants required to submit CSS PROFILE or FAFSA. *Faculty research:* Criminology, cultural sociology; gender, race, and ethics relations; deviant behavior and social control. *Unit head:* Dr. Katharine M. Donato, Chair, 615-322-7501, Fax: 615-322-7505, E-mail: katharine.donato@vanderbilt.edu. *Application contact:* Dr. Mariano Sana, Director of Graduate Studies, 615-322-4004, Fax: 615-322-7505, E-mail: mariano.sana@vanderbilt.edu.

Virginia Commonwealth University, Graduate School, College of Humanities and Sciences, Wilder School of Government and Public Affairs, Department of Sociology, Richmond, VA 23284-9005. Offers applied social research (CASR); sociology (MS). *Students:* 12 full-time (8 women), 9 part-time (4 women); includes 5 minority (2 Black or African American, non-Hispanic/Latino; 2 Hispanic/Latino; 1 Two or more races, non-Hispanic/Latino), 2 international. 14 applicants, 86% accepted, 8 enrolled. In 2010, 9 master's awarded. *Degree requirements:* For master's, thesis optional. *Entrance requirements:* For master's, GRE General Test. Additional exam requirements/recommendations for international students: Required—TOEFL (minimum score 600 paper-based; 250 computer-based; 100 iBT); Recommended—IELTS (minimum score 6.5). *Application deadline:* For fall admission, 7/15 for domestic students; for spring admission, 10/1 for domestic students. Application fee: $50. Electronic applications accepted. *Expenses:* Tuition, state resident: full-time $4308; part-time $479 per credit hour. Tuition, nonresident: full-time $8942; part-time $994 per credit hour. Required fees: $2000; $85 per credit hour. Tuition and fees vary according to course level, course load, degree level, campus/location and program. *Financial support:* Teaching assistantships, career-related internships or fieldwork, Federal Work-Study, institutionally sponsored loans, and tuition waivers (full

Sociology

Virginia Commonwealth University (continued)

and partial) available. Support available to part-time students. *Unit head:* Dr. Niraj Verma, Director, L. Douglas Wilder School of Government and Public Affairs, 804-827-0776, E-mail: nverma2@vcu.edu. *Application contact:* Dr. Sarah Jane Brubaker, Program Chair, 804-827-2400, Fax: 804-828-1027, E-mail: sbrubaker@vcu.edu.

Virginia Polytechnic Institute and State University, Graduate School, College of Liberal Arts and Human Sciences, Department of Sociology, Blacksburg, VA 24061. Offers race and social policy (Certificate); sociology (MS, PhD); women's and gender studies (Certificate). *Faculty:* 26 full-time (12 women), 1 (woman) part-time/adjunct. *Students:* 39 full-time (25 women), 7 part-time (3 women); includes 10 Black or African American, non-Hispanic/Latino; 2 Hispanic/Latino, 2 international. Average age 33. 27 applicants, 22% accepted, 5 enrolled. In 2010, 7 master's, 3 doctorates awarded. *Degree requirements:* For master's, comprehensive exam (for some programs), thesis (for some programs); for doctorate, comprehensive exam (for some programs), thesis/dissertation (for some programs). *Entrance requirements:* For master's and doctorate, GRE. Additional exam requirements/recommendations for international students: Required—TOEFL (minimum score 550 paper-based; 213 computer-based). *Application deadline:* For fall admission, 7/1 for domestic and international students; for spring admission, 12/1 for domestic and international students. Applications are processed on a rolling basis. Application fee: $65. Electronic applications accepted. *Expenses:* Tuition, state resident: full-time $9399; part-time $488 per credit hour. Tuition, nonresident: full-time $17,854; part-time $957.75 per credit hour. Required fees: $1534. Full-time tuition and fees vary according to program. *Financial support:* In 2010–11, 2 research assistantships with full tuition reimbursements (averaging $13,864 per year), 19 teaching assistantships with full tuition reimbursements (averaging $13,074 per year) were awarded; career-related internships or fieldwork, Federal Work-Study, scholarships/grants, health care benefits, and unspecified assistantships also available. Financial award application deadline: 1/15. *Faculty research:* Science and technology, deviance and criminology, social psychology, social organization, demography. Total annual research expenditures: $42,630. *Unit head:* Dr. John W. Ryan, UNIT HEAD, 540-231-6878, Fax: 540-231-3860, E-mail: johnryan@vt.edu. *Application contact:* Jim Hawdon, Contact, 540-231-7476, Fax: 540-231-3860, E-mail: hawdonj@vt.edu.

Washington State University, Graduate School, College of Liberal Arts, Department of Sociology, Pullman, WA 99164. Offers crime and deviance (MA, PhD); environments, community and demographics (MA, PhD); institutions and social organizations (MA, PhD); political sociology (MA, PhD); social inequality (MA, PhD); social psychology and life course (MA, PhD). *Faculty:* 22 full-time (14 women), 8 part-time/adjunct (3 women). *Students:* 42 full-time (23 women), 2 part-time (both women); includes 1 Black or African American, non-Hispanic/Latino; 1 American Indian or Alaska Native, non-Hispanic/Latino, 4 international. Average age 30. 71 applicants, 13% accepted, 9 enrolled. In 2010, 7 master's, 4 doctorates awarded. Terminal master's awarded for partial completion of doctoral program. *Degree requirements:* For master's, thesis; for doctorate, comprehensive exam, thesis/dissertation. *Entrance requirements:* For master's, GRE General Test, minimum GPA of 3.0; for doctorate, GRE General Test, MA in sociology, minimum GPA of 3.0. Additional exam requirements/recommendations for international students: Required—TOEFL (minimum score 550 paper-based). *Application deadline:* For fall admission, 1/15 priority date for domestic students, 1/15 for international students. Application fee: $50. Electronic applications accepted. *Expenses:* Tuition, state resident: full-time $8552; part-time $443 per credit. Tuition, nonresident: full-time $21,650; part-time $1083 per credit. Required fees: $846. *Financial support:* In 2010–11, 5 research assistantships with tuition reimbursements (averaging $12,749 per year), 36 teaching assistantships with tuition reimbursements (averaging $12,749 per year) were awarded; fellowships with tuition reimbursements, Federal Work-Study, institutionally sponsored loans, scholarships/grants, health care benefits, and unspecified assistantships also available. Support available to part-time students. Financial award application deadline: 4/1; financial award applicants required to submit FAFSA. *Faculty research:* Crime/deviance, environmental sociology, social inequality, social psychology, gender. Total annual research expenditures: $101,888. *Unit head:* Dr. Gregory Hooks, Chair, 509-335-4595, Fax: 509-335-6419, E-mail: hooks@mail.wsu.edu. *Application contact:* Dr. Tom Rotolo, Director of Graduate Studies, 509-335-4595, Fax: 509-335-6419, E-mail: rotolo@wsu.edu.

Wayne State University, College of Liberal Arts and Sciences, Department of Sociology, Detroit, MI 48202. Offers MA, PhD. *Faculty:* 10 full-time (6 women), 3 part-time/adjunct (2 women). *Students:* 49 full-time (37 women), 39 part-time (25 women); includes 42 minority (33 Black or African American, non-Hispanic/Latino; 1 American Indian or Alaska Native, non-Hispanic/Latino; 4 Asian, non-Hispanic/Latino; 4 Hispanic/Latino), 8 international. Average age 38. 25 applicants, 48% accepted, 8 enrolled. In 2010, 3 master's, 11 doctorates awarded. *Degree requirements:* For master's, thesis optional; for doctorate, thesis/dissertation. *Entrance requirements:* For master's, GRE General Test, GRE Subject Test, minimum GPA of 3.3; letters of reference; writing sample; for doctorate, GRE General Test, GRE Subject Test, minimum GPA of 3.5 in master's work; letters of reference. Additional exam requirements/recommendations for international students: Required—TOEFL (minimum score 550 paper-based; 213 computer-based); Recommended—TWE (minimum score 6). *Application deadline:* For fall admission, 7/1 for domestic students, 6/1 for international students; for winter admission, 10/1 for international students; for spring admission, 2/1 for international students. Application fee: $30 ($50 for international students). Electronic applications accepted. *Expenses:* Tuition, state resident: full-time $7662; part-time $478.85 per credit hour. Tuition, nonresident: full-time $16,920; part-time $1057.55 per credit hour. Required fees: $571.20; $35.70 per credit hour. $188.05 per semester. Tuition and fees vary according to course load and program. *Financial support:* In 2010–11, 5 fellowships with tuition reimbursements (averaging $14,547 per year), 2 research assistantships with tuition reimbursements (averaging $15,090 per year), 8 teaching assistantships with tuition reimbursements (averaging $15,181 per year) were awarded. *Faculty research:* Social deviance, family, social inequality, medical sociology. *Unit head:* Leon Wilson, Chair, 313-577-8131, E-mail: ab6077@wayne.edu. *Application contact:* Mary Cay Sengstock, Graduate Director, 313-577-3282, E-mail: m.sengstock@wayne.edu.

West Chester University of Pennsylvania, Office of Graduate Studies, College of Arts and Sciences, Department of Anthropology and Sociology, West Chester, PA 19383. Offers gerontology (Certificate); long term health care (MPA, MSA). Part-time and evening/weekend programs available. *Students:* 2 full-time (both women), 4 part-time (all women); includes 3 minority (all Black or African American, non-Hispanic/Latino). Average age 39. 3 applicants, 100% accepted, 1 enrolled. In 2010, 1 other advanced degree awarded. *Degree requirements:* For master's, comprehensive exam. *Entrance requirements:* For master's, MAT, GRE, or GMAT, interview, resume, 2 letters of reference. Additional exam requirements/recommendations for international students: Required—TOEFL (minimum score 550 paper-based; 213 computer-based; 80 iBT). *Application deadline:* For fall admission, 4/15 priority date for domestic students, 3/15 for international students; for spring admission, 10/15 for domestic students, 9/1 for international students. Applications are processed on a rolling basis. Application fee: $35.

Electronic applications accepted. *Expenses:* Tuition, state resident: full-time $6966; part-time $387 per credit. Tuition, nonresident: full-time $11,146; part-time $619 per credit. Required fees: $1614.40; $133.24 per credit. Part-time tuition and fees vary according to campus/location. *Financial support:* Unspecified assistantships available. Support available to part-time students. Financial award application deadline: 2/15; financial award applicants required to submit FAFSA. *Faculty research:* West African communities in the U. S., life-long learning and distance education, comparative religions. *Unit head:* Dr. Douglas McConatha, Chair and Graduate Coordinator, 610-436-2556, E-mail: dmcconatha@wcupa.edu. *Application contact:* Dr. Douglas McConatha, Chair and Graduate Coordinator, 610-436-2556, E-mail: dmcconatha@wcupa.edu.

Western Illinois University, School of Graduate Studies, College of Arts and Sciences, Department of Sociology and Anthropology, Macomb, IL 61455-1390. Offers sociology (MA). Part-time programs available. *Students:* 23 full-time (11 women), 8 part-time (6 women); includes 10 minority (6 Black or African American, non-Hispanic/Latino; 1 Asian, non-Hispanic/Latino; 2 Hispanic/Latino; 1 Two or more races, non-Hispanic/Latino), 2 international. Average age 27. 21 applicants, 57% accepted. In 2010, 9 master's awarded. *Degree requirements:* For master's, thesis or alternative. *Entrance requirements:* Additional exam requirements/recommendations for international students: Required—TOEFL (minimum score 550 paper-based; 213 computer-based; 80 iBT). *Application deadline:* Applications are processed on a rolling basis. Application fee: $30. Electronic applications accepted. *Expenses:* Tuition, state resident: full-time $6370; part-time $265.40 per credit hour. Tuition, nonresident: full-time $12,740; part-time $530.80 per credit hour. Required fees: $75.67 per credit hour. *Financial support:* In 2010–11, 14 students received support, including 13 research assistantships with full tuition reimbursements available (averaging $7,280 per year), 1 teaching assistantship with full tuition reimbursement available (averaging $8,400 per year). Financial award applicants required to submit FAFSA. *Unit head:* Dr. John Wozniak, Chairperson, 309-298-1056. *Application contact:* Evelyn Hoing, Assistant Director of Graduate Studies, 309-298-1806, Fax: 309-298-2345, E-mail: grad-office@wiu.edu.

Western Kentucky University, Graduate Studies, Potter College of Arts and Letters, Department of Sociology, Bowling Green, KY 42101. Offers criminology (MA); sociology (MA). Postbaccalaureate distance learning degree programs offered. *Degree requirements:* For master's, comprehensive exam, thesis optional, final exam. *Entrance requirements:* For master's, GRE General Test, minimum GPA of 3.0. Additional exam requirements/recommendations for international students: Required—TOEFL (minimum score 555 paper-based; 213 computer-based; 79 iBT). *Faculty research:* Criminology/delinquency, quantitative and survey research methodology, occupations/professions, sex and gender, demography.

Western Michigan University, Graduate College, College of Arts and Sciences, Department of Sociology, Kalamazoo, MI 49008. Offers MA, PhD. *Degree requirements:* For master's, thesis, oral exams; for doctorate, one foreign language, thesis/dissertation, oral exams, written exams. *Entrance requirements:* For doctorate, GRE General Test.

West Virginia University, Eberly College of Arts and Sciences, School of Applied Social Sciences, Department of Sociology, Morgantown, WV 26506. Offers applied social research (MA). Part-time programs available. *Degree requirements:* For master's, thesis or alternative. *Entrance requirements:* For master's, GRE General Test, minimum GPA of 2.75. Additional exam requirements/recommendations for international students: Required—TOEFL. *Faculty research:* Applied sociology, stratification, social/complex organization, research methodology criminology.

Wichita State University, Graduate School, Fairmount College of Liberal Arts and Sciences, Department of Sociology, Wichita, KS 67260. Offers MA. Part-time programs available. *Unit head:* Dr. Ronald R. Matson, Chair, 316-978-3280, Fax: 316-978-3281, E-mail: ron.matson@wichita.edu. *Application contact:* Dr. Twyla Hill, Graduate Coordinator, 316-978-3280, E-mail: twyla.hill@wichita.edu.

Wilfrid Laurier University, Faculty of Graduate and Postdoctoral Studies, Faculty of Arts, Department of Sociology, Waterloo, ON N2L 3C5, Canada. Offers health, family and well-being (MA); internationalization, migration and human rights (MA). *Faculty:* 16 full-time (9 women), 2 part-time/adjunct (1 woman). *Students:* 8 full-time (7 women), 1 international. 21 applicants, 62% accepted, 7 enrolled. In 2010, 8 master's awarded. *Entrance requirements:* For master's, honours BA with minimum B+ average and major in sociology. Additional exam requirements/recommendations for international students: Required—TOEFL (minimum score 89 iBT). *Application deadline:* For fall admission, 2/1 priority date for domestic and international students. Application fee: $100. Electronic applications accepted. Tuition and fees charges are reported in Canadian dollars. *Expenses:* Tuition, area resident: Full-time $15,300 Canadian dollars; part-time $1200 Canadian dollars per credit. International tuition: $21,300 Canadian dollars full-time. Required fees: $650 Canadian dollars; $100 Canadian dollars per credit. Tuition and fees vary according to course load, degree level, campus/location and program. *Financial support:* In 2010–11, 14 fellowships, 14 teaching assistantships were awarded; career-related internships or fieldwork, scholarships/grants, health care benefits, and unspecified assistantships also available. *Faculty research:* Internationalization, migration and human rights, health, families, and well-being. *Unit head:* Dr. Garry Potter, Acting Chairperson, 519-884-0710 Ext. 2729, Fax: 519-884-8854, E-mail: gpotter@wlu.ca. *Application contact:* Jennifer Williams, Graduate Admission and Records Officer, 519-884-0710 Ext. 3536, Fax: 519-884-1020, E-mail: gradstudies@wlu.ca.

William Paterson University of New Jersey, College of Humanities and Social Sciences, Wayne, NJ 07470-8420. Offers clinical and counseling psychology (MA); English (MA); history (MA); public policy and international affairs (MA); sociology (MA). Part-time and evening/weekend programs available. Electronic applications accepted.

Yale University, Graduate School of Arts and Sciences, Department of Sociology, New Haven, CT 06520. Offers comparative and historical sociology (PhD); cultural sociology and social theory (PhD); social stratification and the life course (PhD). *Degree requirements:* For doctorate, thesis/dissertation. *Entrance requirements:* For doctorate, GRE General Test.

York University, Faculty of Graduate Studies, Faculty of Arts, Program in Social and Political Thought, Toronto, ON M3J 1P3, Canada. Offers MA, PhD. Part-time programs available. *Degree requirements:* For master's, one foreign language, thesis or alternative, oral exams; for doctorate, one foreign language, comprehensive exam, thesis/dissertation. Electronic applications accepted.

York University, Faculty of Graduate Studies, Faculty of Arts, Program in Sociology, Toronto, ON M3J 1P3, Canada. Offers MA, PhD. Part-time programs available. *Degree requirements:* For master's, thesis or alternative; for doctorate, one foreign language, comprehensive exam, thesis/dissertation, analytical paper. Electronic applications accepted.

Survey Methodology

University of Maryland, College Park, Academic Affairs, College of Behavioral and Social Sciences, Joint Program in Survey Methodology, College Park, MD 20742. Offers MS, PhD. *Faculty:* 3 full-time (2 women), 1 part-time/adjunct (0 women). *Students:* 22 full-time (13 women), 18 part-time (10 women); includes 2 Black or African American, non-Hispanic/Latino; 1 Asian, non-Hispanic/Latino; 1 Hispanic/Latino; 2 Two or more races, non-Hispanic/Latino, 6 international. 47 applicants, 49% accepted, 17 enrolled. In 2010, 11 master's, 2 doctorates awarded. *Degree requirements:* For master's, thesis (for some programs), scholarly paper; for doctorate, thesis/dissertation. *Entrance requirements:* For master's, GRE General Test (recommended), minimum GPA of 3.0, 3 letters of recommendation; for doctorate, GRE General Test, minimum GPA of 3.0, 3 letters of recommendation. *Application deadline:* For fall admission, 1/15 for domestic and international students. Applications are processed on a rolling basis. Application fee: $75. Electronic applications accepted. *Expenses:* Tuition, state resident: part-time $471 per credit hour. Tuition, nonresident: part-time $1016 per credit hour. Required fees: $337 per term. *Financial support:* In 2010–11, 1 fellowship with full tuition reimbursement (averaging $19,386 per year), 5 research assistantships (averaging $15,266 per year), 10 teaching assistantships (averaging $14,248 per year) were awarded; Federal Work-Study also available. Support available to part-time students. Financial award applicants required to submit FAFSA. Total annual research expenditures: $1.9 million. *Unit head:* Roger Tourangeau, Director, 301-314-7911, Fax: 301-314-7912, E-mail: rtourang@umd.edu. *Application contact:* Dean of Graduate School, 301-405-0358, Fax: 301-314-9305.

University of Michigan, Horace H. Rackham School of Graduate Studies, Program in Survey Methodology, Ann Arbor, MI 48109. Offers MS, PhD, Certificate. Part-time programs available. Terminal master's awarded for partial completion of doctoral program. *Degree requirements:* For master's, internships; for doctorate, comprehensive exam, thesis/dissertation. *Entrance requirements:* For master's and doctorate, GRE, 3 letters of recommendation; for Certificate, current enrollment in a graduate degree program at University of Michigan or have completed one within past 5 years. Additional exam requirements/recommendations for international students: Required—TOEFL (minimum score 560 paper-based; 220 computer-based). Electronic applications accepted. *Expenses:* Contact institution. *Faculty research:* Survey methodology, statistics, psychology, sociology, social psychology.

University of Nebraska–Lincoln, Graduate College, Interdepartmental Area of Survey Research and Methodology, Lincoln, NE 68588. Offers MS, PhD. *Degree requirements:* For master's, comprehensive exam. *Entrance requirements:* For master's, GRE General Test or GMAT. Additional exam requirements/recommendations for international students: Required—TOEFL (minimum score 550 paper-based; 213 computer-based). Electronic applications accepted. *Faculty research:* Survey research and data analysis.

BRYN MAWR COLLEGE

Graduate School of Arts and Sciences
Programs in Archaeology, Classics, and History of Art

Programs of Study

The Graduate School of Arts and Sciences at Bryn Mawr College offers the following programs: Ph.D. in Classical and Near Eastern Archaeology; Ph.D. in Greek, Latin and Classical Studies; and Ph.D. in History of Art.

Research Facilities

The award-winning Rhys Carpenter Library, inaugurated in 1997, is a specialized library for history of art, archaeology, and classics. Fully wired carrels are reserved there for all graduate students in these fields. In addition to the more than 135,000 volumes in Carpenter Library, the tri-college library consortium of Bryn Mawr, Haverford, and Swarthmore Colleges contains more than 2 million volumes. Bryn Mawr currently subscribes to more than fifty art history journals. Online reference sources include the Bibliography of the History of Art, Art Index, ARTbibliographies Modern, Avery Index, ARTstor, and JSTOR.

The Ella Riegel Study Collection comprises about 6,500 archaeological items, including Athenian Red-Figure vases; Greek, Cypriot, and Egyptian pottery; Greek and Roman coins; representative artifacts in bronze, glass, terracotta, and wood; lamps; and an extensive collection of pottery samples from Tarsus.

Bryn Mawr's art collection numbers more than 25,000 items and is especially strong in works on paper. The College also owns more than 45,000 rare books, including one of the largest collections of incunabla in the United States, and more than 13,000 photographs illustrating the development of photography since the mid-nineteenth century.

Financial Aid

Bryn Mawr offers a number of fellowships for full-time study, as well as grants, tuition awards, and summer stipends. Fellowship stipends begin at $17,500, including a summer stipend, and can be guaranteed for multiple years. Special awards include Areté (Excellence) Fellowships with a package of $20,000 plus a health insurance subsidy. Each year, the Department offers four teaching assistantships and one collections assistantship, with a stipend of $14,000 and a health insurance subsidy. For students in the Graduate Group in Archaeology, Classics, and History of Art, additional competitive fellowships and curatorial internships for multidisciplinary study are available, with twelve-month stipends of $20,000 plus a health insurance subsidy.

Cost of Study

For the 2011–12 academic year, full-time tuition, consisting of six courses per year, is $34,110; part-time tuition is $5685 per course. Units of supervised work cost $910, and the fee for maintaining matriculation (continuing enrollment) is $460 per semester.

Living and Housing Costs

Students live locally or in Philadelphia. Shared apartments can be rented for $600 to $900 per month, studio apartments begin at $800 per month. Other expenses include transportation (about $165 per month if commuting from Philadelphia) and health insurance (approximately $2500 per year for domestic students and approximately $1500 for international students).

Location

Bryn Mawr is a suburb of Philadelphia, the fifth-largest city in the U.S. It is well served by rail lines and by bus. Philadelphia is renowned for music, museums, and sports, and it is also a culinary mecca, with restaurants serving many cuisines. The metropolitan area has more than 100 museums and fifty colleges and universities, with a total population of 220,000 students.

The College

Bryn Mawr is a liberal arts college for women, founded in 1885. It was the first women's college to offer graduate education through the Ph.D. and the first U.S. institution to offer fellowships to women for graduate study. Throughout its history, the College has been committed first and foremost to providing the most rigorous and challenging education to women and, in the Graduate School of Arts and Sciences, also to men. The current enrollment is 1,300 undergraduate students, 150 graduate students in the Graduate School of Arts and Sciences, and about 250 students in the Graduate School of Social Work and Social Research.

Applying

Application for admission and financial aid should be made on the form available from the Graduate School of Arts and Sciences. Applicants can also download this form from the Graduate School's Web site at http://www.brynmawr.edu/gsas/. The deadline for admission with financial aid is January 4. Applications for admission without financial aid are accepted until June 30.

Correspondence and Information

Teri Lobo, Administrative Assistant to the Dean
Graduate School of Arts and Sciences
Bryn Mawr College
101 North Merion Avenue
Bryn Mawr, Pennsylvania 19010
Phone: 610-526-5072
Fax: 610-526-5076
E-mail: tlobo@brynmawr.edu
Web site: http://www.brynmawr.edu/gsas/

Bryn Mawr College

THE FACULTY AND THEIR RESEARCH

Archaeology

Mehmet-Ali Ataç, Assistant Professor, Department of Classical and Near Eastern Archaeology; Ph.D., Harvard, 2003. Visual and intellectual traditions of the ancient Near East; Neo-Assyrian art and architecture, ancient Near Eastern and Egyptian kingship.

A. A. Donohue, Professor, Department of Classical and Near Eastern Archaeology; Ph.D., NYU, 1984. History and historiography of classical art.

Astrid Lindenlauf, Assistant Professor; Ph.D., University College (London), 2001. Greek art and archaeology, fortifications and warfare, urbanism, disposal and recycling practices.

Peter Magee, Associate Professor, Department of Classical and Near Eastern Archaeology; Ph.D., Sydney, 1996. Archaeology of South Asia, Iran, and Arabia; ancient imperialism; field methods; materials analysis.

James C. Wright, Professor and Chair, Department of Classical and Near Eastern Archaeology; Ph.D., Bryn Mawr, 1978. Prehistory of the Aegean basin, settlement forms and architecture of classical Greece, theory and method in archaeology.

Classics

Annette Baertschi, Assistant Professor; Ph.D., Humboldt, 2006. Post-Augustan poetry, ancient magic, Latin meter, reception.

Catherine Conybeare, Associate Professor; Ph.D., Toronto, 1997. Late antique and early medieval Latin prose, cultural history, critical theory.

Radcliffe G. Edmonds III, Associate Professor; Ph.D., Chicago, 1999. Greek myth, Greco-Roman religion and magic, Greek philosophy.

Russell T. Scott, Doreen C. Spitzer Professor of Latin and Classical Studies; Ph.D., Yale, 1964. Roman history and historiography, Latin literature, Roman archaeology.

History of Art

David J. Cast, Professor; Ph.D., Columbia, 1970. Renaissance art and criticism, architecture post-1400, twentieth-century British art.

Christiane Hertel, Professor; Ph.D., Tübingen, 1985. German, Austrian, and Netherlandish art and architecture; German intellectual history; aesthetics and art theory.

Homay King, Associate Professor; Ph.D., Berkeley, 2003. American film history; film, feminist, psychoanalytic, and rhetorical theory.

Steven Z. Levine, Leslie Clark Professor in the Humanities; Ph.D., Harvard, 1974. Sixteenth- to twentieth-century French painting, psychoanalysis, self-portraiture, visual theory.

Gridley McKim-Smith, Andrew W. Mellon Professor in the Humanities; Ph.D., Harvard, 1974. Seventeenth-century Spanish painting and sculpture, scientific analysis of works of art, costume.

Lisa Saltzman, Professor and Director of the Center for Visual Culture; Ph.D., Harvard, 1994. Post–World War II art and theory, gender and identity, memory and trauma.

APPENDIXES

Institutional Changes
Since the 2011 Edition

Following is an alphabetical listing of institutions that have recently closed, merged with other institutions, or changed their names or status. In the case of a name change, the former name appears first, followed by the new name.

Alliance Theological Seminary (Nyack, NY): now listed as a unit of Nyack College (Nyack, NY)

American InterContinental University (Houston, TX): name changed to American InterContinental University Houston

American InterContinental University Buckhead Campus (Atlanta, GA): closed

American InterContinental University Dunwoody Campus (Atlanta, GA): name changed to American InterContinental University Atlanta

American InterContinental University–London (London, United Kingdom): name changed to American InterContinental University London

Arkansas State University - Jonesboro (State University, AR): name changed to Arkansas State University

Bard Graduate Center for Studies in the Decorative Arts, Design, and Culture (New York, NY): name changed to Bard Graduate Center: Decorative Arts, Design History, Material Culture

Birmingham-Southern College (Birmingham, AL): no longer offers graduate degrees

California School of Podiatric Medicine at Samuel Merritt College (Oakland, CA): name changed to California School of Podiatric Medicine at Samuel Merritt University

Church of God Theological Seminary (Cleveland, TN): name changed to Pentecostal Theological Seminary

Clarke College (Dubuque, IA): name changed to Clarke University

College of Santa Fe (Santa Fe, NM): name changed to Santa Fe University of Art and Design and no longer offers graduate degrees

Dongguk Royal University (Los Angeles, CA): name changed to Dongguk University Los Angeles

Embry-Riddle Aeronautical University (Prescott, AZ): name changed to Embry-Riddle Aeronautical University–Prescott

Embry-Riddle Aeronautical University (Daytona Beach, FL): name changed to Embry-Riddle Aeronautical University–Daytona

Embry-Riddle Aeronautical University Worldwide (Daytona Beach, FL): name changed to Embry-Riddle Aeronautical University—Worldwide

Emily Carr Institute of Art & Design (Vancouver, BC, Canada): name changed to Emily Carr University of Art & Design

Emmanuel School of Religion (Johnson City, TN): name changed to Emmanuel Christian Seminary

Everest University (Clearwater, FL): no longer a campus of Everest University

Framingham State College (Framingham, MA): name changed to Framingham State University

Hannibal-LaGrange College (Hannibal, MO): name changed to Hannibal-LaGrange University

Hebrew Union College–Jewish Institute of Religion (Los Angeles, CA): merged into a single entry for Hebrew Union College–Jewish Institute of Religion (New York, NY) by request from the institution

Hebrew Union College–Jewish Institute of Religion (Cincinnati, OH): merged into a single entry for Hebrew Union College–Jewish Institute of Religion (New York, NY) by request from the institution

Jesuit School of Theology at Berkeley (Berkeley, CA): now listed as a unit of Santa Clara University (Santa Clara, CA)

Johnson Bible College (Knoxville, TN): name changed to Johnson University

Keller Graduate School of Management (Long Island City, NY): now listed as a unit of DeVry College of New York (Long Island City, NY)

Keller Graduate School of Management (New York, NY): now listed as a unit of DeVry University Manhattan Extension Site (New York, NY)

Lancaster Bible College & Graduate School (Lancaster, PA): name changed to Lancaster Bible College

Medical College of Georgia (Augusta, GA): name changed to Georgia Health Sciences University

Mennonite Brethren Biblical Seminary (Fresno, CA): name changed to Fresno Pacific Biblical Seminary and now a unit of Fresno Pacific University (Fresno, CA)

Meritus University (Fredericton, NB, Canada): closed

Mount Mercy College (Cedar Rapids, IA): name changed to Mount Mercy University

Mount Sinai School of Medicine of New York University (New York, NY): name changed to Mount Sinai School of Medicine

Northeastern Ohio Universities College of Medicine and Pharmacy (Rootstown, OH): name changed to Northeastern Ohio Universities Colleges of Medicine and Pharmacy

Polytechnic University of the Americas–Miami Campus (Miami, FL): name changed to Polytechnic University of Puerto Rico, Miami Campus

Polytechnic University of the Americas–Orlando Campus (Winter Park, FL): name changed to Polytechnic University of Puerto Rico, Orlando Campus

Salem State College (Salem, MA): name changed to Salem State University

Sherman College of Straight Chiropractic (Spartanburg, SC): name changed to Sherman College of Chiropractic

Union Theological Seminary and Presbyterian School of Christian Education (Richmond, VA): name changed to Union Presbyterian Seminary

University of Colorado at Boulder (Boulder, CO): name changed to University of Colorado Boulder

University of Phoenix–Western Washington Campus (Tukwila, WA): merged into a single entry for University of Phoenix–Washington Campus (Seattle, WA)

Vassar College (Poughkeepsie, NY): no longer offers graduate degrees

Western New England College (Springfield, MA): name changed to Western New England University

Western States Chiropractic College (Portland, OR): name changed to University of Western States

Westfield State College (Westfield, MA): name changed to Westfield State University

Westminster Choir College of Rider University (Princeton, NJ): name changed to Westminster Choir College and now a unit of Rider University (Lawrenceville, NJ)

West Suburban College of Nursing (Oak Park, IL): name changed to Resurrection University

Worcester State College (Worcester, MA): name changed to Worcester State University

Abbreviations Used in the Guides

The following list includes abbreviations of degree names used in the profiles in the 2012 edition of the guides. Because some degrees (e.g., Doctor of Education) can be abbreviated in more than one way (e.g., D.Ed. or Ed.D.), and because the abbreviations used in the guides reflect the preferences of the individual colleges and universities, the list may include two or more abbreviations for a single degree.

Degrees

A Mus D	Doctor of Musical Arts
AC	Advanced Certificate
AD	Artist's Diploma Doctor of Arts
ADP	Artist's Diploma
Adv C	Advanced Certificate
Adv M	Advanced Master
AGC	Advanced Graduate Certificate
AGSC	Advanced Graduate Specialist Certificate
ALM	Master of Liberal Arts
AM	Master of Arts
AMBA	Accelerated Master of Business Administration Aviation Master of Business Administration
AMRS	Master of Arts in Religious Studies
APC	Advanced Professional Certificate
APMPH	Advanced Professional Master of Public Health
App Sc	Applied Scientist
App Sc D	Doctor of Applied Science
Au D	Doctor of Audiology
B Th	Bachelor of Theology
CAES	Certificate of Advanced Educational Specialization
CAGS	Certificate of Advanced Graduate Studies
CAL	Certificate in Applied Linguistics
CALS	Certificate of Advanced Liberal Studies
CAMS	Certificate of Advanced Management Studies
CAPS	Certificate of Advanced Professional Studies
CAS	Certificate of Advanced Studies
CASPA	Certificate of Advanced Study in Public Administration
CASR	Certificate in Advanced Social Research
CATS	Certificate of Achievement in Theological Studies
CBHS	Certificate in Basic Health Sciences
CBS	Graduate Certificate in Biblical Studies
CCJA	Certificate in Criminal Justice Administration
CCSA	Certificate in Catholic School Administration
CCTS	Certificate in Clinical and Translational Science
CE	Civil Engineer
CEM	Certificate of Environmental Management
CET	Certificate in Educational Technologies
CGS	Certificate of Graduate Studies
Ch E	Chemical Engineer
CM	Certificate in Management
CMH	Certificate in Medical Humanities
CMM	Master of Church Ministries
CMS	Certificate in Ministerial Studies
CNM	Certificate in Nonprofit Management
CP	Certificate in Performance
CPASF	Certificate Program for Advanced Study in Finance
CPC	Certificate in Professional Counseling Certificate in Publication and Communication
CPH	Certificate in Public Health
CPM	Certificate in Public Management
CPS	Certificate of Professional Studies
CScD	Doctor of Clinical Science
CSD	Certificate in Spiritual Direction
CSS	Certificate of Special Studies
CTS	Certificate of Theological Studies
CURP	Certificate in Urban and Regional Planning
D Admin	Doctor of Administration
D Arch	Doctor of Architecture
D Com	Doctor of Commerce
D Couns	Doctor of Counseling
D Div	Doctor of Divinity
D Ed	Doctor of Education
D Ed Min	Doctor of Educational Ministry
D Eng	Doctor of Engineering
D Engr	Doctor of Engineering
D Ent	Doctor of Enterprise
D Env	Doctor of Environment
D Law	Doctor of Law
D Litt	Doctor of Letters
D Med Sc	Doctor of Medical Science
D Min	Doctor of Ministry
D Miss	Doctor of Missiology

D Mus	Doctor of Music	**DH Sc**	Doctor of Health Sciences
D Mus A	Doctor of Musical Arts	**DHA**	Doctor of Health Administration
D Phil	Doctor of Philosophy	**DHCE**	Doctor of Health Care Ethics
D Prof	Doctor of Professional Studies	**DHL**	Doctor of Hebrew Letters
D Ps	Doctor of Psychology		Doctor of Hebrew Literature
D Sc	Doctor of Science	**DHS**	Doctor of Health Science
D Sc D	Doctor of Science in Dentistry	**DHSc**	Doctor of Health Science
D Sc IS	Doctor of Science in Information Systems	**Dip CS**	Diploma in Christian Studies
D Sc PA	Doctor of Science in Physician Assistant Studies	**DIT**	Doctor of Industrial Technology
D Th	Doctor of Theology	**DJ Ed**	Doctor of Jewish Education
D Th P	Doctor of Practical Theology	**DJS**	Doctor of Jewish Studies
DA	Doctor of Accounting	**DLS**	Doctor of Liberal Studies
	Doctor of Arts	**DM**	Doctor of Management
DA Ed	Doctor of Arts in Education		Doctor of Music
DAH	Doctor of Arts in Humanities	**DMA**	Doctor of Musical Arts
DAOM	Doctorate in Acupuncture and Oriental Medicine	**DMD**	Doctor of Dental Medicine
DAST	Diploma of Advanced Studies in Teaching	**DME**	Doctor of Manufacturing Management
DBA	Doctor of Business Administration		Doctor of Music Education
DBH	Doctor of Behavioral Health	**DMEd**	Doctor of Music Education
DBL	Doctor of Business Leadership	**DMFT**	Doctor of Marital and Family Therapy
DBS	Doctor of Buddhist Studies	**DMH**	Doctor of Medical Humanities
DC	Doctor of Chiropractic	**DML**	Doctor of Modern Languages
DCC	Doctor of Computer Science	**DMP**	Doctorate in Medical Physics
DCD	Doctor of Communications Design	**DMPNA**	Doctor of Management Practice in Nurse Anesthesia
DCL	Doctor of Civil Law	**DN Sc**	Doctor of Nursing Science
	Doctor of Comparative Law	**DNAP**	Doctor of Nurse Anesthesia Practice
DCM	Doctor of Church Music	**DNP**	Doctor of Nursing Practice
DCN	Doctor of Clinical Nutrition	**DNS**	Doctor of Nursing Science
DCS	Doctor of Computer Science	**DO**	Doctor of Osteopathy
DDN	Diplôme du Droit Notarial	**DOT**	Doctor of Occupational Therapy
DDS	Doctor of Dental Surgery	**DPA**	Doctor of Public Administration
DE	Doctor of Education	**DPC**	Doctor of Pastoral Counseling
	Doctor of Engineering	**DPDS**	Doctor of Planning and Development Studies
DED	Doctor of Economic Development	**DPH**	Doctor of Public Health
DEIT	Doctor of Educational Innovation and Technology	**DPM**	Doctor of Plant Medicine
DEL	Doctor of Executive Leadership		Doctor of Podiatric Medicine
DEM	Doctor of Educational Ministry	**DPPD**	Doctor of Policy, Planning, and Development
DEPD	Diplôme Études Spécialisées	**DPS**	Doctor of Professional Studies
DES	Doctor of Engineering Science	**DPT**	Doctor of Physical Therapy
DESS	Diplôme Études Supérieures Spécialisées	**DPTSc**	Doctor of Physical Therapy Science
DFA	Doctor of Fine Arts	**Dr DES**	Doctor of Design
DGP	Diploma in Graduate and Professional Studies	**Dr OT**	Doctor of Occupational Therapy
DH Ed	Doctor of Health Education	**Dr PH**	Doctor of Public Health

Dr Sc PT	Doctor of Science in Physical Therapy		**G Dip**	Graduate Diploma
DRSc	Doctor of Regulatory Science		**GBC**	Graduate Business Certificate
DS	Doctor of Science		**GCE**	Graduate Certificate in Education
DS Sc	Doctor of Social Science		**GDM**	Graduate Diploma in Management
DSJS	Doctor of Science in Jewish Studies		**GDPA**	Graduate Diploma in Public Administration
DSL	Doctor of Strategic Leadership		**GDRE**	Graduate Diploma in Religious Education
DSW	Doctor of Social Work		**GEMBA**	Global Executive Master of Business Administration
DTL	Doctor of Talmudic Law		**GEMPA**	Gulf Executive Master of Public Administration
DV Sc	Doctor of Veterinary Science		**GM Acc**	Graduate Master of Accountancy
DVM	Doctor of Veterinary Medicine		**GMBA**	Global Master of Business Administration
DWS	Doctor of Worship Studies		**GPD**	Graduate Performance Diploma
EAA	Engineer in Aeronautics and Astronautics		**GSS**	Graduate Special Certificate for Students in Special Situations
ECS	Engineer in Computer Science		**IEMBA**	International Executive Master of Business Administration
Ed D	Doctor of Education			
Ed DCT	Doctor of Education in College Teaching		**IM Acc**	Integrated Master of Accountancy
Ed L D	Doctor of Education Leadership		**IMA**	Interdisciplinary Master of Arts
Ed M	Master of Education		**IMBA**	International Master of Business Administration
Ed S	Specialist in Education		**IMES**	International Master's in Environmental Studies
Ed Sp	Specialist in Education		**Ingeniero**	Engineer
EDB	Executive Doctorate in Business		**JCD**	Doctor of Canon Law
EDM	Executive Doctorate in Management		**JCL**	Licentiate in Canon Law
EDSPC	Education Specialist		**JD**	Juris Doctor
EE	Electrical Engineer		**JSD**	Doctor of Juridical Science Doctor of Jurisprudence Doctor of the Science of Law
EJD	Executive Juris Doctor			
EMBA	Executive Master of Business Administration			
EMFA	Executive Master of Forensic Accounting		**JSM**	Master of Science of Law
EMHA	Executive Master of Health Administration		**L Th**	Licenciate in Theology
EMIB	Executive Master of International Business		**LL B**	Bachelor of Laws
EML	Executive Master of Leadership		**LL CM**	Master of Laws in Comparative Law
EMPA	Executive Master of Public Administration		**LL D**	Doctor of Laws
EMPP	Executive Master's of Public Policy		**LL M**	Master of Laws
EMS	Executive Master of Science		**LL M in Tax**	Master of Laws in Taxation
EMTM	Executive Master of Technology Management		**LL M CL**	Master of Laws (Common Law)
Eng	Engineer		**M Ac**	Master of Accountancy Master of Accounting Master of Acupuncture
Eng Sc D	Doctor of Engineering Science			
Engr	Engineer			
Ex Doc	Executive Doctor of Pharmacy		**M Ac OM**	Master of Acupuncture and Oriental Medicine
Exec Ed D	Executive Doctor of Education		**M Acc**	Master of Accountancy Master of Accounting
Exec MBA	Executive Master of Business Administration			
Exec MPA	Executive Master of Public Administration		**M Acct**	Master of Accountancy Master of Accounting
Exec MPH	Executive Master of Public Health		**M Accy**	Master of Accountancy
Exec MS	Executive Master of Science		**M Actg**	Master of Accounting

M Acy	Master of Accountancy	M Econ	Master of Economics
M Ad	Master of Administration	M Ed	Master of Education
M Ad Ed	Master of Adult Education	M Ed T	Master of Education in Teaching
M Adm	Master of Administration	M En	Master of Engineering
M Adm Mgt	Master of Administrative Management		Master of Environmental Science
M Admin	Master of Administration	M En S	Master of Environmental Sciences
M ADU	Master of Architectural Design and Urbanism	M Eng	Master of Engineering
M Adv	Master of Advertising	M Eng Mgt	Master of Engineering Management
M Aero E	Master of Aerospace Engineering	M Engr	Master of Engineering
M AEST	Master of Applied Environmental Science and Technology	M Ent	Master of Enterprise
		M Env	Master of Environment
M Ag	Master of Agriculture	M Env Des	Master of Environmental Design
M Ag Ed	Master of Agricultural Education	M Env E	Master of Environmental Engineering
M Agr	Master of Agriculture	M Env Sc	Master of Environmental Science
M Anesth Ed	Master of Anesthesiology Education	M Fin	Master of Finance
M App Comp Sc	Master of Applied Computer Science	M Geo E	Master of Geological Engineering
M App St	Master of Applied Statistics	M Geoenv E	Master of Geoenvironmental Engineering
M Appl Stat	Master of Applied Statistics	M Geog	Master of Geography
M Aq	Master of Aquaculture	M Hum	Master of Humanities
M Arc	Master of Architecture	M Hum Svcs	Master of Human Services
M Arch	Master of Architecture	M IBD	Master of Integrated Building Delivery
M Arch I	Master of Architecture I	M IDST	Master's in Interdisciplinary Studies
M Arch II	Master of Architecture II	M Kin	Master of Kinesiology
M Arch E	Master of Architectural Engineering	M Land Arch	Master of Landscape Architecture
M Arch H	Master of Architectural History	M Litt	Master of Letters
M Bioethics	Master in Bioethics	M Mat SE	Master of Material Science and Engineering
M Biomath	Master of Biomathematics	M Math	Master of Mathematics
M Ch	Master of Chemistry	M Mech E	Master of Mechanical Engineering
M Ch E	Master of Chemical Engineering	M Med Sc	Master of Medical Science
M Chem	Master of Chemistry	M Mgmt	Master of Management
M Cl D	Master of Clinical Dentistry	M Mgt	Master of Management
M Cl Sc	Master of Clinical Science	M Min	Master of Ministries
M Comp	Master of Computing	M Mtl E	Master of Materials Engineering
M Comp E	Master of Computer Engineering	M Mu	Master of Music
M Comp Sc	Master of Computer Science	M Mus	Master of Music
M Coun	Master of Counseling	M Mus Ed	Master of Music Education
M Dent	Master of Dentistry	M Music	Master of Music
M Dent Sc	Master of Dental Sciences	M Nat Sci	Master of Natural Science
M Des	Master of Design	M Oc E	Master of Oceanographic Engineering
M Des S	Master of Design Studies	M Pet E	Master of Petroleum Engineering
M Div	Master of Divinity	M Pharm	Master of Pharmacy
M Ec	Master of Economics	M Phil	Master of Philosophy

M Phil F	Master of Philosophical Foundations
M Pl	Master of Planning
M Plan	Master of Planning
M Pol	Master of Political Science
M Pr Met	Master of Professional Meteorology
M Prob S	Master of Probability and Statistics
M Psych	Master of Psychology
M Pub	Master of Publishing
M Rel	Master of Religion
M S Ed	Master of Science Education
M Sc	Master of Science
M Sc A	Master of Science (Applied)
M Sc AHN	Master of Science in Applied Human Nutrition
M Sc BMC	Master of Science in Biomedical Communications
M Sc CS	Master of Science in Computer Science
M Sc E	Master of Science in Engineering
M Sc Eng	Master of Science in Engineering
M Sc Engr	Master of Science in Engineering
M Sc F	Master of Science in Forestry
M Sc FE	Master of Science in Forest Engineering
M Sc Geogr	Master of Science in Geography
M Sc N	Master of Science in Nursing
M Sc OT	Master of Science in Occupational Therapy
M Sc P	Master of Science in Planning
M Sc Pl	Master of Science in Planning
M Sc PT	Master of Science in Physical Therapy
M Sc T	Master of Science in Teaching
M SEM	Master of Sustainable Environmental Management
M Serv Soc	Master of Social Service
M Soc	Master of Sociology
M Sp Ed	Master of Special Education
M Stat	Master of Statistics
M Sys Sc	Master of Systems Science
M Tax	Master of Taxation
M Tech	Master of Technology
M Th	Master of Theology
M Tox	Master of Toxicology
M Trans E	Master of Transportation Engineering
M Urb	Master of Urban Planning
M Vet Sc	Master of Veterinary Science

MA	Master of Accounting
	Master of Administration
	Master of Arts
MA Missions	Master of Arts in Missions
MA Comm	Master of Arts in Communication
MA Ed	Master of Arts in Education
MA Ed Ad	Master of Arts in Educational Administration
MA Ext	Master of Agricultural Extension
MA Islamic	Master of Arts in Islamic Studies
MA Military Studies	Master of Arts in Military Studies
MA Min	Master of Arts in Ministry
MA Miss	Master of Arts in Missiology
MA Past St	Master of Arts in Pastoral Studies
MA Ph	Master of Arts in Philosophy
MA Psych	Master of Arts in Psychology
MA Sc	Master of Applied Science
MA Sp	Master of Arts (Spirituality)
MA Th	Master of Arts in Theology
MA-R	Master of Arts (Research)
MAA	Master of Administrative Arts
	Master of Applied Anthropology
	Master of Applied Arts
	Master of Arts in Administration
MAAA	Master of Arts in Arts Administration
MAAAP	Master of Arts Administration and Policy
MAAE	Master of Arts in Art Education
MAAT	Master of Arts in Applied Theology
	Master of Arts in Art Therapy
MAB	Master of Agribusiness
MABC	Master of Arts in Biblical Counseling
	Master of Arts in Business Communication
MABE	Master of Arts in Bible Exposition
MABL	Master of Arts in Biblical Languages
MABM	Master of Agribusiness Management
MABS	Master of Arts in Biblical Studies
MABT	Master of Arts in Bible Teaching
MAC	Master of Accountancy
	Master of Accounting
	Master of Arts in Communication
	Master of Arts in Counseling
MACC	Master of Arts in Christian Counseling
	Master of Arts in Clinical Counseling
MACCM	Master of Arts in Church and Community Ministry
MACCT	Master of Accounting

MACD	Master of Arts in Christian Doctrine	**MAH**	Master of Arts in Humanities
MACE	Master of Arts in Christian Education	**MAHA**	Master of Arts in Humanitarian Assistance Master of Arts in Humanitarian Studies
MACFM	Master of Arts in Children's and Family Ministry	**MAHCM**	Master of Arts in Health Care Mission
MACH	Master of Arts in Church History	**MAHG**	Master of American History and Government
MACI	Master of Arts in Curriculum and Instruction	**MAHL**	Master of Arts in Hebrew Letters
MACIS	Master of Accounting and Information Systems	**MAHN**	Master of Applied Human Nutrition
MACJ	Master of Arts in Criminal Justice	**MAHSR**	Master of Applied Health Services Research
MACL	Master of Arts in Christian Leadership	**MAIA**	Master of Arts in International Administration
MACM	Master of Arts in Christian Ministries Master of Arts in Christian Ministry Master of Arts in Church Music Master of Arts in Counseling Ministries	**MAIB**	Master of Arts in International Business
		MAICS	Master of Arts in Intercultural Studies
MACN	Master of Arts in Counseling	**MAIDM**	Master of Arts in Interior Design and Merchandising
MACO	Master of Arts in Counseling	**MAIH**	Master of Arts in Interdisciplinary Humanities
MAcOM	Master of Acupuncture and Oriental Medicine	**MAIOP**	Master of Arts in Industrial/Organizational Psychology
MACP	Master of Arts in Counseling Psychology	**MAIPCR**	Master of Arts in International Peace and Conflict Management
MACS	Master of Arts in Catholic Studies		
MACSE	Master of Arts in Christian School Education	**MAIS**	Master of Arts in Intercultural Studies Master of Arts in Interdisciplinary Studies Master of Arts in International Studies
MACT	Master of Arts in Christian Thought Master of Arts in Communications and Technology	**MAIT**	Master of Administration in Information Technology Master of Applied Information Technology
MAD	Master in Educational Institution Administration Master of Art and Design	**MAJ**	Master of Arts in Journalism
MADR	Master of Arts in Dispute Resolution	**MAJ Ed**	Master of Arts in Jewish Education
MADS	Master of Animal and Dairy Science Master of Applied Disability Studies	**MAJCS**	Master of Arts in Jewish Communal Service
		MAJE	Master of Arts in Jewish Education
MAE	Master of Aerospace Engineering Master of Agricultural Economics Master of Agricultural Education Master of Architectural Engineering Master of Art Education Master of Arts in Education Master of Arts in English	**MAJS**	Master of Arts in Jewish Studies
		MAL	Master in Agricultural Leadership
		MALA	Master of Arts in Liberal Arts
		MALD	Master of Arts in Law and Diplomacy
MAEd	Master of Arts Education	**MALER**	Master of Arts in Labor and Employment Relations
MAEL	Master of Arts in Educational Leadership	**MALM**	Master of Arts in Leadership Evangelical Mobilization
MAEM	Master of Arts in Educational Ministries		
MAEN	Master of Arts in English	**MALP**	Master of Arts in Language Pedagogy
MAEP	Master of Arts in Economic Policy	**MALPS**	Master of Arts in Liberal and Professional Studies
MAES	Master of Arts in Environmental Sciences	**MALS**	Master of Arts in Liberal Studies
MAET	Master of Arts in English Teaching	**MALT**	Master of Arts in Learning and Teaching
MAF	Master of Arts in Finance	**MAM**	Master of Acquisition Management Master of Agriculture and Management Master of Applied Mathematics Master of Arts in Management Master of Arts in Ministry Master of Arts Management Master of Avian Medicine
MAFE	Master of Arts in Financial Economics		
MAFLL	Master of Arts in Foreign Language and Literature		
MAFM	Master of Accounting and Financial Management		
MAFS	Master of Arts in Family Studies		
MAG	Master of Applied Geography		
MAGU	Master of Urban Analysis and Management	**MAMB**	Master of Applied Molecular Biology

MAMC   Master of Arts in Mass Communication
Master of Arts in Ministry and Culture
Master of Arts in Ministry for a Multicultural Church
Master of Arts in Missional Christianity

MAME   Master of Arts in Missions/Evangelism

MAMFC   Master of Arts in Marriage and Family Counseling

MAMFCC   Master of Arts in Marriage, Family, and Child Counseling

MAMFT   Master of Arts in Marriage and Family Therapy

MAMHC   Master of Arts in Mental Health Counseling

MAMI   Master of Arts in Missions

MAMS   Master of Applied Mathematical Sciences
Master of Arts in Ministerial Studies
Master of Arts in Ministry and Spirituality

MAMT   Master of Arts in Mathematics Teaching

MAN   Master of Applied Nutrition

MANP   Master of Applied Natural Products

MANT   Master of Arts in New Testament

MAOL   Master of Arts in Organizational Leadership

MAOM   Master of Acupuncture and Oriental Medicine
Master of Arts in Organizational Management

MAOT   Master of Arts in Old Testament

MAP   Master of Applied Psychology
Master of Arts in Planning
Master of Psychology
Master of Public Administration

MAP Min   Master of Arts in Pastoral Ministry

MAPA   Master of Arts in Public Administration

MAPC   Master of Arts in Pastoral Counseling
Master of Arts in Professional Counseling

MAPE   Master of Arts in Political Economy

MAPL   Master of Arts in Pastoral Leadership

MAPM   Master of Arts in Pastoral Ministry
Master of Arts in Pastoral Music
Master of Arts in Practical Ministry

MAPP   Master of Arts in Public Policy

MAPPS   Master of Arts in Asia Pacific Policy Studies

MAPS   Master of Arts in Pastoral Counseling/Spiritual Formation
Master of Arts in Pastoral Studies
Master of Arts in Public Service

MAPT   Master of Practical Theology

MAPW   Master of Arts in Professional Writing

MAR   Master of Arts in Religion

Mar Eng   Marine Engineer

MARC   Master of Arts in Rehabilitation Counseling

MARE   Master of Arts in Religious Education

MARL   Master of Arts in Religious Leadership

MARS   Master of Arts in Religious Studies

MAS   Master of Accounting Science
Master of Actuarial Science
Master of Administrative Science
Master of Advanced Study
Master of Aeronautical Science
Master of American Studies
Master of Applied Science
Master of Applied Statistics
Master of Archival Studies

MASA   Master of Advanced Studies in Architecture

MASD   Master of Arts in Spiritual Direction

MASE   Master of Arts in Special Education

MASF   Master of Arts in Spiritual Formation

MASJ   Master of Arts in Systems of Justice

MASL   Master of Arts in School Leadership

MASLA   Master of Advanced Studies in Landscape Architecture

MASM   Master of Aging Services Management
Master of Arts in Specialized Ministries

MASP   Master of Applied Social Psychology
Master of Arts in School Psychology

MASPAA   Master of Arts in Sports and Athletic Administration

MASS   Master of Applied Social Science
Master of Arts in Social Science

MAST   Master of Arts in Science Teaching

MASW   Master of Aboriginal Social Work

MAT   Master of Arts in Teaching
Master of Arts in Theology
Master of Athletic Training
Master's in Administration of Telecommunications

Mat E   Materials Engineer

MATCM   Master of Acupuncture and Traditional Chinese Medicine

MATDE   Master of Arts in Theology, Development, and Evangelism

MATDR   Master of Territorial Management and Regional Development

MATE   Master of Arts for the Teaching of English

MATESL   Master of Arts in Teaching English as a Second Language

MATESOL   Master of Arts in Teaching English to Speakers of Other Languages

MATF   Master of Arts in Teaching English as a Foreign Language/Intercultural Studies

MATFL   Master of Arts in Teaching Foreign Language

MATH   Master of Arts in Therapy

MATI	Master of Administration of Information Technology
MATL	Master of Arts in Teacher Leadership Master of Arts in Teaching of Languages Master of Arts in Transformational Leadership
MATM	Master of Arts in Teaching of Mathematics
MATS	Master of Arts in Theological Studies Master of Arts in Transforming Spirituality
MATSL	Master of Arts in Teaching a Second Language
MAUA	Master of Arts in Urban Affairs
MAUD	Master of Arts in Urban Design
MAURP	Master of Arts in Urban and Regional Planning
MAWSHP	Master of Arts in Worship
MAYM	Master of Arts in Youth Ministry
MB	Master of Bioinformatics Master of Biology
MBA	Master of Business Administration
MBA-AM	Master of Business Administration in Aviation Management
MBA-EP	Master of Business Administration–Experienced Professionals
MBAA	Master of Business Administration in Aviation
MBAE	Master of Biological and Agricultural Engineering Master of Biosystems and Agricultural Engineering
MBAH	Master of Business Administration in Health
MBAi	Master of Business Administration–International
MBAICT	Master of Business Administration in Information and Communication Technology
MBATM	Master of Business Administration in Technology Management
MBC	Master of Building Construction
MBE	Master of Bilingual Education Master of Bioengineering Master of Bioethics Master of Biological Engineering Master of Biomedical Engineering Master of Business and Engineering Master of Business Economics Master of Business Education
MBET	Master of Business, Entrepreneurship and Technology
MBiotech	Master of Biotechnology
MBIT	Master of Business Information Technology
MBL	Master of Business Law Master of Business Leadership
MBLE	Master in Business Logistics Engineering
MBMI	Master of Biomedical Imaging and Signals

MBMSE	Master of Business Management and Software Engineering
MBOE	Master of Business Operational Excellence
MBS	Master of Biblical Studies Master of Biological Science Master of Biomedical Sciences Master of Bioscience Master of Building Science
MBT	Master of Biblical and Theological Studies Master of Biomedical Technology Master of Biotechnology Master of Business Taxation
MC	Master of Communication Master of Counseling Master of Cybersecurity
MC Ed	Master of Continuing Education
MC Sc	Master of Computer Science
MCA	Master of Arts in Applied Criminology Master of Commercial Aviation
MCAM	Master of Computational and Applied Mathematics
MCC	Master of Computer Science
MCCS	Master of Crop and Soil Sciences
MCD	Master of Communications Disorders Master of Community Development
MCE	Master in Electronic Commerce Master of Christian Education Master of Civil Engineering Master of Control Engineering
MCEM	Master of Construction Engineering Management
MCH	Master of Chemical Engineering
MCHE	Master of Chemical Engineering
MCIS	Master of Communication and Information Studies Master of Computer and Information Science Master of Computer Information Systems
MCIT	Master of Computer and Information Technology
MCJ	Master of Criminal Justice
MCJA	Master of Criminal Justice Administration
MCL	Master in Communication Leadership Master of Canon Law Master of Comparative Law
MCM	Master of Christian Ministry Master of Church Music Master of City Management Master of Communication Management Master of Community Medicine Master of Construction Management Master of Contract Management Master of Corporate Media
MCMP	Master of City and Metropolitan Planning
MCMS	Master of Clinical Medical Science

MCN	Master of Clinical Nutrition
MCP	Master of City Planning
	Master of Community Planning
	Master of Counseling Psychology
	Master of Cytopathology Practice
	Master of Science in Quality Systems and Productivity
MCPC	Master of Arts in Chaplaincy and Pastoral Care
MCPD	Master of Community Planning and Development
MCR	Master in Clinical Research
MCRP	Master of City and Regional Planning
MCRS	Master of City and Regional Studies
MCS	Master of Christian Studies
	Master of Clinical Science
	Master of Combined Sciences
	Master of Communication Studies
	Master of Computer Science
	Master of Consumer Science
MCSE	Master of Computer Science and Engineering
MCSL	Master of Catholic School Leadership
MCSM	Master of Construction Science/Management
MCST	Master of Science in Computer Science and Information Technology
MCTP	Master of Communication Technology and Policy
MCTS	Master of Clinical and Translational Science
MCVS	Master of Cardiovascular Science
MD	Doctor of Medicine
MDA	Master of Development Administration
	Master of Dietetic Administration
MDB	Master of Design-Build
MDE	Master of Developmental Economics
	Master of Distance Education
	Master of the Education of the Deaf
MDH	Master of Dental Hygiene
MDM	Master of Design Methods
	Master of Digital Media
MDP	Master of Development Practice
MDR	Master of Dispute Resolution
MDS	Master of Dental Surgery
ME	Master of Education
	Master of Engineering
	Master of Entrepreneurship
	Master of Evangelism
ME Sc	Master of Engineering Science
MEA	Master of Educational Administration
	Master of Engineering Administration
MEAP	Master of Environmental Administration and Planning
MEBT	Master in Electronic Business Technologies

MEC	Master of Electronic Commerce
MECE	Master of Electrical and Computer Engineering
Mech E	Mechanical Engineer
MED	Master of Education of the Deaf
MEDS	Master of Environmental Design Studies
MEE	Master in Education
	Master of Electrical Engineering
	Master of Energy Engineering
	Master of Environmental Engineering
MEEM	Master of Environmental Engineering and Management
MEENE	Master of Engineering in Environmental Engineering
MEEP	Master of Environmental and Energy Policy
MEERM	Master of Earth and Environmental Resource Management
MEH	Master in Humanistic Studies
	Master of Environmental Horticulture
MEHS	Master of Environmental Health and Safety
MEIM	Master of Entertainment Industry Management
MEL	Master of Educational Leadership
	Master of English Literature
MELP	Master of Environmental Law and Policy
MEM	Master of Ecosystem Management
	Master of Electricity Markets
	Master of Engineering Management
	Master of Environmental Management
	Master of Marketing
MEME	Master of Engineering in Manufacturing Engineering
	Master of Engineering in Mechanical Engineering
MENG	Master of Arts in English
MENVEGR	Master of Environmental Engineering
MEP	Master of Engineering Physics
MEPC	Master of Environmental Pollution Control
MEPD	Master of Education–Professional Development
	Master of Environmental Planning and Design
MER	Master of Employment Relations
MES	Master of Education and Science
	Master of Engineering Science
	Master of Environment and Sustainability
	Master of Environmental Science
	Master of Environmental Studies
	Master of Environmental Systems
	Master of Special Education
MESM	Master of Environmental Science and Management
MET	Master of Educational Technology
	Master of Engineering Technology
	Master of Entertainment Technology
	Master of Environmental Toxicology

Met E	Metallurgical Engineer	MGM	Master of Global Management
METM	Master of Engineering and Technology Management	MGP	Master of Gestion de Projet
		MGPS	Master of Global Policy Studies
MF	Master of Finance Master of Forestry	MGREM	Master of Global Real Estate Management
MFA	Master of Fine Arts	MGS	Master of Gerontological Studies Master of Global Studies
MFAM	Master in Food Animal Medicine	MH	Master of Humanities
MFAS	Master of Fisheries and Aquatic Science	MH Ed	Master of Health Education
MFAW	Master of Fine Arts in Writing	MH Sc	Master of Health Sciences
MFC	Master of Forest Conservation	MHA	Master of Health Administration Master of Healthcare Administration
MFCS	Master of Family and Consumer Sciences		Master of Hospital Administration Master of Hospitality Administration
MFE	Master of Financial Economics Master of Financial Engineering Master of Forest Engineering	MHA/MCRP	Master of Healthcare Administration/Master of City and Regional Planning
MFG	Master of Functional Genomics	MHAD	Master of Health Administration
MFHD	Master of Family and Human Development	MHB	Master of Human Behavior
MFM	Master of Financial Mathematics	MHCA	Master of Health Care Administration
MFMS	Master's in Food Microbiology and Safety	MHCI	Master of Human-Computer Interaction
MFPE	Master of Food Process Engineering	MHCL	Master of Health Care Leadership
MFR	Master of Forest Resources	MHE	Master of Health Education Master of Human Ecology
MFRC	Master of Forest Resources and Conservation	MHE Ed	Master of Home Economics Education
MFS	Master of Food Science Master of Forensic Sciences Master of Forest Science Master of Forest Studies Master of French Studies	MHEA	Master of Higher Education Administration
		MHHS	Master of Health and Human Services
MFST	Master of Food Safety and Technology	MHI	Master of Health Informatics Master of Healthcare Innovation
MFT	Master of Family Therapy Master of Food Technology	MHIIM	Master of Health Informatics and Information Management
MFWB	Master of Fishery and Wildlife Biology	MHIS	Master of Health Information Systems
MFWCB	Master of Fish, Wildlife and Conservation Biology	MHK	Master of Human Kinetics
MFWS	Master of Fisheries and Wildlife Sciences	MHL	Master of Hebrew Literature
MFYCS	Master of Family, Youth and Community Sciences	MHM	Master of Healthcare Management
MG	Master of Genetics	MHMS	Master of Health Management Systems
MGA	Master of Global Affairs Master of Governmental Administration	MHP	Master of Health Physics Master of Heritage Preservation Master of Historic Preservation
MGC	Master of Genetic Counseling	MHPA	Master of Heath Policy and Administration
MGD	Master of Graphic Design	MHPE	Master of Health Professions Education
MGE	Master of Geotechnical Engineering	MHR	Master of Human Resources
MGEM	Master of Global Entrepreneurship and Management	MHRD	Master in Human Resource Development
MGH	Master of Geriatric Health	MHRIR	Master of Human Resources and Industrial Relations
MGIS	Master of Geographic Information Science Master of Geographic Information Systems	MHRLR	Master of Human Resources and Labor Relations

MHRM	Master of Human Resources Management	**MIR**	Master of Industrial Relations Master of International Relations
MHS	Master of Health Science Master of Health Sciences Master of Health Studies Master of Hispanic Studies Master of Human Services Master of Humanistic Studies	**MIS**	Master of Industrial Statistics Master of Information Science Master of Information Systems Master of Integrated Science Master of Interdisciplinary Studies Master of International Service Master of International Studies
MHSA	Master of Health Services Administration	**MISE**	Master of Industrial and Systems Engineering
MHSM	Master of Health Systems Management	**MISKM**	Master of Information Sciences and Knowledge Management
MI	Master of Instruction	**MISM**	Master of Information Systems Management
MI Arch	Master of Interior Architecture	**MIT**	Master in Teaching Master of Industrial Technology Master of Information Technology Master of Initial Teaching Master of International Trade Master of Internet Technology
MI St	Master of Information Studies		
MIA	Master of Interior Architecture Master of International Affairs		
MIAA	Master of International Affairs and Administration		
MIAM	Master of International Agribusiness Management	**MITA**	Master of Information Technology Administration
MIB	Master of International Business	**MITM**	Master of Information Technology and Management
MIBA	Master of International Business Administration	**MITO**	Master of Industrial Technology and Operations
MICM	Master of International Construction Management	**MJ**	Master of Journalism Master of Jurisprudence
MID	Master of Industrial Design Master of Industrial Distribution Master of Interior Design Master of International Development	**MJ Ed**	Master of Jewish Education
		MJA	Master of Justice Administration
MIE	Master of Industrial Engineering	**MJM**	Master of Justice Management
MIH	Master of Integrative Health	**MJS**	Master of Judicial Studies Master of Juridical Science
MIHTM	Master of International Hospitality and Tourism Management	**MKM**	Master of Knowledge Management
MIJ	Master of International Journalism	**ML**	Master of Latin
MILR	Master of Industrial and Labor Relations	**ML Arch**	Master of Landscape Architecture
MiM	Master in Management	**MLA**	Master of Landscape Architecture Master of Liberal Arts
MIM	Master of Industrial Management Master of Information Management Master of International Management	**MLAS**	Master of Laboratory Animal Science Master of Liberal Arts and Sciences
MIMLAE	Master of International Management for Latin American Executives	**MLAUD**	Master of Landscape Architecture in Urban Development
MIMS	Master of Information Management and Systems Master of Integrated Manufacturing Systems	**MLD**	Master of Leadership Development
MIP	Master of Infrastructure Planning Master of Intellectual Property	**MLE**	Master of Applied Linguistics and Exegesis
MIPER	Master of International Political Economy of Resources	**MLER**	Master of Labor and Employment Relations
		MLHR	Master of Labor and Human Resources
MIPP	Master of International Policy and Practice Master of International Public Policy	**MLI Sc**	Master of Library and Information Science
MIPS	Master of International Planning Studies	**MLIS**	Master of Library and Information Science Master of Library and Information Studies

MLM	Master of Library Media
MLRHR	Master of Labor Relations and Human Resources
MLS	Master of Leadership Studies
	Master of Legal Studies
	Master of Liberal Studies
	Master of Library Science
	Master of Life Sciences
MLSP	Master of Law and Social Policy
MLT	Master of Language Technologies
MLTCA	Master of Long Term Care Administration
MM	Master of Management
	Master of Ministry
	Master of Missiology
	Master of Music
MM Ed	Master of Music Education
MM Sc	Master of Medical Science
MM St	Master of Museum Studies
MMA	Master of Marine Affairs
	Master of Media Arts
	Master of Musical Arts
MMAE	Master of Mechanical and Aerospace Engineering
MMAS	Master of Military Art and Science
MMB	Master of Microbial Biotechnology
MMBA	Managerial Master of Business Administration
MMC	Master of Manufacturing Competitiveness
	Master of Mass Communications
	Master of Music Conducting
MMCM	Master of Music in Church Music
MMCSS	Master of Mathematical Computational and Statistical Sciences
MME	Master of Manufacturing Engineering
	Master of Mathematics Education
	Master of Mathematics for Educators
	Master of Mechanical Engineering
	Master of Medical Engineering
	Master of Mining Engineering
	Master of Music Education
MMF	Master of Mathematical Finance
MMFT	Master of Marriage and Family Therapy
MMG	Master of Management
MMH	Master of Management in Hospitality
	Master of Medical Humanities
MMI	Master of Management of Innovation
MMIS	Master of Management Information Systems
MMM	Master of Manufacturing Management
	Master of Marine Management
	Master of Medical Management
MMME	Master of Metallurgical and Materials Engineering

MMP	Master of Management Practice
	Master of Marine Policy
	Master of Medical Physics
	Master of Music Performance
MMPA	Master of Management and Professional Accounting
MMQM	Master of Manufacturing Quality Management
MMR	Master of Marketing Research
MMRM	Master of Marine Resources Management
MMS	Master of Management Science
	Master of Management Studies
	Master of Manufacturing Systems
	Master of Marine Studies
	Master of Materials Science
	Master of Medical Science
	Master of Medieval Studies
	Master of Modern Studies
MMSE	Master of Manufacturing Systems Engineering
MMSM	Master of Music in Sacred Music
MMT	Master in Marketing
	Master of Management
	Master of Math for Teaching
	Master of Music Teaching
	Master of Music Therapy
	Master's in Marketing Technology
MMus	Master of Music
MN	Master of Nursing
	Master of Nutrition
MN NP	Master of Nursing in Nurse Practitioner
MNA	Master of Nonprofit Administration
	Master of Nurse Anesthesia
MNAL	Master of Nonprofit Administration and Leadership
MNAS	Master of Natural and Applied Science
MNCM	Master of Network and Communications Management
MNE	Master of Network Engineering
	Master of Nuclear Engineering
MNL	Master in International Business for Latin America
MNM	Master of Nonprofit Management
MNO	Master of Nonprofit Organization
MNPL	Master of Not-for-Profit Leadership
MNpS	Master of Nonprofit Studies
MNR	Master of Natural Resources
MNRES	Master of Natural Resources and Environmental Studies
MNRM	Master of Natural Resource Management
MNRS	Master of Natural Resource Stewardship
MNS	Master of Natural Science
MO	Master of Oceanography

MOD	Master of Organizational Development
MOGS	Master of Oil and Gas Studies
MOH	Master of Occupational Health
MOL	Master of Organizational Leadership
MOM	Master of Oriental Medicine
MOR	Master of Operations Research
MOT	Master of Occupational Therapy
MP	Master of Physiology Master of Planning
MP Ac	Master of Professional Accountancy
MP Acc	Master of Professional Accountancy Master of Professional Accounting Master of Public Accounting
MP Aff	Master of Public Affairs
MP Th	Master of Pastoral Theology
MPA	Master of Physician Assistant Master of Professional Accountancy Master of Professional Accounting Master of Public Administration Master of Public Affairs
MPAC	Master of Professional Accounting
MPAID	Master of Public Administration and International Development
MPAP	Master of Physician Assistant Practice Master of Public Affairs and Politics
MPAS	Master of Physician Assistant Science Master of Physician Assistant Studies
MPC	Master of Pastoral Counseling Master of Professional Communication Master of Professional Counseling
MPD	Master of Product Development Master of Public Diplomacy
MPDS	Master of Planning and Development Studies
MPE	Master of Physical Education Master of Power Engineering
MPEM	Master of Project Engineering and Management
MPH	Master of Public Health
MPH/MCRP	Master of Public Health/Mster of Community and Regional Planning
MPHE	Master of Public Health Education
MPHTM	Master of Public Health and Tropical Medicine
MPIA	Master in International Affairs Master of Public and International Affairs
MPM	Master of Pastoral Ministry Master of Pest Management Master of Policy Management Master of Practical Ministries Master of Project Management Master of Public Management
MPNA	Master of Public and Nonprofit Administration
MPO	Master of Prosthetics and Orthotics
MPOD	Master of Positive Organizational Development
MPP	Master of Public Policy
MPPA	Master of Public Policy Administration Master of Public Policy and Administration
MPPAL	Master of Public Policy, Administration and Law
MPPM	Master of Public and Private Management Master of Public Policy and Management
MPPPM	Master of Plant Protection and Pest Management
MPRTM	Master of Parks, Recreation, and Tourism Management
MPS	Master of Pastoral Studies Master of Perfusion Science Master of Planning Studies Master of Political Science Master of Preservation Studies Master of Prevention Science Master of Professional Studies Master of Public Service
MPSA	Master of Public Service Administration
MPSRE	Master of Professional Studies in Real Estate
MPT	Master of Pastoral Theology Master of Physical Therapy
MPVM	Master of Preventive Veterinary Medicine
MPW	Master of Professional Writing Master of Public Works
MQM	Master of Quality Management
MQS	Master of Quality Systems
MR	Master of Recreation Master of Retailing
MRA	Master in Research Administration
MRC	Master of Rehabilitation Counseling
MRCP	Master of Regional and City Planning Master of Regional and Community Planning
MRD	Master of Rural Development
MRE	Master of Real Estate Master of Religious Education
MRED	Master of Real Estate Development
MREM	Master of Resource and Environmental Management
MRLS	Master of Resources Law Studies
MRM	Master of Resources Management
MRP	Master of Regional Planning
MRS	Master of Religious Studies
MRSc	Master of Rehabilitation Science
MS	Master of Science
MS Cmp E	Master of Science in Computer Engineering
MS Kin	Master of Science in Kinesiology

MS Acct	Master of Science in Accounting
MS Accy	Master of Science in Accountancy
MS Aero E	Master of Science in Aerospace Engineering
MS Ag	Master of Science in Agriculture
MS Arch	Master of Science in Architecture
MS Arch St	Master of Science in Architectural Studies
MS Bio E	Master of Science in Bioengineering Master of Science in Biomedical Engineering
MS Bm E	Master of Science in Biomedical Engineering
MS Ch E	Master of Science in Chemical Engineering
MS Chem	Master of Science in Chemistry
MS Cp E	Master of Science in Computer Engineering
MS Eco	Master of Science in Economics
MS Econ	Master of Science in Economics
MS Ed	Master of Science in Education
MS El	Master of Science in Educational Leadership and Administration
MS En E	Master of Science in Environmental Engineering
MS Eng	Master of Science in Engineering
MS Engr	Master of Science in Engineering
MS Env E	Master of Science in Environmental Engineering
MS Exp Surg	Master of Science in Experimental Surgery
MS Int A	Master of Science in International Affairs
MS Mat E	Master of Science in Materials Engineering
MS Mat SE	Master of Science in Material Science and Engineering
MS Met E	Master of Science in Metallurgical Engineering
MS Mgt	Master of Science in Management
MS Min	Master of Science in Mining
MS Min E	Master of Science in Mining Engineering
MS Mt E	Master of Science in Materials Engineering
MS Otal	Master of Science in Otalrynology
MS Pet E	Master of Science in Petroleum Engineering
MS Phys	Master of Science in Physics
MS Poly	Master of Science in Polymers
MS Psy	Master of Science in Psychology
MS Pub P	Master of Science in Public Policy
MS Sc	Master of Science in Social Science
MS Sp Ed	Master of Science in Special Education
MS Stat	Master of Science in Statistics
MS Surg	Master of Science in Surgery
MS Tax	Master of Science in Taxation

MS Tc E	Master of Science in Telecommunications Engineering
MS-R	Master of Science (Research)
MSA	Master of School Administration Master of Science Administration Master of Science in Accountancy Master of Science in Accounting Master of Science in Administration Master of Science in Aeronautics Master of Science in Agriculture Master of Science in Anesthesia Master of Science in Architecture Master of Science in Aviation Master of Sports Administration
MSA Phy	Master of Science in Applied Physics
MSAA	Master of Science in Astronautics and Aeronautics
MSAAE	Master of Science in Aeronautical and Astronautical Engineering
MSABE	Master of Science in Agricultural and Biological Engineering
MSAC	Master of Science in Acupuncture
MSACC	Master of Science in Accounting
MSaCS	Master of Science in Applied Computer Science
MSAE	Master of Science in Aeronautical Engineering Master of Science in Aerospace Engineering Master of Science in Applied Economics Master of Science in Applied Engineering Master of Science in Architectural Engineering Master of Science in Art Education
MSAH	Master of Science in Allied Health
MSAL	Master of Sport Administration and Leadership
MSAM	Master of Science in Applied Mathematics
MSANR	Master of Science in Agriculture and Natural Resources Systems Management
MSAPM	Master of Security Analysis and Portfolio Management
MSAS	Master of Science in Applied Statistics Master of Science in Architectural Studies
MSAT	Master of Science in Accounting and Taxation Master of Science in Advanced Technology Master of Science in Athletic Training
MSB	Master of Science in Bible Master of Science in Business
MSBA	Master of Science in Business Administration Master of Science in Business Analysis
MSBAE	Master of Science in Biological and Agricultural Engineering Master of Science in Biosystems and Agricultural Engineering
MSBC	Master of Science in Building Construction

MSBE	Master of Science in Biological Engineering Master of Science in Biomedical Engineering
MSBENG	Master of Science in Bioengineering
MSBIT	Master of Science in Business Information Technology
MSBM	Master of Sport Business Management
MSBME	Master of Science in Biomedical Engineering
MSBMS	Master of Science in Basic Medical Science
MSBS	Master of Science in Biomedical Sciences
MSC	Master of Science in Commerce Master of Science in Communication Master of Science in Computers Master of Science in Counseling Master of Science in Criminology
MSCC	Master of Science in Christian Counseling Master of Science in Community Counseling
MSCD	Master of Science in Communication Disorders Master of Science in Community Development
MSCE	Master of Science in Civil Engineering Master of Science in Clinical Epidemiology Master of Science in Computer Engineering Master of Science in Continuing Education
MSCEE	Master of Science in Civil and Environmental Engineering
MSCF	Master of Science in Computational Finance
MSChE	Master of Science in Chemical Engineering
MSCI	Master of Science in Clinical Investigation Master of Science in Curriculum and Instruction
MSCIS	Master of Science in Computer and Information Systems Master of Science in Computer Information Science Master of Science in Computer Information Systems
MSCIT	Master of Science in Computer Information Technology
MSCJ	Master of Science in Criminal Justice
MSCJA	Master of Science in Criminal Justice Administration
MSCJPS	Master of Science in Criminal Justice and Public Safety
MSCJS	Master of Science in Crime and Justice Studies
MSCL	Master of Science in Collaborative Leadership
MSCLS	Master of Science in Clinical Laboratory Studies
MSCM	Master of Science in Church Management Master of Science in Conflict Management Master of Science in Construction Management
MScM	Master of Science in Management
MSCM	Master of Supply Chain Management
MSCNU	Master of Science in Clinical Nutrition

MSCP	Master of Science in Clinical Psychology Master of Science in Computer Engineering Master of Science in Counseling Psychology
MSCPE	Master of Science in Computer Engineering
MSCPharm	Master of Science in Pharmacy
MSCPI	Master in Strategic Planning for Critical Infrastructures
MSCR	Master of Science in Clinical Research
MSCRP	Master of Science in City and Regional Planning Master of Science in Community and Regional Planning
MSCS	Master of Science in Clinical Science Master of Science in Computer Science
MSCSD	Master of Science in Communication Sciences and Disorders
MSCSE	Master of Science in Computer Science and Engineering
MSCTE	Master of Science in Career and Technical Education
MSD	Master of Science in Dentistry Master of Science in Design Master of Science in Dietetics
MSDR	Master of Dispute Resolution
MSE	Master of Science Education Master of Science in Economics Master of Science in Education Master of Science in Engineering Master of Science in Engineering Management Master of Software Engineering Master of Special Education Master of Structural Engineering
MSECE	Master of Science in Electrical and Computer Engineering
MSED	Master of Sustainable Economic Development
MSEE	Master of Science in Electrical Engineering Master of Science in Environmental Engineering
MSEH	Master of Science in Environmental Health
MSEL	Master of Science in Educational Leadership
MSEM	Master of Science in Engineering Management Master of Science in Engineering Mechanics Master of Science in Environmental Management
MSENE	Master of Science in Environmental Engineering
MSEO	Master of Science in Electro-Optics
MSEP	Master of Science in Economic Policy
MSEPA	Master of Science in Economics and Policy Analysis
MSES	Master of Science in Embedded Software Engineering Master of Science in Engineering Science Master of Science in Environmental Science Master of Science in Environmental Studies

MSESM	Master of Science in Engineering Science and Mechanics
MSET	Master of Science in Educational Technology Master of Science in Engineering Technology
MSEV	Master of Science in Environmental Engineering
MSEVH	Master of Science in Environmental Health and Safety
MSF	Master of Science in Finance Master of Science in Forestry Master of Spiritual Formation
MSFA	Master of Science in Financial Analysis
MSFAM	Master of Science in Family Studies
MSFCS	Master of Science in Family and Consumer Science
MSFE	Master of Science in Financial Engineering
MSFOR	Master of Science in Forestry
MSFP	Master of Science in Financial Planning
MSFS	Master of Science in Financial Sciences Master of Science in Forensic Science
MSFSB	Master of Science in Financial Services and Banking
MSFT	Master of Science in Family Therapy
MSGC	Master of Science in Genetic Counseling
MSH	Master of Science in Health Master of Science in Hospice
MSHA	Master of Science in Health Administration
MSHCA	Master of Science in Health Care Administration
MSHCI	Master of Science in Human Computer Interaction
MSHCPM	Master of Science in Health Care Policy and Management
MSHE	Master of Science in Health Education
MSHES	Master of Science in Human Environmental Sciences
MSHFID	Master of Science in Human Factors in Information Design
MSHFS	Master of Science in Human Factors and Systems
MSHI	Master of Science in Health Informatics
MSHP	Master of Science in Health Professions Master of Science in Health Promotion
MSHR	Master of Science in Human Resources
MSHRL	Master of Science in Human Resource Leadership
MSHRM	Master of Science in Human Resource Management
MSHROD	Master of Science in Human Resources and Organizational Development

MSHS	Master of Science in Health Science Master of Science in Health Services Master of Science in Health Systems Master of Science in Homeland Security
MSHT	Master of Science in History of Technology
MSI	Master of Science in Information Master of Science in Instruction
MSIA	Master of Science in Industrial Administration Master of Science in Information Assurance and Computer Security
MSIB	Master of Science in International Business
MSIDM	Master of Science in Interior Design and Merchandising
MSIDT	Master of Science in Information Design and Technology
MSIE	Master of Science in Industrial Engineering Master of Science in International Economics
MSIEM	Master of Science in Information Engineering and Management
MSIID	Master of Science in Information and Instructional Design
MSIM	Master of Science in Information Management Master of Science in International Management
MSIMC	Master of Science in Integrated Marketing Communications
MSIR	Master of Science in Industrial Relations
MSIS	Master of Science in Information Science Master of Science in Information Systems Master of Science in Interdisciplinary Studies
MSISE	Master of Science in Infrastructure Systems Engineering
MSISM	Master of Science in Information Systems Management
MSISPM	Master of Science in Information Security Policy and Management
MSIST	Master of Science in Information Systems Technology
MSIT	Master of Science in Industrial Technology Master of Science in Information Technology Master of Science in Instructional Technology
MSITM	Master of Science in Information Technology Management
MSJ	Master of Science in Journalism Master of Science in Jurisprudence
MSJC	Master of Social Justice and Criminology
MSJE	Master of Science in Jewish Education
MSJFP	Master of Science in Juvenile Forensic Psychology
MSJJ	Master of Science in Juvenile Justice
MSJPS	Master of Science in Justice and Public Safety

MSJS	Master of Science in Jewish Studies
MSK	Master of Science in Kinesiology
MSL	Master of School Leadership
	Master of Science in Leadership
	Master of Science in Limnology
	Master of Strategic Leadership
	Master of Studies in Law
MSLA	Master of Science in Landscape Architecture
	Master of Science in Legal Administration
MSLD	Master of Science in Land Development
MSLFS	Master of Science in Life Sciences
MSLP	Master of Speech-Language Pathology
MSLS	Master of Science in Library Science
MSLSCM	Master of Science in Logistics and Supply Chain Management
MSLT	Master of Second Language Teaching
MSM	Master of Sacred Ministry
	Master of Sacred Music
	Master of School Mathematics
	Master of Science in Management
	Master of Science in Mathematics
	Master of Science in Organization Management
	Master of Security Management
MSMA	Master of Science in Marketing Analysis
MSMAE	Master of Science in Materials Engineering
MSMC	Master of Science in Mass Communications
MSME	Master of Science in Mathematics Education
	Master of Science in Mechanical Engineering
MSMFE	Master of Science in Manufacturing Engineering
MSMFT	Master of Science in Marriage and Family Therapy
MSMIS	Master of Science in Management Information Systems
MSMIT	Master of Science in Management and Information Technology
MSMOT	Master of Science in Management of Technology
MSMS	Master of Science in Management Science
	Master of Science in Medical Sciences
MSMSE	Master of Science in Manufacturing Systems Engineering
	Master of Science in Material Science and Engineering
	Master of Science in Mathematics and Science Education
MSMT	Master of Science in Management and Technology
	Master of Science in Medical Technology
MSMus	Master of Sacred Music
MSN	Master of Science in Nursing
MSN-R	Master of Science in Nursing (Research)
MSNA	Master of Science in Nurse Anesthesia
MSNE	Master of Science in Nuclear Engineering
MSNED	Master of Science in Nurse Education
MSNM	Master of Science in Nonprofit Management
MSNS	Master of Science in Natural Science
	Master of Science in Nutritional Science
MSOD	Master of Science in Organizational Development
MSOEE	Master of Science in Outdoor and Environmental Education
MSOES	Master of Science in Occupational Ergonomics and Safety
MSOH	Master of Science in Occupational Health
MSOL	Master of Science in Organizational Leadership
MSOM	Master of Science in Operations Management
	Master of Science in Organization and Management
	Master of Science in Oriental Medicine
MSOR	Master of Science in Operations Research
MSOT	Master of Science in Occupational Technology
	Master of Science in Occupational Therapy
MSP	Master of Science in Pharmacy
	Master of Science in Planning
	Master of Science in Psychology
	Master of Speech Pathology
MSPA	Master of Science in Physician Assistant
	Master of Science in Professional Accountancy
MSPAS	Master of Science in Physician Assistant Studies
MSPC	Master of Science in Professional Communications
	Master of Science in Professional Counseling
MSPE	Master of Science in Petroleum Engineering
MSPG	Master of Science in Psychology
MSPH	Master of Science in Public Health
MSPH/M Ed	Master of Science in Public Health/Master of Education
MSPH/MCRP	Master of Science in Public Health/Msater of City and Regional Planning
MSPH/MSIS	Master of Science in Public Health/Master of Science in Information Science
MSPH/MSLS	Master of Science in Public Health/Master of Science in Library Science
MSPHR	Master of Science in Pharmacy
MSPM	Master of Science in Professional Management
	Master of Science in Project Management
MSPNGE	Master of Science in Petroleum and Natural Gas Engineering
MSPS	Master of Science in Pharmaceutical Science
	Master of Science in Political Science
	Master of Science in Psychological Services
MSPT	Master of Science in Physical Therapy
MSpVM	Master of Specialized Veterinary Medicine

MSR	Master of Science in Radiology Master of Science in Reading
MSRA	Master of Science in Recreation Administration
MSRC	Master of Science in Resource Conservation
MSRE	Master of Science in Real Estate Master of Science in Religious Education
MSRED	Master of Science in Real Estate Development
MSRLS	Master of Science in Recreation and Leisure Studies
MSRMP	Master of Science in Radiological Medical Physics
MSRS	Master of Science in Rehabilitation Science
MSS	Master of Science in Software Master of Social Science Master of Social Services Master of Software Systems Master of Sports Science Master of Strategic Studies
MSSA	Master of Science in Social Administration
MSSCP	Master of Science in Science Content and Process
MSSD	Master of Science in Sustainable Design
MSSE	Master of Science in Software Engineering Master of Science in Space Education Master of Science in Special Education
MSSEM	Master of Science in Systems and Engineering Management
MSSI	Master of Science in Security Informatics Master of Science in Strategic Intelligence
MSSL	Master of Science in School Leadership Master of Science in Strategic Leadership
MSSLP	Master of Science in Speech-Language Pathology
MSSM	Master of Science in Sports Medicine
MSSP	Master of Science in Social Policy
MSSPA	Master of Science in Student Personnel Administration
MSSS	Master of Science in Safety Science Master of Science in Systems Science
MSST	Master of Science in Security Technologies
MSSW	Master of Science in Social Work
MSSWE	Master of Science in Software Engineering
MST	Master of Science and Technology Master of Science in Taxation Master of Science in Teaching Master of Science in Technology Master of Science in Telecommunications Master of Science Teaching
MSTC	Master of Science in Technical Communication Master of Science in Telecommunications
MSTCM	Master of Science in Traditional Chinese Medicine

MSTE	Master of Science in Telecommunications Engineering Master of Science in Transportation Engineering
MSTM	Master of Science in Technical Management
MSTOM	Master of Science in Traditional Oriental Medicine
MSUD	Master of Science in Urban Design
MSW	Master of Social Work
MSWE	Master of Software Engineering
MSWREE	Master of Science in Water Resources and Environmental Engineering
MSX	Master of Science in Exercise Science
MT	Master of Taxation Master of Teaching Master of Technology Master of Textiles
MTA	Master of Tax Accounting Master of Teaching Arts Master of Tourism Administration
MTCM	Master of Traditional Chinese Medicine
MTD	Master of Training and Development
MTE	Master in Educational Technology
MTESOL	Master in Teaching English to Speakers of Other Languages
MTHM	Master of Tourism and Hospitality Management
MTI	Master of Information Technology
MTIM	Master of Trust and Investment Management
MTL	Master of Talmudic Law
MTM	Master of Technology Management Master of Telecommunications Management Master of the Teaching of Mathematics
MTMH	Master of Tropical Medicine and Hygiene
MTOM	Master of Traditional Oriental Medicine
MTP	Master of Transpersonal Psychology
MTPC	Master of Technical and Professional Communication
MTR	Master of Translational Research
MTS	Master of Theological Studies
MTSC	Master of Technical and Scientific Communication
MTSE	Master of Telecommunications and Software Engineering
MTT	Master in Technology Management
MTX	Master of Taxation
MUA	Master of Urban Affairs
MUD	Master of Urban Design
MUEP	Master of Urban and Environmental Planning
MUP	Master of Urban Planning

MUPDD	Master of Urban Planning, Design, and Development
MUPP	Master of Urban Planning and Policy
MUPRED	Master of Urban Planning and Real Estate Development
MURP	Master of Urban and Regional Planning Master of Urban and Rural Planning
MURPL	Master of Urban and Regional Planning
MUS	Master of Urban Studies
MVM	Master of VLSI and Microelectronics
MVP	Master of Voice Pedagogy
MVPH	Master of Veterinary Public Health
MVS	Master of Visual Studies
MWC	Master of Wildlife Conservation
MWE	Master in Welding Engineering
MWPS	Master of Wood and Paper Science
MWR	Master of Water Resources
MWS	Master of Women's Studies Master of Worship Studies
MZS	Master of Zoological Science
Nav Arch	Naval Architecture
Naval E	Naval Engineer
ND	Doctor of Naturopathic Medicine
NE	Nuclear Engineer
Nuc E	Nuclear Engineer
OD	Doctor of Optometry
OTD	Doctor of Occupational Therapy
PBME	Professional Master of Biomedical Engineering
PD	Professional Diploma
PGC	Post-Graduate Certificate
PGD	Postgraduate Diploma
Ph L	Licentiate of Philosophy
Pharm D	Doctor of Pharmacy
PhD	Doctor of Philosophy
PhD Otal	Doctor of Philosophy in Otalrynology
PhD Surg	Doctor of Philosophy in Surgery
PhDEE	Doctor of Philosophy in Electrical Engineering
PM Sc	Professional Master of Science
PMBA	Professional Master of Business Administration
PMC	Post Master Certificate
PMD	Post-Master's Diploma
PMS	Professional Master of Science Professional Master's

Post-Doctoral MS	Post-Doctoral Master of Science
Post-MSN Certificate	Post-Master of Science in Nursing Certificate
PPDPT	Postprofessional Doctor of Physical Therapy
PSM	Professional Master of Science Professional Science Master's
Psy D	Doctor of Psychology
Psy M	Master of Psychology
Psy S	Specialist in Psychology
Psya D	Doctor of Psychoanalysis
Re Dir	Director of Recreation
Rh D	Doctor of Rehabilitation
S Psy S	Specialist in Psychological Services
Sc D	Doctor of Science
Sc M	Master of Science
SCCT	Specialist in Community College Teaching
ScDPT	Doctor of Physical Therapy Science
SD	Doctor of Science Specialist Degree
SJD	Doctor of Juridical Science
SLPD	Doctor of Speech-Language Pathology
SM	Master of Science
SM Arch S	Master of Science in Architectural Studies
SM Vis S	Master of Science in Visual Studies
SMBT	Master of Science in Building Technology
SP	Specialist Degree
Sp C	Specialist in Counseling
Sp Ed	Specialist in Education
Sp LIS	Specialist in Library and Information Science
SPA	Specialist in Arts
SPCM	Special in Church Music
Spec	Specialist's Certificate
Spec M	Specialist in Music
SPEM	Special in Educational Ministries
SPS	School Psychology Specialist
Spt	Specialist Degree
SPTH	Special in Theology
SSP	Specialist in School Psychology
STB	Bachelor of Sacred Theology
STD	Doctor of Sacred Theology
STL	Licentiate of Sacred Theology
STM	Master of Sacred Theology

TDPT	Transitional Doctor of Physical Therapy	**WEMBA**	Weekend Executive Master of Business Administration
Th D	Doctor of Theology	**XMA**	Executive Master of Arts
Th M	Master of Theology	**XMBA**	Executive Master of Business Administration
VMD	Doctor of Veterinary Medicine		

INDEXES

Close-Ups and Displays

Directories and Subject Areas

Following is an alphabetical listing of directories and subject areas. Also listed are cross-references for subject area names not used in the directory structure of the guides, for example, "Arabic (*see* Near and Middle Eastern Languages)."

Graduate Programs in the Humanities, Arts & Social Sciences

Addictions/Substance Abuse Counseling

Administration (*see* Arts Administration; Public Administration)

African-American Studies

African Languages and Literatures (*see* African Studies)

African Studies

Agribusiness (*see* Agricultural Economics and Agribusiness)

Agricultural Economics and Agribusiness

Alcohol Abuse Counseling (*see* Addictions/Substance Abuse Counseling)

American Indian/Native American Studies

American Studies

Anthropology

Applied Arts and Design—General

Applied Behavior Analysis

Applied Economics

Applied History (*see* Public History)

Applied Psychology

Applied Social Research

Arabic (*see* Near and Middle Eastern Languages)

Arab Studies (*see* Near and Middle Eastern Studies)

Archaeology

Architectural History

Architecture

Archives Administration (*see* Public History)

Area and Cultural Studies (*see* African-American Studies; African Studies; American Indian/Native American Studies; American Studies; Asian-American Studies; Asian Studies; Canadian Studies; Cultural Studies; East European and Russian Studies; Ethnic Studies; Folklore; Gender Studies; Hispanic Studies; Holocaust Studies; Jewish Studies; Latin American Studies; Near and Middle Eastern Studies; Northern Studies; Pacific Area/Pacific Rim Studies; Western European Studies; Women's Studies)

Art/Fine Arts

Art History

Arts Administration

Arts Journalism

Art Therapy

Asian-American Studies

Asian Languages

Asian Studies

Behavioral Sciences (*see* Psychology)

Bible Studies (*see* Religion; Theology)

Biological Anthropology

Black Studies (*see* African-American Studies)

Broadcasting (*see* Communication; Film, Television, and Video Production)

Broadcast Journalism

Building Science

Canadian Studies

Celtic Languages

Ceramics (*see* Art/Fine Arts)

Child and Family Studies

Child Development

Chinese

Chinese Studies (*see* Asian Languages; Asian Studies)

Christian Studies (*see* Missions and Missiology; Religion; Theology)

Cinema (*see* Film, Television, and Video Production)

City and Regional Planning (*see* Urban and Regional Planning)

Classical Languages and Literatures (*see* Classics)

Classics

Clinical Psychology

Clothing and Textiles

Cognitive Psychology (*see* Psychology—General; Cognitive Sciences)

Cognitive Sciences

Communication—General

Community Affairs (*see* Urban and Regional Planning; Urban Studies)

Community Planning (*see* Architecture; Environmental Design; Urban and Regional Planning; Urban Design; Urban Studies)

Community Psychology (*see* Social Psychology)

Comparative and Interdisciplinary Arts

Comparative Literature

Composition (*see* Music)

Computer Art and Design

Conflict Resolution and Mediation/Peace Studies

Consumer Economics

Corporate and Organizational Communication

Corrections (*see* Criminal Justice and Criminology)

Counseling (*see* Counseling Psychology; Pastoral Ministry and Counseling)

Counseling Psychology

Crafts (*see* Art/Fine Arts)

Creative Arts Therapies (*see* Art Therapy; Therapies—Dance, Drama, and Music)

Criminal Justice and Criminology

Cultural Anthropology

Cultural Studies

Dance

Decorative Arts

Demography and Population Studies

Design (*see* Applied Arts and Design; Architecture; Art/Fine Arts; Environmental Design; Graphic Design; Industrial Design; Interior Design; Textile Design; Urban Design)

Developmental Psychology

Diplomacy (*see* International Affairs)

Disability Studies

Drama Therapy (*see* Therapies—Dance, Drama, and Music)

Dramatic Arts (*see* Theater)

Drawing (*see* Art/Fine Arts)

Drug Abuse Counseling (*see* Addictions/Substance Abuse Counseling)

Drug and Alcohol Abuse Counseling (*see* Addictions/Substance Abuse Counseling)

East Asian Studies (*see* Asian Studies)

East European and Russian Studies

Economic Development

Economics

Educational Theater (*see* Theater; Therapies—Dance, Drama, and Music)

Emergency Management

English

Environmental Design

Ethics

Ethnic Studies

Ethnomusicology (*see* Music)

Experimental Psychology

Family and Consumer Sciences—General

Family Studies (*see* Child and Family Studies)

Family Therapy (*see* Child and Family Studies; Clinical Psychology; Counseling Psychology; Marriage and Family Therapy)

Filmmaking (*see* Film, Television, and Video Production)

Film Studies (*see* Film, Television, and Video Production)

Film, Television, and Video Production

Film, Television, and Video Theory and Criticism

Fine Arts (*see* Art/Fine Arts)

Folklore

Foreign Languages (*see* specific language)

Foreign Service (*see* International Affairs; International Development)

Forensic Psychology

Forensic Sciences

Forensics (*see* Speech and Interpersonal Communication)

French

Gender Studies

General Studies (*see* Liberal Studies)

Genetic Counseling

Geographic Information Systems

Geography

German

Gerontology

Graphic Design

Greek (*see* Classics)

Health Communication

Health Psychology

Hebrew (*see* Near and Middle Eastern Languages)

Hebrew Studies (*see* Jewish Studies)

Hispanic and Latin American Languages

Hispanic Studies

Historic Preservation

History

History of Art (*see* Art History)

History of Medicine

History of Science and Technology

Holocaust and Genocide Studies

Home Economics (*see* Family and Consumer Sciences—General)

Homeland Security

Household Economics, Sciences, and Management (*see* Family and Consumer Sciences—General)

Human Development

Humanities

Illustration

Industrial and Labor Relations

Industrial and Organizational Psychology

Industrial Design

Interdisciplinary Studies

Interior Design

International Affairs

International Development

International Economics

International Service (*see* International Affairs; International Development)

International Trade Policy

Internet and Interactive Multimedia

Interpersonal Communication (*see* Speech and Interpersonal Communication)

Interpretation (*see* Translation and Interpretation)

Islamic Studies (*see* Near and Middle Eastern Studies; Religion)

Italian

Japanese

Japanese Studies (*see* Asian Languages; Asian Studies; Japanese)

Jewelry (*see* Art/Fine Arts)

Jewish Studies

Journalism

Judaic Studies (*see* Jewish Studies; Religion)

Labor Relations (*see* Industrial and Labor Relations)

Landscape Architecture

Latin American Studies

Latin (*see* Classics)

Law Enforcement (*see* Criminal Justice and Criminology)

Liberal Studies

Lighting Design

Linguistics

Literature (*see* Classics; Comparative Literature; specific language)

Marriage and Family Therapy

Mass Communication

Media Studies

Medical Illustration

Medieval and Renaissance Studies

Metalsmithing (*see* Art/Fine Arts)

Middle Eastern Studies (*see* Near and Middle Eastern Studies)

Military and Defense Studies

Mineral Economics

Ministry (*see* Pastoral Ministry and Counseling; Theology)

Missions and Missiology

Motion Pictures (*see* Film, Television, and Video Production)

Museum Studies

Music

Musicology (*see* Music)

Music Therapy (*see* Therapies—Dance, Drama, and Music)

National Security

Native American Studies (*see* American Indian/Native American Studies)

Near and Middle Eastern Languages

Near and Middle Eastern Studies

Near Environment (*see* Family and Consumer Sciences)

Northern Studies

Organizational Psychology (*see* Industrial and Organizational Psychology)

Oriental Languages (*see* Asian Languages)

Oriental Studies (*see* Asian Studies)

Pacific Area/Pacific Rim Studies

Painting (*see* Art/Fine Arts)

Pastoral Ministry and Counseling

Philanthropic Studies

Philosophy

Photography

Playwriting (*see* Theater; Writing)

Policy Studies (*see* Public Policy)

Political Science

Population Studies (*see* Demography and Population Studies)

Portuguese

Printmaking (*see* Art/Fine Arts)

Product Design (*see* Industrial Design)

Psychoanalysis and Psychotherapy

Psychology—General

Public Administration

Public Affairs

Public History

Public Policy

Public Speaking (*see* Mass Communication; Rhetoric; Speech and Interpersonal Communication)

Publishing

Regional Planning (*see* Architecture; Urban and Regional Planning; Urban Design; Urban Studies)

Rehabilitation Counseling

Religion

Renaissance Studies (*see* Medieval and Renaissance Studies)

Rhetoric

Romance Languages

Romance Literatures (*see* Romance Languages)

Rural Planning and Studies

Rural Sociology

Russian

Scandinavian Languages

School Psychology

Sculpture (*see* Art/Fine Arts)

Security Administration (*see* Criminal Justice and Criminology)

Slavic Languages

Slavic Studies (*see* East European and Russian Studies; Slavic Languages)

Social Psychology

Social Sciences

Sociology

Southeast Asian Studies (*see* Asian Studies)

Soviet Studies (*see* East European and Russian Studies; Russian)

Spanish

Speech and Interpersonal Communication

Sport Psychology

Studio Art (*see* Art/Fine Arts)

Substance Abuse Counseling (*see* Addictions/Substance Abuse Counseling)

Survey Methodology

Sustainable Development

Technical Communication

Technical Writing

Telecommunications (*see* Film, Television, and Video Production)

Television (*see* Film, Television, and Video Production)

Textile Design

Textiles (*see* Clothing and Textiles; Textile Design)

Thanatology

Theater

Theater Arts (*see* Theater)

Theology

Therapies—Dance, Drama, and Music

Translation and Interpretation

Transpersonal and Humanistic Psychology

Urban and Regional Planning

Urban Design

Urban Planning (*see* Architecture; Urban and Regional Planning; Urban Design; Urban Studies)

Urban Studies

Video (*see* Film, Television, and Video Production)

Visual Arts (*see* Applied Arts and Design; Art/Fine Arts; Film, Television, and Video Production; Graphic Design; Illustration; Photography)

Western European Studies

Women's Studies

World Wide Web (*see* Internet and Interactive Multimedia)

Writing

Graduate Programs in the Biological Sciences

Anatomy

Animal Behavior

Bacteriology

Behavioral Sciences (*see* Biopsychology; Neuroscience; Zoology)

Biochemistry

Biological and Biomedical Sciences—General

Biological Chemistry (*see* Biochemistry)

Biological Oceanography (*see* Marine Biology)

Biophysics

Biopsychology

Botany

Breeding (*see* Botany; Plant Biology; Genetics)

Cancer Biology/Oncology

Cardiovascular Sciences

Cell Biology

Cellular Physiology (*see* Cell Biology; Physiology)

Computational Biology

Conservation (*see* Conservation Biology; Environmental Biology)

Conservation Biology

Crop Sciences (*see* Botany; Plant Biology)

Cytology (*see* Cell Biology)

Developmental Biology

Dietetics (*see* Nutrition)

Ecology

Embryology (*see* Developmental Biology)

Endocrinology (*see* Physiology)

Entomology

Environmental Biology

Evolutionary Biology

Foods (*see* Nutrition)

Genetics

Genomic Sciences

Histology (*see* Anatomy; Cell Biology)

Human Genetics

Immunology

Infectious Diseases

Laboratory Medicine (*see* Immunology; Microbiology; Pathology)

Life Sciences (*see* Biological and Biomedical Sciences)

Marine Biology

Medical Microbiology

Medical Sciences (*see* Biological and Biomedical Sciences)

Medical Science Training Programs (*see* Biological and Biomedical Sciences)

Microbiology

Molecular Biology

Molecular Biophysics

Molecular Genetics

Molecular Medicine

Molecular Pathogenesis

Molecular Pathology

Molecular Pharmacology

Molecular Physiology

Molecular Toxicology

Neural Sciences (*see* Biopsychology; Neurobiology; Neuroscience)

Neurobiology

Neuroendocrinology (*see* Biopsychology; Neurobiology; Neuroscience; Physiology)

Neuropharmacology (*see* Biopsychology; Neurobiology; Neuroscience; Pharmacology)

Neurophysiology (*see* Biopsychology; Neurobiology; Neuroscience; Physiology)

Neuroscience

Nutrition

Oncology (*see* Cancer Biology/Oncology)

Organismal Biology (*see* Biological and Biomedical Sciences; Zoology)

Parasitology

Pathobiology

Pathology

Pharmacology

Photobiology of Cells and Organelles (*see* Botany; Cell Biology; Plant Biology)

Physiological Optics (*see* Physiology)

Physiology

Plant Biology

Plant Molecular Biology

Plant Pathology

Plant Physiology

Pomology (*see* Botany; Plant Biology)

Psychobiology (*see* Biopsychology)

Psychopharmacology (*see* Biopsychology; Neuroscience; Pharmacology)

Radiation Biology

Reproductive Biology

Sociobiology (*see* Evolutionary Biology)

Structural Biology

Systems Biology

Teratology

Theoretical Biology (*see* Biological and Biomedical Sciences)

Therapeutics (*see* Pharmacology)

Toxicology

Translational Biology

Tropical Medicine (*see* Parasitology)

Virology

Wildlife Biology (*see* Zoology)

Zoology

Graduate Programs in the Physical Sciences, Mathematics, Agricultural Sciences, the Environment & Natural Resources

Acoustics

Agricultural Sciences

Agronomy and Soil Sciences

Analytical Chemistry

Animal Sciences

Applied Mathematics

Applied Physics

Applied Statistics

Aquaculture

Astronomy

Astrophysical Sciences (*see* Astrophysics; Atmospheric Sciences; Meteorology; Planetary and Space Sciences)

Astrophysics

Atmospheric Sciences

Biological Oceanography (*see* Marine Affairs; Marine Sciences; Oceanography)

Biomathematics

Biometry

Biostatistics

Chemical Physics

Chemistry

Computational Sciences

Condensed Matter Physics

Dairy Science (*see* Animal Sciences)

Earth Sciences (*see* Geosciences)

Environmental Management and Policy

Environmental Sciences

Environmental Studies (*see* Environmental Management and Policy)

Experimental Statistics (*see* Statistics)

Fish, Game, and Wildlife Management

Food Science and Technology

Forestry

General Science (*see* specific topics)

Geochemistry

Geodetic Sciences

Geological Engineering (*see* Geology)

Geological Sciences (*see* Geology)

Geology

Geophysical Fluid Dynamics (*see* Geophysics)

Geophysics

Geosciences

Horticulture

Hydrogeology

Hydrology

Inorganic Chemistry

Limnology

Marine Affairs

Marine Geology

Marine Sciences

Marine Studies (*see* Marine Affairs; Marine Geology; Marine Sciences; Oceanography)

Mathematical and Computational Finance

Mathematical Physics

Mathematical Statistics (*see* Applied Statistics; Statistics)

Mathematics

Meteorology

Mineralogy

Natural Resource Management (*see* Environmental Management and Policy; Natural Resources)

Natural Resources

Nuclear Physics (*see* Physics)

Ocean Engineering (*see* Marine Affairs; Marine Geology; Marine Sciences; Oceanography)

Oceanography

Optical Sciences

Optical Technologies (*see* Optical Sciences)

Optics (*see* Applied Physics; Optical Sciences; Physics)

Organic Chemistry

Paleontology

Paper Chemistry (*see* Chemistry)

Photonics

Physical Chemistry

Physics

Planetary and Space Sciences

Plant Sciences

Plasma Physics

Poultry Science (*see* Animal Sciences)

Radiological Physics (*see* Physics)

Range Management (*see* Range Science)

Range Science

Resource Management (*see* Environmental Management and Policy; Natural Resources)

Solid-Earth Sciences (*see* Geosciences)

Space Sciences (*see* Planetary and Space Sciences)

Statistics

Theoretical Chemistry

Theoretical Physics

Viticulture and Enology

Water Resources

Graduate Programs in Engineering & Applied Sciences

Aeronautical Engineering (*see* Aerospace/Aeronautical Engineering)

Aerospace/Aeronautical Engineering

Aerospace Studies (*see* Aerospace/Aeronautical Engineering)

Agricultural Engineering

Applied Mechanics (*see* Mechanics)

Applied Science and Technology

Architectural Engineering

Artificial Intelligence/Robotics

Astronautical Engineering (*see* Aerospace/Aeronautical Engineering)

Automotive Engineering

Aviation

Biochemical Engineering

Bioengineering

Bioinformatics

Biological Engineering (*see* Bioengineering)

Biomedical Engineering

Biosystems Engineering

Biotechnology

Ceramic Engineering (*see* Ceramic Sciences and Engineering)

Ceramic Sciences and Engineering

Ceramics (*see* Ceramic Sciences and Engineering)

Chemical Engineering

Civil Engineering

Computer and Information Systems Security

Computer Engineering

Computer Science

Computing Technology (*see* Computer Science)

Construction Engineering

Construction Management

Database Systems

Electrical Engineering

Electronic Materials

Electronics Engineering (*see* Electrical Engineering)

Energy and Power Engineering

Energy Management and Policy

Engineering and Applied Sciences

Engineering and Public Affairs (*see* Technology and Public Policy)

Engineering and Public Policy (*see* Energy Management and Policy; Technology and Public Policy)

Engineering Design

Engineering Management

Engineering Mechanics (*see* Mechanics)

Engineering Metallurgy (*see* Metallurgical Engineering and Metallurgy)

Engineering Physics

Environmental Design (*see* Environmental Engineering)

Environmental Engineering

Ergonomics and Human Factors

Financial Engineering

Fire Protection Engineering

Food Engineering (*see* Agricultural Engineering)

Game Design and Development

Gas Engineering (*see* Petroleum Engineering)

Geological Engineering

Geophysics Engineering (*see* Geological Engineering)

Geotechnical Engineering

Hazardous Materials Management

Health Informatics

Health Systems (*see* Safety Engineering; Systems Engineering)

Highway Engineering (*see* Transportation and Highway Engineering)

Human-Computer Interaction

Human Factors (*see* Ergonomics and Human Factors)

Hydraulics

Hydrology (*see* Water Resources Engineering)

Industrial Engineering (*see* Industrial/Management Engineering)

Industrial/Management Engineering

Information Science

Internet Engineering

Macromolecular Science (*see* Polymer Science and Engineering)

Management Engineering (*see* Engineering Management; Industrial/Management Engineering)

Management of Technology

Manufacturing Engineering

Marine Engineering (*see* Civil Engineering)

Materials Engineering

Materials Sciences

Mechanical Engineering

Mechanics

Medical Informatics

Metallurgical Engineering and Metallurgy

Metallurgy (*see* Metallurgical Engineering and Metallurgy)

Mineral/Mining Engineering

Modeling and Simulation

Nanotechnology

Nuclear Engineering

Ocean Engineering

Operations Research

Paper and Pulp Engineering

Petroleum Engineering

Pharmaceutical Engineering

Plastics Engineering (*see* Polymer Science and Engineering)

Polymer Science and Engineering

Public Policy (*see* Energy Management and Policy; Technology and Public Policy)

Reliability Engineering

Robotics (*see* Artificial Intelligence/Robotics)

Safety Engineering

Software Engineering

Solid-State Sciences (*see* Materials Sciences)

Structural Engineering

Surveying Science and Engineering

Systems Analysis (*see* Systems Engineering)

Systems Engineering

Systems Science

Technology and Public Policy

Telecommunications

Telecommunications Management

Textile Sciences and Engineering

Textiles (*see* Textile Sciences and Engineering)

Transportation and Highway Engineering

Urban Systems Engineering (*see* Systems Engineering)

Waste Management (*see* Hazardous Materials Management)

Water Resources Engineering

Graduate Programs in Business, Education, Health, Information Studies, Law & Social Work

Accounting

Actuarial Science

Acupuncture and Oriental Medicine

Acute Care/Critical Care Nursing

Administration (*see* Business Administration and Management; Educational Administration; Health Services Management and Hospital Administration; Industrial and Manufacturing Management; Nursing and Healthcare Administration; Pharmaceutical Administration; Sports Management)

Adult Education

Adult Nursing

Advanced Practice Nursing (*see* Family Nurse Practitioner Studies)

Advertising and Public Relations

Agricultural Education

Alcohol Abuse Counseling (*see* Counselor Education)

Allied Health—General

Allied Health Professions (*see* Clinical Laboratory Sciences/Medical Technology; Clinical Research; Communication Disorders; Dental Hygiene; Emergency Medical Services; Occupational Therapy; Physical Therapy; Physician Assistant Studies; Rehabilitation Sciences)

Allopathic Medicine

Anesthesiologist Assistant Studies

Archival Management and Studies

Art Education

Athletics Administration (*see* Kinesiology and Movement Studies)

Athletic Training and Sports Medicine

Audiology (*see* Communication Disorders)

Aviation Management

Banking (*see* Finance and Banking)

Bioethics

Business Administration and Management—General

Business Education

Child-Care Nursing (*see* Maternal and Child/Neonatal Nursing)

Chiropractic

Clinical Laboratory Sciences/Medical Technology

Clinical Research

Communication Disorders

Community College Education

Community Health

Community Health Nursing

Computer Education

Continuing Education (*see* Adult Education)

Counseling (*see* Counselor Education)

Counselor Education

Curriculum and Instruction

Dental and Oral Surgery (*see* Oral and Dental Sciences)

Dental Assistant Studies (*see* Dental Hygiene)

Dental Hygiene

Dental Services (*see* Dental Hygiene)

Dentistry

Developmental Education

Distance Education Development

Drug Abuse Counseling (*see* Counselor Education)

Early Childhood Education

Educational Leadership and Administration

Educational Measurement and Evaluation

Educational Media/Instructional Technology

Educational Policy

Educational Psychology

Education—General

Education of the Blind (*see* Special Education)

Education of the Deaf (*see* Special Education)

Education of the Gifted

Education of the Hearing Impaired (*see* Special Education)

Education of the Learning Disabled (*see* Special Education)

Education of the Mentally Retarded (*see* Special Education)

Education of the Physically Handicapped (*see* Special Education)

Education of Students with Severe/Multiple Disabilities

Education of the Visually Handicapped (*see* Special Education)

Electronic Commerce

Elementary Education

Emergency Medical Services

English as a Second Language

English Education

Entertainment Management

Entrepreneurship

Environmental and Occupational Health

Environmental Education

Environmental Law

Epidemiology

Exercise and Sports Science

Exercise Physiology (*see* Kinesiology and Movement Studies)

Facilities and Entertainment Management

Family Nurse Practitioner Studies

Finance and Banking

Food Services Management (*see* Hospitality Management)

Foreign Languages Education

Forensic Nursing

Foundations and Philosophy of Education

Gerontological Nursing

Guidance and Counseling (*see* Counselor Education)

Health Education

Health Law

Health Physics/Radiological Health

Health Promotion

Health-Related Professions (*see* individual allied health professions)

Health Services Management and Hospital Administration

Health Services Research

Hearing Sciences (*see* Communication Disorders)

Higher Education

HIV/AIDS Nursing

Home Economics Education

Hospice Nursing

Hospital Administration (*see* Health Services Management and Hospital Administration)

Hospitality Management

Hotel Management (*see* Travel and Tourism)

Human Resources Development

Human Resources Management

Human Services

Industrial Administration (*see* Industrial and Manufacturing Management)

Industrial and Manufacturing Management

Industrial Education (*see* Vocational and Technical Education)

Industrial Hygiene

Information Studies

Instructional Technology (*see* Educational Media/Instructional Technology)

Insurance

Intellectual Property Law

International and Comparative Education

International Business

International Commerce (*see* International Business)

International Economics (*see* International Business)

International Health

International Trade (*see* International Business)

Investment and Securities (*see* Business Administration and Management; Finance and Banking; Investment Management)

Investment Management

Junior College Education (*see* Community College Education)

Kinesiology and Movement Studies

Laboratory Medicine (*see* Clinical Laboratory Sciences/Medical Technology)

Law

Legal and Justice Studies

Leisure Services (*see* Recreation and Park Management)

Leisure Studies

Library Science

Logistics

Management (*see* Business Administration and Management)

Management Information Systems

Management Strategy and Policy

Marketing

Marketing Research

Maternal and Child Health

Maternal and Child/Neonatal Nursing

Mathematics Education

Medical Imaging

Medical Nursing (*see* Medical/Surgical Nursing)

Medical Physics

Medical/Surgical Nursing

Medical Technology (*see* Clinical Laboratory Sciences/Medical Technology)

Medicinal and Pharmaceutical Chemistry

Medicinal Chemistry (*see* Medicinal and Pharmaceutical Chemistry)

Medicine (*see* Allopathic Medicine; Naturopathic Medicine; Osteopathic Medicine; Podiatric Medicine)

Middle School Education

Midwifery (*see* Nurse Midwifery)

Movement Studies (*see* Kinesiology and Movement Studies)

Multilingual and Multicultural Education

Museum Education

Music Education

Naturopathic Medicine

Nonprofit Management

Nuclear Medical Technology (*see* Clinical Laboratory Sciences/Medical Technology)

Nurse Anesthesia

Nurse Midwifery

Nurse Practitioner Studies (*see* Family Nurse Practitioner Studies)

Nursery School Education (*see* Early Childhood Education)

Nursing Administration (*see* Nursing and Healthcare Administration)

Nursing and Healthcare Administration

Nursing Education

Nursing—General

Nursing Informatics

Occupational Education (*see* Vocational and Technical Education)

Occupational Health (*see* Environmental and Occupational Health; Occupational Health Nursing)

Occupational Health Nursing

Occupational Therapy

Oncology Nursing

Optometry

Oral and Dental Sciences

Oral Biology (*see* Oral and Dental Sciences)

Oral Pathology (*see* Oral and Dental Sciences)

Organizational Behavior

Organizational Management

Oriental Medicine and Acupuncture (*see* Acupuncture and Oriental Medicine)

Orthodontics (*see* Oral and Dental Sciences)

Osteopathic Medicine

Parks Administration (*see* Recreation and Park Management)

Pediatric Nursing

Pedontics (*see* Oral and Dental Sciences)

Perfusion

Personnel (*see* Human Resources Development; Human Resources Management; Organizational Behavior; Organizational Management; Student Affairs)

Pharmaceutical Administration

Pharmaceutical Chemistry (*see* Medicinal and Pharmaceutical Chemistry)

Pharmaceutical Sciences

Pharmacy

Philosophy of Education (*see* Foundations and Philosophy of Education)

Physical Education

Physical Therapy

Physician Assistant Studies

Physiological Optics (*see* Vision Sciences)

Podiatric Medicine

Preventive Medicine (*see* Community Health and Public Health)

Project Management

Psychiatric Nursing

Public Health—General

Public Health Nursing (*see* Community Health Nursing)

Public Relations (*see* Advertising and Public Relations)

Quality Management

Quantitative Analysis

Radiological Health (*see* Health Physics/Radiological Health)

Reading Education

Real Estate

Recreation and Park Management

Recreation Therapy (*see* Recreation and Park Management)

Rehabilitation Sciences

Rehabilitation Therapy (*see* Physical Therapy)

Religious Education

Remedial Education (*see* Special Education)

Restaurant Administration (*see* Hospitality Management)

School Nursing

Science Education

Secondary Education

Social Sciences Education

Social Studies Education (*see* Social Sciences Education)

Social Work

Special Education

Speech-Language Pathology and Audiology (*see* Communication Disorders)

Sports Management

Sports Medicine (*see* Athletic Training and Sports Medicine)

Sports Psychology and Sociology (*see* Kinesiology and Movement Studies)

Student Affairs

Substance Abuse Counseling (*see* Counselor Education)

Supply Chain Management

Surgical Nursing (*see* Medical/Surgical Nursing)

Sustainability Management

Systems Management (*see* Management Information Systems)

Taxation

Teacher Education (*see* specific subject areas)

Teaching English as a Second Language (*see* English as a Second Language)

Technical Education (*see* Vocational and Technical Education)

Teratology (*see* Environmental and Occupational Health)

Therapeutics (*see* Pharmaceutical Sciences; Pharmacy)

Transcultural Nursing

Transportation Management

Travel and Tourism

Urban Education

Veterinary Medicine

Veterinary Sciences

Vision Sciences

Vocational and Technical Education

Vocational Counseling (*see* Counselor Education)

Women's Health Nursing

Directories and Subject Areas in This Book

Special Advertising Section

Thomas Jefferson University School of Population Health

University of Medicine & Dentistry of New Jersey

Saint Louis University

St. Mary's University

The Winston Preparatory Schools

Learn from a National Leader in
Population Health

Jefferson School of Population Health

- Master of Public Health (MPH); CEPH accredited
- PhD in Population Health Sciences

Online programs

- Master of Science in Health Policy (MS-HP)
- Master of Science in Healthcare Quality and Safety (MS-HQS)
- Master of Science in Chronic Care Management (MS-CCM)
- Certificates in Public Health, Health Policy, Healthcare Quality and Safety, Chronic Care Management

Population health – putting health and health care together

215-503-0174

www.jefferson.edu/population_health/ads.cfm

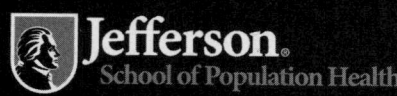

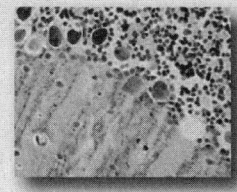

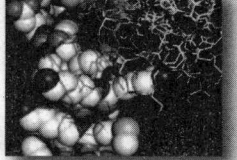
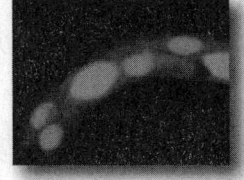
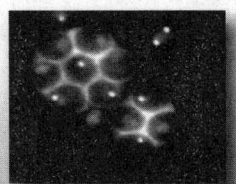

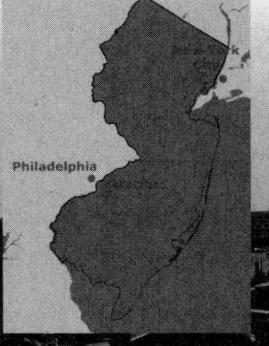

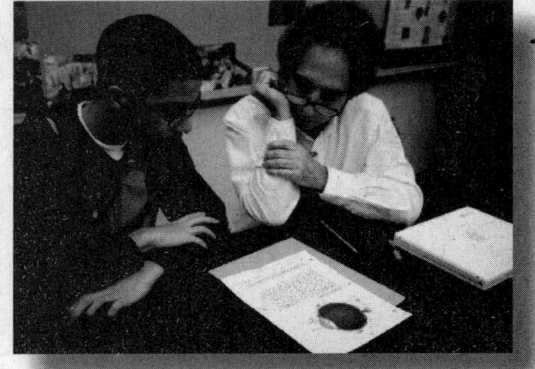

NOTES

NOTES

Sustainability—Its Importance to Peterson's Publishing

What does sustainability mean to Peterson's Publishing? As a leading publisher, we are aware that our business has a direct impact on vital resources—most especially the trees that are used to make our books. Peterson's Publishing is proud that its products are certified by the Sustainable Forestry Initiative (SFI) and that all of its books are printed on paper that is 40 percent post-consumer waste using vegetable-based ink.

Being a part of the Sustainable Forestry Initiative (SFI) means that all of our vendors—from paper suppliers to printers—have undergone rigorous audits to demonstrate that they are maintaining a sustainable environment.

Peterson's Publishing continuously strives to find new ways to incorporate sustainability throughout all aspects of its business.

NOTES

NOTES